The Penguin Encyclopedia

The Penguin

Encyclopedia

Edited by David Crystal

PENGUIN BOOKS

PENGUIN BOOKS

Published by the Penguin Group
Penguin Books Ltd, 80 Strand, London, WC2R ORL, England
Penguin Group (USA) Inc., 375 Hudson Street, New York, New York 10014, USA
Penguin Books Australia Ltd, 250 Camberwell Road, Camberwell, Victoria 3124, Australia
Penguin Books Canada Ltd, 10 Alcorn Avenue, Toronto, Ontario, Canada M4V 3B2
Penguin Books India (P) Ltd, 11, Community Centre, Panchsheel Park, New Delhi – 110 017, India
Penguin Group (NZ) Ltd, Cnr Airborne and Rosedale Roads, Albany, Auckland 1310, New Zealand
Penguin Books (South Africa) (Pty) Ltd, 24 Sturdee Avenue, Rosebank 2196, South Africa

Penguin Books Ltd, Registered Offices: 80 Strand, London, WC2R ORL, England

www.penguin.com

First published 2002
This revised second edition first published 2004
1

Typeset in TheAntiqua and TheSans
Typeset by Tradespools, Frome, Somerset
Printed in Finland by WS Bookwell

Contents

Preface vii

User Guide ix

The Penguin Encyclopedia 1

Ready Reference 1693

Acknowledgements

Crystal Reference

Editor
David Crystal

Assistant Editors
Hilary Crystal
Ann Rowlands
Jan Thomas

Database Assistance
Peter Preston
Todd Warden-Owen

Database Management
Philip Johnstone
Tony McNicholl
Dan Wade

Crystal Reference Administration
Ian Saunders
Rob Phillips

Penguin Books

Publishing Director
Nigel Wilcockson

Publisher
Martin Toseland

Designer
Richard Marston

Production
Andrew Henty

Typesetting
Tradespools

Preface

The Penguin Encyclopedia provides a succinct, systematic and readable guide to the facts, events, issues, beliefs and achievements which make up the sum of human knowledge. Its aim is to act as a standard reference work for use in the home, school, library or office by both adult enquirers and young people of high-school age. Its content derives from a database of information which has been compiled since the mid 1980s, and which has provided the input to other famous reference projects of the past, notably the Cambridge family of encyclopedias and the Chambers factfinders. However, it differs significantly from these works in range, relevance, and presentation. The present book is the largest single-volume encyclopedia it has been my privilege to edit, comprising nearly 2 million words, and representing a much wider range of current topics, issues, locations and personalities than it has been possible to include in earlier publications of this type.

The relevant statistics can be briefly summarized. The encyclopedia contains over 27,000 alphabetically organized entries, and includes a further 4,000 boldface items treated within those entries, all appropriately cross-referenced to anticipate the diverse routes which readers use when they are searching for information. The majority of these entries (nearly 17,000) are general topics. In addition, there are over 7,000 biographical entries, concentrating on persons of international distinction, though not neglecting national personalities within the English-speaking countries that this encyclopedia primarily serves. Some 4,000 gazetteer entries complete the book's alphabetical coverage.

The entries were originally written by a team of over 350 specialist contributors affiliated to universities, museums, and other centres of excellence, and have been regularly revised in an ongoing three-year cycle to ensure a high level of up-to-dateness for the new millennium. The source database is actually updated day-by-day for current affairs, and this, along with a publishing procedure which allows new material to be added right up to just a couple of months before publication, ensures that the present edition of this book, appearing in the second half of 2004, contains information from the first half of that year. Inevitably, events from 2003 loom large, such as SARS and the Iraq war, as well as personalities who have achieved fresh public prominence, such as Ricky Gervais, Jonny Wilkinson, John Kerry, and Hans Blix.

Internationalism is a major focus of *The Penguin Encyclopedia*. There is of course systematic coverage of such traditionally popular areas as flora and fauna, history, art, music, literature, theatre, religion, and mythology. But an encyclopedia for the 2000s has to reflect international issues, especially in politics, economics, technology and current affairs. A further focus is on – for want of a better word – 'intelligent' issues. If I had to identify a single point of difference between this encyclopedia and others, I would single out the many entries in *The Penguin Encyclopedia* devoted to an explanation of important concepts which have shaped the history of ideas in such fields as philosophy, economics, religion, art, linguistics, literature, sociology and politics. Several complex intellectual topics are given a serious yet succinct treatment.

Probably the most noticeable characteristic of the entry treatment in *The Penguin Encyclopedia* relates to its function as a standard reference work. It aims to give rapid answers to specific queries about people, places or topics. The majority of entries are short and to the point: just over half the entries average 125 words, and a further 45 per cent average 50 words; the remaining 5 per cent average 500 words. These longer entries provide a detailed exposition of themes of particular historical contemporary importance – for example, the American Revolution, civil rights, the two World Wars and entries on the nations of the world.

The other important feature of *The Penguin Encyclopedia* – and one which helps to explain the size of the work as a whole – is its concern to present information in an accessible and interesting way. I have paid particular attention to the language of the entries to ensure that they are written in an intelligible style, without losing sight of the stylistic conventions identifying the subject area to which each entry belongs. A particular innovation is the systematic use of a specially condensed style for gazetteer, natural history, and certain other types of entry, which provides information in a clear and direct manner, increases accessibility, and saves a great deal of space (thus permitting an overall increase in coverage). The principle of functional clarity has also been used in the selection of illustrations, where I have avoided the 'pretty picture' approach to encyclopedia compilation, and chosen to rely on a small set of clear, relevant line-drawings. This is very much a text-based encyclopedia, focusing on description and explanation. People need to be able to talk about what they know, and it is text, rather than pictures, which is the only sure means of enabling them to do this. That is also why I give so much guidance on pronunciation, where this is not obvious, using a specially devised phonetic spelling.

The Penguin Encyclopedia, accordingly, presents a knowledge base which is well suited to meeting the information needs of people as we enter the new millennium. At the same time, it is important to recognize not only the strengths, but also the limitations of any general encyclopedia, and to strive to surmount them. Many readers will be more knowledgeable about certain topics than any encyclopedia team could ever be. I therefore very much welcome feedback from readers relating to any inadequacy in our coverage and treatment. The easiest way to do this is to e-mail the database at www.crystalreference.com or through conventional mail at Penguin Press Editorial 1, Penguin Books, 80 Strand, London WC2R ORL. In this way, our knowledge base will grow with the times, and reflect ever more closely the interests and concerns of those wishing to benefit from it.

David Crystal

User Guide

Entry order

- The order of entries follows the English alphabet, ignoring capitals, accents, diacritics, or apostrophes.
- The ordering is letter by letter, ignoring all spaces and hyphens in compound headings, eg **seance** precedes **sea otter**, which precedes **sea pen**, which precedes **seaplane**. Exceptions include all **Mc** names, which are listed as if they were **Mac**, and all **St** names, which are listed as if they were **Saint**.
- When many people have the same name (eg **John**), we list monarchs before saints and popes, followed by others. Compound names (eg **John Paul I**) appear later than single-element names (eg **John, Otto**). Rulers with an identifying byname (eg **John of Austria**, **John the Baptist**) appear after single-element names following the letter-by- letter order of the constituent words (eg **John of Trevisa** precedes **John the Baptist**). The system groups all **John**s together, and occasionally provides an exception to the letter-by-letter convention (eg **John the Baptist** precedes **Johnson**).
- We list phrasal names under their most specific element, eg **Japan, Sea of**, and **Waterloo, Battle of**.
- In cases where headwords have the same spelling, the order is (1) places, (2) people, (3) general topics.
- We list identically spelled topic headwords according to the alphabetical order of their subject areas, eg **depression** (meteorology) precedes **depression** (psychiatry).
- We list rulers chronologically, ordering them by country if titles are the same, eg **Charles I** (of Austria-Hungary) is followed by **Charles I** (of England) then by **Charles II** (of England) and **Charles II** (of Spain). Names of non-English rulers, saints, etc. are anglicized, with a cross-reference used in cases where the foreign name is widely known, eg **Wilhelm >> William**.
- We list places with the same name on the basis of the alphabetical order of their countries, eg **Dover** (UK) precedes **Dover** (USA).
- Parts of a person's name that are not generally used are enclosed in parentheses, eg **Wells, H(erbert) G(eorge)**. Parenthesized elements are ignored in deciding alphabetical sequence, eg **Smith (Robert) Harvey** would precede **Smith, Henry**.

Entry conventions

- Where alternative spellings exist in headwords, we give British usage first, then American usage, eg **colour/color television**. We give cross-references in all cases where spelling variation affects initial letters, eg **esophagus/oesophagus**.
- We transliterate names in non-Roman alphabets, and add a cross-reference in cases where confusion could arise because more than one transliteration system exists. Letter symbols from other languages which do not appear in the English alphabet are given their nearest English equivalents. Chinese names are given in pin-yin (eg **Beijing** for **Peking**). In the case of Arabic names, we have not transliterated the alif and ain symbols. No accent is shown on French capital letters.
- A person's birthplace is usually cited with reference to the present-day town and country (eg Germany rather than Prussia), where this is known. Locations within the UK and USA are usually followed by the name of their country, state, etc., unless the two names are identical (as in the case of New York).
- People mentioned within entries usually have their dates of birth/death following their names; absence of these dates signifies that the person has his/her own entry elsewhere in the encyclopedia.

Other conventions

- Months in parenthesis are abbreviated to the first three letters (16 Sep 1941).
- Chemistry abbreviations are shown in the diagram located under Periodic table.
- A certain number of frequently used abbreviations maintain the succinctness of individual entries.

Abbreviations

AD	Anno Domini
BC	Before Christ
c	century
c.	circa (about)
C	Celsius (Centigrade)
C	Central (in locations)
cc	cubic centimetre(s)
CFA	(for francs) *Communauté financière africaine*
Chin	Chinese
cm	centimetre(s)
Co	County
cu	cubic
d.	died
e	estimate (for populations)
E	east(ern)
eg	for example (*exempli gratia*)
Eng	English
F	Fahrenheit
Finn	Finnish
fl.	flourished
Fr	French
ft	foot/feet
g	gram(s)
Ger	German
Gr	Greek
h	hour(s)
ha	hectare(s)
Hung	Hungarian
I(s)	Island(s)
ie	that is (*id est*)
in	inch(es)
Ir	Irish
Ital	Italian
Jap	Japanese
K	Kelvin
kg	kilogram(s)
km	kilometre(s)
l	litre(s)
L	Lake
Lat	Latin
lb	pound(s)
m	metre(s)
min	minute(s)
mm	millimetre(s)
m/s	metres per second
Mt	Mount(ain)
Mts	Mountains
N	north(ern)
No/ no.	number
oz	ounces
p(p)	page(s)
pop	population
Port	Portuguese
pt	pint(s)
r.	reigned
R	River
Russ	Russian
S	south(ern)
s	second(s)
Span	Spanish
sq	square
St	Saint
Sta	Santa
Ste	Sainte
Swed	Swedish
trans	translation
v.	versus
vol(s)	volume
W	west(ern)
yd	yard(s)

Pronunciation guide

- We give a pronunciation whenever it is unpredictable from the spelling, or where there is a possibility that a reader might choose the wrong form. In foreign words/names we give an approximate foreign pronunciation, unless there is a well-known English version. In cases where both forms are used in English, we give both.
- Bold type is used to show stressed or strongly accented syllables, **Xerxes** [**zerk**seez]. We do not usually show the stress in languages (such as French, Chinese, Japanese) which have a very different rhythmical system to English, and where it would be misleading to identify one of the syllables as most prominent. We make exceptions in cases where there is a widely used or predictable English pronunciation.
- No distinctive symbol is used for unstressed English vowels, in cases where the pronunciation can be intuitively deduced from the spelling, eg **echidna** [e**kid**na].
- The symbol [r] is used to mark cases where an r in the spelling may or may not be pronounced, depending on the accent, eg **Barbarossa** [bah(**r**)ba**ro**sa]. This symbol is not used when the transcription of a sound already contains an [r] symbol, as in [er].

Symbol	Sound	Symbol	Sound	Symbol	Sound	**Non-English sounds**	
a	h**a**t	i	s**i**t	r	**r**ed	ã	French *Nantes*
ah	f**a**ther	iy	l**ie**	s	**s**et	hl	Welsh *llan*
air	h**air**	j	**j**et	sh	**sh**ip	ĩ	French *Saint*
aw	s**aw**	k	**k**it	t	**t**in	õ	French *bon*
ay	s**ay**	l	**l**ip	th	**th**in	kh	Scots *loch*
b	**b**ig	m	**m**an	th	**th**is		German *ich*
ch	**ch**ip	n	**n**ip	u	p**u**t	oe	French *soeur*
d	**d**ig	ng	si**ng**	uh	c**u**p		German *möglich*
e	s**e**t	o	h**o**t	v	**v**an	õe	French *brun*
ee	s**ee**	oh	s**ou**l	w	**w**ill	ü	French *tu*
er	b**ir**d	oo	s**oo**n	y	**y**es		German *müde*
f	**f**ish	ow	c**ow**	z	**z**oo		
g	**g**o	oy	b**oy**	zh	lei**s**ure		

The Penguin Encyclopedia

a

Aachen [ahkhen], Fr **Aix-La-Chapelle** 50°47N 6°04E, pop (2000e) 252 000. Manufacturing city in Cologne district, W Germany; 64 km/40 mi SW of Cologne, near the Dutch and Belgian borders; N capital of Charlemagne's empire; 32 German emperors crowned here; annexed by France, 1801; given to Prussia, 1815; badly bombed in World War 2; railway; technical college; textiles, glass, machinery, chemicals, light engineering, foodstuffs, rubber products; town hall (1350), cathedral (14th-c) is a world heritage site; Bad Aachen hot mineral springs; international riding, jumping, and driving tournament.

Aakjaer, Jeppe [awkyayr] (1866–1930) Novelist and poet, born in Aakjaer, Denmark. A leader of the 'Jutland movement' in Danish literature, his works include the novel *Vredens Børn* (1904, Children of Wrath) and the poems of *Rugens Sange* (1906, Songs of the Rye). He wrote much in the Jutland dialect, into which he translated some of Burns's poems.

Aalto, (Hugo Henrik) Alvar [awltoh] (1898–1976) Architect and designer, the father of Modernism in Scandinavia, born in Kuortane, WC Finland. He studied at Helsinki Polytechnic, and evolved a unique architectural style based on irregular and asymmetric forms and the imaginative use of natural materials. He designed numerous public and industrial buildings in Finland, including the Finlandia concert hall in Helsinki. In the 1930s he also pioneered the use of factory-made laminated birchwood for a distinctive style of Finnish furniture.

Aaltonen, Wäinö (Valdemar) [ahltonen] (1894–1966) Sculptor, born in St Mårtens, SW Finland. He studied at Helsinki, and became one of the leading Finnish sculptors, working in many styles. His best-known works are the bust of Sibelius (in the Gothenburg Museum) and the statue of the Olympic runner Paavo Nurmi (commissioned by the Finnish government in 1924).

aardvark [ah(r)dvah(r)k] A southern African mammal (*Orycteropus afer*); length, 1–1·5 m/3¼–5 ft; long ears, pig-like snout, long sticky tongue, strong claws; digs burrows; inhabits grassland and woodland; eats ants and termites; mainly nocturnal; also known as **ant bear** or **earth pig**. It is the only member of the order Tubulidentata. (Family: Orycteropodidae.)

aardwolf [ah(r)dwulf] A rare southern African carnivore (*Proteles cristatus*) of the hyena family; slender, yellow with black stripes; inhabits dry plains; eats mainly termites; lives in a den (often an abandoned aardvark burrow); nocturnal; also known as **maned jackal**.

Aare, River [ahruh], Fr **Aar** Largest river entirely in Switzerland; emerges from L Grimsel in the Bernese Alps and flows N then W through L Brienz, L Thun, and L Biel to enter the Rhine; length, 295 km/183 mi; navigable from the Rhine to Thun.

Aarhus *Århus*

Aaron [airon] (15th–13th-c BC) Biblical patriarch, the first high priest of the Israelites, and said to be the founder of the priesthood; the elder brother of Moses. He was spokesman for Moses to the Egyptian pharoah in his attempts to lead their people out of Egypt. He later joined rebellious Israelites in making a golden calf for idolatrous worship. He and his sons were ordained as priests after the construction of the Ark of the Covenant and the Tabernacle, and he was confirmed as hereditary high priest by the miracle of his rod blossoming into an almond tree (hence various plants nicknamed 'Aaron's Rod').

Aaron, Hank [airon], popular name of **Henry Louis Aaron**, nickname **Hammerin' Hank** (1934–) Baseball player, born in Mobile, Alabama, USA. A right-handed batting outfielder, he set almost every batting record in his 23-season career with Milwaukee Braves, Atlanta Braves, and Milwaukee Brewers: 2297 runs batted in, 1477 extra-base hits, 6856 total bases, and 755 home runs, still a major league record.

abaca A fibre obtained from the leaf-stalks of a species of banana (*Musa textilis*) native to the Philippines; the oldest, outermost stalks give the strongest, darkest fibres, 0·9–2·7 m/3–9 ft long; also called **Manila hemp**. Strong and buoyant, it is used for cables, carpets, and ships' hawsers. (Family: Musaceae.)

abacus [abakuhs] A device for performing calculations by sliding bead counters, representing various values, along a set of rods or in grooves. It may have originated in Babylonia, and was used in ancient China, Greece, and Rome. It became widespread in Europe in the Middle Ages, as well as in China and Japan, where it is still in use. In Japan, for example, it is taught in primary schools as part of arithmetic, and there is a recognized examination and licence system. However, since the huge growth of the Japanese electronics industry, the abacus is increasingly being replaced by the calculator.

Abadan [abadahn] 30°20N 48°16E, pop (2000e) 418 000. Oil port in Khuzestan province, WC Iran, close to the Iraq border; on Abadan I, in Shatt al-Arab delta, at head of Persian Gulf; terminus of Iran's major oil pipelines; airport; severely damaged in the Iran–Iraq War.

Abailard *Abelard*

abalone [abalohnee] A primitive marine snail which feeds on algae on rocky shores; characterized by a single row of holes extending back from the front margin of its ovoid shell; collected for decoration and for human consumption; also called **ormer**. (Class: Gastropoda. Order: Archaeogastropoda.)

Abarbanel, Isaac ben Jehudah [abah(r)banel] (1437–1508) Jewish writer and philosopher, born in Lisbon, Portugal. His works comprise commentaries on the Bible and philosophical treatises. His eldest son, **Juda Leon** (known as **Leo Hebraeus** in Latin) (c.1460–1535), a doctor and philosopher, wrote *Dialoghi di Amore* (1535, trans Philosophy of Love).

Abba [aba] Swedish pop singing group, formed in 1973 by **Bjorn Ulvaeus** (1945– , guitar, vocals), married to **Agnetha Faltskog** (1950– , vocals), and **Benny Andersson** (1945– , keyboards, vocals), married to **AnniFrid** (known as **Frida**) **Lyngstad** (1945– , vocals). The group's name derives from their first-name initials. They first came to international attention with the winning song in the 1974 Eurovision Song Contest, 'Waterloo', which was followed by hit singles and albums throughout the 1970s and early 1980s. They were perhaps the most successful international group since the Beatles. Ulvaeus and Anderson wrote their songs, and have written a musical, *Mama Mia* (1999), built around many of them, as well as collaborating with Tim Rice in the musical *Chess* (1984). Bjorn and Agnetha divorced in 1979, and Benny and Frida in 1981.

Abbado, Claudio [abahdoh] (1933–) Musical conductor, born in Milan, N Italy. From a distinguished musical family, he began training in piano, composition, and conducting. He made his British debut in Manchester (1965), was conductor and director at La Scala, Milan (1968–86), and principal conductor of the London Symphony Orchestra (1979–87). Other posts include principal conductor of the Vienna Philharmonic Orchestra (1971), musical director of the Vienna State Opera (1986–91), and principal conductor of the Berlin Philharmonic Orchestra (1989–2001). In 1994 he was artistic director of the Salzburg Easter Festival and triumphed with a spectacular postmodern production of Moussorgsky's *Boris Godunov*.

Abbas I [abas], known as **Abbas the Great** (1571–1629) The fifth Safavid shah of Persia. After his accession (1588), he set about establishing a counterweight to the Turkmen tribal chiefs who had constituted the principal political and military powers in the state. From 1598 he was able to recover Azerbaijan and parts of Armenia from the Ottomans, and Khurasan from the Uzbeks. He transferred his capital from Qazvin to Isfahan, and established diplomatic and economic relations with W Europe.

Abbas (c.566–c.652) Ancestor of the Abbasid dynasty of the Islamic empire who ruled as caliphs of Baghdad (750–1258). He was the maternal uncle of the prophet Mohammed. A rich merchant of Mecca, he was at first hostile to his nephew, but ultimately became one of the chief adherents of Islam.

Abbasids [abasidz] A dynasty of caliphs, which replaced that of the Umayyads in 749, establishing itself in Baghdad until its sack by the Mongols in 1258. Early Abbasid power reached its peak under Harun al-Rashid (786–809). The Abbasids came from the family of the Prophet Mohammed's uncle Abbas, and were thus able to claim legitimacy in the eyes of the pious.

Abbe, Cleveland [ahbuh] (1838–1916) Meteorologist, born in New York City, USA. He wrote on the atmosphere and on climate, and was responsible for the introduction of the US system of Standard Time.

Abbe, Ernst [ahbuh] (1840–1905) Professor of optics, born in Eisenach, C Germany. He became professor at the University of Jena in 1870, and in 1878 director of the astronomical and meteorological observatories. He deduced the mathematics of the optics of the microscope and this enabled him and Otto Schott (1851–1935) to design and produce lenses of the highest possible quality for scientific research. He was a partner in the optical works of Carl Zeiss on whose death he became owner in 1888.

abbey A building or group of buildings used by a religious order for worship and living. It houses a community under the direction of an abbot or abbess as head, who is elected for a term of years or for life. Abbeys were centres of learning in the Middle Ages. Examples are La Grande Chartreuse (France), El Escorial (New Castile, Spain), and Fountains Abbey (near Ripon, North Yorkshire, UK).

Abbey Theatre A theatre situated in Dublin's Abbey Street, the centre of the Irish dramatic movement founded by Lady Gregory and W B Yeats. Best known for its championship of Synge and of the early plays of O'Casey, the Abbey was a major theatrical venue (opened 1904) throughout the first 30 years of the 20th-c. The present theatre was opened in 1966 after the earlier building had burnt down in 1951.

Abbott, Bud *Abbott and Costello*

Abbott and Costello Comedy film partners: **Bud Abbott**, originally **William A Abbott** (1896–1974), born in Asbury Park, New Jersey, USA and **Lou Costello**, originally **Louis Francis Cristillo** (1908–59), born in Paterson, New Jersey, USA. Both men had theatrical experience before teaming up as a comedy double act, Costello playing the clown and Abbott his straight man. They began performing on radio (1938), appeared on Broadway (1939), and made a number of successful comedy films, beginning with *Buck Privates* (1941).

ABC Islands An abbreviated name often applied to the three main islands of Aruba, Bonaire, and Curaçao in the S Netherlands Antilles, off the N coast of South America.

Abd al-Aziz ibn Saud *Saud, al-*

Abd-el-Kader [abdulkader] (1807–83) Algerian nationalist hero, born in Mascara, Algiers. After the French conquest of Algiers, the Arab tribes of Oran elected him as their emir, and with great perseverance he waged a long struggle with the French (1832–47). Eventually crushed by overpowering force, he took refuge in Morocco, and began a crusade against the enemies of Islam, but was defeated at Isly in 1844.

Abd-el-Krim [abdulkrim], nickname **the Wolf of the Rif Mountains** (1882–1963) Berber chief, born in Ajdir, N Morocco. He led unsuccessful revolts against Spain and France (1921, 1924–5), formed the Republic of the Rif and served as its president (1921–6), but was brought to surrender by a large Franco-Spanish army under Marshal Pétain. He was exiled to the island of Réunion. Granted amnesty in 1947, he went to Egypt, where he formed the North African Liberation Committee.

Abdias, Book of *Obadiah, Book of*

abdication A political situation which occurs when the ruler of a country gives up the throne or other high office. Most abdications take place under duress: the ruler is forced to abdicate following a wartime defeat, a revolution, or a constitutional crisis. Napoleon Bonaparte was forced to abdicate twice – once in 1814, and again in 1815. Edward VIII of Britain was forced to abdicate in 1936 because of public disapproval of his proposed marriage to a divorcee. Some rulers choose to abdicate, perhaps because of illness or old age, or simply because they feel they have ruled for too long. Queen Wilhelmina of the Netherlands voluntarily abdicated in 1948, as did her daughter, Queen Juliana, in 1980.

Abdim's stork A small stork (*Ciconia abdimii*) native to Africa and the SW Arabian Peninsula; feeds in drier habitats than other storks; eats insects, especially locusts.

abdomen The lower part of the trunk, extending from within the pelvic floor to under the cover of the chest wall. Except for the vertebral column, pelvis, and ribs, it is bounded entirely by muscles. It contains most of the alimentary canal (from stomach to rectum), the liver, pancreas, spleen, kidneys, and bladder, and the internal organs of reproduction. The cavity has a lining (the *peritoneum*) which covers or completely surrounds and suspends the majority of the various contents. Major blood vessels and nerves pass into it from the chest and out of it to the lower limbs.

abdominal thrust *Heimlich manoeuvre*

Abdul-Jabbar, Kareem [abdul jaber], originally **Lewis Ferdinand Alcindor**, known as **Lew Alcindor** (1947–) Basketball player, born in New York City, USA. A talented player from youth, his exceptional height (7 ft 2 in/2 m 5 cm) made him a formidable opponent. He studied at the University of California (1965), then joined the National Basketball Association (NBA) Milwaukee Bucks (1969), leading them to victory in the NBA championships (1971). Already converted to Islam, he took an Arabic name (1971). He moved to the Los Angeles Lakers in 1975, and went on to establish an individual points record of 46 725. He retired in 1989.

à Becket, Thomas *Becket, St Thomas*

Abel [aybel] Biblical character, the second son of Adam and Eve. He is described as a shepherd, whose offering God accepts; but he was then murdered by his brother, Cain.

Abelard, Peter [abelah(r)d] (1079–1142) Theologian, born near Nantes, W France. He studied under Roscellinus and Guillaume de Champeaux (c.1070–1171). As lecturer in the cathedral school of Notre Dame in Paris, he became tutor to Héloïse, the 17-year-old niece of the canon Fulbert. They fell passionately in love, but when their affair was discovered, they fled to Brittany, where Héloïse gave birth to a son. After returning to Paris, they were secretly married. Héloïse's relatives took their revenge on Abelard by castrating him. He fled in shame to the abbey of St Denis to become a monk, and Héloïse took the veil at Argenteuil as a nun. In 1121, a synod at Soissons condemned his Nominalistic doctrines on the Trinity as heretical, and Abelard took to a hermit's hut at Nogent-sur-Seine, where his pupils helped him build a monastic school he named the Paraclete. In 1125 he was elected abbot of St Gildas-de-Rhuys in Brittany, and the Paraclete was given to Héloïse and a sisterhood. In his final years he was again accused of numerous heresies and he retired to the monastery of Cluny. After his death, he was buried in the Paraclete at Héloïse's request, and when she died in 1164 she was laid in the same tomb. In 1817 they were buried in one sepulchre at Père Lachaise.

Abeles, Sir (Emil Herbert) Peter [ayblz] (1924–99) Industrialist, born in Vienna, Austria. He studied in Budapest, then went to Sydney in 1949. The following year he founded Alltrans, which in 1967 merged with Thomas Nationwide Transport (TNT). Under his leadership TNT expanded into all forms of road transport, air courier services, and containerized and bulk shipping. In 1979 TNT and Rupert Murdoch's News Limited gained control of Ansett Airlines, and Abeles became joint managing director of the new company, resigning in 1992. Knighted in 1972, he is known for his friendships with prominent politicians, particularly Bob Hawke.

Aberconwy and Colwyn [aberkonwee, kolwin], Welsh **Aberconwy a Cholwyn** pop (2001e) 109 600; area 1130 sq km/436 sq mi. County (unitary authority from 1996) in NC Wales, UK; renamed **Conwy**, 1998; drained by the R Conwy; administrative centre, Colwyn Bay; other chief town, Llandudno; seaside resorts on north coast; tourism, livestock, light industry; part of Snowdonia National Park; castle at Conwy; Bodnant Garden, Great Orme Cable Railway, Welsh Mountain Zoo.

Aberdeen, ancient **Devana** 57°10N 2°04W, pop (2000e) 223 200. Seaport city council (Aberdeen City), and administrative centre of Aberdeenshire council, NE Scotland, UK; on the North Sea, between Rivers Dee (S) and Don (N), 92 km/57 mi NE of Dundee; royal burgh since 1179; airport; helicopter port; ferries to Orkney and Shetland; railway; university (1494); Robert Gordon University (1992, formerly Institute of Technology); port trade and fishing, finance, oil supply service, granite ('Granite City'), tourism; Art Gallery; Gordon Highlanders Regimental Museum; maritime museum; St Machar's Cathedral (1131); Bridge of Dee (1500); Brig o' Balgownie (c.1320); Aberdeen festival (Jul–Aug).

Aberdeen, George Hamilton Gordon, 4th Earl of (1784–1860) British statesman and prime minister (1852–5), born in Edinburgh, EC Scotland, UK. He studied at Cambridge, succeeding his grandfather as earl in 1801. He was foreign secretary twice, under the Duke of Wellington (1828–30) and then Sir Robert Peel (1841–6). A confirmed free-trader, he resigned with Peel over the repeal of the corn-laws in 1846. In 1852 he was made prime minister of a coalition government that was immensely popular at first, until he reluctantly committed Britain to an alliance with France and Turkey in the Crimean War in 1854. The gross mismanagement of the war aroused popular discontent, and he was forced to resign.

Aberdeen terrier *Scottish terrier*

Aberfan [abervan] 51°42N 3°21W. Village in coal-mining region, Merthyr Tydfil county, S Wales, UK; scene of major disaster in 1966, when a landslip of mining waste engulfed several houses and the school, killing 144, including 116 children.

Abernathy, Ralph D(avid) [abernathee] (1926–90) Baptist clergyman and civil rights activist, born in Linden, Alabama, USA. An early Civil Rights organizer and leading confidante of Martin Luther King, Jr, he was pastor of the West Hunter Street Baptist Church in Atlanta, GA, throughout his civil rights career (1961–90), and became King's chosen successor as head of the Southern Christian Leadership Conference (1968–77). He resigned the leadership to run unsuccessfully for Andrew Young's congressional seat in 1977. Turning away from the Civil Rights movement, he then devoted his attention to the West Hunter Street Baptist Church and the issues of worldwide peace.

aberrations **1** In lens optics, deviations from perfect images, as consequences of the laws of refraction. *Chromatic* aberrations result from the dependence of the bending power of a lens on wavelength, and may produce images having coloured haloes. Colour-independent aberrations (*monochromatic*) deform an image (*distortion, field curvature, coma, astigmatism*) and blur it (*spherical aberration*). Aberrations in cameras, binoculars, and other optical instruments can be minimized using lens combinations. Mirrors have similar monochromatic aberrations to lenses, but no chromatic aberrations.
2 In astronomy, the aberration of starlight is the apparent change in the observed position of a star, caused by a combination of the Earth's velocity in orbit around the Sun, and the finite velocity of light.

Aberystwyth [aberistwith] 52°25N 4°05W, pop (2000e) 12 700. Administrative centre of Cardiganshire county, W Wales, UK; university and resort town, at the mouth of the Ystwyth and Rheidol Rivers, on Cardigan Bay; built around a castle of Edward I, 1227; college of University of Wales (1872); National Library of Wales (1955); railway; boatbuilding, brewing, agricultural trade; university theatre summer season.

Abidjan [abeejan] 5°19N 4°01W, pop (2000e) 3 049 000. Industrial seaport and former capital (1935–83) of Côte d'Ivoire, W Africa; on N shore of Ebrié lagoon; port facilities added in early 1950s; airport; railway; university (1958); farm machinery, metallurgy, car assembly, electrical appliances, plastics, soap, coffee and cocoa trade, timber products, tobacco, food processing, beer, chemicals; Ifan museum.

abiogenesis [aybiyohjenesis] *spontaneous generation*

ablaut [ablowt] Vowel changes in related forms of a word, found in Indo-European languages. Ablaut can be seen in English in several sets of verb forms, such as *drive/drove/driven*.

ABM *antiballistic missile*

Abney level *clinometer*

abnormal psychology The scientific study of the nature and origins of psychologically abnormal states. In contrast to clinical psychology and psychiatry, where the emphasis is on the assessment and treatment of individuals, abnormal psychology seeks more general theories about disorders, in such areas as personality, intelligence, and social behaviour.

Åbo *Turku*

abolitionist movement A 19th-c movement to end slavery in the US South; distinguished from earlier anti-slavery movements by its uncompromising attitude. Blacks as well as whites, and women as well as men took active parts. Abolitionism crystallized around the American Anti-Slavery Society, founded in 1833. Its great achievement was to make slavery an issue that could not be ignored.

A-bomb *atomic bomb*

Abomey [abomay] 7°14N 2°00E, pop (2000e) 90 900. Town in Zou province, S Benin, W Africa; 105 km/65 mi NW of Porto Novo; capital of old Yoruba kingdom of Dahomey; burned by the Portuguese and abandoned to the French, 1892; Royal Palace of Djema, including the tomb of King Gbehanzin (still guarded by women), a world heritage site.

abominable snowman *Bigfoot; Yeti*

Aboriginal art The art of the Australian Aborigines, which originated at least 13 000 years ago – dates of up to 30 000 years have been suggested. Two main stylistic traditions exist: the figurative and the geometric (the latter based on the marks left by animals, humans, and artefacts in the sand). Paints include red ochre, white clay, and charcoal. Carvings on rock and in wood are also common. Much of the art depicts episodes from the 'Dreamtime', the creation period of Aboriginal legend, though sorcery paintings and everyday records of hunting and gathering are also widespread. Aboriginal art is placed on rock, wood, bark, and the human body.

Aboriginal land rights The rights of Australia's indigenous people to the land they inhabited, formerly unrecognized by the white settlers of Australia. Although Aboriginal people and Torres Strait Islanders are spiritually attached to their traditional land, they have been dispossessed of it since 1788. Land rights symbolize the struggle for the autonomy and self-determination of Aboriginal people, and have become a national political issue in Australia since the 1970s. Governments have granted some Aboriginal land claims since then, but the issue attracts controversy because of the opposing interests of mining companies, pastoralists, and the states. The controversy came to a head following the landmark High Court *Mabo* case, named after one of the plaintiffs. In 1992 the Court rejected the doctrine of *terra nullius* – that the land claimed by the colonizers had no prior owners – finding that native title continued to exist after British annexation. While *Mabo* might become the basis for a new relationship between indigenous and non-indigenous Australians, the political difficulties of reconciliation through recognition of native title are immense.

Aborigines [aborijineez] The indigenous inhabitants of Australia, the first of whom reached the continent c.60 000 years ago. By 1788, when European occupation began, there were c.600 territorially defined groups, subsisting on hunting and gathering, with a population of 300 000–1 million. Numbers then fell dramatically, partly through conflict with the Europeans, but mainly through European diseases, especially the smallpox epidemics of 1789 and 1829. By 1933 the population had fallen to c.66 000; it then steadily increased, and now numbers c.250 000.

At first Europeans portrayed Aboriginals as 'noble savages', but this image quickly gave way to contempt, and policies were designed to turn them into Christians with European lifestyles. In the late 19th-c, Social Darwinist ideas were influential, maintaining that Aborigines were an inferior race incapable of self-management and destined to die out. In Van Diemen's Land (Tasmania) the government removed the last survivors of massacre and disease to Flinders I in the late 1820s; the last full-blooded Aborigine, Truganini, died there in 1876. A community of people with mixed descent remains in Tasmania. Elsewhere in Australia, strenuous efforts were made to confine them to government reserves or Christian missions.

Aborigines have not accepted their lot passively. In the 1950s they began moving into the cities of SE Australia and formed advancement groups; but it was not until the mid-1960s that activism became prominent. In 1965 Charles Perkins became the first Aboriginal university graduate, and helped organize 'freedom rides' in New South Wales to protest against discrimination. In 1967 90·8% of Australian voters approved a referendum which granted the federal government the power to count Aborigines in the census and to make laws on their behalf, thus enabling them to be provided with official assistance. Although their condition has since improved significantly, they remain the most disadvantaged group in Australian society. Their disadvantages were the basis for a campaign, begun in 1972, for 'land rights'. Opposition to their claims has come from mining and pastoral interests, and from conservative governments, particularly in Queensland. Nevertheless by the mid-1980s Aborigines had gained freehold title to about 6% of Australia (mostly in the N and C), and were in the process of being granted further areas. The landmark *Mabo* decision in the Australian High Court recognized, for the first time, that Aboriginal people had rights to land in common law based on prior occupancy of the continent. However, a proposal to add a preamble to the constitution recognizing Aborigines as 'the nation's first people' was heavily defeated in a 1999 referendum.

abortion The spontaneous or induced termination of pregnancy before the fetus is viable. In the UK and for legal purposes, this is taken to be the 24th week, although some fetuses expelled before then may survive. In the USA and in some European countries, the time limit may be set some weeks earlier. There is no consensus on the matter in the USA, but the Supreme Court decision in *Roe* v. *Wade* (1973) made abortions legal during the first six months of pregnancy. Spontaneous abortion (*miscarriage*) occurs in about 15% of recognized pregnancies and may occur in up to 50% of all pregnancies. It may be caused by abnormalities of the fetus, placenta, uterus, or maternal environment, such as maternal illness. Abortion can be induced surgically or by the use of drugs (such as prostaglandins and mifepristone). Unless permitted by the Abortion Acts, induced abortion is a criminal offence in the UK. The moral issues surrounding abortion have received increasing publicity in the 1990s, with conflict between extremists from 'pro-life' (anti-abortion) and 'right-to-choose' (pro-abortion) groups leading to violent confrontation, especially in the USA.

abortion pill *contraception*

Aboukir Bay, Battle of **1** (Aug 1798) A naval battle during the War of the Second Coalition, in which Nelson destroyed the French fleet under Brueys off the coast of Egypt; also known as the **Battle of the Nile**. This victory forced Napoleon to abandon his Egyptian campaign, aimed at threatening British territory in India, and return to France.
2 (Jul 1799) The last French victory of the Egyptian campaign, in which Napoleon's Army of Egypt captured Aboukir citadel, NE of Alexandria, defeating an Ottoman Turkish force over twice the size, led by Mustafa Pasha; also known as the **Battle of Aboukir**.

Abrabanel *Abarbanel*

Abraham, Abram, or **Ibrahiz** (after 2000 BC) Revered in the Hebrew Bible as the father of the Hebrew people and of several other nations. According to *Genesis* he came from the Sumerian town of Ur ('Ur of the Chaldees') in modern Iraq, and migrated with his family and flocks to the 'Promised Land' of Canaan, where he settled at Shechem (modern Nablus). He lived to be 175 years old, and was buried with his first wife Sarah in Hebron. By Sarah he was the father of Isaac (whom he was prepared to sacrifice at Moriah at the command of the Lord, as a test of his faith); by Sarah's Egyptian maid, Hagar, he was the father of Ishmael, the ancestor of twelve clans; by his third wife Keturah he had six sons who became the ancestors of the Arab tribes. He is traditionally regarded as the father of Judaism, Christianity, and Islam (*Gen* 22).

Abraham, Plains / Heights of The site of a battle (1759), Quebec City, Canada, in which British forces under Wolfe defeated French, Amerindian, and Canadian forces under Montcalm and Vaudreuil, and gained control over Quebec. Wolfe and Montcalm were both killed in the battle.

Abram *Abraham*

Abramovich, Roman Arkadyevich [abramovich] (1966–) Multi-billionaire businessman and entrepreneur, born in Saratov, S Russia. Orphaned at age two, he was raised by an uncle and his family in Ukhta, N Russia. While still a student at the Moscow Auto Transport Institute (1987), he set up a small company producing plastic toys and its success enabled him to found an oil business in the Omsk region. He later became head of the Sibneft company, completing a merger which made it the fourth biggest oil company in the world. He is now one of the world's richest men with an estimated fortune of £8·2 billion. He became a familiar face in England after his acquisition of Chelsea Football Club in 2003.

abrasives Hard, rough, or sharp textured materials used to wear down, rub, or polish materials which are less hard, as in the traditional grindstone or whetstone. Naturally occurring abrasive substances include various forms of silica (sand, quartz, or flint), pumice, and emery (an aluminium oxide mineral). Artificial abrasives include silicon carbide, synthetic diamond, and boron carbide. They can be used as powders or incorporated in hand or machine tools.

Abravanel *Abarbanel*

Abrikosov, Alexei A (1928–) Physicist, born in Moscow, Russia. He studied at Moscow State University (1948) and the Institute for Physical Problems (1951), and in 1991 joined the Materials Science Division at Argonne National Laboratory, Illinois. He is famous for the discovery of Type II superconductors and their magnetic properties (the **Abrikosov vortex lattice**). In 2003 he shared the Nobel Prize for Physics for pioneering contributions to the theory of superconductors and superfluids.

Abruzzi or **Abruzzo** [abrutsee] pop (2000e) 1 248 000; area 10 794 sq km/4152 sq mi. Region in EC Italy, between the Apennines and the Adriatic Sea, in the valley of the upper Sangro;

cereals, chemicals, foodstuffs processing, fishing, tanning, tourism, textiles, winter sports; resort village of Pescasseroli; national park (400 sq km/150 sq mi) in the S, established in 1922.

abscess A localized collection of pus in an organ or tissue, surrounded by an inflammatory reaction which forms a well-defined wall (an abscess cavity). It is commonly due to infection with pus-forming (*pyogenic*) bacteria, but occasionally a foreign body is responsible.

Abse, Dannie [absee] (1923–) Writer and physician, born in Cardiff, S Wales, UK. He studied at the Welsh National School of Medicine, King's College London, and Westminster Hospital, becoming senior specialist in the chest clinic at the Central Medical Establishment, London, in 1954. His literary output includes several volumes of poetry, four novels, and a number of plays. His autobiographical volumes are *A Poet in the Family* (1974), *A Strong Dose of Myself* (1983), *There was a Young Man from Cardiff* (1991), and the novel *Ash on a Young Man's Sleeve* (1954). Later work includes *Arcadia, One Mile* (1997) and *Twentieth Century Anglo-Welsh Poetry* (1997).

absolute liability *strict liability*

absolute zero The temperature of a system for which a reversible isothermal process involves no heat transfer. It represents the state of lowest possible total energy of a system, and is denoted by 0 K (–273·15°C). It is unattainable, according to the third law of thermodynamics.

absolution A declaration of forgiveness of sins. In Christian worship, it is understood as God's gracious work in Jesus Christ, pronounced by a priest or minister either in private after confession or as part of the liturgy in public worship.

absolutism A theory of kingship elaborated and practised in early modern Europe, associated notably with Louis XIV of France; sometimes equated loosely with systems of government in which one person exercises unlimited power. Absolute power was justified by the belief that monarchs were God's representatives on Earth. Armed with this notion of Divine Right, kings were owed unquestioning obedience by their subjects; as a corollary, the powers of hereditary monarchs were tempered by concepts of fundamental law and responsibility to their subjects and to God.

absorbed dose *radioactivity units*

abstract art A form of art in which there is no attempt to represent objects or persons, but which relies instead on lines, colours, and shapes alone for its aesthetic appeal. It seems to have emerged c.1910, and was partly a reaction against 19th-c Realism and Impressionism. Early abstract artists include Kandinsky, Miró, Pevsner, and Brancusi. Stylistically, abstract art ranges from the 'geometrical' (Mondrian, *De Stijl*, Constructivism) to the 'organic' (Arp, Moore). More recent developments include action painting and Op Art. Historically, abstract tendencies have been present in one form or another in most cultures. Two trends should be distinguished: (a) the simplification, distortion, or reduction of natural appearances, characteristic not only of Cubism, Expressionism, and many other kinds of modern art, but present too in much figurative art in earlier periods (such as Mannerism), which always has its starting-point in objective reality; and (b) the total rejection – in theory, at least – of any dependence on natural appearances. Such works establish their own 'reality' and are intended to appeal in their own right. Only the latter should, strictly speaking, be called 'abstract', but the term is often used imprecisely to cover a wide range of 20th-c art.

abstract expressionism *action painting*

absurdism The expression in art of the meaninglessness of human existence. Originating in France in the early 1950s, it is explored in Camus' *Le Mythe de Sysiphe* (1942, The Myth of Sisyphus), where human efforts are seen as pointless but compulsory. Its potential for comedy and terror has been exploited especially in the theatre (**Theatre of the Absurd**), as in the plays of Ionesco, Beckett, Albee, Stoppard, and Pinter.

Abu-Bakr or **Abu-Bekr** [aboo baker] (c.573–634) The first Muslim caliph, one of the earliest converts to Islam, born in Mecca. He became chief adviser to Mohammed, who married his daughter Aïshah, and on the death of the prophet was elected leader of the Muslim community (632). In his short reign he put down a religious and political revolt, and set in motion the great wave of Arab conquests over Persia, Iraq, and the Middle East. He began the compilation of the Qur'an.

Abu Dhabi or **Abu Zabi** [aboo dabee] pop (2000e) 962 500; area c.67 600 sq km/26 000 sq mi. Largest of the seven member states of the United Arab Emirates; capital Abu Dhabi, pop (2000e) 391 300; main oasis settlement, al-Ayn; vast areas of desert and salt flats; coastline 400 km/250 mi; a major oil region; petrochemical and gas liquefaction industry at Das I; power and desalination complex at Taweelah.

Abuja [aboo ja] 9°05N 7°30E, pop (2000e) 472 000. New capital (from 1991) of Nigeria, in Federal Capital Territory, C Nigeria; planned in 1976, to relieve pressure on the infrastructure of Lagos; under construction at the geographical centre of the country; government offices began moving from Lagos in the 1980s.

abulia A lack of drive or inability to make decisions or to translate decisions into action. The term was considered a cardinal feature of schizophrenia by early psychiatrists, and can be paraphrased as 'the spirit is willing but the energy for action is lacking'.

Abu Mena [aboo mena] A site at Bumma, NW Egypt, sacred to the 3rd-c AD martyr Abu Mena (St Menas). Many miracles were associated with his burial place, which was a centre of pilgrimage for almost 400 years. The ruins of the early 5th-c basilica erected here by Emperor Arcadius are a world heritage site.

abuse of process The unjust or improper use of legal proceedings. In civil law, it includes the bringing of a suit where there is no reasonable prospect of success, or for such reasons as to burden the defendant with an onerous lawsuit. It is also abuse of process to take court proceedings, whether civil or criminal, which are clearly groundless, or doomed to failure. A bankruptcy petition made as a means of extortion or oppression, or a debtor's bankruptcy petition against himself to evade creditors, is an abuse of process. In criminal law, abuse of process covers a wide range of conduct. It most often involves deliberate and sometimes negligent delays in prosecution, so that the defence's chance of a fair trial is significantly prejudiced. When the conduct gives rise to genuine unfairness or prejudice to the preparation or conduct of the defence, a resulting conviction may be overturned.

Abu Simbel [aboo simbel] 22°22N 31°38E. The site of two huge sandstone temples carved by Pharaoh Rameses II (c.1304–1273 BC) out of the Nile bank near Aswan; now a world heritage site. They were dismantled and relocated in the 1960s when the rising waters of the newly-constructed Aswan High Dam threatened their safety.

abyssal hills Low hills which occur on the deep sea floor. Large areas of the Atlantic and Indian Ocean floors and more than three-quarters of the Pacific floor are covered by these hills, no higher than about 1000 m/3000 ft. They tend to occur as series of parallel ridges 1–10 km/½–6 mi across, and represent the rugged topography of mid-ocean ridges subdued by burial beneath thick layers of sediments.

abyssal plains Extremely flat areas of the deep ocean floor which may extend for more than 1000 km/600 mi. They typically have slopes less than 1:1000, and are found off continental margins where sediments can enter the deep sea unobstructed. They are common in the Atlantic and Indian oceans, but rare in the Pacific, where deep trenches and island arcs serve as barriers to the transport of sediment from the continents. Abyssal plains represent thick deposits of primarily land-derived sediments smoothing over more rugged topographic features of the sea floor.

Abyssinia *Ethiopia*

Abyssinian cat A breed of domestic cat, popular in the USA (known as the **foreign short-haired**); reddish-brown, each hair with several dark bands; orange-red nose; two types: **Abyssinian** (**standard Abyssinian** or **ruddy Abyssinian**) and the redder **red Abyssinian**.

acacia *wattle*

Académie Française [akadaymee frõsez] French literary academy founded in 1634 by Cardinal Richelieu for the purpose of maintaining standards of literary taste and to establish the literary language. Its membership is limited to 40 and has included many of the great names of French literature, such as Corneille, Voltaire, Racine, Hugo, Chateaubriand, and Bergson.

academy A place of learning or association formed for scientific, literary, artistic, or musical purposes, the word deriving from the Greek hero *Academus*, who gave his name to the olive grove where Plato taught (387 BC). From the Renaissance the term was applied in Europe to institutions of higher learning (eg the *Accademia della Crusca*, 1587) and advanced teaching (until the term 'university' became widespread in the 18th-c). It was also used to describe societies of distinguished figures and experts in the arts and sciences (eg the *Académie Française*, 1634). Since the 19th-c, the term has been used in many countries for national centres to promote science, literature, and the arts.

Academy of Motion Picture Arts and Sciences An American academy widely known since 1927 for its annual awards for creative merit and craftsmanship in film production, commonly known as the **Oscars**. It has been influential in establishing technical standards. The awards are announced in a widely publicized ceremony in March, and deal with a wide range of categories (*see panel above*), including awards for technical achievement in film science, and special awards to individuals whose contribution to cinema has been preeminent.

Acadia [akaydia] Part of France's American empire; what is today Prince Edward Island, Nova Scotia, and New Brunswick, Canada. The first settlement was established at Port Royal in 1605 by Champlain, and the area was exchanged between France and England until the Treaty of Utrecht (1713) handed most of Acadia to Britain. In 1755, 10 000 Acadians were evicted from the territory by the British for resolving to pursue a policy of neutrality in the conflicts between France and Britain. The last French stronghold, Louisbourg, fell in 1758.

acanthus [akanthuhs] A plant with thick, prickly leaves (*Acanthus spinosus*), stylized representations of which are often used to decorate mouldings or carved parts of a building. It was first used by the Greeks in the 5th-c BC, especially on the capitals of Corinthian columns. In recent centuries it is often found in carved furniture decoration. (Family: Acanthaceae.)

Acapulco [akapulkoh] or **Acapulco de Juárez** 6°51N 99°56W, pop (2000e) 713 000. Port and resort town in Guerrero state, S Mexico; on the Pacific Ocean, 310 km/193 mi SW of Mexico City; airfield; leading Mexican tourist resort ('the Mexican Riviera'); historical town area of Fort San Diego; badly damaged by hurricane Pauline in 1997.

Acari [akariy] *mite*

ACAS [aykas] Acronym for **Advisory, Conciliation and Arbitration Service**, a UK body set up under the Employment Protection Act (1975) under the management of a council appointed by the secretary of state for employment. Its function is to provide facilities for conciliation, arbitration, and mediation in industrial disputes.

acceleration For linear motion, the rate of change of velocity with time; equals force divided by mass; symbol a, units m/s^2; a vector quantity. For rotational motion, the rate of change of angular velocity with time; equals torque divided by moment of inertia; angular acceleration symbol α, units $radians/s^2$; a vector quantity.

acceleration due to gravity The acceleration on an object close to the Earth, due to the Earth's gravitational field; symbol g. Its value is taken as $9{\cdot}806\ 65\ m/s^2$ (standard acceleration of gravity, internationally adopted value), but its actual value varies between 9·76 and 9·83 over the Earth's surface because of geological variations, and decreases with height above sea level.

Academy Award Categories

Best Picture
Best Actor (Leading Role)
Best Actor (Supporting Role)
Best Actress (Leading Role)
Best Actress (Supporting Role)
Best Foreign Language Film
Best Achievement in Animated Short Films
Best Achievement in Art Direction
Best Achievement in Cinematography
Best Achievement in Costume Design
Best Achievement in Directing
Best Achievement in Documentary Features
Best Achievement in Documentary Short Subjects
Best Achievement in Film Editing
Best Achievement in Live Action Short Films
Best Achievement in Makeup
Best Achievement in Music (Original Score)
Best Achievement in Music (Original Song)
Best Achievement in Sound
Best Achievement in Sound Effects Editing
Best Achievement in Visual Effects
Best Screenplay Written Directly for the Screen
Best Screenplay Based on Material Previously Produced or Published

accent 1 The features of pronunciation which mark a speaker's regional background or social class. Accent is to be distinguished from dialect, which involves the study of other linguistic features, such as grammar and vocabulary.
2 The emphasis on a syllable in speech, resulting from a combination of loudness, pitch, and duration. It can be clearly heard in the contrast between the two forms of ***pres**ent* (noun), *pre**sent*** (verb).

accentor A sparrow-like bird native to N Africa, Europe, and Asia; brownish-grey to chestnut above, often streaked; grey beneath; feeds on ground; eats insects in summer, seeds in winter. (Genus: *Prunella*, 12 species. Family: Prunellidae.)

acceptance The act of adding one's signature to a bill of exchange, thus accepting a liability to pay the bill at maturity if the original signatory fails to do so. If the acceptor is of high financial standing, such as a merchant bank, this makes the bill more marketable. The acceptor is taking a risk, and makes a charge for this.

accepting house A merchant bank which 'accepts', ie guarantees, three-month bills of exchange issued by companies. In the UK, the top accepting houses in London form the Accepting Houses Committee.

access course In the UK, a bridging course offered to would-be students not in possession of normal entry requirements which, on successful completion, will permit them to start the course of their choice. It is often provided specifically for students who have been prevented from obtaining formal qualifications, or who have been otherwise disadvantaged.

accessory *accomplice*

access time The length of time required to retrieve information from computer memory or other computer storage media, such as magnetic disks or tapes. Access times from integrated circuit memory are much shorter than those from magnetic disks.

accomplice A person who knowingly, voluntarily, and with a common interest participates with at least one other in committing a crime, either as the person who actually carries out the crime (*principal*), or as *accessory* (or *secondary party*). The accessory is someone who either incites the crime or assists the principal before or after it has been committed.

accordion A portable musical instrument of the reed organ type, fed with air from bellows activated by the player. In the most advanced models a treble keyboard is played with the right hand, while the left operates (usually) six rows of buttons, producing bass notes and chords. The earliest type was patented in Vienna in 1829, since when, despite continuous improvements to its tone and mechanism, it has remained primarily an instrument for popular music, though several major 20th-c composers, including Berg and Prokofiev, have written for it.

accountancy The profession which deals with matters relating to money within an organization. Traditionally its role was that of recording the organization's economic transactions; but it now handles a wide range of activities, including financial planning, management accounting, taxation, and treasury management (managing money), as well as recording and presenting accounts for management, owners, and the tax authorities. The content and form of published accounts are set by company law, stock exchanges, and standards issued by professional accountancy bodies.

Accra [akrah] 5°33N 0°15W, pop (2000e) 1 253 000. Seaport capital of Ghana, on the Gulf of Guinea coast, 415 km/258 mi SW of Lagos; founded as three forts and trading posts, 17th-c; capital of Gold Coast, 1877; capital of Ghana, 1957; airport; railway; university (1948) at Legon 13 km/8 mi W; food processing, fishing, brewing, engineering, scrap metal trade, cacao, gold, timber, fruit, export of zoo animals.

accretion In astronomy, a process in which a celestial body, particularly a star in a binary star system, or a planet, accumulates extraneous matter falling in under gravity often from an orbiting disk. In binary stars this can cause intense X-ray emission.

acculturation A process involving the adoption and acceptance of the ideas, beliefs, and symbols of another society. This may occur by *immigration*, when incoming members of a society adopt its culture, or by *emulation*, when one society takes on cultural features from another, such as happened in colonial contexts.

accumulator A device to store electricity, by accepting a charge and later releasing it; also called a **battery**. It is a lead–acid system, with plates of lead oxides and an electrolyte of sulphuric acid. Each cell produces 2 volts of direct current. Accumulators are widely used to start car engines, and also to propel electric vehicles such as milk floats. Other systems include nickel-iron (*Nife*) and nickel-cadmium (*Nicad*) plates, with alkaline electrolytes, producing 1·5 volts per cell. Some are made in small sizes, to replace torch and other batteries with rechargeable versions.

accusatorial system *prosecution*

acetaldehyde [asitaldihyd] CH_3CHO, IUPAC **ethanal**, boiling point 21°C. The product of gentle oxidation of ethanol, intermediate in the formation of acetic acid; a colourless liquid with a sharp odour. A reducing agent, the compound is actually the one detected in the 'breathalyzer' test.

acetals [asitlz] Substances of the general structure $R_2C(OR)_2$, formed by the reaction of an alcohol with an aldehyde, water also being formed. Internal acetal formation gives most sugars ring structures.

acetate film *safety film*

acetic acid [aseetik] CH_3COOH, IUPAC **ethanoic acid**, boiling point 118°C. The product of oxidation of ethanol. The pure substance is a viscous liquid with a strong odour. Its aqueous solutions are weakly acidic; partially neutralized solutions have a pH of about 5. Vinegar is essentially a 5% aqueous solution of acetic acid.

acetone [asitohn] CH_3COCH_3, IUPAC **propanone**, boiling point 56°C. A volatile liquid with an odour resembling ethers. It is a very widely used solvent, especially for plastics and lacquers.

acetyl [asitiyl] CH_3CO–, IUPAC **ethanoyl**. A functional group in chemistry, whose addition to a name usually indicates its substitution for hydrogen in a compound.

acetylcholine [asitiylkohleen] An acetyl ester of choline ($C_7H_{16}NO_2^+$) which functions as a neurotransmitter in most animals with nervous systems. In mammals it is present in the brain, spinal cord, and ganglia of the autonomic nervous system, as well as the terminals of motor neurones (which control skeletal muscle fibres) and the post-ganglionic fibres of the parasympathetic nervous system.

acetylene [asetileen] $HC\equiv CH$, IUPAC **ethyne**, boiling point −84°C. The simplest alkyne, a colourless gas formed by the action of water on calcium carbide. It is an important starting material in organic synthesis, and is used as a fuel, especially (mixed with oxygen) in the oxyacetylene torch.

Achaeans [akeeanz] **1** The archaic name for the Greeks, found frequently in Homer.
2 In classical Greece, the inhabitants of Achaea, the territory to the S of the Corinthian Gulf.

Achaemenids [akiymenidz] The first royal house of Persia, founded by the early 7th-c BC ruler, Achaemenes. Its capitals included Parsagadae, Susa, and Persepolis.

Achebe, Chinua [achaybay], originally **Albert Chinualumogo** (1930–) Novelist, born in Ogidi, W Nigeria. He studied at the University College of Ibadan, and his early career was in broadcasting. He was in Biafran government service during the Nigerian Civil War (1967–70), and then taught at US and Nigerian universities. His first novel, *Things Fall Apart* (1958), presenting an unsentimentalized picture of the Ibo tribe, was heralded as a fresh voice in African literature, and has since been translated into over 40 languages. Writing exclusively in English, his other novels include *Arrow of God* (1964), *Anthills of the Savanna* (1987), which was short-listed for the Booker Prize, and *A Tribute to James Baldwin* (1989). He has also written short stories, poetry, and children's books. His poetry includes *Beware, Soul Brother* (1971) on his experiences during the War. *Another Africa* appeared in 1998.

Achelous, River [akelohus], Gr **Akhelóös** Second longest river of Greece; rises in the Pindus Mts, flows S through mountain gorges to the fertile Agrinion plain and enters the Ionian Sea opposite Cephalonia I; length 220 km/137 mi.

Achenbach, Andreas [akhenbakh] (1815–1910) Landscape and marine painter, born in Kassel, C Germany. He studied at St Petersburg, then travelled extensively in Holland, Scandinavia, and Italy, where he produced many water-colours. His paintings of the North Sea coasts of Europe had considerable influence in Germany, and he came to be regarded as the father of 19th-c German landscape painting.

achene [akeen] A dry fruit, not splitting to release the single seed. It is usually small, often bearing hooks, spines, or other structures which aid in dispersal.

Achernar [akerna(r)] *Eridanus*

Acheron [akeron] In Greek mythology, the chasm or abyss of the Underworld, and the name of one of the rivers there which the souls of the dead have to cross. It is also the name of a river in Epirus, which disappeared underground, and was thought to be an entrance to Hades.

Acheson, Dean (Gooderham) [achesn] (1893–1971) US statesman and lawyer, born in Middletown, Connecticut, USA. He studied at Yale and Harvard, and joined the Department of State in 1941, where he was under-secretary (1945–7) and secretary of state in the Truman administration (1949–53). He formulated the Truman Doctrine (1947), helped determine the Marshall Plan (1947), and promoted the formation of NATO (1949). His book *Present at the Creation* (1969) was awarded the Pulitzer Prize.

Acheulian [ashoolian] In Europe, Africa, and Asia, a broad term for early prehistoric cultures using symmetrically-flaked stone handaxes. These first appear in E Africa (eg at Koobi Fora, Kenya) c.1·5 million years ago, but were still being made c.150 000 BC. In Europe they are characteristic of N France/England during the Lower Palaeolithic Age, c.300 000–200 000 BC. The name derives from finds made c.1850 at Saint-Acheul, a suburb of Amiens in the Somme Valley, N France.

Achilles [akileez] A legendary Greek hero, son of Peleus and Thetis, who dipped him in the R Styx so that he was invulnerable, except for the heel where she had held him. When the Trojan War began, his mother hid him among girls on Scyros, but he was detected by Odysseus and so went to Troy. The whole story of the *Iliad* turns on his excessive pride; in his anger he sulks in his tent. When his friend Patroclus is killed, he rejoins the battle, kills Hector, brutally mistreats his body, but finally allows Priam to recover it. He was killed by Paris, who shot him in the heel with a poisoned arrow.

achondroplasia [aykondroplayzhuh] An inherited form of dwarfism, in which growth of the limb bones is disproportionately shortened. There is a characteristic bulging of the forehead, and a saddle nose. Circus dwarfs are commonly achondroplastic.

acid Usually, a substance reacting with metals to liberate hydrogen gas, or dissolving in water with dissociation and the formation of hydrogen ions. Acids are classed as strong or weak depending on the extent to which this dissociation occurs. More general concepts of acidity are that an acid is a proton donor or an electron pair acceptor. Strong acids are corrosive.

acidic oxides *oxides*

acid rain A term first used in the 19th-c to describe polluted rain in Manchester, England. Colloquially it is used for polluted rainfall associated with the burning of fossil fuels. Acid pollution can be wet (rain, snow, mist) or dry (gases, particles). A number of gases are involved, particularly sulphur dioxide (SO_2) and oxides of nitrogen (NO). Reactions in the atmosphere lead to the production of sulphuric acid (H_2SO_4) and nitric acid (HNO_3). In Europe c.85% of SO_2 in the air comes from the burning of fossil fuels; chemical plants which remove the sulphurous emissions are being fitted to some power stations. The main emissions of oxides of nitrogen, including (NO) and (NO_2), are from fossil-fuel power generation and the internal combustion engine. Acid rain is implicated in damage to forests and the acidification of soils and lakes. In 1985, 19 countries formed the 'Thirty Percent Club', agreeing to lower their emissions of SO_2 by 30% by 1993, using 1980 emissions as the baseline. European Community states also agreed to reduce emissions of SO_2 by 20% of 1980 levels by 1993, with further reductions of 40% by 1998 and 60% by 2003. The Commission on Long-Range Transboundary Air Pollution also aims to reduce emissions of NO but, like emissions of SO_2, these are the subject of international debate.

acne [aknee] A chronic inflammation of the sebaceous glands in the skin (which secrete a fatty product known as *sebum*), notably affecting the face, upper chest, and back. It is particularly found in adolescents.

Aconcagua, Cerro [akonkagwa] 32°39S 70°01W. Mountain rising to 6960 m/22 834 ft in Mendoza province, W Argentina; in the Andes, E of the Chilean border; 112 km/70 mi NW of Mendoza; the highest peak in the W hemisphere; Uspallata Pass at its S foot; first climbed in 1897 by the Fitzgerald expedition.

aconite *monkshood; winter aconite*

acorn The fruit of the oak tree, actually a specialized nut borne in a cup-shaped structure, the cupule.

acornworm A worm-like, marine invertebrate, length up to 2·5 m/8¼ ft; body soft, divided into a proboscis, collar, and trunk; gill slits supported by skeletal rods; c.70 species, found in soft intertidal and subtidal sediments. (Phylum: Hemichordata. Class: Enteropneusta.)

Acosta, Carlos (1973–) Ballet dancer and choreographer, born near Havana, Cuba. At age nine his father enrolled him in the National Ballet School in Havana. He earned a student placement with the Turin Ballet in Italy (1990), and he went on to win a number of competitions, including the prestigious Prix de Lausanne. After brief spells with the English National Ballet (1991) and the National Ballet of Cuba, he performed to great acclaim with the Houston Ballet. In 1998 he joined the Royal Ballet, where he became guest principal (from 2000). His choreographic debut, *Tocororo – A Cuban Tale*, was performed in 2003.

acouchi [akooshee] A cavy-like rodent; inhabits Amazonian forests; eats plants; resembles a small agouti, but with a longer tail (white, used for signalling). (Genus: *Myoprocta*, 2 species. Family: Dasyproctidae.)

acoustics The study of sound: the production, detection, and propagation of sound waves, and the absorption and reflection of sound. It includes the study of how electrical signals are converted into mechanical signals, as in loudspeakers, and the converse, as in microphones; also, how sound is produced in musical instruments, and perceived by audiences in concert halls; the protection of workers from damaging levels of sound; and the use of detection techniques, such as sonar and ultrasonic scanning.

ACP countries An acronym for a grouping of c.70 developing countries from **Africa, the Caribbean, and the Pacific**. It was established in the 1970s to facilitate the making of agreements with the European Union on economic assistance and trade.

Acre, Hebrew **Akko**, ancient **Ptolemais** 32°55N 35°04E, pop (2000e) 53 000. Ancient town in Northern district, NW Israel; resort centre on the Mediterranean Sea; capital of the Crusader kingdom after capture of Jerusalem in 1187; railway; ancient and modern harbour; fishing, light industry; crypt of the Knights Hospitallers of St John, 18th-c city walls, 18th-c mosque.

acridine [akrideen] $C_{13}H_9N$, melting point 111°C. A coal-tar base structurally related to anthracene. An important class of dyestuffs is derived from it.

acromegaly [akrohmegalee] An adult disorder which arises from the over-secretion of growth hormone by the pituitary gland, usually due to a tumour. There is enlargement of many tissues, with coarsening and thickening of the subcutaneous tissues and the skin, and enlargement of the skull, jaw, hands, and feet.

acronym A word formed from the initial letters of the words it represents, as in *NATO* (=*North Atlantic Treaty Organization*), especially one which can be pronounced as a word. Some authorities distinguish acronyms from **initialisms** (eg *BBC*) which have to be pronounced letter by letter. Both should be distinguished from an **acrostic** – a composition, usually a poem, in which typically the initial letters of the lines make up words. The pattern may also make use of letters from other parts of the lines or combinations of letters (such as the first and last), to produce a wide variety of puzzles and riddles.

Acropolis, The [akropolis] The citadel of ancient Athens. Rising high above the city, the fortified outcrop contained the national treasury and many sacred sites and shrines, most of them (such as the Parthenon and the Erechtheum) associated with the worship of Athene, the patron goddess of Athens. The present ruins date mainly from the second half of the 5th-c BC. The term *acropolis* in its general sense is not restricted to Athens, but applies to any such citadel in ancient Greece.

acrostic *acronym*

acrylic acid [akrilik] CH_2=CH.COOH, IUPAC **prop-2-enoic acid**. The simplest unsaturated carboxylic acid. Its nitrile, CH_2=CH.C≡N, is the monomer of a range of polymers used as fibres and paints. Its methyl ester and the related CH_2=C(CH_3)–$COOCH_3$, **methylmethacrylate**, form other polymers used in paints, adhesives, and safety glass.

acrylic painting An art form using plastic paints, ie colours mixed with a vehicle made from a polymethyl methacrylate solution in mineral spirits; they are quick-drying, with better stability claimed than either oils or watercolours. However, several of the works produced by young painters using this medium in the 1960s have not lasted well, and are now a source of worry to their owners – including many public galleries.

Actaeon [akteeon] A hunter in Greek mythology, whose story epitomizes the fate of a mortal who encounters a god. He came upon Artemis, the goddess of chastity, while she was bathing and therefore naked: she threw water at him, changing him into a stag, so that he was pursued and then killed by his own hounds.

actinides [ak**tin**iydz] Elements with an atomic number between 89 and 104 in which an inner electron shell is filling, the best known being uranium (92) and plutonium (94). Those heavier than uranium are known as the *transuranic elements*. All of their isotopes are radioactive, and most are artificially made. They are chemically similar to lanthanides.

actinomorphic flower A flower which is radially symmetrical or of regular shape so that, if cut through the middle in any plane, each half is identical.

actinomycete [aktinohmiy**seet**] A typically filamentous bacterium. Most have branching filaments, forming a fungal-like network, and require the presence of oxygen for growth. They are usually found in soil and decaying vegetation, feeding as saprophytes. Some species are disease-causing in plants and animals, including the causative agents of tuberculosis and potato scab. (Kingdom: Monera. Order: Actinomycetales.)

actinomycosis [aktinohmiy**koh**sis] A disorder caused by infection with *Actinomyces israeli*. Chronic abscesses are formed in many tissues, notably in and around the face and neck, where they discharge onto the skin. The filaments of the micro-organism form yellow granular masses in the abscesses (*sulphur granules*), which can be seen with the aid of a microscope.

action In mechanics, the difference between kinetic energy K and potential energy V ($K-V$), summed over time; symbol I or S, units J.s (joule.second). Formally, action is the sum over time of the lagrangian. It is crucial to the least-action formulation of mechanics, and to the path-integral formulation of quantum theory.

action painting A form of abstract art which flourished in the USA from the late 1940s, its leading exponent being Jackson Pollock. The snappy term was introduced by the critic Harold Rosenberg in 1952 in preference to the more cumbersome *abstract expressionism*, though the latter has not gone out of use. Many US art historians, for example, consider action painting to be a genre within abstract expressionism. The physical act of applying paint to canvas is emphasized, rather than the picture as a finished artefact; so the paint is thrown or dribbled onto the canvas which may be tacked to the floor. Persons may roll naked or ride bicycles across the wet surface. In France, a similar movement was called *Tachisme* (*tache*, 'blot, mark').

action potential A brief electrical signal transmitted along a nerve or muscle fibre following stimulation. At the site of the action potential, the inside of the fibre temporarily becomes positively charged with respect to the outside, because of a transient change in the permeability of the fibre's plasma membrane to sodium and potassium ions (ie sodium flows in and later potassium flows out of the fibre). It provides the basis for the transmission of information.

actions, limitation of *limitation of actions*

Actium, Battle of [**ak**tium] (31 BC) The decisive victory of Octavian (later the Emperor Augustus) over the forces of Antony and Cleopatra off the coast of NW Greece. It traditionally marks the end of the Roman Republic and the beginning of the Roman Empire.

activated charcoal Wood, carbonized by heating in limited air and treated with acid to make it adsorb large quantities of gases and polymeric materials from solution. It is used in gas masks, unducted cooker hoods, and vacuum technology, and for decolourizing solutions.

activated complex The arrangement of atoms during a chemical reaction involving two or more reacting molecules which is unstable, and which decomposes either to regenerate starting material or to form products.

active galaxy *galaxy*

activity (physics) *radioactivity units*

Act of Congress A bill sanctioned by the US legislature, consisting of the two houses of Congress: the House of Representatives and the Senate. The bill must then be signed by the president to become law.

act of God In law, any natural phenomenon such as an earthquake, hurricane, or flood which, without human intervention, exclusively and directly causes an accident or injury; known in Scots law as a *damnum fatale*. An exceptionally severe gust of wind which directly causes a car to veer off the road constitutes an act of God. Heavy rain or fog to which drivers do not respond appropriately, with the result that their negligence leads to an accident, is not an act of God. The climatic conditions would have to be sufficiently exceptional for the defendant not to have reasonably been expected to anticipate or forsee them.

Act of Parliament A bill which has passed five stages (first reading, second reading, committee stage, report stage, third reading) in both houses of the UK parliament, and received the royal assent. The same kind of procedure applies in other parliamentary systems, although the specific stages through which a bill passes may vary.

Actors' Studio A workshop for professional actors founded in New York City, USA by Elia Kazan, Cheryl Crawford, and Robert Lewis in 1947. Under Lee Strasberg, it was the major centre for US acting – not a school, but a laboratory where trained actors could work on inner resources free from the pressures of a production. His students included Anne Bancroft, Sidney Poitier, Marlon Brando, and Dustin Hoffman. After Strasberg's death, Ellen Burstyn and Al Pacino became artistic co-directors, with Paul Newman as president of the Board of Directors.

Acts of the Apostles A New Testament book, the second part of a narrative begun in Luke's Gospel, which traces the early progress of Jesus's followers in spreading the Christian faith. It begins with the resurrection and ascension of Jesus, but concentrates largely upon the growth of the Jerusalem Church, its spread to Samaria and Antioch, and the missionary journeys of Paul to Asia Minor, the Aegean lands, and Rome.

actual bodily harm *bodily harm*

actuary A statistician specializing in life expectancy, sickness, retirement, and accident matters. Actuaries are employed by insurance companies, pension funds, and the government to calculate probability and risk. They advise on the premiums needed to provide pensions and to cover risks of various types.

actuator A mechanical or electrical device used to bring other equipment into operation; sometimes called a **servomotor**. It commonly refers to the equipment used for the automatic operation of brake valves in car or train brake systems.

acuity [a**kyoo**itee] Acuteness of perception, especially of vision or hearing; the smallest visual features (usually measured in terms of angular size in the retinal image) that can be seen, or auditory difference that can be heard. The bars of a fine grating can just be resolved when the spacing of the bars in the image is approximately equal to the diameter of a single retinal receptor (about a 500th of a millimetre).

acupressure A system of treatment said to be the forerunner of acupuncture. It involves the application of pressure using thumb and fingers, but sometimes also the palms, knees, elbows, and feet, to stimulate acupuncture points and meridians. Practitioners may have a background in martial arts such as tai chi chuan, and the healing aspects of these arts include acupressure techniques together with dietary advice and remedial exercises.

acupuncture (Lat *acus* 'needle' + *punctura* 'piercing') A medical practice known in China for over 3000 years, which has come to attract attention in the West. It consists of the insertion into the skin and underlying tissues of fine needles, usually made of steel, and of varying lengths according to the depth of the target point. The site of insertion of each needle is selected according to the points and meridians related to the tissue or organ believed to be disordered, and several hundred specific points have been identified. Areas which are painful on pressure may also be selected ('trigger point' acupuncture).

Studies are now in progress to establish which disorders benefit from acupuncture, but neuralgia, migraine, sprains, and asthma are claimed to respond, while infectious disease and tumours are unlikely to do so. It is also employed as an analgesic during surgery in the Far East, where skills in local or general anaesthesia are often not easily available. Today, acupuncture is used widely among the general population in China; equipment can be purchased in shops, and used in the way simple pain killers are employed in the West. The efficacy of the method is now being subjected to statistically-controlled trials, but accounts of successes remain anecdotal. Its mechanism of action is also unknown. In the terms of Chinese philosophy it is believed to restore the balance of the contrasting principles of *yin* and *yang*, and the flow of *Qi* in hypothetical channels of the body (*meridians*). Research has shown that brain tissue contains morphine-like substances called *endorphins*, which may be released in increased amounts when deep sensory nerves are stimulated by injury near the body surfaces. A possible mode of action therefore is that these substances are released by acupuncture, and some degree of tranquillity and analgesia is induced.

acyl [asiyl] IUPAC **alkanoyl**. In chemistry, the general name for an organic functional group R.CO–, where R represents H or an alkyl group.

ADA A computer programming language developed for the US Department of Defense which permits the development of very large computer systems, and can cope with complex real-time applications. It was named after Augusta Ada King, Countess of Lovelace, daughter of Lord Byron, who worked with Charles Babbage.

Adad [aydad] The Mesopotamian god of storms, known throughout the area of Babylonian influence; the Syrians called him Hadad, and in the Bible he is Rimmon, the god of thunder. He helped to cause the Great Flood in *Gilgamesh*. His symbol was the lightning held in his hand; his animal was the bull.

Adair, Red [adair], popular name of **Paul Adair** (1915–) Fire-fighting specialist, born in Houston, TX. He is called in as a troubleshooter to deal with major oil fires. In 1984 he and his team put out a major fire on an offshore rig near Rio de Janeiro, and in 1988 they were the first men to board the Piper Alpha oil rig in the North Sea after it was destroyed by an explosion. He was in the public eye again helping to deal with the fires in Kuwait following Operation Desert Storm. He is the subject of a film, *Hellfighter* (1968), starring John Wayne.

Adalbert, St [adalbert], known as **the Apostle of the Prussians** (956–97) Missionary priest, born in Bohemia. In 982 he was appointed the first native Bishop of Prague, but the hostility of the corrupt clergy obliged him to withdraw to Rome in 990. He then took the Gospel to the Hungarians, the Poles, and finally the Prussians, who murdered him. He was canonized in 999; feast day 23 April.

Adam, Adolphe (Charles) [adã] (1803–56) Composer, born in Paris, France. The son of the pianist **Louis Adam** (1758–1848), he wrote some successful operas, such as *Le Postillon de Longjumeau* (1835), but is chiefly remembered for the ballet *Giselle* (1841).

Adam, Robert (1728–92) Architect, born in Kirkcaldy, Fife, E Scotland, UK. He studied at Edinburgh and in Italy (1754–8), and became architect of the king's works (1761–9), jointly with Sir William Chambers. He established a practice in London in 1758, and during the next 40 years he and his brother **James Adam** (1730–94), succeeded in transforming the prevailing Palladian fashion in architecture by a series of romantically elegant variations on diverse classical originals. One of their greatest projects was the Adelphi (demolished 1936), off the Strand, London. Good surviving examples of their work are Home House in London's Portland Square, and Register House in Edinburgh. They also designed furniture and fittings to suit the houses they planned and decorated, strongly influenced by Chinese motifs in wallpapers, carpets, and furniture.

Adam and Eve Biblical characters described in the Book of Genesis as the first man and woman created by God. Adam was formed from the dust of the ground and God's breath or spirit; Eve was made from Adam's rib. Biblical traditions describe their life in the garden of Eden, their disobedience and banishment, and the birth of their sons Cain, Abel, and Seth. Their fall into sin is portrayed as a temptation by the serpent (the Devil) to disobey God's command not to eat the fruit of the tree of the knowledge of good and evil. Many further traditions emerged in later Jewish and Christian writings.

Adamnan, St [adamnan] (c.625–704) Monk, born in Co Donegal, N Ireland. At 28 he joined the Columbian brotherhood of Iona, and was chosen abbot in 679. He came to support the Roman views on the dating of Easter and the shape of tonsure. His works include the *Vita Sancti Columbae* (Life of St Columba), which reveals much about the Iona community. Feast day 23 September.

Adamov, Arthur [adahmof] (1908–70) Playwright, born in Kislovodsk, SW Russia. His family lost their fortune in 1917, and moved to France, where he was educated and met Surrealist artists. His early absurdist plays *L'Invasion* (1950, The Invasion) and *Le Professeur Taranne* (1953) present the dislocations and cruelties of a meaningless world. *Ping-Pong* (1955) sees humanity reduced to mechanism. Later plays, such as *Paolo Paoli* (1957) and *La Politique des restes* (1967, trans The Politics of Waste), show a transition to commitment.

Adams, Abigail, *née* **Smith** (1744–1818) Letter writer, born in Weymouth, Massachusetts, USA. In 1764 she married John Adams, who worked away from home, which prompted her to become a prolific letter writer. Her correspondence became highly valued as a contemporary source of social history and comment during the early days of the republic. Her husband became second president of the USA (1797–1801), and she was the first lady of the newly built White House. Their son, John Quincy Adams, became the sixth president of the USA.

Adams, Ansel (Easton) (1902–84) Photographer, born in San Francisco, California, USA. His work is notable for his broad landscapes of W USA, especially the Yosemite in the 1930s. He was one of the founders with Edward Weston of the f/64 Group (1932), and helped to set up the department of photography at the Museum of Modern Art in New York City (1940). He was a prolific writer and lecturer, always stressing the importance of image quality at every stage of a photographer's work.

Adams, Douglas (Noel) (1952–2001) Writer, born in Cambridge, Cambridgeshire, EC England, UK. He studied at Cambridge, then worked as a writer, producing material for radio and television shows, and also for stage revues. He is known for his humorous science fiction novels, especially *The Hitch-hiker's Guide to the Galaxy* (1979, originally a radio series, 1978, 1980, later televised). Later works include *The Meaning of Liff* (1984, with John Lloyd), *Mostly Harmless* (1992), *The Illustrated Hitch-hiker's Guide to the Galaxy* (1994), *The Hitch-hiker's Guide to the Galaxy: the Primary Phase* (1996), and *The Hitch-hiker's Guide to the Galaxy: the Secondary Phase* (1996). *The Salmon of Doubt*, a collection of unpublished pieces and fragments of an unfinished novel, was published posthumously in 2002.

Adams, Gerry, popular name of **Gerald Adams** (1948–) Northern Ireland politician, born in Belfast, NE Northern Ireland, UK. He joined Sinn Féin, and during the 1970s was interned because of his connections with the IRA. In 1978 he became vice-president of Sinn Féin and later its president. Elected to the Northern Ireland Assembly in 1982, the following year he was also elected to the UK parliament as member for Belfast West (to 1992), but he declined to take up his seat at Westminster. He achieved national prominence as the chief contact with the IRA during the events relating to the IRA ceasefire (1994–6), and regained his seat in the 1997 and 2001 general elections. In 1998 he was elected to the newly formed Northern Ireland Assembly and was a key actor in the implementation of the Good Friday Agreement which led to the transfer of power from London to Belfast in 1999.

Adams, John (1735–1826) US statesman and second president (1797–1801), born in Braintree (now Quincy), Massachusetts,

USA. The son of a farmer, he distinguished himself at Harvard, and was admitted to the bar in 1758. Of strongly colonial sympathies, he led the protest against the Stamp Act (1765), and in 1774 was sent as a delegate to the Continental Congresses. He proposed the election of Washington as commander-in-chief, and was 'the colossus of the debate' on the Declaration of Independence. He retired from Congress in 1777, only to be sent to France and Holland as commissioner from the new republic, and in 1785–8 was minister to England. After eight years as vice-president under Washington (1789–97), he became president in 1797 but his regime was torn by partisan wrangles between Federalists and Democrat-Republicans. Defeated on seeking re-election in 1800, he retired to his home at Quincy.

Adams, John Couch (1819–92) Astronomer, born in Laneast, Cornwall, SW England, UK. He studied at St John's College, Cambridge, and in 1843 became fellow and mathematical tutor there. In 1845 he deduced mathematically the existence and location of the planet Neptune, his prediction occurring almost simultaneously with that of the French astronomer, Leverrier. Adams was appointed professor of astronomy at Cambridge in 1858, and was director of the Cambridge Observatory from 1861.

Adams, John Quincy (1767–1848) US statesman and sixth president (1825–9), born in Quincy, Massachusetts, USA, the son of John and Abigail Adams. He studied at Harvard, and was admitted to the bar in 1790. Successively minister to The Hague, London, Lisbon, and Berlin, he was elected to the US Senate from Massachusetts (1803–6). In 1809 he became minister to St Petersburg, and from 1815 to 1817 was minister at the court of St James. As secretary of state under President Monroe, he negotiated with Spain the treaty for the acquisition of Florida (1819), and was alleged to be the real author of the Monroe Doctrine (1823). He became president in 1825, but failed to win a second term, and was elected to the House of Representatives, where he became noted as a promoter of anti-slavery views.

Adams, Richard (George) (1920–) Novelist, born in Berkshire, S England, UK. He studied at Oxford, and after wartime service in the army worked as a civil servant in the Department of the Environment (1948–74). He made his name as a writer with the best selling *Watership Down* (1972), an epic tale of a community of rabbits. Later books include *Shardik* (1974), *The Plague Dogs* (1977), *The Iron Wolf* (1980), *The Bureaucrats* (1985), *Traveller* (1988), and *Tales from Watership Down* (1996). His autobiography *The Day Gone By* appeared in 1990.

Adams, Samuel (1722–1803) American revolutionary politician, born in Boston, Massachusetts, USA, second cousin to President John Adams. He studied at Harvard, became a tax collector, and was elected a member of the Massachusetts legislature (1765–74). He organized opposition to the Stamp Act in 1765, and was the chief agitator at the Boston Tea Party in 1773. A delegate to the first and second Continental Congress (1774–5), he signed the Declaration of Independence in 1776. He was lieutenant-governor of Massachusetts (1789–94), then governor (1794–7).

Adams, Tony (1966–) Footballer, born in Romford, Essex, SE England, UK. He played for Arsenal's youth team before joining the club as a centre back in 1983, eventually becoming team captain. He was the Professional Footballers' Association Young Player of the Year in 1987. He captained England in 1994, 1995, and during the European Cup in 1996, and had won 66 caps by the time he announced his retirement from international football in 2000. Persistent injuries led to a decision to retire from the game at the end of the 2001–2 season. In 2003 he became manager of second division side Wycombe.

Adams, Will(iam) (1564–1620) Navigator, born in Gillingham, Kent, SE England, UK. He took service with the Dutch in 1598, and reached Japan in 1600. The first Englishman to visit Japan, he was cast into prison as a pirate at the instigation of jealous Portuguese traders, but was freed after building two fine ships for Shogun Ieyasu, receiving a pension, the rank of samurai, and 'living like unto a lordship in England' (1600–20).

Adams–Stokes attacks Brief sudden periods of unconsciousness (*syncope*) resulting from a transient cessation of the action of the heart (*asystole*) or a disorder of rhythm, such as ventricular fibrillation. The patient is pulseless, and extremely pale. Recovery is attended by flushing of the face. Complications include convulsions and sudden death. The syndrome is named after physician William Stokes and surgeon Robert Adams, working in Dublin in the 19th-c.

Adam's needle A species of yucca (*Yucca gloriosa*) native to SE USA with short, woody trunk, stiff erect leaves, and numerous white bell-shaped flowers; commonly grown in gardens. (Family: Agavaceae.)

Adamson, Joy (Friedericke Victoria), *née* **Gessner** (1910–80) Naturalist and writer, born in Austria. Living in Kenya with her third husband, British game warden **George Adamson** (1906–89), she studied and painted wildlife, and made her name with a series of books about the lioness Elsa: *Born Free* (1960), *Elsa* (1961), *Forever Free* (1962), and *Elsa and Her Cubs* (1965). She was murdered in her home by tribesmen.

Adam's Peak, Sinhala **Sri Pada** 6°49N 80°30E. Sacred mountain in Sri Lanka, rising to 2243 m/7359 ft NE of Ratnapura; pilgrimages are made (Dec–Apr) to the foot-shaped hollow found on the mountain's summit, believed to be the footprint of Buddha by Buddhists, of Adam by Muslims, of the god Siva by Hindus, and of St Thomas the Apostle by some Christians.

Adan *Aden*

Adana [adana] 37°00N 35°19E, pop (2000e) 1 103 000. Commercial capital of Adana province, S Turkey, on R Seyhan; fourth largest city in Turkey; railway; airfield; university (1973); centre of a fertile agricultural region.

adaptation (biology) The process of adjustment of an individual organism to environmental conditions. It may occur by natural selection, resulting in improved survival and reproductive success, or involve physiological or behavioural changes that are not genetic. As well as being a process, an adaptation can also be the end product of such a process, ie any structural, behavioural, or physiological character that enhances survival or reproductive success.

adaptation (literature) The process of taking a work of art from one medium and interpreting it in terms of another. The process can be seen in many domains: in the illustration of scenes from classical epic, mythology, and the Bible through the use of painting, statuary, and stained glass; in the dramatization of sacred texts (eg the mediaeval miracle and mystery plays) and historical records (eg 'history plays'); and in prose versions of plays themselves (eg Lamb's *Tales from Shakespeare*). With modern communications technology, adaptation has become a major source of cultural recycling. Film and television (united via the video cassette) are particularly voracious, but radio and audio tapes also reprocess much written material. Shakespeare's plays have been imaged on film, voiced for radio, reduced for television, and even abstracted in cartoon versions (*The Animated Tales*, 1992). Under the repressive regimes of Stalinist Russia and its satellite nations, the plays of Shakespeare, notably *Hamlet*, were adapted to reflect contemporary malaise, and as such became seen as a vehicle for subversiveness. The novels of Dickens have been a magnetic subject for film-makers, with David Lean's *Great Expectations* (1946) a classic example. Epics such as *Ben Hur* and *Quo Vadis?* were soon exploited by the cinema, where biblical subjects have always exerted a fascination – as have the sacred texts of other cultures in their own film industries (the Bombay 'theologicals'). Hollywood became known as 'the writer's graveyard' (Fitzgerald), but adaptation thrived, and the Western proved to be a favourite subject. Meanwhile the relative intimacy of TV has offered scaled-down possibilities. The domestic drama of Chekov, Ibsen, and Shaw has transferred successfully to the small screen, as have the novels of Jane Austen, George Eliot, and Trollope. The adaptation process works both ways, as fictions may also bear the impress of cinematic technique (eg James Joyce, Graham Greene, Salman Rushdie).

adaptive optics The continual adjustment of optical components to counter the effects of distortions introduced during the passage of light from object to imaging device. The field is especially important in astronomy, where adaptive optical techniques allow most distortion due to atmospheric turbulence to be removed, improving the resolution of ground-based optical telescopes by about ten times. Adaptive optical systems have been installed on a number of telescopes, including the William Herschel, La Palma, and the Canada/France/Hawaii Telescope on Mauna Kea, Hawaii.

adaptive radiation A burst of evolution in which a single ancestral type diverges to fill a number of different ecological roles or modes of life, usually over a relatively short period of time, resulting in the appearance of a variety of new forms. This phenomenon may occur after the colonization of a new habitat, such as the radiation of Darwin's finches in the Galápagos Is.

adaptive suspension A pneumatic or hydro-pneumatic suspension system fitted to a motor car or a commercial vehicle that damps out the variations in road surface, and maintains the vehicle at a constant level while in use. This levelling device can be controlled electronically, allowing the suspension system to adapt itself automatically to the road surface conditions and the speed of travel.

adaptogen A substance which maintains or stimulates the body's mechanisms for adapting to change in both the internal and external environment. Health and survival depends upon keeping a physiological balance even in the presence of adverse factors such as infectious organisms, toxins, and radiation. Herbs such as *Eleutherococcus senticosus* are used as general adaptogens, but the term is also applied to more specific adaptors of self-regulation, such as immune stimulants.

Adcock, (Kareen) Fleur (1934–) Poet, born in Papakura, New Zealand. She studied at Victoria University, Wellington, taught at the University of Otago, then held various library posts in New Zealand and the UK, where she has lived since 1963. She published her first collection, *The Eye of the Hurricane*, in 1964. Her poetry is notable for its unsentimental treatment of personal and family relationships, its psychological insights, and its interest in classical themes. She has also edited *The Oxford Book of Contemporary New Zealand Poetry* (1983) and *The Faber Book of Twentieth Century Women's Poetry* (1987), and co-edited *The Oxford Book of Creatures* (1995).

ADD *attention*

Addams, Charles Samuel (1912–88) Cartoonist, born in Westfield, New Jersey, USA. He was a regular contributor to *The New Yorker* from 1935 onwards, specializing in macabre humour and a ghoulish group which was immortalized on television in the 1960s as *The Addams Family*.

Addams, Jane (1860–1935) Social reformer and feminist, born in Cedarville, Illinois, USA. After visiting Toynbee Hall in London she founded in 1889 the social settlement in Hull House, Chicago, which she led for the rest of her life. In 1910 she became the first woman president of the National Conference of Social Work, and in 1911 founded the National Federation of Settlements (president, 1911–35). A committed pacifist and worker for female suffrage, she was president of the Women's International League for Peace and Freedom (1919–35), and shared the Nobel Peace Prize in 1931.

Addams, Vicki *Spice Girls, The*

addax [adaks] A horse-like antelope (*Addax nasomaculatus*) native to N African deserts; resembles the oryx, but has thicker, spiralling horns; pale with clump of brown hair on the forehead; never drinks; lives in herds.

adder A venomous snake of the family Viperidae; three species: *Vipera berus* (**European adder** or **common European viper**, the only venomous British snake) and the puff adders; also Australian **death adders** of family Elapidae (2 species). The name is used in place of 'viper' for some other species, such as the **horned adder/viper** and **saw-scaled adder/viper**.

Adderley, Cannonball, popular name of **Julian Edwin Adderley** (1928–75) Jazz saxophonist and composer, born in Tampa, Florida, USA. Born into a musical family, he directed the local high school band (1948–56) and US army bands (1950–3), then in 1956 formed a combo with his brother Nat (1932–2000), which was soon widely acclaimed. His many recordings include the album *Kind of Blue* (1958–9) with the Miles Davis sextet and John Coltrane, and his film work included *Play Misty for Me* (1971). He died at the height of his career following a stroke.

adder's tongue A fern native to grasslands of Europe, Asia, N Africa, and North America (*Ophioglossum vulgatum*); underground rhizome producing a fertile spike 5 cm/2 in long bearing sporangia and sheathed by a single oval; the entire frond is 10–20 cm/4–8 in long. (Family: Ophioglossaceae.)

Addington, Henry *Sidmouth, 1st Viscount*

Addinsell, Richard [adinsel] (1904–77) Composer, born in Oxford, Oxfordshire, SC England, UK. A student of law at Oxford, he went on to study music in London, Berlin, and Vienna. He composed much film music, including the popular 'Warsaw Concerto' for the film *Dangerous Moonlight* (1941).

Addis Ababa or **Adis Abeba** [adis ababa] 9°02N 38°42E, pop (2000e) 2 157 000. Capital of Ethiopia; altitude 2400 m/7874 ft; founded by Menelik II, 1887; capital, 1889; occupied by Italy, 1936–41, declared capital of Italian East Africa; airport; railway to port of Djibouti; university (1950); tobacco, foodstuffs, textiles, chemicals, cement; national museum, national library, St George's Cathedral, Menelik II's tomb; headquarters of UN Economic Commission for Africa, and of the Organization of African Unity.

Addison, Joseph (1672–1719) Essayist and politician, born in Milston, Wiltshire, S England, UK. A student at Oxford, he was a distinguished Classical scholar and fellow of Magdalen College (1698–1711), beginning his literary career in 1693 with a poetical address to Dryden. In 1699 he obtained a pension to train for the diplomatic service, and spent four years abroad. While under-secretary of state (1706–8) he produced his opera *Rosamond* (1706), and in 1708 was elected to parliament for Lostwithiel and then Malmesbury (1709–19). He became a member of the Kit-Cat Club, and contributed to the *Tatler*, started by his friend Richard Steele in 1709. In 1711 he and Steele founded the *Spectator*, 274 numbers of which were his own work. In 1716 he became a lord commissioner of trade, and married Charlotte, Countess of Warwick. In the Hanoverian cause, he issued (1715–16) a political newspaper, the *Freeholder*, which cost him many of his old friends, and he was satirized as 'Atticus' by Alexander Pope. In 1717 he was appointed secretary of state under Sunderland, but resigned his post because of failing health.

Addison, Thomas (c.1793–1860) Physician, born in Longbenton, Northumberland, NE England, UK. He studied medicine at Edinburgh, settled in London, and in 1837 became physician to Guy's Hospital. His chief researches were on pneumonia, tuberculosis, and especially on the disease of the adrenal glands now known as **Addison's disease**.

Addison's disease A medical condition resulting from the destruction of the adrenal glands by infection (commonly tuberculosis) or by an auto-immune reaction. A fall in the output of corticosteroids causes physical weakness, mental apathy, low blood pressure, and increased skin pigmentation. Without treatment, death is unavoidable. Taking synthetic steroids by mouth restores the patient to normal health, but these must be continued for life.

addition reaction A chemical reaction in which a product contains all atoms of two or more reactants, eg the chlorination of ethylene, $CH_2{=}CH_2{+}Cl_2{\rightarrow}CH_2Cl.CH_2Cl$. Similarly, **addition polymerization** is the formation of a polymer without elimination from the reactants, for example, the formation of polyethylene, $nCH_2{=}CH_2{\rightarrow}(-CH_2.CH_2^-)_n$. The product of an addition reaction is known as an **adduct**.

additives Strictly, any chemical, even a vitamin, added to a food during its processing or preparation; more usually, chemicals which have been added in order to achieve a specific aim. They include (a) *preservatives*, which reduce spoilage by bacteria, (b) *anti-oxidants*, which prevent fats from becoming rancid, (c) *emulsifiers*, which permit a stable mixture of oil and water, (d) *colouring matter*, to vary colour to specifications, (e) *sweeteners*, and (f) *flavouring agents/enhancers*, to achieve a given flavour. Many additives are naturally occurring compounds; others are synthetic. Legislation exists in most countries to ensure that food additives are technologically desirable and at the same time safe. However, in recent years many consumers have come to fear synthetic additives, leading to an increase in the use of natural additives.

adduct *addition reaction*

Adela, Princess [adayla] (c.1062–1137) Princess of England, the youngest daughter of William the Conqueror and Matilda of Flanders. In 1080 she married Stephen-Henry, Count of Blois, and had nine children, the third of whom came to be King Stephen of England. She ruled with skill during her husband's absence on the First Crusade (1095–9) and became regent on his death (1101) until the majority of her eldest son, Theobald, in 1109. In 1118 she effected an alliance between Theobald and Henry I of England.

Adelaide 34°56S 138°36E, pop (2000e) 1 131 000. Port capital of South Australia, on the Torrens R where it meets the St Vincent Gulf; founded, 1837; the first Australian municipality to be incorporated, 1840; airfield; railway; three universities (1874, 1966, 1991); oil refining, motor vehicles, electrical goods, shipbuilding; trade in wool, grain, fruit, wine; fine beaches to the W, including Maslin Beach (the first nude bathing beach in Australia); many parks; two cathedrals; major wine-growing area to the S (McLaren Vale) and to the N (Barossa Valley); Adelaide Festival Centre; South Australian Museum (large collection of aboriginal art); Art Gallery of South Australia; Constitutional Museum; Ayers House (1846), headquarters of the South Australian National Trust; Maritime Museum in Port Adelaide; arts festival, held every two years; Adelaide Cup Day (May).

Adélie Land [adaylee] or **Adélie Coast**, Fr **Terre Adélie** area c.432 000 sq km/167 000 sq mi. Territory in Antarctica 66–67°S, 136–142°E; first seen by the French navy in 1840; explored 1911–14 and 1929–31; French territory, 1938; French research station at Base Dumont d'Urville.

Aden or **Adan** [aydn] 12°50N 45°00E, pop (2000e) 497 500. Commercial capital of Republic of Yemen; port on the Gulf of Aden, at the entrance to the Red Sea; taken by British, 1839; capital of former Aden protectorate; after opening of Suez Canal (1869), an important coaling station and transshipment point; British crown colony, 1937; scene of fighting between nationalist groups in 1960s; capital of former South Yemen, 1968–90; airport; oil refining, shipping.

Aden, Gulf of [aydn] E arm of the Red Sea, lying between Yemen (N) and Somalia (S); connected to the Red Sea by the Strait of Bāb al Mandab; length 885 km/550 mi.

Adenauer, Konrad [adenower] (1876–1967) German statesman, born in Cologne, W Germany. He studied at Freiburg, Munich, and Bonn, before practising law in Cologne, where he became lord mayor in 1917. A member of the Centre Party under the Weimar Republic, he became a member of the Provincial Diet and of the Prussian State Council (president 1920–33). In 1933, he was dismissed from all his offices by the Nazis, and imprisoned in 1934 and again in 1944. In 1945, under Allied occupation, he was again Mayor of Cologne, and founded the Christian Democratic Union. As chancellor from 1949 (re-elected 1953 and 1957), his policy was to rebuild West Germany on a basis of partnership with other European nations through NATO and the European Economic Community, with the ultimate aim of bargaining from strength for the reunification of Germany. He retired in 1963.

adenine [adeneen] $C_4H_5N_5$. A base derived from purine; one of the five found in nucleic acids, where it is generally paired with thymine or uracil.

adenoids An accumulation of lymphoid tissue, arranged as a series of folds behind the opening of the auditory tube in the nasopharynx; also known as the **pharyngeal tonsils**. When enlarged in children they can block or reduce the size of the auditory tube opening and fill the nasopharynx, giving an abnormal resonance to speech.

adenosine triphosphate (ATP) [adenoseen] A molecule formed by the condensation of adenine, ribose, and triphosphoric acid: HO–P(O)OH–O–P(O)OH–O–P(O)OH–OH. It is a key compound in the mediation of energy in both plants and animals. Energy is stored when it is synthesized from **adenosine diphosphate** (ADP) and phosphoric acid, and released when the reaction is reversed.

Ader, Clément [adair] (1841–1926) Engineer and pioneer of aviation, born in Muret, S France. In 1890 he built a steam-powered bat-winged aeroplane, the *Eole*, which made the first powered take-off in history, but it could not be steered, and flew for no more than 50 m/160 ft.

adhesives Materials whose function is to bind one substance to another. Examples are (1) substances of biological origin, generally water soluble, known as *glues*, which are usually proteins or carbohydrates, and (2) synthetic materials, both thermoplastic and thermosetting resins and rubbers.

adiabatic demagnetization *magnetic cooling*

adiabatic process [adiabatik] In thermodynamics, a process in which no heat enters or leaves a system, such as in a well-insulated system, or in some process so rapid that there is not enough time for heat exchange. Sound waves in air involve adiabatic pressure changes. The compression and power strokes of a car engine are also adiabatic.

Adie, Kate [aydee], popular name of **Kathryn Adie** (1945–) News reporter and correspondent, born in Sunderland, Tyne and Wear, NE England, UK. She studied at the University of Newcastle upon Tyne, then joined local BBC radio (1969–76), moving to BBC TV South (1977–8). As a reporter for BBC TV News (1979–81), correspondent (1982), and chief correspondent (1989–2003), she has become a familiar figure presenting reports from the heart of war-torn countries around the world. Among her awards are the Royal Television Society's News Award (1981, 1987), and the BAFTA Richard Dimbleby Award (1989).

Adige, River [ahdije], Ger **Etsch** ancient **Athesis** River in N Italy, rising in three small Alpine lakes at Resia Pass; flows E and S, then E into the Adriatic Sea, SE of Chioggia; length 410 km/254 mi; chief river of Italy after the Po.

Adi Granth [ahdee grahnt] (Hindi 'First Book') The principal Sikh scripture, originally called the **Granth Sahib** (Hindi 'Revered Book'). The name Adi Granth distinguishes it from the Dasam Granth, a later second collection. The text used today is an expanded version of Guru Arjan's original compilation, and is revered by all Sikhs.

adipic acid [adipik] $HOOC–(CH_2)_4–COOH$, IUPAC **hexanedioic acid**, melting point 153°C. It is one of the monomers for nylon, the other being 1,6-diaminohexane.

adipose tissue *fat 2*

Adirondack Mountains [adirondak] Mountain range largely in NE New York State, USA; rises to 1629 m/5344 ft at Mt Marcy; named after an American Indian tribe; source of the Hudson and Ausable Rivers; locations such as L Placid are noted winter resorts; largest state park in USA.

Adis Abeba *Addis Ababa*

adjutant A stork native to tropical SE Asia. There are two species: the **greater adjutant stork** (*Leptoptilos dubius*), and the **lesser**, **haircrested**, or **Javan adjutant stork** (*Leptoptilos javanicus*); grey and white; head nearly naked; eats carrion, frogs or fish; related to the marabou.

Adler, Alfred (1870–1937) Pioneer psychiatrist, born in Vienna, Austria. He trained in Vienna, and first practised as an ophthalmologist, but later turned to mental disease and became a prominent member of the psychoanalytical group which formed around Sigmund Freud in 1900. His most widely referenced work, *Studie über Minderwertigkeit von Organen* (1907, trans Study of Organ Inferiority and its Psychical Compensation), aroused great controversy. In 1911 he broke with Freud and investigated the psychology of the individual person considered to be different from others. His main contributions include the concept of the inferiority complex and his special treatment of neurosis as the exploitation of shock. He moved to the USA to teach in 1932.

administrative law The body of law relating to administrative powers exercised principally by central and local government, including town and country planning, the control of many trades and professions, police powers, and environmental issues. The exercise of such powers can be the subject of scrutiny by the courts or tribunals on legal (but not normally on policy) grounds. In several countries, administrative law is distinguished from constitutional law by being concerned purely with matters of public administration, and not with broad constitutional issues which may impinge on administrative matters.

Admiral's Cup A yacht race for up to three boats per nation, first contested in 1957 and held biennially. Races take place in the English Channel, at Cowes, and around the Fastnet rock. The trophy is donated by the Royal Ocean Racing Club.

Admiralty Court An English court which is part of the Queen's Bench Division of the High Court. Its work deals with maritime claims in civil law, such as salvage and collisions at sea. The commercial court deals with other types of cases, such as those involving marine insurance. In the USA, the federal district courts exercise jurisdiction over maritime actions. In Scotland, the Court of Session and the Sheriff Court have jurisdiction over such matters.

Admiralty Islands pop (2000e) 39 000; area 2000 sq km/800 sq mi. Island group in N Papua New Guinea, part of the Bismarck Archipelago; c.40 islands, main island, Manus; chief town, Lorengau; German protectorate, 1884; under Australian mandate, 1920; fishing, copra, pearls.

adolescence That period of personal development marked by the onset of puberty and continuing through the early teenage years. While it is associated with the process of physical maturation, normally occurring more quickly in girls than in boys, the actual age-range and behavioural patterns involved can vary considerably from one society to another. Adolescence in the Third World, for example, is more likely to mean working in the fields for one's parents and taking on adult responsibilities from as young as age 9 or 10 than a prolonged period of schooling as it does in more prosperous societies. Whatever the differences, adolescents commonly want to be independent of their parents; the conflicts this may generate are sometimes said to reflect 'the generation gap'.

Adonis [adohnis] In Greek mythology, a beautiful young man who was loved by Aphrodite. He insisted on going hunting and was killed by a boar, but Persephone saved him on condition that he spent part of the year with her in the Underworld. There was a yearly commemoration of the event, with wailing and singing. There is a clear connection with the growth and death of vegetation, and similar Eastern ceremonies.

adoption A legal procedure in which a civil court makes an order giving parental rights and duties over a child to someone other than the natural parents. On adoption, the child becomes the legal child of his or her adoptive parents, and the same as any natural child. Natural parents often lose all rights in the child and in his or her property. Contact by the natural parents after adoption is a controversial issue. Adoption law is currently under review in the UK, and it is likely that major reform will take place in the forseeable future, featuring a shift towards a more 'open' system of adoption and the need to dovetail existing laws within the Children Act.

adoptionism In early Christianity, the understanding of Jesus as a human being of sinless life adopted by God as son, usually thought to be at the time of his baptism by John in the R Jordan. Such teaching was declared heretical, in that it implied that Jesus could not have had a fully divine nature. Associated with Arianism, it figured in 4th-c controversies over the person of Christ, in Spain in the 8th-c, and in some scholastic theology (eg Abelard, Lombard).

Adorno, Theodor (Wiesengrund) [adaw(r)noh], originally **Theodor Wiesengrund** (1903–69) Social philosopher and musicologist, born in Frankfurt, WC Germany. He was a student in Frankfurt and later an associate of the Institute for Social Research, becoming a member of the movement known as the 'Frankfurt School'. In 1934 he emigrated to the USA to teach at the Institute in exile, returning to Frankfurt in 1956. His philosophy is most fully presented in *Negative Dialectics* (1966). His sociological writings on music, mass-culture, and art include *Philosophie der neuen Musik* (1949, Philosophy of Modern Music) and *Mahler* (1960).

Adrastea [adrasteea] A tiny natural satellite of Jupiter, discovered in 1979 by Voyager 2; distance from the planet 129 000 km/80 000 mi; diameter 24 km/15 mi.

adrenal glands [adreenl] Paired compound endocrine glands in mammals, one situated above each kidney; also known as the **suprarenal glands**. Each comprises an outer cortex and an inner medulla. The cortex consists of three zones, which produce specific steroid hormones: the outer zone produces mineralocorticoids (eg aldosterone), whereas the intermediate and inner zones produce glucocorticoids (eg cortisol) and sex hormones (androgens, oestrogens, and progestagens). The medulla secretes a specific catecholamine (either adrenaline or noradrenaline). The various groups of hormones are chemically similar in all vertebrates.

adrenaline or **adrenalin** [adrenalin] A hormone released from the adrenal medulla in response to stress, and in some other circumstances; also known as **epinephrine** in the USA. It increases heart rate, raises blood pressure, and causes release of sugar into the blood from liver stores. Thus, in situations of stress the body is prepared for the 'fight or flight reaction'. Therapeutic uses include acute asthma, heart attack, and severe allergic responses.

adrenocorticotrophic hormone (ACTH) [adreenohkaw(r)tikohtrohfik] A chemical substance (a peptide) produced in the front lobe of the pituitary gland; also known as **corticotrophin**. It stimulates the synthesis and release of glucocorticoids from the adrenal cortex, and is released in response to physical, emotional, or chemical stress through a releasing factor produced in the hypothalamus.

Adrian IV, also **Hadrian**, originally **Nicholas Breakspear** (c.1100–59) The first and only Englishman to become pope (1154–9), born in Abbots Langley, Hertfordshire, SE England, UK. He studied at Merton Priory and Avignon, became a monk in the monastery of St Rufus, near Avignon, and in 1137 was elected its abbot. Complaints about his strictness led to a summons to Rome, where the pope recognized his qualities and appointed him Cardinal-Bishop of Albano in 1146. In 1152 he was sent as papal legate to Scandinavia to reorganize the Church, where he earned fame as the 'Apostle of the North'. One of his early acts as pope is said to have been the issue of a controversial bull granting Ireland to Henry II. In 1155 he crowned Frederick I Barbarossa as Holy Roman Emperor in front of his massed army in a show of strength in support of the papacy, but he later engaged in a bitter struggle with him for supremacy in Europe.

Adrian, Edgar Douglas, 1st Baron Adrian (1889–1977) Neurophysiologist, one of the founders of modern neurophysiology, born in London, UK. He became a fellow of Trinity College, Cambridge, where he carried out research on electrical impulses in the nervous system, and later on electrical brain waves. He was appointed professor of physiology at Cambridge (1937–51), Master of Trinity College, Cambridge (1951–6), and Chancellor of the University (1968–75). For his work on the function of neurons, he shared the 1932 Nobel Prize for Physiology or Medicine.

Adrianople, Battle of (AD 378) A battle between the Romans and the Visigoths at present-day Edirne in European Turkey. This was one of the crucial battles of the ancient world, as the crushing Visigoth victory, under Fritigern, opened up Roman territory to Germanic invasion. Two-thirds of the Roman army, including Emperor Valens, were killed.

Adriatic Sea [aydreeatik] Arm of the Mediterranean Sea, between the E coast of Italy and the Balkan Peninsula; Gulf of Venice at its head (NW); separated from the Ionian Sea (S) by the Strait of Otranto; length 800 km/500 mi; width 93–225 km/58–140 mi; maximum depth 1250 m/4100 ft; highly saline; lobster, sardines, tuna; chief ports, Venice, Rijeka, Ancona, Bari, Brindisi; flat, sandy Italian coast; rugged, irregular E coast.

adsorption The extraction of a component from one phase into another phase, usually by chemical interaction (*chemisorption*) between the material adsorbed (the **adsorbate**) and the surface of the adsorbing material (the **adsorbent**). Sometimes, the adsorbate is incorporated into the structure of the adsorbent; an example is the adsorption of hydrogen gas by palladium, which can adsorb several hundred times its own volume of the gas.

adult education The provision of further or continuing educational opportunities for people over the minimum school-leaving age; also known as **continuing education**. Frequently this takes place in institutions specially set up to cater for mature learners, but it is also common for schools and colleges and other centres of learning to be used. A wide network of providers exists. In addition to the formal opportunities offered by institutions, there are numerous informal sources of adult education, such as broadcast programmes on radio and television, as well as correspondence and distance-learning courses, for people who wish to or must learn at home or as part of their job.

Advaita [adviyta] (Sanskrit, 'non-dual') An influential school of Vedanta Hinduism, revived in a modern form during the 20th-c. Associated primarily with the thought of Shankara (8th-c), it holds that there is only one absolute reality, Brahman. All selves are in effect identical, since in essence they are one with Brahman.

Advent In the Christian Church, a period of penitence and preparation for the celebration of the first coming of Christ at Christmas, and for his promised second coming to judge the world. It begins on **Advent Sunday**, the fourth Sunday before Christmas (in effect, the Sunday nearest 30 November).

Adventists Those Christians whose most important belief is in the imminent and literal Second Coming of Christ. Found in most periods of history and in most denominations, a separate movement began in the USA with William Miller (1781–1849), who predicted Christ's return (and the end of the world) in 1843–4, and whose followers eventually formed a denomination called **Seventh Day Adventists**. They believe that the Second Coming of Christ is delayed only by a failure to keep the Sabbath (Friday evening to Saturday evening), which, along with Old Testament dietary laws, is held to rigorously.

adversary politics A political situation said to exist in two-party electoral systems (eg the UK) where the policies of the parties and government are polarized between right and left, resulting in significant reversals in policy when government changes. It is usually associated with a 'first past the post' electoral system. Because the system works against successful challenges from third parties, the views of the majority of the electorate occupying the 'middle ground' are not reflected.

adverse possession The creation of an ownership right in real property through hostile, open, and continuous possession for a period of time, such as when a squatter seizes possession, or a tenant refuses to pay rent. The period required was traditionally 20 years, but is now 12 years in England and Wales (with exceptions for crown land or land owned by charitable institutions), and is fixed by statute from 5 to 20 years in most US jurisdictions.

advertising The practice of informing and influencing others not personally known to the communicator through paid messages in the media; also the advertisements themselves. From humble origins (eg tradesmen's signs), advertising has developed in parallel with modern industrial society and the mass media. News-sheets in the 17th-c carried brief statements (eg announcing the sale of patent medicines), but it was not until the late 19th-c, with the advent of mass production of consumer goods, that the industry developed on the huge scale found today. Advertising for consumer goods, whether of the 'fast moving' variety (eg washing powders) or 'durables' (eg cars) has long been the most conspicuous kind, on poster sites, in the press, and on television. 'Display' ads for such products in newspapers or magazines are characterized by their size and use of graphics (especially photographs), slogans, and large type. In contrast, 'classified' ads are typically single-column width, consisting of words only, and grouped together under headings (eg 'personal', 'situations vacant', or 'wanted'). Other approaches include direct marketing (by post or telephone) and direct response advertising (via tear-off coupons), both of which have resulted from the difficulty mass media advertising has in reaching a target audience and measuring its own effectiveness.

Manufacturers and retailers are not the only groups to realize the value of communicating with the general public through advertising. Governments, political parties, service industries (eg banks and financial institutions), trade unions, employers' associations, pressure groups, and charities also employ advertising as a major means of promoting ideas and causes. Regulations on who may advertise and on the quantity and nature of ads, especially commercials, vary from country to country. In recent years some advertisers have found the sponsorship of sporting and cultural events a convenient way to side-step controls applying elsewhere to the promotion of their products (especially cigarettes) and a means of associating these with healthy or prestigious activities. From being small-scale brokers of advertising space on behalf of newspaper proprietors, many modern **advertising agencies** now offer a 'full service', comprising market research and creative expertise, media planning, and media buying. The influence of the USA in developing advertising techniques (Madison Avenue) has been central. Since the 1960s, however, 'creative shops' have offered specialist design and copywriting services with 'media independents' later doing the same for media planning and buying.

Advertising is only one, though perhaps the most controversial, of the elements of the 'marketing mix'. As such it has always been subject to attack, whether on moral, ideological, or aesthetic grounds. Underlying this criticism is the presumption that advertising has pernicious effects on individuals, social groups, or whole societies. Apologists respond by claiming that advertising merely reflects the values and styles already existing in society.

Advisory, Conciliation, and Arbitration Service *ACAS*

advocacy planning A form of planning in which the planner acts for the interests of a particular group or community in opposition to plans prepared by the official planning authority. It is a means of aiding groups whose interests may be damaged or not represented by the planning authority. The planner is responsible to the group, and not to the authority.

advocate A term frequently applied to lawyers practising in the courts as professional representatives of those who bring or defend a case. Although in the magistrates' courts and county courts both barristers and solicitors have the right to appear, in most higher courts in England and Wales barristers have sole rights to appear for clients. However, the Courts and Legal Services Act 1990 permits solicitors with experience to obtain advocacy qualifications in the higher courts. In Scotland, the term is used as an equivalent to an English barrister, and denotes exclusive right of audience before the superior courts. Also in Scotland, since 1993, a hybrid form of lawyer called a **solicitor advocate** has been created from existing solicitors who, on passing further examinations, is permitted to appear in the High Court or the Court of Session. These senses are not found in other jurisdictions.

aechmea [akmaya] A member of a genus of plants (epiphytes) native to tropical America; rosettes of succulent leaves forming a water-filled cup in the centre, inflorescence produced on a stout, well-developed stalk. Many species are grown as house plants. (Genus: *Aechmea*, 172 species. Family: Bromeliaceae.)

Aedes [ayeedeez] The yellow-fever mosquito, found in coastal and riverside habitats throughout the tropics and subtropics; eggs laid in stagnant water; aquatic larvae colourless except for black respiratory siphon. The adult females feed on blood, transmitting diseases such as yellow fever and dengue. (Order: Diptera. Family: Culicidae.)

Aegean civilization [eejeean] The Bronze Age cultures which flourished in the third and second millennia BC on the islands of the Aegean Sea and around its coasts.

Aegean Islands [eejeean] pop (2000e) 476 000; area 9122 sq km/3521 sq mi. Island group and region of Greece; the name is generally applied to the islands of the Aegean Sea, including Lesbos, Chios, Samos, Lemnos, and Thasos; a major tourist area.

Aegean Sea [eejeean] Arm of the Mediterranean Sea, bounded W and N by Greece, NE and E by Turkey, S by islands of Crete and Rhodes; dotted with islands on which the Aegean civilization of 3000–1000 BC flourished; length (N–S) 645 km/400 mi; width 320 km/200 mi; greatest depth, 2013 m/6604 ft; sardines, sponges; natural gas off NE coast of Greece; tourism.

Aegina [eejiyna], Gr **Aiyna** pop (2000e) 12 000; area 83 sq km/32 sq mi. One of the largest of the Saronic Islands, Greece, SW of Athens; chief town Aiyna; a popular resort; Temple of Aphaia.

aegis [eejis] Originally a goatskin, and then, in Greek mythology, a fringed piece of armour or a shield. Zeus shakes his aegis, which may possibly be the thunder-cloud; Athene's is equipped with the Gorgon's head.

Aegisthus [eegisthuhs, eejisthuhs] In Greek legend, the son of Thyestes; while Agamemnon was absent at Troy he became the lover of Clytemnestra. Together they killed Agamemnon on his return to Argos. Aegisthus was later killed by Orestes.

Ælfric [alfrik, alfrich], also known as **Ælfric Grammaticus** ('The Grammarian') (c.955–c.1020) Anglo-Saxon clergyman and writer, the greatest vernacular prose writer of his time. He became a monk and later abbot at the new monastery of Cerne Abbas in Dorset, S England, and subsequently the first Abbot of Eynsham in Oxfordshire, SC England. He composed two books of 80 *Homilies* in Old English, a paraphrase of the first seven books of the Bible, and a book of *Lives of the Saints*. He also wrote a Latin grammar and Latin–English glossary, accompanied by a Latin *Colloquium* which gives a vivid picture of social conditions in England at the time.

Aelred of Rievaulx *Ailred of Rievaulx*

Aemilian Way [iymeelian] A continuation of Rome's major trunk road to the N, the Flaminian Way. It ran from Rimini on the Adriatic coast to the R Po.

Aeneas [eeneeas] In Roman legend, the ancestor of the Romans. He was a Trojan hero, the son of Anchises and Venus, who escaped after the fall of Troy, bearing his father on his shoulders. After wandering through the Mediterranean, he reached Italy at Cumae and visited the Underworld, where the destiny of Rome was made clear to him. He married the daughter of the King of Latium, and allied himself to the Latins in local wars. His son founded Alba Longa, and a line of kings from whom Romulus was said to be descended.

aeolian harp [eeohlian] A wooden soundbox fitted with strings (usually about a dozen) of various thicknesses, but tuned to a single pitch, which are made to vibrate freely by the surrounding air, producing an ethereal, 'disembodied' sound. It takes its name from Aeolus, god of the winds.

Aeolians [eeohlianz] A sub-group of Hellenic peoples who colonized the NW coast of Asia Minor and the islands of the N Aegean (eg Lesbos) towards the end of the second millennium BC.

Aeolus [eeolus] In Greek mythology, the god of the winds. In the *Odyssey* Aeolus lived on an island, and gave Odysseus the winds tied in a bag so that his ship would not be blown off course. The ship had nearly reached Ithaca when Odysseus' men opened the bag, thinking it contained treasure. As a result, the ship was blown far away.

Aepyornis [eepiaw(r)nis] *elephant bird*

aerial *antenna* (technology)

aerial photography Photography of the ground surface from an aerial viewpoint such as a balloon or aircraft, with application to archaeology, ecology, geology, and wartime reconnaissance. In **aerial survey mapping**, the aircraft flies at a constant height along specified paths, taking pictures at regular intervals to build up a mosaic of overlapping images; ground contour and building heights are measured by viewing pairs of images stereoscopically.

aerobatics Any sequence of turning, looping and rolling movements of an aircraft flown to display the skill of the pilot and the manoeuvrability of the aircraft. Competetive aerobatics are flown in aircraft specially designed to withstand the stresses incurred during the manoeuvres. While performing a set of allowed figures the pilot must keep the aircraft within the lateral and vertical limits of the designated aerobatics box. The flight is assessed by trained judges on the ground and is marked according to the quality of performance and the difficulty of each manouevre. The sport is controlled by the Federation Aeronautique Internationale (FAI).

aerobe [airohb] An organism that requires the presence of oxygen for growth and reproduction. The great majority of all living organisms are aerobic, requiring oxygen for respiration. Some micro-organisms, typically bacteria, are anaerobic, able to grow only in the absence of oxygen; these are known as **anaerobes**.

aerobics [airohbiks] A system of physical training that exercises large muscle groups for long periods. The muscles use oxygen, and the heart and respitratory rates are increased. Regular aerobic exercise improves the performance of the heart, lungs, and muscles, and these improvements can be measured on charts appropriate to different age groups. It includes exercises such as walking, running, swimming, and cycling. In the 1980s the term was particularly used for movement exercises in time to music, which became popular among keep-fit groups.

aerocapture A proposed technique for placing a spacecraft in orbit around a planet, without the expenditure of chemical propellants, by taking advantage of planetary atmosphere. The spacecraft would be equipped with an aerobrake similar to the heat shields on space capsules like Apollo, and would be navigated into the planet's upper atmosphere, where friction would slow it down. The technique offers the prospect of reducing trip times to the outer planets by using less massive spacecraft, and of carrying heavier payloads to Mars for sample return missions and, eventually, human exploration.

aerodynamics The study of the flow of air and the behaviour of objects moving relative to air; a subject which is applicable to other gases, and is part of the larger subject of fluid mechanics. Aerodynamic principles explain flight. The shape and orientation of an aircraft wing (curved upper surface, wing tilted down) mean that the air above the wing travels further than the air beneath. Air above the wing thus travels faster and so has lower pressure (Bernoulli's principle). The pressure difference provides lift to support the aircraft. The available lift increases with wing area, and decreases with altitude. The movement of an aircraft through the air produces a force which impedes motion, called *drag*, dependent on the aircraft size and shape. Air movement across the surface is impeded by friction, which produces additional drag called *frictional drag*; this causes heating, which can sometimes be extreme, as in the case of space re-entry vehicles. Friction losses increase with wing area and velocity, and decrease with altitude. At velocities greater than the speed of sound (Mach 1, approximately 331·5 m/1088 ft per second) air can no longer be treated as incompressible and new rules apply, giving rise to **supersonic aerodynamics**. Passing from subsonic to supersonic speeds, aircraft cross the 'sound barrier', marked by a dramatic increase in drag. Supersonic drag is reduced using thin, swept-back wings typical of military fighter aircraft. Aircraft flying at supersonic speeds produce sonic booms – shock waves in the air around the aircraft, produced because the aircraft's velocity is too great to allow the air pressure to adjust smoothly around it. Vehicles moving through air experience drag forces which increase fuel consumption. Also, buildings and bridges sway due to wind. These effects must be allowed for in design, and can be minimized by attending to the shape of the object as seen by the oncoming air stream. Wind tunnels allow scale models to be exposed to simulated wind conditions, and aerodynamic properties of design can be determined. Of special importance are effects of abnormal air flows such as turbulence and vortices.

aerometry [airometree] The measurement of airflow through the nose and mouth during speech. In the pronunciation of most sounds, air comes through the mouth; but in the case of nasal consonants (eg [m], [n]) and nasal vowels (eg [õ], as in French *bon*) the air travels wholly or partly through the nose. Using an **aerometer**, the variations in the use of the nasal cavity in running speech can be plotted.

aeronautics The broad body of scientifically based knowledge describing aeroplanes as objects subject to the laws of physics. The term is usually taken to mean knowledge which focuses upon the vehicle itself, rather than upon the associated commercial or operational usage, although in practice such a definition is not rigidly adhered to. Thus, aeronautics is taken to cover such topics as the generation of lift to make the aeroplane fly, the physical factors affecting manoeuvring, the production of thrust through the use of propellers and jets, the strength of the structure, and the way these various elements are combined to produce a functioning vehicle.

aerophone Any musical instrument in which air is the main vibrating agent. Aerophones form one of the main categories of instruments in the standard classification of Hornbostel and Sachs (1914). They are subdivided into types according to (a) the main material they are made of, and (b) how the air is set in motion (via a mouthpiece, a reed, or neither).

aeroplane / airplane The general name given to a vehicle whose operational medium is air and which supports itself in the Earth's atmosphere by means of *lift*. Lift is produced through specially shaped fixed wings attached to the aeroplane's body or *fuselage*; these alter the airflow so that the pressure distribution of the air over the wing creates an upward force. The airflow is in turn produced by the aeroplane being 'pushed' or 'pulled' through the air by the propulsion device driven by a motor. By means of design, the lift produced by the wing can be made greater than the weight of the airframe and propulsive system, allowing a payload to be carried.

George Cayley designed a glider in 1853, but the first truly powered flight was made by Orville Wright in December 1903, when he flew 260 m/852 ft. However, it was not until World War 1 that governments on both sides of the conflict put money into the development of engines and airframes. This led to the rapid development of specialized aircraft, particularly the fighter. After the War, the needs of American transcontinental passenger travel produced aircraft with multi-engines, metal skins, and retractable undercarriages to replace the previously fabric-covered types. World War 2 saw a further investment in aircraft by both the Axis and Allied powers, culminating in the world's first operational jet fighter, the Me 262. In the period following the War, jet engines were applied to ever larger passenger aircraft. The first civil jet transport, the British de Havilland Comet, flew in 1949 and regular transatlantic jet services began in 1958 with the Comet 4 and the American Boeing 707. The Boeing 747 Jumbo Jet was introduced in 1970. Similarly, warplanes of all types had jet engines applied to them, the trend being towards ever higher speeds. The first aircraft to fly at supersonic speeds was a Bell X-1 rocket-powered research plane in 1947; the supersonic Concorde passenger aircraft was introduced in 1976. Recent developments in civilian aircraft have been away from higher speed towards more economical and quieter operation, while military and large commercial aircraft are becoming increasingly reliant upon electronics to control and keep them stable in flight.

aerosol An airborne suspension of microscopic particles or liquid droplets, typically formed by forcing a liquid through a fine nozzle under pressure. Aerosol sprays are useful as a means of depositing fine even layers of material, such as in paint sprays.

aerospace medicine The study and prevention of the adverse affects of flight and space travel on the human body. The body is affected during high-altitude flights by low oxygen levels, which deprive the body of oxygen and lead to weakness and drowsiness; low pressure, which causes trapped air within the body to expand, producing pain; and high G-forces produced by rapid accelerations, which force blood away from the brain, leading to blackouts. Preventative measures include oxygen masks, pressurized cabins and suits, and *G-suits* that apply pressure to the legs and maintain blood circulation to vital areas of the body.

Aeschines [eeskineez] (c.390 BC–?) Orator, born in Athens, Greece. Prominent in Athenian politics between 348 and 330 BC, he advocated appeasement of Philip II of Macedon, and was a member of a Greek embassy that negotiated peace with Philip in 346. Demosthenes tried to have him indicted for treason in 343, and in 330 Aeschines tried to prevent Demosthenes from being awarded a golden crown for his services to Athens. Defeated, Aeschines withdrew to Rhodes, where he established a school of eloquence. Of his speeches, only three survive.

Aeschylus [eeskilus] (c.525–c.456 BC) Playwright, known as 'the founder of Greek tragedy', born in Eleusis, near Athens, Greece. He served in the Athenian army in the Persian Wars, and was wounded at Marathon (490). The first and gravest of the great dramatists (winning the victory in 485 BC), he increased the number of characters in the action and introduced new staging. He won 13 first prizes in tragic competitions, before being defeated by Sophocles in 468. This may have induced him to leave Athens and go to Sicily. Out of some 60 plays ascribed to him, only seven are extant: *Persians* (472), *Seven against Thebes* (467), *Prometheus Bound*, *The Suppliants*, and the trilogy of the *Oresteia* (458), three plays on the fate of Orestes, comprising *Agamemnon* (perhaps the greatest Greek play that has survived), *Choephoroe*, and *Eumenides*. Aeschylus' pivotal contribution to the structure of Greek tragedy was the introduction of a second actor, where there had previously been only one actor and the chorus, and the subordination of the chorus to the dialogue of the actors.

Aesculapius [eeskyulaypius] The Latin form of **Asclepius**, the Greek god of healing. His cult was transferred from Epidauros to Rome in 291 BC after a plague.

Aesop [eesop] (?6th-c BC) Legendary Greek fabulist. He is supposed to have been a native of Phrygia and a slave who, after being set free, travelled to Greece. The fables attributed to him are anecdotes which use animals to make a moral point and are, in all probability, a compilation of tales from many sources. The stories were popularized by the Roman poet Phaedrus in the 1st-c AD, and rewritten in sophisticated verse by La Fontaine in 1668.

Aesthetic / Esthetic Movement A view of art based on the theory that art is autonomous and should not be judged by non-aesthetic criteria, whether moral, religious, or political; it flourished in the 19th-c. The French writer Victor Cousin first used the phrase *l'art pour l'art* ('art for art's sake') in 1836, but the doctrine occurs in various forms in the writings of (among others) Kant, Coleridge, and Emerson. Aestheticism was attacked for its exaggerated detachment from everyday life by Ruskin and later by Tolstoy. The view that purely 'formal' rather than associational or 'literary' qualities are paramount has played a major role in 20th-c discussion.

aesthetics / esthetics The philosophical investigation of art, understood to include all the visual arts, music, literature, drama, and dance. The term originally denoted the study of sense-experience generally, and began to emerge as a sub-field of philosophy concerned with beauty and artistic value with the work of Baumgarten and Kant in the 19th-c. Aesthetics now deals with such issues as what it is for an object or a performance to be a work of art; whether there are objective standards for judging it; and what meaning and function can be ascribed to art and the concepts used within it.

aestivation *hibernation*

Æthel- (Anglo-Saxon name) *Athelstan; Ethelbert; Etheldreda; Ethelflaed; Ethelred I; Ethelred II*

aether *ether 2*

Aëtius, Flavius [ayeetius] (c.390–454) Roman general, born in Moesia. In 433 he became patrician, consul, and general-in-chief, and maintained the empire against the barbarians for 20 years. His crowning victory was at Châlons over Attila in 451. Three years later Emperor Valentinian III (reigned 425–55), jealous of his greatness, stabbed him to death.

affenpinscher [afenpinsher] A breed of dog; small with long dark wiry coat; usually black; face like a monkey, with short muzzle and large black eyes; very old breed, originally from Germany, now rare.

affinity A relationship by marriage. Countries generally have rules prohibiting marriage between certain people where there is an affinity – for example between parents and their step-children (subject to certain unusual exceptions, eg when the step-child was not brought up in the same household as the step-parent). Such prohibitions also apply where there is *consanguinity* (a blood relationship).

affirmative action Policies requiring institutions to act 'affirmatively' in employment or other recruitment practices to avoid discrimination on grounds of race, ethnic origin, gender, disability, or sexual orientation; usually found in the USA. Executive Order 10925 issued by President Kennedy contained the first use of the term. Affirmative action policies can range from encouraging the employment of minorities to the setting of quotas of minorities to be employed.

affix A grammatical element which cannot occur on its own, but must always attach to the root or stem of a word. Every language has a limited or closed set of affixes. In English, they may precede the stem (**prefixes**), as in ***im**possible*, or follow it (**suffixes**), as in *form**al***. Some other languages have **infixes**, which are attached within the word.

Affleck, Ben (1972–) Film actor, born in Berkeley, California, USA. He made his feature film debut in *School Ties* (1992), and became internationally known following his appearance in *Good Will Hunting* (1997), for which he shared an Oscar for best original screenplay with fellow co-star Matt Damon. Later films include *Shakespeare in Love* (1998), *Forces of Nature* (1999), *Changing Lanes* (2002), and *Paycheck* (2003).

afforestation The planting of woodland areas. The aim may be to increase the extent of economically useful wood (eg conifer plantations in upland UK) or to protect against soil erosion and desertification by providing shelter belts and vegetation cover on bare ground.

Afghan hound A breed of dog; large, slender, with a bouncing step; hair very long, silky (short-haired forms also exist); long thin muzzle; originated in Middle East; was used for hunting in N Afghanistan; hunts by sight.

Afghanistan *see panel*

Afghan Wars A series of wars (1838–42, 1878–80, 1919) between Britain and Afghanistan, prompted by the British desire to extend control in the region to prevent the advance of Russian influence towards India. The third Afghan War resulted in the country's independence through the Treaty of Rawalpindi (1922).

aflatoxin [aflatoksin] A toxin produced by the mould *Aspergillus flavus* (from Aspergillus *flavus toxin*) commonly found in groundnuts (peanuts), cottonseed, soybeans, wheat, barley, sorghum, and nuts such as pistachios, almonds, and cacao, where the climate favours its growth. The major epidemic of 'Turkey-X disease' in turkeys in the USA in 1960 was caused by feeding with contaminated groundnuts. Symptoms of poisoning include weight loss, loss of co-ordination, convulsions, and death. It also damages the liver, and causes liver tumours when fed long-term at low doses.

AFL/CIO *American Federation of Labor – Congress of Industrial Organisations*

Africa area c.30·97 million sq km/11·6 million sq mi. Second largest continent, extending S from the Mediterranean Sea; bounded W by the Atlantic Ocean and E by the Indian Ocean and the Red Sea; bisected by the Equator; maximum length, 8000 km/5000 mi; maximum width, 7200 km/4500 mi; highest point, Mt Kilimanjaro (5895 m/19 340 ft); major rivers include the Congo, Niger, Nile, Zambezi. *pp.20–1*

Africa, Partition of The division of the continent of Africa into colonial territories, which occurred in the last three decades of the 19th-c. Europeans had traded with Africa for several centuries, using a series of coastal settlements. Portuguese efforts to penetrate the interior in the 16th–17th-c had largely failed,

Afghanistan

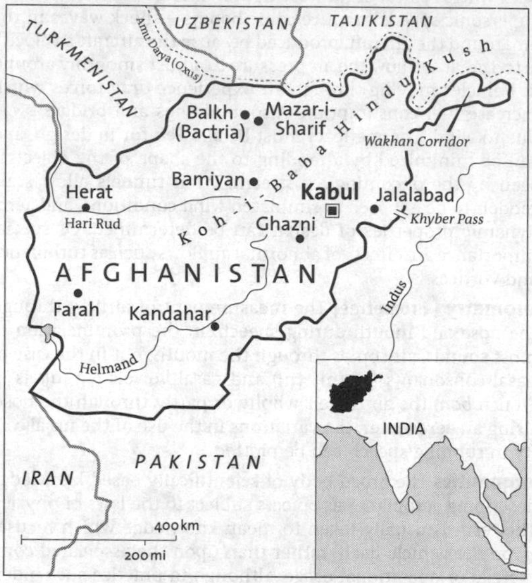

□ International Airport

official name **Islamic Emirate of Afghanistan**, Persian **Dowlat-e-Islami-ye-Afghanestan**

Local name Afghānestān

Timezone GMT +5

Area 647 497 km²/249 934 sq mi

Population total (2002e) 27 756 000, plus an estimated 2·5 million nomadic tribesmen and c.5 million living in Pakistan and Iran as refugees.

Status Democratic republic

Date of independence 1919

Capital Kabul

Languages Pushtu, Dari

Ethnic groups Pathans (50%), Tajik (20%), Uzbek (9%), Hazara (9%), Chahar Aimak (3%), Turkmen (2%), Baluchi (1%)

Religions Muslim (Sunni 84%, Shi'ite 15%)

Physical features Mountainous, landlocked country centred on and divided E-W by the Hindu Kush mountain range which reaches heights of over 7 000 m/24 000 ft. Three distinctive regions: fertile valley of Herat in NW; arid uplands to the S; and 129 495 km2/50 000 sq mi of desert in the SW plateau (including the Rigestan Desert). Amu Darya (Oxus) R forms N border.

Climate Continental climate; summers warm everywhere except on highest peaks; rain mostly during spring and autumn; average annual rainfall 338 mm/12·5 in; winters generally cold, with much snow at higher altitudes (central highlands have a subpolar climate); at lower levels desert or semi-arid climate.

Currency 1 Afghani (Af) = 100 puls

Economy Traditionally based on agriculture, especially wheat, fruit, vegetables, maize, barley, cotton, sugar-beet, sugar cane, sheep, cattle, goats; natural-gas production in the N, largely for export; most sectors have been affected by civil war, especially sugar, carpets, textiles; natural resources also include oil, coal, copper, sulphur, lead, zinc, iron, salt, precious and semi-precious stones; many of these resources remain untapped owing to inaccessibility. Main trading partners: Eastern European and CIS countries, Japan, China.

GDP (2002e) $19 bn, per capita $700

History Nation first formed in 1747, under Ahmad Shah Durrani; seen as a bridge between India and the Middle East. Britain tried but failed to gain control during a series of Afghan Wars (the last in 1919); independence declared in 1919 after World War 1; feudal monarchy survived until after World War 2, when the constitution became more liberal under several Soviet-influenced five-year economic plans; king deposed in 1973, and a republic formed; new constitution, 1977; coup (1979) brought to power Hafzullah Amin, which led to invasion by USSR forces and establishment of Babrak Karmal as Head of State; new constitution in 1987 provided for an executive President, bicameral National Assembly, and council of ministers; Soviet withdrawal implemented 1988–9; new regime met with heavy guerrilla resistance from the Mujahideen (Islamic fghters); resignation of President Najibullah, 1992; Islamic State of Afghanistan declared, 1992; continuing unrest and disunity among Mujahideen groups, hindering implementation of UN-backed peace plans; new conflict, 1994–5, with the *taliban* (army of students), a Muslim force whose military organization emerged in late 1994; Taliban seize Kabul and drive out government forces, imposition of strict Islamic regime, and execution of Najibullah, 1996; government of Burhanuddin Rabbani continued to control part of the country in rebellion against the Taliban government under Mohammad Omar Akhondzada; called Ismalic Emirate of Afghanistan, 1997; following the attack on the World Trade Center in New York (11 Sep 2001), US-led coalition forces launch aerial bombardment of Taliban-controlled military installations linked to Osama bin Laden, Oct 2001; Afghan delegations set up interim administration (under Hamid Karzai) under the auspices of the UN, Dec 2001; International Security Assistance Force (ISAF) established; US-led ongoing operations against remaining Taliban resistance, 2002; ISAF taken over by NATO, Aug 2003.

Democratic Republic of Afghanistan
Revolutionary Council – Head of State
1978–9 Nur Mohammad Taraki
1979 Hafizullah Amin

Soviet Invasion
1979–86 Babrak Karmal
1986–7 Haji Mohammad Chamkani *Acting*
1987 Ahmadzai Najibullah

Islamic Republic of Afghanistan
Head of State
1987–92 Mohammad Najibullah
1992 Seghbatullah Mujjaddedi
1992–6 Burhanuddin Rabbani

Head of Government
1929–46 Sardar Mohammad Hashim Khan
1946–53 Shah Mahmoud Khan Ghazi
1953–63 Mohammad Daoud
1963–5 Mohammad Yousef
1965–7 Mohammad Hashim Maiwandwal
1967–71 Nour Ahmad Etemadi
1972–3 Mohammad Mousa Shafiq
1973–9 *As President*
1979–81 Babrak Karmal
1981–8 Sultan Ali Keshtmand

Republic of Afghanistan from 1987
1988–9 Mohammad Hasan Sharq
1989–90 Sultan Ali Keshtmand
1990–2 Fazl Haq Khaleqiar
1992–3 Abdul Sabur Fareed
1993–4 Gulbardin Hekmatyar
1994–6 Arsala Rahmani *Acting*
1996 Gulbardin Hekmatyar

Interim Council
1996–2001 Mohammad Rabbani *Chairman*

Interim Government
2001–2 Hamid Karzai

Head of State
2002– Hamid Karzai (Interim)

and only the Dutch at the Cape had been able to establish a dynamic permanent settlement. In the course of the 19th-c, efforts to abolish the slave trade, missionary endeavours, and optimistic views of African riches helped to encourage colonial ambitions. The countries involved in the Partition included Britain, France, Germany, Portugal, and Italy, as well as the Boers in the S, and (in his private capacity) King Leopold of the Belgians. When the French and the Italians completed the Partition of N Africa in the years before World War 1, only Liberia and Ethiopia remained independent. At the end of the two World Wars, a repartitioning occurred with the confiscation of German and Italian territories. Most of the countries created by the Partition achieved independence in or after the 1960s, and the Organization of African Unity pledged itself to the maintenance of the existing boundaries.

African art Visual art forms of the Continent of Africa, originally rock painting and drawings, in open shelters rather than caves. Scratched or incised drawings occur more abundantly throughout the Sahara than anywhere else in the world, and extend chronologically from ancient times almost to the present day. Early representations of wild animals, some now extinct, attest to a hunting culture that flourished before c.4000 BC. The style, as in European Palaeolithic art, is naturalistic. Later rock art is more schematic. Horses and chariots, and later camels, appear. In S Africa the Bushmen have practised their own form of rock painting and drawing from early times to the present. The major form of African tribal (as opposed to prehistoric) art, practised mainly in the W Sudan, the Guinea Coast, Middle Africa, and the Congo, has been sculpture, especially masks and small figures, stools and thrones, as well as everyday objects. Materials, apart from wood, include ivory, metal (mostly bronze), terracotta, raffia, and occasionally stone. Painting has been much less important. In the early 20th-c, African sculpture inspired artists such as Picasso to employ 'primitive' forms in reaction against the conventions of 19th-c naturalism. In recent years, especially since c.1960, artists working in independent states have created original forms of art by combining traditional African with modern Western ideas, techniques, and aesthetic attitudes.

African buffalo A member of the cattle family, native to S and E Africa (*Syncerus caffer*); heavy black or brown body; thick horns lying across head like a helmet, with tips curved upwards; large

Africa

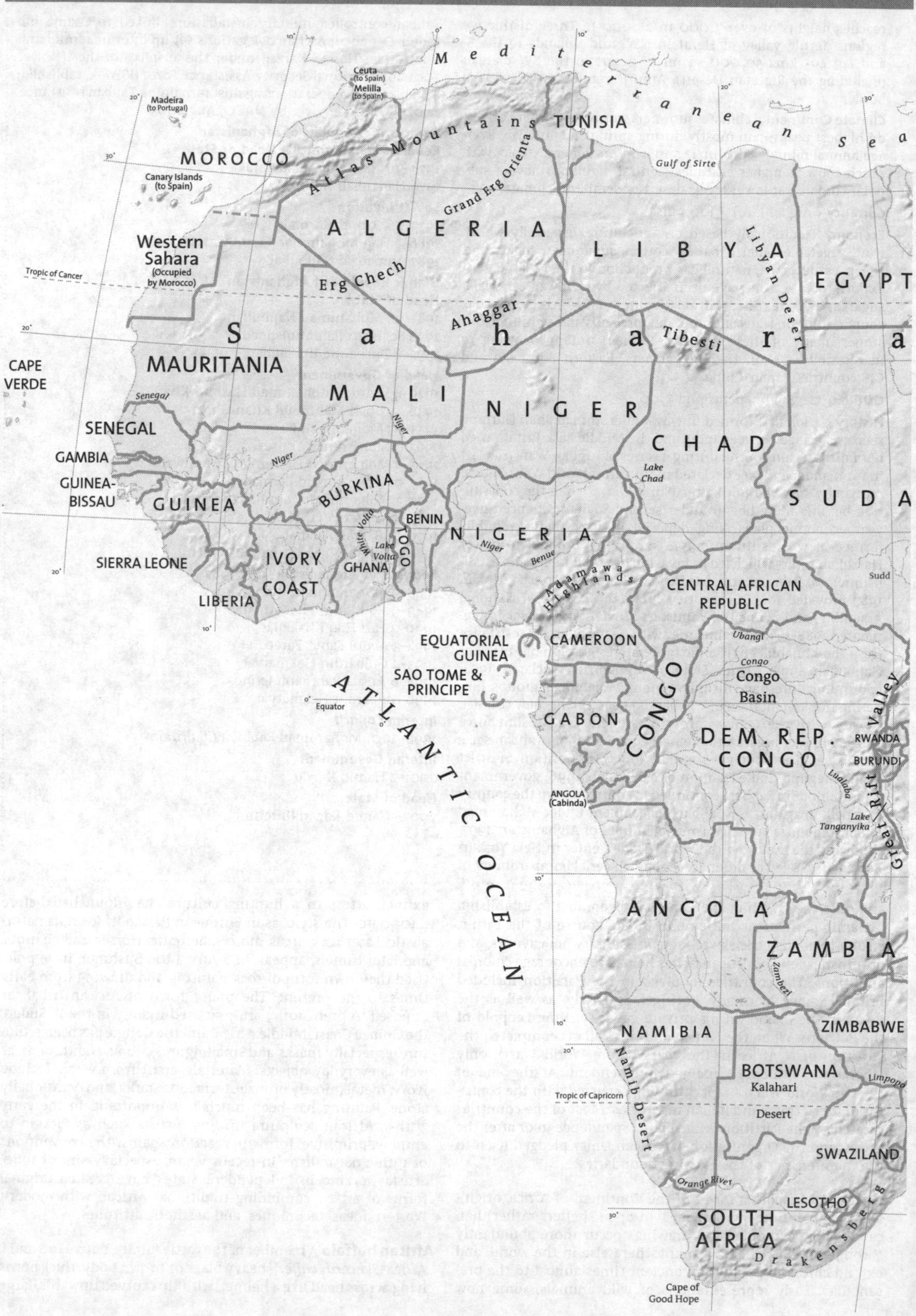
Mediterranean Sea
Ceuta (to Spain)
Melilla (to Spain)
Madeira (to Portugal)
TUNISIA
MOROCCO
Atlas Mountains
Canary Islands (to Spain)
Gulf of Sirte
Grand Erg Oriental
ALGERIA
Western Sahara (Occupied by Morocco)
LIBYA
Libyan Desert
EGYPT
Tropic of Cancer
Erg Chech
Ahaggar
Sahara
Tibesti
CAPE VERDE
MAURITANIA
Senegal
MALI
NIGER
SENEGAL
Niger
CHAD
GAMBIA
Lake Chad
GUINEA-BISSAU
GUINEA
BURKINA
SUDA
BENIN
White Volta
TOGO
NIGERIA
Lake Volta
Benue
SIERRA LEONE
IVORY COAST
GHANA
Adamawa Highlands
LIBERIA
CENTRAL AFRICAN REPUBLIC
Sudd
EQUATORIAL GUINEA
CAMEROON
Ubangi
SAO TOME & PRINCIPE
Congo
Congo Basin
Equator
ATLANTIC OCEAN
GABON
CONGO
DEM. REP. CONGO
RWANDA
BURUNDI
Great Rift Valley
ANGOLA (Cabinda)
Lualaba
Lake Tanganyika
ANGOLA
ZAMBIA
Zambezi
NAMIBIA
ZIMBABWE
BOTSWANA
Kalahari Desert
Limpopo
Tropic of Capricorn
Namib Desert
SWAZILAND
Orange River
LESOTHO
SOUTH AFRICA
Drakensberg
Cape of Good Hope

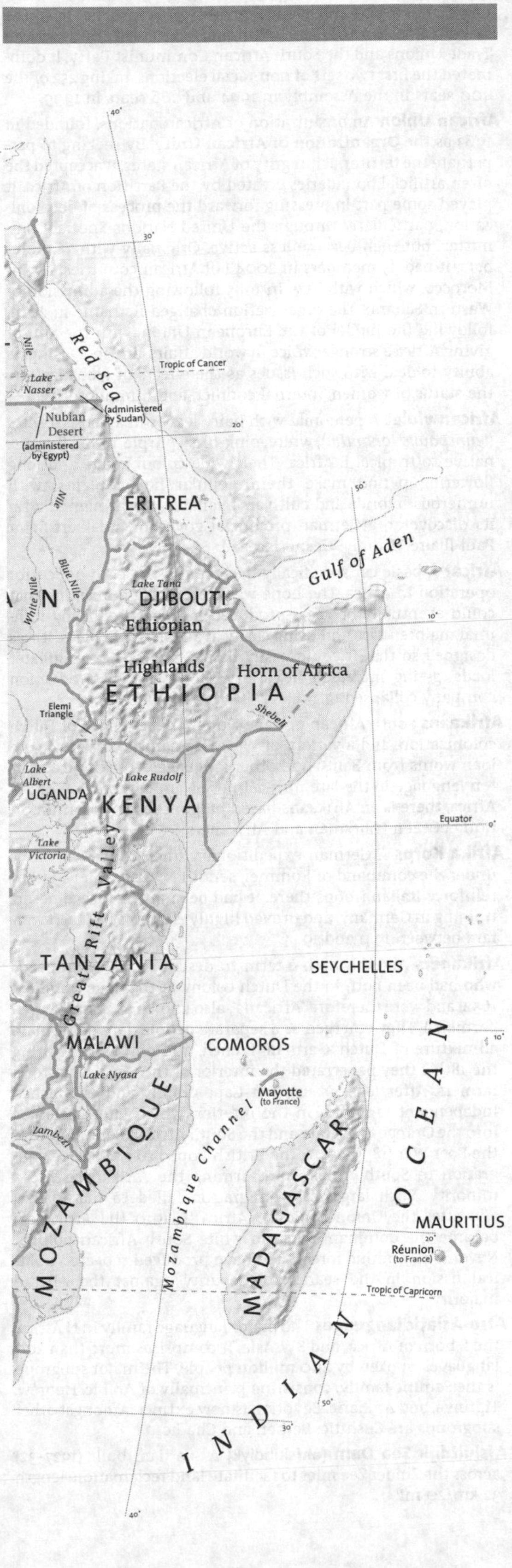

drooping ears; also known as **Cape buffalo** (small form called **dwarf forest buffalo**).

African dance The most common form of dance within the sub-Saharan tradition, performed either in a closed circle or in a linear formation controlled by a team leader. Dance teams may include a soloist, or encourage each team member to leave the circle in turn and improvise freely in the centre. African dances are percussive, employing hand and foot movements and posture to express the rhythmic pulses of their dance. They are often led by musicians playing a flute, drum, xylophone, or bamboo gong. In some traditions, individuals break into an ecstatic trance while in other cultures the dancers may sing either before or during the dance. Dancers may carry staves or horse-tail switches and wear flowing gowns or brief skirts, with girdles or brass bells, and seed pod rattles around their ankles to accentuate their movements. As part of a spiritual ritual, dancers may wear masks, thus assuming the temporary identity of a god or a powerful ancestral spirit. A characteristic of African dance is the encouragement given to improvisation and innovation within the framework of traditional patterns, creating new, intricate, and intertwining rhythms and movements. In the 20th-c the influence of African dance rhythm, music, and gesture on modern and popular dance forms has spread from the Caribbean to the South and North American continents and to Europe.

African history The study of the history of the continent of Africa. Early approaches were bedevilled by the way Europeans regarded history as the study of societies through literacy, the examination of pre-literate societies being dubbed 'pre-history'. Africans themselves, however, though largely non-literate, had a clear conception of history which they maintained through oral traditions. Much could be established about the African past through the archaeological record and through literate sources derived from the ancient world, Islam, and the earliest European travellers. The Portuguese in particular observed, interacted with, and recorded features of several African societies from the 15th-c, and also began the process of collecting traditions. This was developed by explorers, missionaries, administrators, and anthropologists in the 19th-c and early 20th-c. It was only after World War 2 that the professional study of African history was put on a sound footing, and rapid strides were made in the utilization of all available sources, including oral history (often with a chronological depth up to five centuries). There is now a vigorous school of indigenous African historians.

African horse sickness A disease of horses caused by a virus of the Orbivirus group. It affects all Equidae, but asses, mules, and zebra are more resistant than horses. The organism is transmitted by a mosquito and is highly infectious. It causes mainly respiratory signs, often with swelling of the head and neck. There is a high mortality rate, and the disease is notifiable in the UK. A vaccine is available which protects against some strains of the virus.

African hunting dog A member of the dog family (*Lycaon pictus*), native to S Africa; also known as **Cape hunting dog**; the only dog with four toes on each foot; long legs; large rounded ears; mottled light and dark coat; inhabits open plains; packs hunt large grazing mammals.

African languages The languages of the continent of Africa; c.1300, spoken by c.400 million people. They are difficult to classify, because relatively few have been systematically described, and it is not always clear whether two varieties are separate languages or dialects of the same language. Few had written form before the Christian missionary activities of the 19th-c. Many of these languages do not have official status, but are subservient to the languages of colonialism, especially English and French. There are few with more than a million speakers. It is generally agreed, however, that there are four main families: Afro-Asiatic, Niger–Congo, Nilo-Saharan, and Khoisan languages.

African lily An evergreen perennial (*Agapanthus africanus*) with thick, tough rhizomes, native to S Africa; leaves strap-shaped, leathery, growing to 1 m/3 ft; flowers with six perianth-segments, bell-shaped, blue, rarely white, in large umbels on leafless stalks. (Family: Liliaceae.)

African literature The literature of the continent of Africa. Much still belongs to the oral tradition, closely linked to both secular occupation and religious ritual. Throughout the many language groups, there is a wealth of dirges, laments, love songs, chants, celebrations, invectives, and poems inciting warriors to battle, with musical accompaniment. Literature is written in both African and the post-colonial languages. Much vernacular composition tends to be in drama and poetry, such as Kwasi Fiawoo's Ewe play *Toko Atolia* (1937, The Fifth Landing Stage), and Okot p'Bitek's satirical poem in Acholi; whereas Africans writing in English or French will often prefer fiction. Notable examples include the English novels of Chinua Achebe (among them *Things Fall Apart*, 1958), the plays of Wole Soyinka, and the French poetry of Leon Damas (1912–78), Léopold Senghor and Aimé Césaire. *African Literature Today* provides an annual review of the field; while the anthology *Daughters of Africa* (1992) adds women's writing to what is now available. The quite different culture of South Africa has produced a number of distinguished novelists, most recently writing against or despite the apartheid state, among them Olive Schreiner, Nadine Gordimer, J M Coetzee, and Christopher Hope (1944–). During the later decades of the 20th-c, several writers of African and European descent spoke out, often at great danger to themselves, against human rights abuses. Notable among these was the Nigerian writer, Kenule ('Ken') Beeson Saro-Wiwa (1941–95), who was executed in 1995 by his country's military regime.

African marigold A misleading name for *Tagetes erecta*, a popular garden annual originating from Mexico, with deeply cut leaves and showy yellow, orange, or red flower-heads up to 10 cm/4 in diameter. **French marigold**, *Tagetes erecta*, also from Mexico, is very similar but has smaller flower-heads. (Family: Compositae.)

African Methodist Episcopal Church A Church formed at a national meeting of Black Methodists in 1816 in the USA, the culmination of a movement begun in 1787. It expanded rapidly after the Civil War, and today has c.1·2 million members. In 1841 it established the first African-American publishing house in the USA.

African Methodist Episcopal Zion Church An African-American Methodist Church in the USA, dating from 1821, which emerged when a group reacted against the discrimination they experienced as members of a New York City Methodist foundation. The Church grew rapidly after the American Civil War, and in 2004 its membership was c.1·5 million.

African music The indigenous music of the African continent. Generalization is difficult because of the size of the continent, the diversity of its peoples and languages, the profound influence of Arab culture in the N, and the more recent infiltration of Western music in all parts. The most typical features seem to be: the absence, until the 20th-c, of any system of musical notation (except in the ancient chant of the Ethiopian church); the ubiquity of song, especially in a solo–refrain form; the close interaction of language, movement, and music, both vocal and instrumental; the importance of improvisation; and the complexity and sophistication of rhythm.

African National Congress (ANC) The most important of the Black South African organizations opposed to the white regime. It began life in 1912 as the South African Native National Congress, and under the influence of Gandhi organized passive resistance to white power. Banned by the South African government in 1961, it began a campaign of industrial and economic sabotage through its military wing, and in the 1980s started attacking persons as well as property. Based in Zambia for several years, it was estimated to have a force of 6000 guerrillas. It was unbanned in February 1990, and suspended its armed struggle in August 1990, shortly before commencing negotiations with the South African government. It is the senior partner in an alliance with the Congress of South African Trade Unions and the South African Communist Party. It dominated the first two sets of non-racial elections, taking 252 of the 400 seats in the Assembly in 1994 and 266 seats in 1999.

African Union An organization of African nations, founded in 1963 as the **Organization of African Unity**. By seeking to perpetuate the territorial integrity of African states, it accepted the often artificial boundaries created by the Partition of Africa. It played some part in pressing forward the process of decolonization, particularly through the United Nations Special Committee, but then became less active. Originally with 32 members, it had 53 members in 2004 (all African countries except Morocco, which withdrew in 1985 following the admission of Western Sahara). The organization changed its name in 2001, following the model of the European Union, with the aim of giving Africa a stronger voice in world affairs, and increasing its ability to deal with such issues as the effects of globalization, the status of women, internal conflict, and human rights.

African violet A perennial with hairy leaves in a dense rosette (*Saintpaulia ionantha*); white, pink, blue, purple, or red flowers; native to tropical E Africa. Their wide colour range and long flowering period make them popular house plants, with numerous hybrids and cultivars available. It was named after its discoverer, a German provincial governor, Adalbert Saint Paul-Illaire. (Family: Gesneriaceae.)

Africar A basic car specifically designed in the early 1980s for operation in Africa. The hope was to produce a machine that could eventually be mass-produced in Africa, requiring minimal maintenance and using easily available spare parts. It was designed so that it could easily be extended to carry greater loads, giving increased flexibility. However, the production company collapsed in 1988.

Afrikaans South African or Cape Dutch, the language of Dutch colonization, and a variety of West Germanic, but with many loan words from Bantu and other languages. It became a written language in the late 19th-c. In the Namaland region of SW Africa, there is an Afrikaans-based pidgin used in communication between tribesmen and Afrikaners.

Afrika Korps A German expeditionary force of two divisions under the command of Rommel, sent to N Africa (Mar 1941) to reinforce Italian troops there. It had been given special desert training in Germany, and proved highly effective in desert warfare between 1941 and 1944.

Afrikaners An early 18th-c term to describe those Europeans who had been born in the Dutch colony at the Cape (founded 1652) and were therefore 'Africans', also known as **Boers** (Dutch 'farmers'). They emerged as a separate people derived from an admixture of Dutch, German, French, and non-white. During the 18th-c they penetrated the interior of the Cape as pastoral farmers. After 1835, groups left Cape Colony and established independent republics in the interior, which later coalesced into the Orange Free State and the South African Republic. After the Boer War (1899–1902) the British hoped to encourage emigration to South Africa, transforming the Afrikaners into a minority. Such large-scale emigration failed to materialize, and after the Union of South Africa in 1910 the Afrikaners became the dominant force in white South African politics. Never a monolithic force, they have produced repeated political fission in the search for security against the African majority.

Afro-Asiatic languages The major language family in N Africa, the E horn of Africa, and SW Asia. It comprises more than 200 languages, spoken by 200 million people. The major subgroup is the Semitic family, consisting principally of Arabic, Hebrew, Tigrinya, and Amharic. Egyptian is now extinct. Amongst other subgroups are Cushitic, Berber, and Chadic.

Afsluitdijk Sea Dam [ahf**sluhdiyk**] A sea dam built (1927–32) across the Zuider Zee inlet to facilitate land reclamation; length 32 km/20 mi.

afterburning A method of increasing the thrust of a jet engine. Fuel is injected into the hot exhaust gases leaving the engine, thereby igniting the fuel and providing extra thrust.

AFV *armoured fighting vehicle*

Agadir [agad**ee**r] 30°30N 9°40W, pop (2000e) 160 000. Seaport in Sud province, W Morocco; on the Atlantic coast, 8 km/5 mi N of the mouth of the R Sous; named Santa Cruz by the Portuguese, 1505–41; taken by the French in 1913; extensive rebuilding after earthquake in 1960; airport; fishing, tourism; 16th-c kasbah fortress; African People's Arts Festival (Jul).

Aga Khan I, originally **Hasan Ali Shah** (1800–81) Imam of the Nizari Ismailite sect of the Shiite Muslims. He claimed to be descended from Ali, the son-in-law of the Prophet Mohammed. Appointed governor of the Iranian province of Kerman, he was granted the title of Aga Khan in 1818 by the Shah of Iran. In 1838 he rose in revolt against Mohammed Shah but was defeated and fled to India. He helped the British in the first Anglo-Afghan War (1839–42) and in the conquest of Sindh (1842–3), and was granted a pension.

Aga Khan II, originally **Ali Shah** (d.1885) Imam of the Nizari Ismailite sect of Shiite Muslims. In 1881 he succeeded his father, Aga Khan I, and during his short reign sought to improve the conditions of the community.

Aga Khan [ahga **kahn**] Title of the hereditary head of the Ismailian sect of Muslims, who trace their origins to the mediaeval Assassins. The title has been held by four men: **Hasan Ali Shah** (r.1818–81); **Ali Shah** (r.1881–5); **Mohammed Shah** (r.1885–1957), and **Karim**, 49th imam of the line (r.1957–). In the 20th-c the Aga Khans played prominent roles as world statesmen; Aga Khan III served as President of the League of Nations, while Aga Khan IV became a noted philanthropist.

Agamemnon [aga**mem**non] King of Argos and commander of the Greek army in the Trojan War. In the *Iliad*, Homer calls him 'king of men'. On his return home he was murdered by his wife Clytemnestra and her lover Aegisthus.

agamid [**ag**amid] A lizard native to Africa (except Madagascar), S and SE Asia, and Australia; body usually broad, head large, scales with ridges and spines; tongue thick and fleshy; tail cannot be shed; some species able to change colour; also known as **chisel-tooth lizard**. (Family: Agamidae, 300 species.)

Agaña [a**gah**nya] 13°28N 144°45E, pop (2000e) 1400. Port and capital town of Guam, Mariana Is, W Pacific Ocean; taken by Japan, 1941; destroyed during its recapture by the USA, 1944; university (1952); US naval base; cathedral (1669) rebuilt after World War 2; frequent typhoons.

agapanthus *African lily*

agar [**ay**gah(r)] A jelly-like compound produced from seaweed. It is used, after sterilization and the addition of suitable nutrients, for culture of fungi or bacteria for medicinal or research purposes.

Agassi, Andre [**ag**asee] (1970–) Tennis player, born in Las Vegas, Nevada, USA. He turned professional in 1986, won the Association of Tennis Professionals Tour World Championships in 1990, and went on to win Wimbledon (1992), the US Open (1994, 1999), the Australian Open (1995, 2000, 2001, 2003), the French Open (1999), and other titles, leading the world rankings for much of 1995. He is also known for his work in relation to youth community projects, notably the Andre Agassi Foundation (1994). At the beginning of 2004 he had a world ranking of Number 4.

Agassiz, (Jean) Louis (Rodolphe) [**ag**asee] (1807–73) Naturalist and glaciologist, born in Motier, W Switzerland, the father of oceanographer Alexander Agassiz (1835–1910). In 1832 he was appointed professor of natural history at Neuchâtel. *Etudes sur les glaciers* (1840, Studies of Glaciers), showed that glaciers move, thus indicating the existence of an Ice Age. Professor of natural history at the Lawrence Scientific School, Harvard (1847–73), he founded a Museum of Comparative Zoology (1859), to which he gave all his collections. He published four of ten projected volumes of *Contributions to the Natural History of the United States* (1857–62). In his later years he became a US citizen.

agate [**ag**ayt] A form of chalcedony, a fine-grained variety of the mineral quartz. It is formed in cavities, and characterized by fine colour-banding of successive growth layers. Colour variations result in semi-precious stones such as onyx (white/grey), carnelian (red), and chrysoprase (apple-green).

Agatha, St (?–251) Christian martyr from Catania, Sicily. According to legend, she rejected the love of the Roman consul, Quintilianus, and suffered a cruel martyrdom in 251. She is the patron saint of Catania, is invoked against fire and lightning, and is also the patron saint of bell-founders. Feast day 5 February.

agave [a**gah**vee] An evergreen perennial native to S USA, Central America, and N South America; stems very short, tough; leaves sword-shaped, often spiny on margins, thick, fleshy, and waxy, forming a rosette. The plant grows for many years, adding a few leaves and building up reserves each year, finally producing a huge branched inflorescence up to 7 m/23 ft high, with many flowers, after which it dies. Many species produce useful fibres, such as henequen. In Mexico, the sap of several species is fermented to produce pulque; stems and leaf bases are used to make mescal, an alcoholic drink of which tequila is one variety. (Genus: *Agave*, 300 species. Family: Agavaceae.)

Agee, James (Rufus) [**ay**jee] (1909–55) Novelist, poet, film critic, and screen writer, born in Knoxville, Tennessee, USA. He studied at Harvard, and worked for several magazines before being commissioned to rove the Southern states with the photographer Walker Evans, producing *Let Us Now Praise Famous Men* (1941). His film scripts include *The African Queen* (1951) and *The Night of the Hunter* (1955). His novel, *A Death in the Family* (published 1957), was awarded a posthumous Pulitzer Prize. He was also a celebrated film critic, as seen in *Agee on Film* (1958).

ageing *senescence*

Agence France-Press (AFP) [azh**ã**s fr**ã**s] An international news agency, with headquarters in Paris. The direct successor to Havas (established in 1832), AFP is the oldest surviving world agency, and one of the largest. In addition to general news, it offers specialist business, niche, and web services.

agenda setting The presumed power of interest groups, politicians, and the mass media to determine the public's perception of the salience and relative importance of issues. The term was coined in 1972 and has subsequently come to apply to a body of work in the field of mass communications. The agenda-setting hypothesis posits a cognitive correspondence on the part of the media, the public, and politicians (or other elites) on the way issues are seen, which is engineered in part by **spin doctors** and which serves the sectional interests of the powerful. Others argue that agenda setters more commonly respond to the public mood than create it. The available evidence is largely inconclusive, due in part to the difficulty of proving causal links.

Agent Orange (2,4,5-T or 2,4,5-trichlorophenoxy acetic acid) A herbicide used as a defoliant in jungle warfare, for example by the British in Malaya and the USA in Vietnam. Its name derives from the orange rings painted around the containers used in Vietnam. It is toxic to humans because it contains traces of dioxin, which produces severe skin eruptions (*chloracne*), and also birth abnormalities and cancer in laboratory animals.

age-sets Social groups recruited by age. Individuals typically join an age-set at adolescence, passing with their fellow-members through a series of grades such as warrior and elder. Age-sets are best known among E African peoples such as the Masai.

Agesilaus [ajeesi**lay**us] (444–360 BC) King of Sparta (399–360 BC). Called on by the Ionians to assist them in 397 BC against Artaxerxes II, he launched an ambitious campaign in Asia, but the Corinthian War recalled him to Greece. At Coronea (394 BC) he defeated the Greek allied forces, and peace was eventually concluded in favour of Sparta (387 BC). He precipitated the Battle of Leuctra against Thebes (371 BC), a disaster which signified the end of Spartan ascendancy and the beginning of a decade of Theban supremacy in Greece.

Aggeus [agayus] *Haggai, Book of*

aggiornamento [ajaw(r)na**men**toh] The process of making the life, doctrine, and worship of the Roman Catholic Church effective in the modern world. This was initiated by Pope John XXIII at the Second Vatican Council (1962–5).

agglomerate Coarse volcanic rock that consists of a mixture of fragments of various sizes and shapes. It is usually deposited as part of a volcanic cone and derived from the rocks through which the volcanic magma has travelled on its way to the surface.

agglutinating language A type of language in which words are typically made up of sequences of elements, as in English *de-human-ize*. Such languages are at the opposite extreme from *fusional* languages, in which there is no necessary one-to-one correspondence between the string of elements and the total meaning of the word.

Agincourt, Battle of [azhinkaw(r)t] (1415) A battle between France and England during the Hundred Years' War. Henry V of England was forced to fight near Hesdin (Pas-de-Calais) by the French who, ignoring the lessons of Crécy (1346) and Poitiers (1356), pitched cavalry against dismounted men-at-arms and archers. Though heavily outnumbered, the English won another overwhelming victory, and returned in 1417 to begin the systematic conquest of Normandy.

aging *senescence*

Agitprop An abbreviation for the **Department of Agitation and Propaganda**, established in 1920 as a section of the Central Committee Secretariat of the Soviet Communist Party. Its role was to ensure the compatibility of activities within society with Communist Party ideology. The term later came to be widely used in an artistic or literary context for works or cultural activities which adopted an ideological stance.

Agnesi, Maria Gaetana [anyayzee] (1718–99) Mathematician and scholar, born in Milan, N Italy. The daughter of a professor of mathematics at Bologna, she was a child prodigy, speaking six languages by the age of 11. She took her father's place as professor of mathematics at Bologna in 1750, and her mathematical textbook *Istituzioni analitiche* (1784) became famous throughout Italy. A curve, the *witch of Agnesi*, is named after her.

Agnew, Spiro T(heodore) [agnyoo] (1918–96) US vice-president, born in Baltimore, Maryland, USA, the son of a Greek immigrant. After service in World War 2 he studied law at Baltimore University (1947). In 1966 he was elected governor of Maryland on a liberal platform, introducing anti-racial-discrimination legislation that year. As a compromise figure acceptable to most shades of Republican opinion, he was Nixon's running mate in 1968 and 1972, and took office as vice-president in 1969. He resigned in 1973, following an investigation into bribery and other crimes.

Agni [**uhg**ni] The Hindu god of fire, especially important to the priesthood, because in the fire-cult he takes offerings and sacrifices to the gods. More hymns are addressed to him than to any other god. His chariot is drawn by red horses, and clears a way through the jungle by burning: but he is welcome in every home as a principle of life and because he drives away demons.

Agnon, Shmuel Yosef, originally **Shmuel Josef Czaczkes** (1888–1970) Novelist, born in Buczacz, Poland (now Buchach, W Ukraine). He went to Palestine in 1907, studied in Berlin (1913–24), then settled permanently in Jerusalem and changed his surname to Agnon. He wrote in Hebrew an epic trilogy of novels on Eastern Jewry in the early 20th-c: their translated titles are *Bridal Canopy* (1931), *A Guest for the Night* (1939), and *Days Gone By* (1945). He is also known for several volumes of short stories. In 1966 he became the first Israeli to receive the Nobel Prize for Literature.

agnosia [ag**noh**zia] A condition found in some brain-damaged individuals, whereby they are unable to recognize objects despite adequate basic visual and intellectual abilities. It is often specific to a particular sensory modality; for example a patient might be able to recognize by touch but not by sight.

agnosticism Strictly, the view that God's existence cannot be known (*theism*) nor denied (*atheism*). The term was derived from the 'unknown' God in *Acts* 17.23, and first used (by T H Huxley) in 1869: agnostics were contrasted with **gnostics**, or metaphysicians. It was later extended to include the view that knowledge must be restricted to what is available to the senses, and that anything not so available (including therefore religion and God) is irrelevant to life today.

Agostini, Giacomo [agos**tee**nee] (1944–) Motor-cyclist, born in Lóvere, N Italy. He won a record 15 world titles between 1966 and 1975, including the 500 cc title a record eight times (1966–72, 1975); 13 of the titles were on an MV Agusta, the others on a Yamaha. He won 10 Isle of Man TT Races (1966–75), including the Senior TT five times (1968–72). After retirement in 1975, he became manager of the Yamaha racing team.

agouti [a**goo**tee] A cavy-like rodent, native to Central and South America and Caribbean Is; length, 50 cm/20 in; rat-like with long legs and minute black tail. (Genus: *Dasyprocta*, 11 species. Family: Dasyproctidae.)

Agra [**ah**gra] 27°17N 77°58E, pop (2000e) 1 055 000. City in Uttar Pradesh, NE India, 190 km/118 mi SE of Delhi; founded, 1566; Mughal capital until 1659; taken by the British, 1803; seat of the government of North-West Provinces, 1835–62; airfield; railway; university (1927); commerce, glass and leather crafts, carpets; Taj Mahal (1632–54), Pearl Mosque of Shah Jahan (1662), Mirror Palace (Shish Mahal), a world heritage site; Great Mosque, fort (16th-c), tomb of Akbar to the N at Sikandra.

agranulocytosis [aygranyoolohsiy**toh**sis] A clinical condition in which granulocytes (a type of white blood cell) disappear from the blood, leaving the patient vulnerable to infection. It has many causes, including certain drugs and diseases that damage the bone marrow.

agraphia *dysgraphia*

Agre, Peter [ahg ray] (1949–) Biochemist, born in Northfield, Minnesota, USA. He studied at Augsburg College, Minneapolis (1970) and Johns Hopkins University School of Medicine, Baltimore (1974), and after various academic posts became professor of biological chemistry at Johns Hopkins in 1993. He shared the 2003 Nobel Prize for Chemistry for discoveries concerning channels in cell membranes.

agribusiness The combined businesses of: farmers, who produce commodities; input industries, which supply them with equipment, chemicals, and finance; and merchants, processors, and distributors, who convert commodities into foodstuffs, ready for sale to consumers. In many countries the agribusiness sector employs more labour and generates more income than any other sector of the economy.

agrichemicals Farm inputs derived from the chemical industry – in particular, inorganic fertilizers and sprays. Concern about their effect has grown since the 1980s, and led to the development of organic farming methods.

Agricola, Georgius [agrikola], Latin name of **Georg Bauer** (1494–1555) Mineralogist and metallurgist, born in Glauchau, EC Germany. He studied at Leipzig, Bologna, and Padua, and in 1527 was appointed city physician in Joachimstal. After moving to Chemnitz in 1533, he devoted himself to the study of mining. He made the first scientific classification of minerals in *De natura fossilium* (1546, On the Nature of Fossils), based on the observation of their physical properties. Of his many books, the best known is *De re metallica* (1556), a valuable record of the arts of mining and smelting in the 16th-c.

Agricola, Gnaeus Julius [agrikola] (40–93) Roman statesman and soldier, born in Fréjus (formerly Forum Julii). Having served with distinction in Britain, Asia, and Aquitania, he was elected consul in 77, and returned to Britain (78–84) becoming Rome's longest-serving and most successful governor there. In 80 and 81 he extended Roman occupation N into Scotland, defeated Calcagus at Mons Graupius (84), and actively encouraged the development of Roman-style towns in the S. His fleet circumnavigated the coast, for the first time discovering Britain to be an island. The news of Agricola's successes inflamed the jealousy of the emperor, Domitian, and in 84 he was recalled.

Agricola, Johann [agrikola], originally **Schneider** or **Schnitter**, also called **Magister Islebius** (1492–1566) Protestant reformer, born in Eisleben, C Germany. Having studied at Wittenberg and Leipzig, he was sent to Frankfurt by Luther in 1525 to institute Protestant worship there. Appointed in 1536 to a chair at Wittenberg, he resigned in 1540 over his opposition to Luther in the great Antinomian controversy. He later became court preacher in Berlin.

Agricultural Revolution The name popularly given to a series of changes in farming practice occurring first in England and later throughout W Europe. Some historians date these as far back as the end of the 16th-c, but the term usually covers the period 1700–1850. The main changes included: greater intensity of productive land use; the reduction of fallow land and waste lands; the introduction of crop rotation; the development of improved grasses; new crops, such as turnips and potatoes; the use of seed drills; and scientific animal breeding. Many such changes were facilitated by the replacement of open fields by enclosures. They also depended upon tenant farming and market production replacing subsistence and peasant agriculture. The widespread use of mechanized farming techniques, such as threshing machines and mechanical ploughs, mostly post-dated the changes of this agricultural revolution.

agriculture The cultivation of crops and the keeping of domesticated animals for food, fibre, or power. Settled agriculture enabled primitive people, who depended on hunting, fishing, and gathering, to live in communities, which could then grow as their agricultural productivity grew. This was aided by the development of such implements as ploughs, hoes, and sickles – and in drier countries by the construction of irrigation systems that benefitted from the invention of new technology (such as the Archimedes screw, which enabled water to be transported uphill). In mediaeval Britain, agriculture was based on the manorial three-field system, growing two crops of cereals, followed by a year's fallow. Livestock were grazed on the common pastures, but lack of winter feed kept productivity low. Enclosures in the 16th–18th-c made experimentation easier, particularly in the selective breeding of livestock. New rotations, especially the development by 'Turnip' Townshend of the Norfolk four-course rotation, also contributed to a rapid improvement in agricultural productivity. By 2000, 37·3% of the world's land area was in agricultural production – 11·33% in crops and 25·96% in permanent pasture – and 5·4% of this land was irrigated. World agricultural production is dominated by cereals: total world cereal production in 2002 was 2·031 thousand million tonnes. China was the largest producer (402 million tonnes), followed by the USA (334 million tonnes); the EU produced 213 million tonnes. Between 1950 and 1990 world productivity tripled, but by 2002 average annual growth had reduced to 1·7%. Evidence suggests that it is increasingly difficult to sustain rapid growth using traditional crops.

agrimony [agrimonee] An erect perennial (*Agrimonia eupatoria*) growing to 60 cm/2 ft, native to Europe, W Asia, and N Africa; leaves hairy, pinnate with pairs of small leaflets alternating with large ones; flowers 5–8 mm/0·2–0·3 in diameter, 5-petalled, yellow, in a long terminal spike. The fruit is a burr with hooked spines around the top. (Family: Rosaceae.)

Agrippa *Herod Agrippa* **1 / 2**

Agrippa, Marcus Vipsanius [agripa] (c.63–12 BC) Roman commander, statesman, and right-hand man of Octavian (later, the Emperor Augustus). He defeated Sextus, the son of Pompey, at Mylae and Naulochus in 36 BC, and Mark Antony at Actium in 31 BC. He used his great wealth to popularize the new regime by vastly improving the public amenities of Rome. His third wife was Julia, daughter of Augustus.

Agrippina [agripeena], known as **Agrippina the Elder** (c.14 BC–AD 33) Roman noblewoman, the daughter of Marcus Vipsanius Agrippa and grand-daughter of Emperor Augustus. She married Germanicus Caesar (15 BC–AD 19), and was the mother of Caligula and Agrippina the Younger. Regarded as a model of heroic womanhood, she accompanied her husband on his campaigns. Her popularity incurred the anger of the Emperor Tiberius, who banished her in 29 to the island of Pandateria, where she died of starvation in suspicious circumstances.

Agrippina [agripeena], known as **Agrippina the Younger** (15–59) Roman noblewoman, the daughter of Agrippina (the Elder) and Germanicus. She first married Gnaeus Domitius Ahenobarbus, by whom she had a son, the future Emperor Nero. Her third husband was Emperor Claudius, though her own uncle. She persuaded Claudius to adopt Nero as his successor, then proceeded to poison all Nero's rivals and enemies, and finally (allegedly) the emperor himself. Her ascendancy proved intolerable to Nero, who eventually put her to death.

agroforestry The cultivation of tree or bush crops (such as coffee, oil palm, rubber, or tea), sometimes alternating with annual food crops, to give a sustainable and economically viable agricultural cropping system. Such systems are frequently used in place of the climax forest vegetation of the humid or sub-humid tropics.

agronomy The theory and practice of field-crop production and soil management. The subject embraces several disciplines, including plant breeding, plant physiology, plant pathology, and soil conservation.

Aguinaldo, Emilio [aginaldoh] (1870–1964) Filipino revolutionary, born near Cavite, Luzon, Philippines. He led the rising against Spain in the Philippines (1896–8), and then against the USA (1899–1901), but after capture in 1901 took the oath of allegiance to America.

Agulhas, Cape [agulyas] 34°50S 20°00E. The most southerly point of the African continent, 160 km/100 mi SE of the Cape of Good Hope, South Africa; running past it, round the whole S coast, is a reef, the Agulhas Bank, an important fishing ground.

Agutter, Jenny [aguhter] (1952–) Film and stage actress, born in Taunton, Somerset, SW England, UK. She became known following her role in *The Railway Children* (1970). Her other film credits include *The Snow Goose* (1971, Emmy, Best Supporting Actress), *Equus* (1977, BAFTA), *Child's Play 2* (1991), and *Blue Juice* (1995). Television work includes *A Respectable Trade* (1998), a new adaptation of *The Railway Children* (2000), *Spooks* (2003), and *The Alan Clark Diaries* (2004).

Ahab [ayhab] (9th-c BC) King of Israel (c.873–c.852 BC), the son of Omri. He was a warrior king and builder on a heroic scale, extending his capital city of Samaria and refortifying Megiddo and Hazor. He married Jezebel, daughter of the king of Tyre and Sidon, who introduced the worship of the Phoenician god, Baal, in opposition to Yahweh (the God of Israelite religion), and thus aroused the hostility of the prophet Elijah.

Ahaggar Mountains [ahagah(r)] or **Hoggar Mountains** Mountain range in S Algeria, N Africa; rises to 2918 m/9573 ft at Mt Tahat, the highest point in Algeria; peaks rise from a plateau with a mean elevation of c.2000 m/6500 ft; includes the 'mountain of goblins', Garet el Djenoun (2327 m/7634 ft), according to legend a holy mountain.

Aharonov–Bohm effect [aharonof bohm] An effect produced when a single electron beam is divided into two parts, passed either side of a solenoid containing a magnetic field, and recombined at a screen beyond. A quantum mechanical interference pattern is produced which is sensitive to the magnetic vector potential outside the solenoid rather than to the magnetic field within. It reveals the nature of the interaction between wave function and electromagnetic influence. The effect, first described in 1959 by Yakir Aharonov and David Bohm, has been confirmed experimentally.

Ahern, Bertie [ahern] (1951–) Irish politician and prime minister (1997–). He studied at Rathmines College of Commerce and University College Dublin, became a hospital accountant and union organizer, and became a member of the Dáil in 1977. After a series of junior posts, he became minister of state at the departments of Taoiseach and Defence (1982), minister for labour (1987–91) and finance (1991–4), and leader of the opposition and President of Fianna Fáil in 1994. He became head of a coalition government after defeating John Bruton in 1997. He was a key participant in the Northern Ireland peace process following the signing of the Good Friday Agreement. He was elected for a second term in 2002.

Ahimsa [ahimsa] The principle of respect for all life and the practice of non-injury to living things, found in certain Hindu sects, Buddhism, and especially Jainism. It is based on the belief that violence has harmful effects on those who commit it, including an unfavourable future rebirth. The rule of non-violence was applied by Mahatma Gandhi in the political sphere during India's struggle for independence.

Ahmadabad or **Ahmedabad** [ahmadabad] 23°00N 72°40E, pop (2000e) 3 374 000. Commercial centre and industrial city in Gujarat, W India; on the R Sabarmati, 440 km/273 mi N of Mumbai; founded, 1411; fell to the Mughals, 1572; British trading post, 1619; centre of Gandhi's activities during the 1920s and 1930s; airfield; railway; university (1949); textiles; several temples, mosques, forts; Gandhi's Sabarmati Ashram.

Ahmadiyya [ahmahdiya] or **Ahmadis** An Islamic religious movement founded in 1899 in India by Mirza Ghulam Ahmad (c.1839–1908), believed to be the Messiah Mahdi. Rejected by orthodox Islam, the sect is marked by its missionary zeal. It is active in Asia, Africa, and Europe.

Ahmose I [ahmohs] (16th-c BC) Egyptian pharoah (ruled c.1570–1546 BC), who founded the 18th dynasty. He freed Egypt from the alien Shepherd Kings (Hyksos), and established control over Nubia.

Ahriman [ahriman] The supreme evil spirit, Angra Mainyu, the lord of darkness and death in Zoroastrianism. Ahriman is engaged in a continuing struggle with Ahura Mazda, Zoroaster's name for God.

Ahura Mazda [ahura mazda] (Persian 'Wise Lord') The name for God used by Zoroaster and his followers. The world is the arena for the battle between Ahura Mazda and Ahriman, the spirit of evil – a battle in which Ahura Mazda will finally prevail and become fully omnipotent.

Ahvenanmaa [ahvenanmah], Swed **Åland** [awland] pop (2000e) 25 000; area 1550 sq km/600 sq mi. Island group forming a district of Finland, in the Gulf of Bothnia between Sweden and Finland; capital, Mariehamn; 6554 islands, 80 inhabited; first language, Swedish.

AI *artificial intelligence*

Aidan, St [aydn], known as the **Apostle of Northumbria** (?–651) A monk from the Celtic monastery on the island of Iona, born in Ireland. He was summoned in 635 by King Oswald of Northumbria to evangelize the North. He established a church and monastery on the island of Lindisfarne, and was appointed the first bishop there. He later founded several churches throughout Northumbria. Feast day 31 August.

AIDS Acronym for **acquired immuno-deficiency syndrome**, the result of infection with the human immuno-deficiency virus (HIV). The virus is transmitted sexually, or by inoculation with contaminated blood, and can also be passed from mother to baby at birth. In the West, the groups most at risk are homosexual or bisexual men, people with multiple sexual partners, intravenous drug abusers, and people who have had multiple transfusions of blood or blood products prior to 1986, such as haemophiliacs. The infection is endemic in parts of the developing world, such as sub-Saharan Africa and India. Its origin is unknown. It emerged in the 1960s, though the epidemic only became obvious in the 1980s, and one theory is that it spread to humans from African monkeys. The virus damages the immune system, notably T-helper cells, and slowly destroys the body's defence against other infections. Individuals with HIV may remain symptom-free for years; however, after a time illnesses develop, including infections due to micro-organisms that do not normally cause disease. There is also fatigue, weight loss, enlargement of lymph nodes, dementia, and a rare form of skin cancer (Kaposi's sarcoma). In developed countries, survival has been improved by treatment with combinations of powerful anti-retroviral therapies, including AZT. However, these drugs are expensive, and largely unavailable in poor countries. HIV was independently discovered by Luc Montagnier and Robert C Gallo (1983), and later shown by Françoise Barre-Sinoussi and Jean-Claude Chermann to be the virus responsible for AIDS.

Aiken, Conrad (Potter) [ayken] (1889–1973) Poet and novelist, born in Savannah, Georgia, USA. He studied at Harvard, and made his name with his first collection of verse, *Earth Triumphant* (1914). His *Selected Poems* was awarded the 1930 Pulitzer Prize. He also wrote short stories and novels, including the autobiographical novel *Ushant* (1952).

Aiken, Joan (Delano) [ayken] (1924–2004) British writer, the daughter of Conrad Aiken, born in Sussex, SE England, UK. She was educated privately, then worked as a librarian for the UN Information Committee (1943–9) and as features editor for *Argosy* magazine (1955–60). Her many books for children include *All You've Ever Wanted* (1953), *The Kingdom and the Cave* (1960), *Voices Hippo* (1988), and *Dangerous Games* (1999). Among her adult novels are *The Silence of Herondale* (1964), *Mansfield Revisited* (1985), *Cold Shoulder Road* (1995), and *'Moon Cake' and Other Stories* (1998).

aikido [iykeedoh] An ancient Japanese art of self-defence, with ethical and philosophical undertones – a combination of karate and judo deriving from ancient jujitsu. There are two main systems, *tomiki* and *uyeshiba*.

Ailred of Rievaulx, St [aylred, reevoh], also **Aelred** or **Ethelred** (1109–66) Chronicler, born in Hexham, Northumberland, NE England, UK. A Cistercian monk (later abbot) at Rievaulx Abbey, he was a friend and adviser to both David I of Scotland and Stephen of England, and wrote a vivid Latin account of the battle between them at Northallerton, Yorkshire (1138). Feast days 12 January, 3 March.

Ainu [iynoo] The caucasoid aboriginals of Japan, now intermarried with other Japanese and culturally assimilated; their own language and religion has largely disappeared. Traditionally hunters and fishers, today many are factory workers and labourers. Population c.15 000.

air *atmosphere*

Airborne Warning and Control System (AWACS) [aywaks] An aircraft-mounted radar system able to detect and track hostile intruders at long range and direct friendly fighters to intercept them. The US Air Force operates the Boeing E-3 Sentry AWACS. The Sentry is also flown by a joint European NATO unit, has been supplied to Saudi Arabia, and is used by the British and French air forces.

airbrush A miniature spray-gun used to create smoother tonal transitions and more delicate colour effects than are possible with a conventional brush. The technique is mainly used by commercial illustrators.

air conditioning A system which improves the quality of air by purifying it (removing particles of dust, smoke, or pollen) and controlling its temperature and humidity (the amount of water in the air). In an air conditioner, a filter removes the larger particles of matter. Any tiny particles remaining are given a positive electric charge as the air passes over an electric grid. They are then attracted to a negatively charged grid and stick to it. Chemicals which cause smells are removed by passing the air through a charcoal filter. Air temperature is controlled by passing the air over pipes full of hot water to warm it or over pipes full of iced water to cool it. If the air is too dry, steam or water is sprayed into it. Air which is too humid or damp is cooled so that the moisture condenses out and drains away. It can also be passsed through chambers which contain moisture-absorbing chemicals such as silica gel.

aircraft Any vehicle designed to operate within the Earth's atmosphere, supporting itself by means of lift generated by wings or other methods.

aircraft carrier A naval vessel on which aircraft can take off and land, developed during World War 1. The first carrier, HMS

Furious (1918), was a battle-cruiser with forward and after flight-decks. The alighting aircraft had to fly alongside and sideslip onto the deck, forward of the bridge. *Furious* was reconstructed in 1925 and fitted with an island bridge layout on the starboard side of a continuous flight-deck. This became the conventional carrier design. The USA and Japan rapidly developed the carrier to hold many more aircraft, and during World War 2 US supremacy in the use of aircraft carriers was a deciding factor in reversing the fortunes of war in the Pacific. Britain's later significant contributions were the steam catapult, the angled flight-deck, and the mirror landing-sight. The USA now have the five largest carriers. The USS *Nimitz* (91 487 tonnes displacement) has 260 000 shaft horsepower, is 323 m/1092 ft long, has a crew of 5684, and carries over 90 aircraft. The first nuclear-powered carrier, the USS *Enterprise*, was completed in 1961.

air cushion vehicle (ACV) A revolutionary form of sea transport in which the vehicle is supported on a cushion of air; also called a **ground effect machine**, or (following the principle proposed by Christopher Cockerell in 1950) a **hovercraft**. An ACV is propelled by an airscrew, and rides on a cushion of air trapped between the hull and the surface of the water by a flexible skirt, usually made of heavy-duty neoprene, which allows it to surmount obstacles. Cockerell's design was one in which the cushion pressure was maintained by angled peripheral jets; later versions with flexible skirts often had a single plenum chamber supplying the air, which then leaked out under the skirt. The development of Cockerell's craft was delayed for a decade, while funding was found for the project. The success of the concept also depended on the development of the flexible skirt, and this became available only in 1960. As a result, the first regular hovercraft service did not begin until 1962 (across the R Dee estuary, between Rhyl and Wallasey in Britain). Hovercrafts are now in use worldwide in many varied forms.

Airedale terrier The largest breed of terrier; black and tan, thick wiry coat, stiff erect tail, small ears, short beard on chin; developed in Airedale valley (England) by crossing large hunting terriers (now extinct) and otterhounds.

air force The branch of the armed forces which operates aircraft and missiles. The first air forces were founded 1911–14. During World War 1 these fledgling air arms became major military organizations engaged in prosecuting war in the air. Air forces proved decisive to the outcome of World War 2, whether they fought in a tactical role (fighters and short-range ground-attack aircraft), strategically (long-range bombers), or at sea (coastal and carrier-based aviation). The advent of atomic weapons post-1945 changed air forces from being newcomers to warfare into the elite of military establishments. In the USA the US Air Force (USAF) was split from the army in 1947, in the 1950s was given responsibility for the US long-range nuclear missile force, and is now the most powerful air force in the world. The US, Royal, Russian, and French navies maintain separate, sea-warfare oriented air forces with great striking power in their own right.

air miles A consumer incentive scheme which offers the chance of free air travel in return for credits earned by frequent flyers who have joined the scheme. Credits may also be obtained through other means, such as authorized retail transactions, and flights of greater distance become possible as credits accumulate. An 'air mile' is a nautical mile as used by aircraft.

airplane *aeroplane*

air resistance *drag*

airship A self-propelled steerable aircraft whose lift is generated by using lighter-than-air gases to provide buoyancy. The main body is cigar-shaped, with engines and gondolas (cabins) being suspended from it. There are three types of airship construction: *rigid*, *semi-rigid*, and *non-rigid*. In the first type, the body shape is maintained by a rigid frame, with the lift being provided by individual gas cells fitted within the envelope defined by the frame. In the non-rigid (*blimp*) type, the shape of the body is maintained by using the pressure of the gas. A semi-rigid type is similar to a non-rigid type, but with a keel running the length of the airship. The lighter-than-air gas used to provide buoyancy was originally hydrogen, but its highly inflammable nature and poor safety record led to its replacement by helium. Following its heyday in the 1930s, the airship has spasmodically been revived as a cheap observation and patrolling platform, but so far with only limited success.

Air Traffic Control (ATC) The guidance of an aircraft from one airport to another – a procedure which goes on day and night and in almost all weather conditions. From loading ramp to runway threshold, the pilot is directed by a ground controller. At busy airports this controller may use ground radar to make sure that aircraft, maintenance vans, luggage ferries, and other moving vehicles avoid each other. Take-off is directed by air traffic controllers in a control tower. They tell the pilot which runway to use and give them information on weather conditions. Each departing plane has a flight plan which has been agreed before the flight. This includes intended destination, expected flight time, and the altitude at which the plane will be flying. All this information is entered into the ATC computers. Each flight has a unique call sign which identifies it to the ATC officer. Once airborne and away from the airport, control of the aircraft is transferred to **Air Route Traffic Control (ARTC)**. Throughout the journey, the aircraft may be passed through several ARTCs. At all times it will be visible on radar, identified by its call sign, speed, and height. At the end of the journey, an aircraft may have to wait its turn to land. ATC at the destination airport directs the aircraft to circle a radio beacon about 50 km away from the airport. The aircraft forms part of a holding stack, keeping a vertical distance of 300 m/1000 ft between each plane. As an aircraft at the bottom of the stack is called to land, the others spiral down to the next level while they wait their turn. The ATC officer guides the aircraft on its approach to the runway, after which the pilot or the automatic control system locks on to a navigational beam called the **Instrument Landing System (ILS)**. The ILS beam guides the aircraft on to the correct glide slope and down the centre line of the runway. Many large aircraft have completely automatic landing systems.

Aïshah or **Ayeshah** [aeesha] (c.613–78) Third and favourite of the nine wives of the prophet Mohammed, and daughter of Abu-Bakr, the first caliph. When Mohammed died in 632 she resisted the claims to the caliphate of Ali, Mohammed's son-in-law, in favour of her father. She led a revolt against Ali in 656, but was defeated and exiled to Medina. She is known as the 'mother of believers'.

aisles The corridors running lengthways on either side of the W (entrance) part of a church, singly or in pairs. Aisles flank the nave, and are separated from it by a line of arches or columns.

Ait-Ben-Haddou [iyt ben hadoo] A walled village in SC Morocco; a world heritage site. It is a spectacular example of a pre-Saharan ksar, or fortified village, with red earth houses and decorated kasbahs clinging to the steep side of an escarpment.

Aix-en-Provence [eks ã provãs] 43°31N 5°27E, pop (2000e) 130 000. Ancient city in Bouches-du-Rhône department, SE France; 30 km/19 mi N of Marseille in a fertile plain surrounded by mountains; founded as Aquae Sextiae in 123 BC; important centre for Provençal literature since the 15th-c; airport; railway; university (1409); olive oil, fruit, almond processing; many fountains; archbishopric; 11th–16th-c St Saver Cathedral, Baroque town hall (1658), art galleries, thermal springs, casino; home of Cézanne; International Music Festival (Jul–Aug); Saison d'Aix (Jun–Sep).

Ajaccio [azhakseeoh] 41°55N 8°40E, pop (2000e) 62 700. Seaport and capital of the Island of Corsica, France; on the W coast, at the head of Golfe de Ajaccio; founded by the Genoese, 1492; made capital by Napoleon, 1811; Corsica's second largest port; airport; railway; car ferries to Marseille, Toulon, Nice; fishing, timber trade, tourism; casino; Maison Bonaparte (birthplace of Napoleon), now a museum.

Ajanta Caves [ajanta] A group of 29 Buddhist cave-temples and monasteries cut into cliffs over R Wagurna (or Waghora), near Ajanta, Maharashtra, India; a world heritage site. The caves, which were built from the 2nd-c BC onwards, are particularly noted for their wall paintings. They were abandoned in the 7th-c, when building activity was transferred to Ellora, and rediscovered in 1819.

Ajax [ayjaks] The name of two legendary Greek heroes during the Trojan War; the Latin form of Greek **Aias**. **1** The son of Telamon, King of Salamis, therefore known as **Telamonian Ajax**. He was proverbial for his size and strength; in all the worst situations he 'stood like a tower'. When the armour of the dead Achilles was not given to him, he went mad and killed himself.

2 The son of Oileus, King of Locris. When he returned from Troy, he provoked the anger of the gods, and was killed by Poseidon as he reached the shore of Greece.

Ajman [ajman] pop (2000e) 92 000; area c.250 sq km/100 sq mi. Smallest of the seven member states of the United Arab Emirates, entirely surrounded by the territory of Shariqah except on the coast; capital, Ajman; relatively undeveloped, with no significant oil or gas reserves yet discovered.

Akabusi, Kriss (Kezie Uche-Chukwu Duru) [akaboosee] (1958–) Athlete, born in London, UK. He joined the army in 1975, and went on to become one of the leading athletes of the 1990s. His achievements include gold medals in the 4 x 100 m relay at the 1986 European Championships and Commonwealth Games (1986), the 400 m hurdles at the 1990 European Championships (also breaking a 22-year world record) and Commonwealth Games, the 4 x 400 m relay at the 1991 World Championships in Tokyo, and the 4 x 400 m relay in the 1993 European Cup. His Olympic medals include silver in the 4 x 100 m relay (1984) and bronze for the same event in 1994. Since 1993 he has become known as a television presenter.

Akahito, Yamabe no [akaheetoh] (8th-c) Japanese poet. A minor official at the imperial court, he seems to have kept his position largely through his poetic ability. He is known as one of the 'twin stars' – Hitomaro being the other – of the great anthology of classical Japanese poetry called the *Manyoshu* (Collection of a Myriad Leaves).

Akan A cluster of Twi (Kwa)-speaking peoples mostly in Ghana, and in the Côte d'Ivoire and Togo, comprising several kingdoms. The best known and largest is the Asante (Ashanti). All recognize matrilineal descent, and have a long urban and trading tradition. Population c.5 million.

Akashi-Kaikyo Bridge [akashee kiykyoh] Suspension bridge across the Akashi Straits between Honshu and Shikoku, Japan, begun in 1988 and opened in 1998. With a main span of 1991 m/6532 ft (overall length 3911 m/12 831 ft) it is now the longest suspension bridge in the world. It also has the tallest towers of any bridge: 294 m/965 ft.

Akbar the Great [akber], in full **Jalal ud-Din Muhammad Akbar** (1542–1605) Mughal emperor of India, born in Umarkot, near Hyderabad, Sind province, present day S Pakistan. He succeeded his father, Humayun, in 1556, and assumed power in 1560. The early years of his reign were marred by civil war and rebellion, but after triumphing over his enemies within the empire he turned to foreign conquest, extending his control to the whole of N India. He reformed the tax system, promoted commerce, encouraged science, literature, and the arts, and abolished slavery. Although brought up a Muslim, he pursued a tolerant and eclectic religious policy.

à Kempis, Thomas *Kempis, Thomas à*

Akerlof, George A (1940–) Economist, born in New Haven, Connecticut, USA. He studied at Yale University and the Massachusetts of Technology, going on to join the University of California at Berkeley. He shared the Nobel Prize for Economics in 2001 for the analysis of markets with asymmetric information.

Akhenaton [akenaton], also **Akh(e)naten** or **Amenhotep (Amenophis) IV** [amenhohtep] (14th-c BC) Egyptian king of the 18th dynasty. He renounced the worship of the old gods, introduced a monotheistic solar cult of the sun-disc (Aton), and changed his name. He built a new capital at Amarna (Akhetaton), where the arts blossomed while the empire weakened. One of his wives was Nefertiti.

Akhmatova, Anna [akhmahtofa], pseudonym of **Anna Andreeyevna Gorenko** (1889–1966) Poet, born in Odessa, S Ukraine. She studied in Kiev before moving to St Petersburg. In 1910 she married Nicholas Gumilev, and with him started the Neoclassicist Acmeist movement. After her early collections of lyrical poems, including *Evening* (1912) and *Beads* (1914), she developed an Impressionist technique. Her work was condemned by the authorities for its 'eroticism, mysticism, and political indifference', but she continued to write. Following the publication of *Anno Domini* (1922), she was officially silenced until 1940, when she published *The Willow*. Among her best-known works is *Requiem*, written in the late 1930s, an elegy for the prisoners of Stalin, including her son. In 1946 her verse was again banned. She was 'rehabilitated' in the 1950s, and is now recognized as the greatest woman poet in Russian literature.

Akiba ben Joseph [akeeba ben johzef], also spelled **Akiva** (c.50–135) Rabbi and teacher in Palestine. He founded a rabbinical school at Jaffa, and provided the basis for the Mishnah by his codification of the *halakhoth* (legal traditions). He was a supporter of the unsuccessful revolt of bar Kokhba against Hadrian (131–5), and was put to death by the Romans.

Akihito [akiheetoh] (1933–) Emperor of Japan (1989–), born in Tokyo, Japan, the son of Hirohito. He studied among commoners at the elite Gakushuin school, and in 1959 married **Michiko Shoda** (1934–), the daughter of a flour company president, who thus became the first non-aristocrat to enter the imperial family. They have three children: **Crown Prince Naruhito** (1960–), **Prince Fumihito** (1963–), and **Princess Sayako** (1969–). An amateur marine biologist, he is also an accomplished cellist. On becoming emperor in 1989, the new *Heisei* ('the achievement of universal peace') era commenced. In 2001 Crown Prince Naruhito and his wife, Masako, celebrated the birth of a baby daughter.

Akkadian [akaydian] One of the oldest languages in the Semitic (Afro-Asiatic) family, with a substantial literature written in cuneiform script. It is now extinct.

Akmola *Astana*

Akron 41°05N 81°31W, pop (2000e) 217 100. Seat of Summit Co, NE Ohio, USA, on the Little Cuyahoga R; laid out, 1825; city status, 1865; airfield; railway; university (1913); centre of US rubber industry; metal products, tyres, machinery; polymer research centre; Goodyear World of Rubber Museum, E J Thomas Performing Arts Hall, Blossom Music Centre.

Akrotiri [akroteeree] 34°36N 32°57E. Bay on S coast of Cyprus; main port town, Limassol; British base on peninsula separating Akrotiri Bay (E) from Episkopi Bay (W).

Aksakov, Sergei Timofeyevitch [aksahkof] (1791–1859) Novelist, born in Ufa, W Russia. The son of a wealthy landowner, he held government posts in St Petersburg and Moscow before a meeting with Gogol in 1832 turned him to literature. His house became the centre of a Gogol cult. He wrote *The Blizzard* (trans, 1834), *Chronicles of a Russian Family* (trans, 1846–56), and *Years of Childhood* (trans, 1858). His writing shows his love of country sports and deep feeling for nature.

Aksum 14°08N 38°43E. Ancient city in the highlands of N Ethiopia; a world heritage site. During the 1st–7th-c AD it was the capital of a powerful kingdom dominating trade – particularly in ivory and skins – between the Sudanese Nile Valley and the Roman Mediterranean through the Red Sea port of Adulis (near modern Massawa). Its multi-storied stone buildings, massive funeral slabs, and coinage are notable.

Aktyubinsk [aktyoobyinsk] 50°16N 57°13E, pop (2000e) 266 000. Capital city of Aktyubinskaya oblast, NW Kazakhstan; in the S foothills of the Ural Mts, on the left bank of the R Ilek; established, 1869; airport; railway; engineering, agricultural machinery, chemicals, building materials, clothing, furniture, foodstuffs.

Alabama pop (2000e) 4 447 100; area 133 911 sq km/51 705 sq mi. State in SE USA, divided into 67 counties; the 'Heart of Dixie', the 'Camellia State', or 'Yellowhammer'; first permanent settlement by the French at Mobile, 1711; N Alabama became part of the USA in 1783, the remainder being acquired by the Louisiana Purchase in 1803; the 22nd state to be admitted to the Union, 1819; seceded, 1861; slavery abolished, 1865; refused to ratify the Fourteenth Amendment to the US Constitution and placed under military rule, 1867; re-admitted to the Union in 1868, but Federal troops remained until 1876; capital, Montgomery; other chief cities, Birmingham, Mobile, Huntsville; rivers include the Alabama (formed by the confluence of the Tallapoosa and Coosa Rivers), Tombigbee, Mobile, Tennessee, Chattahoochee; highest point Mt Cheaha (734 m/2408 ft); a mountainous NE, separated from the S coastal plain by the rolling plain of the Appalachian Piedmont; diversified agriculture, after the boll weevil blight of 1915; cattle, poultry, cotton, soybeans, peanuts; chemicals, textiles, paper products, processed food; iron and steel industry centred on Birmingham; coal, oil, stone; lumbering, fishing; many civil rights protests in the area in the 1950s and 1960s.

alabaster A fine-grained banded variety of the mineral gypsum; pale and translucent. It is soft enough to be carved and polished by hand for ornamental use.

Alain-Fournier, Henri [alĩ foornyay], pseudonym of **Henri-Alban Fournier** (1886–1914) Writer, born in La Chapelle d'Angillon, Sologne, NC France. He became a literary journalist in Paris, and was killed in the vicinity of Epargue, near Verdun, soon after the outbreak of World War 1. He left a semi-autobiographical fantasy novel, *Le Grand Meaulnes* (1913, trans The Lost Domain), now considered a modern classic.

Alamo [alamoh] A battle fought during the 1836 Texan War of Independence against Mexico, when 180 Texans and US citizens held the old mission/fort of Alamo against a large number of Mexican troops. In an epic of resistance they held out for 11 days until the last survivors were overwhelmed.

Alanbrooke (of Brookeborough), Alan Francis Brooke, 1st Viscount [alanbruk] (1883–1963) British field marshal, born in Bagnères-de-Bigorre, S France. He joined the Royal Field Artillery in 1902, and in World War 1 rose to general staff officer. In World War 2 he commanded the 2nd corps of the British Expeditionary Force (1939–40), covering the evacuation from Dunkirk in France. He became commander-in-chief of home forces (1940–1), Chief of the Imperial General Staff (1941–6), and principal strategic adviser to Winston Churchill. He became a field marshal in 1944, and was created baron in 1945 and viscount in 1946. His war diaries presented a controversial view of Churchill and Eisenhower.

Åland *Ahvenanmaa*

Alarcón (y Ariza), Pedro Antonio de [alah(r)hon] (1833–91) Writer, born in Guadix, S Spain. He served with distinction in the African campaign of 1859–60, and became a radical journalist. He published a war diary, travel notes, and poems, but is best known for his novels, particularly *Sombrero de tres picos* (1874) on which Manuel de Falla based his ballet *The Three-Cornered Hat*.

Alarcón (y Mendoza), Juan Ruiz de [alah(r)hon ee mendohtha] (c.1580–1639) Playwright, born in Taxco, SC Mexico. He trained as a lawyer, and in 1626 became a member of the Council of the Indies in Madrid. He was neglected for generations, but is now recognized as a leading playwright of the Golden Age of Spanish drama. Among his character comedies is *La verdad sospechosa* (c.1619, The Suspect Truth), the model for Corneille's *Le Menteur*.

Alaric I [alarik] (c.370–410) King of the Visigoths (395–410), born in Dacia. After his election as king, he invaded Greece (395), but was eventually driven out by Flavius Stilicho. In 401 he invaded Italy until checked by Stilicho at Pollentia (402). He agreed to join the Western emperor, Honorius, in an attack on Arcadius, but when Honorius failed to pay the promised subsidy Alaric laid siege to Rome, and in 410 pillaged the city, an event which marked the beginning of the end of the Western Roman Empire. Later that year he set off to invade Sicily, but died at Cosenza.

Alas (y Ureña), Leopoldo [alas], pseudonym **Clarín** (1852–1901) Writer, born in Zamora, NWC Spain. He was professor of law at Oviedo, but better known as a forceful literary critic (his pseudonym means 'bugle'). He published short stories (*Cuentos morales*, 1896), a drama *Teresa*, and several novels, including *La regenta* (1885, The Regent's Wife).

Alaska pop (2000e) 626 900; area 1 518 748 sq km/586 412 sq mi. US state, divided into 23 boroughs, in the extreme NW corner of the continent, 'The Last Frontier' or 'The Great Land', separated from the rest of the nation by Canada; first permanent settlement by Russians on Kodiak I, 1784; managed by the Russian-American Fur Company, 1799–1861; period of decline, as Russians withdrew from the area; bought by the USA, 1867 (known as Seward's Folly, after the chief US negotiator); gold discovered in 1889 (at Nome) and 1902 (at Fairbanks); territorial status, 1912; Aleutian islands of Attu and Kiska occupied by the Japanese (Jun 1942–Aug 1943); granted statehood as the 49th state, 1959; large oil reserves discovered in 1968 (Alaska Pipeline from Prudhoe Bay to Valdez completed in 1977); the largest state, but the least populated; capital, Juneau; other chief city, Anchorage; bounded N by the Beaufort Sea and Arctic Ocean, W by the Chukchi Sea, Bering Strait, and Bering Sea, S by the Gulf of Alaska and the Pacific Ocean, and E by Canada (Yukon territory and British Columbia); a third of the area within the Arctic Circle; rivers include the Yukon (with tributaries the Porcupine, Tanana, and Koyukuk), Colville, Kuskokwim, Susitna and Copper; North Slope in the N, rising to the Brooks Range, part of the Rocky Mts; Kuskokwim Mts in the SW; Aleutian Is and Aleutian Range in the SW; Chugach Mts along the S coast; Wrangell Mts in the SE; highest point Mt McKinley (6194 m/20 321 ft); oil, natural gas, wide range of minerals; food processing, paper, lumber, seafood; eight national parks; tourism; balance between industrial development and landscape preservation an ongoing controversy.

Alaska, Gulf of area 1 327 000 sq km/512 000 sq mi. N part of the Pacific Ocean, between the Alaskan Peninsula (W) and the mainland Alaskan Panhandle (E); warm Alaskan Current keeps ports ice-free; main port, Valdez.

Alaska Highway An all-weather road which runs from Dawson Creek in British Columbia, Canada, to Fairbanks in Alaska, linking the state to the North American highway system. It was built in 1942 to supply military forces stationed in Alaska during World War 2.

Alaskan malamute [malamyoot] A breed of dog; spitz bred by the Malamute Eskimos of Alaska as a sledge-dog (*husky*); largest sledge-dog breed; strong and active; thick grey and white coat.

Alastor [alastaw(r)] In Greek mythology, an avenging demon or power. The name was used by Shelley as the title of a poem outlining a myth of his own making, in which a young poet is led through various symbolic states and ultimately to destruction.

Alawi (Islam) Offshoot sect of Shiite Islam, found mainly in the NW mountains of Syria, as well as in Lebanon and Turkey. Persecuted over the centuries for their heterodox beliefs, the Alawis have observed the outward forms of Sunni Islam while observing their own rites in secret. In Syria, where the Alawis (also known as **Nusayris**) represent some 6% of the total population, members of the sect have advanced through the military and the Baath Party to head the national government, particularly since the presidency of Hafez al-Assad (1971–2000), himself an Alawi.

Alawi (rulers) [alahwee] Moroccan royal family, tracing their line to the grandson of the Prophet Mohammed, Hasan bin Ali, from which they derive their name.

Alba, Duke of *Alva, duque de*

Albacete [albathaytay] 30°00N 1°50W, pop (2000e) 131 000. Capital of Albacete province, Castilla-La Mancha, SE Spain; 251 km/156 mi SE of Madrid; bishopric; railway; footwear; clothing, tools, wine, flour, cutlery, souvenir knives; San Juan Bautista Cathedral (16th-c); fairs and fiestas (Sep).

albacore [albakaw(r)] Large tuna fish (*Thunnus alalunga*) with long pectoral fins, widespread in open waters of tropical and warm temperate seas; length up to 1·3 m/4¼ ft, with an iridescent blue band on sides of body; extensively fished commercially, and much prized by sea anglers. (Family: Scombridae.)

Alba Iulia [alba yoolya], Ger **Karlsburg**, Lat **Apulum** 46°04N 23°33E, pop (2000e) 73 300. Capital of Alba county, WC Romania, on the R Mureș; founded by the Romans, 2nd-c AD; former seat of the princes of Transylvania; railway; wine trade, footwear, soap, furniture; 12th-c Romanesque church, Bathyaneum building.

Alban, St [awlbn] (3rd-c) Roman soldier, venerated as the first Christian martyr in Britain. A pagan Romano-Briton living in the town of Verulamium (now St Albans), he was scourged and beheaded in the 3rd-c or early 4th-c for sheltering and changing clothes with a fugitive Christian priest who had converted him. Feast day 22 June.

Albania *p.31*

Albanian The official language of Albania, spoken also by substantial numbers in neighbouring regions of Yugoslavia, Greece, and Italy – in all, some 3 million speakers. It is an idiosyncratic development within the Indo-European group, with no written records earlier than the 15th-c, and much interference with its present-day structure from substantial word-borrowing.

Albany (Australia) 34°57S 117°54E, pop (2000e) 20 800. Resort and seaport in Lower Great Southern statistical division, Western Australia; one of the oldest towns in Australia, founded in 1826; once used as a stopover point for vessels on their way to India; airfield; railway; canning, wool, agricultural trade.

Albany (USA) 42°39N 73°45W, pop (2000e) 95 700. Capital of New York State in Albany Co, E New York, USA; on the Hudson R, 232 km/144 mi N of New York City; the second oldest continuously inhabited settlement in the 13 original colonies, settled by the Dutch, 1624; state capital, 1797; railway; two universities (1844, 1848); State Capitol, Schuyler Mansion; annual Tulip Festival.

Albany Congress (1754) A US colonial gathering of delegates at which Benjamin Franklin proposed a 'plan of union' for the separate British colonies. Both the colonial governments and the British authorities rejected the idea.

Albany Regency A US political faction centred on Martin Van Buren (president, 1837–41), and on the city of Albany, NY, which he made his power base. It was notorious for its use of the 'spoils system' of filling public office.

albatross A large, slender-winged seabird, wingspan up to 3 m/10 ft; glides near water in air currents; lands only to breed. (Order: Procellariiformes (**tubenoses**). Family: Diomedeidae, 14 species.)

albedo [albeedoh] The ratio of the radiation reflected by a surface to the total incoming solar radiation, expressed as a decimal or percentage. The degree of reflectance varies according to the type of surface: snow-covered ice has an albedo of 0·8 (80%), a dry sandy desert 0·37 (37%), a tropical rainforest 0·13 (13%). The average planetary albedo is close to 0·3 (30%).

Albee, Edward (Franklin) [awlbee, albee] (1928–) Playwright, born near Washington, District of Columbia, USA. He studied at Trinity College, CT, and at Columbia University. His major works include *The Zoo Story* (1958), a one-act duologue on the lack of communication in modern society, *The American Dream* (1960), and *Who's Afraid of Virginia Woolf?* (1962, filmed 1966), which won several awards. *A Delicate Balance* (1966), *Seascape* (1975), and *Three Tall Women* (1991) won Pulitzer Prizes. Other plays include *Walking* (1982), *Marriage Play* (1988), and *Fragments* (1993).

Albéniz, Isaac (Manuel Francisco) [albaynith] (1860–1909) Composer and pianist, born in Camprodón, NE Spain. He studied under Liszt, and became a brilliant pianist and composer of picturesque works for piano based on Spanish folk music, notably *Iberia* (1906–9). He also wrote several operas.

Alberoni, Giulio [alberohnee] (1664–1752) Spanish statesman and cardinal, born in Firenzuola, NC Italy. He became prime minister of Spain and was made a cardinal in 1717. His domestic policies were liberal and wise, but in foreign affairs his decisions were often impetuous and irresponsible. He violated the Treaty of Utrecht by invading Sardinia, and was subsequently confronted by the Quadruple Alliance of England, France, Austria, and Holland, resulting in the destruction of the Spanish fleet. Dismissed in 1719, he returned to Italy.

Albert, Lake, Zaire **Lake Mobuto Sésé Seko** area c.6400 sq km/2500 sq mi. Lake in EC Africa; in the W Rift Valley on the frontier between the Democratic Republic of Congo and Uganda; length, c.160 km/100 mi; width, 40 km/25 mi; altitude, 619 m/2031 ft; receives the Victoria Nile (NE) and Semliki (SW) Rivers; Albert Nile flows N; European discovery by Samuel Baker, 1864; originally named after Queen Victoria's consort.

Albert I (1875–1934) King of the Belgians (1909–34), born in Brussels, Belgium, the younger son of Philip, Count of Flanders. At the outbreak of World War 1 he refused a German demand for the free passage of their troops, and after a heroic resistance led the Belgian army in retreat to Flanders. He commanded the Belgian and French army in the final offensive on the Belgian coast in 1918. After the war he took an active part in the industrial reconstruction of the country.

Albert II (1934–) King of Belgium (1983–), born in Brussels, the son of King Leopold III and the brother of King Baudouin. He was educated privately and in Geneva. Between 1962 and his succession to the throne, he took a particular interest in promoting Belgian exports, holding the post of honorary president of the administrative council of the Belgian Office of External Trade.

Albert, Prince, in full **Francis Albert Augustus Charles Emmanuel, Prince of Saxe-Coburg-Gotha** (1819–61) Prince Consort to Queen Victoria, born at Schloss Rosenau, near Coburg, EC Germany, the younger son of the Duke of Saxe-Coburg-Gotha and Louisa, daughter of the Duke of Saxe-Coburg-Altenburg. He studied in Brussels and Bonn, and in 1840 married his first cousin, Queen Victoria – a marriage that became a lifelong love match. Ministerial distrust and public misgivings because of his German connections limited his political influence, although his counsel was usually judicious and far-sighted. He took a keen interest in industry, technology, and the arts, and presided over the Royal Commission that raised support for the Great Exhibition of 1851, whose profits enabled the building of museum sites in South Kensington and the Royal Albert Hall (1871). He died of typhoid in 1861, occasioning a long period of seclusion by his widow. The Albert Memorial in Kensington Gardens was erected to his memory in 1871.

Alberta pop (2000e) 2 851 000; area 661 190 sq km/255 285 sq mi. Province in W Canada, bordered S by the USA; mainly a rolling plain, with edge of Rocky Mts in W; rivers, lakes, and forests in N, with much open prairie; treeless prairie in S; drained (N) by Peace, Slave, and Athabasca Rivers, and (S) by North Saskatchewan, Red Deer, and Bow Rivers (S); largest lakes, Athabasca, Claire, Lesser Slave; several national parks; capital, Edmonton; other chief cities, Calgary, Lethbridge, Medicine Hat; oil, natural gas, grain, cattle, timber products, coal, food processing, chemicals, fabricated metals, tourism; originally part of Rupert's Land, granted to Hudson's Bay Company, 1670; sovereignty acquired by the Dominion, 1869; status as province, 1905; governed by a lieutenant-governor and an elected 83-member Legislative Assembly.

Albert Hall *Royal Albert Hall*

Alberti, Leon Battista [albairtee] (1404–72) Architect, born in Genoa, NW Italy. Influenced by Vitruvius Pollio, he wrote *De re aedificatoria* (10 vols, 1485), which stimulated interest in

Albania

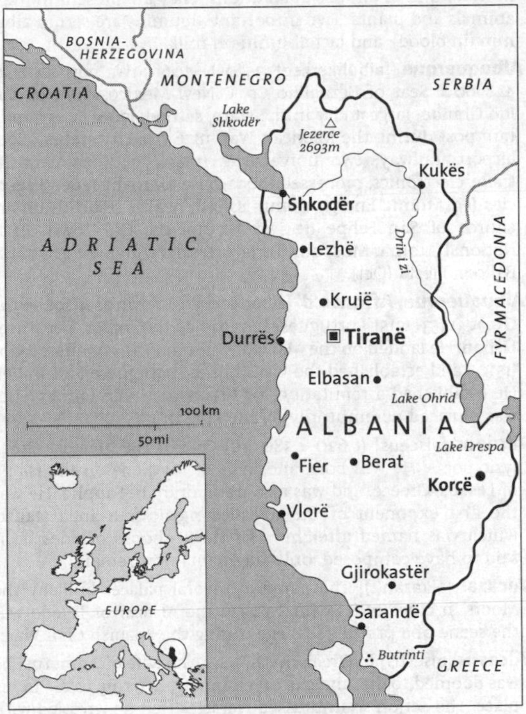

□ International Airport ∴ World heritage site

Albanian **Shqipni**, **Shqipri**, or **Shqipëri**, official name (1991) **Republic of Albania, Republica e Shqipërisë**

Local name Shqīpëri

Timezone GMT +1

Area 28 748 km²/11 097 sq mi

Population total (2002e) 3 108 000

Status Republic

Date of independence 1912

Capital Tiranë

Languages Albanian (official) (Gheg and Tosk, the main dialects), Greek

Ethnic groups Albanian (96%), Greek (2%), Macedonian, Vlach, Gypsy, Bulgarian

Religions Muslim (Sunni 70%), Roman Catholic (5%), Greek Orthodox (2%) (before April 1991, Albania was constitutionally atheist)

Physical features Mountainous country, relatively inaccessible and untravelled; geologically active - earthquakes severe and relatively frequent; N Albanian Alps rise to 2692 m/8 832 ft; mountainous highlands (N, S, and E) account for c.70% of the land; coastal lowland in the W is agricultural; rivers include the Drin i zi, Shkumbin, Seman, Vijosë; 45% of land is forested; 25% is arable, mostly grain-producing; c.20% is permanent pasture land.

Climate Mediterranean climate, hot and dry on the plains in summer; average annual temperatures, 8–9°C (Jan), 24–5°C (Jul); thunderstorms frequent; mild, damp, cyclonic winters.

Currency 1 Lek (L) = 100 qintars

Economy Seventh fve-year plan (1981–5) focused on industrial expansion, especially in oil (new sources were located), mining, chemicals, natural gas; hydroelectric power plans for several rivers (eg the Koman hydroelectric complex on the Drin i zi R); agricultural product processing, textiles, oil products, cement; main crops are wheat, sugar-beet, maize, potatoes, fruit, grapes, oats; all industry is nationalized; progressive transformation of farm cooperatives into state farms; chromate, low-grade iron ore, and soft coal are exported; other natural resources: crude petroleum, asphalt, lignite (brown coal), phosphorus, bauxite, precious metals.

GDP (2002c) $15·69 bn, per capita $4400

Human Development Index (2002) 0·733

History Albanians descended from Illyrians, who occupied W Balkan peninsula c.1000 BC; King Argon and, after him, his wife Teuta conquered many territories, provoking the military might of Rome; despite Roman occupation and invasions by Visigoths, Slavs, and Huns, the Albanians were one of the few peoples to retain their Illyrian language and customs; Turkish invasions, 14th-c; independence after the end of Turkish rule, 1912; occupied by Italian forces, 1914-20; became a republic in 1925, and a monarchy in 1928, under King Zog I; occupied by Germany and Italy during World War 2; a new republic instigated in 1946, headed by Enver Hoxha (until 1985); dispute with the Soviet Union in 1961 led to withdrawal from Warsaw Pact in 1968, but close links with China maintained; People's Socialist Republic instituted, 1976; renamed Republic of Albania, 1991; first free elections, 1991, giving a decisive majority to the communists; however general strike and demonstrations forced government to resign; Communist Party renamed itself the Socialist Party; Democratic Party elected in 1992 elections; collapse of fraudulent pyramid finance schemes, 1997, leading to rebellion in the S, arrival of UN protection force, and early elections, with unrest continuing in 1998; new constitution, 1998; People's Assembly (supreme legislative body) elects the President and Council of Ministers.

People's Socialist Republic of Albania

Head of State

1944–85 Enver Hoxha
1985–91 Ramiz Alia
1991–2 Fatos Nano *Provisional*
1992–7 Sali Berisha
1997–2002 Rexhep Mejdani
2002– Alfred Moisiu

Head of Government

1930–5 Pandeli Evangeli
1935–6 Mehdi Frashëri
1936–9 Koço Kota
1939–41 Shefqet Verlaci
1941–3 Mustafa Merlika-Kruja
1943 Eqrem Libohova
1943 Maliq Bushati
1943 Eqrem Libohova
1943 *Provisional Executive Committee* (Ibrahim Biçakçlu)
1943 *Council of Regents* (Mehdi Frashëri)
1943–4 Rexhep Mitrovica
1944 Fiori Dine
1944–54 Enver Hoxha
1954–81 Mehmed Shehu
1981–91 Adil Carcani
(Republic of Albania)
1991 Ylli Buf
1991–2 Vilson Ahmeti
1992–7 Alexander Meksi
1997 Baskim Fino
1997–8 Fatos Nano
1998–9 Pandeli Majko
1999–2002 Ilir Meta
2002 Pandeli Majko
2002– Fatos Nano

antique Roman architecture. His own designs, which include the churches of S Francesco (Malatesta Temple) at Rimini and S Maria Novella at Florence, are among the best examples of the pure Classical style. One of the most brilliant figures of the Renaissance, he was also skilled as a musician, painter, poet, and philosopher.

Albertina An art gallery founded in 1768 by Duke Albert of Saxony-Tescha. Since 1795 it has been housed in the former Taroucca Palace in Vienna. Its holdings include a vast collection of graphic material.

Albert Medal In the UK, a civilian decoration, instituted in 1866 to commemorate the Prince Consort (1819–61), to reward gallantry in saving life. In October 1971 all surviving holders of the medal exchanged it for the George Cross.

Albert Nile Upper reach of the R Nile in NW Uganda; issues from the NE corner of L Albert, close to the Victoria Nile Delta; flows NE into the Sudan; known in Sudan as the Bahr el Jebel until its meeting point with the Bahr el Ghazal to form the White Nile.

Albertus Magnus, St, Graf von (Count of) **Bollstädt,** known as **Doctor Universalis** ('Universal Doctor') (c.1200–80) Philosopher, bishop, and doctor of the Church, born in Lauingen, S Germany. In 1254 he became provincial of the Dominicans in Germany, and in 1260 was named Bishop of Ratisbon. Of his works the most notable are the *Summa theologiae* and the *Summa de creaturis*. He excelled all his contemporaries in the breadth of his learning, and did more than anyone to bring about that union of theology and Aristotelianism which is the basis of scholasticism. He was canonized in 1931 and named a doctor of the Church by Pope Pius XI. Thomas Aquinas was his most famous pupil. Feast day 15 November.

Albigenses [albijenseez] or **Albigensians** Followers of a form of Christianity which in the 11th-c and 12th-c especially had its main strength in the town of Albi, SW France. It was derived from 3rd-c followers of the Persian religious teacher, Mani, whose ideas gradually spread along trade routes to Europe, especially Italy and France. Also known as **Cathari** or **Bogomils**, they believed life on Earth to be a struggle between good (spirit) and evil (matter). In extreme cases, they were rigidly ascetic, with marriage, food, and procreation all condemned. They believed in the transmigration of souls. Condemned by the Roman Catholic Church, they were devastated in the early 13th-c crusade against them, which also broke down the distinctive civilization of Provence, France.

albinism A common inherited pigmentary disorder of vertebrates: affected individuals lack pigmentation of the skin, hair, eyes (iris), feathers, or scales. The disorder can be harmful, as the missing pigments protect against sunlight and/or provide camouflage against predators. Albinism is found in all human races: the absence of pigment (or *melanin*) results in white hair, pink skin, and pink irises. Varying degrees of non-pigmentation occur. A gene responsible for albinism was discovered in 1990 on chromosome 11; it results in a deficiency of an enzyme called tyrosinase, needed for the production of melanin.

albino horse A breed of horse; white with pale blue or brown eyes; developed in USA by deliberately cross-breeding naturally occurring albino individuals of other breeds.

Albinus *Alcuin*

Albright, Madeleine K(orbel) (1937–) US secretary of state (1997–2000), born in Prague, Czech Republic. Educated at Columbia University, she held an academic post at Georgetown University, then took up a position on the National Security Council until appointed permanent US representative to the UN. In the second Clinton administration she became the first woman to head the State Department. Her book *Madam Secretary: a memoir* appeared in 2003.

Albufeira [albufayra] 37°05N 8°15W, pop (2000e) 25 400. Fishing village and resort, Faro district, S Portugal; 38 km/24 mi W of Faro, in a bay on the S coast; figs, almonds, tourism; Moorish-style architecture; Portugal's busiest seaside resort.

albumins [albyuminz] Part of a system of classification of simple proteins, usually referring to those that are readily soluble in water and in dilute salt solutions. They are present in most animals and plants. Two important albumins are serum albumin (in blood), and lactalbumin (in milk).

Albuquerque [albuhkerkee] 35°05N 106°39W, pop (2000e) 448 600. Seat of Bernalillo Co, C New Mexico, USA, on the Rio Grande; largest city in the state; settled, 1706; later a military post during the Mexican War, 1846–70; city status, 1890; airport; railway; two universities (1889, 1940); agricultural trade, electronics, processed foods; base for many federal agencies (eg Atomic Energy Commission); health resort; tourism; church of San Felipe de Neri (1706), the Old Town Plaza, National Atomic Museum; Feria Artesana (Aug), International Balloon Fiesta (Oct).

Albuquerque, Affonso d' [albookerkay], known as **Affonso the Great** (1453–1515) Portuguese viceroy of the Indies, born near Lisbon. He landed on the Malabar coast in 1502, conquered Goa (1510), and established the basis of the Portuguese East Indies. He established a reputation for his wisdom and fairness, but was replaced peremptorily by the king in 1515.

Alcaeus [alseeus] (c.620–c.580 BC) One of the greatest Greek lyric poets. He was born and lived at Mytilene on the island of Lesbos, Greece, and was a contemporary of Sappho. He was the first exponent of the so-called *Alcaic* four-lined stanza, which was named after him. Of the 10 books of odes he is said to have composed, only fragments now remain.

Alcazar [alkazah(r)] The name of several palaces built by the Moors in cities of S Spain. In 1936 the Alcazar of Toledo was the scene of a protracted siege during the Spanish Civil War.

Alcestis [alsestis] In Greek mythology, the wife of Admetus; he was doomed to die, and she saved him by offering to die in his place. The action so impressed Heracles that he wrestled with the messenger of Death and brought her back to life. Her death and resurrection is depicted on many ancient reliefs and vase paintings and is the subject of Euripides' *Alcestis*.

alchemy The attempt from early times to find an elixir of immortal life. The first reference is by a Chinese Taoist in 140 BC, and a Chinese alchemical text dates from AD 142. The word *alchemy* may be an Arabic derivative from Chinese, and the practice probably spread to Europe via Arab traders, where it was taken up by such scholars as Roger Bacon (1214–92). Alchemists sought to convert base metals into gold – not to create wealth, but as a step towards discovering the recipe for eternity. Chinese Taoists initially sought an immortality pill through refining mercury sulphide: this led to many deaths, including Tang emperors. Later alchemists aimed to promote internal processes towards immortality. Alchemists needed accurate scales, clocks, and temperature control. Their work thus facilitated important discoveries in chemistry, medicine, mineralogy, and pharmacology, including the development of natural drugs, experiments with arsenic, copper, iron, lead and mercury, knowledge of dyeing, and (probably) the invention of fireworks and gunpowder. They also discovered anaesthesia and distillation.

Alcibiades [alsibiyadeez] (c.450–404 BC) Athenian statesman and general, a member of the aristocratic Alcmaeonid family. A ward of Pericles and a pupil of Socrates, he was a leader against Sparta in the Peloponnesian War, and a commander of the Sicilian expedition (415 BC). Recalled from there to stand trial for sacrilege, he fled to Sparta and gave advice which contributed substantially to Athens' defeat in Sicily (413 BC) and her economic discomfiture at home. Falling out with the Spartans in 412 BC, he began to direct Athenian operations in the E Aegean, and won several notable victories; but finding himself unjustly blamed for the Athenian defeat off Notium (406 BC), he went into voluntary exile, where he actively intrigued with the Persians until his assassination in 404 BC.

Alcmaeon (of Croton) [alkmeeon] (6th-c BC) Greek physician and philosopher from Croton, S Italy. The first recorded anatomist, he was the true discoverer of the Eustachian tubes, and a pioneer of embryology through anatomical dissection.

Alcmaeon (mythology) [**alkmeeon**] In Greek mythology, the son of Amphiaraos. To avenge his father's death, he killed his mother, and was pursued by the Furies until he came to a land which had not seen the Sun at the time of his mother's death; he found this recently-emerged land at the mouth of the R Achelous. He was commanded by Apollo to lead the expedition of the Epigoni against Thebes.

Alcmaeonids [**alkmiyonidz**] An aristocratic Athenian family to which many prominent Athenian politicians belonged. It was particularly influential in the period 632–415 BC.

Alcock, Sir John William (1892–1919) Aviator, born in Manchester, Greater Manchester, NW England, UK. He served as a captain in the Royal Naval Air Service in World War 1, then became a test pilot with Vickers Aircraft. On 14 June 1919, with Arthur Whitten Brown as navigator, he piloted a Vickers-Vimy biplane non-stop from St John's, Newfoundland, to Clifden, Co Galway, Ireland, in a time of 16 h 27 min. Soon afterwards Alcock was killed in an aeroplane accident in France.

Alcoholics Anonymous (AA) A self-help group for alcoholics trying to stop drinking. Founded in the USA in 1935 by 'Bill W' (William Griffith Wilson, 1895–1971) and 'Dr Bob S' (Robert Holbrook Smith, 1879–1950), it consists of local groups where members (identified by first names only) meet to give each other support. There are more than 2 million members in over 150 countries. In the early 1990s it influenced the development of several similar programmes for various types of dependencies.

alcoholism An ambiguous term, for some implying a disease, for others a severe form of alcohol dependence. It is also used as a term of opprobrium relating to anyone who has continuing difficulties associated with excessive alcohol consumption. A major limitation of the term is that it suggests a dichotomy between abstinence and moderate drinking, on the one hand, and excessive and uncontrolled drinking, on the other. 'Alcohol abuse' can be found in all social classes, though there is evidence that those suffering from anxiety or depression are most susceptible, with a recent notable increase in the disease among housewives and the young and long-term unemployed.

alcohols IUPAC **alkanols**. Generally organic compounds containing a hydroxyl (–OH) function bonded to a carbon atom which is not itself bonded to further atoms other than carbon or hydrogen. When none or one of these atoms is carbon, the alcohol is called *primary*; with two or three carbon substituents, it is *secondary* or *tertiary* respectively. Compounds in which the hydroxyl group is bonded directly to an aromatic ring are called *phenols*, and are not classed as alcohols. Characteristic reactions of alcohols include dehydration to ethers, and reaction with acids to give esters. In everyday use, the word **alcohol** is often restricted to *ethanol* (**ethyl alcohol**), CH_3CH_2OH.

alcohol strength The measurement of the amount of ethanol (the active constituent) in alcoholic drinks, commonly expressed using either volumetric measures or proof strength. The volumetric measure is becoming increasingly popular: this declares the volume of ethanol present in a unit volume of the alcoholic beverage; for example, an average red wine contains 12% by volume ethanol or 90 millilitres of ethanol per average bottle. *Proof spirit* is a mixture containing a standard amount of ethanol: in the UK it is 57·07% by volume, while in the USA it is 50%. Thus, a bottle of Scotch which claims to be 70° proof is in fact 70% of 57·07% (volume), or 40% ethanol by volume.

alcopops [**alkohpops**] Soft drinks with an alcoholic content, marketed in a wide range of brand names. Known since the 1970s, they became fashionable in the late 1990s, but raised considerable public concern about the wisdom of making alcohol more accessible to young people, and (through the use of terms such as 'alcoholic soft drink') reducing their awareness of its dangers.

Alcott, Louisa M(ay) (1832–88) Writer, born in Germantown, Pennsylvania, USA, the daughter of Amos Bronson Alcott. In 1868 she achieved enormous success with the children's classic, *Little Women*, which drew on her own home experiences. A second volume, *Good Wives*, appeared in 1869, followed by *An Old-Fashioned Girl* (1870), *Little Men* (1871), and *Jo's Boys* (1886).

Alcuin [**alkwin**], originally **Ealhwine**, Lat **Albinus** (c.737–804) Scholar and adviser to the emperor Charlemagne, born in York, North Yorkshire, N England, UK. He studied at the cloister school, of which he became master in 778. In 781, he met Charlemagne at Parma, and joined the court at Aix-la-Chapelle (Aachen). Here he devoted himself first to the education of the royal family, but through his influence the court became a school of culture for the Frankish empire, inspiring the Carolingian Renaissance. His works comprise poems; works on grammar, rhetoric, and dialectics; theological and ethical treatises; lives of several saints; and over 200 letters.

Alcyone *Halcyone*

Alda, Alan [**awlda**] (1936–) Actor and director, born in New York City, USA. He made his Broadway debut in *Only in America* (1959), and his film debut in *Gone Are the Days* (1963), but it was his extensive involvement in the television series *M*A*S*H* (1972–83) that earned him his greatest popularity. He won numerous awards for the series (including five Emmies), which provided a showcase for his talents as a socially conscious writer, director, and performer. His acerbic sense of humour has been uppermost in such films as *The Four Seasons* (1981), *Sweet Liberty* (1985), and *A New Life* (1988). Later films include *Crimes and Misdemeanours* (1990), *Canadian Bacon* (1995), and *The Object of My Affection* (1998).

Aldabra Islands [**aldabra**] 9°25S 46°20E; area 154 sq km/59 sq mi. Coral atoll nature reserve in SW Indian Ocean, NW of Madagascar; 1200 km/750 mi SW of Mahé; outlying dependency of the Seychelles; occupied by scientific staff; habitat of the giant land tortoise; nature reserve, established in 1976; a world heritage site.

Aldebaran [**aldebaran**] *Taurus*

Aldeburgh [**aldeberg**] 52°09N 1°35E, pop (2000e) 2700. Coastal town in Suffolk, E England, UK; developed on the site of a mediaeval fishing centre; received royal charter, 1598; birthplace of Millicent Fawcett and George Crabbe; home of Elizabeth Garrett Anderson; Moot Hall (16th-c), Martello Tower (19th-c); famous for its annual music festival (Jun) founded in 1948; Maltings promenade concerts (Aug), poetry festival (Nov).

aldehydes [**aldihiydz**] IUPAC **alkanals**. Organic compounds containing a (–CHO) function. Aldehydes are readily oxidized (to carboxylic acids) and reduced (to alcohols). The aldehyde function is found in most sugars, notably glucose.

Alder, Kurt [**alder**] (1902–58) Organic chemist, born in Chorzow, S Poland (formerly Konigshütte, Germany). With Otto Diels he discovered in 1928 the Diels–Alder diene reaction, valuable in organic synthesis, and they shared the Nobel Prize for Chemistry in 1950.

alder A small, deciduous N temperate tree, often growing by water or in wet soils; leaves oval or rounded; male and female flowers on separate plants; male catkins long, pendulous; females short, erect, becoming woody and cone-like in fruit. (Genus: *Alnus*, 35 species. Family: Betulaceae.)

alderfly A slow, awkwardly flying insect with two pairs of large, translucent wings held over its body at rest; found around well-aerated, freshwater ponds and streams; larvae aquatic and carnivorous. (Order: Megaloptera. Family: Sialidae, c.50 species.)

Alderney [**awldernee**], Fr **Aurigny**, ancient **Riduna** pop (2000e) 2300; area 8 sq km/3 sq mi. Third largest of the Channel Is, off the coast of French Normandy, W of Cherbourg; separated from France by the Race of Alderney; in the Bailiwick of Guernsey, with its own legislative assembly; chief town, Saint Anne; tourism, dairy farming.

Alderton, John (1940–) Actor, born in Gainsborough, Lincolnshire, EC England, UK. A member of the York Repertory Company, he made his debut in *Emergency Ward 10* (1961), and his West End debut in *Spring and Port Wine* at the Apollo Theatre. From 1969 he has appeared regularly on stage, and became popularly known on television with series such as *Please Sir*, *My Wife Next Door*, and *Forever Green* (with actress wife Pauline Collins). His films include *Please Sir* (1971), *It Shouldn't Happen to a Vet* (1976), *Clockwork Mice* (1995), and *Calendar Girls* (2003).

Aldhelm, St [aldhelm], also spelled **Ealdhelm** (c.640–709) Anglo-Saxon scholar and clergyman. He studied at Malmesbury and Canterbury, and became the first Abbot of Malmesbury about 675, and the first Bishop of Sherborne in 705. A great scholar, he wrote Latin treatises, letters, and verses, as well as some English poems that have perished. Also a skilled architect, he built several churches and monasteries. Feast day 25 May.

Aldington, Richard [awldingtn], originally **Edward Godfree** (1892–1962) Writer, born in Hampshire, S England, UK. He studied at London University, and in 1913 became editor of *The New Freewoman* (renamed *The Egoist* in 1914), the periodical of the Imagist school. His experiences in World War 1 led to his best-known novel, *Death of a Hero* (1929). He published several volumes of poetry, *The Viking Book of Poetry of the English-Speaking World* (1941), and many critical works and biographies. In 1941 his autobiography *Life for Life's Sake* appeared. *Wellington* (1946) was awarded the James Tait Black Memorial Prize. He married Hilda Doolittle ('HD') in 1913 (divorced, 1937).

Aldiss, Brian (Wilson) [awldis] (1925–) Science-fiction writer and novelist, born in East Dereham, Norfolk, E England, UK. He studied at Framlingham College, and his first novel, *The Brightfount Diaries*, appeared in 1955. He is best known as a writer of science fiction, such as *Hothouse* (1962, US title *The Long Afternoon of Earth*) and *The Saliva Tree* (1966). There are two collections of short stories (1988, 1989), and he has produced histories of science fiction such as *Billion Year Spree* (1973) and *Trillion Year Spree* (1986). Among later works are a novel, *Dracula Unbound* (1991), the poetry collections *At the Caligula Hotel* (1995), *The Poems of Makhtumkuli* (1996), and *When the Feast is Finished* (2000).

aldosterone [aldosterohn] A type of hormone (a mineralocorticoid) secreted from the adrenal cortex into the blood. Its primary role in humans is to stimulate sodium reabsorption and potassium excretion by the kidneys, in order to maintain electrolyte and water balance. Excessive secretion is known as **aldosteronism**, indicated by potassium depletion, sodium retention, and hypertension.

Aldrin, Buzz [awldrin], popular name of **Edwin Eugene Aldrin** (1930–) Astronaut, born in Montclair, New Jersey, USA. He trained at West Point, flew combat missions in Korea, and later flew in Germany with the 36th Tactical Wing. In 1966 he set a world record by walking in space for 5 h 37 min during the Gemini 12 mission. He was the second man to set foot on the Moon in the Apollo 11 mission in 1969.

Aldus Manutius [aldus manootius], Latin name of **Aldo Manucci** or **Manuzio** (c.1450–1515) Scholar and printer, born in Sermoneta, Latium, Italy. He was the founder of the Aldine Press, which produced the first printed editions of many Greek and Roman classics. He had beautiful founts of Greek and Latin type made, and was the first to use italics on a large scale.

ale An alcoholic beverage brewed from barley which has been malted (ie softened in water and allowed to germinate). It was a popular drink prior to the introduction of hops as a flavouring agent, thus creating beer. However, the term *ale* is still used to describe the hops-flavoured brew, while *beer* has a broader international interpretation at present, and includes lager and stouts.

aleatory music [ayliatree] Music of which the composition or performance is, to a greater or lesser extent, determined by chance or by whim. The notation may be conventional but indeterminate (ie with the notes but not their sequence composed), or it may take some 'graphic' form which conveys only a general pattern to performers, or elicits an intuitive response from them. The chief proponent of aleatory music has been John Cage.

alecost *costmary*

Aleichem *Sholem Aleichem*

Aleixandre, Vicente [alayksahndray] (1898–1984) Poet, born in Seville, SW Spain. It was the appearance of his collected poems, *Mis poemas mejores* (1937), that established his reputation as a major poet. His later publications include *En un vasto dominio* (1962, In a Vast Domain) and *Antologia total* (1976). He was awarded the Nobel Prize for Literature in 1977.

Alemán, Mateo [aleman] (1547–c.1614) Novelist, born in Seville, SW Spain. His great work is a picaresque novel, *Guzmán de Alfarache* (1599, trans The Spanish Rogue), about a boy running away from home. He emigrated to Mexico in 1608.

Alembert, Jean le Rond d' [alābair] (1717–83) Philospher and mathematician, born in Paris, France. Brought up as a foundling, he was given an annuity from his father and studied law, medicine, and mathematics at the Collège Mazarin. In 1743 he published *Traité de dynamique*, developing the mathematical theory of Newtonian dynamics, including the principle later named after him. Until 1758 he was Denis Diderot's principal collaborator on the *Encyclopédie*, of which he was the scientific editor, and wrote the *Discours préliminaire*, proclaiming the philosophy of the French Enlightenment.

Alentejo [alītezhu] Sparsely populated agricultural area of SEC Portugal, SE of the R Tagus (the name is from Portuguese, 'beyond'); divided in 1936 into the two provinces of **Alto Alentejo** and **Baixo Alentejo**; low-lying plain with cork tree forests, heaths, maquis; prehistoric standing stones and chambered cairns; chief towns, Evora, Beja; corn, cattle, pigs; noted for the Alter Real breed of horse.

Aleppo [alepoh], Arabic **Halab** 36°12N 37°10E, pop (2000e) 1 853 000. Capital city of Halab governorate, NW Syria; 350 km/217 mi N of Damascus; chief commercial and industrial centre of N Syria; airport; road and rail junction; university (1960); industrial refrigeration plant; old city, a world heritage site; Cotton Festival (Sep).

Aletsch [alech] area 117·6 sq km/45·4 sq mi. Glacier in SC Switzerland, W and S of the Aletschhorn; length, 23·6 km/14·6 mi; the largest glacier in Europe.

Aleut [alyoot] Peoples of the Aleutian Is and W Alaska, who are physically, linguistically, and culturally similar to the Eskimo. In the past, they lived in villages and hunted seals, walruses, whales, and bears. Community life and culture were disrupted by Russian occupation of the area in the 18th–19th-c, and the population has since declined from c.25 000 to c.2500 in the 1980s.

Aleutian Islands [alooshn] or **Aleutians**, formerly **Catherine Archipelago** pop (2000e) 14 500; area 18 000 sq km/7000 sq mi. Group of c.150 islands stretching c.1600 km/1000 mi from the Alaskan Peninsula, USA; chief islands Attu, Andreanof, Rat, Umnak, Unimak, Unalaska (chief town, Dutch Harbor); many volcanic peaks over 1000 m/3000 ft; discovered by Russian explorers in 18th-c; purchased by USA, 1867; several military bases; wildlife refuge.

A level An abbreviation for **Advanced level**, the examination taken by British pupils, usually near the age of 18, which qualifies them for entrance to higher education and the professions. It is a single-subject examination at a level representing two further years of study beyond the GCSE. University matriculation requirements normally specify A levels in at least two subjects. One A level is deemed equivalent to two passes in the Advanced Supplementary (*A/S level*) examination.

alewife Deep-bodied, herring-like fish (*Alosa pseudoharengus*), locally abundant along the American Atlantic seaboard; length up to 40 cm/16 in; migrates into rivers (Mar/Apr) to spawn in slow backwaters; commercially fished using traps and nets (seines). (Family: Clupeidae.)

Alexander I (of Russia) (1777–1825) Tsar of Russia (1801–25), born in St Petersburg, NW Russia, the grandson of Catherine the

Great. The early years of his reign were marked by the promise of liberal constitutional reforms and the pursuit of a vigorous foreign policy. His wars with Turkey (1806–12) and Persia (1804–13) brought territorial gains, including the acquisition of Georgia. In 1805 Russia joined the coalition against Napoleon, but after a series of military defeats was forced to conclude the Treaty of Tilsit (1807) with France. When Napoleon broke the treaty by invading Russia in 1812, Alexander's armies forced the French army's retreat. At the Congress of Vienna (1814–15) he laid claim to Poland. He supported Metternich in suppressing liberal and national movements. During the last years of his reign his increased political reactionism and religious mysticism resulted in the founding of the Holy Alliance of European monarchs. His mysterious death at Taganrog caused a succession crisis which led to the attempted revolutionary coup of the Decembrists.

Alexander II (of Scotland) (1198–1249) King of Scots, born in Haddington, East Lothian, E Scotland, UK, who succeeded his father, William I, in 1214. He allied with the disaffected English barons and made an incursion as far S as Dover. The accession of Henry III of England allowed a rapprochement, cemented by his marriage in 1221 to Henry's sister, Joan, and the frontier question was settled by the Treaty of York (1237). Her death without children in 1238, and Alexander's marriage to the daughter of a Picardy nobleman, Marie de Coucy, then strained relations with England. His reign is notable for the vigorous assertion of royal authority in the W Highlands and the SW during the years of peace with England.

Alexander III, originally **Orlando Bandinelli** (c.1105–81) Pope (1159–81), born in Siena, C Italy. He taught law in Bologna, and became adviser to Pope Adrian IV. After his election he was engaged in a struggle with Emperor Frederick I Barbarossa who refused to recognize him, and set up antipopes until compelled to sign the Treaty of Venice (1177). He was also involved in the quarrel between Henry II of England and Thomas Becket. In 1179 he called the third Lateran Council.

Alexander VI, originally **Rodrigo Borgia** (1431–1503) Pope (1492–1503), born in Játiva, E Spain, the father of Cesare and Lucretia Borgia. In 1455 he was made a cardinal by his uncle, Calixtus III, and on the death of Innocent VIII was elevated to the papal chair, which he had previously secured by bribery. He endeavoured to break the power of the Italian princes, and to appropriate their possessions for the benefit of his own family, employing the most execrable means to gain this end. During his pontificate, he apportioned the New World between Spain and Portugal, and despite introducing the censorship of books, he was a generous patron of the arts.

Alexander (Greek mythology) *Paris* (mythology)

Alexander of Hales, known as **Doctor Irrefragabilis** ('Irrefutable Doctor') (c.1170–1245) English theologian and philosopher, born in Hales, Gloucestershire, SWC England, UK. He became a professor of philosophy and theology in Paris, and later entered the Franciscan order. He is known chiefly from the major work ascribed to him, the *Summa theologica*.

Alexander (of Tunis), Sir Harold (Rupert Leofric George) Alexander, 1st Earl (1891–1969) British soldier, born in London, UK. He trained at Sandhurst Military Academy, and in World War 1 commanded a battalion of the Irish Guards on the Western Front. He commanded 1 Corps as rearguard at the Dunkirk evacuation (1940), and was the last man to leave France. In 1942 he commanded in Burma, then became commander-in-chief Middle East (1942–3), his North African campaign being one of the most complete victories in military history. He commanded the invasions of Sicily and Italy (1943), was appointed field marshal on the capture of Rome in June 1944, and became supreme allied commander in the Mediterranean. He was later Governor-General of Canada (1946–52) and minister of defence (1952–4) in the Conservative government.

Alexander the Great (356–323 BC) King of Macedonia (336–323 BC), born at Pella, the son of Philip II and Olympias. He was tutored by Aristotle, and ascended the throne when less than 20 years old. After crushing all opposition at home, he set out to conquer Greece's hereditary enemy, Achaemenid Persia. This he achieved with great rapidity in a series of famous battles: Granicus (334 BC), Issus (333 BC), and Gaugmela (331 BC). By 330 BC, Darius III had fled, and the capitals of Susa, Persepolis, and Ecbatana had been taken. In the next three years, the E half of the empire was also conquered, and Alexander set out for India. He reached the Punjab, and had set his sights on the Ganges, when his troops mutinied and forced his return. He died shortly after at Babylon.

Alexander Archipelago Group of 1100 mountainous islands SE of Alaska, USA; chief islands Chichagof, Baranof (Sitka naval base and national monument), Admiralty, Kupreanof, Kuiu, and Prince of Wales.

Alexander Nevski, St, also spelled **Nevsky** (c.1218–63) Russian hero and saint, prince of Novgorod, born in Vladimir, W Russia. In 1240 he defeated the Swedes in a famous battle on the R Neva, near the site of modern St Petersburg, and in 1242 he defeated the Teutonic knights on the frozen L Peipus. Although a vassal of the Mongol occupation army, he sought to live with them in peace, and suppressed anti-Mongol revolts. He was canonized by the Russian Orthodox Church in 1547. Feast day 30 August or 23 November.

Alexander technique A method of releasing unwanted physical and mental tension from the body by encouraging posture training and self-awareness, developed by the Australian actor Frederick Matthias Alexander (1869–1955). Patients are taught to improve their self-awareness, particularly of bad posture and tension in the neck. Re-educating the muscle system to relax these tensions is said to result not only in a lightness and ease of movement throughout the body but also to have beneficial effects on the mind, emotions, and spirit. The technique is becoming popular as a treatment for headache, backache, anxiety, and depression, and particularly benefits stage performers.

Alexandra, Queen (1844–1925) Consort of King Edward VII of Great Britain, the eldest daughter of King Christian IX of Denmark (r.1863–1906). She married Edward in 1863 when he was Prince of Wales, and became known for her charity work; in 1902 she founded the Imperial (now Royal) Military Nursing Service, and in 1912 instituted the annual Alexandra Rose Day in aid of hospitals.

Alexandra, Princess, the Hon Lady Ogilvy (1936–) Daughter of George, Duke of Kent, and Princess Marina of Greece. In 1963 she married **Sir Angus James Bruce Ogilvy** (1928–). They have a son, **James Robert Bruce** (1964–) and a daughter, **Marina Victoria Alexandra** (1966–). James married Julia Rawlinson and they have a daughter **Flora Alexandra** (1994–), and a son, **Alexander Charles** (1996–). Marina married Paul Mowatt (marriage dissolved) and they have a daughter, **Zenouska May Mowatt** (1990–), and a son, **Christian Alexander Mowatt** (1993–).

Alexandra Feodorovna [fyodorovna] (1872–1918) German princess, and Empress of Russia as the wife of Nicholas II, born in Darmstadt, WC Germany, the daughter of Grand Duke Louis of Hesse-Darmstadt and Alice Maud Mary (the daughter of Queen Victoria). She married Nicholas in 1894. Deeply pious and superstitious, she came under the influence of the fanatical Rasputin. During World War 1, while Nicholas was away at the front, she meddled disastrously in politics. When the revolution broke out, she was imprisoned by the Bolsheviks, and shot in a cellar at Yekaterinburg.

Alexandria, Arabic **al-Iskandariya** 31°13N 29°55E, pop (2000e) 3 958 000. Seaport capital of Alexandria governorate, N Egypt; on the Mediterranean coast, 180 km/112 mi NW of Cairo; second largest city of Egypt and the country's main port; founded in 332 BC by Alexander the Great; capital of the Ptolemies 304–30 BC; former centre of Hellenistic and Jewish culture; noted for its famous royal libraries; airport; railway; university (1942); car assembly, oil refining, natural gas processing, food processing, trade in cotton, vegetables and grain; Catacombs of Kom El Shugafa (1st–2nd-c AD), Graeco-Roman museum, Pompey's Pillar (297), Serapium temple ruins, Abu'l Abbas mosque.

Alexandria, Library of The greatest library in the Ancient World and the most important centre for literary studies; founded by Ptolemy I and greatly extended by Ptolemy II. At one time it was reputed to have contained 700 000 volumes. It was destroyed in the civil wars of the 3rd-c AD. A new library, on the site of Cleopatra's former palace, opened in 2002, aiming to have 5–8 million volumes by 2020.

alexandrine [aligzahndrin] A French term for a line of verse consisting of 12 syllables; known as *tétramètre*. Common in French poetry and dramatic verse since the 12th-c, it is used most often in English for contrast, as in the last line of the Spenserian stanza, or in Pope, who both uses and describes an alexandrine in the line 'That, like a wounded snake, drags its slow length along'. Other English poets who used it successfully were Drayton, Browning, and Bridges.

Alexeyev, Vasiliy [aleksayef] (1942–) Weightlifter, born in Pokrovo-Shishkino, Russia. He set 80 world records (1970–7), more than any other athlete in any sport. Olympic super-heavyweight champion in 1972 and 1976, he won eight world titles and nine European titles. He was made a major in the Russian army, and obtained the title of Master of Sport.

alexia *dyslexia*

Alexius I Comnenus [komneenus] (1048–1118) Byzantine emperor (1081–1118), the founder of the Comnenian dynasty, born in Istanbul. He defeated a major invasion mounted by the Normans of Sicily under Robert Guiscard (1081–2) and later under Bohemond I (1083); in alliance with the Cumans he destroyed the Patzinaks at Mount Levounion (1091). He built up a new fleet with the aim of re-establishing Byzantine rule in Asia Minor. This coincided with the arrival of the First Crusade (1096–1100), with which he co-operated to recover Crete, Cyprus, and the W coast of Anatolia. His reign is well known from the *Alexiad*, the biography written by his daughter, Anna Comnena.

alfalfa *lucerne*

al-Farabi, Mohammed [al farahbee], also known as **Abu Nasr**, **Alfarabius**, and **Avennasar** (c.870–950) Islamic philosopher, known as the 'second master' (Aristotle being the first), born in Farab, Turkmenia. He studied in Baghdad, and travelled widely. He was much influenced by Plato's *Republic*, and can be regarded as the first Islamic Neoplatonist. He also published a utopian political philosophy of his own, known under the title *The Perfect City*.

al-Fatah *PLO*

Al Fayed, Mohamed [al fayed] (1933–) Businessman, born in Egypt. He studied at Alexandria University, and made rapid progress in the international business world, becoming owner of the Ritz Hotel in Paris in 1979, and of Harrods in London in 1985, and one of the world's wealthiest men. One of his children, **Dodi** (1955–97), received worldwide publicity in 1997 when the press discovered his relationship with Princess Diana. A graduate of Sandhurst Military Academy, he briefly became a film producer, but was more renowned for his flamboyant lifestyle. He was killed along with Diana in a car accident in Paris while trying to escape the attentions of paparazzi. A British inquest into his death was opened in 2004.

Alferov, Zhores Ivanovich [alferof] (1930–) Physicist, born in Vitebsk, NE Belarus. He studied at the Leningrad Ulyanov (Lenin) Electrotechnical Institute (1952), and joined the AF Ioffe Physico-Technical Institute in St Petersburg (1953) as an engineer and researcher, becoming director of the institute in 1987. He shared the 2000 Nobel Prize for Physics for his groundbreaking work in the development of semiconductor heterostructures.

Alföld [olfuld] Great Plain region of S Hungary, E of the R Danube, extending into adjoining countries; a flat area covering about half of Hungary, crossed by a system of canals which provide irrigation for grain and fruit; livestock on the arid grasslands (*pusztas*); national parks at Hortobágy, Bükk, and Kiskunság.

Alfonso I or **Alfonso Henriques**, also spelled **Afonso** (c.1110–85) Earliest king of Portugal (1139–85), born in Guimarães, N Portugal. He was only two years old at the death of his father, Henry of Burgundy, the conqueror and first Count of Portugal, so that the management of affairs fell to his mother, Theresa of Castile. Wresting power from her in 1128, he defeated the Moors at Ourique (1139), and proclaimed himself king. He took Lisbon (1147), and later all Galicia, Estremadura, and Elvas.

Alfred, known as **Alfred the Great** (849–99) King of Wessex (871–99), born in Wantage, Oxfordshire, SC England, UK, the fifth son of King Ethelwulf. When he came to the throne, the Danes had already conquered much of Northumbria, parts of Mercia, and East Anglia, and threatened to subdue Wessex itself. He inflicted on them their first major reverse at the Battle of Edington, Wiltshire (878), and began to win back Danish-occupied territory by capturing the former Mercian town of London (886). He stole the military initiative from the Danes by reorganizing his forces into a standing army, building a navy, and establishing a network of burhs (fortified centres). These developments were complemented by his revival of religion and learning, a programme designed to win God's support for victory over the pagan Danes and to consolidate loyalty to himself as a Christian king. He personally translated several edifying Latin works into English. He forged close ties with other English peoples not under Danish rule, and provided his successors with the means to reconquer the Danelaw and secure the unity of England. The famous story of his being scolded by a peasant woman for letting her cakes burn has no contemporary authority, and is first recorded in the 11th-c.

Alfvén, Hannes (Olof Gösta) [alfen] (1908–95) Theoretical physicist, born in Norrköping, SE Sweden. He studied at Uppsala, and joined the Royal Institute of Technology, Stockholm, in 1940, moving to the University of California in 1967. He did pioneering work on plasmas and their behaviour in magnetic and electric fields. In 1942 he predicted the existence of waves in plasmas (*Alfvén waves*), which were later observed. He shared the Nobel Prize for Physics in 1970.

algae An informal grouping of primitive, mainly aquatic plants that have chlorophyll *a* as their primary photosynthetic pigment; body (*thallus*) not organized into root, stem, and leaf; no true vascular system; reproductive organs not surrounded by a layer of sterile cells; range in form from simple unicellular plant plankton to massive seaweeds many metres in length.

Algardi, Alessandro [algah(r)dee] (1598–1654) Sculptor, born in Bologna, N Italy. His chief work is a colossal relief, in St Peter's, Rome, showing Pope Leo I restraining Attila from marching on the city.

Algarve [algah(r)v] area 5072 sq km/1958 sq mi. Region and former province of S Portugal, bounded W and S by the Atlantic Ocean; Moorish kingdom, 1140; capital, Faro; figs, almonds, fishing, fish canning, tourism; **Costa do Algarve** is the S Atlantic coast of Portugal from Cape St Vincent (W) to R Guadiana on the Spanish border; the most popular tourist resort area in Portugal, with resorts at Praia da Luz, Praia da Rocha, Praia do Carvoeiro, Albufeira, Vilamoura.

algebra A branch of mathematics in which unknown quantities are represented by letters or other symbols. It was developed and brought to Europe by the Arabs, from whose word *al-jabr* the name of the subject is derived. In classical algebra (or **arithmetic algebra**), the operations in use are those of arithmetic; whereas in **abstract algebra**, developed in the 19th–20th-c, different operations are defined. In particular, in many abstract algebras, the commutative law does not apply. William Hamilton (1805–65) developed the non-commutative algebra of quaternions, Arthur Cayley and others matrix algebra, and George Boole the algebra of sets that bears his name. *Non-associative* algebras do not follow the associative laws of arithmetic; examples are **Jordan algebras**, named after the German physi-

Algeria

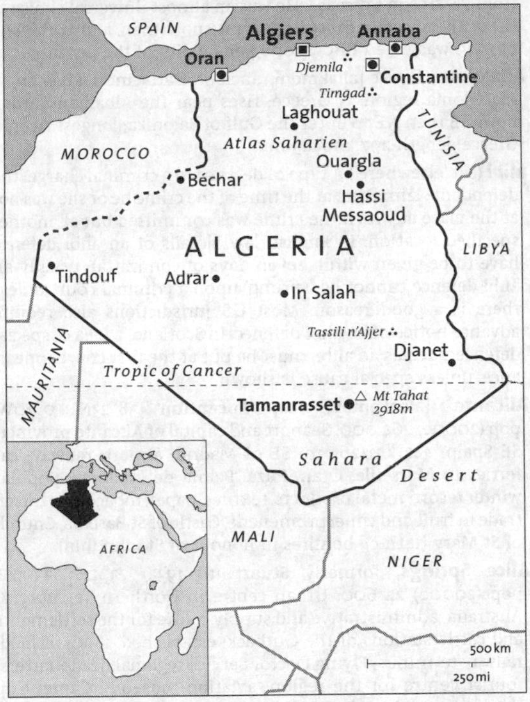

□ International Airport ∴ World heritage site

Fr **L'Algérie**, official name **The Democratic and Popular Republic of Algeria**, Arabic **al-Jumhuriya al-Jazairiya**

Local name(s) Al-Jazā'ir (Arabic), Algérie (French)

Timezone GMT +1

Area 2 460 500 km²/949 753 sq mi

Population total (2002e) 31 261 000

Status Democratic republic

Date of independence 1962

Capital Algiers (Alger)

Languages Arabic (official), Berber, French

Ethnic groups Arab (75%), Berber (25%)

Religions Muslim (Sunni 99%), Roman Catholic (0·5%)

Physical features Mountainous area in N Africa: mountains rise in a series of ridges and plateaux to the Atlas Saharien; Ahaggar Mts in the far S, rising to 2 918 m/9 573 ft at Mt Tahat; 85% of land is Saharan desert.

Climate Mediterranean in N, with cool, rainy winters and hot dry summers; average annual temperatures 12°C (Jan), 25°C (Jul); average annual rainfall 400–800 mm/15·8–31·5 in (mostly Nov–Mar); essentially rainless Saharan climate in S.

Currency 1 Algerian Dinar (AD, DA) = 100 centimes

Economy Petroleum products account for about 30% of national income; natural-gas liquification; jointly built with Italy first trans-Mediterranean gas pipeline; agriculture mainly on N coast: wheat, barley, oats, grapes, citrus fruits, vegetables; also food processing, textiles, clothing.

GDP (2002e) $173·8 bn, per capita $5400

Human Development Index (2002) 0·697

History Islamic Berber empires followed collapse of Numidian, Roman, Vandal, and Byzantine rule; Turkish invasion, 16th-c; French colonial campaign in 19th-c led to French control from 1902; guerrilla war (1954–62) with French forces by the National Liberation Front (FLN) led to independence, 1962; first President of the republic, Ahmed Ben Bella, replaced after coup, 1965; new constitution, 1976; military took control of government in 1992, and a state of emergency declared; continuing violence involving Islamic fundamentalists, including attacks on foreigners from 1993; legislative power shared by the President and National Assembly.

Head of State
1978–92 Chadli Benjedid
1992 Mohamed Boudiaf
1992–4 Ali Kaf
1994–9 Lamine Zeroual
1999– Abdelaziz Bouteflika

Head of Government
1994–5 Mokdad Sifi
1995–8 Ahmed Ouyahia
1998–9 Ismail Hamdani
1999–2000 Ahmed Benbitour
2000–3 Ali Benflis
2003– Ahmed Ouyahia

cist Pascual Jordan in the 1930s, and most of the **Lie algebras** extensive in modern physics.

algebraic geometry The study of geometry by algebraic means. Originally it was the study of curves and surfaces from their equations using algebraic methods, and often avoiding the calculus (thus contrasting it with differential geometry). The subject became part of projective geometry, and once complex numbers were admitted during the 19th-c, deep connections were found by Riemann and Poincaré to complex function theory. Many unresolved questions were reformulated and solved by Oscar Zariski in the 20th-c with the introduction of techniques of modern algebra, leading to a great generalization of the subject. This in turn was overtaken by the methods of Alexandre Grothendieck, which introduce deep geometric ideas into algebraic number theory.

Algeciras [aljeseeras] 36°09N 5°28W, pop (2000e) 103 000. Seaport and resort in Cádiz province, Andalusia, SW Spain; on W side of Algeciras Bay, opposite Gibraltar; founded by the Moors, 713; largely destroyed, 14th-c; rebuilt, 18th-c; scene of Algeciras Conference (over the future of Morocco), 1906; railway; car ferries to Canary Is, Melilla, Tangier, Gibraltar; paper, tourism, trade in oranges, cork; Old Algeciras; watersports; fair and fiestas (Jun), patronal fiestas (Aug), Festival of Spain (Aug).

Alger, Horatio [aljer] (1832–99) Writer and clergyman, born in Revere, Massachusetts, USA. He studied at Harvard, became a Unitarian minister, and wrote highly successful boys' adventure stories on poor-boy-makes-good themes, such as *Ragged Dick* (1867) and *From Canal Boy to President* (1881).

Algeria *see panel*

Algiers [aljeerz], Fr **Alger** [alzhay] 36°50N 3°00E, pop (2000e) 3 545 000. Seaport capital of Algeria, N Africa; 805 km/500 mi SW of Marseille (France); founded 10th-c by Berbers on the site of Roman Icosium; Turkish rule established by Barbarossa, 1518; taken by the French, 1830; Allied headquarters and seat of de Gaulle's provisional government in World War 2; University of Algeria (1879); university of sciences and technology (1974); airport; railway; trade, commerce and administration, wine; Sidi Abderrahman Mosque, Sidi Mohammed Sherif Mosque, Djama Djehid Mosque (16th-c); cathedral; national library; Bardo Museum, Museum of Antiquities, National Museum of Fine Arts.

alginates The calcium salts of alginic acid, found in seaweeds, forming viscous solutions which hold large amounts of water. They are used in food manufacturing as thickening agents in such products as ice-creams and yogurts. They are not digested in the small intestine, but are fermented by the microflora of the large intestine.

Algol An eclipsing binary star in Perseus, the prototype of the Algol-type variable stars. English astronomer John Goodricke suggested in 1782 that the variations were due to an unseen companion revolving around the star with immense velocity, a theory confirmed by spectroscopy in 1889. There is also a third star in orbit. Distance: 28·5 parsec.

ALGOL [algol] Acronym for **ALGOrithmic Language**, a high-level programming computer language developed in Europe in the late 1950s for mathematical and scientific use at approximately the same time as FORTRAN was being developed in the USA.

Algonkin [algongkin] or **Algonquin** Scattered small groups of American Indians speaking Algonkian (Algonquian) languages, living in forest regions around the Ottawa R in Canada. Most were slaughtered by the Iroquois or died from European diseases: only c.2000 survive. They work mainly as trappers, hunters' guides, and market gardeners.

algorithm A set of explicit, finite, and precisely determined rules, the step-by-step application of which to a complex problem will yield a solution or optimal results. The set of rules for doing simple multiplication is an algorithm. Because they are precise and can be applied without judgment, algorithms can be programmed into computers.

Algren, Nelson (Abraham) (1909–81) Novelist, born in Detroit, Michigan, USA. He was a leading member of the Chicago School of Realism, producing a series of uncompromising, powerful novels. These include *Somebody in Boots* (1935) and *The Man with the Golden Arm* (1949), a novel about drug addiction, regarded by some as his best work.

Alhambra [alhambra] The palace-fortress of the Moorish kings, built at Granada, S Spain, in the 13th–14th-c; a world heritage site. It was partially demolished and rebuilt by Charles V in the 16th-c, but retains many beautiful halls and gardens characteristic of mediaeval Islamic architecture.

Alhazen [alhazen], Arabic **Abu al-Hassan ibn al Haytham** (c.965–1039) Mathematician and physicist, born in Basra, SE Iraq. The best known of his many books was the *Treasury of Optics* (first published in Latin in 1270), giving the first account of atmospheric refraction, reflection from curved surfaces, and the nature of vision.

Ali (?–661) Fourth caliph (656–61), the cousin and son-in-law of Mohammed. He converted to Islam when still a boy, and married the prophet's daughter, Fatima. He withdrew, or was excluded from government during the caliphates of Abu-Bakr and Omar, and disagreed with Uthman in the interpretation of the Qur'an. Opposition to his caliphate, led by Muawiyah, began a major division within Islam between Sunni and Shiah Muslims. He was murdered in the mosque at Kufa. He is held by Shiah Muslims to be the only true successor to the prophet.

Ali, Muhammad, originally **Cassius (Marcellus) Clay, Jr** (1942–) Boxer, born in Louisville, Kentucky, USA. As an amateur boxer (1954–60), he became the 1960 Olympic light-heavyweight champion. He won the world heavyweight title in 1964, defeating the purportedly invincible Sonny Liston when he retired at the end of the sixth round. At that time he joined the Black Muslims and adopted the name Muhammad Ali. In 1967, he refused to be drafted into the army on religious grounds, and was stripped of his title and barred from the ring. He took his case to the Supreme Court and had his boxing licence restored in 1970. In 1971 he was beaten by Joe Frazier, but beat him in 1974, and went on to meet George Foreman later that year, knocking him out in eight rounds to regain his title. He was beaten by Leon Spinks in a split decision (Feb 1978), but regained the title the same year – the first man to win the world heavyweight title three times. His flamboyant style has made him a legend, and his slogan 'I am the greatest' became a catch phrase. Ali was President Carter's special envoy to Africa in 1980 (attempting to persuade nations to boycott the Olympics). He has starred in two films, *The Greatest* (1976) and *Freedom Road* (1978), and an Oscar-winning documentary film, *When We Were Kings*, recounting the 1974 Ali v. Foreman fight, appeared in 1996. Ali retired in 1981, since when he has suffered from Parkinson's disease. He was an almost universal choice as the 20th-century's most important sportsman, and at the end of 1999 was voted BBC Sports Personality of the Century.

Aliákmon, River [aliakmon], ancient **Haliacmon** River in W Macedonia region, N Greece; rises near the Albanian border, flows SE then NE to enter the Gulf of Salonika; longest river in Greece; length 297 km/185 mi.

alibi (Lat 'elsewhere') A type of defence to a criminal charge: the defendant claims that at the time of the crime he or she was not at the place at which the crime was committed but at another specified location. In English law, details of an alibi defence have to be given within seven days of committal; usually an alibi defence cannot be 'sprung' upon a criminal court unless there is a good reason. Most US jurisdictions also require advance notice of an alibi defence. In Scotland, a plea of special defence, such as an alibi, must be put at the first court appearance, unless special cause is shown.

Alicante [aleekantay], Lat **Lucentum** 38°23N 0°30W, pop (2000e) 264 000. Seaport and capital of Alicante province, SE Spain; 422 km/262 mi SE of Madrid; airport; railway; car ferries to Marseille, Oran, Ibiza, Palma de Mallorca; popular winter resort; metal products, textiles, paper, tobacco, fertilizer, trade in fruit and wine; promenade, Castle of St Barbara, Church of St Mary (14th-c); bonfires in honour of St John (Jun).

Alice Springs, formerly **Stuart** (to 1933) 23°42S 133°52E, pop (2000e) 22 600. Urban centre in Northern Territory, C Australia; administrative and supply centre for the settlements and cattle stations of the Outback; established, 1890; airfield; railway terminus; Flying Doctor Service regional headquarters; tourist centre for the region; aviation museum; Camel Cup camel races (May); Bangtail Muster with rodeos, parades, and cattle round-ups (May); Alice Springs Show Day (5 Jul); Henley-on-Todd Regatta, with mock yacht races on the dry bed of the Todd R (Aug).

alien A person who is not a citizen of a state. A citizen of country X is usually an alien in country Y and vice versa. In the UK, for example, aliens may hold most kinds of property, but may not vote or hold a public office. The US constitution prohibits discrimination against aliens in jobs that do not require state security. Aliens may acquire citizenship of a country by naturalization or, in some cases, marriage. Within the European Community, citizens of member states may enjoy freedom of movement and other rights under community law. In wartime, a distinction is drawn between alien friends and alien enemies. It has yet to be decided whether any of this applies in the case of the other modern use of the term, referring to visitors from outer space.

Alien and Sedition Acts (1798) US laws passed to crush political opposition, led by Thomas Jefferson, then vice-president. Two Alien Acts gave the president great power over foreigners. The Sedition Act authorized fining and imprisonment for public criticism of the government. They lapsed or were repealed during the period 1800–2.

alienation Until the mid-20th-c, known mainly as a term referring either to the legal transfer of property or to progressive insanity. It then acquired currency as a key term in sociology, deriving from its earlier use by Hegel and Marx, denoting the disorientation, depersonalization, and powerlessness of the individual in an increasingly bureaucratized industrial society.

alienation-effect or **V-effect** A common translation of German *Verfremdungseffekt*, a term coined by Brecht to describe any theatrical means – directorial, histrionic, or literary – used to help an audience see as unfamiliar what they assume to be familiar. These effects inhibit emotional involvement and remind the audience that what they are watching is dramatization and not real life. The audience is thus distanced from what is taking place on the stage. This style of production became known as 'Brechtian' and became very influential.

alimentary canal A tube in which foodstuffs are ingested, digested, and absorbed, and waste products excreted; also known as the **gut**, or the **gastro-intestinal tract**. It may exist as a simple structure with only one opening to the exterior (as in coelenterates, platyhelminths), or as a more complex structure with two openings (as in vertebrates). In the latter case, food is ingested via the mouth, and unassimilated material is expelled from the anus. In many animals the canal is anatomically divided to provide partial separation (eg in invertebrates such as insects and cephalopods), or complete separation (eg in higher vertebrates such as mammals and birds) into regions which secrete different enzymes and absorb digestive products.

aliphatic compound [alifatik] A carbon compound, especially one derived from a fatty acid, containing no aromatic groups.

aliyah [ahleeah] (Heb 'ascend') The name given to the waves of Jewish migration to Palestine. The different waves were inspired by the push of persecution and the pull of Zionism, and drew Jews from Russia, C Europe, and the Middle East. The first two waves, spanning the years 1882–1914, were in response to pogroms in Russia and C Europe as well as the encouragement of the World Zionist Organization, and brought an estimated 60–70 000 Jews to Palestine. The next three waves (1919–39), initially encouraged by the Balfour Declaration and the establishment of the British Mandate in Palestine, incurred opposition from Palestinian Arabs as 365 000 immigrants began to change the demographic balance. To preserve the peace in Palestine with the onset of World War 2, Jewish immigration was halted. The sixth aliyah, coming mostly between 1945 and the establishment of the state of Israel, brought over 118 000 Jews, including many survivors of the Holocaust. By 1948, the Jewish community numbered c.650 000, or one third of the population of Palestine. Since statehood, numerous waves of immigrants have reached Israel, such as the Falashas from Ethiopia (1984) and emigrés from the former Soviet Union, reaching a peak of 10 000 a month in early 1990.

alkali [alkaliy] A strong base, especially sodium and potassium hydroxides. Solutions of alkalis have high values of pH, and are used as cleaning materials, as they dissolve fats. The **alkali metals** are Group I of the periodic table: lithium, sodium, potassium, rubidium, and caesium. They are all characterized by being readily oxidized to compounds in which they exist as singly charged cations, and by having hydroxides which are strong bases.

alkaline-earth Strictly, the elements calcium, strontium, barium, and radium, but often including beryllium and magnesium as well, hence Group II of the periodic table. These elements mainly form compounds in which they occur as doubly charged cations, and are largely responsible for the hardness of water.

alkaloids Organic, nitrogen-containing bases from plants which include complex ring structures. Their functions are not fully understood, but may include protection against grazing animals, and a role in nitrogen assimilation. Many alkaloids have biological activity, and have been used as drugs, such as quinine, morphine, and cocaine. However, they may also be very toxic, as in the case of strychnine.

alkanamides *amides* 2

alkanes [alkaynz] Saturated hydrocarbons, having a general formula C_nH_{2n+2}, derived from methane by the addition of successive $-CH_2-$ groups. Also known as *paraffins*, they are generally unreactive, but make up the major components of petroleum.

alkanet [alkanet] The name given to several plants of the borage family. True alkanet (*Alkanna tinctoria*) is a bristly perennial growing to 15 cm/6 in; leaves oblong; flowers with a red tube and blue lobes; native to S Europe. The roots yield a red dye of the same name. (Family: Boraginaceae.)

alkanoic acids *carboxylic acids*

alkanols *alcohols*

alkanones *ketones*

alkanoyl *acyl*

alkenes [alkeenz] Hydrocarbons containing one or more double bonds; also called **olefins**. With one double bond, their general formula is C_nH_{2n}. They are mainly reactive by addition.

alkyl [alkiyl] A group $C_nH_{2n+1}-$, derived from an alkane, such as methyl (CH_3-), ethyl (C_2H_5-), and propyl (C_3H_7-).

alkynes [alkiynz] Hydrocarbons containing one or more triple bonds; also called **acetylenes**. With one triple bond, the general formula is C_nH_{2n-2}.

Allah [alah] The Islamic name for God. Prior to Mohammed, Allah was the supreme but not the sole deity in Arabia. It was Mohammed's mission to proclaim Allah as the sole God, the creator and sustainer of all things, who in the last days will judge all of humanity. Allah is known to human beings through the revelation of his will in the Qur'an which he delivered piecemeal to his Prophet Mohammed.

Allahabad [ahla-habahd] 25°25N 81°58E, pop (2000e) 947 000. City in Uttar Pradesh, NE India; on N bank of R Yamuna where it joins the R Ganges, 560 km/348 mi SE of New Delhi; founded, 1583; ceded to the British, 1801; airfield; railway; cotton, sugar; centre of Hindi literature; Great Mosque, Sultan Khossor's caravanserai, fort containing the Asoka pillar (240 BC); Hindu religious festival (Kumbh Mela), held every 12 years.

Allais, Maurice [alay] (1911–) Economist and engineer, born in Paris, France. He was professor of economic theory at the Institute of Statistics in Paris (1947–68), and since 1954 has been director of the Centre for Economic Analysis. His primary contributions have been in the reformulation of the theories of general economic equilibrium and maximum efficiency, and in the development of new concepts relating to capital and consumer choice. He received the Nobel Prize for Economics in 1988.

All Blacks The New Zealand national rugby union football team. The term was first applied to the team that toured Britain in 1905.

Allcock, Tony, popular name of **Anthony Allcock** (1955–) British bowls player, born in Leicestershire. His achievements include world outdoor champion (1980, 1984, 1988), world outdoor singles champion (1992, 1996), world indoor singles champion (1986–7, 1998, 2002), and world indoor pairs champion with David Bryant (1986–7, 1989–92). His books include *Improve Your Bowls* (1988) and *Bowl to Win* (1994). He holds a record 15 world bowls titles. He retired in 2003.

Allegheny Mountains [aluhgenee, aluhgaynee] Mountain range in E USA; W part of the Appalachian Mts; extends over 800 km/500 mi from N Pennsylvania SSW through Maryland, West Virginia, and Virginia; forms the watershed between the Atlantic and the Mississippi R; highest point Spruce Knob, 1481 m/4859 ft; rich in timber, coal, iron, and limestone.

allegory A literary device from the Greek *allégoria*, 'speaking otherwise', by which another level of meaning is concealed within what is usually a story of some kind; also, the story itself. Myth and fable are both allegorical. Allegory may therefore be understood as extended metaphor, or a continuous figure of speech. The form allows (indeed, invites) interpretation; it has often been used for works with a religious or political bearing, such as Bunyan's *Pilgrim's Progress* (1678) and Orwell's *Animal Farm* (1945). Two modern examples of allegorical drama have been Karel Čapek's *The Insect Play* (1921) and Edward Albee's *Tiny Alice* (1934).

allele [aleel, aleel] or **allelomorph** One of the alternative forms of a gene which can occur at a given point on a chromosome (a *locus*). Alleles at a given locus controlling a particular character may vary in their effect, and there may be two, three, or more such alleles available in a population, of which each individual carries two – one from the father and one from the mother. The term, introduced in 1902 to apply to Mendelian inheritance, is today increasingly applied to a short variant sequence of DNA, either within or adjacent to a functional gene.

allemande [alemahnd] A dance originating in the 16th-c, probably in Germany. In the 17th-c it became a standard movement in the suite for lute or keyboard. It is in 4/4 time and moderate tempo, and usually begins with a short note before the first main beat.

Allen, Ethan (1738–89) American soldier, born in Litchfield, Connecticut, USA. He spent his career trying to achieve independence for the Green Mountain area that is now the state of Vermont, commanding (1770–5) an irregular force called the Green Mountain Boys. At the outbreak of the War of Independence (1775–83) he helped take Fort Ticonderoga, in the first colonial victory of the war. On an expedition to Canada he was captured by the British at Montreal and held prisoner (1775–8). He continued the campaign for Vermont's statehood, which was not achieved until just after his death. He also published a deist tract, *Reason, the Only Oracle of Man*, often called 'Ethan Allen's Bible'.

Allen, Sir George Oswald Browning, known as **Gubby Allen** (1902–89) Cricketer, born in Sydney, New South Wales, SE Australia. He studied at Cambridge, and played for England in 25 Tests, including the 1932–3 Ashes series, when he refused to bowl 'bodyline'. He led the 1936–7 Ashes party to Australia, and after retiring he became the most powerful figure at the MCC, effectively running Lord's for the best part of half a century. He is the only player to have taken all 10 wickets in an innings at Lord's (10–49 against Lancashire, 1929).

Allen, Red, originally **Henry James Allen** (1908–67) Jazz trumpeter and singer, born in Algiers, New Orleans, Louisiana, USA. As a boy, he marched alongside his father's famous New Orleans Brass Band. In Chicago in 1927, he joined King Oliver's band and travelled with it to New York, where he made his first recordings. He played the Mississippi steamboats (1928–9), then joined Fletcher Henderson's orchestra (1932–4). He recorded prolifically, but when he joined Armstrong's orchestra (1937–40) he was kept in the background. When he finally made it to Europe in 1959, he was lionized, and for the rest of his days he happily played Dixieland either in the raucous band at the Metropole in New York or on European tours.

Allen, William (1532–94) Clergyman, born in Rossall, Lancashire, NW England, UK. He became principal of St Mary's Hall, Oxford, but after the accession of Queen Elizabeth in 1558 he went into exile in Flanders (1561) rather than take the Oath of Supremacy. In 1568 he founded the English college at Douai to train missionary priests for the reconversion of England to Catholicism, and supervised the Reims–Douai translation of the Bible. In 1587 he was created a cardinal.

Allen, Woody, originally **Allen Stewart Konigsberg** (1935–) Film actor, writer, and director, born in Brooklyn, New York City, USA. *What's New, Pussycat?* (1965) saw the start of a prolific film-making career that initially consisted of slapstick lunacy and genre parody in such productions as *Bananas* (1971) and *Love and Death* (1975). *Annie Hall* (1977) marked a shift in style and substance to more concentrated, autobiographical pieces and won him Oscars for writing and direction. Subsequently, he has explored his concerns with mortality, sexual inadequacies, show-business nostalgia, psychoanalysis, and urban living in such films as *Interiors* (1978), *Manhattan* (1979, British Academy Award and New York Film Critics Award), *Broadway Danny Rose* (1984), and *Hannah and Her Sisters* (1986, Oscar). His books include *Getting Even* (1971) and *Without Feathers* (1976). Later films include *Husbands and Wives* (1992) – whose release coincided with the much-publicized breakdown of his long-term relationship with actress **Mia Farrow** – *Bullets over Broadway* (1994, Oscar), *Everyone Says I Love You* (1997), *Celebrity* (1998), and *Sweet and Lowdown* (1999). In 1993 his private life received adverse publicity after losing a court battle for custody of three of their children, following the revelation of an affair with Farrow's adopted daughter, Soon-Yi (whom he married in 1997).

Allenby, Edmund Henry Hynman Allenby, 1st Viscount (1861–1936) British soldier, born in Brackenhurst, near Southwell, Nottinghamshire, C England, UK. He trained at Sandhurst Military Academy, and joined the Inniskilling Dragoons. In World War 1 he commanded the 1st Cavalry Division and then the Third Army in France (1915–17). Thereafter he was appointed commander-in-chief of the Egyptian expeditionary force against the Turks, took Beersheba and Gaza, and entered Jerusalem (1917). In 1918 he routed the Egyptians in the great cavalry battle of Megiddo. He was later high commissioner in Egypt (1919–25).

Allende (Gossens), Salvador [ayenday] (1908–73) Chilean statesman and president (1970–3), born in Valparaíso, Chile. He helped found the Chilean Socialist Party, was elected to the Chamber of Deputies in 1937, served as minister of health for three years, and was a senator (1945–70). He sought, and failed to win, the presidency in 1952, 1958, and 1964. He was finally successful in 1970 but because he lacked a popular majority, his election had to be confirmed by Congress, in which there was strong opposition from the right. He tried to build a Socialist society within the framework of a parliamentary democracy, but met widespread opposition from business interests. He was overthrown by a military junta, led by General Augusto Pinochet, and died in the fighting.

Allende, Isabel [ayenday] (1942–) Novelist, born in Lima, Peru, the niece and god-daughter of Salvador Allende, the former president of Chile. Several months after his assassination and the overthrow of Chile's coalition government in 1973, she fled Chile, seeking sanctuary in Venezuela. Her first novel, *The House of the Spirits* (1985), which arose directly out of her exile, became a worldwide best-seller and critical success. Her later books include *Of Love and Shadows* (1987), *The Infinite Plan* (1993), and *Daughter of Fortune* (1999). Allende's work is written in the style of magic realism, which uses fantasy and myth to override time and place.

allergy An immune reaction to contact with certain foreign substances that are normally harmless and do not provoke a reponse in normal individuals. These substances are called **allergens**. In sensitive individuals they react with antibodies produced within the body by cells of the immune system. The reaction between the allergen and antibodies results in the liberation of substances that damage body cells and tissues, including histamine, hydroxtryptamine, and bradykinin. A large number of substances found in nature (eg pollen) are actual or potential allergens, and are capable of inducing a wide range of illnesses such as asthma and dermatitis.

alley farming An agroforestry system developed to maintain soil productivity, in which rows of fast-growing leguminous trees are planted at intervals of 4–6 m/13–20 ft within fields of annual crops. The trees reclaim nutrients from deep soil layers and fix atmospheric nitrogen. Their branches can be used as nitrogen-rich forage or as green manure, thus making a useful contribution to sustainable agriculture.

Alleyn, Edward [alen] (1566–1626) Actor, born in London, UK, the stepson-in-law of Philip Henslowe. A contemporary of Shakespeare, he was associated with the Admiral's Men, and formed a partnership with Henslowe to run the Bear Garden and build the Fortune Theatre. He founded Dulwich College (1619), and deposited in its library documents relating to his career (including Henslowe's diary), which give a unique insight into the financial aspects of Elizabethan theatre.

All Fools' Day *April Fool*

Allgäu Alps [ahlgoy], Ger **Allgäuer Alpen** Mountain range extending E from L Constance along the Austro-German border to the Lech R valley; highest peak, the Mädelegabel (2645 m/8678 ft); major cattle-rearing area (the Allgäu breed), dairying; many spas and medicinal springs.

Alliance *Liberal Party* (UK); *Social Democratic Party*

Alliance for Progress A 10-year programme of modernization and reform for countries in Latin America, sponsored by the US government in 1961 on the initiative of President Kennedy. Few of its aims were achieved, despite numerous specific development projects.

Allies The term generally applied to the nations that fought the 'Axis' powers during World War 2. By 1942 the combatant countries comprising the Allies included Great Britain and the British Commonwealth, USA, Soviet Union, France, and China, while Costa Rica, Cuba, Brazil, and Mexico had also declared war on Germany and Japan. By March 1945 they had been joined by Bulgaria, Finland, Hungary, Italy (which nations had been previously allied to Nazi Germany), and Turkey.

alligator A crocodile-like reptile of family Alligatoridae; short broad snout; fourth tooth from the front on each side of the lower jaw is hidden when the jaws are closed (unlike the crocodile); two species: **American alligator** (*Alligator mississippiensis*) from SE USA, and the rare **Chinese alligator** (*Alligator chinensis*).

All-India Muslim League A political organization (founded 1906) to protect Indian Muslim rights. During the 1930s and 1940s it campaigned under M A Jinnah's leadership for an independent Muslim state separate from future independent India. It was the dominant party in Pakistan after 1947.

Allingham, Margery (Louise) [alinguhm] (1904–66) Detective-story writer, the creator of the fictional detective Albert Campion, born in London, UK. She wrote a string of elegant and witty novels, including *The Crime at Black Dudley* (1928), *The Tiger in the Smoke* (1952), and *The China Governess* (1963).

alliteration The repetition of a consonantal sound or sounds; to be distinguished from **assonance**, the repetition of a vowel sound. Both are illustrated in these lines by Keats: 'Then in a wailful choir the small gnats mourn/Among the river sallows, borne aloft/Or sinking as the light wind lives or dies'. The dominant consonants here are *l*, *m/n*, and *w*; an example of assonance is the link between *small*, *mourn*, and *borne*. An intrinsic part of the sound-structure of poetry, alliterative effects may also be cultivated in prose, and are common in nonsense verse, tongue-twisters, patter, and jingles.

Allitt, Beverley [alit] (1969–) British convicted murderer. A nurse by profession, she was convicted in 1993 of the murder of four children in her care and of the attempted murder of three others. Dubbed the UK's first female serial killer, she allegedly suffered from a medical condition termed 'Münchhausen's syndrome by proxy'. She is currently detained at Rampton General Hospital for the Criminally Insane.

allium A member of a large genus of perennials, all with a strong, distinctive onion smell, native to the N hemisphere; most form bulbs with a brown papery skin; leaves usually tubular, sometimes elliptical or strap-shaped; flowers with six perianth-segments, bell- or star-shaped, in dense umbels. In many species the flowers are mixed with, or completely replaced by bulbils, which allow the plant to reproduce vegetatively. They include several well-known vegetables and ornamentals. (Genus: *Allium*, 450 species. Family: Liliaceae.)

allopathy [alopathee] (Gr *allos*, 'different' + *pathos*, 'suffering') A term used by Samuel Hahnemann to describe the approach of orthodox medicine, which gives treatment to suppress the symptoms of an illness using the principle of opposites (eg analgesics for pain, purgatives for constipation). This contrasts with the homeopathic approach, which encourages rather than suppresses the body's reaction to a disease process.

allophone *phoneme*

Allosaurus [alosawrus] A large flesh-eating dinosaur reaching 11 m/36 ft in length and two tonnes in weight; bipedal, powerful hindlimbs, and short forelimbs, both with three claws; muscular tail assisted in balancing; teeth with serrated edges; known from the Upper Jurassic period of North America. (Order: Saurischia.)

allotrope One of several forms in which an element may exist. These may be different molecular forms, as O_2 and O_3, or they may be different crystal modifications, as graphite and diamond (allotropes of C).

alloy A blend of a metal with one or more other metals or with a non-metallic substance. Most pure metals lack the properties needed to make them practically useful, and are nearly always used as some alloy. The properties of the alloy may differ considerably from those of any of the constituents, and vary with the proportions used, as with brass. Alloys known since ancient times include bronze (copper with tin), brass (copper with zinc), and pewter (lead with tin). Modern alloys include stainless steels (iron/chromium/nickel), and high temperature-resistant alloys for use in gas turbines (containing titanium).

All Saints' Day A Christian festival commemorating all the Church's saints collectively; held on 1 November in the Roman Catholic and Anglican Churches, and on the first Sunday after Pentecost in the Eastern Churches; formerly known as **All Hallows** (Old English *halga*, 'saint'); the preceding evening is Hallowe'en.

All Souls' Day In the Roman Catholic Church, the day (2 Nov) set apart as a day of prayer for souls in purgatory; also celebrated by some Anglicans, in the Eastern Orthodox Church celebrated about two months before Easter.

allspice An evergreen tree (*Pimenta dioica*) native to tropical America and the West Indies; leaves elliptical; flowers creamy; fruit small, round; also known as **pimento** or **Jamaican pepper**. Spice made from its dried, unripe fruits has a flavour like that of cinnamon, cloves, and nutmeg combined, hence the name. (Family: Myrtaceae.)

Allston, Washington [awlston] (1779–1843) Artist and writer, born at Allston plantation, Brook Green Domain on the Waccamaw R, South Carolina, USA. The earliest US Romantic painter, he studied at Harvard and the Royal Academy in London before going on to Paris and Rome, eventually settling at Cambridgeport, MA, in 1830. He painted large canvases, particularly of religious scenes, such as 'Belshazzar's Feast', 'The Flood', and 'Elijah in the Desert'.

alluvium A geological term for unconsolidated material deposited by a river. The material ranges in size from clay, through silt and sand, to gravel. Alluvium is generally well sorted (ie deposits are of a uniform or narrow size range), and the material is rounded.

Alma-Ata *Almaty*

Almagro, Diego de [almagroh] (c.1475–1538) Conquistador, born in Almagro, SC Spain. He was on the first exploratory expedition from Peru against the Incas led by Francisco Pizarro (1524–8). In the second expedition (from 1532), he joined Pizarro in 1533 at Cajamarca, and occupied the Inca capital of Cuzco. In 1535–6 he led the conquest of Chile, but came back to Cuzco in 1537 and, after a dispute with Pizarro, occupied it by force, thus beginning a civil war between the Spaniards. Early in 1538 he was defeated by an army led by Pizarro's brother, Hernando, and was captured and executed.

Alma-Tadema, Sir Lawrence [alma tadema] (1836–1912) Painter of Classical-genre paintings, born in Dronrijp, The Netherlands. He studied at the Antwerp Academy of Art, and came to specialize in subjects from Greek, Roman, and Egyptian antiquity. He achieved great popularity with such Classical idyllic scenes as 'Tarquinius Superbus' (1867) and 'The Conversion of Paula' (1898). He was a painstaking technician and spared no expense. For 'The Roses of Heliogabalus' (exhibited Royal Academy, 1896), fresh roses were sent weekly from the S of France so that every petal – and the picture contains thousands – could be depicted accurately. He settled permanently in England in 1873, and was knighted in 1899.

Almaty [almatee], formerly **Alma-Ata** (to 1995), **Vernyi** (to 1921) 43°15N 76°57E, pop (2000e) 1 192 000. Former capital city of Kazakhstan (to 1997, now Astana); in the N foothills of the Zailiyskiy Alatau range, c.300 km/185 mi from the Chinese frontier; established in 1854 as a military fortress and trading centre; destroyed by earthquake, 1887; airport; railway; university (1934); Academy of Sciences (1968); engineering, printing, film-making, foodstuffs, tobacco, textiles, leather; noted tourist and athletic centre; Ascension cathedral (1904, world's second highest wooden building).

Almeida, Francisco de [almayda] (c.1450–1510) Portuguese soldier and first viceroy of the Portuguese Indies (1505–9), until he was superseded by Affonso d'Albuquerque. He was killed in South Africa on his voyage home in a skirmish with natives at Table Bay.

Almohads [almuhhadz] *Berber*

almond A small, deciduous, sometimes spiny tree (*Prunus dulcis*) growing to 8 m/26 ft, native to Asia; leaves narrowly oval, toothed; flowers pink fading to white, appearing before the leaves; fruit greyish, velvety, 3·5–6 cm/1½–2½ in, oval; thin, leathery flesh surrounding pitted stone. The **sweet almond** (variety *dulcis*) is the source of edible almond nuts; **bitter almond** (variety *tamara*) is inedible, but provides oil of bitter almonds used in industry; ornamental flowering almonds are other species. (Family: Rosaceae.)

Almoravids [almoravidz] *Berber*

Almquist or **Almqvist, Carl Jonas Love** [almkwist] (1793–1866) Writer, born in Stockholm, Sweden. He had a bizarrely chequered career as a clergyman and teacher; he was accused of forgery and attempted murder, and fled to the USA. From 1865 he lived in Bremen under an assumed name. His prolific literary output, ranging from Romanticism to (from the late 1830s) Social Realism, encompassed novels, plays, poems, and essays, and was published in a 14-volume series, *Törnrosens bok* (1832–51, The Book of the Briar Rose).

aloe [aloh] A member of a large genus of shrub- or tree-like evergreens, native to Africa, especially S Africa, and Arabia; leaves sword-shaped, tough, fleshy, often waxy and toothed, in rosettes at tips of stems; flowers tubular, yellow to red; often planted for ornament. The drug **bitter aloes** is obtained from the sap. (Genus: *Aloe*, 275 species. Family: Liliaceae.)

Alonso, Dámaso [alonsoh] (1898–1990) Poet and philologist, born in Madrid, Spain. He travelled widely in Europe and America as teacher and lecturer, then became professor of romance philology at Madrid University, establishing his reputation as an authority on Góngora y Argote. He also published poetry, of which *Hijos de la ira* (1944, Children of Wrath) is the best known.

alopecia [alopeesha] Hair loss resulting from the failure of hair formation by the hair follicles. It may be patchy (*alopecia areata*) or generalized (*baldness*). It may be inherited, or stem from an underlying general illness or toxin (eg a drug) which disturbs the follicular activity.

Aloysius, St *Gonzaga, Luigi*

alpaca [alpaka] A domesticated member of the camel family, from Peru and Bolivia (*Lama pacos*); resembles a long-haired llama, but with a shorter face, neck, and legs; kept mainly for wool; sheared every two years; two breeds: *huacaya* and *suri*. It may be cross-bred with the vicuña (to produce the finer-woolled *paco-vicuña*) or with the llama.

Alpe Adria [alpay adria] A working association of 11 neighbouring regions in Austria, Germany, Italy, and former Yugoslavia, linked by cultural and economic interests; established in 1978; Oberösterreich, Salzburg, and Steiermark federal states in Austria; Veneto, Lombardy, Trentino–Alto Adige, and Friuli–Venezia Giulia regions in Italy; Bayern in Germany; Croatia; and Slovenia.

alphabet *see panel*

Alpha Centauri [alfa sentawree] *Centaurus*

alpha decay A naturally occurring radioactive decay process in which the atomic nucleus breaks up into a lighter nucleus and an alpha particle, which is ejected. It is governed by the strong nuclear force. Lead-210 is an alpha particle source with a half-life of 21 years.

alphanumeric characters A set of characters which includes all the lower and upper case letters of the alphabet (a to z, A to Z), the digits 0 to 9, and some punctuation characters. The term is widely used in business computing, particularly with languages such as COBOL.

alpha particle A particle emitted in alpha decay. It is composed of two neutrons plus two protons, the same as the helium nucleus, and was identified as such by Ernest Rutherford in 1906; charge +2. It typically travels a few centimetres in the air before being brought to rest by collisions with air molecules. It causes the production of many ions, and in living tissue substantial biological damage.

alphabet

The Development of the Early Alphabet

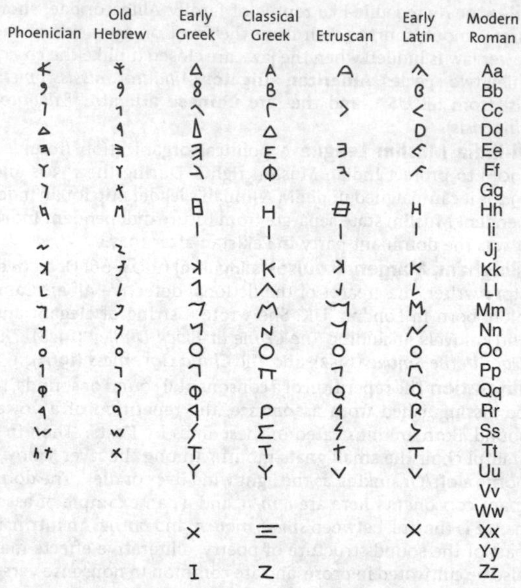

Phoenician
Old Hebrew
Early Greek
Classical Greek
Etruscan
Early Latin
Modern Roman
Aa Bb Cc Dd Ee Ff Gg Hh Ii Jj Kk Ll Mm Nn Oo Pp Qq Rr Ss Tt Uu Vv Ww Xx Yy Zz

The most economical and versatile form of writing system yet devised, because it breaks words down into their phonic components, assigning letters or combinations of letters to represent speech sounds. Thus, in English, the letter (or *grapheme*) *m* represents the sound (or *phoneme*) [m] in such words as *mat*; less obviously, the series *o...e* represents the long [ou] vowel sound in such words as *bone*. The symbols of an alphabetic writing system are not tied to the meanings of the words they represent, and the need for several thousand pictograms, for instance, is avoided. Most alphabets contain less than 30 symbols. However, they differ substantially in the regularity with which they correspond to the sound system: Spanish and Welsh, for instance, have a very regular system, whereas English and Irish Gaelic (particularly in its most traditional form) have many exceptional spelling patterns which can be learned only by special rules. Also, the alphabets of W European languages give vowels and consonants the same status, as full letters; but in the case of *consonantal* alphabets (eg the alphabets of India), the two types of sound are treated differently: the consonants are assigned the function of 'mapping out' the basic form of the word, and the vowels are added as diacritic marks. The Hebrew and Arabic alphabets take this system one step further, and allow the marking of the vowel diacritics to be optional. The model for all Western alphabets was the Etruscan (c.800 BC), itself based on the Greek alphabet, which had modified the Phoenician consonantal alphabet by adding vowel letters to it.

Alpher, Ralph (Asher) (1921–) Physicist, born in Washington, District of Columbia, USA. After studying at George Washington University, he spent World War 2 as a civilian physicist and afterwards worked at Johns Hopkins University and in industry. Together with George Gamow, he proposed in 1948 the 'alpha, beta, gamma' theory (the name of physicist Hans Bethe was added in absentia to the authorship, to make the alphabetical joke work), which suggests the possibility of explaining the abundances of chemical elements as the result of thermonuclear processes in the early stages of a hot, evolving universe.

These ideas became part of the 'big bang' model of the universe. Together with Robert Herman he predicted the cosmic background radiation as a consequence of the 'cooling' of the 'big bang'.

Alphonso *Alfonso*

alphorn A musical instrument found in rural communities, particularly in the Swiss Alps. Most alphorns are about 1·8 m/6 ft long, made of wood, and can sound the first five or six harmonics; but examples up to twice that length are not uncommon.

alpine A botanical term for vegetation growing in mountains above the tree-line; also used for plants naturally occurring in such regions. Alpines are typically low-growing or dome-shaped perennials, adapted to withstand high levels of solar radiation and drought as well as cold.

Alps Principal mountain range of Europe, covering 259 000 sq km/100 000 sq mi in Switzerland, France, Germany, Austria, Liechtenstein, Italy, Slovenia, Croatia, and Yugoslavia; a series of parallel chains over 1000 km/600 mi SW–NE; originally formed by collision of African and European tectonic plates; source of many great European rivers, notably the Rhine, Po, and Rhône; **Western Alps** (highest peaks in parentheses) consist of (1) *Alpes-Maritimes* (Cima Sud Argentera 3297 m/10 817 ft); (2) *Alpes Cottiennes* or *Cottian Alps* (Monte Viso 3851 m/12 634 ft); (3) *Alpes Dauphine* (Barre des Ecrins 4101 m/13 455 ft); (4) *Alpes Graian* or *Graian Alps* (Gran Paradiso 4061 m/13 323 ft); **Middle Alps** consist of (1) *Alpi Pennine* (Mont Blanc 4807 m/15 771 ft, highest peak in the range; Matterhorn 4477 m/14 688 ft); (2) *Alpi Lepontine* (3553 m/11 657 ft); (3) *Alpi Retiche* or *Rhaetian Alps* (Piz Bernina 4049 m/13 284 ft); (4) *Berner Alpen* or *Bernese Alps* (Finsteraarhorn 4274 m/14 022 ft); (5) *Alpi Orobie*; (6) *Ötztaler Alpen* (Wildspitze 3774 m/12 382 ft); (7) *Dolomiti* or *Dolomites* (Marmolada 3342 m/10 964 ft); (8) *Lechtaler Alpen* (3038 m/9967 ft); **Eastern Alps**: (1) *Zillertaler Alpen* or *Alpi Aurine* (3510 m/11 516 ft); (2) *Kitzbühler Alpen* (2559 m/8396 ft); (3) *Karnische Alpen* or *Carnic Alps* (2781 m/9124 ft); (4) *Julijske Alpe* or *Julian Alps* (Triglav 2863 m/9393 ft); (5) *Hohe Tauern* or *Noric Alps* (Grossglockner 3797 m/12 457 ft); (6) *Niedere Tauern* (2863 m/9393 ft); notable passes include the Mont Cenis, St Bernard (Little and Greater), Gemmi, Simplon, St Gotthard, Splugen, Stilfserjoch (Stelvio), and Brenner; railway tunnels at Col de Fréjus, Lotschberg, Simplon, and St Gotthard; summer pasture on many lower slopes; major tourist region, with highly developed facilities; mountaineering and skiing; towns have manufactures concerned with native and imported products such as textiles, clocks, chocolate, wooden goods; in 1911 Karl Blodig was the first to climb all peaks over 4000 m (13 000 ft).

al-Qaeda / al-Qa'ida (Arabic 'The Base') An Islamic network of fundamentalist organizations committed to the use of terrorism for the attainment of their goals. It was formed by Osama bin Laden (see separate entry) in the late 1980s to unite Sunni Arabs who had fought in Afghanistan against the USSR, and was based in Afghanistan until the removal of the Taliban regime in late 2001. Its political agenda is the replacement of 'heretic' governments by Islamic governments based on the rule of Sharia (Islamic law)—a notion which includes several Arab regimes (especially Saudi Arabia) as well as the USA, whose influence throughout the Middle East it wishes to eliminate. Bin Laden has issued three fatwas (religious rulings) calling on Muslims to take up arms against the USA, and a 1998 statement asserted that it was the duty of all Muslims to kill US citizens and their allies.

The numbers of members in the organization is unknown, but probably totals several thousand. Since 1998 it has served as an umbrella organization called 'The Islamic World Front for the struggle against the Jews and the Crusaders' (Al-Jabhah al-Islamiyyah al-'Alamiyyah li-Qital al-Yahud wal-Salibiyyin) which includes several Sunni Islamic extremist groups, such as the Egyptian al-Gama'a al-Islamiyya, the Islamic Movement of Uzbekistan, and the Harakat ul-Mujahidin.

Its most notorious terrorist act was the suicide attack by 19 of its members who hijacked and crashed four US commercial jets into US sites on 11 September 2001 – two into the World Trade Center in New York City, one into the Pentagon, Washington, and one into a field in Shanksville, Pennsylvania, killing over 3,000. It was also responsible for the bombing of US embassies in Nairobi, Kenya and Dar es Salaam, Tanzania (1998), the attack on the USS *Cole* in the port of Aden (2000), other attacks on US military personnel in Kuwait and Yemen (2000–2), and the bombing of a hotel in Mombasa, Kenya (2002), and it may have been implicated in several other terrorist acts, such as the nightclub bombing in Bali, Indonesia (2002).

At the same time, the capture of al-Qaida operatives has foiled several assassination and bombing plots, such as the arrest of Richard Colvin Reid, who attempted to ignite a shoe bomb on a transatlantic flight from Paris to Miami (2001) and the prevention of an attempt to shoot down an Israeli chartered plane with a surface-to-air missile at Mombasa airport (2002). However, the ongoing threat from the organization has led to unprecedented levels of security being put in place all over the world, especially at airports and public buildings in the USA and allied countries, and in areas where US influence is strong.

Al Sabah [saba] The ruling dynasty of Kuwait. Dating their authority in Kuwait to the mid-18th-c, the Al Sabah sheikhs attempted to maintain their independence among the competing rivalries of European, Ottoman, and local powers. **Mubarak the Great** (r.1896–1915) sought British protection to forestall Ottoman intervention into Kuwaiti affairs. Since independence in 1961, Al Sabah rule has twice been challenged by Iraq on the disputed grounds that Kuwait once formed part of the province of Basra. The present emir, Sheikh Jabir al-Ahmad al-Jabir Al Sabah, came to power in 1977. One of the main crises of his rule has been Iraq's invasion of Kuwait (1990). The National Assembly, which had been dissolved by Sheikh Jabir in 1986, was reconstituted in 1992. However, the government of Kuwait remains dominated by members of the Al Sabah family.

Alsace [alsas], Ger **Elsass**, Lat **Alsatia** pop (2000e) 1 699 000; area 8280 sq km/3196 sq mi. Region of NE France, comprising the departments of Bas-Rhin and Haut-Rhin, part of Upper Rhine Plain on frontier with Germany; crossed S–N by Rhine and Ill Rivers; traditional scene of Franco–German conflict; formerly part of Lorraine before becoming part of German Empire; Treaty of Westphalia (1648) returned most of Alsace to France, ceded to Germany, 1871; returned to France, 1919; occupied by Germany in World War 2; chief towns, Strasbourg, Mulhouse, Colmar; several spas, wine towns, and vineyards; fertile and industrially productive region; wine, beer, pottery, chemicals, paper, printed fabrics, textile dyeing and spinning, machinery, car manufacture.

alsatian *German shepherd*

Al Saud [sowd] Royal family and founders of the Kingdom of Saudi Arabia. **Abdul Aziz ibn Saud** (1880–1953), also known as **Ibn Saud**, came out of exile in Kuwait to consolidate his family's rule over a large part of the Arabian peninsula in the 1920s and, naming the country after his family, declared himself king of Saudi Arabia in 1932. The discovery of oil in 1938 and the award of concessions to US oil companies set in motion changes which began to be felt in the reign of his eldest son and successor, **Saud ibn Abd al-Aziz** (1902–69). Ascending the throne in 1953 on the death of his father, Saud found his kingdom under pressure from the revolutionary regime of Nasser in Egypt. In 1964 he was peacefully deposed by the Council of Ministers, and his half-brother **Faisal ibn Abd al-Aziz** (1904–75) became king. Faisal gave the kingdom prominence in Arab and international affairs by the strategic use of its oil power, particularly in the Arab oil embargo of 1973. He was assassinated by a nephew in the royal place in Riyadh, and succeeded by the fourth son of Ibn Saud, **Khaled ibn Abd al-Aziz** (1913–82). Khaled was credited with halting the Lebanese Civil War (1975–89) and moderating OPEC oil pricing. In poor health, he died in Taif. The current ruler of Saudi Arabia is the half-brother of Khaled, **Fahd ibn Abd al-Aziz** (1923–), whose reign has suffered from economic recession and regional insecurity, notably the two Gulf Wars. This turbulence has brought the royal family's monopoly over the country's politics into question, and prompted demands for greater participation and political pluralism.

alsike [alsiyk] A species of clover (*Trifolium hybridum*), probably native to Europe, grown as a fodder crop and now occurring in many temperate countries; a variable perennial growing to 60 cm/2 ft; leaves with three-toothed leaflets, widest towards the tip; pea-flowers white or pink, in lax rounded heads to 3 cm/1¼ in across. (Family: Leguminosae.)

Alston, Richard [awlston] (1948–) Choreographer, born in Stoughton, West Sussex, S England, UK. He was educated at Eton and Croydon College of Art (1965–7), and at the London School of Contemporary Dance (1967–70). He co-founded Strider in 1972 (disbanded 1975), the forerunner of the contemporary dance company Second Stride. He studied in New York with Merce Cunningham (1975–7), then joined Ballet Rambert as resident choreographer (1980–6), and artistic director (1986–92). In 1994 he became artistic director of the Richard Alston Dance Company.

Altaic [altayik] A hypothesized family of languages extending from the Balkan peninsula to the NE of Asia; not accepted as a genetic family by many linguists. About 40 languages fall into three groups: Turkic, of which Turkish is the main member, spoken by c.45 million people in and near Turkey; Mongolian, of which Mongol is the main member, spoken by c.4 million in Mongolia and China; and Manchu-Tungus, of which Evenki (as Tungus is now known) may have 30 000 speakers. Manchu, once a lingua franca between China and the outside world, is now spoken by few of the 3 million who live in the Manchu province of China.

Altai Mountains [ahltiy], Chin **Altai Shan** Major mountain system of C Asia, extending from Russia (NW) SE along the border between NW China and Mongolia, into Mongolia itself; source of the Irtysh and Ob Rivers; highest point, Mt Belukha (4506 m/14 783 ft); major mineral reserves.

Altair [altair] *Aquila*

Altamira [altameera] 43°18N 4°08E. A Palaeolithic limestone cave of c.13 500 BC on the N Spanish coast near Santander, celebrated for its vivid ceiling paintings of game animals (principally bison, bulls, horses, hinds, and boars), some over 2 m/6½ ft long. Though discovered in 1879 by local landowner Marcelino de Sautuola, its authenticity was not established before 1902. It is now a world heritage site.

altarpiece In a Christian church, a carved or painted screen placed above the altar facing the congregation; known as an *ancona* (Ital), *retable* (Fr), or *reredos* (Eng). The earliest examples appeared in the 10th–11th-c. The *pala d'oro* (gold altarpiece) in St Mark's, Venice, commissioned 1105, consists of gold and enamel-work, as well as sculptured figures, and includes images of Christ in Majesty with angels and saints, with scenes from the New Testament and the life of the titular saint, Mark. An altarpiece consisting of two panels is called a *diptych*; three panels make a *triptych*. They vary greatly in size, and were numerous in late mediaeval and Renaissance churches. In Protestant countries this development ended abruptly at the Reformation, and many altarpieces were destroyed, but in Catholic countries their production was encouraged, leading to the luxurious altarpieces of the Baroque period, both painted (Rubens, Caravaggio, van Dyck) and carved (Bernini). The modern preference for plain altars set forward, as in the early Church, has practically ruled out the altarpiece. There is simply nowhere to put it.

altazimuth [altazimuhth] A type of telescope mounting in which the telescope can be moved independently in altitude (swinging on a horizontal axis) and azimuth (swinging on a vertical axis). It is used in very large optical telescopes and radio telescopes, as well as simple amateur telescopes.

Altdorfer, Albrecht [altdaw(r)fer] (c.1480–1538) Painter, engraver, and architect, the leading member of the Danube School of German painting, born in Regensburg, SE Germany. His most outstanding works are biblical and historical subjects set against highly imaginative and atmospheric landscape backgrounds. He was also a pioneer of copperplate etching.

alternating current (AC) An electrical current whose direction of flow reverses periodically; the alternative is **direct current (DC)**, where the flow is in a single direction only. The variation of current with time is usually sinusoidal, as produced naturally by rotating coils in magnetic fields (generators). Household current is AC, with frequencies varying to some extent between countries, eg 50 Hz (UK), 60 Hz (USA). Power transmission and transformers rely on AC.

alternation of generations The progression of the life-cycle of a plant through two reproductive forms. The **sexual generation** or *gametophyte* produces haploid gametes. These fuse and give rise to a diploid *sporophyte*, which produces haploid spores from which grow new gametophytes (**asexual generation**). In algae, the gametophyte is the dominant generation, occupying the major portion of the life-cycle, although the two generations are generally indistinguishable in structure. In bryophytes the gametophyte is also dominant, but is very different in structure from the sporophyte. In ferns, gymnosperms, and flowering plants, the sporophyte is dominant; the gametophyte of flowering plants is represented only by the pollen tube and the embryo-sac. Alternation of generations also occurs in some animals; in coelenterates, for example, a sexual medusa-like stage alternates with an asexual polyp-like stage.

alternative and augmentative communication A means of communicating devised to help severely disabled people who are unable to speak or write normally because of a physical or mental handicap. *Augmentative* systems supplement normal language use; *alternative* systems replace normal language entirely. Examples include the use of sign languages, symbol boards, speech synthesizers, and braille. Typically, users wear or sit in front of a device containing a selection of letters, words, or messages, and type, touch, or point to the element they wish to communicate, using any mobile part of their body (eg foot, mouth, eyebrow) to operate a keyboard, switch, or pointing device. Major advances are in progress, following developments in electronic and computational technology.

alternative energy Sources of energy which do not rely on the burning of fossil fuels (eg coal, gas, oil) or nuclear power to provide energy. With the controversial nature of nuclear power, and the recognition that fossil fuels are a non-renewable resource and contribute significantly to pollution, there is considerable interest in some countries in alternative sources, such as solar power, geothermal power, hydroelectric power, tidal power, and wind power. Such sources are particularly important in countries which lack fossil fuels, and are seen as having potential in economically developing countries. Alternative sources are often seen as being environmentally sound because pollution is rarely a problem. However, their development is not without controversy: schemes to build barrages across estuaries to harness tidal energy are often attacked because of damage to estuarine ecosystems; hydroelectric power projects may require valleys to be flooded and people made homeless; the large number of wind towers needed for wind power are a visual intrusion.

alternative fuel A fuel other than petrol for powering motor vehicles. These fuels include ethanol, methanol, and **biofuels** derived from organic material, such as biodiesel, obtained from various kinds of vegetable oil, and rape methyl esters (RME) from rape-oil. Such fuels are said to be environmentally friendly, but debate continues over whether they are as pollution-free as is claimed, and whether the land devoted to such crops might not be put to better use. The term often includes modifications which have been made to petrol to reduce harmful levels of lead emissions – the unleaded and superunleaded petrols (the latter giving better performance). Research continues into ways of modifying vehicle design to take advantage of such fuels (**alternative fuel vehicles**).

alternative medicine Approaches to the treatment of illness using procedures other than those recommended by orthodox medical science; also known as **complementary medicine**. The demand for such treatment has increased in recent years, as individuals who have not been relieved of their complaints by orthodox methods have become more inclined to look elsewhere for treatment. There are many different approaches, and a recent publication on alternative medicine lists over 600 entries. Some of these procedures are based on theories of disease for which there is scanty evidence, and some invoke principles that most people would recognize as bizarre. The fact that many of these approaches are empirical in their origin is not in itself a fault, as many medical treatments now incorporated into orthodox medical practice began as empirical observations, and only later acquired scientific justification. In fact, many orthodox treatments remain unproven by rigorous scientific investigation. The problem is how to distinguish the genuinely effective from witchcraft and superstition. Hardly any of the therapeutic methods used as alternative medicine have been, or are readily capable of being, rigorously assessed, using the standard scientific techniques of critical assessment and refutation, or of comparison with the natural course of the ailment or with other remedies claimed to influence the ailment. At present, most of the claims for the success of alternative remedies remain anecdotal. However, there is a growing body of evidence to suggest that some alternative therapies may be effective.

Althusser, Louis [alt-hüser] (1918–90) Political philosopher, born in Algiers, Algeria. He studied in Algiers and in France, was imprisoned in concentration camps during World War 2, and from 1948 taught in Paris. He joined the Communist Party in 1948, and wrote influential works on Marxist theory, including *Pour Marx* (1965, For Marx) and *Lénin et la philosophie* (1969, Lenin and Philosophy). In 1980 he murdered his wife, and was confined in an asylum until his death; self-justifying autobiographical pieces were published in 1992.

Altichiero [altikyayroh] (c.1330–c.1395) Painter and possible founder of the Veronese School, born near Verona, N Italy. He worked in Verona and also in Padua, where he painted frescoes (1372–9) in the Basilica of S Antonio, which include a Crucifixion and scenes from the life of St James, and in the Oratory of S Giorgio (1377–84), which depict scenes from the lives of St George and other saints. This work combines the solid Realism of Giotto with a new Gothic elegance typical of the later 14th-c. In S Giorgio he shared the work with a painter called Jacopo Avanzo.

altimeter A device carried by an aircraft to measure its height above the ground. The usual type operates by sending out a radio signal, and measuring the time taken by the signal to return, since the speed at which the radio signal travels is known. When the ground rises below the aircraft, and the aircraft maintains level flight, the altimeter registers a drop in altitude.

Altiplano [altiplahnoh] The arid plateau of W Bolivia and S Peru between the W and E cordilleras; elevation 3000–5000 m/ 9800–16 400 ft. It is covered by widespread alluvial and glacial deposits, and the rivers and streams of the plateau drain into L Titicaca (Bolivia/Peru) and L Poopó (Bolivia). Both are closed lake basins, ie they do not drain to the sea.

altitude sickness Adverse effects experienced by individuals travelling to high altitudes, usually beginning at c.2500 m/ 8000 ft above sea level and getting worse with increasing elevation. The amount of oxygen in the air decreases with altitude, leading to shortness of breath and hyperventilation (rapid breathing). High altitudes also disturb the body's fluid balance and the blood is maintained at a more concentrated level, leading to the production of large amounts of urine and dehydration unless fluid input is maintained. The body is able to gradually adjust to high altitudes by producing more red blood cells to carry oxygen around the body. However if ascent is too rapid there is insufficient time for the body to acclimatize, and acute altitude sickness results, with headache, nausea, fatigue or weakness, dizziness, disturbed sleep, confusion, and even death.

Altman, Sidney (1939–) Biochemist, born in Montreal, Quebec, SE Canada. He became affiliated with Yale in 1971, and holds dual citizenship. He showed that the RNA molecule could rearrange itself, thereby altering the material it produces without requiring an enzyme – a breakthrough in our understanding of genetic processes. He shared the Nobel Prize for Chemistry with Thomas Cech in 1989.

altocumulus clouds Middle-level clouds of the cumulus family at altitudes of c.2000–7000 m/6500–23 000 ft. They are white and/or grey in colour, and usually indicate fine weather. Cloud symbol: Ac.

Alto Paraná, River *Paraná, River*

altostratus clouds Middle-level clouds of the stratus family, similar to stratus clouds but less dense and occurring at higher elevations, typically c.2000–7000 m/6500–23 000 ft. They are greyish in colour with a sheet-like appearance, and give a warning of warm, rainy weather associated with the passage of a warm front. Cloud symbol: As.

altruism The philosophical thesis that people sometimes do or should intentionally promote the interests of others to the detriment of their own interests. It is usually contrasted with *egoism*, which asserts that all actions are really self-interested. Sociobiologists have recently studied how apparently altruistic behaviour in animals can be adaptive for the species.

alum Usually $KAl(SO_4)_2.12H_2O$. Hydrated potassium aluminium sulphate, **common alum**. Other alums have Al substituted by Fe (**iron alum**) or Cr (**chrome alum**). All form large, octahedral crystals. Common alum hydrolyzes in water to give gelatinous $Al(OH)_3$, and can be used as a coagulant in water clarification.

alumina [aloomina] Al_2O_3. Aluminium (III) oxide, the principal ingredient of bauxite. It occurs in various forms, including emery or corundum (used as abrasives), and the coloured forms, rubies and sapphires. Hydrated alumina is used in chromatography.

aluminate [aloominuht] Salt containing an anion derived from $Al(OH)_3$ by the replacement of hydrogen by metal. **Sodium aluminate** ($NaAlO_2$) is used in water purification, coagulating various impurities in a precipitate of hydrated alumina.

aluminium [alyoominyuhm] or **aluminum** [aloominuhm] Al, element 13, melting-point 660°C, density 2·7 g/cm^3. A silvery metal, the third most abundant element in the Earth's crust, occurring mostly as aluminosilicates. It is extracted mainly by electrolysis of alumina from bauxite fused with cryolite (Na_3AlF_6). Although the metal is strongly electropositive, it forms a tough oxide coating and is then passive to further oxidation. Its cheapness, lightness, and corrosion resistance have found it many uses as an alloy in materials ranging from cooking utensils to aircraft components. In its compounds, it mainly shows an oxidation state of +3.

Alva or **Alba, Ferdinand Alvarez de Toledo, duque d'** (Duke of) (1507–82) Spanish general and statesman, born in Piedrahita, WC Spain. A brilliant tactician, he became a general at 26, and a commander-in-chief at 30. After the abdication of Charles V in 1556, he overran the States of the Church, but was obliged by Philip II to conclude a peace and restore all his conquests. On the revolt of the Netherlands, he was sent as lieutenant-general in 1567 to enforce Spanish control there, establishing the 'Bloody Council' which drove thousands of Huguenot artisans to emigrate to England. He defeated William of Orange, and entered Brussels in triumph in 1568. Recalled by his own desire in 1573, he commanded the successful invasion of Portugal in 1581.

alvar [alvah(r)] A particularly fervent devotional Hindu saint of the Vaishava tradition. The word means 'diver', and is attributed to one who enters into the depth of mystical experience. Alvars are closely associated with the Tamils of S India.

Alvarado, Pedro de [alvarahthoh] (c.1485–1541) Conquistador, a companion of Cortés during the conquest of Mexico (1519–21), born in Badajoz, SW Spain. He became governor of Tenochtitlán, where the harshness of his rule incited an Aztec revolt. He was sent by Cortés on an expedition to Guatemala (1523–7), during which he also conquered parts of El Salvador. He returned to Spain, and in 1529 was appointed governor of Guatemala.

Alvarez, Luis W(alter) [alvahrez] (1911–88) Experimental physicist, born in San Francisco, California, USA. He studied at Chicago University, then joined Ernest Lawrence at the University of California, Berkeley, in 1936, becoming professor of physics in 1945. Before World War 2 he did distinguished work in nuclear physics; during the war he developed radar navigation and landing systems for aircraft. In 1947 he built the first proton linear accelerator. He did much to develop the bubble-chamber, using it to discover new sub-atomic particles, for which he was awarded the Nobel Prize for Physics in 1968.

Alvarez Quintero [alvareth keentayroh] Playwrights and brothers: **Serafín Alvarez Quintero** (1871–1938) and **Joaquin Alvarez Quintero** (1873–1944), born in Utrera, SW Spain. They were the joint authors of well over 100 modern Spanish plays, all displaying a characteristic gaiety and sentiment. Some are well known in the translations of Helen and Harley Granville-Barker, such as *Fortunato*, *The Lady from Alfaqueque*, and *A Hundred Years Old* (all produced in 1928), and *Don Abel Writes a Tragedy* (1933).

alveoli *lungs*

alyssum [alisuhm] An annual to perennial, mat-forming or bushy but low-growing, native to Europe and Asia; leaves narrow; flowers cross-shaped, white, blue, or yellow. **Golden alyssum**, a grey-leaved, yellow-flowered perennial, is often grown in gardens, but the popular white garden annual commonly called alyssum is a different, though related, plant. (Genus: *Alyssum*, 150 species. Family: Cruciferae.)

Alzheimer's disease [altshiymer] A common form of generalized cerebral atrophy which results in slowly progressive dementia affecting all aspects of brain function. It leads to memory loss, mood swings, confusion, and ultimately to total disintegration of the personality and loss of independence. The disease was first described in 1906 by a German neurologist, Alois Alzheimer (1864–1915). Current theories as to its cause include a slow viral infection, environmental toxins (eg aluminium), a systemic metabolic illness, and the involvement of a heritable factor in certain forms.

Amado, Jorge [amahdoo] (1912–2001) Novelist, born in Ferradas, near Ilhéus, NE Brazil. He spent part of his childhood on a cacao plantation in NE Brazil, and his early writing focused on the poverty and social conditions of the plantation workers. He became a journalist in 1930, was imprisoned for his political beliefs in 1935, and spent several periods in exile. He was elected a Communist deputy of the Brazilian parliament (1946–7). His novels include *Terras do sem-fin* (1944, trans The Violent Land), *Gabriela, cravo e canela* (1958, Gabriela, Clove and Cinnamon), and *Tenda dos milagres* (1969, Tent of Miracles).

Amal [amal] The first political organization of Lebanon's Shiite Muslims, the country's largest yet economically most disadvantaged community. Founded in the mid-1970s by the charismatic Shiite cleric, the Imam Musa al-Sadr, the party has been led since al-Sadr's 1978 disappearance in Libya by the lawyer Nabih Berri (1938–). Its militia was believed to number over 4000 before the 1991 demobilization of militias in Lebanon.

Amalekites [amalekiyts] An ancient nomadic people, notorious for their treachery, who lived S of Canaan. According to *Gen* 36.12, they were descended from Esau.

amalgam An alloy of mercury with some other metal(s), known since classical times. Copper, zinc, and tin amalgams are used in dentistry. Gold amalgam was used in Renaissance gilding techniques.

Amalthea [amaltheea] The fifth natural satellite of Jupiter, discovered in 1892; distance from the planet 181 000 km/112 000 mi; diameter 270 km/168 mi.

Amanita *fly agaric*

Amanullah Khan [amanula kahn] (1892–1960) Ruler of Afghanistan (1919–29), born in Pagman, E Afghanistan. After an inconclusive religious war against the British in India (1919–22), independence for Afghanistan was recognized by Britain with the Treaty of Rawalpindi (1922). He assumed the title of king in 1926, but his zeal for Westernizing reforms provoked rebellion in 1928. He abdicated and fled the country in 1929, and went into exile in Rome.

amaranth [amaranth] An annual or perennial herb, native to tropical and temperate regions; flowers usually small and forming dense inflorescences, perianth-segments in whorls of three or five, often brightly coloured; also known as **pigweed**. Some Asian species yield edible grain used as a substitute for cereal. (Genus: *Amaranthus*, 60 species. Family: Amaranthaceae.)

Amarillo [amariloh] 35°13N 101°50W, pop (2000e) 173 600. Seat of Potter Co, NW Texas, USA; airport; railway; commercial, banking, and industrial centre for the Texas panhandle; oil refining, meat packing, flour milling, zinc smelting, helicopters.

amaryllis [amarilis] A large bulb, native to tropical America (Genus: *Hippeastrum*, 75 species); flowers flaring, trumpet-shaped, up to 15 cm/6 in long, in a range of bright colours, 1–10 (but usually 2–4) on a hollow stalk, appearing in spring before the strap-shaped leaves. The popular pot plants are mostly complex hybrids increased by bulb division. It is often confused with the belladonna lily (*Amaryllis bella-donna*). (Family: Amaryllidaceae.)

Amaterasu [amaterasu] The principal deity in the Shinto religion of Japan. She is both the Sun-goddess who rules all the gods and the mother-goddess who ensures fertility. Once when she shut herself in her cave, the whole world became darkened and no plants could grow. The other gods played music and offered presents to make her return.

amatol A group of high explosives consisting of mixtures of trinitrotoluene (TNT) and ammonium nitrate. It was much used in World War 1 to economize on TNT, but later fell out of favour because of such faults as the absorption of undesirable water from the air (*hygroscopicity*).

Amazon, River *p.47*

Amazon ant An ant that depends entirely on slaves of other ant species to run its nest and care for its larvae. The workers have sickle-shaped jaws (*mandibles*) used as weapons when raiding other nests. (Order: Hymenoptera. Family: Formicidae.)

Amazons [amaznz] In Greek mythology, a nation of women soldiers, located by Herodotos in Scythia (Russia). Strong and athletic, they were said to mutilate the right breast in order to use the bow. With no apparent basis in fact, this story fascinated the Greeks and was a frequent subject in art, perhaps because of its suggestion of an alternative society.

ambassador An accredited diplomat sent by a state on a mission to a foreign country, or who is its highest-ranking permanent diplomat residing in a foreign country, officially representing his or her state in relations with foreign governments. Ambassadors are to be distinguished from **consuls**, whose chief functions are to protect citizens abroad, and to protect the commercial interests of these citizens.

Ambedkar, Bhimrao Ramji [ambedker] (1893–1956) Indian politician and champion of the depressed castes, born near Mumbai (Bombay), W India. He studied at Bombay, Columbia University in New York City, and the London School of Economics, and practised as a barrister in London. He later became a member of the Bombay Legislative Assembly and leader of 60 million Untouchables. Appointed law minister in 1947, he was the principal author of the Indian Constitution. He resigned in

Amazon, River

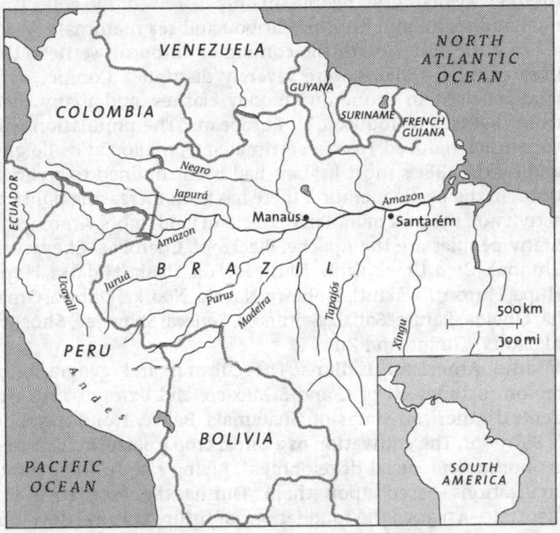

Port **Rio Amazonas** River in N South America, the largest in the world by volume, and the second longest; two major headstreams, the Marañón and the Ucayali, rising in the Andes of Peru (c.150 km/83 mi from the Pacific) and joining S of Iquitos; flows generally W–E across Brazil, entering the Atlantic in a wide delta; drains a basin c.7 000 000 sq km/ 2 700 000 sq mi; more than 1100 tributaries; ocean steamers as far as Iquitos, 3680 km/2287 mi from the Atlantic; deepest point (37 m/121 ft) at the influx of the Trombetas R; large island, Ilha de Marajó, at the delta; length from L Lauricocha (at the headwaters of the Marañón) 6280 km/3902 mi; from L Vilafro following the Ucayali and Apurímac headwaters to the mouth of the Amazon via the Canal do Norte, 6449 km/ 4007 mi; river levels at Manaus fluctuate by over 15 m/50 ft; N channels of the delta made dangerous by a frequent tidal bore (*Pororoca*) moving up river at up to 65 kph/40 mph, with waves sometimes 5 m/16 ft high; cargo launches reach the interior, carrying fish, cedarwood, flour, rubber, and jute; discovered by Europeans, 1500; first descended 1541, ascended 1637; opened to world shipping 1866; free navigation guaranteed by Colombia–Brazil treaty, 1929.

1951, and with some thousands of his followers he publicly embraced the Buddhist faith not long before his death.

ambergris [ambergrees] ('grey amber') A grey waxy substance found in the intestines of the sperm whale, *Physeter catodon*; up to 450 g/1 lb per whale; formerly used in perfumes to make the fragrance last longer.

Ambler, Eric (1909–98) Novelist and playwright, born in London, UK. He studied at Colfe's Grammar School and London University, and worked as an advertising copy-writer before turning to writing thrillers, invariably with an espionage background. He published his first novel, *The Dark Frontier*, in 1936. His best-known books are *Epitaph for a Spy* (1938), *The Mask of Dimitrios* (1939), *Dirty Story* (1967), and *The Intercom Conspiracy* (1970). He received the Crime Writers' Association Award four times, as well as the Edgar Allan Poe Award (1964). Later books include *Here Lies: An Autobiography* (1985) and *The Story So Far* (1993).

Ambrose, St (c.339–97) Roman clergyman and doctor of the Church, born in Trier, W Germany. He practised law in Rome, and in 369 was appointed consular prefect of Upper Italy, whose capital was Milan. When the bishopric fell vacant in 374, he was chosen bishop by universal acclamation, even though he was still only a catechumen undergoing instruction. He was quickly baptized, and consecrated bishop eight days later. He fought for the integrity of the Church at the imperial court, resisting Empress-regent Justina over the introduction of Arian churches. He introduced the use of hymns and made many improvements in the liturgy, notably the *Ambrosian ritual* and *Ambrosian chant*. Feast day 7 December.

ambrosia beetle A small dark beetle that burrows into wood. The adults have cylindrical bodies with short, clubbed antennae. The fleshy, legless larvae feed on fungi that line the walls of tunnels made in the wood. (Order: Coleoptera. Family: Scolytidae.)

ameba *amoeba*

Amen *Amun*

Amenhotep III [amenhohtep] (c.1411–1379 BC) King of Egypt (1417–1379 BC), the son of Thuthmose IV. He consolidated Egyptian supremacy in Babylonia and Assyria. In a reign of spectacular wealth and magnificence, he built his great capital city, Thebes, and its finest monuments, including the Luxor temple, the great pylon at Karnak, and the colossi of Memnon.

Amenhotep IV *Akhenaton*

amenorrhoea / amenorrhea [amenoreea] The absence of menstruation. It may simply be due to pre- or post-menopausal physiological reasons (eg pregnancy) or in the event of substantial weight loss. It may also be due to a variety of disorders including physical obstruction to the flow of menstrual blood and disturbances of the hormonal control of the uterus, ovaries, and pituitary gland.

American Ballet Theatre Renowned ballet company based at the Metropolitan Opera House in the Lincoln Center for the Performing Arts, New York, USA. Originally named **Ballet Theatre**, it was launched in 1939 by Richard Pleasant under the direction (1945–80) of Lucia Chase and Oliver Smith. In 1992 the former American Ballet Theatre's principal dancer, Kevin McKenzie, was appointed artistic director.

American Civil Liberties Union A leading US group which promotes civil rights. It has tended to use the courts to gain changes based on the rights afforded under the Constitution, and is particularly concerned with freedom of speech and maintaining an open society.

American Civil War (1861–5) Sometimes called 'the War Between the States' or 'the Second American Revolution', a conflict in the USA which resolved two great issues: the nature of the Federal Union and the relative power of the states and the central government; and the existence of black slavery.

The war began after Lincoln's accession to the presidency demonstrated that the South could no longer expect to control the high offices of state. Although Lincoln was hostile to slavery, he did not believe that he could interfere where it existed. But to Southerners, he and the Republican Party were intolerable, and 11 Southern states withdrew from the Union, establishing the Confederate States of America. War broke out (12 Apr 1861) when Southern batteries opened fire on a Union emplacement in the harbour of Charleston, SC. At first Lincoln defined the issue as the preservation of the Union, without any reference to slavery. But he broadened the war aims (1 Jan 1863), proclaiming the emancipation without compensation of all slaves in areas then under arms against the government. In practice, the proclamation changed nothing, but it did give the war the semblance of a moral crusade.

Sometimes called the first 'modern' war, the Civil War pitted two different social systems against each other. The free-labour industrial North had greater population, stronger financial, manufacturing, and transportation systems, and international recognition; but initially the South had much better military leaders. Because of slavery, it could also put a larger proportion of its white adult male population under arms. Lincoln's greatest difficulty was finding an effective general; he did not succeed until the emergence from obscurity of Ulysses S Grant.

The winning strategy began in 1863, when Grant won control of the whole Mississippi Valley, isolating the W Confederate States from the rest. Meanwhile Robert E Lee was advancing into Pennsylvania, largely in the hope of winning foreign recognition for the Confederacy. His defeat at Gettysburg ended that possibility. By the autumn, the Chattanooga campaign put Northern troops in a position to bisect the Confederacy E to W, an act accomplished in late 1864 by General Sherman's march through Georgia to the sea. Grant, now the overall Northern commander, adopted a strategy of relentless pressure on Lee's forces, regardless of his own losses. In the single month of June 1864, he lost nearly 60 000, nearly Lee's total strength. But Northern advantages of population and material support, combined with the success of the Mississippi and Chattanooga campaigns, were making the Southern position untenable, particularly after Lincoln defeated the former army commander George B McClellan in the 1864 presidential election. The end came in the spring of 1865, as Sherman marched N through the Carolinas while Grant continued his costly siege of Richmond. Lee finally abandoned the Confederate capital (2 Apr), and a week later he was trapped by the combined forces of Grant and Sheridan. His capitulation at Appomattox Court House left only scattered Southern forces in the field, and the last surrender took place on 26 May.

The cost in death and devastation of the war was enormous. The greatest change was the end of slavery and all that it stood for. With its destruction there emerged the possibility of a modernized South and the long-range hope of a redefinition of the place of African-American people in American life – a hope which was not to be fulfilled until almost a century later.

American Colonization Society A US pre-abolitionist anti-slavery group, aimed at resettling freed slaves in Africa. It was supported by some slaveholders, anxious to keep freed blacks separate from slaves.

American eagle *bald eagle*

American Federation of Labor – Congress of Industrial Organizations (AFL/CIO) A US federation of trade unions, formed in 1955 from the merger of the AFL (mainly craft unions, founded in 1886) with the CIO (mainly industrial workers' unions, founded in 1935). It has c.13 million members. Its aims include educational campaigns on behalf of the labour movement, the settlement of disputes among affiliates, and political support for beneficial legislation. Actual wage bargaining is carried out by member unions. Policy is decided at a biennial convention.

American football *football, American*

American foxhound *foxhound*

American Indians The original inhabitants of the American continent, who arrived during the last glacial period (according to some estimates, 14–40 000 years ago, but the issue is controversial) from Asia, crossing from Siberia over the Bering Strait, perhaps in three waves. They settled in North America, where the earliest sites are now thought to date from c.17 000 years ago, extended into Middle America (Mesoamerica), and reached what is now Chile by c.13 000 years ago. Common origins with the Chinese NE of the Yenisey R have been suggested. There are similarities (eg knife shapes) between Indian and late Palaeolithic/Neolithic Chinese cultures, and there are stylistic resemblances between the totem-pole art of North and South America and Shang dynasty shamanistic motifs.

North American Indians The palaeo-Americans were hunter-gatherers, who established themselves in the forested E coastal zone, on the grassy Great Plains, in the NW, and in the W deserts. The sharp and pronounced climatic changes and over-hunting resulted in a dramatic decline in big-game animals, and the extinction of many species, including the mammoth. Except on the Great Plains, it brought to an end the mobile hunting adaptation based on communal game drives. Instead a new pattern emerged, based largely on sedentary resources such as nuts, seeds, and shellfish.

In the W, a Desert culture developed (at least 7000 years ago) where people settled in densely populated villages, and cultivated plants, produced baskets and other artifacts, and built adobe shelters. On the Plains the people became specialized bison hunters, and (much later) started to grow crops and live in permanent settlements. In the E, which was colder and densely forested, seasonal movement occurred in response to food availability; people mainly survived by collecting nuts and seeds, and hunting caribou and sea mammals.

From the 16th-c, with the coming of European settlers, the lives of most Indians were severely disrupted. Conflict over land resulted in numerous bloody clashes, and many died from diseases introduced by Europeans. The population was very much reduced, from an estimated 1·5 million at its height, and by the 1880s most Indians had been confined to reservations. In the past generation there has been increasing political activity on the part of Indians to reclaim land rights. Among the many peoples are the Apache, Blackfoot, Cherokee, Cheyenne, Chinook, Cree, Creek, Crow, Flathead, Fox, Haida, Hidatsa, Hopi, Hupa, Huron, Kwakiutl, Mohawk, Navajo, Nootka, Ojibwa, Omaha, Oneida, Paiute, Salish, Seminole, Seneca, Shawnee, Shoshoni, Sioux, Tlingit, and Zuñi.

Middle American Indians The cultural and geographical region includes all of C and S Mexico, and extends into the Central American states of Guatemala, Belize, Honduras, and El Salvador. The cultivation of a cereal crop (maize) accelerated economic and social development, giving rise to indigenous civilizations based upon them. During the Formative Era (2500 BC–AD 300) the foundations of future cultural development were laid: the emergence of hieroglyphic writing, calendrics, astronomical observation, monumental architecture, large religious and ceremonial centres, specialization in art and craft, and intensive agriculture. Because of the spread of maize from the highlands and the introduction of new strains more suited to dry areas, people were able to live in more densely concentrated settlements. The area was warm, and an ideal environment for agriculture. The first beginnings of high civilization occurred in the Olmec culture c.1200 BC.

The *Classic Period* (AD 300–900) represented Mesoamerican civilization at its height, during which the Maya civilization flourished in parts of Guatemala, the Yucatán, and the Mexican Chiapas. In the *Post-Classic* period (900–1520), the Mayans were superseded by the Toltecs and then the Aztecs, based in the C highlands of Mexico, who flourished and expanded over several centuries until the arrival of the Spanish. In 1521, Cortés and a small army of soldiers took the last Aztec emperor captive, and the empire ceased to exist. At its height, the Indian population was much larger than in North America – some suggest as many as 20 million. Today most Middle Americans live in small farming and trading village communities, are Roman Catholic and Spanish-speaking, and show a high rate of admixture with the descendants of the Spanish settlers.

South American Indians The earliest peoples were hunter-gatherers, who were gradually replaced by sedentary agricultural societies. Between c.3000 and 1500 BC in most of the region, settled life based on horticulture became the norm. The people probably obtained maize from Middle America, though there is evidence that several local plants (eg the potato tuber) were domesticated as early as 5–7000 BC. Later, from c.1000 BC, larger-scale societies developed, culminating in AD 1000 in one of the world's major civilizations, the Inca. In the century before the Spanish invasion of the region, the Inca state brought together much of the Andean area in the New World's largest empire. In the Amazon basin, tropical forest hunting-and-gathering culture existed from at least 2000 BC. With the European conquest in the 16th-c, some of the groups in the S became extinct, while others were absorbed into colonial society. But in a few remote parts, there are groups which have preserved their culture virtually intact. Apart from the Inca, major ethnic groups include the Araucanians, Arawak, Chimu, and Guaraní.

American Legion In the USA, an association for former members of the armed forces (veterans), the largest in the world. Incorporated in 1919, its aims are to rehabilitate veterans, promote child welfare, ensure a strong national defence, and encourage patriotism.

American literature The first literary works of the English-speaking peoples of North America were sermons, journals, and histories – concerns reflected in the work of the early poets Ann Bradstreet and Edward Taylor (c.1645–1729). In the Revolutionary period the most important work was practical or political, eg Benjamin Franklin's *Poor Richard's Almanac* (1732–58). Franklin's *Autobiography* (1781) is a memorable testament to a Puritan sensibility. The African-born poet, Phillis Wheatley, a Boston servant before her release from slavery, was the first black African to receive critical acclaim with her collection *Poems on Various Subjects: Religious and Moral* (1773, London). After the international impact of Washington Irving's *The Sketch-Book of Geoffrey Crayon, Gent* (1819–20), Fenimore Cooper likewise became a celebrity in the USA and Europe with his *Leatherstocking Tales* (1823–41), which introduced the theme of the problematic relationship between the wilderness and encroaching American civilization. The novelist and playwright William Wells Brown, who escaped from slavery in 1834, wrote the first novel by a black American, *Clotel; or, The President's Daughter* (1853, London). Transcendentalism was enunciated by Ralph Waldo Emerson in *Nature* (1836) and by H D Thoreau in *Walden* (1855). Walt Whitman's free-form *Leaves of Grass* (appearing 1855–92) is the most sustained and successful response to Emerson's call for a literature free from European influence. By contrast, the poetry of Emily Dickinson offers unique concentration and intensity. Another group that spoke for the darker side of existence in the USA included Edgar Allan Poe, Nathaniel Hawthorne, and Herman Melville. Poe's sinister *Tales* (1840, 1845) continue to fascinate; while Hawthorne's *The Scarlet Letter* (1850), and Melville's epic *Moby-Dick* (1852), are central works of the American imagination. But Harriet Beecher Stowe's anti-slavery novel *Uncle Tom's Cabin* (1852) was the best-selling novel of the 20th-c.

Henry James and W D Howells (1837–1920) reacted against the parochialism of American literature, James going to Europe and producing a definitive series of novels on the clash of the two cultures, and Howells editing literary journals that published work by the European realists, James, and himself. Howells also published Mark Twain, whose *Huckleberry Finn* (1885) is one of the few humorous books of the 19th-c whose humour remains uncorroded. Kate O'Flaherty Chopin's brilliant short novel, *The Awakening* (1899), went unregarded for 60 years, while Stephen Crane's *The Red Badge of Courage* (1895) was accepted as a classic. Naturalism was the dominant mode of American fiction until after World War 1, whether in stories like those by Jack London of life in hostile environments, or in the depiction by Theodore Dreiser of the developing industrial centres. The novels of Edith Wharton took New York society as their subject.

T S Eliot and Ezra Pound came to Europe after the war, using experimental verse to express their dismay at the decline of European civilization. Wallace Stevens too adopted the modernist faith in aesthetic values in a world where moral certainties seemed no longer tenable. In the novel, Ernest Hemingway and Scott Fitzgerald represented 'The Lost Generation', while another important innovator, William Faulkner, wrote a series of novels about the South. Sinclair Lewis, the first American writer to win the Nobel Prize for Literature (1930) brilliantly satirized the business culture of the age, while Thornton Wilder, author of *The Bridge of San Luis Rey* (1927) produced urbane comments on human existence. The rigours of the Great Depression were reflected in the novels of John Steinbeck (*The Grapes of Wrath*, 1939) and John Dos Passos (*U.S.A.*, 1930–6) amongst others. American drama made its appearance with the plays of Eugene O'Neill and Tennessee Williams, which rework autobiographical material with classical and expressionist techniques, and Arthur Miller (eg *Death of a Salesman*, 1949). Vladimir Nabokov, born Russian, emerged as one of the greatest masters of English prose style with novels such as *Lolita* (1955), while J S Salinger (*The Catcher in The Rye*, 1951) reflects both the purity of human nature and the hypocritical conformity of his age.

Passionate indignation about the black experience was voiced by, among others, James Baldwin in his novel, *Go Tell it on the Mountain* (1954). The novels of Jewish writers Bernard Malamud and Saul Bellow invoke urban life with subtlety and humour, while Norman Mailer (like Hemingway) saw his writing as a form of action. The enduring popularity of Joseph Heller's *Catch-22* (1961) and Kurt Vonnegut's *Slaughterhouse-Five* (1969) have ensured international recognition for both authors. The most significant post-war poets were Robert Lowell, John Berryman, and Sylvia Plath, who dealt harrowingly with the anguish and madness of the contemporary world, and John Ashbery, who imported the postmodern condition into poetry. Among the outstanding black writers of the latter part of the 20th-c were the poet and novelist Alice Walker (*The Color Purple*, 1982), Toni Morrison (*Beloved*, 1987), and Maya Angelou (*Just Give Me a Cool Drink of Water 'fore I Die*, 1971). Novels tended to polarize between the 'new journalism' represented by Truman Capote and Tom Wolfe, and the postmodern experimentalism of John Barth and Thomas Pynchon; but meanwhile, writers such as Gore Vidal, John Updike, and Philip Roth continued the history of America in fiction. More recently, the novels and dramas of writers such as Don DeLillo, whose epic *Underworld* (1997) offers a spiritual odyssey in the last decades of the 20th-c, continue to make a potent contribution to the world of literature.

American Medical Association (AMA) An association founded in Philadelphia in 1847 'to promote the science and art of medicine and the betterment of public health'. Its membership includes over 300 000 US doctors from all specialties, expressing a corporate view on most aspects of health care.

American Museum of Natural History An institution founded in New York City in 1869. It includes the Hayden Planetarium, as well as the zoo in Bronx Park, run by the American Zoological Society.

American Muslim Mission *Black Muslims*

American ostrich *rhea* (ornithology)

American Revolution (1765–88) The movement that destroyed the first British Empire, establishing the United States and, indirectly, Canada. A much larger event than the War of Independence (1775–83), the revolution developed from the issue of whether Parliament had the power to tax the North American colonies directly. But more was involved than constitutional dispute, and the Revolution left America a transformed place. The Revolution can be divided into three main phases. In the first (1764–5), relations worsened between the colonies and Britain, primarily over the issue of Parliament's right to tax the colonies without reference to the colonial assemblies. During this phase, the American resistance movement was concentrated in the major port towns, with considerable support in the elected assemblies. Major events included the Stamp Act crisis (1765–6), resistance to the Townshend Acts (1767–70), the Boston Massacre (1770), the burning of the customs cruiser *Gaspée* (1772), and the Boston Tea Party (1773). This phase culminated in Parliament's passage of the Intolerable Acts (1774) to punish Massachusetts for the Tea Party, the beginnings of the collapse of the colonial governments, and the calling of the First Continental Congress (1774).

The second phase brought war and independence. Fighting began at Lexington and Concord, MA (Apr 1775), and lasted until the surrender of Lord Cornwallis to Washington at Yorktown, VA, in 1781. Military conflict centred on Boston until the British withdrew (Mar 1776). From August 1776 until the beginning of 1780, the main theatre was the states of New York, New Jersey, and Pennsylvania, with major engagements at Long Island, at such New Jersey sites as Princeton, Monmouth, and Trenton, and at Saratoga in upstate New York. The American victory at Saratoga convinced the French to enter the war officially, bringing badly-needed material support, troops, monetary credit, and a fleet. After 1780, fighting shifted southward, when Sir Henry Clinton led an invasion of South Carolina. Cornwallis, his successor, led his army gradually N until Washington and the French Admiral de Grasse trapped him on the Yorktown peninsula. The defeat resulted in the fall of Lord North, the British prime minister who had prosecuted the war, and ended British will for further fighting. Peace was signed at Paris two years later.

The third phase led to the creation of the modern United States. This process began with the writing of the first state constitutions, immediately after the Declaration of Independence (Jul 1776). At the same time, the Articles of Confederation were prepared by the Continental Congress as a basis for interstate relations, but the document was not adopted until 1781. Its weaknesses, such as an inability to tax or to enforce Congressional decisions and commitments, soon became apparent. These, together with dissatisfaction about developments in the states, led to the Federalist movement. Initially, this sought merely to reform the Articles, but its great achievement, in 1787 and 1788, was to abolish that document completely, and establish the present US Constitution. At that point, the Revolution was effectively over.

The creation of a large republic was one of the most innovative changes that the Revolution brought. Political thinkers had long doubted whether republicanism could govern a large area or even survive at all. The state and federal constitutions adopted between 1776 and 1788 thus defined the most advanced political hopes of their time. Permanent republicanism in the USA opened the way for the long-term decline of monarchy in the world. The Revolution was also a democratic movement. By its end, an ideology of 'equal rights' had taken shape in the USA, largely as a result of pressure from ordinary farmers and artisans who had found their moment to make a political breakthrough. Such people actually seized control in Pennsylvania and in Vermont, which broke free of New York in 1777, and established radically democratic political institutions. The Revolution brought social change as well. One aspect was the transformation of slavery from a fact of life into a political and moral problem. In the Northern states, opposition became strong enough to set slavery on the road to extinction, and even in the upper South, where legal slavery persisted, the number of free blacks grew dramatically.

National independence, declared by the Continental Congress in 1776, thus meant national transformation. But the Revolution was not the work of a united people. In some places there was considerable loyalism, and even civil war. The many loyalists who fled at the war's end became the core of English-speaking Canada. The movement itself developed as a series of coalitions. The initial alliance, which resisted British imperial policy after 1765, centred on the three major seaports (Boston, New York, and Philadelphia) and on the planter class of Chesapeake Bay. But the independence crisis saw the mobilization of large numbers of farmers in the interior, and they, together with urban working people, developed a political programme of their own. The third great coalition enlisted Southern planters and Northern entrepreneurs and professionals in 'Federalism', which created the modern structure of the USA. The movement won wide urban support, but less in rural areas. The Federal Constitution reflected its makers' specific concerns, as well as their large goal of safeguarding American independence and liberty. French support was vital to the Americans' military defeat of Britain. The leadership of a truly remarkable group of men was vital throughout the era. But popular political involvement in unprecedented ways was what made the American Revolution truly revolutionary.

American Samoa *see panel*

American Sign Language (ASL) A sign language widely used by the deaf in the USA; also known as **Ameslan**. The system contains over 4000 signs, and is used by over half a million deaf people – by many, as a first language.

American Society for the Prevention of Cruelty to Animals *RSPCA*

American Veterinary Medical Association *veterinary science*

American whitewood *tulip tree*

American Samoa

[samoha], formerly also **Loanda**, Portuguese **São Paulo de Loanda**

Local name Sao Paulo de Loanda (Portuguese)

Timezone GMT −11

Area 197 km²/76 sq mi

Population total (2000e) 65 500

Capital Fagatogo

Languages English (official), Samoan

Physical features Located in the CS Pacific Ocean, some 3500 km/2175 mi N of New Zealand; five principal volcanic islands (including Tutuila, Aunu'u, Ofu, Olosega, Ta'u, Rose, Swains I) and two coral atolls; main island, Tutuila, 109 km²/42 sq mi, rises to 653 m/2142 ft; islands mostly hilly, with large areas covered by thick bush and forest.

Climate Tropical maritime climate; average annual temperatures 28°C (Jan), 27°C (Jul) in Fagatogo; plentiful rainfall; rainy season (Nov–Apr); dry season (May–Oct); average annual rainfall 5000 mm/200 in; state of emergency declared after heavy rains caused severe flooding over much of the island, May 2003.

Economy Principal crops, taro, breadfruit, yams, bananas, coconuts; tuna fishing; local inshore fishing, handicrafts.

GDP (2000e) $500 mn, per capita $8000

History US acquired rights to American Samoa in 1899 and the islands were ceded by their chiefs, 1900–25; now an unincorporated territory of the USA, administered by the Department of the Interior; bicameral legislature established, 1948, comprising Senate and House of Representatives.

America's Cup Yachting's most famous race, held approximately every 4 years. The trophy was originally called the One Hundred Guinea Cup, and was donated by the Royal Yacht Squadron for a race around the Isle of Wight, S England, UK in 1851. It was renamed the America's Cup after the schooner *America* won the race six years later. The New York Yacht Club offered the cup as a challenge trophy. Between 1870 and 1983 it remained in US ownership until the successful challenge of *Australia II*. The USA won it back in 1987, and then successfully held off a challenge from New Zealand in 1988. New Zealand won the cup in 1995 and defeated an Italian challenge in 2000.

Ameslan *American Sign Language*

amethyst A violet-to-purple form of quartz. It is prized as a precious stone.

Amhara A Semitic-speaking people of the Ethiopian C highlands who, with the Tigray, dominate the country. They are descended from the original Semitic conquerors from S Arabia. The Christian empire of Ethiopia was ruled by Amhara dynasties (1260–1974) which, by intermarriage and cultural assimilation, incorporated people from almost every ethnic group of the empire. *Amharic* is the official language of Ethiopia. Population c.9 million.

Amherst, Jeffrey, 1st Baron Amherst (1717–97) British soldier, born in Sevenoaks, Kent, SE England, UK. Joining the army at the age of 14 he played an important part in the North American phase of the Seven Years' War (1756–63). He was in command of the expedition against the French in Canada, and captured Louisburg (1758). Appointed commander-in-chief of North America in 1759, he captured Montreal in 1760. He was Governor-General of British North America (1760–3), then commander-in-chief of the British army (1772–96).

amicable numbers Two numbers such that each is the sum of all the divisors of the other. Thus 284 and 220 are amicable, for the divisors of 284 are 1,2,4,71,142, whose sum is 220, and the divisors of 220 are 1,2,4,5,10,11,20,22,44,55,110, whose sum is 284. Note that 1 is counted as a divisor. Pythagoras is credited with the discovery of amicable numbers, though he seems only to have known of this pair. Fermat in 1636 announced that 17 296 and 18 416 were amicable. Since then other pairs of amicable numbers have been found. In former times, such numbers were prominent in magic and astrology.

Amichai, Yehuda [amichiy] (1924–2000) Poet, born in Würzburg, SC Germany. In 1936 he went with his family to what was then Palestine. A dozen volumes of verse since *Now and in Other Days* (1955, trans title) are divided in subject-matter between the idyll of childhood and the struggle of Israel to establish and defend its identity. These include *Now in the Turmoil* (1968, trans title), *Amen* (1978, trans by Amichai with Ted Hughes), and *Open, Closed, Open* (1998, trans title).

Amici, Giovanni Battista [ameechee] (1786–1868) Optician, astronomer, and natural philosopher, born in Modena, N Italy. He constructed optical instruments, perfecting his own alloy for telescope mirrors, and in 1827 produced the dioptric, achromatic microscope that bears his name. He became director of the Florence observatory in 1835.

Amidah [ameeda] (Heb 'standing') The principal component of the daily prayers of Talmudic Judaism, recited while standing, and said silently except when in a congregational service. It consists of 19 (originally 18) benedictions, firstly in praise of God, secondly asking for his help (petitions), and closing with thanksgiving. An altered form of the prayer is also recited on sabbaths and festivals.

amides [aymiydz, amidz] **1** Inorganic salts of ammonia, eg sodium amide ($NaNH_2$), strongly basic and hydrolyzed by water to NH_3 and OH^-.
2 Organic compounds containing the function $-CO.NR_2$, also called **alkanamides**, derived from carboxylic acids by substituting NR_2 for OH (R is H or any alkyl group). **Polyamides** include proteins and some artificial polymers, such as nylon.

Amiens [amyĩ], ancient **Samarobriva** 49°54N 2°16E, pop (2000e) 138 000. Agricultural market town and capital of Somme department, N France; 130 km/81 mi N of Paris, on left bank of R Somme; railway; university (1964); bishopric; textiles, food processing, chemicals, market gardening; wartime cemeteries at Arras to the E; Gothic cathedral (13th-c), largest in area in France, a world heritage site.

Amies, Sir (Edwin) Hardy [aymeez] (1909–2003) Couturier, and dressmaker by appointment to Queen Elizabeth II. He worked as a trainee in Birmingham, C England, UK before becoming a managing designer in London in 1934, where he made his name especially with his tailored suits for women. He founded his own fashion house in 1946, and started designing for men in 1959, receiving the British Fashion Council Hall of Fame Award in 1989. His books include *The Englishman's Suit* (1994). He was knighted in 1989.

Amin (Dada), Idi [ameen] (c.1925–2003) Ugandan soldier and dictator (1971–9), born in Koboko, NW Uganda of a peasant family. After a rudimentary education he joined the army, rising from the ranks to become a colonel in 1964. As a friend of prime minister Milton Obote, he was made commander-in-chief of the army and air force, but worsening relations between them resulted in a coup establishing a military dictatorship (1971). He proceeded to expel all Ugandan Asians and many Israelis, seized foreign-owned businesses and estates, and ordered the killing of thousands of his opponents, making his regime internationally infamous. His decision in 1978 to annex the Kagera area of Tanzania gave President Nyerere the opportunity to send his troops into Uganda. Within six months Amin was defeated. He fled to Libya, and later attempted to make his home in several countries, eventually settling in exile in Saudi Arabia.

amines [aymeenz, ameenz] Organic compounds derived from ammonia by the substitution of the hydrogen atoms by one, two, or three alkyl groups; these are *primary*, *secondary*, and *tertiary* amines respectively. They are basic compounds; their solutions, when partially neutralized by strong acids, have pH values of about 9.

amino acids [ameenoh, amiynoh] Aminoalkanoic acids with the general formula $R-CH(NH_2)COOH$. About 24 are involved in protein synthesis; 10 of these cannot be made by the human body, and thus form an essential component of the diet (**essential amino acids**). All amino acids except the simplest, glycine (R=H), are chiral. Nearly all which occur in nature have an arrangement called the *L-configuration*. Examples include alanine (CH_3-), valine ($(CH_3)_2CH-$), phenylalanine ($C_6H_5CH_2-$), cysteine ($HSCH_2-$), histidine ($(C_3N_2H_3)\ CH_2-$), and glutamic acid ($HO(CO)\ CH_2CH_2-$).

aminobenzene *aniline*

aminoethanoic acid *glycine*

Amis, Sir Kingsley (William) [aymis] (1922–95) Novelist and poet, born in London, UK. He studied at Oxford, and became a lecturer in English literature at Swansea (1948–61) and a fellow of Peterhouse, Cambridge (1961–3). He achieved huge success with his first novel, *Lucky Jim* (1954), the story of a comic anti-hero in a provincial university; Jim appeared again as a small-town librarian in *That Uncertain Feeling* (1955), and as a provincial author abroad in *I Like It Here* (1958). After the death of Ian Fleming, he wrote a James Bond novel, *Colonel Sun* (1968), under the pseudonym of **Robert Markham**, as well as *The James Bond Dossier* (1965). His later novels include *Jake's Thing* (1978), *The Old Devils* (1986, Booker), *The Folks that Live on the Hill* (1990), *The Russian Girl* (1992), and *You Can't Do Both* (1994). *The Letters of Kingsley Amis* (ed. Zachary Leader) were published in 2000. He was married (1965–83) to the novelist **Elizabeth Jane Howard** (1923–), and was knighted in 1990.

Amis, Martin (Louis) [aymis] (1949–) Novelist and journalist, born in Oxford, the son of Kingsley Amis. He studied at Exeter College, Oxford, and wrote his first novel, *The Rachel Papers* (1973), when he was 21. Later works include *Other People* (1981), *Money* (1984), *Time's Arrow* (1991), *The Information* (1995), *Night Train* (1997), and *Yellow Dog* (2003). His collected short stories include *Einstein's Monsters* (1986) and *'Heavy Water' and Other Stories* (1999), and he has also produced a great deal of literary journalism. His memoirs, *Experience*, appeared in 2000.

Amman [aman] 31°57N 35°52E, pop (2000e) 1 996 000. Industrial and commercial capital city of Jordan; in Amman governorate, East Bank, on the R Zarqa; capital of the Ammonite kingdom in Biblical times; capital of Transjordan, 1923; many refugees after the Arab–Israeli Wars; airport; railway; university (1962); noted for its locally-quarried coloured marble; food processing, textiles, paper, plastics; Roman amphitheatre (1st-c BC), archaeological museum.

ammine [ameen] Co-ordinated ammonia, or a compound with co-ordinated ammonia. Ammines were among the first identified co-ordination compounds or complex ions, eg $[Co(NH_3)_6]^{3+}$, hexamminecobalt(III).

Ammon *Amun*

ammonia NH_3, boiling point −33°C. A colourless gas with a pungent odour; its molecule is pyramidal with bond angles c.107°C. It is a weak base; aqueous solutions partially neutralized with strong acid have a pH c.9·5. It reacts with acids to form ammonium ions. An important industrial chemical, it is mainly prepared by the Haber process.

ammonia–soda process *Solvay process*

ammonite An extinct, nautilus-like mollusc; found extensively as fossil shells from the Devonian to the Upper Cretaceous periods; shell external in life, typically a flattened spiral, divided internally by transverse walls. (Class: Cephalopoda. Subclass: Ammonoidea.)

Ammonites [amoniyts] An ancient Semitic people who in Old Testament times lived in S Transjordan. Tradition had it that they were descended from Lot.

ammonium NH_4^+. A cation formed by the reaction of ammonia with acid. It is found in many salts, particularly the chloride (*sal ammoniac*) and the carbonate (*sal volatile*). Aqueous solutions of ammonia are often called *ammonium hydroxide*.

amnesia Memory disability, often associated with brain damage or a traumatic event. **Retrograde amnesia** is the inability to remember material learned before the precipitating event. **Anterograde amnesia** is difficulty in learning new material. The most common form of amnesia is one in which short-term memory is adequate, long-term episodic memory (the ability to remember specific past events) is poor, and long-term semantic memory (memory for facts, such as word meanings) is relatively intact.

Amnesty International A human rights organization founded in London in 1961 largely by the efforts of Peter Benenson, a Catholic lawyer. It is based in the UK, but there are several groups in other, mainly industrialized, countries. The fundamental concern of Amnesty is to seek the immediate and unconditional release of prisoners of conscience, as long as they have not advocated violence. It also campaigns against torture and the death penalty, and tries to produce independent, authoritative reports on countries' abuses of human rights.

amniocentesis [amniohsenteesis] A diagnostic procedure performed at 14–18 weeks gestation which involves withdrawal of a small sample of amniotic fluid from within the uterus using a needle inserted through the abdominal wall under ultrasound guidance. Amniotic fluid is in close contact with the fetus, and contains cells that can be analysed to reveal many congenital fetal abnormalities. These include Down's syndrome and spina bifida. The procedure can also reveal the sex of the fetus and other normal features of development. It carries a small risk of inducing an abortion.

amoeba / ameba [ameeba] A naked, single-celled protozoan which moves by protoplasmic flow, changing its shape by the formation of irregular lobes (*pseudopodia*); feeds by engulfing food particles with pseudopodia, or by infolding of the outer surface (*invagination*); c.0·6 mm/0·025 in across; reproduces mainly by splitting in two (*binary fission*). Most are free-living in aquatic habitats; some are parasitic, and can cause amoebic dysentery in humans. (Phylum: Sarcomastigophora. Class: Rhizopoda.)

amoebiasis [ameebiyasis] A disease caused by infection with the protozoan parasite *entamoeba histolytica*, acquired by ingestion of food or water contaminated with faeces containing infected cysts. Once inside the gut, the cysts hatch to release the adult organisms, which irritate the gut lining resulting in severe bloody diarrhoea. They also invade the lining to enter the blood stream, and circulate throughout the body forming cysts in the liver, lungs, and brain.

Amon *Amun*

Amorites [amoriyts] The name borne by various Semitic peoples who lived in Mesopotamia, Syria, and Palestine in Old Testament times.

amorphous solid A solid in which the atoms are in some disordered arrangement, lacking the perfect ordered structure of crystals, as in glass, rubber, and polymers. Many substances may form either amorphous or crystalline states having radically different properties.

amortization [amaw(r)tiyzayshn] A method used in accountancy which reduces the value of a depreciating asset, such as a quarry, over the length of its expected life. It also applies to intangible assets (eg goodwill) and patents which have been acquired at a price, but which may not be resaleable.

Amory, Derick Heathcoat, 1st Viscount Amory [aymoree] (1899–1981) British statesman, born in Tiverton, Devon, SW England, UK. He studied at Oxford, and became a Conservative MP in 1945. He was minister of pensions (1951–3), minister at the board of trade (1953–4), and minister of agriculture (1954–8). He became a viscount during his period as Chancellor of the Exchequer (1958–60). He was also High Commissioner to Canada (1961–3).

Amos (of Brondesbury), Valerie Ann Amos, Baroness [aymos] (1954–) British stateswoman, born in Guyana. She studied at Warwick University (1976), Birmingham University (1977), and the University of East Anglia, and began a career in local government working in various London boroughs (1981–9). In 2001 she became Parliamentary Under-Secretary of State in the Foreign and Commonwealth Office, and took over as International Development Secretary after the resignation of Clare Short in mid-2003, becoming the first black woman to sit in the cabinet. Later that year she was appointed leader of the House of Lords, the third ever woman to hold the post. She was made a life peer in 1997.

Amos, Book of One of the twelve so-called 'minor' prophetic writings in the Hebrew Bible/Old Testament; attributed to the prophet Amos, who was active in the N kingdom of Israel in the mid-8th-c BC. It proclaims judgment on Israel's neighbours for idolatry, and on Israel itself for social injustices and ethical immorality.

Amoy (China) *Xiamen*

amp *ampere*

Ampato, Nevado de [nayvathoh thay ampatoh] Andean massif in the Cordillera Occidental, S Peru; height, 6310 m/20 702 ft; Cañon del Colca nearby, a gorge cut by the R Colca; 60 km/37 mi long and 3000 m/10 000 ft deep, considered to be the deepest canyon in the world.

Ampère, André Marie [ãpair] (1775–1836) Mathematician and physicist, born in Lyon, SC France. He taught at the Ecole Polytechnique in Paris, the University of Paris, and the Collège de France. He laid the foundations of the science of electrodynamics following Oersted's discovery in 1820 of the magnetic effects of electric currents. His name was given to the basic SI unit of electric current (*ampere, amp*).

ampere [ampair] The base SI unit of current; symbol *A*, often called **amp**, named after André Ampère; defined as the constant current which, if maintained in two straight parallel conductors of infinite length, of negligible cross-section, and placed 1 metre apart in vacuum, would produce a force equal to 2×10^{-7} N/m.

Ampère's law [ampair, ãpair] In magnetism, a law which describes the magnetic field resulting from electric current flowing in a wire; formulated by André Ampère in 1827. For any closed loop drawn around the wire, the sum of magnetic flux density contributions at each point along the line is proportional to the current enclosed by the loop.

amphetamine A powerful stimulant of the central nervous system, which causes wakefulness and alertness, elevates mood, increases self-confidence, loquaciousness, and the performance of simple mental tasks, and improves physical performance. Initially, it decreases appetite. It is widely abused to increase energy and alertness, but tolerance often develops after repeated use. Its effects are followed by mental depression and fatigue. It was once used clinically as a slimming aid, but therapeutic use is now restricted to the treatment of narcolepsy because of the problems of addiction and tolerance. It is also used to treat children with attention-deficit-hyperactivity disorder (ADHD). Prolonged use may result in paranoia or clinical psychosis. As a drug of abuse it is called **speed**; it is illegally manufactured as a powder which can be sniffed ('snorted') or injected. Amphetamine sulphate was formerly available medically under the trade name **Benzedrine**. It is now available only as dexamphetamine sulphate, an isomer, under the proprietary name **Dexedrine**.

amphibian A vertebrate animal of class Amphibia (c.4000 species), exhibiting a wide range of characters and lifestyles; usually four legs and glandular skin, lacking scales or other outgrowths; larvae usually live in water and breathe through feathery external gills; undergo a metamorphosis during development, when the gills shrink and disappear; adults breathe using lungs (and partly through the skin); three major groups: salamanders and newts (Order: Urodela or Caudata), frogs and toads (Order: Anura or Salientia), and the legless caecilians (Order: Gymnophiona or Apoda).

amphiboles [amfibohlz] A group of hydrous silicate minerals of considerable chemical complexity, characterized structurally by a double-chain of linked SiO_4 tetrahedra, with iron, magnesium, calcium, sodium, and aluminium among the elements which may be present between the chains. It is widely distributed in igneous and metamorphic rocks. Common varieties include hornblende, actinolite, and tremolite. Fibrous forms belong to the asbestos group of minerals.

amphioxus [amf**iok**suhs] A primitive chordate; body slender, length up to 70 mm/2¾ in, tapered at both ends; notochord present, extending into head; possesses gill slits and segmented muscle blocks, resembling ancestors of vertebrates; 23 species found in shallow marine sediments; also known as **lancelet**. (Subphylum: Cephalochordata.)

amphisbaena [amfis**bee**na] A reptile native to South and Central America, Africa, SW Asia, and SW Europe; body worm-like with encircling rings; no legs or only front legs present; small eyes covered by skin; the only truly burrowing reptile; eats small animals; also known as **worm lizard** or **ringed lizard**. (Order: Squamata. Suborder: Amphisbaenia, 140 species.)

amphitheatre / amphitheater An open-air theatre where tiers of seats are situated round a central circular or oval performance space. The Romans developed this form of building from Campanian (or possibly Etruscan) origins for gladiatorial combats, naval exhibitions, and other events. The earliest amphitheatres were constructed of wood, and later ones of stone. The first Roman amphitheatre was constructed in 59 BC by the Roman pontifex maximus (head of the priests' college), Gaius Scribonius Curio. There are good examples at Pompeii (70 BC), Verona (AD 290) and, most famously, the Colosseum in Rome (AD 72–80) built by the Roman emperor Vespasian to seat 50 000 people.

Amphitrite [amfit**riy**tee] In Greek mythology, a goddess of the sea, married to Poseidon. She is the mother of Triton and other minor deities.

Amphitryon [amf**it**rion] In Greek mythology, the husband of Alcmene. In his absence, Zeus took his shape and so became the father of Heracles.

amphoteric [amfo**te**rik] In chemistry, having two different properties, usually that of being an acid and a base. An example is aluminium hydroxide ($Al(OH)_3$), which forms salts of Al^{3+} in acid and of AlO_2^- in alkali.

amplitude In a wave or oscillation, the maximum displacement from equilibrium or rest position; symbol *A*. It is always a positive number.

amplitude modulation (AM) In wave motion, the altering of wave amplitude in a systematic way, leaving frequency unchanged. In AM radio, an electrical signal is used to modulate the amplitude of the broadcast carrier radio wave. A radio receiver reproduces the signal from the modulated wave by *demodulation*.

amputation The surgical removal of a part of the body because of disease or injury. The operation is carried out when the affected part has been irreparably damaged and is no longer functional, or when there is a risk of the disease (particularly infection) spreading to the rest of the body. Diabetic complications are a common reason for amputations of fingers and toes and even whole limbs. It is sometimes possible to replace the removed part with a prosthesis, such as an artificial leg.

Amr ibn al-As [amribnal**as**] (?–664) Arab soldier. A convert to Islam, he joined the prophet Mohammed in c.629, and took part in the conquest of Palestine in 638. In 639 he undertook the conquest of Egypt, becoming its first Muslim governor (642–44). He helped Muawiyah to seize the caliphate from Ali.

Amritsar [am**rit**ser] 31°35N 74°57E, pop (2000e) 833 000. City in Punjab, NW India; centre of the Sikh religion; founded in 1577 by Ram Das around a sacred tank, known as the pool of immortality; the Golden Temple, found at the centre of the tank, is particularly sacred to Sikhs; under the gold and copper dome is kept the sacred book of the Sikhs, Adi Granth; centre of the Sikh empire in the 19th-c, and of modern Sikh nationalism; massacre of Indian nationalists, 1919; battle between the Indian Army and Sikh militants inside the Golden Temple led to 1000 deaths, including a Sikh leader, 1984; militants re-established in temple, 1986; airport; university (1969); commerce, textiles, silk.

Amritsar Massacre [am**rit**ser] A massacre at Amritsar, Punjab, in April 1919. Local disturbances caused the British army commander, General Dyer, to believe that another Indian Mutiny was imminent. When a public meeting took place in a walled garden (the Jallianwalabagh), he ordered his troops to open fire on an unarmed crowd which had no chance of escape; 380 were killed and 1200 injured. Dyer was censured and resigned, but a public subscription was opened for him in Britain. The massacre was the cue for the opening of Gandhi's Non-Co-operation Movement, and transformed the whole tenor of Indian nationalism.

Amsterdam [**am**sterdam] 52°23N 4°54E, pop (2000e) 746 000. Major European port and capital city of The Netherlands, in North Holland province, W Netherlands; at the junction of the R Amstel and an arm of the Ijsselmeer; chartered, 1300; member of the Hanseatic League, 1369; capital, 1808; airport (Schiphol), railway; two universities (1632, 1880); harbour industry developed after World War 2; major transshipping point; important commercial and cultural centre; banking, shipbuilding, engineering, cars, aircraft, textiles, brewing, foodstuffs, publishing and printing, chemicals, data processing, diamond-cutting; Concertgebouw Orchestra; House of Anne Frank, Rembrandt House (1606), Oude Kerk (consecrated 1306), Nieuwe Kerk (15th-c), royal palace (17th-c), Rijksmuseum, Stedelijk Museum, Van Gogh Museum; international Windjammer Regatta 'Sail Amsterdam' (Aug).

amu *atomic mass unit*

Amudarya, River [amu**dar**ya], ancient **Oxus** River formed by the junction of the Vakhsh and Pyandzh Rivers on the Turkmenia–Afghanistan frontier, forming part of the border; flows W and NW to enter the Aral Sea in a wide delta; length 1415 km/879 mi; largest river of C Asia, and an important source of irrigation.

Amun [**a**mun], also spelled **Amon**, **Ammon**, or **Amen** From the time of the Middle Kingdom, the supreme deity in Egyptian religion. Later he was given the qualities of the sun-god Re, hence the usual title **Amun-Re**. The name means 'the hidden one'.

Amundsen, Roald (Engelbregt Gravning) [**a**mundsen] (1872–1928) Explorer, born in Borge, SE Norway. From 1903 to 1906 he sailed the Northwest Passage from E–W, and located the Magnetic North Pole. In 1910 he set sail in the *Fram* in an attempt to reach the North Pole, but hearing that Peary had apparently beaten him to it, he switched to the Antarctic and reached the South Pole in December 1911, one month ahead of Captain Scott. In 1926 he flew the airship *Norge* across the North Pole with Ellsworth and Nobile. In 1928 he disappeared when searching by plane for Nobile and his airship *Italia*, which had gone missing on another flight to the Pole.

Amur River [a**moor**], Chin **Heilong Jiang** River in NE China and Russia, part of the international border; main source rises in the Greater Khingan Range, Inner Mongolia; flows generally E then NE to enter the Sea of Okhotsk; length, 4350 km/2700 mi; scene of several Sino-Soviet incidents since the 1960s.

amyl [**ay**miyl, **a**mil] $CH_3CH_2CH_2CH_2CH_2$–, IUPAC **pentyl**. A group derived from pentane by removing one hydrogen atom. **Amyl alcohol** is a fraction of fusel oil, boiling point c.130°C, a mixture of several isomers of $C_5H_{11}OH$. **Amylose** is a low molecular weight fraction of starch. **Amyloid** is a combination of protein and polysaccharides deposited as a fibrous substance in some animal organs affected by certain diseases (eg kuru).

amylases [**a**milayziz] A group of enzymes which speed up the breakdown of starch and glycogen into disaccharides and small polysaccharides. They occur widely in plants and animals; for example, α-amylase is found in saliva and the pancreatic secretions of some vertebrates, β-amylase in plants.

amyl nitrite ($C_5H_{11}NO_2$) A drug in the form of a volatile liquid, administered by inhalation, which acts very rapidly and very

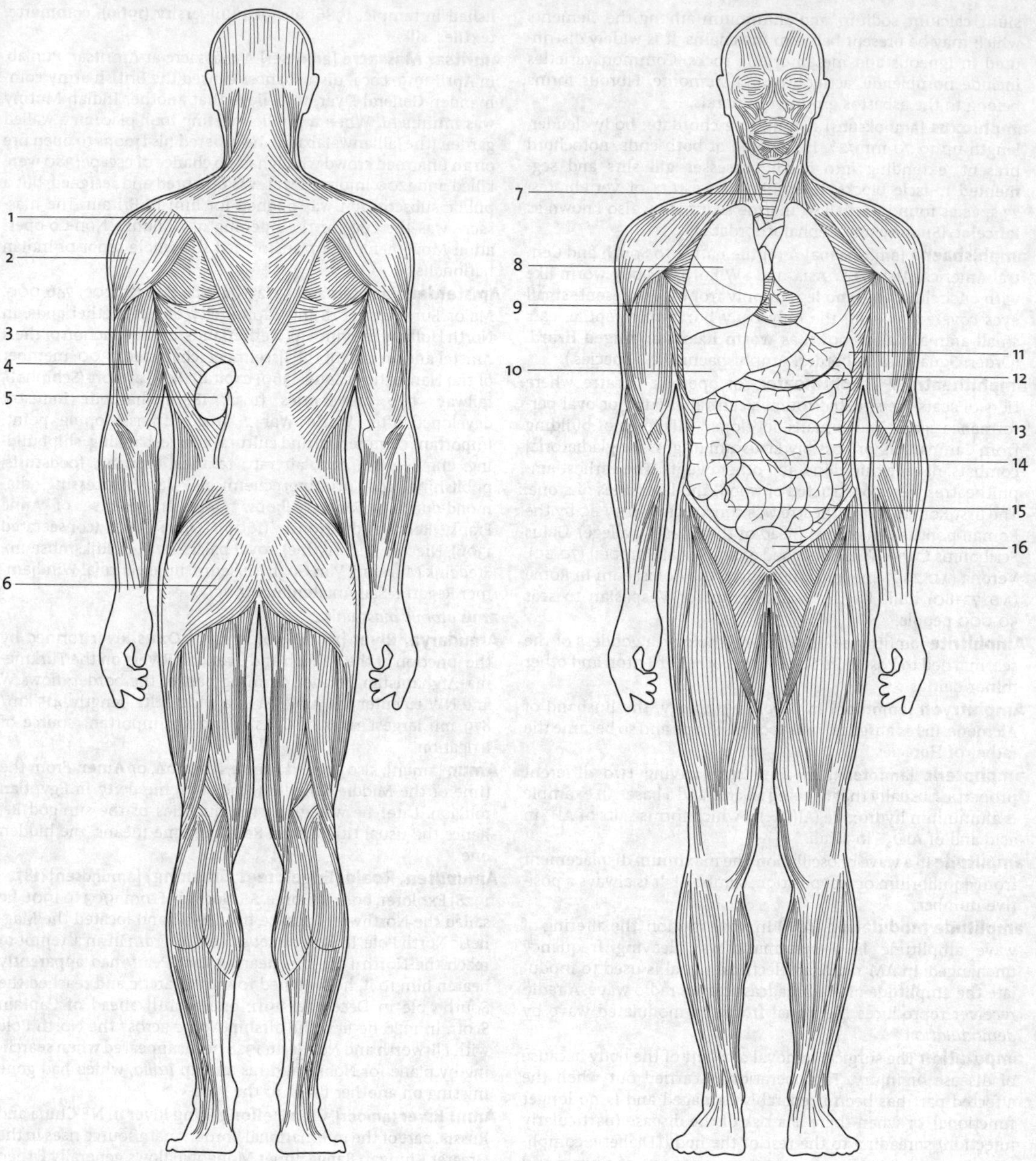

In human beings the musculature normally accounts for some 40% of the total body weight. There are 639 named muscles in the human body.

1 trapezius muscle
2 deltoid muscle
3 latissimus dorsi muscle
4 triceps muscles (the biceps, at the front of the arm, cannot be seen from this view)
5 kidney
6 gluteus maximus muscle (largest muscle in the body)

7 trachea
8 lungs
9 heart
10 liver (only a small part of the liver can be seen in this illustration)
11 spleen

12 stomach
13 small intestine
14 colon
15 appendix
16 bladder

anatomy

The science concerned with the form, structure, and spatial relationships of a living organism, and the relation of structure to function. It originally referred to the cutting up of the body to determine the nature and organization of its parts, but nowadays it includes many other aspects of study. *Topographic* or *gross* anatomy deals with the relative positions of various body parts. *Systemic* anatomy is concerned with the study of groups of related structures (eg the respiratory system). *Applied* anatomy considers anatomical facts in relation to clinical medicine. *Functional* anatomy deals not only with the structural basis of function in the various systems (eg the musculo-skeletal system), but also with the relation of one system to another, and so merges with physiology. *Developmental* anatomy is concerned with the prenatal organization and structural changes within the embryo and fetus (*embryology*), and with postnatal growth and development. *Morbid* or *pathological* anatomy deals with the anatomy of diseased tissues. *Radiological* anatomy is the study of organs and tissues using radiographic techniques (X-rays, computer-assisted tomography, magnetic resonance imaging). *Neuroanatomy* is the study of the structure and function of nervous systems (central, peripheral, autonomic). *Comparative* anatomy describes and compares the form, structure, and function of different animals. *Veterinary* anatomy is the science dealing with the form and structure of the principal domesticated animals. Anatomical science also involves *histology*, the study of the architecture of tissues and organs, and *cell biology*, concerned with the basic elements of the cell.

briefly. It has some use in the treatment of angina but is also sold as a sex aid ('poppers'). It is also used in the emergency treatment of cyanide poisoning.

Anabaptists The collective name given to groups of believers stemming from the more radical elements of the 16th-c Reformation; also known as **Rebaptizers**. They believed in the baptism of believing adults only, refusing to recognize infant baptism. They emphasized adherence to the word of scripture, strict Church discipline, and the separation of Church and state. Being prepared to criticize the state, they frequently suffered savage persecution. They were associated with Thomas Müntzer and the Zwinglian prophets in Wittenberg (1521); the Swiss brethren in Zürich (1525); and Jan Mattys (d.1534) in Münster (1533–4), where the Anabaptists achieved supremacy; and spread to Moravia, N and W Germany, the Low Countries (especially the Mennonites in Holland), and later the USA. They were the forerunners of the Baptists, who are in many respects their spiritual heirs.

anabatic wind A local upslope wind which develops best in a valley. During the day the air in contact with the valley sides is heated to a greater degree than air at the same elevation but above the valley floor. This leads to convectional rising of the heated air, and a circulation pattern of upslope airflow from valley floor to ridge, to replace rising air. Windspeeds of 10–15 m/32–50 ft per second can occur.

anabolic steroids Drugs with structures similar to the male sex hormones (*androgens*) but with reduced androgenic activity and increased anabolic activity to promote weight and muscle development. They are used clinically to accelerate recovery from protein deficiency, in muscle-wasting disorders, and sometimes in breast cancer. They are used illegally to promote the performance of athletes and racing animals, and were first used by weightlifters and bodybuilders. The International Olympic Committee requires that medal winners at major competitions are subject to urine sample analysis to prove themselves drug free. The International Weightlifting Association also has random checks. In women, anabolic steroids can cause masculinization – growth of facial hair, deepening of the voice, etc.

anabolism *metabolism*

anaclitic therapy A form of psychotherapy in which the patient is allowed to regress. The term **anaclitic depression** was introduced by René Spitz (1887–1974), a Hungarian-born US psychoanalyst, who in 1946 described a syndrome of regression in infants separated from their love objects. It has also been used to describe changes in infants in institutions.

anaconda A boa from South America (*Eunectes murinus*), the largest snake in the world; may be more than 11 m/36 ft long, weighing over 500 kg/1100 lb; dull colour with large irregular dark spots; inhabits slow-moving water; may climb low trees; eats birds, mammals, caimans, turtles; also known as the **green anaconda**.

Anacreon [anakreeon] (c.570–c.475 BC) Greek lyric poet, from Teos, modern Turkey. He was invited to Samos by Polycrates to tutor his son, and after the tyrant's downfall, was taken to Athens by Hipparchus, son of the tyrant Pisistratus. He was famous for his satires and his elegant poems on love and wine, of which only fragments of his five books remain.

anaemia / anemia A reduction in the amount of oxygen-carrying pigment, haemoglobin, in the red cells circulating in the blood. The clinical features of the condition are pale skin, fatigue, and breathlessness. There are many causes, including blood loss, excessively rapid destruction of red blood cells, and failure of their normal maturation in the bone marrow, such as in some vitamin deficiencies (eg B_{12}).

anaerobe *aerobe*

anaesthetics / anesthetics, general Drugs which produce a reversible state of unconciousness deep enough to permit surgery. They may be inhaled (eg halothane, nitrous oxide) or given intravenously (eg thiopentone, alphaxalone). *Nitrous oxide* ('laughing gas') was discovered by Joseph Priestley in 1776, and its use in surgical operations was suggested in 1799 by Humphry Davy, who noted its analgesic action. However, for the next few decades it was used only as fairground entertainment. In 1844 the US dentist Horace Wells (1815–48) successfully allowed one of his own teeth to be extracted painlessly under its influence, and in 1846 American William Morton (1819–68) successfully used it in major surgery. After 1860 its use became established. *Ether* was discovered in 1540 by Valerius Cordus (1515–44), and shown to control colic pain in 1795. US surgeon Crawford Williamson Long first used it surgically for minor operations in 1842. *Chloroform* was discovered in 1831 and first used in 1847 as a general anaesthetic by Scottish obstetrician James Young Simpson (1811–70), despite strong opposition from the Church. Today, intravenous anaesthetics are used for short operations only. 'Basal' anesthesia is usually induced before the patient leaves the ward to relieve anxiety and hasten the induction of anaesthesia in the theatre. The medical speciality is known as **anaesthesiology**, and the presence of a specialist (an **anaesthetist**) is required during surgical operations.

anaesthetics / anesthetics, local Drugs which produce a reversible loss of sensation in a localized region of the body by blocking nerve impulses. Regional anaesthesia is achieved by topical application or by injection at the site of an operation (as in tooth extraction), near a main nerve trunk (eg to allow operations in limbs), or between spinal vertebrae (**epidural anaesthesia**). The first local anaesthetic was cocaine, introduced in the 1880s, but this is now obsolete because of problems of addiction and toxicity. Commonly used local anaesthetics include procaine, lignocaine (lidocaine), and benzocaine.

anaglyph A picture for stereoscopic viewing in which the separate right-eye and left-eye images are reproduced in different colours, usually red and blue-green. The observer wears coloured spectacles of complementary colours, so that each eye sees only its appropriate image.

anagram The re-arrangement of the letters of a word or sentence to produce a new form or a puzzle. Often an ingenious analogue to the original word can be found, eg *total abstainers→sit not at ale bars.*

analgesics Drugs which relieve pain. **Narcotic analgesics** (eg codeine, morphine, heroin) act by mimicking the natural brain endorphins responsible for the subjective perception of pain. **Non-narcotic analgesics** (eg aspirin, paracetamol, ibuprofen) act by blocking the synthesis of prostaglandins (substances formed at the site of injury involved in the production of pain responses).

analog computer, also spelled **analogue** Computers which accept, as inputs, continuous electrical or mechanical variables (such as voltage or current or the rotation rate or position of a shaft) and respond immediately to calculate relevant output signals. The processing is generally done by special electrical circuits, usually operational amplifiers, or by complex mechanical arrangements of gears, cogs, etc. Examples range from the automobile speedometer to the anti-aircraft 'predictors' of World War 2. Analog computers are inherently real-time systems, and continue to find special purpose applications, particularly in control systems, although many of their former tasks are now done using the much more versatile digital computers.

analog-to-digital (A/D) conversion, also spelled **analogue** A process of converting analog signals, such as voltage, into a digital form which can be used in a digital computer. It is usually carried out by specialized electronic circuits or discrete integrated circuits called *analog-to-digital converters*. A/D converters and the converse D/A converters are common in computer-controlled processes.

analogue / analog signal *digital techniques*

analogy A type of inference whose form is 'because *x* is like *y* in some respects it will be in other respects'. Analogy can be suggestive, and sometimes works, but it is not a deductive proof. The argument from analogy for the existence of God, popular in the 18th-c and 19th-c, maintained that the universe is like a mechanism; therefore just as a mechanism requires a maker, so does the universe.

analytical chemistry A branch of chemistry dealing with the composition of material. It includes qualitative and quantitative determinations of elements present, as well as structural analysis. The methods used are based either on chemical reactions or on physical properties, generally electrochemical or spectroscopic.

analytic / analytical geometry A method of attacking geometrical problems by referring to a point by its co-ordinates in a system; also known as **Cartesian** or **co-ordinate geometry**. For the plane, the commonest system is of two perpendicular axes, when all points can be identified by a number pair, (x,y). In three-dimensional geometry a number triple is needed (x,y,z). Other systems of co-ordinates, such as polar co-ordinates, have been developed which are more suitable for some types of problems. Descartes is generally credited with inventing this system, but the use of axes in the study of conic sections was known to Apollonius.

analytic language A type of language in which words do not vary their form to show their grammatical function in a sentence; also known as an **isolating language**. In such languages (eg Chinese), the relationships between the words are shown solely by their order. Analytic languages are opposed to **synthetic languages**, in which words typically combine a grammatical meaning with their dictionary meaning; for example, the English word *horses* contains the meaning of 'plural' in addition to the sense of 'animal'. Most languages display features of both systems.

analytic philosophy The dominant tradition in 20th-c Anglo-American academic philosophy, often contrasted with French or German philosophical traditions such as phenomenology or existentialism. Much influenced by Frege, Russell, Moore, and Wittgenstein early in the 20th-c, it emphasized the importance of logical and linguistic analysis to solve or dissolve philosophical problems.

anamorphosis An image drawn or painted in trick perspective so that it appears distorted from a normal viewpoint, but when seen from an extraordinary angle, or through a lens, appears normal. A famous example is the skull in Holbein's *Ambassadors* in the National Gallery, London.

Ananda [ananda] (5th–6th-c BC) The cousin and favourite pupil of the Buddha. Noted for his devotion to the Buddha, and a skilled interpreter of his teachings, he was instrumental in establishing an order for women disciples.

Ananke [anangkee] The 12th natural satellite of Jupiter, discovered in 1951; distance from the planet 21 200 000 km/ 13 174 000 mi; diameter 30 km/19 mi.

anaphylaxis [anafuhlaksis] A severe allergic reaction which occurs when an individual has been previously sensitized by contact with an allergen. It occurs within a few minutes of exposure, and the clinical response depends upon the tissue affected. Examples of local anaphylaxis include asthma, hay fever, red and itching skin weals (urticaria), and swelling of the tissues of the throat. A severe degree of generalized anaphylaxis (**anaphylactic shock**) may result in a sudden attack of wheezing, falling blood pressure, and collapse, and may be fatal.

anarchism A generic term for political ideas and movements that reject the state and other forms of authority and coercion in favour of a society based exclusively upon voluntary co-operation between individuals. To anarchists the state, whether democratic or not, is always seen as a means of supporting a ruling class or elite, and as an encumbrance to social relations. However, they differ in their view of the nature of their future society, their proposals ranging from a communist society based on mutual aid to one based on essentially self-interested voluntary exchange. They reject involvement in political institutions, and support civil disobedience action against the state, and on occasions political violence. Anarchist movements were most prevalent in Europe in the second half of the 19th-c and early 20th-c, but virtually died out apart from fringe groups after the Spanish Civil War.

anarthria *dysarthria*

Anasazi [anasahzee] The prehistoric Indian inhabitants of the arid 'Four Corners' region of the US Southwest (where Arizona, New Mexico, Colorado, and Utah meet), c.200 BC–AD 1500. The name, from Navajo, means 'enemy ancestors'. The villages were of pithouses before c.700, pueblos or cliff dwellings later, while the economy was predominantly horticultural, based on maize, beans, and squashes. The modern descendants are the Hopi of Arizona, and the Rio Grande Pueblo groups of New Mexico.

Anastasia [anastahzia], in full **Grand Duchess Anastasia Nikolaievna Romanova** (1901–?1918) Youngest daughter of Tsar Nicholas II of Russia, born near St Petersburg, NW Russia, believed to have perished when the Romanov family were executed by the Bolsheviks (19 Jul 1918). Various people later claimed to be Anastasia, especially Mrs 'Anna Anderson' Manahan, from the Black Forest, who died in Virginia, USA, in 1984 at the age of 82. For more than 30 years she fought unsuccessfully to establish her identity as Anastasia, and her claim was finally rejected by a Hamburg court in May 1961. Her story has inspired several films and books.

Anatolia [anatohlia], Turkish **Anadolu** Asiatic region of Turkey, usually synonymous with Asia Minor; a mountainous peninsula between the Black Sea (N), Aegean Sea (W), and the Mediterranean Sea (S).

Anatolian [anatohlian] A group of Indo-European languages, now extinct, spoken c.2000 BC in the area of present-day Turkey and Syria. The major language is Hittite, which is recorded on tablets inscribed with cuneiform writing from the 17th-c BC: these are the oldest known Indo-European texts.

anatomy *pp.54–5*

Anaxagoras [anaksagoras] (c.500–428 BC) Greek philosopher, born in Clazomenae. For 30 years he taught in Athens, where he had many illustrious pupils, among them Pericles and Euripides. His scientific speculations led to his prosecution for impiety, and he was banished from Athens. His most celebrated cosmological doctrine was that matter is infinitely divisible into particles, which contain a mixture of all qualities, and that mind (*nous*) is a pervasive formative agency in the creation of material objects.

Anaximander [anakzimander] (c.611–547 BC) Greek philosopher, born in Miletus, the successor and perhaps pupil of Thales. He posited that the first principle was not a particular substance like water or air but the *apeiron*, the infinite or indefinite. He is credited with producing the first map, and with many imaginative scientific speculations, for example that the Earth is unsupported and at the centre of the universe.

Anaximenes [anakzimeneez] (?–c.500 BC) Greek philosopher, born in Miletus. He was the third of the three great Milesian thinkers, succeeding Thales and Anaximander. He posited that the first principle and basic form of matter was air, which could be transformed into other substances by a process of condensation and rarefaction.

Anchises [ankiyseez] In Roman mythology, the Trojan father of Aeneas. The *Aeneid* gives an account of Aeneas's piety in carrying Anchises on his shoulders out of the blazing city of Troy.

anchor A device which prevents a vessel from drifting. The flukes or arms of an anchor dig into the seabed, thus resisting a horizontal pull; it is made fast to the ship by a heavy cable, usually of studded chain. There are two basic types: the old-fashioned anchor with a stock, usually depicted on badges and flags; and the modern, more common, stockless anchor. The stockless anchor consists of a shank and a crown, which are free to move in relation to each other, so that when in use the flukes will adopt an angle of about 45° to the shank. When stowed, the flukes are parallel to the shank.

Anchorage 61°13N 149°54W, pop (2000e) 260 300. City and seaport in SC Alaska, USA, at the head of Cook Inlet; largest city in the state; founded as a railway construction camp, 1914; severely damaged by earthquake, 1964; important transportation hub; administrative and commercial centre; a vital defence centre, with Fort Richardson military base and Elmendorf air force base nearby; airport; railway; university (1957); mining, tourism; Earthquake Park, National Bank Heritage Library; Iditarod Sled Race (Mar), Great Alaska Shootout (Nov), Fur Rendezvous (Nov).

anchovy [anchovee] Any of the small herring-like fishes of the family Engraulidae, widespread in surface coastal waters of tropical and temperate seas; support extensive commercial fisheries, much of the catch being processed before sale. (5 genera, including *Anchoa, Engraulis*.)

ancien régime [ãsyĩ rayzheem] The social and political system of France existing from the late 16th-c to the outbreak of the French Revolution (1789). The term implies a hierarchical, corporative society, bound closely to the dynastic state, and is associated particularly with mechanisms upholding traditional orders and privileges.

ancient lights In English law, an easement acquired through 20 years' uninterrupted use, and not by consent or permission, whereby one property owner can claim the right against another property owner to enjoy at least a reasonable amount of light. Where it exists, this right may restrict building on neighbouring property. A restrictive covenant against building may be more effective, but such a covenant cannot be acquired through long use.

ancona *altarpiece*

Andalusia, Eng [andalooseea], Span **Andalucía** [andalootheea] pop (2000e) 6 950 000; area 87 268 sq km/33 685 sq mi. Large and fertile autonomous region of S Spain; dominated by the great basin of the R Guadalquivir and (S) by the Baetic Cordillera, rising to 3478 m/11 411 ft at Cerro de Mulhacén, Spain's highest peak; S coastal strip known for its tourist resorts on the Costa del Sol and the Costa de la Luz; sugar cane, fruit, bananas, wine, cotton; chief cities, Málaga, Cádiz, Granada, Córdoba; many remains of Moorish rule (8th–15th-c).

Andalusian horse A breed of horse; height, 16 hands/1·6 m/5½ ft; grey (occasionally black); developed in Spain over many centuries by crossing African, Spanish, and German horses; a less refined version is called the **Andalusian-Carthusian** or **Carthusian**.

andalusite [andaloosiyt] One of the three varieties of mineral aluminium silicate (Al_2SiO_5), found in metamorphic rocks, the others being *kyanite* and *sillimanite*. Its importance lies as an indicator of the pressure and temperature of metamorphism in rocks.

Andaman and Nicobar Islands [andaman, nikohbah(r)] pop (2001e) 356 300; area 8300 sq km/3200 sq mi. Union territory of India, comprising two island groups in the Bay of Bengal; separated from Myanmar, Thailand, and Sumatra by the Andaman Sea; over 300 islands, stretching 725 km/450 mi N to S; occupied by Japan in World War 2; part of India, 1950; British penal colony on Andaman Is, 1858–1945; Cellular Jail at Port Blair now a national shrine; Nicobar Is 120 km/75 mi S, a mountainous group of 19 islands; occupied by Denmark, 1756–1848; annexed by Britain, 1869; chief town, Nankauri; tropical forest covers both islands; monsoons frequent (May–Oct); fishing, rubber, fruit, rice, hardwood timber.

Andaman Sea [andaman] area 564 900 sq km/218 000 sq mi. NE arm of the Indian Ocean; bounded E by Myanmar and Thailand, N by the Gulf of Martaban, S by Sumatra, and W by the Andaman and Nicobar Is.

Andean bear *spectacled bear*

Andean Community, also known as the **Andean Group**, Span **Comunidad Andina** An organization modelled on the European Union, with five member countries: Bolivia, Colombia, Ecuador, Peru, and Venezuela, all members of the Latin-American Free Trade Association. It was previously known as the **Andean Pact** (1969–96). Chile, a founding member, withdrew in 1976. Its aims are to facilitate development of the member states through economic and social co-operation. Various subsidiary bodies co-ordinate policy on such matters as commerce, industry, monetary exchange, financial planning, and legislation. Trade between the groups has more than doubled since its foundation.

Anders, Władysław (1892–1970) Polish soldier, born in Blonie, C Poland. He served on the staff of the Russian division and Polish Corps in World War 1 (1914–17). At the outbreak of World War 2 he was captured by the Russians (1939–41), but released to command a Polish ex-POW force organized in Russia, which he led through Iran into Iraq. In 1943 he became commander of the 2nd Polish Corps in Italy, capturing Monte Cassino. After the war, deprived of his nationality by the Polish Communist government, he was a leading figure in the Free Polish community in Britain, and inspector-general of the Polish forces-in-exile.

Andersen, Hans Christian (1805–75) Writer, one of the world's great story-tellers, born in Odense, SC Denmark. The son of a poor shoemaker, after his father's death he worked in a factory, but soon displayed a talent for poetry. He became better known by his *Walk to Amager*, a literary satire in the form of a humorous narrative. In 1830 he published the first collected volume of his *Poems*, and in 1831 a second, under the title of *Fantasies and Sketches*. He wrote many other works, but it is such children's stories as 'The Tin Soldier', 'The Tinderbox', 'The Snow Queen', and 'The Ugly Duckling', collected in *Tales Told for Children* (1835), that have gained him lasting fame and delighted children throughout the world.

Anderson, Benny *Abba*

Anderson, Carl (David) (1905–91) Physicist, born in New York City, USA. He studied at the California Institute of Technology, and became professor there in 1939. In 1932 he discovered the positron. He did notable work on gamma and cosmic rays, and shared the 1936 Nobel Prize for Physics with Victor Hess. Later he confirmed the existence of intermediate-mass particles now called muons.

Anderson, Clive (Stuart) (1953–) Television presenter and barrister, born in London, UK. He studied law at Cambridge, where he was president of Footlights, and was called to the bar in 1976. He wrote scripts for radio and television, began acting as a TV warm-up man, and joined BBC Radio 4 as chairman of the popular *Whose Line Is It Anyway?* (1988). The show later transferred to Channel 4 Television, where he was also given his own chat-show *Clive Anderson Talks Back* (1989–96). Later work includes the BBC documentary series, *Our Man In ...* (1995–), which he also wrote, *Clive Anderson All Talk* (1996–2000), and *What If...?* (2003).

Anderson, Elizabeth Garrett, *née* **Garrett** (1836–1917) Physician, the first English woman doctor, born in London, UK. In 1860 she began studying medicine, in the face of opposition to the admission of women, and eventually (1865) qualified as a medical practitioner by passing the Apothecaries' Hall examination. In 1866 she established a dispensary for women in London (later renamed the Elizabeth Garrett Anderson Hospital), where she instituted medical courses for women. In 1870 she was given the degree of MD by the University of Paris. She married J G S Anderson in 1871, and in 1908 she was elected Mayor of Aldeburgh, the first woman mayor in England. Her daughter **Louisa Anderson** (1878–1943) organized hospitals in France in World War 1, and wrote her mother's biography.

Anderson, Gerry (1929–) British creator of puppet-character programmes for television. He entered the British film industry as a trainee with the Colonial Film Unit, later directing several television series. He enjoyed great success with adventure series that combined a range of popular puppet characters with technologically advanced hardware and special effects. Among the best known are *Fireball XL-5* (1961), *Thunderbirds* (1964–6), *Captain Scarlett and the Mysterons* (1967), and *Terrahawks* (1983–4). He also branched out into live action shows with human actors, such as *The Protectors* (1971), *Space 1999* (1973–6), and *Space Precinct* (1993–5).

Anderson, Gillian (1968–) Actress, born in Chicago, Illinois, USA. Brought up in London, her family returned to the USA, where she became involved in community theatre, and studied at DePaul University. She then found theatre parts in New York City, eventually moving to Los Angeles, where she was offered the part of Dana Scully in the television series *The X-Files* (1993–2002, Golden Globe, Emmy), which has since become a cult classic, and also starred in the feature film *The X-Files: Fight the Future* (1998). Other films include *The Mighty* (1998) She now lives in Vancouver.

Anderson, Lindsay (Gordon) (1923–94) British stage and film director, born in Bangalore, SC India. He studied at Oxford, made short documentary films during the 1950s, and won an Oscar for *Thursday's Children* (1955). He was a leading proponent of the Free Cinema critical movement, with its focus on working-class themes. He joined the English Stage Company at the Royal Court Theatre, London, in 1957. His first feature film was *This Sporting Life* (1963), followed by *If....* (1968), *O Lucky Man!* (1973), *Britannia Hospital* (1982), and *The Whales of August* (1987). He also acted cameo parts on film.

Anderson, Marian (1902–93) Contralto concert and opera singer, born in Philadelphia, Pennsylvania, USA. After a Carnegie Hall recital (1929) she toured in Europe and the USSR. She became the first African-American singer at the New York Metropolitan Opera (1955). President Eisenhower made her a delegate to the UN in 1958, and she received many honours and international awards.

Anderson, Maxwell (1888–1959) Historical playwright, born in Atlantic, Pennsylvania, USA. A verse playwright, he was in vogue in the late 1920s to the early 1940s with numerous plays such as *Elizabeth the Queen* (1930) and *Mary of Scotland* (1933). He also wrote screenplays, most notably that from Remarque's novel *All Quiet on the Western Front* (1930). He was awarded a Pulitzer Prize for *Both Your Houses* in 1933.

Anderson, Philip W(arren) (1923–) Physicist, born in Indianapolis, Indiana, USA. He studied antenna engineering at the Naval Research Laboratories in World War 2, and at Harvard under John H Van Vleck. He was research scientist at Bell Telephone Laboratories (1949–84), visiting professor of physics at Cambridge (1967–75), and professor of physics at Princeton in 1975. He shared the Nobel Prize for Physics in 1977 for his work on the electronic structure of magnetic and disordered systems.

Anderson, Sherwood (1876–1941) Writer, born in Camden, Ohio, USA. He left his family and his lucrative position as manager of a paint factory to devote his entire time to writing. His first novel was *Windy McPherson's Son* (1916), but his best-known work is the collection of short stories, *Winesburg, Ohio* (1919).

Andes [andeez] Major mountain range in South America, running parallel to the Pacific coast from Tierra del Fuego (S) to the Caribbean (N), passing through Argentina, Chile, Bolivia, Peru, Ecuador, Colombia, and Venezuela; extends over 6400 km/4000 mi; rises to 6960 m/22 834 ft in the Cerro Aconcagua (Argentina), the highest point in South America; in N Argentina, Bolivia, Peru, and Colombia, there are several parallel ranges (*cordilleras*) and high plateaux; highest peaks are in the Cordillera Agostini on the Chile–Argentina border, with many lakes and tourist resorts; Puna de Atacama to the N, a desolate plateau, average height 3350–3900 m/11 000–12 800 ft; C Andes in Bolivia covers two-fifths of the country in an elevated plateau (*altiplano*) of 3000–3600 m/9800–11 800 ft, enclosing L Poopó and L Titicaca; Bolivian Andes split into E and W ranges (Cordillera Oriental/Occidental); system divides into many separate ranges in Peru; narrows in Ecuador, and includes such active volcanoes as Chimborazo (6310 m/20 702 ft) and Cotopaxi (5896 m/19 344 ft); three main ranges in Colombia (Cordillera Occidental/Central/Oriental); system continues NE into Venezuela as the Sierra Nevada de Mérida; connects via E Panama to the C American ranges.

andesite [andeziyt] Fine-grained volcanic rock of intermediate composition containing plagioclase feldspar with biotite, hornblende, or pyroxene; chemically equivalent to diorite. Andesites are formed at the continental edge of subduction zones, forming new continental crust, as in the Andes Mts, South America.

Andhra Pradesh [andra pradaysh] pop (2001e) 75 727 500; area 276 814 sq km/106 850 sq mi. State in S India, bounded E by the Bay of Bengal; capital, Hyderabad; made a separate state based on Telugu-speaking area of Chennai (Madras), 1953; unicameral Legislative Assembly with 295 seats; sugar cane, groundnuts, cotton, rice, tobacco; textiles, sugar milling, chemicals, cement, fertilizer, paper, carpets, natural gas, oil refining, shipbuilding, forestry.

Andorra *p.59*

Andorra la Vella [andora la velya], Span **Andorra la Vieja**, Fr **Andorre la Vieille** 42°30N 1°30E, pop (2000e) 28 300. One of the seven parishes of the Principality of Andorra, with a capital town of the same name; on the E side of the Pic d'Enclar (2317 m/7602 ft), 613 km/381 mi NE of Madrid; altitude 1029 m/3376 ft; airports.

Andrássy, Gyula, Gróf (Count) [ondrahshee] (1823–90) Statesman and prime minister (1867–71), born in Kassa, Hungary (now Košice, SE Slovak Republic). A supporter of Kossuth, he was prominent in the struggle for independence (1848–9), after which he remained in exile until 1858. When the Dual Monarchy was formed in 1867, he was made prime minister of Hungary (1871–9).

André, John [ondray] (1751–80) British soldier, born in London, UK, of French-Swiss descent. In 1774 he joined the army in Canada, and became aide-de-camp to Sir Henry Clinton, and adjutant-general. When Benedict Arnold obtained the command of West Point in 1780, André was selected to negotiate with him for its betrayal. While returning to New York he was captured and handed over to the US military authorities. He was tried as a spy, and hanged. In 1821 his remains were interred in Westminster Abbey.

Andrea del Sarto *Sarto, Andrea del*

andrecium [andreesiuhm] *flower; stamen*

Andreotti, Giulio [andrayottee] (1919–) Italian politician and prime minister (1972–3, 1976–8, 1978–9, 1989–92), born in Rome,

Andorra

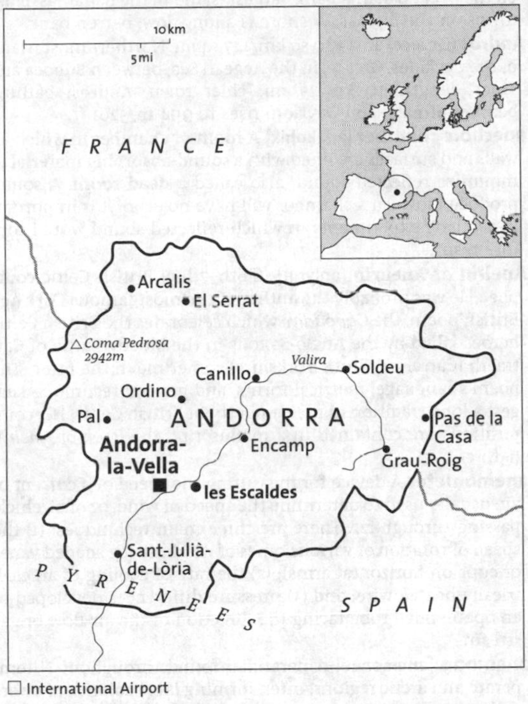

[andora] or **the Valleys of Andorra,** Catalan **Valls d'Andorra,** Fr **Vallée d'Andorre,** official name **Principality of Andorra, Principat d'Andorra**

Local name Vallée d'Andorre (French), Valls d'Andorra (Spanish)
Timezone GMT +1
Area 453 km²/175 sq mi
Population total (2002e) 66 500
Status Independent State
Capital Andorra la Vella
Languages Catalan (official), French, Spanish
Ethnic groups Catalan (50%), Andorran (29%), French (8%), Portuguese (7%)
Religion Roman Catholic (94%)
Physical features Mountainous country, located on the S slopes of the C Pyrénées between France and Spain, peaks reaching 2 946 m/9 665 ft at Coma Pedrosa; two valleys (del Norte and del Orient) of the R Valira.
Climate Alpine climate: heavy snow in winter, warm summers; average annual temperature 2°C (Jan), 19°C (Jul); lowest average monthly rainfall, 34 mm/1·34 in (Jan).
Currency 1 euro = 100 cents (previous to February 2002, 1 French Franc (Fr) = 100 centimes, 1 peseta (Pta, Pa) = 100 céntimos)
Economy No restriction on currency exchange, and no direct value-added taxes, therefore a marketing centre for goods imported from Europe and Asia; commerce, agriculture; skiing at five mountain resorts; in recent years, textiles, publishing, leather, mineral water, tourism.
GDP (2000e) $1·3 bn, per capita $19 000
History One of the oldest states in Europe, under the joint protection of France and Spain since 1278; Co-Princes of Principality are the President of France and the Bishop of Urgel; General Council of the Valley appoints the head of the government; independent state since 1993.
Heads of state (Co-Princes): President of France and Bishop of Urgel, Spain
Head of Government (Chief Executive)
1989–94 Oscar Ribas Reig
1994– Marc Forné Molné

Italy. A Christian Democrat deputy, he played an increasingly important part in post-war Italian politics, and was successively minister of the interior (1954), finance (1955–8), treasury (1958–9), defence (1959–66, 1974), industry and commerce (1966–8), and foreign affairs (1983–7, 1987–9), before becoming prime minister. A life senator since 1991, in 1995 he was accused of connivance with the Mafia and put on trial, and was on trial again in 1996 for ordering the murder of a journalist. In 1999 he was acquitted of both sets of charges, but the acquittal was overturned in 2002 when he was found guilty of murder and given a prison sentence.

Andress, Ursula (1936–) Film actress, born in Bern, Switzerland. She made her international debut in *Dr No* (1963), her later films including *What's New, Pussycat?* (1965), *Casino Royale* (1967), and *The Clash of the Titans* (1981). Television work includes *The Chinatown Murders* (1989). She co-presented the World Music Awards in 1997.

Andrew (Albert Christian Edward), Duke of York (1960–) British prince, the second son of Queen Elizabeth II. He studied at Gordonstoun School, Moray, NE Scotland, UK, and Lakefield College, Ontario, SE Canada, then trained at the Royal Naval College, Dartmouth, where he was commissioned as a helicopter pilot. He saw service in the Falklands War (1982). In 1986 he married **Sarah (Margaret) Ferguson** (1959–), and was made Duke of York. They have two children, **Princess Beatrice Elizabeth Mary** (1988–) and **Princess Eugenie Victoria Helena** (1990–). The couple separated in 1992, and divorced in 1996. He left the navy in 2001, and took up a role as ambassador for British Trade International.

Andrew, St (d.c.60) One of the 12 apostles, the brother of Simon Peter. A fisherman, he was converted by John the Baptist. Tradition says he preached the Gospel in Asia Minor and Scythia, and was crucified in Achaia (Greece) by order of the Roman governor. He is the patron saint of Scotland and of Russia. Feast day 30 November.

Andrewes, Lancelot (1555–1626) Anglican clergyman and scholar, born in Barking, Essex, SE England, UK. He studied at Cambridge, took orders in 1580, and rose to become Dean of Westminster in 1601. He attended the Hampton Court Conference, and took part in the translation of the Authorized Version of the Bible (1607). In 1605 he was consecrated Bishop of Chichester; in 1609 he was translated to Ely, and in 1618 to Winchester. A powerful preacher and defender of Anglican doctrines, he is considered one of the most learned theologians of his time.

Andrews, Eamon (1922–87) Broadcaster, born in Dublin, Ireland. He began sports commentating for Radio Eireann in 1939 and subsequently worked on various programmes for BBC Radio, including *Sports Report* (1950–62). On television he hosted the parlour game *What's My Line?* (1951–63) and *This is Your Life* (1955–87). Active as a chat-show host and children's programmes presenter, as well as being a keen businessman, he later returned to *What's My Line?* (1984–7).

Andrews, Dame Julie, originally **Julia Elizabeth Wells** (1935–) Singer and actress, born in Walton-on-Thames, Surrey, SE England, UK. Radio and stage successes led to her selection for the New York City production of *The Boyfriend* (1954), and several long-running Broadway musicals, notably *My Fair Lady* (1956) and *Camelot* (1960). With her film debut in *Mary Poppins* (1964) she won an Oscar, and this was followed by a further nomination for *The Sound of Music* (1965). Voted the world's most popular star, she broadened her range in *S.O.B.* (1981), *Victor/*

Victoria (1982), *Duet for One* (1987), and *A Fine Romance* (1992). Later films include *Relative Values* (2000) and *Princess Diaries* (2001). Since 1970 she has appeared almost exclusively in films directed by her second husband, Blake Edwards. In 1998 an operation on her vocal cords left her singing voice badly damaged. She became a dame in 1999.

Andrianov, Nikolay [andriahnof] (1952–) Gymnast, born in Vladimir, W Russia. He won 15 Olympic medals (including seven golds) between 1972 and 1980. In addition, he won 12 world championship medals, including the overall individual title in 1978.

Andrić, Ivo [andrich] (1892–1975) Diplomat and writer, born near Travnik, C Bosnia and Herzegovina (formerly in Yugoslavia). A member of the diplomatic service, he was minister in Berlin at the outbreak of war in 1939. His chief works (trans titles), *The Bridge on the Drina* (1945) and *Bosnian Story* (1945), earned him the 1961 Nobel Prize for Literature and the nickname 'the Yugoslav Tolstoy'.

Androcles [androkleez] According to a Roman story, a slave who escaped from his master, met a lion, and extracted a thorn from its paw. When recaptured, he was made to confront a lion in the arena, and found it was the same animal, so that his life was spared.

androgens [androjenz] Chemical substances, usually steroid sex hormones, which induce masculine characteristics. In men the androgen *testosterone* is secreted in the testes by the cells of Leydig, with small amounts of additional androgens secreted by the adrenal cortex. Testosterone may be converted to the more powerful *dihydrotestosterone* by such target organs as the prostate gland. Androgens are necessary for the development of male genitalia in the fetus; during puberty they promote the development of secondary sexual characteristics (growth of the penis and testes; the appearance of pubic, facial, and body hair; an increase in muscle strength; and deepening of the voice); in adults, they are required for the production of sperm and the maintenance of libido. Small amounts of ovarian and adrenal androgens are present in women. They are probably responsible for the adolescent growth spurt in girls.

android *robotics* (cybernetics)

Andromache [andromakee] In Greek legend, the wife of Hector, the hero of Troy. After the fall of the city she became the slave of the Greek Neoptolemus.

Andromeda (astronomy) [andromida] A constellation in the N sky, one of 48 listed by Ptolemy (AD 140), named after the daughter of Cepheus and Cassiopeia. Its brightest stars are Alpheratz and Mirach. It contains the **Andromeda galaxy**, the largest of the nearby galaxies, c.725 kiloparsec away. For centuries, astronomers regarded Andromeda as part of the Milky Way; only in the 1920s did Edwin Hubble establish that it was a separate galaxy. Spiral, about 45 kpc in diameter, it is the most remote object easily visible to the naked eye.

Andromeda (mythology) [andromeda] In Greek mythology, the daughter of Cepheus, King of the Ethiopians, and Cassiopeia. To appease Poseidon, she was fastened to a rock by the sea-shore as an offering to a sea-monster. She was rescued by Perseus, who used the Gorgon's head to change the monster to stone. The persons named in the story were all turned into constellations.

Andropov, Yuri Vladimirovich [andropof] (1914–84) Russian politician, born in Nagutskoye, SW Russia. He began work in the shipyards of the upper Volga at Rybinsk (also called Andropov before 1991), where he became politically active. After World War 2 he was brought to Moscow to work for the Communist Party central committee. He was ambassador in Budapest (1954–7), and came to the notice of the strict ideologist, Mikhail Suslov, for his part in crushing the Hungarian uprising of 1956. In 1967 he was appointed KGB chief, and in 1973 became a full member of the Politburo. His firm handling of dissident movements enhanced his reputation, enabling him to be chosen as Brezhnev's successor in 1983, but he died after less than 15 months in office.

Andros (Bahamas) pop (2000e) 9500; area 5955 sq km/2300 sq mi. Island in the W Bahamas, W of New Providence I, on the Great Bahama Bank; largest island in the Bahamas; chief towns on the E coast; W shore is a long, low, barren bank.

Andros (Greece) area 380 sq km/147 sq mi. Northernmost island of the Cyclades, Greece, in the Aegean Sea, between Euboea and Tinos; length 40 km/25 mi; chief town, Andros; bathing beaches at Batsi and Gavrion; rises to 994 m/3261 ft.

anechoic chamber [anekohik] A room or chamber in which all walls and surfaces are lined with a sound-absorbing material to minimize reflected sound; also called a **dead room**. A sound produced in such a chamber will have no echo. It is important in acoustic experiments in which reflected sound would confuse results.

Aneirin or **Aneurin** [aniyrin] (fl.6th–7th-c) British Celtic court poet. He was probably the author of the most famous Dark Age British poem, the *Gododdin*, which celebrates the British Celtic heroes killed by the Anglo-Saxons in the bloody Battle of Cattraeth (Catterick, North Yorkshire) sometime in the 6th-c. The poem's language, metrical forms, and general technique suggest a long tradition of praise-poetry in British Celtic. His compositions are contained in a manuscript, the *Book of Aneirin* (13th-c).

anemometer A device for measuring the speed of a current of air, usually used to determine the speed of wind, or of a vehicle passing through air. There are three main techniques: (1) the speed of rotation of various types of windmill (eg shaped vanes or cups on horizontal arms); (2) the rate of cooling of an electrically heated wire; and (3) pressure differences developed in an open-ended tube facing the direction of the air-flow or gas stream.

anemone [anemonee] A perennial found throughout N temperate and arctic regions, often forming large colonies; flowers with 5–9 perianth-segments ranging from white to yellow, pink, or blue, but hybrids exhibit an even greater colour range; the flower stalks have a whorl of small, divided leaves two-thirds of the way up; the main, basal leaves appear later. (Genus: *Anemone*, 150 species. Family: Ranunculaceae.)

aneroid barometer *barometer*

anesthetics *anaesthetics*

Aneto, Pico de [peekoh thay anaytoh] 42°37N 0°40E. Highest peak of the Pyrenees Mts, rising to 3404 m/11 168 ft in Huesca province, NE Spain.

aneurysm [anyurizm] The abnormal enlargement of a segment of a blood vessel (usually an artery) due to the weakening or rupture of some of the layers of the wall of the vessel. If the inner layer (*intima*) ruptures, blood passes between the layers of the vessel wall and may escape into surrounding tissues. Rupture of an aneurysm of the aorta or pulmonary trunk often proves fatal.

Anfinsen, Christian B(oehmer) (1916–95) Biochemist, born in Monessen, Pennsylvania, USA. He studied at Harvard, and taught there before moving to the National Institutes of Health in Bethesda, MD (1950–82). His chief work was on the sequence of amino acids which make up the enzyme ribonuclease, for which he shared the Nobel Prize for Chemistry in 1972.

angel A celestial spirit, said to serve God in various capacities, such as acting as a messenger, or as a guardian of individuals. In traditional Christianity, angels were understood to have been created before the world. They feature prominently in Christian art, often depicted with a human body and wings. They are sometimes held to be objects of devotion.

angel dust The street name of the drug **phencyclidine** (1-(1-phenylcyclohexyl) piperidine, or **PCP**) which is a hallucinogen. It was originally introduced in the 1950s as a general anaesthetic, but soon withdrawn; it is still used in veterinary medicine to produce a trance-like anaesthetic state. It was widely abused as a recreational drug in the 1970s and early 1980s, but is no longer fashionable.

Angeles, Victoria de los [anjeles] (1923–) Lyric soprano, born in Barcelona, NE Spain. Her operatic debut was at Barcelona in

1944. She then performed at the Paris Opera and La Scala, Milan (1949), Covent Garden (1950), the New York Metropolitan (1951), and subsequently at all the great houses and festivals throughout the world. She is noted particularly for her 19th-c Italian roles and for her performances of Spanish songs. After retiring from the stage in 1969, she continued to give recitals.

Angel Falls 5°57N 62°33W. Waterfall in SE Venezuela, on a tributary of the R Caroní; highest waterfall in the world, with a total drop of 980 m/3215 ft; named after the US aviator, Jimmy Angel, who crashed nearby in 1937.

angelfish Any of several small, brightly coloured fish found in shallow waters of warm seas, commonly around coral reefs; deep, flattened body; small mouth, with gill cover bearing a spine; very popular in marine aquaria; also called **butterfly fish**. The name is also used for monkfish. (Family: Chaetodontidae.)

angelica [anje**li**ka] A robust herb growing to 2 m/6 ft or more (*Angelica archangelica*), native from N and E Europe to C Asia; stem hollow; leaves divided into oval leaflets up to 15 cm/6 in, the stalks with an inflated base; flowers small, greenish-white, clustered in large rounded umbels. Candied leaf stalks are used for flavouring. Aromatic oil produced from the roots is used in perfumes and herbal liqueurs (eg Chartreuse). (Family: Umbelliferae.)

Angelico, Fra [anje**li**koh], originally **Guido di Pietro**, monastic name **Giovanni da Fiesole** (c.1400–55) Painter, born in Vicchio, NC Italy. He entered the Dominican monastery of San Domenico at Fiesole, and in 1436 was transferred to Florence where he worked for Cosimo de' Medici. In 1445 he was summoned by the pope to Rome, where he worked until his death. His most important frescoes are in the Florentine convent of S Marco (St Mark), which is now a museum. These aids to contemplation are characterized by pale colours, crisp delineation of form, the use of local landscape as background, and an air of mystical piety. In Rome only the frescoes in the chapel of Pope Nicholas V survive. The ethereal beauty of his angelic figures gave him his new name. He died in Rome, and was officially beatified in 1984.

Angell, Sir Norman [aynjl], originally **Ralph Norman Angell-Lane** (1872–1967) Writer and pacifist, born in Holbeach, Lincolnshire, EC England, UK. He wrote *The Great Illusion* (1910) and *The Great Illusion, 1933* (1933) to prove the economic futility of war even for the winners. He was awarded the Nobel Peace Prize in 1933.

Angelou, Maya [anje**loo**], pseudonym of **Marguerite Ann Johnson** (1928–) Writer, singer, dancer, and African-American activist, born in St Louis, Missouri, USA. She has had a variety of occupations in what she describes as 'a roller-coaster life'. She toured Europe and Africa in the musical *Porgy and Bess*, and in New York City joined the Harlem Writers Guild. In the 1960s she was involved in black struggles, then spent several years in Ghana as editor of *African Review*. Her multi-volume autobiography, commencing with *I Know Why the Caged Bird Sings* (1970), was a critical and popular success. Her later books include *All God's Children Need Travelling Shoes* (1986) and *My Painted House, My Friendly Chicken and Me* (1994). She has published several volumes of verse, including *And Still I Rise* (1987) and *Complete Collected Poems of Maya Angelou* (1995).

angelshark *monkfish*

Angevins [anjevinz] Three ruling families of the mediaeval county (and later duchy) of Anjou in W France. (1) Henry II, founder of the Angevin or Plantagenet dynasty in England, was a descendant of the earliest counts of Anjou. He established the 'Angevin empire' by taking control of Normandy, Anjou, and Maine (1150–1), acquiring Aquitaine (1152), and succeeding Stephen in England (1154). (2) The French crown had annexed Anjou by 1205, and in 1246 Louis IX's brother Charles, future king of Naples and Sicily, became count. (3) The third line was descended from Charles of Valois, brother of Philip IV, who married Charles of Anjou's granddaughter in 1290. This family died out in 1481.

angina [anjiyna] A sudden severe pain or sensation of constriction over the front of the chest which occurs when the oxygen demand of the heart muscle exceeds supply (**angina pectoris**). The pain is increased with exercise, and subsides with rest. It may spread to the jaw and arms (usually the left). It usually results from the narrowing or blockage of one or more of the arteries which supply the heart muscle with blood. It can be relieved by the use of drugs which either dilate the blood vessels or reduce the oxygen demands of the heart by reducing the force and frequency of contractions. Severe cases may be treated with surgery to restore the blood supply to the heart.

angiography [anji**og**rafee] A radiological technique used to demonstrate the pathways and configuration of blood vessels in various parts of the body. A radio-opaque solution is injected into a main arterial trunk, which increases the X-ray contrast between the blood vessel and its surrounding tissues. After the injection, a number of X-ray plates are taken in rapid succession to follow the course of the blood. The technique is used to show narrowing or blockage of blood vessels, such as in coronary heart disease. It can also reveal increased vascularity of specific tissue, as in cancer.

angioplasty *balloon angioplasty*

angiotensin *renin*

Angkor Thom [**ang**kaw(r) **tom**] 13°26N 103°50E. The ancient capital of the Khmer Empire, 240 km/150 mi NW of Phnom Penh, Cambodia. The moated and walled city was built on a square plan, extending over 100 sq km/40 sq mi, and completed in the 12th-c. Abandoned in the 15th-c, it was rediscovered in 1861. **Angkor Wat** is the largest of the temples surrounding the site – linked, richly-sculptured sanctuaries on a massive platform 1000 m/3300 ft square, the work of Suryavarman II (1113–50). Its five sandstone towers in the shape of lotus buds rise 65 m/200 ft.

angle A geometrical figure formed by two straight lines meeting at a point. Angles are measured in revolutions (especially per minute [rpm] or per second [rps] when measuring angular velocity), in right angles, degrees (°), radians (rad), or grad. 1 revolution = 4 right angles = 360° = 2π rad = 400 grad.

anglerfish Any of about 13 families of bizarre shallow to deep-sea fishes which have a dorsal fin spine modified as a lure to attract prey; family Lophiidae includes large bottom-dwelling European species (length up to 1·5 m/5 ft) with broad flattened head, capacious mouth, and narrow tail; also called **goosefish**.

Angles A Germanic people thought to have originated from the S Danish peninsula and neighbouring Schleswig-Holstein. With the Saxons, they formed the bulk of the invaders who, in the two centuries following the Roman withdrawal from Britain (409), conquered and colonized most of what became England. Anglian rulers were apparently dominant by the 8th-c, and the Angles ultimately gave their name to England, its language, and people.

Anglesey [**ang**glsee], Welsh **Sir Fôn** or **Ynys Môn** [**uh**nis mohn] pop (2001e) 66 800; area 715 sq km/276 sq mi. Island unitary authority (from 1996) in NW Wales, UK; separated from Gwynedd by Menai Straits, spanned by two bridges; chief towns, Holyhead, Beaumaris, Amlwch, Llangefni, Menai Bridge; linked to Holy I by an embankment (the Cob); ferry link from Holyhead to Dun Laoghaire and Dublin, Ireland; agriculture, aluminium, sheep rearing, marine engineering, tourism; RAF base at Valley; Ucheldre Centre, Oriel Môn, Beaumaris Castle, Sea Zoo, Plas Newydd.

Anglesey, Henry William Paget, 1st Marquess of [**ang**glsee] (1768–1854) British soldier, born in London, UK. He studied at Oxford, and sat in parliament at intervals between 1790 and 1810. He served in the army with distinction in Flanders (1794), Holland (1799), and the Peninsular War (1808), and for his services as commander of the British cavalry at Waterloo (1815), where he lost a leg, he was made Marquess of Anglesey. In 1828 he was appointed Lord-Lieutenant of Ireland, where he advo-

Angola

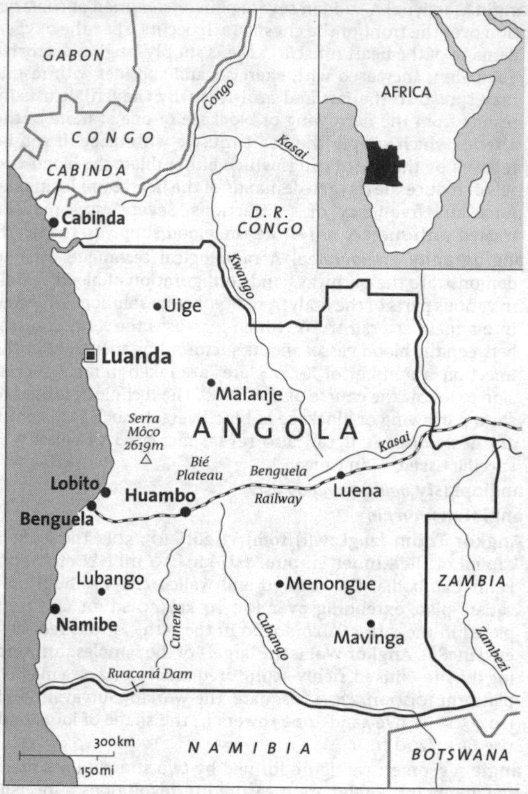

□ International Airport

[anggohla], official name **Republic of Angola**, Port **República de Angola**

Local name Angola

Timezone GMT +1

Area 1 246 700 km²/480 354 sq mi

Population total (2002e) 10 593 000 (excluding more than 400 000 refugees in D.R. of Congo and Zambia)

Status Republic

Date of independence 1975

Capital Luanda

Languages Portuguese (official), Bantu languages, including: Ovimbundu, Kimbundu, Bakongo, Chokwe

Ethnic groups Ovimbundu (37%), Mbundu (22%), Bakongo (13%), Lunda-Tchokwe (5%); also Nganguela, Nyaneka-Humbe, Herero, Ambo, Portuguese

Religions Traditional religions (12%), Roman Catholic (68%), Protestant (20%)

Physical features Located in SW Africa; narrow coastal plain; in S and E the planalto central (central plateau, continuation of great SW African plateau), covers c.60% of the country; in N, highland plateau, mean elevation 1200 m/4000 ft; highest point, Serro Môco 2 619 m/8 592 ft; coastal desert in W; in E, upland escarpments; c.40% of land forested.

Climate tropical plateau climate; at Huambo, on the plateau, average annual rainfall 1450 mm/57 in; rainfall varies greatly from SW to NE (negligible rainfall on SW coastal desert caused by Benguela current); average daily temperatures 24–9°C; temperature much reduced on the coast, which is semi-desert as far N as Luanda.

Currency 1 New Kwanza (kw, kz) = 100 Iweis

Economy Reserves of several minerals; extraction and refining of oil (mainly off the coast of Cabinda Province) provides over 90% of current export earnings; diamond exporter; large producer of honey; principal livestock are cattle, goats, pigs, sheep; agriculture and fishing (mackerel and sardines) industries small; several airfelds and railways.

GDP (2002e) $18·36 bn, per capita $1700

Human Development Index (2002) 0·403

History Became a Portuguese colony in 1482 after exploration; slave trade flourished, causing friction and war (in early 17th-c, c.10 000 slaves were exported from Luanda annually); boundaries formally defined during the Berlin West Africa Congress (1884-5); became an overseas province of Portugal, 1951; Portuguese finally withdrew in 1975, and the People's Republic of Angola achieved full independence; civil war followed independence, involving three internal factions - the Marxist MPLA (Popular Movement for the Liberation of Angola), UNITA (the National Union for the Total Independence of Angola), and the FNLA (National Front for the Liberation of Angola). Cuban combat troops arrived in 1976, at request of MPLA; at the end of 1988, Geneva agreement linked arrangements for independence of Namibia with withdrawal of Cuban troops, and the cessation of South African attacks and support for UNITA; peace agreement in 1991 established a one-party state, governed by a President, Council of Ministers, and National People's Assembly; adopted the name Republic of Angola; first multi-party legislative elections held in 1992. MPLA victory rejected by UNITA led to resumption of conflict in 1993; Lusaka peace protocol, October 1994; withdrawal of UN peace-keeping force (Jan 1999) as fighting resumed between government and UNITA forces; death of UNITA leader Jonas Savimbi, followed by peace agreement, 2002; lifting of UN economic santions against UNITA (Dec, 2002).

Head of State

1975–9 Antonio Agostinho Neto
1979– José Eduardo dos Santos

Head of Government

1992–6 Marcolino José Carlos Moco
1996–9 Fernando José França Van Dúnem
1999–2002 José Eduardo dos Santos
2002– Fernando Da Piedade Dias dos Santos

cated Catholic Emancipation. From 1846 to 1852 he was Master-General of the Ordnance.

Anglican chant *chant*

Anglican Communion A fellowship of some 26 independent provincial or national Churches, several extra-provincial dioceses, and Churches resulting from unions of Anglicans with other Churches, spread throughout the world, but sharing a close ecclesiastical and doctrinal relationship with the Church of England. Most of these Churches are found in the British Commonwealth, and owe their origins to missionary activities of the Church of England in the 19th-c; a major exception is the Episcopal Church in the USA, which was fostered by the Scottish Episcopal Church. Churches from non-Commonwealth countries, such as Brazil, China, and Japan, are also part of the Anglican Communion. The Communion is based on co-operation, since there is no worldwide uniform authority, but every 10 years the Archbishop of Canterbury invites bishops throughout the Anglican Communion to take part in the Lambeth Conference, a consultative body that considers issues of common concern even though it has no decisive policy-making authority. The 1968 Lambeth Conference also set up an Anglican Consultative Council to act during the 10-year intervals. There were over 80 million Anglicans in 2004.

Anglicanism *Church of England*

Anglican–Roman Catholic International Commission *ARCIC*

angling The sport of catching fish, one of the world's most popular pastimes, performed in virtually every country, practised with a rod, line, and hook. Many forms of angling exist: freshwater fishing, fly fishing, game fishing, and deep sea fishing. The oldest fishing club still in existence is the Ellem club in Scotland. Rules governing the time of year when different types of fishing take place are very strict, as are the rules governing the type of, and excessive use of, bait.

Anglo-Burmese Wars Two wars fought largely to advance British trade and the East India Company: the first (1824–6) brought control of Arakan and Tehnasserim; the second (1852–3) led to the occupation of Lower Burma. In 1885 Mandalay was occupied, and in 1886 all Burma was proclaimed a province of British India.

Anglo-Catholicism A movement within the Church of England, the term first appearing in 1838. It stresses the sacramental and credal aspects of Christian faith, and continuity and community with the wider Catholic Church, especially with Roman Catholicism.

Anglo-Irish Agreement A joint agreement allowing the Irish Republic to contribute to policy in Northern Ireland for the first time since 1922, signed (15 Nov 1985) by the British and Irish prime ministers, Margaret Thatcher and Garrett Fitzgerald. It established an intergovernmental conference to discuss political, security, and legal matters affecting Northern Ireland; early meetings focused on border co-operation. Both governments pledged not to change the status of Northern Ireland without the consent of the majority. The Agreement was opposed by the Republic's Opposition party, Fianna Fáil; Unionist leaders withdrew co-operation with ministers and boycotted official bodies. This boycott ended in 1992 when representatives of the main Unionist parties met with the Socialist Democratic and Labour Party, the Alliance Party, and Irish government ministers to discuss the future of talks under the Agreement. The Agreement was instrumental in leading to the 'Downing Street Declaration' of 1993, which argued for self-determination for all the people of Ireland, and also the talks which led to the Good Friday Agreement.

Anglo-Maori Wars A succession of conflicts (1843–7, 1860–70) in which Maori people attempted, unsuccessfully, to resist the occupation of New Zealand by British settlers. Although faced by trained British troops, the Maoris did not suffer a decisive military defeat. The main fighting finished in 1864 after the Kingite Maoris, who had led the resistance, retreated to the C North Island, where the troops could not easily follow them. It is likely that the British learned the art of trench warfare from the Maoris during these conflicts.

Anglo-Saxon *Old English*

Anglo-Saxons A term probably first used to distinguish the Saxons of England from those of the continent; occasionally adopted by the 10th-c English kings for all their subjects, though 'English' was preferred; now commonly employed for the entire Old English people from the incoming of Angles, Saxons, and Jutes in the 5th-c to the Norman Conquest. Among the main themes in Anglo-Saxon history are the emergence of the early kingdoms, their conversion to Christianity, their response to attacks by the Vikings, and their eventual unification into a single realm, England, literally 'land of the Angles'. The Anglo-Saxons left an enduring legacy, including an advanced system of government and a rich economy. One of the main sources of events during the period is the **Anglo-Saxon Chronicle**, first compiled during the reign of Alfred, and then erratically maintained in various locations over the next two centuries (in the case of the Peterborough Chronicle, until 1154).

Angola *p.62*

Angora cat [anggawra] A breed of domestic cat; white long-haired type originated in Turkey (*Angora* is an old name for Ankara); resembles the Persian cat, but with longer body and smaller head; breed not recognized in the UK; name formerly used for all long-haired cats.

Angora goat [anggawra] A breed of domestic goat, originating in Turkey (*Angora* is an old name for Ankara); bred mainly in North America, S Africa, and Australasia for wool; silky hair (length up to 20 cm/8 in), called *mohair*.

angostura [anggostoora] A flavouring agent used in cocktails and some fruit juices, deriving from the bark of a South American tree (*Gallipea aspuria*). It was originally used in medicines.

Angra do Heroísmo [anggra duh eroeezhmu] 38°40N 27°14W, pop (2000e) 11 600. Fortified town and seaport in the Azores; a world heritage site, on S coast of Terceira I; founded, 1464; capital of the Azores until 1832; bishopric; airport; fruit, flax, grain, tobacco, soap, tourism; Sanjoaninas festival (Jun).

Angry Brigade A left-wing group with anarchist sympathies, active in Britain in the 1960s and early 1970s, which took sporadic violent action against representatives of the establishment in the name of the working class. Its leaders were tried and imprisoned for a bomb attack on the secretary of state for employment's home in 1971.

Angry Young Men A term used to describe the authors of some novels and plays of the late 1950s and early 1960s in Britain, who felt a confident contempt for and expressed an energetic rejection of the (apparently) established order. They include Kingsley Amis, John Braine, John Osborne, Alan Sillitoe, and John Wain. The term was also applied to certain characters in their works, notably Jimmy Porter in Osborne's *Look Back in Anger* (1956). Porter, the anti-hero of the play, is the epitome of a young man from a working-class background who had been to university and subsequently found himself alienated from his own social background, while scorning the political and social pretensions of bourgeois society.

Ångström, Anders (Jonas) [angstruhm, ongstroem] (1814–74) Physicist, born in Lögdö, E Sweden. He was keeper of the observatory at Uppsala (1843), and became professor of physics there in 1858. He wrote on heat, magnetism, and especially optics. The *ångstrom* unit, used in crystallography and spectroscopy, is named after him. His son, **Knut Johan Ångström** (1857–1910), was also a noted Uppsala physicist, important for his research on solar radiation.

ångström or **angstrom** [angstruhm] Unit of length common in crystallography or any other subject which studies features of approximately atomic dimensions; symbol Å, named after Anders Ångström; equal to 10^{-10} m; classed as a unit in temporary use with SI units.

Anguilla *p.64*

angular acceleration *acceleration*

angular momentum A vector quantity in rotational motion, equal to the product of moment of inertia with angular velocity; also called the **moment of momentum**; symbol L, units $kg.m^2/s$. The rate of change of angular momentum is called *torque*.

angular velocity *velocity*

angwantibo [anggwantiboh] A West African primitive primate (prosimian); golden brown with pointed face; no tail; first finger reduced to a stump, and second short; grips branches strongly between thumb and remaining fingers; also known as **golden potto**. (*Arctocebus calabarensis*. Family: Lorisidae.)

anhinga *darter*

anhydride [anhiydriyd] (Gk 'without water') In chemistry, often referring to an acid. An inorganic anhydride is usually a non-metal oxide. Organic anhydrides are usually condensation products of two molecules; for example, acetic acid (CH_3COOH) gives acetic anhydride (CH_3–CO–O–CO–CH_3).

anil [anil] A tropical American shrub (*Indigofera anil*), but cultivated in the Old and New World as a source of the blue dye indigo; also called **indigo plant**. (Family: Leguminosae.)

aniline [anileen] $C_6H_5NH_2$, **phenylamine**, or (IUPAC) **aminobenzene**, boiling point 184°C. A liquid with an unpleasant smell, a weaker base than ammonia. It is the starting material for many dyestuffs, known as *aniline dyes*.

Anguilla

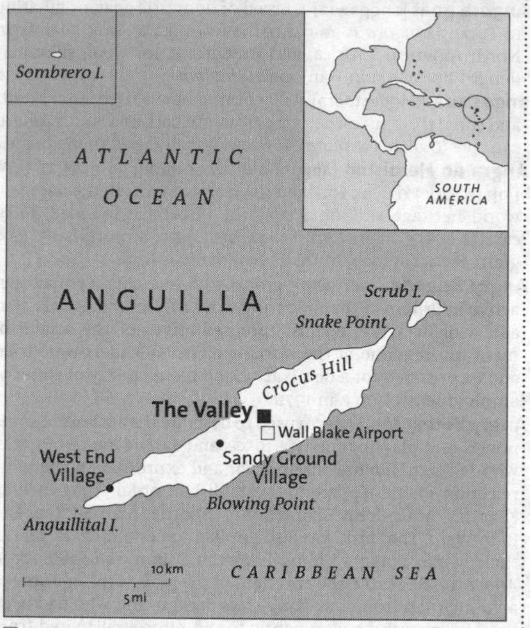

☐ International Airport

[angwila] (UK British Overseas Territory)

Timezone GMT −4

Area 155 km²/60 sq mi

Population total (2000e) 11 900

Capital The Valley

Physical features Most northerly of the Leeward Is, E Caribbean; also includes Sombrero I and several other offshore islets and cays; low-lying coral island, covered in low scrub and fringed with white coral-sand beaches.

Climate Tropical climate; average annual temperature ranges from 24–30°C; low and erratic annual rainfall, 550–1250 mm/22–50 in; hurricane season (Jul–Oct).

Currency 1 East Caribbean Dollar (EC$) = 100 cents

Economy Tourism, fishing, peas, corn, sweet potatoes, salt, boatbuilding.

GDP (2001e) $104 mn, per capita $8600

History Colonized by English settlers from St Kitts in 1650; ultimately incorporated in the colony of St Kitts-Nevis-Anguilla; separated, 1980; Governor appointed by the British sovereign; Legislative Assembly.

animal A living organism; one of the main kingdoms of biological classification, **Animalia**, containing all vertebrates and invertebrates. The term *animal* is sometimes used only for four-legged creatures (mammals, reptiles, and amphibians), but correctly fish and birds are also animals, as are insects, spiders, crabs, snails, worms, starfish, sponges, corals, jellyfish, and many other groups. All animals obtain their nourishment by eating other living organisms or the remains of living organisms, and most can respond quickly to changes in their surroundings by moving part of their body or their entire body.

animal husbandry The keeping of domesticated animals for food, fibre, skins, or to pull loads. Domestication started in the Middle East c.9000 BC with sheep; pigs were domesticated c.6000 BC and cattle c.5500 BC. With the exception of organic farming, modern animal husbandry practices are highly intensive. Pigs and poultry are often raised on factory farms where food intake, temperature, light, and other conditions are controlled to maximize the commercial profitability of each animal unit. A more scientific understanding of the nutritional requirements of animals has made it possible to develop feedstuffs that provide an enhanced, hormone-rich diet throughout the year. Animals are routinely vaccinated and given preventative drugs, including antibiotics, to protect them from disease. These practices have led to steep increases in food production and in some cases to the creation of large surpluses at a regional level. The major concern of animal husbandry today is the extent to which production can be maintained and enhanced. The trend has been to increase animal products by genetic selection (generally through artificial insemination) and genetic engineering, but the latter has met with strong opposition from many consumers.

Animal Protection Society of America *RSPCA*

animal protein factor An essential growth factor found exclusively in animal products, now known to be vitamin B_{12}.

animism A belief in spiritual beings thought capable of influencing human events, based on the idea that animals, plants, and even inanimate objects have souls like humans. The 19th-c anthropologist Edward Tylor (1832–1917) regarded it as the earliest form of religion, a view not accepted by modern anthropologists.

anion [aniyon] A negatively charged atom or group of atoms, such as Cl^- (chloride) or SO_4^{2-} (sulphate). Anions are so called because they migrate towards the anode in an electrochemical cell.

anisotropic *isotropic*

Aniston, Jennifer [aniston] (1969–) Actress, born in Sherman Oaks, Los Angeles, California, USA. She trained at the High School for the Performing Arts in New York City, worked off-Broadway, then went to Hollywood, where she eventually achieved success through her role as Rachel Green in the acclaimed television series *Friends* (1994–2004). Roles in feature films include *Leprechaun* (1993), *She's the One* (1996), *The Object of My Affection* (1998), and *Bruce Almighty* (2003).

Anjou [ãzhoo] Former province in the Paris Basin of NW France, now occupying the department of Maine-et-Loire and small parts of Indre-et-Loire, Mayenne, and Sarthe; former capital, Angers; lost provincial status in 1790; Henry II of England, first of the Plantagenets (or Angevins) was son of Geoffrey Plantagenet, Count of Anjou; Anjou also gave a line of kings to Sicily and Naples.

Ankara [angkara], ancient **Ancyra**, European **Angora** 39°55N 32°50E, pop (2000e) 3 082 000. Capital city of Ankara province and of Turkey, on a tributary of the R Ova; second largest city in Turkey; formerly an important location on the caravan route from Istanbul to the E; conquered by Alexander the Great, 4th-c BC; part of Roman and Byzantine Empires; under Turkish rule, 11th-c; government transferred here from Istanbul, 1923; airport; railway; five universities (1206, 1946, 1956, 1982, 1984); textiles, mohair, leather, cement.

ankh [ank] A cross with a loop for its upper vertical arm. In ancient Egypt it was an emblem of life.

ankle The region of the lower limb between the calf and the foot; specifically, the joint between the tibia and fibula and the talus (one of the tarsal bones). Movement at the joint is important during the stance phase of walking, particularly in ensuring a smooth and controlled contact of the foot with the ground.

ankylosaur [angkilosaw(r)] A small four-legged dinosaur, heavily armoured with rectangular bony plates along body and tail; head small, teeth reduced or absent; fed on vegetation; known from the Cretaceous period of North America. (Order: Ornithischia.)

ankylosing spondylitis [angkilohzing spondiliytis] A progressive inflammatory disease, mainly affecting young men, that attacks the joints of the spine leading to stiffness and pain in the back. Ocasionally other joints such as the hip and shoulder are affected. Some cases are associated with inflammation of the eyes, lungs, and heart valves. Its cause is unknown, but a very high proportion of cases have human leucocyte antigen (HLA) B27.

An Lushan [an looshan], also spelled **An Lu-shan** (?–757) Chinese general under the Tang dynasty in China (618–907), of Turkish origin. He overthrew the crown, and established the short-lived Yan dynasty (755–7). He was patronized by Yang Guifei, mistress to Emperor Xuanzong (ruled 712–55), who adopted him as her son. Controlling 160 000 troops as commandant of three NE regions, he revolted in 755, capturing Luoyang and Changan (Xian). The emperor fled and Yang was executed. An Lushan made himself emperor on Xuanzong's abdication (755), but was murdered by his own son (757).

Anna Comnena [komnayna] (1083–1148) Byzantine princess and historian, the daughter of the Emperor Alexius I Comnenus. In 1097 she married Nicephorus Bryennius, for whom she tried in vain to gain the imperial crown after her father's death in 1118. She took up literature, and after her husband's death (1137) retired to a convent where she wrote the *Alexiad*, a notable account in 15 books of Byzantine history and society for the period 1069–1118.

Annan, Kofi (Atta) (1938–) UN secretary-general (from 1997), born in Kumasi, SC Ghana. He studied in the USA and Switzerland, joining the UN in 1962, and held posts in the High Commission for Refugees and the World Health Organization. After joining the UN secretariat, he became (1993) under-secretary-general for peacekeeping operations. He replaced Boutros Boutros-Ghali to become the first secretary-general from sub-Saharan Africa. Jointly with the UN, he was awarded the 2001 Nobel Peace Prize.

Annapolis [anapolis] 38°59N 76°30W, pop (2000e) 35 800. Capital of state in Anne Arundel Co, C Maryland, USA; port on the S bank of the Severn R; named after Princess (later Queen) Anne, 1695; US capital, 1783–4; railway; business and shipping centre; US Naval Academy (1845); tourist centre; site of the statehouse where the treaty ending the American War of Independence was ratified (1784).

Annapolis Convention (1786) In the American Revolution, a gathering at Annapolis, MD, of delegates from five states to discuss commercial problems. The main result was a call for a meeting the following year to consider changes in the Articles of Confederation. That meeting wrote the present Federal Constitution.

Annapurna, Mount [anapoorna] Mountain massif in the C Himalayas, Nepal; length c.56 km/35 mi; includes Annapurna I (8091 m/26 545 ft), Annapurna II (7937 m/26 040 ft), Annapurna III (7556 m/24 790 ft), Annapurna IV (7525 m/24 688 ft), and several other peaks over 6000 m/20 000 ft; part of the Pokhara trekking region; Annapurna I first climbed in 1950 by Maurice Herzog's French expedition.

Annas [anas] (1st-c) Israel's high priest, appointed in AD 6 and deposed by the Romans in 15, but still described later by this title in the New Testament. He apparently questioned Jesus after his arrest (*John* 18) and Peter after his detention (*Acts* 4). His other activities are described in the works of Flavius Josephus.

Anne (1665–1714) Queen of Great Britain and Ireland (1702–14), born in London, UK, the second daughter of James II (then Duke of York) and his first wife, Anne Hyde. In 1672 her father became a Catholic, but Anne was brought up as a staunch Protestant. In 1683 she married Prince George of Denmark (1653–1708), bearing him 17 children. Probably only six were born alive and only one survived infancy – William, Duke of Gloucester, who died in 1700 at the age of 12. For much of her life she was greatly influenced by her close friend and confidante, Sarah Churchill, the future Duchess of Marlborough. In 1688, when her father James II was overthrown, she supported the accession of her sister Mary and her brother-in-law William, and in 1701, after the death of her own son, signed the Act of Settlement designating the Hanoverian descendants of James I as her successors. Her reign saw the union of the parliaments of Scotland and England (1707), and the War of the Spanish Succession (1701–13). She finally broke with the Marlboroughs in 1710–11, when Sarah was supplanted by a new favourite, Sarah's cousin, Mrs Abigail Masham, and the Whigs were replaced by a Tory administration. She was the last Stuart monarch.

Anne, St (fl.1st-c BC–1st-c AD) Wife of **St Joachim**, and mother of the Virgin Mary, first mentioned in the *Protevangelium* of James, in the 2nd-c. She is the patron saint of carpenters. Feast day 26 July.

Anne (Elizabeth Alice Louise), Princess (1950–) British Princess Royal, the only daughter of Queen Elizabeth II and Prince Philip, born in London, UK. In 1973 she married Lieutenant (now Captain) Mark Phillips of the Queen's Dragoon Guards, but they were divorced in 1992; their children are: **Peter Mark Andrew** (1977–) and **Zara Anne Elizabeth** (1981–). She married **Timothy Laurence** (1955–) in 1992. An accomplished horsewoman, she has ridden in the British Equestrian Team, and was European cross-country champion (1972). She is a keen supporter of charities and overseas relief work; as president of Save the Children Fund she has travelled widely promoting its activities.

Anne Boleyn *Boleyn, Anne*

Anne of Austria (1601–66) Queen of France, born in Valladolid, NWC Spain, the eldest daughter of Philip III of Spain and wife of Louis XIII of France, whom she married in 1615. The marriage was unhappy, and much of it was spent in virtual separation, due to the influence of the king's chief minister Cardinal Richelieu. In 1638, however, they had their first son, Louis, who succeeded his father in 1643 as Louis XIV. Anne was appointed regent for the boy king (1643–51), and wielded power with Cardinal Mazarin as prime minister. After Mazarin's death in 1661, she remained at court, though often visiting the convent of Val de Grâce.

Anne of Bohemia (1366–94) Queen of England, the first wife of Richard II. The daughter of Emperor Charles IV (reigned 1355–78), she married Richard in 1382.

Anne of Cleves (1515–57) German princess and queen consort of England, the fourth wife of Henry VIII, the daughter of John, Duke of Cleves, a noted champion of Protestantism in Germany. She was selected for purely political reasons after the death of Jane Seymour, and was married to Henry in 1540, who found her appearance disappointing. The marriage was annulled by parliament six months later.

Anne of Denmark (1574–1619) Danish princess, and queen of Scotland and England. The daughter of King Frederik II of Denmark (reigned 1559–88), in 1589 she married James VI of Scotland, the future James I of England. She was a lavish patron of the arts and architecture, and appeared in dramatic roles in court masques by Ben Jonson.

annealing The relief of internal stresses in metals after heat treatment or working (hammering, forging, or drawing), or in glass after moulding or blowing. It is effected by maintaining the object at a moderate temperature to allow for molecular or crystalline re-arrangement before allowing it slowly to cool. This improves its properties, or restores its original properties.

Annecy [ansee] 45°55N 6°08E, pop (2000e) 53 500. Industrial town and capital of Haute-Savoie department, E France, in the foothills of the French Alps, on N shore of Lac d'Annecy; railway; bishopric; textiles, watches, paper, bearings; popular tourist centre; on route to Little St Bernard and Mt Cenis passes.

annelid [anelid] A ringed worm; a bilaterally symmetrical worm of phylum Annelida; body divided into cylindrical rings (segments) containing serially arranged organs; body cavity (*coelom*) present; head typically well defined; includes earthworms, bristleworms, and leeches.

Annigoni, Pietro [anigohnee] (1910–88) Painter, born in Milan, N Italy. He was one of the few 20th-c artists to put into practice the technical methods of the old masters. His most usual medium was tempera, although there are frescoes by him in the Convent of S Marco at Florence (executed in 1937). His Renaissance manner is shown at its best in his portraits, such as those of Queen Elizabeth II (1955, 1970) and President Kennedy (1961).

annual A plant which germinates, flowers, sets seed, and dies within one year. The definition is not strict: in mild weather some annuals may germinate late in the season, overwinter as seedlings or young plants, and complete their life-cycle in the next year.

annual ring One of the concentric rings visible when the stem or root of a woody plant is cut across. Each ring is formed by two bands of xylem vessels: large diameter vessels produced early in the year form pale springwood; smaller vessels formed late in the year form darker summerwood. Usually one ring marks one year's growth, providing a means of calculating the age of trees. If there is more than one growing period in the year, there are correspondingly more rings, called *false annual rings*.

annuity [anyooitee] A financial contract by which an insurance company agrees, in exchange for premiums which may be recurrent or lump-sum, to provide a regular income for life. The recipient may be one person, normally retired, or it is possible to contract for full or reduced payments to surviving spouses or other dependents. The payments may be fixed in money terms, or index-linked to a price index. It is also now possible to buy 'with profits' annuities. An annuity enables the recipients to spend their capital as well as the income on it, without the risk of running out of funds before they die.

annulment **1** A judicial declaration of nullity of marriage. A null marriage is one that was never valid (ie it is *void*), for example because it involved parties within the prohibited degrees of affinity or consanguinity, or because it became invalid (*voidable*) due to the behaviour of one of the parties (eg an inability or refusal to consummate the marriage).
2 The term also refers to an incorrectly made bankruptcy order, or a national law set aside by the Court of Justice of the European Communities.

Annunciation The angel Gabriel's foretelling to Mary of the birth of Jesus and of the promise of his greatness (*Luke* 1.26–38). Many of the features of this account are parallel to the annunciation of the birth of John the Baptist (*Luke* 1.5–25). The feast day (25 Mar) is also known as **Lady Day**.

Annunzio, Gabriele d' *d'Annunzio, Gabriele*

anoa [anoha] A rare member of the cattle family, from Sulawesi; height, c.80 cm/30 in; straight backward-pointing horns; inhabits forests; young have thick dark coats; two species: **lowland anoa** (*Bubalus depressicornis*) and **mountain anoa** (*Bubalus quarlesi*); also known as **dwarf buffalo**, **wood ox**, **sapi-utan**, or **sapi-outan**.

anode In electrolysis and gas discharge tubes, the positive electrode from which electrons leave the cell or tube. In a battery, the anode is the negative terminal by which electrons leave the battery. An anion is a negative ion that moves towards the positive anode in electrolysis.

anodizing A metal protection process, usually applied to aluminium or magnesium. The object to be coated is made the anode in an electrolytic bath which produces a thin but dense protective oxide layer. Such a coating can also be made to take dyes, and so produce a decorative effect.

anointing the sick The ritual application of oil performed in cases of (usually) serious illness or preparation for death. In the Roman Catholic and Orthodox Churches, which claim scriptural authority for the practice, it is recognized as a sacrament to be performed by a priest. It was formerly sometimes called **extreme unction**.

anole [anohlee] An iguana found from SE USA to N South America (including the West Indies); can change colour, but this is slow and controlled by chemical changes in the blood; some species signal with a brightly coloured expandable blade of skin under the throat. (Genus: *Anolis*, several species.)

anomia [anohmia] A clinical language disability in which the chief problem is recalling the names of things. It is often found as a symptom of aphasia. While typically involving nouns, the word-finding difficulties can relate to any part of speech.

anomie [anohmee] A personal or wider social condition in which individuals or society at large no longer identify with or feel guided by customary norms and values. In individuals, the concept embraces extreme despair, and a sense of alienation from society, which may lead to suicide. Society at large is said to be 'anomic' when its members no longer agree on a fundamental normative and moral order. The term was introduced by Durkheim in 1897. He considered the condition to be one cause of suicide, indicating the importance of social factors to psychiatric illness.

Anopheles [anofileez] The malaria mosquito, found in all major zoogeographical regions. The adult females transmit a malaria-causing agent when taking blood from vertebrates. The males feed on nectar and plant fluids. The larvae are aquatic, feeding at the water surface using short feeding bristles. (Order: Diptera. Family: Culicidae.)

anorexia nervosa [anoreksia nervohsa] A psychological illness which mainly affects young women, characterized by significant weight loss (usually deliberately induced), an unrealistic fear of being overweight, and a loss of normal menstrual functioning. There is a distortion of body image, and sufferers are frequently hyperactive, have faddish eating habits, and some have depressed mood. The term was first used by the English physician Sir William Gull (1816–90) in 1874, but there are clear historical accounts of a similar condition dating back centuries, indicating that this is not a symptom of modern living. Current views hold that there are both biological and psychological causes, and that early treatment is likely to produce a better outcome than any delay, which may lead to chronicity of the illness and a fatal outcome in a proportion of sufferers.

Anouilh, Jean (Marie Lucien Pierre) [onwee] (1910–87) Playwright, born in Bordeaux, SW France, of French and Basque parentage. His first play, *L'Hermine* (1931), was not a success; but his steady output soon earned him recognition as one of the leading playwrights of the contemporary theatre. He was influenced by the Neoclassical fashion inspired by Giraudoux. His many plays include *Le Voyageur sans bagage* (1938, trans Traveller Without Luggage), *Le Bal des voleurs* (1938, Thieves' Carnival), *La Sauvage* (1938), *L'Invitation au château* (1948) (adapted by Christopher Fry as *Ring Round the Moon*, 1950), *L'Alouette* (1953, The Lark), *Becket* (1959), and *La Culotte* (1978, The Trousers).

Anoura *Anura*

Anquetil, Jacques [ãketeel] (1934–87) Racing cyclist, born in Mont-Saint-Aignan, Normandy, NW France. He was the first man to win the Tour de France five times (1957, 1961–4). He also won the Tour of Italy in 1960 and 1964 and the Tour of Spain in 1963. An outstanding time-trialist, he won the Grand Prix des Nations a record nine times between 1953 and 1965. He retired in 1969.

Anschluss [anshlus] (Ger 'connection') The concept of union between Austria and Germany, prohibited by the Treaty of Versailles (1919), but with some support in both countries after the collapse of the Habsburg Empire and Austria's diminished status. Hitler, himself an Austrian, pursued the idea once in power. In 1938, after the resignation of Austrian Chancellor Schuschnigg, and under the threat of military force, he brought Austria into Germany as the province of Ostmark. The union of Austria and Germany was formally proclaimed on 13 March 1938. In 1943, the Moscow Declaration of the USA, Britain, and the Soviet Union annulled the Anschluss, recognizing Austria's right to independence; an independent government was set up at the end of World War 2.

Anselm, St (1033–1109) Scholastic philosopher and clergyman, born in Aosta, NW Italy. He left Italy in 1056 and settled at the Benedictine abbey of Bec in Normandy. He moved to England to succeed Lanfranc as Archbishop of Canterbury in 1093. His strong principles brought him into conflict both with William II and Henry I, and he was temporarily exiled by each of them. Much influenced by Augustine he sought 'necessary reasons' for religious beliefs, notably the famous ontological argument for the existence of God. He may have been canonized as early as 1163; feast day 21 April.

Ansermet, Ernest (Alexandre) [ansermay] (1883–1969) Conductor and musical theorist, born in Vevey, SW Switzerland. He studied at Lausanne, and gave up teaching mathematics in 1910 to devote his time to music. He was conductor of the Montreux Kursaal in 1912 and of Diaghilev's Russian Ballet (1915–23). In 1918 he founded the Orchestre de la Suisse Romande, whose conductor he remained till 1967. His compositions include a symphonic poem, piano pieces, and songs.

Ansgar or **Anskar, St,** Ger **St Scharies**, known as **the Apostle of the North** (801–65) Frankish clergyman and missionary to Scandinavia, born in Picardy, N France. He became a Benedictine monk, and in 826 he was sent to preach the Gospel in Denmark. In 829 he was allowed to build the first church in Sweden. Consecrated archbishop of the newly founded archdiocese of Hamburg in 832, he was named as papal legate to all the Northern peoples. He is the patron saint of Scandinavia. Feast day 3 February.

Anshan or **An-shan** 41°05N 122°58E, pop (2000e) 1 608 000, administrative region 2 949 000. City in Liaoning province, NE China; organized mining and smelting began here c.100 BC; railway; site of China's largest iron and steel complex, agricultural machinery, construction materials, chemicals, textiles, porcelain, electrical appliances; Qianlian Shan (Thousand Lotuses Hill), 10th-c Buddhist hermitage; Eryijiu (19 Feb) Park; c.10 km/6 mi SE, Tanggangzi hot springs park.

ant A social insect, characterized by a waist of 1–2 narrow segments, forming perennial colonies in nests made in wood, soil, plant cavities, or other constructions. The nest contains one or more fertile queens, many wingless, sterile workers, and winged males that fertilize queens during mass nuptial flights. Most ants scavenge animal remains; some are predators; others feed on fungi, seeds, or honeydew. (Order: Hymenoptera. Family: Formicidae, c.14 000 species.)

Antananarivo [antananareevoh], formerly **Tananarive** or **Tananarivo** (to 1975) 18°52S 47°30E, pop (2000e) 1 076 000. Capital of Madagascar, on a ridge in the EC part of the island; altitude c.1350 m/4400 ft; divided into upper and lower towns; birthplace of François Bayle; airport; railway; university (1955); textiles, tobacco, leather, food processing; two cathedrals, Queen's palace, Ambohitsorahitra palace, museum of art and archaeology, Zoma market, casinos, Mohamasina sports stadium and racecourses.

Antarctica *see panel*

Antarctic Circle Imaginary line on the surface of the Earth at 66°30S, marking the southernmost point at which the Sun can be seen during the summer solstice, and the northernmost point at which the midnight Sun can be seen in S polar regions.

Antarctic Ocean The S regions of the Atlantic, Indian, and Pacific Oceans surrounding Antarctica; narrowest point the Drake Passage between South America and the Antarctic Peninsula (1110 km/690 mi).

Antares [antahreez] *Scorpius*

ant bear *aardvark*

antbird A forest-dwelling bird native to the New World tropics; eats insects, spiders, lizards, frogs; follows army ants, feeding on animals they disturb; includes **antpittas**, **antthrushes**, **antwrens**, **antvireos**, **antshrikes**, and **gnateaters**. (Family: Formicariidae, 236 species.)

anteater A mammal, native to Central and South America, which eats ants and termites; an edentate group, comprising four species: **giant anteaters** (inhabiting grassland), **northern** and **southern tamanduas** (grassland or forest), and **silky anteaters** (forest); numbats are also known as *banded anteaters*, and pangolins as *scaly anteaters*. (Family: Myrmecophagidae.)

antelope A hoofed mammal, found mainly in Africa; classified as gazelles (tribe: Antilopini), four-horned antelopes (tribe: Boselaphini), spiral-horned antelopes (tribe: Strepsicerotini), dwarf (or pygmy) antelopes (tribe: Neotragini), grazing antelopes (subfamily: Hippotraginae, including horse-like ante-

Antarctica

S Polar continent, area nearly 15·5 million sq km/6 million sq mi; surrounded by ice-filled ring of ocean waters containing scattered island groups; mainly S of 65°S, almost entirely within the Antarctic Circle; c.22 400 km/14 000 mi coastline, mainly of high ice cliffs; indented by Ross and Weddell Seas; divided into Greater and Lesser Antarctica, separated by the Transantarctic Mts, highest point 4897 m/16 066 ft at Vinson Massif; no permanent population; no flowering plants, grasses, large land mammals; species of algae, moss, lichen, and sea plankton provide food for fish, birds, whales, and seals; average depth of surface ice sheet 1500 m/5000 ft, overlying rock; inland ice moves slowly towards the periphery, pushing long tongues into the sea and creating shelf ice over large areas; drift ice develops along the whole coastline; many icebergs in adjacent waters, the largest of the tabular type (10–60 m/30–200 ft high); movement of pack ice varies widely in different longitudes; outward blowing winds prevail, often of hurricane force; blizzards common, especially in autumn and winter; lowest temperature on Earth (−88·3°C) recorded at Vostok Station; major scientific explorations since first winter base established in 1899 by Borchgevrink; during International Geophysical Year (1957–8) 12 countries maintained 65 bases in Antarctica; Antarctic Treaty signed by these nations in 1959, providing for international co-operation in scientific research, and prohibiting military operations, nuclear explosions, and disposal of radioactive waste; 50-year ban on mining and mineral extraction, 1991; territorial claims made by the UK (British Antarctic Territory), Norway (Dronning Maud Land), France (Terre Adélie), Australia (Enderby Land, Wilkes Land, George V Coast, part of Oates Coast), New Zealand (160°E to 150°W), Chile (90°W to 53°W), and Argentina (74°W to 25°W); South Pole first reached by Amundsen in 1911; major iceberg losses in Antarctic Peninsula, through global warming, 1987, 1995, 1998, 2000, 2002.

lopes of the tribe Hippotragini, and ox-antelopes of the tribe Alcelaphini), pronghorns (subfamily: Antilocaprinae), duikers (subfamily: Cephalophinae), and goat antelopes (subfamily: Caprinae, which includes goats and sheep). (Family: Bovidae, 116 species.)

antelope goat *Rocky Mountain goat*

antenatal diagnosis *prenatal diagnosis*

antenna (biology) One of a pair of specialized sensory appendages on the head of an invertebrate animal; insects typically have one pair, crustaceans two pairs; varies in shape and size: long and thin in shrimps, feather-like in moths, club-shaped in weevils.

antenna (technology) The component of a radio or television system by which electromagnetic signals are transmitted or received; also known as the **aerial**. In high-frequency practice, additional elements termed *reflectors* and *directors* are included to increase directional efficiency.

Antenor [antaynaw(r)] (6th-c BC) Athenian sculptor, known to have executed bronze statues of 'Harmodius' and 'Aristogiton', and a statue of a kore (a freestanding figure of a maiden) in the Acropolis.

Antheil, George [antiyl] (1900–59) Composer, born in Trenton, New Jersey, USA. He studied in New York City under Ernest Bloch, spending some years in Europe as a professional pianist before becoming known as the composer of the *Jazz Symphony* (1925), the *Ballet Mécanique* (1926), and the opera *Transatlantic* (1930). The sensation caused by the ballet, written for 10 pianos and a variety of eccentric percussion instruments, overshadowed his more traditional later works, which include five symphonies, concertos, operas, and chamber music.

anthelmintics [anthelmintiks] Drugs which paralyse or kill parasitic worms (*helminths*), such as ringworms, tapeworms, and schistosomes. Ancient treatment included antimony compounds and absinthium (wormwood), the leaves and flowers of *Artemesia absinthium*. Galen used aspidium extract of the male fern (*Dryopteris felixmas*) for tapeworms. Many of these treatments were used until quite recently. They are now mostly replaced by safer, more effective drugs such as mebendazole and piperazine.

anthem A sacred vocal composition to an English text, often from the Book of Psalms. 16th-c composers, including Byrd and Tallis, wrote numerous examples, but the anthem was not included in the rubric of the Anglican liturgy until 1662. Purcell excelled in the genre, and also in the instrumentally-accompanied anthem which flourished after the Restoration. The notion later developed a secular sense, referring to a song of praise composed in honour of someone or something, as in the case of **national anthems**.

anther *stamen*

Anthony, St *Antony, St; Antony of Padua*

Anthony, Susan B(rownell) (1820–1906) Social reformer and women's suffrage leader, born in Adams, Massachusetts, USA. Early active in temperance and anti-slavery movements, she became the champion of women's rights in 1854. In 1869, with Elizabeth Cady Stanton, she founded the National American Woman Suffrage Association, becoming its president in 1892. She also organized the International Council of Women (1888) and the International Woman Suffrage Alliance in Berlin (1904).

Anthony Island A provincial park in the Queen Charlotte Is (Haida *G'waii*) off the coast of British Columbia, Canada; a world heritage site. For 2000 years the island was inhabited by the Haida nation. Although it was abandoned in the late 19th-c, their village with its longhouses and totem poles has been preserved.

anthracene [anthraseen] $C_{14}H_{10}$, melting point 216°C. A colourless, cancer-causing, aromatic compound isolated from coal tar. Its blue fluorescence is used in scintillation counters to detect β-particles. Oxidized to **anthraquinone**, it is the raw material for the *alizarin* series of dyestuffs.

anthracite A hard and lustrous variety of coal, containing more than 90% carbon. It is the highest grade of coal, and burns with a very hot, virtually smokeless flame.

anthrax A disease resulting from infection with *Bacillus anthracis*. It predominantly affects animals, but may be contracted by humans in contact with contaminated wool and leather, or pastures used by infected animals, where bacterial spores can remain active for years. There are localized skin lesions which enlarge, ulcerate, and become black ('malignant pustules'). Blood poisoning, pneumonia, and death may occur. There are three types of anthrax, depending on where the infectious spore has arrived on the patient; cutaneous anthrax, is the least serious of the three, intestinal anthrax, caused by the consumption of contaminated meat, and respiratory anthrax, which happens when spores are breathed in by the patient and lodge in the lung. Once anthrax spores have lodged in the lung and caused an infection, nine out of 10 patients die. However, because the disease is not contagious, only those directly exposed to the spores have any chance of falling ill. In October 2001, powdered anthrax spores sent through the post were used in a terrorist attack against US government and media institutions, causing five deaths, the treatment of thousands of possible contacts and locations, much disruption of the postal service, and worldwide concern.

anthropic principle A suggestion, due originally to Fred Hoyle in the 1950s, that humans exist because physical laws governing the universe exhibit special features. For example, if gravitation were stronger relative to electromagnetism than it actually is, stars such as our Sun would burn out too quickly for life to evolve nearby. If the strong nuclear force were slightly weaker relative to electromagnetism, the only stable element would be hydrogen. Some propound the idea of multiple universes which may or may not be stable. Others hold a stronger version of the principle, that a direct link exists between human existence and the actual form of the laws of nature. The anthropic principle is difficult to reconcile with unified theories in physics, which attempt a complete specification of the laws of nature.

Anthropoidea [anthropoydia] A group of primates comprising monkeys and apes; face usually flat; ears small; fingers and toes with nails, not claws; live in complex social groups; also known as **anthropoid apes** (though this term is sometimes used only for apes).

anthropological linguistics The study of language variation and use in relation to the cultural patterns and beliefs of speech communities. It frequently examines linguistic evidence for allegiance to religious, occupational, or kinship groups.

anthropology The scientific study of human beings, traditionally identified as a 'four-field' discipline, encompassing **archaeology**, **social** and **cultural anthropology**, **biological anthropology**, and even **linguistics**. The primary concern of archaeologists is 'digging up history' – recovering and documenting the material remains of past communities. Cultural and social anthropologists study particular living societies, and attempt through comparison to establish the range of variation in human, social, and cultural institutions, and the reasons for these differences. Physical anthropologists study local biological adaptations and human evolutionary history. The fourth field, linguistics, the study of language, is now generally regarded as a separate speciality. Many specialists believe that even the three core disciplines of anthropology are no longer linked in a single scientific enterprise; those who defend the traditional disciplinary range of the subject tend to be concerned above all with questions of human adaptation. Anthropologists are commonly drawn into development projects in Third World countries, to advise on local social conditions. Anthropological expertise has also been applied in the USA (and to some extent elsewhere) in dealing with problems of multi-ethnic communities, nowadays particularly with regard to indigenous rights, medicine, and education. Such developments fall under the heading of **applied anthropology**.

anthropometry The comparative study of the dimensions of the human body and their change with time. The main dimensions examined include weight, height, skinfold thickness, mid-arm circumference, relative limb lengths, and waist-to-hip ratios. Standard charts exist to allow a comparison of an observed anthropometric value with the range of normality within a group (eg the growth of a child). The study also sheds light on human evolution, nutrition, and climatic adaptability, and influences the design of many products, such as clothes, car seats, and space capsules.

anthropomorphism The application to God or gods of human characteristics, such as a body (as in Greek mythology), or the mental, psychological, or spiritual qualities of human beings. It is often used to indicate insufficient appreciation of transcendence and mystery of the divine.

anthroposophy An esoteric system of belief developed by Rudolf Steiner, asserting that the key to understanding the universe lies in new modes of human spiritual development and apprehension.

anti-aircraft gun (AA-gun) A gun firing a shell at high velocity at a high angle designed to shoot down aircraft. AA-guns (sometimes known as 'flak' from the German expression, *Fliegerabwehrkanone*) began to be supplanted by missiles at the end of World War 2. On the modern battlefield, radar-guided 'Triple A' (standing for **Anti-Aircraft Artillery**) has an important role in providing low-level, close-in defence against hostile aircraft, helicopters, and missiles.

anti-anxiety drugs *benzodiazepines*

anti-art An imprecise term sometimes referring to Dada, or to any movement which debunks traditional notions of art, or seeks to undermine its values.

antiballistic missile (ABM) A missile capable of destroying hostile ballistic missiles or their payloads in flight at short, medium, or long ranges inside or outside the atmosphere. Their development was restricted by the US–Soviet ABM Treaty of 1972.

Antibes [ãteeb], ancient **Antipolis** 43°35N 7°07E, pop (2000e) 73 900. Fishing port and fashionable resort on the Riviera, in Alpes-Maritimes department, SE France; facing Nice across a long bay; best known for its luxurious villas and hotels sheltered by the pines of Cap d'Antibes; 3 km/1¾ mi W, Napoleon landed with 1000 men on his return from Elba in 1815; railway; perfumes, flowers, olives, fruit, chocolates; Roman remains; museums, including the Musée Picasso.

antibiotics Substances derived from one micro-organism which can selectively destroy other (infectious) organisms without harming the host. The antibiotic effect has been known for at least 2500 years: the Chinese applied mouldy soybean curd to boils and similar infections. Pasteur recorded that anthrax bacilli grew rapidly in sterile (but not non-sterile) urine (1877). The development of penicillin (1941) was the start of the era of safe and effective antibiotics. Many new antibiotics have since been discovered (over 100), each with a slightly different range of activities. Several are now synthesized. Resistance to antibiotics caused by uncontrolled use represents a serious medical hazard.

antibodies Proteins which help protect against disease-causing micro-organisms (bacteria, viruses, parasites), present mainly in the gamma globulin fraction of serum; also known as **immunoglobulins**. Antibody production is carried out by *B lymphocytes*, and may be regulated by *helper T* and *suppressor T lymphocytes*. The first exposure of the body to a foreign cell or molecule (an *antigen*) produces an immune response which is directed specifically against the antigen that triggered it. Antibodies are produced which eliminate the antigens by a number of mechanisms. Subsequent exposure of the body to the same antigen results in a more rapid and larger immune response. This state of heightened responsiveness is known as a state of *immunity*.

Antichrist A notion found in the Bible only in the Johannine Letters, referring sometimes to a single figure and at other times to many who are adversaries and deceivers of God's people. In later centuries, it was conceived as a supreme evil figure, often identified with one's opponents.

anticline A geological fold structure in the form of an arch, with the younger strata at the top of the succession. It is formed as a result of compressional forces acting in a horizontal plane on rock strata.

anticoagulants Drugs which slow down or prevent the normal process of blood clotting, such as heparin and warfarin. They are used in the treatment and prevention of diseases caused by thrombi (blood clots) which block blood-vessels. Warfarin is also used as a rat poison, where death occurs by internal haemorrhage, but resistance has developed in a number of rat colonies, giving rise to the 'super-rat'.

Anti-Comintern Pact An agreement between Germany and Japan, concluded in 1936, which outlined both countries' hostility to international communism. The Pact was also signed by Italy in 1937, followed by other nations in 1941. In addition to being specifically aimed against Soviet Russia, it also recognized Japanese rule in Manchuria.

anticonvulsants Drugs used in the control of epilepsy. All sedatives are anticonvulsant at high doses, but useful drugs in current use include phenobarbitone, phenytoin, sodium valproate, and clonazepam. The first successful drug treatment for epilepsy was potassium bromide, used in 1857 by English physician Sir Charles Locock (1799–1875), who incorrectly believed it to suppress libido (at the time epilepsy was thought to be associated with sexual activity). The first major advance in the field was the introduction of phenobarbitone in Germany in 1912.

Anti-Corn-Law League An association formed in Manchester (Sep 1838), largely under the patronage of businessmen and industrialists, to repeal the British Corn Laws, which imposed protective tariffs on the import of foreign corn. The League was both an important element in the growing movement for free trade in early 19th-c Britain, and an important political pressure group. The Corn Laws were repealed by Robert Peel in 1846.

anticyclone A meteorological term for a high pressure system. Anticyclones are areas of generally clear skies and stable weather conditions. They occur in a variety of sizes and modes of origin, and warm anticyclones are a semi-permanent feature of subtropical areas (eg the Azores and Hawaiian high pressure zones). A *blocking* anticyclone may persist for several weeks, travelling very slowly and diverting depressions around it. In the N hemisphere, surface winds blow in a clockwise direction out of an anticyclone; in the S hemisphere the direction is anticlockwise.

antidepressants Drugs which cause elevation of mood in depressed patients. There are three major classes: *tricyclics* (eg imipramine, amitriptyline), *monoamine oxidase inhibitors* (eg isocarboxazid, phenelzine) and *serotonin reuptake inhibitors* (SRIs) (eg Prozac). During the clinical investigation of some antihistamine drugs in 1958, Swiss physician Richard Kuhn (1900–67) found that imipramine was beneficial in depressed patients, and this type of drug is widely used today. The second class was also discovered fortuitously in 1952, when the antitubercular drug ipraniazid was noted to have mood-elevating effects. However this type of drug has severe adverse interactions with certain foods, such as cheese and red wine, and its use is therefore quite limited. The third class, which includes a number of drugs similar to Prozac, was mostly developed in the 1990s. Such drugs have relatively few side-effects compared to earlier antidepressants. Lithium is used in manic depression.

antidiuretic hormone (ADH) [anteediyuretik] A chemical substance (a peptide) manufactured in the hypothalamus, but stored in and released from the back part of the pituitary gland of mammals; also known as **vasopressin**. It is one of the most fundamental hormones, being instrumental in conserving body fluids, and has known effects on memory, circadian rhythm, and the control of blood pressure in the brain.

Antietam, Battle of [anteetam] (1862) A battle of the American Civil War, fought in Maryland. It was the bloodiest battle in American history (with over four times the US casualties of D-Day). In military terms the North won a technical victory. This helped dissuade Britain and France from giving diplomatic recognition to the Confederacy and attempting to mediate the conflict, which they were about to do. It also allowed President Lincoln to issue his Preliminary Emancipation Proclamation.

antiferromagnetism *ferromagnetism*

antifreeze A substance added to water in the cooling system of an engine to prevent the system freezing during cold weather. This is necessary since water expands when it freezes, and this can lead to cracking in those parts of the engine where the cooling system is circulated. Substances used as anti-freeze include ethanol and methanol, which can evaporate from water solution; ethylene-glycol does not evaporate, but is more expensive.

antigen *antibodies*

Antigone [antigonee] In Greek mythology, a daughter of Oedipus, King of Thebes. After the Seven Champions had attacked the city, Antigone buried the body of her brother Polynices (one of the attackers), so defying King Creon's order that such a traitor should remain unburied. She was condemned to death by starvation, but hanged herself. In Sophocles' play of the same name, Antigone becomes a symbol of the individual's right to defy the state over a matter of conscience.

Antigonus I [antigonus], known as **Cyclops** or **Monophthalmos** (Gr 'One-eyed') (382–301 BC) Macedonian soldier, one of the generals of Alexander the Great. After Alexander's death, he received the provinces of Phrygia Major, Lycia, and Pamphylia. On Antipater's death in 319 BC, he aspired to the sovereignty of Asia, and waged incessant wars against the other generals, making himself master of all Asia Minor and Syria. In 306 BC he assumed the title of king, together with his son Demetrius Poliorcetes, but was defeated and slain at Ipsus in Phrygia.

Antigua or **Antigua Guatemala** [anteegwa] 14°33N 90°42W, pop (2000e) 40 700. Capital city of Sacatepéquez department, S Guatemala, SW of Guatemala City; founded by the Spanish, 1543; capital, until largely destroyed by earthquake, 1773; old city flourished in the 18th-c, with many churches, university (1680), printing press, and population of c.60 000; now a world heritage site; cathedral (1534); Holy Week processions.

Antigua and Barbuda *see panel*

anti-hero A central character in a novel or play who deviates from or contradicts conventional values and behaviour. Famous examples are Hašek's hero in *The Good Soldier Schweik* (1921–3), and Yossarian in Heller's *Catch-22* (1961).

antihistamines Drugs used in the relief of allergic reactions, such as hay fever (but not asthma). They are so called because they act by blocking the action of the substance histamine, produced in the body during allergies. They are also used in the treatment of motion sickness. Drowsiness is a common side effect, and certain antihistamines are used as sedatives.

antihydrogen *antiparticles*

antiknock A chemical substance added to a spark ignition engine's fuel to improve combustion and prevent knocking. An example is tetra-ethyl lead.

anti-literature A term coined by the poet David Gascoyne (1916–) in 1935 to describe literature which challenges established ideas of what literature should be, on formal, ideological,

Antigua and Barbuda

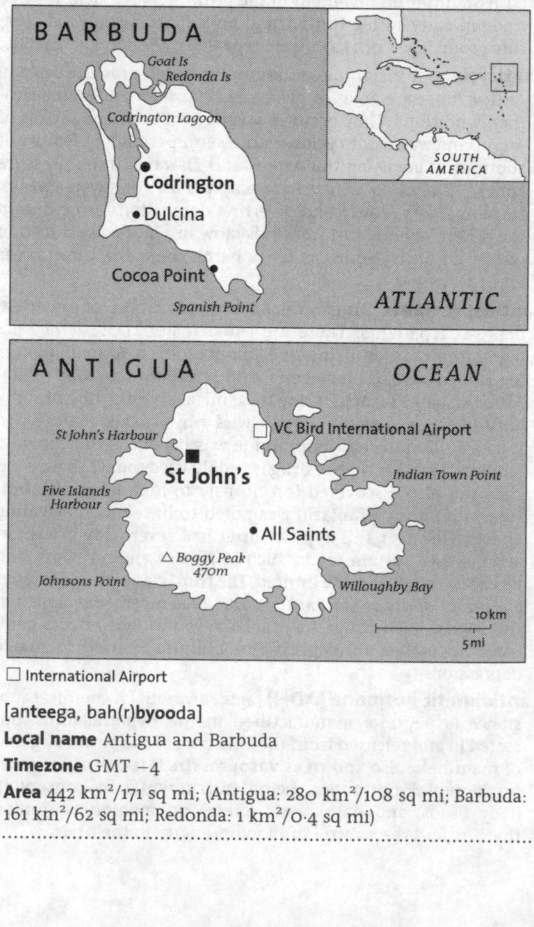

[anteega, bah(r)byooda]

Local name Antigua and Barbuda

Timezone GMT −4

Area 442 km²/171 sq mi; (Antigua: 280 km²/108 sq mi; Barbuda: 161 km²/62 sq mi; Redonda: 1 km²/0·4 sq mi)

Population total (2002e) 76 400

Status Independent republic within the Commonwealth

Date of independence 1981

Capital St John's (on Antigua)

Language English (official)

Ethnic groups African descent (92%), Portuguese, Lebanese, British (4%)

Religions Anglican (80%), Roman Catholic (10%)

Physical features Group of three islands in the Leeward group of the Lesser Antilles, E Caribbean; W part of Antigua rises to 470 m/1542 ft at Boggy Peak. Barbuda is a flat coral island reaching only 44 m/144 ft at its highest point, with a large lagoon on its W side; Redonda is an uninhabited, volcanic island, rising to 305 m/1000 ft at its highest point.

Climate Tropical; temperatures range from 24°C (Jan) to 27°C (Aug–Sep); mean annual rainfall 1000 mm/40 in.

Currency 1 East Caribbean Dollar (EC$) = 100 cents

Economy Tourism; sugar (40% of national income, marked decline in 1960s, now recovering); cotton.

GDP (2002e) $750 mn, per capita $11000

Human Development Index (2002) 0·800

History Antigua claimed for Spain by Columbus, 1493; colonized by British, 1632; ceded to Britain, 1667; Barbuda colonized from Antigua, 1661; administered as part of the Leeward Is Federation, 1871–1956; associated state of the UK, 1967; independence achieved, 1981; legislative power is vested in a bicameral parliament; Governor-General appoints the Prime Minister and Cabinet.

Head of State
(British monarch represented by Governor-General)
1981–93 Sir Wilfred E Jacobs
1993– Sir James Carlisle

Head of Government
1994–2004 Lester Bird
2004– Baldwin Spencer

or other grounds. Much experimental literature, notably in its surrealist form, exhibits these tendencies.

Antilles [antileez] The whole of the West Indies except the Bahamas; **Greater Antilles** include Cuba, Jamaica, Hispaniola (Haiti and the Dominican Republic), and Puerto Rico; **Lesser Antilles** include the Windward Is (S), Leeward Is (N), and the Netherlands Antilles off the coast of Venezuela.

Anti-Masonic Party (1830–6) A US group dedicated to driving Freemasons out of public life, arising from the highly publicized disappearance (1826) of the author of a book revealing Masonic secrets. It was the first 'third party' in the USA, nominating a presidential candidate in 1832 at the first national party convention. It declined after 1836.

antimatter *antiparticles*

antimony [antimonee] Sb (Lat *stibium*), element 51, melting point 631°C. A metalloid in the nitrogen family; common oxidation states 3 and 5; expands on solidifying. It is used in type-metal alloys, and also as an impurity in germanium to make n-type semiconductors.

antinomianism A doctrine in Christian theology to the effect that Christians are exempt from ordinary moral laws and should be governed instead by divine grace and individual conscience. The first 'antinomian controversy' was between Luther and Agricola during the Reformation.

anti-novel A novel which, while still (of necessity) using the conventions of fiction, exposes their artifice in different ways and invites reconsideration of the novel's implicit claim to represent reality. Sterne's *Tristram Shandy* (1760–7) is an early example; 20th-c practitioners include James Joyce, Virginia Woolf, Samuel Beckett, Flann O'Brien, Vladimir Nabokov, Thomas Pynchon, and Michel Butor.

Antioch [anteeok], Turkish **Antakya**, ancient **Hatay** or **Antiochia** 36°12N 36°10E, pop (2000e) 138 000. Capital of Hatay province, S Turkey; near the Mediterranean, 90 km/56 mi W of Aleppo (Syria); founded, 300 BC; centre of early Christianity; destroyed by earthquake, 526; tobacco, olives, cotton, grain; archaeological museum.

Antiochus I [antiohkus], known as **Antiochus Soter** (Gr 'Saviour') (324–261 BC) Seleucid king of Syria (281–261 BC). He was the son of Seleucus I, one of Alexander's generals, whose murder in 280 gave him the whole Syrian empire, but left him too weak to assert his right to Macedonia. He gained his surname for a victory over the Gauls, but fell in battle with them.

Antiochus III [antiohkus], known as **Antiochus the Great** (c.242–187 BC) Seleucid king of Syria, the son of Seleucus II and grandson of Antiochus II, who succeeded his brother, Seleucus III, in 223 BC. He waged war with success against Ptolemy IV Philopator, and though defeated at Raphia near Gaza (217 BC), he obtained entire possession of Palestine and Coele Syria (198 BC). He later became involved in war with the Romans, who had conquered Macedonia. He crossed over into Greece, but was defeated in 191 BC at Thermopylae, and in 190 or 189 BC by Scipio at Magnesia. To raise tribute money, he attacked a rich temple in Elymais, but the people rose against him and killed him.

antioxidants Substances which slow down the oxidation of others (often by being oxidized themselves) which have been implicated as a cause of cancer and a mediator of tissue damage. Aerobic organisms (which cannot survive without oxygen) have evolved protective mechanisms to avoid the lethal effects of oxidation. In human beings, these include enzyme systems (eg superoxide dismutase), and certain vitamins (eg A, C, E), which are beneficial in treating rheumatoid arthritis and Parkinson's disease as well as protecting against carcinoma of the gastro-intestinal tract. Enzyme preparations are available which can be taken in tablet form as a dietary supplement to suppress inflammation in various forms of arthritis, and many foodstuffs have antioxidants added as preservatives. The term is usually applied to additives in foods and plastics, an example being ascorbic acid.

antiparticles Partners of subatomic particles having the same mass and spin but opposite charge, magnetic moment, and other quantum attributes. When antiparticles meet their particle partners the two annihilate, as predicted by Paul Dirac in 1928. The antiparticle is usually denoted by a bar over the symbol for the corresponding particle. Antiparticle partners of electron e^- and proton p are the positron e^+ and antiproton $\bar{p}$, respectively. Antimatter composed of antiparticles is possible, but highly unstable, and not observed naturally. Antihydrogen atoms, comprising an antiproton and a positron, were first created artificially at CERN, Geneva, in 1996. Antiparticles are seen in radioactivity, cosmic rays, and particle physics experiments. Some neutral particles such as photons are identical to their antiparticles.

Antipater (of Idumaea) [antipater] (? 43 BC) A chieftain who dominated Jewish history from the 60s BC until his death. The father of Herod the Great, he was appointed by Julius Caesar procurator of Judaea in 47 BC. He died by poisoning.

Antipater (of Macedon) [antipater] (398–319 BC) Macedonian general. He was highly trusted by Philip II of Macedonia and Alexander the Great, and was left by the latter as regent in Macedonia (334 BC). He discharged his duties with great ability, both before and after the death of Alexander.

Antiphon (orator) [antifon] (c.480–411 BC) The earliest of the ten Attic orators. He belonged to the oligarchical party, and was influential in establishing the government of the Four Hundred (411 BC). On its fall he was condemned to death, in spite of a noble defence.

antiphon (chant) In the Roman Catholic and Greek Orthodox liturgies, a chant with a prose text which precedes or follows a psalm. It is linked with the practice of antiphonal psalmody, in which verses were sung alternately by two groups of singers, or by soloist and choir. A collection of antiphons is known as an **antiphoner**.

antipodes Any two places which are on the opposite sides of the Earth when connected by a straight line passing through the centre of the Earth. For example, the Antipodes Is, New Zealand, 49°42S and 178°50E and the Baie de la Seine, France, 49°45N and 1°W are antipodes. The term is also loosely used by Europeans to refer to Australasia.

antipope In the Roman Catholic Church, a claimant to the office of pope in opposition to one regularly and canonically appointed. Antipopes featured prominently in the period of Great Schism in the Western Church (1378–1417). They included Clement VII and Benedict XIII (in Avignon, France) and Alexander V and John XXIII (in Pisa, Italy).

antiproton The antiparticle partner of the proton; symbol $\bar{p}$. Spin and mass are as for the proton, but the charge is −1. Discovered in 1955, antiprotons are created in particle accelerators by the collisions of protons with nuclei, and can in turn be accelerated and used in particle physics experiments.

antipsychiatry A view that mental illness does not exist, and that therefore the practice of psychiatry is simply a form of social control. This view has been most forcefully propounded by the Hungarian-born US psychiatrist Thomas S Szasz (1920–). A related argument is that every patient is unique and every illness is unique, therefore there is no value in classifying either patients or diseases. These views are now generally considered extreme and of fringe interest only, though they did help to inform more compassionate models of care, particularly addressing problems of institutionalization.

antirrhinum *snapdragon*

Anti-Saloon League A US organization established in 1893 which inaugurated a nation-wide campaign in 1895, with the aim of forbidding alcoholic drink by amending the US Constitution and by state and local anti-alcohol laws. It was primarily responsible for the adoption of Prohibition. The League remained in being during and after the Prohibition period (1920–33), and became part of the National Temperance League in 1950.

antiseptic A substance which kills or prevents the growth of micro-organisms (germs). The practice of using chemicals to control the suppuration of wounds and the spread of disease, and preserving dead bodies (*embalming*) was widespread centuries before micro-organisms were understood. Lister introduced the practice of antiseptic surgery (using phenol) in 1865. Commonly used antiseptics include alcohols, phenols, salts of heavy metals, and chlorine- and iodine-releasing compounds.

Antisthenes [antis**th**eneez] (c.445–c.365 BC) Greek philosopher, thought to be co-founder, with his pupil Diogenes, of the Cynic school. He was a rhetorician and a disciple of Gorgias, and later became a close friend of Socrates. Only fragments of his many works survive.

antisubmarine warfare A practice of warfare aimed at hunting down and destroying hostile submarines. Sonar is the primary means of detecting hostile submarines, while depth charges and homing torpedoes launched by aircraft, surface warships, or hunter-killer submarines are the primary means of destroying them.

antitank gun A gun firing a shell at high velocity, capable of piercing or blasting through the armour of an enemy tank or armoured fighting vehicle.

antitank missile A missile which may be fired by an infantryman, or launched from a helicopter or combat vehicle, aimed at destroying enemy tanks and armoured fighting vehicles. It may be wire or laser guided.

Anti-trust Acts US laws passed to control the development of monopoly capitalism. The Sherman Act (1890) forbade all combinations 'in restraint of trade'. Ambiguities in wording led to its use against labour unions instead of the monopolistic corporations, or *trusts*. The Clayton Act (1914) was intended to close the ambiguities and make enforcement easier.

antivitamin factors Compounds occurring naturally in foods which reduce the availability of a vitamin, or which modify its normal function. For example, avidin, a protein in raw egg white, can bind the B-vitamin, biotin, reducing its absorption. Many of the antivitamin factors are destroyed on cooking.

antlers Bone outgrowths from the head of true deer; only on males, except in reindeer; *water deer* the only species without antlers; used in display, defence, and competition for mates; shed each year (unlike the 'horns' of other ruminants), and grow larger the following year; covered in soft skin ('velvet') when growing; if branched, the number of spikes (*tines*) increases with age; also known as **deer-horn**.

Antlia [ant**lee**a] (Lat 'air pump') A small S hemisphere constellation.

antlion The larva of a nocturnal, damselfly-like insect with a long abdomen and lightly patterned wings. Antlion larvae prey on other insects, typically lying in wait, often at the base of a steep-sided, conical trap into which the prey fall. (Order: Neuroptera. Family: Myrmeliontidae, c.600 species.)

Antofagasta [antofa**gas**ta] 23°38S 70°24W, pop (2000e) 249 100. Port and capital of Antofagasta region, Chile; largest city in N Chile; developed with 19th-c mineral and agricultural trade; airport; railway; 2 universities; exports nitrates and copper; metal refining; huge anchor high in mountains was used as navigational aid by shipping; regional, geological, and anthropological museums; public gardens and beaches, sports stadium.

Antonello da Messina [antone**loh** da me**see**na] (c.1430–79) Painter, born in Messina, Sicily, S Italy. He was the only major 15th-c Italian artist to come from Sicily. An accomplished master of oil painting, he helped popularize the medium, his style being a delicate synthesis of the northern and Italian styles. In 1475 he was working in Venice where his work influenced Giovanni Bellini's portraits. His first dated work, the 'Salvator Mundi' (1465), and a self-portrait are in the London National Gallery.

Antonescu, Ion [antones**koo**] (1882–1946) Romanian general and dictator for the Nazis in World War 2, born in Pitesti, SC Romania. He served as military attaché in Rome and London, and became chief-of-staff and minister of defence in 1937. In September 1940 he assumed dictatorial powers and forced the abdication of Carol II. He headed a Fascist government allied to Nazi Germany until 1944, when he was overthrown and executed for war crimes.

Antonine Wall [anto**niyn**] A defensive barrier built by the Roman Emperor, Antoninus Pius, in AD 142, at the N end of the British province. Constructed of turf upon a foundation of cobbles, the 'wall' ran from the Forth estuary to the Clyde.

Antoninus Pius [anto**niy**nus **piy**us], originally **Titus Aurelius Fulvus** (AD 86–161) Roman emperor, born in Lanuvium. He inherited great wealth, and in 120 was made consul. Sent as proconsul into Asia by Emperor Hadrian, in 138 he was adopted by him, and the same year came to the throne. His reign was proverbially peaceful and happy. In public affairs he acted as the father of his people, and the persecution of Christians was partly stayed by his mild measures. In his reign the empire was extended, and the Antonine Wall, named after him, built between the Forth and Clyde rivers. He was called *Pius* for his defence of Hadrian's memory. Marcus Aurelius was his adopted son and successor.

Antonioni, Michelangelo [antoni**oh**nee] (1912–) Film director, born in Ferrara, NE Italy. After studying political economy at Bologna University, he began as a film critic before becoming an assistant director in 1942. He made several documentaries (1945–50) before turning to feature films, often scripted by himself, and notable for their preoccupation with character study rather than plot. He gained an international reputation with *L'avventura* (1959), followed by other outstanding works, such as *La notte* (1961, The Night), *Blow-up* (1966), *Zabriskie Point* (1969), *Professione: Reporter* (1975, The Passenger), and *Il mistero di Oberwald* (1979, The Oberwald Mystery). He lost the power of speech after a stroke in 1985, but managed to make a further film, *Beyond the Clouds* (1995). He received an Academy lifetime achievement award in 1995.

Antonius, Marcus [an**toh**nius] or **Mark Antony** (c.83–30 BC) Roman triumvir, related on his mother's side to Julius Caesar. After assisting Caesar in Gaul (53–50 BC), he went to Rome to become tribune of the plebians (49 BC). Caesar left him in charge in Italy, and at Pharsalia (48 BC) Antony led the left wing of Caesar's army against Pompey. In 44 BC he was made consul together with Caesar, and on Caesar's assassination, the flight of the conspirators left him with almost absolute power. Besieged and defeated at Mutina by Octavian Augustus (43 BC), he fled beyond the Alps; but in Gaul he visited the camp of Lepidus, and gained the favour of the army, with which he returned to Rome. Augustus, Antony, and Lepidus then established themselves as triumvirs to share the whole Roman world, defeating Brutus and Cassius at Philippi (42 BC). After meeting Cleopatra in Asia, he followed her to Egypt (41–40 BC), until called back by news of a quarrel in Italy between his kinsmen and Augustus. A new division of the Roman world was now arranged, Antony taking the East, and Augustus the West, while Lepidus had to be content with Africa; Antony also married Augustus's sister Octavia (40 BC). Differences grew up between Antony and Augustus, and in 37 BC Antony separated from Octavia and rejoined Cleopatra. His position in the East, his relations with Cleopatra, and his unsuccessful campaigns against the Parthians (36 and 34 BC), were seized upon by Augustus, and in the naval engagement of Actium (31 BC) Antony and Cleopatra were defeated. Antony went back to Egypt, where, deceived by a false report of Cleopatra's suicide, he committed suicide.

Antony or **Anthony, St**, known as **Antony the Great**, also called **Antony of Egypt** (c.251–356) Religious hermit, the father of Christian monasticism, born in Coma, a village near Heracleopolis Magna in Upper Egypt. He sold his possessions for the poor at the age of 20 and withdrew into the wilderness. He spent 20 years in the most rigorous seclusion, during which he withstood a series of temptations by the devil which became famous in Christian theology and art. In 305 he left his retreat to found a monastery, at first only a group of separate and scattered cells near Memphis and Arsinoë – one of the earliest attempts to instruct people in the monastic way of life. Feast day 17 January.

Antony or **Anthony of Padua, St** (1195–1231) Monk, born in Lisbon, Portugal. At first an Augustinian monk, in 1220 he entered the Franciscan order, and became one of its most active propagators. He was canonized by Gregory IX (c.1170–1241) the year after his death. According to legend, he preached to the fishes when people refused to listen to him; hence he is the patron of the lower animals, and is often shown accompanied by an ass. He is also the patron saint of lost property. Feast day 13 June.

antonym *synonym*

Antrim, Ir **Aontroim** pop (2000e) 714 100; area 2831 sq km/ 1093 sq mi. County in NE Northern Ireland, UK, divided into nine districts (Antrim, Ballymena, Ballymoney, Belfast, Carrickfergus, Larne, Lisburn, Moyle, Newtownabbey); the name is also used for one of these districts, pop (2000e) 45 000, and its administrative centre; bounded SW by Lough Neagh, N by the Atlantic Ocean, and E by the Irish Sea; rises N and E to the Antrim Mts; includes the islands of Rathlin, the Skerries, and the Maidens; county town, Belfast; other chief towns, Lisburn, Ballymena, Carrickfergus; Irish linen, textiles, cattle, sheep, potatoes, flax, oats, shipbuilding; basalt rock formation, Giant's Causeway, on N coast.

Antwerp, Flemish **Antwerpen**, French **Anvers** 51°13N 4°25E, pop (2000e) 476 400. Capital city of Antwerpen district, N Belgium; on the right bank of the R Scheldt, 88 km/55 mi from the North Sea; chief port of Belgium and fourth largest port in the world; chartered, 1291; centre of the mediaeval cloth trade with England; airport; railway; colonial university (1920); shipbuilding and repairing, oil refining, synthetic fibres, plastics, petrochemicals, agrochemicals, engineering; foodstuffs, diamonds (major international centre); 16th-c town hall, Cathedral of Our Lady (1352), Church of St Jacob (15th–16th-c), Royal Museum of Fine Arts, famous zoo; home of Rubens and van Dyck.

Anubis [anyoobis] An Egyptian god associated with death. He has the head of a jackal or wild dog of the desert. Guard of the necropolis, he takes part in the process of embalming.

Anura or **Anoura** [anoora] An order of amphibians comprising the frogs and toads (3500 species); adults with no tail; move by thrusting backwards with long hind legs; larvae called *tadpoles*; also known as **Salientia**.

Anuradhapura [anarahdapoora] 8°20N 80°25E, pop (2000e) 45 000. Capital of Anuradhapura district, Sri Lanka, 205 km/ 127 mi N of Colombo; Sri Lanka's first capital; founded, 4th-c BC; Sri Mahabodhi Tree, allegedly the oldest tree in the world (2200 years), all that remains of the Bo tree beneath which Buddha found Enlightenment, a world heritage site; Thuparama Dagaba, built to enshrine the collarbone of Buddha.

anus The terminal part of the gastro-intestinal tract, opening into the natal cleft between the buttocks; the lower limit of the anal canal. In conjunction with the rest of the anal canal, it is guarded by internal and external sphincters under autonomic and voluntary control respectively. It may exhibit bleeding during defaecation, as a result of haemorrhoids.

Anvers [ãvayr] *Antwerp*

anvilhead *hammerkop*

Anville, Jean Baptiste Bourguignon d' [ãveel] (1697–1782) Geographer and map-maker, born in Paris, France. He greatly improved the standards of ancient and mediaeval map-making, and became the first geographer to the King of France.

Anyang *Xiaotun*

ANZAC [anzak] Acronym for **Australia and New Zealand Army Corps**, a unit in which troops from both countries fought during World War 1 in the Middle East and on the Western Front. **Anzac Day** (25 Apr) commemorates the Gallipoli landing in 1915; the fighting lasted until Jan 1916, during which time 7600 were killed and 19 000 wounded. Australian and British law prohibit the word 'Anzac' from commercial use.

Anzengruber, Ludwig [antsengruber] (1839–89) Playwright and novelist, born in Vienna, Austria. He was a bookshop assistant, a touring actor, and a police clerk before the success of his play, *Der Pfarrer von Kirchfeld* (1870, The Pastor of Kirchfeld), enabled him to devote the rest of his life to writing. He was the author of several novels, of which the best is *Der Sternsteinhof* (1885, The Sternstein Farm), and about 20 plays, mostly about Austrian peasant life.

ANZUS [anzuhs] Acronym for the treaty concluded in 1951 between Australia, New Zealand, and the United States for mutual security in the Pacific against armed attack. The treaty, which remains in force indefinitely, encompasses not only the metropolitan territories of the three, but also island territories under their jurisdiction, their armed forces, and their aircraft and shipping.

aorta [ayaw(r)ta] The largest blood vessel in the body, which conveys oxygenated blood from the left ventricle of the heart to the rest of the body. It is conveniently divided into three parts: (1) the **ascending aorta**, passing upwards, backwards, and to the right, giving branches to the heart, (2) the **aortic arch**, running backwards and crossing to the left side, giving major branches to the head and upper limbs, and (3) the **descending aorta**, passing through the thorax and abdomen before terminating as major vessels to the lower limbs. The thoracic branches supply the chest wall, and the abdominal branches supply the contents of the abdomen.

Aosta [ahosta], Fr **Aoste** 45°43N 7°19E, pop (2000e) 37 600. Capital town of Aosta province, Valle d'Aosta, NW Italy; in the fertile valley of the Dora Baltea, ringed by the Alps; Gran Paradiso National park; largely French-speaking; railway; important traffic junction for routes across the Alps; iron and steel, publishing, textiles, tourism, wine making, woodworking; cathedral, old town surrounded by well-preserved Roman walls; traditional handicraft exhibition (Jan).

aoudad [owdad] Wild sheep from the dry mountains of N Africa (*Ammotragus lervia*) (introduced into SW USA); sandy colour, with long fringe along throat; both sexes with curved horns up to 76 cm/30 in long; also known as **Barbary sheep**, **maned sheep**, **udad**, **arui**, or **fechstal**.

Aouita, Said [aweeta] (1960–) Athlete, born in Rabat, Morocco. A middle- and long-distance track athlete, he won the 1984 Olympic 5000 m title, then set world records at 1500 m and 5000 m in 1985 to become the first man for 30 years to hold both records. He went on to break world records at 2 mi, 2000 m, and 3000 m. The overall Grand Prix winner in 1986, 1988, and 1989, he was the 1987 World 5000 m champion. Knighted by King Hassan, the Rabat to Casablanca train was dubbed 'The Aouita'.

Aozou Strip [owzoo] A 100 km/60 mi-wide strip of mountainous desert in N Chad, NC Africa; area 114 000 sq km/ 44 000 sq mi; disputed territory on the frontier with Libya, which occupied the area in 1973; Libya's claim based on an unratified 1935 agreement between France and Italy; returned to Chad by Libya, 1994; area rich in uranium and mineral deposits.

Apache [apahchee] North American Indians who dominated much of the SW during the 19th-c; divided into many smaller groups, lacking any centralized organization. From 1861 they fought against Federal troops in the Apache and Navajo wars, eventually surrendering in 1886. Population c.57 000 (2000 census).

Apaloochy *Appaloosa*

apartheid (Afrikaans 'apartness') The former policy of separate racial development in the Republic of South Africa, supported traditionally by the Nationalist Party, and later by other right-wing parties. The ideology had several roots: Boer concepts of racial, cultural, and religious separation arising out of their sense of national uniqueness; British liberal notions of indirect rule; the need to preserve African traditional life while promoting gradualism in their Christianization and westernization; and the concern for job protection, promoted by white workers to maintain their status in the face of a large and cheaper black workforce. Under the policy, different races were given different rights. In practice the system was one of white supremacy, blacks having no representation in the central state parliament. Many of the provisions of apartheid regarding labour, land segregation (*reserves, Homelands, Bantustans*), municipal segregation, social and educational separation, and a virtually exclusive white franchise, were in place before the Nationalist victory of 1948, but after that date it was erected into a complete political, social, and economic system, down to the provisions of 'petty apartheid' relating to transport, beaches, lavatories, park benches, etc. The whole system was backed by extensive repression. Its principal architect, Hendrik Verwoerd, was assassinated in 1966. The process of dismantling its provisions began in the late 1980s, following the political initiatives of President de Klerk, but its social effects are likely to prove more lasting. Its death knell was sounded when the country's white community voted in favour of a multi-racial society, followed by the signing of a new constitutional agreement by de Klerk and Nelson Mandela in November 1993 and the implementation of free elections in April 1994.

apatite [a**pa**tiyt] A common phosphate mineral widely distributed in minor quantities in many igneous and metamorphic rocks; most varieties can be represented by the formula $Ca_5(PO_4)_3(OH,F,Cl)$. It crystallizes as hexagonal prisms, in various colours, mostly green.

Apatosaurus [a**pa**tosawrus] A giant, semi-aquatic dinosaur that probably ate vegetation around swamps and lakes; four-legged, limbs pillar-like, hindlimbs longer than forelimbs; tail whip-like; neck very long; skull with sloping face; known from the Upper Jurassic period of Colorado; formerly known as ***Brontosaurus***. (Order: Saurischia.)

ape An anthropoid primate; comprises the **lesser apes** (*gibbons*) and **great apes** (*orang-utan, gorilla, chimpanzee*); differs from most monkeys in having no tail and in using arms to swing through trees, not by walking along branches. (Family: Pongidae, 10 species.)

APEC Acronym for **Asia-Pacific Economic Co-operation**, a common market founded in 1989 at the instigation of Australia to promote multilateral trade in the Asia–Pacific region. Its original members were Australia, Brunei, Canada, Chile, China, Hong Kong, Indonesia, Japan, Malaysia, Mexico, New Zealand, Papua New Guinea, Philippines, Singapore, South Korea, Taiwan, Thailand, and USA. Peru, Russia and Vietnam joined in 1998. Member nations comprise more than 2000 million people and account for half of the world's economic production.

Apennines [a**pe**niynz], Ital **Appennino** Mountain range extending down the Italian peninsula into Sicily; length 1400 km/870 mi; width 30–150 km/20–90 mi; N division includes the Appno Ligure, Appno Tosco-Emilliano, and the Appno Umbro-Marchigiano, highest point Monte Cimone (2176 m/7138 ft); C division includes the Appno Abruzzese and the Appno Napoletano, highest point Gran Sasso d'Italia (2914 m/9560 ft); S division includes the Appno Lucano and La Sila, highest point Monte Pollino (2248 m/7375 ft), an earthquake region; typically Mediterranean vegetation in foothills, with olive groves, vineyards, orchards; open forest above, until c.1800 m/6000 ft, then slopes covered with stones and scree; stock-farming (goats and sheep), some arable farming, forestry; marble quarries at Carrara; mineral springs.

aperture **1** The opening, usually circular, through which light enters an optical system, such as a camera lens. It is often adjustable in diameter by means of an iris diaphragm to control the intensity of light transmitted – the 'stop' of a lens system.

2 In cinematography, the rectangular opening in a camera or other projector at which each frame of film is held stationary while it is exposed; also called the **film gate**.

aperture synthesis A method of combining several small telescopes to simulate some properties of very large telescopes. It has been used successfully at radio frequencies to enable astronomers to see fine detail in sources. The technique was developed by UK astronomer Martin Ryle at Mullard Radio Astronomy Observatory, Cambridge, UK.

Apgar, Virginia (1909–74) Physician and anesthesiologist, born in Westfield, New Jersey, USA. Best known for pioneering work in anesthesia relating to childbirth, in 1952 she developed the **Apgar Score** to evaluate newborns. She also created the first department of anesthesiology at Columbia–Presbyterian Medical Center (1938–49) where she was the first woman both to head a department and to hold a full professorship in anesthesiology (1949). A deepening interest in maternal and child health eventually led in 1959 to an executive position with the National Foundation–March of Dimes, where she spent the rest of her life fostering public support for birth defect research.

aphasia A disorder of language caused by brain damage; also (especially in the UK) known as **dysphasia**. The patient appears intellectually and physically capable of using language (eg there is movement of the tongue and lips and no deafness) but suffers from a variety of linguistic disabilities. There are many different types: one important distinction is between **Broca's aphasia** (a disorder of production, characterized by word-finding difficulties and telegrammatic speech) and **Wernicke's aphasia** (a disorder of comprehension, characterized by fluent but largely nonsensical speech). The study of the disorder is known as **aphasiology**.

aphelion *periapsis*

aphid A soft-bodied bug that feeds on plant sap. Aphids have complex life cycles, typically including several asexually reproducing generations of live-bearing females, and one sexually reproducing generation per year. Many species produce wax for protection. Others produce honeydew, and are tended by ants. About 4000 species are known, mainly from the N hemisphere, including some that are serious pests, such as blackfly and greenfly. (Order: Homoptera. Family: Aphididae.)

aphonia *dysphonia*

aphrodisiacs Drugs which induce sexual desire and/or improve sexual performance; named after Aphrodite, the goddess of love. Over 500 substances have been advocated throughout history, notably Spanish fly (responsible for many deaths), rhino horn, and mandrake root.

Aphrodite [afro**diy**tee] The Greek goddess of sexual love, said to have been born from the sea-foam at Paphos in Cyprus. This indication of an Eastern origin to her cult is borne out by resemblances to the worship of Ishtar.

Apia [a**pi**a] 13°48S 171°45W, pop (2000e) 47 700. Capital town of Samoa (formerly Western Samoa), on N coast of Upolu I, SW Pacific Ocean; a rapidly expanding cluster of villages; copra, cocoa, bananas.

apiculture The keeping of bees in hives for honey and wax production. Bees may be also used for pollinating orchards and crops, such as oilseed rape. Bee-keeping is known from the Stone Age, when crude hives were made, probably from wood. European farmers built straw *keps*, which resembled upside-down baskets. Commercial bee-keeping started in the 1880s. As a hobby, collectors (**apiarists**) keep bees both for their honey and to study their habits.

Apis [**ay**pis, **ah**pis] The Egyptian bull-god, representing or incarnating the Ptah of Memphis. An actual bull was selected from the herd, black with a triangular white patch on the forehead, and kept at Memphis; after death it was mummified and placed in a special necropolis, the Serapeum.

APL Abbreviation of **A Programming Language**, a scientific computer programming language, developed in the 1960s. It is of special interest to mathematicians.

Apo, Mount [**ah**poh] Active volcano and highest mountain in the Philippines, near the SE coast of Mindanao I; rises to 2954 m/9691 ft; part of a national park.

apoapsis *periapsis*

apocalypse (Gr 'revelation of the future') A literary genre which can be traced to post-Biblical Jewish and early Christian eras; it especially comprises works in highly symbolic language which claim to express divine disclosures about the heavenly spheres, the course of history, or the end of the world. The most famous example is the Book of Revelation in the New Testament. The notion also includes poems by Blake and Yeats ('The Second Coming'), novels such as Lawrence's *Women in Love* (1920), much science fiction, and cataclysmic films such as Coppola's *Apocalypse Now* (1979).

Apocalypse of John *Revelation, Book of*

Apocrypha, New Testament [apo**k**rifa] Christian documents, largely from the early Christian centuries, which are similar in title, form, or content to many New Testament works, being called Gospels, Acts, Epistles, or Apocalypses, and often attributed to New Testament characters, but not widely accepted as canonical. Some derive from Gnosticism or heretical circles, but others are just of a popular nature.

Apocrypha, Old Testament [apo**k**rifa] (Gr 'hidden things') Usually, a collection of Jewish writings found in the Greek version of the Hebrew Bible (the *Septuagint*), but not found in the Hebrew Bible itself; in a more general sense, any literature of an esoteric or spurious kind. Most of these writings were also in the Latin version of the Christian Bible approved at the Council of Trent (the *Vulgate*), so Roman Catholics tend to consider them as inspired and authoritative, and designate them as **deuterocanonical** (accepted by Catholics as part of the canon, but recognized not to be accepted by all), while Protestants and most others attribute less authority to them, referring to them as **Apocrypha**. Corresponding to this distinction, non-Catholic Bibles tend to locate the Apocrypha as a separate collection between the two Testaments or after the New Testament, while Catholic Bibles tend to place the writings among the Old Testament works themselves.

Agreement is also not complete over which writings are to be included in this collection. Modern studies prefer to limit the Apocrypha to 13 writings found in most Septuagint manuscripts, and to exclude additional works found only in the Vulgate, which are then assigned to a much larger body of writings called the Old Testament **Pseudepigrapha**. The Apocrypha would thus include: 1 Esdras, Tobit, Judith, Additions to the Book of Esther, Wisdom of Solomon, Ecclesiasticus (or Sirach), 1 Baruch, Letter of Jeremiah, Prayer of Azariah and Song of the Three Young Men, Susanna, Bel and the Dragon (the last three being Additions to the Book of Daniel), 1 and 2 Maccabees. Roman Catholics consider all of this list to be deuterocanonical except for 1 Esdras. Most of the Apocrypha were composed in the last two centuries BC.

apogee *periapsis*

Apollinaire, Guillaume [apoli**nair**, gi**yom**], pseudonym of **Wilhelm Apollinaris de Kostrowitzki** (1880–1918) Poet and art critic, born in Rome, Italy. He settled in Paris in 1900, and became a leader of the movement rejecting poetic traditions in outlook, rhythm, and language. His work, bizarre, Symbolist and fantastic, is expressed chiefly in *L'Enchanteur pourissant* (1909, The Decaying Enchanter), *Le Bestiaire* (1911, The Bestiary), *Les Alcools* (1913, The Spirits) and *Calligrammes* (1918). Wounded in World War 1, during his convalescence he wrote the play *Les Mamelles de Tirésias* (1918, The Breasts of Tiresias), for which he coined the term *Surrealist*.

Apollo, (Phoebus) [a**po**loh] In Greek mythology, the god of poetic and musical inspiration; also a destructive force, sending disease with his arrows. He is depicted as an ideal of male beauty, or as an archer. In historic times he was the god who spoke through the Delphic oracle, and his shrine was the island of Delos. Later poetry stresses his connection with the Sun.

Apollo asteroid An asteroid whose orbit crosses that of the Earth, but whose average distance from the Sun is greater than that of the Earth (ie more than 1 astronomical unit, 150 million km/93 million mi).

Apollonius [apo**loh**nius], known as **Dyskolos** ('Bad-tempered') (2nd-c) Greek grammarian, the first to reduce Greek syntax to a system. He wrote a treatise *On Syntax* and shorter works on pronouns, conjunctions, and adverbs.

Apollonius [apo**loh**nius], known as **Apollonius Rhodius** (3rd-c BC) Greek scholar, born in Alexandria, N Egypt, but long resident in Rhodes. He wrote many works on grammar, and an epic poem about the quest for the Golden Fleece, the *Argonautica*, which was greatly admired by the Romans.

Apollonius of Perga [apo**loh**nius], known as **the Great Geometer** (280–210 BC) Greek mathematician, born in Perga, Anatolia. He was the author of the definitive ancient work on conic sections which laid the foundations of later teaching on the subject.

Apollo programme The first crewed mission to the Moon, undertaken by NASA at the direction of President Kennedy in response to the space leadership position established by the USSR. The first landing (20 Jul 1969) was made by the Apollo 11 crew of Neil Armstrong and Edwin Aldrin in the spacecraft *Eagle*. It is by far the most ambitious space achievement to date, and was also a scientific triumph, because of the far-reaching value of lunar sample analysis. Over 300 kg/660 lb of soil, cores, and rocks were returned by all six landed missions. Long duration seismology and space physics experiments were deployed near the landers. The focus of the US space programme for over a decade, it was preceded by Mercury and Gemini manned spaceflight demonstration projects, and Ranger, Surveyor, and Lunar Orbiter robotic lunar exploration missions. Undertaken in an atmosphere of intense competition with the USSR, it required immense technological development in all elements of spaceflight. The Saturn V launch vehicle remains the most powerful ever developed. The three-man crew in each mission was launched inside a Command Module which stayed in lunar orbit, while the Lunar Module with two crew members descended to the surface. Following the surface activities, part of the Lunar Module was launched to rendezvous with the Command Module in orbit. The crew were recovered from an ocean landing after re-entry and parachute descent. Major events of the programme included: the first manned lunar mission (Apollo 8, Christmas 1968); the first landing mission (Apollo 11, Jul 1969); the pin-point landing at Surveyor 3 site (Apollo 12, Nov 1969); the oxygen tank explosion on the aborted Apollo 13; and the first lunar rover excursion (Apollo 15). The last flight was undertaken (Dec 1972) by the Apollo 17 crew, who stayed 75 hours on the lunar surface and travelled 34 km/21 mi in the lunar rover. The landing sites were: 11, Mare Tranquillitatis; 12, Oceanus Procellarum; 14, Mare Imbrium; 15, Hadley Rille; 16, Descartes; and 17, Taurus Littrow. The programme was managed by NASA's Johnson Space Center, using the capabilities of all other NASA Centers.

Apollo–Soyuz project [soy**oos**] A landmark joint space mission conducted by the USA and USSR in 1975, following an agreement signed by President Nixon and Chairman Kosygin in 1972. Intended primarily as a political gesture during a period of US–Soviet detente, Apollo–Soyuz also demonstrated the capability for joint operations between the major space powers and, as such, the potential for on-orbit emergency rescue missions. The rendezvous (17 Jul 1975) lasted 48 hours. The crews (T Stafford, V Brand, D Slayton and A Leonov, V Kubasov) conducted a series of joint experiments. A special adaptor docking module was constructed for the mission.

apologetics (Lat *apologia* 'defence') A branch of theology which justifies Christian faith in the light of specific criticisms or charges. An early example is Justin Martyr's *Apology* (2nd-c).

apomixis [apo**mik**sis] Asexual reproduction without fertilization in plants, in which meiosis and fusion of gametes are suppressed. Apomixis also includes vegetative reproduction, in which part of a plant becomes detached and may develop into a separate individual.

apostle In its broadest sense, a missionary, envoy, or agent; more narrowly used at times in the New Testament to refer to the 12 chosen followers of Jesus (less Judas Iscariot, replaced by Matthias according to *Acts* 1) who witnessed the resurrected Jesus and were commissioned to proclaim his gospel. At times the term also included Paul and other missionaries or itinerant preachers (*Acts* 14.14; *Rom* 16.7).

Apostles' Creed A statement of Christian faith widely used in Roman Catholic and Protestant Churches, and recognized by the Orthodox Churches. It stresses the trinitarian nature of God (as Father, Son, and Holy Spirit) and the work of Christ. In its present form, it dates from the 8th-c, but its origins go back to the 3rd-c.

Apostolic Constitution One of the most solemn documents issued in the name of a pope, concerned with major matters of doctrine or discipline for the Roman Catholic Church at large.

apostolic succession The theory that a direct line of descent can be traced from the original apostles of Christ through episcopal succession to the bishops of the present-day Church which supports it, guaranteeing preservation of the original teaching of the apostles. This is now disputed by most New Testament scholars, but features in Roman Catholic, Orthodox, and Anglican teaching.

apothecary In most countries an old term for a pharmacist at a time when drugs were crude and mostly derived from plants. In England, apothecaries were general medical practitioners; the Society of Apothecaries was founded by James I in 1617 and gained further powers over the next two centuries. As a licensing body, the examinations it sets are subject to approval by the General Medical Council.

Appalachian Mountains [apalayshuhn, apalaychian] Mountain system in E North America extending from the Gulf of St Lawrence SW to C Alabama (2570 km/1600 mi); a series of parallel ranges separated by wide valleys; highest peak Mt Mitchell (2037 m/6683 ft), North Carolina; the **Older Appalachians** in the E include (from N to S) the Shichshock, Notre Dame, White and Green Mts, the Berkshire Hills, and the Blue Ridge Mts; the C band of **Folded** or **Newer Appalachians** includes the Great Appalachian Valley, formed N–S by the St Lawrence lowland, the L Champlain lowland, the Hudson R, and other valleys (notably Shenandoah Valley, Virginia); the **Appalachian Plateau** in the W includes the Catskill, Allegheny, and Cumberland Mts; glaciers in the Canadian and New England areas; rich in minerals, especially coal; a major barrier to westward exploration in early US history; Great Smoky Mountains National Park (Tennessee), Shenandoah National Park (Virginia), the Appalachian Trail (world's longest continuous hiking trail, 3300 km/2050 mi).

Appaloosa A breed of horse; height, 14–15 hands/1·4–1·5 m/4·7–5 ft; short tail; dark with pale spots, or pale with dark spots; sometimes dark with pale hindquarters; name often used for these markings; also called **Apaloochy** or **Palouse**.

apparat The aggregate of full-time officials of the Soviet Communist Party (*apparatchiki*). Originally drawn from professional revolutionaries, and based on Lenin's doctrine of democratic centralism, the role of the apparat was to execute the decisions of the party leadership in a disciplined, bureaucratic manner with little scope for discussion or discretion. The term is also sometimes used to refer to a functionary.

apparition The visual experience of seeing a person or animal (either living or dead) not actually present. The term **crisis apparition** is applied if the person or animal seen is experiencing a crisis at the time, such as death or injury.

appeal A legal procedure whereby a superior court considers an application by a party to a case concerning the decision reached in a lower court or tribunal. In criminal cases, the appeal may concern the verdict and/or the sentence. In civil cases, it may concern a subsidiary factor, such as the amount of damages awarded or the actual decision itself. Appeals may involve matters of fact or law, as in the US appellate court; however, appeals to the House of Lords are solely on points of law. Appeals on questions of European law are heard by the Court of Justice of the European Communities.

appeasement A foreign policy based on conciliation of the grievances of rival states by negotiation and concession to avoid war. The term is most often applied to the British and French unsuccessful attempts before World War 2 to prevent German and Italian expansionism and to satisfy Hitler's demands over German grievances arising out of the Treaty of Versailles. As a result, Hitler remilitarized the Rhineland (1936), secured Anschluss with Austria (1938), and gained the Sudetenland from Czechoslovakia (1938). Neville Chamberlain, who succeeded Baldwin in 1937, used what he called 'active appeasement' to assuage Hitler's demands for the German-speaking Sudeten area of Czechoslovakia. At his last of several meetings with Hitler, the Munich Pact was signed by Chamberlain, Hitler, and also Mussolini and Deladier (of France). Chamberlain called it 'peace in our time': the surrender of several Czechoslovak regions to Hitler, as his last territorial claim in Europe. The policy ended abruptly with Hitler's invasion of Poland (1939) and the subsequent world war.

Appel, Karel Christian (1921–) Painter, born in Amsterdam, The Netherlands. He studied at the Royal College of Art in Amsterdam, and became one of an influential group of Dutch, Belgian, and Danish Expressionists known as 'Cobra'. His work, featuring swirls of brilliant colour and aggressively contorted figures, has many affinities with American abstract expressionism. He settled in New York City in the 1960s.

appendicitis The obstruction and inflammation of the appendix; one of the commonest surgical emergencies. Clinical presentation is with abdominal pain, initially generalized, then localizing to the lower right side of the abdomen and becoming more severe, accompanied by nausea and fever. If the appendix is not removed surgically, it may perforate leading to generalized peritonitis and death.

appendix A blind-ended tube which arises from the caecum at the beginning of the large bowel on the right side of the abdomen; also known as the **vermiform appendix**. In humans, it is variable in length (2–20 cm/$^3/_4$–8 in) and its function is unknown. If its single blood supply is cut off, due often to blockage and swelling, it rapidly becomes infected and inflamed (**appendicitis**) and has to be removed as soon as possible. It is present in apes and numerous other mammals (eg rabbits, rodents), where it is large, and plays a role in digestion.

Appert, Nicolas François [apair] (1752–1841) Chef and inventor, born in Châlons-sur-Marne, NE France. In 1795 he began experiments aimed at preserving food in hermetically sealed containers. His success, which earned him a French government prize in 1810, was due to his use of an autoclave for sterilization. He opened the world's first commercial preserved food factory in 1812, initially using glass jars and bottles, changing to tin-plated metal cans in 1822.

Appia, Adolphe [apia] (1862–1928) Scene designer and theatrical producer, born in Geneva, SW Switzerland. He was one of the first to introduce simple planes instead of rich stage settings, and pioneered the symbolic use of lighting, particularly in the presentation of opera.

Appian Way [apian] The first of Rome's major trunk roads, constructed in 312 BC by Appius Claudius Caecus. It ran initially from Rome SE to Capua. Later it was extended across the peninsula to Brundisium on the Adriatic coast.

apple A small deciduous tree; flowers white or pinkish, in clusters, appearing with the oval leaves; fruit a swollen, fleshy receptacle (or *pome*), containing a core, which is the real fruit. **Crab apples** are wild species native to N temperate regions with smooth leaves and small, sour fruits. All eating and cooking apples – over 1000 cultivars – belong to the cultivated apple of gardens and orchards (*Malus domestica*), a complex hybrid probably derived from several wild species of crab apple, and which has leaves woolly beneath and large sweet fruits. (Genus: *Malus*, 35 species. Family: Rosaceae.)

applet A short progam, written in a language such as JAVA, which can be called from a Web document while the document is being processed by a browser. When the applet is called, it is downloaded from the Web site and run in the user's machine. The JAVA language has been designed to allow applets to operate in user's machines without presenting a threat to user security.

Appleton, Sir Edward (Victor) (1892–1965) Physicist, born in Bradford, West Yorkshire, N England, UK. He studied at Cambridge, and worked at the Cavendish Laboratory from 1920, becoming professor of physics at London University in 1924. In 1936 he returned to Cambridge as professor of natural philosophy, and became secretary of the Department of Scientific and Industrial Research (1939). In 1949 he was appointed Vice-Chancellor of Edinburgh University. In 1947 he was awarded the Nobel Prize for Physics for his contribution towards exploring the ionosphere. His work revealed the existence of a layer of electrically charged particles in the upper atmosphere (the *Appleton layer*) which plays an essential part in making radio communication possible between distant stations.

Appleton layer A strongly ionized region of the upper part of the ionosphere, at heights of about 200–400 km/125–250 mi, which is responsible for the reflection of short radio waves back to Earth. Discovered in 1925 by Edward Appleton, it is also known as the **F layer**.

applied linguistics The application of linguistic theory, practice, and methodology to situations which present language-related tasks or problems. The most well-established field is that of language teaching and learning, particularly with reference to foreign languages. Here, the linguist can contribute such useful background information as a contrastive analysis of the structures of the learner's native language and those of the target language, to enable predictions to be made about likely sources of difficulty and error. Other fields of interest to the applied linguist include interpreting and translating, dictionary-making, the teaching of reading and writing, and the many areas of language pathology (eg stuttering, aphasia, dyslexia).

Appomatox Court House [apomatoks] The site in Virginia, USA, of the surrender of the Confederate army under Robert E Lee to Union forces under Ulysses S Grant, at the end of the American Civil War (9 Apr 1865). Although a few Confederates remained under arms, it marked the effective end of the war.

appulse The seemingly close approach of two celestial objects as perceived by an observer; particularly, the close approach of a planet or asteroid to a star without the occurrence of an occultation.

apraxia [apraksia] Difficulty in controlling voluntary movements of the limbs or vocal organs; also called **dyspraxia**. In particular, there may be an inability to control sequences of sounds or gestures. The intention to act or communicate is present, but the patient cannot carry it out.

apricot A deciduous shrub or small tree (*Prunus armeniaca*) 3–10 m/10–30 ft, native to China and C Asia, and widely cultivated; flowers white or pale pink, appearing before the broadly oval, toothed leaves; fruits globose, velvety, 4–8 cm/1½–3 in, yellow or orange; flesh tart becoming sweet; stone ridged along one edge. (Family: Rosaceae.)

April Fool A person tricked or made a fool of on 1 April (All Fools' Day or April Fools' Day). In origin this may have been the final day of the festivities celebrating the spring equinox, which began on Old New Year's Day (25 Mar until 1564). The custom is also probably linked to the continental festival of Carnival, which takes place prior to Lent, and to the older Feast of Fools celebrated in December.

April Theses A programme of revolutionary action drawn up by Lenin in April 1917 shortly after the February Revolution in Russia. In it he advocated the transformation of the Russian 'bourgeois-democratic' revolution into a 'proletarian-socialist' revolution under the slogan of 'All power to the Soviets'.

apron stage The part of the stage in front of the proscenium. It is often a movable structure and sometimes lower than the main stage. It evolved from the platform stage of the Elizabethan theatre (in front of the proscenium arch), and formed the acting area of the Restoration theatre, with proscenium doors on each side through which the actors entered and exited. In France in 1689 a new theatre for the Comédie Française opened, with an apron stage in front of the proscenium arch.

apse A semi-circular or polygonal vaulted recess in a church, usually at the end of a chapel or chancel. It was originally used to contain the praetor's chair in a Roman basilica.

Apuleius, Lucius [apulayus] (2nd-c) Roman writer, satirist, and rhetorician, born in Madaura, Numidia, N Africa. He studied at Carthage and Athens, travelled widely, and was initiated into numerous religious mysteries. Having married a wealthy widow, Aemilia Pudentilla, he was charged by her relations with having employed magic to gain her affections. His *Apologia* was an eloquent vindication. He settled in Carthage, where he devoted himself to literature and the teaching of philosophy and rhetoric. His romance, *Metamorphoses* or *The Golden Ass*, is a satire on the vices of the age, especially those of the priesthood and of quacks.

Apus [aypus] (Lat 'bird of paradise') A rather small and inconspicuous S hemisphere constellation.

Aqaba [akaba], ancient **Aelana** 29°31N 35°00E, pop (2000e) 77 000. Seaport in Maan governorate, East Bank, SW Jordan, at N end of the Gulf of Aqaba, on the border with Israel; Jordan's only outlet to the sea; airport; railway; an ancient trade route through the Red Sea–Jordan rift valley; container terminal facilities; phosphates, thermal power, fertilizers, timber processing, tourism; popular winter seaside resort.

aquaculture *mariculture*

aquamarine A variety of the mineral beryl, used as a gemstone. It is transparent, usually sea-green or bluish-green.

aquaplaning A phenomenon which can take place when a tyre is operating on a wet road. Under certain circumstances a layer or wedge of water becomes interposed between the tyre and the road, and the tyre 'planes', ie loses adhesion. As a result, steering and braking can become ineffective.

aquarium A building suitably equipped for the display of aquatic plant and animal life. The first public aquarium was the Aquatic Vivarium, in Regent's Park Zoo, London, which opened in 1853. In recent times open-air **dolphinariums** have become popular for the displaying of dolphins, and underwater **oceanariums** can be found in popular tourist resorts, such as Disney World in Florida. Small tanks are available for use as domestic aquariums in which tropical fish can be kept.

Aquarius [akwairius] (Lat 'water bearer') A constellation of the zodiac, lying between Pisces and Capricornus. It contains the Helix Nebula, the closest planetary nebula to us.

aquatint A form of etching which gives a tonal effect like a wash drawing (shaded with diluted ink or watercolour, applied with a brush). The copper plate is dusted with a thin layer of powdered resin, which is fixed to the metal by heating. When immersed in acid, the plate is bitten all over, but as a mass of tiny specks rather than as lines. Gradations of tone from pale grey to deep (but not solid) black are achieved by timing the immersion. The technique was perfected in France in 1768 by Jean-Baptiste Le Prince, but the greatest master to use it was Goya, notably in *Los caprichos* (1799). In the 20th-c, aquatint was revived by Picasso, André Masson (1896–1987), and others.

aquavit A colourless spirit, distilled from potatoes or cereals, and usually flavoured with caraway seeds. It is a popular drink in Scandinavia.

aqueduct An artificial channel for the conveyance of water. The Romans built thousands of miles of aqueducts to bring water to their towns. Many are in the form of arch bridges, and some of these spectacular structures, such as the Pont du Gard at Nîmes, France, still survive.

aquifer Water-bearing rock strata, commonly sandstones or chalk with high porosity and permeability. They provide much of the world's water supply, which may be exploited directly by sinking wells or pumping into a reservoir. The chalk in the London Basin (UK) and the Dakota sandstone (USA) are important aquifers.

Aquila [akwila] (Lat 'eagle') A constellation, the Eagle, on the celestial equator, seen during midsummer in the N hemisphere. Its brightest star is Altair, distance 5·1 parsec.

aquilegia [akwileejuh] *columbine*

Aquinas, St Thomas [akwiynas], known as **Doctor Angelicus** ('angelic doctor') (1225–74) Scholastic philosopher and theologian, born in the castle of Roccasecca, near Aquino, SC Italy. He studied with the Benedictines of Monte Cassino, and at the University of Naples; and, against the bitter opposition of his family, entered the Dominican order of mendicant friars (1244). His brothers kidnapped him and kept him a prisoner in the paternal castle for over a year; in the end he made his way to Cologne to become a pupil of Albertus Magnus. In 1252 he went to Paris, and taught there, until in 1258 he was summoned by the pope to teach successively in Anagni, Orvieto, Rome, and Viterbo. He died at Fossanuova on his way to defend the papal cause at the Council of Lyon, and was canonized in 1323. His prolific writings display great intellectual power, and he came to exercise enormous intellectual authority throughout the Church. In his philosophical writings he tried to combine and reconcile Aristotle's scientific rationalism with Christian doctrines of faith and revelation. His best-known works are two huge encyclopedic syntheses. The *Summa contra Gentiles* (1259–64) deals chiefly with the principles of natural religion. His incomplete *Summa theologiae* (1266–73) contains his mature thought in systematic form, and includes the famous 'five ways' or proofs of the existence of God. *Thomism* now represents the general teaching of the Catholic Church. Feast day 7 March.

Aquino, Cory [akeenoh], popular name of **(Maria) Corazon Aquino**, *née* **Cojuangco** (1933–) Philippines politician and president (1986–92), born in Tarlac province. She studied at Mount St Vincent College, New York, before marrying a young politician, **Benigno S Aquino** (1932–83), in 1956, who became the chief political opponent to Ferdinand Marcos. Imprisoned on charges of murder and subversion (1972–80), he was assassinated by a military guard at Manila airport in 1983 on his return from three years of exile in the USA. Corazon was drafted by the Opposition to contest the 1986 presidential election, and claimed victory over Marcos, accusing the government of ballot-rigging. She took up her husband's cause, leading a non-violent 'people's power' campaign which succeeded in overthrowing Marcos. She survived several coup attempts during her presidency, but did not stand for re-election in 1992.

Aquitaine [akwitayn], Fr [akeeten], ancient **Aquitania** pop (2000e) 2 924 000; area 41 308 sq km/15 945 sq mi. Region of SW France comprising the departments of Dordogne, Gironde, Landes, Lot-et-Garonne, and Pyrénées-Atlantiques; united with Gascony under the French crown, 11th-c; acquired by England on the marriage of Henry II to Eleanor of Aquitaine, 1152; remained in English hands until 1452; chief town, Bordeaux; drained by rivers Garonne, Dordogne, Gironde; several caves with ancient rock paintings; Bergerac and Bordeaux areas noted for wines; Parc des Landes de Gascogne regional nature park; several spas; wine, fruit, resin, tobacco, shipbuilding, chemicals, oil refining.

Ara (Lat 'altar') A small S hemisphere constellation.

arabesque [arabesk] Flowing linear ornament, based usually on plant forms. It occurs widely throughout history, but is especially favoured by Islamic artists.

Arab horse A breed of horse; height, usually 14–15 hands/1·4–1·5 m/4·7–5 ft; grey, brown, or black; wide nostrils and concave face; spirited, with great stamina; three groups: *Kehylan*, *Seglawi*, and *Muniqi*, which are seldom interbred.

Arabia area c.2 590 000 sq km/1 000 000 sq mi. Peninsula of SW Asia, bounded N by the Syrian Desert, E by the Persian Gulf, W by the Red Sea, and S by the Arabian Sea; divided politically into the states of Saudi Arabia, Yemen, Oman, United Arab Emirates, Bahrain, Qatar, and Kuwait; an important world source of petroleum.

Arabian camel *dromedary*

Arabian Gulf *Persian Gulf*

Arabian hound *saluki*

Arabian Sea area 3 863 000 sq km/1 492 000 sq mi. NW part of the Indian Ocean; principal arms include the Gulf of Oman (NW) and the Gulf of Aden (W); bounded N by Pakistan and Iran, E by India, W by Oman and South Yemen; depths of 2895 m/9498 ft in the N to 4392 m/14 409 ft in the SW; trade route between Indian subcontinent, Persian Gulf states, and Mediterranean.

Arabic A language of the S Semitic group within the Afro-Asiatic family, spoken by over 150 millions as a mother-tongue. Its spread outside the Arabian peninsula was concomitant with the spread of Islam in the 7th–8th-c AD. The language has two forms. **Colloquial Arabic** exists as the vernacular varieties of the major Arabic-speaking nation-states, such as Egypt, Morocco, and Syria, which are not always mutually intelligible. **Classical Arabic**, the language of the Qur'an, in its modernized version (known as Standard or Literary Arabic) provides a basis for a common written form, and a common medium for affairs of state, religion, and education throughout the Arabic-speaking world. The language is written from right to left.

Arabic literature The great age of classical Arabic literature was from the 6th-c to the 12th-c, followed by a revival in the 20th-c in poetry and through the introduction of new forms of drama and fiction. The earlier literature was almost exclusively in poetry, with the oral tradition permitting the cultivation of poetic forms of great complexity, such as the pre-Islamic *qasida*, represented in the celebrated *Muallaqat* collection of seven golden odes. The Umayyad period (661–750) saw the introduction of the *ghazal*, a shorter form used for erotic and mystical poetry, in which Omar ibn Abi Rabi'a (644–c.720) excelled, and much political satire. Exposure to Greek and Roman civilization during the Abassid period (750–1055) helped the development of secular prose, best exhibited by Al-Jahiz (776–869); while under the patronage of the 9th-c Baghdad caliphs and at the 10th-c Hamdanid court at Aleppo, historical writing flourished alongside poetry. In the 20th-c Arabic literature again emerged, with works by many hundreds of poets, dramatists, novelists, and short-story writers, active in all Arab countries. International recognition came with the award of the Nobel Prize for Literature in 1988 to Naguib Mahfouz, the Egyptian novelist. In some Arab countries an unofficial censorship has attempted to silence liberal writing, and in 1994 Mahfouz himself was stabbed by Islamic militants as a protest against secularization of Arab society. Arab writers living in exile continue to publish noteworthy works. The Algerian novelist Mohammed Dib, living in France, published *Si Diable vent* (1998), the theme of which was the impossibility of returning to one's homeland; and the Moroccan writer Ahmed Tawfiq has posed questions about the interplay of religion, authority, and politics in his novel *Jarat Abi Musa* (1997, The Neighbours of Abi Musa).

Arab–Israeli Wars Five wars (1948, 1956, 1967, 1973, 1982) fought between Israel and the Arab states over the territorial and strategic consequences of the creation of the Jewish state. In 1948, the end of the British Mandate and the declaration of Israeli statehood on 14 May led to war. By the armistice of 1949, Israel had consolidated its hold over territorial Palestine except for the West Bank and Gaza Strip. These territories, along with the Golan Heights and Egyptian Sinai Peninsula, were occupied in the Six Day War of 1967. In all, some 800 000 Palestinians were made refugees in 1948 and another 300 000 in 1967. The wars of 1956 (the Suez Crisis) and 1973 (the Yom Kippur or Ramadan War) had no territorial consequences as Israel agreed to withdraw from captured land. In 1982, Israel invaded Lebanon in its only engagement primarily with Palestinian forces, and suffered domestic and international criticism for its conduct of the war.

Arab League A League of Arab States, founded in 1945, with the aim of encouraging inter-Arab co-operation. The League's headquarters was established in Egypt, but moved to Tunis after the signing of Egypt's peace treaty with Israel in 1979. It returned to Cairo in 1990. In 2004 the Arab League had 22 member states, including the Palestine National Authority. Its existence has been under pressure since Iraq's invasion of Kuwait (1990).

arable farming Farming which involves regular ploughing and planting of annual crops, such as cereals, potatoes, sugar-beet, and vegetables. It is predominant in flatter and drier areas, where ploughing is easy and where dry summers allow crops to ripen and be harvested.

Arabs A diverse group of people, united by their use of Arabic as a first language, who live primarily in Iraq, Syria, the Arabian Peninsula, the Maghreb region of N Africa, Egypt, and Mauritania. Originating primarily from W Asia, they have in some areas incorporated peoples from sub-Saharan Africa and C Asia. A great unifying force is Islam, the religion of 95% of all Arabs. They played a crucial world-historical role in the East–West diffusion of culture. The majority live in cities and towns; 5% are pastoral nomads living in deserts.

arachidonic acid A polyunsaturated fatty acid with 20 carbons and 4 unsaturated bonds. It is stored in cell membranes, and when released gives rise to the prostaglandins and leukotrienes. Arachidonic acid is synthesized in the body from linoleic acid (18 carbons, 2 double bonds), which is an essential component of the diet in that it cannot be synthesized by humans.

Arachne [araknee] In Greek mythology, an excellent weaver from Lydia, who challenged Athena to a contest. When Arachne's work was seen to be superior, Athena destroyed it, and Arachne hanged herself. Athena saved her, but changed her into a spider.

Arachnida [araknida] A large, diverse class of mostly terrestrial arthropods, comprising c.70 000 species of mites, scorpions, pseudoscorpions, spiders, harvestmen, and whip scorpions; body divided into *prosoma* (fused head and thorax) and *opisthosoma* (abdomen); head lacking antennae and compound eyes; four pairs of legs present, and a pair of fangs (*chelicerae*); breathe by means of specialized regions of the body wall with a thin, highly-folded cuticle (*book lungs*) or by means of internal air tubes (*tracheae*).

arachnodactyly [araknohdaktilee] *Marfan's syndrome*

Arafat, Yasser [arafat], originally **Mohammed Abd al-Ra'uf Arafat** (1929–) Palestinian leader, born in Egypt. He studied at Cairo University (1952–6), and co-founded the Fatah resistance group in 1959. This group gained control of the Palestine Liberation Organization (PLO), founded in 1964, and he became the chairman of its executive committee. In the 1980s the growth of factions within the PLO reduced his power, and in 1982 the Israeli invasion forced him to leave Beirut, and to relocate the PLO executive in Tunis. In 1988, King Hussein of Jordan surrendered his right to administer the West Bank, indicating that the PLO might take over the responsibility. Arafat, to the surprise of many Western politicians, persuaded most of his colleagues to formally acknowledge the right of Israel to co-exist with an independent state of Palestine. Elected president of the PLO Central Committee in 1988, his support for Saddam Hussein in the 1990 Gulf Crisis hurt his international standing, but his reputation was largely restored following his support of Palestinian participation in the Madrid peace talks of 1991. After the negotiations with Israel in 1993, the Palestine National Authority (PNA) was set up in Jericho and Gaza, with Arafat as chairman. He was elected president in 1996 and headed the Legislative Council, working to establish a Palestinian state. He shared the Nobel Peace Prize in 1994.

Arafura Sea [arafoora] area 1 037 000 sq km/400 000 sq mi. Section of the Pacific Ocean, bounded N and NE by Indonesia and New Guinea, and S by Australia; shallow depths (27–55 m/90–180 ft) because of underlying continental shelf.

Aragón [aragon] pop (2000e) 1 194 000; area 47 669 sq km/18 400 sq mi. Autonomous region of NE Spain; featureless upland region largely occupying the basin of the R Ebro; Pyrenees in the N; sparsely populated; almonds, figs, vines, and olives grown by irrigation near rivers; a former kingdom (11th–15th-c), controlling much of N Spain, and conquering parts of S Italy in the 14th–15th-c.

Aragon, Louis [aragõ] (1897–1982) Political activist and writer, born in Paris, France. One of the most brilliant of the Surrealist group, he co-founded the journal *Littérature* with André Breton in 1919. He published two volumes of poetry, *Feu de joie* (1920) and *Le Mouvement perpétuel* (1925), and a Surrealist novel, *Le Paysan de Paris* (1926). After a visit to the Soviet Union in 1930 he became a convert to Communism, wrote a series of social-realistic novels entitled *Le Réel* (1933–51), and later edited the communist weekly *Les Lettres Françaises* (1953–72). Other novels include *La semaine sainte* (1958, Holy Week).

Aragón, House of [aragon] The ruling house of one of Spain's component kingdoms, founded (1035) by Ramiro I, the illegitimate son of Sancho the Great of Navarre. It was united by marriage with the ruling house of Barcelona in 1131. Fernando II of Aragon married Isabel of Castile in 1469, and the crowns of Aragon and Castile were finally united in 1479.

aragonite [aragoniyt] A mineral form of calcium carbonate ($CaCO_3$), occurring in some high-pressure alpine metamorphic rocks, sedimentary carbonate rocks, and in the shells of certain molluscs of which it forms the lining (mother-of-pearl).

Araguaia, River [aragwiya] Main tributary of the Tocantins R, NE Brazil, rising in C Brazil, and flowing NNE; length estimated at 1770–2410 km/1100–1500 mi; separates in mid course into two branches, enclosing Bananal I, world's largest river island (area 20 000 sq km/7700 sq mi), now containing a national park (area 5623 sq km/2170 sq mi); chief tributary (R Garças) noted for its mosquitos.

Arakan Pagoda *Mahamuni Pagoda*

Arakan Yoma [arakahn yohma] Mountain range in SW Myanmar, between the Arakan coast on the Bay of Bengal and the Ayeyarwady (Irrawaddy) R valley; rises to over 1980 m/6496 ft; forms a climatic barrier, cutting off C Myanmar from the effects of the SW monsoon.

Aral Sea [ahral], Russian **Aral'skoye More** Inland sea, E of the Caspian Sea, mainly in Kazakhstan; world's fourth largest lake, originally c.65 000 sq km/25 000 sq mi, c.420 km/260 mi long, 280 km/175 mi wide, maximum depth 70 m/230 ft; contains several small islands; generally shallow, with little navigation; sodium and magnesium sulphate mined along shores; diversion of water from rivers supplying the sea for cotton irrigation projects has seriously upset ecological balance; rapidly decreasing in size (shrunk by over half since 1960 and twice as saline – caused chiefly by irrigation taking too much water from its feeder rivers) sea level dropped by 12 m/40 ft; new desert (the Aralkum) of 2·6 million ha/6·5 million acres; water now heavily polluted, with loss of fishing industry, reduced wildlife, and increased disease. Kazakhstan and neighbouring Uzbekistan share the Aral's waters, and with Turkmenistan, Kyrgyzstan and Tajikistan, they have formed the International Fund for Saving the Aral Sea (Ifas). In 2003 an ambitious plan was launched to restore to health the N part of the Aral by building a massive dam to separate the two parts into which the sea has now split.

Aramaic [aramayik] One of the oldest languages in the Semitic group, still spoken by small communities in the Middle East. It is the basis of Syriac, a present-day dialect spoken by a million people in the Middle East and the USA. A dialect of Aramaic was the language used by Jesus and his disciples.

Aranda [aranda] The language spoken by the Aboriginal people of the region round Alice Springs, Northern Territory, Australia, predominantly associated with the MacDonnel Ranges; c.500–1000 live in Alice Springs, with several thousand others in surrounding settlements.

Araneae [aranee-ee] *spider*

Aran Islands Group of three islands (Inishmor, Inishmaan, Inisheer) off SW coast of Galway Co, Connacht, W Ireland; at the mouth of Galway Bay; each has an airstrip with flights from Carnmore, near Galway; boat service from Rossaveel; several monastic ruins and Dun Aengus fort.

Arany, János [**aw**rony] (1817–82) Poet, born in Nagy-Szalonta, E Hungary. With **Sandor Petöfi** he was a leader of the popular national school, and is regarded as one of the greatest of Hungarian poets. His chief work is the *Toldi* trilogy (1847–54), the story of the adventures of a young peasant in the 14th-c Hungarian court.

Ararat, (Great) Mount [ararat], Turkish **(Büyük) Ağri Daği** 39°44N 44°15E. Highest peak in Turkey; in E Turkey, close to the frontier with Iran and Armenia; height 5165 m/16 945 ft; said to be the landing place of Noah's Ark; **Little Ararat** (**Küçük Ağri Daği**) lies to the SE, rising to 3907 m/12 818 ft.

Araucanians [araw**kay**nianz] A South American Indian group of C Chile. Two divisions, the Picunche and the Huilliche, assimilated into Spanish society in the 17th-c; the Mapuche resisted for over three centuries, but were finally defeated by the Chilean army in the 1880s, and were settled on reservations. They presently number about 200 000, living on reservations and in towns and cities in Chile and Argentina.

araucaria [araw**kair**ia] An evergreen conifer, native to much of the S hemisphere except Africa; branches horizontal, in whorls; leaves usually scale-like, sometimes large; all produce edible seeds and useful timber, often sold as **parana pine**. (Genus: *Araucaria*, 18 species. Family: Araucariaceae.)

Arawak [arawak] American Indians of the Greater Antilles and South America. In the Antilles, they settled in villages and cultivated cassava and maize; frequently attacked by the Caribs, many were later killed by the Spanish. In South America, they lived in isolated small settlements in tropical Amazonian forests, and practised hunting, fishing, and farming. A few survivors live along the coastal strip of Guyana and Suriname. Arawakan languages are still widespread, spoken in parts of an area which extends from Central America to S Brazil.

arbitration The settlement of a dispute by reference to an independent party, the **arbitrator** (in Scotland, the **arbiter**). Contracts may provide for disputes to be settled in this way, in an attempt to avoid proceedings in the courts. There are specialist trade tribunals engaged in settling business disputes, such as the London Maritime Arbitrators Association. The American Arbitration Association helps settle labour disputes. Arbitration and other forms of alternative dispute resolution are increasingly popular alternatives in the UK and the USA to expensive, time-consuming, formal litigation. Both private and public US agencies provide arbitration services; the American Bar Association has a special committee on dispute resolution. Arbitrators, like judges, are immune from action in negligence. English courts attach great weight to arbitration agreements, which are binding. Disputes involving the work of government are often settled by specially created tribunals, such as the Lands Tribunal. Tribunals of Inquiry are appointed to investigate serious allegations of corruption or improper conduct in the public service.

Arbor Day In the USA, New Zealand, and parts of Canada and Australia, a day (whose date varies from place to place) set apart each year for planting trees and increasing public awareness of the value of trees; first observed in the State of Nebraska, USA, in 1872.

arboretum [ah(r)bor**ee**tum] A botanical garden, or a section of a botanical garden, used for the display and study of trees, shrubs, and vines.

arbor vitae [ah(r)baw(r) **vee**tiy] An evergreen coniferous tree or shrub native to North America, China, Japan, and Formosa; leaves scaly, overlapping, in opposite pairs, cones urn-shaped with thin scales. The name is rarely used for individual species, which are called **cedars** or **thujas**, qualified by country of origin or timber colour. (Genus: *Thuja*, 6 species. Family: Cupressaceae.)

Arbuthnot, John [ah(r)**buhth**not] (1667–1735) Physician and writer, born in Inverbervie, Aberdeenshire, NE Scotland. UK. A close friend of Jonathan Swift and all the literary celebrities of the day, he was also a distinguished doctor and writer of medical works, and a physician in ordinary to Queen Anne (1705). In 1712 he published five satirical pamphlets against the Duke of Marlborough, called *The History of John Bull*, which was the origin of the popular image of John Bull as the typical Englishman. He helped to found the Scriblerus Club, and was the chief contributor to the *Memoirs of Martinus Scriblerus* (1741).

arc Part of the curve bounding a region, usually the arc of a circle. The length of an arc of a circle radius r, that subtends an angle θ at the centre of the circle, is $r\theta$. The **minor arc** is the smaller of the two possible arcs AB; the **major arc** is the greater of the two.

Arc, Joan of *Joan of Arc, St*

Arcadia (Ancient Greece) [ah(r)**kay**dia] The mountainous area in the centre of the Peloponnese. Its inhabitants claimed to be pre-Dorian, and the oldest settlers of Hellenic stock in Greece.

Arcadia (mythology) [ah(r)**kay**dia] An ideal pastoral existence; also known as **Arcady**. *Et in Arcadia ego* is a proverbial expression found engraved on a tombstone in a painting by Poussin, usually taken to mean that death is present, even in the ideal world.

Arc de Triomphe [ah(r)k duh **tree**õf] A triumphal arch commemorating Napoleon's victories, designed by Jean Chalgrin (1739–1811) and erected (1806–35) in the Place Charles de Gaulle, Paris. It is 49 m/162 ft high and 45 m/147 ft wide.

Arcesilaus [ah(r)sesi**lay**us] (c.316–c.241 BC) Greek philosopher, born in Pitane, Aeolia. He became the sixth head of the Academy founded by Plato, and under his leadership the school became known as the 'Middle Academy' to distinguish it from Plato's 'Old Academy'. Arcesilaus modelled his philosophy on the critical dialectic of Plato's earlier dialogues but gave it a sharply sceptical turn, directed particularly against Stoic doctrines.

Arc-et-Senans [ah(r)k ay suhnõ] 47°02N 5°46E. A royal saltworks situated N of Arbois, EC France; a world heritage site. The architect, Claude-Nicolas Ledoux, had only partially realized his plan to incorporate a saline extraction plant with an ideal town, when building came to a halt in 1779. The works were abandoned by the end of the 19th-c.

arch *p.81*

Archaean or **Archean eon** [ah(r)**kee**an] The earlier of the two geological eons into which the Precambrian is divided; the period of time from the formation of the Earth (c.4600–2500 million years ago).

Archaebacteria [ah(r)keebak**teer**ia] A recently established kingdom comprising the methane-producing bacteria (*methanogens*). They differ from true bacteria and all higher organisms (the *eucaryotes*, in which the cells have a true nucleus) in numerous detailed characters relating to their ribonucleic acids, enzyme systems, and metabolic pathways. They possibly represent the oldest known life forms, existing more than 3 thousand million years ago.

archaeology / archeology The study of past peoples and societies through the systematic analysis of their material remains. It originated as an aspect of the revival of interest in classical culture during the Renaissance, and was, until the study of human antiquity was established in the 1860s, an almost exclusively European and antiquarian pursuit, interpreting chance survivals of monuments and artefacts by reference to biblical and classical precedent. The emphasis since has shifted firmly to the study of human development over the long period of more than 2 million years in which written records were non-existent (*prehistory*) or at best rudimentary (*protohistory*), and to the recovery of new data through excavation, field survey, laboratory study, and computer analysis. Radiometric dating methods established the discipline on a new and firmer footing in the 1950s and 1960s, and quantification and an increasing

arch

Part of a building, or a structure in its own right, made up of wedge-shaped stones or other pieces over an opening, which support both each other and any weight above. All classical and Norman arches are semicircular; other styles use a variety of shapes, including the elliptical, horseshoe, lancet, ogee, pointed, segmental, and Tudor. A **relieving** or **discharging** arch has no opening, being placed in a wall to direct weight away from an aperture further below.

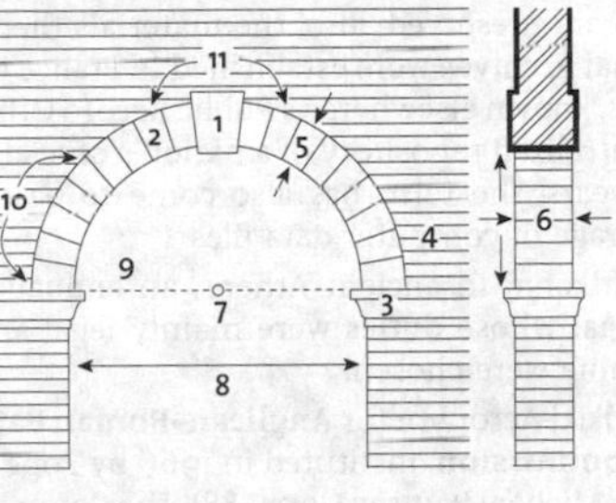

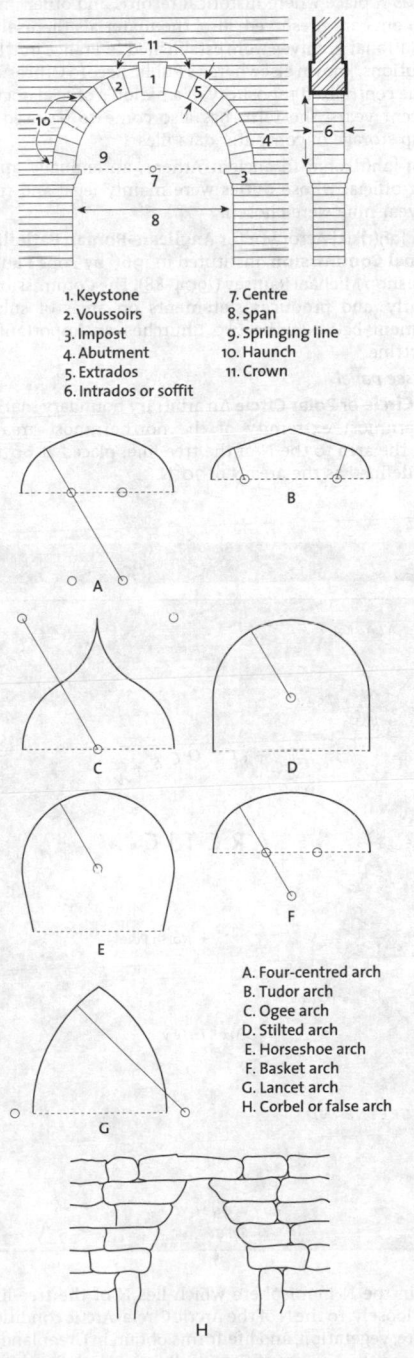

1. Keystone
2. Voussoirs
3. Impost
4. Abutment
5. Extrados
6. Intrados or soffit
7. Centre
8. Span
9. Springing line
10. Haunch
11. Crown

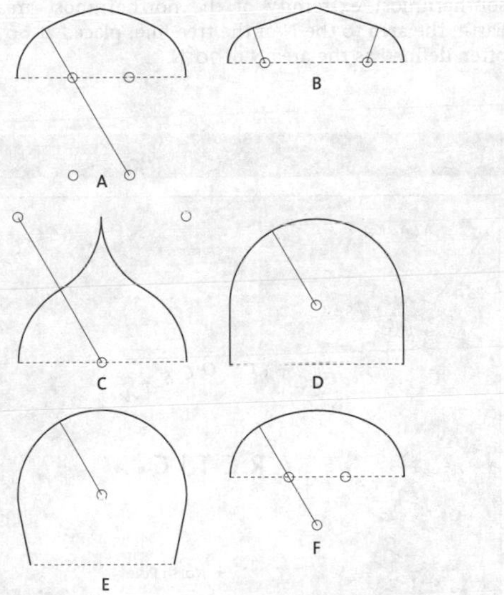

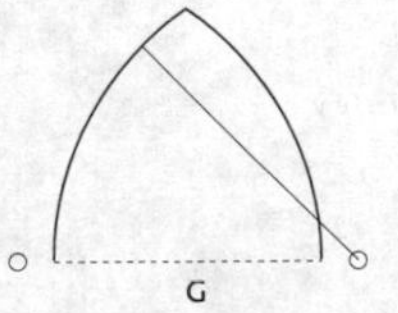

A. Four-centred arch
B. Tudor arch
C. Ogee arch
D. Stilted arch
E. Horseshoe arch
F. Basket arch
G. Lancet arch
H. Corbel or false arch

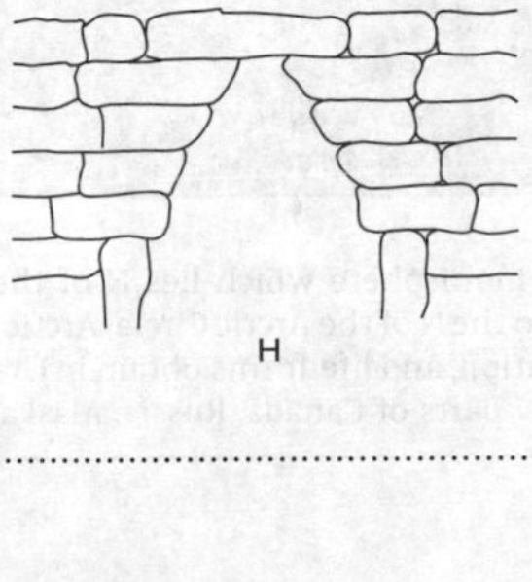

preoccupation with theory wrought an almost equivalent revolution in the 1970s and 1980s. Archaeology has continued throughout to grow in scope, so that it now involves anthropology, ecology, and systematics alongside the more traditional preoccupations of history, art history, and taxonomy. Politically too it has an often potent role to play in the modern world, its finest monuments standing at once as symbols of ancient culture and contemporary nationhood.

Archaeopteryx [ah(r)kiopteriks] The oldest fossil bird, known from the Jurassic period of Europe; characterized by feathers and a wishbone; distinguished from modern birds by reptilian features such as the long bony tail supported by vertebrae, three clawed fingers on wings and sharp teeth on both jaws.

Archangel, Russ **Arkhangelsk** 64°32N 40°40E, pop (2000e) 425 000. Port and capital city of Archangel oblast, European Russia; on R Severnaya Dvina, on an inlet of the White Sea; one of the largest sea and river ports in the state; harbour often icebound in winter; founded, 1584; airfield; railway; fishing, clothing, footwear, shipbuilding, transport equipment, timber; monastery dedicated to the Archangel Michael.

archbishop A bishop appointed to have jurisdiction over other bishops; often, the head of a province. The title sometimes refers to a bishop exercising special functions. In Eastern Churches, a hierarchy of archbishops is recognized.

archdeacon A clergyman in the Anglican Church responsible for the administration of the whole or such part of a diocese as the bishop may authorize. The office formerly existed also in Roman Catholic and Eastern Orthodox Churches.

archegonium [ah(r)kegohnium] The flask-shaped, female gamete-producing organ of bryophytes, pteridophytes, and gymnosperms. It is related to the development of land plants.

Archer, Fred(erick) (1857–86) Champion jockey, born in Cheltenham, Gloucestershire, SWC England, UK. He rode his first race in 1870, and during his career rode 2748 winners, including the Derby five times. His record of 246 winners in one season (1885) remained intact until it was beaten by Gordon Richards in 1933. He was also champion jockey 13 times in succession. He took his own life at age 29.

Archer (of Weston-Super-Mare), Jeffrey (Howard) Archer, Baron (1940–) Writer and former parliamentarian. He became Conservative MP for Louth (1969–74), but resigned after a financial disaster that led to bankruptcy. In order to pay his debts he turned to writing fiction. His first book, *Not a Penny More, Not a Penny Less* (1975), was an instant best-seller. Later books include *Shall We Tell the President?* (1976), *Kane and Abel* (1979), *First Among Equals* (1984), *As the Crow Flies* (1991), and *The Eleventh Commandment* (1998). His plays include *Beyond Reasonable Doubt* (1987) and *Exclusive* (1990). His short stories include *A Twist in the Tale* (1988). Several of his books have been dramatized on television. He was created a life peer in 1992. In 1999 he stood as a Conservative candidate for the London mayoral election, but was forced to stand down following disclosures of malpractice relating to his successful libel action against *The Star* newspaper in 1987. In 2001 he was sentenced to four years imprisonment after being found guilty of perjury and perverting the course of justice, and released on parole in 2003.

Archer, Robyn (1948–) Singer and actress, born in Adelaide, South Australia. She studied at Adelaide University and became a teacher of English until 1974, when she took up a singing career. In 1975 she played Jenny in Weill's *Threepenny Opera*, since when her name has been linked particularly with the German cabaret songs of Weill, Eisler, and Dessau. Her one-woman cabaret *A Star is Torn* (1979) and her 1981 show *The Pack of Women* both became successful books and recordings, the latter also being produced for television in 1986. In 1989 she was commissioned to write a new opera, *Mambo*, for the Nexus Opera, London. She was artistic director of the 1998 and 2000 Adelaide Festivals.

archerfish Any of the Asian marine and freshwater fishes renowned for their ability to dislodge or shoot down insect prey by spitting drops or jets of water over distances up to 3 m/10 ft; body length up to 25 cm/10 in. (Family: Toxotidae.)

archery The use of the bow and arrow, one of the first weapons used in battle. Until the development of gunpowder in the 14th-c, the bowman was the most powerful member of any army. When archery was no longer used in warfare its practice decreased, but in the late 17th-c it gained popularity as a sport. The governing body, the *Fédération Internationale de Tir à l'Arc* was formed in 1931. In competition, a series of arrows is fired from 30, 50, 70, and 90 m (roughly 100–300 ft) for men, and 30, 50, 60, and 70 m (roughly 100–230 ft) for women. The circular target consists of 10 scoring zones. The smallest is gold-coloured and worth 10 points if hit.

archetype (Gr 'original pattern') A prototype or permanent form of an event (birth/death), character (rebel/witch), or disposition. The concept owes much to J G Frazer's study *The Golden Bough* (1890–1915) which traces elemental patterns of myth and ritual, and to the studies in psychology of Carl Jung. Seen as recurring in life, archetypes are a fertile source of images in art and literature.

Archilochus of Paros [ah(r)**kil**okus, **pah**ros] (680–640BC) Greek poet from the island of Paros, Greece, who flourished c.650BC, and is regarded as the first of the lyric poets. Much of his renown is for vituperative satire. Only fragments of his work have survived.

Archimedes [ah(r)ki**mee**deez] (c.287–212 BC) Greek mathematician, born in Syracuse. He probably visited Egypt and studied at Alexandria. In popular tradition he is remembered for the construction of siege-engines against the Romans, the *Archimedes' screw* still used for raising water, and his cry of *eureka* ('I have found it') when he discovered the principle of the upthrust on a floating body. His real importance in mathematics, however, lies in his discovery of formulae for the areas and volumes of spheres, cylinders, parabolas, and other plane and solid figures. He founded the science of hydrostatics, but his astronomical work is lost. He was killed at the siege of Syracuse by a Roman soldier whose challenge he ignored while immersed in a mathematical problem.

Archimedes screw A device to raise water; named after the Greek mathematician Archimedes, who is said to have invented it. It consists of a broad threaded screw inside an inclined cylinder; as the screw is turned, the water is raised gradually between the threads and is run off at the top.

Archipenko, Alexander Porfirievich [ah(r)chi**peng**koh] (1887–1964) Sculptor, born in Kiev, Ukraine. He studied at the Kiev School of Art (1902–5) and in Paris (1908–21), where he was influenced by Cubism, and became famous for his combinations of sculpture and painting, as in 'Medrano II' (1914). After 1923 he settled in New York City, and taught at many institutions, including the New Bauhaus at Chicago (1937–9).

architecture The art or science of building; particularly used to differentiate between building and the art of designing buildings. In the latter context, there has been great division of opinion as to what exactly constitutes architecture. The most usual standpoint is typified by Ruskin in *The Seven Lamps of Architecture* (1849): 'Architecture is the art which so disposes and adorns the edifices raised by man, for whatsoever uses, that the sight of them may contribute to his mental health, power, and pleasure.' Pevsner, in *An Outline of European Architecture* (1943) puts it more succinctly: 'A bicycle shed is a building; Lincoln Cathedral is a piece of architecture.' Traditionally, therefore, architecture has tended to concentrate on aspects of higher culture, looking at ennobling buildings such as the Parthenon (Athens) and the Pantheon (Rome), and studying the work of great artist-architects such as Wren and Schinkel. Nevertheless, the practice of architecture in the 19th-c, and especially in the 20th-c, increasingly involved a larger number and variety of often complex skills and disciplines, ranging from the technical considerations of structural engineering, environmental services, and energy conservation, to the functional considerations of room layout, interior design, and human comfort, as well as the overtly intellectual considerations stressed by Ruskin and Pevsner. Correspondingly, there has been a greater acceptance of the wider concerns and domain of architecture as anything which has been consciously, or even unconsciously, designed and built for the use of people.

architrave In Classical or Renaissance architecture, the lowest and least decorated of the three bands of an entablature. An architrave can also refer to the stone frame surrounding a door or window aperture.

archives A place where historical records and other important documents are preserved; also, the materials themselves. The first National Archives were established in France in 1789. Such institutions, known elsewhere as Public Record Offices, are usually the centralized repository of a nation's official documents. In recent years, the term has also come to be used for the backup storage of computer data files.

archon [**ah(r)**kohn] In ancient Athens, an annually appointed public official whose duties were mainly legal and religious; each year nine were chosen.

ARCIC [**ah(r)**kik] Acronym for **Anglican–Roman Catholic International Commission**, instituted in 1966 by Pope Paul VI and Archbishop Michael Ramsey (1904–88). The Commission meets regularly, and produces statements on areas of substantial agreement between the two Churches on important points of doctrine.

Arctic *see panel*

Arctic Circle or **Polar Circle** An arbitrary boundary marking the southernmost extremity of the northernmost area of the Earth; the area to the N of the tree-line; placed at 66°17N, but often defined as the area N of 70°N.

Arctic

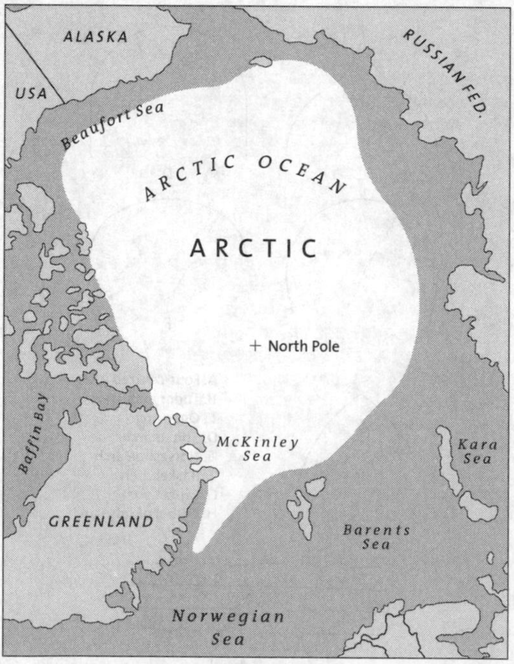

Area in the N hemisphere which lies N of the tree-line or, more loosely, to the N of the Arctic Circle; Arctic conditions of climate, vegetation, and life-forms obtain in Greenland, Svalbard, and the N parts of Canada, Russia, Alaska, and Iceland.

Arctic Council An organization formed in 1996 by seven countries bordering the Arctic Ocean: Canada, Denmark (for Greenland), Iceland, Norway, Sweden, Russia, and the USA, plus Finland. Based in Ottawa for the first two years, it would advise governments on issues to do with the protection and development of the Arctic's aboriginal peoples.

Arctic fox A fox widespread on Arctic land masses (*Alopex lagopus*); hairy feet and small ears; eats lemmings, birds, hares, fish, carrion; coat thickens in winter; two forms: one white in winter, brown in summer; the other (**blue fox** of Greenland) pale blue-grey in winter, darker blue-grey in summer.

Arctic Ocean Body of water within the Arctic Circle; world's smallest ocean, 13 986 000 sq km/5 400 000 sq mi; frozen all year except in marginal areas; greatest depth, Eurasia Basin, 5122 m/16 804 ft; forms the cold East Greenland Current and the Labrador Current; hummocky icefields in winter, pack-ice during summer, carried S by surface currents (generally melting N of the major shipping lanes); unexplored until Amundsen's flight, 1926; research suggests the Ocean is experiencing a period of warming.

Arctic tern A small tern found worldwide (*Sterna paradisaea*); migrates further than any other bird (approximately 36 000 km/22 000 mi per year); spends N summer in the Arctic, and N winter in the Antarctic.

Arcturus *Boötes*

Ardashir I [ah(r)dasheer] or **Artaxerxes** (c.211–41) King of Persia (224–41), and founder of the new Persian dynasty of the Sassanids. He overthrew Artabanus IV, the last of the Parthian kings in AD c.226. He entered into battle with Alexander Severus (232), and though Alexander celebrated victory in Rome, Ardashir took Armenia and Persian power was firmly established. He was succeeded by Shapur I.

Arden, Elizabeth, originally **Florence Nightingale Graham** (?1878–1966) Beautician and businesswoman, born in Woodbridge, Ontario, SE Canada. A nurse by training, she went to New York City in 1907 and opened a beauty salon on Fifth Avenue in 1910, adopting the personal and business name of 'Elizabeth Arden'. She produced cosmetics on a large scale, and developed a worldwide chain of salons. With her rival, Helena Rubinstein, she made make-up acceptable to 'respectable' American women, to whom Arden introduced eyeshadow, mascara, and lipstick tinted to match their outfits. As Elizabeth N Graham she operated Maine Chance Stables in Kentucky, where the 1947 Kentucky Derby winner was bred.

Arden, John (1930–) Playwright, born in Barnsley, South Yorkshire, N England, UK. He studied at King's College, Cambridge, and the Edinburgh College of Art. His first play, the romantic comedy *All Fall Down*, was produced in 1955. His aggressive awareness of N England is particularly evident in *The Workhouse Donkey* (1963), a caricature of northern local politics, and in *Serjeant Musgrave's Dance* (1959), following the tradition of Brecht in its staging. He has continually experimented with dramatic form and theatrical technique. His wife, **Margaretta D'Arcy** (1934–), has collaborated with him in many plays, such as *The Happy Haven* (1960), *The Island of the Mighty* (1972), and *Whose is the Kingdom?* (1988). He has also written television and radio scripts, essays, such as *Awkward Corners* (1988, with his wife), and the novels *Silence Among the Weapons* (1982), *Books of Bale* (1988), and *Jack Juggler and the Emperor's Whore* (1995).

Ardnamurchan Point [ardnamerkhan] 56°44N 6°14W. Cape in SW Highland, W Scotland, UK; N of Mull I; westernmost point on British mainland; lighthouse (1849) has a fixed light visible for 30 km/20 mi.

Area of Outstanding Natural Beauty (AONB) An area in England and Wales which does not merit National Park status, but where special measures are needed to preserve its natural interest and beauty. They are generally smaller than National Parks, and are the responsibility of local authorities and the Countryside Commission.

areca *betel-nut*

Arecibo Observatory [ariseeboh] A radio astronomy observatory in Puerto Rico, opened in 1963. A natural hollow has been lined with metal panels to create the world's largest single radio telescope, 305 m/1000 ft in diameter.

arena stage *theatre in the round*

Arendt, Hannah [arent] (1906–75) Philosopher and political theorist, born in Hanover, NC Germany. She moved to the USA in 1940 as a refugee from the Nazis, becoming a US citizen in 1951. She held several academic posts, notably at the University of Chicago (1963–7) and the New School for Social Research, New York City (from 1967). An active worker in various Jewish organizations, her books include *Origins of Totalitarianism* (1951), *Eichmann in Jerusalem* (1963), and *The Life of the Mind* (1978).

Areopagus [arayopagus] In ancient Greece, the name for the hill in Athens which was the seat of the oldest council of state, and also for the council whose meetings took place there. The name means 'the hill of Ares' (the god of war).

Arequipa [araykeepa] 16°25S 71°32W, pop (2000e) 758 000. Capital of Arequipa department, S Peru; in a valley at the foot of El Misti volcano; altitude 2380 m/7808 ft; built on the site of an ancient Inca city; main commercial centre for S Peru; airfield; railway; two universities (1828, 1964); wool, textiles, soap; cathedral (1612, rebuilt 19th-c), La Companía church, Puente Bolívar, Santa Catalina convent. The historic centre of the city is a world heritage site.

Ares [aireez] The Greek god of war, son of Zeus and Hera, often perceived as hostile, rather than as a national deity, as in other mythologies. He represents the sudden violence of battle, and often helps foreigners rather than the Greeks.

arête [aret] (Fr 'edge') A sharp, jagged mountain ridge separating cirques or valleys. It is formed by glacial erosion, and often further weathered by frost shattering.

Arethusa [arethyooza] In Greek mythology, a nymph who was pursued by the river-god Alpheus from Arcadia in Greece to Ortygia in Sicily. The myth attempts to account for the freshwater fountain which appears in the harbour of Syracuse and was believed to have flowed under the Ionian Sea.

Aretino, Pietro [areteenoh] (1492–1557) Poet, born in Arezzo, NC Italy. In Rome (1517–27) he distinguished himself by his wit, impudence, and talents, and secured the favour of Pope Leo X, which he subsequently lost by writing his 16 salacious *Sonetti lussuriosi* (1524, Lewd Sonnets). A few years later he settled in Venice, there also acquiring powerful friends. His poetical works include five witty comedies and a tragedy.

Arezzo [aretsoh] 43°28N 11°53E, pop (2000e) 93 000. Capital town of Arezzo province, Tuscany, NW Italy; 80 km/50 mi SE of Florence; on the site of an Etruscan settlement; engineering, textiles, furniture, pottery, leather, jewellery making (gold); antiques centre, trade in olive oil and wine; birthplace of Petrarch; Church of Pieve di Santa Maria (12th–14th-c); Gothic cathedral (begun 1277); mediaeval jousting (Sep).

argali [ah(r)galee] A wild sheep (*Ovis ammon*) from the margins of the Gobi Desert; the largest living sheep (1·2 m/4 ft tall at the shoulder); pale brown with white rump; large curling horns on either side of head; also known as **argalis**, **Siberian argali**, or **Marco Polo's sheep**.

Argentina *p.84*

Argentine–Brazilian War (1825–8) A war fought to decide the possession of the Banda Oriental, territory to the E of the R Uruguay occupied by Brazil in 1817. As a result of British pressure and mediation, the province became the independent republic of Uruguay (1828).

Argolid [ah(r)golid] The fertile plain between the mountains and the sea in the E Peloponnese near the town of Argos. It flourished particularly in Mycenaean times: besides Argos itself, Mycenae and Tiryns were located there.

argon Ar, element 18, boiling point −189°C. The commonest of the noble or rare gases, with no known compounds, it makes up about 1% of the Earth's atmosphere, and is fractionally distilled with difficulty from oxygen (boiling-point −183°C). It is used to

Argentina

official name **The Argentine Republic**, Span **La República Argentina**

Local name Argentina

Timezone GMT −3

Area American continent: 2 780 092 km^2/1 073 115 sq mi on Antarctic continent: 964 250 km^2/372 200 sq mi

Population total (2002e) 36 446 000

Status Republic

Date of independence 1816

Capital Buenos Aires

Language Spanish (official)

Ethnic groups European origin (c.85%), mestizo European/Indian origin (15%)

Religions Roman Catholic (90%), Protestant and Jewish minorities

Physical features Divided into four regions: sub-tropical NE plains, the Pampa, Patagonia, and the Andes; the Andes stretch the entire length of Argentina (N–S), forming the boundary with Chile; highest peak, Aconcagua 6960 m/22 831 ft; uneven, semi-desert, arid steppes in the S (Patagonia); grassy, treeless Pampa to E; N drained by the Paraguay, Paraná, and Uruguay rivers, which join in the R Plate estuary; island of Tierra del Fuego off the S tip.

Climate Moderately humid sub-tropical climate in the NE; average annual temperature 16°C; average annual rainfall 500–1000 mm/20–40 in; semi-arid in interior S lowlands; Pampa temperate, dry in W and humid in E, with temperatures ranging from tropical to moderately cool; S directly influenced by strong prevailing westerlies; serious flooding in NE (May 2003).

Currency 1 Peso = 100 centavos (formerly the austral)

Economy Major contribution to economy from agricultural produce and meat processing; deposits of oil and natural gas, chiefly off the coast of Patagonia; important reserves of iron ore, coal, copper, lead, zinc, gold, silver, uranium, manganese.

GDP (2002e) $403·8 bn, per capita $10 500

Human Development Index (2002) 0·844

History Pre-colonially, nomadic Indian hunters lived in S and Inca farmers in NW; after a long battle settled in the 16th-c by the Spanish; declared independence as the federal Republic of Argentina in 1816, and United Provinces of the Río de la Plata established; dictatorship of Juan Manuel de Rosas during 1829–52; federal constitution in 1853; ranchers' oligarchy of 1916 ended by military coup in 1930; acquisition of the Gran Chaco after war with Paraguay, 1865–70; considerable European settlement since the opening up of the Pampas in the 19th-c; Juan Perón elected president (1946 and 1973); eventually succeeded by his wife Isabel (Martínez de Perón) who was deposed in 1976; attempt to control the Falkland Is (1982) failed following war with the UK; successive military governments, until federal constitution re-established in 1983; governed by a President and a bicameral National Congress, with a Chamber of Deputies and a Senate; four presidents resigned amid riots and lootings in protests over stringent economic sanctions (2001–2).

Head of State/Government

1940–3 Ramón S Castillo
1943–4 Pedro P Ramírez
1944–6 Edelmiro J Farrell
1946–55 Juan Domingo Perón
1955–8 Eduardo Lonardi
1958–62 Arturo Frondizi
1962–3 José María Guido
1963–6 Arturo Illia
1966–70 Juan Carlos Onganía
1970–1 Roberto Marcelo Levingston
1971–3 Alejandro Agustín Lanusse
1973 Héctor J Cámpora
1973–4 Juan Domingo Perón
1974–6 María Estela (Isabelita) Martinez de Perón
1976–81 *Military junta* (Jorge Rafaél Videla)
1981 *Military junta* (Roberto Eduardo Viola)
1981–2 *Military junta* (Leopoldo Fortunato Galtieri)
1982–3 Reynaldo Bignone
1983–8 Raúl Alfonsín Foulkes
1988–99 Carlos Saúl Menem
1999–2001 Fernando de la Rua
2001 Ramon Puerta *interim*
2001 Adolfo Rodriquez Saa *interim*
2001 Eduardo Camano *interim*
2002–3 Eduardo Duhalde
2003– Néstor Kirchner

provide inert atmospheres, especially inside incandescent light bulbs.

argonaut *paper nautilus*

Argonauts [ah(r)gonawts] In Greek mythology, the heroes who sailed in the ship *Argo* to find the Golden Fleece. Under Jason's leadership they sailed through the Symplegades (presumably the Dardanelles) and along the Black Sea coast to Colchis. Their return is variously described, and may have included a river-passage to the North Sea.

Argos [ah(r)gohs, -gos] 37°38N 22°43E, pop (2000e) 22 500. Ancient town in Peloponnese region, S Greece, in a fertile plain near the Gulf of Argolikos; involved in wars with Sparta, 7th–4th-c BC; railway; commercial and agricultural centre; many archaeological remains.

argument In mathematics, the angle made with the real axis by the line joining the origin to the point P representing the complex number z. When the complex number is written in the form $r(\cos\theta + i\sin\theta)$, θ is the argument.

Argus [ah(r)gus] In Greek mythology, **1** A watchman with a hundred eyes, appointed by Hera to watch over Io; after Argus was killed by Hermes, the eyes were placed in the tail of the peacock. **2** The name of Odysseus's dog, who greeted his master on his return after 20 years absence, and then died.

Århus or **Aarhus** [aw(r)hoos] 56°08N 10°11E, pop (2000e) 271 300. Capital of Århus county, E Jutland, Denmark; in a wide bay of the Kattegat, S of Ålborg; cultural and educational hub of C Jylland; railway; university (1928); engineering, foodstuffs, machinery, textiles; cathedral (1201).

aria A song with an Italian text, especially one which forms part of a larger work, such as an opera, oratorio, or cantata. The 'da capo' or ternary structure (A–B–A) of most Baroque arias is often referred to simply as 'song form'.

Ariadne [ariadnee] In Greek mythology, the daughter of the King of Crete (Minos). She enabled Theseus to escape from the labyrinth by giving him a ball of thread. He fled with her, but deserted her on the island of Naxos; there she eventually became the wife of Dionysus.

Ariane launch vehicle [areean] A family of launch vehicles developed as a result of a 1973 agreement among member states of the European Space Agency. The first launch of Ariane 1 was in December 1979 from the Kourou launch site in French Guiana and led to operational readiness in 1981. The French National Centre for Space Research was the prime contractor for the Ariane development, which was commercialized in 1980 with the formation of the French private company Arianespace. The latest version is Ariane 5, which has a cryogenic main stage, with a diameter of 5·4 m/17·7 ft, carrying 158·11 tonnes (155·6 UK long tons/143·4 US short tons) of propellant (liquid oxygen and hydrogen). Two large solid boosters provide the bulk of the thrust required at lift-off. The launcher was qualified for operational use in 1998 after an unsuccessful maiden flight in 1996. An enhanced version of Ariane 5 veered off course on its inaugural flight (2002), and was blown up by remote control. Later flights were successful.

Arianism *Arius*

Arica [areeka] 18°28S 70°18W, pop (2000e) 219 400. Port on the Pacific coast of Chile, SW of La Paz, Bolivia, most northerly city in Chile; acquired from Peru after the War of the Pacific, 1883; airport; railway; major trading outlet for Bolivia; oil pipeline with Bolivia; port trade, fishmeal, tourism; Museo Histórico y de Armas (Pacific war museum); San Marcos cathedral built in iron by Eiffel, customs house.

arid zone A climatic zone in which potential evapotranspiration (the maximum loss of water, given an unlimited supply) exceeds precipitation. Geographers use an upper limit of 250 mm/10 in of annual rainfall to define the zone, which is found between latitudes 15° and 30°N and S of the Equator. Most of the world's hot deserts are found in the arid zone.

Ariel [aireeuhl] The fourth-largest satellite of Uranus: distance from the planet 191 000 km/119 000 mi; diameter 1160 km/720 mi. It was discovered in 1851 by British amateur astronomer William Lassell (1799–1880).

Aries [aireez] (Lat 'ram') A constellation in the N sky; brightest star, Hamal. It is a spring sign of the zodiac, lying between Pisces and Taurus. The 'first point of Aries' is the place on the celestial sphere where the vernal equinox lies, but precession has pushed this into the neighbouring constellation Pisces.

aril [aril] The outgrowth surrounding a fertilized seed or ovule. It is often fleshy and brightly-coloured, as in the berry-like arils of the yew and spindle tree, but also hairy or spongy, as in the buoyant seeds of water lilies.

Ariosto, Ludovico [ariostoh] (1474–1533) Poet, born in Reggio nell'Emilia, N Italy. He intended to take up law, but abandoned it for poetry. In 1503 he was introduced to the court of the Cardinal Ippolito d'Este at Ferrara, where he produced his great poem, *Orlando furioso* (1516), the Roland epic that forms a continuation of Boiardo's *Orlando innamorato*. The rich structure of *Orlando* features a main plot and several minor ones, and a stylistic balance which fuses reality and fantasy. When the cardinal left Italy (1518), the duke, his brother, invited the poet to his service. He then composed his comedies, and gave the finishing touch to his *Orlando*. Besides his great work, he wrote comedies, satires, sonnets, and a number of Latin poems.

Aristaeus [aristeeus] In Greek mythology, a minor deity of the countryside, who introduced bee-keeping, vines, and olives. He pursued Eurydice, the wife of Orpheus, who trod on a snake and died; in revenge her sister dryads killed his bees. Proteus told him to sacrifice cattle to appease the dryads, and in nine days he found bees generated in the carcasses.

Aristarchus of Samos [aristah(r)kos], also spelled **Aristarchos** (c.310–230 BC) Alexandrian astronomer who seems to have anticipated Copernicus, maintaining that the Earth moves round the Sun. Only one of his works has survived.

Aristarchus of Samothrace [aristah(r)kos] (c.215–145 BC) Alexandrian grammarian and critic, best known for his edition of Homer. He wrote many commentaries and treatises, edited several authors, and was the founder of a school of philologists. He was in charge of the Library of Alexandria for over 30 years.

Aristides [aristiydeez], known as **Aristides the Just** (c.530–c.468 BC) Athenian soldier and statesman. He became chief archon (489–488 BC), but about 483 BC his opposition to Themistocles' naval policy led to his ostracization. When the Persians invaded in 480 BC Aristides returned from banishment to serve at the Battle of Salamis, and was the Athenian general at Plataea (479 BC). Through him, Athens, not Sparta, became the ruling state of the Delian League.

Aristippus [aristipus] (4th-c BC) Greek philosopher, a native of Cyrene in Africa, hence the name of his followers, the *Cyrenaics*, who became an influential school. Their main doctrines were hedonism and the primacy of one's own immediate feelings. He became a pupil of Socrates at Athens, and taught philosophy both at Athens and Aegina, but lived much of his life as a voluptuary in Syracuse, at the court of Dionysius the tyrant.

Aristophanes [aristofaneez] (c.448–c.388 BC) Greek playwright. He is said to have written 54 plays, but only 11 are extant. His writings fall into three periods. To the first period, ending in 425 BC, belong *The Acharnians*, *The Knights*, *The Clouds*, and *The Wasps*, the poet's four masterpieces, named from their respective choruses, and *Peace*, in all of which full rein is given to political satire. To the second, ending in 406 BC, belong *The Birds*, *Lysistrata*, *Thesmophoriazusae*, and *Frogs*. To the third, ending c.388 BC, belong *The Ecclesiazusae* and *The Plutus*, comedies in which the role of the chorus, which was the distinctive characteristic of the Old Comedy, and political allusions disappear.

Aristotle [aristotl] (384–322 BC) Greek philosopher, scientist, and physician, one of the greatest figures in the history of Western thought, born in Stagira, Macedonia. In 367 he went to Athens, where he was associated with Plato's Academy until Plato's death in 347 BC. He then spent time in Asia Minor and in Mytilene (on Lesbos). In 342 BC he was invited by Philip of Macedon to educate his son, Alexander (later, the Great). He returned to Athens (335 BC) and opened a school (the *Lyceum*); his followers were called *Peripatetics*, supposedly from his practice of walking up and down restlessly during his lectures. After Alexander's death (323 BC), there was strong anti-Macedonian sentiment in Athens; Aristotle was accused of impiety and, perhaps with Socrates' fate in mind, escaped to Chalcis in Euboea, where he died the next year.

Aristotle's writings represented an enormous, encyclopedic output over virtually every field of knowledge: logic, metaphysics, ethics, politics, rhetoric, poetry, biology, zoology, physics, and psychology. The bulk of the work that survives actually consists of unpublished material in the form of lecture notes or students' textbooks; but even this incomplete corpus is extraordinary for its range, originality, systematization, and sophistication, and his work exerted an enormous influence on mediaeval philosophy (especially through St Thomas Aquinas), Islamic philosophy (especially through Averroës), and indeed on the whole Western intellectual and scientific tradition. The works most read today include the *Metaphysics* (the book written 'after the *Physics*'), *Nicomachean Ethics*, *Politics*, *Poetics*, *De anima*, and the *Organon* (treatises on logic).

arithmetic The practical skill of calculating with numbers, in contrast to number theory. The four operations of addition, subtraction, multiplication, and division are defined over the set of all real numbers, and used essentially for practical results. Examples include the total cost of buying two items, one costing 30p and the other 40p (addition); the change received from a $5 bill when buying an item costing $2 (subtraction); the cost of 4 litres of oil at 50 francs a litre (multiplication); and the number of papers that can be bought for $10 if one paper costs $1 (division).

arithmetic average / mean *mean*

arithmetic sequence A sequence in which the difference between any one term and the next is constant; sometimes called an **arithmetic progression**. The term **arithmetic series** is now usually reserved for the sum of the terms of the arithmetic sequence. Thus the terms 1,4,7,10 form an arithmetic sequence; 1+4+7+10 is an arithmetic series. If the first term of an arithmetic sequence is a and the common difference is d, the sequence is $a,a+d,a+2d...$, the nth term is $a+(n-1)d$, and the sum of the terms in the sequence is $\frac{1}{2}n[2a+(n-1)d]$.

Arius [ahrius] (Gr **Areios**) (c.250–336) Founder of Arianism, born in Libya. He trained in Antioch, and became a presbyter in Alexandria. He claimed (c.319) that, in the doctrine of the Trinity, the Son was not co-equal or co-eternal with the Father, but only the first and highest of all finite beings, created out of nothing by an act of God's free will. He won some support, but was deposed and excommunicated in 321 by a synod of bishops at Alexandria. The subsequent controversy was fierce, so the Council of Nicaea (Nice) was called in 325 to settle the issue. Out of this came the definition of the absolute unity of the divine essence, and the equality of the three persons of the Trinity. Arius was banished, but recalled in 334, and died in Constantinople. After his death the strife spread more widely abroad: the West was mainly orthodox, the East largely Arian or semi-Arian; but despite later revivals the doctrine was largely suppressed by the end of the 4th-c.

Arizona pop (2000e) 5 130 600; area 295 249 sq km/ 114 000 sq mi. State in SW USA, divided into 14 counties; the 'Grand Canyon State'; Spanish exploration, 1539; part of New Spain (1598–1821), then included in newly-independent Mexico; acquired by the USA in the Treaty of Guadalupe Hidalgo (1848) and the Gadsden Purchase (1853); a separate territory, 1863; until 1886 frequently attacked by Apache Indians (under Cochise, then Geronimo); joined the Union as the 48th state, 1912; capital, Phoenix; other chief cities, Tucson, Mesa, Tempe; bounded S by Mexico; rivers include the Colorado (forms most of the W border), Gila, and Salt; the Hoover Dam causes the Colorado R to swell into L Mead; several mountain ranges (highest the San Francisco Mts); highest point Humphreys Peak (3862 m/12 670 ft); the Colorado Plateau (N) is a high, dry plain incised by deep canyons (notably the Grand Canyon on the Colorado R); to the S are desert basins interspersed with bare mountain peaks, then relatively low, desert plains; a huge area of national and state forest in the centre; scant rainfall and aridity; cattle on irrigated land; dairy products, cotton, lettuce, hay; computer equipment, aerospace components, timber products, machinery; produces two-thirds of the nation's copper supply; tourism the most important industry (Grand Canyon, Petrified Forest, meteor craters); Kitt Peak National Observatory; Navajo, Hopi, Apache, Papago, and other Indian reservations; largest Indian population in the USA.

Arjan Dev, known as **Guru Arjan Dev** (1581–1606) Sikh leader, the compiler of the Adi Granth in 1604, born in Goindwal, Punjab, India. The text used today is an expanded version of his original compilation and is revered by all Sikhs. He began the construction of the Harimandir, or Golden Temple, at Amritsar, and extended the social reforms and missionary work begun by earlier gurus. After the Mughal emperor Akbar died, his successor, Jahangir, began to oppress the Sikhs and ordered Guru Arjan to eliminate all sections of the Adi Granth that offended Hindus or Muslims. He refused and was tortured to death.

Arjuna [ah(r)juna] An Indian hero. In the *Bhagavadgita*, he hesitates before entering the battle, knowing the killing which will ensue. His charioteer, Krishna, urges him to fulfil the action which is his duty as a warrior, explaining that the whole universe needs the fulfilment of actions which advance God's will.

ark *Ark of the Covenant; Noah*

Arkansas [ah(r)kansaw] pop (2000e) 2 673 400; area 137 749 sq km/53 187 sq mi. State in SC USA, divided into 75 counties; the 'Land of Opportunity'; the first white settlement established by the French as part of French Louisiana, 1686; ceded to the US as part of the Louisiana Purchase, 1803; included in the Territory of Missouri, 1812; became a separate territory, 1819; joined the Union as the 25th state, 1836; seceded, 1861; re-admitted, 1868; capital, Little Rock; other chief cities, Fort Smith, North Little Rock, Pine Bluff; rivers include the Mississippi (forms the E border), Red (part of SW border), and Arkansas; the Boston Mts, part of the Ozark Plateau, rise in the NW, and the Ouachita Mts in the W; highest point, Mt Magazine (860 m/2821 ft); the mountainous region is bisected by the Arkansas R valley; extensive plains in the S and E; over half the state covered by commercial forest; many lakes; poultry, soybeans, rice (the nation's leading producer), cattle, dairy, cotton; processed foods, electrical equipment, paper, timber products, chemicals; the nation's leading bauxite producer; petroleum, natural gas; a major tourist area; resistance to school desegregation made Little Rock a focus of world attention in 1957.

Arkansas River [ah(r)kansaw, ah(r)**kansas**] River in SC USA; rises in the Rocky Mountains, Colorado; flows SE through Kansas, Oklahoma, and Arkansas; joins the Mississippi S of Memphis; length 2330 km/1450 mi; major tributaries the Cimmaron, Canadian, Neosho, Verdigris; navigable for its length in Arkansas.

Ark of the Covenant A portable wooden chest overlaid with gold and having a cherub with extended wings mounted at each end of the golden lid (the 'mercy seat'). In the Hebrew Bible/Old Testament it is described as having many successive functions – containing the two tablets of the Decalogue, serving as a symbol of the divine presence guiding Israel, and acting as a safeguard in war. Biblical traditions suggest it was constructed under Moses, taken into battle in David's time, housed in the Temple under Solomon, and is now lost (though reports of its location in a remote monastery in Ethiopia and in other places have been made in recent years). Torah scrolls are still kept in containers called 'arks' in Jewish synagogues.

ark shell A sedentary bivalve mollusc with two similar, typically trapezoidal shells (valves); adults typically attached to a substrate surface by tough filaments (*byssus* threads); c.250 species, mostly marine. (Class: Pelecypoda. Order: Arcoida.)

Arkwright, Sir Richard (1732–92) Inventor of mechanical cotton-spinning, born in Preston, Lancashire, NW England, UK. He became a barber in Bolton, later (with John Kay) devoting himself to inventions in cotton-spinning. In 1768 he set up his celebrated spinning-frame in Preston – the first machine that could produce cotton thread of sufficient strength to be used as warp. He introduced several mechanical processes into his factories, and many of his rivals copied his designs. Popular opinion went against him on the grounds that his inventions reduced the need for labour, and in 1779 his large mill near Chorley was destroyed by a mob. He was knighted in 1786.

Arles [ah(r)l] or **Arles-sur-Rhône** 43°41N 4°38E, pop (2000e) 55 000. Old town in Bouches-du-Rhône department, SE France; 72 km/45 mi NE of Marseille, at head of the Rhône delta; capital of Gaul, 4th-c; formerly an important crossroads and capital of Provence; railway; boatbuilding, metalwork, foodstuffs, hats; Roman remains, including a huge arena and theatre (a world heritage site), 11th-c cathedral; associations with van Gogh and Gauguin; several art museums.

Arlington pop (2000e) 189 500; area 68 sq km/26 sq mi. County of Virginia, USA, a suburb of Washington, DC; site of the **Arlington National Cemetery** (1920) with a memorial amphitheatre and Tomb of the Unknown Soldier; Pentagon Building; Washington National Airport.

Arlington, Henry Bennet, 1st Earl of (1618–85) English statesman, born in Arlington, N Greater London, UK. He studied at Oxford, becoming secretary of state (1662–74) under Charles II and one of the king's Cabal ministry. In 1674 he was unsuccessfully impeached for popery and self-aggrandizement. He then served as Lord Chamberlain, negotiated the Triple Alliance against France (1668), and helped to develop the English party system.

Arlott, (Leslie Thomas) John (1914–91) Writer, journalist, and broadcaster, born in Basingstoke, Hampshire, S England, UK. Educated there, he worked as a police detective (1934–45) before joining the BBC, where as a cricket commentator on radio and television he became one of the country's most recognizable broadcasting voices. He wrote numerous books about cricket and cricketers, including *How to Watch Cricket* (1949, 1983) and *Arlott on Cricket* (1984). He won the Sports Journalist of the Year Award in 1979, and was Sports Presenter of the Year in 1980.

arm A term commonly used to denote the whole of the upper limb; more precisely, in anatomy, the region between the shoulder and elbow joints, distinguished from the *forearm* (between the elbow and wrist joints), and the *hand* (beyond the wrist joint). The arm articulates with the trunk via the *pectoral girdle* (the scapula, or shoulder blade, and clavicle). The bones are the *humerus* in the arm, the *radius* (on the outside) and *ulna* (on the inside) in the forearm, the *carpals* in the wrist region, and the *metacarpals* and *phalanges* in the hand. The muscles on the front of the arm and forearm cause flexion of the shoulder, elbow, wrist, and digits (fingers and thumb). The muscles on the back of the arm and forearm are *extensors*, causing opposite movements at these places.

armadillo [ah(r)**ma**diloh] A nocturnal mammal (an edentate), found from South America to S USA; long snout and tubular ears; head and body covered with bony plates; large front claws for digging; eats ants, termites, and other small animals. (Family: Dasypodidae, 20 species.)

Armageddon [ah(r)**ma**gedn] A place mentioned in the New Testament (*Rev* 16.16) as the site of the final cosmic battle between the forces of good and evil in the last days. The name is possibly a corruption of 'the mountains of Megiddo' or some other unknown location in Israel.

Armagh (city) [ah(r)**mah**] 54°21N 6°39W, pop (2000e) 14 800. City in Armagh district, Co Armagh, SE Northern Ireland, UK; seat of the kings of Ulster, 400 BC–AD 333; religious centre of Ireland in the 5th-c, when St Patrick was made archbishop here; Protestant and Catholic archbishoprics; city status, 1995; textiles (linen), engineering, shoes, food processing; St Patrick's Cathedral (Roman Catholic, 1840–73), observatory (1791), Royal School (1627); Navan Fort nearby, palace of the kings of Ulster.

Armagh (county) [ah(r)**mah**], Ir **Ard Mhacha** pop (2000e) 132 300; area 1254 sq km/484 sq mi. County in SE Northern Ireland, UK, divided into two districts (Armagh, Craigavon); the name is also used for one of these districts, pop (2000e) 53 000, and its administrative centre; bounded S and SW by the Republic of Ireland; rises to 577 m/1893 ft at Slieve Gullion; county town, Armagh; other chief towns include Lurgan and Portadown; potatoes, flax, apples, linen.

Armani, Giorgio [ah(r)**mah**nee] (1935–) Fashion designer, born in Piacenza, N Italy. He studied medicine for a time in Milan, and after military service worked as a window dresser and menswear buyer in a department store until he became a designer for Nino Cerruti (1930–) in 1961. He set up his own company in 1975, designing first for men, then women, including loose-fitting blazers and jackets. He was appointed a United Nations goodwill ambassador in 2002. In 2003 he became the first fashion designer to be honoured with an exhibition at London's Royal Academy.

armed forces The military organizations which a country officially establishes in order to impose its will onto other countries or to defend itself from attack by other countries. Such forces are to be distinguished from unofficial armed groups (such as brigands) and from the internal law-enforcement agencies (such as the police). The three main branches of the armed forces are the army, navy, and air force; but there may be some overlap between these branches (eg the marines), and the personnel may be of various kinds (eg professionals, conscripts, mercenaries, reserves).

Armenia *p.88*

Armenia (Turkey) [ah(r)**mee**nia], ancient **Minni** Ancient kingdom largely occupying the present-day Van region of E Turkey and parts of NW Iran and the republic of Armenia; SE of the Black Sea and SW of the Caspian Sea; ruled by the Ottoman Turks from 1514; E territory ceded to Persia, 1620; further districts lost to Russia, 1828–9; today Turkish Armenia comprises the NE provinces of Turkey; chief towns, Kars, Erzurum, Erzincan; Armenian nationalist movement developed in the 19th-c.

Armenians A people who came from Armenia, now NE Turkey and the republic of Armenia. Of Indo-European origin, they speak a language of that family with some Caucasian features, and are Christians, affiliated to the Armenian Catholic branch of the Roman Catholic Church, or the Monophysite Armenian Apostolic (Orthodox) Church. Their highly developed ancient culture, particularly in fine art, architecture, and sculpture, reached its zenith in the 14th-c. Highly nationalistic, their resentment of foreign domination during the 19th-c provoked their Russian and Ottoman rulers. During World War 1, the Ottomans deported two-thirds of Armenians (1·75 million) to Syria and Palestine, resulting in many deaths, and Armenian accusations of genocide; later, many settled in Europe, America, and the USSR. Today 4·15 million live in the republics of the former Soviet Union, including 2·7 million in Armenia; very few still live in Turkey.

armillary sphere A celestial globe, first used by the Greek astronomers, in which the sky is represented by a skeleton framework of intersecting circles, the Earth being at the centre. In antiquity, it was of major importance for measuring star positions. The first Chinese sphere dates from the 4th-c BC; they had a 20-ton sphere in the 11th-c.

Arminius, Jacobus [ah(r)**mi**nius], Lat name of **Jakob Hermandszoon** (1560–1609) Theologian, born in Oudewater, The Netherlands. He studied at Utrecht, Leyden, Geneva, and Basel, and was ordained in 1588. Despite early opposition to the strict Calvinistic doctrine of predestination he was made professor of theology at Leyden in 1603. In 1604 his colleague Gomarus attacked his doctrines, and from this time on he was engaged in a series of bitter controversies. In 1608 Arminius asked the States of Holland to convoke a synod to settle the controversy, but he died before it was held. His teaching was formalized in the 'Remonstrance' of 1610, refuted at the Synod of Dort (1618–19); but 'Remonstrants' continued in being, and **Arminianism** influenced the development of religious thought all over Europe.

Armistice Day The anniversary of the day (11 Nov 1918) on which World War 1 ended, marked in the UK by a two-minute silence at 11 o'clock, the hour when the fighting stopped (the armistice agreement having been signed six hours earlier); replaced after World War 2 by **Remembrance Sunday**. The US equivalent is Veterans' Day.

Armitage, Kenneth (1916–2002) Sculptor, born in Leeds, West Yorkshire, N England, UK. He studied at the Royal College of Art and the Slade School of Art, London (1937–9), and became head of sculpture at the Bath Academy of Art (1946–56) and was Britain's first university artist in residence (Leeds University, 1953–6). He exhibited at the Venice Biennale in 1952 and 1958, when he won the prize for best international sculptor under age 45. He became known for his bronzes of semi-abstract fig-

Armenia

□ International Airport

(republic) [ah(r)meenia], official name **Republic of Armenia**, Armenian **Hayastani Hanrapetut'yun**

Local name Hayastan

Timezone GMT +3

Area 29 800 km²/11 500 sq mi

Population total (2002e) 3 800 000

Status Republic

Date of independence 1991

Capital Yerevan

Language Armenian (official)

Ethnic groups (1991) Armenian (90%), Azer (3%), Kurd (2%), Russian (2%) (ethnic conflict since 1990 makes accurate statistical analysis impossible)

Religions Christian (Armenian Church), Russian Orthodox

Physical features Mountainous region in S Transcaucasia, rising to 4090 m/13 418 ft at Mt Aragats (W); rivers include Razdan and Vorotan; largest mountain lake is the Sevan, 1401 km²/541 sq mi - the main source of irrigation system and hydroelectric power.

Climate Varies with elevation; chiefy dry and continental with considerable regional variation.

Currency 1 Dram (Drm) = 100 ioumas

Economy Large mineral resources, chiefy copper; also molybdenum, gold, silver; electrical equipment and machinery, chemicals, textiles, cognac; agriculture based on fruits, wheat, wine grapes, cotton, tobacco.

GDP (2002e) $12·13 bn, per capita $3600

Human Development Index (2002) 0·754

History Proclaimed a Soviet Socialist Republic in 1920; constituent republic of the USSR from 1936; civil war over Nagorno-Karabakh began in 1989; declaration of independence, 1990; independence recognized and joined CIS, 1991; ongoing confict with Azerbaijan over disputed enclave of Nagorno-Karabakh.

Head of State
1991–8 Levon Ter-Petrosian
1998– Robert Kocharyan

Head of Government
1991–2 Gagik Arutynian
1992–3 Khasrov Haroutunian
1993–6 Hrand Bagratian
1996–7 Armen Sarkissian
1997–8 Robert Kocharyan
1998–9 Armen Darpinyan
1999 Vazgen Sarkisyarn
1999–2000 Aram Sarkisyarn
2000– Andranik Markarian

ures, united into a group by stylized clothing. In 1994 he was elected to the Royal Academy.

Armory show An art exhibition, officially entitled **The International Exhibition of Modern Art**, held at the 69th Regiment Armory in New York, 1913. It introduced modern art to the USA.

armoured car Typically a four-wheel-drive, light-armoured fighting vehicle with protection against small-arms fire, armed with a machine gun or small calibre cannon in a rotating turret. The first 'armoured cars' were iron-plated chariots carrying a crossbow on a platform (11th-c China). The first mechanical armoured cars were developed just before 1914, and their roles today on the battlefield are largely unchanged – that of reconnaissance and rear area protection.

armoured fighting vehicle (AFV) A generic term for combat vehicles such as tanks, armoured cars, armoured personnel carriers, and infantry fighting vehicles which have armour protection against hostile fire.

arms, coats of *heraldry*

arms control Any restraint exercised by one or more countries over the level, type, deployment, and use of their armaments, occurring through agreement or unilaterally. Its aim is to reduce the possibility of war and/or reduce its consequences. It is premised on the notion that states can reduce arms to their mutual benefit, including that of reducing the burden of costs, without abandoning their hostile stance. Originating in the USA in the 1950s, it has gained increasing acceptance as a policy: several major agreements have been reached about nuclear missiles, as well as about biological and chemical weapons.

arms race The continual accumulation in terms of numbers and capacity of military weapons by two or more states, in the belief that only by maintaining a superiority will their national security be guaranteed. Many maintain that, in such a situation, the continual growth in weapons becomes a threat to security by increasing international tension and distrust.

Armstrong, Gillian (May) (1950–) Film director, born in Melbourne, Victoria, SE Australia. A student of theatre design and later of film, she won a scholarship to the Film and Television School in Sydney. Early works include the drama *The Singer and the Dancer* (1976), which won the Australian Film Institute (AFI) Award for Best Short. Several of her films focus attention on the difficulties facing independent women, such as *My Brilliant Career* (1979), *High Tide* (1987), *The Last Days of Chez Nous* (1991), *Little Women* (1996), and *Oscar and Lucinda* (1997). She has won many AFI awards, including Best Film and Best Director.

Armstrong, Henry, originally **Henry Jackson**, nickname **Hammerin' Hank** (1912–88) Boxer, born in Columbus, Mississippi, USA. He is the only man to have held three world titles at different weights simultaneously. His first title was at featherweight, which he won in 1937, and the following year he added both the welterweight and lightweight crowns. He lost the featherweight and lightweight titles in 1939, but he successfully defended his welterweight title a record 20 times. He had the last of his 175 fights in 1945, having won 144 and drawn 9. After retirement he became a Baptist minister and died in poverty in Los Angeles.

Armstrong, Lance (1971–) Racing cyclist, born in Plano, Texas, USA. He gained the World Championship title in 1993 and was ranked world number one in 1996 when he became ill with cancer. He later made a remarkable comeback, his achievements including a record-equalling five times winner of the Tour de France (1999–2003) and a bronze medal in the time trial at the Sydney Olympics (2000). In 1996 he established the Lance Armstrong Foundation, a charity to aid the fight against cancer.

Armstrong, Louis, nicknames **Satchmo** and **Pops** (1898/1900–71) Jazz trumpeter and singer, born in New Orleans, Louisiana, USA. Having learned to play the cornet in a waifs' home, he moved to Chicago in 1922 to join King Oliver's band. His melodic inventiveness, expressed with uninhibited tone and range on the trumpet, established the central role of the improvising soloist in jazz, especially in a series of recordings known as the 'Hot Fives' and 'Hot Sevens' (1925–8). Thereafter, every jazz musician emulated Armstrong's melodic style and rhythmic sense. He was also a popular singer (hit recordings include 'When It's Sleepy Time Down South', 'Mack the Knife', 'Hello Dolly!') and entertainer, in such films as *Pennies from Heaven* (1936), *Cabin in the Sky* (1943), and *High Society* (1956), but he remained primarily a jazz musician, touring the world with his New Orleans-style sextet.

Armstrong, Neil (Alden) (1930–) Astronaut, born in Wapakoneta, Ohio, USA. He studied at Purdue University, then became a fighter pilot in Korea and later a civilian test pilot. In 1962 he was chosen as an astronaut and commanded Gemini 8 in 1966. In 1969 with Buzz Aldrin and Michael Collins he set out in Apollo 11 on a successful Moon-landing expedition. On 20 July 1969 Armstrong and Aldrin became in that order the first men to set foot on the Moon. Armstrong later taught aerospace engineering at Cincinnati University (1971–9). He published *First on the Moon* in 1970.

Armstrong-Jones, Antony *Snowdon, 1st Earl of*

army The branch of the armed forces configured and equipped to make war on land. The term *army*, while referring to a nation's land forces, is also conferred on large military formations engaged in a particular theatre of war (the British 'Eighth Army', for example). These are subdivided into Army Corps and Divisions, and may be combined for command purposes into Army Groups.

army ant A tropical ant with very reduced or absent eyes. It forms enormous colonies characterized by group foraging behaviour and frequent changes in nest site. A bivouac nest formed by living ants protects the wingless queen and the brood. (Order: Hymenoptera. Family: Formicidae.)

Arnauld, Antoine [ah(r)noh], known as **the Great Arnauld** (1612–94) French philosopher, lawyer, mathematician, and priest, associated with the Jansenist movement and community at Port Royal, Paris, France. He was a controversialist, and his activities as head of the Jansenists led to his expulsion from the Sorbonne, persecution, and ultimately refuge in Belgium. While at Port Royal he collaborated with Pascal and **Pierre Nicole** (1625–95) on the work known as the *Port Royal Logic* (1662).

Arne, Thomas (Augustine) (1710–78) Composer, born in London, UK. He was educated at Eton, became skilful as a violinist, then turned to composing with his first opera *Rosamond* (1733). He was appointed composer to Drury Lane Theatre, for which he composed famous settings of Shakespearean songs. 'Rule, Britannia' (originally written for *The Masque of Alfred*) is his, as well as two oratorios and two operas.

Arnhem [ah(r)nem] 52°00N 5°53E, pop (2000e) 139 000. Capital city of Gelderland province, E Netherlands; on the right bank of the lower Rhine, 53 km/33 mi SE of Utrecht; seat of the law courts, several government agencies, and the provincial government; on the site of a Roman settlement; charter, 1233; heavily damaged in World War 2; scene of unsuccessful airborne landing of British troops (Sep 1944); railway; tin-smelting, artificial fibres, salt, pharmaceuticals, chemicals, engineering; Grote Kerk (15th-c), town hall (1540), St Walburgisbasiliek (1422), Dutch open-air museum (N), safari park, Burgers Zoo.

Arnhem Land [ah(r)nem] The peninsular plateau in N Australia, E of Darwin; named after the Dutch ship which arrived here in 1618; chief town, Nhulunbuy; now contains Kakadu national park, and a reserve for Aborigines; bauxite and uranium mining.

arni *water buffalo*

Arnold, Benedict (1741–1801) American soldier and turncoat, born in Norwich, Connecticut, USA. On the outbreak of the War of Independence (1775–83) he joined the colonial forces, assisted Ethan Allen in the capture of Fort Ticonderoga (1775), and took part in the unsuccessful siege of Quebec in 1775, for which he was made a brigadier-general. He fought with distinction at L Champlain, Ridgefield, and Saratoga. Though greatly admired by Washington, he had influential enemies, and in 1777 five of his inferiors in rank were promoted over his head. In 1780 he obtained the command of West Point, which, through a conspiracy with John André, he agreed to betray. On the capture of André, he fled to the British lines, and was given a command in the royal army. He went to England in 1781, living in London until his death.

Arnold, Sir Malcolm (Henry) (1921–) Composer, born in Northampton, Northamptonshire, C England, UK. He studied at the Royal College of Music (1938–40) and was principal trumpet player with the London Philharmonic Orchestra until 1948. Of his film scores, *Bridge over the River Kwai* received an Oscar (1957). His works include nine symphonies, the overture *Tam O'shanter*, 18 concertos, five ballets, two one-act operas, and a great deal of vocal, choral, and chamber music. He was knighted in 1993.

Arnold, Matthew (1822–88) Poet and critic, born in Laleham, Surrey, SE England, UK, the eldest son of Dr Thomas Arnold of Rugby. He studied at Oxford, and became one of the lay inspectors of schools in 1851, an office from which he retired in 1886. He made his mark with *Poems: A New Edition* (1853–4), which contained 'The Scholar Gipsy' and 'Sohrab and Rustum', and confirmed his standing as a poet with *New Poems* (1867), which contained 'Dover Beach' and 'Thyrsis'. Appointed professor of poetry at Oxford in 1857, he published several critical works, including *Essays in Criticism* (1865, 1888) and *Culture and Anarchy* (1869), and books on religious themes such as *Literature and Dogma* (1873) and *Last Essays on Church and Religion* (1877).

Arnold, Thomas (1795–1842) Educationist, scholar, and headmaster of Rugby School, born in East Cowes, Isle of Wight, S England, UK the father of Matthew Arnold and Mary Augusta Ward. He studied at Oxford, took deacon's orders in 1818, and in 1828 was appointed headmaster of Rugby. He reformed the school system (especially by introducing sports and ending bullying). The style of teaching he introduced was graphically described in Thomas Hughes's *Tom Brown's Schooldays* (1857). He wrote several volumes of sermons, as well as works on classical and modern history. In 1841 he was appointed professor of modern history at Oxford.

Arnold of Brescia [breshia] (c.1100–55) Clergyman and politician, born in Brescia, N Italy. He adopted the monastic life, but his criticism of the Church's wealth and temporal power led to his banishment from Italy (1139). In France he met with bitter hostility from St Bernard of Clairvaux, and took refuge for five years in Zürich. An insurrection against the papal government in Rome drew him there (1143), and for 10 years he struggled to found a republic on ancient Roman lines. On the arrival of Emperor Frederick I in 1155, he was executed.

aromatherapy A popular form of complementary medicine which uses concentrated essential oils extracted from plants. Some aromatherapists have a background in conventional medicine or in paramedical disciplines such as physiotherapy, but others may use alternative systems such as traditional Chinese medicine or radiesthesia. The application of oil to the skin is an effective way of getting active agents to be absorbed into the bloodstream, and aromatherapy treatment is often combined with massage. Some oils are used topically (eg eucalyptus or tea tree oil as antiseptics); others may be taken internally, either by mouth or in the form of a suppository or pessary. Cosmetic aromatherapy is offered by many beauty salons, sometimes in conjuction with facial massage, usually using proprietary brands of preblended oils.

aromatic compound A compound related to benzene, with bonding usually represented as alternate single and double bonds, but more stable than that arrangement would predict. Unlike an aliphatic compound with multiple bonds, it will react more often by substitution than by addition. Its name is derived from the odour of benzene.

Aroostook War [aroostuk] (1838–9) A US/Canadian boundary dispute between the state of Maine and the province of New Brunswick, leading to near-hostilities. It was resolved by a temporary truce, and permanently settled by the Webster–Ashburton Treaty (1842).

Arp, Jean or **Hans**(1887–1966) Sculptor, born in Strasbourg, NE France. He was one of the founders of the Dada movement in Zürich in 1916. During the 1920s he produced many abstract reliefs in wood, but after 1928 he worked increasingly in three dimensions, becoming a major influence on organic abstract sculpture, based on natural forms. In 1921 he married the artist, **Sophie Tauber** (1889–1943). After World War 2, he wrote several poems and essays.

arquebus [ah(r)kwebuhs] A firearm dating from the 15th-c, a development of the hand cannon, in outline a forerunner of the musket. Fired in action by a flame held to the touch-hole, the weapon was supported by a forked rest holding up the barrel at the operator's chest height.

Arrabal, Fernando [arabal] (1932–) Playwright and novelist, born in Melilla, Spanish Morocco. He studied law in Madrid and drama in Paris, then settled permanently in France. His first play, *Pique-nique en campagne* (1958, trans Picnic on the Battlefield), established him in the tradition of the Theatre of the Absurd. He coined the term *panic theatre*, intended to shock the senses, employing sadism and blasphemy to accomplish its aims. Other plays include *Le Cimetière des voitures* (1958, The Car Cemetery) and *Et ils passèrent des menottes aux fleurs* (1969, And They Put Handcuffs on the Flowers) – a work based on conversations with Spanish political prisoners, which was eventually banned in France and Sweden while becoming his first major success in America in 1971. He writes in Spanish, his work being translated into French by his wife.

Arran area 430 sq km/166 sq mi. Island in North Ayrshire, W Scotland, UK; separated from W coast mainland by the Firth of Clyde; rises to 874 m/2867 ft at Goat Fell; chief centres, Brodick, Lamlash, Lochranza; ferry links between Brodick and Ardrossan and Lochranza and Claonaig; a major tourist area; Brodick castle and country park, Bronze Age Moss Farm Road stone circle, 13th–14th-c Lochranza castle.

arrangement A transcription or reworking of a musical composition, usually (but not always) for a different performing medium. Before c.1600, arrangements (or 'intabulations') of vocal music formed a major part of the keyboard and lute repertory, and in more recent times instruments such as the accordion and the guitar, for which only a limited original repertory exists, have had to rely largely on arrangements. Since the 18th-c at least, publishers have seized on arrangements as a means of increasing their sales of a popular work. Such arrangements often fail to respect the composer's intentions, but the type of arrangement which is perhaps most despised by musicians today is that which aims to bring older music 'up to date' (even though some of the greatest composers have engaged in this practice, as in Mozart's arrangements of some Handel oratorios). Despite its long history, the practice of musical arrangement tends to divide present-day musicians on both aesthetic and ethical grounds, and some look favourably only on those arrangements in which a creative intention is present.

Arras [aras] 50°17N 2°46E, pop (2000e) 44 600. Old frontier town and capital of Pas-de-Calais department, N France, between Lille and Amiens; formerly famous for its tapestries; railway; bishopric; agricultural equipment, engineering, sugar beet, vegetable oil, hosiery; town hall (16th-c), cathedral (18th-c); birthplace of Robespierre; many war cemeteries nearby; Vimy Ridge memorial, 10 km/6 mi N.

Arrau, Claudio [arow] (1903–91) Pianist, born in Chillán, Chile. He studied at the Stern Conservatory, Berlin (1912–18), and taught there (1924–40). He is renowned as an interpreter of Bach, Beethoven, Chopin, Schumann, Liszt, and Brahms. His musical thoughts were collected in *Conversations with Arrau* by Joseph Horowitz (1982).

array processor A particular type of digital computer which allows arrays of numbers to be processed simultaneously. In suitable applications, this can lead to marked increases in computing speeds.

arrest 1 The stopping and detaining by lawful authority of a person suspected of a criminal offence; referred to as **apprehension** in Scotland. Arrests are carried out mainly by the police, but a **citizen's arrest** is possible in certain circumstances; anyone may lawfully arrest without a warrant someone who is committing an **arrestable offence**, or who is reasonably suspected of so doing. A person wrongly arrested may bring civil proceedings for false imprisonment. In English law a distinction is drawn between serious offences for which arrest may be made without a warrant (**arrestable offences**) and relatively minor offences for which a warrant is always required. Arrestable offences include those for which a person not previously convicted might be imprisoned for five years or more. Attempts to commit such crimes are included in the definition. In the USA, **felony arrests** may be made outside the home without a warrant if there is probable cause to believe the accused committed a felony; **misdemeanour arrests** may be made without a warrant only where the offence occurred in the arrestor's presence.
2 A civil remedy in Scotland (arrestment), whereby a court takes control of property owned by a debtor, but in the hands of a third party (eg a bank).

Arrhenius, Svante (August) [araynius] (1859–1927) Scientist, born near Uppsala, E Sweden. He became professor of physics at Stockholm in 1895, a director of the Nobel Institute in 1905, and was awarded the 1903 Nobel Prize for Chemistry. He did valuable work in connection with the dissociation theory of electrolysis, and on reaction rates, and he was the first to recognize the 'greenhouse effect' on climate.

arrhythmia [arithmia] A disturbance of the normal regular rhythm of the heart. There are many types – some of them harmless, some that result in symptoms such as palpitations and shortness of breath, and a few that are a serious threat to life.

Arrian [arian], Lat **Flavius Arrianus** (c.95–180) Greek historian, a native of Nicomedia in Bithynia. An officer in the Roman army, in 136 he was appointed prefect of Cappadocia (legate in 131–7). His chief work is the *Anabasis Alexandrou*, or history of the campaigns of Alexander the Great, which has survived almost entire. His accounts of the people of India, and of a voyage round the Euxine, are valuable for studies of ancient geography.

Arrow, Kenneth J(oseph) (1921–) Economist, born in New York City, USA. He studied at Columbia University, and became professor at Stanford (1949–68) and Harvard (1968–79). His primary field was the study of collective choice based on uncertainty and risk. He also invented the 'learning by doing' model of technical progress. He shared the 1972 Nobel Prize for Economics.

arrow-poison frog A slender frog, native to Central and South America; often brightly coloured; inhabits woodland; eggs laid on ground; adults carry tadpoles to water; skin very poisonous; local Indians rub arrow-heads on live frogs to poison the tips for hunting; also known as **poison-arrow frog**. Some South American true toads of genus *Atelopus* are called **arrow-poison toads**. (Family: Dendrobatidae, 116 species.)

arrowroot A type of starch obtained from the tuberous roots of several plants. The most important is probably **West Indian arrowroot** (*Maranta arundinacea*), a rhizomatous perennial growing to 2 m/6½ ft; leaves with sheathing bases; sepals and petals in threes; native to South America, and cultivated in New World tropics for edible starch. **East Indian arrowroot** is obtained from *Curcuma angustifolia*, a relative of ginger, and from *Tacca pinnatifida*. **Queensland arrowroot** is from a species of canna, *Canna edulis*. **Portland arrowroot**, inedible and formerly used for laundry, was obtained from lords-and-ladies (*Arum maculatum*).

Arrowsmith, Aaron (1750–1823) Cartographer, born in Winston, Durham, NE England, UK. In about 1770 he moved to London, and by 1790 had established a great map-making business. His nephew, **John Arrowsmith** (1790–1873), was also an eminent cartographer.

Arrow War *Opium Wars*

arrow worm A slender invertebrate animal with a translucent body bearing lateral and tail fins; predatory; head armed with several paired spines to catch prey; c.70 marine species, mostly found in open water. (Phylum: Chaetognatha.)

ars antiqua [ah(r)z anteekwa] A term used to distinguish the music of the late 12th-c and 13th-c from that of the succeeding period. It is particularly associated with the theorists and composers of the Notre Dame school in Paris, notably Léonin and Pérotin.

arsenic As, element 33. A grey metalloid in the nitrogen family, usually showing oxidation states 3 and 5. It is used in some lead alloys and in semiconductors, especially gallium arsenide (GaAs). The name is commonly applied to arsenic (III) oxide (As_2O_3), the highly poisonous white arsenic of rodent control and detective novels.

arsenicals [ah(r)seniklz] Drugs developed in the early 20th-c by German scientist Paul Ehrlich, who systematically screened a series of organic arsenic-containing substances in the search for a drug effective in trypanosomiasis (sleeping sickness). Number 606 in the series was most effective, and the drug was often known as '606'. It was called **Salvarsan**, which was subsequently found to be effective against spirochaete infections. In 1910 it was shown to cure syphilis, and was used thus until replaced by penicillin in 1945. Arsenicals have generally been abandoned in favour of newer, safer drugs.

arsine [ah(r)seen] AsH_3, boiling point −55°C. A gaseous hydride of arsenic, formed by reducing solutions of arsenic compounds.

ars nova [ah(r)z nohva] In music, a term for the 'new art' of the 14th-c, as distinct from that of the preceding period. Its principal representatives were the composer Guillaume de Machaut (c.1300–77), and the theorist Philippe de Vitry (1291–1361).

arson The unlawful destruction of, or damage to, property by fire; known as **fire-raising** in Scotland. In English law the Criminal Damage Act 1971 abolished the common law crime of arson, and created another criminal offence covering unlawful damage, however caused. It also preserves the separate statutory crime of arson, even though this seems to add little to the scope of the law. There is also an aggravated offence of damaging property in which someone's life is endangered, which carries a maximum sentence of life imprisonment. In the USA, the definition of arson varies among the states.

art Originally, 'skill' (of any kind), a meaning the word has in everyday contexts. Modern usage referring especially to painting, drawing, or sculpture emerged by c.1700, but significantly Dr Johnson's primary meaning of the word (1755) was still 'The power of doing something not taught by nature and instinct; as to *walk* is natural, to *dance* is an art.' This contrast between art and nature goes back to the Middle Ages. Nor did Johnson's five other meanings of the word make any reference to what we nowadays call 'the visual arts'. However, the modern sense of art as a uniquely significant form of creation, and of an artist as a creative genius of a special kind, does seem to have made headway during Johnson's lifetime. The related concept of **fine arts**, considered as sharing common principles and distinct from science, religion, or the practical concerns of everyday life, also emerged in the 18th-c, together with a new subject, *aesthetics*, the philosophy of art. The artist was now considered distinct from the artisan, or skilled manual worker. By the 19th-c, art was normally (instead of occasionally) associated with the imaginative and creative productions of objects for abstract contemplation, with no useful function. The highly significant phrases 'artistic temperament' and 'artistic sensibility' occur first in the mid-19th-c. The definition of art became controversial again in the 20th-c. New forms, such as film, television, street theatre, pop music, and happenings were claimed by some to be art, by others, not.

Artaud, Antonin [ah(r)toh] (1896–1948) Playwright, actor, director, and theorist, born in Marseille, S France. A Surrealist in the 1920s, in 1927 he co-founded the Théâtre Alfred Jarry. He propounded a theatre that dispensed with narrative and psychological realism, dealing instead with the dreams and interior obsessions of the mind. His main theoretical work is the book, *Le Théâtre et son double* (1938, The Theatre and its Double). As the creator of what has been termed the Theatre of Cruelty, his influence on post-war theatre was profound. A manic depressive, his last years were spent in a mental institution.

Artaxerxes II [ah(r)tazerkseez], Gr **Mnemon** (d.358 BC) King of Persia (404 BC–358 BC), the son and successor of Darius II. Early in his reign, his brother Cyrus the Younger attempted to assassinate him and seize the throne, but Artaxerxes finally crushed him at the Battle of Cunaxa (401 BC), where Cyrus was killed. Artaxerxes was ruled by the will of his wife and mother and relied heavily on his officials. His troubled reign included two failed expeditions against Egypt (385–83 BC and 374 BC), rebellions in Anatolia, and wars against the mountain tribes of Armenia and Iran. He introduced an important change in Persian religious life by reviving the cults of Anahita and Mithra, two deities of the old popular Iranian religion.

Art Brut [ah(r) broo] A term coined by French painter Jean Dubuffet (1901–85) for the art of untrained people, especially mental patients, prisoners, and socially dispossessed persons generally. Dubuffet built up a collection of about 5000 such items, presented in 1972 to the city of Lausanne.

Art Deco [ah(r)t dekoh] A term abbreviated from the Paris Exposition Internationale des Arts Décoratifs et Industriels Modernes ('International Exhibition of Modern Industrial and Decorative Arts'), 1925. It has come to refer to decorative arts of the 1920s and 1930s generally, and the 'modernistic' style associated with them: a mixture of Cubism, Art Nouveau, and the Russian ballet, with a fondness for strident colours and for the streamlining found in aircraft and automobile design, but used nonfunctionally for household objects such as wireless sets, tables, and teapots.

Artemis [ah(r)temis] In Greek mythology, the daughter of Zeus and Leto, twin sister of Apollo, and goddess of the Moon. She was originally a mother-goddess of Asia, with a cult especially at Ephesus; in Greece she was a virgin-goddess, associated with wild creatures and the protector of the young. Being connected with hunting, she is depicted with bow and arrows.

arteriole *artery*

arteriosclerosis [ah(r)teeriohsklerohsis] An umbrella term to describe hardening and thickening of arterial walls caused by a number of pathological processes. The most important is *atheroma*, in which fats and other substances are deposited in the inner wall of the artery.

artery A vessel of the body which usually conveys blood to body tissues. Large, medium, and small arteries (**arterioles**) can be distinguished. Regulation of the blood supply is determined by the activity of a smooth muscle component (under sympathetic control) which changes the diameter of the vessel cavity. With increasing age, arteries tend to become blocked with *atheroma* – porridge-like deposits of cholesterol-based material.

artesian basin A shallow basin-shaped aquifer with impermeable rock strata above and below it, thus confining the groundwater under pressure. Sinking a well into the aquifer allows the water to rise to the surface without pumping. The Great Artesian Basin in E Australia is the largest such aquifer.

art for art's sake *Aesthetic Movement*

art gallery *Hermitage; Louvre; Metropolitan Museum of Art; National Gallery; National Gallery of Art; National Gallery of Australia; National Portrait Gallery; Pitti Palace; Prado; Rijksmuseum; Tate Gallery; Tretyakov Gallery; Uffizi*

arthritis An inflammation of one or more joints resulting in swelling, pain, redness, local heat, and limitation of movement. A large number of different conditions may be responsible, such as degenerative processes (eg osteoarthritis), autoimmune disease (eg rheumatoid arthritis), metabolic disease (eg gout), or infection, and they may involve one or many joints.

arthropod [ah(r)thropod] A member of the largest and most diverse phylum of animals (Arthropoda), characterized by jointed limbs and an external chitinous skeleton. Arthropods have segmented bodies, most segments carrying a pair of limbs variously modified for locomotion, feeding, respiration, or reproduction. The external skeleton (*cuticle*) is moulted periodically to permit growth. Size ranges from 80 μm to 3·6 m/ 11¾ ft. Arthropods have a long fossil history from the Cambrian to the present, and are the most abundant animals on Earth, including the insects, arachnids, crustaceans, trilobites, centipedes, millipedes and several minor groups.

Arthur (?6th-c) Semi-legendary king of the Britons. He may originally have been a Romano-British war leader in W England called **Arturus**; but he is represented as having united the British tribes against the invading Saxons, and as having been the champion of Christendom as well. He is said to have fought against the invaders in a series of momentous battles, starting with a victory at 'Mount Baden' (?516) and ending with defeat and death at 'Camlan' (537), after which he was buried at Glastonbury. The *Anglo-Saxon Chronicle* makes no mention of him, however; he first appears in Welsh chronicles long after the event. The story of Arthur blossomed into a huge literature, interwoven with legends of the Holy Grail and courtly ideas of the Round Table of knights at Camelot, in such writers as Geoffrey of Monmouth, Chrétien de Troyes, and Layamon. Sir Thomas Malory's English version, *Morte d'Arthur*, was the final mediaeval compilation from which most later retellings are derived.

Arthur, Chester A(lan) (1830–86) US statesman, lawyer, and 21st president (1881–5), born in Fairfield, Vermont, USA. He became the head of an eminent law firm and leader of the Republican Party in New York State. He was made vice-president of the USA when Garfield became president in 1881, and president after Garfield's assassination, performing creditably in office.

Arthur, Prince (1187–?1203) Duke of Brittany, and claimant to the throne of England as the grandson of Henry II. He was the posthumous son of Geoffrey, Duke of Brittany, Henry's fourth son, and on the death of his uncle, Richard I (1199) he became a claimant to the throne. The French king, Philip II, upheld Arthur's claim until Richard's brother, John, came to terms with Philip. Arthur was soon in his uncle's hands and was imprisoned, first at Calais and then at Rouen, where he died. It was popularly believed that King John was responsible for his death.

Arthurs, Paul *Oasis*

Arthur's Pass Main mountain pass through the Southern Alps, NC South Island, New Zealand; altitude 924 m/3031 ft; discovered by the explorer, Sir Arthur Dobson in 1864; set in a national park, area 944 sq km/364 sq mi, established in 1929.

artichoke *globe artichoke; Jerusalem artichoke*

Articles of Confederation The organizing document of the USA from 1781 to 1789. It established a single-house Congress, with one vote for each state and with no executive, courts, or independent revenue. Its weaknesses quickly became obvious, and it was replaced by the present Constitution.

articulation The process of modifying the airflow above the larynx to produce a variety of speech-sounds. The jaws open to varying degrees, the tongue makes contact with the palate in various positions, and the lips can be rounded or spread. Sounds are classified according to their *place* of articulation (eg the part of the palate with which the tongue makes contact) and their *manner* of articulation (eg whether the air flows freely, as in the production of a vowel, or is impeded, as with a consonant).

artificial insemination (AI) The instrumental introduction of seminal fluid into the vagina in order to fertilize an ovum. The semen may be that of the husband (**AIH**) or of a donor (**AID**). The technique is also widely used in animal husbandry.

artificial intelligence (AI) A term applied to the study and use of computers that can simulate some of the characteristics normally ascribed to human intelligence, such as learning, deduction, intuition, and self-correction. The subject encompasses many branches of computer science, including cybernetics, knowledge-based systems, natural language processing, pattern recognition, and robotics. Progress has been made in several areas, notably problem-solving, language comprehension, vision, and locomotion.

artificial language An attempt to overcome the difficulties of understanding caused by the diversity of the world's languages, by creating a new, independent language which is no-one's mother tongue, can be learned by anyone, and expresses the most common range of meanings. Special attention is paid to making the grammar, word-formation, and pronunciation as regular and as simple as possible. Over 100 artificial languages have been created, but few have achieved widespread success other than Esperanto.

artificial respiration A procedure to maintain the movement of air into and out of the lungs when natural breathing is inadequate or has ceased. A short-term emergency method is 'mouth-to-mouth' respiration. With the head of the patient bent backwards and the nose pinched, the resuscitator takes a deep breath and expels this into the open mouth and lungs of the victim, either directly or via a mouthpiece, repeating the manoeuvre 10–15 times a minute. When more prolonged assistance is required, a mechanical ventilator supplies a predetermined volume of oxygen at given intervals, usually via a tube inserted in the trachea.

Artigas, José Gervasio [ah(r)teegas] (1764–1850) National hero of Uruguay, born in Montevideo, Uruguay. He became the most important local patriot leader in the wars of independence against Spain, and also resisted the centralizing pretensions of Buenos Aires. He spent the last 30 years of his life in exile in Paraguay.

artillery The heavy ordnance of an army; in particular, its longer-range weapons, as distinct from the small arms that each individual soldier carries. Modern artillery includes guns (known as 'tube' artillery) and missiles, both of which may be used in the traditional artillery role of bringing down destructive firepower on an enemy at a distance. Tube artillery may be mounted on towed carriages or tracked chassis (self-propelled guns) and fire a range of projectiles including small nuclear weapons. Rocket artillery includes simple, unguided bombardment missiles, multi-launch rocket systems, and medium-range, nuclear-armed battlefield missiles.

artiodactyl [ah(r)tiohdaktil] An ungulate mammal; foot with two or four toes (first always absent, second and fifth small or absent); weight carried on the third and fourth toe, which usually form a *cloven hoof*; also known as the **even-toed ungulate**. (Order: Artiodactyla, 192 species.)

Art Nouveau [ah(r) noovoh] (Fr 'new art') A movement which flourished from c.1890 to c.1905, mainly in the decorative arts, characterized by naturalistic plant and flower motifs, and writhing patterns of sinuous, curling lines; called *Jugendstil* in Germany, *Sezessionstil* in Austria, and *Stile Liberty* (after the shop in Regent St, London) in Italy. Typical products include the drawings of Beardsley, the furniture of Mackintosh, the architecture of Gaudí, the jewellery of Lalique, the glassware of Louis Comfort Tiffany (1848–1933), and the Paris Metro stations by Hector Guimard (1867–1942).

Artois [arh(r)twa], Lat **Artesium** Former province of NE France, now occupying the department of Pas-de-Calais; former capital, Arras; belonged to Flanders until 1180; part of Austrian and Spanish Netherlands in Middle Ages; ceded to France, 1659.

Arts and Crafts Movement A predominantly English movement in architecture, art, and the applied arts during the second half of the 19th-c, which advocated the renewed use of handicraft and simple decoration in reaction to industrial machinery and contemporary aesthetic eclecticism. The movement centred on William Morris, whose 'Red House' (1859) by the architect Philip Webb is a good early example of the style. Its origins lie in the writings of Pugin and Ruskin, and its intention was to change both the appearance and the way in which art and architecture were produced. It had a great and lasting effect on British, German, and American architecture, particularly the Garden City town-planning movement.

art therapy The use of self-expression through drawing and painting as a form of treatment for emotional problems. It was introduced to England during the 1940s as a result of a collaboration between artist Adrian Hill and psychotherapist Irene Champernowne. Self-expression through drawing, painting, and collage is combined with psychotherapy as a way of releasing emotional tension, and also to allow the therapist to interpret the meaning of symbols in the work which can give insight into the content of the subject's subconscious mind.

Aruba *see panel*

arum lily [aruhm, airuhm] A fleshy-stemmed perennial (*Zantedeschia aethiopica*) native to S Africa, and widely introduced elsewhere; leaves large, arrowhead-shaped, glossy; 'flower' consisting of a yellow cylindrical spadix surrounded by sheathing; white spathe 15 cm/6 in long; also called **calla lily**. It is often used as a florist's flower. (Family: Araceae.)

Arundel, Thomas [aruhndl] (1353–1414) English clergyman and statesman, the third son of Robert FitzAlan, Earl of Arundel. Chancellor of England (1386–96), he became Archbishop of York in 1388 and Archbishop of Canterbury in 1396. Banished by Richard II in 1397, he returned from exile with Henry IV and crowned him in 1399. He then became Chancellor again, and was a bitter opponent of the Lollards.

Arusha Declaration [aroosha] An important policy statement by President Nyerere of Tanzania in 1967, proclaiming village socialism, self-reliance, nationalization, and anti-corruption measures against politicians. It was a significant attempt to create a socialist route to African development, but for both internal and external reasons it failed.

Arval Brethren [ah(r)val] An ancient priestly college at Rome whose original function was to propitiate the gods of the fields (*arva*). Revived by the first emperor, Augustus, its duties were extended to include prayer and sacrifice for the well-being of the Imperial House.

Aryan [airian] A prehistoric people and their language, an extinct member of the Indo-European language family. Aryans reputedly colonized Iran and N India, and gave rise to the

Aruba

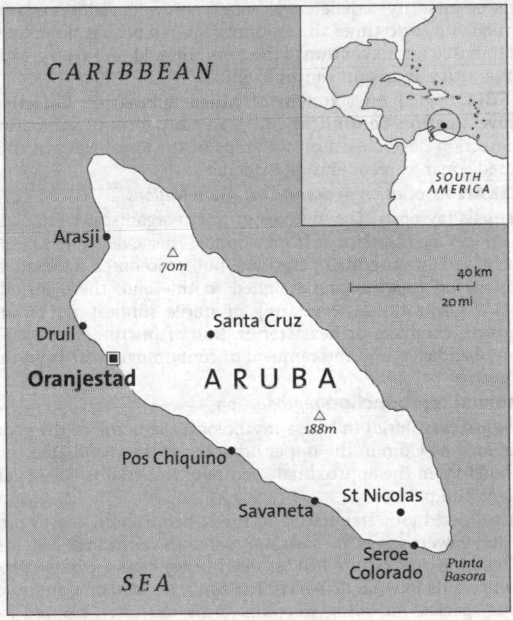

□ International Airport

[arooba]

Timezone GMT

Area 193 km²/74·5 sq mi

Population total (2002e) 100 000

Status Self-governing region of the Netherlands

Date of independence 1996

Capital Oranjestad

Languages Dutch (official) with Papiamento, English, and Spanish widely spoken

Ethnic groups Large majority of mixed European/ Caribbean Indian descent

Religions Christian (Roman Catholic and Protestant), small Hindu, Muslim, Confucian, and Jewish minorities

Physical features Island in the Caribbean, the westernmost of the Lesser Antilles, N of Venezuela; flat, rocky terrain, dry, with little vegetation.

Climate Dry, tropical, with little seasonal temperature variation; average annual temperature 27°C; annual rainfall often falls to below 488 mm/19 in; lies just outside the Caribbean hurricane belt.

Currency 1 Aruban Guilder/Florin = 100 cents

Economy Lack of natural resources limits agriculture and manufacturing; depends heavily on thriving tourist industry.

GDP (2002e) $1·94 bn, per capita $28 000

History Claimed by Dutch in 1634, but remained undeveloped; construction of an oil refinery brought employment and prosperity, 1929; acquired full internal self-government within kingdom of the Netherlands, 1954, as part of the Netherlands Antilles; growing resentment led to a campaign for Aruba's independence; closure of oil refinery, 1985; obtained separate status from the Netherlands Antilles with full internal autonomy in 1986; full independence in 1996; Sovereign of the Netherlands is Head of State, represented by a Governor-General, a Prime Minister, Council of Ministers and a unicameral legislature.

Head of State
(Dutch monarch represented by Governor-General)
1986–92 Felipe B Tromp
1992- Olindo Koolman

Head of Government
1986–89 Henry Eman
1989–94 Nelson Oduber
1994–2001 Henry Eman
2001– Nelson Oduber

Indian subcontinent's Indo-Aryan languages. Nazi Germany embraced unscientific notions of Germanic peoples as the purest members of an Aryan race of Indo-European-speaking peoples responsible for human progress. The term *Aryan* is no longer regarded as scientifically valid within anthropology.

Arya Samaj [ahrya samahj] A dogmatic and militant Hindu sect founded c.1875 by Dyanand Sarasawati (1824–83). He demanded a return to the purity of the Rig Veda and its principles, as opposed to the accretions and corruptions that subsequently entered Hinduism.

Asante *Ashanti*

ASA rating *ISO speed rating*

asbestos The name applied to varieties of fibrous minerals of the serpentine and amphibole groups. Fibres can be separated and woven into cloths or felted into sheets. It is an excellent insulator of heat and electricity, does not burn, and is resistant to chemical attack. The varieties used in manufacture are principally *chrysotile* (white asbestos), a form of serpentine, and *crocidolite* (blue asbestos), an amphibole. Amosite (brown asbestos) has also had fairly widespread use. All forms of asbestos cause asbestosis, and crocidolite and amosite are carcinogenic (the link between chrysotile and cancer is controversial); as a result, several countries have banned their use, either totally or partially.

asbestosis [azbestohsis] A form of fibrosis of the lungs caused by the inhalation of asbestos fibres. Asbestos fibres enter the lung and initiate an inflammatory process that leads to scarring and gradual destruction of lung tissue. Symptoms develop 15–25 years after the exposure, consisting of cough and shortness of breath which can be extremely disabling. Exposure to asbestos can also cause lung cancer and mesothelioma (a cancer of the lining of the chest or abdomen).

Ascaris [askaris] A genus of parasitic roundworm found in vertebrate hosts, typically pigs and humans; usually present in low numbers in the small intestine; sexes separate; length of females up to 250 mm/10 in; eggs resistant, often transmitted in manure. (Phylum: Nematoda.)

ascension *right ascension*

Ascension, Feast of In the Christian calendar, the fifth Thursday (being 40 days – *Acts* 1) after Easter. It commemorates Jesus's last appearance to his disciples, his being 'lifted up' or 'taken away' from them, prior to the attestation of his later presence to them through the Holy Spirit.

Ascension Island 7°56S 14°22W; pop (2000e) 1500; area 88 sq km/35 sq mi. Small, arid, volcanic island in the S Atlantic, 1125 km/700 mi NW of St Helena; highest point, Green Mountain (859 m/2818 ft); discovered by the Portuguese on Ascension Day 1501; British territory, since 1815, administered under the Admiralty; made a dependency of St Helena in 1922; British and US air bases; British forces sent to the island in 1982 in support of the Falkland Islands Task Force; NASA tracking station; Atlantic relay station for the BBC; cable station.

asceticism [asetisizm] A variety of austere practices involving the renunciation or denial of ordinary bodily and sensual gratifications. These may include fasting, meditation, a life of solitude, the renunciation of possessions, denial of sexual gratification, and, in the extreme, the mortification of the flesh.

Asch, Sholem or **Shalom** (1880–1957) Writer, born in Kutno, C Poland. He studied at his local Hebrew school, then moved to Warsaw (1899), where he wrote stories, plays, poems, and novels in Hebrew and Yiddish. He emigrated to New York City (1914) and began as a writer for Yiddish newspapers. His play *The God of Vengeance* (1910) enjoyed great success in Berlin, and several other plays were later produced in the Yiddish theatre in New York. He continued his prolific career as a writer, occasionally in English, but mostly in Yiddish, and although he became a US citizen (1920) and had a home in Florida, he often lived abroad. Most of his works dealt with Jewish subjects, as in *Mottke the Thief* (1917) and *Three Cities* (1933). His most famous books (to English readers) formed a trilogy, *The Nazarene* (1939), *The Apostle* (1943), and *Mary* (1949), in which he attempted to portray Jesus, Paul, and Mary in a way that bridged Christianity and Judaism, but he so antagonized some American Jews that he moved to Israel in 1956.

Ascham, Roger [asham] (1515–68) Humanist, born in Kirby Wiske, North Yorkshire, N England, UK. He studied at Cambridge, where he became reader in Greek (c.1538). In defence of archery he published *Toxophilus* (1545), which ranks among English classics on account of its style. He was tutor to the Princess Elizabeth (1548–50), and later became Latin secretary to Queen Mary I. His principal work was *The Scholemaster*, a treatise on Classical education, published in 1570.

ASCII code [askee] A set of widely used binary codes, defined as the **American Standard Codes for Information Interchange**. ASCII-96, an 8-bit code including a parity check bit, the most common code in use for storing text character strings in computers, allows 96 printing characters to be defined (letters, digits, arithmetic symbols, and punctuation characters) together with a number of control characters, such as printer carriage return and halt processing. An **ASCII keyboard** is a special type of keyboard which allows all the ASCII characters to be coded.

Asclepios or **Asclepius** [askleepius] In Greek mythology, a hero who became a god of healing, the son of Apollo and Koronis, educated by Chiron the centaur. He overreached himself by restoring Hippolytus to life, and was killed by the thunderbolt of Zeus.

Ascomycetes [askohmiyseeteez] A subdivision of the true fungi, characterized by a minute sac-like reproductive structure (*ascus*) within which a complex sexual process results in the formation of eight haploid spores (*ascospores*); asexual reproduction is also common; includes cup fungi, yeasts, truffles, and many parasitic forms. (Division: *Eumycota*.)

ascorbic acid Vitamin C, largely found in citrus fruits, green vegetables, and potatoes. It functions in the body to maintain tissue integrity; a deficiency causes scurvy. Megadoses of vitamin C, up to 20 times the amount required per day, have been promoted for prevention of the common cold, and even greater quantities as an anti-cancer agent.

ASDIC [azdik] An acronym of **Allied Submarine Detection Investigation Committee** (1917), an early form of submarine detection device used on warships of the Royal Navy. ASDIC used sonar as its operating principle.

ASEAN *Association of South-East Asian Nations*

asepsis [aysepsis] The absence of micro-organisms from body surfaces (eg the skin) or from wounds. This ideal state is rarely achieved in surgical operations, but procedures adopted in operating theatres are designed to this end; these include skin sterilization, the wearing of sterile surgical gloves and gowns, chemical or heat sterilization of instruments, swabs, and bandages, and the removal of contaminated air from the theatre.

asexual reproduction *reproduction*

Asgard [azgah(r)d] In Norse mythology, the home of the gods, created by Odin in the upper branches of the World-Tree, and therefore in the approximate centre of things. It is full of gardens and palaces.

ash A deciduous tree native to the N hemisphere; leaves pinnate; flowers sometimes without perianth, borne in dense clusters appearing before leaves; seeds (*keys*) have a papery wing which aids in wind dispersal. The timber is valuable, and various species, including weeping forms, are often planted for ornament. (Genus: *Fraxinus*, 70 species. Family: Oleaceae.)

Ashanti or **Asante** [ashantee] A Kwa-speaking Akan people of S Ghana and adjacent areas of Togo and Côte d'Ivoire. They form a confederacy of chiefdoms, founded by the ruler Osei Tutu in the late 17th-c; the paramount chief was established at Kumasi, and the Golden Stool was the symbol of Ashanti unity. The independent Ashanti state was at the height of its powers in the early 19th-c, and became a major threat to British trade on the coast. The Ashanti defeated a British force in 1824 but made peace in 1831. Conflict arose again in 1863 until the Ashanti were finally defeated (1873) by a force under Sir Garnet Wolseley. The state was annexed by the British in 1902. Traditional culture and religion still flourish, with rich ceremonial and internationally famous art.

Ashbery, John (Lawrence) (1927–) Poet and critic, born in New York City, USA. He studied at Harvard, Columbia, and New York universities, then spent some years as an art critic in Europe. He became associated with the New York School of poetry, publishing his first volume in 1953. *Some Trees* (1956) attracted considerable critical attention, and his 12th collection, *Self-Portrait in a Convex Mirror* (1975) received several prizes, including the Pulitzer Prize. Later volumes include *The Ice Storm* (1987), *Flow Chart* (1991), *Hotel Lautreamont* (1992), and *And The Stars Were Shining* (1994). He is recognized as the major postmodern poet of his generation, and was given a lifetime achievement award by the Academy of American Poets in 2001.

Ashburton, Baron *Dunning, John*

Ashcan School A derisive name given to a group of US Realist painters and illustrators, also called *The Eight*. Formed in 1907, they included Robert Henri (1865–1929), John Sloan (1871–1951), and later George Bellows. They painted everyday, non-academic subjects in an attempt to bring art back into direct contact with ordinary life, especially street life in New York City.

Ashcroft, Dame Peggy, originally **Edith Margaret Emily Ashcroft** (1907–91) Actress, born in London, UK. She first appeared on the stage with the Birmingham Repertory Company in 1926, and scored a great success in London in *Jew Süss* in 1929. She acted leading parts at the Old Vic in the season of 1932–3. Her famous roles included Juliet in Sir John Gielgud's production of *Romeo and Juliet* (1935). Her films include *The Thirty-nine Steps* (1935) and *A Passage to India* (1984), for which she won an Oscar as Best Supporting Actress. She was created a dame in 1956, and a new London theatre was named after her in 1962.

Ashcroft, John (1942–) US attorney general, born in Chicago, IL. He studied at Yale University (1964) and trained as a lawyer at Chicago (1967), then taught business law at Southwest Missouri State University (1968–73). He became Missouri's state auditor (1973–4), assistant attorney general (1975–6), and attorney general (1976–84). Elected governor of Missouri for two terms (1984–92), he then entered the Senate (Republican, 1994–2000). His strongly conservative and religious background made him a controversial appointment as attorney general by George W Bush in 2001.

Ashdod [ashdohd] 31°48N 34°38E, pop (2000e) 110 000. Seaport in Southern district, W Israel; on the Mediterranean Sea, 40 km/25 mi S of Tel Aviv–Yafo; ancient Philistine city; modern city founded in 1956 as the major port of S Israel; railway; ancient and modern harbour; light industry, tourism.

Ashdown, Paddy, popular name of **Lord Jeremy John Durham Ashdown of Norton-sub-Hamdon** (1941–) British politician, born in India. After a childhood and youth spent in India and Ulster, he joined the Royal Marines, serving in the Special Boat Squadron. He then studied Mandarin at Hong Kong University, and spent five years in the diplomatic service. He overturned a large Conservative majority in his constituency of Yeovil and entered the House of Commons as a Liberal in 1983. In 1988 he won the leadership election for the new Liberal and Social Democratic Party. In 1999, having led the Liberal Democrats to their best general election result for over half a century, he resigned as leader. He received a knighthood in the year 2000, and was raised to the peerage in 2001. In 2002 he became the international community's representative in Bosnia and Herzegovina with final responsibility for implementing the terms of the Dayton peace accord, signed by the warring factions in December 1995.

Asher, Jane (1946–) Actress and cake designer, born in London, UK. She studied at North Bridge House and Miss Lambert's Parents' National Educational Union. From 1957 she performed regularly in the theatre and on television, her films including *Alfie* (1966), *Henry VIII and His Six Wives* (1970), *Paris By Night* (1988), and *Closing Numbers* (1994). Later stage work included roles in Alan Ayckbourn's plays *House* and *Gardens* (2000). Among her many books on baking are *Calendar of Cakes* (1989) and *Jane Asher's Complete Book of Cake Decorating Ideas* (1993), and she is proprietor of Jane Asher's Party Cakes Shop and Tea Room in Chelsea, London. She is married to the cartoonist Gerald Scarfe.

Asher, tribe of One of the 12 tribes of ancient Israel, said to be descended from Jacob's eighth son Asher (*Gen* 30.12f). Its territory included the narrow coastal plain from Carmel to the outskirts of Sidon and was bordered on the E by the Galilean hills.

Ashes, the A symbolic trophy contested by the cricket teams of England and Australia. It originated in 1882 after the *Sporting Times* printed a mock obituary to English cricket following the country's first defeat by Australia on home soil. An urn containing the ashes of a stump used in that match remains at Lord's cricket ground.

Ashikaga shogunate [ashikahga] (1338–1569) Second major Japanese shogunate, established by a Kamakura chieftain, Ashikaga Takanji (1305–58) following his seizure of the imperial capital Kyoto in 1336. He established his government at Muromachi, an outlying district of Kyoto. Ashikaga rule was never absolute, extensive castle-building occurred, and a damaging civil war (1467–77) sparked off a century of disorder which ended with the supremacy of Nobunaga (1569). Zen Buddhism spread rapidly during the period, the first Christian mission arrived (1549), and trade with China and Korea flourished.

Ashkenazim [ashkenahzim] Jews of C and E European descent, as distinguished from Sephardim Jews, who are of Spanish or Portuguese descent. The terms arose in the Middle Ages when Europe and W Asia were divided between Christian and Islamic countries. Cut off, the Ashkenazim developed their own customs, traditions of interpretation of the Talmud, music, and language (Yiddish).

Ashkenazy, Vladimir [ashkenahzee] (1937–) Pianist and conductor, born in Nizhni Novgorod (formerly Gorky), W Russia. He graduated from Moscow Conservatory (1960) and in 1962 was joint winner (with John Ogdon) of the Tchaikovsky Piano Competition, Moscow. He left the Soviet Union in 1963 and made his London debut that year. He settled in Iceland in 1973 with his wife, an Icelandic pianist, and became musical director of the Royal Philharmonic Orchestra, London (1987–5), the Radio Symphony Orchestra, Berlin (1989—99), and chief conductor of the Czech Philharmonic Orchestra (1998–).

Ashley, Laura, *née* **Mountney** (1925–85) Fashion designer, born in Merthyr Tydfil, S Wales, UK. She married Bernard Ashley in 1949, and they started a business manufacturing furnishing materials and wallpapers with patterns based upon document sources mainly from the 19th-c. When she gave up work to have a baby, she experimented with designing and making clothes, and this transformed the business into an international chain of boutiques selling clothes, furnishing fabrics, and wallpapers. Her work was characterized by a romantic style and the use of natural fabrics, especially cotton. Ashley Mountney Ltd became Laura Ashley Ltd in 1968.

Ashmolean Museum A museum at Oxford University, England, UK. Elias Ashmole donated the core of the collection to the University in 1675, and the museum was opened eight years later. Its holdings include a distinguished collection of archaeological relics, paintings, prints, and silverware.

Ashmore and Cartier Islands Area c.3 sq km/1½ sq mi. Uninhabited Australian external territory in the Indian Ocean 320 km/200 mi off the NW coast of Australia; consists of the Ashmore Is (Middle, East and West) and Cartier I; formerly administered by the Northern Territory, it became a separate Commonwealth Territory in 1978; Ashmore Reef is a national nature reserve.

ashram [ashram] An Indian religious community whose members lead lives of austere self-discipline and dedicated service in accordance with the teachings and practices of their particular school. A well-known ashram was that of Mahatma Gandhi.

ashrama [ashrama] In Hindu tradition, any of the four stages of life: the pupil, the householder, the forest-dweller and, when all human bonds have been broken, the total renunciation of the world. Seldom followed in practice, these four stages represent the ideal way of life.

Ashton, Sir Frederick (William Mallandaine) (1906–88) British choreographer, born in Guayaquil, Ecuador. Following education at an English public school, he studied under Léonide Massine and Marie Rambert, who commissioned his first piece, *A Tragedy of Fashion* (1926). After a year in America, he returned to Britain to help found the Ballet Club, which later became Ballet Rambert (now the Rambert Dance Company). He joined the Vic Wells Ballet in 1935 as dancer/choreographer, and remained there as the company developed into the Royal Ballet. In 1963 he succeeded Ninette de Valois as director of the company, a post he held for seven years. Famous among his many works are *Façade* (1931), *Ondine* (1958), and *The Dream* (1964). He was knighted in 1962.

Ashura [ashoora] A Muslim fast day observed on the 10th of Muharram, particularly among Shiite Muslims, in commemoration of the death of Husain, grandson of Mohammed (10 Oct 680), with processions in which the faithful beat their breasts or whip themselves. It is a holiday in countries, such as Iran, with mainly Shiite Muslim populations.

Ashurbanipal *Assurbanipal*

Ash Wednesday The first day of Lent. The name derives from the ritual, observed in the ancient Church and continued in Roman Catholic and some Anglican Churches, of making a cross on the forehead of Christians with ashes which have previously been blessed. The ashes are obtained by burning the branches used in the previous year's Palm Sunday service.

Asia area c.44·5 million sq km/17·2 million sq mi. The largest continent; bounded N by the Arctic Ocean, E by the Pacific Ocean, S by the Indian Ocean, and W by Europe; maximum length, 8500 km/5300 mi; maximum width, 9600 km/6000 mi; chief mountain system, the Himalayas, rising to 8848 m/29 028 ft at Mt Everest; major rivers include the Yangtze (Changjiang), Yellow, Brahmaputra, Ayeyarwady (Irrawaddy), Indus, and Ganges. (*see map*)

Asia Minor *Anatolia*

Asian Games A multi-sport competition first held at New Delhi, India in 1951, and since 1954 held quadrennially. The Far Eastern Games, the predecessors of the Asian Games, were first held at Manila in 1913.

Asiatic wild horse *Przewalski's horse*

Asimov, Isaac [azimov] (1920–92) Novelist, critic, and popular scientist, born in Petrovichi, Russia. He was brought to the USA when he was three and grew up in Brooklyn, NY. He studied chemistry at Columbia University and developed a career both as an academic biochemist and as a science fiction writer. Among his leading titles are the 'Foundation' novels – *Foundation* (1951), *Foundation and Empire* (1952), and *Second Foundation* (1953); the so-called Robot novels – *The Caves of Steel* (1954) and *The Naked Sun* (1957); and the short stories which form the collection *I, Robot* (1950). Increasingly regarded as a scientific seer, he added the term *robotics* to the language. He wrote two volumes of autobiography (1979 and 1980), and later novels include *The Disappearing Man and other stories* (1985) and *Nightfall* (1990). Professor of biochemistry at the University of Boston, after 1958 he worked mainly on textbooks and works of popular science.

Asmara or **Asmera** [asmera] 15°20N 38°58E, pop (2000e) 461 300. Capital of Eritrea; altitude 2350 m/7710 ft; occupied by Italians, 1889; regional capital, 1897; occupied by British, 1941; airport; university (1958); meat processing, distilling, textiles; cathedral (1922), mosque (1937), archaeological museum.

Asmoneans [azmoneeanz] *Maccabees*

Aśoka or **Ashoka** [ashohka] (3rd-c BC) King of India (c.264–238 BC), the last ruler of the Mauryan dynasty. After his invasion of the Kalinga country, he renounced armed conquest and became a convert to Buddhism, which subsequently spread throughout

Asia

ARCTIC OCEAN
PACIFIC OCEAN
Bering Sea
East Siberian Sea
Laptev Sea
Kara Sea
Arctic Circle
Kolyma Range
Kamchatka
Sea of Okhotsk
Kurile Islands
Sakhalin
Kolyma
Indigirka
Yana
Lena
Olenek
Anabar
Kheta
Aldan
Vilyuy
Kureyka
Central Siberian Plateau
Siberia
Lower Tunguska
Stony Tungusk
Yenisey
Ob'
SSIAN FEDERATION
West Siberian Plain
Ishim
Irtysh
Chulym
Angara
Vitim
Amur
Argun
Lake Baikal
Hokkaido
JAPAN
Honshu
East Sea (Sea of Japan)
NORTH KOREA
SOUTH KOREA
Liao He
MONGOLIA
Altai Mountains
Gobi
Inner Mongolia
Lake Balkhash
KYRGYZSTAN
Tien Shan
Tarim He
TAJIKISTAN
Takla Makan Desert
Kunlun Mountains
CHINA
Yellow River
Yellow Sea
East China Sea
Ryukyu Islands
Tropic of Cancer
Yangtze
Mekong
Salwee
Plateau of Tibet
Brahmaputra
Himalayas
NEPAL
BHUTAN
INDIA
Ganges
BANGLADESH
BURMA
Narmada
Godavari
Krishna
Irrawaddy
Salween
Xi Jiang
Taiwan Strait
TAIWAN
Philippine Sea
Luzon
Hainan Dao
LAOS
VIETNAM
Bay of Bengal
THAILAND
CAMBODIA
South China Sea
PHILIPPINES
Mindanao
Andaman Islands (to India)
Gulf of Thailand
Andaman Sea
SRI LANKA
Nicobar Islands (to India)
BRUNEI
MALAYSIA
Borneo
New Guinea
Moluccas
Celebes
SINGAPORE
Sumatra
Equator
INDONESIA
Java Sea
Flores Sea
Flores
EAST TIMOR
Timor
Timor Sea
Java

India and beyond. He adopted a policy called *dharma* (principles of right life), advocating toleration, honesty, and kindness, and had his teachings engraved on rocks and pillars at certain sites. With his death the Mauryan empire declined and his work was discontinued.

asp A venomous African snake (*Naja haje*) of family Elapidae; Cleopatra is said to have committed suicide by forcing this species to bite her; also known as the **Egyptian cobra**. The name is also used for venomous African **burrowing asps** (**atractaspid snakes** or **mole vipers**) of family Colubridae, and for the European *Vipera aspis* (**European asp**, **asp viper**, or **aspic viper**) of family Viperidae.

asparagus A perennial native to Europe and Asia; erect or spreading, some species climbers, all with feathery foliage; the true leaves reduced to tiny scales and replaced by tiny modified branches functioning as leaves; flowers tiny, white or yellow, bell- or star-shaped; berries green, red, or black. Young shoots of *Asparagus officinalis* are prized as a vegetable. (Genus: *Asparagus*, 300 species. Family: Liliaceae.)

asparagus fern Not a fern, but a species of asparagus (*Asparagus setaceus*), a perennial with feathery foliage commonly grown as a pot plant and florists' foliage plant. (Family: Liliaceae.)

aspect ratio In visual presentation, especially in cinema and television, the proportion of the picture width to its height, e.g. 4:3, often expressed with the height as unity, 1·33:1. It is usually abbreviated **AR**.

Aspel, Michael (Terence) (1933–) British broadcaster and writer. Following national service, he became a radio actor (1954) and a television announcer (1957), but came to public prominence as a television newsreader (1960–8). In 1968 he became a freelance broadcaster, known for his genial interviewing style in *Aspel and Company* (1984–93), and as presenter of *This is Your Life* (1988–2003) and *The Antiques Roadshow* (from 2000). He writes regularly for magazines, and his books include one for children (*Hang On!*, 1982) and an autobiography (*Polly Wants a Zebra*, 1974).

aspen A species of poplar (*Populus tremula*), also called **trembling aspen**, because the greyish-green, rounded-to-ovoid leaves have flattened stalks, allowing the blades to flutter in the slightest breeze. The movement is accentuated by a flashing of the pale undersurface, giving the impression of constant movement. (Family: Salicaceae.)

Aspen Lodge *Camp David*

Aspergillus [asperjilus] A genus of typically asexually reproducing fungus that can cause food spoilage and produce disease in humans. (Subdivision: Ascomycetes. Order: Eurotiales.)

asphalt A semi-solid bituminous residue of the evaporation of petroleum (formed by slow evaporation in nature or by distillation in industry). It is usually employed mixed with some solid mineral matter for roofing, road-making, etc. Many natural deposits (eg in Trinidad) have a natural mineral content.

asphodel [asfodel] The name applied to two related genera native to the Mediterranean region and Asia, with erect stems, narrow, grass-like leaves, and spikes of flowers each with six perianth-segments. *Asphodelus* (12 species) has leaves V-shaped in cross-section, flowers white or pink. *Asphodeline* (15 species) has leaves triangular in cross-section, flowers yellow. (Family: Liliaceae.)

asphyxia Life-threatening interruption to the passage of air through the airways to the lungs. It is commonly due to physical obstruction to the upper respiratory tract from strangulation or inhaled foreign bodies, vomit, or water, as in drowning. It may also occur due to diseases of the airways or lungs.

aspidistra An evergreen perennial (*Aspidistra elatior*), native to E Asia; leaves long-stalked, elliptical, leathery, lasting several years; flowers bell-shaped with a lid formed by the umbrella-shaped style, dull purple; borne at ground level and pollinated by slugs. It tolerates shade and drought, and is much favoured as a pot-plant. (Family: Liliaceae.)

aspirin or **acetylsalicylic acid**A very widely used drug effective against many types of minor pain (headache, menstruation, neuralgia), inflammation (it is frequently prescribed for rheumatoid diseases), and fever. It has more recently been discovered to prevent the formation of blood clots, and therefore to reduce the incidence of coronary and cerebral thrombosis. The bark of the willow and certain other plants have been used for centuries in the cure of 'agues' (fever). The active ingredient *salicin* is the chemical precursor of aspirin. The German chemist Felix Hoffman (1868–1946) first synthesized aspirin, and it was introduced into medicine in 1899 by German pharmacologist Heinrich Dreser (1860–1924). It owes all its medicinal effects to its ability to prevent the synthesis of prostaglandins, a family of biologically active chemicals found throughout the body. A side-effect of taking aspirin may be gastric bleeding.

Asplund, Erik Gunnar (1885–1940) Architect, born in Stockholm, Sweden. He studied at the Royal Institute of Technology, Stockholm (1905–9). He designed the Stockholm City Library (1924–7), and was responsible for most of the buildings in the Stockholm Exhibition of 1930. Their design was acclaimed for the imagination with which the architect used simple modern forms and methods, such as the cantilever and glass walls.

Asquith, Herbert Henry Asquith, 1st Earl of Oxford (1852–1928) British statesman and prime minister (1908–16), born in Morley, West Yorkshire, N England, UK. He studied at Oxford, was called to the bar in 1876, and was Liberal member for East Fife (1886–1918). He became home secretary (1892–5), Chancellor of the Exchequer (1905–8), and succeeded Campbell-Bannerman as prime minister. He introduced the Parliament Act of 1911, limiting the power of the House of Lords. He was also confronted by the suffragette movement, the threat of civil war over Home Rule for Ireland, and the international crises which led to World War 1. In 1915 he headed a war coalition, but was ousted in 1916 by supporters of Lloyd George and others who thought his conduct of the war was not sufficiently vigorous. He lost his East Fife seat in 1918, then returned to the Commons as MP for Paisley in 1920. His disagreements with Lloyd George weakened the Liberal Party, though he was later recognized as leader again (1923–6). He was created an earl in 1925.

ass A rare wild horse; small, long ears, short erect mane; pale grey or brown; inhabits drier terrain than other horse species; domesticated thousands of years ago for carrying loads; three species: the **African wild ass** (*Equus (Asinus) asinus*); the **Asiatic wild ass** from S Asia (*Equus (Asinus) hemionus*, also called **onager**, **kulan**, and **hemione**); and the **kiang** (*Equus (Asinus) kiang*) from Tibet. The modern *donkey* (or *burro*) is a domesticated form of the African wild ass. (Genus: *Equus*. Subgenus: *Asinus*.)

Assad, Hafez al- [asad] (1928–2000) Syrian general and president (1971–2000), born in Qardaha, NW Syria. A member of the minority Alawi sect of Islam, he rose to high government office through the military and the Arab nationalist Baath Party. He was minister of defence and commander of the air force (1966–70), instigated a coup in 1970, and became prime minister and then president. After the 1973 Arab–Israeli War, he negotiated a partial withdrawal of Israeli troops from Syria. In 1976 he sent Syrian troops into Lebanon, and did so again in early 1987, by 1989 imposing Syrian authority in the greater part of Lebanon. A contender for leadership in the Arab world, he was the only Arab leader to support Iran in its war with rival Iraq. Having long enjoyed Soviet support, he was isolated in the early 1990s by the end of the Cold War and the disappearance of Russian influence in the Middle East.

Assam [asam] pop (2001e) 26 638 400; area 78 523 sq km/30 310 sq mi. State in E India, bounded NW by Bhutan and SE by Bangladesh; almost completely separated from India by Bangladesh; important strategic role in World War 2, during Allied advance into Burma; unicameral legislature of 126 members; crossed by the R Brahmaputra; world's largest river island of Majuli is a pilgrimage centre; capital, Dispur; produces almost half of India's crude oil, oil refining, timber, tea, rice, jute, cotton, oilseeds.

Assamese *Indo-Aryan languages*

assassin bug A small, cone-nosed bug which mostly feeds on the body fluids of small arthropods. The immature stages often conceal themselves with debris and litter. Some suck the blood of vertebrates, and are important medically as carriers of Chagas' disease.

assault An attack upon the person of another, causing them to fear actual injury (battery). Contact is not an essential ingredient of assault: threatening gestures can suffice. In common usage, and in some statutes and jurisdictions, the term *assault* is used to include the related concept of *battery*. Certain kinds of more serious assault, for example assault with intent to resist arrest, are known as *aggravated assault*. The making of a telephone call, followed by silence, can amount to assault.

assaying A chemical analysis which determines the amount of the principal or potent constituent of a mixture. The term usually implies the analysis of precious metals or drugs.

assemblage An imprecise term referring to art objects formed by sticking together bits and pieces to make a three-dimensional whole. Picasso's 'Glass of Absinthe' (1914) pioneered the technique; more recently the term has been stretched to include collages by Jean Dubuffet, readymades by Marcel Duchamp, and a variety of objects made from sacks, crushed automobiles, chairs, old clothes, etc by such artists as Robert Rauschenberg and Edward Kienholz.

Assemblies of God A Christian pentecostalist denomination formed in the USA and Canada in the early 20th-c. It promotes mission work all over the world, and believes baptism by the Holy Spirit to be evidenced by speaking in tongues.

assembly language A set of convenient mnemonics corresponding to the machine-code instructions of a specific central processor unit or microprocessor, defined by the manufacturer. Assembly language is more convenient for the programmer than machine code, and is translated (**assembled**) into machine code by an **assembly program**, usually known as an **assembler**.

Asser [aser] (850–?909) Welsh scholar, bishop, and counsellor to Alfred the Great. He spent his youth in the monastic community at St David's. Gaining a reputation for scholarship, he was enlisted into the royal service by Alfred, and made Bishop of Sherborne sometime before 900. He is best known for his unfinished Latin biography of King Alfred, the earliest biography of an English layman.

Assignats [aseenya] Originally, paper bonds issued by the Constituent Assembly in France (1789). They were later (1790) accepted as currency notes, in view of the shortage of coin, until the abolition of paper currency in 1797.

Assisi [aseezee] 43°04N 12°37E, pop (2001e) 25 500. Town in Umbria region, C Italy; famous religious and tourist centre; birthplace of Francis of Assisi, Agnes of Assisi, Clare of Assisi; Basilica of St Francis (1228–53) has frescoes by Giotto and Cimabue that were damaged in earthquake of 1997; Basilica of St Clare (1257–65); Romanesque Cathedral of San Rufino (9th-c).

assistance dogs Dogs which are trained to assist people with various handicaps, such as the Guide Dogs for the Blind. Dogs are also trained to help deaf people (Hearing Dogs for the Deaf) and the wheelchair-bound, especially paraplegics (Dogs for the Disabled).

Assize Court A legal system in England and Wales, dating from the time of Henry II, which was abolished by the Courts Act, 1971. Assize Courts were presided over by High Court judges, who travelled on circuit to hear criminal and civil cases. In 1972, the civil jurisdiction of the Assize Courts was transferred to the High Court, and the criminal jurisdiction to the Crown Court.

Associated Press (AP) An international news agency, with headquarters in New York City. Founded in 1848, it is the world's oldest and largest news-gathering co-operative, owned by US newspapers. Today the AP serves 1700 newspapers and 6000 television and radio stations in the US, and 8 500 news outlets in 121 countries. It is also on the Internet with The Wire, a 24-hour continuous up-dated multimedia site, and on television with APTN, a video news-gathering agency serving broadcasters around the world.

associated state A former colony that has a free and voluntary arrangement with the UK as the former colonial power. The state enjoys the right of self-government, but recognizes the British sovereign as head. The concept was introduced for states (eg Antigua, Grenada) wishing to be independent, but economically unable to support themselves.

association *dissociation*

Association football *football, Association*

Association of Caribbean States An association created by 25 Caribbean basin countries in 1994, with the aim of promoting a common approach to regional economic and political issues. It included the members of the Caribbean Community and Common Market (CARICOM).

Association of South-East Asian Nations (ASEAN) An association formed in 1967 to promote economic co-operation between Indonesia, Malaysia, the Philippines, Singapore, and Thailand. Brunei joined in 1984 and Vietnam in 1995; Laos, Cambodia, and Myanmar were formally admitted in 1997.

associative operation In mathematics, the principle that the order in which successive operations are performed does not affect the result; for example $(2 + 3) + 4 = 2 + (3 + 4)$. An operation * is associative over a set S if $a^*(b^*c) = (a^*b)^*c$ for all a,b,c in S. Over the set of real numbers, addition and multiplication are associative; subtraction and division are not.

assonance *alliteration*

Assumption The claim concerning the Virgin Mary, mother of Jesus Christ, that on her death she was 'assumed' (taken up, body and soul) to heaven. This was believed by some Christians in the ancient Church, widely accepted thereafter in Roman Catholic and Orthodox Churches, and defined by Pope Pius XII as an article of faith in 1950.

assurance Chiefly in the UK, a general term for insurance related to a person's life. In exchange for recurrent or lump-sum premiums, the insurance company guarantees a fixed sum on the policy-holder's death, or at some agreed date if they survive. Such policies may be *without profits*, ie for a fixed sum, or *with profits*, in which case the amount received reflects the company's success in investing the premiums.

Assurbanipal or **Ashurbanipal** [asoorbanipal] (7th-c BC) King of Assyria (668–627 BC), the last of the great Assyrian kings, the son of Esarhaddon and grandson of Sennacherib. A patron of the arts, he founded at Nineveh the first systematically gathered and organized library in the Middle East, containing a vast number of texts on numerous subjects copied from temple libraries throughout his empire.

Assyria [asiria] The name given first to the small area around the town of Assur on the Tigris in Upper Mesopotamia, and then much later to the vast empire that the rulers of Assur acquired through conquering their neighbours on all sides. At its height in the 9th-c and 8th-c BC, the Assyrian Empire stretched from the E Mediterranean to Iran, and from the Persian Gulf as far N as the mountains of E Turkey. The empire was destroyed in an uprising of Medes and Babylonians in 612 BC.

Assyrian architecture *Sumerian and Assyrian architecture*

Assyrian art The art associated with Assyria, dating from c.1500 BC, to the destruction of Nineveh (612 BC). Stylistically akin to Babylonian art, the best-known examples are the gigantic stone winged and human-headed lions which guarded entrances, and the wall decorations in the form of stone bas reliefs, originally painted, representing battles and hunting-scenes. Human figures tend to be stylized somewhat in the Egyptian manner, but animals are beautifully drawn in lively movement. There is an extensive collection in the British Museum.

Astaire, Fred [astair], originally **Frederick Austerlitz** (1899–1987) Dancer, singer, and actor, born in Omaha, Nebraska, USA. He was teamed up with his elder sister **Adele** (1897–1981) as a touring vaudeville act, rising to stardom with her in the 1920s on Broadway in specially written shows such as

Lady Be Good and *Funny Face*. In Hollywood, with his new partner Ginger Rogers, he revolutionized the film musical with a succession of original tap dance routines in such films as *Flying Down to Rio* (1933), *Top Hat* (1935), and *Swing Time* (1936). He announced his retirement in 1946, but returned to create further classic musicals, such as *Easter Parade* (1948), then turned to straight acting, winning an Oscar nomination for *The Towering Inferno* (1974) and an Emmy for *A Family Upside Down* (1978). He received a special Academy Award in 1949 for his contributions to the musical.

Astana, Kazakh 'capital', formerly **Akmola** (1995–7), **Tselinograd** (1961–95), **Akmolinsk** (to 1961) 51°10N 71°30E, pop (2000e) 300 000. Capital of Kazakhstan (from 1997, as Akmola), on R Ishim; founded as a fortress, 1830; airport; railway junction; agricultural machinery, ceramics, foodstuffs, clothing.

Astarte [astah(r)tay] *Ishtar*

aster A member of a large group of mainly perennials from America, Eurasia, and Africa; flower-heads daisy-like, usually in clusters; outer ray florets blue, purple, pink, or white, often autumn or late-summer flowering. Several are popular ornamentals. (Genus: *Aster*, 250 species. Family: Compositae.)

asterism A conspicuous or memorable group of stars, smaller than a constellation. An example is the Plough.

asteroids Rocky objects generally found in orbits lying between those of Mars and Jupiter, also called **minor planets**. This 'main belt' of asteroids has its inner edge c.100 million km/60 million mi outside Mars' orbit, and is c.165 million km/100 million mi wide. Only a few are large enough to have visible discs (hence the name, meaning 'starlike'), so most sizes are inferred. The orbits of c.10 000 of the larger asteroids are known. The first asteroid, Ceres (diameter 940 km/580 mi) was discovered by Giuseppe Piazzi (1746–1826) in 1801, and has an orbital period of 4·6 years. Other large asteroids are Pallas (540 km/340 mi), Vesta (580 km/360 mi), Hygiea (430 km/270 mi), Interamnia (340 km/210 mi), Davida (320 km/200 mi), and Cybele (310 km/190 mi).

Asteroids are classified according to telescopically measured visible and near-infrared colours, inferences about their composition being based on a comparison with meteorite types. *C* types are thought to be analogous to carbonaceous meteorites; *S* types are thought to be composed of silicates mixed with nickel/iron; and *M* types are thought to be metallic (nickel/iron); there are also several unclassified asteroids. They are believed to have originated in the formation of the Solar System, when planetesimals accreted from solar nebula. The more primitive carbonaceous asteroids may have evolved little since then, while the other types may have been parts of larger bodies first accreted and later broken up by collisions. Recently several hundred small (few km-diameter) asteroids have been discovered in highly elliptical orbits that come inside the orbit of Mars, some crossing the orbit of Earth – the Apollo, Amor, and Aten families. The total number of near-Earth asteroids is thought to be over 100 000; these, and the larger number of unseen boulder-size objects, may collide with the Earth and Moon periodically. Such asteroids are relatively easy to visit by spacecraft, and may in the future represent economically useful resources for an expanding space economy. The first asteroid landing took place in February 2001, when the NEAR Shoemaker spacecraft landed on Eros (32 km/20 mi).

asthenosphere [astheenosfeer] The Earth's upper mantle, extending from the base of the lithosphere at c.72 km/45 mi down to c.250 km/155 mi below the surface. A seismic discontinuity defines the boundary between the upper and lower mantle. The asthenosphere is considerably less rigid than the lithosphere above.

asthma A common condition in which there is narrowing and obstruction of the airways (bronchi and bronchioles) which is partly or completely reversible with time or treatment. Narrowing results from the contraction of the bronchial muscles and inflammation of the bronchial walls. It may be an exaggerated response in hypersensitive individuals to various allergens. Common amongst these are pollen, house dust, and the detritus of house mites that inhabit mattresses, etc. Psychological factors and respiratory chest infection contribute in some cases; however there is often no obvious cause. The first attacks may occur at any age, but are usually early in life. They commonly consist of sudden episodes of breathlessness and wheezing which may last several hours or days. In rare cases, severe persistent asthmatic attacks may be fatal, especially if treatment is delayed. In most patients, treatment involves periodic inhalation of one or more of several available drugs which relax the airways or reduce any inflammation. Exposure to the causative allergen, if known, should be avoided.

Asti 44°54N 8°13E, pop (2001e) 73 100.Town in Piedmont region, NW Italy; at the junction of Tanaro and Borbore rivers; centre of a fertile wine-producing area (Asti Spumante); birthplace of Vittorio Alfieri, Alberto Castigliano, Federigo della Valle, Mikhail Tswett; bishopric; railway; textiles, chemicals, glass, food products; tourism; Palio race (Sep).

astigmatism In vision, an actual asymmetry in the optical system of the eye, so that the eye's ability to focus horizontal and vertical lines is different. In optics, the term refers to aberrations of a lens image due to the position of an object off the lens axis.

Astley, Thea (1925–) Novelist and short-story writer, born in Brisbane, Queensland, NE Australia. Educated in Queensland, she was brought up a Roman Catholic, and much of her writing has been influenced by her Catholicism and the environment of N Queensland. She has won the prestigious Miles Franklin Award three times, for novels including *The Slow Natives* (1965) and *The Acolyte* (1972). An acute observer of contemporary Australia, and a skilled satirist, her novels often focus on misfits, and attack the narrow-mindedness of middle-class life. In 1979 she published a collection of related short stories, *Hunting the Wild Pineapple*, and in 1980 retired from Macquarie University to write full time, her works since then including *Reaching Tin River* (1990) *Vanishing Points* (1992), and *Coda* (1999). In 1996 she won the Age Book of the Year award for *The Multiple Effects of Rainshadow*.

Aston, Francis (William) (1877–1945) Physicist, born in Birmingham, West Midlands, C England, UK. He studied at Birmingham and Cambridge, and was noted for his work on isotopes. He invented the mass spectrograph in 1919, for which he was awarded the Nobel Prize for Chemistry in 1922. The *Aston dark space* in electronic discharges is named after him.

Astor, John Jacob (1763–1848) Fur trader and financier, founder of the America Fur Company and the Astor family, born in Waldorf, W Germany. In 1784 he sailed to the USA and invested his small capital in a fur business in New York City. He founded the settlement of *Astoria* in 1811. He became one of the most powerful financiers in the USA, and at his death left a legacy to found a public library in New York City.

Astor (of Hever), John Jacob Astor, Baron (1886–1971) Newspaper proprietor, born in New York City, USA, the son of William Waldorf Astor, 1st Viscount. He studied at Oxford, was aide-de-camp to the viceroy of India (1911–14), and was elected MP for Dover in 1922. He became chairman of the Times Publishing Company after the death of Lord Northcliffe, resigning his directorship in 1962. He was succeeded as chairman in 1959 by his eldest son, **Gavin Astor** (1918–84).

Astor, Nancy (Witcher) Astor, Viscountess, *née* **Langhorne** (1879–1964) British politician, born in Danville, Virginia, USA. Wife of Waldorf Astor, she succeeded her husband as Conservative MP for Plymouth in 1919, and was the first woman to take a seat in the House of Commons. She was known for her interest in social problems, especially temperance and women's rights.

Astrakhan [astrakhahn], formerly **Khadzhi-Tarkhan** 46°22N 48°04E, pop (2000e) 508 000. Capital city of Astrakhan oblast, SE European Russia; on a huge island in the Volga delta; altitude, 22 m/72 ft below sea-level; protected from floods by

75 km/47 mi of dykes; founded, 13th-c; the most important port in the Volga–Caspian basin; airport; railway; university (1919); fishing, fish processing, metalwork, chemicals, textiles, foodstuffs, river vessels; major transshipment centre for oil, fish, grain, wood; known for astrakhan fur; Kremlin fortress (16th-c).

astral projection The popular interpretation of an out-of-the-body experience in which it is believed that the person's consciousness is contained in a non-physical 'astral body' which temporarily separates from the physical body. People reporting such an experience have said that they can witness events in the vicinity of their astral body (when they claim it is in a different location from their physical body), although the validity of such claims has yet to be established.

astrobiology The multi-disciplinary study of the origin, distribution, and destiny of life in the universe. It addresses the questions of how does life begin and develop, does life exist elsewhere in the universe, and what is life's future on Earth and beyond. It is a major goal of NASA's science programmes.

astrodome An open space or building covered by a vast translucent plastic dome; usually a sports centre or arena. The first and most famous example is the eponymous Astrodome, Houston, TX (1964), officially known as the Harris County Domed Municipal Stadium, architects Lloyd Jones Brewer and Wilson Morris Crain Anderson.

astrolabe [astrolayb] An ancient instrument (c.200 BC) for showing the positions of the Sun and bright stars at any time and date. If fitted with sights, it was also used for measuring the altitude above the horizon of celestial objects, and in this mode was a 15th-c forerunner of the sextant.

astrology A system of knowledge whereby human nature can be understood in terms of the heavens. It relies upon precise measurement and a body of symbolism which has come to be associated with each of the signs of the zodiac and the planets (including the Sun and Moon). It rests on a foundation of ancient philosophy, particularly on the idea that the force which patterns the heavens likewise orders humanity. As with religion, it is a source of both trivial superstition and profound insight. The most significant stages in the development of astrology took place in the first millennium BC in Mesopotamia and Greece. From there it spread worldwide, developing distinct branches and great variation in method. It blossomed most in those periods representing peaks of cultural achievement – Classical Greece, Renaissance Europe, and Elizabethan England. Today it thrives in several Eastern countries, and in the West is undergoing something of a rebirth, though the modern emphasis is on self-knowledge rather than on predicting events. Astrology is the mother of astronomy, although the two parted company in the 17th-c.

astrometry *astronomy*

astronaut The NASA term for a spacecraft crew member; originally applied to pilots, but now including scientists and payload specialists. Over 135 crewed missions were carried out to mid 1998. The longest flight duration was 84 days by the Skylab 4 crew. More than 20 US women have flown in space; and 17 astronauts have lost their lives in accidents directly related to spaceflight.

Astronomer Royal An honorary title awarded to a distinguished British astronomer. Before 1972, the title was given to the director of the Royal Greenwich Observatory, England. The title of Astronomer Royal for Scotland is also honorary, but before 1995 was given to the director of the Royal Observatory, Edinburgh.

astronomical unit (AU) The mean distance of the Earth from the Sun, c.149·6 million km/93 million mi (precise value, $149{\cdot}597870 \times 10^9$ m); a convenient measure of distance within the Solar System. Mean distances of other planets from the Sun are: Mercury 0·39 AU, Venus 0·72 AU, Mars 1·52 AU, Jupiter 5·2 AU, Saturn 9·5 AU, Uranus 19 AU, Neptune 30 AU, Pluto 39·5 AU. There are 63 240 AU in one light year.

astronomy The study of all classes of celestial object, such as planets, stars, and galaxies, as well as interstellar and intergalactic space, and the universe as a whole; the branch of classical astronomy concerned with the precise measurement of the positions of celestial objects is known as **astrometry**. The first known systematic observers were the Babylonians, who compiled the first star catalogues c.1600 BC. From the 9th-c BC they kept dated astronomical records. Around the same time, the Neolithic peoples of W Europe constructed massive observatories of the Sun and Moon at Stonehenge, England, and Carnac, France. Greek philosophers, from c.500 BC, attempted the first cosmologies, models of the ever-changing arrangements of the five visible planets. The influence of Aristotle was especially strong on all later work, to the point of stultifying serious investigations for almost two millennia. Modern astronomy began 450 years ago with Copernicus, who set the scene for the overthrow of the Hellenistic cosmology, asserting that the Sun, not the Earth, is at the centre of the Solar System. Newton described gravitational theory in the 17th-c, and thenceforth planetary astronomy became an exact science. From Newton's time, professional observatories were established, records properly kept, and mathematics was applied to understanding the heavens.

In the 18th-c and 19th-c, techniques to build large telescopes were developed, culminating in the construction of observatories on mountain sites in the USA, such as the Lick and Mt Wilson Observatories. The opening of large telescopes on good sites enabled physics to play a greater role in the interpretation of high-quality observations. In the early 20th-c the main ideas about the evolution of stars became clear, and by the 1950s the theory of nuclear burning in stars, as well as the origin of the chemical elements, was firmly established.

Radio astronomy emerged rapidly after World War 2, taking advantage of antennae and other equipment developed for radar, and was the first of the invisible astronomies. The use of satellites above the blanket of the Earth's atmosphere enabled ultraviolet, X-ray, infrared, and gamma-ray astronomies to be developed from the 1960s on. Opening these new windows on the cosmos produced many unexpected discoveries, such as quasars, pulsars, active galactic nuclei, X-ray binary stars, and the microwave background. Amateurs are also still able to contribute data to astronomy, for example by observing new comets, nova outbursts, supernova explosions in distant galaxies, variable stars, and the visual appearance of the planets.

astrophysics The application of physical laws and theories to stars and galaxies, with the aim of deriving theoretical models to explain their behaviour. Its biggest triumph has been accounting for energy production inside stars, and there have been notable successes in explaining the properties of galaxies and quasars.

Asturias [astoorias] pop (2000e) 1 105 000; area 10 565 sq km/4078 sq mi. Autonomous region and former principality of N Spain, co-extensive with the modern province of Oviedo; mountainous region along the Bay of Biscay; largely occupied by the Cordillera Cantabrica, rising to 2646 m/8681 ft in the Picos de Europa; centre of Christian resistance to Muslim invasion, 8th–9th-c; part of Kingdom of Leon, 911; scene of unsuccessful left-wing revolution, 1934; maize, fruit, livestock; coal (nearly half of Spain's needs), fluorspar, zinc, iron ore.

Asturias, Miguel Angel [astoorias] (1899–1974) Novelist and poet, born in Guatemala City, Guatemala. A law graduate from the National University, he spent many years in exile, particularly in Paris, where he studied anthropology. His novels, many of which reflect Mayan Indian influences, include *El señor presidente* (1946, The President), *Hombres de maíz* (1949, Men of Maize), and a trilogy on the foreign exploitation of the banana trade. In the Guatemalan civil service from 1946, he was ambassador to France, 1966–70. He was awarded the Lenin Peace Prize in 1966 and the Nobel Prize for Literature in 1967.

Asunción [asoonsyohn] 25°15S 57°40W, pop (2000e) 787 000. Federal capital of Paraguay; transport and commercial centre on the E bank of the R Paraguay; established, 1537; capital of La Plata region until 1580; airport; railway; two universities (1890, 1960); food processing, footwear, textiles; cathedral, La Encarnación church, Panteón Nacional de los Héroes.

Aswan [aswahn], ancient **Syene** 24°05N 32°56E, pop (2000e) 255 100. Capital of Aswan governorate, S Egypt; on the E bank of the R Nile, 900 km/560 mi S of Cairo; Aswan Dam to the S, at limit of navigation (1898–1902); Aswan High Dam further S at head of L Nasser (1971); airfield; railway; steel, textiles, winter tourism; Aswan museum, Roman Nilometer, Temples of Ptolemy VII, Seti I, Rameses II; Tombs of the Ancient Nobles, Aga Khan Mausoleum, Coptic monastery of St Simeon (6th-c), Temples of Philae, Temple of Kalabsha (transported 55 km/34 mi from its original site and re-erected near Aswan High Dam).

Aswan High Dam [aswahn] A major gravity dam on the R Nile in Egypt, impounding L Nasser; completed in 1970; situated 6·4 km/4 m upstream from the lesser Aswan Dam; height 111 m/364 ft; length 3600 m/11 811 ft. It has the capacity to generate 2100 megawatts of hydroelectricity.

asymptote [asimtoht] In mathematics, a line (usually straight) which is approached by a curve. This can be shown in a graph where the curve $y = 1/x$ approaches the line $y = 0$ as x becomes large; so $y = 0$ is an asymptote.

asynchronous transmission A protocol for the transmission of data between one computer and another, in which each character of information is transmitted by itself. A signal is sent to say the character is coming (a *start bit*), the bits of the character are sent, then another signal (the *stop bit(s)*) is sent to say the character has completed.

Atacama Desert [atakahma], Span **Desierto de Atacama** Arid desert area in N Chile, claimed to be the world's driest area; a series of dry salt basins, extending 960 km/596 mi S from the Peru border to the R Copiapó; bounded W by the Pacific coastal range and E by the Cordillera de Domeyko; average altitude 600 m/2000 ft; almost no vegetation; town of Calama recorded a 400-year drought up to 1971; water is piped to the towns and nitrate fields from the Cordillera; ceded to Chile by Peru and Bolivia, 1883–4; copper, nitrates, iodine, borax deposits.

Atahualpa [atawalpa] (?–1533) Last Inca ruler of Peru. On the death of his father, he received the N half of the Inca empire, and in 1532 overthrew his brother, Huascar, who ruled the S half. A year later he was captured by invading Spaniards under Francisco Pizarro. Although his subjects paid a vast ransom to secure his release, Atahualpa was executed.

Atalanta [atalanta] In Greek mythology a heroine, nurtured by a she-bear, who grew up to be a strong huntress. She refused to marry any man who would not take part in a foot-race with her: those who lost were killed. Eventually Hippomenes (or Milanion) threw three golden apples of the Hesperides at her feet, so that her attention was diverted and she lost.

Atatürk [ataterk], originally **Mustafa Kemal** (1881–1938) Turkish army officer, politican, and president (1923–38), born in Salonika, Greece. He raised a nationalist rebellion in Anatolia in protest against the post-war division of Turkey, and in 1921 established a provisional government in Ankara. In 1922 the Ottoman Sultanate was formally abolished, and in 1923 Turkey was declared a secular republic, with Kemal as president. He ruled as a dictator, supported by the bureaucracy and rising middle class. He successfully launched a social and political revolution introducing Western forms of dress, the emancipation of women, educational reform, the replacement of Arabic script with the Latin alphabet, and the discouragement of traditional Islamic loyalties in favour of a strictly Turkish nationalism. He transformed Turkey into a modern, secular state, even abandoning the constitutional requirement that Islam be the state religion. In 1935 he assumed the surname Atatürk ('Father of the Turks').

ataxia [ataksia] Inco-ordination of the arms or legs, arising from a failure of the central nervous system to control the movement of muscles in the limbs, or because the brain is deprived of information about the position of the limbs in space (**sensory ataxia**).

ATC (Automatic Train Control) *train protection systems*

atelier [atelyay] (Fr 'artist's studio') An abbreviation of *atelier libre* (literally 'free studio' – in the sense that anyone can attend, on payment of a fee), which provides a nude model for artists to work from, but no instruction. The most famous, the Atelier Suisse in Paris, opened c.1825 and was attended by Delacroix, Courbet, Manet, Monet, Cézanne, and others. They exist throughout Europe.

Aten or **Aton** In Ancient Egypt, originally the name of the Sun's disc, and then that of the sun-god. In the reign of the Pharaoh Akhenaton, the cult of Aten temporarily replaced that of Amun-Re; this is sometimes interpreted as an early form of monotheism.

Athabascan or **Athapascan** [athabaskn] A language family spoken by various American Indian groups living in Alaska and NW Canada, W of Hudson Bay; the term is often used for the Indians themselves. Before the arrival of Europeans, some groups migrated S, and settled in the Great Plains and New Mexico (Apaches and Navajo are of Athabascan origin). They lived mainly in small independent hunting-and-gathering bands, and there was little tribal unity. They engaged in the fur trade after Europeans reached North America. Today some supply trapped animals for the fur trade and are hunters' guides, and a few are assimilated into the dominant US culture: but most still live by hunting and fishing.

Athanasian Creed [athanayzhn] A statement of Christian faith, written in Latin probably in the 5th-c AD. Called *Quicunque vult* after the opening words, it remains a historic statement of Trinitarian doctrine, still sometimes used liturgically. The Greek text is known in Eastern Churches, but with the omission of the *filioque* clause.

Athanasius, St [athanayzius] (c.296–373) Christian theologian and prelate, born in Alexandria. A distinguished participant at the Council of Nicaea (325), he was chosen Patriarch of Alexandria and Primate of Egypt. As a result of his stand against the heretic Arius, he was dismissed from his see on several occasions by emperors sympathetic to the Arian cause. However, his teaching was supported after his death at the Council of Constantinople (381). His writings include works on the Trinity, the Incarnation, and the divinity of the Holy Spirit. The *Athanasian Creed* (representing his beliefs) was little heard of until the 7th-c. Feast day 2 May.

atheism The denial of the existence of God or gods. It includes both the rejection of any specific belief in God or gods, and the view that the only rational approach to claims about divine existence is one of scepticism. Justification of atheism is often made on the grounds that some branch of science or psychology has rendered belief in God or gods superfluous, or that experiential verification of religious belief is lacking. Theists argue that such justification has not proved to be logically grounded.

Athelstan or **Æthelstan** [athelstan] (c.895–939) Anglo-Saxon king, the grandson of Alfred the Great, and the son of Edward the Elder, whom he succeeded as King of Wessex and Mercia in 924. A warrior king of outstanding ability, he extended his rule over parts of Cornwall and Wales, and kept Norse-held Northumbria under control. In 937 he defeated a confederation of Scots, Welsh, and Vikings from Ireland in a major battle (Brunanburh), and his fame spread far afield. At home, he improved the laws, built monasteries, and promoted commerce.

Athene or **Athena** [atheena] The Greek goddess of wisdom. She was not born, but sprang fully armed from the head of Zeus; she was the patron of Athens, and her emblem was the owl.

Athens, Gr **Athínai**, ancient **Athenae** 38°00N 23°44E, pop (2000e) Greater Athens 3 235 000. Capital city of Greece, in a wide coastal plain between the Ilissus and Cephissus Rivers, surrounded by hills; ancient Greek city-state extending over Attica by the 7th-c BC; great economic and cultural prosperity under Pericles, 5th-c BC; taken by the Romans, 146 BC; part of the Ottoman Empire, 1456; capital of modern Greece, 1835; occupied by Germans in World War 2; two airports; railway; three universities (1836, 1837, 1984); port and main industrial area at Piraeus; textiles, machine tools, shipbuilding, chemicals, food processing, tourism; hill of the Acropolis (156 m/ 512 ft), with the Parthenon (5th-c BC), Propylaea (437–432 BC), Temple of Athena Niki (432–421 BC), Ionic Erechtheion (421–406 BC), and Acropolis museum; to the S, the Odeon of Herod Atticus (2nd-c BC), portico of Eumenes, remains of the Asklepieion (4th-c BC), and site of the Odeum of Pericles; to the N, the excavated area of the Ancient Agora (market-place); Olympieion, Arch of Hadrian (AD 131–2), Stadion; Parliament Building, National Garden, National Archaeological Museum; Carnival (Feb), *son et lumière* (Apr–Oct), folk dancing in open-air theatre (May–Sep), Athens Festival of Music and Drama (Jul–Sep).

atherosclerosis [atherohsklerohsis] The irregular deposition of fats (mainly cholesterol and triglycerides) and other substances in the inner wall of arteries; seen as sharply-defined, raised, cream-coloured patches. Together with the associated scarring, this causes narrowing of the affected blood vessel. It also predisposes to the formation of thrombus at the affected site. Common sites are the aorta and blood vessels to the heart and brain, but any artery can be affected. The disorder increases with age, and the consequences to health depend on the blood vessel affected. Thus angina pectoris, stroke, or gangrene of the limb may arise when the coronary arteries, cerebral arteries, or arteries to the lower limbs respectively are affected. Contributing causes include high fat (particularly saturated fat) dietary intake, high blood pressure, obesity, and lack of exercise.

Atherton, David (1944–) Conductor, born in Blackpool, Lancashire, NW England, UK. He studied at Cambridge, and was founder and musical director of the London Sinfonietta (1967–73). In 1968 he became the youngest ever conductor of the Henry Wood Promenade Concerts, later joining the Royal Liverpool Philharmonic Orchestra as principal conductor and artistic adviser (1980–3) and principal guest conductor (1983–6). He was principal guest conductor of the BBC Symphony Orchestra (1985–9), and has been musical director and principal conductor with the Hong Kong Philharmonic Orchestra since 1989.

Atherton, Mike, popular name of **Michael Andrew Atherton** (1968–) Cricketer, born in Manchester, Greater Manchester, NW England, UK. He studied at Cambridge and made his first-class debut for the University v. Essex in 1987, his debut for Lancashire the same year, and his debut for England in 1989 against Australia. He captained England in a record 51 Tests (1993–8), leading tours to the West Indies (1994–8), Australia (1994–5), South Africa (1995–6), and Zimbabwe and New Zealand (1996–7). Awards include Cricket Writers' Young Cricketer of the Year (1990) and the Cornhill Player of the Year (1994). Latterly bedevilled by back trouble, his best-remembered innings was an 11-hour, match-saving 188 against South Africa in Johannesburg in 1996. He announced his retirement from first-class cricket in 2001.

athlete's foot A common form of ringworm infection (*tinea pedis*) in which a fungus causes itching and fissuring of the skin of the soles of the feet and between the toes. It is usually acquired in swimming baths and from shower floors.

athletics Tests of running, jumping, throwing, and walking skills for trained athletes, also known (especially in the USA) as **track and field**. The track events are divided into six categories: *sprint races* (100 m, 200 m, and 400 m); *middle distance races* (800 m and 1500 m); *long distance races* (5000 m and 10 000 m); *hurdle races* (110 m – 100 m for women – and 400 m); *relay races* (4 × 100 m and 4 × 400 m); and the men-only *steeplechase* (3000 m). In addition there is the endurance test of the *marathon*. The field events involve jumping and throwing. *Jumping events* consist of the high jump, long jump, triple jump, and pole vault. The *throwing events* are the discus, shot put, javelin throw, and hammer throw. *Walking races* take place on either the road or the track. In addition, two-day multi-event competitions exist in the form of the *decathlon* (10 events) for men and *heptathlon* (7 events) for women. Such competitions date to Egypt in c.3800 BC and they formed part of the ancient Olympic Games. The athletics events are now the most important part of the Modern Olympics. The governing body is the International Amateur Athletic Federation, founded in 1912.

Athletics Congress *USA Track and Field*

Athlone [athlohn] 53°25N 7°56W, pop (2000e) 15 500. Town in Co Westmeath, Leinster, C Ireland; on R Shannon, W of Dublin; railway; technical college; barracks; radio transmitter; textiles, industrial and electrical cable; remains of town wall, 13th-c Franciscan abbey, 13th-c castle; river boating centre; all-Ireland amateur drama contest (Jul).

Atiyah, Sir Michael (Francis) [ateeah] (1929–) Mathematician, born in London, UK. He studied at Trinity College, Cambridge (1952), lectured at Cambridge and Oxford, became professor of mathematics at Oxford (1963–9), and was appointed Master of Trinity College, Cambridge, in 1990. He has worked on algebraic geometry, algebraic topology, index theory of differential operators, and the mathematics of quantum field theory, where he has been particularly concerned with bridging the gap between mathematicians and physicists. In 1966 he was awarded the Fields Medal.

Atkins, Chet, popular name of **Chester Burton Atkins** (1924–2001) Guitarist and record producer, born near Luttrell, Tennessee, USA. In the 1940s he performed with the Carter Family and Red Foley, and first appeared in the 'Grand Ole Opry'. In Nashville in the 1950s he made the electric guitar popular as a solo instrument for country music. He became a producer for RCA, reviving country music in the 1960s and 1970s, and in 1982 began recording for CBS records. He won a total of 14 Grammy Awards during his career and was posthumously inducted into the Rock and Roll Hall of Fame in 2002.

Atkins, Robert C (1930–2003) Cardiologist and businessman, born in Ohio, USA. He studied at the University of Michigan (1951) and graduated in medicine from Cornell University (1955), then moved to New York City, where he opened the Atkins Center for Complementary Medicine (closed Oct 2003). He developed a dietary system based on the theory that people can lose weight by following a high-protein, high-fat diet with a significant restriction of dietary carbohydrate, published in *Dr. Atkins' Diet Revolution* (1972), revised as *Dr. Atkins' New Diet Revolution* (1992). The approach ran against most nutritional opinion of the time, but its continuing controversial status has done nothing to reduce its popularity.

Atkinson, Rowan (Sebastian) (1955–) British comic actor and writer, born in Newcastle upon Tyne, Tyne and Wear, NE England, UK. He studied electrical engineering at the universities of Newcastle upon Tyne and Oxford, first appeared in Oxford University revues at the Edinburgh Festival Fringe, and in 1981 became the youngest performer to have had a one-man show in the West End. Subsequent appearances include *The Nerd* (1984), *The New Revue* (1986), and *The Sneeze* (1988). Television roles include *Not the Nine O'Clock News* (1979–82), *Blackadder* (1983–9), *The Thin Blue Line* (1995–6), and *Mr Bean* (from 1990–4, 1996 in the USA). Film credits include *Four Weddings and a Funeral* (1994), *The Lion King* (voiceover, 1994), *Bean: the Ultimate Disaster Movie* (1997), and *Johnny English* (2003).

Atlanta 33°45N 84°23W, pop (2000e) 416 500. State capital in Fulton Co, NW Georgia, USA; largest city in the state, near the Appalachian foothills; founded at the end of the railway in 1837 (named Terminus); renamed Atlanta, 1845; a Confederate supply depot in the Civil War; burned by General Sherman, 1864; capital, 1887; airport; railway; four universities (1835, 1836, 1865, 1913); industrial, transportation, commercial, and cultural centre; aircraft, automobiles, textiles, food products, steel, furniture, chemicals; professional teams, Braves (baseball), Hawks (basketball), Falcons (football); High Museum of Art, Alliance

Theatre, Oakland Cemetery, Martin Luther King Jr historic site, Grant Park.

Atlanta Campaign *Sherman, William Tecumseh*

Atlantic, Battle of the (1940–3) The conflict arising out of German attacks on shipping in the Atlantic during World War 2. The German strategy was to cut off Britain's supplies of food and munitions by submarine action. Only at the end of 1943 were the attacks countered, and the threat brought under control.

Atlantic Charter A declaration of common objectives by Roosevelt and Churchill after a secret meeting off Newfoundland (Aug 1941). It announced agreement on principles which should govern post-war settlements, several of which paralleled Wilson's Fourteen Points of 1918. The Charter was endorsed by the USSR and 14 other states at war with the Axis Powers, and served as an ideological basis for Allied co-operation during the war and for the post-war United Nations Organization.

Atlantic City 39°21N 74°27W, pop (2000e) 40 500. Town in Atlantic Co, SE New Jersey, USA; on the Atlantic coast, 96 km/60 mi SE of Philadelphia; railway; popular seaside resort with famed boardwalk (over 9 km/5½ mi long) and piers; many casinos; convention centre; Miss America Pageant (Sep).

Atlantic Intracoastal Waterway *Intracoastal Waterway*

Atlantic Ocean Body of water extending from the Arctic to the Antarctic, separating North and South America (W) from Europe and Africa (E); area c.82 217 000 sq km/31 700 000 sq mi; depths of 5725 m/18 783 ft reached in Argentine abyssal plain; average depth 3700 m/12 000 ft; maximum depth, Puerto Rico Trench, 8648 m/28 372 ft; principal arms (W), Labrador Sea, Gulf of Mexico, Caribbean Sea; (E), North Sea, Baltic Sea, Mediterranean and Black Sea, Bay of Biscay, Gulf of Guinea; (S), Weddell Sea; continental shelf narrow off coast of Africa and Spain, broader in NW Europe and off Americas; 'S' shaped, submarine Mid-Atlantic Ridge between Iceland and the Antarctic Circle, centre of earthquake and volcanic activity; sea-floor spreading, such that North and South America are moving away from Africa and Europe, rate of 2 cm/0·8 in per year (N), 4·1 cm/1·6 in (S); major surface circulation, clockwise in N, counterclockwise in S; main currents include the Gulf Stream (N Atlantic Drift), and the N Equatorial, Canary, S Equatorial, Brazil, Benguela, and Equatorial Counter Currents; Sargasso Sea, a sluggish region at centre of movement in the N Atlantic; main islands include Iceland, Faeroes, British Is, Newfoundland, Azores, Bermuda, Madeira, Canary Is, Cape Verde Is, Trinidad and Tobago, Ascension, St Helena, Tristan da Cunha, Falkland Is, S Georgia; mineral resources include manganese nodules, offshore oil and gas, and metal-rich sediments; several major fishing areas; important international communications highway, particularly from Middle East to Europe.

Atlantic Provinces *Maritime Provinces*

Atlantic Wall An incomplete network of coastal fortifications, supplemented by beach-obstacles and minefields, constructed in 1942–4 between the Pas-de-Calais and the Bay of Biscay as part of Hitler's plans for an impregnable 'Fortress Europe' capable of repelling any Allied landings. On D-Day its 'invincibility' was shown to be a myth.

Atlantis [atlantis] According to Plato, an island in the ocean W of Spain, whose armies once threatened Europe and Africa, and which disappeared into the sea. Plato claimed to have heard of the island from the Egyptians, and this has generated many speculative books and expeditions; but it was simply a fictional place where he could locate his ideas of social organization.

Atlas (astronomy) The 15th natural satellite of Saturn, discovered in 1980; distance from the planet 138 000 km/86 000 mi; diameter 40 km/25 mi.

Atlas (mythology) In Greek mythology, a Titan who was made to hold up the heavens with his hands, as a punishment for taking part in the revolt against the Olympians. When books of maps came to be published, he was often portrayed as a frontispiece, hence the name *atlas*.

Atlas Mountains A system of folded mountain chains in Morocco, Algeria, and Tunisia, NW Africa; includes (1) the volcanic **Anti-Atlas** range in SW Morocco which runs SW–NE for 250 km/155 mi and rises to heights over 2500 m/8000 ft; (2) the **Haut Atlas** range, the largest in the group, running SW–NE for 650 km/400 mi from Morocco's Atlantic coast, rising to Mt Toubkal (4165 m/13 665 ft); (3) the **Moyen Atlas** (N) rising to 3343 m/10 968 ft at Caberral; (4) E–W along Morocco's Mediterranean coast, the **Er Rif Mts**, rising to over 2000 m/6500 ft; (5) the **Atlas Saharien** which extends NE of the Haut Atlas across N Algeria; (6) the **Tell Atlas**, a smaller coastal range running along Algeria's Mediterranean seaboard.

atman [ahtman] (Sanskrit, 'soul' or 'self') In Hinduism, the human soul or essential self. In the teaching of the Upanishads, it is seen as being one with the absolute, and identified with Brahman.

atmosphere *see panel*

atmospheric physics The application of physical principles to the layer of gas surrounding planets, especially Earth. The Earth's atmosphere is a dynamic cloud of approximately 5×10^{15} tonnes of gas. The atmosphere's temperature drops with altitude to a minimum of about −100°C, rising at greater heights to 1200°C in the thermosphere 600 km above the Earth's surface. The Sun heats the Earth's surface, warming the air which then moves by convection, resulting in heat transfer and wind. This air movement combined with the Coriolis force gives rise to large-scale wind patterns, such as the trade winds. The Earth's rotation causes air temperature and hence pressure changes, giving rise to 'tidal' movement of the atmosphere (*atmospheric tides*). Absorption and radiation principles govern the uptake and re-emission of solar radiation by the Earth and its atmosphere, ensuring an overall energy bal-

atmosphere

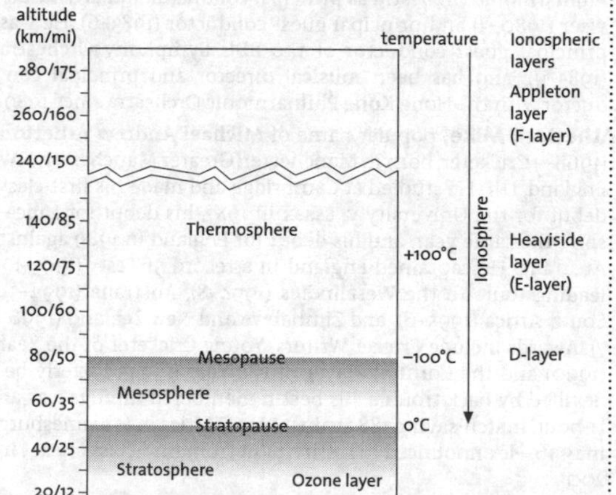

The layer of gas surrounding any planet or star. Earth's atmosphere is composed of air, which on average is made up of 78% nitrogen, 21% oxygen, and 1% argon, with traces of other rare gases, carbon dioxide, and hydrogen. Moist air may contain up to 31% water vapour. Earth's atmosphere is divided into several concentric shells, the lowest being the *troposphere*, followed by the *stratosphere*, *mesosphere*, and *thermosphere*. The outer shell of the atmosphere, at c.400 km/250 mi, from which light gases can escape, is termed the *exosphere*. The atmosphere contains the gases vital to life, and shields the Earth from harmful ionizing radiation.

ance; X-rays and ultraviolet radiation incident on the upper atmosphere create ions. These can influence radio waves, and in the upper reaches of the atmosphere the movement of these ions is governed by the Earth's magnetic field. The presence of ions makes the atmosphere an electrical conductor, and atmospheric electrical currents flow constantly. Thunder clouds are positively charged on top, and current flows upwards into the ionosphere (*Wilson current*). Current also flows from the Earth's surface to the negative base of thunder clouds (lightning). Positive charge flows back to Earth via 'fair-weather currents', due to the atmosphere's positive charge relative to Earth. Evaporation deposits water vapour into the atmosphere; condensation followed by precipitation returns it to Earth. The interplay of chemical and physical processes is necessary to understand ozone depletion and the greenhouse effect.

atmospheric pressure The pressure or force exerted by the atmosphere on the Earth's surface. The average pressure at sea level is taken as standard, and it is usual to modify measurements taken at different elevations so that they refer to this level. Pressure varies with elevation (decreases with altitude) and temperature. Units of measurement vary: at sea level, average pressure is 1013·25 mb (millibars, the units generally used by meteorologists), 101 325 Pa (pascals), 760 mm of mercury (760 torr), 29·92 in of mercury, or 14·7 lb/sq in. Pressure is measured using a barometer.

atoll A roughly circular structure of coral reefs enclosing a lagoon. Atolls occur in warm, clear, tropical oceanic waters where corals and coralline algae can flourish. Darwin first theorized that they are the final stage in a progression of reef formations. In the first stage, a *fringing reef* grows adjacent to land with little or no lagoon separating it from the shore. The second stage, a *barrier reef*, lies offshore with a lagoon separating it from the land. An *atoll* is the third and most mature stage, where the original land is no longer present. Darwin theorized that as volcanic islands subsided below sea level, reefs might continue to grow upward towards the surface. Drilling on several atolls has shown them to be supported by volcanic pedestals, confirming Darwin's hypothesis.

atom The smallest portion of a chemical element. Each atom comprises a positively charged nucleus surrounded by negatively charged electrons, whose number equals that of the protons contained within the nucleus. Electrons are attracted to the nucleus by electromagnetic force. They determine the chemistry of an atom, and are responsible for binding atoms together. Atoms are described using quantum mechanics; the diameter of an atom is approximately 10^{-10}m, and the number of atoms of a substance is given in terms of Avogadro's constant.

atomic bomb A nuclear explosive device (the **A-bomb**) which achieves its destructive effects through energy released during the fission of heavy atoms (as in uranium-235 or plutonium-239). The bombs were developed in the USA from 1942 onwards under the code-name 'Manhattan', and used to destroy the Japanese cities of Hiroshima and Nagasaki (Aug 1945). Atomic weapons have been supplanted by the very much more destructive thermonuclear weapons, but a fission weapon trigger is an essential component of these devices. Fission devices are also used for low-yield 'tactical' weapons, and in 'enhanced radiation' or neutron weapons. They can be delivered by submarines, artillery, or aircraft.

atomic clock *clock*

atomic force microscope A microscope using a mechanical sensor to form an image of a surface fine enough to see the individual atoms. The sample is moved under a very sharp tip mounted on a soft cantilever spring. A detector, often optical, monitors deflections of the cantilever and passes this information to an electronic display system. Unlike the scanning tunnelling microscope, the atomic force microscope can image non-conducting surfaces. One of a class of *scanning probe microscopes*, it was invented by Gerd Binnig, Christopher Gerber, and Calvin Quate in 1986.

atomic mass unit (amu) Unit of mass; symbol *u*; also termed **unified atomic mass unit**; defined as 1/12 of the mass of the carbon-12 atom; value $1u = 1{\cdot}66 \times 10^{-27}$ kg; used to express relative atomic masses of atoms; sometimes called a **dalton**.

atomic number *proton number*

atomic physics The study of the structure and properties of atoms, and of their interactions with electromagnetic radiation and with other atoms. In 1911 Ernest Rutherford interpreted the scattering of alpha particles passing through gold foil as demonstrating that atoms contain a hard central nucleus, c.10^{-14}m in diameter, complete atoms being c.10^{-10} m across. He visualized the atom as a central positively-charged nucleus with negatively-charged electrons orbiting round it, rather like planets orbiting the Sun. However, such atoms would be unstable, according to the laws of classical mechanics, decaying by the emission of electromagnetic radiation. Further, they would not exhibit observed atomic spectra. These problems were solved by the improved atomic model of Niels Bohr (1913), in which an electron in a particular orbit around the nucleus had a specific energy depending on the orbit radius. Since only certain orbits were allowed, electrons could only have certain energies, giving rise to a pattern of discrete allowed energy levels. Electrons in an allowed orbit would not radiate electromagnetic energy, but electron jumps from one orbit to another would correspond to the emission or absorption of well-defined quantities of light, in agreement with observed atomic spectra.

Though the Bohr model still provides a useful visual model, current atomic theory is an extension which incorporates quantum mechanics. Electrons have wave properties, and the Bohr orbits can then be explained as the requirement of fitting a whole number of electron waves round the nucleus. Electrons in atoms are better represented as distributions of electric charge each labelled by a particular set of quantum numbers, rather than by point particles in circular orbits. Every possible set of quantum numbers corresponds to an energy level, though not all can be occupied at once. Whereas Bohr's theory allowed a partial understanding of atomic spectra, modern quantum theory allows their explicit detailed calculation.

The quantum numbers required to specify electrons in (unexcited) atoms of elements determine exactly the position of those elements in the periodic table; and electron structure determines the type of chemical bond that will be formed with other atoms. The properties of hydrogen atoms can be calculated with great precision; but for more complicated atoms, the problems of predicting properties become severe. Spectroscopy and collisions between atoms are used to test predictions of energy levels and other properties. Exotic atoms (eg negative calcium ions) can now be produced and studied. The direct technological applications of atomic physics include lasers and atomic clocks.

atomic radius The effective size of an atom: in a metal, half the distance between the nuclei of the two nearest neighbour atoms in the solid (also called the **metallic radius**); in non-metals, half the distance of the closest approach of the nuclei of two identical non-bonded atoms.

atomic spectra A set of specific frequencies of electromagnetic radiation, typically light, emitted or absorbed by atoms of a certain type. A given spectral line corresponds to the transition of an electron between two specific energy levels. **Emission spectra** are produced by applying energy to atoms, for example by heating or electrical discharge, raising the electrons to a higher energy level; the excited electrons emit light upon returning to an unexcited state. **Absorption spectra** are observed by passing light through a substance. Spectra in infrared correspond to molecular vibrations and rotations; X-ray spectra correspond to the transitions of electrons deep inside heavy atoms. The study of spectra is called **spectroscopy**, a major analytic technique in physics and chemistry. The study of hydrogen spectra by Swiss physicist Johann Balmer (1825–

98) and others was important to the development of quantum mechanics.

atomic weight *relative atomic mass*

atomism A tradition dating back to the 5th-c BC, associated particularly with Democritus and Leucippus, which maintains that matter is composed ultimately of indivisible particles and that all its properties must be explained in terms of them. Classical atomism anticipated the 17th-c corpuscularian philosophy of Locke, Boyle, and Gassendi; but modern particle physics has a very different origin and approach.

atom laser A device which creates a beam of atoms having properties akin to those of the light beam from a laser. In particular, the waves associated with the atoms are coherent, or in step, and the beam of an atom laser is much brighter than that of an ordinary (incoherent) atomic beam. An atom laser which created pulses of atoms was first demonstrated in 1997 by Wolfgang Ketterle's team at the Massachusetts Institute of Technology. Continuous atom laser beams were first produced by Theodor Hänsch and his team in Munich, Germany, in 1999. They may have a major impact on atom optics, atom lithography, and precision measurements via atom interferometers.

atom optics The manipulation of beams of neutral atoms, in a way that parallels the manipulation of light in conventional optical systems, using atom optical equivalents of mirrors, lenses, beam splitters, and other elements. Conventional lenses and mirrors will not work for atoms, which are absorbed by the lens material or stick to the mirror surface. Standing wave patterns of laser light act as atom lenses and beam splitters. Atom optics can be used to fabricate microstructures directly via atom lithography, as an atom microscope, and as the basis for high-precision gyroscopic and gravitational measurements.

atom trap A device for trapping atoms whose velocity has been greatly slowed using laser cooling. The trapping is performed either by magnetic fields or by an intense laser beam focused to a spot. Magneto-optical atom traps, using combined magnetic fields and lasers, first appeared in 1987 and quickly became the most widely used optical trap. The trapped atoms allow a detailed study of their properties, and can be used in atomic optics experiments.

atonality The property of music which is not written in a key. While any music not written in the tonal system, which prevailed between c.1600 and c.1920, might be described as 'atonal', the term is most commonly applied to music written in the post-tonal but pre-serial style of Schoenberg's *Ewartung* (1909) and other compositions of that period.

atonement [atohnmnt] In Christian theology, the process whereby sinners are made 'at one' with God, through the life, death, and resurrection of Jesus Christ. No one theory is recognized as authoritative, but the theories of Irenaeus (stressing 'victory' over evil), Anselm (stressing 'satisfaction' made to God), and Abelard (stressing the force of example of Christ) have been commonly held.

Atonement, Day of *Yom Kippur*

ATP (Automatic Train Protection) *train protection systems*

atractaspid snake *asp*

Atreus [aytryoos] In Greek mythology, a king of Argos who quarrelled with his brother Thyestes, and placed the flesh of Thyestes' children before him at a banquet. Atreus was the father of Agamemnon and Menelaus.

atrial natriuretic factor [aytrial naytriuretik] A chemical substance (a peptide) isolated from granules found within the muscle cells of the atrium of the heart in various mammals (eg humans, rats). It inhibits the re-absorption of sodium by the kidney tubules, and the secretion of renin and antidiuretic hormone, and also lowers blood presssure. It possibly acts as a hormone involved in the regulation of body salt, water, and blood pressure.

atrium [aytrium] (plural **atria**) The entrance hall or open inner court of a Roman house; in mediaeval architecture, an open court in front of a church; generally, any cavity or entrance in a building. Atria became particularly fashionable in late-20th-c hotels and office blocks, sometimes rising to great height.

atropine [atropeen, atropin] A drug extracted from deadly nightshade (*Atropa belladonna*), used as a poison during the Roman Empire and later. It acts by blocking nerve transmission mediated by acetylcholine. Safer derivatives are now used in a wide variety of disorders, commonly in motion-sickness preparations, and also in ophthalmology, to dilate the pupil during eye examinations.

Atropos [atropos] *Moerae*

attachment In psychology, the infant–care-giver relationship, and the actions (eg crying, cuddling) which promote this relationship. The dominant explanation for attachment is the ethological theory of British psychiatrist John Bowlby (1907–90), which argues that early reciprocity between parent and child is determined by genetic factors in both participants, modified by the parent's own attachment history. Experience of disrupted relationships thus may be repeated in successive generations.

Attalids [atalidz] The flamboyant Hellenistic dynasty which ruled over large parts of W Asia Minor from the 3rd-c to the 2nd-c BC. Keen patrons of the arts, they made their beautiful capital, Pergamum, one of the main cultural centres of the Graeco-Roman world.

attar A fragrant essential oil distilled from plants; also called **otto**. The best known is attar of roses, obtained from the petals of the damask rose (*Rosa damascena*), cultivated in the Balkans.

Attenborough, Sir David (Frederick) [atenbruh] (1926–) Naturalist and broadcaster, born in London, UK, the brother of Richard Attenborough. After service in the Royal Navy (1947–9) and three years in an educational publishing house, he joined the BBC in 1952 as a trainee producer. The series *Zoo Quest* (1954–64) allowed him to undertake expeditions to remote parts of the globe to capture intimate footage of rare wildlife in its natural habitat. He was the controller of BBC 2 (1965–8) and director of programmes (1969–72) before returning to documentary-making with such series as *Life on Earth* (1979), *The Living Planet* (1984), *The First Eden* (1987), and *The Private Life of Plants* (1995). Later series include *Life of Birds* (1998), *The Blue Planet* (2001), and *Life of Mammals* (2002). He was knighted in 1985 and made a Companion of Honour in 1996.

Attenborough, Sir Richard (Samuel), Baron [atenbruh] (1923–) Actor and film director, born in Cambridge, Cambridgeshire, EC England, UK, the brother of David Attenborough. He trained at the Royal Academy of Dramatic Art, London, before making his film debut in *In Which We Serve* (1942). Initially typecast as weak and cowardly youths, he was seen to chilling effect as Pinkie in *Brighton Rock*, on stage in 1943 and on film in 1947. He won British Academy Awards as the kidnapper in *Seance on a Wet Afternoon* (1964) and the bombastic sergeant major in *Guns at Batasi* (1964). He became a producer in partnership with Bryan Forbes, and directed such large-scale epics as *A Bridge Too Far* (1977). A 20-year crusade to film the life of Mahatma Gandhi led to an Oscar for *Gandhi* (1982) and BAFTAs for best film and best director. In 1987 he made *Cry Freedom*, a biography of the black activist Steve Biko, and in 1992 a biography of Charles Chaplin. The following year he directed *Shadowlands* (BAFTA best British film), the story of C S Lewis's marriage, and later appeared in *In Love and War* (1996) and *Elizabeth* (1998). He married actress Sheila Sim (1922–) in 1944, was knighted in 1976, and became a baron in 1993. In 1999 he was honoured with a BAFTA Lifetime Achievement Award for his contribution to film.

attention A phenomenon where the processing capacity of the brain is directed towards a particular type of incoming, competing information. The classic example is the 'cocktail party phenomenon', where we are able to listen successfully to a single speaker in a room full of other speakers. *Early selection* theories suppose that we can filter out unwanted material at an early stage of processing; *late selection* theories suppose that most material is fully processed, and selection occurs only when we come to make a response. Sustained attention is difficult to maintain, and substantial decrements in performance are often obtained in vigilance tasks (eg detecting rare signals on a radar screen), if attention is to be maintained for more than 20 minutes. **Attention deficit (hyperactivity) disorder**, or **ADD**, includes a range of behaviour disorders, especially in children, with such symptoms as poor concentration, hyperactivity, and learning difficulties.

attenuation The reduction in magnitude of some quantity, caused either by absorption when passing through a medium or by increasing distance from its source. Sunlight is attenuated by clouds; sounds die away with distance from their source.

Attersee [aterzay] or **Kammersee** [kamerzay], Eng **Lake Atter** or **Lake Kammer** 47°55N 13°32E. Largest Alpine lake in Austria, in Vöcklabruck district, Oberösterreich, N Austria; area 45·9 sq km/17¾ sq mi; length 20 km/12 mi; width 2–3 km/1¼–1¾ mi; maximum depth 171 m/561 ft; lakeside summer resorts at Seewalchen, Kammer, Weyregg, Steinbach, Weissenbach.

Attica [atika] The SE promontory of C Greece, and the most easterly part of the Greek mainland. In Classical Greece, it was the territory which made up the city-state of Athens.

Attila [atila], known as **the Scourge of God** (c.406–53) King of the Huns (434–53). He ruled with his elder brother until 445, his dominion extending over Germany and Scythia from the Rhine to the frontiers of China. In 447 he devastated all the countries between the Black Sea and the Mediterranean, defeating Emperor Theodosius II (ruled 408–50). In 451 he invaded Gaul, but was routed by Aëtius, the Roman commander, and Theodoric I, King of the Visigoths, on the Catalaunian Plain. He retreated to Hungary, but then made an incursion into Italy (452), devastating several cities, Rome itself being saved only by the personal mediation of Pope Leo I. The Hunnish empire decayed after his death.

Attis or **Atys** [atis] In Greek mythology, the young male vegetation god connected with the Asiatic cult of Cybele; he died after castrating himself, and was resurrected. The story was later associated with the spring festival.

Attlee, Clem, popular name of **Clement Richard Attlee, 1st Earl Attlee** (1883–1967) British statesman and prime minister (1945–51), born in London, UK. He studied at Oxford, and was called to the bar in 1905. He became a Labour MP in 1922, Ramsay MacDonald's parliamentary secretary (1922–4), under-secretary of state for war (1924), and postmaster-general (1931). He succeeded Lansbury as Leader of the Opposition in 1935. In Churchill's war cabinet, he was dominions secretary (1942–3) and deputy prime minister (1942–5). As Leader of the Opposition he accompanied Eden to the San Francisco and Potsdam conferences (1945), and after the Labour victory returned to Potsdam as prime minister. He carried through a vigorous programme of reform, nationalizing several industries, and introducing the National Health Service. Independence was granted to India (1947) and Burma (1948). He was again Leader of the Opposition (1951–5), then resigned and accepted an earldom.

attorney **1** A person who has power to act for another in all or a specified number of matters; **power of attorney** refers to the authority so given. In England and Wales, the Enduring Powers of Attorney Act (1985) provides a method whereby such a power may survive a loss of the other person's mental capacity. This overcomes a crucial shortcoming of the earlier law, which invariably ended the power at a time when it was sometimes most needed. US law provides for an analogous durable power of attorney. A power to sign a deed on behalf of another person must itself be given formally by deed.
2 The term used in some jurisdictions as a general label for lawyers. In England and Wales, the title 'attorney (at law)' was abolished by the Supreme Court of Judicature Act 1873, and all attorneys, solicitors, and proctors became solicitors of the Supreme Court.

attorney general The chief legal officer of a number of nations or states, who represents the government in its legal actions. In England and Wales, the attorney general is a member of the House of Commons and of the government, politically responsible for the Crown Prosecution Service, and head of the English Bar. It is his or her duty to represent the public interest with complete detachment. In the USA, the federal attorney general is an appointed member of the president's cabinet. In Australia, the USA, and several other countries, each constituent state has its own attorney general. The chief law officer in Scotland is termed the *Lord Advocate*, and is likewise a member of the government.

Attwell, Mabel Lucie (1879–1964) Artist and writer, born in London, UK. She studied at Heatherley's and other art schools, and married cartoonist **Harold Earnshaw**. She was noted for her child studies, both humorous and serious, with which she illustrated her own and other stories for children. Her immensely popular 'cherubic' style was continued in annuals and children's books by her daughter, working under her mother's name.

Atwood, Margaret (Eleanor) (1939–) Novelist, short-story writer, poet, and critic, born in Ottawa, Ontario, SE Canada. She studied at the University of Toronto and Radcliffe College, becoming a lecturer in English literature. Her first published work, a collection of poems entitled *The Circle Game* (1966), won the Governor-General's Award. Since then she has published many volumes of poetry and short stories, but is best known as a novelist. Her controversial *The Edible Woman* (1969) is one of several novels focusing on women's issues. Her futuristic novel, *The Handmaid's Tale* (1985, filmed with a script by Pinter, 1990), was short-listed for the Booker Prize, as was *Cat's Eye* in 1989. Later books include *The Robber Bride* (1994), *Alias Grace* (1996), *The Blind Assassin* (2000, Booker), and *Oryx and Crake* (2003). Her *Survival* (1972) is widely considered to be the best book on Canadian literature.

aubergine [ohberzheen] A bushy perennial (*Solanum melea-grum*) with funnel-shaped, violet flowers and large, edible berries, native to New World tropics; also its fruit, variable in shape and colour, but typically egg-shaped and purple; also called **egg-plant**. It is widely cultivated as an annual vegetable in temperate regions. (Family: Solanaceae.)

aubretia [awbreesha] A mat-forming perennial (*Aubretia deltoidea*); slightly greyish leaves; pink to purple or blue cross-shaped flowers; native to SE Europe. (Family: Cruciferae.)

Aubrey, John [awbree] (1626–97) Antiquary and folklorist, born in Easton Percy, Wiltshire, S England, UK. He studied at Oxford and London, training as a lawyer, but was never called to the bar. Only his quaint, credulous *Miscellanies* (1696) of folklore and ghost-stories was printed in his lifetime, but he left a large mass of unpublished materials. He also collected biographical and anecdotal material on celebrities of his time, which appeared in *Letters by Eminent Persons* (1813), better known as *Brief Lives*.

Aubusson, Pierre d' [ohbüsõ] (1423–1503) French soldier and clergyman, and Grand Master of the Knights Hospitallers from 1476, born in Monteil-au-Vicomte, France. His outstanding achievement was his defence of Rhodes in 1480 against a besieging army of Turks under Sultan Mohammed II. In 1481 he made a treaty with the Turks under Sultan Bayezit II by agreeing to imprison the sultan's rebellious brother, Djem; and in 1489 was created cardinal for handing Djem over to Pope Innocent VIII.

Auch [ohsh] 43°39N 0°36E, pop (2000e) 25 900. Ancient town and capital of Gers department, S France, on R Gers; important city of Roman Gaul; former capital of Gascony and Armagnac; railway; archbishopric; furniture, hosiery, brandy, pâté; folk museum, Gothic cathedral.

Auchinleck, Sir Claude (John Eyre) [okhinlek] (1884–1981) British soldier, born in Aldershot, Hampshire, S England, UK. He studied at Wellington College, and joined the 62nd Punjabis in 1904. In 1941 he became commander-in-chief in India, then succeeded Wavell in N Africa. He made a successful advance into Cyrenaica, but was later thrown back by Rommel. His regrouping of the 8th Army on El Alamein paved the way for ultimate victory, but at the time he was made a scapegoat for the retreat, and was replaced by General Alexander in 1942. In 1943 he returned to India, and was created field-marshal in 1946.

Auckland [**awk**land] 36°55S 174°43E, pop (2000e) 931 000 (urban area). Seaport city in North Island, New Zealand; principal port of New Zealand; founded, 1840; capital, 1840–65; airport; railway; university (1883); textiles, footwear, clothing, chemicals, steel, electronics, carpets, plastics, food processing, vehicle assembly; Waitemata Harbour spanned by Auckland Harbour Bridge (1959); two cathedrals, New Zealand Heritage Park, Howick colonial village, art gallery, Auckland War Memorial Museum, Museum of Transport and Technology.

auction bridge *bridge* (recreation)

Auden, W(ystan) H(ugh) [**aw**den] (1907–73) Poet and essayist, born in York, North Yorkshire, N England, UK. He studied at Oxford, and in the 1930s wrote passionately on social problems from a far-left standpoint, especially in his collection of poems *Look, Stranger!* (1936). He went to Spain as a civilian in support of the Republican side, and reported on it in *Spain* (1937), followed by a verse commentary (with prose reports by Christopher Isherwood) on the Sino-Japanese war in *Journey to a War* (1939). He also collaborated with Isherwood in three plays in the 1930s: *The Dog Beneath the Skin* (1935), *The Ascent of F6* (1936), and *On the Frontier* (1938). He emigrated to New York early in 1939, and became a US citizen in 1946. There he became converted to Anglicanism, tracing his conversion in *The Sea and the Mirror* (1944) and *For the Time Being* (1944). Later works include *Homage to Clio* (1960) and *City Without Walls* (1969). He was also professor of poetry at Oxford (1956–61).

Audenarde [ohd**nah(r)d**] *Oudenaarde*

audiogram A widely used profile of hearing ability, used in the diagnosis of hearing impairment. It is a graph showing the absolute threshold for the intensity of pure tones as a function of their frequency. It is commonly represented as a hearing loss, which is the difference (in decibels) between the measured threshold and the average of thresholds obtained from a large number of young, healthy ears.

audiology The study of the physiology of hearing, and of diseases that affect the external, middle and inner ear and the associated nerve. It is specifically concerned with assessing the nature and degree of hearing loss and conservation, and with the rehabilitation of people with hearing impairment. The scientific measurement of hearing is known as **audiometry**. Audiometric testing is carried out using an **audiometer**.

audiometry *audiology*

audio-visual aids Sources other than print which are used to help people teach and learn. These may include pieces of equipment such as still, overhead, and film projectors, tape recorders, and radio or television sets, as well as pictures, graphics, charts, films, videotapes, and audiotapes. They may be used singly or in combination, as with a synchronized tape–slide sequence, or the interactive video-disk which can be linked with a microcomputer to provide moving or still pictures as well as screen text and graphics.

audit The process of checking that the accounts of an organization have been kept in accordance with good practice and with relevant laws (eg the Companies Acts, in the UK), and that the accounts fairly reflect the activities of the organization and its state of affairs at a certain date. All limited companies must have accounts audited. Auditors are appointed by shareholders and report to them. They are usually members of professional accountancy firms. In the USA, government audits are performed by the Central Accounting Office. Companies also employ internal auditors, whose duty is to ensure that records are properly kept and that accounts are produced in a form which external auditors can approve.

Audit Commission In the UK, an independent body set up by the government in 1982 to monitor local authority spending. It has also carried out reviews in the areas of education, health, and the police.

auditory perception The ability to detect and respond appropriately to sounds; and the study of this ability. It encompasses a range of specializations distinguished by the type of sound considered (eg music perception, speech perception), the theory and methods employed in the study (eg psychoacoustics, auditory psychophysics), and by the different aspects of the ability considered (eg sound localization, pitch perception).

auditory tube A tube connecting the middle ear to the nasopharynx, made partly of bone and cartilage, and lined with mucous membrane; also known as the **Eustachian tube** [yus**tay**shn], after Italian physician Bartolommeo Eustachio (1520–74). It enables air to enter or leave the middle ear, so balancing the pressure on either side of the tympanic membrane, thus allowing it to vibrate freely. In aeroplanes, failure to equalize pressure during take-off and landing leads to popping sounds (and occasional pain) in the ear; chewing helps to keep the auditory tube open and so reduce this tendency. In the young child (up to age 7) the tube is more horizontal than in the adult, leading to a greater incidence of ear infections.

Audubon, John James [**aw**duhbon] (1785–1851) Ornithologist and bird artist, born in Les Cayes, SW Haiti. He was sent to the USA in 1804 to look after his father's property near Philadelphia, and married Lucy Bakewell, the daughter of an English settler. He spent several years seeking out every species of bird in America in order to catalogue them. In 1826 he took his work to Europe, where he cultivated a rugged backwoodsman image that went down well with fashionable society. In 1827 he published the first of the 87 portfolios of his massive *Birds of America* (1827–38). Between 1840 and 1844 he produced a 'miniature' edition in 7 volumes, which became a best-seller. The National Audubon Society, dedicated to the conservation of birds in the USA, was founded in his honour in 1866.

Auger effect [**oh**zhay] In atoms, the filling of a vacancy in an inner electron energy level by an electron from an outer energy level of the same atom. The excess energy evolved causes emission of another electron. The effect, discovered by French physicist Pierre-Victor Auger in 1925, forms the basis of Auger spectroscopy.

augmentative communication *alternative and augmentative communication*

Augsburg [**owgz**berg], Ger [**owgz**boork], ancient **Augusta Vindelicorum** 48°22N 10°54E, pop (2000e) 263 000. Industrial and commercial city in Schwaben district, S Germany; at the confluence of the Lech and Wertach Rivers, 48 km/30 mi NW of Munich; founded by the Romans, 15 BC; influential commercial centre in 15th-c; seat of the famous Diets of 1530 and 1555; railway; university (1970); textiles, aircraft, machinery, heavy engineering, chemicals, cars, construction; birthplace of Brecht and Holbein; Renaissance town hall (1615–20), St Ulrich's Minster (1500), Rococo Schaezler Palais; Mozart Summer Festival.

Augsburg, League of [**owgz**berg] (1686) A defensive alliance formed by the Holy Roman Emperor, Bavaria, Spain, Sweden, and several German states, to defend the Treaties of Nijmegen (1678–9) and Ratisbon (1684), and to challenge Louis XIV's legalistic pursuit of territory, especially in disputed border areas (his *réunion* policy). However, continuing mutual provocation between France and the League resulted in the **War of the League of Augsburg** (1689–97), also known as the **War of the Grand Alliance**.

Augsburg, Peace of [**owgz**berg] A compromise settlement agreed by Protestant and Catholic representatives at the Diet of Augsburg in 1555. The Peace adopted the notable principle of *cuius regio eius religio*, establishing the right of princes to determine their subjects' faith and enforce religious uniformity, while condemning dissent.

Augsburg Confession [**owgz**berg] A statement of faith composed by Luther, Melanchthon, and others for the Diet of Augsburg (1530), the official text being written by Melanchthon in 1531. The earliest of Protestant Confessions, it became authoritative for the Lutheran Church.

augury [awgyuree] In ancient Rome, the principal means of divining the will of the gods. It involved observing natural phenomena such as lightning, the flight patterns of wild birds, or the feeding habits of sacred chickens. It was taken very seriously, since success in any enterprise was believed to be dependent on knowing the will of the gods and acting in accordance with it. The augurs themselves were not professional priests, but distinguished public men who had undergone training in traditional augural lore and been admitted to the college of augurs – a select body of 16.

Augusta (Georgia) [awguhsta] 33°28N 81°58W, pop (2000e) 54 000. Seat of Richmond Co, E Georgia, USA, on the Savannah R; founded as a river trading post; established in 1735; changed hands many times during the War of Independence; state capital, 1786–95; housed Confederate powder works in the Civil War; airfield; railway; popular resort with a notable golf club; trade and industrial centre.

Augusta (Maine) [awguhsta] 44°17N 69°50W, pop (2000e) 18 600. State capital of Maine, USA, in Kennebec Co, S Maine; on the Kennebec R 72 km/45 mi from its mouth; established as a trading post, 1628; city status, 1849; airfield; wood products, fabrics, shoes.

Augustan age The age of the Emperor Augustus in Rome (27 BC–AD 14), graced by the poets Horace, Ovid, and Virgil; hence, the classical period of any national literature. Examples include the half-century after the revolution settlement in England (1689), during which Dryden, Pope, Addison, Steele, Swift, and (later) Johnson were active; and in France, the earlier age of Corneille, Racine, and Molière under Louis XIV (1643–1715).

Augustine, St [awguhstin], also known as **Augustine of Canterbury** (?–604) Clergyman, the first Archbishop of Canterbury, born probably in Rome. He was prior of the Benedictine monastery of St Andrew in Rome, when in 596 he was sent, with 40 other monks, by Pope Gregory I to convert the Anglo-Saxons to Christianity. Landing in Thanet (597), the missionaries were kindly received by Æthelbert, King of Kent, whose wife was already a Christian. A residence was assigned to them at Canterbury, where they devoted themselves to monastic exercises and preaching. The conversion and baptism of the king contributed greatly to the success of their efforts. In 597 Augustine went to Arles, and there was consecrated Bishop of the English. He died at Canterbury, and in 612 his body was transferred to the abbey of Saints Peter and Paul, now the site of St Augustine's Missionary College (1848). Feast day 26/27 May.

Augustine, St [awguhstin], originally **Aurelius Augustinus**, also known as **Augustine of Hippo** (354–430) The greatest of the Latin Fathers of the Church, born in Tagaste, Numidia (modern Algeria). His father was a pagan, but he was brought up a Christian by his devout mother, Monica. He went to Carthage to study, and had a son (Adeonatus) by a mistress there. He became deeply involved in Manicheanism, which seemed to offer a solution to the problem of evil, a theme which was to preoccupy him throughout his life. In 383 he moved to teach at Rome, then at Milan, and became influenced by Scepticism and then by Neoplatonism. After the dramatic spiritual crises described in his autobiography, he finally became converted to Christianity and was baptized (together with his son) by St Ambrose in 386. He returned to N Africa and became Bishop of Hippo in 396, where he was a relentless antagonist of the heretical schools of Donatists, Pelagians, and Manicheans. The *Confessions* (400) is a classic of world literature and a spiritual autobiography, as well as an original work of philosophy. *The City of God* (412–27) is a work of 22 books presenting human history in terms of the conflict between the spiritual and the temporal. Feast day 28 August.

Augustinians A religious order united in 1255 following the monastic teaching and 'rule' of St Augustine; also known as the **Augustinian** or **Austin Friars**; in full, the **Order of the Hermit Friars of St Augustine** (**OSA**). It established missions and monasteries throughout the world, and was responsible for founding many famous hospitals. There are also Augustinian nuns of second or third orders ('tertiaries').

Augustus, (Gaius Julius Caesar Octavianus) (63 BC–AD 14) Founder of the Roman Empire, the son of Gaius Octavius, senator and praetor, and great nephew (through his mother, Atia) of Julius Caesar. On Caesar's assassination (44 BC), he abandoned student life in Illyricum and returned to Italy where, using Caesar's money and name (he had acquired both under his will), he raised an army, defeated Antony, and extorted a wholly unconstitutional consulship from the Senate (43 BC). When Antony returned in force from Gaul later that year with Lepidus, Octavian made a deal with his former enemies, joining the so-called Second Triumvirate with them, and taking Africa, Sardinia, and Sicily as his province. A later redivision of power gave him the entire western half of the Roman world, and Antony the eastern. While Antony was distracted there by his military schemes against Parthia, and his liaison with Cleopatra, Octavian consistently undermined him at home. Matters came to a head in 31 BC, and the Battle of Actium followed, Octavian emerging victorious as the sole ruler of the Roman world. Though taking the inoffensive title *princeps* ('first citizen'), he was in all but name an absolute monarch. His new name, Augustus ('exalted'), had historical and religious overtones, and was deliberately chosen to enhance his prestige. His long reign (27 BC–AD 14) was a time of peace and reconstruction at home, sound administration and steady conquest abroad. In gratitude the Romans awarded him the title *Pater Patriae* ('Father of his Country') in 2 BC, and on his death made him a god (*divus Augustus*).

Augustus I (1526–86) Elector of Saxony, born in Freiberg, modern Germany, who succeeded his brother Maurice as leader of the German Protestant princes. He first favoured the Calvinistic doctrine of the sacraments, and then, becoming Lutheran, persecuted the Calvinists (from 1574). He gave a great impetus to the arts, education, and commerce, reorganizing Saxony into a model state. The Dresden library and most galleries owe their origin to him.

Augustus II, known as **Augustus the Strong** (1670–1733) King of Poland (1697–1706, 1710–33) and elector of Saxony, born in Dresden, E Germany (formerly Saxony). He succeeded to the electorship as Frederick Augustus I in 1694, and became a Roman Catholic in order to secure his election to the Polish throne as Augustus II in 1697. In alliance with Peter the Great of Russia and Frederik IV of Denmark, he planned the partition of Sweden, invading Livonia in 1699. Defeated by Charles XII of Sweden, he was deposed in 1706 and replaced by Stanislaus Leszczynski. After the defeat of the Swedes by Peter the Great at Poltava (1709), he recovered the Polish throne.

Augustusburg The 18th-c Baroque residence of the former electors of Cologne at Brühl, NW Germany; a world heritage site. It was designed by Konrad Schlaun, and later Francois Cuvillié (architect of the Rococo hunting lodge of Falkenlust, which lies across the park) for Elector Clemens August (1700–61).

auk A small, black-and-white, short-winged seabird, the N hemisphere equivalent to the penguin (which it superficially resembles); inhabits cool seas; excellent swimmer; breeding colonies contain millions of birds. (Family: Alcidae, 21 species.)

Auld Lang Syne [ohld lang ziyn] A Scottish song, sung communally with arms crossed and hands linked at moments of leave-taking or at the end of the year. The words were adapted by Robert Burns in 1791 from an earlier lyric, and later fitted to the pentatonic tune (of uncertain origin) to which they are sung today. The title (literally 'old long since') refers to past times.

Aung San Suu Kyi, Daw [owng san soo kyee] (1945–) Political leader, born in Yangon, Myanmar (formerly Rangoon, Burma), the daughter of the assassinated General Aung San, who was hailed as the father of Burmese independence. She studied in India and at Oxford, and came to be committed to the cause of democracy in her country. Social unrest forced dictator General Ne Win (1911–2002) to resign in 1988, and the military took power. In response, she co-founded the National League for Democracy (NLD), but was later arrested along with many NLD members (1989). The NLD won a resounding victory in the ensuing elections, but she was to remain under house arrest. She was awarded the Nobel Peace Prize in 1991. She was released in July 1995, but refused to leave the country (for fear she would not be allowed to return), and remained there despite the death of her husband, **Michael Aris**, in Britain in 1999. She continued to campaign for human rights in her country, and a further period of house arrest followed (Sep 2000–May 2002). In 2003, she was detained at Insein Prison near Rangoon despite worldwide criticism, and later placed under house arrest.

aura The energy field which radiates from all living organisms, and which some people claim to see in the form of a luminous glow of various colours. The aura may also be revealed by such techniques as Kirlian photography. The shape, colour, and strength of the aura may be affected by a person's emotional, mental, and physical well-being, and therapists claim to be able to detect dysfunction in the internal organs through analyzing its appearance. There is current research interest in the computer analysis of Kirlian images for diagnostic purposes.

Aurangzeb or **Aurungzib** [awrangzeb] ('ornament of the throne'), kingly title **Alamgir** (1618–1707) Last of the Mughal emperors of India (1658–1707), the third son of Emperor Shah Jahan. When Shah Jahan became seriously ill in 1657, Aurangszeb defeated his brothers and confined his father, beginning his rule without formal coronation in 1658. During his long reign, the empire remained outwardly prosperous and extended its boundaries, but his puritanical and narrow outlook alienated the various communities, particularly the Hindus, whom he treated with great harshness. Opposed by his own rebellious sons and by the Mahratta empire in the S, he died a fugitive at Ahmadnagar.

Aurelian [awreelian], in full **Lucius Domitius Aurelianus** (c.215–75) Roman emperor (270–5), born of humble origins in Dacia or Pannonia. Enlisting early as a common soldier he rose rapidly to the highest military offices. On the death of Claudius II (270), he was elected emperor by the army. By restoring good discipline in the army, order in domestic affairs, and political unity to the Roman dominions, he merited the title awarded him by the Senate, *Restitutor Orbis* ('Restorer of the World'). He was assassinated by his own officers during a campaign against the Persians.

Aurelian Way *Roman roads*

Aurelius [awreelius], in full **Caesar Marcus Aurelius Antoninus Augustus**, originally **Marcus Annius Verus** (121–80) One of the most respected emperors in Roman history, born in Rome, Italy. When only 17, he was adopted by Antoninus Pius, who had succeeded Hadrian and whose daughter Faustina was selected for his wife. From 140, when he was made consul, till the death of Antoninus in 161, he discharged his public duties with great conscientiousness, at the same time devoting himself to the study of law and philosophy, especially Stoicism. Peaceful by temperament, his reign suffered from constant wars, and though in Asia, Britain, and on the Rhine the barbarians were checked, permanent peace was never secured. His death was felt to be a national calamity, and he was retrospectively idealized as the model of the perfect emperor.

Auric, Georges [ohrik] (1899–1983) Composer, born in Lodève, S France. He studied under Vincent d'Indy, and became one of *Les Six*. His compositions range widely from full orchestral pieces and ballets to songs and film scores, such as *Passport to Pimlico* (1949) and *Moulin Rouge* (1952). In 1962 he was appointed director of the Paris Opéra and Opéra-Comique, but in 1968 resigned most of his official positions in order to compose.

auricula [arikyula] A European alpine (*Primula auricula*) displaying a rosette of fleshy leaves with a mealy white bloom; flowers in clusters on a common stalk. Numerous hybrids are cultivated, some with intricately patterned flowers. (Family: Primulaceae.)

auricular therapy [awrikyuler] A form of acupuncture which developed outside China, using points on the ear which relate to remote areas of the body. The entire body is said to be represented on the surface of the ear, and more than 200 ear acupuncture points have now been described on a comprehensive map constructed by Dr Paul Nogier in 1951. The application of needles, electronic stimulation, or laser to these points is said to cure disease in the related part. Ear acupuncture is now widely used to treat addictions (eg to tobacco, drugs, and alcohol) and for pain relief during childbirth and dentistry.

Auriga [awriyga] (Lat 'charioteer') A prominent N hemisphere constellation in the Milky Way, containing many star clusters. Its brightest star is Capella (Lat 'she-goat'), sixth-brightest in the sky, actually a close pair of giant yellow stars, distance 13 parsec.

Aurignacian [awrignayshn] In European prehistory, a division of Upper Palaeolithic culture, named after the cave site at Aurignac, Haute Garonne, SW France, excavated in 1852–60 by French archaeologist Edouard Lartet (1801–71). Aurignacian stone scrapers, blades, and bone points occur throughout France/Germany c.38 000–28 000 BC, less frequently in Hungary/Austria.

Auriol, Vincent [ohreeol] (1884–1966) French statesman, the first president of the Fourth Republic (1947–54), born in Revel, S France. He studied law at Tolouse, and was elected to the Chamber of Deputies in 1914, later becoming leader of the Socialist Party. He served as a minister in 1936 and 1945, and resigned from politics in 1960.

aurochs [awroks] (plural, **aurochsen**) An extinct large wild ox (*Bos primigenius*), formerly widespread in Europe, Asia, and N Africa; the ancestor of domestic cattle; bulls large with long forward-pointing horns; females smaller with shorter horns; last individual killed in Poland in 1627; also known as **urus**, or **wild ox**; name formerly used for the European bison.

aurora (astronomy) [awrawra] A diffuse coloured light in the upper atmosphere (100 km/60 mi) over polar regions, visible at night. It is caused by charged particles from the Sun colliding with oxygen and nitrogen atoms in the atmosphere. It is seen most frequently in the **auroral zones**, which have a radius of c.22° around the geomagnetic poles. In the N it is known as the *aurora borealis* or *northern lights*; in the S as the *aurora australis*.

Aurora (mythology) [awrawra] The Roman name of the goddess of the dawn, equivalent to the Greek Eos.

Aurungzeb(e) *Aurangzeb*

Auschwitz [owshvitz] The largest Nazi concentration and extermination camp, on the outskirts of Oświęcim, SW Poland. Heinrich Himmler, the chief of the SS, ordered the establishment of the first camp in 1940. It was supplemented in 1941 by **Auschwitz II** or Birkenau, a nearby village where the SS developed a huge extermination complex with *Badeanstalten* ('bathhouses') in which prisoners were gassed to death and *Einäscherungsöfen* ('cremation ovens'). Another camp, **Auschwitz III**, became in 1942 a labour camp supplying workers for the nearby chemical and synthetic rubber works of IG Farben. Among these was the Italian-Jewish chemist, Primo Levi, who wrote an account of life there in his book, *Se questo e un uomo* (1947, If This is a Man). Auschwitz became the nexus of a complex of 45 subcamps, in some of which camp doctors such as Josef Mengele conducted medical experiments on the prisoners. Estimates of the number of men, women, and children who died at Auschwitz vary greatly, but it is believed that about 1·6 million people were killed there, 1·3 million of whom were Jewish, the remainder consisting mainly of Poles, Soviet prisoners-of-war, and gypsies. Designated a world heritage site in 1979, its gas chambers, watch towers, and prison huts are preserved at the camp, part of which is now a museum.

auscultation [awskuhltayshn] The process of listening to and analyzing the audible sounds within the body, usually with the aid of a stethoscope. These include the sounds (vibrations) in blood vessels, heart, lungs, airways, and intestines, made by the flow of blood, air, or gas within the various organs.

Ausgleich [owsgliykh] (Ger 'compromise') The arrangement in 1867 which created the Dual Monarchy of Austria–Hungary. Following the defeat of Austria in Italy and Germany (1866), it was drawn up by Francis Deák for Hungary and ratified by the Austrian emperor Francis Joseph, granting Hungary its own parliament and constitution, but retaining Francis Joseph as King of Hungary. A dual monarchy was thus created, in which the Magyars were permitted to dominate their subject peoples to the detriment of their own ethnic minorities, while Austria retained the remaining 17 (mainly non-German-speaking) provinces of the empire. The Austro-Hungarian empire was finally dissolved by the Treaty of St Germain-en-Laye (1919) as part of the Versailles peace settlement.

Ausonius, Decimus Magnus [awsohnius] (c.309–92) Latin poet, born in Burdigala (Bordeaux, France). He taught rhetoric there for 30 years, and was then appointed by Emperor Valentinian I to be tutor to his son Gratian. He later held the offices of quaestor, prefect of Latium and consul of Gaul. His works include epigrams, poems on his deceased relatives and on his colleagues, epistles in verse and prose, and idylls.

Austen, Jane (1775–1817) Novelist, born in Steventon, near Basingstoke, Hampshire, S England, UK, where her father was rector. She spent the first 25 years of her life there, and later lived in Bath, Southampton, Chawton, and Winchester. The fifth of a family of seven, she began writing for family amusement as a child. *Love and Friendship* (published 1922) dates from this period. Her early published work satirized the sensational fiction of her time, and applied common sense to apparently melodramatic situations – a technique she later developed in evaluating ordinary human behaviour. Of her six great novels, four were published anonymously during her lifetime and two under her signature posthumously. *Sense and Sensibility*, published in 1811, was begun in 1797; *Pride and Prejudice* appeared in 1813; *Mansfield Park*, begun in 1811, appeared in 1814; *Emma* in 1816. Her posthumous novels were both published in 1818; *Persuasion* had been written in 1816, and *Northanger Abbey*, begun in 1797, had been sold in 1803 to a publisher, who neglected it, and reclaimed it in 1816.

Auster, Paul [awster] (1947–) Novelist, born in Newark, New Jersey, USA. He studied at Columbia University, then lived in France for four years. Since 1974 he has published poems, essays, novels and translations. His use of detective-story techniques to explore modern urban identity is evident in *The New York Trilogy* (1985–6). Later books include *The Music of Chance* (1990), *Leviathan* (1992), and *Timbuktu* (1999).

Austerlitz, Battle of [owsterlits] (1805) Napoleon's most decisive victory, also known as **the Battle of the Three Emperors** (Alexander I of Russia, Francis I of Austria, and Napoleon Bonaparte), fought in Moravia against a larger combined Austro-Russian army under Kutuzov. It forced Austria to make the Treaty of Pressburg (1805), in which it recognized Napoleon as king of Italy, and ceded considerable territories in N Italy, the Alpine regions, and on the Adriatic coast. Austria then withdrew from the Third Coalition.

Austin [awstin] 30°17N 97°45W, pop (2000e) 656 600. Capital of state in Travis Co, SC Texas, USA, on the Colorado R; settled, 1835; capital of the Republic of Texas, 1838; Texas government moved to Houston (1842) for fear of marauding Mexicans and Indians; returned in 1845 when Texas joined the Union; airfield; railway; two universities (1876, 1881); commercial centre for an extensive agricultural region; electronic and scientific research; tourism; Aqua Festival (Aug); famous for its moonlight tower lights, since 1895; underwent remarkable growth during the economic boom of the 1980s.

Austin (of Longbridge), Herbert Austin, Baron (1866–1941) Car manufacturer, born in Little Missenden, Buckinghamshire, SC England, UK. He studied at Brampton College, went to Australia in 1884, and worked in engineering shops there. He returned to England in 1893, and in 1895, with the Wolseley Company, produced his first three-wheeled car. In 1905 he opened his own works near Birmingham, its enormous output including the popular 'Baby' Austin 7 (1921). He was also Conservative MP for King's Norton (1918–24).

Austin, John (1790–1859) Jurist, born in Creeting Mill, Suffolk, E England, UK. In 1818 he was called to the bar at the Inner Temple, London, and was appointed professor of jurisprudence in the University of London (1826–32). His *Province of Jurisprudence Determined* (1832), defining the sphere of ethics and law, came to revolutionize English views on the subject.

Austin, J(ohn) L(angshaw) (1911–60) Philosopher, born in Lancaster, Lancashire, NW England, UK. He studied at Oxford, where he was a leading figure in the Oxford Philosophy movement, and became professor there in 1952. His distinctive contribution was the meticulous examination of ordinary linguistic usage to resolve philosophical perplexities, pioneering the analysis of speech acts. His best-known works are *Philosophical Papers* (1961), *Sense and Sensibilia* (1962), and *How to Do Things with Words* (1962).

Austin, Stephen Fuller (1793–1836) Founder of the state of Texas, born in Austinville, Virginia, USA. He served in the Missouri legislature, then moved to Texas, where his father had obtained a grant of land from the Mexican government. In 1822 he founded a colony on the Brazos R, and became leader of the movement for Texan independence.

Austin Friars *Augustinians*

Australasia A term used loosely to include Australia and the islands of Tasmania, New Zealand, New Guinea (including New Britain), New Caledonia, and Vanuatu; often described as equivalent to all of Oceania below the Equator and N of 47°S; the name is not commonly used in these areas.

Australia *pp.112–13*

Australia, Order of An order established by Queen Elizabeth II in 1975, to accord recognition to Australian citizens (and others). The order comprises the sovereign, the Governor-General of Australia, and the Prince of Wales. Appointments to the order are recommended by a Council, which researches nominations. The ribbon is of royal blue silk, with a central band of golden mimosa blossoms.

Australia Day A public holiday in Australia commemorating the founding of the colony of New South Wales on 26 January 1788; held annually on 26 January if a Monday, otherwise on the Monday following that date.

Australian Alps Chain of mountains in SE Australia forming the S part of the Great Dividing Range; extends c.300 km/185 mi SW from Australian Capital Territory to the Goulburn R, Victoria; includes the Snowy Mts, Bowen Mts, and Barry Mts; rises to 2228 m/7310 ft at Mt Kosciusko; much used for winter sports.

Australian Antarctic Territory area 6 043 852 sq km/2 332 927 sq mi of land, 84 798 sq km/32 732 sq mi of ice shelf. Situated S of 60°S and lying between 142° and 136°E (excluding Terre Adélie); claimed by Australia, 1936; scientific station at Mawson, 1954; Davis Base, 1957; Australia assumed custody of the US Wilkes Station on the Budd Coast in 1959, replacing it by the Casey Station in 1961.

Australian art The art of Europeans in Australia began in the late 18th-c. Single-storied colonial houses with verandahs reflected English Georgian and Regency styles. In the 1830s, Gothic was employed for Anglican churches (eg St Andrew's Cathedral, Sydney, 1837) and Greek for public buildings. From the earliest years, graphic artists drew native flora and fauna for scientific purposes, while landscape painters such as John Glover (1767–1849) and Conrad Martens (1801–78) tried to reconcile the Picturesque approach favoured in Europe with the harsh realities of local scenery. Later painters such as Tom Roberts and Frederick McCubbin (1855–1917), while influenced by current European styles (eg Impressionism), developed an independent and distinctively Australian vision of nature. Abstract and Surrealist art was slow to reach Australia; an adherence to traditional figurative forms has helped artists like Roberts, William Dobell (1899–1970), Sydney Nolan, and Russell Drysdale to

Australia

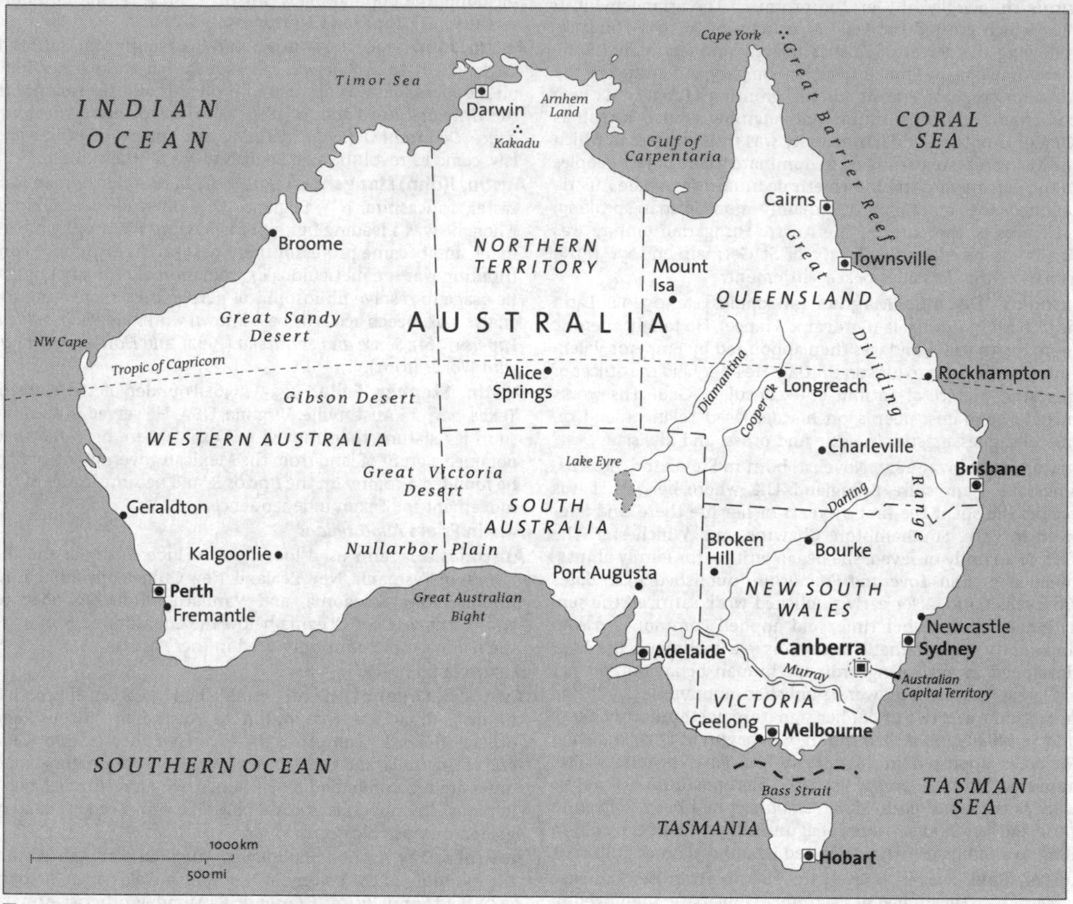

☐ International Airport ∴ World heritage site

official name **Commonwealth of Australia**

Local name Australia

Timezone GMT +8 (Western Australia); GMT +10 (New South Wales, Queensland, Tasmania, Victoria, Australian Capital Territory); GMT +9·5 (South Australia, Northern Territory)

Area 7 692 300 km^2/2 969 228 sq mi

Population total (2002e) 19 702 000

Status Independent state within the Commonwealth

Date of independence 1901

Capital Canberra

Language English (official)

Ethnic groups European descent (95%), Asian and Pacific (2%), Aboriginal (1%)

Religions Christian (74%, including Roman Catholic 27%, Anglican 24%)

Physical features Variously viewed as the smallest continent or largest island; consists largely of plains and plateaux, most of which average 600 m/ 2000 ft above sea level; four main regions: Western Craton (or Western Shield), the Great Artesian Basin, the Great Dividing Range (or Eastern Uplands), and the Flinders-Mt Lofty ranges; W Australian Plateau occupies nearly half of the country; MacDonnell Ranges lie in the centre, highest point Mt Liebig, 1525 m/5000 ft; most of the plateau is dry, barren desert; Nullarbor Plain in the S is crossed by the Trans-Australian Railway; Great Dividing Range parallel to the Great Barrier Reef, rising to 2228 m/7310 ft at Mt Kosciusko, Australia's highest point; Great Barrier Reef off NE coast stretches for over 1900 km/ 1200 mi; island of Tasmania rises to 1617 m/5305 ft at Mt Ossa; separated from the mainland by the Bass Strait; longest river is the Murray; chief tributaries, the Darling, Murrumbidgee, Lachlan; Lake Eyre occupies 8800 km^2/3400 sq mi; c.18% of area forested; c.6% arable.

create a highly expressive art distinct from the fashions of the Western avant garde.

Australian Ballet Company The national ballet company of Australia. Founded in Melbourne in 1962, it grew out of the Borovansky Ballet Company and School founded by Edouard Borovansky in 1942. The British dance teacher, Peggy van Praagh, jointly became its artistic director with Robert Helpmann, and together they created ballets such as *Yugen* (1965) and *Sun Music* (1968), based on Australian themes. Ross Stretton was its artistic director (1997–2001).

Australian Capital Territory pop (2000e) 309 300; area 2400 sq km/925 sq mi. Territory in SE Australia, created

Climate More than a third of Australia receives under 260 mm/10 in mean annual rainfall; less than a third receives over 500 mm/20 in; prolonged drought and frequent heatwaves in many areas; average daily temperature 26–34°C (Nov) and 19–31°C (Jul) in N; rainfall varies from 286 mm/15·2 in (Jan) to zero (Jul); fertile land with a temperate climate and reliable rainfall only in the lowlands and valleys near the E and SE coast, and a small part of the SW corner; Tasmania and Mt Kosciusko have snowfields in winter.

Currency 1 Australian Dollar ($A) = 100 cents

Economy Free-enterprise economy; world's largest wool producer, and a top exporter of veal and beef; most important crop is wheat; major mineral producer; petroleum reserves. Coal, bauxite, nickel, lead, zinc, copper, tin, uranium, iron ore, and other minerals in early 1960s; manufacturing industry expanded rapidly since 1945, especially engineering, shipbuilding, car manufacture, metals, textiles, clothing, chemicals, food processing, wine; self-sufficient in lumber; marine fishing (especially tuna) important, as are tourism and winter sports.

GDP (2002e) $525·5 bn, per capita $26 900

Human Development Index (2002) 0·939

History Aboriginal people thought to have arrived in Australia from SE Asia c.40 000 years ago; first European visitors were the Dutch, who explored the Gulf of Carpentaria in 1606 and settled in 1616; became known as New Holland in 1644; Captain James Cook arrived in Botany Bay in 1770, and claimed the E coast for Britain; New South Wales established as a penal colony in 1788; gold discovered in New South Wales and Victoria in 1851, and in Western Australia in 1892; transportation of convicts to E Australia ended in 1840, but continued until 1853 in Tasmania and 1868 in Western Australia; during this period the colonies drafted their own constitutions and set up governments: New South Wales (1855), Tasmania and Victoria (1856), South Australia (1857), Queensland (1860), and Western Australia (1890); Commonwealth of Australia established in 1901, with Canberra subsequently chosen as capital, (1901); policy of preventing immigration by non-whites remained in force from the end of the 19th-c until 1974; the issue of Aboriginal civil rights has been a major issue since the 1960s. Northern Territory self-governing since 1978; divided into six states and two territories: each state has its own legislature, government, and constitution; legislature comprises a bicameral Federal Parliament with a Prime Minister and Cabinet; British monarch is Head of State, represented by a Governor-General; republican movement growing since the late 1980s; proposal on the issue rejected by referendum, late 1999.

Head of State

(British monarch represented by Governor-General)
1982–9 Sir Ninian Stephen
1989–96 Bill Hayden
1996–2001 Sir William Deane
2001–3 Peter Hollingworth
2003 Sir Guy Green *Acting*
2003– Michael Jeffery

Head of Government

1901–3 Edmund Barton *Prot*
1903–4 Alfred Deakin *Prot*
1904 John Christian Watson *Lab*
1904–5 George Houstoun Reid *Free/Prot**
1905–8 Alfred Deakin *Prot*
1908–9 Andrew Fisher *Lab*
1909–10 Alfred Deakin *Fusion*
1910–13 Andrew Fisher *Lab*
1913–14 Joseph Cook *Lib*
1914–15 Andrew Fisher *Lab*
1915–16 William Morris Hughes *Lab*
1916–17 William Morris Hughes *Nat Lab*
1917–23 William Morris Hughes *Nat*
1923–9 Stanley Melbourne Bruce, Viscount Bruce of Melbourne *Nat/Co**
1929–32 James Henry Scullin *Lab*
1932–8 Joseph Aloysius Lyons *UAP*
1938–9 Joseph Aloysius Lyons *UAP/Co**
1939 Earle Christmas Grafton Page *UAP/Co**
1939–40 Robert Gordon Menzies *UAP*
1940–1 Robert Gordon Menzies *UAP/Co**
1941 Arthur William Fadden *UAP/Co**
1941–5 John Joseph Curtin *Lab*
1945 Francis Michael Forde *Lab*
1945–9 Joseph Benedict Chifley *Lab*
1949–66 Robert Gordon Menzies *Lib/Co**
1966–7 Harold Edward Holt *Lib/Co**
1967–8 John McEwen *Lib/Co**
1968–71 John Grey Gorton *Lib/Co**
1971–2 William McMahon *Lib/Co**
1972–5 Gough Whitlam *Lab*
1975–83 John Malcolm Fraser *Lib/Co**
1983–91 Robert Hawke *Lab*
1991–6 Paul Keating *Lab*
1996– John Howard *Lib*

Co *Country* Nat Lab *National Labor*
Free Free Trade *Prot* Protectionist
Lab Labor *UAP* United Australia Party
Lib Liberal * Coalition
Nat Nationalist

Australian States

Name / Area (km² / sq mi) / State capital
Australian Capital Territory / 2400 / 930 / Canberra
New South Wales / 801 400 / 309 400 / Sydney
Northern Territory / 1 346 200 / 519 800 / Darwin
Queensland / 1 727 200 / 666 900 / Brisbane
South Australia / 984 000 / 379 900 / Adelaide
Tasmania / 67 800 / 26 200 / Hobart
Victoria / 227 600 / 87 900 / Melbourne
Western Australia / 2 525 500 / 975 000 / Perth

External territories

Name / Area (km² / sq mi) / Population / Date under Australian administration
The Ashmore and Cartier Islands / 3·0 / 2·0 / Uninhabited / 1931
Australian Antarctic Terr / 6 043 852·0 / 2 332 927·0 / Uninhabited / 1936
Christmas Island / 155·0 / 60·0 (2000e) / 2700 / 1958
Cocos (Keeling) Islands / 14·2 / 5·5 / (2000e) 780 / 1955
Coral Sea Island / 2·0* / 0·8* Uninhabited / 1969
Heard Island and McDonald Islands / 412·0 / 159·0 / Uninhabited / 1947
Norfolk Island / 35·0 / 13·0 / (2000e) 2200 / 1913

* Land figure only. Islands cover 1 000 000 km²/286 000 sq mi of ocean.

in 1911 to provide a location for the national capital, Canberra; bordered on all sides by New South Wales; Jervis Bay on the E coast ceded (1915) for its use as a port; mountainous in the S; urbanized floodplains of the Murrumbidgee and Molonglo Rivers in the N; c.50% of the workforce employed by the government; electronics, computing; state holidays Canberra Day (Mar), Bank Holiday (Aug), Labour Day (Oct).

Australian Council of Trade Unions (ACTU) Australia's national trade union organization, formed in 1927. Its prestige has come from representing the unions' case before the Australian Conciliation and Arbitration Commission, and in helping to settle industrial disputes. In 1992, there were 227 unions in the country, with a claimed total membership of 3·1 million. Trade union membership in Australia declined from 50% in 1982 to 40% in 1992.

Australian East Coast Temperate and Sub-Tropical Rainforest Parks A series of national parks, and nature and flora reserves, which extends along the length of the New South Wales coast; a world heritage area. The region provides a representative sample of the whole animal and plant life of E Australia, as well as striking examples of landscape diversity, including the Mt Warning volcano and segments of the Great Escarpment.

Australian gold rush Traces of gold were first found in Australia in 1823, but the first significant find was in 1851, when Edward Hargraves publicized his find and attracted 2000 to the site at Ophir in New South Wales. In the same year, large gold finds were made in Victoria, which accounted for 35% of world gold production 1851–60. Gold was also found in Queensland (1867) and Western Australia (1893). The discovery transformed Australia. It drew thousands of immigrants (342 000 arrived from overseas 1852–61), created a mass movement for democracy, and gave a tremendous boost to the economy. Cities, in particular Melbourne (which grew from 29 000 to 473 000, 1851–91), symbolized the new-found prosperity. Although some miners struck it rich, most did not, and this led to pressure to open pastoral land for farming. Gold also attracted thousands of Chinese miners, who were greatly resented by the Europeans; this led to anti-Chinese laws and the beginning of the 'White Australia' Policy.

Australian Imperial Force (AIF) The volunteer military forces raised in Australia in both world wars. In World War 1, 330 770 men served overseas in the first AIF, of whom 54 000 were killed and 155 000 were wounded. In World War 2, 690 000 men and 35 000 women served in the second AIF.

Australian Labor Party (ALP) Australia's oldest political party, founded in 1891 in New South Wales following the defeat of the trade unions in the 1890 strike. The party spread to all States by the mid-1900s and formed the world's first labour government in Queensland in 1899 for one week. It has always been a social democratic party, committed to evolutionary not revolutionary change. Despite a commitment to 'socialism', it has generally been moderate and pragmatic when in government. Two major splits in the ALP occurred: in 1916–17 over conscription, and in 1955 over attitudes to communism. ALP has had varied success in winning federal government (1908–9, 1910–13, 1914–15, 1929–32, 1941–9, 1972–4, 1983–96), but managed to stay in office in the recession of the early 1990s. Its most important national figures have been Prime Ministers W M ('Billy') Hughes (1915–16), James Scullin (1929–32), John Curtin (1941–5), Ben Chifley (1945–9), Gough Whitlam (1972–4), R J L ('Bob') Hawke (1983–91), and Paul Keating (1991–6). The party has always had fewer members than its main rival, the Liberal party.

Australian languages The aboriginal languages of Australia. About 50 survive, spoken by fewer than 50 000 people, and with vastly differing degrees of fluency. Most speakers are bilingual in their indigenous language and English, though there are now some bilingual school programmes, which will ensure the immediate survival of some languages. The majority of the languages, however, are near extinction, and only five have more than 1000 speakers. Some of the languages are used as lingua francas, one of the most vigorous being Warlpiri, spoken in the Northern Territory.

Australian literature After a number of convict and gold-rush novels in the mid-19th-c (eg Marcus Clarke's *For the Term of his Natural Life*, 1870–2), Australian literature began to assume its own identity at the beginning of the 20th-c with distinctive bush ballads and short stories, many published in the Sydney *Bulletin*. The Australian past was explored in historical novels and family sagas between the wars, which also saw the home-spun Jindyworobak movement, though neither of these managed to incorporate the aboriginal experience. Since 1945, Australian literature has been enriched and diversified by many influences, and with novelists such as Nobel prize-winner Patrick White (eg *Voss*, 1957), Booker prize-winner Thomas Keneally (eg *Schindler's Ark*, 1982), and Peter Carey (eg *Illywhacker*, 1985), poets such as Les Murray (1938–), Chris Wallace-Crabbe (1934–), and A D Hope, and a vigorous and inventive drama, it now has a recognized international standing.

Australian republicanism The desire to sever ties with Britain and install an Australian, non-hereditary head of state. An intermittent theme in Australian history since the 19th-c, republicanism has gained prominence since the late 1980s, and the Australian Republican Movement, supported by the Labor government of Paul Keating, aimed for a republic by 2001, the centenary of Australian federation. Opinion polls have suggested that republicans outnumber monarchists in Australia. Debate about a republic focuses not only on the monarchy, however, but addresses issues of nationalism, increased executive power, reconciliation with Aboriginal people, a new flag, Australia's place in Asia, the country's identity as a multicultural nation, and its opportunity for radical political reform, such as the abolition of the states. Many argue that a republic is inevitable, but whatever its form, such a change will necessitate constitutional amendments which depend on successful referenda. In 1998 the Constitutional Convention voted in favour of a republican system and a president; the proposals were placed before the electorate in late 1999, and defeated (55% no, 45% yes).

Australian Rules football *football, Australian Rules*

Australian Workers' Union (AWU) The largest Australian trade union from the early 1900s to 1970, and still one of the largest. It was formed in 1894 by the amalgamation of the shearers' union (formed 1886) and the rural labourers' union (formed 1890), and has traditionally recruited lesser-paid workers. It has always been a conservative force in trade union and labour politics.

Australia Telescope An array of radio telescopes at three locations in New South Wales, the largest being the 64 m dish at Parkes, which use aperture synthesis to achieve very high resolving power. It is the most important radio telescope in the S hemisphere.

Austral Islands [**o**stral] *Tubuai Islands*

Australopithecus [ostral**oh**pithekus] Early hominids known from fossils found in Ethiopia, Kenya, Tanzania, and South Africa; dated c.5·5–1·0 mya (million years ago); although most finds are c.4·0–1·5 mya. They were truncally erect and bipedal, narrow-chested, and pot-bellied, with long powerful arms, and short legs. Face and jaws were strongly constructed and projecting; braincases were small. Overall they probably resembled upright chimpanzees, but living in open savannah environments, not forest or woodland, as do present apes. Features such as erect bipedalism, reduced canines, parabolic tooth rows, and rotary chewing reveal their close evolutionary links with humans. Several australopithecine species are known, all showing marked size variation (30–70+ kg/66–155+ lb), with males much larger than females. *Australopithecus afarensis* lived in E Africa 4+–2·8 mya; *Australopithecus africanus* lived in S Africa 3·0–2·5 mya; *Australopithecus robustus* lived in S Africa c.2·0–?1·0 mya; *Australopithecus boisei* lived in E Africa 2+–1·4 mya. Another species, *Australopithecus aethiopicus*, is identified on a 2·6 my-old skull from L Turkana, Kenya, and may represent an early stage in the evolution of *A. boisei* from an *A. afarensis*-like ancestor. Compared with other primates, all australopithecines have relatively large cheek teeth (premolars and molars), but in *A. robustus* and *A. boisei* they are enormous, suggesting much crushing and grinding of hard food objects. Bigger-brained hominids (*Homo*), probably evolved from *A. afarensis* or *A. africanus*; later species (*A. robustus* and *A. boisei*) persist well after earliest *Homo*, showing that they are not direct ancestors. A new species, *Australopithecus garhi*, discovered in Ethiopia, was announced in 1999 (lived c.2·5 mya).

Austria *p.115*

Austria–Hungary, Dual Monarchy of, also known as the **Austro–Hungarian Empire** A constitutional arrangement created by the Ausgleich ('compromise') of 1867. In Austria–Hungary

Austria

Ger **Österreich**, official name **Republic of Austria**, Ger **Republik Österreich**

Local name Österreich

Timezone GMT +1

Area 83 854 km^2/32 368 sq mi

Population total (2002e) 8 077 000

Status Republic

Date of independence 1955

Capital Vienna (Wien)

Languages German (official), Croatian, Slovene

Ethnic groups Austrian (99%), Croatian, Slovakian, Turkish, German

Religions Roman Catholic (85%), Protestant (12%), Muslim (1%), Jewish (1%)

Physical features One of the most mountainous countries in Europe; lies at E end of the Alps; highest point, Grossglockner, 3797 m/12 457 ft; largest lake, Neusiedler See; divided into three regions: Alpine; the highland Bohemian Massif; and the hilly lowland region, including the Vienna basin; R Danube drains whole country; most densely forested country in central Europe (40% of land is forested).

Climate Three climatic regions: the Alps (often sunny in winter, but cloudy in summer); the Danube valley and Vienna basin (driest region); and the SE, a region of often severe winters but warmer summers; average annual temperature: 2°C (Jan), 20°C (Jul) in Vienna; most rain in summer months; average annual rainfall 868 mm/34 in; winters cold, especially with winds from the E or NE; humid, continental climate in NE.

Currency 1 euro = 100 cents (previous to 2002, 1 Schilling (S, Sch) = 100 Groschen)

Economy Mixed free market; principal agricultural areas to the N of the Alps, and along both sides of the Danube; principal crops: cereals; dairy cattle and pigs; wine industry; wide range of metal and mineral resources; tourism (summer and winter); well-developed transportation networks; river ports at Linz and Vienna; airports at Vienna, Graz, Linz, Klagenfurt, Salzburg, Innsbruck; much power produced hydroelectrically.

GDP (2002e) $227·7 bn, per capita $27 900

Human Development Index (2002) 0·926

History Early Iron-Age settlement at Hallstatt; later Illyrian settlers driven out by the Celts; part of Roman Empire until 5th-c, then occupied by Germanic tribes, most signifcantly Bavarians; Charlemagne drove out the Slavic Avars who also settled in the region; area became a duchy and passed to the Habsburg family in 1282, who made it the foundation of their Empire; Hungarian nationalism and Habsburg defeats in 19th-c led to the dual monarchy of Austria-Hungary from 1867; nationalist protest resulted in assassination of Archduke Ferdinand in 1914 and World War 1, which ended the Austrian Empire; republic established, 1918; annexed by the German Reich in 1938 (the Anschluss) and named Ostmark; occupied by British, American, French, and Russian troops from 1945; obtained independence, 1955; neutrality declared, since when Austria has been a haven for many refugees; governed by a Federal Assembly; Federal President appoints a Federal Chancellor.

Head of State (Federal President)

1945–50 Karl Renner
1950–7 Theodor Körner
1957–65 Adolf Schärf
1965–74 Franz Jonas
1974–86 Rudolf Kirchsläger
1986–92 Kurt Waldheim
1992– Thomas Klestil

Head of Government (Federal Chancellor)

1945 Karl Renner
1945–53 Leopold Figl
1953–61 Julius Raab
1961–4 Alfons Gorbach
1964–70 Josef Klaus
1970–83 Bruno Kreisky
1983–6 Fred Sinowatz
1986–97 Franz Vranitzky
1997–2000 Viktor Klima
2000– Wolfgang Schüssel

the Habsburg emperors Francis Joseph (until 1916), and Charles (1916–18), ruled over the twin kingdoms of Austria (incorporating German-, Czech-, Polish-, Slovenian-, and Ruthenian-speaking regions of their empire) and Hungary (incorporating Magyar, Romanian, Slovak, and South Slav regions). The separate kingdoms possessed considerable autonomy over internal policy, with overall foreign and financial policy remaining in the hands of the Imperial government in Vienna. The Dual Monarchy provided a temporary solution to the internal problems of the Habsburg Empire, but was ultimately destroyed by defeat in World War 1.

Austrian School (economics) A school of economics which has its roots in the work of late 19th-c Austrian economists, Carl Menger (1840–1921), Eugen von Böhm Bawerk (1851–1914), Friedrich von Wieser (1851–1926), and later, Ludwig Von Mises (1881–1973) and Friedrich A Hayek, who developed the major tenets of marginalism, diminishing marginal utility, opportunity cost, and time preferences of saving, consumption, and production. In recent years, the school's followers have opposed governmental planning, and stressed the importance of markets and relative prices in coordinating individuals' actions.

Austrian Succession, War of the (1740–8) The first phase in the struggle between Prussia and Austria for mastery of the German states, developing after 1744 into a colonial conflict between Britain and the Franco-Spanish bloc. Hostilities were prompted by Frederick II of Prussia's seizure of the Habsburg province of Silesia on the accession of the Archduchess Maria Theresa (1740). Subsequently the war demonstrated the volatility of European alliances, and the ineffectiveness of much military campaigning. Prussia repeatedly deserted its allies; and relations between the 'Pragmatic Army' states were strained by conflicting interests. The fighting spread from C Europe to the Austrian Netherlands, the Mediterranean, and Italy, embroiling the New World and India before peace was concluded at the Treaty of Aix-la-Chapelle (1748).

Austro-Asiatic languages A group of over 100 languages spoken in SE Asia. Few of them had written forms until recent times, and their connections with other languages in the region are uncertain. The major group is the Mon–Khmer, which has three main languages: Mon (Tailang), Khmer, and Vietnamese.

Austronesian languages The most numerous and (after Indo-European) the most widely dispersed of the world's great language families; also called **Malayo-Polynesian languages**. Extending from Taiwan to Madagascar and from Malaysia, the Philippines, and Indonesia E through the Pacific Islands, it contains over 700 separate languages.

Austro–Prussian War (1866) A war between Austria and Prussia occasioned by a dispute over the duchies of Schleswig and Holstein. It was declared on 14 June, decided by the Prussian victory at Königgrätz (sometimes known as Sadowa) on 3 July, and ended by the Treaty of Prague on 23 August. By the end of the seven-week conflict, Prussia had become the dominant power in Germany. By interfering with Austrian control of Holstein, Bismarck provoked the war to achieve that dominance, bringing Austrian-Prussian rivalry for leadership to a head. Prussian military superiority was personified by their general, Count Helmuth von Moltke, whose well-organized forces crushed the Austrians at Königgrätz (now Hradec Králové, Czech Republic). Austria's defeat hastened German unification; allowed Italy, Prussia's ally, to acquire Venetia; and precipitated the creation of Austria–Hungary. The German Confederation was dissolved; Prussia annexed Hanover and Hesse-Kassel; Austria ceded Holstein to Prussia. Austria was excluded from the North German Confederation.

autarky [awtah(r)kee] A self-sufficient economy, with no external trade. The term is often used in economics to describe policies of decreasing reliance on external trade by tariffs or quotas.

***auteur* theory** [ohter] A concept, arising in France in the late 1940s and popularized in the 1960s, of the film director as the major creative artist, imposing a personal viewpoint on every aspect of the production, rather than co-ordinating the work of many contributors. The director's personality is thus consistently expressed throughout a series of films. The theory of director-as-author was principally advanced by André Bazin in his periodical *Cahiers du cinéma*. It became the foundation store of the *nouvelle vague* film school, notably through François Truffaut and Jean-Luc Godard.

authoritarianism A form of government, or a theory advocating such government, which is the opposite of democracy, in that the consent of society to rulers and their decisions is not necessary. Voting and discussion are not usually employed, except to give the appearance of democratic legitimacy to the government, and such arrangements remain firmly under the control of the rulers. Authoritarian rulers draw their authority from what are claimed to be special qualities of a religious, nationalistic, or ideological nature, which are used to justify their dispensing with constitutional restrictions. Their rule, however, relies heavily upon coercion.

authority The right to issue commands without that right being questioned. In effect, authority is a form of legitimate power, in that those subject to it voluntarily consent to its exercise. Sources of authority are rational-legal (eg elections, qualifications), tradition (eg the monarchy), and charisma (eg authoritarian rulers such as Hitler). Included in most cases of authority is the right to use coercion against those who do not consent.

Authorized Version of the Bible The English translation of the Bible commissioned by James I and accomplished by a panel of leading scholars of the day; widely called the **King James Bible**. They used Greek and Hebrew texts, but were indebted also to earlier English translations. Noted for its literary excellence, the 'Authorized Version' gained wide popular appeal after its first publication in 1611, but was never formally 'authorized' by king or Parliament.

autism A condition characterized by abnormal functioning in social interaction together with repetitive behaviour and poor communication, almost always commencing before three years of age. One in 2000 children suffer from this disorder, which is four times more common in males. It was first described by Leo Kanner (1894–1981), an Austrian-born US child psychiatrist, in 1943. Intelligence is very variable in autistic children, and outcome is crucially dependent on the facilities for teaching. In the best facilities, up to 80% of children are eventually able to look after themselves. The cause is unknown.

autobiography A narrative of a life written by the subject. There are examples from antiquity in the *Meditations* of Marcus Aurelius (2nd-c) and the *Confessions* of St Augustine (4th-c), and some remarkable early modern instances, such as the arresting autobiography by Benvenuto Cellini (c.1560) and the self-searching *Essays* of Montaigne (from 1580). The 17th-c puritan 'spiritual autobiography' influenced the early novel. However, autobiography proper implies a self-creation as well as self-criticism on the part of the author, and as such is a post-Romantic art (the term was first used by Southey in 1809), though heralded by Rousseau's *Confessions* (1781–8). Among celebrated autobiographers are Goethe, de Quincey, Stendhal, Benjamin Franklin, George Sand, Hector Berlioz, J S Mill, Ulysses S Grant, Anthony Trollope, T E Lawrence, Robert Graves, H G Wells, and Leonard Woolf. Among novelists who have successfully borrowed the autobiographical form of confession is Charlotte Brontë in *Jane Eyre: An Autobiography* (1847).

autochthony [awtokthonee] The notion that, upon independence, members of the Commonwealth were not only no longer subordinate to the British, but that the status of their independent constitution was rooted in their own soil, not drawn from the UK. The term was popularized by British political scientist, Sir Kenneth Clinton Wheare (1907–79).

auto-da-fé [awtohdafay] (Port 'act of faith') The public burning at the stake of heretics and sinners condemned by the Spanish Inquisition. It was last carried out in Spain in 1781, and in Mexico in 1815.

auto-destructive art An artefact, typically a painting or piece of sculpture, deliberately constructed in a way guaranteed to self-destruct almost immediately. Examples include pictures executed with acid, and disintegrating kinetic machines.

autofocus The automatic focusing of a camera lens by electronic means on a chosen part of the subject to ensure a sharp image. Various methods are used; for example, a sound-ranging system measures distance from the return time of the echo of an emitted ultrasonic pulse. Single lens reflex cameras use a phase (separation) detection method. The apex of the cone of light from the camera lens is judged to be in focus, convergent, or divergent by its separation into two beams, using small lenses in front of a linear charge-coupled device array, and the spread (phase) is then measured from the response of the array. The data controls a small motor which drives the lens to correct focus.

autogiro A non-fixed-wing aircraft whose lift is provided (unlike a helicopter) by non-powered horizontal blades, which are brought into action by means of an engine providing horizontal thrust propelling the aircraft forward. This type of aeroplane was popular in the 1930s, but nowadays is mainly used for sport.

auto-immune diseases A group of apparently unrelated disorders which possess a common underlying immunological mechanism. The body is unable to distinguish accurately between 'self' and 'not-self' proteins, and mounts an immune response against its own cells. Antibodies are produced that damage the body's own tissues, producing a variety of illnesses. Disorders include rheumatoid arthritis, diabetes mellitus, pernicious anaemia, haemolytic anaemia, some forms of kidney and thyroid disease, systemic lupus erythematosus, systemic sclerosis, and Addison's disease.

Autolycus [awtolikus] In Greek mythology, the maternal grandfather of Odysseus, who surpassed all men in thieving. He was said to be a son of Hermes. The name was also used by Shakespeare for a pedlar, 'a snapper-up of unconsidered trifles', in *The Winter's Tale*.

autolysis [awtoluhsis] The process of breakdown and disintegration of tissues or cells due to the action of their own self-dissolving (**autolytic**) enzymes. It occurs after the death of an organism, and sometimes in pathological conditions (eg pancreatitis in humans).

automated teller machine (ATM) The formal name for the 'service tills' now common outside most banks and building societies, through which money can be withdrawn and other transactions carried out. The ATMs are linked to the banks' computers to enable on-line monitoring of customer's accounts to take place through the machines.

automatic exposure The automatic setting of the shutter speed and lens aperture (f-number) of a camera to give the optimum exposure for a subject, as determined by the measurement of its brightness using a photocell, and taking into account the speed of the film in use. In *aperture priority* mode, the user chooses an f-number to give the depth of field required, and the corresponding shutter speed is automatically selected. In *shutter priority* mode, the appropriate shutter speed is chosen and the lens aperture is then set automatically. In *program* mode, both shutter speed and aperture are selected by the metering system according to a pre-set program.

automatic pilot A device that automatically controls a vehicle (aircraft, ship, land vehicle) so that it will follow a preset course. It makes suitable adjustments to the vehicle's control systems to compensate for the offsetting effects of the environment or terrain.

automatic writing The production of written text without the writer's conscious predetermination of the content, if any, of the message produced. It is sometimes associated with mediums, who claim the messages come from spirits of the deceased.

automation The control of a technical process without using a human being to intervene to make decisions. The result of one operation is fed back to control the next. Central heating is a simple automatic system: the thermostat is a sensor, feeding information back to the heater, which then adjusts automatically, switching on and off as necessary. Computers are the most widespread example of automation, controlling systems which humans would find too time-consuming. A widely-known example is in aviation, where the automatic pilot system ('George') relieves the pilot of the routine tasks of flying.

automaton [awtomatn] A mechanical device that imitates the actions of a living creature, human or animal. Such devices, constructed in the ancient world and in the Middle Ages, benefited from the development of clock mechanisms during the 17th-c. Some are made as toys, but others are useful as research or control mechanisms, and in the remote handling of hazardous materials.

automobile *car; motor insurance*

autonomic nervous system (ANS) That part of the nervous system which supplies the glands (eg the salivary and sweat glands), heart muscle, and smooth muscle (eg the walls of blood vessels and the bladder). It consists of groups of nerve cells outside the central nervous system, interposed between it and the target organs. The *sympathetic* (S) system is distributed throughout the whole body, particularly to the blood vessels. The *parasympathetic* (P) system is distributed to the gastro-intestinal, respiratory, and urogenital systems, and to the eye. Where S and P fibres supply the same structure, their effects are often opposite, to produce a balance with multiple gradations: for example, S nervous activity increases heart rate, P decreases it; S dilates the pupil, P constricts it. In general terms, the S system prepares the body for action, while the P is concerned with the conservation of energy.

autorad *DNA profiling*

autoradiography A technique for recording the positions of radioactive atoms in a specimen, by placing it over a fine-grain photographic emulsion. The radiation then produces a latent image corresponding to the site of each radiation source. The developed emulsion shows the distribution of the radioactive content of the specimen (eg a biological tissue containing a radioactive isotope).

autosomes Chromosomes other than the X and Y chromosomes. The term was coined in genetics at a time (1906) when sex-determination was little understood. Distinguishing the sex chromosomes from the autosomes cleared the way for the understanding of a wide variety of sex-determining mechanisms.

autotrophic organism [awtohtrofik] An organism that is capable of synthesizing complex organic substances from simple inorganic substrates. These organisms include the photosynthetic green plants that use atmospheric carbon dioxide as their main source of carbon in the synthesis of organic compounds, and the micro-organisms that obtain energy for metabolism by the oxidation of inorganic substrates such as iron, sulphur, and nitrogen (*chemotrophic* organisms).

autumnal equinox *equinox*

autumn crocus *meadow saffron*

Auvergne [ohvairn] pop (2000e) 1 381 000; area 26 013 sq km/ 10 041 sq mi. Region and former province of C France, comprising the departments of Allier, Cantal, Haute-Loire, and Puy-de-Dôme; Roman province, later a duchy and (10th-c) principality, united to France in 1527; **Haute-Auvergne** a mountainous area (W), **Basse-Auvergne** in R Allier valley; highest peaks in the Monts Dore, with Puy de Sancy at 1886 m/6188 ft; source of the Loire, Cher, Allier, Dordogne, and Lot Rivers; capital, Clermont-Ferrand; agriculture, mineral springs, cattle, wheat, wine, cheese.

Auxerre [ohzair], Lat **Autissiodorum** 47°48N 3°32E, pop (2000e) 42 400. Market town and capital of Yonne department, C France; on the R Yonne, surrounded by orchards and vineyards; one of the oldest towns in France; railway; bishopric; wine, paints, metal goods; Gothic cathedral (13th–16th-c); abbey church of St Germain with 9th-c frescoes.

auxiliary language A natural language adopted by people of different speech communities for the needs of trade, education, and communication, though it may not be the native language of any of them. English and French are used in this way in many parts of Africa.

auxiliary store *backing store*

auxins [awksinz] A large group of plant hormones vital to many processes, produced in meristems, and principally involved in controlling the growth of shoots and roots, as well as in fruit formation, leaf and fruit fall, tropisms, and nastic movement. They play an important role in the function of other hormones. The precise effects vary with the concentration of auxin in the tissues, low levels promoting growth, high levels inhibiting it. They are used commercially as rooting compounds, weedkillers, and to induce parthenocarpy.

Auyuittuq [owyooituk] National park in Northwest Territories, N Canada, on SE Baffin I; dominated by the Penny Highlands, rising to over 2094 m/6870 ft, capped by the Penny Ice Cap; glaciers in the surrounding valleys; established in 1972.

Auzangate [owsanggatay] 13°47S 71°15W. Andean peak in a spur of the Cordillera de Carabaya, part of the Cordillera Occidental, SE Peru; height, 6394 m/20 977 ft.

avadavat [avadavat] An Asian bird of the waxbill family. There are two species: the **green avadavat** (*Amandava formosa*), from India, and the **red avadavat/strawberry finch** (*Amandava amandava*), from Pakistan to SE Asia (introduced on many Indo-Pacific islands).

Avadh [avad] A semi-independent N Indian province within the Mughal Empire, annexed in 1856 by the British East India Company. Loss of rights by hereditary land revenue receivers caused resentment, and contributed towards the 1857 uprising.

avahi [avahhee] *indri*

Avalon [avalon] In Celtic mythology, the land of the dead, the place to which King Arthur was taken after his death. The name possibly means 'land of apples'.

avant garde [avã gah(r)d] (Fr 'vanguard') A term first used to describe the radical artists of mid-19th-c France and Russia, often with political associations. Since then it has been applied to the innovative, experimental artists of any time; described by W H Auden as 'the antennae of the race'.

avatar [avatah(r)] In Hinduism, the descent to Earth of deity in a visible form. The idea derives from the tradition associated with the deity Vishnu, who from time to time appears on Earth in animal or human form in order to save it from destruction or extraordinary peril.

Avebury [ayvbree] 51°27N 1°51W. Village in North Wiltshire district, Wiltshire, S England, UK; on the R Kennet, c.110 km/70 mi W of London; the largest megalithic monument in England, a world heritage site; in use c.2600–1600 BC; consists of a 427 m/1400 ft diameter earthwork, with a 9 m/30 ft-deep ditch and a 5 m/16 ft-high outer bank; entrances at the cardinal points, and approached by a 2·4 km/1½ mi avenue of 100 paired stones; three stone circles within the enclosure, the largest of nearly 100 boulders; nearby Silbury Hill is the largest prehistoric construction in Europe; also nearby, West Kennet long barrow, containing 30 burials in five chambers, the largest chambered tomb in England; Windmill Hill, one of the oldest known Neolithic sites, with remains dating back to about 3100 BC.

Ave Maria [ahvay mareea] *Hail Mary*

avens [avinz] Either of two plants from genus *Geum*, both native to temperate regions. **Wood avens** (*Geum urbanum*), also called **herb Bennet**, is an erect perennial growing to c.60 cm/2 ft; leaves divided into small, unequal lateral leaflets and a large, lobed terminal leaflet; flowers 5-petalled, erect, yellow, petals spreading; fruits with hooked beak, forming burr-like head. **Water avens** (*Geum rivale*) is similar, but flowers are bowl-shaped, drooping, petals pinkish. (Family: Rosaceae).

Averroës [averoheez], Latin form of **Ibn Rushd** (1126–98) The most famous of the mediaeval Islamic philosophers, born in Córdoba, S Spain. He was a judge successively at Córdoba, Seville, and in Morocco, and wrote on jurisprudence and medicine. In 1182 he became court physician to Caliph Abu Yusuf, but in 1185 was banished in disgrace (for reasons now unknown) by the caliph's son and successor. Many of his works were burnt, but after a brief period of exile he was restored to grace and lived in retirement at Marrakesh until his death. The most important of his works were the *Commentaries on Aristotle*, many of them known only through their Latin (or Hebrew) translations, which greatly influenced later Jewish and Christian writers and offered a partial synthesis of Greek and Arabic philosophical traditions.

aversion therapy A process in which an unpleasant experience is induced (eg by pharmacological, physical, or electrical means) in association with an undesirable behaviour, in an attempt to inhibit or eliminate by this conditioning the undesirable behaviour. The technique has been used in a wide range of conditions, including smoking and alcohol dependence; some have tried to use it in changing sexual orientation.

Avery, Oswald (Theodore) [ayveree] (1877–1955) Bacteriologist, born in Halifax, Nova Scotia, SE Canada. He studied medicine at Colgate University, then spent his career at the Rockefeller Institute Hospital, New York City (1913–48). He showed in 1944 that genetic transformation in bacteria can be caused by deoxyribonucleic acid (DNA), a key result in the development of molecular biology.

Avesta [avesta] The scriptures of Zoroastrianism, written in Avestan, a language of the E branch of the Indo-European family. Traditionally believed to have been revealed to Zoroaster, only the Gathas, a set of 17 hymns, may be attributed to him. Few portions of the original survive.

aviation All forms of flying, and the uses to which aircraft are put. Aviation is divided into two principal areas. **Military aviation** deals with the use of aircraft by military forces, either as a weapon in its own right, or as a platform from which to launch other weapons, together with the aircraft's use as a reconnaissance vehicle and military transport. **Civil aviation** deals with the organization and use of aircraft as a means of commercial transportation. The principal interest is the use of aircraft on scheduled and chartered flights to carry passengers and cargo, but the subject also covers the use of aircraft for pleasure, business, and medical services. Because of the international character of civil aviation, governments play a major role in its conduct and regulation, through both national legislation and international agreements. This governmental influence was a major factor in commercial airline operation until the early 1980s, when the US domestic market was deregulated. The result was a massive increase in competition, which led in turn to a reorganization of the airlines into larger groupings. It seems likely that this process will continue in the international market, which will lead to an increase in air travel, and increased pressure on airports and air traffic control.

Avicebron [avisebron], Arabic **Solomon ben Judah ibn Gabirol** (c.1020–c.1070) Poet and philosopher of the Jewish 'Golden Age' in Moorish Spain, born probably in Málaga, S Spain. He lived much of his life in Zaragoza, crippled by disease. He fused the heritage of Hebrew literature contained in the Bible, Talmud and other rabbinical writings with that of the dominant Arab culture of Andalusia, drawing on the Koran, Arab poetry, philosophy, and ethics. His most famous work is *Yanbu' al-hayya* (Source of Life), familiar in the West under its Latin title *Fons vitae*, and important for passing on the neo-Platonic and particularly Plotinian tradition. His secular poetry includes love poems, portraits of nature and praise of the seasons, and wine songs, as well as panegyrics about his patrons. His poetry became part of the mystical tradition of the Kabbalah.

Avicenna [avisena], Arabic **Ibn Sina** (980–1037) Philosopher and physician, born near Bokhara, SW Uzbekistan. Renowned for his learning, he became physician to several sultans, and for some time vizier in Hamadan, Persia. He was one of the main interpreters of Aristotle to the Islamic world, and the author of some 200 works on science, religion, and philosophy. His medical textbook, *Canon of Medicine*, long remained a standard work.

avidin *antivitamin factors*

Avignon [aveenyõ], Lat **Avenio** 43°57N 4°50E, pop (2000e) 93 600. Walled capital of Vaucluse department, SE France, on left bank of R Rhône; papal residence 1309–76; railway; archbishopric; chemicals, soap, paper, artificial fibres; popular tourist centre; Gothic Palais des Papes; ruins of 12th-c Pont St Benezet, subject of the folk-song 'Sur le Pont d'Avignon'; many churches and museums; centre of school of painting; John Stuart Mill died here.

Avignon School [aveenyõ] A group of artists, mostly Italian, who worked for the papal court in exile in Avignon (1309–77), especially Martini. Their influence continued after the popes returned to Italy. The 'Pietà', c.1460, by an unknown artist (Louvre) is considered the masterpiece of the school.

Ávila [aveela], also **Avila de los Caballeros**, ancient **Avela**, **Abula**, or **Abyla** 40°39N 4°43W, pop (2000e) 46 500. Ancient walled city, capital of Ávila province, Castilla-León, C Spain; 115 km/71 mi W of Madrid; altitude, 1126 m/3694 ft; bishopric; railway; wine, livestock, tourism; birthplace of Queen Isabella and St Teresa; cathedral (11th-c), Monastery of St Thomas, Churches of St Peter and St Vincent, town walls; old town and churches are a world heritage site; Holy Week, Fiesta of St John (Jun), summer fiesta (Jul), Fiesta of St Teresa (Oct).

Avila, El [el aveela] area 851 sq km/328 sq mi. National park in N Venezuela; on the Caribbean, directly E of Caracas; established in 1958.

avocado [avohkahdoh] An evergreen tree growing to 18 m/60 ft (*Persea americana*), covered with aromatic oil glands, thought to be native to Central America; leaves oval, leathery; flowers 2 cm/0·8 in, greenish-white, 6-lobed; berry pear-shaped, leathery, growing to 15 cm/6 in long, green, yellow, or purplish, with thick yellowish-green edible flesh surrounding a single large stone. It is cultivated on a large scale in many warm regions such as Mexico and the Mediterranean: the cultivated plants are smaller and bushier than wild ones, with fruits of various colours and sizes, ripening at different times of the year. (Family: Lauraceae.)

avocet [avoset] A long-legged wading bird, found in fresh and saline waters worldwide; catches small animals by sweeping a long, slender, up-curved bill from side to side on the surface of submerged mud. (Genus: *Recurvirostra*, 4 species. Family: Recurvirostridae.)

Avogadro, Amedeo [avohgadroh] (1776–1856) Scientist, born in Turin, NW Italy. In 1811 he formulated the hypothesis, known as *Avogadro's law*, that equal volumes of gases contain equal numbers of molecules, when at the same temperature and pressure. The principle did not come to be accepted until the work of Cannizzaro in the 1850s. Avogadro became professor of physics at Turin (1834–59).

Avogadro's constant [avohgadroh] The physical quantity of molecules in a mole or of electronic charges in a faraday. It is defined as the number of atoms in a sample of carbon with a mass of 12 g in which all atoms have nucleon number = 12. Its approximate value is $6 \cdot 023 \times 10^{23}$.

Avon [ayvn] pop (2000e) 989 800; area 1346 sq km/520 sq mi. Former county in SW England, UK; created in 1974 from parts of Somerset and Gloucestershire; replaced in 1996 by the unitary authorities of Bath and NE Somerset, Bristol, South Gloucestershire, and NW Somerset.

Avon, River [ayvn] *England*

Avon, 1st Earl of *Eden, Sir Anthony*

AWACS [aywaks] *Airborne Warning and Control System*

Awash [awash] National park in Lower Awash Valley, Ethiopia, in the East African Rift Valley; area 13 000 sq km/4000 sq mi; noted for its wildlife, including leopards, lions, and crocodiles; a world heritage site.

Awe, Loch Picturesque loch in Argyll and Bute, W Scotland, UK; length 37 km/23 mi; SE of Oban; drained by R Awe; many early lake dwelling-sites (*crannogs*); Ben Cruachan rises to 1124 m/3688 ft (N); Inverliever Forest (W); hydroelectric power station; 15th-c Kilchurn castle, Inshail chapel.

AWS (Automatic Warning System) *train protection systems*

Axelrod, Julius [akselrod] (1912–) Pharmacologist, born in New York City, New York, USA. He was a chemist at the Laboratory of Industrial Hygiene (New York City) (1935–45), and a research associate at Goldwater Memorial Hospital (New York City) (1946–9). He became a biochemist for the National Heart Institute (1949–55), then joined the National Institute for Mental Health (1955–84), remaining as a guest worker (1984). His studies of neurotransmission of adrenalin and amphetamines led to his investigations into psychoactive drugs for treatment of mental illness, including schizophrenia. He shared the 1970 Nobel Prize for Physiology or Medicine for his work on chemical neurotransmission and pharmacological interactions.

axiom A proposition that is assumed to be true, on which later studies may be developed. The most famous axioms are those on which Euclidean geometry was developed. (1) A straight line may be drawn from any one point to any other point. (2) A finite straight line may be extended at each end. (3) A circle can always be drawn with any point as centre and with any radius. (4) All right angles are equal to each other. (5) If a straight line meets two other straight lines so that the two adjacent angles on one side of it are together less than two right angles, the other lines when extended will meet on that side of the first line. This fifth axiom has been recast in many different, consistent forms. A more complete and rigorous set of axioms for Euclidian geometry was developed by Hilbert in 1899. Axiomatic foundations are now conventional in all of mathematics.

axis deer *chital*

Axis Powers The name given to the co-operation of Nazi Germany and Fascist Italy (1936–45), first used by Mussolini to proclaim the creation of a Rome–Berlin 'axis round which all European states can also assemble'. In May 1939 the two countries signed a full military and political treaty, the *Pact of Steel*. In September 1940, Germany, Italy, and Japan signed a tripartite agreement, after which all three were referred to as Axis Powers. The alliance was subsequently joined by Hungary, Romania, and Bulgaria, as well as by the Nazi-created states of Slovakia and Croatia.

axolotl [aksolotl] A rare Mexican salamander (*Ambystoma mexicanum*) from high altitude in L Xochimilco; pale with three pairs of feathery gills; large fin around tail; usually breeds as juvenile form and never leaves water, but some individuals do become land-dwelling adults; family also known as **mole salamanders**. (Family: Ambystomatidae.)

axon *neurone*

axonometric and isometric projection A system for producing a three-dimensional drawing of an object without perspective and in which all lines are drawn to scale. Isometric projection is a particular case of axonometric projection, in which the three axes of height, width, and depth are drawn at 120° to each other, with width and depth axes at 30° to the horizontal. The method is widely used in engineering and architectural drawings.

Axum A Greek-influenced Semitic trading state on the Eritrean coast, founded about the beginning of the Christian era and trading with Meroe. From its port at Adulis it dominated the trade of the Red Sea, and in the 3rd-c extended its power to Yemen. At the height of its influence under King Ezana (c.320–50), who accepted Christianity, it later became the basis of the Christian kingdom of Ethiopia.

Ayacucho, Battle of [iyakoochoh] (1824) The final major battle of the Spanish–American Wars of Independence, fought in the Peruvian Andes. It was a notable victory for the Venezuelan general, Sucre.

ayatollah [iyatola] (Persian 'sign of God') A Shiite Muslim religious title: a clergyman who has reached the third level of Shiite higher education, is recognized as a mujtahid, and is over 40. The word is particularly associated today with the Islamic Republic of Iran.

Ayckbourn, Sir Alan [aykbaw(r)n] (1939–) Playwright, born in London, UK. He began his theatrical career as an acting stage manager in repertory before joining Stephen Joseph's Theatre-in-the-Round company at Scarborough. After his first success, *Relatively Speaking* (1967), he was quickly established as a master of farce. He has made considerable experiments with staging and dramatic structure: *The Norman Conquests* (1974) is a trilogy in which each play takes place at the same time in a different part of the setting, and *Way Upstream* (1982) is set on and around a boat and necessitates the flooding of the stage. Among his most successful farces are *Absurd Person Singular* (1973) and *Joking Apart* (1979). He has also collaborated in musicals, notably *Jeeves* (with Andrew Lloyd Webber, 1975), and is recognized as a theatre director. His later plays include *Woman in Mind* (1986), *Man of the Moment* (1990), *Communicating Doors* (1995), *Things We Do For Love* (1998), and *Damsels in Distress* (2002). He was knighted in 1997.

aye-aye [iyiy] A nocturnal primitive primate (prosimian) from Madagascar (*Daubentonia madagascariensis*); shaggy coat, long bushy tail, and large ears; fingers extremely long and slender, especially the third finger (used to probe for wood-boring insects); inhabits trees. (Family: Daubentoniidae.)

Ayer, Sir A(lfred) J(ules) [air] (1910–89) Philosopher, born in London, UK. He studied at Oxford, where he was a pupil of Gilbert Ryle. He became professor at University College London, then at Oxford (1947–59). His first and best book was *Language, Truth and Logic* (1936), a concise and forceful account of the antimetaphysical doctrines of the Vienna Circle of philosophers he had become acquainted with in the 1930s. His later publications include *The Problem of Knowledge* (1956) and *The Central Questions of Philosophy* (1972). He was knighted in 1970.

Ayers, Sir Henry [airz] (1821–97) Politician, born in Portsea, Hampshire, S England, UK. He emigrated to South Australia in 1841 and took up a post with the South Australia Mining Association, with which he was associated for 50 years. Elected in 1863 to the first Legislative Council for the state under responsible government, he was a member of the Council for 36 years, and premier on several occasions. *Ayers Rock* was named after him in 1873.

Ayers Rock [airz], Aboriginal name **Uluru** 25°18S 131°18E. A huge red rock in SW Northern Territory, Australia, 450 km/280 mi SW of Alice Springs; within the Uluru National Park (1325 sq km/511 sq mi); rises from the desert to a height of 348 m/1142 ft; 3·6 km/2¼ mi long, 2·4 km/1½ mi wide, 8·8 km/5½ mi in circumference; resort town of Yulara 20 km/12 mi NW; the largest monolith in the world; named after South Australia premier, Sir Henry Ayers.

Ayeshah *A'ishah*

Ayeyarwady, River, formerly **Irrawaddy** Major river dissecting Myanmar N–S, formed in Kachin state, N Myanmar, by the meeting of the Mali Hka and Nmai Hka; flows S through gorges, then W and S to form a delta beginning 290 km/180 mi from the sea; empties into Andaman Sea in a broad front of tidal forests spreading for 260 km/160 mi; easternmost arm of delta linked to Yangon (Rangoon) by canal; chief tributary, R Chindwin; navigable to Bhamo (1300 km/800 mi inland); length c.1600 km/1000 mi; with the Nmai Hka, c.2000 km/1300 mi; large proportion of population in valley and delta; major rice-growing region.

Ayia Napa [ahya napa] 34°59N 34°00E, pop (2000e) 1000. Old fishing village in Famagusta district, SE Cyprus; with nearby Paralimni, the second most important tourist area on the island; monastery (16th-c).

Aykroyd, Dan (1952–) Actor, born in Ottawa, Canada. He studied at Carleton University, Ottawa, joined the Second City Comedy improvisation group in Toronto, made a name for himself as a stand-up comedian, then joined the cast of the anarchic television show *Saturday Night Live* (1975–9). He wrote the screenplay for and starred in *The Blues Brothers* (1980), appeared in *Ghostbusters* (1984), and earned a Best Supporting Actor Oscar nomination for his first dramatic role in *Driving Miss Daisy* (1989). Later films include *Exit to Eden* (1994), *Feeling Minnesota* (1996), *Grosse Pointe Blank* (1997), *Antz* (voice, 1999), and *Bright Young Things* (2003). His albums include *Briefcase Full of Blues*, *Made in America*, *The Blues Brothers*, and *Best of the Blues Brothers*.

Aylesbury [aylzbree] 51°50N 0°50W, pop (2000e) 61 400. County town of Buckinghamshire, SC England, UK; N of the Chiltern Hills, 60 km/37 mi NW of London; railway; furniture, chemicals, food processing, engineering; 13th-c St Mary's Church.

Aylward, Gladys [aylwerd] (1902–70) Missionary in China, born in London, UK. In 1930, she spent her entire savings on a railway ticket to Tientsin in N China. With a Scottish missionary, Mrs Jeannie Lawson, the pair founded an inn, the famous Inn of the Sixth Happiness, in an outpost at Yangcheng. From there, in 1938, she trekked across the mountains leading over 100 children to safety when the war with Japan brought fighting to the area. She returned to England in 1948, preached for five years, then in 1953 settled in Taiwan as head of an orphanage. Ingrid Bergman played her in the popular film, *The Inn of the Sixth Happiness* (1958).

Ayn, al- [iyn] 24°11N 55°45E, pop (2000e) 163 500. Rapidly developing new city in Abu Dhabi emirate, United Arab Emirates; 150 km/93 mi E of the city of Abu Dhabi; former oasis village; E terminus of the highway from Abu Dhabi; university (1977); small industrial areas to the S; date and palm plantations; fort, archaeological sites; al-Ayn National Park, 16 km/10 mi S.

Ayodhya [ayodya] Town in the N Indian state of Uttar Pradesh, and the location of the ancient Babri Masjid shrine. During the 1980s the shrine became the target of intense agitation by the Hindu followers of the Bharatiya Janata Paksh and related Hindu fundamentalist organizations. These asserted that the shrine lay over the birthplace of the god Rama, and that a temple to the god should be built on the site. In December 1992 a group of militant Hindus stormed the site, destroyed the shrine, and began to erect a temple. This sparked off intense communal violence in many parts of India, and plunged the minority Congress government of Narasimha Rao into crisis.

Ayr [air] 55°28N 4°38W, pop (2000e) 49 800. Administrative centre of South Ayrshire, SW Scotland, UK; on the Firth of Clyde, at mouth of R Ayr, 48 km/30 mi SW of Glasgow; railway; metal products, machinery, carpets, agricultural trade, tourism; Loudoun Hall (15th–16th-c), Tam o' Shanter Museum; Alloway, 3 km/1¾ mi S, birthplace of Burns; Culzean castle (1777), 19 km/12 mi SW.

Ayub Khan, Mohammad [ayub kahn] (1907–74) Pakistani soldier and president (1958–69), born in Hazara, EC Pakistan (formerly India). He studied at Aligarh Moslem University, trained at Sandhurst Military Academy, and became commander-in-chief of Pakistan's army (1951) and a field marshal (1959). He became president after a bloodless army coup, and established a stable economy and political autocracy. In 1969, after widespread civil disorder, he relinquished power and martial law was re-established.

ayurveda [ayoorvayda] (Hindi *ayur* 'life' + *veda* 'knowledge') A sacred system of medicine from ancient India, originating c.5000 BC. Good health is seen as a state of harmony between the air (*vata*) which governs movement, fire (*pitta*) which governs digestion and warmth, and water (*kapha*) which governs cohesion, growth, and lubrication. A practitioner will take a history which includes an astrological assessment, and emphasis is placed on the prevention of disease and a patient's own responsibility for curing any illness. Treatment may include fasting, bathing, diets, and enemas to purify the body, followed by massage, prayers, and yogic breathing, as well as prescriptions from a large herbal pharmacopoeia.

azalea [azaylia] A deciduous species of rhododendron. The name is used in horticulture to distinguish it from the evergreen species. (Genus: *Rhododendron*. Family: Ericaceae).

Azaña (y Díaz), Manuel [athanya] (1880–1940) Spanish statesman and president (1936–9), born in Alcalá de Henares, C Spain. A barrister, author, and lecturer in Madrid University, in 1925 he founded a political party, *Acción Republicana*. He became war minister in 1931, then prime minister (1931–3), and leader of the Republican Left (1936). He was elected president of the Second Republic and held office throughout most of the Spanish Civil War, but was forced into exile by General Franco.

Azande [azanday] A cluster of ethnically mixed Sudanic-speaking agricultural people of SW Sudan, Democratic Republic of Congo, and the Central African Republic. In the 18th-c, they were formed into a series of kingdoms by the Ambomu, led by the ruling Avongara clan, and are known for their elaborate system of beliefs in witchcraft, divination, and magic. Population c.800 000.

Azariah, Prayer of [azariya] One of three additions to the Book of Daniel in the Old Testament Apocrypha or in Catholic versions of the Bible, usually linked with the Song of the Three Young Men; known also as the *Benedictus es* in Catholic forms of worship. It depicts a lamentation for the sins of Israel on the mouth of Azariah (Abednego in *Dan* 1.6ff), one of those cast into the furnace for their faithful adherence to Israel's religion.

Azerbaijan *p.121*

Azhar, al- [azhah(r)] Islamic mosque and university founded in Cairo, Egypt, in 970, the oldest school of higher learning in continuous operation in the world. It has traditionally trained the *ulama* (Muslim scholars) who teach Islamic sciences and interpret the religious law (*sharia*). Graduates of al-Azhar are respected and have taught throughout the Muslim world. The curriculum has gradually been modernized and brought under Egyptian government control. In 1961 a secular campus was added at a new site. Al-Azhar offers an alternative to the state educational system and perpetuates traditional Islamic learn-

Azerbaijan

☐ International Airport ⌜⌟ Nagorno-Karabakh

[azerbiyjahn], Azerbaijani **Azärbayjan Respublikasi**, official name **Republic of Azerbaijan**

Local name Azerbaijan

Timezone GMT +3

Area 86 600 km²/33 428 sq mi

Population total (2002e) 8 176 000

Status Republic

Date of independence 1991

Capital Baku

Languages Azeri (official), Russian

Ethnic groups Azeri (83%), Russian (6%), Armenian (6%) (ethnic conflict since 1990 makes accurate statistical analysis impossible)

Religion Shi'ite Muslim

Physical features Mountainous country in E Transcaucasia: 10% of country is above 1494 m/4900 ft; 40% of land is lowland, 396–1494 m/1300–4900 ft; Bazar-Dyuzi rises to 4480 m/14 698 ft; rivers include the Kara and Araks.

Climate Central and eastern Azerbaijan dry and sub-tropical with mild winters and long, hot summers (often as hot as 43°C); SE is humid with annual rainfall of 1193–1396 mm/47–55 in.

Currency 1 Manat = 100 gopik

Economy Once the former Soviet Union's most important oil-producing region, but now in decline; manufacturing industries include building materials, chemicals, textiles; mineral resources include natural gas, iron, copper, lead, zinc; exports include cotton, wheat, tobacco.

GDP (2002e) $28·61 bn, per capita $3700

Human Development Index (2002) 0·741

History Proclaimed a Soviet Socialist Republic, 1920; constituent republic of the USSR, 1936; declaration of independence, 1991; became a member of UN, 1992; ongoing conflict with Armenia over disputed enclave of Nagorno-Karabakh.

Head of State
1991–2 Ayaz Mutalibov
1992 Yagub Mamedov *Interim*
1992–3 Abulfaz Elchibey
1993–2003 Geidar Aliyev
2003– Ilham Aliyev

Head of Government
1991–2 Gasan Gasanov
1992–3 Feirus Mustafayev *Acting*
1993–4 Rakhim Guseinov
1994 Ali Masimov *Acting*
1994 Panakh Guseinov
1994–5 Surat Guseinov
1995–6 Fuad Guliyev
1996–2003 Artur Rasizade
2003 Ilham Aliyev
2003 Artur Rasizade *Acting*

ing. Its students number c.90 000, and women, who attend segregated academic faculties, are admitted.

azidothymidine *AZT*

Azikiwe, Nnamdi [azeekeeway] (1904–96) Nigerian statesman and president (1963–6), born in Zungeru, WC Nigeria. He studied at US universities, and in 1937 began to take a leading part in the Nigerian nationalist movement, becoming president of the National Council of Nigeria and the Cameroons. He became prime minister of the E region (1954–9), Governor-General of Nigeria (1960–3), and was elected the first president of the Nigerian republic. While in Britain during the military uprising of 1966 his office was suspended, although he returned privately to Nigeria.

azimuth The direction of an object measured in degrees clockwise around the horizon from N point to a point on the horizon vertically beneath the object. The notion is used in astronomy, navigation, gunnery, and other contexts where it is important to determine a bearing as well as an altitude.

Aznar, (López) José Maria [aznah(r)] (1953–) Spanish statesman and prime minister (1996–), born in Madrid, Spain. Educated at Madrid, he became a civil servant before his election to the Cortes (Spanish parliament) in 1982. He was prime minister of the autonomous region of Castilla y León, and has been president of the PP (Popular Party, formerly Popular Alliance) since 1990.

azo-dyes [azoh] An important class of dyes originally made (1861) by Peter Griess (1829–88), a German-born chemist who worked mainly as a brewery chemist at Burton-on-Trent, Staffordshire, UK. All have two nitrogen atoms joined: –N=N–.

azolla [azola] An aquatic, free-floating fern, native to tropical and subtropical regions, and widely naturalized even in cooler areas such as Europe, despite suffering badly in winter; stem only a few cm long, branched with scale-like, overlapping fronds covered with non-wettable hairs, reddish in autumn. It often covers the surface of water in lakes, ponds, and ditches. (Genus: *Azolla*, 6 species. Family: Azollaceae.)

Azores *p.122*

Azorín [athorin], pseudonym of **José Martínez Ruiz** (1874–1967) Novelist and critic, born in Monóvar, SE Spain. He studied law, then became a writer, his novels including *Don Juan* (1922) and *Dona Inés* (1925). He was also one of the leading literary critics of his time.

Azov, Sea of [azof], Russ **Azovskoye More** Gulf in NE of Black Sea; connected to the Sea by the Kerch Strait; main arms, Gulf of Taganrog (NE) and Sivash or Putrid Sea (W); latter mostly swamp, almost completely cut off from the Sea of Azov by a sandspit (Tongue of Arabat); shallow water, tending to freeze (Nov–Mar); maximum depth 15·3 m/50·2 ft; river deposits cause further shallowing and silting of harbours; important source of freshwater fish.

Azores

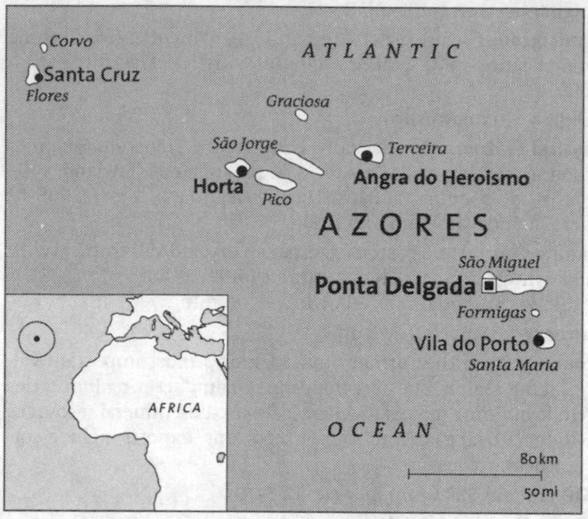

☐ International Airport

[azaw(r)z], Port **(Arquipélago dos) Açôres**

Local name Ilhas dos Açôres Port (Arquipélago dos) Açôres

Timezone GMT −1

Area 2300 km²/900 sq mi

Population total (2000e) 239 000

Status Semi-autonomous region of Portugal

Capital Ponta Delgada (on São Miguel Island)

Physical features Island archipelago of volcanic origin, 1400–1800 km/870–1100 mi W of mainland Portugal; three widely separated groups of nine islands; Flores and Corvo (NW), Terceira, Graciosa, São Jorge, Faial (Fayal), Pico (C), and Santa Maria with the Formigas Islands and São Miguel, the principal island (E); highest point, Pico, 2351 m/7713 ft; volcanic terrain.

Economy Agriculture; grain, fruit, tea, tobacco, wine.

History Settled by the Portuguese in 1439; under Spanish rule, 1580–1640; new constitution established in 1832, when islands were grouped into three administrative districts; given limited autonomous administration, 1895; has no central government, but a General Council.

AZT An abbreviation for **azidothymidine**, a drug which inhibits replication of viruses, including the AIDS virus, HIV. Developed as **zidovudine**, it was granted a licence unusually rapidly, in response to pressure from AIDS patients. Clinical trials have demonstrated the drug to be of limited use in therapy: it can slow the progress of the disease, but it cannot cure AIDS symptoms. In addition, it has inherent toxicity, and resistance develops rapidly.

Aztec–Tanoan languages A group of North American Indian languages which form a bridge between the indigenous languages of North and South America, most of which have few speakers today. An exception is Aztec itself, spoken in Mexico, which has about a million speakers.

Aztecs The most powerful people of Central America during the 15th–16th-c. Their main city, Tenochtitlan (present-day Mexico City), near L Texcoco, became the most densely populated city of the region. They built up a great and powerful despotic state, with a strong military force, subjugating nearly all the people of C Mexico, and eventually ruling 400–500 small tribute-paying states (probably 5–6 million people), which provided them with raw materials and produce. People captured in wars were offered for human sacrifice to the Aztec gods. The Aztecs were famous for their agriculture, cultivating all available land, introducing irrigation, draining swamps, and creating artificial islands in the lakes. Their best-known ruler was Montezuma II. They developed a form of hieroglyphic writing, a complex calendar system, and built famous pyramids and temples. The Aztec empire was finally destroyed by the Spanish under Cortés in 1521.

Azuero [aswayroh] Peninsula in WC Panama, on the Pacific Ocean coast, forming the W side of the Gulf of Panama; length 80 km/50 mi; rises to 829 m/2720 ft at Cerro Canajagua.

b

Baader–Meinhof [bahder miynhof] The popular name for *Rote Armee Fraktion* (RAF), after leaders Andreas Baader (1943–77) and Ulrike Meinhof (1934–76); a left-wing German revolutionary terrorist group which carried out political bombings in Germany in the early 1970s. Baader, Meinhof, and 18 other members were arrested in 1972. On a much smaller scale, RAF continued into the 1980s.

Baal [bayl] (Heb 'lord') The Phoenician god of rain and fertility, his voice being the thunder; in the Bible, used for gods of various localities in Syria and Canaan, and eventually for the great god of the Canaanites, whose cult was often associated with the goddess Asherah or Ashtoreth. He also features in the Ugaritic Ras Shamra texts in conflicts with the gods Yam (the sea) and Mot (death).

Baalbek [bahlbek], ancient **Heliopolis** 34°00N 36°12E, pop (2000e) 17 000. Town in E Lebanon where the Phoenicians built a temple to the Sun-god, Baal; a world heritage site; Temple of Jupiter, Temple of Bacchus; centre of Muslim Shiite activity; arts festival.

Baath or **Ba'ath** [bahth] (Arabic 'resurgence') The ideology of the Baath (or Ba'ath) Arab Socialist Party, founded in 1940 by a Christian, Michel Aflaq, and a Muslim, Salah al-Din Bitar, synthesizing Marxism with a pan-Arab nationalism that aims to unite Arab nations. The party was most prominent in Syria and Iraq, where it had a close relationship with the military. In Iraq, the party seized power in the coup of 1968 which installed Saddam Hussein as leader.

Baba Malay *Malay* (language)

Babar or **Babur** (Arabic 'tiger'), originally **Zahir-ud-din Muhammad** (1483–1530) First Mughal Emperor of India, born in Ferghana, E Uzbekistan. After failing to establish himself in Samarkand, he invaded India, defeating Ibrahim Lodi decisively at the Battle of Paniput in 1526, and laying the foundation for the Mughal Empire. The following year he defeated the Hindu Rajput confederacy. A soldier of genius, he was also a cultured man with interests in architecture, music, and literature. Himself a Muslim, he initiated a policy of toleration towards his non-Muslim subjects. He was succeeded by his son, Humayun.

Babbage, Charles (1791–1871) Mathematician and inventor, born in London, UK. He studied at Cambridge, where he became professor of mathematics (1828–39), and spent most of his life attempting to build two calculating machines. His assistant was Byron's daughter, Augusta Ada, Lady Lovelace. His 'difference engine' was intended for the calculation of tables of logarithms and similar functions by repeated addition performed by trains of gear wheels. An unfinished portion of the machine is now in the Science Museum, London. His 'analytical engine' was designed to perform many different computations, using punched cards. The idea was too ambitious to be realized by the mechanical devices available at the time, but can now be seen to be the essential germ of the electronic computer of today, and Babbage is thus regarded as the pioneer of modern computers.

Babbitt, Bruce (Edward) (1938–) US statesman, born in Flagstaff, Arizona, USA. He trained as a lawyer, served as Arizona's attorney-general (1975–8), and became state governor (1978–87). An unsuccessful candidate for the Democratic presidential nomination in 1988, he was appointed secretary of the interior in 1993, and was reappointed in the 1997 administration.

Babbitt, Milton (1916–) Composer and theorist, born in Philadelphia, Pennsylvania, USA. He studied at New York University and then Princeton, where he later taught (1938). He was a leading proponent of total serialism, and composed many works for the electronic synthesizer. In recognition, The Columbia-Princeton Music Center made him a director.

babbler A songbird native to warmer regions of the Old World; soft, fluffy plumage and short wings; eats insects, fruit, seeds, and nectar; usually found in small groups. The name is also used for the **sooty babbler** (a chat of the family Turdidae). (Family: Timaliidae, over 280 species.)

Babel, Isaac (Emmanuilovich) [babel] (1894–1941) Short-story writer, a protégé of Maxim Gorky, born in the Jewish ghetto of Odessa, S Ukraine. He worked as a journalist in St Petersburg, then served in the tsar's army and in various Bolshevik campaigns. He wrote stories of the Jews in Odessa in *Odesskie rasskazy* (1916, Odessa Tales), and tales of the brutality and heroism of the post-revolutionary Russian Civil War in *Konarmiya* (1926, Red Cavalry). He was exiled to Siberia in the mid-1930s, and died in a concentration camp.

Babel, Tower of Probably the site of an important temple shrine in the ancient city of Babylon. In the Bible (*Gen* 11.1–9) the legend is related of how its construction led to the confusion of languages, and the consequent dispersion of peoples, as a punishment by God for human pride.

Babeuf, François-Noël [baboef], originally **Gracchus Babeuf** (1760–97) Political agitator in revolutionary France, born in St Quentin, N France. During the Revolution, he helped organize a conspiracy aiming to destroy the Directory (1796) and establish an extreme democratic and communistic system. When this was discovered, he was guillotined.

Babi *Baha'i*

Babington, Antony (1561–86) Conspirator, born in Dethick, Derbyshire, C England, UK. In 1586 he was induced by Ballard and other Catholic emissaries to put himself at the head of a conspiracy aiming to murder Queen Elizabeth I and release Mary, Queen of Scots (the **Babington Plot**). Cipher messages were apparently intercepted by Walsingham in which Mary was implicated by her approval of the plot, and these were later used against her. Babington fled, was captured at Harrow, and executed with the others.

Babinski, Joseph (François Felix) [babinskee] (1857–1932) Neurologist, born in Paris, France. He is known for his description of an abnormal foot reflex which is symptomatic of upper motor neurone disease, and a reflex of the forearm believed to be due to a lesion in the spinal cord. Both reflexes are known as **Babinski's Sign**. Independently of **Alfred Fröhlich** (1871–1953), a Viennese pharmacologist, he investigated an endocrine disorder, adiposogenital dystrophy, or **Babinski–Fröhlich disease**.

babirusa [babiroosa] A wild pig native to Sulawesi (*Babyrousa babyrussa*); pale, almost hairless body; long lower tusks; upper canines in the male grow from the top of the snout, and curl towards the eyes; inhabits riverbanks; swims well.

Babi Yar A huge ravine near Kiev in Ukraine into which over 30 000 Jews were herded and massacred by Nazi German troops in 1941. It is also the title of a poem by Yevgeny Yevtushenko (1961) and a novel by Anatoly Kuznetsov (1966) dedicated to the victims.

baboon A ground-dwelling African monkey; long dog-like muzzle with large teeth; males with swollen, naked buttocks; troops contain up to 100 individuals. (Genera: *Papio*, 5 species; *Mandrillus*, 2 species; *Theropithecus*, 1 species.)

Babylon 32°33N 44°25E. From the 18th-c BC, the capital of the Babylonian Empire, situated on the R Euphrates S of Baghdad, modern Iraq. Its massive city walls and 'hanging gardens', attributed by classical tradition to Semiramis, wife of Shamshi-Adad V (823–811 BC), regent (811–806 BC), were one of the wonders of the ancient world. Semi-subterranean vaulted rooms provided with hydraulic lifting gear in the later Palace of Nebuchadnezzar (604–562 BC) have been claimed as remains of the gardens, but their site is not definitely known.

Babylonia [babilohnia] The region in Lower Mesopotamia around the ancient city of Babylon, which formed the core twice in antiquity of extensive but short-lived empires. The first, covering the whole of Mesopotamia, was created by the great Amorite king Hammurabi (c.1795–1750 BC) but destroyed by the Hittites c.1595 BC. The second came into being with the Babylonian overthrow of Assyria in 612 BC and lasted until the Persian conquest in 539–538 BC. Under its greatest ruler Nebuchadnezzar (605–562 BC), it stretched as far W as the Mediterranean. Although the Persians ended Babylonian political power for good, culturally Babylonian influence lasted for centuries, particularly in the fields of astrology, astronomy, and mathematics.

Babylonian art The art associated with ancient Babylonia (the S part of modern Iraq), dating from c.2500 BC, until the conquest of the country by Alexander (331 BC). What survives is religious and courtly, such as the stylized stone statues of Gudea (eg in the Louvre) made c.2100 BC, the wall-paintings and coloured bas-reliefs representing religious sacrifices, royal ceremonies, and (as in neighbouring Assyria) comparatively realistic hunting scenes. Figures follow the typical Ancient Near-Eastern conventions, with frontal bodies, profile heads and legs, and large staring eyes. Precious metals occur in the objects from the royal cemetery at Ur, made c.2500 BC.

Babylonian exile The mass deportation of the Jews from Palestine to Babylonia in 587–586 BC, after the failure of their revolt against Nebuchadnezzar.

baby talk The way in which adults talk to very young children, mimicking what are perceived to be the main features of child language. It includes simplified sentence structures (eg *Mummy gone*) and word pronunciations (eg *doggie*). Many parents lapse naturally into this style of speech, though some are critical of it, and try to avoid it. However, there is no evidence that the use of baby talk does any harm to the process of language acquisition, and the use of simplified structures may actually facilitate it.

Bacall, Lauren [bakawl], originally **Betty Joan Perske** (1924–) Actress, born in New York City, USA. A student at the American Academy of Dramatic Arts, she made her stage debut in 1942. She married her co-star Humphrey Bogart in 1945, appearing with him in such thrillers as *The Big Sleep* (1946) and *Key Largo* (1948). After Bogart's death in 1957, she turned to the stage, her Broadway successes including the musical *Applause!* (1970–2, Tony). Later films include *Murder on the Orient Express* (1974), *The Shootist* (1976, BAFTA), *The Mirror Has Two Faces* (1996), and *Diamonds* (1999). She was also married (1961–9) to the actor Jason Robards Jr. Her autobiography, *By Myself* (1979), was an international best-seller, and in 1994 appeared *Lauren Bacall Now*.

baccarat A casino card game, the most popular version being *baccarat banque*, in which the bank plays against the players. Another variant is *chemin de fer*, whereby all players take it in turn to hold the bank. Baccarat is derived from popular 15th-c games, and is thought to have been introduced into France from Italy during the reign of Charles VIII. The object is to assemble, either with two or three cards, a points value of 9. Picture cards and the ten count as 0. The ace counts as 1, and other cards according to their face value. If the total is a double figure then the first figure is ignored, eg 18 would count as 8.

Bacchanalia [bakanaylia] The orgiastic rites of Bacchus (Dionysus), the god of nature, fertility, and wine. They were banned from Rome in 186 BC on the grounds that they were a threat to morality and public order.

Bacchylides [bakilideez] (5th-c BC) Greek lyric poet, the nephew of Simonides of Ceos, and a contemporary of Pindar in Hiero's court at Syracuse. Fragments of his Epinician Odes (written to celebrate victories in the great athletic festivals) were discovered in 1896.

Bach, C(arl) P(hilipp) E(manuel), known as **the Berlin Bach** or **the Hamburg Bach** (1714–88) Composer, born in Weimar, C Germany, the second surviving son of J S Bach. He studied at the Thomasschule, Leipzig, where his father was cantor, and at Frankfurt University. In 1740 he became cembalist to the future Frederick II, and later became *Kapellmeister* at Hamburg (1767). He was famous for his playing of the organ and clavier, for which his best pieces were composed. He published *The True Art of Clavier Playing* (1753), the first methodical treatment of the subject, introduced the sonata form, and wrote numerous concertos, keyboard sonatas, church music, and chamber music.

Bach, J(ohann) C(hristian), known as **the London Bach** or **the English Bach** (1735–82) Composer, born in Leipzig, EC Germany, the 11th son of J S Bach. He studied under his brother C P E Bach in Berlin, and from 1754 worked in Italy. After becoming a Catholic, he was appointed organist at Milan in 1760, and for a time composed only ecclesiastical music, including two Masses, a requiem, and a 'Te Deum', but later he began to compose opera. In 1762 he was appointed composer to the London Italian opera, and became musician to Queen Charlotte.

Bach, Johann Sebastian (1685–1750) Composer, one of the world's greatest musicians, born in Eisenach, C Germany. He was orphaned by the age of 10, and brought up by his elder brother, **Johann Christoph Bach** (1671–1721), organist at Ohrdruf, who taught him the organ and clavier. He attended school in Lüneburg, before in 1703 becoming organist at Arnstadt. He found his duties as choirmaster irksome, and angered the authorities by his innovative chorale accompaniments. In 1707 he married a cousin, **Maria Barbara Bach** (1684–1720), and left to become organist at Mühlhausen. In 1708 he transferred to the ducal court at Weimar, and in 1711 became *Kapellmeister* to Prince Leopold of Anhalt-Cöthen, where he wrote mainly instrumental music, including the 'Brandenburg' Concertos (1721) and *The Well-tempered Clavier* (1722). Widowed in 1720, and left with four children, he married in 1721 **Anna Magdalena Wilcke** (1701–60), and had 13 children by her, of whom six survived. In 1723 he was appointed cantor of the Thomasschule in Leipzig, where his works included perhaps c.300 church cantatas, the *St Matthew Passion* (1727), and the *Mass in B Minor*. Almost totally blind, he died in Leipzig. One of his main achievements was his remarkable development of polyphony. Known to his contemporaries mainly as an organist, his genius as a composer was not fully recognized until the following century.

Bach, W(ilhelm) F(riedemann), known as **the Halle Bach** (1710–84) Composer, born in Weimar, C Germany, the eldest and most gifted son of J S Bach. He studied at the Thomasschule and Leipzig University, and in 1733 became organist at Dresden and in 1747 at Halle. His way of life became increasingly dissolute, and from 1764 he lived without fixed occupation at Brunswick, Göttingen, and Berlin, where he died. He was the greatest organ player of his time, but very few of his compositions were published, as he rarely bothered to write them down.

Bacharach, Burt (1929–) Composer, born in Kansas City, Missouri, USA. He studied piano and composition at Mannes

School of Music, Berkshire Music Center, and McGill University (Montreal), and after army service worked as accompanist. In 1957 he met Hal David, and they teamed up to write such hits as 'Magic Moments' (1957) and 'The Story of My Life' (1957). 'Raindrops Keep Fallin' on My Head' (1969, Oscar Best Song) was another popular hit, while *Promises, Promises* (1968) was their most successful musical. In the late 1970s he revived his career as a composer with lyricist and wife (1982–90) **Carol Bayer Sager**.

Bacher, Ali [bakher] (1942–) Cricketer and sports administrator, born in Roodepoort, NE South Africa. His career was deeply intertwined with South Africa's exclusion from and subsequent return to international sport. He captained Transvaal and South Africa with great success, but his Test career was cut short by international sports boycotts of South African teams. He was a leading figure in organizing the 'rebel' tours to South Africa in the 1980s, but rapidly adjusted to political change, and emerged as a key figure in the new non-racial administrative structures by the end of that decade. In 1990 he received the Jack Cheetham Memorial Award for his efforts to normalize sport in South Africa. In 1997, now the managing director of the United Cricket Board of South Africa, he became the first chairman of the International Cricket Council's development committee.

Bach flower remedies A system of flower remedies for illnesses, and especially for disharmonies of the personality and emotional state, devised by British medical microbiologist Edward Bach (1880–1936). Bach theorized that the dew condensing on a plant would, when exposed to sunlight, absorb the energy of the plant into the water molecules. From this premise he developed a system of herbal remedies prepared from 38 different species of flower. He believed that every disorder arises as a result of an imbalance of inner energy, and that nature has a cure for all illnesses in the form of healing plants.

bacillus [basiluhs] Any rod-shaped bacterium; also a large and diverse genus of rod-shaped bacteria, typically motile by means of flagella. They are widely distributed as saprophytes in soil and aquatic habitats. Some are disease-causing, including the causative agent of anthrax. (Kingdom: Monera. Family: Bacillaceae.)

Back, Sir George (1796–1878) Arctic explorer, born in Stockport, Greater Manchester, NW England, UK. He sailed with Sir John Franklin on Polar expeditions (1818–22, 1825–7), and in 1833–5 went in search of explorer Sir John Ross, discovering Artillery Lake and the Great Fish River (now *Back's River*), which he traced to the Frozen Ocean. In 1836–7 he further explored the Arctic shores. He was knighted in 1839, and made admiral in 1857.

backcross In experimental genetics, the mating of a first generation hybrid with an individual that is genetically identical with one of its parents. Such experiments are used to detect linkages between genes.

backgammon A board game for two players. Equipment similar to that used in backgammon was excavated from Tutankhamen's tomb. Introduced to Britain by the Crusaders, it became known as backgammon from c.1750. Each player has 15 round, flat pieces of a particular colour, which are moved around the board on the throw of two dice. The board is divided into two halves; the inner table and the outer table. The object is to move your own pieces around the board and 'home' to your own inner table. You win by being the first to remove all your pieces from the board.

background processing A lower priority task carried out on a computer while it is also engaged in doing other tasks. For example, many computers operate their printer(s) in this way, without apparently interrupting the user.

background radiation Naturally occurring radioactivity which can be detected at any place on Earth. It results from cosmic rays reaching the Earth from outer space, and from the radioactive decay of materials in the ground.

backing store A general term used in computing to describe the place where the computer stores the long term data needed to carry out its tasks (eg to calculate a payroll the computer needs to have available the employee records together with the current tax tables); also known as **bulk store** or **secondary store**. It has a higher capacity but lower access time than the main memory of a computer, and is normally in the form of magnetic tape storage or magnetic disk storage, but could be a card with a magnetic stripe which is updated each time the card is used.

back projection The technique of projecting an image on to a translucent screen to be viewed from the opposite side, advantageous when the audience area cannot be darkened, as in museums and exhibitions and for large-screen television. In a form of composite cinematography, the performance of actors is photographed to appear against a moving background scene projected from the rear on to such a screen.

back slang A type of secret language used mainly by children, in which words are spelled backwards and pronounced according to the new spelling: for example, *week* might be pronounced as *kew*. Some children train themselves to reach high speeds in speaking backwards.

back translation A test of the quality of a foreign language translation. The translated text is re-translated into the original language, and the two versions compared. The closer the correspondence, the better the translation.

Bacon, Francis, Viscount St Albans (1561–1626) Philosopher and statesman, born in London, UK, the younger son of Sir Nicholas Bacon. He studied at Cambridge and Gray's Inn (1576), and was called to the bar in 1582. Becoming an MP in 1584, he was knighted by James I in 1603. He was in turn solicitor general (1607), attorney general (1613), privy counsellor (1616), Lord Keeper (1617), and Lord Chancellor (1618). He became Baron Verulam in 1618, and was made viscount in 1621. However, complaints were made that he accepted bribes from suitors in his court, and he was publicly accused before his fellow peers, fined, imprisoned, and banished from parliament and the court. Although soon released, and later pardoned, he never returned to public office, and he died in London, deeply in debt. His philosophy is best studied in *The Advancement of Learning* (1605) and *Novum Organum* (1620). His stress on inductive methods gave a strong impetus to subsequent scientific investigation.

Bacon, Francis (1909–92) Artist, born in Dublin, Ireland. He settled permanently in England in 1928. After working as an interior designer he began painting in c.1930 without any formal training, making a major impact in 1945 with his 'Three Figures at the Base of a Crucifixion'. Although the initial inspiration for his work was Surrealism, he made frequent use of imagery annexed from old masters, usually translated into blurred and gory figures imprisoned in unspecific, architectural settings. A technical perfectionist, Bacon destroyed a great deal of his prolific output. He is widely regarded as Britain's most important post-war artist.

Bacon, Kevin (1958–) Actor and musician, born in Philadelphia, Pennsylvania, USA. He studied acting at the Circle in the Square Theater in New York, and gained his first feature film role in *National Lampoon's Animal House* (1981). Later films include *JFK* (1991), *Apollo 13* (1995), *Hollow Man* (2000), and *Mystic River* (2003). Since the mid-1990s he has performed with The Bacon Brothers, a folk-rock group formed with his brother Michael.

Bacon, Nathaniel (1647–76) American colonial leader, born in Suffolk, E England, UK. He emigrated to Virginia in 1673, and made himself prominent by his raids against the Indians. His activities prompted the English governor to declare him a rebel in 1676, whereupon Bacon captured and burned Jamestown. For a time he controlled most of Virginia, but died suddenly, and the rebellion ended.

Bacon, Roger, known as **Doctor Mirabilis** ('Wonderful Doctor') (c.1220–92) Philosopher and scientist, probably born in Ilchester, Somerset, SW England, UK. He studied at Oxford and Paris, and gained a reputation for diverse and unconventional learning in philosophy, magic, and alchemy. He seems to have returned to Oxford in 1247 to develop his interests in experimental science and, more surprisingly, to become a Franciscan. But he suffered censorship and eventually imprisonment from the Order for the heresy of his 'suspected novelties', and he died in Oxford soon after his eventual release from prison. He has been associated with scientific inventions such as the magnifying glass and gunpowder, and with speculations about lighter-than-air flying machines, microscopes, and telescopes. His views on experimentalism have often seemed strikingly modern, and despite surveillance and censorship from the Franciscans he published many works on mathematics, philosophy, and logic whose importance was recognized only in later centuries.

bacteria *see panel*

bacteria

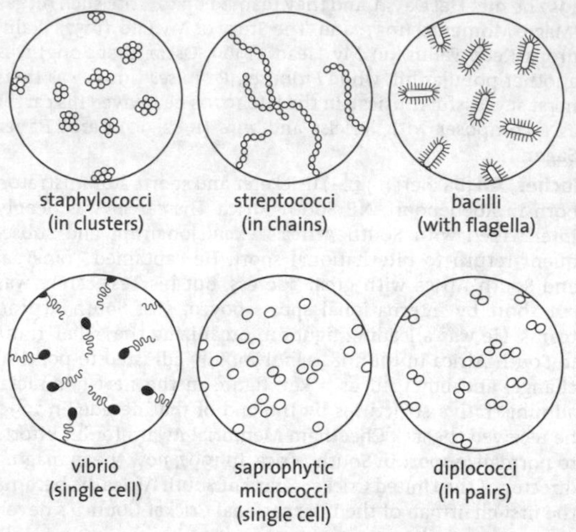

(sing **bacterium**) A diverse division of microscopic organisms that all share a *procaryotic* cellular organization, ie each cell lacks a true nucleus bounded by a nuclear membrane. The genetic information is carried on a loop of deoxyribonucleic acid (DNA) in the cytoplasm. Most bacteria are single-celled. Basic bacterial shapes are spherical (*coccus*), rod-like (*bacillus*), and spiral (*spirillum*). These may occur singly, or in chains, pairs, clusters, or other groupings. Some (the actinomycetes) have a branching, filamentous structure, and may form a mycelium. Most have a rigid cell wall containing peptidoglycan, the exceptions being the mycoplasms and halobacteria. Cell division typically occurs by symmetrical binary fission; some form spores; mitosis never occurs. Bacteria range in size from less than 1 μ (*Chlamydia*) to about 0·5 mm (spirochaete), but most are between 1 and 10 μ; a bacterium *Thiomargarita namibiensis*, with a cell up to 0·75 mm, was reported in 1999. They differ greatly in their growth requirements. Some can grow only in the presence of oxygen (**aerobic bacteria**), while others grow only in the absence of oxygen (**anaerobic bacteria**). They occur in soil, water, and air, as well as in symbiotic associations with other organisms, and as parasites or disease-causing agents. They cause many human diseases, including anthrax, plague, pneumonia, syphilis, tetanus, and tuberculosis. The scientific study of bacteria is known as **bacteriology**.

bacteriological warfare A form of warfare using organic agents such as micro-organisms and viruses which cause disease and death in humans. Many such agents have been investigated, including anthrax, plague, and botulinus toxin. Fears of bacteriological warfare surfaced in the aftermath of the terrorist attack on the United States of America on 11 Sep 2001 when a number of individuals were infected after coming into contact with anthrax-tainted letters and packages received through the postal service.

bacteriology The study of the biology of bacteria and of the diseases they cause. It involves identifying and classifying bacteria according to their characteristics, growing them in artificial media to determine the conditions under which they thrive, observing the disease processes they induce in human and animal subjects, and collecting and testing specimens to develop cures and vaccinations.

bacteriophage A virus that infects bacteria, reproducing only inside living bacteria. Bacteriophage virions (complete infective virus particles) are typically very small, and may contain either ribonucleic or deoxyribonucleic acid.

Bactria [**bak**tria] The name given in antiquity to the area roughly corresponding to N Afghanistan and the adjacent parts of S Russia. It was ruled for centuries by foreign conquerors, notably the Achaemenids and the Seleucids. In the second half of the 3rd-c BC Bactria at last became an independent state, and under a series of able Indo-Greek rulers went on to establish an empire that at its height covered not only all Afghanistan but large parts of Russian Central Asia and Pakistan.

Badajoz [**bad**ajoz], Span [ba*th*a**hoth**], ancient **Pax Augusta** 38°50N 6°59W, pop (2000e) 124 000. Capital of Badajoz province, SW Spain, on R Guadiana, 401 km/249 mi SW of Madrid; bishopric; former Moorish capital; scene of a battle in the Peninsular War, 1812; airport; railway; tinned vegetables, textiles; cathedral (13th-c).

Baden [**bah**dn], ancient **Thermae Pannonicae** 48°01N 16°14E, pop (2000e) 25 800. Capital of Baden district, Niederösterreich, NE Austria; 30 km/19 mi S of Vienna, on the R Schwechat; connected to Vienna by tram; principal Austrian spa, with sulphurous waters, known since Roman times; tourism, casino.

Baden-Powell, Robert Stephenson Smyth Baden-Powell, Baron [**bay**dn **pow**el] (1857–1941) British general and founder of the Boy Scout movement, born in London, UK. He studied at Charterhouse, joined the army in 1876, served in India and Afghanistan, and won fame during the Boer War as the defender of Mafeking (1899–1900). He is best known as the founder in 1908 of the Boy Scouts and in 1910, with his sister **Agnes** (1858–1945), of the Girl Guides, known as Girl Scouts in the USA after 1912. In 1916 he organized the Wolf Cubs in Britain (known as Cub Scouts in the USA) for boys under the age of 11. In 1920 he was made world chief scout at the first international Boy Scout Jamboree, and in 1929 was created Baron Baden-Powell. He published *Scouting for Boys* in 1908.

Bader, Sir Douglas (Robert Stuart) [**bah**der] (1910–82) Wartime aviator, born in London, UK. Commissioned from Cranwell in 1930, he lost both legs in a flying accident in 1931 and was invalided out, but overcame his disability and returned to the RAF in 1939. He commanded the first RAF Canadian Fighter Squadron, evolving tactics that contributed to victory in the Battle of Britain, but was captured in August 1941 after a collision with an enemy aircraft over Béthune. A great pilot and leader of what Churchill called 'the Few', he set an example of fortitude and heroism that became a legend. He was knighted in 1976.

badger A nocturnal mammal, usually grey-brown with a black and white head; pointed face; length 0·5–1 m/1½–3¾ ft; lives in burrows; species include the **Old World badger** (*Meles*), **hog badger** (*Arctonyx*), **stink badger** (*Mydaus*), **ferret badger** (*Melogale*), all native to European and Asian woodlands; also the **American badger** (*Taxidea*) from open country in North America. (Family: Mustelidae, 8 species.)

Badlands Arid region of SW South Dakota and NW Nebraska, USA; an area of barren, eroded landscapes and fossil deposits E of the Black Hills; Badlands National Monument; several other areas in these states are also described in this way.

badminton An indoor court game played by two or four people using rackets and a shuttlecock. Its name derives from Badminton House, the seat of the Duke of Beaufort, where the Duke's family and guests played in the 19th-c; but a similar game was being played in China over 2000 years ago. It developed from the children's game of *battledore and shuttlecock*. The object is to volley the shuttle over the central net. Points are won by forcing errors when you are the server.

Badoglio, Pietro [bahdolyoh] (1871–1956) Italian soldier and prime minister (1943–4), born in Grazzano Monferrato, N Italy. He served in World War 1, and was promoted field-marshal in 1926. He was Governor-General of Libya (1928–33) and directed the conquest of Abyssinia, now Ethiopia (1935–6). On Italy's entry into World War 2 in 1940 he was made commander-in-chief, but resigned during the Greek humiliation of Italian arms in Albania. Following Mussolini's downfall (1943) he formed a non-Fascist government, negotiated an armistice with the Allies, declared war on Germany, and held power till 1944.

Baedeker, Karl [baydeker] (1801–59) Publisher, born in Essen, W Germany. He started his own publishing business at Koblenz in 1827, and is best known for the authoritative guidebooks which still bear his name, published since 1872 at Leipzig.

Baeyer, Johann (Friedrich Wilhelm Adolf) von [bayer] (1835–1917) Organic chemist, born in Berlin, Germany. He studied at Heidelberg, and became professor of chemistry at Strasbourg (1872) and Munich (1875–1915). His researches covered many aspects of chemistry, notably the synthesis of the dye indigo and the elucidation of its structure, the mechanism of photosynthesis, the condensation of phenols and aldehydes, the polyacetylenes, the stability of polymethylene rings, the terpenes, and the basicity of organic oxygen compounds. He was awarded the 1905 Nobel Prize for Chemistry.

Baez, Joan [biyez] (1941–) Folksinger, born in Staten Island, New York City, USA. During the revival of traditional folk music in the 1960s she became popular with young audiences for her songs and political views. She gave free concerts supporting civil rights, UNESCO, and anti-Vietnam war rallies, and was imprisoned briefly (1967) for refusing to pay tax towards war expenses. In 1968 she published an autobiography, *Daybreak*, and a further volume *And A Voice To Sing With* appeared in 1987. A legendary protest figure for over three decades, she continues to perform at fund-raising events around the world.

Baffin, William (c.1584–1622) Navigator, probably born in London, UK. From 1612 to 1616 he was pilot on several expeditions in search of the Northwest Passage. The most significant of these were the voyages under the command of Robert Bylot in the *Discovery*, during which they visited Hudson Strait (1615), and were the first Europeans to find Baffin Bay (1615) and Lancaster, Smith, and Jones Sounds (1616). He was possibly the first person to determine a degree of longitude at sea by lunar observation. Thereafter he carried out extensive surveys of the Red Sea (1616–21), and was killed at the siege of Ormuz.

Baffin Bay Ice-blocked Arctic gulf between Greenland (E) and Baffin, Bylot, Devon, and Ellesmere Is (W); length c.1125 km/700 mi; width 110–650 km/70–400 mi; depth over 2400 m/8100 ft; navigation only in summer; first entered by John Davis, 1585; explored by William Baffin, 1615; important whaling area in the 1800s; seafowl and fur-bearing animals along coast.

Baffin Island Largest island in the Canadian Arctic Archipelago, in the Arctic Ocean; separated from Labrador by the Hudson Strait, and from Greenland to the E by the Davis Strait and Baffin Bay; became part of new Nunavut territory in 1999; area 318 186 sq km/122 820 sq mi; length c.1600 km/1000 mi; width 209–725 km/130–450 mi; irregular coastline, with several peninsulas and deep bays; mostly a plateau rising to c.915 m/3000 ft; first visited by Frobisher, 1576–8; Iqaluit (formerly Frobisher Bay) is capital of Nunavut; other chief settlements are Lake Harbour, Pond Inlet; population mainly Inuit.

BAFTA *British Academy of Film and Television Arts*

bagatelle [bagatel] A restricted form of billiards, played on a table with nine numbered cups instead of pockets. Popular in the UK, especially in the N of England, the Midlands, and N Wales, it is played in many different forms on a rectangular table, with measurements varying according to local conditions.

Bagehot, Walter [bajuht] (1826–77) Economist and journalist, born in Langport, Somerset, SW England, UK. He graduated in mathematics at University College London, was called to the bar in 1852, and succeeded his father-in-law, James Wilson (1805–60), as editor of the *Economist* in 1860. His *English Constitution* (1867) is still a standard work. His *Physics and Politics* (1872) applied the theory of evolution to politics. He advocated many constitutional reforms, including the introduction of life peers.

Bagerat [bageraht] The former city of Khalifatabad, founded in the 15th-c by General Ulugh Khan Jahan in the S Ganges delta, present-day Bangladesh; a world heritage site. Its mosques and palaces spring from a unique marriage of local architectural styles with that of imperial Delhi.

Baggara *Baqqarah*

Baghdad [bagdad] 33°20N 44°26E, pop (2000e) 6 247 000. Capital city of Iraq, on R Tigris; a commercial and transportation centre; founded, 762; enclosed on three sides by ancient walls; sacked by Mongols, 1258; later under Mongol, then Turkish rule; independent capital, 20th-c; badly damaged through bombing during the Gulf War, 1991; attacked by US-led coalition forces (Mar 2003) during the Iraq War; UN headquarters damaged in terrorist bomb attack (Aug 2003); Red Cross headquarters damaged during series of bomb blasts in city centre (Oct 2003); airport; railway; university (1958); oil refining, distilling, tanning, tobacco, textiles, gum, brick, tiles, metal industry, cement; Abbasid palace, Mustansiriyah law college (13th-c).

Baghlan [baglahn] pop (2000e) 1 080 000 area 17 109 sq km/6604 sq mi. Province in NEC Afghanistan; N of Kabul; capital, Baghlan Jadid, pop (2000e) 82 000; Salang Pass and Tunnel, on the main Russian supply route to Kabul, the focus of resistance by Mujahideen guerrillas during the Russian occupation of Afghanistan (1979–89).

Bagley, Sarah (1806–47) Labour leader, of whose early life nothing is known. She was active during the 1830s and 1840s in the mills of Lowell, Massachusetts, where she led 'turn-outs' (strikes) and organized the Female Labor Reform Association. She played a major role in the successful campaign for a 10-hour working day in Massachusetts.

bagpipes A musical instrument of great antiquity consisting of a bag (usually of sheepskin) which the player fills with air through a blow-pipe or bellows, and squeezes with his arm so that the air then passes through the sounding pipes. One of these, the chanter, is fitted with a reed and finger-holes, and is used for playing melodies; two or three other pipes supply the continuous accompanimental drone which is a distinctive (and to some ears maddening) feature of the bagpipes. The Highlands and Lowlands of Scotland have their different types of bagpipes, as also do Ireland and Northumberland, and various types of bagpipes are found throughout Europe.

Baguio [bagioh] 16°25N 120°37E, pop (2000e) 191 000. Summer capital of the Philippines, in Benguet province, NW Luzon I; mountain resort town and official summer residence of the president; two universities (1911, 1948); military academy; gold, copper; summer festival.

Baha'i [bahiy] A religious faith arising out of a 19th-c anti-clerical movement in Iran, when Mirza Husayn-Ali (1817–92), known as Baha'u'llah ('Glory of God'), declared himself the prophet foretold by the founder of the Babi movement, Mirza Ali-Mohammed (1819–50). Baha'ism teaches the oneness of God, the unity of all faiths, the inevitable unification of humankind, the harmony of all people, universal education, and obedience to government. It has no priesthood, and its adherents are expected to teach the faith. Local assemblies meet for informal devotions in homes or rented halls. There is little formal ritual, but there are ceremonies for marriage, funerals,

Bahamas

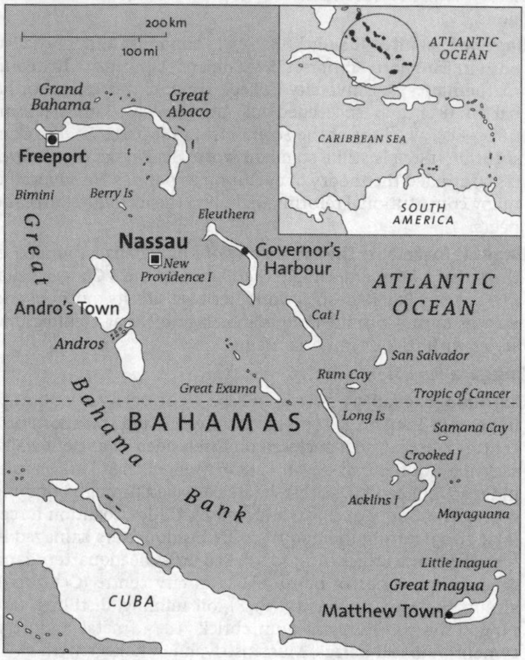

☐ International Airport

official name **Commonwealth of the Bahamas**

Local name Bahamas

Timezone GMT −5

Area 13 934 km²/5378 sq mi

Population total (2002e) 309 000

Status Independent state within the Commonwealth

Date of independence 1973

Capital Nassau

Language English (official)

Ethnic groups African (85%), European/N American descent (15%)

Religions Baptist (29%), Anglican (29%), Roman Catholic (23%)

Physical features Coral archipelago of 700 islands and 2400 uninhabited cays, forming a chain extending c.800 km/500 mi SE from the coast of Florida; population centres on the two oceanic banks of Little and Great Bahama; highest point, Mt Alvernia, 120 m/394 ft.

Climate Sub-tropical; average temperatures 21°C (Jan) and 27°C (Jul); mean annual rainfall 750–1500 mm/30–60 in; hurricanes frequent (Jun–Nov).

Currency 1 Bahamian Dollar (BA$, B$) = 100 cents

Economy Market economy based on tourism; important financial centre (no income tax); oil refining, fishing, rum and liqueur distilling; cement; pharmaceuticals.

GDP (2002e) $4·59 bn, per capita $15 300

Human Development Index (2002) 0·826

History Visited by Columbus in 1492, but first permanent European settlement not until 1647 by British and Bermudan religious refugees; British Crown Colony from 1717; independence, 1973; governed by a bicameral Parliament.

Head of State
(British monarch represented by governor-general)
1988–92 Sir Henry Taylor
1992–5 Clifford Darling
1995– Orville Turnquest

Head of Government
1973–92 Sir Lynden O Pindling
1992–2002 Hubert Alexander Ingraham
2002– Perry Christie

and the naming of babies. Its headquarters is in Haifa, Israel. There were around 7.5 million adherents in 2004.

Bahamas *see panel*

Bahasa Indonesia [bahasa] The Malay dialect of the S Malay Peninsula, which has been the standard language of Malaysia since 1949; also called **Bahasa Malaysia**. It was first given official status by the Japanese occupiers during World War 2. It is often referred to simply as **Indonesian**.

Bahia [baeea] pop (2000e) 13 536 000; area 561 026 sq km/216 556 sq mi. State in Nordeste region, NE Brazil, bounded E by the Atlantic; capital Salvador; agriculture, chemical and petrochemical industries, oil; Brazil first claimed for Portugal by Cabral in 1500, when he stepped ashore N of Pôrto Seguro in SE Bahia.

Bahía Blanca [baeea blangka] 38°45S 62°15W, pop (2000e) 302 500. City in Buenos Aires province, E Argentina; at the head of the Bahía Blanca Bay, SW of Buenos Aires; includes five ports on R Naposta, including naval base of Puerto Belgrano; founded in 1828; university (1956); airport; railway; oil refining, wool and food processing, timber trade, fishing.

Bahrain *p.129*

Baikal or **Baykal, Lake** [biykal] area 31 500 sq km/12 160 sq mi. Crescent-shaped lake in S Siberia, Russia; largest freshwater lake in Eurasia, and deepest in the world; length (SW–NE) 636 km/395 mi; width 24–80 km/15–50 mi; maximum depth 1620 m/5315 ft; in a deep tectonic basin, fed by over 300 rivers and streams; only outlet, the R Angara; contains 22 islands, the largest being Ostrov Ol'khon (length 51 km/32 mi); hot springs on the shores; earthquakes frequent; freezes over (Jan–Apr); Trans-Siberian railway passes the S shore; measures to control serious pollution introduced since 1971.

Baikonur or **Baykonyr Cosmodrome** [biykonoor] A Russian space centre constructed in the 1950s in Karaganda oblast, Kazakhstan. It was from here that the first artificial satellite and manned space flights were launched, and in 1998 the first element of the International Space Station, the Russian-built Zarya control module, was launched from there. Russia is to lease part of this complex for 20 years, and a new Cosmodrome is planned for Svobodnyy in the far East.

bail The freeing from custody of a person charged with a crime and awaiting trial. There are often conditions imposed to secure the person's attendance at a court on a future date, and, in certain circumstances, these conditions may relate to other matters (such as the non-interference with witnesses). Frequently the security involves a sum of money pledged by the person or a guarantor (a *surety*) with the police or a court. This money is liable to be forfeited in the event of the accused person's non-appearance. There are several differences in the operation of the bail procedure between legal systems; for example, in Scotland bail may be granted only on conditions which do not (except in special circumstances) include a pledge or a deposit of money. Breach of any such condition is itself an offence.

Bailey, David (Royston) (1938–) Photographer, born in London, UK. Originally specializing in fashion photography as a freelance from 1959, his creative approach soon extended to portraits expressing the spirit of the 1960s and to some outstanding studies of the nude. He writes extensively on all aspects of his craft and has been a director of televison commercials and documentaries since the 1970s. His publications include *Nudes 1981–84* (1984) and *The Lady is a Tramp* (1995). In 1999 a major retrospective of his work, 'Birth of the Cool', opened in London.

Bahrain

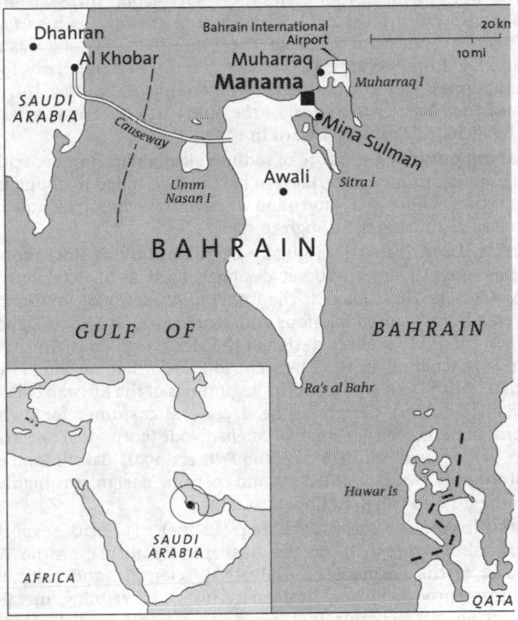

☐ International Airport

official name **State of Bahrain**

Local name al-Bahrayn

Timezone GMT +3

Area 678 km^2/262 sq mi

Population total (2002e) 672 000

Status Independent state

Date of independence 1971

Capital Manama

Languages Arabic (official), Farsi, Urdu, and English

Ethnic groups Bahraini Arab (63%), Asian (13%), Arab (10%), Iranian (9%)

Religions Muslim (Shi'ite 65%), Sunni 35%)

Physical features Island of Bahrain c.48 km/30 mi long, 13–16 km/8–10 mi wide, area 562 km^2/217 sq mi; highest point Jabal Dukhan, 135 m/443 ft; largely bare and infertile.

Climate Temperate (Dec–Mar); hot and humid (particularly Jun–Sep); cool N/NE winds with a little rain (Dec–Mar); average annual rainfall 35 mm/1·4 in; average annual temperature 19°C (Jan), 36°C (Jul).

Currency 1 Bahrain Dinar (BD) = 1000 fils

Economy Major centre for oil trading, banking, commerce.

GDP (2002e) $9·91 bn, per capita $15 100

Human Development Index (2002) 0·831

History Flourishing centre of trade during 2000–1800 BC; treaty of protection with the UK, 1861; independence in 1971, with a constitutional monarchy governed by an Emir; National Assembly dissolved in 1975 and not yet revived; historic territorial dispute with Qatar over the Hawar Is began with the brief occupation of Fasht al-Dibal by Qatari troops, 1986; joined UN coalition during the Iraqi invasion of Kuwait, 1990; became monarchy, 2002.

Head of State (Emir; King, from 2002)
1869–1935 Isa I
1923–42 Hamad
1942–61 Salman II
1961–9 Shaikh Isa II bin Sulman al-Khalifa
1999– Shaikh Hamad II bin Isa al-Khalifa

Head of Government
1971– Shaikh Khalifa bin Sulman al-Khalifa

Bailey bridge A prefabricated bridge used by combat engineers, which can be rapidly constructed on the battlefield. The system was devised by British engineer Sir Donald Bailey (1901–85) during World War 2, and consists of a basic diamond braced unit of welded steel, 3 × 1·5 m/10 × 5 ft square, which can be easily manipulated by a squad of six men and joined together to make complex bridging structures.

bailiff An officer of the sheriff or the county court who is responsible for executing warrants, processes, and writs. He may also seize goods under a 'warrant of execution' as a method of obtaining payment, such as for unpaid rent. The equivalent position in Scotland is that of the Sheriff officer whose duty is to serve, process, and execute writs and warrants of the Sheriff Court. Many Sheriff officers are also messengers-at-arms, which empowers them to carry out the same duties for the Court of Session and the High Court of Justiciary.

Baillie, Dame Isobel [**bay**lee] (1895–1983) Soprano, born in Hawick, Scottish Borders, SE Scotland, UK. She worked as an assistant in a music shop, then as a clerk in Manchester Town Hall, and made her debut with the Hallé Orchestra in 1921. After studies in Milan, she won immediate success in her opening season in London in 1923. Regarded as one of the 20th-century's greatest oratorio singers, she gave over 1000 performances of the *Messiah*. She was made a dame in 1978.

Baily, Francis (1774–1844) Astronomer, born in Newbury, West Berkshire, S England, UK. He made a large fortune as a stockbroker, and on his retirement in 1825 devoted himself to astronomy. In 1936 he detected the phenomenon known as *Baily's beads* – a broken ring of bright points around the edge of the Moon, formed in a total solar eclipse by the Sun's rays shining through the Moon's valleys at the moment of totality. He also calculated the mean density of the Earth.

Bainbridge, Dame Beryl (Margaret) (1934–) British writer, born in Liverpool, Merseyside, NW England, UK. She began writing in the 1960s, and became known for her terse, black comedies, such as *The Dressmaker* (1973, filmed 1979), *Filthy Lucre* (1986) and *An Awfully Big Adventure* (1989, filmed 1995). Several novels tackle historical subjects, notably *Young Adolf* (1978), *Watson's Apology* (1984), and *The Birthday Boys* (1991). She has also written several plays, both for theatre and television. Later works include collections of her journalistic essays (1993) and stories (1994), and the novels *Every Man for Himself* (1996, Whitbread), *Master Georgie* (1998), and *According to Queeney* (2001). She was made a dame in 2000.

Baird, John Logie (1888–1946) Electrical engineer and television pioneer, born in Helensburgh, Argyll and Bute, W Scotland, UK. He studied electrical engineering at Glasgow University, later settling in Hastings (1922), where he began research into the possibilities of television. In 1926 he gave the first demonstration of a television image. His 30-line mechanically scanned system was adopted by the BBC in 1929, being superseded in 1936 by his 240-line system. In the following year the BBC chose a rival 405-line system with electronic scanning made by Marconi-EMI. Other lines of research initiated by Baird in the 1920s included radar and infra-red television (*Noctovision*); he also succeeded in producing three-dimensional and coloured images (1944), as well as projection onto a screen and stereophonic sound.

Baisakhi [biy**sah**ki] A Sikh festival (generally celebrated on 13 Apr) commemorating the founding in 1699 of the Khalsa order of baptized Sikhs by the tenth guru of Sikhism, Guru Gobind Singh.

Baja California [**ba**ha], Eng **Lower California** A long peninsula in NW Mexico, bounded E by the Gulf of California, S and W by the Pacific Ocean, and N by the USA; length 1220 km/760 mi; area c.144 000 sq km/55 000 sq mi; divided into the states of Baja California Norte (pop (2000e) 1 998 000) and Baja California Sur (pop (2000e) 383 000); San Pedro Mártir Mts rise to 3095 m/10 154 ft; Colorado R flows into the N of the Gulf; geographical isolation much eased by highway completed in 1970s down the whole peninsula; chief towns, Mexicali, Ensenada, La

Paz; cotton, wheat, grapes, olives, sugar, cattle, food processing, fish packing, copper, tourism.

Bajazet *Bayezit I*

Baker, Sir Benjamin (1840–1907) Civil engineer, born in Keyford, Somerset, SW England, UK. In 1861 he entered into a long association with John Fowler as consulting engineer. They together designed the London Metropolitan Railway, Victoria Station, and many bridges, including the Forth Rail Bridge (1883–90) built on the cantilever principle, for which Baker was knighted. He was also consulting engineer for the Aswan Dam in Egypt (1902) and the Hudson River Tunnel in New York (1888–91).

Baker, Chet, popular name of **Chesney H Baker** (1929–88) Jazz trumpeter and singer, born in Yale, Oklahoma, USA. He played in US army bands (1946–52), then joined the Gerry Mulligan Quartet, and his brilliant interplay with Mulligan brought critical and popular success. As a leader, his signature tune became 'My Funny Valentine', which epitomized his image as a lonely, searching wanderer. His boyish good looks led to minor movie roles in the 1950s, but his erratic personal life made him a perpetual outsider. A full-length documentary film, *Let's Get Lost* (1987), shadowed him on his incessant round of European jazz clubs, with juxtaposed clips of his bright-eyed youth. He died in Amsterdam, purportedly by leaping from his hotel window, but suspicions remain that he was pushed.

Baker, James A(ddison), III (1930–) US secretary of state (1989–92), born in Houston, Texas, USA. He studied at Princeton and the University of Texas Law School, saw service in the US Marines, and became a successful corporate lawyer. He was appointed under-secretary of commerce (1975–6) in the Gerald Ford administration, and managed Ford's 1976 presidential and George Bush's 1979 Republican Party nomination campaigns. President Reagan appointed him White House chief-of-staff in 1981 and treasury secretary in 1985. After directing Bush's victorious presidential campaign in 1988, he became secretary of state in 1989, and in 1992 returned to the White House as chief-of-staff, to run Bush's re-election campaign.

Baker, Dame Janet (Abbott) (1933–) Mezzo-soprano, born in Hatfield, South Yorkshire, N England, UK. She studied music in London in 1953, making her debut in 1956 at Glyndebourne. She has enjoyed an extensive operatic career, especially in early Italian opera and the works of Benjamin Britten; she retired from opera in 1982. As a concert performer, she is noted for her interpretations of Mahler and Elgar. She became a Companion of Honour in 1994.

Baker (of Dorking), Kenneth (Wilfred), Baron (1934–) British Conservative statesman. He studied at Oxford, in 1960 entered local politics, and in 1968 was elected an MP. After holding junior posts (1970–4) he became parliamentary private secretary to Edward Heath as Leader of the Opposition. In the Margaret Thatcher administration he rose from minister of state in the Department of Trade to become secretary of state for the environment (1985–6) and for education (1986–9), responsible for introducing a controversial education reform bill. He was later appointed chairman of the Conservative Party (1989–90) and home secretary (1990–2). He was made a Companion of Honour in 1992, and a life peer in 1997.

Baker, Richard (Douglas James) (1925–) Broadcaster and author, born in London, UK. He studied in Cambridge, worked as an actor and teacher, and joined the BBC as an announcer in 1950. He became known as a television newsreader (1954–82), and as a commentator on major state occasions. He also introduced the television productions of BBC Promenade Concerts (1960–95), and has presented many radio series, such as *Start the Week with Richard Baker* (1970–87). He was BBC radio personality of the year in 1984. His books include *The Magic of Music* (1975), *London, a theme with variations* (1989), and *Richard Baker's Companion to Music* (1993).

Bakewell, Joan (Dawson) (1933–) Broadcaster and writer, born in Stockport, Greater Manchester, NW England, UK. She studied at Cambridge, and became known for her regular contributions and series on BBC television, such as *Late Night Line Up* (1965–72), *Holiday* (1974–8), and *Heart of the Matter* (1988–2000). Her ITV work included four series of *Reports Action* (1976–8), and she also did a great deal of radio broadcasting, such as *PM* (1979–81). Television critic of *The Times* (1976–81), she was a *Sunday Times* columnist (1988–90), and writes regularly for magazines. Her books include *The Complete Traveller* (1977) and *The Heart of the Heart of the Matter* (1996). She received the Richard Dimbleby Award in 1994.

baking powder A mixture of sodium bicarbonate, tartaric acid, and potassium tartrate, used in baking. It is added to dough (a mixture of flour and water), and when heated, carbon dioxide is released, causing the dough to rise.

Bakst, Léon [bahkst], originally **Lev Samuilovich Rosenberg** (1866–1924) Painter and set designer, born in St Petersburg, NW Russia. He studied at the Imperial Academy of Arts in St Petersburg, painted religious and genre works in Moscow, and then turned to scenery design at the Hermitage Court Theatre in St Petersburg. In 1908 he went to Paris, where he was associated with Diaghilev from the beginnings of the Russian ballet (Ballets Russes), designing the decor and costumes for their productions such as *Carnaval*, *Shéhérazade* (both 1910), *Spectre de la Rose* (1911), and *The Sleeping Princess* (1921). Bakst's innovatory work, which unified set and costume design, was highly influential in ballet and opera staging.

Baku [bakoo] 40°22N 49°53E, pop (2000e) 1 174 000. Seaport capital of Azerbaijan; on the Apsheron Peninsula, on the W coast of the Caspian Sea; industrial, scientific, and cultural centre; airport; railway; university (1919); oil refining, metal-working, petrochemicals, tyres, solar research and development; oil pipeline to Batumi on the Black Sea; Kiz-Kalasyi (Virgin's Tower, 12th-c), Shirvan Shah's Palace. The walled city is a world heritage site.

Bakunin, Mikhail Aleksandrovich [bakoonin] (1814–76) Anarchist, born near Moscow. He took part in the German revolutionary movement (1848–9) and was condemned to death. Sent to Siberia in 1855, he escaped to Japan, and arrived in England in 1861. In September 1870 he attempted an abortive rising at Lyon. As a leading anarchist, he was the main opponent of Karl Marx in the Communist International, and at the Hague Congress in 1872 was outvoted and expelled.

Balabanov, Aleksei (1959–) Film director, born in Yekaterinburg, W Russia (formerly Sverdlovsk, USSR). In 1983, after studying languages in Gorky and working as a translator for the Soviet Army, he began working as a jobbing director at Sverdlovsk Film Studios. His directorial debut came in 1989 with *Yegor and Nastya*. Later films include *Brat* (1997, The Brother), the award-winning *Pro urodov i lyudej* (1998, Of Freaks and Men), and *Brat II* (2000, The Brother II). Balabanov's films are a dark portrayal of post-communist Russian society, focusing on his country's abuse of capitalism and endemic racketeering.

Balaclava, Battle of (1854) A battle fought between British and Russian forces during the early stages of the Crimean War. The Russian attack on the British base at Balaclava was unsuccessful, but the British sustained the heavier losses.

Balakirev, Mili Alekseyevich [balakiryef] (1837–1910) Composer, born in Nizhni Novgorod, W Russia. He turned to composing after an early career as a concert pianist, and became the leader of the national Russian school of music. He founded the Petersburg Free School of Music (1862), and was director of the Imperial Capella (1883). His compositions include two symphonies, a symphonic poem *Tamara*, and the oriental fantasy for piano, *Islamey*.

balalaika [balaliyka] A Russian musical instrument: a lute with a triangular body, flat back, long neck, and three strings which are strummed by the player's fingers. It is used to accompany singing and dancing, or as a member of larger ensembles.

balance of payments The difference, for a country, between the income and expenditure arising out of its international trading activities. The *current account* includes the country's income from selling goods abroad (exporting), offset by its expenditure on goods imported. The difference between these two totals is the **trade balance**. Also included are 'invisible' services bought and sold abroad, such as air transport, banking, insurance, shipping, and tourism. The *capital account* deals with private and corporate investment abroad, borrowing and lending, and government financial transactions. **A balance of payments deficit** drains a nation's reserves of convertible currency and gold, and can lead to a devaluation of its currency.

balance sheet A statement of the assets and liabilities of a firm or organization at a moment in time, normally the end of a financial year. Assets include physical objects including land and buildings, plant and equipment, stocks of materials, work in progress and inventories of output not yet sold, and financial assets including cash and bank balances, securities held, and trade credit extended. Liabilities include long- and short-term debt, taxes due for payment, and trade credit. A solvent company's liabilities are less than these assets; to equate the two sides of the balance sheet the difference is treated as a debt to the shareholders of a company or members of an organization. Some assets and liabilities, such as bank balances and securities held, can be objectively valued. For others, such as buildings or inventories, and debts owing from other firms which are not certain to pay up, values have to be estimated using professional judgement. The accountancy bodies provide guidelines on how accounts should be drawn up. Balance sheets, which show the state of affairs at one time, should not be confused with profit-and-loss accounts, which show income and expenditure over a long period such as a financial year.

Balanchine, George [baluhncheen], originally **Georgi Melitonovich Balanchivadze** (1904–83) Ballet dancer and choreographer, born in St Petersburg, NW Russia. He studied at the ballet school of the Imperial Theatres, then formed his own small company. In 1924 he defected with a group of dancers during a European tour, and after performing in London as the Soviet State Dancers, Diaghilev took them into his Ballets Russes in Paris, when he changed his name to Balanchine. In 1925 he succeeded Nijinska as choreographer and ballet-master. He helped to found Les Ballets Russes de Monte Carlo in 1932, and Les Ballets the following year, then opened the School of American Ballet in New York City in 1934. After the war he directed a private company, the Ballet Society, which in 1948 emerged as the New York City Ballet. With that company he created over 90 works of enormous variety. He was also a successful musical comedy and film choreographer.

Balaton, Lake [boloton] area 598 sq km/231 sq mi. Lake in WC Hungary; length 77 km/48 mi; width 8–14 km/5–9 mi; largest and shallowest lake in C Europe; Hungary's largest recreation area, with resorts at Siófok, Keszthely, and Balatonfüred (spa with carbonic waters).

Balboa, Vasco Núñez de [balboha] (1475–1519) Explorer, born in Jerez de los Caballeros, SW Spain. In 1511 he joined an expedition to Darién as a stowaway. Taking advantage of an insurrection, he took command, founded a colony at Darién, and extended Spanish influence into neighbouring areas. On one of these expeditions he climbed a peak and sighted the Pacific Ocean (1513), the first European to do so, and took possession for Spain. The governorship was granted in 1514 to Pedro Arias Dávila (?1440–1531), for whom Balboa undertook many successful expeditions, but after a disagreement in 1519 Balboa was beheaded.

bald cypress *swamp cypress*

bald eagle A large eagle (length 80–100 cm/30–40 in), native to North America (*Haliaeetus leucocephalus*); numbers now declining; found near water; eats fish, birds, and mammals. The name refers to the white plumage on its head and neck. The national symbol of the USA, it is also known as the **American eagle**. (Family: Accipitridae.)

Balder, Baldur, or **Baldr** [bawlder, balder] Norse god, the most handsome and gentle of the children of Odin and Frigga; the name means 'bright'. He taught human beings the use of herbs for healing. Frigga made a spell so that nothing which grew out of or upon the Earth could harm him, but Loki made Hodur (Balder's blind brother) throw a dart of mistletoe at him. Balder died, to return after Ragnarok to the new Earth.

baldness Commonly described as permanent loss of hair from the front and/or top of the head, usually in men, because of the degeneration and reduction in the size of hair follicles. Genetic factors, ageing, and androgens (eunuchs are seldom bald) may be causative agents. There is no effective cure. An improper diet, certain endocrine and skin disorders, as well as some chemical or physical agents may damage the hair follicles leading to either permanent or temporary baldness in either sex at any age. Some other primates also develop baldness, such as the oukari monkey of South America.

baldpate *wigeon*

Baldwin I (1172–c.1205) Emperor of Constantinople, born in Valenciennes, N France. He succeeded his father as Count of Flanders (in 1194) and Hainault (in 1195). In 1202 he joined the fourth Crusade, and in 1204 was chosen the first Latin emperor of Constantinople. The Greeks, invoking the aid of the Bulgarians, rose and took Adrianople. Baldwin laid siege to the town, but was defeated in 1205 and died in captivity.

Baldwin, James (Arthur) (1924–87) Writer, born in Harlem, New York City, USA. After a variety of jobs he moved to Europe, where he lived (mainly in Paris) from 1948 to 1957, before returning to the USA as a civil rights activist. His novels, in which autobiographical elements appear, include *Go Tell it on the Mountain* (1954), *Giovanni's Room* (1957), and *Just Above My Head* (1979). Other works include collections of essays and plays – *The Amen Corner* (1955), *Blues for Mr Charlie* (1964), and *The Women at the Well* (1972).

Baldwin, Mark (Phillip) (1954–) Choreographer and dancer, born in Fiji. Raised in New Zealand, he studied at the University of Auckland, New Zealand, and became a dancer with the New Zealand Ballet and Australian Dance Theatre before joining the Rambert Dance Company in London (1982–92), also as choreographer (1992–4). He became resident choreographer with Sadlers Wells (1994–5), established the Mark Baldwin Dance Company (1993–2001), then became artistic director of the Rambert (2002–). In 1996 he received the Time Out Dance Award and the Grand Prix International Special Judges' Prize for his video *Danse 8*.

Baldwin (of Bewdley), Stanley Baldwin, 1st Earl (1867–1947) British statesman and prime minister (1923–4, 1924–9, 1935–7), born in Bewdley, Hereford and Worcester, WC England, UK. He studied at Cambridge, and became vice-chairman of the family iron and steel business. A Conservative MP in 1908, he became President of the Board of Trade (1921), and unexpectedly succeeded Bonar Law as premier. His period of office included the General Strike (1926) and was interrupted by the Ramsay MacDonald coalition (1931–5), in which he served as Lord President of the Council. He skilfully avoided a party split by his India Act (1935), but the Hoare-Laval pact and the policy of non-intervention in Spain (1936) came to be regarded as betrayals of the League of Nations. He displayed considerable resolution during the constitutional crisis culminating in Edward VIII's abdication (1937). He had the party politician's sure touch in domestic matters, but was criticized for his apparent failure to recognize the threat from Nazi Germany. He resigned and was made an earl in 1937.

Balearic Islands *p.132*

baleen A fibrous material from the mouth of some species of whale; forms a sieve during feeding; formerly used in manufacturing, when strong, light, flexible material was needed (eg to strengthen women's corsets); also known as **whalebone** (though it is not in fact bone).

Balenciaga, Cristóbal [balenthiahga] (1895–1972) Fashion designer, born in Guetaria, N Spain. He trained as a tailor, and in 1915 opened dressmaking and tailoring shops of his own in Madrid and Barcelona. He left Spain for Paris in 1937 because of the Spanish Civil War, and became a fashion

Balearic Islands

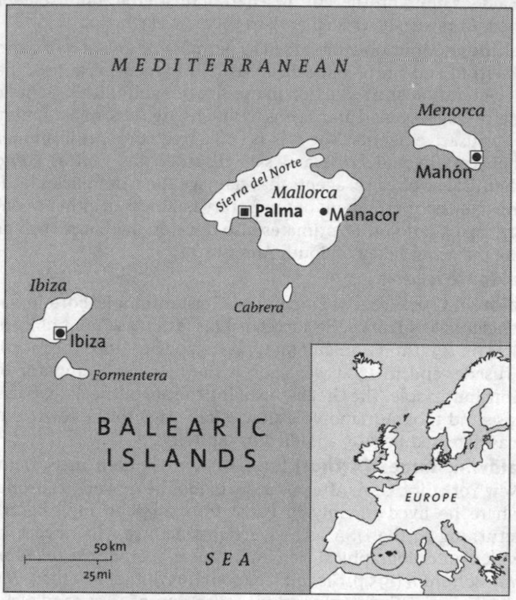

□ International Airport

[baliarik], Span **Islas Baleares**
Local name Islas Baleares
Area 5014 km²/1935 sq mi
Population total (2000e) 712 000
Status Province of Spain
Capital Palma de Mallorca
Physical features Archipelago of five major islands and 11 islets in the Mediterranean, near the E coast of Spain; E group of islands consists of Mallorca (Majorca), Menorca, Cabrera; Ibiza and Formentera (W group); popular tourist resorts.
Climate Continental; average annual temperatures 11°C (Jan), 25°C (Jul); average annual rainfall 347 mm/14 in.
Currency 1 euro = 100 cents (formerly, 1 Peseta (Pta, Pa) = 100 céntimos).
Economy Tourism; fruit, wine, grain, cattle, fishing, textiles, chemicals, cork, timber.

designer, producing clothes noted for dramatic simplicity and elegant design. He retired in 1968.

Balewa, Sir Abubakar Tafawa [balaywa] (1912–66) Nigerian statesman and first federal prime minister (1957–66), born in Bauchi, C Nigeria. A member of the Northern People's Congress, he entered the Federal Assembly in 1947, was minister of works (1952–3) and of transport (1953–7), then became premier. He was knighted when Nigeria became independent in 1960, and was assassinated in the military uprising of 1966.

Balfour, Arthur James Balfour, 1st Earl [balfer] (1848–1930) British statesman and philosopher, born in Whittingehame, East Lothian, E Scotland, UK. He studied at Cambridge, and entered parliament in 1874 as a Conservative MP for Hertford. He was returned for East Manchester (1885), was secretary for Scotland (1886), chief secretary for Ireland (1887), and First Lord of the Treasury and Leader of the House of Commons (1892–3). His premiership saw the end of the Boer War (1902), the Education Act (1905), and the establishment of the Committee of Imperial Defence. In 1911 he resigned the leadership of the House owing to the constitutional crisis. He followed Churchill to the Admiralty (1915) and served under Lloyd George as foreign secretary (1916–19). He was responsible for the famous *Balfour declaration* (1917) which promised Zionists a national home in Palestine, and as Lord President of the Council (1921) was responsible for the controversial note cancelling Allied war debts to America.

Bali [bahlee] pop (2000e) 3 265 000; area 5561 sq km/2146 sq mi. Island province of Indonesia, between Java (W) and Lombok (E); mountainous, with peaks rising to 3142 m/10 308 ft at Gunung Agung (E); chiefly Hindu population; Dutch control by 1908; capital, Denpasar; rice, cattle, coffee, copra, salt, onions, handicrafts; major tourist area, but tourism badly affected following terrorist bomb attack which killed 180 in Kuta (Oct 2002).

balkanization (*balkan*, Turkish 'mountain') The fragmentation of a region into smaller, often hostile, political units; specifically in the Balkans, where division is enhanced by their often mountainous geography. As the Ottoman empire weakened its hold on the Balkans in the 19th-c, ancient power struggles emerged. During the Ottoman period, most Albanians had converted to Islam, while most Serbs had adhered to a form of Christian orthodoxy. New political boundaries were drawn up after World Wars 1 and 2; a degree of autonomy and national independence was allowed to some groups, furthering ethnic separatism. This contributed to the polarization of ethnic groups into religious, cultural, geographic, and economic factions. On Tito's death in 1980, his presidency was replaced by an 8-man collective state presidency, but after the collapse of communism in 1990 the Balkans fragmented once again, leading to economic collapse, military offensives, and the 'ethnic cleansing' of the 1990s.

Balkans (Turkish, 'mountains') Mountainous peninsula in SE Europe (the **Balkan Peninsula**), and the countries it contains; lies between the Adriatic Sea (W), Ionian Sea (SW), Black Sea (E), Aegean Sea (SE), and Mediterranean Sea (S); partly bounded N by the Danube R and its tributaries; area c.500 000 sq km/200 000 sq mi; chief ranges are the Carpathian, Balkan, Rhodope, and Pindus Mountains, and branches of the Dinaric Alps; chief land pathway (via the Bosphorus) between E and C Europe and the Middle East; Balkan countries (some of which extend to the N of the peninsula proper) are Albania, Bosnia-Herzegovina, Bulgaria, Croatia, Greece, Macedonia, Romania, Slovenia, Yugoslavia; the ethnic, religious, and political mix in the region, chiefly comprising Slavs (C), Turks (SE), Romanians (NE), Albanians (SW), and Greeks (S), has brought a history of conflict recorded since classical times; Ottoman Empire supreme 15th–18th-c; partition of region into modern states, especially in 19th-c, with much subsequent instability, notably the Balkan Wars (1912–13) and the 1990s conflict in former Yugoslavia.

Balkan Wars (1912–13) A series of complex military campaigns fought in the Balkans. In 1912, Bulgaria, Serbia, Greece, and Montenegro attacked Turkey, securing swift victories. A preliminary peace was drawn up by the Great Powers (Britain, France, Germany, Austro-Hungary, Russia) in May 1913, in which Turkey surrendered most of her European territories on condition that a new state of Albania was created. Disputes between the Balkan allies over the spoils of war led to a second war (June–July 1913), in which Bulgaria attacked her former allies, and was defeated. As a result of the two wars, Turkish territory in Europe was reduced to an area around Adrianople and Constantinople, Albania was established, Serbia and Montenegro almost doubled in size, and tension among the Great Powers in Europe was considerably increased. The Balkan Wars prepared the way for World War 1 by giving impetus to Serbian desires to annex parts of Austria-Hungary, by stiffening Austrian resolution to crush Serbia, and by giving causes of dissatisfaction to Bulgaria and Turkey.

Balkhash, Lake [balkash] area 17 000–22 300 sq km/6500–8500 sq mi. Crescent-shaped lake in SE Kazakhstan, 160 km/100 mi W of the Chinese border; length 605 km/376 mi; maximum width 74 km/46 mi; maximum depth 26 m/85 ft; no outlet; salt extraction, fishing, copper; chief harbours, Burylbaytal, Burlyu-Tobe; gradually shrinking.

Ball, Michael (Ashley) (1962–) Actor and singer, born in the West Midlands, C England, UK. He studied at the Guildford School of Acting (1981–4), then made his professional debut. His first starring role was in *The Pirates of Penzance* (1985, Manchester Opera House), and he made his West End debut in *Les Miserables* later that year. Other major productions include *Phantom of the Opera* (1987), *Aspects of Love* (1989, Broadway debut 1990), and *Passion* (1996). Television work includes his own series (1993, 1994) and he has made many recordings. The Variety Club of Great Britain voted him Most Promising Artiste in 1989 and he later received their award for Best Recording Artiste of 1998.

Balla, Giacomo (1871–1958) Artist, born in Turin, NW Italy. Largely self-taught, he was the master of the Futurists Boccioni and Severini. After a visit to Paris in 1900 he was strongly influenced by Impressionism and Divisionism. He was one of the founders of Futurism and a signatory to the 1910 Futurist Manifesto. Primarily concerned with conveying movement and speed in painterly terms, he achieved this by imitating time-lapse photography. By 1930, he was painting in a more conventional style.

ballad An elementary poetic form, found in many languages, which tells and/or dramatizes a story in a lyrical stanza apt for oral transmission (and singing). Ballads have been created in many verse forms, but the most typical form in English has been the four-line stanza of varying length, rhyme scheme *abab*. This pattern of a four-beat line followed by a three-beat line is called *common measure*. The traditional, anonymous ballad sang of wars, feuds, and fatal love stories, often with chilling power and great pathos; the modern 'literary' ballad has been used by many 19th-c and 20th-c poets (eg Coleridge, Keats, D H Lawrence, Auden). Some popular American singers, including Johnny Cash and Bob Dylan, have composed their own ballads.

ballade [balad] An Old French form, consisting normally of three eight-line stanzas and a concluding four-line section, strictly rhymed. Used by de Machaut and Villon in the 14th–15th-c, and adopted in England by Chaucer and Gower, it was resurrected by a few sophisticated poets in the 19th–20th-c, notably Swinburne, Chesterton, and Belloc.

ballad opera A musical play with songs written to fit existing popular tunes. A peculiarly English form of theatrical entertainment, it consisted of a spoken play with up to 70 songs, the music of which was borrowed from popular songs of the day. The form was fashionable in England for a decade after John Gay's *The Beggar's Opera* (1728). After the vogue of the full-length ballad opera had died down, shorter works in the same style (sometimes misleadingly called 'farces') became popular as after-pieces to spoken plays.

Ballantyne, R(obert) M(ichael) (1825–94) Writer of boys' books, born in Edinburgh, EC Scotland, UK, a nephew of James and John Ballantyne. He studied at the Edinburgh Academy, joined the Hudson's Bay Company in 1841, and worked as a clerk at the Red River Settlement in the backwoods of N Canada until 1847, before returning to Edinburgh in 1848. He wrote his first stories on his experiences in Canada, with books such as *The Young Fur Traders* (1856). *The Coral Island* (1858) is his most famous work.

Ballarat or **Ballaarat** [balarat] 37°36S 143°58E, pop (2000e) 38 100. City in SWC Victoria, Australia, NW of Melbourne; railway; centre of a wool-producing district; largest gold reserves in the country discovered here, 1851; scene of the Eureka Stockade, the gold-diggers' rebellion against state authority, 1854; textiles, brewing, metal products; Eureka Stockade reconstruction; Sovereign Hill historic park; gold museum; vintage trams.

Ballard, J(ames) G(raham) (1930–) Writer, born in Shanghai, E China. He studied at Cambridge, and became a science fiction writer, fashioning a series of novels at once inventive, experimental, and often bizarre. His early novels, including his first, *The Drowned World* (1962), offer a view of the world beset by elemental catastrophe. He has been admired chiefly for his short stories, particularly those included in such collections as *The Terminal Beach* (1964), *The Disaster Area* (1967), and *Vermilion Sands* (1973). His 1973 novel *Crash* was made into a controversial film by David Cronenberg in 1996. *Empire of the Sun* (1984; filmed by Spielberg, 1987), a mainstream novel which is portentously autobiographical, was short-listed for the Booker Prize. A sequel, *The Kindness of Women*, appeared in 1991. Later works include *Rushing to Paradise* (1994), *Super-Cannes* (2000), and *Millennium People* (2003).

Ballesteros, Sevvy [ba-yestayros], popular name of **Severiano Ballesteros** (1957–) Golfer, born in Pedrena, N Spain. A highly combative, adventurous player, he has continually set records. Professional since 1974, when he won the (British) Open in 1979 he was the youngest player to do so in the 20th-c, and he took the title again in 1984 and 1988. Other wins include the US Masters (1980, 1983) and the World Matchplay (1981–2, 1984–5, 1991), and he has also been an inspirational captain of the European Ryder Cup team. The leading money winner in Europe in the years 1976–8, 1986, and 1988, he was the first man to win 50 European golf tournaments. His brothers Manuel, Baldomero, and Vicente are also all top golfers.

ballet A theatrical form of dance typically combined with music, stage design, and costume in an integrated whole, based around a scenario. Italian Renaissance court spectacles developed into the French *ballet de cour* under Louis XIV. Ballet became a professional theatre form in the 18th-c, gradually formalizing its technique in the early 19th-c. It can be divided roughly into historical periods; mid-19th-c Romantic ballets such as *La Sylphide*, *Giselle*, and the late 19th-c Russian classics (eg *Swan Lake*, *The Sleeping Beauty*); 20th-c neoclassical works, such as Balanchine's *Apollo*; and modern ballets, such as Ashton's *Monotones* and MacMillan's *Gloria*. Recent works may incorporate modern and jazz elements. The ballet technique is based on turn out from the hip socket. There are five positions of the feet and a codified system of arm positions (*port de bras*). Exercises at the barre (the horizontal support found in studios) move to extended phrases (*enchainements*) in the centre of the space. Intensive training is required from a young age, often in specialist schools.

Ballet Company *New York City Ballet*

Ballet Rambert *Rambert Dance Company*

Ballets Russes [balay roos] A ballet company created by Diaghilev, composed of the best dancers of Moscow and St Petersburg, and active in Europe 1909–29. It was famous for nurturing new talents and for collaborations between great painters (Bakst, Benois, Picasso), composers (Rimsky-Korsakov, Satie, Stravinsky), and choreographers (Fokine, Nijinsky, Massine, Nijinska, Balanchine). It had a repertoire of 20th-c classics including *Les Sylphides*, *Le Sacre du printemps* (The Rite of Spring) and *Petrushka*. Colourful Russian spectacles were set alongside experimental European modern art, for example using backdrops created by Cocteau, Massine, Picasso, and Satie in *Parade* (1917). The 1987 reconstruction of Nijinsky's long-lost 1913 version of *Le Sacre du printemps* was based on detailed historical evidence, and performed by the Joffrey Ballet in the USA and Europe.

Ballet Theatre *American Ballet Theatre*

ballistic missile A missile which acquires its energy during its launch phase, flying on a trajectory dictated by its initial velocity added to the factors of gravity and aerodynamic drag, until it reaches the target. A **cruise missile**, by contrast, flies with wings through the atmosphere under continuous power. A rifle bullet is in effect a ballistic missile, but more specifically the term applies to the big intercontinental and submarine-launched ballistic missiles which carry nuclear warheads. They may be propelled by a single rocket or several stages of rocket booster which fall away as the fuel they carry is expended. The missile's 'payload' is then free to fly on, arcing through space on its ballistic trajectory, before re-entering the atmosphere to impact on the target.

ballistics The study of what takes place when a projectile is fired from a firearm. Ballistics has three aspects: (1) *internal*, concerning the way the object is thrown into the air; (2) *external*, investigating the way it moves in flight; (3) *terminal*, analyzing its impact on the target. **Forensic ballistics** helps in the investigation of gun crimes.

balloon A flexible envelope filled with a lighter-than-air gas which provides the buoyancy force to rise upwards. A popular children's toy, large balloons are also used for meteorological and scientific research as well as for pleasure. The envelope of a modern hot-air balloon is made from either nylon or Dacron, which is then coated with polyurethane applied under pressure to make the material more airtight.

balloon angioplasty [anjiohplastee] The insertion of a catheter into an artery that has narrowed pathologically. A balloon at the tip of the catheter is expanded at the site of the constriction, which causes the blood vessel to dilate. The procedure is successful in many cases of narrowing of the arteries to the limbs, kidney, and heart.

ballooning Sailing through the air in a basket attached to a fabric bag filled with gas that is lighter than air. The first manned flight was by Pilâtre de Rozier and Marquis d'Arlandes at Paris in 1783 in a balloon designed by the Montgolfier brothers. The first to circumnavigate the world by balloon were Bertrand Piccard (1958–), a Swiss psychiatrist, and Brian Jones (1948–), from Wiltshire, England. They took off in the *Breitlingen Orbiter 3* on 1 March 1999 from Château d'Oex in the Swiss Alps and crossed the finishing line in Mauritania, NW Africa, 19 days 21 hours later, having covered 46 759 km at an average speed of 97 km/h.

ballroom dance A social dance form developed in the early 20th-c, revealing the strong influence of American ragtime, syncopated rhythms producing the foxtrot, quickstep, and tango. Also popular were animal dances (such as the Turkey Trot, Bunny Hug) and Latin-American dances (such as the cha-cha-cha and samba). The 1960s rock 'n roll era moved young people's dance out of the ballroom and into the club or disco. Since then, ballroom dancing has reasserted its popularity. In most Western countries, contemporary ballroom dancing is rewarded with dance titles and prizes at area, national, European, and world championship level, and is broadcast on television.

balm A name applied to various plants, but especially to **bee balm** or **lemon balm** (*Melissa officinalis*), a member of the mint family, Labiatae.

Balmain, Pierre (Alexandre Claudius) [balmĩ] (1914–82) Fashion designer, born in St Jean-de-Maurienne, E France. He studied architecture in Paris, but turned to dress designing, working for Edward Molyneux and Lucien Lelong, and in 1945 opened his own house. Famous for elegant simplicity, his designs included evening dresses, tailored suits, sportswear, and stoles. He also designed for the theatre and cinema.

Balmoral Castle A castle and estate of 9700 ha/24 000 acres located on Upper Deeside, Aberdeenshire, NE Scotland, UK. It has been in the possession of the British Royal family since 1852, and is used by them as a holiday home. The 19th-c castle was rebuilt under the direction of Prince Albert.

balsa A fast-growing tree (*Ochroma pyramidale*), reaching 25 m/80 ft or more, with very light, soft timber, native to lowland areas of tropical America; leaves broadly oval to circular, 30 cm/12 in or more in diameter; flowers 15 cm/6 in long, white. (Family: Bombacaceae.)

balsam An annual with a translucent stem; leaves alternate, opposite or in threes; flowers 2-lipped with funnel-shaped tube and curved spur, the capsule exploding to scatter seeds, especially when touched. The **Himalayan balsam** (*Impatiens glandulifera*) has flowers 2·5–4 cm/1–1½ in, purplish-pink; native to the top Himalayas. The **orange balsam** (*Impatiens capensis*) has flowers 2–3 cm/0·8–1·2 in, orange with brown blotches within; native to E North America. The **touch-me-not** (*Impatiens noli-tangere*) has flowers 3·5 cm/1½ in, orange with brown spots; native to Europe and Asia. (Family: Balsaminaceae).

balsam poplar *poplar*

Balthus, in full **Count Balthasar Klossowski de Rola** (1908–2001) Painter, born in Paris, France. He had no formal training, but received early encouragement from Bonnard and Derain. He held his first one-man exhibition at the Galerie Pierre, Paris, in 1934, and later became director of the French School in Rome. His work includes landscapes and portraits, but he is chiefly known for his interiors with adolescent girls, painted in a highly distinctive naturalistic style with a hint of Surrealism. He had grown in fame and popularity in recent years, despite the fact that he lived for many years as a virtual recluse.

Baltic Exchange An abbreviation for the **Baltic Mercantile and Shipping Exchange**, a major world market for cargo space on sea and air freight, which originated in the London coffee houses, and is still found in the City of London. It was known as the Virginia and Baltic from 1744, reflecting the growth of trade with America. The Exchange also handles the market in some commodities, such as grain. Its headquarters are in London.

Baltic languages A branch of the Indo-European family of languages, principally comprising Latvian and Lithuanian. Both have written records from the 14th-c, and each has a standard form and official status in its country. There are striking similarities between the Baltic and Slavic languages, but it is not certain whether these derive from their common origin, or from prolonged contact.

Baltic Sea [bawltik], Ger **Ostsee**, ancient **Mare Suevicum** area 414 000 sq km/160 000 sq mi. An arm of the Atlantic Ocean enclosed by Denmark, Sweden, Germany, Poland, Estonia, Latvia, Lithuania, Russia, and Finland; connected to the North Sea by the Kattegat, Skagerrak, Danish Straits, and the Kiel Canal; chief arms, the Gulfs of Bothnia, Finland, Riga; main islands, Hiiumma, Saaremaa, Åland, Gotland, Öland, Bornholm, Rüdgen, Fehmarn; mean depth 55 m/180 ft; deepest point, Gotland Deep (c.463 m/1519 ft); low salinity; generally shallow, with large areas frozen in winter; navigation impossible for 3–5 months yearly; main ports include Kiel, Gdańsk, St Petersburg, Riga, Copenhagen, Stockholm, Helsinki.

Baltic Shield The geological name for the continental mass made up of Precambrian crystalline rocks exposed in parts of Norway, Sweden, and Finland, and forming the underlying basement of the continent. They are the oldest rocks in Europe, and are made up predominantly of granites and gneisses.

Baltic states The countries of Estonia, Latvia, and Lithuania on the E shore of the Baltic Sea. They were formed in 1918 from the Russian Baltic provinces or governments of Estonia, Livonia, and Courland, and parts of the governments of Pskov, Vitebsk, Kovno, Vilna, and Suvalki. The states remained independent until 1940, when they were annexed by the USSR. They became independent again in 1990, following the collapse of communism.

Baltimore [boltimaw(r)] 39°17N 76°37W, pop (2000e) 651 200. Port in N Maryland, USA, on the Patapsco R, at the upper end of Chesapeake Bay; established, 1729; developed as a seaport and shipbuilding centre (Baltimore clippers); city status, 1797; rebuilt after 1904 fire; largest city in the state; airport; railway (first in the USA); six universities; trade in coal, grain, metal products; shipbuilding, food processing, copper and oil refining, chemicals, steel, aerospace equipment; major centre for culture and the arts; professional team, Orioles (baseball); first Roman Catholic cathedral in the USA (1806–21); Inner Harbour, Edgar Allan Poe House; Preakness Festival (May).

***Baltimore* Incident** A brief but serious dispute (1891) between the USA and Chile, stemming from the death of two American sailors from the cruiser *Baltimore* in a brawl in Valparaiso. A war between the two countries was averted by a Chilean apology.

Baluchi [baloochee] Baluchi-speaking peoples of Baluchistan (Pakistan), Iran, Afghanistan, Punjab (India), and Bahrain; divided into Sulaimani and Makrani groups. Once nomads, most are now settled agriculturalists, with cattle, goats, camels, etc. They are well known for their carpets and embroidery.

Baluchistan [baloochis**tahn**] pop (2000e) 7 039 000; area 347 190 sq km/134 015 sq mi. Province in W and SW Pakistan; bounded W by Iran, N by Afghanistan, and S by the Arabian Sea; ancient trading centre between India and Middle East; treaties of 1879 and 1891 brought the N section under direct British control; incorporated into Pakistan in 1947–8; capital, Quetta; mountainous terrain, with large areas of desert; cotton, natural gas, fishing, salt, mineral reserves.

Baluchitherium [baloochi**theer**ium] *Indricotherium*

Balzac, Honoré de, originally **Honoré Balssa** (1799–1850) Novelist, born in Tours, WC France. He studied at the Collège de Vendôme and the Sorbonne. From 1819 to 1830 he led a life of frequent privation and incessant industry, incurring a heavy burden of debt which harassed him to the end of his career. His first success was *Les Chouans* (1829, The Chouans). After writing several other novels, he formed the idea of presenting in *La Comédie humaine* (1827–47, The Human Comedy) a complete picture of mankind, employing a cast of over 2000 characters. Among the masterpieces which form part of his vast scheme are *Le Père Goriot* (Father Goriot), *Les Illusions perdues* (Lost Illusions), *Les Paysans* (The Peasants), *La Femme de trente ans* (The Thirty-Year-Old Woman), and *Eugénie Grandet*, in which detailed observation and imagination are the main features. His industry was phenomenal, writing 85 novels in 20 years, whose theme was predominantly the corrupting power of money and the over-riding force of self-interest. His work did not bring him wealth. During his later years he lived principally in his villa at Sèvres. In 1849, when his health had broken down, he travelled to Poland to visit Eveline Hanska, a rich Polish lady, with whom he had corresponded for more than 15 years. In 1850 she became his wife, and three months later, Balzac died.

Bamako [bama**koh**] 12°40N 7°59E, pop (2000e) 910 000. River-port capital of Mali, on the R Niger; mediaeval centre of Islamic learning; capital of French Sudan, 1905; airport; railway; power plant, ceramics, food processing, pharmaceuticals, metals, textiles, cycles, chemicals, tobacco; zoo, botanical gardens.

Bambara [bam**bah**ra] A Mande-speaking agricultural people of Mali, W Africa, divided into several small chiefdoms. Many are now urbanized and intermingled with other groups. They are known for their elaborate cosmology and metaphysics, their indigenous writing, and religious sculptures. They founded two important states, at Segu (c.1650) and at Kaarta (now in Mali, c.1753–4). Population c.2·5 million.

bamboo A giant woody grass, mostly tropical or subtropical, with a few temperate species; usually forming large clumps growing rapidly – up to 40 cm/15 in a day – and reaching heights of 36 m/120 ft. Some species flower annually; others only once after several to many years, and then all together, after which the entire population dies. They provide edible shoots and light timber, including garden canes. (Genera: *Bambusa* and others. Family: Gramineae.)

Bamian, Buddhas of [**bam**ian] Two enormous images of Buddha cut into the cliffs of the Bamian Valley, Afghanistan, in the 6th-c. The figures, which were 53 m/174 ft and 35 m/115 ft high, were defaced by Iranian conqueror Nader Shah's troops in the 18th-c. They were destroyed by the fundamentalist Islamic Taliban regime in March 2001.

Bampton, Deborah (Ellen) (1961–) British football player and manager. She joined Arsenal Ladies' Football Club as player-manager (1992–3), where her honours included the Women's Football Association Cup, League Cup, and National League (1992–3). She is a former captain of the England Women's Football Team (82 caps), and player-manager of Croydon Women's Football Club.

banana A giant perennial herb, superficially resembling a tree. The true stem lies underground, at intervals bearing buds which produce large, oar-shaped leaves. It is the closely sheathing bases of the leaves which form the soft, hollow, trunk-like 'stem' rising to a height of several metres above ground. The underground bud also produces the inflorescence, which grows up the hollow centre of the stem, emerging from the crown of leaves to droop towards the ground. The male flowers are borne towards the tip of the inflorescence, protected by large, reddish bracts. The female flowers are borne in clusters or hands in the lower part of the inflorescence; as the fruits develop after fertilization, they bend backwards to point away from the ground. Wild bananas are native to SE Asia, and produce inedible fruit with numerous seeds but little pulp. Cultivated bananas are grown throughout the tropics as a staple food, producing a higher yield per acre than potatoes. Fruit for export is cut while still green, and ripened on the voyage. They are often sold as unblemished yellow fruits, but are not fully ripe until flecked with brown spots. Cooking bananas are referred to as **plantains**. Banana leaves also yield useful fibre and thatch, and some species are planted for their ornamental flowers. (Genus: *Musa*, 35 species. Family: Musaceae.)

Banares *Benares*

Bancroft, Sir Squire (1841–1926) Actor-manager, born in London, UK. He made his debut at Birmingham (1861), and in 1867 married **Marie Wilton** (1840–1921), a distinguished actress. From 1865 to 1880 the Prince of Wales's Theatre witnessed their triumphs in a wide range of comedies, and until 1885 they were successful lessees of the Haymarket. He was knighted in 1897.

Banda, Hastings (Kamuzu) (c.1906–97) Malawi statesman, prime minister (1963–6) and first president (1966–94), born in Kasungu, WC Malawi. He studied medicine in the USA and in Britain. His opposition to the Central African Federation caused him to give up his successful London practice (1955) and return via Ghana to Nyasaland (1958). Leader of the Malawi African Congress, he was jailed in 1959, became minister of national resources (1961), then prime minister and president of the Malawi (formerly Nyasaland) Republic (1966). Made life president in 1971, he established a strong, one-party control of Malawi, but following growing opposition he was defeated in a referendum for multi-party democracy in 1993, and was defeated in the 1994 elections.

Band Aid *Geldof, Bob*

Bandaranaike, S(olomon) W(est) R(idgeway) D(ias) [ban-da**rah**niykuh] (1899–1959) Sri Lankan (Ceylonese) statesman and prime minister (1956–9), born in Colombo, W Sri lanka. He studied at Oxford, and was called to the bar in 1925. He became president of the Ceylon National Congress, then helped to found the United National Party, which formed the government of Ceylon in 1948–56. In 1951 he resigned from the government and organized the Sri Lanka Freedom Party, which returned him to parliament as Leader of the Opposition, and in 1956 he became prime minister on a policy of nationalization and neutralism. He was assassinated by a Buddhist monk.

Bandar Seri Begawan [**bahn**dah seree be**ga**wan], formerly **Brunei Town** 4°56N 114°58E, pop (2000e) 90 600. Capital of Brunei, SE Asia, 20 km/12 mi from mouth of Brunei R; airport; town wharf used mainly for local vessels since opening of deep-water port at Muara in 1972; Mesjid Sultan Omar Ali Saifuddin mosque (1958), Churchill Museum, Sultan Hassanal Bolkiah Aquarium.

Bandeira (Filho), Manuel (Carneiro de Sousa) [ban**dai**ra] (1886–1968) Poet, born in Recife, Brazil. His first books of poetry, *A Cinza das Horas* (1917, Destruction of the Hours) and *Carnaval* (1919, Carnival), identified him with the contemporary Modernist movement. Later works include *Ritmo dissoluto* (1924, Rhythm in Dissolution) and *Estrelha da tarde* (1963, Evening Star). Highly influential among aspiring Brazilian writers, he became a much respected national figure.

bandeirante [bandayr**an**tay] A 17th-c Brazilian slave-raider and explorer. Based on São Paulo, parties of bandeirantes (*bandeiras*) opened up much of the interior of Brazil, including the Amazon basin. They are today seen in Brazil as a heroic pioneering myth.

Banderas, Antonio [bandayras], in full **José Antonio Domínguez Banderas** (1960–) Actor, born in Málaga, S Spain. He studied drama, then moved to Madrid where he met Pedro Almodóvar, who gave him a small part in the film *Laberinto de Pasiones* (1982). From then on he worked exclusively with Almodóvar in such films as *Matador* (1985) and *La ley del deseo* (1986). In the 1990s he began a film career in Hollywood, his films including *Philadelphia* (1993), *Never Talk to Strangers* (1994), *Evita* (1996), and *Frida* (2002). He divorced his wife Ana Leza in 1995 and married actress Melanie Griffith.

bandicoot An Australasian marsupial (family: Peramelidae, 17 species); superficially rat-like, but larger with longer snout and ears; digs in soil with front claws; eats invertebrates; also includes the Australian **rabbit-eared bandicoots** (or **bilbies**) of family Thylacomyidae (2 species) from dry areas.

Bandung [bandung] 0°32N 103°16E, pop (2000e) 2 065 000. Capital of Java Barat province, W Java, Indonesia; 180 km/112 mi SE of Jakarta; founded, 1810; former administrative centre of Dutch East Indies; **Bandung Conference** (1955), at which 29 non-aligned countries met to facilitate joint diplomatic action; airport; railway; two universities (1955, 1957); nuclear research centre (1964); chemicals, plastics, textiles, quinine; Sundanese cultural centre.

band-width In radio and television transmission, the range of frequencies required for the satisfactory reproduction of a signal. For television, it is determined by the field frequency, the number of scanning lines, and the colour-coding system, typically requiring 5·5 mHz for 625-line 50-field systems but considerably more for high-definition TV.

Bangalore [banggalaw(r)] 12°59N 77°40E, pop (2000e) 3 113 000. Capital of Karnataka, SC India, 290 km/180 mi W of Chennai (Madras); founded, 1537; former military headquarters of the British-administered district of Mysore (1831–1947); airfield; railway; university (1964); aircraft, machine tools, light engineering, electronics, trade in coffee.

Banghazi *Benghazi*

Bangkok [bangkok] 13°44N 100°30E, pop (2000e) 6 746 000. Capital city of Thailand; on Chao Praya R, 25 km/15 mi from its mouth on the Bight of Thailand; capital, 1782; old city noted for its many canals; accessible to small ocean-going vessels; since 1955, headquarters of the SE Asia Treaty Organization; airport; railway; eight universities; commerce, paper, ceramics, textiles, timber, aircraft, matches, food processing, cement; Grand Palace, Temples of the Golden Buddha and Reclining Buddha; Phra Pathom Chedi, world's tallest Buddhist monument, 60 km/37 mi W.

Bangladesh *p.137*

Bangor [bangger] 53°13N 4°08W, pop (2000e) 48 700. City in Gwynedd, NW Wales, UK; opposite the island of Anglesey; railway; university (1884); cathedral (founded 6th-c); chemicals, engineering, electrical goods; tourism; Theatre Gwynedd.

Bangui [bahngwee] 4°23N 18°37E, pop (2000e) 767 800. Capital of Central African Republic; on the R Ubangi, 1030 km/640 mi NE of Brazzaville; founded, 1889; airport; university (1969); handles Chad trade; cotton, coffee, timber products, cigarettes, metal products, office machinery, beer; Boganda Museum.

Bani-Sadr, Abolhassan [banee sadr] (1935–) Iranian politician, and first president of the Islamic Republic of Iran (1980–1), associated with Ayatollah Khomeini from 1966. He studied economics and sociology at the Sorbonne in Paris, having fled there in 1963 after a brief imprisonment in Iran for involvement in riots against the Shah's regime. An important figure in the Iranian Revolution of 1978–9, he was soon criticized by the fundamentalists and dismissed by Ayatollah Khomeini (mid-1981). He fled to France where he was granted asylum.

Banjalang One of the principal Aboriginal communities of NE New South Wales, Australia. The Banjalang language is currently the object of a revival programme.

banjo A plucked string instrument developed in the 19th-c from earlier similar instruments used by W African slaves in the USA. It has a long neck and fingerboard, fretted like a guitar's, and five metal strings (gut, in older instruments). These pass over a bridge which presses against a parchment (or plastic) membrane stretched over a circular frame. It is played either with a plectrum or with the fingers.

Banjul [banjul], formerly **Bathurst** (to 1973) 13°28N 16°35W, pop (2000e) 68 700. Seaport capital of The Gambia, W Africa; on Island of St Mary in R Gambia estuary, 195 km/121 mi SE of Dakar; established in 1816 as a settlement for freed slaves; airport; peanuts, crafts, tourism; Fort Bullen (1826).

bank An organization which offers a wide range of services to do with the handling of money. Most banks are *commercial banks*, which keep money on behalf of their customers, lend it to them, and offer them such facilities as currency exchange, money transfer, credit facilities, mortgages, and investment advice. A *central bank* in a country (such as the Bank of England or the Banque de France) is the banker for the government, issuing money on its behalf and setting the chief interest rate for loans; it is much involved in the country's monetary policy. Merchant banks offer specialized services to businesses, such as managing shares, dealing in gold or foreign currencies, and providing funds to finance a new business. Savings banks were founded in the 19th-c to encourage people to save, small deposits being placed in interest-bearing accounts. There are also several international banks, which regulate currency matters between countries and handle international loans, notably the World Bank.

bank base rate A base lending rate for UK clearing banks, used as the primary measure for interest rates since 1981. It is decided by the Bank of England, on the advice of the Monetary Policy Committee.

bank card *cheque card*

Bankhead, Tallulah (1903–68) Actress, born in Huntsville, Alabama, USA. She was brought up in New York City and Washington, and made her stage debut in 1918. She won Critic awards for her two most famous stage roles, Regina in *The Little Foxes* (1939) and Sabina in *The Skin of Our Teeth* (1942). Her most outstanding film portrayal was in *Lifeboat* (1944).

Bank of England The central bank of Britain. The concept of a national bank was put forward by William Paterson (1658–1719), a Scottish merchant, after the Stuart kings' abuse of the royal prerogative to borrow from the Royal Mint (founded in AD 825) had severely damaged government credit. It was based on the concept of a national debt, whereby the government could raise money 'upon a Fund of perpetual interest'. The Bank began business in Mercers' Hall, London, in 1694, then moved to Grocers' Hall, where it stayed until 1734. In 1725 the first fixed notes were issued, for £20, £30, £40, and £100. In 1734 the Bank moved to Threadneedle Street in a building designed by George Sampson. A major reconstruction of the Bank began in 1788 under the direction of Sir John Soane, who designed a neoclassical building surrounded by a windowless wall. In the 1920s and 1930s, rebuilding by Sir Herbert Baker left only a few interiors and the outside walls intact. During the Napoleonic Wars the Bank earned a nickname when Sheridan, speaking in the House of Commons in 1797, called it 'an elderly lady in the city', as a result of which it became known popularly as 'The Old Lady of Threadneedle Street'. In 1844 the Bank Charter limited the issue of notes by other banks, and by the end of the 19th-c the Bank was acting as the government and bankers' bank only, and was no longer accessible to the public. In 1946 the Bank of England Act brought the Bank into public ownership. Today the main functions of the Bank are to act as a note-issuing authority, as the government and bankers' bank, as manager of the National Debt, and as custodian of the nation's gold reserves. The monetary policy of the Bank of England used to be subject to control by the Treasury, but the Bank is now independent, advised by a nine-member Monetary Policy Committee. In 1997 the Treasury ceded its power to set interest rates to the Bank of England.

bank rate A former interest rate at which the Bank of England would lend to discount houses, and an important instrument

Bangladesh

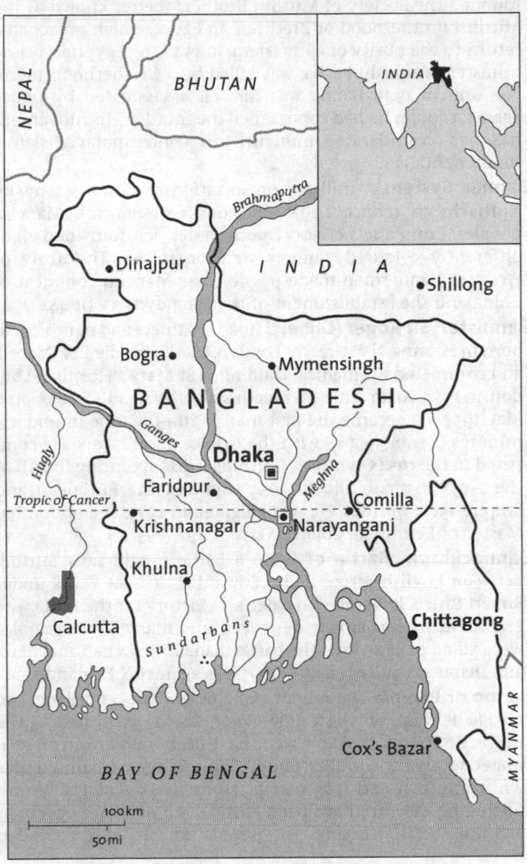

□ International Airport ∴ World heritage site

[banggladesh], formerly **East Pakistan**, official name **People's Republic of Bangladesh, Gana Prajatantri Bangladesh**

Local name Bangladesh

Timezone GMT +6

Area 143 998 km²/55 583 sq mi

Population total (2002e) 133 377 000

Status Republic

Date of independence 1971

Capital Dhaka

Languages Bengali (official), also local dialects and English widely spoken

Ethnic groups Bengali (98%), Bihari (1%), tribal: Garo, Khasi, Santal (1%)

Religions Muslim (86%), Hindu (12%), Buddhist (1%), small Christian majority

Physical features Mainly a vast, low-lying alluvial plain, cut by a network of rivers, canals, swamps, marshes; main rivers the Ganges (Padma), Brahmaputra (Jamuna), Meghna; joining in the S to form the largest delta in the world, subject to frequent fooding; Chittagong Hill Tracts in the E rise to 1200 m/3900 ft.

Climate Tropical climate; monsoon season (Jun–Oct).

Currency 1 Taka (TK) = 100 paisa

Economy Agriculture, especially rice (employs 86% of population); and supplies 80% of the world's jute; also paper, aluminium, textiles, glass, shipbuilding, fishing, natural gas

GDP (2002e) $238·2 bn, per capita $1800

Human Development Index (2002) 0·478

History Part of the State of Bengal until Muslim East Bengal created in 1905, separate from Hindu West Bengal; reunited, 1911; partitioned again in 1947, with West Bengal remaining in India and East Bengal forming East Pakistan; rebellion in 1971 led to independence as the People's Republic of Bangladesh; political unrest led to suspension of constitution, and assassination of first President, Sheikh Mujib, 1975; further coups in 1975, 1977, and 1982; constitution restored, 1986; last military dictator, Hossain Mohammad Ershad, overthrown, 1990; constitutional amendments in 1991 restricted powers of President to ceremonial and restored full powers to unicameral legislature, *Jatiya Sangsad*.

Head of State

1971–2 Sayed Nazrul Islam *Acting*
1972 Mujibur Rahman
1972–3 Abu Saeed Chowdhury
1974–5 Mohammadullah
1975 Mujibur Rahman
1975 Khondaker Mushtaq Ahmad
1975–7 Abu Saadat Mohammad Sayem
1977–81 Zia Ur-Rahman
1981–2 Abdus Sattar
1982–3 Abdul Fazal Mohammad Ahsanuddin Chowdhury
1983–90 Hossain Mohammad Ershad
1990–1 Shehabuddin Ahmed *Acting*
1991–6 Abdur Rahman Biswas
1996–2001 Shehabuddin Ahmed
2001–2 A.Q.M. Badruddoza Chowdhury
2002– Iajuddin Ahmed

Head of Government

1971–2 Tajuddin Ahmed
1972–5 Mujibur Rahman
1975 Mohammad Monsur Ali
1975–9 Martial Law
1979–82 Mohammad Azizur Rahman
1982–4 Martial Law
1984–5 Ataur Rahman Khan
1986–8 Mizanur Rahman Chowdhury
1988–9 Moudud Ahmed
1989–91 Kazi Zafar Ahmed
1991–6 Begum Khaleda Zia
1996–2001 Hasina Wajed
2001 Latifur Rahman *Interim*
2001– Begum Khaleda Zia

of government economic policy. It was abandoned in 1973, and replaced by the minimum lending rate (MLR). A change in bank rate was the signal to other lending institutions to follow suit.

bankruptcy The state of being reduced to financial ruin through being unable to meet one's debts. A debtor may be insolvent without becoming bankrupt, and may become a bankrupt without being insolvent. Legally, individuals and partnerships are in this state when a court in bankruptcy proceedings declares them to be bankrupt, the debtor's property being thereafter administered for the benefit of the creditors. These proceedings are started by a creditor (or sometimes the debtor) petitioning a court for bankruptcy (in England or Wales) or 'sequestration' (in Scotland). In the USA, bankruptcy is a legal concept through which a debtor seeks refuge from creditors through federal statutes that allow the debtor to formulate a schedule of payments to creditors. An analogous notion, **liquidation**, applies to companies; this may be either compulsory (as when a company is unable to pay its debts) or voluntary (as when its members have decided to cease trading).

Banks, Don (1923–80) Composer, born in Melbourne, Victoria, SE Australia. He attended the Melbourne Conservatory (1947–9), then studied in London, Salzburg, and Florence. Having settled in England, he became music director of Goldsmith's College (1969–71). He returned to Australia in 1973, became head of Composition and Electronic Music Studies at Canberra School of Music in 1974, and head of the School of Composition Music Studies at the Sydney Conservatory in 1978. His work was particularly influenced by Milton Babbitt and by jazz. His compositions include a horn concerto, a violin concerto, a trilogy for orchestra, *An Australian Entertainment* (1979), and many film and TV scores.

Banks, Iain (Menzies) (1954–) Novelist, born in Fife, E Scotland, UK. He worked as a testing technician in Scotland and as a solicitor's clerk in England before attracting equal measures of fame and notoriety with his first novel, a gruesome Gothic fantasy, *The Wasp Factory* (1984). Later books include *The Bridge* (1986), *Whit* (1995), *Inversions* (1999), and *Dead Air* (2002).

Banks, Sir Joseph (1743–1820) Botanist, born in London, UK. He studied at Oxford, and in 1766 made a voyage to Newfoundland collecting plants. He then accompanied James Cook's expedition round the world in the *Endeavour* (1768–71). In 1778 he was elected president of the Royal Society, an office he held for 41 years. An important patron of science, he founded the African Association, and the colony of New South Wales owed its origin mainly to him. Through him the bread-fruit was transferred from Tahiti to the West Indies, and the mango was introduced from Bengal, along with many fruits of Ceylon and Persia.

Banks, Lynne (Reid) (1929–) British writer and actress. She studied in Canada, and in London at the Italia Conti Stage School and the Royal Academy of Dramatic Art. After a brief career as an actress (1949–54), she joined ITN as a reporter (1955–62), taught English in Israel (1963–71), and became a full-time lecturer from 1971. Her best-known novel is *The L-Shaped Room* (1960, filmed 1962), and she has also written plays and biographical novels. Her many books for children include *The Adventures of King Midas* (1977), *The Indian in the Cupboard* (1980, filmed 1995), *The Mystery of the Cupboard* (1993), *Angela and Diabola* (1997), and *Alice By Accident* (2000).

Banks, Tony, popular name of **Anthony Lewis Banks** (1945–) British Labour statesman, born in Belfast, NE Northern Ireland, UK. Educated at London, York, and the London School of Economics, he worked as a full-time trade union official and served on the Greater London Council (1970–7, 1981–6) before being elected MP for Newham North West (1983–97) then West Ham (1983–). A former chair of the London Group of Labour MPs, and an avid association football fan, he served in a number of minor opposition posts before being a surprise appointment as minister for sport in the 1997 Blair government. In 1999 he relinquished the post to lead the English bid for the 2006 association football World Cup competition.

banksia A low shrub or small tree, native to Australia; leaves sometimes very small, usually narrow, sharply toothed, leathery; flowers commonly cream, also orange, red, or purplish with four perianth segments and protruding style; up to 1000 in spectacular globular or cylindrical heads up to 40 × 18 cm/ 15 × 7 in, which become cone-like in fruit with woody capsules, shaggy with persistent remains of flowers. Typical of dry bush country, most species are adapted to withstand fires, re-sprouting from woody tubers or trunks protected by thick fibrous bark; in many the capsules open only after experiencing strong heat, remaining closed for years before releasing seeds onto ground newly cleared by fire. It is named after Sir Joseph Banks. (Genus: *Banksia*, 58 species. Family: Proteaceae.)

Bann, River Major river in Northern Ireland; rises in the Mourne Mts, and flows 40 km/25 mi NW to enter the S end of Lough Neagh; flows N for 53 km/33 mi through Lough Beg to enter the Atlantic.

Banna, Hassan al- [bana] (1906–49) Islamic leader and reformer, born in Mahmudiya, near Cairo, Egypt. In 1928 he founded the Society of Muslim Brothers (better known as the Muslim Brotherhood or Brethren) in Egypt, which preached a return to the purity of early Islam. In 1948 the Egyptian prime minister, Nuqrashi-Pasha, was killed by a Brotherhood member, and in 1949 Banna was himself assassinated by police agents, though he had condemned the murder. His movement has had considerable influence on contemporary Islamic fundamentalism.

Banner System A military organization in China set up by Nurhachi to reduce tribal divisions between the Manchu peoples. Companies of 300 troops under first four then eight differently coloured banners were organized. The army of 170 000 bannermen made possible the Manchu conquest of China and the establishment of the Qing dynasty (1644).

Bannister, Sir Roger (Gilbert) (1929–) Athlete and neurologist, born in Harrow, NW Greater London, UK. He studied at Oxford, and completed his medical training at St Mary's Hospital, London, in 1954. At an athletics meeting at Iffley Road, Oxford, on 6 May 1954, he became the first man to run the mile in under 4 minutes (3 min 59·4 s), with the help of pacemakers. He competed in the 1952 Olympics, finishing a disappointing fourth in the 1500 m final, and in 1954 captured the European and Empire 1500 m titles. He was knighted in 1975, and appointed Master of Pembroke College, Oxford, 1985–93.

Bannockburn, Battle of (1314) A battle fought near Stirling between English forces under Edward II and the Scots under Robert Bruce. It resulted in a decisive victory for the Scots. The English army was largely destroyed, and many English nobles were killed or captured. The battle made Bruce a national hero, and inspired Scottish counter-attacks against N England.

Banpo or **Pan-p'o** The remains of a 6000–4000 BC Yangshao village at Xian, on the Yellow River, China. Excavated in the 1960s, 46 round, sunken houses have been found from an estimated total of 200. Millet, pottery kilns, Yangshao painted pots with bird, fish and frog motifs, stone tools, and 174 burials (including a coffin) have been found, with evidence of a hierarchical social structure. The population probably exceeded 600.

banteng or **banting** A rare SE Asian ox (*Bos javanicus*); long upward-curving horns; male black with white rump and 'stockings'; females brown; inhabits forests and dry regions; often nocturnal; shy; domesticated form called **Bali cattle**; can be cross-bred with zebu; also known as **tsaine** or **tembadau**.

Banting, Sir Frederick Grant (1891–1941) Physiologist, the discoverer of insulin, born in Alliston, Ontario, SE Canada. He studied medicine at Toronto University and later became professor there (1923). Working under J J R Macleod, in 1922 he discovered (with his assistant Charles H Best) the hormone insulin, used in the control of diabetes. For this discovery he was jointly awarded, with Macleod, the Nobel Prize for Physiology or Medicine in 1923, voluntarily sharing his own part of the award with Best. He established the Banting Research Foundation in 1924 and the Banting Institute at Toronto in 1930. He was knighted in 1934, and died in a plane crash during a war mission.

Bantu-speaking peoples Ethnically diverse groups who speak one of 500 Bantu languages or dialects (which belong to the Benue–Congo sub-group of the Niger–Congo family). They comprise altogether about 60 million people living in the S part of Africa, occupying a third of the continent. They may well have had their origins in the region of modern Cameroon, with a second nucleus of dispersal in the Katanga area. From there they spread S interacting with Khoisan peoples, E as far as Madagascar, and NE where they mingled with coastal Arab traders. Generally regarded as iron-working cultivators, their dispersal occurred in the early years of the Christian era. In South Africa, the term **Bantu** has been used as a racial classification.

Bantustans *apartheid*

Banville, (Etienne Claude Jean Baptiste) Théodore (Faullain) de [bãveel] (1823–91) Poet and playwright, born in Moulins, C France. He was given the title *roi des rimes* (King of Rhymes) for his ingenuity in handling the most difficult forms of verse – the mediaeval ballades and rondels. His *Gringoire* (1866) holds an established place in French repertory.

banyan A large evergreen species of fig (*Ficus benghalensis*), native to the Old World tropics. It is notable for its aerial roots, which grow from the horizontal branches to the ground, becoming trunk-like, so that an apparent group of trees may in fact be only one. (Family: Moraceae.)

baobab [bayohbab, **bow**bab] A deciduous tree (*Adansonia digitata*) native to arid parts of C Africa; its short but massive barrel- or bottle-shaped trunk 9–12 m/30–40 ft high and up to 9 m/ 30 ft in girth contains large stores of water. The edible pulp of its woody fruits is called *monkey bread*. (Family: Bombacaceae.)

baptism A sacramental practice involving water, symbolizing initiation into a church. The Christian ritual is usually traced to the New Testament, where new converts were immersed in water (*Acts* 8.38–9) and where the rite was linked with the imparting of the Spirit and with a confession of repentance and faith (*Acts* 2.38, 10.47). Jesus Christ's baptism by John marked the start of his ministry. Today, Church practices vary over infant and adult baptism, and over the use of immersion or sprinkling.

baptistery / baptistry A church or part of a church used to administer baptism, and containing the font.

Baptists A worldwide communion of Christians, who believe in the baptism only of believers prepared to make a personal confession of faith in Jesus Christ. They have certain links with the 16th-c Anabaptists, but mainly derive from early 17th-c England and Wales, where Baptist churches spread rapidly, and in the USA, where the first Baptist church was established in 1639, at Providence, RI. A rapid increase took place in the late 18th-c and 19th-c in the USA, especially among the Southern black population. Black Baptist churches, and their ministers, played an important role in the civil rights movement of the 1960s, led by Martin Luther King. Strongly biblical, the emphasis in worship is on scripture and preaching. Individual congregations are autonomous, but usually linked together in associations or unions. The Baptist World Alliance was formed in 1905. In 2004 there were 210 member denominations, representing over 47 million baptized members.

Baqqarah or **Baggara** [bagara] A nomadic Arabic-speaking people of the Sudan, possibly descended from Arabs who migrated during the Middle Ages from Egypt to Chad and then eastwards. They lack any centralized political authority. Cattle are kept in the arid region between the Nile and L Chad, migrating seasonally in search of water. Population c.5 million.

bar Unit of pressure; symbol bar; equal to 10^5 Pa (pascal, SI unit); 1 bar is approximately atmospheric pressure. The **millibar** (mb; 1 bar = 1000 mb) proves to be of greater use for practical measurements. At sea level, atmospheric pressure is c.1013·25 mb; classed as a unit in temporary use with SI units.

Bar, Confederation of (1768) A military alliance of Polish gentry established at Bar, Podolin, directed against the Russian-backed king, Stanislas Poniatowski. The Confederation advocated the preservation of the privileges of the Polish aristocracy and the Catholic Church. Its suppression in 1772 led to the first partition of Poland.

Barabbas [barabas] (1st-c) Political rebel and murderer (as described in *Mark* 15, *Luke* 23), who was arrested but apparently released by popular acclaim in preference to Pilate's offer to release Jesus of Nazareth. He was possibly also called 'Jesus Barabbas' (in some manuscripts of *Matt* 27.16-17).

Barak, Ehud (1942–) Israeli statesman and Labour prime minister (1999–2001), born in Kibbutz Mishmar Hasharon, Israel. Educated in Jerusalem and Stanford University, USA, he joined the Israeli army in 1959 and saw active service in both the Six-Day War and the Yom Kippur War, becoming a major-general in 1982. In 1991 he was appointed chief of the general staff and, following the signing of the Gaza–Jericho agreement with the Palestinians, he oversaw the Israeli Defence Force's redeployment in those areas. He served as minister of the interior (1995) and minister of foreign affairs (1995–6), being elected to the Knesset in 1996. As prime minister, he retained the defence portfolio to himself.

Barba, Eugenio (1936–) Theatre director, born in Brindisi, S Italy. He was the founder (1964) of Odin Teatret, an experimental theatre company and centre for collective research in performance. In 1979 he established the International School of Theatre Anthropology. His theoretical writings include *The Floating Islands* (1984), *Beyond the Floating Islands* (1986), and *The Paper Canoe* (1994).

Barbados *p.140*

Barbarossa [bah(r)barosa] ('Redbeard'), nickname of **Khair-ed-Din** (16th-c) **1** Barbary pirate, born in Lesbos, Greece. With his brothers he became a Turkish corsair, attacking shipping in the Mediterranean. After the execution of his brother **Aruj** (1518), he captured Algiers (1529) and was made admiral of the Ottoman fleet (1533), conquering Tunisia, and defeating the Holy Roman Emperor (Charles V) at Preveza (1538). He became one of the great figures at the Court of Constantinople until his death. **2** »Frederick 1 (Emperor).

Barbary ape A monkey (macaque) native to N Africa (*Macaca sylvanus*), and maintained artificially on the Rock of Gibraltar; not an ape; stocky with no tail; spends much time on the ground; lives in troops of up to 30 individuals; also known as **magot** or **rock ape**.

Barbary Coast The coast of N Africa from Morocco to Tripolitania (Libya), famous for piracy between the 16th-c and 18th-c. This coast and the Barbary States of Morocco, Algeria, Tunisia, and Tripolitania take their name from the Berbers who inhabited this region.

Barbary sheep *aoudad*

barbastelle [bah(r)bastel] A bat, native to Europe, Asia, and N Africa; fur extends onto wings and tail membrane; ears large and broad; flies with slow wingbeats; eats insects. (Genus: *Barbastella*, 2 species. Family: Vespertilionidae.)

barbel Slender-bodied fish (*Barbus barbus*) of the carp family Cyprinidae, widespread in European rivers on clean gravel beds; body length up to 90 cm/3 ft; lips fleshy, bearing four long barbels; migrate upstream to spawn (Apr–Jun); fine sport fish. The name is also used for other species of the genus.

Barber, Chris (1930–) Jazz musician, born in Welwyn Garden City, Hertfordshire, SE England, UK. A trombonist and vocalist, he joined the Ken Colyer band, taking it over in 1954. By the end of the decade the Chris Barber Jazz Band was well established, and had made several hit singles, notably 'Petite Fleur', with soloist Monty Sunshine (1928–). Several successful albums followed, including *Best of Chris Barber* (both 1960). He is married to the blues singer **Ottilie Patterson**.

Barber, Samuel (1910–81) Composer, born in West Chester, Pennsylvania, USA. He studied at the Curtis Institute, Philadelphia, and won the American *Prix de Rome*. His early music includes the overture to *The School for Scandal* (1931) and the popular *Adagio for Strings*, and is in traditional neo-Romantic vein. His later works lay more emphasis on chromaticism and dissonance, and include the *Capricorn Concerto* (1944) and the ballet *Medea* (1946). His first full-length opera *Vanessa* was performed at the Salzburg Festival (1958, Pulitzer), followed by *Antony and Cleopatra* (1966).

Barbera *Hanna-Barbera*

barberry A deciduous or evergreen shrub, native to N temperate regions and South America; long shoots with 3-pointed spines; leaves often spiny; flowers yellow, orange, or reddish; berries red, black, blue, yellow or purple, globose or cylindrical; several species grown as ornamentals, especially purple-leaved forms. The common barberry (*Berberis vulgaris*) is a necessary host in the life-cycle of the cereal disease *black rust*; in some countries, especially the USA, attempts to break the life-cycle

Barbados

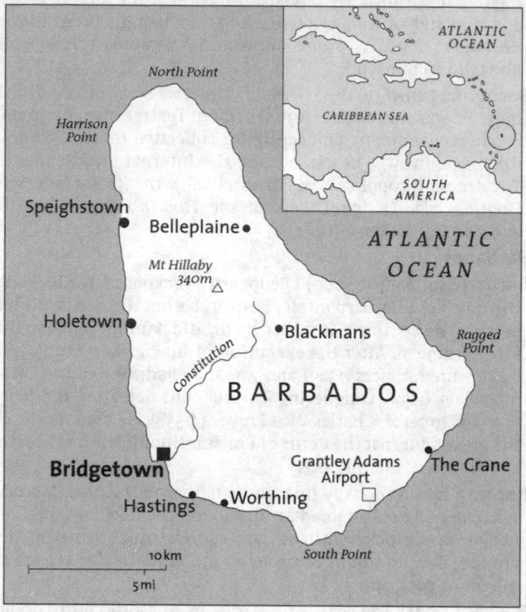

□ International Airport

[bah(r)baydos]

Local name Barbados

Timezone GMT −4

Area 430 km²/166 sq mi

Population total (2002e) 270 000

Status Independent state within the Commonwealth

Date of independence 1966

Capital Bridgetown

Language English (official)

Ethnic groups African (80%), mixed race (16%)

Religions Anglican (40%), Protestant (15%), Roman Catholic (4%)

Physical features Small, triangular island in the Atlantic Ocean; length 32 km/20 mi (NW–SE); rising to 340 m/1115 ft at Mt Hillaby; ringed by a coral reef.

Climate Tropical climate, with average annual temperature 27°C; mean annual rainfall 1420 mm/56 in.

Currency 1 Barbados Dollar (Bds$) = 100 cents

Economy Market economy based on tourism and sugar cane; cotton, bananas; natural gas; textiles.

GDP (2002e) $4·153 bn, per capita $15 000

Human Development Index (2002) 0·871

History Colonized by the British, 1627; self-government, 1961; independent within the Commonwealth, 1966; executive power rests with the Prime Minister, appointed by a Governor-General, the Senate, and the House of Assembly.

Head of State
(British monarch represented by Governor-General)
1984–90 Hugh Springer
1990–5 Dame Nita Barrow
1996– Sir Clifford Husbands

Head of Government
1966–76 Errol Walton Barrow
1976–85 J M G (Tom) Adams
1985–6 H Bernard St John
1986–7 Errol Walton Barrow
1987–94 L Erskine Sandiford
1994– Owen Seymour Arthur

of the rust have involved the eradication of barberry populations. (Genus: *Berberis*, 450 species. Family: Berberidaceae.)

barbershop quartet A group of singers who perform four-part 'close-harmony' arrangements of popular sentimental songs in a suave, nostalgic style. It is particularly associated with the USA, where it originated in the late 19th-c.

barbet A plump, brightly-coloured bird, inhabiting the tropics worldwide (especially Africa); usually a forest-dweller; named after its 'beard' of feathers, at the base of a large bill; eats fruit, flowers, and insects. (Family: Capitonidae, over 70 species.)

Barbie, Klaus, known as **the Butcher of Lyon** (1913–91) Nazi leader, born in Bad Godesberg, W Germany. He joined the Hitler Youth in 1931, graduating to the SS, and worked for the Gestapo in the Netherlands, Russia, and finally Lyon, where he sent thousands of people to Auschwitz. After the War, he fled to South America with his family under an assumed name, but was traced by Nazi hunters, and extradited from Bolivia in 1983. He was tried in France on 177 crimes against humanity, found guilty, and sentenced to life imprisonment.

Barbirolli, Sir John (Giovanni Battista) [bah(r)birolee] (1899–1970) Conductor and cellist, born in London, UK of French and Italian parents. He served in World War 1, played in several leading string quartets (1920–4), and succeeded Toscanini as conductor of the New York Philharmonic (1937). He returned to England as permanent conductor (1943–58) of the Hallé Orchestra in Manchester, later becoming its principal conductor (1959–68). In 1939 he married oboist **Evelyn Rothwell** (1911–). He was created a knight in 1949, and awarded the Gold Medal of the Royal Philharmonic Society in 1950.

barbiturates Drugs derived from barbituric acid, itself first prepared on St Barbara's Day, 1863. *Barbitone* (US *barbital*) was introduced into medicine in 1903; *phenobarbitone* (US *phenobarbital*) in 1912. Over 50 different barbiturates have been used at some time as sedatives, sleep inducers, and anti-epileptic drugs. They cause severe tolerance, ie increasingly higher doses are required to produce the same effect. The doses are progressively more dangerous, and poisoning becomes a major risk; they are also addictive. As sedatives and sleeping pills they have generally been replaced by the safer benzodiazepines.

Barbizon School [bah(r)bizon] A group of French landscape painters working c.1830–80 at Barbizon, a village in the Forest of Fontainbleau. Pioneers of *plein air* painting, they sketched out-of-doors, directly from nature, in a way that foreshadowed the Pre-Raphaelites in England and the Impressionists in France. Leading members were Théodore Rousseau (1812–67), Charles François Daubigny (1817–78), Narciso-Virgilio Díaz (1807–76), and Constant Troyon (1810–65).

Barbour, John [bah(r)ber] (c.1320–95) Poet, clergyman, and scholar, probably born in Aberdeen, NE Scotland, UK. He was Archdeacon of Aberdeen from 1357, or earlier, till his death. His national epic, *The Brus*, written in the 1370s, is a narrative poem on the life and deeds of King Robert I, the Bruce, preserving many oral traditions.

Barbuda *Antigua and Barbuda*

barcarolle An instrumental or vocal piece in a lilting 6/8 metre, evoking the songs of the Venetian gondoliers. A well-known example is the Barcarolle in Offenbach's opera *Les Contes d'Hoffman* (The Tales of Hoffman).

Barcelona [bah(r)selohna], Span [barthelohna], ancient **Barcino** or **Barcinona** 41°21N 2°10E, pop (2000e) 1 645 000. Major seaport and capital of Barcelona province, NE Spain, 621 km/386 mi NE of Madrid; second largest city in Spain; airport; railway; car ferries to Mahón, Palma de Mallorca, Ibiza, Canary Is; two universities (1440, 1968); centre of Catalan art and literature, and of the separatist political movement; textiles, petrochemicals, oil refining, engineering, aircraft; Gothic Quarter, cathedral

(13th-c), Ramblas Palace, Church of the Holy Family, Museum of Catalan Art, Maritime Museum, Bishop's Palace, Palace of la Virreina art gallery; Casa Mila (1906–10), Casa Güell (1900–14), and Parque Güell (1900–14), architectural creations by Antonio Gaudí, now world heritage sites; Palau de la Música Catalana and Hospital de Sant Pau, world heritage sites; Fiesta of St George (Apr), Fiesta Mayor (Sep); location of the 1992 Summer Olympic Games.

Barclay, Robert (1843–1913) British banker, under whom in 1896 the merger of 20 banks took place to form Barclay & Co Ltd. In 1917 the name was changed to Barclay's Bank Ltd.

Barclay de Tolly, Mikhail Bogdanovich, Knaz (Prince) [bah(r)**kliy** duh **tol**yuh] (1761–1818) Russian soldier of Scottish descent, born in Luhda-Grosshof, Livonia (modern Estonia and Latvia). He entered a Russian regiment in 1786 and gained rapid promotion. In the war against Finland he defeated the Swedes, and forced a surrender by crossing the frozen Gulf of Bothnia in strength (1808). Tsar Alexander I appointed him minister of war in 1810. Forced to give battle to Napoleon at Smolensk (1812), he was defeated and was superseded by Kutuzov. He fought at Borodino (1812), was again promoted commander-in-chief after the Battle of Bautzen (1813), served at Dresden and Leipzig (1813), and took part in the capture of Paris (1814). In 1815 he was made a prince.

barcode A pattern of black vertical lines, with information coded in the relative widths of the lines. This type of coding is very widely used in the retail market, such as on food packages. The barcoded labels can be read by special barcode scanners, and the output entered into a computer to link the product with such factors as price and stock level. There are standards for barcodes, such as the European Article Numbering Code and, in North America, the Universal Product Code.

bard Among ancient Celtic peoples, a poet-minstrel who held a privileged place in society, singing the praises of chiefs and celebrating heroic deeds, historical events, genealogies, and the passing of laws. The bards of Gaul disappeared under the Roman Empire, but in Ireland, Wales, and the Gaelic-speaking area of Scotland they survived until the 18th-c. In Wales, the bardic tradition was revived in the Romantic period, and contestants today for the Chair at the National Eisteddfod must compose their poems in the classical bardic verse-form, in strict metre, with alliteration and internal rhyming.

Bardeen, John [bah(r)**deen**] (1908–91) Physicist, born in Madison, Wisconsin, USA. He studied electrical engineering at Wisconsin University, and mathematical physics at Princeton (1936). After World War 2, he joined a new solid-state physics group at Bell Telephone Laboratories, where with Walter Brattain and William Shockley he developed the point-contact transistor (1947), for which they shared the Nobel Prize for Physics in 1956. Professor at Illinois University (1951–75), with Leon Cooper and John Schrieffer he received the Nobel Prize for Physics again in 1972 for the first satisfactory theory of superconductivity (the *Bardeen–Cooper–Schrieffer* or *BCS theory*), thereby becoming the first person to receive the Nobel Prize for Physics twice.

Bardot, Brigitte [bah(r)**doh**], originally **Camille Javal** (1934–) Film actress, born in Paris, France. A ballet student and model, her appearance on the cover of *Elle* led to her film debut in Jean Boyer's *Le Trou Normand* (1952, Crazy for Love). *Et Dieu créa la femme* (1956, And God Created Woman) established her reputation as a sex kitten. Her roles exploited an image of petulant sexuality that was reinforced by a much publicized off-camera love life. Her many screen credits include *La Vérité* (1960, The Truth), *Le Mépris* (1963, Contempt), *Viva Maria* (1965), and *Si Don Juan était une Femme* (1973, If Don Juan Were a Woman). She retired from the screen in 1973 and has devoted herself to campaigning for animal rights.

Barebone's Parliament The British 'Parliament of Saints' (4 Jul–12 Dec 1653), nominated by the Council of Officers of the Army to succeed the Rump Parliament; named after radical member Praise-God Barebone. It instituted civil marriage and sought legal reforms; but collapsed after disagreements over the abolition of tithes and lay patronage in the Church.

Barenboim, Daniel [barenboym] (1942–) Pianist and conductor, born in Buenos Aires, Argentina. Educated at Santa Cecilia Academy in Rome, he studied with his father, then with Nadia Boulanger and others. He made his debut with the Israel Philharmonic Orchestra in 1953. A noted exponent of Mozart and Beethoven, he gained his reputation as pianist/conductor with the English Chamber Orchestra. He was musical director of the Orchestre de Paris (1975–87), and musical director-designate of the new Paris Opéra at the Place de la Bastille in 1987. He became musical director of the Chicago Symphony Orchestra in 1991. In 1967 he married the cellist Jacqueline du Pré.

Barents, Willem [baruhnts], also spelled **Barentz** (c.1550–97) Dutch navigator. He was pilot to several Dutch expeditions in search of the Northeast Passage, and died off Novaya Zemlya. His winter quarters were found undisturbed in 1871, and in 1875 part of his journal was recovered by another expedition. The *Barents Sea* was named after him.

Barents Euro-Arctic Council An international organization established in 1993 to renew trade and economic co-operation in the Barents Sea region. Its members are Denmark, Finland, Iceland, Norway, Russia, and Sweden, with one Sami (Lapp) representative.

Barents Sea [barents], Russian **Barentsovo More**, Norwegian **Barents Havet** area 1 405 000 sq km/542 000 sq mi. Shallow arm of the Arctic Ocean, lying N of Norway and European Russia; warm North Cape Current disperses pack-ice in the S; Murmansk and Vardö ports are ice-free; fishing area.

Barère (de Vieuzac), Bertrand [barair] (1755–1841) Revolutionary and regicide, born in Tarbes, S France. He was originally a moderate in the National Convention, but later helped form the Committee of Public Safety, which he defended with great eloquence. After the fall of Robespierre (1794) he was imprisoned, but escaped. He served under Napoleon, was later exiled at the Restoration, but returned to Paris under an amnesty in 1830.

Bari [baree] 41°07N 16°52E, pop (2000e) 357 000. Seaport and capital town of Bari province, Puglia, SE Italy; on a peninsula in the Adriatic Sea, NW of Brindisi; archbishopric; airport; car ferries; university (1924); naval college; industrial and commercial centre; petrochemicals, textiles, shipbuilding, food processing, printing, paper making, glass; site of Italy's first atomic power station; Cathedral of San Nicola (begun 1087); annual Levante Fair (Sep).

barite [bairiyt] The mineral form of barium sulphate ($BaSO_4$), the chief ore of barium. Found in hydrothermal vein deposits, it is used in paints, paper making, and drilling muds; earlier known as **barytes**.

barium [bairium] Ba, element 56, in Group II of the periodic table, melting point 725°C. It is a very reactive metal. In most of its compounds, it occurs as Ba^{2+}, eg BaO_2 is barium (II) peroxide. Its soluble compounds are highly poisonous, but the very insoluble sulphate, $BaSO_4$, is used in the so-called **barium meal** to provide material opaque to X-rays.

bark In its everyday sense, the rough, protective outer layer of the woody parts of trees and shrubs; in botany, the term also embraces several inner tissues, including cork and phloem. Continued growth causes the bark to stretch, often cracking, flaking, or peeling in distinctive patterns as it is replaced by new growth from the cambium layers.

bark beetle A small, dark beetle whose egg chamber is excavated by adults under tree bark. The fleshy, legless larvae tunnel away from the chamber after hatching. Some species carry fungal diseases of trees. (Order: Coleoptera. Family: Scolytidae.)

Barker, George Granville (1913–91) Poet, born in Loughton, Essex, SE England, UK. He lived abroad, teaching at universities in the USA and Japan, but has lived mainly by his writing. He published his first book of poetry in 1933, his early career suffering by comparison with his contemporary Dylan Thomas.

He wrote prolifically in the following decades, a major work being *The True Confession of George Barker* (1950). He also published essays, plays, scripts, and novels, and his *Collected Poems* appeared in 1987.

Barker, Pat(ricia Margaret) (1943–) Novelist, born in Thornby-on-Tees, Cleveland, NE England, UK. She started to write after attending Angela Carter's writing classes. *Regeneration* (1991), the first of her acclaimed trilogy about World War 1, is based on the real-life encounter between the poet Siegfried Sassoon and the medical psychologist W H R Rivers. *The Eye in the Door* (1993, Guardian Fiction Award), shows how conscientious objectors of the time were treated; *The Ghost Road* (1995, Booker), tells of one soldier's traumatic return to the Front. Later novels include *Another World* (1998) and *Double Vision* (2003).

Barker, Ronnie, popular name of **Ronald William George Barker** (1929–) Comic actor, born in Bedford, Bedfordshire, SC England, UK. An amateur performer, he made his professional debut at Aylesbury Repertory Theatre in *Quality Street* (1948). An affable figure, adept at precisely detailed characterizations, tongue-twisting comic lyrics, and saucy humour, his many radio and television appearances include *The Frost Report* (1966–7), the widely popular *Porridge* (1974–7), *Open All Hours* (1976, 1981–5) and, in partnership with Ronnie Corbett, the long-running *The Two Ronnies* (1971–87). His film roles include *Wonderful Things* (1958), *Robin and Marian* (1976), and *Porridge* (1979). He retired in 1987 and his autobiography, *Dancing in the Moonlight*, appeared in 1993.

barking deer *muntjac*

barking wolf *coyote*

bar Kokhba, Simon [kokhba], also spelled **bar Kochba** (?–135) Jewish leader in Palestine. With the rabbi Akiba ben Joseph, he led a rebellion of Jews in Judaea from 132 in response to the founding of a Roman colony (Aelia Capitolina) in Jerusalem. It was suppressed by Hadrian with ruthless severity, and he was killed at the Battle of Bethar. In 1960 some of his letters were found in caves near the Dead Sea.

bark painting A traditional product of Australian Aboriginal art: human and animal figures, sometimes geometrically stylized but occasionally naturalistic, painted on irregularly-shaped pieces of bark. They were created mainly for use in magical and initiation ceremonies, but sometimes, apparently, for aesthetic delight.

barley A cereal of Middle Eastern origin (*Hordeum vulgare*), cultivated in temperate regions; inflorescence a dense head with long, slender bristles; grains in 2, 4, or 6 rows. It is more tolerant of drought, cold, and poor soil than wheat, and an important crop in such regions as N Europe. Germinated grains produce malt used in brewing beer and making whisky; its flour is used in cakes and porridge. It is also an important animal feed. (Family: Gramineae.)

Bar Mitzvah [bah(r) mitsva] (Heb 'son [*bar*]/daughter [*bat*] of the commandment') Jewish celebrations associated with reaching the age of maturity and of legal and religious responsibility, being 13 years plus one day for boys. The child reads a passage from the Torah or the Prophets in the synagogue on the Sabbath, and is then regarded as a full member of the congregation. Non-Orthodox synagogues have a **Bat Mitzvah** ceremony for girls at 12 years plus one day.

barn *cross section*

Barna, Victor, originally **Gyözö Braun** (1911–72) Table tennis player, born in Budapest, Hungary. He won a record 20 English titles between 1931 and 1953, including five singles titles (1933–5, 1937–8), and also won 15 world titles, including five singles (1930, 1932–5). One of the game's greatest players, he emigrated to France before becoming a British citizen in 1938. After retirement, he played exhibitions and formed the Swaythling Club, a social club for ex-table tennis internationals.

Barnabas [bah(r)nabas] (1st-c) Christian missionary, originally a Levite from Cyprus called Joseph (*Acts* 4.36). He was a companion and supporter of Paul during Paul's early ministry to the Gentiles, but later separated from him after a dispute over John Mark (*Acts* 15.36) and went to Cyprus. The so-called *Letter of Barnabas* is a spurious 2nd-c work.

barnacle A marine crustacean that lives attached by its base to hard substrates or to other organisms; body enclosed within a shell formed of calcareous plates; typically feeds by filtering food particles from the water with modified thoracic limbs (*cirri*); c.1000 species, found from the intertidal zone to deep sea; some parasitic on crabs. (Subclass: Cirripedia.)

barnacle goose A goose native to the N Atlantic (*Branta leucopsis*). In the Middle Ages it was thought these geese hatched from goose-necked barnacles. They were thus considered fish, not birds, and were eaten on Friday when only fish was permitted. (Family: Anatidae.)

Barnard, Christiaan (Neethling) (1922–2001) Surgeon, born in Beaufort West, SW South Africa. He graduated from Cape Town medical school, and after research in America returned to Cape Town in 1958 to work on open-heart surgery and organ transplantation. In December 1967 at Groote Schuur Hospital he performed the first successful human heart transplant. The recipient, Louis Washkansky, died of pneumonia 18 days later, drugs given to prevent tissue rejection having heightened the risk of infection. A second patient, Philip Blaiberg, operated on in January 1968, survived for 594 days. Barnard retired in 1983.

Barnardo, Thomas John [bah(r)nah(r)doh] (1845–1905) Physician and philanthropist, the founder of homes for destitute children, born in Dublin, Ireland. A clerk by profession, he was converted to Christianity in 1862 and, after a period spent preaching in the Dublin slums, moved to London in 1866 to study medicine with the aim of becoming a medical missionary. Instead he founded in 1867, while still a student, the East End Mission for destitute children in Stepney and a number of homes in Greater London, which came to be known as the *Dr Barnardo's Homes*. The present-day organization is responsible for over 140 schools, hostels, and youth centres, with branches in such countries as Australia, New Zealand, and Kenya.

Barnard's star One of the very few stars which is named after the astronomer who studied it. In June 1916, Edward Emerson Barnard (1857–1923) of Yerkes Observatory, USA, measured a proper motion of 10·31 seconds of arc per year, still the largest known. In about 180 years this star moves through our sky by a distance equal to the diameter of the full Moon. The second-nearest star to the Sun, distance 1·82 parsec, it is a red dwarf, too faint to see with the naked eye.

Barnave, Antoine (Pierre Joseph Marie) [bah(r)nahv] (1761–93) French revolutionary, born in Grenoble, E France. He studied law, and became a member of the new National Assembly (1789), where he established a reputation as an orator, and helped to carry through the Civil Constitution of the Clergy. He brought back the royal family from their abortive flight to Varennes (1791), but subsequently developed royalist sympathies, advocated a constitutional monarchy, and was guillotined.

Barnburners A faction within the US Democratic Party in New York State (in the 1840s), which arose through opposition to extending slavery into Western territory conquered during the Mexican War. Many Barnburners, led by former President Van Buren, joined the Free Soil Party in 1848. Their name derived from the story of a Dutch farmer who burned down his barn (the Democratic Party) in order to drive out rats (slavery).

Barnes, John (Charles Bryan) (1963–) Footballer, born in Kingston, Jamaica. He played for Watford, moving to Liverpool in 1988, to Newcastle in 1997, and on loan to Charlton in 1998. He won 79 caps playing for England. He joined Kenny Dalglish at Celtic Football Club as team coach (1999–2000).

Barnes, Peter (Henry) (1931–) Playwright and writer of screenplays, born in London, UK. His only major commercial success has been *The Ruling Class* (1968). Later plays, which include *The Bewitched* (1974), *Laughter* (1978), *Red Noses* (1985), and *Sunset and Glories* (1990), show him to be a master of non-naturalistic techniques drawn from Elizabethan theatre, mediaeval and 19th-c farce, German Expressionist drama, and the *commedia* *dell'arte*. Other plays include *Lunar Park Eclipsis* (1995) and *Corpsing* (1996).

Barnes, William (1801–86) Pastoral poet, born in Sturminster Newton, Dorset, S England, UK. He taught in a school at Dorchester, then went to Cambridge and took holy orders. He became curate of Whitcombe in 1847, and rector of Winterborne Came, Dorset, in 1862. His three volumes of poetry were collected in 1879 as *Poems of Rural Life in the Dorset Dialect*. He also wrote several philological works.

Barney, Natalie (Clifford) (1876–1972) Socialite and writer, born in Dayton, Ohio, USA. Born into a wealthy family, she was educated in France and New York City (1894), before settling in Paris (1898), where she established an international salon at her home. She wrote poetry, plays, and novels, and became notorious for her love affairs with women. Her memoirs include *Souvenirs indiscrets* (1960, Indiscreet Memories) and *Traits et portraits* (1963).

barn owl An owl of worldwide distribution; legs feathered; inhabits forests, open country, and habitation; eats small vertebrates, especially mammals and insects; nests in crevices high above ground (or in buildings); sometimes called **screech owl**. (Genus: *Tyto*, 6 species. Family: Tytonidae.)

Barnum, P(hineas) T(aylor) (1810–91) Showman, born in Bethel, Connecticut, USA. He ran a museum in New York City, introducing freak shows, and in 1842 sponsored the famous dwarf 'General Tom Thumb' (Charles Stratton), using flamboyant publicity. He managed the US tour of Jenny Lind in 1847, and in 1881 joined with his rival **James Anthony Bailey** (1847–1906) to found the famous Barnum and Bailey circus, calling it 'The Greatest Show on Earth'. It is known today as the Ringling Brothers and Barnum and Bailey Circus.

barograph *barometer*

Baroja (y Nessi), Pío [baroha] (1872–1956) Writer, born in San Sebastián, N Spain. In 1913 his sister, Carmen Baroja, married Rafael Caro Raggio, founder of the Baroja family publishing house (1917). His first book of short stories, *Vidas sombrías* (1900, Sombre Lives), was the prelude to more than 70 volumes of novels and essays, distinguished by quiet humour and a vivid style derived from the 19th-c Russian and French masters. His best novels are those with a Basque setting.

barometer A meteorological instrument used to measure atmospheric pressure, invented in 1643 by Torricelli. It was based on the principle that the height of a column of mercury in a tube sealed at one end and inverted in a dish of mercury will change according to the atmospheric pressure exerted on the dish of mercury. This is still in common use, and several types exist. Another method of measuring pressure is the **aneroid barometer**, a metallic box containing a vacuum, and with flexible sides which act as a bellows expanding and contracting with changing atmospheric pressure. Changes of pressure through time are recorded on a **barograph**.

baron / baroness In the UK, a title of nobility, ranking below viscount; the title held by most life peers. Originally the term was used for a tenant-in-chief (one who held his land direct from the sovereign).

baronet (abbreviation **bart**) In the UK, a hereditary title, not part of the peerage and not a knighthood, although baronets and knights are both styled 'Sir'. The form, which was originally purchased by the holder, was created by James I in 1611 to raise money to pay the troops in Ireland.

Barons' Wars The wars in England during the reigns of John and Henry III. **1** (1215–17) Despite the granting of Magna Carta, many barons still defied John, and offered the crown to Prince Louis of France. After John's death, the French and baronial army was routed at Lincoln (May 1217), and the war was effectively ended by the Treaty of Kingston-on-Thames (Sep 1217).

2 (1264–7) After the Provisions of Oxford failed to achieve a settlement, some barons led by Simon de Montfort captured Henry III at Lewes (1264). Earl Simon was killed at Evesham (1265), and the king was restored to power by the Dictum of Kenilworth (1266).

Baroque (art and architecture) [barok, barohk] A style prevalent in the 17th-c and part of the 18th-c, characterized by curvilinear forms and ornate decoration arranged in dramatic compositions, often on a large scale and in a complicated fashion. Its principal exponents included architects Borromini and Le Vau, and the sculptor Bernini. In painting, the style is epitomized by the dramatic chiaroscuro of Caravaggio and Rubens. Baroque art was especially associated with Louis XIV, but spread over most of W Europe until it was transformed into Rococo in the early 18th-c.

Baroque (music) [barok, barohk] A period in musical history extending from c.1580 to c.1730. Its features include a gradual replacement of modality by tonality, a love of melodic ornamentation, the enrichment of harmony by more essential chromaticism, the prominence accorded to instrumental music, and the formation of the orchestra. Genres originating in the Baroque period include the opera, oratorio, cantata, sonata, and concerto. Composers of this period include Johann Sebastian Bach, Handel, Monteverdi, Purcell, and Vivaldi.

Barossa [barosa] pop (2000e) 37 000. A NE suburb of Outer Adelaide, South Australia; the Barossa Valley is a noted wine-producing area; wine festival every two years celebrates the grape harvest (alternating with Adelaide Festival of Arts).

Barotse *Lozi*

barque [bah(r)k] A sailing vessel with three or more masts. The aftermost mast is fore- and aft-rigged and the remainder square-rigged – a style which was especially prevalent in the last decade of the 19th-c, when sail made its last stand against competition from steamships.

barracuda [barakooda] Any of the voracious, predatory fishes widespread in tropical and warm-temperate seas; body slender, length up to 1·8 m/6 ft, jaws armed with many short teeth; feeds on other fish; some species important commercially and as sport fish. (Genus: *Sphyraena*. Family: Sphyraenidae.)

Barranquilla [barankeelya] 11°00N 74°50W, pop (2000e) 1 053 000. Modern industrial capital of Atlántico department, N Colombia; on R Magdalena, 18 km/11 mi from its mouth; Colombia's principal Caribbean port; founded, 1721; airport; three universities (1941, 1966, 1967); bull ring; commerce, foodstuffs, footwear, drinks, tobacco, furniture, textiles, petrochemicals; modern cathedral; 5 sports stadia; 4-day carnival.

Barras, Paul François Jean Nicolas, comte de (Count of) [bara] (1755–1829) French revolutionary, born in Fox-emphoux, SE France. An original member of the Jacobin Club, he voted for the king's execution. He conducted the siege of Toulon, and suppressed the revolt in the S of France. Hated by Robespierre, he played the chief part in the tyrant's overthrow, and was appointed virtual dictator by the terrified Convention. In 1795, faced with a royalist rising, he called his young friend Napoleon to his aid, who assured his own future with the historical 'whiff of grape-shot'. The Directory being appointed, Barras was nominated one of the five members. Once more dictator in 1797, he guided the state almost alone, until his covetousness had rendered him so unpopular that Napoleon overthrew him easily in the coup of 18 Brumaire (9 Nov) 1799.

Barrault, Jean-Louis [baroh] (1910–94) Actor, mime, and producer, born in Le Vesinet, NC France. He was a member of the Comédie Française (1940–6), then with his actress wife, **Madeleine Renaud** (1903–94), founded his own company, le Troupe Marigny, which became celebrated for its performances of Molière, Claudel, and the Gide translation of *Hamlet*. He became director of the Théâtre de France (1959–68), the Théâtre des Nations (1965–7, 1972–4), and first director of the Théâtre d'Orsay (1974). His films include *La Symphonie fantastique* (1942), *La Ronde* (1950), and *The Longest Day* (1962). His theories of dramatic art are expressed in his autobiographical *Réflexions sur le théâtre* (1949, Reflections on the Theatre). As a mime-actor he is best known through his appearance as Deburau in *Les Enfants du paradis* (1945, The Children of Paradise), set in 19th-c France.

Barré, (Mohammed) Siad [baray] (1919–95) Somali soldier and president (1969–91). Educated at a military academy in Italy, he served as a police officer in the British and Italian trust administrations (1941–50). He joined the Somali army as a colonel in 1960, and became president after a military coup. Towards the end of his rule, the country broke up into warring factions, and he was deposed, leaving behind civil war, famine, and an international crisis in which many aid agencies, the UN, and the USA became involved.

barrel A measure of volume, its value depending on the substance contained. A barrel of alcohol is 189 litres; a barrel of petroleum is 159 litres.

barrel organ A mechanical musical instrument. By turning a handle at the side, the player both feeds a bellows and operates a rotating cylinder fitted with metal pins which allow air access to a set of pipes; the placing of the pins determines which pipes sound and when. The instrument is of great antiquity. It was widely used to play hymns in churches in the 18th–19th-c, and also as a street instrument, often with a pet monkey perched on top.

Barren Grounds The name given to the tundra region of N Canada, dominated by muskeg or sphagnum bog. It is an area of marshy depressions and meandering rivers, with an abundance of mosquitoes, and is a major range for caribou.

Barrie, Sir J(ames) M(atthew) (1860–1937) Novelist and playwright, born in Kirriemuir, Angus, E Scotland, UK. He studied at Edinburgh University, then wrote a series of autobiographical novels, and from 1890 wrote for the theatre, beginning with the successful *Walker, London* (1893), *Quality Street* (1902), *The Admirable Crichton* (1902), and *What Every Woman Knows* (1908), which established his reputation. It is, however, as the creator of *Peter Pan* (1904) that he will be chiefly remembered. An unfailing romantic, he continued his excursions into fairyland in such later plays as *Dear Brutus* (1917) and *Mary Rose* (1920). He became a baronet (1913), was awarded the Order of Merit (1922), and was rector of Edinburgh University (1930–7).

barrier islands Long, straight, narrow islands or peninsulas which generally parallel the coast and are separated from the mainland by a lagoon or salt marsh. Though barrier islands may have been formed in several ways, many appear to have been created as sea level rose between 5000 and 6000 years ago, moving large masses of sand across the continental shelf. Around 4000 years ago, sea level temporarily stabilized, and many barrier islands acquired their current shape. During the last 1000 years, sea level has again been rising, causing these islands to continue to migrate towards the mainland.

barrier reef *atoll*

barrigudo *woolly monkey*

Barringer Crater *Meteor Crater*

barrister A member of the legal profession in England and Wales whose work is mainly concerned with advocacy in the courts. Barristers have right of audience in the High Court and superior courts as well as in all other courts. In addition to trials and preparation for trials, they write advisory opinions. They are either **Queen's** (or **King's**) **Counsel** (leaders or leading counsel) or **junior barristers**. To be a barrister, it is necessary to be a member of one of the four Inns of Court. Not all barristers are in practice; many use the qualification for work in education, industry, or administration.

Barry, Sir Charles (1795–1860) Architect, born in London, UK. He was apprenticed to a firm of surveyors before going to Italy (1817–20). On his return, he designed the Travellers' Club (1831), the Manchester Athenaeum (1836), the Reform Club (1837), and the new Palace of Westminster (Houses of Parliament, 1840–70), completed after his death by his son **Edward Middleton Barry** (1830–80). His work showed the influence of the Italian Renaissance. He was knighted in 1852. His fifth son, **Sir John Wolfe-Barry** (1836–1918), was engineer of the Tower Bridge and Barry Docks.

Barrymore, Ethel, originally **Ethel Blythe** (1879–1959) Stage and film actress, born in Philadelphia, Pennsylvania, USA. The daughter of **Maurice Barrymore**, and a member of the famous family of actors. In 1897–8 she scored a great success in London with Sir Henry Irving in *The Bells*, had her first Broadway success in *Captain Jinks of the Horse Marines* (1901), and made some early silent films. In 1944 she won an Oscar for best supporting actress in *None But the Lonely Heart*. She was admired for her portrayal of lovable eccentrics.

Barrymore, John, originally **John Blythe**, known as **the Great Profile** (1882–1942) Stage and film actor, born in Philadelphia, Pennsylvania, USA. Brother of Ethel Barrymore and Lionel Barrymore of the great acting family, he made his debut in 1903 and became a matinee idol. He triumphed on stage as Hamlet (1922), then turned to films and radio. Married four times, he caricatured his own decadent, alcohol-ridden life in a series of minor comedies, including *The Great Profile* (1940).

Barrymore, Lionel, originally **Lionel Blythe** (1878–1954) Actor, born in Philadelphia, Pennsylvania, USA, the elder brother of Ethel and John Barrymore. He made a name for himself in *Peter Ibbetson* (1917) and *The Copperhead* (1918), thereafter taking many roles in films and radio plays, notably *Free Soul* (1931, Oscar), *Grand Hotel*, *Captains Courageous* (1937), and *Duel in the Sun* (1947). In the USA he played Scrooge annually for many years on radio. After twice breaking a hip he was confined to a wheelchair, but undeterred he scored a great success as Dr Gillespie in the original *Dr Kildare* film series.

Barstow, Dame Josephine (Clare) (1940–) Soprano, born in Sheffield, South Yorkshire, N England, UK. She studied at Birmingham University and the London Opera Centre (1965–66), making her debut with Opera for All (1964). Resident principal with Sadlers Wells (1967–8) and the Welsh National Opera (1968–70), she made her Covent Garden debut in 1969 and her US debut in 1977. She continued to perform with major opera houses around the world, and was made a dame in 1995.

Bart, Lionel (1930–99) Composer and lyricist, born in London, UK. In 1959, *Lock Up Your Daughters* ended the US domination of the musical theatre in London. He followed it with *Fings Ain't Wot They Used T'be* (1959), *Oliver!* (1960, adapted from Dickens's *Oliver Twist*), and *Blitz!* (1962), a cavalcade of East End life during World War 2. *Maggie May*, a between-the-wars story of a Liverpool prostitute, followed in 1964, but his Robin Hood musical, *Twang!!* (1965), was a flop, as was *La Strada* (1969). *Oliver!* enjoyed several successful revivals in later years.

barter Trade conducted without the use of currency. Goods are directly exchanged for one another, each party to the exchange seeking to make a profit. In the absence of a currency, the relative value of goods must often be negotiated through haggling.

Barth, John (Simmons) (1930–) Novelist and short-story writer, born in Cambridge, Maryland, USA. He studied at Johns Hopkins University, and was a professional drummer before turning to literature and teaching. Much admired by academic critics, his novels include *The Floating Opera* (1956), *Giles Goat-Boy* (1966), *The Tidewater Tales* (1987), and *The Last Voyage of Somebody the Sailor* (1991). Later works include *On with the Story* (1996) and *Coming Soon!!!* (2003).

Barth or **Bart, Jean** [bah(r)t] (1650–1702) Privateer, born in Dunkirk, NW France. He served first in the Dutch navy, but on the outbreak of war with Holland joined the French service. In 1691, in command of a small squadron in the North Sea, he destroyed many English vessels. In 1694, after a desperate struggle with a superior Dutch fleet, he recaptured a convoy of 96 ships and brought them to Dunkirk. Soon after he was taken prisoner and carried to Plymouth, but escaped in a fishing-boat to France. King Louis XIV received him with distinction at Versailles, and in 1697 appointed him to the command of a squadron.

Barth, Karl [bah(r)t] (1886–1968) Theologian, born in Basel, N Switzerland. He studied at Bern, Berlin, Tübingen, and Marburg. While pastor at Safenwil, Aargau, he wrote a commentary on St Paul's Epistle to the Romans (1919) which established his theological reputation. He became professor at Göttingen (1921), Münster (1925), and Bonn (1930), refused to take an unconditional oath to Hitler, was dismissed, and so became professor at

Basel (1935–62). His theology emphasized the finiteness of man, and God's unquestionable authority and 'otherness'. His many works include the monumental *Kirchliche Dogmatik* (4 vols, 1932–67, Church Dogmatics, incomplete).

Barthes, Roland (Gérard) [bah(r)t] (1915–80) Writer, critic, and teacher, born in Cherbourg, NW France. After researching and teaching he began to write, and his collection of essays entitled *Le Degré zéro de l'écriture* (1953, trans Writing Degree Zero) immediately established him as France's leading critic of Modernist literature. Other works include *Mythologies* (1957). His literary criticism avoided the traditional value judgments and investigation of the author's intentions, addressing itself instead to analysis of the text as a system of signs whose underlying structure forms the 'meaning' of the work as a whole. For 16 years he was a member of the faculty of the Ecole Pratique des Hautes Etudes in Paris, and from 1976 was professor of literary semiology at the Collège de France, gaining international recognition as a developer of semiology and structuralism.

Bartholdi, (Frédéric) Auguste [bah(r)tholdee], Fr [bah(r)toldee] (1834–1904) Sculptor, born in Colmar, E France. He specialized in enormous monuments, such as the 'Lion of Belfort', and created the colossal bronze Statue of Liberty, 'Liberty Enlightening the World', in New York harbour, unveiled in 1886.

Bartlett, Sir Frederic (Charles) (1886–1969) Psychologist, born in Stow-on-the-Wold, Gloucestershire, SWC England, UK. Professor of experimental psychology at Cambridge (1931–52), he wrote on practical (ergonomic) problems in applied psychology, but is best-known for his pioneering cognitive approach to understanding human memory.

Bartlett, John (1820–1905) Publisher and bookseller, born in Plymouth, Massachusetts, USA. He was for many years owner of the University Book Store at Harvard (1849–63). He is best known as the compiler of *Bartlett's Familiar Quotations* (1855).

Bartók, Béla [bah(r)tok] (1881–1945) Composer, born in Nagyszentmiklós, SE Hungary. He studied in Pressburg and at the Budapest Academy of Music, then toured widely as a pianist. He first collected folksongs in 1904, discovering a treasury of national material, which he recorded and classified. From 1907 he was professor of piano at the Budapest Academy, a post relinquished only in 1934 in order to devote more time to ethnomusicological research. He left Hungary in 1939, and settled in the USA. His works include the opera *Duke Bluebeard's Castle*, the ballets *The Wooden Prince* and *The Miraculous Mandarin*, two violin and three piano concertos, orchestral music including the *Concerto for Orchestra*, chamber music including six string quartets, works for violin and piano, songs, choruses, and folksong arrangements.

Bartoli, Cecilia [bah(r)tohlee] (1966–) Mezzo-soprano, born in Rome, Italy. She studied at the Conservatorio di Santa Cecilia in Rome and was also coached by her parents, Silvana Bazzoni and Angelo Bartoli, both professional singers. Her debut performance was in Zurich in 1988. She has won four Grammy Awards, and received the Outstanding Contribution to Music award at the Classical Brits in 2003. Her albums include *The Vivaldi Album* (1999), *Gluck Italian Arias* (2001), and *The Salieri Album* (2003).

Bartolommeo, Fra [bah(r)tolomayoh], originally **Baccio della Porta** (1472–1517) Painter, leading artist of the High Renaissance, born near Florence, NC Italy. Under the influence of Savonarola he publicly burnt many of his paintings and in 1500 became a Dominican novice, but Raphael's visit to Florence in 1504 encouraged him to take up painting again. He worked in Venice (1507), then in Florence (c.1509–12), before going to Rome. His work is distinguished by controlled composition, delicate drawing, and the use of colour.

Bartolozzi sounds Special musical sounds (including microtones and chords) employed by woodwind players following techniques developed by Italian composer Bruno Bartolozzi (1911–80), and set out in his *New Sounds for Woodwind* (1967).

Barton, Clara, popular name of **Clarissa Harlowe Barton** (1821–1912) Founder of the American Red Cross, born in Oxford, Massachusetts, USA. She worked as a schoolteacher (1836–54), and during the Civil War (1861–5) helped to obtain supplies and comforts for the wounded. In Europe, she worked for the International Red Cross in the Franco-Prussian War (1870–1), and established the US branch of the Red Cross in 1881, becoming its first president (1881–1904). As a result of her campaigning, the USA signed the Geneva Convention in 1882.

Barton, John (1928–) Stage director, born in London, UK. He studied at King's College, Cambridge, where he was a fellow (1954–60), and joined the Royal Shakespeare Company at Stratford-upon-Avon in 1960, where he became associate director (1964–91) and then advisory director. He wrote and directed *The Hollow Crown* (1961), an anthology about English monarchs, and is the author of *Playing Shakespeare* (1984), based on the television series he made in 1982. In 1990 he wrote *The War That Never Ends* for BBC2. *Tantalus*, a 10-part epic drama based on the Trojan Wars, was produced in 2000 by the Denver Center Theatre Company in association with the Royal Shakespeare Company, and directed by Peter Hall.

Baruch [barukh] (7th–6th-c BC) Biblical character, described as the companion and secretary of the prophet Jeremiah (*Jer* 36), possibly of a wealthy family. His name became attached to several Jewish works of much later date, known as: 1 Baruch (the Book of Baruch); 2 (the Syriac Apocalypse of) Baruch; and 3 (the Greek Apocalypse of) Baruch. There is also a Christian Apocalypse of Baruch in Ethiopic.

barycentre For a group of objects, such as the Solar System or a cluster of stars, the point at which total mass may be considered to be concentrated ('the centre of gravity') for the purposes of calculating its gravitational effect on other objects.

baryon [barion] In particle physics, a collective term for heavy matter particles which experience strong interactions. Baryons are composed of three quarks. The least massive baryon is the proton, into which other baryons decay.

Baryshnikov, Mikhail Nikolaievich [barishnikof] (1948–) Dancer, born in Riga, Latvia. He trained at the Riga Choreography School, then with the Kirov Ballet in St Petersburg. In 1974 he defected to the West while on tour in Canada, joining the American Ballet Theatre, and later the New York City Ballet, where he worked with George Balanchine. He returned to American Ballet Theatre, taking over as artistic director (1980–9), and in 1990 formed the White Oak Dance Project with Mark Morris. He has taken part in several Hollywood films, including *The Turning Point* (1977).

barytes *barite*

baryton An obsolete musical instrument resembling a bass viol, with (usually) six strings which were bowed and a further 10–15 which were plucked. Between 1765 and 1778 Haydn wrote numerous pieces for the instrument.

basalt [basawlt] The most common extrusive igneous rock, characterized by low silica content, and composed essentially of plagioclase feldspar and pyroxene. It is a dark, fine-grained rock, solidified from lava erupted from fissures or craters. Submarine basalts, extruded along mid-ocean ridges, form the oceanic crust. Subaerial eruptions produce extensive flows, the largest of which form the Deccan Plateau, India, and the Columbia–Snake R Plateau, USA. It is commonly used as a building stone and road-stone aggregate.

base (chemistry) A substance liberating hydroxide ions in water, an acceptor of protons, or a donor of electron pairs: each of these definitions includes the previous one. The term is thus the opposite of an acid, whatever definition of acid is used. In water, strong bases include the hydroxides of the alkali metals, while weak bases include ammonia and the amines.

base (mathematics) The number on which a system of counting is constructed (**number-base**). The numbers in common use are in base ten, which uses ten symbols 0–9, and expresses numbers in multiples of powers of ten; thus 'three hundred and forty-two' is written 342, since it is $3 \times 10^2 + 4 \times 10 + 2$. A

baseball

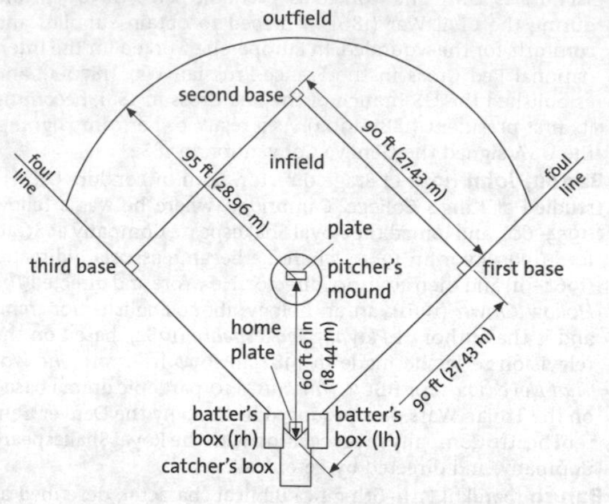

Minimum distance along each foul line is 250 ft (72.2 m)
Distance to the farthest point in centre field is at least 400 ft 122 m)

A team game played on a wedge-shaped field, with a diamond-shaped infield (the *diamond*), by two sides of players with a bat and ball. One team, on offence or *at bat*, tries to score the most runs by having their players circle the bases before they are put *out* by the other team which is *in the field*. An out is made when the batter fails to hit a legally pitched ball on three successive occasions (a *strikeout*, see below), or when the fielding team catches a batted ball before it touches the ground, tags a member of the offensive team between the bases, or touches a base before an offensive player reaches that base. The defensive team is aided in stopping the offensive team by fielding batted balls with an oversized glove or *mitt*. Each game is made up of nine innings unless the score is tied, in which case the game is extended into *extra innings* until one team outscores the other in a particular inning. Each inning is divided into two parts - the *top* and *bottom*. The visiting team always bats first (the top) and the home team always bats last (the bottom). Each team at bat is allowed three outs in its half inning. The major confrontation of the game centres on the *pitcher* and *batter*. The pitcher hurls the ball (at upwards of 145 kph/90 mph) towards the batter, who stands alongside the home plate poised to strike the ball. If the batter swings at the ball and fails to hit it, or if the pitcher throws the ball into a designated strike zone without the batter swinging at the ball, a *strike* is called. Three strikes causes a batter to be declared out. Conversely, if the pitcher fails to throw the ball into the strike zone and the batter does not swing, a *ball* is called. Four balls allow the batter to take first base. The home plate umpire, who stands behind the catcher, determines if the ball is within the strike zone (which comprises the area over home plate extending from the midway point between the top of the batter's shoulders to the top of his pants, down to the top of his knees). If the batter slices the ball outside the foul lines, the umpire call a 'ball'. If the batter strikes the ball beyond the playing area's limits (within the foul lines), or if he circles the bases before being put out, he has hit a *home run* (or *homer*).

Baseball is called the *national pastime* in the USA. Professional teams usually consist of 25 players. The *Major League* of North America is divided into the American League and National League, each consisting of an Eastern, Western, and (since 1994) Central division. In the National League 9 players can participate at one time for each team, while in the American League 10 take part because that league employs the designated hitter rule allowing a team to replace the pitcher in its batting order with a player who bats but does not play the field. The culmination of the season, which runs from April through October, is a best-of-seven game *World Series* between the champions of each league. The origins of the game are unclear. The person most widely cited as the game's inventor is a West Point cadet, Abner Doubleday, who in 1839 laid out a diamond at Cooperstown, NY, where the modern day Baseball Hall of Fame stands. However, there is evidence that the game was played much earlier, and gradually evolved into its present form. The first formal set of baseball rules were drawn up by Alexander Cartwright in 1845. Baseball is becoming increasingly popular in Japan and Latin America, and in 1992 a Canadian team (the Toronto Blue Jays) won the World Series for the first time.

number in base five, which uses five symbols 0–4, would be written as the sum of multiples of powers of five; thus 'seventy-three' (in base ten) is $2 \times 25+4 \times 5+3=2 \times 5^2+4 \times 5+3=243_{five}$: other than base ten, base two is the commonest base.

baseball *see panel*

Basel [bahzl], Eng **Basle** [bahl], Fr **Bâle** 47°35N 7°35E, pop (2000e) 179 000. Capital of Basel-Stadt demicanton and of Basel canton, N Switzerland; on the R Rhine, 69 km/43 mi N of Bern; centre of the Regio Basiliensis 'natural region'; second largest city in Switzerland; river port at the terminus of Rhine navigation; on the site of a Roman fort; mediaeval centre for silk, dyeing, and printing; joined the Swiss Confederacy, 1501; influential centre during the Reformation; scene of the first Zionist conference, 1897; airport (Basel-Mulhouse, on French territory, shared with France); railway junction; oldest Swiss university (1460); major European communications crossroads; Switzerland's leading centre for transshipment and international commerce; pharmaceuticals, salt, synthetics, chemicals, textiles, metallurgy, engineering, foodstuffs, tourism; Gothic minster (11th-c, largely rebuilt 14th-c), town hall (1504–14), Spalentor (1400), European World Trade and Convention Centre, zoological and botanical gardens, many museums and theatres; space-age pylon (symbolizing the city's location at the junction of France, Germany, and Switzerland); annual Swiss Industries Fair, 3-day Basel Carnival (Fasnacht).

Basel, Council of (1431–49) A controversial Council of the Church. It was intended to continue the work of the Council of Constance, against heresy, and initiating reform, but fell into dispute with Pope Eugenius IV for asserting the authority of the Council over that of the pope. When the pope attempted to dissolve it, the Council appointed Felix V, the last of the antipopes.

basenji [basenjee] A spitz breed of dog developed in C Africa for hunting; pale brown and white; short coat; keeps itself meticulously clean; cannot bark, but makes a yodelling noise.

Basho, Matsuo, pseudonym of **Matsuo Munefusa** (1644–94) Poet, born in Ueno (Iga), C Japan. He was raised in an atmosphere of poetry. Becoming master of the haiku, he started his own school, but later retired to a hermitage. Influenced by Zen Buddhism, he then journeyed extensively, and composed his celebrated book of travels *The Narrow Road to the Deep North* (1689) in a mixture of poetic prose and haiku.

BASIC [baysik] Acronym for **Beginner's All-purpose Symbolic Instruction Code**, a high-level computer programming language developed in the late 1950s at Dartmouth College in the USA, which has the advantage of being relatively simple to learn and implement. It has since been widely adopted as a standard language by microcomputer manufacturers, though there are now a large number of 'dialects' of BASIC for different types of computer which are not readily interchangeable. More recently BASIC has been overtaken by C as a programming language for microcomputers, but Microsoft has developed Visual Basic as a fourth generation language for programming client applications.

basic oxides *oxides*

Basidiomycetes [basidiohmiyseeteez] A subdivision of the true fungi, characterized by a sexual reproduction process that forms a club-shaped structure (*basidium*) bearing four haploid spores (*basidiospores*); basidia arranged on fruiting body (mushroom); includes edible mushrooms, agarics, puffballs, and many parasitic forms. (Division: Eumycota.)

Basie, Count [baysee], popular name of **William Allen Basie** (1904–84) Jazz pianist, organist, and bandleader, born in Red Bank, New Jersey, USA. After several years touring the vaudeville circuit as a soloist and accompanist to blues singers, he reached Kansas City, where he became pianist and co-arranger with the Bennie Moten band. He formed his own band in 1935, which became established in New York City as the Count Basie Orchestra until 1950, when big bands appeared to be no longer viable. But after two years of leading an octet, he re-formed a 16-piece orchestra and continued to lead it until his death. Over nearly 50 years as a bandleader, he remained true to music rooted in the Kansas City style, recognized for his highly distinctive piano playing. Among his most popular compositions are 'One O'Clock Jump' and 'Jumpin' at the Woodside'.

Basil I, known as **Basil the Macedonian** (c.812–886) Byzantine emperor (867–86), born in Thrace. He rose in the imperial service from obscure origins to become co-ruler in 867 with Michael III, whom he murdered in the same year. He formulated the Greek legal code, in a text known as the *Basilica*.The dynasty he founded ruled Constantinople until 1056.

Basil, St, known as **Basil the Great** (c.329–79) One of the greatest of the Greek fathers, born in Caesarea, Cappadocia, the brother of Gregory of Nyssa. He studied at Byzantium and Athens, lived for a time with hermits in the desert, and in 370 succeeded Eusebius of Caesarea as bishop of his native city. A fierce opponent of Arianism, he improved monastic standards and wrote many seminal works. Feast day 1 Jan (E), 2 Jan (W).

basil A bushy aromatic annual or perennial (*Ocimum basilicum*), growing to 1 m/3¾ ft, but often less; stems square; leaves oval, pale, glossy, in opposite pairs; flowers 2-lipped, white or purplish, in whorls; probably native to SE Asia, but widely cultivated in Europe and USA as a culinary herb and for use in perfumery. (Family: Labiatae.)

basilica [bazilika] Originally a royal palace or large oblong hall with double colonnades, for the administration of justice and commerce. It was later adopted by early Christians as a similarly arranged church with two or more aisles, timber roof, and apse. The name derives from Greek *basileus*, 'king'.

Basiliensis, Regio [rejioh basilyensis] area 234 sq km/90 sq mi. Transnational 'natural region' encompassing the frontier districts of France, Switzerland, and Germany, in the Upper Rhine Valley, between the Jura Mts and the Black Forest; administrative centre, Basel; regional centres at Mulhouse and Freiburg; international co-operation between local governments, industries, and universities promoted since 1963.

basilisk (mythology) A fabulous beast, a small dragon-like creature combining features of the snake and the cockerel. Its eye could freeze and kill, hence the expression 'If looks could kill'. It is equivalent to the **cockatrice**, which was hatched by a serpent from the egg of a cock.

basilisk (zoology) An iguana native to South America; male with bony projections on head and prominent sail-like crests along back; tail long; may run upright on long hind legs; can even run on water for short distances. (Genus: *Basiliscus*, 5 species.)

Basinger, Kim [baysinjer] (1953–) Film actress, born in Athens, Georgia, USA. She appeared in television commercials and was a top model before making her feature film debut in *Hard Country* (1981). Other films include *Nine ½ Weeks* (1986), *The Real McCoy* (1993), *The Getaway* (1994), and *I Dreamed of Africa* (2000). She won an Oscar for Best Supporting Actress in *L.A. Confidential* (1997). Her second marriage (1993–2001) was to actor Alec Baldwin.

Baskerville, John (1706–75) Printer, born in Wolverley, Hereford and Worcester, WC England, UK. He became a writing master in Birmingham, and from 1740 carried on a successful japanning (varnishing) business there. In c.1750 he began to make experiments in letter founding, and produced the types named after him. His works include editions of Virgil, Milton, and the Bible. In 1758 he became printer to Cambridge University.

basketball A five-a-side team ball game, invented by James Naismith in 1891 in Springfield, MA; but a similar game was played by the Olmecs in Mexico in the 10th-c BC. It is especially popular as a professional sport in the USA. Played on a court, the object is to throw the ball through your opponent's basket, situated at the end of the court, and 10 ft (3·05 m) above the ground. Virtually all professional basketball players are well over 6 ft (1·8 m) tall.

basking shark Extremely large, inoffensive shark (*Cetorhinus maximus*), second only to the whale shark as the largest living fish; length up to 10 m/33 ft, weight c.6000 kg/13 200 lb; lives in oceanic surface waters feeding entirely upon plankton filtered by stiff bristles on its long gill arches. (Family: Cetorhinidae.)

Basle *Basel*

Basov, Nikolai Gennadiyevich [basof] (1922–2001) Physicist, the inventor of masers and lasers, born in Usman, near Voronezh, SC Russia. At the Lebedev Physics Institute in Moscow (deputy director 1958–73, director from 1973), his work provided the theoretical basis for the development of the maser in 1955, for which he shared the 1964 Nobel Prize for Physics. In 1958 he invented the laser.

Basque Provinces [bask], Span **País Vasco** or **Provincias Vascongadas**, Basque **Euskadi** pop (2000e) 2 121 000; area 7261 sq km/2803 sq mi. Autonomous region of N Spain, comprising the provinces of Álava, Guipúzcoa, and Vizcaya; coastal hills, separated from the main ridge of the Cordillera Cantabrica to the S by valleys growing wheat; rivers provide hydroelectric power; industries centred around Bilbao and San Sebastian include metallurgy, paper, furniture.

Basques [basks] A people living in northern parts of Spain and neighbouring areas in France, and now thought to originate from local Mesolithic peoples; population c.805 000 in Spain, 130 000 in France, and 170 000 elsewhere, mainly in South America and the USA. They are physically similar to their neighbours, and are Roman Catholics, but their language, Basque, spoken by c.500 000, does not relate to any other European language, and is thought to be a remnant of the languages spoken in W Europe before the advent of the Indo-European family. Despite extensive cultural and linguistic assimilation, urbanized Basques retain strong ethnic identity, and their main city Bilbao is a centre of Basque nationalism. Most Basques sided with the Spanish Republic during the Spanish Civil War (1931–6), and an autonomous Basque Republic resisted Franco's Nationalists until crushed in 1937. Many thereafter went into exile. Since the death of Franco (1975), the new liberal Spanish monarchy has granted Basques some local autonomy (1978–9), but the more militant continue to agitate for a separate Basque state, engaging in terrorism for this end. The Basque Homeland and Freedom movement (Euzkadi Ta Azkatasuna, ETA) was founded in 1959, and its political wing, Herri Batasuna, was founded in 1978.

Basra [bazra], Arabic **al-Basrah** 30°30N 47°50E, pop (2000e) 954 000. Port capital of Basra governorate, SE Iraq, at head of the Shatt al-Arab, c.120 km/75 mi from the Persian Gulf; major centre of literature, theology, and scholarship in 8th–9th-c; modern administrative and commercial centre; airport; railway; university (1967); oil refining, fertilizers; port badly affected in 1980s by Iran–Iraq war and again in 1991 during and after the Gulf War; attacked by US-led coalition forces (Mar 2003) during the Iraq War.

bas-relief [bah ruhleef] Low relief sculpture, in which the design projects only very slightly from the background, as on a coin.

Masters of the technique include Donatello and Desiderio da Settignano.

bass [bas] Marine and brackish-water fish (*Dicentrarchus labrax*) found in the surf zone around rocks and beaches of the NE Atlantic; body blue-grey with silver sides, length up to 1 m/ 3¼ ft; valuable commercial and sport fish. (Family: Serranidae.) The name is also used for other species of the families Serranidae and Centrarchidae.

Bassae [basay] A temple dedicated to Apollo Epicurius on the slopes of Mt Lykaion, SW Arcadia, Greece; a world heritage site. It was built in the 5th-c BC by Ictinos for the people of Phigalia after their city escaped a plague epidemic. Rediscovered in 1763, it has since been largely re-erected.

Bassani, Giorgio [basahnee] (1916–2000) Novelist and poet, born in Bologna, N Italy. He lived until 1943 in Ferrara, where much of his fiction is set. His first major success was *Cinque storie ferraresi* (1956, Five Stories of Ferrara), most of them composed in the aftermath of World War 2. A sensitive chronicler of Italian Jews and their suffering under Fascism, other major works include *Il giardino dei Finzi-Contini* (1962, The Garden of the Finzi-Continis, filmed in 1971) and *L'airone* (1968, The Heron, Campiello Prize).

Bassano, Jacopo da [basahnoh], also known as **Giacomo da Ponte** (c.1510–92) Founder of genre painting in Europe, born in Bassano, Venice, NE Italy. His best paintings are of peasant life and biblical scenes, and include the altarpiece of the Nativity at Bassano, 'Calvary' (c.1538, Cambridge), and 'Pastoral' (c.1565–70, Lugano). His four sons were also painters.

basse taille enamel [bas tiy] A technique of enamelling on silver, or occasionally gold, where the metal is carved and engraved, and translucent coloured enamel is applied on top with the image shining through. It was introduced about the end of the 13th-c, probably in Paris.

Basse-Terre [bas tair] pop (2000e) 178 000; area 848 sq km/ 327 sq mi. One of the two main islands of the French Overseas Department of Guadeloupe, Lesser Antilles, E Caribbean; separated from Grande-Terre I by the narrow Rivière Salée; mountainous, with active volcano Grande Soufrière rising to 1484 m/ 4869 ft; national park in C of island; capital, Basse-Terre, pop (2000e) 14 500; tourism.

Basseterre [bastair] 17°17N 62°43W, pop (2000e) 15 200. Capital and chief port of St Kitts-Nevis, N Leeward Is, E Caribbean, on SW coast of St Kitts I; airport; distribution centre; electrical components, garments, data processing, beverages; cathedral.

basset-horn An 18th-c musical instrument belonging to the clarinet family, with a lower compass than that of the normal clarinet. It was much used by Mozart, but fell into disuse in the 19th-c.

basset hound A breed of dog formerly used in France and Belgium for hunting; long, solid body, with very short legs; muzzle long and broad; ears long and pendulous; short-haired coat of white, black, and tan.

Bassey, Dame Shirley (Veronica) (1937–) Singer and entertainer, born in Tiger Bay, Cardiff, S Wales, UK. The youngest of seven children, she left school at 15 and worked in a factory while performing at local working men's clubs at the weekends. She soon turned professional, had a number of UK hit singles, and went on to international success spanning four decades. Her best-known songs include 'As Long as He Needs Me' (1960), 'What Now My Love' (1962), 'Goldfinger' (1964), 'Big Spender' (1967), and 'Diamonds are Forever' (1971). She was voted Show Business Personality of the Year in 1995 by the Variety Club of Great Britain. She was made a dame in 2000.

bassoon A musical instrument consisting of a jointed wooden pipe, about 2 m 54 cm/8 ft 4 in long, doubled back on itself, and fitted with metal keys and a curved crook with a double reed. It is, in effect, a bass oboe. The larger **double bassoon**, or **contrabassoon**, sounds one octave lower than the standard instrument.

Bass Strait [bas] A channel separating Tasmania from Victoria, Australia, maximum width 240 km/150 mi, depth 50–70 m/ 180–240 ft; named in 1798 after the British explorer George Bass (1771–1803); oil and natural gas.

basswood An American species of lime (*Tilia americana*), producing useful timber and bass/bast, the stringy inner bark used for mats and ropes. (Family: Tileaceae.)

Bastia [basteea] 42°40N 9°30E, pop (2000e) 40 500. Port and capital of Haute-Corse department, NW Corsica, France; in NE corner on narrow Cap Corse between mountains and sea; founded by the Genoese, 1380; capital of Corsica until 1811; largest port and chief town of the island; airport; railway; fishing, wine, tobacco, shipping trade, tourism.

Bastille [basteel] (Fr 'strongly fortified structure') A mediaeval fortress and prison in E Paris, France. King Charles V built the Bastille of Paris as a fortress in c.1370. For centuries it was used as a political prison by French monarchs, the symbol of Bourbon despotism. Stormed by a Parisian mob on 14 July 1789, its destruction came to have a unique place in French Revolutionary ideology as marking the end of the *ancien régime* and the beginning of the French Revolution. The anniversary of the day is a French national holiday.

bat A nocturnal mammal, widespread in tropical and temperate regions; hibernates in winter in cold areas; usually hangs head-down at rest; the only mammal capable of sustained flight (the wing is a web of skin stretched between elongated fingers and joined to the rear legs and tail); probably evolved to exploit night-flying insects. Most members of the suborder Microchiroptera eat insects; some also eat fish, frogs, birds, or other bats. They use echolocation to detect prey and avoid obstacles, and have a nose and ears which are often complex in shape. In contrast, **fruit bats** (or *flying foxes*) of the Old World tropics (suborder: Megachiroptera, 170 species) eat fruit and flowers detected by smell. They include the largest bats, with large eyes and a dog-like head (small ears and a long muzzle). They have better vision than other bats, and few use echolocation. A quarter of living mammal species are bats. The name **fruit bat** is also used for genus *Artibeus* (14 fruit-eating species) from the New World tropics (suborder: Microchiroptera; family: Phyllostomidae). (Order: Chiroptera, 951 species.)

Batak Six closely-related ethnic groups of C Sumatra, Indonesia, speaking Austronesian languages. Their ancestors were Proto-Malayan people fairly isolated in the Sumatran highlands until the early 19th-c. Indian cultural influences date back to the 2nd–3rd-c AD. The most literate and Christianized group are the Toba Batak, well-known for trade and their key role in national government. They are one-third Muslim, one-third Christian, and the rest adhering to traditional religion.

Batalha, Monastery of [batalya] A Dominican abbey, in Batalha, W Portugal, one of the great examples of Christian Gothic architecture; a world heritage site. It was founded in 1388 by King João I (r.1385–1433) in fulfilment of a vow made at the Battle of Aljubarrota, where Portuguese independence was established.

Batavian Republic [batayvian] The name given to Holland 1795–1806, after that country had been conquered by Revolutionary French forces in 1794–5. Between 1806 and 1810 the Kingdom of Holland was ruled by Napoleon's brother, Louis Bonaparte, but Holland was incorporated into France between 1810 and the collapse of French rule in 1813.

batch processing A defined series of tasks which are submitted to larger computers and executed only when time becomes available on the computer. This is in contrast to **interactive computing**, where the user accesses the computer in a conversational mode.

bateleur [bateler] An aerobatic hawk of the group known as **snake eagles** or **snake hawks** (*Terathopius ecaudatus*); native to Africa S of the Sahara; very long wings and short tail; eats reptiles, mammals, and carrion; robs other carrion-feeding birds; flies about 300 km/190 mi each day. (Family: Accipitridae.)

Bates, H(erbert) E(rnest) (1905–74) Novelist, playwright, and short-story writer, born in Rushden, Northamptonshire, C England, UK. He began his working life as a solicitor's clerk, provincial journalist, and warehouse clerk. His first play, *The Last Bread*, and his first novel, *The Two Sisters*, appeared in 1926. He is one of the greatest exponents of the short-story form. His best-known works are *Fair Stood the Wind for France* (1944), *The Jacaranda Tree* (1949), and *The Darling Buds of May* (1958), which became a popular television series in the UK.

Bates, H(enry) W(alter) (1825–92) Naturalist and traveller, born in Leicester, Leicestershire, C England, UK. He explored the valley of the Amazon (1848–59), accompanied by his friend Alfred Russel Wallace for the first four years, returning with 8000 species of hitherto unknown insects. In 1861 he published his distinctive contribution to the theory of natural selection in a paper explaining the phenomenon of mimicry in animals (later known as **Batesian mimicry**).

Bates, (Michael) Jeremy (1962–) Tennis player, born in Solihull, West Midlands. He was educated at Strodes Grammar School and Solihull Sixth Form College, and after winning national tennis titles at junior level turned professional in 1980. A member of the Davis Cup team (1984–95), his achievements include the Wimbledon mixed doubles title (1987), the mixed doubles champion Australian Open (1991), and the singles title Korean Open (1994). A former British number one, he retired in 1996.

Bates, William Horatio (1860–1931) Physician and ophthalmologist, born in Newark, New Jersey, USA. He studied at Cornell University (1881) and graduated from the College of Physicians and Surgeons (1885). Establishing a practice in New York City, he worked as clinical assistant at the Manhattan Eye and Ear hospital and was attending physician at Bellevue hospital (1886–8) and the New York Eye Infirmary. He was also a lecturer in ophthalmology at the New York Medical School and Hospital (1886–91). His book, *Better Eyesight Without Glasses* (1919), explained poor sight as a disturbance of normal mind–body co-ordination which results from mental, emotional, or other disturbances. He developed a series of exercises to achieve healthy eyesight which emphasize relaxation, memory, imagination, and perception to improve the communication between the eyes and the brain.

Bateson, William (1861–1926) Geneticist, born in Whitby, North Yorkshire, N England, UK. He studied at Rugby School and Cambridge, became Britain's first professor of genetics at Cambridge (1908–10) and director of the new John Innes Horticultural Institution there (1910–26), as well as professor of physiology at the Royal Institution (1912–26). He produced the first translation of the heredity studies of Gregor Mendel (1900), and played a dominant part in establishing Mendelian ideas. He is known as 'the father of genetics', a term he himself coined.

batfish Any of two groups of fishes with wing-like extensions; the deep-bodied Indo-Pacific genus *Platax* (Family: Ephippidae), and the bizarre Ogcocephalidae (including *Ogcocephalus*) with flattened triangular bodies and elbow-like pectoral fins; both sold as curios.

Bath, Lat **Aquae Calidae**, Old English **Akermanceaster** 51°23N 2°22W, pop (2000e) 84 400. Spa town, part of Bath and North East Somerset unitary authority (from 1996), SW England, UK; on R Avon, 19 km/12 mi ESE of Bristol; noted since Roman times for its hot springs; chartered in 1189; fashionable spa centre in 18th-c; railway; university (1966); tourism, printing, plastics, engineering; Roman baths, 15th-c Roman bath museum, abbey church, notable Georgian crescents; City of Bath a world heritage site; Mid-Somerset festival (Mar), Festival of the Arts (May).

Bath, Most Honourable Order of the A British order of chivalry, formally created by George I in 1725, but traditionally founded by Henry IV in 1399 at the Tower of London, when he conferred the honour on the 46 esquires who had attended him at his bath the night before his coronation. The order comprises the sovereign and three classes: Knights and Dames Grand Cross (GCB), Knights and Dames Commander (KCB), and Companions (CB). The ribbon is crimson, and the motto *Tria juncta in uno* ('three joined in one'), namely England, Scotland, and Ireland.

batholith A very large igneous rock mass, typically granite, intruded while molten into the surrounding country rock, outcropping over at least 100 sq km/40 sq mi and extending to unknown depth. It is characteristic of orogenic belts and subduction zones, such as the Andean batholith in South America or the Coast Range of W Canada and Alaska.

Bathurst *Banjul*

Bathurst and Melville Islands pop (2000e) 2200; area 7487 sq km/2890 sq mi. Islands off the NW coast of Northern Territory, Australia, c.80 km/50 mi N of Darwin; Aboriginal communities; town of Nguiu on Bathurst I (population 1000) founded as a Catholic mission in 1911; wood-carving and pottery.

bathymetry The measurement of the depths of sea-bottom features in large bodies of water. **Bathymetric charts** indicate the depths of water in feet, fathoms, or metres, and are used to show the morphology of submarine topographic features. Detailed bathymetric mapping was only possible with the advent of continuous echo-sounding, which was first extensively used during the German Meteor Expedition (1925–7).

bathypelagic zone The open ocean environment lying beneath the mesopelagic zone, extending from a depth of 1000 m/3300 ft down to 4000 m/13 200 ft. It lies above the **abyssal pelagic** (4000–6000 m/13 200–19 800 ft) and the **hadal pelagic** (6000 m–11 000 m/19 800 ft–36 300 ft) zones, but in common usage these zones are sometimes included under bathypelagic. All three environments are aphotic (without sunlight) and with few exceptions must depend on a continuous rain of organic detritus from above to support life. All three are characterized by nearly constant salinity, cold water temperatures, and high levels of dissolved nutrients. The bathypelagic zone includes the water overlying the continental slope and rise, whereas the abyssal pelagic zone encompasses the water overlying the abyssal hills and plains. The hadal pelagic zone is reserved for the waters isolated in deep ocean trenches.

bathyscaphe [**bathiskayf**] Any free-moving vessel designed for underwater exploration, consisting of a flotation compartment with an observation capsule underneath. Originally designed by Piccard in 1948, they have proved capable of reaching depths of over 10 000 m/32 000 ft. Modern submersibles (such as *Alvin*, which explored the *Titanic*) are much more manoeuvrable.

bathysphere [**bathisfeer**] A specially strengthened spherical vessel in which observers may be lowered to great depths by a parent vessel. First used in 1930, it achieved 923 m/3028 ft in 1934. Other forms of underwater exploration craft have made them obsolescent.

batik [**bateek**] A form of dyeing in which parts of the fabric are left undyed because of wax printed or painted onto it. The fabric is then crushed to crack the wax, and dyed. Removal of the wax leaves undyed areas covered in fine lines. This method, a form of *resist dyeing*, originated in Indonesia.

Batista (y Zaldívar), Fulgencio [**bateesta**] (1901–73) Cuban soldier and dictator, born in Oriente province. A labourer's son, he rose from sergeant-major to colonel in the army coup against President Machado (1931–3) and was later elected president (1940–4), fostering a major programme of social and economic reform. He stepped down in 1944, and travelled abroad, but returned to power following another army revolt in 1952, overthrowing President Prio Socorras. This regime was marked by oppression and corruption, and he was overthrown by Fidel Castro in 1959. He then found refuge in the Dominican Republic.

Bat Mitzvah *Bar Mitzvah*

Baton Rouge [**baton roozh**] 30°27N 91°11W, pop (2000e) 227 800. Capital of state in East Baton Rouge parish, SE Louisiana, USA; a deep-water port on the Mississippi R; founded, 1719; governed successively by France, Britain, and Spain; ceded to the USA as part of the Louisiana Purchase, 1803; declared its independence under the name Feliciana, 1810; incorporated as a town within Louisiana, 1817; state capital, 1849–61 and since 1882; airfield; railway; university (1860); oil refining, petrochemical industries, machinery; State Museum, Riverside Museum, the old capitol, Huey Long grave and memorial; during its history, it has been ruled by seven different governments: French, British, Spanish, West Floridan, Louisiana, Confederate, USA.

Batten, Jean (1909–82) Pioneer aviator, born in Rotorua, New Zealand. In 1934, in a Gypsy Moth, she broke Amy Johnson's record for the flight from England to Australia by nearly five days. She became the first woman to complete the return journey, and in 1936 made a record-breaking flight from England to New Zealand.

battered baby / child syndrome *child abuse*

battery (electricity) A device that converts chemical energy into electrical energy. The first battery, made by Alessandro Volta in c.1800, was the basis of the *voltaic cell* – two chemicals immersed in an electrolyte, enabling electrons to travel from one to the other along a circuit. *Primary cells* only discharge electricity, whereas *secondary cells* (or *accumulators*) can also be recharged. The batteries commonly encountered in torches, toys, cameras, etc are 'dry' primary cells, in which the electrolyte has been treated so that it will not spill out of the battery. 'Wet' primary cells are used in telephone and railway signalling systems. Secondary cells are used in motor vehicles.

battery (law) In several legal systems, the intentional touching of another person without that person's consent. It involves physical contact beyond that customary in everyday life, but not necessarily physical damage or force. Also, the person need not be aware that a battery is to take place (as in the case of a blow from behind) or has taken place (they might suffer a battery while unconscious). Consent may sometimes be implied, such as in the context of lawful and properly organized sporting activity such as a boxing match or rugby football, or reasonable surgery. However, a doctor who gave blood transfusions to a Jehovah's Witness, knowing that he carried a card stating no blood was to be given to him, was found guilty of battery in 1991.

battery farming *factory farming*

battle cruiser A powerful warship capable of defeating an enemy cruiser squadron. Originally a cross between an armoured cruiser and a battleship, it evolved to be of battleship size but lightly armoured and very fast.

battleship The most powerful warship capable of engaging an enemy; the word is derived from 'line-of-battle ship'. All other vessels originally served subsidiary purposes which aided the battleship in its role. The largest battleships ever built were the Japanese *Musashi* and *Yamato* (72 800 tonnes), each mounting 18·1-inch guns; both were sunk in World War 2. The largest battleship now in service is the USS *New Jersey* (58 000 tonnes), mounting nine 16-inch guns. Gun armament is now supplemented by cruise missile batteries.

baud [bawd] A unit used to measure the capacity of a communications channel to carry digital data; named after the French inventor, J M E Baudot. The baud rate of a communications channel is the number of signal changes per second with which the channel can cope. Using an analog link and current modem technology, up to 16 bits can be coded into each signal change; hence a 2400 baud channel can (but rarely does) carry 38 Kbps (kilobauds per second) of digital information. Even with digital transmission, the baud rate is not the same as the number of bits per second that can be transmitted. *Manchester encoding* requires two signal changes for each bit of data, so the maximum bit rate is only half the baud rate.

Baudelaire, Charles (Pierre) [bohduhlair] (1821–67) Symbolist poet, born in Paris, France. He was sent on a voyage to India, but stopped off at Mauritius. On his return to Paris in 1842, he met Jeanne Duval, a half-caste, who became his mistress and inspiration. He spent much of his time in the studios of Delacroix, Manet, and Daumier. His masterpiece is a collection of poems, *Les Fleurs du mal* (1857), for which author, printer, and publisher were prosecuted for impropriety in 1864, but which earned the praise of critics and was to exert an influence far into the 20th-c. Later works include *Les Paradis artificiels* (1860) and *Petits Poèmes en prose* (1869). His preoccupation with the macabre, the perverted, and the horrid was an essential feature of his work.

Baudot, Jean-Maurice-Emile [bawdoh] (1845–1903) Electrical engineer, born in Magneux, France. In 1874 he patented the Baudot code, used in telegraph systems, and in 1894 a system which allowed several messages to be sent along the same wire simultaneously (*multiplexing*).

Baudot code [bawdoh] A code for transmitting verbal messages in telegraph systems, devised by Jean-Maurice-Emile Baudot in 1874, and originally known as the **International Telegraph Code 1**. Unlike Morse code, which uses short dots and long dashes, the Baudot code uses equal length electrical pulses, either on or off. Every letter, number or figure can be represented by a five-bit combination of these pulses. Two sets of 32 combinations were devised – one to represent letters and the other containing figures and punctuation. It is still in use today for international wire communications and for press and weather systems. Modern versions of the Baudot code usually operate with groups of seven or eight 'on' and 'off' signals. A later system (*multiplexing*) allowed several messages to be sent along the same wire simultaneously. In multiplexing, each operator is connected to the wire for the exact amount of time it takes to transmit one letter of the Baudot code. By synchronizing the outgoing signals, it is possible to separate them and correctly read them when they are received. With the advent of digital computers in the 1960s, a new coding scheme, the **American Standards Code for Information Interchange (ASCII)** was developed and came to be widely used.

Baudouin I [bohdwĩ] (1930–93) King of the Belgians (1951–93), born at Stuyvenberg Castle, near Brussels, the elder son of Leopold III and his first wife, Queen Astrid. He succeeded to the throne in July 1951 on the abdication of his father over the controversy of the latter's conduct during World War 2. In 1960 he married the Spanish **Doña Fabiola de Mora y Aragón**. A Roman Catholic, in 1990 he resigned his throne for a day to overcome a constitutional crisis caused by his refusal to sign a law legalizing abortion.

Bauhaus [bowhows] An influential school of arts and crafts founded in Weimar by Walter Gropius in 1919. The aim was for artists and architects to work together to create a new unity in the arts. At first expressionist in style, the Bauhaus quickly championed the stark simplicity of functionalism. Students and teachers included Feininger, van Doesburg, Moholy-Nagy, Kandinsky, Klee, and Mies van der Rohe. The school was constantly troubled by opposition from local people and politicians, and by divisions amongst its own members. It moved to Dessau in 1925, but was closed by Hitler in 1933, many members living thereafter in the USA. A new director was appointed in 1987, and the renamed Bauhaus Dessau Foundation now contains a collection, studio, academy, and workshop.

Baum, Vicki [bowm], originally **Vicki Hedvig** (1888–1960) Novelist, born in Vienna, Austria. After writing several novels and short stories in German, she made her name with *Grand Hotel* (1930), which became a best-seller and a popular film. She emigrated to the USA in 1931, where her later novels included *Falling Star* (1934), *Headless Angel* (1948), and *The Mustard Seed* (1953).

Baumgarten, Alexander Gottlieb [bowmgah(r)tn] (1714–62) Philosopher of the school of Christian von Wolff, born in Berlin, Germany. In 1740 he became professor of philosophy at Frankfurt-an-der-Oder. His main works were *Metaphysica* (1739) and *Aesthetica* (1750–58), a long unfinished treatise which pioneered this field and helped establish the modern term *aesthetics*.

Baur, Ferdinand Christian [bowr] (1792–1860) Theologian and New Testament critic, born in Schmiden, SW Germany. He held the Tübingen chair of theology from 1826, and founded the 'Tübingen School' of theology, the first to use strict historical research methods in the study of early Christianity.

Bausch, Pina [bowsh], popular name of **Philippine Bausch** (1940–) Choreographer and dancer, born in Solingen, W Germany. She trained first at the Essen Folkwangschule and then in New York City. After a season with the Metropolitan Opera Ballet Company and another with US choreographer Paul Taylor, she returned to Essen, where she staged several operas for the Wuppertal Theatre. Her success led to an invitation to found her own company, and she began to produce her own work in the 1970s, including *Rite of Spring* (1975), *Café Muller* (1978), and *1980* (1980). Her choreography and particularly her unusual stagings mark a turning point in contemporary dance, and remain a powerful influence. In 1996 her company performed at the Edinburgh International Festival's 50th anniversary celebrations.

bauxite [bawksiyt] A natural mixture of hydrated aluminium oxide minerals produced by the weathering of rocks in hot, humid climates in which more soluble constituents are leached out. It is the chief ore of aluminium.

Bavaria, Ger **Bayern** pop (2000e) 11 677 000; area 70 553 sq km/ 27 233 sq mi. Province in SE Germany; bounded (E) by Czech Republic and (S) by Austria; largest province in former West Germany, and Europe's oldest existing political entity; capital, Munich; chief towns, Augsburg, Passau, Nuremberg, Würzburg, Regensburg; chief rivers, the Danube, Isar, Lech, Main; surrounded by the Bavarian Forest (E), Fichtelgebirge (NE), Bavarian Alps (S); a third of the area is forested; agriculture, electrical and mechanical engineering, clothing, timber, tourism; many spas and climatic health resorts.

Bavarian Alps, Ger **Bayerische Alpen** Mountain range extending E and W from L Constance to Salzburg; highest peak, the Zugspitze (2962 m/9718 ft); Allgäu Alps form W section; called the **Tirol Alps** in Austria.

Bavarian Forest, Ger **Bayerische Wald** Mountain range bounded NW by Chamb and Regen Rivers and SW by the Danube valley; merges N into the Bohemian Forest in the Czech Republic; highest peak, the Einodriegel (1126 m/3694 ft); largest continuous forest in Europe; contains Germany's first national park.

Bavarian Succession, War of the (1778–9) A short episode in the political rivalry between Austria and Prussia for hegemony among the German states. Military manoeuvring gave way to stalemate; the Habsburg acquisition of Innviertel further tarnished Frederick the Great's prestige.

Bax, Sir Arnold (Edward Trevor), pseudonym **Dermot O'Byrne** (1883–1953) Composer, born in London, UK. He studied piano at the Royal Academy of Music, London. His love of all things Celtic was expressed early in Irish short stories, which he wrote under his pseudonym, and musically in orchestral pieces (1912–13), songs set to the words of revival poets, the choral *St Patrick's Breastplate* (1923–4), and *An Irish Elegy* (1917), for English horn, harp, and strings. Between 1921 and 1939 he wrote his seven symphonies. Other works include tone poems, such as *In the Faery Hills* (1909) and *Tintagel* (1917), chamber music, and piano concertos. In 1942 he was made Master of the King's (from 1952 Queen's) Musick.

Baxter, James Keir (1926–72) Poet, playwright, and critic, born near Dunedin, New Zealand. He worked as a labourer, journalist, and teacher and led a bohemian life until he was converted to Roman Catholicism. He later founded a religious community on the Wanganui R. He published more than 30 books of poetry, notably *In Fires of No Return* (1958), *Howrah Bridge* (1961), and *Autumn Testament* (1972).

Bayazid I *Bayezit I*

Bayeux Tapestry [biyuh, biyoe] An embroidered wall-hanging in coloured wool on linen, narrating events leading up to the invasion of England by William of Normandy, and the Battle of Hastings in 1066. Probably commissioned by William's half-brother Odo, Bishop of Bayeux in N France, and embroidered in S England c.1067–77, its length is 68 m/224 ft, and its height 46 cm–54 cm/18–21 in. The contemporary social, military, architectural, and iconographic information the tapestry provides is of unparalleled importance.

Bayezit I [bajazet], also spelled **Bajazet** or **Bayazid**, nickname **Yildrim** ('Thunderbolt') (c.1354–1403) Sultan of the Ottoman empire. He succeeded his father (1389), and conquered Bulgaria, with parts of Serbia, Macedonia, and Thessaly, and most of Asia Minor. His rapid conquests earned him his nickname. For 10 years he blockaded Constantinople, defeating a large army of crusaders under Sigismund of Hungary (1396). He would have entirely destroyed the Greek empire if he had not been defeated by Timur near Ankara (1402).

Baykonyr Cosmodrome *Baikonur Cosmodrome*

Bayle, Pierre (1647–1706) Protestant philosopher and critic, born in Carlat, S France. In 1675 he took the chair of philosophy at Sedan until forced into exile at the University of Rotterdam in 1681, where he published a strong defence of liberalism and religious toleration. He was dismissed from the university in 1693 following the accusation that he was an agent of France and an enemy of Protestantism. In 1696 he completed his major work, the *Dictionnaire historique et critique*, a sceptical analysis of philosophical and theological arguments, which came to be influential in the 18th-c Enlightenment.

Baylis, Lilian Mary (1874–1937) Theatrical manager, born in London, UK. In 1890 the family emigrated to South Africa, where she became a music teacher in Johannesburg. Returning to England in 1898, she helped with the management of the Royal Victoria Hall. In 1912 she founded the Old Vic Theatre there; it became the only London theatre permanently to stage Shakespeare, as well as other classics. She also re-opened Sadler's Wells Theatre in 1931, making it the home for the Vic Wells Ballet (later the Royal Ballet) and the English National Opera.

Baylis, Trevor (1937–) Engineer and inventor, born in Kilburn, NW London, UK. He studied structural engineering at Southall Technical College, and started a successful swimming pool company while working at home on inventions to help the physically handicapped. In 1993 he began work on a clockwork ('wind-up') radio that dispensed with batteries and electric power, which could be used by isolated communities where energy resources were scarce or non-existent. By 1996 the radio was being commercially marketed, and has since been in demand globally, notably in rural Africa and by people working in disaster areas.

Bay of Pigs The attempted invasion of Cuba (Apr 1961) by Cuban exiles supported by the USA. The invasion force of 1300 men landed at Bahía de Cochinos (Bay of Pigs) on the S coast, but was rapidly overwhelmed and defeated by Cuban troops commanded by Fidel Castro.

bayonet A steel blade, thought to have been invented in Bayonne, France, in the 17th-c, which turns an infantryman's firearm into a thrusting weapon. Originally plugging into the end of the musket, by the early 19th-c bayonets were designed to fit into a slot beneath the muzzle, allowing the weapon to be fired at will. The bayonet was sheathed in a short scabbard when not in use. Modern infantry weapons still retain a facility for taking a bayonet, and modern bayonets have become more universally functional, including such tools as wirecutters.

bayou [biyoo] A section of still or slow-moving marshy water cut off from a main river channel. It is often in the form of an oxbow lake. Bayous are typical of the Mississippi R delta in Louisiana, USA.

bay owl An owl native to Africa and SE Asia; inhabits wet tropical forest; eats insects and vertebrates. (Genus: *Phodilus*, 2 species. Family: Tytonidae.)

Bayreuth [biyroyt] 49°56N 11°35E, pop (2000e) 73 500. Industrial and marketing town, capital of Oberfranken district, Germany, on a tributary of R Main; world famous as a festival city committed to the operas of Wagner; railway; university (1975); textiles, machinery, electricity supply; 16th-c old palace, new palace (1753), Wagner theatre (1872–6); Wagner Festival (Jul–Aug).

bay tree *sweet bay*

Bazaar Malay *Malay* (language)

bazooka A US infantry weapon developed during World War 2 which fires a small rocket projectile from a simple launching tube. The projectile's warhead is effective against light tank armour.

bazouka *kazoo*

BBC Abbreviation of **British Broadcasting Corporation**, the UK organization responsible for local, regional, national, and international television and radio services. It began radio broadcasts in November 1922 as the British Broadcasting Company, and received a Royal Charter in 1927, thereafter maintaining a national radio service (a monopoly until 1973). It began its television service in 1936 (a monopoly until the creation of the Independent Television Authority in 1954). Financed almost wholly by viewers' licence fees, it is formally independent of government, and committed to a public-service ethos. It is widely respected for its news service, its world external services, its patronage of the arts (especially music and drama), and its educational broadcasting, and has been instrumental in promoting a standardized form of spoken English.

BBC World Service A part of the British Broadcasting Corporation (BBC), providing radio services in English and 42 other languages. Based in London, it is funded by a grant from the Foreign and Commonwealth Office, but is editorially independent of the UK government. More than 900 national and local radio stations in over 90 countries rebroadcast World Service programmes.

BCD *binary coded decimal*

BCG An abbreviation of *Bacille Calmette-Guérin*, a vaccine used to protect against tuberculosis named after French bacteriologists Albert Calmette (1863–1933) and Camille Guérin (1872–1961). It consists of attenuated living tubercle bacteria.

BCS theory A quantum theory of superconductivity; developed by John Bardeen, Leon Cooper, and Robert Schrieffer in 1957. Bound states of two electrons (*Cooper pairs*) form, which account for zero electrical resistance and the Meissner effect. There has been experimental verification of the prediction that magnetic fields through a superconducting ring should have values that are multiples of a basic magnetic unit (the *fluxoid*).

beach Unconsolidated earth materials ranging in size from silt to boulders, which occur along a shore. Broadly defined, a beach extends from the upper landward limit of wave effects (usually the base of a sea cliff or dune) offshore to the greatest depths normally affected by wave activity (where storm waves break). Beaches of fine sand and silt-size particles normally occur where gentle wave action dominates, whereas pebbles, cobbles, and boulders are characteristic of beaches with high wave energy. Beaches can be divided into a breaker zone, surf zone, beach face, and berm (the almost horizontal area at the top). A beach is among the most dynamic of earth surface features, often changing profile on a seasonal or even daily basis.

Beach Boys, The US singing/instrumental group, formed in California in 1961, consisting originally of brothers **Brian Wilson** (1942– , vocalist, bass guitar, keyboards, songwriter), **Carl Wilson** (1946–98, vocalist, guitar) and **Dennis Wilson** (1944–83, vocalist, drums), with cousin **Mike Love** (1941– , vocalist) and **Al(an) Jardine** (1942– , vocalist, bass guitar, guitar); later also **Bruce Johnston** (1944–) and others. They found fame in the 1960s with Brian's cheerful songs of teenage West Coast life, surfing, fast cars and motorcycles, and all-American girls, including 'I Get Around', 'California Girls', and 'Good Vibrations'. In 1966, with the technically innovative album *Pet Sounds*, an increasingly reclusive Brian Wilson emulated the Beatles' imaginative use of recording techniques in a 'concept album'. Later, more pensive hit singles included 'I Can Hear Music' and 'Darling'. *Smile*, unfinished in the 1960s, was performed for the first time in 2004.

Beachcomber *Morton, John Cameron*

Beaconsfield, Earl of *Disraeli, Benjamin*

Beadle, George (Wells) (1903–89) Biochemical geneticist, born in Wahoo, Nebraska, USA. He taught at Stanford University (1937–46) and California Institute of Technology (1946–61), and was president of Chicago University (1961–8). He studied the genetics of maize, the fruit fly (*Drosophila*), and the bread mould (*Neurospora*). In association with Edward Laurie Tatum, he developed the idea that specific genes control the production of specific enzymes. Beadle and Tatum shared the Nobel Prize for Physiology or Medicine in 1958 with Joshua Lederberg.

beagle A breed of dog developed in Britain; a medium-sized hound with a sturdy body and short coat (coarse-haired forms exist); white, tan, and black; broad pendulous ears, deep muzzle; formerly used to track hares by scent.

Beaglehole, John Cawte (1901–71) Writer and historian, born in Wellington, New Zealand. He graduated from Victoria University College, to which he returned in 1936 as lecturer in history, remaining there as professor of British Commonwealth history (1963–6). His life's work was the masterly Hakluyt Society edition of *The Journals of Captain James Cook on his Voyages of Discovery* (1955–67), associated with which was his *The Endeavour Journal of Sir Joseph Banks* (1962). He was awarded the Order of Merit in 1970.

Beaker culture A prehistoric culture defined archaeologically by finely-made, pottery drinking vessels for mead or beer, often burnished and geometrically decorated. Found in graves of the 3rd millennium BC from Spain, Czech Republic, and Hungary to Italy and Britain, Beakers have often been taken as evidence for trans-European migrations perhaps originating in Spain. Equally, they could be no more than a status symbol disseminated widely by trade, and copied locally.

Beale, Dorothea (1831–1906) Pioneer of women's education, born in London, UK. She was principal of Cheltenham Ladies' College (1858–1906), and in 1885 founded St Hilda's College, Cheltenham, as the first English training college for women teachers. She sponsored St Hilda's Hall in Oxford for women teachers in 1894.

beam weapons *directed energy weapons*

bean A general name applied to the seeds of many plants, but particularly those belonging to the pea family, Leguminosae, many of which are edible.

bear A carnivorous mammal, widespread in the N hemisphere; head large with short, rounded ears and long muzzle; body bulky with thick (usually shaggy) coat and very short tail; eats meat (**polar bear**), or meat and plants (other species). It may rest for long periods during winter months, but this is not true hibernation as the body temperature does not fall. (Family: Ursidae, 7 species.)

bearbaiting A popular sport in Britain in the 16th-c, forbidden by law in 1835. The bear was chained to a stake or put into a pit, and then attacked by dogs. Betting took place on the performance of individual dogs. The Master of Bears was a crown office with a daily stipend.

bearberry A low, mat-forming evergreen shrub (*Arctostaphyllos uva-ursi*), native to arctic moorland in the N hemisphere; leaves 1–2 cm/0·4–0·8 in, elliptic or widest above middle, dark green above, pale beneath; flowers drooping, 4–6 mm/$\frac{1}{8}$–$\frac{1}{4}$ in, almost globular, white tinged with pink; berry round, glossy red. (Family: Ericaceae.)

Beard, Dan(iel Carter), nickname **Uncle Dan** (1850–1941) Illustrator and youth leader, born in Cincinnati, Ohio, USA. He was a surveyor (1874–8) before he became an illustrator. He wrote *What to Do and How to Do It: The American Boy's Handy Book* (1882), the first of his 16 books on handicrafts, and was praised by Mark Twain for his illustrations in *A Connecticut Yankee in King Arthur's Court* (1889). To promote magazines that he edited, he organized the Sons of Daniel Boone (1905) and the Boy Pioneers of America (1909), precursors of the Boy Scouts. When the Boy Scouts of America were formed (1910), he designed the Scout hat, neckerchief, and shirt. As National Scout Commissioner (1910–41), he argued for voluntary leadership within the Scouts, and became known as 'Uncle Dan' to a generation of American boys.

bearded lizard An Australian agamid lizard; group of large spines behind each ear; body with numerous small spines; throat with deep pouch which can be enlarged as a threat display (hence 'beard'); also known as **bearded dragon**. (Genus: *Amphibolurus*, 3 species.)

bearded tit *reedling*

bearded vulture *lammergeier*

Beardsley, Aubrey (Vincent) [beerdzlee] (1872–98) Illustrator, born in Brighton, East Sussex, SE England, UK. He became famous through his fantastic posters and illustrations for *Morte d'Arthur* (1893), *Salomé*, *The Rape of the Lock*, and other works, as well as for the *Yellow Book* magazine (1894–96) and his own *Book of Fifty Drawings*, mostly executed in black and white, in a highly individualistic asymmetrical style. With Wilde he is regarded as leader of the 'Decadents' of the 1890s.

beardworm A sedentary marine worm that lives in a vertical tube buried in fine oceanic sediments; feeds by absorbing nutrients through tentacles on head; mouth, gut and anus absent in adults; body slender, length up to 0·8 m/2·6 ft; c.100 species found from shallow water to deep sea. (Phylum: Pogonophora.)

bearings Mechanical devices supporting rotating shafts with a minimal amount of frictional resistance. A large number of different bearings exist to meet special circumstances, although the best known is probably the **ball bearing**. In this type the rotating shaft is supported by a number of balls which are interposed in a cage between it and the fixed mounting.

bear market A stock market term for a situation when stock prices have fallen and it is feared that they will fall further. 'Bears' will sell shares in the hope of buying them back when the prices has fallen; they may even contract to sell shares they do not yet own.

bear's breech A stout perennial native to S Europe (*Acanthus mollis*); 30–80 cm/12–30 in high; leaves large, deeply divided, spiny; flowers in a long spike, zygomorphic, 2-lipped, white with purple veins. The leaves of this or similar species are thought to provide a common decorative motif in classical art and architecture. (Family: Acanthaceae.)

beat generation A group of US writers of the 1950s who rejected conventional society and its values for a life and writing based on an authentic individual experience, according to the poet Allen Ginsberg (*Howl*, 1957), 'of God, sex, drugs, and the absurd'. Besides Ginsberg, novelist Jack Kerouac (*On the Road*, 1957) and poets Gregory Corso (1930–2001) and Laurence Ferlinghetti (1919–) were principal beat writers. Their 'outsider' lifestyle was taken over by the hippies of the 1960s.

beating the bounds In England, at Rogationtide, a traditional ceremonial walk round the boundaries of a parish, during which boundary marks are beaten with sticks, sometimes willow wands, and/or bumped by lifting up boys for the purpose. The aim is to establish the boundaries and to ensure well-being.

Beatitudes The common name for the opening pronouncements of blessing upon the poor, the hungry, and others in Jesus's great Sermon on the Mount, reported in Matthew's gospel (nine listed in *Matt* 5.3–10) and the Sermon on the Plain in Luke's gospel (four listed in *Luke* 6.20–3).

Beatles, The (1960–70) British pop group, formed in Liverpool, NW England, UK in 1960, consisting at that time of **John Lennon** (1940–80, rhythm guitar, keyboards, vocals), **Paul McCartney** (1942– , bass guitar, vocals), **George Harrison** (1943–2001, lead guitar, sitar, vocals), and **Pete Best** (1941– , drums). In 1962 Best was replaced by **Ringo Starr** (1940– , real name Richard Starkey), and the band signed a record contract. 'Love Me Do' became a hit in the UK, and their appearances at the Cavern Club in Liverpool and elsewhere in the UK overflowed with idolizing fans. 'Beatlemania' spread around the world in 1964, buoyed by international hits such as 'She Loves You' and 'I Want to Hold Your Hand', and by the overwhelming success of a concert tour in American stadiums. At press conferences and interviews, the Beatles projected a fey, carefree, somewhat cynical image that influenced the attitudes of their teenage admirers just as their long hair and 'granny' glasses influenced their looks. The image was sustained in their films *A Hard Day's Night* (1964) and *Help!* (1965). The string of early hits, all written by Lennon and McCartney, also included 'Please Please Me', 'Can't Buy Me Love', 'And I Love Her', and 'Yesterday'. In 1966 the Beatles stopped performing in public. They then produced *Sergeant Pepper's Lonely Hearts Club Band* (1967), a loose programme of songs on the theme of alienation: at its best (as in 'Mr Kite', 'She's Leaving Home', 'A Day in the Life') it uses the devices of pop music to express a poetic vision. The group dissolved acrimoniously in 1970, and each member pursued a solo career (see separate entries). The then three surviving members of the group sang together again in 1994 to record Lennon's 'Free as a Bird', and were all involved in the issue of the Beatles anthology in 1995.

Beaton, Sir Cecil (Walter Hardy) (1904–80) Photographer and designer, born in London, UK. He studied at Cambridge, and became an outstanding photographer of fashion and high-society celebrities, including royalty. He also designed scenery and costumes for many ballet, operatic, theatrical, and film productions, including *My Fair Lady* and *Gigi*. His publications include *My Royal Past* (1939), *The Glass of Fashion* (1959), and *The Magic Image* (1975), and he also wrote several volumes of autobiography (1961–78). He was knighted in 1972.

Beaton or **Bethune, David** (1494–1546) Scottish statesman and Roman Catholic clergyman, born in Balfour, Fife, E Scotland, UK. He studied at the universities of St Andrews, Glasgow, and Paris, and was at the French court (1519) as Scottish 'resident' and twice later as ambassador to negotiate James V's marriages. In 1525 he took his seat in the Scots Parliament as Abbot of Arbroath and was appointed Privy Seal. Made a cardinal in 1538, he became Archbishop of St Andrews. On James's death, he produced a forged will, appointing himself and three other regents of the kingdom during the minority of Mary, Queen of Scots. The nobility, however, elected the Protestant Earl of Arran regent. Beaton was arrested, but soon regained favour and was made chancellor (1543). He was assassinated by a band of conspirators in his castle of St Andrews.

Beatrix, in full **Beatrix Wilhelmina Armgard** (1938–) Queen of The Netherlands (1980–), born in Soestdijk, The Netherlands, the eldest daughter of Queen Juliana and Prince Bernhard Leopold. In 1966 she married West German diplomat **Claus-Georg Wilhelm Otto Friedrich Gerd von Amsberg** (1926–2002); their son, **Prince Willem-Alexander Claus George Ferdinand** (1967–) is the first male heir to the Dutch throne in over a century. There are two other sons, **Johan Friso Bernhard Christiaan David** (1968–) and **Constantijn Christof Frederik Aschwin** (1969–). She acceded to the throne on her mother's abdication in 1980.

beats In physics, regular low-frequency variations in amplitude, resulting from an interference effect between waves of similar wavelength. The effect is exploited in piano tuning and in heterodyne radio receivers.

Beatty, David Beatty, 1st Earl (1871–1936) Naval commander, born in Nantwich, Cheshire, NWC England, UK. He entered the navy in 1884, and by 1912 had been appointed to command the 1st Battle Cruiser Squadron. At the outbreak of World War 1 he steamed into Heligoland Bight and destroyed three German cruisers. In 1915 he pursued German battle cruisers near the Dogger Bank, sinking the *Blücher*, and in 1916 fought in the Battle of Jutland. He succeeded Lord Jellicoe as commander-in-chief of the Grand Fleet in 1916, and became First Sea Lord in 1919.

Beatty, Warren [baytee], originally **Henry Warren Beaty** (1937–) Actor and film-maker, born in Richmond, Virginia,

USA, the younger brother of actress Shirley MacLaine. He made his film debut in *Splendor in the Grass* (1961). A broodingly handsome leading man, his enduring Casanova image has done a disservice to his many political interests and consistent efforts to expand the scope of his talents. At the same time as acting, he produced *Bonnie and Clyde* (1967), co-wrote *Shampoo* (1975), and co-directed *Heaven Can Wait* (1978). He was the producer, co-writer and star of *Reds* (1981), which won him an Oscar as Best Director. Later films include *Dick Tracy* (1990), *Bugsy* (1991), *Love Affair* (1994), and *Bulworth* (1998). Television includes *A Salute to Dustin Hoffman* (1999). He received the Irving G Thalberg Memorial Award at the Academy Awards in 2000, and a BAFTA Fellowship for outstanding contributions to world cinema in 2002.

Beaufort, Henry [**boh**fert] (1377–1447) English clergyman, the second illegitimate son of John of Gaunt and his mistress Catherine Swynford, and half-brother of Henry IV. He was chancellor three times (1403–4, 1413–17, and 1424–6), and in 1426 was made a cardinal. In 1431 he conducted the young King Henry VI to Paris, to be crowned as King of France and England, and for several years was the dominant figure in his government.

Beaufort, Lady Margaret, Countess of Richmond [**boh**fert] (1443–1509) Daughter of John Beaufort, 1st Duke of Somerset, and great-granddaughter of John of Gaunt, Duke of Lancaster. She married Edmund Tudor, Earl of Richmond (1455), and became the mother of Henry VII, to whom she conveyed the Lancastrian claim to the English crown. She was twice widowed before her third husband, Thomas, Lord Stanley, was instrumental in helping Henry VII assume the crown. She was a benefactress of William Caxton, and of Oxford and Cambridge.

Beaufort Scale [**byoo**fert, **byoo**faw(r)t] A scale of windspeed, ranging from 0 to 12, devised by Admiral Francis Beaufort (1774–1857) in the mid-19th-c, which uses descriptions of the way common outdoor features (eg smoke, trees) respond to different wind conditions. *(see p.155)*

Beaufort Sea [**boh**fert] Region of the Arctic Ocean, N of Alaska and W of the Canadian Arctic archipelago; covered with pack-ice; major oil deposit discovered at Prudhoe Bay (1968), linked by pipeline to Valdez.

Beauharnais, Alexandre, vicomte de (Viscount of) [bohah(r)-**nay**] (1760–94) French soldier, son of the governor of Martinique, where he was born. In 1779 he married Joséphine de Tascher de la Pagerie who later became the wife of Napoleon. He became president of the Constituent Assembly in Paris in June 1791, and was given command of the army of the Rhine in 1793. During the Reign of Terror he was arrested as an aristocratic 'suspect' and guillotined.

Beaujolais [**boh**zholay] Sub-division of the old province of Lyonnais in EC France, now forming part of Rhône and Loire departments; granite upland on edge of Massif Central; major wine-growing region; N part known as Beaujolais Villages; centre Villefranche.

Beaumarchais, Pierre Augustin Caron de [bohmah(r)**shay**], originally **Pierre Augustin Caron** (1732–99) Comic playwright, born in Paris, France. He married the wealthy widow of a court official, whereupon he assumed the title by which he was known thereafter. He is best known for his two satirical comedies (considered politically subversive in their time), *Le Barbier de Séville* (1775, The Barber of Seville) and *La Folle Journée ou le mariage de Figaro* (1784, The Marriage of Figaro). Both are still popular plays in France, but in England are chiefly known through Mozart's and Rossini's operatic adaptations. The Revolution cost Beaumarchais his fortune, and, suspected of an attempt to sell arms to the *émigrés*, he had to take refuge in Holland and England (1793).

Beaumaris 53°16N 4°05W, pop (2001e) 1600. Resort town on the Menai Straits, Anglesey, North Wales, UK; former capital of Anglesey, the town prospered during 17th–18th-c from fishing and shipbuilding; now a popular tourist resort with yachting centre and pier (1826); castle (late 13th-c) built by Edward I is a designated world heritage site; courthouse and gaol; Church of St Mary and St Michael (late 13th-c, restored 1500); Henllys Hall (13th-c, rebuilt 1852); Tudor Rose house (15th-c); Museum of Childhood.

Beaumont, Francis [**boh**mont] (c.1584–1616) Playwright, born in Gracedieu, Leicestershire, C England, UK. He studied at Oxford, and entered the Inner Temple in 1600. He became a friend of Ben Jonson, and worked closely with John Fletcher, with whom he wrote several plays. Modern research finds Beaumont's hand in only about 10 plays, but these include the masterpieces. *The Woman Hater* (1607) is attributed solely to Beaumont, and he had the major share in *The Knight of the Burning Pestle* (1609), a play in which he ridicules the naivety of middle-class Londoners, their pride in their merchant guilds, and their taste for romance. *Philaster, The Maid's Tragedy*, and *A King and No King* established their joint popularity.

Beauregard, P(ierre) G(ustave) T(outant) [**boh**regah(r)d] (1818–93) Confederate general, born near New Orleans, Louisiana, USA. He trained at West Point (1838), and was appointed to the command at Charleston, SC. He was virtually in command at the first Battle of Bull Run (1861). In the spring of 1862 he was defeated at Shiloh, and in 1864 commanded the military division of the West, defeating Butler at Drewry's Bluff.

beauty (physics) *bottom*

Beauvais [boh**vay**] 49°25N 2°08E, pop (2000e) 58 900. Market town and capital of Oise department, N France; on R Thérain, 76 km/47 mi N of Paris; railway; bishopric; former tapestry-making centre; agricultural equipment, rayon, tiles, fruit, dairy produce; cathedral (13th–16th-c), with highest Gothic vault in existence (48 m/156 ft).

Beauvoir, Simone de *de Beauvoir, Simone*

Beaux-Arts [boh**zah**(r)] A decorative classical architectural style of the late 19th-c, particularly popular in France. The name derives from the Ecole des Beaux-Arts in Paris. It is typified by the grandeur of the Opéra, Paris (1861–75), architect J L C Garnier.

Beaux-Arts, Ecole des [boh**zah**(r), ay**kol** day] The main official art school in Paris. It dates from 1648, when the first class was taught by Charles Le Brun. Abolished at the Revolution, but refounded in 1796, it was installed in its present quarters on the left bank of the Seine by 1830. It was immensely important throughout the 19th-c, but became notoriously conservative in the 20th-c.

beaver A large squirrel-like rodent from North America, N Europe, and Asia; semi-aquatic; hind feet webbed; tail broad, flat, and scaly; builds a 'lodge' from logs and mud in woodland ponds; often dams streams to create ponds; was formerly hunted for fur; young called *kits*. (Family: Castoridae, 2 species.)

Beaverbrook (of Beaverbrook and of Cherkley), (William) Max(well) Aitken, Baron (1879–1964) Politician and newspaper magnate, born in Maple, Ontario, SE Canada. He moved to Britain in 1910, entered parliament (1911–16), and became private secretary to Bonar Law. When Lloyd-George became premier, he was made minister of information (1918). In 1919 he took over the *Daily Express*, which he made into the most widely-read daily newspaper in the world. He founded the *Sunday Express* (1921) and bought the *Evening Standard* (1929). In World War 2 Churchill successfully harnessed Beaverbrook's dynamic administrative powers to the production of much-needed aircraft. He was made minister of supply (1941–2), minister of production (1942), Lord Privy Seal (1943–5), and lend-lease administrator in the USA.

beaver scout *scouting*

Beazley, Kim (Christian) (1948–) Politician, born in Perth, Western Australia, Australia. He was educated at the University of Western Australia and Oxford University as a Rhodes Scholar, returning to take up an academic post at Murdoch University. In 1980 he was elected as an MP for the West Australian seat of Swan, but transferred to the seat of Brand in 1996. He held a number of portfolios, including defence, employment, education, and training, during the Australian Labor Party's 13 years in power, and became deputy Prime Minister

Wind Force And Sea Disturbance

Beaufort number	Windspeed kph	Windspeed mph	Wind name	Observable wind characteristics	Sea disturbance number	Average wave height m	Average wave height ft	Observable sea characteristics
0	<1	<1	Calm	Smoke rises vertically	0	0	0	Sea like a mirror
1	1–5	1–3	Light air	Wind direction shown by smoke drift but not by wind vanes	0	0	0	Ripples like scales, without foam crests
2	6–11	4–7	Light breeze	Wind felt on face; leaves rustle; vanes moved by wind	1	0·3	0–1	More definite wavelets, but crests do not break
3	12–19	8–12	Gentle breeze	Leaves and small twigs in constant motion; wind extends light flag	2	0·3–0·6	1–2	Large wavelets; crests beginning to break; scattered white horses
4	20–28	13–18	Moderate	Raises dust, loose paper; small branches moved	3	0·6–1·2	2–4	Small waves becoming longer; fairly frequent white horses
5	29–38	19–24	Fresh	Small trees begin to sway; crested wavelets on inland waters	4	1·2–2·4	4–8	Moderate waves with longer form; many white horses; some foam spray
6	39–49	25–31	Strong	Large branches in motion; whistling heard in telegraph wires; difficult to use umbrellas	5	2·4–4	8–13	Large waves forming; more white foam crests; spray
7	50–61	32–38	Near gale	Whole trees in motion; difficult to walk against wind	6	4–6	13–20	Sea heaps up; streaks of white foam blown along
8	62–74	39–46	Gale	Breaks twigs off trees; impedes progress	6	4–6	13–20	Moderately high waves of greater length; well-marked streaks of foam
9	75–88	47–54	Strong gale	Slight structural damage occurs	6	4–6	13–20	High waves; dense streaks of foam; sea begins to roll; spray affects visibility
10	89–102	55–63	Storm	Trees uprooted; considerable damage occurs	7	6–9	20–30	Very high waves with overhanging crests; generally white appearance of surface; heavy rolling
11	103–17	64–72	Violent storm	Widespread damage	8	9–14	30–45	Exceptionally high waves; long white patches of foam; poor visibility; ships lost to view behind waves
12–17	≥118	≥73	Hurricane		9	14	>45	Air filled with foam and spray; sea completely white; very poor visibility

Beaufort Scale

(1995–6). Since 1996 he had been leader of the Australian Labor Party Opposition, but he resigned after the election defeat in 2001.

bebop A jazz style, also known as **bop**, characterized by fast tempos, extended chordal harmonies, and agitated rhythms. It was cultivated in the 1940s by small groups of musicians, among them Charlie Parker, Dizzy Gillespie, and Thelonious Monk.

bèche de mer [besh duh **mair**] A French culinary term, referring to the food obtained from a marine animal found in the SW Pacific, also known as a **sea cucumber**; the name derives from Portuguese *bicho da mar* 'sea worm'. It is a part of some Chinese cuisine, but rarely appears on Western menus.

Bechet, Sidney [**be**shay, be**shay**] (1897–1959) Jazz musician, born in New Orleans, Louisiana, USA. He took up the soprano saxophone in 1919, his forceful style making him the first significant saxophone voice in jazz. He re-emerged in 1940 as a figurehead of the traditional jazz revival. The warmth of his reception during many tours in Europe led him to make his permanent home in Paris.

Bechstein, Karl [**bek**stiyn], Ger [**bekh**shtiyn] (1826–1900) Piano manufacturer, born in Gotha, C Germany. He founded his famous factory in Berlin in 1856.

Beck, Aaron T(emkin) (1921–) Psychiatrist, born in Rhode Island, USA. He became professor of psychiatry and director of the Center for Cognitive Therapy at the University of Pennsylvania. He introduced cognitive therapy as a treatment approach for neurotic disorders, particularly depression. His books include *Depression: Causes and Treatment* (1972) and *Love is Never Enough* (1988).

Beck, Julian (1925–85) Actor, producer, and director, born in New York City, USA. With **Judith Malina** (1926–) he was cofounder of the Living Theater. Known for his experimental and improvisatory approach, among his publications is *The Life of the Theater* (1972).

Beckenbauer, Franz [**bek**enbower], nickname **the Kaiser** (1945–) Footballer, born in Munich, SE Germany. As player, coach, manager, and administrator, he became a dynamic force in German football during the 1970s. He captained the West German national side to European Nations Cup success in 1972 and to the World Cup triumph of 1974. In 1972 and 1976 he was voted European Footballer of the Year. He became manager of Germany in 1986, and in 1990 became the first person to have won the World Cup both as a captain and a manager. He is currently president of Bayern Munich.

Becker, Boris [**bek**er] (1967–) Tennis player, born in Leimen, SW Germany. He first came to prominence in 1984 when he finished runner-up in the US Open. In 1985 he became the youngest ever winner of the men's singles at Wimbledon, as well as the first unseeded winner. He successfully defended his title in 1986, and won it for a third time in 1989. He won the US Open in 1989, the Australian Open in 1991 and 1996, and the Association of Tennis Professionals world title in 1992, as well as inspiring Germany's Davis Cup triumphs of 1988 and 1989. In 2003 he was inducted into the Tennis Hall of Fame.

Becker, Gary (Stanley) (1930–) Economist, born in Pottsville, Pennsylvania, USA. Except for a period at Columbia University (1957–69), he has worked at the University of Chicago as an active participant in the 'Chicago school' of economics. After the mid-1960s, he concentrated on his 'new economics of the family', his controversial ideas challenging the singular consumptive nature of the family, viewing it instead as a multiperson unit which produces 'joint utility' from the skills and knowledge of different family members. He was awarded the Nobel Prize for Economics in 1992.

Becket, St Thomas, also called **Thomas à Becket** (1118–70) Saint and martyr, Archbishop of Canterbury, born in London, the son of a wealthy Norman merchant. He studied in London and Paris, then took up canon law at Bologna and Auxerre. In 1155, he became Chancellor, the first Englishman since the Conquest to hold high office. A skilled diplomat and brilliant courtly figure, he changed dramatically when created Archbishop of Canterbury (1162), resigning the chancellorship, and becoming a zealous ascetic, serving the Church as vigorously as he had the king. He thus came into conflict with Henry II's aims to keep the clergy in subordination to the state. He unwillingly consented to the Constitutions of Clarendon (1164) defining the powers of Church and state, but remained in disfavour. He fled the country after having his goods confiscated and the revenues of his sees sequestered. After two years in France, he pleaded personally to the pope, and was reinstated in his see. In 1170 he was reconciled with Henry, and returned to Canterbury, amid great public rejoicing. New quarrels soon broke out, however, and Henry's rashly-voiced wish to be rid of 'this turbulent priest' led to Becket's murder in Canterbury cathedral (29 Dec 1170) by four of the king's knights. He was canonized in 1173, and Henry did public penance at his tomb in 1174. In 1220 his bones were transferred to the Trinity Chapel, for many years a popular place of pilgrimage, as described by Chaucer in the prologue to *The Canterbury Tales*. Feast day 29 December.

Beckett, Margaret (Mary) (1943–) British stateswoman, born in Ashton-under-Lyne, Greater Manchester, NW England, UK. She studied at Manchester College of Science and Technology, became a metallurgist, then became a research assistant for the Labour party (1970–4). Elected an MP in 1974, she went on to hold a number of political posts, eventually becoming deputy leader of the Labour Party (1992–4, including a short term as leader in 1994). She held shadow ministerial posts in social security (1984–9), the Treasury (1989–92), health (1994–5), and trade and industry (1995–7), and became president of the Board of Trade and secretary of state for trade and industry (1997–8). She was appointed Leader of the House of Commons (1998–2001), and secretary of state for environment, food and rural affairs (2001–).

Beckett, Samuel (Barclay) (1906–89) Writer and playwright, born in Dublin, Ireland. He became a lecturer in English at the Ecole Normale Supérieure in Paris and later in French at Trinity College, Dublin. From 1932 he lived mostly in France and was, for a time, an associate of James Joyce. His early poetry and first two novels, *Murphy* (1936) and *Watt* (c.1943, published 1953), were written in English, but not the trilogy *Molloy* (1951), *Malone Meurt* (1951, Malone Dies), and *L'Innommable* (1953, The Unnamable), or the plays *En attendant Godot* (1954, Waiting for Godot), which took London by storm, and *Fin de partie* (1956, End Game), all of which first appeared in French. His later works include *Happy Days* (1961), *Not I* (1973), and *Ill Seen Ill Said* (1981). He was awarded the 1969 Nobel Prize for Literature. Although there were one or two increasingly short pieces in later years, he wrote very infrequently towards the end, though his *Teleplays* appeared in 1988.

Beckham, David (Robert Joseph) (1975–) Footballer, born in Leytonstone, Greater London, UK. A midfield player, he joined Manchester United in 1993, and the England team in 1996. He was a member of the 1998 World Cup team and the Euro 2000 squad, and was made captain in the lead-up to the 2002 World Cup. By the end of the 2003 season he had won 63 caps playing for his country. His many honours with United include the treble of FA Cup, Premier League Championship, and European Cup in the 1998–9 season, the first British side to achieve this feat. His move to Real Madrid at the start of the 2003–4 season attracted much publicity and coincided with the publication of his bestselling autobiography, *My Side*. In 2001 he was voted BBC Sports Personality of the Year. He married Victoria Adams ('Posh Spice') in 1999.

Beckmann, Max (1884–1950) Expressionist painter, draughtsman, and printmaker, born in Leipzig, EC Germany. He trained at Weimar, and in 1904 moved to Berlin where he began painting large-scale, dramatic works. The suffering he witnessed as a hospital orderly in World War 1 led him to develop a highly individual style influenced by Gothic art, which he used to give voice to the disillusionment he saw around him in post-war Germany. When he learnt that his work was to be included in an exhibition of Degenerate Art to be mounted by the Nazis in 1937, he fled to Holland, where he lived until emigrating to the USA in 1947.

Becquerel, (Antoine) Henri [bekerel] (1852–1908) Physicist, born in Paris, France. An expert on fluorescence, he discovered the *Becquerel rays*, emitted from the uranium salts in pitchblende (1896), which led to the isolation of radium and to the beginnings of modern nuclear physics. For his discovery of radioactivity he shared the 1903 Nobel Prize for Physics with the Curies.

becquerel [bekerel] The activity of a radioactive source as the number of disintegrations per second; SI unit; symbol *Bq*; named after Henri Becquerel.

bed bug A flattened, flightless bug. Adults and developing nymphs are nocturnal, emerging from concealment to suck blood mainly from mammals, including humans. They are a pest of human dwellings, but are not known to transmit diseases.

Bedchamber Crisis A British political crisis which occurred in May 1839, after Melbourne, prime minister in the Whig government, offered to resign, and advised the young Queen Victoria to appoint Peel and the Tories. The Queen refused to dismiss certain Ladies of the Bedchamber with Whig sympathies, whereupon Peel refused office and the Whig government continued.

Bede or **Baeda, St,** known as **the Venerable Bede** (c.673–735) Anglo-Saxon scholar, theologian, and historian, born near Monkwearmouth, Durham, NE England. At the age of seven he was placed in the care of Benedict Biscop at the monastery of Wearmouth, and in 682 moved to the new monastery of Jarrow in Durham, where he was ordained priest in 703 and remained a monk for the rest of his life, studying and teaching. His devotion to Church discipline was exemplary and his industry enormous. He wrote homilies, lives of saints, lives of abbots, hymns, epigrams, works on chronology, grammar and physical science, and commentaries on the Old and New Testaments; and he translated the Gospel of St John into Anglo-Saxon just before his death. His greatest work was his Latin *Historia ecclesiastica gentis anglorum* (Ecclesiastical History of the English People), which he finished in 731, and which is the single most valuable source for early English history. He was buried at Jarrow but in the 11th-c his bones were removed to Durham. He was canonized in 1899; feast day 25 May.

Bedford 52°08N 0°29W, pop (2001e) 147 900. County town of Bedfordshire, SC England, UK; a residential town 32 km/20 mi SE of Northampton and 75 km/47 mi N of London; railway; foodstuffs, engineering; John Bunyan (1628–88) was imprisoned here for 12 years, during which time he wrote *The Pilgrim's Progress*.

Bedford, John of Lancaster, Duke of (1389–1435) English prince, the third son of Henry IV. In 1414 his brother, Henry V, created him Duke of Bedford, and during the war with France he was appointed Lieutenant of the Kingdom. After Henry's death (1422), Bedford became Guardian of England, and Regent of France during the minority of his nephew, Henry VI. He defeated the French in several battles, but in 1428 failed to capture Orléans. In 1431 he had Joan of Arc burned at the stake in Rouen, and crowned Henry VI King of France in Paris; but in 1435 a treaty was negotiated between Charles VII and the Duke of Burgundy, which ruined English interests in France. He died at Rouen, and was buried in the cathedral there.

Bedford Level *Fens, the*

Bedfordshire pop (2001e) 381 600; area 1235 sq km/477 sq mi. County in SC England, UK; drained W–E by the R Ouse; county town, Bedford; Luton a new unitary authority from 1997; distribution centre, motor vehicles, bricks, wheat, barley.

Bedlington terrier A British breed of dog, with a tapering muzzle, and no obvious forehead in side view; coat curly, usually pale, but may be grey or brown. The original short-legged breed was crossed with the whippet to produce the longer-legged modern form.

Bednorz, (Johannes) Georg [bednaw(r)ts] (1950–) Physicist, born in Germany. He studied at Münster and Zürich universities, then joined K Alexander Müller at the IBM Zürich Research Laboratory at Rüschlikon (1982). Their work was chiefly directed to finding novel superconductors which would show superconductivity at higher temperatures than the near-absolute zero level previously observed. Following the success of this project in 1986–7, they shared the 1987 Nobel Prize for Physics.

Bedouin Arabic-speaking nomads of Arabia, Syria, Jordan, Iraq, and other desert areas in the Middle East. They mainly herd animals in the desert during winter months – camels, sheep, goats, and (in the case of the Baqqarah) cattle – and cultivate land in summer; camel herders have the highest prestige. Many have been forced to settle in one locality, because of political or economic moves, such as restrictions on their grazing land, or nationalization of their land. They are divided into largely independent, endogamous patrilineal tribal groups, each controlled by its sheikh and council of male elders. There are also several vassal tribes, whose members work for others as artisans, blacksmiths, entertainers, etc.

bed sore An area of ulcerated skin and subcutaneous tissue, usually over a bony prominence, that can develop in bed-ridden or unconscious patients if their care is inadequate. The lesion is due to pressure which reduces the blood supply to the affected part.

bedstraw An annual or perennial, found almost everywhere; weak, 4-angled stem, often with tiny hooks, narrow leaves in whorls; flowers tiny, white, yellow, or greenish, 4-petalled, in open clusters; fruits often burrs. (Genus: *Galium*, 400 species. Family: Rubiaceae.)

bee A winged insect that builds and provisions a nest for its young; the common name of several different types of hymenopteran, including solitary mining bees (Family: Andrenidae), carpenter bees (Family: Anthophoridae), bumblebees, orchid bees, stingless bees, and honeybees (all Family: Apidae). Social structure ranges from the solitary bees, in which each queen effectively raises her own brood, to honeybees, which form a complex society with a caste system and overlapping, co-operating generations. (Order: Hymenoptera.)

beech A deciduous, shallow-rooted tree native to the N hemisphere; leaves oval, margins wavy; flowers tiny, males in long-stalked clusters, females (and later, nuts) in pairs enclosed in 4-lobed, spiny case. The leaves are very resistant to decay, forming deep, nutrient-poor litter in beech woods, discouraging the growth of other plants. Young beech trees retain dead leaves throughout the winter, and make good hedges. In the S hemisphere, it is replaced by the closely related **roble beech**. (Genus: *Fagus*, 10 species. Family: Fagaceae.)

Beecham, Sir Thomas (1879–1961) Conductor and impresario, born in St Helens, Merseyside, NW England, UK. He studied at Oxford, travelled extensively, and began his career as conductor with the New Symphony Orchestra in 1906. He soon branched out as a producer of opera, introducing British audiences to Diaghilev's Russian ballet. He was principal conductor (1932) and artistic director (1933) of Covent Garden, and in 1943 was conductor at the Metropolitan Opera, New York. In 1944 he returned to Britain, having married **Betty Humby** (d.1958), the pianist. In 1947 he founded the Royal Philharmonic Orchestra and conducted at Glyndebourne (1948–9). He did much to foster the works of Delius, Sibelius, and Richard Strauss, and was noted for his candid pronouncements on musical matters, his 'Lollipop' encores, and his after-concert speeches.

Beecher, Catharine Esther (1800–78) Educator and writer, born in East Hampton, New York, USA, the daughter of Lyman Beecher. She was educated at home and private school (1810–16), then founded the Hartford Female Seminary, launching a lifelong campaign as a lecturer, author, and advocate for women's education. In 1852, to promote female education in the W states, she founded the American Women's Education Association. Among her publications was *Treatise of Domestic Econ-*

omy (1841), and in 1869 she and her sister Harriet Beecher Stowe collaborated on a new edition, retitled *The American Woman's Home*, which became an influential guide for generations of US houswives. Although she was in the forefront on many social issues of her day, she did not believe that women should be involved in political affairs, and she opposed women's suffrage.

Beecher, Henry Ward (1813–87) Congregationalist clergyman, orator, and writer, born in Litchfield, Connecticut, USA, the son of Lyman Beecher. He studied at Amherst College, MA, and in 1847 became the first pastor of Plymouth Congregational Church, New York City, where in his preaching he contended for temperance and denounced slavery. On the outbreak of the Civil War in 1861 his Church raised and equipped a volunteer regiment, and in 1865 he became an earnest advocate of reconciliation. For many years he wrote for *The Independent*, and after 1870 edited *The Christian Union* (later *Outlook*).

Beecher, Lyman (1775–1863) Presbyterian minister and revivalist, born in New Haven, Connecticut, USA. He studied at Yale, and was ordained in 1799. He preached at East Hampton, Long Island, NY (1799–1810), then at Litchfield, CT (1810–26), his brand of Calvinism calling for constant church services and strong opposition to drinking. He then worked in Boston, and in 1832 went to Cincinnati as head of the newly founded Lane Theological Seminary, and to serve as pastor of the Second Presbyterian Church. His evangelical zeal and arrogance led to years of strife with more conservative Presbyterians, but he stayed until 1859, when he retired to the Brooklyn home of his son Henry.

Beecher Stowe, Harriet *Stowe, Harriet (Elizabeth) Beecher*

Beeching, Richard, Baron (1913–85) Engineer and administrator, born in Maidstone, Kent, SE England, UK. He studied at Imperial College, London, became chairman of the British Railways Board (1963–5), and deputy chairman of ICI (1966–8). He is best known for the scheme devised and approved under his chairmanship (the *Beeching Plan*) for the substantial contraction of the rail network of the UK. He was created a life peer in 1965.

bee dancing The patterned movements of honey-bees used to signal the direction and distance of pollen and nectar to other members of the colony. The phenomenon was first documented by the Austrian biologist Karl von Frisch, who plotted the way in which worker bees perform circling or tail-wagging 'dances' depending on the distance of the food from the hive.

bee-eater A brightly-coloured bird native to the Old World, especially Africa and S Asia; slender, pointed bill; eats ants, bees, and wasps caught in flight. Some species migrate thousands of kilometres. (Family: Meropidae, 24 species.)

beefeater *Yeomen of the Guard*

bee-keeping *apiculture*

Beelzebub [bee-elzebuhb] (Gr **Beelzebul**) In the New Testament Gospels, the 'prince of demons', the equivalent of Satan. He is possibly linked with the Old Testament figure *Baal-zebub* ('lord of flies'), the god of Ekron, or with the Canaanite *Baal-zebul* ('lord of the high place').

bee orchid The name for various species of the genus *Ophrys*, widespread throughout Europe, W Asia, and N Africa; remarkable for their flowers which mimic insects. The lower lip (*labellum*) of the flower resembles a female insect in both colour and texture, and the flower emits a powerful pheromone-like scent to attract males of the same species. The males are induced to attempt copulation with the mimic, and in doing so pollinate the flower. In *Ophrys apifera*, which mimics bumblebees, the flowers are also capable of self-pollination. Other species of *Ophrys* resemble flies, wasps, sawflies, and even spiders. (Genus: *Ophrys*, 30 species. Family: Orchidaceae.)

beer An alcoholic beverage made from ale (malted barley) which has been flavoured with hops – a drink popular since ancient Egyptian times. It is currently an umbrella term covering a wide range of drinks, distinguished by the type of yeast used, such as *bitter* (a beer brewed with more hops and a lighter malt than *mild*), *lager* (a light beer which matures over a long period of time at a low temperature), and *stout* or *porter* (types of dark ale produced from the brewing of roasted malt).

Beerbohm, Sir (Henry) Max(imilian) [beerbohm], nickname **the Incomparable Max** (1872–1956) Writer and caricaturist, born in London, UK, the half-brother of Sir Herbert Beerbohm Tree. He studied at Oxford, and published his first volume of essays under the title *The Works of Max Beerbohm* (1896). In 1910 he married US actress Florence Kahn (d.1951), and went to live, except during the two World Wars, in Rapallo, Italy. His caricatures were collected in various volumes beginning with *Twenty-five Gentlemen* (1896) and *Poet's Corner* (1904). His best-known work was his only novel, *Zuleika Dobson* (1911), a parody of Oxford undergraduate life. He was knighted in 1939. His ashes are buried in St Paul's Cathedral.

Beerbohm Tree, Herbert *Tree, Sir Herbert (Draper) Beerbohm*

Beersheba [beersheeba] 31°15N 34°47E, pop (2000e) 154 000. Industrial town in South district, S Israel; on N edge of Negev desert; important centre for development of Negev; railway; airfield; university (1965); desert farming research; oil pipeline; ruins of ancient city to the E.

Beeston 52°56N 1°12W; pop (2000e) 70 000. Town linked with Stapleford in Broxtowe district, Nottinghamshire, C England, UK; 5 km/3 mi SW of Nottingham; railway; engineering, pharmaceuticals, textiles.

beeswax Wax secreted by bees of the family Apidae, including bumblebees, stingless bees, and honeybees. It is produced by glands beneath the abdominal body plates (*sterna* or *terga*), and used in nest construction.

beet An annual, biennial, or perennial native to Europe and Asia; leaves shiny, often tinged dark red. Cultivated beets, all derived from the wild beet (*Beta vulgaris*), are divisible into two groups: **leaf beets**, including spinach beets and chards, are grown as leaf vegetables; **root beets**, including beetroot and mangel-wurzel, are biennials grown for their edible, swollen roots. **Sugar-beet**, containing up to 20% sugar in the root, has largely replaced sugar-cane as the source of sugar in W Europe. (Genus: *Beta*, 6 species. Family: Chenopodiaceae.)

Beethoven, Ludwig van [baytohvn] (1770–1827) Composer, born in Bonn, W Germany. Miserably brought up by a father who wanted him to become a profitable infant prodigy, he joined the Elector of Cologne's orchestra at Bonn. In 1787 he had lessons from Mozart in Vienna, and in 1792 returned to that city for good, apart from a few excursions. He first joined Prince Lichnowsky's household and studied under Haydn, Albrechtsberger, and possibly Salieri. His music is usually divided into three periods. In the first (1792–1802), which includes the first two symphonies, the first six quartets, and the 'Pathétique' and 'Moonlight' sonatas, his style gradually develops its own individuality. His second period (1803–12) begins with the 'Eroica' symphony (1803), and includes his next five symphonies, the difficult 'Kreutzer' sonata (1803), the Violin Concerto, the 'Archduke' trio (1811), and the 'Razumovsky' quartets. His third great period begins in 1813, and includes the Mass, the 'Choral' symphony (1823), and the last five quartets. Beethoven was tolerated by Vienna society despite his physical unattractiveness and arrogance. Just as he was developing a reputation as a composer, he began to go deaf, but stoically accepted the fact. None of this stopped him from falling in love with his pupils, including Giulietta Guicciardi and Josephine von Brunswick. From 1812 he was increasingly assailed by ill health, business, and family worries, which included prolonged litigation to obtain custody of his dead brother's son, Karl. His last work was completed at Gneixendorf in 1826, where he developed a severe chill (exacerbated by returning to Vienna in an open chaise), from which he died.

beetle A winged insect with forewings modified as rigid, horny cases covering membranous hindwings and abdomen beneath; hindwings used in flight, sometimes missing; biting mouthparts; range in size from less than 0·5 mm/0·2 in to c.170 mm/7 in; development includes distinct larval and pupal phases; c.350 000 species known, including many pests. Most feed on live plants or plant material, but some are carnivorous or carrion-feeders. (Order: Coleoptera.)

Beeton, Isabella Mary, *née* **Mayson**, known as **Mrs Beeton** (1836–65) Cookery writer, born in London. She studied in Heidelberg and became an accomplished pianist. In 1856 she married **Samuel Orchard Beeton**, a publisher. She became a household name after the publication of her *Book of Household Management*, first published in parts (1859–60) in a women's magazine founded by her husband, and covering cookery and other branches of domestic science. She died of puerperal fever at the age of 28.

beetroot *beet*

Begin, Menachem (Wolfovitch) [**bay**gin] (1913–92) Israeli statesman and prime minister (1977–83), born in Brest-Litovsk, SW Belarus. He studied law at Warsaw University, and as an active Zionist became head of the Betar Zionist movement in Poland in 1931. At the invasion of Poland in 1939 he fled to Lithuania, where he was arrested by the Russians. Released in 1941, he enlisted in the Free Polish Army in exile, and was sent to British-mandated Palestine in 1942. Discharged from the army the following year, he became commander-in-chief of the Irgun Zvai Leumi resistance group. In 1948 he founded the right-wing Herut Freedom Movement, becoming chairman of the Herut Party, and in 1973 led the Likud front, a right-of-centre nationalist party, forming a coalition government in 1977. In the late 1970s he initiated peace negotiations with the Egyptians, and attended peace conferences in Jerusalem (1977), and at Camp David at the invitation of President Carter (1978). He shared the 1978 Nobel Peace Prize with President Sadat of Egypt.

begonia A tuberous or rhizomatous perennial, sometimes a shrub or climber, native to warm regions, especially America; leaves asymmetric, one side larger than the other, often spotted or marked with white or red; male flowers with two large and two small petals, females with 4–5 more petals; fruit a winged capsule; sometimes called **elephant's ear**, from the shape of its leaves. It reproduces readily from leaf-cuttings placed on damp soil, a technique much used in horticulture. Many species are grown for ornament. (Genus: *Begonia*, 900 species. Family: Begoniaceae.)

Behan, Brendan (Francis) [**bee**an] (1923–64) Writer, born in Dublin, Ireland. He left school at 14 to become a house painter, and soon joined the IRA. In 1939 he was sentenced to three years in Borstal for attempting to blow up a Liverpool shipyard, and soon after his release given 14 years by a Dublin military court for the attempted murder of two detectives, but was released by a general amnesty (1946). He was in prison again in Manchester (1947), and deported in 1952. His first play, *The Quare Fellow* (1956; filmed 1962), starkly dramatised the prison atmosphere prior to a hanging. His exuberant Irish wit, spiced with balladry and bawdry and a talent for fantastic caricature, found rein in his next play *The Hostage* (1958, first produced in Irish as *An Giall*, 1957). It is also evident in the autobiographical novel, *Borstal Boy* (1958), and in *Brendan Behan's Island* (1963).

Behar *Bihar*

behaviourism / behaviorism The view that psychology is most effectively pursued by analyzing the overt behaviour of people and animals, in preference to subjective states, thoughts, or hypothetical internal dynamics. It has had an important influence on modern psychology, but is now rarely held in its extreme form.

behaviour / behavior modification Techniques for changing an individual's behaviour by controlling the consequences of the behaviour and/or the environmental conditions in which the behaviour occurs. It is employed to develop new behaviours or to eliminate existing ones. The approach is controversial, being viewed by some as a form of 'manipulation'; but it is a potentially valuable tool within applied psychology.

behaviour / behavior therapy A type of psychological treatment, formulated by psychotherapist Joseph Wolpe, which emphasizes the alteration of thoughts by altering behaviour. It is often applied to neurotic illnesses (eg phobias) on the presumption that these are learned forms of behaviour which can be 'unlearned'. The term was coined by Hans Eysenck in the 1950s. The range of techniques now used include processes of desensitization and flooding for anxiety responses, and the use of rewards and punishments for patients suffering from mental handicap.

Behn, Aphra [ben], *née* **Amis** (1640–89) Writer and adventurer, born in Wye, Kent, SE England, UK. She was brought up in Suriname, where she claimed to have made the acquaintance of the enslaved negro prince Oroonoko, the subject afterwards of one of her novels, in which she anticipated Rousseau's 'noble savage'. She returned to England in 1663, then became a professional spy for Charles II in Antwerp, sending back political and naval information. Using the pen name **Astraea** she turned to writing, as perhaps the first professional woman author in England, and wrote many coarse but popular Restoration plays, such as *The Rover* (1678), and later published *Oroonoko* (1688).

Behrens, Peter [**bair**enz] (1868–1940) Architect and designer, born in Hamburg, N Germany. Trained as a painter, he was appointed director of the Düsseldorf Art and Craft School (1903–7). In 1907 he became artistic adviser to Walther Rathenau at the AEG electrical company in Berlin, for whom he designed a turbine assembly works (1909) of glass and steel, a landmark in industrial architectural style. He was professor at Düsseldorf and Vienna, and trained several notable modern architects, including Le Corbusier, Ludwig Mies van der Rohe, and Walter Gropius.

Behring, Emil (Adolf) von [**bay**ring] (1854–1917) Bacteriologist and pioneer in immunology, born in Hansdorf, W Poland (formerly Prussia). He was professor of hygiene at Halle (1894–5) and Marburg (from 1895), and discovered antitoxins for diphtheria and tetanus. He was awarded the first Nobel Prize for Physiology or Medicine (1901).

Beiderbecke, (Leon) Bix [**biy**derbek] (1903–31) Cornettist and composer, born in Davenport, Iowa, USA. He was largely self-taught on piano and cornet, playing in local bands as a teenager. When expelled from a military academy, he began the short career that made him one of the most celebrated jazz performers of the 1920s. His bell-like tone and lyrical solo improvisations were heard to best effect in various small groups. His later career ravaged by alcoholism, he succumbed to pneumonia at the age of 28.

Beijing [bay**zhing**] or **Peking**, formerly **Beiping (Pei-p'ing)** 39°55N 116°25E; pop (2000e) 8 208 000, administrative region 12 062 000; municipality area 17 800 sq km/6900 sq mi. Capital city and municipality of NE China; as Yenching, principal city of NE China, and secondary capital of Liao dynasty (10th-c); seized by Mongols (1215); as Khanbaligh, capital of the Yuan dynasty (1271–1368), and fully described by Marco Polo (late 13th-c); extensively rebuilt by Ming dynasty (1368–1644); capital of Qing dynasty (1644–1912); looted by Western armies, 1860, 1900; government moved to other cities after fall of Qing, 1912; named Beiping ('Northern Peace') by Nationalists, 1928; occupied by Japanese, 1937–45; capital of People's Republic of China, 1949; airport; railway; two universities (1898, 1950); important industrial centre – electricity, textiles, petrochemicals, light and heavy engineering; major tourist location – Imperial Palace (formerly the Forbidden City); Tiananmen (Gate of Heavenly Peace, 1417, restored 1651), Tiananmen Square, Mao Zedong Memorial Hall (1977), Niu Jie (oldest Muslim temple, 996), Fayuan Si Temple (696), Tiantan (Temple of Heaven, 1406–20), Yiheynan (Summer Palace, rebuilt 1888 after Anglo-French sacking in 1860), Lugouqiao Bridge (Marco Polo Bridge); to the N, tombs of 13 Ming emperors; 75 km/47 mi NW, part of the Great Wall of China.

Beira [**bay**ra] 19°46S 34°52E, pop (2000e) 379 000. Seaport capital of Sofala province, Mozambique, SE Africa, at the mouth of the Buzi and Pungué Rivers, 725 km/450 mi NNE of Maputo; Mozambique's main port; occupied by the Portuguese, 1506;

Belarus

[belarus], official name **Republic of Belarus**, also spelled **Byelarus**, formerly (to 1991) **Belorussian SSR** or **White Russia**, Russ **Belorusskaya**

Local name Belarus

Timezone GMT +3

Area 207 600 km²/80 134 sq mi

Population total (2002e) 9 933 000

Status Republic

Date of independence 1991

Capital Minsk (Mensk)

Languages Belorussian (official), Russian

Ethnic groups (1989) Belorussian (78%), Russian (13%), Polish (4%), Ukrainian (3%), Jewish (1%)

Religions Roman Catholic, Orthodox

Physical features Hilly lowlands with marshes, swamps; Dzyarzhynskaya Mt rises to 346 m/1135 ft; largest lake, Narach; Belaruskaya Hrada, largest glacial ridge, runs NW into Minsk Upland; rivers include the Pripyat and Dnepr; Pripyat marshes in E.

Climate Varies from maritime, near Baltic, to continental and humid; average annual temperatures, 18°C (Jul), -6°C (Jan); average annual rainfall 550–700 mm/22–8 in.

Currency Belorussian Rouble = 100 kopec (in parallel with the Russian Rouble); currency coupons for food, alcohol, tobacco

Economy Main exports include textiles, timber, chemical products, fertilizers, electrical goods; valuable resource: peat marshes.

GDP (2002e) $90·19 bn, per capita $8700

Human Development Index (2002) 0·788

History Neolithic remains widespread; colonized by E Slavic tribes, 5th-c; Mongols conquered Slavs, 13th-c; Catherine the Great of Russia acquired E Belorussia (White Russia) in the first Polish partition in 1772; gained Minsk in 1793 and the remainder in 1795; W Belorussia ceded to Poland in 1921 as part of the Treaty of Riga which ended Soviet-Polish War; regained by Soviet Union as part of Nazi-Soviet Non-aggression Pact of 1939, and Belorussia became Belorussian Soviet Socialist Republic; admitted to UN, 1945; declared independence, 1991; co-founder of Commonwealth of Independent States (CIS), 1991.

Chairman of Supreme Council
1991–4 Stanislav Shushkevich
1994–6 Mechislav Grib
1996– Syamyon Sharetski

Head of State
1994– Alexander Lukashenko

Head of Government
1991–4 Vyacheslav Kebich
1994–6 Mikhail Chigir
1996–2000 Syargey Ling
2000–1 Uladzimir Yarmoshyn
2001–3 Henadz Navitski
2003– Syarhey Sidorski *Acting*

founded as the seat of the Mozambique Company, 1891; airport; railway; minerals, cotton, foodstuffs.

Beirut [bayroot], Arabic **Bayrut**, Fr **Beyrouth**, ancient **Berytus** 33°52N 35°30E, pop (2000e) 1 690 000. Seaport capital of Lebanon, on a promontory which juts into the Mediterranean Sea; airport; railway; American University (1866), Lebanese University (1953), Arab University (1960); Grand Seraglio, Cathedrals of St Elie and St George, national museum; the 'Green Line' refers to the division of the city during the 1975–6 civil war into Muslim (W) and Christian (E) sectors; Israeli attack on Palestinian and Syrian forces in 1982 led to the evacuation of Palestinians to camps such as Sabra, Chatila, and Bourj Barajneh; severely damaged by continued fighting; restoration work begun following reduction of tension and release of foreign hostages, 1991.

Béjart, Maurice [bayzhah(r)], originally **Maurice Jean de Berger** (1927–) Choreographer, born in Marseille, S France. He trained at the Marseille Opéra Ballet and then in Paris, where he formed (1953) the Ballets de l'Étoile (later known as the Ballet of the 20th Century). In 1960 he moved to the Théâtre Royal de la Monnaie in Brussels, where he worked as choreographer and director, returning to France in 1979. He became director of Béjart Ballet Lausanne (1987–92) and Rudra Béjart Ballet School, Lausanne (1992–), producing dance spectacles on a grand scale often in non-traditional settings such as sports arenas and circuses. In his choreographies he has pioneered the use of multimedia elements.

Békésy, Georg von [baykayshee] (1899–1972) Aural physiologist, born in Budapest, Hungary. He studied physics there, then worked as a telephone research engineer in Hungary (1924–46). His research, first in Stockholm (1946–7), then at Harvard (1947–66), led to a study of the human ear and how it analyses and transmits sounds to the brain. He was awarded the Nobel Prize for Physiology or Medicine in 1961.

Bekka, the *Beqaa, el*

bel *decibel*

Bel and the Dragon An addition to the Book of Daniel, part of the Old Testament Apocrypha, or Chapter 14 of Daniel in Catholic versions of the Bible. It contains two popular tales, probably from the 2nd-c BC: one of how Daniel discredited Bel (patron god of Babylon) and its priests, and the other of Daniel in the lion's den.

Belarus *see panel*

Belau *p.161*

Belém [belem], also called **Pará** 1°27S 48°29W, pop (2000e) 1 388 000. Port capital of Pará state, Norte region, N Brazil; at the mouth of the Tocantins R; founded, 1616; airport; railway; university (1957); trade in jute, nuts, rubber, black pepper, cassava, aluminium; cathedral (1748); Teatro da Paz, Santo Aleix-

Belau

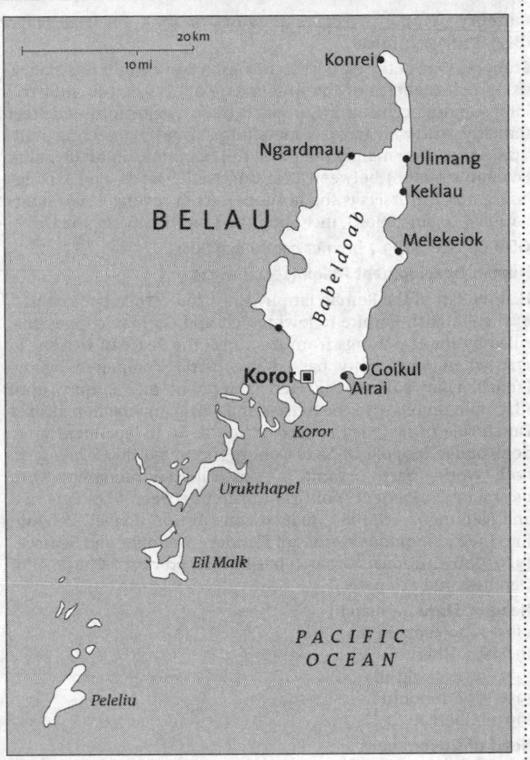

☐ International Airport

[below], also **Palau** or **Pelau**, official name **Republic of Belau**

Local names Belau, also Pelau, Palau

Timezone GMT +10

Area 494 sq km/191 sq mi

Population total (2002e) 19 900

Status Republic

Date of independence 1994

Capital Koror

Languages Palauan, English

Ethnic groups Palauan (83%)

Religions Christianity (66%), traditional beliefs (25%)

Physical features A group of c.350 small islands and islets, c.960 km/600 mi E of the Philippines; most W group of the Caroline Is; largest island, Babeldoab ((367 sq km/142 sq mi). Climate Warm all year, with high humidity; average annual temperature 27°C; average annual rainfall, 3810 mm/150 in; typhoons common.

Currency 1 US dollar = 100 cents

Economy Tourism, taro, pineapple, breadfruit, bananas, yams, citrus fruit, coconuts, pepper, fishing.

GDP (2001e) $174 mn, per capita $9000

History Smallest of the four political units to emerge out of the US Trust Territory of the Pacific Islands; organized into 16 states; held by Germany, 1899–1914; mandated to Japan by League of Nations, 1920; invaded by USA, 1944; compact of free association with the USA, signed in 1982, but not confirmed until 1993; independence, 1994; member of the UN, 1995; governed by a president and a National Congress consisting of a Senate and a House of Delegates.

Head of State

1993–2001 Kuniwo Nakamura
2001– Tommy Remengesau

andre church; Emilio Goeldi Museum, 17th-c Mercês Church, Basilica of Nossa Senhora de Nazaré (1909).

Belém Monastery A magnificent monastery of the Hieronymite hermit order founded in 1499 by Emmanuel I in Belém, a present-day suburb of Lisbon, Portugal. It commemorates Vasco da Gama's discovery of a sea-passage to India, and was built on the site of the chapel in which he is said to have prayed. The complex includes a museum and the Church of Santa Maria.

belemnite An extinct, squid-like mollusc; found extensively as fossil shells from the Upper Carboniferous period to the Eocene epoch; shell internal in life, typically bullet-shaped. (Class: Cephalopoda. Order: Belemnoidea.)

Belfast, Ir **Beal Feirste** 54°35N 5°55W, pop (2000e) 285 800. Capital of Northern Ireland in Belfast district, Antrim, NE Northern Ireland; at the mouth of the Lagan R, on Belfast Lough; original settlement and castle destroyed in 1177; settled in the 17th-c by English, Scots, and Huguenots, becoming a centre of Irish Protestanism; capital, 1920; well-defined Nationalist (Catholic) and Unionist (Protestant) areas; disrupted by civil unrest since 1969; two airports (Aldergrove, City); railway; university (1908); shipyards, aircraft, linen, engineering, footwear, food processing; city hall (1900), St Anne's Cathedral (begun 1898), Ulster Museum, Parliament House at Stormont.

Belgian Congo *Congo, Democratic Republic of*

Belgium *p.162*

Belgrade, Serbo-Croatian **Beograd**, ancient **Singidunum** 44°50N 20°30E, pop (2000e) 1 574 000. Capital city of Serbia in the Union of Serbia and Montenegro (former federation of Yugoslavia), at the junction of the Danube and Sava Rivers; damage from NATO bombing in Kosovo crisis (Apr–Jun 1999); airport; railway; university (1863); arts university (1957); communications centre; machine tools, electrical equipment, light engineering, vehicles, pharmaceuticals, textiles, foodstuffs; Kalemegdan fortress, Prince Eugene's Gate (1719), Palace of Princess Ljubica, St Mark's Church, tomb of Sheikh Mustapha, cathedral, several museums; international film festival (Feb), international festival of modern dramatic art (Sep), Belgrade Music Festival (Oct).

Belgrano, General [belgrahnoh] An Argentinian cruiser, formerly owned by the US Navy in World War 2, sunk by HM submarine *Conqueror* during the Falklands conflict in 1982, with great loss of life. Her armament of fifteen 6-inch guns posed a serious threat to the ships of the British task force, but her sinking proved to be one of the most controversial incidents of the war.

Belisarius [belisairius] (505–65) Byzantine general under Emperor Justinian, born in Germania, Illyria. He defeated the Persians (530), suppressed an insurrection in Constantinople (532), and defeated the Vandals in Africa (533–4) and the Ostrogoths in Italy (535–40). He later again drove back the Persians (542), and repelled an assault of the Huns on Constantinople (559). Falsely accused of conspiracy against the emperor, he was imprisoned (562), but was restored to favour soon after.

Belize *p.163*

Belize City 17°29N 88°10W, pop (2000e) 66 500. Seaport in Belize district, Belize, Central America; at the mouth of the Belize R where it meets the Caribbean Sea; capital of Belize until 1970; occasionally badly damaged by hurricanes; airport; timber, coconuts, fishing, commerce, tourism; 19th-c cathedral; Government House.

Bell, Acton / Currer / Ellis *Brontë, Anne / Charlotte / Emily*

Bell, Alexander Graham (1847–1922) Educationist and inventor, born in Edinburgh, EC Scotland, UK, the son of Alexander Melville Bell. He studied at Edinburgh and London, and worked as assistant to his father in teaching elocution (1868–70). In 1870 he went to Canada, and in 1871 moved to the USA and became professor of vocal physiology at Boston (1873), devoting himself to the teaching of deaf-mutes and to spreading his father's system of 'visible speech'. After experimenting with various acoustical devices he produced the first intelligible telephonic transmission with a message to his assistant

Belgium

□ International Airport

official name **Kingdom of Belgium**, Fr **Royaume de Belgique**, Flemish **Koninkrijk België**

Local names Belgique (French), België (Flemish)

Timezone GMT +1

Area 30 518 km^2/11 780 sq mi

Population total (2002e) 10 280 000

Status Kingdom

Date of independence 1830

Capital Brussels

Languages Flemish/Dutch (56%), French (32%), German (1%); (Brussels officially bilingual Flemish/French)

Ethnic groups Flemish (Teutonic origin) (55%), Walloon (French Latin) (33%)

Religions Roman Catholic (75%), Muslim (1%), Protestant (0·4%)

Physical features Mostly low-lying, with some hills in the SE region (Ardennes), average elevation 300–500 m/1000–1600 ft; large areas of fertile soil, intensively cultivated for many centuries; main river systems linked by complex network of canals; low-lying, dune-fringed coastline.

Climate Cool and temperate with strong maritime infuences; average annual temperatures 2°C (Jan), 18°C (Jul) in Brussels; average annual rainfall 825 mm/35 in.

Currency 1 euro = 100 cents (previous to 2002, 1 Belgian Franc (BFr) = 100 centimes)

Economy One of the earliest countries in Europe to industrialize, using rich coalfelds of the Ardennes; Flanders textile industry; long-standing centre for European trade; major iron and steel industry, with wide range of metallurgical and engineering products; agriculture mainly livestock; full economic union (Benelux Economic Union) between Belgium, Netherlands, and Luxembourg, 1948. Brussels is the headquarters of several major international organizations, including the Commission of the EU.

GDP (2002e) $299·7 bn, per capita $29 200

Human Development Index (2002) 0·939

History Part of the Roman Empire until 2nd-c; then became part of the Frankish Empire following Celt and Germanic invasions; ruled by the Habsburgs from 1477 until the Peace of Utrecht in 1713, when sovereignty passed to Austria; conquered by the French, 1794; part of the French Republic and Empire until 1815, then united with the Netherlands; Belgian rebellion against Dutch rule in 1830, led to recognition as an independent kingdom under Leopold of Saxe-Coburg; occupied by Germany in both World Wars; became a constitutional monarchy with bicameral Parliament; political tension between Walloons in S and Flemings in N, 1980; federal constitution divided Belgium into the autonomous regions of Flanders, Wallonia, and Brussels, 1989; Constitutional Monarch has limited powers; a Chamber of Deputies and a Senate.

Head of State (Monarch)
1865–1909 Leopold II
1909–34 Albert I
1934–50 Leopold III
1950–93 Baudouin I
1993– Albert II

Head of Government
1950 Jean Pierre Duvieusart
1950–2 Joseph Pholien
1952–4 Jean van Houtte
1954–8 Achille van Acker
1958–61 Gaston Eyskens
1961–5 Théodore Lefèvre
1965–6 Pierre Harmel
1966–8 Paul Vanden Boeynants
1968–72 Gaston Eyskens
1973–4 Edmond Leburton
1974–8 Léo Tindemans
1978 Paul Vanden Boeynants
1979–81 Wilfried Martens
1981 Marc Eyskens
1981–92 Wilfried Martens
1992–9 Jean-Luc Dehaene
1999– Guy Verhofstadt

on 5 June 1875, and patented the telephone in 1876. He defended the patent against Elisha Gray, and formed the Bell Telephone Company in 1877. In 1880 he established the Volta Laboratory, and invented the photophone (1880) and the graphophone (1887). After 1897 his principal interest was in aeronautics. He became an American citizen in 1874.

Bell, Alexander Melville (1819–1905) Educationist, born in Edinburgh, EC Scotland, UK, the father of Alexander Graham Bell. A teacher of elocution at Edinburgh University and University College London, he moved to Canada in 1870, then settled in Washington, DC. In 1867 he published *Visible Speech*, a system showing the position of the vocal organs for each sound.

Bell, Martin (1938–) Television journalist and politician, born in Cambridge, Cambridgeshire, EC England, UK. He studied at Cambridge and joined the BBC in 1962, becoming overseas reporter (1964–76), diplomatic correspondent (1976–7), chief North American correspondent (1977–89), Berlin correspondent (1989–93), Vienna correspondent (1993–4), and foreign affairs correspondent (1994–6). Awards include the Royal Television Society's Reporter of the Year (1976, 1992) and the Radio and Television Industries Club Newscaster of the Year (1995). He fought an 'anti-sleaze' campaign in the 1997 general election, and was returned – much to his own surprise, describing himself as an 'accidental MP' in his maiden speech – as Independent MP for Tatton. He failed to repeat his success in Brentwood and Ongar in the 2001 general election.

bell A hollow vessel of bronze or other material which, when struck, vibrates to produce a ringing sound (or rather, a complex of sounds) which, if the bell is tuned, may be heard as a musical note of definite pitch. Bells have been made for some 4000 years for a variety of uses and in many different shapes and sizes. A bell fastened to a cat's collar as a warning to birds may be no larger than a small gooseberry; the enormous 'Tsar

Belize

[beleez], formerly **British Honduras** (to 1973)

Local name Belice (Spanish)

Timezone GMT −6

Area 22 963 km²/8864 sq mi

Population total (2002e) 251 000

Status Independent state within the Commonwealth

Date of independence 1981

Capital Belmopan

Languages English (official), Spanish, Garifuna, Maya

Ethnic groups Creole (40%), mestizo (33%), Mayan (9·5%), Carib (8%), Garifuna (8%)

Religions Roman Catholic (62%), Protestant (30%)

Physical features Located in Central America; extensive coastal plain; swampy in the N, fertile in the S; Maya Mts extend almost to the E coast, rising to 1120 m/3674 ft at Victoria Peak; Belize R fows W–E; inner coastal waters protected by world's second longest barrier reef.

Climate Generally sub-tropical, but tempered by trade winds; average annual temperature 24°C (Jan), 27°C (Jul); variable rainfall; average annual rainfall 1295 mm/51 in (N), 4445 mm/175 in (S); hurricanes frequent.

Currency 1 Belize Dollar (Bz$) = 100 cents

Economy Developing free-market economy based on timber and forest products, more recently on agriculture; banana industry devastated by Hurricane Iris (Oct 2001).

GDP (2002e) $1·28 bn, per capita $4900

Human Development Index (2002) 0·784

History Evidence of early Mayan settlement; colonized in the 17th-c by shipwrecked British sailors and disbanded soldiers from Jamaica; created a British colony, 1862; administered from Jamaica until 1884; internal self-government, 1964; changed name from British Honduras to Belize, 1973; full independence, 1981; Guatemalan claims over Belize territory have led to a continuing British military presence; Guatemala accord, respecting Belize self-determination, 1991; bicameral National Assembly.

Head of State
(British Monarch represented by Governor-General)
1981–93 Dame Minita Elvira Gordon
1993– Colville Norbert Young

Head of Government
1981–4 George Cadle Price
1985–9 Manuel Esquivel
1989–93 George Cadle Price
1993–8 Manuel Esquivel
1998– Said Musa

Kolokol' bell in the Kremlin, Moscow is about 6·9/22 ft 8 in in diameter and weighs over 200 000 kg/190 tons. These two examples also illustrate the two basic types of bell. The cat's bell is of the *closed* (or *crotal*) variety: a hollowed sphere, with one or more slits in the surface, which is shaken to cause a loose pellet inside to strike against the inner surface. The Kremlin monster is an example of the open bell, cast (like most ship's bells and church bells) in the shape of an upturned cup; such bells are usually sounded by means of a clapper suspended from the inside of the bell, but in some cases (such as the huge bells of some Buddhist temples) they are struck externally with a ramrod.

belladonna (Ital 'fair lady') A liquid extract of the deadly nightshade plant (*Atropa belladonna*), so called because Italian ladies used to apply it to their eyes to make the pupils dilate, an effect deemed attractive. The main active constituent is atropine.

belladonna lily A large bulb (*Amaryllis bella-donna*), native to S Africa; leaves strap-shaped; flowers trumpet-shaped, 7–9 cm/2¾–3½ in long, white to pink, 6–12 on a solid stalk appearing in autumn after the leaves have died. A popular ornamental, it is often confused with *Hippeastrum*, which is the amaryllis of horticulture. (Family: Amaryllidaceae.)

Bellamy, David (James) (1933–) British botanist, writer, and broadcaster. He studied at London University, taught at Durham (1960–80), and became a professor at Nottingham in 1987. He established the Conservation Foundation in 1988. The writer of numerous conservation-oriented books, he is best known for his eccentric manner in TV programmes designed to create a greater awareness and understanding of the natural environment. Working as both presenter and scriptwriter, his many programmes include *Life in Our Sea* (1970), *Bellamy's Britain* (1975), *Bellamy's Birds' Eye View* (1988), *Bellamy's Border Raids: The Peak District* (1994), and *A Welsh Herbal* (1998–9).

Bellarmine, St Robert [belermin], originally **Roberto Francesco Romolo Bellarmino** (1542–1621) Jesuit theologian, born in Montepulciano, C Italy. He entered the order of Jesuits at Rome in 1560, and studied theology at Padua and Louvain. In 1570 he was appointed to the chair of theology at Louvain, but returned to Rome in 1576 to lecture at the Roman College. In 1592 he became rector there, was made a cardinal in 1599 against his own inclination, and in 1602 Archbishop of Capua. After the death of Clement VIII, he evaded the papal chair, but was induced by Paul V to hold an important place in the Vatican from 1605 until his death. He was canonized in 1930, and was the chief defender of the Church in the 16th-c. In the 17th-c, stone beer jugs with a caricature of his likeness, called *bellarmines*, were produced by Flemish Protestants to ridicule him. Feast day 17 May.

Bellay, Joachim du [belay] (1522–60) Poet and prose writer, born in Lire, NW France. After his friend and fellow-student, Ronsard, he was the most important member of the *Pléiade*. His *Défense et illustration de la langue Française* (1549, The Defence and Illustration of the French Language), the manifesto of the *Pléiade*, advocating the rejection of mediaeval linguistic traditions and a return to Classical and Italian models, had a considerable influence at the time.

Bellerophon [belerofon] In Greek mythology, a hero who was sent to Lycia with a letter telling the king to put him to death. The king set him impossible adventures, notably the killing of the Chimera. In later accounts it is said that Athena helped him to tame Pegasus.

bell-flower A member of a large variable genus of mostly annuals and herbaceous perennials, low and spreading to tall and erect, often forming clumps, native throughout N temperate regions; leaves very narrow to almost circular; flowers 5-lobed bells, usually large and showy, and almost always blue, sometimes pink or white, solitary or in long inflorescences; fruit a capsule opening by pores, shedding seeds like a pepper-pot when shaken. Many species are cultivated for ornament. (Genus: *Campanula*, 300 species. Family: Campanulaceae.)

Bellingshausen, Fabian Gottlieb Benjamin von [belingshowzn] (1778–1852) Explorer, born in Ösel, SW Estonia. In 1819–21 he led an expedition around the world which made several discoveries in the Pacific, and sailed to 70°S, probably discovering the Antarctic continent. The *Bellingshausen Sea* was named after him.

Bellini [beleenee] A family of 15th-c Venetian painters. **Jacopo Bellini** (c.1400–70) studied under Gentile da Fabriano, painting a wide range of subjects, but only a few of his works remain. His son **Gentile Bellini** (c.1429–1507) worked in his father's studio, and painted many portraits, especially that of Sultan Mohammed II in Constantinople (now in the National Gallery, London). His other son, **Giovanni Bellini** (c.1430–1516), was the greatest Venetian painter of his time. He painted many 'Pietà' and 'Madonna' themes, altarpieces, and pagan allegories, notably 'The Feast of the Gods' (1514). His innovations of light and colour became the hallmark of Venetian art, continued by his pupils Giorgione and Titian.

Bello, Andrés [bayoh] (1781–1865) Venezuelan writer and polymath, born in Caracas, Venezuela. He studied in Caracas, then lived in London (1810–29), before finally settling in Chile, where he became a senior public servant, senator, and first rector of the University (1843). The most remarkable Latin-American intellectual of the 19th-c, his writings embrace language, law, education, history, philosophy, poetry, drama, and science.

Belloc, (Joseph) Hilaire (Pierre René) [belok] (1870–1953) Writer, born in Saint-Cloud, near Paris, NC France, the son of a French barrister and his English wife. The family moved to England during the Franco-Prussian war, and he studied at the Oratory School, Birmingham, under Newman, and at Oxford. He became a naturalized British subject in 1902, and a Liberal MP in 1906, but, disillusioned with politics, did not seek re-election in 1910. He was a close friend of G K Chesterton, who illustrated many of his books. He is best known for his nonsensical verse for children: *The Bad Child's Book of Beasts* (1896) and the *Cautionary Tales* (1907). He also wrote many travel books, including *Path to Rome* (1902) and *The Old Road* (1910), reconstructing the Pilgrim's Way; several historical studies such as *Robespierre* (1901) and *Napoleon* (1932); and religious works, including *Europe and the Faith* (1920) and *The Great Heresies* (1938). He was an energetic Roman Catholic apologist.

Bellotto, Bernardo [belotoh] (1720–80) Painter, born in Venice, NE Italy, the nephew of Antonio Canaletto. He attained high excellence as a painter, and also as an engraver on copper. He is known for his detailed views of many European cities, renowned for their accuracy and realism. His paintings of Warsaw were used after World War 2 in the restoration of the historic areas of the city.

Bellow, Saul (1915–) Writer, born in Lachine, Quebec, SE Canada. In 1924 his family moved to Chicago, and he attended university there and at Northwestern University. He abandoned his postgraduate studies at Wisconsin University to become a writer, and his first novel, *The Dangling Man*, appeared in 1944. Other works include *The Victim* (1947), *Henderson the Rain-King* (1959), *Herzog* (1964), *Humboldt's Gift* (1975; Pulitzer, 1976), *A Theft* (1989), and *The Actual* (1997). Other works include a collection of essays *It All Adds Up* (1994). He was awarded the Nobel Prize for Literature in 1976.

Bellows, George (Wesley) (1882–1925) Painter and lithographer, born in Columbus, Ohio, USA. He was a leading figure in the movement known as The Eight, which sought to break away from Postimpressionism into the vivid harshness of social realism. He delighted in prize fights, festivals, and the teeming life of the cities. Probably his most famous work is 'Dempsey and Firpo' (1924, Museum of Modern Art, New York City).

bell-ringing The art of ringing church bells, also known as **campanology**. Its two popular forms are **change ringing**, a hand-pulled method, and the **carillon** method, performed with the use of a keyboard connected to the clappers of the bells.

Bell's palsy Paralysis of the muscles of one side of the face innervated by the VIIth cranial nerve (the facial nerve). Damage to the nerve may be caused by trauma, virus infection, or undue pressure as the nerve emerges through its canal at the base of the skull. The condition is named after Scottish surgeon Charles Bell (1774–1842).

Belmopan [belmohpan] 17°18N 88°30W, pop (2000e) 6600. Capital of Belize, Central America, between the Belize and Sibun Rivers, 80 km/50 mi inland, W of Belize City; made capital in 1970, following major hurricane damage to Belize City in 1961; airfield; new settlement at the Valley of Peace for refugees from El Salvador and Guatemala was made permanent in 1985.

Belo, Carlos (Felipe Ximenes) (1948–) Roman Catholic bishop, born in East Timor, Indonesia. Ordained bishop in 1983, he became an outspoken critic of the Indonesian regime's actions in East Timor, and shared the Nobel Prize for Peace in 1996.

Belo Horizonte [beloh oreezontay] 19°54S 43°54W, pop (2000e) 2 786 000. Commercial and industrial capital of Minas Gerais state, Sudeste region, SE Brazil; N of Rio de Janeiro, altitude 800 m/2625 ft; Brazil's first planned modern city, founded, 1897; International (39 km/24 mi) and National (8 km/5 mi) airports; railway; three universities (1927, 1954, 1958); industrial area (c.10 km/6 mi from city centre) third largest in Brazil; commerce, mining, steel, cars, textiles, agricultural processing; Minascentro Convention Centre, Mineirão sports stadium (second largest in Brazil), Museum of Modern Art, monument in the Parque de Mangabeiras commemorating pope's visit of 1982; notable modern architecture in suburb of Pampulha.

Belorussia *Belarus*

Belshazzar [belshazer], Gr **Balt(h)asar** (?–539 BC) Son of Nabonidus, King of Babylon (556-539 BC), and ruler after his father was exiled in 550 BC. In the Book of Daniel, mysterious writing appears on the wall of his palace, which Daniel interprets as predicting the fall of the empire to the Persians and Medes. He died during the capture of Babylon.

Beltane An ancient Celtic festival held at the beginning of May, and also in late June, when bonfires were lit on the hills. The custom of lighting bonfires continued in many localities, especially in the N of Scotland, into the 19th-c, and is still celebrated in Peebles.

beluga (fish) [belooga] Very large sturgeon (*Huso huso*) found in the Caspian Sea, Black Sea, and adjacent rivers; body length up to 5 m/16 ft; weight over 1000 kg/2200 lb; fished commercially for caviar, but numbers now much reduced by over-fishing and pollution; one of the largest freshwater fish known. (Family: Acipenseridae.)

beluga (mammal) [belooga] A small toothed whale (*Delphinapterus leucas*), native to shallow Arctic seas and rivers; white when adult; no dorsal fin; eats fish, squid, crustaceans, and molluscs; also known as the **white whale** or **sea canary**. (Family: Monodontidae.)

Belukha, Mount [byilookha] 49°46N 86°40E. Highest peak in the Altai range; height 4506 m/14 783 ft; gives rise to 16 glaciers.

Bembo, Pietro [bemboh] (1470–1547) Poet and scholar, born in Venice, NE Italy. In 1513 he was made secretary to Pope Leo X, and in 1539 a cardinal by Paul III, who appointed him to the dioceses of Gubbio and Bergamo. Bembo was the restorer of good style in both Latin and Italian literature, especially with his treatise on Italian prose (*Prose della volgar lingua*, 1525), which marked an era in Italian grammar.

Bemis Heights, Battle of [beemis] A preliminary conflict during the Saratoga campaign, in the US War of Independence.

Benares or **Banares** [benahres], also **Varanasi**, ancient **Kasi** 25°22N 83°08E, pop (2000e) 1 087 000. City in Uttar Pradesh state, N India; on N bank of R Ganges, 120 km/75 mi E of Allahabad; one of the seven most sacred Hindu cities, reputed to be Shiva's capital while on Earth; also a holy city of Buddhists, Sikhs, and Jains; Hindu city since the 6th-c; invaded by Afghans, 1033; ceded to Britain, 1775; airfield; railway; two universities (1916, 1958); textiles, brassware, jewellery; over 1400 Hindu temples and shrines, including the Golden Temple (1777) and Durga Temple; stairs (*ghats*) along c.7 km/4 mi of the high bank of the Ganges, used by pilgrims to bathe in the sacred waters; mosque dedicated to Muslim emperor Aurangzeb.

Benaud, Richie [benoh], popular name of **Richard Benaud** (1930–) Cricketer, broadcaster, and international sports consultant, born in Penrith, New South Wales, SE Australia. He played in 63 Test matches for Australia (captain in 28), including three successful tours of England (1953, 1956, 1961). An all-rounder, he scored 2201 Test runs, including three centuries, and took 248 wickets with subtle leg-spin bowling. He is now a well-known cricket commentator.

Ben Bella, (Mohammed) Ahmed [ben bela] (1918–) A key figure in the Algerian War of Independence against France, and Algeria's first prime minister (1962–3) and president (1963–5), born in Maghnia, NW Algeria. He fought with the Free French in World War 2, and in 1949 became head of the Organisation Spéciale, the paramilitary wing of the Algerian nationalist Parti du Peuple Algérien. In 1952 he escaped from a French-Algerian prison to Cairo, where he became a key member of the Front de Libération Nationale (FLN). Captured by the French in 1956, he spent the remainder of the war in a French prison. Following independence (1962) he became president, but was deposed in 1965. After 15 years of imprisonment, he went into voluntary exile in 1980, returning to Algeria in 1990.

Benbow, John (1653–1702) English naval commander, born in Shrewsbury, Shropshire, WC England, UK. He was master of the fleet at Beachy Head (1690), and at Barfleur and La Hague (1692). He commanded squadrons off Dunkirk (1693–5), and as a rear-admiral was commander-in-chief West Indies from 1698. In 1702, he came up against a superior French force off Santa Marta. For four days he kept up a running fight, almost deserted by the rest of his squadron, until his right leg was smashed by a chain shot and he was forced to return to Jamaica, where he died.

benchmark A surveyor's mark placed permanently on some buildings and rock outcrops. Their elevations are surveyed with respect to a fixed datum level, and can be used in further topographical surveys.

Bendigo [bendigoh] 36°48S 144°21E, pop (2000e) 33 300. City in NC Victoria, Australia, NNW of Melbourne; centre of a wine-producing area; gold mined here until the 1950s; railway; agricultural trade, textiles, rubber, railway engineering; the Central Deborah gold mine; wax museum; reconstructed Sandhurst Town; the Bendigo Pottery (1858), Australia's oldest pottery; the only surviving Chinese Joss House of the 1860s; Chinese Dragon Festival at Easter.

Benedict of Nursia, St (c.480–c.547) The founder of Western monasticism, born in Nursia near Spoleto, C Italy. He studied at Rome, and became convinced that the only way of escaping the evil in the world was in seclusion and religious exercise; so as a boy of 14 he withdrew to a cavern or grotto near Subiaco, where he lived for three years. The fame of his piety led to his being appointed the abbot of a neighbouring monastery at Vicovaro, but he soon left it, as the morals of the monks were not strict enough. Multitudes still sought his guidance; and from the most devoted he founded 12 small monastic communities. He ultimately established a monastery on Monte Cassino, near Naples, afterwards one of the richest and most famous in Italy. In 515 he is said to have composed his *Regula monachorum*, which became the common rule of all Western monasticism. He was declared the patron saint of all Europe by Pope Paul VI in 1964. Feast day 11 July.

Benedict XV, originally **Giacomo della Chiesa** (1854–1922) Pope (1914–22), born in Pegli, Sardinia, Italy. He studied at the University of Genoa, and the Collegia Capranica in Rome, and was ordained in 1878. He became secretary to the Papal Embassy, Spain, in 1883, then secretary to Cardinal Rampolla, bishop (1900), Archbishop of Bologna (1907), and cardinal (May, 1914). Although a junior cardinal, he was elected to succeed Pius X in September 1914, soon after the outbreak of World War 1. He made repeated efforts to end the war, and organized war relief on a munificent scale.

Benedict, Ruth, *née* **Fulton** (1887–1948) Anthropologist, born in New York City, USA. She studied philosophy and English literature at Vassar College, NY, before going on to study anthropology under Franz Boas at Columbia University. She became a leading member of the culture-and-personality movement in American anthropology of the 1930s and 1940s. Her most important contribution lay in her 'configurational' approach to entire cultures, according to which each culture tends to predispose its individual members to adopt an ideal type of personality. Her best-known work is *Patterns of Culture* (1934).

Benedictines A religious order following the 'rule' of St Benedict of Nursia; properly known as the **Order of St Benedict** (**OSB**). The order consists of autonomous congregations, and has a long tradition of scholarship and promotion of learning.

Benelux A customs union between Belgium, The Netherlands, and Luxembourg which came into existence in 1947 as the result of a convention concluded in London in 1944. Despite the difficulties of achieving economic integration and the exclusion of agriculture from the union, mutual trade between the three countries expanded. A treaty established a more ambitious economic union between the three in 1958.

Beneš, Edvard [benesh] (1884–1948) Czech statesman and president (1935–8, 1941–5 in exile, 1945–8), born in Kožlany, WC Czech Republic. He studied law and became professor of sociology at Prague. As a refugee during World War 1 he worked in Paris with Toměš Masaryk for Czechoslovak nationalism, and was foreign minister of the new state (1918–35) and also premier (1921–2). He succeeded Masaryk as president in 1935, but resigned in 1938 and left the country, resuming office in 1941 on the setting up of a government in exile in England. He returned to his country in 1945, and was re-elected president, but resigned after the Communist coup of 1948.

Benesh, Rudolph (1916–75) and **Joan Benesh** (1920–) [benesh], *née* **Rothwell** Dance notators, husband and wife, born in London, and Liverpool, Merseyside, NW England, UK, respectively. Rudolph was a painter and Joan a former member of the Sadler's Wells Ballet. Together they copyrighted (1955) a dance notation system, called Choreology, that has been included in the syllabus of London's Royal Academy of Dancing and is used to document all important Royal Ballet productions. They opened their own institute in 1962, and have been a major influence on many notators and educators.

Benét, Stephen (Vincent) [binay] (1898–1943) Writer, born in Bethlehem, Pennsylvania, USA, the brother of writer William Benét (1886–1950). He published a number of novels, short stories, and volumes of poetry, his first book appearing at the age of 17. His long narrative poem on the Civil War, 'John Brown's Body', was awarded the Pulitzer Prize in 1929.

Bengal, Bay of area 2 172 000 sq km/839 000 sq mi. Arm of the Indian Ocean, on S coast of Asia; bounded by India and Sri Lanka (W), Bangladesh (N), and Myanmar, Andaman Is, and Nicobar Is (E); c.2000 km/1300 mi long, 1600 km/1000 mi wide, depth 2390 m/7850 ft (N) to 4150 m/13 600 ft (S); receives many large rivers, such as the Krishna, Ganges, Brahmaputra, Ayeyarwady (Irrawaddy); main ports include Chennai (Madras), Kolkata (Calcutta), Chittagong; subject to heavy monsoon rains and cyclones.

Bengali *Indo-Aryan languages*

Benghazi or **Banghazi** [bengahzee] 32°07N 20°05E, pop (2000e) 610 000. Seaport in Benghazi province, N Libya; on the Gulf of Sirte, 645 km/400 mi E of Tripoli; first settled by Greeks; modern town partly situated on Hellenistic and Roman towns of Berenice; controlled by Turks, 16th-c–1911; Italian rule, 1911–42; military and naval supply base during World War 2; second largest city in Libya; airport; university (1955); oil, engineering.

Ben-Gurion, David [ben gurion], originally **David Gruen** (1886–1973) Israeli statesman and prime minister (1948–53, 1955–63), born in Plonsk, C Poland. Attracted to the Zionist Socialist movement, he emigrated to Palestine in 1906, working as a farm labourer and forming the first Jewish trade union in 1915. Expelled by the Ottomans for pro-Allied sympathies, he helped to raise the Jewish Legion in America and served in it in the Palestine campaign against Turkey in World War 1. He was general secretary of the General Federation of Jewish Labour (1921–33), and in 1930 became leader of the Mapai (Labour) Party, which became the ruling party in the state of Israel, whose birth he announced in May 1948. He played the chief role in establishing the young state and came to symbolize its newfound authority and power.

Benidorm [benidaw(r)m] 38°33N 0°09W, pop (2000e) 42 600. Resort town in Alicante province, E Spain, on the Mediterranean Costa Blanca; two beaches on either side of a rocky promontory; a leading centre of low-cost package holidays.

Benigni, Roberto [beneenee] (1952–) Film director, actor, writer, and producer, born in Arezzo, Tuscany, Italy. At the age of 10 he became a member of a troubadour act in Tuscany, improvising songs and poetry. His film debut as an actor came with *Berlinger ti Volgio Bene* (1976, Have You Berliner). Later films as an actor include *The Son of the Pink Panther* (1993) and Astérix et Obélix Contre César *(1999,* Asterix and Obelix Take on Caesar). In 1982 he made his directorial debut with *Tu Mi Turbi* (You Disturb Me), a television monologue which criticized Pope John Paul II and brought Benigni widespread fame. In 1997 he made his most successful film to date, *La Vita e Bella* (Life is Beautiful, Oscars for Best Actor and Best Foreign Language Film), which he wrote, starred in, and directed.

Benin *p.167*

Benin (former kingdom) **[beneen]** A powerful kingdom in the S Nigerian rainforest, founded in the 13th-c AD, which survived until the 19th-c. The Portuguese turned to Benin as a source of cloth, beads, and slaves in the 15th–16th-c, and it was later involved in the slave trade. The culture is renowned for the life-size brass heads and human/animal plaques cast for its ruler, the Oba, from the 15th-c onwards. Benin was conquered by the British in 1897, and many of its treasures were taken to London. In 1975, the name was adopted by the former French colony of Dahomey.

Benjamin, tribe of One of the 12 tribes of ancient Israel, said to be descended from Jacob's youngest son by Rachel (*Gen* 35.16–18, 24). Its ancient territories included the land between the hill country of Ephraim and the hills of Judah. Saul, first King of Israel, and the prophet Jeremiah were of this tribe.

Ben Macdhui [muhkdooee], Gaelic **Ben Muich-Dhui** 57°04N 3°40W. Second highest mountain in the UK; in Cairngorm Mts, NC Scotland; 29 km/18 mi NW of Braemar; height 1309 m/4295 ft.

Benn, Anthony (Neil) Wedgwood, known as **Tony Benn** (1925–) British statesman, born in London, UK, the son of Viscount Stansgate. He studied at Oxford, and became a Labour MP (1950–60). He was debarred from the House of Commons on succeeding to his father's title, but was able to renounce it in 1963 having fought a campaign to introduce a law allowing such an action, and was re-elected to parliament the same year. He was postmaster-general (1964–6), minister of technology (1966–70), and assumed responsibility for the ministry of aviation (1967) and ministry of power (1969). He was Opposition spokesman on trade and industry (1970–4), and on Labour's return to government became secretary of state for industry, minister for posts and telecommunications, and secretary of state for energy. Representing the left wing of Labour opinion, he unsuccessfully stood for the deputy leadership of the party in 1981. He lost his seat in the general election of 1983, but returned to represent Chesterfield from 1984 until he stepped down at the general election in 2001. He unsuccessfully challenged Neil Kinnock for the party leadership in 1988. Among his many publications on politics is *The Benn Diaries 1940–90* (1995).

Benn, Gottfried (1886–1956) Poet and physician, born in Mansfeld, EC Germany. He embraced the philosophy of Nihilism as a young man, and later became one of the few intellectuals to favour Nazi doctrines. Trained in medicine as a venereologist, he began writing Expressionist verse dealing with the uglier aspects of his profession, such as *Morgue* (1912). After 1945 his poetry became more versatile though still pessimistic, as in *Statische Gedichte* (Static Poems, 1948), and he became recognized as a leading poet of the 20th-c.

Bennett, Alan (1934–) Playwright, actor, and director, born in Leeds, West Yorkshire, N England, UK. He came to prominence as a writer and performer in *Beyond the Fringe*, a revue performed at the Edinburgh Festival in 1960, and wrote a television sketch show, *On the Margin* (1966), before his first stage play, *Forty Years On* (1968). Despite his own self-effacing qualities, he has remained in the public eye. A great deal of his writing is political comedy, a number of plays displaying a preoccupation with British institutions. There is an ambitious treatment of monarchy in *The Madness of George III* (1991, film 1995). Other plays include *Enjoy* (1980), *Kafka's Dick* (1986), and *Single Spies* (1988). He has also written much for television, including *An Englishman Abroad* (1983), *The Insurance Man* (1986), *Talking Heads* (1988, adapted for the stage in 1992), and the documentary *Portrait or Bust* (1994). The autobiographical *Writing Home* appeared in 1994, and 1999 saw the staging of the similarly autobiographical *The Lady in The Van*.

Bennett, (Enoch) Arnold (1867–1931) Novelist, born near Hanley, Staffordshire, C England, UK. He studied locally and at London University, and was a solicitor's clerk in London, but quickly transferred to journalism, and in 1893 became assistant editor (editor in 1896) of the journal *Woman*. He published his first novel, *The Man from the North*, in 1898. In 1902 he moved to Paris for 10 years and from then on was engaged exclusively in writing. His claims to recognition as a novelist rest mainly on the early *Anna of the Five Towns* (1902), the more celebrated *The Old Wives' Tale* (1908), and the *Clayhanger* series – *Clayhanger* (1910), *Hilda Lessways* (1911), *These Twain* (1916), subsequently issued (1925) as *The Clayhanger Family* – all of which feature the 'Five Towns', centres of the pottery industry. He was an influential critic, and as **Jacob Tonson** on *The New Age* he was a discerning reviewer. His *Journals* were published posthumously.

Bennett, James Gordon (1795–1872) Journalist, born in Keith, Moray, NE Scotland, UK, the father of James Gordon Bennett. He emigrated to America in 1819, and became a journalist in New York City in 1826. In 1835 he started the *New York Herald*, which he edited until 1867, pioneering many journalistic innovations.

Bennett, Michael, originally **Michael Bennet Difiglia** (1943–87) Dancer, choreographer, director, and producer, born in Buffalo, New York, USA. He began his career as a chorus boy before turning to Broadway show choreography. His first hit, *Promises, Promises* (1968), was followed by *Coco* (1970), *Company* (1970), *Follies* (co-director, 1971), *Seesaw* (1973), and the popular masterpiece *A Chorus Line* (1975) for which he shared the Pulitzer Prize. Later works include *Ballroom* (1978) and *Dreamgirls* (1981).

Bennett, Richard Bedford Bennett, 1st Viscount (1870–1947) Canadian statesman and prime minister (1930–5), born in New

Benin

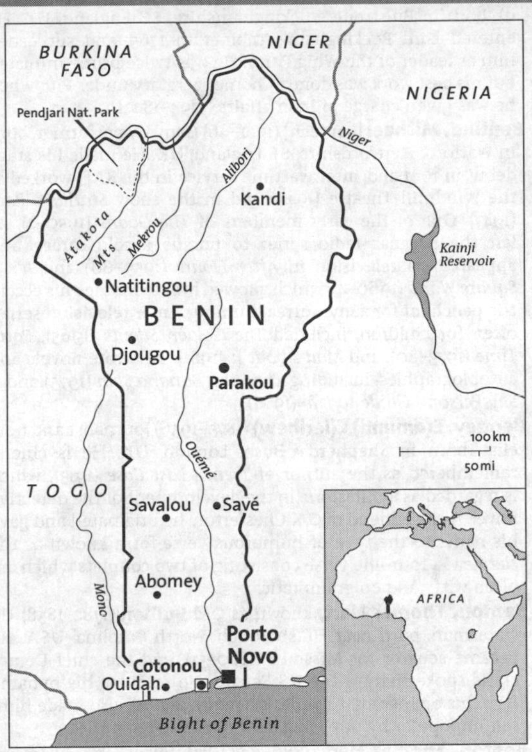

□ International Airport

(republic) [beneen], formerly **Dahomey** (to 1975), official name **Republic of Benin**, Fr **République du Benin**, formerly (to 1990) **The People's Republic of Benin**

Local name Bénin

Timezone GMT +1

Area 112 622 km^2/43 484 sq mi

Population total (2002e) 6 788 000

Status Republic

Date of independence 1960

Capital Porto Novo (nominal), Cotonou (political and economic)

Languages French (official), Fon (47%), Adja (12%), Bariba (10%), Yoruba (9%), Fulani (6%), Somba (5%), Aizo (5%)

Ethnic groups Fon (40%), Yoruba (10%), Bariba (20%), minority of Fulani nomads

Religions Traditional beliefs (c.70%), Christian (15%), Muslim (13%)

Physical features Located in N Africa; rises from a 100 km/62 mi-long, sandy coast with lagoons to low-lying plains; savannah plateau, c.400 m/1300 ft, in N; descend to forested lowlands in S fringing the Bight of Benin; Atakora Mts rise to over 500 m/1000 ft in NW; rivers include Ouémé, Alibori, Mekrou; Pendjari National Park in NW.

Climate Tropical climate divided into three zones: in the S, rain throughout the year, especially during the Guinea Monsoon (May–Oct); in C, two rainy seasons (peaks in May–Jun and Oct); in the N, one rainy season (Jul–Sep); dry season in N (Oct–Apr); hot, with low humidity, subject to the dry harmattan wind from the NE.

Currency 1 CFA Franc (CFAFr) = 100 centimes

Economy Agriculture, especially palm-oil products, cashew nuts, maize, cassava, rice, cotton, coffee; no known natural resources in commercial quantity; small offshore oilfield.

GDP (2002e) $7·38 bn, per capita $1100

Human Development Index (2002) 0·420

History Pre-colonially a collection of small, warring principalities, including the Fon Kingdom of Dahomey (founded 17th-c); Portuguese colonial activities centred on slave trade; subjugated by French, becoming the French Protectorate of Dahomey, 1892; territory within French West Africa from 1904; independent from 1960; Marxist-Leninist regime gained power, 1972; name changed from Dahomey to the People's Republic of Benin, 1975; Marxism-Leninism abandoned in 1989, and a new multi-party constitution approved, 1990; changed name to Republic of Benin, 1990; multi-party elections held, 1991; President elected for five-year term, and a National Assembly.

Head of State

1990–1 Ahmed Kerekou
1991–6 Nicéphore Soglo
1996– Ahmed Kerekou

Head of Government

1958–9 Sourou Migan Apithy
1959–60 Hubert Coutoucou Maga
1960–4 *As President*
1964–5 Justin Tométin Ahomadegbé
1965–7 *As President*
1967–8 Maurice Kouandete
1968–96 *As President*
1996–8 Adrien Houngbedji

Brunswick, E Canada. A lawyer by training, he was elected to parliament in 1911, and became Conservative leader from 1927. As prime minister, he convened the Empire Economic Conference in Ottawa in 1932, out of which came a system of empire trade preference known as the Ottawa Agreements. He retired to Britain in 1939, and was made a peer in 1941.

Bennett, Sir Richard Rodney (1936–) Composer, born in Broadstairs, Kent, SE England, UK. He studied at the Royal Academy of Music, London, and in Paris under Pierre Boulez. Well known for his music for films, he has also composed operas, orchestral works, chamber music, and experimental works for one and two pianos. Some of his music uses the 12-tone scale, and his interest in jazz has prompted such works as *Jazz Calendar* (1963) and *Jazz Pastoral* (1969). His more recent work shows a growing emphasis on internal rhythmic structure. Among his other works are the two operas commissioned by Sadler's Wells, *The Mines of Sulphur* (1965) and *A Penny for a Song* (1968), the opera commissioned by Covent Garden, *Victory* (1970), and the choral work, *Spells* (1975). His work *Rondel* (for large jazz ensemble) was premiered in 1999. He was appointed Professor of Composition at the Royal Academy of Music in 1995, and was knighted in 1998.

Bennett, William J(ohn) (1943–) US Federal official, born in Brooklyn, New York, USA. He was educated at the University of Texas and Harvard. Outspoken and controversial, as chairman of the National Endowment for the Humanities (1981–5) he reversed Liberal policies. He became secretary of education (1985–8) promoting a conservative agenda, cutting federal student aid, and urging schools to become a force for moral education. As President Bush's 'drug tzar' (1989–91) he co-ordinated the campaign against drugs, but resigned in frustration. He went on to become a senior editor of the *National Review*, and wrote *The Book of Virtues* (1997).

Ben Nevis 56°48N 5°00W. Highest mountain in the UK; in Grampian Mts, Highland, W Scotland; 7 km/4 mi E of Fort William; height 1344 m/4409 ft.

Benny, Jack, originally **Benjamin Kubelsky** (1894–1974) Comedian, born in Waukegan, Illinois, USA. A child prodigy violinist, he performed as part of a vaudeville double-act. After navy service during World War 1, he returned to the stage, making his film debut in the short *Bright Moments* (1928). Following his Broadway success in *The Earl Carroll Vanities* (1930) and his radio debut in *The Ed Sullivan Show* (1932), he earned his own radio series which, combined with its subsequent television incarnation, *The Jack Benny Show* (1950–65), won him the loyalty and warm affection of a mass audience. A gentle, bemused, self-effacing figure, his humour lacked malice, relying for its effect on his mastery of timing and an act based on his ineptitude as a fiddler, his claiming of perennial youth, and an unfounded reputation as the world's cheapest man.

Benoît de Sainte-Maure [benwah] (12th-c) Poet, born in either Sainte-Maure near Poitiers, or Sainte-More near Tours, France. His vast romance *Le Roman de Troie* (The Romance of Troy) was a source book to many later writers, notably Boccaccio, who in turn inspired Chaucer and Shakespeare to use Benoît's episode of Troilus and Cressida.

Benson, E(ward) F(rederic) (1867–1940) Scholar, novelist, and sportsman, born at Wellington College, Berkshire, S England, UK. He studied at King's College, Cambridge and, after a brief period at the British School of Archaeology in Athens, took up a life-long career as man-of-letters. His first successful novel, *Dodo*, appeared in 1893, and from the 1890s he published over 100 books, including 70 novels as well as biographies of Charlotte Brontë and Alcibiades. He is best remembered for his *Lucia* novels and ghost stories.

Bentham, Jeremy (1748–1832) Philosopher, jurist, and social reformer, born in London, UK. He entered Oxford at the age of 12, and was admitted to Lincoln's Inn at 19. He is best known as a proponent of utilitarianism in his pioneering works *A Fragment on Government* (1776) and *Introduction to the Principles of Morals and Legislation* (1789), which argued that the proper objective of all conduct and legislation is 'the greatest happiness of the greatest number', and developed a 'hedonic calculus' to estimate the effects of different actions. He was made an honorary citizen of the French Republic in 1792, and published copiously on penal and social reform, economics, and politics. He also founded University College London, where his clothed skeleton is preserved on public view.

benthic or **benthonic environments** The marine life zone at the sea floor; distinguished from the **pelagic environments**, in the water itself. There are two major divisions. **Shallow benthic environments** are those towards the shore from the edge of the continental shelf. They comprise three sub-divisions. The *supralittoral* zone lies just above the mean high tide line, sometimes called the 'splash zone', because the organisms are exposed to sea water mainly from the wave splashes, periodic storm waves, and spring tides. The *littoral* zone lies between the mean high and low tide lines, also called the 'intertidal' zone. The *sublittoral* zone extends from below the mean low tide line to the edge of the continental shelf, and has been called the 'shelf' zone. **Deep benthic environments** are those of the continental margin and deep ocean seaward of this boundary. They have been subdivided into the *bathyl benthic* (shelf edge to 4000 m/13 000 ft), the *abyssal benthic* (4–6000 m/13–20 000 ft), and the *hadal benthic* (6 11 000+ m/20–36 000+ ft). At the sea floor itself, the various benthic habitats can be divided into those where the organisms live primarily on the surface of the bottom (**benthic epifauna**) and those where they actually inhabit the sediment (**benthic infauna**).

Bentinck, Lord William (Henry Cavendish) (1774–1839) British statesman and Governor-General of India (1828–35), born in Bulstrode, Buckinghamshire, SC England, UK. He became Governor of Madras (1803–7), but was recalled when his prohibition of sepoy beards and turbans caused the massacre at Vellore (1806). He served in the Peninsular War (1808–14), in 1827 became Governor-General of Bengal, and in 1828 first Governor-General of India. His administration resulted in better internal communications, brought about many educational reforms with the help of Thomas Macaulay, and prohibited *suttee*.

Bentinck, William Henry Cavendish, 3rd Duke of Portland (1738–1809) British statesman and prime minister (1783, 1807–9), born in Bulstrode, Buckinghamshire, SC England, UK. He entered Lord Rockingham's cabinet in 1765, and succeeded him as leader of the Whig Party. He was twice prime minister, but his best work was done as home secretary under Pitt, when he was given charge of Irish affairs (1794–1801).

Bentine, Michael [benteen] (1921–96) Comedy performer, born in Watford, Hertfordshire, SE England, UK. He made his stage debut in 1941 and, after wartime service in the RAF, worked at the Windmill Theatre (1946) and in the show *Starlight Roof* (1947). One of the early members of *The Goons* (1950–2), he left the popular radio series to pursue a solo career, and appeared on television in *After Hours* (1959–60) and *It's a Square World* (1960–4), which allowed him to indulge his eccentric penchant for zany, surreal humour. Later television series, often for children, included *The Golden Silents* (1965), *Potty Time* (1973–80), and *Mad About It* (1981). He wrote novels and autobiographies, including *The Long Banana Skin* (1975) and *A Shy Person's Guide to Life* (1984).

Bentley, E(dmund) C(lerihew) (1875–1956) Journalist and novelist, born in Shepherd's Bush, London, UK. He is chiefly remembered as the author of *Trent's Last Case* (1913), which is regarded as a milestone in the development of the detective novel. A close friend of G K Chesterton, he originated and gave his name to the type of humorous verse-form known as the *clerihew*, a four-line verse consisting of two couplets which are often witty and epigrammatic.

Benton, Thomas Hart, known as **Old Bullion** (1782–1858) US statesman, born near Hillsborough, North Carolina, USA. He became senator for Missouri (1820–51), and the chief Democratic spokesman in the US Senate. He received his byname from his opposition to paper currency, and he also made himself unpopular by opposing slavery in the territories.

Benton, Thomas Hart (1889–1975) Painter of large historical murals on American themes and realistic genre scenes, born in Neosho, Missouri, USA. He admired the Cubists in Paris (1909–11), but after returning to the USA he reacted against European modernism, and in the late 1920s set about creating a populist American art based on ordinary Middle-Western experience: cowboys, gamblers, oil wells, and native Americans (eg 'Independence and the Opening of The West', 1959–62, Truman Library, Independence, MO).

Bentsen, Lloyd Millard, Jr (1921–) US statesman, born in Mission, Texas, USA. He studied law at Texas University, Austin, and served as a combat pilot during World War 2. He was a member of the US House of Representatives (1948–54), then built up a substantial fortune as president of the Lincoln Consolidated insurance company in Houston. He returned to Congress as a senator for Texas in 1971, and was vice-presidential running-mate to Michael Dukakis in the Democrats' 1988 presidential challenge. In Bill Clinton's administration he served as secretary to the treasury (1993–4).

Benue, River [baynway], Fr **Beboué** Major tributary of the R Niger in Nigeria; rises in Cameroon, and flows generally W across E and SC Nigeria; navigable below Garoua; joins the R Niger at Lokoja; length 1295 km/805 mi.

Benue–Congo languages [baynway konggoh] *Niger–Congo languages*

Benz, Karl (Friedrich) (1844–1929) Engineer and car manufacturer, born in Karlsruhe, SW Germany. He developed a two-stroke engine (1877–9) and founded a factory for its manufacture, leaving in 1883 when his backers refused to finance a mobile engine. He then founded a second company, Benz & Co, Rheinisch Gasmotorenfabrik, at Mannheim. His first car – one of the earliest petrol-driven vehicles – was completed in 1885 and sold to a French manufacturer. In 1926 the firm was merged with the Daimler-Motoren-Gesellschaft to form Daimler-Benz & Co.

benzaldehyde [benzaldihiyd] C_6H_5CHO, IUPAC **phenylmethanal**, boiling point 179°C. A colourless liquid, with the odour of almonds, used as a flavouring. It is readily oxidized to benzoic acid.

Benzedrine *amphetamine*

benzene [benzeen] C_6H_6, melting point 5°C, boiling point 80°C. An aromatic liquid obtained from coal tar, which may be synthesized by dehydrogenation of petroleum hydrocarbons. It is the simplest of the large series of aromatic compounds. Although the bonds in the benzene ring are often represented as alternating single and double, they are in fact all equivalent, this fact usually being described by the misleading name 'resonance'. Benzene does not easily undergo addition reactions, but has a large number of substitution reactions, giving a wide range of aromatic compounds. It is used in dyestuffs, plastics, insecticides, detergents, and several other products.

benzodiazepines [benzohdiyayzepeenz] A group of drugs each of which exerts, to varying degrees, anti-anxiety, anti-epilepsy, hypnotic (sleep-inducing), muscle-relaxant, and sedative properties. The two tranquillizers *chlordiazepoxide* (Librium) and *diazepam* (Valium) were the first to be introduced, in 1960 and 1962 respectively. *Nitrazepam* (Mogadon) and *temazepam* (Normison) are commonly used as hypnotics, and *alprezalam* is widely prescribed to suppress anxiety. They are very safe drugs, with fatal overdose being very uncommon, and therefore they took over from the more dangerous barbiturates. Some concern is now being expressed at their very wide use, which has been criticized as inappropriate. Evidence of addiction following long-term use is accumulating, and the UK Committee on the Safety of Medicines now recommends that treatment should be restricted to severe anxiety and insomnia for a maximum of four weeks.

benzoic acid [benzohik] C_6H_5COOH, melting point 122°C. A white crystalline compound obtained by the oxidation of toluene. It is the simplest aromatic acid, a weak acid. Its sodium salt, *sodium benzoate*, is used as a preservative.

benzoin [benzohin] $C_6H_5.CHOH.CO.C_6H_5$, melting point 137°C. A fragrant solid, a condensation product of benzaldehyde. It also occurs naturally in the resin known as balsam, from trees of the genus *Styrax*.

Ben-Zvi, Itzhak [ben tsvee], original name **Isaac Shimshelevich** (1884–1963) Israeli statesman and president (1952–63), born in Poltava, EC Ukraine. Having migrated to Palestine in 1907 he became a prominent Zionist, and in 1920 helped create the Histadrut, The General Federation of Labour. He signed Israel's Declaration of Independence in 1948, and was elected president of Israel on the death of Weizmann in 1952. A prominent scholar and archaeologist, he wrote on Jewish and Zionist history.

benzyl [benziyl, benzil] $C_6H_5CH_2$–, IUPAC **phenylmethyl**. A functional group containing a phenyl ring, whose addition to a name usually indicates its substitution for hydrogen in a compound.

Beqaa, al- [bekah], Eng **the Bekka** Governorate of E Lebanon, bounded NE and E by Syria; capital, Zahle; poultry, sheep, wheat, vineyards; al-Beqaa valley of strategic importance to both Israel and Syria, and a centre of Muslim Shiite activity.

Bérain, Jean (the Elder) [bayrĩ] (1639–1711) Artist, born in Lorraine, NE France. He was the leading designer of stage scenery, costumes, fêtes, and displays at the court of Louis XIV. His arabesques, grotesques, and *singeries* (monkey designs), often combined with Chinese motifs, herald the lighter Rococo style of the early 18th-c.

Berber Afro-Asiatic-speaking peoples of Egypt, Algeria, Libya, Tunisia, and Morocco. They were originally settled in one area, but the Bedouin Arabs who invaded N Africa in the 12th-c turned many of them into nomads. Most Berber tribes ultimately accepted Islam, and in the 11th-c formed themselves into a military federation known as the Almoravids, who conquered the mediaeval states of Ghana, Morocco, Algeria, and S Spain. In the 12th-c their power began to wane, and the Almohads, a new group influenced by Sufism, by 1169 came to command the entire Maghreb to Tripoli, as well as Muslim Spain. The Almohad Empire declined in the 13th-c. Today, some Berbers are sedentary farmers, while others are nomadic or transhumant pastoralists. Many work as migrant labourers in S Europe. The best-known groups include the Kabyle, Shluh, and Tuareg. They comprise 40% of the population of Morocco (10 million) and 30% of that of Algeria (7 million).

Berberian, Cathy *Berio, Luciano*

berberis *barberry*

Berenson, Bernard or **Bernhard** [berenson] (1865–1959) Art critic, born in Vilnius, Lithuania. He moved to the USA in 1875, studied at Harvard, and became a leading authority on Italian Renaissance art. He became a US citizen, but in 1900 went to live in Italy, producing a vast amount of critical literature. He bequeathed his villa and art collection to Harvard University, which turned it into the Center for Italian Renaissance Culture.

Beresford, Bruce (1940–) Film director, born in Sydney, New South Wales, SE Australia. He studied in Sydney and worked at the British Film Institute (1966–71) before directing his first feature, *The Adventures of Barry McKenzie* (1972). He was a key figure in the revival of the Australian film industry, and won the Australian Film Institute's Best Director award for *Don's Party* (1976) and *Breaker Morant* (1979). He has since received international recognition for *Tender Mercies* (1982), *Driving Miss Daisy* (1989, Oscar), and *Black Robe* (1991). Later films include *Last Dance* (1995), *Double Jeopardy* (1999), and *Evelyn* (2002). In 1991 he directed *Elektra* for the South Australian State Opera.

Beresford, Jack (1899–1977) British oarsman. He competed for Great Britain at five Olympics (1920–36) as sculler and oarsman, winning three gold and two silver medals, and received the Olympic Diploma of Merit in 1949. He won the Diamond Sculls at Henley four times, and was elected president of the Thames Rowing Club in 1971.

Berg, Alban (1885–1935) Composer, born in Vienna, Austria. He studied under Schoenberg (1904–10), and after World War 1 taught privately in Vienna. With the last of his *Four Songs* (1909–10) he displays a free harmonic language tempered wih Romantic tonal elements which remained his characteristic style. He is best known for his opera *Wozzeck* (1925), his violin concerto, and the *Lyric Suite* for string quartet. His unfinished opera, *Lulu*, was posthumously produced.

Bergama [bergahma], ancient **Pergamon** or **Pergamum** 39°08N 27°10E, pop (2000e) 55 000. Town in Izmir province, W Turkey, N of Izmir; former capital of the ancient Kingdom of Pergamum, and of the Roman province of Asia; parchment is supposed to have been invented here; carpet making, tourism; Acropolis, Temples of Trajan and Dionysos, Sanctuary of Athena, Altar of Zeus.

Bergamo [bairgamoh] 45°42N 9°40E, pop (2000e) 122 000. Capital town of Bergamo province, Lombardy, N Italy; between the Brembo and Serio Rivers, NE of Milan; first seat of the Republican fascist government set up in N Italy by Mussolini after his fall from power, 1943; airport; railway; textiles, cement, printing, electrical switches, bottling plant; Romanesque basilica (1137–1355), 15th-c cathedral; annual trade fair (Nov).

bergamot [bergamot] **1** An aromatic perennial, native to North America and Mexico; stem square; leaves oval, toothed, in opposite pairs; flowers 2-lipped, hooded, purple or red, in crowded whorls around stem; visited by bees and humming-birds. The leaves provide medicinal Oswega (or Oswego) tea. (Genus: *Monarda*, 12 species. Family: Labiatae.)
2 *orange*

Bergen (Belgium) [berkhen] *Mons*

Bergen (Norway) [bergn] 60°23N 5°20E, pop (2000e) 223 000. Seaport and administrative capital of Hordaland county, SW Norway; on a promontory at the head of a deep bay; old shipping and trading town; second largest city in Norway; founded, 1070; capital, 12th–13th-c; occupied by Germans in World War 2; bishopric; airport; railway; university (1948); shipyards, engineering, paper, fishing, fish products, pottery, offshore oil services; tourist and cultural centre; birthplace of Grieg; restored 13th-c cathedral, Hanseatic museum, Håkonshall (13th-c palace), Mariakirke (12th-c), art gallery, museums.

Berger, Samuel R, known as **Sandy Berger** (1945–) US public official and lawyer. Educated at Cornell and Harvard, he practised law with a Washington firm (1973–7, 1981–92), and also served as the State Department's deputy director of policy and planning (1977–80). Formerly the Deputy Assistant to the President for National Security Affairs (1993–6), he was appointed Assistant in Clinton's second administration. He is the author of *Dollar Harvest* (1971) on American rural politics.

Bergerac, Savinien Cyrano de *Cyrano de Bergerac, Savinien*

Bergius, Friedrich [bergius] (1884–1949) Organic chemist, born in Goldschmieden, Germany. He researched into coal hydrogenation for the production of motor fuels under high pressure, and the hydrolysis of wood to sugar, for which he shared the 1931 Nobel Prize for Chemistry. After World War 2 he left Germany for Argentina.

Bergman, Hjalmar (Fredrik Elgérus) (1883–1931) Novelist, poet, and playwright, born in Örebro, SC Sweden. His plays include *Maria, Jesu moder* (1905) and the comedy *Swedenhielms* (The Swedenhielm Family, 1925). His novels, including the broadly comical *Markurells i Wadköping* (1919, trans God's Orchid), were often popular satires on his native Örebro.

Bergman, (Ernst) Ingmar (1918–) Film and stage director, born in Uppsala, E Sweden. A trainee director in the Stockholm theatre, he began his film career in 1943, making his film debut with *Kris* (1945, Crisis). His explorations of personal torment won many international prizes for such films as *Det sjunde inseglet* (1957, The Seventh Seal), *Smultronstället* (1957, trans Wild Strawberries), *Jungfrukällan* (1960, The Virgin Spring, Oscar), and *Såsom i en spegel* (1961, Through a Glass Darkly, Oscar), which are outstanding for their photographic artistry, haunting imagery, and subtle exploration of facial characteristics. Preoccupied with guilt, anguish, emotional repression, and death, he created a succession of bleak masterpieces including *Viskningar och rop* (1972, Cries and Whispers) and *Höstsonaten* (1978, Autumn Sonata). His later film, *Fanny och Alexander* (1982, Fanny and Alexander, Oscar), was an unexpectedly life-affirming evocation of autobiographical elements from his own Dickensian childhood. He then largely retired from the film-making scene, but later work includes the script for *Private Confessions* (1996). Publications include his autobiography *Laterna Magica* (1987, The Magic Lantern) and *Images: My Life in Film* (1994).

Bergman, Ingrid (1915–82) Film and stage actress, born in Stockholm, Sweden. After studying at the Royal Dramatic Theatre, she made her film debut in *Munkbrogreven* (1934). Unaffected and vivacious, she became an immensely popular romantic star in such films as *Casablanca* (1942), *Spellbound* (1945), and *Notorious* (1946). In 1950 she gave birth to the illegitimate child of director Roberto Rossellini. The ensuing scandal led to her ostracization from the US film industry. She continued her career in Europe, and was welcomed back by Hollywood on her return in 1956. Nominated seven times for an Academy Award, she won Oscars for *Gaslight* (1944), *Anastasia* (1956), and *Murder on the Orient Express* (1974).

Bergson, Henri (Louis) [bergsõ] (1859–1941) Philosopher, born in Paris, France. He became professor at the Collège de France (1900–21), a highly original thinker who became something of a cult figure. He contrasted the fundamental reality of the dynamic flux of consciousness with the inert physical world of discrete objects, which was a convenient fiction for the mechanistic descriptions of science. The *élan vital*, or 'creative impulse', not a deterministic natural selection, is at the heart of evolution; and intuition, not analysis, reveals the real world of process and change. His own writings are literary, suggestive, and analogical rather than philosophical in the modern sense. His most important works are *Essai sur les données immédiates de la conscience* (1889, trans Time and Free Will), *Matière et mémoire* (1896, Matter and Memory), and *L'Evolution créatrice* (1907, Creative Evolution). He was awarded the Nobel Prize for Literature in 1927.

Beria, Lavrenti Pavlovich [beria] (1899–1953) Soviet secret police chief, born in Mercheuli, NW Georgia. He served as a member of the OGPU (the forerunner of the KGB) in the Caucasus (1921–31), before becoming first secretary of the Georgian Communist Party. He was appointed minister for internal affairs (1938) by his patron, Stalin, and served as vice-president of the State Committee for Defence during World War 2, being accorded the title of marshal in 1945. On Stalin's death in March 1953, he attempted to seize power, but was foiled by fearful military and party leaders. Following his arrest he was tried for treason, and was executed in December 1953. He was a plotter of ruthless ambition, and a notoriously skilled organizer of forced labour, terror, and espionage.

beri beri A nutritional disease due to an inadequate dietary intake of vitamin B_1, as occurs in alcoholism and starvation. Peripheral nerves are affected (*polyneuritis*), resulting in weakness and loss of sensation in the hands and feet. It also causes heart failure and oedema.

Berigan, Bunny, originally **Roland Bernard** (1908–42) Swing trumpeter and singer, born in Hilbert, Wisconsin, USA. He epitomized the Jazz Era, starring in dance bands at the University of Wisconsin as an undergraduate – tall, dark, and handsome playing love songs in a raccoon coat. He won featured billing with several orchestras including Benny Goodman (1935–6, where he had his first hits 'Sometimes I'm Happy' and 'King Porter Stomp'), and twice with Tommy Dorsey (1937 and 1940). Before and after the stints with Dorsey, he led his own band, but in spite of a huge hit playing and singing 'I Can't Get Started With You', his business sense was hopeless, even when he was sober. His health disintegrated, and he died at 34.

Bering, Vitus (Jonassen) [bayring], also spelled **Behring** (1681–1741) Navigator, born in Horsens, C Denmark. He led an expedition in the Sea of Kamchatka (1728) to determine whether the continents of Asia and America were joined. In 1733 he was given command of the 600-strong Great Northern Expedition to explore the Siberian coast and Kuril Is, and in 1741 sailed from Ohkotsk towards the American continent, finally sighting Alaska. He was wrecked on the island of Avatcha (now *Bering I*), where he died. *Bering Sea* and *Bering Strait* are named after him.

Bering Sea [bayring] area 2 304 000 sq km/890 000 sq mi. Part of the Pacific Ocean between Siberia (W) and Alaska (E), bounded S by the Aleutian Is and Trench; connected to the Arctic by the Bering Strait (90 km/56 mi wide at narrowest point); often ice-bound (Nov–May); contains boundary between Russia and USA; depths reach 4000 m/13 000 ft (SW), but 25–75 m/90–240 ft over continental shelf in NE; explored first in 17th-c; seal herd threatened with extinction because of over-exploitation, but herds built up after 1911 agreement by UK, USA, Russia, and Japan.

Berio, Luciano [berioh] (1925–2003) Composer and teacher of music, born in Oneglia, NW Italy. He studied at the Music Academy in Milan, and founded an electronic studio. He moved to the USA in 1962, taught composition at the Juilliard School, New York City, and returned to Italy in 1972. In 1950 he married the US soprano **Cathy Berberian** (1925–83), for whom he wrote several works; the marriage was dissolved in 1966. His particular interest was in the combining of live and pre-recorded sound, and the use of tapes and electronic music, as in his compositions *Mutazioni* (1955, Mutations) and *Omaggio a James Joyce* (1958, Homage to James Joyce). His *Sequenza* series for solo instruments (1958 onwards) are striking virtuoso pieces. Other works included *Passaggio* (1963), *Laborintus II* (1965), *Opera* (1969–70), and *Continuo* (1991).

Berkeley, Busby [berklee], originally **William Berkeley Enos** (1895–1976) Choreographer and director, born in Los Angeles, California, USA. He worked as an actor, stage manager, and dance director, directing his first Broadway show, *A Night in Venice*, in 1928. He became one of the cinema's most innovative choreographers, noted for his mobile camerawork and dazzling kaleidoscopic routines involving spectacular multitudes of chorus girls. His work enhanced such films as *Forty Second Street* (1933), *Gold Diggers of 1933* (1934), and *Dames* (1934). In later years, ill health restricted his opportunities, but he enjoyed a Broadway triumph as the supervising producer of the 1971 revival of *No, No, Nanette*.

Berkeley, George [bah(r)klee] (1685–1753) Anglican bishop and philosopher, born at Dysert Castle, Kilkenny, SE Ireland. He studied at Trinity College, Dublin, where he remained, as fellow and tutor, until 1713. His most important books were published in these early years: *Essay towards a New Theory of Vision* (1709), *A Treatise concerning the Principles of Human Knowledge* (1710), and *Three Dialogues between Hylas and Philonous* (1713). In these works he developed his celebrated claim that 'to be is to be perceived' – that the contents of the material world are 'ideas' that only exist when they are perceived by a mind. He became Dean of Londonderry (1724), but became obsessed with a romantic scheme to found a college in the Bermudas to promote 'the propagation of the Gospel among the American savages'. After years of intensive lobbying in London for support he sailed for America with his newly married wife (1728) and made a temporary home in Rhode Island. He waited there nearly three years: the grants did not materialize, and the college was never founded. He returned first to London and then in 1734 became Bishop of Cloyne. His remaining literary work was divided between questions of social reform and of religious reflection.

Berkeley, Sir Lennox (Randall Francis) [bah(r)klee] (1903–89) Composer, born in Boars Hill, Oxfordshire, SC England, UK. A pupil of Nadia Boulanger, his early compositions, the largest of which is the oratorio *Jonah* (1935), show the influence of his French training. Later works, notably the 'Stabat Mater' (1947), the operas *Nelson* (1953) and *Ruth* (1956), and the orchestral *Windsor Variations* (1969) and *Voices of the Night* (1973), have won him wide recognition for their combination of technical refinement with lyrically emotional appeal. He was knighted in 1974.

Berkoff, Steven [berkof] (1937–) Playwright, actor, and director, born in London, UK. After studying at the Ecole Jacques Lecoq in Paris, he founded the London Theatre Group, for whom he directed his own adaptations from the classics, including Kafka's *Metamorphosis* (1969). His own plays include *Greek* (1979), *Decadence* (1982), *West* (1983), *Kvetch* (1987), and *Acapulco* (1992). His publications include *Graft: Tales of an Actor* (1998) and *Richard II in New York* (1999). An autobiography, *Free Association*, appeared in 1996. In 1998 he wrote, directed, and acted in *Shakespeare's Villains*, a one-man show.

Berkowitz, David [berkohvits] (c.1953–) Convicted US murderer, who dubbed himself 'Son of Sam' in a note to the New York Police Department. He terrorized the city for a year (1976–7), preying on courting couples and lone women. He was finally caught because of a parking ticket: he watched as it was stuck on his car, and then went and tore it to pieces. A woman witnessed this, noticed a strange smile on his face, and reported him to the police. Berkowitz's car was traced and he was arrested. In pursuit of a plea of insanity he claimed at his trial that Satanic voices told him to kill. Deemed sane, he received a prison sentence of 365 years in 1977.

Berkshire [bah(r)ksheer], also known as **Royal Berkshire** pop (2000e) 781 700; area 1259 sq km/486 sq mi. Former county of S England, UK; replaced in 1998 by the unitary authorities of Windsor and Maidenhead, Wokingham, Reading, Slough, West Berkshire, and Bracknell Forest; continues to receive widespread cultural recognition.

Berlin [berlin] 52°32N 13°25E, pop (2000e) 3 530 000; area 883 sq km/341 sq mi. Capital of Germany, partitioned in 1945 into East Berlin and West Berlin; founded in the 13th-c; former residence of the Hohenzollerns and capital of Brandenburg; later capital of Prussia, becoming an industrial and commercial centre in the 18th-c; in 1949 West Berlin became a province of the Federal Republic of Germany (pop (1991) 2 146 300; area 480 sq km/185 sq mi) and East Berlin a county of the German Democratic Republic (pop (1991) 1 272 600, area 403 sq km/156 sq mi); the two halves of the city separated by the Berlin Wall (1961); contact between East and West was restored in 1989, following government changes in East Germany; capital-designate of unified Germany, 1990; railway; two airports; Humboldt University (1809), Free University (1948), Technical University (1946); engineering, motor vehicles, office equipment, pharmaceuticals, chemicals, brewing, soft drinks, food processing, toys, electronics, electrical cables, clothing, steel construction, publishing; Kaiser Wilhelm Church (preserved ruins), Tiergarten, Charlottenburg Palace; Brandenburg Gate, Unter den Linden, Pergamum museum, national gallery, Rotes Rathaus (red town hall); festival of dramatic art and music, film festival (Feb).

Berlin, Irving [berlin], originally **Israel Baline** (1888–1989) Composer who helped to launch 20th-c American popular music, born in Temun, N Russia. Taken to the USA as a child, he worked for a time as a singing waiter in a Bowery beer hall, introducing some of his own songs, such as 'Alexander's Ragtime Band'. The 1940s saw him at the peak of his career, with the hit musicals *Annie Get Your Gun* (1946) and *Call Me Madam* (1950). 'God Bless America'(1939) and 'White Christmas' (1942) achieved worldwide popularity. In 1954 he received a special presidential citation as a composer of patriotic songs, and in all he wrote the words and music for over 900 songs. He retired in 1962, and lived as a recluse in Manhattan.

Berlin, Sir Isaiah (1909–97) Philosopher and historian of ideas, born in Riga, Latvia. Most of his academic career was at Oxford, where he became a fellow of All Souls (1932), professor of social and political theory (1957), and Master of Wolfson College (1966). His philosophical works included *Karl Marx* (1939), *Historical Inevitability* (1954), *Two Concepts of Liberty* (1959), and *Vico and Herder* (1976). Later works included *The Crooked Timber of Humanity* (1990) and *The Magus of the North* (1993). He was widely recognized as one of the leading intellectual voices of his generation.

Berlin, Congress of (1878) An international congress following the Russian defeat of Ottoman Turkey (1877–8). Under the chairmanship of the German chancellor, Otto von Bismarck, the Congress limited Russian naval expansion; Serbia, Romania, and Bulgaria achieved independence from Turkey; Austria–Hungary occupied Bosnia-Herzegovina; Russia retained gains in S Bessarabia and the Caucasus, but conceded a reduction in the size of her satellite, Bulgaria; and Britain occupied Cyprus. Bismarck's handling of the Congress antagonized Russia; and the claim of Disraeli, that it had achieved 'peace with honour', proved unfounded.

Berlin Airlift (1948–9) A massive airlift of essential supplies flown in to post-war Berlin by British and US aircraft in round-the-clock missions. The airlift was carried out in response to the action of the Soviet military authorities in Berlin, who had attempted to isolate the city (pop 2 million) from the West by severing all overland communication routes (Jun 1948). Post-war West Berlin was a Western outpost surrounded by the Soviet zone (East Germany). More than 270 000 flights were conducted. Stalin lifted the blockade in May 1949.

Berliner Ensemble [berliner] A theatre company in East Berlin which was formed by Brecht in 1949. In its early years it had an enormous influence on Western theatre, chiefly through Brecht's own productions of his mature plays written during his years in exile from Nazi Germany. After Brecht's death in 1956, his widow Helene Weigel took over as director, and the company later extended its repertoire to include other playwrights, including Shaw and Wedekind, on its tours to the West.

Berlin Wall A concrete wall built by the East German government in 1961 to seal off East Berlin from the part of the city occupied by the three main Western powers. Built largely to prevent mass illegal emigration to the West, which was threatening the East German economy, the wall was the scene of the shooting of many East Germans who tried to escape from the Eastern sector. The wall, seen by many as a major symbol of the denial of human rights in E Europe, was unexpectedly opened in November 1989, following increased pressure for political reform in East Germany. It has now been taken down.

Berlioz, (Louis-)Hector [ber**lioh**z] (1803–69) Composer, born in La Côte-Saint-André, SE France. He entered the Paris Conservatoire in 1826, where he fell in love with the actress **Harriet Smithson**, whom he subsequently married (1833, d.1854); the *Symphonie Fantastique* expresses his devotion to her. Gaining the Prix de Rome in 1830, he spent two years in Italy. After 1842 he won a brilliant reputation in Germany, Russia, and England, but on his return to France he failed to gain a hearing for his major works. The deaths of his second wife (**Maria Recio**, 1862) and his son, ill health, and his fruitless struggle to win a regular place in French music, clouded his later years. His compositions include the *Grande messe des morts* (1837), the dramatic symphony *Roméo et Juliette* (1839), the overture *Le Carnival romain* (1843), the cantata *La Damnation de Faust* (1846), and his comic opera *Béatrice et Bénédict* (1860–2). One of the founders of 19th-c programme music, he also produced seven books, including a treatise on orchestration and an autobiography.

Berlusconi, Silvio [berlus**koh**nee] (1936–) Italian politician, prime minister (1994, 2001–), and entrepreneur, born in Milan, Lombardy, N Italy. After building a thriving property business, he expanded his activities to include, in his Fininvest group of companies, media, publishing, sport (he owns AC Milan Football Club), and finance. In 1993 he entered politics, founding the right-wing party *Forza Italia*, which was successful at the 1994 elections. In 2003 he faced corruption allegations relating to his business affairs and became the first serving Italian prime minister to appear in court at his own trial. The trial was halted when parliament approved a controversial law giving serving prime ministers immunity from prosecution while in office, but the ruling was annulled in January 2004.

Bermuda *see panel*

Bermuda Triangle An area of the North Atlantic Ocean, roughly delimited by Bermuda, the Greater Antilles, and the US coast, which has become part of maritime mythology. Reports of vessels which have been abandoned or disappeared, vanishing aircraft, and other inexplicable events have been known for over a century, and have attracted diverse explanations involving extraterrestrial beings, force fields, crippling sea vegetation, sea monsters, and other such factors. Although objective evidence, such as wreckage, is conspicuous by its absence, the Triangle continues to attract a great deal of imaginative writing.

Bern, Fr **Berne** 46°57N 7°28E, pop (2000e) 140 000. Federal capital of Switzerland and of Bern canton, W Switzerland; on R Aare 94 km/58 mi SW of Zürich; founded, 1191; joined the Swiss Confederation, 1353; capital, 1848; airport (Belpmoos); railway junction; university (1834); textiles, machinery, chocolate, pharmaceuticals, foodstuffs, graphic trades, electrical equipment, engineering, tourism; Gothic cathedral (1421–1573), mediaeval town hall, clock tower, many museums; old city is a world heritage site; 'Zibelemärit' old market (Nov); headquarters of several international organizations.

Bernadette of Lourdes, St, originally **Marie Bernarde Soubirous** (1844–79) Visionary, born in Lourdes, S France, the daughter of François Soubirous, a miller. She claimed in 1858 to have received 18 apparitions of the Blessed Virgin at the Massabielle Rock in 1858, which has since become a notable place of pilgrimage. She became a nun with the Sisters of Charity at Nevers, and was canonized in 1933. Feast day 18 February or 16 April.

Bernadotte, Folke, Greve (Count) [berna**dot**] (1895–1948) Humanitarian and diplomat, born in Stockholm, Sweden, the nephew of King Gustav V of Sweden. He acted as a mediator during World War 2, succeeding in obtaining the release of many concentration-camp prisoners to Sweden, via the Red Cross. Appointed by the UN to mediate in Palestine, he produced a partition plan, but was assassinated by Jewish terrorists in Jerusalem.

Bernadotte, Jean *Charles XIV* (of Sweden)

Bernanos, Georges [bair**na**nos] (1888–1948) Writer, born in Paris, France. He did not begin to write seriously until he was 37 and had taken degrees in law and letters. A Catholic polemicist, he attacked indifference and was preoccupied with problems of sin and grace. His most memorable novels are *Sous le soleil de Satan* (1926, trans The Star of Satan) and *Le Journal d'un curé de campagne* (1936, The Diary of a Country Priest).

Bernard of Clairvaux, St [klair**voh**], known as **the Mellifluous Doctor** (1090–1153) Theologian and reformer, born in Fontaines, NE France. He entered the Cistercian monastery of Cîteaux (1113), and became the first abbot of the newly-founded monastery of Clairvaux, in Champagne (1115). His studious,

Bermuda

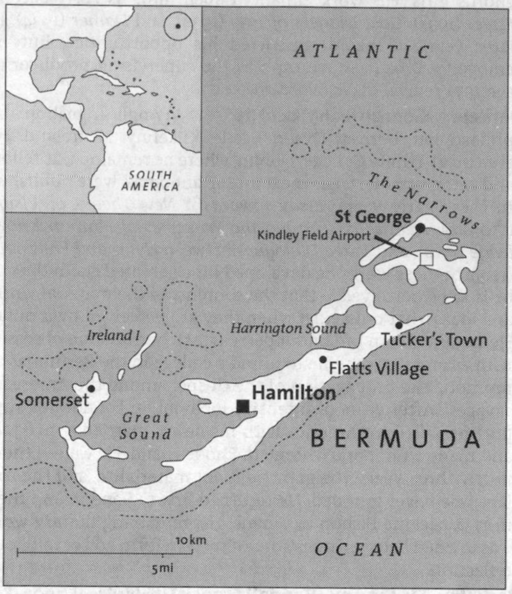

formerly **Somers Is** (UK British Overseas Territory)

Timezone GMT –4

Area 53 km²/20 sq mi

Population total (2000e) 62 900

Capital Hamilton

Physical features Archipelago in W Atlantic, c.900 km/560 mi E of Cape Hatteras, N Carolina; c.150 low-lying coral islands and islets, 20 inhabited, 7 linked by causeways and bridges; largest island, (Great) Bermuda; highest point, Gibb's Hill, 78 m/256 ft.

Climate Subtropical climate; generally humid; rain throughout year; warm summers, mild winters.

Currency 1 Bermuda Dollar = 100 cents

Economy Mainly year-round tourism; increasingly an international company business centre; petroleum products, pharmaceuticals, aircraft supplies, boatbuilding, ship repair, vegetables, citrus fruits; fish-processing centre.

GDP (2002c) $2·25 bn, per capita $35 200

History Formerly called Somers Is, discovered by Spanish mariner, Juan Bermudez, in early 16th-c; colonized by English settlers, 1612; important naval station, and (to 1862) penal settlement; internal self-government, 1968; movement for independence caused tension in the 1970s, including assassination of the Governor-General; bicameral legislature.

ascetic life and stirring eloquence made him the oracle of Christendom; he founded more than 70 monasteries; and he is regarded by the Catholic Church as the last of the Fathers. His preaching kindled the enthusiasm of France for the second Crusade (1146). His writings comprise more than 400 epistles, 340 sermons, a Life of St Malachy, and distinct theological treatises. He was canonized in 1174. The monks of his reformed branch of the Cistercians are often called *Bernardines*. Feast day 20 August.

Bernard of Menthon, St [mãtõ], known as **the Apostle of the Alps** (923–1008) Clergyman, born in Savoy, Italy. As archdeacon of Aosta he founded the hospices in the two Alpine passes that bear his name. *St Bernard dogs* are named after him. He was canonized in 1115; feast day 28 May or 15 June.

Bernardines *Bernard of Clairvaux, St*

Berners-Lee, Sir Tim (1955–) Network designer, the inventor of the World Wide Web, born in London, UK. He studied physics at Oxford (1973–6), then worked for various companies in telecommunications and computing. In 1984 he took up a fellowship at CERN, Geneva, to work on distributed real-time systems for scientific data acquisition and system control. In 1989 he proposed a global hypertext project, initially with the international physics community in mind, which was implemented on the Internet in 1991. He joined the Massachusetts Institute of Technology in 1994, becoming the first holder of the 3 Com (Computer Communications Compatability) chair in 1999. He is also director of the World Wide Web Consortium and his book, *Weaving the Web*, appeared in 1999. He became a fellow of the Royal Society in 2001, and was knighted in 2004.

Bernese Alps, Ger **Berner Alpen**, Fr **Alpes Bernoises** Mountain range in Switzerland, a N division of the Central Alps, extending from L Geneva to the Grimsel Pass; highest peak, the Finsteraarhorn (4274 m/14 022 ft); also includes the Aletschhorn and Jungfrau; numerous tourist resorts, including Interlaken and Grindelwald.

Bernhard Leopold [bernhah(r)t] (1911–) Prince of The Netherlands, born in Jena, EC Germany, the son of Prince Bernhard Casimir of Lippe. In 1937 he married Juliana, the only daughter of Wilhelmina, Queen of The Netherlands; they have four daughters. During World War 2, he commanded the Netherlands Forces of the Interior (1944–5). In 1976 he was involved in a bribery scandal, in which he was found to have received money for promoting the Dutch purchase of aircraft from the Lockheed Aircraft Corporation.

Bernhardt, Sarah [bernhah(r)t], originally **Henriette Rosine Bernard** (1844–1923) Actress and theatre producer, born in Paris, France. She entered the Paris Conservatoire in 1859, and in 1867 won fame as Zanetto in Coppée's *Le Passant* (1869), and as the Queen of Spain in *Ruy Blas* (1872). After 1876 she made frequent appearances in London, the USA, and Europe. She also managed several theatres, including the Théâtre Sarah-Bernhardt (founded, 1899), and wrote poetry and plays. In 1882 she married **Jacques Daria** or **Damala** (d.1889), a Greek actor, from whom she was divorced shortly afterwards. In 1915 she had a leg amputated, but did not abandon the stage.

Bernini, Gian Lorenzo [berneenee] (1598–1680) Baroque sculptor, architect, and painter, born in Naples, SW Italy, the son of a sculptor, **Pietro Bernini** (1562–1629). He went to Rome at an early age and was introduced to the papal court. He completed the bronze baldacchino in St Peter's (1633), and the fountain of the four river gods in the Piazza Navona (1647). In 1656 he decorated the apse of St Peter's with the so-called Cathedra Petri, designed the colonnade in front of the cathedral, and in 1663 the grand staircase to the Vatican.

Bernoulli, Daniel [bernoolee] (1700–82) Mathematician, born in Groningen, The Netherlands, the son of Johann Bernoulli. He studied medicine and mathematics, and became professor of mathematics at St Petersburg in 1725. In 1732 he returned to Basel to become professor of anatomy, then botany, and finally physics. He worked on trigonometric series, mechanics, vibrating systems, and hydrodynamics (anticipating the kinetic theory of gases), and solved a differential equation proposed by Jacopo Riccati, now known as *Bernoulli's equation*.

Bernoulli disk [bernoolee] A form of computer magnetic disk storage where, unlike the Winchester disk, the disk can be removed and replaced. It is named after the mathematician, Daniel Bernoulli, who developed the theory of fluid mechanics.

Bernoulli's principle [bernoolee] In physics, the principle that as the speed of a moving fluid increases, its pressure decreases; stated by Daniel Bernoulli in 1738. For example, when water flows down a pipe of varying cross-section, the water velocity is greatest at the narrowest point; the force required to accelerate the water to this greatest velocity is provided by the higher pressure in the slower-moving portion upstream. Bernoulli's principle explains the curved flight of a spinning cricket ball, and the lift on aircraft wings.

Bernstein, Carl [bernstiyn] (1944–) Journalist and writer, born in Washington, District of Columbia, USA. With Bob Woodward (1943–) he was responsible for unmasking the Watergate cover-up, which resulted in a constitutional crisis and the resignation of President Richard Nixon. For their coverage of the acknowledged investigative story of the 20th-c, Bernstein and Woodward won for the *Washington Post* the 1973 Pulitzer Prize for public service. Together they wrote the best seller, *All the President's Men* (1974), which became a successful film (1976), and *The Final Days* (1976), an almost hour-by-hour account of President Nixon's last months in office.

Bernstein, Leonard [bernstiyn] (1918–90) Conductor, pianist, and composer, born in Lawrence, Massachusetts, USA. He studied at Harvard and the Curtis Institute of Music, and achieved fame suddenly in 1943 by conducting the New York Philharmonic as a substitute for Bruno Walter. His compositions include three symphonies – *Jeremiah* (1942), *The Age of Anxiety* (1949), and *Kaddish* (1961–3) – a television opera, *Trouble in Tahiti*, and the musicals *On the Town* (1944) and *West Side Story* (1957). Later works include a Mass commissioned for the opening of the John F Kennedy Center of the Performing Arts (1971), the ballet *The Dybbuk* (1974), *Songfest* (1977), *Halil* (1981), and a revision of his operetta *Candide* (1956/88).

Berra, Yogi, popular name of **Lawrence Peter Berra** (1925–) Baseball player and coach, born in St Louis, Missouri, USA. He played with the New York Yankees (1946–63), including 14 World Series (a record). He also set the record for most World Series hits (71), and for most home runs by a catcher in the American League (313). After winning three Most Valuable Player awards (in five seasons), he went on to manage and coach the Yankees, then did the same for their arch-rivals, the New York Mets. In 1986 he went on to coach the Houston Astros. His comment that 'It ain't over 'til it's over' has become part of the game's legend.

Berruguete, Pedro [beroogetuh] (c.1450–1504) Painter, born near Valladolid, NWC Spain, the father of Alonso Berruguete. He became court painter to Ferdinand and Isabella, and visited Italy (c.1447), where he helped to decorate the palace library at Urbino. The new, Venetian-inspired feeling for light and colour, and the interest in perspective which he acquired in Italy, made him the first truly Renaissance painter in Spain. His later work can be seen in the cathedrals of Toledo and Avila.

Berry, Chuck, popular name of **Charles Edward Anderson Berry** (1926–) Rock singer, born in St Louis, Missouri, USA. The biggest influence on pre-Beatles rock, he learnt to play the guitar at high school. He served three years in a reform school for armed robbery (1944–7), then worked in a factory and trained as a hairdresser before moving to Chicago in 1955 and launching his professional career. His successes include 'Maybellene' (1955), 'Rock And Roll Music' (1957), and 'Johnny B Goode' (1958). In 1959 he was charged with transporting a minor over state lines for immoral purposes and was jailed for two years in 1962. After his release his creativity never fully recovered, although 'My Ding A Ling' (1972) was one of the most successful singles of his career.

Berry, Halle [halee] (1966–) Actress, born in Cleveland, Ohio, USA. She began modelling at age 16 and, after coming runner-up in the 1986 Miss USA pageant, decided on a career in acting. She joined the Second City comedy theatre in Chicago before moving to New York City. Her first feature film was *Jungle Fever* (1991), and later films include *The Flintstones* (1994), *Bulworth* (1998), and *Die Another Day* (2002). In 2002 she made Hollywood history as the first black woman to win an Academy Award for Best Actress for her role in *Monster's Ball* (2001).

Berry, Wendell (Erdman) (1934–) Poet, novelist, essayist, philosopher, and farmer, born in Port Royal, Kentucky, USA. He studied at the University of Kentucky, Lexington, taught at various institutions, and at one time was an editor for Rodale Press, Pennsylvania. An ardent defender of the countryside and rural communities, his writing is concerned with the abuse of land and human responsibility to the Earth. His earliest collection of poetry on this theme was *The Broken Ground* (1964). Novels include *The Memory of Old Jack* (1974). Non-fiction works include *The Unsettling of America* (1977), *What Are People For?* (1990), and *Another Turn of the Crank* (1995).

Berryman, John (1914–72) Poet, biographer, novelist, and academic, born in McAlester, Oklahoma, USA. He studied at Columbia and Cambridge (UK) universities, and taught at several universities before becoming professor of humanities at the University of Minnesota (1955–72). Often pigeon-holed as a confessional poet, he disparaged the label. *Homage to Mistress Bradstreet* (1956), established his reputation. His major work is *Dream Songs*, which he began in 1955; *77 Dream Songs* (1964) won the Pulitzer Prize in 1965. He became a severely disturbed alcoholic, and committed suicide in Minneapolis.

Berry's phase An extra factor needed in the quantum description of systems undergoing certain changes, dependent on the system's geometry; identified in 1983 by UK physicist Michael Berry (1941–). The effect is observed in the rotation of the polarization plane of light passing along a helical optical fibre, and in certain chemical reactions, such as $H+H_2 \rightarrow H_2+H$ exchange reaction. It provides an interpretation of the Aharonov–Bohm effect.

berserker [berserker] In Norse mythology, a warrior in a 'bear-shirt' who fought in such a frenzy that he was impervious to wounds. The name is the origin of the phrase 'to go berserk'.

Berthelot, (Pierre Eugène) Marcellin [bairteloh] (1827–1907) Chemist and French statesman, born in Paris, France. He became the first professor of organic chemistry at the Collège de France (1865), and was foreign minister (1895–6). He helped to found the study of thermochemistry, introducing a standard method for determining the latent heat of steam. His syntheses of many fundamental organic compounds helped to destroy the classical division between organic and inorganic compounds.

Berthollet, Claude Louis, comte (Count) [bairtolay] (1748–1822) Chemist, born in Talloires, E France. He studied at Turin, moving to Paris in 1772. He aided Antoine Lavoisier in his research into gunpowder and in forming the new chemical nomenclature. In 1785 he showed the value of chlorine for bleaching, and showed ammonia to be a compound of hydrogen and nitrogen. He was made a senator and a count by Napoleon, yet voted for his deposition in 1814, and on the Bourbon restoration was created a peer.

Bertillon, Alphonse [berteeyõ] (1853–1914) Police officer, born in Paris, France. As chief of the identification bureau in Paris, in 1882 he devised a system of identifying criminals by anthropometric measurements (later superseded by fingerprints).

Bertolucci, Bernardo [bertohloochee] (1941–) Film director, born in Parma, N Italy. He became an assistant to Pier Paolo Pasolini on *Accatone* (1961). His collection of poetry, *In cerca del mistero* (1962, In Search of Mystery), won the Premio Viareggio Prize, and he made his directorial debut the same year with *La commare seca* (The Grim Reaper). The success of *Il conformista* (1970, The Conformist) and *Ultimo tango a Parigi* (1972, Last Tango in Paris) allowed him to make the Marxist epic *Novecento* (1976, 1900). After a number of unrealized projects during the 1980s, *The Last Emperor* (1987) won nine Oscars. Later films include *Stealing Beauty* (1996), *Besieged* (1998), and *Training Day* (2001).

Bertrand, Henri Gratien, comte (Count) [bairtrã] (1773–1844) French soldier and military engineer, one of Napoleon's generals, born in Châteauroux, C France. Aide-de-camp to the emperor from 1804, he shared the emperor's banishment to both Elba and St Helena. After Napoleon's death he returned to France, where he was appointed commandant of the Polytechnic School (1830). His shorthand diary gave a detailed account of Napoleon's life in exile.

Berwick-upon-Tweed [berik] 55°46N 2°00W, pop (2000e) 13 500. Town in Berwick-upon-Tweed district, Northumberland, NE England, UK; on the North Sea at the mouth of the R Tweed, on the Scottish–English border; disputed by England and Scotland, changed ownership 14 times, but part of England since 1482; railway; foodstuffs, salmon fishing, engineering; 16th-c ramparts; Church of the Holy Trinity (1652); 16 km/10 mi SW is Flodden Field (1513); 12 km/7 mi SW is 15th-c Norham Castle.

beryl A beryllium, aluminium silicate mineral ($Be_3Al_2Si_6O_{18}$), occurring in granite pegmatites as greenish hexagonal prisms. Gemstone varieties are aquamarine and emerald. It is the commercial ore of beryllium.

beryllium [berilium] Be, element 4, melting point 1278°C. An element chemically similar to aluminium, but showing an oxidation state of 2 in most of its compounds. The metal forms an unreactive coat of BeO in air, making it inert to further oxidation. Its low density (1·85 g/cm^3) makes it a valuable component of alloys, but the poisonous nature of its compounds limits its use. It is mainly found in nature in the mineral beryl.

Berzelius, Jöns Jakob, Baron [berzaylius] (1779–1848) Chemist, born near Linköping, SE Sweden. He studied at Uppsala, becoming professor at Stockholm (1807–32). His accurate determination of atomic weights established the laws of combination and John Dalton's atomic theory. He introduced modern symbols (1828), an electrochemical theory, discovered the elements selenium, thorium, and cerium, and first isolated others. Among the standard laboratory equipment that he introduced are wash bottles, filter paper, and rubber tubing. He was made a baron in 1835.

Bes In Egyptian mythology, a dwarf god, bandy-legged and horrific in appearance, but congenial in temperament. He was the protector in child-birth, and guardian of the family.

Besançon [bezãsõ], ancient **Vesontio** or **Besontium** 47°15N 6°00E, pop (2000e) 118 000. Industrial town and capital of Doubs department, NE France, on R Doubs; former capital of Franche-Comté; railway; university (1485); archbishopric; strategic site between Vosges and Jura Mts since Gallo-Roman times; watches, clocks, artificial silk, cars; cathedral (11th–13th-c), citadel on high rock overlooking river, Roman remains, museums; birthplace of Victor Hugo.

Besant, Annie [beznt], *née* **Wood** (1847–1933) Theosophist, born in London, UK, the sister-in-law of Sir Walter Besant. After her separation in 1873 from her husband, the Rev Frank Besant, she became vice-president of the National Secular Society (1874). A close associate of Charles Bradlaugh, she was an ardent proponent of birth control and Socialism. In 1889, after meeting Madame Blavatsky, she developed an interest in theosophy, and went out to India, where she became involved in the independence movement.

Beskids or **Beskydy** Mountain group in the Carpathians on the Polish–Czech frontier; rises to 1725 m/5659 ft at Babia Góra.

Bessemer, Sir Henry [besemer] (1813–98) Inventor and engineer, born in Charlton, Hertfordshire, SE England, UK. A self-taught man, he learned metallurgy in his father's type foundry, and made numerous inventions. In 1855–6, in response to the need for guns in the Crimean War (1853–6), he took out a series of patents covering an economical process in which molten pig-iron can be turned directly into steel by blowing air through it in a tilting converter (the *Bessemer process*). He established a steelworks at Sheffield in 1859, specializing in guns and, later, steel rails. He was knighted in 1879.

Bessemer process [besemer] A process for converting pig iron (high carbon iron from the blast furnace) into steel (low carbon iron alloy). Air is blown through the molten iron; the oxygen of the air converts the carbon in the iron into carbon dioxide, which escapes. This reaction produces heat which keeps the iron molten. The principle was known to Chinese and Japanese ironmasters by the 17th-c, and to US ironmaster William Kelly (1811–88) as early as 1846, but the process is named after Henry Bessemer, who introduced it successfully into Britain in 1856. It was an invention of the greatest importance, because it led to many industrial processes being greatly changed or inaugurated by the easy availability of steel. It did not work well with some ores, for which the open-hearth process was devised.

Best, Charles H(erbert) (1899–1978) Physiologist, born in West Pembroke, Maine, USA. As a research student at Toronto University he helped Sir Frederick Banting to isolate the hormone insulin (1922), used in the control of diabetes. He was head of the department of physiology at Toronto from 1929 and director of medical research from 1941. He discovered choline (a vitamin that prevents liver damage) and histaminase (the enzyme that breaks down histamine), and introduced the use of the anti-coagulant, heparin.

Best, George (1946–) Footballer, born in Belfast, NE Northern Ireland, UK. He was the leading scorer for Manchester United in the Football League First Division (1967–8), and won a European Cup Medal and the title of European Footballer of the Year (1968). Becoming increasingly unable to cope with the pressure of top-class football, his career was virtually finished by the time he was 25 years old. Attempted come-backs with smaller clubs in England, the USA, and Scotland were unsuccessful.

best boy *gaffer*

bestiary A didactic literary form popular in classical and mediaeval times which presents human characteristics in the guise of animal behaviour: the Greek *Physiologus* is the model. Many animals such as the lion, the eagle, and the fox owe their symbolic associations to these works, of which the 13th-c Middle English Bestiary is a late example. Stories such as George Orwell's *Animal Farm* (1945) and Richard Adam's *Watership Down* (1972) are sometimes seen as modern developments of the bestiary.

beta-blockers A group of drugs, introduced in the early 1960s, which lower heart rate and blood pressure. *Propranolol*, the first clinically useful beta-blocker, and *atenolol* are also widely used in acute stress and panic, where they prevent symptoms such as racing of the heart, sweating, and tremor. They are therefore prescribed for situations such as public performances and driving tests. There is current controversy over their use in some sports (eg snooker), where they may improve performance.

Betacam The trade name of a videotape cassette recorder and camera system of TV broadcast standard, introduced by Sony in 1981, initially for electronic news-gathering but widely adopted internationally for all forms of video production. It uses component recording with separate luminance and chrominance tracks on ½ in (12·7 mm) tape at a speed of 10·15 cm/s in compact cassettes, 156 × 96 × 25 mm. **Betacam SP** is an improved version using metal-particle tape for higher bandwidth and better picture quality.

beta decay A naturally occurring radioactive decay process in which a neutron in an atomic nucleus spontaneously breaks up into a proton, which remains in the nucleus, and an electron (beta particle), which is emitted. The process is always accompanied by the emission of an antineutrino, and is governed by the weak nuclear force. Strontium-90, for example, is a beta emitter with a half-life of 28·1 years.

Betamax The trade name for a videotape cassette recorder system developed by Sony in 1975 for the domestic market, using ½ in (12·7 mm) tape at a speed of 1·87 cm/s in a compact Beta cassette with a playing time up to 3 hours. Although economical, it never achieved the popularity of the competitive VHS system.

beta particle A charged particle emitted in beta decay. It is usually a high-energy electron, but positrons are also sometimes called beta particles. These particles are emitted with a wide range of energies from any particular source; the typical particle range in air is several metres.

betatron [baytuhtron] A particle accelerator in which electrons are held in a circular orbit by a magnetic field, and accelerated by a varying electric field superimposed. Very high particle energies have been attained. It is used for research on high-energy electron behaviour or to produce high-energy X-rays.

Betelgeuse [beetlzherz, betljooz] A red supergiant star, prominent in Orion, over 500 times the diameter of the Sun. Distance: 131 parsec.

betel-nut A slender tree (*Areca catechu*) reaching 30 m/100 ft, native to SE Asia; leaves 8 m/26 ft, feathery; seeds 4–5 cm/1½–2 in, red or orange; also called the **tareca palm**. The nuts are boiled with lime, then dried, and wrapped in betel leaf from the climbing species of pepper, *Piper betle*. The 'plug' is habitually chewed in the Indian subcontinent and SE Asia for its intoxicating effects, which are similar to alcohol. The juice stains teeth and saliva bright red. (Family: Palmae.)

Bethe, Hans (Albrecht) [baytuh] (1906–) Physicist, born in Strasbourg, NE France (formerly Germany). He studied at the universities of Frankfurt and Munich, and taught in Germany until 1933. He moved first to England, then to the USA, where he held the chair of physics at Cornell University until his retirement (1937–75). During World War 2 he was director of theoretical physics for the atomic bomb project based at Los Alamos. In 1939 he proposed the first detailed theory for the generation of energy by stars through a series of nuclear reactions. He was awarded the 1967 Nobel Prize for Physics.

Bethlehem, Arabic **Beit Lahm** 31°42N 35°12E, pop (2000e) 25 000. Biblical town in Jerusalem governorate, Israeli-occupied West Bank, W Jordan; 8 km/5 mi SW of Jerusalem; birthplace of Jesus and the home of David; trade centre for surrounding agricultural area; university (1973); Church of the Nativity, built by Constantine, 330 (scene of a 39-day siege by Israeli troops when a group of Palestinian men took refuge inside, 2002); Monastery of Elijah (6th-c, restored).

Bethmann-Hollweg, Theobald (Theodor Friedrich Alfred) von [baytman holvayk] (1856–1921) German statesman, born in Hohenfinow, NE Germany. He studied law, and rose in the service of Brandenburg, Prussia, and the empire, becoming imperial chancellor in 1909. He described the Belgian neutrality treaty as 'a scrap of paper', and played an important role before and after the outbreak of war in 1914. He was dismissed in 1917.

Betjeman, Sir John [bechuhman] (1906–84) Poet, broadcaster, and writer on architecture, born in London, UK. He studied at Magdalen College, Oxford, but left university without a degree. He began to write for the *Architectural Review* and became general editor of the *Shell Guides* (1934). His first collection of verse was *Mount Zion; or In Touch with the Infinite* (1933). Other collections include *New Bats in Old Belfries* (1945), *A Few Late Chrysanthemums* (1954), and *Collected Poems* (1958). His *Summoned by Bells* (1960) is an autobiography in verse. Nostalgic and wary of change, he preferred the countryside to the city, loved railways and churches, and was impassioned in his abhorrence of modern architecture. He was knighted (1969), and succeeded Cecil Day-Lewis as poet laureate in 1972.

betony [betonee] A perennial related to woundworts (*Betonica officinalis*), native to Europe; stems square; long-stalked basal leaves in a rosette, upper in opposite pairs; flowers 2-lipped with long tube, bright reddish-purple, in whorls. It is an old medicinal and magical herb. (Family: Labiatae.)

Better Business Bureau One of many local organizations, mainly in the USA and Canada, formed to protect communities against unfair or misleading advertising and selling practices. Established in the early years of the 20th-c by advertising men, it nowadays sets standards for business practice, and investigate complaints.

Betti, Ugo (1892–1953) Playwright and poet, born in Camerino, EC Italy. He studied law and became a judge in Rome (1930–44), and librarian of the ministry of justice (1944–53). He is best known for his 26 plays, notably *La padrona* (The Mistress, 1927). Collections of verse include *Il re pensieroso* (1922, The Thoughtful King), and he also wrote three books of short stories.

Beuys, Joseph [boys] (1921–86) Avant-garde artist, born in Krefeld, W Germany. He studied art at Düsseldorf Academy, where he later became professor of sculpture (1961–71). His sculpture consisted mainly of 'assemblages' of bits and pieces of rubbish; for one typical exhibit he smeared frankfurters with brown shoe polish. He also staged multimedia 'happenings'. He was much admired and imitated by the younger avant-garde from the 1960s onwards. A prominent political activist, he was one of the founders of the Green Party in Germany.

Bevan, Aneurin, known as **Nye Bevan** (1897–1960) British statesman, born in Tredegar, Blaenau Gwent, SE Wales, UK. One of 13 children of a miner, he began work in the pits at 13. Active in trade unionism in the South Wales coalfield, he led the Welsh miners in the 1926 General Strike. He joined the Labour Party (1931), establishing a reputation as an irreverent and often tempestuous orator. He was Labour MP for Ebbw Vale (1929–60). In 1934 he married **Jennie Lee**. Appointed minister of health and housing in the 1945 Labour government, he introduced the revolutionary National Health Service (1948). He became minister of labour in 1951, but resigned the same year over the National Health charges proposed in the Budget. From this period dated *Bevanism*, the left-wing movement to make the Labour Party more socialist and less 'reformist', which made him the centre of prolonged disputes with his party leaders. He ceased to be a *Bevanite* at the 1957 Brighton party conference, when he opposed a one-sided renunciation of the hydrogen bomb by Britain.

Bevan, Brian, nickname **the Galloping Ghost** (1924–91) Rugby league player, born in Sydney, New South Wales, SE Australia. A wing-threequarter, he scored a record 796 tries in 18 seasons (1945–64). He played for Blackpool Borough and Warrington, and was one of the inaugural members of the Rugby League Hall of Fame in 1988.

bevatron [bevatron] A thousand million electron volt proton accelerator, designed and built at Berkeley Radiation Laboratory, University of California, USA.

Beveridge, William Henry Beveridge, Baron (1879–1963) Economist and social reformer, born in Rangpur, W India. He studied at Oxford, and became a leading authority on unemployment insurance. He entered the Board of Trade (1908) and became director of labour exchanges (1909–16). In 1909 he published a notable report, *Unemployment*, and was instrumental in drafting the Labour Exchange Act (1909) and the National Insurance Act (1911). In 1941 he was commissioned by the government to chair an inquiry into the social services, and produced the report *Social Insurance and Allied Services* (1942), popularly known as the *Beveridge Report*, which became the foundation of the British Welfare State. He was director of the London School of Economics (1919–37) and Master of University College Oxford (1937–45). Elected to parliament as a Liberal (1944), he was defeated in 1945, and became a peer in 1946.

Beverley 53°51N 0°26W, pop (2000e) 21 100. Administrative centre of East Riding unitary authority, NE England, UK; 12 km/7 mi NW of Hull; former administrative centre of Humberside; railway; market town, engineering; Beverley Minster (13th-c).

Beverly Hills 34°04N 118°25W, pop (2000e) 33 800. Residential city in Los Angeles Co, SW California, USA; surrounded by Los Angeles; the home of many television and film celebrities.

Bevin, Ernest (1881–1951) British statesman, born in Winsford, Somerset, SW England, UK. Orphaned at seven, and self-taught, he early came under the influence of trade unionism and the Baptists, and was for a time a lay preacher. A paid official of the dockers' union, he gained a national reputation in 1920 when he won most of his union's claims against an eminent barrister, earning the title of 'the dockers' KC'. He built up the National Transport and General Workers' Union, and became its general secretary (1921–40). In 1940 he became a Labour MP, minister of labour and national service in Churchill's coalition government, and in the Labour government was foreign secretary (1945–51). In this role he played a decisive part in extricating Britain from Palestine in 1948, and involving the USA in rebuilding Europe through the Marshall Plan and NATO.

bézique [bezeek] A card game believed to have originated in Spain, and brought to England in 1861. The rules were drawn up by the Portland Club in 1887. Played with at least two players, each has a pack of cards but with the twos, threes, fours, fives, and sixes taken out. The object is to win tricks, and score points on the basis of the cards won. A variation is **rubicon bézique**.

bezoar *goat*

Bhadgaon [badgown], also **Bhaktapur** 27°41N 85°26E, pop (2000e) 183 000. City and religious centre in C Nepal, 14 km/9 mi E of Kathmandu, in the Kathmandu Valley; altitude 1400 m/4600 ft; probably founded in AD 889; shaped like a conch-shell, urban area occupying c.10 sq km/4 sq mi; processing of grain and vegetables, pottery, weaving; Lion Gate, Golden Gate, Palace of 55 Windows, Bell of Barking Dogs, Batsala Temple, replica of Pashupatinath Temple.

Bhagavadgita or **Bhagavad Gita** [bahgavadgeeta] (Sanskrit 'The Song of the Lord') A philosophical poem forming part of the Hindu epic, the Mahabharata, consisting of an eve of battle dialogue between the warrior prince Arjuna and Lord Krishna (in the person of his charioteer). It was probably written in the 1st-c or 2nd-c AD. Krishna, revealing his divinity, preaches absolute devotion (*bhakti*) to the all-loving Supreme Being incarnated from age to age to save mankind. Most Hindus regard the poem, with its teaching that there are many valid ways to salvation, but that not all are universally appropriate, as the supreme expression of their religion.

bhakti [bahktee] Loving devotion to God, recommended as the most effective path to God in most of the religious texts of popular Hinduism. Devotees are drawn into a close personal relationship to God and, in surrender to God, receive grace however lowly their station.

bhangra [banggra] Originally traditional Punjabi dance music, developed by South Asian communities in the UK and elsewhere from the 1970s onwards into a hugely popular genre, at least within those communities. The term may derive from *bhang*, for hemp or cannabis, perhaps because the music was originally associated with the hemp and wheat harvest festival Baisakhi. Prominent UK bhangra bands have included Alaap, Holle Holle, Heera, the Sahotas, and Pardesi. The singer Apache Indian (real name Steve Kapur, 1967–) has had some success in the mainstream UK pop charts with his 'bhangramuffin' fusion of bhangra with rap and reggae/ragga.

Bharata Natyam The oldest form of classical Indian temple dance found in SE India. It has many different types, but is primarily a dramatic interpretation of philosophical teachings combining acting with dancing. Its technical brilliance is found in intricate patterns of footwork set against the graceful design of arm movements. It retains strict codes of performance that denote mood and sentiment.

Bharatiya Janata Paksh (BJP) [bahratya janata paksh] Hindu political party, formed in April 1980, with the aim of transforming a secular and multicultural India into an organic Hindu nation. Taking advantage of the decline of the Indian National Congress, the fragmentation of opposition parties, and the increasing communalization of Indian politics during the 1980s, the BJP has promoted its vision of *Hindutva* with increasing success. From its base in the Hindi-speaking states of N India, it climbed to national prominence in the elections of 1989, capturing 12% of the popular vote. In 1991 it took power in

Bhutan

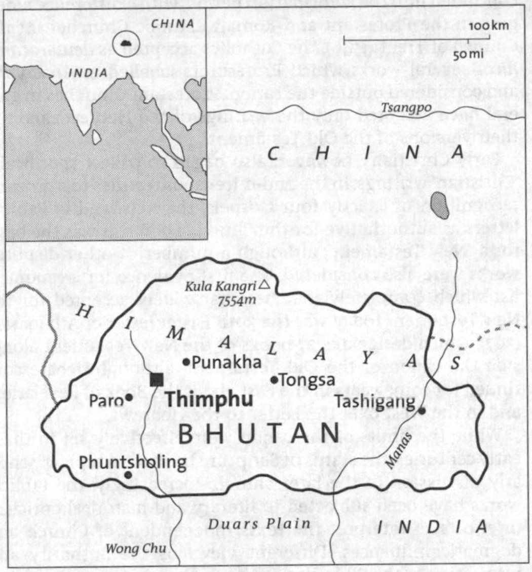

□ International Airport

[bootahn], Dzongkha **Druk-yul**, official name **Kingdom of Bhutan**

Local name Druk-yul

Timezone GMT +5·5

Area 46 600 km²/18 000 sq mi

Population total (2002e) 1 996 000

Status Kingdom

Capital Thimphu

Languages Dzongkha (official) (60%), Nepalese (25%), English

Ethnic groups Bhote (60%), Nepalese (25%), indigenous or migrant tribes (15%)

Religions Lamaistic Buddhist (75%), Hindu (20%), Muslim (5%)

Physical features High peaks of E Himalayas in the N, over 7 000m/23 000 ft; forested mountain ridges with fertile valleys descend to low foothills in the S; rivers include Wong Chu, Manas; permanent snowfields in the mountains; sub-tropical forest in S.

Climate Affected by altitude; snowcapped in glaciated N; average monthly temperatures 4°C (Jan), 17°C (Jul); torrential rain common, average 1000 mm/40 in (C valleys) and 5 000 mm/200 in (S).

Currency 1 Ngultrum (Nu) = 100 chetrum

Economy Largely based on agriculture, mainly rice, wheat, maize, mountain barley, potatoes, vegetables, fruit (especially oranges); also timber (large area of plantation forest).

GDP (2002e) $2·7 bn, per capita $1300

Human Development Index (2002) 0·494

History British involvement since treaty of 1774 with the East India Company; S part of the country annexed, 1865; Anglo-Bhutanese Treaty signed, in which Britain agreed not to interfere in internal affairs of Bhutan, 1910; similar treaty (Indo-Bhutan Treaty of Friendship) signed with India, 1949; governed by a maharajah from 1907; now addressed as King of Bhutan; National Assembly (Tsogdu) established, 1953; constitutional monarchy with power shared between the King, the Council of Ministers, the National Assembly, and the monastic head of the kingdom's Buddhist priesthood; king devolved executive powers to the Council of Ministers, 1998; separatist movements associated with Assam and Bodoland located in the S.

Head of State (Monarch)
1907–26 Uggyen Wangchuk
1926–52 Jigme Wangchuk
1952–72 Jigme Dorji Wangchuk
1972– Jigme Singye Wangchuk

Chairman of the Council of Ministers
1999–2000 Sangay Ngedup
2000–1 Yeshey Zimba
2001–2 Khandu Wangchuk
2002–3 Kinzang Dorji
2003– Lyonpo Jigme Yoser Thinley

the state of Uttar Pradesh and a share of power in other states. With the fundamentalist Vishwa Hindu Parishad, the Party made a disputed shrine at Ayodhya a major focus for agitation. The destruction of the shrine in December 1992 precipitated communal violence in many parts of India.

Bharatpur [baratpoor] *Keoladeo*

Bhil [beel] An ethnic group in W India stretching from Rajasthan to Maharashtra; mostly agriculturalists. They have adopted kinship patterns and features of Hinduism from their Hindu neighbours, but some are Muslim.

Bhopal [bohpahl] 23°20N 77°53E, pop (2000e) 1 248 000. Capital of Madhya Pradesh, C India, 170 km/106 mi NE of Indore; founded, 1723; scene of a major industrial disaster in December 1984, when poisonous isocyanate gas escaped from the Union Carbide factory, killing c.2500 people and leaving 100 000 homeless; airfield; railway; university (1970); cotton, electrical goods, jewellery; Taj-il Masajid mosque (unfinished).

Bhutan *see panel*

Bhutia [bootia] A Buddhist mountain people in the Himalayas, followers of the Dalai Lama. They speak a Tibetan dialect, and probably came from Tibet in the 9th-c. They practise terrace farming on mountains, and some breed cattle and yaks. The largest population group is in Bhutan (500 000); others live in Sikkim, Nepal, and elsewhere in India.

Bhutto, Benazir [bootoh] (1953–) Pakistani stateswoman and prime minister (1988–91, 1993–6), born in Karachi, SE Pakistan, the daughter of the former prime minister, Zulfikar Ali Bhutto. She studied at Oxford, returned to Pakistan, and was placed under house arrest (1977–84) after the military coup led by General Zia ul-Haq. She moved to England (1984–6), becoming the joint leader in exile of the Opposition Pakistan People's Party, then returned to Pakistan to launch a nationwide campaign for 'open elections'. She married a wealthy landowner, **Asif Ali Zardari**, in 1987 and was elected prime minister barely three months after giving birth to her first child. She was defeated in the 1991 election, and found herself in court defending herself against several charges of misconduct while in office. She continued to be a prominent focus of Opposition discontent, and won a further election in 1993, but was replaced in 1996. In 1999 she was convicted in absentia of corruption and sentenced (2002) to three years in prison. She continues to lead her party from abroad, being re-affirmed as PPP leader in 2002.

Bhutto, Zulfikar Ali [bootoh] (1928–79) Pakistani statesman, president (1971–3), and prime minister (1973–7), born in Larkana, Sind, SE Pakistan. He graduated from the universities of California and Oxford, and lectured in law at Southampton (1952–3) and in Pakistan. He became minister of commerce (1958), and foreign minister (1963), then founded the Pakistan People's Party (1967), which won the army-supervised elections in West Pakistan (1971). As president and prime minister he did much to rebuild national morale, introducing constitutional, social, and economic reforms. Opposition to his government strengthened among right-wing Islamic parties, and he was ousted by the army (1977). The military leader, General Zia ul-Haq, instituted proceedings against corruption, under which Bhutto was convicted of conspiring to murder and was sentenced to death in 1978. In spite of worldwide protest and appeals for clemency, the sentence was carried out.

Biafra [biafra] The SE province of Nigeria, inhabited by the Igbo people. Under the leadership of Colonel Ojukwu, it attempted to break away from the federation, thus precipitating the civil war of 1967–70. After the war Nigeria was reorganized into a new provincial structure in an attempt to avert continuing instability.

Bialik, Hayyim Nahman [beealik], also known as **Chaim Hachman** (1873–1934) Poet, born in the Ukraine. He studied the Talmud in Odessa, becoming literary editor of the weekly *Hashiloah* and active in literary circles. His first poem 'To a Bird' was published at this time. In 1921 Maxim Gorky helped him to emigrate to Berlin, where he set up the Dvir Publishing House. In 1924 he resettled in Tel Aviv, taking the publishing house with him. Regarded by many as the greatest Hebrew poet of modern times, his works include the posthumously published *The Writings of H N Bialik* (1938), *Collected Poems – Critical Edition* (1983), and a collection of stories about the Bible and Jewish history, *The Book of Legends* (1992).

Białystok [byawistok] 53°09N 23°10E, pop (2000e) 267 000. Industrial capital of Białystok voivodship, E Poland, on the Polasie plain; largest city in NE Poland; developed as a textile centre, 19th-c; city devastated in World War 2; railway; medical academy; cotton, wool, tools, food processing, power; Revolutionary Movement Museum, residence of the Branicki family, Church of St Roch (1924), town hall; national festival of music and poetry (Apr).

Biarritz [beearits] 43°29N 1°33W, pop (2000e) 30 200. Fashionable resort town in Pyrénées-Atlantiques department, SW France, on Bay of Biscay; noted for its mild climate and beaches.

biathlon A combined test of cross-country skiing and rifle shooting. It is used as a form of military training and is based on the old military patrol race. Men's individual competitions are over 10 km and 20 km (6·2 mi and 12·4 mi), while women's are over 5 km and 10 km (3·1 mi and 6·2 mi). At designated points on the course, competitors have to fire either standing or prone at a fixed target. The biathlon was introduced into the Winter Olympic programme in 1960.

Bible Either the Christian Scripture or the Jewish Scripture, those works recognized as sacred and authoritative writings by the respective faiths. The Christian Scriptures are divided between two *testaments*: the Old Testament (which corresponds roughly to the canon of Jewish Scriptures), and the New Testament. The Old Testament, or **Hebrew Bible**, is a collection of writings originally composed in Hebrew, except for parts of Daniel and Ezra that are in Aramaic. These writings depict Israelite religion from its beginnings to about the 2nd-c BC. The New Testament is so-called in Christian circles because it is believed to constitute a new 'testament' or 'covenant' in the history of God's dealings with his people, centring on the ministry of Jesus and the early development of the apostolic churches. The New Testament writings were in Greek.

The process of determining precisely which writings were to be accepted in the Jewish or Christian Scriptures is known as the formation of the *canon* of Scripture. The earliest step towards establishing the canon of Jewish Scriptures was probably the fixing of the *Law*, viz the Pentateuch (the Books of Genesis, Exodus, Leviticus, Numbers, and Deuteronomy), in about the 4th–3rd-c BC. In addition, a group of writings known as the *Prophets* appear to have been recognized by the grandson of Ben Sira (c.117 BC). The remaining books of the Hebrew Bible are called the *Writings* (eg the Books of Psalms, Proverbs, Job) and were seemingly the last to be settled. It was only AD c.100 that the final selection of authorized Jewish Scriptures was complete, following a decision taken by the council at Jabneh. The Greek translations of the Hebrew Bible (the Septuagint) contained some other writings which were not accepted at Jabneh.

The early Christians largely accepted the Jewish Scriptures, but frequently had access to the larger collection of writings in the Septuagint and some other translations of the Hebrew Bible. Debates about the precise limits of the 'Old Testament' continued into the Reformation period, with a difference emerging in the Protestant and Roman Catholic Churches. At the Council of Trent (1546), the Catholics accepted as *deuterocanonical* several works which Protestants labelled as *Apocrypha* and considered outside the canon. Protestant Churches in general have accepted only the writings of the Hebrew canon in their versions of the Old Testament.

Early Christians, however, also began to collect specifically 'Christian' writings. In the 2nd-c, Irenaeus testifies to a growing recognition of exactly four Gospels, the Acts, and 13 Pauline letters as authoritative for the Church. Soon this was the basis for a 'New Testament', although a number of other disputed works were also considered. The first evidence for a canonical list which completely matches that widely accepted for the New Testament today was the 39th Easter letter of Athanasius (367), which designates 27 books of the New Testament alongside the canon of the Old Testament, although debate continued for some years in the East about the Book of Revelation, and in the West over the Letter to the Hebrews.

While the limits of the canon were effectively set in these early centuries, the status of Scripture has been a topic of scholarly discussion in the later church. Increasingly, the Biblical works have been subjected to literary and historical criticism in efforts to interpret the texts independent of Church and dogmatic influences. Different views of the authority and inspiration of the Bible also continue to be expressed in liberal and fundamentalist churches today. What cannot be denied, however, is the enormous influence which the stories, poetry, and reflections found in the Biblical writings have had, not only on the doctrines and practices of two major faiths, but also on Western culture, its literature, art, and music.

Bible Society An agency for the translation and dissemination of the Bible. The first was the Van Canstein Bible Society, formed in Germany in 1710, but the modern movement really began with the British and Foreign Bible Society, formed in London in 1904. The United Bible Society now provides a world-wide network of autonomous societies, protestant and evangelical in the main, responsible for the translation of the Bible in well over 1500 languages, and distributing copies at subsidized prices.

bibliography **1** The study of the history, identification, and description of books, seen as physical objects, including the materials used and the methods of production (**critical** or **analytical bibliography**).
2 A book, or a list in a book, containing systematic details of an author's writings, or of publications on a given subject or period (**descriptive** or **enumerative bibliography**). Each entry normally consists of an author's name, the title of the work, its publisher, and its place and date of publication. Details of format, binding, number of illustrations, and other characteristics may also be included.

Bibliothèque Nationale [bibliohtek nashuhnahl] The national library of France, located in Paris. It evolved from the libraries of the French monarchs, and was designated a national depository in 1537. Its holdings include over 10 million volumes and 170 000 manuscripts. There is also a Bibliothèque Nationale in Quebec.

bicameral system A parliament of two chambers, which usually have different methods of election or selection. In some countries (such as the USA) the two chambers enjoy equal powers, which necessitates a means of reconciling differences; but commonly one chamber enjoys supremacy over the legislative process, with the other enjoying powers of revision and delay (as in the UK).

bicarbonate HCO_3^-, IUPAC **hydrogen carbonate**. The anion corresponding to half-neutralized carbonic acid. **Sodium bicarbonate** $NaHCO_3$, or baking soda, is used with weak acids as a source of carbon dioxide. Aqueous solutions of soluble bicarbonates are mildly alkaline, with pH values of 8–9.

Bichat, (Marie-François) Xavier [beesha] (1771–1802) Physician, born in Thoirette, E France. He studied at Lyon and Paris, and in 1801 was appointed physician to the Hôtel-Dieu. He was the first to simplify anatomy and physiology by reducing the complex structures of the organs to their elementary tissues. His work largely founded the study of histology.

Bickerdyke, Mary Ann, *née* **Ball**, known as **Mother Bickerdyke** (1817–1901) Nurse and humanitarian, born in Knox Co, Ohio, USA. A farmer's daughter with little formal education, at age 42 she was left a widow with three children. She supported herself by practising 'Botanic' medicine, and when the Civil War broke out she volunteered to work in the hospitals at the Union army base at Cairo, IL. From then until the surrender at Appomattox, she worked as a nurse and caregiver both in battle and behind the lines, taking time out only to give speeches and gain support for the Sanitary Commission. After the war, she worked for various social service causes. She received a special pension from Congress in 1886, and retired to Kansas in 1887.

bicycle A light-framed vehicle possessing two wheels fitted with pneumatic tyres, the rear wheel being propelled by the rider through a crank, chain, and gear mechanism. The major uses to which bicycles are put are personal transport, particularly in underdeveloped countries, and sport. It is generally held that the modern pedal bicycle was invented by Kirkpatrick Macmillan of Dumfriesshire, Scotland, and first ridden by him in 1840. The pneumatic tyre was invented by Robert William Thomson in 1845 and first successfully applied to the bicycle in 1888 by John Boyd Dunlop.

Bidault, Georges (Augustin) [beedoh] (1899–1983) French statesman and prime minister (1946, 1949–50, 1958), born in Paris, France. He became a professor of history and edited the Catholic newspaper *L'Aube*. He was leader of the MRP (Movement Républicaine Populaire), and in addition to becoming prime minister, also served as deputy prime minister (1950, 1951) and foreign minister (1944, 1947, 1953–4). He opposed de Gaulle over the Algerian War, and was charged with plotting against the security of the state. He went into exile in 1962, returning in 1968.

Biedermeierstil [beedermiyershteel] A satirical name for the simple, plain ('bourgeois philistine') style of furniture and decoration popular in Austria and Germany 1815–48. The term is sometimes extended to architecture. Biedermeier painting tends to a mild sentimentalism and homely naturalism.

Biennale [bee-enahlay] An international art exhibition held in Venice regularly since 1895, and imitated at Paris, Tokyo, and elsewhere. It was originally conservative, but since 1948 has been a major showcase for the avant garde.

biennial A plant which flowers, sets seed, and dies in its second year. In the first year it produces only vegetative growth, usually a rosette of leaves which build up food reserves for the onset of flowering.

Bierce, Ambrose (Gwinett) [beers] (1842–?1914) Journalist and writer, born in Meigs Co, Ohio, USA. He fought in the Civil War, then became a journalist, working in both the USA and England. He was the author of such collections of sardonically humorous tales as *The Fiend's Delight* (1872), *In the Midst of Life* (1898), and *The Devil's Dictionary* (1906). A misanthrope, he disappeared in Mexico.

Bierstadt, Albert [beershtat] (1830–1902) Painter, born near Düsseldorf, W Germany. He studied art at Düsseldorf (1853–7), then settled in New York City. He became associated with the Hudson River School, painting Romantic panoramic landscapes in which truth to topographical detail was secondary to dramatic and awe-inspiring effect. His paintings of the Rocky Mts gained him great popularity.

Biffen, Sir Rowland Harry (1874–1949) Botanist and geneticist, born in Cheltenham, Gloucestershire, SWC England, UK. He studied at Cambridge, and became the first professor of agricultural botany there (1908). Using Mendelian genetic principles, he pioneered the breeding of hybrid rust-resistant strains of wheat. Appointed the first director of the Cambridge Plant Breeding Institute in 1912, he was largely responsible for the foundation of the modern science of plant breeding.

bigamy A criminal offence committed when someone who is already lawfully married enters into 'marriage' with another person. The offence is not committed where the first marriage has been ended by divorce or death, where the accused honestly believed that his or her spouse was dead, or where the first marriage has been declared void. In some jurisdictions, there is also a good defence if the accused has, for a period of time (7 years, in England and Wales and in most US states, 5 years in other states), not known that his or her first marriage partner was alive. The onus of proving that the defendant knew the partner was alive during that time lies on the prosecution. Even if the accused can successfully defend an action for bigamy, the second marriage will still be void if the first spouse was living at the time.

'big bang' A hypothetical model of the universe which postulates that all matter and energy were once concentrated into an unimaginably dense state, or primaeval atom, from which it has been expanding since a creation event some 12 thousand million years ago. The main evidence favouring this model comes from cosmic background radiation and the redshifts of galaxies. Evidence for an expanding universe was announced by Edwin Hubble in 1929, and is now generally accepted.

Big Ben Originally the nickname of the bell in the clock tower of the Houses of Parliament, London, UK, and now by association the clock and its tower. The bell, 2·7 m/9 ft in diameter and weighing 13 tonnes, was cast in 1858.

Big Dipper *Plough, the*

Bigfoot or **Sasquatch** In the mountaineering folklore of North America, a creature the equivalent of the abominable snowman or yeti, said to be 2–3 m/7–10 ft tall; its footprints are reported to be 43 cm/17 in long.

Biggs, Ronald (1929–) Convicted thief and member of the gang who perpetrated the Great Train Robbery (England, 1963). He was among the first five to be arrested for the theft, having been traced by fingerprints left at the gang's farm hideout. Convicted and sentenced to 25 years for conspiracy and 30 years (to run concurrently) for armed robbery, he escaped from Wandsworth Prison in 1965 and fled to Australia. Pursued by the police, he eventually settled in Brazil. There, he was saved from extradition because his girlfriend was pregnant (under Brazilian law, fathers of Brazilian children cannot be extradited). He lived in Brazil, with an income generated largely by press interviews. The question of his extradition arose again in 1997, after his son came of age, but he was allowed to stay. Suffering from bad health he finally returned to Britain voluntarily in 2001 and was imprisoned.

bighorn A wild sheep, inhabiting mountains, especially cliffs; males with large curling horns; two species: **American bighorn sheep** (*Rocky Mountain sheep* or *mountain sheep*) from North America (*Ovis canadensis*), and **Siberian bighorn** or **snow sheep** from NE Siberia (*Ovis nivicola*).

Bihar or **Behar** [beehah(r)] pop (2001e) 82 878 800; area 173 876 sq km/67 116 sq mi. State in E India, bounded N by Nepal; crossed by the R Ganges; Rajmahal Hills in the S; capital, Patna; governed by a 325-member Legislative Assembly; major mineral deposits, including coal, copper, mica; rice, jute, sugar cane, oilseed, wheat, maize; iron and steel, machine tools, fertilizers, electrical engineering, paper milling, cement.

Bikini [bikeenee] Atoll in the Marshall Is, W Pacific, 3200 km/2000 mi SW of Hawaii; site of 23 US nuclear tests, 1946–58; first H-bomb tested here (1952); inhabitants evacuated in 1946, many returned in 1972, but were evacuated again when it was discovered that they had ingested the largest dose of plutonium ever monitored in any population.

Biko, Stephen (Bantu) [beekoh], known as **Steve Biko** (1946–77) South African political activist, founder and leader of the Black Consciousness Movement, born in King William's Town, Cape Province. He became involved in politics while studying medicine at Natal University, and was one of the founders (and first president) of the all-black South African Students Organization (1969). In 1972 he became honorary president of the Black People's Convention, a coalition of over 70 black organizations. The following year he was served with a banning order severely restricting his movements and freedom of speech and association, and in 1975 the restrictions were increased. He was detained four times in the last few years of his life, and died in police custody, allegedly as a result of beatings received. He was the subject of a film made by Richard Attenborough (*Cry Freedom*, 1987).

bilateralism *multilateralism*

Bilbao [**bil**bow] 43°16N 2°56W, pop (2000e) 374 000. Major seaport and industrial capital of Vizcaya province, N Spain; on R Nervión, 395 km/245 mi N of Madrid; founded, 1300; bishopric; airport; railway; university (1886); commercial centre of the Basque Provinces; iron, steel, chemicals, shipbuilding, fishing, wine trade; cathedral (14th-c), art museum, Churches of St Anton and St Nicholas de Bari; machine tool fair (Mar), Semana Grande (Aug).

bilberry A small deciduous shrub (*Vaccinium myrtillus*), native to acid soils in Europe and N Asia, especially on high ground where it may form bilberry moors; leaves 1–3 cm/0·4–1·2 in, oval, toothed; 1–2 flowers in leaf axils, drooping, 4–6 mm/⅛–¼ in, globose, greenish-white; berry c.8 mm/½ in, black with bluish-white bloom, sweet, edible. Alternative names are **blaeberry**, **whortleberry**, and (in the USA) **huckleberry**. (Family: Ericaceae).

bilby *bandicoot*

Bildungsroman [**bil**dungksrohman] (Ger 'education novel') A novel which deals principally with the formative stages of its hero(ine)'s life – childhood, education, adolescence. The term comes from Germany, where Goethe's *Wilhelm Meister's Apprenticeship* (1795–6) set the pattern for later *Bildungsromane*. Other examples are Rousseau's *Emile* (1762), Dickens's *David Copperfield* (1850), Musil's *Young Torless* (1906), and Joyce's *A Portrait of the Artist as a Young Man* (1914).

bile A golden-yellow fluid produced by the liver, and stored and concentrated in the gall bladder, until released into the duodenum in response to certain dietary substances (eg fats) in the duodenal cavity. In humans it contains sodium and potassium salts of certain organic acids (which facilitate the digestion and absorption of fats, and the absorption of fat-soluble vitamins), excretory products (bile pigments, cholesterol), and other alkaline dissolvable substances.

bilharziasis [bilhah(r)**tsiy**asis] *schistosomiasis*

biliary system [**bil**yaree] A physiological system for the production, storage, and transport of bile, comprising the liver, gall bladder and various ducts. Bile produced in the liver drains into the hepatic ducts and usually into the gall bladder (for storage and concentration) via the cystic duct. Ingestion of fatty food leads to the release of bile from the gall bladder into the duodenum via the cystic and common bile ducts, when it joins with digestive enzymes from the pancreas. Gallstones are occasionally formed in the gall bladder or bile ducts, affecting the flow of bile through the duct system, resulting in pain and discomfort (*biliary colic*).

bilingualism The ability to speak two languages. Research studies in linguistics have focused on the diversity of bilingual situations which exist, and on the varying degrees of ability which bilinguals can have in their two languages (eg what level of proficiency does a person need, to be regarded as a speaker of a language?). There may also be important differences between those who are bilingual from an early age and those who become so through education or as adults. And an interesting question is whether bilinguals have separate conceptual systems in their two languages, or whether they have the same 'world view' when using either. Contrary to popular belief, it is more common throughout the world as a whole to be bilingual than monolingual. People with more than two languages are said to be **multilingual**.

Bilk, Acker, popular name of **Bernard Stanley Bilk** (1929–) Jazz musician, composer, and band leader, born in Pensford, Somerset, SW England, UK. He took up the clarinet while doing National Service, later joining Ken Colyer's Band as clarinettist, and forming the Bristol Paramount Jazz Band in 1951. Hit singles include 'Somerset' (1960), 'Stranger on the Shore' (1961, first Number 1 simultaneously in UK and USA), and 'Aria' (1976). Still performing and recording into the 1990s, his later albums include *That's My Home* (1994) and *Three in the Morning* (1995).

bill, parliamentary A draft of a proposed new law that is to be considered by a legislature. A bill may be amended before it is finally enacted in law. The procedures for a legislature to consider a bill vary considerably from country to country.

billfish Any of a group of large and very agile surface-living fishes (Family: Istiophoridae) in which the snout is prolonged to form a slender pointed bill used for stunning prey; all are adapted for fast swimming, with elongate streamlined bodies and short wide tail fin; includes sailfish and marlins. Most are exploited commercially, and are amongst the most highly prized of all sport fishes.

billiards An indoor table game played in many different forms. The most popular is that played on a standard English billiard table measuring c.12 ft × 6 ft (3·66 m × 1·83 m). Originally an outdoor game, its exact origins are uncertain; an early reference is 1429, when Louis XI of France owned a billiard table. It is played with three balls; one red and two white. Scoring is achieved by *potting* balls, *going in-off* another ball, and *making cannons* (hitting your white ball so that it successively strikes the two others). **Carom** is another form, popular in Europe; it is played on a pocketless table with the object of making cannons. In the USA, the name *billiards* can also refer to pool and snooker.

Billingsgate Market A fish-market in C London, UK, dating from the 9th-c. Its name derived from a river-gate in the nearby city wall. The market was closed in 1982, and relocated further E, on the Isle of Dogs.

billion In earlier British usage, a million million (10^{12}); in US (and increasingly in technical international) usage, a thousand million (10^9). Because both senses are still encountered, however, many specialists avoid the term (and also *trillion* and other derivatives), preferring to state the numbers involved using superscripts, or in such a form as 'thousand million'. The latter usage is standard in this book.

bill of exchange or **commercial bill** A document ordering someone to pay a certain sum of money to another on a specific date, or when certain conditions have been fulfilled. Bills of exchange are used mainly in foreign trade; their legal status in the UK is laid down by the Bills of Exchange Act (1882).

bill of rights A list of citizens' rights set out in constitutional documents. Usually accompanying the document is an elaboration of the institutional means and powers by which such rights may be enforced. The best-known example is the first ten amendments to the US Constitution, adopted in 1791. This protects the liberties of private citizens in relation to the federal and state governments in such matters as freedom of speech, religion, the press and assembly, and legal procedure. It was adopted because of popular pressure during the campaign to ratify the Constitution (1787–8), and its meaning has been expounded in many cases decided by the Supreme Court.

Billy the Kid *Bonney, William H, Jr*

Biloxi [bi**lok**see] 30°24N 88°53W, pop (2000e) 50 600. Town in Harrison Co, SE Mississippi, USA; on the Gulf of Mexico at the mouth of the Biloxi R; named after an Indian tribe; settled, 1699; the first permanent white settlement in the Mississippi valley; railway; tourism, boatbuilding, shrimp and oyster fisheries; Keesler Air Force Base.

bimetallic strip Two strips of different metals welded or riveted together face to face, which expand to different extents on heating because of their different coefficients of thermal expansion. One can become longer than the other only if the whole takes up a curved shape, with the metal which expands the more on the outer face. This phenomenon can be used to actuate indicators or electric switches in response to changes in temperature.

bimetallism The proposal that a country with a metallic currency should use both gold and silver, rather than either of these alone. Under a metallic standard, a country's currency would expand until the metals used as currency were just worth producing. Geographical discoveries and technical progress cause variations in the costs of mining. It is argued that under a bimetallic system the rate of inflation a country could expect would be higher but less variable than under a single metallic standard. In the long run, however, a bimetallist country would come to have a currency consisting only of whichever metal could be produced more cheaply. The rise of paper and credit-based fiat money has meant that bimetallism has long been as obsolete as metallism itself.

binary code A code derived from the binary number system, using only two digits (0 and 1), in comparison with the decimal system, which has ten digits (0 to 9). The advantage of the binary system for use in digital computers is that only two electronic states, off and on, are required to represent all the possible binary digits. All digital computers operate using various binary codes to represent numbers, characters, etc.

binary coded decimal (BCD) A computer coding system where each decimal numeral (0–9) is represented by a set of four binary digits, or bits.

binary number A number written in base two, using the two symbols 0,1, in which every number is expressed as the sum of powers of 2; thus 'seven' (in base ten) is $4+2+1=1 \times 2^2+1 \times 2^1+1$; thus $7_{ten} = 111_{two}$.

binary star Two stars revolving around their common centre of mass. Perhaps half of all stars in our Galaxy are members of binaries. Astronomers study orbital motions in binaries because this gives the only direct way of finding out what the mass of a star is. In some rare and exotic cases, one star in a binary can be a black hole or a neutron star, and mass transfer takes place from the other, normal star with intense X-ray emission.

binary weapon An expression describing how a munition used in chemical warfare can be configured. Two individually harmless chemicals are packed separately into, for example, an artillery shell; these are combined on detonation to form a deadly toxic agent.

Binchy, Maeve (1940–) Writer, born in Dublin, Ireland. She studied history at University College Dublin, then became a teacher, travel writer, and columnist, joining the *Irish Times* in 1969. She has written plays for television and the stage, but is most widely known as a romantic novelist. Her books include *Light a Penny Candle* (1982), *Circle of Friends* (1990), *The Glass Lake* (1994), *Tara Road* (1998), and *Scarlet Feather* (2000). Other work includes several volumes of short stories.

binding sites *receptors*

bindweed Any of several related climbers with fleshy, rope-like roots, fast-growing twining stems, and large funnel-shaped flowers, all native to temperate regions; often pernicious weeds. *Convolvulus arvensis* is a coastal plant; leaves arrowhead-shaped; flowers 3 cm/1¼ in diameter, pink, striped white above, maroon beneath. **Sea bindweed** (*Calystegia soldanella*) has kidney-shaped leaves; flowers 5 cm/2 in diameter, pink with white stripes; calyx hidden by two bracts. **Hedge bindweed** (*Calystegia sepium*) has arrowhead- or heart-shaped leaves; flowers 3·5 cm/1½ in diameter, white; calyx hidden by two bracts. **Large bindweed** (*Calystegia sylvatica*) is similar, but its flowers are 7·5 cm/3 in diameter. (Family: Convolvulaceae.)

Binet, Alfred [beenay] (1857–1911) Psychologist, the founder of intelligence tests, born in Nice, SE France. Director of physiological psychology at the Sorbonne from 1892, his first tests were used on his children; later, with Théodore Simon, he expanded the tests (1905) to encompass the measurement of relative intelligence amongst deprived children (the *Binet–Simon* tests).

Binford, Lewis (Roberts) (1930–) US archaeologist, pioneer of the anthropologically-oriented 'processual' school of archaeology ('New Archaeology'). He studied at Michigan University and taught at Ann Arbor, Chicago, Santa Barbara, and Los Angeles before becoming professor of anthropology at the University of New Mexico, Albuquerque. His original manifesto *New Perspectives in Archaeology* (1968, with Sally R Binford) has subsequently been elaborated in such works as *Bones* (1981) and *In Pursuit of the Past* (1983).

Bing, Sir Rudolf (1902–97) Opera administrator, born in Vienna, Austria. He worked in Berlin and Darmstadt (1928–33) before managing the opera at Glyndebourne (1935–49). He was co-founder and director (1947–9) of the Edinburgh Festival, and general manager of the Metropolitan Opera, New York City (1950–72). He took British nationality in 1946, and was knighted in 1971.

bingo A game played by any number of people, using cards normally containing 15 squares numbered between 1 and 90. The caller picks numbers at random, and if players have the corresponding number on their card they eliminate it, usually by crossing it through. The first person(s) to eliminate all numbers is the winner, and is usually identified by calling out 'bingo'. Known as **lotto** or **housey-housey** for many years, it became popularized as bingo in the 1960s.

bin Laden *Osama bin Laden*

Binoche, Juliette [binosh] (1964–) Film actress, born in Paris, France. She attended acting school in the late 1970s and later took classes at the Paris Conservatoire. After various roles in French films and theatrical productions she received international success with the film version of Milan Kundera's novel, *The Unbearable Lightness of Being* (1988). She then went on to make films, including *Fatale* (1992) and *Hussard sur le Toit* (1995, Horseman on the Roof). Later films include *The English Patient* (1996, Oscar for Best Supporting Actress), *Chocolat* (2000), and *La Veuve de Saint-Pierre* (2000, The Widow of Saint-Pierre).

binoculars A magnifying optical instrument for use by both eyes simultaneously; also known as **field-glasses**. Two optical systems are mounted together, each consisting of two convex lenses (an eyepiece and an object lens) plus prisms to produce an upright image. Focusing is achieved by varying the distance between eyepiece and object lens. Some instruments, such as opera glasses, use a concave eyepiece to produce an upright image without prisms.

binomial nomenclature The modern system of naming and classifying organisms, established by the Swedish naturalist Carl Linnaeus (1707–78) in the mid-18th-c. Every species has a unique scientific name (*binomen*) consisting of two words: a generic name and a specific name. For example, the scientific name of a lion is *Panthera leo* and that of the tiger *Panthera tigris*. They belong to the same genus, but are different species.

Bintley, David (Julian) (1957–) British choreographer and dancer. He studied at the Royal Ballet School, then joined Sadler's Wells Royal Ballet (1976–86), becoming resident choreographer and principal dancer (1983–6). During 1986–93 he was resident choreographer and principal dancer with the Royal Ballet before joining the Birmingham Royal Ballet as artistic director (1995–).

binturong [bintoorong] A carnivorous mammal (*Arctictis binturong*), native to SE Asia; dense black fur, thickest on its grasping tail, tips of ears with prominent tufts; inhabits dense forests; eats birds, carrion, vegetation; catches fish by swimming; easily tamed. (Family: Viverridae.)

Binyon, (Robert) Laurence (1869–1943) Poet and art critic, born in Lancaster, Lancashire, NW England, UK. On leaving Oxford, he joined the British Museum, and became keeper of Oriental prints and paintings (1913–33). His poetic works include *Lyric Poems* (1894), *Odes* (1901), and *Collected Poems* (1931). He also wrote plays, and translated Dante into *terza* *rima*. He was professor of poetry at Harvard (1933–4). Extracts from his poem 'For the Fallen' (set to music by Elgar) adorn war memorials throughout the British Commonwealth.

bioassay [biyohasay] The measurement of amounts or activities of substances using the responses of living organisms or cells; an abbreviation of **biological assay**. For example, the concentration of pollutants can be estimated by determining the growth rate of particular organisms exposed to them under a range of controlled conditions.

biochemistry The branch of biology dealing with the chemistry of living organisms, especially with the structure and function of their chemical components.

bioclimatology The study of climate as it affects humans, for example calculation of wind chill and degree days. A *degree day* is the difference in actual mean temperature for a day and a pre-determined threshold temperature; if actual temperatures are consistently below the chosen threshold, then the provision of heating might be necessary.

biodegradable substance Any substance that can be decomposed by natural processes, particularly microbial decay, so that its constituents are rendered available for use within the ecosystem. Many modern materials are non-biodegradable, accumulating in the ecosystem.

biodiversity A term used to cover the total variety of genetic strains, species, and ecosystems in the world, which change with evolution. Human activity is accelerating the process of change, leading to the depletion and extinction of species. A treaty to preserve biodiversity, including the sustainable development of biological resources, was signed at the Earth Summit in 1992.

bioengineering The design and production of mechanical and electronic medical devices that apply the latest technological developments to solving medical problems. Examples include machines for helping diagnosis, such as new forms of medical imaging; instruments to assist medical practice, such as computer-assisted surgery; and systems to enable more efficient delivery of drugs to disease sites.

biofeedback A technique by which an individual can learn to control autonomic responses (ie those not usually under conscious control) by using monitoring devices to give information about the results of current and past performance. Training in this way using a sphygmomanometer allows reduction in blood pressure, and using an electroencephalogram can encourage the production of alpha brain waves which are associated with well-being and relaxation. Various machines are marketed as 'relaxation meters', and are said to facilitate relaxation and to be useful in treating stress-induced disorders. The effects are usually small and transitory.

biogas A gas produced by the fermentation of organic waste. Decomposition of animal manure, crop residues, and food processing wastes in an airtight container produces a methane-rich gas which can be used as a source of energy. Small biogas plants are used in developing countries, and some farms in Europe and the USA produce biogas for farm use.

biogenesis The principle that a living organism can arise only from another living organism. It contrasts with notions such as the spontaneous generation of living organisms from non-living matter by natural processes.

biogenetic law The generalization that early stages of development in animal species resemble one another, and that differences between species become increasingly apparent as development proceeds.

biogeography The geographical study of the distribution of animals and plants at global, regional, and local scales. In particular it examines the factors responsible for their changing distribution in both time and space.

biography The narrative of a person's life: as we know it, a form proper to the modern centuries (post-17th-c). In classical and mediaeval times, such biographical writing as existed tended to be summary and exemplary lives of kings, heroes, and saints, with little concern for the personal subject. But the Protestant and democratic spirit conferred greater value on the individual; and the subject of Boswell's great biography (published in 1791), Dr Johnson, maintained that the narrative of any person's life would be worth reading. Most well-known figures in the last 200 years have found a biographer: latterly, even while still alive. Beginning in the 20th-c, biographical treatments are also to be found on audiotape, radio, film, television, and the Internet.

Bioko [beeokoh], formerly **Fernando Po** or **Póo** (to 1973), **Macías Nguema Bijogo** (to 1979) pop (2000e) 93 400; area 2017 sq km/ 779 sq mi. Island in the Bight of Biafra, off coast of Cameroon, W Africa; province of Equatorial Guinea; volcanic origin, rising to 3007 m/9865 ft at Pico de Basilé; chief town, and capital of Equatorial Guinea, Malabo; other towns include Luba and Riaba; visited by Portuguese, 1471; originally named after Portuguese navigator; occupied at various times by British, Portuguese, and Spanish; coffee, cocoa, copra.

biolinguistics The study of the ways in which human biology is predisposed to the development of language and use. It is particularly concerned with the genetic transmission of language and with neurophysiological studies of the way spoken language is produced and understood.

biological assay *bioassay*

biological control The control of populations of plant or animal species by natural enemies such as predators or parasites. In particular, biological control refers to the introduction or encouragement of natural enemies for use in the regulation of numbers of a pest species. Recently developed techniques for biological control include methods of disrupting reproductive behaviour of the pest, such as the release of sterilized males, the strategic dispersal of pheromones important in pest mating behaviour, and the use of attractants to bait traps.

biological psychiatry That area of psychiatry which sees mental illness as resulting from disorders of the physiological system. It emphasizes biochemical, pharmacological, and neurological aspects of mental illness and psychiatric treatments.

biological rhythm or **biorhythm** The rhythmical change in a biological function of a plant or animal. The frequency of rhythms varies from short (eg less than a second) to long (eg more than a year). Many rhythms arise from within organisms (*endogenous rhythms*); others (*exogenous rhythms*) are entirely dependent upon external environmental factors (such as the alternation of light and dark). Endogenous rhythms are usually synchronized to follow periodic changes in the environment. Examples of biological rhythms in humans are breathing, sleep, and waking, and the daily rise and fall of cortisol production; these are controlled by the brain (eg the pineal gland and parts of the hypothalamus). Important biological rhythms in higher plants are photosynthesis and the daily opening and closing of flowers.

biological sciences Specialized study areas which have developed to study living organisms and systems. All biological sciences are based on **taxonomy**, the description, naming, and classification of living organisms as a means of creating order out of the diversity of the natural world. The study of the distribution of organisms throughout the world is known as **biogeography**. How organisms work is the subject of a number of biological sciences. The chemical processes that occur within living systems are studied as a whole (**biochemistry**) or at the level of interactions between large organic molecules such as proteins and nucleic acids (**molecular biology**). Functional aspects of living systems are the subject of disciplines such as **physiology** and **biophysics**, and these are frequently subdivided further into topics such as **endocrinology** (the study of the production and actions of hormones) and **neurophysiology** (the study of the function of the nervous system). The study of the comparative behaviour of animals is known as **ethology**. **Genetics** encompasses heredity and variation. The study of the relationship between organisms and their environment is **ecology**. Finally, each major group of organisms is the basis of its own special study area, including bacteria (**bac-**

teriology), plants (**botany**), viruses (**virology**), animals (**zoology**), fungi (**mycology**), parasitic worms (**helminthology**), parasites (**parasitology**), shells (**malacology**), birds (**ornithology**), insects (**entomology**), fishes (**ichthyology**), crustaceans (**carcinology**), organisms living in the sea (**marine biology**), fossils (**palaeontology**), amphibians and reptiles (**herpetology**), pollen (**palynology**), and seaweeds (**phycology**).

biological shield A protective enclosure around the radioactive core of a nuclear reactor, to prevent the escape of radiation capable of damaging biological tissue. It usually consists mainly of massive concrete walls.

biological value The nutritional value of a protein, which depends upon the balance of amino acids it contains. A protein with a low concentration of one or more essential amino acids relative to requirements will be of little biological value. Biological value can be quantified as the proportion of truly absorbed nitrogenous material (amino acids) truly retained. Animal proteins such as egg have a high value, while vegetable proteins such as gluten have a low value.

biological warfare An expression that embraces *bacteriological warfare*, which uses naturally-occurring micro-organisms as a weapon of war, and *toxins*, which are poisonous chemicals derived from natural sources. The manufacture and stockpiling of such agents is forbidden by a UN Convention of 1972, although research is allowed to continue.

biology The study of living organisms and systems. The beginnings of biology as a science are the natural history observations made by curious amateurs, travellers, farmers, and all those in contact with the natural world. Its rapid development during the 20th-c led to the increasing subdivision of biology into a variety of specialized disciplines, although the most recent trend is towards more integrated interdisciplinary studies.

bioluminescence The light produced by living organisms through a chemical reaction, and the process of emitting such biologically produced light. The phenomenon can be found in some bacteria, fungi, algae, and animals, including many marine organisms such as deep-sea fishes, squid, and crustaceans, and some terrestrial organisms such as fireflies. Bioluminescence serves a variety of functions, such as signalling during courtship rituals, deterring predators, or locating prey in the dark.

biomass The total mass of living organisms (including producers such as plants, as well as consumers and decomposers) in an ecosystem, population, or other designated unit, at a given time; equivalent to the term **standing crop**. It is usually expressed as dry weight per unit area.

biome [biyohm] A major regional subdivision of the Earth's surface, broadly corresponding to the dominant ecological communities of the main climatic regions, as characterized by their principal plant species and distinctive life forms. Biomes are the largest recognized living communities classified on a geographical basis, such as tundra biome, desert biome, and tropical rainforest biome. Artificial biomes have also been created, as in the Eden Project in Cornwall, UK.

biomechanics A system of exercises devised by the Russian theatre director, Vsevolod Meyerhold, to extend the physical resources of the actor. It is based on rhythm, the elimination of superfluous movements, and awareness of the body's centre of gravity both in stillness and in motion. Actors were required to suppress their individuality and the settings were minimal. It was eventually condemned by the Stalinist regime and its supporters were suppressed.

biomorphic art A type of abstract art based on shapes which vaguely resemble plants and animals. The most celebrated exponent was Hans Arp.

Biondi, Matt(hew) [byondee] (1965–) Swimmer, born in Morago, California, USA. At the 1986 world championships he won a record seven medals, including three golds, and at the 1988 Olympics won seven medals, including five golds. He set the 100 m freestyle world record of 48·24 s in Austin, TX, in 1988.

bionics The construction of artificial mechanisms, models, circuits, or programs imitating the responses or behaviour of living systems. Its purpose is to adapt observed living functions to practical purposes in useful machines. It contrasts with **cybernetics**, which is concerned with the study of communication within the living system, and **automation**, which is concerned with the mere outward imitation of the appearance of living things.

bionomics The study of organisms in relation to their environment. The term is used particularly with reference to ecological studies of single species.

biophysics The application of physics to the study of living organisms and systems. It includes the study of the mechanical properties of biological tissues such as bone and chitin, and the interpretation of their functional significance.

biopsy [biyopsee] The removal by surgical operation or a needle of a small piece of tissue (eg from the skin, intestine, breast, or kidney) in order to assist the diagnosis of a suspected disease process.

biorhythms (alternative medicine) Three biological cycles thought to govern human life and behaviour. The *physical cycle* is 23 days, and is concerned with strength, vitality, endurance, and sex drive. The *emotional cycle* is 28 days, and governs mood, sensitivity, creative ability, and nervous reactions. The *intellectual cycle* spans 33 days, and governs memory, learning ability, and decision making. The biorhythms can be calculated by extrapolating these various cycles from the date of birth, and can be used to predict 'critical days' when exceptionally good or exceptionally poor performance might be expected, and also to understand behaviour patterns which are the result of the interaction of these cyclical influences.

biosphere That part of the Earth's surface and atmosphere in which living organisms are found, and with which they interact to form the global ecosystem.

biotechnology The application of biological and biochemical science to large-scale production. Isolated examples have existed since early times, notably brewing, but the first modern example was the large-scale production of penicillin in the 1940s. Other pharmaceutical developments followed. Research in genetic engineering is prominent in current studies and has led to the production of hormones and enzymes by recombinant DNA technology, with important clinical implications. Human cells have also been genetically manipulated to replace faulty genes in diseased tissues.

bioterrorism *terrorism*

biotin One of the B vitamins, found in yeast and in the bacteria which inhabit the human gut. It acts as a co-factor in the synthesis of fatty acids and the conversion of amino acids to glucose. It is made unavailable for absorption if it combines with the protein, avidin, found in raw egg white. Biotin deficiency has been produced in human volunteers by feeding them large amounts of raw egg white, resulting in such symptoms as dermatitis, nausea, muscle pain, cholesterol increase, and depression.

biotite *micas*

Biot–Savart law [beeoh savah(r)] In physics, a law which expresses the magnetic field resulting from an electric current; stated in 1820 by French physicists Jean Biot (1774–1862) and Félix Savart (1791–1841). The magnetic flux density B is proportional to the current, divided by the distance from the current. The Biot–Savart result is less general than Ampère's law, from which it can be deduced, but is easier to use.

bipolar disorder *manic depressive psychosis*

bipolarity (politics) *multipolarity*

birch A slender deciduous tree, occasionally a dwarf shrub, native to the N hemisphere, often colonizing poor soils and reaching the tree line in the arctic; branches often pendulous, leaves ovoid, toothed; catkins pendulous, males long, females shorter, becoming cone-like in fruit; nutlets tiny with papery wings. (Genus: *Betula*, 60 species. Family: Betulaceae.)

Bird, Dickie, popular name of **Harold Dennis Bird** (1933–) Cricket umpire, born in Barnsley, South Yorkshire, N England, UK. He played county cricket for Yorkshire (1956–9) and Leicestershire (1960–4) before establishing himself as a popular and respected umpire. During his career he umpired many major events, including 68 Test matches and three World Cup Finals (1975, 1979, 1983), retiring as a Test umpire in 1996 and leaving the first-class list in 1998. His books include *From The Pavilion End* (1988) and an autobiography that in 1998 was the best-selling hardback book in British publishing.

bird A vertebrate animal assignable to the class Aves; any animal in which the adult bears feathers (only birds have feathers, and all adult birds have feathers). The fore-limbs of birds are modified as wings; teeth are absent; and the projecting jaws are covered by horny sheaths to produce a bill or 'beak'. The female lays eggs with hard chalky shells. Other characters shared by most living birds are the pronounced vertical blade, or 'keel', on the breastbone, and the joining of the collar bones to form a 'wishbone'. The keel acts as an attachment for the large muscles moving the wings (the breast muscles), and the wishbone acts as a strut to support the wings in flight.

Flight has dominated the evolution of the birds, and their bodies are adapted accordingly. The bones of most birds are hollow, reducing weight; much of the wing and all of the tail is composed entirely of long feathers, these being strong but very light. The body is streamlined with a smooth covering of short overlapping feathers. Flight has also controlled size. Most birds are small. No bird capable of horizontal flight in still air weighs more than 13 kg/30 lb. Even flying birds close to this weight, such as the condor or the albatross, spend much time gliding in air currents. This weight level is very light compared to large mammals or reptiles.

That flight is the factor limiting size is indicated by the largest known birds, living or extinct: these are flightless forms, such as the modern ostrich (up to 150 kg/330 lb) or the extinct elephant bird (457 kg/1000 lb). Such flightless running birds, or *ratites*, evolved from flying ancestors, but with the loss of flight the keel has disappeared from the breastbone, and the wishbone has become two separate bones again. The wings of ratites may be very reduced (as in the kiwi), and the feathers may become fluffy, rather than streamlined, and may even be absent from large areas of the body (as in the ostrich). The power of flight has also been lost by the penguins, whose wing feathers have become small and scale-like. However, penguins have kept the keel on the breastbone and now use their wings for 'flying' under water.

Whether capable of flight or flightless, birds have spread to cover almost the entire globe. They are absent today only from the true polar wastes (in common with most other animals) and the deep-sea. They have adapted to fill virtually every habitat and lifestyle, and their shapes, sizes, colours, and behaviours reflect this diversity. There are approximately 8600 living species of birds, and specialists indicate their relationships by grouping them into 29 orders and 181 families. Birds evolved from reptiles approximately 150 million years ago, and the birds' closest living relatives are the crocodiles. The exact reptile ancestor of the birds is not known, but it has been suggested that they evolved from a group of small dinosaurs. If that is true, then not all dinosaurs became extinct: some merely changed their shape, and are flying around our gardens today.

bird of paradise A stout-billed, strong-footed bird native to SE Asian forests. The males use spectacular plumage to attract females, and may take several mates during the breeding season. (Family: Paradisaeidae, 43 species.)

bird of paradise flower An evergreen perennial (*Strelitzia reginae*) growing to c.1 m/3 ft, forming clumps of long-stalked oblong leaves, native to Cape Province, South Africa, and cultivated elsewhere for its striking flowers. Each 'flower' represents a complete inflorescence of several flowers, enclosed in a sheathing bract. Adapted to pollination by sunbirds, the flowers have orange sepals and blue petals, emerging from the bract at weekly intervals. (Family: Strelitziaceae.)

bird of prey Any bird that hunts large animals (especially mammals and birds) for food; also known as a **raptor**. They have a strong, curved bill and sharp claws. The category includes members of the orders Accipitriformes (hawks, eagles, Old World vultures, and the secretary bird), Falconiformes (falcons), and Cathartiformes (New World vultures, including condors); some authorities include the order Strigiformes (owls).

Birdseye, Clarence (1886–1956) Businessman and inventor, born in New York City, USA. He is best known for developing a process for freezing food in small packages suitable for retailing. He founded the General Seafoods Company in 1924, later becoming president of Birdseye Frosted Foods (1930–4) and of Birdseye Electric Company (1935–8). Some 300 patents are credited to him; among his other inventions were infrared heat lamps, the recoilless harpoon gun, and a method of removing water from food.

bird's-foot trefoil A perennial growing to 40 cm/15 in (*Lotus corniculatus*), native to Europe, Asia, and Africa; leaves with five oval leaflets up to 1 cm/½ in long; pea-flowers in stalked, rather flat-topped clusters of 2–8, yellow often tinged with red; pods up to 3 cm/1¼ in long, many-seeded; also called **eggs and bacon**. (Family: Leguminosae.)

bird's-nest fern A species of spleenwort (*Asplenium nidus*); an epiphyte native to Old World tropical forests, in which the bright green, undivided fronds form a basket or nest-like rosette which accumulates humus. The roots then grow into the humus, obtaining nutrients and water. (Family: Polypodiaceae.)

birdwing butterfly A large to very large butterfly, found in the Indo-Australian region; long wings; in male, wings black with iridescent colours; in female, wings dull. (Order: Lepidoptera. Family: Papilionidae.)

birefringence A property exhibited by certain crystals, in which the speed of light is different in different directions because of the crystal structure; also called **double refraction**. Birefringent crystals such as calcite and quartz are characterized by two refractive indices, and can form double images.

bireme [**biy**reem] A galley, usually Greek or Roman, propelled by two banks of oars, rowed by slaves or criminals. It was also equipped with a square sail for use with a favourable wind.

Birgitta, St *Bridget, Brigit*, or *Birgitta (of Sweden), St*

Birkbeck, George (1776–1841) Physician and educationist, born in Settle, North Yorkshire, N England, UK. As professor of natural philosophy at Anderson's College, Glasgow, he delivered his first free lectures to the working classes (1799). In 1804 he became a physician in London. He was the founder and first president of the London Mechanics' or Birkbeck Institute (1824), the first in the UK, which developed into Birkbeck College, a constituent college of London University.

Birkenhead, Frederick Edwin Smith, 1st Earl of (1872–1930) Lawyer and statesman, born in Birkenhead, Merseyside, NW England, UK. He studied at Oxford (becoming a fellow of Merton in 1896), and was called to the bar in 1899. He entered parliament in 1906 as a Conservative and established himself as a brilliant orator and wit. He was attorney general in 1915, and Lord Chancellor in 1919. He played a major part in the Irish settlement of 1921 and was created earl. He was also secretary of state for India (1924–8). His greatest achievement as a lawyer was the preparation of the series of Acts reforming land law.

Birkenhead [**ber**kenhed] 53°24N 3°02W, pop (2002e) 91 800. Town in Wirral borough, Merseyside, NW England, UK; located on the Wirral peninsula, opposite Liverpool, to which it is linked under the R Mersey by road and rail tunnels; railway; shipbuilding, engineering, food processing, clothing.

Birmingham (UK) [**ber**mingm] 52°30N 1°50W, pop (2001e) 977 100. City and chief town in West Midlands, C England, UK; part of West Midlands urban area and Britain's second largest city; 175 km/109 mi NW of London; noted centre for metalwork since the 16th-c; developed rapidly in the Industrial

Revolution in an area with a large supply of iron ore and coal; heavily bombed in World War 2; railway; airport; motorway complex to the N at 'Spaghetti Junction'; three universities (Birmingham, 1900; Aston, 1966; Central England, formerly Birmingham Polytechnic, 1992); Aston Science Park; regional media centre for television and radio; engineering, vehicles, plastics, chemicals, electrical goods, machine tools, glass; 18th-c Church of St Philip, Cathedral of St Chad (1839), Aston Hall (1618–35), art gallery, symphony orchestra, theatre, museums, Bull Ring shopping complex, National Exhibition Centre; football league teams, Aston Villa (Villa), Birmingham City (Blues), nearby West Bromwich Albion (Baggies), Walsall (Saddlers); international show-jumping championships (Apr).

Birmingham (USA) **[bermingham]** 33°31N 86°48W, pop (2000e) 242 800. Seat of Jefferson Co, NC Alabama, USA; settled, 1813; largest city in the state; airfield; railway; university (1842); canal connection to Gulf of Mexico; leading iron and steel centre in the S; iron, coal and limestone mined; metal products, transportation equipment, chemicals, food products; centre for commerce, banking and insurance; civil rights protests in the 1960s; Alabama Symphony, Sloss Furnaces, iron statue of Vulcan; Festival of the Arts (Apr).

Birmingham Six Six men convicted and sentenced to life imprisonment in 1975 for the bombing of two public houses in Birmingham, England, in which 21 people died. After a lengthy campaign by their supporters, they were freed by the Court of Appeal for England and Wales in 1991 and had their convictions quashed. The release of the Birmingham Six and the Guildford Four led to the British Government setting up a Royal Commission on Criminal Justice, which made various recommendations in 1993.

Biró, Lazlo [biro] (1899–1985) Hungarian inventor. Working with a magazine, he realized the advantage of quick-drying ink, and in 1938 he went to Argentina with his ideas for developing a ballpoint pen, which eventually became a great success (the *biro*). He was responsible for several other inventions, including a lock, a heat-proof tile, and a device for recording blood pressure.

Birt, John, Baron (1944–) Broadcasting executive, born in Liverpool, Merseyside, NW England, UK. He studied engineering at Oxford, joined Granada Television (1968), and worked on the public affairs programme *World in Action* before moving to London Weekend Television (1971) as producer of *The Frost Programme*. Directly responsible for the political programme *Weekend World*, he became noted for his rigorous professionalism. British television was undergoing a critical period of change when the BBC's director general, Michael Checkland, appointed him deputy director (1987). During his time as director-general (1993–2000), he initiated a radical and controversial programme of reforms ('Birtism'), including a market-driven approach to programme-making. He received an Emmy in 1995, was knighted in 1998, and was created a life peer in 2000.

birth control *contraception*

birthmark A skin blemish present at birth; also known as a **naevus/nevus**. There are two main causes: an accumulation of melanocytes (skin pigment cells) known as *moles*, which vary in colour from light brown to black; and a benign enlargement of blood and lymph vessels, the most common of which are 'strawberry marks' and 'port-wine stains'.

Birtwistle, Sir Harrison (1934–) Composer, born in Accrington, Lancashire, NW England, UK. He studied at the Royal Manchester College of Music and the Royal Academy of Music in London. While in Manchester he formed with other young musicians the New Manchester Group for the performance of modern music. In 1967 he formed the Pierrot Players with Peter Maxwell Davies; much of his work being written for them and for the English Opera Group. In 1975 he was appointed musical director of the National Theatre, and in 1993 became composer in residence to the London Philharmonic Orchestra at the South Bank Centre. Two works of 1965, the instrumental *Tragoedia* and vocal/instrumental *Ring a Dumb Carillon*, established him as a leading composer. Among his later works are the operas *Punch and Judy* (1966–7), *The Masque of Orpheus* (1973–84), *Gawain* (1990), and *The Second Mrs Kong* (1994). Other works include *The Fields of Sorrow* (1971), *Pulse Sampler* (1981), *Panic* (1995), and *The Woman and the Hare* (1999). He was knighted in 1988 and made a Companion of Honour in 2001.

Biscay, Bay of, Span **Golfe de Vizcaya**, Fr **Golfe de Gascogne** area 220 000 sq km/85 000 sq mi. Arm of the Atlantic Ocean, bounded E by France and S by Spain; irregular coasts with many harbours; known for strong currents and sudden storms; major fishing region; resorts such as Biarritz on straight, sandy shores of SE French coast; major ports include St Nazaire, La Rochelle, San Sebastian, Santander.

biscuit A term derived from Old French *bescuit* 'twice cooked', a process which produced small flat cakes that were truly crispy. Today, biscuits are many and varied, ranging from sweet to plain. In the USA, the term is often used for what in the UK would be called a *scone*; the nearest equivalent to UK *biscuit* is *cookie*.

Bishkek, formerly **Pishpek** (to 1926), **Frunze** (to 1991) 42°54N 74°46E, pop (2000e) 680 000. Capital city of Kyrgyzstan; in the Chu valley, at the foot of the Kirgizskiy Khrebet; altitude, 750–900 m/2500–3000 ft; founded, 1864; airport; railway; university (1951); major transportation, industrial, and cultural centre; agricultural machinery, textiles, foodstuffs, tobacco products.

Bishop, Elizabeth (1911–79) Poet, born in Worcester, Massachusetts, USA. A graduate of Vassar College, she received a Pulitzer Prize for her first two collections, *North and South* (1946) and *A Cold Spring* (1955). She lived for some time in Brazil (1952–67), and taught at Harvard from 1970. *Complete Poems* was published in 1969. She fought a long battle against asthma and alcoholism.

bishop An ecclesiastical office, probably equivalent to pastor or presbyter in the New Testament, and thereafter generally an ordained priest consecrated as the spiritual ruler of a diocese in Orthodox, Roman Catholic, and Episcopal Churches. In some other Churches (eg certain Methodist Churches), the term is equivalent to 'overseer', or supervising minister. The office was abolished by many Protestant Churches at the 16th-c Reformation, but in many churches which retain it, it is considered to be essential for the identity of the Church and the transmission of the faith. The issue of whether women as well as men may be consecrated bishop aroused great controversy at the end of the 1980s, especially following the first such appointment (Rev Barbara Harris, as Bishop of Massachusetts) by the Episcopal Church of the United States in 1989.

Bishops' Wars (1639–40) Two brief conflicts between Charles I of England and the Scottish Covenanters, caused by his attempt to impose Anglicanism on the Scots and to take back former church lands from Scottish noblemen. In 1637 a modified version of the English Prayer Book was introduced in Scotland, spurring the Covenanters to abolish the episcopacy. They resulted in English defeats, and bankruptcy for Charles, who was then forced to call the Short Parliament in 1640 to petition for funds, bringing to an end his 'personal rule' (1629–40). His army was routed by the Covenanters at Newburn and Charles was forced to make peace. Bankrupted by the conflicts, Charles summoned the Long Parliament (1640–60).

Bismarck (USA) 46°48N 100°47W, pop (2000e) 55 500. Capital of state in Burleigh Co, C North Dakota, USA, on the Missouri R; established, 1873 (named after the German statesman); territorial capital, 1883; state capital, 1889; airfield; railway; trade and distribution centre for agricultural region; oil refining, food products, machinery; Camp Hancock Museum, Heritage Centre; 18-story state capitol, completed in 1934; Folkfest (Sep).

Bismarck, Otto Eduard Leopold, Fürst von (Prince of) (1815–98) The first chancellor of the German Second Empire (1871–90), born in Schönhausen, EC Germany. A member of the Brandenburg nobility, he studied law and agriculture at Göttingen, Berlin, and Greifswald. In the new Prussian parliament (1847) he became known as an ultraroyalist, resenting Austria's predominance and demanding equal rights for Prussia. During the Revolutions of 1848 he opposed demands for constitutional reform and opposed democratization of the political system. He was ambassador to Russia (1859–62), and was appointed prime minister of Prussia in 1862. He enlarged and reorganized the Prussian army. In 1864, in partnership with Austria, he led the German states in the defeat of Denmark, acquiring Schleswig-Holstein, whose Kiel Canal became of strategic importance to Germany. In 1866 he provoked a confrontation with Austria, known as the 'seven weeks's war', from which he emerged victorious. He annexed Hanover and united most of the other German states in the North German Confederation (1867–71). Uniting German feeling, he deliberately provoked the Franco–Prussian War (1870–1) subjecting Paris to a long and terrible siege. He was made a count in 1866, and created a prince and chancellor of the new German Empire. After the Peace of Frankfurt (1871) in which France ceded Alsace and Lorrain to Germany, his policies aimed at consolidating and protecting the young Empire. His domestic policy included universal male suffrage, a common currency, a central bank, a scheme of social insurance against unemployment, sickness, and old age, and the codification of the law. He engaged in a lengthy conflict with the Vatican (known as the *Kulturkampf*) for the control of schools and church appointments, which proved to be a failure. In foreign affairs, he initiated the Three Emperors League (1872–87) between Prussia, Austria, and Russia. He presided with great success over the Congress of Berlin (1878). As a result of his protective tariffs, German industry and commerce flourished and new colonies were acquired overseas. To counteract Russia and France, he formed the Austro–German Treaty of Alliance (1879), which was later joined by Italy. Called the 'Iron Chancellor', he clashed with Emperor William II, who saw him as a rival for power, and was forced to resign from the chancellorship (1890). In the same year he was made Duke of Lauenburg.

Bismarck Archipelago pop (2000e) 473 000; area 49 709 sq km/ 19 188 sq mi. Island group, part of Papua New Guinea, NE of New Guinea, SW Pacific; main islands, New Britain, New Ireland, Admiralty Is, and Lavongai; mountainous, with several active volcanoes; annexed by Germany, 1884; mandated territory of Australia, 1920; occupied by Japan in World War 2; part of UN Trust Territory of New Guinea until 1975; chief town, Rabaul, on New Britain; copra, cocoa, oil palm.

Bismarck Sea SW arm of the Pacific Ocean, NE of New Guinea; c.800 km/500 mi E–W; contains many islands; Battle of the Bismarck Sea (1943) saw destruction of Japanese naval force by USA.

bismuth [**biz**muhth] Bi, element 83. The heaviest element with stable isotopes, a metalloid which melts at 271°C, but forms alloys with much lower melting points. It is in the nitrogen family, and commonly shows oxidation states of +3 and +5. The main natural source is the sulphide, Bi_2S_3.

bison A large mammal which inhabits forest and grassland; stocky; large hairy hump on shoulders; short upcurved horns; chin with beard; two species: the **American bison** – technically also called **boss**, and popularly **buffalo** – with two subspecies, **plains bison** and **wood** (or **mountain**) **bison** from North America (*Bison bison*); and the **European bison** or **wisent** (*Bison bonasus*). The American bison has been crossbred with cattle to produce the hybrid *cattalo*; male hybrids are sterile. Regarded as 'the staff of life' by Plains Indians, the prairie bison was hunted by natives and settlers to virtual extinction in the 19th-c. (Family: Bovidae.)

Bissau [**bee**sow] 11°52N 15°39W, pop (2000e) 160 000. Seaport capital of Guinea-Bissau, W Africa; on Bissau I in the R Geba estuary; established as a fortified slave-trading centre, 1687; free port, 1869; capital moved here from Bolama, 1941; airport; national museum, cathedral.

Bissoondath, Neil (1955–) Novelist, born in Trinidad, West Indies, of Indian descent, the nephew of V S Naipaul. He emigrated to Canada in 1973 to study French at York University, Toronto. His first book, a collection of short stories, *Digging Up the Mountains* (1985), deals with the themes of immigration and exile. His acclaimed first novel, *A Casual Brutality* (1988), about the violent decline of a Caribbean island state was shortlisted for the Guardian Fiction Prize. The stories in his third book, *On the Eve of Uncertain Tomorrows* (1990), are set in Canada and Spain. A second novel, *The Worlds Within Her* (2000), returns to a Caribbean setting.

bistort [**bis**taw(r)t] The name for several species of the genus *Polygonum*, related to knotgrass and mostly N temperate; some aquatic; stems erect, nodes enclosed in papery sheaths; leaves lance-shaped to oblong; small flowers white, pink, or red, in terminal spikes. (Genus: *Polygonum*. Family: Polygonaceae.)

bisynchronous transmission A shortened form of **binary synchronous transmission**, a form of data communication in a network of computers in which one or more remote devices communicate with a mainframe. The terminology is used particularly by IBM.

bit An abbreviation of **Binary digIT**. A bit may take only one of the two possible values in the binary number system, 0 or 1. All operations in digital computers take place using the binary number system.

Bithynia [bi**thin**ia] The name in antiquity for the area to the SW of the Black Sea. Inhabited mainly by warlike Thracians, it eluded Achaemenid and Seleucid control, becoming an independent kingdom under a Hellenizing dynasty of Thracian stock c.300 BC. In 75–74 BC, under the will of its last king, Nicomedes IV, it passed to Rome. Initially a rather unimportant province, Bithynia's strategic status rose during the imperial period. In the late 3rd-c AD, its leading city, Nicomedia, even became for a while the capital of the entire E half of the Empire.

biting midge A minute, biting fly that feeds on the blood of vertebrates; also known as **punkie** and **noseeum**. There are c.1200 species, some of which have medical and veterinary importance as carriers of disease. (Order: Diptera. Family: Ceratopogonidae.)

Bitola or **Bitolj** [**bee**tola], Turkish **Monastir** 41°01N 21°21E, pop (2000e) 164 000. Town in the Former Yugoslav Republic of Macedonia, 112 km/70 mi S of Skopje; under Turkish rule until 1912; second largest town in the republic; railway; carpets, textiles, tourism; nearby national park in the Palister range, 120 sq km/46 sq mi, established in 1949; Ajdar Kadi mosque; festival of folk music (Jul–Aug).

bitonality The property of music written in two keys simultaneously. The piquant dissonances that usually result were cherished particularly by *Les Six* in France during the first half of the 20th-c.

bittern A marsh-dwelling bird, widespread; heron-like but stouter, with shorter legs and neck; mottled brown plumage; usually solitary; eats diverse animal prey. When threatened, it stands immobile with its bill raised. (Family: Ardeidae, 12 species.)

bittersweet *woody nightshade*

bitumen 1 A mixture of tar-like hydrocarbons derived from petroleum either naturally or by distillation. It is black or brown and varies from viscous to solid, when it is also known as **asphalt**. It is used in road-making.

2 In art, a transparent, brown pigment made from tar, popular with painters in the 18th-c for the rich 'Rembrandtesque' transparent tones which it gives when first applied. Unfortunately, it never dries, but turns black and develops wide traction-cracks which are difficult to repair.

bivalve An aquatic mollusc with a body compressed sideways, and enclosed within a shell consisting of two valves joined by a flexible ligament along a hinge line; the valves are closed by one or two adductor muscles, and opened by an elastic ligament; head not defined; typically feeds on small particles collected by large gills covered with tiny hairs (*cilia*); class contains over 20 000 species with varied life-styles including burrowing, boring, free-swimming, and base-attached (*sessile*); life-cycle often includes a planktonic larval stage (the *veliger*);

many species of great economic importance, such as oysters, clams, and mussels; also known as **lamellibranchs** and **pelecypods**. (Class: Pelecypoda.)

Biwa, Lake [beewa], Jap **Biwa-ko**, also **Lake Omi** area 670 sq km/ 261 sq mi. Largest lake in Japan; in Kinki region, C Honshu, 8 km/ 5 mi NE of Kyoto; 64 km/40 mi long; 3–19 km/1¾–12 mi wide; 103 m/315 ft deep; connected by canal to Kyoto.

Bizerte or **Bizerta** [bizertuh], Lat **Hippo Diarrhytus** 37°18N 9°52E, pop (2000e) 170 000. Capital of Bizerte governorate, N Tunisia, 60 km/37 mi NW of Tunis; strategically important on the Mediterranean coastline; occupied by Romans, Vandals, Arabs, Moors, Spanish, and French (1881); German base in World War 2, heavily bombed; French naval base until 1963; railway; kasbah in old city; Bizerte Festival (Jul–Aug).

Bizet, Georges [beezay], originally **Alexandre César Léopold Bizet** (1838–75) Composer, born in Paris, France. He studied at the Paris Conservatoire under Halévy, whose daughter he married in 1869, and in Italy. Although he won the Prix de Rome in 1857 with *Le Docteur miracle*, his efforts to achieve a reputation as an operatic composer were largely unsuccessful. His incidental music to Daudet's play *L'Arlésienne* (1872) was remarkably popular and survives in the form of two orchestral suites. His masterpiece was the four-act opera *Carmen*, completed just before his untimely death from heart disease. A symphony in C was first performed in 1935.

Bjerknes, Jakob (Aall Bonnevie) [byerknes] (1897–1975) Meteorologist, born in Stockholm, Sweden, the son of Norwegian physicist Vilhelm Bjerknes. Professor at the Geophysical Institute, Bergen, with his father he formulated the theory of cyclones on which modern weather-forecasting is based. He moved to the USA in 1939, and in 1940 was appointed the first professor of meteorology at the University of California, Los Angeles. He became a US citizen in 1946.

Björling, Jussi [byerling], originally **Johan Jonaton Björling** (1911–60) Tenor, born in Stora Tuna, SC Sweden. From 1928 he studied at the Stockholm Conservatory, making his debut as principal with the Royal Swedish Opera in 1930. Although his repertoire was mainly Italian he sang rarely in Italy, but became a favourite in the USA, especially at the Metropolitan Opera, New York City, and made numerous recordings.

Bjørnson, Bjørnstjerne (Martinius) [byernsn] (1832–1910) Writer and Norwegian statesman, born in Kvikne, C Norway. He studied at Molde, Kristiania (now Oslo) and Copenhagen, was a playwright and novelist of wide-ranging interests, and a lifelong champion of liberal causes. A friend of Ibsen and an ardent patriot, he sought to free the Norwegian theatre from Danish influence and revive Norwegian as a literary language. He was named Norway's national poet, and his poem, 'Ja, Vi Elsker Dette Landet' (1870, trans Yes, We Love This Land of Ours) became the national anthem. His other major works include the novel *Fiskerjenten* (1868, The Fisher Girl), the epic poem *Arnljot Gelline* (1870), and his greatest plays, *Over Aevne I og II* (1883, 1895, trans Beyond Our Power, Beyond Human Might). He was awarded the 1903 Nobel Prize for Literature.

Black, Sir James (1924–) Pharmacologist, born in Uddingston, South Lanarkshire, WC Scotland, UK. He studied medicine at St Andrews, Scotland, then taught at various universities, in 1984 becoming professor of analytical pharmacology at King's College, London. His reasoning on how the heart's workload could be reduced led to the discovery of beta-blockers in 1964, and his deductions in 1972 on acid secretion in the stomach resulted in the introduction of cimetidine in the treatment of stomach ulcers. He shared the Nobel Prize for Physiology or Medicine in 1988.

Black, Joseph (1728–99) Chemist, born in Bordeaux, SW France. He studied at Belfast, Glasgow, and Edinburgh, and in 1756 showed that the causticity of lime and alkalis is due to the absence of the 'fixed air' (carbon dioxide) present in limestone and the carbonates of the alkalis. He evolved the theory of 'latent heat', on which his scientific fame chiefly rests, and founded the theory of specific heats. In 1766 he became professor of medicine and chemistry at Edinburgh.

Black and Tans Additional members of the Royal Irish Constabulary, recruited by the British government to cope with Irish national unrest in the Irish War of Independence (1919–21), which reached a climax in 1920. The shortage of regulation uniforms led to the recruits being issued with khaki tunics and trousers and very dark green caps, hence their name. Unemployed veterans of World War 1 and ex-prisoners were recruited. Republican guerrilla tactics instigated by the IRA under Michael Collins provoked severe reprisals by the Black and Tans. These included the Croke Park Gaelic football ground massacre, in which a skirmish between IRA gunmen and Black and Tans turned into a stampede, resulting in 12 deaths and hundreds of injured. Whole towns were terrorized, most notably Drogheda and Balbriggan (the 'sack of Balbriggan'). These actions caused an outcry in Britain and the USA, and had the unintended effect of galvanizing the Republican cause. The Black and Tans were withdrawn following the signing of the Anglo-Irish Treaty (1921).

black bear Either of two species of bear, usually black but sometimes brown in colour; the **American black bear** from North America (*Ursus americanus*), and the **Asiatic black bear**, **Himalayan bear**, or **moon bear** from S and E Asia, with a white chin and white 'V' on chest (*Selenarctos thibetanus*).

black beetle A beetle found in cellars and outhouses; larvae cylindrical; adults move clumsily; feeds on plant material. (Order: Coleoptera. Family: Tenebrionidae.)

blackberry A scrambling prickly shrub (*Rubus fruticosus*) with arching, biennial stems rooting at the tips; also known as **bramble**. It is native to Europe, Mediterranean region, but has been introduced elsewhere, often forming extensive thickets. The leaves are divided into 3–5 toothed leaflets, flowers numerous, in terminal inflorescences, 5 petals, white or pale pink. The 'berry' is an aggregate of 1-seeded carpels, not separating from the core-like receptacle when ripe. The plants are highly variable; many reproduce without cross-fertilization, and form clonal populations regarded as microspecies, of which c.400 have been identified in Britain alone. (Family: Rosaceae.)

blackbird A thrush native to Europe, N Africa, and S and W Asia, and introduced in New Zealand (*Turdus merula*); inhabits woodland, scrub, and habitation; eats fruit, insects, and worms; male black with yellow bill; female brown. The name is also used for some American orioles.

blackbirding The recruiting of Pacific islanders ('Kanakas'), mostly for work on plantations in Queensland and Fiji, from the 1860s to 1910. About 61 000 islanders were taken to Queensland between 1863 and 1904. Despite criticisms, the trade was not a form of slavery. Most came voluntarily, and under contract; about a quarter were tricked or forced.

blackbody A perfect emitter of heat and light radiation. A blackbody is a perfect absorber of radiation, and so appears black, since no light is reflected; but once in equilibrium it must emit as much radiant energy as it absorbs, so it is both a perfect absorber and emitter. A good approximation to a blackbody is formed by a small hole in a box, where the hole is the blackbody, since light incident on the hole is lost inside the box. When the box is heated, blackbody radiation in the form of light is emitted from the hole. At room temperature, energy emitted as blackbody radiation is invisible infrared, so the hole appears black.

blackbody radiation Light and heat radiation emitted by a blackbody having a frequency distribution that depends only on the temperature of the blackbody. At higher temperatures, higher frequency light predominates. According to the law independently formulated by Josef Stefan in 1879 and Ludwig Boltzmann in 1889, the total energy emitted is $E = \sigma T^4$, where σ is the Stefan–Boltzmann constant. The study of blackbody radiation led Max Planck to suggest the quantization of light (1900). Blackbody radiation is the basis of optical pyrometry.

black box A complete unit in an electronics or computer system whose circuitry need not be fully understood by the user. The name is commonly used for the flight data recorder in an aircraft: this collects information about the aircraft's performance during a flight, which can be used to help determine the cause of a crash.

blackboy *grass tree*

black bryony A perennial climber (*Tamus communis*) with a large, black tuber, related to the yam, native to Europe, W Asia, and N Africa; stems grow to 4 m/13 ft, twining; leaves heart-shaped, dark, glossy green with prominent curving veins; flowers tiny, 6-lobed, yellowish-green, males and females on separate plants; berry 12 mm/½ in diameter, red. (Family: Dioscoriaceae.)

blackbuck A gazelle native to India and Pakistan (*Antilope cervicapra*); inhabits plains and scrubland; adult males blackish brown with white chin, white disc around eye, and white underparts; horns long, spiralling, ringed with ridges; females pale brown, hornless.

blackcap A warbler found in mature deciduous woodland from Europe to C and S Siberia (*Silvia atricapilla*); eats insects, fruit, and nectar. Many European birds migrate to African forests for the winter. (Family: Silviidae.)

blackcock *black grouse*

black comedy A kind of comedy (whether in narrative or dramatic form) which derives its often bitter humour from exposing and facing up to the grotesque accidents and meaningless misfortunes to which human life is liable. The term is a translation of *comédie noire*, first coined by Jean Anouilh, who divided his early plays into *pièces roses* and *pièces noires*. Examples include Evelyn Waugh's *Black Mischief* (1932), Nathanael West's *The Day of the Locust* (1939), and Joe Orton's *Loot* (1965).

black consciousness An attitude, particularly in the USA, which asserts that African-Americans, by virtue of their ethnicity and history, possess a cultural tradition distinct from the wider population. It rejects the notion that they have been totally absorbed into white society, only distinguishable by colour. Proponents of black consciousness aim to raise the awareness of blacks by espousing and publicizing these cultural traditions and values.

Black Consciousness Movement (South Africa) A movement formed by Steve Biko in 1969, when he led African students out of the multi-racial National Union of South African Students and founded the South African Students Organization. From this emerged the Black Peoples' Convention, which sought to create co-operation in social and cultural fields among all non-white peoples. Most of its leaders were imprisoned in 1977, and Biko died in police custody. The film *Cry Freedom* (1988) was based on these events.

Black Country The industrial area of the English Midlands during and after the Industrial Revolution. It lies to the NW of Birmingham, in SW Staffordshire and N Worcestershire, England, UK.

blackcurrant An aromatic species of currant (*Ribes nigrum*) native to Europe and temperate Asia. It is widely cultivated, producing edible black berries on new wood. (Family: Grossulariaceae).

black dance A term used in the mid-1980s to describe British forms of dance that owe some allegiance to African or Caribbean influences; there are black consciousness overtones emphasizing non-white, non-Western forms of dance. The Black Dance Development Trust was briefly active from 1985, offering summer schools and short courses to examine ways in which cultural traditions of Africa and the Caribbean relate to black people's dance in Britain.

Black Death The name given to the virulent bubonic and pneumonic plague which swept through W and C Europe from Asia (1347–51). Approximately 25 million people, about a third of the population, perished; some 13 million Chinese also died. The disease was caused by diseased rats carrying the plague bacillae, which infected humans via the rats' infected fleas. Merchants may have carried the disease along trade routes to the Middle East and Mediterranean countries. Pneumonic plague was 95 per cent fatal. Up to half the population of Europe died, including almost everyone in Florence. The Church believed it to be God's punishment, and survivors joined self-punishment movements such as the Flagellants. Many blamed the Jews, who suffered brutal oppression This catastrophe was not solely responsible for causing or accelerating important socio-economic changes; probably more decisive was the subsequent pandemic recurrence of the plague (eg in 1361–3, 1369–71, 1374–5, 1390, and 1400). The consequences varied from region to region, and the economies of S England, the Netherlands, and S Germany continued to prosper, due partly to lack of labour and rising wages.

black economy In the UK, a term used for economic activities not reported to tax and other public authorities; also referred to as the **underground economy** or (in the USA) as 'off the books' activities. This allows one or both parties to avoid paying tax and/or social security contributions, and may conceal breaches of laws concerning such matters as job security, employer's liability, health and safety, and work permits for aliens. Lack of records of such activities makes economic statistics on output and employment less reliable than they might otherwise be.

Blackett, Patrick M(aynard) S(tuart) Blackett, Baron (1897–1974) Physicist, born in London, UK. He studied at Cambridge University. He was the first to photograph nuclear collisions involving transmutation (1925), and in 1932, independently of Carl Anderson, he discovered the positron. He pioneered research on cosmic radiation, for which he was awarded the Nobel Prize for Physics in 1948. He was professor at London (1933–7), Manchester (1937–53), and the Imperial College of Science and Technology (1953–74). He became a life peer in 1969.

black-eyed Susan **1** A slender annual climber (*Thunbergia alata*) native to S Africa; stems twining to 2 m/6½ ft; leaves opposite, heart-shaped; flowers tubular with five spreading bright-yellow lobes, and a dark purplish or black central eye. (Family: Acanthaceae.)

2 In North America, a member of the genus *Rudbeckia*.

blackfish *pilot whale*

blackfly A black-bodied aphid which feeds by sucking plant sap. (Order: Homoptera. Family: Aphididae.)

black fly A small biting fly found near running water; larvae aquatic, feeding by filtering plankton and detritus; also known as **buffalo gnat**. The females of some species are blood-suckers, and serious cattle pests. One species is the carrier of filarial river blindness. (Order: Diptera. Family: Simuliidae.)

Blackfoot Three Algonkin-speaking Indian Groups (Blackfoot, Blood, Piegan) originally from the E who settled in Montana, USA and Alberta, Canada. Famous hunters and trappers, many died of starvation after the bison were exterminated; others turned to farming and cattle rearing. Population now c.32 000 (1990 census), chiefly on reservations.

Black Forest, Ger **Schwarzwald** Mountain range in Germany; extends 160 km/100 mi from Pforzheim (N) to Waldshut on the Upper Rhine (S); highest peak, the Feldberg (1493 m/4898 ft); divided by R Kinzig into Lower (N) and Upper (S) Schwarzwald; source of Danube and Neckar Rivers; crafts, tourism; many medicinal baths and spas.

Black Friars *Dominicans*

Black Friday (24 Sep 1869) A US financial crisis: the date of a severe fall in the price of gold as a result of an attempted fraud by financiers Jay Gould (1836–92) and James Fisk (1834–72). Many speculators lost their fortunes in the ensuing panic.

black grouse A grouse native to upland areas of N Europe and N Asia (*Tetrao tetrix*); the male (**blackcock**) black with a red comb above each eye; the female (**greyhen**) brown. The males display to females at a traditional site (known as a *lek*); successful males take several mates. (Family: Phasianidae.)

black gum *tupelo*

Black Hand A symbol and name for a number of secret societies which flourished in the 19th-c and early 20th-c. It was the name adopted by a secret organization formed in Serbia in 1911, led by army officers, whose objective was the achievement of Serbian independence from Austria and Ottoman Turkey. It is best known for planning the assassination of Archduke Francis Ferdinand of Austria in Sarajevo in June 1914, an event which led directly to the outbreak of World War 1. The name and symbol were adopted by organizations controlled by the Mafia in the USA and Italy, which used intimidation and murder to achieve their ends.

Black Hawk War (1832) A military conflict between the USA and Sauk and Fox Indians, which led to the completion of the policy of removing Indians from 'the Old Northwest' to beyond the Mississippi R.

black hole A region of spacetime from which matter and energy cannot escape; in origin, a star or galactic nucleus that has collapsed in on itself to the point where its escape velocity exceeds the speed of light. Its boundary is known as the *event horizon*: light generated inside the event horizon can never escape. Black holes are believed to exist on all mass scales. Some binary stars which strongly emit X-rays may have black hole companions.

Black Hole of Calcutta A small, badly-ventilated room in which surviving British defenders were imprisoned overnight in an incident following Calcutta's capture (June 1756) by Siraj ud Daula, Nawab of Bengal. It was claimed that only 23 out of 146 prisoners survived. The incident became famous in the history of British imperialism, but its status is controversial, as the total number involved was probably much smaller.

blackjack A popular casino card game, derived from 15th-c European games. The object is to accumulate a score of 21 with at least two cards. Picture cards count as 10, the ace as either 1 or 11, and other cards according to their face value. A score of 21 with a picture card and an ace is called a blackjack. Multiple packs of cards are shuffled together and dealt face up from a mechanical 'shoe'. The original bets are placed before the first card is dealt. Some cards are dealt face down in the casino game. There are several variations.

blackleg A debilitating disease of cattle and sheep, characterized by swollen legs; can be fatal; also known as **black legs** or **black quarter**.

black letter writing A style of writing, common in the mediaeval period, which formed the basis of early models of printers' type in Germany; sometimes called **Gothic**. It had relatively straight strokes in its letters.

blackmail The making of an unwarranted demand with menaces. The demand must be made with a view either to ensure gain for the person demanding or someone else or to ensure loss to another person. The menaces may include a threat of violence or of some detrimental action, for example exposure of past immorality. The demand is unwarranted unless the accused believes that he or she has reasonable grounds for the demand, and that the menaces are appropriate to reinforce the demand. In England and Wales, blackmail is an offence under the Theft Act of 1968. In many US states, and also in Scotland, the crime of obtaining money or any other advantage by threats is termed *extortion*.

black market An illegal trade in goods or currencies. The practice is well known in countries where there is rationing or restriction on the availability of food, petrol, clothing, and other essential commodities. These may be difficult or impossible to obtain using legal channels, but may be available (at a much higher price) 'on the black market'. In countries where strict currency exchange controls exist, there is invariably a black market economy which can make foreign currency available above the official rate.

black Mass A blasphemous caricature of the Roman Catholic Mass, in which terms and symbols are distorted, and Satan is worshipped instead of God.

Blackmore, R(ichard) D(oddridge) (1825–1900) Novelist, born in Longworth, Oxfordshire, SC England, UK. He studied at Oxford, and was called to the bar in 1852, but poor health made him take to market gardening and literature in Teddington. *Clara Vaughan* (1864) was the first of 15 novels, mostly with a Devonshire background, of which *Lorna Doone* (1869) is his masterpiece and an accepted classic of the English West Country.

Black Mountain College An experimental college in the USA founded in 1933 by John Andrew Rice, Theodore Dreier, and others. Originally located south of the village of Black Mountain, near Ashville, NC, the college sought to educate the 'whole' student through a combination of study, communal living, and manual work. An appreciation of the arts was central to its unorthodox curriculum. In 1933 the artist Josef Albers and his wife, both former Bauhaus teachers, joined the faculty and the college became a centre for the Bauhaus movement. The college relocated to its own campus at Lake Eden in 1941, where it remained until its closure in 1957.

Black Mountain poetry A school of poetry started in the 1950s by Charles Olson (1910–70), one-time rector of Black Mountain College in North Carolina, USA, and including such names as Robert Creeley and Robert Duncan (1919–88). The aim was greater physicality and immediacy, as exemplified in the *Black Mountain Review* (1954–7).

Black Muslims A black separatist movement in the USA, founded in 1930 by W D Fard, Elijah Muhammad (1925–75); also known at different times as the **Nation of Islam**, the **American Muslim Mission**, and the **World Community of Islam in the West**. The movement holds that black Americans are descended from an ancient Muslim tribe. Members of the movement adopted Muslim names, avoided contact with whites, and demanded a separate state for blacks, and reparation for injustices. Malcolm X (*né* Little) was one of their foremost preachers, while Cassius Clay (Muhammad Ali) is undoubtedly the most famous member of the movement. They now repudiate their early separatism, and have adopted orthodox Muslim beliefs.

black-necked stork *jabiru*

Black Pagoda *Sun Temple*

Black Panthers A militant, revolutionary African-American organization in the USA, founded in the late 1960s after the murder of Martin Luther King, Jr. The organization preached violence and acted as a protector of blacks, although much of what it advocated was simply rhetoric. It went into rapid decline with the killing, arrest, and exile of many of its leaders, and also because of internal divisions. A particular target of the FBI, the organization had ceased to exist by 1974.

Blackpool 53°50N 3°03W, pop (2001e) 142 300. Town in NW Lancashire, NW England, UK; on the Irish Sea coast, 25 km/15 mi W of Preston; unitary authority from 1998; the largest holiday resort in N England, with an estimated 8·5 million visitors annually; railway; tourism, electronics, engineering, transport equipment; conference centre; Tower (1894, based on Eiffel Tower), Grundy Art Gallery; ballroom dancing championships (summer); musical festival (summer); agricultural show (summer); football league team, Blackpool (Tangerines); illuminations (autumn).

black power The term used by African-American activists in the USA from the late 1950s to reflect the aspiration of increased black political power. It formed part of the more radical wing of the civil rights movement, was against integrationist policies, and used force to advance the black cause. Some political results were achieved in terms of registering black voters.

Black Prince *Edward the Black Prince*

black quarter *blackleg*

Black Rod In the UK, since 1552, the chief gentleman usher of the Lord Chamberlain's department of the Royal Household, who is also an official of the House of Lords. One of his chief ceremonial functions is to act as the official messenger from the Lords to the House of Commons. In a tradition dating from 1643, the door of the Commons is shut on his arrival to summon the MPs to hear the Monarch's speech. To gain entrance to the Commons he must knock three times with his ebony staff of office (the black rod). This tradition represents the independence of the Commons.

black rust *barberry*

Black Sea, ancient **Pontus Euxinus** (Euxine Sea), Bulgarian **Cherno More**, Romanian **Marea Neagra**, Russian **Chernoye More**, Turkish **Karadeniz** area 508 900 sq km/196 000 sq mi. Inland sea between Europe and Asia, connected to the Mediterranean (SW) by the Bosporus, Sea of Marmara, and Dardanelles; 1210 km/752 mi long by 120–560 km/75–350 mi wide, maximum depth 2246 m/7369 ft; bounded N and E by republics of the former USSR, S by Turkey, and W by Bulgaria and Romania; largest arm, Sea of Azov; steep, rocky coasts in S and NE, sandy shores N and NW; fishing important, especially N; main ports include Burgas, Varna, Odessa, Sebastopol, Trabzon; navigated since ancient times; opened by Treaty of Paris (1856) to commerce of all nations, and closed to ships of war; now increasingly polluted; states bordering Black Sea met in Istanbul, 1992, to establish a new trading zone (Black Sea Economic Co-operation Project).

Blackshirts The colloquial name for members of Oswald Mosley's British Union of Fascists (BUF), formed in October 1932. It derived from the colour of the uniforms worn at mass rallies and demonstrations organized by the BUF on the model of European Fascist parties. After clashes and disturbances in Jewish-inhabited areas of E London in 1936, the Public Order Act prohibited the wearing of uniforms by political groups, and the Blackshirts went into decline. Mosley was interned from 1940 until 1943.

black snake A venomous Australian snake of genus *Pseudechis* (Family: Elapidae, 4 species). The name is also used for several species of North American **racers** (Genus: *Coluber*; Family: Colubridae) and for the Jamaican water-snake (*Natrix atra*).

Blackstone, Sir William (1723–80) Jurist, born in London, UK. He studied at Oxford, and in 1746 was called to the bar. He became the first holder of the Vinerian chair of common law at Oxford (1758), where he delivered the first lectures in English law ever given in a university. MP for Hindon, Wiltshire (1761–70), and Principal of New Inn Hall, Oxford, he was made solicitor general to the Queen (1763) and a judge of the Court of Common Pleas (1770–80). From 1765 to 1769 he published his celebrated *Commentaries on the Laws of England*, based on his lectures, which became the most influential and comprehensive exposition of English law.

black swan A swan native to Australia and Tasmania (*Cygnus atratus*); now introduced in New Zealand; nests in reed beds. Its name reflects its unusual colour. (Family: Anatidae.)

blackthorn A deciduous spiny shrub (*Prunus spinosa*) growing to 6 m/20 ft; flowers white, appearing before ovoid, toothed leaves; fruits (**sloes**) globular, blue-black with waxy bloom, edible but very tart, used for jams and wines. Native to Europe, it is probably one of the parents of plum. (Family: Rosaceae.)

Black Thursday (24 Oct 1929) The date of the crash of the New York stock market that marked the onset of the Great Depression.

Black Watch The name of a famous Highland regiment of the British Army; first raised in 1704, it derives from their distinctive, very dark tartan. The two battalions known as the 42nd and 73rd Foot were amalgamated in 1881, and given the traditional title.

blackwater fever A complication of untreated or inadequately treated malaria, particularly due to *Plasmodium falciparum*. The name arises from the breakdown of red blood cells in the circulation, allowing the pigment haemoglobin to pass into the urine, darkening its colour.

Blackwell, Sir Basil (Henry) (1889–1984) Publisher and bookseller, born in Oxford, Oxfordshire, SC England, UK, the son of **Benjamin Henry Blackwell**, who founded the famous Oxford bookshop in 1846. He studied at Oxford, and joined the family bookselling business in 1913, but also published independently, founding the Shakespeare Head Press (1921). He succeeded to the chairmanship in 1924, and from that time joined the family bookselling interest with that of publishing. He was knighted in 1956.

Blackwell, Elizabeth (1821–1910) The first woman doctor in the USA, born in Bristol, SW England, UK, the sister of Emily Blackwell. Her family emigrated to the USA in 1832. After fruitless applications for admission to various medical schools, she entered that of Geneva, NY, and graduated in 1849. She next visited Europe and, after much difficulty, was admitted into La Maternité in Paris, and St Bartholomew's Hospital in London. In 1851 she returned to New York City, where she established a successful practice. From 1869 she lived in England, founding the London School of Medicine for Women in 1874.

black widow A medium-sized, dark-coloured spider, found in warm regions world-wide. Its bite is venomous, containing a neurotoxin causing a set of symptoms known as *lactrodectism*, including severe pain, nausea, and breathing difficulties. It is occasionally fatal. (Order: Araneae. Family: Theridiidae.)

Blackwood, Algernon Henry (1869–1951) Writer, born in Shooters Hill, Kent, SE England, UK. He studied at Edinburgh University before working his way through Canada and the USA, as related in his *Episodes before Thirty* (1923). His best-known novels are *The Centaur* (1911) and *Julius Le Vallon* (1916). His works reflect his taste for the supernatural and the occult, seen especially in his books of short stories, such as *John Silence* (1908), *Tongues of Fire* (1924), and *Tales of the Uncanny and Supernatural* (1949).

Black Zionism The term applied to quasi-nationalist, messianic movements founded among African-Americans and West Indians who look to Africa as a land from which their ancestors came as slaves. To them Africa is held in reverence, black history is held in pride, and there is a desire to return to the land of their forefathers.

bladder A rounded muscular organ situated in the pelvic cavity behind the front of the pelvic bone (the *pubis*), but in children extending upwards into the main abdominal cavity. The bladder receives urine from the kidneys via the ureters for temporary storage and eventual expulsion via the urethra (its capacity is c.600 ml/1·05 UK pt/1·3 US pt). In males it is anatomically related to the prostate gland, seminal vesicles, and *vas deferens*; in females it is related to the vagina and uterus.

bladder campion A species of campion (*Silene vulgaris*) native to Europe, Asia, and N Africa, in which the calyx-tube is inflated and bladder-like. (Family: Caryophyllaceae.)

bladderwort A mostly aquatic carnivorous plant with finely divided leaves, the segments bearing tiny bladders; flowers 2-lipped, spurred, borne on a slender spike projecting above the water surface. The prey are insects or crustacea such as *Daphnia*, trapped in the tiny bladders; each bladder has a trap-door triggered when sensitive hairs are touched and springing inwards, sucking in the prey before the door closes again. The traps reset themselves after the plant has absorbed any nutrients from the breakdown of the prey. The species native to temperate regions are all free-floating aquatics, but those native to the tropics may be land plants or epiphytes. (Genus: *Utricularia*, 120 species. Family: Utriculariaceae.)

Bladud [**blay**duhd] A legendary king of Britain, who discovered the hot spring at Bath and founded the city. One story is that he was a leper who found that the mud cured him.

blaeberry *bilberry*

Blaenau Gwent [**bliy**niy **gwent**] pop (2001e) 70 100; area 109 sq km/42 sq mi. County (unitary authority from 1996) in SE Wales, UK; administrative centre, Ebbw Vale; other chief towns, Tredegar, Abertillery; former coal mining area.

Blaine, David [blayn] (1973–) Illusionist, born in Brooklyn, New York. He worked as a street magician in New York and got his break into showbusiness when ABC TV offered him his own show (1997). Modelling himself on Harry Houdini, he began to perform seemingly impossible feats of endurance. In 1999 he was buried alive for one week beneath a glass tank filled with 4000 pounds of water. Further such feats followed, and in 2003 he apparently endured starvation in solitary confinement for 44 days in a perspex box suspended by a crane over the River Thames. The stunt gained worldwide media coverage and thousands gathered at the site near Tower Bridge to witness his release.

Blainey, Geoffrey Norman (1930–) Social historian, born in Melbourne, Victoria, SE Australia. He studied at Melbourne University, where he became professor of economic history (emeritus since 1988). In 1966 *The Tyranny of Distance* showed how geographical isolation had shaped the history and the people of Australia. *Triumph of the Nomads* (1975) and *A Land Half Won* (1980) completed his trilogy, *A Vision of Australian History*. He reached a wide popular audience through his books, as well as a television programme *The Blainey View*, and became well known in the 1980s for his controversial views on immigration to Australia.

Blair, Tony, popular name of **Anthony Charles Lynton Blair** (1953–) British politician and prime minister (1997–), born in Edinburgh, EC Scotland, UK. Educated in Edinburgh, he studied law at Oxford, and was called to the bar in 1976. He was elected Labour MP for Sedgefield in 1983, becoming his party's spokesperson on Treasury affairs (1985–7) and trade and industry (1987–8). He joined the shadow cabinet in 1988, becoming responsible for energy (1988), employment (1989), and home affairs (1992). He was elected leader of the Labour Party in 1994 and led it to power in a landslide victory in 1997 and 2001, the first Labour prime minister to win a second full term. His wife, **Cherie Blair**, is also a barrister. Following his victory, he pledged to modernize Britain and to continue to modernize the (New) Labour Party. His political and economic policies have given rise to the term **Blairism**, which combines a concern for social issues with market-based economics, including an emphasis on the economic aspirations of the individual. He encountered much public opposition over Britain's involvement in the invasion of Iraq (Mar 2003) by US-led coalition forces.

Blake, Nicholas *Day-Lewis, Cecil*

Blake, Sir Peter (1932–) Artist, born in Dartford, Kent, SE England, UK. From the mid-1950s, while still a student at the Royal College of Art, he became a pioneer of the Pop Art movement in Britain, using media imagery from sources such as comics, advertisements, and popular magazines. His most widely known work is the cover design for the Beatles' LP *Sergeant Pepper's Lonely Hearts Club Band* (1967). In 1980 he became a member of the Royal Academy. He was knighted in 2002.

Blake, Quentin (Saxby) (1932–) Children's writer and illustrator, born in London, UK. He read English at Cambridge, and became a freelance illustrator, producing cartoons for *Punch* and other periodicals. Acclaimed for his illustrations in the books of Russell Hoban, Roald Dahl, and other children's authors, he also produced books of his own, such as *Mister Magnolia* (Kate Greenaway Medal), and *The Quentin Blake Book of Nonsense Verse* and ... *Nonsense Stories* (both 1996). He was head of the Department of Illustration at the Royal College of Art (1978–86), and became a visiting professor there in 1989. He became the first ever Children's Laureate (1999–2001).

Blake, Robert (1599–1657) English naval commander, born in Bridgwater, Somerset, SW England, UK. He studied at Oxford, and led the life of a quiet country gentleman until he was 40. Returned for Bridgwater in 1640 to the Short Parliament, he cast in his lot with the parliamentarians. In the Civil War his defence of Taunton (1644–5) against overwhelming odds proved a turning point in the war. Appointed admiral in 1649, he destroyed Prince Rupert's fleet and captured the Scilly Is and Jersey. In the first Dutch War (1652–4) he defeated Tromp at the Battle of Portland (1653) and shattered Dutch supremacy at sea. He destroyed the Barbary Coast pirate fleet off Tunis (1655), and destroyed a Spanish treasure fleet at Santa Cruz off Tenerife (1657).

Blake, William (1757–1827) Poet, painter, engraver, and mystic, born in London, UK. After studying at the Royal Academy School he began to produce watercolour figure subjects and to engrave illustrations for magazines. His first book of poems, *Poetical Sketches* (1783), was followed by *Songs of Innocence* (1789) and *Songs of Experience* (1794), which contain some of his best-known lines (such as 'Tyger! Tyger! burning bright') and express his ardent belief in the freedom of the imagination and his hatred of rationalism and materialism. His mystical and prophetical works include the *Book of Thel* (1789), *The Marriage of Heaven and Hell* (1791), and *The Song of Los* (1795), which mostly have imaginative designs interwoven with their text, printed from copper treated by a peculiar process, and coloured by his own hand or that of his wife, **Catherine Boucher**. Among his designs of poetic and imaginative figure subjects are a series of 537 coloured illustrations to Edward Young's *Night Thoughts* (1797). His finest artistic work is to be found in the 21 *Illustrations to the Book of Job* (1826), completed when he was almost 70. Subsequent poets, among them Swinbourne and Yeats, have been much influenced by him.

Blakemore, Colin (Brian) (1944–) British physiologist. He studied at Cambridge, California, and Oxford universities, then worked at Cambridge (1968–79), and has been professor of physiology at Oxford since 1979. He also holds posts in Oxford as director of the Centre for Cognitive Neuroscience (1989) and associate director of the Centre in Brain and Behaviour (1991). He gave the BBC Reith lectures in 1976, and was the presenter of the BBC TV series *The Mind Machine* in 1988. He received the Royal Society's Michael Faraday Award in 1989.

Blakey, Art [blaykee], popular name of **Arthur Blakey**, also known as **Abdulla Ibn Buhaina** (1919–90) Jazz drummer and bandleader, born in Pittsburgh, PA. He emerged from big band work in the 1930s to become a leading exponent of the attacking 'hard bop' style from the 1950s. From 1954 he led the Jazz Messengers, a sextet or septet which he constantly renewed with outstanding young players.

Blamey, Sir Thomas Albert [blaymee] (1884–1951) Australian field marshal, born in Wagga Wagga, New South Wales, SE Australia. He joined the regular army in 1906, attended Staff College at Quetta, and became chief-of-staff of the Australian Corps in 1918. At the outbreak of World War 2 he was given command of the Australian Imperial Forces in the Middle East. On the establishment of the SW Pacific Command he led Allied land forces in Australia (1942), and received the Japanese surrender in 1945.

Blanc, Mont *Mont Blanc*

Blanc, Mel (1908–89) Entertainer, born in Los Angeles, California, USA. For over fifty years he provided the voices for some of the most famous cartoon characters including Bugs Bunny, Daffy Duck, Sylvester, and Tweety Pie. In 1933 he had his own radio show *Cobwebs and Nuts*, and because of cash constraints provided most of the character voices himself. He took over the voice of the stammering Porky Pig ('Th-th-th-that's all, folks') in 1937, and in 1940 created the laugh for Woody Woodpecker. While his voice was heard in many films he made his only two appearances in *Neptune's Daughter* (1949), and *Kiss Me Stupid* (1964). He was the voice of Barney Rubble in the television cartoon series *The Flintstones* (1960–66). His autobiography *That's Not All, Folks* appeared in 1989.

Blanchard, Jean Pierre François [blãshah(r)] (1753–1809) Balloonist, and inventor of the parachute, born in Les Andelys, NW France. With John Jeffries he was the first to cross the English Channel by balloon, from Dover to Calais, in 1785. He was killed during practice parachute jumps from a balloon.

Blanchett, Cate (1969–) Actress, born in Melbourne, Victoria, Australia. She studied at the National Institute of Dramatic Art in Sydney and began her career with the Sydney Theatre Company. Television roles followed which led to her feature film debut in *Paradise Road* (1997). Further successes include *Oscar* *and Lucinda* (1997), *Elizabeth* (1998, Golden Globe, BAFTA, Oscar nomination), *An Ideal Husband* (1999), *The Talented Mr Ripley* (1999), and *Veronica Guerin* (2003).

Blanda, (George) Frederick (1927–) Player of American football, born in Youngwood, Pennsylvania, USA. He studied at the University of Kentucky before joining the National Football League Chicago Bears (1949). He moved to the American Football League Houston Oilers (1960), and was traded to the Oakland Raiders (1967) before retiring (1976). His 27 years as an active player with 340 matches played and 2002 points scored, are all-time NFL records. He was elected to the Football Hall of Fame in 1981.

blank verse Regular but unrhymed verse, in any metre but most usually the iambic pentameter of Shakespeare's plays, Milton's *Paradise Lost*, and Wordsworth's *Prelude*.

Blanqui, (Louis) Auguste [blãkee] (1805–81) Revolutionary socialist leader, born in Puget-Théniers, SE France. An extremist, he worked from 1830 at building up a network of secret societies committed to violent revolution. He spent 33 years in prison, and was in prison in 1871 when he was elected president of the revolutionary Commune of Paris. In 1881 his followers, known as *Blanquists*, joined the Marxists.

Blantyre [blantiyr] 14°46N 35°00E, pop (2000e) 480 000. Town in Southern region, S Malawi; altitude 1040 m/3412 ft; Church of Scotland mission founded here, 1876; named after David Livingstone's birthplace in Scotland; airport; railway; Malawi's main commercial and industrial centre; trade in tea, coffee, rubber; brewing, distilling, hides and skins, crafts; museum, two cathedrals, Kapachira Falls nearby.

Blarney 51°56N 8°34W, pop (2000e) 2100. Small village in Cork county, Munster, S Ireland; 8 km/5 mi NW of Cork; visitors to Blarney Castle are supposed to gain the power of eloquent speech as they hang upside down to kiss the Blarney Stone; legend dates from the 16th-c, when Lord Blarney, by pure loquaciousness, avoided acknowledging to Queen Elizabeth's deputy that the lands of Blarney were held as a grant from the Queen and not as a chiefship.

Blasco Ibáñez, Vicente [blaskoh eevahnyeth] (1867–1928) Novelist, born in Valencia, E Spain. He dealt in realistic fashion with provincial life and social revolution. Notable works are *Sangre y arena* (1909, Blood and Sand), and *Los cuatro jinetes del Apocalipsis* (1916, The Four Horsemen of the Apocalypse), which vividly portrays World War 1 and earned him world fame.

Blasis, Carlo [blasees] (1797–1878) Dancer, choreographer, and teacher, born in Naples, SW Italy. He danced in France, Italy, London, and Russia, and became director of the Dance Academy at La Scala in Milan in 1837. He was the author of noted treatises on the codification of ballet technique (1820, 1840, 1857), and is regarded as the most important ballet teacher of the 19th-c.

blasphemy Any word, sign, or action which intentionally insults the goodness of or is offensive to God. Until the Enlightenment, it was punishable by death. Blasphemy was classed as heretical if it openly asserted something contrary to faith, and as non-heretical if it involved careless or insulting speech about God. In many Christian countries, it is technically a crime, and is extended to include the denial or ridicule of God, Christ, or the Bible; but the law is seldom if ever invoked. It is also a crime in certain non-Christian (eg Islamic) countries. The contemporary relevance and range of application of the law of blasphemy became a particular issue in the UK in 1989, following the publication of Salman Rushdie's book, *The Satanic Verses*.

blast furnace A furnace used for the primary reduction of iron ore to iron. Ore, coke, and limestone (which acts as a flux to remove silica) are loaded into the top of a tall furnace lined with mineral heat-resisting substances (such as fire-clay), in which the combustion of the coke is intensified by a pre-heated blast of air. At the temperature produced by the several chemical reactions taking place, the iron ore is reduced to iron, which runs to the bottom of the furnace, where it is either tapped off and solidified as pig-iron, or conveyed while still molten to other plant for steel-making. This iron contains a high proportion of carbon, and is the starting material for other steel-making and iron-founding processes. The complete blast furnace layout includes other structures for heating the blast and utilizing combustible furnace gases. The world's first recorded blast furnace was built in China, 28 BC.

blastula [blastyula] An early embryonic stage in the development of multicellular animals. It typically consists of a hollow sphere of cells.

Blattaria *cockroach*

Blatter, (Joseph) Sepp (1936–) Sports administrator, born in Visp, Switzerland. He studied business administration and economics at Lausanne University, and went on to pursue a career in journalism and public relations in the fields of sport and industry. He has served the Fédération Internationale de Football Association (FIFA) in a variety of posts, including technical director (1975–81) and general secretary (1981–98), and in June 1998 was elected FIFA president (re-elected in 2002). Also an active footballer (1948–71) for the Swiss amateur league, he was made an honorary member of the Swiss Football Association, and has been a member of the International Olympic Committee since 1999.

Blaue Reiter, der [blower riyter] (Ger 'blue rider') The name adopted by a group of avant-garde artists in Munich in 1911. It was apparently inspired by a coloured illustration of a horseman on the cover of a book. Members of the group included Wasily Kandinsky, Paul Klee, August Macke and Franz Marc.

Blavatsky, Helena Petrovna [blavatskee], *née* **Hahn**, known as **Madame Blavatsky** (1831–91) Theosophist, born in Yekaterinoslav (now Dnepropetrovsk), SC Ukraine. She had a brief marriage in her teens to a Russian general, but left him and travelled widely in the East. She moved to the USA in 1873, and in 1875, with Henry Steel Olcott, founded the Theosophical Society in New York City, later carrying on her work in India. Her psychic powers were widely acclaimed by her large following that included Annie Besant.

blazar [blayzah(r)] A type of extremely luminous extragalactic object, similar to a quasar except that the optical spectrum is almost featureless.

blazonry The science of describing the pictorial devices used in heraldry. The basic colour (*tincture*) or background of the shield is known as the *field*, and this is overlaid with heraldic signs (*charges*). At their simplest, charges are broad bands, such as the vertical *pale*, or narrower stripes, such as the horizontal *fess*. The basic charges are called *ordinaries*; more fanciful ones depict a vast range of subjects, from real and mythological creatures to scientific instruments. The *helm* or helmet appears above the shield, and denotes the rank of the bearer.

bleaching The removal of the colour of textiles or other materials, such as paper. It was traditionally carried out on textiles by exposure to sunlight (until the late 18th-c.) After the discovery of chlorine by Scheele (1774), and its bleaching power by Berthollet (1785), most bleaching was done by chemical means. **Bleaching powder** was used in immense quantities until its eventual replacement in the 1920s by cheap pure chlorine and sodium hypochlorite. So-called **optical bleaches** do not remove colour, but add a fluorescent emission to the basic colour of the textile.

bleaching powder A crude mixture of calcium hypochlorite ($Ca(ClO)_2$) and calcium chloride ($CaCl_2$), made by reacting chlorine with calcium hydroxide: $2Ca(OH)_2 + 2Cl_2 \rightarrow Ca(ClO)_2 + CaCl_2 + 2H_2O$. It is used as a bleach and as a disinfectant.

bleak Small freshwater fish (*Alburnus alburnus*) with a slender compressed body, common in lowland rivers of Europe; length up to c.15 cm/6 in; lives in shoals feeding at the surface on crustaceans and insects. The silvery crystals from their scales were once used in the manufacture of artificial pearls. (Family: Cyprinidae.)

Bleasdale, Alan [bleezdayl] (1946–) Playwright, born in Liverpool, Merseyside, NW England, UK. He was a schoolteacher before he turned to writing. He became known through the popular TV series, *The Boys from the Blackstuff* (1982), about a group of unemployed Liverpudlians, which won several awards. Later television series include the World War 1 drama *The Monocled Mutineer* (1986), *GBH* (1991), *Melissa* (1997), and his adaptation of *Oliver Twist* (1999). He has written several stage plays, including *Are You Lonesome Tonight?* (1985), a respectful musical about Elvis Presley.

bleeding heart An erect, brittle-stemmed perennial (*Dicentra spectabilis*), native to China, named from its pendulous, heart-shaped flowers, two outer petals pink, two inner white, in long, drooping spikes; also called **Dutchman's breeches**, similarly inspired. It is cultivated for ornament. (Family: Fumariaceae.)

Blenheim, Battle of [**blen**im] (1704) The greatest military triumph of Marlborough and Prince Eugene in the War of the Spanish Succession. Fought on the Danube to prevent a combined Franco-Bavarian thrust on Vienna, it marked the first significant defeat of Louis XIV's armies, and the first major English victory on the European mainland since Agincourt.

Blenheim Palace [**blen**im] A Baroque palace designed by Vanbrugh, and built (1705–24) at Woodstock, near Oxford, Oxfordshire; a world heritage site. The palace, with its estate of 809 ha/2000 acres, was a gift from the nation to the 1st Duke of Marlborough after his victories at the Battle of Blenheim.

blenny Any of the large family Blennidae (11 genera), of mostly small bottom-dwelling fishes of coastal waters; found worldwide in tropical to temperate seas, rarely in freshwater lakes; many live intertidally in pools and under rocks; body stout, devoid of scales; jaws bearing many small teeth.

Blériot, Louis [**blay**ryoh] (1872–1936) Airman, born in Cambrai, N France. He made the first flight across the English Channel from Baraques to Dover on 25 July 1909 in a small 24-hp monoplane.

blesbok *bontebok*

blesmol *mole rat*

Blessed Virgin (Mary) *Mary* (mother of Jesus)

Blessington, Marguerite Gardiner, Countess of (1789–1849) Writer and socialite, born near Clonmel, Co Tipperary, SC Ireland. After her husband's death (1829), she held a salon at her Kensington mansion, Gore House, where she wrote many sketches of London life, and formed a relationship with the Comte d'Orsay (1801–57). Her best-known work was *Conversations with Lord Byron* (1834). Her lavish tastes left her deep in debt, and with d'Orsay she fled to Paris (1849), where she died two months later.

Blethyn, Brenda (1946–) Theatre and film actress, born in Ramsgate, Kent, SE England, UK. After graduating from the Guildford School of Acting she gained early stage experience with the touring *Bubble Theatre Company* and the Belgrade Theatre, Coventry, and in 1975 joined the Royal National Theatre. She worked widely in British television in such programmes as *Chance In A Million* (1983–5), *The Buddha of Suburbia* (1993), *Outside Edge* (1994–6), and *Between the Sheets* (2003). During the 1990s she concentrated on her film career, and received international acclaim for her portrayal as Cynthia in Mike Leigh's *Secrets and Lies* (1996), for which she won the Palme d'Or for Best Actress at Cannes. Later films include *Girls' Night* (1998), *Little Voice* (1998), and *Saving Grace* (2000).

Bleuler, Eugen [**bloy**ler] (1857–1939) Psychiatrist, born in Zollikon, N Switzerland. Professor at Zürich (1898–1927, he carried out research on epilepsy, then turned to psychiatry, and in 1911 published a study on what he called *schizophrenia* or 'splitting of the mind'. Jung was one of his pupils.

Bligh, William [**bliy**] (c.1754–c.1817) British Naval officer, born in Plymouth, Devon, SW England, UK. He went to sea at the age of 15, sailed under Captain Cook on his third world voyage, and in 1787 was chosen by Sir Joseph Banks to command HMS *Bounty* on a voyage to Tahiti to collect plants of the bread-fruit tree. During a six-month stay on the island the men became demoralized, and on 28 April 1789 the first mate, Fletcher Christian, led a mutiny; Bligh and 18 of his men were cast adrift in an open boat with a small stock of provisions and no chart. They reached Timor, in the East Indies, on 14 June, having travelled nearly 4000 mi. In 1805 he was appointed Governor of New South Wales, and was imprisoned by mutinous soldiers during the so-called 'Rum Rebellion' (1808–10). Exonerated of all blame, he was promoted admiral on his retirement in 1811.

blight A general term applied to any of a variety of plant diseases, especially those caused by fungal infection.

blimp *airship*

blindness A substantial or total loss of vision in both eyes. It can be caused by degeneration of the retina of the eye (*macular degeneration*), cataract, glaucoma, or diabetes. In developing countries it can also be caused by infections, including trachoma, gonorrhoea, and onchocerciasis.

blindworm *slowworm*

Bliss, Sir Arthur (Edward Drummond) (1891–1975) Composer, born in London, UK. He studied at the Royal College of Music, and in 1921 became professor of composition there, but resigned his post after a year to devote himself to composing. He was music director of the BBC (1942–4), and on the death of Bax in 1953 became Master of the Queen's Musick. His compositions include the ballets *Checkmate* (1937) and *Miracle in the Gorbals* (1944), the opera *The Olympians* (1949), chamber music, and piano and violin works. He was knighted in 1950.

Blissymbolics A communication system designed for children unable to use normal spoken or written language; devised by Canadian chemical engineer Charles Bliss (1897–1985) in the 1970s. The system uses a set of simple symbols expressing important everyday concepts, printed on a board along with their written equivalents. It has been used with several clinical populations, such as cerebral palsied, mentally handicapped, and autistic children.

blister beetle A brightly coloured beetle, usually from warm, dry regions; larvae minute, clawed, feeding as parasites, or on insect nests and food provisions. The adults produce a chemical (*cantharidin*) that causes skin blisters. (Order: Coleoptera. Family: Meloidae, c.3000 species.)

blister blight A serious airborne disease of tea (*Exobasidium vexans*), endemic in SE Asia. It reached Sri Lanka in 1946, but has not yet been reported from Africa because of stringent quarantine regulations. The disease attacks young leaves, spreading very rapidly and rendering them economically useless. It can be controlled only by the application of expensive fungicidal sprays. (Order: Basidiomycetes.)

blitzkrieg [**blitz**kreek] (Ger 'lightning war') A term coined (Sep 1939) to describe the German armed forces' use of fast-moving tanks and deep-ranging aircraft in techniques which involved by-passing resistance and aiming the focus of effort at the enemy's rear areas rather than making frontal attacks. Blitzkrieg tactics were used with great success by the Germans 1939–41, and by the Israelis in 1982 during the invasion of Southern Lebanon.

Blix, Hans (1928–) Diplomat, born in Uppsala, Sweden. He studied at Uppsala, Columbia, and Cambridge universities, qualified as a lawyer at Stockholm University (1959), and in 1960 was appointed associate professor in International Law. He was head of department in the Ministry for Foreign Affairs (1963–76), becoming under-secretary of state then minister (1978), and served as director-general of the International Atomic Energy Agency (1981–97). He has written several books on international and constitutional law. He became widely known following his appointment in 2000 as head of the UN Monitoring, Verification and Inspection Commission, leading the investigation into the whereabouts of Iraq's weapons of mass destruction. In July 2003 he was appointed head of a Sweden-sponsored international commission on such weapons.

Blixen, Karen, Baroness, pseudonym **Isak Dinesen**, *née* **Karen Christentze Dinesen** (1885–1962) Writer and story teller, born in Rungsted, E Denmark. She and her sisters were taught at home, though she spent a little time in a Swiss school when she was thirteen, and later studied for several semesters at the Royal Academy of Fine Arts in Copenhagen. In 1914 she married her cousin, **Baron Bror Blixen Finecke**, and went with him to

Kenya. They were divorced in 1921, and in 1931 she returned to Denmark. She wrote *Seven Gothic Tales* (1934), in English, later translating it into Danish. Other works include her memoir, *Out of Africa* (1937, filmed 1985) and *Last Tales* (1957).

Blobel, Günter (1936–) Cell and molecular biologist, born in Waltersdorf, Germany. He studied at the Rockefeller University, New York City, joining the staff in 1969 and spending his career there. He received the 1999 Nobel Prize for Physiology or Medicine for the discovery that proteins have intrinsic signals that govern their transport and localization in the cell.

Bloch, Ernest [blokh] (1880–1959) Composer, born in Geneva, SW Switzerland. He studied in Brussels, Frankfurt, and Munich, eventually teaching at the Geneva Conservatory (1911–15). In 1916 he went to America, where he held several teaching posts, and became a US citizen (1924). His compositions include the *Israel* symphony (1912–16), *Trois Poèmes juifs* (1913), the 'epic rhapsody' *America* (1926), and the Hebrew *Sacred Service* (1930–3).

Bloch, Felix [blokh] (1905–83) Physicist, born in Zürich, N Switzerland. He studied at Leipzig, left Germany for the USA in 1933, and became professor of theoretical physics at Stanford University (1934–71). During World War 2 he worked on radar, and shared the 1952 Nobel Prize for Physics for work on magnetic resonance. The **Bloch bands** are sets of discrete but closely adjacent energy levels arising from quantum states when a nondegenerate gas condenses to a solid.

Bloc Québecois [kaybekwah] A separatist political organization in Quebec, Canada, formed in 1990 when Lucien Bouchard and other Conservative MPs from Quebec deserted the Mulroney government. In the October 1993 federal election the *Bloc* won the second largest number of seats (all in Quebec) and became the official Opposition in Ottawa.

Bloemfontein [bloomfon**tayn**] 29°07S 26°14E, pop (2000e) 350 000. Capital of Free State province, EC South Africa; 370 km/230 mi SW of Johannesburg; judicial capital of South Africa; founded as a fort, 1846; seat of government of Orange River Sovereignty and of Orange Free State Republic, 1849–57; taken by Lord Roberts in Boer War, 1900; airfield; railway; university (1855); trade centre for Free State province and Lesotho; railway engineering, food processing, glassware, furniture, plastics, fruit canning; Anglican cathedral, national museum (1877), war museum (1931).

Blok, Alexander Alexandrovich (1880–1921) Poet, born in St Petersburg, NW Russia. In 1903 he married the daughter of Mendeleyev. His first book of poems, *Songs about the Lady Fair* (1904), was influenced by the mysticism of Solovyev. He welcomed the 1917 Revolution and in 1918 wrote two poems, 'Dvenadtsat' (trans The Twelve), a symbolic sequence of revolutionary themes, and 'Skify' (The Scythians), an ode, inciting Europe to follow Russia.

Blondel or **Blondel de Nesle** [blõdel] (12th-c) French minstrel. According to legend he accompanied Richard I to Palestine on the Crusades, and located him when imprisoned in the Austrian castle of Dürrenstein (1193) by means of the song they had jointly composed.

Blondin, Charles [blõdĩ], originally **Jean François Gravelet** (1824–97) Acrobat and tightrope-walker, born in Hesdin, N France. In 1859 he crossed Niagara Falls on a tightrope, and later did the same with variations (eg blindfolded, with a wheelbarrow, with a man on his back, on stilts). He was still performing in his early 70s.

Blood, Thomas, known as **Colonel Blood** (c.1618–80) Irish adventurer. A parliamentarian during the English Civil War, he was deprived of his estate at the Restoration. He put himself (1663) at the head of a plot to seize Dublin Castle, but the plot was discovered and his chief accomplices executed. In 1671, with three accomplices he entered the Tower and stole the crown, while one of his associates took the orb. They were pursued and captured; but Blood was pardoned by King Charles, who took him to court and restored his estate.

blood An animal tissue composed of cells, cell-like bodies, and fluid plasma that circulates around the body within vascular channels or spaces by the mechanical action of the channels or their specialized parts (primarily the heart). Present in many major classes of animals, it usually contains respiratory pigment, and transports oxygen, nutrients, waste-products, and many other substances around the body. In humans, the cells (red, *erythrocytes*, and white, *leucocytes*), cell-like bodies (*platelets*), and plasma constitute about 8% of total body weight; in an average-sized adult male, blood volume is c.5·5 l/9·7 UK pt/11·6 US pt; in an equivalent female, it is c.4·5 l/7·9 UK pt/9·5 US pt. The haemoglobin-containing erythrocytes (which bind and carry oxygen) are produced in bone marrow and released into the circulation, where they remain for about 120 days before being destroyed in the liver. Platelets (which have important roles in blood clotting) are also produced in bone marrow, but are destroyed after about seven days. Various types of leucocyte are important in protecting the body against disease and infection; these circulate within the vascular system, and are produced in bone marrow and lymphoid tissue. Examples of blood disorders, diseases, and infections are AIDS, anaemia, haemophilia, leukaemia, and septicaemia.

Blood, Council of A council established 1567–76 by the Duke of Alva, the Spanish Habsburg military commander in the Low Countries, on Philip II's orders, to suppress heresy and opposition during the Revolt of the Netherlands. Also known as the **Council of Troubles**, it comprised seven members (three of them Spaniards). The Council's proceedings 1567–73 included some 12 200 trials, 9000 convictions, and 1000 executions, which caused widespread fear and alienation among the population.

blood bank A depository for refrigerated whole blood taken from donors. The 1939–45 war revealed the need for blood transfusion following serious injury. This led to the development of ways of storing blood withdrawn from donors for later use.

blood-bark *gum tree*

blood–brain barrier A selective barrier to the exchange of substances between the blood and brain cells, dependent on the differential permeability of brain capillaries. Water, oxygen, and carbon dioxide cross the barrier rapidly, whereas salts, protein, and dopamine cross it slowly. Its function is possibly to protect the brain against blood-borne toxins.

blood coagulation (clotting) *haemostasis*

blood fluke A parasitic flatworm, found as an adult in the blood of some mammals, including humans; causes bilharzia, a common disease in tropical areas; complex life-cycle involves a fresh-water snail as intermediate host, within which asexual reproduction occurs; larvae (*cercaria*) released from the snail into fresh water, infecting the final host by skin penetration. (Phylum: Platyhelminthes. Class: Trematoda. Genus: *Schistosoma*.)

blood group systems A series of genetically determined systems of substances on the plasma membranes of red blood cells, which act as *agglutininogens* and which, when in contact with the complementary *agglutinin* in plasma cause the red cells to stick together. In humans, the most prominent system is the ABO. Everybody belongs to four main subdivisions of this system (A, B, AB, or O) determined by the presence or the absence of A and/or B substances on the red cell membrane. The absence of A or B antigen is usually associated with the presence of corresponding natural anti-A or anti-B antibodies in the plasma. Before a blood transfusion, the recipient's and donor's blood are cross-matched, otherwise antibodies of the recipient may combine with antigens of the donor, causing clumping of foreign erythrocytes and possible fatal consequences. Other well-known systems are the Rh (Rhesus) and MNSs.

bloodhound A breed of dog, known for its keen sense of smell; used for tracking; large powerful body with loose-fitting skin; short coat; tan or black and tan; long pendulous ears and jowls;

long, deep muzzle. Originally French, the breed was perfected in Britain.

Bloodless Revolution *Glorious Revolution*

blood–testis barrier A physical barrier which creates the optimum environment for the maturation of germ cells into spermatozoa; it comprises the Sertoli cells of the seminiferous tubules of the testis, and the impermeable junctions between them. It also prevents antigenic material formed after immune competence is attained from 'leaking' back into the circulation and reacting with the body's immune system (which recognizes it as 'not-self') to produce testis-damaging antibodies. If the barrier is damaged (eg by mumps in adults), such leakage and antibody formation may occur, and a consequent immune inflammation of the testis (*orchitis*) may result in destruction of germ cells and consequent sterility.

blood poisoning *septicaemia*

blood pressure The hydrostatic pressure of the blood within the blood vessels. It usually refers to the pressure within arteries, the pressure within capillaries and veins being much lower. Arterial blood pressure depends on heart rate, the volume of blood ejected by the heart with each beat, and the *peripheral resistance* to the flow of blood through the arteries. It is measured, using a sphygmomanometer, as the height in millimetres of a column of mercury (mmHg). In health, the arterial blood pressure reaches a peak of around 120 mmHg with each heartbeat (*systolic pressure*) and falls to around 70 mmHg as the heart relaxes (*diastolic pressure*).

blood products The constituent elements of the blood, separated into relatively pure and concentrated form so they can be transfused separately. Blood is separated into cells and plasma using a centrifuge. Blood cells include platelets (needed for the clotting of blood), and white cells (concerned with the control of infection). Fractionation of plasma yields albumin (for use in shock) and other proteins, such as Factor VIII and fibrinogen (for use in disorders of bleeding such as haemophilia). These may be preserved in dried powder form over many years.

Blood River, Battle of *Great Trek*

blood sports The killing of animals for sport, such as fox-hunting, hare-coursing, or bullfighting. Cockfighting, once popular in Britain, and still practised illegally in certain parts of the country, is a popular sport in many continental countries and in Asia. Blood sports, often referred to as **field sports**, have come under increasing attack in recent years from those concerned with animal welfare.

bloodstone A type of chalcedony, a fine-grained variety of the mineral quartz. It is dark-green with red flecks.

blood test The analysis of a sample of blood withdrawn from a living person to determine its characteristics or detect abnormalities in its composition. Blood tests are often carried out for diagnostic purposes, such as to determine the levels of physiological solutes or cells in the blood, or to detect drugs and poisons, or antibodies which have developed in response to infection. They are used in a number of legal contexts. For example, following a positive breath test which indicates an alcohol level in excess of that permitted for driving a vehicle, a blood (or urine) test may be required to determine the precise blood alcohol level. In addition, blood tests have been used in disputed paternity cases (to exclude the possibility of a particular person having fathered the child), and in the detection and identification of criminals.

blood transfusion The transfer of blood from one person to another, for example in the event of blood loss due to injury. It was first carried out early in the 19th-c, but usually resulted in serious reactions. Clinically useful and safe blood transfusions were possible only after the discovery of blood groups: blood taken from one individual can be given only to another person with a compatible blood group. Blood for transfusion is carefully screened to prevent transmission of infectious agents.

blood vessels A closed system of tubes whereby blood permeates through all the tissues of the body, comprising the arteries, arterioles, capillaries, venules, and veins. In general, arteries and arterioles carry oxygenated blood from the heart, and venules and veins return deoxygenated blood back to it. However, the pulmonary arteries convey deoxygenated blood to the lungs from the heart, while the pulmonary veins return oxygenated blood to it from the lungs. Gaseous exchange (oxygen and carbon dioxide) and nutritional requirements pass between the blood and body tissues in the capillaries. Disorders of the circulatory system include aneurysm, embolism, haemorrhage, and thrombosis.

bloodworm The aquatic larva of a midge; body worm-shaped, up to 20 mm/0·8 in long, with 12 segments; coloured red with haemoglobin as an adaptation to life in poorly oxygenated water. (Order: Diptera. Family: Chironomidae.)

Bloody Assizes The name given to the western circuit assizes in England in the summer of 1685, presided over by Lord Chief Justice George Jeffreys after the defeat of the Duke of Monmouth at the Battle of Sedgemoor. About 150 of Monmouth's followers, mostly poorer farmers and clothworkers, were executed, and 800 transported to the West Indies. The severity of the sentences greatly increased support for William of Orange in the West Country in 1688.

Bloody Mary *Mary I*

Bloom, Claire (1931–) Actress, born in London, UK. She was educated in Bristol and made her debut at the Oxford Repertory Theatre (1946). A distinguished Shakespearean actress on stage and television, she has acted major roles in other classic and modern plays, including *A Street Car Named Desire* (1974) and *The Cherry Orchard* (1981). Her many films include *Limelight* (1952), *Look Back in Anger* (1959), *The Spy Who Came in From the Cold* (1966), *Sammy and Rosie Get Laid* (1987), *Crimes and Misdemeanours* (1990), and *Wrestling with Alligators* (1999). Among her roles in television drama are *Brideshead Revisited* (1981), *Shadowlands* (1985, BAFTA), *Shadow on the Sun* (1988), *Family Money* (1997), and *Imogen's Face* (1998).

Bloom, Ursula, pseudonym of **Mrs Gower Robinson** (1892–1984) Novelist and playwright, born in Chelmsford, Essex, SE England, UK. Her novels, which include *Pavilion* (1951) and *The First Elizabeth* (1953), are mainly historical romances. Most of her plays were written for radio production.

Bloomer, Amelia, *née* **Jenks** (1818–94) Champion of women's rights and dress reform, born in Homer, New York, USA. She founded and edited the feminist paper *The Lily* (1849–55). In her pursuit of dress equality she wore her own version of trousers for women, which came to be called *bloomers*.

Bloomsbury Group An informal association of intellectuals taking their name from the Bloomsbury area of London, UK who were active around the time of World War 1: among them Leonard and Virginia Woolf, Clive and Vanessa Bell, Maynard Keynes, Lytton Strachey, Roger Fry, Duncan Grant, and E M Forster. In reaction against Victorian values, they had no single position on any issue, but subscribed to the spirit of George Moore's *Principia Ethica* (1903), with its privileging of art and intuition. They had a significant influence on the Modernist movement in England.

Bloor, Ella (Reeve), known as **Mother Bloor** (1862–1951) Radical and feminist, born on Staten Island, New York City, USA. Married at the age of 19, she became interested in women's rights, her political interests leading to her divorce in 1896. Following a second unsuccessful marriage she moved into politics as an activist. In 1901 she joined the Socialist Party, and in 1919 was one of the founders of the American Communist Party.

Blow, John (c.1649–1708) Composer, born in Newark, Nottinghamshire, C England, UK. He became organist at Westminster Abbey (1668), Master of the Children at the Chapel Royal (1674), and Master of the Children at St Paul's (1687). He is known for his vast output of anthems and church services, and also for his masque, *Venus and Adonis* (1680–5), which was performed before Charles II.

blowfly An alternative common name for the bluebottle. It refers to the habit of laying eggs on exposed meat, which is then termed 'blown', and unfit for human consumption.

Blücher, Gebhard Leberecht von, Fürst von (Prince of) **Wahlstadt** [**bloocher, blooker**], nickname **Marshal Forward** (1742–1819) Prussian field marshal, born in Rostock, N Germany. He fought against the French in 1793 and 1806, and in 1813 took chief command in Silesia, defeating Napoleon at Leipzig, and entering Paris (1814). In 1815 he assumed the general command, suffered a severe defeat at Ligny, but saved Wellington from defeat at Waterloo by his timely appearance on the field.

Blue, Lionel (1930–) British rabbi and broadcaster. He studied at Oxford and London universities, was ordained a rabbi in 1960, and joined Leo Baeck College in London in 1967. He was convener of the ecclesiastical court of the Reform Synagogues of Great Britain (1971–88). He is well known for his humorous and off-beat comments on life, both on radio (notably his weekly contribution to the *Today* programme on BBC Radio 4) and in such books as *A Taste of Heaven* (1977), *Bolts from the Blue* (1986), *Blue Horizons* (1989), and *Tales of Body and Soul* (1994).

blue In the UK, a sporting honour awarded at Oxford and Cambridge universities to students who represent their university against the other in the annual matches of certain sports. Ribbons of dark blue (Oxford) or light blue (Cambridge) were first awarded to competitors after the second Boat Race in 1836, but now holders may wear ties, blazers, and sweaters in the appropriate colour.

blue-backing shot A method of combining images in cinematography and television in which one or more components of the foreground action is shot against a uniform bright blue backing, and superimposed on a background scene recorded by another camera. In motion pictures this involves subsequent complex printing at the laboratory, but in television it can be done continuously at the time of shooting by colour keying ('chromakey'), each area of blue being replaced by the corresponding portion of the background scene. The technique enables an extremely wide range of effects to be achieved, typically studio actors appearing in exotic locations, children playing within a story-book illustration, or the fantastic flights of Superman.

Bluebeard A character in a European folk or fairy tale, who gives his new wife charge of the keys of his castle, forbidding her to enter one room; she unlocks it out of curiosity, to discover the bodies of six previous wives. Her brothers arrive just in time to save her from becoming Bluebeard's seventh victim, and kill him. The story inspired Bartók's opera *Duke Bluebeard's Castle* (1911).

bluebell A small herb with an annually renewed bulb (*Hyacinthoides non-scriptus*), native to W Europe; leaves strap-shaped; inflorescence 1-sided, flowers 1·5–2 cm/½–¾ in, bell-shaped, drooping, blue, sometimes pinkish or white. It often forms large colonies in woods or on cliff tops. (Family: Liliaceae.)

blueberry A deciduous shrub, native to North America (c.20 species), and cultivated for fruit; flowers bell-shaped; berries c.8 mm/¼ in, blue-black, edible. The low bush blueberry (*Vaccinium angustifolium*) grows to 30 cm/12 in; lance-shaped leaves; narrow white flowers with red markings. The high bush blueberry (*Vaccinium corymbosum*) grows to 3 m/10 ft; elliptic leaves; broader, pinkish flowers. (Family: Ericaceae.)

bluebird A thrush native to North and Central America; male with bright blue plumage on back; inhabits open country, forest clearings, and cultivation; eats fruit and insects; nests in holes in trees. (Genus: *Sialia*, 3 species.)

blue book A UK government publication of official documents, presented to parliament, bound in a blue cover. Unlike other command papers, which put forward government proposals, blue books are more concerned with the provision of information.

bluebottle (botany) *cornflower*

bluebottle (entomology) A large fly with a metallic blue abdomen; lays eggs on decaying animal matter; legless larvae feed by liquefying food; adults feed by exuding digestive juices onto food and imbibing dissolved material. (Order: Diptera. Family: Calliphoridae.)

bluebuck / blue bull *nilgai*

blue fish Predatory fish widespread in tropical and warm-temperate seas; length up to 1·2 m/4 ft; body blue above, sides silvery; lives in large shoals feeding voraciously on anchovies, sardines, and other small shoaling fish; valuable food fish, and prized as sport fish.

blue fox *Arctic fox*

blue grass The name applied to several different grasses of a bluish-green colour. The Kentucky blue grass of the USA is a bluish form of meadow grass. (Family: Gramineae).

bluegrass US 'hillbilly' country music. It features mandolins, banjos, fiddles, guitars, 'dobro' guitars (fitted with a metal resonator), and high ('high lonesome') singing in harmony, with its roots in black and European folk music. Originating from the Appalachian mountain regions, its virtuoso exponents have included singer and mandolin player Bill Monroe (1911–96) and his Blue Grass Boys, with banjoist Earl Scruggs (1924–) and guitarist Lester Flatt (1914–79), the Dillards, and Jimmy Martin (1927–).

blue-green algae *blue-green bacteria*

blue-green bacteria Single-celled, colonial or filamentous organisms with an alga-like body and a bacterium-like (*prokaryotic*) cellular structure; nucleus not delimited by a nuclear membrane; photosynthetic pigment chlorophyll *a* found on a special membrane (*thylakoid*) not enclosed within chloroplasts as in true algae; very ancient organism, believed to have been responsible for enriching the Earth's atmosphere with oxygen as a by-product of its photosynthesis; over 1000 living species known, found mostly in aquatic habitats, also in soil and on rock surfaces; formerly known as **blue-green algae**. (Division: Cyanophycota.)

blue jay *jay*

blue moon **1** A phrase often used to refer to the second full moon in a calendar month in which two full moons occur – a rare event, only once every 2·7 years on average (though happening twice in one year in 1999 and 2018). However, research reported in 1999 suggested that this definition derives from an almanac misinterpretation of the 1940s, and that the phrase only makes sense in relation to a season of the year containing four (not the usual three) full moons.
2 A rare visual effect in which the Moon's disc actually appears blue. If the atmosphere has particles 0·8–1·8 microns in diameter, for example from volcanoes or forest fires, red light gets scattered out of the line of sight, but the blue is allowed through. The result is a blue moon, or even a blue sun.

Blue Mountain Mountain peak in Jamaica; height 2256 m/7401 ft; highest point on the island.

Blue Mountains Mountain range in E New South Wales, Australia; part of the Great Dividing Range; rises to 1180 m/3871 ft at Bird Rock; contains a national park, area 2159 sq km/833 sq mi; tourist area; becoming a popular dormitory area for Sydney.

Blue Nile, Ethiopia **Abay Wenz**, Sudan **Bahr El Azraq** Upper reach of R Nile, NE Africa; length 1450 km/901 mi; issues from SE corner of L Tana, in Gojam region of Ethiopia; flows SE, then S and W, crossing into Sudan at Bumbadi; joins White Nile at Khartoum, forming the R Nile proper; during period of high flood, provides almost 70% of R Nile's flow; during low water, less than 20%.

Blue Riband A notional honour awarded to the fastest passenger ship on the North Atlantic run. A trophy was designed for it, but was never accepted by Cunard Line, whose ships held the record for longer than any others. The final holder (1952) was the SS *United States* in a time of 3 days 11 hours and 20 minutes at an average speed of 35·39 knots for the distance of 4745 km/2949 mi. The trophy returned to Britain after *Hoverspeed Great Britain* crossed the Atlantic at an average speed of 36·966 knots on 23 June 1990. The award was controversial, since this vessel was not a conventional North Atlantic passenger liner.

Blue Rider *Blaue Reiter, der*

Blue Ridge Mountains Mountain range, SE USA; E part of the Appalachian Mts; extends NE–SW for c.1050 km/650 mi from S Pennsylvania, through Maryland, Virginia, and North Carolina to Georgia; includes the Black Mts and Great Smoky Mts; highest point Mt Mitchell (2037 m/6683 ft); other high points Brasstown Bald (1458 m/4783 ft), Mt Rogers (1746 m/5728 ft) and Sassafras Mt (1083 m/3553 ft); Great Smoky Mountains and Shenandoah national parks; famous for its wooded scenery; timber.

blues A form of US African-American music, originating in the 19th-c. Blues songs may have a number of verses, but the standard pattern for each is one of three lines of 4 bars each, the second being lyrically a repetition of the first. The '12-bar blues', as it is known, has a standard chord progression, too, which never varies in its essentials but allows every opportunity for spontaneous vocal and instrumental variations. The origins and early period of the blues are associated particularly with the Mississippi region, and many of the most influential early singers, such as Bessie Smith, 'the Empress of Blues', and Leadbelly were from the S States. In the 1930s, Chicago emerged as the centre for a more aggressive type of urban blues, typified in the singing and guitar playing of the Mississippi-born Big Bill Broonzy (1893–1958). After World War 2, the authentic tradition was represented by Muddy Waters (1915–83) and others, while new departures were seen in the 'rhythm and blues' of the 1950s, and a great deal of rock 'n roll. Blues music is also now found in a wide range of instrumental manifestations, especially using the guitar.

blue shark Powerful, slender-bodied shark (*Prionace glauca*) found worldwide in open tropical to temperate seas, and common around W coasts of the British Isles; length up to 3·8 m/12½ ft; pectoral fins elongate; deep blue dorsally, white underneath; large numbers taken by sea anglers. (Family: Carcharhinidae.)

blueshift An astronomical effect observed when an object emitting electromagnetic radiation is moving towards an observer, increasing the observed frequency of its radiation. This is called a blueshift because, in the case of visible light, spectral lines move to the blue end of the spectrum. Blueshifts are unusual, because almost all galaxies are moving away from us, and hence have redshifts.

bluestockings A nickname, usually with derogatory connotations, for pedantic, educated women. The term was widely used when opportunities expanded for the education of middle-class women in the late 19th-c, but it originated in the Blue Stocking Club at Montagu House, London, c.1750.

bluetit A small typical tit common in gardens (*Parus caeruleus*); native to Europe, N Africa, and SW Asia; eats insects, seeds, and fruit; may hang upside down to feed; nests in hole in tree or wall; also known as **tomtit** (a name additionally used for the great tit). (Family: Paridae.)

blue whale A rare baleen whale (*Balaenoptera musculus*) of the rorqual family; the largest animal that has ever existed, length up to 30 m/100 ft; blue with pale spots (may have yellow micro-organisms on undersurface); in summer, eats shrimp-like *krill* (40 million a day for each whale); in winter, breeds near the Equator, but does not eat; also known as the **sulphur-bottom whale**.

Blum, Léon [blum] (1872–1950) French statesman and prime minister (1936–7, 1938, 1946–7), born in Paris, France. A lawyer, he was elected to the chamber in 1919, becoming one of the leaders of the Socialist Party. He led 'popular front' governments in 1936 and 1938, achieving a series of labour reforms. During World War 2 he was interned in Germany. He remained the leader of the Socialists on his return, and in 1946 was elected prime minister of the six-week caretaker government.

Blunden, Edmund (Charles) (1896–1974) Poet and critic, born in Yalding, Kent, SE England, UK. He studied at Oxford, was professor of English literature at Tokyo (1924–7), and fellow of Merton College, Oxford (from 1931). He joined the staff of *The Times Literary Supplement* (1943), and from 1953 lectured at the University of Hong Kong. He later became professor of poetry at Oxford (1966–8). A lover of the English countryside, he is essentially a nature poet, as is evident in *Pastorals* (1916) and *The Waggoner and Other Poems* (1920), but his prose work *Undertones of War* (1928) is widely considered his best.

blunderbuss A type of firearm, dating from the late 18th-c, with a large bore and a trumpet mouth. It is able to discharge 10 or 12 balls in one shot designed for very short-range use.

Blunkett, David (1947–) British statesman, born in Sheffield, South Yorkshire, N England, UK. He received his early education in special schools for the blind, and went on to study at Sheffield University, then to lecture in industrial relations and politics at Barnsley College of Technology (1973–81). A member of Sheffield City Council (1970–88), he became an MP in 1987. He was opposition spokesman for the environment (1988–92), joined the shadow cabinet (1992), and was spokesman on health (1992–4), education (1994–5), education and employment (1995–7), and chairman of the Labour Party (1993–4). He became secretary-of-state for education and employment in the 1997 Labour government, and Home Secretary in 2001.

Blunt, Anthony (Frederick) (1907–83) Art historian and Soviet spy, born in Bournemouth, Dorset, S England, UK. In 1926 he went to Trinity College, Cambridge, and became a fellow there in 1932. Influenced by Guy Burgess, he acted as a 'talent-spotter', supplying to him the names of likely recruits to the Communist cause, and during his war service in British Intelligence with MI5 was in a position to pass on information to the Soviet government. In 1964, after the defection of Philby, a confession was obtained from Blunt in return for immunity from prosecution, and he continued as surveyor of the Queen's pictures, a post he held from 1945 to 1972. His full involvement in espionage was made public only in 1979. A distinguished art historian, he had been director of the Courtauld Institute of Art (1947–74). His knighthood (1956) was annulled in 1979.

Blyth, Chay, popular name of **Charles Blyth** (1940–) Yachtsman, born in Hawick, SE Scotland, UK, the first to sail single-handed 'the hard way' round the world (1970–1). Educated at Hawick, he joined the Parachute Regiment of the Royal Army (1958–67). In 1966 he rowed the Atlantic from W to E with John Ridgeway (1938–), before making his epic voyage westward around the globe. With a crew of paratroopers he won the Whitbread Round the World Yacht Race (1973–4), travelling eastwards. He has set further ocean-sailing records, and was a key figure in the organization of the British Steel Challenge, Round World Yacht Race (1992–3), retracing his original westward voyage.

Blyton, Enid (Mary) (1897–1968) Children's writer, born in London, UK. She trained as a Froebel kindergarten teacher, then became a journalist. In 1922 she published her first book, *Child Whispers*, a collection of verse, but it was in the late 1930s that she began writing her many children's stories featuring such characters as Noddy, the Famous Five, and the Secret Seven. She identified closely with children, and always considered her stories highly educational and moral in tone, but in the 1980s her work was criticized in some quarters for racism, sexism, and snobbishness. She published over 600 books, and is one of the most translated British authors.

BMD A software package for computers for undertaking statistical analysis. It was developed originally for medical applications.

B'nai B'rith [bniy brith] (Heb 'sons of the covenant') The oldest and largest Jewish service organization, founded in the USA in 1843. It pursues educational and community activities, and concerns itself with the rights of Jews throughout the world. Included in the organization are the Hillel Foundation (for Jewish college students), the Anti-Defamation League (a civil rights group), and B'nai B'rith Women.

boa A snake native to the New World, N Africa, SW Asia, and Australasian islands; a constrictor; minute remnants of hind limbs; females give birth to live young (up to 80 at one time); includes the anaconda. (Family: Boidae, 39 species.)

Boadicea *Boudicca*

Boal, Augusto [**boh**al] (1931–) Brazilian theatre director, playwright, and theorist. His revolutionary models of political theatre-making have gained an international reputation, especially through his book *Teatro do Oprimido* (1975, Theatre of the Oppressed).

boar *pig*

board games *backgammon; chess; draughts; go; mah-jong*

Boas, Franz [**boh**as] (1858–1942) Anthropologist, born in Minden, NW Germany. Having studied geography at Kiel, his expeditions to the Arctic and to British Columbia shifted his interest to the tribes there, and motivated his emigration to the USA in 1886. Professor at Columbia from 1899, he became the dominant figure in establishing modern anthropology in the USA. He and his pupils established new and less simple concepts of culture and of race, as outlined in his collection of papers, *Race, Language and Culture* (1940).

boatbill A heron found from Mexico to Peru and Brazil (*Cochlearius cochlearius*); also known as the **boat-billed heron**; short, scoop-like bill, unlike other herons; inhabits wetlands; nocturnal; hides in mangroves during day. (Family: Ardeidae, but some authorities place it in a separate family, Cochleariidae.)

Boat People Vietnamese who fled Vietnam by boat after the communist victory in 1975, travelling to Australia, Hong Kong, Japan, and several other parts of SE Asia (c.110 000 by the end of 1990). Many died on the long voyages, or were killed by pirates. Voluntary repatriation schemes gained momentum in 1989, and the first involuntary repatriation operation was carried out by the Hong Kong authorities that December. Over 31 000 were resettled in 1990, and over 8000 repatriated. The UK suspended forced repatriation in 1990, but this began again in 1991. The term has since been applied to other groups who try to flee from a country using small craft.

Boat Race The annual rowing race between the crews of Oxford and Cambridge Universities. First held 10 June 1829 from Hambledon Lock to Henley Bridge, it is now raced over 6 km 780 m/ 4 mi 374 yd from Putney to Mortlake.

bobcat A nocturnal member of the cat family native to North America (*Felis rufus*); resembles a small lynx; length up to 1 m/ $3\frac{1}{4}$ ft; brown with dark spots; tail very short; inhabits scrubland and forest; eats birds, rodents, rabbits, and (in winter) deer.

bobolink An oriole native to North America (*Dolichonyx oryzivorus*); spends winter in South America; has the longest migration (8000 km/5000 mi) of any bird in its family; eats insects and grain; in breeding season, male mates with many females.

Bobrowski, Johannes [bo**brof**skee] (1917–65) Poet, born in Tilsit, Germany. His early poems appeared in *Das Innere Reich*, the Nazi journal. He served on the E front in World War 2, and was taken prisoner. He returned to East Germany in 1949, when his poems began to appear in the communist magazine *Sinn und Form*. He published only two volumes: *Sarmatische Zeit* (1961, Sarmatian Times) and *Schattenland Ströme* (1962, Shadowland Rivers), but his generous historical vision has ensured a growing reputation.

bobsledding The art of propelling oneself along snow or ice on a sled (or sledge). The earliest known sled was used in Finland c.6500 BC. As a sport it became popular amongst Britons in Switzerland in the late 19th-c; a special luge run was created at Davos, Switzerland in 1879. The most popular forms of competitive bobsledding are **luge tobogganing** on a small sled, **bobsleighing** in a sophisticated streamlined sled, and the **skeleton**, which is similar to the luge but the athletes descend headfirst.

bobwhite A quail native to North and Central America, and introduced in the West Indies (*Colinus virginianus*); inhabits farmland, open woodland, and brush; eats seeds, grains, and insects; usually lives in groups of 30 or more. (Family: Phasianidae.)

Boccaccio, Giovanni [bo**kah**chioh] (1313–75) Poet and scholar, born in Tuscany or Paris. He abandoned a career in commerce, and at Naples (1328) turned to story-writing in verse and prose. He mingled in courtly society, and fell in love with the noble lady whom he made famous under the name of Fiammetta. Until 1350 he lived alternately in Florence and Naples, producing prose tales, pastorals, and poems. The *Teseide* was partly translated by Chaucer in the *Knight's Tale*. The *Filostrato*, dealing with the loves of Troilus and Cressida, was also in great part translated by Chaucer. After 1350 he became a diplomat entrusted with important public affairs, and a humanist devoted to the cause of the new learning. In 1353 he completed his great collection of tales, the *Decameron*, begun some 5 years before. A huge fresco of life in the late Middle Ages, *Decameron* represents all social classes in situations ranging from comic to dramatic, linked together by exuberant sensuality. During his last years he lived principally in retirement at Certaldo, and would have entered into holy orders, allegedly moved by repentance for the follies of his youth, had he not been dissuaded by Petrarch. Boccaccio is a seminal figure in the history and development of narrative fiction, providing inspiration to Chaucer and Shakespeare, among many others.

Boccherini, Luigi (Rodolfo) [boke**ree**nee] (1743–1805) Composer, born in Lucca, NW Italy. He was a cellist and prolific composer at the courts of the Infante Don Luis in Madrid and Frederick II of Prussia. He is best known for his chamber music, and for his cello concertos and sonatas.

Boccioni, Umberto [bo**choh**nee] (1882–1916) Artist and sculptor, born in Reggio di Calabria, S Italy. He was the most original artist of the Futurist school, and its principal theorist. An important bronze sculpture, 'Unique Forms of Continuity in Space' (1913), is in the Museum of Modern Art, New York City.

Bocelli, Andrea [bo**chel**ee] (1958–) Tenor, born in Lajatico, Tuscany, NW Italy. Interested in music from an early age, he learned to play the piano, flute, and saxophone, and was often asked to sing at family gatherings. Visually impaired from birth, he became blind at the age of 12 following a football injury. He later studied law at the University of Pisa, spent a year working as a lawyer, then decided to try a singing career, financing himself by playing piano in bars. His lucky break came in 1992 when he recorded a demo tape of a duet, *Miserere*, that was heard by Pavarotti, who was persuaded to record the song with him. The duo scored a Europe-wide smash hit. International success followed with the single *Time To Say Goodbye* (1996), recorded with Sarah Brightman, and his albums include *Romanza* (1997), *Sueno* (1999), and *Cieli di Toscana* (2001).

Bochum [**bokh**um] 51°28N 7°12E, pop (2000e) 410 000. Industrial and commercial city in the Ruhr valley, Düsseldorf district, W Germany; 59 km/37 mi SSW of Münster; originally developed around the coal and steel industries; railway; university (1965); vehicles, textiles, radio and television sets; home of the German Shakespeare Society.

Bock, Fedor von (1880–1945) German soldier, born in Kostrzyn, WC Poland. He studied at Potsdam Military School, served as a staff officer in World War 1, and commanded the German armies which invaded Austria (1938), Poland (1939), and the Lower Somme, France (1940). Promoted to field marshal in 1940, he participated in the invasion of Russia with remarkable success (1941), but was dismissed by Hitler for failing to capture Moscow (1942). He was killed in an air-raid.

bodegón [bo*th*ay**gon**] (Span 'tavern') A type of genre painting featuring still life, especially food in a kitchen setting. Velazquez's 'Old Woman Cooking Eggs' (1618, Edinburgh) is a well-known example.

Bodensee *Constance, Lake*

Bode's law or **Titius–Bode law** A numerical relationship linking the distances of planets from the Sun, discovered in 1766 by German astronomer Johann Daniel Titius (1729–96), and published in 1772 by Johann Elert Bode (1747–1826), but now considered to be an interesting coincidence. The basis of this relationship is the series 0,3,6,12,...,384, in which successive numbers are obtained by doubling the previous one. If 4 is then added to create the new series 4,7,10,16,...,388, the resulting numbers correspond reasonably with the planetary distances on a scale, with the Earth's distance equal to ten units.

Bodh Gaya *Buddh Gaya*

Bodhidharma [bodhi**dah(r)**ma] (6th-c) Monk and founder of the Ch'an (or Zen) sect of Buddhism, born near Chennai (Madras), SE India. He travelled to China in 520, where he had a famous audience with the Emperor. He argued that merit applying to salvation could not be accumulated through good deeds, and taught meditation as the means of return to Buddha's spiritual precepts.

bodhisattva [bodhi**sat**wa] (Sanskrit, 'enlightened existence') In Mahayana Buddhism, one who has attained the enlightenment of a Buddha but chooses not to pass into Nirvana; voluntarily remaining in the world to help lesser beings attain enlightenment. This example of compassion led to the emphasis in Mahayana on charity and comfort towards others.

bodily harm A criminal offence against the person, being an aggravation of a simple assault and battery. **Grievous bodily harm** (GBH) involves serious physical injury, such as wounding with a knife, although the injury may be self-inflicted and need not be permanent. **Actual bodily harm** involves a less serious attack, involving any hurt or injury which causes ill health or discomfort. These terms are not used in all jurisdictions.

Bodleian Library [**bod**lian] The university library and national depository at Oxford. It was founded in 1595 by Sir Thomas Bodley (1545–1613), who restored the disused 14th-c library and laid the foundations of its now extensive holdings. It was opened in 1602.

Body art A type of modern art which exploits the artist's – or someone else's – physical presence as a work of art in its own right. Artists may stand in the gallery like a living statue, perhaps singing; photograph themselves performing some banal action, such as smiling; or may deliberately injure themselves. A typical fad of the 1960s, it emerged again in the 1990s, with people using paint, tattoo, rings, and a variety of attachments.

body colour *gouache*

body language *nonverbal communication*

body mass index *weight for height*

body popping *street dance*

Boehm or **Böhm, Theobald** [boem] (1794–1881) Flautist and inventor, born in Munich, SE Germany. In 1828 he opened a flute factory in Munich, and determined to make a flute which would be acoustically perfect. As this involved making holes in places where they could not be fingered, he devised a key mechanism to overcome the problem, and in 1847 produced the model on which the modern flute is based. Certain features of his system have also been applied to the clarinet.

Boehme, Jakob *Böhme, Jakob*

Boeing, William E(dward) [**boh**ing] (1881–1956) Aircraft manufacturer, born in Detroit, Michigan, USA. He formed the Pacific Aero Products Co in 1916 to build seaplanes he had designed with Conrad Westerfelt. Renamed as the Boeing Airplane Company in 1917, it eventually became the largest manufacturer of military and civilian aircraft in the world.

Boeotia [bee**oh**sha] In antiquity, the area in C Greece bordering on Attica. Its chief city-state was Thebes. Its inhabitants were largely of Aeolian stock, and proverbial for their stupidity.

Boers *Afrikaners*

Boer Wars Two wars fought by the British and the Boers for the mastery of S Africa. The British had made several attempts to re-incorporate the Boers, who had left the Cape Colony in the Great Trek (1836), within a South African confederation. The first Boer War (1880–1) ended with the defeat of the British at Majuba Hill, and the signing of the Pretoria and London Conventions of 1881 and 1884. In 1896 the Jameson Raid was a clumsy private effort to achieve the same objective. The second Boer War (1899–1902) can be divided into three phases: (1) (Oct 1899–Jan 1900) a series of Boer successes, including the sieges of Ladysmith, Kimberley, and Mafeking, as well as victories at Stormberg, Modder River, Magersfontein, Colenso, and Modderspruit; (2) (Feb–Aug 1900) counter-offensives by Lord Roberts, including the raising of the sieges, the victory at Paardeberg, and the capture of Pretoria; (3) (Sep 1900–May 1902) a period of guerrilla warfare when Kitchener attempted to prevent Boer commandos raiding isolated British units and lines of communication. The Boers effectively won the peace. They maintained control of 'native affairs', won back representative government in 1907, and federated South Africa on their terms in 1910. On the other hand, British interests in South Africa were protected and, despite internal strains, the Union of South Africa entered both World Wars 1 and 2 on the British side.

Boesak, Allan (Aubrey) [**bu**sak] (1945–) Clergyman, born in Kakamas, W South Africa. Lecturer and student chaplain at Western Cape University, president of the alliance of Black Reformed Christians in South Africa (1981), and president of the World Alliance of Reformed Churches (1982–97), he sees the Christian Gospel in terms of liberation of the oppressed. An outspoken opponent of apartheid, he is leader of the coloured (mixed-race) community in South Africa. In 1999, after a controversial trial, he was jailed for six years for embezzlement of funds sent to his organization. On appeal the sentence was reduced to three years.

Boethius, Anicius Manlius Severinus [boh**ee**thius] (c.AD 480–524) Roman philosopher and statesman, born of a patrician Roman family. He studied at Athens, and there gained the knowledge which later enabled him to produce the translations of Aristotle and Porphyry that became the standard textbooks on logic in mediaeval Europe. He became consul in 510 during the Gothic occupation of Rome, and later chief minister to the ruler Theodoric; but in 523 he was accused of treason and after a year in prison at Pavia was executed. It was during his imprisonment that he wrote the famous *De consolatione philosophiae* (Consolation of Philosophy), in which the personification of Philosophy solaces the author by explaining the mutability of all earthly fortune. The *Consolation* was for the next millennium probably the most widely read book after the Bible.

Bogarde, Sir Dirk [**boh**gah(r)d], originally **Derek Niven van den Bogaerde** (1921–99) Actor and novelist, born in London, UK. He began acting in repertory theatre and made his film debut as an extra in *Come On George* (1940). After war service, he was signed to a long-term contract with Rank Films, spending many years playing small-time crooks, military heroes, and breezy comic leads (notably in the 'Doctor in the House' series) until he was voted Britain's top box-office star (1955, 1957). His major films include *A Tale of Two Cities* (1958), *Victim* (1961), *The Servant* (1963), *Death in Venice* (1971), and *Providence* (1977). He published several volumes of autobiography, and his novels include *A Gentle Occupation* (1980) and *A Period of Adjustment* (1994). He was knighted in 1992. In 1996 he suffered a stroke, but continued to work by means of dictation.

Bogart, Humphrey (DeForest) [**boh**gah(r)t] (1899–1957) Film actor, born in New York City, USA. He made his film debut in *Broadway's Like That* (1930). Alternating between stage and screen, he was frequently cast as a vicious hoodlum, most memorably in *The Petrified Forest* (1936), but eventually attained stardom with his roles in *High Sierra* (1941), *The Maltese Falcon* (1941), and *Casablanca* (1942, with Ingrid Bergman). *To Have and Have Not* (1944) also marked the debut of **Lauren Bacall**, who became his fourth wife in 1945. Over the next 12 years he created an enduring screen persona of the lone wolf, as in *The Big Sleep* (1946). Later films include *The African Queen* (1951, Oscar) and *The Caine Mutiny* (1954).

bog asphodel A rhizomatous perennial (*Narthecium ossifragum*), growing to 40 cm/15 in, native to boggy regions of NW Europe; leaves rigid, curved, V-shaped in cross-section; flowers with six perianth-segments, yellow, turning deep orange after fertilization, stamens woolly. (Family: Liliaceae.)

bog burials Ancient human bodies recovered from N European peat bogs, their soft tissues and hair remarkably preserved by waterlogged, anaerobic conditions (known finds: Denmark 166, Germany 215, Netherlands 48, Britain and Ireland 120). Notable

Iron Age examples are *Tollund Man* (c.200 BC), *Grauballe Man* (c.50 BC), both in Denmark, and the 25–30-year-old, 1·7 m/5 ft 7 in tall *Lindow Man*, buried naked c.300 BC in Lindow Moss, Cheshire, UK, and discovered in 1984. All three were murdered, presumably sacrificial victims or criminals.

Bogdanov, Michael [bogdahnov] (1938–) Stage director, born in London, UK. He studied at the universities of Dublin, Munich, and the Sorbonne, and went on to direct several major productions for the Royal Shakespeare Company and the National Theatre. In 1986 he became co-founder and artistic director of the touring English Shakespeare Company. Recent productions include *The Hostage* (1995), *Timon of Athens* (1997), and *Chicago* (1997). For television he devised and presented *Shakespeare Lives* (1983) and directed *Shakespeare on the Estate* (1995).

bog myrtle A reddish deciduous shrub (*Myrica gale*), native throughout cooler N temperate regions; foliage aromatic, dotted with yellowish oil-glands; flowers tiny, in spike-like catkins; also called **sweet gale**. Males and females are usually on separate plants, but plants may change sex from year to year. (Family: Myricaceae.)

Bognor Regis [**bog**ner **ree**jis] 50°47N 0°41W, pop (2000e) 60 500. Coastal resort town in West Sussex, S England, UK; on the English Channel, 20 km/12 mi W of Worthing; the title 'Regis' dates from 1929, when King George V came here to recuperate; railway; tourism, electrical engineering.

Bogomils [**bo**gohmilz] *Albigenses; Cathars*

Bogotá [bohgohta], official name **Santa Fe de Bogotá** 4°38N 74°05W, pop (2000e) 4 796 000. Federal capital of Colombia, and capital of the Department of Cundinamarca; on a plateau at 2650 m/8694 ft in C Colombia; former centre of Chibcha culture; founded by Spanish, 1538; former capital of Greater Colombia and of New Granada; airport (El Dorado); railway; several universities and colleges; cathedral, Museum of Colonial Art, Palace of San Carlos, Municipal Palace, National Capitol, Churches of San Ignacio, Santa Clara, and San Agustín; Quinta de Bolivar (museum, once Bolivar's home), Gold Museum; linked to Monserrate National Park by funicular railway and cable car.

Bohemia [boh**hee**mia], Czech **Čechy**, Ger **Böhmen** Historic province of W Czech Republic, bounded E by Moravia, W and S by Germany and Austria, and N by Germany and Poland; a plateau enclosed by mountains; natural boundaries include the Erzgebirge (N), Bohemian Forest (SW), and Sudetes Mts (NE); chief rivers include the Elbe (Labe), Vltava (Moldau), Ohre (Eger), Jihlava, and Jizera; major towns include Prague, České Budějovice, Plzeň, Ústí nad Labem; highly industrialized area; coal, iron ore, uranium; mineral springs; part of Moravian Empire, 9th-c; at its peak in early Middle Ages, especially in 14th-c under Charles I; Hussite religious dissension; Habsburg rule from early 16th-c; became a province of Czechoslovakia, 1918; part of Czech Socialist Republic of W Czechoslovakia, 1968; part of Czech Republic, 1993.

Bohemian Forest, Ger **Böhmerwald**, Czech **Český Les** Forested mountain range along the boundary between Germany and Bohemia, Czech Republic; highest German peak, Grosser Arber (1457 m/4780 ft); source of Bayern, Vltava, Regen, and Ilz Rivers.

Bohemond I [**boh**imond] (c.1056–1111) Prince of Antioch, the eldest son of Robert Guiscard. He led his father's army against Alexius I Comnenus in Thessaly in 1083 but was defeated. He joined the First Crusade (1096), and took a prominent part in the capture of Antioch (1098). While the other crusaders advanced to storm Jerusalem, Bohemond established himself as prince in Antioch. He was taken prisoner by the Turks (1100–3), then returned to Europe to marry Constance, the daughter of Philip I of France (1106). He then collected troops to wage war against Alexius, who agreed to hand over lands to Bohemond in return for peace in 1107.

Böhm, Karl [boem] (1894–1981) Conductor, born in Graz, SE Austria. He studied in Vienna and held permanent posts as an opera conductor in Dresden (1934–43), Vienna (1943–5, 1954–6), and elsewhere, and also appeared frequently in London, New York City, and Bayreuth. Remembered chiefly for his Mozart performances, he also conducted premieres of operas by Richard Strauss, a personal friend.

Böhm, Theobald *Boehm, Theobald*

Böhme or **Boehme, Jakob** [**boe**muh] (1575–1624) Theosophist and mystic, born in Altseidenberg, Germany. He became a shoemaker, but in 1600 had a mystical experience which led him towards meditation on divine things. *Aurora* (1612) contains revelations upon God, humanity, and nature, and shows considerable knowledge of Scripture and of the writings of alchemists. It was condemned by the ecclesiastical authorities of Gürlitz, and he was cruelly persecuted, but in 1623 he published *The Great Mystery* and *On the Election of Grace*, and his influence spread beyond Germany to Holland and England.

Bohm–Aharonov effect *Aharonov–Bohm effect*

Bohr, Niels (Henrik David) [baw(r)] (1885–1962) Physicist, born in Copenhagen, Denmark. He studied at Copenhagen University, went to England to work at Cambridge and Manchester, and in 1920 founded the Institute of Theoretical Physics in Copenhagen, which he directed until his death. He greatly extended the theory of atomic structure when he explained the spectrum of hydrogen by means of an atomic model and quantum theory (1913). During World War 2 he assisted atomic bomb research in America, returning to Copenhagen in 1945. He was awarded the Nobel Prize for Physics in 1922.

Bohr magnetron The magnetic moment of the electron, as given by relativistic quantum mechanics, treating the electron as a point particle; named after Niels Bohr; symbol μ_B; $\mu_B = eh/(4\pi m)$, where e and m are electron charge and mass, and h is Planck's constant; value $\mu_B = 9{\cdot}274 \times 10^{-24}$ J/T (joules per tesla); measured value of magnetic moment slightly different, suggesting the need for corrections to quantum mechanics. The nuclear magnetron μ_N is the corresponding expression for the proton, with proton mass replacing electron mass: $\mu_N = 5{\cdot}051 \times 10^{-27}$ J/T.

Boiardo, Matteo Maria, conte di (Count of) **Scandiano** [boy**ah(r)**doh] (c.1441–94) Poet, born in Scandiano, N Italy. He studied at Ferrara, and in 1462 married the daughter of the Count of Norellara. He lived at the court of Ferrara where he was employed on diplomatic missions, and was appointed governor in 1481 of Modena, and in 1487 of Reggio. His fame rests on the unfinished *Orlando Innamorato* (1486), a long narrative poem in which the Charlemagne romances are recast into *ottava rima*. Ariosto finished the story in *Orlando Furioso*.

boil An abscess at the base of a hair follicle, which results in a raised, reddened, and often painful swelling in the skin. It usually results from infection with *Staphylococcus aureus*.

Boileau(-Despréaux), Nicolas [bwahloh] (1636–1711) Poet and critic, born in Paris, France. He studied law and theology at Beauvais, but, as a man of means, devoted himself to literature. In 1677 the king appointed him, with Racine, official royal historian. *L'Art poétique* (Poetic Art), imitated by Pope in the *Essay on Criticism*, was published in 1674, along with the first part of the serio-comic *Lutrin*. His influence as a critic has been profound. He set up good sense, sobriety, elegance, and dignity of style as the cardinal literary virtues.

boiling point The point at which heat added to a liquid is no longer used to increase temperature but instead to form gas from the liquid. Formally, the boiling point temperature is reached when a liquid's vapour pressure equals external pressure. Boiling points thus decrease with altitude. Water may be boiled at room temperature by decreasing the pressure around it.

boiling water reactor *nuclear reactor*

Bois de Boulogne [bwah duh booloyn] A park of 962 ha/2380 acres situated on the W outskirts of Paris, France. Originally a royal hunting forest, it became a popular recreation area for Parisians in the 17th-c, and in 1852 was relandscaped along the lines of London's Hyde Park. The Longchamp racecourse was opened there in 1857.

Boise [boyzee] 43°37N 116°13W, pop (2000e) 185 800. State capital in Ada Co, SW Idaho, USA, on the Boise R; founded after the 1862 gold rush; airfield; railway; largest city in the state; contains several thousand people of Basque origin (largest Basque group in USA); trade and transportation centre; food processing and light manufacturing; Old Idaho Penitentiary, Idaho State museum.

Bolden, Buddy, popular name of **Charles Joseph Bolden** (1877–1931) Jazz cornetist, born in New Orleans, Louisiana, USA. He is a putative founder of jazz, a figure of mythic significance. He reputedly played his trumpet so powerfully that he could be heard for 10 miles in all directions. No recorded evidence survives, though scholars spent decades searching for an Edison cylinder said to have been made at the beginning of the 20th-c. In 1907, his uncontrollable fits of violence led to his incarceration for life, and he died in a fire at an asylum.

bolete [bohleet] A fungus with a typically mushroom-shaped fruiting body; fertile spore-producing layer present as a lining of tubes on underside of cap; commonly found on ground under trees; some species edible, others poisonous. (Subdivision: Basidiomycetes. Order: Agaricales.)

Boleyn, Anne [bolin], also spelled **Bullen** (c.1507–36) English queen, the second wife of **Henry VIII** from 1533–6. Daughter of Sir Thomas Boleyn by Elizabeth Howard, she secretly married Henry (Jan 1533), and was soon declared his legal wife (May); but within three months his passion for her had cooled. It was not revived by the birth (Sep 1533) of a princess (later Elizabeth I), still less by that of a stillborn son (Jan 1536). She was arrested and brought to the Tower, charged with treason, and beheaded (19 May). Henry married Jane Seymour 11 days later.

bolide [bohleed] An exceptionally brilliant meteor, or fireball, which explodes in our atmosphere. It makes a very loud bang, and in some cases scatters stony debris over a wide area.

Bolingbroke *Henry IV* (of England)

Bolingbroke, Henry St John, 1st Viscount (1678–1751) English statesman and writer, born in London, UK. He was educated at Eton, and may have gone to Oxford. After travelling in Europe, he entered parliament (1701), becoming secretary for war (1704), foreign secretary (1710), and joint leader of the Tory Party. He was made a peer in 1712. On the death of Queen Anne (1714), his Jacobite sympathies forced him to flee to France, where he wrote *Reflections on Exile*. He returned for a while to England (1725–35), but unable to attain political office he went back to France (1735–42). His last years were spent in London, where his works included the influential *Idea of a Patriot King* (1749).

Bolívar, Simón [boleevah(r), bolivah(r)], known as **the Liberator** (1783–1830) The national hero of Venezuela, Colombia, Ecuador, Peru, and Bolivia, born in Caracas. Having travelled in Europe, he played the most prominent part in the wars of independence in N South America. In 1819, he proclaimed and became president of the vast Republic of Colombia (modern Colombia, Venezuela, and Ecuador), which was finally liberated in 1822. He then took charge of the last campaigns of independence in Peru (1824). In 1826 he returned N to face growing political dissension. He resigned office (1830), and died on his way into exile.

Bolívar, Pico Andean peak in Mérida state, W Venezuela; height, 5007 m/16 427 ft; highest peak of the Cordillera de Mérida and of Venezuela; crowned with a bust of Bolívar.

Bolivia *p.202*

Böll, Heinrich (Theodor) [boel] (1917–85) Writer, born in Cologne, W Germany. A trilogy, *Und sagte kein einziges Worte* (1953, trans Acquainted with the Night), *Haus ohne Hüter* (1954, The Unguarded House), and *Das Brot der frühen Jahre* (1955, The Bread of our Early Years), depicting life in Germany during and after the Nazi regime, gained him a worldwide reputation. His later novels, characteristically satirizing modern German society, included *Die vorlorene Ehre der Katherina Blum* (1974, The Lost Honour of Katherina Blum). He was awarded the 1972 Nobel Prize for Literature.

boll weevil A small weevil that prevents the normal development of cotton flowers by its feeding activities. It is an economically important pest of cotton. (Order: Coleoptera. Family: Curculionidae.)

Bologna [bolohnya] 44°30N 11°20E, pop (2000e) 411 000. Capital city of Bologna province, Emilia-Romagna, N Italy; 83 km/52 mi N of Florence, at the foot of the Apennines; ancient Etruscan city, enclosed by remains of 13th–14th-c walls; archbishopric; airport; rail junction; university (11th-c); pasta, chocolate, sausages, shoes, chemicals, engineering, precision instruments, publishing, furniture; birthplace of Marconi, Pasolini; Church of San Petronio (14th-c), Church of San Domenico (13th-c), Pinacoteca Nazionale; two leaning towers (12th-c), the Asinelli and the Garisenda; music festival (summer).

Bolsheviks (Russ 'majority-ites') Members of the hard-line faction of the Marxist Russian Social Democratic Labour Party, formed by Lenin at the party's second congress in 1903; the forerunner of the Communist Party of the Soviet Union (abolished in 1991). After they split into two factions in 1912, the two parties competed for the leadership of the revolution against the Tsar. The Bolsheviks wanted revolution above all else; the Mensheviks, however, preferred reformism. In October 1917 the Bolsheviks led the revolution in Petrograd which established the first Soviet government.

Bolshoi Ballet [bolshoy] (Russian 'Great Ballet') The leading ballet company of Russia and, formerly, of the Soviet Union. Based in Moscow, it traces its origins back to its foundation (1773) as the dancing school for the Moscow Orphanage. In 1825 the newly formed Bolshoi Theatre took over the ballet company of the Petrovsky Theatre and moved into its premises. Throughout the 19th-c such renowned and influential choreographers as Petipa, Blasis, and Saint-Léon worked there. By the mid-20th-c the Bolshoi Ballet was one of the world's foremost ballet companies. After the collapse of communism, its subsidies were drastically cut and it fell into decline. Under the current directorship of Vladmir Vasiliev a new building, near the site of the present Bolshoi Theatre, is under construction.

Bolt, Robert (Oxton) (1924–95) Playwright, born in Sale, Greater Manchester, NW England, UK. He studied at Manchester University, served in the RAF and worked as a teacher before achieving success with *A Man for All Seasons* (1954). Other plays included *The Tiger and the Horse* (1960) and *State of Revolution* (1977). He also wrote screenplays, including *Lawrence of Arabia* (1962), *Dr Zhivago* (1965), *Ryan's Daughter* (1970), and *The Mission* (1986). He was an anti-nuclear activist in the 1960s, joining the 'Committee of 100', and was jailed for a month in 1961. He continued writing, despite being partly paralysed and left with speech difficulties, following a stroke in 1979.

Boltzmann, Ludwig (Eduard) [boltsman] (1844–1906) Physicist, born in Vienna, Austria. He studied at Vienna, where he became professor in 1895. He did important work on the kinetic theory of gases and established the principle of the equipartition of energy (*Boltzmann's law*). He laid the foundations of statistical mechanics by applying the laws of mechanics and the theory of probability to the motion of atoms, and his name was given to the *Boltzmann constant*, a fundamental constant of physics.

Boltzmann constant [boltsman] Symbol k, units J/K (joules per kelvin), value $1{\cdot}381 \times 10^{-23}$ J/K, defined as R/N_A, where R is the molar gas constant and N_A is Avogadro's constant; appears throughout the study of the statistical properties of gases; named after Ludwig Boltzmann.

Bolzano [boltsahnoh], Ger **Bozen** 46°30N 11°20E, pop (2000e) 106 000. Capital town of Bolzano province, Trentino-Alto Adige, N Italy; on R Isarco, SW of the Brenner Pass; chief commercial, industrial, and tourist centre of the region; mainly German-speaking; steel production, textiles, distilling, wine, canning, pianos; winter sports.

bomb A device used to cause an explosion, usually consisting of a container, an explosive substance (eg TNT, RDX), and a fuse.

Bolivia

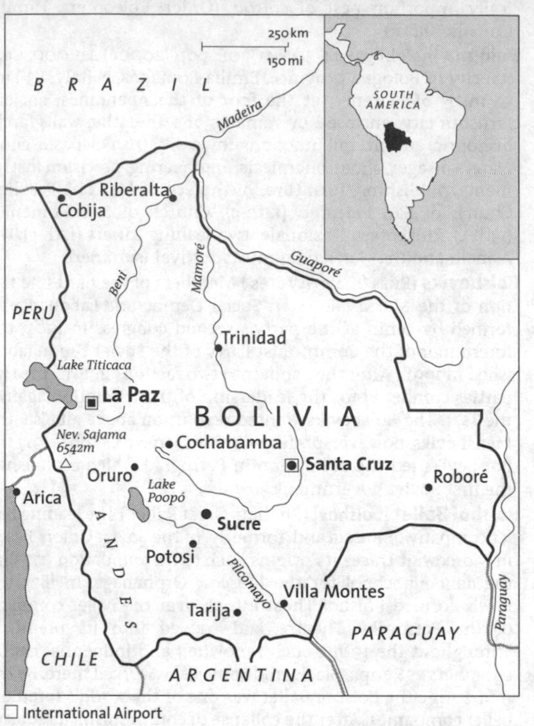

official name **Republic of Bolivia**, Span **República de Bolivia**
Local name Bolivia
Timezone GMT −4
Area 1 098 580 km²/424 052 sq mi
Population total (2002e) 8 401 000
Status Republic
Date of independence 1825
Capital La Paz (administrative), Sucre (legal)
Languages Spanish, Quechua, Aymará (all used offcially)
Ethnic groups Mestizo (31%), Quechua (25%), Aymará (25%), white (14%)
Religions Roman Catholic (95%), Baha'i (3%)
Physical features Landlocked country, bounded W by the Cordillera Occidental of the Andes, rising to 6542 m/21 463 ft at Sajama; separated from the Cordillera Real to the E by the flat, 400 km/250 mi-long Altiplano plateau, 3600 m/11 800 ft; major lakes, Titicaca and Poopó.
Climate Varies with altitude, ranging from consistently warm (26°C) and damp conditions (1800 mm/71 in of rainfall per year) in NE rainforests of Amazon Basin, to drought conditions in S; over 500 m/16 000 ft, conditions become sub-polar.
Currency 1 Boliviano (Bs) = 100 centavos
Economy Dependent on minerals for foreign exchange; silver largely exhausted, but replaced by tin (a fifth of world supply); oil and natural-gas pipelines to Argentina and Chile; illegally-produced cocaine.
GDP (2002e) $21·15 bn, per capita $2500
Human Development Index (2002) 0·653
History Part of Inca Empire, conquered by Spanish in 16th-c. Independence after war of liberation in 1825; much territory lost after wars with neighbouring countries; several changes of government and military coups during 1964–82; returned to civilian rule in 1982; governed by a bicameral Congress and an elected President and a Cabinet.
Head of State/Government
1982 Guido Vildoso Calderón
1982–5 Hernán Siles Suazo
1985–9 Victor Paz Estenssoro
1989–93 Jaime Paz Zamora
1993–7 Gonzalo Sánchez de Lozada
1997–2001 Hugo Bánzer Suárez
2001–2 Jorge Quiroga Ramírez
2002–3 Gonzalo Sánchez de Lozada
2003– Carlos Mesa

Generally bombs are distinguished from other explosive devices by means of delivery, in that they are not propelled towards their target. They normally use gravity (when dropped from aircraft) or are placed in position (as in the case of car bombs). Common types include blast, fragmentation, general purpose, anti-armour, and incendiary bombs. They can vary in size from the World War 2 'grand slam' bombs (10 000 kg of explosive) to car bombs (as little as 1 kg of explosive). Gravity and release speed determine an ordinary aircraft bomb's flight-path, although so-called **smart bombs** have a target-seeking guidance package in the nose which can pick up signals from targets on the ground ('illuminated' by laser energy, for example), and generate steering commands to guide the bomb onto a target.

Bombard, Alain Louis [bombah(r)] (1924–) Physician and marine biologist, born in Paris, France. In 1952, after preliminary trials in the Mediterranean, he set out across the Atlantic alone in his rubber dinghy *L'Hérétique* without food or water to prove his claim that shipwreck castaways could sustain life on nothing more than fish, plankton, rain water and controlled drinking of small amounts of sea water. He landed at Barbados 62 days later. He started a marine laboratory at Saint-Malo for the study of the physiopathology of the sea.

bombardier beetle A small beetle of genus *Brachinus*. As a protective mechanism, adults fire clouds of caustic vapour, expelled by an explosion caused by mixing chemicals in glands at the rear end of the body. It can fire repeatedly at short intervals. (Order: Coleoptera. Family: Carabidae.)

Bombay *Mumbai*

Bombay duck Slender-bodied fish (*Harpadon nehereus*) with large jaws and barb-like teeth; common in the tropical Indian Ocean, especially the Bay of Bengal; length up to 40 cm/16 in; flesh soft and translucent; important food fish, caught in fixed nets in brackish waters, and sun-dried. (Family: Harpadontidae.)

Bonaire [bonair] pop (2000e) 11 500; area 288 sq km/111 sq mi. Island of the S Netherlands Antilles, E Caribbean, 60 km/37 mi N of Venezuela; composed of coralline limestone; rises to 241 m/791 ft in the hilly NW; low-lying coastal plain in the S; length 35 km/22 mi; capital, Kralendijk; airport; tourism, salt, textiles; Washington-Slagbaai National Park, area 59 sq km/23 sq mi, established in 1969; underwater park, area 60 sq km/23 sq mi.

Bonaparte, Jérôme [bohnapah(r)t] (1784–1860) King of Westphalia (1807–13), born in Ajaccio, Corsica, the youngest brother of Napoleon. He served in the navy (1800–2) and lived in New York (1803–5), marrying **Elizabeth Patterson** (1785–1879) in Baltimore in 1803, a marriage which Napoleon declared null and void. Jérôme was given a high military command by Napoleon in the Prussian campaign of 1806, led an army corps at Wagram in 1809, incurred his brother's displeasure during the invasion of Russia in 1812, but fought with tenacity at Waterloo (1815). After accepting exile in Rome, Florence, and Switzerland, he returned to Paris in 1847. His nephew Napoleon III appointed him governor of the Invalides, and created him a marshal of France.

Bonaparte, Joseph [**boh**napah(r)t] (1768–1844) King of Naples and Sicily (1806–8) and of Spain (1808–13), born in Corte, Corsica, the eldest surviving brother of Napoleon I. He served Napoleon on diplomatic missions and was a humane sovereign in S Italy, but faced continuous rebellion as a nominated ruler in Spain, where his army was decisively defeated by Wellington at Vittoria (1813). He spent much of his life in exile in New Jersey, but settled in Florence for the last years of his life.

Bonaparte, Napoleon [**boh**napah(r)t] *Napoleon I / III*

Bonaventure or **Bonaventura, St** [**bon**avencher], known as **Doctor Seraphicus** ('Seraphic Doctor'), originally **Giovanni di Fidanza** (c.1221–74) Theologian, born near Orvieto, C Italy. He became a Franciscan (1243), a professor of theology at Paris (1253), general of his order (1257), and Cardinal Bishop of Albano (1273). He was canonized by Sixtus IV (1482), and in 1587 was declared by Pope Sixtus V the sixth of the great Doctors of the Church. Feast day 15 July.

Bond, Alan (1938–) Businessman, born in London, UK. He emigrated to Fremantle, Western Australia, in 1951, and formed a company dealing in insurance, property, and resources. The Bond Corporation developed extensive interests in Australian newspapers and television, brewing, oil and gas, and gold mining. In 1983 his syndicate's yacht *Australia II* was the first since 1870 to challenge the USA successfully for the America's Cup. With the ending of the economic boom in 1987, his empire began to fall: receivers were appointed to Bond Brewing in 1989, and in 1992 he was declared bankrupt and convicted on a charge of dishonesty in business dealings with a merchant bank. He was acquitted after spending six months in jail, but in 1996 he was sentenced to three years' imprisonment for failing to declare assets, and in 1997 received an additional 4-year sentence on charges of fraud.

Bond, Edward (1934–) Playwright and director, born in London, UK. His first play, *The Pope's Wedding*, was given a Sunday night reading at the Royal Court Theatre, London, in 1962 and aroused great controversy. *Saved* (1965) achieved notoriety through a scene in which a baby in a pram is stoned to death. Later plays such as *Narrow Road to the Deep North* (1968) use historical themes to look at broad contemporary issues. Other plays include a reworking of Shakespeare's play *Lear* (1971), a trilogy *The War Plays* (1985), and *At the Inland Sea* (1996), sub-titled 'a play for young people'.

bond A loan to a company or a government. The loan carries interest payments and is repaid after several years. It can be bought and sold on the stock market, and is a relatively secure investment often held by insurance companies and pension funds.

Bondi [**bon**diy] A well-known resort beach in the Sydney suburb of Waverley, New South Wales, SE Australia.

Bondi, Sir Hermann (1919–) Mathematical physicist and astronomer, born in Vienna, Austria. He studied at Cambridge, where he held academic posts (1945–54) after working for the British Admiralty during World War 2. He was appointed professor of mathematics at King's College, London (1954), director-general of the European Space Research Organisation (1967–71), chief scientific adviser, Ministry of Defence (1971–7), chief scientist, Department of Energy (1977–80), chairman of the Natural Environment Research Council (1980–4), and Master of Churchill College, Cambridge (1983–90). He is best known as one of the originators of the steady-state theory of the universe.

bone The hard tissue component of the vertebrate skeleton. It is composed of two functionally important principal components physically blended together: an organic element (mainly collagen), 25% of the weight of the fully formed bone, and a mineral matrix (calcium, phosphate, and variable amounts of magnesium, sodium, carbonate, citrate, and fluoride), having a crystalline structure. It basically consists of many cylindrical units (*osteons*), each with a central canal, containing bone-forming cells (*osteoblasts*), blood vessels, and nerve filaments, surrounded by bony tissue. Long bones consist of a shaft (a hollow tube surrounded by compact bone) and the ends (a network of spongy bone). Growth in length occurs in the region between shaft and ends (the *epiphyseal growth plate*). Growth in width occurs by deposition of bone from the surface membrane (*periosteum*). When the growth plate disappears (between puberty and 25 years) growth in length ceases, as the shaft has fused with the ends. As bones grow, they increase in size and also change shape. Bone shape and dimensions are genetically determined, but are also influenced by hormonal, nutritional, mechanical, and neural factors. Calcium, phosphorus, and vitamins A, C, and D are all required for normal bone growth and development. Abnormal pressures on bone (from a tumour or aneurysm) may cause bone erosion. Bone deprived of a nerve supply and muscular paralysis result in poor bone development and atrophy. Examples of bone disorders, diseases, and infections are dislocation, fracture, osteoarthritis, osteoporosis, Paget's disease, and rickets.

bone-black Animal charcoal obtained by heating bones in closed retorts. It contains calcium and magnesium phosphates as well as carbon, and is used as an adsorbent to remove colouring matter from food liquids such as raw sugar syrup.

bone marrow An accumulation of cells and supporting tissues found within the central cavity of all bones. *Yellow marrow* consists of fat cells, blood vessels, and a minimal framework of reticular cells and fibres. *Red marrow* consists of numerous blood cells of all kinds, as well as the substances from which these cells are formed. At birth all bones contain highly cellular red marrow; with increasing age the marrow becomes fattier, until in adults red marrow is present only in the vertebrae, sternum, ribs, flat bones of the skull and pelvis, and upper ends of the femur and humerus. The functions of red marrow are (1) the formation of red blood cells (*erythrocytes*), blood platelets, granulocytes, and to a lesser extent monocytes and lymphocytes, and (2) the destruction of old (c.120 days), worn-out erythrocytes.

Bonfire Night *Guy Fawkes Night*

bongo A spiral-horned antelope (*Tragelaphus euryceros*) native to equatorial Africa; brown with thin vertical white stripes; stiff erect hairs along spine; each cheek with two white spots; white line joining eyes; usually inhabits dense forest.

bongos A pair of wooden conical or cylindrical drums with single heads of skin or plastic, played with the hands. The shells are usually joined together, and in some varieties the heads may be tuned to different pitches. Originating in Cuba c.1900, they are used throughout Latin America, and frequently elsewhere.

Bonham-Carter, Helena [**bon**am] (1966–) Actress, born in London, UK. Her gift for playing quintessential English heroines brought her early fame; she made her cinematic debut as Lady Jane Grey in *Lady Jane* (1985). Later film credits include *Hamlet* (1990), *Howard's End* (1992), *Mary Shelley's Frankenstein* (1994), *Twelfth Night* (1996), and *The Heart of Me* (2003). Television work includes her role as Anne Boleyn in ITV's *Henry VIII* (2003).

Bonhoeffer, Dietrich [**bon**hoefer] (1906–45) Lutheran pastor and theologian, and opponent of Nazism, born in Wrocław, SW Poland (formerly Breslau, Prussia). He studied at Tübingen and Berlin, and left Germany in 1933 in protest against the Nazi enforcement of anti-Jewish legislation. He worked in London until 1935, then returned to Germany to combat anti-Semitism, becoming head of a pastoral seminary of the German Confessing Church until its closure by the Nazis in 1937. He became deeply involved in the German resistance movement and in 1943 was imprisoned until 1945, when he was hanged at Flossenbürg. His writings include *Ethik* (1949, Ethics) and *Widerstand und Ergebung* (1951, trans Letters and Papers from Prison) on the place of Christian belief in the modern world.

Boniface, St [bonifas], originally **Wynfrith**, known as **the Apostle of Germany** (c.680–c.754) Anglo-Saxon missionary, born in Wessex, England. A Benedictine monk, he taught in the monastery of Nursling near Romsey. He set out in 718 to preach the Gospel to all the tribes of Germany, assisting Willibrord (719–22), and was consecrated Bishop (723), Archbishop, and Primate of Germany (732). He was killed at Dokkum by heathens. Feast day 5 June.

Bonington, Sir Chris(tian John Storey) (1934–) Mountaineer and photo-journalist, born in London, UK. He trained at Sandhurst Military Academy. His first mountaineering ascents include Annapurna II (1960), Nuptse (1961), and the first British ascents of the North Wall of the Eiger (1962) and Mt Vinson in Antarctica (1983). He led or co-led many successful expeditions, including Annapurna South Face (1970) and Everest (1972, 1975 SW face), and reached the summit of Everest himself in 1985. He was knighted in 1996.

Bonington, Richard Parkes (1802–28) Painter, born near Nottingham, Nottinghamshire, C England, UK. About 1817 his family moved to Calais, and there and at Paris he studied art, and became a friend of Delacroix. His first works were exhibited in the Salon in 1822, mostly sketches of Le Havre and Lillebonne. He excelled in light effects achieved by the use of a large expanse of sky, broad areas of pure colour, and the silhouetting of dark and light masses, as well as his rich colouring of heavy draperies and brocades.

Bonin Islands, Jap **Ogasawara-shoto** area 104 sq km/40 sq mi. Group of 27 volcanic islands in the W Pacific Ocean, c.965 km/600 mi S of Tokyo, Japan; largest island, Chichijima; first colonized by Europeans and Hawaiians, 1830; annexed by Japanese, 1876; taken by USA, 1953; returned to Japan, 1968; sugar cane, bananas, cocoa.

Bonino, Emma [boneenoh] (1949–) Politician, born near Turin, NW Italy. Born into a poor farming family, at the age of 28 she became pregnant and chose to have an abortion, then illegal in Italy. To draw attention to the squalid conditions of underground abortions, she made hers public, was sent to jail, went on hunger strike, and helped to change the law. She then joined the small Radical Party and campaigned successfully for the introduction of a divorce law. In 1995 she was chosen European Commissioner for fisheries, consumer affairs, and humanitarian aid, with responsibility for the controversial Common Fisheries Policy. In 1999, along with all the other commissioners, she resigned following criticism of the European Commission's administration. In the same year she was elected to the European Parliament.

bonito [boneetoh] Medium-sized tuna widely distributed in open ocean surface waters, living in compact schools; length up to 90 cm/3 ft; body steel blue to olive dorsally, with oblique black stripes, sides silver to yellow; important commercially and prized as sport fish. (Genus: *Sarda*. Family: Scombridae.)

Bonn 50°43N 7°06E, pop (2000e) 300 000. Capital city of former West Germany, in Cologne district; on R Rhine, 25 km/15 mi SSE of Cologne; early Roman fort on the Rhine; seat of Electors of Cologne (13th–16th-c); part of Prussia, 1815; badly bombed in World War 2; capital status since 1949; airport at Cologne; railway; university (1818); service industries, plastics, packaging materials, aluminium; birthplace of Beethoven; spa resort at Bad Godesberg; 11th–13th-c minster, Beethovenhalle; International Beethoven Festival every three years (Sep).

Bonnard, Pierre [bonah(r)] (1867–1947) Painter and lithographer, born in Paris, France. He trained at the Académie Julien, then joined the group called *Les Nabis*, which included Denis and Vuillard, with whom he formed the Intimist group. Ignoring the movement towards abstraction, he continued to paint interiors and landscapes, in which everything is subordinated to the subtlest rendering of light and colour effects.

Bonner, Neville Thomas (1922–99) Australian politician, born in Tweed Heads, New South Wales, SE Australia. He had little formal education, but was president of the One People of Australia League (1967–73). He filled a casual Senate vacancy in 1971, becoming the first Aboriginal member of the Australian parliament. The following year, standing for the Liberal Party, he was elected as a representative for Queensland. He stood unsuccessfully as an independent member in 1983 and just before his death became involved in the pro-monarchist movement.

Bonner, Yelena (1923–) Civil rights campaigner, born in Moscow, Russia. After the arrest of her parents in Stalin's 'great purge' of 1937, she was brought up in Leningrad by her grandmother. She joined the Soviet Communist Party in 1965, but became disillusioned after the invasion of Czechoslovakia (1968) and drifted into dissident activities. She married **Andrei Sakharov** in 1971 and resigned from the party a year later. During the next 14 years she and her husband led the Soviet dissident movement. Following a KGB crackdown, Sakharov was banished to internal exile in Gorky (Nizhni Novgorod) in 1980, and Bonner suffered a similar fate in 1984. The couple were finally released in 1986 by the Gorbachev administration, and remained prominent campaigners for greater democratization.

Bonney, William H, Jr, known as **Billy the Kid**, originally (?) **Henry McCarty** (1859–81) Bandit and gunfighter, born in New York City, USA. His family moved West, eventually to New Mexico. A killer from the age of 12, he achieved legendary notoriety for his part in the Lincoln County 'War' that pitted rival cattle barons against each other. He was captured by Sheriff Pat Garrett in 1880, and sentenced to hang, but escaped from jail, to be tracked down and shot by Garrett some months later. His brief life has formed the subject for numerous films.

Bonnie and Clyde Notorious robbery partners: **Clyde Barrow** (1909–34), born in Telico, Texas, USA, and **Bonnie Parker** (1911–34), born in Rowena, Texas. Despite the popular romantic image of the duo, they and their gang were also responsible for a number of murders. The pair met in 1932. When Barrow first visited Parker's house, he was arrested on seven accounts of burglary and car theft, convicted, and sentenced to two years in jail. Parker smuggled a gun to him and he escaped. With their gang, which included Barrow's brother and wife, they continued to rob and murder until they were betrayed by a friend and shot dead at a police road-block in Louisiana.

Bonnie Prince Charlie *Stuart, Charles*

bonobo *chimpanzee*

bonsai The technique or practice of growing dwarfed plants in which all parts – stems, leaves, flowers – are in proportion. The effect is achieved by growing the plants in small pots, and by careful pruning of the roots to restrict growth. It is a Japanese speciality.

bontebok [bontebok] An ox-antelope (*Damaliscus dorcas*) native to S Africa; long face; lyre-shaped horns ringed with ridges; dark brown with white face and underparts; two subspecies: **bontebok** (with white rump) and **blesbok** (with brown rump).

bonxie *skua*

bony fish Any of the very large group Osteichthyes, comprising all true bony fishes (18 000 species; 450 families); includes both the ray-finned fishes (Actinopterygii) and the fleshy-finned fishes (Sarcopterygii), the latter containing the lungfishes (Dipnoi) and tassel-finned fishes (Crossopterygii); endoskeleton made of bone; with air bladder or lungs.

booby A bird related to gannets, native to tropical and subtropical seas; streamlined, with a colourful pointed bill. It catches fish by diving vertically into the water; air sacs beneath the skin of its face absorb the shock of impact. (Genus: *Sula*, 6 species. Family: Sulidae.)

book A handwritten or printed document, comprising at least 25 leaves of paper, vellum, or parchment bound together along one edge, generally affixed within a protective cover, and usually intended for non-periodical publication. The earliest books can be traced back to China in the 3rd-c BC, in the form of wood or bamboo leaves bound with cords. In the West the papyrus roll used by the Egyptians and Greeks was superseded in Greece and Rome by the codex (bound, handwritten leaves of vellum or parchment). Superbly written and illuminated manuscript books were made in the monasteries of W Europe from the 'Dark Ages' until well after the development of European printing in c.1450.

The earliest known printed book is Chinese (868). All the world's printed books before the 15th-c were Chinese, Korean, or Japanese; and between 1450 and 1750 Chinese printed books exceeded those of the rest of the world. In Europe, printing, along with the introduction of paper in the 14th-c, led to a very large increase in book production. Books from this period, known as *incunabula*, number some 35 000. The earliest printed books, such as Gutenberg's '42-line' Bible of 1456, were set in black-letter type and closely modelled on the design of mediaeval manuscript books. New features, such as title-pages and page numbers, began to appear towards the end of the 15th-c. Aldus Manutius, working in Venice, introduced a revolution in book production in 1501: pocket-size editions of Latin classics set in compact italic types in print-runs as long as 1000 copies. Following the Reformation, censorship became increasingly repressive: the mid-16th-c saw the publication of the *Index* of prohibited books, and in England a royal charter giving the Stationers' Company a virtual monopoly over who might print what. The first book printed in America was the *Whole Booke of Psalmes* ('Bay Psalm Book') in 1640. The 19th-c brought many technical innovations, such as mechanical typesetting and cheaper paper, and several changes in retailing and use, following the mushroom growth of railway bookstalls and the development of public libraries. With the 20th-c came the heyday of the private press movement, the steady development of book clubs, new techniques in printing, and a notable growth in the numbers of new titles published, particularly in paperback.

bookbinding Techniques for the joining of leaves along one edge and casing them in a cover to form a codex or book. All bookbinding was done by hand until the 19th-c, and the craft tradition lives on for the production of single copies and *editions de luxe*. Single leaves and folded sections of two or more leaves are stitched together with thread around cords attached to the cover boards; the spine and boards are covered with leather or cloth, and titling is stamped on the spine. Modern mechanical bookbinding automates these processes, though eliminating the cords. Various techniques such as adhesive or 'perfect' (cut-off, glued backs) and 'burst' (glue forced through the backs of folded sections) binding have replaced the thread. In paperback binding, light boards are glued around adhesive-bound books.

Booker Prize Britain's most prestigious literary prize, sponsored by Booker McConnell Ltd and administered by the National Book League in the UK. Established in 1969 and worth £20 000, it is awarded annually to the best full-length novel written in English during the preceding 12 months by a citizen of the UK, the Commonwealth, Eire, Pakistan, or South Africa. The judging panel, consisting of prominent critics, writers, publishers, and academics, draws up a shortlist from which a winner is chosen.

book fairs International collaborative occasions for the buying and selling of books and the right to publish translations of books. The principal fairs include those held at Frankfurt, Bologna (children's books), London, Moscow, and Jerusalem, and that of the American Booksellers' Association, which is held at various locations in the USA.

booklouse A small flattened insect which typically feeds on old books or dried organic material. It can cause extensive damage in libraries.

Book of Changes, Chin **Yijing** or **I-ching** One of Chinese literature's oldest and most treasured works, possibly dating in part from the 11th-c BC, with additions in the 7th-c and 1st-c BC. It comprises 64 hexagrams, each formed by combining two out of eight trigrams of three broken (*yin*) or unbroken (*yang*) lines. Each hexagram has a commentary, and there are appendices (incorrectly attributed to Confucius). The trigrams were by tradition devised by the mythological dragon-emperor Fuxi. The *Yijing* could yield guidance on problems and imminent decisions, since each hexagram supposedly corresponded to typical human issues and life-change patterns, and the underpinning assumption was a unification of nature and humanity in the cosmos. It has been studied throughout Chinese history.

Book of Common Prayer The official directory of worship or service-book of the Church of England, widely honoured and followed in churches of the Anglican Communion. Largely composed by Archbishop Cranmer, it was first introduced in 1549, and revised in 1552, 1604, and finally 1662. Until 1975, revisions in England required the approval of Parliament. It is generally considered a landmark of English prose.

book of hours A prayer book, popular in the Middle Ages, and known in England as a **primer**. It typically contained the Little Office of Our Lady, psalms of penitence, and the Office of the Dead (usually in Latin).

Book of Songs, Chin **Shijing** A collection of 311 Chinese odes, some antedating 600 BC. Used freely in teaching by Confucius, it later became a classic memorized by all scholars as a primer of socio-political morality. It gives rich evidence on early China and the Chinese view of life, yielding more detail on the lives of ordinary people than any other ancient world text. Its poems preceded Europe by a millennium in using rhyme, and influenced the style and subject-matter of Chinese poetry for 2000 years.

Book of the Dead An ancient Egyptian collection of magical and religious texts. Copies were often buried with the dead as a protection and comfort in the after-life.

bookworm The common name of various larval and adult insects that damage books by feeding on the paper and binding, and by burrowing activity. It is used particularly of the booklouse and silverfish.

Boole, George (1815–64) Mathematician and logician, born in Lincoln, Lincolnshire, EC England, UK. He was largely self-taught, and though without a degree was appointed professor of mathematics at Cork in 1849. He did important work on finite differences and differential equations, but is primarily known for his *Mathematical Analysis of Logic* (1847) and *Laws of Thought* (1854), pioneering works in modern symbolic logic.

Boolean algebra An algebra on sets, devised by Boole, developed as an algebra of symbolic logic. The differences from arithmetic algebra can be illustrated by the absorption laws on sets A, B and C: $A + A = A$ and $(A + B)(A + C) = A + BC$. The similarities between the algebra of sets and that of logic can be seen by comparing $A \cap A = A$ and $p \wedge p = p$, the latter being read 'p and p implies p', where p is a statement. The laws of Boolean algebra derive from those relating to the union and intersection of sets. There is a similar algebra governing the use of 'and' and (inclusive) 'or' with propositions; indeed if p and q are propositions and $P = \{x{:}px\}$ (the set of x such that p is true when applied to x) and $Q = \{x{:}qx\}$,,, then 'p and q' is true of the x in the intersection of P and Q and 'p or q' is true of the set of x which are in the union of P and Q.

boomer *mountain beaver*

boomerang A throwing stick, so shaped as to fly great distances and strike a severe blow; mainly Australian, but known elsewhere (eg among certain American Indian groups). Some are made to take a curved path and return, and are used mainly for play or training.

boomslang A venomous African snake (*Dispholidus typus*); long thin green or dark brown body; length, up to 2 m/6½ ft; three fangs; lives in trees adjoining grassland; eats lizards, birds, frogs. (Family: Colubridae.)

Boone, Daniel (c.1734–1820) Pioneer, born in Berks Co, Pennsylvania, USA. His family moved to North Carolina, and from there he went to Kentucky. From 1769 he lived in the forest, exploring much of the country with his brother, and helping to open up a trail through the Cumberland Gap in the Appalachian Mts. He was twice captured by Indians, and (1775–8) repeatedly repelled Indian attacks on a stockade fort which he had erected, now Boonesborough. He was a legend even in his lifetime.

Boot, Sir Jesse, Baron Trent (1850–1931) Drug manufacturer, born in Nottingham, Nottinghamshire, C England, UK. At 13 he inherited his father's herbalist shop, and in 1877 opened his first chemist's shop in Nottingham. He began large-scale drug manufacture (1892), and soon after the beginning of the 20th-c was controlling the largest pharmaceutical retail trade in the world, with over a thousand branches by 1931. He was made a peer in 1929.

Boötes [bohohteez] (Lat 'herdsman') A large N hemisphere constellation. It contains Arcturus, a red giant, the brightest star in the N sky, radius 28 times the Sun. Distance: 11 parsec. Doubtless one of the first stars to be named, it is mentioned in literature from the earliest times.

Booth, Edwin (Thomas) (1833–93) Actor, born near Bel Air, Maryland, USA, the brother of John Wilkes Booth. He played Tressel at the age of 16 to his father's Richard III, and rose to the top of his profession, touring abroad on several occasions. In 1864 he produced *Hamlet* in New York City for a record run.

Booth, John Wilkes (1839–65) Assassin, born near Bel Air, Maryland, USA, the brother of Edwin Thomas Booth. He became an actor, and though less well-known than his brother, was popular in the South during the early 1860s. A strong supporter of the Southern cause, in 1865 he entered into a conspiracy to avenge the defeat of the Confederates, and shot President Lincoln at Ford's Theatre, Washington, DC, on 14 April. He managed to escape to Virginia, but was tracked down and shot.

Booth, William (1829–1912) Religous leader, founder and general of the Salvation Army, born in Nottingham, Nottinghamshire, C England, UK. In 1844 he was converted and became a Methodist New Connexion minister on Tyneside. He began 'The Christian Mission' in London's East End (1865), which in 1878 developed into the Salvation Army. The Army spread throughout the world, with a whole new network of social and regenerative agencies. His book, *In Darkest England and the Way Out* (1890), tells of his philosophy and motivation. His eldest son, **William Branwell Booth** (1856–1929), was chief-of-staff from 1880 and succeeded his father as general (1912). His second son, **Ballington Booth** (1857–1940), was commander of the army in Australia (1883–5) and the USA (1887–96), but resigned after disagreement with his father, and founded a similar organization, Volunteers of America. One of his daughters, **Evangeline Cora Booth** (1865–1950), became a US citizen and was elected general in 1934. A grand-daughter, **Catherine Branwell Booth** (1884–1987), was a commissioner in the Army.

Boothe, Clare *Luce, Clare Boothe*

Booths, Feast of *Sukkoth*

bootlegging The illegal manufacture or distribution of alcoholic drink or other highly taxed goods, such as cigarettes. The term is mainly used with reference to the smuggling of alcohol into the USA during the Prohibition era (1920–33). This became a major illegal industry, which led to the development of organized crime on a large scale. Bootlegging still exists in those parts of the USA where the sale of alcoholic drinks is prohibited.

bop *bebop*

Bophuthatswana [bopootatswahna], locally **Bop** Former independent black homeland in South Africa; comprised seven separate units of land in Cape, Free State, and Transvaal provinces; self-government, 1971; second homeland to receive independence from South Africa (not recognized internationally), 1977; incorporated into North West province in the South African constitution of 1994.

boracic acid *boric acid*

borage A robust annual (*Borago officinalis*), growing to 60 cm/24 in, covered in stiff, white bristles, native to C Europe and the Mediterranean region; leaves oval, rough; flowers 2 cm/¾ in diameter, bright blue, drooping, with five spreading petals and black anthers. Cultivated as a herb, its bruised leaves smell of cucumber. (Family: Boraginaceae.)

boranes [bohraynz] Compounds of boron and hydrogen, the simplest being diborane (B_2H_6). They are high-energy compounds, and have been used as rocket fuels. They are oxidized to boric acid. The reaction is $B_2H_6 + 1\frac{1}{2}O_2 \rightarrow 2H_3BO_3$. Compounds with CH^+ replacing BH are called *carboranes* or *carbaboranes*.

borate *boric acid*

borax [bohraks] $Na_2B_4O_7.10H_2O$; a hydrated salt of boric acid. It forms insoluble salts with Ca^{2+} and Mg^{2+} ions, and thus is useful as a water softener and cleanser. Borax in a less hydrated form ($4H_2O$) is the most important source of boron. It is an important ingredient in borosilicate (Pyrex®) glasses.

Bordeaux [baw(r)doh], Lat **Burdigala** 44°50N 0°36W, pop (2000e) 222 000. Inland port and capital of Gironde department, SW France, on R Garonne; major port, and cultural and commercial centre for SW; 480 km/298 mi SW of Paris and 100 km/60 mi from the Atlantic; held by the English, 1154–1453; centre during the wars of the Fronde; temporary seat of government in 1870, 1914, and 1940; centre of wine-growing region, Médoc (N), Graves and Sauternes (S), and Entre-deux-Mers (between Garonne and Dordogne Rivers); airport; railway; archbishopric; university (1441); cathedral; shipbuilding, chemicals, wine trade (claret), oil refining, fishing; Church of St Seurin (12th–15th-c), Grand Theatre (1773–80), Pont de Pierre (1813–21).

Borden, Lizzie (Andrew) (1860–1927) Alleged murderess, born in Fall River, Massachusetts, USA. In one of the most sensational murder trials in US history, she was accused of murdering her wealthy father and hated step-mother with an axe in 1892. She claimed to have been outside in the barn at the time of the murder, and despite a wealth of circumstantial evidence she was acquitted. She lived out her life in Fall River, and was buried alongside her father and step-mother. The case is immortalized in the rhyme *Lizzie Borden took an axe and gave her mother forty whacks; And when she saw what she had done; she gave her father forty one.*

Borden, Sir Robert (Laird) (1854–1937) Canadian statesman and prime minister (1911–20), born in Grand Pré, Nova Scotia, SE Canada. He practised as a barrister, became leader of the Conservative Party (1901), overthrew Laurier's Liberal government over the issue of reciprocity with the USA (1911), and became prime minister. He organized Canada for war, and was influential in arranging a separate Canadian membership in the League of Nations.

Border, Allan (Robert) (1955–) Cricketer, born in Sydney, New South Wales, SE Australia. Educated in Sydney, he became a professional cricketer in 1977, made his Test debut against England in 1978–9, and was captain 1984–94. The Australian team regained much of its lustre under his leadership, regaining the Ashes in 1989 and retaining them in 1990–1 and 1993. A left-hander, he was Australia's most prolific batsman since Don Bradman, and on his retirement in 1994 held Test records for the most Test appearances (156), and having captained Australia in more Tests than anyone (93). His most outstanding achievement is as the highest run-scorer in the history of Test cricket: in 1993 he beat Sunil Gavaskar's record with 10 123 runs, and he increased this record to a final 11 174 runs. He was Australian of the Year in 1990.

Border terrier A breed of dog, developed in the Scottish/English border hills to hunt foxes; small and active; solid, flat-ended muzzle; small ears; thick, stiff, wiry coat; usually golden or reddish brown.

Bordet, Jules (Jean Baptiste Vincent) [baw(r)day] (1870–1961) Physiologist, born in Soignies, S Belgium. He became director of the Pasteur Institute, Brabant (1901), professor at Brussels (1907), and recognized the immunity factors in blood serum. He discovered alexine and (1906) the microbe of whooping cough (Bordetella). He was awarded the 1919 Nobel Prize for Physiology or Medicine.

bore A nearly vertical wall of water that may be produced as a result of a tide, tsunami, or seiche. Bores usually occur in funnel-shaped estuaries with sloping bottoms. Bottom friction slows the advancing wave front, and water piles up behind to produce a nearly vertical bore face. The rapidly moving wall of water is followed by a less steep rise in sea level accompanied by swift upstream currents.

boreal forests The dense, coniferous forests of North America, Europe, and Asia. Characteristic tree species include fir, hemlock, spruce, and pine in more open areas. It is sometimes regarded as synonymous with *taiga*, though the vegetation canopy in the boreal forest is less open, with relatively little light reaching the forest floor.

borecole [baw(r)kohl] *kale*

Borg, Björn (Rune) (1956–) Tennis player, born in Södertälje, SE Sweden. He left school at 14 to concentrate on tennis, and at 15 was selected for the Swedish Davis Cup team. He was Wimbledon Junior Champion at 16. In 1976 he won the first of his record five consecutive Wimbledon singles titles (1976–80). He also won the Italian championship twice and the French Open six times between 1974 and 1981. His Wimbledon reign ended in 1981 when he lost in the final to John McEnroe. He retired in 1983, having written his autobiography, *My Life and Games* (1980).

Borgå *Porvoo*

Borge, Victor [baw(r)guh], originally **Børge Rosenbaum** (1909–2000) Entertainer and pianist, born in Copenhagen, Denmark. He studied at the Royal Danish Academy of Music, Copenhagen, and in Vienna and Berlin. He made his debut as a pianist in 1926, and as a revue actor in 1933. From 1940 he worked in the USA for radio, television, and theatre, and performed with leading symphony orchestras on worldwide tours since 1956. He was best known for his comedy sketches combining music and narrative.

Borges, Jorge Luis [baw(r)khes] (1899–1986) Writer, born in Buenos Aires, Argentina. He studied there and at Geneva and Cambridge. From 1918 he was in Spain, where he was a member of the avant-garde Ultraist literary group, returning to Argentina in 1921. His first book of poems, *Fervor de Buenos Aires*, was published in 1923, and in 1941 appeared the first collection of the intricate and fantasy-woven short stories for which he is famous. Later collections include *Ficciónes* (1944, 1946, Fictions), *El Aleph* (1949), and *El Hacedor* (1960, trans Dreamtigers).

Borghese [baw(r)gayzay] A great 13th-c family of ambassadors and jurists of Siena, afterwards (16th-c) at Rome. Their members include **Camillo Borghese** (1552–1621), who ascended the papal throne in 1605 as Paul V, and **Prince Camillo Filippo Ludovico Borghese** (1775–1832), who joined the French army, married Napoleon's sister Marie Pauline (1803), and became Governor-General of Piedmont. The Borghese Palace and the Villa Borghese still contain one of the finest collections of paintings in Rome.

Borgia [baw(r)ja] Italian form of **Borja**, an ancient family in the Spanish province of Valencia. Their members include **Alfonso Borja** (1378–1458), who accompanied Alfonso of Aragon to Rome, and was elected pope as Calixtus III. **Rodrigo Borgia** (1431–1503), his nephew, became pope as Alexander VI (1492). Two of Rodrigo's children became especially notorious. **Cesare Borgia** (1476–1507) was a brilliant general and administrator, succeeding his brother (whom he may have murdered) as Captain-General of the Church. In two campaigns he became master of Romagna, Perugia, Siena, Piombino, and Urbino, and planned a Kingdom of Central Italy. After the death of Alexander (1502), his enemies rallied. He surrendered at Naples, was imprisoned, escaped (1506), but soon after died while fighting for the King of Navarre. **Lucrezia Borgia** (1480–1519) was married three times by her father, for political reasons, finally becoming the wife of Alfonso d'Este, Duke of Ferrara. She has been represented as a person of wantonness, vices, and crimes; but she died enjoying the respect of her subjects, a patroness of learning and of the arts.

Borglum, (John) Gutzon (de la Mothe) [baw(r)gluhm] (1867–1941) Sculptor, born in St Charles, Idaho, USA. He won renown for works of colossal proportions, such as the famous Mt Rushmore National Memorial, hewn out of the mountainside (completed in 1939). Other huge works include the head of Lincoln in the US Capitol Rotunda. His brother **Solon Hannibal Borglum** (1868–1922) also won fame as a sculptor.

boric acid H_3BO_3; a weak acid, with antiseptic properties. Dilute solutions have a pH of about 6, while partially neutralized solutions have a pH of about 9. Salts of boric acid are called **borates**. Hydrated boron(III) oxide (B_2O_3) is also called **boracic acid**.

Borlaug, Norman (Ernest) [baw(r)log] (1914–) Agricultural scientist, born in Cresco, Iowa, USA. He studied at the University of Minnesota, and was research scientist at the Rockefeller Foundation's Co-operative Agriculture Program in Mexico (1944–60). During this period he developed strains of grain that greatly increased crop production, notably the tripling of Mexico's wheat yields. Dedicated to the alleviation of world hunger, he was director of both the Inter-America Food Crop Program (1960–3) and the International Maize and Wheat Improvement Center (1964–79). He was awarded the Nobel Peace Prize in 1970.

Bormann, Martin (1900–?45) Nazi politician, born in Halberstadt, C Germany. He participated in the abortive Munich putsch of 1923 and became one of Hitler's closest advisers. He was made *Reichsminister* (party chancellor) in 1941, and was with Hitler to the last. His own fate is uncertain, but he was possibly killed by Russian snipers in the mass breakout by Hitler's staff from the Chancellery (1945). A skeleton accidentally uncovered by an excavator in Berlin in 1972 has been officially recognized as his by forensic experts.

Born, Max (1882–1970) Physicist, born in Wrocław, SW Poland (formerly Breslau, Prussia). He became professor of theoretical physics at Göttingen (1921–33), lecturer at Cambridge (1933–6), and professor of natural philosophy at Edinburgh (1936–53). In 1954 he shared the Nobel Prize for Physics with Walter Bothe for work in the field of quantum physics.

Borneo [baw(r)neeoh] area 484 330 sq km/186 951 sq mi. Island in SE Asia, E of Sumatra, N of Java, W of Sulawesi; comprises the Malaysian states of Sarawak and Sabah and the former British protectorate of Brunei (N); remainder comprises the four provinces of Kalimantan, part of Indonesia; formerly divided between the British and the Dutch; mountainous (N), rising to 4094 m/13 432 ft at Mt Kinabalu in Sabah; interior densely forested; rice, pepper, copra, tobacco, oil, bauxite, iron.

Born–Haber cycle [baw(r)n hahber] A thermochemical cycle relating the lattice energy of an ionic solid to its heat of formation, in terms of properties of the single atoms. Since the total consumption of energy for any process is independent of the path taken, any single unknown quantity in the cycle may be estimated if the others are known.

Bornholm [baw(r)nholm] pop (2000e) 46 700; area 588 sq km/227 sq mi. Danish island in the Baltic Sea, 40 km/25 mi S of Sweden, 168 km/104 mi SE of Copenhagen; length 37 km/23 mi; rises to 162 m/531 ft; taken by Sweden, 1645; returned to Denmark, 1660; administrative capital and chief port, Rønne; fishing, fish-processing, farming, pottery, tourism.

Borobudur [borohbooder] A Buddhist sanctuary built between 750 and 850 in Java, Indonesia. The vast temple is built of stone blocks on terraces cut into a natural mound and originally consisted of 10 terraces, two of which have become covered over. Built by the Sailendra dynasty of the Srivijaya kingdom, it is the world's largest stupa and includes depictions of the god Shiva as well as the life of Buddha. It is renowned for the abundance and intricacy of its relief sculptures.

Borodin, Alexander Porfiryevich [borodeen] (1833–87) Composer and scientist, born in St Petersburg, NW Russia. He showed a precocious aptitude for music, but was trained for medicine and distinguished himself as a chemist. His first systematic musical studies were undertaken in 1862, under Balakirev, who conducted his first symphony in 1869. His compositions include the unfinished opera, *Prince Igor* (edited and published by Rimsky-Korsakov), three symphonies, and the symphonic sketch *In the Steppes of Central Asia*.

borohydride [borohhiydriyd] An anion containing boron and hydrogen, especially BH_4^-. **Sodium borohydride** ($NaBH_4$) is an important reducing agent.

boron [bohron] B, element 5; melting point 2300°C. A hard, non-metallic solid, which as a pure element does not occur free in nature. It forms many compounds in which it is bound to oxygen, and shows an oxidation state of +3. Although a relatively rare element, it is found in large concentrations, especially as boric acid and borax.

borough In general terms, the second tier of local government in England and Wales, based on charters granted at different times by the monarchy. **Borough councils** were first elected in 1835, when their main function was law and order. The name has survived all subsequent reforms of local government, but now is largely indistinguishable from the equivalent unit of *district*. The Scottish equivalent is **burgh**, but this term is no longer used in official designations, *district* being preferred. In the USA, it has a special use identifying the five counties comprising New York City.

Borromeo, St Charles [boromayoh] (1538–84) Cardinal and archbishop, born in Arona, N Italy. In 1560, at the age of 22, he was appointed Cardinal of Milan by his uncle, Pope Pius IV. He did much to bring the Council of Trent (1545–63) to a successful conclusion, and had the principal part in drawing up the famous *Catechismus romanus* (1566). He was renowned for his determined efforts to maintain ecclesiastical discipline and for his poor relief during the famine of 1570 and the plague of 1576. He also introduced the confessional box. In 1578 he founded the community later known as the Oblates of St Ambrose. He was canonized in 1610; feast day 4 November.

Borromini, Francesco [boromeenee], originally **Francesco Castello** (1599–1667) Baroque architect and sculptor, born in Bissone, N Italy. He spent all his working life in Rome, where he was associated with his great rival Bernini in the Palazzo Berberini (1620–31) and the baldacchino in St Peter's (1631–3). His own chief buildings include the S Carlo alle Quattro Fontane (1641) and the oratorio of S Philippo Neri (1650). Although now considered one of the great Baroque architects, his influence was felt only after his death, and then more in N Italy and C Europe than in Rome.

Borrow, George (Henry) (1803–81) Writer and traveller, born in East Dereham, Norfolk, E England, UK. He was educated at Norwich, began to train as a solicitor, then worked for a publisher in London. From 1825 to 1832 he wandered in England, sometimes in gypsy company, as described in *Lavengro* (1851) and *The Romany Rye* (1857). As agent of the Bible Society he visited St Petersburg (1833–5), Portugal, Spain, and Morocco (1835–9), and later visited SE Europe (1844) and Wales (1854).

borstal *young offender institution*

borzoi [baw(r)zoy] A breed of dog, developed in Russia, where aristocrats used groups of borzois to hunt wolves; an athletic breed, tall and slender; long thin muzzle; long tail; coat long, straight or curly; also known as **Russian wolfhound**.

Bosch, Carl [bosh] (1874–1940) Chemist, born in Cologne, W Germany, the brother-in-law of Fritz Haber. He became president of I G Farbenindustrie in 1925. He shared the Nobel Prize for Chemistry in 1931 for his part in the invention and development of chemical high-pressure methods, notably the *Haber–Bosch process*, by which hydrogen is obtained from water gas and superheated steam.

Bosch, Hieronymus, originally **Jerome van Aken** (c.1450–1516) Painter, named after the town in which he was born, 's Hertogenbosch in N Brabant, The Netherlands, and in which he seems to have spent the whole of his life. He is noted for his allegorical pictures displaying macabre devils, freaks, and monsters. Among his best-known works are 'The Garden of Earthly Delights' (Prado) and 'The Temptation of St Anthony' (Lisbon). He had considerable influence on the Surrealists.

Bose–Einstein statistics [bohs] In quantum statistical mechanics, the description of collections of many non-interacting bosons; named after Indian physicist **Satyendra Nath Bose** (1894–1974), who collaborated with Einstein. The Bose–Einstein distribution expresses the partition of energy amongst bosons, and is important in, for example, the description of photons in laser action and of superfluidity in liquid helium.

Bosman, Jean-Marc (1964–) Footballer, born in Belgium. A youth international, his name entered football's vocabulary after he challenged the game's contract and transfer rules at the European Court of Justice after his club, FC Liège, refused to allow him a transfer to the French club Dunkerque. Bosman won a judgment in 1995 which made players free agents at the end of contracts and prevented limitations on the number of overseas players at clubs in the European Union.

Bosnia and Herzegovina *p.209*

boson [bohson] A subatomic particle having integer spin; named after Indian physicist **Satyendra Nath Bose** (1894–1974). Unlike fermions, bosons have no exclusion principle limiting the number occupying some state. Force-carrying particles, such as photons, gluons, and gravitons, are all bosons.

Bosporus or **Bosphorus** [bospuhruhs], Turkish **Karadeniz Boğazi** Narrow strait separating European from Asiatic Turkey, and connecting the Black Sea and the Sea of Marmara; length 32 km/20 mi; minimum width 640 m/2100 ft; at its narrowest point are two famous castles, Anadolu Hisar (1390) on the Asian side, and Rumeli Hisar (1452) on the European side; an area of great strategic importance.

Bosporus Bridge [bosporus] A major steel suspension bridge across the Golden Horn at Istanbul, Turkey; completed in 1973; length of main span 1074 m/3524 ft.

Bosques Petrificados [boskays petreefeekathohs], Eng **Petrified Forests** Natural monument in E Santa Cruz province, Patagonia, Argentina; area 100 sq km/39 sq mi; established in 1954; contains 70 000-year-old araucaria trees, averaging 3 m/10 ft in circumference and 15–20 m/50–65 ft in length; Monumento Natural closed indefinitely in 1989, though other areas still open.

Bosra An ancient Syrian city 117 km/73 mi S of Damascus; a world heritage site. Originally an Arab fortress, Bosra was conquered by the Nabataeans, and became almost as important as Petra. It was annexed by the Romans in AD 105, and subsequently flourished as capital of the province of Arabia.

boss (zoology) *bison*

Bossuet, Jacques Bénigne [bosway] (1627–1704) Catholic churchman, and pulpit orator, born in Dijon, E France. He studied at Dijon and Paris, received a canonry at Metz (1652), and in 1661 preached before Louis XIV. His reputation as an orator spread over France, and he became tutor to the Dauphin. As Bishop of Meaux (1681) he took a leading part in the Gallican controversy, asserting the king's independence from the Roman Catholic Church in secular matters.

Boston 42°22N 71°04W, pop (2000e) 589 100. Capital of Massachusetts state, USA; in Suffolk Co, on Massachusetts Bay, at the mouth of the Charles R; largest city in New England; settled, 1630; capital of the Massachusetts Bay Colony, 1632; city status, 1822; a centre of opposition to British trade restrictions and scene of the Boston Tea Party (1773); centre of the Unitarian Church movement; airport; railway; noted for its colleges and universities (1869, 1898, 1906); large immigrant population; commerce, finance, electronics, printing and publishing; professional teams, Red Sox (baseball), Celtics (basketball), Bruins (ice hockey); Boston Tea Party ship and museum, Christ Church (1723), Paul Revere's house, Faneuil Hall (1742); Conservatory of Music; Museum of Fine Arts; Boston Marathon run on Patriot's Day (Apr).

Boston Massacre (5 Mar 1770) The first bloodshed of the American Revolution, as British guards at the Boston Customs House opened fire on a crowd, killing five. Among the issues involved were the general presence of troops, competition between sol-

Bosnia and Herzegovina

☐ International Airport

[boznia, hertzegovina], Serbo-Croatian **Bosna-Hercegovina**, official name **Republic of Bosnia and Herzegovina**

Local name Bosnia i Hercegovina

Timezone GMT +2

Area 51 129 km²/19 736 sq mi

Population total (2002e) 3 964 000

Status Republic

Date of independence 1992

Capital Sarajevo

Languages Serbian, Croatian

Ethnic groups (Pre-civil war) Slav (44%), Serbian (31%), Croatian (17%)

Religions Muslim (Sunni), Serbian Orthodox, Roman Catholic

Physical features Mountainous region in the Balkan peninsula, noted for its stone gorges, lakes, rivers, mineral springs; reaches heights of 1800 m/6000 ft above sea level; principal rivers are Bosna, Una, Drina, Neretva, Sava; in the SW lies the dry, limestone plateau (karst).

Climate Ranges from Mediterranean to mildly continental; sirocco wind brings rain from SW; strong NE wind (bora) affects coastal area in winter.

Currency 1 Convertible Mark (KM) = 100 convertible pfennigs

Economy Highly industrialized, particularly iron and steel; large cellulose factory at Banja Luka; forestry strong in Bosnia; inflation rate high; war (1992–3) disrupted all economic activity.

GDP (2002e) $7·3 bn, per capita $1900

History Annexed by Austria in 1908; Serbian opposition to the annexation led to the murder of Archduke Francis Ferdinand and World War 1; ceded to Yugoslavia, 1918; declaration of sovereignty, 1991; Bosnian Serbs proclaimed three autonomous regions (Bosanska Krajina, Romanija, and Northern Bosnia), 1991; declaration of independence in 1992 led to ongoing military confict between formerly integrated communities of Bosnians, Croats, and Serbs; UN peace-keeping forces deployed, and air-exclusion ('no-fly') zone imposed, 1992; conflict continued until ceasefire in Oct 1995; peace accord leaves Bosnia-Herzegovina a single state, comprising the Bosnian-Croat Federation (in the west) and the Bosnian Serb Republic (in the east), with Sarajevo a united city, centrally governed by a national parliament and president, and people allowed freedom of movement; NATO peace implementation force established.

Head of State
1992–8 Aliya Izetbegovic

Collective Presidency (Chairman)
1996–8 Alija Izetbegovic (Bosniak)
1998–9 Zivko Radisic (Serb)
1999–2000 Ante Jelavic (Croat)
2000 Alija Izetbegovic (Bosniak)
2000–1 Zivko Radišic (Serb)
2001–2002 Jozo Krizanovic (Croat)
2001–2 Beriz Belkic (Bosniak)
2002– Sulejman Tihic (Bosniak)
2002– Dragan Covic (Croat)
2002–3 Mirko Sarovic (Serb)
2003– Borislav Paravac (Serb)

Head of Government
1992 Jure Pelivan
1992–3 Mile Akmadzic
1993–6 Haris Silajdzic
1996–7 Hasan Muratovic
1997–9 Boro Bosic (co-PM)
1997–2000 Haris Silajdzic (co-PM)
1999–2000 Svetozar Mihajlovic (co-PM)
2000 Spasojc Tuscvljak
2000–1 Martin Raguz
2001 Bozidar Matic
2001–2 Zlatko Lagumdzija
2002– Adnan Terzic

diers and civilians for jobs, and the shooting of a Boston boy by a customs official.

Boston Strangler *Desalvo, Albert*

Boston Tea Party (1773) During the American Revolution, the climax of resistance to British attempts at direct taxation, resulting in the destruction in 1773 of 342 chests of dutied tea by working men disguised as Mohawks. Other ports had refused to let the tea ships enter.

Boston terrier A breed of dog, developed in the USA by crossing existing terriers and bulldogs; small, deep-chested; large ears, spherical head, thick neck; coat short; white and brown or white and black.

Boswell, James (1740–95) Man of letters and biographer, the son of Lord Auchinleck, born in Edinburgh, EC Scotland, UK. He studied at Edinburgh High School and University, then studied civil law at Glasgow and Utrecht, and on his travels through Europe met Voltaire and Rousseau. At 18 he began his private, often scandalous journal, published in 18 volumes as *The Private Papers of James Boswell from Malahide Castle* (1928–34), and in 1760 ran away to London where, according to his own accounts, he led a debauched life. He first met Johnson in 1763, and took him on the memorable journey to the Hebrides. His *Journal of a Tour to the Hebrides* (1785) appeared after Johnson's death. He had, with Johnson's agreement, been storing up material for his great work, the *Life of Johnson*, since 1763, and he completed it in 1791.

Bosworth Field, Battle of (22 Aug 1485) The battle which put Henry Tudor on the English throne after victory over Richard III, who died in the conflict. The battle was fought close to the English town of Bosworth in Leicestershire. Henry Tudor's forces were possibly inferior in number, but proved more loyal; they received crucial support from the Stanley family, who had a foot in both camps.

botanical garden A collection of living plants usually arranged by geographic or taxonomic principles, and maintained for the purposes of scientific research, education and, with increased urbanization, recreation. In China, gardens of medicinal and economically valuable plants were cultivated and used for the introduction and acclimatization of foreign flora 3000 years ago; the Aztecs and Incas also established extensive gardens of useful plants. The first European botanical gardens were collections of medicinal plants used for study in monasteries, and later in the medical schools of the early universities. The first such garden in the USA was established at St Louis, MO, in 1860.

botany The study of all aspects of plants, principally their structure, physiology, relationships, and biogeography, but embracing many aspects of other disciplines. Important areas in modern botanical research include genetics and plant breeding; vegetative reproduction and tissue culture, especially the use of microtechniques in which plants are propagated from small amounts of excised tissue such as meristems rather than from seeds; ecology and conservation, especially of endangered habitats such as tropical rain forests and wetlands; and, increasingly, the use of plants as indicators of pollution.

Botany Bay A shallow inlet 8 km/5 mi S of Sydney, New South Wales, Australia; now a residential part of Sydney; Captain Cook made his first landing here in 1770, naming the bay after the number of new plants discovered there; chosen as a penal settlement in 1787, but found to be unsuitable, and a location at Sydney Cove used instead; the name Botany Bay, however, was for many years synonymous with Australian convict settlements.

bot fly A robust, hairy fly, whose larvae are parasites beneath the skin of mammals, feeding on fluids exuding from tissues. The mature larvae bore out through the skin and pupate on the ground. The sheep bot fly deposits its eggs in the nostrils of sheep. (Order: Diptera. Family: Oestridae.)

Botha, Louis [**boh**ta] (1862–1919) South African soldier, statesman, and prime minister (1910–19), born in Greytown, Natal, E South Africa. He succeeded Joubert (1900) as commander-in-chief of the Boer forces during the war, and in 1907 became prime minister of the Transvaal colony under the new constitution. In 1907 and 1911 he attended imperial conferences in London, and in 1910 became the first premier of the Union of South Africa.

Botha, P(ieter) W(illem) [**boh**ta] (1916–) South African statesman, prime minister (1978–84), and first state president (1984–9), born in Paul Roux, Orange Free State, C South Africa. The longest-serving member of the South African Assembly (which he first entered in 1948), in his 14 years as minister of defence (1966–80) he presided over the controversial military intervention in Angola. He attempted to introduce constitutional reforms, but his plans led to wide international condemnation. In 1989 he suffered a stroke which compelled him to cede the state presidency to his party successor, F W de Klerk. In 1998 he was put on trial, and found guilty of contempt for refusing to appear before the country's Truth and Reconciliation Committee.

Botha, Roelof Frederik [**boh**ta], known as **Pik Botha** (1932–) South African politician. After a career in the diplomatic service (1953–70), he entered politics and was elected to parliament. He became South Africa's permanent representative at the UN, then ambassador to the USA. He returned to domestic politics in 1977, becoming foreign minister in the government of P W Botha and that of F W de Klerk. In 1994–6 he served as minister for minerals and energy in Nelson Mandela's first cabinet.

Botham, Ian (Terence) [**boh**tham] (1955–) Cricketer, born in Heswall, Merseyside, NW England, UK. An all-rounder, he appeared in 102 Test matches for England, 65 of them consecutively, and including 12 as captain (1980–1). He held the record number of Test wickets (383 wickets at an average of 28·40 runs) until overtaken by Richard Hadlee, and on four occasions took 10 wickets in a match. He scored 5200 runs in Tests (average 33·54), including 14 centuries. Off-the-field brushes with authority alternated with successful charity fund-raising campaigns such as his walk from John o' Groats to Land's End and his re-enactment of Hannibal's crossing of the Alps. He first played for Somerset in 1974, joined Worcestershire in 1987, and moved to Durham in 1992. He retired from first-class cricket in 1993, best remembered as the architect of improbable wins against Australia at Leeds and Edgbaston in 1981.

Bothe, Walther (Wilhelm Georg) [**boh**tuh] (1891–1957) Physicist, born in Oranienburg, NE Germany. From 1934 he was head of the Max Planck Institute for Medical Research at Heidelberg. His work on the development of the coincidence technique in counting processes brought him a share of the Nobel Prize for Physics in 1954.

Bothnia, Gulf of [**both**neea] N arm of Baltic, between Sweden and Finland; length c.650 km/400 mi; width 80–240 km/50–150 mi; maximum depth c.100 m/330 ft; islets and sandbars impede navigation; generally freezes over in winter.

Bothwell, James Hepburn, 4th Earl of (c.1535–78) Third husband of **Mary, Queen of Scots**. One of the greatest nobles in Scotland, he was held responsible for the abduction and murder of Mary's second husband, Lord Darnley (1567). He was made Duke of Orkney, then married Mary, but faced opposition from the nobles. He fled to Denmark after Mary's surrender to rebel forces at Carberry Hill, and was imprisoned in Dragsholm, where he died insane.

Botrange [**boh**trãzh] 50°30N 6°05E. Mountain in the Hohe Venn, E Liège province, E Belgium; 8 km/5 mi NNE of Malmédy; the highest mountain in Belgium; 694 m/2277 ft.

bo-tree *peepul*

Botswana *p.211*

bottega [bot**ay**ga] (Ital 'shop') An artist's workshop or studio in which assistants trained, and helped the master to produce works bearing his signature. Ghirlandaio and Verrocchio ran important *botteghe* in Renaissance Florence.

Botticelli, Sandro [boti**che**lee], originally **Alessandro Filipepi** (1445–1510) Painter of the early Renaissance, born in Florence, NC Italy. He trained, probably, under Filippo Lippi (c.1458), and from c.1470 worked from his own studio. He is best known for his treatments of mythological subjects, notably 'Primavera' (Spring) and 'Birth of Venus', both in the Uffizi. His work includes illustrations for Dante's *Divina commedia*, which he executed in pen and ink and silverpoint. Among his numerous devotional pictures are the 'Coronation of the Virgin' (Florence Academy) and the large circular 'Madonna and Child' (Uffizi). He also painted frescoes for the Sistine Chapel at the Vatican, and in his later years was much influenced by the teaching of Savonarola, producing works of a more deeply religious character.

bottlebrush An evergreen shrub native to Australia; leaves narrow; flowers small, crowded in dense cylindrical spikes, stamens red or yellow, far exceeding length of petals, and giving inflorescence a brush-like appearance. (*Callistemon*, 25 species. Family: Myrtaceae.)

bottle gourd *calabash*

bottlenose A toothed whale with a narrow projecting 'beak'; name used for **bottlenosed dolphins** (genus: *Tursiops*, 3 species), **bottlenosed whales** (genus: *Hyperoodon*, 2 species) and **giant bottlenosed whales** (genus: *Berardius*, 2 species).

bottom In particle physics, an internal additive quantum number conserved in strong and electromagnetic interactions, but not in weak interactions. Its symbol is usually B, sometimes called **bottomness** or **beauty**. Bottom quarks are those having $B = -1$, and bottom particles contain at least one bottom (or b) quark or antiquark. The b quark was discovered in 1977 as a b quark and b antiquark pair called the *upsilon meson*. Members of the B meson family contain a bottom quark or antiquark.

bottom-up/top-down processing In cognitive psychology, a distinction drawn between two forms of information processing. The contrast is made between the passive processing of environmental information, in which current expectations and past knowledge play no role (*bottom-up*), and its active processing, which makes use of such higher-level information (*top-down*).

Botswana

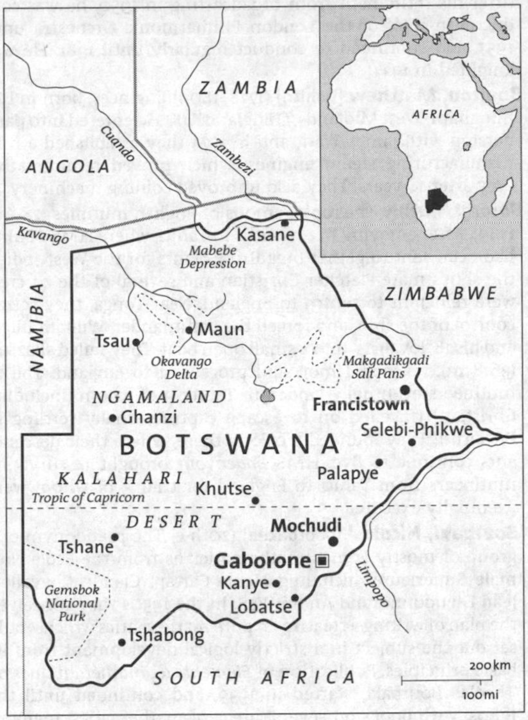

☐ International Airport

[botswahna], official name **Republic of Botswana**

Local name Botswana

Timezone GMT +2

Area 581 730 km^2/224 711 sq mi

Population total (2002e) 1 679 000

Status Independent republic within the Commonwealth

Date of independence 1966

Capital Gaborone

Languages English (official), Tswana

Ethnic groups Tswana (75%), Shona (12%), San (Bushmen) (3%), Khoikhoin (Hottentot) (3%), Ndebele (1%)

Religions Mainly local beliefs; Christian (20%)

Physical features Landlocked S African republic; undulating, sand-filled plateau, part of the S African Plateau; mean elevation c.1000 m/3300 ft; N–S plateau divides country into two regions: hilly grasslands (velt) to E, and Okavango Swamps to W; most of the population lives in fertile, hilly E; SE terrain hilly, 1402 m/4600 ft; dry scrubland, savannah, and the Kalahari Desert in W; salt lakes in N.

Climate Largely sub-tropical; rainfall in N and E almost totally in summer (Oct–Apr); average annual temperature 26°C (Jan), 13°C (Jul) in Gaborone; average annual rainfall 450 mm/17·7 in.

Currency 1 Pula (P, Pu) = 100 thebes

Economy Mainly subsistence farming, especially livestock; continual problems of drought and disease; some crops, especially sorghum; main minerals, nickel, diamonds (jointly mined by the government and De Beers Consolidated Mines of South Africa), cobalt; tourism, especially wildlife observation; Central Kalahari Game Reserve (54 388 km^2/21 000 sq mi) attracts tourists; principal trading partners, members of South African Customs Union.

GDP (2002e) $13·48 bn, per capita $8500

Human Development Index (2002) 0·572

History San (Bushmen) were the earliest inhabitants, followed by Sotho peoples who migrated to Botswana c.1600; explored by Europeans, 1801; visited by missionaries during 19th-c; London Missionary Society established a mission on the Kuruman R, 1813; Ndebele raided Botswana; Boers arrived, 1835; gold was discovered, 1867; under British protection from 1885; S became a Crown Colony, then part of Cape Colony, 1895; N became the Bechuanaland Protectorate; self-government from 1964; independence and change of name to Botswana, 1966; governed by a legislative National Assembly, President, and Cabinet; House of Chiefs considers chieftaincy matters but has no right of veto.

Head of State/Government

1966–80 Seretse Khama

1980–98 Quett K J Masire

1998– Festus Mogae

botulism [botyoolizm] A serious and often fatal illness resulting from the ingestion of a poisonous toxin produced by the *Clostridium botulinum* bacteria. It is one of the most severe forms of food poisoning, which affects the nervous system, and gives rise to rapidly developing paralysis and respiratory failure. The toxin is found in inadequately cooked non-acid fruit, meat, or fish without any apparent spoilage, and is destroyed by cooking for 10 minutes at 80°C.

Bouchard, Lucien [booshahr(r)] (1938–) Canadian and Québecois statesman, and prime minister of Québec (1996–2001), born in Saint-Coeur-de-Marie, Lac-Saint-Jean, Québec, Canada. Educated in Jonquière and Laval, he practised law before being appointed Canadian ambassador to France (1970–80), entering parliament as a Conservative (1988). He became minister of the environment (1989–90) before resigning from both post and party to form and lead the Bloc Québecois. Following the 1993 elections, the Bloc became the official Opposition in the House of Commons. An active campaigner for Québecois sovereignty, he became chairman of the Parti Québecois in 1996, a position he resigned from in 2001.

Boucher, François [booshay] (1703–70) Painter, born in Paris, France. He worked on a range of material from stage design to tapestry, and from 1755 was director of the Gobelins factory. He is recognized as a leading Rococo painter at the court of Louis XV, where he produced several portraits of Madame de Pompadour. His work is usually considered, along with that of his pupil, Fragonard, as being wholly representative of the frivolous spirit of his age.

Boucicault, Dion [booseekolt, -koh], originally **Dionysius Lardner Boursiquot** (1820–90) Playwright, actor, and theatre manager, born in Dublin, Ireland. A versatile theatrical personality, he wrote or adapted some 130 plays, including *London Assurance* (1841) and *The Poor of New York* (1857), becoming one of the most popular playwrights of his era. Most of his plays are now forgotten, but *The Octoroon* (1860) is notable for its condemnation of slavery. He moved to America in 1853, where, along with George Henry Boker (1823–90) and others, he worked to pass the first American Copyright Law of 1856. He was later based in London (1862–72), then returned to the USA.

Boudicca [boodika, boodika], also known as **Boadicea** (1st-c) British Celtic warrior-queen, wife of **Prasutagus**, king of the Iceni, a tribe inhabiting what is now Norfolk and Suffolk, E England. On her husband's death (60), the Romans seized her territory and treated the inhabitants brutally. She gathered a large army, destroyed the Roman colony of Camulodunum (Colchester), Londinium (London), and Verulamium (St Albans), putting to death as many as 70 000 Romans and Romano-Britons. Defeated in battle by Suetonius Paulinus, she took poison.

Boudin, (Louis) Eugène [boodī] (1824–98) Painter, born in Honfleur, NW France. A precursor of Impressionism, he is noted for his seascapes, which include 'On the Beach of Deauville' (1869, Louvre).

Bougainville [bohguhnvil] 6°12S 155°15E; pop (2000e) 160 000; area c.10 000 sq km/4000 sq mi. Mountainous volcanic island in Papua New Guinea, SW Pacific; length, 190 km/118 mi; width, 50 km/31 mi; rises to 2743 m/9000 ft at Mt Balbi; chief port, Kieta; independence movement and guerrilla fighting from 1988, badly affecting economy; fragile ceasefire, 1998; peace agreement, 2001, providing for autonomy and an eventual referendum on independence; copper mining, copra, cocoa, timber.

Bougainville, Louis Antoine, comte de (Count of) [booganveel] (1729–1811) Navigator, mathematician, and French soldier, born in Paris, France. He studied law and then mathematics, publishing an important treatise on integral calculus. Entering the French navy in 1763, he was responsible for colonizing the Falkland Is for France, and for their transfer to Spain. In command of the ships *La Boudeuse* and *L'Etoile*, he accomplished the first French circumnavigation of the world (1766–9), which he described in his *Voyage autour du monde* (1771, A Voyage round the World). The largest of the Solomon Is is named after him, as is the plant *bougainvillaea*. After the outbreak of the Revolution he devoted himself solely to scientific pursuits. Napoleon I made him a senator, count of the empire, and member of the Légion d'Honneur.

bougainvillea [booguhnvilia] A shrub, tree, or woody climber, native to South America; leaves oval; flowers tubular, in threes, surrounded by three lilac, purple, magenta, red, orange, pink, or white petal-like bracts; grown as ornamentals in warm areas everywhere. (Genus: *Bougainvillea*, 18 species. Family: Nyctaginaceae.)

Boulanger, Nadia [boolãzhay] (1887–1979) Composer, born in Paris, France. She studied at the Conservatoire (1897–1904), where she won several prizes, and went on to write many vocal and instrumental works, winning second prize at the Grand Prix de Rome in 1908 for her cantata, *La Sirène* (The Siren). After 1918 she devoted herself to teaching, first at home, and later at the Conservatoire and the Ecole Normale de Musique, where she had international influence. She was also a noted organist and conductor. Her sister, **(Marie-Juliette Olga) Lili Boulanger** (1893–1918), was also a composer.

boulder clay *till*

Boulder Dam *Hoover Dam*

boules [bool] A French ball game similar to bowls, played between two players or teams, also known as **pétanque**. The object is to place the ball nearer to a target ball, or jack, than the opposing player or team. It is thought to have first been played in 1910.

Boulez, Pierre [boolez] (1925–) Conductor and composer, born in Montbrison, SC France. He studied at the Paris Conservatoire (1943–5), and became musical director of Barrault's Théâtre Marigny (1948), where he established his reputation as an interpreter of contemporary music. During the 1970s he devoted himself mainly to his work as conductor of the BBC Symphony Orchestra (1971–5) and of the New York Philharmonic (1971–7), before becoming director of the Institut de Recherche et de Coordination Acoustique Musique (Ircam) at the Pompidou Centre in Paris (1977–91). His early work as a composer rebelled against what he saw as the conservatism of such composers as Stravinsky and Schoenberg. Of his later works, *Le Marteau sans maître* (1955, The Hammer Without a Master) gained him a worldwide reputation, confirmed by *Pli selon pli* (Fold according to Fold) and his third piano sonata.

boulle *buhl*

Boulogne Eng [booloyn], Fr [boolon] or **Boulogne-sur-Mer** 50°43N 1°37E, pop (2000e) 46 300. Seaport in Pas-de-Calais department, NW France; on coast of English Channel, S of Calais; principal commercial harbour and fishing port of France; boatbuilding, textiles, engineering; ferry and hovercraft links with Dover and Folkestone.

Boult, Sir Adrian (Cedric) [bohlt] (1889–1983) Conductor, born in Chester, Cheshire, NW England, UK. After studying at Oxford and Leipzig, he conducted the City of Birmingham Orchestra (1924–30), and was then appointed musical director of the BBC and conductor of the newly formed BBC Symphony Orchestra. After his retirement from broadcasting in 1950, he was conductor-in-chief of the London Philharmonic Orchestra until 1957, and continued to conduct regularly until 1981. He was knighted in 1937.

Boulton, Matthew [bohltn] (1728–1809) Engineer, born in Birmingham, West Midlands, C England, UK. He entered into partnership with James Watt, and in 1774 they established a firm manufacturing steam engines, which proved remunerative only after 18 years. They also improved coining machinery.

***Bounty* Mutiny** The most famous of English mutinies (28 Apr 1789). After enjoying five months in Tahiti, where HMS *Bounty* had been sent to gather breadfruit plants for the West Indies, the ship's mate Fletcher Christian and several of the 44 crew were reluctant to return to England. Near Tonga, they seized control of the ship, and forced the commander, William Bligh, and his 18 'loyalists' into a small open boat. They sailed 5822 km (3618 m), reached Timor, and proceeded to England. The 25 mutineers eventually landed in Tahiti, 9 of whom (including Christian) travelled on to escape capture, finally settling in Pitcairn I. They founded a colony there, where their descendants continue to live. HMS *Endeavour* brought 14 surviving mutineers from Tahiti to England for trial, 3 of whom were eventually executed.

'Bourbaki, Nicolas' [boorbakee] (20th-c) The pseudonym of a group of mostly French mathematicians from the Ecole Normale Supérieure, including Henri Cartan, Claude Chevalley, Jean Dieudonné, and André Weil. In the 1930s they conceived the plan of writing a treatise on pure mathematics which would set out the subject in a strictly logical development from its basic principles. Publication of *Eléments de mathématiques* by 'Nicolas Bourbaki' started in 1939, and continued until the 1980s, with books on several areas of mathematics, many of them highly influential.

Bourbon, Charles de [boorbõ], known as **Constable de Bourbon** (1490–1527) French soldier, born in Montpensier, C France. As son of the Count of Montpensier and of the only daughter of the Duke of Bourbon, he united the estates of both these branches of the Bourbon family. For his bravery at the Battle of Marignano (1515) he was made Constable of France; but losing the favour of Francis I he concluded a private alliance with the Emperor Charles V and Henry VIII of England. He invaded France in 1524, and was chief imperial commander at Pavia, in which Francis I was taken prisoner. He was made Duke of Milan, and commanded in N Italy, but was killed while attacking Rome in 1527.

bourbon [berbn] A dark-coloured American whiskey, a distillate of at least 51% corn, which originated in Bourbon Co, KY. It is aged in barrels of white oak, charred on the inside, from two to eight years. *Straight bourbon* is the product of a single distillery in a given year, ie an unblended bourbon.

Bourbons [boorbõ] A French royal house descended from the Capetian St Louis IX (1215–70), associated with absolutist traditions at home and the extension of French influence abroad. Succeeding the last Valois, Henry IV (r.1589–1610) firmly established the dynasty. Under his son (Louis XIII) and grandson (Louis XIV), the long-standing rivalry between France and the Spanish Habsburgs came to a climax; it was concluded when a descendant, Philip of Anjou, ascended the Spanish throne (Philip V, r.1700–46), thereby founding the Spanish House of Bourbon. Under Louis XV (1715–74) and Louis XVI (1774–93), the prestige of the French Bourbons gradually declined; with the latter's execution (1793) the line was interrupted, to be briefly restored (1814–30).

bourgeoisie [boorzhwahzee] In mediaeval times, a member of a free city or *bourg* who was neither a peasant nor a landlord – essentially, a member of the 'middle class'. Later it referred to an employer or merchant. In the 19th-c the bourgeoisie was associated with leading revolutionary change, the demise of the aristocracy, the beginnings of liberal democracy, and the development of industrial capitalism. Alongside this went a view, which still persists, that the bourgeoisie are culturally reactionary and small-minded, being primarily concerned with commercial matters. In recent times the term **bourgeois** has been applied to those with rather narrow views about cultural and moral issues. In Marxist theory, the *bourgeoisie* are defined as a class by their ownership and control of capital.

Bourges [boorzh] 47°09N 2°25E, pop (2000e) 82 400. Ancient ducal town and capital of Cher department, C France; at confluence of rivers Auron and Yèvre; capital of Berry, 12th-c; railway; bishopric; hardware, linoleum, textiles, armaments, agricultural equipment; cathedral (13th-c), Palais Jacques Coeur (1443), many fine Renaissance houses.

Bourget or **Lac du Bourget** [lak dü boorzhay] Lake in Savoie department, E France; area 45 sq km/17 sq mi; length 18 km/11 mi, width 2–3 km/1¼–1¾ mi; depth 60–100 m/200–325 ft; largest lake in France; overlooked by Aix-les-Bains (E); major tourist area; Benedictine abbey.

Bourke-White, Margaret [berk], originally **Margaret White** (1906–71) Photo-journalist, born in New York City, USA. She studied at Columbia University, and started as an industrial and architectural photographer. She became a staff photographer and associate editor on *Life* magazine when it started publication in 1936. She covered World War 2 for *Life*, and was the first woman photographer to be attached to the US armed forces, producing reports of the siege of Moscow (1941) and the opening of the concentration camps in 1944. She was also an official UN war correspondent during the Korean War.

Bourne, Matthew (1960–) Choreographer and dancer, born in London, UK. He studied at London's Laban Centre, and in 1987 he co-founded and became artistic director (resigned 2003) of the dance company Adventures in Motion Pictures. He gained a reputation for his unconventional interpretations of classical ballets, and aroused controversy with his 1995 production of *Swan Lake* in which the 'swans' were replaced by dozens of bare-chested male dancers with wings. It received the Laurence Olivier Award for the best new dance production (1996) and also won a Tony on Broadway (1999). Later works include his staging of *Cinderella* (1997), set in London during the Blitz, and *My Fair Lady* (2001).

Bournemouth [baw(r)nmuhth] 50°43N 1°54W, pop (2001e) 163 400. Unitary authority (from 1997) and resort town in S England, UK; on Poole Bay, 40 km/25 mi SW of Southampton; railway; Bournemouth University (1992, formerly Bournemouth Polytechnic); conference centre; tourism, printing, engineering; symphony orchestra; football league team, Bournemouth (Cherries).

bourse [boors] A market for stocks, shares, and government bonds. In many countries, it refers to the place where these activities take place, as in the Paris Bourse.

Boussingault, Jean-Baptiste (Joseph) [boosīgoh] (1802–87) Agricultural chemist, born in Paris, France. He studied at the School of Mines and at St Etienne, and became professor of chemistry at Lyon. He demonstrated that plants absorb nitrogen from the soil, and showed that carbon is assimilated by plants from the carbon dioxide of the atmosphere.

boustrophedon [boostrofeedn] An ancient method of writing, particularly in early Greek, in which the lines go alternately from left to right and right to left. The name comes from the Greek words for 'ox' and 'turn' – hence, following the path taken by a plough.

Boutros-Ghali, Boutros [galee] (1922–) Egyptian diplomat, who took office as the sixth secretary-general of the United Nations (1992–7). The former deputy prime minister of Egypt, he was the first to hold the post from the Continent of Africa. He became head of La Francophonie in 1997.

Bouts, Dierick [bowts], also spelled **Dirk**, or **Thierry** (c.1415–75) Painter, born in Haarlem, The Netherlands. He is usually placed with the Flemish school. He worked at Louvain and Brussels, coming under the influence of Rogier van der Weyden, and produced austere religious paintings, with rich and gem-like colour.

bouzouki [buhzookee] A plucked string instrument of Greece, used in folk music and more recently in urban contexts. It has a very long neck, a fretted fingerboard, and three or four courses of metal strings played with a plectrum.

Bovet, Daniel [bohvay] (1907–92) Pharmacologist, born in Neuchâtel, W Switzerland. He studied chemistry at Geneva, and conducted research at the Pasteur Institute in Paris (1929–47), where he developed the first antihistamine drug and the first synthetic muscle-relaxants, for which he was awarded the 1957 Nobel Prize for Physiology or Medicine. In 1947 he emigrated to Italy, where later he was appointed professor of psychology at the University of Rome (1971–82).

Bovidae [bohvidee] A family of ruminant artiodactyl mammals (128 species), including cattle and antelopes; feed by grasping vegetation with their tongue, and cutting it with the lower incisor teeth; adult male (and usually female) with horns; horns have a bone centre and a sheath of horny material.

bovine mastitis The inflammation of mammary tissue in cattle, which results in serious loss of milk production. Acute cases are usually obvious and may affect the whole or just part of the mammary gland. A wide variety of micro-organisms is involved, and can usually be detected from milk samples. Subclinical cases are diagnosed from cell counts in milk samples. Prevention requires a very high standard of dairy hygiene and husbandry practice.

bovine milk fever A metabolic disturbance due to a lack of circulating calcium following calving; the term *fever* is a misnomer, as there is not usually a rise in body temperature. There are muscle tremors and a general weakness leading to collapse and partial paralysis (*downer cow syndrome*) and the danger of heart changes. Most cases respond to prompt administration of calcium solutions. Veterinary attention is needed to establish a definite diagnosis and to prevent complications.

bovine spongiform encephalopathy (BSE) [bohviyn spuhnjifaw(r)m ensefalopathi] A progressive, fatal disease of the central nervous system of cattle (*encephalopathy*: disease affecting the structure of the brain); usually referred to by its abbreviation, but also widely called **mad cow disease**. BSE appeared in the UK in 1985, after a post mortem analysis of the brain tissue of a cow from a farm in West Sussex; the disease was identified in 1986, and clinical cases peaked in late 1992–early 1993 (100,000th case in July 1993) and have declined steadily since, following control measures. Affected cattle may show behavioural changes and lack of co-ordination. There is no known treatment or cure. BSE is probably caused by a type of protein organism (a *prion*) resistant to high temperatures and disinfectants. The BSE agent is unique amongst the transmissible spongiform encephalopathies in that it may have crossed the species barrier: it is believed that cattle may have become infected by eating feed containing tissue from scrapie-infected sheep. Fear that BSE may be transmitted to humans by eating the nervous tissue of affected cattle, possibly causing the comparable spongiform encephalopathy, Creutzfeldt-Jakob disease (CJD), has led to control measures being enforced. These have included the banning of certain meat and bone meals of ruminant origin, the destruction of specified bovine offals, and the selective slaughter of cattle. The indications are that the policies adopted will see the early elimination of BSE.

Bow, Clara [boh] (1905–65) Film actress, born in New York City, USA. After winning a beauty contest at 17, she went on to Hollywood stardom. She was chosen by Elinor Glyn to star in *It* (1927), the film adaptation of her novel, and Bow became popularly known as 'the It Girl'. Her films were box-office hits (1927–30), but her strong Brooklyn accent and vocal delivery prevented her successful transition to sound, and she subsequently retired (1933).

bow (music) An implement for playing musical instruments such as the violin, consisting essentially of a wooden stick to each end of which lengths of horsehair are attached. Early bows had convex sticks, bent away from the hair, which was gripped by the player's fingers to keep it taut. Gradually sticks were made straighter to increase the tension, and from c.1700 this could be adjusted by means of a movable nut (*frog*) at the lower end. The modern bow, with its strongly sprung concave stick, its ample width of hair, and its easily adjustable frog, was perfected and standardized c.1785 by French bowmaker François Tourte (1747–1838).

bow (weaponry) *crossbow; longbow*

Bowdler, Thomas [bowdler] (1754–1825) Doctor and man of letters, born in Ashley, Somerset, SW England, UK. He retired from medical practice and settled in the Isle of Wight to devote himself to literary pursuits. He is immortalized as the editor of *The Family Shakespeare* (10 vols, 1818), in which 'those words and expressions are omitted which cannot with propriety be read aloud in a family' and which are 'unfit to be read by gentlemen in the company of ladies'. *Bowdlerizing* has since become a synonym for prudish expurgation.

Bowen, Elizabeth (Dorothea Cole) (1899–1973) Novelist and short-story writer, born in Dublin, Ireland. She moved to England when she was seven, and later lived in London and Italy. In 1923 she published her first collection of short stories, *Encounters*. Her best-known novels are *The Death of the Heart* (1938) and *The Heat of the Day* (1949).

bowerbird A bird native to New Guinea and Australia; related to birds of paradise. Males usually attract females by building ornate structures (*bowers*) on the ground, decorated with colourful objects. (Family: Ptilonorhynchidae, 18 species.)

bowfin Primitive freshwater fish (*Amia calva*) found in weedy backwaters of E North America; swim bladder serves as a lung to use atmospheric oxygen; length up to 90 cm/3 ft, dorsal fin long, tail fin rounded; sole representative of family Amiidae; also called **mudfish**.

bowhead *right whale*

Bowie, David [bowee], originally **David Robert Jones** (1947–) Rock singer, born in London, UK. He changed his name in 1966 ('Bowie', a Western knife) to avoid confusion with another pop singer (David Jones of the Monkees). His early career was undistinguished and he came close to becoming a Buddhist monk before the success of 'Space Oddity' (1969) – a song derived from the Kubrick film *2001: a Space Odyssey*. His career blossomed throughout the 1970s as he adopted a range of extreme stage images to suit a variety of musical styles. His albums have included *Hunky Dory* (1971), *Heroes* (1977), *Hours* (1999), and *Reality* (2003). He has also acted in films, including *The Man Who Fell to Earth* (1976), had a leading role in the animated film *Labyrinth* (1986), and starred in a long Broadway run of *The Elephant Man*. Later films include *Basquiat* (1996).

Bowie, Jim [booee, bohee], popular name of **James Bowie** (c.1796–1836) US pioneer, born in Logan Co, Kentucky, USA. After settling in Texas, he became a naturalized Mexican citizen. As a colonel in the Texan army, he was killed at the Battle of the Alamo. He may have been the inventor of the curved dagger or sheath-knife, that was later named after him.

Bowles, Erskine [bowlz] (1945–) US public official, born in North Carolina. Educated at the University of North Carolina and Columbia University, he became an investment banker (1975–93) and administrator of the US Small Business Administration (1993–4). He joined the White House as deputy chief-of-staff (1994–5), and after returning to his business career (1995–6) became chief-of-staff in Clinton's second administration (1997–2000).

bowling The act of delivering a ball at pins (as opposed to a target, as in bowls); a popular indoor sport and pastime, with an ancient history. It was popularized by German churchgoers in the 3rd–4th-c, who would roll a ball at a *kegel*, a club used for protection, and if hit they would be absolved from sin. The game of **ninepins** was taken to the USA by Dutch and German immigrants in the latter part of the 19th-c. When the sport was outlawed, a tenth pin was added as a way around the legislation. Mechanical devices for replacing the pins on their spots were developed in the 1950s, which helped the game's growth, and **ten-pin bowling** is now the most popular form. Its international organization is the Federation International des Quilleurs.

bowls An indoor and outdoor game played as singles, pairs, triples, or fours. A similar game was believed to have been played by the Egyptians as early as 5200 BC. Glasgow solicitor William Mitchell (1803–84) drew up the rules for modern bowls in 1848. There are two main variations: **lawn bowls** (also known as **flat green bowls**) is played on a flat, level rink, whereas **crown green bowls** is played on an uneven green raised at the centre. Triples and fours are rarely played in the crown green game. In both varieties the object is to deliver your ball nearer to the *jack* (a smaller target ball) than your opponent(s). Bowls have a bias which causes them to curve, imparted by flattening one side of the bowl. The Waterloo Handicap crown green championship, first held in 1907, takes place annually at the Waterloo Hotel, Blackpool (the Waterloo Cup). In the USA, the main organization is the American Lawn Bowling Association.

Bow porcelain [boh] A London porcelain factory founded by Irish painter Thomas Frye (1710–62) and a glass merchant Edward Heylyn (1695–1765), which flourished from c.1747 until 1776. Their most notable productions were figures, often derived from Meissen models, but also from contemporary theatrical life (eg Kitty Clive). They also made expensive tableware.

bow wave [bow] In fluid mechanics, the wave disturbance emanating from the leading edge of an object moving through fluid, especially the V-shaped surface wave associated with boats moving through water. It is caused by displacement of the fluid by the moving object.

box An evergreen shrub or small tree (*Buxus sempervirens*) growing to 10 m/30 ft, often less, native to Europe and N Africa; leaves small, leathery, paired; flowers green, lacking petals, clusters of several males around one female; fruit a woody capsule. It is a popular bush for formal clipped hedges and for topiary. (Family: Buxaceae.)

box camera The simplest form of camera for amateur photography: a rectangular box containing holders for paper-backed roll film advanced by an external winder, a fixed-focus lens, and a shutter for instantaneous exposure. Early examples are the original Kodak camera of 1888 and the Box Brownie of 1900 which popularized snapshot photography.

box elder A species of maple (*Acer negundo*) with leaves pinnately divided into 3–5 separate leaflets; male and female flowers on separate trees, the males with conspicuous red anthers; native to E North America. Forms with yellow and green variegated leaves are common street trees. (Family: Aceraceae.)

boxer A breed of dog; large muscular body; rounded compact head; ears soft, pendulous; muzzle short and broad, with pronounced jowls and prominent lower jaw; developed from the bulldog in Germany (late 19th-c).

Boxer Rising An anti-foreign movement in China (1898–1900). Its name derives from the secret society to which the rebels belonged, the 'Righteous and Harmonious Fists', whose members adopted boxing and other rituals, convinced by their mixture of magical beliefs that foreign weapons could not harm them. It originated in N China, as a reaction to economic distress and Western territorial seizures. Christian missionaries, churches and Chinese converts were attacked, 200 foreigners were killed, and foreign legations in Tianjin and Beijing were besieged. With Tianjin's relief by a force of the combined Treaty powers, the siege of Beijing's foreign quarter intensified, aided by a Chinese army following the dowager empress Cixi's declaration of war. The siege was raised by an American force, and the Boxers were suppressed in a welter of executions without trial. The Boxer Protocol (1901) imposed massive indemnities on China, which continued into the 1940s.

boxing Fighting with fists, a sport recorded from the earliest times. The Greeks and Romans used to entertain themselves by staging fist fights between their gladiators. The first known boxing match in Britain was in 1681, when the Duke of Albemarle organized a match between his butler and his butcher at his home in New Hall, Essex. The sport began to develop in the early part of the 18th-c, when James Figg, a renowned swordsman and cudgel fighter, opened his school of arms in Oxford Road, London. Figg came to be regarded as the first champion of bare-knuckle boxing. The first rules were drawn up by John Broughton in 1743; each round lasted until one fighter was knocked down. The *Queensberry Rules*, as drawn up in 1867 by John Sholto Douglas, the 8th Marquess of Queensberry, changed boxing completely. It legislated for fighting with gloves, stipulated the length of each round at three minutes, and laid the foundation of the modern sport. Officially recognized world championship contests started in 1884, early world champions including John L Sullivan (heavyweight) and Jack 'Nonpareil' Dempsey (middleweight – to be distinguished from heavyweight fighter Jack Dempsey). Over the years the different boxing authorities have had difficulty in agreeing upon recognition of some fighters as champions, and today four primary bodies recognize world champions; the *World Boxing Council (WBC)*, founded in 1963; the *World Boxing Association (WBA)*, founded in 1927 as the National Boxing Association; the *International Boxing Federation (IBF)*, founded in 1983; and the *World Boxing Organization (WBO)*, founded in 1988. In the USA, each state has a governing commission. Different weight divisions exist, and fighters can compete only within the appropriate category, although they can move up, or down, depending upon weight change. In 2004 there were 17 different weight divisions, ranging from straw-weight for fighters under 105 lb (48 kg), to heavyweight, which is any weight, but normally over 190 lb (88 kg). Professional championship bouts comprise twelve 3-minute rounds. Amateur contests are over three rounds, and all fighters must wear a vest and, in the Olympics, a headguard. All fights last until one fighter is knocked out or retires, the referee halts the fight, a fighter is disqualified, or the designated number of rounds is reached. If the fight goes the distance, judges then mark the fighters according to winning punches, etc. It is possible to have a draw. *(see panel)*

Boxing Day In the UK and the Commonwealth, the day after Christmas Day, so called because traditionally on that day gifts from boxes placed in church were distributed to the poor, and apprentices took a box round their masters' customers in the hope of getting presents of money from them. Christmas 'boxes' or gifts of money are still sometimes given to tradespeople, postal workers, etc.

box set Theatre scenery representing the interior of a room by a three-dimensional arrangement of painted flats, with practicable doors and windows, to form three of the walls, and covered by a cloth to form the ceiling. It was first used in 1841 when the style and content of stage production shifted from spectacle and sensation to bourgeois drama. The plays of Edward Bulwer-Lytton and Dion Boucicault were of this school, requiring new staging practices and laying the groundwork for much modern stagecraft.

box turtle A North American terrapin; spends little time in water; eats invertebrates and fruit. The lower surface of its shell has hinged ends which close against the upper shell when the head and legs have been withdrawn (forming a closed box). *Cuora amboiensis* of the same family is called the **Malayan box turtle**. (Genus: *Terrapene*, several species.)

Boyana Church A world heritage monument comprising three churches situated in the former village of Boyana, a present-day suburb of Sofia, Bulgaria. The buildings date from the 10th-c, 13th-c and 19th-c, but despite their differing styles, combine to form a notable architectural unit.

boyars Members of the highest stratum of the Russian feudal aristocracy from the 10th-c to the early 18th-c. The *Boyarskaya Duma* ('Boyars' Council') was a major legislative and deliberative assembly under the mediaeval tsars. During the reign of Ivan IV, the boyars' authority was ruthlessly curtailed; the *Boyarskaya Duma* was finally abolished by Peter I in 1711, and replaced by an appointed Senate.

Boyce, William (1710–79) Composer, born in London, UK. In 1736 he was appointed composer to the Chapel Royal and, in 1758, organist. He held a high rank as a composer of choral and orchestral music, and his works include the song 'Hearts of Oak', the serenata of *Solomon* (1743), and a valuable collection of *Cathedral Music* (1760).

Boycott, Charles Cunningham (1832–97) British army captain and estate manager, born in Burgh St Peter, Norfolk, E England, UK. He was the agent for Lord Erne in Co Mayo, Ireland, when bad harvests in 1879 made famine likely, and the Land League under Parnell requested lower rents to ease the tenants' burden. When Boycott ruthlessly evicted tenants in 1880, Parnell suggested they avoid any form of contact or communication with Boycott. His name thus became the source of the verb *to boycott*.

Boycott, Geoffrey (1940–) Cricketer and broadcaster, born in Fitzwilliam, West Yorkshire, N England, UK. He gained his county cap for Yorkshire in 1963, and was capped for England the following year. An opening batsman, he played 108 times for England (1964–82), scoring 8114 runs (average 47·72), in 1981 overtaking Gary Sobers' world record of 8032 Test runs. His 22 Test centuries constitute an English record, matched by Colin Cowdrey and Walter Hammond. Total runs in his career were 48 426 (average 56·83). Captain of Yorkshire (1971–8), he was a controversial batsman, and the county was divided about the value of his contribution to the club. After retiring from first-class cricket in 1986, he gained renown as a cricket commentator. Among his books is *Boycott on Cricket* (1990).

boycott A collective refusal to have dealings – usually in relation to trade – with a person, company, or country. A trade union may boycott talks with a company as a negotiating ploy. Individuals may refuse to buy a country's goods as a gesture of political protest – for example, during the late 1980s, goods from South Africa in protest against apartheid. Boycotts have also been used in international sporting events, such as by the USA at the 1980 Moscow Olympic Games in protest over the Soviet invasion of Afghanistan the previous year. They are often effective only if legally enforced – for example, the ban on the import of Cuban cigars into the USA.

The Weight Divisions In Professional Boxing

name	*maximum weight*
heavyweight	any weight
cruiserweight / junior-heavyweight	88 kg / 195 lb
light-heavyweight	79 kg / 175 lb
super-middleweight	77 kg / 170 lb
middleweight	73 kg / 160 lb
light-middleweight / junior-middleweight	70 kg / 154 lb
welterweight	67 kg / 147 lb
light-welterweight / junior welterweight	64 kg / 140 lb
lightweight	61 kg / 135 lb
junior-lightweight / super-featherweight	59 kg / 130 lb
featherweight	57 kg / 126 lb
super bantamweight / junior-featherweight	55 kg / 122 lb
bantamweight	54 kg / 118 lb
super-flyweight / junior-bantamweight	52 kg / 115 lb
fly weight	51 kg / 112 lb
light-flyweight / junior-flyweight	49 kg / 108 lb
mini-flyweight / straw-weight / minimum weight	under 48 kg / 105 lb

Boyd, Michael (1955–) Stage director, born in Belfast, NE Northern Ireland, UK. He studied at Edinburgh University, before commencing his training at the Malaya Bronnaya Theatre, Moscow. He began his career at the Belgrade Theatre, Coventry (1980–2), became an associate director at the Crucible, Sheffield (1982–4), and was founding artistic director of the Tron Theatre, Glasgow (1985–9). He became an associate director of the Royal Shakespeare Company (RSC) in 1996, and won an Olivier Award for best director for the *Henry VI* trilogy (2000). In 2003 he succeeded Adrian Noble as artistic director of the RSC.

Boyd Orr (of Brechin Mearns), John Boyd Orr, Baron (1880–1971) Biologist, born in Kilmaurs, East Ayrshire, SW Scotland, UK. He studied at Glasgow University, became director of the Rowett Research Institute and professor of agriculture at Aberdeen (1942–5), and was the first director of the UN Food and Agriculture Organization (1945–8). His pessimistic reports on the world food situation got him a reputation as an apostle of gloom, but his great services in improving that situation brought him the Nobel Peace Prize in 1949, in which year he was made a peer.

Boyer, Charles [boyay] (1899–1978) Actor, born in Figeac, SC France. He studied at the Sorbonne and the Paris Conservatoire. Having become established as a star of the French stage and cinema, he settled in Hollywood in 1934, and was known as the screen's 'great lover' from such romantic roles as *Mayerling* (1936), *The Garden of Allah* (1936), and *Algiers* (1938). His later appearances included *Barefoot in the Park* (1967) and *Stavisky* (1974). In 1943 he received a special Academy Award for his work in promoting Franco–American cultural relations.

Boyer, Paul D (1918–) Chemist, born in Provo, Utah, USA. He graduated from the University of Wisconsin in 1943, and taught at the University of California, Los Angeles. He shared the 1997 Nobel Prize for Chemistry for his contribution towards the elucidation of the enzymatic mechanism underlying the synthesis of adenosine triphosphate.

Boyer, Sir Richard (James Fildes) [boyer] (1891–1961) Broadcasting administrator, born in Taree, New South Wales, SE Australia. He was a member of the Australian delegation to the League of Nations in 1939, and was appointed to the Australian Broadcasting Commission in 1940. After Prime Minister Curtin affirmed the independence of the Australian Broadcasting Company, Boyer accepted the chairmanship in 1945. The ABC Lectures were renamed the *Boyer Lectures* in his honour after his death.

Boy George, popular name of **George O'Dowd** (1961–) Pop singer and songwriter, born in Eltham, Kent, SE England, UK. In 1981 he formed his own band, Culture Club, and had a string of hit records including a Number 1 single, 'Karma Chameleon' (1983). A flamboyant cross-dresser and admitted drug user, controversy dogged his career. Culture Club disbanded and he underwent successful treatment for drug dependence, re-emerging as a solo artist with the hit single 'Everything I Own' (1987). During the 1990s he forged a new career as a DJ on the club scene and gained international recognition. His album *Essential Mix* appeared in 2001. In January 2002, his musical *Taboo*, charting his own life-story in the world of pop music, opened in London. The Broadway version (2003) opened to mixed reviews.

Boylan, Clare (1948–) Writer, born in Dublin, Ireland. Educated in Dublin, she worked as a journalist, winning in 1983 the Dublin Journalist of the Year Award. Her first novel, *Holy Pictures*, appeared in 1983, and a book of short stories, *A Nail in the Head* (1983), confirmed her reputation. Later books include *Concerning Virgins* (1990), *That Bad Women* (1995), *Black Baby* (1998), and *Beloved Stranger* (2000). Non-fiction works include *The Agony or the Ego* (1993) and *The Literary Companion to Cats* (1994).

Boyle, Danny, popular name of **Daniel Boyle** (1956–) Director, born in Bury, Greater Manchester, NW England, UK. He was artistic director of London's Royal Court Theatre Upstairs (1982–7), an experimental venue for new writing, then moved into television directing, where he made his name with *Mr Wroe's Virgins*, a period drama. His directorial film debut was *Shallow Grave* (1994, BAFTA), followed by *Trainspotting* (1996), which was a critical and box-office success. More recent films include *A Life Less Ordinary* (1997), *The Beach* (2000), and *Alien Love Triangle* (2000). In all of his films he has worked in close partnership with producer Andrew MacDonald (1966–) and screenwriter John Hodge (1964–).

Boyle, Robert (1627–91) Chemist and natural philosopher, born at Lismore Castle, Co Waterford, S Ireland. He was educated at Eton, went to the European mainland for six years, then devoted himself to science. Settling at Oxford in 1654, with Robert Hooke as his assistant, he carried out experiments on air, vacuum, combustion, and respiration. In 1661 he published his *Sceptical Chymist*, in which he criticized the current theories of matter, and defined the chemical element as the practical limit of chemical analysis. In 1662 he arrived at *Boyle's law*, which states that the pressure and volume of gas are inversely proportional. He also researched into calcination of metals, properties of acids and alkalis, specific gravity, crystallography, and refraction, and first prepared phosphorus. As a director of the East India Company (for which he had procured the Charter) he worked for the propagation of Christianity in the East, circulated at his own expense translations of the Scriptures, and by bequest founded the *Boyle Lectures* in defence of Christianity.

Boyle, T(homas) C(oraghessan) (1948–) Novelist and storyteller, born in Peekshill, New York, USA. He joined the Iowa Writers' Workshop in 1972, and published in 1979 his first collection of short stories, *Descent of Man* (St Lawrence Award for Short Fiction). Later books include *World's End* (1988, PEN/Faulkner Award) and his satirical novel *The Road to Wellville* (1993), which was made into a film. *Friend of the Earth* (2000) is a darkly humorous novel about the future of the planet.

Boyne, River River in E Ireland, rising in the Bog of Allen, Kildare county, Leinster; flows 110 km/68 mi NE to the Irish Sea near Drogheda.

Boyne, Battle of the (1690) A battle fought near Drogheda, Co Louth, Ireland, between Protestant forces under William of Orange (of the Netherlands), and smaller Catholic forces led by the exiled James II. After William had been proclaimed William III, king of England, Scotland, and Ireland, James tried to regain his crown but was overwhelmed by the army William brought to Ireland, which numbered c.35 000 men. William's decisive victory on the Boyne enabled him to capture Dublin, and marked a critical stage in the English reconquest of Ireland. It ended James's campaign to regain the English throne. James returned to exile in France. The Protestant Orange Order (first called the Orange Society) was established in Co Armagh, Ireland, in 1795. The Orangemen have commemorated William of Orange's victory ever since – with parades every 12 July through Belfast and other towns in Northern Ireland, as well as in Liverpool and Glasgow.

Boy Scouts *scouting*

Brabham, Jack [brabuhm], popular name of **Sir John Arthur Brabham** (1926–) Motor-racing driver and constructor, born in Sydney, New South Wales, SE Australia. He served with the Royal Australian Air Force, and started his racing career in 1947. After winning the Australian Grand Prix in 1955, he went to the UK, where he joined the successful Cooper team. He won his first Formula 1 World Drivers' Championship at Sebring, FL, in 1959 by pushing his car over the finishing-line, and won the title again the following year. In 1962 he set up his own team and won his third world title and the Constructor's Championship in a car of his own design, the only driver to have done so. He won the Constructor's Championship again in 1967. He retired from racing in 1970, and was knighted in 1979.

Brachiopoda [brakiopoda] *lamp shell*

bracken A perennial fern (*Pteridium aquilinum*) with far-creeping rhizomes; fronds solitary, up to 2–4 m/6½–13 ft; tri-pinnate, with sori continuous around edges of leaf-segments. It is common on acid soils, especially in woods and heaths where it may cover extensive areas by means of the rhizomes. It is poisonous, and not grazed by animals such as sheep and rabbits. Fire does not seriously damage it, the deeply buried rhizomes remaining unharmed. Bracken can be an aggressive invader of grassland. (Family: Polypodiaceae.)

bract A modified leaf immediately below a flower or inflorescence. It is usually green, but may be brightly coloured and petal-like, as in *Poinsettia*.

Bracton, Henry de (?–1268) English jurist, a 'justice itinerant' for Henry III. He was also a priest, like most lawyers of his time. In 1264, he became archdeacon of Barnstaple and chancellor of Exeter Cathedral. His *De legibus et consuetudinibus Angliae* (On the Laws and Customs of England) is the earliest attempt at a systematic treatment of the body of English law. He enlarged the English common law with principles both from Canon and Roman law.

Bradbury, Sir Malcolm (Stanley) (1932–2000) Writer and critic, born in Sheffield, South Yorkshire, N England, UK. He studied at Leicester, and taught there at the university, before becoming professor of American studies at the University of East Anglia in 1970. The travels and travails of an academic have provided material for several of his novels, such as *Eating People is Wrong* (1959), *Stepping Westward* (1965), *The History Man* (1975, also a television series), and *Rates of Exchange* (1982). His work for television inspired the novella *Cuts* (1987); these worlds collide in *Dr Criminale* (1992). In his critical writing, he sponsored Modernist and post-Modernist ideas, and his books include monographs on Evelyn Waugh (1962) and Saul Bellow (1982), and *The Modern American Novel* (1983). Later works include the comic fiction anthology *Present Laughter* (1994), *The Atlas of Literature* (1996), and *To the Hermitage* (2000). He was knighted in 1999.

Bradbury, Ray(mond Douglas) (1920–) Writer of science fiction, born in Waukegan, Illinois, USA. An avid reader of sensational fiction and comics, he began early to contribute to magazines and short-story anthologies. While he has written notable novels – *Fahrenheit 451* (1953), *Dandelion Wine* (1957), and *Death is a Lonely Business* (1985) – he is primarily a short-story writer, and has created some of the finest examples in the genre. Well-known stories include *The Day It Rained Forever*, *R is for Rocket*, and those collected as *The Martian Chronicles* (1950, filmed 1966). Later novels include *A Graveyard for Lunatics* (1990), *Green Shadows, White Whale* (1992), and *Ahmed and the Oblivion Machines* (1998).

Bradford 53°48N 1°45W, urban area pop (2001e) 467 700. Town in West Yorkshire, N England, UK; part of West Yorkshire urban area; 15 km/9 mi W of Leeds and 310 km/193 mi NW of London; 19th-c development was based on the wool textile industry; railway; university (1966); textiles, textile machinery, coal, engineering, micro-electronics; scene of major disaster (1985) when wooden stand of Bradford City Football Club caught fire, killing 56; City Hall (1873), Wool Exchange (1867), art gallery (1904), 15th-c cathedral; football league team, Bradford City (Bantams).

Bradford, Barbara Taylor (1933–) Journalist and novelist, born in Leeds, West Yorkshire, N England, UK. She joined the *Yorkshire Evening Post* as reporter (1949–51) and women's editor (1951–3), became fashion editor of *Woman's Own* (1953–4), a columnist on *The London Evening News* (1955–7), and executive editor of *The London American* (1959–62). Moving to the USA, she worked as a columnist for leading newspapers, including the Chicago Tribune/New York Daily News Syndicate (1970–5) and the Los Angeles Times Syndicate (1975–81). She gained success with her first novel, *A Woman of Substance* (1980), and later books include *Hold the Dream* (1985), *The Women in his Life* (1990), *Her Own Rules* (1996), and *Where You Belong* (2000). *Emma's Secret*, a sequel to *A Woman of Substance*, appeared in 2003.

Bradford, William (1590–1657) Colonist and religious leader, born in Austerfield, South Yorkshire, N England, UK. A Nonconformist from boyhood, he joined a separatist group in 1606 and went with them to Holland in 1609. One of the moving spirits in the Pilgrim Fathers' expedition to the New World in 1620, he sailed on the *Mayflower*, and in 1621 took over from John Carver as elected governor of Plymouth Colony.

Bradlaugh, Charles [**brad**law] (1833–91) Social reformer and free-thinker, born in London, UK. He became a busy secularist lecturer and pamphleteer under the name of 'Iconoclast'. In 1880 he was elected MP for Northampton but, as an unbeliever, he refused to take the oath, and was expelled and re-elected regularly until 1886, when he took the oath and his seat. In 1886 he was prosecuted, with Annie Besant, for republishing a pamphlet advocating birth control (*The Fruits of Philosophy*); the conviction was subsequently quashed on appeal.

Bradlee, Benjamin (Crowninshield) (1921–) Journalist and writer, born in Boston, Massachusetts, USA. A founder of the *New Hampshire Sunday News*, he subsequently joined the *Washington Post* and worked for *Newsweek*. His book *Conversations with Kennedy* appeared in 1975. In 1965 he became managing editor of the *Washington Post*, and encouraged the investigative journalism which reached its high point in the Watergate scandal.

Bradley, F(rancis) H(erbert) (1846–1924) Philosopher, born in Clapham, Surrey, SE England, UK. He became a fellow of Merton College, Oxford (1870), but a kidney disease caused him to live as a semi-invalid most of his life. He was probably the most important figure in the British idealist movement of this period, and was much influenced by Kant and Hegel. His most important works are *Ethical Studies* (1876), *Principles of Logic* (1883), and the highly original and influential *Appearance and Reality* (1893).

Bradley, James (1693–1762) Astronomer, born in Sherborne, Gloucestershire, SWC England, UK. He studied at Oxford, and became professor of astronomy there in 1721. In 1742 he succeeded Edmond Halley as professor of astronomy at Greenwich. He published his discovery of the aberration of light (1729), providing the first observational proof of the Copernican hypothesis. In 1748 he discovered that the inclination of the Earth's axis to the ecliptic is not constant.

Bradley, Omar N(elson) (1893–1981) US general, born in Clark, Missouri, USA. He trained at West Point, and entered the army in 1915. A brigadier in 1941, he commanded II Corps in Tunisia and Sicily (1943). In 1944 he commanded the US forces at the Normandy invasion, and later the US 12th Army Group through France. He became the first permanent chairman of the US joint chiefs-of-staff (1949–53), and in 1950 was promoted to five-star general.

Bradman, Sir Don(ald George) (1908–2001) Cricketer, born in Cootamundra, New South Wales, SE Australia. The most prolific batsman in the history of the game, he played for Australia from 1928 to 1948 (captain, 1936–48). He made the highest aggregate and largest number of centuries in Tests against England, and jointly with Mark Taylor holds the record for the highest Australian Test score (334 against England at Leeds in 1930). His batting average in Test matches was 99·94 runs per innings; nobody else has attained 70. The first Australian cricketer to be knighted (1949), he was chairman of the Australian Cricket Board (1960–3, 1969–72), and also published a number of books about cricket.

Bradstreet, Anne, *née* **Dudley** (1612–72) Puritan poet, born probably in Northampton, Northamptonshire, C England, UK. In 1628 she married a Nonconformist minister, **Simon Bradstreet** (1603–97), who later became Governor of Massachusetts. In 1630 they emigrated to New England with the Winthrops. Her first volume of poems, *The Tenth Muse Lately Sprung Up in America*, was published by her brother-in-law in London in 1650 without her knowledge. She is considered the first English poet in America.

Brady, Ian (1938–) Convicted murderer, born in Glasgow, W Scotland, UK. He was found guilty of the murder of two children, John Kilbride (12) and Lesley Ann Downey (10), and a 17-year-old boy, Edward Evans, in 1966. In a case which horrified the public, it was revealed that Brady, with his lover **Myra Hindley** (1942–2002), from Gorton, lured young children into their home in Manchester and subjected them to torture before killing them. The lovers were described as the 'Moors Murderers' because they buried most of their victims on Saddleworth Moor in the Pennines. Hindley confessed to two other murders in 1986. Brady remains a patient at Ashworth Special Hospital, Merseyside

Brady Bill A gun control measure in the USA mandating a five-day waiting period and background checks before a handgun can be purchased, enacted in 1993. The law is named after James Brady, Ronald Reagan's press secretary, who was severely wounded in the assassination attempt on the president in 1981. The law has been bitterly opposed by the National Rifle Association and other opponents of gun control, but the overall impact of the law has been positive in reducing the flow of guns to criminals.

Braemar [braymah(r)] 57°01N 3°24W. Village in Aberdeenshire, NE Scotland, UK, 10 km/6 mi W of Balmoral Castle; tourism; Highland games (Aug).

Braga [brahga], ancient **Bracara Augusta** 41°32N 8°26W, pop (2000e) 90 000. Industrial capital of Braga district, 361 km/224 mi N of Lisbon, N Portugal; former capital of the old region of Entre Minho and Douro; seat of the Primate of Portugal; university; electrical appliances, leather, cutlery, textiles; cathedral (11th-c); midsummer celebrations, São Miguel fair and agricultural show (Sep).

Braganza [braganza], Port **Bragança** [bragansa], ancient **Juliobriga** 41°47N 6°46W, pop (2000e) 16 400. Capital of Braganza district, NE Portugal, 15 km/9 mi from the Spanish border; original seat of the House of Braganza, rulers of Portugal, 1640–1910; bishopric; agricultural centre, silk weaving, olive oil; castle (1187), cathedral, town hall (12th-c), Baçal Abbey; Cantarinhas fair (May), São Mateus fair (Sep).

Bragg, Billy, popular name of **Steven William Bragg** (1957–) Rock singer, musician, and songwriter, born in Barking, Essex, SE England, UK. Generally regarded as one of the most committed left-wing political performers working in popular music, he began performing in the 1970s with the punk group Riff Raff, then briefly joined the British army. Starting a solo career, he became known as the leading figure of the anti-folk movement of the 1980s and appeared regularly at political rallies, strikes, and benefits. His albums include *Brewing Up With Billy Bragg* (1984), *Talking to the Taxman About Poetry* (1986), *Don't Try This at Home* (1991), and *Mermaid Avenue* (1998, 2000).

Bragg (of Wigton), Melvyn Bragg, Baron (1939–) Novelist and broadcaster, born in Wigton, Cumbria, NW England, UK. He studied at Oxford, and joined the BBC as a producer in 1961, publishing his first novel, *For Want of a Nail*, in 1965. Later novels include *The Silken Net* (1974), *Love and Glory* (1983), *A Time to Dance* (1990), *Credo* (1996), *A Son of War* (2001), and *Crossing the Lines* (2003). His other writing includes screenplays and musicals. He has been presenter and editor of ITV's *The South Bank Show* since 1978, and presenter of BBC Radio 4's *Start the Week* (1988–98). He was head of arts (later, controller) at London Weekend Television (1982–90), became chairman of Border Television in 1990, and was reappointed as controller of arts and features at London Weekend Television in 2000. He received a life peerage in 1998.

Bragg, Sir William (Henry) (1862–1942) Physicist, born in Wigton, Cumbria, NW England, UK. With his son, William Lawrence Bragg (1890–1971), he founded X-ray crystallography. After studying at Cambridge, he became professor of mathematics at Adelaide, Australia (1886), and professor at Leeds in 1909, where from 1912 he worked in conjunction with his son. They were awarded a joint Nobel Prize for Physics in 1915, the only father–son partnership to share this honour. Bragg moved to University College London the same year, and became director of the Royal Institution in 1923.

Brahe, Tycho [brahhoe, tiykoh] (1546–1601) Astronomer, born in Knudstrup, Sweden. In 1573 he discovered serious errors in the astronomical tables, and commenced work to rectify this by observing the stars and planets with unprecedented positional accuracy. He rejected the Copernican theory, but it fell to Kepler to show this model to be essentially correct, using Brahe's data.

Brahma [brahma] The personified creator god of Hinduism. The deities Vishnu, Shiva, and Brahma form the *Trimurti* of classical Indian thought. As Vishnu and Shiva represent opposite forces, Brahma represents the balance between them. Brahma is the all-inclusive deity behind all the gods of popular Hinduism.

Brahman [brahman] In Hinduism, the eternal, impersonal Absolute Principle. It is the neuter form of Brahma, and is equated with cosmic unity.

Brahmanas [brahmanas] Priestly Indian texts appended over time to each of the Vedas. They describe, set out the grounds for, and enunciate the principles of the Brahmins' system of sacrifice.

Brahman cattle *zebu*

Brahmanism [brahmanizm] An early religion of India (though not the earliest), to which, historically, Indians have looked as the source of their religious traditions. It came to dominance during the Vedic Period (c.1200–500 BC) and was a religion of ritual and sacrifice. It gave supremacy to the Brahmin class, which exercised priestly authority over all aspects of life through their responsibility for the transmission of the sacred traditions and the performance of sacrifical rituals.

Brahmaputra, River [bramapootra], Chin **Yalu Zangbu**, Bangla **Jamuna** River in SW China and India, rising in the Tibetan Himalayas as the Maquan He R; flows E then S into Assam, becoming the Brahmaputra near Sadiya; then flows S into Bangladesh, joining the R Ganges before entering the Bay of Bengal through a vast delta; length c.2900 km/1800 mi.

Brahmins [brahminz] The highest of the four Hindu social classes. A priestly class, the Brahmins dominated Indian society for many centuries. Owing to modern economic and social changes, many of their descendants took up secular occupations. Recently they have come under critical attack by some lower-caste movements.

Brahmo Samaj [brahmoh samahj] (Hindi, 'divine Society') A theistic movement founded by Ram Mohan Roy in 1828 which argued that reason should form the true basis of Hinduism. Influenced by Islam, Christianity, and modern science, it sought a return to the purity of Hindu worship through an emphasis on monotheism, the rejection of idol-worship, and the reform of Hindu social practices.

Brahms, Johannes (1833–97) Composer, born in Hamburg, N Germany. The son of a poor orchestral musician, he earned his living as a pianist until 1853, when he was able to concentrate on composition. He toured with the Hungarian violinist Reményi, meeting Joachim and Liszt, and then Schumann, who helped Brahms publish his piano sonatas. He settled in Vienna, making occasional public appearances in Austria and Germany. Firmly based on classical foundations, his works contain hardly any programme music. His great orchestral works are comparatively late, the first, *Variations on a Theme of Haydn*, appearing when he was 40. His main works include four symphonies, two piano concertos, a violin concerto, a large amount of chamber and piano music, and many songs. His greatest choral work is the *German Requiem* (first performed complete in 1869).

Braille, Louis [brayl] (1809–52) Educationist, born in Coupvray, NC France. Blind from the age of three, at 10 he entered the Institution des Jeunes Aveugles in Paris. He studied organ playing, and became professor of the Institute in 1826. In 1829 he devised a system of raised-point writing which the blind could both read and write.

brain

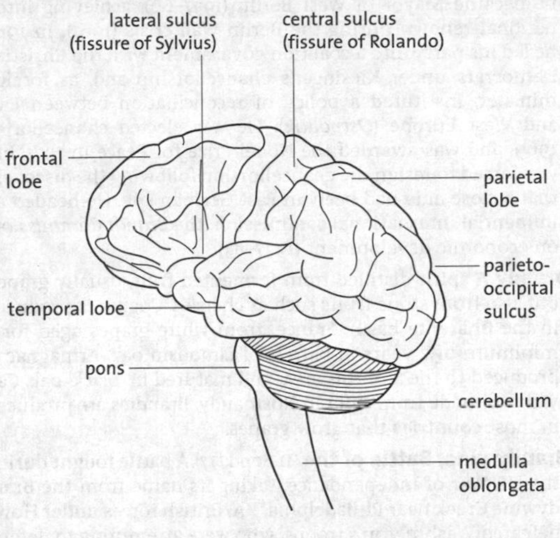

The part of the central nervous system of bilaterally symmetrical animals which co-ordinates and controls many bodily activities to an extent that depends upon the species. In humans, in addition to the control of movement, sensory input, and a wide range of physiological processes, it acts as the organ of thought, with several areas being specialized for specific intellectual functions (eg language, calculation). It occupies the cranial cavity, and can be divided into the **forebrain** (the *cerebral hemispheres* and *diencephalon*), **midbrain**, and **hindbrain** (the *cerebellum*, *pons*, and *medulla oblongata*). It is continuous with the spinal cord at the medulla oblongata (part of the **brain stem**). The cerebral hemispheres and brain stem contain cavities (the *ventricles*) which are continuous with the central canal of the spinal cord, and within which cerebrospinal fluid is produced. The brain also gives rise to the 12 pairs of cranial nerves. Examples of brain disorders, diseases, and infections are cerebral palsy, dementia, encephalitis, epilepsy, hydrocephalus, and meningitis.

braille [brayl] A communication system designed to enable blind people to have access to written language; devised in 1829 by Louis Braille. It consists of a sequence of cells, each of which contains a 3 × 2 matrix of embossed dots, whose patterns can be sensed through the fingers. In the basic system, the patterns represent letters, numbers, punctuation marks, and several short words. Computer-assisted systems are now available which can turn written text into braille.

Brain, Dennis (1921–57) Horn player, born in London, UK. He studied under his father **Aubrey Brain** (1893–1955) at the Royal Academy of Music, also becoming an organist, then worked with the Royal Philharmonic and Philharmonia Orchestras as chief horn player. Amongst the composers who wrote works especially for him were Britten, Hindemith, and Malcolm Arnold.

brain *see panel*

brain death The cessation of brain activity, in particular in the parts of the brain stem concerned with respiration and other vital functions. It must be certified by two doctors who can demonstrate the absence of electrical impulses from the brain surface (a flat EEG) and the failure of brainstem reflexes, including the reaction of pupils to light and oscillation (*nystagmus*) in response to the introduction of warm and cold water into the external ear canal. The diagnosis is usually made on an individual in a coma whose respiration is being artificially sustained and whose heart has not ceased to beat.

Braine, John (Gerard) (1922–86) Writer, born in Bradford, West Yorkshire, N England, UK. The success of his first book, *Room at the Top* (1957), enabled him to become a full-time novelist. The theme of aggressive ambition and determination to break through social barriers identified him with the 'Angry Young Men' of the 1950s. His novels deal mostly with the north of England and northerners, and include *The Vodi* (1959), *Life at the Top* (1962), and *One and Last Love* (1981). Many of his writings have been adapted for television.

brain stem That part of the nervous system between the spinal cord and the forebrain, consisting of (from above) the *midbrain*, *pons*, and *medulla oblongata*. Through it the cerebral hemispheres communicate with the rest of the central nervous system. The cardiac, respiratory, vasomotor, and other 'vital' physiological centres are located in the medulla. On the rear surface of the midbrain are four rounded projections (*colliculi*) arranged in pairs; these receive and transmit impulses for the reflex rotatory movements of the eyes, head, body, and limbs away from or towards light and sound stimuli.

brake A device used to apply a force to an object to retard its motion. The most common method is to bring the moving surface into contact with a fixed surface, thereby generating friction which opposes the direction of movement. The two types of brake most commonly used on motor cars are **drum brakes** and **disc brakes**.

brake horsepower (bhp) The power delivered by an engine to its output shaft, immediately prior to its transmission to other devices for useful work. For example, the brake horsepower of a medium-sized family car engine would be c.60–80 bhp, while a very large tanker's marine diesel engine would produce c.40 000 bhp.

Bramah, Joseph [brama] (1748–1814) Inventor, born in Stainborough, South Yorkshire, N England, UK. He made numerous inventions, including a beer machine used at the bar of public-houses, a safety lock, an improved water-closet (1778), a hydraulic press (1795), and a machine for printing bank-notes (1806). He was one of the first to propose the application of the screw-propeller.

Bramante, Donato [bramantay], originally **Donato di Pascuccio d'Antonio** (c.1444–1514) High Renaissance architect, born near Urbino, EC Italy. He started as a painter, and worked in Milan (1477–99), where he executed his first building projects, such as Sta Maria delle Grazie. He was employed in Rome from 1499 by Popes Alexander VI and Julius II. He designed the new Basilica of St Peter's (begun in 1506), as well as the Belvedere courtyard, the Tempietto di Sta Pietro in Montorio (1502), the Palazzo dei Tribunale (1508), and the Palazzo Caprini (1514).

bramble *blackberry*

brambling A finch native to the N Old World (*Fringilla montifringilla*); inhabits forests; eats seeds and insects; migrates to the Mediterranean and N Africa for winter. (Family: Fringillidae.)

bran The protective coat surrounding a cereal seed which, because of its high fibre content, is becoming increasingly common as a component of human foods. It comprises about 12% of the seed.

Branagh, Kenneth (Charles) [brana] (1960–) Actor and director, born in Belfast, NE Northern Ireland, UK. He studied at the Royal Academy of Dramatic Art, London, and joined the Royal Shakespeare Company in 1984. In 1987 he co-founded and became co-director of the Renaissance Theatre Company, starring in successful tours in 1988 and 1989, and in 1998 co-founded the Shakespeare Film Company. His film credits as director/actor include the remake of *Henry V* (1989, BAFTA best actor), *Much Ado About Nothing* (1993), a 4-hour film production of *Hamlet* (1997), and a musical version of *Love's Labour's Lost* (2000). Other films include *In the Bleak Midwinter* (1995) and *Wild, Wild West* (1999). Television work includes *Shackleton* (2002) and *Conspiracy* (2002, Emmy). Among his many awards are European Actor of the Year (1990), the Gielgud Award (2000), and an honorary Doctor of Letters (2001) by the Shakespeare Institute for his work in bringing Shakespeare to a popular audience. In 2001 he directed *The Play What I Wrote*, a comedy tribute to Morcambe and Wise. He returned to the stage after an absence of 10 years to play the lead in *Richard III* at the Crucible Theatre, Sheffield (2002), and later starred in David Mamet's *Edmond* at the National Theatre (2003). He was married to actress Emma Thompson (1989–96).

Branchiopoda [brangkiopoda] A diverse class of aquatic crustaceans found mostly in inland waters, from fresh to hypersaline, and occasionally in the sea; characterized by leaf-like trunk limbs that act as food-gathering apparatus and as gills; contains c.820 living species, including tadpole shrimps, fairy shrimps, clam shrimps, and water fleas.

Brancusi, Constantin [brankoozee] (1876–1957) Sculptor, born in Pestisani, W Romania. He won a scholarship to the Bucharest Academy and arrived in Paris in 1904. 'The Kiss' (1908) was his most abstract sculpture of the period, representing two block-like figures. His 'Sleeping Muse' (1910) shows Rodin's influence, but is the first of his many characteristic, highly polished egg-shaped carvings. Other works include several versions of 'Mademoiselle Pogany' (1913–31), 'Bird in Space' (1925), and 'The Sea Lions' (1943).

Brandeis, Louis (Dembitz) [brandiys] (1856–1941) Judge, born in Louisville, Kentucky, USA. He studied at Louisville, Dresden, and Harvard, and practised in Boston. He conducted many labour arbitrations, and was frequently involved in cases challenging the power of monopolies and cartels. He formulated the economic doctrine of the New Freedom adopted by Woodrow Wilson for his 1912 presidential campaign, and was appointed to the US Supreme Court in 1916. Brandeis University in Waltham, MA, is named after him.

Brandenburg or **Brandenburg an der Havel** [brandnberg] 52°25N 12°34E, pop (2000e) 99 200. Industrial city in Brandenburg district, Potsdam, EC Germany; on R Havel, W of Berlin; former centre of the Prussian province of Brandenburg, part of which is now in Poland; much rebuilding after severe damage in World War 2; railway; steel, textiles, machinery.

Brandenburg Gate An arch designed by Carl Langhans (1733–1808) and erected in Berlin in 1788–91. The monument, which was badly damaged during World War 2, was restored in 1958.

Brando, Marlon (1924–) Film and stage actor, born in Omaha, Nebraska, USA. A product of the New York Actors' Studio, he made his debut in 1943, and appeared in several plays before achieving fame in *A Streetcar Named Desire* (1947). His many films include *The Wild One* (1953), *Julius Caesar* (1953), *One-Eyed Jacks* (which he also directed, 1961), *Mutiny on the Bounty* (1962), and *Last Tango in Paris* (1972). An Oscar winner for *On the Waterfront* (1954) and *The Godfather* (1972), he refused the latter honour in protest at the film industry's treatment of American Indians, and has been a prominent campaigner for the Civil Rights movement. He ended a period of absence from the screen with the anti-apartheid drama *A Dry White Season* (1988), the comedy *The Freshman* (1990), *Don Juan de Marco* (1995), *The Brave* (1997), *Free Money* (1998), *Autumn of the Patriarch* (1999), and *The Score* (2001).

Brandt, Bill [brant], popular name of **William Brandt** (1904–83) Photographer, born in London, UK. He studied with Man Ray in Paris in 1929 and returned to London in 1931. Later in the 1930s he made a series of striking social records, contrasting the lives of the rich and the poor, and during World War 2 he worked for the ministry of information recording conditions in London in the Blitz. His greatest creative work was his treatment of the nude, in which his essays in pure form, as published in *Perspective of Nudes* (1961) and *Shadows of Light* (1966), approached the surreal.

Brandt, Willy [brant], originally **Karl Herbert Frahm** (1913–92) West German statesman and chancellor (1969–74), born in Lübeck, N Germany. He joined the Social Democrats at 17 and, as a fervent anti-Nazi, fled to Norway (1933), where he changed his name. In 1940 he went to Sweden, working as a journalist in support of the German and Norwegian resistance movements. In 1945 he returned to Germany, and was a member of the Bundestag (1949–57). A pro-Western, anti-Communist leader, he became Mayor of West Berlin (1957–66), achieving international renown during the Berlin Wall crisis (1961). In 1966 he led his party into a coalition government with the Christian Democrats under Kiesinger's chancellorship and, as foreign minister, instituted a policy of reconciliation between East and West Europe (*Ostpolitik*). He was elected chancellor in 1969, and was awarded the Nobel Prize for Peace in 1971, but was forced to resign the chancellorship following the discovery that a close aide had been an East German spy. He headed an influential international commission (the *Brandt Commission*) on economic development (1977–83).

brandy A spirit distilled from fermented fruit, usually grapes, but also from stone fruits such as cherries. Cognac is produced in the Charente basin, France, from white grapes aged for a minimum of 2 years in barrels of Limousin oak. Armagnac is produced to the S of this area, and matured in 'black' oak. Calvados is made from cider in Normandy. Brandies are produced in most countries that grow grapes.

Brandywine, Battle of the (11 Sep 1777) A battle fought during the US War of Independence, taking its name from the Brandywine Creek near Philadelphia, PA. British forces under Howe defeated Washington's troops, who were attempting to defend Pennsylvania.

Branson, Sir Richard (Charles Nicholas) (1950–) Businessman, born in Sharnley Green, Surrey, SE England, UK. He launched a mail-order business in discount records in 1969, opening his first shop in London in 1971, under the name Virgin. This was followed by a series of highly successful business enterprises, including a recording company, various retailing operations, the travel company Voyager Group (1980), the airline Virgin Atlantic (1984), Virgin Radio (1993), Virgin Direct (1995), V2 Music (1996), and Virgin Trains (1996). He is also known for his sporting achievements, notably the record-breaking Atlantic crossing in *Virgin Atlantic Challenger II* in 1986, and the first crossing by hot-air balloon of the Atlantic (1987) and Pacific (1991). He was knighted in 1999.

Brant, Joseph, Mohawk name **Thayendanegea** (1742–1807) Mohawk Indian chief, and brother-in-law of the Irish fur trader, Sir William Johnson. He served the British in the French and Indian War, and in Pontiac's War (1763–6), and in the American War of Independence (1775–83) commanded the Mohawks on the British side. In 1785 he went to England to persuade the British government to indemnify the Indians for their losses in the war, and in London was received at court and lionized by society. In later years an earnest Christian, he founded the first Episcopal Church in Upper Canada.

brant *brent goose*

Braque, Georges [brak] (1882–1963) Painter, born in Argenteuil, NC France. He was one of the founders of classical Cubism, and worked with Picasso (1908–14). After World War 1 he developed a personal nongeometric, semi-abstract style. His paintings are mainly of still-life, the subject being transformed into a two-dimensional pattern, and they are among the outstanding decorative achievements of our time, with a pervasive influence on other painters. Two of his paintings are 'The Port of La Ciotat' (1907, John Hay Whitney Collection, New York) and 'The Black Birds' (1957, Aimé Maeght Collection).

Brasília [brazilia] 15°45S 47°57W, pop (2000e) 2 080 000. Capital of Brazil in Centro-Oeste region, WC Brazil; construction began in 1956; capital moved from Rio de Janeiro in 1960; principal architect Oscar Niemeyer (1907–); laid out in the shape of a bent bow and arrow; residential areas lie along the curve of the bow; at right angles to these is the arrow (8 km/5 mi), with the Congress buildings, the president's office, and the Supreme Court at the tip; to the W lie the cathedral and the Ministry buildings; the cultural and recreational zones and the commercial and financial areas lie on either side of the intersection of the bow and arrow; airport; university (1961); light industry;

famous for its modern sculpture; designated a world heritage site.

Braşov [brashov], formerly **Kronstadt** (to 1918), **Stalin** (1950–60) 45°39N 25°35E, pop (2000e) 319 000. Industrial capital of Braşov county, C Romania; founded, 13th-c; important mediaeval trade centre; ceded by Hungary after World War 1; railway junction; university (1971); textiles, lorries, tractors, metallurgy, ball bearings, chemicals, machinery; summer resort and winter sports centre.

brass An alloy composed of copper and zinc; yellowish, malleable, and ductile. Its properties and applications may be altered by varying the proportions of copper and zinc. It is the most widely-used non-ferrous alloy.

Brassaï [brasaee], professional name of **Gyula Halasz** (1899–1984) Painter and photographer, born in Brasso, Hungary. Coming to Paris in 1923, he worked as a journalist, and from 1930 used photography to record the underworld and night-life of 1930s Paris. His first collection, *Paris de nuit* (1933, Paris by Night), caused a sensation. He became a French citizen in 1948.

brasses Ornamental objects made from brass, an alloy of zinc and copper. Monumental brasses were a less expensive substitute for carved stone tomb slabs. Particularly popular in England in the Gothic period, they could be very elaborate, with engraved portraits and heraldry in architectural framing, or simply inscriptions.

brassica A member of a genus of plants containing numerous economically important vegetables, including turnip and mustard, but often in a gardening sense referring more specifically to cabbages, cauliflower, broccoli, and Brussels sprouts, all derived from the wild cabbage, *Brassica oleracea*. (Genus: *Brassica*, 30 species. Family: Cruciferae.)

brass instrument A musical instrument made of brass or other metal, in which air is made to vibrate by means of the player's lips and breath, usually through a narrow mouthpiece. In simple instruments, such as the bugle, the notes available are restricted to the lower end of a single harmonic series; in others, valves or slides enable the fundamental note to be altered, and consequently a greater number of pitches to be obtained. The main orchestral brass instruments are the horn, trumpet, trombone, and tuba.

Bratby, John (1928–92) Artist and writer, born in London, UK. He studied at Kingston Art School and the Royal College of Art. A leading protagonist of English 'New Realism', in the mid-1950s he was associated with the 'kitchen sink' school because of his preoccupation with working-class domestic interiors, as in 'Baby in Pram' (Liverpool). He represented Britain at the 1956 Vienna Biennale, but after that his reputation declined. He also wrote several novels, including *Breakdown* (1960), with his own illustrations.

Bratislava [bratislahva], Ger **Pressburg**, Hung **Pozsony**, ancient **Posonium** 48°10N 17°08E, pop (2000e) 450 000. River port and capital of Slovak Republic; on R Danube; stronghold of Great Moravian Empire, 9th-c; capital of Hungary, 1541–1784; Hungarian monarchs crowned here until 1830; centre of emergent Slovak national revival; incorporated into Czechoslovakia in 1918; airport (Vajnory); railway; university (1919); technical university (1938); food processing, petrochemicals, agrochemicals, oil refining, textiles, paper, electrical equipment, mechanical engineering, agricultural trade; 13th-c cathedral, castle, Mirbach Palace, Lenin's museum, pharmaceutical museum; Slovak National Theatre, Slovak National Gallery and Museum, musical festivals.

Bratsk Dam A major gravity earth-fill dam on the Angara R, Russia; completed in 1967; height 125 m/410 ft. It has the capacity to generate 4500 megawatts of hydroelectricity.

Brattain, Walter H(ouser) (1902–87) US physicist, born in Amoy, SE China, where his father was a teacher. He grew up on a cattle ranch in the State of Washington, and studied at the universities of Oregon and Minnesota. In 1929 he joined Bell Telephone Laboratories, where he worked as a research physicist on the surface properties of semiconductors. With Bardeen and Shockley he developed the point-contact transistor, using a thin germanium crystal. He shared the Nobel Prize for Physics in 1956.

Braun, Eva [brown] (1910–45) Mistress of Adolf Hitler, born in Munich, SE Germany. She was secretary to Hitler's staff photographer, became Hitler's mistress in the 1930s, and is said to have married him before they committed suicide together in the air-raid shelter (the bunker) of the Chancellery during the fall of Berlin.

Braun, Wernher von [brown] (1912–77) Rocket pioneer, born in Wyrzysk, NWC Poland (formerly Wirsitz, Germany). He studied engineering at Berlin and Zürich, and founded in 1930 a society for space travel which maintained a rocket-launching site near Berlin. By 1936 he was director of a rocket research station at Peenemünde. Hitler personally released him when he was imprisoned on espionage charges for refusing to co-operate with Himmler over the V-2 project. He never approved of the military use of the rocket, and surrendered willingly to US troops in 1945. He became a US citizen in 1955 and a director of the US army's Ballistic Missile Agency at Huntsville, AL, where in 1958 he was chiefly responsible for the launching of the first US artificial Earth satellite, Explorer 1. He was also director of the Marshall Space Flight Center (1960–70), where he developed the Saturn rocket for the Apollo 11 Moon landing (1969).

Brautigan, Richard (Gary) [brawtigan] (1933–84) Novelist and poet, born in Tacoma, Washington, USA. He performed public readings in San Francisco, becoming an inspiration to the 'flower children'. His writing is highly imaginative and often surreal. His first novel was the humorous *A Confederate General from Big Sur* (1964). This was followed by the critically acclaimed *Trout Fishing in America* (1967) and the collected poems, *The Pill Versus the Springhill Mine Disaster* (1968). A very private man, he travelled throughout the USA and spent his later years in Tokyo. After his suicide, an obituary in the Los Angeles *Times* described him as 'the literary guru of the '60s.

Brazil *p.222*

Brazil nut An evergreen tree (*Bertholletia excelsa*) growing to 30 m/100 ft, native to the jungles of Brazil; leaves oblong; flowers white, in large panicles; fruit a woody or rounded capsule to 15 cm/6 in across, containing 12–15 tight-packed, woody, 3-sided seeds familiarly called by the same name. Not cultivated, the nuts sold in shops are gathered from wild trees. (Family: Lecythidaceae.)

brazing The joining of two pieces of metal (the same or different) by heating, then filling in the junction with a metal of lower melting point than those being joined. A flux is generally necessary. Brazing differs from soldering, in that a soldered joint is not expected to stand any mechanical strain (as in electrical unions), whereas a brazed joint can be very strong.

Brazos River River in S USA, formed in W Texas by the Double Mountain Fork and Salt Fork Rivers; enters the Gulf of Mexico at Freeport; length 1947 km/1210 mi; major tributaries the Clear Fork, Little, Navasota; used for irrigation, hydroelectricity, and flood-control.

Brazzaville [brazavil] 4°14S 15°14E, pop (2000e) 1 098 000. River-port capital of the Congo, W Africa, on right bank of R Congo (opposite Kinshasa, Democratic Republic of Congo); founded, 1880; capital of French Equatorial Africa, 1910; headquarters of Free French forces in World War 2; capital of Congo, 1960; airport; railway terminus from coast; university (1972); banking, chemicals, metallurgy, food processing, textiles, timber; cathedral.

bread A widely used staple food made by baking a mixture of flour and water; the flour used is most commonly wheat, which may be mixed with flour from oatmeal, rye, or barley. The mix results in a dough which may be kneaded, a process that stretches and aligns the protein molecules of the wheat. The product is then either immediately baked to give **unleavened bread**, or allowed to rise, through the production of carbon dioxide, to give **leavened bread**. The carbon dioxide can be

Brazil

□ International Airport ∴ World heritage site

Port **Brasil**, official name **The Federative Republic of Brazil**, Port **República Federativa do Brasil**

Local name Brasil

Timezone GMT −2 (Atlantic Islands); GMT −3 (E); GMT −4 (mid-W); GMT −5 (extreme W)

Area 8 511 965 km²/3 285 618 sq mi

Population total (2002e) 174 619 000

Status Republic

Date of independence 1822

Capital Brasília

Language Portuguese (official)

Ethnic groups White (53%), mixed (34%), black (6%)

Religions Roman Catholic (89%), Protestant, Spiritualist

Physical features Located in E and C South America; low-lying Amazon basin in the N; where forest canopy cleared, soils susceptible to erosion; Brazilian plateau in the C and S, average height 600–900 m/2000–3000 ft; Guiana Highlands (S) contain Brazil's highest peak, Pico da Neblina, 3014 m/9888 ft; eight river systems, notably Amazon (N), Sao Francisco (C), Paraguay, Paraná, and Uruguay (S); 30% of population concentrated on a thin coastal strip on the Atlantic, c.100 km/325 mi wide.

Climate Almost entirely tropical, equator passing through the N region, and Tropic of Capricorn through the SE; Amazon basin, annual rainfall 1500–2000 mm/60–80 in; no dry season; average midday temperatures 27–32°C; dry region in the NE, susceptible to long droughts; hot, tropical climate on narrow coastal strip, with rainfall varying greatly N–S; S states have a seasonal temperate climate.

Currency 1 Cruzeiro real (Cr$) = 100 centavos

Economy One of the world's largest farming countries, agriculture employing 35% of population; world's largest exporter of coffee, second largest exporter of cocoa and soya beans. Iron-ore reserves (possibly world's largest). Timber reserves, the third largest in the world; but continuing destruction of the Amazon rainforest is causing much concern; road network being extended through the Amazon rainforest.

GDP (2002e) $1·376 tn, per capita $7600

Human Development Index (2002) 0·757

History Claimed for the Portuguese by Pedro Alvares Cabral, 1500, first settlement at Salvador da Bahia; King of Portugal moved seat of government to Brazil, 1808; his son, Dom Pedro, declared himself emperor, 1818; independence established, 1822; Dom Pedro forced to abdicate in 1831 and succeeded by his 14-year-old son, Dom Pedro II, 1840; abolition of slavery in 1888, persuaded former slave-owners in declining sugar-plantation areas to join Republican opposition to the king, who was overthrown in the coup of 1889; ruled by dictator, Getúlio Vargas, 1930–45; Vargas deposed by military, and liberal republic restored, 1946; returned to office, 1950, but committed suicide, 1954; capital moved from Rio de Janeiro to Brasília, 1960; another coup in 1964 led to a military-backed presidential regime; President da Costa e Silva resigned and military junta took control, 1969; new elections, 1985; new constitution approved, transferring power from the President to the Congress, 1988; bicameral National Congress.

Head of State/Government

1945–51 Eurico Gaspar Dutra
1951–4 Getúlio Dornelles Vargas
1954–5 Joïo Café Filho
1955 Carlos Coimbra da Luz
1955–6 Nereu de Oliveira Ramos
1956–61 Juscelino Kubitschek de Oliveira
1961 Janio da Silva Quadros
1961–3 Joïo Belchior Marques Goulart
1963 Pascoal Ranieri Mazilli
1963–4 Joïo Belchior Marques Goulart
1964 Pascoal Ranieri Mazilli
1964–7 Humberto de Alencar Castelo Branco
1967–9 Artur da Costa e Silva
1969–74 Emílio Garrastazu Médici
1974–9 Ernesto Geisel
1979–85 Joïo Baptista de Oliveira Figueiredo
1985–90 José Sarney
1990–2 Fernando Collor de Mello
1992–5 Itamar Franco
1995–2003 Fernando Henrique Cardoso
2003– Luiz Inacio Lula da Silva

produced either chemically or by using yeast. Much of today's bread is made using a short fermentation process called the Chorleywood Bread Process.

breadfruit An evergreen tree (*Artocarpus altilis*) growing to 12–18 m/40–60 ft, probably native to Malaysia; glossy leaves oval, deeply lobed towards tips; male flowers in short catkins, females in prickly heads, achenes, and spongy receptacle, enlarging to form a rounded, multiple fruit, 10–20 cm/4–8 in diameter, and green to brownish when ripe, filled with a white, fibrous pulp. It was introduced in prehistoric times to the S Pacific, where it is a staple food; and was carried via the HMS *Bounty* to the West. (Family: Moraceae.)

bread mould Any mould found growing on bread; more specifically used for the fungus *Mucor* (Class: Zygomycetes), which forms a colourless hair-like covering over bread surface; produces dark spores (*zygospores*) at the tips of its upright branches; and *Neurospora*, which is reddish in colour and causes bread spoilage in bakeries.

break dancing *street dance*

breaking radiation *bremsstrahlung*

breaking stress *tensile strength*

Breakspear, Nicholas *Adrian IV*

breakwater An artificial barrier to wave activity. Breakwaters are constructed to intercept incoming waves and provide a sheltered area, usually for marine recreation or port facilities. Most are built offshore and parallel to the shoreline. Because breakwaters reduce wave energy and modify the direction of wave propagation in their lee, they alter the natural near-shore circulation of sand and other sediments, and frequently produce silting in the very harbours and channels they are designed to protect.

Bream, Julian (Alexander) [breem] (1933–) Guitarist and lutenist, born in London, UK. A protégé of Andrés Segovia, he made his debut in London in 1950. He has edited much music for guitar and lute, and among the composers who have written for him are Britten, Henze, Tippett, and Walton. He formed the Julian Bream Consort in 1961, specializing in early ensemble music. In 1990 he performed at his 40th anniversary concert at the Wigmore Hall, London.

bream Deep-bodied freshwater fish (*Abramis brama*) found in quiet lowland rivers and lakes of N Europe; length up to c.60 cm/2 ft. The name is also used for various similarly deep-bodied fishes in other families, both freshwater and marine. (Family: Cyprinidae.)

breast The milk-producing organ of the female reproductive system; also known as the **mammary gland**. It is composed of glandular tissue enclosed in thick masses of fat, supported by fibrous tissue and covered by skin. The two breasts in humans are found on the front of the chest: they are small in children, but at puberty the female breasts increase rapidly in size, whereas in males they remain rudimentary. Size and appearance is variable both within an individual as well as between individuals and different races. During pregnancy the breasts enlarge, being largest during milk secretion (*lactation*). At the apex of the breast is the *nipple*, surrounded by the darker *areola*.

breastbone *sternum*

breast cancer One of the commonest malignant tumours in women. It first appears as a lump within breast tissue, and spreads locally to the skin, which may ulcerate, and to the lymph nodes. Blood-borne spread also occurs to bones, lungs, liver, and other organs. Treatment includes surgical removal of the tumour or breast (*mastectomy*) and a combination of hormonal and anti-cancer drugs. Some countries routinely screen women for breast cancer with *mammograms*, X-rays that allow visualization of the breast tissue.

breast feeding The suckling of an infant by its mother for a time after birth. The secretion of breast milk (*lactation*) takes two to three days to become established. The early transfer of maternal antibodies to the baby which helps to prevent infections is one advantage of this form of feeding. Breast feeding an infant for the first six months of its life confers significant health benefits over bottle feeding. The number of mothers who breastfeed in the developed countries has increased steadily since the 1960s, when bottle feeding was the norm.

breast milk The product of the female milk-producing (*mammary*) gland of humans and other mammals. Its composition is variable, both during a feed and throughout lactation. Human breast milk is rich in the antibodies of the secretory class (immunoglobulin A) and in other antimicrobial factors. Its iron content is in a highly absorbable form. Its quality remains more or less constant, despite quite marked variation in the mother's diet, and is widely held to be the preferred sole food for infants during the first three to four months of life.

breathalyzer / breathalyser A device used with a driver suspected of having drunk an excessive amount of alcohol or having committed a moving traffic offence. Formerly, the breathalyzer was based on a tube through which the driver blew; crystals in the device changed colour if there was alcohol present; and the extent of the change indicated whether the driver had exceeded the alcohol limit, which in the UK is 80 mg per 100 ml of blood, and varies by jurisdiction in the USA. Modern devices, such as the Lion Alcometer 7410, are battery-operated; the suspect blows through a tube, and lights indicate the alcohol level. The initial test is given by a uniformed police officer; if positive, the driver may be arrested, and given a further blood or urine test at a police station with a doctor present. Many US jurisdictions do not use the field breathalyzer, but the driver is taken directly to the police station, where a choice of blood, urine, or breath sample (on an 'intoxilyzer' or other breath test machine) is given.

breathing *respiration*

breccia [brechia] Coarse sedimentary rock made up of a mixture of angular rock cemented by a finer-grained matrix. It usually results from local processes such as landslides and geological faulting, in which rock fracturing occurs.

Brecht, (Eugene) Bertolt (Friedrich) [brekht] (1898–1956) Poet, playwright, and theatre director, born in Augsburg, S Germany. His early plays, marked by a revolt against bourgeois values, won him success, controversy, and the Kleist Prize in 1922. Popularity came with *Die Dreigroschenoper* (1928, The Threepenny Opera), an adaptation of Gay's *The Beggar's Opera* (1728), and from then until 1933 his work was particularly concerned with encouraging audiences to think rather than identify, and with experimentation in epic theatre and alienation effects. Hitler's rise to power forced him to leave Germany, and he lived in exile for 15 years, chiefly in the USA. During this period, he wrote some of his greatest plays, including *Mutter Courage und ihre Kinder* (1938, Mother Courage and her Children) and *Der Kaukasische Kreidekreis* (1945, The Caucasian Chalk Circle). After his return to East Berlin in 1948, his directorial work on these and other plays with the Berliner Ensemble firmly established his influence as a major figure in 20th-c theatre. In 1955 he received the Stalin Peace Prize.

Breckinridge, Mary (1881–1965) Nurse, midwife, and organization founder, born in Memphis, Tennessee, USA. Founder and director of the Frontier Nursing Service in Kentucky and pioneer in American midwifery, she fought successfully to lower infant mortality rates in the South. An effective fundraiser and crusader for women and children, she combined administrative and practical skills with deep spirituality.

Breckland, The A sandy region of heathland on the border of Norfolk and Suffolk, E England, UK. It was an important area of Neolithic flint mining. Today large areas are covered in conifer plantations.

Brecon Beacons [brekn] National park in S Wales, UK; area 1434 sq km/553 sq mi; established in 1957; three main peaks of 'the Beacons', Pen-y-Fan, Corn Du, and Cribyn, rise to c.900 m/2950 ft; includes Brecon cathedral, Llanthony Priory, Llangorse Lake.

Breda [brayda] 51°35N 4°45E, pop (2000e) 132 000. Industrial city in North Brabant province, S Netherlands, at confluence of Mark and Aa Rivers; bishopric; important cultural centre, headquarters of many educational institutes; charter, 13th-c; known for the **Compromise of Breda**, a protest against Spanish tyranny (1566), and Charles II's **Declaration of Breda** before his restoration (1660); railway; engineering, synthetic fibres, foodstuffs, matches, brewing, power tools, tourism; Breda castle (1350, now a military academy), town hall (18th-c), Gothic cathedral (1510).

Breeches Bible A name sometimes applied to the **Geneva Bible**, because of the rendering of *Gen* 3.7, which refers to Adam and Eve having sewn fig leaves together 'and made themselves breeches'. This translation, though, is not unique to the Geneva Bible.

breeder reactor *nuclear reactor*

brehon laws [breehuhn] The corpus of ancient Irish customary law written down by the 8th-c; the name derives from Irish *breitheamh* 'judge'. Following the Anglo-Norman invasion of Ireland in the late 12th-c, Irish law gave much ground to English common law. It was finally abolished by statute in the early 17th-c.

Bremen [braymen] 53°05N 8°48E, pop (2000e) 569 000. Commercial city, seaport, and capital of Bremen province, NW Germany; on both banks of the lower R Weser, 94 km/58 mi SW of Hamburg; railway; university (1970); trade in grain, cotton, tobacco; shipbuilding and repairing, machinery, oil refining, chemicals, electrical equipment, electronics, aerospace, vehicles, textiles; 11th-c cathedral, Gothic town hall (1405–10).

Bremerhaven [braymerhahvn] 53°34N 8°35E, pop (2000e) 134 000. Seaport in Bremen province, NW Germany; on E bank of Weser estuary, 56 km/35 mi N of Bremen; city status, 1851; united with Wesermunde, 1938; railway; Europe's largest fishing port for many years, declining in 1990s; trawling, fish processing, shipbuilding and repairing, machinery.

Bremner, Rory (Keith Ogilvy) (1961–) British satirical impressionist, writer, and performer. He studied at King's College, London, and began performing in tours and one-man shows in 1985. He made several series for BBC television (1986–92) and *Rory Bremner – Who Else?* for Channel 4 (from 1992), as well as a number of videos. Awards include the Top Male Comedy Performer BAFTA (1994, 1995, 1996) and the Royal Television Society's Award (1995).

bremsstrahlung [bremshtrahlung] (Ger 'braking radiation') Electromagnetic radiation emitted by decelerating charged particles passing through matter. For example, electrons fired into lead produce bremsstrahlung in the form of X-rays. It is the principal means of energy loss for high energy particles.

Brendan, St, known as **the Navigator** (?–c.577) Abbot and traveller, born in Tralee, SW Ireland, traditionally the founder of the monastery of Clonfert in Co Galway (561), and other monasteries in Ireland and Scotland. The Latin *Navigation of St Brendan* (7th–8th-c) recounts his legendary voyage to a land of saints far to the W and N, possibly the Northern Isles, Iceland, or even N America. He should not be confused with another Irish saint and a contemporary – St Brendan, abbot of Birr. Feast day 16 May.

Brendel, Alfred (1931–) Pianist, born in Wiesenberg, NE Czech Republic. He made his debut in Graz (1948), and has since performed widely throughout Austria, where he lives. He is known for his interpretations of Mozart, Beethoven, Schubert, Liszt, and Schoenberg. He tours internationally, and has written many essays on music.

Bren gun A light machine-gun, the standard section weapon of the British Army during World War 2. The name derives from Brno, Czech Republic, where the gun was first designed, and Enfield in Britain, where it was manufactured in large quantities.

Brennan, William J(oseph), Jr (1906–97) Judge, born in Newark, New Jersey, USA. He studied at Harvard, joined a Newark law firm, and specialized in labour law. He was appointed to the New Jersey Superior Court (1949) and the state Supreme Court (1952), and President Eisenhower appointed him to the US Supreme Court in 1956, where he took an active role in the 'liberal' decisions it handed down under the chief justiceship of Earl Warren. He continued to favour liberal policies until his retirement in 1990.

Brenner, Sydney (1927–) Molecular biologist, born in Germiston, NE South Africa. He studied at Witwatersrand University and Oxford, and joined the MRC Molecular Biology Laboratory in Cambridge (1957), becoming its director in 1980. He did notable work on the information code of DNA, and in the 1970s moved to basic studies designed to relate, in detail, an animal's nervous system to its genetic make-up.

Brenner Pass [brenuh], Ger **Brenner Sattel**, Ital **Passo del Brennero** 47°02N 11°32E. Mountain pass in the C Tirol Alps on the border between Italy and Austria; altitude 1371 m/4498 ft; on the main route between Bolzano and Innsbrück; the lowest pass over the main chain of the Alps; open at all seasons of the year.

Brentano, Clemens von [brentahnoh] (1778–1842) Poet, born in Ehrenbreitstein, WC Germany, the uncle of Franz and Lujo Brentano. He became a Roman Catholic in 1818 and withdrew to the monastery of Dülmen, near Münster (1818–24), where he recorded the revelations of the nun Anna Katharina Emmerich. One of the founders of the Heidelberg Romantic school, he was mostly successful in his novellas, particularly in the *Geschichte vom braven Kasperl und dem schönen Annerl* (1817, The Story of Just Caspar and Fair Annie), and with his brother-in-law Achim von Arnim (1781–1831) he edited *Des Knaben Wunderhorn* (1805–8), a collection of folk songs that was of seminal influence in the Romantic movement in Europe.

Brentano, Franz [brentahnoh] (1838–1917) Psychologist and philosopher, born in Marienberg, E Germany. He became a Catholic priest (1864), and taught philosophy at Würzburg until 1873. He then abandoned the priesthood, and moved to teach at Vienna until his retirement (1895). In his most important work, *Psychologie vom empirischen Standpunkt* (1874, Psychology from an Empirical Standpoint), he developed the doctrine of 'intentionality', characterizing mental events as involving the 'direction of the mind to an object'.

brent goose A goose native to the N hemisphere, also known as **brant** (*Branta bernicla*); breeds in the high Arctic; migrates to temperate N coasts in winter; eats primarily the marine grass *Zostera*; unusually for geese, rarely nests in captivity if caught. (Family: Anatidae.)

Brescia [braysha] 45°33N 10°13E, pop (2000e) 209 000. Industrial town and capital of Brescia province, Lombardy, N Italy; rail junction; textiles, clothing, shoes, iron and steel, metal products, transport equipment, marble quarrying, precision engineering, firearms; market centre for local agricultural produce; Tempio Capitolino (AD 73), and other Roman remains; cathedrals (11th-c, 17th-c), Renaissance town hall (1492–1508).

Bresson, Robert [bresõ] (1907–99) Film director, born in Bromont-Lamothe, C France. At first a painter and photographer, he started serious work in the cinema with *Les Anges du péché* (1943, The Angels of Sin), but it was his next production *La Journal d'un curé de campagne* (1951, Diary of a Country Priest) which brought international acclaim, subsequently repeated with *Un Condamné à mort s'est echappé* (1956, trans A Man Escaped) and *Le Procès de Jeanne d'Arc* (1962, The Trial of Joan of Arc). Later productions are *Lancelot du lac* (1974), *Le Diable, probablement* (1977, The Devil, Probably), and *L'Argent* (1983, Money).

Brest (Belarus), formerly **Brest-Litovsk**, Pol **Brześć nad Bugiem** 52°08N 23°40E, pop (2000e) 279 600. River-port capital city of Brestskaya oblast, Belarus; on the R Mukhavets at its junction with the R Bug, on the Polish border; founded by Slavs, 1017; railway; major transportation centre; foodstuffs, electrical engineering, electronics.

Brest (France) 48°23N 4°30W, pop (2000e) 154 000. Fortified port and naval station in Finistère department, NW France; on the Atlantic coast; natural harbour on the Penfeld estuary; used as a German submarine base in World War 2; rebuilt after heavy bombing; railway; extensive dockyards, naval stores, arsenals; fishing, textiles, chemicals, metallurgy.

Brest-Litovsk, Treaty of (1918) A bilateral treaty signed at Brest between Soviet Russia and the Central Powers (Germany, Austria–Hungary, Bulgaria, and the Ottoman Empire). Under its terms, Russia withdrew from World War 1, hostilities ceased on Germany's E front, and the new Soviet government ceded nearly half of its European territory: Finland, the Baltic provinces, Belorussia, Poland, Ukraine, and parts of the Caucasus. Lenin said that Russia must 'sacrifice space in order to gain time'. The German armistice in the West (November 1918) annulled the treaty, but at Versailles Russia regained only Ukraine.

Brethren (in Christ) A Church founded in the late 18th-c in Pennsylvania, USA, deriving from Mennonite tradition; also known as **River Brethren**. Pietistic, evangelical, and missionary, it soon spread to Canada, and in the 20th-c, although numerically small, supported missionary churches in Asia, Africa, and Central America.

Breton, André [bruhtõ] (1896–1966) Poet, essayist, and critic, born in Tinchebray, NW France. In 1916 he joined the Dadaist group, and in 1922 turned to Surrealism. He published his first Surrealist manifesto in 1924, and became editor of *La Révolution surréaliste*. His major novel, *Nadja*, was published in 1928, and his collected poems in 1948.

Breton The Celtic language of Brittany, introduced by migration from Cornish-speaking S England in the 5th-c AD. It is thought the two languages were mutually intelligible until the 15th-c, but Breton is marked by increasing influence from French, especially in pronunciation and vocabulary. Breton was not recognized as a school subject until the 1950s, nor was it legal to christen a child with a Breton name. There are no official figures for Breton speakers, but it is thought they are now less than 250 000. There is a substantial body of literature from the mediaeval period onwards.

Bretton Woods Conference An international conference held at Bretton Woods, NH, USA, in 1944, to consider the stabilization of world currencies and the establishment of credit for international trade in the post war years. It led to the establishment of the International Monetary System, including the International Monetary Fund (IMF) and the World Bank. The agreement, signed by the USA, UK, and 42 other nations, aimed to control exchange rates, which were fixed for members in terms of gold and the dollar. This system was used until 1973, when floating exchange rates were introduced.

Breuer, Marcel (Lajos) [broyer] (1902–81) Architect and designer, born in Pécs, S Hungary. A student at the Bauhaus in Germany from 1920, he took charge of the furniture workshop by 1924, and designed probably the first modern tubular steel chair. In 1937 he joined Walter Gropius in the USA, and became associate professor of architecture at Harvard (1937–46). Working independently after 1947, his work includes the UNESCO building in Paris. A significant figure in the 'Modern Movement', his classic furniture designs, in particular, represented major developments in materials and techniques.

Breughel *Brueghel*

Breuil, Henri (Edouard Prosper) [broey] (1877–1961) Archaeologist, born in Mortain, NW France. He trained as a priest, became interested in cave art in 1900, and was responsible for the discovery of the decorated caves at Combarelles and Font-de-Gaume in the Dordogne the following year. Professor at the Collège de France (1929–47), his work marked the beginning of the study of palaeolithic art.

breviary A book of liturgical material (psalms, hymns, lessons, prayers) used in the Daily Office, and required to be recited by all priests and clerics in major orders of the Roman Catholic Church. It was revised by Pope Paul VI in 1971, to incorporate the recommendations of Second Vatican Council.

brewing The art and technique of producing an alcoholic beverage (most often a variety of beer) from cereals. Grain is steeped in water, and allowed to germinate. The germination is halted by heating (*malting*), and after *milling* to crush the grain and expose the contents, the malt is *mashed* (leached with hot water) to give a solution of fermentable carbohydrates (the *wort*). Sugar may be added. The wort is boiled in a *copper* with hops (to give aroma and flavour). When cool, a brewer's yeast is added. Traditional British beers are fermented at the top of the vessel. Bottom fermentation with a different kind of yeast yields the lager type of beer.

Brezhnev, Leonid Ilich [brezhnyef] (1906–82) Russian statesman, general secretary of the Soviet Communist Party (1964–82), and president of the Supreme Soviet (1977–82), born in Kamenskoye (present-day Dniprodzerzhyns'k), EC Ukraine. He trained as a metallurgist, and became a political commissar in the Red Army in World War 2. After the war, he was a party official in the Ukraine and Moldavia, becoming a member (1952–7) and then chairman (1960–4) of the Presidium of the Supreme Soviet. He was general secretary of the Party Central Committee after Khrushchev, and gradually emerged as the most powerful figure in the Soviet Union, the first to hold simultaneously the position of general secretary and president.

Brezhnev Doctrine [brezhnef] The term applied to the policies of Leonid Brezhnev, general secretary of the Soviet Communist Party (1964–82), which combined strict political control internally with peaceful co-existence and détente abroad. It also justified intervention (including military) in the internal affairs of other socialist states, as in Czechoslovakia (1968). The Brezhnev period was later referred to in the USSR as the 'years of stagnation'.

Brian [breean], known as **Brian Boroimhe** or **Boru** ('Brian of the Tribute') (c.926–1014) King of Ireland (1002–14). In 976 he became chief of Dál Cais, and after much fighting made himself King of Leinster (984). After further campaigns in all parts of the country, his rule was acknowledged over the whole of Ireland. He was killed after defeating the Vikings at Clontarf.

Briand, Aristide [breeã] (1862–1932) French statesman and prime minister (1909–11, 1913, 1915–17, 1921–2, 1925–6, 1929), born in Nantes, W France. He was founder (with Jean Jaurés) of *L'Humanité*, and framer of the law for the separation of Church and state (1905). A socialist, he was 11 times elected French premier, and also served as foreign minister (1925–32), helping to conclude the *Kellogg–Briand Pact* (1928), outlawing war as a means of solving disputes. He shared the Nobel Prize for Peace in 1926, and advocated a United States of Europe.

briar The woody root of two species of heath, *Erica scoparia* and *Erica arborescens*, used to make tobacco pipes. (Family: Ericaceae.)

Brickhill, Paul (Chester Jerome) (1916–91) Writer, born in Sydney, New South Wales, SE Australia. He studied at Sydney University, and worked in journalism before serving with the Royal Australian Air Force during World War 2. Shot down in North Africa, he was for two years a prisoner-of-war in Stalag Luft III, Germany; he described his escape from the camp in *The Great Escape* (1951). He became the most successful non-fiction writer of the post-war period, with *The Dam Busters* (1951), *Escape or Die* (1952), and *Reach for the Sky* (1954).

bricks Blocks, usually of clay or a clay mixture, baked by the Sun or by fire. Bricks have been made for thousands of years, and are still one of the most widely used building materials. Most are now made by machine, and fired in kilns. The fixing of bricks in place to provide a strong wall is called **bricklaying**. Bricks are laid in mortar, a mixture of cement or lime with sand and water. The patterns are formed by laying the bricks end-on (*headers*) or lengthwise (*stretchers*). The bonds are selected for both their degree of strength and aesthetic value.

Bride, St *Bridget, Brigid,* or *Bride, St*

bridewealth Wealth given by a husband or his kin to the bride's family, in compensation for the loss of the bride, who goes to join the husband's household. Bridewealth is distinct from a **dowry**, which is wealth provided by the bride's family, and taken with her at her marriage.

bridge (engineering) A structure carrying a road, path, or railway over an obstacle. The principal types are **arch bridges**, **girder bridges**, and **suspension bridges**. The simplest consist of slabs of stone or branches laid across a stream. Bridges may be built of timber, stone, iron, steel, brick, or concrete, different materials being suited to different forms of construction. The greatest spans are achieved by suspension bridges, the longest at present being the Akashi-Kaikyo, Japan (1991 m/6532 ft). The greatest single span arch bridge is the New River Gorge, W Virginia, USA (518 m/1700 ft). China had iron-chain suspension and segmental arch bridges by the early 7th-c. Famous bridges include the Golden Gate Bridge (California, USA), Tower Bridge (UK), Sydney Harbour Bridge (Australia), and the Rialto (Venice).

bridge (recreation) A popular card game developed from whist, using the full set of 52 playing cards, and played by two pairs of players. It may have originated in Turkey, Russia, or India, but the first published reference to the game was found in a 1529 sermon by an Englishman, Bishop Latimer. **Auction bridge** was brought to England by a British officer serving in India (c.1894) and became popular at the Portland Club. Trumps are decided by a preliminary bid or auction that is intended to be low, because the declarer is given credit for all tricks, whether contracted or not. In the more aggressive **contract bridge**, the side winning the contract, and so naming trumps, scores towards game only the number of tricks contracted for in the bidding. Auction bridge was displaced by contract bridge in the 1920s, and is now rarely played. The game's scoring system was devised by US businessman and yachtsman Harold Stirling Vanderbilt (1884–1970) in 1925. Important innovators in the USA were Ely Culbertson (1891–1955) and Charles H(enry) Goren (1901–91).

Bridgend [brijend] pop (2001e) 128 600; area 246 sq km / 95 sq mi. County (unitary authority from 1996) in S Wales, UK; administrative centre, Bridgend; castle (12th-c), resort at Porthcawl.

Bridge of Sighs An enclosed 16th–17th-c bridge in Venice, through which condemned prisoners would pass from the Doge's Palace to the Prigioni prison.

Bridges, Robert (Seymour) (1844–1930) Poet, born in Walmer, Kent, SE England, UK. He studied at Oxford, qualified in medicine, and practised in London. He published three volumes of graceful lyrics (1873, 1879, 1880), wrote several plays, the narrative poem *Eros and Psyche* (1885), and other works, including a great deal of literary criticism. He was also an advocate of spelling reform. From 1907 he lived in seclusion at Oxford, publishing comparatively little; then in 1929, on his 85th birthday, he issued his most ambitious poem, *The Testament of Beauty*. He became poet laureate in 1913.

Bridget, Brigid, or **Bride, St** (453–523) Abbess, said to be the daughter of an Ulster prince. She entered a convent at Meath in her 14th year, and founded four monasteries for women, the chief at Kildare, where she was buried. She was regarded as one of the three great saints of Ireland, the others being St Patrick and St Columba, and was held in great reverence in Scotland (as St Bride). Feast day 1 February.

Bridget, Brigit, or **Birgitta (of Sweden), St** (c.1302–73) Visionary, born in Finsta, Sweden. At the age of 13 she was married to a young nobleman, **Ulf Gudmarsson**, by whom she had eight children. After his death in 1344, she founded the monastery of Vadstena, which became the cradle of the new order of *Bridgettines* as a branch of the Augustinian order. In 1349 she travelled to Rome where she founded a Swedish hospice. She made a pilgrimage to Palestine and Cyprus in 1372 and died in Rome on her return. She was canonized in 1391; feast day 23 July or 8 October. Her daughter, **St Katarina of Sweden** (1335–81), was canonized in 1489; feast day 22 March.

Bridgetown 13°06N 59°36W, pop (2000e) 6100. Seaport and capital city of Barbados, West Indies, on Carlisle Bay in the SW of the island; a new deep-water harbour built to the NW; resort of Paradise Beach to the N; University of the West Indies (1963); tourism, sugar manufacturing; cathedral; one of the earliest monuments commemorating Lord Nelson.

Bridgewater Canal An inland waterway in England commissioned by Francis Egerton, 3rd Duke of Bridgewater (1736–1893), and constructed (1762–72) by James Brindley. The canal links Worsley to Manchester, crossing the Irwell valley by viaduct, and continues to Liverpool. It is 64 km/40 mi long.

Bridgman, P(ercy) W(illiams) (1882–1961) Physicist, born in Cambridge, Massachusetts, USA. He studied at Harvard, and became professor of physics and mathematics there in 1919. He obtained under high pressure a new form of phosphorus, proved experimentally that viscosity increases with high pressure, and was awarded the Nobel Prize for Physics in 1946 for his work on high-pressure physics and thermodynamics.

Bridgnorth 52°33N 2°25W, pop (2001e) 52 500. Market town in E Shropshire, C England, UK; originally a mediaeval crossing place on the R Severn; formerly a commercial river port, now a busy town and commuter area for Wolverhampton; N terminus of the Severn Valley Railway; has Britain's only inland cliff railway; Aircraft and Missile Museum at RAF Cosford; many fine half-timbered buildings including Bishop Percy's house and stilted Town Hall; annual international food festival.

brig Any two-masted, square-rigged sailing vessel. Brigs became common in the mid-18th-c as colliers supplying London from the northern coal fields. They are still fairly common as sail-training vessels.

brigantine [briganteen] A two-masted sailing vessel, square-rigged on the foremast and fore- and aft-rigged on the after-mast. Used mainly in the late 19th-c, a few are still in commission.

Briggs (of Lewes), Asa Briggs, Baron (1921–) Educationalist and historian, born in Keighley, West Yorkshire, England, UK. He was educated at Sidney Sussex College, Cambridge, and London University. Professor of modern history at Leeds University (1955–61), he was the first professor of history, then Vice Chancellor (1967), of the University of Sussex, and became provost of Worcester College, Oxford, in 1976. A pioneer in distance learning, he was instrumental in the establishment of Britain's Open University (1969), and became its Chancellor in 1978. Of his more than 70 books, important titles include *Victorian People* (1954), *A Social History of England* (1983, 1994), and *Modern Europe 1789–1989* (1997).

Briggs, Barry (1934–) Speedway rider, born in Christchurch, New Zealand. He appeared in a record 17 consecutive world championship finals (1954–70), and a record 18 all told, during which he scored a record 201 points and took part in 87 races, winning the title in 1957–8, 1964, and 1966. He won the British League Riders' championship six times in succession (1965–70). His career started with Wimbledon (1952), and he also rode for New Cross, Southampton, Swindon, and Hull. After retiring (1976), he ran a motorcycle business in Southampton, and was a co-promoter of the 1982 world championships in Los Angeles.

Bright, Bill, popular name of **William Rohl Bright** (1921–) Businessman and evangelist, born in Coweta, Oklahoma, USA. He studied economics at Northeastern State University, and later moved to Los Angeles where he launched a successful business career. He became a Christian (1945) and studied for five years at Princeton and Fuller theological seminaries. At UCLA he began sharing New Testament scriptures with students on campus, an activity that led to his Campus Crusade for Christ International. He was awarded the Templeton Prize for Progress in Religion in 1996.

Bright, John (1811–89) Radical British statesman and orator, born in Rochdale, Greater Manchester, NW England, UK. When the Anti Corn-Law League was formed in 1839 he was a leading member, and engaged in free trade agitation throughout the country. In 1843 he became MP for Durham, and strongly opposed the corn laws until they were repealed (1846). Elected in 1857 for Birmingham, his name was closely associated with the Reform Act of 1867. He accepted office as President of the Board of Trade (1868), but retired through illness in 1870, returning in 1881 as Chancellor of the Duchy of Lancaster. He was regarded as one of the most eloquent speakers of his time.

Bright, Richard (1789–1858) Physician, born in Bristol, SW England, UK. He studied at Edinburgh, London, Berlin, and Vienna, and from 1820 was connected with Guy's Hospital. **Bright's disease** of the kidneys is named after him.

brightness *luminous intensity*

Brighton 50°50N 0°10W, pop (2000e) 144 400. Resort city in Brighton and Hove unitary authority, SE England, UK; on the English Channel, 77 km/48 mi S of London; in 1782 the Prince of Wales (later George IV) took up residence here; city status, 2000; railway; University of Sussex (1961), 5 km/3 mi NE; University of Brighton (1992, formerly Brighton Polytechnic); food processing, furniture; conference centre; marina; Royal Pavilion (1811), designed by John Nash; pier (built 1866) badly damaged by fire in 2003; Brighton Festival (May); football league team, Brighton and Hove Albion (Seagulls); London–Brighton veteran car run (Nov).

Brigid, St *Bridget, Brigid,* or *Bride, St*

Brigit or **Brighid** An Irish goddess of fire and the hearth; also of poetry and handicrafts. In the Christian era a number of her attributes were taken over by St Brigid. The name means 'the exalted one'.

Brigit, St *Bridget, Brigit,* or *Birgitta (of Sweden), St*

Brihadisvara Temple [brihadisvahra] A Hindu temple at Thanjavur (formerly Tanjore), Tamil Nadu, India; a world heritage monument. The temple was founded by the Chola king Rajaraja I (985–1014) in the late 10th-c. It is renowned for its frescoes and for its 60 m/200 ft tower, encrusted with shrines and relief sculptures.

brill Large flatfish (*Scophthalmus rhombus*) found mainly on sandy bottoms in shallow waters (10–75 m/30–250 ft) of NE Atlantic and Mediterranean; body length up to c.60 cm/2 ft; both eyes on left side, mouth large and curved; sandy brown with dark and light flecks; good food fish. (Family: Scophthalmidae.)

Brillat-Savarin, (Jean) Anthelme [breeyah savarĩ] (1755–1826) French politician, gastronome, and writer, born in Belley, EC France. He was a deputy in 1789, and Mayor of Belley in 1793. During the French Revolution he took refuge in Switzerland, and afterwards in America. His *Physiologie du goût* (1825, The Physiology of Taste), an elegant and witty compendium of the art of dining, has been repeatedly republished and translated; an English form is *A Handbook of Gastronomy*, with 52 etchings by Lalauze (1884).

brimstone (chemistry) *sulphur*

brimstone (entomology) A wide-winged butterfly; wings lemon-yellow in male, greenish-white in female, each with an orange spot; caterpillars blue-green, with fine hairs; found on buckthorn; adult remains dormant under leaves during winter. (Order: Lepidoptera. Family: Pieridae.)

Brindisi [breendisee], ancient **Brundisium** 40°37N 17°57E, pop (2000e) 90 000. Seaport and capital of Brindisi province, Puglia, S Italy; 100 km/62 mi SE of Bari, on the Adriatic; inner and outer harbour; centre of trade with E Mediterranean from ancient times; used by Crusaders as a naval base; archbishopric; airport; railway; Virgil died here; cathedral (11th-c, rebuilt 18th-c), Castello Svevo (1227).

Brindley, James (1716–72) Engineer and canal builder, born in Thornsett, Derbyshire, C England, UK. Apprenticed to a millwright, he became an engineer, and contrived a water engine for draining a coalmine (1752). Francis Egerton, 3rd Duke of Bridgewater, employed him to build the canal between Worsley and Manchester (1759), a difficult enterprise completed in 1772. He also commenced the Grand Trunk Canal, and completed the Birmingham, Chesterfield, and other canals. He was illiterate, solving most of his problems without writings or drawings.

Brinell hardness test [brinel] A test for the hardness of metal, named after Swedish engineer, Johann August Brinell (1849–1925). A hard steel ball is pressed into the test piece with a known and reproducible force, producing a depression. The dimensions of the depression provide a measure of hardness.

brine shrimp A fairy shrimp found in inland salty or hypersaline waters; swims upside down, beating its leaf-like legs; eggs resistant to desiccation, sold as fish food and hatched in salt water when required. (Class: Branchiopoda. Order: Anostraca.)

Brink, André (Philippus) (1935–) Novelist, short-story writer, playwright, critic, and translator, born in Vrede, E South Africa. An Afrikaner dissident, he emerged as a writer in the 1950s, but it was not until his seventh novel – which he later translated into English as *Looking on Darkness* (1974) – was banned by the South African authorities that he began to attract international attention. Later books include *Rumours of Rain* (1978), *Chain of Voices* (1982), *Imaginings of Sand* (1996), *The Devil's Valley* (1998), *The First Voice of Adamastor* (1999), and *The Rights of Desire* (2001). He received the Martin Luther King Memorial Prize and the French Prix Medicis Etranger in 1980, and has twice been runner-up for the Booker Prize.

briquette A fuel made into uniformly shaped lumps, formed by compressing small coal, previously carbonized to render it smokeless, and consolidated by a combustible binder. The term is also used for the uniform lumps of brown coal formed by extrusion or compression.

Brisbane [brizbn] 27°30S 153°00E, pop (2000e) 1 506 000. State capital of Queensland, Australia, on the Brisbane R; founded as a penal colony, 1824; state capital, 1859; third largest city in Australia; the only Australian city with one central metropolitan government; airport; railway; two universities (1909, 1975); commerce, oil refining, chemicals, engineering, shipbuilding, food processing, textiles; City Hall (1930); Lone Pine Koala Sanctuary; botanical gardens; Government House; maritime museum; Brisbane Royal Show (Aug); scene of World Expo (1988), since redeveloped as entertainment and cultural venue.

brisling Small Norwegian fish, *Sprattus sprattus*, usually canned in oil.

Brissot (de Warville), Jacques Pierre [breesoh] (1754–93) French revolutionary politician, born near Chartres, NC France. After completing his studies in Paris he abandoned the legal profession for that of journalism. He was imprisoned for four months in the Bastille on the false charge of having written a brochure against the queen. In 1789 he was present at the storming of the Bastille, and was elected representative for Paris in the National Assembly. He exercised a predominant influence over all the early movements of the revolution, and was recognized as the head of the Girondins or Brissotins. In the Convention his moderation made him suspect, and with 20 other Girondins he was guillotined.

bristletail A primitive wingless insect with long tail filaments; the group includes the silverfish. **Two-pronged bristletails** (Order: Diplura, 660 species) are blind, mostly minute, and found in the soil, feeding on decaying organic matter. **Three-pronged bristletails** (Order: Thysanura, 600 species) are minute, mostly found in the soil and forest leaf litter.

bristleworm An aquatic annelid worm; body segmented, segments typically with paired lateral lobes (*parapodia*) bearing various bristles and scales; body length from 1 mm–3 m/0·04 in–10 ft; c.8000 species, including sedentary, tube-living, free-swimming, and parasitic forms. (Class: Polychaeta.)

Bristol, Anglo-Saxon **Bricgstow** 51°27N 2°5W, pop (2001e) 380 600. Unitary authority in SW England; former (to 1996) administrative centre of Avon county; county status 1373; major port in 17th–18th-c, much involved in the slave trade; 187 km/116 mi W of London; an important shipping centre, ports at Avonmouth, Royal Portbury, Portishead; 2 airports; railway; university (1909); University of the West of England (1992, formerly Bristol Polytechnic); shipbuilding, aircraft construction, engineering, tobacco processing; trade in food, petroleum products, metals; 12th-c cathedral, Roman Catholic cathedral (1973), 14th-c St Mary Redcliffe, Theatre Royal (1766), Clifton suspension bridge (1864); Brunel's SS *Great Britain* rests restored where she was launched in 1843; football league teams, Bristol City (Robins), Bristol Rovers (Pirates).

Bristol Channel An inlet of the Atlantic Ocean and an extension of the R Severn estuary, between Wales and England, UK; extends 128 km/79 mi E–W, with a varying width of 5–80 km/3–50 mi at its mouth; the greatest tidal range in England; chief towns on the Welsh (N) coast include Cardiff and Swansea, and on the English (S) coast Ilfracombe and Weston-super-Mare.

Bristow, Eric, nickname **the Crafty Cockney** (1957–) Darts player, born in London, UK. World professional champion a record five times (1980–1, 1984–6), he was also the beaten finalist twice. His other major championships include the World Masters (1977, 1979, 1981, 1983–4), the World Cup individual (1983, 1985), and the *News of the World* Championship (1983–4).

Britain *United Kingdom*

Britain, Battle of The name given to the air war campaign of late summer 1940 in which the German Luftwaffe attempted to destroy the Royal Air Force (RAF) as a prelude to the invasion of Great Britain. The aerial offensive began in August, the German bomber aircraft and fighter escorts concentrating on wiping out the RAF both by combat in the air and by bombing their vital airfields in the S of the country. British resistance proved stubborn, with the Spitfires and Hurricanes of RAF Fighter Command being directed by radar onto the incoming bomber streams. Badly mauled, the Luftwaffe switched their offensive from attacks on airfields to attacks on British cities (the 'Blitz'), losing their opportunity to gain true air superiority. Between 1 July and 31 October the Luftwaffe lost 2848 aircraft to the RAF's 1446.

Britain, Roman Known to the Graeco-Roman world from the late 4th-c BC, Britain escaped invasion until the time of Julius Caesar (55–54 BC) and conquest until the time of Emperor Claudius (AD 43); Roman military occupation then followed, the main garrison towns being Lincoln, York, Caerleon on the Usk, and Chester. Conquest of the whole island was initially intended, but the fierce resistance of the tribes in the N (Caledonia) ruled this out. Instead, defensive barriers were erected in N England and S Scotland (Hadrian's Wall and the Antonine Wall). To the S, control was exerted through the army and the policy of Romanizing the natives. Military occupation lasted until c.400, when troubles elsewhere in the Empire forced the withdrawal of the garrison troops.

Britannia metal A tin alloy used for tableware, containing 90% tin, 7% antimony, and 2% copper; lustrous, hard, and malleable. It was initially used as a substitute for pewter, but has now been largely displaced by *nickel-silver*, an alloy of nickel, copper, and zinc.

Brit Awards British popular music awards established in 1977 by the British Music Industry to mark the Queen's silver jubilee. That year the ceremony honoured the best in popular music over the previous 25 years, and since 1982 the awards have been presented annually. Nominees in various categories are voted for by an academy of over 1000 members from business and the media. Some winners are voted for by the public, while the Outstanding Contribution to British Music Award is gifted by the British Record Industry. In 2000 the spin-off Classical Brit Awards were established.

British *Celtic languages*

British Academy of Film and Television Arts (BAFTA) A media academy which began in 1947 as the British Film Academy, becoming the Society of Film and Television Arts in 1959, and changing its name to its present title in 1975. The BAFTA award, a bronze theatrical mask, was originally nicknamed a 'Stella'. Over the years the categories have varied and widened and currently include awards for best film, director, actor/actress, screenplay, cinematography, music, and production design. Special categories include the Richard Dimbleby Award for outstanding personal contribution to factual television.

British Antarctic Survey A division of the Natural Environment Research Council which has responsibility for research in atmospheric, earth, and life sciences in the Antarctic and surrounding oceans. It supports a number of research stations on the continent, including permanent stations at Signy (60°43S 45°36W), Faraday (65°15S 64°16W), Rothera (67°34S 68°08W), and Haley (75°36S 26°41W). Research includes the continued investigation of changes in atmospheric ozone concentrations, analyses of ice cores for climatic information, the modelling of ice-sheet behaviour, and the dynamics of the terrestrial, freshwater, and marine ecosystems.

British Antarctic Territory British colonial territory 20–80°W and S of 60°S; includes South Orkney Is, South Shetland Is, Antarctic Graham Land Peninsula, and the land mass extending to the South Pole; area 5·7 million sq km/2·2 million sq mi; land area (660 000 sq km/170 000 sq mi) covered by ice and fringed by floating ice shelves; population solely of scientists of the British Antarctic Survey; territory administered by a High Commissioner in the Falkland Is.

British Association for the Advancement of Science An organization whose aims are to promote interest and progress in science. At its annual conference the social, political, and economic implications of scientific advances are considered. It was founded in 1831 by a group of scientists disillusioned with the elitist and conservative attitude of the Royal Society.

British Athletic Federation (BAF) The former governing body for athletics in England and Wales. It was formed in 1991 as a result of a merger between the Amateur Athletic Association, founded in 1880, and the Women's Amateur Athletic Association, founded in 1922. Bankruptcy led to its reconstitution in 1998 as UK Athletics.

British Broadcasting Corporation *BBC*

British Columbia pop (2000e) 3 675 000; area 947 800 sq km/365 945 sq mi. Mountainous province in SW Canada, bordered S by USA, E by Alberta, N by Yukon, and W by the Pacific; several mountain chains, including Rocky Mts, Monaghee Range, Coast Mts; largest islands, Queen Charlotte, Vancouver; ranges cut by fertile valleys of Fraser, Thompson, and Columbia Rivers; many lakes, largest Williston, Okanagan, Kootenay, Shuswap and Arrow; capital, Victoria; major cities, Vancouver, Kamloops, Kelowna, Prince George; timber products, hydroelectric power, mining (coal, copper, silver, gold, molybdenum), tourism, oil and natural gas, fishing, dairy products, cattle; Captain Cook landed at Vancouver I, 1778; sea otter fur trade flourished; border with USA settled by Oregon Treaty, 1846; gold rush to Fraser R, 1858; entered federation of Canada, 1871; Canadian Pacific Railway completed, 1885; opening of Panama Canal (1915) increased trade with Europe; governed by a lieutenant-governor and an elected 57-member Legislative Assembly.

British Commonwealth *Commonwealth* (British)

British Council A London-based organization founded in 1934, with (in 2004) offices in 110 countries throughout the world. The UK's international organization for educational and cultural relations, it works along with the Foreign Office to enhance the UK's reputation in the world as a valued partner. Among its objectives are the promotion of the country's creativity, cultural diversity, and achievements; the challenging of outmoded stereotypes of the UK abroad; the provision of educational and cultural services for people overseas; and the promotion of English teaching and learning. It also aims to strengthen ties within Europe; to encourage a greater international awareness in the UK, especially among young people; and to position the UK overseas as a committed partner in tackling reform agendas and promoting sustainable development.

British currency The basic units of the present British currency are the pound (£) and the (new) **penny**. 100p = £1. Coins are issued for 1p, 2p, 5p, 10p, 20p, 50p, £1, and £2 (with £5 struck for special occasions). The British currency was decimalized in 1971. The basic unit, the pound or pound sterling, survived, the symbol £ deriving from the Latin *libra* (originally a pound weight of silver). The pre-decimal currency units include the penny, abbreviated to *d* from the Latin *denarius*, with 240 pence equal to £1 and 12 pence equal to one shilling. The Norman design for the penny showed a crossed indentation on one side, allowing the coin to be broken in half to serve as a **halfpenny**, and into quarters to become a **farthing**. The first round farthing and halfpenny coins were struck in 1279. The shilling (abbreviated to *s*), was introduced under Henry VII, 20 shillings equalling £1. This combination of entities is the source of the term *Lsd* for money. The farthing was withdrawn from circulation in 1960. Other old units were the halfpenny coin (two halfpence equalling 1 penny, 480 halfpence equalling £1); the threepence ('threepenny bit') and the sixpence coins, both introduced under Edward III; the florin or two-shilling piece (equalling 24 pence, with ten florins equalling £1); the **half-crown**, equalling 30 pence, with eight half-crowns equalling £1; the **crown**, with one crown equalling five shillings and four crowns equalling £1, and the **guinea**, whose value was fixed at 21 shillings in 1717 and which was last coined in 1813. This guinea is still used as a unit of account, for example, in art auctions. Archaic terms include the **groat**, with one groat equalling 4 pence, coined in 1351–2 and remaining in circulation until 1662.

British Empire There were in fact several British Empires: the empire of commerce and settlement in the Caribbean and North America, founded in the 17th-c and partly lost when the 13 colonies declared their independence in 1776; the empire in the East, founded in the 17th-c but developed through the extensive conquest of India (1757–1857) and the acquisition of islands, trading posts, and strategic positions from Aden to

Hong Kong; the empire of white settlement in Canada, Australia, New Zealand and the Cape in South Africa, each of which had been federated as 'dominions' by 1910; and the 'dependent territories' in Africa and elsewhere acquired during the 'New Imperialism' of the last few decades of the 19th-c. To this must be added the British 'informal empire' – territories which she did not rule directly, but which fell under her influence because of her industrial and commercial power. These included parts of S America, the Middle East, the Persian Gulf, and China. In 1919 the Empire reached its fullest extent through the acquisition of mandates over German and Ottoman territories in Africa and the Middle East. It was this diversity which gave rise to such famous phrases as 'the empire on which the sun never sets'. By the late 19th-c the Empire was bonded together not only by industrial strength but by a vast merchant marine and powerful navy. After World War 1 it was apparent that Britain could not control such an extensive empire: the dominions secured effective independence in 1931; the Middle Eastern mandates were virtually lost by World War 2; India gained her independence in 1947, and the other Asian colonies soon followed; while most of the rest of the Empire was decolonized in the 1960s. Many of the countries of the Empire remained in the British Commonwealth of Nations.

British Empire, Most Excellent Order of the In the UK, an order of chivalry, the first to be granted to both sexes equally, instituted in 1917 by George V. It has five classes: Knights and Dames Grand Cross (GBE), Knights and Dames Commander (KBE/DBE), Commanders (CBE), Officers (OBE), and Members (MBE). Appointments are made on the recommendations of government ministers, but recipients may come from any walk of life. The ribbon is pink edged with grey (civil division), with a central narrow stripe (military division).

British Expeditionary Force (BEF) An army, first established in 1906, sent to France (Aug 1914 and Sep 1939) to support the left wing of the French armies against German attack. In World War 2 its total strength was 394 000, of whom 224 000 were safely evacuated, mainly from Dunkirk, in May–June 1940.

British Indian Ocean Territory *see panel*

British Isles Group of islands off the NW coast of Europe. It consists of two main islands (Great Britain and Ireland), and many smaller islands, notably the Isle of Man, Isle of Wight, Channel Is, Western Is, Orkney, and Shetland.

British Legion *Royal British Legion*

British Library The national depository created by the British Library Act of 1972 through the amalgamation of the British Museum Library, the National Central Library, and the National Lending Library for Science and Technology. Its reference division is based in London; its lending division in West Yorkshire. A new site for the Library in Euston Rd, London, opened in 1997 after many delays.

British Lions The name used by representative touring rugby teams: British Isles in Rugby Union, Great Britain in Rugby League. British RU teams first went to New Zealand and Australia in 1888, although they were only fully representative from 1910. The 'Lions' nickname has been used by 18 teams since its adoption on the 1924 tour of South Africa. They were always popular, crowd-pulling visitors, but enjoyed only limited playing success until the 1970s, when the 1971 team beat New Zealand, and the 1974 team won in South Africa. Further wins came in Australia (1989) and in South Africa (1997). The first British RL team went to Australia and New Zealand in 1910, but the name was not adopted until players formed the British Rugby League Lions Association in 1945. They won in Australia in 1946, 1958, 1962, and 1970, and in New Zealand in 1954, 1966, 1970, 1974, 1979, and 1990.

British Medical Association (BMA) An association founded in 1832 in Worcester to promote medical and allied sciences, and to maintain the honour of the profession. It is now concerned with issues such as standards of practice, medical education, and conditions of service for doctors. It is listed as a trade union, but is not affiliated to the Trades Union Congress.

British Indian Ocean Territory

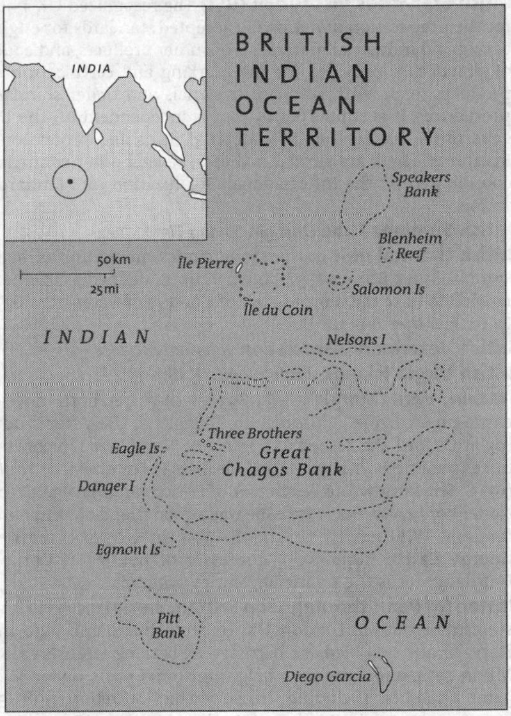

pop (2000e) 2900 (no permanent inhabitants); land area 60 sq km/23 sq mi. British territory in the Indian Ocean, 1900 km/1180 mi NE of Mauritius, comprising the Chagos Archipelago; the islands cover c.54 400 sq km/21 000 sq mi of ocean, in six main island groups; largest island, Diego Garcia; acquired by France, 18th-c; annexed by Britain, 1814; dependency of Mauritius until 1965; established to meet UK and US defence requirements in the Indian Ocean; UK–US naval support facility on Diego Garcia; copra plantations.

British Museum The national museum of archaeology and ethnography in Bloomsbury, London, UK. It dates from 1753, when the collection of Sir Hans Sloane was acquired for the nation. To the Sloane collection were added the Harleian and Cotton manuscript collections, forming the nucleus of the British Library, which is still partly housed in the British Museum. Since 1881 the natural history collection has been housed separately. The Library moved to a new site on Euston Road, London, in 1997. In 2003 the museum celebrated its 250th anniversary with special exhibitions throughout the year and the re-opening of newly restored galleries.

British North America Act An act passed by the British Parliament in 1867 which brought about the Confederation of Nova Scotia, New Brunswick, Quebec, and Ontario, thus giving rise to Canada. In 1981 it was renamed the Constitution Act (1867).

British South Africa Company A company, formed by Cecil Rhodes, which used a series of concessions from C African chiefs to secure a Royal Charter from the British government in 1889. In 1923–4, its territories were divided into Northern Rhodesia (Zambia after 1964) and Southern Rhodesia (Zimbabwe after 1980).

British Sports Association for the Disabled An organization, founded in 1961, which aims to provide sports and recreation opportunities for people with disabilities throughout the UK. Its membership of c.50 000 is represented in over 500 clubs, schools, and associations, participating in over 20 different sports.

British Standards Institution (BSI) The recognized UK body for the preparation of nationally accepted standards for engineering and industrial materials, consumer products, and codes of practice. It provides for the marking and certification of products made with standard materials and under standard procedures. It is supported by (but is independent of) the UK government, as well as by industrial firms and professional institutes. There are similar bodies in several other countries, coordinated by the International Organization for Standardization.

British Summer Time *Daylight Saving Time*

British thermal unit In thermodynamics, an old unit of heat; symbol *Btu*; 1 Btu = 1055 J (joule, SI unit); defined as the heat needed to raise the temperature of a pound of water from 63°F to 64°F; a *therm* is 10^5 Btu.

British Veterinary Association *veterinary science*

British Virgin Islands *Virgin Islands, British*

Brittain, Vera (Mary) [britn] (1893–1970) Writer, born in Newcastle-under-Lyme, Staffordshire, C England, UK. After studying at Oxford she served as a nurse in World War 1, recording her experiences with war-found idealism in *Testament of Youth* (1933). She later wrote *Testament of Friendship* (1940) and *Testament of Experience* (1957). She was a good friend of writer and feminist Winifred Holtby (1898–1935). In 1925 she married **George Catlin** (1896–1979), professor of politics at Cornell. Her daughter is the politician, Shirley Williams.

Brittan (of Pennithorne), Leon Brittan, Baron (1939–) British statesman, born in London, UK. He studied at Cambridge and Harvard, and qualified as a barrister. He became a Conservative MP in 1974, and from 1979 held ministerial posts under Margaret Thatcher, including Treasury chief secretary (1981–3), home secretary (1983–5), and trade and industry secretary (1985–6). He resigned from the cabinet in 1986 because of his involvement in a political dispute over the sale of the Westland Helicopter Co. In 1989 he was nominated as a vice-president of the European Commission with special responsibility for competition policy. He resigned from the Commission in 1999 along with all his fellow commissioners following the publication of a report severely critical of European administration. He was knighted in 1989, and created a life peer in 1999.

Brittany, Fr **Bretagne** pop (2000e) 2 923 000; area 27 208 sq km/ 10 502 sq mi. Region and former province of NW France, comprising departments of Côtes-du-Nord, Finistère, Ille-et-Vilaine, and Morbihan; prominent NW peninsula, bounded N by the English Channel, S by the Bay of Biscay; rugged and striking coastline; large tracts of heathland rising to 391 m/1283 ft at Monts d'Arrée and 326 m/1069 ft at Montagne Noire; part of Roman Empire, following Julius Caesar's invasion, 56 BC; arrival of Celts from Britain 5th–6th-c AD, from which came a distinctive culture and language (Breton); chief towns, Nantes, Rennes, Lorient, Quimper, Brest; high concentration of megaliths; area noted for its seafood, onions, artichokes, strawberries, Breton Muscadet wine; major tourist area.

Brittany spaniel A breed of dog, developed in France from British spaniels; thick orange-brown and white coat; virtually no tail; the only spaniel that 'points'; good stamina.

Britten (of Aldeburgh), (Edward) Benjamin Britten, Baron (1913–76) Composer, born in Lowestoft, Suffolk, E England, UK. During the 1930s he wrote incidental music for plays and documentary films. He then moved to the USA (1939–42), where he wrote his violin concerto and the *Sinfonia da Requiem*. Back in the UK, his works were largely vocal and choral – exceptions include the famous *Variations and Fugue on a Theme of Purcell* (also known as *The Young Person's Guide to the Orchestra*). He then wrote three operas: *Peter Grimes* (1945), *Billy Budd* (1951), and *Gloriana* (1953), as well as several chamber operas and children's operas. His later operas include *A Midsummer Night's Dream* (1960) and *Death in Venice* (1973). He was also an accomplished pianist, often accompanying Peter Pears. He helped to found the annual Aldeburgh Festival in 1948, and became a life peer in 1976.

brittle bone syndrome A hereditary disease of the skeleton, characterized by the deficient formation of bone and connective tissue, resulting in excessive skeletal fragility; also known as **osteogenesis imperfecta**. Seriously afflicted babies suffer multiple fractures and die in infancy. Less severely affected children may survive into adult life and suffer only an occasional fracture, often in the lower limbs. Dwarfing and a blue colour to the sclerae of the eye are associated features.

brittle material *plastic deformation*

brittle star A starfish-like marine invertebrate (echinoderm) which typically has five slender arms sharply demarcated from the central disc; arms sometimes branched; c.2000 species, found from the intertidal zone to deep sea; most feed as scavengers. (Class: Ophiuroidea.)

Brittonic *Celtic languages*

Brno [bernoh], Ger **Brünn** 49°11N 16°39E, pop (2000e) 390 000. Industrial capital of Jihomoravský region, Czech Republic; at junction of Svratka and Svitava Rivers; third largest city in Czechoslovakia; founded in 10th-c; part of Bohemia, 1229; free city, 1243; formerly capital of Austrian crownland of Moravia; airport; railway; university (1919); technical university (1899); university of agriculture (1919); music conservatory; machinery, textiles, armaments, chemicals, trade in vegetables; Bren gun was developed here; Špilberk fortress, 15th-c cathedral.

broadband A data communications service which has been developed by telecommunications agencies throughout the world to allow data to be transferred digitally at very high speed. Baud rates 600 Mbps (megabauds per second) were introduced in the 1990s, with much higher rates following. Such speeds allow computers to send video sequences, synchronized in such a way that very sophisticated videoconferencing could be supported, at the same time as all the usual forms of data.

broad bean An annual growing to 80 cm/30 in (*Vicia faba*); stems square in cross-section, erect; leaves with 2–6 oval bluish-green leaflets; pea-flowers in small clusters, white with purplish-black wings; pods up to 20 cm/8 in long, hairy, black; containing few large seeds each 2–3 cm/¾–1¼ in across; also called **horse bean**. Of unknown origin, it has been cultivated since prehistoric times for its edible seeds and for animal fodder. (Family: Leguminosae.)

broadbill A bird native to Africa and S Asia; small with bright plumage, wide bill and short legs; inhabits woodland; pear-shaped nests often suspended from branches over water; eats insects, fruit, and seeds. (Family: Eurylaimidae, 14 species.)

broadcasting The provision of television and radio programmes and commercials for the general public; also, the technical transmission of television and radio signals. Starting in the 1920s, broadcasting, whether of the commercial or 'public-service' variety, quickly established itself at regional, national, and international levels as a popular source of entertainment, information, and education. The medium has always been subject to controls, the severity of which has varied according to the political character of the country concerned. In recent years **narrowcasting** has been introduced for services geared to special interest groups. The USA has been a particularly important area for the development of broadcasting, both in terms of the number of radio and television stations, and the number of sets used (over 2000 million radio and over 1500 million TV receivers in use in the early 2000s).

Broadmoor A hospital for mental patients who have committed crimes and who require treatment under conditions of security (formerly known as the *criminally insane*). Established in 1863 near Crowthorne, Berkshire, S England, UK, it is the prototype special hospital, and has lent its name to the generic description **Broadmoor institutions**.

Broads, The, also known as **The Norfolk Broads** An area (c.2000 ha/5000 acres) of low-lying and shallow lakes in Norfolk, E England, UK. The lakes are flooded peat pits, excavated during the 11th-c and 12th-c. Flooding occurred during a period of climatic deterioration from the 13th-c. It is a popular holiday area, especially for sailing. The Broads does not bear the title National Park but is part of the Association of National Park Authorities.

Broadway The name of a street in New York City (25 km/15·5 mi long, within the city limits) which since the 1890s has become famous as a symbol of commercial theatre in the USA, though the number of Broadway theatres has declined as production costs have soared. In the 1950s the label **Off-Broadway** emerged to distinguish those theatrical enterprises in New York which operated outside the crippling economics of Broadway. By the mid-sixties the rising economic pressures of Off-Broadway in their turn spawned an off-Off-Broadway movement, where lower overheads enabled risks to be taken with experimental drama.

broccoli A type of cultivated cabbage (*Brassica oleracea*) grown for the immature flowers, which are edible. **Winter broccoli** has large, white heads similar to cauliflower, **sprouting broccoli** (**calabrese**) produces numerous small, purplish, green, or white spears. (Family: Crucifereae.)

Broch, Hermann [brokh] (1886–1951) Novelist and essayist, born in Vienna, Austria. He spent his early adult life working in his father's textile business, and was over 40 when he began to study philosophy and mathematics at Vienna University. When the Nazis invaded Austria in 1938 he was imprisoned, but influential friends obtained his release and facilitated his emigration to America in 1940. Major works include *Der Tod des Vergil* (1945, The Death of Virgil) and *Die Schlafwandler* (3 vols, 1931–2, The Sleepwalkers).

Brockhouse, Bertram N (1918–2003) Physicist, born in Lethbridge, Alberta, W Canada. He studied at the University of Toronto, joined Chalk River Nuclear Laboratories in Ontario (1950–9), later moving to McMaster University as professor of physics (1962–84). He shared the Nobel Prize for Physics in 1994 for his work in developing the field of neutron spectroscopy.

Broderick, Matthew (1962–) Actor and director, born in New York City, USA. He starred as the computer hacker who nearly starts World War 3 in *War Games* (1983), and gained commercial success in *Ferris Bueller's Day Off* (1986). He earned a Tony award for the Broadway production of the Neil Simon comedy hit *Brighton Beach Memoirs* (1982–3), and another for the musical *How to Succeed in Business Without Really Trying* (1995). Later films include *Godzilla* (1998), *Election* (1999), *Inspector Gadget* (1999), and *You Can Count On Me* (2000). He made his directorial debut with *Infinity* (1996). He returned to the stage in a musical adaptation of the Mel Brook's cult film *The Producers* (2001).

Brodkey, Harold (Roy), originally **Aaron Roy Weintraub** (1930–96) Novelist and short-story writer, born in Staunton, Illinois, USA. He studied at Harvard University, and joined the *New Yorker* in 1987. The short stories he wrote for the magazine were collected in *First Love and Other Sorrows* (1957). His long-awaited autobiographical novel *The Runaway Soul* (1991) was compared to Marcel Proust's *Remembrance of Things Past*, though it was criticized by some for its difficult prose.

Brodsky, Joseph (1940–96) Poet, born in St Petersburg, NW Russia, of Jewish parents. Convicted as a 'social parasite', he was exiled, moved to the USA, and was naturalized in 1977. He wrote in both Russian and English. Collections include *Ostanovka v pustynie* (1970, A Halt in the Wilderness), *Chast rechi* (1977, A Part of Speech), and *Uraniia* (1984, To Urania). He was awarded the Nobel Prize for Literature in 1987, and later published essays and a prose meditation on Venice, *Watermark* (1992).

Brogan, Sir Denis (William) (1900–74) Historian, born in Rutherglen, Glasgow, W Scotland, UK. He studied at Glasgow, Oxford, and Harvard, and became a fellow of Corpus Christi College, Oxford (1934), and professor of political science at Cambridge (1939). He is chiefly known for his work on historical and modern America. He was knighted in 1963.

Broglie, Louis (Victor Pierre Raymond), 7^e^ duc de (7th Duke of) [broy, brolee] (1892–1987) Physicist, born in Dieppe, NW France. He studied at the Sorbonne, where he later became professor of theoretical physics (1928). In 1929 he was awarded the Nobel Prize for Physics for his pioneer work on the wave nature of the electron (*de Broglie waves*).

Broglie, (Louis César Victor) Maurice, 6e duc de (6th Duke of) [broy, brolee] (1875–1960) Physicist, born in Paris, France. He founded a laboratory in Paris, where he made many contributions to the study of X-ray spectra, and was professor at the Collège de France (1942–6).

Broken Hill 31°57S 141°30E, pop (2000e) 26 200. Mining town in New South Wales, Australia; centre of silver, lead, and zinc mining; a centre of the trade union movement, and now administered by the Barrier Industrial Council; School of the Air founded here (1956); Royal Flying Doctor Service based here (1938); 19th-c Afghan Mosque.

bromeliad Any member of the pineapple family; typically fleshy, spiny-leaved epiphytes, especially common in the canopy of tropical forests, and notable for the reservoir of water which collects in the cup-shaped centre of the leaf rosette. This can be very large, holding up to five gallons of water which is absorbed by the plant via hairs on the leaves. It also provides a habitat for a host of other life forms, often in areas where there is little or no other standing water, including insects, amphibians, and aquatic plants, some of which live and breed only in these reservoirs. (Family: Bromeliaceae.)

Bromfield, Louis (Brucker) (1896–1956) Writer, born in Mansfield, Ohio, USA. He studied at Cornell Agricultural College and Columbia University, joined the French army in 1914, then returned to journalism in the USA. He moved to France in 1923, where he wrote his most highly acclaimed novels, such as *Early Autumn* (1926, Pulitzer) and *A Good Woman* (1927). Later works include *Until the Day Break* (1942) and *Mr Smith* (1951).

bromine [brohmeen] Br, element 35, freezing point −7°C, boiling point 58·8°C. A corrosive brown liquid containing diatomic molecules (Br_2) with an unpleasant and irritating odour. In nature, it does not occur as the free element, and is mainly extracted from brines containing its salts. In its compounds, it shows oxidation states ±, +3, +5, and +7. Its main uses are in 1,2-dibromoethane, a petrol adduct, and silver bromide, used in photographic emulsions.

bromoil process A method of making photographic prints in which the silver image formed by original development is bleached out, and an oil-pigment ink manually applied with a brush to the corresponding gelatine areas. The linked image may be in any colour, and can be transferred by pressure to another support sheet.

Bron, Eleanor (1938–) Actress and writer, born in Stanmore, N Greater London, UK. She studied at Cambridge, and from the early 1960s has made regular stage appearances, including a one-woman show, *Desdemona – If You Had Only Spoken* (1991). On television she became known in *Not So Much a Programme, More a Way of Life* (1964) and her films include *Alfie* (1966), *Black Beauty* (1994), and *A Little Princess* (1995). She has written several series for television (with John Fortune), and her books include *The Pillow Book of Eleanor Bron* (1985) and a novel, *Double Take* (1996).

bronchi [brongkee] A series of branching tubes which gradually decrease in size, conveying air from the trachea to the lungs. The larger bronchi contain cartilage rings or plates to keep the tubes open. The smaller tubes, known as *respiratory bronchioles*, have sac-like dilatations (*atria, alveolar sacs, alveoli*) where gaseous exchange occurs. Disorders of the bronchi include asthma, bronchiectasis, and bronchitis.

bronchiectasis [brongkee-ektasis] A chronic condition in which the airways (*bronchi*) are dilated, and become obstructed with mucus and recurrently infected. This leads to a cough producing purulent sputum, and repeated bouts of pneumonia. It may be caused by a number of diseases including cystic fibrosis, measles, whooping cough, and tuberculosis.

bronchitis [brong**kiy**tis] Inflammation of the airways (bronchi). Acute bronchitis is a serious disease in infants, usually caused by viruses such as influenza which produce intense inflammation of the respiratory tract that may lead to asphyxia. **Chronic bronchitis** affects adults who smoke cigarettes. Excessive bronchial mucous secretion follows, inducing a chronic cough productive of sputum.

bronchodilators Agents which produce dilation of the bronchi in the lungs, and which can therefore be helpful in the treatment of asthma, eg adrenaline, isoprenaline, salbutamol. Not all bronchodilators are sufficiently safe for use in asthma; salbutamol (usually in aerosol form) is used clinically, as are salmeterol and aformeterol, which are longer-acting. Use of bronchodilators alone, ie without steroids, is controversial. Some studies have shown that, because bronchodilators suppress symptoms but do not stop the disease progressing, they may be partly responsible for the increasing morbidity from asthma seen in Western countries.

bronchopneumonia *pneumonia*

bronchoscopy [brong**kos**kopee] The direct inspection of the trachea and bronchi with a flexible fibre-optic bronchoscope introduced under local or general anaesthetic into the respiratory passages. It permits tissue biopsies to be taken.

Brontë, Anne [brontee], pseudonym **Acton Bell** (1820–49) Poet and novelist, born in Thornton, West Yorkshire. She went as governess to the Inghams at Blake Hall in 1839 and to the Robinsons at Thorpe Green (1841–5), a post she had to leave because of her brother's Branwell's unfortunate love for Mrs Robinson. She shared in the publication, under pseudonyms, of the three sisters' *Poems* (1846). Her two novels, *Agnes Grey* (1848) and *The Tenant of Wildfell Hall* (1848), were unsuccessful at the time.

Brontë, Charlotte [brontee], pseudonym **Currer Bell** (1816–55) Novelist and poet, born in Thornton, West Yorkshire. She worked as a teacher at her old school, but gave up this post and two others as governess. Back at Haworth, she and her two sisters planned to start a school of their own and, to augment their qualifications, Charlotte and Emily attended the Pensionnat Héger in Brussels (1842). Their plans foundered, however, and Charlotte returned to Brussels as an English teacher (1843–4). Her chance discovery of Emily's remarkable poems led to the joint publication under pseudonyms of the three sisters' *Poems* (1846). Her first novel, *The Professor*, did not achieve publication until after her death (1857). Her masterpiece, *Jane Eyre* (1847), received instant acclaim. It was followed by *Shirley* (1849), and *Villette* (1853). She married her father's curate, Arthur Bell Nicholls, in 1854, and died during pregnancy in the following year, leaving the fragment of another novel, *Emma*. Two stories, *The Secret* and *Lily Hart*, were published for the first time in 1978.

Brontë, Emily (Jane) [brontee], pseudonym **Ellis Bell** (1818–48) Novelist and poet, born in Thornton, West Yorkshire. In 1837 she became a governess in Halifax, then attended the Pensionnat Héger in Brussels with Charlotte (1842), and in 1845 embarked upon a joint publication of poems after the discovery by the latter of her Gondal verse. She is known for her personal visionary poems and for her masterly novel, *Wuthering Heights* (1847). The most noted of the sisters, her writings have received widespread praise for their depth of feeling, courageous realism, and terse language.

Brontosaurus Apatosaurus

Brontotherium [bronto**thee**rium] An extinct, browsing, hoofed mammal, known from the Oligocene epoch of North America; very large, rhinoceros-like body standing up to 2·5 m/8 ft at the shoulder; head with pair of bony nasal horns; probably ate soft vegetation. (Class: Mammalia. Order: Perissodactyla.)

Bronx or **the Bronx** 40°50N 73°52W, pop (2000e) 1 332 600, area 109 sq km/42 sq mi. A mainland borough of N New York City and County of New York State, USA; Fordham University (1841); named after Jonas Bronck, an early Dutch settler; Yankee Stadium; New York Zoological Park.

bronze One of the earliest known alloys; two parts copper and one part tin. Hard and resistant to corrosion, it is traditionally used in bell casting, and is the most widely used material for metal sculpture. The sculptor first prepares a clay model which is cast by means of a plaster mould. Ornamented bronzes of high quality were made in China by the 16th-c BC.

Bronze Age *Three Age System*

Bronzino, Il [bron**zee**noh], originally **Agnolo di Cosimo di Mariano** (1503–72) Mannerist painter, born in Monticelli, N Italy. He was a pupil of Rafaello del Garbo and of Pontormo, who adopted him. He decorated the chapel of the Palazzo Vecchio in Florence, and painted the 'Christ in Limbo' in the Uffizi (1552). His 'Venus, Folly, Cupid and Time' is in the National Gallery, and his portraits include most of the Medici family, as well as Dante, Boccaccio, and Petrarch. His nephew, Alessandro Allori, and his nephew's son, both Florentine painters, adopted his name.

Brook, Peter (Stephen Paul) (1925–) Theatre and film director, born in London, UK. He studied at Oxford, and his involvement in the theatre began while at university. He directed many classical plays at the Birmingham Repertory Theatre, went to Stratford in 1947, and was also director of productions at the Royal Opera House, Covent Garden (1947–50). Famous for his innovatory approach, during the 1950s he worked on many productions in Britain, Europe, and the USA, and in 1962 returned to Stratford to join the newly established Royal Shakespeare Company for which he directed, among other productions, *King Lear* (1962) and Peter Weiss's *Marat/Sade* (1964). Most of his work in the 1970s was done with the Paris-based Centre for Theatre Research, which he founded. Later Paris productions include an adaptation of *The Mahabharata* (televised in 1989), *The Tempest* (1990), and *Hamlet* (2001). Among his films are *The Beggar's Opera* (1952), *Lord of the Flies* (1962), and *King Lear* (1969). His publications include *The Shifting Point* (1988, autobiography), *Threads of Time* (1998, a memoir), and *Evoking Shakespeare* (1999). He became a Companion of Honour in 1998.

Brooke, Rupert (Chawner) (1887–1915) Poet, born in Rugby, Warwickshire, C England, UK. He studied at Cambridge, travelled in Germany, and visited the USA and Tahiti. He died a commissioned officer on Skyros on his way to the Dardanelles, and was buried there. His *Poems* appeared in 1911, and *1914 and Other Poems* in 1915, after his death. His handsome appearance and untimely death made him a favourite poet among young people in the interwar period.

Brookeborough, Basil Stanlake Brooke, 1st Viscount (1888–1973) Northern Ireland statesman and prime minister (1943–63), born in Fermanagh, SW Northern Ireland, UK. Elected to the Northern Ireland parliament in 1929, he became minister of agriculture (1933), of commerce (1941), and prime minister of the province, resigning in 1963. He was a staunch supporter of Unionist policy, determined to preserve the ties between Northern Ireland and the UK. He was created a viscount in 1952.

Brooklyn 40°40N 73°58W, pop (2000e) 2 465 300. Borough of New York City, co-extensive with Kings Co, New York State, USA; area 182 sq km/70 sq mi; incorporated into New York City, 1898; a major port, at the SW corner of Long Island; linked to Staten I by the Verrazano-Narrows Bridge, and to Manhattan by the Brooklyn Bridge; Brooklyn Institute of Arts and Sciences (1823); New York Naval Shipyard (1801), now in civilian use; Long Island University (1926).

Brooklyn Bridge A suspension bridge built (1869–83) across East R from Brooklyn to Manhattan I, New York City, USA; first in the world to use steel cables; length of main span 486 m/1595 ft.

Brookner, Anita (1928–) Writer and art historian, born in London, UK. An authority on 18th-c painting, she was the first woman Slade professor at Cambridge University (1967–8), and has been a reader at the Courtauld Institute of Art since

1977. As a novelist she was a late starter, but in eight years (1981–8) she published as many novels, winning the Booker Prize with *Hôtel du Lac* (1984). Other titles include *Family and Friends* (1985), *A Friend from England* (1987), *Incidents in the Rue Laugier* (1995), *Undue Influence* (2000), and *The Rules of Engagement* (2003).

Brooks, Mel, originally **Melvin Kaminsky** (1926–) Film actor and director, born in New York City, USA. After some years as a gag-writer and comic, he turned to film-making with *The Producers* (1967), following this with a number of zany comedies satirizing established movie styles, among them *Blazing Saddles* (1974) and *Silent Movie* (1976). He usually writes the script, and acts in his productions, as well as directing them. Other films include *High Anxiety* (1977) and *History of the World Part One* (1980), and he co-produced *The Fly* (1986) and *84 Charing Cross Road* (1986). Later films include *Spaceballs* (1987), *Robin Hood: Men in Tights* (1993), *Dracula: Dead and Loving It* (1995), and *Svitati* (1999). He married actress **Anne Bancroft** (1931–) in 1964.

broom The name applied to several different shrubs in the pea family, *Leguminosae*, but particularly to the common broom (*Cytisus scoparius*), native to Europe, a shrub growing to 2·5 m/ 8 ft; branches numerous, green, straight, and stiff; leaves mostly trifoliate, soon falling; pea-flowers golden yellow, up to 2 cm/$^3/_4$ in long, in loose, leafy clusters at the ends of the branches; pods up to 4 cm/1$^1/_2$ in long, black. (Family: Leguminosae.)

Broome, David (1940–) Show jumper, born in Cardiff, S Wales, UK. He won the World Championship on *Beethoven* in 1970, was three times European champion, on *Sunsalve* (1961) and *Mister Softee* (1967, 1969), and was the individual bronze medallist at the 1960 and 1968 Olympics. He returned to the British Olympic team in 1988 after a 20-year absence.

broomrape An annual or perennial, parasitic and lacking chlorophyll; only densely-flowered spikes appear above ground; leaves reduced to scales; flowers 2-lipped, in subdued colours, mainly browns; mainly native to Old World warm temperate regions. All food is obtained via haustoria attached to the roots of the host. Despite the name, broom is not the only host: others include ivy and members of the daisy family; however most broomrapes are specific to a single, or to very few, host species. (Genus: *Orobanche*, 140 species. Family: Orobanchaceae.)

Brosnan, Pierce [broznan] (1951–) Actor, born in Navan, Co Meath, E Ireland. After an unsettled childhood, he moved to London, where he joined an experimental theatre group and studied at the Drama Centre. After several stage roles in London, he moved to Los Angeles, where he was offered the lead in the detective series *Remington Steele* (1982–7). Although early singled out as a possible James Bond, it was not until 1995 that he finally played the role, in *Goldeneye*, followed by *Tomorrow Never Dies* (1997), *The World is Not Enough* (1999), and *Die Another Day* (2002). Other films include *The Long Good Friday* (1980), *Mrs Doubtfire* (1993), *The Thomas Crown Affair* (1999), and *Evelyn* (2003).

Brougham, Henry Peter, Baron Brougham and Vaux [broom] (1778–1868) Jurist and politician, born in Edinburgh, EC Scotland, UK. He studied at Edinburgh University, helped to found the *Edinburgh Review* (1802), was called to the English bar in 1808, and entered parliament in 1810. His eloquence and boldness made him a popular hero for some time (1820–30). He accepted a peerage and the chancellorship (1830), assisted materially in carrying the Reform Bill, and introduced several law reforms. He designed the *brougham* (carriage), which is named after him.

Brouwer or **Brauer, Adriaen** [brow*er*] (c.1605–38) Painter, born in Oudenaarde, W Belgium. He studied at Haarlem under Frans Hals, and settled at Antwerp (c.1630). His favourite subjects were scenes from tavern life, country merrymakings, card players, smoking and drinking groups, and roisterers generally.

Browder, Earl (Russell) (1891–1973) Writer and communist leader, born in Wichita, Kansas, USA. After an elementary schooling he entered trade-union and socialist politics. He was general secretary of the US Communist Party (1930–44) but was expelled in 1946 for his views supporting the peaceful coexistence of socialism and capitalism. He served several prison sentences for his beliefs and activities.

Brown, Sir Arthur Whitten (1886–1948) Aviator, born in Glasgow, W Scotland, UK. As navigator with Sir John William Alcock he made the first non-stop crossing of the Atlantic in a Vickers-Vimy biplane on 14 June 1919, and shared a £10 000 prize given by the London *Daily Mail*. Both men were knighted after the flight.

Brown, Capability *Brown, Lancelot*

Brown, Charles Brockden (1771–1810) Novelist, born in Philadelphia, Pennsylvania, USA. He was the first professional American writer, and is often called 'the father of the American novel'. *Wieland* (1798), *Ormund* (1799), and *Jane Talbot* (1804) are among his Gothic Romances.

Brown, Ford Madox (1821–93) British historical painter, born in Calais, NW France. He studied art at Bruges, Ghent, and Antwerp. In Paris he produced his 'Manfred on the Jungfrau' (1841), a work intensely dramatic in feeling, but sombre in colouring. A visit to Italy (1845) led him to seek a greater richness of colouring, as in 'Chaucer Reciting his Poetry' (1851). He was a close associate of William Morris, and in 1861 was a founder member of Morris, Marshall, Faulkner & Co, for which he produced designs for furniture and stained glass. He completed 12 frescoes for Manchester Town Hall just before his death.

Brown, George (Alfred) *George-Brown, Baron*

Brown, George Mackay (1921–96) Poet, novelist, and short-story writer, born in Stromness, Orkney, Scotland, UK. He published his first collection of poems, *The Storm* (1954), while studying at Edinburgh University. He lived most of his life on Orkney, and his first collection of stories, *A Calendar of Love* (1967), is about the lives of Orkney farmers and fishermen. His second collection, *A Time to Keep* (1969), won the Katherine Mansfield Memorial Prize. In 1988 he was awarded the James Tait Black Memorial Prize, and a novel *Beside the Ocean of Time* was nominated for the 1994 Booker Prize. *Selected Poems* was published in 1991, and *Travellers* posthumously in 2001.

Brown, (James) Gordon (1951–) Scottish politician, born in Glasgow, W Scotland, UK. He studied history at Edinburgh University, and while still a student there was elected rector (1972–5). He lectured at Glasgow College of Technology, and entered the House of Commons in 1983 as Labour member for Dunfermline East. Despite losing the sight of one eye in a sporting accident, he rose swiftly within the Labour Party, becoming Opposition chief secretary to the Treasury (1987–9), Opposition trade and industry secretary (1989–92), Shadow Chancellor (1992–7) under the leadership of John Smith, then Tony Blair, and Chancellor of the Exchequer (1997–2001, 2001–) in the Labour government.

Brown, Jim, popular name of **James Nathaniel Brown** (1936–) Player of American football, born in St Simon Island, Georgia, USA. An All-American halfback at Syracuse University (1956), he had nine outstanding years with the Cleveland Browns in the National League (1957–66), during which he led the league eight times in rushing. His 126 career touchdowns remained an NFL record for almost 30 years until overtaken by Jerry Rice. He was elected to the Football Hall of Fame in 1971. Later he had a successful film career in Hollywood.

Brown, John (1800–59) Militant abolitionist, born in Torrington, Connecticut, USA. He supported himself with many different jobs while wandering through the country advocating antislavery. He was twice married, and had 20 children. In 1859 he led a raid on the US Armory at Harper's Ferry in Virginia, with the intention of launching a slave insurrection. The raid failed, and after being convicted of treason against Virginia, he was hanged at Charlestown. The song 'John Brown's Body' commemorates the Harper's Ferry raid, and was popular with Northern soldiers in the Civil War.

Brown, John (1826–83) Manservant, born in Crathie, Deeside, NE Scotland, UK. He was raised on a farm, and was employed at Balmoral Castle at the time of its purchase (1852) by Queen Victoria and Prince Albert. He was ghillie to Albert and favourite servant to Victoria, and after Albert's premature death (1861) he became a great support to the grieving queen. She came to depend on him as loyal servant, groom, and friend, and awarded him two medals in recognition of his devoted service. But the unlikely relationship fuelled gossip, and he became resented by the royal family and gained many enemies. He died at the age of 56 as the result of a chill. In his memory, Victoria commissioned a life-sized statue of him to be erected in the grounds of Balmoral. After her death (1901), her son Edward VII had the statue removed from public view.

Brown, Lancelot, known as **Capability Brown** (1715–83) Landscape gardener, born in Kirkharle, Northumberland, NE England, UK. He established a purely English style of garden layout, using simple artifices to produce natural effects, as in the laid-out gardens at Blenheim, Kew, Stowe, Warwick Castle, and others. He acquired his nickname from telling clients that their gardens had excellent 'capabilities'.

Brown, Melanie *Spice Girls, The*

Brown, Robert (1773–1858) Botanist, born in Montrose, Angus, E Scotland, UK. He studied at Aberdeen and Edinburgh, and in 1798 visited London, where his ability so impressed Sir Joseph Banks that he was appointed naturalist to Matthew Flinders's coastal survey of Australia (1801–5). He brought back nearly 4000 species of plants for classification. In 1810 he received charge of Banks' library and collections, and when they were transferred to the British Museum in 1827 he became botanical keeper. He was the first to note that, in general, living cells contain a nucleus, and to name it. In 1827 he first observed the *Brownian movement* of fine particles in a liquid.

brown algae A large group of predominantly marine seaweeds, characterized by their photosynthetic pigments which include chlorophylls *a* and *c*, *β*-carotene, and fucoxanthin; reproduction usually sexual, involving a sperm with two whip-like flagella; over 1500 species known; mainly from intertidal and sublittoral zones; body form ranges from filament-like to large blades. (Class: Phaeophyceae.)

brown bear A bear widespread in the N hemisphere (*Ursus arctos*, many subspecies); thick brown coat and pronounced hump on shoulders; in North America prefers open habitats, in Old World inhabits forest; includes the **big brown bear** and **grizzly bear** (also called **silvertip** or **roachback**) from the Rocky Mts, and the **Kenai bear** and **Kodiak bear** (both from S Alaska); Kodiak bear is the largest living carnivore (length 2·7 m/9 ft; weight up to 780 kg/1720 lb).

brown dwarf A hypothetical very large planet, which is just below the critical mass (0·08 Suns) needed to ignite a stellar nuclear reaction in its interior. There is evidence for brown dwarfs as companions to a handful of stars.

Browne, Charles Farrar, pseudonym **Artemus Ward** (1834–67) Humorist, born in Waterford, Maine, USA. In 1858 he wrote for the *Cleveland Plain Dealer* a description of an imaginary travelling menagerie, followed by letters in which grotesque spelling and a mixture of business platitudes and sermonizing served to convey sound sense and shrewd satire. In 1861, as Artemus Ward, he became a lecturer, giving performances whose artistic wretchedness gave rise to countless jokes. In 1866 he travelled to London, where he contributed to *Punch*, and became popular as 'the genial showman'.

Browne, Hablot Knight, pseudonym **Phiz** (1815–82) Illustrator, born in London, UK. He was apprenticed to a line engraver, but soon took to etching and watercolour painting, and gained a medal from the Society of Arts for an etching of 'John Gilpin' (1833). In 1836 he became illustrator of *The Pickwick Papers*, and maintained his reputation by his designs for other works by Dickens.

Browne, Robert (c.1550–1633) Clergyman, founder of the *Brownists*, born in Tolethorpe, Leicestershire, C England, UK. After graduating from Cambridge (1572), he became a schoolmaster in London, and an open-air preacher. In 1580 he began to attack the established Church, and soon after formed a distinct Church on congregational principles at Norwich. Reconciling himself to the Anglican Church, he became master of Stamford grammar school (1586), and rector of Achurch, Northamptonshire (1591). Of a very violent temper, he was sent to Northampton jail at the age of 80 for an assault on a constable, and died there.

Browne, Sir Thomas (1605–82) Writer and physician, born in London, UK. He studied at Oxford, then travelled in Ireland, France, and Italy, and settled in Norwich (1637). His greatest work is his earliest, the *Religio medici*, written about 1635 – a confession of faith, revealing a deep insight into the mysteries of the spiritual life. His other works include *Pseudodoxia epidemica* (1646), *Hydriotaphia; Urn Burial* (1658), and the *Garden of Cyrus* (1658). Writing during what has been called the Golden Age of the English language, he is particularly noted for the beauty of his sonorous prose. He was knighted in 1671.

Brownian movement or **motion** The ceaseless erratic motion of fine particles in suspension, first observed by Robert Brown in 1827 using pollen grains in water. The effect was explained by Einstein in 1905 as the result of the irregular bombardment of the suspended matter by invisible, thermally-agitated molecules of solution. It provided support for the atomic view of matter.

Browning, Elizabeth Barrett, *née* **Barrett** (1806–61) Poet, born in Durham, Co Durham, NE England, UK, the wife of Robert Browning. She seriously injured her spine (c.1821), and was long an invalid. Her first poems were published at 19, and other volumes appeared in 1838 and 1844. In 1845 she met **Robert Browning**, with whom she eloped in 1846. Her best-known work is *Sonnets from the Portuguese* (1850), 'Portuguese' being Browning's pet name for her. Her major work, the verse novel *Aurora Leigh* (1857), speculates with wit and force on social responsibilities and the position of women. During her lifetime she was criticized for her progressive social ideas and her audacious metrical experiments. In her later years she developed an interest in spiritualism, and also in Italian politics.

Browning, Robert (1812–89) Poet, born in London, UK, the husband of **Elizabeth Barrett**. The son of a clerk, he received scant formal education. His early work attracted little attention until the publication of *Paracelsus* (1835). *Bells and Pomegranates* (1841–6) included several of his best-known dramatic lyrics, such as 'How they Brought the Good News from Ghent to Aix'. In 1846 he married Elizabeth Barrett, and with her settled in Florence, where he wrote *Men and Women* (1855) and began *Dramatis Personae* (1864). Their son, **Robert Barrett Browning** (1849–1912), the sculptor, was born there. After the death of his wife (1861) he settled in London, where he wrote his masterpiece, *The Ring and the Book* (1869), a series of dramatic monologues for which he received widespread acclaim. His technical virtuosity and his experiments in poetic form and content considerably influenced later poets, notably Eliot and Pound.

browning A brown colour produced in some foods under certain chemical circumstances. *Non-enzymatic browning* occurs when foods containing protein and carbohydrate are heated, the result of the amino acid lysine reacting with free sugars. *Enzymatic browning* occurs with some fruits, such as apples, when exposed to oxygen.

Browning automatic rifle A gas-operated light machine-gun designed by US gunsmith John Moses Browning (1855–1926) in 1917, and produced in various countries until 1950. The weapon had a 20-round magazine and an effective range of 600 m/2000 ft.

Brown judgment *civil rights*

Brownshirts Members of an early Nazi paramilitary organization, officially the *Sturmabteilungen*, or *SA* ('assault division'). Formed in 1920 by Adolf Hitler, it had expanded to over 2 million members by 1933, double the size of the army, its chief rival for power. Under the leadership of Ernst Röhm, it developed a radical, pseudo-socialist outlook which appealed to the masses. The Brownshirts' methods of violent intimidation of political opponents and of Jews was widely endorsed and played a key role in Hitler's rise to power. After Hitler's accession (1933), the SA challenged the ascendancy of the German army. In a bid to retain control, Hitler ordered the slaughter of Röhm and other Brownshirts by the SS in what came to be known as the 'Night of the Long Knives' (29–30 Jun 1934). Nevertheless, Hitler chose a reunion of Brownshirt veterans in Munich on 9–10 November 1938 to unleash a random attack on Jewish property and persons across Germany in what became known as the *Kristallnacht* ('night of crystal' or 'broken glass'), thereby signalling a major escalation in the Nazi programme of Jewish persecution.

Brown University *Ivy League*

browser A type of computer program which uses the Internet to locate and transfer documents held on Web sites, and presents the documents to the user of the program in a way which makes them easy to read and understand. The two most common browsers in use are Netscape Communicator and Microsoft Internet Explorer.

Brubeck, Dave, popular name of **David Warren Brubeck** (1920–) Pianist, composer, and bandleader, born in Concord, California, USA. He studied music at the College of the Pacific, CA, leading a 12-piece jazz band and at the same time studying composition under Darius Milhaud. Towards the end of World War 2 he was stationed in Europe, leading a service band, but in 1946 he began to make his reputation as an experimental musician with his Jazz Workshop Ensemble. He reached a wider public with the Dave Brubeck Quartet, featuring saxophonist Paul Desmond, formed in 1951. He has also composed larger works such as ballets, a Mass, and pieces for jazz group and orchestra, and continued to tour and record with small groups through the 1980s. His best-known pieces are 'Take Five', 'Unsquare Dance', and 'Blue Rondo à la Turk'.

Bruce, Christopher (1945–) Dancer and choreographer, born in Leicester, Leicestershire, C England, UK. He studied tap, acrobatics, and ballet, and on graduating from the Ballet Rambert School (1963) immediately joined the company. In 1967 he established his reputation in Glen Tetley's *Pierrot lunaire*. His work is a fusion of classical and modern dance idioms, with a strong undercurrent of social consciousness. He became associate choreographer of English National Ballet (formerly London Festival Ballet) (1986–91), resident choreographer at Houston Ballet (from 1989), and artistic director at Rambert Dance Company (1994–2002).

Bruce, James, nickname **the Abyssinian** (1730–94) Explorer, born in Larbert, Falkirk, C Scotland, UK. He became consul-general in Algiers (1763–5), and in 1768 journeyed to Abyssinia by the Nile, Aswan, the Red Sea, and Massowah. In 1770 he reached the source of the Abbai, or headstream of the Blue Nile. His *Travels to Discover the Sources of the Nile* was published in 1790.

Bruce, Lenny, originally **Leonard Alfred Schneider** (1925–66) Satirical comedian, born in New York City, USA. He first appeared as a night-club performer in Baltimore. The satire and 'black' humour of his largely improvised act often overstepped the bounds of what was considered respectable; in 1961 he was imprisoned for obscenity, and in 1963 was refused permission to enter Britain. In 1963 he was found guilty of illegal possession of drugs, and it was his use of these which contributed to his death three years later.

Bruce, Robert (1274–1329) King of Scots (1306–29) as Robert I, and hero of the Scottish War of Independence. As Earl of Carrick, in 1296 he swore fealty to Edward I of England, but soon joined the Scottish revolt under Wallace. In 1306 he quarrelled with John Comyn, his political rival, stabbing him to death; then assembled his vassals and was crowned king at Scone. He was forced to flee to Ireland, but returned in 1307 and defeated the English at Loudoun Hill. After Edward's death (1307), the English were forced from the country, and all the great castles were recovered except Berwick and Stirling. In 1312 the Hebrides were ceded to him by the king of Norway. Raids on the N of England led to the Battle of Bannockburn (1314), when the English were routed. Sporadic war with England continued until the Treaty of Northampton (1328), which recognized the independence of Scotland, and Bruce's right to the throne. He was recognized by the pope as king of Scotland (1323), and died of leprosy six years later. He was succeeded by David II, the son of his second wife.

Bruce (of Melbourne), Stanley Melbourne Bruce, 1st Viscount (1883–1967) Australian statesman and prime minister (1923–9), born in Melbourne, Victoria, SE Australia. He entered parliament in 1918, and represented Australia in the League of Nations Assembly. After serving as prime minister, he was high commissioner in London (1933–45), and represented Australia at meetings of Churchill's war cabinet. He settled in England for the last 20 years of his life.

brucellosis [brooselohsis] A disease of animals, especially cattle, caused by micro-organisms of genus *Brucella*, named after British bacteriologist Sir David Bruce (1855–1931); also known as **contagious abortion**. It can be caught by humans, commonly after eating infected cheese or drinking infected cow's or goat's milk, in which case it is called **undulent fever** or **Malta fever**.

Bruch, Max [brukh] (1838–1920) Composer, born in Cologne, W Germany. He became musical director at Koblenz in 1865, and conducted the Liverpool Philharmonic Society (1880–3), introducing many of his choral works. He is best known for his violin concerto in G minor, the *Kol Nidrei* variations in which he employs the idioms of Hebrew and Celtic traditional melodies, and the *Konzertstück*.

Brücke, die [brüker] (Ger 'bridge') The name adopted by a group of avant-garde artists active in Dresden, 1905–13, including Ernst Ludwig Kirchner, Karl Schmitt-Rottluff, Erich Heckel (1883–1970), and slightly later, Emil Nolde and Max Pechstein. Unlike the more abstract *Blaue Reiter* group, they painted portraits, landscapes, and figurative subjects in a crude, harsh style based on van Gogh and Gauguin, and influenced by Oceanic art in Dresden Ethnological Museum. Their most striking works are prints, especially bold and expressive woodcuts.

Bruckheimer, Jerry [brukhiymer] (c.1944–) Film producer, born in Detroit, Michigan, USA. He studied at the University of Arizona, and took up a career in advertising. He moved into film production, and in 1983 teamed up with Don Simpson to head a company that produced such successful films as *Beverley Hills Cop* (1984), *Top Gun* (1986), and *Dangerous Minds* (1995). The partnership ended shortly before Simpson's death in 1996. Bruckheimer's later productions include *Armageddon* (1998), *Pearl Harbor* (2001), and *Pirates of the Caribbean* (2003).

Bruckner, Anton [brukner] (1824–96) Composer and organist, born in Ansfelden, N Austria. He held several posts as organist, and became professor of composition at the Vienna Conservatory (1868–91). His fame chiefly rests on his nine symphonies (the last unfinished), but he also wrote four impressive Masses, several smaller sacred works and many choral works. His music, which shows the influence of Wagner and Schubert, was given a mixed reception during his lifetime.

Brueghel, Pieter [broygl], also spelled **Bruegel** or **Breughel**, known as **the Elder** (c.1520–69) The most original of all 16th-c Flemish painters, probably born in the village of Brueghel, near Breda, North Brabant, The Netherlands. He studied under Pieter Coecke van Aelst (1502–50), and was much influenced by Bosch. In about 1551 he began to travel through France and Italy, later settling in Brussels, where he painted his major works. His genre pictures of peasant life reach their finest expression in 'The Blind Leading the Blind', (1568, Naples), the 'Peasant Wedding', and the 'Peasant Dance' (c.1568, Vienna). His eldest son, **Pieter Brueghel the Younger** (c.1564–1637), is known as 'Hell' Brueghel, because of his paintings of devils, hags, and robbers. His younger son, **Jan Brueghel** (1568–

1625), known as 'Velvet' Brueghel, painted still-life, flowers, landscapes, and religious subjects on a small scale.

Bruges [broozh], Flemish **Brugge** 51°13N 3°14E, pop (2000e) 119 600. Port and capital town of Brugge district, West Flanders province, NW Belgium; 12 km/7 mi S of Zeebrugge; known as 'the Venice of the north'; chief market town of the Hanseatic League and a major centre of the woollen and cloth trade; connected by canals to several cities and the North Sea; railway; port handles crude oil, coal, iron ore, general cargo, fish; traditional centre for lace; steel, cotton, furniture, brewing, paints, light engineering; one of the best-preserved mediaeval European cities; a world heritage site. Gothic town hall (1376–1420), Chapel of the Holy Blood, Church of Our Lady (12th–13th-c), 13th–14th-c market hall, with a 13th–15th-c belfry; Procession of the Holy Blood (every Ascension Day), Pageant of the Golden Tree (every 5th year).

Brugge [brooguh] *Bruges*

Bruijn, Inge de [brown] (1973–) Swimmer, born in Barendrecht, W Netherlands. She won two gold medals and set a European record in the 100 m butterfly event at the European championships in 1999. In 2000 she set world records in the 50 m and 100 m freestyle and the 50 m and 100 m butterfly. She then won gold medals in the 50 m and the 100 m freestyle and the 100 m butterfly at the Sydney Olympics (2000) and set new world records in each of these events.

bruise Damage to the skin and subcutaneous tissues, but without breaking the skin, usually caused by a blow from a blunt instrument or object. Damage to the underlying local blood vessels allows blood to escape into the tissues, resulting in swelling and the red, blue, and yellow discolouration over the affected area.

bruitisme [brweeteezm] French futuristic music of the 1920s which used percussion and electronics to suggest machinery. Antheil's *Ballet mécanique* (1926, Mechanical Ballet) was performed by eight pianos, player piano, four xylophones, two electric bells, two aeroplane propellors, tam-tam, four bass drums, and siren.

Brummell, George Bryan, known as **Beau Brummell** (1778–1840) Dandy, born in London, UK. At Eton, and during a brief sojourn at Oxford, he was less distinguished for studiousness than for the exquisiteness of his dress and manners; and after four years in the army, having come into a fortune, he entered on his true vocation as arbiter of elegancies. A close friend and protégé of the prince regent (the future George IV), they quarrelled in 1813, and gambling debts forced Brummell to flee to France (1816). He died in the lunatic asylum in Caen.

Bruna, Dick [broona] (1927–) Artist and writer, born in Utrecht, The Netherlands. The creator of a highly successful series of picture books for young children, he started in the book-trade but gave this up to concentrate on graphic art. His first book was *The Apple*, published in England in 1966, 13 years after it appeared in Holland. His books include such characters as Miffy the rabbit, and the small dog Snuffy.

Brundage, Avery (1887–1975) International athletics administrator, born in Detroit, Michigan, USA. He was a member of the US decathlon team in the 1912 Olympic Games at Stockholm, but was far more influential in his long spell as president of the US Olympic Association (1929–53), and in his 20 years as president of the International Olympic Committee (1952–72).

Brundtland, Gro Harlem [bruntland], *née* **Harlem** (1939–) Norwegian stateswoman and first woman prime minister of Norway (1981, 1986–9, 1990–6), born in SE Bærum, Norway. She studied medicine at Oslo and Harvard, qualifying as a physician. In 1960 she married a leader of the Opposition Conservative Party, **Arne (Olav) Brundtland**, and they have four children. She joined the Labour Party and entered politics (1969), after working in public medicine services in Oslo. She was appointed environment minister (1974–9) and, as leader of the Labour Party group, became prime minister for the first time. In 1987 she chaired the World Commission on Environment and Development which produced the report *Our Common Future*. Awarded the Third World Foundation Prize for leadership in environmental issues in 1998, she also served as director-general of the World Health Organization (1998–2003).

Brunei *p.237*

Brunel, Isambard Kingdom [broonel] (1806–59) Engineer, born in Portsmouth, Hampshire, S England, UK, the son of **Marc Brunel**. He worked in his father's office, and helped to plan the Thames Tunnel, opened in 1843. He himself planned the Clifton Suspension Bridge (1829–31, completed 1864), and the Hungerford Suspension Bridge (1841–5) over the Thames. He designed the *Great Western* (1837), the first steamship built to cross the Atlantic, the *Great Britain* (1843), the first ocean screw-steamer, and the *Great Eastern* (1853–8), then the largest vessel ever built. He was also appointed engineer to the Great Western Railway (1833) and constructed many docks.

Brunel, Sir Marc Isambard [broonel] (1769–1849) Engineer and inventor, born in Hacqueville, NW France. He fled from the French Revolution in 1793, going first to the USA, where he was architect and chief engineer in New York. He settled in England in 1799, constructed many public works, and solved many of the problems of underwater tunnelling. His main achievement was the 460 m/503 yd Thames Tunnel from Rotherhithe to Wapping (1825–43). He was knighted in 1841.

Brunelleschi, Filippo [brooneleskee] (1377–1446) Architect, goldsmith, and sculptor, born in Florence, NC Italy. One of the figures responsible for the development of the Renaissance style in Florence, his chief work is the dome of the cathedral there. Erected between 1420 and 1461, it is (measured diametrically) the largest in the world, and served as the model for Michelangelo's design for St Peter's in Rome. Other well-known buildings by him in Florence are the Church of San Lorenzo (1418–29) and the Ospedale degli Innocenti (1419–44). He is also noted for his innovations in the use of perspective.

Brunhild, Brunhilde, or **Brynhild** [broonhild(uh)] In Norse mythology, a Valkyrie who has assumed human form. Odin places her behind a wall of flame where she lies in an enchanted sleep; she is woken by Sigurd, who is able to leap the barrier on his horse Grani. Tricked into marrying Gunnar, she finally kills herself on Sigurd's funeral pyre. In the similar Nibelungen legend, she is the wife of Gunther.

Bruno, Giordano, originally **Filippo Bruno**, nickname **Il Nolano** (1548–1600) Renaissance philosopher, born in Nola, S Italy. At first a Dominican, his unorthodox interests in hermeticism caused him to leave the order, and he travelled widely throughout Europe. His philosophy was an extreme pantheism, and he was sympathetic to Copernicus's theory of the universe. This led to his arrest by the Inquisition and, after a 7-year trial, he was burned in Rome. He published dialogues in Italian and many Latin treatises on a vast range of topics in philosophy, science, mathematics, religion, and magic.

Bruno of Cologne, St (c.1030–1101) Clergyman, the founder of the Carthusian order, born in Cologne, W Germany. He became rector of the cathedral school at Reims, but withdrew in 1084 to the wild mountains of Chartreuse, near Grenoble. Here with six friends he founded the austere Carthusian order on the site of the present Grande Chartreuse. In 1091, at the invitation of Pope Urban II, he established a second Carthusian monastery at Della Torre in Calabria. Feast day 6 October.

Brunswick [brownshviyk], Ger **Braunschweig** 52°17N 10°28E, pop (2000e) 268 000. Manufacturing and commercial city in NC Germany; capital of former duchy of Braunschweig; railway; technical university (1745); cathedral (12th-c), castle (12th-c).

brush turkey A bird native to Japan and Australasia; solitary; seldom flies; plumage black; tail folded vertically; head and neck naked except for some hair-like feathers; eats fruit and insects. (Family: Megapodiidae, 6 species.)

Brussels, Flemish **Brussel**, Fr **Bruxelles**, ancient **Broucsella** 50°50N 4°21E, pop (2000e) 1 069 000 (including suburbs). Commercial and cultural city in Brabant province, Belgium;

Brunei

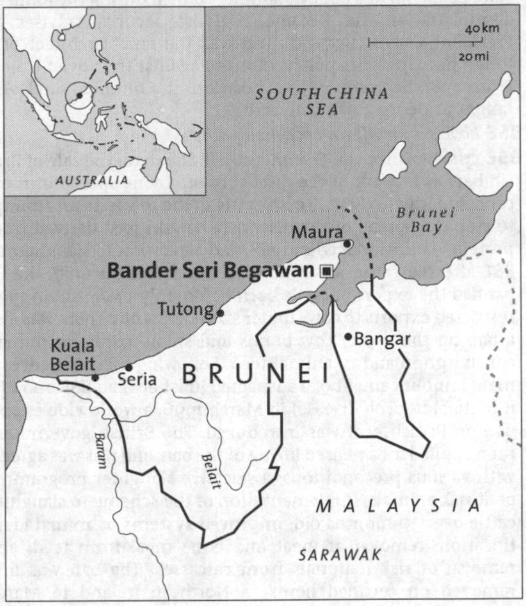

□ International Airport

[brooniy], official name **State of Brunei Darussalam** (Islamic Sultanate of Brunei)

Local name Negara Brunei Darussalam

Timezone GMT +8

Area 5765 km²/2225 sq mi

Population total (2002e) 351 000

Status Independent state

Date of Independedce 1984

Capital Bandar Seri Begawan

Languages Malay (official), English

Ethnic groups Malay (65%), Chinese (20%)

Religions Muslim (Sunni 65%), Buddhist (12%), Christian (9%)

Physical features Swampy coastal plain; equatorial rainforest covers 75% of land area; rivers include Belait, Tutong Brunei; mountainous tract on Sarawak border, average height 500 m/1640 ft.

Climate Tropical; high temperatures and humidity and no marked seasons; average daily temperature 24–30°C; average annual rainfall 2540 mm/100 in on coast, doubling in the interior.

Currency 1 Brunei Dollar (Br$) = 100 cents

Economy Largely dependent on oil (discovered 1929) and gas resources.

GDP (2002e) $6·5 bn, per capita $18 600

Human Development Index (2002) 0·856

History Formerly a powerful Muslim sultanate, with dominion over all of Borneo, its neighbouring islands, and parts of the Philippines by early 16th-c; under British protection from 1888; occupied by Japanese, 1941; liberated and reverted to former status as a British residency, 1945; internal self-government in 1971 and full independence, 1984; a constitutional monarchy with the Sultan as Head of State, who presides over a Council of Cabinet Ministers, a Religious Council, and a Privy Council.

Head of State/Government (Sultan)
1885–1906 Hashim Jalil-ul-Alam Akam-ud-Din
1906–24 Muhammad Jamal-ul-Alam II
1924–50 Ahmad Taj-ud-Din
1950–67 Umar Ali Sa if-ud-Din III
1967– Muda Hassan al Bolkiah Mu'izz-Din-Waddaulah

capital of Belgium, lying at the geographical mid-point of the country; divided into the Lower Town, intersected by several branches of the R Senne, and the Upper Town, set on the crest of the hills to the E; inner city surrounded by 18 suburbs with independent administrations; major mediaeval wool centre; capital of Spanish and Austrian Netherlands; headquarters of many international organizations, such as the European Union and NATO; linked to the North Sea by the Willebroek Canal; linguistic frontier between Flemings and Walloons runs just S of the city; officially Brussels is bilingual, but French predominates in the centre, Flemish in the suburbs; archbishopric; Brussels National Airport (Zaventem); railway; underground system; Free University of Brussels (1834); St Louis and St Aloysius private universities; industry largely outside the city, leaving the centre to the service sector; textiles, lace, carpets, porcelain, glass, metals, cement, chemicals, engineering, electronics and electrical goods, vehicles, publishing, brewing, tobacco, foodstuffs; Royal Military School; several royal academies of fine arts and royal conservatories; town hall (15th–18th-c), royal palace (1827–9, rebuilt 1905); Palais de la Nation (1779–83); cathedral (13th–15th-c), Church of Notre-Dame de la Chapelle (begun 1210); Ommegang (processions, Jul).

Brussels, Treaty of **1** (1948) A treaty of economic, social, and cultural collaboration and collective self-defence signed by Belgium, France, Luxembourg, the Netherlands, and the UK. It set up the so-called **Brussels Treaty Organization**, with the principal aim of joint action to resist aggression. It was superseded by the Treaty of Paris and the Western European Union. The treaty set out the prime aims of the union, originally as a 50-year pact, to provide economic and social collaboration as well as 'collective self-defence'.
2 (1973) A treaty which enabled Britain, Denmark, and Ireland to join the European Economic Community. These three countries and Norway had applied to join in 1961, but further negotiations had been vetoed by President de Gaulle in 1963. After his resignation, it was agreed to hold fresh negotiations. Following signature of the treaty, Norway failed to ratify after a referendum.

Brussels sprout A type of cultivated cabbage (*Brassica oleracea*), thought to have been first grown in Belgium; also spelled **brussel sprout**; produces shoots or sprouts in all the axils of the leaves on the main stem; sprouts resemble miniature cabbages, and can be harvested over a long period, especially in winter. (Family: Crucifereae).

Brussig, Thomas [broosikh] (1965–) Novelist, born in East Berlin, German Democratic Republic (now Germany). He worked as a removal man, museum attendant, and hotel porter before studying sociology and drama. His first novel, *Watercolours* (1994), was published under the pseudonym **Cordt Berneburger**. His best-selling satirical novel *Heroes Like Us* (1998) comments on the downfall of former East Germany, and chronicles the farcical fortunes of the fictional Klaus Uhltzscht, the man who breached the Berlin Wall.

Brutalism or **New Brutalism** An architectural concept of the 1950s, in which the buildings often have large distinct blocks of exposed concrete. It is typified by the work of Le Corbusier at Chandigarh, India, and at Marseille, France, and by his British followers James Stirling, William Gowan, and Alison and Peter Smithson.

Bruton, John (1947–) Irish statesman and prime minister (1994–7), born in Dublin, Ireland. He studied economics under Garret FitzGerald at University College, Dublin. When only 22, he was elected to the Dáil Éireann in 1969. He was minister of finance under FitzGerald (1981–2, 1986–7), and became leader of Fine Gael (1990–2001). In 1994, he formed a coalition with the

Labour and Democratic Left parties. He maintained the momentum of the Northern Ireland peace process, producing with British prime minister John Major a joint framework document to set up all-party talks on the decommissioning of terrorist arms (1995).

Brutus, Marcus Junius [**broo**tus] (c.85–42 BC) Roman politician. He sided with Pompey when the civil war broke out, but submitted to Caesar, and was appointed Governor of Cisalpine Gaul. He divorced his wife to marry **Portia**, the daughter of his master, Cato. Cassius persuaded him to join the conspiracy against Caesar (44 BC); but, defeated by Mark Antony and Octavian at Philippi, he killed himself.

Bruxelles [brüksel] *Brussels*

Bryant, William Cullen (1794–1878) Poet and journalist, born in Cummington, Massachusetts, USA. He graduated in law, and from 1816 practised in Great Barrington, MA, but in 1817 achieved fame as a poet following the publication of 'Thanatopsis'. He continued to practise at the bar until 1825, but more and more turned to newspaper contributions in prose and verse, becoming co-owner and editor of the New York *Evening Post* in 1829. He was a resolute opponent of slavery.

Bryggen [**brüg**gen] A world heritage site in Bergen, SW Norway. Probably founded in the 11th-c, it retains a large number of wooden gabled buildings, and is the best surviving example of the traditional wooden towns of N Europe.

bryophyte A spore-bearing, non-vascular plant belonging to the division Bryophyta, which includes some 25 000 species of moss, liverwort, and hornwort. Bryophytes have conducting cells but lack true vascular tissue; they have rhizoids, thread-like outgrowths which anchor the plant and conduct water, but no true roots. Leaves, if present, are simple structures, usually one cell thick, with a slightly thicker central strand. The dominant generation is the gametophyte, consisting of either a thallus or a small, leafy plant. The gametes are produced in *antheridia* (male) and *archegonia* (female), borne either directly on the surface of the plant or on erect, fleshy-stalked, and often complex structures called *gametangiophores*. The sporophyte generation consists simply of a long-stalked spore capsule growing directly from a fertilized archegonium. It is very short-lived, and is so dependent on the gametophyte that it is termed parasitic. Asexual reproduction can also occur by means of *gemmae* – multicellular dics or filaments produced in special cups, either on leaf tips or on stalks (*pseudopodia*), and able to grow into new plants in the same way that small bulbs of flowering plants do. Bryophytes are mainly terrestrial plants, often epiphytic, but very vulnerable to desiccation, and require water for the transfer of gametes from antheridium to archegonium; they are mostly restricted to damp or humid habitats. They are increasingly regarded as important indicator plants (eg in pollution studies). (Division: Bryophyta.)

Bryozoa [briyo**zo**ha] A phylum of small, aquatic animals that typically form colonies comprising a few to a million individuals (*zooids*); each zooid typically has a tentacle-like feeding apparatus around its mouth; colony forms a calcareous, chitinous, or gelatinous skeleton; c.4000 living species, mostly marine, and attached to hard substrates or seaweeds, rarely to soft sediments; some found in fresh water; abundant as fossils; also known as **moss animals**.

Bryson, Bill (1951–) Writer, born in Des Moines, Iowa, USA. In 1977 he moved to England and settled in North Yorkshire. His travel books include the best-sellers *The Lost Continent* and *Neither Here Nor There* (1991), and among his books on the English language are *Mother Tongue* (1990) and *Made in America* (1994). *Notes From A Small Island* (1995) recounts his last trip around Britain before returning to America, when he produced *Notes From a Big Country* (1998). He returned to England again with his family in 2003, settling in Norfolk.

Brythonic *Celtic languages*

Brzezinski, Zbigniew [bzhuh**zin**skee] (1928–) Academic and politician, born in Poland. He settled in the USA and became a US citizen in 1958. He taught at Harvard's Russian Research Center during the 1950s and then, as professor of public law and government, at Columbia University. A member of the state department's policy planning council during the Johnson administration, he became national security adviser to President Carter (1977–80) and was the chief architect of a tough human rights policy, directed against the Soviet Union. From 1981 he resumed his position at Columbia, and also taught at Georgetown University.

BSE *bovine spongiform encephalopathy*

BSE crisis A European Commission (EC) ban on the sale of British beef as a result of the discovery of bovine spongiform encephalopathy (BSE) in British cattle in the 1980s. In an attempt to stop the spread of the disease, a ban on feed derived from protein was introduced in 1988, and a decision to slaughter all BSE-affected cattle was made the same year. In 1989, the EC banned the export of cattle born before July 1988, and in 1990 restricted exports to cows under six months old. There was also a ban on the use of cow brains and spinal cords for human consumption and in animal feed. Following a British government announcement of a suspected link between BSE and CJD (Creutzfeldt-Jacob disease) in March 1996, a worldwide export ban on British beef was introduced. The British government then applied for a phased lifting of the ban, and this was agreed, with various preconditions: a selective slaughter programme of at-risk animals; implementation of the scheme to slaughter cattle over 30 months old; improved systems of animal identification; removal of meat and bone meal from feed; and removal of risk materials from carcasses. The ban was first removed on certified herds in Northern Ireland in March 1998, and the following November was lifted for the whole of the UK.

BSI *British Standards Institution*

BTU *British thermal unit*

bubble chamber A device for detecting the paths of sub-atomic particles, devised in 1952 by Donald Glaser. The chamber contains a liquid prevented from boiling by pressure. The pressure is briefly released. Before general boiling can take place, the passage of a particle produces a local instability which initiates boiling, forming visible bubbles of gas along its path. The phenomenon is very brief and is operated cyclically. The track patterns are photographed for later analysis. In the 1970s the large Gargamelle bubble chamber at CERN, Geneva, containing 18 tonnes of liquid Freon, saw important discoveries in weak nuclear interactions.

bubble jet printer A form of printer for a computer, usually a personal computer, in which small bubbles of ink are deposited on the paper. This type of printer can offer quite high quality at very little cost.

bubble memory A type of computer memory first produced as a storage medium in the mid-1970s. These devices operate as read/write memories by circulating very small polarized magnetic bubbles which represent single bits. They have the advantage of being extremely sturdy, both mechanically and in terms of their ability to operate over large temperature ranges, but they are relatively slow and expensive. They find some applications in harsh environments.

Buber, Martin [**boo**ber] (1878–1965) Jewish theologian and philosopher, born in Vienna, Austria. He studied philosophy at Vienna, Berlin, and Zürich, then became attracted to Hasidism, founding and editing a monthly journal *Der Jude* (1916–24). He taught comparative religion at Frankfurt (1923–33), and directed a Jewish adult education programme until 1938, when he fled to Palestine to escape the Nazis. He became professor of social philosophy at Jerusalem, where he wrote on social and ethical problems. He is best known for his religious philosophy, expounded most famously in *Ich und Du* (1923, I and Thou), contrasting personal relationships of mutuality and reciprocity with utilitarian or objective relationships.

bubonic plague *plague*

Bucaramanga [bookaramangga] 7°08N 73°10W, pop (2000e) 401 900. Capital of Santander department, NC Colombia; NE of Bogotá, in the Cordillera Oriental at 1018 m/3340 ft; 'the garden city of Colombia'; founded, 1622; university (1947); coffee, cacao, tobacco, cotton; Parque Santander, Parque García Roviro, El Paragüitas gardens (Jardin Botanico) in Floridablanca suburb; international piano festival (Sep).

buccaneers Pirates and adventurers who preyed upon Spanish and other shipping in the West Indies and along the Spanish Main in the 17th-c; mainly Dutch, English, and French. The name derived from *boucan* (native American for 'barbecue'), because they roasted meat on board ship in Caribbean style. Referred to by the Spanish as *corsarios* ('corsairs'), by the Dutch as *vrijbuiter* ('freebooters'), and by the English as *privateers*, they flourished between 1630 and 1689. Privateering was accepted as illegal by most European powers in 1856 (Declaration of Paris), and universally outlawed by the Hague Convention of 1907.

Bucer or **Butzer, Martin** [**but**ser] (1491–1551) Protestant reformer, born in Sélestat, NE France (formerly Schlettstadt, Germany). He entered the Dominican order, and studied theology at Heidelberg. In 1521 he left the order, married a former nun, and settled in Strasbourg (1523). In the disputes between Luther and Zwingli he adopted a middle course. At the Diet of Augsburg he declined to subscribe to the proposed Confession of Faith, and afterwards drew up the *Confessio tetrapolitana* (1530). He became professor of theology at Cambridge in 1549. His chief work was a translation and exposition of the Psalms (1529).

Buchan, John, Baron Tweedsmuir [**buh**kn] (1875–1940) Writer and statesman, born in Perth, Perth and Kinross, E Scotland, UK. He studied at Glasgow and Oxford, and in 1901 was called to the bar. During World War 1 he served on HQ staff (1916–17), when he became director of information. He was MP for the Scottish Universities (1927–35), was made a baron, and became Governor-General of Canada until 1940. In 1937 he was made a privy councillor and Chancellor of Edinburgh University. Despite his busy public life, he wrote over 50 books, especially fast-moving adventure stories, such as *Prester John* (1910) and *The Thirty-nine Steps* (1915). His biographical works include *Montrose* (1928) and *Sir Walter Scott* (1932).

Buchanan, James [byoo**kan**an] (1791–1868) Fifteenth president of the USA (1857–61), born near Mercersburg, Pennsylvania, USA. He studied at Dickinson College, and in 1812 was admitted to the bar. He became secretary of state in 1845, and succeeded in settling the Oregon boundary question. Receiving the nomination of the Democratic Party, he was elected president in 1856, and during his administration the slavery question came to a head. He was strongly in favour of the maintenance of slavery, and he freely supported the attempt to establish Kansas as a slave state. After his retirement in 1861, he took no part in public affairs.

Buchanan, James M(cGill) [byoo**kan**an] (1919–) Economist and educator, born in Murfreesboro, Tennessee, USA. He studied at universities in Tennessee and in Chicago, and taught at the University of Virginia from 1956. He became director of the Center for Study of Public Choice in 1969, and joined George Mason University in 1983. He was awarded the Nobel Prize for Economics in 1986 for his work on the theory of public choice, a unique method of analyzing economic and political decision-making.

Bucharest [buka**rest**], Romanian **București**, ancient **Cetatea Dambovitei** 44°25N 26°07E, pop (2000e) 2 066 000. Capital and largest city of Romania, on the R Dambovit; founded, 14th-c; important commercial centre on the trade route to Constantinople; capital of Wallachia, 1698; capital of Romania, 1861; badly damaged by German bombing in World War 2; airport (Baneasa); railway; university (1864); technical university (1819); oil pipeline link with Ploești; engineering, metallurgy, machinery, oil refining, textiles, chemicals, food processing, vehicles; Domnita Baleasa Church (18th-c), St George Church (17th-c), Palace of the Republic, Palace of St Synod, Athenaeum arts and music centre.

Buchman, Frank (Nathan Daniel) [**buhk**man] (1878–1961) Evangelist, founder of the 'Group' and 'Moral Rearmament' movements, born in Pennsburg, Pennsylvania, USA. He was a Lutheran minister in charge of a hospice for under-privileged boys in Philadelphia (1902–7), travelled extensively in the East, and in 1921, believing that there was an imminent danger of the collapse of civilization, founded at Oxford the 'Group Movement'. It was labelled the 'Oxford Group' until 1938, when it rallied under the slogan 'Moral Re-armament'. After World War 2 the movement emerged in a more political guise as an alternative to capitalism and communism.

Büchner, Georg [**bük**hner] (1813–37) Playwright and pioneer of Expressionist theatre, born in Goddelau, WC Germany. He studied medicine and science, became involved in revolutionary politics, and to escape arrest fled to Zürich, where he died of typhoid at the age of 24. His best-known works are the poetical dramas *Dantons Tod* (1835, The Death of Danton) and *Woyzeck* (1837), used by Alban Berg as the basis for his opera *Wozzeck*.

Buck, Pearl (Comfort) S(ydenstricker), pseudonym **John Sedges** (1892–1973) Novelist, born in Hillsboro, West Virginia, USA. She lived in China from infancy, and her earliest novels are coloured by her experiences there. *The Good Earth* (1931) earned her the 1932 Pulitzer Prize and the 1938 Nobel Prize for Literature. In 1935 she returned to the USA and wrote many novels about the contemporary American scene, such as *The Patriot* (1939) and *Dragon Seed* (1942). Five novels were written under her pseudonym.

Buck, Sir Peter (Henry), originally **Te Rangi Hiroa** (1879–1951) Maori scholar and writer, born in Urenui, New Zealand. He practised medicine, was an MP (1909–14), served in World War 1, then became an anthropologist. In 1927 he joined the Bishop Museum in Honolulu, Hawaii, and was director there from 1936 until his death. He was knighted in 1946.

buckhound *deerhound*

Buckingham, George Villiers, 1st Duke of [**buhk**ingam] (1592–1628) English statesman and court favourite, born in Brooksby, Leicestershire, C England, UK. He was knighted by James I, and raised to the peerage as Viscount Villiers (1616), Earl of Buckingham (1617), Marquess (1618), and Duke (1623). In 1623 he failed to negotiate the marriage of Prince Charles to the daughter of the Spanish king, but later arranged the marriage to Henrietta Maria of France. The abortive expedition against Cadiz (1625) exposed him to impeachment by the Commons, and only a dissolution rescued him. An expedition against France failed (1627), and while planning a second attack he was assassinated at Portsmouth by John Felton, a discontented subaltern.

Buckingham, George Villiers, 2nd Duke of [**buhk**ingam] (1628–87) English statesman and playwright, born in London, UK. After his father's assassination, he was brought up with Charles I's children, and went into exile after the Royalist defeat in the Civil War. His estates were recovered at the Restoration, and he became a member of the Cabal of Charles II. He was instrumental in Clarendon's downfall (1667), but lost power to Arlington, and was dismissed in 1674 for alleged Catholic sympathies. He wrote poetry, religious tracts, and plays, among them a celebrated satire on heroic drama, *The Rehearsal* (1671).

Buckingham Palace The 600-room residence of the British sovereign in London, UK, built for George IV on the site of his parents' home, Buckingham House. The architect, John Nash, was dismissed on the king's death in 1830, and the palace remained unused until Queen Victoria's accession in 1837. The famous east facade was added by Sir Aston Webb in 1913. Some rooms were opened to the public for the first time in summer 1993.

Buckinghamshire pop (2001e) 479 000; area 1883 sq km/727 sq mi. County in SC England, UK; drained by the Ouse and Thames Rivers; crossed in the S by the Chiltern Hills; extensive woodland; county town, Aylesbury; chief towns include Bletchley, High Wycombe, Buckingham; Milton Keynes a unitary authority from 1997; mainly agriculture, also furniture, bricks, printing, high technology.

buckler fern A perennial fern, found almost everywhere; rhizomatous; fronds form a tuft or crown; bi- or tri-pinnate, scaly; sori with kidney-shaped indusia, borne near the midrib. (Genus: *Dryopteris*, 150 species. Family: Polypodiaceae.)

Buckley, William F(rank), Jr (1925–) Writer, born in New York City, USA. After briefly attending the University of Mexico, he served in the US army during World War 2. He entered journalism, and founded the conservative journal *National Review* (1955), a platform for his influential political views. He worked for the Information Agency Advisory 1 Commission (1969–72), and was delegate to the UN General Assembly (1973). His books dealt with contemporary politics, and in the 1970s he turned to writing spy novels.

buckminsterfullerene [buhkminsterfulereen] C_{60}. An almost spherical molecule, thought to be an ingredient of soots; also called **soccerene**.

buckthorn A thorny, spreading, deciduous shrub or small tree (*Rhamnus catharticus*) 4–10 m/13–30 ft, native to Europe and the Mediterranean region; leaves oval, toothed, in opposite pairs; flowers tiny, green, parts in fours; berries 5–10 mm/0..2–0..3 in, black, mildly poisonous, and purgative. (Family: Rhamnaceae.)

buckwheat An erect annual (*Fagopyrum esculentum*) with spear-shaped leaves and a terminal cluster of tiny pink or white flowers; fruit a triangular nut c.6 mm/¼ in long; native to C Asia and cultivated as a substitute for cereals. (Family: Polygonaceae.)

Budaeus, Guglielmus [budayus], Latin name of **Guillaume Budé** (1467–1540) Scholar, born in Paris, France. He studied in Paris and Orléans, and held several diplomatic posts under Louis XII and Francis I. At his suggestion Francis founded the Collège de France. As royal librarian he founded the collection which later became the Bibliothèque Nationale. Of his works on philology, philosophy, and jurisprudence, the two best known are on ancient coins (1514) and the *Commentarii linguae Graecae* (1519, Commentaries on the Greek Language).

Budapest [boodapest] 47°29N 19°05E, pop (2000e) 1 966 000. Capital and largest city of Hungary, on R Danube where it enters the Great Plain; old-world Buda on W bank hills, modern Pest on E bank, unified in 1873; Buda on site of Roman colony of Aquincum; major cultural and trading centre in the 15th-c; scene of popular uprising, crushed by Soviet troops, 1956; Eötvös Loránd University (1635); universities of medicine (1769), economic science (1948), horticulture (1853); Hungarian Academy of Sciences; airport (Ferihegy); railway; underground; iron, steel, chemicals, pharmaceuticals, textiles; St Matthias Church (13th-c), Royal Palace, Parliament Building, museum of fine arts, national theatre, opera house, thermal baths; Buda castle and banks of the Danube are a world heritage site; location for World Fair (Expo) in 1996.

Budd, Zola, married name **Pieterse** (1966–) Athlete, born in Bloemfontein, EC South Africa. Dogged by controversy, she set a world record time of 15 min 1·83 sec for the 5000 m while still a South African citizen. In 1984 she was accorded British citizenship on the strength of her parental background, and became eligible to participate in the 1984 Olympic Games. Her presence was not universally welcomed, and her disappointing performance was best remembered for the incident in which she accidentally tripped the American Mary Decker during the 3000 m. She set further world records for the 5000 m (1984, 1985), then dropped out of international running until South Africa was re-admitted to international sports in 1992. A hip injury and public attitudes caused her to retire in 1988.

Buddha ('the enlightened one') (c.563–c.483 BC) The title of Prince **Gautama Siddhartha**, the founder of Buddhism, born the son of the rajah of the Sakya tribe ruling in Kapilavastu, Nepal. When about 30 years old he left the luxuries of the court, his beautiful wife, and all earthly ambitions for the life of an ascetic; after six years of austerity and mortification he saw in the contemplative life the perfect way to self-enlightenment. According to tradition, he achieved enlightenment when sitting beneath a peepul tree near Buddh Gaya, Bihar. For the next 40 years he taught, gaining many disciples and followers, and died at the age of about 80 in Kusinagara, Oudh. His teaching is summarized in the *Four Noble Truths*, the last of which affirms the existence of a path leading to deliverance from the universal human experience of suffering. The goal is *Nirvana*, which means 'the blowing out' of the fires of all desires, and the absorption of the self into the infinite.

Buddh Gaya or **Bodh Gaya** [bud gahya] A sacred Buddhist site in Bihar, India. Since the 3rd-c BC, shrines have marked the spot where Gautama Buddha attained enlightenment.

Buddhism A tradition of thought and practice originating in India c.2500 years ago, and now a world religion, deriving from the teaching of Buddha (Siddhartha Gautama), who is regarded as one of a continuing series of enlightened beings. The teaching of Buddha is summarized in the *Four Noble Truths*, the last of which affirms the existence of a path leading to deliverance from the universal human experience of suffering. A central tenet is the law of *karma*, by which good and evil deeds result in appropriate reward or punishment in this life or in a succession of rebirths. Through a proper understanding of this condition, and by obedience to the right path, human beings can break the chain of karma. The Buddha's path to deliverance is through morality (*sila*), meditation (*samadhi*), and wisdom (*panna*), as set out in the *Eightfold Path*. The goal is *Nirvana*, which means 'the blowing out' of the fires of all desires, and the absorption of the self into the infinite. All Buddhas are greatly revered, and a place of special importance is accorded to Gautama.

There are two main traditions within Buddhism, dating from its earliest history. **Theravada Buddhism** adheres to the strict and narrow teachings of the early Buddhist writings: salvation is possible for only the few who accept the severe discipline and effort necessary to achieve it. **Mahayana Buddhism** is more liberal, and makes concessions to popular piety: it teaches that salvation is possible for everyone, and introduced the doctrine of the *bodhisattva* (or personal saviour). As Buddhism spread, other schools grew up, among which are Ch'an or Zen, Lamaism, Tendai, Nichiren, and Soka Gakkai. Recently Buddhism has attracted growing interest in the West. The only complete canon of Buddhist scripture is called the Pali canon, after the language in which it is written. It forms the basic teaching for traditional Theravada Buddhism, but other schools have essentially the same canon written in Sanskrit. Mahayana Buddhists acknowledge many more texts as authoritative.

Underlying the diversity of Buddhist belief and practice is a controlling purpose. The aim is to create the conditions favourable to spiritual development, leading to liberation or deliverance from bondage to suffering. This is generally seen as involving meditation, personal discipline, and spiritual exercises of various sorts. This common purpose has made it possible for Buddhism to be very flexible in adapting its organization, ceremony, and pattern of belief to different social and cultural situations. Reliable figures are unobtainable, but there were over 360 million Buddhists estimated in 2004, and over 1000 million people live in lands where Buddhism is a significant religious influence.

budding The formation of buds by cell division within a localized area of a shoot. Budding is also a method of sexual reproduction in which a new individual develops as a direct growth off the body of the parent, and may subsequently become detached and lead a separate existence.

buddleia or **buddleja** [buhdlia] A deciduous shrub or small tree, native to warm regions, and widely cultivated and naturalized in many areas; flowers small, various colours, often scented, crowded in dense spikes or globular clusters. It is very attractive to insects, especially butterflies, hence the name **butterfly bush** given to *Buddleia davidii*, the most commonly cultivated species. (Genus: *Buddleia*, 100 species. Family: Loganiaceae.)

Budé, Guillaume *Budaeus, Guglielmus*

Budge, (John) Don(ald) (1915–2000) Tennis player, born in Oakland, California, USA. In 1938 he became the first player to win all four Grand Slam events in the same year. He was at his peak in 1937–8: in both years he won the Wimbledon singles, the men's doubles (with his compatriot Gene Mako) and, with fellow-American Alice Marble (1913–90), the mixed doubles. He then turned professional.

budgerigar A small parrot native to C Australia, and introduced in Florida (*Melopsittacus undulatus*); common; lives in nomadic flocks; eats grass seeds; nests in tree stumps or logs. It is a popular cage-bird, with many colour variations, but is usually green in the wild. (Family: Psittacidae.)

budget A monetary plan for a specified period of future time. A government budget is a statement of forecast expenditure in the following financial year, and of how the revenue needed will be raised (eg by taxation or borrowing). Most commercial organizations of any size prepare budgets to forecast sales revenue, operating costs, capital expenditure, and cash flow. They may also be prepared several years in advance, and amended annually.

Buenaventura [bwenaven**too**ra] 3°51N 77°06W, pop (2000e) 189 400. Pacific seaport in Cauca department, SW Colombia; on Island of Cascajal in the Bahia de Buenaventura; Colombia's most important Pacific trading port; founded, 1540 (on different site); shrimp fishing, fish canning; trade in coffee, hides, gold, platinum, sugar.

Buenos Aires [**bway**nos **iy**rees] 34°40S 58°30W, pop (2000e) 3 333 000. Federal capital of Argentina in Gran Buenos Aires federal district, E Argentina; on S bank of R Plate; founded in 1535 as the city of the 'Puerto de Santa Maria del Buen Aire'; destroyed by Indians, and refounded 1580; formerly capital of the Spanish viceroyalty of La Plata; suburbs include Avellaneda (industrial), Olivos (residential), San Isidro (sporting and leisure resort), Quilmes (industrial), Tigre, and the old port district of La Boca; nine universities; international (Ezeiza) and domestic airports; two airfields; railway; metro; trade in beef and wool; brewing, textiles, ironware, glass; national gallery, Teatro Colón; Plaza de Mayo, town hall (Cabildo), presidential palace (Casa Rosada), cathedral; horse-racing course.

Buerk, Michael (Duncan) [berk] (1946–) Television journalist and presenter, born in Solihull, West Midlands, C England, UK. He began his career with the *Daily Mail* and joined the BBC in 1970. His posts have included special correspondent (1981–2) and Africa correspondent (1983–7). Since 1990 he has presented Radio 4's *The Moral Maze*, and for television *999* (from 1993), the new format *Ten O'Clock News* (2000–2), and *The Hand of God* (2003).

Buffalo 42°53N 78°53W, pop (2000e) 292 600. Seat of Erie Co, W New York, USA; port on the Niagara R at the NE end of L Erie; second largest city in the state; railway; two universities (1846, 1867); motor vehicles and vehicle parts, machinery, steel; professional teams, Bills (football), Sabres (ice hockey); Albright-Knox art gallery, science museum.

buffalo *African buffalo; bison; water buffalo*

Buffalo Bill *Cody, William F*

buffalo gnat *black fly*

buffalo-weaver *weaverbird*

buffer (chemistry) A system which resists change. In chemistry, usually a solution whose pH is not greatly affected by small additions of strong acids or bases. This is most effective when an acid and its conjugate base are present in approximately equal amounts. Some important buffer systems and the approximate pH at which they operate are: acetate (CH_3COOH and CH_3COO^-), 4–5; carbonate (H_2CO_3 and HCO_3^-), 6–8; and ammonia (NH_4^+ and NH_3), 9–10. Biological systems are particularly dependent upon buffers to maintain constant pH values.

buffer (computing) A temporary storage area in memory for data. Buffers are often used when transmitting data between two devices with different working speeds, such as between a keyboard and the central processor, or the central processor and a printer.

buffer state A small state lying between two or more larger and potentially belligerent states, as a means of reducing border friction between them; often specially created for the purpose, though seldom successful. For example, after World War 1, attempts were made to create a buffer state between Germany and France involving Belgium, the Saar, the Rhine area, and Alsace-Lorraine.

Buffet, Bernard [bufay] (1928–99) Painter, born in Paris, France. He made his name in the early 1950s with murky still-lifes, and interiors with skinny, miserable figures painted in a sharp linear style and a neutral, almost monochromatic palette which seemed to catch the mood ('existential alienation') of post-war Paris. He has exhibited regularly in Paris and occasionally in London. In 1973 a Buffet Museum was established in Japan.

Buffon, Georges-Louis Leclerc, comte de (Count of) [bufõ] (1707–88) Naturalist, born in Montbard, EC France. He studied at Dijon, then devoted himself to science. In 1739 he was made director of the Jardin du Roi, and formed the design of his *Histoire naturelle* (1749–67, Natural History). His wide-ranging ideas led to fresh interest in natural science, and foreshadowed the theory of evolution. He was made a count in 1773.

Buffon's needle [büfõ] A problem first set and solved by French scientist Georges Buffon in 1777. If a straight thin needle length l is thrown at random onto a plane ruled with parallel lines a distance $a>l$ apart, what is the probability that the needle will cross one of the lines? Buffon showed that this probability was $\frac{2l}{\pi a}$.

bug (computing) An error in a computer program or a fault in computer hardware. The process of detecting and correcting errors is known as **debugging**.

bug (entomology) An insect with forewings leathery at base, membranous near the tip, and folded over membranous hindwings at rest; diverse in form and feeding habits; mouthparts modified into a snout for piercing and sucking; includes many crop pests and disease carriers. (Order: Heteroptera.)

Bugatti, Ettore (Arco Isidoro) [boogatee] (1881–1947) Car manufacturer, born in Milan, N Italy. He began designing cars in 1899, and set up his works in Strasbourg (1907). In World War 1 he moved to Italy and later to France, where his racing cars won international fame in the 1930s.

Buginese or **Bugi** A major ethnic group of Celebes (Sulawesi), Indonesia, who live as rice cultivators, traders, and seafarers. They came from Makasar, in SW Celebes, but migrated into the Malay Archipelago after the Dutch East India Company took the city (1667). They established settlements and a state at Selanger (1710), were defeated by the Dutch in the 18th-c, were further weakened by conflict with the Malay states, and lost supremacy in the 19th-c.

bugle (botany) A perennial with creeping, rooting stolons, native to Europe, the Mediterranean, and SW Asia (*Ajuga reptans*); flowering stems square, erect; leaves in opposite pairs; flowers blue, 2-lipped, upper lip very short, lower 3-lobed, in whorls forming loose spikes; the whole plant often bronze-tinged. (Family: Labiatae.)

bugle (music) A musical instrument made of brass or copper, curved elliptically and ending in a large bell. It normally has no valves and can therefore produce only those notes forming the first half-dozen harmonics above the fundamental (usually B♭). It has been used above all for sounding military calls.

bugloss [byooglos] A bristly annual or biennial (*Anchusa arvensis*) growing to 50 cm/20 in, native to Europe and Asia; leaves narrowly oblong with wavy margins; infloresence coiled; flowers 5 mm/¼ in diameter with curved white tube, spreading bright-blue lobes, and white eye. (Family: Boraginaceae.)

buhl or **boulle** [bool] A technique of furniture decoration involving very elaborate inlays of brass, tortoiseshell, mother-of-pearl, and coloured wood, introduced into France in the 16th-c from Italy, but perfected by André Charles Boulle (1642–1732) and his sons. The spelling *Buhl* is a 19th-c distortion.

building biology The study of the interaction between a building and its environment, especially with respect to the effects upon the health of the occupants. It deals with the location and geometry of the building, its colour scheme, lighting, and furnishings, and the selection of non-toxic and ecologically 'friendly' building materials.

building society An institution which lends money to enable people to buy property (via a mortgage loan). Their funds are derived from investors who obtain interest on the sum deposited. Interest paid to the society by the borrower is higher than the rate paid out. In the UK there were once some 150 societies, but their numbers have been falling through amalgamations. Following the Building Societies Act (1986) societies are permitted to provide other services. They are also allowed to become limited companies, and several of the largest ones have done so. The US equivalent is the **savings and loan association**.

Bujumbura [bujumboora], formerly **Usumbura** 3°22S 29°21E, pop (2000e) 400 000. Port and capital of Burundi, C Africa, at NE end of L Tanganyika; altitude 805 m/2641 ft; founded in 1899 by German colonists; airport; university (1960); coffee and cotton processing, brewing, cement, textiles, soap, shoes, metal working; Museum of African Civilization.

Bukharin, Nikolay Ivanovich [bookharin] (1888–1938) Russian Marxist revolutionary and political theorist, born in Moscow, Russia. Called by Lenin 'the darling of the Party', he was active in the Bolshevik underground (1905–17), and after the Febuary Revolution returned to Russia, playing a leading role in the organization of the October Revolution in Moscow. As a member of the Politburo (1924–9) he was a firm supporter of Lenin's New Economic Policy, and opposed Stalin's collectivization campaign. In 1937 he was arrested in Stalin's Great Purge, expelled from the Party, tried on trumped-up charges, and shot. In 1987 he was officially rehabilitated by a board of judicial inquiry, and posthumously readmitted to the Party in 1988.

Bukkyo [bukyoh] The Japanese conception of Buddhism, which came to Japan from China via Korea in the 6th-c. Today, the 'Pure Land' sects are the most popular; Zen is respected but not widespread. For many Japanese, Buddhism primarily means funeral ceremonies and remembering ancestors. Several of the 'new religions' claim to be Buddhist.

Bulawayo [boolawayoh] 20°10S 28°43E, pop (2000e) 612 100. Capital of Matabeleland North province, Zimbabwe, 370 km/230 mi SW of Harare; second largest city in Zimbabwe; founded, 1893; airport; railway junction; commercial, industrial, and tourist centre; asphalt, agricultural equipment, confectionery, electrical equipment, tyres, cement; national parks nearby.

bulb A highly modified shoot forming an underground storage organ. It is composed of overlapping leaves or leaf bases, swollen with food reserves which nourish early growth. The bulbs usually persist from year to year, the reserves being replenished before the plant dies back.

bulbil A small organ resembling a bulb, but produced above ground, either in a leaf axil or in the inflorescence in place of some flowers. It produces a new plant after falling from the parent.

bulbul A bird native to tropical Africa, Madagascar, and S Asia; short wings, long tail; stiff bristles at base of pointed bill; noisy and gregarious; inhabits woodland or cultivation; eats fruit and insects. (Family: Pycnonotidae, 120 species.)

Bulfinch, Charles (1763–1844) Architect, born in Boston, Massachusetts, USA. America's first native-born architect, he graduated from Harvard and was inspired by Neoclassical buildings on a European tour (1785–7). He sought to make Boston a US model of Classical elegance through town planning and the development of the Federal Style, his buildings include the Massachusetts State House (1795–7), India Wharf (1803–7), and Massachusetts General Hospital (1818–23). Succeeding Latrobe as architect of the US Capitol (1817–30), he completed the W portico, original dome, and landscaping before retiring to Boston. His domed capitol buildings influenced the design of state capitals across the country throughout the 19th-c.

Bulgakov, Mikhail Afanasievich [bulgakof] (1891–1940) Writer, born in Kiev, Ukraine. He studied medicine, but in 1920 worked as a journalist in Moscow, where he wrote several plays, novels, and short stories. His major novels include *Belaya gvardiya* (1925, The White Guard, rewritten as a play, 1926) and the deeply satirical *Master i Margerita* (1938, The Master and Margarita). Several of his works were considered too outspoken, were withdrawn, and re-emerged only in the 1960s.

Bulganin, Nikolay Alexandrovich [bulgahnin] (1895–1975) Soviet statesman and prime minister (1955–8), born in Nizhni Novgorod, W Russia. An early member of the Communist Party, he was Mayor of Moscow (1933–7), a member of the Military Council in World War 2, and minister of defence in 1946. After Stalin's death he became vice-premier in Malenkov's government, and was made premier after Malenkov resigned (1955), with Khrushchev wielding real power. 'B and K' travelled extensively abroad, conducting propaganda through lengthy letters to Western statesmen. He was dismissed in 1958, and retired into obscurity.

Bulgaria *p.243*

Bulgarian *Slavic languages*

Bulge, Battle of the (1944) The last desperate German armoured counter-offensive through the Ardennes in World War 2 (beginning 16 Dec), to prevent the Allied invasion of Germany. It achieved early success, but ground to a halt, and by the end of January 1945 the Germans were forced to retreat by the Allies.

bulimia nervosa [byoolimia nervohsa] A condition typified by repeated episodes of binge eating and frequent vomiting and purging, associated with a preoccupation with control of body weight and a feeling of lack of control over eating behaviour. The vast majority of patients are female, and patients report a high incidence of relatives who are obese and/or who have had a depressive illness. It is the reverse of anorexia nervosa, with which curiously it is occasionally associated in cycles. In rare cases it results from disturbance of the hypothalamus.

bulked yarn A yarn made of fibres, usually synthetic, whose properties have been modified to induce a high volume to the yarn by crimping the fibres during processing.

bulker A vessel designed to carry cargoes in bulk; grain, coal, iron ore, and bauxite are the commonest. The type has grown steadily since World War 2. The world total in 1991 was 116·3 million gross tonnes, or 206·7 million gross tonnes deadweight.

bulk modulus The negative ratio of a change in pressure applied to a block of some material to the resulting fractional change in volume of the block; symbol *K*, unit Pa (pascal); also called the **modulus of compression**. It is constant for a given material, eg for glass, $K = 0{\cdot}37 \times 10^{11}$Pa. The higher the value of *K*, the more difficult is the material to compress. Compressibility is $1/K$.

bulk store *backing store*

Bull, John (c.1562–1628) Musician, born in Somerset, SW England, UK. He was appointed organist in the Queen's Chapel (1586), first music lecturer at Gresham College (1597), and organist to James I (1607). A Catholic, he fled abroad to escape persecution in 1613, and in 1617 became organist of Antwerp Cathedral. A virtuoso player, he was one of the founders of contrapuntal keyboard music. He has been credited with composing the air 'God Save the King'.

Bull, Deborah (Clare) (1963–) Ballerina, born in Derby, Derbyshire, C England, UK. She trained at the Royal Ballet School, and in Monte Carlo with Marika Besobrasova. In 1981 she joined the Royal Ballet (principal dancer from 1992), and retired in 2001. Her repertoire ranged from classical ballet to contemporary choreography, and she has appeared in the television shows *Dance Night* (1998) and *Travels With My Tutu* (2000). In 2001 she was appointed artistic director of the Linbury Studio Theatre and Clore Studio Upstairs at the Royal Opera House.

Bulgaria

□ International Airport

[buhlgaireea], official name **Republic of Bulgaria**, Bulgarian **Republika Bulgariya**, formerly **People's Republic of Bulgaria** (1941–90)

Local name Bălgarija

Timezone GMT +2

Area 110 912 km^2/42 812 sq mi

Population total (2002e) 7 890 000

Status Republic

Date of independence 1908

Capital Sofia

Languages Bulgarian (official), Turkish

Ethnic groups Bulgarian (85%), Turkish (9%)

Religions Bulgarian Orthodox (85%), Muslim (13%)

Physical features Traversed W–E by the Balkan Mts, averaging 2000 m/6500 ft; in the SW, Rhodope Mts, rising to 3000 m/9600 ft; rivers include Maritsa, Iskur, Danube.

Climate Continental climate, with hot summers, cold winters; average annual temperatures -2°C (Jan), 21°C (Jul); average annual rainfall 635 mm/25 in.

Currency 1 Lev (Lv) = 100 stotinki

Economy Mainly agricultural produce; coal, iron ore; offshore oil (Black Sea), natural gas; tourism; tobacco, wine exports.

GDP (2002e) $49·23 bn, per capita $6500

Human Development Index (2002) 0·779

History Bulgars crossed the Danube in the 7th-c; their empire continually at war with Byzantines until destroyed by Turks, 14th-c; remained under Turkish rule, 1396-1878; full independence, 1908; became a kingdom, 1908–46; aligned with Germany in both World Wars; occupied by USSR, 1944; Socialist People's Republic founded, 1946; unicameral National Assembly established, 1971; proclaimed Republic of Bulgaria in 1990; new constitution, 1991, with a directly elected President, and a 250-member National Assembly.

Head of State
1991–6 Zhelyu Zhelev
1996–2001 Petar Stoyanov
2001– Georgi Parvanov

Head of Government
1995–6 Zhan Videnov
1997 Stefan Sofianski *Interim*
1997–2001 Ivan Kostov
2001– Simeon Borisov Sakskoburggotski

bull (religion) An important, formal communication or edict from a pope, originally sealed with his signet-ring (Lat *bulla*, 'seal') and identified by the opening Latin words. It is often used to promulgate major doctrines (eg infallibility, Immaculate Conception).

bull (zoology) A male mammal belonging to one of several species; female usually called *cow*; young called *calf*; used especially for uncastrated male cattle (male castrated when young called a *bullock*, *ox*, or *steer*; if castrated when fully grown, called a *stag*). The name is also used with several other species, including large whales, walrus, elephant seal, elephant, and moose.

bullace [**boo**lis] A type of small, wild plum (*Prunus domestica*), usually a thorny shrub with spherical black fruit with waxy bloom; native to Europe. (Subspecies *institia*. Family: Rosaceae.)

bulldog A breed of dog, used in mediaeval Britain for the sport of bull-baiting; heavy body with short, bowed legs and short tail; large round head with flat upturned muzzle; ears and eyes small; short brown or brown and white coat.

bulletin board A form of electronic notice board which occurs frequently in data communications networks, particularly those linking academic institutions; also called a **bulletin board system (BBS)**. The bulletin board hosts notices of meetings, technical papers, or even computer programs. The special feature of bulletin boards is that, since the networks are worldwide, the readership is worldwide.

bullfighting The national sport in Spain, also popular in some regions of S France, and in Latin-American countries. Known as the *corrida de toros* (Span 'running of the bulls') it is regarded as an art in Spain. Leading bullfighters (*matadors*) are treated as national heroes. Picadors are sent into the bull-ring to weaken the bull before the matador enters the arena to make the final killing. It is perhaps misnamed as a 'fight' because of its one-sidedness.

bullfinch A bird native to Europe, Scandinavia, and Asia E to Japan and the Philippines; inhabits woodlands and gardens; eats buds, seeds, and fruit; causes serious damage in orchards. (Genus: *Pyrrhula*, 6 species. Family: Fringillidae.) The name is also used for several species of genus *Loxigilla* in the family Emberizidae, and for the **bullfinch cardinal** in the family Cardinalidae.

bullfrog Any large frog; name used especially for North American *Rana catesbeiana* (**bullfrog** or **American bullfrog**); also for *Rana tigrina* (**Asian bullfrog**) and *Pyxicephalus adspersus* (**South African bullfrog**), all of the family Ranidae. *Leptodactylus pentadactylus* of the family Leptodactylidae is called the **South American bullfrog**.

bullhead Small, bottom-dwelling fish found in clear streams and lakes of N Europe; body stout, length up to 10 cm/4 in, with broad flattened head; eggs laid under stones and guarded by the male; feeds on invertebrates, especially crustaceans; also called **sculpin** or **miller's thumb**. The name is also used for others of this genus, the similar-looking marine Icelidae, and some North American catfishes of family Ictaluridae. (Genus: *Cottus*. Family: Cottidae.)

bull market A stock market term which signifies that the prices of stocks and shares are on a rising trend, due to buying demand. A 'bull' buys shares hoping that the price will rise, so that they can be sold later at a profit. Since the early 18th-c the terms 'bull' and 'bear' have been broadly used on the Stock Exchange to describe an optimist or a pessimist in share-dealing.

bull-mastiff A breed of dog, developed in Britain by crossing bulldogs and mastiffs; thick-set body; brown short-haired coat; soft ears and powerful muzzle; aggressive but controllable; used by gamekeepers in the 19th-c to deter poachers.

bullroarer A primitive musical instrument made from a wooden blade, often with serrated edges and sometimes elaborately carved, attached to a length of string and whirled around in the open air. It was known to the ancient Greeks and is still found in many countries.

Bull Run, Battles of Major victories by Confederate forces in the American Civil War; also known as the **Battles of Manassas**. The first battle pitted untrained Northern troops attempting to capture Richmond, VA (the Southern capital), against well-commanded Southerners. It turned into a Northern rout. In the second battle, a large Northern force under John Pope was trapped by combined Confederate forces under 'Stonewall' Jackson (1824–63) and James Longstreet (1821–1904).

bull terrier A breed of dog, developed for bull-baiting in Britain by crossing bulldogs and terriers; powerful body; long tail; ears pointed, erect; head broad with small eyes; coat short; **English bull terrier** usually white; **Staffordshire bull terrier** usually reddish fawn. The **American pit bull terrier** attracted widespread publicity during the 1980s, following several attacks on people; it became subject to controls and registration in the UK in 1991, along with the *tosa fila Brazileira* and *dogo Argentina*. The small form is known as the **miniature bull terrier**.

Bülow, Bernhard (Heinrich Martin Karl), Fürst von (Prince of) [**bü**loh] (1849–1929) German statesman and chancellor (1900–9), born in Flottbeck, N Germany. He was foreign secretary (1897) before becoming chancellor, and was made a count (1899) and a prince (1905). He was identified with an aggressive foreign policy in the years before World War 1.

Bülow, Hans (Guido), Freiherr von (Baron) [**bü**loh] (1830–94) Pianist and conductor, born in Dresden, E Germany. He studied law, but under the influence of Wagner made himself the musico-political spokesman of the new German School. In 1851 he took pianoforte lessons from Liszt, married Liszt's daughter, **Cosima** (1857), and became an outstanding conductor. In 1864 he became court pianist and director of the music school at Munich, but resigned when his wife deserted him for Wagner in 1869, and thereafter became an opponent of Wagner and his School.

bulrush An aquatic, rush-like perennial (*Scirpus lacustris*), found almost everywhere; stems to 3 m/10 ft; leaves in tufts; flowers tiny, perianth reduced to six rough bristles, in oval, brown spikelets. The name is sometimes misapplied to reedmace. (Family: Cyperaceae.)

bulrush millet *millet*

Bultmann, Rudolf (Karl) (1884–1976) Lutheran theologian, Hellenist, and New Testament scholar, born in Wiefelstede, NW Germany. He studied at Tübingen, taught at Marburg, Wrocław, (formerly Breslau, Prussia), and Giessen, then became professor of New Testament at Marburg (1921). An early exponent of form criticism (*History of the Synoptic Tradition*, 1921) he is best known for his highly influential programme (1941) to 'demythologize' the New Testament and interpret it existentially, employing the categories of the earlier work of Heidegger.

Bulwer-Lytton, Edward George Earle *Lytton, Edward George Earle Bulwer-Lytton*

bumblebee A large bee found mainly in the temperate N hemisphere. The adults transport pollen on the modified outer surface of the hindleg. They are organized into primitive societies, in which only the queen overwinters to produce the next generation of workers. (Family: Apidae. Genus: *Bombus*.)

Bunche, Ralph (Johnson) [buhnch] (1904–71) US diplomat, born in Detroit, Michigan, USA. He studied at Harvard and the University of California in Los Angeles, then taught political science at Howard University, Washington (1928–50). He directed the UN Trusteeship department (1947–54), and became UN mediator in Palestine, where he arranged for a ceasefire. Awarded the Nobel Peace Prize (1950), he became an under-secretary for Special Political Affairs (1954–67), and later under-secretary-general (1968–71).

Bundestag [**bun**destag] (Ger 'Federal Diet') The more powerful of the two houses of parliament of the German Federal Republic, the other being the Bundesrat ('Federal Council'). Elections for the Bundestag are held every four years in the autumn. It is possible for the Bundestag to be dissolved and elections held before the end of the fixed term, and this has happened twice (in 1972 and 1983). In addition to legislating, the Bundestag selects the Chancellor and supports his government. Following the reunification of East and West Germany in 1990, the Bundestag was enlarged to 656 members, and the Bundesrat to 68 members. After World War 2, the Bundesrat was opened in Bonn in 1949 and remained in session there until 1999. It then moved to the Reichstag building in Berlin, where all plenary meetings are now held. The Reichstag building, destroyed in a fire in 1933, was restored and redesigned by British architect Sir Norman Foster in the 1990s.

Bundy, McGeorge (1919–96) US government administrator, born in Boston, Massachusetts, USA. He studied at Yale, and became a junior fellow at Harvard (1941). After working in intelligence during World War 2, he joined Harvard as dean of arts and sciences (1953). He is remembered for his major role in foreign policy decisions during the Kennedy and Johnson administrations, notably in the Vietnam War. After resigning (1966), he became president of the Ford Foundation, and was later appointed history professor at New York University.

Bundy, Ted (1954–89) US convicted murderer. He was a law student who is believed to have killed at least 36 females, both adults and children, over a number of years. Convicted in 1979 on several charges, including the murder of a 12-year-old girl, he was sentenced to death. He was executed in Florida in 1989 after a string of unsuccessful appeals.

bungee jumping The activity of jumping from a high point to which the jumper is attached by a strong rubber cable fastened to the ankles. The length and tension of the cable is calculated to ensure that the jumper bounces up before reaching the ground. The activity became popular in the early 1990s, and is now practised as a sport in several countries.

Bunin, Ivan Alexeyevich [**boo**nin] (1870–1953) Writer, born in Voronezh, W Russia. He worked as a journalist and clerk, writing lyrics and novels of the decay of the Russian nobility and of peasant life. His best-known work is *Gospodin iz San-Francisco* (1922, The Gentleman from San Francisco). He was the first Russian to receive the Nobel Prize for Literature (1933). After the Revolution, he lived in Paris.

bunion A painful, inflamed hardening and thickening of the skin of the sole of the foot at the base of the great toe. It is often induced by ill-fitting footwear.

Bunker Hill, Battle of (1775) The first pitched battle of the US War of Independence, fought during the siege of Boston. It was technically an American defeat, as New England troops were dislodged from the position overlooking occupied Boston; but very high British casualties demonstrated American fighting capacity, and forbade attempts on other American emplacements. The eventual result was the British evacuation of Boston. It was actually fought on Breed's Hill, above Charlestown, not on nearby Bunker Hill.

bunraku [bun**ra**koo] The classical Japanese puppet theatre. Puppets are two-thirds life size, hand-held by a puppet master, generally with two 'invisible' assistants in black. The movements are accompanied by a singer-narrator, who voices all the roles, and musicians. Bunraku's greatest popularity was in the 17th–18th-c.

Bunsen, Robert Wilhelm (1811–99) Chemist and physicist, born in Göttingen, C Germany. After studying at Göttingen, Paris, Berlin, and Vienna, he became professor of chemistry at Heidelberg (1852). He shared with Gustav Robert Kirchhoff the discovery of spectrum analysis (1859), which facilitated the discovery of new elements, including caesium and rubidium. He invented the *Bunsen burner*, the grease-spot photometer, a galvanic battery, an ice calorimeter and, with Sir Henry Roscoe, the actinometer.

Bunsen burner A gas burner, used mainly in chemistry laboratories. Gas enters through a jet at the lower end of a tube, and is drawn through a side tube whose aperture can be controlled. The controllable gas–air mixture makes possible a flame of quality, ranging from luminous to hot non-luminous. The idea is attributed to German scientist Robert Wilhelm Bunsen, but its first practical construction should be credited mainly to his technical assistant, C Desaga.

Bunting, Basil (1900–85) Poet, born in Scotswood, Northumberland, NE England, UK. He worked as a journalist in Paris, was much influenced by Pound and the American Modernists, and published his early poetry abroad. After some years in Paris, where he worked on translation, he returned to Britain and established his reputation with *Briggflatts* (1966), a semi-autobiographical poem deeply rooted in the North East.

bunting A small seed-eating bird, usually dull in colour with a short stout bill. It belongs to a widespread family, thought to have evolved in the Americas, spread across the Bering Straits to Asia, then colonized Europe and Africa. (Family: Emberizidae, c.290 species.)

Bunton, Emma *Spice Girls, The*

Buñuel, Luis [buhnwel] (1900–83) Film director, born in Calanda, NE Spain. He studied at Madrid University, and his first films (made with Salvador Dali) were a sensation with their Surrealistic, macabre approach: *Un Chien andalou* (1928, An Andalusian Dog) and *L'Age d'or* (1930, The Golden Age). His career then went into eclipse until he settled in Mexico (1947), where he directed such major films as *Los olvidados* (1950, trans The Young and the Damned), *Viridiana* (1961), *The Discreet Charm of the Bourgeoisie* (1972), and *That Obscure Object of Desire* (1977). His work is characterized by a poetic, often erotic, use of imagery, a black humour, and a hatred of Catholicism, often expressed in blasphemy.

Bunyan, John (1628–88) Writer, born in Elstow, Bedfordshire, SC England, UK. He worked as a tinker, and fought in the parliamentary army during the English Civil War (1644–5). In 1653 he joined a non-conformist Christian fellowship, preaching around Bedford. In 1660 he was arrested for preaching without a licence and spent 12 years in Bedford county gaol, where he wrote prolifically, including his impassioned and tormented autobiography, *Grace Abounding* (1666). Briefly released after the Declaration of Indulgence (1672), he was reimprisoned for six months in the town gaol, and there wrote the first part of the *The Pilgrim's Progress* (published 1678), a vision of salvation told allegorically as if it were a journey through life. Returning to his career, he acted as pastor in Bedford for 16 years, where he wrote the second part of *The Pilgrim's Progress* (1684).

Bunyan, Paul In American folklore, a lumberjack of superhuman size and strength, stories of whose prowess began to circulate early in the 20th-c. Not only could he break up log-jams with spectacular ease; he could also refashion geography, creating lakes, rivers, and even the Grand Canyon.

bunyip In the mythology of the Australian aborigines, the source of evil. He is not to be thought of as a spirit or as a human. The Rainbow Serpent, the mother of life, confined bunyip to a waterhole: he haunts dark and gloomy places.

bunyip aristocracy An unsuccessful local attempt in Australia to create an upper house elected from an order of hereditary baronets for the government of New South Wales in 1853. The proposal was associated with W C Wentworth, and was designed to counter the 'spirit of democracy' unleashed by the gold rushes, and to stabilize society with the granting of self-government. The name was first used with witty cynicism in a political speech in 1853.

Buonaparte *Naploeon*

buoy A fixed, floating object attached by a cable or chain to the seabed to mark safe channels, approaches to harbours, and dangers to navigation. Buoys made of wood are known to have been used in the Middle Ages and are probably much older; modern buoys are generally made of steel or fibre-glass reinforced plastic. Buoys may be fitted with bells or whistles, usually operated by the motion of the waves. There are also mooring buoys, used for the anchoring of ships. In addition to a battery-powered light which allows recognition at night, a buoy may be fitted with a fog signal and a *racon* (a radar beacon that can be identified and located by its response to a radar signal). The colour, shape, markings, and flash pattern of a buoy convey information to navigators.

buoyancy The upward thrust on an object immersed in liquid or gas, equal to the weight of the displaced fluid. The human body is more buoyant in salt water than in fresh water, as the former is 3% denser.

Burakumin [burakoomin] An outcaste group in Japanese society, concentrated in about 6000 ghetto communities and numbering 1–3 million; the target of extreme discrimination with regard to employment, marriage, and residential segregation. Their origins go back to the Edo feudal period of the 17th-c, when impoverished Japanese in lowly occupations were segregated. The class was officially abolished in 1871, but to no great effect: some militancy within the group since the 1920s has also had little impact.

Burbage, Richard [berbij] (c.1569–1619) Actor, born in London, UK. He was the leading performer with Shakespeare's company, the Chamberlain's (later the King's) Men, from 1594 until his death, and was the first creator on stage of many of Shakespeare's greatest roles, including Hamlet, Othello, Richard III, and Lear. He performed at the first permanent public playhouse (The Theatre) built by Richard's father James in 1576, then from 1599 at the Globe, which Richard and his brother Cuthbert built on the south bank of the R Thames. Burbage also played leading roles in dramas by Jonson and others.

Burbank, Luther (1849–1926) Horticulturalist, born in Lancaster, Massachusetts, USA. He developed the *Burbank potato* on a farm near Lunenberg, MA, and in 1875 moved to Santa Rosa, CA, where he bred over 800 new strains of fruits and flowers.

burbot Elongate, slender-bodied fish (*Lota lota*) widespread in rivers and lakes of N Eurasia and North America; the only freshwater species in the cod family Gadidae; length up to 1 m/3¾ ft; single barbel beneath mouth; fished commercially in Russia; also called **eelpout**.

Burckhardt, Jacob (Christopher) [berkhah(r)t] (1818–97) Historian, born in Basel, N Switzerland. He studied theology and later art history in Berlin and Bonn, became editor of the *Basler Zeitung* (1844–5), and was professor of history at Basel University (1858–93). He is known for his works on the Italian Renaissance and on Greek civilization.

Bureau of Indian Affairs A US government agency, established in 1836, which was notorious in the late 19th-c for its extreme corruption, both in the provision of supplies for client Indians and in the redistribution of Indian lands. It was responsible for implementing the long-term policy of removing Indians from areas of possible white occupation, and destroying indigenous Indian culture. It operated under the Department of War until 1849, when it was transferred to the Department of the Interior. It now operates as the Indian Service.

Burford, Eleanor *Hibbert, Eleanor*

Burgess, Anthony, pseudonym of **John Anthony Burgess Wilson** (1917–93) Writer and critic, born in Manchester, Greater Manchester, NW England, UK. He studied at Xaverian College and Manchester University, lectured at Birmingham University (1946–50), worked for the Ministry of Education, and taught at Banbury Grammar School (1950–4). He then became an education officer in Malaya and Brunei (1954–9), where his experiences inspired his *Malayan Trilogy* (1965). His many novels include *A Clockwork Orange* (1962), *1985* (1978), *Earthly Powers* (1980), and *Any Old Iron* (1989). He wrote several critical studies and film scripts, including *Jesus of Nazareth* (1977). His musical compositions include symphonies, a ballet, and an opera. He also wrote under the name of **Joseph Kell** as well as under his original name. In his later years he lived in Monaco.

Burgess, Guy (Francis de Moncy) (1910–63) British traitor, born in Devonport, Devon, SW England, UK. He studied at Eton, Dartmouth, and Cambridge, where he became a communist. Recruited as a Soviet agent in the 1930s, he worked with the BBC (1936–9), wrote war propaganda (1939–41), and again joined the BBC (1941–4) while working for MI5. Thereafter, he was a member of the Foreign Office, and second secretary under Philby in Washington in 1950. Recalled in 1951 for 'serious misconduct', he and Maclean disappeared, re-emerging in the Soviet Union in 1956. He died in Moscow.

Burgh, Hubert de [ber] (?–1243) English statesman. He was the patriotic justiciar of England (1215–32), and virtual ruler for the last four years of this period, but now is chiefly remembered as the jailer of Prince Arthur. He was created Earl of Kent in 1227.

burgh *borough*

Burghley or **Burghleigh, Lord** *Cecil, William*

burglary In some legal systems, a crime which involves entering a building as a trespasser with the intent to commit theft, grievous bodily harm, rape, or cause criminal damage; or, having entered, stealing or attempting to steal anything, or committing or attempting to commit grievous bodily harm. In England and Wales, *aggravated burglary*, in which the accused is carrying a firearm, imitation firearm, offensive weapon, or explosive, may carry a maximum sentence of life imprisonment. In the USA, the entry must be with the intent to commit theft or a felony; the crime occurs at the moment of entry. A 'building' is a roofed structure with some measure of permanence: caravans and houseboats are included. In the USA the definition of structure has been extended in some jurisdictions as far as including automated teller machines. The term *burglary* is not used in Scottish law, which has its own forms of aggravated theft (eg theft by housebreaking and theft by opening lockfast places).

Burgos [boorgos] 42°21N 3°41W, pop (2000e) 163 000. Capital of Burgos province, NC Spain; on R Arlanzón, 243 km/151 mi N of Madrid; former capital of Old Castile; archbishopric; railway; a world heritage site; home and burial site of El Cid; textiles, motor accessories, silk, chemicals, nails, clothes; Santa Maria de Gerona nuclear power station (1971); cathedral (13th–16th-c), castle; fair and fiestas of St Peter (Jun).

Burgoyne, John, nickname **Gentleman Johnnie** (1722–92) British general and playwright, born in Sutton, Bedfordshire, SC England, UK. He entered the army in 1740, and gave distinguished service in the Seven Years' War (1756–63). He then sat in parliament as a Tory, and in 1777 was sent to America, where he led an expedition from Canada into New York State, taking Ticonderoga, but being forced to surrender at Saratoga. He later joined the Whigs, and commanded in Ireland (1782–3). His best-known work was his comedy, *The Heiress* (1786).

Burgundy, Fr **Bourgogne** pop (2000e) 1 683 000; area 31 582 sq km/12 191 sq mi. Region and former province of EC France, comprising departments of Côte-d'Or, Nièvre, Saône-et-Loire, and Yonne; former kingdom of Burgundia (5th–10th-c); famous wine-producing area (eg Beaujolais, Beaune, Chablis); wooded Monts du Morvan (902 m/2959 ft) in C; chief town, Dijon; industry centred on Le Creusot; caves at Arcy-sur-Cure; Parc de Morvan regional nature park; several spas.

burials *bog burials; Hochdorf; Kofun; Maes Howe; Mount Li; New Grange; Pazyryk; shaft graves; Ship of Cheops; Sutton Hoo ship burial*

Buridan, Jean [booreedã] (c.1300–c.1358) Scholastic philosopher, probably born in Béthune, N France. He studied under William of Ockham and taught in Paris, publishing works on mechanics, optics, and logic. He gave his name to the famous problem of decision-making called *Buridan's ass*, where an ass faced with two equidistant and equally desirable bales of hay starves to death because there are no grounds for preferring to go to one bale rather than the other.

burin [byoorin] A tool used in engraving; also called a **graver**. It has a rounded wooden handle to fit into the palm of the hand, and a pointed metal blade for cutting into the woodblock or metal plate.

Burke, Edmund (1729–97) British statesman and political philosopher, born in Dublin, Ireland. Educated at a Quaker boarding-school and at Trinity College, Dublin, he began studying law (1750), but then took up literary work. His early writing includes his *Philosophical Inquiry into the Origin of Our Ideas of the Sublime and Beautiful* (1756). He became secretary for Ireland, and entered parliament in 1765. His main speeches and writings belong to the period when his party was opposed to Lord North's American policy (1770–82). His *Reflections on the French Revolution* (1790) was read all over Europe.

Burke, Robert O'Hara (1820–61) Traveller and explorer of Australia, born in St Clerans, Co Galway, W Ireland. He studied in Belgium, served in the Austrian army (1840), joined the Irish constabulary (1848), and emigrated to Australia in 1853. As leader of the Burke and Wills expedition (1860), he was one of the first white men to cross the Australian continent from S to N. Both Burke and Wills died of starvation on the return journey.

Burke, William (1792–1829) Murderer, born in Orrery, Ireland. With his partner, **William Hare** (c.1790–c.1860), born in Londonderry, he carried out a series of infamous murders in Edinburgh in the 1820s, with the aim of supplying dissection subjects to Dr Robert Knox, the anatomist. Hare, the more villainous of the two, turned king's evidence, and died a beggar in London in the 1860s; Burke was hanged, to the general satisfaction of the crowd. In his confession, Burke exonerated Knox from all knowledge of his crimes. The incident caused the Anatomy Act (1832) to be passed, which regulated the supply of bodies to medical schools.

Burke's Peerage A reference guide to the aristocratic and titled families of Great Britain, first published by John Burke (1787–1848) in 1826 under the title *Genealogical and Heraldic Dictionary of the Peerage and Baronetage of the United Kingdom*.

Burkina Faso *p.247*

burlesque In Europe, a play satirizing contemporary theatre or theatrical fashion; originally the critical aspect was strong but, by the 19th-c, fantasy and travesty often predominated. It was the training ground for many famous stage, screen, and radio comedians, and was popular up to World War 2. In the USA, the term is used for a sex and comedy show created around 1865 for mainly male audiences.

Burlington, Richard Boyle, 3rd Earl of (1694–1753) Architect and patron of the arts, born in London, UK. A great admirer of Palladio, he was himself an enthusiastic architect. He refashioned the Burlington House in Piccadilly of his great-grandfather, the 1st earl, and by his influence over a group of young architects was responsible for fostering the Palladian precept which was to govern English building for half a century.

Burma *Myanmar*

Burma Road A road linking the Burmese railhead at Lashio with Kunming, 1150 km/700 mi distant in Yunnan province, China. Completed by the Chinese in 1938, it was of great strategic importance to the Allies during World War 2 until the Japanese conquest of Burma (1942).

Burmese cat A breed of domestic cat, of the *foreign short-haired* type; many breeds (not all recognized in USA): brown (or zibelines), blue, blue-cream, cream, chocolate (or champagne), tortoiseshell (or tortie), chocolate tortie, lilac (or platinum), lilac tortie (or lilac cream), and red.

burn A wound in which tissues are damaged or destroyed by heat or electricity. Burns are classified into *partial* or *full* thickness, and then according to what percentage of the body's surface area has been affected. In a partial thickness burn, enough

Burkina Faso

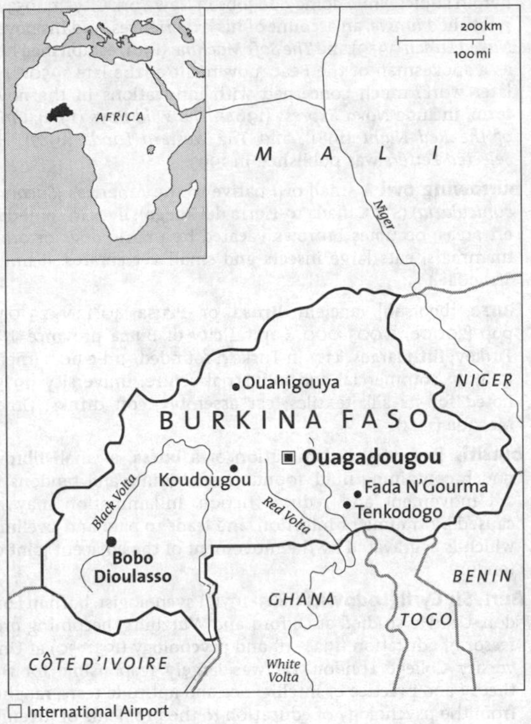

[berkeena fasoh], formerly **Upper Volta** (to 1984), then (Fr) **République de Haute-Volta**

Local name Burkina Faso

Timezone GMT

Area 274 200 km^2/105 870 sq mi

Population total (2002e) 12 603 000

Status Republic

Date of independence 1960

Capital Ouagadougou

Languages French (official), with Moré, Mossi, Mande, Fulani, Lobi, and Bobo also spoken

Ethnic groups Mossi (48%), over 50 other groups

Religions Traditional beliefs (45%), Muslim (43%), Christian (12%)

Physical features Landlocked republic in W Africa; low-lying plateau, falling away to the S; tributaries of the Volta and Niger unnavigable in dry season; wooded savannahs in S; semi-desert in N.

Climate Tropical; average annual rainfall 894 mm/35 in; dry season (Dec–May), rainy season (Jun–Oct); average annual temperature 24°C (Jan), 28°C (Jul) in Ouagadougou; violent storms (Aug); subject to drought conditions.

Currency 1 CFA Franc (CFAFr) = 100 centimes

Economy Based on agriculture, largely at subsistence level; millet, corn, rice, livestock, peanuts, sugar cane, cotton.

GDP (2002e) $14·51 bn, per capita $1100

Human Development Index (2002) 0·325

History Mossi empire in 18th–19th-c; Upper Volta created by French, 1919; abolished in 1932, with most land joined to Ivory Coast; original borders reconstituted, 1947; autonomy within French community, 1958; independence, 1960, with several military coups since; changed name from Upper Volta to Burkina Faso ('land of upright men'), 1984; end of military rule, 1991; governed by a president and an appointed Council of Ministers; new constitution, 1991, which promulgated an Assembly of People's Deputies (from 1997, with 111 members).

Head of State

1984–7 Thomas Sankara (Chairman)
1987– Blaise Compaoré

Head of Government

1992–4 Youssouf Ouedraogo
1994–6 Roch Christian Kabore
1996–2000 Kadre Desire Ouedraogo
2000– Paramanga Ernest Yonli

of the surface layer is preserved to allow spontaneous regeneration. Full thickness burns usually require skin grafts.

Burne-Jones, Sir Edward Coley (1833–98) Painter and designer, born in Birmingham, West Midlands, C England, UK. He studied at Oxford, where he met William Morris, and through the encouragement of Rossetti, relinquished the Church for art. His later oils, inspired by the early Italian Renaissance, are characterized by a Romantic and contrived Mannerism. His subjects, drawn from the Arthurian romances and Greek myths, include 'The Days of Creation', 'The Beguiling of Merlin', and 'The Mirror of Venus', exhibited in 1877. He also designed stained glass and tapestries, and illustrated several books for William Morris, notably Chaucer. He was made a baronet in 1894.

burnet An erect, tuft-forming perennial, native to Europe, W Asia, and North Africa; leaves mostly basal, slightly bluish, pinnate with oval, toothed leaflets; flowers in a globular head, four sepals, petals absent. The **salad burnet** (*Sanguisorba minor*) grows to 40 cm/15 in, flowers green or purple-tinged; crushed foliage smelling of cucumber. The **great burnet** (*san guisorba officinalis*) is a larger plant growing to 60 cm/2 ft; flowers dull red. (Family: Rosaceae.)

Burnet, Alastair [bernet], popular name of **Sir James William Alexander Burnet** (1928–) British journalist and television news presenter. He studied at Worcester College, Oxford, then became editor of *The Economist* (1965–74) and *The Daily Express* (1974–6). He became a nationally known personality when he joined ITN as a news presenter (1976–91), and he later became associate editor for *News at Ten* (1982–91). He was knighted in 1984.

Burnet, Sir (Frank) Macfarlane [bernet] (1899–1985) Physician and virologist, born in Traralgon, Victoria, SE Australia. Director of the Institute for Medical Research, Melbourne, he became a world authority on viral diseases, perfecting the technique of cultivating viruses in living chick embryos. He shared the 1960 Nobel Prize for Physiology or Medicine for researches on immunological intolerance in relation to skin and organ grafting. He was knighted in 1951.

Burnett, Frances (Eliza) Hodgson (1849–1924) Writer, born in Manchester, Greater Manchester, NW England, UK. In 1865 her family emigrated to Tennessee, where she married (1873, divorced 1898), and had her first literary success with *That Lass o' Lowrie's* (1877). She wrote several plays and over 40 novels, notably *Little Lord Fauntleroy* (1886) and *The Secret Garden* (1911).

Burnett, Ivy Compton *Compton-Burnett, Ivy*

Burney, Fanny, popular name of **Frances Burney**, married name **Madame d'Arblay** (1752–1840) Writer and diarist, born in King's Lynn, Norfolk, E England, UK. She educated herself by reading English and French literature and observing the distinguished people who visited her father. Her first and best novel, *Evelina*, was published anonymously in 1778, and influenced Jane Austen. She was given a court appointment in 1786, but her health declined; she retired on a pension and married a French emigré, **General d'Arblay**, in 1793. Her *Letters and Diaries* (1846) show her skill in reporting events of her time.

burning bush *dittany; summer cypress*

Burns, George, originally **Nathan Birnbaum** (1896–1996) Comedian and actor, born in New York City, USA. He made his debut at the age of 13 as a singer, later performing as a dancer, skater, and comic. In 1923 he teamed up with **Gracie Allen** (1905–64) and they became a husband and wife comedy duo popular in the United States for more than three decades in vaudeville, radio, films, and television. He later co-starred in the film *The Sunshine Boys* (1975), for which he received an Oscar. Well known for his omnipresent cigar, dry wit, and comic timing, other films included *Oh God* (1977), *Going in Style* (1979), and *Oh God! You Devil* (1984).

Burns, Robert (1759–96) Scotland's national poet, born in Alloway, South Ayrshire, SW Scotland, UK. The son of a poor farmer, his education was thoroughly literary, and he studied the technique of writing, influenced also by the popular tales and songs of Betty Davidson, an old woman who lived with his family. On his father's death (1784) he was left in charge of the farm. At the same time his entanglement with **Jean Armour** (1767–1834) began, and as the farm went to ruin, his poverty, passion, and despair produced in 1785 an extraordinary output of poetry, including 'The Jolly Beggars'. Looking for money to emigrate to Jamaica, he published the famous Kilmarnock edition of his *Poems, Chiefly in the Scottish Dialect* (1786), which brought such acclaim that he was persuaded to stay in Scotland. Going to Edinburgh, where he was feted, he began the epistolary flirtations with 'Clarinda' (Agnes Maclehose). He collaborated with the musicologists James Johnson and George Thomson in collecting Scottish songs. His own songs, many of which were published in *The Scots Musical Museum* (1787–1803), include *Auld Lang Syne*. In 1788 he married Jean Armour and leased a farm near Dumfries, in 1789 being made an excise officer. By 1790, when he wrote 'Tam o' Shanter', the farm was failing. He left for Dumfries, briefly adopting Radical views and becoming an ardent supporter of the French Revolution, but he turned patriot again in 1795.

Burnside, Ambrose Everett (1824–81) Union general in the US Civil War, born in Liberty, Indiana, USA. He trained at West Point, and in the Civil War commanded a brigade at the first Battle of Bull Run, capturing Roanoke I. He was repulsed at Fredericksburg (1862), but held Knoxville (1863), and led a corps under Grant through the Battles of the Wilderness and Cold Harbor (1864). After the war he became Governor of Rhode Island, and a US senator in 1875. He lent his name to a style of side whiskers, later known as *sideburns*.

Burns Night The evening of 25 January, anniversary of the birth (in 1759) of the Scottish poet Robert Burns, celebrated in Scotland and many other parts of the world with a special meal (**Burns Supper**) featuring haggis, potatoes, and swedes, followed by a set formula of toasts and performances of Burns's works.

Burr, Aaron (1756–1836) US statesman, born in Newark, New Jersey, USA. He studied at Princeton, was called to the bar in 1782, and became attorney general (1789–91), US senator (1791–7), and Republican vice-president (1800–4). In 1804 he killed his political rival, Alexander Hamilton, in a duel, and fled to South Carolina. He then prepared to raise a force to conquer Texas, and establish a republic. He was tried for treason (1807), acquitted, spent some wretched years in Europe, and in 1812 resumed his law practice in New York City.

Burra, Edward (1905–76) Artist, born in London, UK. He studied at the Chelsea School of Art and the Royal College of Art, and travelled widely in Europe and the USA. Well known as a colourist, his Surrealist paintings of figures against exotic (often Spanish) backgrounds are invariably in watercolour, as in 'Soldiers' (1942, Tate, London). He also designed for the ballet.

Burroughs, Edgar Rice [buhrohz] (1875–1950) Writer, born in Chicago, Illinois, USA. He had many unsuccessful jobs before making his name with the 'Tarzan' adventure stories, beginning with 'Tarzan of the Apes' (1914). In later years he became a war correspondent.

Burroughs, William S(eward) [buhrohz] (1914–97) Writer, born in St Louis, Missouri, USA. He studied at Harvard, and became a heroin addict while doing odd jobs in New York City. In 1953 he published *Junkie*, an account of his experiences, and his novels *Naked Lunch* (1959) and *The Soft Machine* (1961) established him as a spokesman of the Beat movement of the late 1950s. His later work, much concerned with innovations in the novel form, include *Nova Express* (1964), *The Wild Boys* (1971), *Cities of the Red Night* (1981), and *The Western Lands* (1987). His *Selected Letters* was published in 1993.

burrowing owl A small owl native to the Americas (*Speotyto cunicularia*) (SW Canada to Tierra del Fuego); lives in semi-desert areas; occupies burrows vacated by prairie dogs or other mammals; eats large insects and small vertebrates. (Family: Strigidae.)

Bursa [boorsah], ancient **Brusa** or **Prusa** 40°12N 29°04E, pop (2000e) 1 005 000. Capital city of Bursa province, NW Turkey; fifth largest city in Turkey; founded, 3rd-c BC; airfield; railway; commercial and industrial centre; university (1975); noted for its silk textiles; car assembly, soft drinks; Green Mosque (1421).

bursitis [bersiytis] Inflammation of a **bursa**, a small fibrous pouch containing fluid, found around joints and tendons to aid movement and reduce friction. Inflammation may be caused by trauma or infection, and leads to pain and swelling, which is aggravated by the movement of the adjacent joint or tendon.

Burt, Sir Cyril (Lodowic) (1883–1971) Psychologist, born in London, UK. He studied at Oxford and Würzburg, becoming professor of education (1924–31) and psychology (1931–50) at University College London. He was largely responsible for the theory and practice of intelligence and aptitude tests, ranging from the psychology of education to the problems of juvenile delinquency. He was knighted in 1946. In the 1980s, the validity of some of his findings was called into question.

Burton, Richard, originally **Richard Walter Jenkins** (1925–84) Stage and film actor, born in Pontrhydfen, Neath and Port Talbot, SC Wales, UK. The 12th child (possibly grandchild) of a coalminer, Richard Jenkins, he was brought up in his sister's house after his mother's death. He was befriended by his English teacher, Philip H Burton, who encouraged his acting and study of English, and eventually adopted him. He went to Oxford, and in 1943 changed his name to Burton. He acted in Liverpool and Oxford, served in the RAF, and returned to the stage in 1948, when he made his film debut. He made his stage reputation in Fry's *The Lady's Not for Burning* (1949), and had a triumphant season at Stratford (1951). He acted in Shakespearean productions at the London Old Vic in 1953–6, and gave a memorable performance of Hamlet in John Gielgud's Broadway production of that play in 1964. His early Hollywood films include *My Cousin Rachel* (1952) and *The Robe* (1953) for which he received one of his six Oscar nominations. In 1954 he was the narrator in the famous radio production of Dylan Thomas's *Under Milk Wood*. His romance with Elizabeth Taylor during the making of *Cleopatra* (1962) and their eventual marriage (1964–74) projected them both into the 'superstar' category. Among his later films were *Becket* (1964), *Equus* (1977), and *1984* (released after his death). In his later years, interest in his social life grew, especially after his remarriage to Elizabeth Taylor (1975–6).

Burton, Sir Richard (Francis) (1821–90) Explorer and language expert, born in Torquay, Devon, SW England, UK. He studied in Europe and Oxford, where he was expelled in 1842. In 1856 he set out with Speke on the journey which led to the discovery of L Tanganyika (1858), and afterwards travelled in North America, holding consular posts in Fernando Pó, Santos, Damascus, and Trieste. He wrote over 80 volumes on the sociology and anthropology of the countries he visited, and became famous for his translations of Arab literature. He was knighted in 1886. **Lady Burton**, *née* **Isabel Arundell** (1831–96), who shared in much of his travelling and writing, burned most of her husband's papers after his death.

Burton, Robert (1577–1640) Writer, born in Lindley, Leicestershire, C England, UK. He studied at Oxford, then taught there, taking orders in 1614. His great work was the *Anatomy of Melancholy* (1621), a satire on the inefficacy of human learning and satire, which influenced many subsequent authors.

Burundi *see panel*

burying beetle A medium to large beetle; adults bury corpses of small animals by excavating soil beneath them; eggs laid in tunnels off burial chamber; larvae typically feed on carrion. (Order: Coleoptera. Family: Silphidae.)

bus (computing) A form of wiring within or between computers in which any electronic message to be transferred is sent down the wire and is taken off the wire only by the particular device to which the message is being sent. Inside a computer there are usually an **address bus**, a **data bus**, and an **input–output bus**.

Busan *Pusan*

Busby, Sir Matt(hew) (1909–94) Footballer and football manager, born in Bellshill, North Lanarkshire, C Scotland, UK. After a comparatively undistinguished playing career with Manchester City and Liverpool, he became manager of Manchester United in 1945. Almost immediately the club won the FA Cup in 1948 and the League shortly afterwards. Rebuilding the team, he seemed likely to bring the European Cup to Britain for the first time in 1958, but his young side was largely wiped out in an air crash at Munich airport. He himself was severely injured, but patiently reconstructed the team until European Cup success eventually came in 1968.

Bush, Alan (Dudley) (1900–95) Composer and pianist, born in London, UK. He studied at the Royal Academy of Music (1918–22), where he was a notable composition teacher (1925–78), and also at Berlin University (1929–31). In 1924 he became active in the British working-class movement and founded the Workers' Music Association (1936), becoming its president in 1941. His works include four operas, four symphonies, concertos for violin and piano, choral works, chamber works, and songs.

Burundi

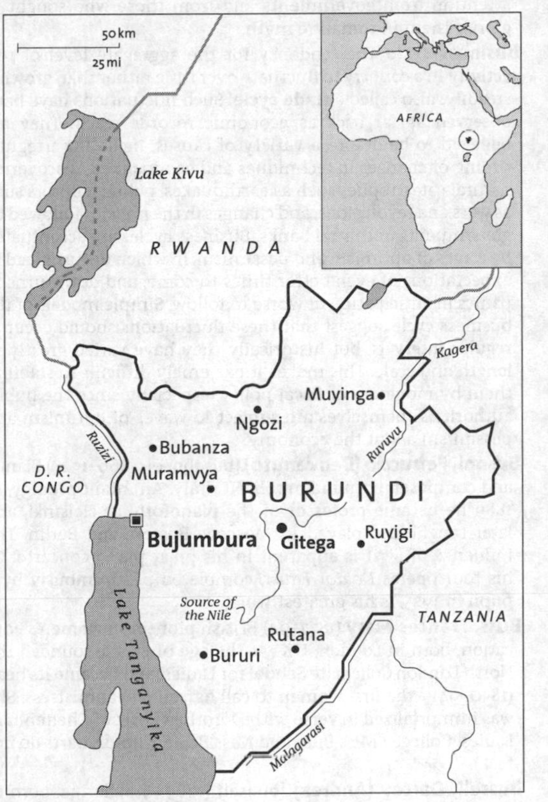

[burundee], official name **Republic of Burundi**

Local name Burundi

Timezone GMT +2

Area 27 834 km²/10 747 sq mi

Population total (2002e) 6 373 000

Status Republic

Date of independence 1962

Capital Bujumbura

Languages French and Kirundi (official), Swahili

Ethnic groups Hutu (82%), Tutsi (14%), Twa Pygmy (1%)

Religions Roman Catholic (62%), traditional beliefs (32%)

Physical features Located in C Africa; lies across Nile-Congo watershed; interior plateau, c.1500 m/5000 ft; highest point, Mt Karonje 2685 m/8809 ft; R Ruzizi forms part of NW frontier with Zaire and links Lake Kiki in Rwanda, with Lake Tanganyika in S and E; river Malagarasi valley in E.

Climate Equatorial; moderately wet; dry season (Jun–Sep); average annual temperature 23°C; average annual rainfall at Bujumbura, 850 mm/33·5 in.

Currency 1 Burundi Franc (BuFr, FBu) = 100 centimes

Economy Mainly agriculture; cash crops include coffee, cotton, tea; light consumer goods, shoes, blankets; reserves of rare-earth metals.

GDP (2002e) $3·146 bn, per capita $500

Human Development Index (2002) 0·313

History Ruled by the Tutsi kingdom, 16th-c; occupied by Germany in 1890, and included in German East Africa, 1890; League of Nations mandated territory, administered by Belgians, 1919; joined with Rwanda to become the UN Trust Territory of Ruanda-Urundi, 1946. Independent, 1962; full republic following the overthrow of the monarchy, 1966; civil war, 1972; military coup, 1976; new constitution provided a National Assembly, 1981; Assembly dissolved and constitution suspended after 1987 coup; Military Council for National Salvation disbanded, 1990; new constitution, 1992; political instability following assassination of president, 1993; inter-ethnic (Hutu/Tutsi) conflict, 1993– ; transitional government agreed, 1994–8; ongoing conflict led to a further period of transitional governance, 2001; ceasefire agreement signed (Dec 2002) by President Pierre Buyoya and the leader of the main Hutu rebel group (CNDD-FDD); talks on political and military power sharing began early 2003; in April 2003 Buyoya handed power over to Domitien Ndayizeye, a Hutu, for 18-month term as agreed; government signed peace agreement with FDD, November 2003; demobilization of the FDD planned for early 2004; peace talks with the Hutu rebel group NFL began January 2004.

Head of State
1993 Melchior Ndadye
1994 Cyprien Ntaryamina
1994–6 Sylvestre Ntibantunganya
1996–2003 Pierre Buyoya *Military coup*
2003– Domitien Ndayizeye

Head of Government
1993–4 Sylvie Kinigi
1994–5 Anatole Kanyenkiko
1995–6 Antoine Nduwayo
1996–8 Pascal-Firmin Ndimira

Bush, George (Herbert Walker) (1924–) US statesman and 41st president (1989–93), born in Milton, Massachusetts, USA. He joined the US navy in 1942, as its youngest pilot. After the war he studied economics at Yale and went into business in the Texas oilfields. In 1964 he lost a senate race, but was elected to the US House of Representatives. Unsuccessful for the US Senate in 1970, he became US permanent representative to the UN. During the Watergate scandal he was chairman of the Republican National Committee. Under President Ford he headed the US Mission to Beijing, then became director of the CIA. In 1980 he campaigned for the Republican nomination, but lost to Reagan, later becoming his vice-president. In 1988 he won the Republican nomination for the presidency, and defeated Governor Michael Dukakis of Massachusetts in the general election. He lost to Bill Clinton in the 1992 election.

Bush, George W(alker), also known as **George Bush Jr** (1946–) US statesman and 43rd president (2001–), born in New Haven, Connecticut, USA, the eldest child of president George Bush. He graduated from Yale University and Harvard Business School and entered the oil business in West Texas in the 1970s. He made an unsuccessful run for the US Congress in 1978. During the late 1980s and into the early 1990s he was managing general partner of the Texas Rangers baseball team. In 1994 he defeated incumbent governor Ann Richards to become the 46th governor of Texas, and easily won re-election in 1998 as an exponent of 'compassionate conservatism'. In 2000 he was declared president following five weeks of complex legal argument over the voting procedure in the presidential election. His domestic policies centred on economic growth and job creation, improved health care, the promotion of energy independence while improving the environment, and encouraging acts of compassion. Following a terrorist attack on the World Trade Center in New York City (11 Sep 2002), he created the Department of Homeland Security responsible for coordinating a national strategy against terrorism. Key defence initiatives include guarding against bio-terrorism through Project BioShield, improving intelligence capabilities through the Terrorist Threat Integration Center, and disarming Saddam Hussein. Iraq's apparent failure to comply with UN resolution 1441 to eliminate its weapons of mass destruction led to the Iraq War (Mar–Apr 2003) and the removal and eventual capture of Saddam Hussein.

Bush, Laura Welch (1946–) US First Lady (2001–), born in Midland, Texas, USA. She attended Southern Methodist University (1968), studied library science at the University of Texas, Austin (1973), and worked as a librarian in public schools in Texas until 1977, when she married future president George W Bush. In her role as First Lady, she promotes the importance of libraries and reading for children, and is a member of many education advisory boards. She also supports the Texas Health Department, the American Cancer Society, and other organizations in the battle against breast cancer.

bushbaby A primitive primate (*prosimian*), whose cry sounds like a human baby; large eyes and ears; thick coat, very long tail; long hind legs; agile; leaps through trees; on ground may hop upright using only hind legs; also known as **galago**. (Family; Lorisidae, 7 species.)

bushbuck A spiral-horned antelope (*Tragelaphus scriptus*) native to Africa S of the Sahara; reddish-brown with white spots or thin white lines; females without horns; inhabits thick undergrowth near water; lives in pairs; nocturnal.

bush cat *genet*

bush cricket A true cricket, with a well-developed sound-producing mechanism for auditory communication; box-like forewings bent down at sides of body; egg-laying tube cylindrical; c.2000 species, including some important pests. (Order: Orthoptera. Family: Gryllidae.)

bush dog A member of the dog family native to Central and South America (*Speothos venaticus*); dark brown with pale brown head; short ears, legs, and tail; inhabits woodland and grassland near water; eats mainly rodents.

bushido [busheedoh] The Japanese notion of 'way of the warrior'. The samurai code until 1868, which taught personal loyalty to a master, death rather than capture/surrender, and stoic indifference to material goods – a product of Confucian ethics. Like European knights, samurai rode into battle in armour. The bushido tradition is still seen in modern times, eg Japanese officers carried swords in World War 2. Its more positive influence is seen in the ethics of Japan's popular martial arts.

bushmaster A rare pit viper (*Lachesis muta*), native to Central and South America; largest venomous snake in the New World; length, up to 3·5 m/11½ ft; the only New World viper to lay eggs; inhabits forests; nocturnal; eats mammals (including small deer); shakes its tail when alarmed, causing loud rustling in undergrowth.

Bushmen *Khoisan*

bushrangers Australian rural outlaws who operated from 1790 to 1900. Concentrated in New South Wales, Victoria, and Van Dieman's Land, the first bushrangers were ex-convicts, but the opportunities of the gold-rushes led to a revival in the 1860s and 1870s. They were a product of frontier society. Some attained folk hero status, such as Ben Hall (killed 1865), and Ned Kelly (hanged 1880). Never numerous, they attracted great attention from governments and from those who sought to glorify them in romantic myth.

business cycle The tendency for the aggregate level of real activity in a country to fluctuate over time rather than growing steadily; also called a **trade cycle**. Such fluctuations have been observed as far back as economic records reach. They are believed to be due to a variety of causes, including irregular timing of changes in techniques and geographical discoveries, natural catastrophes such as earthquakes, political upsets such as wars and revolutions, and changes in the policies followed by governments or central banks. Business cycles are accentuated by waves of optimism and pessimism, in which upturns lead to expectations of even better times to come, and downturns to panics in anticipation of worse to follow. Simple models of the business cycle suggest that these fluctuations should occur at regular intervals, but historically they have varied greatly in length and scale. This makes it extremely difficult to stabilize them by monetary or fiscal policy, especially since the public authorities themselves are subject to waves of optimism and pessimism about the economy.

Busoni, Ferruccio (Benvenuto) [busohnee] (1866–1924) Pianist and composer, born in Empoli, NC Italy. An infant prodigy, in 1889 he became professor of the pianoforte at Helsinki, and later taught and played in Moscow, Boston, and Berlin. The influence of Liszt is apparent in his great piano concerto. Of his four operas *Doktor Faust*, completed posthumously by a pupil in 1925, is his greatest work.

Buss, Frances Mary (1827–94) British pioneer in women's education, born in London, UK. At the age of 23 she founded the North London Collegiate School for Ladies, and became its head (1850–94) – the first woman to call herself a headmistress. She was immortalized in verse with Dorothea Beale of Cheltenham Ladies' College ('Miss Buss and Miss Beale, Cupid's darts do not feel').

Bussell, Darcey (Andrea) [buhsel] (1969–) Ballerina, born in London, UK. She studied at the Arts Educational School and the Royal Ballet School, joining Sadler's Wells Royal Ballet (now Birmingham Royal Ballet) in 1987. The following year she moved to the Royal Ballet as soloist, becoming first soloist (1989), then principal dancer (1989). Kenneth MacMillan created roles for her, such as Masha in *Winter Dreams* (1991), and in 1995 Twyla Tharp created a principal role for her in *Mr Worldly Wise*. She has made guest appearances internationally for various companies. In 1997 the choreographer Glen Tetley created *Amores* for her.

bussing A government policy adopted in the 1960s (particularly in the USA) to promote social integration among school children in ethnically divided urban communities. Children (especially black and Asian) were taken by bus from disadvantaged urban contexts to schools elsewhere. In the USA, bussing became controversial when the Supreme Court determined to force the integration against widespread opposition from whites, and to a lesser extent from blacks as well: the policy was abandoned in 1972.

bustard A large, long-legged, ground-living bird native to Africa, S Europe, Asia, and Australia; prefers open country; walks rather than flies (but flies well); eats large insects (especially locusts and grasshoppers), lizards, and small birds. Permission for the reintroduction of the bird to Britain (on to Salisbury Plain, Wiltshire), was granted in 2003. (Family: Otididae, 24 species.)

bustard quail *button quail; quail*

busy Lizzie *impatiens*

butadiene [byootadiyeen] $CH_2=CH-CH=CH_2$, **buta-1,3-diene**, boiling point $-4°C$. A gas, an important monomer of synthetic rubbers; also important as the simplest example of a conjugated double-bond system.

butane [byootayn] $CH_3CH_2CH_2CH_3$, boiling point 0°C. An easily liquefied alkane gas, obtained as a petroleum fraction. It is supplied as a liquid under pressure for use as a fuel, as in Calor® gas. It has one structural isomer, $(CH_3)_2CH-CH_3$, isobutane or methylpropane.

butanedioic acid *succinic acid*

Butcher, Rosemary (1947–) Choreographer, born in Bristol, SW England, UK. The first dance graduate of Dartington College in Devon, she went to New York City, and began choreographing her own work in 1976. Her work is minimal and often made in conjunction with other artists. An example is the fast-moving *Flying Lines* (1985), which incorporates music by Michael Nyman and an installation by Peter Noble.

butcherbird *shrike*

butcher's broom A stiff, leathery, dark-green shrub (*Ruscus aculeatus*) native to Europe and the Mediterranean; true leaves reduced to scales; white flowers and red berries borne in the centre of apparent leaves, which are really flattened, leaf-like branches. (Family: Liliaceae.)

Bute, John Stuart, 3rd Earl of (1713–92) British statesman and prime minister (1762–3), born in Edinburgh, EC Scotland. UK. After early court appointments, he became a favourite of George III, who made him one of the principal secretaries of state (1761). As prime minister, his government was highly unpopular. Its principal objective was the supremacy of the royal prerogative, and he was soon forced to resign. From 1768 his life was chiefly spent in the country, where he engaged in scientific study.

Buthelezi, Mangosuthu Gatsha [bootuhlayzee], known as **Chief Buthelezi** (1928–) South African Zulu leader and politician, born in Mahlabatini, KwaZulu Natal, E South Africa. He studied at the University of Natal, and in 1953 was installed as chief of the Buthelezi tribe. He was assistant to the Zulu king Cyprian (1953–68) before being elected leader of Zululand in 1970. He became chief minister of KwaZulu, the black South African homeland, in 1976. He is founder-president of Inkatha, a politico-cultural body which has the aim of achieving a non-racist democratic political system, and which in the 1980s developed paramilitary tendencies. In 1994 he was appointed minister for home affairs in Nelson Mandela's first cabinet.

Butler, Joseph (1692–1752) Moral philosopher and theologian, born in Wantage, Oxfordshire, SC England, UK. He studied at Oxford, took orders, and was appointed preacher at the Rolls Chapel, London (1718). While holding various church appointments, he wrote his major work, *The Analogy of Religion* (1736), in which he argued that objections against revealed religion may also be levelled against the whole constitution of nature. He was made Bishop of Bristol (1738), Dean of St Paul's (1740), and Bishop of Durham (1750).

Butler, Reg(inald Cotterell) (1913–81) Sculptor, born in Buntingford, Hertfordshire, SE England, UK. He studed architecture, taught at the Architectural Association School in London (1937–9), then practised as an engineer (1939–50). He turned to sculpture in 1951, and soon became recognized as one of the leading exponents of 'linear' constructions in wrought iron, but in his later years turned to a more realistic style.

Butler, R(ichard) A(usten), Baron Butler, known as **Rab Butler** (1902–82) British statesman, born in Attock Serai, India. He studied at Cambridge, and became Conservative MP for Saffron Walden in 1929. After a series of junior ministerial appointments, he became minister of education (1941–5), introducing the forward-looking Education Act of 1944, and then minister of labour (1945). He became Chancellor of the Exchequer (1951), Lord Privy Seal (1955), Leader of the House of Commons (1955), home secretary (1957), first secretary of state and deputy prime minister (1962). He narrowly lost the premiership to Douglas-Home in 1963, and acted as foreign secretary (1963–4) in his administration. He then became Master of Trinity College, Cambridge (1965–78), and was made a life peer.

Butler, Samuel (1612–80) Poet and satirist, baptized at Strensham, Hereford and Worcester, WC England, UK. He was educated at Worcester grammar school, and perhaps Oxford or Cambridge. He held several secretarial posts before becoming steward of Ludlow Castle (1661) and in later years was secretary to the Duke of Buckingham. His great poetic work, *Hudibras*, appeared in three parts (1663, 1664, 1678). A burlesque satire on Puritanism and on human failings in general, it secured immediate popularity, and was a special favourite at the court of Charles II.

Butler, Samuel (1835–1902) Writer, painter, and musician, born at Langar Rectory, Nottinghamshire, C England, UK. He studied at Cambridge, and became a sheep farmer in New Zealand (1859–64). On returning to England, he worked on his Utopian satire, *Erewhon* (1872) – the word is an inversion of 'nowhere' – in which many conventional practices and customs are reversed. Its supplement, *Erewhon Revisited* (1901), dealt with the origin of religious belief. His musical compositions include two oratorios, gavottes, minuets, fugues, and a cantata. He is best known for his autobiographical novel *The Way of All Flesh* (1903), an ironic and witty study of the stultifying effects of Victorian family traits and attitudes.

Butlin, Billy, popular name of **Sir William (Edmund) Butlin** (1899–1980) Holiday camp promoter, born in South Africa. He moved with his parents to Canada, and after serving in World War 1, worked his passage to England with only £5 capital. After a short period in a fun fair he went into business on his own. In 1936 he opened his first camp at Skegness, followed by others at Clacton and Filey. During World War 2 he served as director-general of hostels to the ministry of supply. After the War more camps and hotels were opened, both at home and abroad. He was knighted in 1964.

Butor, Michel (Marie François) [bütaw(r)] (1926–) Writer and critic, born in Lille, N France. He studied at the Sorbonne, and taught at Manchester (1951–3), Thessaloniki (1954–5), and Geneva (1956–7). One of the popular writers of the *roman nouveau* ('new novel'), his works include *L'Emploi du temps* (1959, Passing Time), *Degrés* (1960, Degrees), and the non-fiction *Mobile* (1962). He has also written several volumes of poetry, his collection *A la frontière* appearing in 1996.

Butskellism A compound of the names of UK Conservative politician R A Butler and the Labour leader Hugh Gaitskell, used in the 1950s and early 1960s to imply a high degree of similarity between the policies of the two main parties. 'Mr Butskell' was first referred to in *The Economist* (Feb 1954).

butte [byoot] Isolated, flat-topped, steep-sided residual hills formed by erosion of a mesa, when a remnant of hard rock protects the softer rock underneath.

butter A pale yellow foodstuff derived from the churning of cream, typically used in baking, cooking, or for spreading on bread. Milk fat exists as globules of fat each surrounded by an outer core of protein. This creates the emulsion of oil in water seen in milk. If milk is churned or beaten, collision of the fat globules allows them to gradually increase in size; they lose their protective protein coat and consequently their solubility in water. The result is butter, which comprises c.82% fat and c.16% water.

buttercup A member of a large and diverse genus of annuals or perennials, some aquatic, common throughout most of the world, but especially in the N hemisphere; leaves narrow and entire, or broad and divided; flowers cup-shaped, 5-petalled, glossy yellow, sometimes white or red; bitter-tasting and poisonous to animals, which avoid them, hence the abundance of buttercups in pastures. (Genus: *Ranunculus*, 400 species. Family: Ranunculaceae.)

butterfish *gunnel*

butterfly An insect belonging to the order Lepidoptera, which comprises the butterflies and moths. Butterflies are usually distinguished from moths by being active during the daytime, by folding their wings upright over their bodies when at rest, and by having small knobs at the tips of their antennae; but there are exceptions.

butterfly bush *buddleia*

butterfly diagram A diagram which plots the location of sunspots on the Sun as a function of date, and is useful for tracking the 11-year solar cycle of activity. It is sometimes referred to as a **Maunder diagram**, after British astronomer E W Maunder of the Royal Greenwich Observatory, who started systematic solar observations in 1873, and published the original version of this chart in 1904.

butterflyfish *angelfish*

Butterley, Nigel Henry (1935–) Composer and pianist, born in Sydney, New South Wales, SE Australia. He studied at the New South Wales Conservatory, and later in London. He worked as a producer and planner for the music department of the Australian Broadcasting Commission from 1955, and in 1966 won the prestigious Italia Prize with *In the Head the Fire*, a musical work for radio commissioned by the ABC. Other compositions include a violin concerto, *Explorations for Piano and Orchestra*, and a two-act opera, *Lawrence Hargrave Flying Alone* (1987). *From Sorrowing Earth*, his first major orchestral work in more than a decade, was considered the best work from an Australian composer by the Australian Music Centre in 1992.

butter-nut A deciduous conical tree (*Juglans cinerea*) growing to 30 m/100 ft, native to North America; leaves with 11–19 oval leaflets; male flowers in catkins; fruit 4–6·5 cm/1½–2½ in, ovoid, hairy, containing ridged, nut-like seed. (Family: Juglandaceae.)

butterwort A small carnivorous perennial native to the N hemisphere and the mountains of South America. It has a rosette of oval, slightly inrolled leaves; flowers solitary on leafless stems, 2-lipped, spurred; white, lilac, or violet. Insects are trapped by a sticky coating on the leaves, then washed by rain towards the leaf-margins which inroll over them, secrete digestive enzymes, absorb the products, and finally unroll. (Genus: *Pinguicula*, 46 species. Family: Lentibulariaceae.)

button quail A small, plump, ground-living bird of genus *Turnix*, also *Ortyxelos meiffrenii* (the **lark quail** or **quail plover**), native to the warm grasslands of the Old World; unusually for birds, the female actively courts males and takes several mates; the less colourful males incubate the eggs; also known as the **bustard quail** or **hemipode**. (Family: Turnicidae, 14 species.)

buttress A mass of masonry built against a wall, usually on the outside of a building to oppose the lateral thrust of an arch, roof, or vault. Varied in form, the most notable type is the **flying buttress**, which consists of a segment of an arch, stretching from a higher wall (sometimes, from a detached pier) to an external buttress.

Buttrose, Ita (Clare) (1942–) Journalist, publisher, and broadcaster, born in Sydney, New South Wales, SE Australia. She was educated in Sydney, and joined Australian Consolidated Press at age 15 as a copy girl, going on to become editor of the *Australian Women's Weekly*, Australia's leading women's magazine. In 1981 she moved to News Limited as editor-in-chief of the *Sunday Telegraph*, becoming the first woman in Australia to edit either a daily or a Sunday paper. In 1988 she became editor of that paper's opposition, *The Sun Herald*, and by 1989 had started her own magazine, called *Ita*. She is chairman of the National Advisory Committee on AIDS, and one of the best-known women in Australia.

butyl [**byoo**tiyl, **byoo**til] $CH_3CH_2CH_2CH_2$–. A four-carbon aliphatic group. In addition to the form given, there are three other isomers: isobutyl $(CH_3)_2CH–CH_2$–; secondary butyl $(CH_3)(C_2H_5)CH$–; and tertiary butyl $(CH_3)_3C$–.

Buxtehude, Diderik or **Dietrich** [**buks**tehooduh] (1637–1707) Organist and composer, born in Oldesloe or Helsingborg, Sweden (formerly in Denmark). In 1668 he was appointed organist at the Marienkirche, Lübeck, where he began the famous *Abendmusiken* – Advent evening concerts of his own sacred music and organ works. In 1705 Bach walked c.200 mi across Germany, and Handel travelled from Hamburg, to attend his concerts.

Buys Ballot, Christoph H(endrick) D(iederick) [**biyz balot**] (1817–90) Meteorologist, born in Kloetinge, The Netherlands. He studied and taught at the University of Utrecht, and founded the Royal Netherlands Meteorological Institute in 1854. He was the inventor of the aeroklinoscope and of a system of weather signals. He stated the law of wind direction in relation to atmospheric pressure in 1857 (*Buys Ballot's law*).

buzzard A large hawk found worldwide (except Australasia and Malaysia); brown, grey, and white; soaring flight, but spends much time perching; kills prey on ground; inhabits woodlands or open country; territorial. (Genus: *Buteo*, 25 species.)

buzz-bomb *V-1*

Byatt, Dame A(ntonia) S(usan), *née* **Drabble** (1936–) Writer and critic, born in Sheffield, South Yorkshire, N England, UK, the sister of Margaret Drabble. She studied at Cambridge, and became a lecturer in English at University College London. Her novels include *Virgin in the Garden* (1978) and *Still-Life* (1985), the first two parts of a projected sequence tracing English life from the mid-1950s to the present day, and *Possession* (1990, Booker). Later works include *Angels and Insects* (1992), *Babel Tower* (1996), *The Biographer's Tale* (2000), and *A Whistling Woman* (2002). Among her short story collections are *The Djinn in the Nightingale's Eye* (1994) and *Elementals: Stories of Fire and Ice* (1999), and her several critical works include a monograph on Iris Murdoch. She was made a dame in 1999.

Byblos [**bib**los] 34°07N 35°39E. An ancient trading city on the Lebanese coast N of Beirut; a world heritage site. It was the chief supplier of papyrus to the Greeks, which they accordingly nicknamed 'byblos' – hence the word 'bible' (literally, 'the papyrus book').

Byelarus; Byelorussia *Belarus*

Byers, Stephen (John) (1953–) British statesman, born in Wolverhampton, West Midlands, C England, UK. He studied at Liverpool University, and was a university lecturer before becoming Labour MP for Wallsend (1992–). A former deputy leader of North Tyneside council and leader of the Council of Local Education Authorities, he was an opposition whip (1994–5) and spokeman on education and employment (1995–7) before becoming secretary of state for trade and industry (1997–2001) and for transport, local government and the regions (2001–2), resigning after a period of personal upheaval within his department and heavy criticism of his handling of the country's rail problems.

Bygraves, Max (Walter) (1922–) Entertainer, born in Rotherhithe, SE Greater London, UK. Educated there, he worked for an advertising agency before joining the RAF (1940–5), where he became involved in entertainment for the troops. A professional entertainer since 1946, he has performed all over the world, and is among the best-selling recording artists. His catchphrase, 'I wanna tell you a story', is also the title of his autobiography (1976). Since then he has published several more autobiographical works, including *I Wanna Tell You A Funny Story* (1992) and *In His Own Words* (1997).

Byng, George, 1st Viscount Torrington (1663–1733) English sailor, born in Wrotham, Kent, SE England, UK. He joined the navy at 15, and gained rapid promotion as a supporter of William of Orange. Made rear-admiral in 1703, he captured Gibraltar, and was knighted for his gallant conduct at Màlaga. In 1708 he defeated the French fleet of James Stuart, the Pretender, and in 1718 destroyed the Spanish fleet off Messina. He was created viscount in 1721.

Byng (of Vimy), Julian Hedworth George Byng, 1st Viscount (1862–1935) British general, born in Wrotham Park, Hertfordshire, SE England, UK. He commanded the 9th Army Corps in Gallipoli (1915), the Canadian Army Corps (1916–17), and the 3rd Army (1917–18). After World War 1 he became Governor-General of Canada (1921–6) and Commissioner of the Metropolitan Police (1928–31), and was made a viscount in 1928 and a field marshal in 1932.

Byrd, Richard E(velyn) (1888–1957) Aviator, explorer, and rear-admiral, born in Winchester, Virginia, USA, the brother of Harry Byrd. He was navigator on the first aeroplane flight over the North Pole (9 May 1926), and was awarded the Congressional Medal of Honor. He organized the largest and best-equipped expedition to date to explore Antartica, and flew as navigator over the South Pole (28–29 Nov 1929). He carried out further Antarctic explorations in 1933–4 and 1939–41, using aircraft, radio, and modern technology to support, rather than replace, traditional methods of exploring on foot with dogs and sledges.

Byrd, William (1543–1623) Composer, probably born in Lincoln, Lincolnshire, EC England, UK. His early life is obscure, but it is likely that he was one of the Children of the Chapel Royal, under Tallis. He was organist of Lincoln Cathedral until 1572, when he was made joint organist with Tallis of the Chapel Royal. In 1575 Byrd and Tallis were given an exclusive licence for the printing and sale of music. A firm Catholic, Byrd was several times prosecuted as a recusant, but he wrote music of great power and beauty for both the Catholic and the Anglican services, as well as madrigals, songs, keyboard pieces, and music for strings.

Byron (of Rochdale), George (Gordon) Byron, 6th Baron, known as **Lord Byron** (1788–1824) Poet, born in London, UK. His first 10 years were spent in poor surroundings in Aberdeen, but then he inherited the title of his great-uncle, and went on to Dulwich, Harrow, and Cambridge, where he led a dissipated life. An early collection of poems, *Hours of Idleness* (1807) was badly reviewed, and after replying in satirical vein, he set out on his grand tour, visiting Spain, Malta, Albania, Greece, and the Aegean. He then published the popular *Childe Harold's Pilgrimage* (1812), and several other works, becoming the favourite of London society, and giving to Europe the concept of the 'Byronic hero'. He married **Anne Isabella (Annabella) Milbanke** (1792–1860) in 1815, but was suspected of an incestuous love for his half-sister, **Augusta Leigh** and was ostracized. He left for Europe, where he met Shelley, and spent two years in Venice. Some of his best works belong to this period, including *Don Juan* (1819–24). He gave active help to the Italian revolutionaries, and in 1823 joined the Greek insurgents who had risen against the Ottoman Turks. He died of malaria at Missolonghi.

byte A fixed number of bits (binary digits), usually defined as a set of 8 bits. An 8-bit byte can therefore take 256 different values corresponding to the binary numbers 00000000, 00000001, 00000010, through to 11111111. A **kilobyte** is one thousand bytes (actually 1024); a **megabyte** is one million bytes (actually 1024 × 1024); a **gigabyte** is one thousand million bytes (actually 1024 × 1024 × 1024). ($1024 = 2^{10}$.)

Byzantine art [bizantiyn] The art which flourished from AD 330, when Constantinople (modern Istanbul) became the capital of the Roman Empire, to 1453 when that city fell to the Turks. It was conservative in form, stylized and overwhelmingly theological in content. The church of St Sophia at Istanbul (6th-c), the greatest work of early Byzantine architecture, combines the axial Roman basilican plan with a huge dome; later churches adopted the Greek-cross plan, with four equal arms and a small dome carried on a high drum. Churches were adorned with richly-coloured marble inlay, stained glass windows, and with mosaics and wall-paintings of subjects chosen from the Bible and apocryphal literature.

Byzantine Empire [bizantiyn] The E half of the Roman Empire, centred upon Constantinople, formerly Byzantium. Founded in AD 324 by Constantine the Great as the New Rome, and formally inaugurated in AD 330, Constantinople, with its Senate and traditionally named magistracies (eg consuls, praetors), its 14 regions, and its state corn dole, was directly modelled on old imperial Rome. But in two respects it was always different: it was a Christian, not a pagan, city, and its culture was predominantly Greek, not Latin. Though initially subordinate to the Old Rome, in due course it outstripped it in importance, becoming both the capital of an independent state and a major centre of learning, law, and culture. The two most comprehensive codifications of Roman Law – Justinian's Code and the Theodosian Code – were carried out here, the former under Byzantium's greatest ruler, Justinian (527–65). A bastion against the barbarian hordes, Byzantium for centuries fought off marauding Goths, Huns, and others. In 1453 she finally succumbed to the Ottoman Turks, having survived old imperial Rome by nearly a thousand years.

C

C A computer programming language, developed by AT&T in the USA to be used with the Unix operating system. It has since been adopted much more widely, and is now available on personal computers. It is seen as a major contribution to achieving open systems interconnection.

Cabal [kabal] An acronym taken from the initials of the five leading advisers of Charles II of England between 1667 and 1673: Clifford, Arlington, Buckingham, Ashley Cooper (Shaftesbury), and Lauderdale. The name is misleading, since these five were by no means Charles's only advisers; nor did they agree on a common policy. Arlington and Buckingham were bitter rivals. The overtones of conspiracy and intrigue found in the general use of the word *cabal* made the acronym attractive.

Caballé, Montserrat [kabayay] (1933–) Soprano, born in Barcelona, NE Spain, where she studied at the Liceo. She made her operatic debut in Basel (1956), and soon earned an international reputation, especially in operas by Donizetti and Verdi. In 1964 she married the tenor **Bernabé Marti**.

cabbage A vegetable (*Brassica oleracea*) grown for its dense leafy head, which is harvested before the flowers develop and the head elongates. There are numerous cultivars, all derived from wild cabbage, a biennial or perennial with woody, leafy stems and yellow cross-shaped flowers, native to W Europe and the Mediterranean. (Family: Cruciferae.)

cabbage white butterfly A large butterfly, found in Europe, N Africa, and North America; wings mainly white with black markings, and yellow on undersides of hindwings, also known as **large white**. The caterpillars are pests of cabbage family crops. (Order: Lepidoptera. Family: Pieridae.)

Cabbala *Kabbalah*

Cabell, James Branch [kabl] (1879–1958) Writer and critic, born in Richmond, Virginia, USA. He made his name with his novel *Jurgen* (1919), the best known of a sequence of 18 novels, collectively called *Biography of Manuel*. They are set in the imaginary mediaeval kingdom of Poictesme and written in an elaborate, sophisticated style showing the author's fondness for archaisms.

caber tossing The art of tossing a tree trunk (**caber**), practised in Scotland, UK. The competitor has the caber, about 3–4 m/12–18 ft in length, placed vertically into the palms of his hands. He then runs with it and tosses it; the caber should revolve longitudinally, its base landing away from him. The tradition is popular at Highland Games gatherings.

Cabinda [kabeenda] area 7270 sq km/2800 sq mi. Province of Angola on the SW coast of Africa, N of the R Congo; bounded W by the Atlantic and surrounded by the Congo, it is separated from the rest of Angola; attached to Angola in 1886 by agreement with Belgium; seaport and chief town Cabinda, 5°35S 12°12E, 55 km/34 mi N of the R Congo estuary; offshore oil fields; oil refining.

cabinet In a parliamentary system, a group of senior ministers usually drawn from the majority party. In Britain (where cabinet government originated), the cabinet has no constitutional status other than the conventions by which it operates. It forms the link between the executive and legislative branches of government, as its members must be drawn from the legislature. Cabinet members are bound by the doctrine of collective responsibility: ministers must publicly support decisions taken by the cabinet, or its committees, or else resign. The importance and role of the cabinet varies across political systems, some (eg Britain) attaching greater importance than others (eg Germany) to co-ordination in decision-making. A cabinet may also be found in a non-parliamentary system, such as that of the USA, where it provides the president with an additional consultative body.

cabinet picture A small easel painting, carefully executed, intended for close viewing, and suitable for display in a small private room. The Dutch masters of the 17th-c specialized in this type of picture.

Cable, George Washington (1844–1925) Writer, born in New Orleans, Louisiana, USA. He earned a precarious living in New Orleans before taking up a literary career in 1879. In 1884 he went to New England. His Creole sketches in *Scribner's Magazine* made his reputation. Among his books are *Old Creole Days* (1879), *The Grandissimes* (1880), and *Lovers of Louisiana* (1918).

cable An insulated conductor used to carry power or signals overhead, underground, or under the sea. The simplest type has a core of conducting material, such as copper, surrounded by an insulating sheath of plastic or rubber. **Coaxial cables** have another sheath of wire braid under the outer insulation. Telephone communications between countries use multicore cables, although fibre optic cables are now replacing copper cables.

cable television The distribution of video programmes to subscribers by coaxial cable or fibre-optic links, rather than by broadcast transmission, providing a wide range of choice to individual homes within a specific area. Programmes may originate from satellite transmission to a master antenna installed at the cable centre, as well as from recorded sources.

Cabot, John [kabot], Ital **Giovanni Caboto** (1425–c.1500) Navigator, born possibly in Genoa, NW Italy, who discovered the mainland of North America. Little is known about his life. About 1490 he settled in Bristol, and set sail in 1497 with two ships, accompanied by his three sons, sighting Cape Breton I and Nova Scotia on 24 June. He set out on another voyage in 1498, and died at sea.

Cabot, Sebastian [kabot] (1474–1557) Explorer and navigator, the son of John Cabot, born in Venice, NE Italy, or Bristol, SW England. He accompanied his father to the American coast, then entered the service of Ferdinand V of Spain as a cartographer (1512). In 1526 he explored the coast of South America for Emperor Charles V, but failed to colonize the area, and was imprisoned and banished to Africa. He returned to Spain in 1533, and later to England, where he was made inspector of the navy by Edward VI.

Cabral or **Cabrera, Pedro Alvarez** [kabral] (c.1467–c.1520) Explorer, born in Belmonte, EC Portugal. In 1500 he sailed from Lisbon bound for the East Indies, but was carried to the unknown coast of Brazil, which he claimed on behalf of Portugal. He then made for India, but was forced to land at Mozambique and provided the first description of that country. He made the first commercial treaty between Portugal and India, and returned to Lisbon in 1501. He was given no further missions, and remained for the rest of his life at Santarém.

Cabrera [kabrayra] 39°15N 2°58E. Small Spanish island in the Balearic Is, Mediterranean Sea; 15 km/9 mi S of Majorca; no permanent population; declared a national park in 1991; tourism.

Cabrini, St Frances Xavier [kabreenee] (1850–1917) Nun, born near Lodi, N Italy. She founded the Missionary Sisters of the Sacred Heart (1880), emigrated to the USA in 1889, and became renowned for her social and charitable work. Canonized in 1946, she was the first US saint. Feast day 13 November.

cacao An evergreen tree native to Central America (*Theobroma cacao*), widely cultivated elsewhere and of great economic importance; leaves oblong; flowers pink, borne in clusters directly on trunks and older branches; fruit an ovoid yellow pod, leathery and grooved, enclosing up to 100 beans embedded in soft pulp. The beans are dried, roasted, and ground to produce cocoa powder, used in drinks and chocolate. Pressed beans yield cocoa butter. (Family: Sterculiaceae.)

Cáceres [katheres], Arabic **Qazris** 39°26N 6°23W, pop (2000e) 72 400. Walled town and capital of Cáceres province, W Spain; on R Cáceres, 297 km/185 mi SW of Madrid; railway; pharmaceuticals, chemicals, textiles, leather; a world heritage site; Roman settlement, 1st-c BC; Plaza Santa Maria, Lower Golfines Palace, Church of San Mateo, Maltravieso cave paintings.

cachalot [kashalot] *sperm whale*

cache memory [kash] A very high-speed buffer memory which operates between a computer processor and main memory in high performance computer systems.

cacomistle [kakomisl] A mammal native to S USA and Central America; pale brown with lighter underparts; long bushy tail with black bands; inhabits rocky areas or forest; also known as **cacomixl** or **ringtail**. (Genus: *Bassariscus*, 2 species. Family: Procyonidae.)

cactus A member of a large family of plants typical of arid zones but found in a number of habitats: some occur as epiphytes in the canopy of tropical rainforests where water can also be in short supply; others in high mountains; but almost all are confined to the New World. In the Old World they are paralleled by various members of the spurge family (Euphorbiaceae), remarkably similar in appearance, and sometimes mistaken for cacti. Cacti exhibit a wide variety of size, form, and adaptations to dry conditions, some very sophisticated. All species are succulents and store water, sometimes in the roots but usually in swollen, often barrel-like, stems which may be of huge capacity and capable of sustaining the plant over several years without rain; the stem often has pleat-like ribs which allow it to expand or contract as the water content changes. Water loss is reduced in various ways. The plants are leathery with a thick waxy cuticle. In some species the surface area is reduced by assuming a globose shape, and the vulnerable leaves are absent or reduced to spines, photosynthesis being carried out by the green stem. The spines can be very intricate, ranging from simple prongs to parasols and long, soft hairs; they shade or insulate the cactus, protect it from animals, reflect light, and collect and absorb droplets of dew – an important source of water. Cacti show a wide range of flowers, often large and conspicuous, pollinated by bees, hawk-moths, hummingbirds, and bats. Bird-pollinated day flowers are predominantly reds and yellows and scentless; moth- and bat-pollinated night flowers are predominantly white, often strongly perfumed, sometimes unpleasantly so. The fruits are usually fleshy and sometimes edible. (Family: Cactaceae, c.2000 species.)

cactus hybrid A type of cactus (*Schlumbergera* × *buckleyi*); an epiphyte, with spineless, arching stems made up of flattened, jointed segments and magenta flowers, appearing in winter. (Family: Cactaceae.)

cactus moth A small, dull moth with narrow forewings and broad hindwings (*Cactoblastis cactorum*); introduced successfully into Australia in 1925 as a measure to control the spread of prickly pear cactus. The caterpillars destroy cactus plants by burrowing into stems. (Order: Lepidoptera. Family: Pyralidae.)

CAD *computer-aided design*

Cadbury, George (1839–1922) Businessman, born in Birmingham, West Midlands, C England, UK, the son of **John Cadbury**. In partnership with his brother **Richard Cadbury** (1835–99), he expanded his father's cocoa and chocolate business, and established for the workers the model village of Bournville (1879), a prototype for modern methods of housing and town planning. He also became proprietor of the *Daily News* (1902), and was an ardent Quaker.

caddis fly A dull-coloured, moth-like insect; aquatic larvae build silken protective cases incorporating sand, twigs, and leaves; feed on algae, fungi, or plant material; adults live near water; forewings hairy, held at oblique vertical angle at rest. (Order: Trichoptera.)

Cade, Jack [kayd] (?–1450) Irish leader of the insurrection of 1450 against Henry VI. After an unsettled early career he lived in Sussex, possibly as a physician. Assuming the name of Mortimer, and the title of Captain of Kent, he marched on London with a great number of followers, and entered the city. A promise of pardon sowed dissension among the insurgents; they dispersed, and a price was set upon Cade's head. He attempted to reach the coast, but was killed near Heathfield, East Sussex.

cadence A melodic or (more commonly) harmonic formula marking the end of a phrase or longer section of music. The 'perfect' cadence, formed by dominant–tonic chords, is the one that most often ends a piece. The word (from Lat *cadere* 'to fall') originates from the tendency for a plainchant (or, in early polyphony, a tenor line) to fall to its final note from the one above.

cadenza An improvised (or improvisatory) passage, usually of a virtuoso and rhythmically free character, which the soloist in a concerto plays as a kind of adjunct to the main body of the piece. In the concertos of Mozart and Beethoven, the main cadenza is heard towards the end of the first movement; later composers, such as Liszt, introduced them at various unpredictable points. During the cadenza the orchestra is usually silent, but some composers (eg Strauss, Elgar, Walton) have written accompanied cadenzas.

Cader Idris [kader idris] (Welsh 'chair of Idris') 52°42N 3°54W. Mountain ridge in NW Wales, UK; in Snowdonia National Park, SW of Dolgellau; rises to 892 m/2928 ft at Pen-y-Gader.

Cádiz [kadiz], Span [kadeeth], ancient **Gadier** or **Gades** 36°30N 6°20W, pop (2000e) 156 000. Seaport and capital of Cádiz province, Andalusia, SW Spain; in the Bay of Cádiz, 663 km/412 mi SW of Madrid; base for Spanish treasure ships from the Americas, 16th–18th-c; Francis Drake burned the ships of Philip II at anchor here, 1587; bishopric; airport; railway; car ferries to Casablanca and Canary Is; university; naval harbour of La Carraca; shipbuilding, trade in sherry, fish, salt, olives; cathedral (18th-c), Chapel of Santa Catalina; Fiestas Tipicas Gaditanas (May), Festival of Spain (Aug), Trofeo Internacional Ramon (football competition, Aug).

cadmium Cd, element 48, density 8·7 g/cm^3, melting point 321°C, colour bluish-white. A metal, normally occurring with other metals, especially copper and zinc, as the sulphide, CdS. The metal is recovered for use in low-melting alloys and as an absorber for neutrons in atomic reactors. Cadmium compounds are used as phosphors in colour television tubes. Its commonest oxidation state is +2; its compounds are very toxic.

Cadmus [kadmus] According to Greek legend the son of Agenor, King of Tyre; he set off in pursuit of his sister Europa, arrived in Greece, and founded the city of Thebes, teaching the natives to write. He sowed dragons' teeth, from which sprang up armed men.

caduceus [kadyoosius] In classical mythology, the name of the wand carried by Mercury. It is usually depicted as a central staff with two serpents entwined around it which cross at seven points, representing the seven chakras. In mythology the staff was said to have power over sleep, dreams, happiness, and health, and it has been adopted by the medical profession as their emblem.

caecilian [seesilian] An amphibian of worldwide tropical order Gymnophiona (163 species); length, up to 1·5 m/5 ft; body worm-like with encircling rings and no legs; some species with fish-like scales; burrows on forest floors or in riverbeds; eats invertebrates.

Caedmon [kadmon] (?–c.680) The first English poet of known name, to whom the *Song of Caedmon* is attributed. Bede reports that, unlearned till mature in years, Caedmon became aware in a semi-miraculous way that he was called to exercise the gift of religious poetry. The name Caedmon cannot be explained in English, and has been conjectured to be Celtic. He became a monk at Whitby, N Yorkshire, and spent the rest of his life composing poems on the Bible histories and on religious subjects. The *Song* influenced much later Anglo-Saxon poetry.

Caelum [kiyluhm] (Lat 'chisel') An inconspicuous S hemisphere constellation.

Caen [kã] 49°10N 0°22W, pop (2000e) 118 000. Port and capital of Calvados department, NW France; on R Orne, 15 km/9 mi S of R Seine; airport; railway; university (1432, refounded 1809); principal seat of William the Conqueror; badly damaged during Normandy campaign in World War 2; tourism, commerce, steel, horse breeding, silk, leather; abbey church of St-Etienne, with tomb of William the Conqueror; Church of St-Pierre, with famous clock tower.

Caernarfon [kiyrnarvon], Eng **Caernarvon** [kuhnah(r)vn] 53°08N 4°16W, pop (2000e) 9800. County town of Gwynedd, NW Wales, UK; on Menai Straits; yachting centre; agricultural trade, plastics, metal products; tourism; castle (1284), birthplace of Edward II is a world heritage site; investiture of Prince Charles as Prince of Wales, 1969.

Caernarfonshire *Gwynedd*

Caerphilly [kiy(r)filee], Welsh **Caerffili** pop (2001e) 169 500; area 279 sq km/108 sq mi. County (unitary authority from 1996) in S Wales, UK; administrative centre, Hengoed; original home of Caerphilly cheese; Caerphilly Castle (13th-c), the largest in Wales.

Caesar, in full **Gaius Julius Caesar** (c.101–44 BC) Roman politician of patrician origins but slender means, whose military genius, as displayed in the Gallic Wars (58–50 BC), enabled Rome to extend her empire permanently to the Atlantic seaboard, but whose ruthless ambition led to the breakdown of the Republican system of government at home. Never one to allow himself to be blocked by constitutional niceties, in 60 BC he joined with Pompey and Crassus (the so-called First Triumvirate) to protect his interests in the state, and in 49 BC, to avoid being humbled by his enemies at Rome, he led his army across the R Rubicon into Italy and plunged the state into civil war. Victory over the Pompeian forces at Pharsalus (48 BC), Zela (47 BC), Thapsus (46 BC), and Munda (45 BC) left him in sole control at Rome. He did not disguise his absolute power, taking the title 'Dictator for Life' in 44 BC, and allowing himself to be paid extravagant honours which suggested he was aiming at regal and even divine status. This was too much for many Republican-minded Romans, and under the leadership of Brutus and Cassius they conspired to murder him. His brief period of power left him with little time to carry through the many reforms, social, economic, and administrative, that he had intended. It was left to his great-nephew and heir, Octavian (the future Emperor Augustus) to reap where he had sown, and also to learn from his mistakes.

caesarian / cesarian section [seezairian] The surgical removal of the fetus from the uterus. It is undertaken when normal labour and vaginal delivery is causing or is likely to cause significant harm to the mother or fetus. Indications include obstructed labour, excessively prolonged labour without cervical dilatation, uncontrollable maternal hypertension, and impaired fetal blood supply. The fetus is removed through an incision in the lower abdomen. The name is derived from Julius Caesar, who is supposed to have been born in this way.

caffeine $C_8H_{10}N_4O_2$. An alkaloid, also called **theine**, a weak stimulant of the central nervous system. It is found in both coffee and tea, from which it may be removed by extraction with organic solvents, acidic aqueous solutions, or liquified carbon dioxide.

Cage, John (Milton) (1912–92) Composer, born in Los Angeles, California, USA. A pupil of Schoenberg, he was associated with ultra-Modernism. He variously exploited the 'prepared piano' (distorting the sound of the instrument with objects placed inside); unorthodox musical notation in the form of pictures or graphics; indeterminacy in music, or 'aleatory' (chance-dependent) music, in which (following one method) a dice would be thrown to determine the elements of a composition; and silence as an art form. He wrote copiously about music, and was also an authority on mushrooms.

Cage, Nicolas, originally **Nicholas Coppola** (1964–) Film actor, born in Long Beach, California, USA. He made his film debut in a small role in *Fast Times at Ridgemont High* (1982), and became well known after his appearances in *The Cotton Club* (1984) and *Peggy Sue Got Married* (1986). He won critical acclaim for his performance as a suicidal alcoholic in *Leaving Las Vegas* (1995, Oscar). Later films include *The Rock* (1996), *City of Angels* (1998), *Bringing Out the Dead* (1999), *Captain Corelli's Mandolin* (2001), *Adaptation* (2002, Oscar nomination), and *Matchstick Men* (2003).

Cagliari [kalyahree], ancient **Carales** 39°13N 9°08E, pop (2000e) 236 000. Seaport and capital of Cagliari province, S Sardinia, Italy; on the S coast, in the Gulf of Cagliari; archbishopric; airport; railway; ferries to mainland Italy; university (1956); oil terminal, petrochemicals, milling, fishing, trade in minerals; cathedral (1312), Roman amphitheatre, museum of archaeology; Sagra di Sant' Efisio costume festival (May).

Cagliostro, Alessandro, conte di (Count of) [kalyohstroh], originally **Giuseppe Balsamo** (1743–95) Adventurer and charlatan, born in Palermo, Sicily, S Italy. He learned some chemistry and medicine at a monastery, married the beautiful **Lorenza Feliciani**, and from 1771 they visited many centres in Europe as Count and Countess Cagliostro. Successful as physician, philosopher, alchemist, and necromancer, he carried on a lively business in his 'elixir of immortal youth', and founded lodges of 'Egyptian freemasons'. In 1789 he was imprisoned for life in San Leo, near Urbino.

Cagney, James (1899–1986) Film actor, born in New York City, USA. He studied at Columbia, and after 10 years as an actor and dancer in vaudeville, his film performance as the gangster in *The Public Enemy* (1931) brought him stardom. His ebullient energy and aggressive personality kept him in demand for the next 30 years, including such varied productions as *A Midsummer Night's Dream* (1935), *Angels with Dirty Faces* (1938), and *Yankee Doodle Dandy* (1942), for which he was awarded an Oscar. He retired to his farm in New York State in 1961, but returned for a brief appearance in *Ragtime* (1981).

Cahokia [kahohkia] A prehistoric city of Middle Mississippi Indians in E St Louis, IL, USA, founded c.600 and, at 13 sq km/5 sq mi, the largest such settlement in North America; a world heritage site. At its height (c.1050–1250), the population reached c.10 000. The central plaza has 17 platform mounds, notably Monks Mound (c.1200), a 6000 cu m/7850 cu yd earthen pyramid, 316 m/1030 ft by 241 m/790 ft at the base, still standing 30 m/100 ft high.

CAI *computer-aided instruction*

Caiaphas [kiyafas] (1st-c) Son-in-law of Annas, eventually appointed by the Romans to be his successor as high priest of Israel (c.18–36). In the New Testament he interrogated Jesus after his arrest (*Matt* 26; *John* 18) and Peter after his detention in Jerusalem (*Acts* 4).

Caicos Islands [kaykos] Island group in the W Atlantic, SE of the Bahamas, forming a British overseas territory with the Turks Is; settled by Loyalist planters from the S States of America after the War of Independence; after the abolition of slavery (1838), the planters left the islands to their former slaves.

Caillaux, Joseph (Marie Auguste) [kiyoh] (1863–1944) French statesman, financier, and prime minister of France (1911–12), born in Le Mans, NW France. He trained as a lawyer, was elected to the Chamber of Deputies in 1898, and became finance minister in several governments. His brief term as prime minister ended when he was overthrown for showing too conciliatory an attitude towards Germany. In 1914, his second wife shot Gaston Calmette, editor of *Figaro*, who had launched a campaign against him and published a number of their private letters; after a famous trial, she was acquitted. He stayed in politics until France fell in 1940, when he retired.

caiman or **cayman** [kayman] A member of the alligator family (5 species), native to Central and South America; length, up to 2 m/6½ ft; inhabits rivers and swamps; eats fish and other water-dwelling vertebrates.

Cain [kayn] Biblical character, the eldest son of Adam and Eve, brother of Abel and Seth. He is portrayed (*Gen* 4) as a farmer whose offering to God was rejected, in contrast to that of his herdsman brother Abel. This led to his murder of Abel, and Cain's punishment of being banished to a nomadic life.

Caine, Sir Michael [kayn], properly **Sir Maurice Micklewhite** (1933–) Film actor, born in London, UK. He spent many years as a struggling small-part actor in a variety of media, before winning attention for his performance as an aristocratic officer in *Zulu* (1963). His stardom was consolidated with roles such as down-at-heel spy Harry Palmer in *The Ipcress File* (1965) and its two sequels, and as the Cockney Romeo in *Alfie* (1966). Later films include *Sleuth* (1972), *California Suite* (1978), and *Educating Rita* (1983, BAFTA best actor). Nominated four times for the Academy Award, he won an Oscar for *Hannah and Her Sisters* (1986). Later films include *Dirty Rotten Scoundrels* (1988), *Noises Off* (1992), *Little Voice* (1998), *The Cider House Rules* (1999, Oscar for Best Supporting Actor), *The Quiet American* (2002, Oscar nomination), and *Secondhand Lions* (2003). He received a knighthood in the year 2000.

ca(a)'ing whale *pilot whale*

Cainozoic era *Cenozoic era*

Cairngorms or **Cairngorm Mountains** Mountain range in NEC Scotland, UK, part of Grampian Mts; granite mountain mass in SE Highland and SW Grampian regions; rises to 1309 m/4295 ft in Ben Macdhui; between the rivers Dee (S) and Spey (N); winter sports region, centre at Aviemore.

Cairns [kairnz] 16°51S 145°43E, pop (2000e) 54 500. Resort and seaport on the NE coast of Queensland, Australia; especially popular with Japanese tourists; starting point for tours to the Great Barrier Reef and the Cape York Peninsula; offshore are Green I, Fitzroy I, and Arlington Reef; railway; international airfield; agricultural trade, timber, mining, sugar, deep-sea fishing.

Cairns Group An informal association of agricultural exporting countries, established in Cairns, Australia, in 1986. Its aims are to introduce reforms in international agricultural trade, such as the reduction of export subsidies and internal support measures. It had 17 members in 2004.

cairn terrier A breed of dog, developed in N Scotland for driving foxes out of their burrows; small with short legs; thick shaggy brown coat; ears erect and expression alert.

Cairo [kiyroh], Arabic **al-Qahira** 30°03N 31°15E, pop (2000e) 7 630 000. Capital of Egypt and Cairo governorate; at head of R Nile delta, 180 km/112 mi SE of Alexandria; largest African city; originally founded as El Fustat in AD 642; occupied by British, 1882–1946; airport; railway; four universities (1908, 1919, 1950, and Muslim university in Mosque of al-Azhar, 1972); tourism, cement, chemicals, leather, textiles, brewing, food processing; Islamic Cairo a world heritage site; mosques of Amur (7th-c), Kait Bey (15th-c), Ibn Touloun (878), Sultan Hassan (14th-c); major archaeological sites nearby, including Heliopolis, pyramids at El Giza, ruins of Memphis; Egyptian museum of antiquities, Coptic museum, museum of Islamic art, royal library.

caisson [kaysn] A permanent structure for keeping water or soft ground from flowing into the site when building foundations. There are several types: **open caissons**, open at the top and bottom; **box caissons**, open at the top and closed at the bottom; and **pneumatic caissons**, containing a working chamber in which compressed air excludes the water.

caisson disease [kaysn] *decompression sickness*

CAL *computer-aided instruction*

calabash A trailing or climbing vine (*Lagenaria siceraria*), native to warm Old World regions, with white flowers and woody, bottle-shaped fruits; also called **bottle gourd**. It was the source of the earliest containers, and is still used in this way today. (Family: Cucurbitaceae.)

calabash tree An evergreen tree (*Crescentia cujete*) growing to 12 m/40 ft, native to tropical America; clusters of lance-shaped leaves; flowers bell-shaped, borne directly on trunk and branches; fruit a woody berry up to 30 cm/12 in long or more, flask-shaped and used as a container. (Family: Bignoniaceae.)

calabrese [kalabrayzee] *broccoli*

Calabria [kalaybria], Ital [kalabria] pop (2000e) 2 008 000; area 15 079 sq km/5820 sq mi. Region of S Italy, occupying the 'toe' of the country, between the Ionian and Tyrrhenian Seas; capital, Catanzaro; chief towns, Cosenza, Crotone, Reggio di Calabria, Locri; underdeveloped area with mixed Mediterranean agriculture; wheat, olives, figs, wine, citrus fruit; subject to earthquakes, floods, and erosion; Calabria national park, area 170 sq km/66 sq mi, established in 1968.

Calais [kalay] 50°57N 1°52E, pop (2000e) 79 300. Seaport in Pas-de-Calais department, NW France; on the Straits of Dover, at the shortest crossing to England; 34 km/21 mi SE of Dover and 238 km/148 mi N of Paris; captured by England, 1346 (commemorated in Rodin sculpture); retaken by France, 1558; British base in World War 1; centre of heavy fighting in World War 2; airport; railway; ferry services to Dover and Folkestone; tulle and machine-made lace, shipping services.

calamine [kalamiyn] A mixture of zinc carbonate and ferric oxide, used as an ointment for many skin conditions. It was formerly a common name for the mineral *smithsonite* (zinc carbonate).

Calamity Jane, popular name of **Martha Jane Burke**, *née* **Cannary** (c.1852–1903) Legendary frontier figure, born in Princeton, Missouri, USA. Raised in Virginia City, MT (1864), she became an expert markswoman and rider and (dressed as a man) held her own in rough, mining-town society. Allegedly a pony-express rider and then a scout for General George Custer in Wyoming (1870s), she was companion to **'Wild Bill' Hickok** (1837–76), and was a heroine during the smallpox epidemic (1878) in the gold-rush town of Deadwood, SD. She is said to have threatened 'calamity' for any man who tried to court her, but in 1891 she married **Clinton Burk(e)** in El Paso, TX, who soon left her. She died in poverty, and is buried beside Hickok in Deadwood.

calceolaria [kalsiohlairia] A member of a large genus of annuals, perennials, or shrubs native to Central and South America; wrinkled leaves in opposite pairs; characteristic 2-lipped flowers with lower lip inflated and pouch-like. Commonly grown ornamentals are mainly hybrids with yellow, orange, or red spotted flowers up to 5 cm/2 in diameter. (Genus: *Calceolaria*, 300–400 species. Family: Scrophulariaceae.)

Calchas [kalkas] A seer on the Greek side during the Trojan War. He advised that Iphigeneia should be sacrificed at Aulis; at Troy he told Agamemnon to return Chryseis, the daughter of the priest of Apollo, to stop the plague. He died in a combat of 'seeing' with Mopsos.

calcite [kalsiyt] A mineral form of calcium carbonate ($CaCO_3$), and the main constituent of limestone and marble. It can occur by precipitation from carbonate-rich solutions to form stalactites and stalagmites, and forms the structure of coral reefs. Good crystals formed in vein deposits are transparent, and termed *Iceland spar*. It is used in the manufacture of Portland cement.

calcitonin [kalsi**toh**nin] A hormone (a polypeptide) synthesized and secreted by 'C' cells in the thyroid gland in mammals, and in the ultimobranchial bodies in other vertebrates; sometimes called **thyrocalcitonin**. It is released in response to elevated blood calcium levels, and lowers extracellular calcium levels.

calcium Ca, element 20, melting point 839°C. A very reactive, silvery metal only found combined in nature; the metal is obtained by electrolysis. It is the fifth most common element in the Earth's crust, occurring mainly in fluorite (CaF_2), gypsum ($CaSO_4.2H_2O$), and limestone ($CaCO_3$). It shows an oxidation state of +2 in almost all of its compounds, which are mainly ionic. Ca^{2+} ions are largely responsible for hardness in water. Calcium is an essential element in biology, being used in the structural tissue of both plants and animals; its compounds are common components of agricultural fertilizers, and are ingredients of both glass and cement. The oxide (CaO, or *quicklime*) is widely used as a strong base. Other important compounds include the hypochlorite ($Ca(OCl)_2$) and the carbide (CaC_2).

calculator A machine designed to perform a range of mathematical operations automatically. Early calculators include devices by Pascal (1647) and Leibniz, and the mechanical and electrically driven adding machines of the early 20th-c. Since the early 1960s, the electronic revolution has seen the development of high-speed calculators of diminishing size and increasing functions for pocket or desk-top use. They all handle the arithmetical functions of add, subtract, multiply, and divide, and most provide additional functions, such as squares, roots, percentages, and other statistical or trigonometric functions, typically showing the results as a one-line liquid-crystal display. Several now have the capabilities of a small computer, including a memory in which intermediate results can be stored, a set of programming options, the insertion of software modules, and the ability to make results available through a printout or screen.

calculi [**kal**kyooliy] In medicine, small stone-like concretions which form within certain organs and ducts. They are formed mainly by calcium salts, but other constituents include uric acid, cholesterol, and xanthine. The most common sites include the salivary glands, urinary tract, and biliary tract.

calculus *differential calculus; integral calculus*

calculus, fundamental theorem of If a function $f(t)$ meets certain conditions, $\frac{d}{dx}\int_0^x f(t)dt = f(x)$. This theorem unites differential calculus and integral calculus. It is usually credited to Isaac Newton, and independently to Gottfried Leibniz.

Calcutta [kal**kuh**ta], official name **Kolkata** (Jan 2001) 22°36N 88°24E, pop (2000e) 12 750 000. Port capital of West Bengal, E India; on the R Hugli in the R Ganges delta, 128 km/79 mi from the Bay of Bengal; third largest city in India; chief port of E India; founded by the British East India Company, 1690; capital of British India, 1773–1912; airport (Dum Dum); railway; three universities; textiles, chemicals, paper, metal, jute, crafts; Queen Victoria Memorial Museum, Ochterlony Monument, Raj Bhavan, St John's Cathedral (1787), Nakhoda Mosque (1926), Marble Palace (1835), Jain temples (1867), Hindu Bengali Temple of Kali (1809).

Caldecott, Randolph [**kawl**dikot] (1846–86) Artist and illustrator, born in Chester, Cheshire, NWC England, UK. He began as a bank-clerk in Whitstable and Manchester, and moved to London to follow an artistic career. He illustrated Washington Irving's *Old Christmas* (1876) and numerous children's books, such as *The House that Jack Built* (1878) and Aesop's Fables (1883). The Caldecott Medal has been awarded annually since 1938 to the best US artist-illustrator of children's books.

Calder, Alexander [**kawl**der], known as **Sandy Calder** (1898–1976) Artist and pioneer of kinetic art, born in Philadelphia, Pennsylvania, USA. He trained as an engineer (1915–19) before studying art at the School of the Art Students' League in New York City (1923). He specialized in abstract hanging wire constructions, some of which were connected to motors (Marcel Duchamp christened them 'mobiles' in 1932). His best-known works, however, were unpowered, relying upon air currents to set them rotating and casting intricate shadows.

caldera [kal**dair**a] A large volcanic crater formed when the remains of a volcano subside down into a magma chamber, emptied after a violent eruption. The caldera may subsequently fill with water, and become a crater lake – a notable example being Crater Lake in Oregon, USA.

Calderón de la Barca, Pedro [kolduh**ron** duh la **bah(r)**ka] (1600–81) Playwright, born in Madrid, Spain. He studied law and philosophy at Salamanca, and in 1635 was appointed to the court of Philip IV, where he began to write plays. He served in the army in Catalonia (1640–2), and in 1651 entered the priesthood. Recalled to court, he became chaplain of honour to Philip and continued to write plays, masques, and operas for the court, the Church, and the public theatres until his death. He wrote over 100 plays on secular themes, such as *El príncipe constante* (1629, The Constant Prince) and *El alcalde de Zalamea* (1640, The Mayor of Zalamea). From 1648 he wrote mostly religious plays, including over 70 one-act religious dramas performed in streets during the annual Corpus Christi processions.

Caldwell, Erskine (Preston) [**kawld**wel] (1903–87) Writer, born in White Oak, Georgia, USA. He worked amongst the 'poor whites' in the Southern states, where he absorbed the background for his best-known work, *Tobacco Road* (1932). Other books include *God's Little Acre* (1933), *Love and Money* (1954), and *Close to Home* (1962).

Caldwell, Sarah [**kawld**wel] (1924–) Opera director and conductor, born in Maryville, Missouri, USA. She studied violin, and while affiliated to Boston University formed her own opera company in Boston (1958). Overseeing every detail of the productions, staging, and music, she was notorious for just meeting last-minute deadlines and averting financial crises, but she made her opera company one of the most distinguished and innovative in the USA, especially noted for its productions of modern works such as Schoenberg's *Moses and Aaron*. In the 1970s she began to appear as a guest conductor of major orchestras.

Caledonian Canal A line of inland navigation following the Great Glen (Glen More) in Highland, Scotland, UK; extends from Inverness (NE) to Loch Eil near Fort William (SW), thus linking North Sea and Irish Sea; passes through Lochs Ness, Oich, and Lochy and 35 km/22 mi of man-made channels (1803–47); 29 locks; total length 96 km/60 mi; built by Telford.

calendar *French Republican / Gregorian / Julian calendar; month / year equivalents (p.259)*

calendar customs Traditional celebrations which mark turning-points in the seasons and the agricultural and religious years, usually forming a cycle. The celebrations involve eating special food, gift exchange, and merrymaking. Examples include New Year's Day, Easter, Thanksgiving, and Christmas.

calf scour Acute diarrhoea in calves, especially neonates. There is usually profuse, watery, foul-smelling faeces, which characteristically become caked around the rear quarters, and the calf becomes severely dehydrated. Collapse soon follows, and the condition rapidly becomes life-threatening once the calf stops eating. Although a number of micro-organisms (*Escherichia coli, Salmonella*) may be associated with calf scour, the condition is usually a result of poor husbandry and housing. Urgent treatment is required to control the diarrhoea and rehydrate the animal.

Calgary 51°05N 114°05W, pop (2000e) 795 500. Town in S Alberta, Canada, on the Bow R, near foothills of Rocky Mts; centre of rich grain and livestock area; rapid growth following arrival of Canadian Pacific Railway, 1883; oil found to the S, 1914; airport; communications and transport centre; university (1945); meat packing, oil refining; ice hockey team, Calgary Flames; football team, Calgary Stampeders; Glenbow Alberta art gallery and museum, Heritage Park open-air museum, Dinosaur Park, Calgary Zoo; Calgary Tower (1967, 190 m/623 ft), Centennial Planetarium; Calgary Stampede rodeo (Jul).

Calendar Year Equivalents

Jewish[1] (AM)	*Islamic*[2] (H)	*Hindu*[3] (SE)
5761 (30 Sep 2000–17 Sep 2001)	1421 (6 Apr 2000–25 Mar 2001)	1922 (21 Mar 2000–21 Mar 2001)
5762 (18 Sep 2001–6 Sep 2002)	1422 (26 Mar 2001–14 Mar 2002)	1923 (22 Mar 2001–21 Mar 2002)
5763 (7 Sep 2002–26 Sep 2003)	1423 (15 Mar 2002–4 Mar 2003)	1924 (22 Mar 2002–21 Mar 2003)
5764 (27 Sep 2003–15 Sep 2004)	1424 (5 Mar 2003–21 Feb 2004)	1925 (22 Mar 2003–21 Mar 2004)
5765 (16 Sep 2004–3 Oct 2005)	1425 (22 Feb 2004–9 Feb 2005)	1926 (22 Mar 2004–21 Mar 2005)

Gregorian equivalents are given in parentheses and are AD (= Anno Domini).
[1] Calculated from 3761 BC, said to be the year of the creation of the world, AM = Anno Mundi.
[2] Calculated from AD 622, the year in which the Prophet went from Mecca to Medina, H = Hijra.
[3] Calculated from AD 78, the beginning of the Saka era (SE), used alongside Gregorian dates in Government of India publications since 22 Mar 1957. Other important Hindu eras include: Vikrama era (58 BC), Kalacuri era (AD 248), Gupta era (AD 320), and Harsa era (AD 606).

Calendar Month Equivalents

Gregorian equivalents to other calendars are given in parentheses; the figures refer to the number of solar days in each month.

Gregorian (Basis: Sun)	*Jewish* (Basis: Moon)	*Islamic* (Basis:Moon)	*Hindu* (Basis:Moon)
January (31)	Tishri (Sep–Oct) (30)	Muharram (Sep–Oct) (30)	Caitra (Mar–Apr) (29 or 30)
February (28 or 29)	Heshvan (Oct–Nov) (29 or 30)	Safar (Oct–Nov) (29)	Vaisakha (Apr–May) (29 or 30)
March (31)	Kislev (Nov–Dec) (29 or 30)	Rabi I (Nov–Dec) (30)	Jyaistha (May–Jun) (29 or 30)
April (30)	Tevet (Dec–Jan) (29)	Rabi II (Dec–Jan) (29)	Asadha (Jun–Jul) (29 or 30)
May (31)	Shevat (Jan–Feb) (30)	Jamada I (Jan–Feb) (30)	Dvitiya Asadha *certain leap years*
June (30)	Adar (Feb–Mar) (29 or 30)	Jumada II (Feb–Mar) (29)	Svrana (Jul–Aug) (29 or 30)
July (31)	Adar Sheni *leap years only*	Rajab (Mar–Apr) (30)	Dvitiya Sravana *certain leap years*
August (31)	Nisan (Mar–Apr) (30)	Shaban (Apr–May) (29)	Bhadrapada (Aug–Sep) (29 or 30)
September (30)	Iyar (Apr–May) (29)	Ramadan (May–Jun) (30)	Asvina (Sep–Oct) (29 or 30)
October (31)	Sivan (May–Jun) (30)	Shawwal (Jun–Jul) (29)	Karttika (Oct–Nov) (29 or 30)
November (30)	Tammuz (Jun–Jul) (29)	Dhu al-Qadah (Jul–Aug) (30)	Margasirsa (Nov–Dec) (29 or 30)
December (31)	Av (Jul–Aug) (30)	Dhu al-Hijjah (Aug–Sep) (29 or 30)	Pausa (Dec–Jan) (29 or 30)
	Elul (Aug–Sep) (29)		Magha (Jan–Feb) (29 or 30)
			Phalguna (Feb–Mar) (29 or 30)

Calhoun, John C(aldwell) [kalhoon] (1782–1850) US statesman, born in Abbeville County, South Carolina, USA. He studied at Yale, and became a successful lawyer. In Congress he supported the measures which led to the war of 1812–15 with Great Britain, and promoted the protective tariff. In 1817 he joined Monroe's cabinet as secretary of war, and was vice-president under John Quincy Adams (1825–9), and then under Jackson. In 1832 he entered the US Senate, becoming a leader of the states-rights movement, and a champion of the interests of the slave-holding states. In 1844, as secretary of state, he signed a treaty annexing Texas; but, once more in the Senate, he strenuously opposed the war of 1846–7 with Mexico.

Cali [kalee] 3°24N 76°30W, pop (2000e) 1 561 000. Capital of Valle department, W Colombia; on Rio Cali; at centre of rich sugar-producing region; founded, 1536; airport; two universities (1945, 1958); coffee, sugar, cotton; colonial ranch-house of Cañas Gordas; church and 18th-c monastery of San Francisco; church and convent of La Merced; cathedral, national palace, modern art museum; national art festival (Jun); fair, with bullfights, masquerades, and sports (Dec).

calibration The verification or rectification of a measure or mark by comparison with a known standard or by experiment. For example, the scale on a thermometer may be checked by subjecting it to standard conditions, such as the freezing point and boiling point of water. The term also applies to determining points on a blank scale.

calico bush *mountain laurel*

calico cat *tortoiseshell cat*

Calicut *Kozhikode*

California pop (2000e) 33 871 600; area 411 033 sq km/ 158 706 sq mi. State in SW USA, divided into 58 counties; the 'Golden State'; originally populated by several Indian tribes; discovered by the Spanish, 1542; colonized mid-18th-c; developed after gold discovered in the Mother Lode, 1848; ceded to the USA by the treaty of Guadalupe Hidalgo, 1848; joined the Union as the 31st state, 1850; major US growth area in the 20th-c; now the most populous US state; capital, Sacramento; other chief cities, San Francisco, Los Angeles, Oakland, San Diego; bounded S by Mexico and W by the Pacific Ocean; mountainous in the N, W and E, with dry, arid depressions in the S (Mojave and Colorado Deserts) and SE (Death Valley); Klamath Mts in the N; Coast Ranges in the W run parallel to the Pacific; Sierra Nevada in the E, rising to 4418 m/14 495 ft at Mt Whitney (state's highest point); foothills of the Sierra Nevada contain the Mother Lode, a belt of gold-bearing quartz; the Sierra Nevada and Coast Ranges are separated by the Central Valley, drained by the San Joaquin and Sacramento Rivers, a major fruit-producing area; climate gives a wet and a dry season, with most rainfall November–March; vegetables, grain, livestock; a zone of faults (the San Andreas Fault) extends S from N California along the coast; earth tremors commonplace; major earthquakes in San Francisco, 1906, 1989, and in Los Angeles, 1993; devastating wildfires in the south, October 2003; centre of the US microelectronics industry in Silicon Valley; oil, natural gas, and a wide range of minerals; food processing, machinery, defence industries, transportation equipment, fabricated metals, cotton, wine (vineyards in over 40 Californian counties); increasing Hispanic and Asian populations; a major tourist state, with several national monuments and parks (Yosemite, Kings Canyon, Sequoia, Redwood), the film industry, Disneyland.

California, Gulf of Arm of the Pacific Ocean between Mexican mainland (E) and Baja California (W); Colorado R delta (N); broadens and deepens towards the S; maximum depth 2595 m/8514 ft; 1130 km/700 mi long by 80–130 km/50–80 mi wide; tourism, fishing, harvesting of sponge, pearl, oyster.

Californian Indians Once a very large concentration of many distinct American Indian groups, including the Yurok, Maidu, Cahuilla, Miwok, Pomo, Mojave, Hupa, and Chumash. The first groups migrated there at least 7000 years ago, and before the Spanish conquest in the 18th-c there were an estimated 105 tribes, speaking many different dialects, and mostly hunter-gatherers. Later, influenced by Indians in neighbouring territories, they developed pottery and basketry, elaborate ceremonials, and a maritime culture. With the Spanish conquest, their population was reduced from an estimated 350 000 to 100 000, and during the 19th-c many groups became extinct.

Californian lilac An evergreen shrub, rarely deciduous, native to North America; leaves lance-shaped to oval; flowers in dense clusters, 5 sepals incurved, 5 petals longer and spreading, blue, lilac, or white. (Genus: *Ceanothus*, 55 species. Family: Rhamnaceae.)

Californian poppy A grey-green annual or perennial (*Eschscholzia californica*), 20–45 cm/8–18 in, native to California and Oregon, USA; leaves finely divided; flowers bright yellow-orange, also creamy and scarlet in cultivars; the 4 petals roll up longitudinally in dull weather; grown in gardens, and often escaping into the surrounding area. (Family: Papaveraceae.)

California redwood *mammoth tree*

California sorrel *palomino*

Caligula [kaligyula], nickname of **Gaius Julius Caesar Germanicus** (12–41) Roman emperor (37–41), the youngest son of Germanicus and Agrippina, born in Antium. Brought up in an army camp, he was nicknamed Caligula from his little soldier's boots (*caligae*). His official name, once emperor, was Gaius. Extravagant, autocratic, vicious, and mentally unstable, he wreaked havoc with the finances of the state, and terrorized those around him, until he was assassinated. Under him, Hellenistic court practices, such as ritual obeisance, made their first (though not last) appearance in Rome.

calimanco cat *tortoiseshell cat*

caliph, also spelled **calif** (Arabic *khalifa*, 'deputy of God', or 'successor to his Prophet') A Muslim ruler, the title given to the temporal and spiritual head of the Muslim community after the death of Mohammed (632). Following Mohammed's death, his friend and disciple Abu-Bakr became the first caliph. The first four caliphs, Abu-Bakr, Omar, Uthman, and Ali, along with Mohammed, are regarded by Sunni Muslims as the 'rightly guided' caliphs. The title then became hereditary, and was used by the Umayyads at Damascus and later at Córdoba, by the Abbasids at Baghdad, by the Fatimids and Mamluks in Egypt, and by other Muslim chieftains. The title was taken over by the Ottoman sultans in the 16th-c, following their conquest of the last caliph in Cairo in 1517, and abolished when the Republic of Turkey was established in 1924. It was also used in India. Disagreement over the status and legitimate line of caliphs lies at the root of the division between Shiite and Sunni Muslims. The caliphate has throughout history been an important symbolic focus of unity for Muslims, and since its abolition several pan-Islamic congresses have attempted to establish a rightful caliph.

calisthenics The art and practice of bodily exercises designed to produce beauty and grace rather than muscular development. They are often performed with the aid of hand-held apparatus, such as rings and clubs. Similar exercises were first seen in Germany in the 19th-c.

Callaghan (of Cardiff), (Leonard) James Callaghan, Baron [kalahan], known as **Jim Callaghan** (1912–) British statesman and prime minister (1976–9), born in Portsmouth, Hampshire, S England, UK. He joined the Civil Service (1929), served in naval intelligence in World War 2, and in 1945 was elected Labour MP for South Cardiff. As Chancellor of the Exchequer under Harold Wilson (1964–7), he introduced the controversial corporation and selective employment taxes. He was home secretary (1967–70) and foreign secretary (1974–6), and became prime minister on Wilson's resignation. He resigned as Leader of the Opposition in 1980, and became a life peer in 1987. His autobiography, *Time and Chance*, was published in 1987.

Callaghan, Morley (Edward) [kalahan] (1903–90) Novelist, short-story writer, and memoirist, born in Toronto, Ontario, SE Canada. He studied at Toronto University, and was befriended by Hemingway. He was called to the bar in 1928, but while in Paris Hemingway encouraged him to give up law for literature, and helped him get some of his stories published in expatriate literary magazines. His first novel was *Strange Fugitive* (1928) and his first collection of stories *A Native Argosy* (1930). He returned to Toronto in 1929. Later novels include *The Loved and the Lost* (1951), *The Many Colored Coat* (1960), and *A Time for Judas* (1983).

calla lily *arum lily*

Callao [kalyahoh] 12°05S 77°08W, pop (2000e) 688 000. Port province contiguous with Lima, W Peru; handles 75% of Peru's imports and c.25% of its exports; occupied by Chile (1879–84); linked by rail and road to Lima (one of the first railways in South America, 1851); Real Felipe fortress (1774).

Callao Painter *El Niño*

Callas, Maria (Meneghini) [kalas], originally **Maria Kalogeropoulos** (1923–77) Operatic soprano, born in New York City, USA of Greek parents. She studied at Athens Conservatory, and in 1947 appeared at Verona in *La Gioconda*, winning immediate recognition. She sang with great authority in all the most exacting soprano roles, excelling in the intricate *bel canto* style of pre-Verdian Italian opera.

calligraphy The art of penmanship, or writing at its most formal. Chinese emperors were expected to practise calligraphy. It is a major art form in many countries of E Asia and in Arabic-speaking countries, and there has been a revival of interest in Europe and America since the 19th-c. In painting or drawing, 'calligraphic' means linear, freely-handled, and rhythmic, resembling a fine piece of formal handwriting.

Callimachus [kalimakus] (5th-c BC) Greek sculptor, working in Athens in the late 5th-c BC. Vitruvius says he invented the architectural Corinthian capital. Several statues have been identified as his, including the 'Draped Venus' in the Boston Museum of Fine Arts.

Callimachus [kalimakus] (299–210 BC) Greek poet, grammarian, and critic, born in Cyrene, N Libya. He became head of the Alexandrian Library, and prepared a catalogue of it, in 120 volumes. He wrote numerous prose works which have not survived, a number of *Hymns* and *Epigrams*, and a long elegiac poem, *Aitia*, among others.

calliope [kaliyopee] A steam organ patented by J C Stoddard of Worcester, MA, in 1855. Most calliopes had about 15–30 whistles, operated by a keyboard, but some had many more. They were fitted to the top decks of river showboats, and could be heard for miles around playing popular tunes. They are also heard as part of some merry-go-rounds in amusement parks.

Calliope [kaliyopee] In Greek mythology, the Muse of epic poetry. She is sometimes said to be the mother of Orpheus.

Callisto (astronomy) [kalistoh] The fourth natural satellite of Jupiter, discovered in 1610 by Galileo; distance from the planet 1 883 000 km/1 170 00 mi; diameter 4800 km/3000 mi; orbital period 16·689 days. Its dark surface is a mixture of ice and rocky material, and is heavily cratered.

Callisto (mythology) [kalistoh] In Greek mythology, an Arcadian nymph attendant upon Artemis. Loved by Zeus, she became pregnant, and was sent away from the virgin band. Hera changed her into a she-bear; and after 15 years had passed, her son tried to spear her. Zeus took pity on them, and changed her into the constellation Ursa Major and her son into Arctophylax.

callus 1 An acquired area of localized thickening of the epidermal layer of skin, due to continued physical trauma.
2 The tissue formed during the repair of a fracture. Fibrocartilage and hyaline cartilage are formed to seal and unite the ends of the bone (a *provisional* callus), being gradually replaced by mature bone (a *permanent* callus).

Calmar *Kalmar*

Calmette, (Léon Charles) Albert [kalmet] (1863–1933) Bacteriologist, born in Nice, SE France. A pupil of Pasteur and founder of the Pasteur Institute at Saigon, where he developed an anti-snakebite and anti-plague serum. In 1895 he founded the Pasteur Institute at Lille (director, 1895–1919). He is best known for the vaccine BCG (*Bacille Calmette–Guérin*), which provides protection against tuberculosis, jointly developed with **Dr Camille Guérin** (1872–1961). He was the brother of newspaper editor Gaston Calmette.

calmodulin [kalmodyulin] One of a group of intracellular proteins widely distributed in plants and animals. It binds with calcium to form the calmodulin–calcium complex, which activates enzymes involved in basic cellular processes (eg mitosis, motility, and neurotransmitter release).

caloric *thermodynamics*

calorie In thermodynamics, an old unit of heat, symbol *cal*; 1 cal = 4·184 J (joule, SI unit); defined as the quantity of heat required to raise the temperature of a gram of water from 14·5°C to 15·5°C. The calorie is an extremely small unit of energy, the average person requiring 2·5 million calories per day. To overcome the obvious problem in counting such small units, the preferred term in scientific literature is the **kilocalorie**, symbol *kcal* or *Cal*, where 1 Cal = 1000 cal, and this is the term commonly used in describing the energy content of foodstuffs. However, the public have continued to use the familiar word; so, in popular usage, 1 kilocalorie is often thought of as 1 Calorie.

calorimetry The measurement of energy transferred in some physical or chemical process, such as the energy absorbed from its surroundings by a solid melting to a liquid, or the energy evolved by burning some substance. In nutrition, **calorimeters** are used to measure the number of calories in a given substance, or to measure the heat output of humans, equivalent to caloric expenditure. Some of these are sufficiently large for people to live in for several days, while fulfilling reasonably normal lives, thus enabling the energy needs of daily living to be recorded.

Calotype A very early method of photography patented by Fox Talbot in 1841, using paper sensitized with silver iodide to produce a negative image.

Calvaert, Denis [kalvairt], known as **Il Fiammingo** (1540–1619) Flemish Mannerist painter. He studied in Antwerp and then in Bologna under Prospero Fontana, and while a student he worked on frescoes in the Vatican. Later, he set up a school in Bologna where his pupils included Guido Reni and Domenichino. Much of his work is in the churches and national museum of Bologna.

Calvary [kalvaree] (Lat *calvaria*, 'skull', translating Semitic *Golgotha*) The site where Jesus was crucified, presumed to be a place of execution just outside Jerusalem. The term appears in the Authorized Version of the Bible (*Luke* 23.33).

Calvin, John (1509–64) Protestant reformer, born in Noyon, N France. He studied Latin at Paris, then law at Orléans, where he developed his interest in theology. In Bourges and other centres he began to preach the reformed doctrines, but was forced to flee from France to escape persecution. At Basel he issued his influential *Christianae religionis institutio* (1536, Institutes of the Christian Religion), and at Geneva was persuaded by Guillaume Farel to help with the reformation. The reformers proclaimed a Protestant Confession of Faith, under which moral severity took the place of licence. When a rebellious party, the Libertines, rose against this, Calvin and Farel were expelled from the city (1538). Calvin withdrew to Strasbourg, where he worked on New Testament criticism, and married **Idelette de Bure** (1540). In 1541 the Genevans recalled him, and he founded a theocracy which controlled almost all the city's affairs. By 1555 his authority was confirmed into an absolute supremacy. The father-figure of Reformed theology, he left a double legacy to Protestantism by systematizing its doctrine and organizing its ecclesiastical discipline. His commentaries, which embrace most of the Old and New Testaments, were collected and published in 1617.

Calvin, Melvin (1911–97) Chemist, born in St Paul, Minnesota, USA. He studied at the universities of Minnesota and Manchester (UK), then became professor of chemistry at the University of California, Berkeley (1947–71) and head of the Lawrence Radiation Laboratory there (1963–80). He was best known for his research into the role of chlorophyll in photosynthesis, for which he received the Nobel Prize for Chemistry in 1961.

Calvinism [kalvinizm] A term with at least three applications.
1 The theology of the 16th-c Protestant reformer, John Calvin.
2 The principal doctrines of 17th-c Calvinist scholars, including the 'five points of Calvinism' affirmed by the Synod of Dort (1618–19).
3 More broadly, the beliefs of those Churches in the Reformed tradition which arose under the influence of Calvin, and the impact they had on the societies and cultures in which they took root. Historically, Calvinism has emphasized the sovereignty of God, the Bible as the sole rule of faith, the doctrine of predestination, and justification by faith alone. The movement greatly influenced the Pilgrims of New England. There has been a Neo-Calvinist renewal in the 20th-c under the influence of the theologian Karl Barth.

Calvino, Italo [kalveenoh] (1923–85) Writer, essayist, and journalist, born in Santiago de las Vegas, N Cuba, of Italian parents. He spent his early years in San Remo, and studied at Turin, where he worked as a publisher. His first novel, *Il sentiero dei nidi di ragno* (1947, The Path to the Nest of Spiders), described resistance against Fascism in a highly naturalistic manner. In later works, such as *I nostri antenati* (1960, Our Ancestors), he adopted a more condensed style of story-telling, hovering between allegory and pure fantasy, while *Se una notte d'inverno un viaggiatore* (1979, If On a Winter's Night a Traveller) tests the limits of experiment in fiction.

Calypso (astronomy) The 14th natural satellite of Saturn, discovered in 1980, moving along the same orbit as Tethys; distance from the planet 295 000 km/183 000 mi; diameter 30 km/19 mi.

calypso (music) A song tradition from Trinidad, with roots in West African music. It regularly features satirical, social, political, or other topical comment sung to the accompaniment of guitar and maracas, or steel drums, with a syncopated beat. Among the best known calypsonians are (Mighty) Sparrow (real name Slinger Francisco, 1935–), (Mighty) Shadow (real name Winston Bailey, born late 1930s), David Rudder (1953–), and Lord Kitchener (real name Aldwyn Roberts, 1922–2000). The music has been one of several influences on the development of reggae and its variants, and has itself developed (some would say degenerated) into soca.

calyx *flower; sepal*

CAM *computer-aided manufacture*

Camargue [kamah(r)g] area 750 sq km/290 sq mi. District in R Rhône delta, SE France; alluvial island, mainly saltmarsh and lagoon; Etang de Vaccares nature reserve for migratory birds; information centre at Ginès; rice and vines on reclaimed land (N); centre for breeding bulls and horses; chief locality, Saintes-Maries-de-la-Mer; tourism, with boating and riding.

Cambacérès, Jean Jacques Régis de [kābasayres] (1753–1824) Lawyer, born in Montpellier, S France. He became arch-chancellor of the French Empire (1804) and Duke of Parma (1808). As Napoleon's chief legal adviser he was a moderating influence;

Cambodia

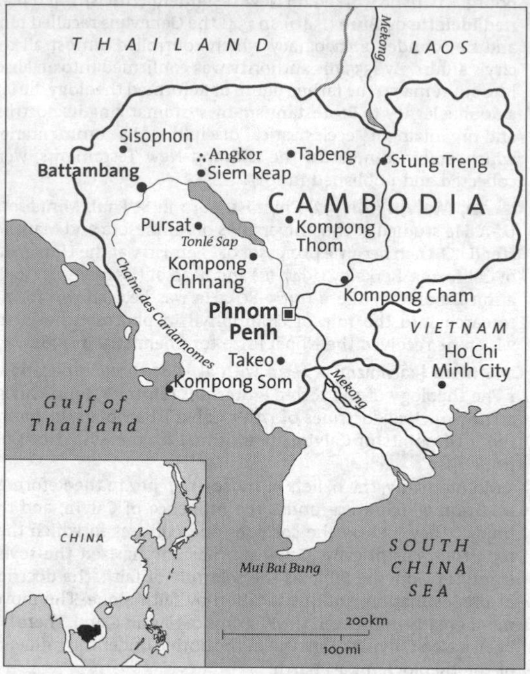

□ International Airport ∴ World heritage site

[kambohdia], formerly **Kampuchea** (1975–89) and **Khmer Republic** (1970–5), official name (from 1993) **Kingdom of Cambodia**, Khmer **Preah Reach Ana Pak Kampuchea**

Local name Cambodia

Timezone GMT +7

Area 181 035 km²/69 879 sq mi

Population total (2002e) 13 414 000

Status Kingdom

Date of independence 1953

Capital Phnom Penh

Languages Khmer (official), French

Ethnic groups Khmer (93%), Chinese (3%), Cham (2%)

Religions Theravada Buddhist (88%), Muslim (2%)

Physical features Kingdom in SE Asia. Crossed E by floodplain of Mekong R; Cardamom mountain range 160 km/100 mi across Thailand border, rising to 1813 m/5948 ft at Phnom Aural; Tonlé Sap (Greek Lake) in NW.

Climate Tropical monsoon climate, with a wet season (May–Sep). High temperatures in lowland region throughout the year; average annual temperature 21°C (Jan), 29°C (Jul); average annual rainfall 5000 mm/71 in (SW), 1300 mm/51 in (interior lowlands).

Currency 1 Riel (CRl) = 100 sen

Economy Most of population employed in subsistence agriculture, rice and corn; industrial development disrupted by the civil war.

GDP (2002e) $20·42 bn, per capita $1600

Human Development Index (2002) 0·543

History Originally part of Funan Kingdom, then part of the Khmer Empire, 6th-c; in dispute with Vietnamese and Thais from 15th-c; French Protectorate, 1863; formed French Indo-Chinese Union with Laos and Vietnam; 1887; independence, 1953; Prince Sihanouk deposed and Khmer Republic formed in 1970; fighting throughout the country involved troops from N and S Vietnam and the USA; surrender of Phnom Penh to the Khmer Rouge, and country renamed Kampuchea, 1975; attempt to reform economy on cooperative lines by Pol Pot (1975–8) caused the deaths of an estimated 3 million people; further fighting 1977–8; Phnom Penh captured by the Vietnamese, causing Khmer Rouge to flee, 1979; 1981 constitution established a Council of State and a Council of Ministers; name of Cambodia restored, 1989; Vietnamese troops completed withdrawal, 1989; UN peace plan agreed, with ceasefire and return of Sihanouk as Head of State, 1991; Sihanouk crowned King, 1993; further conflict following Khmer Rouge refusal to take part in 1993 elections.

Head of State (Monarch)

1993– Norodom Sihanouk II (*restored*)

Head of Government

1993–7 Norodom Ranariddh (*joint*)

1993–8 Hun Sen (*joint*)

1997–8 Ing Huot (*joint*)

1998– Hun Sen

his civil code formed the basis of the *Code Napoléon* or *Code Civil* (1894), and subsequent codes.

Camberwell beauty A colourful butterfly; wings velvet brown with yellow margin and line of blue spots; caterpillar mainly black, with black spike; found on willow, birch, and other trees; pupa hangs by tail. (Order: Lepidoptera. Family: Nymphalidae.)

cambium A layer of actively dividing cells, producing an increase in the girth of woody plants by additional growth of vascular tissue and cork, after these tissues have been formed by the meristem.

Cambodia *see panel*

Cambodian *Austro-Asiatic languages; Khmer*

Cambrian period The earliest geological period of the Palaeozoic era, lasting from c.590 to 505 million years ago. Characterized by widespread seas, its rocks contain a large variety of marine invertebrate fossils, including trilobites and brachiopods. Present exposures include N Wales, Scotland, Norway, Spain, and the Appalachians.

Cambridge (UK), Lat **Cantabrigia** 52°12N 0°07E, pop (2000e) 121 200. County town of Cambridgeshire, EC England, UK; on the R Cam (Granta); 82 km/51 mi N of London; Roman settlement AD 70; airfield; railway; radio, electronics, printing, publishing, scientific instruments, tourism; one of the world's great universities, established 13th-c (Peterhouse, 1284); Churches of St Benedict and the Holy Sepulchre, King's College Chapel, university colleges; football team, Cambridge United ('U's).

Cambridge (USA), formerly **New Towne** (to 1638) 42°22N 71°06W, pop (2000e) 101 400. Seat of Middlesex Co, E Massachusetts, USA; on one side of the Charles R, with Boston on the other; founded, 1630; city status, 1846; the first printing press in the USA set up here in 1640; Harvard University (1636) is the oldest US college; Massachusetts Institute of Technology (1859) moved from Boston in 1915; railway; electronics, glass, scientific instruments, photographic equipment, printing and publishing.

Cambridge Platonists A group of 17th-c philosophers and theologians centred on Cambridge University. Their most prominent members were Benjamin Whichcote, Henry More, Nathanael Culverwel, Richard Cumberland, and Ralph Cudworth. The movement looked in a general way to the Platonic and Neoplatonic traditions of thought, and tried to establish a strictly rational basis for ethics and religion.

Cambridge ring One of the early types of computer local area network which was pioneered at Cambridge University, UK, by R M Needham (1925–); also called a **slotted ring**.

Cambridgeshire pop (2001e) 552 700; area 3409 sq km/1316 sq mi. County of EC England, UK; drained by the Nene, Ouse, and Cam Rivers; flat fenland to the N; county town, Cambridge; chief towns include Peterborough (unitary authority, 1998), Ely, Huntingdon; grain, vegetables, food processing, electronics, engineering.

Cambridge University The second oldest university in England, after Oxford. Informal groups of scholars and masters were probably present in Cambridge at the end of the 12th-c. The first college, Peterhouse, was founded in 1284 and further colleges were founded after the Pope formally recognized Cambridge as a *universitas* (1318). Prestigious university institutions include the Fitzwilliam Museum, the Cavendish Laboratory of experimental physics, the Cambridge University Press (founded 1534), and the University Library, a national depository. (*see panel*)

camcorder A small, portable video camera with an integral narrow-gauge videotape recorder, also known as the **camera cassette recorder** (CCR). It offers immediate play-back through a domestic television receiver.

Camden (UK) 51°33N 0°09W, pop (2001e) 198 000. Borough of N Greater London, UK; includes suburbs of Hampstead, St Pancras, and Holborn, named after an 18th-c Lord Chancellor, university (1826); railway stations at Euston (1849), King's Cross (1852), St Pancras (1874); British Museum, John Keats House, Gray's Inn, Lincoln's Inn, Post Office Tower (1964).

Camden (New Jersey) 39°56N 75°07W, pop (2000e) 79 900. Seat of Camden Co, W New Jersey, USA; a port on the E bank of the Delaware R, opposite Philadelphia; city status, 1828; railway; university (1934); oil refining, textiles, food processing, radio and television equipment; formerly a major shipbuilding port (yards closed in 1967); home of Walt Whitman (1873–92).

Camden, William (1551–1623) Antiquarian and historian, born in London, UK. He studied at Oxford, and became second master of Westminster School (1575), then headmaster (1593). A dedicated scholar, he compiled a pioneering topographical survey of the British Isles in Latin, *Britannia* (1586, English trans, 1610). The *Camden Society* (founded 1838), which promoted historical publications, was named after him.

Camden, Battle of (1780) A battle of the US War of Independence, fought in South Carolina. After the British capture of Charleston, Camden was the first major battle of the Southern campaign. Americans under Horatio Gates were defeated by British troops under Lord Cornwallis.

Camden Town Group A group of artists who flourished 1905–13 in London, UK. Sickert was the leading member, but the group also included Harold Gilman (1878–1919) and Spencer Gore (1878–1914). They shared an enthusiasm for recent French painting.

Camdessus, Michel (Jean) [kãdesy] (1933–) Civil servant, and managing director and chairman of the International Monetary Fund (1987–99), born in Bayonne, SW France. Educated in Paris, he served in the Treasury (1960–6) before spending two years as part of the French delegation to the EEC. Returning to the Treasury in 1968, he became its director in 1982 and also chairman of the monetary committee of the EEC (1982–4). Deputy-director of the Bank of France from 1982, he became its director in 1984, a post he held until he was appointed managing director of the IMF.

camel A mammal of the family Camelidae (2 species): the **Bactrian** (or **two-humped**) **camel** (*Camelus bactrianus*) from cold deserts in C Asia, and domesticated elsewhere, and the **dromedary** (*Camelus dromedarius*); eats any vegetation; drinks salt water if necessary; closes slit-like nostrils to exclude sand; humps are stores of energy-rich fats. The two species may interbreed: the offspring has one hump; males are usually sterile, while females are fertile.

Camelidae [kamelidee] The camel family of mammals (6 species), found from N Africa to Mongolia (*camels*), or in the Andes (*llama, alpaca, guanaco, vicuña*); artiodactyls; unusual walk (move both right legs, then both left); mate lying down; upper lip cleft; the only mammals with oval (not round) red blood cells.

camellia [kameelia] An evergreen shrub or tree, native to China, Japan, and SE Asia; leaves alternate, leathery, glossy green; flowers usually large and showy, often scented, 4–7 petals, but often numerous in cultivars, white, pink, or crimson; popular ornamentals. The genus includes the tea plant. (Genus: *Camellia*, 82 species. Family: Theaceae.)

camel(e)opard [kameluhpah(r)d] *giraffe*

Camelopardalis [kamelopah(r)dalis] (Lat 'giraffe') A large constellation in the N hemisphere, also known as **Camelopardus**. It lacks any bright stars.

Camelot [kamelot] The legendary capital of King Arthur's Britain. It is variously located at Cadbury in the West Country, Colchester (Camulodunum), and Winchester.

cameo A method of carving a relief image into a shell or semi-precious stone with different coloured layers. It was popular in the Roman Empire, and has been used ever since in W European art, often copied in glass and ceramic.

camera An apparatus which produces an image of an external scene. In the early **camera obscura** (literally 'darkened room'), first developed in 11th-c China, light passing through a small hole or lens formed a picture on the opposite wall. Portable versions in boxes served as artist's guides in landscape drawing, and early 19th-c attempts to record the image led to the first photographic camera: a light-tight box containing a glass or metal plate with a light-sensitive surface on which the image was formed by a lens. The long exposure time was controlled simply by removing and replacing a cap on the lens. During the 1850s more sensitive plates greatly reduced exposure time, and

Cambridge University

College	*Founded*
Peterhouse	1284
Clare	1326
Pembroke	1347
Gonville (refounded as Gonville and Caius 1558)	1348
Trinity Hall	1350
Corpus Christi	1352
King's	1441
Queen's	1448
St Catharine's	1473
Jesus	1496
Christ's	1505
St John's	1511
Magdalene	1542
Trinity	1546
Emmanuel	1584
Sidney Sussex	1596
Homerton*	1768
Downing	1800
Girton	1869
Newnham[1]	1871
Selwyn	1882
Hughes Hall[3]	1885
St Edmund's[3]	1896
New Hall[1]	1954
Churchill	1960
Lucy Cavendish[1]	1964
Darwin[2]	1964
Wolfson	1965
Clare Hall[2]	1966
Fitzwilliam	1966
Robinson	1977

[1] Women's colleges
[2] Graduate colleges
[3] Graduate and affiliated graduate colleges
* Only offers education courses leading to BEd or PGCE

mechanical shutters became essential, with adjustable lens aperture and the body formed by folding leather bellows. In the 1880s photographic film in continuous strips revolutionized camera design, first with the Kodak box-camera and later with pocket cameras having collapsible bellows folding into a metal body when not in use. The first miniature camera to use perforated film 35 mm wide was the Leica in 1925, and this compact cassette-loaded form was widely adopted for other sizes. Camera operation has become increasingly simplified with automatic focus setting and exposure; built-in synchronized electronic flash and motor drive for film advance and repeated operation are also now available, as is within-camera film processing (Polaroid®). Of many early cameras for cinematography, the *Kinetograph* developed by Dickson, working for Edison in 1891, had the most lasting influence, establishing the use of film 35 mm wide in long rolls moved intermittently by holes perforated along both edges. Early cameras were hand-cranked, relying on the operator's skill to maintain a steady 16 pictures per second; but clockwork and electric motors were used later, with rolls of film being fed into the camera and taken up after exposure in detachable magazines. With the introduction of sound-films in 1927, the picture rate was increased to 24 per second, and precisely controlled speed became essential for synchronization with the sound recording. In a **video camera** the lens image is formed on the photo-cathode surface of an electronic tube, where it is scanned to produce the signal for transmission. Early TV cameras had large pick-up tubes, with an image diagonal of 55 mm, but from the 1960s much smaller camera tubes were developed, 25 mm or 17 mm in diameter. In the 1980s the very compact charge-coupled device (CCD) sensor was introduced in place of the photo-conductive tube, and camcorders with self-contained videotape recording became available. The use of a single zoom lens has become standard, focused and set under the operator's control with automatic exposure and colour balance.

camera obscura *camera*

camera operator The member of a film production crew, formerly termed **lighting cameraman** or **cinematographer**, responsible under the director for the artistic and technical quality of the picture. Camera operators choose the camera viewpoint and lens angle, and direct the character and distribution of lighting for both set and artists to create the dramatic mood required. During rehearsal and shooting they decide the composition of the action and any camera movement needed, and approve the resulting prints of each day's work.

Camerarius, Rudolf Jakob [kamerairius] (1665–1721) Botanist, born in Tübingen, SW Germany. He followed his father in becoming professor of medicine at Tübingen. He showed by experiment in 1694 that plants can reproduce sexually, and identified the stamens and carpels as the male and female sexual apparatus, respectively. He also described pollination.

Cameron, James (1954–) Film director, screenwriter, and producer, born in Kapuskasing, Ontario, Canada. His family moved to California, while he was a teenager. He dropped out of California State University at Fullerton, and had a variety of jobs before immersing himself in film techniques, and making a home-made short film. Hired by New World Pictures as a production designer, he graduated to directing. His credits as writer/director include *The Terminator* and its sequel (1984, 1991), *Aliens* (1986), *The Abyss* (1989), *True Lies* (1994), and *Titanic* (1997, 11 Oscars, including Best Film and Best Director).

Cameroon *p.265*

Cameroon, Mount or **Mongo-Ma-Loba** 4°14N 9°10E. Volcanic massif in S Cameroon, W Africa; runs inland for 37 km/23 mi from Gulf of Guinea; main peak, 4070 m/13 353 ft; highest mountain group in W Africa; last eruption, 1999.

Camisards The last major Protestant rebellion in early modern Europe, centred on the Cévennes Mts in N Languedoc (1700–4), fought between French Protestants and troops of the monarch Louis XIV. It was provoked by the Revocation of the Edict of Nantes (1685), which had guaranteed limited toleration of Protestantism, and the failure of the Treaty of Ryswick (1697) to safeguard French Protestants. The uprising was put down with difficulty by royal troops under Marshal Villars, and was followed by a period of savage persecution.

Camoens or **Camões, Luís Vaz de** [kamohenz] (1524–80) The greatest Portuguese poet, born in Lisbon, Portugal. He studied for the Church at Coimbra, but declined to take orders. He became a soldier, and during service at Ceuta lost his right eye. He went to India (1553) and Macao (1556), and was shipwrecked while returning to Goa (1558), losing everything except his major poem, *Os Luciados* (The Lusiads, or Lusitanians). After returning to Portugal in 1570, he lived in poverty and obscurity. *The Lusiads* was published in 1572, and was an immediate success, but did little for his fortunes, and he died in a public hospital. The work has since come to be regarded as the Portuguese national epic.

camomile *chamomile*

Camorra [kamohra] In Naples and S Italy, a generic term applied to practices based in corporate institutions and practices of the poor, which developed during the 19th-c into a complex network of patronage, clientelism, protection, and ultimately crime. As with the Sicilian Mafia, which it resembles, no single Camorra organization has ever existed.

Campaign for Nuclear Disarmament *CND*

campanile [kampaneelay] The Italian name for a bell tower, usually tall and detached from the main building. The earliest known campanile was square, and attached to St Peter's, Rome, in the mid-8th-c AD. The most famous example is the circular Leaning Tower of Pisa, with eight arcaded storeys.

campanology *bell-ringing*

campanula *bell-flower; Canterbury bell*

Campbell, Sir Colin, Baron Clyde (1792–1863) British field marshal, born in Glasgow, W Scotland, UK. He fought in the Peninsular War against Napoleon, where he was twice badly wounded, and after 30 years of duty in various garrisons fought in China (1842) and in the second Sikh war (1848–9). In the Crimean War (1854–6) he commanded the Highland Brigade in a campaign which included the renowned repulse of the Russians by the 'thin red line' at Balaclava. During the Indian Mutiny he commanded the forces in India, and effected the final relief of Lucknow. He was created baron in 1858.

Campbell, John W(ood), Jr, pseudonym **Don A Stuart** (1910–71) Science-fiction writer, born in Newark, New Jersey, USA. His first published novel, *When the Atoms Failed* (1930), was one of the earliest to make reference to computers. He developed in his stories the new idea that machines could dominate humans, notably in *Twilight* (1934). His works were highly influential, and he has come to be regarded as the father of modern science-fiction.

Campbell, Kim (Avril Phaedra Douglas) (1947–) Canadian stateswoman, and Canada's first woman prime minister (1993), born in British Columbia, SW Canada. Her first public office was as school trustee with the Vancouver School Board (1980). She later ran unsuccessfully as a Social Credit candidate in the British Columbia provincial election, then was elected for the province in 1988 as a federal conservative. She served as minister of justice and defence in Brian Mulroney's cabinet, before becoming leader of the party and prime minister in spring 1993, but disastrously lost the general election some months later. She returned to university lecturing, holding a fellowship at Harvard.

Campbell, Sir Malcolm (1885–1948) Land and water speed-record contestant, born in Chislehurst, Kent, SE England, UK. He held both speed records from 1927 onwards. In 1935 he became the first man to break 300 mph on land with 301·1292 mph at Bonneville Salt Flats, UT. In 1939 he achieved his fastest speed on water with 141·74 mph. He called all his cars and boats *Bluebird*, after the symbol of unattainability in the play of that name by Maurice Maeterlinck. His son, **Donald Campbell** (1921–67) was killed when his turbo-jet hydroplane crashed on Coniston Water, England (salvaged in 2001). Do-

Cameroon

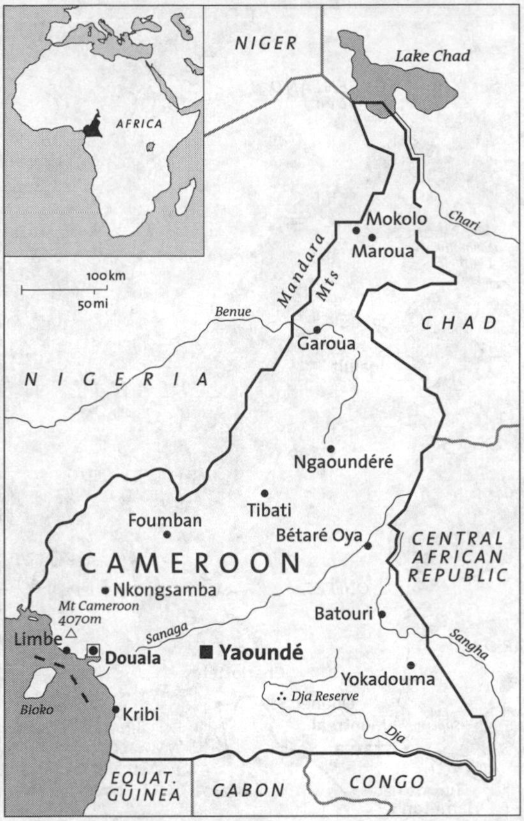

□ International Airport ∴ World heritage site

[kameroon], official name **Republic of Cameroon**, Fr **République du Cameroon**

Local name Cameroun

Timezone GMT +1

Area 475 442 km²/183 569 sq mi

Population total (2002e) 16 185 000

Status Republic

Date of independence 1960

Capital Yaoundé

Languages French and English (official); 24 major African languages including Fang, Bamileke, Luanda, Fulani, Tika, Maka

Ethnic groups Highlanders (31%), Equatorial Bantu (19%), Kirdi (11%), Fulani (10%)

Religions Christian (40%), traditional beliefs (39%), Muslim (21%)

Physical features Located in W Africa. Equatorial forest, with low coastal plain. C plateau 1300 m/4200 ft. W forested and mountainous; Mt Cameroon, 4070 m/13 353 ft (active volcano and the highest peak in W Africa). Low savannah, semi-desert towards L Chad; rivers include Sanaga and Dja.

Climate Rain all year in equatorial S; daily temperature in Yaoundé 27–30°C; average annual rainfall 4030 mm/159 in.

Currency 1 CFA Franc (CFAFr) = 100 centimes

Economy Agriculture (employs c.80% of workforce); world's fifth largest producer of cocoa; tourism, especially to national parks.

GDP (2002e) $26·84 bn, per capita $1700

Human Development Index (2002) 0·512

History First explored by Portuguese navigator Fernando Po; later by traders from Spain, Netherlands, Britain. German protectorate of Kamerun from 1884. Divided into French and British Cameroon in 1919; confirmed by League of Nations mandate in 1922; UN trusteeships, 1946. French Cameroon independent as Republic of Cameroon in 1960: N sector of British Cameroon voted to become part of Nigeria, S sector part of Cameroon; became Federal Republic of Cameroon, with separate parliaments, 1961. Federal system abolished in 1972, and name changed to United Republic of Cameroon. Changed name to the Republic of Cameroon in 1984; multiparty legislative and presidential elections, 1992; governed by a President, an executive Prime Minister, Cabinet, and national assembly.

Head of State

1960–82 Ahmadou Ahidjo

1982– Paul Biya

Head of Government

1991–2 Sadou Hayatou

1992–6 Simon Achidi Achu

1996– Peter Mafany Musonge

nald's daughter, **Gina Campbell** (1948–) broke the women's water speed record in 1984.

Campbell, Mrs Patrick, *née* **Beatrice Stella Tanner** (1865–1940) Actress, born in London, UK. She married in 1884, and went on the stage in 1888. Though her mercurial temperament made her the terror of managers, she possessed outstanding charm and talent, and leapt to fame in *The Second Mrs Tanqueray* (1893). She played Eliza in Shaw's *Pygmalion* (1914), and formed a long friendship with the author.

Campbell, (Ignatius) Roy(ston) (Dunnachie) (1901–57) Poet and journalist, born in Durban, E South Africa. He became an ardent admirer of all things Spanish, and fought with Franco's armies during the Civil War. His books of poetry include *The Flaming Terrapin* (1924), *The Wayzgoose* (1928), and *Flowering Rifle* (1939). A collected edition of his poems appeared in 1949, and the autobiographical *Light on a Dark Horse* in 1951.

Campbell-Bannerman, Sir Henry (1836–1908) British statesman and prime minister (1905–8), born in Glasgow, W Scotland, UK. He studied at Glasgow and Cambridge, became a Liberal MP (1868), was chief secretary for Ireland (1884), war secretary (1886, 1892–5), Liberal leader (1899), and prime minister. A 'pro-Boer', he granted the ex-republics responsible government, and his popularity united the Liberal Party. He supported the Lib-Lab pact of 1903, which played a part in the Liberal landslide of 1906.

Camp David The US presidential retreat established in 1942 by President Roosevelt in Catoctin Mountain Park, Maryland, USA. Originally known as 'Shangri La', it was renamed in 1953 after President Eisenhower's grandson. The retreat covers 81 ha/200 acres and includes a main residence (Aspen Lodge), conference hall, and office. It has been used for a number of historic meetings between heads of state.

Camp David Accords The framework for 'a just, comprehensive, and durable settlement of the Middle East conflict', reached by Egyptian President Sadat, Israeli Prime Minister Begin, and US President Jimmy Carter at Camp David, MD, in September 1978. Based on the principle of exchanging land for peace embodied in UN Security Council Resolution 242, the accords laid the foundation for the March 1979 peace treaty between Egypt and Israel. Other elements of the accord, including a settlement of the Palestinian–Israeli dispute, were still being negotiated at the beginning of the 2000s.

Campese, David (Ian) [kampeezee], nickname **Campo** (1962–) Rugby union player, born near Queanbeyan, New South Wales, SE Australia. A fast, flamboyant wing, between 1982–96 he set a world record 64 tries as an international, and an Australian record for the most matches played, 101. The star of Australia's

Canada

□ International Airport

formerly **British North America** (to 1867)

Local name Canada

Timezone GMT W -9, to E -3

Area 9 971 500 km^2/3 848 900 sq mi

Population total (2002e) 31 244 000

Status Independent nation within the Commonwealth

Date of independence 1867 (Dominion of Canada)

Capital Ottawa

Languages English and French (official)

Ethnic groups British origin (45%), French origin (29%), other European, Indian, and Inuit (23%)

Religions Roman Catholic (49%), United Church (18%), Anglican (12%)

Physical features Dominated in the NE by the Canadian Shield; flat prairie country S and W of the Shield, stretching to the Western Cordillera, which includes the Rocky, Cassiar, and Mackenzie Mts; coast Mts flank a rugged, heavily indented coastline; Mt Logan in the Yukon, 5950 m/19 521 ft, the highest peak in Canada; major rivers; the Mackenzie (W), and St Lawrence (E); Great Bear, 31 330 km^2/11 030 sq mi, and Great Slave, 28 570 km2/11 030 sq mi, are lakes in NW Territories.

Climate N coast permanently ice-bound or obstructed by ice floes, but for Hudson Bay (frozen c.9 months each year); mild winters and warm summers on Pacific coast and around Vancouver Island; average annual rainfall 145 mm/57 in.

Currency 1 Canadian Dollar (C$, Can$) = 100 cents

Economy Traditionally based on natural resources and agriculture: world's second largest exporter of wheat; world's largest producer of asbestos, zinc, silver, nickel; second largest producer of potash, gypsum, molybdenum, sulphur; hydroelectricity, oil (especially Alberta), natural gas; major industrial development in recent decades.

GDP (2002e) $934·1 bn, per capita $29 300

Human Development Index (2002) 0·940

History Evidence of Viking settlement c.1000; Newfoundland claimed for England, 1583; Champlain founded Quebec, 1608; Hudson's Bay Company founded, 1670; conflict between British and French in late 17th-c; Britain gained large areas from Treaty of Utrecht, 1713, after Seven Years' War, during which British

1991 World Cup victory, he was one of the early year-round players, spending the southern winter in the Sydney club competition and the northern winter in Italy. After retiring in 1998, he was appointed national coach to the Singapore Rugby Union.

camphor $C_{10}H_{16}O$, melting point 179°C. A colourless, waxy material (a terpene), occurring especially in the tree *Cinnamomum camphora*, and also synthesized from α–pinene. It is used in many lotions, mainly for its characteristic odour. **Camphorated oil** is a 20% solution of camphor in olive oil.

General James Wolfe captured Quebec from Louis Montcalm's forces in 1759, Treaty of Paris gave Britain almost all France's possessions in North America; Province of Quebec created, 1774; migration of loyalists from USA (1783) after War of Independence led to division of Quebec into Upper and Lower Canada; reunited as Canada, 1841; Dominion of Canada created (1867) by confederation of Quebec, Ontario, Nova Scotia, and New Brunswick; Rupert's Land and Northwest Territories bought from Hudson's Bay Company, 1869–70; joined by Manitoba (1870), British Columbia (1871), Prince Edward I (1873), Alberta and Saskatchewan (1905), and Newfoundland (1949); recurring political tension in recent decades arising from French-Canadian separatist movement in Quebec; Canada Act, 1982, gave Canada full responsibility for constitution; bicameral Federal Parliament includes Senate and a House of Commons; British monarch is Head of State, represented by a Governor-General; referendum on Quebec separation narrowly defeated in 1995.

Head of State
(British monarch represented by Governor-General)
1999– Adrienne Clarkson

Head of Government
1867–73 John Alexander MacDonald *Con*
1873–8 Alexander Mackenzie *Lib*
1878–91 John Alexander MacDonald *Con*
1891–2 John J C Abbot *Con*
1892–4 John Sparrow David Thompson *Con*
1894–6 Mackenzie Bowell *Con*
1896 Charles Tupper *Con*
1896–1911 Wilfrid Laurier *Lib*
1911–20 Robert Laird Borden *Con*
1920–1 Arthur Meighen *Con*
1921–6 William Lyon Mackenzie King *Lib*
1926 Arthur Meighen *Con*
1926–30 William Lyon Mackenzie King *Lib*
1930–5 Richard Bedford Bennett, 1st Viscount Bennett *Con*
1935–48 William Lyon Mackenzie King *Lib*
1948–57 Louis Stephen St Laurent *Lib*
1957–63 John George Diefenbaker *Con*
1963–8 Lester Bowles Pearson *Lib*
1968–79 Pierre Elliott Trudeau *Lib*
1979–80 Charles Joseph Clark *Con*
1980–4 Pierre Elliott Trudeau *Lib*
1984 John Napier Turner *Lib*
1984–93 (Martin) Brian Mulroney *Con*
1993 Kim Campbell *Con*
1993–2003 Jean Chrétien *Lib*
2003– Paul Martin *Lib*
Con Conservative *Lib* Liberal

Canadian provinces and territories
Name / Area (km^2 / sq mi) / Capital
Alberta / 661 190 / 255 285 / Edmonton
British Columbia / 947 800 / 365 945 / Victoria
Manitoba / 649 950 / 250 945 / Winnipeg
New Brunswick / 73 440 / 28 355 / Fredericton
Newfoundland / 405 720 / 156 648 / St John's
Northwest Territories / 3 426 320 / 1 322 902 / Yellowknife
Nova Scotia / 55 490 / 21 424 / Halifax
Nunavut / 2 093 190 / 807 971 / Iqaluit
Ontario / 1 068 580 / 412 578 / Toronto
Prince Edward Island / 5 660 / 2 185 / Charlottetown
Quebec / 1 540 680 / 594 856 / Quebec City
Saskatchewan / 652 380 / 251 883 / Regina
Yukon Territory / 483 450 / 186 660 / Whitehorse

camphor tree A name applied to several different trees, principally *Cinnamonium camphora*, a small evergreen growing to 6 m/20 ft with greenish-white flowers, native to Japan. Camphor is obtained by distillation of the bark. (Family: Lauraceae.)

Campi, Giulio [kampee] (c.1502–72) Architect and painter, born in Cremona, N Italy. He was influenced by Giulio Romano, and founded the Cremonese school of painting, to which his brothers **Vincenzo Campi** (1539–91) and **Antonio Campi** (1536–c.1591) also belonged. His work includes a fine altarpiece at Cremona.

Campin, Robert [kãmpīn] (c.1378–1444) Artist, born in Tournai, W Belgium. He was called **the Master of Flémalle** from his paintings of Flémelle Abbey near Liège. About 1400 he settled in Tournai, where Rogier van der Weyden was one of his pupils.

Campinas [kampeenas] 22°54S 47°60W, pop (2000e) 1 108 000. Town in São Paulo state, Sudeste region, SE Brazil; NW of São Paulo; agricultural institute; international and national airports; railway; two universities (1941, 1962); cotton, maize, sugar cane, coffee; cathedral, old market, colonial buildings.

campion An annual or perennial herb with opposite leaves and usually cymose inflorescences, of the same genus as catchflys, and native to the temperate N hemisphere; calyx tubular, 5 petals, notched or bifid, red or white depending on species. (Genus: *Silene*. Family: Caryophyllaceae.)

Campion, Edmund, St (1540–81) The first of the English Jesuit martyrs, born in London, UK. He studied at Oxford, and although made a deacon in the Church of England (1569) he leaned towards Roman Catholicism. Fearing arrest, he escaped to Douai, and in 1573 joined the Jesuits in Bohemia. In 1580 he was recalled from Prague, where he was professor of rhetoric, for a Jesuit mission to England. He circulated his *Decem rationes* (Ten Reasons) against Anglicanism in 1581, and was arrested, tortured, tried on a charge of conspiracy, and hanged in London. He was beatified in 1886, and canonized in 1970; feast day 1 December.

Campion, Jane (1954–) Film director, born in Waikanae, New Zealand. She studied at art school in Wellington and at the Australian Film, Television, and Radio School in Sydney, the city where she is now based. Her films include *Peel* (1984), which won the 1986 Cannes Palme d'Or for best short film, her highly original first feature *Sweetie* (1989), and *An Angel at My Table* (1990), based on Janet Frame's autobiographies. *The Piano* (1993), a love story set in colonial New Zealand, which she wrote as well as directed, shared the Palme d'Or at the 1993 Cannes Film Festival, the first such award for an Australian production and the first for a woman director. Later films include *The Portrait of a Lady* (1996), *Holy Smoke* (1999), and *In the Cut* (2003).

Campoli, Alfredo [kampohlee] (1906–91) Violinist, born in Rome, Italy. He went to London in 1911, and quickly won a reputation as a soloist. During the lean years of the 1930s he became better known for his salon orchestra. This was disbanded at the outbreak of World War 2, after which he emerged as one of the outstanding violinists of his time.

camshaft A rotating shaft upon which **cams** are fixed. A cam is a flat plate cut to a defined shape which rotates about an axis perpendicular to the plane of the plate. The shape of the cams and their relative orientation actuate and time the lifting of valves as part of an engine's operating cycle.

Camulodunum [kamulodoonum] The name for ancient Colchester, the capital first of the Belgic kingdom of Cunobelinus and then of the Roman province of Britain. Destroyed in the revolt of Boudicca in AD 60, it later recovered, but yielded its capital status to Londinium (London).

Camus, Albert [kahmü] (1913–60) French existentialist writer, born in Mondovi, NE Algeria. He studied philosophy at Algiers, and worked as an actor, teacher, playwright, and journalist there and in Paris. Active in the French resistance during World War 2, he became co-editor with Sartre of the left-wing newspaper *Combat* after the liberation until 1948. He earned an international reputation with his nihilistic novel, *L'Etranger* (1942, The Outsider). Later novels include *La Peste* (1947, The Plague) and *La Chute* (1956, The Fall), and he also wrote plays and several political works. He received the Nobel Prize for Literature in 1957.

Canaan [kaynan, kanayan] The land of the ancient Semitic-speaking peoples, living in the coastal areas of modern Israel and Syria, but perhaps also extending inland to the Jordan R and the Dead Sea. It was divided into various city-states during the early 2nd millennium BC, but mostly fell under the control of Israelites and other powers from the late 13th-c BC. The name can be traced to one of the sons of Ham (*Gen* 9–10).

Canada *pp.266–7*

Canada, Order of A decoration established in Canada in 1967, with three categories: Companion, Medal of Courage, and Medal of Service. The Medal of Courage was converted to three decorations in 1972: the Cross of Valour, the Star of Courage, and the Medal of Bravery. Three levels of membership were created: Companions, Officers, and Members, with the Governor-General of Canada as the Chancellor and principal Companion of the Order.

Canada Company A colonization company established in Upper Canada (Ontario) in 1824. It sold more than a million acres of land to settlers in the area around L Huron, and laid foundations for the towns of Guelph, Galt, and Goderich.

Canada Day A public holiday in Canada (observed 1 Jul), the anniversary of the union of the provinces in 1867; formerly known as **Dominion Day**.

Canada First Movement A political movement in Canada, founded in Ontario in 1868. Its objectives were to ensure that the newly-confederated Dominion of Canada would not collapse over regional disputes. It increasingly promoted a policy of Canadian self-determination and autonomy in international relations. Its view of Canadian nationality was aggressively anglophone and Protestant.

Canada goose A goose native to North America, and introduced in Europe and New Zealand (*Branta canadensis*); head and neck black with white chin; eats grass and water plants; migrates; females often return to own birthplace to breed, producing many local races and variations. (Family: Anatidae.)

Canadian art The art associated with Canada which, since the 17th-c, has mixed European – especially French – and local folk elements. Late 18th-c churches reflect the styles of Georgian Britain and the American colonies. The Parliament building in Ottawa, by Thomas Fuller (c.1859), is Gothic Revival. The late 19th-c saw the foundation of the Royal Canadian Academy and the National Gallery of Canada (both 1880), and the first major private collections. By the early 20th-c, Canadians who had studied in Paris began painting Canadian scenery in an Impressionist style, but European avant-garde movements made little impact before the 1940s.

Canadian literature Canadian literature is written in both English and French. The two traditions are overlapping but distinct, not least because the French is older and more embattled within an idealized past. This may be why it is more noted for its poetry, much of it in late Symbolist style, following Saint-Denis-Garneau. Writers in English have generally preferred prose. Humorists such as Stephen Leacock, novelists such as the popular Mazo de la Roche (eg *Jalna*, 1927) and the realist Frederick Grove (1879–1948), Morley Callaghan, and Mordechai Richler, and cultural critics Northrop Frye (1912–91) and Marshall McLuhan have established a world-wide readership. Another important author, Margaret Atwood, provides a guide in her *Survival: A Thematic Guide to Canadian Literature* (1972).

Canadian National Railway *Canadian Pacific Railway*

Canadian National Tower *C N Tower*

Canadian Pacific Railway (CPR) A transcontinental railway, constructed 1881–5, linking the Dominion of Canada with British Columbia. Carried out with large government cash subsidies and enormous land grants to the railway company, the project represented an act of political will and an engineering triumph. It produced a chain of western railway towns terminating in Vancouver on the Pacific coast. In 1922 a second transcontinental system was introduced, the **Canadian National Railway (CNR)**, running from Halifax, Novia Scotia, to Vancouver. There followed a period of intense competition, which was ended only by government intervention in 1933. Canadian National's passenger services were taken over by VIA Rail Canada in 1978. The company has since diversified into a wide range of communication and service industries.

Canadian Rocky Mountain Parks A group of five national parks (Banff, Jasper, Waterton Lakes, Kootenay, Yoho) in Alberta and British Columbia, Canada. Together with the Burgess Shale site – an important geological fossil region in the Selkirk Mts of British Columbia – these constitute a world heritage site.

Canadian Shield or **Laurentian Shield** Vast area of ancient pre-Cambrian rocks, forming a low plateau covering over half of Canada; S boundary runs from the Labrador coast around Hudson Bay, through Quebec and Ontario to the Arctic near the Mackenzie R mouth; extends into parts of N USA; many lakes and swamps, remnants of Pleistocene glaciation; generally infertile, but a rich source of minerals, forest products, and hydroelectricity.

Canadian waterweed A submerged aquatic plant native to North America (*Elodea canadensis*); stems growing to 3 m/10 ft, brittle, with whorls of narrow, dark-green leaves; flowers 5 mm/¼ in, floating, three greenish-purple sepals, three translucent white petals. Introduced to Europe, where male plants are quite rare, they spread by vegetative reproduction, for a while becoming a nuisance, blocking waterways. (Family: Hydrocharitaceae.)

canal An artificial watercourse for inland navigation or for connecting seas. The first modern canal in the UK was the Sankey Brook from the Mersey to St Helens, built by Henry Berry between 1755 and 1772. Rather more famous was the canal from Worsley to Manchester built by James Brindley for the Duke of Bridgewater, opened in 1761. Thousands of miles of canal were built, and they were the major method of transporting goods until the mid-19th-c, when the railways superseded them. After a long period of decline, more recently many canals have been restored, and nowadays are principally used for leisure activities. Many larger canals are in use throughout Europe, North America, and Asia, such as the 1000 mi Grand Canal in China (the world's longest artificial inland waterway), built in AD 610. The Romans also built canals. The chief sea-connecting canals are those of Suez and Panama.

Canaletto [kanal**e**toh], originally **Giovanni Antonio Canal** (1697–1768) Painter, born in Venice, NE Italy. He studied at Rome, then painted a renowned series of views in Venice, many as souvenirs for foreign visitors. He spent most of the years 1746–56 in England, where his views of London and elsewhere proved extremely popular. He later returned to Venice and was elected to the Venice Academy in 1763.

canary A small finch, native to the Old World; prized as a songbird; also known as **serin**. All domestic varieties of the cage canary were developed from one species, *Serinus canaria*, from the Canary Is. (Genus: *Serinus*, 32 species. Family: Fringillidae.)

Canary Islands *p.269*

Canary whitewood *tulip tree*

canasta A card game similar to rummy. It derives from the Spanish word *canasta* ('basket'), probably referring to the tray into which cards were discarded. The game originated in Uruguay in the 1940s. Its most popular form is played with two standard packs of playing cards and four jokers. The object is to collect as many cards of the same denomination as possible. All cards have points value, but jokers and deuces (twos) are 'wild' (ie can take any value). Cards are picked up and discarded.

Canaveral, Cape [kan**a**veral], formerly **Cape Kennedy** (1963–73) 28°28N 80°28W. Cape in Brevard Co, E Florida, USA, on the E coast of the Canaveral peninsula; US crewed space flights launched from here since 1961.

Canberra [k**a**nbera] 35°18S 149°08E, pop (2000e) 308 300. National and regional capital in Australian Capital Territory, SE Australia, on the Molonglo R; planned by US architect Walter Burley Griffin (after a competition, 1911); building started in 1913; has extensive parks and gardens; Commonwealth Parliament moved from Melbourne, 1927; airport; railway; two universities (1946, 1989); Australian War Memorial, National Library, National Museum, National Gallery, High Court, Par-

Canary Islands

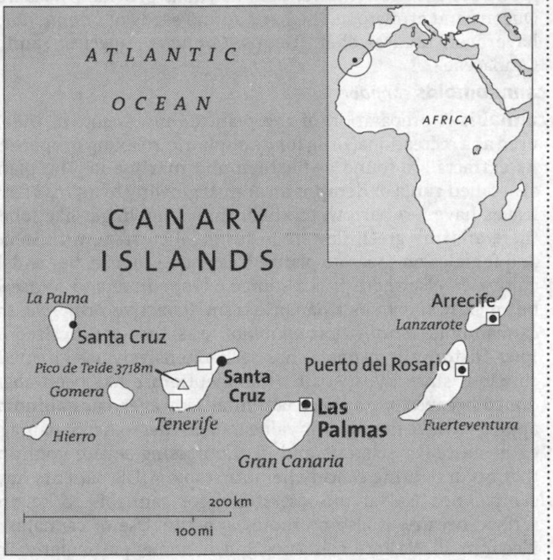

☐ International Airport

Span **Islas Canarias**

Local name Islas Canarias

Area 7273 km²/2807 sq mi

Population total (2000e) 1 475 000

Status Forms two provinces of Spain

Chief town Las Palmas

Physical features Island archipelago, located in the Atlantic, 100 km/60 mi off the NW coast of Africa; includes the islands of Tenerife, La Palma, Gomera, Hierro, Grand Canary (Gran Canaria), Fuerteventura, Lanzarote, and several uninhabited islands; major ports, Las Palmas, Santa Cruz; volcanic and mountainous, the Pico de Teide rises to 3718 m/12 198 ft on Tenerife; tourist resorts on main islands.

Climate Continental; average annual temperature 18°C (Jan), 24°C (Jul); average annual rainfall 196 mm/8 in.

Currency 1 euro = 100 cents (previous to February 2002, 1 Peseta (Pta, Pa) = 100 céntimos)

Economy Tourism; agriculture, fishing, canning, textiles, leatherwork, footwear, cork, timber, chemical and metal products.

liament House (1927, new building opened in 1988 by the Queen); devastating bush fires in suburbs (Jan 2003).

cancan (Fr 'scandal') A high kicking and risqué dance popularized in the Paris music-halls c.1830. It is normally danced by four women in 4/4 time. Although danced to many tunes, it is associated with Offenbach's *Orpheus in the Underworld* (1858).

Cancer (Lat 'crab') An inconspicuous N constellation of the zodiac, lying between Gemini and Leo. It contains an open star cluster, Praesepe, just visible by eye.

cancer A general term to denote all forms of malignant tumour. Tumours occur when the cells of a tissue or organ multiply in an uncontrolled fashion unrelated to the biological requirements of the body and not to meet the needs of repair or of normal replacement. In contrast to *benign* tumours, which enlarge in a specific place, and cause damage by pressure on adjacent tissues, *malignant* tumours invade, destroy, and spread to other tissues. The cells of a malignant tumour may also be carried in the blood stream and lymphatics, and lodge in distant organs where they continue to spread and enlarge (*metastases*). Cancer kills by destroying vital tissues, by interfering with the performance of their functions through ulceration, bleeding, and infection, and by affecting bodily nutrition.

Microscopic examination of the cells of malignant tumours often reveals the special characteristics of the cells of its tissue of origin. Sometimes the cells lose these characteristics and are totally undifferentiated (*anaplastic*). Tumours of this cell type tend to be rapidly growing and highly malignant. Identification of the tissue of origin is important, as it may give a clue to the possible origin of the tumour, its natural course, the outlook for the patient, and the most appropriate treatment. Each cell or tissue type of malignancy has its own profile of age and sex occurrence. Thus one specific cancer of the back of the eye occurs equally in both sexes and occurs only in infancy, while cancer of the stomach is twice as common in men as in women and its frequency rises with age from adolescence. The cause of cancer is unknown, but appears to depend upon an interplay between factors in the environment and the genetic component of body cells. Only a small number of cancers are determined solely by inherited factors. The great majority are related to exposure to one or more environmental factors which predisposes to the cancer. These factors are known as *carcinogenic agents*, with cigarette smoking being the most important known. Both chemotherapy and radiotherapy treatments for cancer are available.

candela [kandayla] Base SI unit of luminous intensity; symbol *cd*; defined as the luminous intensity, in a given direction, of a source that emits monochromatic radiation of frequency 540×10^{12} Hz, and has a radiant intensity in that direction of 1/683 watt per steradian; obsolete name **candle**.

Candida [kandida] A genus of fungi known from its yeast-like vegetative state; parasitic in animals; includes *Candida albicans*, the causative agent of thrush in humans. (Family: Cryptococcaceae.)

candidiasis [kandidiyasis] A disease caused by *Candida albicans*, a yeast which normally inhabits the gut and vagina without causing symptoms. In debilitating conditions and when the immune system is depressed, it may invade the surface of the skin and the mucous membranes of the vagina and gastro-intestinal tract, including the mouth, where white patches can be seen with the naked eye. This is known as **thrush**. In rare cases it can invade the blood stream and prove fatal.

candle A light source typically consisting of a wax cylinder (stearic acid, paraffin wax, etc) with a central fibrous wick, known from ancient times (at least 3000 BC). Light is generated by burning liquid wax melted by the flame and drawn up the wick by capillary action. The **International Standard Candle** was a measure of light-source intensity, now replaced by the *candela*.

Candlemas A Christian festival (2 Feb) commemorating the purification of the Virgin Mary after the birth of Jesus, and the presentation of Jesus in the Jerusalem Temple (*Luke* 2). The name is derived from the lighted candles carried in procession on that day. It is also a Scottish quarter-day.

Candolle, Augustin Pyrame de [kãdol] (1778–1841) Botanist, born in Geneva, SW Switzerland. He studied medicine in Geneva, and from 1798 botany in Paris, and by 1813 had developed a general scheme of plant taxonomy which was to dominate plant classification for 50 years, his *Théorie élémentaire de la botanique*. He used the scheme in a major series of volumes on botany, completed by his son **Alphonse de Candolle** (1806–93). He also did much to establish plant geography and to relate vegetation to soil type, a study supported by his extensive expeditions.

candytuft An annual, biennial, or evergreen perennial, native to Europe and Asia; leaves narrow; flowers white or mauve, in flattened heads, cross-shaped with outer two petals of outermost flowers enlarged. Several large-flowered species and cultivars are ornamentals. (Genus: *Iberis*, 30 species. Family: Cruciferae.)

cane *bamboo; sugar cane*

Canea *Chania*

cane rat An African cavy-like rodent; large (length, up to 75 cm/30 in; weight, 9 kg/20 lb); short tail and broad blunt snout; lives near water; may damage sugar-cane plantations. (Family: Thryonomyidae.)

cane sugar *sugar cane*

Canes Venatici [**kan**eez vena**t**isiy] (Lat 'hunting dogs') An inconspicuous constellation in the N hemisphere which includes the famous Whirlpool Galaxy.

Canetti, Elias [kanetee] (1905–94) Writer, born in Rustschuk, Bulgaria. He was educated at schools in England, Austria, Switzerland, and Germany, and lived in England from 1938, though continued to write in German. His interest in crowd psychology produced two important works: the novel *Die Blendung* (1936, trans as both Auto da Fé and The Tower of Babel) and the study *Masse und Macht* (1960, Crowds and Power). He was awarded the Nobel Prize for Literature in 1981.

Cange, seigneur du *du Cange, Charles du Fresne*

Canidae [**kan**idee] The dog family of carnivores (36 species), usually with slender legs, lean muzzles, large erect ears, and bushy tails; four toes on hind feet, usually five on front; blunt claws not retractable; colour usually without stripes or spots; small canids may hunt alone by stalking then pouncing; larger may hunt in packs and run prey to exhaustion.

canine hip dysplasia (HD) A disorder in the development of the hip joint in dogs. The head of the femur becomes flattened, and its seating remains shallow, so that the joint fails to engage properly. Complications include boney outgrowths around the joint, and arthritis. The normal 'ball and socket' arrangement thus becomes ineffective and fails to articulate effectively, leading to lameness. There is a characteristic rolling gait and some hip pain, especially on rising. Treatment may be medical and palliative for mild cases, with surgical procedures for more severe cases. There is a high degree of inheritance in a number of dog breeds, especially the larger gundogs and German shepherd dogs, but it is virtually unknown in greyhounds. Several control schemes are run by kennel clubs and veterinary associations around the world.

canine parvovirus A serious viral infection of dogs and other canids, which emerged in the late 1970s. Its highly infectious nature was evidenced by its appearance in most countries around the world within a very short time. The most characteristic feature of the disease is very severe persistent diarrhoea with blood, and there may be vomiting and a high fever. Puppies may die of shock and dehydration very soon after signs appear. Other cases may have serious heart changes. The disease is now well controlled by effective vaccines.

canine progressive retinal atrophy (PRA) An inherited disease of the retina affecting a wide variety of dog breeds, especially certain working and gundog varieties. The condition also occurs in cats, with the Abyssinian breed apparently the most affected. Clinical signs vary with the location of the degeneration on the retina. Central PRA is seen in older dogs, and mainly affects day vision. Night blindness is associated with a more peripheral atrophy of the retina. Control schemes are operated by veterinary associations working with kennel clubs and breed societies.

Canis Major [**kan**is] (Lat 'great dog') A constellation in the S hemisphere, partly in the Milky Way. It includes Sirius, the brightest star in our sky.

Canis Minor [**kan**is] (Lat 'little dog') A small N hemisphere constellation. Its brightest star is Procyon, just 3·5 parsec away, and the eighth brightest star in the sky. It has a faint white dwarf companion.

canker (botany) A general term for a localized disease of woody plants, in which bark formation is prevented; typically caused by bacteria or fungi.

canker (zoology) A disease of animals, characterized by open sores or ulcers; name used for several conditions, such as inflammation of a horse's foot involving a fluid discharge, eczema on a dog's ear, an abscess on a bird, or an infestation of mites in the ear of a cat (*ear canker*, or *otodectic mange*).

canna A tuberous perennial, native to Central and tropical North America; leaves broadly lance-shaped, stalks sheathing stem; flowers in a spike, three sepals, three petals, 4–6 stamens, petal-like and brightly coloured; fruit a warty capsule; often grown for the showy flowers. *Canna edulis* provides the starch Queensland arrowroot. The hard, round seeds of *Canna indica* have been used as shot. (Genus: *Canna*, 55 species. Family: Cannaceae.)

cannabinoids *cannabis*

cannabis A preparation of the plant *Cannabis sativa*, widely used as a recreational drug for its euphoric, relaxing properties: its extracts are found as **hashish** and **marijuana**. The plant, also called **ganja** or **hemp**, is an annual growing to 2·5 m/8 ft; its leaves have 5–7 narrow, toothed, spreading, finger-like lobes; there are tiny green flowers in terminal clusters, with males and females on separate plants. It is native to Asia, but widely cultivated elsewhere. It is a source of rope fibre and birdseed, but is best known as a narcotic resin. Its active principle, the cannabinoid *tetrahydrocannabinol*, was first synthesized in 1967. Historically, cannabis has been extensively used in medicine, but since the 1930s its therapeutic use has been abandoned because of its abuse potential. However, **cannabinoids** appear to have therapeutic value in pain due to nerve damage, eg in muscular sclerosis and in suppressing severe vomiting that occurs during cancer chemotherapy. AIDS patients have campaigned (so far unsuccessfully) for cannabis to be prescribed because it also promotes appetite. Use of cannabis is illegal in all Western countries, but in some, particularly The Netherlands, it has been decriminalized and its sale is tolerated. In 1991 a receptor for cannabis was discovered in the human brain, and since then several molecules have been identified in the brain which bind to them. These molecules are believed to be the brain's own 'cannabis'. They probably act as neurotransmitters to modify mood, memory, and muscle function, and may also have other functions. (Family: Cannabidaceae.)

Cannadine, David (1950–) Historian, born in Birmingham, West Midlands, C England, UK. He studied at Cambridge and Oxford universities, and became a fellow of Christ's College, Cambridge (1977). In 1998 he was appointed professor of history at Columbia University, New York, and also became director of the Institute of Historical Research at London University. His books include *The Decline and Fall of the British Aristocracy* (1990), *G M Trevelyan* (1992), *Class in Britain* (1998), and *Ornamentalism: how the British saw their Empire* (2001).

Cannes [kan] 43°33N 7°00E, pop (2000e) 72 600. Fashionable resort town on the French Riviera in Alpes-Maritimes department, SE France, on the Golfe de la Napoule; airport; railway; fruit, flowers, textiles; major tourist centre, with many beaches and yachting harbours; mild winter and temperate summer climate; casinos; International Film Festival (May), International Fireworks Festival (Aug).

Cannes Film Festival Awards One of the world's leading film festivals, established in 1939. Now held annually in May, over the years the categories have varied and widened and awards are currently given for best film, which receives the Palme d'Or (inaugurated 1955), director, actor and actress.

Canning, George (1770–1827) British statesman, born in London, UK. He studied at Oxford and Lincoln's Inn, and entered parliament for Newport, Isle of Wight (1794) as a supporter of Pitt. He became under-secretary of state (1796), treasurer of the navy (1804–6), and minister for foreign affairs (1807). His disapproval of the Walcheren expedition led to a misunderstanding with Castlereagh, which resulted in a duel. He became MP for Liverpool (1812), ambassador to Lisbon (1814), President of the Board of Control (1816), and MP for Harwich (1822). Nominated Governor-General of India (1822), he was on the eve of departure when Castlereagh's suicide saw him installed as foreign secretary. In this post he gave a new impetus to commerce by advocating tariff reductions. He was the first to recognize the free states of Spanish America; promoted the union of Britain, France, and Russia in the cause of Greece (1827); protected Portugal from Spanish invasion; contended earnestly for Catholic Emancipation; and prepared the way for a repeal of the Corn Laws. In 1827 he formed an administration with the aid of the Whigs, but died the same year.

canning A food preservation process relying on the sterilization of foods by heating in a container sealed before or immediately after the heat treatment. The idea was first applied in 1810 by Nicolas Appert (c.1750–1841) to foods sealed in bottles and heated, but since 1839 in cans made of tinned thin steel sheet. Aluminium or plastic sometimes now replaces steel. Internal coatings are chosen to resist the chemical properties of different contents. The processes are now highly automated, and food growing is usually closely associated with a canning plant.

Cannizzaro, Stanislao [kaneedzahroh] (1826–1910) Chemist, born in Palermo, Sicily, S Italy. He was professor of chemistry at Genoa, Palermo, and Rome. In 1860, while at Genoa, he marched with Garibaldi's Thousand. He was the first to appreciate the importance of Amedeo Avogadro's work in connection with atomic weights. He co-ordinated organic and inorganic chemistry, and discovered the reaction named after him.

Cannon, Annie Jump (1863–1941) Astronomer, born in Dover, Delaware, USA. She became deaf through contracting scarlet fever, entered Radcliffe College to study astronomy, and was appointed to the staff of the Harvard College Observatory in 1896. She reorganized the classification of stars in terms of surface temperature, and developed great skill in cataloguing them. Her classification of over 225 000 stars brighter than 9th or 10th magnitude was a major contribution.

Cannon, W(alter) B(radford) (1871–1945) Physiologist, born in Prairie du Chien, Wisconsin, USA. He studied medicine at Harvard, where he taught (1899–1942), becoming renowned for his use of X-rays in the study of the alimentary tract, and for his work on the effects of haemorrhage and shock. He went on to study hormones and nerve transmission, and developed the concept of a constant internal physiological environment, which he named *homoeostasis*.

Cano, Juan Sebastian del [kahnoh] (?–1526) The first man to circumnavigate the globe, born in Guetaria on the Bay of Biscay. In 1519 he sailed with Magellan in command of the *Concepción*. After Magellan's death in the Philippines, he safely navigated the *Victoria* home to Spain, arriving in 1522.

canoe A small, double-ended open craft propelled with paddles. There are two main types: a vessel carrying three or four people, made from a light wooden framework, traditionally covered with birch bark or hides, but latterly using thin wooden planks; and the Pacific dugout canoe, often fitted with an outrigger, which could be made capable of ocean voyages. Maori war canoes were up to 20 m/70 ft long, fashioned from a single pine tree, fitted with one inverted-triangle-shaped sail, and propelled by c.60 paddlers. Many modern canoes are made from aluminium or plastics.

canoeing A water sport practised in canoes, developed by British barrister John Macgregor (1825–92) in 1865. The Canoe Club was formed the following year. Two types of canoe are used in competition: the *kayak*, which has a keel, with the canoeist sitting in the boat, and the *Canadian canoe*, which has no keel, with the canoeist kneeling. The number of persons per craft varies between one and four.

canon (music) A strictly ordered texture in which polyphony is derived from a single line by imitation of itself at fixed intervals of time and pitch. In other words, all the canonic parts are the same, but they overlap each other. The term *canon* originally referred to the verbal, symbolic, or cryptic 'rule' by which the imitations are formed.

canon (religion) **1** In Christianity, a list of the inspired writings regarded as comprising Holy Scripture. The precise limits of the Old and New Testament canons were debated in the early Christian centuries, and Protestants and Roman Catholics still differ regarding the inclusion of some works. The term is also sometimes used to comprise the rules regarding liturgy, the life and discipline of the Church, and other decisions of the Councils. **2** The prayer of consecration in the Roman Catholic Mass. **3** The ecclesiastical title of clergy attached to cathedrals or certain endowed churches; either **secular** or, if living under semi-monastic rule, **regular** (eg Augustinian). In the Church of England, **residentiary** canons are the salaried staff of a cathedral, responsible for the upkeep of the building; **non-residentiary** canons are unsalaried, but have certain privileges, including rights with regard to the election of bishops.

canonization The culmination of a lengthy process in the Roman Catholic Church whereby, after a long process of enquiry, a deceased individual is declared a saint, or entitled to public veneration. It confers various honours, such as a festival day, and the dedication of churches to his/her memory. In the Orthodox Church, there is a similar but less formal procedure.

canon law In the Roman Catholic Church, a body of rules or laws to be observed in matters of faith, morals, and discipline. It developed out of the decisions of the Councils of the Church, and the decrees of popes and influential bishops. A notable compilation was made by Gratian in his *Decretum* (1140), which, with later additions, formed the *Corpus juris canonici* (completely revised in 1917 and 1983). Pre-Reformation canon law is observed in the Church of England, subject to revisions such as the Book of Canons (1604–6) and Code (1964–9).

Canopus [kanohpus] *Carina*

Canova, Antonio [kanohva] (1757–1822) Sculptor, born in Possagno, NE Italy. He studied at Venice and Rome, and came to be regarded as the founder of a new Neoclassicist school. His best-known works are the tombs of popes Clement XIII (1787–92) and XIV (1783–7), several statues of Napoleon, and one of his sister Princess Borghese reclining as Venus Victrix (1805–7). In 1802 he was appointed by Pius VII as curator of works of art.

Cantabria [kantabria] pop (2000e) 531 000; area 5289 sq km/2041 sq mi. Autonomous region of N Spain, co-extensive with the modern province of Santander; stretches across the Cordillera Cantabrica (1382 m/4534 ft) to the headwaters of the R Ebro; capital, Santander.

Cantabrian Mountains, Span **Cordillera Cantabrica** Mountain range in N Spain, extending 500 km/310 mi W–E from Galicia along the Bay of Biscay to the Pyrenees, and forming a barrier between the sea and the C plateau (Meseta) of Spain; highest point, the Picos de Europa massif (2648 m/8688 ft); rich in minerals, and a source of hydroelectric power.

cantata Music which is 'sung'. The Italian solo cantata of the 17th–18th-c was a setting of secular (usually amatory) verses, alternating recitative and aria. Lutheran cantatas (eg those of Bach) were church compositions for soloists, choir, and instruments. More recent cantatas, whether sacred or secular, are usually choral and orchestral pieces, with or without soloists; many are festival or commemorative pieces.

Canterbury, Lat **Durovernum**, Anglo-Saxon **Cantwaraburh** 51°17N 1°05E, pop (2001e) 135 300. Market town in Kent, SE England, UK; St Augustine began the conversion of England to Christianity here, 597; Archbishopric founded 602; Thomas Becket murdered (1170) in Canterbury Cathedral; seat of the Primate of the Anglican Church; important literary associations with Chaucer, Marlowe, Defoe, Dickens, and Maugham; railway; University of Kent (1965); tourism, engineering, glass; cathedral (11th–15th-c); Churches of St Dunstan, St George, St Martin, St Mildred, and St Peter; St Augustine's College; the Weavers, half-timbered Tudor houses; city walls; cricket festival (Aug).

Canterbury bell A robust hairy biennial (*Campanula medium*), native to Italy, introduced elsewhere; flowers 4–5 cm/1½–2 in, bell-shaped, dark blue, in long spikes; popular ornamental; garden forms in many colours. (Family: Campanulaceae.)

Canterbury Tales A series of linked narrative poems (and prose pieces) by Geoffrey Chaucer, composed during the last two decades of the 14th-c: the most important English work of literature from mediaeval times. Modelled on Boccaccio's *Decameron*, the tales are told by a group of pilgrims on the road to Canterbury. The Prologue, introducing the 29 pilgrims, is a gallery of contrasting characters, including the Knight, the Squire, the prim Prioress, the bawdy Miller, and the much-married Wife of Bath. Their 24 tales (the plan is incomplete) are told in a remarkable variety of poetic styles, from the romance to the comic fabliau.

Canticles *Song of Solomon*

cantilever A horizontal building element where the part hidden within the building bears a downward force, and the other part projects outside without external bracing, and so appears to be self-supporting. It is often used to dramatic effect in modern architecture.

Canton (China) *Guangzhou*

Canton (USA) 40°48N 81°23W, pop (2000e) 80 800. Seat of Stark Co, E Ohio, USA; railway; iron and steel industry; home and burial place of President McKinley, 25th US president; National Professional Football Hall of Fame.

canton A territorial division of land. In Switzerland, cantons have their own separate governments; in France, cantons are sub-divisions of *arrondissements*, which are themselves sub-divisions of the regional *départements*.

Cantona, Eric [kantona] (1966–) Footballer, born in Paris, France. Brought up in Marseille, he made his professional debut for Auxerre in 1983, and won his first French International cap in 1987. He moved to Leeds United in 1991 and to Manchester United in 1993, becoming the first foreigner to win the Professional Footballers' Association Player of the year award in 1994. An aggressive and tempestuous player, his career was interrupted by a series of suspensions, and his temperament became a focus of public debate when he was sentenced to 120 hours community service after kicking out at a Crystal Palace fan who had been insulting him. A football idol for a generation of fans, he announced his retirement in 1997, and began a career in films. In 2003 he received the Overseas Player of the Decade award, presented by the FA Premier League to mark the first 10 years of the Premiership.

Cantonese *Chinese*

Cantor, Georg (Ferdinand Ludwig Philipp) (1845–1918) Mathematician, born in St Petersburg, NW Russia. He studied at Berlin and Göttingen, and in 1877 became professor of mathematics at Halle. He worked out a highly original arithmetic of the infinite which resulted in a theory of infinite sets of different sizes, adding a new and important branch to mathematics. He suffered a nervous breakdown in 1884, and died in an asylum.

Canute or **Cnut**, sometimes known as **the Great** (c.995–1035) King of England (from 1016), Denmark (from 1019), and Norway (from 1028), the younger son of Sweyn Forkbeard. He first campaigned in England in 1013, and after his father's death (1014) became king of Denmark. He successively challenged Ethelred the Unready and his successor Edmund Ironside for the English throne. He defeated Edmund in 1016 at the Battle of Assandun (possibly Ashdon, Essex), secured Mercia and Northumbria, and became King of all England after Edmund's death. In 1017 he married **Emma of Normandy**, the widow of Ethelred. He ruled England according to the accepted traditions of English kingship, and maintained the peace throughout his reign. A story is told by the 12th-c historian, Henry of Huntingdon, that Canute rebuked his flatterers by showing that even he, as king, could not stop the incoming tide nor, by implication, the might of God.

canyon A deep valley with almost vertical sides which have been cut by a river, often in arid or semi-arid regions. Submarine canyons form on continental slopes, and are thought to have been eroded by turbidity currents.

Canyon de Chelly [shay] National monument in NE Arizona, USA; established in 1931 to protect notable Indian cliff dwellings, dating from c.350 AD; area 339 sq km/131 sq mi.

Capa, Robert, originally **Andrei Friedmann** (1913–54) Photojournalist, born in Budapest, Hungary. He recorded the Spanish Civil War (1935–7), covered China under the Japanese attacks of 1938, and reported World War 2 in Europe from the Normandy invasion onwards. He was killed by a landmine in the Indo-China fighting which preceded the war in Vietnam.

capacitance The measure of a system's ability to store electric charge; symbol *C*, units F (*farad*); for a capacitor comprising two separate parallel conductors, the capacitance is equal to the charge on one conductor divided by the potential difference between the two. For an electrical circuit, elements are usually quoted as μF (*microfarad*, 10^{-6} F) or pF (*picofarad*, 10^{-12} F).

Cape Breton Island pop (2000e) 200 500; area 10 295 sq km/3974 sq mi. Island in Nova Scotia, Canada; separated from mainland by the Strait of Canso; almost bisected by Bras d'Or Lake (arm of the sea); chief towns, Sydney, Glace Bay, Louisburg; Cape Breton Highlands National Park in NW (1936); many people of Scottish descent, with Gaelic still spoken; dairy farming, fishing, timber, coal mining, gypsum, tourism; originally French (Ile Royale), taken by British, 1758; joined to Nova Scotia, 1820.

Cape buffalo *African buffalo*

Cape Cod A sandy peninsula of SE Massachusetts, USA; length 105 km/65 mi; width up to 32 km/20 mi; bounded E by the Atlantic and W by Cape Cod Bay; crossed by the 13 km/8 mi Cape Cod Canal; on 15 May 1602 Bartholomew Gosnold recorded, 'Near this cape...we took great store of codfish...and called it Cape Cod'; pilgrims from the *Mayflower* landed near Provincetown in November 1620; airfield at Provincetown; a popular resort area.

Cape Coloured or **Coloured** A term used in South Africa to refer to a group of people of mixed descent, arising from the unions of Europeans with slaves (from Madagascar, Mozambique, or the East) or Khoikoi (Hottentots). They number about 3·2 million people (c.8·5% of the total population), mainly living in the towns and rural areas of the Western Cape province. Culturally akin to White South Africans, most Coloureds speak Afrikaans and are Christian, with a small Muslim minority (Cape Malays). In South Africa's former racial hierarchy, they were ranked between Europeans and Black Africans living in separate areas on city outskirts, with their own schools and other facilities, and with limited rights within the country's political system. They are mostly farm labourers, factory workers, and artisans, with a small middle class.

Cape gooseberry A perennial native to South America (*Physalis peruviana*), related and very similar to Chinese lantern; yellow flowers; calyx bladder-like, enclosing an edible yellow berry. (Family: Solanaceae.)

Cape hunting dog *African hunting dog*

Cape jasmine A species of gardenia (*Gardenia jasminoides*) with large flowers up to 10 cm/4 in diameter. A double-flowered form is a popular pot plant and corsage. (Family: Rubiaceae.)

Čapek, Karel [chapek] (1890–1938) Writer, born in Schwadonitz, W Czech Republic, the brother of Josef Čapek (1887–1945). He is remembered above all for his play *R.U.R.* (Rossum's Universal Robots), produced in 1921, showing mechanization rampant. With his brother he wrote the comic fantasy *Ze Života hmyzu* (1921, The Insect Play), one of several pieces foreshadowing totalitarianism, as well as short stories on crime and mystery, prophetic science-fiction, and travel-books.

Capella [kapela] *Auriga*

Cape Provinces, Afrikaans **Kaapprovinsie** Former province in South Africa; founded, 1652; formally ceded to Britain (Cape Colony), 1814; separate parliament, 1850; joined Union of South Africa, 1910; since the 1994 constitution, divided into three provinces: Northern, Western, and Eastern.

caper A sprawling, deciduous, spiny shrub (*Capparis spinosa*), native to S Europe; leaves alternate, oval, slightly fleshy; flowers 5–7 cm/2–2¾ in in diameter, 4-petalled, white with numerous long purple stamens. The young flower buds are pickled as **capers**. (Family: Capparidaceae.)

capercaillie [kaperkaylee] A large grouse native to Europe and N Asia, also known as **capercailzie**; usually solitary; forest-dwelling; males have special mating calls, and display by leaping into

Cape Verde

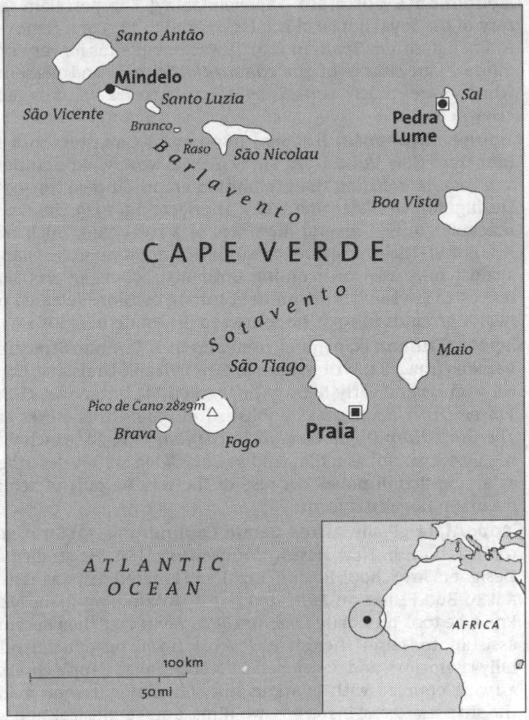

☐ International Airport

[kayp vaird], official name **Republic of Cape Verde**, Port **República de Cabo Verde**
Local name Cabo Verde
Timezone GMT −1
Area 4033 km²/1557 sq mi
Population total (2002e) 453 000
Status Island group
Date of independence 1975
Capital Praia (on São Tiago Island)
Languages Portuguese (official), Crioulo (Portuguese-based creole)
Ethnic groups Creole (mulatto) (60%), African (28%), European (2%)
Religion Roman Catholic (80%), others (20%)
Physical features Island group in the Atlantic Ocean off W Coast of Africa, c.500 km/310 mi W of Dakar, Senegal; Barlavento (windward) group in N, Sotavento (leeward) group in S; mostly mountainous islands of volcanic origin; highest peak, Pico do Cano, 2829 m/9281 ft; active volcano on Fogo I; fine sandy beaches on most islands.
Climate Arid climate; located at N limit of tropical rain belt; low and unreliable rainfall (Aug Sep); small temperature range throughout year; average annual temperature 23°C; average annual rainfall 250 mm/10 in.
Currency 1 Escudo (CVEsc) = 100 centavos
Economy Suffering because of drought; substantial emigration in early 1970s; c.70% of workforce are farmers occupying irrigated inland valleys; increase in fishing since 1975.
GDP (2002e) $600 mn, per capita $1400
Human Development Index (2002) 0·715
History Colonized by Portuguese in 15th-c, also used as a penal colony; administered with Portuguese Guinea until 1879; overseas province of Portugal, 1951; independence, 1975; governed by a President, Council of Ministers, and People's National Assembly; multi-party elections held, 1991.
Head of State
1975–91 Aristides Pereira
1991–2001 Antonio Mascarenhas Monteiro
2001– Pedro Verona Rodrigues Pires
Head of Government
1975–91 Pedro Pires
1991–2000 Carlos Viega
2000–1 António Gualberto do Rosário
2001– José Maria Pereira Neves

the air, flapping their wings. (Genus: *Tetrao*, 2 species. Family: Tetraonidae.)

Capet, Hugo or **Hugh** [kapet] (c.938–96) King of France, founder of the third Frankish royal dynasty (the Capetians), which ruled France until 1328. Son of Hugh the Great, whom he succeeded as Duke of the Franks in 956, he was elected king and crowned at Noyon (987). His 40 years in power were marked by constant political intrigue and struggle, both among the feudal aristocracy and with his Carolingian rivals, but his position was invariably saved by the disunity of his enemies.

Capetians A French ruling dynasty for over 300 years (987–1328), founded by Hugh Capet in succession to the Carolingians. Two dynamic royal descendants were Philip II Augustus (r.1180–1223) and Louis IX or St Louis (r.1226–70). By increasing territorial control, enforcing the right to inherit of an eldest son, and devoting themselves to administration and justice, the Capetians laid the foundations of the French nation-state.

Cape Town, Afrikaans **Kaapstad** 33°56S 18°28E, pop (2000e) Greater Cape Town 1 285 000. Seaport capital of Western Cape province, South Africa, on Table Bay at the foot of Table Mt; legislative capital of South Africa; founded as a victualling station for the Dutch East India Company, 1652; occupied by the British, 1795; airport; railway; university (1829); cathedral; commerce, vehicles, chemicals, textiles; trade in wool, mohair, grain, fruit, wine, oil; Castle of Good Hope (1666), oldest colonial building in South Africa; Koopmans de Wet House (1777), Groote Kerk, Union Houses of Parliament, national gallery.

Cape Verde *see panel*

capillarity A surface tension effect in which liquids rise up narrow tubes or spread through porous solids; caused by the difference in attraction between liquid and air molecules for the material of the solid; also called **capillary action**. Examples include the movement of blood through the smallest blood vessels (*capillaries*), and ink soaking into blotting paper.

capillary [kapilaree] A minute, thin-walled blood vessel situated between arterioles and venules. It is the site of the exchange of materials (oxygen, nutrients, carbon dioxide, and other waste products) between capillary blood and surrounding tissues, which occurs by diffusion across the capillary wall. The term is also used to denote a small lymphatic channel.

capital (accountancy) Business sources of finance to buy assets, such as buildings, machinery, stocks, or investment in other firms. **Equity capital** is supplied by shareholders, either by buying shares or by ploughing back profits into the business. **Loan capital** or **debt** is borrowed from a financial institution or individual, and interest is paid. **Capital gearing** or (US) **leverage** is the ratio of capital raised by debt to equity; a high gearing means a heavy reliance on debt.

capital (architecture) The top part of a column, pilaster, or pier, identifiable in classical architecture as one of the five main orders: Doric, Tuscan, Ionic, Corinthian, and Composite. Romanesque and Gothic types include basket, bell, crocket, cushion, protomai (with animal figures), scalloped, and waterleaf.

capital (economics) Productive assets. These include **fixed capital** (ie buildings, machinery, and equipment) and **circulating capital** (ie stocks of inputs and finished products, and work in progress). It also includes **intellectual capital**, such as patents and copyright. In discussing the whole economy, land would not be included, and net credit is zero. In discussing a particular firm, land would be included with fixed capital, and net credit extended with circulating capital.

capital gains tax (CGT) A tax on the increase in the value of assets. This is usually payable only when an asset is realized by sale or bequest. CGT is levied in various countries – in the UK since 1965. It is usually payable only on gains in any year in excess of some minimum amount, and in the UK only on gains on excess of the rise in the Retail Price Index since the asset was acquired. In the UK, CGT is not payable in respect of a taxpayer's principal residence. In the USA it is a federal income tax, with lower rates for long-term holdings, and is politically controversial.

capitalism A set of economic arrangements which developed in the 19th-c in Western societies following the Industrial Revolution, though with antecedents in other societies, notably 11th-c China. The concept derives from the writings of Marx, and rests upon the private ownership of the means of production by the capitalist class, or *bourgeoisie*. The workers, or *proletariat*, own nothing but their labour, and although free to sell their labour in the market, they are dependent upon the capitalist class which exploits them by appropriating the surplus value created by their labour. Non-Marxist economists define capitalism as an economic system in which most property is privately owned and goods are sold freely in a competitive market, but without reference to exploitation, except where monopoly situations occur. Capitalism may be an ideological stance: Marx saw it as one stage in a historical process, finally being replaced by socialism. It has been the most productive economic system to date, although it has brought with it massive environmental (eg pollution) and social (eg unemployment) problems.

capital punishment Sentence of death passed by a judicial body following trial. Capital punishment for murder has been abolished in the UK since 1969, although proposals for its reinstatement are regularly debated by parliament, and it theoretically remains the penalty for high treason and certain other statutory offences, such as piracy with violence. It is still available in several states of the USA, and in many other countries. When the sentence is available, it is not invariably carried out; a head of state or other authority can recommend a reprieve. Countries employ a variety of procedures in carrying out executions, including lethal injection, electrocution, hanging, gassing, and shooting.

capital transfer tax (CTT) A former UK tax arising when individuals gave assets to others (excluding small gifts), including the transfer of ownership on death (originally called **estate** or **death duties**). The tax was not payable on small estates. It was replaced in 1986 by the inheritance tax.

Capitol The building on Capitol Hill, Washington, District of Columbia, USA, in which the US Congress meets. It was designed in 1792 by William Thornton (1759–1828), but a succession of architects supervised its construction. In 1814 the British set fire to the unfinished structure, and it was not until 1827 that it was finally completed by Benjamin Latrobe and Charles Bulfinch. The dome was added by Thomas Walter (1804–87).

Capitoline Hill The highest of the seven hills upon which Rome was built. Once the political and religious centre of Ancient Rome, it is now the site of the Piazza del Campidoglio, designed by Michelangelo, and of the city's administrative offices.

capitulum An inflorescence typical of the daisy family, Compositae, consisting of many stalkless florets packed onto a flattened receptacle cupped by bracts. The florets are often of two kinds: small disc florets in the centre; petal-like ray florets around the edge. The whole inflorescence gives the impression of being a single flower.

Capodimonte porcelain [kapohdimontay] The porcelain factory of the royal house of Naples, started in 1743 and removed to Buen Retiro in Spain in 1759. It was notable for its very fine figures, particularly of the *commedia dell'arte* and peasants, which were much copied by later factories in Italy and elsewhere.

Capone, Al(phonse) [kapohn] (1899–1947) Gangster, born in Brooklyn, New York, USA. He achieved worldwide notoriety as a racketeer during the prohibition era in Chicago (1925–31). During the St Valentine's day massacre in 1929, his men machine-gunned several members of a rival gang. Such was his power that no evidence sufficient to support a charge against him was forthcoming until 1931, when he was sentenced to 11 years' imprisonment for tax evasion. Released on health grounds in 1939, he retired to his estate in Florida.

Capote, Truman [kapohtee], pseudonym of **Truman Streckfus Persons** (1924–84) Writer, born in New Orleans, Louisiana, USA. He won several early literary prizes, and his first novel, *Other Voices, Other Rooms*, was published in 1948. Other works are *The Grass Harp* (1951), *Breakfast at Tiffany's* (1958), which was highly successful as a film, and *In Cold Blood* (1966), described as a 'non-fiction novel' because of the way he tells of actual events in novelistic form.

Capp, Al, originally **Alfred Gerald Caplin** (1909–79) Strip cartoonist, born in New Haven, Connecticut, USA. He studied at Designers Art School, Boston (1929), and entered strips as assistant to Bud Fisher on *Mutt and Jeff* (1930). Joining Associated Press, he took on a daily joke, *Mr Gilfeather* (1932), then became assistant to Ham Fisher on *Joe Palooka* (1933), introducing hill-billy characters, and developed *L'il Abner* (1934). Capp's chunky artwork coupled with hilarious hill-billy dialogue soon made the strip a success, inspiring two films, a stage musical, and an animated series.

Cappadocia [kapadohshia], Turkish **Kapadokya** Ancient name for the mountainous region of C Turkey, between the Black Sea and the Taurus Mts; a poor area without good natural defences, it tended to be ruled by whatever power was dominant in Asia Minor; a province of the Roman Empire from AD 17; noted for its eroded landscape features and cave dwellings in the Göreme valley; carpet making; largest town, Nevşehir.

Capra, Frank (1897–1991) Film director, born in Palermo, Sicily, S Italy. When he was six, his family emigrated to California, where he studied at the Institute of Technology. He began in film work in 1921, and had several box-office hits. Among his best-known films are *It Happened One Night* (1934), *Mr Deeds Goes to Town* (1936), *You Can't Take It with You* (1938), all of which won Oscars, and *Lost Horizon* (1937), *Arsenic and Old Lace* (1942), *It's A Wonderful Life* (1946), and *State of the Union* (1948). He retired for some years before his later films, *A Hole in the Head* (1959) and *A Pocketful of Miracles* (1961).

Capri [kapree], Ital [**kap**ree], ancient **Capreae** area 10·5 sq km/4 sq mi. Island in Napoli province, Campania, Italy, in the Tyrrhenian Sea; length 6 km/4 mi; maximum width 2·5 km/1·5 mi; rugged limestone crags rise to 589 m/1932 ft; capital, Capri; Blue Grotto on N coast; major tourist centre; home of Emperor Tiberius.

Capriati, Jennifer (Marie) [kapriahtee] (1976–) Tennis player, born in New York City, New York, USA. Hailed as a tennis phenomenon at the age of 13, she turned professional in 1990 and went on to win a gold medal at the Barcelona Olympics in 1992. In 1994 personal problems resulted in an extended break from tennis, but in 2001 she made a successful comeback, winning the French Open and Australian Open singles titles that year. She retained the Australian title in 2002. At the beginning of 2004 she had a world ranking of Number 6.

capriccio (music) [kaprichioh] A short musical composition, usually of a light or fanciful kind and often (though not necessarily) for piano. There are several famous examples in the work of Brahms.

capriccio (art) [kaprichioh] (Ital 'caprice') In art, an imaginative picture or print. In the 18th-c, the term refers specifically to landscapes by such artists as Canaletto or Giovanni Pannini (1691–1765), combining buildings from different places. Goya and Tiepolo produced outstanding sets of etched fantasies, with bizarre or grotesque subjects.

Capricornus (Lat 'goat') A S constellation of the zodiac, lying between Sagittarius and Aquarius.

capsid A small to medium-sized bug that typically feeds on plants; occasionally predatory; c.10 000 species, distributed worldwide. (Order: Heteroptera. Family: Miridae.)

capsule 1 A dry, many-seeded fruit derived from more than one carpel. When ripe it opens by means of valves, pores, or a lid, or by irregular fracturing.

2 A stalked structure containing spores in ferns, mosses, and liverworts, rupturing when ripe to release the contents.

capuchin [**ka**puchin] A New World monkey, the most numerous captive monkey in the USA and Europe; tail partly adapted for grasping (*prehensile*), often carried curled at the tip; acrobatic and intelligent; once a popular pet for street musicians; also known as **ring-tailed monkey** or **organ-grinder's monkey**. (Genus: *Cebus*, 4 species.)

Capuchins [kapyoochinz] (Ital *capuche*, a kind of cowl) A monastic order stemming from the Franciscans; in full, the **Order of Friars Minor of St Francis Capuccinorum**; abbreviated as **OM Cap** or **OSFC**. It was formed in 1528 by Matteo di Bassi (c.1495–1552), and observes a very strict rule, stressing poverty and austerity.

Cap Vert [kap **vair**] or **Cape Verde** [**vair**dee] The most westerly point of the African continent, in Dakar region, W Senegal; 2980 km/1850 mi ENE of Natal (Brazil).

capybara [kapi**bah**ra] A cavy-like rodent (*Hydrochoerus hydrochaeris*), native to Central and South America; largest living rodent (length, over 1 m/3¼ ft); dog-like with deep square snout; no tail; lives in or near water; part-webbed toes; eats vegetation. (Family: Hydrochoeridae.)

car, also **motor car** (UK), **automobile** (USA) The general name used in the UK for a passenger-carrying, self-propelled vehicle designed for normal domestic use on roads. The vehicle itself is made up of a number of systems, all of which may be discussed and constructed in isolation, but whose combined functioning produces the final vehicle. Thus the motive power system includes the engine (of whatever type), and its fuel supply, and the lubrication, exhaust, and cooling systems. The power developed by the engine is transmitted to the wheels by the transmission system, which includes gears, clutches, shafts, axles, and brakes. The engine and transmission are housed in the carriage unit, which also provides the compartment for the driver and passengers to sit, and in which the steering, engine controls, suspension, and electrical components can be mounted. Although there had been much experimenting with steam vehicles during the late 18th-c and early 19th-c, the basic feature that allowed the motor car to become a reality was the invention in 1884 of the medium-speed internal combustion engine by Daimler in Germany. However, it was not until the early 1900s, and the application in the USA of mass production techniques to the motor car by Henry Ford, that mass motoring started to become a reality. Over the years, the size of the domestic market ensured US dominance in the field of mass production, although the European manufacturers (particularly in the 1930s) also produced cheap 'people's' cars, such as the Volkswagen and the Citroen 2CV. The emergence of small Japanese cars in the 1970s challenged the US and European manufacturers in their own countries. This led in the early 1980s to a series of amalgamations of companies into ever larger multinationals, including the Japanese, which began to co-operate with each other. This process has continued, in an attempt to offset the massive costs of design and mass production by exploiting economies of scale and global marketing.

carabao [karabow] *water buffalo*

caracal [karakal] A member of the cat family, native to Africa and S Asia (*Felis caracal*); reddish-brown; slender with long legs, short tail, long tufted ears; inhabits savannah and dry woodland; eats birds, rodents, and small antelopes; easily tamed.

caracara [kahra**kah**ra] A large, broad-winged falcon; native to S USA and South America; inhabits open country to considerable altitudes; eats many types of animal or carrion; will rob other birds of prey. (Family: Falconidae, 10 species.)

Caracas [karakas] 10°30N 66°55W, pop (2000e) 2 208 000. Federal capital of Venezuela; altitude, 960 m/3150 ft; founded in 1567; often damaged by earthquakes; major growth since the 1940s, greater than any other Latin-American capital; airport; airfield; railway; metro; three universities (1725, 1953, 1970); mountain pass gives access to port (La Guaira) and airport; commercial, cultural, and industrial centre; birthplace of Bolívar; many museums, Plaza Bolívar, Panteón Nacional (with Bolívar's tomb), Casa Natal del Libertador, Capitolio Nacional, cathedral (1674); Ciudad Universitaria de Caracas is a world heritage site.

Caractacus [karaktakus], **Caratacus**, or **Caradoc** (1st-c) A chief of the Catuvellauni, the son of Cunobelinus. He mounted a gallant but unsuccessful guerrilla operation in Wales against the Romans in the years following the Claudian conquest (43). Betrayed by the Brigantian queen, Cartimandua, he was taken to Rome (51), where he was exhibited in triumph, and pardoned by Claudius.

caracul *karakul*

Caradoc *Caractacus*

carat or (US) **karat 1** A measure of the purity of gold in some alloy. A gold carat is a 24th part of the whole, and the purity of a gold alloy is stated by the number of such parts it contains. Pure gold is 24-carat gold. A 12-carat ring is one in which half the metal is gold.

2 A unit of mass for precious stones, equal to 200 mg.

Caratacus *Caractacus*

Caravaggio [karavajioh], originally **Michelangelo Merisi** (1573–1610) Baroque painter, born in Caravaggio, N Italy, whence his nickname. He studied in Milan and Venice, and went to Rome, where Cardinal del Monte became his chief patron. His works include several altarpieces and religious paintings, using dramatic contrasts of light and shade, notably several paintings of St Matthew (1599–1603) and 'Christ at Emmaus' (c.1602–3, National Gallery, London). In 1606, his temper led him to kill a man, and he fled to Naples and Malta.

caravel [karavel] A sailing vessel with up to four masts developed by the Portuguese in the 15th-c. It had lateen rig sails with long curved spars.

caraway A much-branched annual (*Carum carvi*), growing to 1 m/3¼ ft, native to Europe; leaves finely divided into narrow lance-shaped lobes; flowers small, borne in umbels 2–4 cm/¾–1½ in across, petals whitish, deeply notched; fruit (the 'seeds') 3–6 mm/⅛–¼ in, ribbed, strong-smelling when crushed. The fruits are widely used as a spice and for flavouring bread, cakes, and cheese; they are also an essential ingredient of Kümmel liqueur. (Family: Umbelliferae.)

carbamide *urea*

carbide Any compound of carbon, especially those in which carbon is ionic. It is often used specifically for **calcium carbide**, CaC_2, a salt of acetylene, which may be regenerated by the addition of water: $CaC_2 + 2H_2O \rightarrow Ca(OH)_2 + C_2H_2$.

carbohydrate A non-nitrogen-containing compound based on carbon, hydrogen, and oxygen, generally with two hydrogen atoms per atom of oxygen. The molecules may be small (glucose) or large (cellulose, starch). Most carbohydrates comprise one or more 6-carbon units, of which glucose is by far the most abundant. Starch is a polymer of glucose which is digestible by humans. Cellulose, another glucose polymer, is not digestible by higher animals, but is fermented by bacteria in the gut. Carbohydrates are not nutritionally essential, but prolonged intake of carbohydrate-free diets can cause a type of abnormal body metabolism (*ketosis*).

carbolic acid *phenol*

carbon C, element 6. It has two main forms: **graphite** (the stable form, very soft and black with a density of c.2 g/cm^3) and **diamond** (the hardest substance known, density 3·5 g/cm^3). Various molecular forms called **fullerenes** have recently been discovered. Both graphite and diamond melt above 3500°C. Coal is mainly graphite, but also contains amorphous (non-crystalline) carbon, occurring as well as 'carbon black' (soot). Graphite can be grown into **carbon fibres**, used for strengthening plastics. Carbon also occurs naturally in compounds, particularly as **carbonates**, and in the atmosphere as carbon dioxide. In virtually all its compounds, it is covalently bonded, and shows a valency of 4. Carbon compounds are the basis of all living matter, and form the subject matter of organic chemistry. There are two simple oxides, **carbon monoxide** (CO), a very poisonous gas, boiling point −191°C, formed from the incomplete combustion of carbon and hydrocarbons, and **carbon dioxide** O=C=O, the product of complete combustion. Carbon dioxide is in turn the raw material for photosynthesis, regenerating combustibles. Solid carbon dioxide, or *dry ice*, sublimes at −78°C without passing through a liquid phase. It accounts for less than 0·03% of the gases of the atmosphere.

Carbonari [kah(r)bonahree] (Ital 'charcoal burners') Neapolitan secret societies, linked with freemasonry and probably founded under Napoleonic occupation. Liberal and loosely nationalist in outlook, they played a major role in the Neapolitan revolution of 1820 (by which time membership may have numbered 300 000–500 000) and in the early stages of the Risorgimento.

carbonates Salts of carbonic acid, containing the ion CO_3^{2-}. Important natural carbonates include the almost insoluble **calcium carbonate** ($CaCO_3$), or limestone; **magnesium carbonate** ($MgCO_3$); and **dolomite** ($CaMg(CO_3)_2$). **Sodium carbonate**, known as 'washing soda' in its hydrated form ($Na_2CO_3.10H_2O$), is a cleansing agent because of its basicity, and a water softener because it precipitates calcium and magnesium carbonates.

carbon cycle The cycle through which carbon is transferred between the biological (*biotic*) and nonbiological (*abiotic*) parts of the global ecosystem. It involves the fixation of gaseous carbon dioxide during photosynthesis to form complex organic molecules, as well as the subsequent processes through which it ultimately returns to the atmosphere by respiration and decomposition.

carbon dating *radiocarbon dating*

carbon dioxide *carbon*

carbon fibre A high-strength material made by the controlled heat treatment of acrylic fibre. Woven as a fabric, it has the property of absorbing poisonous gas, and is used for protective underwear for military personnel, and for firehoods. The fibres are several times stronger than steel, and are extensively used where laminates of great strength and low weight are needed, as in components for rockets and aeroplanes. As carbon fibre reinforced plastic (or graphite epoxy), it is widely used for sports equipment such as fishing rods, rackets, and skis.

carbonic acid H_2CO_3; the hydrated form of carbon dioxide (CO_2). It is a weak acid, dissociating in two stages to give hydrogen carbonate (HCO_3^-) and carbonate (CO_3^{2-}) ions. Natural waters are generally saturated with carbon dioxide from the atmosphere, and their pH is generally determined by the amount of bicarbonate and carbonate ions present. Rain water containing pure carbonic acid has a pH of about 5.

Carboniferous period A geological period of the Palaeozoic era, extending from 360 to 286 million years ago, and characterized by extensive swampy forests with conifers and ferns which now form most of the present-day coal deposits. It was also marked by widespread coral reefs and limestone deposits, and the first appearance of reptiles and seed-bearing plants. In the USA, the period is termed the **Mississippian** (earlier) and the **Pennsylvanian** (later).

carbonyl [kah(r)boniyl] The group CO, (1) in organic compounds, found in aldehydes, ketones, carboxylic acids, esters, and amides; (2) in inorganic compounds, found as co-ordinated carbon monoxide.

carborundum The trade name for silicon carbide (SiC), a highly refractory material formed by fusing together sand and coke. It is almost as hard as diamond, and is used in grinding wheels and cutting tools.

carboxylic acids [kah(r)boksilik] Organic compounds containing the group –COOH; formed by the oxidation of alcohols or aldehydes; IUPAC **alkanoic acids**. Weaker than mineral acids, partially neutralized solutions have pH values of about 5. Many are found in nature, particularly as part of fats (*fatty acids*).

carbro process A photographic printing procedure in which a pigmented gelatine tissue is differentially hardened by contact with a developed print on bromide paper to produce an image which can be transferred to another support. Black-and-white prints using carbon as a pigment have great permanence, and colour prints can be made by superimposition of three layers in yellow, cyan and magenta.

carbuncle An infection in sweat glands and under the skin. It forms multiple confluent abscesses that discharge pus onto the surface through two or more tracts.

carburettor / carburetor A device fitted to a spark ignition engine that mixes its fuel of air and petrol in suitable proportions for combustion. As the engine draws in its air/petrol mixture, the carburettor ensures that small droplets of petrol are carried along with the airstream. These droplets then vaporize on their way to the engine to form the highly inflammable mixture used in the engine's power stroke. A number of different types of carburettor exist, but most of them work upon a floating valve system that detects when the air is to be drawn into the engine.

Carcassonne [kah(r)kason], ancient **Carcaso** 43°13N 2°20E, pop (2000e) 47 100. Ancient city and capital of Aude department, S France, on R Aude and Canal du Midi, in foothills of Pyrenees; railway; bishopric; hosiery, tanning, wine; the Cité (altitude 200 m/650 ft) is the best preserved example of a French mediaeval fortified town, with a double circuit of walls and towers (world heritage site); basilica of St Nazaire (5th-c, rebuilt 11th–13th-c), cathedral (late 13th-c, restored 1840), Gothic Church of St Vincent (late 13th-c).

Carchemish [kah(r)kemish] An ancient trading city in N Syria controlling one of the main crossing points of the Euphrates. It was ruled by the Hittites in the second millennium BC, survived the destruction of the Hittite empire (c.1200 BC), and remained an important centre of Hittite culture until its conquest by Assyria in 716 BC.

carcinogen [kah(r)sinojn] An agent which is capable of inducing cancer in tissues exposed to it. Several carcinogens have been identified by studies of the frequency of specific tumours in relation to different occupations, lifestyles, exposure to injurious chemical agents, drugs, ionizing radiations, ultraviolet light, and certain tumour-inducing (*oncogenic*) viruses. Exposure to such agents does not cause cancer immediately, but only after a period which may be months or years. The dose or duration of exposure to the agent is also critical: an example is cancer of the lung and cigarette smoking, where both the duration of smoking and the number of cigarettes smoked increase the probability of developing lung cancer some time in the future.

carcinoma *sarcoma*

Card, Andrew (1947–) US Republican politician, born in Brockton, MA. He studied engineering at the University of South Carolina (BS 1971), then worked as a structural design engineer. He entered politics, serving four terms in the Massachusetts House of Representatives (Republican, 1975–83), then served under Ronald Reagan as a special assistant for intergovernmental affairs (1983–7) and under George Bush as deputy chief-of-staff (1989–92) and as secretary of transportation (1992–3). In the Democrat years, he was president and chief executive officer of the American Autombile Manufacturers Association (1992–9), then vice-president of intergovernmental affairs at

General Motors. He was appointed White House chief-of-st[aff] by George W Bush in 2001.

cardamom [kah(r)damom] A perennial native to India (*Elett[ari]a cardamomum*), also cultivated in Sri Lanka; rhizomatous; s[t]em to 3·5 m/11½ ft; leaves in two rows, stalks sheathing; flowers small, white with blue and yellow markings, in clusters 60 cm/2 ft long on leafless stems near the ground; fruit a capsule 2 cm/¾ in long. The dried ripe fruits are used as spice, especially in curries. (Family: Zingiberaceae.)

Cardan, Jerome [kah(r)dan, kah(r)**dah**noh], Ital **Geronimo Cardano**, Lat **Hieronymus Cardanus** (1501–76) Mathematician and physician, born in Pavia, N Italy. He became professor of mathematics at Padua, and of medicine at Pavia and Bologna. He wrote over 100 treatises on physics, mathematics, astronomy, astrology, rhetoric, history, ethics, dialectics, natural history, music, and medicine. His *Ars magna* (1545, Great Art) was influential in the development of algebra, giving the first published algebraic solution of cubic and quartic equations.

Cárdenas, Lázaro [kah(r)thenas] (1895–1970) Mexican soldier and political leader, president of the Mexican Republic (1934–40), born in Jiquilpan, WC Mexico. He joined the revolutionary army in 1913, was a general by 1923, and Governor of Michoacán (1928–32). He rose from relative obscurity through the patronage of former president Plutarco Calles. Cárdenas wrested control of the government from Calles and instituted a broad programme of social and economic reforms. Often wrongly accused of being a Communist, he carried out the long overdue promises of the 1910 revolution, ensuring Mexico's stability.

card games *playing cards*

cardiac resuscitation Emergency treatment following cardiac arrest (the sudden complete cessation of heart function); also known as **external cardiac massage**. It must be started within three minutes if the brain is not to suffer irreversible damage. It involves administering regular, firm compressions to the chest over the sternum, at a rate of about 70 per minute, in order to force blood round the body artificially. The procedure is usually combined with mouth-to-mouth ventilation, and five compressions are given for each breath. Resuscitation needs to be continued until either the heart starts beating spontaneously, or until facilities are available to attempt to restart it using an electric shock applied to the chest (*defibrillation*).

Cardiff, Welsh **Caerdydd** 51°30N 3°13W, pop (2001e) 305 300. Capital of Wales, in Cardiff county, S Wales, UK; also administrative centre of Rhondda Cynon Taff county council; at the mouth of the Taff, Rhymney, and Ely Rivers, on the Bristol Channel; Roman fort, 1st-c AD; Norman castle, c.1090; city charter, 1147; expansion in 19th-c as trade in coal grew; decline with the loss of coal and steel industries in recent decades; Tiger Bay quayside area now redeveloping as a suburb; capital of Wales, 1955; airport (Rhoose); railway; university college (1893); registry for University of Wales; general services, steel, car components, cigars, tourism; Welsh National Opera; Cathays Park public buildings, Llandaff Cathedral, Welsh National Folk Museum (St Fagans), Cardiff Castle, Millennium Stadium (1999); football league team, Cardiff City (Bluebirds).

Cardiff Arms Park Welsh rugby and cricket ground, the home ground of Cardiff Rugby Club from 1876. It became the venue for the Welsh national team in 1884 (sharing the matches with St Helen's Swansea until 1954) and for Glamorgan County Cricket Club in 1888. It has also been used for athletics, boxing, greyhound racing, and international football. While redeveloped in the 1960s into the National Stadium, it was still popularly known as the Arms Park. The National Stadium was demolished in 1997, to be replaced by the Millennium Stadium (on the same site) for the 1999 Rugby World Cup.

Cardiff Singer of the World International singing competition founded by BBC Wales in 1983 to celebrate the opening of St David's Hall in Cardiff, S Wales, UK. Generally regarded as the world's leading vocal contest, it is a showcase for singers of opera and Lieder who are on the threshold of professional careers. The overall winner receives £10 000 and a specially commissioned trophy. A Song Prize worth £2000 is awarded to the singer of the best performance of Lieder, art song, or folksong during the entire competition.

Cardigan, James Thomas Brudenell, 7th Earl of (1797–1868) British general, born in Hambleden, Buckinghamshire, SC England, UK. He studied at Oxford, entered the army in 1824, and purchased his promotion, commanding the 15th Hussars (until 1833), then the 11th Hussars (1836–47). He commanded a cavalry brigade in the Crimea, and led the fatal charge of the Light Brigade at Balaclava (25 Oct 1854). He then became inspector-general of cavalry (1855–60). The woollen jacket known as a *cardigan* is named after him.

Cardiganshire, Welsh **Sir Aberteifi** pop (2001e) 75 400; area 1797 sq km/694 sq mi. County (unitary authority from 1996) in W Wales, UK; administrative centre, Aberystwyth; other chief town, Cardigan; tourism, crafts, agriculture; Aberystwyth university and National Library of Wales; Devil's Bridge (12th-c).

Cardin, Pierre [kah(r)dĩ] (1922–) French fashion designer, born in Venice, NE Italy. After working during World War 2 for a tailor in Vichy, he went to Paris in 1944. He worked in fashion houses and on costume design, notably for Cocteau's film *Beauty and the Beast* (1947). He opened his own house in 1953, and has since been prominent in fashion for both women and men.

cardinal (ornithology) Either of two species of bird of genus *Cardinalis*, native to the Americas: the **red** or **northern cardinal** (*Cardinalis cardinalis*), and the **vermilion cardinal** (*Cardinalis phoeniceus*); males bright red. The name is sometimes used for other (unrelated) red birds. (Family: Emberizidae.)

cardinal (religion) A name originally given to one of the parish priests, bishops, or district deacons of Rome, then applied to a senior dignitary of the Roman Catholic Church, being a priest or bishop nominated by a pope to act as counsellor. His duties are largely administrative, as head of a diocese, a curial office, an ecclesiastical commission, or a Roman congregation. The office carries special insignia, such as the distinctive red cap (*biretta*).

Cardinals, College of An institution consisting of all the cardinals of the Roman Catholic Church, technically of threefold structure: bishops, priests, and deacons. It originates from the reforms of Pope Urban II (r.1088–99). In 1586 its number was restricted to 70, but this limit was removed by Pope John XXIII in 1958. It is responsible for the government of the Church during a vacancy in the papacy, and since 1179 has been responsible for the election of a pope.

cardinal vowels A set of reference points devised by Daniel Jones for identifying the vowel sounds of a language, based on the movements of the tongue and jaws, and separated by roughly regular acoustic intervals from each other. Eighteen main tongue positions are recognized on a grid representing vertical and horizontal tongue movement.

carding The blending and disentanglement of fibres prior to subsequent spinning processes. The fibres are passed between a series of rollers covered in projecting steel wires and rotating at different speeds.

cardioid The path of a point on a circle rolling around another circle of the same radius. The equation of a cardioid is best expressed in polar co-ordinates: $r = a(1 + \cos \theta)$.

care proceedings The procedure adopted by a court or tribunal in relation to children, taken with a view to ensuring their protection and, if necessary, their reception into care. Care proceedings encompass children who are or may be the victims of abuse or neglect, those who are beyond the control of their parents, and those who are failing to receive a proper education. Many jurisdictions also include children and young persons who are committing offences in this category, though there has been an increasing tendency in certain countries (eg England and Wales) to separate child offenders from other children in need of care, protection, or control.

caretaker speech *motherese*

Carew, Thomas [karoo] (1595–1639) Poet, born in West Wickham, Kent, SE England, UK. He studied at Oxford and the Middle Temple, and became a diplomat. A friend of Jonson and

Donne, he wrote polished lyrics in the Cavalier tradition, and a masque *Coelum britannicum* (1634) which was performed at court.

Carey, George (Leonard) [**kai**ree] (1935–) Anglican clergyman, born in London, UK. After service in the RAF, he studied divinity at King's College, London. He held Church posts in London and Durham, then became Principal of Trinity Theological College, Bristol (1982–7). He was appointed Bishop of Bath and Wells in 1987 and Archbishop of Canterbury (1991–2002).

Carey, Peter [**kai**ree] (1943–) Writer, born in Bacchus Marsh, Victoria, SE Australia. He attended Geelong Grammar School before beginning a career as an advertising copywriter. His first book, *The Fat Man in History* (1974), was a collection of short stories, and he was quickly regarded as an innovative force in Australian writing. Later books include *Bliss* (1981), *Illywhacker* (1985), *Oscar and Lucinda* (1988, Booker), *The Tax Inspector* (1991), *The True History of the Kelly Gang* (2001, Booker; Commonwealth Writers Prize), and *My Life as a Fake* (2003). He co-wrote the screenplays for *Bliss* (1985) and *Until the End of the World* (1990).

cargo cult The Melanesian variety of a widely occurring type of social movement (millenarianism) in which people look to some supernatural event to bring them prosperity. It is so-called because in Melanesia, in numerous instances, people performed rituals in an effort to obtain European material goods (referred to as 'cargo'). The movement first appeared in the late 19th-c, and was popular in the 1930s.

cariama *seriema*

Carib American Indian groups of the Lesser Antilles and neighbouring South America (the Guianas and Venezuela); also the name of the largest family of South American Indian languages. The island Caribs were maritime people and warriors, who drove the Arawak from the area. Most were slaughtered by Spaniards in the 15th-c, and the survivors mixed with Spanish conquerors and later Negro slaves. The mainland Caribs led a more peaceful existence in small autonomous settlements in the tropical forests. Population c.5000.

Caribbean Community (CARICOM) An association chiefly of former British colonies in the Caribbean Sea, some of which (Barbados, Jamaica, and the Leeward Is except for the Virgin and Windward Is) existed as the Caribbean Federation, with the aim of full self-government, until the establishment of the West Indies Federation (1958–63). When Jamaica became independent in 1962, the Federation was dissolved. In 1969 certain of the remaining islands in the Windward and Leeward Is were offered associated status within the Commonwealth, and in 1969 the West Indies Associated States was formed. In 1968 many of the islands agreed to the establishment of the **Caribbean Free Trade Area (CARIFTA)**. Suriname joined CARICOM in 1995 and Haiti in 2000, making its membership 15.

Caribbean dance A mixture of dance styles basically of African origin but influenced by the Spanish conquest of the West Indies and later by French and English dance styles of the colonial era. It shows the merging of African body movements with formal European set dances. Its vivid rhythmic form profoundly influenced jazz dance in the USA, and was being revived in England during the 1990s.

Caribbean literature Caribbean literature begins with the rejection of colonial status by the West Indian islands. Influenced by the Harlem Renaissance, Claude McKay asserted the black viewpoint in *Banana Bottom* (1933); C L R James's *Minty Alley* (1936) led to a new realism. The post-war years brought a number of important novelists, among them Roger Mais (1905–55), eg *Brother Man* (1954); George Lamming (1932–), eg *In the Cell of my Skin* (1953); V S Naipaul, eg *A House for Mr Biswas* (1961); and Wilson Harris (1921–), eg *Guyana Quartet* (1960–3). Several of these writers moved to England in the 1950s, where they were encouraged by the BBC's 'Caribbean Voices' programme. Meanwhile Derek Walcott published several volumes of poetry and created the Trinidad Theatre Workshop: poet/historian Edward Brathwaite (1930–) set new voices to old rhythms in his trilogy *The Arrivants* (1967–9), which has been influential on the performance poetry of Bongo Jerry and Linton Kwesi Johnson (1952–). Other writers include the poets James Berry (1924–) and Fred d'Aguiar (1960–), and the novelist/dramatist Caryl Phillips (1958–).

Caribbean Sea area 2 515 900 sq km/971 000 sq mi. Arm of the Atlantic Ocean between the West Indies and Central and South America; linked to the Pacific by the Panama Canal; depth 6 m/20 ft on continental shelf off Nicaragua to 5058 m/16 594 ft on floor of Venezuelan Basin; deepest point, Cayman Trench, 6950 m/22 802 ft; visited by Columbus, 1493; main island groups, Greater and Lesser Antilles; major trade route and tourist area.

caribou *reindeer*

caricature A mock portraiture, usually graphic rather than painted, in which features are exaggerated for humorous or satirical effect. Early practitioners included the Carracci in late 16th-c Bologna. Bernini was a brilliant caricaturist. Modern political caricature was invented in mid-18th-c England (Gillray, Rowlandson), and has flourished ever since. Modern US practitioners include David Levine and Al Hirschfeld.

CARICOM *Caribbean Community*

caries (dentistry) [**kai**reez] A non-specific bacterial disease in which infecting organisms penetrate the enamel coating of a tooth. They may proceed to the centre or pulp of the tooth, which may be destroyed, and if unchecked reach the root of the tooth to produce an apical tooth abscess. A high consumption of sugar predisposes to the development of caries, while an adequate amount of fluoride in drinking water (one part in a million) increases the resistance of the enamel to bacteria.

CARIFTA *Caribbean Community*

carillon A set of bells, usually with a compass of two octaves or more, installed in a tower or other high construction, and operated mechanically or by hand to play melodies or more complex polyphonic music. Many carillons are incorporated into elaborate public clocks, especially on the European mainland.

Carina [ka**riy**na] (Lat 'keel') A S hemisphere constellation, formerly part of the huge ancient constellation of Argo Navis. It contains Canopus, the second-brightest star in our sky, a supergiant. The Greek Stoic scientist Poseidonius used sightings of Canopus near the horizon in his estimation of the size of the earth. Distance: 96 parsec.

carinatae [kari**na**tiy] (Lat 'with a keel', referring to the keel on a bird's breastbone) A generally obsolete term used for birds which fly. The group Carinatae was distinct from the group Ratitae.

Carl XVI Gustaf (1946–) King of Sweden since 1973, born in Stockholm, Sweden, the grandson of King Gustav VI. His father died in an air accident (1947), and he became crown prince from his grandfather's accession (1950). A new constitution restricting monarchical powers was approved by the Swedish parliament just before his accession. In 1976 he married **Silvia Sommerlath**, the daughter of a West German businessman. They have three children: **Victoria** (1977–), **Carl Philip** (1979–), and **Madeleine** (1982–). He is a keen all-round sportsman, proficient in yachting, skiing, and shooting.

Carling, Will, popular name of **William David Charles Carling** (1965–) Player of rugby union football, born in Bradford-on-Avon, Wiltshire, S England, UK. He studied at Durham University, where he played for the university, and later for Harlequins, then joined the army, but resigned his commission to devote more time to rugby. In 1988 at the age of 22 he made his England debut against France, was appointed captain (1988–96), and played a major role in the Grand Slam victories of 1991, 1992, and 1995. He retired in 1998. His 73 international appearances (72 England, 1 British Lions) are a record for an English centre. His 59 appearances as captain are a record for any country. He received national publicity in 1995 when the media focused on rumours of a possible relationship with Princess Diana.

Carlisle [kah(r)liyl], Lat **Luguvallum** 54°54N 2°55W, pop (2001e) 100 700. County town in Cumbria, NW England, UK; at the W end of Hadrian's Wall, at the confluence of the Eden and Caldew Rivers; important fortress in Scots–English border wars; airfield (Crosby); railway junction; foodstuffs, metal goods, textiles, engineering; cathedral (11th–12th-c), castle (11th-c), Church of St Cuthbert (18th-c); Great Fair (last Saturday in Aug); football league team, Carlisle United.

Carlism A Spanish dynastic cause and political movement, officially born in 1833, but with origins in the 1820s. Against the claim to the Spanish throne of Isabella II, daughter of Ferdinand VII, Carlists supported the claim of the latter's brother, Don Carlos (1788–1855). In the 19th-c, Carlism attracted widespread popular support chiefly in conservative, Catholic districts of rural N Spain. In 1833–40, 1846–9, and 1872–6, Carlists fought unsuccessful civil wars against Spanish liberalism. After 1876 Carlism became a political party espousing ultra-rightist, 'traditionalist' principles. It took the Nationalist side in the Spanish Civil War (1936–9), providing c.100 000 volunteers. Since 1939, under the Franco regime and after, the cause has suffered division and serious decline, though small Carlist groups persist.

Carlow (county) **[kah(r)loh]**, Ir **Cheatharlach** pop (2000e) 41 000; area 896 sq km/346 sq mi. County in Leinster province, SE Ireland; between the Slieve Ardagh Hills (W) and the Wicklow Mts (E) where the Barrow and Slaney Rivers water rich farm land; Blackstairs Mts rise in the S; capital, Carlow; wheat, barley, sugar beet.

Carlow (town) **[kah(r)loh]** 52°50N 6°55W, pop (2000e) 14 400. Capital of Carlow county, Leinster, SE Ireland; railway; technical college; barley malting, sugar beet, footwear; Carlow Castle (12th-c), cathedral (19th-c), Browne's Hill tumuli.

Carlson, Chester (Floyd) (1906–68) Physicist, born in Seattle, Washington, USA. He graduated in physics at the California Institute of Technology, and worked in electronics, later specializing also in patent work. By 1938 he had devised a basic system of electrostatic copying on plain paper, which after 12 years' work by assistants became the xerographic method, the basis of modern photocopiers.

Carlsson, Arvid (1923–) Pharmacologist, born in Uppsala, Sweden. He studied at the University of Lund (1951), and became professor of pharmacology at the University of Göteborg, Sweden (1959, emeritus 1989). He shared the 2000 Nobel Prize for Physiology and Medicine with Paul Greengard and Eric Kandel for their discoveries concerning signal transduction in the nervous system.

Carluccio, Antonio (Mario Gaetano) [kah(r)loochioh] (1937–) Restaurateur, born in Vietri Sul Mare, Italy. He studied at the Roland Matura Schule, Vienna, and became a wine merchant in England (1975–81). He joined the Neal Street Restaurant in London as restaurateur (1981–), became proprietor (1989–), and joint proprietor (with his wife) of Carluccio's food retailers (1992–). His numerous television appearances include BBC's *Food and Drink* (from 1986), *Hot Chefs* (1991), and the series *Antonio Carluccio's Italian Feasts* (1996) with accompanying book. Among other books are *An Invitation to Italian Cooking* (1986) and *A Passion for Pasta* (1993).

Carlyle, Jane Baillie, *née* **Welsh** (1801–66) Diarist, born in Haddington, East Lothian, E Scotland, UK, the wife of Thomas Carlyle. She was tutored by the revivalist minister Edward Irving, and he introduced her in 1821 to his friend Carlyle, whom she married in 1826. Forthright and quick-witted, she declined to become a writer, despite Carlyle's promptings. She supported Carlyle loyally through his depressions and chronic ill health, and after her death he retired from public life, writing an anguished memoir of her in his *Reminiscences* (1881). He also edited her letters and diaries, which are full of vivid insights and quality writing, and show her to have been one of the most accomplished women of her time.

Carlyle, Robert (1961–) Actor, born in Glasgow, W Scotland, UK. At age 21 he enrolled in acting classes at the Glasgow Arts Centre and formed his own acting group called Raindog. He became known for his role in the television series *Hamish Macbeth* (1995–7), and his film credits include *Trainspotting* (1996), *The Full Monty* (1996), *Angela's Ashes* (1999), *The World is Not Enough* (1999), and *The Beach* (2000).

Carlyle, Thomas (1795–1881) Man of letters, born in Ecclefechan, Dumfries and Galloway, SW Scotland, UK. The son of a stonemason, he studied at Edinburgh University, and taught for several years before beginning to write articles for the *Edinburgh Encyclopaedia*, and becoming absorbed in German literature, notably Goethe. In 1826 he married **Jane Baillie Welsh** (1801–66). His best-known work is *Sartor Resartus* (1833–4). He then moved to London, where he wrote his other major works on the French Revolution (3 vols, 1837) and Frederick the Great (1858–65). After his wife's death, he retired from public life, and wrote little.

Carmarthen [ka(r)mah<u>th</u>en] 51°52N 4°19W, pop (2000e) 15 800. County town of Carmarthenshire, SW Wales, UK; on R Towy, 13 km/8 mi N of the Bristol Channel; chartered, 1227; railway; dairy products, pharmaceuticals, flour milling, agricultural trade.

Carmarthenshire, Welsh **Sir Caerfyrddin** pop (2001e) 173 600; area 2398 sq km/926 sq mi. County (unitary authority from 1996) in SW Wales, UK; drained by R Teifi and R Tywi; administrative centre, Carmarthen; other chief towns, Llanelli, Ammanford; tourism, crafts, agriculture; Laugharne (home of Dylan Thomas); Carreg Cennen and Kidwelly castles; early motor speed trials on Pendine sands.

Carme [kah(r)mee] The 11th natural satellite of Jupiter, discovered in 1938; distance from the planet 22 600 000 km/14 044 000 mi; diameter 40 km/25 mi.

Carmelites A Roman Catholic monastic order originating in the 12th-c from the Hermits of Mount Carmel (Israel), seeking the way of life of the prophet Elijah; properly known as the **Order of the Brothers of the Blessed Virgin Mary of Mt Carmel**, or **White Friars**; abbreviated **OCarm**. They flourished as mendicant friars in Europe. Carmelite nuns were officially recognized in 1452, reformed by Teresa of Ávila in Spain (1562) as strictly cloistered **Discalced Carmelites** (**ODC**). (The term 'discalced' derives from the practice of wearing sandals instead of shoes and stockings.) The male order was similarly reformed by St John of the Cross, and in 1593 was recognized as a separate order. The older order specialized in teaching and preaching; the Discalced mainly in parochial and foreign mission work.

Carmichael, Hoagy, popular name of **Hoagland Howard Carmichael** (1899–1981) Jazz pianist and composer, born in Bloomington, Indiana, USA. While at Indiana University he met and was influenced by jazz musicians, notably Bix Beiderbecke, to whom Carmichael dedicated his first composition, 'Riverboat Shuffle' (1924). During the 1930s he wrote many compositions, several of which became classics. He later worked in Hollywood, and won an Oscar for 'In the Cool Cool Cool of the Evening' (1951). His most successful composition was 'Stardust' (1927).

Carmichael, Stokely, after 1969, also known as **Kwame Ture** (1941–98) Radical activist, born in Port-of-Spain, Trinidad. He emigrated to the USA in 1952, and was shocked by the racism he encountered. Involved in Civil Rights while attending Howard University (1960–4), he was elected leader of the Student Nonviolent Co-ordinating Committee, and changed the group's focus from integration to black liberation. He popularized the phrase 'black power', and as a Black Panther came to symbolize black violence to many whites. He later favoured forging alliances with radical whites, which led to his resignation from the Panthers in 1968. He and his wife, **Miriam Makeba**, moved to Guinea in 1969, where he supported Pan-Africanism, and changed his name (after Kwame Nkrumah of Ghana and Sekou Toure of Guinea).

Carnac A peninsula on the S coast of Brittany, N France, renowned for its megalithic alignments, stone circles, and chambered tombs of Neolithic date. The alignments, unsurpassed elsewhere, run E–W with 7–13 parallel rows each: the best preserved, at Kermario, has seven principal lines up to c.1100 m/3700 ft long with 1029 stones. In all, c.3000 stones survive, extending over some 5 km/3 mi.

Carnap, Rudolf (1891–1970) Philosopher, born in Wuppertal, W Germany. He studied at Freiburg and Jena, becoming lecturer at Vienna (1926–31), and professor of philosophy at Prague (1931–5), Chicago (1936–52), and California, Los Angeles (1954–70). He was one of the leaders of the 'Vienna Circle' of logical positivists. His writings include *Der logische Aufbau der Welt* (1928, The Logical Construction of the World), *Logische Syntax der Sprache* (1934, Logical Syntax of Language), and *Meaning and Necessity* (1947), as well as semantic studies of induction and probability.

carnation A perennial species of pink (*Dianthus caryophyllaceus*), native to the Mediterranean; leaves tufted; flowers with spreading, slightly frilly petals. Wild carnations have pink, strongly-scented flowers. Ornamental hybrids and garden cultivars are various colours, and may have multiple petals. (Family: Caryophyllaceae.)

Carné, Marcel [kah(r)nay] (1909–96) Film director, born in Paris, France. He trained as a film technician, later working as an assistant to René Clair. From 1931 his collaboration as director with the poet and scriptwriter Jacques Prévert resulted in a series of outstanding productions, including *Quai des brumes* (1938, trans Port of Shadows), *Le Jour se lève* (1939, Daybreak) and *Les Enfants du paradis* (1944, Children of Paradise). After the break-up of the partnership in 1949, his late work was irregular and less distinguished.

Carneades [kah(r)neeadeez] (c.214–129 BC) Greek philosopher, born in Cyrene. He became head of the Academy, which under his very different, sceptical direction became known as the 'New Academy'. He had the reputation of a virtuoso dialectician, who could argue equally persuasively for quite opposing points of view.

Carnegie, Andrew [kah(r)naygee, or **karnegee**] (1835–1919) Industrialist and philanthropist, born in Dunfermline, Fife, E Scotland, UK. His family emigrated to Pittsburgh in 1848, and after several jobs he invested in the business which grew into the largest iron and steel works in the USA. He retired in 1901, a multimillionaire, to Skibo Castle in Sutherland. He gave millions of dollars to libraries and public institutions in the UK and USA, and several buildings are named after him.

Carnegie Hall International concert venue located in New York City, USA. Originally the idea of composer Leopold Damrosch, it was left to his son Walter to establish a concert hall in New York City. Walter found a patron in industrial tycoon Andrew Carnegie, and the building was inaugurated in May 1891 with a five-day music festival at which Tchaikovsky conducted several of his works. Today, concerts are performed either in the main auditorium or in the Weill Recital Hall. The building was designated a national historic landmark in 1964.

Carney, Art, popular name of **Arthur William Matthew Carney** (1918–2003) Television comedian and actor, born in Mount Vernon, New York, USA. He served in the US Army and was wounded during the Normandy landing (1944). He later performed on Broadway and television, gaining his greatest success in *The Honeymooners* (1955–6). He created the role of slovenly Oscar in Broadway's *The Odd Couple* (1960), and after recovering from a mental breakdown he returned to work on stage, television, and films, winning an Oscar for *Harry and Tonto* (1974).

Carnic Alps, Ger **Karnische Alpen**, Ital **Alpi Carniche** S Alpine mountain range on the border between Italy and Austria; highest peak is Hohe Warte (2780 m/9121 ft); crossed by the Plöcken Pass.

carnitine A chemical substance (an *amine*) derived from the essential amino acid, lysine. The oxidation of fatty acids by mammalian cells requires carnitine as an intermediary in the intracellular transport of fatty acids. Although it was once considered a vitamin, carnitine is probably not an essential component of the diet. Most infant formulae based on cow's milk are supplemented with carnitine to the level normally found in breast milk.

Carnival A traditional festive period prior to Lent, celebrated in the Catholic countries of S Europe and their former colonies, and characterized by feasting, sexual licence, dancing, processions, masking, satire, and social levelling. Well known examples are those of Rome, Venice, New Orleans, and Rio de Janeiro. The term is applied by extension to other similar festivals, such as the Notting Hill Carnival in London.

carnivore [**kah(r)nivaw(r)**] A primarily meat-eating mammal, preying on other vertebrates; lower jaw moves only up and down; canine teeth long; some cheek teeth (*carnassials*) specialized for cutting flesh; 4–5 clawed toes on each foot. (Order: Carnivora, 7 families, 238 species.)

carnivorous plant A plant which traps animals, usually insects and small invertebrates, and secretes digestive enzymes which break down the prey, allowing the resulting products to be absorbed; also known as an **insectivorous plant**. Carnivorous plants grow in nutrient-poor habitats, and food obtained from prey, especially organic nitrogen, augments that produced by photosynthesis. The carnivorous habit has arisen independently in several unrelated groups, principally in the families Droseraceae (sundews), Nepenthaceae and Sarraceniaceae (pitcher plants), and Lentibulariaceae (butterworts and bladderworts). The traps are invariably formed from modified leaves, sometimes with very sophisticated features. The simplest, found in butterworts, are merely covered with a viscous substance to which insects stick; in sundews, long, mobile sticky hairs and even the leaf itself move in response to the struggles of the prey and enfold it. The leaves of pitcher plants form tubular or jug-shaped traps filled with fluid, in which the victims drown before being digested. The largest are said to be capable of trapping small rodents. The pitchers are often brightly and attractively coloured, and bear honey glands on the inner surface to entice animals towards a smooth, glossy 'slip zone'; further down, the surface is covered with downward projecting hairs to prevent escape. Equally sophisticated are the underwater traps of bladderworts which suck in the prey, but the most spectacular is the Venus's fly-trap, in which a trigger mechanism causes the jaw-like traps to snap closed around the prey.

Carnot, Lazare (Nicolas Marguerite) [kah(r)noh] (1753–1823) French statesman, known as 'the organizer of victory' during the Revolutionary Wars, born in Nolay, E France. He entered the army as an engineer, and became a member of the Legislative Assembly (1791). He survived the Terror, and became one of the Directors (1795), but in 1797, suspected of Royalist sympathies, he escaped to Germany. Back in Paris, he became minister of war (1800), and helped to organize the Italian and Rhenish campaigns. He commanded at Antwerp in 1814, and during the Hundred Days was minister of the interior.

Carnot, (Nicholas Léonard) Sadi [kah(r)noh] (1796–1832) Scientist, born in Paris, France. He became a captain of engineers in the army, and spent much of his life investigating the design of steam engines. In 1824 he published his essay *Réflexions sur la puissance motrice du feu*. His findings were the foundation of the science of thermodynamics.

Carnot cycle *p.281*

Carnot's law *Carnot cycle*

carob An evergreen tree or shrub (*Ceratonia siliqua*), growing to 10 m/30 ft, native to the Mediterranean region; leaves with 2–5 pairs of leathery oval leaflets; flowers lacking petals, borne in short catkin-like inflorescences; pods to 20 cm/8 in long, pendent, violet-brown when ripe; also called **locust tree**. It is cultivated for fodder, the pods containing a nutritious pulp rich in protein. The seeds are said to be the original carat weights used by goldsmiths. (Family: Leguminosae.)

Carol I (1839–1914) The first King of Romania (1881–1914), born in Hohenzollern-Sigmaringen. He was elected Prince of Romania in 1866 and became king when his country received independence from the Ottoman Empire. He promoted economic devel-

Carnot cycle

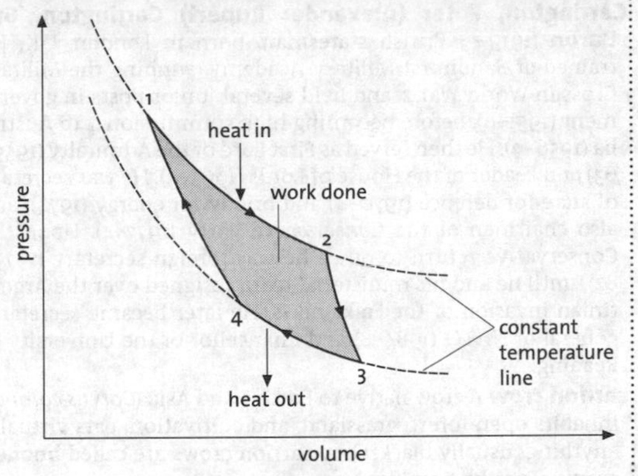

[kah(r)noh] The fundamental thermodynamic cycle proposed by French engineer Sadi Carnot in 1824, in an attempt to explain the working of the steam engine. It comprises four stages: isothermal then adiabatic expansions, followed by isothermal and adiabatic compressions. A **Carnot engine** is the most efficient heat engine possible (**Carnot's law**). For intake temperature T_i and exhaust temperature T_o, thermal efficiency e is $e = (T_i - T_o)/T_i$. Because of physical and metallurgical problems, the Carnot cycle is not practical, and other cycles have been developed that meet the needs of real engines. Such cycles reflect more closely the way heat is actually added to and taken from the gases of a real engine.

opment and military expansion, and brutally crushed a peasant rebellion in 1907. He married **Princess Elizabeth of Wied** (1869), a prolific writer under the pseudonym Carmen Sylva. At the outset of World War 1, he declared Romanian neutrality, but his successor (his nephew King Ferdinand I) declared for the Allies in 1916.

Carol II (1893–1953) King of Romania (1930–40), born in Sinaia, C Romania. He renounced his right of succession (1925) as a result of a love affair (he divorced his second wife, **Princess Helen of Greece** (1928), mother of his son **Michael**, to live with **Elena (Magda) Lupescu**) and went into exile in Paris. He returned through a coup in 1930, proclaiming a dictatorship in 1938. He was forced to abdicate in 1940 in favour of his son and went into exile in Portugal where he later married Lupescu (1947). In 2003, fifty years after his death, his remains were brought back to Romania for reburial with full national honours.

Caroline of Ansbach, Wilhelmina (1683–1737) Queen of George II of Great Britain, born in Ansbach, SC Germany, the daughter of a German prince. She exercised a strong influence over her husband, and was a leading supporter of his chief minister, Robert Walpole.

Caroline, Radio The best-known UK pirate radio station of the 1960s. Operating illegally from a ship off the Essex coast, and financed by advertising, Radio Caroline broke the BBC's monopoly of domestic radio broadcasting and 'created' a youth audience through non-stop pop music, thus prompting the creation of BBC Radio 1.

Caroline of Brunswick, Amelia Elizabeth (1768–1821) Wife of George IV of Great Britain, born in Brunswick, NC Germany, the daughter of George III's sister, Augusta. She married the Prince of Wales in 1795, but the marriage was disagreeable to him, and although she bore him a daughter, **Princess Charlotte**, they lived apart. When George became king (1820), she was offered an annuity to renounce the title of queen and live abroad; when she refused, the king persuaded the government to introduce a Divorce Bill. Although this failed, she was not allowed into Westminster Abbey at the coronation (1821).

Carolingian or **Carlovingian architecture** [karohlinjian, kah(r)lohvinjian] A form of architecture prevalent from the 8th-c to the 10th-c AD, named after Emperor Charlemagne, and common to France, Germany, and the Netherlands. It was composite in character, made up of late Roman forms mixed with heavier, indigenous elements such as prominent towers.

Carolingian art A style of art named after Charlemagne, which flourished in what is now France and W Germany from the mid-8th to the early 10th-c. Graeco-Roman and Byzantine stylistic elements were fostered as part of a deliberate classical revival.

Carolingians A Frankish ruling dynasty which rose to power as mayors of the palace, and ultimately replaced the Merovingians when Pepin II became King of the Franks in 751. The Carolingian Empire created by Charlemagne embraced most of the former territory of the Roman Empire in the West. In 843 it was divided into E Francia, W Francia, and the 'Middle Kingdom' stretching from the North Sea to Italy, and these soon dissolved into smaller states.

carom *billiards*

carotene A class of plant pigments which provide the natural colours of carrots, green vegetables, algae, shrimps, and tomatoes. The carotene of carrots and green vegetables is rich in beta-carotene, of which about 16% is converted to vitamin A in the digestive tract.

carotenoid [karoteenoyd] A non-water-soluble pigment, usually red to yellow in colour, found in many higher plants, algae, and bacteria. It functions as an accessory photosynthetic pigment.

carp Deep-bodied freshwater fish (*Cyprinus carpio*) native to Black Sea coasts but now introduced worldwide; thrives in warm pools, lakes, and rivers with rich vegetation; length up to 1 m/3¾ ft; two pairs of barbels on upper jaw; important food fish, used extensively in aquaculture and very popular with anglers; broadly, any member of the large family Cyprinidae.

Carpaccio, Vittore [kah(r)pachioh] (c.1460–c.1525) Painter, born in Venice, NE Italy. His most characteristic work is seen in the nine subjects from the life of St Ursula (1490–5). In 1510 he executed for San Giobbe his masterpiece, 'The Presentation in the Temple', now in the Accademia.

carpal tunnel syndrome A weakness of the thumb and hand, with numbness or tingling in the thumb and adjacent two or three fingers. It is caused by pressure on the nerve that supplies the muscles and skin in this area (the *median nerve*) as it passes through a band of tissue that encircles the wrist (the *carpal tunnel*). The carpal tunnel is inflexible, and so the median nerve becomes compressed if there is swelling of other tissues within it. This occurs with repetitive use of the wrist, such as during typing, driving, and some sports, and it is also associated with a variety of conditions including pregnancy and menopause, rheumatoid arthritis, diabetes mellitus, and hypertension. Symptoms can often be relieved by rest and splinting of the wrist, but surgery may be required to release the pressure on the nerve.

Carpathian Mountains Mountain system of EC Europe, forming the E wing of the great Alpine uplift; extends 1400 km/870 mi in a semi-circle from the Czech Republic to Romania, forming in the middle a boundary with Poland; main divisions (W–E) are the Little Carpathians, White Carpathians, Beskids, Low Tatra, High Tatra, E or Romanian Carpathians, and the Transylvanian Alps; highest point, Mt Gerlach (2655 m/8711 ft); rich in minerals and coal deposits; generally forested to 1200 m/4000 ft.

carpel Part of the innermost whorl of a flower, collectively forming the *gynecium*: it typically consists of an ovary, style, and stigma, which together are sometimes called the **pistil**. More primitive flowers generally have many carpels; more advanced flowers tend to have fewer, and often fused, carpels.

Carpentaria, Gulf of [kah(r)pen**tay**ria] Major inlet on N coast of Australia between Cape Arnhem and Cape York; bounded N by the Arafura Sea; 595 km/370 mi long by 491 km/305 mi wide; shallow depths of 25–55 m/80–180 ft; contains several islands; named by Tasman in honour of the Governor-General of Dutch East Indies, 1642; bauxite, manganese.

carpenter bee A tropical bee that bores into solid wood or plant pith to make a nest; most species are solitary; a few show a primitive degree of sociality. (Order: Hymenoptera. Family: Anthophoridae.)

carpet A floor covering made from wool, silk, jute, mohair, or other fibres, traditionally woven but currently produced by other methods such as bonding or machine-stitching the pile to a base. The technique is thought to have originated in Persia in ancient times, and spread to C Asia, the Caucasus, and Anatolia, where characteristic forms developed as folk art and in court workshops. In the 18th-c, carpet-making became a widely distributed craft in Britain, France, and other West European countries, and the former led the way in mechanization.

Carpetbaggers A derogatory term for US Northerners who went to the defeated South after the Civil War to aid freed blacks and take part in rebuilding. Supposedly they carried all their belongings in bags made of carpet. Collectively they have had a bad press, but are now recognized as well-intentioned.

carpet beetle A small, rounded, black beetle with zigzag markings around margins; larvae known as **woolly bears**, covered with long hairs, feeding on woollen carpets, furs, and animal skins; adults common on fruit trees, feeding on pollen. (Order: Coleoptera. Family: Dermestidae.)

Carr, Philippa *Hibbert, Eleanor*

Carrà, Carlo [**ka**ra] (1881–1966) Painter, born in Quargnento, NW Italy. Largely self-taught, he adopted a Futurist style, then in 1917 met Giorgio di Chirico and for some years was influenced by his 'metaphysical painting' movement. His best-known work is 'Le canal' (Zürich).

Carracci [ka**rah**chee] A family of painters, born in Bologna, N Italy. The most famous was **Annibale Carracci** (1560–1609), whose style was much influenced by Correggio and Raphael. With his brother, **Agostino Carracci** (1557–1602), he painted the gallery of the Farnese Palace, Rome. Together with their cousin, **Ludovico Carracci** (1555–1619), they founded an influential academy of painting in Bologna (1582).

carrack [**ka**rak] A 15th-c development of the Portuguese caravel, distinguished by having square sails in addition to lateen sails.

Carrantuohill [karan**too**uhl] Mountain in SW Ireland in the Macgillycuddy's Reeks range, rising to 1041 m/3415 ft; highest peak in Ireland.

Carrel, Alexis (1873–1944) Biologist, born in Ste Foy-lès-Lyon, France. He studied at Lyon University, and moved to the Rockefeller Institute for Medical Research in New York City in 1906. He discovered a method of suturing blood-vessels which made it possible to replace arteries, and was awarded the 1912 Nobel Prize for Physiology or Medicine. He did much research on the prolongation of the life of tissues, and helped Henry Dakin (1880–1952) develop *Dakin's solution* for sterilizing deep wounds.

Carreras, José Maria [ka**rair**as] (1946–) Lyric tenor, born in Barcelona, NE Spain. He made his debut at Covent Garden and at the Metropolitan Opera (1974), La Scala (1975), and Salzburg (1976). After severe illness in the mid-1980s, he returned to the stage.

Carrey, Jim, popular name of **James Eugene Carrey** (1962–) Actor and entertainer, born in Newmarket, Ontario, Canada. He moved to Los Angeles in 1981, where he worked in nightclubs as a stand-up comedian and impressionist. He gained a role in the TV comedy sketch series *In Living Color* (1990–3) and appeared in the feature film *Earth Girls Are Easy* (1989), for which he also co-wrote the script. Known for his extrovert personality, later films include *Ace Ventura: Pet Detective* (1994), *The Mask* (1994), *Batman Forever* (1995), *The Truman Show* (1998), and *Bruce Almighty* (2003).

Carrington, Peter (Alexander Rupert) Carrington, 6th Baron (1919–) British statesman, born in London, UK. He trained at Sandhurst Military Academy, winning the Military Cross in World War 2, and held several junior posts in government (1951–6), before becoming high commissioner to Australia (1956–9). He then served as First Lord of the Admiralty (1959–63) and Leader of the House of Lords (1963–4). He was secretary of state for defence (1970–4) and briefly for energy (1974), and also chairman of the Conservative Party (1972–4). Upon the Conservative return to office he was foreign secretary (1979–82), until he and his ministerial team resigned over the Argentinian invasion of the Falkland Is. He later became secretary-general of NATO (1984–8) and Chancellor of the University of Reading.

carrion crow A crow native to Europe and Asia (*Corvus corone*); inhabits open forest, grassland, and cultivation; eats virtually anything; usually black. Grey carrion crows are called **hooded crows**. (Family: Corvidae.)

carrion flower A flower which attracts pollinating insects, usually flies, by giving off an odour of rotting meat. The flowers or associated parts are usually livid reddish-brown in colour to complete the disguise. Such plants occur in several unrelated families.

Carroll, Lewis, pseudonym of **Charles Lutwidge Dodgson** (1832–98) Writer, mathematician, and photographer, born in Daresbury, Cheshire, NWC England, UK. He studied at Oxford, took orders in 1861, and became a lecturer in mathematics (1855–81). His nursery tale, *Alice's Adventures in Wonderland* (1865), and its sequel, *Through the Looking-Glass* (1872), both describe a child's dream adventures, and quickly became classics. 'Alice', to whom the surreal and satirical story was originally related during boating excursions, was the second daughter (who died in 1934) of Henry George Liddell, the head of his Oxford college. He wrote a great deal of humorous and nonsense verse, such as 'The Hunting of the Snark' (1876), as well as several mathematical works. He was also a respected portrait photographer. He lived much of his life in the N of England. 'The Walrus and the Carpenter' was written on Whitburn Sands, Sunderland, and most of 'Jabberwocky' was also composed in Whitburn, where there is a statue in his memory.

carrot A biennial herb (*Daucus carota*) growing to 1 m/3·3 ft, native to Europe, temperate Asia, and N Africa; leaves divided, leaflets with toothed oval segments; flowers white or pink, borne in dense, rather flat-topped umbels, the central flower usually dark purple; fruits spiny. Wild carrots have tough roots, but the cultivated carrot (subspecies *sativus*), with a large fleshy orange or whitish tap root, has been grown since ancient times as a root vegetable and fodder for animals, and is also an important human dietary food. (Family: Umbelliferae.)

Carrott, Jasper, originally **Bob Davies** (1945–) Comedy entertainer, born in Acocks Green, Birmingham, West Midlands, UK. He had a variety of jobs before starting his own folk club in Solihull. He had a hit record with 'Funky Moped' (1975), and in 1978 starred in his own television show *An Audience with Jasper Carrott*. Later series include *Carrott's Lib* (1982–3), *Carrott Confidential* (1987–9), *Canned Carrott* (1990–1), and *The Detectives* (1992–4). In 2002 he took on a more serious acting role in the TV sit-com *All About Me*.

carroway thyme *thyme*

Carson, Johnny, popular name of **John William Carson** (1925–) Television personality and businessman, born in Corning, Iowa, USA. He studied journalism at Nebraska University, then worked in local radio and television from 1950. He hosted *Carson's Cellar* (1951) and wrote and performed on *The Red Skelton Show* (1954). Following *The Johnny Carson Show* (1955–6) and a stage appearance in *Tunnel of Love* (1958), he was engaged as an occasional host of *The Tonight Show*, a position that was made permanent in 1962. Consistently top of the ratings, his breezy, relaxed manner, comic monologue, and selection of guests made him an American institution. He retired from the show in 1992.

Carson, Kit, popular name of **Christopher Carson** (1809–68) Frontiersman, born in Madison Co, Kentucky, USA. A Missouri trapper and hunter, his knowledge of Indian habits and languages led to his becoming guide in John Frémont's explorations (1842). He was Indian agent in New Mexico (1853), and fought for the Union in the Civil War. Several places are named after him.

Carson, Rachel (Louise) (1907–64) Naturalist and publicist, born in Springdale, Pennsylvania, USA. She studied at Johns Hopkins University, and worked in marine biology in the US Fish and Wildlife Service (1936–49). She was an effective writer, and during the 1940s her books on marine ecology became influential. In 1962 her *Silent Spring* directed much public attention to the problems caused by agricultural pesticides, and she became a pioneer in the conservationist movement of the 1960s.

Carson City 39°10N 119°46W, pop (2000e) 52 500. State capital and independent city, W Nevada, USA, near L Tahoe; founded, 1858; named after the frontiersman Kit Carson; trade centre for a mining and agricultural area; tourism; a gambling centre; Nevada State Museum; Nevada Day (Oct).

Cartagena (de los Indes) (Colombia) [kartakhayna] 10°24N 75°33W, pop (2000e) 590 200. Port capital of Bolívar department, NW Colombia; on Caribbean coast SW of Barranquilla; founded, 1533; sacked by Francis Drake, 1586; airfield; university (1824); oil-refining, chemicals, plastics; the old colonial quarter is a world heritage site; several forts; Festival of the Virgin of La Candelaria (Jan–Feb); Independence of Cartagena (Nov), Caribbean Music Festival (Mar), Film Festival (Apr).

Cartagena (Spain) [kah(r)tajeena], Span [kartakhayna], Lat **Carthago Nova** 37°38N 0°59W, pop (2000e) 169 000. Fortified seaport and naval base in Murcia province, SE Spain, 48 km/30 mi S of Murcia; Spain's leading commercial port and naval base; formerly the largest naval arsenal in Europe; founded by the Carthaginians, 221 BC; two airports; railway; food processing, clothes, metallurgy, glass, oil refining; watersports; Castle of la Concepción, Church of Santa Maria la Vieja (13th-c); Virgen del Monte Carmel patronal festival (Jul).

Carte, Richard D'Oyly *D'Oyly Carte, Richard*

cartel [kah(r)tel] An agreement by a number of companies in the same industry to fix prices and/or quantities, thus avoiding cut-price competition or overproduction. It is often seen as not being in the public interest, since it does not allow market forces to operate freely. Many countries have made cartels illegal.

Carter, Angela (1940–92) Writer, born in Eastbourne, East Sussex, SE England, UK. She studied at Bristol University, and her first novel, *Shadow Dance*, was published in 1966. She then wrote novels and short stories characterized by feminist themes and fantasy narratives, including *The Magic Toyshop* (1967, screenplay 1986), *The Infernal Desire Machines of Dr Hoffman* (1972), *Nights at the Circus* (1984), and *Wise Children* (1991).

Carter, Benny, popular name of **Bennet Lester Carter** (1907–2003) Alto saxophonist and composer, born in New York City, USA. Although also a trumpeter and clarinettist, it was the warm tone of the alto saxophone that set the swing era style. He was among the outstanding early writers of big band arrangements, composing for the Fletcher Henderson and Benny Goodman orchestras, among others. He led big bands of his own, though none gained particular recognition. A spell in London in 1936 as musical director of the Henry Hall Orchestra had significant influence on the development of British jazz. He was composer-in-residence to the first Glasgow Jazz Festival in 1987.

Carter, Betty, originally **Lillie Mae Jones** (1930–98) Jazz singer and arranger, born in Flint, Michigan, USA. She was perhaps the major jazz singer of the 1980s and 1990s. In her younger days she sang with Charlie Parker and Dizzy Gillespie, and became known as 'Betty Bebop'; later she worked with Ray Charles and other blues artists, and continued performing into her sixties. She modelled her singing style more on jazz instrumentalists than on other vocalists, and projected it with an authoritative, prowling stage presence.

Carter, Elliott Cook, Jr (1908–) Composer, born in New York City, USA. He studied at Harvard University, and with Nadia Boulanger in Paris. Prizes and fellowships enabled him to alternate further periods of study with teaching at St John's College, Annapolis (1940–2), Peabody Conservatory (1946–8), Columbia University (1948–50), Queens College, New York City (1955–6), and Yale (1960–2). His second string quartet won a Pulitzer Prize in 1960. His other works, often of great complexity, include two symphonies, four concertos, and several sonatas.

Carter, Howard (1874–1939) Archaeologist, born in Swaffham, Norfolk, E England, UK. He joined Flinders Petrie's archaeological survey of Egypt as an artist in 1891, from 1907 conducting his own research under the patronage of George Herbert. His discoveries included the tombs of Hatshepsut (1907), Thutmose IV and, most notably, Tutankhamen (1922), a find on which he worked for the remainder of his life.

Carter, Jimmy, popular name of **James (Earl) Carter** (1924–) US statesman and 39th president (1977–81), born in Plains, Georgia, USA. He trained at the US Naval Academy, and served in the US navy until 1953, when he took over the family peanut business and other enterprises. As Governor of Georgia (1970–4) he expressed an enlightened policy towards the rights of African-Americans and women. In 1976 he won the Democratic presidential nomination, and went on to win a narrow victory over Gerald Ford. He arranged the peace treaty between Egypt and Israel (1979), and was much concerned with human rights at home and abroad. His administration ended in difficulties over the taking of US hostages in Iran and the Soviet invasion of Afghanistan, and he was defeated by Ronald Reagan in the 1980 election. He has been much involved in international diplomacy in several parts of the world, notably in relation to the crisis in Haiti in 1994. He was awarded the Nobel Prize for Peace in 2002.

Carteret, John, 1st Earl Granville [kah(r)tuhret] (1690–1763) British statesman and chief minister (1742–4), born in London, UK. He entered the House of Lords in 1711, and became ambassador to Sweden (1719), secretary of state (1721), and Lord-Lieutenant of Ireland (1724–9). As Earl Granville, he was driven from power by the Pelhams (1744) because of his pro-Hanoverian policies, though from 1751 was president of the Council under Henry Pelham, and twice refused the premiership.

Cartesian co-ordinates A method developed by Descartes of determining the position of a point by its distances from two fixed (and usually) perpendicular straight lines, called the *axes of co-ordinates*. The development of analytic geometry by Descartes and others enabled great advances to be made in the study of geometry, and was most convenient for the application of the calculus.

Cartesian geometry *analytic geometry*

Cartesian product In mathematics, the set of all possible ordered pairs from two sets, A and B, formed by taking one element of A and one of B. If $A = \{1,2\}$ and $B = \{a,b\}$, the Cartesian product $A \times B$ is the set $\{(1,a),(2,a),(1,b),(2,b)\}$.

Carthage 36°54N 10°16E. Ancient town in Tunisia, N Africa, now a suburb of Tunis; a world heritage site; reputedly founded by the Phoenicians in 814 BC; destroyed by Rome following the Punic Wars, 146 BC; refounded by Caesar and Octavian (29 BC); restored as capital by the Vandals, AD 439–533, but destroyed again by the Arabs, 698; the few remains include the Roman baths of Antonius, the old harbour, and an aqueduct of Hadrian; cathedral (1866); International Festival of Carthage (Jul–Aug).

Carthusian horse *Andalusian horse*

Carthusians A Roman Catholic monastic order founded in 1084 by Bruno of Cologne in Chartreuse, near Grenoble, France; properly known as the **Order of Carthusians**; abbreviated **OCart**. The monks practise strict abstinence and live as solitaries; lay brothers live in a community. Membership is small, but the order maintains houses in many parts of Europe. At the mother-house, 'La Grande Chartreuse', a famous liqueur is distilled, the profits being distributed to local charities.

Cartier, Jacques [ka(r)tyay] (1491–1557) Navigator, born in St-Malo, W France. He made three voyages of exploration to North America (1534–42), surveying the coast of Canada and the St Lawrence R, and providing the basis for later French claims in the area.

Cartier-Bresson, Henri [ka(r)tyay bresõ] (1908–) Photographer, born in Paris, France. He studied painting and literature before taking up photography after a trip to Africa (1930). His first pictures were published in 1933. In the later 1930s he worked as assistant to the film director Jean Renoir, and after the war was a co-founder of the independent photographic agency, Magnum Photos. He works only in black-and-white, concerned exclusively with the capturing of visual moments illustrating contemporary life. His books include *The World of Henri Cartier-Bresson* (1968). In the mid-1970s he gave up photography, and returned to his earlier interests of painting and drawing.

cartilage Tissue supplementary to bone in the skeleton, which may be temporary (as in the process of endochondrial ossification) or permanent (as in the nose, ear, and larynx); sometimes called **gristle**. It is composed of living cells surrounded by an intercellular substance containing collagen and/or elastin fibres. It is not hard or strong (so can be easily cut or damaged by high pressure), and is relatively nonvascular, being nourished by tissue fluids (particularly at joint surfaces). There are three main types. **Hyaline cartilage** forms the temporary cartilage model of bone, epiphyseal growth plates, the costal cartilages of the ribs, and is also found in the respiratory system (larynx, trachea, bronchi) and nasal septum. **White fibrocartilage** contains bundles of white fibrous tissue (giving it great tensile strength), present in intervertebral discs, the pelvis, the joint surfaces of the clavicle and the lower jaw, and the knee. **Yellow fibrocartilage** contains bundles of elastic fibres with little or no white fibrous tissue, present in the external ear, auditory tube, and epiglottis.

cartilaginous fish [kah(r)tilajinuhs] Any fish of the Class Chondrichthyes (800 species), having a cartilaginous endoskeleton that may be calcified but not ossified (true bone), and lacking air bladder or lungs; comprises the sharks and rays (Elasmobranchii) and ratfishes (Holocephalii).

Cartimandua [kah(r)timandyooa] (1st-c) Pro-Roman queen of the Brigantes, the British Celtic tribe that inhabited what is today the N of England. She protected the N borders of the Roman province of Britain after the conquest (43), until her overthrow by her husband, the anti-Roman Venutius, in 68–9.

Cartland, Dame (Mary) Barbara (Hamilton) (1901–2000) Popular romantic novelist, born in Edgbaston, West Midlands, C England, UK. She published her first novel, *Jigsaw*, in 1923, and produced a total of 723 novels, mostly dictated to a team of secretaries. Their theme was one of chaste romantic love in which only the scenery and names of characters changed. She wrote a further series of biographies, books on food, health, and beauty, and several volumes of autobiography. She earned a place in the *Guinness Book of Records* for writing 26 books in 1983. She married first, in 1927, **Alexander George McCorquodale** (d.1964), whom she divorced in 1933; then in 1936 his cousin, **Hugh McCorquodale** (d.1963). By her first marriage she was the mother of **Raine, Dowager Countess Spencer**, step-mother of the Princess of Wales (d.1997). She was an ardent advocate of health foods, and fitness for the elderly. She became a dame in 1991.

cartography The method of construction of maps and charts. Through the use of symbols, lettering, and shading techniques, data concerning an area (eg its relief, land use, and population density) are portrayed on a map in such a way that it can be interpreted by the user to find out information about a place. Data for mapping come from many sources, such as fieldwork, surveying, and remote sensing. Increasingly, computer-assisted cartography is being used in map production.

cartoon Originally, a full-size outline drawing which would be transferred to the wall or panel ready for painting; used in this way by painters since the Middle Ages, the word comes from the Italian *cartone* 'thick paper'. Raphael's famous cartoons, in the Victoria and Albert Museum, are in full colour, being designed for tapestries. When in 19th-c London a competition was held for frescoes in the Houses of Parliament, the cartoons submitted by candidates were parodied in *Punch*, and since then the word has had its popular meaning of a humorous drawing. A wide range of sub-genres have since developed, such as the caricature, political cartoon, and cartoon strip, and there has been a highly successful adaptation into the medium of film.

cartridge tape drive *magnetic tape 2*

Cartwright, Edmund (1743–1823) Inventor of the power loom, born in Marnham, Nottinghamshire, C England, UK. He studied at Oxford, became a clergyman (1779), and after visiting Arkwright's cotton-spinning mills devised his power loom (1785–90), and also a wool-combing machine (1790). Attempts to use the loom at Doncaster and Manchester met with fierce opposition, and it was not until the 19th-c that it came into practical use. In 1809 the government awarded him a grant of £10 000 for his achievements.

Caruso, Enrico [karoozoh] (1873–1921) Operatic tenor, born in Naples, SW Italy. He was born into a poor family, the 18th of 20 children, and received little formal education. He made his debut in Naples in 1894, in London in 1902, and in New York City in 1903. The extraordinary power of his voice, combined with his acting ability, won him worldwide recognition.

Carver, George Washington (1861–1943) Scientist, born near Diamond Grove, Missouri, USA. He was born into an African-American slave family, and received little formal education in his early years. He finally graduated from Iowa State Agricultural College in 1894, and became renowned for his research into agricultural problems and synthetic products, especially from peanuts, sweet potatoes, and soybeans. For much of his life he worked to make Tuskegee Institute, Alabama, a means of education for the disadvantaged black farmers of the South, and became famous as a teacher and humanitarian.

Cary, John [kairee] (c.1754–1835) English cartographer. He began as an engraver in London, UK, and became a publisher and land surveyor (c.1783). His *New and Correct English Atlas* appeared in 1787, followed by county atlases, and the *New Universal Atlas* of 1808. In 1794 he undertook a road survey of England and Wales, published as *Cary's New Itinerary* (1798).

Cary, (Arthur) Joyce (Lunel) [kairee] (1888–1957) Writer, born in Londonderry, Co Londonderry, NW Northern Ireland, UK. He studied art in Edinburgh and Paris, then law at Oxford, and fought in West Africa in World War 1. Injuries and ill health dictated his early retirement to Oxford, where he took up writing. Out of his African experience came several novels, such as *Mister Johnson* (1939). His best-known work is his trilogy, *Herself Surprised* (1941), *To be a Pilgrim* (1942), and *The Horse's Mouth* (1944).

caryatid [kareeatid, kariatid] A sculptured female figure, used as a column or support for an entablature or other building element. The name derives from the ancient Greek women of Caryae sold into slavery. It is also used in a general sense for any column or support carved in human form.

Casablanca [kasablangka], Arabic **Dar el Beida** 33°20N 71°25W, pop (2000e) 3 141 000. Seaport in Centre province, W Morocco; on the Atlantic coast 290 km/180 mi SW of Tangiers; founded by the Portuguese as Casa Branca, 1515; seriously damaged by an earthquake in 1755 and rebuilt; French occupation, 1907; meeting place of Churchill and Roosevelt, 1943; airport; railway; university; tourism, banking, fishing, textiles, food processing, glass, soap, phosphates, manganese; handles over 75% of Morocco's trade; world's second largest mosque (King Hassan II

Mosque) opened, 1993; target of terrorist suicide bomb attacks, May 2003.

Casablanca Conference A meeting in N Africa between Roosevelt and Churchill during World War 2 (Jan 1943), at which it was decided to insist on the eventual unconditional surrender of the Axis states. No agreement was reached on the claims for leadership of the rival French generals, Henri H Giraud and Charles de Gaulle, who also attended the conference. The combined chiefs of staff settled strategic differences over the projected invasion of Sicily and Italy.

Casals, Pablo [kasals], Catalan **Pau** (1876–1973) Cellist, conductor, and composer, born in Vendrell, NE Spain. He studied at the Royal Conservatory, Madrid, became professor of cello at Barcelona, and in 1899 began to appear as a soloist. In 1919 he founded the Barcelona Orchestra, which he conducted until he left Spain at the outbreak of the Civil War (1936). In 1950 he founded an annual festival of classical chamber music in Prades, France. His own compositions consist of choral and chamber works. During his later years, he conducted master classes.

Casanova (de Seingalt), Giacomo Girolamo [kasanohva] (1725–98) Adventurer and author, born in Venice, NE Italy. By 1750 he had worked as a clergyman, secretary, soldier, and violinist in various countries, and in 1755 was imprisoned for being a magician. He escaped in 1756, and for nearly 20 years wandered through Europe, visiting most of its capitals, and meeting the greatest men and women of the day. Alchemist, cabalist, and spy, he was everywhere introduced to the best society, and had always to 'vanish' after a brief period of felicity. In 1785 he established himself as librarian with the Count of Waldstein, in Bohemia, where he died. His main work is his autobiography, first published in complete form in 1960. His seductions are the first things many think of in connection with his name.

Cascade Range Mountain range in W North America; extends over 1120 km/700 mi from N California, through Oregon and Washington to British Columbia; named after the cascades of the Columbia R where it passes through the range in a canyon c.1200 m/4000 ft deep; highest point, Mt Rainier (4392 m/14 409 ft), Washington; other high peaks, Mts Adams (3742 m/12 277 ft), Baker (3285 m/10 777 ft), Hood (3424 m/11 233 ft), Jefferson (3200 m/10 498 ft) and Shasta (4317 m/14 163 ft); many are snow-covered volcanic cones; Mt St Helens (2549 m/8363 ft) erupted 1980; many glacial lakes (largest L Chelan); glaciers on the higher peaks, notably Mt Rainier; Crater Lake National Park in the S; Klamath and Columbia Rivers cut through the range from E to W; a 13 km/8 mi-long railway tunnel goes through the range E of Seattle; heavily forested; hydroelectricity.

case A grammatical category, associated primarily with nouns and pronouns, which registers the syntactic relations between words in a sentence. In inflectional languages, nouns have a range of variant forms, with affixes marking the various cases, as in Latin *mensa* ('table', nominative), *mensam* (accusative), and *mensae* (genitive). The cases have important grammatical functions: the nominative typically identifies a word that is the subject of a sentence; the accusative marks the object; while the genitive marks the possessor of something. Some languages have many case forms: Finnish, for example, has 15.

case-control study A scientific method used in medicine to determine the cause of a disease. Two groups of people, one with the disease under investigation and the other without, are analysed to see whether the diseased group has had a statistically greater exposure to the suspected risk factor. An example is the relationship between smoking and lung cancer: comparisons of groups of people with and without the disease have revealed a significantly greater history of smoking in the affected group.

case hardening A method of hardening tool steels or components subject to hard wear, such as gears. The object is heated in an atmosphere, or in contact with some substance (eg in a hydrocarbon oil), which alters its surface composition to that of a harder alloy. Aluminium steels are heated in an atmosphere of ammonia, which introduces nitrogen into the surface layer.

casein [kayseen] The main protein in milk and cheese, rich in associated calcium and phosphorus. Casein is heat-stable, but is precipitated at a pH of about 4·2 (mildly acid). This is exploited in cheese-making, where the initial step is the precipitation of the curd (casein and fat) from the whey. Casein can also be precipitated by rennet, the digestive enzyme of the calf.

Casement, Roger (David) [kaysment] (1864–1916) British consular official, born in Dun Laoghaire (formerly Kingstown), Co Dublin, E Ireland. He acted as consul in various parts of Africa (1895–1904) and Brazil (1906–11). Knighted in 1911, ill health caused him to retire to Ireland in 1912. An ardent Irish nationalist, he tried unsuccessfully to obtain German financial help for the cause. In 1916 he was arrested on landing in Ireland from a German submarine to head the Sinn Féin rebellion. He was tried in London, found guilty of high treason, stripped of his knighthood, and hanged. His controversial 'Black Diaries', revealing, among other things, homosexual practices, were long suppressed by the British government, but ultimately published in 1959. In 1965 his remains were taken to Ireland and reinterred at Glasnevin, Dublin, after a state funeral.

cashew A small evergreen tree (*Anacardium occidentale*), native to South America; leaves oval, alternate; flowers in terminal clusters, petals red, narrow, and reflexed; the receptacle thick, fleshy, pear-shaped in fruit, and bearing the curved nut. It is cultivated in Africa and Asia for cashew nuts and cashew apples (the receptacles). (Family: Anacardiaceae.)

cashmere The highly-prized fine warm undercoat fibres from the Kashmir goat; principally produced in China and Iran. One of the most luxuriant and expensive fibres, it is used mainly in knitwear.

Casimir, Hendrik [kazimeer] (1909–2000) Physicist, born in The Hague, The Netherlands. He studied physics at Leyden, Copenhagen, and Zürich, and became director of the Philips Research Laboratories in 1946. In 1934 he helped to devise a general theory of superconductivity; the later theory by Bardeen and others both includes and extends Casimir's work. The **Casimir effect** is a weak attractive force between conducting plates in a vacuum, predicted by Casimir in 1948 using quantum electrodynamics.

casino An establishment where gambling takes place, the best-known casino games being roulette, blackjack, and craps. The first legal casino opened in Baden-Baden in 1765, and rules governing their operation are very strict in most countries. Among the world's most famous casino locations are the US cities of Las Vegas, NV, and Atlantic City, NJ.

Čáslavská, Vera [kaslavska] (1942–) Gymnast, born in Prague, Czech Republic. She switched from ice skating to gymnastics as a 15 year-old, and went on to win 22 Olympic, world, and European titles. She won three Olympic gold medals in 1964, and four in 1968. She donated her medals one each to the four Czech leaders (Dubcek, Svoboda, Cernik, Smrkorsky) deposed following the Russian invasion. She married Josef Odložil, the Olympic 1500 m silver medallist in the Mexico City Olympics (1968).

Casper 42°51N 106°19W, pop (2000e) 49 600. Seat of Natrona Co, EC Wyoming, USA, on the North Platte R; largest city in the state; town expanded rapidly after oil discovered in the 1890s; airfield; railway; distributing, processing and trade centre in a farming, sheep/cattle ranching and mineral-rich area; oil refineries, oil-related industries; coal and open-pit uranium mining nearby; tourist centre; Old Fort Casper Museum.

Caspian Sea [kaspian], ancient **Mare Caspium** or **Mare Hyrcanium** area 371 000 sq km/143 200 sq mi. Largest inland body of water on Earth, surrounded on three sides by republics of the former USSR, and in the S by Iran; c.28 m/90 ft below sea-level, but much variation in level; maximum depth, 980 m/3215 ft in S; shallow N area, average depth 5·2 m/17 ft; low salinity; frozen in N for several months in severe winters; no outlet and no tides; pollution an increasing problem; UN-sponsored Caspian

Sea pact (agreed Nov 2003) aims to reduce amount of sewage and industrial waste pumped into sea; chief ports, Astrakhan, Baku; freight trade, especially oil from Baku; Beluga caviar.

Cassander [kasander] (c.358–297 BC) Ruler of Macedon after the death of his father Antipater in 319 BC, and its king from 305 BC. An active figure in the power struggle after Alexander's death (323 BC), he murdered Alexander's mother, widow, and son, and contributed to the defeat of Antigonus I Monophthalmos at Ipsus in 301 BC.

Cassandra [kasandra] In Greek legend, the daughter of Priam, King of Troy. She was favoured by Apollo, who gave her the gift of prophecy. Because she did not return his love, he decreed that while she would always tell the truth, she would never be believed. After the fall of Troy she was allotted to Agamemnon, and murdered on her arrival in Argos.

Cassatt, Mary [kasat] (1844–1926) Impressionist painter, born in Allegheny, Pennsylvania, USA. She studied in Spain, Italy, and Holland, but worked mainly in France, where she was a pupil and close follower of Degas. She was renowned for her etching and drypoint studies of domestic scenes.

cassava A food plant (*Manihot esculenta*), also called **manioc**, probably first cultivated by the Maya of Mexico, and now an important crop throughout the tropics. It ranges from low herbs to shrubs or slender trees, with fleshy, tuberous roots and fan-shaped, 5–9-lobed leaves. The raw roots are poisonous, containing a cyanide-producing sugar which must be destroyed by a complex process of grating, pressing, and heating. It can then be made into a wide range of products, including cassava flour, bread, tapioca, laundry starch, and an alcoholic drink. (Family: Euphorbiaceae.)

Cassegrain telescope [kasuhgran] A telescope designed by French scientist Laurent Cassegrain (c.1629–93) in 1672, and now the commonest optical system for a telescope. It has a paraboloid primary mirror with a central hole, a hyperboloid secondary mounted inside the focus of the primary, and the eyepiece behind the primary. Most of the world's largest optical telescopes currently use this arrangement. A variant of it, the Schmidt-Cassegrain, has a thin correcting lens as well, and is popular for amateur astronomy.

Cassel *Kassel*

Cassidy, Butch, originally **Robert LeRoy Parker** (1866–?1909) Outlaw, born in Beaver, Utah, USA. As a youth he learned cattle rustling and gunfighting. After serving time in Wyoming State Prison (1894–6) he joined the infamous Wild Bunch and was partner with the Sundance Kid. Together they roamed America, robbing banks, trains, and mine stations with the law in constant pursuit. From 1901 they lived mainly in South America, where (according to one theory) they were trapped and killed.

Cassini, Giovanni Domenico [kaseenee], also known as **Jean Dominique Cassini** (1625–1712) Astronomer, born in Perinaldo, NW Italy. In 1650 he became professor of astronomy at Bologna, and in 1669 the first director of the observatory at Paris. He greatly extended knowledge of the Sun's parallax, the periods of Jupiter, Mars, and Venus, and was the first to record observations of zodiacal light. In 1684 he discovered two natural satellites of Saturn, Dione and Tethys. *Cassini's division* (the gap between two of Saturn's rings) is named after him, and *Cassini's laws*, describing the rotation of the Moon, were formulated in 1693. He was succeeded as director at Paris by a dynasty of Cassinis.

Cassini–Huygens mission A spacecraft mission to Saturn and Titan undertaken as an international project by NASA, the European Space Agency (ESA), the Italian Space Agency (ASI), and several European academic and industrial partners. The mission has two main components: an orbital spacecraft (Cassini, supplied by NASA and powered by a radioisotope thermoelectric generator) that also serves as a carrier for a Titan atmospheric probe (Huygens, supplied by ESA). Launched in October 1997 on a Titan IVB-Centaur, the spacecraft requires several gravity assists (Venus–Earth–Jupiter) to reach Saturn in November 2004. The probe will take more than two hours to descend through the atmosphere of Titan, and the orbital tour of the many moons and the rings is planned to last four years.

Cassiodorus (Flavius Magnus Aurelius) [kasiohdawrus] (c.490–c.580) Roman writer and monk, born in Scylaceum (Squillace), Calabria. He was secretary to the Ostrogothic king, Theodoric, quaestor and praetorian prefect, sole consul in 514, and after Theodoric's death (526) chief minister to Queen Amalasontha. His *Institutiones* is an encyclopedic course of study for the monks of the Vivarium, which he founded and to which he retired.

Cassiopeia (astronomy) [kasiohpeea] A large N constellation that includes rich star fields in the Milky Way. A supernova of 1572 appeared in this constellation. It contains **Cassiopeia A**, the strongest radio source in the sky after the Sun. About 3 kiloparsec away, it is the remnant of a supernova estimated to have exploded c.1667, but which went unseen.

Cassiopeia (mythology) [kasiohpaya] In Greek mythology, the beautiful daughter of Arabus who gave his name to the country called Arabia. She is said to have been the wife of King Cepheus of Ethiopia by whom she bore Andromeda. Cassiopeia was turned into a constellation.

Cassirer, Ernst [kaseerer] (1874–1945) Philosopher, born in Wrocław, SW Poland (formerly Breslau, Prussia). He studied at Berlin, Leipzig, Heidelberg, and Marburg, where he was attracted to neo-Kantianism. He worked as a tutor and civil servant, then became professor of philosophy at Hamburg (1919), and rector (1930), but he resigned when Hitler came to power, and taught at Oxford (1933–5), Göteborg (1935–41), Yale (1941–4) and Columbia (from 1944 until his death). His best-known work, *Die Philosophie der symbolischen Formen* (1923–9, The Philosophy of Symbolic Forms), analyses the symbolic functions underlying all human thought, language, and culture.

cassiterite [kasiteriyt] The mineral form of tin oxide (SnO_2), a black, hard, dense material originally formed in hydrothermal veins associated with igneous rocks, though many deposits are alluvial. It is the main ore of tin.

Cassius [kasius], in full **Gaius Cassius Longinus** (?–42 BC) Roman soldier and politician. An opponent of Caesar during the civil war with Pompey, he was pardoned by him after Pharsalus (48 BC). Despite gaining polical advancement through Caesar and the promise of the post of Governor of Syria, he later turned against him again, and played a leading part in the conspiracy to murder him (44 BC). He raised an army in Syria, defeated Dolabella, and marched against the Triumverate, but was defeated by Caesar's avengers at Philippi (42 BC), and committed suicide.

Cassivellaunus [kasivelawnus] (1st-c BC) British chief of the Catavellauni, a British tribe living in the area of modern Hertfordshire, SE England, UK. He led the British resistance to Julius Caesar on his second invasion, 54 BC.

Casson, Sir Hugh (Maxwell) [kasn] (1910–99) British architect. He studied at Cambridge, and was professor of interior design at the Royal College of Art (1953–75). He directed the architecture of the Festival of Britain (1951), and was president of the Royal Academy (1976–84). He was knighted in 1952.

cassowary [kasohwairee] A large flightless bird native to S Australasia; eats seeds and fruit; inhabits forests; naked head has a bony outgrowth (*casque*), used as a shovel to uncover food; feet with long claws; its kick may be fatal. (Genus: *Casuarius*, 3 species. Family: Casuariidae.)

Castagno, Andrea del [kastanyoh], originally **Andrea di Bartolo de Simone** (c.1421–57) Painter, born in Castagno, NW Italy. After early privations he attracted the attention of Bernardetto de' Medici, who sent him to study in Florence. In c.1440 he painted some effigies of men hanged by their heels, which established his reputation as a painter of violent scenes. His celebrated 'Last Supper', painted for S Apollonia, is now in the Castagno Museum, as are his series of 'Famous Men and Women', painted for a villa at Legnaia. In his own time he was praised as a draughtsman.

castanets Pairs of wooden (usually chestnut) discs, slightly concave, worn on the thumbs and clicked together rhythmically to accompany dancing, especially in Spain. Orchestral castanets are normally mounted on a wooden stick.

caste A system of inequality, most prevalent in Hindu Indian society, in which status is determined by the membership of a particular lineage and associated occupational group into which a person is born. The groups are ordered according to a notion of religious purity or spirituality; thus, the Brahmin or priest caste, as the most spiritual of occupations, claims highest status. Contact between castes is held to be polluting, and must be avoided.

Castiglione, Baldassare, conte di (Count of) **Novilara** [kasteelyohnay] (1478–1529) Writer and diplomat, born near Mantua, N Italy. He studied at Milan, began a career at court, and in 1505 was sent by the Duke of Urbino as envoy to Henry VII of England, who made him a knight. His chief work, *Il cortegiano* (1528, The Courtier), is a manual for courtiers. He also wrote Italian and Latin poems, and many letters illustrating political and literary history.

Castile or **Castille** [kasteel] (Span **Castilla**) Central region and a component kingdom of Spain. The United County of Castile was formed in 970, and during the 11th-c and most of the 12th-c was subject to the suzerainty of Léon or Navarre. Hegemony over Léon was established in 1188, and the union of Castilian and Leonese crowns took place in 1230. The union of crowns with the Kingdom of Aragon (1469–79), the conquest of Granada (1492), and the annexation of Navarre (1512) created the basis of the modern Spanish state.

Castilho, Antonio Feliciano, Viscount [kasteelyoh] (1800–75) Poet, blind from childhood, born in Lisbon, Portugal. His volumes, *Cartas de Echo e Narciso* (1821, Letters from Echo and Narcissus) and *Amor e melancholia* (1828, Love and Melancholy), inaugurated the Portuguese Romantic movement. He also translated Virgil, Ovid, Shakespeare, and Goethe.

casting The pouring of molten metal into a mould, where it solidifies into an ingot of manageable size for further processing, or into a desired final shape. Some metals can be **continuously cast**, solidified metal being removed at one end of a continuous length as more molten metal is added at the beginning. Some alloys (often containing zinc) can be **die-cast**, ie cast under pressure into a complex re-usable mould to give intricate shapes. Some of these processes can be applied to certain plastics.

cast iron The primary product of the blast furnace: iron with about 4% carbon (**pig iron**). It has a low melting point and solidifies well into the shape of the mould. It is therefore valuable for casting, but has to be purified or modified before being used for manufacture. It machines well, but its defects are brittleness and lack of tensile strength. Cast iron can be treated to modify the form of the carbon inclusions (**spheroidal cast iron**) so as to improve its properties. In the past cast iron was used as a building or construction material, as it is very strong in compression.

Castle (of Blackburn), Barbara (Anne) Castle, Baroness, *née* **Betts** (1911–2002) British stateswoman, born in Bradford, West Yorkshire, N England, UK. She studied at Oxford, in 1944 married a journalist, **Edward Cyril Castle**, later Baron Castle (1907–79), and became Labour MP for Blackburn in 1945. She was chairman of the Labour Party (1958–9), minister of overseas development (1964–5), and a controversial minister of transport (1965–8), introducing a 70 mph speed limit, and the 'breathalyser' test for drunken drivers. She became secretary of state for employment and productivity (1968–70) and for social services (1974–6). She then returned to the back benches, but was later elected to the European Parliament, where she became vice-chair of the Socialist group (1979–86). She became a life peer in 1990. Her writing includes *The Castle Diaries* (1980, 1984), *Sylvia and Christabel Pankhurst* (1987), and a volume of autobiography, *Fighting All the Way* (1993).

Castle, Roy (1932–94) Entertainer, born in Scholes, West Yorkshire, N England, UK. A talented musician, dancer, and actor, he starred in cabaret, theatre, film, and television, becoming known for such programmes as BBC television's *Record Breakers*. Following his death from lung cancer, the Roy Castle Cause for Hope Foundation, a research centre into the disease, was launched in Liverpool in 1994, with building completed in 1997.

castle Castles were the products of feudal society as it spread across Europe and into the Crusader kingdoms. Found in France from the mid-10th-c, they reached England as a result of the Norman Conquest, where they were built in large numbers by the new Norman elite. The earliest English castles were normally earthen mounds surrounded by ditches and topped by wooden towers. In 12th-c England, castle-builders increasingly used stone for towers and walls, and in the 13th-c Edward I built a fine series of castles in Wales (eg Caernarfon, Conwy, Harlech). Castles served as residences, seats of justice, administrative centres, and symbolic manifestations of lordly authority. Despite their defensive features, the main value of castles in war was their offensive role in mastering the surrounding countryside. They were often ineffective in frontier defence, and from c.1200 advances in siege warfare and, especially important, the 16th-c development of firearms further reduced their defensive capacity. Later in the Middle Ages, especially in England, increasing emphasis was placed on their non-military roles, with greater concessions to domestic comfort and ornamental display, while growing to accommodate large royal retinues. Many beautiful examples of European castles survive as testimony to their country's history, such as Hradčany Castle, Prague, which was a 9th-c fortress and is now a vast presidential residence.

Castlebar [kaslbah(r)], Ir **Caisleán an Bharraigh** 53°52N 9°17W, pop (2000e) 7800. Capital of Mayo county, Connacht, W Ireland, on R Castlebar; residential and agricultural market town; Irish Land League founded here in 1879; airfield; railway; linen, hats, bacon; international song contest (Oct).

Castlereagh, Robert Stewart, Viscount [kaslray] (1769–1822) British statesman, born in Dublin, Ireland. He studied at Cambridge, and became Whig MP for Co Down (1790), turning Tory in 1795. He was created Viscount Castlereagh in 1796, and became Irish secretary (1797), President of the Board of Control (1802), and minister of war (1805–6, 1807–9). His major achievements date from 1812, when, as foreign secretary under Lord Liverpool, he was at the heart of the coalition against Napoleon (1813–14). He represented England at Chaumont and Vienna (1814–15), Paris (1815), and Aix-la-Chapelle (1818). He advocated 'Congress diplomacy' among the great powers, to avoid further warfare. Believing that he was being blackmailed for homosexuality, he committed suicide at Foots Cray, his Kentish seat.

Castner–Kellner process A process for the manufacture of sodium hydroxide and chlorine by the electrolysis of brine in a tank with barriers separating compartments. The brine lies over a mercury bath, which acts as a cathode, and can be made to flow from one compartment to another. Chlorine is liberated at iron anodes. Sodium liberated at the mercury cathode forms an amalgam, which flows to another compartment where it reacts with water to form sodium hydroxide free of sodium chloride.

Castor and Pollux, Gr **Kastor** and **Polydeuces** Two heroes of classical mythology, known as the **Dioscuri**, usually pictured as twin brothers on horseback. They were children of Leda, at least one being fathered by Zeus. After death they became divine beings, and were turned into the constellation Gemini. They appear in the form of St Elmo's Fire to help mariners, and were an important early cult at Rome.

castor-oil plant An evergreen plant (*Ricinus communis*), in its native tropics forming a tall shrub or tree, in temperate regions only a stout herb; leaves each with 5–12 deep lobes, often bronze-green; flowers tiny, green, in dense male and female clusters; oil-rich seeds poisonous, but when processed yield castor oil. (Family: Euphorbiaceae.)

castration The surgical removal of the sex glands (testes or ovaries). When carried out in children, secondary sexual characteristics do not develop. In adults, physical changes are less marked, but the individuals are sterile. In contrast with surgical castration, medical castration consists of giving drugs that block the normal effects of male or female sex hormones. It is used in the treatment of some forms of cancer.

castrato A male singer who underwent castration before puberty in order to preserve his treble voice. The practice probably originated at the Vatican in the 16th-c to compensate for the absence of women's voices from the choirs. Castrati took many of the leading roles in Italian opera during the 17th-c and 18th-c, the most famous being Carlo Broschi, known as Farinelli (1705–82). They ceased to be used in opera after c.1825, but were employed at the Sistine Chapel until the end of the 19th-c. The last castrato there, Alessandro Moreschi, died in 1922.

Castries [**kas**trees] 14°01N 60°59W, pop (2000e) 56 500. Port and capital town of St Lucia, Windward Is, E Caribbean, on NW coast; founded, 1650; rebuilt after a fire in 1948; airport; foodstuffs, beverages, tobacco, textiles, wood, rubber and metal products, printing, chemicals, tourism.

Castro (Ruz), Fidel (1927–) Cuban revolutionary, prime minister (1959–), and president (1976–), born near Birán, S Cuba. He studied law in Havana. In 1953 he was imprisoned after an unsuccessful rising against Batista, but released under an amnesty. He fled to the USA and Mexico, then in 1956 landed in Cuba with a small band of insurgents. In 1958 he mounted a full-scale attack and Batista was forced to flee. As prime minister he proclaimed a 'Marxist–Leninist programme', and set about far-reaching reforms. His overthrow of US economic dominance, and the routing of the US-connived emigré invasion at the Bay of Pigs (1961), was balanced by his dependence on Russian aid.

casuarina *she-oak*

cat A carnivorous mammal of the family Felidae; name popularly used for the domestic cat, *Felis catus*, other species having individual names (lion, tiger, etc); domestic cats known in Egypt 4000 years ago and may have evolved there from the **wild cat** (or **caffre cat**); numerous modern breeds, classed as **hairless**, **long-haired**, **British short-haired** (stocky breeds, descended from European ancestors – called 'British' because the first cat show was held in Britain), **American** (or **domestic**) **short-haired** (descended from the British), and **foreign short-haired** (smaller, more slender breeds, with ancestors from the Middle-East and elsewhere); male called a *tom*, female a *queen*, young are *kittens*.

catabolism *metabolism*

catacombs Subterranean Jewish or early Christian cemeteries found in certain parts of the Roman world – notably Rome itself – where soft rocks made the tunnelling of passages and carving of burial niches easy. The practice is believed to have been derived from ancient Jewish cave burials.

Catalan *Romance languages*

Catalaunian Plains, Battle of the [katal**aw**nian] (451) The decisive defeat in E France suffered by Attila the Hun at the hands of the Romans and Visigoths. Deflected from France, he turned S to Italy, which he ravaged the following year.

catalepsy The adoption of a body posture which would normally be unsustainable; also referred to as **waxy flexibility**. It occurs in serious psychotic illness or as a hysterical reaction.

Çatal Hüyük [cha**tahl** hoo**yuk**] A prehistoric riverside settlement of c.6500–5500 BC in S Turkey, c.50 km/30 mi SE of Konya, the largest Neolithic site known in the Near East. The *tell* (mound) is 20 m/65 ft high, and covers 13 ha/32 acres, its 12 successive levels being packed with rectangular mudbrick houses, courtyards, and shrines; its estimated population was c.5000. Spectacular cult fittings include wall paintings, plastered reliefs, and numerous bull's head effigies.

Catalonia [kata**loh**nia], Span **Cataluña**, Catalan **Catalunya** pop (2000e) 6 038 000; area 31 932 sq km/12 320 sq mi. Autonomous region of NE Spain, comprising the provinces of Barcelona, Girona, Lleida, and Tarragona, and formerly including Roussillon and Cerdana; area with a distinctive culture and Romance language; united with Aragon, 1137; created a mediaeval trading empire, 13th–14th-c; part of Spain following union of Castilian and Aragonese crowns, 1469–79; strong separatist movement since the 17th-c; Catalan republic established in 1932, abolished by Franco during the Civil War, 1936–9; new government established, 1979; cereals, olives, almonds, hazelnuts, grapes; industry centred on Barcelona; hydroelectric power from R Ebro; major tourist resorts on the Costa Brava.

catalpa *Indian bean tree*

catalysis [ka**tal**isis] The acceleration or slowing of a chemical reaction by the action of a material (**catalyst**) which is recovered unchanged at the end of the reaction. It is of immense importance in chemistry and biology, accelerating reactions that otherwise proceed very slowly, although they are energetically favourable. Catalysts include iron in the Haber process for ammonia, and chlorophyll in photosynthesis. Catalysis within a single phase (eg a solution) is called *homogeneous*, that in more than one phase *heterogeneous*.

catalytic converter An antipollution device fitted to a car exhaust system, now standard in Japan and the USA, and becoming quite common in Europe. It contains a platinum catalyst for chemically converting unburned hydrocarbons and nitrogen oxides to compounds harmless to the environment.

catalytic cracking The breaking down (*cracking*) of the hydrocarbon molecules of petroleum, which in their initial state are too large to be useful. When the petroleum is distilled, the way the large molecules are made to break down can be induced to follow desired paths by several means, one being the use of *catalysts* – substances which intervene in the chemical process without being consumed by the product.

catamaran [**kat**amaran, katama**ran**] A twin-hulled vessel of Tamil origin, offering advantages in speed and stability. Propelled nowadays either by sail or power, it has become very popular as a yacht design in the past 25 years, and the advantages of the design have also proved attractive to firms introducing a new generation of car/passenger ferries.

catamount *cougar*

Catania [ka**tah**nia] 37°31N 15°06E, pop (2000e) 364 000. Port and capital of Catania province, Sicily, S Italy; 160 km/100 mi SE of Palermo, at foot of Mt Etna, on E coast; archbishopric; airport; railway; university (1444); agricultural trade, shipbuilding, textiles, paper, footwear, sulphur processing, tourism.

cataplexy The sudden loss of all muscle tone. It is usually associated with narcolepsy.

cataract Opacities in the lens of the eye which cause slowly progressive loss of vision. Senile cataract is the most common type, but cataracts may also follow excessive exposure to ultraviolet light, or injury to the eye, as well as being a complication of diabetes and other conditions associated with rapid changes in the solute concentration of body fluids. Congenital cataracts occur as a rare genetic disease, and also following maternal rubella. When severe, the lens can be removed and the vision corrected with the aid of spectacles and an artificial lens implantation.

catastrophe theory The mathematical study of sudden change, such as the bursting of a bubble, in contrast to continuous change. For example, in Necker's cube, the location of a dot appears first either in the centre of one face or in a corner of another face, then suddenly changes. It is not possible to say in which face any one viewer will first see it, but it always changes suddenly. Catastrophe theory was created in the late 1950s and early 1960s by French mathematician René Thom (1923–) and developed in particular by Stephen Smale, Vladimir Arnold, Christopher Zeeman, and others. There are many applications to economics and behavioural sciences as well as to the natural sciences.

catastrophism (geology) *uniformitarianism*

catatonia A psychiatric state in which there is stupor associated with catalepsy, or overactivity associated with stereotyped behaviour. This condition was first described by the German physician Karl Ludwig Kahlbaum (1828–99) in 1874, and is seen particularly in manic-depressive illnesses and schizophrenia. There may be repetitive movements, the repetition of sounds or phrases the patient has heard (echolalia), automatic obedience, and negativism.

cat bear *panda*

Catch-22 The title of a novel by Joseph Heller, published in 1961. US airmen seeking to be excused bombing missions in World War 2 on grounds of mental derangement are judged ineligible to apply, since such a request proves their sanity. Hence 'Catch-22' signifies any logical trap or double bind.

catchfly An annual or perennial herb, part of the same genus as campions, but with hairy, sticky stem; native to the temperate N hemisphere; leaves opposite; calyx tubular, five petals, notched or bifid, white, pink, or yellow. (Genus: *Silene*. Family: Caryophyllaceae.)

catechism A manual of Christian doctrine, in question-and-answer form. It derived from the early Church period of instruction for new converts, and was later applied to the instruction of adults baptized in infancy. Such manuals became popular after the Reformation, eg the Heidelberg Catechism (1563). These were intended for instruction, preparation for confirmation, and confessional purposes. Some have avoided the question-and-answer format, such as the Roman Catholic 'New Catechism' of 1966 and the 'Universal Catechism' of 1992.

catechol [**kat**ekohl] $C_6H_4(OH)_2$, 1,2-dihydroxybenzene, melting point 105°C. A colourless solid which can form strong complexes with metals by chelation. Important derivatives include adrenaline and dopa.

catecholamine [katekohlameen] The chemical classification of a group of biologically important components widely distributed among animals and plants. Those occurring in mammalian tissues are dopamine, noradrenaline, and adrenaline, all of which have important roles in the functioning of the sympathetic and central nervous systems. They are crucial in the control of blood pressure, and in the 'flight or fight' response.

Categorical Imperative A principle introduced into ethics by Kant to distinguish the overriding, objective force of moral injunctions (eg 'do not lie') from the **hypothetical imperatives** of other prescriptions (eg 'if you want to avoid cancer, stop smoking'). He formulated the principle as 'act so that you can will the principle of your action to become a universal law' or 'act so that you treat humanity as an end, never merely a means'.

catenary (Lat *catena*, 'chain') In mathematics, the plane curve in which an 'ideal' chain hangs under its own weight. The simplest Cartesian equation is $y = \frac{a}{2}(e^{\frac{x}{a}} + (e^{\frac{-x}{a}})$.

catenation In chemistry, chain formation by bonding between atoms of the same element. It is seen most strikingly in carbon compounds, but is also found with other elements, especially sulphur.

caterpillar The larval stage of butterflies and moths (Order: Lepidoptera), usually feeding on plants; occasionally also used for the larvae of sawflies (Order: Hymenoptera).

caterpillar bird *cuckoo shrike*

Catesby, Robert [**kayts**bee] (1573–1605) Chief conspirator involved in the Gunpowder Plot, born in Lapworth, Warwickshire, C England, UK. A Catholic of wealth and lineage, he had suffered much as a recusant both by fines and imprisonment. He was imprisoned in 1601 for his part in the abortive uprising of Robert Devereux, 2nd Earl of Essex, and again in 1603 for promoting a Spanish invasion. He was shot dead while resisting arrest after the failure of the Gunpowder Plot (1605).

catfish Any of about 28 families of typically elongate bottom-living fishes; flattened head, smooth skin, long barbels around mouth; habits often sluggish, nocturnal; several important as food fish and in the aquarium trade; includes freshwater families Siluridae, Bagridae, Clariidae, Ictaluridae, and marine Ariidae, Plotosidae.

cat flu A disease of the upper respiratory tract of cats. Of the organisms involved, *feline viral rhinotracheitis* (FVR) and *feline calici virus* (FVC) are the commonest, causing varying degrees of inflammation with oculo-nasal discharge. Ulceration of the tongue and palate as well as obstruction of the nasal passages leads to lack of appetite and further debility. Other infections may supervene, and pneumonia may result. A great deal of supportive nursing is needed to aid treatment. The disease is highly infectious. Recovered cats can remain as carriers, and may start to shed the virus when stressed. Cats may be protected by the use of vaccines, and most cat-boarding establishments require evidence of up-to-date vaccination before accepting an animal. A different condition, **feline infectious enteritis** is occasionally called by the same name.

catgut A tough cord prepared from the intestines of sheep (sometimes horse or ass, but never a cat). The intestine is cleaned, steeped in alkali, and sterilized by sulphur fumes. It has been used for musical instrument strings and surgical sutures (now replaced for the most part by synthetic fibres). *Cat* seems to be derived from *kit* 'fiddle'.

Cathars [**kath**ah(r)z] (Gr *kathari* 'pure ones') Originally, 3rd-c separatists from the Church, puritan and ascetic, following the teaching of the 3rd-c Roman bishop, Novatian. In the Middle Ages, as a sect, they were known in Bulgaria as **Bogomils** and in France as **Albigenses**. Celibate, they rejected sacraments and held 'good' and 'evil' to be separate spheres ('dualism'). They survived until the 14th-c, when they were finally exterminated by the Inquisition.

cathartid vulture *vulture*

cathedral (Lat *cathedra*, 'chair') The chief church of a bishop of a diocese; originally, the church which contained the throne of the bishop, then the mother church of the diocese. The most famous are the W European Gothic cathedrals built in the Middle Ages, such as those at Reims and Chartres, France (both 13th-c). In many towns, they were the centre around which social and cultural as well as religious life developed. The largest cathedral in the world is thought to be New York City's Episcopalian Cathedral of St John the Divine, which has been under intermittent construction since 1892. Famous cathedrals include St Mark's (Venice, Italy), St Paul's (London, UK), Notre Dame (Paris, France), and St Peter's Basilica (Rome, Italy).

Catherine, Mount, Arabic **Katherina, Gebel** 28°30N 33°57E. Mountain in S Sinai governorate, NE Egypt; height 2637 m/8651 ft; highest point in Egypt; St Catherine's monastery (6th-c), altitude 1500 m/4921 ft.

Catherine II, known as **Catherine the Great**, originally **Princess Sophie Friederike Auguste von Anhalt-Zerbst** (1729–96) Empress of Russia (1762–96), born in Szczecin (Stettin), NW Poland. A German princess, she was the daughter of Christian Augustus, prince of Anhalt-Zerbst. In 1745 she was married to the heir to the Russian throne (later Peter III, r.1761–2). Their marriage was an unhappy one, and Catherine (now baptized into the Russian Orthodox Church under that name) spent much of her time in political intriguing, reading, and extramarital affairs. In 1762 a palace coup overthrew her unpopular husband; he was murdered, and she was proclaimed empress. She carried out an energetic foreign policy and extended the Russian Empire S to the Black Sea as a result of the Russo–Turkish Wars (1774, 1792) while in the W she brought about the three partitions of Poland (1772, 1793, 1795). Despite pretensions to enlightened ideas, her domestic policies achieved little for the mass of the Russian people, though great cultural advances were made among the nobility. In 1774 she suppressed the popular rebellion led by Pugachev, and later actively persecuted members of the progressive-minded nobility while curtailing the rights of serfs. She increased Russian control over the Baltic provinces and Ukraine. She secured the largest portion of Poland in successive partitions of that country. Russia became the dominant power in the Middle East through the Treaty of Kuchuk Kainarji (1774). In 1783 she annexed the Crimea and cemented Russia's hold on the N Coast of the Black Sea. An active patron of the arts and education, she wrote memoirs, comedies, and stories, and corresponded with the French encyclopedists, notably Voltaire, Diderot, and d'Alembert. Of her many lovers, Orlov, Potemkin, and P L Zubor (1767–1822) were the most influential in government affairs. She was succeeded by her son, Paul I.

Catherine de' Medici [maydeechee] (1519–89) Queen of France, the wife of Henry II, and regent (1560–74), born in Florence, NC Italy, the daughter of Lorenzo de' Medici, Duke of Urbino. Married at 14, she was slighted at the French court, but during the minority of her sons, Francis II (1559–60) and Charles IX (1560–3), she assumed political influence which she retained as queen mother until 1588. She tried to pursue moderation and toleration, to give unity to a state increasingly torn by religious division between the Catholic Guise faction and the Huguenots, but she nursed dynastic ambitions, and was drawn into political and religious intrigues, conniving in the infamous Massacre of St Bartholomew (1572). After the accession of her third son, Henry III, she continued to rule the court, and unsuccessfully attempted religious reconciliation between the Protestant and Catholic factions.

Catherine of Aragon [aragon] (1485–1536) Queen of England, the first wife of Henry VIII (1509–33), born in Alcalá de Henares, C Spain, the fourth daughter of Ferdinand and Isabella of Spain. She was first married in 1501 to Arthur (1486–1502), the son of Henry VII, and following his early death was betrothed to her brother-in-law Henry, then a boy of 11. She married him in 1509, and bore him five children, but only the Princess Mary survived. In 1527 Henry began a procedure for annulment of the marriage, which was refused by Pope Clement VII. Henry then proceeded on his own; a court presided over by Thomas Cranmer pronounced his marriage to Catherine invalid (1533), thereby breaking with the pope, and starting the English Reformation. Catherine then retired to lead an austere religious life until her death.

Catherine of Braganza [braganza] (1638–1705) Wife of Charles II of England, born in Vila Viçosa, E Portugal, the daughter of King John IV of Portugal. She was married to Charles in 1662 as part of an alliance between England and Portugal, but failed to produce an heir. She helped to convert him to Catholicism just before his death, after which she returned to Portugal (1692).

Catherine of Siena, St [syayna], originally **Caterina Benincasa** (1347–80) Nun and mystic, born in Siena, C Italy. She became a Dominican, and gained a great reputation for holiness, writing many devotional pieces, letters, and poems. She prevailed on Pope Gregory XI to return the papacy from Avignon to Rome. Christ's stigmata were said to have been imprinted on her body. She was canonized in 1461, and is the patron saint of Italy. Feast day 29 April.

catheter [katheter] A fine tube made of rubber or synthetic material for insertion into parts of the body cavities, such as the bladder, blood vessels, the chambers of the heart, and the respiratory passages. It is used either to introduce drugs and fluids, to withdraw blood and body fluids for analysis, or to measure pressure or rates of flow.

cathode In electrolysis and gas discharge tubes, the negative electrode by which electrons enter the cell or tube. In a battery, the cathode is the positive terminal by which electrons enter the battery. For a circuit connected to a battery, conventional current flows from the positive cathode of the battery through the circuit to the negative anode. A cation is a positive ion that moves towards the negative cathode in electrolysis; metals are removed from the anode and deposited at the cathode in electrolysis.

cathode rays *electron*

cathode-ray tube (CRT) An electronic device in which an image is formed on a phosphor screen in a vacuum tube by a beam of electrons deflected in electric or magnetic fields. It is used in oscilloscopes, display screens, and television receivers.

Catholic Church (Gr *katholikos*, 'general', 'universal') **1** As in the Apostles' Creed, the universal Church which confesses Jesus Christ as Lord.
2 Christian Churches with episcopal order and confessing ancient creeds.
3 Specifically, the Roman Catholic Church and other Churches recognizing the primacy of the Pope, as distinct from Protestant and Orthodox Churches.

Catholic Emancipation Act A reluctant religious concession to Roman Catholics in the British Isles, granted by the British Tory government of the Duke of Wellington in 1829, following mounting agitation led by Daniel O'Connell and the Catholic Association. Earlier civil disabilities suffered by Roman Catholics had gradually been lifted in the 18th-c and 19th-c. Priest-hunting in general had ceased by the mid-18th-c. In 1778 English Catholics were relieved of the restrictions on land inheritance and purchase. In 1793 the army, the navy, the universities, and the judiciary were opened to Catholics. In 1829 Roman Catholics were permitted to become MPs; and all offices of state except Viceroy and Chancellor, were also opened to Catholics. However, Roman Catholics remain excluded from the British throne.

Catiline [katiliyn], in full **Lucius Sergius Catilina** (c.108–62 BC) An impoverished Roman politician of patrician extraction who tried to exploit the economic unrest of Rome and Italy in the 60s BC for his own political ends. His conspiracy against the state was foiled by Cicero late in 63 BC, and he fell in battle early in 62 BC.

cation [katiyon] An ion bearing a positive charge, so called because it will migrate towards the cathode in an electrochemical cell.

catmint A square-stemmed perennial (*Nepeta cataria*), growing to 1 m/3¾ ft, native to Europe and Asia, often on chalky soils; oval, toothed leaves in opposite pairs; flowers 2-lipped, white spotted with purple, in whorls forming spikes; also called **catnip**. A relative of true mints, its strong scent is attractive to cats. (Family: Labiatae.)

catnip *catmint*

Cato, Marcus Porcius [kaytoh], known as **Cato the Elder** or **Cato the Censor** (234–149 BC) Roman statesman, orator, and man of letters, born in Tusculum, Latium. Deeply conservative, and strongly opposed to the contemporary fashion of all things Greek, when made censor (184 BC) he conducted such a vigorous campaign that he was thereafter known by this name. Sent on a mission to Carthage (175 BC), he was so impressed by the power of the Carthaginians that afterwards he ended every speech in the Senate with the words: 'Carthage must be destroyed'. His treatise on agriculture is the oldest extant literary prose work in Latin.

Cato, Marcus Porcius [kaytoh], known as **Cato the Younger** or **Cato Uticensis** (95–46 BC) Roman statesman, the great-grandson of Cato the Censor. A man of uncompromising principles and deep conservatism, his career was marked by an unswerving opposition to Caesar. A supporter of Pompey in the Civil War, after Pharsalus (48 BC) he escaped to Africa. On hearing of Caesar's overwhelming victory at Thapsus (46 BC), he killed himself.

Cato Street conspiracy [kaytoh] A plot in February 1820, formulated by Arthur Thistlewood (1770–1820) and fellow radical conspirators, to blow up the British Tory cabinet as it attended a dinner at the house of the Earl of Harrowby. The plot was infiltrated by a government agent, and the leaders were arrested and hanged.

CAT scanning *computerized tomography*

cat's eyes In the UK, rubber road studs fitted with a pair of light reflectors, designed to mark road lanes at night by reflecting a vehicle's headlights; devised by UK inventor Percy Shaw in 1934. The device can be compressed by the vehicle's wheels without doing damage to itself or the wheel. It also cleans itself when it is compressed.

Catskill Mountains Mountain group in SE New York State, USA; part of the Appalachian system; rises to 1282 m/4206 ft at Slide Mt; New York recreational area.

cat's tail *reedmace*

cattalo *bison*

cattle Domesticated mammals, developed from wild aurochs (*Bos taurus*); now worldwide with numerous breeds; kept for milk and/or meat or for hauling loads; also known as **oxen**. The world's cattle population doubled, 1960–80. The name *cattle* is sometimes used to include other species (eg banteng, gaur, yak, bison, buffalo, anoa). (Family: Bovidae.)

cattle plague *rinderpest*

cattleya [katlia] An orchid (mainly an epiphyte) native to the forests of Central and South America. Most kinds have swollen, bulb-like stems (*pseudobulbs*) bearing 1–3 leaves, and spikes of up to 47 large, showy flowers. Widely cultivated with numerous hybrids, they are one of the most widely used orchids of floristry. (Genus: *Cattleya*, 30 species. Family: Orchidaceae.)

Catullus, Gaius Valerius [katuhlus] (c.84–c.54 BC) Lyric poet, born in Verona, Italy. He settled in Rome (c.62 BC), where he met 'Lesbia' whom he addressed in his verses. He entered as an aristocrat into the contest of parties, and several of his poems attack Caesar and other political enemies. His extant works comprise 116 pieces, many of them extremely brief, while the longest contains only some 400 lines. He was admired and imitated by Renaissance poets.

Caucasus Mountains [kawkasus], Russ **Kavkaz** Major mountain system between the Black Sea and the Caspian Sea; bounded S by Turkey and Iran; comprises the **Greater Caucasus** and the **Lesser Caucasus**; generally accepted as the physical boundary between Europe (N) and Asia (S); extends c.1120 km/700 mi SE; in the W is Mt Elbrus (5642 m/18 510 ft), highest point in the Kavkaz range; in the E the range widens to over 160 km/100 mi.

caucus A meeting, public or private, restricted to persons sharing a common characteristic, usually membership of a political party, held to formulate decisions or nominate candidates in forthcoming elections. It is most often applied to the USA, where the caucus-convention system is significant in selecting presidential and vice-presidential candidates, and where caucuses are the authoritative voice of the parties in Congress.

cauliflower A type of cultivated cabbage (*Brassica oleracea*) grown for the immature inflorescence which forms the edible white head. If left to mature, the head eventually elongates greatly, producing numerous yellow cross-shaped flowers. (Family: Cruciferae.)

causation The relationship between two things whereby the first is necessary or sufficient to bring about the second. Philosophers have debated whether all events must have causes (quantum theory suggests not) and whether a causal connection is more than just an experienced regularity in nature.

Causley, Charles (Stanley) [kawzlee] (1917–2003) Poet, born in Launceston, Cornwall, SW England, UK. He left school at 15, joined the navy, and trained as a teacher after World War 2. He wrote his first poetry while in the navy, publishing his first collection, *Hands to Dance*, in 1951. He became known as a poet of the sea, and also as a children's poet. Later volumes include *Union Street* (1957), *Figgie Hobbin* (1970), and *Early in the Morning* (1988), and his *Collected Poems 1951–1997* were published in 1997. Among his many awards was the Queen's Gold Medal for Poetry (1967).

caustic In chemistry, descriptive of substances (normally strongly alkaline) which are destructive, particularly to biological tissue. **Caustic soda** is sodium hydroxide; **caustic potash** is potassium hydroxide.

caution *right to silence*

Cavalcanti, Guido [kavalkantee] (c.1230–1300) Poet, born in Florence, NC Italy. He was a friend of Dante, and wrote about 50 poems in the 'new style' of the period. A member of the Papal Party (the Guelphs), he married the daughter of Farinata degli Uberti, the leader of the rival, Imperial Party (the Ghibellines), and was banished.

Cavalier poets Poets of the mid-17th-c who supported Charles I in the Civil War, noted for their lyrical poetry and courtly sentiments. The best known are Carew, Lovelace, Herrick, and Waller. Indebted to Ben Jonson, their (mostly love) poems are characterized by urbanity, elegance, and wit. Typical themes were love, honour, the transience of beauty, and gallantry.

Cavaliers Those who fought for Charles I in the English Civil War. The name was used derogatorily in 1642 by supporters of Parliament to describe swaggering courtiers with long hair and swords, who reportedly welcomed the prospect of war. Similarly, the Parliamentarians were labelled 'Roundheads' by Cavaliers, dating from the riotous assemblies in Westminster during Strafford's trial in 1641, when short-haired apprentices mobbed Charles I's supporters outside the House of Lords.

Cavallini, Pietro [kavaleenee] (c.1250–c.1330) Painter and artist in mosaic, born in Rome, Italy. A contemporary of Giotto, whom he influenced, his best-known work is the series of mosaics in the Church of Santa Maria at Trastevere, Rome.

Cavan (county) [kavn] pop (2000e) 53 000; area 1891 sq km/730 sq mi. County in Ulster province, NC Ireland; bounded N by N Ireland; drained by Analee, Boyne, and Erne Rivers; capital, Cavan; oats, potatoes, dairy farming.

Cavan (town), Ir **Cabháin** 54°00N 7°21W, pop (2000e) 5300. Agricultural market town and capital of Cavan county, Ulster, NC Ireland; NW of Dublin; bishopric; crystal; international song contest (Apr).

cave A natural cavity in the Earth's surface, generally hollowed out by the action of water, and most spectacularly developed in limestones (soluble in mildly acid rainwater), in which huge vaults and interconnected river systems may form. Caves are also made by the action of sea water against cliffs, as in Fingal's Cave in the Scottish Hebrides. Ice caves may form in glaciers by streams of meltwater.

cave art *Palaeolithic art*

cavefish Small, blind North American fish confined to limestone caves of SE states; body lacking pigment (Genera: *Amblyopsis*, *Typhlichthys*, 4 species); also two species (Genus: *Chologaster*) with small eyes and pigmented skin from coastal swamps. (Family: Amblyopsidae.)

Cavell, Edith [kavel] (1865–1915) Nurse, born in Swardeston, Norfolk, E England, UK. She became a nurse in 1895, and matron of the Berkendael Medical Institute, Brussels, in 1907. She tended friend and foe alike in 1914–15, yet was executed by the Germans for helping Belgian and Allied fugitives to escape capture.

Cavendish, Henry (1731–1810) Physicist and chemist, born in Nice, SE France. He studied at Cambridge, but left to devote himself to science after being bequeathed a fortune. In 1760 he studied the 'inflammable air', now known as hydrogen gas, and later ascertained that water resulted from the union of two gases. The *Cavendish experiment* was an ingenious means of estimating the density of the Earth.

Cavendish, Spencer Compton, 8th Duke of Devonshire, known (1858–91) as the **Marquess of Hartington** (1833–1908) British statesman, born in Lower Holker, Lancashire, NW England, UK. He studied at Cambridge, entered parliament (1857), and between 1863 and 1874 was a Lord of the Admiralty, under-secretary for war, war secretary, postmaster-general, and chief secretary for Ireland. In 1875 he became Leader of the Liberal Opposition during Gladstone's temporary abdication, later serving under him as secretary of state for India (1880–2) and as war secretary (1882–5). He disapproved of Irish Home Rule, and having led the breakaway from the Liberal Party became head of the Liberal Unionists from 1886, serving in the Unionist government as Lord President of the Council (1895–1903). His younger brother, **Lord Frederick Cavendish** (1836–82), also a Liberal MP from 1865, was appointed chief secretary for Ireland, but immediately after his arrival in Dublin was murdered by 'Irish Invincibles' in Phoenix Park.

Cavendish, William, 4th Duke of Newcastle (1592–1676) English soldier and patron of the arts. He studied at Cambridge, was created Knight of the Bath (1610), Viscount Mansfield in 1620, and Earl (1628), Marquess (1643), and Duke (1665) of Newcastle. He gave strong support to Charles I in the Civil War, and was general of all forces north of the Trent. After Marston Moor (1644) he lived on the European mainland, at times in great poverty, until the Restoration. A noted patron of poets and playwrights, he was himself the author of several plays, and of two works on horsemanship.

caviar The prepared roe (eggs) of the female sturgeon, beluga, sevruga, and sterlet. These fish are caught in the winter months in the rivers flowing into the Baltic Sea and the Danube. Sturgeon roe is black, and is considered superior.

cavitation A form of localized boiling in a liquid, caused by sudden dramatic reductions in pressure, giving rise to pockets of gas. Cavitation can occur at the trailing edge of ship propellers, and in liquids subject to powerful sound waves.

Cavour, Camillo Benso, conte di (Count of) [kavoor] (1810–61) Piedmontese statesman and premier (1852–9), who brought about the unification of Italy (1861), born in Turin, NW Italy. As premier, he greatly improved economic conditions, and brought the Italian question before the Congress of Paris. He resigned over the Peace of Villafranca (which left Venetia Austrian), but returned in 1860, and secretly encouraged the expedition of Garibaldi, which gained Sicily and S Italy. He believed church and state should be separate ('libera chiesa in libero stato', trans 'free church in a free state'), and was negotiating a solution to the Roman question when he died.

cavy A rodent native to South America; includes **guinea pigs** (Genus: *Cavia*), and a wide range of cavy-like rodents. The **domestic guinea pig** (*Cavia porcellus*) was bred as food by the Incas, and is still eaten in South America. (Family: Caviidae, 15 species.)

Cawley, Evonne (Fay), *née* **Goolagong** (1951–) Tennis player, born in Barellan, New South Wales, SE Australia, of Aboriginal descent. A popular and relaxed player, she won the Wimbledon singles championship in 1971, and made a comeback to win it again in 1981. She won the Australian Open four times, and many other championships during her career, including the Italian Open and the South African Open. In 1988 she was elected to the International Tennis Hall of Fame.

Caxton, William (c.1422–c.1491) The first English printer, born possibly in Tenterden, in the Weald of Kent, SE England, UK. He was trained in London as a cloth merchant, and lived in Bruges (1441–70). In Cologne he probably learned the art of printing (1471–2), and soon after printed the first book in English, *The Recuyell of the Historyes of Troye* (1475). About the end of 1476 he set up his wooden press at Westminster, and produced the *Dictes or Sayengis of the Philosophres* (1477), the first book printed in England. Of about 100 books printed by him, including the *Canterbury Tales*, over a third survive only in unique copies or fragments.

Cayenne [kayen] 4°55N 52°18W, pop (2000e) 60 000. Federal and district capital of French Guiana, NE South America; major port on Cayenne I at mouth of R Cayenne, on the Atlantic coast; founded, 1643; used as penal settlement, 1854–1938; airport; source of Cayenne pepper; timber, sugar cane, rum, pineapples; Jesuit-built residence (1890) of the prefect.

cayenne *pepper 1*

Cayley, Arthur [kaylee] (1821–95) Mathematician, born in Richmond, SW Greater London, UK. He studied languages and mathematics at London and Cambridge, graduated with distinction, but on failing to find a position in mathematics, took up law and was called to the bar in 1849. In 1863 he became professor of pure mathematics at Cambridge. He originated the theory of invariants and covariants, and worked on the theories of matrices and analytical geometry, and on theoretical astronomy.

Cayley, Sir George [kaylee] (1771–1857) Pioneer of aviation, born in Scarborough, North Yorkshire, N England, UK. In 1808 he constructed and flew a glider, probably the first heavier-than-air machine, and made the first successful man-carrying glider (1853). He also interested himself in railway engineering, allotment agriculture, and land reclamation methods, and invented a new type of telescope, artificial limbs, the caterpillar tractor, and the tension wheel. He helped to found the Regent Street Polytechnic, London (1839).

cayman *caiman*

Cayman Islands *see panel*

Cazaly, Roy [kazaylee] (1893–1963) Legendary Australian Rules footballer, born in Melbourne, Victoria, SE Australia. Leaping master of the high mark (jumping high in the air above other players to catch the ball), the call 'Up there Cazaly' was chanted by South Melbourne crowds and became a rallying cry for Australian troops in World War 2. A star player for St Kilda (1913–20), he was named Champion of the State in 1920, and transferred to South Melbourne in 1921 before moving to Tasmania.

Cayman Islands

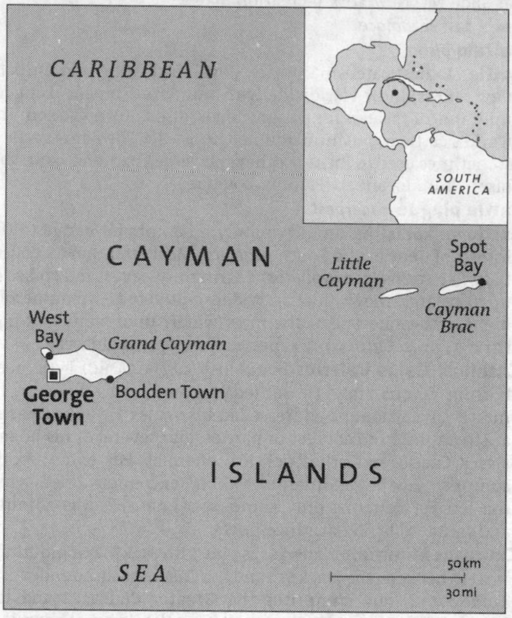

□ International Airport

[kayman] (UK British Overseas Territory)

Timezone GMT –5

Area 260 km^2/100 sq mi

Population total (2000e) 41 000

Capital George Town

Physical features Located in W Caribbean, comprising the islands of Grand Cayman, Cayman Brac, and Little Cayman, c.240 km/150 mi S of Cuba; low-lying, rising to 42 m/138 ft on Cayman Brac plateau; ringed by coral reefs.

Climate Tropical climate; average temperatures 24–32°C (May–Oct), 16–24°C (Nov–Apr); average annual rainfall 1420 mm/56 in; hurricane season (Jul-Nov).

Currency 1 Cayman Island Dollar (CI$) = 100 cents

Economy Tourism; international finance, property development; over 450 banks and trust companies established on the islands; oil transshipment; crafts, jewellery, vegetables, tropical fish.

GDP (2002e) $1·27 bn, per capita $35 000

History Visited by Colombus, 1503; ceded to Britain, 1670; colonized by British settlers from Jamaica; British Crown Colony, 1962; a Governor represents the British sovereign, and presides over a Legislative Assembly.

CBE *British Empire, Order of the*

CBI *Confederation of British Industry*

CD *compact disc*

CDC *Commonwealth Development Corporation*

CD-ROM [seedeerom] An acronym for **Compact Disk Read Only Memory**, a computer storage medium based on the use of the standard 5 in (25 mm) compact disk, licensed by Sony and Philips, and usually used for digital audio. One CD-ROM disk can store more than 600 megabytes of computer information, which is considerably more than a comparable size of hard magnetic disk. Most CDs are read-only, and data is installed during manufacture; unlike the hard disk, the data on such a CD-ROM cannot be altered. The main applications have been in providing access to large volumes of information such as encyclopedias and databases. A **CD-writer** is a device, approximately the size of an external disk drive, which can be used to write data to writable CD-ROMs, thus allowing the CD-ROM to be used in a similar way to a floppy disk.

CD-writer *CD-ROM*

Ceanannus Mór, formerly **Kells** 53°44N 6°53W, pop (2000e) 3600. Urban district in Meath county, Leinster, E Ireland; on R Boyne NW of Dublin; noted for its monastery (founded by St Columba) and the remains of five Celtic crosses; **Book of Kells** (now in Trinity College, Dublin) produced there c.800.

ceanothus *Californian lilac*

Ceaușescu, Nicolae [chowsheskoo] (1918–89) Romanian statesman and president (1967–89), born in Scornicești, S Romania. He studied at Bucharest, joined the Communist Party at 15, and held several junior political posts before becoming President of the State Council (1967) and general secretary of the Romanian Communist Party (1969). Under his leadership, Romania became increasingly independent of the USSR, and for many years was the only Warsaw Pact country to have cordial relations with China. He became the first president of the Republic in 1974, and established a strong personality cult. His policy of replacing traditional villages by collectives of concrete apartments caused much controversy and distress in the late 1980s. A ruthless and unpopular leader, he was deposed in 1989 when the army joined a popular revolt against his repressive government. Following a cursory trial by military tribunal, he and his wife, **Elena**, were shot on Christmas Day 1989.

Cebu or **Cebu City** [sayboo] 10°17N 123°56E, pop (2000e) 749 000. Seaport in Cebu province, E coast of Cebu I, Philippines; founded, 1565 (first Spanish settlement in the Philippines); airfield; four universities (1595, 1919, 1946, 1949); commerce, tobacco, copra, food processing, textiles; Spanish fort, Santo Niño Church; Santo Niño de Cebu festival (Jan).

Cech, Thomas R [chek] (1947–) Biochemist, born in Chicago, Illinois, USA. At the University of Colorado (1977–) he showed that RNA could have an independent catalytic function aiding a chemical reaction without being consumed or changed. This had major implications for genetic engineering, as well as for understanding how life arose. He and Sidney Altman shared the 1989 Nobel Prize for Chemistry.

Cecil, Robert (Arthur Talbot Gascoyne), 3rd Marquess of Salisbury [sesil] (1830–1903) British statesman and prime minister (1885–6, 1886–92, 1895–1902), born in Hatfield, Hertfordshire, SE England, UK. He studied at Oxford, and became a Conservative MP in 1853. In 1865 he was made Viscount Cranborne, and in 1868 Marquess of Salisbury. He was twice Indian secretary (1866, 1874), became foreign secretary (1878), and on Disraeli's death (1881) was Leader of the Opposition. He was prime minister on three occasions, much of the time serving as his own foreign secretary. He resigned as foreign secretary in 1900, but remained as head of government during the Boer War (1899–1902). He retired in 1902.

Cecil, William, 1st Baron Burghley or **Burghleigh** [sesil] (1520–98) English statesmen, born in Bourn, Lincolnshire, EC England, UK. He studied at Cambridge and Gray's Inn, London, served under Somerset and Northumberland, became secretary of state (1550), and was knighted (1551). During Mary I's reign he conformed to Catholicism. In 1558 Elizabeth appointed him chief secretary of state, and for the next 40 years he was the chief architect of Elizabethan greatness, influencing her pro-Protestant foreign policy, securing the execution of Mary, Queen of Scots, and preparing for the Spanish Armada. He used an army of spies to ensure security at home. In 1571 he was created Baron Burghley, and in 1572 became Lord High Treasurer – an office he held until his death.

Cecilia, St (2nd-c or 3rd-c) Christian martyr, and patron saint of music. According to tradition, she was a Roman maiden of patrician birth compelled to marry a young pagan, Valerian, despite a vow of celibacy. She succeeded in persuading him to respect her vow, and converted him to Christianity. They were both put to death for their faith. Later tradition made her a singer, hence her association with music-making. Feast day 22 November.

Cecrops or **Kekrops** [kekrops] In Greek mythology, the ancestor and first king of the Athenians. He was born from the earth, and formed with snakelike appendages instead of legs. During his reign Athena and Poseidon fought for the possession of Athens. He was buried in the Erechtheum.

cedar An evergreen conifer with a massive trunk and flat, wide-spreading crown, native to the mountains of N Africa, the Himalayas, and the E Mediterranean; needles sometimes bluish, in tufts; timber fragrant and oily. It should not be confused with the 'cedar' of commerce, which is obtained from other conifers. (Genus: *Cedrus*, 4 species. Family: Pinaceae.)

Ceefax [seefaks] A UK alphanumeric teletext system operated by the BBC since 1974. It is broadcast on the BBC's two terrestrial channels and forms part of its News and Current Affairs Directorate. The name derives from 'see facts'.

celandine *lesser celandine*

Celebes *Sulawesi*

Celebes Sea [selebeez], Indonesian **Laut Sulawesi** area 280 000 sq km/110 000 sq mi. Sea of SE Asia, bounded by islands of Indonesia (W and S), Malaysia (NW), and the Philippines (NE); maximum depth 5090 m/16 700 ft; fishing, local trade.

celeriac A variety of celery (*Apium graveolens*, variety *rapaceum*), also called **turnip-rooted celery**, with a tuberous base to the stems, cooked as a vegetable or used in salads. (Family: Umbelliferae.)

celery A strong-smelling biennial herb (*Apium graveolens*), growing to 1 m/3¼ ft, native to Europe, SW Asia, and N Africa; stems deeply grooved; leaves shiny, divided into triangular or diamond-shaped segments; flowers minute, greenish-white, borne in umbels 3–5cm/1¼–2 in across. Forms with swollen leaf stalks (variety *dulce*) are widely cultivated as a vegetable. (Family: Umbelliferae.)

celesta A musical instrument resembling a small upright piano, but with metal plates instead of strings and a shorter (five-octave) compass. It was invented in 1886 by French instrument maker Auguste Mustel (1842–1919) and used a few years later by Tchaikovsky in his ballet *The Nutcracker* ('Dance of the Sugar Plum Fairy').

celestial equator The great circle in which the plane of the Earth's equator cuts the celestial sphere. This is the primary circle for the co-ordinates' right ascension and declination.

celestial mechanics The study of the motions of celestial objects in gravitational fields. Founded by Isaac Newton, it deals with satellite and planetary motion within the Solar System, using Newtonian gravitational theory.

celestial sphere An imaginary sphere surrounding the Earth, used as a reference frame to specify the positions of celestial objects on the sky. Its N and S poles lie over those of Earth, and its equator is the projection of the terrestrial Equator.

Céline, Louis-Ferdinand [sayleen], pseudonym of **Louis-Ferdinand Destouches** (1894–1961) Writer, born in Paris, France. He was invalided out of the army early in World War 1, travelled widely during the war years, then practised medicine. His reputation is based on the two autobiographical novels he wrote during the 1930s: *Voyage au bout de la nuit* (1932, Journey to the End of the Night) and *Mort à crédit* (1936, trans Death by Instalments). During World War 2 he collaborated with the Vichy government and, a declared anti-semite, fled to Germany and Denmark in 1944. He later returned to Paris.

cell (biology) The basic unit of plant and animal bodies; it comprises, at least, a nucleus or nuclear material and cytoplasm enclosed within a cell membrane. Some cells, such as the mature red blood corpuscles of mammals, lack a nucleus, but possessed one at an earlier stage of development. Many cells are more complex, and contain other specialized structures (*organelles*), such as mitochondria, chloroplasts, Golgi bodies, and flagella. Many simple organisms comprise a single cell, and may lack a membrane separating nuclear material from cytoplasm. Advanced organisms consist of a variety of co-operating cells, often specialized to perform particular functions and organized into tissues and organs. Plant cells are typically surrounded by an outer cell wall containing cellulose. Cell division may occur by splitting into two parts (*fission*), by mitosis, and (in the case of reproductive cells) by meiosis. All nucleated cells contain within their nuclei the entire inherited genetic information of that individual, but in specialized cells, such as a liver or brain cell, only a minute fraction of their genetic database is operational.

cell (electricity) *accumulator; battery* (electricity)

Cellini, Benvenuto [che**lee**nee] (1500–71) Goldsmith, sculptor, engraver, and writer, born in Florence, NC Italy. He is particularly known for his autobiography (1558–62). By his own account, it seems he had no scruples about murdering or maiming his rivals, and at the siege of Rome (1527) he killed the Constable de Bourbon. He was several times imprisoned. His best work includes the gold saltcellar made for Francis I of France, and his bronze 'Perseus'. He lived at times in Rome, Mantua, Naples, and Florence.

cello or **violoncello** [**chel**oh] The bass instrument of the violin family, with four strings tuned one octave below the viola's. Until the 19th-c it was usually gripped between the player's knees; the modern instrument is fitted with an adjustable endpin which rests on the floor.

cellophane *cellulose*

cellular radio *mobile communications*

cellulite According to certain beauty experts, the dimpled fat around the thighs and buttocks, which is said to resist dieting. However, available scientific evidence shows that when an individual diets, fat is lost from all fat deposits in the body.

cellulitis [selyoo**liy**tis] Inflammation of the connective tissue that supports organs and structures in the body, usually caused by a bacterial infection. It may arise following wounds and after surgical operations. It is potentially dangerous, as the infection may enter the bloodstream or affect adjacent organs, and is best treated by an appropriate antibiotic.

celluloid The earliest commercial plastic (c.1865–9), consisting of cellulose nitrate plasticized with camphor. It had the great virtue of dimensional stability, which kept it in vogue for photographic film in spite of its dangerous inflammability, long after other plastics had been contrived. It was eventually superseded as a film base by dimensionally stable forms of cellulose acetate.

cellulose $(C_6H_{10}O_5)_n$. A structural polysaccharide found mainly in the cell walls of woody and fibrous plant material, such as cotton. It is a condensation polymer with glucose, and isomeric with starch. It is the main raw material for paper. Many important derivatives are formed by esterifying some of the hydroxyl groups; these include rayon (**cellulose acetate**) and guncotton (**cellulose nitrate** or **nitrocellulose**). **Cellophane** (a trade mark in some countries) is a form of cellulose which has been stretched into thin transparent sheets; it is used in the packaging of food and other perishable products.

celostat *coelostat*

Celsius, Anders [**sel**sius] (1701–44) Astronomer, born in Uppsala, E Sweden. He became professor at Uppsala (1730), and devised the centigrade scale (*Celsius scale*) of temperature in 1742. He advocated the introduction of the Gregorian calendar, and made observations of the aurora borealis. In 1740 he became director of the observatory at Uppsala that had been built in his honour.

Celsius (temperature) A temperature scale that takes the triple point of water to be 0·01°C, which corresponds roughly to taking the freezing point of water as 0°C and the boiling point as 100°C; named after Anders Celsius; a change in temperature of one degree Celsius is equal to a change in temperature of one Kelvin; a temperature in degrees Celsius is still often called by the old name *degrees Centigrade*.

Celtiberia [keltibee**ria**] The territory in NC Spain inhabited by the Celtiberians, a warlike people of mixed Celtic and Iberian ancestry. Staunch opponents of the Romans, they were pacified in 133 BC after decades of intermittent but fierce resistance.

Celtic art [**kel**tic] The art which emerged in 5th-c BC in S Germany and E France, spread throughout Europe for 500 years, and affected much subsequent mediaeval art, especially decorative gold and bronze-work. Greek motifs such as rosettes and lyre-shapes were combined with arabesques and strongly stylized human and animal forms traceable to the art of nomadic tribes on the E Steppes. Ceremonial metal vessels took their shapes from Etruscan and S Italian models.

Celtic languages [**kel**tik] The languages of the Celts, the first Indo-European peoples to spread throughout Europe. The dialects spoken on the continent are known as **Continental Celtic**; traces remain in several inscriptions and place-names in *Gaulish* (from the tribal name *Galli* or *Gaul*), and in *Celtiberian* (from *Celtiberi*, the name given to the Celtic tribes of Spain). **Insular Celtic** is the name given to the Celtic languages of the British Is and Brittany. There are two branches: *Goidelic* comprises the Gaelic spoken in Ireland, which spread to the Isle of Man (Manx) and Scotland; *Brythonic* (also called *Brittonic* or *British*) comprises Welsh, Cornish, and Breton. The two branches of Insular Celtic are labelled **Q-Celtic** (Goidelic) and **P-Celtic** (Brythonic), because of a distinctive divergence in the development of the Indo-European sound system: the consonant sequence *kw* became *q* or *c* in Goidelic, and *p* in Brythonic, as is evidenced in the final consonant of the surnames *Mac* (Gaelic) and *Ap* (Welsh).

Celtic literature [**kel**tik] The indigenous literatures of Ireland, Scotland, and Wales, as well as some Cornish texts from the 15th-c (including the three biblical plays comprising the *Ordinalia*). There is also an extensive literature in the Breton language, consisting of saints' lives, plays, comic pieces, folk tales, and ballads. This comes mainly from the Middle Breton (12th–17th-c) and Modern Breton periods, the latter dating from 1659 with the regularization of Breton spelling by Julien Maunoir. Despite 18th-c and 19th-c neglect and even opposition, in the 20th-c there was a revival of interest in the Celtic languages and literatures, which has continued to grow.

Celtic Sea [**kel**tik] Part of the Atlantic Ocean S of Ireland; separated from the Irish Sea by St George's Channel; main inlet, Bristol Channel; average depths of 100–200 m/330–650 ft.

Celts Different groups of peoples who all spoke Celtic languages and lived in most parts of Europe from the Balkan regions to Ireland. Most powerful during the 4th-c BC, they probably originated in present-day France, S Germany, and adjacent territories during the Bronze Age. Celtic-speaking societies developed in the later first millennium BC, expanding through armed raids into the Iberian Peninsula, British Is, C Europe, Italy, Greece, Anatolia, Egypt, Bulgaria, Romania, Thrace, and Macedonia. They were finally repulsed by the Romans and Germanic tribes, and in Europe withdrew into Gaul in the 1st-c BC. Celtic tradition survived most and for longest in Ireland and Britain. They were famous for their burial sites and hill forts, and their bronze and iron art and jewellery. Their modern descendents are found chiefly in Ireland, Scotland, and Wales.

cement In general, any substance used to adhere to each of two materials which cannot themselves adhere, and therefore to effect a join. More usually, it refers to **Portland cement**, an artificial mineral substance used in building and engineering construction. This is made by heating clay and limestone in retorts to form a clinker which is then finely ground. The addition of water produces a soft manageable substance which sets hard, through the formation of hydrated silicates. It is commonly mixed with other mineral substances (sand, stone) to form various grades of concrete, or used as a mortar for joining brickwork.

cementation The modification of the surface layer of a metal by heating it in a packing of some substance which will diffuse into it. This was the oldest method of making steel: heating iron packed in charcoal.

Cenozoic era [see**no**zohik], or **Cainozoic** [kayno**zoh**ik] The most recent of the four eras of geological time, beginning c.65 million years ago and extending to the present day; subdivided into the *Tertiary* and *Quaternary* periods. It was characterized by widespread changes in the fauna, with the dominance of mammals and flowering plants, and the development of present-day geographical features.

censors In Republican Rome (5th-c–1st-c BC), two officials (usually ex-consuls) elected every five years to compile a register of citizens and their property for military, legislative, electoral, and fiscal purposes. Though prestigious, the office was not part of the *cursus honorum*.

censorship The controlling of access to and dissemination of information, especially on political and moral grounds. In its extreme form, it involves the wholesale banning of information, including works of fiction, enforced by the imposition of penalties against offenders. As such it is a characteristic of authoritarian states, which seek to regulate the flow of information, opinion, and expression. This is usually justified by reference to state security, the public interest, and good taste. In contemporary democracies, the term usually has wholly negative connotations. Such societies pride themselves on the freedoms enjoyed by their people, including the right of free expression, often enshrined in law (eg the First Amendment to the US Constitution). But censorship plays a part in even the most enlightened and progressive of societies, its legitimacy deriving from an assumed consensus on what is and is not acceptable at a particular time. Organizations of all kinds have certain secrets which need to be protected for reasons of security, confidentiality, and personal privacy. Such information will be 'classified' to some degree, and be restricted to those authorized to receive it. Problems arise when the censoring of information is believed to be against the wider public interest, insofar as it is used to conceal incompetence, corruption, and crime.

Art in all its forms has always been prone to censorship, often due to the desire of artists to extend the boundaries of taste and to challenge authority. For example, in the British theatre it was not until 1968 that managements ceased having to submit manuscripts of plays for approval by the official censor, the Lord Chamberlain. Formal pre-censorship of this kind is uncommon today in the West. One major exception is film and video recordings, which are usually previewed by a board of censors, before being released for public consumption, with cuts if required. Since 1972 the monthly periodical *Index on Censorship* has campaigned against abuses of the fundamental right of free expression throughout the world.

census A count of the population resident in an area at a given time, together with the collection of social and economic data, made at regular intervals. In many countries census data form the basis for the planning of service provisions, and a census is taken every 10 years. The USA conducted its first national census in 1790, and France and the UK began to collect census data in 1801. The first Chinese census was AD 2, when the population was recorded at 59 594 978. The United Nations has tried to ensure some comparability between the questions asked in different countries, and has been partially successful.

centaur [sentaw(r)] In Greek mythology, a creature combining the upper half of a man and the rear legs of a horse (as shown on vases); later and more popularly imagined as having the entire body of a horse. Centaurs came from Thessaly, and most were beastly and wild, fighting with the Lapiths and with Heracles.

Centaurus [sen**taw**rus] (Lat 'centaur') A large and rich S constellation. Its brightest star, **Alpha Centauri**, is actually three stars, the faintest of which, **Proxima Centauri**, is the closest star to the Sun, 1·29 parsec away from Earth. Omega Centauri is the largest and brightest globular cluster, 5·2 kiloparsec away. **Centaurus A** is a huge radio galaxy (600 kiloparsec across) and one of the nearest (4 megaparsec away). It is a strong source of X-rays and infrared radiation, and is thought to include a supermassive black hole in its nucleus.

centaury An annual, sometimes perennial, found almost everywhere; opposite entire leaves; flowers pink, tubular with 4–5 spreading lobes, borne in dense heads. (Genus: *Centaurium*, c.50 species. Family: Gentianaceae.)

centigrade *Celsius* (temperature)

centimetre *metre* (physics)

centipede A carnivorous, terrestrial arthropod, commonly found in soil, leaf litter, and rotting wood; body up to 30 cm/12 in long, divided into head (bearing feelers and mouthparts) and many-segmented trunk; each trunk segment has one pair of legs; c.2500 species, some venomous. (Class: Chilopoda.)

CENTO *Central Treaty Organization*

Central (Scotland) pop (2000e) 274 700; area 2631 sq km/1016 sq mi. Former (to 1996) region in C Scotland, UK; replaced in 1996 by Stirling, Clackmannanshire, and Falkirk councils; N part in the Highlands, including the Trossachs (W); S part encloses the Forth river valley; drained by the Forth, Carron, and Devon Rivers; contains several lochs, including Katrine, Lubnaig, Venachar (W) and part of Earn (NE); capital, Stirling; other chief towns, Falkirk, Alloa, Grangemouth (all in SE, region's industrial area); brewing and distilling, engineering, agriculture; Stirling castle, Loch Lomond, Bannockburn battle site.

Central African Republic *p.296*

Central America area 596 000 sq km/230 000 sq mi. A geographical region that encompasses the independent states to the S of Mexico and to the N of South America; includes Guatemala, El Salvador, Belize, Honduras, Nicaragua, Costa Rica, and Panama; the area gained independence from Spain in 1821.

Central American Common Market (CACM) An economic association initiated in 1960 between Guatemala, Honduras, El Salvador, Nicaragua, and (from 1963) Costa Rica. Its early apparent success was offset by growing political crisis in the late 1970s.

Central American Federation A federation formed in 1823, following independence from Spain, by Costa Rica, Nicaragua, Honduras, El Salvador, and Guatemala. Despite vigorous leadership by Francisco Morazán (1792–1842) of Honduras, internal tensions brought about the collapse of the federation by 1838.

Central Committee Under Soviet Communist Party rules, the highest decision-making authority in the former USSR, apart from Congress, which elected it. Except in rare circumstances, however, it exercised little influence, partly because of its unwieldy size and partly because of the concentration of power in the Politburo.

Central Computer and Telecommunications Agency (CCTA) The department of government in the UK which is responsible for advising on all aspects of using computers and telecommunications in government departments. The advice of the CCTA is also usually sought by other public bodies, such as the National Health Service and universities.

Central Criminal Court *Old Bailey*

Central Intelligence Agency (CIA) The official US intelligence analysis organization responsible for external security, established under the National Security Act (1947). Often involved in subversive activities, and suspected of internal subversive activities from time to time, it suffered a loss of credibility

Central African Republic

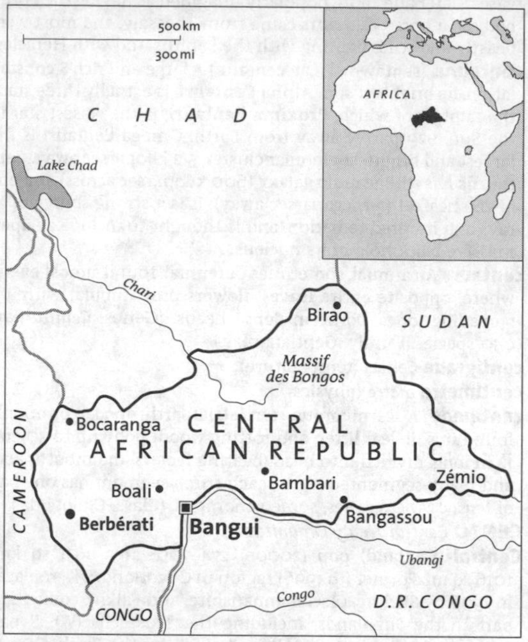

International Airport

Fr **République Centrafricaine**

Local name République Centrafricaine

Timezone GMT +1

Area 622 984 km²/240 535 sq mi

Population total (2002e) 3 643 000

Status Republic

Date of independence 1960

Capital Bangui

Languages French (official), Sangho

Ethnic groups Baya (34%), Banda (28%), Sara (10%), over 80 other groups

Religions Christian (50%), (Protestant 25%, Roman Catholic 25%), also Muslim and traditional beliefs

Physical features Located in C Africa; plateau forming a watershed between Chad and Congo river basins; Massif des Bongos rises 1400 m/4593 ft in NW; granite ranges of Mont Karre, 1220 m/4003 ft in W.

Climate Tropical; single rainy season in N (May–Sep); average annual rainfall 875–1000 mm/34–9 in; more equatorial climate in S; rainfall 1500–2000 mm/60–80 in.

Currency 1 CFA Franc (CFAFr) = 100 centimes

Economy Agriculture employs c.85% of working population; also sawmilling, brewing, diamond splitting, leather and tobacco processing.

GDP (2002e) $4·296 bn, per capita $1200

Human Development Index (2002) 0·375

History Part of French Equatorial Africa (Ubangi Shari); autonomous republic within the French community, 1958; independence, 1960; coup deposed country's first President, David Dacko, 1965; Jean-Bédel Bokassa declared himself emperor for life, and country's name changed to the Central African Empire, 1976; Bokassa deposed and country reverted to a republic, 1979; military coup established Committee for National Recovery, 1981–5; Committee dissolved and National Assembly established, 1987; movement toward multi-party democracy, 1991; multiparty legislative and presidential elections, 1993, elected Ange-Félix Patasse; President Patasse overthrown in coup, 2003, by Gen.Bozize; governed by a president, prime minister, and 85-member National Assembly.

Head of State
1981–93 André Kolingba
1993–2003 Ange-Félix Patasse
2003 *Military Coup*
2003– General François Bozize

Head of Government
1992–3 Thimothée Malendoma
1993 Enoch Derant Lakoue
1993–5 Jean-Luc Mandaba
1995–6 Gabriel Koyambounou
1996–7 Jean-Paul Ngoupandé
1997–8 Michel Gbezera-Bria
1999–2001 Anicet Georges Dologuélé
2001–3 Martin Ziguele
2003 Abel Goumba
2003– Célestin Gaombalet

following the investigation into the Watergate affair in the mid-1970s.

central nervous system (CNS) A collection of nerve cells, connected in an intricate and complex manner, which is involved in the control of movement and the analysis of sensation, and in humans also subserves the higher-order functions of thought, language, and emotion. In vertebrates it consists of the brain and spinal cord, enclosed within the meninges within the skull and vertebral column. Diseases of the CNS include Parkinson's, motor neurone, and prion disease.

Central Powers Initially, the members of the Triple Alliance (Germany, Austria–Hungary, Italy) created by Bismarck in 1882. As Italy remained neutral in 1914, and joined the Allies in 1915, the term was later used to describe Germany, Austria–Hungary, their ally Turkey, and later Bulgaria in World War 1.

central processing unit (CPU) *digital computer*

Central Valley or **Great Central Valley** Valley in California, USA, between the Sierra Nevada (E) and the Coast Range (W); the Sacramento and San Joaquin Rivers feed the Central Valley Project, a series of dams and reservoirs for flood-control, irrigation and hydroelectricity.

centre, the The centre ground in political opinion and action which avoids the extremism and idealism of right and left, and advocates compromise or consensus solutions to societal problems. It is often characterized by pragmatic responses – more concerned with 'getting things done' than with 'fruitless' searching for the means of achieving ideal objectives.

Centre Beaubourg [sãtruh bohboorg] The popular name for the Centre National d'Art et de Culture, or **Pompidou Centre**, situated on the Plateau Beaubourg in Paris. Designed by Renzo Piano and Richard Rogers, and opened in 1977, the 6-storey building houses a modern art gallery and a centre for industrial design. Display space has been maximized by placing all services – conduits, elevators, etc – on the outside of the transparent exterior walls.

centre of gravity In mechanics, the point in some object upon which the action of gravity is equivalent to the sum of the action of gravity on the object's component parts. The centre of gravity of the object is identical to its centre of mass.

centre of mass In mechanics, a point whose motion represents that of an entire object or group of objects. The product of the velocity of this point with the total mass of the system equals the sum of the momentum contributions of the individual parts. For example, the centre of mass of the fragments of an exploding bomb is the position that the bomb would have had if it had not exploded. Should a force act on the system, the centre of mass undergoes an acceleration as though the force were acting on the entire mass concentrated at the centre of mass.

centrifuge A device for separating the components of a mixture (solid-in-liquid or liquid-in-liquid) by applying rapid rotation and consequent centrifugal force. It may be equipped for the technical separation of materials (eg cream) or for scientific observation (eg the **ultracentrifuge**, which separates particles of macromolecular size).

centripetal force An inward-directed radial force required to keep an object on a circular path; gravity, for example, provides a centripetal force, causing the Moon to orbit the Earth. Corresponding to a centripetal force is a centripetal acceleration due to that force, and acting in the same direction as it. For an object moving in a circle at a constant speed, the rate of change of velocity (the direction changes continuously, but magnitude is constant) is the centripetal acceleration and is directed towards the centre of the circle. The term **centrifugal force**, denoting an outward-acting force, is common in everyday use, but is best avoided. It is a fictitious force; such a force balancing the centripetal force is applicable only to rotating observers, for whom the object appears at rest.

centrography In geography, the study of descriptive statistics for the determination and mapping of measures of central tendency. For example, the mean centre of population distribution can be mapped to show the main focus of a country's population distribution.

centromere The point on a chromosome, usually a constriction, by which it is attached to the spindle during the division of the cell nucleus. It orchestrates the division of the chromosome into its two daughter chromosomes.

century The smallest unit in a Roman legion, under the command of a **centurion**. Probably consisting originally of 100, under the Empire there were 80 soldiers in a century.

century plant A species of agave (*Agave americana*), so-called from the length of time once thought to pass between germination and flowering – up to 100 years. In Mexico the great flow of sap during the final burst of flowering – up to 1000 litres per plant – is collected, and is one of the sources of the national drink, pulque, as well as a spirit, mescal. (Family: Agavaceae.)

ceorl [chayaw(r)l] An ordinary freeman of Anglo-Saxon England, who normally held between one and five hides of land (1 hide = c.120 acres). By the 10th-c, wealthy ceorls could become thegns; but after the Norman Conquest many ceorls lost personal freedom. The Middle English derivative *churl* has the sense of serf or ill-bred person.

cephalic index A head's breadth as a percentage of its length. Heads of different relative breadths are termed *brachycephalic* (broad), *mesocephalic* (intermediate), and *dolichocephalic* (long). The **cranial index** expresses comparable ratios on the skull, rather than the living head. The notion is especially used in anthropological classification.

Cephalonia [kefalohnia], Gr **Kefallinía** pop (2000e) 33 700; area 780 sq km/300 sq mi. Largest of the Ionian Is, Greece, in the Ionian Sea, off the W coast of Greece; length 48 km/30 mi; hilly island, rising to 1628 m/5341 ft; capital, Argostolion; devastated by earthquakes in 1953; olives, grapes.

Cephalopoda [sefalopoda] A class of carnivorous, marine molluscs characterized by the specialization of the head-foot into a ring of tentacles, typically armed with hooks or suckers, and by their method of swimming using jets of water squirted out of a funnel; mouth typically with a powerful beak; eyes usually well developed; includes octopus, squid, cuttlefish, and nautilus, as well as large fossil groups such as ammonites and belemnites.

Cephas [seefas] *Peter, St*

Cepheid variable [seefeeid] A class of variable star with a period of 1–50 days, characterized by precise regularity. There is a direct correlation between the period and luminosity (the longer the period, the more luminous the star). The observed brightness of a Cepheid indicates its distance from Earth, and is consequently of great importance in determining the distance scale of the universe.

Cepheus (astronomy) [seefyoos] A N constellation which includes the famous star **delta Cephei**, the prototype of regular variables used for calibrating the distance scale of the universe.

Cepheus (mythology) [seefyoos] In Greek mythology, the son of Belus. He became the husband of Cassiopeia and was the father of Andromeda. He ruled over the Cephenes who were said to live partly on the banks of the Euphrates and partly in Ethiopia. At his death he was succeeded by his grandson, Perses.

ceramics The products of the baking of clay, giving hard, strong, non-conducting, brittle, heat-resistant substances. They are useful for technical purposes (eg abrasives, cutting tools, refractory linings) and for decoration. The initial value of clay arises from its plasticity, so that ceramics can be made in an unlimited variety of forms, by moulding, casting, spinning, or pressing. Clays of many kinds are used, from the coarse clay used for bricks to the fine white clay used for porcelain. Ceramics may be made in stages, such as the many ways of producing a *glaze*, a coating of a second clay or glass-like substance, which confers impermeability (as in making pipes) or decorative colours.

ceramic stratus A method of creating large electronic circuits from chips by sealing them in a ceramic tile. It is akin to the printed circuit board, but much more reliable.

Ceratopsia [seratopsia] The horned dinosaurs; typified by enormous bony frill extending back over neck from posterior part of skull; usually with median horns in nasal region and paired horns behind eyes; evolved during the Upper Cretaceous period. (Order: Ornithischia.)

Cerberus [serberus] In Greek mythology, the dog which guards the entrance to the Underworld, originally 50-headed, later with three heads. Any living souls visiting Hell gave 'a sop to Cerberus', ie a honey-cake, to quieten him. Heracles carried him off as one of his labours.

cereals Grain-bearing grasses which provide staple foods for most of the world's population. The grains are much larger than those of other grass species, including wild cereal ancestors, and are rich in protein and carbohydrates. There are eight major cereals: rice, wheat, oats, barley, rye, sorghums, millets, and maize (corn). A number of minor types grow where conditions will not support major crops, and these assume local importance, especially in the Third World. All cereals derive from wild species, and their domestication in early times (c.8000 BC in the case of wheat and barley) marks a turning-point in human history. The replacement of *ramassage* (the gathering of wild grains) by a more dependable crop allowed the development of a more settled lifestyle, and all of the great early civilizations were based on the cultivation of one or more major cereals. With domestication came selection for desirable characteristics, such as larger grains. The development of modern cereals is very sophisticated, with strains tailored for specific purposes and conditions, such as rapid ripening for areas with short growing seasons, or high disease-resistance. (Family: Gramineae.)

cerebellum [serebelum] A part of the brain which occupies the lower back part of the cranial cavity within the skull, consisting of two hemispheres united in the midline by the *vermis*. It is connected to the brain stem by three pairs of structures called *peduncles*, and forms part of the wall of the fourth ventricle. Its principal function is the control of posture, repetitive movements, and the geometric accuracy of voluntary movements; it also appears to have an important role in learning. Damage to the cerebellum in both animals and humans results in *cerebellar ataxia* (inco-ordination of movement).

cerebral haemorrhage / hemorrhage An episode of acute bleeding within the substance of the brain. It tends to occur when the blood pressure is high, or when the wall of the cerebral blood vessel is weakened by degenerative change (eg atherosclerosis) or is the site of a localized distension (*aneurysm*). The neurological disability that follows depends on the severity and site of the haemorrhage.

cerebral palsy A disorder resulting from damage to the brain during fetal development or in infancy. It is characterized by weakness, paralysis, rigidity, and lack of co-ordination of movement; the muscular spasms involved have led to the use of the term **spastic** for these children. A high proportion of children also suffer from epilepsy, and some are retarded mentally. Several types of brain injury are responsible, including maternal diseases during pregnancy, lack of oxygen during birth, and viral infections during infancy, but the cause is unknown in many cases.

cerebrospinal fluid (CSF) In vertebrates a clear, colourless, protein-free fluid circulating through the ventricles of the brain, the central canal of the spinal cord, and the subarachnoid space. It surrounds the brain and spinal cord, and provides them with mechanical support and nutrients. In humans, CSF is sometimes collected (by *lumbar puncture*) and analysed for diagnostic purposes: an excess of CSF around the brain in the fetus and young child (through overproduction or blockage within the circulating system) leads to hydrocephalus, unless it is drained off.

cerebrum [serebruhm] The largest part of the brain, occupying most of the cranial cavity within the skull. It is separated into right and left halves (the right and left **cerebral hemispheres**), connected by a body of nerve fibres known as the *corpus callosum*. Each hemisphere can be divided into four *lobes* which are named according to the skull bone that they are most closely related to (ie *frontal*, *parietal*, *temporal*, and *occipital*). The surface of each hemisphere is formed by a layer of *grey matter* known as the *cerebral cortex*, containing the cell bodies of the neurones responsible for the functions of the cerebrum. Within the cortex the hemispheres are formed by a large mass of *white matter* consisting largely of the axons of the neurones in the cerebral cortex.

The surface of the cerebrum is thrown into a series of folds (*gyri*) separated by troughs (*sulci*): the *lateral sulcus* separates the temporal lobe from the frontal and parietal lobes; the *central sulcus* separates the frontal and parietal lobes; and the *parieto-occipital sulcus* separates the parietal and occipital lobes. Immediately in front of the central sulcus is the *motor cortex*, in which the opposite half of the body is represented upside down: the face lies lowest, then the hand (a very large area), then the arm, trunk, and leg. Stimulation here results in contraction of the appropriate voluntary muscles on the opposite side of the body. Below the area of the brain representing the face, on the left side, lies the speech area (*Broca's area*). Immediately behind the central sulcus is the *sensory cortex*, which receives sensory information from the opposite side of the body via the brain stem and thalamus.

The occipital lobe is involved with vision. The parietal lobe is in general responsible for sensory functions such as the perception of touch, pressure, and body position, as well as three-dimensional perception, the analysis of visual images, language, geometry, and calculations. The frontal lobe subserves motor functions, and also governs the expression of the intellect and personality. The upper part of the temporal lobe is involved in the perception of sound, with the remainder being concerned with memory and various emotional functions.

Čerenkov, Pavel (Alexeyevich) [cherengkof], also spelled **Cherenkov** (1904–90) Physicist, born in Novaya Chigla, Russia. He studied at Voronezh, and worked at the Academy of Sciences. In 1934 he noted the emission of blue light from water and other transparent media when atomic particles, moving at a speed greater than light in that medium, are passed through it. Subsequent researches by Tamm and Frank led to a definite explanation of this *Čerenkov effect*, for which all three shared the Nobel Prize for Physics in 1958.

Čherenkov radiation [cherengkof], also spelled **Cherenkov** Electromagnetic radiation produced by charged particles passing through some material at a velocity greater than the velocity of light in that material; discovered in 1934 by Pavel Čerenkov. It is a type of electromagnetic shock wave, analogous to a sonic boom, and is used to measure particle velocities in particle physics experiments.

Ceres (astronomy) [seereez] The first asteroid to be found, discovered by Giuseppe Piazzi of the Palermo Observatory, Italy, on the first night of the 19th-c. Much the largest known asteroid in the Solar System, its diameter is 940 km/580 mi (over one-quarter of the Moon's).

Ceres (mythology) [seereez] The ancient Italian corn-goddess, an early cult at Rome. She was given characteristics and stories associated with Demeter.

CERN *European Laboratory for Particle Physics*

Cerne Abbas [sern abas] 50°49N 2°29W, pop (2000e) 800. Village in Dorset, S England, UK; 10 km/6 mi N of Dorchester; ruins of 10th-c abbey where Ælfric was abbot; tithe barn (14th-c), church (15th-c); famous tourist attraction is the Cerne Giant, a 45 m/150 ft high figure cut into the chalk downs overlooking the village.

certificate of deposit A certificate representing a fixed-term, interest-bearing deposit in large denominations, which can be bought and sold. The concept was first introduced by Citibank in New York City in 1961; sterling certificates were introduced in 1968.

Cervantes (Saavedra), Miguel de [servanteez], Span [thairvantes] (1547–1616) Writer of *Don Quixote*, born in Alcalá de Henares, C Spain. He entered the army in Italy, being wounded in the Battle of Lepanto. He was captured by Barbary pirates on his way back to Spain and enslaved in Algiers until ransomed in 1580. His first major work was the *Galatea*, a pastoral romance (1585), and he wrote many plays, only two of which have survived. He became a tax collector in Granada (1594), but was imprisoned for failing to make up the sum due to the treasury. Tradition maintains that he wrote *Don Quixote* in prison at Argamasilla in La Mancha. When the book came out (1605), it was hugely popular. He wrote the second part in 1615, after several years of writing plays and short novels.

cervical cancer [serviykl] A malignant tumour arising from the lining of the cervical canal. It is one of the leading causes of cancer death among women. Its occurrence is related to frequent sexual intercourse with several partners, and most cases arise in association with genital infection by the human papilloma virus. Early stages of the cancer can be detected by the cervical smear test and effectively treated.

cervix [serviks] The lower tapering third of the uterus (womb). Its lower, blunt part projects into the vagina; its upper part communicates with the body of the uterus through a slight constriction (the *isthmus*). The vaginal part is firm in the non-pregnant uterus, and relatively soft in the pregnant uterus. A small opening at the lower end of the cervix (the *external os*) allows communication between the uterine cavity and the vagina.

Césaire, Aimé (Fernand) [sayzair] (1913–) Poet, novelist, and Martinique politician, born in Basse-Pointe, Martinique. He studied there and in Paris, returning to Martinique as a teacher. The influential *Cahier d'un retour au pays natal* (1947, Notebook of a Return to my Native Land) records his conscious adoption of an African identity. This theme is returned to in later poems and plays, such as *Une saison au Congo* (1967, A Season in the Congo) and an African version of Shakespeare's *The Tempest* (1969). He has represented the progressive element in the politics of Martinique since 1945.

cesarian section *caesarian section*

Cestoda [sestoda] *tapeworm*

Cetacea [seetayshia] *whale*

cetane number An index defining the ignition quality of fuel for diesel internal combustion engines. The number is the cetane percentage in a mixture of cetane and alpha-methyl napthalene, adjusted to match the characteristics of the fuel under test.

Cetewayo or **Cetshwayo** [ketewayoh] (c.1826–84) Ruler of Zululand from 1873, born near Eshowe, E South Africa. In 1879 he defeated the British at Isandhlwana, but was himself defeated at Ulundi. He presented his case in London, and in 1883 was restored to part of his kingdom, but soon after was driven out by an anti-royalist faction.

Cetus [seetus] (Lat 'whale') The fourth largest constellation, lying on the celestial Equator, but inconspicuous because it has few bright stars.

Ceuta [thayoota] 35°52N 5°18W, pop (2000e) 69 000. Freeport and military station, at E end of the Strait of Gibraltar, on the N African coast of Morocco; administered by Cádiz province, Spain; car ferries to Algeciras; became Spanish in 1580; trade in tobacco, oil products; old fortress at Monte Hacho, cathedral (15th-c), Church of Our Lady of Africa (18th-c).

Cévennes [sayven], ancient **Cebenna** Chief mountain range in the S of France, on the SE edge of the Massif Central; general direction NE–SW; highest peak, Mt Mézenc (1754 m/5754 ft); varied landscape, including forest, barren grassland, and deep gorges, such as Gorges du Tarn near Les Vignes.

Cézanne, Paul [sayzan] (1839–1906) Postimpressionist painter, born in Aix-en-Provence, SE France. He studied law at Aix, then was persuaded by his friend Emile Zola to go to Paris (1862), where he began to paint. He was influenced by Pissarro, with whom he worked at Auvers and Pontoise (1872–3). He abandoned his early sombre Expressionism for the study of nature, and began to use his characteristic glowing colours. In his later period (after 1886), he emphasized the underlying forms of nature – 'the cylinder, the sphere, the cone' – by constructing his pictures from a rhythmic series of coloured planes, thus becoming the forerunner of Cubism. He obtained recognition only in the last years of his life. Among his best-known paintings are 'L'Estaque' (c.1888, Musée d'Orsay, Paris), 'The Card Players' (1890–2, Musée d'Orsay, Paris), and 'The Gardener' (1906, Tate, London). Picasso called him 'the father of us all'.

CFCs An abbreviation of **chlorofluorocarbons**, also called **Freons**; derivatives of methane and ethane containing both chlorine and fluorine. Important examples are CCl_2F_2 and $CClF_2$–$CClF_2$. They are inert, volatile compounds, used as refrigerants and aerosol sprays. Their decomposition in the atmosphere damages the Earth's ozone layer. International agreements propose replacing them with less harmful substances.

Chabrier, (Alexis) Emmanuel [shabreeyay] (1841–94) Composer, born in Ambert, SC France. He studied law in Paris, and devoted himself to music in 1879 after hearing Wagner's *Tristan und Isolde*. He wrote operas, piano works, and songs, but his best-known pieces were inspired by the folk music of Spain, notably his orchestral rhapsody *España* (1883).

Chabrol, Claude [shabrol] (1930–) Film critic and director, born in Paris, France. He financed his own first production *Le Beau Serge* (1958, Handsome Serge), and with *Les Cousins* (1959) became identified with the French *Nouvelle Vague*, a style which had become more publicly acceptable when he produced *Les Biches* (1968, The Does). His most widely-known films are dramas of abnormality in the provincial bourgeoisie, notably *Le Boucher* (1970, The Butcher), *Les Noces rouges* (1973, Red Wedding), and *Inspector Lavardin* (1986). Later films include *L'Enfer* (1993, Torment), *Rien ne va plus* (1997), and *Au Coeur du mensonge* (1999).

chacma baboon A baboon native to S Africa (*Papio ursinus*); large but slender body; dark brown with dark face; inhabits grassland and rocky regions; troops contain up to 100 individuals.

Chaco Canyon A remote desert canyon in New Mexico, 160 km/100 mi NW of Albuquerque, the hub in AD c.950–1300 of the Anasazi Indian culture of the American SW; now a world heritage site. A National Monument since 1907, its 650 km/400 mi road network links c.125 D-shaped pueblos or planned villages. The best known is Pueblo Bonito, a compact five-storey settlement covering 1 ha/2·5 acres, with c.600 rooms housing 1000 people.

chaconne A dance of Latin-American origin. The harmonies and basses traditionally associated with it were widely used as material for arias and instrumental variations in the 17th–18th-c.

Chaco War (1932) A territorial struggle between Bolivia and Paraguay in the disputed Northern Chaco area. Owing to the brilliant tactics of Col José Félix Estigarribia (1888–1940), Paraguay won most of the area, and a peace treaty was signed in 1938. Around 50 000 Bolivians and 35 000 Paraguayans died in the war.

Chad *p.300*

Chad, Lake, Fr **Tchad, Lac** Shallow freshwater lake in NC Africa at meeting point of Chad, Nigeria, Cameroon, and Niger; remnant of former inland sea; area 10 000 sq km/4000 sq mi (low water), 26 700 sq km/10 000 sq mi (high water); no visible outlets; chain of inhabited islands along E coast; fishing, mineral extraction (natron); first reached by Europeans in 1823; Douguia Wildlife Reserve nearby; oil discovered nearby in Niger.

Chadic [chadik] A group of 100 languages, spoken by over 25 million people in parts of Ghana and the Central African Republic. It is assigned to the Afro-Asiatic family, though its position there is unclear.

Chadwick, Sir James (1891–1974) Physicist, born in Manchester, Greater Manchester, NW England, UK. He studied at Cambridge, and in Berlin under Geiger. He then worked at the Cavendish Laboratory with Rutherford, investigating the structure of the atom, and discovered the neutron (1932), for which he received the Nobel Prize for Physics in 1935. He led the UK's work on the atomic bomb in World War 2, and was knighted in 1945.

Chadwick, John *Ventris, Michael*

Chadwick, Lynn (Russell) (1914–2003) Sculptor, born in London, UK. He studied architecture, but after war service began making mobiles (c.1946), then rough-finished solid metal sculptures. In 1956 he won the International Sculpture Prize at the Venice Biennale.

Chaetognatha [keetognatha] *arrow worm*

chafer A large, nocturnal beetle; adults feed on leaves; larvae fleshy, C-shaped, burrow in soil eating roots, often taking 3–4 years to develop. Chafers are diverse, and some are pests. The family includes the cockchafer. (Order: Coleoptera. Family: Scarabaeidae.)

chaffinch Either of two species of bird of genus *Fringilla*. *Fringilla coelebs* is native to Europe, N Africa, the Azores, and SW Asia; inhabits forest and human habitations; colour varies over range; N populations move S for winter. The **blue chaffinch** (*Fringilla teydea*) is from the Canary Is. (Family: Fringillidae.)

Chagall, Marc [shagal] (1887–1985) Artist, born in Vitebsk, NE Belarus. He studied at St Petersburg and Paris, left Russia in 1922, and settled near Paris. During World War 2 he moved to the USA, where he began to design ballet sets and costumes. He illustrated several books, but is best known for his paintings of animals, objects, and people from his life, dreams, and Russian folklore. The word *Surrealist* is said to have been coined by Apollinaire to describe the work of Chagall.

Chaikin, Joseph [chiykin] (1935–) Actor and theatre director, born in New York City, USA. His early work as an actor was with the Living Theater, notably in *The Connection* (1960) and *Man is Man* (1962). In 1963 he founded The Open Theater, which for a decade produced some of the most original work in the US theatre, such as *America Hurrah* (1965), *Terminal* (1969), and *Nightwalk* (1973). He suffered a stroke in 1984 but went on to co-write *The War in Heaven* (1991) with Sam Shepard.

Chain, Sir Ernst Boris [chayn] (1906–79) Biochemist, born in Berlin, Germany. After studying physiology and chemistry in Berlin, he fled from Nazi Germany to Britain, where he taught at Cambridge (1933–5) and Oxford (1935–48). With Sir Howard Florey at Oxford he was a key figure in the successful isolation of penicillin (discovered earlier by Sir Alexander Fleming), and all three shared the 1945 Nobel Prize for Physiology or Medicine. He was director of the International Research Centre for Chemical Microbiology in Rome (1948–61), and professor of biochemistry at Imperial College, London (1961–73). He was knighted in 1970.

Chad

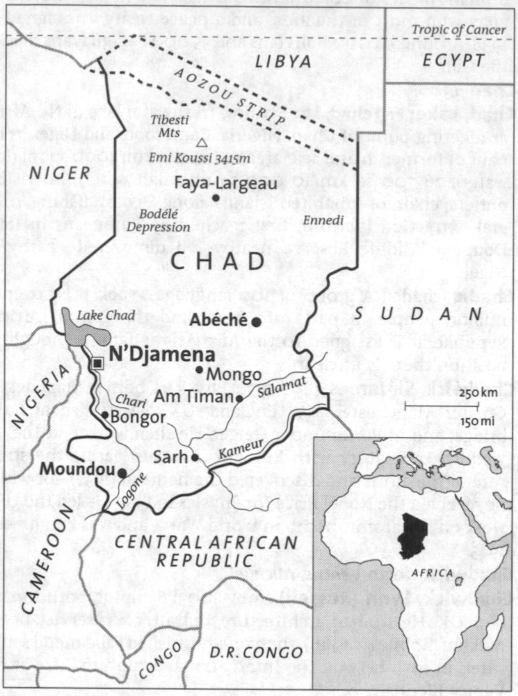

□ International Airport

Fr **Tchad**, official name **Republic of Chad**, Fr **République du Tchad**

Local name Tchad

Timezone GMT +1

Area 1 284 640 km²/495 871 sq mi

Population total (2002e) 8 997 000

Status Republic

Date of independence 1960

Capital N'djamena

Languages Arabic and French (official), many local languages spoken

Ethnic groups Sara, Bagirmi, and Kreish (30%); Sudanic Arab (26%), Teda (17%), Masalit, Maba, Mimi (6%), over 200 groups

Religions Muslim (50%), Christian (Roman Catholic 21%, Protestant 12%), and local religions

Physical features Landlocked in C Africa; mostly arid, semi-desert plateau at edge of Sahara Desert; average altitude of 200–500 m/650–1650 ft; Tibesti Mts (N) rise to 3415 m/11 204 ft at Emi Koussi; rivers in S (Chari and Logne) flow NW to Lake Chad.

Climate Tropical, moderately wet in S (May–Oct); hot, arid N, almost rainless; C plain hot, dry, with brief rainy season (Jun–Sep).

Currency 1 CFA Franc (CFAFr) = 100 centimes

Economy Severely damaged in recent years by drought, locusts, and civil war; export of cotton, kaolin, animal products; salt mined around L Chad.

GDP (2002e) $9·297 bn, per capita $1000

Human Development Index (2002) 0·365

History Part of French Equatorial Africa, 1908; colonial status, 1920; independence, 1960; Libyan troops occupied the Aozou Strip in extreme N, 1973; fighting between Libyan-supported rebels and French-supported government until ceasefire agreed, 1987; continuing civil war with some further periods of ceasefire during the 1990s; new constitution adopted, 1991; transitional charter, 1993; Aouzou strip returned to Chad by Libya, 1994; peace agreement with northern rebel movement, 2002; draft peace agreement signed with rebels of National Resistance Army (ANR), 2003; governed by a president, prime minister, Council of Ministers, and a 57-member Higher Transitional Council.

Head of State

1982–90 Hissne Habré
1990– Idriss Déby

Head of Government

1991–2 Jean Alingue Bawoyeu
1992–3 Joseph Yodemane
1993 Fidèle Moungar
1994–5 Delwa Kassire Koumakoye
1995–7 Koibla Djimasta
1997–9 Nassour Ouaidou Guelendouksia
1999–2002 Negoum Yamassoum
2002–3 Haroun Kabadi
2003– Moussa Faki Mahamat

chain reaction In nuclear physics, a reaction in which nuclear fission induced by a neutron releases further neutrons that in turn may cause further fission through some material. For a large enough block of material, enough neutrons will undergo collisions, rather than escaping from the material, to sustain the reaction. Nuclear power and atomic bombs rely on chain reactions in uranium or plutonium.

chakras The seven centres of energy in the yogic system. Roughly equivalent to the autonomic nervous system and endocrine glands of Western medicine, they are important for channelling vital energy and consciousness. In ascending order they are the Base Chakra (*Muladhara*), Abdominal Chakra (*Swadhistana*), Solar Plexus Chakra (*Manipura*), Heart Chakra (*Anahata*), Throat Chakra (*Vishuddi*), Commend Chakra (*Ajna*), and Crown Chakra (*Sahasra*). They may be visualized as vortices in the body's energy field, and an imbalance of, or interference with, the energy associated with these centres may lead to physical, mental, emotional, or spiritual disharmony.

Chalcedon, Council of [kalseedn] (451) A Council of the Church which agreed that Jesus Christ is truly God and truly man, two natures in one person (the *Chalcedonian definition*). The definition is generally accepted by the Churches, though from the beginning there was uneasiness about its interpretation, and recently it has come under sustained criticism.

chalcedony [kalsedonee] A group name for the compact varieties of mineral silica (SiO_2) composed of very fine-grained crystals of quartz. It occurs in massive form with a wax-like lustre, often filling cavities in volcanic rocks. Banded varieties are agate and onyx, and coloured varieties include carnelian, jasper, bloodstone, and chrysoprase.

Chalcis [kalsis], Gr **Khalkis** 38°27N 23°42E, pop (2000e) 48 600. Capital of Euboea, Greece; railway; local ferries; commerce, tourism; Aristotle died here.

Chalcolithic *Three Age System*

chalcopyrite [kalkopiyriyt] A copper iron sulphide mineral ($CuFeS_2$) found in veins associated with igneous rocks; brass-coloured and metallic. It is the main ore of copper.

Chaldaeans [kaldeeanz] Originally the name of a Semitic people (*Kaldu*) from Arabia who settled in the region of Ur in Lower Mesopotamia. By the 7th-c and 6th-c BC, it had become a generic term for Babylonians. In Roman times, it referred to practitioners of the Babylonian science of astrology.

Chaliapin [shalyapeen] *Shalyapin, Fyodor Ivanovich*

chalk A fine-grained limestone rock, mainly of calcite, formed from the shells of minute marine organisms. Often pure white in colour, it is characteristically seen in rocks of the Upper Cretaceous period of W Europe, its most famous exposures being on either side of the English Channel. Blackboard chalk is calcium sulphate.

***Challenger* expedition** The first major oceanographic expedition (1872–6), carried out aboard the British steam corvette, HMS *Challenger*. The voyage circumnavigated the globe, carrying out studies in the Atlantic, Indian, and Pacific Oceans, and covering nearly 69 000 nautical miles in the process. The expedition laid the groundwork for the modern science of oceanography, discovered 4417 new species and 715 new genera of marine organisms, and proved the existence of life at all depths in the sea.

Challoner, Richard [chaloner] (1691–1781) Roman Catholic clergyman and writer, born in Lewes, East Sussex, SE England, UK. He studied at Douai (1704) and was ordained in 1716, remaining there as a professor until 1730. He then served as a missionary priest in London, becoming Bishop of Debra (1741) and Vicar Apostolic of the London district (1758). His best-known works are the prayer book, *The Garden of the Soul* (1740), and his revision of the Douai version of the Bible (5 vols, 1750).

Chalmers, Judith (1937–) British television presenter. She studied in Manchester and the London Academy of Music and Dramatic Art, then began broadcasting with BBC Manchester, moving to BBC London in 1960. In 1972 she joined Thames Television, where she presented the long-running holiday programme *Wish You Were Here...?* (from 1973). She hosted her own daily programme for Radio 2 (1990), and has been commentator for many royal and state occasions.

Chalmers, Thomas (1780–1847) Theologian and reformer, born in Anstruther, Fife, E Scotland, UK. He studied at St Andrews, was ordained in 1803, and became a minister in Glasgow (1815), where his oratory took the city by storm. He became professor of moral philosophy at St Andrews (1823), and of theology at Edinburgh (1827). In the Disruption of 1843 he led 470 ministers out of the Established Church of Scotland to found the Free Church of Scotland.

chalone [kalohn] A small to medium-sized protein that inhibits mitosis in cells when adrenalin is present. When injury occurs, the loss of chalones from damaged cells stimulates and directs wound healing.

Chamaeleon [kameelion] A faint S constellation.

chambered tomb In European prehistory, megalithic monuments usually constructed of uprights (*orthostats*) and capstones beneath a cairn or mound of earth, the burial chamber sometimes being provided with a corbelled vault; also known as a **dolmen**. Originating in the Neolithic period, they were often used for collective burial over generations. Two famous examples are Maes Howe (on Orkney, N Scotland, UK) and New Grange (in the Boyne R valley, Ireland).

Chamberlain, Sir (Joseph) Austen (1863–1937) British statesman, born in Birmingham, West Midlands, C England, UK, the eldest son of Joseph Chamberlain. He studied at Cambridge, was elected a Liberal Unionist MP (1892), and sat as a Conservative MP until his death. He was Chancellor of the Exchequer (1903–6, 1919–21), secretary for India (1915–17), Unionist leader (1921–2), foreign secretary (1924–9), and First Lord of the Admiralty (1931). He shared the 1925 Nobel Peace Prize for negotiating the Locarno Pact.

Chamberlain, Joseph (1836–1914) British statesman, born in London, UK. He entered the family business at 16, became Mayor of Birmingham (1873–5), and a Liberal MP (1876). He became President of the Board of Trade (1880), but resigned over Gladstone's Home Rule Bill (1886), which split the Liberal Party. From 1889 he was leader of the Liberal Unionists, and in the coalition government of 1895 took office as secretary for the Colonies. In 1903 he resigned office to be free to advocate his ideas on tariff reform, and in 1906 withdrew from public life after a stroke.

Chamberlain, Lindy (Alice Lynne) (1948–) Mother of the 'dingo baby', born in Whakatane, New Zealand. The disappearance of her nine-week-old daughter, Azaria, at Uluru (Ayers Rock), in 1980, made her the subject of national obsession in Australia. Married to pastor **Michael Chamberlain** (who was tried with her, and whom she has since divorced), she claimed the baby was taken by a dingo. She was found guilty of murder, and gaoled, but released in 1986 when a baby's jacket was found at the base of the rock. A judicial inquiry found that forensic evidence used in the 1982 trial was unreliable, and that the dingo story was probably correct. In 1988 the Northern Territory Court of Criminal Appeal quashed all convictions against the couple, and they received A$1 million in compensation. The saga is recounted in John Bryson's *Evil Angels* (1985), and was later filmed, and her autobiography *Through My Eyes* appeared in 1990.

Chamberlain, (Arthur) Neville (1869–1940) British statesman and prime minister (1937–40), born in Birmingham, West Midlands, C England, UK, the son of Joseph Chamberlain. He studied at Rugby and Birmingham, was Mayor of Birmingham (1915–16), and a Conservative MP from 1918. He was a skilful Chancellor of the Exchequer (1923–4, 1931–7), steering the country back towards prosperity with a policy of low interest rates and easy credit. Three times minister for health (1923, 1924–9, 1931), he was responsible for the reform of the Poor Law, the promotion of council-house building, and the reorganization of local government. He played a leading part in the formation of the National Government (1931). As prime minister, he advocated 'appeasement' of the German and Italian dictators in order to avoid war, returning from Munich with a written undertaking by Hitler amounting to 'peace for our time' (1938). While giving orders for the immediate stepping up of the armaments programme, Chamberlain did not, in fact, prevent Hitler's invasion of the Czech Sudetenland in March 1939. When Germany invaded Poland later in the year, he offered Hitler an ultimatum to withdraw or force a war between Britain and Germany. Ignored by Hitler, Chamberlain announced to the nation that war between the two powers had broken out. Criticism of his war leadership and initial military reverses led to his resignation as prime minister (1940), followed by his death a few months later.

Chamberlain, Wilt(on) Norman, nickname **Wilt the Stilt** (1936–99) Basketball player, born in Philadelphia, Pennsylvania, USA. He studied at Kansas University. Height 1·85 m/7 ft 1 in, he played for the Philadelphia 76ers against the New York Knickerbockers in 1962, and scored 100 points in one game, a National Basketball Association (NBA) record. He scored a record 4029 points that season, and was seven times the NBA leading scorer (1960–6). During his career (1960–73) he scored 31 419 points at an average of 30·1 per game. He had a brief spell playing for the Harlem Globetrotters.

Chamberlain, Lord In the UK, the chief official of the royal household, overseeing all aspects of its management, and bearing responsibility for matters ranging from the care of works of art to the appointment of royal tradesmen. The office should be distinguished from the **Lord Great Chamberlain**, whose duties are largely ceremonial; in particular, at coronations, he presents the sovereign to the people.

chamber music Music for two or more players intended for performance in a room rather than a concert hall, with only one player to a part. The term is a translation of the Italian 'musica da camera' and, by convention, applies only to instrumental music, and therefore mainly to music since c.1600. Until c.1750 the main type of chamber music was the trio sonata (typically for two violins and continuo). Since then the string quartet has been looked upon as the chamber ensemble *par excellence*, but any wind, string, or keyboard instrument might participate in chamber music.

chamber of commerce An association of business enterprises in a district, whose aims are to promote the area and its members' businesses. The Chambers of Commerce of the USA (established 1912) represent, through member organizations, some five million business firms and individuals. The International Chamber of Commerce (ICC), based in Paris, was set up in 1920, and has the affiliation of over 40 national institutions. It operates a court of arbitration providing conciliation and arbitration facilities for the settlement of commercial disputes among different nationalities.

chamber opera Opera which employs a small cast and (especially) a small orchestra. Many 18th-c operas and intermezzos fit this description, but the term is applied particularly to 20th-c works such as Britten's *The Turn of the Screw*.

Chambers, Ephraim (c.1680–1740) Encyclopedist, born in Kendal, Cumbria, NW England, UK. While apprenticed to a globe-maker in London he conceived the idea of a *Cyclopaedia, or Universal Dictionary of Arts and Sciences* (2 folio vols, 1728). A French translation inspired Diderot's *Encyclopédie*.

Chambers, Robert (1802–71) Publisher and writer, born in Peebles, Scottish Borders, SE Scotland, UK, the brother of William Chambers. He began as a bookseller in Edinburgh (1818), and gave his leisure to literary composition, writing many books on Scottish history, people, and institutions, and contributing regularly to *Chambers's Edinburgh Journal*. His son **Robert Chambers** (1832–88) became head of the firm in 1883, and conducted the *Journal* until his death.

Chambers, William (1800–83) Publisher and writer, born in Peebles, Scottish Borders, SE Scotland, UK. He was apprenticed to a bookseller in Edinburgh (1814), and in 1819 went into business for himself. In 1832 he started *Chambers's Edinburgh Journal*, and soon after united with his brother Robert Chambers in founding the printing and publishing firm of W & R Chambers. As Lord Provost of Edinburgh (1865–9), he promoted a successful scheme for improving the older part of the city. Shortly before his death he received the offer of a baronetcy.

Chambord [shãbaw(r)] 47°37N 1°31E, pop (2000e) 220. A village 18 km/11 mi E of Blois, C France, noted for its chateau and estate; a world heritage site. Once a hunting lodge of the counts of Blois, the chateau was reconstructed (1519–33) by Francis I and Henry II as a royal residence.

chameleon [kameelion] A lizard native to Africa, the Middle East, S Spain, India, and Sri Lanka; body flattened from side to side; can change colour rapidly (controlled by nerves in skin); tail clasping, cannot be shed; eyes move independently of one another; tongue longer than head and body, with sticky tip that shoots out to hit insect prey; usually lives in trees. (Family: Chamaeleontidae, 85 species.)

chamois [shamwah] A goat-antelope from S Europe (*Rupicapra rupicapra*) (introduced in New Zealand); brown with pale patches on face or neck; horns short, vertical, with backward-hooked tips; inhabits rugged mountains; skin formerly used to make 'shammy leather' (this now obtained from goats and sheep).

chamomile or **camomile** [kamomiyl] A perennial growing to 30 cm/12 in (*Chamaemelum nobile*), native to W Europe and N Africa; leaves oblong in outline, divided into narrow, fine-pointed segments; flower-heads up to 2·5 cm/1 in across, solitary; outer ray florets spreading, white; inner disc florets yellow. It is widely used to make chamomile tea, and is a popular additive to shampoos, hair washes, etc. Chamomile lawns were formerly very popular, especially in England during Elizabethan times, giving off a pleasant aromatic smell when walked on. (Family: Compositae.)

champagne A sparkling wine produced in the Champagne region of NE France, using either a mixture of black and white grapes, or white grapes only. The effervescent nature of champagne is due to the fact that some of the fermentation takes place in the bottle. Sweet (*sec*), slightly sweet (*demi-sec*), and dry (*brut*) varieties are made.

Champagne-Ardenne [shãpanyah(r)den] pop (2000e) 1 410 000; area 25 606 sq km/9884 sq mi. Region of NE France comprising the departments of Ardennes, Aube, Marne, and Haute-Marne; a long-standing scene of conflict between France and Germany; noted for the production of champagne wine; 120 km/75 mi-long 'Route du Champagne' through the vine-growing areas, starting at Reims.

Champlain, Samuel de [shãplĩ] (1567–1635) Governor of Canada, born in Brouage, W France. In a series of voyages he travelled to Canada (1603), exploring the E coast (1604–7), and founding Quebec (1608). He was appointed Lieutenant of Canada (1612), and established alliances with several Indian nations. When Quebec fell briefly to the British, he was taken prisoner (1629–32). From 1633 he was Governor of Quebec. L Champlain is named after him.

champlevé [shomluhvay] A technique of enamelling on metal, which involves engraving the image out of the metal surface, and filling it with vitreous pastes of different colours, which are then fired. Popular throughout the Middle Ages, it was produced on an almost industrial scale at Limoges in France.

Champollion, Jean François [shãpolyõ] (1790–1832) Founder of Egyptology, born in Figeac, SC France. He studied at Grenoble, and went to Paris (1807), subsequently becoming professor of history at Grenoble (1809–16). Best known for his use of the Rosetta Stone to decipher Egyptian hieroglyphics (1822–4), he was the first to place the study of early Egyptian history and culture on a firm footing. In 1831 a chair of Egyptology was founded for him at the Collège de France.

Chan or **Ch'an** [chan] A general term for meditation in Chinese Buddhism, referring to a school which dates from perhaps the 6th-c. It combines Mahayana Buddhist teachings with those of Taoism to form an outlook emphasizing meditative experience as opposed to an intellectual approach. It is called **Zen** in Japanese.

chancel The E end of a church, containing the altar, choir, and clergy; more generally, the body of the church to the E of the nave. The name is derived from the Latin *cancellus*, the screen separating the chancel from the rest of the church.

Chancellor, Lord (High) *Lord Chancellor*

Chancellor of the Exchequer The senior minister in charge of the UK Treasury, and a senior minister in the cabinet. The Chancellor takes responsibility for the preparation of the budget, and (in contrast to most other countries) is economic as well as finance minister. In 1997, however, the new Labour government gave responsibility for fixing interest rates to the Bank of England, thus reducing the Chancellor's ability to manage the economy.

Chancery Division A division of the High Court of England and Wales created by the Judicature Acts (1873–5) to replace the Court of Chancery. It is mainly concerned with real property, trusts and probate matters, but also includes cases involving company law, patents, and intellectual property cases. The effective head of the Chancery Division is the Vice Chancellor, although the Lord Chancellor is nominally its president. In the USA, most courts of general jurisdiction combine law and equity. In Scotland, the Court of Chancery is part of the Sheriff Court, and deals with the issue of land titles for heirs of deceased persons.

Chan Chan An ancient Chimu capital in the Moche Valley, Peru, occupied from c.1000 to the Inca conquest c.1470; a world heritage site. Its residential area covered 19 sq km/7¼ sq mi, with a population of c.30 000. The monumental centre 6 sq km/2¼ sq mi in area is notable for its 10 huge rectangular enclosures, administrative centres of the kingdom during successive reigns.

chancroid A sexually transmitted disease common in Africa and South Asia, resulting from infection with *Haemophilus Ducreyi*. It causes ulceration of the genital organs.

Chandigarh [chandigah(r)] pop (2001e) 901 000; area 114 sq km/44 sq mi. City and union territory (1966) in NW India; serves as the joint state capital of the Punjab and Haryana; airfield; railway; university (1947); city designed by Le Corbusier, includes an 8 km/5 mi green belt; Asia's largest rose garden.

Chandler, Raymond (Thornton) (1888–1959) Writer, born in Chicago, Illinois, USA. He studied in England, France, and Germany, then worked as a freelance writer in London. In World

War 1 he served in the Canadian army in France and in the Royal Flying Corps. During the Depression he began to write short stories and novelettes for the detective-story pulp magazines of the day, later turning to 'private-eye' novels, such as *The Big Sleep* (1939) and *Farewell, My Lovely* (1940), several of which were filmed. He is the creator of the cynical but honest detective antihero, Philip Marlowe.

Chandragupta II [chandra**gup**ta], also known as **Vikramaditya** (Sanskrit 'sun of valour') (4th-c) Indian emperor (c.380–c.415), the third of the imperial Guptas of N India. He extended control over his neighbours by both military and peaceful means. A devout Hindu, he tolerated Buddhism and Jainism, and patronized learning. During his reign, art, architecture, and sculpture flourished, and the cultural development of ancient India reached its climax.

Chandrasekhar, Subrahmanyan [chandra**say**ker] (1910–95) Astrophysicist, born in Lahore, NE Pakistan (formerly India). He studied at the Presidency College, Madras, before going to Cambridge University. In 1936 he went to America and worked at the University of Chicago and the Yerkes Observatory, becoming a US citizen in 1953. He studied the final stages of stellar evolution, showing that the final fate of a star (as a supernova or as a white dwarf), depends on its mass. Massive stars will be unable to evolve into white dwarfs, and this limiting stellar mass (about 1·4 solar masses) is called the *Chandrasekhar limit*. He was awarded the Nobel Prize for Physics in 1983.

Chanel, Coco [sha**nel**], popular name of **Gabrielle Chanel** (?1883–1971) Fashion designer, born in Saumur, W France. She worked as a milliner until 1912, and after World War 1 opened a couture house in Paris. She revolutionized women's fashions during the 1920s, her designs including the 'chemise' dress and the collarless cardigan jacket. Many of the features she introduced, such as the vogue for costume jewellery and the evening scarf, still retain their popularity. She retired in 1938, but made a surprisingly successful come-back in 1954.

Chaney, Lon [**chay**nee], originally **Alonso Chaney** (1883–1930) Film actor, born in Colorado Springs, Colorado, USA. He was famous for spine-chilling deformed villains and other horrific parts, as in *The Hunchback of Notre Dame* (1923) and *The Phantom of the Opera* (1925), and came to be called 'the man of a thousand faces'. His son, **Lon Chaney, Jr** (1907–73), was also an actor in horror films, and starred in a film version of Steinbeck's *Of Mice and Men* (1939).

Changchun or **Ch'ang-ch'un** [chang**chun**] 43°50N 125°20E, pop (2000e) 2 444 000, administrative region 6 679 000. Capital of Jilin province, NE China; on the Yitong R in C of China's NE plain; developed during Japanese military occupation (1933–45) as capital of Manchukuo; airfield; railway; university (1958); electric furnaces, vehicles, light engineering, textiles, food processing, chemicals; Changchun film studio.

change ringing A British form of bell-ringing devised by 17th-c Cambridge printer Fabian Stedman. A set of differently tuned bells, usually those in a church tower, are rung in various permutations so that no sequence (or **change**) is sounded more than once. A full diatonic scale of eight bells allows 40 320 changes. A 'peal' of about 5000 changes takes about three hours to ring. Change ringers belong to Guilds, the oldest being the Ancient Society of College Youths, founded in 1637.

Changjiang *Yangtze River*

Changsha or **Ch'ang-sha** [chang**shah**] 28°10N 113°00E, pop (2000e) 1 536 000, administrative region 5 712 000. River port and capital of Hunan province, SE China; on the lower Xiang R, in intensively cultivated lowlands; early craft, industrial, and educational centre; foreign trade port, 1904; airfield; railway; university (1959); textiles, food-processing, chemicals, light engineering, electronics; Hunan Provincial Museum; Yuelushan Park, containing Lushan Temple (founded, 268); Kaifu Temple (896).

Chania [**khan**ya] or **Cania** 35°31N 24°01E, pop (2000e) 139 000. Capital town of Chania department, Crete; on N shore of Crete I; founded, 13th-c; capital of Crete until 1971; airport; fruit, olives, leather, crafts, tourism; dance festival to commemorate the battle for Crete (May).

Channel Islands *see panel*

channelling The process by which a person can act as a vehicle or channel through which an external energy source can be harnessed and directed. The term is usually applied to directing healing energies to sick patients in order to cure their disease. It may also be a way of transmitting ideas or other communications from external sources of intelligence, which some people believe to be of divine or extraterrestrial origin.

channel swimming Swimming the English Channel, first achieved on 24–25 August 1875 by Captain Matthew Webb (1848–83), who covered the 34 km/21 mi from Dover to Calais Sands in 21 h 45 min. The record is now 7 h 40 min. The Channel Swimming Association was founded in 1927.

Channel Islands

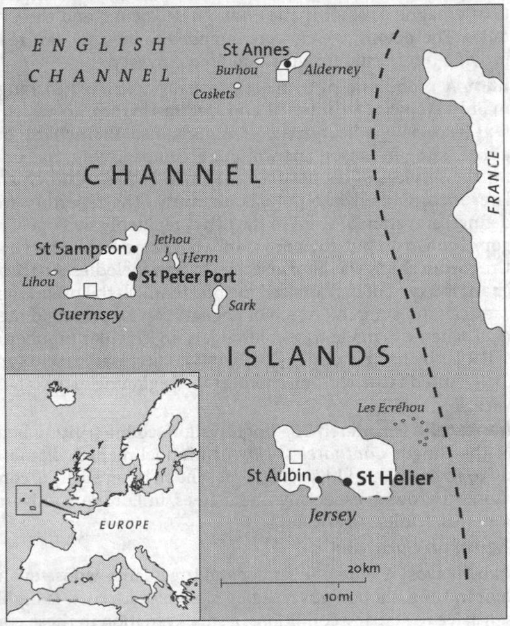

□ International Airport

Fr **Iles Anglo-Normandes** (UK British Islands)

Timezone GMT

Area 194 km²/75 sq mi

Population total (2000e) 151 600

Status Crown dependency of the United Kingdom

Capital St Helier (on Jersey), St Peter Port (on Guernsey)

Languages English and Norman-French

Physical features Island group of the British Isles in the English Channel, W of Normandy; comprises the islands of Guernsey, Jersey, Alderney, Sark, Herm, Jethou, Brechou, and Lihou.

Economy Tourism, fruit, vegetables, flowers, dairy produce, Jersey and Guernsey cattle; used as a tax haven; not part of the European Community.

History Granted to the Dukes of Normandy, 10th-c; only British possession to have been occupied by Germany during World War 2; a dependent territory of the British Crown, with individual legislative assemblies and legal system; divided into the Bailiwick of Guernsey and the Bailiwick of Jersey; Bailiff presides over the Royal Court and the Representative Assembly (the States).

Channel Tunnel A tunnel linking France and Britain, first proposed in 1802. Excavations begun in 1882 were soon abandoned due to fears about defence, and a state-financed venture by the French and British governments was scrapped in the 1970s. In 1985 Eurotunnel, an Anglo-French consortium, was set up to finance the tunnel and operate it once it opened. The tunnel, built by the Anglo-French Transmanche Link, consists of twin rail tunnels between Cheriton near Folkestone and Fréthun near Calais. Completed in 1994, it is 50 km/31 mi long (38 km/23 mi of this under the sea). In November 1996 a fire in a freight train caused serious damage and temporary closure.

chanoyu [**chahnohyoo**] The Japanese tea ceremony. It first became popular among priests and warriors in the Middle Ages as a means of concentration. The tea is made from a strong green powder, and drunk in small quantities. The bowls and utensils are prized as art objects. The detailed etiquette is often learnt by young women before marriage. Teachers must have a recognized licence.

chansons de geste [shãsõ duh **zhest**] (Fr 'poems of action') French poems from the 12th–13th-c, celebrating historical figures and events on an epic scale. Different cycles centre on Charlemagne (including the *Chanson de Roland*) and the Crusades. The poems, which were intended to be sung, not read, provide interesting insights into feudal society.

chant A monotone or a melody, usually restricted in range, mainly stepwise in interval and free in rhythm, to which a text (especially a liturgical one) is declaimed. **Plainchant**, originally sung in unison and without accompaniment, was used for the services of the mediaeval Roman Catholic Church and later incorporated into polyphonic music. The repertory was defined and standardized in the 6th-c, reputedly by Pope Gregory the Great, but the corpus of what came to be known as **Gregorian chant** was later enriched by new melodies. **Anglican chant** is a type of harmonized melody to which the psalms and canticles are sung in Church of England services. Its rigid metrical scheme is made to accommodate an irregular number of syllables by having as many of them as is necessary freely sung (or 'chanted') to a 'reciting chord' at the beginning of each half-verse.

chanterelle [shanterel] The bright yellow, edible fruiting body of the fungus *Cantharellus cibarius*; funnel-shaped, diameter up to 10 cm/4 in; gill-like ridges present on lower surface; common on ground, especially under trees, in Europe and North America. (Order: Agaricales.)

Chanukah *Hanukkah*

chaos [**kay**os] A state of disorder and irregularity whose evolution in time, though governed by simple exact laws, is highly sensitive to starting conditions: a small variation in these conditions will produce wildly different results. Long-term behaviour of chaotic systems cannot be predicted. Chaos is an intermediate stage between highly ordered motion and fully-random motion. For example, in fluid flow, a slowly moving fluid exhibits perfectly regular flow; as the fluid velocity increases, the flow becomes chaotic; and as the velocity increases still further, the flow becomes fully turbulent (random). In a chaotic system, the values of some quantity at two points maintain their relationship as time passes, even though the exact value of each cannot be predicted in the future. In truly random motion, there exist no such relationships. Chaos is present in most real systems, such as in weather patterns and the motion of planets about the Sun; the stable classical motion widely accepted as the norm in physics is now known to be the exception rather than the rule. The underlying structure of chaos exhibits universal features, regardless of the system in question. The modern theory of chaos is based on the work of US meteorologist Edward Lorenz (1917–) in 1963, arising from the study of convection in the atmosphere. Some degree of non-linearity is necessary for chaotic behaviour. *Fractals* feature in a comprehensive description of chaos.

Chaos [**kay**os] In Greek mythology, the primaeval state of emptiness (according to Hesiod), but in later Greek philosophy a universe of muddled forms and elements which separated out into our world. It can be personified, as in Milton's 'reign of Chaos and old Night'.

Chapala, Lake [cha**pah**la] area 3370 sq km/1300 sq mi. Lake in SW Mexico; 77 km/48 mi long E–W; c.16 km/10 mi wide; largest lake in Mexico, on the C plateau, 48 km/30 mi S of Guadalajara; resort town of Chapala on the N shore.

chaparral [shapa**ral**] (Span *chaparro* 'scrub oak') The evergreen scrub vegetation of semi-arid areas with a Mediterranean-type climate in SW USA and NW Mexico. It is a plant community adapted to frequent fires. Without fire every few years the chaparral would degrade. Typical vegetation species include evergreen scrub oak, laurel sumac, and ceanothus.

chapati [cha**pah**tee] A thin, flat, unleavened bread, made from a mixture of water and wheat flour containing c.95% of the original wheat. It is a traditional accompaniment to many Asian dishes, especially those of India, Pakistan, and Bangladesh.

chapel Originally, a place to house sacred relics; now generally a church. In England and Wales, the term is used of Nonconformist places of worship; in N Ireland and Scotland, of Roman Catholic churches. It may also be a place of worship belonging to a college or institution, and may further denote the chancel of a church or cathedral, or part of a cathedral containing a separate altar.

Chaplin, Charlie, popular name of **Sir Charles Spencer Chaplin** (1889–1977) Film actor and director, born in London, UK. His skill in comedy developed under Fred Karno, with whom he went to Hollywood in 1914. In his early comedies he adopted the bowler hat, out-turned feet, moustache, and walking-cane which became his hallmark, as in *The Kid* (1921), *The Gold Rush* (1925), and many others. His art was essentially suited to the silent film, and when sound arrived he experimented with new forms, as in *City Lights* (1931), with music only, and *Modern Times* (1936), part speech and part mime. His first sound film was *The Great Dictator* (1940). In *Limelight* (1952) he acted, directed, and composed the music and dances. His left-wing sympathies caused him to leave the USA for Switzerland in 1952. He was married four times, was awarded an Oscar in 1972, and was knighted in 1975.

Chapman, George (c.1559–1634) Poet and playwright, born near Hitchin, Hertfordshire, SE England, UK. He studied at Oxford, then worked in London. He is best known for his translations of Homer's *Iliad* (1598–1611) and *Odyssey* (1616), followed by the minor works (c.1624). He joined Jonson and Marston in the composition of *Eastward Ho* (1605), and in 1607 *Bussy d'Ambois* appeared, which had a sequel in 1613.

Chapman horse *Cleveland bay*

Chappaquiddick [chapa**kwid**ik] (Algonquian 'separated-island-at') Island to the E of Martha's Vineyard I, USA; in the Nantucket Sound, off the SE coast of Massachusetts; briefly achieved worldwide fame in 1969, as the site of a car accident involving US senator Edward Kennedy.

Chappell, Greg(ory Stephen) (1948–) Cricketer, born in Unley, South Australia, the brother of Ian Chappell. A middle-order batsman, slip fielder, and seam bowler, he played 88 times for his country (1970–84), 48 as captain, and scored 24 Test centuries. He also played in England for Somerset for two years.

Chappell, Ian (Michael) (1943–) Cricketer, born in Unley, South Australia, the brother of Greg Chappell. He played 75 times for Australia (1976–80), scoring over 5000 runs and 14 Test centuries. His pugnacious, driving style of captaincy made Australia a side universally respected in the 1970s. He is now a well-known sports commentator.

characin [**kar**asin] Any of a large family of colourful carp-like freshwater fishes common in South and Central America and Africa; mostly carnivorous; important as a food fish and in the aquarium trade; 40 genera, including piranhas, tigerfish, headstanders, tetras, and penguinfish. (Characidae.)

character (computing) In a computer system, the representation of a printed character, used for recording information on paper. There are two common ways of coding characters in a computer system: ASCII and EBCDIC.

character recognition The technology associated with the ability of computer-based systems to recognize specific patterns; sometimes referred to as **pattern recognition**. In particular, the ability to read printed characters from ordinary printed material is known as **optical character recognition (OCR)**. Another common type is **magnetic ink character recognition (MICR)**, used worldwide to read automatically such things as account numbers and serial numbers on cheques.

Charadriiformes [karadriuhfaw(r)meez] An order of essentially water-loving birds (18 families). It includes gulls, terns, skuas, auks, and many waders.

charcoal An impure form of carbon made by heating animal or vegetable substances (usually wood) in the absence of air to drive off the volatile constituents. It is porous and hence used as an adsorbent and filter. It burns without flame or smoke. Coke is a variety formed from coal. Animal charcoal is known as *bone-black*.

Charcot, Jean Martin [shah(r)koh] (1825–93) Pathologist, one of the founders of neurology, born in Paris, France. He worked at the Salpêtrière, and had Freud among his pupils. He contributed much to the knowledge of chronic neurological diseases, and made hypnotism a scientific study. The way joints deteriorate in some types of neurological disease was named after him (**Charcot's joint**).

chard A type of cultivated beet (*Beta vulgaris*, variety *cicla*) lacking a swollen root but with swollen midribs and leaf-stalks; also called **Swiss chard**. (Family: Chenopodiaceae.)

Chardin, Pierre Teilhard de *Teilhard de Chardin, Pierre*

Chargaff, Erwin [chah(r)gaf] (1905–) Biochemist, born in Czernowitz, S Czech Republic. He studied at Vienna, Yale, Berlin, and Paris, and worked at Columbia University, New York City, from 1935. His pioneer work on nucleic acids showed that the DNA of an organism has a composition characteristic of the organism; and his work on the ratio of bases present in DNA (the *Chargaff rules*) provided a fundamental contribution to the double helix structure for DNA advanced in 1953.

charge A quantity of electricity (**electrical charge**), the source of an electric field; symbol Q, units C (*coulombs*). The elementary unit of charge $e = 1{\cdot}602 \times 10^{-19}$ C, equal in size but opposite in sign to the electron's charge, cannot be subdivided and is a fundamental constant. Charge occurs only in multiples of e, a simple additive quantity which is always conserved. Two types of charge are possible: **positive** and **negative**. Like-sign charges repel, opposite-sign charges attract; the force between charges is expressed by Coulomb's law. Moving charges constitute a *current*. The study of stationary charges and the forces between them is called **electrostatics**. The Coulomb force between charged electrons and protons holds atoms together. The charge on an object refers to the excess of one type of charge over the other. The charge of an elementary particle is always the same for a given particle, and is one of its fundamental properties.

charge card *credit card*

charge-coupled device (generally abbreviated **CCD**) An image sensor which in a video camera comprises a mosaic of minute photo-conductive diodes corresponding to the pixels and lines of a television system. Charges produced in each element by incident light are stored until read off in the required scanning sequence.

Charge of the Light Brigade An incident during the Battle of Balaclava (25 Oct 1854) in the Crimean War, when a British cavalry division, the Light Brigade, under the command of Lord Cardigan, charged the main Russian artillery. The charge involved massive loss of life. It resulted from the misunderstanding of an order given by the commanding officer, Lord Raglan, to stop guns captured by the Russians being carried away during their retreat.

Charing Cross An area in C London, UK. It takes its name from a cross erected to mark the site of the resting-place of the body of Queen Eleanor, who died in 1290. Traditionally Charing Cross is viewed as the centre of London, when measuring distances to and from the city.

Chari, River [shahree] River in SW Chad, NC Africa; flows 800 km/500 mi NW to join R Logone at N'djamena, where it forms the border between Chad and Cameroon before entering L Chad; length including main headstream (R Bamingui), 1060 km/660 mi.

charismatic movement [karizmatik] A movement of spiritual renewal, rooted in Pentecostalism, which takes a variety of forms in Roman Catholic, Protestant, and Eastern Orthodox Churches. It emphasizes the present reality and work of the Holy Spirit in the life of the Church and the individual. It is sometimes accompanied by speaking in tongues.

charivari [sharivahree] (Lat *caribaria* 'headache') A traditional ritual which involves blowing horns and banging pots and pans in order to express disapproval, for example of a cuckolded husband or an elderly bridegroom. The custom was practised in much of Europe under different names; in England it was known as 'rough music' or 'the skimmington'. Such forms of community 'policing' died out mainly during the 19th-c.

Charlemagne or **Charles the Great** [shah(r)luhmayn] (742–814) King of the Franks (joint ruler with his brother from 768; sole ruler, 771–814), and emperor of the West (800–14), the eldest son of Pepin the Short. He defeated the Saxons (772–804) and the Lombards (773–4), fought the Arabs in Spain, and took control of most of Christian W Europe. In 800 he was crowned emperor by Pope Leo III. In his later years he consolidated his vast empire, building palaces and churches, and promoting Christianity, education and learning, agriculture, the arts, manufacture, and commerce, so much so that the period has become known as the *Carolingian Renaissance*. His reign was an attempt to consolidate order and Christian culture among the nations of the West, but his empire did not long survive his death, for his sons lacked both his vision and authority.

Charleroi [shah(r)lrwah] 50°25N 4°27E, pop (2000e) 210 000. Town in Hainaut province, SW Belgium, on the R Sambre; formerly a fortress; location of World War 1 German attack against the French (Aug 1914); centre of coal-mining area; iron, wire and cables, cutlery.

Charles I (of Austria-Hungary) (1887–1922) Emperor of Austria (1916–18, as **Karl I**) and king of Hungary (1916–19, as **Kâroly IV**), born at Persenbeug Castle, C Austria. The last of the Habsburg emperors, he succeeded his grand-uncle, Francis Joseph, in 1916, and became heir presumptive on the assassination at Sarajevo (1914) of his uncle, Archduke Francis Ferdinand. In 1919 he was deposed by the Austrian parliament and exiled to Switzerland. Two attempts to regain his Hungarian throne in 1921 failed.

Charles I (of England) (1600–49) King of Britain and Ireland (1625–49), born in Dunfermline, Fife, E Scotland, UK, the second son of **James I**. He failed in his bid to marry the infanta Maria of Spain (1623), marrying instead the French princess, **Henrietta Maria**, and thus disturbing the nation, for the marriage articles permitted her the free exercise of the Catholic religion. Three parliaments were summoned and dissolved in the first four years of his reign; then for 11 years he ruled without one, using instead judges and prerogative courts. He warred with France (1627–9), and in 1630 made peace with Spain, but his continuing need for money led to unpopular economic policies. His attempt to anglicize the Scottish Church brought active resistance (1639), and he then called a parliament (1640). In 1642, having alienated much of the realm, he entered into the Civil War, which saw the annihilation of his cause at Naseby (14 Jun 1645), and his surrender to the Scots at Newark (1646). After many negotiations, during which his attempts at duplicity exasperated opponents, and a second Civil War (1646–8), he came to trial at Westminster, where his dignified refusal to plead was interpreted as a confession of guilt. He was beheaded at Whitehall (30 Jan 1649).

Charles II (of England) (1630–85) King of Britain and Ireland (1660–85), born in London, UK, the son of Charles I. As Prince of Wales, he sided with his father in the Civil War, and was then forced into exile. On his father's execution (1649), he assumed the title of king, and was crowned at Scone, Scotland (1651). Leading poorly organized forces into England, he met disastrous defeat at Worcester (1651). The next nine years were spent in exile until an impoverished England, in dread of a revival of military despotism, summoned him back as king (1660). In 1662 he married the Portuguese princess, **Catherine of Braganza**. It was a childless marriage, though Charles was the father of many illegitimate children. His war with Holland (1665–7) was unpopular, and led to the dismissal of his adviser, Lord Clarendon (1667), who was replaced by a group of ministers (the Cabal). He negotiated skilfully between conflicting political and religious pressures, including the trumped-up 'Popish Plot', and refused to deny the succession of his brother James. For the last four years of his life, he ruled without parliament.

Charles II (of Spain) (1661–1700) King of Spain (1665–1700), the last ruler of the Spanish Habsburg dynasty, born in Madrid, Spain. The congenitally handicapped son of Philip IV (reigned 1621–65), he presided over the final decline of Spanish hegemony. Under him Spain joined the League of Augsburg (1686) and the ensuing hostilities against France. To prevent the dismemberment of his patrimony, he bequeathed the entire Spanish Habsburg inheritance to Louis XIV's younger grandson, Philip of Anjou, in 1700, although his intentions were subsequently thwarted by the War of the Spanish Succession and the territorial settlement of Utrecht (1713).

Charles III (of Spain) (1716–88) King of Naples and Sicily (1734–59) before becoming King of Spain (1759–88), born in Madrid, Spain. Generally regarded as an archetypal enlightened despot, he was driven by the belief that the Spanish monarchy and the colonial empire were in need of political, economic, and cultural reform. He encouraged commercial reforms in the colonies, and encouraged an ambitious building programme at home, undertook agricultural improvements, and brought the Roman Catholic Church under state control. In the Seven Years' War (1756–63) he sided with France and against Great Britain, receiving Louisiana from his ally while conceding Florida to Britain in return for Havana and Manila (1763). Later, however, by joining the anti-British coalition in support of the Americans, he regained Florida by the Treaty of Paris (1783).

Charles IV (of Spain) (1748–1819) King of Spain (1788–1808), born in Portici, S Italy, the son of Charles III (reigned 1759–88). His government was largely in the hands of his wife, **Maria Luisa** (1751–1819) and her favourite, Manuel de Godoy. Nelson destroyed his fleet at Trafalgar (1805), and in 1808 he abdicated under pressure from Napoleon. He spent the rest of his life in exile.

Charles V (of France), known as **Charles the Wise** (1338–80) King of France, born in Vincennes, NC France. He came to the throne in 1364, and in a series of victories regained most of the territory lost to the English in the Hundred Years' War.

Charles V (Emperor) (1500–58) Holy Roman Emperor (1519–56), born in Ghent, NW Belgium, the son of Philip of Burgundy and Joanna of Spain. He was made joint ruler of Spain (as **Charles I**) with his mother (1517), and was elected to the Holy Roman Empire (1519). His rivalry with Francis I of France dominated west European affairs, and there was almost constant warfare between them. In 1525 the defeat of Francis led to the formation of the Holy League against Charles by Pope Clement VII, Henry VIII, Francis, and the Venetians. In 1527 Rome was sacked and the pope imprisoned, and although Charles disclaimed any part of it, the Peace of Cambrai (1529) left him master of Italy. At the Diet of Augsburg (1530) he confirmed the 1521 Edict of Worms, which had condemned Luther, and the Protestants formed the League of Schmalkald. After further battles, in 1538 the pope, Francis, and Charles agreed at Nice to a 10 years' truce. Charles's league with the pope drove the Protestants to rebellion. They were crushed at Mühlberg (1547); but in 1552 Charles was defeated by Maurice of Saxony, and Protestantism received legal recognition. In 1555 he divided the empire between his son (Philip II of Spain) and his brother (Emperor Ferdinand I), retiring to the monastery of Yuste in Spain.

Charles VI (of France), known as **Charles the Foolish** (1368–1422) King of France, born in Paris, France, who came to the throne as a young boy in 1380. He was defeated by Henry V at the Battle of Agincourt (1415). From 1392, he suffered from fits of madness.

Charles VII (of France), known as **Charles the Victorious** (1403–61) King of France (1422–61), born in Paris, France. At his accession, the N of the country was in English hands, with Henry VI proclaimed King of France, but after Joan of Arc roused the fervour of both nobles and people, the siege of Orléans was raised (1429), and the English gradually lost nearly all they had gained in France. Under his rule France recovered in some measure from her calamities.

Charles IX (of France) (1550–74) King of France (1560–74), born in St Germain-en-Laye, NC France. The second son of Henry II and Catherine de' Medici, he succeeded his brother Francis II. His reign coincided with the Wars of Religion. He was completely subject to his mother, whose counsels drove him to authorize the massacre of Huguenots on St Bartholomew's Day (1572), the memory of which was said to have haunted him until his death.

Charles X (of France) (1757–1836) The last Bourbon king of France (1824–30), born at Versailles, NC France. The grandson of Louis XV, he received the title of Comte d'Artois, and in 1773 married Maria Theresa of Savoy. He lived in England during the French Revolution, returning to France in 1814 as lieutenant-general of the kingdom. He succeeded his brother Louis XVIII, but his repressive rule led to revolution, and his eventual abdication and exile after the July Revolution (1830).

Charles XII (of Sweden) (1682–1718) King of Sweden (1697–1718), born in Stockholm, Sweden, the son of Charles XI. Following an alliance against him by Denmark, Poland, and Russia, he attacked Denmark (1699), and compelled the Danes to sue for peace. He then defeated the Russians at Narva (1700), and dethroned Augustus II of Poland (1704). He invaded Russia again in 1707, and was at first victorious, but when Cossack help failed to arrive, he was defeated at Poltava (1709). He escaped to Turkey, where he stayed until 1714. He then formed another army and attacked Norway, but was killed at the siege of Halden. After his death, Sweden, exhausted by his wars, ceased to be numbered among the great powers.

Charles XIV (of Sweden), originally **Jean Baptiste Jules Bernadotte** (1763–1844) King of Sweden (1818–44), born a lawyer's son in Pau, SW France. He joined the French army in 1780, and fought his way up to become marshal (1804). In 1799 he was minister of war, and for his conduct at Austerlitz was named Prince of Pontecorvo (1805). He fought in several Napoleonic campaigns (1805–9), then was elected heir to the throne of Sweden (1810), turning Protestant, and changing his name to Charles John. He refused to comply with Napoleon's demands, and was soon involved in war with him, taking part in the final struggle at Leipzig (1813). In 1814 he was rewarded with the Kingdom of Norway, recreating the union of the two countries. Thereafter he had a peaceful reign, though his conservative rule led to opposition at home in the 1830s.

Charles (Philip Arthur George), Prince of Wales (1948–) Eldest son of Queen Elizabeth II and Prince Philip, Duke of Edinburgh, and heir apparent to the throne, born at Buckingham Palace, London, UK. Duke of Cornwall as the eldest son of the monarch, he was given the title of Prince of Wales in 1958, and invested at Caernarfon (1969). He studied at Cheam and Gordonstoun, and entered Trinity College, Cambridge, in 1967. He served in the RAF and Royal Navy, (1971–6), and in 1981 married **Lady Diana Frances**, younger daughter of the 8th Earl Spencer. They had two sons: **Prince William Arthur Philip Louis** (1982–) and **Prince Henry Charles Albert David** (1984–). The couple separated in 1992, and divorced in 1996. During this period he was, along with Princess Diana, the focus of continual media interest, attracting unprecedented attention from biographers. Diana was killed in a car crash in 1997. Charles is noted for his views on conservation and community architecture. In 1976 he founded the Prince's Trust, which provides training opportunities for young people.

Charles, Jacques Alexandre César [shah(r)l] (1746–1823) Physicist, born in Beaugency, C France. A clerk with an interest in science, which led eventually to a chair in physics at Paris, he became famous by making the first manned ascent by hydrogen balloon, reaching 3000 m/9800 ft in 1783. His interest in gases subsequently led him to formulate *Charles's law*, which relates the volume of a gas at constant pressure to its temperature.

Charles, Ray, originally **Ray Charles Robinson** (1930–) Singer, pianist, and composer, born in Albany, Georgia, USA. Blind from the age of six, he attended a special school and studied music. Influenced by jazz and blues, he became a versatile performer, developing an original blend of music identified as 'soul'. He had many hit records, 'What'd I say' (1959) being his first million-seller. He has received eight Grammy Awards, and co-wrote an autobiography *Brother Ray: Ray Charles' Own Story* (1978). Still performing into his seventies, in 2002 he released the album *Thanks For Bringing Love Around*, and gave his 10 000th concert in 2003.

Charles Edward Stuart *Stuart, Charles Edward*

Charles Martel [mah(r)tel] (Old French, 'the hammer') (c.688–741) Mayor of the palace for the last Merovingian kings of the Franks, the illegitimate son of Pepin of Herstal, and the undisputed head of the Carolingian family by 723. He conducted many campaigns against the Frisians and Saxons, as well as in Aquitaine, Bavaria, and Burgundy. He halted Muslim expansion in W Europe at the Battle of Poitiers (732). Established as effective ruler of much of Gaul, but never crowned king, he left the kingdom to his sons, Carloman and Pepin, and in 751 Pepin was anointed as the first Carolingian king of the Franks.

Charles's law A law discovered by and named after Jacques Charles, but first published by Joseph Gay-Lussac: at constant pressure, the volume of a given mass of an ideal gas is directly proportional to a constant plus its temperature measured on any scale. The value of this constant fixes the zero of the absolute scale of temperature, ie if temperature is given in K then at constant pressure volume is directly proportional to temperature.

Charleston (South Carolina) 32°46N 79°56W, pop (2000e) 96 600. Seat of Charleston Co, SE South Carolina, USA; a port on the Atlantic Ocean, at the mouths of Ashley and Cooper Rivers; the oldest city in the state, founded in 1670; survived attacks by a British fleet in 1776 and 1779; finally captured and held by the British, 1780–2; the Confederate attack on nearby Fort Sumter (12–13 Apr 1861) began the Civil War; evacuated by Confederate forces in 1865 after a 2-year siege; devastated by an earthquake in 1886; badly damaged by hurricane Hugo in 1989; airfield; railway; fertilizers, chemicals, steel, asbestos, cigars, paper products, textiles; site of a US naval and air force base; tourist centre; Charleston Museum, Old Slave Mart Museum and Gallery, Gibbes Art Gallery, several old colonial buildings.

Charleston (West Virginia) 38°21N 81°38W, pop (2000e) 53 400. Capital of state in Kanawha Co, W West Virginia, USA, at the confluence of Elk and Kanawha Rivers; developed around Fort Lee in the 1780s; city status, 1870; capital of West Virginia, 1870–5 and from 1885; largest city in the state; airfield; railway; an important transportation and trading centre; chemicals, glass, primary metals; various other products based on the salt, coal, natural gas, clay, sand, timber, and oil found in the region; Sternwheel Regatta (Aug).

Charleston (dance) A jazz dance of black origin popularized in the 1920s. It was, however, first seen at Charleston, SC, in 1903, and was named after the city. It can be danced either solo, with a partner, or in a group. Music is in 4/4 time and with syncopated rhythms.

Charleston, Battles of (11 Feb–12 May 1780) During the US War of Independence, the victorious British siege of Charleston, South Carolina, USA, which marked the beginning of the Southern phase of British strategy. At a small cost, the troops of Sir Henry Clinton (c.1738–95) captured a 5400-strong American garrison and a squadron of four ships.

Charlestown 17°08N 62°37W, pop (2000e) 1790. Capital and port of Nevis I, St Kitts-Nevis, N Leeward Is, E Caribbean; formerly famous for its thermal springs; tourism, garments.

charlock A roughly hairy annual (*Sinapis arvensis*), 30–80 cm/12–30 in, found in most temperate regions; leaves toothed and lobed; flowers yellow, cross-shaped, capsule cylindrical, long-beaked. Related to mustard, and once grown as a leaf vegetable, it is nowadays a pernicious weed of arable land. (Family: Cruciferae.)

Charlotte 35°13N 80°51W, pop (2000e) 540 800. Seat of Mecklenburg Co, S North Carolina, USA; settled c.1750; incorporated, 1768; the Mecklenburg Declaration of Independence was signed here, 1775; largest city in the state; airfield; railway; two universities (1867, 1946); textiles, chemicals, machinery, food, printed materials; birthplace of President Polk; professional team, Hornets (basketball).

Charlotte Amalie [shah(r)lot amalyuh], formerly **St Thomas** (1921–36) 18°22N 64°56W, pop (2000e) 13 300. Port and capital city of the US Virgin Is, Lesser Antilles, Caribbean, on S coast of St Thomas I; founded by the Danes, 1672; important cruise ship port; tourism.

Charlottenburg Palace A palace in Berlin, built (1695–1796) by Elector Frederick for his wife, Sophie Charlotte. The building houses a museum.

Charlottesville 38°02N 78°30W, pop (2000e) 45 000. Independent city and seat of Albemarle Co, C Virginia, USA, on the Rivanna R; settled in the 1730s; named after the wife of King George III; railway; university (1819); electronics, navigational systems, communications equipment; Ash Lawn (home of James Monroe); Monticello (home of Thomas Jefferson) and University of Virginia are world heritage sites.

Charlottetown 46°14N 63°09W, pop (2000e) 17 200. Provincial capital of Prince Edward Island, Canada; on Hillsborough Bay; founded by the French in the 1720s; capital since 1765; university (1969); fishing, trades in textiles, potatoes, dairy products, timber, tourism.

Charlottetown Accord A Canadian constitutional package for a new federal structure, put together by the prime minister (Brian Mulroney), provincial and territorial leaders, and First Nations representatives in August 1992. The essential difference between the 'Consensus Report on the Constitution' and the failed Meech Lake Accord of 1990 was that it recognized aboriginal demands as legitimate, and promised to integrate First Nations' leadership in future constitutional discussions. Nonetheless, the Charlottetown Accord was also rejected, this time in a national referendum in October 1992.

Charlottetown Conference A meeting of colonial representatives from New Brunswick, Nova Scotia, and Prince Edward Island (1864) to discuss Maritime Union. A delegation from the province of Canada (present-day Ontario and Quebec) successfully promoted the idea of a larger federation with the rest of mainland British North America. It was followed by the Quebec Conference, and led to Confederation in 1867.

Charlton, Bobby, popular name of **Sir Robert Charlton** (1937–) Footballer, born in Ashington, Northumberland, NE England, UK, the brother of Jack Charlton. He spent most of his career playing with Manchester United, making his debut in 1956. He survived the Munich air disaster (1958), winning three League Championship medals, an FA Cup-winner's medal (1963), and a European Cup-winner's medal (1968). He won 105 caps for England, scored 49 goals for the national team (an English record), and was a member of the World Cup-winning side of 1966. He joined Preston North End (1973–5), before retiring. He is now a director of Manchester United, and was knighted in 1994.

Charlton, Jack(ie), popular name of **John Charlton** (1935–) Footballer, born in Ashington, Northumberland, NE England, UK, the brother of Bobby Charlton. He was a part of the great Leeds United side of 1965–75 under Don Revie's management. He was almost 30 before he was capped for England, but then retained his place for five years. He later became manager of Middlesborough (1973), Sheffield Wednesday (1977), and Newcastle United (1984). He became manager of the Republic of Ireland team (1986–96), taking them to the last stages of the World Cup in 1990 and 1994. He retired as manager in 1996.

charm In particle physics, an internal additive quantum number conserved in strong and electromagnetic interactions, but not in weak interactions; symbol *C*. Charmed quarks are those having $C = +1$; charmed particles contain at least one charmed quark. It was postulated in 1964, and used to to account for the J/ψ particle discovered 10 years later. Members of the D meson family contain a charmed quark or antiquark.

Charminar [chah(r)minah(r)] A famous city landmark at Hyderabad, Andhra Pradesh, India. The imposing archway, surmounted by four minarets 56 m/182 ft high, was built under Mohammed Quli Qutab Shah in 1591.

Charon (astronomy) [**kairon**] Pluto's only known satellite, discovered photographically in 1978 by James W Christy and Robert S Harrington at the US Naval Observatory in Washington, DC. Its distance from the planet is 19 600 km/12 200 mi; diameter 1200 km/745 mi. It is unusually large, relative to its planet, and has a surface of mainly water ice.

Charon (mythology) [**kairon**] The ferryman of the Underworld, who carried the shades or souls of the dead across the R Acheron. Sometimes other rivers are substituted in literature, such as Styx and Lethe. The Greeks placed a small coin in the mouth of a corpse as Charon's fee.

Charpentier, Gustave [shah(r)pãtyay] (1860–1956) Composer, born in Dieuze, NE France. He studied at the Lille Conservatory, and the Paris Conservatoire under Massenet. He founded a free school of music for the poor, the Conservatoire Populaire de Mimi Pinson, wrote dramatic and choral works, and composed both the music and libretti for the operas *Louise* (1900) and *Julien* (1913).

charr Freshwater or anadromous (ascending rivers to breed) fish with circumpolar distribution in lakes and rivers of N hemisphere; length up to 1 m/3¾ ft; valuable food fish; popular with anglers as sport fish; includes the **Arctic charr** (*Salvelinus alpinus*) and **brook charr** or **brook trout** (*Salvelinus fontinalis*). (Family: Salmonidae.)

chartering Hiring a vessel (boat, ship, or aeroplane) and crew for a commercial activity between particular locations (a **voyage charter**) or over a particular period (a **time charter**). Most business charters are negotiated on the Baltic Exchange in London.

Charteris, Leslie [chah(r)teris], originally **Leslie Charles Bowyer Yin** (1907–93) Crime-story writer, born in Singapore. He studied at Cambridge, then worked in a wide variety of jobs, changed his name in 1928, and settled in the USA (1932), working as a Hollywood screenwriter. He became a US citizen in 1941. He is especially known as the creator of Simon Templar, 'the Saint'.

Chartier, Alain [shah(r)tyay] (c.1385–c.1435) Writer, born in Bayeux, NW France. His preoccupation with the plight of France in the Hundred Years' War formed the background to his two best works, the *Livre des quatre dames* (1415–16, Book of the Four Ladies) and the *Quadrilogue invectif* (1422), a four-part debate on the ills of France. He also wrote the allegorical poem, *La Belle Dame sans merci* (1424).

Chartism A largely working-class radical movement which achieved substantial but intermittent support in Britain between the late 1830s and the early 1850s. Its objective was democratic rights for all men, and it took its name from 'The People's Charter', first published in 1838. Its six points were: universal male suffrage; the abolition of property qualifications for MPs; parliamentary constituencies of equal size; a secret ballot; payment for MPs; and annual general elections by ballot. Chartist petitions were presented to parliament in 1839 and 1842 and on both occasions were rejected by huge majorities. Despite its immediate failure, Chartism had long-term influence on the direction of working-class political and economic organizations later in the 19th-c.

Chartres [shah(r)truh], ancient **Autricum**, **Civitas Carnutum** 48°29N 1°30E, pop (2000e) 43 700. Capital city of Eure-et-Loire department, NC France, on left bank of R Eure, 100 km/62 mi SW of Paris; railway; bishopric; agricultural centre and wheat market; abbey church of St Pierre-en-Vallée (11th–13th-c); Gothic cathedral (1195–1220), a world heritage site; students' pilgrimage (Apr–May).

Chartres Cathedral [shah(r)truh] The cathedral of Notre Dame, built (1195–1220) at Chartres, NC France, and widely recognized as a masterpiece of Gothic architecture. It is now a world heritage site.

Chartreuse, La Grande [la grãd chah(r)troez] The principal monastery of the Carthusian order, founded in 1084 by St Bruno in the Dauphin Alps of SE France. The monastery has been destroyed and rebuilt several times, and the present structure (which is now a museum) dates from the 17th-c. Chartreuse liqueur was first distilled here in 1607.

Charybdis [karibdis] In Greek mythology, a whirlpool which swallowed ships whole, encountered by Odysseus on his wanderings, and sometimes placed in the Straits of Messina – incorrectly, since there is no whirlpool there.

Chase, James Hadley, pseudonym of **René Raymond** (1906–85) Novelist, born in London, UK. He started the vogue for tough realism in gangster stories in the UK with his *No Orchids for Miss Blandish* (1939), the first of a number in similar vein.

Chase, Salmon P(ortland) (1808–73) Jurist and statesman, born in Cornish, New Hampshire, USA. In 1830 he settled as a lawyer in Cincinnati, where he acted as counsel for the defence of fugitive slaves and the white persons who had helped them. He was twice Governor of Ohio (1855–9), and became secretary of the Treasury (1861–4). In 1864 Abraham Lincoln appointed him Chief Justice of the USA; as such he presided at the impeachment trial of President Andrew Johnson (1868), which ended in an acquittal.

chat The name given to numerous birds: 51 species of thrush (family: Turdidae), 5 species of New World warblers (Family: Parulidae), and 5 species of Australian chats (Family: Ephthianuridae).

chateau Originally, a mediaeval fortified residence in France, acting as the focus of the feudal community in the same way as the contemporaneous English castle. By the 15th-c chateaux had become private seignoral residences, while the 16th-c saw the emergence of the less fortified *château de plaisance*, of which Ambois, Chambord, Chenonceaux, and Azay-le-Rideau are the most notable examples.

Chateaubriand, François Auguste René, vicomte de (Viscount of) [shatohbreeã] (1768–1848) French politician and writer, born in St Malo, W France. *Atala* (1801) established his literary reputation, and *Le Génie du christianisme* (1802, The Genius of Christianity) made him prominent among men of letters. A founder of Romanticism, he lived in exile in England during the French Revolution. He held various political and diplomatic posts after the Restoration, but was disappointed in his hope of becoming prime minister. In his later years, he wrote his celebrated autobiography, *Mémoires d'outre-tombe* (Memoirs from Beyond the Tomb), not published as a whole until 1902.

Château Gaillard [giyah(r)] A massive castle at Les Andelys, Normandy, NW France, sited on a promontory overlooking the R Seine, and controlling the approach to Rouen. Built 1196–8 by Richard I, King of England (1157–99) and Duke of Normandy, it was inspired by the Crusader castles of Syria and Palestine. Physically impregnable, it was captured by the French king, Philip Augustus, only after a long siege in 1203–4.

Chatham, 1st Earl of *Pitt, William, 1st Earl of Chatham*

Chatham Islands [**chat**m] pop (2000e) 800; area 963 sq km/ 372 sq mi. Islands of New Zealand in the SW Pacific Ocean; 850 km/528 mi E of South Island; comprises Chatham I (Wharekauri) and Pitt I (Rangiaotea), and some rocky islets; visited in 1791 by the British brig *Chatham*; chief settlement, Waitangi; sheep-rearing, sealing, fishing.

Chatsworth One of the great English country houses, built (1687–1707) for the 1st Duke of Devonshire near Edensor village, Derbyshire, C England, UK. The original design by William Talman (1650–1719) was altered and extended by successive architects. The gardens, laid out in 1688 by George London (d.1714), were re-landscaped by Capability Brown and Sir Joseph Paxton.

Chattanooga Campaign (Sep–Nov 1863) A series of battles in Tennessee, during the American Civil War, leading to Southern victory at Chickamauga, and Northern victories at Lookout Mountain and Missionary Ridge. It was of military importance, because it placed Northern troops in a position to bisect the Confederacy on an E–W axis.

chattels *property*

Chatterton, Thomas (1752–70) Poet, born in Bristol, SW England, UK. In 1768 he hoaxed the whole city with a description, 'from an old manuscript', of the opening of Bristol Bridge in 1248. His poems, purporting to be by Thomas Rowley, a 15th-c monk, were sent to Horace Walpole, but (though Walpole was taken in) were soon denounced as forgeries. He then went to London, where he wrote many successful stories, essays, and other works. When his patron, Lord Mayor William Beckford, died, his publishers ceased to support him. Starving and penniless, he took poison. The debate over the authenticity of the Rowley poems waged for 80 years, and he received posthumous tributes from many poets including Byron, Keats, and Shelley. His collected works appeared in 1803.

Chau [chow] A traditional theatre of E India with three regional styles: *mayurbhanj*, dance-drama without masks, *seraikala*, dance with masks, and *purulia*, dance-drama with masks.

Chaucer, Geoffrey (c.1343–1400) Poet, probably born in London, the son of a tavern keeper, perhaps the John Chaucer who was deputy to the king's butler. He may have gone to Oxford or Cambridge. In 1357 and 1358 he was a page to the wife of Lionel, Duke of Clarence, and then transferred to the king's household. In 1359 he served in France, and was taken prisoner, but ransomed with the king's help. In 1367 the king granted him a pension. In 1368 a Philippa Chaucer appears amongst the ladies of the queen's bedchamber, very probably his wife, and she seems to have had two sons and a daughter. In 1369 Chaucer wrote his *Book of the Duchess*, on the death of John of Gaunt's wife. Travelling extensively abroad on the king's service, he also held royal posts at home, including that of Comptroller of the Petty Customs (1382). In 1386 he was elected a knight of the shire for Kent. During this time he wrote *Troilus and Criseyde*, one of the great poems on love in the English language, and several other major works. His early writings followed French trends, but were greatly influenced by Italian authors, notably Boccaccio and Petrarch. Losing his offices in 1386, he fell upon hard times, though in 1399 he was awarded a pension. He died in London and was buried in Westminster Abbey. It was during this last period that he wrote his most famous work, the unfinished *Canterbury Tales*, which is unique for its variety, humour, grace, and realism. Chaucer strongly influenced the development of Middle English; he was the first great poet of the English nation, and in the Middle Ages he stands supreme.

Chautauqua movement [shuh**tawk**wuh] A late 19th-c and early 20th-c US adult education movement, organized under Methodist auspices by Lewis Miller (1829–99) and Bishop John H Vincent (1832–1920), with home reading programmes and summer gatherings. At its peak it attracted up to 60 000 participants annually to regional centres in the USA and elsewhere. The original centre at L Chautauqua, New York, continues its activities.

Chavez, Cesar (Estrada) [**chav**ez, **chah**vez] (1927–93) Labour leader, born in Yuma, Arizona, USA. A migrant farmworker in his youth (he attended 65 elementary schools, and never graduated from high school), he became a community and labour organizer of agricultural workers in the 1950s. In 1962 he started the National Farm Workers Association, based in the SW among the mainly Chicano and Filipino farmworkers; in 1966 this union was chartered by the AFL/CIO as the United Farm Workers of America, and he remained its president until his death. He became widely known for organizing a series of national grape boycotts that helped the union to gain improved wages and working conditions for its members.

Chavín de Huantar [cha**veen**, hwan**tah(r)**] A prehistoric ceremonial centre at 3200 m/10 000 ft in the Mosna Valley of the E Andes, the focus c.400–200 BC of an expansive religious cult embracing all C and N Peru; a world heritage site. Its buildings cover 50 ha/125 acres, the 6-ha/15-acre civic centre being notable for its carved stone deities, the 75-m/225-ft square, and the 13-m/42-ft high New Temple, internally a maze of galleries, ramps, and stairways.

Chechnya [**chech**nya] Republic in the C Caucasus, bordered S by the main Caucasus range and Georgia; capital, Grozny (also named Dzhoxhar Ghala, 1997); economy based on oil, with major refining centre at Grozny; population largely Chechen (c.60%, Muslim); history of resistance to Russian rule, especially in 19th-c; became an administrative region (*oblast*) within the Soviet Union; amalgamated with Ingushetiya (**Checheno-Ingushetiya**) as an autonomous republic (ASSR) in 1934, dissolved by Stalin in 1944, with its population deported, but re-established in 1957; area 19 300 sq km/7400 sq mi; pop (2002e) 1 080 000, but uncertain numbers of deaths and refugees in ongoing war; Chechnya declared independence from Russia, 1991; Chechnya and Ingushetiya separated, 1992; civil war between forces loyal to Chechen president Dzhokar Dudayev and former leader of the opposition Ruslan Khasbulatov; invasion of Russian troops with aim of restoring Moscow control, December 1994; continued fighting in 1995; Dudayev killed, peace accord signed between Yeltsin and new Chechen leadership, but hostilities renewed, 1996; Russian troops finally withdrawn by end of 1996, with fresh elections in early 1997; renewed Russian invasion against Chechen rebels, following a series of terrorist bombings in Russian cities and incursions into Dagestan, 1999; major assault on the capital by Russian troops, with displacement of most of the population and widespread destruction; tentative peace negotiations, 2001, but conflict still ongoing into 2004.

check *cheque*

checkers *draughts*

Cheddar 5°17N 2°46W, pop (2000e) 4400. Market town in Somerset, SW England, UK; 16 km/10 mi SE of Weston-super-Mare; famous for the limestone features of the Cheddar Gorge and for the Cheddar cheese originally made here.

cheese A dairy foodstuff made from milk, originally used as a means of preserving food from periods of plenty during leaner times. Milk proteins are soluble in water at a neutral pH, but when the pH falls to a critically low level of about 4·6, the proteins no longer remain soluble. They precipitate out to form the curd of sour milk, which is the basis of cheese manufacture. The most basic cheese is known as cottage cheese, where skimmed milk (ie milk with all the fat removed) is allowed to coagulate. The wide variety of cheeses is achieved by allowing particular strains of bacteria to cause the fall in pH by fermenting lactose. The curd is then processed into cheese by a variety of methods, some of which require quite lengthy maturation in the presence of moulds. Others are matured in a smoky atmosphere, and others mixed with cream to form very creamy cheeses. The hardness of a cheese is determined by both its water content and its fat content.

Many regions of Europe have produced cheeses for which they are famous. France alone has more than 400 varieties, including Brie, Camembert, and Roquefort. Other well-known cheeses include Swiss Gruyère and Emmenthal; English Cheddar, Cheshire, and Stilton; Italian Parmesan and Gorgonzola;

and Dutch Gouda and Edam. Versions of these cheeses are now made in many other countries.

cheetah A member of the cat family (*Acinonyx jubatus*), native to Africa and SW Asia; fastest land animal (can reach 110 kph/ 70 mph); only cat unable to retract its claws completely; pale with solid dark spots; lean with long legs and tail; inhabits dry grassland and scrub; eats birds, hares, and antelopes; easily tamed.

Cheka An acronym from the Russian letters **che** + **ka**, for the All-Russian Extraordinary Commission for Combating Counter-Revolution and Sabotage, established in 1917. It was in effect a political police force whose duties were to investigate and punish anti-Bolshevik activities. During the Civil War it was responsible for executing thousands of political opponents in what came to be called the 'Red Terror'.

Chekhov, Anton (Pavlovitch) [chekof] (1860–1904) Playwright and master of the short story, born in Taganrog, SW Russia. He studied medicine at Moscow, and began to write while a student. His first book of stories (1886) was successful, and gradually he adopted writing as a profession. His early full-length plays were failures, but when *Chayka* (1896, The Seagull) was revived in 1898 by Stanislavsky at the Moscow Art Theatre, it was a great success. He then wrote his masterpieces: *Dyadya Vanya* (1900, Uncle Vanya), *Tri sestry* (1901, The Three Sisters), and *Vishnyovy sad* (1904, The Cherry Orchard). Meanwhile he continued to write many short stories, the best of which are unsurpassed in their medium. In 1897 he fell ill with tuberculosis and lived thereafter either abroad or in the Crimea. In 1901 he married the actress **Olga Knipper** (1870–1959), who remained for many years the admired exponent of female roles in his plays.

chelate [keelayt] A complex of two or more components in which one is joined to another by two or more points of attachment. In co-ordination compounds, a chelating ligand such as diaminoethane complexes metal ions more completely than do similar ligands such as ammonia with only one point of attachment to the metal.

chelation therapy [keelayshn] A treatment for heavy metal poisoning in which biochemical substances are given to a patient intravenously to bind the poisonous metal so that it is inactivated and can be removed from the body. The substances administered are known as **chelating agents** and vary according to the toxic substance to be inactivated. There have been attempts to use this form of treatment to remove calcium deposits from the walls of blood vessels for patients suffering with atherosclerosis, in the hope that this will improve blood flow. Some claims have been made for this technique as a non-invasive alternative to cardiac surgery for treating patients at risk from coronary thrombosis.

Chelmsford 51°44N 0°28E, pop (2001e) 157 100. County town of Essex, SE England, UK; on the R Chelmer, 48 km/30 mi NE of London; railway; Anglia Polytechnic University (1992); electronics, furniture; cathedral (15th-c).

Chelonia [kelohnia] An order of reptiles (244 species); body encased in a domed shell of bones covered by large horny scales (*scutes*); no teeth; jaws form a hard *beak*; most withdraw head and legs into the shell for protection; head may be pulled backwards into the shell (species of suborder Cryptodira or **hidden-necked turtles**), or bent sideways (suborder: Pleurodira or **side-necked turtles**). In the USA, all species are called **turtles** (with **tortoise** used for a terrestrial **turtle** and marine forms called **sea turtles**); in the UK there is no single common name for all species, and only marine forms are called **turtles**.

Chelsea *Kensington and Chelsea*

Chelsea pensioners Occupants of the hospital for old and disabled soldiers in Chelsea, London. Founded by Charles II in 1682, the Royal Hospital takes in about 420 men, usually aged over 65. Chelsea pensioners wear distinctive uniforms, navy blue in winter and scarlet in summer.

Chelsea porcelain A London porcelain factory which flourished 1744–84, and was almost certainly the first to make soft-paste porcelain in the British Is. It was founded by a silversmith from Liège, Nicholas Sprimont (1716–71) and Charles Gouyn (d.1781). It produced both figures and finely-painted tableware. In 1770 the factory was bought by William Duesbury (1725–86) of Derby.

Cheltenham [cheltnm] 51°54N 2°04W, pop (2001e) 110 000. Residential town in Gloucestershire, SWC England, UK; on W edge of Cotswold Hills, 12 km/7 mi NE of Gloucester; famous spa in 18th-c; railway; schools (Cheltenham College, Cheltenham Ladies' College); Cheltenham Gold Cup horse-race (Mar); National Hunt steeplechases in Prestbury Park; festival of contemporary music (Jul).

Chelyabinsk [chilyabinsk], also **Tchelyabinsk** 55°12N 61°25E, pop (2000e) 1 142 000. Industrial capital city of Chelyabinskaya oblast, W Siberian Russia; on E slopes of the S Ural Mts; founded in 1736 as a frontier outpost; airport; road and rail junction; iron and steel, machines, foodstuffs, chemicals.

chemical analysis The determination of the composition of a material. It may be qualitative or quantitative, and may refer to the relative amounts of different elements present, or the extent to which particular properties, such as acidity or oxidizing power, are present.

chemical bond The electric forces linking atoms in molecules and non-molecular solid phases. Three types of bond may be identified: (1) **ionic**, as in sodium chloride (NaCl), in which electrons are lost and gained so that the structure is held together by the mutual attraction of Na^+ and Cl^- ions; (2) **covalent**, as in chlorine (Cl_2), where some electrons are associated with two atomic nuclei; and (3) **metallic**, as in sodium (Na), where the valence electrons are delocalized and associated with many nuclei, giving rise to electrical conductivity. Covalent bonds involving 2, 4, and 6 electrons are called *single*, *double*, and *triple*, and are represented by –, =, and ≡, respectively. The energy required to break a chemical bond (eg to convert a chlorine molecule to two chlorine atoms) is called the **bond energy**.

chemical elements The simplest substances into which matter can be broken without nuclear reactions. Each element is characterized by the number of protons in the nuclei of its atoms, the atomic number of the element, and is identified by a one- or two-letter symbol. There are about 90 elements which have been found in nature. Several more have been artificially made, with those greater than atomic number 112 being referred to as superheavy elements. The most common elements in the crust of the Earth are: oxygen (O), 49%; silicon (Si), 26%; aluminium (Al), 8%; iron (Fe), 5%.

chemical energy Energy potentially or actually liberated by a chemical reaction, also called **heat of reaction**. This energy may be converted to or from electrical energy, heat, or light. Normally, energy *absorbed* in chemical change is considered positive; energy *released* is negative. It is generally expressed on the molar scale.

chemical engineering The theory and practice of designing, setting up, and operating apparatus for the large-scale manufacture of the products of chemical reactions. The earliest chemical manufacture (to the mid-19th-c) was based on personal skills and on tradition. From then on, the application of mathematics and physics to chemical problems, and an increased demand for chemical products, led to the study of the ways in which known chemical and physical principles applied to large quantities, the demands for heat supply, and the control of the movement of chemicals in bulk through large systems. The various problems in manufacturing a wide variety of substances are studied in the light of common principles that apply to unit processes. University departments, professional training, and professional institutions devoted to chemical engineering have developed in all industrialized countries since 1900.

chemical equation The quantitative expression of a chemical reaction. It must balance, in terms of both the numbers of atoms of all elements involved, and the electric charge. The example given below is the reaction of manganate(VII) (permanganate) ions with iron(II) to give manganese(II) and iron(III). The reaction also consumes acid (H+) and produces water: $MnO_4^- + 5Fe^{2+} + 8H^+ \rightarrow Mn^{2+} + 5Fe^{3+} + 4H_2O$.

chemical finishing A general term used for the treatment of fabrics by chemical processing, such as bleaching, mercerizing, resin treatment, or waterproofing. It is carried out to 'finish' the fabric after weaving, knitting, etc has taken place.

chemical formula The representation of a substance in terms of the symbols of its elements. Molecular compounds are written as the full molecule; thus benzene is C_6H_6 and acetylene is C_2H_2. Non molecular compounds are written as the simplest ratio of elements, also called the **empirical formula**; thus calcium fluoride is CaF_2, and diamond is C.

chemical laser A laser in which a chemical reaction provides the energy for laser action. For example, in a laser containing carbon dioxide with hydrogen and fluorine, the laser action would take place in the carbon dioxide, powered by the reaction of hydrogen and fluorine to give hydrogen fluoride. Chemical lasers with powers in excess of 10^6 W are possible.

chemical reaction A process in which one or more compounds are converted into others, by the breaking and forming of chemical bonds (usually with the gain or loss of energy by the system).

chemical warfare The use of deadly or disabling substances in warfare. It was forbidden by a declaration of the Hague Conference in 1899, but one of the signatories, Germany, was the first to use such weapons, the first attack being made against British troops at Ypres in April 1915. Since 1918 chemical weapons have been used in many conflicts, but not on European battlefields, although the Germans manufactured large quantities of deadly nerve gases during World War 2. Such weapons are not forbidden by treaty, and large quantities were stockpiled by the USA and the former Soviet Union. Other agents of chemical warfare include non-lethal harassing and incapacitating agents, hallucinogenic substances, and herbicides.

chemiluminescence *bioluminescence*

chemin de fer [shuhmĩ duh **fair**] A casino card game, often referred to as 'chemmy'. A variant of *baccarat banque*, it is played by up to 12 players. The object is to obtain a total as near as possible to 9 with two or three cards. If the total is a double figure then the first figure is ignored, eg 16 would count as 6. The ace counts as 1, face cards their value, and picture cards 10.

chemisorption *adsorption*

chemistry The study of the composition of substances and the changes that they undergo. Its origins lie partly in ancient technology (eg metallurgy and soap manufacture), partly in mediaeval speculation on methods of obtaining gold (*alchemy*), and partly in early attempts to improve medicines (*iatrochemistry*). Antoine Lavoisier is usually considered the father of modern chemistry, with his distinction between *elements* and *compounds* formed from elements, and his insistence that chemical reactions are quantitative in nature. With the development of the atomic theory of John Dalton, chemistry evolved rapidly in the 19th-c. **Organic chemistry** originated from the isolation of medicinal compounds from animals and plants, and **inorganic chemistry** from the study of minerals. They developed mainly into the synthesis and study of molecular compounds and of ionic compounds respectively, but are now often indistinguishable. **Physical chemistry** (studying the relationship of physical properties to chemical composition, structure, and reactivity) and **analytical chemistry** (studying the composition of material) also developed in parallel, particularly with 20th-c developments in spectroscopic and electrochemical methods. Modern chemistry has also been advanced by the elucidation of the nature of chemical bonding. Chemistry today is the basis of a worldwide industry concerned with almost every aspect of life, including food, fuel, clothing, building materials, and medicines. While the growth of this industry has had some undeniably bad ecological effects, chemistry provides the key to the improvement of the environment and world living standards.

chemoreception The perception of chemical stimuli by living organisms; usually performed by specialized receptor cells or organs. Chemoreception includes both olfaction (the perception of smells) and gustation (the perception of taste).

chemotaxis [keemoh**tak**sis] The process by which cells or organisms move in response to a chemical stimulus towards the most appropriate region of their environment. Examples include the movement of leucocytes towards the sites of inflammation, infection, or tissue damage; and the movement of bacteria towards areas that are nutritionally rich.

chemotherapy The drug treatment of infectious diseases (using antibiotics), parasitic diseases, and cancer. Cancer chemotherapy usually involves the administration of a cocktail of cytotoxic drugs (ie which kill or damage cells). Although designed to attack preferentially the rapidly growing cells of a tumour, they also attack normal cells (especially bone marrow) causing reduced resistance to infection, loss of hair, and sterility. Supportive therapy can now help with these problems. They also cause severe nausea and vomiting, which can prevent completion of a course of treatment, so drugs are included in the cocktail to combat this. Examples of cytotoxic drugs include alkylating agents (eg cisplatin), antimetabolites (eg methotrexate), and *Vinca* alkaloids. Hormones are also used to suppress the growth of some tumours.

Chenab, River [**chay**nab] River in Kashmir and Pakistan; one of the five rivers of the Punjab; rises in the Himalayas and flows NW into Kashmir, then S into Pakistan; joined by the R Sutlej E of Bahawalpur to form the R Panjnad, which then joins the R Indus to the NE of Chachran; length 1087 km/675 mi.

Chen-chiang *Zhenjiang*

Cheney, Dick [**chay**nee], popular name of **Richard B(ruce) Cheney** (1941–) US Republican politician, born in Lincoln, Nebraska. After a short time at Yale, he studied political science at the University of Wyoming (MA 1966), went to Washington as a congressional intern, and became special assistant to Donald Rumsfeld in the Nixon administration (1969–70). Appointed Gerald Ford's chief-of-staff (1975–6), he was the youngest man to have held that post. He then worked in the private sector until elected to the House of Representatives in 1978, becoming minority whip in 1988. Secretary of defence under George Bush (1989–93), he formed the coalition to execute Operation Desert Storm. In the Democrat years he was chief executive officer of Halliburton Co, but returned to politics as George W Bush's running-mate in 2000, and became vice-president in 2001.

Chengchow; Cheng-chou *Zhengzhou*

Chengdu or **Cheng-tu** [cheng**doo**] 30°37N 104°06E, pop (2000e) 3 295 000, administrative region 10 331 000. Capital of Sichuan province, SWC China; founded 200 BC as Zhou dynastic capital; population exceeded 1·3 million by 1st-c AD; regional industrial base since 1949; airfield; railway; university (1931); rice, wheat, sweet potatoes, tea, medicinal herbs, tobacco, silk, handicrafts, coal, metallurgy, electronics; home of Sichuan opera; home of Tang poet, Du Fu (712–70); Dujiang Yan irrigation works (250 BC), 40 km/25 mi NW is a world heritage site; Qingyanggong Temple; flower festival (Feb–Mar).

Cheng-hsien *Zhengzhou*

Chennai *Madras*

Cheops, Ship of *Ship of Cheops*

cheque (UK) or **check** (US) An order in writing to a bank to pay the person or institution named the sum of money specified. Cheques are commonly printed by banks for the use of their customers, but may be written on anything; examples include a tablecloth and (in legal fiction) a cow. If a bank refuses to accept a cheque, it will be marked 'R.D.', signifying 'Refer to Drawer'.

cheque card In the UK, a flexible plastic card (c.54 × 85 mm/ 2⅛ × 3⅜ in) issued by banks to customers who have a cheque book; in the USA usually called a **bank card**. It shows the customer's name and account number, and guarantees that the bank will honour a cheque (up to a specified sum) where the name and number correspond. Some may also be used in bank cash-dispensing machines.

chequerberry *service tree*

Chequers [chekerz] The official country residence of British prime ministers, donated to the nation by Viscount Lee of Fareham in 1921. The estate is located in the Chiltern Hills, Buckinghamshire, SC England, UK. It is mentioned in the Domesday Book.

Cher, in full **Cherilyn La Piere Sarkisian** (1946–) Singer and actress, born in El Centro, California, USA. She was originally paired in a singing act with her husband **Salvatore 'Sonny' Bono** (1935–98) as Sonny and Cher, and was later married briefly to rock guitarist Greg Allman (1947–). Sonny and Cher were best known for the rock anthem 'I Got You Babe' (1965). Cher found greater success on her own, both as a singer and as a stage and film actress, notably in *Moonstruck* (1987, Oscar). Later films include *Tea With Mussolini* (1999).

Cherbourg [sherboorg], Fr [shairboor], ancient **Carusbur** 49°38N 1°37W, pop (2000e) 30 000. Fortified seaport and naval base in Manche department, NW France; at head of the Cotentin peninsula; harbour protected by a long breakwater, 1853; France's third largest naval base; shipbuilding and dockyards; used by transatlantic shipping; ferry services to Southampton, Weymouth, Rosslare.

Cherenkov *Čerenkov*

Chernenko, Konstantin Ustinovich [chernyengko] (1911–85) Soviet statesman and president (1984–5), born in Bolshaya Tes, C Russia. He joined the Communist Party in 1931, and held several local posts. An associate of Brezhnev for many years, he became a member of the Politburo in 1978, and the Party's chief ideologist after the death of Suslov. Regarded as a conservative, Chernenko was a rival of Andropov in the Party leadership contest of 1982, and became Party general secretary and head of state after Andropov's death in 1984. He suffered from ill health, and died soon after, to be succeeded by Gorbachev.

Chernobyl [chernobil] 51°16N 30°15E. City in Ukraine; near the junction of the Pripyat and Ushk Rivers, N of Kiev; scene of the world's largest known nuclear disaster in 1986; nuclear power station projected to close in 2000, though the only operable unit was restarted following repairs (Nov 1999).

chernozem [chernozem] A dark, rich and fertile soil found in cool, low-humidity regions. It is typical of the Russian steppes.

Cherokee [cherokee] A North American Indian people, originally from the Great Lakes, who migrated to the SE after their defeat by the Iroquois and Delaware. Evicted from their land when gold was discovered on it, 15 000 were force-marched W by 7000 US troops (the 'trail of tears', 1838–9). The survivors were settled in Oklahoma with Creeks and other SE tribes who were moved there by the US government in the 1830s. They speak an Iroquoian language. They are now the largest Indian group in the USA, numbering c.730 000 (2000 census).

cherry A deciduous, mostly N temperate tree closely related to the plum, peach, and blackthorn; often with distinctive shiny reddish-brown banded bark; oval, finely toothed leaves; clusters of white flowers and bright red or purplish fruits which are sour or sweet, depending on the species or variety. The well-known orchard fruits are mostly the **sour** or **morello cherry** (*Prunus cerasus*), a species of unknown origin, with white flowers and bright red, acid fruit; and the **sweet cherry**, probably a hybrid between gean and sour cherry with sweet, red or purplish fruits. Various other species and hybrids, especially pink-flowered Japanese ones, are popular ornamentals. (Genus: *Prunus*. Subgenus: *Cerasus*. Family: Rosaceae.)

cherry laurel An evergreen shrub or small tree (*Prunus laurocerasus*), native to the Balkans but cultivated since the 16th-c, and widely naturalized; leaves oblong, leathery; flowers white, fragrant, c.30 in a spike; berries red or green, turning black when ripe, poisonous. (Family: Rosaceae.)

cherry plum A deciduous, occasionally spiny, shrub or small tree (*Prunus cerasifera*), growing to 8 m/26 ft, probably one of the parents of plum; flowers white, appearing with or before ovoid, toothed leaves; fruit globular, 2–3·5 cm/0·8–1·5 in, red or yellow; native to the Balkans, and cultivated elsewhere; also called **myrobalan**. (Family: Rosaceae.)

chert A very fine-grained form of silica (SiO_2), in which the quartz crystals are too small to be observed by optical microscopy. It is characteristically formed on the ocean bed by the accumulation and subsequent recrystallization of the silica shells of diatoms and Radiolaria. It also occurs as concretions in limestones.

cherubim [cheruhbim], singular **cherub** In the Hebrew Bible/Old Testament, winged celestial creatures or beasts of various descriptions. Their roles include guarding the tree of life in the Garden of Eden (*Gen* 3.24), being stationed on the cover of the Ark of the Covenant (*Ex* 25.18–22), adorning Solomon's temple (1 *Kings* 6.23ff), and accompanying the throne chariot of God (*Ezek* 1, 10).

Cherubini, (Maria) Luigi (Carlo Zenobio Salvatore) [keru**beenee**] (1760–1842) Composer, born in Florence, NC Italy. He studied at Bologna and Milan, and wrote a succession of operas, at first in Neapolitan, later (having moved to Paris) in French style. His best-known opera is *Les Deux Journées* (1880, The Two Days, or The Water-Carrier). His later work was mainly ecclesiastical. In 1822 he became director of the Paris Conservatoire.

chervil A hollow-stemmed annual (*Anthriscus cerefolium*), growing to 70 cm/27 in, native to Europe and Asia, and often introduced elsewhere; leaves divided, the lobes dissected into narrow oblong segments; flowers small, white, borne in umbels up to 5 cm/2 in across; fruits oblong, smooth. It is often grown for its aromatic leaves, used as a flavouring. (Family: Umbelliferae.)

Cherwell, Frederick Alexander Lindemann, 1st Viscount [chah(r)wel] (1886–1957) Scientist, born in Baden-Baden, SW Germany. He was brought up in England, but went to university at Berlin and the Sorbonne. In 1914 he became director of the Experimental Physics Station at Farnborough, where he evolved the mathematical theory of aircraft spin, and tested it in a daring flight. In 1919 he became professor of experimental philosophy at Oxford, and later director of the Clarendon Laboratory. A close friend of Churchill, he became his scientific adviser in 1940. He was created a baron in 1941, and was paymaster-general on two occasions (1942–5, 1951–3).

Chesapeake Bay [chesapeek] 38°40N 76°25W. An inlet of the Atlantic Ocean in Virginia (S) and Maryland (N) states, USA; over 300 km/185 mi long; at the mouth of the Susquehanna, Patuxent, Potomac, Chester, Choptank, Nanticoke, Rappahannock, and James Rivers; part of the Intracoastal Waterway; an early area of US settlement (explored 1607); wide range of seafood; increasing pollution.

Cheshire pop (2001e) 673 800; area 2328 sq km/899 sq mi. County of NWC England, UK, bounded W by Wales; drained by the Mersey, Weaver, Dee, Gowy, and Wheelock Rivers; Delamere Forest between Chester and Northwich; county town, Chester; chief towns include Crewe, Warrington, Widnes, Runcorn, Macclesfield; Warrington and Halton new unitary authorities from 1998; dairy farming, petrochemicals, motor vehicles.

Cheshire (of Woodhall), (Geoffrey) Leonard Cheshire, Baron (1917–92) British bomber pilot and philanthropist. He studied at Oxford, and was repeatedly decorated (including the VC, 1944) for his leadership and bravery during World War 2. He was one of the official British observers of the destruction caused by the atomic bomb over Nagasaki (1945). This experience, together with his new-found faith, Catholicism, made him determine to establish co-operative communities for ex-servicemen dedicated to living in peace. His initial venture failed, but he found himself looking after a homeless, cancer-stricken ex-serviceman who urged him to welcome others in a similar situation, and from this grew the Cheshire Homes for the Disabled. In 1959 he married **Sue Ryder**, and he was created a life peer in 1991.

chess A game for two players played on a board containing 64 squares alternately black and white. Each player has 16 pieces, either black or white, consisting of eight *pawns*, two *rooks* (also known as *castles*), two *knights*, two *bishops*, a *queen*, and a *king*. The game is one of strategy, the object being to attack the opponent's king in such fashion that it cannot move safely. That attacking move is called *checkmate*. All pieces have set moves, and the most versatile is the queen. The game was probably first played in ancient India, where it was known as *chaturanga*, then spread E to China and W to Persia. The earliest documentary references are in Persian and Chinese texts in c.600. A Chinese bibliography of that date includes books on chess, and a 10th-c Chinese encyclopedia dates it to 568.

The international body which supervises the game is the World Chess Federation (*Fédération Internationale des Echecs*, or FIDE). It traditionally organizes the world chess championships and other international competitions, though in 1987 a disagreement between Russian grandmaster Gary Kasparov and FIDE over levels of prize funding and FIDE's alleged autocratic methods led Kasparov to promote a breakaway body (the *Professional Chess Association*, or PCA). This body mounted an independent championship match in 1993 between Kasparov and his official challenger, UK grandmaster Nigel Short. Both players were then stripped of their right to contest the World Chess Federation title by FIDE, who invited Russian grandmaster Anatoly Karpov and Dutch grandmaster Jan Timman to play in their place. Kasparov and Karpov won their respective matches, and the division continues to this day, with Karpov holding the official FIDE title, but most experts regarding Kasparov as the world's top player. Karpov beat Gata Kamsky of the USA in 1996, and the year after, Kasparov beat Vishwanathan Anand of India. Following the collapse of the PCA, and the subsequent collapse of the *World Chess Council* set up to replace it, the 2000 world championship was contested under the aegis of Braingames Network, an Internet company, and won by Vladimir Kramnik. Anand regained the FIDE championship in 2000, but lost it to Ruslan Ponomariov (Ukraine) in 2002. An agreement was signed in Prague (May, 2002) to unify the various competing federations under FIDE with a reunification contest in 2003, but the event had still not taken place by the end of that year.

Chessman, Caryl (Whittier), nickname **The Red Light Bandit** (1921–60) Convict and writer, born in St Joseph, Michigan, USA. He was sentenced to death in 1948 on 17 charges of kidnapping, robbery, and rape, but was granted eight stays of execution by the Governor of California amounting to a record period of 12 years under sentence of death, without a reprieve. During this period he maintained his innocence and conducted a brilliant legal battle from prison, learned four languages, and wrote the best-selling books against capital punishment *Cell 2455 Death Row* (1956), which was also filmed, *Trial by Ordeal* (1956), and *The Face of Justice* (1958). His execution provoked worldwide criticism of US judicial methods.

chest *thorax*

Chester, Lat **Deva**, **Devana Castra**, Welsh **Caerleon**, Anglo-Saxon **Legaceaster** 53°12N 2°54W, pop (2001e) 118 200. County town of Cheshire, NWC England, UK; on the R Dee, 305 km/189 mi NW of London; important Roman port and military centre; railway; airfield (Hawarden), commercial centre, light engineering, tourism, car components; 13th–15th-c cathedral, city walls, two-tiered shopping arcades, 11th-c St John's Church; town hall (1869); football league team, Chester City; Chester Zoo.

Chesterfield, Philip Dormer Stanhope, 4th Earl of (1694–1773) English statesman, orator, and man of letters, born in London, UK. He studied at Cambridge, travelled in Europe, and became an MP (1715). In 1726 he succeeded his father as earl and became ambassador to Holland. He returned to England and parliament as a bitter antagonist of Robert Walpole, joined the Pelham ministry (1744), and became Irish lord-lieutenant (1745), and one of the principal secretaries of state (1746–8). Intimate with Swift, Pope, and other contemporary authors, his own best-known work was his guide to men's manners and worldly success, *Letters to his Son* (1774).

Chesterton, G(ilbert) K(eith) (1874–1936) Critic, novelist, and poet, born in London, UK. He studied at the Slade School of Art, London, then turned to writing. Much of his best work took the form of articles for periodicals, including his own *G.K.'s Weekly*. He wrote a great deal of poetry, as well as literary critical studies and works of social criticism. The amiable detective-priest who brought him popularity with a wider public first appeared in *The Innocence of Father Brown* (1911). Chesterton became a Catholic in 1922, and thereafter wrote mainly on religious topics, including lives of Francis of Assisi and Thomas Aquinas.

Chetniks (Serbo-Croatian *četnici*) Yugoslav, mainly Serbian, guerrillas during World War 2. Under the leadership of Drazha Mihailovic, they fought Tito's communist Partisans rather than the Axis occupiers. Abandoned by the Allies in 1944, they were defeated by the Partisans, and Mihailovic was tried and executed in 1945. Since 1990 the name has been adopted by Serb irregular forces in the former state of Yugoslavia.

Chevalier, Maurice [shevalyay] (1888–1972) Film and vaudeville actor, born in Paris, France. He began as a child singer and dancer in small cafes, then danced at the Folies Bergères (1909–13). He often appeared with the revue singer and dancer Mistinguett. His first Hollywood film was *The Innocents of Paris* (1929), and 30 years later his individual, straw-hatted, *bon-viveur* personality, with his distinctive French accent, was still much acclaimed, as in the musical *Gigi* (1958). He received a special Academy Award in 1958.

chevet [shevay] The circular or polygonal E end of a church. It is surrounded by an aisle, normally called an *ambulatory*. There are usually chapels radiating outwards.

Cheviot Hills [cheeviuht] Hill range on the border between Scotland and England, UK; extends 56 km/35 mi SW along the frontier between Scottish Borders council and Northumberland; rises to 816 m/2677 ft at The Cheviot; gives its name to a famous breed of sheep.

Chevreul, Michel Eugène [shevroei] (1786–1889) Chemist, born in Angers, NW France. He studied chemistry at the Collège de France in Paris, then lectured at the Collège Charlemagne, and became a director of the Gobelins tapestry works. In 1830 he became professor and then director (1864–79) of the Museum of Natural History. His best-known work is on animal fats, soap-making, candle-making, waxes, and natural dyes. Between 1828 and 1864 he studied the psychology of colour, and (when he was over 90) the psychological effects of ageing.

chevrotain [shevrotin] A ruminant artiodactyl mammal, native to tropical forest in Africa, India, Sri Lanka and SE Asia; small with stocky bodies and short slender legs; no horns or antlers; male with long protruding canine teeth; also known as **mouse deer** or **deerlet**. (Family: Tragulidae, 4 species.)

Chewa [chaywa] A Bantu-speaking agricultural people of Malawi, Zambia, and Zimbabwe who speak Chinyanja, the lingua franca of Zambia and Malawi. They belong to a cluster of Bantu-speaking peoples known as the Maravi. Like many other groups in the area, descent and succession is matrilineal. Population c.2 million.

chewing gum A sugared and flavoured product made from the concentrated juice of latex of the sapodilla tree, especially popular in the USA. It is chewed for its flavour, but not swallowed.

Cheyenne (Wyoming) [shiyan] 41°08N 104°49W, pop (2000e) 53 000. State capital in Laramie Co, SE Wyoming, USA; founded at a railway junction, 1867; territorial capital, 1869; prospered with gold mining in the Black Hills in the 1870s; railway; livestock market and shipping centre; Frontier Days Museum; Frontier Days (Jul).

Cheyenne (Indians) [**shi**yan] North American Plains Indians, speaking an Algonquian language, divided since the 1830s into N and S groups. Buffalo hunters on horseback, they were pushed W by various groups (such as the Ojibwa and Sioux), and their population was reduced by fighting and disease. They were involved in conflict with European prospectors and settlers (1857–9), and in the 1870s participated in the uprisings of other Plains tribes against the whites. They live mainly in Montana and Oklahoma, numbering c.18 200 (2000 census).

Chiang Ch'ing *Jiang Qing*

Chiang Kai-shek *Jiang Jieshi*

Chiang Mai [jee-eng **miy**] 18°48N 98°59E, pop (2000e) 191 000. City in NW Thailand, 700 km/435 mi N of Bangkok; N Thailand's principal city since 1296, when it was founded as the capital of Lan Na Thai kingdom; airfield; railway; university; tea, rice, groundnuts, corn, teak; flower festival (Feb), Songkran water-throwing festival (Thai New Year), Loy Krathong (Nov).

chiaroscuro [keearos**koo**roh] (Ital 'light-dark') In painting, the use of strong light and shadow to define forms in space. The technique was developed in Italy by Leonardo da Vinci and Caravaggio, and perfected by Rembrandt in 17th-c Holland.

Chiba [**chee**ba] 35°38N 140°07E, pop (2000e) 839 000. Port capital of Chiba prefecture, Kanto region, E Honshu, Japan; commuter town 40 km/25 mi E of Tokyo, on Tokyo Bay; railway; eight universities; steel, textiles, paper; Buddhist temple (8th-c).

Chicago [shi**kah**goh] 41°53N 87°38W, pop (2000e) 2 896 000. Third largest city in the USA; seat of Cook Co, NE Illinois, on L Michigan; built on the site of Fort Dearborn; settled in the 1830s; city status, 1837; developed as a result of its strategic position linking the Great Lakes with the Mississippi R after the Illinois and Michigan Canal was completed (1848), and after the railway to the E was opened (1853); much of the city destroyed by fire, 1871; notorious gangster activity in the Prohibition years (1920s), notably by Al Capone; now the major industrial, commercial, financial and cultural centre for the US interior; electrical machinery, metal products, steel (one-quarter of the nation's steel produced in and around the city), textiles, chemicals, food products, printing and publishing; commerce and finance centred upon 'The Loop' area; transport centre of the USA, with one of the busiest airports in the world; major rail network and inland port; seven universities; Sears Tower (1974), the world's second tallest building in 1999 (443 m/1454 ft); professional teams, Cubs, White Sox (baseball), Bulls (basketball), Bears (football), Black Hawks (ice hockey); Lyric Opera, Art Institute, Museum of Science and Industry, Shedd Aquarium, Planetarium; Chicago Film Festival (Nov).

Chicago School (architecture) The name given to a group of Chicago architects and office buildings in the late 19th-c. The buildings were the forerunners of 20th-c skyscrapers, and are characterized by the pioneering use of steel frame construction, clothed in masonry and with large expanses of windows, often to a great height. A prime example is the Stock Exchange (1893–4), architects Sullivan & Adler.

Chicago School (economics) A group of economists at Chicago University, led by Milton Friedman from 1948 to 1979. They hold the monetarist view that competition and market forces should be allowed to act freely, and with minimal government interference, for the best results.

Chichén Itzá [chee**chen** eet**za**] Toltec/Maya capital of the Yucatan peninsula, Mexico, AD c.1000–1200, reputedly established by the Toltec ruler Topílitzin after his expulsion from Tula c.987. Its monumental centre (area 3 km/1¾ mi by 2 km/1¼ mi) contains temple pyramids, the largest known Meso-American ballcourt, and a *tzompantli* (skull platform). From the Great Plaza, a 275-m/900-ft causeway leads N to the Cenote (Well) of Sacrifice, a massive water-filled pit sacred to the Rain God into which votive offerings and human sacrifices were cast.

Chichester [**chi**chester] 50°50N 0°48W, pop (2001e) 106 400. County town of West Sussex, S England, UK; 26 km/16 mi E of Portsmouth; founded by the Romans; later taken by the Saxons and named after their leader, Cissa; railway; engineering, furniture, agricultural trade, tourism; cathedral (11th–12th-c), bishop's palace (12th-c), St Mary's hospital (13th-c), market cross (15th-c), theatre (1962), remains of Roman villa at Fishbourne (3 km/1¾ mi W); Chichester Festival Theatre season (Aug–Sep).

Chichester, Sir Francis (Charles) [**chi**chester] (1901–72) Pioneer air navigator, adventurer, and yachtsman, born in Barnstaple, Devon, SW England, UK. He studied at Marlborough, and emigrated to New Zealand in 1919, where he made a fortune as a land agent. He became interested in flying, and made several pioneer flights, but was badly injured by a crash in Japan (1931) while attempting a solo flying circumnavigation. He served in Britain as an air-navigation expert during World War 2. In 1953 he took up ocean sailing, winning the first solo transatlantic yacht race (1960) in *Gipsy Moth III*, sailing from Plymouth to New York City in 40 days; he repeated the success in 1962 in 33 days. He made a successful solo circumnavigation of the world (1966–7) in *Gipsy Moth IV*, sailing from Plymouth to Sydney in 107 days, and from there back to Plymouth, via Cape Horn, in 119 days. He was knighted in 1967.

chickadee A name used in the USA for certain small birds of the tit family. (Family: Paridae, 7 species.)

chickaree *red squirrel*

chicken *domestic fowl*

chickenpox A highly infectious and usually benign disease of childhood (and sometimes adults), caused by *herpes zoster*, the same virus that is responsible for shingles. It causes characteristic blister-like (vesicular) eruptions on the skin, which may become infected by bacteria.

chick-pea A branching annual (*Cicer arietinum*), growing to 50 cm/20 in or more; leaves pinnate with 7–17 oval, toothed, glandular-hairy leaflets; pea-flowers white or bluish, solitary on long stalks; pods inflated, usually 2-seeded; also called **garbanzos**. Probably native to Asia, it has been cultivated since ancient times as a fodder plant and for its large, wrinkled, edible seeds. (Family: Leguminosae.)

chickweed A slender, spreading, often pale-green annual (*Stellaria media*); a very common weed, often flowering throughout the year; leaves oval, opposite; flowers tiny, white, five petals, shorter than sepals, deeply cleft into two parts. (Family: Caryophyllaceae.)

chicle An evergreen tree (*Achras zapota*) growing to 18 m/60 ft, native to Central America, cultivated elsewhere; leaves elliptical; flowers tiny, greenish-white, 6-petalled; fruit 5–10 cm/2–4 in, greyish to reddish-brown with yellow flesh. The copious white latex, collected as for rubber, provides the elastic base for chewing gum; the edible fruit is called **sapodilla plum**. (Family: Sapotaceae.)

chicory A perennial growing to 120 cm/4 ft (*Cichorium intybus*), with a long stout tap root, native to Europe, W Asia, and N Africa, and widely introduced elsewhere; leaves spear-shaped, lobed or toothed, the upper clasping the stem; flower-heads nearly stalkless, 2·5–4 cm/1–1½ in across, bright blue, rarely pink or white. It is locally grown as a vegetable and as a medicinal plant. Dried and ground roots are used as a coffee substitute. (Family: Compositae.)

Chief Justice The presiding justice of the United States Supreme Court, nominated by the US president and confirmed by a majority of the Senate. The Chief Justice serves for life (along with the eight associate justices), presides in both public session and at private court conferences, assigns the task of writing majority opinions, and administers the oath of office to the US president. The Chief Justice can dynamically shape the direction of the court's opinions, as demonstrated by John Marshall (served 1801–35), who established the principle of judicial review and enhanced the prestige and power of the court, and Earl Warren, who presided from 1953–69 over major court decisions from desegregating the nation's schools to giving more protection to criminal defendants.

chiffchaff A bird belonging to a group of Old World warblers (*Phylloscopus collybita*); native to Europe, N Africa, and Asia;

inhabits forest edges with thick undergrowth; eats insects; N birds move S in winter. (Family: Silviidae.)

Chifley, (Joseph) Ben(edict) (1885–1951) Australian statesman and prime minister (1945–9), born in Bathurst, New South Wales, SE Australia. In early life an engine driver, he entered parliament in 1928, and became defence minister in 1929. As Labor prime minister, he expanded social services and reformed the banking system. He continued as leader of the Labor Party until his death.

chigger *harvest-mite*

Chihuahua [chiwahwa] 28°40N 106°06W, pop (2000e) 639 000. Capital of Chihuahua state, N Mexico; altitude 1428 m/ 4685 ft; centre of Pancho Villa's revolutionary activities; railway; university (1954); mining, cattle raising, smelting; cathedral (18th-c); famous for its hairless small dog.

chihuahua [chiwahwa] The smallest domestic breed of dog, developed in Mexico; tiny body; head disproportionately large with bulbous forehead, large widely-spaced eyes, and large ears; constant body temperature of 40°C; two forms: the **long-coat chihuahua** and **smooth-coat chihuahua**.

Chikatilo, Andrei [chikateeloh] (1938–94) Russian convicted murderer. He was convicted and sentenced to death in Russia in 1992 for the murders of 52 adults and children committed over a 12-year period. He was executed in 1994.

chi kung [chee kung] (Chin 'energy' + 'practice') A system of Taoist physical and breathing exercises, practised as a form of meditation, with the object of increasing vital energy and directing its circulation. The exercises clear blockages in the meridians through which the energy circulates, and regular practice is said to promote health, harmonize physical and spiritual energy, and allow communiction with the cosmic energy which pervades the universe. Many practitioners of the Chinese healing arts practise chi kung in order to improve their own energy, so that this can be used for the benefit of their patients.

chilblains Bluish and slightly swollen areas of the skin of fingers and toes, caused by exposure to excessive cold. The lesions become red and itchy on warming.

child abuse The treatment of a child by an adult in a way unacceptable in a given culture at a given time; also referred to technically as **non-accidental injury of childhood** and popularly as **battered baby/child syndrome**. Abuse may be physical (soft and bony tissue injury, burns and scalds, poisoning and suffocation), sexual, emotional, or through neglect – though these varieties may overlap. Most abuse is perpetrated by parents, particularly non-related cohabitants. The precise frequency is unknown, but up to 4% of children under 12 are brought to the notice of professional agencies. There has been an increasing awareness since the 1960s of the scale and nature of this behaviour and of the need to protect children from it. Such activities may result in both criminal proceedings being taken against the adult concerned, and care proceedings in respect of the victim.

childbirth *labour*

Childe, (Vere) Gordon [chiyld] (1892–1957) Archaeologist, born in Sydney, New South Wales, SE Australia. He studied at Sydney and Oxford universities, and his early books, notably *The Dawn of European Civilisation* (1925), and *The Most Ancient Near East* (1928), established him as the most influential archaeological theorist of his generation. He was professor of archaeology at Edinburgh (1927–46) and director of the University of London Institute of Archaeology (1946–56). He returned to Australia on retirement, where he committed suicide.

Childers, (Robert) Erskine [childerz] (1870–1922) Irish nationalist and writer, born in London, UK. He studied at Cambridge, fought in the South African and First World Wars, and wrote a popular spy story, *The Riddle of the Sands* (1903), and several works of non-fiction. After the establishment of the Irish Free State, he joined the Irish Republican Army, and was active in the Civil War. He was captured and executed. His son **Erskine Hamilton Childers** (1905–74) was president of Ireland (1973–4).

childhood, non-accidental injury of *child abuse*

Children's Crusade A movement in 1212 of thousands of children (some as young as six) from Germany and France, aiming to reach the Holy Land and recapture Jerusalem from the Turks. Some reached Genoa, Italy, but did not embark; some reached Marseille, France, whence they were shipped to N Africa and sold into slavery.

Child Support Agency (CSA) In the UK, a government agency responsible for assessing and collecting obligatory child maintenance payments from non-resident parents. Introduced in 1993, it took over its role from the courts, and became part of the Department of Social Security. Although its aim of alleviating single-parent poverty was welcomed, widespread complaints in the mid-1990s about its practices made its work controversial, and led to several procedural reforms.

Chile *p.316*

Chile pine *monkey-puzzle*

chili *pepper 1*

Chilopoda [keelopoda] *centipede*

Chiltern Hills Low chalk hill range in SE England; extends 88 km/55 mi NE from S Oxfordshire, through Buckinghamshire, Hertfordshire, and Bedfordshire; continued SW as the Berkshire Downs and NE as the East Anglian Ridge; rises to 260 m/853 ft at Coombe Hill.

Chiltern Hundreds In the UK, a legally fictitious office of profit under the Crown: Steward or Bailiff of Her Majesty's Chiltern Hundreds (that is, districts) of Stoke, Desborough, and Burnham. To accept this office disqualifies an MP from the House of Commons. As an MP cannot resign, application to be appointed to the Chiltern Hundreds is the conventional manner of leaving the Commons.

Chi-lung *Jilong*

Chimaera *Chimera*

chimaera (botany) [kimeera] A mosaic organism, usually a plant, composed of tissues of two genetically different types, or a tissue composed of cells of genetically different types. It is formed either by a mutation that affects cell type, or by the artificial grafting together of parts of different individuals.

chimaera (zoology) [kimeera] Cartilaginous fish (*Chimaera monstrosa*) with robust body, large pelvic fins, and long tapering tail; teeth fused into plates; common in deeper waters (100–500 m/300–1600 ft) of N Atlantic and Mediterranean; length up to 1·5 m/5 ft; cream with brown patches and metallic sheen; also called **ratfish** or **rabbitfish**. (Family: Chimaeridae.)

Chimborazo [cheemborasoh] 1°28S 78°48W. Inactive Andean volcano in C Ecuador; height 6310 m/20 702 ft; highest peak in Ecuadorean Andes; cone partly covered by glaciers.

Chimbote [cheembohtay] 8°59S 78°38W, pop (2000e) 356 000. Port in Ancash department, N Peru; one of the few natural harbours on the W coast and Peru's largest fishing port; a new port has been built to serve the national steel industry; exports fishmeal.

Chimera [kiymeera, kimeera], also **Chimaera** In Greek mythology, a fabulous monster with the head of a lion, the body of a goat (the name means 'she-goat'), and the tail of a serpent, which breathed fire.

chimpanzee An ape native to equatorial Africa, believed to be the closest living relative to humans; height, 1–1·7 m/3¼–5½ ft; black coat; hair on head parted or directed backwards; face and ears naked; skin pale or dark; spends most time on the ground; eats fruit and some insects, but may kill small vertebrates; uses twigs, etc as tools to obtain food; two species: **chimpanzee** (*Pan troglodytes*) and the smaller, black-faced **pygmy chimpanzee** or **bonobo** (*Pan paniscus*).

Chimu [cheemoo] A South American Indian people of Peru, the most important political and cultural group before the Incas in the 14th-c, with a highly stratified social system. They built cities with huge buildings, pyramids, and streets, and developed sophisticated irrigation systems. They were con-

Chile

[chilee], official name **Republic of Chile**, Span **República de Chile**

Local name Chile

Timezone GMT −4

Area 756 626 km²/292 058 sq mi (excluding territory claimed in Antarctica)

Population total (2002e) 15 082 000

Status Republic

Date of independence 1818

Capital Santiago

Language Spanish (official)

Ethnic groups Mestizo (92%), Indian (6%), European (2%)

Religions Roman Catholic (89%), Protestant (10%), small Jewish and Muslim minority

Physical features Coastal Cordillera, Pampa Central, and the Chilean Andes are parallel regions running almost the entire length of the country; narrow coastal belt, backed by Andean mountain ridges rising in the NW to 6910 m/22 660 ft at Ojos del Salado; Atacama Desert in far NW, rich in minerals; arable land and forest in the S; S Andes still experiences volcanic activity; main river, the Bío-Bío; Punta Arenas located on southern tip of Chile's mainland; Chilean possessions include a rock measuring 424 m/1390 ft on Horn Island in the Wollaston group, and 1 250 000 km²/482 628 sq mi of Antarctic territory.

Climate Varied climate (spans 37° of latitude, with altitudes from Andean peaks to coastal plain); extreme aridity in N Atacama Desert, temperatures averaging 20°C; cold, wet, and windy in far S; Mediterranean climate in C Chile, with warm wet winters and dry summers; average temperature at Santiago 19°C (Jan), 8°C (Jul); average annual rainfall 375 mm/14·8 in.

Currency 1 Chilean Peso (Ch$) = 100 centavos

Economy Based on agriculture and mining; wheat, corn, potatoes, sugar beet, fruit, livestock; fishing in N, timber in S; copper, iron ore, nitrates, silver, gold, coal, molybdenum; oil and gas discovered in far S (1945); steel, wood pulp, cellulose, mineral processing.

GDP (2002e) $156·1 bn, per capita $10 100

Human Development Index (2002) 0·831

History Originally occupied by South American Indians; arrival of Spanish in 16th-c; part of Viceroyalty of Peru; independence from Spain declared in 1810, with a provisional government set up in Santiago; Spain reasserted its authority, 1814; patriot leader, Bernardo O'Higgins, escaped and returned, with military help of José de San Martín, to defeat the Spanish at Chacabuco, 1817; O'Higgins became first president and independence was declared, 1818; border disputes with Bolivia, Peru, and Argentina brought Chilean victory in War of the Pacific, 1879–84; economic unrest in late 1920s led to military dictatorship under Carlos Ibáñez until 1931; Marxist coalition government of Salvador Allende Gossens ousted in 1973, and replaced by military junta under Augusto Pinochet Ugarte, which banned all political activity; constitution providing for eventual return to democracy came into effect, 1981; plebiscite held in 1988 resulted in a defeat for Pinochet's candidacy as President beyond 1990, and limited political reforms; National Congress restored, comprising a Senate and a Chamber of Deputies in 1990; 6-year term for president agreed in 1994.

Head of State/Government

1910–15 Ramón Barros Luco
1915–20 Juan Luis Sanfuentes
1920–4 Arturo Alessandri
1924–5 *Military juntas*
1925 Arturo Alessandri
1925 Luis Barros Borgoño *Vice President*
1925–27 Emiliano Figueroa
1927–31 Carlos Ibáñez
1931 Pedro Opaso Letelier *Vice President*
1931 Juan Esteban Montero *Vice President*
1931 Manuel Trucco Franzani *Vice President*
1931–2 Juan Estaban Montero
1932 *Military juntas*
1932 Carlos G Dávila *Provisional President*
1932 Bartolomé Blanche *Provisional President*
1932 Abraham Oyanedel *Vice President*
1932–8 Arturo Alessandri Palma
1938–41 Pedro Aguirre Cerda
1941–2 Jerónimo Méndez Arancibia *Vice President*
1942–6 Juan Antonio Ríos Morales
1946–52 Gabriel González Videla
1952–8 Carlos Ibáñez del Campo
1958–64 Jorge Alessandri Rodríguez
1964–70 Eduardo Frei Montalva
1970–3 Salvador Allende (Gossens)
1973–90 Augusto Pinochet Ugarte
1990–4 Patricio Aylwin Azócar
1994–9 Eduardo Frei Ruíz-Tagle
1999– Ricardo Lagos Escobar

quered by the Incas (1465–70), who absorbed many aspects of their culture.

China *p.318*

china clay *kaolin*

Chi-nan *Jinan*

chinch bug A small, short-winged bug that feeds by sucking juices from grasses; an important corn and grain pest in America; overwinters as hibernating adult; reproduces rapidly, with two generations each year. (Order: Heteroptera. Family: Lygaeidae.)

chinchilla A South American cavy-like rodent; small (length, 35 cm/14 in); thick soft grey coat, bushy tail, large round ears. It is widely farmed for its fur, which is the most expensive in the world. (Genus: *Chinchilla*, 2 species. Family: Chinchillidae.)

chinchilla cat A breed of domestic cat, of the long-haired type; round head with short face; very dense white coat; each hair tipped with black (one colour form, the *blue chinchilla*, has the hairs tipped with blue-grey); also known as **silver Persian** or **silver**.

chinchilla rabbit A breed of domestic rabbit with thick soft grey fur resembling that of a chinchilla.

Chindits Members of the 3rd Indian Division, raised in 1942 by Brigadier Orde Wingate for long-range guerrilla operations, supported by air-supplied bases, in Japanese-occupied Burma. High casualties were sustained on the two deep penetrations of the Burmese jungle in 1943 and 1944, and their military value has been questioned.

Ch'in dynasty *Qin dynasty*

Chinese The Sinitic branch of the Sino–Tibetan group of languages, comprising eight major varieties, commonly called 'dialects'. This classification is an artifact of the writing system of Chinese, which is used by all varieties. Although the orthography transfers from one variety to another, the varieties themselves are, in some cases, not mutually intelligible, and on linguistic criteria would be classed as different languages. The two best-known varieties are *Cantonese*, spoken in the S, and *Mandarin*, spoken in the N, C, and W, the Beijing form being the basis of the modern standard language. Chinese writing originated in Shang period pictographs (16th-c BC), which closely resemble the modern ideographs. There have been numerous attempts to romanize the Chinese writing system, and in 1958 the *pinyin* 'phonetic spelling' system of 58 symbols was officially adopted, with the further aim of popularizing the grammar, vocabulary, and pronunciation of the codified standard Mandarin, now known as *putonghua* ('common language'). Chinese has the largest number of mother-tongue speakers of all the world's languages, at over 1000 million.

Chinese archaeology China's oldest anthropoid remains were discovered near Xian in 1964. The world's oldest hominoid remains giving any evidence of the way of life were found near Beijing in the 1920s. Adjacent Mesolithic remains suggest ancestry to the Chinese (25 000–8000 BC). Neolithic finds (6000–4000 BC) in 1921 between Xian and Luoyang led to over 100 similar excavations. The Shang capital near Anyang (16th–11th-c BC) has been excavated since the 1930s. Zhou period chariot burials were excavated in 1955 (11th–5th-c BC). The 6000 life-size ceramic guards at the Xian tomb of Qin Shihuangdi (3rd-c BC) have been famous since 1974. Tomb archaeology is a major form of information on the Han dynasty period (3rd-c BC–3rd-c AD) and important 5th-c Buddhist shrines have been excavated. Objects from Byzantium, Japan and Persia have been found in 8th-c Tang royal tombs. The products of Chinese archaeology can be matched only by Pharaoic treasures; paradoxically, the greatest activity accompanied the Cultural Revolution.

Chinese architecture The architecture of China, until the 20th-c, consistently based on the column, with walls used as screens rather than as load-bearing structures. Apart from pagodas, buildings were mostly made from wood. The earliest surviving buildings are the Tang dynasty pagodas (AD 618–907), such as the Wild Goose pagoda, Ch'ang-an, Shensi (701–5). Most buildings date from the Ming dynasty (1368–1644) and later, including the Imperial City and Forbidden City of Beijing (Peking), with complex symmetrical plans, colourful pavilions, and curved roofs. European styles and multi-storey structures have been increasingly used since the 1911 revolution, particularly the International Style in recent decades.

Chinese art The art associated with ancient China, dating from before 4000 BC, which influenced all Far Eastern countries, and reached Europe in the late 17th-c. It is characterized by technical innovation (silk, porcelain, paper, printing) and great stylistic refinement. Decorated bronze vessels and jade carvings date from 1000 BC; the interconnected traditions of painting and calligraphy were established during the Han period (206 BC–AD 220). High-quality porcelain was produced under the Tang (618–906) and later dynasties. Landscape painting emerged in the Song period (960–1279), and the Ming period (1368–1644) saw the production of refined cloisonné, lacquer, and porcelain. Important schools emerged under the Qing dynasty (1644–1912), including early Impressionistic painting, and the various types of Qing period porcelain were in demand worldwide.

Chinese astronomy Among the many achievements of early Chinese astronomy (which developed independently of that in the West) are: the first lunar eclipse recordings (1361 BC, four more by 1279 BC); solar measurement and a 12-monthly calendar (before 1100 BC); algebraic stellar calculations (by 5th-c BC); observation of Halley's comet (possibly 611 BC, definitely 467 BC); the compilation of star catalogues (5th-c BC); the year calculated to 365¼ days (444 BC); the movements of Jupiter and Saturn noted (350 BC); 1080 stars catalogued in six brightness categories (1st-c BC); sunspots recorded (28 BC); lunar tidal influences discovered (AD 80); lunar eclipses and revolution understood (2nd-c); stellar navigation (2nd-c); direction of comet tails away from the Sun observed (635); supernova observation (1054, never recorded in Europe); and a water-powered astronomical clock, armillary sphere, and celestial globe (1080). A great observatory (1280 on) anticipated European innovations by 300 years. By 1700, 90 supernovae and 581 comet observations had been documented. The star co-ordinates used worldwide today are Chinese in origin.

Chinese block *wood block*

Chinese gooseberry *kiwi fruit*

Chinese historical writing A Chinese cultural tradition from earliest times, unsurpassed in any civilization. The vast corpus of documentation includes: commentaries on social practices, such as the 5th-c BC *Book of Etiquette*; documentary collections starting with the 7th-c BC *History Classic*; works on geographical issues, starting with the 4th-c BC *River Mountain Classic*; catalogues of inventions, such as the *Book of Origins* (1st-c BC); collections, such as the official Ming encyclopaedia of Chinese culture (1408, 11 095 vols) or the Qing encyclopaedia (1726, 5000 vols); and 11 000 closely detailed local gazetteers for 2500 prefectures (AD 347 on). In historical writing, China stands apart in the volume, detail, and continuous length of the record. The BC era alone shows: court historians from 753 BC; historical writings from the 5th–4th-c BC (eg the *Spring and Autumn Annals*); and major Han period histories, such as Sima Qian's unprecedented *Historical Records* (2nd-c BC). For the whole period, there are 26 major official dynastic histories, equivalent to 45 million English words.

Chinese lantern A perennial (*Physalis alkakengi*) native to SE Europe and Asia; rhizomatous; flowers white with dark spots in centre; persistent bladdery calyces 5 cm/2 in long, becoming papery and bright red in fruit – the 'lanterns' often seen in dried floral displays – enclosing an edible red berry. (Family: Solanaceae.)

Chinese literature The literature of China goes back 3000 years. The earliest works under the Zhou dynasty (1028–256 BC) were the Nine Classics, an admixture of history, poetry, ethics, and commentary on ritual and divination, used by Confucius in his teachings. Closely associated are the 20 books of Confucius's own *Analects*, and the *Mencius* by a disciple. Late in

China

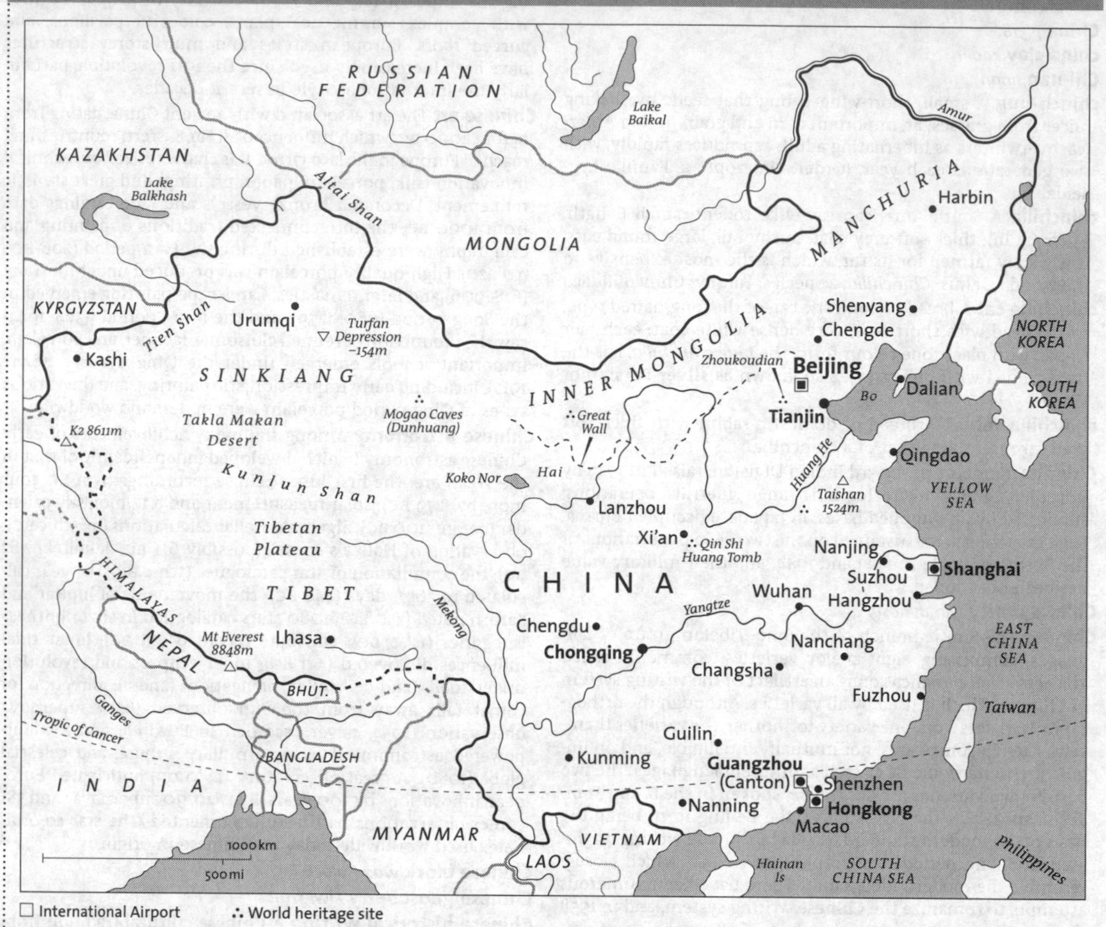

official name **People's Republic of China**, Chin **Zhonghua Renmin Gonghe Guo** or **Zhongguo**

Local name Zhongguo

Timezone GMT +8

Area 9 597 000 km²/3 705 000 sq mi (also claims island of Taiwan)

Population total (2002e) 1 284 211 000

Status People's republic

Capital Beijing (Peking)

Languages Standard Chinese (Putonghua) or Mandarin, also Yue (Cantonese), Wu, Minbei, Minnan, Xiang, Gan and Hakka

Ethnic groups Han Chinese (92%), over 50 minorities, including Chuang, Manchu, Hui, Miao, Uighur, Hani, Kazakh, Tai and Yao

Religions Officially atheist; widespread Confucianism and Taoism (20%), Buddhism (6%)

Physical features Over two-thirds of country are upland hills, mountains, and plateaux; highest mountains in the W, where the Tibetan plateau rises to average altitude of 4000 m/13 000 ft; Mt Everest rises to 8848 m/29 028 ft on the Nepal-Tibet border; land descends to desert/semi-desert of Xinjiang and Inner Mongolia (NE); broad and fertile plains of Manchuria (NE); further E and S, Sichuan basin, drained by Yangtze R (5980 km/3720 mi in

the Zhou dynasty we have the 'Hundred Schools of Thought', and the poetry of Qu Yuan, whose lyrical and allegorical *Li Sao* influenced poets in the Han dynasty (206 BC–AD 220). The introduction of Buddhism into China at this time enhanced the popularity of personal poetry, exemplified by the work of the Cao family; and the political instability of the Six Dynasties that followed (221–581) further encouraged an 'escapist' or idealist literature. The following Tang dynasty (618–907) is known as the Golden Age of Chinese Poetry, providing 2000 poets from all ranks of society, the best known being the Taoist Li Po (701–62), his friend the Confucian Du Fu (712–70), Li Ho ('the Chinese Keats', 790–816), and the populist Bo Juji (772–846). At the same time, Han Yu (768–824) replaced the elaborate 'parallel prose' of earlier dynasties with a more flexible medium. The poetry of the Song dynasty (960–1216) was likewise more versatile than Tang; Su Shi and others experimenting with irregular metres. This period also produced a good deal of historical writing. The Yuan dynasty (1279–1368) was celebrated for its musical drama, a form favoured by the Mughal ruling class, with Ma Zhiyuan's *Autumn in the Han Palace* typical of their plots from legend and romance.

There were developments in drama in the Ming dynasty (1368–1644), with plays of historical and political significance; but this was primarily the age of the Chinese novel. Developing out of the *hua-pen* or short story, the earlier novels often dealt with historical and heroic subjects; famous examples are *The Romance of the Three Kingdoms*, and *The Water Margin*. The personalized novel arrived with the last, Qing dynasty (1644–

length); Huang He (Yellow) R runs for 4840 km/3010 mi; heavily populated S plains and E coast, with rich, fertile soils.

Climate Varied, with seven zones; (1) NE China: cold winters, with strong N winds, warm and humid summers, unreliable rainfall; (2) C China: warm and humid summers, sometimes typhoons or tropical cyclones on coast; (3) S China: partly within tropics; wettest area in summer, frequent typhoons; (4) SW China: summer temperatures moderated by altitude, winters mild with little rain; (5) Xizang autonomous region: high plateau surrounded by mountains; winters severe with frequent light snow and hard frost; (6) Xinjiang and W interior: arid desert climate, cold winters; rainfall well distributed throughout year; (7) Inner Mongolia: extreme continental climate; cold winters, warm summers.

Currency 1 Renminbi Yuan (RMBY, $, Y) = 10 jiao = 100 fen

Economy Since 1949, economy largely based on heavy industry; more recently, light industries; special economic zones set up to attract foreign investment; rich mineral deposits; largest oil-producing country in Far East; major subsistence crops include rice, grain, beans, potatoes, tea, sugar, cotton; economy hit by SARS epidemic (2003).

GDP (2002e) $5·989 tn, per capita $4700

Human Development Index (2002) 0·726

History Chinese civilization believed to date from the Xia dynasty (2200–1799 BC); Qin dynasty (221–207 BC) unified warring states and provided system of centralized control; expansion W during Western and Eastern Han dynasties (206 BC– AD 220), and Buddhism introduced from India; split into Three Kingdoms (Wei, Shu, Wu, 220–65); period of Six dynasties (221–581); from 4th-c, series of N dynasties set up by invaders, with several dynasties in S; gradually reunited during the Sui (590–618) and Tang (618–906) dynasties; partition into the Five Dynasties (907–60); Song (Sung) dynasty (960–1279), remembered for literature, philosophy, inventions; Kublai Khan established Mongol Yuan dynasty which ruled China 1279–1368; visits by Europeans, such as Marco Polo, 13th-14th-c; Ming dynasty (1368–1644) increased contacts with West; overthrown by Manchus, who ruled China during 1644–1911 under the Qing dynasty, and enlarged empire to include Manchuria, Mongolia, Tibet, Taiwan; opposition to foreign imports led to Opium Wars 1839–42, 1858–60; Sino-Japanese War, 1895; Hundred Days of Reform movement, 1898; Boxer Rising, 1900; Qing dynasty overthrown, 1911; Republic of China founded by Sun Yatsen, 1912; May Fourth Movement, 1919; unification under Jiang Jieshi (Chiang Kai-shek), who made Nanjing capital in 1928; conflict between Nationalists and Communists led to the Long March, 1934–5, with Communists moving to NW China under Mao Zedong (Mao Tse-tung); Nationalist defeat by Mao and withdrawal to Taiwan in 1950; People's Republic of China proclaimed, 1949, with capital at Beijing; first Five-Year Plan (1953–7) period of nationalization and collectivization; Great Leap Forward, 1958–9, emphasized local authority and establishment of rural communes; Cultural Revolution initiated by Mao Zedong, 1966; many policies reversed after Mao's death in 1976, and drive towards rapid industrialization and wider trade relations with West; after 1980, Deng Xiaoping became the dominant figure within the ruling Chinese Communist Party; he retired from his last official post in 1990, but remained influential until his death in 1997; governed by elected National People's Congress who elect a State Council; Hong Kong returned to China, 1997.

President of the Executive Council
1928–30 Tan Yankai
1930 Song Ziwen (T V Soong) *Acting*
1930 Wang Jingwei (Wang Ching-wei)
1930–1 Jiang Jieshi (Chiang K'ai-shek)
1931–2 Sun Fo
1932–5 Wang Jingwei
1935–7 Jiang Jieshi (Chiang K'ai-shek)
1937–8 Wang Chonghui (Wang Ch'ung-hui) *Acting*
1938–9 Kong Xiangxi (K'ung Hsiang-hsi)
1939–44 Jiang Jieshi (Chiang K'ai-shek)
1944–7 Song Ziwen (T V Soong)
1945–9 *Civil war*
1948 Wang Wenhao (Wong Wen-hao)
1948–9 Sun Fo
1949 He Yingqin (Ho Ying-ch'in)
1949 Yan Xishan (Yen Hsi-shan)
People's Republic of China

Head of State
1949–59 Mao Zedong (Mao Tse-tung)
1959–68 Liu Shaoqi
1968–75 Dong Biwu
1975–6 Zhu De
1976–8 Song Qingling
1978–83 Ye Jianying
1983–8 Li Xiannian (Li Hsien-nien)
1988–93 Yang Shangkun
1993–2003 Jiang Zemin
2003– Hu Jintao

Head of Government
1949–76 Zhou Enlai (Chou En-lai)
1976–80 Hua Guofeng
1980–7 Zhao Ziyang (Chao Tzu-yang)
1987–98 Li Peng
1998–2003 Zhu Rongji
2003– Wen Jibao

Communist Party Chairman
1935–76 Mao Zedong
1976–81 Hua Guofeng
1981–2 Hu Yaobang (Hu Yao-pang)

General Secretary
1982–7 Hu Yaobang
1987–9 Zhao Ziyang
1989–2002 Jiang Zemin (Chiang Tse-min)
2002– Hu Jintao

1912), new ground being broken by Cao Xueqin's partly autobiographical *The Dream of the Red Chamber*. This was followed by satirical works (often directed at the abuses of bureaucracy) and fine examples of the ever-popular ghost story. After 1911, Western influence completely transformed Chinese literature, which experienced its own force-fed modernist movement before Mao Zedong imposed a new discipline and encouraged folk art. The Cultural Revolution of 1966 was hostile to outside influences, but there are now signs that Chinese literature is in creative dialogue with the rest of the world.

Chinese mathematics, science, and technology China played a leading world role in these areas from earliest times until the 17th-c, anticipating European developments often by many centuries. Among its contributions (to the 10th-c) are the following: *Prehistoric*: World's earliest evidence of deliberate use of fire in cooking. *Shang* (16th-c BC): Bronzes by multipart mould casting; chariots with axled 15-spoke wheels; weather records kept (1216 BC). *Zhou* (11th–3rd-c BC): Iron (512 BC); cast-iron agricultural implements (4th-c BC); crossbows with 4-part trigger; mustard gas blown with bellows (possibly 4th-c BC); chariots with 30-spoke wheels (European equivalents, 15th-c); salt production (7th-c BC); dam construction (6th-c BC); irrigation (560 BC); canals (3rd-c BC). *Han* (3rd-c BC–3rd-c AD): paper (AD 105) (Europe, 1150); conversion of rotary to rectilinear motion (1st-c AD); simple porcelain; furrow plough (3rd-c); artesian wells (1st-c) (Europe, 1126); steam condensation (3rd-c

BC); square pallet chain pump (for irrigation, 1st-c BC); crank handle (2nd-c AD); wheelbarrow (AD 300); brine extraction by deep drilling; iron smelting in cupola furnaces (28 BC) (Europe, 1380); water-powered piston bellows (AD 31) (Europe, 1565); coal in smelting (4th-c); steel manufacture (6th-c, possibly 1st-c BC); stirrup (AD 300); breast strap and collar harness (by 5th-c); 6-man chariots; rudder (1st-c, possibly 1st-c BC) (Europe, c.1200); watertight bulkheads (Europe, 18th-c); multiple-masted ships (Europe, 15th-c); tacking sails (3rd-c) (Europe 16th-c); snowflake symmetry observed (135 BC) (Europe, 15th-c); weather forcasting (2nd-c BC); abacus (2nd-c AD); seismograph (AD 132) (Europe, 1703); proof of 'Pythagoras's theorem' (2nd-c); concept of negative number (2nd-c BC) (Europe, 16th-c); π calculated (2nd-c). *Sui-Tang* (6th–10th-c): printing (by 593) (Europe, 1375); first printed book (868); toilet paper (590); fireworks (600); gunpowder (900) (Europe, 1327); true porcelain; clockwork escapement (724); crossbow with 700 m range; long stirrups; 30-man military carriages (7th-c); iron-chain suspension bridges (7th-c) (Europe, 1595); segmental arch bridges (7th-c) (Europe, 1340); 5-deck ships; paddlewheel warships (780) (Europe, 15th-c); use of acids described (860) (Europe, 1295); alcohol distillation (8th-c) (Europe, 13th-c); dictionary of chemical synonyms (806) (Europe, 18th-c).

Chinese medicine and public health China played a leading world role from the earliest times until the 18th-c, as the following contributions (to the 10th-c) illustrate: *Zhou* (11th-c–3rd-c BC): Royal physicians and dieticians (6th-c BC), state-employed doctors, public health officials; importance of pure drinking water realized; connection between physical and mental illness known. *Qin/Han* (3rd-c BC–3rd-c AD): Biography of a doctor (*Shi Chi*, 1st-c BC); first hospital (491), state hospitals (by 6th-c); 360 acupuncture points known (1st-c BC); dissection (1st-c AD); caesarians (5th-c); connection established between sweet food and diabetes (1st-c) (Europe, 18th-c); value of seaweed in goitre (1st-c) (Europe, 1180); medicinal tea-drinking; culinary and insect-borne causes of food-poisoning noted; piped drinking water in Qin palaces (3rd-c BC); piped drinking water from limed wells via pottery conduits to cities (2nd-c AD); public bath-houses; public rat/insect catchers, with use of pyrethrum; first Chinese pharmacopoeia (365 drugs) and first medical treatise (1st-c BC). *Sui/Tang* (6th–10th-c AD): Imperial Medical College founded (620), including specialist courses (dentistry, opthalmics); 10 compulsory final examinations (759); legal requirement of 20 medical students in every large city; state supply of medicines, provincial drug distribution centres, experimental herb-culture, 400 medicinal plants used (7th-c); dictionary of prescriptions (723); 27 seaweed treatments for goitre (7th-c); circulatory system studied.

Chinese music The music of China is both ancient and varied, with a correspondingly rich instrumentation. The *qin*, a type of zither, the *dizi*, a bamboo flute, and the *pipa*, a pear-shaped lute, are among the oldest and most highly regarded of Chinese instruments. Until the end of the Qing dynasty (1911) most types of Chinese music were transmitted orally, although notation systems had existed for centuries. Historical writings and contemporary accounts yield much information about music among the people, at the courts, and, above all, in the theatre, where a kind of opera developed before the earliest Western operas were staged in Florence c.1600. The Beijing opera has been of central importance in Chinese music and culture for two centuries, and since 1949 a vital mouthpiece for socialist propaganda. The Cultural Revolution of the late 1960s halted performances of traditional opera, as well as the scholarly study of ancient Chinese music that had begun in the Qing dynasty. Since the fall of Mao Zedong's wife in 1976, many traditional features have returned, and performances of Western music have also increased.

Chinese philosophy Intellectual inquiry in China dates back at least to the time of Confucius in the 6th-c BC, and until the consolidation of empire in the 2nd-c BC a number of different schools engaged in vigorous rivalry. Since argument was primarily directed at competing rulers rather than fellow-citizens, early Chinese thought has a strongly social, non-speculative emphasis, but modern researchers have come to respect the coherence of its culturally and linguistically unfamiliar modes of debate. Three early schools were particularly influential: *Confucians* stressed the importance of the cultural heritage – at best as humanists, at worst as pedants; *Taoists* stressed the *tao* 'way', underlying and sustaining the natural world, as a surer guide than human institutions; *Legalists* stressed the ruler's need to promulgate laws, setting out rewards and punishments to mould his kingdom into an effective power against his rivals. Legalism created the Chinese empire, but Confucianism sustained it, though the decline of empire from the 2nd-c AD onward allowed more mystical philosophies based on the surviving Taoist texts to flourish, paving the way for the acceptance of Buddhism. The rejection of Buddhism in favour of Neo-Confucianism from the 11th-c onward marks a major turning point. Buddhism was accused of denying the reality of the world of our experience, which for Neo-Confucians was composed of *ch'i*, the material element, ordered by *li*, abstract norms patterning this material. Comprehension of these norms was for some, following Chu Hsi (1130–1200), a matter of studying the cultural heritage; for others, following Wang Yang-ming (1472–1529), a matter of looking within the mind. The ramifications of Neo-Confucian debate provoked a shift from the 17th-c onwards towards the more philological study of the authoritative early texts. The wholesale rejection of traditional thought in the early 20th-c has now yielded to attempts at defining a modern Confucianism in parts of E Asia, even as Marxism remains the official philosophy of the homeland of Confucius himself.

Chinese water deer *water deer*

Ch'ing dynasty *Qing dynasty*

Chingis Khan *Genghis Khan*

Ching-tao *Qingdao*

Ch'in-huang-tao *Qinhuangdao*

Chinkiang *Zhenjiang*

chinoiserie [sheenwazeree] Silks, porcelain, and lacquer from China, which were very much admired in Europe from the time they were first imported in the late Middle Ages, and consequently much imitated. From the work of the 17th-c japanners and the productions of the early European porcelain makers, which directly copied Oriental art, a separate Western style evolved, using Chinese and Japanese motifs in an original manner in a completely Western decorative context. It reached its height in the 18th-c (with Louis XIV's court celebrating the first day of the century Chinese-style), and was used throughout the decorative arts, as well as in such fields as book illustration, furniture, architecture, the theatre, and gardening. Tea-drinking, imported in 1658, became universal within a century. Chinoiserie was the artistic manifestation of *Le Rêve chinois* ('The Chinese dream'), a broader phenomenon which embraced philosophical, religious, legal, and social issues, attracting many thinkers of the age.

Chinook A North American Indian people of Washington and Oregon, one of the NW Indian groups with an artistic tradition. They were successful middlemen in the trade between coastal Indians and interior Plateau Indians, their language being widely used as a lingua franca. They fished salmon, and traded in dried fish, slaves, canoes, and shells. White contact, dating back to 1805, eventually eroded their culture; most Chinook were moved to reservations. Their language was widely used as a trade lingua franca throughout the Pacific Northwest.

chinook wind *Föhn wind*

Ch'in Shih Huang-ti *Qin Shihuangdi*

Chios [keeos], Gr **Khíos**, Ital **Scio** pop (2000e) 55 000; area 842 sq km/325 sq mi; length 48 km/30 mi. Greek island in the Aegean Sea, off the W coast of Turkey; fifth largest of the Greek islands; crossed N–S by hills rising to 1298 m/4258 ft; fertile plain in SE; chief town, Chios, pop (2000e) 32 400; ferry to mainland and islands; noted for its wine and figs; tanning, boatbuilding, tourism; Navy Week (Jun–Jul).

chip A commonly used name for an integrated circuit. Strictly, the term refers to the small 'chip' of silicon on which the electronic circuits reside, rather than the encapsulated package.

chipmunk A type of squirrel; all species native to North America except *Eutamias sibiricus* from W Asia; back with alternating pale and dark longitudinal stripes; cheeks with internal pouches for carrying seeds. (Genera: *Tamias*, 1 species; *Eutamias*, 22 species.)

Chipp, Don(ald) Leslie (1925–) Australian politician, born in Melbourne, Victoria, SE Australia. He studied at the University of Melbourne, and entered the federal parliament as the Liberal member for Higinbotham, Victoria, in 1960. He remained in the House of Representatives until he became a senator for Victoria in 1977. He founded the Australian Democrats in 1977, a party which aimed to be a centre group that would 'keep the bastards honest'. He was the Democrats' parliamentary leader from 1978 until 1986, when he retired.

Chippendale, Thomas (1718–79) Furniture-maker and designer, baptised at Otley, West Yorkshire, N England, UK. He set up a workshop in St Martin's Lane, London, UK, in 1754, in partnership with a merchant, James Rannie (d.1766). He soon became famous for his graceful Neoclassical furniture, especially chairs, which he made mostly from mahogany in the Rococo, chinoiserie, and Gothic Revival styles. *The Gentleman and Cabinet-maker's Director*, which he published in 1754, was the first comprehensive trade catalogue of its kind. He was succeeded by his second partner, Thomas Haig, and his son **Thomas** (c.1749–1822).

Chippewa *Ojibwa*

Chirac, Jacques (René) [shirak] (1932–) French prime minister (1974–6, 1986–8) and president (1995–). Educated in Paris, he became a civil servant, and was first elected to the National Assembly in 1967. He gained extensive governmental experience before being appointed prime minister by Giscard d'Estaing. He resigned over differences with d'Estaing and broke away to lead the Gaullist Party. Mayor of Paris since 1977, he was an unsuccessful candidate in the 1981 and 1988 presidential elections, but won in 1995. His presidency began controversially when, in June 1995, France resumed nuclear testing in the French atoll of Mururoa during a worldwide moratorium, bringing international condemnation and committing Chirac to a future test-ban treaty. Strikes and rulings over corruption while Chirac was mayor of Paris increased his and his government's unpopularity and, in the 1997 election, the Juppé government was rejected in favour of the Socialists under his political rival, Lionel Jospin. In 2000 he campaigned for a Franco-German 'top-tier' alliance within the European Union, and called for a European constitution. He won a landslide victory in the second round of the 2002 presidential election after voters surged to the polls to keep out the far-right candidate, Jean-Marie Le Pen.

chirality [kiyralitee] Asymmetry resulting in an object not being superimposable upon its mirror image. Chemical chirality is usually associated with a carbon atom having four different substituents. Two isomers which are mirror images of one another are called *enantiomers*. Towards symmetrical environments, enantiomers behave identically, but towards other chiral molecules they are different. Thus they will have identical melting points, but may have different tastes and smells.

Chirico, Giorgio de [kireekoh] (1888–1978) Artist, born in Volos, Greece. He studied at Athens and Munich, working later in Paris, and with Carrà in Italy. About 1910 he began to produce a series of dreamlike pictures of deserted squares, which had considerable influence on the Surrealists. His whole style after 1915 is often called 'metaphysical painting', including semi-abstract geometric figures and stylized horses. In the 1930s he reverted to an academic style.

chirography [kiyrografee] The various forms and styles of handwriting, which differ between the writing systems of the major language families. Early Western styles included *majuscule*, as seen in the chiselled capital letters of early Greek and Roman inscriptions from c.300 BC; *minuscule*, the use of small letters found in Greek from the 8th-c AD; *uncial* writing, large rounded letters found in Latin and Greek manuscripts from the 4th-c AD; *cursive*, used from c.4th-c BC, in which the letters are joined together in rounded strokes to promote speed; and *italic*, developed in Italy in c.1500, a forerunner of italic letters in printing.

Chiron [kiyron] In Greek mythology, a good and wise centaur, the son of Kronos and Philyra the Oceanid, who kept a school for princes in Thessaly. He educated Asclepius in the art of medicine and music, Jason the Argonaut, and Achilles. He was wounded with a poisoned arrow of Heracles, and gladly gave up his immortality to be rid of pain.

chiropody [chiropodee] The study of the structure and function of the foot in health, and of its disorders and deformities. It is also known as **podiatry**.

chiropractic [kiyrohpraktik] The study of health and disease from a structural point of view, with special emphasis on the alignment of the bones of the skeleton and of the anatomical relation of nerves and muscles of the body to them. The discipline was founded in 1895 by US physician Daniel David Palmer (1845–1913), and is probably now the most widely recognized alternative medical practice in the Western world. It is mainly concerned with the bones of the spine, and with pain or discomfort held to be the result of malposition, bony pressure, or muscle spasm in the neck, back, and pelvis. Chiropractors treat these disorders by manipulation without the use of drugs or surgery, and aim to correct distortion of posture, restore function to spinal and pelvic joints, and relieve pressure or irritation on nerves which might be causing discomfort or disturbed function.

Chiroptera [kiyroptera] *bat*

Chirripó Grande [chiripoh granday] 9°50N 83°25W. Highest peak of Costa Rica and S Central America; in the Cordillera de Talamanca; height 3819 m/12 529 ft; Chirripó National Park, area of 437 sq km/169 sq mi.

chiru [chiroo] A goat-antelope (*Pantholops hodgsoni*) native to the high plateau of Tibet and China; pale pinkish brown; nose swollen at tip; male with black face and long slender vertical horns growing apart towards tips; female without horns, also known as **Tibetan antelope**.

chisel-tooth lizard *agamid*

Chisholm, Melanie *Spice Girls, The*

Chisholm Trail A cattle trail in the USA from Texas across Oklahoma to the railheads at Abilene, Kansas. It is named after Jesse Chisholm, who pioneered the route in 1866. The trail fell into disuse with the spread of enclosure and the growth of a rail network.

chi-square test [kiy] A statistical test to measure how well the values 'expected' from a model agree with the 'observed' values. If e_i is an 'expected' value and o_i the corresponding 'observed' value, the statistic $\chi^2 = \sum(o_i - e_i)^2/e_i$ is calculated, and its significance deduced by comparing it with values given in tables.

chital [cheetl] A true deer (*Axis axis*), native to India and Sri Lanka (introduced in Australia); pale brown with white spots; antlers long, lyre-shaped; inhabits woodland; often gather under trees occupied by langur monkeys, feeding on leaves the monkeys drop; also known as **axis deer** or **spotted deer**.

chitarrone [kitarohnay] A long-necked lute or theorbo, used in the 16th–17th-c to accompany singing. There were usually six pairs of gut or metal strings running over a fretted keyboard, and eight longer bass strings which were not stopped (ie each produced one note only). The instrument might be as long as 1 m 90 cm/6 ft 3 in.

chitin [kiytin] A long chain-like molecule (a linear homopolysaccharide of N-acetyl-D-glucosamine) found as a major constituent of the horny covering (cuticle) of insects and cell walls of fungi. When cross-linked, these chains produce a lightweight but strong material.

chiton [**kiy**tn] A marine mollusc characterized by a dorsal shell consisting of eight overlapping calcareous plates; muscular foot used for attachment to, and movement over, a substrate; several pairs of gills present in a groove around the foot; most species in shallow water; also known as **coat-of-mail shell**. (Class: Polyplacophora.)

Chittagong [chi**ta**gong] 22°20N 91°48E, pop (2000e) 2 386 000. Seaport capital of Chittagong district, SE Bangladesh; principal port of Bangladesh on the R Karnafuli, flowing into the Bay of Bengal; conquered by Nawab of Bengal, 1666; ceded to British East India Company, 1760; damaged during 1971 Indo-Pakistani War; many Hindu and Buddhist temples; university (1966); trade in tea, jute, skins, hides; cotton, iron, steel, fruit canning, matches, shipbuilding, oil refining; offshore oil installations in the 1960s.

Chittagong Hill Tracts area 8680 sq km/3350 sq mi. Region in SE Bangladesh, bounded E by Burma; hilly area enclosed by rivers; reaches heights of 500–1000 m/1500–3000 ft in the SE; divided into four fertile valleys, covered with thick planted forest; L Kaptia (686 sq km/265 sq mi) formed when Karnafuli hydroelectric dam built at Kaptia; capital, Rangamati.

Chitwin or **Royal Chitwin** area 932 sq km/360 sq mi. National park in SC Nepal; between the Sumesar Range (E) and the R Gandak (W); established in 1973; a world heritage site.

chive A perennial growing to 40 cm/15 in (*Allium schoenoprasum*); tufts of narrow, tubular leaves; dense umbels of pink or purple flowers; native to the N hemisphere. It is cultivated for its leaves, which are used as flavouring. (Family: Liliaceae.)

Chlamydia [kla**mi**dia] A genus of spherical, non-motile bacteria that multiply only within the cytoplasm of true nucleated (*eukaryotic*) cells. Virulent strains can cause eye, mouth, genital, and other diseases of humans and other animals. (Kingdom: Monera. Family: Chlamydiaceae.)

chloracne [klaw**rak**nee] Acne-like lesions on the skin with pimple-like (*papular*) formations which may become infected (*pustular*). Its occurrence is linked to industrial exposure to chlorinated hydrocarbons.

chloral CCl_3CHO, IUPAC **2,2,2-trichloroethanal**, boiling point 97°C. **Chloral hydrate** is a sedative.

chlorates Salts of an oxyacid of chlorine, usually a chlorate(V), containing the ion ClO_3^-, including the weedkiller **sodium chlorate** ($NaClO_3$). Chlorate(I) or **hypochlorite** is ClO^-; chlorate(VII) or **perchlorate** is ClO_4^-.

chlordiazepoxide *benzodiazepines*

Chlorella [klo**re**la] A genus of non-motile, single-celled green algae containing a cup-shaped chloroplast; very common in a variety of freshwater habitats.

chlorides Compounds containing chlorine, especially those containing the ion Cl^-. Common salt is **sodium chloride** (Na^+Cl^-).

chlorine [**klaw**reen] Cl, element 17, boiling point −35°C. A greenish-yellow gas, containing diatomic molecules (Cl_2). A very reactive substance, it does not occur free in nature, but is recovered from deposits of NaCl or KCl by electrolysis. It may also be recovered from sea water, which contains about 2% chlorine as dissolved Cl^-. The gas has an intense odour and is very poisonous. Industrially, chlorine is mainly used in reactions with organic compounds to form propellants, cleaning fluids, and monomers for rubber production. It is also widely used as a powerful disinfectant, such as in swimming pools.

chlorofluorocarbons *CFCs*

chloroform $CHCl_3$, IUPAC **trichloromethane**, boiling point 62°C. A dense liquid (1·4 g/cm³), it has found use as a solvent and one of the first modern anaesthetics. It is somewhat toxic, and this has led to its progressive disuse.

Chlorophyceae [klorohfi**y**see-ee] *green algae*

chlorophyll [**klo**rohfil] The green pigment (a magnesium-porphyrin derivative) found in plants, which absorbs radiant energy from sunlight, mainly in blue (wavelength 435–438 nm) and red (wavelength 670–680 nm) regions of the spectrum. Several variants occur, the principal ones being chlorophylls *a* and *b* in land plants, and *c* and *d* in seaweeds.

Chlorophyta [klo**ro**fita] The green algae that form zoospores or gametes having cup-shaped grass-green chloroplasts and at least two anterior flagella; classified as a phylum of the kingdom Protoctista.

chloroplast [**klo**rohplast] A specialized structure found within plant cells. It is typically biconvex in shape, and comprises stacks of membraneous discs bearing photosynthetic pigments embedded in a matrix. It contains some genetic material (DNA), and partly controls the synthesis of its own proteins.

chlorpromazine *phenothiazines*

Chobham armour *reactive armour*

chocolate and **cocoa** A foodstuff derived from the cacao bean, cultivated mainly in W Africa; it was introduced to Europe by the Spanish, who discovered its use during their conquest of Mexico. **Cocoa butter** is rich in fat, and **cocoa powder** contains a mixture of protein (25%), fat (30%), and carbohydrate (45%). **Drinking chocolate** is a blend of cocoa powder, sugar, and dried milk powder. **Milk chocolate** is produced by mixing finely ground cocoa powder with some cocoa butter, sugar, and dried milk. The USA is the world's leading processor of chocolate products.

choir The part of a church for the singers; usually part of the chancel, and separated from the nave by a screen or a rail.

Choiseul(-Amboise), Etienne François, duc de (Duke of) [shwa**zoel**] (1719–85) French statesman and minister of Louis XV, born in Lorraine, NE France. He served with credit in the Austrian Wars of Succession, and became Duc de Choiseul and foreign minister in 1758. He arranged the alliance between France and Austria against Frederick the Great (1756), and obtained good terms for France at the end of the Seven Years' War (1763). He improved the army and navy, and developed trade and industry. Madame du Barry alienated Louis from his able minister, who retired in 1770.

cholecystitis [kohlesis**tiy**tis] Acute inflammation of the gall bladder, often induced by a blockage or partial blockage of the flow of bile by gallstones. It presents with severe upper right-sided abdominal pain accompanied by vomiting and fever. To prevent recurrence the gall bladder is often removed surgically (cholecystectomy) after the inflammation has settled.

cholera [**ko**lera] An acute infection of the gastro-intestinal tract by *Vibrio cholerae*, acquired by drinking contaminated water. The bacteria cause profuse watery diarrhoea, which so depletes the body of water and electrolytes as to induce shock and death within 24–48 hours. Adequate treatment involving the replacement of body fluids can prevent death and allow a full recovery.

cholesterol [ko**les**terol] The most abundant steroid in animals, an essential component of plasma membranes, and the substance from which bile salts and the adreno-cortical and sex hormones are formed. It is ingested in the diet as a constituent of egg-yolk, meats (particularly offal), and some shellfish; transported in the blood; and synthesized in the liver, gastro-intestinal tract, and other tissues. It is implicated as a cause of atherosclerosis.

choline [**koh**leen] The most common form of the variable part of phospholipids, which play a key role in the structure of biological membranes. It is an essential component of the diet of some species, and is therefore often linked with vitamins; but it is not an essential dietary component for humans. Phospholipids containing choline are also known as *lecithin*, commonly sold in health-food shops to reduce cholesterol absorption, a feat which it does not achieve.

Chomsky, (Avram) Noam (1928–) Linguist and political activist, born in Philadelphia, Pennsylvania, USA. He studied at Pennsylvania and Harvard universities, and became professor of linguistics at the Massachusetts Institute of Technology, where he wrote *Syntactic Structures* (1957), introducing a new theory of language called transformational generative grammar. Later works include *Aspects of the Theory of Syntax* (1965), *Language and Mind* (1968), *Knowledge of Language* (1986), and *On Nature and Language* (2002). His opposition to the Vietnam War involved him in the radical movement, and in 1969 he published *American Power and the New Mandarins*, attacking politically liberal intellectuals who force their ideology on other nations.

Chongqing or **Chungking** [chungching], also **Pahsien** 31°08N 104°23E, pop (2000e) 3 486 000, administrative region 15 289 000. City in Sichuan province, SWC China; at confluence of Jialing Jiang and Yangtze Rivers; founded 12th-c; treaty port, 1891; Nationalist capital of Republic of China, 1937–46, during the Japanese war; most important industrial city in SW; airfield; railway; river transport; steel, machinery, chemicals, textiles, light industry; hot springs nearby; US–Chiang Kai-shek Criminal Acts Exhibition Hall, former prison in World War 2; Sichuan Fine Arts Academy; Chongqing Museum.

Chopin, Frédéric (François) [shohpĩ] (1810–49) Composer and pianist, born in Zelazowa Wola, C Poland, where his French father had settled. He played in public at the age of eight, and published his first work at 15. He studied at the Warsaw Conservatory under Elsner (1826–9), made his adult debut in Warsaw (1830), then visited Vienna and Paris, becoming the idol of the *Salons*. He lived with the novelist George Sand (Madame Dudevant) from 1838 until 1847, when they became estranged. Chopin wrote mainly for the piano, including 50 mazurkas, 27 études, 25 préludes, 19 nocturnes, 13 waltzes, 12 polonaises, four ballades, three impromptus, three sonatas, two piano concertos, and a funeral march. Long enfeebled by tuberculosis, he died in Paris.

Chopin, Kate [shohpin], *née* **Katherine O'Flaherty** (1851–1904) Novelist, short-story writer, and poet, born in St Louis, Missouri, USA. Educated in St Louis, she married **Oscar Chopin**, a Creole cotton trader from Louisiana, by whom she had six children. After her husband died of swamp fever (1882), she returned with her children to St Louis, where she began to compose sketches of her life, collected in *Bayou Folk* (1894) and *A Night in Acadie* (1897). This work gives no indication of the furore she aroused with the publication of a realistic novel of sexual passion, *The Awakening* (1899), which was harshly condemned by the public. Interest in her work was revived largely by Edmund Wilson, and she has since been embraced by feminists because of her concerns about the freedom of women.

chopsticks A pair of slender sticks used in several Far Eastern countries for eating food, first documented in China during the 3rd-c. Chinese chopsticks are generally round and are not pointed. Most Japanese chopsticks (*hashi*) have square sides, and when lacquered, are usually pointed. In Japan, lacquered chopsticks are normally used at home. Restaurants often provide plain wooden chopsticks in a paper wrapper, which are thrown away afterwards. Knives, forks, and spoons are used for Western food.

chorale 1 A hymn of the Lutheran church. The qualities most associated with its music – harmonic strength and a firm, regular metre – are those of Bach's harmonizations; he wrote few original hymn melodies himself. Like most other hymns, chorales are strophic, ie the same music is used for each stanza.
2 The term *chorale* is also used for a choir, especially in the USA.

chord In music, two or more notes sounded simultaneously. In tonal music of the period c.1600–1920 a chord functions as a unit in a harmonic progression related to (or diverging from) a particular key centre. Before then, chord progressions (though not the chords themselves) were largely determined by the direction of the individual melodic lines. In post-tonal music, chords have been formed on serial or other principles, without reference to a key centre.

Chordata [kaw(r)**dah**ta] or **chordates** A phylum of animals having bilateral symmetry, a stiffening rod (*notochord*) running along the back, a hollow dorsal nerve cord, a tail extending backwards beyond the anus, and gill slits. Some of these characters may be present only in the embryo. There are three subphyla: Cephalochordata (*lancelets*), Tunicata (*sea squirts* and *salps*), and Vertebrata (*vertebrates*). Vertebrates are chordates in which the dorsal nerve cord is surrounded by *vertebrae* made from cartilage or bone (includes fish, amphibians, reptiles, mammals, birds).

chordophone Any musical instrument in which the sound is produced by the vibrations of one or more strings. Chordophones form one of the main categories of instruments in the standard classification of Hornbostel and Sachs (1914). They are divided into (i) those without resonators, or with resonators that can be detached while leaving the strings in place (**simple chordophones**: piano, zither, etc), and (ii) those in which an integral resonator serves to keep the strings in place (**composite chordophones**: violin, lute, etc). Each type may be further subdivided (eg according to whether the strings are bowed, plucked, or struck); but in the perception of most people the main divisions are between those with keyboards, those with bows, and those with neither. However, some keyboard instruments (such as the organ) and some bowed instruments (such as the musical saw) are not chordophones.

chorea [koreea] Involuntary jerky movements caused by damage to the part of the brain that controls muscular co-ordination. It may occur due to genetic disease (Huntington's chorea), stroke, or in children as a complication of rheumatic fever due to streptococcal infection (Sydenham's chorea).

choreography Originally, as 'chorégraphie', the writing of dances in notation; in its current general use, the making of dances by the selection of movements for a particular dance purpose, linked together to form a whole. The maker of the dance, the **choreographer**, was barely mentioned by name before the 19th-c, the dance being simply an adjunct to the musical and dramatic act. The choreographic structure is often derived from music but can also be independent of it, based directly on the rhythm of movement. Sometimes the dance is written down in dance notation, but it is frequently passed from one generation to the next orally and by demonstration.

chorionic villus sampling [korionik viluhs] A technique for obtaining samples of placental tissue, ideally at 8–12 weeks gestation. A needle is introduced through the mother's abdominal and uterine walls under ultrasound guidance. It is advanced to the edge of the placenta, a small piece of which is removed. The tissue can be used for chromosome analysis, enzyme assay, and DNA analysis, thereby identifying the presence of Down's syndrome and such genetically-determined disorders as cystic fibrosis. The procedure carries a small risk of inducing an abortion.

chorus The collective or impersonal voice in a drama (as distinct from the individual characters), which serves to introduce and comment on the action. It was an essential feature in classical drama, but less common later (where another character often assumes this role, as with Enobarbus in Shakespeare's *Antony and Cleopatra*). However, the chorus is used by Shakespeare in *Henry V*, and by Eliot in *Murder in the Cathedral*, and is restored to a central role in the epic drama of Brecht, and other plays in this tradition.

Chouans [shooã] Peasant guerrilla bands from the W provinces of France, who rose against the Republican government in Paris (1793), opposing attempts to enforce conscription and subdue the clergy. Their name comes from the Breton word for 'screech-owl', allegedly the nickname of their leader, Jean Cottereau.

Chou dynasty *Zhou dynasty*

Chou En-lai *Zhou Enlai*

chough [chuhf] A crow-like bird, especially the **red-billed** or **Cornish chough** (*Pyrrhocorax pyrrhocorax*), native to Europe and Asia. (Family: Corvidae, 3 species.) The name is also used for the Australian **white-winged chough** (*Corcorax melanorhamphos*) in Family Corcoracidae.

chow chow or **chow** A breed of dog, developed in China before 1000 BC; heavy body with thick coat and lion-like mane; blue tongue; tail curled over back; kept in temples, and bred with stern expressions to frighten away evil spirits; introduced to Europe in the 18th-c.

Chrétien, (Joseph Jacques) Jean [kraytyen] (1934–) Canadian statesman and prime minister (1993–2003), born in Shawinigan, Quebec, SE Canada. He studied at Laval University, was called to the bar, and elected to the House of Commons as a Liberal in 1963. He has occupied a range of portfolios, including minister of state and minister of national revenue in Lester B Pearson's cabinet, and minister of finance, justice, and others in Pierre Trudeau's cabinet. Known as 'the little guy from Shawinigan', and making use of a folksy and engaging style, he was a popular politician, and an opponent of Quebec separatism. In 1990 he became leader of the Liberal Party, and prime minister when his party won the 1993 general election. He was returned to power for a second term in 1997, and again in the general election of 2000, and announced his retirement in 2003.

Chrétien de Troyes [kraytī duh trwah] (?–c.1183) Mediaeval poet, born in Troyes, NEC France. He enjoyed the patronage of Marie de Champagne, the daughter of Louis VII. His best-known works are the great metrical Arthurian romances, such as *Lancelot* and *Perceval*, which employ all the traditional ingredients of Celtic legend, and introduce into European literature the theme of the mystical Holy Grail. *Erec et Enide* (c.1160) is the earliest known Arthurian romance.

Christ *Jesus Christ*

Christadelphians [kristadelfianz] A Christian sect, founded by John Thomas (1805–71) in the USA, which teaches a return to primitive Christianity and that Christ will soon come again to establish a theocracy lasting for a millennium. Christadelphians are congregational in organization, and there are no ordained ministers. The name means 'Brothers of Christ'.

Christchurch 43°33S 172°40E, pop (2000e) 334 000. City in Canterbury, South Island, New Zealand; on the R Avon, on the E coast, NW of its port, Lyttelton Harbour; founded, 1850; airport; railway; university (1873); corn and sheep trade from the Canterbury Plains; food processing, wool, chemicals, fertilizers, furniture; Canterbury Museum, Ferrymead Historic Park, McDougall Art Gallery; scene of 1974 Commonwealth Games.

Christian X (1870–1947) King of Denmark (1912–47), born in Charlottenlund, E Denmark. During his reign, Denmark's link with Iceland was severed (1918, 1944), but North Sleswig was recovered from Germany (1920). During the German occupation (1940–5), he attracted great acclaim by remaining in Denmark, seeking with some success to save the country, without undue collaboration, from the harshest effects of occupation.

Christian, Fletcher (18th-c) Seaman and ringleader of the mutiny against Captain William Bligh on the *Bounty* in 1789, born in Cockermouth, Cumbria, NW England, UK. Educated at Cockermouth Grammar School, he declined to go to university, and joined the navy instead at the age of 18. He served with Bligh on various ships, and was selected by him as midshipman on the *Britannia* sailing to the West Indies in 1787. A close friendship developed, and Bligh appointed him as first mate on the *Bounty*. After the mutiny, Christian and eight other mutineers took refuge on Pitcairn I, where his descendents were found in 1808. In all probability, he was killed by the Tahitians.

Christian Aid A large UK-based charity supported by most Churches in Britain. It pays for development projects in the poorest countries of the world, particularly in agriculture, water supply, and health, using its own experts as advisors.

Christian art The art associated with the development of Christianity, emerging c.300 in Italy, using the formal style of late Roman art for new spiritual purposes; technically mediocre, but with a new iconography. Frescoes in the Roman catacombs, relief-sculptured panels on sarcophagi, and ivory carvings already in the 4th-c show basic motifs, such as the Good Shepherd, Jonah and the Whale, and scenes from Christ's Passion. The Crucifixion does not appear until the 5th-c. Christian manuscript illustration combined classical naturalism and oriental abstraction. The earliest panel paintings date from the 7th-c, representing the Virgin and Saints.

Christian Democratic Union *Christian Democrats*

Christian Democrats Members of Christian Democratic political parties, most of which were formed in W Europe after 1945, and which have since become a major political force. The Christian Democratic philosophy is based upon strong links with the Catholic Church and its notions of social and economic justice. It emphasizes the traditional conservative values of the family and Church, but also more progressive, liberal values such as state intervention in the economy and significant social welfare provision. Christian Democrat parties emerged to fill the vacuum created by the general disillusionment with parties of the right and left after World War 2, a major exception being the UK, which has no such party. Electorally, the most successful example was the West German Christian Democratic Union (CDU), which polled nearly 50% of the votes in 1983.

Christianity (Gr *christos* 'anointed') A world religion (with over 2 000 million adherents in 2004) centred on the life and work of Jesus of Nazareth in Israel, and developing out of Judaism. The earliest followers were Jews who, after the death and resurrection of Jesus, believed him to be the Messiah or Christ, promised by the prophets in the Old Testament, and in unique relation to God, whose Son or 'Word' (*Logos*) he was declared to be. During his life he chose 12 men as *disciples*, who formed the nucleus of the Church as a society or communion of believers, called together to worship God through Jesus Christ, Lord of history, who would come again to inaugurate the 'Kingdom of God'. The Gospel ('Good News') of Jesus was proclaimed first by word-of-mouth, but by the end of the 1st-c it was reduced to writing and accepted as authoritative scriptures of the New Testament, understood as the fulfilment of the Jewish scriptures, or Old Testament. Through the witness of the 12 earliest leaders (*Apostles*) and their successors, the Christian faith or 'Way', despite sporadic persecution, quickly spread through the Greek and Roman world, and in 315 was declared by Emperor Constantine to be the official religion of the Roman Empire. It survived the break-up of the Empire and the 'Dark Ages' through the life and witness of groups of monks in monasteries, and formed the basis of civilization in the Middle Ages in Europe.

Major divisions, separated as a result of differences in doctrine and practice, are the *Eastern* or *Orthodox Churches*, the *Roman Catholic Church*, acknowledging the Bishop of Rome as head (the *Pope*), and the *Protestant Churches* stemming from the split with the Roman Church in the 16th-c Reformation. All Christians recognize the authority of the Bible, read at public worship, which takes place at least every Sunday, the first day of the week, to celebrate the resurrection of Jesus Christ. Most Churches recognize at least two sacraments (Baptism, and the Eucharist, Mass, or Lord's Supper) as essential. The impetus to spread Christianity to the non-Christian world in missionary movements, especially in the 19th-c and 20th-c, resulted in the creation of numerically very strong Churches in the developing countries of Asia, Africa, and South America. A powerful ecumenical movement in the 20th-c, promoted by, among others, the World Council of Churches, sought to recover unity among divided Christians.

Christian Science A movement, founded by Mary Baker Eddy, which seeks to reinstate the original Christian message of salvation from all evil, including sickness and disease as well as sin. The first Church of Christ, Scientist, was established in 1879 in Boston, MA, followed in 1892 by the present worldwide organization, with its headquarters at Boston. Eddy's *Science and Health with Key to the Scriptures* (1875) and the Bible are the principal texts of the movement. They believe that God is Spirit and the good creator; accordingly, sin, sickness, death, and matter itself only seem real to mistaken human belief. Health is restored, not by recourse to medical treatment, which they decline, but by applying to all aspects of life practices in keeping with the principle of divine harmony. The internationally known newspaper, *The Christian Science Monitor*, is published by the society.

Christian Socialism A range of movements aiming to combine Christian and socialist, or collectivist, ethical principles. They attempt to promote socialism through enlisting Christ's help, and though undoctrinal in nature are most commonly found in the Protestant church. Originating in 19th-c Britain, they have since spread to Scandinavia, Switzerland, France, Germany, and the USA. The New Labour government (UK) of Tony Blair contains a number of ministers claiming to be influenced by these principles.

Christian Social Union *Christian Democrats*

Christie, Dame Agatha (Mary Clarissa), *née* **Miller** (1890–1976) Writer, born in Torquay, Devon, SE England, UK. Under the surname of her first husband (**Colonel Archibald Christie**, divorced 1928), she wrote more than 70 detective novels, featuring the Belgian detective, Hercule Poirot, or the enquiring village lady, Miss Marple. In 1930 she married archaeology professor **Max Mallowan**, with whom she travelled on several expeditions. Her play *The Mousetrap* opened in 1952, and holds the record for the longest unbroken run in a London theatre. Several of her stories have become popular films, such as *Murder on the Orient Express* (1974) and *Death on the Nile* (1978). She was made a dame in 1971.

Christie, John Reginald Halliday (1898–1953) Murderer, born in Yorkshire, N England, UK. He was hanged at London for the murder of his wife, and confessed to the murder of six other women, including the wife of **Timothy John Evans**, who lived in the same house. Evans had been convicted and hanged for the murder of his infant daughter in 1950, and also charged with his wife's murder. After a special inquiry, Evans was granted a free pardon in 1966. The trial of Christie thus played an important part in altering British legislation affecting the death penalty.

Christie, Julie (1940–) British actress, born in Chukua, Assam. She studied at the Central School of Music and Drama, London, and worked in repertory, becoming known through her role in *Billy Liar* (1963). In 1965 she won an Oscar for *Darling*. She consolidated her career with *Dr Zhivago* (1965), *Far From the Madding Crowd* (1967), and *The Go-Between* (1971). Subsequent films have highlighted her involvement with a variety of political issues, although she returned to more mainstream productions with *Heat and Dust* (1982), *Power* (1985), *Fools of Fortune* (1990), *Hamlet* (1996), *Afterglow* (1997), *The Miracle Maker* (2000, voice), and *I'm with Lucy* (2002).

Christie, Linford (1960–) Sprinter, born in Jamaica, now living in Britain. The most successful of all British athletes, and the oldest Olympic 100 m champion, in 1993 he held the World, Olympic, Commonwealth, and European Cup titles for the 100 m, achieving 9·87 seconds at the world championships in Stuttgart, Germany (a European record). He retired in 1997.

Christmas The Christian festival commemorating the birth of Jesus, observed by most branches of the Church on 25 December but by some denominations in January. The practice of celebrating Christmas on 25 December began in the Western Church early in the 4th-c; it was a Christian substitute for the pagan festival held on that date to celebrate the birth of the unconquered Sun. Many Christmas customs are of non-Christian origin; for example, Christmas trees (introduced into Britain from Germany) and holly and mistletoe decorations are of N European pagan origin, belonging to the midwinter festival of Yule. The name is often abbreviated to **Xmas**, *X* being the first letter (*chi*) of the Greek word **Christos**. The first Christmas cards were produced in the 1840s.

Christmas cactus A hybrid cactus (*Schlumbergera × buckleyi*); an epiphyte with spineless, arching stems made up of flattened, jointed segments and magenta flowers. It appears in winter. (Family: Cactaceae.)

Christmas disease *haemophilia*

Christmas Island (Kiribati) *Kiritimati*

Christmas Island (Indian Ocean) 10°25S 105°39E, pop (2000e) 2700; area 140 sq km/54 sq mi. Island in the Indian Ocean 360 km/225 mi S of Java Head and 1310 km/815 mi from Singapore; administered by Australia as an external territory; annexed by the UK, 1888; sovereignty passed to Australia, 1958; population includes Europeans, Chinese, and Malays; wet season Nov–Apr; annual rainfall c.2040 mm/80 in; main source of income (recently threatened by reduced demand) the export of rock phosphate and phosphate dust; technical school; airport.

Christmas rose A species of hellebore (*Helleborus niger*), with white flowers blooming in winter. (Family: Ranunculaceae.)

Christmas tree *Norway spruce*

Christology The orderly study of the significance of Jesus Christ for Christian faith. Traditionally, the term was restricted to the study of the person of Christ, and in particular to the way in which he is both human and divine. Latterly, an emphasis on the inseparability of Christ's person and work has meant that Christology often encompasses enquiry into his saving significance (*soteriology*) as well.

Christophe, Henry [kri**stof**] (1767–1829) Haitian revolutionary, born a slave on the island of Grenada. He joined the black insurgents on Haiti against the French (1790), and became one of their leaders, under Toussaint L'Ouverture. He was appointed resident in 1807, and despite civil war was proclaimed king in the N part of the island as Henry I in 1811. He ruled with vigour, but his avarice and cruelty led to an insurrection, and he shot himself.

Christopher, St (3rd-c) Syrian Christian martyr. According to tradition, he was a man of gigantic stature. His name in Greek (*Christophoros*) means 'Christ-bearing', which gave rise to the legend that he had carried the Christ-child across a river. He is said to have suffered martyrdom under Emperor Decius (reigned 249–251). He is the patron saint of wayfarers, and now motorists. Feast day 25 July.

Christopher, Warren M(inor) (1925–) Lawyer and government official, born in Scranton, North Dakota, USA. In 1950, he joined the Los Angeles law firm O'Melveny & Myers, and in the 1960s analysed race riots and aided international textile negotiations. Deputy attorney general (1967–9) and deputy secretary of state (1977–81), in 1989–91 he led successful US negotiations for the release of 52 hostages held in Iran. He remained a respected voice in the Democratic Party in the following years, and President Clinton appointed him secretary of state in 1993. He resigned after the 1996 election.

Christ's Hospital An independent co-educational boarding school, founded in London, UK in 1552. It is known as the **Blue Coat School**, because of the distinctive long blue coat which was worn by the boys. The school moved to Horsham, West Sussex in 1902, and in 1985 the girls' school (formerly at Hertford), was merged with the boys school. The boys still wear their traditional blue coat as part of the everyday uniform.

chromakey An image-combination process in video production where an area of strong colour in one scene is replaced ('keyed') by the picture from another source; also termed **colour separation overlay** (CSO). A typical application is a blue-backing shot.

chromaticism An attribute of music which uses notes, intervals, and chords outside the prevailing key; a note which does not belong to the diatonic scale is called a **chromatic note**. It was the move towards extremes of chromaticism in the 19th-c (eg by Wagner) that eventually led to the abandoning of tonality in the music of Schoenberg and others.

chromatids [**kroh**matidz] The two longitudinal halves into which each chromosome appears to split at cell division, which separate to become daughter chromosomes. Studying the exchange of segments between the chromatids (*sister chromatid exchange*) is useful in diagnosing some human hereditary diseases.

chromatin [**kroh**matin] The complex formed by the association of genetic material (DNA) with large numbers of different pro-

chromosome

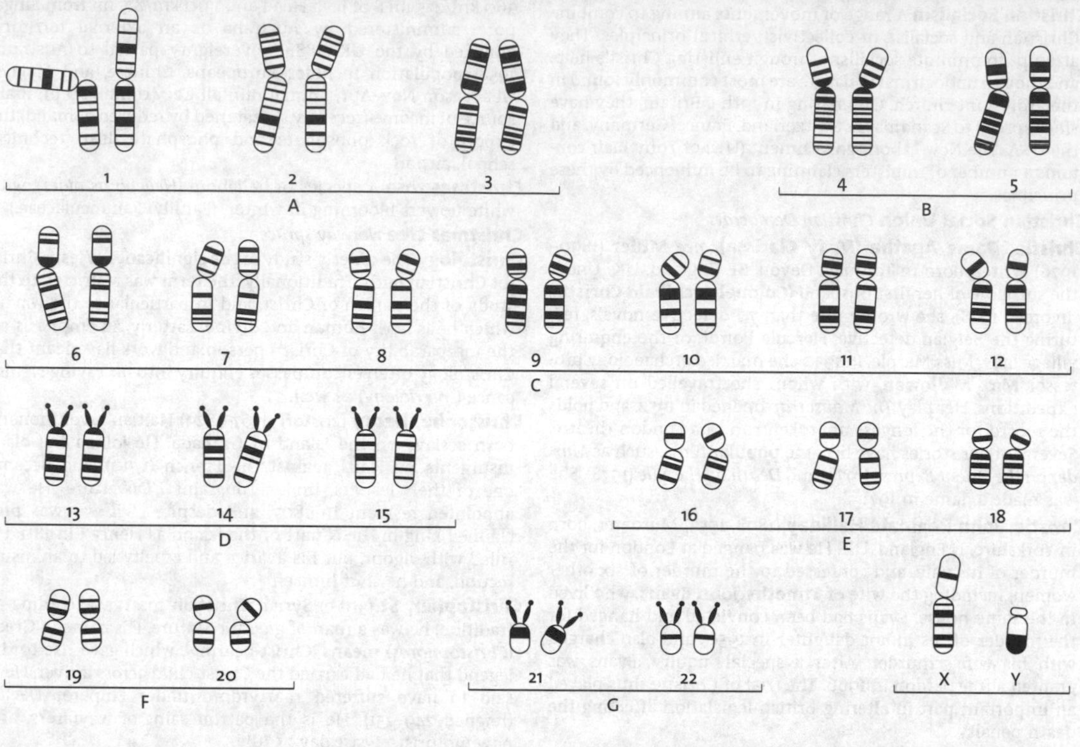

The threads within the nucleus of a cell which become visible during cell division. The chromosomes were postulated to be the carriers of inherited information in 1903, after a study of the close correspondence between their behaviour and Mendelian factors. They occur in pairs - one member of maternal and one of paternal origin. They are the major carriers of genetic material, consisting of chromatin (DNA and various types of proteins, mostly histones). The position of a particular gene on a chromosome is called its *locus*. The number of chromosomes differs from species to species. A normal human cell has 46 chromosomes: 22 pairs of autosomes together with (in females) one matching pair of X chromosomes and (in males) one nonmatching pair, the X and Y chromosomes. By the end of 2003, the genetic map of four human chromosomes (14, 20, 21, 22) had been published.

teins within the cell nucleus. The role of chromatin is to assist in the compaction of DNA to fit within the nucleus and to control the function of genes. Chromatin takes up stain, and thus can be made visible under the microscope during the process of cell division. It is organized into distinct bodies (the chromosomes). Distinctive parts of each chromosome that stain very darkly consist of **heterochromatin**; those that stain lightly, of **euchromatin**.

chromatography The separation of components of a mixture (the *mobile phase*) by passing it through another phase (the *stationary phase*), making use of the different extents to which the various components are adsorbed by the stationary phase. Many systems have been developed. One is **paper chromatography**, illustrated by the separation of the constituent dyes of an ink when it is spilled on a paper tissue. Another is **gas–liquid chromatography (GLC)**, used to separate mixtures of gases.

chromatophore [krohmatofaw(r)] A pigment-bearing cell, or structure within a cell. In many animals, chromatophores are cells containing pigment granules. By dispersing or contracting these granules, the animal is able to change colour.

chrominance The component of a video signal which determines the hue and saturation of a reproduced colour. The term is sometimes abbreviated to 'chroma'.

chromium Cr, element 24, density 7·2 g/cm^3, melting point 1857°C. A hard, lustrous metal, found combined with oxygen, especially in chromite (Cr_2FeO_4), and generally prepared as a metal by reduction of the ore with aluminium. It reacts readily with atmospheric oxygen, but, like aluminium, forms a tough oxide coat, preventing further reaction. Its principal uses are in plating and as a component of steels, to which it gives corrosion resistance. Its compounds mainly show oxidation states +3 (salts containing Cr^{3+} ions, usually coloured green or violet) or +6 (chromate or dichromate salts containing CrO_4^{2-} or $Cr_2O_7^{2-}$ ions, and coloured yellow or orange).

chromophore That part of a molecule giving rise to colour. Most chromophores in dyestuffs involve double bonds, especially conjugated ones. These lower the energy of radiation absorbed, so that visible radiation as well as ultraviolet radiation is absorbed by the compound.

chromosome *see panel*

chromosphere Part of the outer gaseous layers of the Sun (and other stars), a few thousand km deep. It is visible as a thin crescent of pinkish light during a total eclipse of the Sun.

chronic fatigue syndrome *ME syndrome*

chronicle plays Plays (from any period) based upon historical events, often using the written record as both source and structure. Marlowe and Shakespeare used Holinshed's chronicles for their plays from English history; and Hardy wrote *The Dynasts* (1904–8) after extensive research on the Napoleonic wars. Epic theatre (after Brecht) has revived this mode of drama.

Chronicles or **Paralipomenon, Books of** Two books of the Hebrew Bible/Old Testament, originally a single work, perhaps also linked with the books of Ezra and Nehemiah, thereby presenting a history of Judah from its beginnings to its restoration under Ezra and Nehemiah. It has many parallels with the Books of Samuel and Kings, but the Chronicler's interests are mainly in the Temple and its cult.

chronogram The practice of hiding a date within a series of words, by using the letters for Roman numerals (C = 100, V = 5, etc); often used on tombstones and foundation stones to mark the date of the event being commemorated. The numeral letters are usually written in capitals, eg *DoMVs* 'domus' ('house').

chrysalis *pupa*

chrysanthemum A name applied in a broad sense to various members of the family Compositae. The well-known large-flowered 'chrysanthemums' of gardens (Genus: *Dendranthema*) have a long history of cultivation, especially in China and Japan, and modern plants are derived from complex hybrids whose exact parentage is uncertain. Numerous cultivars have been developed, varying in flower colour, shape, and size, popularly grown as cut flowers and also as pot plants, often chemically treated to produce bushy, short-stemmed plants.

Chrysippus [kriysipus] (c.280–c.206 BC) Stoic philosopher, born in Soli, Cilicia. He went to Athens as a youth, and studied under Cleanthes to become the third and greatest head of the Stoa. He wrote over 700 works, of which only fragments remain.

chrysoprase [krisoprayz] The apple-green form of chalcedony.

Chrysostom, St John [krisostom] (c.347–407) Church Father, born in Antioch, S Turkey (formerly Syria). His name comes from the Greek, 'golden-mouthed', on account of his eloquence. He spent six years as a monk in the mountains, but returned in 381 to Antioch, where he was ordained, and gained a reputation as the greatest orator of the Church. In 398 he was made Archbishop of Constantinople, where he carried out many reforms, but his reproof of vices moved the Empress Eudoxia (ruled 395–404) to have him deposed and banished (403). His body was brought to Constantinople and reburied with honour in 438. Feast day 13 September.

chrysotile [krisotiyl] The fibrous form of serpentine. It is a member of the asbestos group of minerals.

Chu, Steven (1948–) Physicist, born in St Louis, Missouri, USA. He was a member of the technical staff at Bell Telephone Laboratories (1976–8) and head of the quantum electronics and research department of AT & T Bell Laboratories (1983–7) before becoming a physics professor at Stanford. He has made major contributions to laser spectroscopy, the analysis of positronium atoms, and studies of gaseous sodium at temperatures approaching absolute zero. He shared the 1997 Nobel Prize for Physics with Claude Cohen-Tannoudji and William D Phillips for work on cooling and trapping atoms with laser light.

chub Fish of European streams and rivers (*Leuciscus cephalus*), also found in lakes and in the Baltic Sea; body elongate, rather cylindrical, length up to 60 cm/2 ft; greenish-grey above, sides silver, underside white; popular as fine sport fish; a relative of orfe and dace; in the USA the term is used for a type of minnow. (Family: Cyprinidae.)

Chubb Crater A meteorite crater c.410 m/1350 ft deep in Quebec, Canada; occupied by Crater Lake, 260 m/850 ft deep; discovered in 1949 by a prospector, F W Chubb; also known as **Ungava–Quebec Crater**.

chuckwalla An iguana (*Sauromalus obesus*) from North America, found in rocky deserts; dark body with thick blunt yellow tail; no crest along back; eats plants; rests in rock crevices; if disturbed, may wedge itself in the crevice by inflating its lungs.

Chukchi or **Chuckchee** A people of NE Siberia in the Chukchi Autonomous Okrug of Russia. They were placed on collective farms during the Russian Revolution (1917), and are divided into **maritime Chukchi**, who are hunters and fishers of the Arctic and Bering Sea, and the previously nomadic **reindeer Chukchi**, who live inland and herd reindeer.

Chukchi Peninsula [chukchee], Russ **Chukotskiy Poluostrov** NE extremity of Asia, in Russia; bounded N by the Chukchi Sea, E by the Bering Strait, and S by the Anadyrskiy Zaliv gulf of the Bering Sea; rises to heights above 1000 m/3300 ft; its E point is Cape Dezhnev.

Chu-kiang *Zhu Jiang*

Chungking *Chongqing*

church *see panel*

Church, Charlotte (1986–) Soprano, born in Cardiff, S Wales, UK. She began singing lessons at age 9, and at 11 performed 'Pie Jesu' from Andrew Lloyd Webber's *Requiem* on a television talent show. The Sony Music Corporation immediately signed her to a recording contract, and she has gone on to international success. With her debut album, *Voice of an Angel* (1998), she became the youngest ever artist to make Number 1 in the UK classical charts. Later albums include *Dream A Dream* (2001) and *Enchantment* (2001). She made her acting debut in the film *I'll Be There* (2003).

Church Army An Anglican organization of volunteer lay workers, founded in 1882. Its aims are evangelical, but it concentrates on social welfare and rehabilitation work, mainly in cities.

Churcher, Betty, popular name of **Elizabeth Ann Churcher** (1931–) Arts administrator, born in Brisbane, Queensland, NE Australia. She studied in London at the Courtauld Institute and the Royal College of Art. She held a range of academic positions in Australia, wrote the award-winning book *Understanding Art* (1974), and was chairman of Australia Council's Visual Arts

church

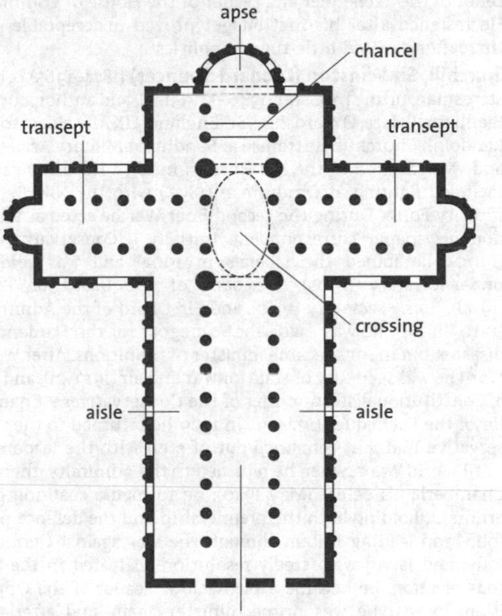

In architecture, a building used for public religious worship, especially Christian. First adapted by the early Christians from the Roman basilicas and martyrs' shrines, it was later developed in the Romanesque architecture of the 11th-c and 12th-c into the now more usual Latin cross plan, typically consisting of nave with side aisles, transepts, chancel, and apse, such as Pisa Cathedral (mainly 1063–1118) and the Panthéon (Sainte Geneviève), Paris (1757–90), architect J G Soufflot. The centrally-planned circular or Greek cross plan was briefly favoured in Renaissance Italy, such as Santa Maria della Consolazione, Todi (1508–1604). In the 20th-c, church design has become increasingly eclectic, most famously the Chapel of Notre Dame, Ronchamp, France (1950–5), architect Le Corbusier; the Roman Catholic Cathedral, Liverpool, UK (1960–7), architect Frederick Gibberd; and also in numerous smaller, usually urban churches.

Board (1983–7) and director of the Art Gallery of Western Australia (1987–9). She was director of the Australian National Gallery (1990–7), during which time the Gallery received critical praise, broke attendance records, and mounted such acclaimed exhibitions as 'The Age of Angkor', from the National Museum of Phnom Penh.

Churches of Christ A religious movement whose origins lie in the work of Thomas and Alexander Campbell and Barton Stone in the 19th-c in the USA. It preaches a restoration of New Testament Christianity, and rejects all creeds and confessions. Later there was a split which led to the Disciples of Christ being distinguished from the Churches of Christ.

Churchill, Caryl Lesley (1938–) Playwright, born in London, UK. She began writing while a student at Oxford, and her first play was *Light Shining in Buckinghamshire* (1976), about the Levellers. Her greatest commercial success has been *Serious Money* (1987), satirizing the world of city financial brokers. Other plays include *Cloud Nine* (1979), *Top Girls* (1982), *Mad Forest* (1990), *Skriker* (1994), *Blue Heart* (1997), and *A Number* (2002).

Churchill, Lord Randolph (Henry Spencer) (1849–95) British statesman, born in Blenheim Palace, Oxfordshire, SC England, UK, the third son of the 7th Duke of Marlborough, and the father of Winston Churchill. He studied at Oxford, entered parliament in 1874, and became conspicuous in 1880 as the leader of a guerrilla band of Conservatives known as the 'Fourth Party'. He was secretary for India (1885–6), and for a short while Chancellor of the Exchequer and Leader of the House of Commons. He resigned after his first budget proved unacceptable, and thereafter devoted little time to politics.

Churchill, Sir Winston (Leonard Spencer) (1874–1965) British statesman, prime minister (1940–5, 1951–5), and author, born in Blenheim Palace, Oxfordshire, SC England, UK, the eldest son of Randolph Churchill. He trained at Sandhurst Military Academy, and was gazetted to the 4th Hussars in 1895. His army career included fighting at Omdurman (1898) with the Nile Expeditionary Force. During the second Boer War he acted as a London newspaper correspondent. Initially a Conservative MP (1900), he joined the Liberals in 1904, and was colonial under-secretary (1905), President of the Board of Trade (1908), home secretary (1910), and First Lord of the Admiralty (1911). In 1915 he was made the scapegoat for the Dardanelles disaster, but in 1917 became minister of munitions. After World War 1 he was secretary of state for war and air (1919–21), and – as a 'Constitutionalist' supporter of the Conservatives – Chancellor of the Exchequer (1924–9). In 1929 he returned to the Conservative fold, but remained out of step with the leadership until World War 2, when he returned to the Admiralty; then, on Chamberlain's defeat (May 1940), he formed a coalition government, holding both the premiership and the defence portfolio, and leading Britain through the war against Germany, Italy, and Japan with steely resolution. Defeated in the July 1945 election, he became a pugnacious Leader of the Opposition. In 1951 he was prime minister again, and after 1955 remained a venerated backbencher. In his last years, he was often described as 'the greatest living Englishman'. He achieved a world reputation not only as a great strategist and inspiring war leader, but as the last of the classic orators with a supreme command of English; as a talented painter; and as a writer with an Augustan style, a great breadth of mind, and a profound sense of history. He was knighted in 1953, and was awarded the Nobel Prize for Literature the same year. He left a widow, **Clementine Ogilvy Hozier** (1885–1977), whom he had married in 1908, and who was made a life peer in 1965 for her charitable work (**Baroness Spencer-Churchill of Chartwell**).

Church of England The official state Church of England, a national Church having both Protestant and Catholic features, based on episcopal authority, and with the monarch of England formally as its head. It originated when Henry VIII broke with the Roman Catholic Church (c.1532–4) and was declared by Parliament to be 'the supreme head on earth of the English Church'. The Church remained largely Catholic in character, however, until reforms of doctrine and liturgy under Edward VI, when the new Book of Common Prayer appeared (1549, 1552), the later edition being significantly more Protestant in its features. Further revisions were made in 1604 and 1662. Under Elizabeth I the moderately Protestant set of doctrinal statements known as the 39 Articles emerged. She and James I resisted competing efforts towards a Catholic revival on the one hand and Puritan attempts to take a more Calvinist stance on the other; but under Charles I a presbyterian form of government was temporarily established until the episcopacy and Prayer Book were restored under Charles II. While a general attitude of toleration now exists, the tension of Catholic and Protestant inclinations tends to persist in the Church of England, as well as the tensions introduced by the newer influences of evangelicalism and liberalism.

The Church of England today consists of 44 dioceses in the two provinces of Canterbury and York, with over 16 000 churches and other places of worship. Local parishes are arranged into rural deaneries and dioceses, with each diocese led by a bishop and sometimes assisted by a suffragan or assistant bishop. The parish structure is fundamental to the organization of the church, but increasingly team ministries, priests-in-charge, and non-stipendiary priests have found a place in addition to parish priests and curates. The Church also supports its own missionary organizations and societies. The largest societies are the Mothers' Union and the Church Army, the latter being engaged in social welfare work.

In 1970 the General Synod was established for the purpose of reaching decisions and expressing views on issues of interest to the Church. It also appoints several committees, boards, and councils to advise it. There are over 500 members, divided between the three houses: the Houses of Clergy, of Bishops, and of Laity. It meets three times a year and is presided over by the Archbishops of Canterbury and York. In addition, there are synods of clergy and laity at diocesan level. In 1992 the General Synod voted to ordain women to priesthood – an event which took place for the first time in 1994. In 2003, the first consecration of an openly gay minister as bishop, in New Hampshire, USA, took place amid much controversy. The appointment was condemned by some Anglican leaders, who warned that the issue would lead to a split in the Church.

The Church of England has especially close relations in Britain with the Church in Wales and the Scottish Episcopal Church. The spread of Anglicanism more widely through the world (over 82 million in 2004), especially in Commonwealth countries has given the Church of England a prominent role in the Anglican Communion at large.

Church of Scotland The national Church in Scotland, founded at the Reformation of 1560 under the leadership of John Knox. It comprises a larger proportion of the population than most Protestant Churches in the English-speaking world, with a strong missionary tradition, especially in Africa and India. It maintains links with and supports many Churches in developing countries. Presbyterian in its governing organization and discipline, laymen or *elders* (ordained) play a leading part with ministers in church courts at local, congregational level (in *kirk session*), district level (*presbyteries*, overseeing congregations in a given area), and in the General Assembly. Ministers (women and men), who are ordained by presbytery, are alone authorized to administer the sacraments of baptism (of infants as well as adults) and the Lord's Supper (*communion*). Historically renowned for scholarship in Reformed theology, it has occupied a position in the world Reformed community out of proportion to its size.

Church Slavonic *Slavic languages*

Chu-teh *Zhu De*

Chuuk *Truk*

CIA *Central Intelligence Agency*

Ciano, Galeazzo, conte di (Count) **Cortellazzo** [chyahnoh] (1903–44) Italian politician, born in Livorno, W Italy, the son-in-law of Mussolini. A leading Fascist, he became minister of propaganda (1935) and of foreign affairs (1936–43), supporting his father-in-law's expansionist and war policy. He was nevertheless unenthusiastic about Mussolini's alliance with Germany, and from 1942 openly opposed it. Having participated in Mussolini's deposition (Jul 1943), in 1944 he was put on trial by Mussolini's supporters, and shot.

Cibber, Colley [siber] (1671–1757) Actor and playwright, born in London, UK. He spent most of his career at the Theatre Royal in Drury Lane. In 1696, his first comedy, *Love's Last Shift*, established his fame both as a dramatist and actor. As a manager and playwright, he greatly improved the decency of the theatre. From 1730 he was poet laureate. He is now principally remembered for his autobiography, *Apology for the Life of Mr Colley Cibber, Comedian* (1740), on account of the perceptive theatrical portraits of his contemporaries that it contains.

cicada [sikahda] A large, typically tropical insect that spends most of its long life-cycle as a nymph burrowing underground, feeding on sap from roots; adults live in trees; males typically have well-developed sound-producing organs. (Order: Homoptera. Family: Cicadidae.)

Cicero, Marcus Tullius [siseroh], also known in English as **Tully** (106–43 BC) Roman orator, statesman, and philosopher, born in Arpinum, Latium. At Rome he studied law, oratory, philosophy, and literature, and embarked upon a political career, attaining the consulship in 63 BC. He foiled Catiline's revolutionary plot, survived an attempt on his life, and persuaded the Senate to execute Catiline. He spoke against Clodius in 61 BC, and was exiled when Clodius became tribune in 58 BC. In 57 BC he was recalled by the people, but lost the esteem of both Caesar's and Pompey's factions by vacillating between the two. Living in retirement (46–44 BC), he wrote most of his chief works on rhetoric and philosophy. Cicero greatly expanded the vocabulary of the Latin language, enabling later writers to adopt a more fluent style to expound their doctrines and thought. In 43 BC he delivered his famous speeches against Antony, the so-called 'Philippics', urging the Senate to declare war on Antony. He was murdered near Caieta by Antony's soldiers as he tried to escape after the triumvirate of Antony, Lepidus, and Octavian was formed.

cichlid [siklid] Any of a large family of freshwater fishes found in South and Central America, Africa, and India; many species in African Great Lakes; body usually perch-like; feeding and breeding habits extremely diverse; important as a food fish and in the aquarium trade. (20 genera, including *Haplochromis*, *Tilapia*. Family: Cichlidae.)

CID An abbreviation of **Criminal Investigation Department**, formed in 1878 as a branch of the London Metropolitan Police, and responsible for the investigation and prevention of crime and the gathering of criminal intelligence. From its inception, the officers in the CID have operated as detectives and do not wear uniform. The CID of the Metropolitan Police is based at New Scotland Yard, and may assist other forces, but most provincial forces in Scotland, England, and Wales now have their own CIDs.

Cid, El [sid], Span [theed], popular name of **Rodrigo** or **Ruy Díaz de Vivar** (c.1043–99) Spanish hero, born in Burgos, NC Spain. A soldier of fortune in the service of both Christian and Muslim kings, he soon became known as the *Cid* (from the Moorish *Sidi*, 'lord'); *Campeador* ('warrior') is often added. He was constantly fighting from 1065, his great achievement being the capture of Valencia in 1094, which he ruled until his expulsion and death in 1099.

cider An alcoholic drink produced from the fermentation of apples, traditionally made in SW England and Normandy, France. Its alcoholic content varies widely, from 3% to 9% ethanol. Most modern ciders are artificially carbonated. In the USA, ciders are either 'sweet' (non-alcoholic) or 'hard' (containing alcohol).

Cienfuegos [syenfwaygohs] 22°10N 80°27W, pop (2000e) 132 600. Port and capital of Cienfuegos province, WC Cuba; on S coast, 337 km/209 mi SE of Havana; founded, 1819; important industrial centre; tobacco, citrus, cattle products; naval base; botanical garden, Castillo de Jagua museum (1738–45).

cigar *cigarette*

cigarette A thin roll of finely-cut tobacco, wrapped in paper, used for smoking. The origins of the cigarette lie in Central and South America, where native Indians wrapped crushed tobacco leaves in a reed or vegetable casing. Spanish explorers then introduced the practice to Europe in the form of the *cigar*. By the 16th-c, *cigarillos* ('little cigars') had emerged, re-using the tobacco found in discarded cigar butts by wrapping it in paper. *Cigarettes* (the term is French) spread throughout Europe in the following century. The first-cigarette making machine was devised by James Bonsack in the USA in 1880.

cilantro *coriander*

ciliate [siliuht] A microscopic, single-celled organism typically possessing short hair-like appendages (**cilia**) on its surface; contains two types of nucleus (macronucleus and micronucleus); commonly also with a specialized mouth region (*cytostome*); found free-living in all kinds of aquatic and terrestrial habitats, and as parasites. (Phylum: Ciliophora.)

Cilicia [siylisia, silisha] The ancient name for the S coastal part of Turkey around the Taurus Mts. It was famous for its timber and its pirates.

Cimabue [cheemabooay], originally **Cenni di Peppi** (c.1240–c.1302) Painter, born in Florence, NC Italy. He adopted traditional Byzantine forms at first, but soon turned to nature, and led the way to the naturalism of his great pupil, Giotto. He executed several important frescoes in the Church of St Francis at Assisi; these were destroyed or severely damaged in an earthquake in 1997.

Cimarosa, Domenico [cheemarohsa] (1749–1801) Composer of operas, born in Aversa, S Italy. He studied music at Naples, and produced his first opera there in 1772. He was court musician at St Petersburg (1787) and *Kapellmeister* at Vienna (1791) succeeding Salieri, where his comic opera *Il Matrimonio segreto* (1792, The Secret Marriage) was a great success, then in 1793 he returned to Naples. He wrote many other works, including church and chamber music.

cimbalom [simbalom] A kind of dulcimer, native to Hungary but found also in other E European countries. The smaller types are portable, carried on a strap round the player's shoulders. The concert cimbalom has been used as an orchestral instrument by Liszt, Kodály, Bartók, and others.

Cimbri [kimbree] A Germanic people from N Europe who migrated S towards the end of the 2nd-c BC in search of new lands. They were defeated and destroyed by the Romans (101 BC) in the Po valley.

cimetidine *H2 blockers*

Cimmerians [kimairianz] A nomadic people of S Russia who were driven out by the Scythians in the 8th-c BC. They migrated through the Caucasus Mts to Assyria and Asia Minor, where they caused widespread havoc and destruction.

Cimon [siymon] (?–449 BC) Athenian commander, the son of Miltiades, particularly prominent in the 470s and 460s BC. Active in the mopping-up operations in the Aegean after the Persian Wars, his greatest exploit was the defeat, on the same day, of the Persian land and naval forces at the R Eurymedon (c.469 BC). In politics, he was less successful. His opposition to democracy at home and support for Sparta abroad brought him into conflict with Pericles, and he was ostracized in 461 BC.

Cincinnati [sinsinatee] 39°06N 84°01W, pop (2000e) 331 300. Seat of Hamilton Co, SW Ohio, USA, on Ohio R; Fort Washington built here, 1789; city status, 1819; large numbers of German immigrants in the 1840s; airport; railway; two universities (1819, 1831); aircraft engines, vehicles, chemicals, machinery, food, metal products; several centres for culture, music, and the arts; professional teams, Reds (baseball), Bengals (football); birthplace of William Howard Taft; Taft Museum, Contemporary Arts Centre, Kings Island Park; Oktoberfest (Sep).

Cincinnatus, Lucius Quinctius [sinsinahtus] (5th-c BC) Roman statesman, farmer, and folk hero. Called from the plough and given absolute power to rescue the Roman army of the consul Minucius, which had been trapped by the Aequi (458 BC), he voluntarily gave up this power and returned to his farm, as soon as the crisis was over.

cinema At the first shows of 1895, audiences were satisfied to see single short scenes of real life in movement, but these were soon supplemented by music hall turns, fantastic trick films, and stories told in continuous action, including historical reconstruction. By 1900 cross-cutting between scenes was used, as well as close shots to establish detail. A practical syntax of film drama evolved rapidly, and by 1912 productions lasting longer than a single reel of film (12–15 min) were acceptable – the Italian *Quo Vadis* of 1913 ran for two hours. The star system of publicized named artistes was developed soon after, and by the 1920s the silent cinema was recognized as an established international medium for entertainment, instruction, and propaganda, with contributions to its art from many sources (eg from Méliès, Griffith, Eisenstein). Sound was added to motion pictures in 1927, and although the static staging of some of the first talkies was a retrograde step, technical limitations on movement were soon overcome, and directors were quick to realize the vast additional scope offered by dialogue, sound effects, and background music. Colour was available from the 1930s, but did not become universal until the late 1950s. Also in the 1950s, various forms of wide-screen presentation were introduced, and this format is now general. Despite competition, feature films made for the cinema still form a major source of popular entertainment, in the motion picture theatre, on broadcast television, over the Internet, and on videocassettes, laserdiscs, digital videodiscs, and CD-ROM in the home.

CinemaScope A system of wide-screen cinematography, based on Henri Chrétien's invention of 1927 and adopted by 20th Century Fox in 1953. An anamorphic lens on the camera produces a laterally compressed image on 35 mm film, which is expanded on projection by a similar optical system. A squeeze factor of 2:1 horizontally is used, resulting in a screened picture of aspect ratio (width:height) 2·35:1.

cinematheque, Fr 'cinémathèque' An archive of motion picture films, especially one presenting cinema classics and international, archival, and cultural productions to a public or specialized audience. The first cinémathèque was founded in Paris in 1937 by Georges Franju (1912–87), himself a documentary film director. It was expanded into a full museum where the art of film-making and film technology could be studied. Similar museums were opened in other countries, notably the National Museum of Photography (1983) in the UK.

cinematographer *camera operator*

cinematography The presentation of moving pictures as a series of photographic images recorded and reproduced in rapid succession, the eye's persistence of vision giving the impression of continuous movement. Film in continuous strips provided the material for Edison's pioneer Kinetoscope camera of 1891, but projecting the image on a screen for a large audience originated with the Lumière brothers in 1895, establishing the film production and cinema industries. Pictures were exposed in the camera at a rate of 16 per second, the film being held stationary for each exposure and then advanced one frame at a time while a shutter obscured the lens. After developing this film as a negative, a positive print was made for projection, again with an intermittent mechanism and shutter. In the late 1920s synchronized sound was added to the picture presentation, at first from separate disc records but after 1927 from a sound track on the film itself, the frame rate being increased to 24 pictures per second. Colour cinematography developed in the 1930s but did not become general for another 20 years, when various forms of wide-screen presentation in the cinema were extensively adopted.

cinéma vérité (Fr 'truth cinema') A style of film production stressing realistic documentary treatment even for fictional drama. The approach prefers non-professional actors and minimal script and rehearsal, using the mobile viewpoint of a hand-held camera and natural sound. The movement took shape in France in the 1960s; outstanding examples are Jean Rouch's *Chronique d'un été* (1961, Chronicle of a Summer) and Chris Marker's *Le joli mai* (1962). Leading American practitioners were Ricky Leacock (*Primary*, 1960) and Don Pennebaker (*Monterey Pop*, 1968).

Cinerama One of the first systems of wide-screen cinema presentation in 1952, using three synchronized projectors to cover a very large curved screen in three blended panels. Its cost and complexity limited its use to showing travelogues in specially adapted theatres, and it ceased after 1962.

cineraria A dwarf shrub growing to 60 cm/2 ft or more, native to Africa and Madagascar; stem much-branched from the base; leaves rounded, shallowly lobed, thickly white-haired beneath; flower-heads numerous, daisy-like, in dense flat-topped clusters, red to deep blue-violet. The popular garden cinerarias are derived from a related species, *Pericallis hybrida*, native to the Canary Is. (Genus: *Cineraria*, c.50 species. Family: Compositae.)

Cinna, Lucius Cornelius [**si**na] (?–84 BC) Prominent Roman politician of the turbulent 80s BC. Driven from Rome and illegally deposed while consul in 87 BC, he recaptured the city with the help of Marius amid much bloodshed, and was all-powerful there until his murder in 84 BC.

cinnabar (entomology) [**si**nabah(r)] A medium-sized, nocturnal tiger moth; forewings dark grey with carmine patches, hindwings carmine with black margins; caterpillar yellow and black, feeding on ragwort (Family: Compositae); overwinters as pupa; also called **cinnabar moth**. (Order: Lepidoptera. Family: Arctiidae.)

cinnabar (metallurgy) [**si**nabah(r)] A mineral of mercury sulphide (HgS), the chief ore of mercury. It consists of small, red, soft crystals formed in hydrothermal veins and volcanic deposits, and is used in the mineral pigment vermilion.

cinnamon A small evergreen tree (*Cinnamomum zeylanicum*) growing to 6 m/20 ft, native to SE Asia; leaves ovoid to oblong; flowers greenish; berries black. The spice is obtained from the bark of young trees. (Family: Lauraceae).

cinquefoil [**singk**foyl] The name of various species of *Potentilla*, with 5-petalled, white, yellow, or purple flowers. (Genus: *Potentilla*. Family: Rosaceae.)

Cinque Ports [singk] Originally, the five S English coast ports of Dover, Hastings, Hythe, Romney, and Sandwich, associated by royal authority (under Edward the Confessor) to provide ships for naval defence; Rye and Winchelsea were added later. They received royal privileges, including (from 1265) the right to send barons to Parliament, and charters, the first dating from 1278; they were governed by a Lord Warden who was also Constable of Dover castle. Their role declined with the growth of the navy under the Tudors and Stuarts, and the status was abolished in 1835.

CIO *American Federation of Labor*

cipher A secret way of writing; also, anything written in such a manner. The letters comprising a message in ciphers are normally either replaced by others (*substitution*) or re-ordered (*transposition*) according to a frequently changing scheme. In either case the appropriate key is needed to decipher and understand the message.

circadian rhythm [ser**kay**dian] (Lat *circa* 'about' + *dies* 'day') A biological rhythm that has a periodicity of about one day. This periodicity can be seen, for example, in the sleep cycle in animals and the growth cycles of plants.

Circassians A people from the Caucasus, speaking a NW Caucasian language, who are divided into Adyghians (Lower Circassians) and Kabardians (Upper Circassians). Most live in Russia, but there are also Circassian communities in Syria and Turkey, and small groups in Iraq, Jordan, and Israel. They are Sunni Muslims; most are farmers and pastoralists, hierarchically organized, with princes, nobles, and (until recently) also slaves.

Circe [sersee] In the *Odyssey*, an enchantress who detained Odysseus and his followers on the island of Aeaea. Her house was full of wild beasts. She transformed Odysseus's men into swine with a magic drink, but he was able to defeat her charms through the protection of the herb *moly*.

Circinus [sersinus] (Lat 'compasses') A small obscure S constellation.

circle The locus of a point that is a constant distance from a fixed point. The constant distance is called the *radius*, and the fixed point the *centre*. From this definition are obtained all the properties of the circle. Thus if *A* and *B* are two points on a circle centre *O*, triangle *OAB* is isosceles, and so the perpendicular bisector of any chord of a circle passes through the centre of the circle. By the use of two isosceles triangles, it can be proved that the angle subtended by an arc of a circle at the centre of a circle is twice the angle subtended by that arc at a point on the circumference of the circle. The area of a circle radius r is πr^2; the circumference is $2\pi r$. Archimedes c.240 BC showed that $223/71 < \pi < 22/7$.

circotherm oven An oven with a fan to circulate internal hot air. It is designed to achieve uniformity of heating and to economize in heating or cooking time.

circuit An administrative division of the judicial system of England and Wales. Each circuit has a circuit administrator and two presiding judges, one senior, one junior. It is based upon the traditional regional groupings adopted by the bar, and consists of the South-Eastern, Western, Midland and Oxford, Welsh, Northern, and North Eastern circuits. In the USA, federal and state judicial systems have similar administrative divisions, also known as circuits. In Scotland, the High Court of Justiciary operates in three circuits for trials outside Edinburgh.

circuit riders Early itinerant Methodist preachers on horseback who regularly covered a circuit of churches and also carried their messages to new settlements. They were instrumental in the rapid expansion of early Methodism.

circulation In physiology, the vertebrate system in which blood is pumped intermittently from the heart, and flows continuously around the body (**systemic circulation**) or to the lungs (**pulmonary circulation**) and back to the heart by a network of blood vessels. By means of the systemic circulation, tissues are provided with oxygen (taken up in the lungs), nutrients (absorbed from the alimentary canal), hormones, and enzymes for controlling metabolic processes and eliminating waste products (eg carbon dioxide carried to the lungs, urea to the kidneys). The pulmonary circulation is concerned with the exchange of oxygen and carbon dioxide with the environment. In mammals and birds the circulatory system also functions in body temperature regulation.

circumcision The widespread practice of removing all or part of the foreskin of the penis. The age of circumcision varies; male Jewish babies, for example, are circumcised eight days after birth, while other groups circumcise just before or at puberty as part of an initiation ceremony which marks the changing status from childhood to adulthood. In female circumcision, some or all external genitalia are removed. Circumcision may also be carried out for health reasons.

Circumcision, Feast of the A Christian festival (1 Jan) in honour of the circumcision of Jesus eight days after his birth (*Luke* 2).

circumference The boundary, or length of the boundary, of a closed curve, usually a circle. The circumference of a circle is $2\pi r$, where r is the radius of the circle. The circumference of an ellipse can be expressed only in terms of an integral.

circumpolar star A star which never sets when viewed from a particular location. In Europe and North America the stars of Ursa Minor and Ursa Major are always visible. In Australia, Crux is a circumpolar constellation.

circumstantial evidence *evidence*

circus Historically, games in ancient Rome involving horse and chariot races, gladiatorial combat, and wild animals; in modern times, a travelling show featuring animals and feats of human endurance and skill. Acts of bareback horse riding and lion taming formed the basis of early circuses, but other animals, such as chimpanzees, dogs, seals and elephants, became popular features (less so in recent years, with the growth in the animal rights movement). Human feats such as sword swallowing, fire eating, trapeze, and juggling are also common. Most have a comedy routine carried out by clowns. The modern-day circus was initiated in 1768 by trick horseback rider Philip Astley (1742–1814), who built his own 'arena' in which to display his skills. Charles Hughes built his famous *Royal Circus* in 1782, and this was the first modern-day use of the word *circus*. The most famous 19th-c circuses were Barnum and Bailey's in the USA, Astley's and Spengler's. In the 20th-c the shows of Bertram Mills, Billy Smart, and David Chipperfield were popular, though suffering a decline in recent years. European and Asian circuses, such as those of Moscow and China, continue to provide spectacular shows, and tour regularly, as does Canada's Cirque du Soleil.

Cirencester [**siy**rensester, **si**sister], ancient **Corinium Dobunorum** 51°44N 1°59W, pop (2000e) 15 700. Market town in Gloucestershire, SWC England, UK; in the Cotswolds, on the R Churn, 22 km/14 mi NW of Swindon; second largest town in Roman Britain during 2nd-c AD; electrical goods, engineering; Royal Agricultural College; 14th-c Church of St John the Baptist, Corinium museum.

cire perdue [seer perdoo] or **'lost wax' process** A technique for casting metals, mainly for sculpture. The desired shape is formed (eg in clay), and a mould is made, the inside of which is then coated in wax. The inside of the wax is coated with further heat-resisting material, giving a gap filled with wax. The wax is then melted out, leaving a hollow into which molten metal can be poured. There are variants of this process; for example, the wax shape can be perfected by the sculptor before the two moulds are re-assembled for pouring.

cirque [serk] A bowl-shaped, steep-sided hollow formed at the head of a mountain valley by the erosion of ice in glaciated regions; termed **corrie** or **cwm** in Scotland and Wales respectively. Two cirques cutting back into a ridge form an *arete*, while three or more result in pyramidal peaks such as the Matterhorn in the Alps.

cirrhosis [sirohsis] A chronic diffuse disorder of the liver, in which liver cells are destroyed and progressively replaced by scar tissue (*fibrosis*). The most common cause is long-continued excessive consumption of alcohol. Other causes include an auto-immune disorder, primary biliary cirrhosis, obstruction of the common bile duct (eg due to gallstones), and viral infections such as hepatitis B and C. It eventually leads to liver failure with jaundice, bleeding, accumulation of fluid in the peritoneal cavity within the abdomen, and eventually coma and death.

Cirripedia [siripeedia] *barnacle*

cirrocumulus clouds [sirohk**yoo**myuluhs] High-level clouds above c.5000 m/16 000 ft, composed of ice crystals. They are white in thin sheets or layers, but have the rounded appearance of cumulus clouds. Their similarity to fish markings in appearance has given them the name 'mackerel sky'. Cloud symbol: Cc.

cirrostratus clouds [sirohstratuhs] High-level stratus or layered clouds, in which there is a transition from supercooled water droplets to ice crystals. Found at altitudes above c.5000 m/16 000 ft, they are sheet-like and white/grey in colour. Their arrival precedes the warm front of a depression. Ice and water droplets in the clouds may refract light to produce a halo or ring of light. Cloud symbol: Cs.

cirrus clouds [siruhs] High-level clouds above c.5000 m/16 000 ft, composed of ice crystals. They are white and wispy in appearance, producing 'mares' tails', a hooked shape, as the wisps are elongated by strong winds in the upper atmosphere. They are an indication of the leading edge of a warm front at altitude. Cloud symbol: Ci.

CIS *Commonwealth of Independent States*

Cisalpine Gaul [sizalpiyn gawl] *Gaul*

Cisalpine Republic [sizal**piy**n] N Italian state created by Napoleon I at the Peace of Campoformio (1797), comprising Milan and Lombardy, the Valtellina, the Romagna, the Venetian territories of Brescia and Bergamo, and the Duchy of Massa Carrara. By the Treaty of Lunéville (1802), it became the Italian Republic, with Bonaparte as president.

***cis*-butenedioic acid** *maleic acid*

Ciscaucasia The N Caucasus territory of Kuban, Stavropol, Terek, and the Black Sea, formed in 1924. It existed until 1934.

Ciskei [**sis**kiy] Former independent black homeland in NE Cape province, South Africa; bounded SW by the Indian Ocean; fourth homeland to gain independence from South Africa (not recognized internationally), 1981; military takeover in bloodless coup, 1990; incorporated into Eastern Cape province in the South African Constitution of 1994.

Cisneros, Henry (Gabriel) [siz**nair**ohs] (1947–) Mayor and cabinet official, born in San Antonio, Texas, USA. As mayor of his native city (1982–90) he gained a national reptutation for being a progressive. In 1992, President Clinton named him secretary of housing and urban affairs, a post he left in 1996 to head Univision Communications, the US's dominant Spanish-language broadcaster.

Cistercians [sis**ter**shnz] A religious order formed by Benedictine monks by St Robert of Molesme in Citeaux, France, in 1098, under a strict rule, with an emphasis on solitude, poverty, and simplicity. The order was prominent in the Middle Ages, with leaders including Bernard of Clairvaux. By the 13th-c it had over 500 houses in Europe, but thereafter declined. In the 17th-c it was divided into communities of **Common Observance** (now abbreviated **SOCist**) and of **Strict Observance** (in full, the **Order of the Reformed Cistercians of the Strict Observance**, abbreviated **OCSO**). The latter were revived in France after the Revolution by *Trappists* (former members of the monastery of La Trappe). Common Observance is now prominent in the USA and parts of W Europe, with an abbot-general in Rome; Strict Observance, with a mother-house in Citeaux and an abbot in Rome, is active in France, Switzerland, England, and Poland.

citation analysis The quantitative analysis of the use of bibliographical citations in academic publications. The number of times a research study or a journal is cited by others can be interpreted as a valid indicator of its productivity and/or importance.

cithara *kithara*

Citizen's Advice Bureaux (CAB) In the UK, a national network of information offices, set up in 1939 to inform the public about the emergency wartime regulations. It has remained in operation since the end of the war to provide free and confidential information, particularly concerning the social services, housing, legal aid, consumer services, and family matters. Its 900 offices are staffed by 13 500 trained counsellors, 90% of whom are volunteers, and each office is funded by the local authority.

citizens' band (CB) radio A short-range two-way radio communication system for use by members of the public, typically consisting of a transceiver (a combined transmitter-receiver) and aerial. CB originated in the USA in the 1940s, and is particularly associated with long-distance truck drivers, who evolved a special language of codes and jargon to keep their messages from being understood by the police and public, such as *10–1* 'poor reception', *10–4* 'message understood', *smokey* 'policeman'. Many CB clubs were formed, especially in the 1970s. In the UK, the use of CB was illegal until 1981, when a special channel was authorized. The technology has now been largely replaced by cellular phones.

Citlaltépetl [seetlal**tay**petl] or **Pico de Orizaba** 19°02N 97°02W. Highest peak in Mexico, rising to 5699 m/18 697 ft in E Mexico; a dormant volcano, inactive since 1687; in the Pico de Orizaba National Park, area 197 sq km/76 sq mi, established in 1936.

citric acid cycle *Krebs cycle*

citron A citrus fruit (*Citrus medica*), 10–25 cm/4–10 in diameter; ovoid, with thick, rough, yellowish-orange rind, and green or yellow flesh. (Family: Rutaceae.)

citrus A member of a group of plants bearing distinctive juicy, acid-tasting fruits of great economic importance. The majority belong to the genus *Citrus*, but a few come from close relatives. All species are spiny evergreen shrubs or trees; ovoid, dark green, glossy leaves with an articulated joint at the junction of blade and stalk; the stalk often winged, sometimes to the extent of appearing as a second blade attached end-to-end to the first. The leaves of side shoots become modified to form spines. Flowers and fruits are borne on the tree at the same time; the fragrant flowers solitary or in small clusters in the axils of the leaves, with 4–5 sepals and 4–8 white fleshy petals. The fruit is a type of berry, in which the carpels (the familiar segments containing the seeds or pips buried in a pulpy flesh composed of specialized hair-cells) are enclosed in a thick, leathery rind. Both the foliage and rind of the fruit have numerous glands containing aromatic essential oils.

Most *Citrus* species are cultivated, along with numerous cultivars. They include well-known species such as orange, lemon, lime, grapefruit, as well as more local fruits, such as the shaddock. Citrus fruits originated in China and SE Asia, but have been cultivated in many areas since early times, and a number are of obscure parentage. They are now grown in the tropics and warm temperate regions throughout the world, mainly the Mediterranean, S USA, S Africa, and Australia, and have become a major export crop for several countries. Breeding experiments to produce improved varieties and new and exotic hybrids are common. Although many citrus fruits are grown for eating, either as fresh fruit or in marmalade and preserves, some (eg bergamot orange) are grown for their essential oils, important in the perfume industry. (Genus: *Citrus*, 12 species. Family: Rutaceae.)

cittern A plucked string instrument of great antiquity, particularly popular in the 16th–17th-c. It resembled a lute, but with a smaller, pear-shaped body, a flat (or slightly convex) back, and usually four, five, or six courses of strings played with a plectrum.

city A settlement larger than a town or village, the definition of which varies according to national conventions. In Britain the term is used of cathedral towns (eg Ely) and certain other towns upon which the title has been conferred by royal authority (eg Birmingham, 1889); in the USA it is used of those urban centres which have a particular local government structure.

City, the A square mile of C London, UK housing some of the world's major financial institutions, including the Stock Exchange, money markets, commercial and merchant banks, the insurance institutions, and commodity exchanges. An important source of overseas investment and earnings, its major rival is Wall Street in the USA. The term is also used as a collective noun to denote the major British financial institutions and their interests.

city-state *polis*

city technology college (CTC) A type of secondary school in the UK, established by the 1988 Education Act, which specializes in science and technology. It is independent of the local education authority and receives its annual grant direct from the government.

Ciudad del Este [syoodad del estay], formerly **Ciudad Presidente Stroessner** 25°32S 54°34W, pop (2000e) 144 000. Capital of Alto Paraná department, N Paraguay, on the R Paraná; centre for the construction of the Itaipú dam, the largest hydroelectric project in the world; a bridge links the city with Brazil and the town of Foz do Iguaçu; earlier named after the former President of Paraguay, and renamed after his death.

Ciudad Guayana [syoodad gwayana] 8°22N 62°37W, pop (2000e) 656 400. New city in Bolívar state, E Venezuela, on the Orinoco and Caroní Rivers; founded in 1961 to link the towns of San Félix, Puerto Ordaz, Palúa, and Matanzas; population of 1 million is planned; airfield; railway (freight); commercial port at San Félix; iron-ore loading at Puerto Ordaz; iron-ore terminal at Palúa; hydroelectric power nearby.

Ciudad Juárez [syoodad hwares] 31°42N 106°29W, pop (2000e) 960 000. Town in Chihuahua state, N Mexico; on US border, opposite El Paso, Texas, on the Río Grande; altitude 1133 m/ 3717 ft; headquarters of Benito Juárez in 1865; railway; university (1973); cotton trade.

civet A carnivorous mammal of the family Viverridae, comprising 17 (mostly Asian) species; grouped as *oriental civets, palm civets, otter civet, African civet*, and *Malagasy civet*; also known as **civet cat** or **bush dog**, but the name *civet* is often used for any member of this family. A musky extract from the glandular secretions of some species (*civettone* or *civet*) is added to perfumes to prolong their scent.

Civic Trust A charitable organization in the UK which exists to promote conservation and improvement of the environment in town and country, through encouraging high standards in architecture and planning, and the preservation of buildings of historic and architectural interest. Its concerns include urban wasteland, industrial dereliction, damage from heavy lorries, and town improvement schemes. There are separate Civic Trusts for England, Scotland, and Wales.

civil aviation *aviation*

civil defence (CD) The organization of civilian defences, able to limit damage and keep communications and production moving. It became a vital part of a nation's defences during the bombing campaigns of World War 2. In the age of nuclear weapons, however, faced with the prospect of massive casualties, Britain has largely disbanded its Civil Defence operations. Countries which maintain active organizations include Switzerland, Sweden, and the USA, where Civil Defense copes with natural disasters.

civil disobedience A political strategy adopted by M K Gandhi and his followers in India's Congress Party in 1930, in opposition to Britain's imperial rule, involving a non-violent, mass, illegal protest intended to discredit the authority of the state. The movement was banned, and many were arrested, including Gandhi; but a pact was reached in 1931, and Congress then participated in the second Round Table Conference on India's government. The strategy was later used by Martin Luther King Jr to good effect, and was a path sometimes advocated by opponents of nuclear weapons.

civil engineering A branch of engineering which deals with the design and construction of public works: buildings, bridges, tunnels, waterways, canals, streets, sewerage systems, railways, and airports. The subject includes structural, sanitary, and hydraulic engineering. Civil engineers must be familiar with the materials used in the structures and with construction equipment. They also study soils and rocks, so that they can design suitable foundations, and manufactured products such as cars, aeroplanes, and missiles. The name was first used in 1750 by the English engineer, John Smeaton (1724–94). Civil engineers nowadays are able to use the computer simulation technique of virtual reality to 'walk' around the building and 'see' how they will look before they are constructed.

civil law 1 A branch of law regulating relationships between private citizens, in contrast to criminal law, administrative law, military law, and ecclesiastical law. An aggrieved person must generally initiate proceedings personally in order to obtain a remedy. In a narrower sense, it refers to domestic law, seen in contrast with international law.

2 Civil law systems based on Roman law, such as those of continental Europe and Japan, where law is codified. The *Code Napoléon* (1804) is an influential example. The contrast here is with **common law** systems, where the emphasis is on the development of law through individual cases under a system of precedent. It was also adopted by the state of Louisiana in the USA.

civil liberties Individual freedoms that are thought to be essential to the operation of liberal democratic societies. These include freedom of speech, association, religion, conscience and movement, freedom before the law, and the right to a fair trial. In some political systems (eg the USA) the freedoms are constitutionally guaranteed in a bill of rights, while in others (eg the UK) they form part of the ordinary law.

civil list In the UK, since 1760, a payment made from public funds for the maintenance of the senior members of the royal family (except the Prince of Wales, who derives his income from the revenues of the Duchy of Cornwall). It covers the salaries of the household staff, travel, entertaining, and public engagements at home and abroad. A sum payable from the Treasury is fixed by Act of Parliament at the beginning of each reign; in exchange, the new sovereign surrenders to the Exchequer the revenues from the Crown Estates. During the reign of Queen Elizabeth II (1952–), the original sum has had to be reviewed upwards several times because of inflation. For 1991–2000 the annual sum was fixed at £10 420 000, of which £7 900 000 was intended for the Queen; for the decade to 2011, the annual sum is fixed at £8.9 million. In 1992 it was decided that only the Queen, the Queen Mother, and the Duke of Edinburgh would receive payments from the civil list. In that year the income from the Crown Estates was £113 693 000. The Queen has paid tax since 1993.

civil list pension In the UK, pensions originally paid from the sovereign's civil list, but now granted separately. They are awarded by the monarch on advice from the prime minister to persons who have given service to the Crown or public.

civil rights The rights guaranteed by the state to its citizens. It incorporates the belief that governments should not arbitrarily act to infringe these rights, and that individuals and groups, through political action, have a legitimate role in determining and influencing what constitutes them. In common usage, the term is taken to mean the rights of groups, as opposed to the rights of the individual, although there is a clear element of overlap. Women's rights, gay rights, ethnic and racial minority rights, and others are all commonly cited in this connection, but the term has come to be especially associated with movements in the USA, especially 1954–68, which aimed to secure the legal enforcement of the guarantees of racial equality contained in the 13th, 14th, and 15th Amendments to the US Constitution. Beginning as an attack on specific forms of racial segregation in the Southern states, it broadened into a massive challenge to all forms of racial subordination, and achieved considerable success, especially at the level of legal and juridical reform. It was less successful in allaying black/white economic disparity, which was the central problem outside the Southern states.

If the movement had any definite beginning, it was in the law school of the black-oriented Howard University (Washington, DC) and in the councils of the National Association for the Advancement of Colored People (NAACP). At Howard a generation of black lawyers received the training that would be vital during a long, well-planned assault against the legal structure of segregation. Among the most important was Thurgood Marshall (1908–93), who presented the argument against school segregation in the epochal Supreme Court case of *Brown* v. *Board of Education of Topeka, Kansas* (1954). Marshall would eventually become the first black justice on the court. The NAACP, founded early in the 20th-c, provided the funding and organizational support for the many cases in which the courts tested the constitutional validity of segregation statutes. Throughout the movement's history, the justices of the Supreme Court proved important allies.

The movement began at the level of law, but developed into a popular confrontation with the segregationist political and social order. The first major event (1955) was a boycott of the bus system of Montgomery, AL. It arose from a driver's victimization of Mrs Rosa Parks after she refused to yield her seat to a white, as the law required. The boycott saw the emergence to leadership of Martin Luther King Jr, who was to be the foremost black spokesman until his assassination in 1968. During his career King was denounced in the strongest terms by enemies of the movement. Now his birthday is a holiday in most States.

King had a major hand in establishing the Southern Christian Leadership Conference (SCLC). This joined in coalition with the NAACP and such other organizations as the Urban League, the Congress of Racial Equality (CORE) and the Student Non-Violent Co-ordinating Committee (SNCC). Strongly influenced by the teachings of Mahatma Gandhi, King led a campaign aimed at the desegregation of all public facilities, including schools, restaurants, stores, and transport services, and at winning the rights to vote and hold public office. Major instances included: the struggle to desegregate the schools of Little Rock, AR (1957); the 'Freedom Rides' of 1961 aimed at ending discrimination in long-distance bus transport; specific campaigns in many S cities, especially Albany, GA (1961–2), Birmingham, AL (1963), and Selma, AL (1965); and the Mississippi 'Freedom Summer' of 1964. On many occasions participants in the movement were arrested and/or injured. Some lost their lives.

The movement did benefit from growing white support, made manifest in the Freedom Rides, at the national March on Washington (1963), and in Selma and Mississippi. Whites likewise suffered arrest, injury, and death. But at all levels the driving force was the energy and anger of African-Americans, whether it was expressed in legal briefs, in strategic planning, or in direct protest. By 1965 the original goals seemed won. Court decisions, major legislation, and the actions of Presidents Eisenhower, Kennedy, and especially Johnson put the power of the federal government on the black side in the Civil Rights Act (1964) and the Voting Rights Act (1965). The result can be seen in the fact that Southern communities which were once bastions of segregation now have African-American mayors and other officials. But even as the civil rights legislation of the mid-1960s was being passed, issues were arising that proved too great to be resolved.

The new problem was the quality of life in the ghettos of the N cities, where during 1964–7 there was massive rioting in black neighbourhoods. Sometimes it was directed against the local police, and sometimes against the whole ghetto situation of poverty and permanent unemployment. The most articulate exponent of the situation was Malcolm X (1925–65, born Malcolm Little), who entered the Nation of Islam (Black Muslims) while in prison for youthful crimes. Malcolm X began his public career with wholly separatist ideas, but by the time of his assassination his position was changing towards a more inclusive attitude. Neither he, nor King, who turned his attention northward during the last three years of his life, nor anyone else succeeded in working out a strategy comparable to the winning one that had been developed in the South.

Nonetheless, considerable gains were made. New York City, Philadelphia, Chicago, and Los Angeles, have all elected African-American mayors and other public officials. Virginia has elected an African-American governor. The powerful candidature of the Rev. Jesse Jackson for the Democratic presidential nomination in 1988 demonstrated that an African-American could become a serious figure in national politics. No African-American need now endure the sort of discrimination that was written into the law until the middle of the 20th-c, though informal discrimination and social justice remain serious problems. It may fairly be said that the Civil Rights Movement ranks with the American Revolution and the era of the Civil War as one of the major formative epochs in American public life.

civil service Civilian personnel or officials employed on behalf of the state to administer central governmental policies, as distinct from the wider generality of public officials employed in such areas as local government, public corporations, and education, or as civilian staff of the armed forces. Most civil servants are permanent, in that they remain in post upon a change in government, though in some countries such as the USA and Germany a significant number of top positions do change hands. Civil services are hierarchically organized, operate according to established rules of procedure, and are accountable through ministers to the Crown or the state.

civil war *American / English / Irish / Lebanese / Russian / Spanish / Yugoslavian Civil War*

Ci-Xi or **Tz'u-hsi** [tsoe shee], **Xiaogin** or **Hsiao-ch'en**, family name **Yehonala**, known as **the Empress Dowager** (1835–1908) Chinese consort of the Xianfeng emperor (1851–62), born in Beijing, China, who rose to dominate China by manipulating the succession to the throne. She bore the Xianfeng emperor his only son, who succeeded at the age of five as the T'ung Chih emperor, but kept control even after his majority in 1873. After his death (1875), she flouted the succession laws of the imperial clan to ensure the succession of another minor, aged three, as the Guangxu emperor, and continued to assert control even when the new emperor reached maturity. In 1898 she put down the Hundred Days of Reform movement initiated by Kang Youwei, seizing the emperor and executing six of his young supporters. In 1900 she took China into war against the combined treaty powers in support of the Boxer movement. Only after her death was it possible to begin reforms.

CJD *Creutzfeldt-Jakob disease*

cladistics A method of classifying organisms employing evolutionary hypotheses as the basis for classification. It uses recency of common ancestry as the criterion for grouping species together, rather than data on apparent similarity between species.

Cladocera [kladosera] *water flea*

Clair, René, pseudonym of **René Chomette** (1898–1981) Film producer, born in Paris, France. He was a soldier, journalist, critic, and actor, before he wrote and directed his first film in 1923. He produced both silent and talking films, in France and the USA, which were noted for a light touch and whimsical irony. His major works include *Sous les toits de Paris* (1930, Under the Roofs of Paris), *The Ghost Goes West* (1935), and *It Happened Tomorrow* (1944). He returned to France in 1946, and continued to make films for nearly 20 years.

Clairvaux [klairvoh] A Cistercian abbey founded in 1115 by St Bernard near Ville-sous-la-Ferté, Champagne, NE France. The site is now occupied by a prison.

clairvoyance The gaining of information about an object or a contemporaneous external physical event by alleged paranormal means. The term **precognitive clairvoyance** is used to refer to the supposed paranormal gaining of information about an external physical source which will come into existence at some time in the future. Together with telepathy and precognition, clairvoyance makes up one of the three main categories of extrasensory perception, and as such is a major topic of current parapsychological research.

clam The common name for a variety of bivalved molluscs; includes the giant clams, soft-shelled clams, and venus clams. (Class: Pelecypoda.)

Clampitt, Amy (1920–94) Poet, born near New Providence, Iowa, USA. Raised on a farm in Iowa, she attended Columbia University but dropped out before graduating. She worked for Oxford University Press and the National Audubon Society in New York before winning a trip to England for an essay competition. It was there that she started writing poetry, her first major collection, *The Kingfisher* (1983), being immediately successful. Other collections include *What the Light was Like* (1985), *Archaic Figure* (1987), *Westward* (1990), and *A Silence Opens* (1994).

clan *descent*

Clapham Sect A movement for evangelical reform of the Church of England, active in the 1780s and 1790s; also known as **the Saints**. Its members were all Anglicans, the name deriving from the estate at Battersea Rise, Clapham, owned by English economist Henry Thornton (1760–1815), where he and his cousin William Wilberforce lived. John Venn (1759–1813), Vicar of Clapham, was also a prominent evangelical.

clapper board In motion picture production, a board or 'slate' with subject details, photographed at the beginning of each scene for identification. A hinged arm is 'clapped' to mark a synchronization point in the separate picture and sound records.

Clapton, Eric (1945–) Rock guitarist and singer, born in Ripley, Surrey, SE England, UK. In the 1960s he was in British rhythm-and-blues bands The Yardbirds and John Mayall's Bluesbreakers, then 'supergroups' Cream and Blind Faith. He has since played and recorded with most of the great names of rock music. 'Layla', recorded in 1970 with Duane Allman and others under the name of Derek and the Dominoes, is considered a rock classic by many, as are 'I Shot the Sheriff', 'Lay Down Sally', and 'Wonderful Tonight'. His album *Eric Clapton: Unplugged* reached number 3 in the UK charts in 1992, and he was voted Variety Club Best Recording Artist the same year.

Clare, Ir **An Chláir** pop (2000e) 92 000, area 3188 sq km/ 1231 sq mi. County in Munster province, W Ireland; bounded W by Atlantic Ocean and E by Slieve Aughty Mts; Cliffs of Moher on Atlantic coast; limestone outcrops at the Burren; capital, Ennis; cattle, dairy farming, fishing; 3-day folk festival at spa town of Lisdoonvarna (Jul).

Clare of Assisi, St (1194–1253) Abbess, born of a noble family in Assisi, C Italy. She gave up her possessions and joined a Benedictine convent (1212), and in 1215 founded with St Francis the order of Franciscan nuns, known as the Poor Clares. She was canonized in 1255. In 1958 she was designated patron saint of television, on the grounds that at Christmas 1252, while in her cell at the Convent of San Damiano, she both saw and heard the Mass in the Church of St Francis in Assisi. Feast day 11 August.

Clare, Anthony (Ward) (1942–) British psychiatrist and broadcaster. He studied at University College, Dublin, and London University, became registrar at St Patrick's Hospital, Dublin (1967–9), then was appointed professor in the Department of Psychological Medicine at St Bartholomew's Hospital Medical College, London (1982–8), and professor of clinical psychiatry, Trinity College, Dublin (1985–95). His many broadcasts include BBC's *In the Psychiatrist's Chair* (1982–), and among his books are *Let's Talk About Me* (1981), *Depression and How to Survive It* (1993, with Spike Milligan), *In the Psychiatrist's Chair II* (1995), and *On Men* (2000).

Clare, John (1793–1864) Poet, born in Helpston, Cambridgeshire, EC England, UK. Though almost without schooling, he began to cultivate verse writing, and his *Poems Descriptive of Rural Life* (1820) and *Shepherd's Calendar* (1827) had a good reception. Despite some patronage, he was forced to live in poverty. Pronounced insane in 1837, he spent the last 23 years of his life in an asylum at Northampton, where he wrote some of his best poetry. He is appreciated for his highly personal evocations of landscape and for his lament at the death of an earlier rural England and a vanished innocence.

Clarendon, Edward Hyde, 1st Earl of (1609–74) English statesman and historian, born near Salisbury, Wiltshire, S England, UK. He trained as a lawyer, and in 1640 became a member of the Short Parliament. At first he supported the popular party, but in 1641 became a close adviser of Charles, and headed the Royalist Opposition in the Commons until 1642. He was knighted in 1643, and made Chancellor of the Exchequer. He became High Chancellor (1658), and at the Restoration was created Baron Hyde (1660) and Earl of Clarendon (1661). In 1660 his daughter **Anne** (1638–71) secretly married the king's brother, James (later James II). Unpopular as a statesman, Clarendon irritated Cavaliers and Puritans alike, and in 1667 he fell victim to a court cabal. Impeached for high treason, he left the country for France. His major work is the *History of the Rebellion in England* (3 vols, 1704–7).

Clarendon Code A series of British Acts passed between 1661 and 1665 named after Edward Hyde, Earl of Clarendon, chief minister at the time of their passage, which re-asserted the supremacy of the Church of England after the collapse of the 'Puritan Revolution' in 1660. The most important were the Corporation Act (1661), which required all servants of the state to take communion according to the rites of the Church of England, and the Act of Uniformity (1662), which required all ministers in England and Wales to use and subscribe to the Book of Common Prayer, the Conventicle Act (1664) forbade the assembly of five or more persons for religious worship other than Anglican, the Five Mile Act (1665) forbade any nonconforming preacher or teacher to come within 5 miles (8 km) of a city or town where he had served as minister. Nonconformity was recognized as lawful, but many restrictions were placed on the activities of Nonconformists. Nearly two thousand ministers resigned rather than submit to the code.

Clarendon, Constitutions of (1164) A written declaration of rights claimed by Henry II of England in ecclesiastical affairs, with the purpose of restoring royal control over the English Church. Promulgated at Clarendon, near Salisbury, the Constitutions – especially Clause 3, which attempted to curb the growth of ecclesiastical power and threatened clerical criminals with secular penalties – brought the Archbishop of Canterbury Thomas Becket and Henry II into open conflict.

claret *wine*

clarinet A woodwind instrument, with a cylindrical bore and a single reed. It evolved from the chalumeau, a somewhat coarse-toned instrument with a single reed, two keys, and seven finger-holes, developed at the end of the 17th-c; the term *chalumeau* is still used for the clarinet's lowest register. The clarinet came into regular use as a solo and orchestral instrument in the late 18th-c, since when the major development has been the addition of the Boehm key-mechanism. It is a transposing instrument, the most common models being pitched in A or B♭. The larger **bass clarinet** (in B♭) sounds one octave lower than the standard instrument.

Clark, Alan (Kenneth McKenzie) (1928–99) British politician, military historian, and diarist. He studied at Oxford and was called to the bar in 1955. He was elected Conservative MP for Plymouth Sutton (1974–92) and brought into government by Mrs Thatcher where he held posts at employment (1983–6), trade (1986–9), and defence (1989–92). He left parliament before the 1992 general election but returned in 1997 as MP for Kensington and Chelsea. Three volumes of his diaries have been published (1994, 2000, 2002).

Clark, Helen (Elizabeth) (1950–) New Zealand politician and prime minister (1999–), born in Hamilton, New Zealand. A former lecturer in political studies at Auckland University, she became an MP in 1981, and served in Labour administrations in the 1980s. She became deputy prime minister (1989), leader of the party (1993), and New Zealand's first elected woman prime minister (1999). She won a second term in office in 2002.

Clark, Jim, popular name of **James Clark** (1936–68) Motor-racing driver, born in Kilmany, Fife, E Scotland, UK. He won his first race in 1956, becoming Scottish National Speed Champion (1958–9). After joining the Lotus team in 1960, he went on to become World Champion Racing Driver (1963, 1965), and respected by all in the industry as a gentleman. He won in all 25 Grands Prix. He was killed during a Formula Two race in Hockenheim, Germany.

Clark, Joe, popular name of **(Charles) Joseph Clark** (1939–) Canadian statesman and prime minister (1979–80), born in High River, Alberta, W Canada. At first a journalist, then professor of political science, he was elected to the Federal parliament in 1972, becoming leader of the Progressive Conservative Party (1976) and of the Opposition. In 1979 he became Canada's youngest ever prime minister. His minority government lost the general election the following year, and he was deposed as Party Leader in 1983. After 1984 he was Canada's minister for external affairs, and retired from politics to take up a post with the UN in 1993.

Clark, Kenneth (Mackenzie) Clark, Baron (1903–83) Art historian, born in London, UK. He studied at Oxford, became keeper of the Department of Fine Art in the Ashmolean Museum (1931–3), director of the National Gallery (1934–45), and professor of fine art at Oxford (1946–50). He was also chairman of the Independent Television Authority (1954–7). In addition to his acclaimed scholarly work on Leonardo da Vinci, he wrote many popular books on his subject, and became widely known through his television series *Civilisation* (1969). He was given a life peerage in 1969.

Clark, Michael (1962–) Dancer and choreographer, born in Aberdeen, NE Scotland, UK. He trained at the Royal Ballet School, and went on to dance with the Royal Ballet and Ballet Rambert (now Rambert Dance Company). After studying with Merce Cunningham in New York for a short time, he began to choreograph. While developing his own style he worked as a dancer with Karole Armitage in Paris, starting his own company, Dance Umbrella, with Ellen Van Schuylenbruch in 1984. In the 1990s he worked in the USA with Stephen Petronio before returning to Britain.

Clark, William (1770–1838) Explorer, born in Caroline Co, Virginia, USA. He joined the army in 1789, and became joint leader with Meriwether Lewis of the successful transcontinental expedition to the Pacific coast and back (1804–6). He later became superintendent of Indian affairs in Louisiana Territory, and the Governor of Missouri Territory.

Clarke, Sir Arthur C(harles) (1917–) Writer of science fiction, born in Minehead, Somerset, SW England, UK. He studied at King's College, London, and worked in scientific research before turning to fiction. He was a radar instructor in World War 2, and originated the idea of satellite communication in a scientific article in 1945. A prolific writer, his themes are exploration – in both the near and distant future – and the position of humanity in the hierarchy of the universe. His first book was *Prelude to Space* (1951), and while he is credited with some of the genre's best examples – *Rendezvous with Rama* (1973), *The Fountains of Paradise* (1979) – his name will always be associated first with *2001: a Space Odyssey* (1968) which, under the direction of Stanley Kubrick, became a highly successful film. Later works include the sequels to *2001*, *2010: Space Odyssey II* (1982, film 1984), *2062: Odyssey III* (1988), and *3001: the Final Odyssey* (1997). Other books include *The Garden of Rama* (1991) and *The Snows of Olympus* (1994). Non-fiction publications include *Arthur C Clarke's Mysterious World* (1980, also a TV series) and *Arthur C Clarke's Chronicles of the Strange and Mysterious* (1987). He emigrated to Sri Lanka in the 1950s, and was knighted in 1998.

Clarke, Jeremiah (c.1674–1707) Composer, probably born in London, UK. He studied under John Blow at the Chapel Royal, and became organist of Winchester College in 1692, and of St Paul's Cathedral three years later, following his master at the Chapel Royal in 1704. The real composer of the Trumpet Voluntary long attributed to Purcell, Clarke wrote operas, theatre music, religious and secular choral works, and music for harpsichord. He committed suicide as the result of an unhappy love affair.

Clarke, Kenneth (1940–) British statesman. He studied at Cambridge, was called to the bar in 1963, and became a Conservative MP in 1970, representing Rushcliffe, Nottinghamshire. After junior posts in the Heath administration (1971–4), he entered Margaret Thatcher's government in 1979, in 1988 was appointed secretary of state for health, then became home secretary under John Major in 1992, and Chancellor of the Exchequer (1993–7). Following the party's defeat in the 1997 general election, he stood for party leadership, but was beaten in the final ballot by William Hague. He then retired to the back benches. He entered the leadership race again in 2001 following William Hague's resignation, but was defeated by Iain Duncan Smith in the final ballot.

Clarke, Marcus (Andrew Hislop) (1846–81) Novelist, born in London, UK. The son of a London barrister, he emigrated to Australia at the age of 18, where he became a journalist. His best-known work is a story of the convict settlements, *For the Term of his Natural Life* (1874). He also wrote plays and pantomimes.

clarkia An annual native to W North America and Chile; leaves narrow to oblong; flowers in spikes, 4-petalled, white, pink, or violet; cultivated as ornamentals. (Genus: *Clarkia*, 36 species. Family: Onagraceae.)

Clarkson, Jeremy (Charles Robert) (1960–) Journalist and television presenter, born in Doncaster, S Yorkshire, N England, UK. A junior reporter on the Rotherham Advertiser (1978–83), he founded the Motoring Press Agency (1983), then joined the BBC as presenter on *Top Gear* (1989–1998) and *Jeremy Clarkson's Motorworld* (1995–). He is a regular columnist for leading newspapers and for *Top Gear* magazine, which he founded in 1993. In 1999 he hosted his own television chat show, *Clarkson*, and returned as presenter of a new-look *Top Gear* in 2002.

class A set or group of people sharing the same socio-economic position. A **class society** is a system of social inequality based on the unequal distribution of income and wealth. A person's class position is ascribed at birth via that of their parents (typically, the class income of the father), and is measured in terms of the income and wealth they enjoy. Classes can be differentiated in terms of occupational groups in a labour market, or (as in Marxism) in terms of different groups' ownership and control of property – such as the 'bourgeoisie' (the owner class) and the 'proletariat' (the non-owning working class) of capitalism.

classical architecture *Greek architecture; Neoclassicism* (art and architecture)

classical art *Greek art; Roman art*

classical literature *Greek literature; Latin literature*

classical music Music which is part of a long written tradition, which lends itself to sophisticated study and analysis in conservatories and universities, and which is heard in concert halls, opera houses, and churches (rather than in dance halls, public houses, and discotheques). The term *classical* (with a small *c*) is a popular but vague description; *Classical* (usually with a capital *C*) is best reserved for the historical period c.1770–1830, which embraces the mature works of Haydn, Mozart, Beethoven, and Schubert. These days, the distinction between classical music on the one hand and folk music, light music, jazz, pop, etc on the other is felt to be largely unnecessary, and even injurious.

classical revival A recurrent phenomenon in Western art. The major revivals occurred in the Carolingian period (8th-c), 13th-c France, 15th-c Italy, 17th-c France, and 18th-c Rome, spreading to the rest of Europe and America. This last revival is known as the **Neoclassical** movement. These periods are usually characterized by a return to the classical orders in architecture, a reaffirmation of the human figure, nude or draped, as a central motif, with proportions based on Roman sculpture, and an interest in themes from classical literature.

classicism An adherence, in any period, to the standards of Greek and Roman art, traditionally understood in terms of 'correct' proportions of the figure, dignified poses and gestures (as in Raphael, Poussin), but also powerful expression of feeling (as in Donatello, David). The French Academy in the 17th-c laid down elaborate rules, and in the mid-18th-c Winckelmann stressed the importance of 'noble simplicity and calm grandeur'. In Western art the pendulum seems to swing between 'classical' and 'non-classical' (eg Gothic, Mannerist, Baroque, Romantic), although in certain periods a tension between the two is maintained. In literature, classicism is associated especially with Latin poets such as Horace and Virgil. It implies the skilful imitation and adaptation of permanent forms and themes, rather than new departures and 'originality'.

Classics The name given to horse-racing's leading races in several countries. In England there are five Classics. The *One Thousand Guineas* is traditionally the first, run over 1 mi (1·6 km) at Newmarket; first run in 1814, it is open to fillies only. The *Two Thousand Guineas* is also early in the season, run over 1 mi (1·6 km) at Newmarket; first run in 1809, it is open to colts and fillies. *The Derby* or *Derby Stakes*, named after the 12th Earl of Derby, is run over 1½ mi (2·4 km) at Epsom Downs; first run in 1780, it is open to 3-year-old colts and fillies. The *Oaks*, named after the Epsom home of the 12th Earl of Derby, is run three days after the Derby over 1½ mi (2·4 km) at Epsom; first run in 1779, it is open to fillies only. The *St Leger* is the last Classic of the season, run over 1 mi 6 furlongs 127 yd (2 km 932 m) at Doncaster; first held in 1776, it is open to both colts and fillies. In the USA, there are three Classic races comprising the Triple Crown: the *Kentucky Derby*, run over 1¼ mi (2 km) at Louisville, KY, in May; the *Preakness Stakes*, run over 1⅜ mi (1·9 km) at Baltimore, MD, also in May; and the *Belmont Stakes*, run over 1½ mi (2·4 km) at Belmont, NY, in early June.

classification (biology) *systematics; taxonomy*

clathrate [**klath**rayt] A substance in which one type of molecule (the *guest*) is held in clefts in a matrix of the other (the *host*) without specific chemical bonding. The noble gases and some hydrocarbons form clathrates with water, occupying cavities in an open ice structure.

Claudel, Paul (Louis Charles Marie) [klohdel] (1868–1955) Catholic poet, essayist, and playwright, born in Villeneuve-sur-Fin, France. A convert at the age of 18, he joined the diplomatic service, and held posts in many parts of the world. His plays, such as *L'Annonce faite à Marie* (1912, The Annunciation to Mary) and his poetry, such as *Cinq grandes odes* (1910, Five Great Odes), are remarkable for their spiritual intensity.

Claude Lorrain [klohd], originally **Claude Gellée** (1600–82) Landscape painter, born in Chamagne, Lorraine region, NE France. He studied with various Italian painters, then settled in Rome (1627). He painted about 400 landscapes, including several with biblical or Classical themes, such as 'The Sermon on the Mount' (1656, Frick Collection, New York City). His compositions, if rather formal, are always graceful and well considered, and his colour is singularly mellow and harmonious. He also produced many drawings and etchings.

Claudianus, Claudius [**klaw**dius] (340–410) The last of the great Latin poets, born in Alexandria, N Egypt. He went to Rome in AD 395, and obtained patrician dignity by favour of Stilicho. He wrote first in Greek, then in Latin. Several of his works have survived, notably his epic poem *De raptu Proserpinae* (The Rape of Proserpine), the work for which he was famed in the Middle Ages.

Claudius [**klaw**dius], in full **Tiberius Claudius Caesar Augustus Germanicus** (10 BC–AD 54) Roman emperor (41–54), the grandson of the Empress Livia, the brother of Germanicus, and the nephew of the Emperor Tiberius. Kept in the background because of his physical disabilities, he devoted himself to historical studies, and thus survived the vicious in-fighting of the imperial house. Becoming emperor largely by accident in the chaos after Caligula's murder, he proved to be an able and progressive ruler, despite his gross and sometimes ridiculous indulgence of his wives and freedmen. Through his lavish public works and administrative reforms, he made a lasting contribution to the government of Rome and the empire, and through the annexation of Britain, Mauretania, and Thrace, a significant extension of its size. He died poisoned, it was widely believed, by his fourth wife **Agrippina**.

Claudius, Appius [**kloh**dius], nickname **Caecus** ('the blind') (4th–3rd-c BC) Aristocratic Roman statesman, general, and law-giver, the first clear-cut figure in Roman history. His fame rests primarily on his great reforming censorship (c.312–307 BC), during which he opened up the political process to the lower orders, and inaugurated a number of life-enhancing public projects at Rome, such as the building of the city's first aqueduct, the Aqua Appia, and Rome's first trunk road, the Appian Way. A fervent expansionist, he fought in many of Rome's early wars. He was regarded by the Romans as the father of Latin prose and oratory. He became blind in his old age, hence his byname.

Clause Four *New Labour*

Clausewitz, Karl (Philip Gottlieb) von [**klow**zevits] (1780–1831) General, born in Burg, EC Germany. He served with distinction in the Prussian and Russian armies, and ultimately became director of the Prussian army school, and Gneisenau's chief-of-staff. His posthumously published *Vom Kriege* (1833, On War), advocating a policy of total war, revolutionized military theory, and was extremely influential in Germany and beyond.

Clausius, Rudolf (Julius Emanuel) [**klow**zius] (1822–88) Physicist, born in Koszalin, NW Poland (formerly Köslin, Germany). He studied at Berlin, and in 1869 became professor of natural philosophy at Bonn. He worked on optics and electricity, formulated the second law of thermodynamics, and was influential in establishing thermodynamics as a science.

clavichord A keyboard instrument used from the 15th-c to the late 18th-c and revived in recent times, mainly for performing early music. The keys, when depressed, cause metal tangents to strike the strings, which run at right angles to the keys and are tuned in pairs. They are dampened at one end by means of cloth or felt. In early 'fretted' clavichords, one pair of strings served to produce several different notes depending on where the tangent struck them; in later 'unfretted' models, each key sounded only one pair of strings. The tone was slight but variable, and within its dynamic range capable of great sensitivity and nuance.

clavicle The curved bone, also known as the **collar bone**, lying almost horizontally at the base of the neck between the breastbone (*sternum*) and the shoulder blade (*scapula*); part of the pectoral girdle. It acts as a strut preventing the shoulder falling inwards and downwards – hence the position of the shoulder and upper limb when the clavicle is broken.

clawed toad An African or South American frog; claws on three hind toes; aquatic, seldom found on land; no tongue; may catch prey with its hands; most lack movable eyelids; also known as **clawed frog**. (Genera: *Xenopus*, *Hymenochirus*, or *Pseudhymenochirus*. Family: Pipidae.)

Clay, Cassius *Ali, Muhammad*

Clay, Henry (1777–1852) US statesman and orator, born in Hanover Co, Virginia, USA. The son of a Baptist preacher, he became a lawyer (1797), entered the US House of Representatives in 1811, and was chosen its speaker, a post he held for many years. He was active in bringing on the War of 1812 with Britain, and was one of the commissioners who arranged the Treaty of Ghent which ended it. In 1824, 1831, and 1844 he was an unsuccessful candidate for the presidency, and he served in the US Senate (1831–42). He made several attempts to hold the Union together in the face of the issue of slavery, for which he earned the title of 'the great pacificator'.

clay A fine grained sedimentary deposit composed mainly of clay minerals with some quartz, feldspar, and gypsum. Wet clay can be shaped into bricks, pottery, or sculpture, and when fired forms a durable solid due to the recrystallization of clay minerals into anhydrous silicates. Clay-rich soils are characteristically sticky, with poor drainage when wet, or cracked and hard when dry.

clay minerals Hydrous sheet silicates which form fine, flaky crystals, and which can absorb water, giving clay its characteristic plasticity when wet. They are formed as the product of the weathering of rocks, and are often deposited by rivers. Kaolinite, montmorillonite, and illite are important clay mineral groups. They are used as fillers for paper, rubber, and paint.

claymore (Gael 'great sword') A large, double-edged sword used by Scottish Highlanders in the 17th-c. It had a broad, flat blade, and was wielded with both hands. An 18th-c development was a single-edged broadsword with a basket hilt.

clay-pigeon shooting A pastime and sport in which clay targets are released into the air using an automatic machine. The 'clays' simulate the flight of birds, and are fired at with shotguns. It is also known as **trap shooting**.

clay tokens Small clay artifacts of several distinctive shapes, used in the Middle East since at least the 9th millennium BC as a system of accounting. Some of the symbols used on the earliest known writing tablets from the same area (c.3500 BC) show a striking resemblance in shape to those of the clay tokens.

Clayton, Lisa (1959–) Yachtswoman, born in Birmingham, West Midlands, C England, UK. In 1995 she became the first British woman to circumnavigate the globe, in a single, unaided, continuous journey. Her voyage, in a 39 ft sloop, *Spirit of Birmingham*, took 285 days.

Clayton–Bulwer Treaty (1850) A US/British agreement on the terms for building a canal across Central America; it remained in effect until 1901. The major provision was to forbid either party to exercise exclusive control or to build fortifications. The parties involved were US secretary of state John M Clayton and the British minister to Washington, Sir Henry Lytton Bulwer.

Cleanthes [kleeantheez] (c.331–232 BC) Greek Stoic philosopher, born in Assos, Troas. He studied under Zeno of Citium in Athens for 19 years and succeeded him as head of the Stoa in 262. His own contributions to Stoicism were especially in the areas of theology and cosmology, and his principal extant writing is the *Hymn to Zeus*.

Clear Grits The name given to a Radical political reform group in Upper Canada (Canada West/Ontario) in the 1850s and 1860s. The term derived from the group's attitude of uncompromising determination. It promoted major constitutional reform, including direct election to executive posts, and secularization of Clergy Reserves. After 1867 it formed the core of the Canadian Liberal Party.

clearing house In economics, any institution whose function is to co-ordinate and settle the debts owed by its various members; in particular, a place where cheques from different banks are sorted, and the amounts owed by and to each bank are calculated. Since 1984, the process has been mainly automated in the UK through the Clearing House Associated Payments System (CHAPS). Several million cheques and credit transfers are handled every day. In the USA, the equivalent organization is the Clearing House Interbank Payments System (CHIPS). Similar systems exist in many other countries.

clearwing moth A small moth in which scales are absent over much of the wings, leaving clear, transparent areas; mimics of bees and wasps; daytime fliers, flight rapid; larvae often tunnel into plant stems. (Order: Lepidoptera. Family: Sesiidae.)

cleavage The process by which a fertilized egg cell (*zygote*) divides to give rise to all the cells of an organism. In animals, cleavage results in the formation of a blastula. The animal kingdom can be divided into two major groups on the basis of cleavage pattern: the *deuterostomes*, which include vertebrates and echinoderms, with radial cleavage, and the *protostomes*, which include molluscs and arthropods, with spiral cleavage.

cleavers *goosegrass*

Cledwyn (of Penrhos), Cledwyn Hughes, Baron [kledwin] (1916–2001) British statesman, born in Holyhead, Anglesey, NW Wales, UK. He studied at the University College of Wales, Aberystwyth, and became a solicitor in 1940. Elected Labour MP for Anglesey (1951–79), he became minister of state for the Commonwealth (1964–6), secretary of state for Wales (1966–8), and minister of agriculture, fisheries and food (1968–70). He later served as leader of the Opposition in the Lords (1982–92) and Opposition spokesman on the Civil Service, foreign affairs, and Welsh affairs (1983–92). He was made a Companion of Honour in 1977, and a life peer in 1979.

Cleese, John (Marwood) [kleez] (1939–) Comic actor and writer, born in Weston-super-Mare, Somerset, SW England, UK. As a student at Cambridge he joined the Footlights Revue (1963), and began to write and perform in such television series as *The Frost Report* (1966). He joined *Monty Python's Flying Circus* (1969–74), an anarchic series that changed the face of British television humour with its inspired lunacy, surreal comedy, and animated graphics. The troupe subsequently collaborated on such films as *The Life of Brian* (1979), and *The Meaning of Life* (1983). Tall and angular, he specialized in explosive, manic eccentricity and physical humour. He enjoyed spectacular success as the co-writer and star of the series *Fawlty Towers* (1975, 1979) and the film *A Fish Called Wanda* (1988, BAFTA best actor). Later films include *Splitting Heirs* (1993), *Fierce Creatures* (1997), *The World is Not Enough* (1999), and *Isn't She Great* (2000). He also founded Video Arts Ltd, producing industrial training films, and with **Robin Skynner** (1922–2000), wrote the best-seller *Families and How to Survive Them* (1983). He married the actress **Connie Booth** in 1968 (dissolved, 1978).

cleft lip and palate A congenital abnormality of development of the lips and palate, occurring in about 1 in 1000 live births, and sometimes accompanied by other abnormalities. It consists of a fissure or cleft on one or both sides of the upper lip, occurring either alone or associated with a cleft in the palate. Cleft lip alone seldom causes feeding difficulties, but cleft palate usually results in inhalation of milk or food. The use of a special palatal teat which covers the defect during feeding is useful until surgical repair can be carried out.

Cleisthenes [kliystheneez] (6th-c BC) Prominent Athenian politician of the Alcmaeonid family, and founder of Athenian democracy. His constitutional reforms (c.508 BC) paved the way for the radical democracy established by Ephialtes and Pericles (c.461 BC).

Cleland, John [klayland] (1709–89) Novelist, born in London, UK. He studied at Westminster School, and after working and travelling abroad, published *Fanny Hill, or the Memoirs of a Woman of Pleasure* (1750). A best-seller in its time, it achieved a second *succès de scandale* on its revival and prosecution under the Obscene Publications Act in 1963. He also practised journalism and playwriting, excelling at neither, and dabbled in Celtic philology.

clematis [klemaytis] A member of a genus of woody climbers native throughout temperate regions; stems sometimes thick and liane-like; leaves pinnate, the stalk sensitive on the lower side, acting as a tendril and bending around supports on contact; flowers with four petaloid perianth-segments, styles long and feathery, aiding wind dispersal of the seeds, and giving seed-heads a white, hoary appearance. Many garden forms have brightly-coloured flowers. (Genus: *Clematis*, 250 species. Family: Ranunculaceae.)

Clemenceau, Georges [klemãsoh] (1841–1929) French statesman and prime minister (1906–9, 1917–20), born in Mouilleron-en-Pareds, France. He trained as a doctor, worked as a teacher in the USA (1865–9), then returned to France, where he became a member of the National Assembly, and in 1876 a leader of the extreme left in the Chamber of Deputies. He fought for justice for Dreyfus (1897), but as minister of the interior and prime minister (1906–9) he ruthlessly suppressed popular strikes and demonstrations. Known as 'the tiger', he presided at the Versailles Peace Conference in 1919, showing an intransigent hatred of Germany, demanding the restoration of Alsace-Lorraine to France, the acquisition of the industrial Saar basin, and the permanent separation of the Rhine left bank from Germany, in addition to financial reparations which Germany found impossible to meet. A brilliant journalist, he founded *L'Aurore*, and other papers.

Clemens, Samuel Langhorne *Twain, Mark*

Clement I, St, known as **Clemens Romanus** or **Clement of Rome** (late 1st-c) One of the apostolic Fathers of the Church, reckoned variously as the second or third successor of St Peter at Rome, possibly 88–97 or 92–101. He may have been a freedman of Jewish parentage belonging to Caesar's household. The first of two epistles attributed to him is generally accepted as his (written c.96); it is written to the Corinthian Church, and treats of social dissensions, the nature of early Christian ministry, and the resurrection. He was probably martyred. Later, several spurious works were circulated in his name, such as the *Clementine Homilies*. Feast day 23 November.

Clement V, originally **Raymond Bertrand de Got** (c.1260–1314) Bishop and pope (1305–14), born in Bordelais, SW France. He became Archbishop of Bordeaux in 1299. As pope, he suppressed the Templars, and removed the seat of the papacy to Avignon (1309), a movement disastrous to Italy.

Clement VII, originally **Robert of Geneva** (1342–94) The first antipope (1378–94) of the Great Schism. He became a cardinal (1371) and served as the legate in Italy of Pope Gregory XI. In 1378, Urban VI was elected pope but later a conclave nullified his election and chose Clement to replace him. While Urban remained at the Vatican, Clement established his papal residence at Avignon. On his death (1394) he was succeeded by antipope Benedict XIII.

Clement VII, originally **Giulio de' Medici** (1478–1534) Pope (1523–34), born in Florence, NC Italy. He allied himself with Francis I of France against the Holy Roman Emperor Charles V, was besieged by the Constable de Bourbon, and for a while became his prisoner. His indecisiveness, along with his refusal to sanction Henry VIII's divorce from Catherine of Aragon, hastened the Reformation. He was also a patron of artists and scholars.

Clement of Alexandria, St, Lat **Clemens Alexandrinus** (c.150–c.215) Theologian and Father of the early Church, probably born in Athens, Greece. He first studied philosophy, then became head of the celebrated Catechetical school in Alexandria, where he related Greek philosophical thought to Christian belief. In 203 the persecution under Severus compelled him to flee to Palestine. His most distinguished pupil was Origen. Feast day 5 December.

Clementi, Muzio [klementee] (1752–1832) Composer and pianist, born in Rome, Italy. In 1766 he was brought to England, where he conducted the Italian Opera in London (1777–80), toured as a virtuoso pianist (1781), and went into the piano-manufacturing business. He wrote the *Gradus ad Parnassum* (1817–26), on which subsequent piano methods have been based. He composed mainly piano and chamber music.

Cleon [kleeon] (?–422 BC) The first Athenian of rich, bourgeois stock to play a prominent role in 5th-c BC politics. Routinely dismissed as an upstart, demagogue, and warmonger, it was his capture of the Spartans on the island of Sphacteria (425 BC) that gave Athens her trump card in the peace negotiations of the late 420s BC.

Cleopatra VII (69–30 BC) Queen of Egypt (51–48 BC, 47–30 BC), the daughter of Ptolemy Auletes. A woman of great intelligence, she made the most of her physical charms to strengthen her own position within Egypt, and to save the country from annexation by Rome. Thus, Julius Caesar, to whom she bore a son **Caesarion**, supported her claim to the throne against her brother (47 BC), while Antony, by whom she had three children, restored to her several portions of the old Ptolemaic empire, and even gave to their joint offspring substantial areas of the Roman East (34 BC). Defeated along with Antony at Actium (31 BC), she preferred suicide to being captured and exhibited at Rome in Octavian's victory parade. The asp, which she used to cause her death, was an Egyptian symbol of royalty.

clerestory or **clear-storey** [kleerstawree] The upper part of a wall in a building with windows above adjacent roofs. The term is usually applied to windows in a church above the aisle roofs. The name is derived from French *clair*, 'light'.

clergy *abbey; archbishop; archdeacon; bishop; canon 3; cardinal* (religion)*; curate; deacon; dean; priest; rector; vicar*

Clergy Reserves A seventh of the public land in Upper and Lower Canada (Ontario and Quebec), set aside for the future use of Protestant clergy; established under the Constitutional Act (1791). In practice the Reserves became bastions of wealth and power for the predominantly Anglican elite in Upper Canada, drawing fierce criticism from Methodists and disestablishmentarians. They were secularized in 1854.

Clerk Maxwell, James *Maxwell, James*

Clermont-Ferrand [klairmõ ferã] 45°46N 3°04E, pop (2000e) 142 000. Capital of Puy-de-Dôme department, C France; capital of Auvergne, 16th-c; Clermont merged with Montferrand, 1630; railway; bishopric; university (1896); geographical and economic centre of the Massif Central; Michelin tyres, chemicals, textiles, foodstuffs; major source of mineral water; Gothic Cathedral of Notre-Dame (begun 1248), basilica of Notre-Dame-du-Port (11th–12th-c); birthplace of Pascal.

Cleveland (UK) [kleevland] pop (2000e) 567 600; area 583 sq km/225 sq mi. Former county of NE England, UK; created in 1974 from parts of Yorkshire and Durham; replaced in 1996 by Hartlepool, Redcar and Cleveland, Middlesbrough, and Stockton-on-Tees unitary authorities.

Cleveland (USA) [kleevland] 41°30N 81°42W, pop (2000e) 478 400. Seat of Cuyahoga Co, NE Ohio, USA; port on L Erie at the mouth of the Cuyahoga R; developed with the opening of the Ohio and Erie Canal, 1827; city status, 1836; largest city in Ohio; airfield; railway; three universities (1826, 1886, 1923); machinery, metals and metal products, electronics, transportation equipment; medical research centre; professional teams, Indians (baseball), Cavaliers (basketball), Browns (football); Cleveland Symphony Orchestra; Play House, Holden Arboretum, Museum of Art.

Cleveland, (Stephen) Grover (1837–1908) US statesman and the 22nd and 24th president (1885–9, 1893–7), born in Caldwell, New Jersey, USA. The son of a Presbyterian minister, he became a lawyer, Mayor of Buffalo, and in 1882 Democratic Governor of New York. In his first term as president, he strongly advised a readjustment of the tariff on various imports. In 1895 he evoked intense excitement throughout the world by applying the Monroe Doctrine to Britain's dispute with Venezuela over the frontier question with what is now Guyana. His second term was a disaster for his party because of his unpopularity arising from his response to the hard times of the 1890s.

Cleveland bay One of the oldest English breeds of horse; height, 15–16 hands/1·5–1·6 m/5–5 ft 4 in; reddish-brown with long body, shortish legs, muscular hindquarters; also known as the **Chapman horse**. Crossing with thoroughbreds in the 18th-c produced the rare *Yorkshire coach horse*.

Cleveland Way Long-distance footpath in North Yorkshire, England, UK; length c.150 km/90 mi; stretches from Helmsley to near Filey.

Clewlow, Warren (Alexander Morten) (1936–) Businessman, born in KwaZulu Natal, E South Africa. He studied at Natal University, Durban, and became a chartered accountant. Executive chairman of the Barlow Rand Group of Companies (now Barloworld), South Africa's largest industrial corporation, he is also chairman of the State President's Economic Advisory Council, and president of the South Africa Foundation. He was named 'Marketing Man of the Year' in 1988.

click beetle An elongate, usually dark-coloured beetle; an adult lying on its back can right itself with a jack-knifing movement that produces a loud click; long, cylindrical larvae live in soil, feeding on roots; can be serious crop pests, known as **wireworms**. (Order: Coleoptera. Family: Elateridae.)

click language A language in which 'click' sounds are a systematic part of the consonant system, as in such African languages as Zulu and Xhosa. Clicks are produced by an air-stream which begins at the back of the mouth, and typically involve the kind of sounds made when 'tut-tutting', or in 'gee-upping' a horse.

client-centred / centered therapy An approach developed by US psychologist Carl Rogers, sometimes referred to as **non-directive therapy**. It is based on the belief that a human being is an innately good, rational, and socialized person who continually strives to realize his/her potential (known as *self-actualization*). Psychological maladjustment is thought to occur when individuals experience situations in a way which conflicts with their self-concept. Therapy is 'non-directive', in that the therapist does not tell the client what to do, say, think, or feel. The therapist's role is to be warm, empathic, and genuine in dealing with the client, thus providing a climate of psychological safety within which clients can attempt to change their self-concept.

client/server architecture A term used in computing to describe the situation today where computers, instead of doing one task centrally as they used to do, connect with each other to carry out a task. For example, a computer program wishing to compute an employee's pay (the **client**) would ask the central personnel computer (the **server**) for the employee's details in order to work out how much should be paid.

cliff dwellings Houses of the Pueblo Indians in SW USA from the Pueblo III cultural period (AD c.1100–1300). Made with stone blocks and adobe mortar, some were several storeys high, and built in arched recesses of cliff walls. They were deserted by 1300, when people moved further S and established pueblo villages, where they still live. Some cliff dwellings are preserved, such as Cliff Palace at Mesa Verde, Colorado.

climacteric *menopause*

climate The long-term prevailing weather conditions in a region or place. There are a number of different schemes for dividing the Earth into climatic regions, the majority of which are based on a combination of indices of mean annual temperature, mean monthly temperature, annual precipitation totals, and seasonality. The climate of a place is influenced by several factors. Latitude determines the amount of solar radiation received, with the greatest in equatorial regions and the least in polar regions. Elevation affects both temperature and precipitation; mountainous areas are generally cooler and wetter. Location close to the sea or large bodies of water moderates temperature; continental areas are generally more arid and affected by greater extremes of temperature. Aspect is of local importance; in the N hemisphere, S- and W-facing slopes are warmer than N- and E-facing slopes. The scientific study of climate, describing and attempting to explain climatic differences from place to place, is known as **climatology**.

climax vegetation A botanical term for the final stage of plant succession which has developed without disturbance. Where climate is the major factor in determining vegetation, a climatic climax results. In most regions of the Earth, the climatic climax is dominated by trees: tropical rainforest in the humid tropics; deciduous woodland at temperate latitudes. Acceptance of the concept is not universal, and factors other than climate (eg soil type) may be important.

climbing perch Asiatic freshwater fish common in rivers, canals, and lakes; body length up to 25 cm/10 in; possesses special respiratory organ above gills for air breathing; able to move overland by jerky thrusts of tail fin; good food fish. (3 genera, including *Ariabas*. Family: Anabantidae.)

climbing plant A plant which reaches towards the light by clinging to neighbouring plants, walls, or other supports, sometimes referred to by the general term **vine**. Various means are used, including twining stems and leaf-stalks, tendrils, and aerial roots. **Ramblers** merely grow against and lean on their supports, but often have thorny hooks to help grip. **Lianes** have long, woody stems which reach high into the forest canopy, and are found especially in the tropics.

clingfish Small marine fish found worldwide in rocky inshore habitats of tropical to temperate seas; head triangular; body smooth, flattened on underside with large sucking disc formed from pelvic fins and used for clinging to rocks; includes *Lepadogaster lepadogaster*, the Cornish sucker. (Family: Gobiesocidae; 9 genera.)

clinical linguistics The application of linguistics to the analysis of disorders of spoken, written, or signed language. It emerged in the 1970s as an ancillary subject to speech pathology, and has since developed into a separate academic field, investigating the nature of the problems of pronunciation, grammar, vocabulary, and language use in adults and children.

clinical psychology The application of psychological knowledge to the assessment, prevention, and treatment of a variety of psychological disorders, involving behavioural, emotional, or cognitive disturbances.

clinometer A hand-held surveying instrument, also known as an **Abney level**. It is used to measure the angles of a slope by bringing a level-bubble on a graduated circle into coincidence with a wire in a sighting tube.

Clinton, Bill, popular name of **William Jefferson Clinton**, born **William Jefferson Blythe** (1946–) US statesman and 42nd president (1993–2000), born in Hope, Arkansas, USA. He studied at Georgetown University, Oxford, and Yale Law School, and was elected attorney general (1977–9), then governor of Arkansas (1979–81, 1983–93). In 1992 he became the first Democratic Party candidate to win a presidential election since 1976. He was re-elected in 1996. From the outset of his national career, he was dogged by stories of financial improprieties and sexual misconduct. Despite the efforts of two special prosecutors, charges of criminality in his Whitewater real estate investments and other ventures proved groundless. In 1998 his sexual relations with Monica Lewinsky came to light and led, along with the sexual harassment charges of Paula Jones, to his impeachment by the House of Representatives in December. A Senate trial followed, and he was acquitted of perjury and of obstruction of justice in February 1999. Despite the controversies that culminated in his impeachment, Clinton governed from the centre of American politics. His economic policies helped to produce a balanced budget, he joined Republicans in reforming the welfare system and saw a reduction of the crime rate. Sustained prosperity helped to keep his job ratings at a high level during his second term. In foreign policy, Clinton pushed for peace initiatives in Haiti, Ireland, and the Middle East. He maintained the existing policy towards Iraq, and oversaw the expansion of the North Atlantic Treaty Organization (NATO) into Eastern Europe. Few major foreign policy crises occurred during his administrations. His historical reputation will depend on how his personal life is viewed in the perspective of his political career.

Clinton, De Witt [duh wit] (1769–1828) US politician, born in Little Britain, New York, USA. He became a lawyer in 1788, sat in the New York state legislature (1797) and US Senate (1798–1802) as a Democratic–Republican, was appointed Mayor of New York City (1802), but was defeated by Madison in the presidential contest of 1812. He planned the Erie Canal scheme ('Clinton's ditch'), which he opened in 1825.

Clinton, Hillary (Rodham) (1947–) Lawyer and US first lady (1993–2000), born in Park Ridge, Illinois, USA. She graduated from Wellesley College (1969) and Yale University Law School (1973), marrying fellow law graduate Bill Clinton in 1975. She practised as a lawyer in Arkansas, gaining a national reputation for her contributions to issues of women's and children's rights and public education. She led the drive for statewide school reforms, and was twice named one of the nation's top 100 lawyers. She emerged as a dynamic and valued partner of her husband amid the allegations of extramarital affairs which surfaced during his 1992 presidential nomination campaign, and performed an active political role following his election, heading a task force on national health reform in 1993, and later focusing on children's and women's issues. Her defence of her husband during the Lewinsky affair was widely admired, and her personal political presence was greatly enhanced following her effective role supporting Democratic candidates during the mid-term elections in November 1998. In 2000 she won a senate seat representing New York state, making her the first wife of a president to seek and win national office. A volume of memoirs, *Living History*, appeared in 2003.

Clio [kliyoh] In Greek mythology, the Muse of history, and of lyre-playing.

clipper ship A mid-19th-c revolutionary US design of sailing ship. Its principal features were finer bow and stern lines, greater rake to the masts, and greater beam than in traditional vessels, resulting in faster ships with improved windward performance.

clitellum [klitelum] The saddle or swollen glandular part of the skin of earthworms and leeches. It functions during reproduction, and is responsible for the formation of the cocoon containing the eggs.

clitoris [klitoris] Part of the female external genitalia, composed of erectile tissue partly surrounded by muscle. It is the equivalent of the male penis (though it does not convey the urethra), and enlarges upon tactile stimulation. In seals and some other animals it contains a small bone (the *os clitoridis*).

Clive (of Plassey), Robert Clive, Baron (1725–74) Soldier, and administrator in India, born in Styche, Shropshire, WC England, UK. In 1743 he joined the East India Company, and took part in the campaigns against the French. In 1755 he was called to avenge the so-called Black Hole of Calcutta, and at Plassey (1757) defeated a large Indian–French force. For three years he was sole ruler of Bengal in all but name. In 1760, he returned to England, entered parliament, and was made a baron (1762). He returned to Calcutta (1765), effectively reformed the civil service, and re-established military discipline. His measures were seen as drastic, and he became the subject of a select committee enquiry upon his return to England in 1767.

cloaca [klohayka] In some species (eg reptiles, birds, but not placental mammals), the terminal region of the gut. The alimentary canal, urinary system, and reproductive system all open into the cloaca and discharge their products via a single common aperture.

clock A mechanism for measuring and indicating the passage of time, and for recording the duration of intervals. Its essential elements are a source of energy to drive the mechanism, and a device to maintain a regular (usually stepwise) rate of motion. (In the earliest mechanical clocks, the striking of bells was a primary function.) The first clockwork escapement was Chinese, AD 724, and water-powered clocks are noted in China from the 760s. In mediaeval and many later clocks, the drive was a falling weight; from the 16th-c, it was the coiled mainspring; and from the late 19th-c, it was electric current from batteries or mains. Steady rate was provided first (very inadequately) by a verge escapement (projections on a freely oscillating arm engaging intermittently in the teeth of a crown wheel); then during the 17th-c by a pendulum, the accuracy of which was increased by successive refinements and corrections (eg for temperature change). From c.1670 a balance wheel was used for small clocks and watches. In modern times, clocks are powered by electric synchronous motors maintained by the mains frequency, by a maintained tuning fork, or by the oscillation of a quartz crystal. Observatory clocks use one of two methods: (i) the constancy of the difference in energy levels of different states of the cesium atom, a beam of the atoms divided by a magnetic field forming part of an electric circuit with self-correcting feedback; (ii) the natural frequency of inversion of the pyramidal ammonia molecule, the excitation radiation of the correct frequency being locked in by a feed-back circuit.

clock paradox A phenomenon resulting from an experiment involving two identical clocks, initially together and showing the same time, one of which is carried off on a round-trip journey. Upon returning, the clock which moved will have lost time relative to the motionless clock by an amount prescribed by special relativity. Such effects have been observed using a pair of atomic clocks, one of which is flown around the world. However, a principle of relativity which claims that all observers are equal appears violated. The apparent paradox is resolved within special relativity by noticing that any clock undergoing a round-trip journey must be accelerated at some stage. The clock paradox was first discussed by Einstein (1905). It is sometimes expressed in terms of identical twin brothers, one of whom undertakes a journey and finds himself younger than his brother upon returning (the **twin paradox**).

Clodion [klodyõ], pseudonym of **Claude Michel** (1738–1814) Sculptor, born in Nancy, NE France. He was trained in Paris and Rome, where he stayed from 1762 to 1771. One of the most brilliant Rococo sculptors, he specialized in small terracottas and low reliefs of dancing nymphs and satyrs, unmistakably erotic.

cloisonné [klwazonay] A method of enamelling on metal, and occasionally ceramic, in which the different fields of colour are separated by metal wires soldered to the surface to be decorated. Principally an oriental technique, it was much used in Byzantine and Mediaeval art.

cloisters Covered walkways around an open space or court, with a colonnade or arcaded inner side and a solid outer wall. Cloisters are normally used in a monastery or convent to connect the church to other parts of the building. They are usually placed S of the nave and W of the transept.

Cloisters, the A complex in Fort Tryon Park, New York City, USA, incorporating several mediaeval structures. The Cloisters were opened as a branch of the Metropolitan Museum of Art in 1938, and house George Grey Barnard's notable collection of mediaeval art.

clone (computing) Hardware or software products manufactured by one company which completely mimic the behaviour of products originally devised by another manufacturer. It is usually cleverly designed to avoid patent and licence restrictions.

cloning (genetics) The process of asexual reproduction observed, for example, in bacteria and other unicellular micro-organisms which divide by simple fission, so that the daughter cells are genetically identical to each other and to the parent (except when mutation occurs). In higher organisms, genetically identical individuals may be produced by cloning. A body (*somatic*) cell is taken from an embryo in an early stage of development or from an adult, the nucleus transferred to an unfertilized ovum from which the nucleus has been removed, and the product grown in culture; daughter cells from the earliest divisions are removed, and grown in culture or implanted into host mothers to give genetically identical offspring. The successful cloning of a sheep (named Dolly, 1996–2003) was reported by scientists from the Roslin Institute, Edinburgh, UK, in February 1997. There is considerable potential application in animal rearing, but its application to humans is extremely unlikely (except in some rare instances of *in vitro* fertilization). The term *molecular cloning* is used in recombinant DNA technology, where a section of foreign DNA is inserted into an artificial bacterial chromosome (plasmid) and divides with it, thus 'cloning' the DNA. In 1998, a Council of Europe protocol banning the cloning of human beings was signed in Paris by 19 states – the first international treaty on the issue. However, in 1999, predictions were being made about the application of the technique in other areas, such as bone-marrow grafting in leukaemia, and transplant medicine in general, and the controversy surrounding the ethics of human cloning continued to exercise professional and public opinion.

Clonmel [klonmel], Ir **Cluain Meala** 52°21N 7°42W, pop (2000e) 15 700. Capital of Tipperary county, South Riding, Munster, S Ireland; on R Suir; centre of Irish greyhound racing and salmon fishing; railway; agricultural trade, food processing, tourism, footwear, cider.

clonorchiasis [klono(r)**kiy**asis] A disease caused by infection with *Clonorchis sinensis*, a fluke which lies in the bodies of freshwater fish in tropical climates. Affected individuals may show no symptoms, but some develop liver abscesses and cirrhosis.

Clooney, Rosemary (1928–2002) Singer, born in Kentucky, USA. She joined Tony Pastor's orchestra in 1945, singing duets with her younger sister, Betty. In 1950, she recorded a dialect song, 'Come On-a My House' and became a pop star, following it with a string of hits including 'Hey There' (1951) and 'This Ole House' (1952). She co-starred in the film *White Christmas* (1954) and for television hosted *The Rosemary Clooney Show* (1956–7). Personal problems in the aftermath of divorce from actor Jose Ferrer silenced her for almost 20 years, but she began appearing in nostalgia shows in the 1970s, and to record regularly. In 2002 she received a Grammy Award for lifetime achievement.

Clooney, George (1961–) Actor, born in Lexington, Kentucky, USA. The son of former television presenter, Nick Clooney, he studied journalism at Northern Kentucky University before heading for Los Angeles to try his luck at acting. He became well-known for his role as Dr Doug Ross in the TV series *ER* (1994–9), and his film credits include *Batman and Robin* (1997), *Wild, Wild West* (1998), *O Brother, Where Art Thou?* (2000, Best Comedy Actor Golden Globe), and *Intolerable Cruelty* (2001). In 2003 he made his directorial debut with *Confessions of a Dangerous Mind*. His aunt was singer Rosemary Clooney.

closed circuit television (CCTV) Any system of image presentation in which a video camera and its display screen are directly linked, even at a considerable distance, rather than by broadcast transmission or intermediate recording. Applications include surveillance, surgical and scientific demonstration, and industrial remote examination.

closed shop A company or works where some grades of worker are required to belong to a recognized trade union; the opposite situation is known as an **open shop**. Unions prefer the closed shop, as it gives them more members, and gives their members a better chance of getting any available jobs. They also feel that non-members benefit from agreements on pay and working conditions, and that it is unfair for them not to share in the costs of achieving them. Employers accept the closed shop for the sake of industrial peace, though they know it weakens their bargaining position in the event of an industrial dispute. Some workers resist union membership on conscientious grounds; others because they do not think the benefits of union membership are worth the subscription. Closed shops are banned in many US states.

closer settlement The name given to Australian colonial and state government laws (1894–1906) designed to settle individuals or groups of unemployed persons on small farm blocks. Based on New Zealand's example (1892), the laws provided for the re-purchase of land by the government, either by arrangement or compulsorily at a fair price, and its sale in small blocks to settlers on easy terms. The principles of closer settlement and goverment assistance for land settlement were also applied to soldier settlement schemes after both world wars.

Clostridium A genus of rod-shaped bacteria that are typically motile by means of flagella, and produce spores (*endospores*). They are widespread in the soil and in the intestinal tract of humans and other animals. The genus includes the causative agents of botulism, gas gangrene, and tetanus. (Kingdom: Monera. Family: Bacillaceae.)

clothes moth A small drab moth; larvae feed on dried organic matter, including woollen materials and fur; can be household pests. (Order: Lepidoptera. Family: Tineidae.)

Clotho *Moerae*

Clotilde or **Clotilda, St** [klohtilduh] (474–545) Queen consort of Clovis I, king of the Franks, and daughter of Chilperic, king of Burgundy. She married in 493, and after Clovis's death lived a life of austerity and good works at the Abbey of St Martin at Tours. Feast day 3 June.

cloud A visible collection of particles of ice and water held in suspension above the ground. Clouds form when air becomes saturated and water vapour condenses around nuclei of dust, smoke particles, and salt. Four main categories of clouds are recognized: **nimbus clouds**, which produce rain; **stratus clouds**, which resemble layers; **cumulus clouds**, which resemble heaps; and **cirrus clouds**, which resemble strands or filaments of hair. These names are further modified by an indication of cloud height: *strato* – low level clouds; *alto* – middle level clouds; *cirro* – high level clouds. Fog can be considered as cloud close to ground level.

cloud chamber A device for detecting subatomic particles; invented by Charles Wilson in 1912. It comprises a chamber containing vapour prone to condensing to liquid. The passage of particles forms ions, which act as centres for condensation, and the particle paths become visible as trails of mist. The cloud chamber was important in the early days of radioactivity, but has been superseded by other particle detectors.

clouded leopard A member of the cat family (*Neofelis nebulosa*), native to SE Asia; has the longest canine teeth of any living cat; coat with large brown blotches separated by thin yellow lines; inhabits forest; may leap on prey from trees; eats birds, monkeys, pigs, and grazing animals.

clouded tiger *tortoiseshell cat*

Clough, Arthur Hugh [kluhf] (1819–61) Poet, born in Liverpool, Merseyside, NW England, UK. He studied at Rugby and Oxford, travelled in Europe, and espoused progressive social views. Experimental techniques in his long poem *The Bothie* (1848), and the ironic narrative *Amours de Voyage* (1849), have influenced modern poets. His best-known poem, beginning 'Say not the struggle nought availeth', was published posthumously in 1862.

clover A low-growing annual or perennial, occurring in both temperate and subtropical regions, but mainly in the N hemisphere; leaves with three toothed leaflets; small pea-flowers, white, pink, or red, clustered into often dense, rounded heads; pods small, remaining enclosed by the calyx. The flowers are visited by hive bees, providing an important source of nectar for bee-keepers. Several species are extensively grown as fodder for cattle, and they are also valuable pasture plants, often grown with grasses, enriching the soil through the presence of nitrogen-fixing bacteria in small nodules on the root system. Yellow-flowered species are generally called **trefoils**. (Genus: *Trifolium*, 250 species. Family: Leguminosae.)

clove tree An evergreen tree (*Syzygium aromaticum*) growing to 12 m/40 ft, native to Indonesia but cultivated elsewhere; leaves lance-shaped; flowers yellow, 4-petalled, in terminal clusters. The flower buds are dried to form the spice cloves. (Family: Myrtaceae.)

Clovis [klohvis] The earliest identifiable Indian culture of North America – hunter-gatherers exploiting the mammoth herds of the plains towards the end of the last glaciation, c.10 000–9000 BC. It is characterized archaeologically by bifacially-flaked spear points found across the USA, notably near Clovis, New Mexico, in 1963.

Clovis I [klohvis], Ger **Chlodwig** or **Chlodovech** (c.465–511) Merovingian king, who succeeded his father, Childeric (481), as king of the Franks. He overthrew the Gallo-Romans, and took possession of the whole country between the Somme and the Loire by 496. In 493 he married (St) **Clotilde**, and was converted to Christianity along with several thousand warriors after routing the Alemanni. In 507, he defeated the Visigoth, Alaric II, captured Bordeaux and Toulouse, but was checked at Arles by the Ostrogoth, Theodoric. He then took up residence in Paris.

clown An archetypal comic figure (part anti-social trickster, part clumsy innocent child) found as a popular entertainer in diverse cultures. A long and varied tradition of professional exponents in European theatre has created such distinct clowns as *Pickleherring*, *Hanswurst*, *Harlequin*, *Pierrot*, *Auguste*, and *Joey*. When Grimaldi was creating *Joey*, he was shaping both a unique figure and a specific tradition of clowning that in Tudor times had been much influenced by the cognate figure of the court fool. The hallmark of the 17th-c clowns was a costume of oversized shoes, waistcoats, pointed hats, and giant neck ruffs. The white-faced clown is said to have been introduced in France. In the 1860s a clown under the name of Auguste introduced the red nose, exaggerated eyebrows, and tuffs of hair.

cloze testing A test widely used in foreign language teaching to establish a learner's comprehension of a reading passage. The passage is presented with words omitted at regular intervals: the reader must try to supply the missing words, or plausible substitutes.

club An establishment where people associate to pursue social, political, or sporting activities. In the US, country clubs and women's clubs are well-established. In London, clubs for men developed in the 17th-c from the taverns and coffee houses where men met to do business. These clubs (Whites, founded 1693, Boodles 1767, Brooks's 1764, Portland 1816, Athenaeum 1824, Garrick 1831, Carlton 1832, Reform 1836, Savages 1857, Press 1882, Royal Automobile 1897) were used by members of the aristocratic and professional classes, and excluded women. Some have relaxed their rules; most continue to provide meals, library facilities, and overnight accommodation.

club foot A congenital deformity of one or both feet, in which the child cannot stand on the sole of the affected foot (technically called **talipes** [**tal**ipeez]. The sole of the foot is turned inwards. The deformity is readily seen at birth, and cannot be manipulated, but improvement may be achieved by the application of a series of graded splints, or in severe cases by surgical operation.

clubmoss A spore-bearing plant related to ferns and horsetails; stem long, regularly branched, clothed with numerous small leaves; sporangia in leaf-axils, often arranged in a terminal, cone-like strobilus. It is found almost everywhere, many in heathland or similar habitats. Clubmoss, selaginella, and quillwort form the only living members of an ancient group, the *Lycopsida*. Formerly much more diverse, especially during the Carboniferous period, its fossils include giant tree-forms. (Genus: *Lycopodium*, 450 species. Family: Lycopodiaceae.)

clubroot A disease of cabbage-family plants (the Brassicaceae) that causes gall-like swellings of roots and discoloration of leaves; caused by the parasitic slime mould *Plasmodiophora brassicae*.

Cluj-Napoca or **Cluj** [kloozh napoka], Ger **Klausenburg** 46°47N 23°37E, pop (2000e) 323 000. Capital of Cluj county, NEC Romania, on the R Someș; founded on the site of a former Roman colony, 12th-c; a former capital of Transylvania; ceded from Hungary, 1920; chief cultural and religious centre of Transylvania since the 16th-c; airfield; railway; university (1872), technical university (1948); electrical equipment, metallurgy, chemicals, machinery, textiles, footwear; St Michael Church, Austrian fort, Franciscan monastery, botanical gardens; winter sports facilities nearby.

Clune, Frank [kloon], popular name of **Francis Patrick Clune** (1893–1971) Writer of biography, history, and travel, born in Sydney, New South Wales, SE Australia. His early life was one of travel and adventure at sea. He served with the Australian Imperial Forces in World War 1, and was wounded at Gallipoli. At the age of 40 he decided to write the story of his early years, published as *Try Anything Once* (1933). He wrote over 60 books, often in collaboration with P R ('Inky') Stephensen, and was one of Australia's best-selling writers. Stories such as *Ben Hall the Bushranger* (1947), and *Wild Colonial Boys* (1948) aroused interest in Australian history.

Cluny Abbey [klúnee] A Benedictine abbey founded in 910 at Cluny, EC France, known for the monastic reforms it introduced, promoting a stricter observance of the Benedictine rule. The basilica of St Peter and St Paul (11th–12th-c) was the largest church in the world at the time. The abbey was forced to close in 1790, during the French Revolution.

Clurman, Harold (Edgar) [kloorman] (1901–80) Theatre director and critic, born in New York City, USA. He was playreader for the Theater Guild (1929–31), co-founder of the Group Theater (1931–40), and one of its directors. His book *The Fervent Years* (1946) is a history of the Group. He later worked as a director in Hollywood and on Broadway. An influential drama critic, his writings include *Lies Like Truths* (1958) and *The Divine Pastime* (1974).

clustered wax flower *stephanotis; wax plant*

Cluster project A space project undertaken by the European Space Agency (ESA), launching in 2000 after the destruction of the original Cluster spacecraft on the first Ariane 5 launch in 1996. Four identical satellites are designed to study the interaction of the solar wind and the Earth's magnetic field. Two launches, each carrying two spacecraft, were carried out by Russian Soyuz rockets from Baikonur Cosmodrome in Kazakhstan. They were inserted into highly elliptical polar orbits which vary from 25 500–125 000 km/16 000–78 000 mi above the Earth. The spacecraft fly in formation to provide the first three-dimensional study of the interaction between the solar wind and Earth's magnetosphere.

clutch A mechanical device that allows an engine to be connected and disconnected from its load while the engine is running. A clutch is necessary when the power characteristics of an engine's output do not match naturally the power characteristics of the load. In such cases a gearbox has to be interposed between engine and load, together with a clutch, to allow the engine to be disconnected and a new gear to be substituted. The most common application of a clutch is in the motor car, where normally a plate covered with high friction material is sandwiched and held in place between a disc attached to the engine's flywheel and a disc fixed to the gear-box.

Clutha, River [klootha] Longest river of South Island, New Zealand; rises in L Wanaka, W South Island, and flows SE to enter the Pacific near Kaitangata; length from its source, the Makarora R, c.320 km/200 mi; major hydroelectric schemes near Alexandra.

cluttering A disorder of speech fluency, in which the main symptom is excessive rapidity while speaking. Clutterers seem unable to control their speech rate, and as a result introduce disturbances of rhythm and articulation into their speech, with sounds becoming displaced, mispronounced, or omitted, and syllables telescoping into each other. The cause is unknown, though a physical explanation in terms of the brain's motor control of speech has been suggested.

Clwyd [klooid] pop (2000e) 422 200; area 2426 sq km/937 sq mi. Former county in NE Wales, UK; created in 1974, and replaced in 1996 by the counties of Denbighshire, Flintshire, and Wrexham.

Clyde, Lord *Campbell, Sir Colin*

Clyde, River River in S Scotland, UK; main headstream, Daer Water, rises in the Southern Uplands, and flows generally N and NW; waterfalls near Lanark (**Falls of Clyde**); passes through Scotland's most important industrial area, including Glasgow, then expands into the **Firth of Clyde** estuary (2–30 km/1¼–20 mi wide, increasing to c.60 km/40 mi at mouth), leading to the Atlantic Ocean; length 170 km/100 mi; Glasgow head of navigation for ocean-going vessels; hydroelectricity; Clyde valley noted for breeding of Clydesdale horses.

Clydesdale A breed of horse, produced in Scotland by crossing local mares with large Flemish stallions; a heavy horse, developed in the 18th-c for hauling coal; height c.16·1 hands/1·7 m/5 ft 5 in; reddish-brown with white face and legs.

Clydeside pop (2000e) 1 624 100. Urban area in WC Scotland, UK, focused on the R Clyde; comprises the 11 districts of Bearsden and Milngavie, Clydebank, Cumbernauld and Kilsyth, East Kilbride, Eastwood, Glasgow City, Hamilton, Monklands, Motherwell, Renfrew, and Strathkelvin; airport; railway; major industrial area of Scotland.

Clytemnestra [kliytemnestra] or **Clytemestra** In Greek legend, the twin sister of Helen and the wife of Agamemnon. She murdered him on his return from Troy, assisted by her lover, Aegisthus. She was killed in revenge by her son, Orestes.

CND An abbreviation of **Campaign for Nuclear Disarmament**, a mass organization founded in the UK in 1958 to mobilize public opinion against the nuclear-weapons programme and for unilateral disarmament. It organized peaceful mass marches between London and Aldermaston, where the Atomic Weapons Research Establishment was based, and was successful in securing acceptance of a resolution at the 1960 Labour Party Conference for Britain's unilateral disarmament. Partly because of a split over non-violent direct action favoured by the Committee of 100, and the course of other events such as the Cuban missile crisis (1962), the signing of the Test-Ban Treaty (1963) and detente, its appeal and activities declined. During the 1980s it underwent a revival, and membership rose again as concern over the proliferation of nuclear weapons grew. However, following disarmament agreements between the USA and USSR, and the end of the Cold War, the organization again declined in numbers and was given less prominence on the political stage.

Cnidaria [nidaria] *coelenterate*

CNS *central nervous system*

C N Tower or **Canadian National Tower** The world's tallest self-supporting tower, erected in Toronto, Ontario, Canada (1973–5); 555·3 m/1822 ft high.

Cnut *Canute*

coal A black or brown sedimentary rock found in beds or seams, and formed by heat and pressure over millions of years on vegetation accumulated in shallow swamps; used as a fuel.

Successive stages in the formation of coal involve an increase in carbon content or 'rank': **peat** is the first stage, followed by **lignite** or **brown coal** (60–70% carbon), **bituminous coal** (more than 80% carbon), and **anthracite** (more than 90% carbon).

coalfish *saithe*

coal gas A mixture, mainly consisting of hydrogen and methane, resulting from the distillation of coal as part of the process of conversion to coke.

coalition An interparty arrangement established to pursue a common goal, most obviously government. Coalition governments are relatively common in electoral systems using proportional representation and/or in multiparty systems. The nature of the coalition is defined by those parties with seats in the cabinet.

coal mining Extracting coal from beneath the ground. In **opencast mining**, the coal is near the surface: the overburden is stripped away, the coal removed, and the overburden restored for environmental conservation. In **drift mining**, the coal lies within a slope: a horizontal tunnel is driven into the side of the slope, and the coal removed on level railways or conveyors. **Deep mining** relies on vertical shafts with horizontal approaches to the seams. Coal is dug (mainly now by mechanical means) and removed by conveyors to the shaft bottom for haulage to the surface. Coal mining presents special hazards: explosion may occur from gas or fine coal dust, so ventilation must be constant and efficient; shafts and tunnels must be protected against collapse. Coal is the most abundant fossil fuel on earth. Reserves are estimated at around 1 million million tonnes. World production in 2001 was c.4780 million tonnes, the leading producers (in million tonnes) being China (1323), the USA (1023), Russia (272), Germany (205), Australia (324), South Africa (233), Poland (162), and India (307). The UK produced 31 million tonnes in 2001.

Coalsack The finest visual example of an obscuring cloud of dust in space, 180 parsec away. It is in the constellation Crux, where it causes a gaping hole in the Milky Way.

coal tar A volatile by-product of heating coal in the absence of air to form coke; a black viscous liquid consisting of a complex mixture of organic compounds. Further distillation of coal tar produces a large number of chemicals which form the basis of explosives, dyes, and drugs.

coal tit A small bird native to Europe, Asia, and Africa (*Parus ater*); head and throat black, cheeks and back of neck white; inhabits woodland, especially coniferous, and gardens; eats seeds, and often takes insects from tree bark. (Family: Paridae.)

Coase, Ronald (Harry) [kohs] (1910–) Economist, born in London, UK. Educated in England, he worked as a statistician in the British war cabinet before emigrating to the USA in 1951. He taught at the universities of Virginia (1958–64) and Chicago (1964–79). Two journal articles in particular are the basis of his widespread influence: 'The Nature of the Firm' (1937), which analysed the economics of 'transaction costs', and 'The Problem of Social Cost' (1960), which led to the development of the economics of property rights and the economics of law. He was awarded the Nobel Prize for Economics in 1991.

Coastal Command A separate functional Command within the British Royal Air Force (1936–69). Moves to transfer it to the Royal Navy caused a political storm in 1958–9. During World War 2, the Command destroyed 184 German U-boats and 470 000 tonnes of enemy shipping, and played a decisive role in winning the Battle of the Atlantic.

coastguard An institution whose duty is to keep watch on the coastline and organize rescue and lifeboat services to help those in trouble. The nature of these services varies widely; some nations use their naval forces, whereas others operate through voluntary organizations. The largest service is the US Coastguard, responsible for search and rescue, lighthouses and lightships, pilotage, fishery protection, security at ports, enforcement of maritime legislation, and oceanography. It uses 550 craft, 100 helicopters, and over 30 long-range aircraft to cover a 16 000 km/10 000 mi coastline. The Canadian Coastguard operates similarly, but also has 20 icebreakers, and mounts ice rescue missions and ice warning patrols. The UK Coastguard was formed in 1822 to combat smuggling, and was so successful that it adopted a new role as a naval reserve in addition to revenue protection; in 1925 it was taken over by the Board of Trade. The service enjoyed a major rejuvenation in 1972 due to increased yachting activity. Australia operates a similar service, while the New Zealand service carries out additional rescue operations in mountain and bush areas.

Coast Mountains Mountain range in W British Columbia and Alaska, extending about 1600 km/1000 mi NW–SE; rises to 4042 m/13 261 ft in Mt Waddington, British Columbia; rugged terrain with several glaciers.

Coast Range Mountain belt in W North America, extending along the coast of the Pacific Ocean from Alaska through British Columbia, Washington, Oregon, California, and Baja California (Mexico); includes the Kenai, Chugach, St Elias, Olympic, and Klamath Mts; highest point Mt Logan (5950 m/19 521 ft); the Central Valley lies to the E in California.

coast redwood A massive evergreen conifer (*Sequoia sempervirens*), the tallest tree in the world at over 100 m/325 ft high and 8 m/26 ft thick; bark almost 1 m/3¼ ft thick, reddish, fibrous, spongy. Formerly widespread, with fossils in Greenland and China, it is now confined to the misty bottomlands of coastal California and SW Oregon. (Family: Taxodiaceae.)

coated fabrics Fabrics made by combining traditional textile fabric with a strongly adhering layer (coat) of plastic or other material. They are commonly used in protective clothing, such as rainwear.

Coates, Eric (1886–1957) Composer, born in Hucknall, Nottinghamshire, C England, UK. He studied in Nottingham and at the Royal Academy of Music, London, working as a violinist. Sir Henry Wood performed several of his early works at Promenade Concerts. Success as a composer of attractive light music enabled him to devote himself to composition after 1918. Among his best-known compositions are the *London Suite* (1933), *The Three Elizabeths* (1944), and a number of popular waltzes and marches.

coati [kohahtee] A raccoon-like mammal, found from S USA to South America; reddish-brown; long banded tail; long narrow muzzle with overhanging tip; inhabits woodland; eats fruit and small animals; solitary males called *coatimundis* (or *koatimundis*). The name is also used for the Andean **mountain coati** (*Nasuella olivacea*). (Genus: *Nasua*, 2 species. Family: Procyonidae.)

coat of arms *heraldry*

coat-of-mail shell *chiton*

coaxial cable A form of electrical wiring with relatively low loss which is used in the home as a connector from a television aerial to the television set. In computer systems it is the standard form of inter-connection wiring for local area networks. It is now being replaced in many places by fibre-optic cable, and in many computer networks by unshielded twisted pair (UTP) cabling.

cob A type of horse, often produced when crossing a heavy carthorse with a racing horse; height, 14·2–15·2 hands/1·5–1·6 m/4 ft 10 in–5 ft 2 in; short deep body; calm natured; lacks speed; also known as **rouncy** or **roncey**. The name is also used specifically for the **Irish cob**, **Norman cob**, **Welsh cob**, and extinct **Powys cob**.

cobalt Co, element 27, density 9 g/cm^3, melting point 1495°C. A hard metal, which occurs in ores as its sulphide (CoS), along with copper and nickel. It is used mainly as a metal in steel alloys, especially for permanent magnets. Most of its compounds show +2 oxidation state. Hydrated salts are usually light red, but many anhydrous ones are bright blue, and are used as pigments.

Cobb, Ty(rus Raymond), nickname **the Georgia Peach** (1886–1961) Baseball player, born in Narrows, Georgia, USA. An outstanding base runner and batter, in a 23-year career with Detroit and Philadelphia he had over 4000 base hits, a record which survived 57 years until broken in 1985. His career batting average was an all-time record at ·367, and he led the American League 12 times in batting.

Cobb and Co An Australian company which operated the largest coach service in E Australia (1853–1924). Famous for the reliability of its service, it was based in Victoria to 1862, and then in Bathurst, New South Wales. By 1890, Cobb and Co had 6400 km/4000 mi of coach routes, but from then on found itself less able to compete with the railways. It continues today as a motor transport company.

Cobbett, William (1763–1835) Journalist and social reformer, born in Farnham, Surrey, SE England, UK. The son of a farmer, he moved on impulse to London (1783), spent a year reading widely, and joined the army, serving in New Brunswick (1785–91). In 1792 he married and went to the USA, where he wrote fierce pieces against democratic government under the name 'Peter Porcupine'. Returning to England in 1800, he was welcomed by the Tories, and started his famous *Weekly Political Register* (1802), which continued until his death, changing in 1804 from its original Toryism to an uncompromising Radicalism. Deeply concerned at the condition of the working classes, especially the rural workers in the rapidly industrialized English population, he campaigned for reform. In 1810 he was imprisoned for two years for criticizing the flogging of militiamen by German mercenaries, and in 1817 he went again to the USA, fearing a second imprisonment. Returning in 1819 he travelled widely in Britain, and finally became an MP (1832). His works include a *History of the Protestant Reformation* (1824–7) and *Rural Rides* (1830), a classic portrayal of the situation of the rural workers of the time.

Cobden, Richard (1804–65) Economist and politican, 'the apostle of free trade', born in Heyshott, West Sussex, S England, UK. He worked as a clerk and commercial traveller in London, then went into the calico business, settling in Manchester. In 1835 he visited the USA, and the Levant (1836–7), after which he published two pamphlets preaching free trade, nonintervention, and speaking against 'Russophobia'. In 1838 he helped to found the Anti-Corn-Law League, becoming its most prominent member. He became an MP in 1841. His lectures and parliamentary speeches focused opinion on the Corn Laws, which were repealed in 1846.

Coblenz *Koblenz*

COBOL [kohbol] Acronym for **COmmon Business Orientated Language**, a high-level computer language widely used in the business community. It uses statements written in English which are relatively easy to understand; for example, the statement ADD VAT TO NET-PRICE could be used in a COBOL program.

cobra A venomous snake, native to S Asia and Africa; neck has loose folds of skin which can be spread as a 'hood' when alarmed; fangs short; venom (more poisonous than that of vipers) attacks the nervous system; usually inhabits forests, but also open country. Some species (**spitting cobras**) can squirt venom up to 3 m/10 ft into the eyes of threatening animals, and may leave them permanently blinded. The **king cobra** is the largest venomous snake. Cobras are the snakes of Indian 'snake charmers'. (Family: Elapidae, many species, most in genus *Naja*.)

coca *cocaine*

cocaine $C_{17}H_{21}NO_4$, melting point 98°C. A white alkaloid extracted from the leaves of the South American shrub *Erythroxylon coca*, and used for its stimulant properties, similar to those of amphetamine. Freud used it 'to boost the flagging human spirit' of his patients, and his physician colleague Carl Koller (1857–1944) discovered its local anaesthetic actions. It is still used as a topical local anaesthetic, mainly in ophthalmology. It is widely abused; the powder is sniffed and when converted to **crack** it can be smoked (*freebasing*). It causes addiction, particularly when freebased. Street names include 'Charlie', and 'charge'.

coccus Any spherical bacterium. It varies in size, and may occur in chains, clusters, or other groupings. Examples are *Staphylococcus*, and *Streptococcus*.

coccyx [koksiks] The lowest part of the vertebral column, forming the tail in many animals. In humans it is small and triangular, comprising three to five rudimentary vertebrae, and is situated in the groove between the buttocks.

Cochabamba [kochabamba] 17°26S 66°10W, pop (2000e) 517 000. Capital of Cochabamba department, C Bolivia; altitude 2500 m/8200 ft; country's third largest city; founded, 1542; airfield; railway; university (1832); important agricultural centre; oil refining, furniture, footwear; cathedral, Palacio de Cultura, Los Portales museum, monument to War of Independence, markets; golf club at L Alalay; Carnival (before Lent).

Cochin [kochin] 9°55N 76°22E, pop (2000e) 663 000. Naval base and seaport in Kerala, SW India; on the Malabar coast of the Arabian Sea, 1080 km/671 mi SE of Mumbai; Portuguese trading station, 1502, Fort Cochin, first European settlement in India; shipbuilding, trade in fruit and cattle; tomb of Vasco da Gama.

cochineal [kochineel] A dye (**carminic acid**) obtained from the dried bodies of a female bug, *Dactylopus coccus*. The bug feeds on cacti, and is native to Peru and Mexico. (Order: Homoptera. Family: Coccidae.)

cochlea [koklia] The spiral cavity in the internal ear, which is concerned with hearing. It consists of a bony part with a central pillar (the *modiolus*) and a spiral duct (part of the *membranous labyrinth*). The space between the bony and membranous parts is filled with *perilymph* (a fluid similar to cerebrospinal fluid). A thin spiral shelf projects from the modiolus, on which lies the *basilar membrane*. Sound waves in the air are transmitted from the middle ear to the cochlea through the *oval window*, making the basilar membrane vibrate. The basal part of the basilar membrane responds with nerve impulses to both high and low frequencies, while the apical part responds to low frequencies only. Vibrations of the membrane stimulate a set of hair cells, which trigger impulses in the cochlear part of the eighth cranial nerve. These signals are then transmitted to the auditory areas of the brain for interpretation.

cockatiel [kokateel] An Australian parrot of the cockatoo family (*Nymphicus hollandicus*); long tapering crest on head; male with colourful facial markings; inhabits open country; eats grass seeds or fruit. (Family: Cacatuidae.)

cockatoo An Australasian parrot, separated from other parrots mainly by features of its skull, and in having an erectile crest of feathers on the head. (Family: Cacatuidae, 18 species.)

cockatrice *basilisk* (mythology)

cockchafer A large, dark-coloured chafer; adults nocturnal, feeding on leaves; fleshy, C-shaped larvae burrow in ground for 3–4 years, feeding on roots before emerging as flying adults, typically in May, hence alternative name of **maybug**. (Order: Coleoptera. Family: Scarabeidae.)

Cockcroft, Sir John Douglas (1897–1967) Nuclear physicist, born in Todmorden, West Yorkshire, N England, UK. He studied at Manchester and Cambridge, and became professor of physics at Cambridge (1939–46). With E T S Walton (1903–95) he succeeded in disintegrating lithium by proton bombardment (the first artificial transmutation) in 1932, pioneering the use of particle accelerators, and they shared the Nobel Prize for Physics (1951). During World War 2 he was director of Air Defence Research (1941–4). He became the first director of Britain's Atomic Energy Establishment at Harwell in 1946. He was knighted in 1948, and in 1959 appointed the first Master of Churchill College, Cambridge.

Cockerell, Sir Christopher (Sydney) (1910–99) Engineer, born in Cambridge, Cambridgeshire, EC England, UK. He studied at Cambridge and worked on radio and radar, before turning to hydrodynamics. In the early 1950s, experimenting with air as a lubricant between a boat's hull and the water, he invented the amphibious hovercraft. The first full-scale machine was built in 1958, and its prototype first crossed the English Channel successfully in 1959. In the course of his long life he patented more than 70 inventions, though the patent for the hovercraft went to a marketing corporation. He was knighted in 1969.

cocker spaniel or **American cocker spaniel** A breed of dog, developed in the USA from the **English cocker spaniel**; recognized as a separate breed in 1941; smaller than ancestral stock; longer coat; black or golden brown; popular as pets.

cockfighting A blood sport in which *gamecocks*, aged 1–2 years, wearing steel spurs on their legs, are set against each other. Betting takes place on the performance of the birds. It probably originated in Asia 3000 years ago, and was a popular sport in England until 1849, when it was banned. It survives elsewhere (eg in parts of the USA), though often illegal.

cockle A marine bivalve mollusc whose shell comprises two more or less equal valves closed by two adductor muscles; an active burrower in intertidal sediments; fished extensively for human consumption. (Class: Pelecypoda. Order: Veneroida.)

cock of the rock A bird native to tropical South America; male with brilliant red or orange plumage and large crest on head; male poses on ground to attract females. (Genus: *Rupicola*, 2 species. Family: Cotingidae, sometimes placed in a separate family, Rupicolidae.)

cockroach An active, typically nocturnal insect; body depressed; legs long and adapted for running; forewings hard and leathery; hindwings membranous, sometimes lost; eggs laid in crevices, litter, caves, and other habitats; will eat almost any organic matter; common household pest. (Order: Blattaria, c.3700 species.)

cock's comb An annual (*Celosia cristata*), native to tropical Asia, related to amaranth; the peculiar inflorescence, a thick fleshy crest resembling a cock's comb, is the result of mutation-induced fasciation; the normal form has a plume-like inflorescence. Both forms are grown as pot plants. (Family: Amaranthaceae.)

Cockscomb Basin area 14·6 sq km/5·6 sq mi. Region of the Maya mountains, Belize; a forest reserve, part of which was designated the world's first jaguar reserve in 1986.

cocktail party effect The technique of selective listening, whereby people surrounded by a number of different conversations cut off attention from all but one. It is often triggered by someone in the nearby conversation uttering a word which has some special significance to the listener, such as the listener's name, or the town he/she comes from.

cocoa *chocolate*

coco de mer [**koh**koh duh mair] A species of palm endemic to the Seychelles (*Lodoicea maldavica*). The fruit is one of the largest known, up to 20 kg/45 lb, taking 10 years to ripen; buoyant and often washed ashore, it was well known before the tree itself was discovered. The palm is sometimes called the **double coconut**, because the nut as fruit resembles two coconuts fused side by side. (Family: Palmae.)

coconut crab *robber crab*

coconut palm A tree with a characteristic curved trunk (*Cocos nucifera*), growing to 30 m/100 ft, with feathery leaves up to 6 m/20 ft long; the large, single-seeded fruits (**coconuts**) have a fibrous outer husk and a hard inner shell enclosing a layer of white flesh and a central cavity filled with milky fluid; at the base of the fruit are three round marks which correspond to the three chambers of the ovary, and under one of which lies the embryo. The coconut palm is probably native to Polynesia. It flourishes near the sea, and the buoyant fruit is capable of floating long distances in sea water without harm, so it is a characteristic tree of oceanic islands. It has long been cultivated throughout the tropics. Like many other palms it provides a remarkable range of products. The trunk provides timber. The leaves are woven into mats and baskets and are used for thatching; the leaf-stalks are sufficiently stout to provide poles for fencing and other uses. The bud at the top of the stem is eaten as a vegetable, and the young inflorescence can be tapped to provide a sugary liquid which can be fermented and distilled into alcoholic drinks and vinegar. The coconuts themselves form the basis of many tropical island economies. They are rarely seen in natural form outside the regions where the trees grow, as the outer husk is removed before the nuts are exported to make coir, a tough fibre used for matting. Coconut milk is a refreshing drink, and the white flesh is eaten raw or cooked, sold as desiccated coconut, or dried to form copra, the world's principal source of vegetable fat. The oil obtained from pressed copra is used in margarine, and the residual cake is a valuable animal food. (Family: Palmae.)

cocoon *pupa*

Cocos Islands [**koh**kohs] or **Keeling Islands** 12°05S 96°53E, pop (2000e) 780, total land area 14·2 sq km/5½ sq mi. Two separate groups of atolls in the Indian Ocean, 3685 km/2290 mi W of Darwin, Australia; an Australian external territory comprising 27 small, flat, palm-covered coral islands, notably **West I** (pop 240), 10 km/6 mi long, airport, mostly occupied by Europeans, and **Home I** (pop 400) occupied by the Cocos Malay community; discovered 1609 by Captain William Keeling of the East India Company; first settled 1826, and developed by the Clunies-Ross family; annexed to the British Crown, 1857; granted by Queen Victoria to George Clunies-Ross, 1886; incorporated with the Settlement of Singapore, 1903; placed under Australian administration (1955) as the Territory of Cocos (Keeling) Islands; Australia purchased Clunies-Ross interests in the islands (1978), and the inhabitants voted to be part of Northern Territory, 1984; islands council advises the administrator on all issues; copra plantation; meteorological station.

Cocteau, Jean [kok**toh**] (1889–1963) Poet, playwright, and film director, born in Maisons-Lafitte, NC France. He had early success with his poems, which he fully exploited, and figured as the sponsor of Picasso, Stravinsky, Giorgio de Chirico, and the musical group known as *Les Six*. He was an actor, director, scenario writer, novelist, critic, and artist, all of his work being marked by vivacity and a pyrotechnic brilliance. His best-known works include his novel *Les Enfants terribles* (1929, Children of the Game), his play *Orphée* (1926, Orpheus), and his films *Le Sang du poète* (1932, The Blood of the Poet) and *La Belle et la bête* (1945, Beauty and the Beast).

cod Any of the family Gadidae (15 genera; 100 species) of marine fishes, found mainly in cool temperate shelf waters of N hemisphere; body with 2–3 dorsal and 1–2 anal fins; includes the **common cod** (*Gadus morhua*); length up to 120 cm/4 ft; greenish to reddish, freckled, with a pale lateral line; adults feed mainly on crustaceans and small fishes; supports very important trawl and net (seine) fisheries.

coda The final section of a piece of music (eg a sonata-form movement or a fugue), not strictly integral to the structure, but required for a satisfactory peroration.

CODASYL [**koh**dasil] Acronym for **COnference on DAta SYStems Language**, a committee of computer experts meeting in the USA which reports on aspects of computer programming. It was responsible for the development of a technique (known as the *network model* of data, and also as the CODASYL model) for storing in a computer system not only data items but also the relationships between these data items.

code A system of rules for matching signs, linguistic or otherwise, which makes communication possible. It may be governed by informal, unwritten conventions (eg body language) or by officially agreed rules (eg some types of sign language), and may be culturally specific or universal in its use. Computer programmers may apply an alphanumeric code, while linguists often view language as a code or set of rules pairing sounds with meaning.

codec Acronym for **coder/decoder**, a device for converting the analogue signals used by audio and video equipment to digital form so that the signals can be sent over digital telecommunications networks such as ISDN. Pulse Code Modulation is used for the conversion.

codeine A painkiller related to morphine that is used for treating mild types of pain (eg headache); it is rarely addictive. It does cause constipation and can be used to treat diarrhoea. It is also used in some cough mixtures, since it suppresses the cough reflex.

Code Napoléon The French Civil Code, introduced (though not devised) by Napoleon Bonaparte as First Consul in 1804, to fill the void left by the abolition of the legal and social customs of pre-revolutionary France. It established the principles of equality between people, liberty of person and contract, and the inviolability of private property. From 1804 to 1810 the Code was introduced into those areas of Europe under direct French control, and also in the state of Louisiana. The Civil Code of the newly-united Italian state (1865) bore close affinity to it, and it was widely emulated in South America. It is still substantially extant in France, Belgium, Luxembourg, and Monaco today. It was revised in 1904. In addition to the Civil Code, Napoleon introduced the Code of Civil Procedure (1807), the Commercial Code (1808), the Code of Criminal Procedure (1811), and the Penal Code (1811).

Codex Alimentarius A code of practice intended to set worldwide standards for food production and processing. It was established in 1963 by the Food and Agricultural Organization (FAO) of the United Nations and the World Health Organization.

Codex Juris Canonici [**kohdeks jooris kanonikiy**] (Lat 'code of canon law') A code of canon or church law regulating the Roman Catholic Church. The codification, authorized by Pope Pius X in 1904, was completed in 1917, with revisions recommended by a commission set up in 1963.

codling moth A small, drab-coloured moth that lays eggs on apples and other fruit; the caterpillars feed inside the fruit, before emerging to pupate in a silken cocoon. They can be a serious pest of cultivated apples. (Order: Lepidoptera. Family: Tortricidae.)

cod-liver oil An oil obtained from the fresh liver of the cod and refined. It provides a rich source of vitamins A and D. It is now believed to be protective in heart disease because of its high content of unsaturated fatty acids.

codon [**kohdon**] The sequence of three nucleotides in DNA or RNA which determine (or 'code for') the particular amino acid to be inserted into a polypeptide chain, or the beginning or end of a protein chain.

Cody, William F(rederick) [**kohdee**], known as **Buffalo Bill** (1846–1917) Showman, born in Scott Co, Iowa, USA. He received his nickname after killing nearly 5000 buffalo in eight months for a contract to supply workers on the Kansas Pacific Railway with meat. He served as a scout in the Sioux Wars, but from 1883 toured with his Wild West Show. The town of Cody in Wyoming stands on part of his former ranch.

Coe, Kelvin (1946–92) Ballet dancer, born in Melbourne, Victoria, SE Australia. He joined the Australian Ballet for its inaugural season in 1969, and went on to dance virtually every lead role in its repertoire. He appeared as a guest with the Sydney Dance Company, American Ballet Theatre, Bolshoi Ballet, and London Festival Ballet. He retired as the Australian Ballet's principal dancer in 1981, but continued dancing on a more restricted basis. A popular performer in classical and contemporary pieces, he is widely considered to have been Australia's best male dancer.

Coe (of Ranmore), Sebastian (Newbold) Coe, Lord [**koh**] (1956–) Athlete, born in London, UK, the world's outstanding middle-distance runner of the 1980s. He studied at Loughborough College, won the bronze medal in the 800 m at the 1978 European Championships, and the following year broke his first world records (800 m and 1 mi). Altogether he broke eight world records including the mile three times; uniquely, he held the 800 m, 1000 m, 1500 m, and mile records simultaneously. At the 1980 Olympics he won the gold medal in the 1500 m and the silver in the 800 m, repeating the achievement four years later despite a career-threatening infection. Fitness problems followed, and he was omitted from the British team that went to the 1988 Olympics. He retired from running after the 1990 Commonwealth Games to pursue a career in politics, becoming a Conservative MP in 1992, but lost his seat in the 1997 general election. In 2000 he was given a life peerage.

coeducation The education of boys and girls in the same school or college. In some countries, for religious or cultural reasons, schools are predominantly for children of the same sex; but in others coeducation is the norm. In many countries the 20th-c trend has been away from single-sex education. At the same time, there has been a sustained debate about whether girls in particular are disadvantaged by coeducation.

coelacanth *Crossopterygii*

coelenterate [**seelenteruht**] A simple, multicellular animal with a body plan comprising two primary layers separated by a layer of gelatinous material (*mesoglea*); few found in fresh water; most are marine, and all are carnivorous; most exhibit radial symmetry, and possess stinging cells (*nematocysts*) for prey capture and defence; life-cycle typically involves two phases: an attached polyp, which may be solitary, and a disc-shaped medusa; includes the corals, sea anemones, and jelly-fish. (Phylum: Cnidaria.)

coeliac / celiac disease [**seeliak**] A disorder of the small intestine, which develops in childhood, caused by a hypersensitivity reaction to gluten, a protein found in wheat and cereals. This damages the lining of the intestine, preventing absorption of nutrients, particularly fats, and leading to retarded growth, anaemia, and the passage of pale bulky stools (*steathorrea*). A gluten-free diet, maintained for life, will reverse these adverse features.

coelom [**seeluhm**] The principal body cavity in multicellular animals, arising during embryological development, and typically forming the cavity around the gut in annelid worms, echinoderms, and vertebrates. The coelom is present, but reduced in size, in molluscs and arthropods.

coelostat / celostat [**seeluhstat**] A flat mirror driven by a clock mechanism in such a way as to project the same part of the heavens into a fixed telescope. This is particularly used for solar telescopes, which in any case do not need to survey the whole sky, as a means of controlling costs.

Coelurus [**seeloorus**] A lightly built, flesh-eating dinosaur; slender neck and long tail; skull long, with large orbits; two-legged; forelimbs short with three digits, one facing the other two; known from the Upper Jurassic period of Wyoming; formerly known as *Ornitholestes*. (Order: Saurischia.)

co-enzyme An organic, non-protein molecule that associates with an enzyme in catalysing a biochemical reaction. It usually acts by accepting or donating certain chemical groups.

Coetzee, J(ohn) M(axwell) [**kootzee**] (1940–) Writer and critic, born in Cape Town, SW South Africa. The political situation in his native country provides him with the base from which to launch his allegories and fables, attacking colonialism and demythologizing historical and contemporary myths of imperialism. His first work of fiction was *Dusklands* (1974), followed by *In the Heart of the Country* (1977), *Waiting for the Barbarians* (1980), *Life and Times of Michael K* (1983, Booker), *Foe* (1986), *Age of Iron* (1990), and *The Master of Petersburg* (1994). In 1999 he became the first writer to win the Booker Prize twice, with *Disgrace*, and later novels include *Elizabeth Costello* (2003). He became professor of English Literature at the University of Cape Town (1984), and in 2002 he moved to Australia where he is attached to the University of Adelaide. He received the 2003 Nobel Prize for Literature.

coffee An evergreen shrub, leaves oval, in opposite pairs; flowers white, fragrant, 5-petalled, in axils of leaves; cherry-like fruits, red, fleshy, containing two seeds (the coffee beans) rich in caffeine; used worldwide as a beverage. **Arabian coffee** (*Coffea arabica*) is native to Ethiopia, and was introduced first to Arabia, later the East Indies, West Indies, South America, and Africa. During the 16th-c and 17th-c coffee was introduced into one European country after another. The major world producer is now Brazil. **Robusta coffee** (*Coffea canephora*) and **Liberian coffee** (*Coffea liberica*) are inferior species grown mainly in Africa and Asia. Commercial names (eg 'Kenya') often indicate the origin of different types. (Genus: *Coffea*, 40 species. Family: Rubiaceae.)

coffee berry disease A serious disease (*Colletotrichum africanum*) which attacks the berries of *Arabica* coffee plants, turning them black and rendering them economically useless. It was first identified in Kenya in the 1920s, and has since spread rapidly throughout Africa, though it is not serious in other continents. The disease is spread by rain splash, particularly from residues of a previous crop, and is difficult to control by fungicidal sprays. Resistant varieties are being developed. (Order: Fungi imperfecti.)

cofferdam A temporary structure designed to keep water or soft ground from flowing into a site when building foundations. A cofferdam usually consists of a dam or sheet piling. More elaborate structures may consist of two rows of sheet piling with an earth fill or of walls made of steel 'cells'.

Coggan (of Canterbury and of Sissinghurst), (Frederick) Donald Coggan, Baron (1909–2000) Clergyman, born in London, UK. He studied at Cambridge, was a lecturer in Semitic languages at Manchester (1931–4), professor of the New Testament at Wycliffe College, Toronto (1937–44), Principal of London College of Divinity (1944–56), Bishop of Bradford (1956–61), Archbishop of York (1961–74), and finally Archbishop of Canterbury (1974–80), when he was made a life peer. He was the author of several theological works, including *Sure Foundation* (1981) and *A New Way for Preaching* (1996).

cognates Languages or language forms which derive from the same historical source. For example, Welsh, Breton, and Cornish are all derived from Brythonic, a branch of the Celtic language family.

cognitive anthropology The branch of anthropology which studies cultural differences in perception, reasoning, and the construction of knowledge. The best-known project of cognitive anthropology has been *ethnoscience*, the study of the bodies of knowledge and theory developed by non-Western societies in such fields as botany or human physiology.

cognitive psychology A branch of psychology which studies the higher mental processes (memory, attention, language, reasoning, etc). In contrast to behaviourists, cognitive psychologists are more ready to posit mechanisms and processes that are not directly observable, such as memory stores and switches of attention. Many cognitive psychologists subscribe to the 'computer metaphor', in which the brain and the computer are seen as having the same essential characteristics.

cognitive science The formal study of mind, in which models and theories originating in artificial intelligence (AI) and in the human sciences (particularly cognitive psychology, linguistics, and philosophy) are subject to interdisciplinary development. For example, a grammar written by a linguist might be implemented on a computer by an AI scientist, and its predictions tested by a psychologist observing human subjects. The dominant partner in this enterprise is often the AI scientist, since the major criterion for success is usually whether a program can be written and successfully implemented on a computer.

cognitive therapy A form of behaviour therapy based on the supposition that the manner in which individuals cognitively perceive themselves and the world about them determines their feelings and emotions, and that restructuring of the former can lead to changes in the latter. This form of treatment was described by US psychotherapist Aaron T Beck, and has been championed in Europe by British clinical psychologist Ivy Marie Blackburn (1939–).

Cohan, George Michael (Keohane) (1878–1942) Actor, dramatist, and director, born in Providence, Rhode Island, USA. He began in vaudeville as a child in his family's act, the Four Cohans, and was writing for the act by the age of 15. As an actor he is remembered in such roles as the father in O'Neill's *Ah, Wilderness!* (1933), and as a writer of such songs as 'Yankee Doodle Dandy', which featured in his musical *Little Johnny Jones* (1904), and which gave the title of the film made of his life in 1942.

Cohan, Robert [**koh**han] (1925–) Dancer, choreographer, teacher, and director, born in New York City, USA. He trained with Martha Graham and danced with her company, becoming co-director in 1966. He moved to London as artistic director of the new London Contemporary Dance Theatre in 1967, choreographing works with a wide range of subject matter. He then started the London Contemporary Dance School with Robin Howard, and developed a British version of Graham's expressive dance technique, before retiring in 1988.

Cohen, William S (1940–) US statesman. He was educated at Bowdoin College and Boston University Law School. He became Republican senator for Maine in 1973, serving three terms before retiring in 1996. A leading critic of the administration in the Watergate and Iran-Contra scandals, he was made secretary of defense in the 1997 administration, following Clinton's election promise to appoint a Republican to his cabinet.

Cohen-Tannoudji, Claude [koh**ī** ta**noo**jee] (1933–) Physicist, born in Constantine, NE Algeria. He graduated in 1962 from the Ecole Normale Supérieure, Paris, where he went on to work. In 1997 he shared the Nobel Prize for Physics for his contribution to the development of methods to cool and trap atoms with laser light.

coherence A relationship between waves. Two waves of the same frequency are described as coherent if their relative displacements are constant in time, ie if one wave lags behind the other at one moment, and at some later time lags by the same amount. Such waves have a constant phase difference; they are 'in step'. Light from lasers is coherent, but from ordinary bulbs it is incoherent.

cohort A term used especially in demographic studies to describe a group of people living at the same time whose life histories overlap, and who can be traced through the birth, death, marital, educational, and other experiences they have.

cohort study A scientific method used in medicine to determine the cause of a disease. A group of people exposed to a suspected risk factor is followed up over time and compared to a group not exposed, to determine whether there is a statistically significant difference in the proportion of each group that develop the disease under investigation. An example is the relationship between smoking and lung cancer: follow-ups of groups of smokers and non-smokers have revealed significant higher rates of lung cancer in the smoking group.

Coimbatore [kohimba**taw(r)**] 11°00N 76°57E, pop (2000e) 1 002 000. City in Tamil Nadu, S India, 425 km/264 mi SW of Chennai (Madras); stronghold of successive Tamil kingdoms, 9th–17th-c; ceded to Britain, 1799; airfield; railway; university (1971); agricultural centre; tea, cotton, hides, teak; glass, electrical goods, fertilizer.

Coimbra [**kweem**bra], ancient **Conimbriga** 40°12N 8°25W, pop (2000e) 95 000. Capital of Coimbra district, C Portugal; on R Mondego, 173 km/107 mi NE of Lisbon; former capital of Portugal, 12th–13th-c; oldest university in Portugal (founded at Lisbon in 1290, transferred here in 1537); bishopric; paper, tanning, pottery, biscuits, food processing, fabrics, wine; two cathedrals, São Sebastião aqueduct, Monastery of the Holy Cross, national museum, Conimbriga Roman site and Children's Portugal village nearby; Queima das Fitas student festival (May).

coins *money; numismatics*

Coke, Sir Edward [kook], commonly called **Lord Coke of Cooke** (1552–1634) Jurist, born in Mileham, Norfolk, E England, UK. He was educated at Norwich and Trinity College, Cambridge, was called to the bar in 1578, and rose to become Speaker of the House of Commons (1593), attorney general (1594), Chief Justice of the Common Pleas (1606), Chief Justice of the King's Bench (1613), and privy councillor. He brutally prosecuted for treason Essex, Raleigh, and the Gunpowder conspirators, but after 1606 stands out as a vindicator of national liberties against the royal prerogative. He was dismissed in 1617, and from 1620 led the popular party in parliament, serving nine months in prison in the Tower of London. The Petition of Right (1628) was largely his doing. Most of his epoch-making Law Reports were published during his lifetime (1600–15).

Coke, Thomas William *Leicester of Holkham, Thomas, William Coke*

coke A form of charcoal, first used in 13th-c China, made by heating coal to over 1000°C in the absence of air to remove the volatile constituents. It is a brittle, porous substance consisting mainly of carbon, and used chiefly in steelmaking for fuelling blast furnaces.

Cola [chola] An ancient Tamil dynasty, which ruled much of S India between the 8th-c and 13th-c. The height of power was under Rajaraja (985–1014) and Rajendra (1014–44), who extended the kingdom to include Ceylon. It introduced highly-developed revenue administration, village self-organization, and irrigation systems. Tamil architecture and literature flourished.

cola *kola*

Colbert, Claudette [kolbair], originally **Lily Claudette Chauchoin** (1903–96) Film actress, born in Paris, France. She went to the USA as a child, and started in films with spirited comedy roles, becoming a star with *It Happened One Night* (1934), which won her an Oscar. This was followed by 10 years of romantic comedy successes, including *Tovarich* (1937) and *The Palm Beach Story* (1942), and varied character parts up to the 1960s, such as in *Parrish* (1960). On the stage her career continued into the 1980s.

Colbert, Jean Baptiste [kolbair] (1619–83) French statesman, born in Reims, NE France. In 1651 he entered the service of Mazarin, and became the chief financial minister of Louis XIV (1661). He found the finances in a ruinous condition, and introduced a series of successful reforms, doubling the revenue in 10 years. He reorganized the colonies, provided a strong fleet, improved the civil code, and introduced a marine code. The Academies of Inscriptions, Science, and Architecture were founded by him, and he became a patron of industry, commerce, art, science, and literature. However, his successes were undone by wars and court extravagance, and he died bitterly disappointed.

Colchester, Lat **Camulodunum**, Anglo-Saxon **Colneceaster** 51°54N 0°54E, pop (2001e) 155 800. Town in Essex, SE England, UK; S of the R Colne, 82 km/51 mi NE of London; University of Essex (1961); claimed to be the oldest town in England, founded by Cunobelinus AD c.10; railway; light industry, printing, oysters, rose growing; city walls, castle (12th-c); oyster festival (Oct); football league team, Colchester United ('U's).

colchicine [kolchiseen] A drug effective against gout, extracted from the corm and seeds of the meadow saffron, *Colchicum autumnale* ('autumn crocus'), so called because it grows in Colchis on the Black Sea. The plants were used in Europe to treat gout in the 17th-c; pure colchicine was first prepared in 1820. It is still widely used.

cold An infection of the upper respiratory tract caused by several different viruses, usually a rhinovirus; also known as the **common cold** or **coryza** [koriyza]. It is characterized by a sore throat and profuse nasal secretions, initially watery and then thicker. In severe cases, infection may spread to the sinuses and lower respiratory tract, causing sinusitis, bronchitis, and exacerbating underlying respiratory disease. It spreads rapidly around the population in infected droplets (hence its designation as the 'common cold'). Colds are more common in winter months, though the reasons for this are unclear: cold weather as such does not cause a cold, but may lower the body's resistance to infection, and in cold weather people tend to spend more time indoors in close contact. In view of the frequency of the problem (with its hidden effects on the economy of workdays lost), a great deal of research has been devoted – so far with limited success – to finding an effective treatment, although there are many popular 'remedies'.

cold-bloodedness *poikilotherm*

cold front A meteorological term for the leading edge of a parcel of cold or polar air. In a depression, the passage of a cold front is often preceded by heavy rainfall, and as it passes there is a sharp fall in temperature together with a veering of the wind (a clockwise change in direction, eg from south to southwest or west) followed by cold unstable air.

cold fusion Nuclear fusion occurring at room temperature. In March 1989, US chemist Stanley Pons and British chemist Martin Fleischmann claimed to have observed nuclear fusion in an electrolytic cell comprising platinum and titanium electrodes in heavy water. Their claims are now known to be false. The way in which Pons and Fleischmann announced their results to the media so soon, the lack of independent checking by other experimental groups, and the claims and counter-claims that followed their announcement created a scientific incident without parallel in recent times.

Cold Harbor, Battles of (1–3 Jun 1864) Battles of the American Civil War, fought in Virginia as part of General Grant's strategy of unrelenting pressure on the South. Grant lost 12 000 men in one day's fighting.

cold sore (*Herpes labialis*) A localized blister-like rash affecting the lips and adjoining skin around the mouth, the lining of the mouth, and the tongue. The lesions are due to a virus (*Herpes simplex*, Type 1) that is widespread throughout the population. It usually lies dormant but is activated by intermittent illness or debility.

cold storage Storage for perishable foodstuffs at a temperature just above freezing point. This process minimizes deterioration from chemical or biological action, but does not subject the food to damage by ice crystal formation on freezing. It is carried on in large buildings with cold air or brine circulated from a central refrigeration plant, and is often associated with manufacturing or packing plant, or large central markets. It is sometimes installed in ships, trucks, or aircraft.

Cold War A state of tension or hostility between states that is expressed in economic and political terms, and stops short of a 'hot' or shooting war. The policies adopted are those which attempt to strengthen one side and weaken the opposition, particularly those relating to military and weapon superiority. Thus the term was often used to describe the relationship between the USSR and the major Western non-communist powers – especially the USA – between 1945 and the mid-to-late 1960s, when the nuclear 'arms race' intensified. The process of detente, begun in the late 1960s, led to a 'thaw' in relations between the major powers. This continued in the relationship between US President Reagan and USSR President Gorbachev. Following the breakup of the communist system in the Soviet Union, the West declared that it had won the Cold War.

Cole, George (1925–) Actor, born in London, UK. Educated in Morden, Greater London, he joined the cast of *White Horse Inn* (1939). He has had many parts on stage, screen, and television, in serious works such as *The Three Sisters* (1967) as well as comedy. His many films include the *St Trinian's* series and other comedies, but he is probably best known in the UK as Arthur Daly from the long-running television series, *Minder*. Other television work includes *The Bounder*, *Blott on the Landscape*, *My Good Friend* (1995–6), and *Dad* (1997–9).

Cole, Nat King, originally **Nathaniel Adams Cole**, family name formerly **Coles** (1919–65) Entertainer, born in Montgomery, Alabama, USA. During the 1930s he became popular as a jazz pianist and singer, forming his own instrumental trio of piano, guitar, and double bass in 1937 which set the pattern for many later jazz trios. Among many hit records were 'Route 66' and 'Walking My Baby Back Home', but probably his best-known song is 'Unforgettable', which enjoyed a recent revival in a posthumous electronically arranged duet with his daughter, **Natalie Cole** (1950–).

Coleoptera [kolioptera] *beetle*

Coleridge, Samuel Taylor (1772–1834) Poet and man of letters, born in Ottery St Mary, Devon, SE England, UK. He studied at Cambridge, imbibed revolutionary ideas, and left to enlist in the Dragoons. His plans to found a communist society in the USA with Robert Southey came to nothing, and he turned instead to teaching and journalism in Bristol. Marrying **Sara Fricker** (Southey's sister-in-law), he went with her to Nether Stowey, where they made close friends with William and Dorothy Wordsworth. From this connection a new English Romantic poetry emerged, in reaction against Neoclassic artificiality. The publication of *Lyrical Ballads* (1798), which opens with his magical 'Rime of the Ancient Mariner', achieved a revolution in literary taste and sensibility. After visiting Germany (1798–9), he developed an interest in German philosophy and was instrumental in introducing German thought to England. In 1800 he moved to the Lake District, but his career prospects were blighted by his moral collapse, partly due to the opium-based drug laudanum. He rejected Wordsworth's animistic views of nature, and relations between them became strained. He began a weekly paper, *The Friend* (1809), and settled in London, writing and lecturing. In 1816 he published 'Christabel' and the fragment, 'Kubla Khan', both written in his earlier period of inspiration. His small output of poetry proves his gift, but he is known also for his critical writing, and for his theological and politico-sociological works.

Colet, John [**kol**et] (c.1467–1519) Theologian and Tudor humanist, born in London, UK. He studied at Oxford, travelled in Italy, then returned to England where he became a priest. While lecturing at Oxford (from 1496), he worked with Thomas More and Erasmus. In 1505 he became Dean of St Paul's, where he continued to deliver controversial lectures on the interpretation of Scripture, and founded St Paul's School (1509–12).

Colette, Sidonie Gabrielle [kolet] (1873–1954) Novelist, born in Saint-Sauveur-en-Puisaye, France. Her early books were written in collaboration with her first husband, **Henri Gauthier-Villars** (pseudonym **Willy**); after their divorce in 1906 she appeared in music halls in dance and mime, then settled as a writer. Her novels include the 'Claudine' series (1900–3), *Chéri* (1920), and *Gigi* (1944). In 1912 she married **Henry de Jouvenel**, and in 1935, **Maurice Goudeket**. She won many awards for her work, and became a legendary figure in Paris.

coleus A perennial native to Java (*Coleus blumei*); stems square; leaves oval, toothed, in opposite pairs; small flowers pale blue or white, in whorls forming slender spikes. A very popular pot plant, it is grown for its foliage, which is variegated in a range of bright colours. (Family: Labiatae.)

coley *saithe*

colic [**kol**ik] Excessive contraction and spasm of smooth (involuntary) muscle, tending to occur in waves, and giving rise to severe short-lived but recurring bouts of pain. It particularly affects the smooth muscle of the gut (**intestinal colic**), the common bile duct (**biliary colic**), and the renal pelvis and ureters (**renal colic**). Calculi in the ducts are the common causes of colic. Babies are prone to develop intestinal colic as a result of swallowing air during feeding, or of other feeding difficulty.

Coligny, Gaspard II de, seigneur de (Lord of) **Châtillon** [ko**leenyee**] (1519–72) Huguenot leader, born in Châtillon-sur-Loing, C France. He fought in the wars of Francis I and Henry II, and in 1552 was made Admiral of France. In 1557 he became a Protestant, and commanded the Huguenots during the second and third Wars of Religion. Catherine de' Medici made him one of the first victims in the St Bartholomew's Day massacre in Paris.

colitis [ko**liy**tis] Inflammation of the large bowel (*colon*) leading to diarrhoea, abdominal pain, and bleeding. It may be due to infection with micro-organisms, auto-immune processes (ulcerative colitis and Crohn's disease), or inadequate blood supply (ischaemic colitis). Ulcerative colitis affects young adults; the lining of the colon and rectum ulcerate and may perforate, leading to peritonitis. Ischaemic colitis tends to arise in elderly people, often as a result of thrombosis of the arteries that supply the bowel.

collage [kol**ahzh**] A technique of picture-making introduced by the Cubists c.1912 in which pieces of paper, fabrics, or other materials are glued to the surface of the canvas. It was much used by the Surrealists in the 1920s.

collagens [**kol**ajenz] A family of fibrous proteins found in all multicellular animals, constituting 25% of the total protein in mammals. They have a stiff, triple-stranded structure, and play an essential role in providing tissue strength. Several major types (depending on the sequence of amino acids) are known, notably Type I, found in skin, tendon, bone, ligaments, the cornea, and internal organs, which accounts for 90% of total body collagens.

collar bone *clavicle*

collateral [ko**lat**eral] A valuable item used as security for a loan – often land, shares, or an insurance policy. A mortgage is a loan in which a house or other property is the collateral. If the borrower fails to repay the debt, the collateral can be sold and the debt (along with any costs) deducted from the proceeds.

collective bargaining Trade union negotiations on behalf of a group of workers in relation to pay and conditions of employment. If the negotiations break down, the dispute may result in industrial action (such as a strike), or the matter may be referred to arbitration by another body.

collective farm A large co-operative farm, at one time commonly found in socialist countries, where many small peasant holdings have been pooled to create a single unit capable of exploiting the economies of scale associated with mechanized agriculture. Technically the ownership of the land may still be retained by the peasants, but their income inside the collective is proportional to their labour services and to their needs. In addition, a high proportion of the families are allocated small private plots where they can keep livestock and grow fruit and vegetables for market. In communist E Europe, collectives could encompass several villages, thousands of hectares, and a population of hundreds or even thousands. They were first introduced on a large scale during Stalin's campaign for the enforced collectivization of the Russian peasantry (1928–33). The peasants initially resisted the new policies, which resulted in millions of deaths from famine, armed resistance, or execution.

collective security The concept of maintaining security and territorial integrity by the collective actions of nation states, especially through international organizations such as the League of Nations (where the principle is embodied in its Covenant) and the United Nations (in its Charter). Individual member states must be prepared to accept collective decisions and implement them, if necessary, through military action. Because of the difficulty of obtaining such agreements, collective security has never been fully established.

collectivism A set of doctrines asserting the interests of the community over the individual, and the preference for central planning over market systems. It advocates that economic and political systems should be based upon co-operation, a significant amount of state intervention to deal with social injustice, and central planning, decision-making, and administration to ensure uniformity of treatment. Although often treated as synonymous with socialism, collectivism is a broader term which encompasses other doctrines that justify state intervention and state or collective control, such as co-operativism, workers' control, and corporatism.

college *university*

College of Arms *heraldry*

college of education A college specializing in the initial and in-service training of teachers. In the UK, such colleges were formerly called **training colleges**, and since the 1970s many have diversified into different fields, or merged with other colleges and become known as **colleges of higher education**. Such colleges may offer BA as well as BEd degrees. Other colleges merged with universities or polytechnics during the 1970s and 1980s, when the numbers of pupils in British schools fell, and the demand for teachers dropped accordingly. In the USA there are **teachers' colleges**, such as the one at Columbia University in New York City. Such colleges began in the late 18th-c in Europe, and were at first called **normal schools** (eg the *Ecole Normale Supérieure* in Paris); they arrived in the USA in the 1830s. The term is still occasionally found as a college title, as in *Coleg y Normal* (Welsh, 'Normal College') in Bangor, N Wales.

collegiate church A church which has a group (chapter) of canons attached to it, but which is not a cathedral; examples in the Church of England are Westminster Abbey and St George's Chapel, Windsor. The term is also used (in the USA and Scotland) for a church which has ministers of equal rank.

collie A medium-sized domestic dog; several breeds developed in Scotland as sheepdogs; **collie**, usually brown and white, with a long pointed muzzle (two forms: the long-haired *rough collie* and the rarer *smooth collie*); black and white **Border collie** similar; smaller **Welsh collie** not recognized as a true breed; **bearded collie** (or **Highland collie**), with a long shaggy coat, resembles a small untidy Old English sheepdog with a tail.

colligative properties [**ko**ligativ] Properties of a solution which vary directly with the concentration of a solute. They include depression of the vapour pressure, elevation of the boiling point, depression of the freezing point, and osmotic pressure.

collimator [**ko**limayter] **1** An optical device for changing a divergent beam of light (from a point source) into a parallel beam, which is required for control of the optical behaviour of the beam (as in a spectroscope). Generally, light passes through a converging lens, then through a slit. The collimator in X-radiography uses slits only, in order to give a beam which will cast a sharp shadow.
2 A small telescope fixed to a large one, to help in preliminary alignment. It is a device for changing the diverging light or other radiation from a point source to a parallel beam.

Collingwood, Cuthbert, Baron (1750–1810) British admiral, born in Newcastle upon Tyne, Tyne and Wear, NE England, UK. He joined the navy at 11, and from 1778 his career was closely connected with that of Nelson. He fought at Brest (1794), Cape St Vincent (1797), and Trafalgar (1805), where he succeeded Nelson as commander. He was created baron after Trafalgar, and is buried beside Nelson in St Paul's Cathedral.

Collingwood, R(obin) G(eorge) (1889–1943) Philosopher, historian, and archaeologist, born in Coniston, Cumbria, NW England, UK. He studied at Oxford, where he became professor of philosophy (1934–41). He was an authority on the archaeology of Roman Britain, and much of his philosophical work was concerned with the relationship between history and philosophy.

Collins, Joan (Henrietta) (1933–) Actress, born in London, UK. She made her film debut in *Lady Godiva Rides Again* (1951) and used her sultry appeal and headline-catching private life to build a career as an international celebrity. By the 1970s she was appearing in low-budget horror films and softcore pornography, but her fortunes were revitalized with a leading role in the universally popular television soap opera *Dynasty* (1981–9). Married four times, she has written one volume of autobiography, *Past Imperfect* (1978), and her novels include *Prime Time* (1988), *My Secrets* (1994), and *Second Act* (1996). Her recent films include *Clandestine Marriage* (1999). Her sister is the best-selling novelist **Jackie Collins** (1942–).

Collins, Michael (astronaut) (1930–) Astronaut, born in Rome, Italy. He trained at West Point, became a test pilot, and joined the space programme in 1963. He was one of the members of the Gemini 10 project, and remained in the command module during the successful Apollo II Moon-landing expedition. He became under-secretary of the Smithsonian Institution in 1978.

Collins, Michael (politician) (1890–1922) Irish politician and Sinn Féin leader, born near Clonakilty, County Cork, E Ireland. He became an MP (1918–22), and with Arthur Griffith was largely responsible for the negotiation of the treaty with Great Britain in 1921. He was killed in an ambush by his former compatriots, between Bandon and Macroom.

Collins, Pauline (1940–) Actress, born in Exmouth, Devon, SW England, UK. She studied at the Central School of Speech and Drama in London, and after regular stage appearances she became known in the popular television series *Upstairs, Downstairs* (1971–3). Later series include *Forever Green* (1989–91), with actor husband John Alderton (married 1969), and *The Ambassador* (1998). Her film credits include *Shirley Valentine* (1989, Best Actress Oscar nomination), *City of Joy* (1992), and *Paradise Road* (1997).

Collins, (William) Wilkie (1824–89) Novelist, born in London, UK. He spent four years in business, then entered Lincoln's Inn to train as a lawyer, but gradually took to literature, becoming a master of the mystery story. His best-known works are *The Woman in White* (1860) and *The Moonstone* (1868), the first full-length detective story in the English language.

colloid [**ko**loyd] A state midway between a suspension and a true solution. It is classified in various ways, particularly into **sols** (eg milk), in which liquid properties predominate, and **gels** (eg gelatine), which are more like solids.

colobus [**ko**lobuhs] An Old World monkey, native to tropical Africa; slender with long tail; thumbs absent; three groups: **black and white colobus** (with very long silky hair), **red colobus**, and **olive colobus**; inhabits forest; eats leaves; also known as **guereza**. (Genus: *Colobus*, c.6 species.)

Cologne [ko**lohn**], Ger **Köln** 50°56N 6°58E, pop (2000e) 986 000. Manufacturing and commercial river port in Cologne district, W Germany, on W bank of R Rhine; capital of N Roman Empire (3rd-c); influential centre in Middle Ages; badly bombed in World War 2; major traffic junction and commercial centre, noted for its trade fairs; archbishopric; railway; university (1388); oil refining, chemicals, wine, foodstuffs, vehicles, machinery, cosmetics, perfumes, medicaments, tools; Gothic cathedral (begun 1248) is a world heritage site; Rhineland Carnival (Feb).

Colombia *p.352*

Colombo [ko**lom**boh], originally **Kalan-Totta** 6°55N 79°52E, pop (2000e) 689 000. Chief city and seaport of Sri Lanka; on the W coast, S of the R Kelani; outer suburb, Sri-Jayawardenapura, the official capital since 1983; settled by the Portuguese in 1517 and by the Dutch in 1656; under British control, 1796; large artificial harbour; British defence base, 1942–5; location of the 1950 Commonwealth Conference which established the Colombo Plan; road and rail centre; university (1972); oil refining, iron and steel, trade in tea, rubber, cocoa, spices; national museum, Independence Hall, many Hindu shrines and Moorish mosques.

Colombo Plan A plan drawn up by British Commonwealth foreign ministers in Colombo, Sri Lanka (Jan 1950), whose purpose was the co-operative development of the countries of S and SE Asia. Colombo also houses the headquarters of the Council for Technical Co-operation, which assists with planning agriculture and industry, health services, scientific research and the training and equipping of personnel. Significant contributions to the aid programme are made by the USA, along with the assisted countries themselves, other Commonwealth countries, Japan, and the International Bank.

Colón [ko**lon**], formerly **Aspinwall** 9°21N 79°54W, pop (2000e) 157 000. Port and capital city of Colón province, N Panama, at the Caribbean end of the Panama Canal; second largest free port in World (after Hong Kong); founded, 1850; originally named after William Aspinwall, railway builder; railway; commerce, oil refining.

colon *intestine*

Colonial and Imperial Conferences A series of conferences at which representatives of the British colonies and dominions discussed matters of common imperial concern; usually held in London. The first Colonial Conference was held in 1887, and this was followed by others in 1894, 1897, 1902 and 1907. They were particularly concerned with defence, although they also dealt with issues of trade and communications. The first Imperial Conference was held in 1911, the change of name implying a new status for the colonies, and was followed by others in 1921, 1923, 1926, 1930, and 1937, mainly concerned with constitutional changes and economic matters. After World War 2

Colombia

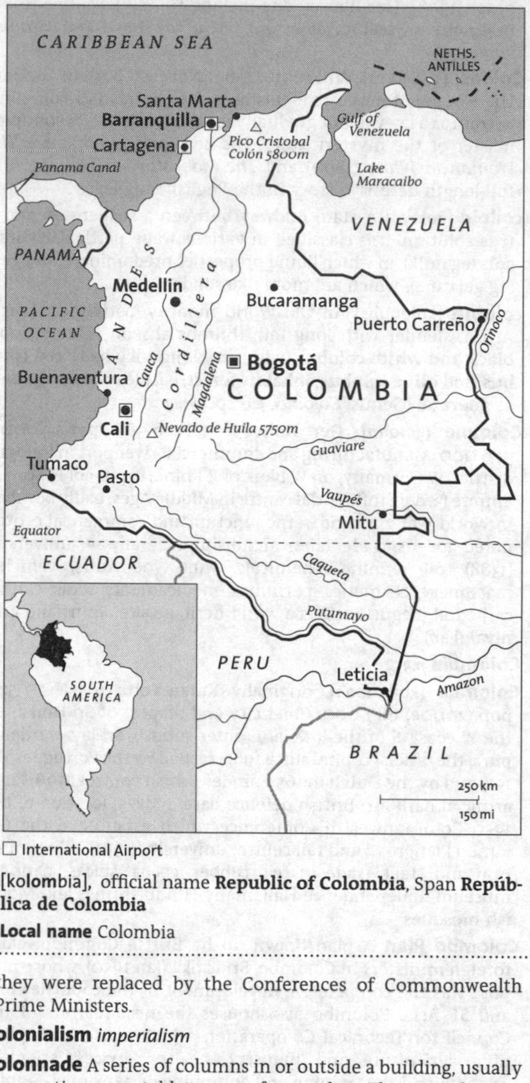

☐ International Airport

[kolombia], official name **Republic of Colombia**, Span **República de Colombia**

Local name Colombia

Timezone GMT −5

Area 1 140 105 km^2/440 080 sq mi

Population total (2002e) 41 008 000

Status Republic

Date of independence 1819

Capital Bogotá

Language Spanish (official)

Ethnic groups Mestizo (58%), European descent (20%), mulatto (14%)

Religion Roman Catholic (95%), other (5%)

Physical features Located in NW South America, includes several island possessions (Providencia, San Andrés and Mapelo); Andes run N–S, dividing narrow coastal plains from forested lowlands of Amazon basin; Cordillera Central rises 5000 m/16 000 ft to the high peak of Huila, 5750 m/18 865 ft; rivers include Vaupés, Magdalena, Cauca, and Guaviare.

Climate Hot, humid coastal plains (NW and W); annual rainfall over 2 500 mm/100 in; drier period on Caribbean coast (Dec–Apr); hot, humid tropical lowlands in E.

Currency 1 Colombian Peso (Col$) = 100 centavos

Economy Virtually self-sufficient in food; major crops include coffee, bananas, cotton; leather; gold, silver, emeralds, coal, oil; widespread illegal cocaine trafficking.

GDP (2002e) $251·6 bn, per capita $6100

Human Development Index (2002)0·772

History Spanish occupation from early 16th-c, displacing Amerindian peoples; governed by Spain within Viceroyalty of Peru, later Viceroyalty of New Granada; independence in 1819, after the campaigns of Simón Bolívar; Union with Ecuador, Venezuela, and Panama as Gran Colombia, 1821–30. Civil war in 1950s; considerable political unrest in 1980s; new constitution, 1991; ongoing conflict with FARC (Colombian Revolutionary Armed Forces) led to establishment of a FARC-controlled zone in S Colombia, 1998, as part of peace negotiations, but conflict continuing into 2004; governed by a President, bicameral Congress and Cabinet.

Head of State/Government

1994–8 Ernesto Samper Pizano

1998–2002 Andrés Pastrana Arango

2002– Alvaro Uribe Velez

they were replaced by the Conferences of Commonwealth Prime Ministers.

colonialism *imperialism*

colonnade A series of columns in or outside a building, usually supporting an entablature, roof, or arches. The most famous example is the enormous 284-column colonnade that forms the Piazza of St Peter's, Rome (1655–67), architect Bernini.

Colonsay [kolonsay] or **St Columba's Isle** Island in Argyll and Bute, W Scotland, UK; N of Islay and W of Jura; separated from Oronsay by a low channel which is dry at low water; rises to 142 m/468 ft at Carn Eoim; islet of Eilean nan Ron (SW) is a nature reserve with a breeding colony of grey seals; Augustinian priory.

colony An area of land or a country held and governed by another country, usually for the purpose of economic or other forms of exploitation. It was only in the 20th-c that colonialism became generally regarded as illegitimate, capable of justification only where it was deemed by the international community to be in the longer-term interests of the colonial territory, which usually meant preparation for independence. The present Commonwealth comprises the former colonies and the **Crown Colonies** (those still directly administered by Britain), which made up the British Empire.

colophony *rosin*

color (entries) *colour / color*

Colorado pop (2000e) 4 301 000; area 269 585 sq km/104 091 sq mi. State in WC USA, divided into 63 counties; the 'Centennial State'; E part included in the Louisiana Purchase, 1803; W part gained from Mexico by the Treaty of Guadalupe Hidalgo, 1848; settlement expanded after the gold strike of 1858; became a territory, 1861; joined the Union as the 38th state, 1876; contains the Ute Indian reservation (SW); capital, Denver; other chief cities, Colorado Springs, Aurora, Lakewood, Pueblo; rivers include the Colorado, Arkansas, Rio Grande, S Platte; Rocky Mts run N–S through the centre, divided into several ranges (Front Range, Sangre de Cristo Mts, Park Range, Sawatch Mts, San Juan Mts); over 50 peaks above 4000 m/13 000 ft; highest point Mt Elbert (4399 m/14 432 ft); forms part of the High Plains in the E, the centre of cattle and sheep ranching; the Colorado Plateau (W) has many canyons cut by the Colorado and Gunnison Rivers; several notable national parks and monuments (Rocky Mountain National Park, Dinosaur National Monument, Great Sand Dunes National Monument); wheat, hay, corn, sugar-beet, livestock; food processing, printing and publishing, electrical and transportation equipment, defence industries, fabricated metals, chemicals; lumber, stone, clay, and glass products; oil, coal, uranium; world's largest deposits of molybdenum; growing tourist industry.

Colorado beetle A small leaf beetle; yellow back with 10 longitudinal black stripes on wing cases; females lay eggs on potato plants; larvae fat, reddish-yellow with black side spots;

pupates in ground; causes great damage to potato crops. (Order: Coleoptera. Family: Chrysomelidae.)

Colorado Desert Depressed arid region in SE California and N Baja California, USA; part of the Great Basin; area 5000–8000 sq km/2000–3000 sq mi; contains the Salton Sea, a shallow saline lake, situated 71 m/233 ft below sea-level.

Colorado River River in SW USA; rises in the Continental Divide, N Colorado; flows through Utah and Arizona (via Marble Canyon and the Grand Canyon), and forms part of the Nevada–Arizona, California–Arizona and Arizona–Mexico borders; empties into the Golfo de California; length c.2350 km/1450 mi; major tributaries the Gunnison, Green, San Juan, Little Colorado, Gila, Virgin; used extensively for irrigation, flood-control, and hydroelectric power (Hoover, Davis, Parker and Imperial Dams).

Colorado Springs 38°50N 104°49W, pop (2000e) 360 900. Seat of El Paso Co, C Colorado, USA; a residential and all-year resort city at the foot of Pikes Peak; established, 1872; city status, 1886; railway; university; electronic and aerospace equipment; the nearby mineral springs make it a popular health resort; known for its high average annual sunshine (over 300 days); also nearby is the US Air Force Academy; Easter Sunrise Service.

coloratura Florid ornamentation, or 'colouring', of a melody, especially in vocal music. A **coloratura soprano** is one with a high voice who specializes in such music.

colorization The addition of colour by electronic means to the videotape transfer of a motion picture originally photographed in black-and-white. The intention is to make the picture more attractive to a modern television audience, but sometimes the former picture quality is sacrificed, and the technique has therefore proved to be controversial.

Colossians, Letter to the [koloshnz] New Testament writing attributed to Paul while he was in prison. It bears many similarities to the Letter to the Ephesians, but there is much current debate about whether the work is genuinely from Paul. It was apparently written to counter false teachers at Colossae who claimed a higher spiritual knowledge associated with an ascetic and ritualistic way of life and with the worship of angels (*Col* 2.8–23).

Colossus of Rhodes A huge, bronze statue of the Sun-god, Apollo, which bestrode the harbour entrance of the seaport of Rhodes. Built c.280 BC, it was considered to be one of the Seven Wonders of the Ancient World.

colostrum [kolostruhm] In mammals, the yellowish milky fluid secreted by the mammary glands immediately before and after giving birth, which is followed by the secretion of the true milk.

colour / color *complementary colour; light; primary colour; quark; spectrum*

colour / color blindness *colour / color vision*

colour / color cinematography Regular black-and-white films were hand-tinted or chemically toned even before 1900, but true motion-picture photography in colour was slow to develop. Most of the processes originated in the USA. Kinemacolor (1906) had some success as a novelty, taking and projecting successive black-and-white frames through red and blue-green filters, relying on the eye's persistence of vision to provide an additive two-colour mixture. Additive systems with three separation images on one frame, optically superimposed in colour on projection, had limited use (Francita, Opticolor, 1930–7), as did the Dufay mosaic (1931–40), but were inconvenient and inefficient in the cinema. From 1928 Technicolor made two-colour subtractive prints by dye-transfer, which readily produced multiple copies for cinema release, and in 1932 introduced a three-colour camera exposing three black-and-white separation colour negatives, with prints in three-colour dye-transfer. By the end of the 1930s this process was firmly established as the dominant medium for professional colour cinematography. It was not until Kodak produced their masked Eastmancolor negative that Technicolor's process was challenged. By 1955 the three-strip camera was obsolete, but dye-transfer printing continued into the 1970s. Eastmancolor negative/positive films opened the way to a vast expansion of colour cinematography, and similar materials are now manufactured worldwide.

Coloured *Cape Coloured*

colour / color filter A transparent material which transmits light from only a selected portion of the visible spectrum, partially or completely absorbing the remainder. Colour filters are used to provide light of a required spectral composition, or to give an overall colour balance to a colour photograph. In black-and-white photography, their use can change the tonal values of coloured objects, such as emphasizing the depth of a blue sky.

colouring / coloring agents Dyes used for colouring food which are either natural, nature identical, or synthetic. Tartrazine is an example of a synthetic colouring agent, while carotene is a natural colourant. Hypersensitivity to colours has been reported. The incidence of perceived hypersensitivity (c.7%) is far higher than the true incidence (0·1%).

colourization *colorization*

colour / color negative An intermediate photographic image used for the production of a colour print, and characterized by a reversal of subject tones and subject colours recorded as their complementary colours. Colour negative or print film uses a basic arrangement of three light-sensitive emulsion layers superimposed to form an 'integral tripack'. The layers are sensitive to blue, green, and red light, and after colour processing give dye images in yellow, magenta, and cyan colours, respectively. An overall yellow/orange appearance is due to other dyes in the emulsions whose function is to improve colour reproduction in the print.

colour / color photography The photographic reproduction of colour from negatives recording separately the red, green, and blue light components of a scene. A positive picture is formed by the superimposition of three corresponding images, either projected in the light of the same hues (*additive*) or printed in the complementary colours, cyan, magenta, and yellow (*subtractive*). Cameras exposing three plates simultaneously through colour filters and beam-splitting prisms or mirrors were made from the 1880s onwards, with subtractive prints by the carbro process or by dye-transfer. A major advance was the integral *tripack*, recording in three separate photographic layers on a common base and developed with colour couplers. The first was Kodachrome (1935), the film exposed in the camera being reversal-processed to a subtractive colour positive transparency. In 1939 Agfa introduced a multi-layer colour negative from which positives could be printed on a corresponding tripack, either as transparencies on film or on paper. Integral masking in the negative emulsions (Ektacolor 1949) greatly improved the colour quality of the resultant prints and is now incorporated by all manufacturers. Modern tripack films embody two or more separate coatings in each of the three colour-sensitive layers, and provide high sensitivity combined with high resolution and low grain.

colourpoint / colorpoint *Himalayan cat*

colour / color printer (computing) A computer printer which can print in full colour, enabling computers to print maps, pictures, and other illustrations. Cheaper models are based on the ink-jet principle. Colour laser printers are now becoming less costly, and hence increasingly common.

colour / color separation overlay *chromakey*

colour / color television When television broadcasting in colour was introduced in the 1950s, it was essential that a compatible picture should be obtained on existing monochrome sets, and all current systems were established on that basis. The image formed by the lens of a camera is divided into its components of red, green, and blue light, either by a beam-splitting prism with colour filters and three separate sensors, or by a filter with fine stripes of the three colours and a single sensor. Scanning the image provides separate red, green, and blue signals (RGB) and these are combined in the proportions of 30% R, 59% G, and 11% B to form the *luminance* signal, Y, which represents the picture in neutral tones from white to black. The colour information, *chrominance*, is handled as two colour-difference signals, B–Y and R–Y, which are coded in phase relationship and added to the luminance signal for transmission, in what is termed the *composite mode*. The colour coding details vary in different systems – NTSC in America and Japan, and PAL or SECAM in Europe and elsewhere. In the late 1980s, the alternative *component* mode was developed, in which the chrominance signals are kept separate from the luminance, but compressed in time to occupy the same period. This provides improved picture quality, and is widely used in the latest generation of videotape recorders. It could also be employed for high-definition TV broadcasting, as in the MAC (multiple analogue component) system. In the receiver, scanning controlled by the luminance signal alone provides a black-and-white image on the screen of a monochrome cathode ray tube, but in a colour set both chrominance and luminance are decoded to give separate RGB signals controlling the three electron guns of a shadow-mask tube. As these beams are scanned across the screen they stimulate groups of minute phosphor dots which glow in the corresponding colour, red, green and blue, to form the elements of the complete picture by additive colour mixture.

colour / color therapy The use of psychological and physical effects of coloured light for healing purposes. Colour therapists use a variety of techniques such as astrology, medical history, physical examination, and examination of a patient's aura to arrive at a diagnosis which is usually expressed in terms of an excess or deficiency of a particular colour. Since both infrared and ultraviolet radiation are used in orthodox medicine for healing purposes, the protagonists of colour therapy claim that the intervening wavelengths of visible light may also have healing properties, since the body is thought to absorb electromagnetic radiation as well as to emit it. An unhealthy body emits an unbalanced vibration pattern, and colour therapy is designed to restore balance using such methods as exposure to coloured light, wearing particular colours of clothing, or eating coloured foods (eg beetroot for patients deficient in the colour red). Therapists may also be asked to advise on the selection of colours in buildings, for example calming colours such as blue in prison cells and hospital wards, and cheerful, energetic colours such as yellow and red in the workplace.

colour / color vision The ability to detect differences between light of various wavelengths reaching the retina by converting them into colours. It is dependent on the presence of light-sensitive pigments in the cones (*retinal photoreceptors*), each being sensitive to light of a specific wavelength. The cones send coded information to the brain (via certain retinal neurones and the optic nerve) for processing and colour appreciation. In humans, the cones contain pigments most sensitive to red, green, or blue light. Absence of one or more of these pigments results in **colour blindness**: red-blindness (*protanopia*) affects the ability to distinguish red and green; blue-blindness (*deuteranopia*) affects blue and yellow; and green-blindness (*tritanopia*) affects the green range of the spectrum. Colour blindness is a sex-linked characteristic, about 20 times more common in men; women cannot suffer from the defect unless both parents possess the defective gene.

Colt, Samuel (1814–62) Inventor, born in Hartford, Connecticut, USA. He ran away to sea in 1827, and c.1832 travelled throughout the USA, lecturing on chemistry. In 1835 he took out his first patent for a revolver, which after the Mexican War was adopted by the US army, founding the fortunes of his company, Colt's Patent Fire-Arms.

Coltrane, John (William) (1926–67) Saxophonist and composer, born in Hamlet, North Carolina, USA. He emerged in the 1950s as one of the most influential jazz performers of the post-bebop era. After working with the Dizzy Gillespie Big Band and with such modernists as pianist Bud Powell, he began to shape his distinctive style when he joined the influential Miles Davis Quintet (1955). The intensity of his attack and dense flow of notes influenced a generation of future saxophone players, as did his adoption of the soprano saxophone as a second instrument to the tenor. He led his own small groups after 1960, remaining a controversial avant-garde figure.

coltsfoot A perennial with long whitish rhizomes (*Tussilago farfara*), native to Europe, W and N Asia, and N Africa; leaves all basal, up to 30 cm/12 in across, rounded to shallowly lobed, white-felted beneath; flower-heads bright yellow, solitary on stems to 15 cm/6 in, appearing before the leaves. It is an old herbal medicine for chest complaints. (Family: Compositae.)

colugo [koloogoh] A nocturnal mammal, native to SE Asia; face lemur-like; large gliding membrane along each side of body, extending to tips of fingers, toes, and long tail; lives in trees; eats plant material; closely related to insectivores; only member of the order Dermoptera; also known as **flying lemur**. (Family: Cynocephalidae, 2 species.)

Colum, Padraic (1881–1972) Poet and playwright, born in Co Longford, C Ireland. He studied at Trinity College, Dublin, and was a leader of the Irish literary revival. He wrote several plays for the Abbey Theatre, and helped to found the *Irish Review* (1911). From 1914 he lived in the USA, and published two studies on Hawaiian folklore (1924, 1926). He wrote several volumes of poetry, and also children's stories.

Columba, St, also **Columcille** or **Colm** (521–97) Missionary and abbot, born in Gartan, Co Donegal, N Ireland. He founded monasteries at Derry (546), and Durrow (553), and then at Iona, in the Inner Hebrides (c.563), from where he and his followers brought Christianity to Scotland. In his system, bishops were subordinate to abbots, and Easter was kept on a different day from the Roman churches. He is said to have copied 300 books with his own hand. Feast day 9 June.

Columba (Lat 'dove') A small S constellation.

Columbae *Columbiformes*

Columban or **Columbanus, St** (c.543–615) Missionary and abbot, 'the younger Columba', born in Leinster, E Ireland. About 585 he went to Gaul and founded the monasteries of Anegray, Luxeuil, and Fontaine in the Vosges. His adherence to the Celtic Easter involved him in controversy, and the courage with which he rebuked the vices of the Burgundian court led to his expulsion. He later went to Lombardy, and in 612 founded the monastery of Bobbio, in the Appenines. Feast day 23 November.

Columbia 34°00N 81°03W, pop (2000e) 116 300. State capital in Richland Co, C South Carolina, USA; at the confluence of the Broad and Saluda Rivers, which join to form the Congaree R; settled, early 1700s; state capital, 1786; city status, 1854; burned by General Sherman, 1865; airfield; railway; two universities (1801, 1870); commercial and trading centre in a rich farming area; printing; textiles, plastics, electrical equipment, machinery.

Columbia River River in NW USA and SW Canada; rises in the Rocky Mts in E British Columbia, flows into Washington state, USA, and enters the Pacific at Cape Disappointment, SW of Vancouver, Washington; length 1953 km/1214 mi; many rapids and falls; major gorge through the Cascade range; source of irrigation and hydroelectric power.

Columbia University *Ivy League*

Columbiformes [koluhmbi**faw(r)**meez] An order of birds encompassing the pigeons, sandgrouse, the extinct dodo, and dodo-like solitaires; also known as **Columbae**.

columbine A perennial (*Aquilegia vulgaris*) native to Europe, N Africa, and Asia; leaves divided into three segments, each again divided into three; flowers blue, rarely white, each of the five petals with a curved backward-pointing spur containing nectar. The popular garden forms, often called **aquilegias**, include hybrids with long straight spurs and more colourful flowers. (Family: Ranunculaceae.)

Columbus 39°58N 83°00W, pop (2000e) 711 500. Capital of state in Franklin Co, C Ohio, USA, at the confluence of the Olentangy and Scioto Rivers; laid out opposite the earlier settlement of Franklinton, 1812; state capital, 1824; city status, 1834; railway; three universities (1850, 1870, 1902); air force base; electronics, machinery, fabricated metals, aircraft and automobile parts; centre for research in science and information technology; Centre of Science and Industry, Ohio Historical Centre, Ohio Railway Museum, Ballet Metropolitan.

Columbus, Christopher, Ital **Cristoforo Colombo**, Span **Cristóbal Colón** (1451–1506) European discoverer of the New World, born in Genoa, NW Italy. He went to sea at 14, was shipwrecked off Portugal, and settled there c.1470. His plans to reach India by sailing W were rejected by John II of Portugal, but finally supported by Ferdinand and Isabella of Spain. He set sail from Saltes (3 Aug 1492) in the *Santa Maria*, with 50 men, and attended by the *Pinta* and the *Niña*. He reached the Bahamas (12 Oct), then visited Cuba and Hispaniola (Haiti), where he left a small colony. He returned (15 Mar 1493) to be received with the highest honours by the court. His second voyage (1493–6) led to the discovery of several Caribbean islands. On his third voyage (1498–1500) he discovered the South American mainland, but after a revolt against his command, he was sent home in irons by a newly appointed royal governor. Restored to favour in Spain, he went on his last great voyage (1502–4) along the S side of the Gulf of Mexico. He died at Valladolid, in Spain, but in 1536 his remains and those of his son Diego were removed to Santo Domingo, in Hispaniola. They were returned to Spain in 1899, and interred in Seville Cathedral.

Columbus Day A national holiday in the USA, held in most states on the Monday nearest the 12 October, in commemoration of Christopher Columbus's discovery of America (12 Oct 1492). It is also celebrated in several countries of Central and South America.

column A vertical support in a building, usually made up of a base, circular shaft, and spreading capital, and designed to carry an entablature or arch. It is also used as an aesthetic device to add ornament or to divide a space. Occasionally it is built in total isolation as a free-standing object.

Colwyn *Aberconwy and Colwyn*

Colwyn Bay [kolwin] 53°18N 3°43W, pop (2001e) 32 000. Seaside resort town in NW Wales; administrative centre of Aberconwy and Colwyn unitary authority; railway; theatre; mountain zoo; annual summer fishing festival; tourism.

coly [kohlee] A bird native to Africa S of the Sahara, also known as **mousebird**; small, greyish; head crest, short curved bill, long tail; outer toe reversible; lives in groups. It is placed in a separate order, Coliiformes. (Genus: *Colius*, 6 species. Family: Coliidae.)

coma (medicine) A state of unconsciousness from which individuals cannot be roused. Brain functions are progressively depressed, but the vital activities of respiration and constriction of the heart continue. The causes include trauma to the brain, meningitis, alcohol and drug overdosage, and metabolic disorders such as severe kidney and liver failure and complications of diabetes.

coma (physics) *aberrations 1*

Coma Berenices [kohma bereniyseez] (Lat 'Berenice's hair') A faint N constellation established in 1551 by Gerardus Mercator. It includes the huge Coma cluster of galaxies, located 100 megaparsec away.

COMAL [kohmal] Acronym for **COMmon ALgorithmic language**. An enhanced version of the BASIC computer language which combines aspects of both BASIC and PASCAL. It was developed by Danish computer scientist Borge Christiansen in 1974.

Comanche [komanchee] Shoshonean-speaking North American Plains Indians who migrated S from Wyoming and became a powerful group, raiding and displacing others (eg the Apache), and challenging white settlers. They were one of the first to acquire horses from the Spanish, and hunted buffalo. The S Comanche were settled on reservations in the mid-19th-c, but the N Comanche held out against the white settlers, finally agreeing to settle on a reservation in Oklahoma in 1867.

Comaneci, Nadia [komaneech] (1961–) Gymnast, born in Onesti, C Moldova. Representing Romania, she was the star of the 1976 Olympic Games, when at the age of 14 (coached by Bela Karolyi) she won gold medals in the beam, vault, and floor disciplines. She retained the beam and floor exercise gold medals in 1980. In 1976 she became the first gymnast to obtain a perfect score of 10 for her performance on the parallel bars and beam. Later she became an international judge, and coach to the Romanian national team. In 1989, amid much publicity, she defected to the USA via Hungary.

combassou *whydah*

Combination Acts British legislation passed in 1799 and 1800 which prohibited the coming together (*combination*) of workers in trade unions. The Acts were part of anti-reformist legislation passed by the Pitt government during the French wars, though combinations in many trades were already illegal. The Acts were repealed in 1824–5, and trade unions, though under severe restrictions, legalized.

Combined Operations Command A British force established in 1940 when Churchill appointed Admiral of the Fleet Lord Keyes to co-ordinate British commando raids against German-occupied Europe. Keyes' successor Lord Mountbatten (1941–3) directed larger operations involving all three Services, and prepared for the eventual Allied invasion of France, in which Combined Operations techniques were to play a crucial role.

combine harvester An agricultural machine which cuts, threshes, and cleans all types of cereals, oilseeds, and legumes. Most combines are now self-propelled, and are equipped for handling grain and seed in bulk. The machine combines four functions: it gathers the crop, threshes the seed from the ear, separates the seed from the straw, and cleans the seed of the chaff, weed seeds, and other unwanted material. There are two major types of combine: the most common type is based on a drum and concave threshing mechanism; the axial flow type has higher work rates, but is more suited to dry conditions such as those experienced in parts of the USA. *Forage harvesters* are used to cut and gather grass and other crops used for animal feed, afterwards chopping and blowing them into high-sided trailers.

combing In spinning, a post-carding process which removes unwanted short fibres, termed *noil*, and straightens and aligns the remaining fibres (*sliver*). The sliver may then be spun into fine smooth yarns.

comb jelly *ctenophore*

combustion A burning, usually in a supply of oxygen to form oxides. The complete combustion of a hydrocarbon yields carbon dioxide and water. The energy associated with the combustion of a mole of a substance is called its **heat of combustion**.

COMECON *Council for Mutual Economic Assistance*

Comédie-Française, La [komaydee frãsez], official name *Le Théâtre Français* The oldest surviving theatre company in France, founded by Louis XIV in 1680. Having been formed seven years after the death of Molière by a combination of troupes which included his former company, it was soon referred to as *La Maison de Molière*. During the French Revolution, the company split into Revolutionary and Royalist factions. After the Revolution it was reconstituted and installed in its present home in the rue de Richelieu. Its constitution, originally regulated by royal command, was redrafted by Napoleon himself on a basis that has fundamentally remained the same. Its members are known as *pensionnaires* while still on probation, and thereafter as *sociétaires* (ie full members). Despite various vicissitudes it has continued to the present to be the guardian of the French classical tradition and is subsidized by the state. It is organized as a co-operative society, with its longest serving actor as the Doyen or head of the company. All full members of the society, as shareholders, are eligible for a pension on retirement.

comedy The formal embodiment of a 'comic' view of experience in literary (or other artistic) form: typically, the drama.

Although humour and laughter are often involved, comedy need not necessarily be funny. The term is contrasted with tragedy to indicate a play (or other work) with a happy ending, provided by clarification and reconciliation and often symbolized by marriage. Comedy derives from fertility rituals, which had a positive and celebratory function involving the whole community; hence despite proliferating forms in all cultures its general commitment is to the continuity and self-regulation of human society – to which (by contrast with tragedy) the individual interest is always subservient. The **Old Comedy** of Aristophanes and Menander exposed the weakness and wickedness of individuals and cliques against the social sanity of the chorus; the more tolerant if mechanical **New Comedy** of Plautus and Terence added a love interest to the stock comic deviations from the norm. The mediaeval miracle and morality plays had a crude, corrective, comic aspect. Ben Jonson recreated the best of classical comedy in Jacobean England, with intellectual but festive satires such as *The Alchemist* (1610); while the contemporary comedies of Shakespeare, such as *Twelfth Night* (1600) and *Measure for Measure* (1604), are formally and ethically more complex, at once profound and problematical. The succeeding **Restoration comedies** of Wycherley (1670s) and Congreve (1690s) were coarse in comparison, and the later 'sentimental' comedies of Goldsmith and Sheridan (1770s) superficial, although structurally accomplished. Meanwhile the prolific Lope de Vega and his successor in Madrid, Calderón, delineated the contradictions of the Spanish character, and Molière brought the **comedy of manners** to perfection at the court of Louis XIV in France. The rationalist 18th-c and idealizing Romantic age were not productive of comedy, but the dark dramas of Ibsen and the ambiguities of Chekhov introduce the modern 'problem' comedy of relativistic values. In the 20th-c the **comedy of ideas** (Shaw), the **theatre of the absurd** (Ionesco, Beckett, Pinter), and **black comedy** (Orton, Albee) took the form in new directions.

Comenius, John Amos [komeenius], Czech **Komenský, Jan Ámos** (1592–1670) Educational reformer, born in Moravia, S Czech Republic. He studied at Herborn and Heidelberg, became rector of the Moravian school of Prerau (1614–16) and minister at Fulnek, but fled to Poland at the beginning of the Thirty Years' War. Settling at Lissa (1628), he worked out his new theory of education, and was chosen Bishop of the Moravian Brethren in 1632. He visited England and Sweden, and in 1650 went to Hungary, where he composed his *Orbis sensualium pictus* (1658, The Visible World in Pictures), the first picture book for children. He then settled in Amsterdam.

comet A small Solar System body made of ice and dust. Comets are asteroidal in appearance at distances of many astronomical units from the Sun (when they consist of a bare, inactive nucleus) and are often spectacularly active when nearer to the Sun. The characteristic bright head (*coma*) and streaming tails (both dust and ions) are created by solar heating, which causes sublimation of the ices (and entrainment of the dust) with subsequent solar-induced emission of light from gas molecules and scattered light from the dust. The source of comets of long orbital periods is believed to be a spherical halo cloud about the Sun called the *Oort Cloud* – representing a region to which cometary planetesimals scattered gravitationally after their formation 4·6 thousand million years ago. Oort Cloud comets are loosely bound in a solar orbit at distances of c.50 000 astronomical units. Comets with orbital periods shorter than about 200 years are thought to originate in an inner extension of the Oort Cloud, termed the *Kuiper Belt*.

Observable comets are occasionally scattered into the inner Solar System by the gravitational fields of nearby stars and giant molecular clouds. There are about 50 known periodic comets in the 'Jupiter' family whose aphelion distance is near Jupiter's, their orbits having been affected by gravitational interactions with that planet. These are potential targets for spacecraft missions, and represent the most primitive material, dating back to the origin of the Solar System. International Cometary Explorer encountered Comet Giacobini–Zinner in 1985, and a small 'armada' of spacecraft (Sakigake and Suisei, VEGA 1 and 2, Giotto) encountered Halley's comet in 1986.

From spacecraft and telescopic measurements it is now known that the nucleus of a typical comet is a few km in size, irregularly shaped and very dark; dust in the coma contains carbon and silicate; there is evidence of polymerized organic molecules; the gases of the coma include water, carbon monoxide, carbon dioxide, ammonia, methane, and hydrocarbons; the 'dirty snowball' hypothesis of astronomer Fred Whipple (1906–) is basically confirmed. Cometary impacts on Earth over geologic time may have been an important source of volatile material and organics contributing to the pre-biotic environment. Cometary and asteroidal impacts may also have contributed to periodic extinctions of species in the past.

comfrey A bristly perennial, native to Europe and the Mediterranean region; leaves grow to 30 cm/12 in, narrowly oval, rough, the upper with stalks forming wings on the stem; inflorescence coiled; flowers drooping, tubular, or funnel-shaped, white, yellow, or pink in bud, and opening blue. (Genus: *Symphytum*, 25 species. Family: Boraginaceae.)

comic opera A light, amusing opera, particularly one which (like those of Gilbert and Sullivan) alternates songs and ensembles with spoken dialogue. The modern equivalent is the **musical**.

Cominform An abbreviation for the former USSR's **Communist Information Bureau**, and a successor to the Comintern. It was established upon Stalin's orders at a meeting in Poland (Sep 1947), its purpose being the co-ordination of the 'voice' and activities of the communist parties of Bulgaria, Czechoslovakia, France, Hungary, Italy, Poland, Romania, the USSR, and Yugoslavia. Its headquarters were moved from Belgrade to Bucharest following the break between Stalin and Tito which culminated in Yugoslavia's expulsion in 1948. Cominform reflected a new hard line, expressing hostility towards the capitalist camp of the world, and was used by Stalin as an instrument for Soviet domination of E Europe. After the rapprochement of the USSR and Yugoslavia in 1956, the Cominform was dissolved.

Comino [komeenoh] 36°00N 14°20E; area 2·7 sq km/1·04 sq mi. Smallest of the three main islands of the Maltese group, midway between Malta and Gozo; highest point, 247 m/810 ft; harbour for pirates until the 1700s; 20-minute boat trip from the main island; no cars allowed; Blue Lagoon.

Comintern An abbreviation for the **Communist International**, founded in Moscow (Mar 1919) at the behest of the Russian Communist Party, its purpose being the rallying of left-wing Socialists and Communists. It adopted Leninist principles in its policies, rejecting reformism in favour of revolutionary action, which it encouraged against capitalist governments. It was disbanded in May 1943.

Commagene [komajeenee] An area in N Syria, ruled in Seleucid and Roman times by a Hellenized dynasty of Persian (Achaemenid) origin. The Romans suppressed the dynasty in AD 72 because of its pro-Parthian leanings, and made Commagene part of the Syrian province.

command economy *market economy*

commedia dell'arte [komaydia delah(r)tay] (Ital 'comedy of the profession') A distinctive form of theatre which flourished in Italy from about the middle of the 16th-c to the 18th-c. Its performance was the prerogative of professional troupes, unlike that of the literary comedies, which was open to learned amateurs. The skills of the form were performance skills passed on from player to player. The dialogue and comic business was not written down, but the storyline, its division into acts, and the entrances and exits of the characters were. The comedy relied on stock characters, many represented by masks. The popularity of the *commedia* spread throughout Europe, and many of these masks developed an independent stage history, among them Arlechino (Harlequin), Pulcinella (Punch), Columbina (Columbine), and Pedrolino (Pierrot). The tradition survives in puppetry, the harlequinade, mime, and pantomime.

commensalism A type of interaction between two different species in which one species (the **commensal**) derives benefit from a common food supply, while the other species (the **host**) is not adversely affected.

commercial bill *bill of exchange*

commercial paper A short-term negotiable instrument for payment of money, such as a bill of exchange. In the USA the term is used to describe a short-term note (between four and twelve months) issued by a company with a very high credit-rating.

Commission for Racial Equality A body of between 8 and 15 individuals set up in England and Wales under the Race Relations Act (1976) to work towards the elimination of discrimination because of colour, race, nationality, or ethnic origin. The Commission also works to promote equality of opportunity and good relations between racial groups. It is an offence to incite racial hatred, which includes using threatening behaviour or publishing threatening words, whether in writing, images, or sounds. *Positive discrimination* is a call to offset the effects of past bias by weighting opportunity in favour of ethnic minority groups.

Committees of Correspondence In the American Revolution, an informal network linking communities and provinces for the purpose of sharing political information. Committees began to appear in 1772, and during the independence crisis (1775–6) they assumed full power in many places.

commodity market A market where buyers and sellers of commodities – mainly agricultural crops and metals – trade (**commodity trading**); also called a **commodity exchange**. Often prices are fixed on a bargain-by-bargain basis. The dealers who negotiate on behalf of clients are known as **commodity brokers**. Commodities can be traded 'spot', ie for immediate delivery, or 'futures', for delivery at an agreed future date. A major centre is the Chicago Mercantile Exchange.

Common Agricultural Policy (CAP) One of the most important of the common policies of the European Union (EU). The basic principles behind the CAP (established 1962), or farm-support plan, are free trade for agricultural commodities within the EU, EU preference for domestic production, control of imports from the rest of the world, regional aid policies, and common financing. The objectives of the CAP were stated in the Treaty of Rome (1957) to be increased agricultural productivity, a fair standard of living for farmers, reasonable consumer prices, stability of markets, and secure food supplies. Most of these objectives have been met, through the use of high price-support measures, which in turn have generated surpluses in most major commodities (eg the 'butter mountain' and 'wine lake'). An important additional objective for the CAP is now to contain these surpluses, limit the huge cost associated with their disposal, and prepare for the admission of central and east European countries into the EU.

common law A source of the law of many countries, derived largely from custom. The system of common law (general) replaced over a period of centuries local courts and customs. In England, Henry II was particularly influential in developing the common law by, for example, sending out royal representatives on circuit. The tradition is one which emphasizes the development of law through individual cases rather than prescriptive codes, and is also the foundation of most US law. Common law, accordingly, tends to be judge-made law rather than statute law. It was defined by Blackstone as 'the common sense of the community, crystalized and formulated by our forefathers'.

Common Market *European Economic Community*

common seal A true seal native to N Pacific and N Atlantic Oceans (*Phoca vitulina*); usually grey with dark blotches; may dive deeper than 90 m/300 ft; eats fish, squid, and crabs; also known as **harbour seal** or **hair seal**.

Commons, House of The lower, and effectively the ruling, chamber of the bicameral legislature of the UK. It contains 659 members, elected by universal adult suffrage in plurality (first-past-the-post) elections, each representing a single constituency. The Commons is elected for a maximum period of five years, though the prime minister may call an election at any time within that period, and the government is drawn from the party that wins the majority of seats. The ascendancy of the House of Commons over the House of Lords began during the 16th-c, and was completed with the passage of the Parliament Acts of 1911 and 1949. The Commons is dominated by a disciplined party system, which means that governments are generally assured of a majority in the passage of legislation. In this sense the Commons serves a legitimizing rather than a legislating function. The presiding office of the Commons is the *Speaker*, who functions in a strictly non-partisan way.

Commonwealth (British) A free association of independent nations formerly subject to British imperial government, and maintaining friendly and practical links with the UK, whose total population comprises 30 per cent of the human race. In 1931 the Statute of Westminster established the **British Commonwealth of Nations**; the adjective 'British' was deleted after World War 2. Most of the states granted independence, beginning with India in 1947, chose to be members of the Commonwealth. There are annual meetings between finance ministers, and biannual meetings between Commonwealth heads of government, as well as various committees concerned with education, agriculture, and science. Burma resigned from the association in 1947, Ireland in 1948, South Africa in 1961, Pakistan in 1972, and Fiji in 1987; Pakistan re-entered in 1989, South Africa in 1994, and Fiji in 1997; Nigeria was suspended in 1995 and re-admitted in 1999. Mozambique, although not formally part of the British Empire, was admitted as a member in 1995. There were 54 members in 2002, but Zimbabwe was suspended for a year in March 2002, and withdrew after the 2003 conference reaffirmed its suspension.

Commonwealth (English history) English republican regime, established in 1649 after the execution of Charles I, and lasting until the Instrument of Government created a Protectorate in 1653. It failed to achieve political settlement at home, but its armies pacified Scotland and Ireland. The Navigation Acts (1650, 1651) and war with the Dutch (1652–4) fostered overseas trade and colonies.

Commonwealth Conference An annual meeting of prime ministers of the independent nations that evolved from the former British Empire and now comprise the Commonwealth. Its role is somewhat elusive, but it acts as a forum for maintaining political and economic links between the member countries.

Commonwealth Day The second Monday in March, celebrated with receptions, educational events, etc throughout the Commonwealth; originally instituted as **Empire Day** (by which name it was known until 1960) and held on 24 May, Queen Victoria's birthday; from 1967, celebrated in June on the official birthday of Queen Elizabeth II; changed to its present date in 1977.

Commonwealth Development Corporation (CDC) An organization established by the British government under the 1948 Overseas Resources Development Act, until 1963 known as the Colonial Development Corporation. Its functions were to develop trade and defence in former British colonial territories and countries through a loans programme, which lasted until the early 1970s. The 1997 Labour government stated that it seeks to increase the CDC's role in encouraging sustainable development in the Third World.

Commonwealth Games A multi-sport gathering every four years by representatives of the nations of the Commonwealth. The first Games were in Hamilton, Canada in 1930. Edinburgh is the only city to have staged two Games. The 2002 games held in Manchester was the first major multi-sport event to include Elite Athletes with a Disability (EAD).

Commonwealth of Independent States (CIS)

Russ **Sodruzhestvo Nezavisimykh Gosudarstv** Organization formed to replace Gorbachev's Union of Sovereign States, which was thwarted by the abortive political coup of 19–22 August 1991; administrative centre, Minsk. The agreement on the creation of the CIS declares that 'the USSR no longer exists as a subject of international law and geopolitic reality'. The initiative was taken by Belarus, the Russian Federation, and the Ukraine at a meeting in Minsk, and signed by the three parties on 8 December 1991. The Alma-Ata Declaration (21 Dec 1991) saw the original three members joined by the independent republics of Armenia, Azerbaijan, Kazakhstan, Kyrgyzstan, Moldova, Tajikistan, Turkmenistan, and Uzbekistan. Georgia joined in 1993. The aims of the CIS include: to cement historical ties; to build democracy on the rule of law; to recognize the sovereignty and territorial integrity of individual states within their existing borders; to promote mutually beneficial co-operation in the spheres of economy, transport, and communications; and to recognize the rights of the individual. There was to be an agreement on the joint command of strategic forces and the central control of nuclear weapons.

Commonwealth Institute An organization founded in 1959 to replace the Imperial Institute, itself founded in 1886 to promote commerce and industry between the countries of the British Empire. Based in London and Edinburgh, its main activity is the promotion of the heritage and culture of its member nations.

Commonwealth of Independent States *see panel*

Commonwealth Scientific and Industrial Research Organization (CSIRO) Australia's leading government science organization, formed in 1920; its present name dates from 1949. It grew out of a national conference held in 1916 on the role of science in industrial development. Its early work was in primary industry, but after 1936 its role was extended to secondary industry, and further broadened by legislation in 1978. It remains Australia's foremost centre of non-medical scientific research.

commune A settlement of people at village or household level, usually based on the common ownership of material goods. Communes often have a tradition of self-government; this was most clearly expressed in the formation of the **Paris Commune** in 1871 which challenged the authority of the national government of France. During China's Great Leap Forward after 1958, 98% of the peasantry were organized into 26 000 communes.

Commune of Paris An uprising by Parisian Republicans (18 Mar–28 May 1871) following France's humiliating defeat in the Franco-Prussian War. The insurgents rose against the Versailles government, personified by the veteran Thiers and a conservative Assembly. The climax came amid vicious fighting and destruction: the Communard rump was cornered and shot, leaving an unprecedented legacy of bitterness.

communicable disease A disease caused by a micro-organism which can be transmitted to humans from infected animals, other people, or the environment. The infection may be by direct contact (eg venereal diseases), via the air (eg influenza), by ingestion (eg dysentery), or by insect transmission (eg malaria).

communication 1 The sharing of meaning by individuals, groups, or organizations through the conveying of facts, ideas, feelings, values, etc from one party to another. The codes used may be linguistic (as in speech, writing, or signing) or those of non-verbal communication (eg gestures or clothes), but they require to be common to both parties for the most complete sharing of meaning or the fullest communication to take place. The act of communicating may be direct and face-to-face (**interpersonal** communication) or indirect and at a distance, using technical means such as television, radio, cinema, books, newspapers, or magazines (**mass** communication). The aim may be to inform someone, or to warn, persuade, or give pleasure with immediate effect; it may also be intended to serve wider and longer-term purposes, such as the maintenance of social cohesion or cultural identity. Though usually considered as a deliberate process, communication can also take place unintentionally; sweating, for instance, may be a sign of embarrassment, fear, or simply being overheated. As with every sign, its interpretation will depend to a degree on the context in which it is produced and received. The central role that communication plays in all human life is indicated by the fact that it is a major area of interest in psychology, sociology, anthropology, linguistics, and several other disciplines.

2 The technical means by which links are established between individuals, organizations, countries, etc for the purpose of the transfer of messages. These involve an *initiator*, who formulates a message and sends it as a signal (by means of a particular *channel*) to a *receiver*, who decodes and interprets the meaning. **3** A system of routes (road, rail, sea, air) for transporting people and goods from one place to another. Historically used for the movement of troops and supplies, the notion is now more often associated with commercial transactions.

communication theory The application of information theory to human communication in general. Communication is seen to involve an information source encoding a message which is transmitted via a channel to a receiver, where it is decoded and has an effect. Efficient, error-free transmission is assumed to be the primary goal, especially in engineering contexts. Attempts to apply this model more generally have been criticized for neglecting the importance of other factors, such as feedback, social context, and the active role played by human receivers in the production of meaning.

communicative competence The ability to communicate with another person about the whole range of everyday situations and events. In foreign language teaching, this emphasis led to courses being based principally on contemporary spoken and written language about topics such as shopping, travel, leisure, and family life. In examinations, it produced marking schemes where more of the marks were given for oral and written fluency.

Communion, Holy *Eucharist*

communism A political doctrine based on Marxism–Leninism (also called *scientific communism*) which has as its central tenet the communal ownership of property used in productive processes, and thereby the abolition of private property. While many social and religious communities based on communally shared property have been recorded throughout history, the origins of contemporary communism are associated with the theoretical writings of Karl Marx. In these writings, communism is seen as the final stage in human historical development, a process which sees societies move through feudalism, capitalism, and socialism (a transitional stage involving the dictatorship of the proletariat) before reaching this highest stage. According to Marx, social class (the fundamental social division) is determined by an individual's economic relationship to the means of production. In a society in which productive property is communally owned, every person has the same relationship to the means of production, and is thus of the same social class. Communal ownership therefore logically entails the abolition of social class. Similarly, because the State is seen by Marx as an instrument of class oppression, with the abolition of classes the function performed by the State is no longer necessary and, as a result, Marx predicted that it would 'wither away'. The transition to socialism and then communism was to be brought about by the overthrow of the capitalist system and the seizing of the means of production by the proletariat (or working class). This new socio-economic system would allow for the liberation of human potential and for the development of a new social ethic of 'from each according to his ability, to each according to his need'.

Marx's theories have been developed and adopted by many communist and socialist parties, and these developments have been used to legitimize both the policies and the internal organization of these parties. Thus, the Communist Party of the Soviet Union (CPSU), initially under the leadership of Lenin and later of Stalin, reinterpreted Marxism as, first, Marxism–Leninism and then Stalinism. The Party itself was regarded as the 'vanguard of the working class' and, after the socialist revolution, acquired the 'leading role' in society. The major features of this reinterpretation were the communalization of property and the means of production through the agency of the State, and the development of the doctrine of democratic-centralism. This doctrine meant that the CPSU became a highly centralized, monolithic, and secretive organization bearing little resemblance to the spontaneous, decentralized forms of organization envisaged under communism by Marx. Under Lenin and Stalin, the party became an instrument in the development of a brutal, totalitarian dictatorship. During the first half of the 20th-c, the CPSU provided the ideological lead for European communist parties, with only those which accepted this lead being able to join the *Third International* or Comintern (established 1919, dissolved 1943, *Cominform* founded in 1947). Latterly, however, the CPSU's leadership was both questioned and challenged for a variety of reasons. These include the economic inefficiencies associated with rigid central planning, the resentment of the leading role of the CPSU by the Yugoslav communist party (1948), and the neo-imperialist military crushing of attempts to liberalize communist regimes in Hungary and Poland (1956) and Czechoslovakia (1968). The emergence of a challenge to Soviet-style communist rule in Poland in the late 1970s, which involved demands for political reforms and the lack of any military response by the USSR, further diminished the leading role of the CPSU.

Outside the communist world, some parties, such as the Italian Communist Party, had developed a new variant, **Eurocommunism**, which contained elements drawn more from social democracy than from Marxism–Leninism, as a response to the changing nature and aspirations of the working class in advanced industrial societies. The fall from a position of dominance of the Communist Party in Poland and the holding of multiparty elections was the first of a series of events which led to the institution of political reform and free elections throughout Eastern Europe, and also in the USSR under the leadership of Secretary-General Gorbachev. This change was symbolized best by the breaching (1989) and demolition of the Berlin Wall, a structure which had stood from 1961 for the division of Europe into two ideologically opposed, armed camps. Following the failure of a military coup against Gorbachev in 1991, in which the CPSU was implicated, the Party was banned. Although the ban was later declared unconstitutional by the Russian Supreme Court, following the breakup of the former USSR, it lost all hold on power in the country which it ruled absolutely for 70 years. There remain a number of countries in which communist parties continue to rule, most notably the People's Republic of China, North Korea, Vietnam, Laos, and Cuba. However, even in these the system is showing signs of strain, and in China the aging rulers (adherents to the variant of communism known as Maoism) had to resort to force to crush demands for reform in the Tiananmen Square Massacre in 1989 and the banning of the Falun Gong sect in 1999. Only in North Korea and Cuba does a fully-blown totalitarian democratic-centralist regime continue in power.

The experience of communist regimes over the seven and a half decades following the Russian Revolution of 1917 gives rise to two types of assessment of applied Marxism. On the one hand there are those who say that Marxism has failed because of its economic inefficiencies and because, contrary to theory, communist states have seen an inexorable growth in the power of the State rather than the withering away predicted by Marx. On the other hand there are those who say that the regimes that call themselves communist are not really Marxist, but rather some dictatorial misinterpretation of Marxism and that, therefore, Marxism has not yet been tested in practice.

Communism Peak, Russ **Pik Kommunizma**, formerly **Mt Garmo** (to 1933), **Mt Stalin** (1933–62) 39°00N 72°02E. Highest peak in the former USSR, in the Pamir range, N Tajikistan; height, 7495 m/24 590 ft; first climbed in 1933.

Communist Party of the Soviet Union (CPSU) The party which controlled political, economic, and social life in the former USSR. It was the only party with the right to put forward candidates in elections, and most of the country's important jobs were controlled by the party. Many posts were confined to party members, who comprised only c.10% of the population. The party was ruled illegal by Boris Yeltsin following the failed

1991 coup, but Russia's constitution court reinstated the legality of at least some of their activities.

community charge A flat-rate charge on every adult resident in a particular area to contribute towards the provision of local government services. As the **poll tax**, it was first levied as a national tax on each adult or 'head' (Middle English, *polle*) in 1377, and periodically reimposed (eg in 1513, 1641, and during the reign of Charles II). In the USA, it was used in the late 19th-c in the South as a means of disenfranchising blacks and poor whites. Most tax systems have abandoned the poll tax, but in the UK it was revived as a way of overcoming weaknesses in the domestic rating system, because it would apply to all adults who use the services in a district, not just to those who own property. The charge came into operation in Scotland in 1989 and in England and Wales in 1990, with the actual levels fixed by local authorities. The intention was to induce voters to impose greater financial responsibility on local authorities. In practice, the level had to be 'capped' (ie limited by central government) in some cases. The system proved to be extremely unpopular and difficult to enforce, with claims that it was unjust in its impact on the poorer members of society. Following a campaign of non-payment and increasing dissatisfaction, the tax was replaced in 1993 by a **council tax**, which reverts to the system of basing local taxation on property values.

community dance The widespread participation in dance in community, arts, and dance centres in a particular locality. It started in Britain in the 1970s based on the French notion of the cultural 'animateur' to devise educational and outreach programmes, drawing its philosophy and practices from the theories of modern dance pioneers such as Rudolf von Laban and Margaret Morris to involve the wider community in artistic creativity. The Community Dance and Mime Foundation was founded in Britain in 1989.

community medicine A branch of medicine which assesses and meets the health needs of populations rather than individuals; also known as **social medicine** and **public health**. It includes epidemiology, preventive medicine, planning the delivery of health care, communicable disease control, and environmental health.

community politics An ongoing emphasis by candidates in general and parliamentary elections upon local, rather than national, issues and policies, the suggestion being that national parties pay insufficient attention to local concerns and campaign only during the formal campaign period. The term became popular in the UK following the successful adoption of such tactics by the Liberal Party in the Sutton and Cheam by-election (Dec 1972), and the general election of 1974.

community property A legal theory of property ownership in which all of a couple's earnings and property acquired during marriage, subject to certain exceptions (eg gifts and inheritance), are owned jointly by the 'community' and divided equally in the event of a divorce; as opposed to **separate property**, in which each spouse owns his or her own property individually. Many US states have adopted community property laws, which are seen as more equitable to women, though the separate system is still used in England and Wales.

community school / college A school or college which is open to the whole community, not just to those of school age. It may therefore be open seven days a week, during evenings as well as through the day, and in some cases children and adults may study in the same class or take part in the same recreational activities. In the USA, there are community colleges offering 2-year programmes leading to an associate's degree.

community service order A sentence of the criminal courts in England and Wales whereby an offender, who must be aged at least 16 and consent to the order, can be required to perform constructive unpaid work in the community, rather than being detained or paying a fine; also known as a **community sentence**. Breach of the order may be punished either by a fine or punishment of the original offence.

commutative operation In mathematics, an operation where the order of combination does not affect the result. Thus addition is commutative, because $a + b = b + a$ for all values of a and b; but subtraction is not commutative, because $a - b \neq b - a$ for all a,b.

Como, Perry, nickname **Mr C** (1912–2001) Popular singer, born in Canonsburg, Pennsylvania, USA. He sang with the Ted Weems band for six years and recorded many hit records in the 1940s and 1950s. His popularity on radio and on his television show, *The Kraft Music Hall*, earned him his nickname. Known for his smooth baritone crooning, he released the hit song 'It's Impossible' in 1970, and was one of the most commercially successful popular singers during a career that lasted over six decades.

Como 45°49N 9°06E, pop (2000e) 96 000. Capital town of Como province, Lombardy, NW Italy, at SW end of L Como; railway; silk, motor cycles, glass, furniture, printing, marble quarrying, food processing, finance and service industries, tourism; marble cathedral (1396), 11th-c twin-towered church of Sant'Abbondio (11th-c), old town largely encircled by mediaeval wall; some Roman remains.

Como, Lake (Ital **Lago di**) or **Lario**, ancient **Larius Lacus** area 146 sq km/56 sq mi. Narrow lake in Como province, Lombardy, N Italy, at the foot of the Bernese Alps; length 50 km/31 mi; 4 km/2½ mi wide at its half-way point; maximum depth 412 m/1353 ft, the deepest of the N Italian lakes; promontory of Bellagio divides it into two branches, with Como at the S end of the SW branch; lake resorts include Tremezzo and Menaggio.

Comodoro Rivadavia [kohmohdohroh reevadavia] 45°50S 67°30W, pop (2000e) 135 300. Seaport and largest city in Chubut province, Patagonia, S Argentina; on the Golfo San Jorge, on the Atlantic coast; railway; airfield; university (1961); natural gas pipeline linked to Buenos Aires; oil, petrochemicals.

Comoé [komohay] National park, largely in Bouna department, NE Côte d'Ivoire; crossed by R Comoé; area 11 500 sq km/4450 sq mi; established in 1968; a world heritage site.

Comoros *p.361*

compact camera *miniature camera*

compact disk (CD) A plastic disk of 120 mm/4·7 in diameter, holding on a single side up to 70 min of digitally encoded sound recording, stored as a succession of pits and plateaux in tracks 1·6 μm wide. The disk is coated in a reflective material (usually aluminium), which either scatters or reflects back into a photoelectric detector a laser beam used to read (play) the encoded sound when the disk is rotated at high constant linear speed. Launched in 1982–3 by Philips and Sony jointly, digital compact disks are free of stylus wear, are essentially immune to surface blemishes, and thus appear near to perfection in sound recording.

Companions of Honour, Order of the (CH) In the UK, an award instituted in 1917, made to members of either sex for outstanding service to the nation. It now consists of the sovereign and a maximum of 65 members. The ribbon is carmine with gold edges.

company An association existing for a commercial or business purpose, considered to be a legal entity independent of its members. It may be formed by Act of Parliament, by Royal Charter, or by registration under company law (referred to as a **limited liability** or **joint-stock company**). The main regulating law in England is the Companies (Consolidated) Act (1985). A company registered under this Act has limited liability: its owners (the shareholders) have no financial liability in the event of winding up the affairs of the company, but they might lose the money already invested in it. *Ltd* after the company's name signifies *limited*, and *PLC* (**public limited company**) indicates that its shares are widely held. In the USA, companies are registered in a particular state – Delaware being especially favoured – and become *Incorporated* (*Inc*).

comparative history A form of historical enquiry reacting against an excessive concentration on accounts of national development. Comparative historians usually study the devel-

Comoros

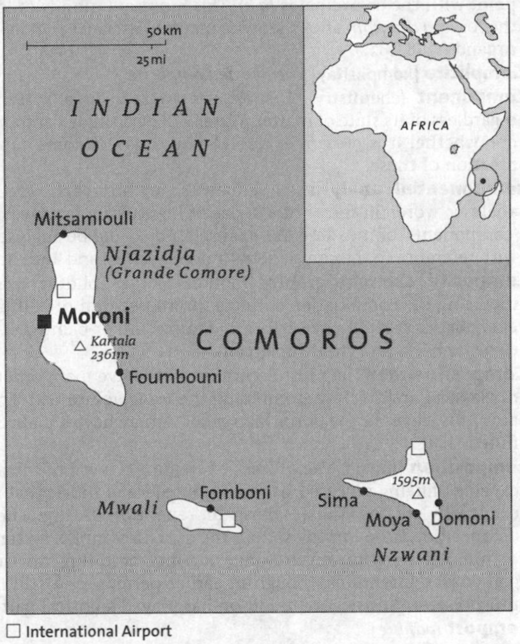

[komoros], official name **Federal and Islamic Republic of the Comoros, République Fédérale Islamique des Comores**

Local name Comores

Timezone GMT +3

Area 1 862 km^2/719 sq mi

Population total (2002e) 583 000

Status Federal republic

Date of independence 1975

Capital Moroni (on Njazidja Island)

Languages Arabic, French (official), Kiswahili

Ethnic groups Comorian (97%), Makua (2%)

Religions Sunni Muslim (86%), Roman Catholic (14%)

Physical features Located in the Mozambique Channel between mainland Africa and Madagascar; a group of three volcanic islands: Njazidja (Grande Comore), Nzwani (Anjouan), and Mwali (Mohéli); largest island, Njazidja, with an active volcano, Mt Kartala, 2361 m/7746 ft.

Climate Tropical; dry season (May–Oct), hot, humid season (Nov–Apr); average temperatures, 20°C (Jul), 28°C (Nov).

Currency 1 Comorian Franc (CFr) = 100 centimes

Economy Largely agricultural economy: vanilla, copra, cacao, sisal, coffee, cloves, vegetable oils; perfume.

GDP (2002e) $441 mn, per capita $700

Human Development Index (2002) 0·511

History Under French control, 1843–1912; French overseas territory, 1947; internal political autonomy, 1961; unilateral independence declared, 1975; Mayotte, island in the archipelago, has remained under French rule; established as a Federal Islamic Republic, 1978; a one-party state, governed by a President, Council of Ministers, and unicameral Federal Assembly; new constitution, 2001, provided for the creation of a new federation, the Comoros Union, with greater autonomy for each of the three islands; a president, elected for a 4-year term, heads a central government, and a 33-member legislature.

Head of State/Government
1999–2002 Azali Assoumani
2002 Hamada Madi (Interim)
2002– Azali Assoumani

Prime Minister
1999–2000 Tarmidi Bianrifi
2000– Hamada Madi

opment of different societies within a similar period. Their techniques can be used, for example, to help explain why Britain industrialized in the late 18th-c and early 19th-c, when European competitors did not. More recently, some comparative studies have looked at similar phenomena across very different periods. For example, attempts have been made to identify the similarities between European peasant societies in the later Middle Ages, and underdeveloped agrarian societies in Africa and India in the 20th-c. It is characteristic of comparative history that it tends to concentrate on specific themes or problems, rather than attempting to provide narrative accounts of the societies studied.

comparative linguistics The comparison of the features of different languages or dialects, or the different historical states of a language. In the 19th-c, the concern was exclusively historical, as linguists explored the similarities and differences between languages, and tried to set up common antecedents on the basis of the correspondences they observed to exist between their sounds. In this way, Greek, Latin, and the Germanic languages were all shown to belong to the Indo-European language family. This field of study was known as **comparative philology**, and the process of deducing the characteristics of the antecedent or parent language as **comparative reconstruction**.

comparative literature The study of literature across national and linguistic boundaries. This developed during the 19th-c in the spirit of Schlegel's *Universalpoesie* and Goethe's *Weltliteratur*, and studies by Madame de Staël. Abel François Villemain (1790–1870) introduced the term *littérature comparée* in 1829; it was taken up by Sainte-Beuve, and there are clear influences on Matthew Arnold in his pursuit of 'the best that is known and thought in the world'. During the 20th-c, comparative literature was cultivated especially in Europe and the USA, its admixture of historical and synthetic methods producing some fine works of scholarship and interpretation. Notable contributions were made by Rene Wellek (1903–95), Leo Spitzer (1887–1960), Erich Auerbach (1892–1957), and George Steiner (1929–). There are several journals devoted to the discipline.

comparative method In anthropology, initially an attempt to locate individual human societies within the framework of an evolutionary history of mankind. The aim was to classify societies into types, corresponding to a particular evolutionary level. The term may now apply to any method for comparing different cultures or social institutions.

comparative philology *comparative linguistics*

comparative psychology Studies of the differences among animal (including human) species in behaviour and psychological capacities. It is traditionally concerned with attempts to rank groups of vertebrates in terms of 'intelligence', and to relate intelligence to relative brain size and other characteristics. However, it is now accepted that different species cannot be ordered on a single scale of intelligence, but that each species' capacities partly reflect specialized adaptations to particular environmental conditions.

comparative religion The objective investigation of the religions of the world by scientific and historical methods. Its approach is descriptive and comparative, and is not concerned with questions of the truth or falsity of the beliefs it examines. Friedrich Max Müller (1823–1917), often called 'the father of comparative religion', did much to bring a knowledge of the world's religions to the notice of the English-speaking world. The discipline has contributed greatly to our knowledge of religions by identifying recurring patterns of belief and practice among religions widely separated by culture and geography, as well as by indicating what is distinctive in each religion.

compass A device for determining a horizontal geographical direction or bearing; invented in China in 1117, and in Europe in 1190. The **magnetic compass** depends on a magnet, free to rotate in a horizontal plane, locating itself in line with the Earth's magnetic field. It is subject to the irregularity and to the short- and long-period variation of the Earth's field.

compensation order In British law, an order, made by a criminal court to someone convicted of an offence which has caused personal injury, loss, or damage, to pay a specified amount of compensation to the victim, in addition to or instead of any other sentence imposed by the court (typically a fine). Courts have certain restrictions placed on them, such as the obligation to consider the means of the offender in setting the level of repayment, and they may not order compensation in certain types of cases (eg most offences involving motor vehicles). Any later award to the victim by the Criminal Injuries Compensation Board or by a civil court in an action for damages is reduced by the amount of compensation ordered to be paid by the criminal court. Compensation may also be paid for the wrongful conviction for a criminal offence, for sexual or racial discrimination, or for unfair dismissal. Many other jurisdictions have introduced similar restitution arrangements, some of which are restricted to financial compensation while others involve an element of service either to the victim or to the community in general.

compensatory education A form of enrichment for learners thought in some way to be deprived. It was specially popular during the 1960s in US programmes such as Project Head Start, or British initiatives such as the establishment of educational or social priority areas. The emphasis was often on the development of language and communication skills which would help children benefit more from their lessons. The notion was sometimes criticized for not sufficiently respecting the cultural values of the groups at whom it was aimed.

competence In linguistics, an idealized conception of language, representing the system of grammatical rules which any speaker of a language subconsciously knows. It is contrasted with **performance**, the way in which sentences actually appear, containing 'imperfections' such as hesitations, false starts, and grammatical errors.

compiler A computer program which translates (**compiles**) the source code of a high-level computer language program, such as BASIC, into a set of machine-code instructions which can be understood by the central processing unit. Compilers are very large programs, and contain error-checking and other facilities.

complementary colour / color Colours located opposite to each other, if the hues of the spectrum are arranged in a circle in their natural order, eg red–green, blue–orange, yellow–violet.

complementary medicine *alternative medicine*

complementation (genetics) The process by which two recessive mutant genes at different loci in a chromosome can supply each other's deficiency. An individual carrying both genes (a double heterozygote) appears phenotypically normal. For example, if two dwarfs marry they may have normal children as their genetic deficiencies are at different loci.

complex A psychiatric term coined by Jung to indicate a set of feelings or ideas which influence (usually unconsciously) our behaviour and attitudes. The term also refers to a series of childhood fantasies underlying a neurotic process.

complex ion *co-ordination compounds*

complex number A number that is a pair of real numbers, (a,b). The algebra of complex numbers obeys these laws of addition: $(a,b) + (c,d) = (a + c, b + d)$ and multiplication: $(a,b)(c,d) = (ac - bd, ad + bc)$. The real part, a, and the imaginary part, b, may be zero. The real numbers are the subset of complex numbers which arise on setting the imaginary part = 0: $(a,0)$. Since $(0,1)(0,1) = (-1,0)$, it is possible to regard $(0,1)$ as a square root of -1, often denoted i, and complex numbers can be written in the form $a + bi$. In the same way that real numbers are represented on the number-line, complex numbers are represented in the plane, so the complex number (a,b) is represented by the point with the co-ordinates (a,b). This representation is called the *Argand diagram* after the Swiss mathematician Jean Robert Argand (1768–1822).

Complicite [komplisitay] *Theatre de Complicite*

component (chemistry) A substance present in a system, regardless of its state of matter. Water will be a single component, whether it is present as a solid, liquid, gas, or some combination of these.

componential analysis In semantics, an approach which analyses words in terms of a series of identifying features or 'components' of meaning. For example, *boy* could be analysed with reference to the components 'male', 'young', and 'human'.

composite cinematography Motion picture photography involving the combination of images from two or more different sources, typically live actors and miniature or painted settings, or back- and front-projection.

Composite order The most decorative of the five main orders of classical architecture, combining the Ionic volute with the acanthus leaves of the Corinthian order. It may have a plain or fluted shaft.

composition (music) The process of creating a piece of music capable of being repeated, as well as the piece of music that is eventually created. The emphasis on repetition distinguishes composition from improvisation. The use of a complex system of musical notation ensures repeatability according to the composer's intentions, though in earlier periods (and still in much Eastern music) oral tradition has played a critical part.

compost *manure*

compound In chemistry, an entity with a definite composition, containing atoms of two or more elements.

comprehensive school A school catering for the whole of the ability range; opposed to a **selective school**, which takes only a section of the population. In countries such as Sweden and the USA, these schools were commonplace for most of the 20th-c. In other places, such as the UK, the non-selective school did not become widespread until the 1960s. Some countries have no comprehensive schools at all, and others operate both comprehensive and selective schools in different places. According to some definitions, a school would be truly comprehensive only if it really did take all pupils, losing none to private, selective, or special schools.

compressibility *bulk modulus*

Compromise of 1850 A US attempt to resolve conflict over the expansion of slavery by legislation. Its major terms were the admission of California as a free state, and the passage of a strong Fugitive Slave Law to placate the South.

Compton, Arthur (Holly) (1892–1962) Physicist, born in Wooster, Ohio, USA. He studied at Princeton University, and became professor of physics at Chicago (1923). He was a leading authority on nuclear energy, X-rays, and quantity production of plutonium. He observed and explained the **Compton effect**, the increase in wavelength of X-rays scattered by collisions with electrons, for which he shared the Nobel Prize for Physics in 1927. He became Chancellor of Washington University in 1945, and also professor of natural history there (1953–61).

Compton, Denis (Charles Scott) (1918–97) Cricketer, born in London, UK. He played cricket for England 78 times, and scored 5807 runs at an average of 50·06. His county team was Middlesex. In the 1947 season he scored a record 3816 runs, including a record 18 centuries. During his career (1936–57) he made 38 942 runs and took 622 wickets. A winger at soccer, he won an England cap during the war years. His career was spent with Arsenal, and along with his brother, **Leslie Compton** (1912–84), he won a Football Association Cup-winner's Medal in 1950. He became a journalist and broadcaster when he retired from active sport.

Compton, Fay (1894–1978) Actress, born in London, UK, the daughter of the actor **Edward Compton** (1854–1918), and the sister of Sir Compton Mackenzie. She first appeared on the stage in 1911, and won acclaim in London in *Peter Pan* (1918). She later played many famous parts, especially in plays by Barrie.

Compton-Burnett, Dame Ivy [bernet] (1884–1969) Novelist, born in Pinner, NW Greater London, UK. She studied classics at London, and became a prolific writer. Her rather stylized novels have many features in common, being set in upper-class Victorian or Edwardian society; the characters usually belong to a large family, spanning several generations. Her first novel was *Pastors and Masters* (1925), later works including *Brothers and Sisters* (1929) and *Mother and Son* (1955, James Tait Black). She was made a dame in 1967.

computational linguistics The application and development of statistical and computational techniques as part of the study of language. Areas of interest include analyzing the frequency of occurrence of particular words to investigate the authorship of a text, the use of computers in speech analysis and synthesis, the study of techniques of automatic ('machine') translation, and the development of computational models of linguistic structure and interaction as part of research into artificial intelligence.

computer The modern electronic digital computer is the result of a long series of developments, which started some 5000 years ago with the abacus. The first mechanical adding device was developed in 1642 by the French scientist-philosopher, Pascal. His 'arithmetic machine', was followed by the 'stepped reckoner' invented by Leibnitz in 1671, which was capable of also doing multiplication, division, and the evaluation of square roots by a series of stepped additions, not unlike the methods used in modern digital computers. In 1835, Charles Babbage formulated his concept of an 'analytical machine' which combined arithmetic processes with decisions based on the results of the computations. This was really the forerunner of the modern digital computer, in that it combined the principles of sequential control, branching, looping, and storage units.

In the later 19th-c, George Boole developed the symbolic binary logic which led to Boolean algebra and the binary switching methodology used in modern computers. Herman Hollerith (1860–1929), a US statistician, developed punched card techniques, mainly to aid with the US census at the beginning of the 20th-c; this advanced the concept of automatic processing, but major developments awaited the availability of suitable electronic devices. J Presper Eckert (1919–95) and John W Mauchly (1907–80) produced the first all-electronic digital computer, ENIAC (Electronic Numerical Integrator and Calculator), at the University of Pennsylvania in 1946, which was 1000 times faster than the mechanical computers. Their development of ENIAC led to one of the first commercial computers, UNIVAC I, in the early 1950s, which was able to handle both numerical and alphabetical information. Very significant contributions were made around this time by Johann von Neumann, who converted the ENIAC principles to give the EDVAC computer (Electronic Discrete Variable Automatic Computer) which could modify its own programs in much the same way as suggested by Babbage.

The first stored program digital computer to run an actual program was built at Manchester University, UK and first performed successfully in 1948. This computer was later developed into the Ferranti Mark I computer, widely sold. The first digital computer (EDSAC) to be able to be offered as a service to users was developed at Cambridge University, UK, and ran in the spring of 1949. The EDSAC design was used as the basis of the first business computer system, the Lyons Electronic Office. Advances followed rapidly from the 1950s, and were further accelerated from the mid-1960s by the successful development of miniaturization techniques in the electronics industry. The first microprocessor, which might be regarded as a computer on a chip, appeared in 1971, and nowadays the power of even the most modest personal computer can equal or outstrip the early electronic computers of the 1940s. The key elements in computing today are miniaturization and communications. Hand-held computers, with input via a stylus, can be linked to central systems through a mobile telephone.

computer-aided design (CAD) The use of computers in various design activities, such as designing the interconnections on printed circuit boards and optimizing the aerodynamic shapes of aeroplanes. CAD makes great use of computer graphics, and generally requires relatively fast computers.

computer-aided instruction (CAI) The use of computers as teaching aids or substitute teachers. Through the use of suitable programs the computer can provide information, ask questions, react appropriately to the student's response, and score multiple-choice tests. It is also known as **computer-assisted learning** (CAL) or **computer-based learning** (CBL).

computer-aided manufacture (CAM) The use of computers in controlling and supervising various manufacturing activities, usually involving robotics, such as the assembly of complex mechanical units and the welding or spraying of motor cars. CAM forms the basis of the fully automatic production line.

computer-aided software engineering (CASE) The use of computer-based tools to assist with the process of designing and implementing computer programs and larger software suites. The acronym CASE also stands for **computer-aided systems engineering** – the use of computer-based tools to assist with the process of analyzing manual business information systems and designing new computer-based systems to replace them.

computer art An art style begun after 1945 when wartime analogue computers were adapted to make abstract drawings; for example, the work of English artist and philosopher, Desmond Paul Henry (1921–), included in the 'Cybernetic Serendipity' exhibition, London, in 1968. However, since the mid-1960s, modern digital computers have been used to produce drawings, paintings, and even sculpture (eg Charles Csuri, Robert Mallory). Typically, the artist designs programmes, which may include some randomizing element, and the results are printed out by machine; but it is possible to incorporate light and sound input, and frequently the artist intervenes during the production of the image.

computer-assisted learning (CAL) *computer-aided instruction*

computer-based learning (CBL) *computer-aided instruction*

computer game A small personal computer supplied with a computer program which allows one or more users to play some game. The game could be chess, in which case a single user plays against the computer, or it could be driving a car, in which case two users could compete against each other in a race. In some cases the game is just a computer program which runs on a mainframe computer where there are many users – as with business games, used for management training. Many games are concerned with a series of trials (eg fighting a dragon) in which the player has to win the trial before being allowed to proceed. Increasingly, computer games require the user to wear a visor (in order that the player sees only the computer display) and gloves (in order that the computer can record arm and hand movements) – a technique known as *virtual reality*. The companies dominating the home computer-games market are Nintendo and Sega.

computer generations Different eras of technical development of digital computers, defined as different 'generations'. **First-generation** computers were the early devices in the 1940s and 1950s, built using thermionic valves. **Second-generation** computers replaced these valves by discrete transistors. **Third-generation** computers replaced transistors by integrated circuits. **Fourth-generation** computers were built with very large scale integrated circuits (VLSI). **Fifth-generation** computers are those showing artificial intelligence with which we can communicate in natural language.

computer graphics The use of computers to display information in graphical or pictorial form, usually on a visual display unit (VDU), a printer, or a plotter. Computer graphics are now used in an increasing number of applications, ranging from the manipulation of highly detailed engineering drawings to computer games, from high definition views in aircraft simulators to automatic production of animated film, even indeed as an art form in its own right. Computer graphics can make very heavy demands on computing power, and many of the faster computers have been designed with graphics very much in mind.

computer-integrated manufacture (CIM) The use of computers in a factory to combine computer-aided design, computer-aided manufacture, just-in-time component delivery, and production scheduling.

computerized tomography (CT), also **computerized axial tomography (CAT)** A medical X-ray scanning technique which makes a series of pictures that are then reconstructed by computer programs to represent a 'slice' through the patient. The X-ray tube rotates round the patient and produces images in sequence on a number of detectors. The system has been developed since the 1970s and nowadays it is possible to produce multicoloured images showing great detail. The data stored in the computer can be further analysed in many different ways to produce information about a variety of tissues. These machines are now widely available, and have a special use in setting up radiotherapy treatment for precise action on small target areas in the patient.

computer language *programming language*

computer management The discipline of understanding how to use computers effectively in commerce, industry, and public administration. It also involves the study of how to implement and run the systems which are devised to achieve the required effect.

computer memory A part of a computer which stores, either permanently or temporarily, programs and data. There are two basic types of internal memory used in digital computers: **Random Access Memory** (RAM) and **Read-Only Memory** (ROM) or variants thereof. All are available as integrated circuits which allow very rapid data transfer between the memory and the central processing unit.

computer network A group of computers, linked together by telecommunications lines, for the purpose of working together. For example, the banks are linked by computer networks so that transactions involving more than one bank can be processed between them. During the preparation of this encyclopedia, several computer terminals in one building were linked through a network to a computer containing the encyclopedia database, thus enabling different editorial tasks to be carried out simultaneously.

computer package A computer program, or group of computer programs, sold as a 'package' for the performance of a specific function. An example is an accounting package, which contains all the routines and calculations necessary for the analysis and presentation of accounts.

computer peripheral Any device which can be connected to a computer. It may be an input device or an output device. Examples include printers, magnetic disks, scanners, visual display units, and plotters.

computer printer A computer output device which produces characters or graphics on paper. Many different types exist, and the optimum choice for any given situation depends on the acceptable cost, printing speed, print quality, and operating noise.

computer program A complete structured sequence of statements in a programming language or languages which directs a computer to carry out a specific task. The task of writing computer programs is known as **programming**, and the specialists who carry out this task are **computer programmers**.

computer science The whole area of knowledge associated with the use and study of computers and computer-based processes. It encompasses computer design and programming, and intercomputer communication, and intersects with a number of other established disciplines such as mathematics, information theory, and electronic engineering.

computer supported co-operative work (CSCW) The use of computers and data communications to support groups of people working together, usually at some distance apart. Using the techniques of virtual reality it is possible to create an imaginary environment in which all the participants in a conference appear to be in the same room.

computer terminal Any device which can be attached to a computer, possibly over a telecommunications line, to allow a user to interact with the computer. Examples are visual display units and some kinds of personal computers using appropriate software while linked to another computer.

computer virus A term applied to computer programs which can spread from computer to computer, usually via shared software, and damage other programs stored on the computers. The 'virus' program is often attached, by the human perpetrator, to a genuine program and is not readily detectable.

Comte, Auguste [kõt] (1798–1857) Philosopher and sociologist, the founder of Positivism, born in Montpellier, S France. He studied for a while at Paris, and was for some years a disciple of Saint-Simon. He published his lectures on positivist philosophy in six volumes (1830–42). He taught mathematics privately, and in his later years was supported by his friends. His *Système de politique positive* (4 vols, 1851–4, System of Positive Polity), shows the influence of his brief relationship with Clothilde de Vaux. In his philosophy, all sciences are regarded as having passed through a theological and then a metaphysical stage into a positive or experiential stage; the sociological development is from militarism to industrialism. In positive religion, the object of reverence is humanity, and the aim the well-being and progress of the race.

Conakry [konakree] 9°30N 13°43W, pop (2000e) 966 000. Seaport capital of Guinea, W Africa; on Tumbo island, 710 km/441 mi SE of Dakar (Senegal); linked to the mainland by a causeway; established in 1889; airport; railway terminus; technical college (1963); textiles, trade in fruit, iron ore, alumina.

Conan Doyle *Doyle, Arthur Conan*

concentration In chemistry, the number of atoms, molecules, or ions of a substance present in a given volume. It is generally measured in moles per litre or per cubic metre.

concentration camp Originally, a compound where non-combatants were detained. First instituted by Lord Kitchener during the Second Boer War (1900–2), Boer civilians were placed in camps to protect them from the British 'scorched earth' policy inflicted on their farmlands, and to prevent partisans from aiding Boer guerrillas. Some 20 000 Boer women and children died, largely from disease. During the Nazi regime in Germany (1933–45), the term was applied to places of internment for unwanted people, specifically Jews, but also for religious dissidents, communists, gypsies, and the handicapped. At least 22 camps (*Konzentrazionslager* or *KZ*) were operated by the Nazis. Administered by the SS, these were divided into *Arbeitslager* such as Buchenwald, where prisoners were organized into labour batallions, and *Vernichtungslager* such as Auschwitz, set up for the extermination and incineration of men, women and children. Among Jews alone, some 4 million died in the camps and a further estimated 1 million died in ghettos from starvation and disease, while over a million were shot by mobile killing squads (the Holocaust). Half a million gypsies met their death in the camps (the 'Devouring'). In the Soviet Union, Lenin greatly expanded the Tsarist forced-labour camps in Siberia (1919), which were renamed *Gulags* in 1930. An estimated 15 million prisoners were sent to the Gulags during Stalin's purges, among them Christians, Jews, intellectuals, dissidents, and those peasants who resisted collectivization. Concentration camps were widely used in China under Mao. More recent examples of civilian incarceration include the Serb and Croat camps set up during the Yugoslav civil war of the early 1990s, where 'ethnic cleansing' of the Muslim population was carried out.

Concepción [konsepsyohn] 36°49S 73°03W, pop (2000e) 351 900. Industrial capital of Bío-Bío region, C Chile; 15 km/

9 mi up the R Bío-Bío; port of Talcahuano; founded, 1550; often damaged by earthquakes; airfield; railway; university (1919); coal, steel, textiles, paper, oil refining, ship repairing; Cerro Caracol (SE), with major views at Mirador Chileno and Cerro Alemán; craft fair (Feb).

Conceptual Art A movement, dating from the 1960s, where the artist, instead of producing a physical object (eg a painted canvas) presents ideas, often in the form of a written text, a map, or a sound cassette. For example, Claes Oldenburg (1929–) had a hole dug in Central Park, New York City, then had it filled in again. Others have buried themselves, the event being recorded by photographs taken at various stages.

concertina A portable reed organ similar in principle to the accordion, but hexagonal in vertical cross-section, smaller, and without a keyboard. The English type, fully chromatic, was patented in 1844: it was largely superseded by the fully developed piano accordion early in the 20th-c.

concertino [konsher**tee**noh] **1** A musical work for soloist(s) and orchestra, shorter than a concerto and usually with a lighter accompaniment.
2 The solo group in a concerto grosso.

concerto A musical work for one or more solo instruments and orchestra. The earliest examples, such as those written by Corelli in the 1680s, were of the concerto grosso type, contrasting two instrumental groups of unequal size. The early concerto with a single soloist is associated above all with Vivaldi, whose three-movement form (fast–slow–fast) was adopted by J S Bach, and remained standard in the concertos of Mozart, Beethoven, and most later composers. The cult of virtuosity in the 19th-c placed most Romantic concertos (such as those for piano or violin by Liszt, Brahms, Tchaikovsky, and Rachmaninov) beyond the capabilities of all but the most brilliant technicians, but some 20th-c composers (such as Bloch and Stravinsky) treated the soloist more as 'first among equals' in the Baroque manner, while others (such as Bartók and Kodály) wrote 'concertos for orchestra' in which the orchestral instruments are treated as soloists in turn.

concerto grosso A musical work in which a small group of instruments (*concertino*: typically two violins and cello) is contrasted with the full string orchestra (*ripieno*). The Baroque concerto grosso, in four or more movements, was cultivated with particular distinction by Corelli and Handel. It later declined in favour of the solo concerto, but the title of 'concerto grosso' was used by some 20th-c composers (such as Bloch) for works based in some measure on Baroque models.

conch A large marine snail found in shallow seas around coral reefs; the queen conch, *Strombus gigas*, is abundant in the Caribbean, and is gathered for food and the curio trade. (Class: Gastropoda. Order: Mesogastropoda.)

conciliarism The theory that the General Council (consisting of all bishops) has supreme authority in the Church. It gained prominence in disputes concerning the authority of the papacy in the W Church in the Middle Ages, but declined after 1460 when Pope Pius II forbade appeals from a pope to a General Council. Interest revived with the recognition of corporate or collegial authority of bishops at the Second Vatican Council (1962–5).

conclave (Lat *cum clave*, 'with a key') A meeting of cardinals of the Roman Catholic Church. Its original purpose was to elect a pope; by a tradition dating from 1271, the cardinals are locked into an apartment to hasten election.

Concord (Massachusetts) 42°28N 71°21W, pop (2000e) 17 000. Town in Middlesex Co, E Massachusetts, USA; on the Concord R, 8 km/5 mi NW of Boston; railway; in April 1775 British soldiers attempted to seize military stores in Concord but were resisted by minutemen; battles at Concord (19 Apr) and Lexington marked the start of the American War of Independence; home of Alcott, Emerson, Hawthorne, and Thoreau.

Concord (New Hampshire) 43°12N 71°32W, pop (2000e) 40 700. Capital of New Hampshire state, USA; in Merrimack County, S New Hampshire, on the Merrimack R; established, 1727; city status, 1853; state capital, 1808; railway; New Hampshire Technical Institute (1964); electrical goods; home of Mary Baker Eddy.

concordance / discordance The degree to which identical (monozygotic) twins share attributes. It is used as a measure of how much their genetic make-up contributes to any particular characteristic. For example, 80% of identical twins are very similar in height, and would thus be said to have 80% concordance for height. However, for diseases such as diabetes and schizophrenia, in 50% of identical twin pairs one will have the disorder and one will not; they are thus said to be 50% concordant (or 50% discordant) for the disease. In such cases it is probable that environmental factors play as great a role as the genes.

Concorde The world's first supersonic airliner, built jointly by the British Aircraft Corporation and the French company, Aérospatiale. It entered full-time operational service in January 1976. Its maximum speed was 2·2 times the speed of sound, though normal cruising speed was reduced to twice the speed of sound, ie c.2000 kph/1300 mph. The maximum range was c.6400 km/4000 mi, and the time taken to cross the Atlantic was 3½ hours. The record crossing between London and New York is 2 hrs 52 min 59 sec (7 Feb 1996). It was temporarily withdrawn from service in July 2000 after an Air France Concorde crashed shortly after take-off in Paris killing 113 people. After undergoing a complete overhaul including bullet-proof fuel tank linings and reinforced tyres, it became operational once more in November 2001 but British Airways later decided to retire the aircraft as it was no longer profitable. Concorde was finally withdrawn from service on 24 October 2003 and crowds of spectators gathered at Heathrow Airport to witness the arrival of her last flight from New York.

concrete art An art form defined by the Dutch artist Theo van Doesburg (1883–1931) in 1930 as a totally abstract art 'constructed entirely from purely plastic elements, that is to say planes and colours'. After van Doesburg's death, the term was used by Max Bill (1908–94) and Jean Arp (1887–1966), Bill staging several exhibitions, such as in Zürich in 1964.

concrete music *musique concrète*

concrete poetry Poetry which emphasizes the visual presentation of the poem on the page. Classical inscriptions provide a model, and 17th-c emblem poems are simple examples; Lewis Carroll's 'Mouse' in Alice is more playful. The French poets Mallarmé (*Un Coup de dés*, 1897), and Apollinaire (*Calligrammes*, 1918) considerably extended visual techniques. Later experiments (notably in South America) have been very various, including the use of different typefaces, colour, collage, and more recently computer graphics.

concussion A state of reversible unconsciousness which may immediately follow a severe blow to the head, but which outlasts the trauma. On regaining consciousness there is impaired memory of the accident or of immediately preceding events (*retrograde amnesia*). There is no gross damage to the brain, but microscopic examination reveals some reversible neuronal damage.

Condé [kõday] The junior branch of the French royal line, the House of Bourbon, which played a prominent role in French dynastic politics, particularly in the 16th–17th-c. Ten generations bore the title of **Prince de Condé**, the most eminent being Louis II de Bourbon (1621–86), better known as the **Great Condé**.

Condé, Louis I de Bourbon, Prince de [kõday] (1530–69) Leader of the Huguenots during the French Wars of Religion, born in Vendôme, C France, the younger brother of **Antony of Bourbon** (1518–61), king of Navarre. He fought in the wars between Henry II and Spain (1551–7), and joined the Huguenots on the accession of Francis II (1559). He was defeated at Dreux during the first civil war (1562); and in the second war (1567–9) was defeated at Jarnac, taken prisoner, and shot.

Condé, Louis II de Bourbon, Prince de [kõday], known as **the Great Condé** (1621–86) French military leader, born in Paris,

France. During the Thirty Years' War he defeated the Spaniards (1643, 1648) and Bavarians (1645–6). The court party came to terms with the Fronde by his help; but his arrogance led to his imprisonment, and when he was released he joined the rebels. Defeated at the Battle of the Dunes, near Dunkirk (1658), he was then pardoned, and became one of Louis XIV's greatest generals, defeating the Spanish in Franche-Comté (1668) and William of Orange at Seneffe (1674). Ill health led to his retirement to Chantilly.

condensation (chemistry) The combination of two or more substances to form a product, with the elimination of a relatively small side-product. *Condensation polymerization* usually involves the elimination of water, and is important in the production of synthetic fabrics of the polyester and polyamide varieties.

condensation (physics) The process by which water changes from a gaseous state (*water vapour*) to a liquid state. It occurs either when a parcel of air becomes saturated, or is cooled to below its dew point temperature. Cooling can result from uplift of air, radiation cooling on a calm cloudless night, or when warm moist air comes into contact with a cooler surface. In such situations, vapour condenses around condensation nuclei, such as salt, dust, and smoke particles in the air. When condensation occurs at altitude, clouds form; close to the ground, it results in fog or dew.

condensed matter physics *solid-state physics*

Condillac, Etienne Bonnot de [kõdeeyak] (1715–80) Philosopher, born in Grenoble, E France. He was ordained a Catholic priest in 1740, and was a tutor to the Duke of Parma, and Abbé de Mureaux. He became an associate of Diderot and other Enlightenment secularists, and was an admirer of John Locke. He based all knowledge on the senses, his works including *Essai sur l'origine des connaissances humaines* (1746, Essay on the Origin of Human Knowledge), and *Traité des sensations* (1754, Treatise on Sensations).

condition In law, a relatively important term in a contract. In English law, breach of condition gives the innocent party the right to treat the contract as terminated. Contracts may also contain express or implied **warranties**, which may (eg in Scotland), in the event of a breach, justify repudiating the contract. Breach of a warranty in England is considered less important, and does not give the innocent party the right to end the contract, though a claim for damages may be possible. In some contracts (eg sale of goods) certain warranties are implied. In English law, condition can also mean a provision which does not form part of the contract, but operates either to suspend the contract until a specified event has happened (a **condition precedent**) or to end it in certain circumstances (a **condition subsequent**). In both US and Scottish contract law, a condition usually specifies some future event which, should it occur or in some cases not occur, will trigger, terminate, or modify the contractual obligations.

conditionality The practice of lenders, in particular the International Monetary Fund (IMF), to impose conditions on the recipients of loans. These conditions include measures such as reducing budget deficits, currency devalution, or liberalization of trade controls. The argument for the IMF imposing conditions when making loans is that it only has finite funds available to help member countries in balance of payments difficulties, and there is no point in using them on borrowers who do not adopt policies to ensure eventual recovery from their problems. Objectors to conditionality argue that the actual conditions imposed may be based on economic dogmas rather than a full understanding of the real problems affecting borrowing countries, and in particular that they may be too deflationary.

conditioning Two types of elementary associative learning process, seen in many invertebrates and all vertebrates.
1 In **Pavlovian**, **classical**, or **respondent conditioning**, a stimulus which reliably precedes another stimulus of biological significance (eg food, pain, a potential mate) comes to evoke a new pattern of reaction (a *conditioned response*) similar to that evoked by the biologically significant (*unconditioned*) stimulus. For example, salivation, normally evoked by the taste of food, comes to be evoked by the sight of food or the sound of a dinner gong.
2 In **instrumental** or **operant conditioning**, an individual's action reliably causes a change in stimulation of biological significance, and this alters the way the individual performs the action. If the consequence is an increase in a 'positive' stimulus, such as food, or a decrease in a 'negative' stimulus, such as pain, the action is performed more frequently than before; if the consequences are of the opposite kind, the action will be performed less frequently. An example would be waiting for a pigeon to select a particularly coloured object from a group of objects, and then rewarding (eg with food) this random event; in due course the pigeon will selectively pick out only objects of the colour rewarded.

condominium 1 In government, the joint rule, tenancy, or co-ownership of a territory by two or more countries, often suggested as appropriate where ownership of a territory is disputed. For example, the former New Hebrides (now the republic of Vanuatu) was, until 1980, jointly administered by Britain and France.
2 A type of co-operative ownership of a domestic dwelling. A person owns a unit (an apartment, or flat) in the building, and typically enters into an arrangement with other unit-owners to share the responsibility for the services to the building and the general upkeep of the site. The concept has a long European history, but is particularly associated with property dealing in the USA, where the term is used both for the building as a whole and for the units within it.

condor Either of two species of New World vulture; the **Californian condor** (*Gymnogyps californianus*) and the **Andean condor** (*Vultur gryphus*). The Andean condor, which inhabits the mountains, has the largest wingspan of any living bird (up to 3 m/10 ft). The Californian condor is in danger of extinction. (Family: Cathartidae.)

Condorcet, Marie Jean Antoine Nicolas de Caritat, marquis de (Marquess of) [kõdaw(r)say] (1743–94) French statesman, philosopher, and mathematician, born in Ribemont, N France. He studied at Paris, and his work in mathematics became highly regarded in the 1760s. At the Revolution he made eloquent speeches and wrote famous pamphlets on the popular side, was sent to the Legislative Assembly (1791), and became its president, siding usually with the Girondists. Accused and condemned by the extreme party, he was captured, and found dead in prison. In his philosophy, he proclaimed the ideal of progress, and the indefinite perfectibility of the human race.

condottiere [kondottyayray] A leader of mercenary soldiers in 14th–15th-c Italy; from Italian *condotta* 'contract'. Hired by city-states and the papacy, they were often of foreign origin (eg Englishman Sir John Hawkwood or Giovanni Acuto), but they also included Italian noblemen (eg the d'Este dukes of Ferrara, Gonzaga marqueses of Mantua, and Sforza dukes of Milan).

conductance *resistance*

conducting The task of directing an orchestra, choir, or other musical group in the performance of a musical work. The conductor establishes a musical rhythm and interpretation, signalling this in a performance by conventional hand and arm movements, as well as by movements of the body and facial expression. A thin stick, or baton, held in the right hand, became widely used only in the mid-19th-c to give a clearly visual emphasis to the basic rhythm, the left hand being used for special functions, such as signalling the entry of different parts; but many modern conductors have dispensed with the baton, and use only their hands. A printed score may be followed, but conductors who have memorized a piece of music often dispense with it in public performances. The special role of the conductor emerged only in the 19th-c; previously, the task of keeping the musicians together was performed by one of the leading players. The prestige now associated with the role developed with the emergence of composers (such as Berlioz and Mendelssohn) who also conducted, and with the serious intellectual and aesthetic demands of major works (such as those by Wagner and Mahler) in which as much effort had to be devoted to the context of the work and the interpretation of the score as to the accuracy of the playing. As their musical stature grew, many world-famous conductors of the 20th-c (such as Sir Thomas Beecham) became known as much for their personalities as for their musicianship.

conduction *electrical conduction; thermal conduction*

conductivity *resistivity*

cone In gymnosperms, a spike-like structure formed of woody, overlapping scales bearing seeds. Clubmosses and horsetails have similar structures bearing spores. The term is also used for the cone-like fruits of some flowering plants.

coneflower *rudbeckia*

cones *rods and cones*

cone shell A typically predatory marine snail; length up to 30 cm/12 in; its shell has a pronounced canal for a front-placed organ (siphon) for drawing in fluid; over 400 species, many producing poison to paralyse prey; occasionally causes human fatalities. (Class: Gastropoda. Order: Neogastropoda.)

coney *pika; rabbit*

Coney Island [**koh**nee] (Dutch 'rabbit') 40°35N 73°59W. Public beach and amusement park in the borough of Brooklyn, New York City, USA; on the Atlantic Ocean, near the mouth of the Hudson R; developed as a pleasure resort since the 1840s; New York Aquarium.

Confederacy *Confederate States of America*

Confederate States of America The official name of the states that seceded in 1860–1, precipitating the American Civil War: Virginia, North Carolina, South Carolina, Georgia, Florida, Tennessee, Alabama, Mississippi, Louisiana, Texas, and Arkansas. The Confederacy's constitution was modelled on the US Constitution, and its only president was Jefferson Davis of Mississippi. It never won foreign recognition, and collapsed in 1865. The other four slave states (Delaware, Maryland, Kentucky, and Missouri) did not secede, and neither did the NW counties of Virginia, which became West Virginia.

Confederation (Canada) A movement in the 1860s devoted to the unification of the British North American colonies within a federal framework. New Brunswick, Nova Scotia, Quebec, and Ontario were so joined in 1867. The stimulus for confederation included threats emanating from the USA, declining British interests in the colonies, ambitions to link up with British Columbia, and proposals for an expensive railway building programme. Confederation marked the birth of modern Canada, and it is celebrated annually on 1 July.

Confederation, Articles of *Articles of Confederation*

Confederation of British Industry (CBI) A federation of UK employers, founded in 1965, with a membership of over 250 000 companies. Its role is to ensure that the needs, intentions, and problems of business organizations are generally understood. It carries out surveys and research into matters affecting business, and expresses opinions to government on matters that affect its members.

Confederation of the Rhine (1806–14) A union of all the German states except Prussia and Austria, established by Napoleon I on the dissolution of the Holy Roman Empire in 1806. The 18 states were placed under French control to assist the French war effort, although the long-term effect was to stimulate the movement for German unification. After Napoleon's defeat in Russia (1813), its members, by changing their allegiance in the war, caused the collapse of the confederation.

Conference on Security and Co-operation in Europe *Organization for Security and Co-operation in Europe*

Confessing Church A Church formed in Germany by Evangelical Christians opposed to Nazism and the Nazi-supported 'German Christian Church Movement'. Its Synod of Barmen published the Barmen Declaration (1934), which became influential in Germany and beyond as a basis for resistance to oppressive civil authorities. It was succeeded in 1948 by the 'Evangelical Church in Germany'.

confession 1 A declaration or profession of faith, originally by an individual martyr, later by a group or church. Such a document became common after the Reformation.
2 An acknowledgment of sin, made either corporately in the course of public worship or privately and individually as *auricular* confession, 'into the ear' of a priest.

confessional poetry Poetry which takes as its subject the intimate details of the poet's own life, often disparaged by critics for this reason (Coleridge argued that such material offers 'a fallacious pledge of literary power'). Generally considered a recent phenomenon, it has been encouraged by US poets such as Robert Lowell and Sylvia Plath; but the songs of Sappho (6th-c BC) and the sonnets of Shakespeare (1598) indicate that lyric poetry at all times has included confessional elements.

confinement In particle physics, the postulate that quarks and gluons interact in such a way that they are always constrained to remain inside larger subatomic particles, and so may never be observed directly. It accounts for the continuing failure to observe quarks directly. Understanding the nature of confinement continues to present difficulties.

confirmation The Christian sacrament of initiation, the nature and theology of which have been understood in varying ways in Christian history. In early usage, it was difficult to distinguish baptism from confirmation as acts of initiation into Christian belief, but by the Middle Ages there was a tendency in the West to separate the two, so that confirmation was performed only by the laying on of hands (or by anointing with oil, or both) by a bishop. Children are not usually confirmed before reaching seven years of age, and many Churches prefer them to reach adolescence. In Anglicanism it is often seen as the young person assuming personal responsibility for earlier baptismal vows. The Second Vatican Council ordered that the rite should be revised so as to emphasize more clearly its character of initiation.

conformation In chemistry, the arrangement of atoms of a molecule relative to other atoms to which they are not bonded. For example, the structure of ethane illustrates its most stable conformation, in which the hydrogen atoms interact as little as possible.

conforming In film and video production, the final assembly of original material to match the approved continuity resulting from editing. With films this is done by the physical cutting and joining of the picture negative, while in video it involves the transfer of selected portions of the original videotapes in sequence to form the master record.

Confucius [kon**fyoo**shuhs], Lat name of **Kongfuzi** or **K'ung Futse** (Chin 'Venerated Master Kong') (551–479 BC) Chinese philosopher, born in the state of Lu (modern Shantung). Largely self-educated, he married at 19, became a local administrator, and in 531 BC began his career as a teacher. In 501 BC he was appointed Governor of Chung-tu, then minister of works, and later minister of justice. His ideas for social reform made him the idol of the people; but his enemies caused him to leave Lu, and he travelled widely, followed by many disciples. He later edited the ancient writings, and the *Confucian Analects*, memorabilia compiled soon after his death, are a collection of his sayings and doings. His moral teaching stressed the importance of the traditional relations of filial piety and brotherly respect. No writings can definitely be attributed to him. His teachings later inspired a cult of veneration. Confucianism became the state religion of China, but he was denounced as a class-exploiter during the Cultural Revolution (1966–76). There are now thought to be over 6 million Confucians.

conga An Afro-Cuban dance usually performed (often with singing) in a long line, using simple and repetitive steps. It was popular in Western ballrooms in the mid-20th-c, and continues to be danced spontaneously at informal parties.

Congo

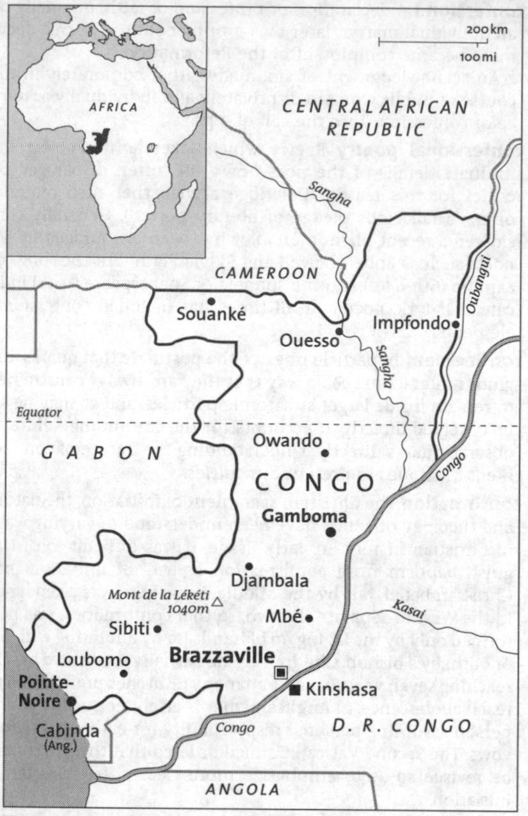

□ International Airport

[konggoh], official name **Republic of the Congo** (1991), formerly **People's Republic of the Congo** (from 1968), Fr **République du Congo**

Local name Congo

Timezone GMT +1

Area 341 945 km²/132 047 sq mi

Population total (2002e) 2 899 000

Status Republic

Date of independence 1960

Capital Brazzaville

Language French (official), with local languages, including Kongo and Téké

Ethnic groups Kongo (45%), Sangha (15%), Téké (20%)

Religions Roman Catholic (40·5%), Protestant (9·5%), local traditional beliefs

Physical features Niari valley rises to 1040 m/3412 ft at Mont de la Lékéti; mainly covered by dense grassland, mangrove, and tropical rainforest; rivers include Sangha and Alima in N.

Climate Hot, humid equatorial climate; annual rainfall 1250–1750 mm/50–70 in, annual daily temperature 28–33°C in Brazzaville; dry season (Jun–Sep).

Currency 1 CFA Franc (CFAFr) = 100 centimes

Economy Mainly agriculture and forestry; sugar cane, coffee, cocoa, palm oil, tobacco; oil, timber, diamonds; sugar-refining.

GDP (2002e) $2·5 bn, per capita $900

Human Development Index (2002) 0·512

History Visited by Portuguese, 14th-c; part of French Equatorial Africa, known as 'Middle Congo', 1908–58; independence as Republic of Congo, 1960; military coup created first Marxist state in Africa, renamed People's Republic of the Congo, 1968; Congolese Labour Party (PCT), the single ruling party in Congo, renounced Marxism, 1990; transitional government formed, 1991, and country renamed the Republic of Congo; new constitution, 1992, recognized a multi-party system; violence following disputes over the election process, 1993; new constitution, 2001; executive authority vested in the President, elected for a 7-year term, and a bicameral legislature.

Head of State

1992–7 Pascal Lissouba

1997– Denis Sassou-Nguesso

Head of Government

1992–3 Claude Antoine Dacosta

1993–6 Jacques-Joachim Yhombi-Opango

1996–7 Charles David Ganao

1997–2002 Bernard Kolelas

congenital abnormality An anatomical or physiological abnormality found at birth or within a few weeks of birth. They are a common occurrence, affecting 5% of the population, and may be so severe as to be incompatible with life, such as failure of the brain to grow (*anencephaly*), or mild, such as an extra finger or toe. Some are caused by chromosome abnormalities or genetic defects. Others are caused by environmental factors such as infections (eg rubella) and drugs given to the mother (eg thalidomide). Some have no obvious cause, such as failure of the testicles to descend, malformations of the heart, and cleft lip and palate.

conger eel Predatory marine fish (*Conger conger*) found in shallow coastal waters of N Europe and Mediterranean, usually within cover of rocks, jetties, or wrecks; body cylindrical, length up to 2·7 m/8¾ ft; jaws powerful, teeth conical and close-set; feeds mainly on fishes, crustaceans, and cephalopods; may be dangerous to divers. (Family: Congridae.)

conglomerate (economics) A company conducting a variety of business activities with little or nothing in common. Advantages claimed are that some inputs, especially finance, may be shared; that expertise may be transferred between the parts; and that the spread of activities reduces risk. Disadvantages are that management effort may be spread too widely, often into areas where specialist knowledge is inadequate.

conglomerate (mineralogy) Sedimentary rock composed of rounded pebbles of pre-existing rocks and embedded in a fine matrix of sand and silt. It is commonly formed along beaches or on river beds.

Congo *see panel*

Congo, Democratic Republic of *p.369*

Congonhas do Campo [kongohnyas] 23°38S 46°38W, pop (2000e) 30 100. A town in the Brazilian highlands, noted for its Sanctuary of Bom ('good') Jesus do Matozinho (1773), an imposing church with chapels and gardens; a world heritage site. The sanctuary, which contains Antônio Francisco (Aleijadinho) Lisboa's (1738–1814) sculptures of the 12 Apostles, is a major centre of pilgrimage.

Congo, River [zaheer] (1971–97, known as **River Zaire**) River in C and W Africa; length c.4670 km/2900 mi, second longest in Africa; rises as the R Lualaba, which drains L Deleommune (S Democratic Republic of Congo), and flows N, crossing the Equator SE of Kisangani, where it becomes known as R Congo; flows NW in an arc across C Africa, then SW, with capitals of Brazzaville and Kinshasa on opposite banks; makes a narrow trench in the Crystal Mts into the extreme W of the Democratic Republic of Congo, then enters the Atlantic Ocean SSE of Pointe-Noire; affected by ocean tide for 100 km/60 mi upstream; hydroelectricity from several dams; first European discovery of river mouth by Portuguese explorer, Diogo Cão, 1482; its extent

Congo, Democratic Republic of

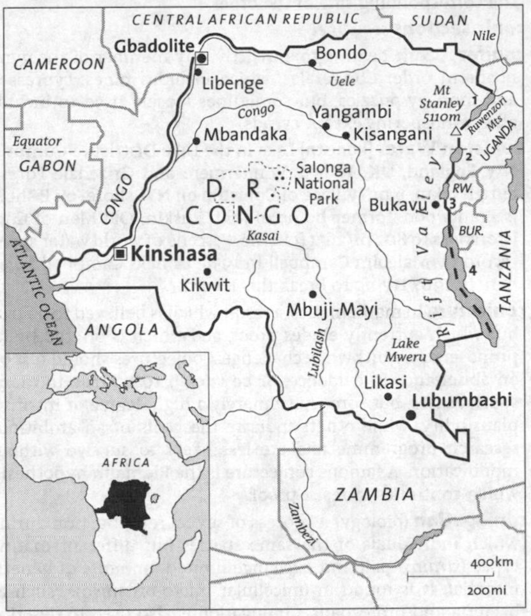

□ International Airport ∴ World heritage site
1 Lake Albert 2 Lake Edward 3 Lake Kivu 4 Lake Tanganyika

formerly **Congo Free State** (1885–1908), **Belgian Congo** (1908–60), **Democratic Republic of the Congo** (1960–71), **Republic of Zaire** [zaheer] (1971–97)

Local name République Démocratique du Congo

Timezone GMT +1 (W) to +2 (E)

Area 2 234 585 km²/905 365 sq mi

Population total (2002e) 52 557 000

Status Republic

Date of independence 1960

Capital Kinshasa

Languages French (official), English, with various Bantu dialects (including Swahili, Lingala, Ishiluba, and Kikongo) spoken

Ethnic groups Bantu, with Sudanese, Nilotes, Pygmies, Hamite and Angolan minorities

Religions Christian (70%) (Roman Catholic 50%, Protestant 20%), Kimbanguist (10%), Muslim (10%), traditional beliefs (10%)

Physical features Located in C Africa, land rises E from a low-lying basin to a densely forested plateau; Ruwenzori Mts (NE) rise to 5110 m/16 765 ft in the Mt Stanley massif; Mitumba Mts further S; Rift Valley chain of lakes, Albert, Edward, Kivu, and Tanganyika; Congo R.

Climate Equatorial, hot and humid; average annual temperature, 26°C (Jan), 23°C (Jul) in Kinshasa; average annual rainfall 1125 mm/44 in; dry coastal region; dry season (May–Sep) S of the Equator, (Dec–Feb) N of the Equator.

Currency 1 Congolese franc (CDF) = 100 centimes

Economy Subsistence farming employs c.80% of population; palm oil, rubber, quinine, fruit, vegetables, tea, cocoa; extensive mineral reserves; world's biggest producer of cobalt; industrial diamonds, copper; coffee, petroleum, cotton, tobacco processing, chemicals, cement.

GDP (2002e) $34 bn, per capita $600

Human Development Index (2002) 0·431

History Visited by the Portuguese, 1482; expeditions of Henry Morton Stanley, 1874–7; claimed by King Leopold of Belgium, recognized, 1885; Congo Free State ceded to the state, 1907, and renamed Belgian Congo; independence as the Democratic Republic of the Congo, 1960; shortly after, mineral-rich Katanga (later, Shaba) province claimed independence, leading to civil war; UN peace-keeping force present until 1964; renamed the Republic of Zaïre, 1971; further conflict, 1977–8, as Katangese rebels invaded Shaba province from Angola; President Mobutu announced proposals for the introduction of a new constitution in 1990, including the adoption of a three-party system; dissatisfaction with proposals resulted in boycotting of elections scheduled for 1992; conflict between president and opposition party over appointment of prime minister, 1993; new constitutional act, and period of transition established, 1994; further conflict, 1996; Alliance of Democratic Forces for the Liberation of Congo-Zaire, led by Laurent Kabila, take control; formation of new transitional government, May 1997, with president assuming full executive, legislative, and military powers; further fighting with rebel movements, 1998, with troops from Uganda and Rwanda supporting rebels, and troops from Zimbabwe, Angola, and Namibia supporting government; assassination of Laurent Kabila, 2001; peace negotiations disrupted by ongoing fighting, 2002; peace agreement signed with Rwanda and Uganda, 2002; power-sharing agreement signed between the government and key rebel groups (Dec 2002); agreement signed with Uganda providing for withdrawal of Ugandan forces from the NE (Feb 2003); emergency UN peacekeeping force deployed in Bunia (Ituri province) after heavy fighting broke out (May 2003); interim government named, and leaders of main rebel groups sworn in as vice-presidents (Jul 2003).

Head of State

1960–5 Joseph Kasavubu
1965–97 Mobutu Sese Seko (formerly Joseph Mobutu)
Democratic Republic of Congo
1997–2001 Laurent Kabila
2001– Joseph Kabila

Head of Government

1961 Joseph Ileo
1961–4 Cyrille Adoula
1964–5 Moïse Tshombe
1965 Evariste Kimba
1965–6 Mulamba Nyungu wa Kadima
1966–77 *As President*
1977–80 Mpinga Kasenga
1980 Bo-Boliko Lokonga Monse Mihambu
1980–1 Nguza Karl I Bond
1981–3 Nsinga Udjuu
1983–6 Kengo wa Dondo
1986–8 *No Prime Minister*
1988 Sambwa Pida Nbagui
1988–9 Kengo wa Dondo
1989–91 Lunda Bululu
1991 Mulumba Lukeji
1991 Etienne Tshisekedi
1991 Bernardin Mungul Diaka
1991–2 Jean Nguza Karl-I-Bond
1992–3 Etienne Tshisekedi
1993–4 Fouistin Birindwa *Acting*
1994–7 Kengo Wa Dondo
1997 Etienne Tshisekedi
1997 Likulia Bolongo
1997–2003 *As President*
2003– Yerodia Abdoulaye Ndombasi (*Vice President*)

appreciated only in the 19th-c, with explorations by Stanley, Livingstone, and others.

Congregationalism A movement which sees the Christian Church as essentially a gathered community of believers, covenanting with God, keeping God's law, and living under the Lordship of Christ. It derived from the Separatists of the 16th-c Reformation in England, of whom Robert Browne was an early leader. Persecution drove the Congregationalists to Holland and the USA (the Pilgrim Fathers, 1620). Church affairs, including calling a minister and appointing deacons to assist, are regulated by members at a 'Church Meeting'. As a world denomination, it has a strong missionary tradition. One denomination formed the International Congregational Council in 1949, which merged with Presbyterians as the World Alliance of Reformed Churches in 1970. With a strong tradition of tolerance and freedom of belief, its major contribution to ecumenism has been its insistence on the importance of the local church in the event of union with other denominations.

Congress The national, or federal, legislature of the USA, consisting of two elected chambers: the Senate and the House of Representatives. Unusually powerful for a modern legislature, Congress can initiate legislation, and significantly amend or reject presidential legislative proposals. The constitution endows it with the 'power of the purse', as all revenue bills must originate in the House. For a bill to become law it must be passed in identical form by both chambers and signed by the president. A presidential veto may be overturned by a two-thirds majority in both chambers. Legislation receives detailed consideration in the powerful Congressional committees. Although the chambers are organized along party lines, there is seldom a strong party majority, and when such a majority does occur it is often not of the president's party. There are signs that this may be changing with an increase in voting along party lines. The majority party leader of the House occupies the influential position of Speaker.

Congress Kingdom of Poland The name of that part of Poland given to Russia at the Congress of Vienna (1815). Tsar Alexander I granted a constitution (Nov 1815) which established the country as a constitutional monarchy united to Russia. After the Polish uprising of 1830 (known as the November Revolution) the constitution was suspended, and after that of 1863 (the so-called January Revolution) Congress Poland was fully absorbed into the Russian Empire and subjected to a campaign of russification. Large estates were divided and given in freehold to peasants.

Congress of Racial Equality A prominent US civil rights organization which campaigns for the rights of African-Americans, and which was particularly involved in the attack on discrimination and racism in the 1960s. It still exists, and is regarded as one of the more militant black rights organizations.

Congreve, William **[konggreev]** (1670–1729) Playwright and poet, born in Bardsey, West Yorkshire, N England, UK. He studied at Trinity College, Dublin, and became a lawyer in London, but then took up a career in literature. His first comedy, *The Old Bachelor*, was produced under Dryden's auspices in 1693, and was highly successful, as were *The Double Dealer* (1693), *Love for Love* (1695), and *The Way of the World* (1700). His one tragedy, *The Mourning Bride* (1697), was much admired by his contemporaries. He largely ceased writing after 1700.

congruence In mathematics, a type of equivalence between expressions. Numbers *b* and *c* are said to be congruent relative to a number *a* if *a* divides the difference of *b* and *c*: *a* is called the *modulus* (mod) of the congruence. We write *b*Ù*c* mod *a*, eg 12Ù2 mod 5. The algebra of congruences was devised by Gauss.

congruent triangles Triangles such that one could be superimposed on the other. Two triangles are congruent if either (1) each side of one triangle is equal to a side of the other; or (2) each of two sides of one triangle is equal to the corresponding side of the other, and the angles between the two sides are equal; or (3) one side of one triangle is equal to a side of the other triangle, and two angles of one are equal to two angles of the other; or (4) each triangle contains a right angle, the hypotenuses are equal, and one other side of one triangle is equal to the corresponding side of the other.

conic sections *see panel*

conifer A cone-bearing tree; strictly, any member of the gymnosperm order Coniferales, which includes pines, cypresses, and monkey-puzzles, but sometimes loosely used to include all gymnosperms except cycads.

Coniston Water **[konistn]** Lake in the Lake District of Cumbria, NW England, UK; W of L Windermere and Grizedale Forest; length 9 km/6 mi; village of Coniston on NW shore; on E shore is Brantwood, former home of John Ruskin; Old Man of Coniston rises to 802 m/2631 ft in the W; scene of world water speed record by Malcolm Campbell in 1939; Donald Campbell killed here in 1967 trying to break this record.

conjecture In mathematics, a result which is believed to be true but which currently eludes proof, and which is offered by its proposer as a worthwhile challenge. Conjectures should rest on an abundance of evidence, or be known to be true in many special cases, but some have merely a high degree of intrinsic plausibility, while others indicate the goals of an ambitious research programme and are less likely to survive without modification. A famous conjecture is the Riemann hypothesis, which continues to resist proof.

conjugation (biology) A process of sexual reproduction during which individuals of the same species but different mating types (*strains*) pair and exchange limited amounts of genetic material. It is found in unicellular micro-organisms, such as bacteria and protozoans. Conjugation is also used to describe related processes, such as the union of similarly-sized gametes in some green algae (eg *Spirogyra*) and some fungi.

conjugation (chemistry) The real or apparent alternation of single and double bonds in a compound.

conjugation (linguistics) The scheme of inflections which mark contrasts of tense, person, and number in verbs. Latin and

conic sections

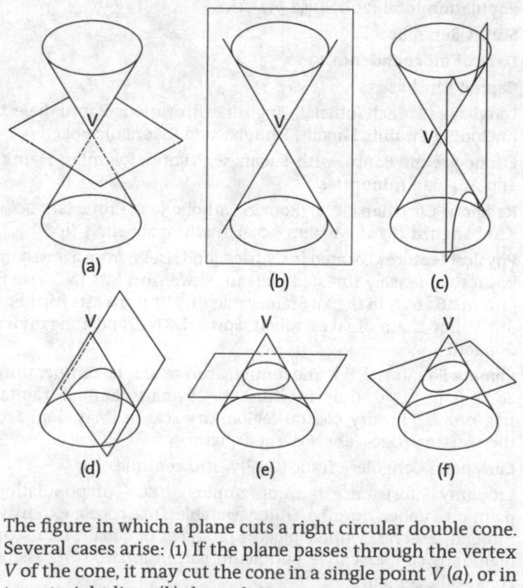

The figure in which a plane cuts a right circular double cone. Several cases arise: (1) If the plane passes through the vertex *V* of the cone, it may cut the cone in a single point *V* (*a*), or in two straight lines (*b*) through *V*, generators of the cone. (2) If the plane is at right angles perpendicular to the axis of the cone, and not through *V*, it cuts the cone in a circle (*e*). (3) If the plane is parallel to a generator of the cone, it cuts the cone in a parabola (*d*); otherwise it cuts the cone in an ellipse (*f*) or a hyperbola (*c*).

Greek had complex conjugational systems; English has very few verbal inflections (eg *-ing*, *-ed*, *-en*); by comparison, French and German are intermediate in complexity.

conjunction (astronomy) The alignment of two celestial bodies seen from Earth, for example a planet with the Sun. The outer planets, further than we are from the Sun, are at conjunction when they lie directly behind the Sun. Mercury and Venus, the planets closer than Earth to the Sun, have two types of conjunction. They are said to be at **inferior conjunction** when they lie between us and the Sun, and at **superior conjunction** when directly behind the Sun. In all cases, the exact moment of conjunction occurs when the two bodies have the same celestial longitude.

conjunctivitis Inflammation of the membrane covering the inner surface of the eyelids and the front surface of the eye (the **conjunctiva**). It may be caused by infections, foreign bodies, or chemicals. It results in a feeling of grittiness in the eyes, and is associated with stickiness of the eyelids and a discharge. The whites of the eyes are red and bloodshot.

Connacht or **Connaught** [**kon**awt] pop (2000e) 428 000; area 17 121 sq km/6609 sq mi. Province in W Ireland, comprising counties of Sligo, Leitrim, Mayo, Roscommon, Galway; chief towns include Sligo, Galway, Castlebar; agriculture, livestock.

Connaught *Connacht*

Connecticut [kuh**net**ikuht] pop (2000e) 3 405 000; area 12 996 sq km/5018 sq mi. A state in NE USA, divided into eight counties; the 'Constitution State', 'Nutmeg State' or 'The Insurance State'; densely populated; explored by Adriaen Block, 1614; one of the original states of the Union, fifth to ratify the Federal Constitution, 1788; capital, Hartford; other chief cities, Bridgeport, New Haven, Waterbury, Stamford; the Thames, Connecticut, and Housatonic Rivers flow S through the state to empty into Long Island Sound; highest point, Mt Frissell (725 m/ 2379 ft); coast largely urbanized, with many industries; interior mainly woodland and forest, with some cropland producing dairy produce, poultry, and tobacco; machinery, transport equipment, electrical goods, firearms, metal products.

connectionism A form of computer modelling in which information-processing is carried out by a network of inter-connected units, with some similarity to information-processing in the brain. It is sometimes called **parallel distributed processing**, because information is processed in many parts of the network simultaneously, and specific information is not localized at a particular point in the network.

connective tissue Tissue which binds together and is the ground substance of various parts and organs of the body. The character of the tissue depends on the organization of its constituent cells and fibres (eg the amount of collagen it contains). In the embryo, it forms a loose cellular network known as *mesenchyme*, from which develop such specialized connective tissues as bone, cartilage, blood cells, and fat. Diseases that affect the connective tissue include Marfan's syndrome and cellulitis.

Connemara [kone**mah**ra] Mountainous region in W Galway county, W Ireland; W of L Corrib; rocky coastline with mountains rising to 765 m/2510 ft at Croagh Patrick in the Twelve Bens; peat bogs; numerous lakes.

Connery, Sir Sean, originally **Thomas Connery** (1930–) Film actor, born in Edinburgh, EC Scotland, UK. After a succession of jobs, his powerful physique won him a role in the chorus line of the London stage production of *South Pacific* (1951). Sporadic film work followed, although there were more significant opportunities in television drama, particularly *Requiem for a Heavyweight* (1956). In 1963 he was cast in *Dr No* as Ian Fleming's secret agent James Bond, a part he subsequently played on seven occasions. The film's unexpected success established him as an international box-office attraction. Later films include *The Man Who Would Be King* (1975), *Highlander* (1986), *Indiana Jones and the Last Crusade* (1989), *The Russia House* (1991), *Just Cause* (1995), *The Rock* (1996), and *Entrapment* (1999). He won an Oscar as an aging Irish cop with true grit in *The Untouchables* (1987). In 1998 he received a BAFTA Fellowship award for his lifetime achievements in film. He was knighted in 1999.

Connolly, Billy (1942–) Comedian, actor, and television presenter, born in Glasgow, W Scotland, UK. After leaving school, he worked as an apprentice welder in Glasgow, then entered show business, becoming well known during the 1980s for his one-man theatre comedy performances. Television appearances increased during the 1990s, including several documentary series, such as his tours of Scotland (1994) and Australia (1996). His film credits date from 1979, with *Absolution*, and include *The Big Man* (1989), *Pocahontas* (1995), *Deacon Brodie* (1996, BBC TV), *Mrs Brown* (1997), *Still Crazy* (1998), and *The Man Who Sued God* (2003).

Connolly, James (1868–1916) Irish political leader and insurgent, born in Edinburgh, EC Scotland, UK. He joined the British army at the age of 14, and was stationed in the Curragh and Dublin, but deserted to get married to an Irish girl in Scotland. Returning to Ireland in 1896, he organized the Irish Socialist Republican Party and founded *The Workers' Republic*, the first Irish Socialist paper. He toured the USA as a lecturer (1902–10), and helped found the Industrial Workers of the World ('Wobblies'). Back in Ireland, he organized Socialist 'citizen armies', and after taking part in the Easter rebellion (1916) he was arrested and executed.

Connolly, Maureen (Catherine), nickname **Little Mo** (1934–69) Tennis player, born in San Diego, California, USA. She won the US championship in 1951 at the age of 16, and thereafter lost only four matches in her career. She won the Wimbledon singles title (1952–4), the US title (1951–3), the French Open (1953–4), and the Australian title (1953), thus becoming the first woman to win all four major titles in the same year (1953). She married **Norman Brinker** in 1954, broke her leg in a riding accident the same year, and was forced to retire. She died of cancer.

Connors, Jimmy, popular name of **James Scott Connors**, nickname **Jimbo** (1952–) Tennis player, born in Belleville, Illinois, USA. The All-American and National Intercollegiate champion from the University of California in 1971, he went on to become Wimbledon champion in 1974 (against Ken Rosewall) and 1982 (against John McEnroe). He won the US Open in 1974, 1976, 1978, and 1982–3. A left-handed player, he was one of the first to use the two-handed backhand. He was elected to the International Tennis Hall of Fame in 1998

connotation In linguistics, the emotional associations connected with the meanings of words; for example *green* carries implications of 'youth' and 'inexperience'. It is contrasted with **denotation**, the objective reference a word has to an object ouside language, such as the physical properties of a colour.

conquistador [kon**kee**stadaw(r)] (Span 'conqueror') The standard term for the leaders of the Spanish expeditions of the early 16th-c that undertook the invasion and conquest of America.

Conrad, Joseph, originally **Józef Teodor Konrad Nalecz Korzeniowski** (1857–1924) Novelist, born in Berdichev, WC Ukraine. He joined the British merchant navy, and became a British national in 1886. He sailed to many parts of the world, married in 1896, and settled in Ashford, Kent. His first novel was *Almayer's Folly* (1895). His best-known works are *The Nigger of the Narcissus* (1897), *Lord Jim* (1900), *Nostromo* (1904), *The Secret Agent* (1907), *Under Western Eyes* (1911), and *Chance* (1914). He also wrote many short stories; and the short novel *Heart of Darkness* (1902) anticipates many 20th-c themes and effects. His fiction has been a favourite subject for film and television adaptation.

Conran, Jasper (1959–) Fashion designer, born in London, UK, the son of Sir Terence Conran. He trained at the Parsons School of Art and Design in New York City, leaving in 1977, when he joined Fiorucci briefly as a designer. In 1978 he founded his own company in London, producing his first collection of easy-to-wear, quality clothes. Awards include the British Fashion Council Designer of the Year (1986–7) and the British Fashion Collections Award (1991).

Conran, Sir Terence (Orby) (1931–) Designer and businessman, born in Esher, Surrey, SE England, UK. He founded and ran the Habitat Company (1971), based on his own success as a furniture designer and the virtues of good design and marketing. He has since been involved in the management of several related businesses and has won many design awards. His many books include *The Soft Furnishings Book* (1986) and *Terence Conran on Design* (1996). He was knighted in 1983.

consanguinity *kinship*

conscientious objection A refusal to accept a particular policy, plan, or course of action, because to do so would go against one's conscience. It is often invoked by pacifists or others objecting to military service, though the State may not always recognize conscientious objection as a citizen's 'right'.

consciousness The psychological state of being aware. Several different meanings can be distinguished, including the state of being awake (in contrast to *unconscious*) and the state in which mental experiences are directly accessible and reportable (in contrast to *subconscious* or *preconscious*). William James stressed the continuity of consciousness (the 'stream of thought'). Cognitive psychologists have emphasized that consciousness may be restricted to certain levels of processing; for example, we may be conscious at a high level of what someone has said, but not be aware (nor be capable of being aware) of the low-level processing details of the acoustic signal that conveyed the message.

conscription The practice, dating from the Napoleonic era, of compelling young men of eligible age and fitness to serve by statute in the armed forces of a nation. To meet the huge manpower needs of World War 1, conscription was introduced in Great Britain in early 1916 and then in the USA under the Selective Service Act (May 1917). Conscription was again enforced in Britain from 1939–45, continuing in peacetime as **National Service**, which was finally abolished in 1962. Women are also required to perform military service in certain countries, such as Israel. In popular US usage, conscription is often referred to as **the draft**, last time invoked during the Vietnam war.

consensus politics An emphasis, usually contained in the prescriptions of centrist political parties, upon the need to formulate policies that avoid or resolve conflict, and build consensus in society. Consensus refers to the sharing by individuals of a set of norms, values, and beliefs. A policy's correctness tends to be judged less by whether it conforms to some ideal aim, and more by whether it is capable of furthering consensus and thereby social cohesion. The term is also used to describe the nature of British politics in the period 1951–74.

Consentes Dii or **Di** [**konsenteez dee-ee, dee**] The Roman name for the 12 major gods, whose statues, grouped in male/female pairs, stood in the Forum. They were probably Jupiter/Juno, Neptune/Minerva, Mars/Venus, Apollo/Diana, Vulcan/Vesta, and Mercury/Ceres.

conservation (earth sciences) The protection and preservation of the Earth's resources (eg plants, animals, land, energy, minerals) or of historical artefacts (eg books, paintings, monuments) for the future. The term is most widely used with reference to the environment, where several reasons are given for conservation. The World Conservation Strategy (1980) concluded that conservation of living resources was needed to preserve genetic diversity, to maintain essential ecological processes, and to ensure the sustainable use of species and ecosystems. This would maintain viable stocks of all animal and plant species, pure air and water, and fertile soil for future use, and allow animals, plants, and land to be there indefinitely. In this way conservation ensures that both present and future generations will be able to make maximum sustainable use of available resources. This definition is essentially economic. Some non-economic, though not necessarily non-utilitarian, reasons for conservation include the enjoyment and spiritual nature of wildlife and the land, the continued use of the land for recreation, and the moral responsibility to future generations to conserve the Earth and its resources.

conservation (psychology) The hallmark of the concrete operations stage in Piagetian psychology. It is the ability to understand the invariance of such properties as number or volume, despite a change in appearance, eg that a row of counters which is lengthened by increasing the space between them represents the same number.

conservation laws Sets of rules describing quantities which are the same before and after some physical process. The identification of these laws is central to physics; all physical laws express conservation principles. A conservation law is related to a symmetry of the system. The most important such law is the **conservation of energy**, which is related to the symmetry of physical systems under translation in time. **Conservation of momentum** results from symmetry under translation in space. In particle physics, complex interactions are expressed in terms of conserved but unfamiliar quantum numbers.

conservatism A set of political ideas, attitudes, and beliefs which stress adherence to what is known and established in the political and social orders, as opposed to the innovative and untested. Generally associated with right-wing political parties, conservatives view humanity as inherently imperfect, emphasizing the need for law and order and the value of tradition. Society is often seen as an organic whole, and as it is only imperfectly understood, change should rarely, or only gradually, be attempted. It implies the acceptance of inequality in society and limited state intervention. Conservatives reject the notion that conservatism is an ideology, and indeed in some cases it can become highly reactionary. Burke's conception of conservatism was developed as an attack upon revolutionary action.

Conservative Party, nickname **Tories** One of the two main political parties in the UK, its full name being the **Conservative and Unionist Party** due to its adherence to union of the countries making up the UK. In common with other conservative parties it is on the right of the political spectrum, though in the 1980s it fused conservative with radical neo-liberal ideas. It developed out of the Tory Party in the 1830s, and spent long periods in power 1886–1905, and 1922–45. Later periods in office are 1951–64 (under Churchill, Eden, Macmillan, and Home), 1970–4 (under Heath), and 1979–97 (under Thatcher and Major), when it was defeated by the Labour Party.

conservatory (music) An institution dedicated to the training of musicians. Conservatories originated as charitable foundations for the care of poor or orphaned children. In the 17th-c the *conservatorii* for boys at Naples and the *ospedali* for girls at Venice found that a concentration on musical training could be educationally and financially profitable. Later they began to attract fee-paying pupils, and the idea of the modern conservatory, as exemplified by the Paris Conservatoire (1795), began to take shape.

consols [konsolz] Loan-stock issued by the British government, first introduced in 1751; the name derives from *consolidated fund*. It is a form of gilt-edged stock, but 'undated' – no redemption date is given for the return of the capital.

consonant A sound made with a closure or narrowing of the vocal tract, so that the airflow is either momentarily impeded or restricted. For example the lips close to produce a [p], and the tongue contacts the palate in producing an [s]. Consonants occur at the beginning or end of a syllable, eg *cup*. The notion is also used with reference to the written language: in English, for example, all letters apart from A, E, I, O, and U, and in some circumstances W and Y, are classed as consonants.

Constable, John (1776–1837) Landscape painter, born in East Bergholt, Suffolk, E England, UK. He trained at the Royal Academy (1799). In 1816 he married **Maria Bicknell**; and in 1828 received an inheritance which enabled him to continue as a painter. Among his best-received works were 'Haywain' (1821, National Gallery, London) and 'The White Horse' (1819, Frick Collection, New York City), which both gained gold medals in

France. Although his work was not especially popular in Britain, he continued to exhibit regularly at the Royal Academy, becoming a member in 1829. His later years were saddened by the death of his wife, and by ill health. He is today considered, along with Turner, as the leading painter of the English countryside.

Constance, Ger **Konstanz**, ancient **Constantia** 47°39N 9°10E, pop (2000e) 77 400. Lake port in Tübingen district, SW Germany, on L Constance, on the Swiss border; former episcopal see and imperial city; railway; university (1966); tourism, commerce, wine, computers, metals, pharmaceuticals, textiles; council hall (1388), cathedral (15th-c).

Constance, Council of, Ger **Konzil von Konstanz** The 16th ecumenical council of the Roman Catholic Church (1414–18) that met in Constance, SW Germany, to settle the question of papal succession, claimed by antipope John XXIII, Pope Gregory XII, and antipope Benedict XIII. The most important results were that its rulings were binding, even on the pope, and that such councils must be held regularly. The voting procedure for papal elections was regularized and the council members chose Ottone Cardinal Colonna as Pope Martin V. His selection ended the schism between the popes of Rome and Avignon. The council also condemned as heretical the doctrines of John Wycliffe and Jan Huss.

Constance, Lake, Ger **Bodensee**, ancient **Lacus Brigantinus** area 541 sq km/209 sq mi. Lake on the N side of the Swiss Alps, forming a meeting point of Switzerland, Austria, and Germany; length, 64 km/40 mi; part of the course of the R Rhine; contains the island of Mainau and the monastic island of Reichenau, which is a world heritage site; NW arm known as the **Überlingersee**; chief towns on the shore, Constance, Friedrichshafen, Lindau, Bregenz.

constancy In the study of perception, the tendency to perceive the intrinsic properties of objects correctly, despite dramatic changes in, for example, the size (as a function of distance), the shape (as a function of viewpoint), or the brightness (as a function of illumination) of their image on the retina.

Constant (de Rebeque), (Henri) Benjamin [kõstã duh rebek] (1767–1830) French politician and novelist, born in Lausanne, W Switzerland. He studied at Oxford, Erlangen, and Edinburgh, and settled in Paris as a publicist (1795). He supported the Revolution, but was banished in 1802 for his opposition to Napoleon. He returned in 1814, and became Leader of the Liberal Opposition. His best-known work is the novel *Adolphe* (1816), based on his relationship with Madame de Staël.

Constanța [konstantsa], Eng **Constantza**, ancient **Tomis** or **Constantinia** 44°10N 28°40E, pop (2000e) 307 000. Major port and capital of Constanța county, SE Romania, on the W shores of the Black Sea; third largest city in Romania; established as a Greek colony, 7th-c BC; under Roman rule from 72 BC; Ovid lived in exile here; named after Constantine I (4th-c AD); ceded to Romania, 1878; airport; railway; naval shipyards, tourism, textiles, foodstuffs, metal products, soap, oil refining.

Constantine [konstanteen], ancient **Ciria**, **Qacentina** 36°22N 6°40E, pop (2000e) 549 200. Chief town of Constantine department, NE Algeria, N Africa; 320 km/200 mi SE of Algiers; oldest city in Algeria, important since the 3rd–4th-c BC; Roman provincial capital of Numidia; destroyed in AD 311 during a civil war, rebuilt by Constantine I; seat of successive Muslim dynasties in Middle Ages; prospered under Turks in the 18th-c; French occupation in 1837; university (1969); airport; railway; tourism, handicrafts; Old Town.

Constantine I (Emperor), known as **the Great**, originally **Flavius Valerius Constantinus** (c.274–337) Roman emperor, born in Naissus, Moesia, the eldest son of Constantius Chlorus. Though proclaimed emperor by the army at York on his father's death in 306, it was not until his defeat of Maxentius at the Milvian Bridge in Rome (312) that he became emperor of the West; and only with his victory over Licinius, the emperor of the East, that he became sole emperor (324). Believing that his victory in 312 was the work of the Christian God, he became the first emperor to promote Christianity, from which came the byname 'Great'. His Edict of Milan (313), issued jointly with Licinius, brought toleration to Christians throughout the empire, and his new capital at Constantinople, founded on the strategically important site of Byzantium (324), was from the outset a Christian city.

Constantine I (of Greece) (1868–1923) King of Greece (1913–17, 1920–2), born in Athens, Greece. He played a leading part in Greece's victories in the Balkan Wars (1912–13), and succeeded his father, George I, as king. During World War 1, his policy of neutrality led to bitter conflict with interventionist forces led by liberal politician Venizelos, culminating (1916–17) in virtual civil war, Anglo-French intervention, and his abdication. Restored after the War, he abdicated once again (1922) following Greece's defeat by Turkey and an internal military revolt.

Constantine II (of Greece) (1940–) King of Greece (1964–73), born near Athens, Greece, who succeeded his father Paul I. In 1964 he married **Princess Anne-Marie of Denmark** (1946–), and has two sons and a daughter. He fled to Rome in 1967 after an abortive coup against the military government which had seized power, and was deposed in 1973. The monarchy was abolished by a national referendum in 1974.

Constantinople, Latin Empire of, also known as the **Latin Empire of the East** A 13th-c empire based at Constantinople (ancient Byzantium, modern Istanbul), the capital of the mediaeval (Eastern) Roman or Byzantine Empire. During the Fourth Crusade, diverted from Palestine, Constantinople was taken from the Greeks after a fierce attack by Western Crusaders (1204) and a Latin Empire created, with Baldwin count of Flanders as the first emperor. This Crusade shocked Europe for its brutality, discredited the papacy and the crusading movement, and facilitated the advance of the Ottoman Turks. It succumbed in 1261 to the Greek emperor Michael VIII after a precarious existence.

constellations *pp.374–5*

constipation A condition in which there is infrequent and difficult emptying of the bowel. The interval between bowel movements varies widely in healthy individuals. However, a period of more than three days, especially if followed by difficult defaecation, suggests constipation. It results from the delayed transit of faeces through the colon, or its retention in the rectum, and may be due to inadequate dietary fibre, immobility, diseases of the intestine (eg diverticulosis), or other disorders such as hypothyroidism.

constituency A territorial division that in many countries serves as a unit in the election of one or more political representatives to national assemblies. Population usually serves as the main criterion in determining the size of each constituency, but variations exist across political systems. For example, in the USA 435 people are elected to the House of Representatives from constituencies with roughly equivalent populations, while two senators are elected from each state, regardless of population size. The UK contains 659 single-member constituencies, most with electorates of c.65 000.

constituent analysis In linguistics, the analysis of linguistic forms into the components ('constituents') from which they are made. Sentences can be analysed into subjects and predicates (eg *John slept*) and words into stems and affixes (eg *de/nation/al/ize*). In more complicated sentences, several 'layers' of grammatical analysis can be shown.

constitution Usually a written document which contains the rules determining the way that a country may be governed in terms of the sources, purpose, use, and limits upon the exercise of political power. The UK is one of a few exceptions in having an unwritten constitution, although in all countries the identification of constitutional principles include reference to statute law, judicial interpretation, tradition, and other constitutional practices. Written constitutions normally include: a preamble; a description of governmental institutions and their powers, including the processes for amending the constitution

constellations: northern sky

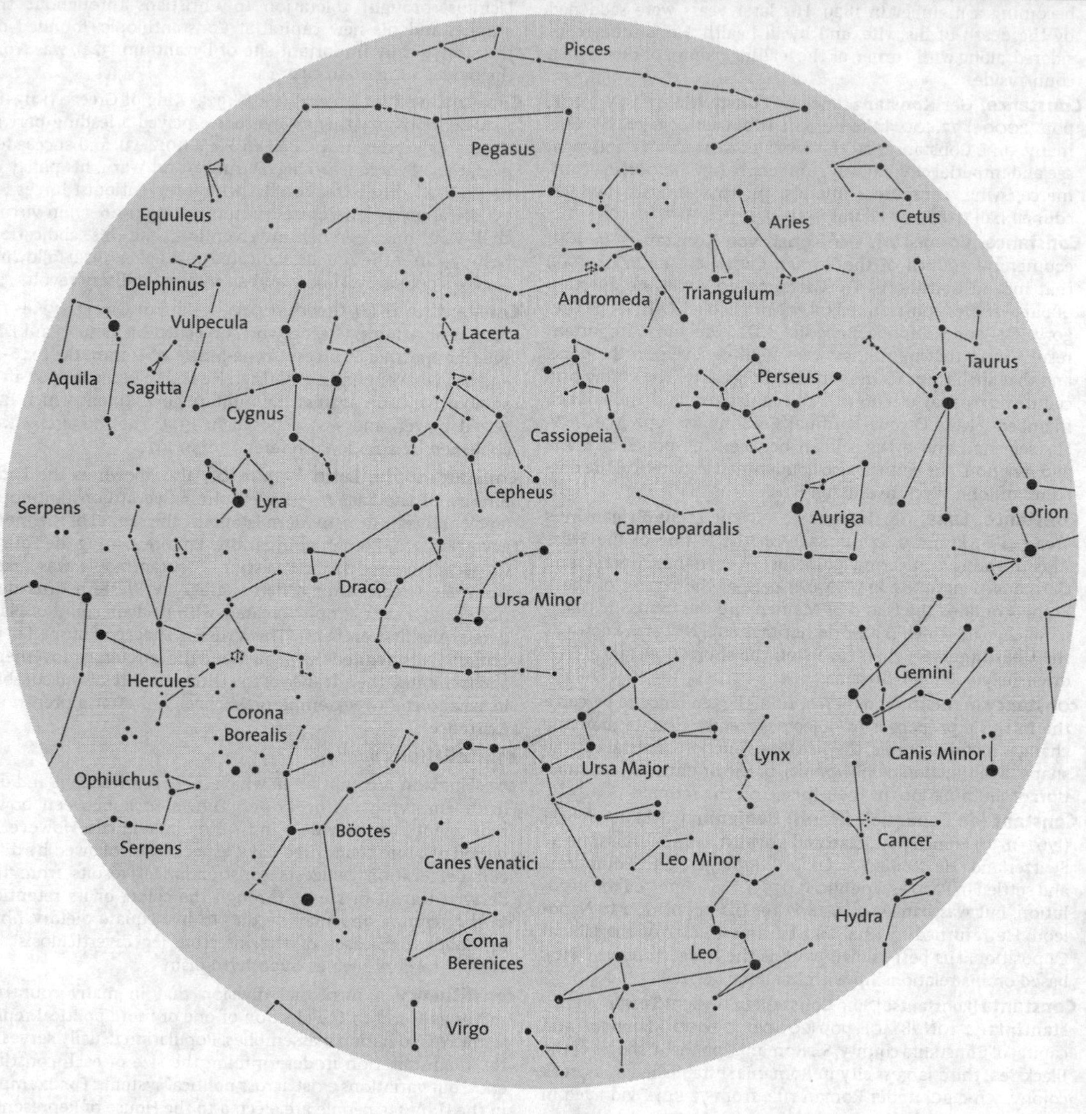

From ancient times, a group of stars that form a recognizable shape or picture. The stars in most constellations are not genuinely related, but lie at greatly different distances from the Solar System. Different cultures have their own ways of delineating the constellations. The system in use by astronomers today has its origins in ancient Mesopotamia, and still includes many names from Greek mythology. Until the 20th-c, the traditional mythological figures were still used to illustrate star atlases.

The boundaries of the constellations were at first drawn using arbitrary curves. This led to great confusion until half of them were agreed along lines of right ascension and declination in 1875, with the remainder being adopted by the International Astronomical Union in 1930. The whole patchwork

and reviewing decisions that are claimed to infringe the constitution; a bill of rights; and amendatory articles.

Constitutional Convention (1787) A gathering at Philadelphia during the American Revolution that produced the present US Constitution; 12 of the original 13 states were represented. The term, by extension, is also used for any political meeting empowered to write a state or national constitution.

Constitution of the United States A constitution, ratified in 1787, founded upon the principles of the Declaration of Independence, and based upon the concepts of limited and responsible government, and federalism. Power is divided amongst three independent branches of government: legislative; executive; judicial. The constitutional document comprises a short preamble followed by seven articles which include: the organization, powers and procedures of the legislative branch (Congress); the powers of the president and executive; the powers of the judiciary, including the Supreme Court; the rights of the states; and procedures for amending the constitution. The articles are then followed by 26 amendments, the first 10 of which are known as the *bill of rights* (although later amendments also deal with civil rights issues), while the others cover such matters as the election, death or removal of the president, and eligibility to stand for election to Congress.

constellations: southern sky

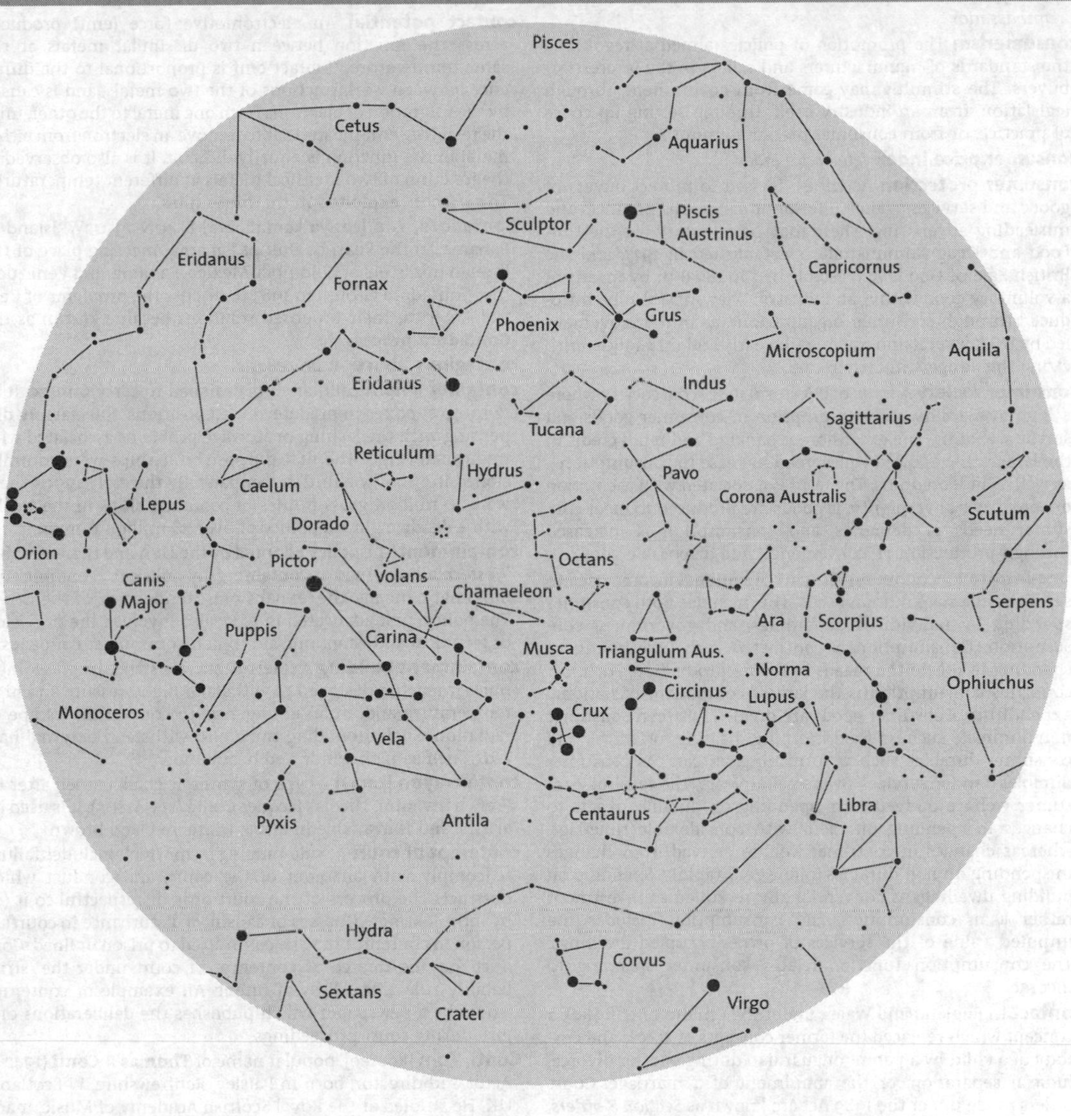

quilt now includes 88 constellations, which vary enormously in size and shape: the largest, Hydra, is 20 times bigger in area than the smallest, Crux. The Egyptian astronomer Claudius Ptolemy listed 48 constellations in *Almagest* AD c.140; the modern ones were mostly invented in the 16th–18th-c. The brightest stars are named after the constellation in which they are found, using the Greek alphabet and the Latin genitive or possessive form for the constellation: *alpha Ursae Majoris* is thus the brightest star in Ursa Major. Modern astronomers use numerical co-ordinates that computers can readily interpret, to map the sky.

Constitutions of Clarendon *Clarendon, Constitutions of*

constrictor A snake which wraps its body tightly around its prey and, by squeezing, induces suffocation, teeth carry no venom; lips often have heat-sensitive pits.

Constructivism An imprecise term usually applied to a form of abstract art that began in Russia in 1917, using machine-age materials such as steel, glass, and plastic. Leading practitioners were Vladimir Tatlin (1885–1953), who projected the gigantic spiral monument to the Third International, and the brothers Antoine Pevsner and Naum Gabo. In Russia this impetus was soon channelled into industrial design (**Soviet Constructivism**), and Pevsner and Gabo left Russia in the early 1920s. Their ideas subsequently exerted a deep influence on abstract artists in the West (**International Constructivism**).

consubstantiation A theory attributed to Luther, describing the presence of Christ in the Eucharist 'under or with the elements of bread and wine'. It is to be contrasted with the Roman Catholic doctrine of transubstantiation.

consul 1 In Republican Rome (5th-c–1st-c BC), a chief executive officer of state, with military and judicial functions. Two consuls were elected annually. The consulship was the highest office in the *cursus honorum* and could not be held before the age of 36. Under the Empire, it became mainly honorific. **2** *ambassador*

consumerism The promotion of policies aimed at regulating the standards of manufacturers and sellers in the interests of buyers. The stimulus may come from government, through legislation, from an industry itself, through setting up codes of practice, or from consumer pressure groups.

consumer price index *retail price index*

consumer protection Activities devised to protect buyers of goods and services against inferior or dangerous products and misleading advertising. These may be statutory (eg the USA Food and Drug Administration, established in 1927, and the British Sale of Goods Act, established in 1893) or by means of a voluntary code within an industry. They may also be introduced through consumer organizations, as in the movement led by US lawyer Ralph Nader in the early and mid-1960s, criticizing the dangers in certain cars.

consumer society A stage of (Western) industrial society where a high availability and consumption of consumer goods and services obtains. The extension of banking and retail credit in the late 20th-c allowed widespread increase in consumption – as well as indebtedness. The term is associated with the notion of **consumer sovereignty**, ie goods are produced to meet consumer needs or demands, and consumption is increased through production of 'convenience' and disposable goods.

consumption (economics) The part of national income used to satisfy immediate human needs. This includes both consumer spending by individuals or families, and government consumption. Consumption is contrasted with investment, or spending to create the means of future production. For most countries consumption is the largest component of national expenditure. Consumer goods are divided between consumer non-durables, such as food, clothing, heating, or travel, and consumer durables such as furnishings or cars. As consumer durables render services over several years, the level of consumer welfare derived from spending on durables reacts to changes in spending on them with considerable time-lags, whereas changes in consumer welfare derived from changes in spending on non-durables follow very rapidly. Spending on building dwellings is conventionally reckoned as investment rather than consumption, and consumption includes the imputed value of the services of owner-occupied dwellings. The consumption function relates consumer spending to income.

contact In England and Wales, under the Children Act (1989), a concept which replaced the former concepts of access and custody of a child by a parent or guardian during or after divorce, judicial separation, or the annulment of a marriage. Court orders made under the 1989 Act are known as *Section 8 orders*, and include *residence orders*, which formalize arrangements about where a child is to live, and *contact orders*, which permit a parent or anyone with whom the child has lived for the last three years to communicate with or stay with the child regularly. The contact may be for any length of time, from a short telephone call to a long holiday, but may be refused if it is not in the child's best interests.

contact lens A disc of plastic which fits over the front of the eye, usually to correct vision problems, in the same way as spectacles. Coloured contact lenses can change the apparent colour of the eye, generally for theatrical or cosmetic reasons. Contact lenses first became available in the 1930s. Early devices, called *scleral* or *haptic* lenses, covered the complete front of the eyeball. Modern lenses are the much smaller *corneal* lenses, and fit over the coloured part of the eye (the iris). Contact lenses can be *hard* or *soft*, offering different possibilities with respect to such features as visual improvement, maintenance, length of wear, comfort, convenience, and side-effects. Hard lenses are made from perspex (polymethylmethacrylate, or PMMA). Those which allow oxygen to pass through are called *rigid gas permeable* (RGP) and are made from cellulose acetate butyrate (CAB). Soft lenses are made from hydroxyethylmethacrylate – a plastic which contains water and is like a gel.

contact potential An electromotive force (emf) produced across the junction between two dissimilar metals at the same temperature. Contact emf is proportional to the difference between workfunctions of the two metals, and is caused by the migration of electrons from one metal to the other, until the resulting emf means that to remove an electron from either metal in the junction is equally difficult. It is also observed in the junction of two identical metals at different temperatures. The effect is exploited in thermocouples.

Contadora, Isla [eeslya kontadohra] 8°40N 79°02W. Island of Panama, in the Pearl Is, Gulf of Panama; meeting place of the foreign ministers of Colombia, Mexico, Panama, and Venezuela (the Contadora Group) in 1983 to discuss the problems of Central America; their proposed solutions became known as the **Contadora process**.

contagious abortion *brucellosis*

container ship A cellular ship, designed to carry 6 m/20 ft or 12 m/40 ft boxes in predetermined positions, thus largely dispensing with the lashing or stowage problems associated with traditional cargo. The first purpose-built ships were commissioned in 1966 by a British company. By the early 1990s there were 26 million gross tonnes of container ships in the world, with a deadweight capability of over 28 million tonnes.

containment The policy adopted by the USA and thereafter her Western allies aimed at containing, by political, economic, and diplomatic means, the 'expansionist tendencies' of the USSR. The policy, first advocated in 1947, also involved the provision of technical and economic aid to non-communist countries.

containment building A steel or concrete structure enclosing a nuclear reactor, designed to withstand high pressure and high temperature and, in an emergency, to contain the escape of radiation. Such a building must also withstand external hazards, such as high winds and heavy snow.

conté crayon [kõtay] A type of synthetic chalk named after its French inventor, Nicolas Jacques Conté (1755–1805). It is used by artists, and is available in black, white, red, and brown.

contempt of court A wide-ranging term which includes failure to comply with an order of the court, and conduct which obstructs the process of the court or is disrespectful to it (eg by intimidating witnesses or causing a disturbance in court). A person in contempt may be committed to prison or fined. Conduct may be treated as contempt of court under the 'strict liability rule', regardless of intent. An example of contempt would be a newspaper which publishes the deliberations of a jury during court proceedings.

Conti, Tom [kontee], popular name of **Thomas A Conti** (1942–) Actor and director, born in Paisley, Renfrewshire, W Scotland, UK. He studied at the Royal Scottish Academy of Music, made his acting debut in 1960, and has since performed and directed regularly in London theatres. Television appearances include *The Norman Conquests* and *Glittering Prizes*, and the later *Donovan* (2004). Among his films are *Galileo* (1974), *Merry Christmas, Mr Lawrence* (1982), *Shirley Valentine* (1989), and *Don't Go Breaking My Heart* (1998). He was voted Best Stage Actor by the Variety Club of Great Britain in 1978, and he received a Tony Award for Best Actor in 1979. Later theatre productions include *Chapter Two* (1996) and *Jesus My Boy* (1998).

continent A term applied to the seven large land masses on the Earth's surface: Asia, Africa, North America, South America, Antarctica, Europe, and Australia, in decreasing order of size. The continents (including the submerged continental shelves) make up about 35% of the Earth's crust, the rest being made up of the oceanic plates. The thickness of the crust below the continents is 30–40 km/15–25 mi, and is composed of lower density rocks enriched in silica and aluminium compared to the oceanic crust.

Continental Congress (1774–88) The gathering that declared and led the struggle for American independence. Each of the 13 colonies (states after 1776) had one vote. The First Congress met

Continents

Name	Area km²	Area sq mi	% of total	Lowest point below sea level	m	ft	Highest elevation	m	ft
Africa	30 293 000	11 696 000	20.2	Lake Assal, Djibouti	156	512	Kilimanjaro, Tanzania	5 895	19 340
Antarctica	13 975 000	5 396 000	9.3	Bently subglacial trench	2 538	8 327	Vinson Massif	5 140	16 864
Asia	44 493 000	17 179 000	29.6	Dead Sea, Israel/Jordan	400	1 312	Mt Everest, China/Nepal	8 848	29 028
Oceania	8 945 000	3 454 000	6.0	Lake Eyre, S Australia	15	49	Puncak Jaya (Ngga Pulu), Indonesia	5 030	16 500
Europe	10 245 000	3 956 000	6.8	Caspian Sea, Russia	29	94	Elbrus, Russia	5 642	18 510
North America	24 454 000	9 442 000	16.3	Death Valley, California	86	282	Mt McKinley, Alaska	6 194	20 320
South America	17 838 000	6 887 000	11.9	Peninsular Valdez, Argentina	40	131	Aconcagua, Argentina	6 959	22 831

for six weeks in 1774. The Second (convened Apr 1775) did not formally dissolve until replaced by the government under the present Constitution, adopted in 1788.

Continental Divide or **Great Divide** A line of mountain peaks in North America extending SSE from NW Canada down the W USA into Mexico, Central America, and South America where it meets the N end of the Andes; a major watershed, with rivers running to the Atlantic and the Pacific; includes the Rocky Mts in Canada and the USA and the Sierra Madre ranges in Mexico.

continental drift A theory which proposes that the present positions of the continents and oceans results from the breaking up of a single large land mass or 'supercontinent', termed *Pangaea*, c.200 million years ago. The idea is generally ascribed to Alfred Wegener (1910) but gained little support until the 1960s, when the theory of plate tectonics was established.

continental margin The boundary province between the deep ocean basins and continents, which makes up c.20% of the ocean area. Though continental margins vary considerably, there are two main groups: the *passive* (or *aseismic*) and the *active* (or *seismic*). Atlantic Ocean margins are dominantly of the passive type, sometimes referred to as *Atlantic-type margins*. Active margins are typical of the Pacific Ocean and are sometimes called *Pacific-type margins*. The margins of the Indian Ocean are of the Atlantic type, except in the NE, where the boundary is an active margin.

Passive continental margins consist typically of three parts: a shelf, slope, and rise. The **continental shelf** is a seaward extension of the continent, usually with low relief and a gentle gradient, averaging less than 1:1000. At the edge of the shelf (the *shelf break*), there is a marked increase in steepness. The depth of the break is 20–500 m/65–1600 ft, averaging 130 m/425 ft in most areas. The width of the shelf ranges from a few km to more than 400 km/250 mi, averaging just over 75 km/45 mi. The **continental slope** lies seaward of the continental shelf, and extends to 1500–3500 m/5000–11 000 ft), with a much steeper gradient, averaging 1:40. It is a relatively narrow zone, usually 20–100 km/12–60 mi in width. The continental shelf and slope together form the **continental terrace**. In many areas of the ocean, this is cut by submarine canyons, which serve to carry sediment from the continent to the continental rise and the deep ocean. The **continental rise** lies between the slope and the ocean basin. It has a gentle gradient between 1:100 and 1:700, and a width of 100–1000 km/60–600 mi, averaging about 600 km/375 mi. The rise is formed by sediment eroded from the continents accumulating at the base of the slope. It too may be cut by submarine canyons which allow the transport of sediment beyond the rise to the ocean basin. A **continental borderland** is a continental terrace consisting of a series of basins and ridges. The true shelf is a few km wide only, but the adjacent zone of basins, banks, and islands may extend up to 200 km/125 mi in width. An example is the continental margin off S California.

Continental System The process of economic warfare introduced by Napoleon to destroy British commercial power, after Trafalgar put paid to his invasion plans. The Decrees of Berlin (1806) and Milan (1807) established a blockade of European and neutral trade with Britain and her colonies. Britain responded by issuing Orders in Council which blockaded the ports of France and her allies and allowed them to trade with each other and neutral countries only if they did so via Britain.

contingency fee In law, an arrangement by which a lawyer's fee is a percentage of the sum awarded by the court to the attorney's client. If no sum is awarded, no payment is made to the lawyer. Many jurisdictions do not permit payment by contingency fee. In England and Wales, contingency fees are illegal, but conditional fee agreements are allowed in certain cases which are not criminal proceedings.

continuing education *adult education*

continuo The practice, common to most Baroque music, of filling out the harmonic texture by reference to a specially notated bass line (a *figured bass*). The continuo is usually supplied by a harmony instrument (harpsichord, organ, lute, etc) reinforced by a melodic bass instrument (cello, double bass, bassoon, etc).

continuous assessment The appraisal of students' work on a regular basis rather than exclusively by final examination. Essays, practical work, projects, and assignments done during the course might form all or part of the final assessment, which can be based on marks, grades, or a profile.

continuous representation In art, the practice of including several consecutive stages of a story in one picture. For example, in a Nativity, the shepherds who adore the Child in the foreground may also be shown in the distance watching their flocks.

contrabassoon *bassoon*

contraception The prevention of pregnancy following sexual intercourse; also known as **birth control** or **family planning**. For centuries its practice was opposed by the Church and the medical profession, but it has come to be widely advocated in order to control populations, protect against venereal disease, and regulate the size of families.

The earliest methods adopted did not involve chemical or mechanical devices. Cleaning the vagina with water (*douching*), although widely practised, has never been effective. Avoiding intercourse during a 'safe period' – the **rhythm method** – is based on the fact that both spermatozoa and ova survive for only a day or two after release. Attractive to the Roman Catholic Church, it is fallible because of the difficulty in timing ovulation, and the variability of the duration of the menstrual cycle. The most fertile period is between 10–17 days of a regular 28-day menstrual cycle, but in practice for most women this period is considerably longer, as few follow a sufficiently regular pattern. Thus, other than for religious grounds, the rhythm method is best avoided in couples for whom an unwanted pregnancy would be a disaster, but it can be acceptable to those for whom an unplanned pregnancy would merely be an inconvenience. *Coitus interruptus* involves withdrawal of the penis from the vagina just prior to ejaculation. Formerly popular, its effectiveness depends on self-control on the part of the male and is comprised by release of sperm prior to ejaculation.

The use of a condom was first described in the 16th-c as a protection against syphilis; it consisted of a linen sheath. The modern condom is made of siliconed latex with an expanded part or teat on the end. It is appropriately and widely advocated because its mechanical protection guards not only against pregnancy but also against AIDS and other sexually transmitted diseases. It is probably the most widely used contraceptive method in the Western world; however, condom failure remains a problem. Other **mechanical devices** include shields, diaphragms, or caps inserted into the vagina over the cervix. These require proper insertion some time before intercourse, and should be retained for 6–8 hours afterwards. Their effectiveness can be improved by the use of spermicidal agents. **Intra-uterine devices** (IUD) are coils or hooks made out of plastic or metal that are inserted by a trained person into the uterus. They do not prevent ovulation and are not spermicidal, but appear to act by preventing the products of conception becoming embedded in the wall of the uterus. They have found great use in the control of population in some developing countries. They may cause complications such as infection or bleeding in the uterus, which can result later in permanent infertility.

The most important development in contraception has been the introduction of the **contraceptive pill**. This contains synthetic steroids similar to the female sex hormones oestrogen and progesterone, either together or progesterone alone. They inhibit ovulation and induce changes in the lining and secretions of the cervix, uterus, and uterine tubes that makes them hostile to sperm. Combined oestrogen and progesterone pills are the most effective, and are taken for 21 days followed by a 7-day interval during which menstrual bleeding occurs. The use of combined oestrogen/progesterone pills carries a small risk of thrombosis, especially in women over 35 years. The progesterone-only pill (the 'minipill') taken daily without a break has a higher failure rate, but is safer in older women. Synthetic progesterone can also be administered as an injection. **Post-coital contraceptives** (the 'morning-after pill') contain the synthetic oestrogen stilboestrol, which prevents implantation of any fertilized egg. It is insufficiently safe to be used as an ordinary contraceptive device, and is reserved for emergencies (eg if a condom splits, or in the event of unplanned unprotected intercourse). Substance RU-486 (mifepristone, often referred to as the 'abortion pill') was launched in 1988, surrounded by considerable controversy; designed for use in the early stages of pregnancy, it causes the womb lining to shed as in normal menstruation.

An alternative approach to the avoidance of pregnancy is sterilization.

contract An agreement intended either expressly or by implication to be legally enforceable. A contract has certain essential features. It arises from an offer which has been accepted in identical terms. Unless there is (in the terminology of English law) a promise under seal (ie a covenant), there must (in English but not Scots law) be *consideration* – that is, the promisee must confer some benefit or suffer some detriment in return for the promise made. There must be an intention to create *legal relations* (ie to enter into a legally enforceable agreement), and the parties must have *legal capacity* (ie be legally able to enter into the agreement – for example, by being old enough). There is no general rule that a contract must be in writing – buying something in a shop is a contractual agreement – but there are exceptions (eg by statute, a contract to buy land must be evidenced in writing). Many specific types of contract, such as a contract of employment, are governed by specific statutes.

contract bridge *bridge* (recreation)

contrapposto [kontrapostoh] In art, a pose in which the top half of the body is turned in a different direction from the lower. It occurs in classical sculpture, and was much used in 16th-c Italy, for example by Michelangelo and the Mannerists.

Contras *Nicaragua*

contrast In the visual medium, the relation between the light and dark areas of a scene or their reproduction by photographic or electronic means. It is expressed numerically as the *brightness range* of the subject or the *gamma value* of a process.

contre-jour [kõtruh zhoor] In cinematography, a term describing a scene taken with the camera pointing in the direction of the main source of light. This tends to show foreground objects in silhouette, often with a bright halo effect at their edges.

control *seance*

control character A non-printing character or code which, when sent to a computer peripheral, causes a specific operation to take place. Examples are carriage return and line feed characters which make the printer operate in a particular way.

control engineering The branch of engineering concerned with the control and adjustment of systems. A human operator need not be involved. Control is achieved by using closed loop systems: when an error is detected, the information is returned to the input and used to correct the error – a system known as *feedback*. Control engineering uses servo-mechanisms as automatically-operating control devices, as found in measuring instruments, detectors, amplifiers, and power units. Advances in nanotechnology have allowed control systems to be built with sensors and actuators made from individual atoms. Biomedical engineering uses the electrical impulses from transmitted thoughts (from nerves) to control external processes.

control group A group of subjects in an experiment, similar in all relevant respects to the experimental group, and submitting to the same conditions and changes except those specifically under investigation. The effect of the experimental treatment is assessed by taking the difference after treatment between experimental and control group on whatever measure is being used.

contrology *Pilates*

convection The flow of heat by the actual movement of a gas or liquid. For example, air warmed by a fire expands, becomes less dense, and so rises, creating a **convection current** as fresh cool air is drawn in to replace the warmed air. Convection currents spread heat round a room. **Forced convection** takes place when heated fluid is forced to move, as in hot water heating systems.

convective rain A type of rain commonly associated with equatorial climates, and with the cold front of unstable polar air masses; also known as **convectional rain**. When a parcel of air is heated from below, it expands and rises; as it cools, condensation occurs to form cumulonimbus clouds from which heavy rainfall is produced.

convergence (biology) The independent evolution of a structural or functional similarity, not based on an inherited similarity of genetic material, in two or more unrelated organisms as an adaptation to a particular way of life. For example, the similarities between a bird and a bat that are related to their ability to fly are the result of convergent evolution.

convergence (linguistics) The process whereby variant forms of a language become more alike, as in the 'levelling' of dialect differences under the influence of a standard language. When varieties come increasingly to differ in structure, the process is known as **divergence**.

conversation analysis *discourse analysis*

conversation piece A type of small group portrait which flourished in 18th-c England, representing a family and/or friends grouped informally either indoors or in a landscape or garden setting. Hogarth, Philippe Mercier (c.1689–1760), and Francis Hayman (1708–76) were masters of this genre.

conversion (law) The tort of intentionally dealing with goods so as to deny the true owner's rights by 'converting' the goods to the defendant's own use. An example would be the taking of someone's credit card without the owner's consent; even if the taker does not make use of the card, the act is still an instance of conversion, as it has deprived the rightful owner of the benefits which belong to possession of the card. The term is not recognized in all jurisdictions (eg in Scotland). The remedy is damages for the full value of the goods at the time and place of conversion.

conversion (linguistics) The potential for words to alternate between different grammatical categories without any change in their form. For example, *smell* can be both noun (*there's a smell*) and verb (*I can smell something*). The English language coins many new words in this way, eg *an impact→to impact*; *round→a round* (of drinks).

conversion (psychiatry) A loss or alteration of physical functioning which gives the impression of a physical disorder, but which is in fact the result of psychological mechanisms. For example, a patient might describe a sensation of back pain and paralysis of the legs when there is no organic disease and following an argument with his/her spouse who has asked him/her to leave home.

conversion (religion) A change in affiliation from one religion to another, or the transition from non-involvement to belief in a religion. It also designates a change involving a transformation and reorientation affecting every aspect of a person's life, which can occur suddenly or gradually.

convertibility The right of holders of a country's currency to change it into foreign currency without permission from the authorities. A **fully convertible** currency can be changed for any purpose. **Current account convertibility** is when a currency can be changed for current but not capital account purposes. Inconvertible currencies were common in the period after World War 2, and are still common in less-developed countries and in parts of the former Soviet bloc. Current account convertibility spread in Europe in the 1950s and 1960s, reaching the UK in 1958. Full convertibility spread later, reaching the UK in 1979.

conveyance A legal document which when signed, sealed, and delivered transfers ownership of real property (eg in England and Wales) or heritable property (eg in Scotland) such as houses or land (specified in the document) from one party to another. In the USA, the document is usually a deed (a seal is no longer required in most US jurisdictions). In England and Wales, in the case of land which has been registered, the procedure is modified: a completed form transferring the land must be lodged at the district Land Registry in order to transfer the legal estate. In England and Wales, there is now compulsory registration on the sale of freehold land, or leasehold with at least 40 years to run. Evidence of title is provided by a land certificate. The Solicitors Act (1974) preserved the monopoly of solicitors with regard to preparing a conveyance of land for a fee. As a modification of this privilege, the Administration of Justice Act (1985) permits licensed conveyancing to be carried on for payment by a class of persons who are not solicitors. These **licensed conveyancers** are subject to the professional controls of the Council for Licensed Conveyancers. In the USA, private parties may convey land.

Convocation A gathering of Church of England clergy, originally in the provinces of Canterbury and York, to regulate affairs of the Church. The **Upper House** consists of the archbishop and bishops; the **Lower House** of representatives of the lower clergy. Since the early 20th-c, the two convocations meet together, all now forming the Church Assembly, which meets two or three times a year, with powers regulated by Parliament.

convolvulus *bindweed*

convulsion An involuntary contraction of all the muscles in the body, with widespread muscle spasms, rolling eyeballs, laboured breathing, and tightly clenched teeth. It may be due to epilepsy or metabolic disturbances, and can occur as a reaction to fever in children (*febrile convulsion*).

Conwy, Eng **Conwy** 53°17N 3°50W, pop (2000e) 13 900. Historic market town and resort in Conwy borough council, NC Wales, UK; at head of R Conwy (Conway); engineering, market, tourism; 13th-c castle (a world heritage site), with walls around the town; road tunnel beneath river.

cony *hyrax; pika; rabbit*

Cook, Mount 43°37S 170°08E. Mountain in W South Island, New Zealand, in the Southern Alps; height, 3764 m/12 349 ft; highest peak in New Zealand; in Mount Cook National Park, area 944 sq km/364 sq mi, established in 1953, a world heritage site; park contains 22 of the 27 peaks in the country over 3000 m/10 000 ft; Tasman Glacier; landslide in 1991 lowered its summit by 11 m to 3753 m/12 313 ft.

Cook, James (1728–79) Navigator, born in Marton, North Yorkshire, N England, UK. He spent several years as a seaman in North Sea vessels, then joined the navy (1755), becoming master in 1759. He surveyed the area around the St Lawrence River, Quebec, then in the *Endeavour* carried the Royal Society expedition to Tahiti to observe the transit of Venus across the Sun (1768–71). He circumnavigated New Zealand and charted parts of Australia, landing in Botany Bay in 1770. In his second voyage he sailed round Antarctica (1772–5), and discovered several Pacific island groups. Thanks to his dietary precautions, there was only one death among the crew. His third voyage (1776–9) aimed to find a passage round the N coast of America from the Pacific; but he was forced to turn back, and on his return voyage was killed by natives on Hawaii.

Cook, Peter (Edward) (1937–95) Comedian and actor, born in Torquay, Devon, SW England, UK. He studied at Cambridge and first achieved prominence as one of the writers and performers of *Beyond the Fringe* (1959–64), and a sequel *Behind the Fridge* (1971–2). He invented the stage character E L Wisty, a forlorn figure perplexed by the complexities of life. From 1965 to 1971 he collaborated with Dudley Moore in the irreverent television programme, *Not Only... But Also*. He made regular film appearances, notably in *The Bed-Sitting Room* (1970), and was long associated with the satirical magazine, *Private Eye*.

Cook, Robin, popular name of **Robert Finlayson Cook** (1946–) British statesman, born in Bellshill, North Lanarkshire, C Scotland, UK. He studied at Edinburgh University, trained as a teacher, then became an MP in 1974. He was opposition spokesman for the Treasury and economic affairs (1980–3), then held various posts in the shadow cabinet, including spokesman on health and social security (1987–92). He managed the leadership campaigns of Neil Kinnock (1983) and John Smith (1992). Other posts include chief opposition spokesman on trade and industry (1992–4) and foreign affairs (1994–7), and chair of the Labour Party (1996–8). He became secretary of state for foreign and commonwealth affairs (1997) and Leader of the Commons (2001), but resigned in March 2003 over his opposition to war in Iraq.

Cook, Sue, popular name of **Susan Lorraine Cook** (1949–) British broadcaster. She studied at Leicester University, then joined Capital Radio as a producer and presenter (1974–6). She moved to the BBC, working on a wide range of radio documentaries and topical features, then took up a role as a reporter and presenter on BBC television's *Nationwide* (1979–83). She became well known for her later television work, including *Breakfast Time*, *Holiday*, and *Crimewatch UK*, while also working with several charities to do with children, animals, and the elderly.

Cook, Thomas (1808–92) Railway excursion and tourist pioneer, born in Melbourne, Derbyshire, C England, UK. He became a Baptist missionary in 1828. In 1841 he arranged an excursion railway trip between Leicester and Loughborough to attend a temperance meeting, and this later became a regular event. In the 1860s he became an agent for the sale of travel tickets, and built up the business of Thomas Cook & Son.

Cooke, (Alfred) Alistair (1908–2004) Journalist and broadcaster, born in Manchester, Greater Manchester, NW England, UK. He studied at Cambridge, and won a scholarship to study at Yale and Harvard. He returned to England, working as a film critic for the BBC, and as London correspondent for a US broadcasting company (NBC). He returned to the USA in 1937, and became a US citizen in 1941. A sympathetic and urbane commentator on current affairs and popular culture in the USA, he has reported for several British newspapers, written numerous books, including *One Man's America* (1952), and edited *The Vintage Mencken* (1954). His 'Letter from America', broadcast by the BBC from 1946 to 2004, was the longest-running solo radio feature programme. He is also well-known for his BBC TV series *America* (1972–3), which produced a best-selling book. In 2003 he was inducted into the newly established Radio Hall of Fame. He retired from broadcasting in 2004.

Cooke, Sam, originally **Sam Cook** (1935–64) Soul singer, born in Chicago, Illinois, USA. He started his career as a Gospel singer, but from 1956 onwards recorded many rhythm-and-blues and soul classics, much covered by other artists, including 'You Send Me', 'Cupid', and 'Twistin' the Night Away'. He was shot dead in a motel room in 1964.

cooking fats Solid fats derived from vegetable oils, used in cooking; often referred to as **shortening**. Vegetable oils with the exception of coconut or palm oil tend to be unsaturated and liquid at room temperature. They are treated with hydrogen to produce the solid fat used in cooking.

Cook Islands pop (2000e) 20 400; area 238 sq km/92 sq mi. Widely scattered group of 15 volcanic and coral islands, c.3200 km/2000 mi NE of New Zealand, S Pacific Ocean; self-governing country in free association with New Zealand; capital, Avarua (on Rarotonga); timezone GMT −10; mainly Polynesian population; main religion, Christianity; official language, English, with local languages widely spoken; unit of currency, New Zealand dollar; airport at Avarua; highest island, Rarotonga, rises to 650 m/2132 ft; climate damp and tropical, with rainfall heavy on forested volcanic slopes of S islands; hurricane season (Nov–Apr); placed under British protection, 1888–1901; New Zealand dependency, 1901; internally self-governing, 1965; elected 24-member Legislative Assembly, with a premier as head of state; a high commissioner represents British sovereign and New Zealand interests; economy mainly agriculture and fishing, especially copra, citrus fruits, pineapples, tomatoes, bananas; fruit processing, tourism (especially in Rarotonga and Aitutaki).

Cookson, Dame Catherine (Ann) (1906–98) Novelist, born in East Jarrow, Tyne and Wear, NE England, UK. She did not begin to write until in her 40s, publishing her first novel, *Kate Hannigan*, in 1950. Most of her novels are set in the NE of England, several of them belonging to a series tracing the fortunes of a single character or family, such as *Tilly Trotter* (1981). Other novels include *Rooney* (1957), *The Round Tower* (1968), *The Moth* (1986), *Branded Man* (1997), and *The Thursday Friend* (1998). Her *Kate Hannigan's Girl* was published posthumously in 2000. A national survey showed that in 1988 a third of all fiction borrowed from public libraries in the UK was by this author. She was made a dame in 1993.

Cook Strait Channel of the Pacific Ocean separating North Island from South Island, New Zealand; 23–130 km/14–80 mi wide; visited by Captain Cook in 1770.

Coolidge, (John) Calvin (1872–1933) US statesman and 30th president (1923–9), born in Plymouth, Vermont, USA. He became a lawyer, was Governor of Massachusetts (1919–20), vice-president (1921–3), then president on Harding's death. A strong supporter of US business interests, he was triumphantly re-elected by the Republicans in 1924, but refused to be renominated in 1928. His economic policies were later questioned because of the depression that followed his administration.

cool jazz A jazz movement, in which emphasis was placed on light, unforced playing, originated in the 1940s by Miles Davis in opposition to **hot jazz**. It is also exemplified in the music of Gerry Mulligan, Stan Getz, and John Lewis.

Coombs, Herbert Cole, nickname **Nugget Coombs** (1906–97) Australian public servant, born in Perth, Western Australia. He studied at the London School of Economics, and joined the [Australian] Commonwealth Bank as an assistant economist, moving to the Treasury in 1939. He became governor of the bank in 1949, and in 1959 the inaugural governor of the Reserve Bank of Australia, a position he held until he retired in 1968. He became Pro-Chancellor of the Australian National University (ANU) in 1959, and Chancellor in 1968. On his 'retirement' he worked with Aboriginal people in C Australia and the Kimberley region of Western Australia, and had written extensively on resource allocation and the environment. The personal adviser to seven Australian prime ministers, he was widely acknowledged as one of the most influential figures in his country since World War 2.

Cooper, Gary (Frank) (1901–61) Film actor, born in Helena, Montana, USA. A newspaper cartoonist in Los Angeles before working as an extra in silent films, his first leading role came in *The Winning of Barbara Worth* (1926). With the coming of sound, he continued as a star for more than 30 years, not only as the archetypal hero of Westerns, notably in *High Noon* (1952), and in the Hemingway epics *A Farewell to Arms* (1932) and *For Whom the Bell Tolls* (1943), but also representing the best of American small-town virtues in *Mr Deeds Goes to Town* (1936) and *Meet John Doe* (1941). In addition to two Oscars for Best Actor, he received a special Academy Award in 1960 for his many memorable performances.

Cooper, Sir Henry (1934–) Boxer, born in Bellingham, Kent, SE England, UK, the only man to win the Lonsdale Belt outright on three occasions. He beat Brian London to win his first British heavyweight title in 1959, and won his first Lonsdale Belt in 1961 when he beat Joe Erskine. After flooring Cassius Clay at Wembley in 1963, he had his only world title fight at Highbury Stadium in 1966, when a bad cut against Muhammad Ali (formerly Cassius Clay) forced his early retirement. He lost his British heavyweight title in a disputed contest against Joe Bugner in 1971, and announced his retirement. He does much work for charity, and is a popular television personality. He was knighted in 1999.

Cooper, James Fenimore (1789–1851) Novelist, born in Burlington, New Jersey, USA. Expelled from Yale, he joined the navy in 1806, but in 1811 resigned his commission, married, and began to write novels. He is best known for his frontier adventures such as *The Last of the Mohicans* (1826, filmed 1936 and 1992) and *The Pathfinder* (1840). He also wrote novels and historical studies about the sea. After visiting England and France, he was US consul at Lyon (1826–9). His later years were much disturbed by literary and newspaper controversies and actions for libel.

Cooper, Jilly, *née* **Sallitt** (1937–) Writer and journalist, born in Yorkshire, N England, UK. She was educated in Salisbury, became a reporter on a local paper (1957–9), and tried many other occupations before becoming a writer. She produced a regular column for the *Sunday Times* (1969–82) and *The Mail on Sunday* (1982–7), and has written a number of general interest works, including *How To Stay Married* (1969), *Jolly Marsupial* (1982), and *Angels Rush In* (1990). Her novels, always among the best sellers, include *Riders* (1978), *Polo* (1991), *Score!* (1999), and *Pandora* (2002).

Cooper, Leon Neil (1930–) Physicist, born in New York City, USA. He studied at Columbia University, and taught at Ohio State and (from 1958) Brown University, RI. His theory of the behaviour of electron pairs (*Cooper pairs*) in certain materials at low temperatures was a major contribution to the theory of superconductivity, which he helped to develop. He shared the Nobel Prize for Physics in 1972.

Cooper, Susie, popular name of **Susan Vera Cooper** (1902–95) Ceramic designer and manufacturer, born in Burslem, Staffordshire, C England, UK. After designing for A E Gray (1922–9), she founded a decorating studio at Tunstall, known as Susie Cooper Pottery. In 1931 she moved to Burslem and used earthenware supplied mainly by Wood & Sons. She became famous for functional shapes with simple hand-painted patterns, and in 1940 was appointed a Royal Designer for Industry. In 1950 she acquired a bone-china factory, renamed Susie Cooper China Ltd, which became part of the Wedgwood group in 1966 and closed in 1980.

Cooper, Dame Whina (1895–1994) Maori leader, born in Hokianga, New Zealand. After experience as a local community organizer and businesswoman, from the 1930s she became nationally known for her efforts to help her people recover from the problems caused by European settlement. In 1951 she became the founding president of the Maori Women's Welfare League, and in 1975 led a historic march to publicize Maori land claims. She was made a dame in 1981.

Cooper, William, pseudonym **H(arry) S(ummerfield) Hoff** (1910–2002) Novelist, born in Crewe, Cheshire, C England, UK. He studied at Cambridge. In the 1930s he published four novels under his own name, but it was *Scenes from Provincial Life* (1950) that established his reputation and was an influence on the 'Angry Young Men' of the 1950s. Three further novels charting the adventures of the same anti-hero followed: *Scenes from Married Life* (1961), *Scenes from Metropolitan Life* (1982), and *Scenes from Later Life* (1983). In 1960 he published *Genji*, a play based on Lady Murasaki's 11th-c novel, *The Tales of Genji*. A volume of memoirs, *From Early Life*, appeared in 1990.

co-operative *collective farm; farmer co-operative*

Co-operative Party A British political party which grew out of the ideas of voluntary mutual economic assistance developed in the 19th-c by Robert Owen. Established in 1917, one candidate, who joined with the Parliamentary Labour Party, was elected to the House of Commons in 1918. Thereafter it became closely integrated with the Labour Party, with which it still elects MPs jointly.

co-operative society A business venture owned by its members, who share the profits. These ventures may be shops, as with the original 'Rochdale Pioneers', who set up a co-operative shop in 1844. They may be producers, as in the co-operative businesses of many countries. Agricultural co-operatives in various countries, notably Denmark, often both buy inputs for their members and market their produce. The Co-operative Wholesale Society (CWS), set up in the UK in 1862 to manufacture and distribute goods to its members, was a co-operative of co-operatives. Advantages claimed for co-operatives are that the absence of outside shareholders maximizes the incentive for members to collaborate, and provides an outlet for idealism. The disadvantages are that business success demands capital, willingness to take risks, and business acumen, any of which the members may not possess. In adverse economic conditions a democratic structure may make decisions to retrench difficult to take. Many manufacturing co-operatives have failed, often however having been tried only after other forms of organization had already failed.

Cooper pairs *BCS theory*

co-ordinated universal time *Greenwich Mean Time*

co-ordinate geometry *analytic geometry*

co-ordination compounds Compounds containing metal atoms to which other atoms, molecules, or ions are bonded by means of the donation of lone pairs of electrons; also called **complex ions**. Most common for the transition metals, they are very widespread. Examples range from simple ions such as the brilliant blue salt tetra-amminecopper(II) sulphate, $[Cu(NH_3)_4]^{2+}SO_4^{2-}$, to enzymes including haemoglobin (iron) and chlorophyll (magnesium).

coot A bird of the rail family, inhabiting fresh waters; widespread; front of head with horny shield; sides of toes lobed, to assist swimming; pelvis and legs modified for diving. The name is sometimes misapplied to related birds. (Genus: *Fulica*, 9 species.)

copal *kauri gum*

Copán [kopahn] 14°52N 89°10W. An ancient Mayan city in the Motagua Basin of W Honduras, noted for its three-dimensional stone carving; flourished in the 8th-c AD; area 39 sq km/15 sq mi; now a world heritage site; town of Copán (or Santa Rosa de Copán) nearby. In 1839 the US explorer John Lloyd Stephens (1805–52) and artist Frederick Catherwood (1799–1856) bought the site for $50 from the local inhabitants so they could uncover and record the monuments uninterrupted.

Cope, Wendy (Mary) (1945–) Poet, writer, and journalist, born in Kent, SW England, UK. Educated at St Hilda's College, Oxford, she went on to become a teacher in London. Her first, best-selling collection of poems, *Making Cocoa for Kingsley Amis*, was published in 1986. She won the Cholmondeley Award for poetry in 1987, and the Michael Braude Award for Light Verse in 1995. Her poems have appeared in many anthologies and she has also written many books for children.

Copenhagen [kohpnhaygn], Danish **København**, Lat **Hafnia** 55°43N 12°34E, pop (2000e) 478 400. Capital city of Denmark, on E coast of Zealand and N part of Amager I; developed around 12th-c fortifications; charter, 1254; capital, 1443; birthplace of Martin Andersen-Nexø; airport (Kastrup); railway; university (1479); technical university of Denmark (1829); shipping and commercial centre; engineering, foodstuffs, brewing; old citadel of Frederikshavn; Tivoli amusement park (May–Sep); Amalienborg Palace (residence of Danish monarch since 1794); Christiansborg Palace; town hall (1894–1905); national (Thorwaldsen) museum; cathedral; Little Mermaid sculpture (1913); 17th-c Trinitatiskirke; Rosenborg Castle (1610–24), now a museum.

Copenhagen Interpretation In quantum mechanics, the view expressed by Neils Bohr and others that any quantum system must be considered in conjunction with relevant measuring equipment, since the act of making a measurement is part of the system. A definite quantum state does not exist until some measurement is performed. This is the current orthodox interpretation of quantum measurement.

copepod [kohpepod] A small aquatic arthropod; free-living forms extremely abundant in most marine and freshwater habitats, forming a vital link in the food chain by feeding on minute plant plankton; subclass contains c.9000 species, many being commensals or parasites of other animal groups. (Subphylum: Crustacea. Subclass: Copepoda.)

Copernican system A model of the Solar System in which the Sun is at the centre, with the Earth and other planets moving in combinations of circular movements around it (a *heliocentric* system). Prior to the publication of this theory in 1543, it was held by European astronomers that the Earth lay at the centre of the universe. To reproduce the observed planetary motions in that system, a complex arrangement of circular orbits was needed. The simpler heliocentric viewpoint gave the first modern view of our place in the universe. It fell to Kepler to demonstrate that the orbits of the planets were actually ellipses, not circles, and to Newton to explain the orbits through gravitational theory.

Copernicus, Nicolas [kopernikus], Polish **Mikolaj Kopernik** (1473–1543) The founder of modern astronomy, born in Toruń, C Poland. He studied mathematics and optics at Kraców, then canon law at Bologna, before becoming canon of Frombork. His 400-page treatise, *De revolutionibus orbium coelestium* (On the Revolutions of the Celestial Spheres, completed 1530) in which he put forward the theory of the Earth rotating daily about its own axis and annually about the Sun, had a hostile reception when it was published (1543), as it challenged the ancient teaching of the Earth as the centre of the universe.

Copland, Aaron [kohpland] (1900–90) Composer, born in New York City, USA. He studied under Rubin Goldmark, and in France under Nadia Boulanger, returning to the USA in 1924. A series of early works influenced by Stravinsky, Neoclassical in outlook and employing jazz idioms, was followed by compositions in which he tapped a deeper vein of US tradition and folk music, as in the ballets *Billy the Kid* (1938) and *Appalachian Spring* (1944). He also composed film scores, two operas, and three symphonies.

Copleston, Frederick (Charles) [kohplston] (1907–94) Jesuit philosopher, born near Taunton, Somerset, SW England, UK. He studied at Oxford, was ordained in 1937, and became professor of the history of philosophy at Heythrop College (1939) and of metaphysics at the Gregorian University, Rome (1952). He wrote several books on individual philosophers and movements, as well as an eight-volume *History of Philosophy* (1946–66).

copper Cu, element 29, density 9 g/cm^3, melting point 1080°C. The only brown metal, known from ancient times; its name derives from Cyprus, the main source in Roman times. It occurs free in nature, but more commonly as CuS and $CuCO_3$. It corrodes slowly, conducts electricity well, and is used mainly in electrical apparatus. Compounds show oxidation states +1 and, more commonly, +2. Copper(II) sulphate ($CuSO_4.5H_2O$) is used as an antiseptic and pesticide.

Copper Age *Three Age System*

Copperbelt pop (2000e) 2 119 400; area 31 328 sq km/12 093 sq mi. Province in C Zambia; economic centre of the country because of its vast copper and cobalt reserves, the world's largest known deposits; capital, Ndola; chief mines at Mufulira, Nkana, and Chibuluma; mining area extends into the N of the country and into S Democratic Republic of Congo.

Copperhead The name given to a member of the US Democratic Party who opposed the Civil War, derived from the name of a poisonous snake. In the election of 1864, Copperheads included a peace plank in their party platform, but this was repudiated by the presidential candidate, George McClellan. The name also applied more broadly to any Northerner with Southern sympathies.

copperhead A pit viper (*Agkistrodon contortrix*) native to SE USA; top of head reddish-brown; bites more people in North America than any other venomous snake, but venom is weak and deaths are rare. The name is also used for the SE Australian *Austrelaps superbus* of family Elapidae. The Asian pit viper *Agkistrodon acutus* is called the **Chinese copperhead**.

coppice Woodland in which the trees are periodically cut to near ground-level to encourage new growth. The cutting is usually done in rotation, and the regular opening up of the canopy encourages woodland flowers. The practice was widespread in the management of woods in the UK until the 19th-c.

Coppola, Francis Ford [kopohla] (1939–) Film director and screenwriter, born in Detroit, Michigan, USA. He studied the theatre in New York City, and film-making in Los Angeles. His first feature as director was *Dementia 13* (1963), and this was followed by the musical *Finian's Rainbow* (1967). Among his outstanding productions were *The Godfather* (1972; *Part II*, 1974; *Part III*, 1990) and his controversial study of the Vietnam War, *Apocalypse Now* (1979). Later films include *The Cotton Club* (1984), *Peggy Sue Got Married* (1987), *Tucker, the Man and His Dream* (1988), *Bram Stoker's Dracula* (1992), and *The Rainmaker* (1997).

copra The dried kernel of the coconut. In the 1860s, to supplement supplies of animal fats, manufacturers of soap, margarine, and lubricants turned to tropical vegetable oils, especially coconut oil. At first traders bought oil from local people, but later plantations were set up to produce copra, from which the oil is extracted by crushing. The Philippines, Indonesia, Sri Lanka (Ceylon), Malaysia, and the Pacific islands have been the largest producers.

co-processor A second computer processor, an optional extra processor on most personal computers, which allows the computer to carry out specific tasks more quickly. Examples are mathematics co-processors and graphics co-processors.

coprolalia The uncontrolled verbalization of obscenities. It occurs rarely in a variety of psychiatric disorders.

Coptic art A style of art which flourished in Egypt, 5th–8th-c. The Copts were Christians, and their wall-paintings, woven textiles, and stone carvings reflected late-Roman, Syrian, and Byzantine influences. After the 9th-c Islamic influence predominated.

Coptic Church (Gr *aigyptos* 'Egyptian') The Christian Church in Egypt of ancient origin, claiming St Mark as founder, and scholars and bishops of Alexandria in the early centuries of Christianity as fathers (eg Clement, Athanasius). With the condemnation of Patriarch Dioscuros and the Monophysite doctrine by the Council of Chalcedon (451), the Copts split from the rest of the Church, and by the 6th-c included almost all Egypt. This Church was gradually weakened by religious strife, invasions by Arabs in the 7th-c and 11th-c, and Turks in the 16th-c, accompanied by mass conversions to Islam. It preserves the Coptic (ancient Egyptian) language, and observes the liturgy and sacraments of the ancient Alexandrian rite. It maintains a monastic tradition and structure, its head (called a *pope*) being elected by a religious tribunal and confirmed by the Egyptian government.

copyright Ownership of and right of control over all possible ways of reproducing a 'work', ie the product of an original creative act by one or more people, in a form which makes it possible to be copied. In particular, copyright protection is given to literary, dramatic, and artistic works (paintings, drawings, photographs, etc), sound recordings, films, television and sound broadcasts, and various productions of new technology. All major countries (except for China) and most minor ones have copyright laws, and international protection is given via two major conventions. The laws of each country differ, but there are important characteristics common to most. Copyright is a property owned by the creator (unless working under a contract of employment), but it is transferrable: the creator can either assign full copyright to another party or, retaining copyright, lease out (directly or through a publisher or agent) any of the separate rights (eg to translate) which make up the copyright. It extends to all 'works': the hurried private letter receives as much protection as the great novel. It is finite: at some time or other the work falls into public ownership and can be copied without permission: in the UK, since 1996, the period is 70 years after the creator's death (previously, 50); in the USA, since 1978, the period is 50 years for most works (previously 28, once renewable). It is divisible: copyright in a novel, for example, will include the right to publish in translation, to turn into a film, to anthologize, etc. It is independent of the work as a physical object: ownership of a manuscript or painting does not in itself constitute ownership of the copyright. The 1988 Copyright, Designs and Patents Act introduced for the first time in the UK the concept of authors' and illustrators' moral rights. These include the *right of paternity* (the right of the author or creator to be identified as such) and the *right of integrity* (the right not to have work subjected to unjustified modification). These rights are retained by the creator and not assigned along with copyright.

coracle A small circular craft first constructed from reeds in basket form by ancient Britons. Watertightness was achieved originally with hides, but latterly with pitch. It was light enough to be carried on a man's back. The tradition mainly survives in Wales, where coracles are still used by salmon fishermen.

coral A typically massive hydroid, found in colonies in warm shallow seas; many produce a calcareous external skeleton forming coral reefs; polyp phase of life-cycle dominant, with many specialized types of individuals; medusa often small and transparent. (Phylum: Cnidaria. Class: Hydrozoa.)

Coral Sea or **Solomon Sea** area 4 791 000 sq km/1 850 200 sq mi. Arm of the Pacific Ocean, bounded W by NE Australia, N by Papua New Guinea and the Solomon Is, and E by Vanuatu and New Caledonia; many coral islands; maximum depth in New Hebrides Trench, 9175 m/30 101 ft; Great Barrier Reef along W edge; scene of US victory over Japanese (1942).

Coral Sea Islands, Territory of the Uninhabited territory in the Coral Sea off the NE coast of Australia, administered by the Australian government since 1969; comprises scattered reefs and islands (including the Great Barrier Reef) over a sea area of about 1 million sq km; manned meteorological station on Willis I.

coral snake A venomous snake native to the New World (Genera: *Micrurus* and *Micruroides*) and E Asia (Genus: *Calliophis*); usually with bold alternating bands of black, yellow, and red; strong venom, but not aggressive; short fangs do not inject venom easily, and snake either grips prey in mouth after strike, or bites several times. (Family: Elapidae.)

coral tree A tropical tree and shrub armed with spines; leaves with three leaflets; pea-flowers red or orange, often waxy-looking, showy, in dense clusters, borne when the tree is bare of leaves. The flowers are an important source of nectar and water for birds and animals during the dry season, and also attract ants, which guard the tree. Coral trees are grown as ornamentals in warmer countries, and provide shade in crop plantations. (Genus: *Erythrina*, 100 species. Family: Leguminosae.)

cor anglais [kawr onggIay] (Fr 'English horn') A woodwind instrument with a slightly conical bore, a double reed, and a distinctive bulb-shaped bell. Neither English nor a horn, it is in effect a tenor oboe, a transposing instrument (in F) sounding a 5th below the written pitch.

corbelling A prehistoric method of constructing a vault, using courses of dry stone stepped successively inwards until they come close enough together to span with a single slab or capstone. The chambered tombs of Maes Howe and New Grange afford notable early examples in N Europe. In the Aegean, the so-called Treasury of Atreus of c.1300 BC at Mycenae is the widest single-span chamber known ever to have been built before Hadrian's Pantheon, its corbelled dome measuring 14·5 m/48 ft in diameter, and standing 13 m/43 ft high.

Corbet, Christian Cardell (1966–) Painter and art historian, born in Ajax, Ontario, SE Canada. He studied at the University of Guelph, was appointed artist to Elizabeth the Queen Mother in 1966, and received international recognition for 'Elizabeth Holding her Ribbon' (1995). An authority on Canadian women in the fine arts, he is the author of several works on Canadian women artists, and founder of the Corbet Collection of Canadian Women Artists (1993). The first president of the Canadian Portrait Society (1996), he is also noted for his abstract works representing botanical-fragmented studies.

Corbett, Ronnie, popular name of **Ronald Balfour Corbett** (1930–) Comedian, born in Edinburgh, EC Scotland, UK. After national service in the Royal Air Force, and 18 months as a civil servant, he entered showbusiness. Spotted in Danny La Rue's nightclub by David Frost, he appeared on television in *The Frost Report* (1966–7) and *Frost on Sunday* (1968–9). His diminutive stature, impish sense of fun, and comic monologues soon gained him national popularity. His television series include *Sorry!* (1981–8), *Small Talk* (1994–6), and a fruitful partnership with Ronnie Barker led to the long-running *The Two Ronnies* (1971–87). Film appearances comprised *Casino Royale* (1967) and *No Sex Please, We're British* (1972). A keen amateur golfer, he wrote *Armchair Golf* (1986).

Corbières [kaw(r)byair] Sparsely populated upland district in Aude department, S France, lying between the Massif Central and the Pyrenees; highest point, Pic de Bugarach (1231 m/4039 ft); lower-lying area known for its red wine; chief locality, Quillan.

Corbin, Margaret, *née* **Cochran** (1751–c.1800) Revolutionary heroine, born in Franklin Co, Pennsylvania, USA. When she was five, her father was killed in an Indian raid in which her mother was taken captive, and she was raised by an uncle. Her husband, **John Corbin**, enlisted in the Revolution, and she accompanied him as cook, laundress, and nurse for the troops. During the Battle of Harlem Heights in 1776, Corbin was mortally wounded; she took over his battle station and was wounded, suffering the permanent loss of the use of one arm. After the battle, she was accorded some of the benefits accorded to veterans, thereby becoming the first woman pensioner of the USA. She apparently remarried, but vanished from view c.1783.

Corbusier, Le *Le Corbusier*

Corday (d'Armont), (Marie) Charlotte [kaw(r)day] (1768–93) Noblewoman, born in St Saturnin, W France. She sympathized with the aims of the Revolution, but was horrified by the acts of the Jacobins. She managed to obtain an audience with the revolutionary leader, Jean Paul Marat, while he was in his bath, and stabbed him. She was guillotined four days later.

Cordeliers, Club of the [kaw(r)delyay] An extreme revolutionary club founded in Paris (1790) by Danton and Marat; also called the **Society of the Friends of the Rights of Man and Citizen**. Under Hébert's leadership its programme became increasingly radical (1792–4), contributing to the downfall of the Girondins (1793).

cord grass A perennial marine grass, native to coasts in temperate regions, mainly North America. *Spartina × townsendii*, a fertile hybrid between a British and an American species, is often planted as a mud-binder, and is spreading rapidly in the wild in Britain. (Genus: *Spartina*, 16 species. Family: Gramineae.)

Córdoba (Argentina) **[kaw(r)dohba]**, Span **[korthoba]** 31°25S 64°11W, pop (2000e) 1 327 000. Capital of Córdoba province, C Argentina; Argentina's second largest city; on the R Primero, near the foothills of the Sierra de Córdoba; founded by Cabrera in 1573; renowned as a Jesuit mission centre; 3 universities (including Argentina's first, 1613); airport; railway; vehicles, textiles, cement, glass; cathedral (1697–1787). The Jesuit Block in Córdoba is a world heritage site.

Córdoba (Spain) **[kaw(r)dohba]**, Span **[korthoba]** 37°50N 4°50W, pop (2000e) 305 000. Capital of Córdoba province, Andalusia, S Spain; on R Guadalquivir, 400 km/250 mi SW of Madrid; capital of Moorish Spain, 8th-c; bishopric; airport; railway; tourism, brewing, wine, olives, textiles, paper, tools, copper; cathedral, old Jewish quarter, Moorish Alcazar; Great Mosque (completed 990) is a world heritage site; Festival of los Patios Cordobeses (May), fair of Our Lady of la Salud (May), autumn fiestas (Sep).

Córdoba Cathedral Originally a mosque built (785–6) by Abd-er-Rahman I (731–88) in Córdoba, S Spain, and extended in the 9th-c and 10th-c. It has been used as a Christian cathedral since 1238, when the Moors lost control of the area. It is now a world heritage site.

core curriculum A basic central provision for all pupils, as opposed to a set of options taken only by some. It usually contains subjects like mathematics, science, and the pupil's native language, though in some schools and in some countries the core may be larger.

core electrons Electrons closer to the nucleus than the valence electrons. They usually play no part in chemical reactions.

Corelli, Arcangelo [korelee] (1653–1713) Composer, born in Fusignano, N Italy. From c.1675 he lived in Rome, where he was in great demand as a violinist, spending the last 22 years of his life in the service of Cardinal Ottoboni. His Concerti grossi, and his solo and trio sonatas for violin, mark an epoch in chamber music, and greatly influenced a whole generation of composers.

Corelli, Marie [korelee], pseudonym of **Mary Mackay** (1855–1924) Novelist, born in London, UK. She trained for a musical career, but then became a writer of romantic melodramas which proved to be extremely popular, such as *A Romance of Two Worlds* (1886), *Barabbas* (1893), and *The Sorrows of Satan* (1895).

Corfu **[kawfoo]**, Gr **Kérkira** pop (2000e) 110 000; area 592 sq km/228 sq mi. Northernmost and second largest of the Ionian Is, Greece, off NW coast of Greece; seventh largest Greek island; length 64 km/40 mi; semi-mountainous terrain (highest point 907 m/2976 ft), dense vegetation; chief town, Corfu, pop (2000e) 36 500; airport; local ferries to mainland Greece and to Italy, Turkey, and ports in the Balkan Peninsula; textiles, fishing, tourism, olive oil, fruit; Church of St Spyridon, old fortress (1386); Navy Week (Jun–Jul).

corgi The only British spitz breed of dog; small with short legs, pointed muzzle, large erect ears; two varieties: short-tailed **Pembroke** and long-tailed **Cardigan**; also known as **Welsh corgi**.

coriander An annual (*Coriandrum sativum*), growing to 50 cm/20 in, native to N Africa and W Asia; leaves with narrow linear lobes; flowers white or pink, petals unequal, in umbels 1–3 cm/

0·4–1·2 in across; fruit 3–4 mm/0·12–0·16 in, globular; also known as **cilantro** in North and South America. It is cultivated for the leaves, which are used in Chinese, Indian, and Mexican cooking, and for the fruits, used as a spice in sausages, curries, confectionery, and liqueurs. (Family: Umbelliferae.)

Corinth, Gr **Kórinthos** 37°56N 22°55E, pop (2000e) 30 200. Capital town of Corinth department, Greece; on an isthmus separating the Adriatic Sea from the Aegean; founded before 3000 BC; influential Greek city-state of Dorian origins, often at odds with Ionian Athens; famous in antiquity for its commercial and colonizing activities; destroyed by Romans 146 BC; ancient Kórinthos, 7 km/4 mi SW; transferred to new site in 1858, after a severe earthquake; railway; ferry to Italy; wine trade, tourism; extensive remains, including Archaic Temple of Apollo and several basilicas; Navy Week (Jun–Jul).

Corinth Canal An artificial waterway bisecting the Isthmus of Corinth in Greece; built 1881–93, although excavation of a canal through the Isthmus was begun as early as AD 67; length 6·5 km/4 mi.

Corinthian order One of the five main orders of classical architecture, characterized by a fluted shaft and a decorative acanthus capital. It was first invented in Athens in the 5th-c BC, later developed by the Romans, and used extensively in the Renaissance period.

Corinthians, Letters to the Two New Testament writings, widely accepted as from the apostle Paul to the church that he founded in Corinth. The first describes his efforts to deal with the first phase of a crisis involving a variety of ethical and doctrinal problems dividing the church at Corinth, such as the use of spiritual gifts, claims to special knowledge, attitudes towards pagan practices of eating meat offered to idols, marriage, celibacy, and sexual behaviour; the second is his response to later developments in this church, to the efforts to collect funds for the Jerusalem church, and to charges against him by opponents.

Corinto [kohreentoh], formerly **Punta Icacos** 12°29N 87°14W, pop (2000e) 22 000. Port in Chinandega department, Nicaragua; chief Pacific port of Nicaragua; founded, 1840; railway; trade in sugar, coffee, hides, timber.

Coriolanus, Gaius or **Gnaeus Marcius** [koriolaynus] (5th-c BC) Roman folk hero, so named from his capture of the Volscian town of Corioli. Banished by the Romans for tyrannical behaviour (491 BC), he took refuge with the Volscians, and proceeded to lead them against his native city. After entreaties from his mother and wife, he spared Rome, and was executed by the Volscians.

Coriolis force [koriohlis] An apparent force acting on objects moving across the Earth's surface; named after French mathematician Gustave Gaspard Coriolis (1792–1843). It results from the Earth's rotation, and is distinct from centripetal force. In the N hemisphere, the path of an object appears deflected to the right, in the S hemisphere to the left. It is responsible for wind and ocean current patterns, and is applicable to rotating systems generally.

Cork (city), Ir **Chorcaigh** 51°54N 8°28W, pop (2000e) 176 000. Commercial seaport, county borough, and capital of Cork county, Munster, S Ireland; on R Lee near its mouth on Lough Mahon; third largest city in Ireland; airport; docks and ferry terminal; railway; university (1845); shipbuilding, brewing, tanning, food processing; St Finbarr's Cathedral, St Mary's Cathedral; cattle shows (Feb); international folk dance and choral festival.

Cork (county), Ir **Chorcaigh** pop (2000e) 415 000; area 7459 sq km/2880 sq mi. County and county borough, Munster, S Ireland; prosperous agricultural and industrial county bounded S by Atlantic Ocean and watered by the Lee, Bandon and Blackwater Rivers; the Boggeragh and Nagles Mts rise to the NW and N; capital, Cork; fishing, agriculture; natural gas and oil off Old Head of Kinsale, with terminal facilities at Whiddy I; Blarney Castle; Fastnet Lighthouse.

cork A spongy, protective layer just beneath the outer bark in trees, made up of thin-walled cells impregnated with a waxy substance (*suberin*). The cork layer may be built up over several years, becoming very thick.

cork oak An evergreen tree (*Quercus suber*) growing to 20 m/ 65 ft, native to the Mediterranean region; leaves holly-like, glossy, with spiny margins; bark produces very thick cork layer which can be removed in cylindrical sheets from the trunk without harming the tree. It is cultivated as a commercial source of cork. (Family: Fagaceae.)

corm A short underground shoot containing food reserves. Early growth of foliage and flowers totally depletes the reserves, and a new corm is formed on top of the old one at the end of each year before the plant dies back.

Cormack, Allan Macleod (1924–98) Physicist, born in Johannesburg, NE South Africa. He worked at the Groote Schuur Hospital in Johannesburg after graduating in physics at Cape Town University. There he developed a technique for computer-assisted X-ray imaging (*CAT scanning*) which has proved valuable in diagnostic medicine. He shared the Nobel Prize for Physiology or Medicine in 1979.

cormorant A large gregarious seabird, found worldwide; dark plumage, often with bright naked facial skin; flies fast, usually close to water surface; swims underwater using feet; eats fish. Some species are called **shags**. Cormorants are important guano producers in the S hemisphere. (Family: Phalacrocoracidae, 31 species.)

corn A generic term usually referring to the most widely cultivated cereal crop in a country or region. In North America, corn normally refers to maize, in Britain to wheat, and in Scandinavia to barley.

corn belt The major agricultural region of the US Midwest. It is centred on the states of Iowa and Illinois, and includes parts of S Dakota, Minnesota, Nebraska, Kansas, Missouri, Ohio, and Indiana. Its main products are corn (maize) and other feed-grain. Livestock raising is also common.

corn borer A small, dull-coloured moth with long snout-like mouthparts; caterpillars feed on plants, especially maize, burrowing into stalks, leaves, and ears; an important pest of maize worldwide. (Order: Lepidoptera. Family: Pyralidae.)

corncockle An annual with a little-branched stem (*Agrostemma githago*), 30–100 cm/12–40 in, clothed in white hairs; flowers 3–5 cm across with stalks and calyx-tube woolly, petals reddish-purple, slightly notched. Once a common weed of cornfields everywhere, it is now decreasing, and is rare in places. The seeds are thought to be poisonous; when numerous, they reduce the quality of flour. (Family: Caryophyllaceae.)

corncrake A bird of the rail family (*Crex crex*), native to Europe and W Asia, also known as the **landrail**; migrates to tropical Africa in winter, otherwise seldom seen flying or in groups; inhabits grassland and cultivation; eats seeds and insects.

cornea [kaw(r)nia] The transparent front part of the outer protective coat of the eyeball. The degree of its curvature varies from person to person, and also with age (greater in youth than in old age). A large inequality in its vertical and horizontal curvatures is known as *astigmatism* (an inability to focus vertical and horizontal lines at the same point). The cornea is largely responsible for the refraction of light entering the eye, focusing it approximately on the retina, so that the lens can make the final fine adjustment. It is devoid of blood vessels in the adult (except at its margins), which presumably explains why corneal grafts escape rejection.

Corneille, Pierre [kaw(r)nay] (1606–84) Playwright, born in Rouen, NW France. He trained as a lawyer, but in 1629 went to Paris, where his comedy *Mélite* was highly successful, and he became a favourite of Cardinal Richelieu. Other comedies followed, then in 1636 *Le Cid*, a classical tragedy, took Paris by storm. Other major tragedies were *Horace* (1639), *Cinna* (1639), and *Polyeucte* (1640). *Le Menteur* (1642, The Liar) entitles him to be called the father of French comedy as well as of French tragedy. A master of the alexandrine verse form, he wrote many other plays, and in 1671 he joined Molière and Quinault in writing *Psyché*, a play employing music, incorporating ballet sequences and written in lyrical language. After his marriage in 1640 he lived in Rouen until 1662, then settled in Paris.

cornelian cherry A deciduous shrub or tree (*Cornus mas*), growing to 8 m/26 ft, native to Europe and W Asia; leaves oval, opposite; flowers appearing before leaves in small clusters 2 cm/¾ in diameter, 4-petalled, yellow; berries bright red, acid but edible. (Family: Cornaceae.)

Cornelius, Peter von [kaw(r)**nee**lius] (1783–1867) Painter, born in Düsseldorf, W Germany. He influenced the revival of fresco painting in 19th-c Germany. In 1811 he joined a group of painters (the Nazarenes) in Rome, and helped in the decoration of the Casa Bartoldi. He went to Munich in 1819, where he executed the large frescoes of Greek mythology in the Glyptothek and the New Testament frescoes in the Ludwigskirche. In 1841 he became director of the Academy in Berlin.

Cornell, Eric A (1961–) Physicist, born in Palo Alto, California, USA. He studied at Stanford University and the Massachusetts Institute of Technology, and went on to work at the National Institute of Standards and Technology at the University of Colorado. He shared the 2001 Nobel Prize for Physics for the achievement of Bose–Einstein condensation in dilute gases of alkali atoms, and for early fundamental studies of the properties of the condensates.

cornet A musical instrument made of brass. The modern cornet, resembling a small trumpet with three valves, is used above all in brass bands. It is sometimes used in symphony orchestras, especially in France.

cornetfish Colourful tropical marine fish found around reefs and sea-grass beds; head and body very slender, length up to 1·8 m/6 ft; scaleless, tail bearing a whip-like process; predatory, feeding on other small fishes; also called **flutemouth**. (Family: Fistulariidae.)

cornett A musical instrument in use from the 15th-c to the mid-18th-c, made from two pieces of hollowed wood, glued together and covered with leather to form a tube, usually curved, with a conical bore. This was provided with fingerholes and a cup-shaped mouthpiece like that of a brass instrument. The cornett has been revived in modern times for performing older music, including Bach's cantatas, in which it often doubles the highest voice part.

cornflour The flour of the maize seed, favoured by cooks as a thickening agent in sauces and soups.

cornflower A branched annual (*Centaurea cyanus*) growing to 80 cm/30 in, native to SE Europe; leaves narrowly lance-shaped, with grey cottony hairs, the lower lobed; flower-heads 1·5–3 cm/½–1½ in across, solitary, long-stalked; outer florets bright blue, spreading, larger than the inner red-purple florets; also called **bluebottle**. It was once widely introduced as a cornfield weed, but is now rare because of the improved cleaning of seed grain. Its petals were used to produce a blue pigment used by artists. (Family: Compositae.)

cornice [**kaw(r)**nis] In classical or Renaissance architecture, the crowning, projecting part of an entablature. In a general sense, it may refer to any crowning ornamental projection along the top of a building or wall.

Cornish The Celtic language once spoken to the W of the R Tamar in Cornwall. It shares some features with dialects of S Welsh, with which it was originally geographically contiguous. There is some religious literature, mainly translations from English, from the 15th–16th-c, showing vast lexical borrowing from English. The last speakers died in c.1800, but there is growing interest in a modern revival of the language.

Corn Laws British legislation regulating the trade in corn. This was common in the 18th-c, but the most famous Corn Law was that enacted by Lord Liverpool's government in 1815. Passed at a time when market prices were dropping rapidly, it imposed prohibitively high duties on the import of foreign corn when the domestic price was lower than 80 shillings (£4) a quarter, giving British farmers a domestic monopoly. Widely criticized by radical politicians as legislation designed to protect the landed interest at the expense of the ordinary consumer, the Corn Law was amended in 1828, with the introduction of a sliding scale, and duties were further reduced by Peel in 1842. Bread price increases led to civil unrest, to which the government responded with legislation suspending the rights of *habeas corpus* and freedom of assembly. Demands for free trade grew; John Bright and Richard Cobden set up the Anti-Corn Law League. In 1846 Peel managed to bring in a free trade policy, leading to the abolition of export duties. Later in 1846 the Corn Laws were repealed, but a low temporary wheat tax was introduced. In 1849 the import tax was further reduced; this nominal duty was finally abolished in 1869. The Irish famine in 1845 and 1846, in which 25% of the population died, hastened repeal of the Corn Laws but their removal brought the Irish little immediate relief.

corn marigold An annual (*Chrysanthemum segetum*) native to Europe and W Asia; leaves toothed or divided, somewhat fleshy, the upper clasping the stem; flower-heads golden yellow. Once a troublesome cornfield weed, it is still found on arable land. (Family: Compositae.)

corn poppy An erect annual (*Papaver rhoeas*), growing to 60 cm/2 ft, producing white latex, native to Europe and Asia, and introduced elsewhere; leaves divided, bristly; flowers round, four petals, bright scarlet, with or without dark basal patch; capsule pepper-pot shaped with a ring of pores around the rim. It was formerly a widespread weed, with seeds lying dormant in the soil for many years, rapidly reappearing when soil is freshly turned, as in arable or disturbed land; now declining because of improved farming techniques. It is a poignant symbol of World War 1, when fields bloomed with poppies after being churned by battle. (Family: Papaveraceae.)

corn spurrey A slender annual (*Spergula arvensis*), 7–40 cm/ 2¾–15 in; leaves very narrow, fleshy, in clusters; flowers 4–7 mm/⅛–¼ in diameter, white, five petals; seeds 1·2–1·5 mm/ 0·5–0·7 in, black. It is a cosmopolitan weed, but was a crop plant grown for its seeds from pre-Roman to mediaeval times, and is occasionally used today for fodder. (Family: Caryophyllaceae.)

cornucopia [kaw(r)nyu**koh**pia] A classical motif of a ram's horn overflowing with fruit and flowers, symbolizing abundance and plenty. It was much used in Renaissance and later decorative schemes to do with eating and drinking.

Cornwall, Celtic **Kernow** pop (2001e) 499 100; area 3564 sq km/ 1376 sq mi. County in SW England, UK, divided into six districts and the Isles of Scilly; bounded S by the English Channel, and W by the Atlantic Ocean; county town, Truro; tin mining, dairy farming, market gardening, fishing, tourism; Cornish nationalist movement revived the Stannary (Tinners' Parliament) in 1974, and there is renewed interest in the Cornish language.

Cornwallis, Charles Cornwallis, 1st Marquess [kaw(r)n**wo**lis] (1738–1805) British general and statesman, born in London, UK. He studied at the Military Academy of Turin, and served in the Seven Years' War. Though personally opposed to taxing the American colonists, he accepted a command in the war, and defeated Gates at Camden (1780), but was forced to surrender at Yorktown (1781). In 1786 he became Governor-General of India, where he defeated Tippoo Sahib, and introduced the series of reforms known as the *Cornwallis Code*. He returned in 1793, to be made marquess. He was Lord-Lieutenant of Ireland (1798–1801), and negotiated the Peace of Amiens (1802). He was re-appointed Governor-General of India in 1804.

Cornwell, Patricia (Daniels) (1957–) Novelist, born in Miami, Florida, USA. After an unsettled childhood, she studied at Davidson College, North Carolina. Working as a police reporter, and (from 1984) in the Virginia medical examiner's office, she gained a wide range of experience which she put to use in her novels. In the 1990s she became one of the world's best-selling women novelists, producing a book each year, and known especially for the character of medical examiner Dr Kay Scarpetta introduced in her first novel *Postmortem* (1990). Later books include *Body of Evidence* (1991), *Cause of Death* (1996), the first non-Scarpetta mystery, *Hornet's Nest* (1997), and *Blow Fly* (2003). Her very first book was *A Time for Remembering* (1983), a biography of Ruth Bell Graham (wife of Billy Graham), with whom she was in close contact as a child.

corolla *flower; petal*

Coromandel Coast [korohmandl] The E coast of India, extending more than 650 km/400 mi from Point Calimere in the S to the mouth of the Krishna R in the N.

coromandel screen [korohmandl] A screen made of wood, lacquered and incised with coloured decoration. Such screens were imported in large numbers for the European luxury trade in the later 17th-c from the Far East.

corona (astronomy) [korohna] The outermost layers of the Sun's atmosphere, visible as a pearly halo of light during a total eclipse, temperature c.1–2 million K. It is a source of strong X-rays.

corona (botany) [korohna] An extension of the corolla (petals) of a flower, such as the central trumpet of a daffodil.

Corona Australis [korohna awstralis] (Lat 'southern crown') A small but prominent S constellation on the fringes of the Milky Way.

Corona Borealis [korohna borialis] (Lat 'northern crown') A small N constellation, the stars forming a striking semicircle.

corona discharge An electrical discharge accompanied by the emission of blue light that sometimes occurs in the air surrounding the sources of an intense electric field. Electrons and ions in the air are accelerated by the field, giving rise to further ions; light is produced by the recombination of ions with electrons.

coronagraph An optical instrument for producing an artificial eclipse inside a telescope. Real eclipses last only a few minutes, and most take place far from any observatory. With a coronagraph, it is possible to study the outer layers of the solar atmosphere without waiting for the next eclipse.

coronary heart disease Atherosclerosis of the coronary arteries, the most important cause of death over 40 in the West, and the commonest cause of angina pectoris and myocardial infarction; also known as **ischaemic/ischemic heart disease**. There are large differences in the prevalence of coronary artery disease between countries and communities. Risk factors include family history, smoking, diabetes, high blood pressure, high levels of cholesterol in the blood, and stress. In developed countries, people from deprived areas have higher rates of disease.

coroner A public officer who investigates the cause of a death, especially one where there is reason to suspect that it was due to violent or unnatural causes, in some cases holding an official inquiry, or *inquest*, to investigate the facts surrounding the death. Inquests into treasure trove are also held in the coroner's court, which may sit with a jury. Coroners are appointed by the Crown, or elected or appointed as a county or state office in the USA, and are typically qualified as a medical doctor or a lawyer (though not all US jurisdictions have this requirement). In Scotland, it is the responsibility of the procurator fiscal to investigate all sudden, suspicious, unexplained, or accidental deaths, to commence fatal accident inquiries, and if necessary to conduct a public enquiry before a sheriff.

Corot, (Jean Baptiste) Camille [koroh] (1796–1875) Landscape painter, born in Paris, France. He studied at Rouen, took up art in 1822, and after visiting Italy, settled in Paris (1827). His main sketching ground was at Barbizon, in the Forest of Fontainebleau; but he made two other visits to Italy in 1835 and 1843. Several of his masterpieces, such as 'La Danse des nymphes' (1850) are in the Louvre.

corporate state *corporatism*

Corporation Act A British Act passed by the Cavalier Parliament in 1661, soon after the Restoration of Charles II. Office in municipal corporations was restricted to those who took the sacrament according to the usage of the Church of England. Part of the re-assertion of Anglican supremacy represented by the Clarendon Code, the Act remained on the statute book until 1828.

corporation tax A tax levied on company profits after the deduction of operating expenses. Created in the UK in 1966, its predecessor was the **profits tax**. The tax rate payable has been changed over the years, and small firms pay the tax at a lower rate. In the USA there are federal, state, and local taxes on corporations.

corporatism Arrangements where the authority to decide and implement economic and social policies is either shared with or delegated to groups of producers who are expected to abide by principles laid down by the state. Failure to do so may lead to a withdrawal of decision-making and representational rights. It produces a quasi-private system of government. Corporatism (often termed **corporativism** in the 1920s and 1930s) is found in authoritarian countries, which are sometimes referred to as **corporate states**, where the freedom of producers' associations is severely curtailed, and they act largely as agents of the state. Less formalized, but often widespread corporatist arrangements can also be found in many liberal democracies which operate by negotiation; the term **neo-corporatism** is usually applied, and such developments were held to have become increasingly prominent in the post-World War 2 period (eg in Japan and parts of W Europe). In the UK, the Thatcherite agenda was largely a response to these perceived developments.

Corpus Christi, Feast of [kaw(r)pus kristee] A festival of the Roman Catholic Church in honour of the Eucharist, observed on the Thursday after Trinity Sunday. This was the first available Thursday after the natural date for the festival, Maundy Thursday, which was unsuitable because of the proximity of Easter.

Corpus Juris Canonici [kaw(r)pus jooris kanonikiy] (Lat 'body of canon law') The chief collection of church or canon law of the Roman Catholic Church and, to an extent, of the Anglican Churches. It includes the decrees of popes and canons, and rules formulated by the Councils, eg the Decretals of Gregory IX. Canon law exercised considerable influence on the development of civil and international law. The 'Corpus' was succeeded in the Roman Catholic Church by the **Codex Juris Canonici** (1918).

Corpus Juris Civilis *Justinian Code*

corpus luteum [kaw(r)pus lootium] The mass of yellowish tissue remaining after ovulation, when a mature ovarian follicle ruptures from the ovary of a mammal. If fertilization does not occur after ovulation, the corpus luteum rapidly breaks down.

Correggio [korejioh], originally **Antonio Allegri** (c.1494–1534) Renaissance painter, born in Correggio, N Italy. In 1518 he began his great series of mythological frescoes for the convent of San Paolo at Parma, and between 1521 and 1524 was engaged upon 'The Ascension' in the cupola of San Giovanni. The decoration of the cathedral of Parma was commissioned in 1522. He also painted many easel pictures on religious themes, such as 'The Adoration of the Shepherds', known as 'The Night' (c.1530, Dresden). He returned to Correggio in 1530.

correlation In mathematics, a measure of the extent to which there is a linear relation between two variables. Given a set of data (x_i,y_i), standard deviation of x and y s_x and s_y, and covariance s_{xy}, a **correlation coefficient** r is defined by s_{xy}/s_xs_y. If r is close to 1, there is said to be good positive correlation: y increases as x increases. If r is close to -1, there is good negative correlation: y decreases as x increases. **Rank correlation** compares orders, not numerical values, using different statistics.

Correns, Karl (Franz Joseph) Erich (1864–1933) Botanist, born in Munich, SE Germany. He taught at Tübingen (1892–1902), Leipzig (1902–9), and Münster (1909–14) universities, and from 1914 was director of the Kaiser Wilhelm Biological Institute at Berlin. He rediscovered the neglected results reported in Mendel's paper on the principles of heredity, and confirmed them by his research on the garden pea.

correspondence principle The requirement that the quantum theory of submicroscopic systems, when applied to macroscopic systems, gives results consistent with those of classical mechanics. The principle ensures that classical and quantum mechanics are compatible.

corrie *cirque*

Corrigan-Maguire, Mairead (1944–) Roman Catholic woman who, with **Betty Williams** (1943–), founded the movement for peace in Northern Ireland known as the 'Peace People' (1976). The movement involved people from both the Catholic and Protestant communities who wished to see an end to the sectarian violence plaguing the province. They shared the Nobel Peace Prize in 1976.

corroboration Credible evidence which confirms or supports evidence already given in court by an independent source. Corroboration may involve the testimony of another witness or may relate to documents or certain forensic findings. The requirement for evidence to be corroborated varies between jurisdictions, though there is usually no requirement that evidence in civil proceedings be corroborated. In English law, corroboration is not generally required, and any fact may be proved by a single item of credible evidence. The risk that an innocent person may be convicted is reduced if the testimony of more than one sound witness is available.

corroboree [koroboree] A term used by 19th-c settlers in New South Wales, Australia, for any Aboriginal ceremonial or festive gathering which included singing and dancing. Later it came into common use among non-Aborigines, but it fails to mark the distinction between religious ceremonies and non-religious performance practised by Aboriginal peoples.

corrosion Destructive oxidation, usually by air in the presence of water; most marked for metals, especially iron. It is an electrochemical process, occurring most rapidly when two different metals are in contact with one another and with air and water, the more reactive metal being oxidized while the other provides a surface for the reduction of O_2. Corrosion prevention is best carried out by isolating the reactive metal surface from air and water. Some metals, including aluminium and zinc (*passive* metals), form adherent oxide coatings which serve this purpose.

corsairs Dutch, English, and French privateers licensed by governments to prey upon enemy shipping in the Channel and Atlantic during the Wars of the League of Augsburg (1689–97) and the Spanish Succession (1702–13). The most famous were Captain Kidd, who turned to piracy, and Frenchman Jean Barth, who was enobled. In a broader sense, corsairs were privateers of the Barbary Coast of North Africa, and especially Algiers. After the Moorish expulsion from Spain (1491), individuals began attacks on Christian shipping. The early 17th-c saw the peak of their activity. Britain and France frequently attacked the corsairs, and from 1800 to 1815 the USA declared war on Tripoli and Algiers. Privateering in the Mediterranean ceased with the French occupation of Algiers in 1830.

Corsica [kawsikuh], Fr **Corse** pop (2000e) 261 000; area 8680 sq km/3350 sq mi. Mountainous island and region of France in the Mediterranean Sea, comprising the departments of Corse-du-Sud and Haute-Corse; length 183 km/114 mi; width up to 84 km/52 mi; separated from Sardinia (S) by the Strait of Bonifacio; part of France since 1768; France's largest island; mountainous interior, rising to 2710 m/8891 ft at Mont Cinto; fertile alluvial plains (E), edged with lagoons and swamps; airport; car ferries from Nice, Toulon, Marseille; capital, Ajaccio; chief towns Bastia, Calvi, Corte, Bonifacio; corks, asbestos, vines, olives, fruit, sheep, goats; major scenic area, with a wide range of tourist activities; birthplace of Napoleon; the 'Calanches' (above Gulf of Porto), granite pinnacles worn into bizarre forms resembling fabulous animals; Parc de la Corse regional nature park, area 1483 sq km/572 sq mi.

Cort, Henry (1740–1800) Ironmaster, born in Lancaster, Lancashire, NW England, UK. He became a navy agent in London, then in 1775 bought an ironworks near Plymouth, inventing the 'puddling' process for converting pig iron into wrought iron (1784), as well as a system of grooved rollers for the production of iron bars. Ruined by a prosecution for debt, he was ultimately pensioned.

Cortes [kaw(r)tes] The representative assembly in Spain, which became the Spanish parliament after the fall of the monarchy in 1931. It continued to exist under Franco, but with little or no powers. In 1977 it became a two-chamber parliament, elected upon universal suffrage, and its powers were extended in 1978 after a national referendum.

Cortés, Hernán [kaw(r)tez], Span [kawrtays], also spelled **Cortéz** (1485–1547) The conqueror of Mexico, born in Medellín, W Spain. He studied at Salamanca, then accompanied Velázquez in his expedition to Cuba (1511). In 1519 he commanded an expedition against Mexico, fighting his first battle at Tabasco. He founded Vera Cruz, marched to Tlaxcala, and made allies of the natives. He then marched on the Aztec capital, capturing the king, Montezuma; but the Mexicans rose, and Cortés was forced to flee. He then launched a successful siege of the capital, which fell in 1521. He was formally appointed governor and captain-general of New Spain in 1522, but his authority was later superseded. He spent the years 1530–40 in Mexico, then returned to Spain.

cortex An outer layer of an organism or biological system. For example, the adrenal cortex is the outer layer of the adrenal gland. In the brain of vertebrates, the cerebral cortex is a layer of grey matter lying above each cerebral hemisphere. In plants, the cortex is the tissue lying just below the epidermis.

corticosteroids Steroid hormones produced and secreted by the adrenal glands, including **hydrocortisone**, **corticosterone**, and **aldosterone**. They have numerous effects in the body, influencing metabolism, salt and water balance, and the function of many organs. Preparations of natural and synthetic corticosteroids (eg cortisol, prednisolone) are used to treat a wide range of diseases, including arthritis and cancer.

corticotrophin *adrenocorticotrophic hormone*

cortisol [kaw(r)tisol] A steroid hormone found in the adrenal cortex of vertebrates; also known as **hydrocortisone**. In some mammals (eg humans, dogs), it is the major glucocorticoid hormone. It promotes the conversion of protein and fat into glucose (*gluconeogenesis*), and has an important role in the body's resistance to physical and psychological stress, especially after trauma. Its synthesis and release are primarily controlled by adrenocorticotrophic hormone.

Cortona, Pietro (Berrettini) da [kaw(r)tohna] (1596–1669) Painter and architect, born in Cortona, C Italy. With Bernini he ranks as one of the great figures of the Baroque in Rome. With Lanfranco and Guercino he was the founder of the Roman High Baroque style in painting. He specialized in highly illusionistic ceiling painting in which paint is combined with stucco and gilt, notably in his 'Allegory of Divine Providence' and 'Barberini Power' (1633–39) in the Palazzo Barberini in Rome.

corundum [korundum] A mineral formed from aluminium oxide (Al_2O_3); extremely hard and used as an abrasive. Gemstone varieties are ruby and sapphire.

Corunna [koruhna], Span **La Coruña**, Galician **A Coruña**, ancient **Caronium** 43°20N 8°25W, pop (2000e) 248 000. Seaport and capital of La Coruña province, Galicia, NW Spain; on the Atlantic coast, 609 km/378 mi NW of Madrid; base of the Spanish Armada, 1588; city sacked by Drake, 1589; scene of British victory during the Peninsular War (1809), and the death of Sir John Moore; airport; railway; car ferries to the Canary Is; watersports; oil, iron and steel, shipbuilding, clothes, food canning, fishing; Hercules Tower, Church of Santiago; Fiesta of the Virgen del Monte Carmel (Jul), Fiesta of Maria Pita (Aug), Galician Pilgrimage (Sep).

corvette [kaw(r)vet] A small single-screw warship designed for convoy escort duties in World War 2. In former times, it was a single gun-decked, three-masted, square-rigged sailing vessel, originally of French design and adopted by the British.

Corvus [kaw(r)vus] (Lat 'crow') A small S constellation, named in ancient times.

Corybantes [koreebantayz] The attendants and eunuch priests of the Phrygian nature goddess, the Cybele, whose orgiastic cult was officially introduced into Rome towards the end of the Punic Wars.

coryphaena [korifeena] *dolphinfish*

coryza [kuhriyza] *cold*

Cos, Gr **Kós**, Ital **Coo** area 290 sq km/112 sq mi. Island of the Dodecanese, E Greece, in the Aegean Sea, off the SW coast of Turkey; length 43 km/27 mi; width 2–11 km/1¼–7 mi; hilly E region, rising to 846 m/2776 ft at Mt Dikaios; severely damaged by earthquakes in 1933; capital, Cos, pop (2000e) 15 300; cereals, olive oil, wine, fruit, tourism; famous in antiquity for its wine, amphorae, and 'Coan garments', and for the cult of Asclepius and its doctors, notably Hippocrates; sanctuary of Asclepios, 15th-c Castle of the Knights of St John; Plane Tree of Hippocrates; Navy Week (Jun–Jul).

Cosby, Bill [kozbee], popular name of **William Henry Cosby** (1937–) Comedian, born in Philadelphia, Pennsylvania, USA. After service in the US navy (1956–60), he began performing as a nightclub comic, abandoning his studies to pursue this career full time. An appearance on *The Tonight Show* in 1965 led to him being cast in the television series *I Spy* (1965–8), where his role won him three consecutive Emmy Awards. He made his film debut in *Hickey and Boggs* (1971), and has appeared in *Uptown Saturday Night* (1974), *California Suite* (1978), and *Leonard: Part VI* (1987). His TV series *The Cosby Show* (1984–92) consistently topped the ratings, and he returned with a further series *Cosby* in 1996. He has recorded more than 20 albums and won eight Grammy Awards, and his book *Fatherhood* (1986) was a best seller.

Cosgrave, William Thomas [kozgrayv] (1880–1965) Irish statesman and first president of the Irish Free State (1922–32), born in Dublin, Ireland. He joined the Sinn Féin movement at an early age, and took part in the Easter Rising (1916). He was elected a Sinn Féin MP (1918–22), and after his years as president became Leader of the Opposition (1932–44).

Cosmas and **Damian, Saints** (3rd-c) Arabian twin brothers, said to have been physicians at Aegaea, Cilicia, who were cast into the sea as Christians, but rescued by an angel. Thereafter, burning and stoning having proved ineffectual, they were beheaded by Diocletian. They are the patron saints of physicians. Feast day 26 September (W), 1 July/1 November (E).

cosmetics Preparations for artificially beautifying the human hair and complexion, used at various historical periods by both men and women. Fashionable women in W Europe have painted their faces since the Greek and Roman periods, to conform to a sequence of youthful ideals. The effects were formalized and unnatural in the later mediaeval period and during the 16th-c; in the 17th-c and 18th-c, black 'patches' representing moles or beauty spots were popular, to contrast with the flawless effect of the rest of the complexion: for most of the 19th-c, detectable 'make-up' was considered the mark of the fast or theatrical rather than the respectable woman. Many of the preparations used until recent times were dangerous to the health, or even potentially fatal (eg white lead).

Cosmic Background Explorer (COBE) A NASA satellite launched in November 1989 to study the cosmic background radiation from the universe. COBE precisely measured the temperature of this radiation as 2·73 K. In 1992 it also discovered minuscule temperature variations of 30 millionths of a degree in the background radiation, which are attributed to slight fluctuations in the density of the early universe that led to the formation of the galaxies.

cosmic background radiation A weak radio signal that comes from the entire universe; also called **microwave background radiation**. It has a spectrum identical to a perfect black body a mere 2·73 degrees above absolute zero. This is the temperature of our universe, measured far from any stars. The character of the radiation is almost the same in every direction, apart from a slight asymmetry due to the motion of our galaxy relative to the radiation. The microwave background is a relic of an early very hot phase in the universe, a fossil of the 'big bang' itself. In 1992, satellite observations showed slight 'ripples' in the strength of this radiation (of c.1/100 000 of a kelvin), corresponding to 'hot' and 'cold' patches in space, believed to be due to differences in density in the early universe which gave rise to the formation of galaxies. The radiation was discovered in 1965 by Arno Penzias and Robert Wilson of the AT&T Bell Laboratories, NJ, for which they shared the 1978 Nobel Prize for Physics.

cosmic dust Microscopic grains of dust of extraterrestrial origin: also called **Brownlee particles**, after the original collector. It enters Earth's atmosphere at high velocity, and is slowed down by friction in the uppermost atmosphere. It spends months floating in the stratosphere, and can be collected by high-flying research aircraft or in space at space stations. The particles are a few microns in size, often with porous structure. Some are believed to be dust from comets.

cosmic rays High energy electrons and ions moving through space, thought to be produced by exploding stars. When the particles strike the Earth's atmosphere, secondary rays comprising mostly pions and muons are produced. Cosmic rays are a useful source of high-energy particles for experiments. They also contribute to natural background radiation. Cosmic rays with energies exceeding 10^{20} eV (electron volts) are known.

cosmic string Hypothetical massive filaments of matter (10^{19} kg/cm) predicted in supersymmetry theory as an important component of the very early universe.

cosmogony [kozmoguhnee] *cosmology*

cosmological argument One of the traditional arguments for the existence of God, championed especially by Aquinas. The basic argument is that the existence of the universe cannot be explained by things *in* the universe, and that there must be one first cause, itself uncaused.

cosmological constant A constant introduced by Einstein into equations of general relativity to give a static model of the universe, later claimed by him to be a mistake; symbol Λ; sign unknown; size uncertain, but less than 10^{-25} kg/m^3; often assumed to be zero. In cosmology, the value and sign are related to the expansion or contraction of the universe.

cosmology The study of the universe on the largest scales of length and time, particularly the propounding of theories concerning the origin, nature, structure, and evolution of the universe. A cosmology is any model said to represent the observed universe. The currently favoured cosmological model is the 'big bang' hypothesis. The study of the origin and mode of formation of various celestial objects is known as **cosmogony**.

cosmonaut The Russian term for a spacecraft crew member. Over 70 crewed flights, including three women (one British), were carried out by the Soviet (later, Russian) space programme to the beginning of 1992. The longest flight duration by two individuals was that of Vladimir Titov and Musa Manarov, who spent 366 days in the space station Mir (Dec 1987–Dec 1988). Cosmonauts (some paying customers) have included numerous individuals from other nations. Four cosmonauts have lost their lives as a direct result of spaceflight-related accidents.

Cossacks Originally, members of semi-independent communities of fugitive peasants and military adventurers inhabiting the steppelands of S Russia and Ukraine. Attempts to limit Cossack freedom led to several large-scale rebellions against the Russian government in the 17th–18th-c. In the 18th–19th-c they were formed into military organizations (*hosts*), and earned a reputation for ferocious fighting and skilled horsemanship. Towards the end of the 19th-c and the first years of the 20th-c, the Tsar used Cossacks to carry out pogroms against the Jews and to suppress the 1905 Revolution. Following the 1917 Revolution, most Cossacks fought against the Red revolutionaries. However, Cossack traditions continued in some areas during the Soviet Communist period.

Cossington-Smith, Grace (1892–1984) Painter, born in Neutral Bay, Sydney, New South Wales, SE Australia. She studied at Dattilo Rubbo's Art School in Sydney, and in England and Germany. A pioneer of Modernist painting in Australia, she was instrumental in introducing Postimpressionism to Australia. Her 1915 painting, 'The Sock Knitter', is seen as a key work in the Australian Modernist movement. Her painting is characterized by individual, square brush strokes and radiant colours. Her many paintings of Sydney landscapes, still-lifes, and interiors include 'Kuringai Avenue' (1943) and 'The Lacquer Room' (1935). She received acclaim rather late in her career, and in 1973 a major retrospective exhibition of her work toured Australia.

Costa Azul [azul] Atlantic coastline of W Portugal between the Ponta da Arrifana and the mouth of the R Sado; chief resorts, Vila Nova de Milfontes, Porto Covo; the name means 'blue coast'.

Costa Blanca [blangka] The coastal resort regions of Murcia, Alicante, and part of Almeria provinces, E Spain; on the Mediterranean coast extending S from Cabo San Antonio to the Punto Almerimar; summer and winter tourism; the name means 'white coast'.

Costa Brava [brahva] The Mediterranean coastal resort region of Catalonia, E Spain, between Barcelona and the French border; the name means 'wild coast'.

cost-accounting A branch of accountancy which seeks to calculate the cost of a product, operation, department, or activity, both historically and as planned, thereby establishing a current standard or norm. The actual cost can be compared against the standard to determine whether costs are getting out of line with expectations.

Costa de la Luz [loos] Resort region on the Atlantic coastline of Huelva and Cádiz provinces, S Spain; from the Portuguese border to the most S tip of Spain at Tarifa on the Strait of Gibraltar; the name means 'coast of light'.

Costa del Azahar [asakhahr, athakhahr] Mediterranean coastal resort region of Castellón de la Plana and Valencia provinces, E Spain; between the Costa Dorada (N) and Costa Blanca (S); longest stretch of coast in Spain; the name means 'orange-blossom coast'.

Costa del Sol [sol] Mediterranean coastal resort region, Andalusia, S Spain, extending from Punto Almerimar to the most S point in Spain at Tarifa; the name means 'coast of the sun'.

Costa Dorada [dorahda] Mediterranean coastal resort region S of the Costa Brava, Barcelona, and Tarragona provinces, E Spain; the name means 'golden coast'.

Costa Dourada [dorada] Atlantic coastline of W Portugal between the Ponta da Arrifana and the mouth of the R Sado; chief resorts, Aljezur, Vila Nova de Milfontes, Porto Covo; the name means 'golden coast'.

Costa Rica *see panel*

cost–benefit analysis An attempt to compare in money terms the total costs and benefits of economic activities, including not only direct pecuniary costs and benefits, but also 'externalities'. These would include costs not traded in a market, such as noise from airfields or disturbance to wildlife, and non-marketed benefits such as reduction in travel times and accidents from transport improvements. If total benefits exceed costs this may be used to justify carrying out public works, such as motorway building, or subsidizing private projects that are not commercially profitable. If total costs exceed benefits this may justify refusing private firms permission to undertake projects, such as building in a green belt, which would be privately profitable. The difficulty of valuing non-marketed costs and benefits means that the results of cost–benefit studies are often controversial.

Costa Rica

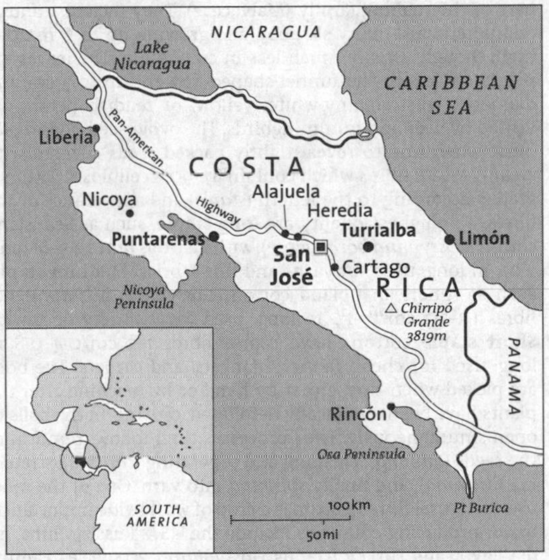

□ International Airport

[kosta reeka], official name **Republic of Costa Rica**, Span **República de Costa Rica**

Local name Costa Rica

Timezone GMT –6

Area 51 022 km^2/19 694 sq mi

Population total (2002e) 3 960 000

Status Republic

Date of independence 1821

Capital San José

Language Spanish (official)

Ethnic groups European (87%), mestizo (7%), black/mulatto (3%), E Asian (mostly Chinese) (2%), Amerindian (1%)

Religions Roman Catholic (85%), Protestant (15%)

Physical features Second smallest republic in Central America; formed by series of volcanic ridges: Cordillera de Guanacaste (NW), Cordillera Central, and Cordillera de Talamanca; highest peak, Chirripó Grande, 3819 m/12 529 ft. C plateau; swampy land near coast, rising to tropical forest.

Climate Tropical; small temperature range; abundant rainfall; dry season (Dec–May); average annual temperature 26–8°C.

Currency 1 Costa Rican Colón (CRø) = 100 céntimos

Economy Primarily agriculture, mainly coffee (especially in Meseta Central), bananas, sugar, cattle; silver, bauxite; exploration for oil in collaboration with Mexico.

GDP (2002e) $32 bn, per capita $8300

Human Development Index (2002) 0·820

History Visited by Columbus, 1502; named Costa Rica ('rich coast') in the belief that vast gold treasures existed; independence from Spain, 1821; member of Federation of Central America, 1824–39; new constitution, 1949, established Costa Rica as a democratic state; governed by an executive President, legislative assembly, and Cabinet.

Head of State/Government

1962–6 Francisco José Orlich Bolmarcich
1966–70 José Joaquín Trejos Fernández
1970–4 José Figueres Ferrer
1974–8 Daniel Oduber Quirós
1978–82 Rodrigo Carazo Odio
1982–6 Luis Alberto Monge Alvarez
1986–90 Oscar Arias Sánchez
1990–4 Rafael Angel Calderón Fournier
1994–8 José María Figueres
1998–2002 Miguel Angel Rodríguez Echeverría
2002– Abel Pacheco

Costello, Elvis, originally **Declan Patrick McManus** (1955–) Singer and songwriter, born in London, UK. The son of big-band singer **Ross McManus**, he started his own career with the unrecorded band Flip City and as a solo folk club singer. Signed to Stiff Records in 1977, his debut album *My Aim Is True* established his reputation. For his second album, *This Year's Model* (1978), he was joined by The Attractions – a three-piece group consisting of Steve Nieve, Pete Thomas, and Bruce Thomas, who worked with Costello on most of his albums over the next eight years. Later albums include *Mighty Like A Rose* (1991), *All This Useless Beauty* (1996), and *North* (2003). In 1999 he had a hit single with 'She' from the *Notting Hill* film soundtrack. He was inducted into the Rock and Roll Hall of Fame in 2003.

Costello, Lou *Abbott and Costello*

costmary A sweetly aromatic perennial (*Balsamita major*) growing to 90 cm/3 ft, native to W Asia; leaves elliptical, minutely toothed; flower-heads numerous, in flat-topped clusters; spreading outer florets white, inner disc florets yellow; also called **alecost**. Its strong-smelling foliage was formerly used for flavouring ales. (Family: Compositae.)

Costner, Kevin (1955–) Motion-picture actor and director, born in Compton, California, USA. He studied at California State University (1978), became an actor, and established a reputation in the critically acclaimed films *Bull Durham* (1988) and *Field of Dreams* (1989). He directed and starred in the epic film *Dances With Wolves* (1990), a major triumph which won seven Oscars. Further successes followed with starring roles in *Robin Hood: Prince of Thieves* (1991), *JFK* (1991), *The Bodyguard* (1992), and *Waterworld* (1995). *The Postman* (1997), which he also directed, *Message in a Bottle* (1999), and *For the Love of the Game* (1999), were less favourably received. Later films include *Beyond Borders* (2000) and *Open Range* (2003).

cost of living (index) *retail price index*

Cosway, Richard (1742–1821) Miniaturist, born in Tiverton, Devon, SW England, UK. He studied with **Thomas Hudson** (1701–79) in London, and became a fashionable painter of portraits, patronized by the Prince of Wales. The use of watercolour on ivory is a notable feature of his work. In 1781 he married the artist **Maria Hadfield** (1759–1838), also a miniaturist.

cot death *sudden infant death syndrome*

Côte d'Ivoire *p.391*

cotinga [kotingga] A bird native to the New World tropics; inhabits woodland. Most species eat fruit; some catch insects in flight. (Family: Cotingidae, 65 species.)

Cotman, John Sell (1782–1842) Watercolourist, born in Norwich, Norfolk, E England, UK. He studied art in London, and returned to Norwich in 1806, where he became a leading member of the Norwich School. At Yarmouth (1811–23) he executed some fine oil paintings and etchings, but lack of success made him sell his pictures and possessions and return to London (1834), where he became drawing master of King's College. His best work shows a masterly arrangement of masses of light and shade, with a minimum of modelling, as in 'Greta Bridge' (c.1805). His two sons were also landscape painters.

cotoneaster [kotohniaster] A deciduous or evergreen shrub or small tree, native to N temperate regions; variable in size and shape, branches arching, spreading or erect; leaves oval to rounded, often with bright autumn colours; flowers usually in clusters, 5-petalled, white or pink; berries yellow, red, or black. They are widely used as ornamental and amenity plants. (Genus: *Cotoneaster*, 50 species. Family: Rosaceae.)

Cotonou [kohtonoo] 6°24N 2°31E, pop (2000e) 831 800. Port in Ouémé province, S Benin, W Africa; on a sandspit between the Bight of Benin and L Nokoué; largest city in Benin, and its political and economic centre, though not the official capital; seat of the Presidency, most ministries, the National Assembly, and all embassies; centre for most commercial activities; airport; railway; university (1970); vegetable oils, soap, brewing, textiles, power plant.

Cotopaxi [kohtopaksee] 0°40S 78°26W. Active Andean volcano in NC Ecuador; 48 km/30 mi S of Quito; height 5896 m/19 344 ft; national park, area 340 sq km/131 sq mi established in 1975; llama breeding station and Clirsen satellite tracking station nearby.

Cotswold Hills or **Cotswolds** [kotzwohld] Hill range mainly in Gloucestershire, SE England, UK; extends 80 km/50 mi NE from Bath to Chipping Camden, separating the lower R Severn from the source of the R Thames; rises to 333 m/1092 ft at Cleeve Cloud, near Cheltenham; gives its name to a breed of sheep; district noted for its mellow-coloured limestone, used in many picturesque villages.

Cottee, Kay (1954–) Yachting record holder, born in Sydney, New South Wales, SE Australia. She was the first woman to complete a solo, nonstop, unassisted circumnavigation of the world, arriving in Sydney harbour in June, 1988. She sailed 25 000 nautical miles in her 12-m Cavalier 37 sloop *First Lady* in 189 days, a record time for a woman. She was named Australian of the Year in 1989.

Cotten, Joseph (1905–94) Film actor, born in Los Angeles, California, USA. A member of Orson Welles Mercury Theater radio ensemble from 1937, he appeared in the Broadway production of *The Philadelphia Story* (1939–40), before starring in *Citizen Kane* (1941), *The Magnificent Ambersons* (1942), and *Journey into Fear* (1942). His many later films include *Gaslight* (1944), *The Third Man* (1949), and *Heaven's Gate* (1980).

Cottian Alps, Fr **Alpes Cottiennes** Division of the W Alps in SE France along the French–Italian frontier, from the Alpes Maritimes at Maddalena Pass to the Alpes Graian at Mont Cenis; highest peak, Monte Viso (3851 m/12 634 ft).

Cotton, John (1585–1652) Puritan clergyman, born in Derby, Derbyshire, C England, UK. He was a tutor at Cambridge, and from c.1612 held a post at Boston, Lincolnshire. Cited for his Puritan views before Laud, in 1633 he emigrated to Boston, MA, where he became the head of Congregationalism in the USA.

cotton The name of both a plant and the fibre it produces. Cotton is related to mallows, hollyhocks, and hibiscus, all members of the mallow family (Malvaceae). They include annuals and perennials, many shrubby and growing up to 6 m/20 ft high, though usually much less in cultivation. The leaves are palmately lobed; the funnel-shaped flowers, up to 5 cm/2 in diameter, with creamy-white, yellow, or reddish petals, are visited by bees and hummingbirds. The ovoid seed pods (*bolls*) burst when ripe to reveal tightly packed seeds covered with creamy-white fibres which contain 87–90% cellulose. Cotton is graded according to the length (*staple*) and appearance of the fibres. The highest quality are **long staple**, such as Sea Island cotton (*Gossypium barbadense*), with lustrous fibres 2·5–6·5 cm/1–2½ in long, used for yarns and fine fabrics. **Medium staple**, such as American upland cotton (*Gossypium hirsutum*) has fibres 1·3–3·3 cm/½–1¼ in long, used for a variety of fabrics. **Short staple** cottons have coarse fibres 1–2 cm/0·4–0·8 in long, used for cheap fabrics, blankets, and carpets. The bolls are picked when ripe, either by hand or by machine after the plants have been chemically defoliated, causing all the bolls to open simultaneously. Four processes then follow: removal of the seeds (*ginning*), cleaning and separating (*carding*), stretching (*drawing*), and finally *spinning* into yarn. One of the most useful natural fibres, cotton is a crop of worldwide importance; major producing countries include the USA, Russia, China, India, Egypt, and Turkey. (Genus: *Gossypium*, c.20 species. Family: Malvaceae.)

cotton gin A machine, reputedly invented in 1793 by Eli Whitney in the USA (a cotton gin was used in 11th-c China), which separated the seeds from the cotton boll quickly and efficiently. It greatly increased productivity, meant that the short staple cotton grown in the USA could be used, and provided a large, cheap supply of raw cotton for the world.

cottongrass A grass-like perennial, native to cool and arctic parts of N temperate regions; stem leafy; flower spikes brownish, perianth consisting of numerous white hairs which elongate in fruit, forming a conspicuous cottony head. (Genus: *Eriophorum*, 21 species. Family: Cyperaceae.)

Côte d'Ivoire

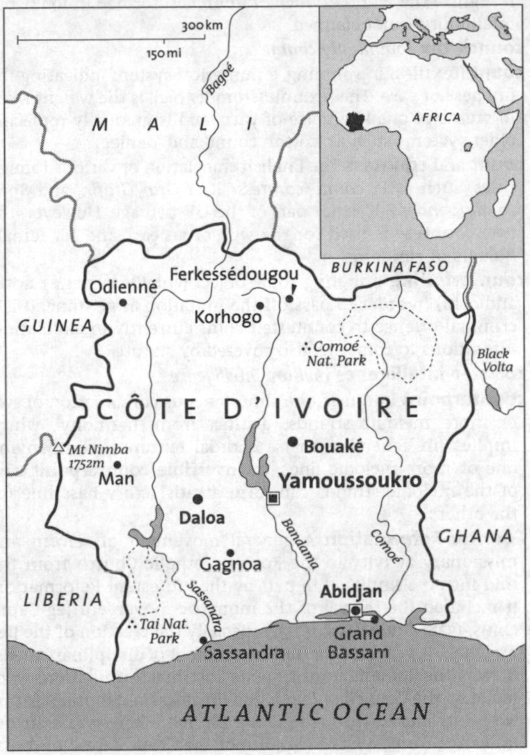

□ International Airport ∴ World heritage site

[koht deevwah(r)], official name **Republic of Côte d'Ivoire** (Eng **Ivory Coast**), Fr **République de Côte d'Ivoire**

Local name Côte d'Ivoire

Timezone GMT

Area 322 462 km²/124 503 sq mi

Population total (2002e) 16 805 000

Status Republic

Date of independence 1960

Capital Yamoussoukro (formerly Abidjan)

Languages French (official), Akan, Kru

Ethnic groups Akan (41%), Kru (17%), Voltaic (16%), Malinke (15%), Southern Mande (10%)

Religions Traditional beliefs (63%), Muslim (25%), Christian (12%)

Physical features Sandy beaches and lagoons backed by broad forest-covered coastal plain; Mt Nimba massif in NW, 1752 m/5748 ft; rivers include Comoé, Sassandra, Bandama.

Climate Tropical, varying with distance from coast; average annual rainfall at Yamoussoukro 2100 mm/83 in; average annual temperatures 25–7°C.

Currency 1 CFA Franc (CFAFr) = 100 centimes

Economy Largely based on agriculture (employs c.82% of the population): palm oil, rice, maize, ground nuts, bananas; world's largest cocoa producer, third largest coffee producer.

GDP (2002e) $24·03 bn, per capita $1400

Human Development Index (2002) 0·428

History Explored by Portuguese, 15th-c; declared a French protectorate, 1889; colony, 1893; territory within French West Africa, 1904; independence, 1960; constitution provides for a multiparty system, however, opposition parties only allowed to function since 1990; post of Prime Minister created, 1990; governed by a National Assembly, executive President, and Council of Ministers; during 2002 fighting escalated between emerging rebel groups in W of country; ceasefire agreed (Oct 2000) but breached, leading to intervention by French troops (Dec 2002); rebels agree to attend peace talks (Jan 2003); peace plan drawn up but tensions continue; UN mission to facilitate peace plan (May 2003).

Head of State
1993–9 Henri Konan Bédié
1999–2000 Robert Guéi
2000– Laurent Gbagbo

Head of Government
1993–9 Daniel Kablan Duncan
2000 Seydou Diarra
2000–3 Affi N'Guessan
2003 Seydou Diarra

cottonmouth A pit viper (*Agkistrodon piscivorus*) native to SE USA; inside of mouth white; lives near water; mainly nocturnal; eats vertebrates (especially fish and frogs); one of the few snakes to eat carrion; venom very dangerous, coagulates the blood (collected for this purpose in medicine); also known as **water moccasin**.

cotton stainer A plant-feeding bug that feeds by sucking sap; its habit of piercing the bolls of cotton plants transmits a fungus that stains the cotton fibres. (Order: Heteroptera. Family: Pyrrhocoridae.)

cottontail A type of rabbit, native to the New World; inhabits open country or woodland clearings; only one species digs burrows; remainder shelter in burrows of other animals or under vegetation. (Genus: *Sylvilagus*, 13 species.)

cotton tree *kapok tree*

cottonwood *poplar*

cottony cushion scale A small scale insect that lives on stems and leaves of citrus trees; adult females immobile, covered by protective scale; eggs laid in mass of waxy fibres resembling cotton wool; a serious pest of citrus orchards. (Order: Homoptera. Family: Margarodidae.)

cotyledons [kotileednz] Embryo leaves present in a seed. Usually very different in appearance to the true leaves, they are either fleshy and remain underground as a food store, or are thin and raised above ground to act as the first leaves of the seedling.

Coubertin, Pierre de [koobairtĩ] (1863–1937) Educator, born in Paris, France. One of the first French advocates of physical education, he toured the USA and Europe to study educational methods, and visited Greece, where excavators were uncovering the ancient Olympic site. The visit inspired his proposal to revive the Olympic Games, and in 1894 the delegates at an international athletics conference in Paris voted to hold an Olympic competition at Athens in 1896. He became the first president (1896–1925) of the International Olympic Committee.

couch grass [kooch, kowch] A dull-green perennial grass (*Elymus repens*) with numerous creeping rhizomes, native to temperate regions; spikelets set edge-on to stem in a stiff, erect spike; a tenacious weed, difficult to eradicate; also called **twitch grass**. (Family: Gramineae.)

Coué, Emile [kooay] (1857–1926) Pharmacist, hypnotist, and pioneer of 'auto-suggestion', born in Troyes, NEC France. A pharmacist in Troyes from 1882, he became a psychotherapist, and in 1910 opened a free clinic in Nancy. His system became world-famous as *Couéism*, expressed in the famous formula 'Every day, in every way, I am becoming better and better'.

cougar A member of the cat family (*Felis concolor*), found from Canada to South America; grey or reddish-brown; solitary; territorial; lives in diverse habitats; eats mainly deer; also known as **puma**, **mountain lion**, **catamount**, **panther**, **painter**.

Coulomb, Charles (Augustin de) [koolõ] (1736–1806) Physicist, born in Angoulême, W France. After serving as a military engineer for nine years, he retired to a small estate and devoted himself to scientific research. He experimented on friction, and invented the torsion balance for measuring the force of magnetic and electrical attraction. The *coulomb*, the unit of electrical charge, is named after him.

coulomb [**koo**lom] SI unit of electric charge; symbol *C*; named after Charles Coulomb; defined as the quantity of electricity transported by a current of 1 ampere in 1 second.

Coulomb's law In physics, a law expressing the force *F* between two electrical charges *p* and *q* separated by a distance *d* as $F = \frac{pq}{4\pi\varepsilon_0 d^2}$, where ε_0 is the permittivity of free space, $8{\cdot}854 \times 10^{-12} C^2/(N.m^2)$; stated by Charles Coulomb in 1785. The direction of force is along the line joining the charges, and is repulsive for like charges, attractive for opposite charges.

council A political body appointed or elected to perform specific functions or provide services, whose powers may be advisory or executive. It may be locally, nationally, or internationally based; for example, at local level, county and district councils exist in England and Wales, while Scotland has only district councils.

Council for Mutual Economic Assistance (COMECON) A body founded in 1949 by Stalin, and dominated by the Soviet Union; its purpose was ostensibly the economic integration of the Eastern bloc as a means of counteracting the economic power of the EEC and EFTA. The 10 member states were the USSR, Bulgaria, Cuba, Czechoslovakia, Hungary, Poland, Romania, East Germany, Mongolia, and Vietnam. It was disbanded in 1991, and replaced by the Organization for International Economic Co-operation.

Council for the Protection of Rural England A pressure group founded in 1926 as the Council for the Preservation of Rural England. With 42 county branches, it aims to promote the protection and improvement of the countryside and rural amenities. Subjects of recent campaigns include afforestation, new towns, motorways, and energy policy. The Council for the Protection of Rural Wales is a similar organization.

Council of Baltic States A grouping of Baltic countries established at a meeting in Copenhagen in 1992. Its members are Denmark, Estonia, Finland, Germany, Iceland, Latvia, Lithuania, Norway, Poland, Russia, and Sweden. Its aim is regional co-operation, specifically to create a community in which assistance could be given to enable Russia, Poland, Estonia, Latvia, and Lithuania to transform into free market economies.

Council of Constance *Constance, Council of*

Council of Europe A loose association now including most of the states of Europe, established in 1949. Membership was originally limited to Western Europe (including Scandinavia), but since the collapse of communism (1991) it has been extended to Central and Eastern Europe, including Russia. The Council's institutions include a Committee of Ministers and a representative at the parliamentary assembly, whose role is essentially advisory. The Council has furthered European co-operation through a number of international conventions, notably the European Convention on Human Rights. It had 45 members in 2004. Several other nations have observer status.

Council of Ministers The body (established 1974) which allows the expression of national interest within the European Union, the minister involved depending on the subject under consideration. There are around 20 different types of council meetings; agriculture and foreign affairs have the most regular meetings.

Council of the Church In the Orthodox and Roman Catholic Churches, a meeting of bishops of the whole Church to regulate doctrine and discipline. The last Ecumenical Council (of the undivided Church) is generally held to be the Second Council of Nicaea (787). The Roman Catholic Church recognizes a Council if called by a pope, and its decisions, if approved by the pope, as infallible, with guaranteed assistance of the Holy Spirit, and binding on the whole Church. Non-Roman Catholic Churches recognize the World Council of Churches (formed in 1948), but infallibility is not claimed.

council tax *community charge*

count (textiles) In spinning, a numerical system indicating the fineness of yarn. The *tex* unit (from *textile*), is the weight mass in grams of one kilometre of yarn, and is gradually replacing older systems such as 'cotton count' and 'denier'.

count and **countess** The English translation of various foreign titles, such as Fr *comte/comtesse*, Ger *Graf/Gräfin*, and Span *conde/condesa*. It is not part of the UK peerage. However, the title **countess** is used for the wife of an earl, and for female holders of earldoms.

counterfeiting Imitating some object (chiefly, currency notes and coin) in order to pass off the imitation as genuine. It is a criminal offence to counterfeit coins currently in circulation. Alterations to coins are also covered by statute.

counter-intelligence *military intelligence*

counterpoint In music, the simultaneous combination of two or more melodic strands; distinct from 'harmony', which implies (in general terms) a chordal texture accompanying one or more melodic lines. In **invertible counterpoint**, any of the melodic strands can form a satisfactory bass line for the others.

Counter-Reformation A general movement of reform and missionary activity in the Roman Catholic Church from the mid 16th-c, stimulated in part by the Protestant Reformation. It included the revival of the monastic movement (eg Capuchins, 1528; Oratorians, 1575), especially the creation of the Jesuit Order. It provided for the enforcement of disciplinary measures by the Roman Inquisition; its doctrinal formulations were made by the Council of Trent; and liturgical and moral reforms were introduced throughout the Church. There was a strong influence from mystics (eg John of the Cross, Teresa of Ávila) and devotional teachers (eg Francis of Sales). In a secular sense, the term also refers to the success of Roman Catholic powers in Europe in the late 16th-c and early 17th-c.

countertenor The falsetto voice of the adult male, trained and developed to sing alto parts, especially in sacred polyphony. The revival of interest in the countertenor as a solo voice has been largely due to the artistry of Alfred Deller.

countries of the world Estimates of the number of countries in the world vary, depending on how a 'country' ('nation', 'state') is defined. At the beginning of 2004 there were 191 countries in the United Nations. A further three clearly independent countries do not have UN membership: Republic of China (Taiwan), Switzerland, Vatican City. Another seven claim independence, most having some degree of sovereignty – Northern Cyprus, Somaliland, Abkhazia, Bougainville, Chechnya, Dniestria, and Sahara. Several other territories (eg Aruba, Greenland, Isle of Man) have some degree of identity, with their own flags, postage stamps, uniforms, etc, and there are many groups claiming territorial autonomy amidst conflict in various parts of the world (eg Nagorno Karabakh, Krajina, Kosovo). The situation continues to change, as fresh political realities emerge (eg in South Africa, Palestine, and former USSR and Yugoslavia).

country and western A type of popular US music stemming from the hillbilly tradition of the years between the two World Wars. The country music of that time was identified with white communities in the rural areas of the Southern states; it was played at barn dances, fairs, and similar gatherings, typically on a violin, banjo, and guitar. After World War 2 it absorbed influences from the more sophisticated country music of the SW, and developed a more urbanized, pan-American style, popularized by such performers as Merle Haggard (1937–), Johnny Cash (1932–), Charley Pride (1938–), and Tammy Wynette (1942–98). The influence of rock has also been felt, as in the music of Kris Kristofferson (1937–). The recognized centre of country and western music is Nashville, TN.

country dance Historic social dances based on John Playford's *The English Dancing Master* (1651). They spread across Europe, taught by travelling dancing masters, adding 19th-c forms such as the waltz, quadrille, and polka. The emphasis was on spatial design, with couples in long or circular sets, using simple walking steps. Their decline is associated with the Industrial Revolution and the growth of towns. In a broader sense, country dancing is a popular social activity involving pairs or circles of dancers performing dance patterns to traditional folk music.

Country Party (Australia) *National Party* (Australia)

Countryside Commission, formerly (to 1991) **Countryside Commission for England and Wales** A UK government amenity agency set up in 1968 to replace the National Parks Commission. It advises the government on matters of countryside interest, and formulates policy for National Parks. It provides grants for nature reserves, wardens, footpaths, and for public access to open countryside. The Commission now covers England only; there is a separate Countryside Council for Wales.

Country Women's Association (CWA) Australia's largest and oldest women's organization. Based on Canadian (1890s) and British examples (1913), the CWA began in New South Wales and spread to the other States. Non-sectarian and non-political, its aims are to improve welfare of rural women and children. Its many achievements include rest rooms and baby health centres in country towns. The CWA is represented at three-yearly conferences of the Associated Country Women of the World.

county council The body elected to carry out such responsibilities as may be statutorily determined, within a defined geographical boundary. In areas of England and Wales without all-purpose local authorities, it is the higher in a two-tier local government system whose powers are delegated by parliament. Actions beyond these powers may be declared by the courts to be *ultra vires* (outside its authority).

County Court A court system of England and Wales, concerned with civil disputes, established in 1846. The County Courts deal with cases of contract and tort, landlord and tenant disputes, and matrimonial cases (including divorce) also come within its jurisdiction, as does the relatively informal small-claims procedure, where the sum in dispute generally does not exceed £1000. The County Court ranks lower in the hierarchy of courts than the High Court. The High Court and County Court Jurisdiction Order 1991 abolished many of the former financial limits on the jurisdiction of the County Court. Instead, there are new rules on the allocation of cases between the High Court and the County Court. Each court has a circuit judge and district judge. The nearest US equivalent is the **municipal court**, which in most jurisdictions may hear misdemeanours, small claims (cases between civilians representing themselves up to a set monetary limit) and civil cases with a set monetary limit.

Couperin, François [kooperĩ] (1668–1733) Composer, born in Paris, France. He was taught by his father, whom he eventually followed as organist of Saint-Gervais (1685). In 1693 he also became organist to Louis XIV, and in 1717 composer-in-ordinary of chamber music to the king. Known mainly as a harpsichord composer (whose influence on Bach was profound), he also composed chamber concertos and church music.

couple In physics, two forces equal in magnitude, acting in opposite directions, whose lines of action are not coincident, causing a turning motion. The magnetic forces on a compass needle illustrate a couple.

couplers In photographic processing, chemicals which combine with the oxidized developing agent to form coloured transparent dyes adjacent to the silver image. They can form part of the developing solution, but are normally incorporated in the photographic emulsion layers.

courante [koorahnt] A Baroque dance in triple metre; it became a standard movement of the instrumental suite.

Courbet, Gustave [koorbay] (1819–77) Painter, born in Ornans, E France. He was sent to Paris to study law, but turned to painting. The founder of Realism, in 1844 he began exhibiting pictures in which everyday scenes were portrayed with complete sincerity and absence of idealism, such as 'Burial at Ornans' (1849, Musée d'Orsay, Paris). His best-known work is the large 'Studio of the Painter: an Allegory of Realism' (1855, Musée d'Orsay, Paris). Republican in sympathies, he joined the Commune in 1871, and on its suppression was imprisoned. Released in 1873, he fled to Switzerland.

coureurs de bois [koorer duh bwah] French fur traders or voyageurs who ranged throughout the interior of America from the 1660s. They played a significant role in the exploration of NW Canada.

courgette [koorzhet] (UK) or **zucchini** (US) A variety of marrow with small, green or yellow fruits (*Cucurbita pepo*). (Family: Cucurbitaceae.)

Courrèges, André [koorezh] (1923–) Fashion designer, born in Pau, SW France. He studied civil engineering, but later turned to fashion in Paris, where he was trained by Balenciaga, and opened his own house in 1961. Famous for stark, futuristic, 'Space Age' designs, he has featured trouser suits, white boots, and short skirts. He produces ready-to-wear as well as couture clothes.

courser A long-legged, short-winged, running bird, native to Africa and SW Asia; inhabits deserts; dull-coloured plumage; long curved bill; three forward-pointing toes only on each foot; seldom flies; nests on ground. (Family: Glareolidae; subfamily: Cursoriinae, 7 species.)

coursing A blood sport involving greyhounds, which seek out their prey by sight and not scent. The dogs pursue in pairs, as opposed to being in packs, and the performance of one dog against another is judged. The most popular coursing event is the Waterloo Cup at Altcar, near Formby, Merseyside. First held in 1836, it takes its name from the nearby Waterloo Hotel.

Court, Margaret (Jean) [kaw(r)t], *née* **Smith** (1942–) Tennis player, born in Albury, New South Wales, SE Australia. She was the winner of more Grand Slam events (66) than any other player: 10 Wimbledon (including the singles in 1963, 1965, 1970), 22 US, 13 French, and 21 Australian titles. In 1970 she became the second woman (after Maureen Connolly) to win all four major titles in one year. She retired in 1977.

courtly love The conception of an ideal and exalted relation between the sexes, which developed in the West in mediaeval times from sources as various as Plato's *Phaedrus*, Ovid's *Ars Amatoria*, and the cult of the Virgin Mary. Before the 12th-c women were for the most part considered inferior to men, but courtly love idealized women, placing them on a pedestal, and the lover's feelings for his mistress were supposed to ennoble him and lead him towards moral excellence. Mediaeval love poetry was deeply infused by the idea, which also influenced Renaissance sonneteers, although by this time the convention was treated with some irony.

court martial A court which tries members of the armed forces for offences against national law, in some instances, and offences against naval, military (ie army), and air force law. The court is composed of three to five serving officers advised if necessary on the law by a judge advocate, a barrister. The Armed Forces Act (1996) updated the laws of court martial and reinforced their independence. The Lord Chief Justice presides over the Courts Martial Appeal Court. Courts martial in the USA have jurisdiction only over service-related offences committed by active members of the armed forces. Some countries make a distinction between a **general** and a **special court martial**: the former is convened by a senior military authority, deals with any offences, and can impose any penalty; the latter is convened by a lower authority (eg at regimental level) and is limited to a restricted range of penalties (eg short-term imprisonment).

Court of Appeal An English court, with civil and criminal divisions, which hears appeals from the High Court, and most county court decisions. The civil division hears appeals from the High Court and the county court; its head is the Master of the Rolls. The criminal division hears appeals from the Crown

Court; its head is the Lord Chief Justice. Appeal on a point of law may be allowed from the Court of Appeal to the House of Lords. The Court of Appeal is bound to follow decisions of the House of Lords and its own previous decisions. Most US states have a Court of Appeals which generally hears appeals on points of law from the trial courts (ie the municipal and superior courts), and a state Supreme Court (sometimes with a different name) which hears appeals on points of law from the intermediate appellate courts. The federal courts have their own appellate system. The US Supreme Court, in addition to its original jurisdiction, may hear appeals from federal intermediate courts or state Supreme Courts where a federal constitutional issue is decisive.

Court of Auditors The body within the institutions of the European Union which is responsible for overseeing the implementation of the budget. Its role is to counter fraud and inefficiency.

Court of Justice of the European Communities The Court for the European Union (EU); also known as the **European Court of Justice (ECJ)**. It sits at Luxembourg, and its judges are appointed by the member states. It has 15 judges, one from each member state, and a president of the Court. Its functions involve the interpretation of EU treaties and legislation, and it can decide whether the conduct of any member state, the European Commission, or the Council of Ministers breaches EU law. The court also gives rulings on relevant points of law under Article 177 of the Treaty of Rome (known as a '177 reference') referred to it by domestic courts of member states, Community institutions, firms, or individuals. Its decisions are directly binding in the member countries.

court of law A forum for settling legal disputes. There are two broad categories of courts as traditionally distinguished: **civil courts**, dealing with disputes between private persons; and **criminal courts**, dealing with offences against society generally.

Court of Session The supreme civil court in Scotland, which sits in Edinburgh, and which deals primarily with civil appeals and some civil trials. It has an Outer House and a more senior Inner House, headed by the Lord President, Scotland's senior judge. Appeal lies to the House of Lords on matters of law.

Cousin, Jean [koozĩ], known as **Jean Cousin the Elder** (c.1490–c.1560) Engraver, glass-stainer, and painter, born in Soucy, C France. He was probably responsible for two stained glass windows in Sens Cathedral, and a picture of a nude woman ('Eva Prima Pandora') in the Louvre. His son, **Jean Cousin (the Younger)** (c.1522–c.1594), was also a versatile artist, who continued many aspects of his father's work.

Cousin, Victor [koozĩ] (1792–1867) Philosopher, born in Paris, France. After the 1830 revolution, he became a member of the Council of Public Instruction, and in 1832 a peer of France and director of the Ecole Normale. In 1848 he aided the government of Cavaignac, but after 1849 left public life. His eclectic philosophy can be seen in his *Fragments philosophiques* (1826) and *Du vrai, du beau, et du bien* (1854, On the True, the Beautiful, and the Good).

Cousins, Frank [kuhzinz] (1904–86) Trade-union leader, born in Nottingham, C England, UK. He worked in the pits at 14, turned lorry driver, and by 1938 was a full-time union organizer. In 1955 he became general secretary of the Transport and General Worker's Union. He was minister of technology (1964–6) until he resigned over the prices and incomes policy, MP for Nuneaton (1965–6), and chairman of the Community Relations Commission (1968–70).

Cousins, Robin (1957–) Ice skater, born in Bristol, SW England, UK. He trained at the Bristol Ice Dance and Figure Skating Club (1968–80), and in 1980 became only the second British male to win an Olympic figure-skating gold medal. Other achievements include the European Championship gold (1980) and World Championship silver medals (1979, 1980), and he was World freeskating champion for three successive years (1978–80). He turned professional in 1980, and has been artistic director of the Ice Castle International Training Center in California since 1989. He later returned to England and in 1997 co-founded the company Adventure! on Ice, creating and producing programmes for television. He later began his own production company, Cousins Entertainment Ltd. In 2000 he announced his retirement from professional ice skating, and now runs his own production company.

Cousteau, Jacques (Yves) [koostoh] (1910–97) Naval officer and underwater explorer, born in Saint-André, SW France. He invented the aqualung diving apparatus (1943) and a process of underwater television. In 1945 he founded the French Navy's Undersea Research Group, and commanded the research ship *Calypso* in 1950. He became director of the Oceanographic Museum of Monaco in 1957. He wrote widely on his subject, and his films included the Oscar-winning *The Golden Fish* (1960).

covalent *chemical bond*

covariance A term describing mathematical equations whose form is identical in different co-ordinate systems; also called **form invariance**. It is an essential property of the equations of theories of gravitation and nuclear forces.

covenant **1** A term used in certain legal systems (eg in England and Wales, but not in Scotland) for a written document under seal; also known as a **deed**. It contains a promise to act in a certain way, which is signed, sealed, and takes effect on delivery (in the USA, the requirement of seal is now largely abolished). A transfer of property may be made by deed. In England and Wales, most documents transferring freehold or leasehold land contain covenants which are said to 'run with the land'. A covenant may be *positive*, providing for the performance of some act or the payment of money, or *negative* or *restrictive*, forbidding some act. In some cases there may be a tax advantage: the term **deed of covenant** is often used in the UK for members of charities to covenant their membership subscriptions or donations (it being assumed that the subscription is paid after tax has been deducted). The charity claims back from the tax authorities a sum equal to the tax paid by the member. **2** In the Hebrew Scriptures, the agreement between God and his chosen people which was the basis of Jewish religion; especially identified with the giving of the law to Moses on Mt Sinai, but preceded by covenants with Noah and Abraham. Some New Testament writers portray the death of Jesus as a 'new covenant'.

Covenanters Originally, signatories (and their successors) of the **National Covenant** (1638) in Scotland, who resisted the theory of the 'Divine Right of Kings' and the imposition of an episcopal system on the Presbyterian Church of Scotland. When declared rebels, they resorted to open-air preaching. Until Presbyterianism was established in 1690, they were savagely persecuted, with imprisonment, execution without trial, and banishment (eg to Holland or America).

Covent Garden [kovnt] A square in C London, UK, known for the fruit and vegetable market that operated there for nearly three centuries; it also gives its name to the Royal Opera House close by. Once the garden of a convent in Westminster, the site was developed in the 17th-c. It was initially a fashionable area, but with the growth of the market wealthy families moved away, and cheap coffee houses and lodging houses sprang up. The market was relocated in 1974, and the buildings restored by the Greater London Council.

Coventry [kovntree], Middle Eng **Couentrey** 52°25N 1°30W, pop (2001e) 300 800. Modern industrial city in West Midlands, C England, UK; 150 km/93 mi NW of London; Benedictine priory founded in 1043, around which the town grew; important centre of clothing manufacture from 17th-c; University of Warwick (1965); Coventry University (1992, formerly Polytechnic); railway; vehicles, machine tools, agricultural machinery, telecommunications equipment, artificial fibres; old cathedral (1433) destroyed during World War 2; new cathedral designed by Sir Basil Spence (consecrated 1962); 15th–16th-c Church of Holy Trinity; St Mary's Hall (1343), built for the merchants' guild; museum of British road transport; football league team, Coventry City (Sky Blues).

cover crop A crop which protects the crop planted beneath it. Cereals are often used as a cover crop for newly sown grass and clover seeds. The term may also refer to crops, such as kale, which provide cover for game birds.

Coverdale, Miles (1488–1568) Bible scholar, born in York, North Yorkshire, N England, UK. He studied at Cambridge, was ordained priest in 1514, and joined the Augustinian Friars at Cambridge, but was converted to Protestantism. His own translation of the Bible appeared in 1535 (the first complete one in English), and he then superintended the work which led to the 'Great Bible' (1539). He also edited the work known as 'Cranmer's Bible' (1540). Forced to live abroad for several years, he returned to England in 1548 and became Bishop of Exeter in 1551. On Queen Mary's accession he went abroad again, but returned in 1559 to live in London.

covered wagon *prairie schooner*

cow *bull* (zoology)

Coward, Sir Noel (Pierce) (1899–1973) Actor, playwright, and composer, born in London, UK. An actor from the age of 12, his first play, written with Esme Wynne, was produced in 1917. Among his many successes were *The Vortex* (1924), *Hay Fever* (1925), *Private Lives* (1930), and *Blithe Spirit* (1941), all showing his strong satirical humour, and his gift for witty dialogue. He wrote the music as well as the lyrics for most of his works, including the musical *Bitter Sweet* (1929), the play *Cavalcade* (1931), and the revue *Words and Music* (1932), with its 'Mad Dogs and Englishmen'. He was also an accomplished singer, produced several films based on his own scripts, and published two volumes of autobiography, *Present Indicative* (1937) and *Future Indefinite* (1954). He was knighted in 1970.

cowberry A small evergreen shrub (*Vaccinium vitis-idaea*) growing to 30 cm/12 in, native to N temperate regions; leaves oval, often notched at tip; flowers in terminal clusters, drooping, bell-shaped, pinkish-white; berry red, edible but acid; also called **red whortleberry**. (Family: Ericaceae.)

cowbird A strong-billed bird, native to the Americas; eats seeds and insects; may seek food by using bill to lift stones or cow dung. Few species build nests; most lay eggs in the nests of unrelated birds. (Family: Icteridae, 7 species.)

Cowell, Henry (Dixon) [kowel] (1897–1965) Composer, born in Menlo Park, California, USA. He studied in New York City and Berlin, and earned his living as a pianist, lecturer, and writer. As a composer he was noted for his experimental techniques, including note-clusters produced on the piano by using the fist or forearm. He founded *The New Musical Quarterly* in 1927. His works include two ballets, an unfinished opera, and 20 symphonies.

Cowes [kowz] 50°45N 1°18W, pop (2000e) 17 500. Town in the Isle of Wight, S England, UK; on R Medina estuary; a notable yachting centre; ferries and hydrofoil to Southampton; boat and hydrofoil building, radar, tourism; Osborne House (East Cowes), summer residence of Queen Victoria and Prince Albert; Cowes Castle, built by Henry VIII (1543), home of the Royal Yacht Squadron; Cowes Week (Aug).

Cowley, Abraham (1618–67) Poet, born in London, UK. He studied at Cambridge, and was publishing poetry at the age of 15. During the Civil War he went with the queen to Paris, was sent on Royalist missions, and carried on her correspondence in cipher with the king. After the Restoration (1660), he retired to Chertsey. His main works were the influential *Pindarique Odes* (1656), and his unfinished epic on King David, *Davideis* (1656).

cow parsley A biennial or perennial (*Anthriscus sylvestris*), growing to 1·5 m/5 ft, native to Europe, temperate Asia, and N Africa; stems hollow, grooved; leaves divided, leaflets with toothed oval segments; flowers small, white, in umbels 2–6 cm/¾–2½ in across; fruit 7–10 mm/0·28–0·39 in, smooth; also called **Queen Anne's lace** and **keck**. It is often the most common and early flowering of the umbellifers. (Family: Umbelliferae.)

cow parsnip *hogweed*

cow pea A sprawling annual (*Vigna unguiculata*), growing to 2 m/6½ ft, native to Africa; leaves with three leaflets; pea-flowers white or yellow, pinkish at the base; pods to 30 cm/12 in long. Numerous varieties cultivated in warmer countries for the edible seeds and young pods, eaten like French beans; also commonly grown for pasturage. (Family: Leguminosae.)

Cowpens, Battle of (1781) During the US War of Independence, an engagement in S Carolina in which a small American army under Daniel Morgan (1736–1802) defeated a British force under Banastre Tarleton (1754–1833).

Cowper, William [kooper] (1731–1800) Poet, born in Berkhamsted, Hertfordshire, SE England, UK. He studied at Westminster School, and was called to the bar in 1754. He suffered frequently from mental instability, and attempted suicide several times. While living in Olney, he collaborated with the clergyman John Newton to write the *Olney Hymns* (1779). His ballad of John Gilpin (1783) was highly successful, as was his long poem about rural ease, *The Task* (1785).

cow pox A virus disease of cattle characterized by small blisters (*pocks*) on the teats; also known as **kine pox**. The contents of these blisters were used by Edward Jenner in 1798 to vaccinate humans against the related *smallpox*.

cowrie A marine snail with a glossy, smooth, and often highly patterned shell, largely covered by lobes of mantle; used as decorations and even as currency on Pacific Islands; mostly tropical in distribution, living on coral reefs. (Class: Gastropoda. Order: Mesogastropoda.)

cowslip A perennial (*Primula veris*) with rosette of oblong, slightly crinkled leaves, native to Europe and Asia; flowers 1–30 at the tip of a common stalk, drooping, calyx tubular, petals yellow with orange spots at base. (Family: Primulaceae.)

Cox, (Charles) Brian (1928–) British academic. He studied at Cambridge, taught English at Hull University (1954–66), then became professor at Manchester and pro-Vice-Chancellor (1987). A member of the Kingman Committee on the English Language, he became chairman of the National Curriculum English Working Group (1988–9). As well as a series of *Black Papers on Education* (1969–77), his publications include *The Free Spirit* (1963) and *Joseph Conrad: the Modern Imagination* (1974). He has also written books of poetry, *Collected Poems* appearing in 1993. His name is most widely known in UK English circles as the author of the report produced on the teaching of English in the National Curriculum (the *Cox Report*).

Cox (Arquette), Courtenay (1964–) Actress, born in Birmingham, Alabama, USA. She studied architecture for a year at Mount Vernon College, became a model in New York City, then took a range of parts in films and television, and became well known through her role as Monica Geller in the acclaimed television series *Friends* (1994–2004). Roles in feature films began with *Down Twisted* (1986), and include *Ace Ventura: Pet Detective* (1994), *Scream* and its sequel (1996, 1998), and *Commandments* (1997). She married actor David Arquette in 1999.

coyote [koyohtee] A member of the dog family (*Canis latrans*), native to North and Central America; inhabits grassland and open woodland; eats hares, rodents, other animals, berries; also known as **prairie wolf**, **barking wolf**, **little wolf**, or (in fur trade) **cased wolf**. Coyotes have been subject to bounties, and are still often hunted by ranchers and farmers.

coypu [koypoo] A cavy-like rodent (*Myocastor coypus*), native to South America (introduced elsewhere); large (length over 1 m/3¼ ft); rat-like with broad blunt muzzle; inhabits wetlands; burrows may damage dykes, etc; farmed for soft underfur; also known as **nutria**. (Family: Myocastoridae.)

C++ [see pluhs pluhs] A computer programming language, developed from C, to enable the programmer to carry out object-oriented programming.

CPU *digital computer*

CP violation The violation of a fundamental symmetry principle, observed in 1964 by US physicists James Watson Cronin and Val Logsdon Fitch (1923–), using subatomic particles called *kaons* (a type of meson). *C* stands for *charge conjugation* (in quantum mechanics, the operation of turning a particle into its antiparticle) and *P* for parity (the operation of changing left- to right-hand co-ordinates). CP violation allows an absolute definition of right- and left-handedness in the universe, and is related to the preponderance of matter over antimatter in the universe; but its mechanism and role is not understood. Kaons violate time reversal symmetry T in such a way that the fundamental combination CPT is preserved. The first evidence for CP violation in B mesons was reported in 1999.

crab A typically marine crustacean with a front pair of legs specialized as pincers (*chelipeds*) and used for food capture, signalling, and fighting; usually walks sideways, using four pairs of walking legs; also capable of swimming; body broad, flattened, with a hard outer covering (*carapace*); abdomen permanently tucked up beneath body; eyes usually movable on stalks; some species terrestrial, some found in fresh water; eggs carried by females, usually hatching into a planktonic larval stage (*zoea*); many species exploited commercially for food. (Class: Malacostraca. Order: Decapoda.)

Crabbe, George (1754–1832) Poet, born in Aldeburgh, Suffolk, E England, UK. He trained as a surgeon, but turned to literature. He was ordained in 1782, and held livings in Suffolk and Wiltshire. His best-known work from this early period is *The Village* (1783), a realistic portrait of rural life. He then wrote nothing for over 20 years. His later narrative poems include *The Parish Register* (1807), *The Borough* (1810), and other volumes of *Tales*.

crabeater seal A true seal (*Lobodon carcinophagus*), native to the Antarctic and sub-Antarctic; teeth with deeply notched margins, forming a sieve when mouth is shut; eats krill (despite its name); fastest true seal on land (up to 25 kph/15 mph); one of the world's most numerous large mammals (may be 15 million individuals).

Crab nebula The remnant of a star seen by Chinese astronomers to explode spectacularly on 4 July 1054 (unrecorded in the West). The nebula itself was named in 1848 by the 3rd Earl of Rosse. Photographs show a tangled web of filaments threading a luminous nebula. The explosion which triggered the nebula was a supernova, which expelled its outer layers and left a dense neutron star at the centre, now observed as a pulsar rotating 30 times a second.

crab-plover *plover*

Crabtree, Joseph [**krab**tree, ?krab**tray**] (1754–1854) Poet and polymath, born in Bristol, SW England, UK. According to the records of the Crabtree Foundation, he was a precocious child, who travelled as flute boy in Cook's first voyage (1768). He spent some time at Oxford University (1773) before joining his family wine firm (1783) and travelling in Europe, where he met and developed a great friendship with Wordsworth, inspiring several of his poems. Crabtree went on to become a latter-day Renaissance man, making contributions to science, engineering, and mathematics, as well as achieving recognition as a traveller, translator, and lawyer. He is thought to have met virtually all the leading figures of his time, often suggesting ideas and inventions later attributed to them, and is himself considered to have been the first inventor of several products and devices, such as soda water and the beer pump. Little was known of him until the 20th-c, partly due to his own wish that no biographical account should be published after his death. Nonetheless, the Crabtree Foundation was founded in 1954 at University College London, dedicated to research into and exposition of his life and work, and continues to organize annual orations in his memory.

crack The free base of cocaine, produced by mixing with baking powder and water. The cocaine hardens to white cinder chunks which can be smoked in a small pipe. The effect is immediate. This form of cocaine is held to be extremely addictive.

Cracow *Kraków*

Cradock, Fanny, *née* **Phyllis Primrose-Pechey** (1909–94) British writer and television cook. From 1955 she became known for her 'bon viveur' television cookery programmes, dressed in a ball gown, and presented with her monocled husband, Johnny. Her writing included cookery books, children's books, several novels (under the pen name **Frances Dale**), and columns on cookery and restaurants in the daily press, which became notorious for their social pretension and outspoken opinions.

Craig, Edward (Henry) Gordon (1872–1966) Stage designer, actor, director, and theorist, born in Stevenage, Hertfordshire, SE England, UK. He worked for nine years as an actor in Irving's company, but left the Lyceum in 1897 to be both a director and a designer. He settled in Italy in 1906, where he published the theatre journal, *The Mask* (1908–29), which together with his scene designs and his books, *On the Art of the Theatre* (1911) and *The Theatre Advancing* (1921), had a profound influence on modern theatre practice. A pioneer of modern theatre, he replaced the decorative pseudo-realism of his time with a simple, structured stage defined by the expressive use of lighting.

Craigie, Sir William Alexander [**kray**gee] (1867–1957) Scholar, born in Dundee, E Scotland, UK. He studied at St Andrews, and became professor of Anglo-Saxon at Oxford (1916–25), and of English at Chicago (1925–35). He was joint editor of the *New English Dictionary* (1901–33), and also editor of dictionaries on Scots and on American English.

crake The name often given to any smallish rail with a short, chicken-like bill (45 species).

Cram, Steve, popular name of **Stephen Cram** (1960–) Athlete, born in Gateshead, Tyne and Wear, NE England, UK. The European junior champion at 3000 m in 1979, he won senior titles at 1500 m in 1982 and 1986. He won the World Championship gold medal at 1500 m in 1983, and the Commonwealth Games gold medals at 1500 m (1982, 1986) and 800 m (1986). In 1985 he set three world records in 20 days at 1500 m, 1 mi, and 2000 m. His time for the mile was 3 min 46·32 s. He is now a television commentator.

cramp The involuntary spasm of a muscle, or a group of skeletal muscles, which causes pain. Cramp tends to occur in the elderly and in pregnancy. The calf muscles are particularly affected.

Cranach, Lucas [**krah**nakh], known as **Lucas Cranach the Elder** (1472–1553) Painter, born in Kronach, EC Germany, from where he took his name. In 1504 he became court painter at Wittenberg to the Elector Frederick. His paintings include sacred and a few classical subjects, hunting scenes, and portraits. He was closely associated with the German Reformers, many of whom (including Luther and Melanchthon) were portrayed by himself and his pupils. A 'Crucifixion' in the Stadkirche, Weimar, is his masterpiece. Of three sons, all painters, the second, **Lucas Cranach the Younger** (1515–86), painted so like his father that their works are difficult to distinguish.

cranberry A dwarf, creeping, evergreen shrub (*Vaccinium oxycoccos*), native to N temperate regions on boggy, acid soils; stems very slender, rooting; leaves 4–8 mm/0·15–0·3 in, oblong-oval, pointed, bluish beneath, margins inrolled; flowers on long, slender stalks, 5–6 mm/0·2–0·25 in, pink, four petals, curling backwards; berry round or pear-shaped, red- or brown-spotted, edible. (Family: Ericaceae.)

Crane, (Harold) Hart (1899–1932) Poet, born in Garrettsville, Ohio, USA. After an unhappy childhood, he settled in New York City as a writer in 1923. His work is contained in *White Buildings* (1926), a collection on New York life, and *The Bridge* (1930), an epic using Brooklyn Bridge as its focal point. He drowned himself by jumping overboard while returning from a visit to Mexico.

Crane, Stephen (Townley) (1871–1900) Writer and war correspondent, born in Newark, New Jersey, USA. He began as a journalist in New York City, and became known as a novelist through *Maggie: A Girl of the Streets* (1893) and *The Red Badge of Courage* (1895), a vivid story of the Civil War. He also wrote poems and short stories, and worked as a war correspondent in Greece and Cuba.

crane (engineering) A machine which can lift and position loads. It essentially consists of an arm (or *jib*) carrying a pulley, attached to a post round which it can rotate, and with a rope which can be wound round a barrel. In antiquity, cranes might lift 5 tons, and be worked by a treadmill. Steam cranes in the later 1800s could often lift 20 tons, and some very large floating cranes now can lift 200 tons. They are much used in docks (with special designs used for container traffic), in construction (**tower cranes**), and in engineering (often as **gantry cranes**).

crane (ornithology) A long-legged, long-necked bird, height 0·6–1·5 m/2–5 ft; worldwide except South America, New Zealand, and the Pacific; adult usually with head partly naked; inhabits flat wetlands and wet plains; eats small animals, grain, and other plant material. (Family: Gruidae, 15 species.)

cranefly A long-legged, true fly; adult body slender, legs fragile, readily discarded if trapped; female egg-laying tube prominent; larvae known as **leatherjackets**, typically ground-dwelling, feeding on roots, rarely predaceous; adults also known as **daddy longlegs**; c.13 500 species. (Order: Diptera. Family. Tipulidae.)

cranesbill An annual or perennial of the genus *Geranium*, native to temperate regions; leaves with lobes radiating from central point; flowers usually white to purple or blue, 5-petalled; fruit with long beak resembling a bird's bill, exploding when ripe, the beak of each seed rolling up and flicking seed away; many of the so-called geraniums of horticulture belong to the genus *Pelargonium*. (Genus: *Geranium*, 400 species. Family: Geraniaceae.)

cranial index *cephalic index*

Cranko, John [**krang**koh] (1927–73) Dancer, choreographer, and director, born in Rustenburg, N South Africa. He studied at the Cape Town University ballet school, and at Sadler's Wells School in London. He choreographed for both Sadler's Wells and the Royal Ballet companies, and in 1961 became ballet director of the Stuttgart Ballet. He is known chiefly for his full-length dramatic works, such as *Romeo and Juliet* (1962) and *Onegin* (1965).

Cranmer, Thomas (1489–1556) Archbishop of Canterbury, born in Aslockton, Nottinghamshire, C England, UK. He studied at Cambridge, took orders in 1523, and became a divinity tutor. His suggestion that Henry VIII appeal for his divorce to the universities of Christendom won him the king's favour and he was appointed a royal chaplain. He was made Archbishop of Canterbury in 1533, making allegiance to the pope 'for form's sake'. He later annulled Henry's marriages to Catherine of Aragon and to Anne Boleyn (1536), and divorced him from Anne of Cleves (1540). He was largely responsible for the Book of Common Prayer (1549, 1552). On Henry's death, Cranmer rushed Protestant changes through. He had little to do with affairs of state, but agreed to the plan to divert the succession from Mary to Lady Jane Grey (1553), for which he was arraigned for treason. Accused later of heresy, and sentenced to death, he retracted the seven recantations he had been forced to sign, before being burned alive.

craps A casino dice game of American origin, adapted from the game *hazard* by Bernard de Mandeville in New Orleans in 1813. Using two dice, a player loses throwing on the first roll 2, 3, or 12 (*craps*), but wins with 7 or 11. If the player's first throw makes 4, 5, 6, 8, 9, or 10, this number is called the *point*; the player then continues to throw until the same number is rolled again (*making the point*), thus giving a win, or throws a 7 and thus loses (*craps out*).

craquelure [krakuh**lür**] The distinctive pattern of fine cracks on the surface of a painting or glazed pottery. Normally the result of aging, craquelure can be faked.

Crashaw, Richard [**kray**shaw] (c.1613–49) Religious poet, born in London, UK. He studied at Cambridge, went to Paris, became a Catholic (1644), and in 1649 was given a Church post in Loretto, Italy. He is best known for his volume of Latin poems, *Epigrammatum sacrorum liber* (1634, A Book of Sacred Epigrams), and *Steps to the Temple* (1646).

Crassus, Marcus Licinius, nickname **Dives** (Lat 'wealthy') (c.115–53 BC) Roman politician. As praetor he defeated Spartacus at the Battle of Lucania (71 BC), and in 70 BC was made consul with Pompey. The richest of Roman citizens, he became a friend of Caesar, and formed the first triumvirate with him and Pompey (60 BC). In 53 BC, as Governor of Syria, he attacked the Parthians, but was routed and killed at the Battle of Carrhae.

Crater (Lat 'cup') A small, faint constellation in the S sky. One of the 48 constellations known to the ancient Greeks, in mythology it represents the cup in which Corvus, the Crow, was supposed to bring water to Apollo.

crater A circular depression on the surface of a planetary body. Those on Mercury, the Moon, and most of the natural satellites of planets have been formed by impacts with meteorites and comets in the remote past. The Moon, Mars, Venus, and Io (one of Jupiter's satellites) also have volcanic craters. Craters on Earth have been caused by meteorites (eg Meteor Crater, Arizona) and by volcanic explosions (eg Crater Lake, Oregon).

Crater Lake (Canada) *Chubb Crater*

Crater Lake (USA) Circular crater lake in SW Oregon, USA, in the Cascade Range; 9·5 km/6 mi across; area 52 sq km/20 sq mi; 604 m/1982 ft deep; altitude 1879 m/6165 ft; in a large pit formed by the destruction of the summit of a prehistoric volcano.

Craven, Dan(iel Hartman), known as **Danie** (1911–93) Rugby union player and administrator, born in Lindley, EC South Africa. He won 16 caps for South Africa in four different positions, captaining them against the 1938 British Lions. After coaching and managing Springbok touring teams, he became chairman of the South African Rugby Board in 1956, and worked for over 30 years to keep South Africa within the Rugby Union fold.

crawfish *spiny lobster*

Crawford, Joan, originally **Lucille Fay Le Sueur** (1904–77) Film actress, born in San Antonio, Texas, USA. At first a nightclub dancer, she started in silent films in 1925, taking the lead in *Our Dancing Daughters* (1928). She became an established star in the 1930s and 1940s, winning an Oscar for *Mildred Pierce* (1945); her last great role was in *Whatever Happened to Baby Jane?* (1962), in which she co-starred with her long-standing rival, Bette Davis. After her death, a very critical biography, *Mommie Dearest*, by her adopted daughter Christine, was filmed in 1981.

Crawford, Michael (1942–) Actor and singer, born in Salisbury, Wiltshire, S England, UK. His performance in *No Sex Please, We're British* (1971) established him as a comedy actor. In the 1970s the television series *Some Mothers Do 'Ave 'Em*, in which he played the accident-prone misfit Frank Spencer, made him a household name in Britain. He went on to star in such musicals as *Billy* (1974), *Flowers for Algernon* (1979), *Barnum* (1981), and *The Phantom of the Opera* (1986, Tony). His films include *The Knack* (1964), *How I Won the War* (1966), *Hello Dolly* (1968), *Condorman* (1980), and *Once Upon a Forest* (1993). In 1999 he published his autobiography, *Parcel Arrived Safely: Tied With String*.

Craxi, Bettino [**krak**see] (1934–2000) Italian statesman and prime minister (1983–7), born in Milan, N Italy. He was active in the Socialist Youth Movement, and joined the Central Committee of the Italian Socialist Party in 1957. A member of the National Executive in 1965, he became deputy secretary (1970–6), general secretary (1976), and Italy's first Socialist prime minister. He was involved in a major corruption scandal in 1992 which ended his political career.

crayfish A typically freshwater, lobster-like crustacean with a well-developed abdomen and front pair of legs modified as powerful pincers (chelipeds); many species exploited commercially for food. (Class: Malacostraca. Order: Decapoda.)

Crazy Horse, Sioux name **Tashunka Witco** (c.1842–77) Oglala Sioux chief, born near the Black Hills, South Dakota, USA. He participated in all the major Sioux actions to protect the Black Hills against white intrusion, believing himself immune from battle injury. In 1876 he was named supreme war and peace chief of the Oglalas, uniting most of the Sioux still free. He led the Sioux and Cheyenne to victory at the Battle of Rosebud, and defeated Custer's forces at Little Bighorn (1876). Pursued by US forces, with his band of some 1000 facing starvation, he surrendered the following year. He died at the hands of a US soldier, allegedly while resisting being forced into a jail cell. He is regarded as a symbol of Sioux resistance and as their greatest leader, and a gigantic figure of Crazy Horse has been sculpted (by Korczak Ziolkowski) out of a mountain in the Black Hills of South Dakota.

cream of tartar *tartaric acid*

creamware A hard durable type of earthenware which was developed in Staffordshire by the middle of the 18th-c. A much-refined version of it was perfected by Josiah Wedgwood. In 1765 he sold a service of creamware to Queen Charlotte, who was so satisfied with it that she permitted Wedgwood to market it as **Queensware**. High quality creamware was also produced in Leeds.

creationism Originally, the belief that God creates a soul for each human individual at conception or birth. It is now commonly applied to the belief that the Genesis account of creation in the Bible accurately describes the origins of the world and humanity. It is opposed to the theory of evolution, and some evangelical conservative Christians claim there is scientific evidence to support creationism, though this has not been supported by other scientists.

Crécy, Battle of [kraysee] (1364) A battle between France and England in the Hundred Years' War. Using tactics perfected against the Scots, Edward III routed Philip VI of France and his larger army, mainly cavalry, near Abbeville (Somme). It was a classic demonstration of the superiority of a numerically outnumbered co-ordinated force of dismounted men-at-arms, and archers providing offensive fire-power, over mounted knights armed with crossbows. English longbows, effective up to c.180 m/600 ft, could dispatch 10 flights a minute. The victory enabled the English to reach Calais.

credibility An element in strategic defence strategies, in particular deterrence, originating in the USA. It was designed to demonstrate to the East that the West had a sufficient number of accurate and dependable weapons which it would be prepared to use in the event of a first strike by the other side.

credit card A plastic card which is used instead of cash or cheque to pay for goods or services. Card holders present their card when making a payment. The credit-card company sends a statement of account monthly to each account holder, listing their purchases and showing the sum of money owed. If the statement is settled in full by a specified date, no interest is payable. The best-known companies are *Visa*, *Mastercard*, and *American Express*. Credit cards differ from **charge cards**, in that there is a specified credit limit. Charge cards have no limit, but full repayment is to be made each month.

credit insurance An insurance taken out where a business sells on credit terms (ie asks for payment at a later date). In this way the insurer provides a safeguard against the possibility of a customer not paying, thus creating a 'bad debt'.

credit rating A system used to assess the ability of a company (or individual) to pay for goods and services, or the ability to borrow and repay. Some rating firms suggest a maximum amount of credit to be allowed. Popular rating systems in the USA are *Moody*, *Standard and Poor*, and *Dun & Bradstreet*. All companies are assigned a rating code: the highest is AAA, next is AA, and so on.

credits The recognition given to someone who has successfully completed a part of a modular course. American education is firmly based on the notion of accumulated credits, whereas in some countries the principle does not exist at all. The advantages are that students know from the beginning how many credits they must acquire in order to obtain the qualification they seek, and that the transfer of credit for partially-completed courses is useful for someone who wishes to study at more than one institution.

credit union A co-operative venture where members save together and lend to each other, mainly short-term consumer loans. The system is popular in North America, where there are some 50 000 credit unions.

Cree A North American Algonkin Indian group from the Canadian Subarctic region, originally hunters and fishermen. With guns acquired from French fur traders in the 17th-c, they began to expand: one group, the **Plains Cree**, moved W, adopting the culture of the Plains Indian; the **Woodland Cree** remained in forested areas, where they continued to hunt.

Creek A North American Indian people, originally from Georgia and Alabama, speaking a language of the Hokan–Siouan family, c.71 000 (2000 census). The Spanish invaded their territory in the 16th-c. They were defeated in the Creek War (1813–14) against US troops, and forced to cede much of their land. Finally they were forcibly moved to Oklahoma (1837), where they became one of the so-called 'Five Civilized Tribes'.

Creeley, Robert (White) (1926–) Poet and novelist, born in Arlington, Massachusetts, USA. He studied for a while at Harvard, then worked at a variety of jobs until he began to write. Influenced by the Black Mountain school, he developed a spare, minimalist style evident in *For Love: Poems 1950–60* (1960). His manner becomes even more fragmentary in later volumes, notably *Words* (1965), *Pieces* (1969), *Hello: A Journal* (1978), and *Memory Gardens* (1986). *Life and Death* and *The Dogs of Auckland* appeared in 1998.

creep The gradual deformation of a solid subjected to continual stress, such as the lengthening of a wire under load. In crystalline materials such as metals, creep is caused by the movement of dislocations through the material.

cremation Burning the remains of a dead person. The practice was recorded in ancient Greece for soldiers killed in battle, and was later adopted by the Romans. Discouraged in the past by Christians because of its pagan associations, it is the regular form of disposal by Hindus. Today cremation is becoming more common in many countries, because of lack of space in cemeteries.

creodont An extinct flesh-eating mammal; known from the early Tertiary period around the world except Australia and South America; distinguished from true carnivores by their shorter limbs, unfused wrist bones, cleft claw bone, and shearing teeth (*carnassials*) formed from molars. (Order: Creodonta.)

creole A pidgin language which has become the mother-tongue of a speech community, as has happened with Jamaican creole. A creole develops a wider range of words, grammatical structures, and styles than is found in a pidgin.

Creon or **Kreon** [**kree**on] A name (meaning 'ruler') given to several legendary Greek kings, but especially to the brother of Jocasta, regent of Thebes, who awarded the throne to Oedipus. Later, after the siege of the city by the seven Champions, he commanded that Polynices should not be buried, and condemned Antigone for disobedience.

creosote [kreeosoht] A fraction of coal tar, boiling point c.250°C, containing a variety of toxic aromatic compounds giving it strong antiseptic and preservative properties.

cresol [kreesol] $(CH_3)C_6H_4(OH)$, three isomeric compounds: 2-, 3-, and 4-hydroxytoluene, oils with boiling point c.200°C. They are ingredients of coal tar, and are important raw materials for plastics.

cress The name given to several different members of the cabbage family, often small weeds, some cultivated as salad plants. (Family: Cruciferae.)

Cressida [kresida] In mediaeval accounts of the Trojan War, the daughter of Calchas, a Trojan priest; probably the story was a misunderstanding of Calchas and Chryseis in the *Iliad*. Beloved by Troilus, a Trojan prince, she deserted him for Diomedes when transferred to the Greek camp.

crested tit A small bird (*Parus cristatus*), native to Europe and E to the Urals; inhabits coniferous and mixed woodlands; often found with coal tits. (Family: Paridae.)

Cretaceous period [kretayshuhs] The last geological period of the Mesozoic era, lasting from 144 to 65 million years ago, characterized by the emergence of flowering plants and the dominance and extinction of dinosaurs. It was also a period of marine transgressions and the deposition of widespread chalk deposits in NW Europe.

Crete, Gr **Kríti**, Ital **Candia**, ancient **Creta** pop (2000e) 561 000; area 8336 sq km/3218 sq mi. Island region of Greece, in the Mediterranean Sea, S of the Cyclades island group; length 256 km/159 mi; width 14–60 km/9–37 mi; largest of the Greek islands and fifth largest in the Mediterranean; White Mts (W) rise to 2452 m/8044 ft; Idhi Oros (C) rise to the highest point of the island, Psiloritis (2456 m/8058 ft); N coastline deeply indented; evidence of settlement from c.6000 BC; important Minoan civilization, c.2000 BC; ruled at various times by Greeks, Romans, Turks, and Arabs; passed to Greece in 1913; German occupation in World War 2, after airborne invasion (1941); capital, Heraklion; other chief towns, Chania, Agios Nikolaos; two universities (1973, 1977); fruit, olive oil, wine, sheep, goats, tourism; ancient sites at Knossos, Gortys, Lato, Phaistos.

cretinism A condition affecting children who suffer from inadequate production of thyroid hormones (*thyroxine*). The thyroid gland is enlarged in some forms only. There is failure of normal growth and development, with short stature, puffiness of the skin, notably of the face, enlarged tongue, hairloss, and mental deficiency. Infants can be screened shortly after birth to ensure they are producing adequate thyroid hormone.

Creus, Cape [krayoos], ancient **Aphrodisium** 42°19N 3°19E. The most E point on the Iberian peninsula; picturesque fishing village of Cadaques nearby, preserved by local artists.

Creutzfeldt-Jacob Disease [kroytsvelt yakob] A prion disease involving degeneration of the nervous system; named after German neuropathologists Heinz Creutzfeldt and Andreas Jacob. Hereditary and sporadic cases have been documented since the 1920s, characterized by an onset between 45 and 60 years of age, and neurological symptoms including dementia, problems with speech and balance, abnormal movements, and paralysis. There are typical electroencephalographic changes and pathological changes in the brain identifiable at post-mortem. The disease progresses steadily, with death occurring within 12 months. More recently, a new form of the disease has been described, thought to be due to an infectious agent. It affects younger people, and has a more aggressive course. It is possible that infection may occur following inoculation with infected tissue, eg during medical procedures. There is also concern that transmission may occur from animals by the consumption of infected meat, particularly beef products.

cribbage A card game popular in public houses in the UK, played by two, three, or four people with a standard pack of 52 cards and a holed board known as the **cribbage board** or *peg board*. The number of cards dealt to each player varies according to the number of players, but will be five, six, or seven. Cards are discarded into a dummy hand, which each player has in turn. Points are scored according to cards dropped (ie for playing a card that makes a pair, a run of three or more, etc). Cards are discarded in each round until a total of 31 is reached. Play continues until the players have each discarded all their cards. The value of the hand is then calculated. All scores are marked on the peg board.

Crick, Francis (Harry Compton) (1916–) Biophysicist, born in Northampton, Northamptonshire, C England, UK. He studied at London and Cambridge, and from 1949 carried on research in molecular biology at the Cavendish Laboratory. In 1953, with the help of X-ray diffraction photographs taken by Maurice Wilkins and Rosalind Franklin (1920–58), he and J D Watson constructed a molecular model of the genetic material DNA. In 1958 he proposed that the DNA determines the sequence of amino acids in a polypeptide through a triplet code. He shared the 1962 Nobel Prize for Physiology or Medicine with Watson and Wilkins.

cricket (sport) *p.400*

cricket (entomology) A large, grasshopper-like insect; forewings box-like and bent down round sides of body; female egg-laying tube (*ovipositor*) cylindrical; many species have a well-developed sound-producing mechanism for auditory communication; c.2000 species, including some pests. (Order: Orthoptera. Family: Gryllidae.)

Crimea [kriymeea], Russ **Krym** area 25 900 sq km/10 000 sq mi. Peninsula in S Ukraine; bounded S and W by the Black Sea, and E by the Sea of Azov; separated from the mainland (N) by the narrow Perekop Isthmus, and from the Taman Peninsula (E) by the Kersh Strait; length 320 km/200 mi; Greek colonization, 7th-c BC; invaded by Goths (AD 250), Huns (373), Khazars (8th-c), Byzantine Greeks (1016), Kipchaks (1050), Tatars (13th-c), Ottomans (late 15th-c), and Russians, 1736; scene of the Crimean War, 1854–6; an autonomous Soviet republic, 1921; an oblast of the Russian SFSR, 1946; transferred to the Ukraine SSR, 1954; rich in minerals (iron, gypsum, limestone); chief cities include Simferopol, Sevastopol, Kerch; subtropical Black Sea coast is a major tourist attraction, notably at Yalta.

Crimean War (1854–6) A war fought in the Crimean peninsula by Britain, France, Turkey, Piedmont, and Austria against Russia, whose origins lay in Russian successes against the Turks in the Black Sea area, and the British and French desire to prevent further westward expansion by the Russians, which threatened the Mediterranean and overland routes to India. Major battles were fought in 1854 at the R Alma (20 Sep), Balaclava (25 Oct), and Inkerman (5 Nov). The fall of the Russian fortress at Sebastopol (Sep 1855) led to peace negotiations, finally agreed at the Treaty of Paris (Mar 1856). Russia ceded S Bessarabia to neighbouring Moldavia. The war was an ineptly run, costly conflict. The commanders on both sides wasted their troops' lives, as in the Charge of the Light Brigade during the Battle of Balaclava, (1854) in which many British troops died. Medical care was primitive, but the war was notable for the nursing achievements of Florence Nightingale at Scutari. The pioneer war reports of the Irishman W H Russell in *The Times*, the first journalist in history to write as a war correspondent, using the newly invented telegraph, made people in Britain increasingly critical of the war. Most significantly, it ended the 40-year post-Napoleonic coalition of Britain, Russia, Austria, and Prussia, who together had tried to maintain peace in Europe.

Crime Writers' Association A British literary association open to all published writers who write about crime – fiction or non-fiction – with the aim of promoting the prestige and appreciation of crime writing. The first meeting was convened by John Creasey in 1953, and past chairs include HRF Keating, PD James, Lady Antonia Fraser, Dick Francis, and Ian Rankin. Annual awards include the categories of Gold Dagger for the best novel published in the English language that year, and the Silver Dagger for the runner-up. The Debut Dagger is awarded to the best new writer previously unpublished.

Criminal Injuries Compensation Scheme A British scheme whereby the state pays compensation to certain victims who have suffered personal injury attributable to a crime of violence. First established in 1964, and now governed by the Criminal Injuries Compensation Act (1995), the system is administered by the Criminal Injuries Compensation Authority. The 1995 Act sets out new rules for assessing compensation, which is made on the basis of a tariff of awards that band together injuries of comparable severity plus, in some cases, an amount to cover loss of earnings and special expenses. Certain classes of victims, offences, and injuries are excluded from the scheme, and any payment made under the scheme is reduced by the amount of damages or compensation awarded by a civil or criminal court. The first such scheme was established in New Zealand in 1963, and since then similar schemes have been adopted in a large number of jurisdictions, including Hong Kong, Australia, Canada, France, The Netherlands, and most states in the USA. The scheme is carried out on an *ex gratia* (Lat 'as a favour') basis; there is no appeal to the courts.

Criminal Investigation Department *CID*

cricket

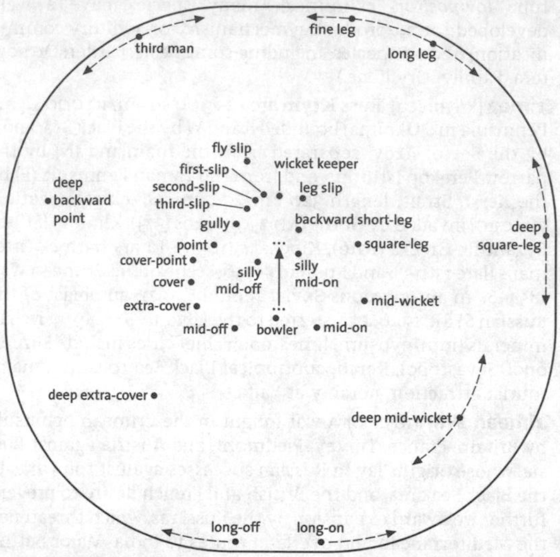

A bat-and-ball team game of 11-a-side. A wicket consisting of three stumps surmounted by a pair of bails is placed at each end of a grassy pitch 22 yd (20·1 m) in length. Each team takes it in turn to bat and bowl. The aim of the batting team is to defend the two wickets while trying to score as many runs as possible before being dismissed. Each member of the team must bat, and two batsmen are on the field at any one time, one in front of each wicket (unless one is injured, and a 'runner' is needed). After the captains of the two sides have tossed a coin to decide who bats first, the fielding team assembles on the field. At any one time it will consist of a bowler, a wicket-keeper (who stands behind the wicket that the bowler is attacking), and nine fielders, who are placed at strategic positions around the field. A bowler delivers an 'over' of (usually) six balls to one wicket, before a different bowler attacks the other wicket.

If the batsman hits a ball (and in certain other circumstances, such as the bowler bowling too wide or the wicket-keeper missing the ball), he may decide it is safe to run between the two wickets, exchanging places with the other batsman, in which case he scores a 'run'. Several runs may be scored following a single hit, but if the ball reaches the boundary of the field, four runs are scored automatically, and six if it has not bounced on the way. A batsman is out if he is 'bowled' (the ball from the bowler knocks his wicket down), 'caught' (the batsman hits the ball so that it is caught by a fielder without bouncing), 'stumped' (the wicket-keeper knocks the wicket down with the ball while the defending batsman is standing outside his 'safe ground' or 'crease'), 'run out' (the wicket towards which one of the batsmen is running is knocked down before the batsman reaches the safe ground), and 'leg before wicket', or 'lbw' (the batsman's body obstructs the ball's path to the wicket without the bat having first made contact). He may also be out if he hits his own wicket while playing a shot, hits the ball twice, prevents a fielder taking a catch ('obstructing the field'), uses a hand to prevent the ball hitting the wicket ('handled the ball') or takes more than three minutes to replace the previous batsman once the wicket has fallen ('timed out'). Once 10 batsmen have been dismissed, the innings comes to a close, but a team can stop its innings ('declare') at any time before that, if it thinks it has made enough runs. In first-class cricket, the pre-eminent form of the game, each team has two innings, and the one with the greater number of runs at the end of the match is the winner, provided the other side has completed - or declared - both its innings. It is possible, however, to forfeit innings in order to obtain a definite result.

The game has been traced back to 1300, but the first known county match was in 1719. The earliest known laws of cricket were drawn up in 1744, and the Marylebone Cricket Club (MCC) was founded in 1787. The first Test match was played in Melbourne in March 1877. Principal domestic competitions in the UK consist of the County Championship, Cheltenham and Gloucester Trophy, Benson and Hedges Cup, and the Norwich Union National League. In 1998 the counties voted to introduce two championship divisions from 2000. The Pura Milk Cup (previously the Sheffield Shield) is the principal competition in Australia. Test matches are staged over five days, county championship matches over four days. Limited-over competitions are normally concluded in one day, and last for a specific number of overs per side. For practical reasons, the World Cup (1975 to date) is strictly limited-overs.

criminal law A branch of law which deals with offences against society generally. A crime may also constitute a breach of the civil law. Investigation of breaches of the criminal law is generally the responsibility of the police. The responsibility for prosecution varies between jurisdictions: for example, in England and Wales, it belongs to the Director of Public Prosecutions and the Crown Prosecution Service; in Scotland, to the Lord Advocate and, in practical terms, to the procurator fiscal; in most US jurisdictions, to a local district attorney or county prosecutor; and in federal jurisdictions, to a US attorney. Private prosecutions are possible in some jurisdictions, but uncommon.

crimp The waviness which occurs naturally in wool fibres, imparting a soft bulkiness to yarns. Crimping of synthetic fibres extends their range of uses into knitting and carpet yarns, and the manufacture of softer woven fabrics.

crinoid [**kriy**noyd] A primitive marine invertebrate (echinoderm), typically attached to the sea bed by a long stalk; occasionally base-attached (*sessile*) or free-swimming; mouth and arms on upper surface; most feed on suspended particles transported to the mouth via food grooves on arms; long fossil record; c.650 living species found from shallow waters to deep sea; also known as **sea lilies** and **feather stars**. (Phylum: Echinodermata. Class: Crinoidea.)

Crippen, Hawley Harvey, known as **Dr Crippen** (1862–1910) Murderer, born in Michigan, USA. He studied medicine and dentistry, eventually settling in London, UK (1900) with his second wife, Cora Turner. Having transferred his affections to his secretary, Ethel le Neve, he poisoned his wife, dissected the body, and interred the remains in the cellar. He and his mistress attempted to escape to Canada on board the SS *Montrose* as Mr and Master Robinson. The suspicious captain contacted Scotland Yard by radiotelegraphy (the first use of radio for a murder case). They were arrested, and Crippen was hanged in London.

Cripps, Sir (Richard) Stafford (1889–1952) British statesman, born in London, UK. He studied at London University, was called to the bar in 1913, and made a fortune in patent and compensation cases. In 1930 he was appointed solicitor general in the second Labour government, and became an MP in 1931. During the 1930s he was associated with several extreme left-wing movements, and was expelled from the Labour Party in 1939 for his 'popular front' opposing Chamberlain's policy of appeasement. He sat as an independent MP during World War 2, was ambassador to the Soviet Union (1940–2), and in 1942 became Lord Privy Seal, and later minister of aircraft production. In the 1945 Labour government, he was readmitted to the Party and appointed President of the Board of Trade. In 1947 he became minister of economic affairs and then Chancellor of the

Exchequer, introducing a successful austerity policy. In 1950 he resigned due to illness.

crisis apparition *apparition*

crisis management A term first employed by Robert McNamara shortly after the 1962 Cuban missile crisis. It implies, given the limited availability of information about other actors, and their unpredictability, that long-term strategic planning cannot provide the basis for action. Crises between states can be resolved only by managing them as they arise.

crisis theology A type of Protestant theology initiated after World War 1 under the inspiration of Karl Barth (1886–1968), and very influential during the 1920s and 1930s. The term 'crisis' essentially applied to the judgment (Gr *krisis*) of God upon all merely human social, moral, and religious endeavours. The approach exercised a decisive influence on the Declaration of Barmen (1934) which, in opposition to the readiness of the so-called 'German Christians' to integrate the racialist ideology of the German National Socialists into Christian doctrine, affirmed Jesus Christ as God's sole and sufficient revelation and denied any revelations in nature, history, or race apart from him.

Cristóbal Colón, Pico [peekoh kreestohbal kohlon] Snow-capped Andean peak in N Colombia; rises to 5800 m/19 029 ft, 113 km/70 mi E of Barranquilla; highest peak in Sierra Nevada de Santa Marta and in Colombia.

Cristofori, Bartolomeo [kristoforee] (1655–1731) Harpsichord-maker, born in Padua, NE Italy. He is usually credited with the invention of the pianoforte in c.1710.

criterion-referenced test A test which requires the candidate to meet a set of criteria, as opposed to a **norm-referenced test** which simply ranks students alongside others. Thus a criterion-referenced test in mathematics might list for each grade what a student must do to obtain that grade, eg be able to convert a fraction to a decimal, or multiply two three-digit numbers.

critical mass The smallest mass of material of a given type and formed into a given shape able to sustain a nuclear-fission chain reaction. For a mass of material greater than the critical mass, large amounts of energy are released via the fission-chain reaction in a small fraction of a second. For a sphere of uranium-235, the critical mass is 52 kg/114·6 lb, corresponding to a radius of 8·7 cm/3·4 in.

critical phenomena The physical properties of systems at their critical points, ie at the temperature where the distinction between two phases vanishes. They are typified by dramatic changes in the parameters used to describe the system; for example, the spontaneous magnetization of iron is reduced to zero when its temperature is raised beyond the critical temperature (the *Curie point*). Critical phenomena are observed in many systems, such as the superfluid, superconducting, ferroelectric, and ferromagnetic transitions. Certain aspects are nevertheless common to all.

critical point (physics) *critical phenomena*

critical theory *Frankfurt School*

Crittenden Compromise (1860) In the months preceding the American Civil War, an attempt by Senator John J Crittenden of Kentucky to resolve the crisis between North and South by formally recognizing slavery in territories S of 36°30. This proved unacceptable to Abraham Lincoln, whose election as president was causing secession by the slave-holding South.

croaker *drumfish*

Croatia *p.402*

Croce, Benedetto [krohchay] (1866–1952) Philosopher, historian, and critic, born in Pescasseroli, EC Italy. He studied at Rome, and in Naples devoted himself at first to literature and antiquarian studies, founding the review, *La Critica* (1903), and making major contributions to idealistic aesthetics in his *Estetica* (1902, Aesthetic) and *La Poesia* (1936, Poetry). In 1910 he became senator, and was minister of education (1920–1) when, with the rise of Mussolini, he had to resign his professorship at Naples. He was opposed to totalitarianism, and with the fall of Mussolini (1943) helped to resurrect Liberal institutions in Italy.

crocket [krokit] In Gothic architecture, a decorative leaf shaped carving, projecting from the raking lines of spires, pinnacles, canopies, etc. It is particularly common in English Decorated style churches.

Crockett, Davy, popular name of **David Crockett** (1786–1836) Backwoodsman, born in Green Co, Tennessee, USA. He distinguished himself against the Creek Indians in Jackson's campaign of 1814, and was elected to the Tennessee state legislature (1821) and to the Congress (1826). He died fighting for Texas at the Battle of the Alamo. Highly embellished stories of his exploits have assumed mythological proportions.

Crockford, William (1775–1844) British founder of a famous gaming club in London (1827). He was previously a fishmonger, but his successes at gambling led to a change in his fortunes. He is reputed to have won over £1 million at the game of hazard.

crocodile A reptile native to tropical rivers and estuaries worldwide (estuarine species sometimes cross open sea); length, up to 7·5 m/25 ft; fourth tooth from the front on each side of the lower jaw is visible when the jaws are closed (unlike the alligator); snout long and slender, or short and broad; eats a range of vertebrate prey; eggs have hard shells (like birds' eggs). Crocodilians (crocodiles, alligators, and the gharial) are the descendants of an ancient reptile group, the *archosaurs* (which included the extinct dinosaurs and pterodactyls) and have changed little in appearance during the last 65 million years. (Order: Crocodilia. Family: Crocodilidae, 14 species.)

crocodile-bird The name used for birds reported to feed on parasites and food residue found in the mouths of basking crocodiles. It is not certain that such feeding occurs, but the name is sometimes used for any birds frequently found associating with crocodiles, such as certain plovers or the **common sandpiper** (*Actitis hypoleucos*).

crocus A perennial producing corms, native to Europe and Asia; leaves grass-like with distinctive silvery stripe down centre; stalkless flowers, goblet-shaped with long, slender tube, mainly white, yellow, or purple, closing up at night; many cultivated for ornament. The autumn-flowering species produce flowers before leaves appear in the spring. They are often attacked by birds, which prefer the yellow flowers, reason unknown. (Genus: *Crocus*, 75 species. Family: Iridaceae.)

Croesus [kreesuhs] (?–c.546 BC) The last king of Lydia (c.560–546 BC), who succeeded his father, Alyattes. He made the Greeks of Asia Minor his tributaries, and extended his kingdom E from the Aegean to the Halys. His conquests and mines made his wealth proverbial. Cyrus II defeated and imprisoned him (546 BC), but his death is a mystery.

crofting A form of small-scale subsistence farming once characteristic of the Highlands and Islands of Scotland. A croft usually comprised a house, a few hectares of arable land, and grazing rights on the hill. It has long been economically unviable unless combined with part-time or full-time jobs, such as fishing, weaving, and tourism.

Crohn's disease [krohn] A persisting but fluctuating disorder affecting any part of the alimentary canal. The lining of the mouth, stomach, and especially the small intestine becomes inflamed and ulcerated. Affected individuals suffer chronic diarrhoea and weight loss, with episodes of abdominal pain and fever. It is named after US physician Burrill Crohn (1884–1983).

Cro-Magnon Man [krohmanyon] The earliest fully modern humans (*Homo sapiens sapiens*) from late Pleistocene Europe (40 000–10 000 BC), named after a rock shelter near Les Eyzies, Dordogne, France, which in 1868 yielded skeletons with stone tools and extinct arctic animals. Often tall and well-muscled, Cromagnons were specialist hunters (mammoth, reindeer) occupying rock shelters in W Europe and hut campments on the steppe and tundra of C Europe and Russia. They created figurines, fine engravings, and cave art.

Crome, John, known as **Old Crome** (1768–1821) Landscape painter, chief of the Norwich School, born in Norwich, Norfolk, E England, UK. He was apprenticed to a house painter (1783),

Croatia

[krohaysha], official name **Republic of Croatia**, Serbo-Croatian **Republika Hrvatska**

Local name Hrvatska

Timezone GMT +1

Area 56 538 km²/21 824 sq mi

Population total (2002e) 4 405 000

Status Republic

Date of independence 1991

Capital Zagreb

Language Croatian

Ethnic groups (1990) Croat (75%), Serb (12%), Slovenes (1%)

Religions Roman Catholic, Eastern Orthodox

Physical features Fertile Pannonian Plain in C and E; mountainous, barren coastal region near Dinaric Alps; Adriatic coast to W; one third of country is forested; main rivers: Drava, Danube, Sava. Coastal Velebit and Velika Kapela ranges reach heights of 2200 m/7200 ft; islands include Korčula, Lŏsinj, Dugi Otok, Cres, Krk.

Climate Continental in Pannonian Basin: average temperatures 19°C (Jul), -1°C (Jan); average annual rainfall 750 mm/30 in; Mediterranean climate on Adriatic coast: average temperatures 24°C (Jul), 6°C (Jan).

Currency 1 kuna (hrk) = 100 lipa

Economy Agriculture; corn, oats, sugar-beet, potatoes, meat and dairy products; tourism on Adriatic coast. Electrical engineering; metal-working; machinery manufacture; lumber; aluminium, textiles, petroleum refining, chemicals, rubber; natural resources include bauxite, coal, copper, iron; all economic activity adversely affected by war of independence.

GDP (2002e) $43·12 bn, per capita $9800

Human Development Index (2002) 0·809

History Slavic Croat tribes (Chrobati, Hrvati) migrated to White Russia (now Ukraine) during 6th-c; converted to Christianity between 7th and 9th-c and adopted Roman alphabet; Frankish and Byzantine invaders repelled, and Croat kingdom reached its peak during 11th-c; Lázló I of Hungary claimed Croatian throne, 1091; Turkish defeat of Hungary in 1526 placed Pannonian Croatia under Ottoman rule; rest of Croatia elected Ferdinand of Austria as king and fought Turkey; Croatia and Slovenia became part of Hungary until collapse of Austria-Hungary in 1918; formed the Kingdom of Serbs, Croats and Slovenes with Montenegro and Serbia, 1918; Yugoslavia, 1929; proclaimed an independent state during occupation by the Axis Powers, 1941–5; became a republic of Yugoslavia again in 1945; nationalist upsurges during 1950s against Communist rule, culminating in a bloody war with Serbian-dominated Yugoslav army, 1991; declaration of independence, 1991; autonomy claimed by Serb-dominated Krajina area; UN peacekeeping forces deployed, 1992; continued fighting between Croatian forces and Bosnian Serbs in the civil war in Bosnia-Herzegovina; 1995 offensive restored territorial balance in Bosnia; ceasefire followed by peace treaty (Nov) recognized Bosnian-Croat Federation in W Bosnia; governed by an Assembly consisting of a Chamber of Deputies and a Chamber of Districts.

Head of State

1991–9 Franjo Tudjman

1999 Vlatko Pavletic *acting*

2000– Stipe Mesic

Head of Government

1995–2000 Zlatko Matesa

2000–3 Ivaca Racan

2003– Ivo Sanader

then became a drawing master, and founded the Norwich Society of Artists (1803). His subjects derived from the scenery of Norfolk, such as 'Poringland Oak' and 'Mousehold Heath' (Tate, London).

cromlech *megalith*

cromoglycate or **sodium cromoglycate** [krohmohgliysayt] An anti-allergy drug used in the prevention of asthma, also known as **cromolyn** or **Intal**®. It is administered using a special inhaler which dispenses very fine powder into the inspired air. Chromoglycate under various proprietary names is also used in other allergic conditions, such as hay fever and allergic rhinitis.

Crompton, Richmal, pseudonym of **Richmal Samuel Lamburn** (1890–1969) Writer of children's books, born in Bury, Greater Manchester, NW England, UK. She studied at London, and taught Classics at Bromley High School until she contracted poliomyelitis in 1923. She wrote the first of the 'William' books (*Just William*) in 1922, and had written 40 of them before her death.

Crompton, Samuel (1753–1827) Inventor of the spinning-mule, born in Firwood, Greater Manchester, NW England, UK. In 1779 he devised a machine which produced yarn of such astonishing fineness that the house was beset by persons eager to know the secret. He had no funds to obtain a patent, so he was forced to sell his idea to a Bolton manufacturer for very little return. The mule was such a great success that he was awarded a national grant of £5000 in 1812. His later ventures, in bleaching and cotton, were failures.

Cromwell, Oliver (1599–1658) English soldier and statesman, born in Huntingdon, Cambridgeshire, EC England, UK. Educated at Huntingdon and Cambridge, he studied law in London. A convinced Puritan, he sat in both the Short and the Long Parliaments (1640), and when war broke out (1642) fought for the parliament at Edgehill. He formed his unconquerable Ironsides, combining rigid discipline with strict morality, and it was his cavalry that secured the victory at Marston Moor (1644), while under Fairfax he led the New Model Army to decisive success at Naseby (1645). He ruthlessly quelled insurrection in

Wales in support of Charles I, and defeated the invading army of Hamilton. He then brought the king to trial, and was one of the signatories of his death warrant (1649). Having established the Commonwealth, Cromwell suppressed the Levellers, Ireland (1649–50), and routed the Scots (under Charles II) at Dunbar (1650) and Worcester (1651). In Ireland, he was reponsible for widespread and harsh repression, culminating in massacres following the siege of the Drogheda and Wexford garrisons (1649). He then initiated a policy of systematic dispossession of the Irish, transferring their lands to English landlords. He dissolved the Rump of the Long Parliament (1653), and after the failure of his Barebone's Parliament, established a Protectorate (1653). Although in effect a dictator, he refused the offer of the crown in 1657. At home he reorganized the national Protestant Church, and gave Scotland and Ireland parliamentary representation at Westminister. Under him the Commonwealth became, figuratively, the head and champion of Protestant Europe. His wars with the Netherlands (1652–4) and Spain (1655–8) were a strain on the nation's finance. He was succeeded by his son **Richard Cromwell** (1626–1712), who was forced into French exile in 1659.

Cromwell, Thomas, Earl of Essex (c.1485–1540) English statesman, born in London, UK, known as *malleus monachorum*, 'the hammer of the monks'. He served as a soldier on the European mainland (1504–12), then entered Wolsey's service in 1514, and became his agent and secretary. He arranged Henry VIII's divorce from Catherine of Aragon, and put into effect the Act of Supremacy (1534) and the dissolution of the monasteries (1536–9). He became privy councillor (1531), Chancellor of the Exchequer (1533), secretary of state and Master of the Rolls (1534), vicar-general (1535), Lord Privy Seal and Baron Cromwell of Oakham (1536), Knight of the Garter and Dean of Wells (1537), Lord Great Chamberlain (1539), and finally Earl of Essex (1540). In each of his offices, he proved himself a highly efficient administrator and adviser to the king; but Henry's aversion to Anne of Cleves, consort of Cromwell's choosing, led to his ruin. He was sent to the Tower and beheaded.

Cronenberg, David (1943–) Film director and screenplay writer, born in Toronto, Ontario, SE Canada. He studied at the University of Toronto, and went on to become one of the most prolific and acclaimed exponents of the horror film genre to have emerged in recent years. His work is often stylish and experimental, with plots typically concerning the aftermath of some disastrous biological mishap, as in the highly successful *The Dead Zone* (1983) and *The Fly* (1986), which gave him cult status. Other films include *Rabid* (1977), *Scanners* (1981), *Dead Ringers* (1988), the controversial *Crash* (1996), *eXistenZ* (1998), and *Spider* (2002). In 1999 he appeared in the film *Last Night*.

Cronin, A(rchibald) J(oseph) [**kroh**nin] (1896–1981) Novelist, born in Cardross, Argyll and Bute, W Scotland, UK. He studied medicine at Glasgow (1919), but in 1930 took up literature, and at once was successful with *Hatter's Castle* (1931). Subsequent works include *The Citadel* (1937) and *The Keys of the Kingdom* (1942). Several of his books were filmed, and the television series *Dr Finlay's Casebook* was based on his stories.

Cronin, James Watson [**kroh**nin] (1931–) Physicist, born in Chicago, Illinois, USA. He studied at Southern Methodist and Chicago universities, then worked at Brookhaven National Laboratory, NY. He taught at Princeton (1958–71), then became professor at Chicago University. In 1964 with Val Fitch (1923–) he demonstrated the non-conservation of parity and charge conjugation in certain subatomic particle reactions. This surprising result is of fundamental interest in particle physics, and they shared the Nobel Prize for Physics in 1980.

Cronje, Piet [**kron**yay] (1835–1911) Boer general, born in Colesberg, SC South Africa. He was a leader in the Boer Wars (1881, 1899–1900), defeated Methuen at Magersfontein, but surrendered to Lord Roberts at Paardeberg (1900).

Cronkite, Walter (Leland), Jr [**krong**kiyt] (1916–) Journalist and broadcaster, born in St Joseph, Missouri, USA. A student at Texas University (1933–5), he became a radio news and sports reporter in Kansas City. Employed by the United Press (1939–48), he provided vivid eye-witness accounts of the war in Europe. At CBS from 1950, he hosted a number of shows and narrated *You Are There* (1953–6), but became a national institution as the anchorman of the *CBS Evening News* (1962–81), where his studious impartiality and straightforward reporting earned him a reputation for honesty and trust.

Cronus [**kro**nus] or **Kronos** In Greek mythology, the second ruler of the universe, a Titan, the youngest son of Uranus, who rebelled against his father. During his rule people lived in the Golden Age. Because it was foretold that one of his own children would dethrone him, he devoured them all as soon as they were born – with the exception of Zeus, who escaped because of a trick played by his mother, Rhea. Probably a pre-Greek deity, he is incorrectly, but popularly, confused with *chronos* 'time'.

Crookes, Sir William (1832–1919) Chemist and physicist, born in London, UK. He studied at London, then superintended the meteorological department of the Radcliffe Observatory, Oxford, and from 1855 lectured on chemistry at Chester. In 1859 he founded the *Chemical News*, and edited it until 1906. He was an authority on sanitation, discovered the metal thallium (1861), improved vacuum tubes and promoted electric lighting, and invented the radiometer (1873–6). He was knighted in 1897.

crop rotation A system of farming which involves growing crops in sequence. The aim is to control pests and weeds, and to maintain fertility. Modern sprays and chemical fertilizers now make it possible to farm successfully with intermittent or even no rotations, but soil structure may suffer. Most farmers still practise some form of rotation, but it is not usually as rigid as the famous 18th-c Norfolk four-course rotation of roots, barley, clover, wheat, and then back to roots.

croquet [**kroh**kay] A ball-and-mallet game for two to four players, played on a lawn 32 m/35 yd long and 25 m/28 yd wide, on which have been arranged six hoops and a central peg. The four balls are coloured blue, red, black, and yellow. The object is to strike your own ball through the hoops in a prescribed order before finally hitting the central peg.

Crosby, Bing, popular name of **Harry Lillis Crosby** (1904–77) Singer and film star, born in Tacoma, Washington, USA. He began his career while still at school, playing the drums in the evenings, and later became one of the trio known as Paul Whiteman's Rhythm Boys. He began to make films, specializing in light comedy roles, and his distinctive style of crooning made him one of the best-known names in the entertainment world. His recordings of 'White Christmas' and 'Silent Night' were the hits of the 20th-c. He starred in many films, notably the *Road* films with Bob Hope and Dorothy Lamour (1914–96), and he won an Oscar for *Going My Way* (1944). Later films include *The Bells of St Mary's* (1945), *White Christmas* (1954), and *High Society* (1956). A keen golfer, he continued to perform and give concerts until his death on a golf course in Spain.

Crosland, Tony, popular name of **(Charles) Anthony Raven Crosland** (1918–77) British statesman, born in St Leonards, East Sussex, SE England, UK. He studied at Oxford, where he also taught after serving in World War 2. He was elected a Labour MP in 1950 and became secretary for education and science (1965–7), President of the Board of Trade (1967–9), secretary for local government and regional planning (1969–70), environment secretary (1974–6), and foreign secretary (1976–7). A strong supporter of Hugh Gaitskell, he was a key member of the revisionist wing of the Labour Party, and wrote one of its seminal texts, *The Future of Socialism* (1956).

Cross, Amanda *Heilbrun, Carolyn*

cross The main symbol of Christianity, but a widespread religious symbol even in pre-Christian times. For Christians, it signifies the execution of Jesus by crucifixion, an especially demeaning ancient Roman form of capital punishment which was closely associated with the display of corpses or heads of enemies on poles. Many popular variations of the cross-symbol have appeared in Christian worship and art (eg the Jerusalem cross, the St Andrew's cross or Saltire, the Celtic cross).

cross-bencher The name given to a member of the House of Lords who sits as an independent peer rather than accepting a party whip. The name comes from the position in the Lords chamber of the benches upon which this group of peers sit.

crossbill A finch native to the N hemisphere, especially N regions; inhabits coniferous forests. The tips of its bill cross over, an adaptation for extracting seeds from pine cones. (Genus: *Loxia*, 4 species. Family: Fringillidae.)

crossbow A form of bow mounted in a stock, with a crank to wind back and tension the bow itself, and a trigger to discharge the arrow, or 'bolt'. Crossbows were fired more slowly than longbows, but were especially useful in sieges. They were much used in the Crusades and by troops of mercenary expert bowmen. China had crossbows before the 4th-c BC.

cross-country running An athletic running event using a predetermined course over natural terrain. The length of race varies, but world championships are over 12 km/7·5 mi for men and 5 km/3·1 mi for women. The first recorded international race was in May 1898, and covered a 14·5 km/9 mi course at Ville D'Avray near Paris.

Cross Fell Highest peak of the Pennine Chain in Cumbria, NW England, UK; rises to 893 m/2930 ft, 32 km/20 mi SE of Carlisle.

cross-hatching *hatching*

Crossman, Richard (Howard Stafford) (1907–74) British statesman, born in Cropredy, Oxfordshire, SC England, UK. He studied at Oxford, where he became a philosophy tutor, and was leader of the Labour group on Oxford City Council (1934–40). In 1938 he joined the staff of the *New Statesman*. In 1945 he became a Labour MP, and under Wilson was minister of housing and local government (1964–6), then secretary of state for social services and head of the Department of Health (1968–70). He was editor of the *New Statesman* (1970–2). His best-known work is his series of political diaries, begun in 1952, keeping a detailed record of the day-to-day workings of government. They were published in four volumes (1975–81), despite attempts to suppress them.

Crossopterygii [krosopterijeeiy] A subclass of bony fishes comprising the tassel-finned (or lobe-finned) fishes, having an extensive fossil record from the Devonian to Cretaceous periods. The only living representative is the coelacanth, *Latimeria*.

cross-section In the scattering experiments of atomic, nuclear, and particle physics, the area presented by a target to an oncoming beam of particles. Its value depends on the particle energy and the type of interaction; symbol σ; units m^2; sometimes expressed in barns, 1 barn = $10^{-28} m^2$.

croup [kroop] A hollow crowing noise during respiration and on coughing. It occurs in children due to swelling and narrowing of the vocal cords due to infection with one of several viruses. It may arise following a cold. In severe cases, respiration may be compromised.

Crow North American Sioux-speaking Plains Indians. They separated from the Hidatsa in the 18th-c, and lived between the Missouri and Yellowstone Rivers, becoming nomadic buffalo hunters on horseback, and traders. They allied with whites in the Indian wars of the 1860s and 1870s; and in 1868 were settled on reservations in Montana, where most Crow still live.

crow A bird of the worldwide family Corvidae. It can be a common name for the whole family, or just for the 40 species of the genus *Corvus* (other genera being jays, magpies, choughs, nutcrackers, and the piapiac), or just for some species of *Corvus* (others being ravens, rooks, and jackdaws). The name is also sometimes misapplied to birds not belonging to Corvidae.

crowberry A spreading, evergreen, heather-like shrub (*Empetrum nigrum*), native to arctic and N temperate moors; leaves 4–6 mm/⅛–¼ in; alternate, separate male and female flowers, three sepals, three petals; berry 5 mm/0·2 in diameter, black. (Family: Empetraceae.)

Crowe, Russell (1964–) Actor, born in New Zealand. At age four he settled with his parents in Sydney, Australia. He entered the pop music scene as singer/musician Russ Le Roc (1980), and in 1985 made his acting debut on the Australian television soap *Neighbours*. His early film credits include *Proof* (1992) and *Romper Stomper* (1993, Australian Film Institute Best Actor), and in 1995 he made his US debut in *The Quick and the Dead*. Later films include *The Insider* (1999, Oscar nomination), *Gladiator* (2000, best actor Oscar), *A Beautiful Mind* (2001, Golden Globe best actor; BAFTA best actor), and *Master and Commander* (2003).

Crowley, Aleister, originally **Edward Alexander Crowley** (1875–1947) British writer and 'magician', born in Leamington Spa, Warwickshire, C England. He became interested in the occult while an undergraduate at Cambridge, and was initiated into the occult society of the Golden Dawn (1898). He travelled widely, settling for some years in Sicily with a group of disciples at the Abbey of Thelema, near Cefalù. Rumours of drugs, orgies, and magical ceremonies led to his expulsion from Italy. Back in England, he co-founded the order of the Silver Star (1906) based on the mystical Law of Thelema that he developed. He liked to be known as 'the great beast' and 'the wickedest man alive' – and certainly many who associated with him died tragically.

Crown In the UK and many former colonial countries, an alternative legal definition to that of the state, representing the organs of government, and reflecting the former power of the monarchy. It is now a legal fiction, in that such powers are largely exercised by the government of the day, though they are carried out in the name of the Crown.

Crown Agents (for Overseas Governments and Administrations) A UK agency which provides professional, financial, and commercial services to governments and other public authorities in developing countries and to international agencies. It also acts on behalf of the World Bank.

Crown Colony *colony*

Crown Court A court in England and Wales, established by the Courts Act (1971), which abolished the Assizes and Quarter Sessions. Crown Courts have unlimited power to deal with indictable offences, and also hear most appeals from magistrates' courts. In addition to the criminal jurisdiction, a High Court judge may hear civil cases in this court. When sitting in London, it is known as the Central Criminal Court.

Crown Estate Property belonging by heredity to the British sovereign, comprising over 120 000 ha/300 000 acres in England, Scotland, and Wales. Over half of Britain's foreshore is included, together with the sea bed within territorial waters. Revenue from the Crown Estate is made over to the government at the beginning of each reign.

crown jewels Regalia and jewellery belonging to a sovereign. The English crown jewels have been displayed at various sites in the Tower of London for 300 years, since 1967 in the Jewel House. After the abolition of the monarchy in 1649, much of the regalia was sold or broken up, with the exception of the gold anointing spoon (12th-c) and eagle-headed ampulla (14th-c). Most of the crown jewels date from the Restoration (1660). They include St Edward's Crown, used in most coronations since that of Charles II; the Imperial State Crown; the gold spurs made for Charles II's coronation; the armills (gold-enamelled bracelets); the King's Orb; the King's Sceptre with the Cross (since 1909 containing the Star of Africa, the largest cut diamond in the world at 530 carats); the King's Sceptre with the Dove; the jewelled Sword of State and four other ceremonial swords; the Imperial Crown of India; and Queen Elizabeth the Queen Mother's crown, which is set with the Koh-i-Noor (Persian 'mountain of light') diamond. The Scottish crown jewels (or 'Honours of Scotland') are located in Edinburgh Castle.

crown of thorns A large starfish up to 60 cm/2 ft in diameter, with 9–23 arms; body and arms with long spikes on upper surface; found in shallow waters on coral reef areas in tropical Indo-West Pacific; feeds on live coral polyps; when abundant, can cause massive damage to reefs. (Phylum: Echinodermata. Subclass: Asteroidea.)

Crown Proceedings Act A UK act (1947) which permits ordinary civil actions against the Crown. It had been possible before this date for someone to take certain proceedings against the Crown by personal petition (*petition of right*), as in breach of contract cases. The significance of the 1947 Act is that it permitted action in tort (delict, in Scotland) in respect of conduct by Crown servants. The Crown had enjoyed a special status by virtue of the doctrine that the monarch could do no wrong. The extension of the activities of the state in the 20th-c necessitated a revision of this immunity. *Crown Privilege*, now known as *public interest immunity*, which is the right of the Crown to withhold documents on certain grounds (such as national security), is still claimed in some cases. However, the monarch remains personally immune from civil or criminal liability. The analogous act in the USA is the Federal Tort Claims Act (1946).

Crown Prosecution Service In England and Wales, a body of lawyers responsible for assessing the evidence collected by the police, and for deciding whether to prosecute an individual or a corporate body and what the particular charge should be. Established in 1985, it is independent of the police, and is headed by the Director of Public Prosecutions. Although certain other bodies or individuals may initiate a prosecution, the Crown Prosecution Service is responsible for the majority of cases prosecuted in the criminal courts of England and Wales. It is organized on a regional basis, and each region has its own Chief Crown Prosecutor.

crucifixion A common form of capital punishment in the Roman world, in which a person was nailed or bound to a wooden cross by the wrists and feet, and left to die. The method, probably borrowed from the Carthaginians, was inflicted only upon slaves and people of low social status (*humiliores*). It was regularly preceded by flagellation, as happened in the case of Christ himself.

Cruden, Alexander [**kroo**den] (1701–70) Scholar and bookseller, born in Aberdeen, NE Scotland, UK. He worked as a tutor, then started as a bookseller in London. In 1737 appeared his *Concordance of the Holy Scriptures*. He suffered from bouts of insanity and, assuming the title of 'Alexander the Corrector', from 1755 went through the country reproving Sabbath-breaking and profanity.

Cruelty, Theatre of A notion developed during 1931–6 by French poet, actor, and theorist Antoine Artaud to describe his vision of a metaphysical theatre in which both actors and audience could experience, without any avoidance or illusion, existential realities. Using gesture, movement, sound, and rhythm, rather than words, he aimed to release the audience's inhibitions.

Cruft, Charles (1852–1939) British showman who organized the first dog show in London, UK in 1886. He was for many years general manager of James Spratt. The annual shows have since become world-famous, and have helped to improve standards of dog-breeding.

Cruikshank, George [**krook**shangk] (1792–1878) Caricaturist and illustrator, born in London, UK. He often contributed to topical magazines, and illustrated several children's books. His best-known work includes Grimm's *German Popular Stories* (1824–6) and Dickens's *Oliver Twist* (1837–9). In his later years he used his etchings and oil paintings in a vigorous protest against drunkenness, as in the series for 'The Bottle' (1847).

Cruise, Tom [krooz] (1962–) Film actor, born in Syracuse, New York, USA. After an itinerant childhood, his plans for a professional wrestling career were abandoned through injury. He tried his hand at acting, struggling through night classes and auditions, and went on to make many successful films including *Top Gun* (1985), *Rain Man* (1988), *Days of Thunder* (1990), *A Few Good Men* (1992), *The Firm* (1993), and *Interview with the Vampire* (1995). He received Golden Globe Awards and Oscar nominations for best actor for both *Born on the Fourth of July* (1989) and *Jerry Maguire* (1996). In 1999 he co-starred with his wife, Nicole Kidman (divorced, 2001), in *Eyes Wide Shut*. Later films include *Mission Impossible 2* (2000), *Vanilla Sky* (2001), *Minority Report* (2002), and *The Last Samurai* (2003).

cruise missile A type of missile which flies continuously on wings, and is propelled continuously by an engine using air from the atmosphere as its oxidant to mix with the fuel it carries. The German V-1 of 1944 was a cruise missile, but the weapon came to prominence again 30 years later when it was revived by US weapon scientists to provide a comparatively cheap means of delivering a nuclear or conventional warhead over a long distance, using onboard computer power to provide pinpoint accuracy. The US armed forces have deployed a range of cruise missile systems including *ground-launched* (GLCMs), *sea-launched* (SLCMs, capable of being launched from small warships and submarines), and *air-launched* weapons (ALCMs).

cruiser A medium-sized warship designed to protect trade routes and to act as a scout for a battle fleet. Size, speed, and armament varied enormously with the passing years, depending upon the strength of enemy cruisers.

crumhorn A musical instrument made from wood with a small cylindrical bore, and curved at the end like a hockey stick. It had a double reed and a wind-cap (so that the player's lips did not touch the reed), and was made in various sizes. There were seven fingerholes and a thumbhole, and the larger instruments had metal keys. It was widely used in Europe in the 16th–17th-c, and revived in the 20th-c for performing early music.

Crusades Holy Wars authorized by the Pope in defence of Christendom and the Church. They were fought against the Muslims in the East, Germany, and Spain, against heretics and schismatics who threatened Catholic unity, and against Christian lay powers who opposed the papacy. Crusaders committed themselves with solemn vows, and by the 13th-c were granted the full Indulgence, ie remission of all punishment due for sin and an assurance of direct entry into heaven. Papal authorizations of war against Islam continued to be made until the 18th-c. There were eight numbered crusades: First (1096–9), Second (1147–8), Third (1189–92), Fourth (1202–4), Fifth (1217–21), Sixth (1228–9), Seventh (1248–54), Eighth (1270-2). The Crusaders captured Jerusalem in 1099 and massacred its inhabitants, establishing a kingdom there under Godfrey of Bouillon (c.1061–1100). The fall of Acre in 1291 ended the Crusader presence in the Levant. In the long term the Crusades deepened the hostility between Christianity and Islam, but they also stimulated economic and cultural contacts of lasting benefit to European civilization, for example in astronomy, architecture, literature, music, and mathematics. (*see also pp.406–7*)

crustacean [kruh**stay**shn] A typically aquatic arthropod possessing a pair of jaws (*mandibles*) and two pairs of antennae situated in front of the mouth in adults; group contains c.40 000 species, mostly marine, but also in freshwater and terrestrial habitats; great diversity of forms; life-cycle commonly involves a larval stage with three pairs of limbs (the *nauplius*). (Subphylum: Crustacea.)

Crutzen, Paul (1933–) Chemist, born in Amsterdam, The Netherlands. He studied at Stockholm University, then joined the Max Planck Institute for Chemistry in Mainz, Germany. In 1970 he was among the first to draw attention to the vulnerability of the ozone layer, and demonstrated that the presence of nitrogen oxides increase the rate of ozone's decomposition. He shared the 1995 Nobel Prize for Chemistry with Mario Molina (1943–) and Sherwood Rowland (1927–).

Crux (Lat 'cross') The smallest constellation in the sky, and one of the most distinctive, better known as **the Southern Cross**. It features on the national flags of Australia and New Zealand. Originally part of Centaurus, it received a separate identity in the 16th-c.

Cruyff, Johann [kriyf] (1947–) Footballer, born in Amsterdam, The Netherlands. He joined his first club, Ajax, at the age of 10, and at 19 made his debut in the Dutch League. He won 11 Dutch League and Cup medals with Ajax, and helped them to three consecutive European Cup successes (1971–3). In 1973 he joined

The Main Crusades To The East

	Background	Leader(s)	Outcome
First Crusade (1096–9)	Proclaimed by Urban II to aid the Greeks against the Seljuk Turks in Asia Minor, liberate Jerusalem and the Holy Land from Seljuk domination, and safeguard pilgrim routes to the Holy Sepulchre.	Bohemond I Godfrey of Bouillon Raymond, Count of Flanders Robert Curthose, Duke of Normandy Stephen, Count of Blois	Capture of Nicaea in Anatolia (Jun 1097); Turks vanquished at Battle of Dorylaeum (Jul 1097); capture of Antioch in Syria (Jun 1098), Jerusalem (Jul 1099). Godfrey of Bouillon became ruler of the new Latin Kingdom of Jerusalem, and defeated the Fatimids of Egypt near Ascalon in Palestine (Aug 1099). Three other crusader states were founded: Antioch, Edessa, Tripoli.
Second Crusade (1147–8)	Proclaimed by Eugenius III to aid the crusader states after the Muslim reconquest of Edessa (1144).	Conrad III of Germany Louis VII of France	German army heavily defeated by Turks near Dorylaeum (Oct 1147), and the French at Laodicea (Jan 1148); Damascus in Syria invested, but siege abandoned after four days (Jul 1148). The crusaders' military reputation was destroyed, and the Syrian Muslims united against the Latins.
Third Crusade (1189–92)	Proclaimed by Gregory VIII after Saladin's defeat of the Latins at the Battle of Hattin (Jul 1187) and his conquest of Jerusalem (Oct 1187). (By 1189 all that remained of the Kingdom of Jerusalem was the port of Tyre).	Frederick Barbarossa Philip II Augustus of France Richard I of England	Cyprus conquered from Greeks (May 1191), and established as new crusader kindgom (survived until 1489); capture of Acre in Palestine (Jul 1191); Saladin defeated near Arsuf (Sept 1191); three-year truce guaranteeing safe-conduct of Christian pilgrims to Jerusalem. Most cities and castles of the Holy Land remained in Muslim hands.
Fourth Crusade (1202–4)	Proclaimed by Innocent III to recover the Holy Places.	Boniface of Montferrat	Despite papal objections, crusade diverted from Egypt or Palestine (1) to Zara, a Christian town in Dalmatia, conquered for Venetians (Nov 1202); (2) to Byzantium, where embroilment in dynastic struggles led to sack of Constantinople (Apr 1204) and foundation of Latin Empire of Constantinople (survived until 1261). The crusading movement was discredited; the Latins in Palestine and Syria were hardly helped at all; the Byzantine empire never fully recovered; and the opportunity was lost of a united front between the Latins and Greeks against the Muslims.

Barcelona (Spain) and won Spanish League and Cup medals with them. He captained Holland in the 1974 World Cup final (beaten by West Germany). He returned to Holland as a player in 1983, joining Feyenoord in 1984, but moved back to Barcelona as manager (1988–96), guiding the Spanish champions to the European Cup for the first time in 1992. His son, Jordi (1974–), joined Manchester United Football Club (1996–2000).

Cruz, Penélope (1974–) Actress, born in Madrid, Spain. She trained in classical ballet at the National Conservatory in Madrid, and also studied jazz dancing. She turned to acting, and her work for the Spanish cinema includes *Belle Epoque* (1993) and *All About My Mother* (1999), both of which won Best Foreign Film Oscars. In the USA her films include *The Hi-Lo Country* (1998), *All the Pretty Horses* (2000), *Blow* (2001), and *Captain Corelli's Mandolin* (2001).

crwth [krooth] A Celtic (especially Welsh) lyre, played with a bow or plucked. The earliest types, known from the 12th-c onwards, had three strings, but by the 18th-c, when it became obsolete, the crwth had acquired a further three, tuned in unison with the others or at the octave.

cryogenics The study of physical systems at temperatures less than c.90 K (−183°C). Many processes are more easily understood and measured at low temperatures, where unwanted

	Background	Leader(s)	Outcome
Fifth Crusade (1217–21)	Proclaimed by Innocent III when a six-year truce between the Kingdom of Jerusalem and Egypt expired.	Andrew II of Hungary John of Brienne, King of Jerusalem Leopold, Duke of Austria	Three indecisive expeditions against Muslims in Palestine (1217); capture of Damietta in Egypt after protracted siege (May 1218–Nov 1219); further conquests attempted, but crusaders forced to relinquish Damietta (Aug 1221) and withdraw.
Sixth Crusade (1228–9)	Emperor Frederick II, who first took the Cross in 1215, married the heiress to the Kingdom of Jerusalem in 1225. Excommunicated by Gregory IX for delaying his departure, he finally arrived at Acre in Sept 1228.	Frederick II	Negotiations with Egyptians secured Jerusalem and other places, including Bethlehem and Nazareth (Feb 1229); Frederick crowned King of Jerusalem in church of Holy Sepulchre (Mar 1229). Jerusalem was held until recaptured by the Khorezmian Turks in 1244.
Seventh Crusade (1248–54)	Proclaimed by Innocent IV after the fall of Jerusalem and defeat of the Latin army near Gaza by the Egyptians and Khorezmians (1244).	Louis IX of France	Capture of Damietta (June 1249); defeat at Mansurah (Feb 1250); surrender of crusaders during attempted withdrawal; Damietta relinquished and large ransoms paid (May 1250). Louis spent four years in Palestine, refortifying Acre, Caesarea, Joppa and Sidon, and fruitlessly attempting to regain Jerusalem by alliances with the Mameluks and Mongols.
Eighth Crusade (1270–2)	Proclaimed after the Mameluk conquest of Arsuf, Caesarea, Haifa (1265), Antioch and Joppa (1268).	Charles of Anjou, King of Naples-Sicily Edward of England (later Edward I) Louis IX of France	Attacked Tunisia in N Africa (Jul 1270); Louis died in Aug; Charles concluded treaty with Tunis and withdrew; Edward negotiated 11-years truce with Mameluks in Palestine. By 1291 the Latins had been driven from the Holy Land.

thermal effects are reduced. Some processes can be observed only at low temperatures, either because of masking by thermal effects or because the phenomena (eg superconductivity, superfluidity) exist only at low temperature.

cryolite [kriyoliyt] A mineral composed of sodium, aluminium, and fluorine (Na_3AlF_6), used in the smelting of aluminium ores. It occurs in important quantities in Russia and Greenland.

cryoscopic [kriyoskopik] In chemistry, to do with melting point; especially the determination of molecular weight of a solute by the depression of the freezing point of a solvent.

crypt Part of a building below the main floor and usually underground. In particular, it refers to the part of a church containing graves and relics.

cryptanalysis The deciphering or codebreaking of messages intended for others. The use of codes and ciphers to protect sensitive information from falling into the hands of enemies or rivals creates a reciprocal demand for cryptanalysis. This involves firstly intercepting a message, then analyzing it to reveal its contents. Since languages can be distinguished by the different frequencies with which the letters of the alphabet occur, the prime task is to search for such enciphered patterns. The use of computers has greatly facilitated this process, but

Cuba

□ International Airport

official name **Republic of Cuba**, Span **República de Cuba**

Local name Cuba

Timezone GMT −5

Area 110 860 km²/42 792 sq mi

Population total (2002e) 11 267 000

Status Republic

Date of independence 1902

Capital Havana

Language Spanish (official)

Ethnic groups Mulatto (50%), Spanish (37%), African origin (11%)

Religions Roman Catholic (40%), Protestant (3%), Afro-Cuban syncretist (2%), non-religious (55%): Castro regime discourages religious practice

Physical features Archipelago in the Caribbean Sea, comprising the island of Cuba, Isla de la Juventud, and c.1600 islets and cays; main island of Cuba, 1250 km/777 mi; three mountainous regions range E–W, the Oriental, including Cuba's highest peak, Pico Turquino, 2005 m/6578 ft, Central, and Occidental ranges; longest river is Rio Cauto in E.

Climate Subtropical climate, warm and humid; average annual temperature 25°C; dry season (Nov–Apr); mean annual rainfall, 1375 mm/54 in; hurricanes (Jun–Nov).

Currency 1 Cuban Peso (Cub$) = 100 centavos

Economy World's second largest sugar producer (accounting for 75% of export earnings); world's fifth largest producer of nickel; fish, coffee, tobacco, citrus fruits, rice.

GNP (2002e) $30·69 bn, per capita $2700

Human Development Index (2002) 0·795

History Visited by Columbus, 1492; Spanish colony until 1898, following revolution under José Martí with support of USA; independence, 1902; struggle against dictatorship of General Batista led by Fidel Castro Ruz finally successful in 1959, and a Communist state was established; invasion of Cuban exiles with US support defeated at Bay of Pigs, 1961; US naval blockade, after Soviet installation of missile bases discovered in Cuba (Cuban Missile Crisis), 1962. Communist Party of Cuba established as the sole legal party, 1965; President of the State Council is Head of State; State Council, appointed by National Assembly of People's Power.

Head of State/Government
1902–6 Tomas Estrada Palma
1906–9 *US rule*
1909–13 José Miguel Gómez
1913–21 Mario García Menocal
1921–5 Alfredo Zayas y Alfonso
1925–33 Gerardo Machado y Morales
1933 Carlos Manuel de Céspedes
1933–4 Ramón Grau San Martín
1934–5 Carlos Mendieta
1935–6 José A Barnet y Vinagres
1936 Miguel Mariano Gómez y Arias
1936–40 Federico Laredo Bru
1940–4 Fulgencio Batista
1944–8 Ramón Grau San Martín
1948–52 Carlos Prío Socarrás
1952–9 Fulgencio Batista
1959 Manuel Urrutia
1956–76 Osvaldo Dorticós Torrado
1976 Fidel Castro Ruz *Prime Minister and First Secretary*
1976– Fidel Castro Ruz *President*

even they have major problems with the more arbitrary nature of highly sophisticated modern codes.

cryptography The alteration of the form of a message by codes and ciphers to conceal its meaning. Codewords, normally from a code book, stand for one or more words of the *plaintext* (the original message). With ciphers, the letters of the plaintext are individually substituted or transposed (re-ordered), according to a secret key.

cryptomeria *Japanese cedar*

cryptomonad *cryptophyte*

cryptophyte [kriptofiyt] A single-celled alga with two ribbon-like flagella located in a front oral groove; typically with various pigments (*phycobilins*) in addition to chlorophylls *a* and *c*; also called **cryptomonad**. (Class: Cryptophyceae.)

Crystal, Billy (1947–) Film actor, born in Long Beach, New York, USA. A successful stand-up comic, he played television's first openly gay character in the comedy series *Soap*, before becoming established as a feature film actor in films such as *Throw Momma From The Train* (1987), and *When Harry Met Sally* (1989). Later films include *City Slickers* and its sequel (1991, 1994), *Forget Paris* (1995), which he also directed, *Fathers' Day* (1997), *Analyze This* (1999), and *America's Sweethearts* (2001).

Crystal 1 A computer package for the development of expert systems. 2 An inexpert package for the development of encyclopedias (see title page).

crystal defects Irregularities in otherwise perfectly regular crystals. Some, such as cracks and dislocations, strongly influence crystal mechanical properties, typically causing weakness. Others, such as impurities, affect electrical properties (eg the semiconductor crystals used in electronics) or give colour to crystals (eg chromium in red ruby).

crystal growth The formation of crystals when a saturated solution of a suitable substance is either cooled or some solvent removed by evaporation. The growth usually starts on small introduced 'seed' crystals. The shape of the final crystals reflects the underlying crystal structure of the substance.

crystallography The study of crystals, both of their external form and of their internal structure. The symmetries shown by natural crystals strongly suggested an atomic theory to Nicolaus Steno in the 17th-c, and the application of the diffraction of X-rays by crystals acting as optical gratings has given a great deal of information about the arrangements and bonding of atoms in crystals, and, by analogy, in other environments.

Crystal Palace An iron-framed, prefabricated, glass building designed by Sir Joseph Paxton to house the Great Exhibition of 1851. The structure, dubbed the 'Crystal Palace' by *Punch* magazine, was erected in London's Hyde Park. It was re-erected in S London, but destroyed by fire in 1936.

crystals True solids, made up of regularly repeating groups of atoms, ions, or molecules. In contrast with liquids and other amorphous materials, the properties of crystals vary with the direction in which they are measured. A complete crystal structure is defined by giving both a lattice of points, of which only 14 types are possible, and the group of atoms associated with each lattice point.

crystal therapy In alternative medicine, a technique which uses precious and semi-precious stones, credited with particular astrological, esoteric, and physical properties. Each stone has a particular vibration pattern which some believe can act upon the body's energy field to increase the available energy and also to correct any imbalance or blockages. Crystals have been used to transmit healing energy from a healer or other external energy source to a patient, and treatment can be given by placing the relevant crystal on a specific part of the body such as an associated chakra or acupuncture point. Particular crystals are credited with special healing properties (eg amethyst is said to ease pain and encourage sleep, and haematite to purify and detoxify the blood). There are no references in orthodox medical literature to any of these beneficial effects.

CS gas US military designation for a chlorinated compound, 1-*o*-chlorophenyl-2,2-dicyanoethylene, $Cl{-}C_6H_4{-}CH{=}C(C{\equiv}N)_2$. It causes irritation and watering of the eyes, and has been widely used in riot control.

ctenophore [tenofaw(r)] A marine animal with a transparent, jelly-like (gelatinous) body, which swims using eight comb-like rows of plates (**ctenes**); carnivorous, using paired tentacles armed with stinging cells to catch prey; c.80 species, found mostly in open sea; known as **comb jellies** or **sea gooseberries**. (Phylum: Ctenophora.)

CT scanning *computerized tomography*

Cuauhtémoc [kwowtaymok] (c.1495–1525) The last Aztec ruler, successor to Montezuma, who resisted the Spaniards under Cortés at the siege of Tenochitilán (now Mexico City) in 1521. He was later executed while on an expedition with Cortés to Honduras.

Cuba *p.408*

Cuban Missile Crisis A period of acute international tension and potential military confrontation between the USA and USSR in October 1962, following the USA's discovery of Soviet nuclear missile sites in Cuba. The crisis pushed the world to the brink of a nuclear war. Amazingly, Soviet leader Khrushchev assumed that the USA would take no action, but President Kennedy demanded the dismantling of the base and the return of the missiles, and threw a naval blockade around the island. The crisis ended on 28 October, when Khrushchev agreed to Kennedy's demands. Kennedy also secretly promised to withdraw US missiles that had recently been stationed in Turkey, a NATO country. An outcome of the crisis was the establishment of a direct, exclusive line of communication (the 'hot line'), to be used in an emergency, between the president of the USA and the leader of the Soviet Union.

Cubism A modern art movement out of which grew most of the early forms of abstraction. About 1907 Picasso and Braque rejected Renaissance perspective and Impressionist attention to light and atmosphere. Objects, painted in sombre shades of brown and grey, were analysed into geometrical planes with several views depicted simultaneously (**analytic cubism**). After c.1912 a flatter, more colourful and decorative hard-edged style emerged (**synthetic cubism**), using collage and painted relief constructs.

Cubitt, Thomas (1788–1855) Builder, born in Buxton, Norfolk, E England, UK. He revolutionized trade practices in the building industry, working with his brother **Lewis Cubitt** (1799–1883) until 1831. They worked together on the development of Belgravia, London; later, Thomas's buildings included Osborne House and the E front of Buckingham Palace; Lewis's best-known building is Kings Cross Station.

Cuchulain [kuhoolin] Ir **Cu Chulainn** The hero of many Irish legends, the chief warrior of Ulster, who obtained his name (meaning 'the hound of Culaan') after killing a huge dog. He took its place in guarding the property of its owner.

cuckoo A bird of the worldwide family Culculidae (130 species), mostly inhabiting woodland; some (eg roadrunners) inhabit desert. About 50 species do not build nests, but lay eggs in the nests of other birds, with the young reared by 'foster' parents. The name is sometimes misapplied to birds not belonging to this family.

cuckoo flower An erect perennial (*Cardamine pratensis*), 15–60 cm/6–24 in, native to temperate N hemisphere; rosette leaves pinnate with oval leaflets, stem leaves with narrower leaflets, flowers cross-shaped lilac, sometimes white; also called **lady's smock**. (Family: Cruciferae.)

cuckoo-pint *lords-and-ladies*

cuckoo-roller *roller*

cuckoo shrike A bird native to the Old World, especially the tropics; also known as the **caterpillar bird**; dull, greyish plumage; inhabits trees; eats insects and some fruit. It is neither a true cuckoo nor a shrike. (Family. Campephagidae, 70 species.)

cuckoo-spit insect *froghopper*

cucumber A vine (*Cucumis sativa*), trailing or climbing by means of tendrils, probably native to Africa but cultivated from early times as a salad vegetable; leaves heart-shaped, palmately lobed; male and female flowers 2·5 cm/1 in diameter, yellow, funnel-shaped; fruit up to 45 cm/18 in or more, green, fleshy, cylindrical or oval. (Family: Cucurbitaceae.)

Cúcuta [kookoota] 7°55N 72°31W, pop (2000e) 441 300. Capital of Norte de Santander department, NE Colombia; 16 km/10 mi from Venezuelan frontier; within a Tax Free Zone; founded, 1734; destroyed by earthquake, 1875, then rebuilt; gateway to Venezuela, and a focal point in Colombia's fight for independence; airfield; university (1962); coffee, tobacco, cattle trade.

Cudworth, Ralph (1617–88) Philosopher and theologian, born in Aller, Somerset, SW England, UK. He studied at Cambridge, where he became a tutor, and leader of the 'Cambridge Platonists'. He was professor of Hebrew (1645), rector of North Cadbury, Somerset (1650), and Master of Christ's College (1654). His best-known work, *The True Intellectual System of the Universe* (1678), aimed to establish the reality of a supreme divine intelligence against materialism.

Cuenca [kwenka] 2°54S 79°00W, pop (2000e) 234 400. Capital of Azuay province, SC Ecuador; founded by Spanish, 1557; airfield; railway; two universities (1868, 1970); tobacco, dairy products, meat packing, fruit canning, textiles, leatherworks, motor vehicles, agricultural machinery, chemicals; La Concepción convent (1599), now religious art museum; old and new cathedrals, modern art museum, Instituto Azuayo de Folklore, Pumapungo archaeological museum, sulphur baths nearby; Carnival (pre-Lent), New Year and Easter festivals.

Cukor, George D(ewey) [kooker] (1899–1983) Film director, born in New York City, USA. He worked first on Broadway, but went to Hollywood in 1929, starting a career of 50 years directing with *Girls About Town* (1931) and *Little Women* (1933). He was particularly successful with the great actresses of the star system – Garbo, Crawford, Hepburn – but his range was wide, including *Gaslight* (1944), *A Star is Born* (1954), and *My Fair Lady* (1964, Oscar). His last film was *Rich and Famous* (1981).

cu lan *loris*

Culicidae [kyoolisidee] A family containing c.3000 species of true flies, including mosquitoes and gnats. Many species are of primary medical and veterinary importance as carriers of diseases such as malaria, yellow fever, dengue, and elephantiasis. (Order: Diptera.)

Cullinan diamond [kuhlinan] The largest gem diamond ever found, weight 3255 carats (650 grams/22·9 avoirdupois ounces). It was found in Premier Diamond Mine, Transvaal in 1905 and named after Sir Thomas Cullinan, who had discovered the mine. It was cut into 9 large and 96 small stones, the largest of which (the Star of Africa) is in the Royal Sceptre of the British Crown Jewels.

Culloden Moor, Battle of [kuhlodn] (1746) A battle fought near Inverness, the last major battle on British soil, which marked the end of the Jacobite rebellion of 1745 led by Charles Edward Stuart. His force, mainly of Scottish highlanders, was crushed by a superior force of English and lowland Scots under the Duke of Cumberland.

Culpeper, Nicholas (1616–54) Astrologer and physician, born in London, UK. He studied at Cambridge, and in 1640 began to practise astrology and medicine in Spitalfields. In 1649 he published an English translation of the College of Physicians' Pharmacopoeia, *A Physical Directory*, for which he was virulently lampooned, and in 1653 appeared *The English Physician Enlarged, or the Herbal*. Both books had an enormous sale.

Culpeper's Rebellion (1677–80) An attempt by settlers in North Carolina to establish a government in opposition to 'proprietors' who claimed control of the province on effectively feudal terms. It was named for John Culpeper, the settlers' chief spokesman, who was subsequently acquitted on a charge of treason, and who died, as he was born, in obscurity.

cult Any set of beliefs and practices associated with a particular god or group of gods, forming a distinctive part of a larger religious body. The focus of the worship or devotion of a cult is usually a god or gods, spirit or spirits, associated with particular objects and places. The focus of devotion may be an animal (eg the whale cult in Eskimo religions), a particular deity (eg the Hindu cult devoted to Shiva), or even a deified human being (eg the emperor cult in ancient Rome).

cultivar A contraction of **cultivated variety**; in names further abbreviated to **cv**. It refers to any distinct type of plant produced in cultivation but not growing in the wild. Many cultivars do not breed true, and are propagated vegetatively.

cultivator An agricultural implement carrying rows of prongs (*tines*); some versions carry blades. It is used for breaking up soil and creating a seed-bed before planting, and is also used in the control of weeds.

cultural anthropology *anthropology*

cultural evolution (anthropology) A theory popular among Victorian anthropologists that human cultures could be ranked on an evolutionary scale, and even that every community was fated to pass through a fixed series of stages of cultural evolution. This view is now discredited, but the term is still used to describe the cultural adaptation of a particular community to its human and natural environment.

cultural history An approach to the study of history, dating from the work of Hegel, who argued that all epochs are characterized by a certain 'spirit', culture, or *Zeitgeist*. The most notable practitioner of this brand of history was Burckhardt, who was influenced by Hegelian historical thought and whose influential book *Die Kultur der Renaissance in Italien* (The Civilization of the Renaissance in Italy) appeared in 1860. In later generations the Burckhardt approach fragmented into the more limited fields of the history of art, intellectual history, and the history of science; but more recently there has been a return to cultural history, including the history of popular culture.

cultural pluralism *pluralism* (politics)

Cultural Revolution An abbreviation for the Great Proletarian Cultural Revolution, a radical Maoist mass movement initiated as a rectification campaign in 1966, which ended only with the death of Mao Zedong and the arrest of the Gang of Four in the autumn of 1976. To prevent the Chinese revolution from stagnating and to avoid 'revisionism', Mao aimed at replacing the old guard, including Liu Shaoqi (died in prison in 1969), Peng Zhen, and Deng Xiaoping (both disgraced in 1966), with a new generation of fervent revolutionaries. He appealed directly to the masses, in particular to young students, the Red Guards, who with the support of the People's Liberation Army overthrew not only party leaders but all so-called 'bourgeois reactionaries' and 'capitalist-roaders' in authority in schools, universities, factories, and the administration. The '10 lost years' of social and political turmoil saw the closure of schools and universities, factories at a standstill, tens of thousands of deaths, and millions of people sent to undertake manual labour in the countryside as re-education. The Cultural Revolution was however important in promoting archaeological investigation throughout China.

culture (anthropology) The way of life of a group of people, consisting of learned patterns of behaviour and thought passed on from one generation to the next. The notion includes the group's beliefs, values, language, political organization, and economic activity, as well as its equipment, techniques, and art forms (referred to as **material culture**).

culture (microbiology) An artifically maintained population of micro-organisms, or of dissociated cells of a tissue, grown in a nutrient medium and reproducing by asexual division. The process is used in experimental microbiological research and also in medical applications, chiefly as part of the task of diagnosis.

Cumae [kyoomee] The oldest Greek colony in Italy, founded c.750 BC near present-day Naples. It was famous in Roman times as the home of the oracular prophetess, the Sibyl.

Cumberland A former county of NW England, UK; part of Cumbria since 1974.

Cumberland, William Augustus, Duke of (1721–65) British general, born in London, UK, the second son of George II. He adopted a military career and, in the War of the Austrian Succession (1740–8), was wounded at Dettingen (1743) and defeated at Fontenoy (1745). He crushed the Young Pretender's rebellion at Culloden (1746), and by his harsh policies afterwards earned the lasting title of 'Butcher'. In the Seven Years' War (1756–63), he surrendered to the French (1757), and thereafter retired.

Cumberland Gap Pass through the Allegheny Mts, E USA; altitude 500 m/1640 ft; European discovery, 1750; named after the Duke of Cumberland (son of George II); major migration route to the West in the 18th-c; strategic point during the American Civil War; Cumberland Gap National Historical Park (1955), area 83 sq km/32 sq mi.

Cumbria pop (2001e) 487 600; area 6810 sq km/2629 sq mi. County in NW England, UK; bounded W by the Irish Sea, NW by the Solway Firth, N by Scotland; Pennines in the E; 40% of the county within the Lake District and Yorkshire Dales national parks; created in 1974 from the former counties of Westmorland and Cumberland, and parts of Lancashire and Yorkshire; county town, Carlisle; chief towns include Penrith, Kendal, Barrow-in-Furness; agriculture, tourism, shipbuilding, marine engineering, chemicals; atomic energy at Sellafield and Calder Hall (operational 1956–2003).

cumin A slender annual (*Cuminum cyminum*) growing to 50 cm/20 in, native to N Africa and SW Asia; leaves divided into narrow thread-like lobes; flowers white or pink, petals notched; fruit oblong with slender ridges. It is cultivated for the aromatic fruits, used for spice, is an ingredient of curry powder, and is much used in Mexican cooking. (Family: Umbelliferae.)

Cummings, E(dward) E(stlin) (1894–1962) Writer and painter, born in Cambridge, Massachusetts, USA. He studied at Harvard, served in World War 1 in France, then studied art at Paris. His writings attracted more interest than his paintings (though a collection of his work was published in 1931). His several successful collections of poetry, starting with *Tulips and Chimneys* (1923), are striking for their unorthodox typography and linguistic style. *Complete Poems* appeared in 1968. He also wrote a travel diary, a morality play, *Santa Claus* (1946), and a collection of six 'non-lectures' delivered at Harvard entitled *i* (1953). His best-known prose work, *The Enormous Room* (1922), describes his wartime internment in France.

cumquat *kumquat*

cumulonimbus clouds [kyoomyulohnimbuhs] Clouds of the cumulus family which rise to great heights (up to 10 km/6 mi). They are often dark and threatening when seen from below, and are associated with thunderstorms and the arrival of a cold front during the passage of a depression. At the top, the cloud may form an 'anvil' shape. Cloud symbol: Cb.

cumulus clouds [**kyoomyuluhs**] A family of clouds with a predominantly vertical extent but relatively horizontal base. They range from small, white fluffy clouds, typical of summer afternoons, to black and threatening storm or cumulonimbus clouds. Convection is responsible for their vertical extent, and the cloud base occurs c.450–2000 m/1500–6500 ft. Cloud symbol: Cu.

Cunard, Sir Samuel [**kyoonah(r)d**] (1787–1865) Ship-owner, born in Halifax, Nova Scotia, SE Canada. He succeeded early as a merchant and shipowner, and emigrated to Britain in 1838. For the new steam rail service between Britain and America, he joined with George Burns in Glasgow and David McIver in Liverpool to found (1839) the British and North American Royal Mail Steam Packet Company, later known as the Cunard Line. With a British government loan, he built two rival superliners in 1906, the *Lusitania* and *Mauritania*, which were fitted with powerful new turbines. Cunard ships were renowned for their beautiful decoration; they included the *Queen Mary* (1936) and *Queen Elizabeth* (1940), which was replaced by the *Queen Elizabeth II* (1967). The modern Cunard Line runs luxury cruises and officially launched *Queen Mary 2* in January 2004.

cuneiform A form of writing used throughout the Middle East for over 3000 years until about the 1st-c BC. Originally derived from pictograms, the symbols were later used to represent words, syllables, and phonetic elements. The earliest examples were written from top to bottom, but later the symbols were turned on their sides and written from left to right. At first, the symbols took the form of impressions made on soft clay with a stylus, but subsequently a harder writing surface was used. Cuneiform writing was not deciphered until the 19th-c.

Cunningham, Jack, popular name of **John Cunningham** (1939–) British statesman, born in Felling, Durham, NE England, UK. Educated at Jarrow and Durham, he was a university lecturer and full-time trade union official before becoming a Labour MP (1970). He was minister for energy (1976–9) in the Callaghan government before holding a number of shadow posts under a succession of party leaders. In the Blair government he became minister of agriculture (1997–8) before becoming minister for the cabinet office and chancellor of the Duchy of Lancaster (1998–9). His abrasive manner and his ability to bring colleagues to heel led to his nickname as 'the cabinet enforcer'.

Cunningham, Merce (1919–) Dancer, choreographer, teacher, and director, born in Centralia, Washington, USA. He experienced a range of dance forms before attending the Bennington School of Dance to study modern dance. He danced with the Martha Graham Company (1939–45), and started his own company in 1952. He is one of the major figures in the development of a concern with form and abstraction in modern dance and has received many awards. Among his many works are *Summerspace* (1958), *Scramble* (1967), *Rain Forest* (1968) and *Duets* (1980).

Cunobelinus *Cymbeline*

Cuomo, Mario [**kwohmoh**] (1932–) US politician, born in New York City, USA. He studied at St John's University, NY, and became Governor of New York State (1983–94). His keynote address at the 1984 Democratic Convention made him a national figure, and he was mentioned as a possible Democratic presidential candidate in 1988 and 1992.

cup fungus A fungus producing a cup-shaped fruiting body that opens at maturity to expose the fertile layer; most grow on decaying organic matter, some are parasitic. (Subdivision: Ascomycetes. Class: Discomycetes.)

Cupid The Roman god of Love, son of Venus, depicted as a naked winged boy with bow and arrows. Apuleius tells the story of *Cupid and Psyche*. He is equivalent to Greek Eros.

cupola [**kyoopohla**] A small dome over a circular, square, or polygonal part of a building, usually above a roof or turret; more loosely, a dome of any size.

cupping A technique common to traditional Eastern and Western medicine in which a vacuum is created inside a cup or jar, usually with a flame, while the cup is applied to the body. In traditional Chinese medicine the process of cupping is thought to draw perverse energy to the surface of the body for dispersal, and in Western medicine the technique was usually used to relieve congestion, such as the swelling which follows trauma. The partial vacuum created by the flame draws flesh into the cup, fixing it in place, and this is usually left in position for up to 15 minutes before removal. The technique is still widely practised by acupuncturists, but is no longer popular in orthodox medical circles.

cuprite [**kyoopriyt**] A red copper oxide (Cu_2O) mineral, which is widely distributed. It is an important source of copper.

cupronickel [**kyooprohnikl**] An alloy of copper and nickel, silver in colour. It is used extensively for coinage.

Curaçao [**koorasahoh**] pop (2000e) 150 000; area 444 sq km/ 171 sq mi. Largest and most populous island of the Netherlands Antilles, E Caribbean, 60 km/37 mi N of Venezuela; composed of coralline limestone; generally flat, but rises to 373 m/1224 ft in the NW; length 58 km/36 mi; width 13 km/8 mi; visited by Europeans, 1499; Dutch colony, 1634; capital, Willemstad; airport; tourism, oil refining, phosphate mining, ship repairing, liqueur.

curare [**kyoorahree**] An extract of the South American plants *Chondrodendron tomentosum* or *Strychnos toxifera*, used as an arrow poison for hunting by South American Indians. The active principle, tubocurarine, is widely used to induce muscle paralysis during surgery.

curassow [**kyoorasoh**] A large, tree-dwelling, turkey-like bird, native to C and N South America; head with a conspicuous crest of curved feathers; legs long, strong; eats buds, leaves, and small animals. (Family: Cracidae, 13 species.)

curate Strictly, a Christian clergyman admitted to the 'cure of souls' and having the 'cure' or charge of a parish. Popularly, the term is used of an assistant or unbeneficed clergyman, helping or temporarily replacing the priest, rector, vicar, or other incumbent of the parish.

curia In ancient Rome, the Senate house. It stood on the NW side of the forum, adjacent to the site of the legislative assembly.

Curia Romana *Roman Curia*

Curie, Marie [**kyooree**], *née* **Manya Sklodowska** (1867–1934) Physicist, born in Warsaw, Poland, who worked in Paris with her French husband **Pierre Curie** (1859–1906) on magnetism and radioactivity. She emigrated to France in 1891, and studied at the Sorbonne where she met and married Pierre Curie (1895), who became professor of physics there in 1901. Together they discovered and isolated polonium and radium in 1898. Pierre and his brother, **Jacques Curie**, discovered piezoelectricity. For her thesis she studied the 'rays' earlier discovered by Becquerel, and the Curies shared the 1903 Nobel Prize for Physics with Becquerel for the discovery of radioactivity. After her husband's death in a road accident (1906), Madame Curie succeeded to his chair. She published her fundamental treatise on radioactivity in 1910 and was awarded the Nobel Prize for Chemistry in 1911. She died of leukaemia, probably caused by long exposure to radiation.

curie [**kyooree**] In radioactivity, defined as $3{\cdot}7 \times 10^{10}$ disintegrations per second; symbol *Ci*; 1 Ci = $3{\cdot}7 \times 10^{10}$ Bq (becquerel, SI unit); original definition related to the activity of radioactive radon; named after Pierre and Marie Curie; classed as a unit in temporary use with SI units.

Curie point *Curie temperature*

Curie's law A law for paramagnetic materials which states that the magnetization is proportional to B/T, where B is magnetic flux density and T is temperature in kelvins; stated by physicist Pierre Curie in 1895. Physically, increasing B serves to align individual atomic magnetic moments; increasing T gives more thermal agitation, which upsets alignment.

Curie temperature In ferromagnetism, the material-dependent temperature above which a ferromagnetic material becomes merely paramagnetic; symbol T_c, units K; introduced by Pierre Curie in 1895; also called **Curie point**. It results from the increased thermal agitation of atoms, which overcomes the aligning force between neighbouring atoms. For iron, T_c = 1043 K.

Curitiba [kooreecheeba] 25°24S 49°16W, pop (2000e) 1 604 000. Commercial and industrial capital of Paraná state, S Brazil; SW of São Paulo, altitude 900 m/2950 ft; two universities (1912, 1959); railway; airfield; commercial centre; tobacco, furniture, paper, textiles, cars, maté, cattle; cathedral (1894), Palácio Iguaçu, Paranaense Museum, Passeio Público park, temple in Egyptian style on L Bacacheri to the N.

Curl, Robert, Jr (1933–) Chemist, born in Alice, Texas, USA. He studied at the University of California, Berkeley, moving to Rice University, Houston, in 1958. He shared the Nobel Prize for Chemistry in 1996 for his contribution to the discovery of fullerenes (1985).

curlew A long-legged sandpiper; breeds in the N hemisphere, but flies S (some as far as Australia) during the N winter; has long, down-curved bill; probes for food in sediments. (Genus: *Numenius*, 8 species.)

curling A game played usually by teams of four on an ice rink, using special stones fitted with handles. The object is similar to that of bowls, to deliver the stones nearest to a target object, known as the *tee*. The ice is swept with brooms in front of the running stone to help it travel further. It is popular in Scotland, Canada, the Nordic countries, and the USA.

currant A deciduous shrub, native to N temperate regions and the Andes; leaves palmately lobed; flowers borne in clusters on short lateral shoots, 4–5 sepals and petals, petals slightly shorter and rounded; berries juicy; cultivated for ornament and as soft fruit. The currants used for 'fruit' cakes are dried grapes. (Genus: *Ribes*, 150 species. Family: Grossulariaceae.)

currency A country's money. A currency is *convertible* if it can be changed into other currencies without restriction. A currency *depreciates* if it becomes cheaper relative to other currencies. For example, if £1 can be exchanged for $2, but subsequently the rate falls to £1 for $1.50, the pound has depreciated against the dollar; the dollar, by comparison, has *appreciated*.

current (electricity) The flow of electric charge, symbol i or I, units A (amp). A current of one amp means that a charge of one coulomb flows every second. Current flows positive to negative by convention. **Current density**, symbol j or J, is the total current divided by the cross-sectional area of the conductor.

current (oceanography) *p.413*

curriculum *core curriculum; education; national curriculum*

curry A spiced dish of fish, meat, poultry, or vegetables, originating in the East. Among the spices used in curries are coriander, cumin, chili, cinnamon, cardamom, cloves, fenugreek, ginger, and turmeric. These spices may act as a preservative in the cuisine of hot climates. Other common ingredients are garlic, yogurt, and coconut milk.

cursus honorum [koorsus onawrum] Literally, (Lat) 'the course of honours'; the ordered career structure which was obligatory for any man in ancient Rome who wished to hold high public office. Under the cursus, the major offices of state – such as the quaestorship, praetorship, and consulship – had to be held in a strict order, and not before a certain age.

curtain wall A non-loadbearing wall used as a protective screen over the structural frame of a building. The materials used are varied: they include aluminium, steel, and especially glass. In mediaeval military architecture, the term referred to the defensive outer wall of a castle.

Curtin, John (Joseph) (1885–1945) Australian statesman and prime minister (1941–5), born in Creswick, Victoria, SE Australia. He was active in trade union work, and edited a Perth newspaper. In 1928 he entered parliament, became leader of the Labor Party (1934), and was prime minister during most of World War 2. He organized national mobilization during the Japanese war, and died in office.

Curtis, Tony, originally **Bernard Schwarz** (1925–) Actor, born in New York City, USA. After many small film parts early in his career, he proved he could play light comedy roles as in *Some Like It Hot* (1959) while also displaying his dramatic ability in *The Boston Strangler* (1968). His many films include *The Vikings* (1958), *Spartacus* (1960), *The Great Imposter* (1961), *The Mirror Crack'd* (1980), and *The Continued Adventures of Reptile Man* (1996). He is the father of actress **Jamie Lee Curtis** (1958–).

Curtiss, Glenn (Hammond) (1878–1930) Air pioneer and inventor, born in Hammondsport, New York, USA. Originally a bicycle mechanic, he established a motorcycle factory in Hammondsport in 1902, and in 1905 set a world speed record of 137 mph on a motor-cycle of his own design. He also designed motors for airships, and with Alexander Graham Bell formed the Aerial Experiment Association (1907). In 1908 he achieved the first public one-kilometre flight in the USA. In 1911 he invented the aileron, and also flew the first practical seaplane (hydroplane), as well as the flying boat. During World War 1 he produced military aircraft such as the JN-4 (Jenny), the Navy-Curtiss flying boat, speedboats, and Liberty engines.

curvature of space–time An expression of the effect of mass and energy on space and time. This is zero for Newtonian mechanics and special relativity, corresponding to flat space–time. It is known from observation of the bending of star light by the Sun that space–time is not flat. In the general relativity theory of gravitation, space–time curvature is due to the presence of mass. Regions of infinite curvature are predicted (black holes). At a large distance from massive bodies, space–time is almost flat, corresponding to weak gravity.

Curwen, John (1816–80) Music educationist, born in Heckmondwike, West Yorkshire, N England, UK. He became a Nonconformist minister in 1838, but devoted himself to promoting the tonic sol-fa musical system. His method came to be widely used, and in 1864 he left his ministry, having established a publishing house for music.

Curzon, Sir Clifford (1907–82) Pianist, born in London, UK. He studied at the Royal Academy of Music in London, and in Berlin (1928–30). He taught for some years at the Royal Academy, but resigned in 1932 to devote himself to concert work, specializing in Mozart and other Viennese classics. He was knighted in 1971.

Curzon (of Kedleston), George Nathaniel Curzon, Marquess (1859–1925) British statesman, born in Kedleston Hall, Derbyshire, C England, UK. He studied at Oxford, became an MP in 1886, and travelled widely in Eastern countries. He became under-secretary for India (1891–2), and for foreign affairs (1895), and in 1898 was made Viceroy of India and given an Irish barony. He introduced many social and political reforms, established the North West Frontier Province, and partitioned Bengal. He resigned after a disagreement with Lord Kitchener (1905), returning to politics in 1915 as Lord Privy Seal. He became foreign secretary (1919–24), and was created a marquess (1921).

Curzon Line A line of territorial demarcation between Russia and Poland proposed in 1920 by the British foreign secretary, Lord Curzon. Poland rejected the proposal, subsequently gaining larger territories. In September 1939 a boundary similar to the Curzon Line became the border between German- and Soviet-occupied Poland, and in 1945 was recognized as the frontier between Poland and the USSR.

cuscus [kuskus] *phalanger*

Cush *Kush*

Cushing, Harvey Williams (1869–1939) Neurosurgeon and physiologist, born in Cleveland, Ohio, USA. He studied at Johns Hopkins, Yale, and Harvard universities, graduating in medicine in 1895, then taught at Harvard (1912–32) and Yale (from 1933). His main research field was the brain and the pituitary gland, describing the symptoms of the pituitary malfunction now called **Cushing's syndrome**.

Cushing, Peter (1913–94) Actor, born in Kenley, Greater London, UK. He studied at the Guildhall School of Music and Drama, making his stage debut in 1935. A trip to the USA resulted in his

current

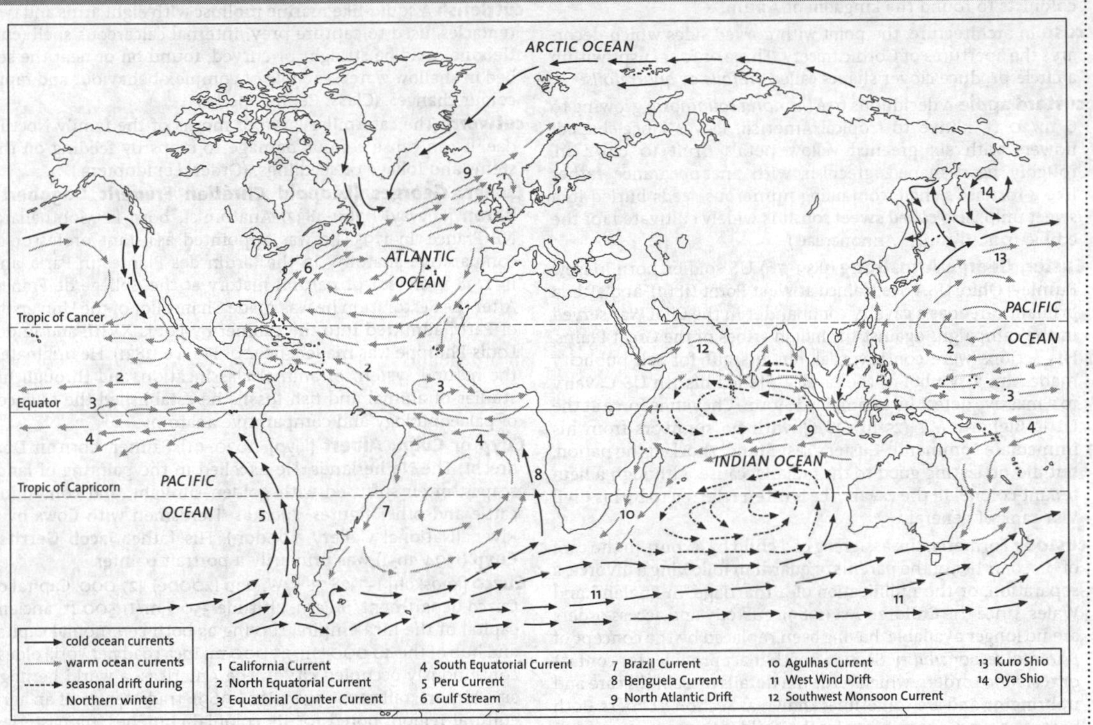

Flowing water in the ocean. The surface currents depicted on atlases of the seas are long-term averages of the direction of water motion at the sea surface, driven primarily by the winds. Because most do not extend deeper than 300–500 m/1000–1600 ft, they can be conveniently separated from the circulation of intermediate and deep waters, driven by varying densities of sea water caused by differences in temperature and salinity. (The situation is more complex, in fact, because the Antarctic Circumpolar Current and even parts of the Gulf Stream system do extend all the way to the sea floor.)

The surface circulation has certain similarities in each of the major ocean basins. The strong, persistent *trade winds*, blowing out of the NE in the N hemisphere and out of the SE in the S hemisphere, produce major W-flowing **equatorial currents**. These currents flow along bands of latitude until, deflected by continents, they form **boundary currents** flowing N or S. In the Atlantic and Pacific Oceans these equatorial and boundary currents are parts of semi-enclosed circulation cells called *gyres*. The gyres are oval-shaped, elongated E–W, and centred in the subtropics (30°N and S). Their centres are displaced towards the W side of ocean basins because of the rotation of the Earth, which results in an intensifying of boundary currents on the W side and a weakening of E boundary currents.

In general, a subtropical gyre has four components. (1) An equatorial current travelling W in response to the Trade Winds. (2) A W boundary current flowing towards the Poles; these currents are important in transporting heat from lower to higher latitudes; they are narrow, swift, and deep. (3) An E-flowing current pushed along by the bands of W winds at temperate latitudes. (4) An E boundary current flowing towards the Equator; these currents transport cool water from higher to lower latitudes, and are broad, shallow, and weak. Smaller subpolar gyres, turning in the opposite direction to the subtropical gyres, are present especially in the N hemisphere where continents deflect current flow.

The W-flowing N and S equatorial currents of the N and S subtropical gyres are separated by an E-flowing equatorial counter-current. **Counter-currents** are developed at the inter-tropical convergence (ITC), the area of weak and variable winds known as *the Doldrums*. The ITC is not found at the geographic equator, but is shifted to c.5°N in the Atlantic and Pacific and to c.7°S in the Indian Ocean. The shift of this 'climatic equator' away from the geographic equator is the result of the unequal distribution of land and sea between the N and S hemispheres.

Hollywood film debut in *The Man in the Iron Mask* (1939). After the war he established himself as a classical actor with the Old Vic Company (1948–9). He was chiefly known for his long association with the Gothic horror films produced by Hammer Studios, such as *The Curse of Frankenstein* (1956), *Dracula* (1958), and *The Mummy* (1959). His numerous other films include *Hamlet* (1948), *Dr Who and the Daleks* (1965), and *Star Wars* (1977). He also enjoyed a long screen association with the character of Sherlock Holmes. His writing includes *An Autobiography* (1986) and *Past Forgetting* (1988).

Cushing's syndrome A disorder caused by excessive levels of glucocorticoid hormones. It may be a result of steroid treatment, or excessive secretion of glucocorticoids by the adrenal glands, due to a benign adrenal tumour or overstimulation of the adrenal glands by hormones secreted by the pituitary gland. It produces a range of characteristic clinical features, including a round red face, thin easily bruised skin, obesity, muscle wasting, osteoporosis, amenorrhoea, and hypertension.

Cushites A group of peoples in NE Africa, including the Somali and Oromo. Their economies are primarily pastoral. It may be that in the early part of the Christian era they inhabited a wider area of E Africa. On the Red Sea coast they fused with Semitic colonists to found the kingdom of Axum.

cusp In architecture, the point with curved sides which decorates the apertures of Gothic tracery. Three or four cusps within a circle produce clover shapes called *trefoils* or *quatrefoils*.

custard apple A deciduous tree (*Annona squamosa*) growing to 6 m/20 ft, native to tropical America; leaves lance-shaped; flowers with six greenish-yellow petals; fruit 10 cm/4 in, roughly heart-shaped, greenish, with an appearance rather like a tortoise's shell, containing numerous seeds buried in a sweet pulp; also called **sweet sop**. It is widely cultivated for the edible fruit. (Family: Annonaceae.)

Custer, George Armstrong (1839–76) US soldier, born in New Rumley, Ohio, USA. He trained at West Point (1861), and after a brilliant career as a cavalry commander in the Civil War served in the campaigns against the Indian tribes of the Great Plains. His actions were controversial, but his gift for self-publicity made him a symbol of the cavalry. He led his 7th US Cavalry to a massive defeat by a combined Sioux–Cheyenne force at the Little Bighorn, MT (25 Jun 1876), with no survivors from his immediate command. 'Custer's Last Stand' shocked the nation, but did no lasting good to the Indians' cause. Although a lieutenant-colonel in the cavalry, he is often referred to by his Civil War rank of general.

custody Formerly, the assigning of a child by a court to the care of one or other of the parents or guardian following a divorce, a separation, or the nullification of a marriage. In England and Wales, since the Children Act (1989), custody and access orders are no longer available, having been replaced by the concept of *parental responsibility*. Section 8 of that act provides for contact or residence orders, which settle the details of a child's care and upbringing and are sometimes known as *Section 8 Orders*. Both parents have responsibility for the child if they are married to each other; and if not, the parental responsibility is conferred on the mother. However, the court may order parental responsibility to be given to someone other than the natural parents, such as a local authority or guardian. In Scotland, the terms *custody* and *access* have been superseded by the terms *residence* and *contact*.

customs and excise The UK government department charged with collecting taxes due on specified goods and services, and controlling imports into a country where there are tariffs or quota restrictions, or where the imports are illegal. It is most visible at airports and ports checking goods imported, and charging tax (*duty*) as appropriate. It also ensures that goods in bonded warehouses (ie where dutiable products are held before tax is paid) are properly managed. The department also handles value-added tax.

customs union A group of countries with a common external tariff and free trade between its members. Examples include Benelux, set up in 1948, and the European Economic Community (now the European Union), set up in 1958.

Cuthbert, St (c.635–87) Missionary, born in Ireland or Northumbria. He became a monk (651), prior of Melrose (661), and prior of Lindisfarne (664). In 676 he left to become a hermit, but in 684 was persuaded to take the bishopric of Hexham, then of Lindisfarne. After two years he returned to his cell, on the island of Farne, where he died. His body was moved to many places, and finally buried at Durham in 999. Feast day 20 March.

Cutner, Solomon *Solomon* (music)

cutter A single-masted, fore-and-aft-rigged sailing vessel with more than one headsail, usually requiring a bowsprit. Although sailing cutters are fairly uncommon today, the term is still in use, especially in compounds (eg **revenue cutter**). It is also applied to a ship's boat which is rigged for sailing and rowing, and in the USA it applies to vessels which would elsewhere be called **sloops**.

cutting A portion of a plant, usually a side shoot but also a leaf or root which, when removed from the parent, will grow to form a new individual. It is commonly used by gardeners as a means of propagation.

cuttlefish A squid-like marine mollusc with eight arms and two tentacles, used to capture prey; internal calcareous shell (**cuttlebone**) may be straight or curved; found on or near the sea bed in shallow water; capable of complex behaviour and rapid colour changes. (Class: Cephalopoda.)

cutworm The caterpillar larva of moths of the family Noctuidae. It can cause serious damage to crops by feeding on the stems and foliage of seedlings. (Order: Lepidoptera.)

Cuvier, Georges (Léopold Chrétien Frédéric Dagobert), Baron [küvyay] (1769–1832) Anatomist, born in Montbéliard, NE France. In 1795, he was appointed assistant professor of comparative anatomy in the Jardin des Plantes in Paris, and in 1798 professor of natural history at the Collège de France. After the Restoration he was made Chancellor of the University of Paris, admitted into the cabinet by Louis XVIII, and under Louis-Philippe was made a peer of France (1831). He originated the natural system of animal classification, and through his studies of animal and fish fossils he established the sciences of palaeontology and comparative anatomy.

Cuyp or **Cuijp, Albert** [kiyp] (1620–91) Painter, born in Dordrecht, The Netherlands. He excelled in the painting of landscapes, often suffused with golden sunlight, and containing cattle and other figures, such as 'Herdsmen with Cows by a River' (National Gallery, London). His father **Jacob Gerritsz Cuyp** (1594–1651) was primarily a portrait painter.

Cuzco [**koos**koh] 13°32S 71°57W, pop (2000e) 327 000. Capital of Cuzco department, S Peru; altitude 3500 m/11 500 ft; ancient capital of the Inca empire, serving as both ceremonial capital and hub of the 40 000 km/25 000 mi Inca road network; oldest continuously occupied city in the Americas; a world heritage site; airport; railway; university (1969); trade centre of an agricultural region; noted for its colonial churches, monasteries, convents, and extensive Inca ruins; cathedral (17th-c), Church of La Compañía de Jesús (17th-c), Church of Santo Domingo (17th-c).

cwm *cirque*

cyanide A compound containing the group –CÙN in a molecule, or salts of hydrocyanic acid containing the ion CN^-. It is a very rapidly acting poison, which can kill within minutes. Cyanide gas has been used in gas chambers, and was used for more than 900 religious 'suicide-murders' in Guyana in 1978. It acts by preventing oxygen from being used by cells. Amyl nitrite (by inhalation) can treat cyanide poisoning if administered in time.

cyanide process A process for extracting gold and silver from ores. The finely divided ore is treated with a dilute solution of sodium or potassium cyanide. The gold or silver forms a soluble complex, from which it is regenerated by treatment with zinc dust.

cyanocobalamin [siyanohkoh**bal**amin] The chemical name for vitamin B_{12}. This vitamin is involved in cell division and in the manufacture of the sheath surrounding nerve cells. It is found predominantly in animal-derived food, so that a true deficiency rarely occurs except among vegans, who eat no animal food. A secondary deficiency can occur if there is a deficiency of the *intrinsic factor*, a substance in the gut which aids B_{12} absorption. In individuals where the intrinsic factor is low or absent, pernicious anaemia develops.

cyanogen [siyanojen] N–C–C–N, boiling point −21°C. A colourless, inflammable, poisonous gas, with a bitter almond smell. It bears the same relation to cyanide ion (CN^-) as chlorine (Cl_2) does to chloride ion (Cl^-).

Cyanophycota [siyanoh**fiy**kuhta] *blue-green bacteria*

Cybele [siy**bee**lee] In Greek mythology, a mother-goddess, especially of wild nature, whose cult originated in Phrygia, and was taken over by the Greeks. She was depicted with a turreted mural crown, and was attended by lions.

cyberintelligence The (usually covert) gathering of information via computer networks and databases, and the subsequent analysis and evaluation of this information in a useable form. With organizations now increasingly dependent on computer systems for the conduct and recording of business, cyberintelligence is undertaken by third parties in order to gain access to these systems. Those involved are mainly national and international intelligence agencies, including criminal agencies, which apply information-warfare techniques to obtain their aim. Private-sector firms also seek cyberintelligence about clients and competitors, forcing the latter to install more powerful critical infrastructure protection. Target systems are accessed by hacking, with their contents typically copied rather than altered or destroyed. **Intelligent agents** are computer programs associated with browsers which search the Web for specific information on behalf of the user and then analyse it.

cybernetics The study of control systems that exhibit characteristics similar to those of animal and human behaviour. The term was coined by Norbert Wiener in the 1940s, based on a Greek word meaning 'steersman'. Although the term has tended to fall into disuse with the expansion of the computer field, cybernetics is essentially a broad-based discipline which includes information, message, and noise theories, and can reconcile the work of neurophysiologists, psychologists, and computer engineers.

cyberspace *Internet*

cycad [**siy**kad] A tropical or subtropical gymnosperm, palm-like in appearance, trunk usually unbranched, armoured with old leaf bases or scar-like remains, with a crown of tough, feathery leaves; flowers borne in separate male and female cones, the female very large. Cycads are considered to be the most primitive living seed-plants, appearing in the late Palaeozoic era, and thought to be related to seed-ferns, a fossil group dominant during the Triassic period. The slow-growing trunks have a large, starchy central pith which in some species yields sago. (Family: Cycadaceae, 100 species.)

Cyclades [**sik**ladeez], Gr **Kikládhes** pop (2000e) 99 300; area 2572 sq km/993 sq mi. Island group in the Aegean Sea, Greece, between the Peloponnese (W) and the Dodecanese (E); chief islands are Tinos, Andros, Mikonos, Milos, Naxos, Paros, Kithnos, Serifos, lying in a circle around Siros; capital, Siros; several now popular holiday resorts.

cyclamate [**sik**lamayt] A derivative of cyclohexylsulphamic acid. It has c.30 times the sweetening power of sucrose, and was previously used widely in sweetening 'diet foods'. It is less used now because of possible health risks.

cyclamen [**sik**lamen] A perennial with leaves growing direct from fleshy corm, native to Europe and Asia; flowers nodding, white, pink, or purple, corolla lobes bent back; after flowering, stalk coils to bring ripening fruit to the soil. Pot plants are derived mainly from *Cyclamen persicum*. (Genus: *Cyclamen*, 15 species. Family: Primulaceae.)

cycling The riding of a bicycle for fitness, pleasure, or as a sport. The first cycle race was in Paris in 1868, and won by James Moore of England. There are several popular forms of cycling as a sport. In *time trials* cyclists race against the clock. *Cyclo-cross* is a mixture of cycling and cross-country running, with the bike on the shoulder. *Track racing* takes place on purpose-built concrete or wooden velodromes. *Criteriums* are races around towns or cities. *Road races* are normally in excess of 150 km/100 mi in length, and take place either from one point to another, or involve several circuits around a predetermined road course. *Stage races* involve many days' racing, each consisting of 100 mi or more. The most famous cycle race is the *Tour de France*.

cycloid The path traced out by a point on the circumference of a circle as the circle rolls along a straight line. Using the angle θ through which the circle has turned as parameter, the equation of the cycloid is $x = a(\theta - \sin\theta)$, $y = a(1 - \cos\theta)$.

cyclone *depression* (meteorology); *hurricane*

cyclophosphamide [siyklohfosfamiyd] An important drug in the treatment of cancers. It belongs to a class of drug called the *nitrogen mustards*, developed from mustard gas which was used in the first world war. Nitrogen mustards are so-called *alkylating* agents, which work by binding to the DNA of cells, thus stopping them from dividing. Cyclophosphamide is the most widely prescribed nitrogen mustard. It has severe side-effects, including nausea and vomiting and hair loss, and resistance to its anti-cancer actions can develop. It is usually given in a cocktail of different classes of anti-cancer drug to optimize therapy and minimize side effects.

Cyclops [**siy**klops], plural **Cyclopes** In Greek mythology, a race of one-eyed giants who worked as smiths and were associated with volcanic activity. In the *Odyssey*, the Cyclops Polyphemus is outwitted and blinded by Odysseus, and hurls rocks into the sea at the departing ship. The Greeks called any pre-Greek structures incorporating huge stones 'Cyclopean'.

cyclops [**siy**klops] A freshwater copepod named after its conspicuous single eyespot; abundant in lake plankton, but also found on mud and in damp semiterrestrial habitats; feeds on fine particulate matter, or as a carnivore on insect larvae and other invertebrates. (Subphylum: Crustacea. Class: Copepoda.)

cyclostome [**siy**klohstohm] Any of a group of jawless fishes with a large sucking mouth.

cyclothymia [siyklohthiymia] In psychiatry, a persistent instability of affect, with repeated periods of mild elation and mild depression. This may be a feature of an individual's personality or a forerunner of manic-depressive illness. It usually commences in adolescence or early adulthood and runs a chronic course.

cyclotron A machine for accelerating charged particles, typically protons; developed by Ernest Lawrence and others in 1931, and now largely superseded in particle physics by the synchrotron. Acceleration is provided by an oscillating electric field. A large constant magnetic field guides particles in a spiral path, having a radius that increases as particle velocity increases. Cyclotrons are used in nuclear physics, and in nuclear medicine, such as in cancer therapy.

Cygnus [**sig**nus] (Lat 'swan') A large N constellation, associated by the ancient Greeks with the swan into which Zeus changed to seduce Queen Leda of Sparta. Its brightest star is Deneb, a supergiant, distance 990 parsec. Of all the stars visible to the naked eye, this is the most luminous, 250 000 times the Sun's light. **Cygnus X-I**, a strong X-ray source, is a prime candidate for a black hole. **Cygnus A**, a strong radio source, is identified with a distant peculiar galaxy that is also an X-ray source. It is one of the most powerful radio galaxies known. Cygnus is popularly known as the Northern Cross because of its distinctive shape.

cymbals Musical instruments of great antiquity. Modern orchestral cymbals are made in pairs, from an alloy of copper and tin, with a diameter of about 40–50 cm/16–20 in. They are clashed together, or suspended from a stand and played with a drumstick. They are of no definite pitch, but the small 'antique cymbals' or *crotales*, are tuned to precise pitches. An array of free-standing cymbals is also an important part of the jazz drummer's kit.

Cymbeline [**sim**beleen], also known as **Cunobelinus** (?–c.43) Pro-Roman king of the Catuvellauni, who from his capital at Camulodunum (Colchester) ruled most of SE Britain. Shakespeare's character was based on Holinshed's half-historical Cunobelinus.

cymbidium [simbidium] A member of a genus of orchids (epiphytes) native to tropical forests from Asia to Australia. They are widely cultivated for the spikes of large, showy flowers much used in floristry and the cut-flower trade. (Genus: *Cymbidium*, 40 species. Family: Orchidaceae.)

cyme [siym], **cymose** *inflorescence*

Cynewulf [**kin**ewulf] (8th-c) Anglo-Saxon poet, identified by some with Cynewulf, Bishop of Lindisfarne (737–80). Four poems, 'Juliana', 'Christ', 'Elene', and 'The Fates of the Apostles', have his name worked into the text in runes.

Cynics (Gr 'dogs') A loose sect of philosophers founded by Antisthenes and Diogenes of Sinope, influential discontinuously in Greece and Rome, particularly in the 3rd-c BC and the 1st-c AD.

Cyprus

☐ International Airport

[siypruhs], Gr **Kypros**, Turkish **Kibris**; official name **Republic of Cyprus**, Gr **Kypriaki Dimokratia**, Turkish **Kibris Cumhuriyeti**

Local names Kipros (Greek), Kibris (Turkish)

Timezone GMT +2

Area 9251 km²/3571 sq mi

Population total (2002e) 802 000

Status Republic

Date of independence 1960

Capital Nicosia (Lefkosia to Greek Cypriots, Lefkosa to Turkish Cypriots)

Languages Greek and Turkish (official), English

Ethnic groups Greek (78%), Turkish (18%), other (4%)

Religions Greek Orthodox (78%), Sunni Muslim (18%), other Christian (4%)

Physical features Third largest island in Mediterranean; Kyrenia Mts extend 150 km/90 mi along N coast, Mt Kyparissovouno, 1024 m/3360 ft; forest-covered Troödos Mts in SW, rising to 1951 m/6401 ft at Mt Olympus; fertile alluvial Mesaoria plain extends across island centre; SE plateau region slopes towards indented coastline, with several long, sandy beaches; major rivers include the Pedios, Karyota, Kouris.

Climate Mediterranean, with hot, dry summers and warm, wet winters; average annual rainfall ranges from 300–400 mm/12–16 in on the Mesaoria Plain to 1200 mm/47 in in the Troödos Mts; mean daily temperatures in Nicosia 10°C (Jan), 28°C (Jul); temperatures range from 22°C on Troödos Mts, to 29°C on Central plain (Jul–Aug); snow on higher land in winter.

Currency 1 Cyprus Pound (ĖC) = 100 cents

Economy Main exports include cement, clothing, footwear, citrus, potatoes, grapes, wine; tourism also recovering (now accounting for c.15% of national income); Famagusta (chief port prior to 1974 Turkish invasion) now under Turkish occupation, and declared closed by Cyprus government; Turkish Cypriot economy heavily dependent on agriculture.

GDP (2001) Greek $9·4 bn, per capita $15 000
Turkish $787 mi, per capita $6000

Human Development Index (2001) 0·891

History Recorded history of 4000 years; rulers included Greeks, Ptolemies, Persians, Romans, Byzantines, Arabs, Franks, Venetians, Turks (1571–1878), and British; British Crown Colony from 1925; Greek Cypriot demands for union with Greece (enosis) led to guerrilla warfare, under Grivas and Makarios, and four-year state of emergency, 1955–9; independence, 1960, with Britain retaining sovereignty over bases at Akrotiri and Dhekelia; Greek-Turkish fighting throughout 1960s, with UN peacekeeping force sent in 1964; Greek junta engineered coup d'Õtat, 1974; Turkish invasion in 1974 led to occupation of over a third of the island; island divided into two parts by the Attila Line, cutting through Nicosia where it is called the Green Line; almost all Turks now live in N sector (37% of island); governed by a president (head of state), elected for a 5-year term by the Greek community, and a House of Representatives of 80 elected members (including 24 seats nominally reserved for Turkish Cypriots); Turkish members ceased to attend in 1983, when the Turkish community declared itself independent (as 'Turkish Republic of Northern Cyprus', with Raul Denktas as president, recognized only by Turkey); UN peace proposals rejected, 1984; summit meeting between Kyprianou (Greek president of Cyprus) and Denktas failed, 1985; president Georgios Vassiliou renewed talks with Denktas, 1988, but soon abandoned; UN-sponsored peace negotiations, 1997; representatives of both sides in a new series of talks, 2002; Green Line border opened for daytime crossings (Apr 2003); restrictions eased further with lifting of travel ban on Greek Cypriots to Turkey (May 2003); accession of Greek Cyprus as EU member (from 1 May 2004) ratified, July 2003.

Head of State/Government
1960–77 Archbishop Makarios III
1977–88 Spyros Kyprianou
1988–93 Georgios Vassiliou
1993–2003 Glafkos Clirides
2003– Tassos Papadopoulos

They espoused an ascetic life in conformity with nature, ignoring all social conventions and artificially-induced desires. Their thought was influential on Stoicism.

cypress An evergreen conifer, native to the temperate N hemisphere; leaves small, scale-like; cones like the head of a mace, with 4–12 woody scales joined at their margins, sometimes remaining on the branches for years. The timber is insect-repellant. It is susceptible to extreme cold, and is most common in warm climates. (Genus: *Cupressus*, 15–20 species. Family: Cupressaceae.)

Cyprian, St [siprian], originally **Thascius Caecilius Cyprianus** (c.200–58) One of the great Fathers of the Church, probably born in Carthage. He became a Christian c.245, and was made Bishop of Carthage in 248, when his zealous efforts to restore strict discipline brought him a host of enemies. He was forced to flee from Roman persecution, and eventually suffered martyrdom under Valerian (reigned 253–60). At a synod in Carthage in 256 he argued for a notion of Church unity as expressed through the consensus of bishops. His writings remained influential. Feast day 16 September.

Cyprus *see panel*

Cyrano de Bergerac, Savinien [siranoh duh berzherak] (1619–55) Satirist and playwright, born in Paris, France. In his youth he fought more than a thousand duels, mostly on account of his extremely large nose. His works include satirical accounts of visits to the Moon and Sun, *Histoire comique des états et empires de la lune* and ... *du soleil*, published posthumously in 1656 and 1662, which suggested 'Gulliver' to Swift. His life was the subject of the play by Edmond Rostand (1897).

Cyrenaics [sirenayiks] A school of 4th-c and 3rd-c BC Greek philosophers, whose founder was Aristippus of Cyrene. They espoused a radical hedonism, contrasted (but often confused) with that of Epicureanism. They believed that the immediate sensation of pleasure is the only good, that all such sensations are equal in worth, and that past and future pleasures have no present value.

Cyrene [siyreenee] 32°49N 21°52E. A prosperous Greek city-state in N Africa, famous in antiquity for the export of silphium, a plant used in ancient medicine. Ruled over by the Ptolemies, it became part of the Roman province of Cyrene in 74 BC. It is now a world heritage site, and the location of the village of Shahhat, E Libya.

Cyril, St (c.827–69) Christian missionary and saint, born in Thessaloniki, Greece, who with his brother **St Methodius** (c.825–85), also born in Thessaloniki, became missionaries to the Slavs. Cyril first worked among the Tartar Khazars, and Methodius among the Bulgarians of Thrace and Moesia. Together they went to Moravia, where they prepared a Slavonic translation of the Scriptures and the chief liturgical books. Cyril died in Rome, leaving Methodius to complete the evangelization of the Slavs as Bishop of Moravia. Called to Rome in 879 to justify his celebration of the Mass in the native tongue, he gained the approval of Pope John VIII. The Cyrillic alphabet, modified out of the Greek by Cyril, superseded a more ancient Slavonic alphabet. Feast day 14 February (W), 11 May (E).

Cyril of Alexandria, St (376–444) Theologian, one of the Fathers of the Church, born in Alexandria, N Egypt. He became Patriarch of Alexandria in 412, and vigorously implemented orthodox Christian teaching. He expelled the Jews from the city (415), and relentlessly persecuted Nestorius, whose doctrine was condemned at the Council of Ephesus (431). Feast day 9 June (E) or 27 June (W).

Cyril of Jerusalem, St (c.315–86) Theologian, and Bishop of Jerusalem, who took a leading part in the doctrinal controversies concerning Arianism. Twice expelled from his see, he regained it and spoke for the Orthodox churchmen at the Council of Constantinople (381). Feast day 18 March.

Cyrillic alphabet [si**ril**ik] An alphabet attributed to St Cyril, and used for Slavonic languages, such as Russian and Bulgarian. It is also used for many non-Slavonic languages in the republics of the former USSR.

Cyrus II [**siy**rus], known as **the Great** (?–529 BC) The founder of the Achaemenid Persian empire, the son of Cambyses I. He defeated the Medes (549 BC), became King of Persia (548 BC), and took Lydia (c.546 BC) and Babylon (539 BC). His empire eventually ran from the Mediterranean to the Hindu Kush. He had a policy of religious conciliation: the nations which had been carried into captivity in Babylon along with the Jews were restored to their native countries, and allowed to take their gods with them.

Cyrus [**siy**rus], known as **Cyrus the Younger** (424–401 BC) The second son of Darius II of Persia (reigned 423–404 BC). He was accused of conspiring against his brother, Artaxerxes II, and sentenced to death (404 BC), but was afterwards pardoned and restored as satrap of Asia Minor. In 401 BC he led an army of Greek mercenaries against his brother, but was killed at Cunaxa.

cyst (biology) [sist] Any relatively thick-walled resting cell formed by an organism as a means of dispersal or as a way of surviving a period of adverse conditions. Eggs and spores are often protected in cysts, but whole organisms may also encyst, to re-emerge when favourable conditions return.

cyst (medicine) [sist] A benign (non-malignant) swelling within a tissue, very often containing fluid. It is sometimes caused by the blockage of a duct (eg a sweat-gland cyst in the skin), by abnormal embryological development (eg a renal cyst), or by infection (eg an amoebic or hydatid cyst).

cystic fibrosis [**sis**tik fiy**broh**sis] A genetically determined disorder that causes the mucous secretions in many parts of the body to become thickened and viscid. One in 25 Caucasians carry the cystic fibrosis gene, and a child will be affected if it inherits the gene from both parents. The thick mucus particularly affects the respiratory and digestive symptoms. It accumulates in the airways, which dilate and are prone to recurrent infection. It also blocks ducts in the pancreas, preventing pancreatic secretions, which are essential for digestion, from reaching the intestines. Daily physiotherapy can reduce the build-up of mucus in the airways, and oral supplements are available to replace pancreatic enzymes. However, even with treatment, affected individuals die prematurely.

cystitis [si**stiy**tis] Inflammation of the wall of the urinary bladder, usually due to an infection. It induces frequency of urination, with a burning sensation on passing urine.

cytochrome [**siy**tokrohm] An iron-containing protein (*haemoprotein*) found in virtually all aerobic organisms. It functions as an electron-carrier in a variety of oxidation–reduction reactions that take place within living cells during normal metabolism.

cytokines [**siy**tokiynz] Messenger molecules within the immune system which are involved in modulating the immune response. Some (eg IL-2, TNF, interferon, GMCSF) have been genetically engineered, and tested (though not with particular success) in diseases such as cancer. Cytokine gene therapy is currently being tested and appears to be a more promising approach.

cytokinin [siyto**kiy**nin] A hormone found in plants which acts in combination with other hormones (*auxins*) to promote cell division.

cytology [siy**tol**ojee] The study of the structure and function of cells. Microscopic studies of cells, using a variety of staining techniques to identify cell types, are important in the diagnosis of some diseases, especially cancer. The use of the electron microscope enables detailed study of the fine structures within cells.

cytoplasm [**siy**toplazm] That part of an animal or plant cell enclosed by the cell membrane (*plasma membrane*) but excluding the nucleus. The cytoplasm contains a range of organelles, such as mitochondria, ribosomes, and golgi bodies, each with a specialized function.

cytosine [**siy**toseen] $C_4H_5N_3O$. A base derived from pyrimidine, one of the four found in nucleic acids, where it is generally paired with guanine.

cytotoxic drugs *chemotherapy*

czar *tsar*

Czech and Slovak literature From its chronicle beginnings in the 11th-c, Czech literature has always looked to the West, and the late 13th-c *Alexandreida* also signals an endemic political awareness – evident in the Chaucerian *Groom and Student*, and the *New Council of Animals* by Flaška z Pardubic (died 1403). The verse legend, courtly romance, and love lyric also flourished from the 14th-c, alongside the publication of the first Czech dictionary and the foundation of Prague University (1348). The early Renaissance brought many translations and travelogues, while the Reformation stimulated the vigorous prose writings of the martyr John Huss (1372–1415), and the philosophy of Petr Chelčický (1390–1460), who influenced Tolstoy.

The publication of the Kraliká Bible (1579–93, 6 vols) helped create the modern Czech language, and it was the Czech National Revival, heralded by the scholar Josef Dobrovský (1753–1829) which laid the foundation for modern Czech literature. Prominent writers were the historical novelist Josef Linda (1789–1834), the poet Jan Kollár (1793–1852), who promoted the Pan-Slav idea at this time; and Karel Mácha (1810–36), who is regarded as the greatest of Czech poets. The influential almanacs *May* (begun 1858), *Ruch* (begun 1868), and *Lumír* (begun c.1875) directed a predominantly patriotic taste, publishing writers such as Jan Neruda (1834–91), Svatopluk Çech (1846–1908), Julius Zeyer (1841–1901), and Jaroslav Vrchlický (1853–1912); and 'the Czech Walter Scott', Alois Jirásek (1851–1930). World War 1 produced Hašek's satirical masterpiece *The Good Soldier Šwejk* (1921–3); Karel Çapek, who invented the word for 'robot', foresaw the dangers of advanced technology. Czech literature veered left with Vladislav Vançura (1891–1942), Vítĕzslav Nezval (1900–58), and the poet Jaroslav Seifert before succumbing to stagnation under communist rule. Writers such as the poet Miroslav Holub, the novelists Bohumil Hrabal (1914–97) and Milan Kundera, and the dramatist Václav Havel maintained a courageous witness until the liberation of 1989.

Czech Republic

[chek], Czech **Česká Republika**

Local name Ccaron;eská republika

Timezone GMT +1

Area 78 864 km²/30 441 sq mi

Population total (2002e) 10 210 000

Status Republic

Date of independence 1993

Capital Prague

Languages Czech (official), with several minorities

Ethnic groups Czech (94%), Slovak (4%), Hungarian, Polish, German, and Ukrainian minorities

Religions Roman Catholic (39%), Protestant (2%)

Physical features Landlocked in C Europe; Bohemian Massif, average height, 900 m/2953 ft, surrounds the Bohemian basin in W; Elbe-Moldau river system flows N into Germany; fertile plains of the Morava R divide Czech from Slovak Republic; c.40% land is arable.

Climate Continental, with warm, humid summers and cold, dry winters; average annual temperatures 2°C (Jan), 19°C (Jul) in Prague; average annual rainfall, 483 mm/19 in.

Currency 1 Koruna (Kcs) = 100 haléř

Economy Steel production around Ostrava coalfields; machinery, iron, glass, chemicals, motor vehicles, cement; wheat, sugar beet, potatoes, rye, corn, barley.

GDP (2002e) $157·1 bn, per capita $15 300

Human Development Index (2002) 0·849

History From 880 ruled by the Premyslid dynasty; rise of Bohemian royal power, 14th-c; ruled by Austrian Habsburgs, early 17th-c; Czech lands united with Slovakia to form separate state of Czechoslovakia, 1918; occupied by Germany, 1938; government in exile in London during World War 2; Czechoslovakian independence, with loss of some territory to USSR, 1946; communist rule imposed by Russia following 1948 coup; attempt at liberalization by Dubcvek terminated by intervention of Warsaw Pact troops, 1968; fall from power of the Communist Party, 1989; 1992 agreement to divide Czechoslovakia into its constituent republics, Czech and Slovak, by Jan 1993; Czech Republic now comprises former provinces of Bohemia, Silesia, Moravia; governed by a Chamber of Deputies and (1996) 81-member Senate.

Head of State

1993–2003 Václav Havel

2003– Václav Klaus

Head of Government

1997–8 Josef Tosovsky

1998–2002 Miloš Zeman

2002– Vladimir Spidla

But Kundera remains a self-exile in France; and Havel, prolific under persecution, has been lost to literature as president, first of Czechoslovakia and later of the Czech Republic.

Slovak literature existed only in oral tradition before the 19th-c. The 'National Awakening' produced the poets L'udovit Štúr (1815–56) and Janko Král' (1822–76), and Ján Botto's lyrical epic *The Death of Jánošík* (1862); also novels by Ján Kalinčiak (1822–71) and Jonáš Záborský (1812–76). More sophistication is apparent in the works of the poet Hviezdoslav (pseudonym of Pavol Országh, 1849–1921), the novelist Martin Kukučín (1860–1928), and the later Symbolist Ivan Krasko (1876–1958). Slovak literature endured the same trials as Czech until 1989, preserving its tradition nevertheless in the work of several fine lyric poets; among them Vojtěch Mihálik (1926–), Ivan Kupec (1922–), L'ubomír Feldek (1936–), and Miroslav Pius (1942–).

Czech Legion A corps of 40 000 Czech and Slovak volunteers and ex-prisoners-of-war in Russia, who rose in revolt against the Bolsheviks (May 1918) while being transported home along the Trans-Siberian railway. They seized many towns along the railway, and soon controlled much of Siberia. The Czech Legion's revolt sparked off the first phase of the Russian Civil War.

Czechoslovakia [chekoslovahkia], Czech **Československo**, official name **Czech and Slovak Federative Republic** pop (1992e) 15 605 000; area 127 899 sq km/49 369 sq mi. Former federal state consisting of the Czech Republic (W) and the Slovak Republic (E); capital, Prague; official languages, Czech and Slovak; population, 65% Czech, 30% Slovak, with several minorities; unit of currency, the koruna or crown of 100 haler; formerly ruled by Austrian Habsburgs; Czech lands united with Slovakia to form separate state, 1918; Masaryk elected first president of parliamentary democracy; communist rule followed 1948 coup; attempt at liberalization by Dubček terminated by intervention of Warsaw Pact troops, 1968; strong dissident protest movement led to fall of communism in 1989, and election of President Havel; each republic was governed by a National Council, with overall power vested in the Federal Assembly, which elected the president, and comprised the Chamber of Nations (75 Czech and 75 Slovak delegates) and Chamber of the People (200 elected deputies); agreement to divide into the two constituent republics made in 1992, effective 1 January 1993.

Czech Republic *see panel*

Czestochowa [chestokhova] 50°49N 19°00E, pop (2000e) 260 000. Industrial city in SC Poland; on R Warta; railway; airfield; technical university (1949); steel, iron ore, chemicals, textiles; Paulite Monastery (1382) on Jasna Góra (Hill of Light), chief pilgrimage centre in Poland, with icon of the Black Madonna; museum of iron ore mining; annual national violin festival.

d

dab European flatfish (*Limanda limanda*) abundant on sandy bottoms in inshore waters to 150 m/500 ft depth; feeds on crustaceans and other invertebrates; both eyes on right side of head; scales rough; body length up to 40 cm/16 in; valuable food fish, exploited commercially using trawls and nets (seines). Family: Pleuronectidae.)

dabbling duck A duck of the tribe Anatini; obtains food from water surface, or turns vertically 'tail up' to feed on vegetation on shallow lake beds, rivers, etc. One species, the **mallard**, has given rise to various domestic forms. (Subfamily: Anatinae.)

dabchick The common name for some smaller birds of the grebe family.

Dacca *Dhaka*

dace Freshwater fish (*Leuciscus leuciscus*) widespread in rivers of Europe and Russia; length up to 30 cm/1 ft, body slim; olive-green above, underside silvery white; feeds on aquatic invertebrates and plants, including flying insects at surface; close relative of chub and orfe. (Family: Cyprinidae.)

dachshund A breed of dog, developed from small terriers in Germany; small, with long back, short legs; long muzzle, pendulous ears; used for hunting (sent into burrows); several sizes: *standard*, *miniature*, and *rabbit*, each with *smooth-haired*, *wire-haired*, and *long-haired* varieties; also known as **sausage dog**.

Dacia [daysha] In antiquity, the name given to the area N of the Danube roughly corresponding to modern Romania. Conquered by the Romans in the early 2nd-c AD, its rich deposits of silver, iron, and gold were actively exploited by them.

dactylology [daktilolojee] A means of communication in which the fingers are used to sign the different letters of the alphabet; also known as **finger-spelling**. The system has been documented from the 17th-c, and is widely used among the adult deaf population. Both two-handed and one-handed manual alphabets have been devised.

dactyloscopy *fingerprint*

Dada (Fr 'rocking horse') or **Dadaism** A modern art movement founded in Zürich in 1916 which, against the background of disillusionment with World War 1, attacked traditional artistic values. The name was chosen at random from a dictionary. The founders included poets such as Tristan Tzara (1896–1963) as well as artists such as Jean Arp. Important contributors included Duchamp (whose *Fountain*, 1917 – a porcelain urinal – is perhaps the best-known 'work' of Dada), Ernst, Picabia, and Ray. The Dadaists influenced the Surrealists, and their deliberate shock-tactics were revived by some artists in the 1960s.

daddy longlegs *cranefly; harvestman*

Daedalus [deedalus] A legendary Athenian inventor, who worked for King Minos in Crete and constructed the labyrinth. Later he escaped to Sicily with wings he had made for himself and Icarus; there he made the golden honeycomb kept at Mt Eryx. Any archaic work of skill was ascribed to him, and he was a patron saint of craftsmen in Ancient Greece.

daffodil A species of narcissus (*Narcissus pseudonarcissus*), yellow, with a central trumpet up to 2·5 cm/1 in long, and darker than the six surrounding perianth-segments; native to Europe, the widely-grown garden plants are mainly large-flowered hybrids; name used for many species of *Narcissus*, but not for the whole genus. (Family: Amaryllidaceae.)

Dafoe, Willem [dafoh] (1955–) Film actor, born in Appleton, Wisconsin, USA. He joined an avant garde theatre group and toured extensively with them for two years in the USA and Europe, then became a founding member of the Wooster Group. He made his film debut with a small part in *Heaven's Gate* (1980), and went on to the Oscar-nominated role of Sergeant Elias in *Platoon* (1986) and the controversial title role in *The Last Temptation of Christ* (1988). Later films include *Tom and Viv* (1994), *The English Patient* (1996), *Speed 2* (1997), *eXistenZ* (1999), and *Animal Factory* (2003).

Dafydd ap Gwilym [davith ap gwilim] (c.1320–c.1380) Poet, born probably in Brogynin, Cardiganshire, W Wales, UK. He wrote love songs, satirical poems, and nature poems in the complex *cywydd* metre which he perfected, much extending the range of such poetry. His work may be compared with that of the troubadours.

Dagda, the [dagda] Irish spirit being found throughout Ireland, variously represented as benign, good, and the father of all. He is noted for his enormous club on wheels which both kills and restores to life, for his cauldron which inspires and rejuvenates, and for his effective harp. Oengus and Brigit were his children.

Daguerre, Louis Jacques Mandé [dagair] (1789–1851) Photographic pioneer, born in Cormeilles, NW France. He had been a scene painter in Paris, when, from 1826 onwards, and partly in conjunction with Nicéphore Niepce, he perfected the photographic process named after him.

daguerreotype [dageruhtiyp] An early system of photography established by Louis Daguerre in France in 1839. A silver-plated sheet was sensitized by iodine vapour, and after a long exposure in the camera the image was developed over heated mercury and fixed in a solution of common salt. It became obsolete in the 1850s.

Dahl, Roald (1916–90) Writer, born in Llandaff, Cardiff, S Wales, UK, of Norwegian parents. Educated at Repton School, he worked for the Shell Oil Co in London and Africa, then served as a fighter pilot in the RAF during World War 2. He specialized in writing short stories of unexpected horror and macabre surprise, such as in *Someone Like You* (1953) and *Kiss, Kiss* (1960). His children's books display a similar taste for the grotesque, such as *James and the Giant Peach* (1961), *Charlie and the Chocolate Factory* (1964), and *BFG* (1982); several have been made into successful films.

dahlia [daylia] A tuberous perennial up to 8 m/26 ft high, sometimes an epiphyte, native to mountains from Mexico to Colombia. Several species with large, showy, chrysanthemum-like flower-heads were introduced into cultivation, originally for the tubers, which were eaten as a vegetable; but they are now commonly grown as garden ornamentals. Extensive hybridization has resulted in a great variety of flower colour and form. (Genus: *Dahlia*, 28 species. Family: Compositae.)

Dahmer, Jeffrey (1960–94) US convicted murderer. He confessed to 17 killings, committed in the USA over several years, and was found guilty in 1992 of 15 of these murders. His insanity plea having been rejected by the jury, he was sentenced to life imprisonment. He was killed in prison by a fellow prisoner.

Dahomey [dahohmee] W African kingdom based on its capital at Abomey, which in the late 17th-c and early 18th-c extended its authority from the coast to the interior, to the W of the Yoruba states. In the 1720s the cavalry of the Oyo kingdom of the Yoruba devastated Dahomey, but when the Oyo Empire collapsed in the early 19th-c, Dahomey regained its power. The state was annexed by the French in 1883, and regained its independence (later renaming itself Benin) in 1960.

Daibutsu [diybutsoo] A Japanese statue of Buddha, the finest example in Japan being the bronze figure cast in 1252 at Kamakura, 11·5 m/37 ft high.

Dáil Éireann [doyl airan] (Gaelic 'Assembly of Ireland') The lower house of the parliament of the Republic of Ireland. Unlike the upper house, the Senate (*Seanad Éireann*), which is appointed, the Dáil is elected by universal suffrage by proportional representation for a period of 5 years. It nominates the prime minister for appointment by the president. There are 166 members, who are called *Teatcha Dala*. It was first established in 1919 when the Irish republicans, elected to Westminister in the 1918 election, proclaimed an Irish state.

Daimler, Gottlieb (Wilhelm) [daymler], originally [diymler] (1834–1900) Engineer, born in Schorndorf, SW Germany. He worked from 1872 on improving the gas engine, and in 1885 patented a high-speed internal combustion engine. With W Maybach (1846–1929) he produced an engine-driven bicycle (1885, perhaps the first motorcycle), converted a horse-drawn carriage into a petrol-engined vehicle (1886), and designed one of the earliest roadworthy motor cars (1889). In 1890, he founded the Daimler Automobile Co in Cannstatt, near Stuttgart.

daimyo [diymyoh] A Japanese feudal lord, equivalent to a mediaeval baron in Europe. Powerful under the Tokugawa shoguns (1603–1868), daimyo lost power at the Meiji Restoration. They had responsibility for keeping the peace. The amount of rice their domains produced showed their prestige.

Dairen *Dalian*

dairy farming A farming system specializing in the production of milk – usually from cows, but in some regions from sheep, goats, yaks, buffalo, or reindeer. Specialist dairy-cow breeds include Friesians, Ayrshires, and Jerseys; there are also dual beef-and-dairy herds, such as the US shorthorn. Dairy farming is most common in the wetter, temperate parts of the world, where grass grows well and where cows can graze outside for all or part of the year. In hotter climates dairy cows tend to be confined all year round, and fodder is harvested and carried to them. Most farmers specializing in dairy husbandry sell their milk to dairy manufacturers, who make butter, cheese, cream, yogurt, and skimmed milk. These foods are **dairy products**. European Union policy has been to encourage high production from fewer cows, which under a quota regime ultimately means fewer dairy farmers. In recent years, many dairy farms in the developed world have become unviable and have ceased production.

daisy A perennial native to Europe and W Asia (*Bellis perennis*), with a basal rosette of oval or spoon-shaped leaves; leafless flowering stems up to 20 cm/8 in, each bearing a solitary flower-head; outer ray florets white often tinged red, inner disc florets yellow. It grows in short grassland and garden lawns where regular mowing prevents it from being smothered by taller vegetation. It spreads by short rhizomes, often becoming a pernicious weed. Forms with double flowers are grown for ornament. (Family: Compositae.)

daisy-wheel printer A type of impact printer, used in computer systems and in typewriters, in which the individual print characters are carried on separate 'petals' of a segmented disk called the **daisy-wheel**. The daisy-wheel is rotated to bring the relevant character in front of a striking hammer. Daisy-wheel printers are relatively slow, but are capable of producing high quality typescript.

Dakar [dakah(r)] 14°38N 17°27W, pop (2000e) 2 183 000. Seaport capital of Senegal, at the S extremity of the Cape Verde peninsula; W Africa's second largest port, serving Senegal and Mauritania; founded, 1857; capital of French West Africa, 1902; part of Dakar and Dependencies, 1924–46; held by Vichy forces during World War 2; capital of Senegal, 1958; airport; railway terminus; university (1957); commerce, soap, sugar, leather products, pharmaceuticals, textiles, metal products, plastics, food processing; Great Mosque, cathedral (consecrated, 1936), ethnographical museum, notable markets.

Daladier, Edouard [daladyay] (1884–1970) French statesman and prime minister (1933, 1934, 1938–40), born in Carpentras, SE France. In 1927 he became leader of the Radical Socialists, and in 1933 minister of war, and prime minister of a short-lived government, a pattern which was repeated in 1934. In 1936 he was minister of war in the Popular Front cabinet, and as premier (1938) supported appeasement policies and signed the Munich Pact. In 1940 he resigned, became successively war and foreign minister, and on the fall of France was arrested and interned until 1945. After the war he continued in politics until 1958.

Dalai Lama [daliy lahma], (Mongolian, 'ocean-like guru') Spiritual and temporal head of Tibet, currently **Tenzin Gyatso** (1935–), born in Taktser, China, into a peasant family. He was designated the 14th Dalai Lama in 1937, but his rights were exercised by a regency until 1950. He fled to Chumbi in S Tibet after an abortive anti-Chinese uprising in 1950, but negotiated an autonomy agreement with the People's Republic the following year, and for the next eight years served as nominal ruler of Tibet. After China's suppression of the Tibetan national uprising of 1959, he was forced into permanent exile, settling at Dharamsala in Punjab, India, where he established a democratically-based alternative government. He was awarded the 1989 Nobel Prize for Peace in recognition of his commitment to the nonviolent liberation of his homeland.

Daldry, Stephen [doldree] (1960–) Film and theatre director, born in Dorset, S England, UK. He studied at Sheffield University, and began his career with the Crucible Theatre, Sheffield (1986–8). He later moved to London where he became artistic director of the Gate Theatre (1990–2) and the English Stage Company (1992–9), and directed *An Inspector Calls* (1992, Tony Award) for the National Theatre. In 1999 he was appointed associate director of the Royal Court. He received best director Oscar nominations for the films *Billy Elliot* (2000) and *The Hours* (2002), and later films include *Hiding Room* (2002).

d'Alembert, Jean le Rond *Alembert, Jean le Rond d'*

Dales pony A breed of horse, developed in N England; height, 14–14½ hands/1·4–1·5 m/4 ft 8 in–4 ft 10 in; black or brown; sturdy with short legs; strong; formerly used for farm work and carrying loads; now popular for pony trekking.

Dalglish, Kenny [dalgleesh], popular name of **Kenneth Mathieson Dalglish** (1951–) Footballer and manager, born in Glasgow, W Scotland, UK. He joined Glasgow Celtic in 1967, transferring to Liverpool in 1977 for a then record fee between two British clubs of £440 000. He won 102 caps for Scotland, in addition to three European Cups. Unexpectedly invited to manage Liverpool while still a player, he confounded the pundits by being an instant success. In his first season, Liverpool won both Cup and League. He is the only player to have scored 100 goals in both English and Scottish football. He joined Newcastle United as manager (1997–8), returning to Celtic as director of football in 1999.

Dalhousie, James Andrew Broun Ramsay, 1st Marquess of [dalhowzee] (1812–60) British Governor-General of India (1847–56), born at Dalhousie Castle, Midlothian, EC Scotland, UK. He studied at Oxford, and became an MP (1837), Earl of Dalhousie (1838), and President of the Board of Trade (1845). In India (1847) he encouraged the development of railways and irrigation works. He annexed Satara (1847) and Punjab (1849), but the annexation of Oudh (1856) caused resentment which fuelled the 1857 rebellion. He was made a marquess in 1849, and retired through ill health in 1856.

Dali, Salvador (Felipe Jacinto) [dahlee], Span **Dalí** (1904–89) Artist, born in Figueras, NE Spain. After studying at the Academy of Fine Arts, Madrid, he moved to Paris and joined the

Surrealists (1928), becoming one of the principal figures of the movement. His study of abnormal psychology and dream symbolism led him to represent 'paranoiac' objects in landscapes remembered from his Spanish boyhood. In 1940 he settled in the USA, became a Catholic, and devoted his art to symbolic religious paintings. He wrote *The Secret Life of Salvador Dali* (1942), and collaborated with Luis Buñuel in the Surrealist films *Un Chien andalou* (1928, An Andalusian Dog), and *L'Age d'or* (1930, The Golden Age). One of his best-known paintings is 'The Persistence of Memory' (known as 'The Limp Watches', 1931, Museum of Modern Art, New York City).

Dalian [dalyan], also **Lüda, Lü-ta, Dairen, Ta-lien** 38°53N 121°37E, pop (2000e) 2 770 000, administrative region 5 456 000. Port city in Liaoning province, NE China; port built (1899–1930) by Japanese; Soviet occupation (1945–54); deep natural harbour, silt-free and ice-free; resort beaches nearby; airfield; railway; designated a special economic zone; diesel engines, shipbuilding, machine tools, chemicals, textiles, glass, fishing (especially shellfish); centre of fruit-growing area (well-known apples).

Dallapiccola, Luigi [dalapeekohla] (1904–75) Composer, born in Pazin, W Croatia (formerly Pisino, Italy). He studied at Florence, becoming a pianist and music teacher. After World War 2 he taught composition in the USA for several years. His compositions make wide use of 12-note technique, and include songs, a piano concerto, three operas, a ballet, and choral works such as *Canti di prigionia* (1938–41, Songs of Prison).

Dallas 32°47N 96°49W, pop (2000e) 1 188 600. Seat of Dallas Co, NE Texas, USA, on the Trinity R; ninth largest city in the USA; commercial and financial centre of the SW; founded, 1841; city status, 1871; President Kennedy assassinated here (22 Nov 1963); airport (Dallas–Fort Worth); railway; two universities (1910, 1956); electronic and transportation equipment, machinery, textiles, clothing, leather goods, oil refining; cultural, educational and artistic centre; tourism; scene of the television series *Dallas*; professional teams, Mavericks (basketball), Cowboys (football); Texas State Fair (Oct).

Dalmatia [dalmaysha] A name applied since early times to the strip of territory in the Balkan Peninsula bordering the Adriatic Sea in SW Croatia from the S end of Pag I to Cavtat, S of Dubrovnik; largely mountainous and barren, with few lines of communication to the interior; formerly part of the Greek province of Illyria, settled 6th-c BC; occupied by Slavs, 7th-c AD; harbours at Zadar, Split, Dubrovnik; wine, tourism.

dalmatian A breed of dog, officially from the Balkans W coastal region, but probably developed in India many centuries ago; large, lightly built, with long legs, tail, and muzzle; ears short, pendulous; coat short, white with black or brown spots.

Dalton, (Edward) Hugh (John Neale) Dalton, Baron (1887–1962) British statesman, born in Neath, SC Wales, UK. He studied at Cambridge and the London School of Economics, and was a Labour MP (1924–31, and from 1935). He became minister for economic warfare (1940) and President of the Board of Trade (1942) in Churchill's wartime coalition. As Labour Chancellor of the Exchequer (1945–7), he nationalized the Bank of England (1946), but resigned as a result of 'budget leakages' to a journalist. He was made a life peer in 1960.

Dalton, John [dawltn] (1766–1844) Chemist, born in Eaglesfield, Cumbria, NW England, UK. After 1781 he became assistant in a boarding-school kept by a cousin in Kendal, where in 1787 he commenced a meteorological journal, continued all his life, recording 200 000 observations. In 1793 he was appointed teacher of mathematics and science in New College, Manchester. He first described colour blindness (*Daltonism*) in 1794, exemplified in his own case and that of his brother. His chief physical researches were on mixed gases, the force of steam, the elasticity of vapours, and the expansion of gases by heat, his law of partial pressures being also known as *Dalton's law*. In chemistry he worked on the absorption of gases, and his atomic theory (c.1810) was able to interpret the laws of chemical combination and the conservation of mass, and gave a new basis for all quantitative chemistry. One of the leading early scientists, he remained a man of quiet demeanour and simple habits, reflecting his Quaker beliefs. He 'never found time' to marry.

dalton *atomic mass unit*

Dalton's law of partial pressures A law in chemistry, formulated by John Dalton: in a mixture of gases, each gas exerts the same pressure as it would if it were the only gas present in the given volume. For example, as the atmosphere contains roughly 80% nitrogen, the pressure exerted by nitrogen is 80% of the total pressure.

dam A barrier constructed to control the flow of water, thus forming a reservoir. Dams are built to allow storage of water, giving a controlled supply for domestic or industrial consumption, for irrigation, to generate hydro-electric power, or to prevent flooding. Large dams are built of earth, rock, concrete or of some combination of these materials (eg earth and rockfill). They are built either as **gravity dams**, where the strength is due entirely to the great weight of material; as **arch dams**, where abutments at either side support the structure; or as **arch gravity dams**, a combination of the two. The earliest known dams were in China, 6th-c BC. Modern examples are Aswan High Dam (Egypt), Grand Coulee Dam (NE Washington, USA), and Hoover Dam (Arizona, USA).

damages A remedy providing compensation in the form of money for a civil wrong or breach of duty. In breach of contract cases, the compensation aims to put the innocent party in the same position he or she would have been in had the contract been performed as agreed. In tort (delict, in Scotland), the aim is to compensate the plaintiff for the injury, loss, or damage actually suffered. In certain cases, exemplary damages can be awarded in addition to compensatory damages as a punishment and a deterrent. Nominal damages may be given for a breach of contract and some torts (eg trespass) when no damage has been caused. The innocent person must do whatever possible to minimize his or her losses, for example a travel company must try to re-book a cancelled holiday. Damages must be reasonably forseeable by the defendant, and may be reduced by the plaintiff's *contributary negligence*.

daman *hyrax*

Daman and Diu [damahn, deeoo] pop (2001e) 158 100; area 456 sq km/176 sq mi. Union territory in W India; chief town, Daman; island of Diu taken by Portugal, 1534; Daman area N of Mumbai ceded to Portugal, 1539; occupied by India, 1961; part of Union Territory of Goa, Daman and Diu until 1987.

Damascus [damaskus], Arabic **Dimashq** 33°30N 36°19E, pop (2000e) 1 860 000. Capital city of Syria, on the R Barada; claimed to be the world's oldest continuously inhabited city; a world heritage site; in ancient times a great trade and commercial centre; satellite city Dimashq ad-Jadideh; airport; railway; university (1923); famous for its crystallized fruits, brass and copper ware, silks, woodwork; mediaeval citadel (1219), Great Mosque (8th-c, burned 1893, then restored); ancient Via Recta, runs E–W for 1500 m/5000 ft with Roman gateways at either end; international fair (Aug).

Damavand, Mount [damavand] 35°56N 52°08E. Volcanic cone in the Elburz Mts, N Iran; height 5670 m/18 602 ft; highest peak in Iran, with a permanent snowcap; Damavand resort at its S foot.

Damien, Father Joseph [damyĩ], originally **Joseph de Veuster** (1840–89) Missionary, born in Tremelo, N Belgium. He was renowned for his great work among the lepers of the Hawaiian island of Molokai, where he lived from 1873 until his death from the disease. He became internationally known after Robert Louis Stevenson published a passionate defence of his character and work. He was beatified in 1995.

Damocles [damokleez] (4th-c BC) Legendary courtier of the elder Dionysius, tyrant of Syracuse (405–367 BC). He extolled the happiness of royalty, but the tyrant showed him the precarious nature of fortune in a singular manner. While seated at a richly-spread table, Damocles looked up to see a keen-edged sword suspended over his head by a single horse-hair.

Damon, Matt (1970–) Film actor, born in Cambridge, Massachusetts, USA. He studied English at Harvard but left early to pursue a career in acting. He went on to gain starring roles in the films *The Rainmaker* (1997), and *Good Will Hunting* (1997), for which he shared an Oscar for best original screenplay with fellow co-star Ben Affleck. Later films include *The Talented Mr Ripley* (1999), and *Ocean's Eleven* (2001).

Damon and Pythias [daymon, pithias], also found as **Phintias** (4th-c BC) Two Pythagoreans of Syracuse, remembered as the models of faithful friendship. Condemned to death by the elder Dionysius, tyrant of Syracuse (405–367 BC), Pythias begged to be allowed to go home to arrange his affairs, and Damon pledged his own life for his friend's. Pythias returned just in time to save Damon from death. Struck by so noble an example, the tyrant pardoned Pythias, and desired to be admitted into their sacred fellowship.

Dampier, William [dampeer] (1652–1715) Navigator and buccaneer, born in East Coker, Somerset, SW England, UK. He journeyed to Newfoundland and the West Indies, then joined a band of buccaneers along the Pacific coast of South America (1679). In 1683 he sailed across the Pacific, visiting the Philippines, China, and Australia. On his return to England, he published his *New Voyage round the World* (1697). He then led a voyage of discovery to the South Seas (1699), exploring the NW coast of Australia, and giving his name to the *Dampier Archipelago* and *Strait*. He made further journeys there in 1703 and 1708.

damping Reduction of the size of oscillations by the removal of energy. For example, the indicator needles of gauges are often immersed in oil to give frictional damping; and resistive circuit components reduce electrical oscillations.

damselfish Any of the family Pomacentridae; small brightly coloured marine fishes widespread in tropical and temperate seas around reefs and rocky shores; body length 10–25 cm/4–10 in; includes anemonefish, which lives in close association with sea anemones. (7 genera, including *Chromis* and *Pomacentrus*.)

damselfly A large, long-bodied insect with two pairs of slender wings typically held together over the abdomen at rest. Damselflies are powerful predators, both as aquatic larvae and as flying adults. (Order: Odonata. Suborder: Zygoptera, c.3000 species.)

damson A type of plum (*Prunus domestica*, subspecies *institia*) in which the small, ovoid fruit is purplish with a waxy bloom; thought to be a cultivated form of bullace. (Family: Rosaceae.)

Danae [danayee] In Greek mythology, the daughter of King Acrisius of Argos. When an oracle prophesied that her son would kill his grandfather, Acrisius imprisoned her in a bronze tower, where Zeus visited her in the form of a golden shower. She gave birth to a son, Perseus, who accidentally killed Acrisius with a discus.

Danakil Depression [danakil] Desert area in NE Ethiopia and Eritrea; low-lying region bounded by Red Sea (N, E) and Rift Valley (S, W); mountainous in parts, rising to 1000 m/3000 ft; land also dips to 116 m/381 ft below sea-level; extremely hot area, temperatures close to 60°C; major salt reserves; inhabited by the Afar; crossed by Djibouti–Addis Ababa railway.

Da Nang [dah nang], formerly **Tourane** 16°04N 108°13E, pop (2000e) 445 100. Seaport in Quang Nam-Danang province, C Vietnam; on the South China Sea; site of an important US military base during the Vietnam War; textiles.

Dance, George, known as **George Dance the Elder** (1695–1768) Architect, born in London, UK. He designed the Mansion House (1739) and many other London buildings, and was surveyor to the City of London (1735–68). His son, **George Dance, the Younger** (1741–1825), was also an architect, and succeeded his father as surveyor. An exponent of Neoclassicism, deriving from his studies in Italy, his best-known building was Newgate Prison (1770–83). He was one of the original Royal Academicians.

dance *African / Black / British Ballroom / Caribbean / community / country / disco / European court / Indian / jazz / modern / morris / National Youth / Oriental / postmodern / step / street / sword / traditional dance; allemande; ballet; conga; courante; dance notation; fandango; farandole; flamenco; gavotte; gigue; hornpipe; jig; London Contemporary Dance Theatre; mazurka; maypole; minuet; pavane; polka; polonaise; quadrille; Rambert Dance Company; rumba; samba; sarabande; tarantella; waltz*

dance notation The recording of dance movement through symbols. More than 100 systems have been created, using letter abbreviations (15th-c), track drawings (18th-c), stick figure and music note systems (19th-c), and abstract symbol systems. Three are in current use; Benesh, Eshkol, and Labanotation. Labanotation is the most widely used system outside the UK; Benesh is used chiefly by the Royal Ballet (London). They are used in dance education, the documentation of choreography, movement behaviour in work and therapy, and anthropology. Recently, systems have been developed to computerize notation.

dance of death A common theme in late mediaeval art: the allegorical representation of a dance or procession in which the living and the dead take part. Holbein the Younger designed a famous set of woodcuts on this theme (published 1538).

dance therapy A form of group psychotherapy, with or without music, which encourages spontaneous movements rather than teaching formal dance sequences. It is particularly used as a way of enabling people who have difficulty in talking about their feelings to express their emotions through body movements. The technique is also used to encourage the elderly to keep their joints and spines supple, and can improve mobility in patients suffering from nervous and muscle disorders.

D and C *dilatation and curettage*

dandelion A perennial, native to Europe and W Asia; leaves in a basal rosette, entire or variably lobed and toothed; flower-heads solitary, borne on leafless hollow stems, florets yellow; fruits with a parachute of white hairs attached by a long stalk, the whole fruiting head forming the familiar 'clock'. Many dandelions reproduce from fruits formed without fertilization having taken place, resulting in many distinct populations or microspecies, with over a thousand described from Europe alone. The best-known species, *Taraxacum officinale*, is a cosmopolitan weed, its young leaves eaten as a salad vegetable, tap roots ground into a coffee substitute, and flower-heads sometimes used for wine-making. (Genus: *Taraxacum*, c.60 species. Family: Compositae.)

Dandie Dinmont A breed of dog, developed in Britain in the 19th-c from wire-haired hunting terriers; small terrier with long body and short legs; long soft hair, especially on the head; ears pendulous; tail long.

Dandolo, Enrico [dandoloh] (c.1110–1205) Italian statesman, born in Venice, NE Italy. In 1173 he was ambassador to Constantinople, and in 1192 became Doge of Venice. In 1202 he marched at the head of the Fourth Crusade, subduing Trieste and Zara, the coasts of Albania, the Ionian Is, and (1205) Constantinople, where he established the empire of the Latins.

dandruff Fine dry scales which fall from an eruption of the skin of the scalp, usually noticed when the scales fall on to clothing around the shoulders. It possibly results from infection with the fungus *Pityrosporum*.

Dane, Clemence, pseudonym of **Winifred Ashton** (1888–1965) Novelist and playwright, born in Greenwich, EC London, UK. Her novels include *Regiment of Women* (1917), *Legend* (1919), and *The Flower Girls* (1954). Many of her plays achieved long runs, notably *A Bill of Divorcement* (1921), and the ingenious reconstruction of the poet's life in *Will Shakespeare* (1921).

Danelaw That part of England where Danish conquest and colonization in the late 9th-c left an imprint not only on legal and administrative practices, but on place-names, language, and culture. Danish-derived customs survived even the Norman Conquest, and in the 12th-c all E England from the Thames to the Tees was so designated.

Dangerfield, Thomas (1650–85) Conspirator, born in Waltham, Essex, SE England, UK. A thief, vagabond, and soldier, in 1679 he accused the Presbyterians of plotting to destroy the government. Imprisoned when this was shown to be a lie, he claimed he had been deceived by Catholics plotting against the life of Charles II. Convicted of libel, he was whipped and pilloried, and on returning from Tyburn was killed by a blow from a bystander.

Daniel, Glyn (Edmund) (1914–86) Archaeologist, born in Barry, Vale of Glamorgan, S Wales, UK. He studied at Cardiff and at Cambridge, where he lectured (1945–74) and became professor of archaeology (1974–81). His career was devoted less to excavation and research than to stimulating popular interest in archaeology through writing, editing, and broadcasting. He was a pioneer historian of archaeology and an energetic editor, both of the journal *Antiquity* (1958–86) and of the book series *Ancient Peoples and Places* published from 1955. On television he achieved particular popularity in the 1950s as chairman of the archaeological panel game, *Animal, Vegetable, Mineral.*

Daniel, Book of A book of the Hebrew Bible/Old Testament named after Daniel, its main character. It falls into two parts: chapters 1–6 contain narrative accounts about Daniel and his three companions, ostensibly set during the Babylonian Exile in the 6th-c BC; chapters 7–12 describe apocalyptic revelations of Daniel recorded as first-person visions. Although some date the work in the 6th-c BC, many prefer a later date of the 3rd–2nd-c BC, with several stages of compilation. The **Additions** are three works found joined to the Book of Daniel in some ancient Greek versions and in modern Roman Catholic Bibles, but forming part of the Protestant Apocrypha.

Danilova, Alexandra Dionysievna [danilohva] (1904–97) Dancer and teacher, born in Peterhof, NW Russia. She studied at the Imperial and State Ballet Schools in St Petersburg, and in 1924 toured Europe, joining Diaghilev and his Ballets Russes Company until his death. She danced as prima ballerina with the Ballet Russe de Monte Carlo (1938–52), and created leading parts in the works of Balanchine and Massine. She then taught at the School of American Ballet.

danio [daynioh] Colourful freshwater fish (*Danio malabaricus*) from India and Sri Lanka, extremely popular among aquarists; body with blue and golden side stripes, length up to c.13 cm/5 in. (Family: Cyprinidae.)

Danish *Danish literature; Germanic languages; Scandinavian languages*

Danish literature The first written evidence of Danish may be found in runic transcriptions dating from 800 to 1100. The important *Gesta Danorum* (Deeds of the Danes) was written in Latin by Saxo Grammaticus in the 12th-c. There was an oral tradition of epic balladry (13th–15th-c) but Danish literature begins with the translation of the Bible in 1550. Classical imitations marked the 17th-c, and the influence of English and French literature was strongly felt in the 18th-c, while the Norwegian-born dramatist Ludwig Holberg (1684–1754) was the first significant Danish writer. The 19th-c brought radicals and Romantics, including the poets Adam Oehlenschlager (1779–1850), Steensen Blicher (1782–1848), and Henrik Hertz (1798–1870). The early existentialist Søren Kierkegaard wrote at this time, as did Hans Christian Andersen, whose fairy tales appeared from 1835. The critic Georg Brandes (1842–1927) led the 'modern breakthrough' of the 1870s, when Jens Peter Jacobsen (1847–85) introduced naturalist fiction (*Niels Lyhne*, 1880), and Holger Drachmann (1846–1908) became Denmark's finest poet. The 20th-c saw a peasant movement, Expressionism, and inter-war restlessness, notably the fantasies of Karen Blixen (1885–1962, eg *Six Gothic Tales* 1934), and the novels and plays of Hans Christian Branner (1903–66) and Martin Hansen (1909–55), which are much concerned with World War 2. One of Denmark's internationally best-known modern authors, Henrik Stangerup (1937–98) wrote eloquently of late-20th-c society's feeling of alienation, in novels such as *Forføreren eller det er svaert at dø i Dieppe* (1985, The Seducer: it is hard to die in Dieppe, 1988).

Dannay, Frederic, originally **Daniel Nathan** (1905–82) Novelist, born in New York City, New York, USA. First cousin to **Manfred B Lee** (originally Manford Lepofsky (1905–71)), also born in New York City, they grew up as neighbours. In the 1920s they collaborated to win a detective short-story contest, and decided to become full-time writers. They adopted the joint pseudonyms **Ellery Queen and Barnaby Ross**, and in 1929 published their first 'Ellery Queen' novel, *The Roman Hat Mystery*. They went on to publish 33 Ellery Queen detective novels (with Ellery Queen also the name of their detective), and four others under the name of Barnaby Ross, featuring the detective Drury Lane. In 1941 they founded *Ellery Queen's Mystery Magazine* and later co-founded Mystery Writers of America. They always refused to disclose their exact writing methods, but evidently they took turns in developing the plots and writing the stories.

d'Annunzio, Gabriele [danuntseeoh] (1863–1938) Writer, born in Pescara, E Italy. He studied at Rome, and during the 1890s wrote several novels, influenced by the philosophy of Nietzsche, notably *Il trionfo della morte* (1894, The Triumph of Death). His best-known poetic work is *Laudi del cielo del mare della terra e degli eroi* (1899, In Praise of Sky, Sea, Earth, and Heroes), and his major plays include *La figlia di Iorio* (1904, The Daughter of Jorio) and the tragedy *La gioconda* (1899), which he wrote for the actress Eleonora Duse. Their tempestuous relationship was exposed in his erotic novel, *Il fuoco* (1900, trans The Flame of Life). An enthusiastic patriot, he urged Italian entry into World War 1, and served as a soldier, sailor, and finally airman. In 1919 he seized and held Fiume, despite the opposition of the Italian government and the rest of Europe, and ruled as dictator until he was removed by the Italian government (1920). He became a strong supporter of the Fascist Party under Mussolini.

Dante (Alighieri) (1265–1321) Poet, prose writer, literary theorist, philosopher, and political thinker, born in Florence, NC Italy. A lawyer's son, he was baptized Durante, later contracted into Dante. In 1274, when he was nine, a meeting with **Beatrice** (c.1265–90), possibly the daughter of the Florentine aristocrat Folco Portinari, influenced the rest of his life. His platonic devotion to her continued despite her marriage, and despite his own marriage (after her death) to Gemma Donati, daughter of a powerful Guelph family. In 1300, he became one of the six priors of Florence. His sympathy for the moderate 'White Guelphs' led to his exile in 1302, when the Black faction became dominant. His travelling after this date is unclear, but he never returned to his native city. He may have visited Paris and Oxford. Some believe he was recalled to Italy when Henry of Luxembourg became emperor, but when Henry died (1313), he took refuge in Ravenna, where he stayed until his death. Dante had six sons and one daughter. The dates and sequence of his various works are not known. The lyric poems, *Vita nuova*, which tells of his boyish passion for Beatrice, are probably the earliest. By far the most celebrated is the *Divina commedia* (1307–21, Divine Comedy), a vision of hell, purgatory, and heaven which gives an encyclopedic view of the highest culture and knowledge of his age. He also wrote several shorter poems, as well as treatises on government and language. Of the latter, his *Eloquence in the Vernacular Tongue* was of major importance in establishing the Italian vernacular in place of Latin as the literary language, which in turn was to revolutionize the literary tradition of other European cultures.

Danton, Georges (Jacques) [dãtõ] (1759–94) French revolutionary politician, born in Arcis-sur-Aube, NEC France. He became a lawyer, and was practising in Paris at the outbreak of the Revolution. In 1790 he formed the Cordelier's Club, a rallying point for revolutionary extremists, and in 1792 became minister of justice. He voted for the death of the king (1793), and was one of the original members of the Committee of Public Safety. He tried to abate the pitiless severity of his own Revolutionary Tribunal, but lost the leadership to Robespierre. He was arrested, brought before the Tribunal, and charged with conspiracy. Despite a heroic and eloquent defence, he was guillotined.

Dan, tribe of One of the 12 tribes of ancient Israel, said to be descended from the fifth son of Jacob, Dan's mother having been Bilhah, Rachel's maid. Its territory was vaguely defined, but was initially a coastal plain surrounded by the territories of Ephraim, Benjamin, and Judah; later they were forced to migrate N near the sources of the Jordan R.

Danu In Celtic religion, a mother-goddess who is associated with hills and the earth.

Danube, River, Ger **Donau**, Bulgarian **Dunav**, Russian **Dunai**, Romanian **Dunarea** River in C and SE Europe, rising in the Black Forest, SW Germany; flows generally E and S through Austria, the Slovak Republic, and Hungary, forming most of the Romania–Bulgaria border; enters the Black Sea through a wide, swampy delta; second longest river in Europe (2850 km/1770 mi); important commercial route, linked by canals to other major rivers (part of the Trans-Europe Waterway); flows through Vienna, Budapest, and Belgrade.

Danube School Pioneers of imaginative landscape painting who worked in the Danube region in the early 16th-c. Their members included Altdorfer and Cranach.

Danzig *Gdańsk*

Daoism *Taoism*

Daphne In Greek mythology, the daughter of a river-god, Ladon (or, in another story, Peneios). Pursued by the god Apollo, she was saved by being turned into a laurel, which became Apollo's sacred tree.

Daphnia [dafnia] A genus of water flea, commonly found in freshwater bodies. (Class: Branchiopoda. Order: Cladocera.)

Daphnis In Greek mythology, a Sicilian shepherd, half-brother of Pan, who was loved by a nymph. He did not return her love, so she blinded him. He became the inventor of pastoral poetry. In another story he would love nobody; when he died, all the beings of the island mourned him.

Da Ponte, Lorenzo [da pontay], originally **Emanuele Conegliano** (1749–1838) Poet, born in Ceneda, NE Italy. He was professor of rhetoric at Treviso until political and domestic troubles drove him to Vienna, where as a poet to the Court Opera he wrote the libretti for Mozart's operas *The Marriage of Figaro* (1786), *Don Giovanni* (1787), and *Così fan tutte* (1790). In 1805 he moved to New York City, where he became professor of Italian literature at Columbia College in 1825.

d'Arc, Joan *Joan of Arc*

Dardanelles or **Hellespont** [dah(r)danelz], Turkish **Çanakkale Boğazi**, ancient **Hellespontus** Narrow strait in NW Turkey, connecting the Aegean Sea (W) and the Sea of Marmara (E), and separating the Gallipoli peninsula of European Turkey from Anatolia; length 65 km/40 mi; width varies from 1·6–6·4 km/1–4 mi; scene of an unsuccessful Allied campaign in World War 1.

Dar es Salaam [dahr es salahm] 6°51S 39°18E, pop (2000e) 1 800 000. Seaport and capital of Dar es Salaam region, E Tanzania; on the Indian Ocean, 45 km/28 mi S of Zanzibar; founded, 1882; occupied by German East Africa Company, 1887; capital of German East Africa, 1891; occupied by the British in World War 1; capital of Tanganyika, 1916–64; capital of Tanzania until 1974; chief port and industrial, commercial, and financial centre; airport; university (1970); food processing, glass, crafts, car parts, printing, oil products, chemicals, aluminium, steel, polystyrene, textiles, timber, machinery; national museum (contains the Olduvai Gorge fossils), Tanzanian State House; Saba Saba festival (Jul).

Darién [daryen] pop (2000e) 51 000; area 16 803 sq km/6486 sq mi. Province of E Panama, bounded SE by Colombia and W by the Gulf of Panama; capital, La Palma; chief towns, Yaviza and El Real; attempted settlement by the Scots in the 1690s (the **Darién Scheme**) is still remembered in local place-names such as Punta de Escoces and Caledonia Bay.

Darío, Rubén [dareeoh], pseudonym of **Félix Rubén García Sarmiento** (1867–1916) Poet, born in Metapa, WC Nicaragua. He lived a wandering life of journalism, amours, and diplomatic appointments. His *Azul* (1888, Blue) and *Prosas Profanas* (1896, Profane Hymns) gave new vitality to Spanish poetic Modernism. After 1898 he worked mainly in Europe, where he wrote *Cantos de vida y esperanza* (1905, Songs of Life and Hope). Influenced by French Symbolism, he established the Spanish-American modernist literary movement which abandoned Spanish provincialism.

Darius I [dariyus, dahrius], known as **the Great** (548–486 BC) King of Persia (521–486 BC), one of the greatest of the Achaemenids. He is noteworthy for his administrative reforms, military conquests, and religious toleration. His division of the empire into provinces called *satrapies* outlasted the Achaemenids. His conquests, especially in the East and Europe (Thrace and Macedonia) consolidated the frontiers of the empire. Patriotic Greek writers made much of the failure of his two punitive expeditions against Athens, the first miscarrying through the wreck of his fleet off Mt Athos (492 BC), the second coming to grief at Marathon (490 BC); but in Persian eyes they were probably not very important. Although a worshipper himself of Ahura Mazda, turning Zoroastrianism into a state religion, he showed an unusual respect for the religions of his subjects.

Darius III, also known as **Codommanus** (d.330 BC) King of Persia (336–330 BC), the last ruler of the Achaemenid dynasty. He was placed on the throne by the eunuch Bagoas, who had poisoned the two previous kings, Artaxerxes III and his son, Arses. When Darius asserted his independence, Bagoas tried to poison him too, but Darius forced him to drink it himself. In 334 BC, Alexander the Great invaded Persia; Darius was unprepared, and his army was defeated at Issus (333 BC) and at Gaugamela (331 BC). He fled to Ecbatana and then to Bactria, where he was murdered by Bessus, satrap of Bactria.

Darjeeling or **Darjiling** [dah(r)jeeling] 27°02N 88°20E, pop (2000e) 80 000. Hill station in West Bengal, NE India, in Himalayan foothills, near the Sikkim state frontier; population mainly Bhutanese and Nepalese; centre of a tea-growing region; tourism; former summer residence of the Bengal government.

Dark, Eleanor, *née* **O'Reilly**, pseudonym **Patricia O'Rane** or **P O'R** (1901–85) Writer, born in Sydney, New South Wales, SE Australia. Employed briefly as a stenographer, she married a general practitioner in 1922, and a year later moved to Katoomba in the Blue Mountains. From 1921 she wrote short stories and verse for various magazines, mostly under her pen name. Her novels include *Slow Dawning* (1932), *The Little Company* (1945), and the historical trilogy, *The Timeless Land* (1941), *Storm of Time* (1948), and *No Barrier* (1953). She was awarded the Australian Literature Society's gold medal in 1934 and 1936, and in 1978 received the Australian Society of Women Writers' Alice Award.

Dark Ages A term once used to describe the period of Western European history from c.500 to c.1000, but misleading because of its negative implications, probably due to the fall of the Roman empire, the subsequent migrations and invasions by Goths and other peoples, and the supposed lack of learning during the period. Knowledge from the ancient Romans survived only in a few monasteries and cathedral schools, while knowledge acquired from ancient Greek almost disappeared. Many of the artistic and technical skills (such as road- and bridge-building) were neglected. Nevertheless, the 'Dark Ages' left a rich legacy of Ottonian and Celtic art and scholarship in N and W Europe, while in the E and S of the continent Byzantine and Arab civilizations flourished. Historians usually describe the whole period c.500–c.1500 as the **Middle Ages**.

darkling beetle A small to medium-sized ground beetle; most species brown or black; many flightless with vestigial wings; well-adapted for living in dry conditions; feeds mostly on plant material, including stored products such as flour. (Order: Coleoptera. Family: Tenebrionidae, c.25 000 species.)

dark matter Material in space which does not emit light, and which therefore cannot be seen with conventional astronomical instruments; also known as the **missing mass**. Over 95% of the universe is thought to be composed of dark matter. According to one view, most of this matter consists of *machos* (*massive compact halo objects*) – large structures which do not emit light (such as black holes and brown dwarfs). An opposing view conceives of dark matter as consisting of new kinds of subatomic particle which have so far not been detected, known as *wimps* (*weakly interacting massive particles*). Research published in 1993 reported evidence indicating the existence of brown dwarfs, but the issue remains controversial.

Darling, Grace (1815–42) Heroine, born in Bamburgh, Northumberland, NE England, UK. She lived with her father, **William** (1795–1860), the lighthouse keeper on one of the Farne Islands. On 7 September 1838, she braved raging seas in an open rowing boat to rescue the survivors of the *Forfarshire* steamboat, which was stranded on one of the other islands in the group.

Darling Range Mountain range in Western Australia, near Perth; extends 320 km/200 mi S along the SW coast, and rises to 582 m/1909 ft at Mt Cooke.

Darling River Longest tributary of the Murray R; formed by the Dumaresq and Macintyre Rivers at the New South Wales–Queensland border; flows generally SW to join the Murray R; length 3070 km/1908 mi; major tributaries the Gwydir, Namoi, Castlereagh, Macquarie, Bogan, and Warrego Rivers; used for irrigation in New South Wales.

Darnley, Henry Stewart, Lord (1545–67) Nobleman, the second husband of Mary, Queen of Scots and father of James I of England, born at Temple Newsom, Yorkshire, N England, UK. He married **Mary** (his cousin) in 1565, and was made Earl of Ross and Duke of Albany. His debauchery and arrogance made him unpopular, and his part in the murder (1566) of the Queen's secretary, David Rizzio, caused his downfall. He became estranged from the Queen, and during an illness was killed at Edinburgh when Kirk O'Field, the house in which he was sleeping, was destroyed by gunpowder – the result of a plot probably organized by the Earl of Bothwell, perhaps with Mary's knowledge.

Darrow, Clarence (Seward) (1857–1938) Lawyer, born in Kinsman, Ohio, USA He was admitted to the bar in 1878, and practised in Ohio and Illinois. When 37, he became counsel for Chicago and North Western Railways, but left this post when a strike of the American Railway Union occurred, and defended Eugene Debs who had called it. He took on further labour cases, and after World War 1 was involved in several notable defences, including the murder case against Nathan Leopold and Richard Loeb (1924), saving them from the death penalty, and the trial of John T Scopes (1925) for the teaching of Darwinian evolution in school. He was noted for his liberal views on segregation.

Dart, Raymond (Arthur) (1893–1988) Palaeoanthropologist, born in Brisbane, Queensland, NE Australia. He studied at the universities of Queensland and Sydney, and taught at University College London (1919–22), before becoming professor of anatomy at Johannesburg (1923–58). His discovery in a quarry at Taung, near the Kalahari Desert, of *Australopithecus africanus* in 1924 substantiated Darwin's view of Africa as the cradle of the human species.

Dart, Thurston (1921–71) Keyboard player, conductor, and musical scholar, born in London, UK. He studied at the Royal College of Music and London University, became professor of music at Cambridge (1962) and at London (1964), and was also director of the Philomusica of London (1955–9). A specialist in early music, he edited several editions of 16th-c and 17th-c English works.

darter A slender bird native to warm regions worldwide; spears fish underwater with long pointed bill; swims with only head and long neck out of water; inhabits still water; called **anhinga** in the New World, **darter** in the Old World; also known as **snake bird** and **water turkey**. (Genus: *Anhinga*, 1 or 2 species; experts disagree. Family: Anhingidae.)

Dartmoor National park in Devon, S England, UK; area 913 sq km/352 sq mi; established in 1951; noted for its granite tors and hanging oak woods; highest point, High Willhays, 621 m/2039 ft, several Bronze and Iron Age settlements; prison (1806–13); popular area for walking and riding.

Dartmoor pony A small pony, developed on Dartmoor, England; tough and sure-footed; calm-natured; height, up to 12·2 hands/1·3 m/4 ft 2 in; usually brown or black; slim legs, long bushy tail and mane, short erect ears.

Dartmouth College *Ivy League*

darts An indoor game played by throwing three darts (or 'arrows') at a circular board. The throwing distance is normally 8 ft (2·4 m), and the height from the floor to the centre of the board (known as the *bull*) is 5 ft 8 in (1·7 m). The standard dartboard is divided into 20 segments, numbered 1–20, but not in numerical order. Within each segment are progressively smaller segments which either double or treble that number's score if hit. The centre ring (*the bull*) is worth 50 points, and the area around it (*the outer*) is worth 25 points. The most popular game in the UK is 501, in which players start at that figure and deduct all scores from it; the final shot must consist of a double. The modern game is credited to a Lancashire carpenter Brian Gamlin (1852–1903) who devised the present-day board and scoring system.

Darwin (Australia), formerly **Palmerston** (to 1911), **Port Darwin** 12°23S 130°44E, pop (2000e) 86 300. Seaport capital of Northern Territory, Australia, on the Beagle Gulf, Clarence Strait; an important communications centre serving Arnhem Land (E) and the surrounding mining districts; first European settlement (1869) destroyed by hurricane in 1879; bombed by the Japanese, 1942; destroyed by cyclone Tracy, 1974; airport; railway; university (1989); Government House (1869); Overland Telegraph Memorial; Stuart Memorial (John McDouall Stuart crossed Australia from Adelaide to Darwin 1861–2); Ross and Keith Smith memorial (first flight from England, Dec 1919); cathedral (1902); Fannie Bay Gaol Museum; S of Darwin is Australia's first commercial crocodile farm; Darwin Beer Can Regatta for craft made almost entirely of beer cans (Jun); Darwin Royal Show Day (Jul).

Darwin (Falkland Is) 51°48S 58°59W. Settlement on East Falkland, Falkland Is; at the head of Choiseul Sound, on the narrow isthmus that joins the N half of East Falkland to Lafonia in the S; c.70 km/43 mi from Stanley.

Darwin, Charles (Robert) (1809–82) Naturalist, the discoverer of natural selection, born in Shrewsbury, Shropshire, WC England, UK. He studied medicine at Edinburgh (1825), then biology at Cambridge (1828). In 1831 he became the naturalist on HMS *Beagle*, which was to make a scientific survey of South American waters, and returned in 1836, having travelled extensively throughout the S Pacific. By 1846 he had published several works on his geological and zoological discoveries, and become one of the leading scientists of his day. In 1839 he married his cousin, Emma Wedgwood (1808–96). From 1842 he spent his time at Downe, Kent, working in his garden and breeding pigeons and fowls, and here he devoted himself to his major work, *On the Origin of Species by Means of Natural Selection* (1859). An epoch-making work, it was given a mixed reaction throughout Europe, but in the end received widespread recognition. He then worked on a series of supplemental treatises, including *The Descent of Man* (1871), which postulated the descent of the human race from the anthropoid group. He wrote many other works on plants and animals, but is remembered primarily as the leader in the field of evolutionary biology. He is buried in Westminster Abbey.

Darwin, Erasmus (1731–1802) Physician, born in Elton, Nottinghamshire, C England, UK, the grandfather of Charles Darwin. He studied at Cambridge and Edinburgh universities, and at Lichfield became a popular physician and prominent figure, known for his freethinking opinions, poetry, large botanical garden, mechanical inventions, and position in the Lunar Society. Many of his ideas on evolution anticipated later theories.

His chief prose work is *Zoonomia, or the Laws of Organic Life* (1794–6). After his second marriage (1781), he settled in Derby.

Darwinism The theory of evolution proposed jointly by Charles Darwin and Alfred Russel Wallace, and later expanded upon by Darwin in *On the Origin of Species by Means of Natural Selection*. Individuals of a species show variation. On average, more offspring are produced than are needed to replace the parents, but population size remains more or less stable in nature. There must therefore be competition for survival, and it is the best adapted (the fittest) variants which survive and reproduce. Evolution occurs by means of natural selection acting on individual variation, resulting in the survival of the fittest. The discovery of the genetic mechanism causing variation has resulted in a modified version of the theory, known as **neo-Darwinism**.

Darwin's finches A closely related group of birds, native to the Galapagos Is (off Ecuador); also known as **Galapagos finches**. Thought to have evolved from one ancestral species, 14 species are now recognized, differing in diet (and related bill shapes), habitat preferences, and distribution. The classification of the group is currently uncertain; they may be put in the family Fringillidae (**finches**) or the family Emberizidae (**buntings** and their allies). Charles Darwin's observations on this group were important to his ideas about natural selection.

dasheen *taro*

Dassanowsky, Elfriede von [dasanofskee] (1924–) Operatic singer, pianist, and music educator, born in Vienna, Austria. At age 15, she was then the youngest female student admitted to the Vienna Academy of Music and Art. Her anti-fascist stance halted her career, and she did not make her debut until 1946, when she became known as a pianist and a mezzo-soprano operatic singer. To promote the rebuilding of democratic cultural institutions in post-war Austria and Germany, she directed and performed in concerts for the Allied High Command (1947–9), founded new musical theatre ensembles in Vienna, and was instrumental in the revival of German-language cinema, founding Belvedere Film Productions in 1946. She moved to the USA in 1955, where she was a vocal coach in the film world of the 1960s, and became a US citizen in 1962. She has since come to be recognized as a leading figure of post-war European culture.

dassie *hyrax*

dasyure [dasyoor] A marsupial native to Australia and New Guinea; most superficially resembles the mouse, but some are larger; comprises most Australian carnivorous marsupials; includes quolls, dunnarts, and the Tasmanian devil. (Family: Dasyuridae, 51 species.)

data In computing, the stored facts and figures on which computers operate in order to perform their assigned task. For example, in a payroll operation the data would be the employee details, the details of the hours worked, absences, etc, and the national insurance, pension, and taxation rules to be applied. The task of taking facts (eg names, addresses) and figures from a form and entering them into a computer system is known as **data entry**. In the early days of computers, this was usually done by coding the information in patterns of holes on a card and reading the cards into the computer. Nowadays it is normally done by teams of data entry clerks keying the data directly into the computer using visual display units, though some data entry is done by optical character recognition and by magnetic ink character recognition. Character recognition is usually used where the bulk of the data to be read has previously been printed by the computer, such as the payment slips arising from credit-card statements. Some data entry is now done by reading handwriting, such as the letter-sorting equipment used by the post office for reading postal codes.

database A file of computer data structured in such a way that it can be of general use and is independent of any specific application. This information can be managed by a **database management system (DBMS)**, a software system or program which allows data to be modified, deleted, added to, and retrieved from one or more databases.

data communications The tools and techniques used to allow computers to communicate with each other over telephone lines, coaxial cables, or even by radio.

data processing (DP) A general term used to describe various uses of computers in business. These include clerical functions (eg scheduling and stock control), financial functions (eg salaries and budget management), and many other aspects of business management and planning.

data protection The techniques of maintaining the privacy and the integrity of computer-based information. The UK Data Protection Act (1987), with subsequent amendents, requires formal registration of all computer users who store information on individuals, and gives certain rights to the individual if they wish to obtain access to this information. There is similar legislation in several other countries.

data warehousing The use of special techniques and database software to interrogate selected company data, with the aim of identifying business trends and patterns. Because databases are being used for decision-support, they are optimized for queries rather than transactions. Typically, data are exported from a company's main database to a more accessible secondary database which has been specially designed to handle user queries from company managers.

Date Line *p.427*

date palm A tree reaching 30 m/100 ft (*Phoenix dactylifera*); thick trunk covered with old, spiny leaf bases; leaves feathery; inflorescence large; native to Near East, and widely cultivated since 6000 BC. A single tree produces up to 250 kg/550 lb of deep orange, sugary dates each year for up to 100 years or more. (Family: Palmae.)

date plum *persimmon*

Datong or **Ta-t'ung** [dahtoong] 40°12N 113°12E, pop (2000e) 1 424 000. City in Shanxi province, NEC China, W of Beijing; founded in the 4th-c as capital of N Wei dynasty; railway; livestock, fur, coal mining, cement, locomotives, soda; Jiulong Bi (Nine Dragon Screen), Yungang Caves, 16 km/10 mi W (earliest Buddhist stone-carvings in China, AD 460–94).

Daubigny, Charles François [dohbeenyee] (1817–78) Artist, born in Paris, France. He studied for a while in Italy (1835–6), but worked mainly in Paris. He was a member of the Barbizon School, painting landscapes, especially moonlight and river scenes, such as 'The Banks of the Oise' (1872, Reims).

Daudet, Alphonse [dohday] (1840–97) Writer, born in Nîmes, S France. He moved to Paris in 1857, where he devoted himself to literature. He wrote a book of poems and several theatrical pieces, including *L'Arlésienne*, for which Bizet composed incidental music. Some of his best work appears in the journals, notably his sketches of Provençal subjects, collected as *Lettres de mon moulin* (1866, Letters from My Mill), and the extravaganza *Tartarin de Tarascon* (1872), with its two sequels.

Daughters of the American Revolution A patriotic society organized in the USA in 1890. Members must be directly descended from soldiers or patriots of the Revolutionary period.

Daumier, Honoré (Victorin) [dohmyay] (1808–79) Painter and caricaturist, born in Marseille, S France. He won contemporary fame for satirical cartoons about government corruption, and was imprisoned for caricaturing the king. An opponent of artificial Classicism, he painted strongly realistic subject pictures, such as *The Third Class Carriage* (c.1862, New York City).

Dauphin [dohfĩ] The title of the eldest son of the reigning French monarch in the period 1350–1830, acquired in 1349 when the future King Charles V purchased the lands known as Dauphiné.

Dauphiné [dohfeenay] Former province in SE France, now occupying the departments of Drôme, Isère, and Hautes-Alpes; part of Holy Roman Empire; passed to Philip V of France in 1349, both lands and title becoming the property of the king's eldest son.

daurian jackdaw *jackdaw*

Date Line

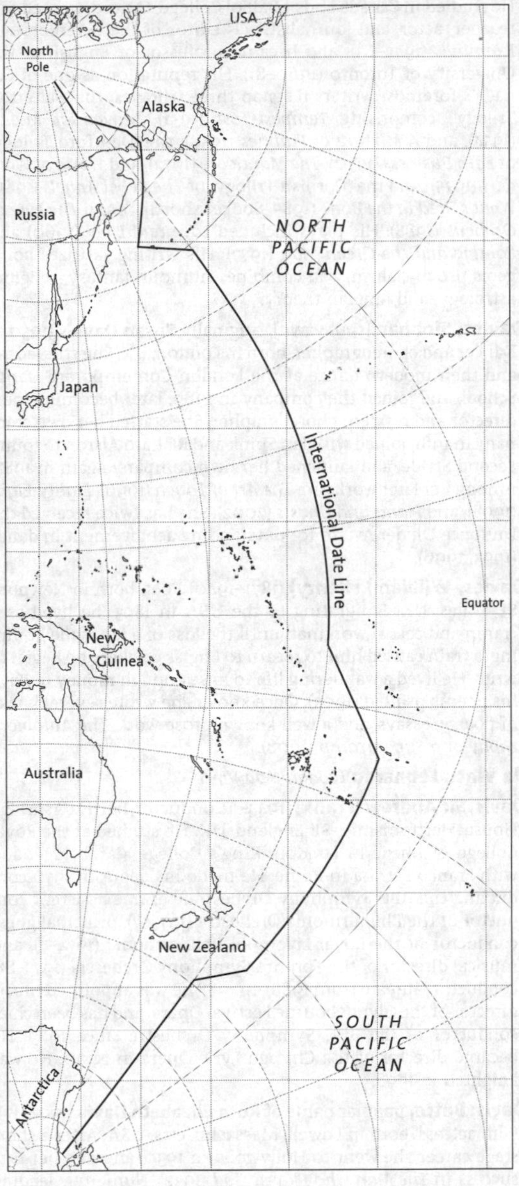

An imaginary line, based by international agreement on the meridian of 180° (with deviations to keep certain islands in the same zone as their respective mainlands); the date is altered to compensate for the gain or loss of time (1 hour per 15°) which occurs when circumnavigating the globe.

Dausset, Jean [dohsay] (1916–) Immunologist, born in Toulouse, S France. After studying medicine in Paris, service during World War 2 in a blood transfusion unit developed his interest in haematology and the immune response to transfusion. His work in this field led to 'tissue typing', which has since helped to reduce the risk of rejection in organ transplant surgery. He shared the Nobel Prize for Physiology or Medicine in 1980.

Davao or **Davao City** [davow] 7°05N 125°38E, pop (2000e) 1 043 000. Seaport in Davao del Sur province, S Mindanao, Philippines, at the head of Davao Gulf; founded, 1849; formerly held by the Japanese; airfield; university (1965); commercial centre; rice, copra, corn trade, pearls, fishing, timber; tribal festival (Oct).

Davenant or **d'Avenant, Sir William** [davenant] (1606–68) Poet and playwright, born in Oxford, Oxfordshire, SC England, UK. His father kept the Crown at Oxford, at which Shakespeare used to stop between London and Stratford – hence the rumour that he was Shakespeare's illegitimate son. In 1628 he took to writing for the stage, his most successful work being *The Wits* (1636), a comedy. In 1638, he became poet laureate, and was later manager of the Drury Lane Theatre. He was knighted in 1643 for services to the Crown during the Civil War. In 1656, he helped to revive drama, banned under Cromwell, and brought to the stage *The Siege of Rhodes* (1656), 'the story sung in recitative music', composed by Charles Coleman (d.1664) and George Hudson. It was generally regarded as the first attempt at public opera in England.

Davenport, Lindsay (1976–) Tennis player, born in Palos Verde, California, USA. In 1996 she won the Olympic gold medal and finished the season ranked ninth, her second top-ten finish in three years. In 1997, she won four titles, and in 1998 three, including the US Open. In the same year, she reached the quarter finals of the Wimbledon championship, the competition she won in 1999, beating Steffi Graf, which advanced her world ranking to number one. She won the Australian Open title in 2000. At the beginning of 2004 she had a world ranking of Number 5.

David (?–c.962 BC) Second king of Israel, and the first of the dynasty that governed Judah and Israel until the exile, the youngest son of Jesse of Bethlehem. According to Jewish tradition he is the author of several of the Psalms, and according to some Christian traditions he is the ancestor of Jesus. He was a warrior under King Saul (and his son-in-law), but his successes against the Philistines (including the killing of Goliath) caused the king's jealousy, and he was forced to become an outlaw. After Saul's death, he became king over Judah in Hebron, and later was chosen king of all Israel. He made Jerusalem the political and religious centre of his kingdom, building a palace for himself on its highest hill, Zion (the 'city of David'), and placing the Ark of the Covenant there under a tent. He united the many tribes of Israel, and extended his territory from Egypt to the Euphrates. The later part of his reign was troubled by the revolts of his sons **Absalom** and **Adonijah**. He was succeeded by Solomon, his son by Bathsheba.

David I (c.1085–1153) King of Scots (1124–53), the youngest son of Malcolm Canmore and Queen (later St) Margaret. Educated at the court of Henry I of England, he became Earl of Huntingdon through his marriage to **Maud de Senlis** (c.1113). Once king, he emphasized his independence, systematically strengthened royal power, and firmly secured the foundations of the mediaeval Kingdom of Scotland. In 1136, as a nominal supporter of the claims of his niece, Empress Matilda, to the English crown, he embarked on wars of territorial conquest against Stephen. He was defeated in 1138 at the Battle of the Standard, near Northallerton, but from 1141 occupied the whole of N England to the Ribble and the Tees.

David II (1324–71) King of Scots (1329–71), the only surviving son of Robert Bruce, born in Dunfermline, Fife, E Scotland, UK. He became king at the age of five. In 1334, after the victory of Edward III of England at Halidon Hill (1333) he fled to France. He returned in 1341, and later invaded England, but was defeated and captured at Neville's Cross (1346), and was kept prisoner for 11 years. After his death he was succeeded by his sister's son, Robert II.

David or **Dewi, St** (?–601) Patron saint of Wales, born near St Bride's Bay, Pembrokeshire, SW Wales, UK. He was Bishop of Moni Judeorum, or Menevia (afterwards St David's), presided over two Welsh Synods, at Brefi and Caerleon, and founded many churches in S Wales. He died at Menevia, which became a shrine in his honour. Feast day 1 March.

David, Hal (1921–) Lyricist, born in Brooklyn, New York, USA. He teamed up with composer Burt Bacharach in 1957 and among their many successful songs are '24 Hours From Tulsa' (1964), 'Walk On By' (1964), 'What's New Pussycat?' (1965), 'What the World Needs Now is Love' (1965), 'The Look of Love' (1968), and 'Close To You' (1970). His work for films includes 'Alfie' (1966, Oscar nomination), and he received an Academy Award for 'Raindrops Keep Falling On My Head' (1969, *Butch Cassidy and the Sundance Kid*). In 1999 he was the first non-Briton to receive the Ivor Novello Award.

David, Jacques Louis [dahveed] (1748–1825) Painter, born in Paris, France. He won the Prix de Rome in 1774, and studied in Italy until 1780. Returning to France, he became known for his paintings of classical themes and historical events, such as 'The Oath of the Horatii' (1784, Louvre). He entered with enthusiasm into the Revolution, and painted several of its leaders. After Robespierre's death he was twice imprisoned, and narrowly escaped with his life. Released in 1795, he produced his masterpiece, 'Les Sabines' (1799, commonly known as 'The Rape of the Sabines', Louvre), and in 1804 was appointed court painter by Napoleon. After the Bourbon restoration, he was banished in 1816 as a regicide, and died in Brussels.

Davies, Clement (Edward) (1884–1962) British politician, leader of the Liberal Party (1945–56), born in Llanfyllin, Powys, E Wales, UK. He studied at Cambridge, and was called to the bar in 1909. Elected MP for Montgomeryshire in 1929, he held his seat until his death. Although offered a post as education secretary in Churchill's 1951–5 government, he declined, and saved the Liberal Party from being subsumed in the Conservative Party (as had the National Liberals). In doing this, he lost his only chance of holding office, but put Party above career.

Davies, (Edward) Hunter (1936–) Writer, journalist, and broadcaster, born in Renfrew, Renfrewshire, W Scotland, UK. He studied at Durham University, joined the *Sunday Times* as a reporter (1960), and became chief feature writer (1967) and editor of the *Sunday Times Magazine* (1975–7). He is well known for his 'Father's Day' column in *Punch* (1979–89, televised 1983), and as presenter of the radio programme *Bookshelf* (1983–6). He has written several novels, including *A Very Loving Couple* (1971) and *Saturday Night* (1989), as well as a great deal of non-fiction, such as *The Joy of Stamps* (1983), *The Good Guide to the Lakes* (1984), and *Living on the Lottery* (1996). He is married to Margaret Forster.

Davies, Paul (Charles William) (1946–) Physicist and popularizer of science, born in London, UK. He studied at University College London, and became professor of theoretical physics at Newcastle (1980–90), then professor of mathematical physics at Adelaide, Australia (professor of natural philosophy, 1993). His numerous popular books on science, such as *God and the New Physics* (1983), *Superforce* (1995), and *About Time* (1995) reflect his research interests in cosmology, the origin of the universe, and quantum gravity. The connections between science and religion are explored in several works, notably *The Mind of God* (1992), and he received the Templeton Prize for Progress in Religion in 1995. He retired from Adelaide in 1997.

Davies, Sir Peter Maxwell (1934–) Composer, born in Manchester, Greater Manchester, NW England, UK. He studied at Manchester, Rome, and Princeton, and was composer-in-residence at the University of Adelaide in 1966. He founded and co-directed the Pierrot Players (1967–70) and was founder/artistic director of The Fires of London (1971–87). A prolific composer, his works include *Taverner* (1972) and three other operas, *Eight Songs for a Mad King* (1969), symphonies, concertos, works for individual instruments and instrumental ensembles, songs, and a considerable amount of chamber music (for which he received the Cobbett Medal in 1989). Since 1970 he has worked mainly in Orkney, frequently using Orcadian or Scottish subject matter for music. He became associate composer/conductor with the Scottish Chamber Orchestra in 1985, composer laureate in 1994, and Master of the Queen's Musick in 2004. He was knighted in 1987.

Davies, (William) Robertson (1913–95) Writer, playwright, essayist, and critic, born in Thamesville, Ontario, SE Canada. He studied in Canada and at Balliol College, Oxford, worked as a teacher, actor, and journalist, was editor of the Peterborough *Examiner* (1942–63), and became professor of English at the University of Toronto (1960–81). His reputation as one of Canada's foremost writers rests on three trilogies: the 'Salterton Trilogy', comprising *Tempest-Tost* (1951), *Leaven of Malice* (1954), and *A Mixture of Frailties* (1958); the 'Deptford Trilogy' of *Fifth Business* (1970), *The Manticore* (1972), and *World of Wonders* (1975); and the 'Cornish Trilogy' of *The Rebel Angels* (1981), *What's Bred in the Bone* (1985, Booker shortlist), and *The Lyre of Orpheus* (1988). His plays included *Love and Libel* (1960) and *Pontiac and the Green Man* (1977). His writing satirizes bourgeois provincialism, and combines humour, fantasy, religion, astrology, and Jungian theory.

Davies, Siobhan [shuhvawn], originally **Susan Davies** (1950–) Dancer and choreographer, born in London, UK. She studied art and then modern dance at the London Contemporary Dance School, and joined the company in 1969, later becoming joint director and resident choreographer. She started her own company in 1981, joined with Ian Spink and Richard Alston to found Second Stride, and launched her own company again in 1988. Among her later works are *The Art of Touch* (1996), *Eighty-Eight* (1998), and *Plants and Ghosts* (2002). She has twice received the Laurence Olivier Award for outstanding achievement in dance (1993, 1996).

Davies, W(illiam) H(enry) (1871–1940) Poet, born in Newport, SE Wales, UK. Emigrating to the USA in 1893, he lived as a tramp and casual workman until the loss of a leg while 'jumping' a train caused him to return to England, where he began to write. He lived a wandering life to raise enough money to have his poems printed (1905). Once known, he wrote several books of poetry, essays, and a well-known prose work, *The Autobiography of a Super-tramp* (1908).

da Vinci, Leonardo *Leonardo da Vinci*

Davis, Sir Andrew (Frank) (1944–) Conductor, born at Ashridge House, Hertfordshire, SE England, UK. He studied at the Royal College of Music in London, King's College, Cambridge, and with Franco Ferrara in Rome. He made his debut in 1970 conducting the BBC Symphony Orchestra, became assistant conductor of the Philharmonia Orchestra (1973–7), principal guest conductor of the Royal Liverpool Philharmonic (1974–7), and musical director of the Toronto Symphony Orchestra (1975–88, conductor laureate from 1988). In 1988 he was appointed music director of the Glyndebourne Festival Opera, and has been chief conductor of the BBC Symphony Orchestra since 1989. He became director of the Chicago Lyric Opera in 2000. He was knighted in 1998.

Davis, Bette, popular name of **Ruth Elizabeth Davis** (1908–89) Film actress, born in Lowell, Massachusetts, USA. After a short stage career she went to Hollywood in 1930, and had her first success in *The Man who Played God* (1932). Numerous leading roles followed, among them *Of Human Bondage* (1934), *Dangerous* (1935, Oscar), and *Jezebel* (1938, Oscar), which established her as a major star for the next three decades. She was outstanding in *Whatever Happened to Baby Jane?* (1962), in which she co-starred with her long-term rival, Joan Crawford. Later appearances included *Death on the Nile* (1979), *The Whales of August* (1987) opposite Lillian Gish, and many television productions.

Davis, Carl (1936–) Composer and conductor, born in New York City, USA. He studied in New York and Copenhagen, and in 1958 became assistant conductor of New York City Opera. A prolific composer, among his works for ballet are *Liaison Amoureuses* (1988, Northern Ballet Theatre), *The Savoy Suite* (1993, English National Ballet), and *Alice in Wonderland* (1995, English National Ballet). His music for television includes *The World at War* (1972, Emmy), *The Accountant* (1989, BAFTA), and *Pride and Prejudice* (1995), and for film *The French Lieutenant's*

Woman (1981, BAFTA), *Scandal* (1988), and *Waterloo* (1995). He has also written for the theatre, as well as concert works.

Davis, Sir Colin (Rex) (1927–) Conductor, born in Weybridge, Surrey, SE England, UK. He studied at Christ's Hospital and the Royal College of Music, and became assistant conductor of the BBC Scottish Orchestra (1957–9), then moved to Sadler's Wells as a conductor and (1961–5) musical director. He was chief conductor of the BBC Symphony Orchestra (1967–71) and musical director at Covent Garden (1971–86). At Covent Garden he gained his reputation as a Wagner conductor of international standing with a new production of the *The Ring*. He became chief conductor of the Bavarian Radio Symphony Orchestra (1983–92) and was appointed principal conductor of the London Symphony Orchestra in 1995. He was knighted in 1980, and became a Companion of Honour in 2001.

Davis, Geena (1957–) Film actress, born in Wareham, Massachusetts, USA. She studied at Boston University and was a model before she made her film debut with a small role in *Tootsie* (1982). She won an Oscar for Best Supporting Actress for *The Accidental Tourist* (1988), and critical acclaim for her role as Thelma in the controversial film *Thelma and Louise* (1991). Other films include *Beetlejuice* (1989), *Angie* (1994), *The Long Kiss Goodnight* (1996), and *Stuart Little* (1999).

Davis, Jack (1917–) Writer and actor, born in Perth, Western Australia. He is a prominent Aboriginal writer who draws much from the traditions of his own people, the Nyoongarah of the SW of Western Australia. Director of the Aboriginal Centre (1967–71), he began to publish relatively late in his life. His poetry includes *The Firstborn* (1970), *Jagardoo* (1978), and *Black Life: Poems* (1992). His plays include *Kullark* (1979, Home), *The Dreamers* (1982), *No Sugar* (1986), and *Wahngin Country* (1992).

Davis, Jefferson (1808–89) US statesman, president of the Confederate States during the Civil War (1861–5), born in Christian Co, Kentucky, USA. After training at West Point, he served in several frontier campaigns. He entered Congress for Mississippi (1845), fought in the Mexican War (1846–7), and became secretary of war (1853–7). In the US Senate he led the extreme States' Rights Party, and supported slavery, in 1861 being chosen president of the Confederacy. At the close of the Civil War he was imprisoned for two years, then released on bail. Though indicted for treason, he was never brought to trial, and was included in the amnesty of 1868.

Davis, Joe, popular name of **Joseph Davis** (1901–78) Billiards and snooker champion, born in Whitwell, Derbyshire, C England, UK. The first great snooker player, he popularized the game in the 1920s. Responsible for inaugurating the World Championship in 1927, he won every title between then and 1946, when he retired from world championship play. He retired from all competitive play in 1964. In 1955 at the Leicester Square Hall he became the first man to compile an officially recognized maximum snooker break of 147. His brother, **Fred Davis** (1913–98), followed the same career, winning the first of his 10 world titles in 1948.

Davis, John (c.1550–1605) Navigator, born in Sandridge, Devon, SW England, UK. In 1585–7 he undertook three Arctic voyages in search of a Northwest Passage, in the last of which he reached 73°N, and discovered the Strait later named after him. He discovered the Falkland Is in 1592. On a journey to the East Indies he was killed by Japanese pirates at Bintang, near Singapore.

Davis, Miles (Dewey) (1926–91) Trumpeter, composer, and bandleader, born in Alton, Illinois, USA. He became the most influential stylist and most admired instrumentalist of the post-war era, from 1948 leading a nonet that introduced the style known as 'cool jazz'. He displayed a wistful, introverted, expressive lyricism (as in 'Round About Midnight', 1955), introduced new modal structures ('Milestones', 1958), soloed in elegant orchestrations ('Porgy and Bess', 1958), and fused jazz harmonies with rock instrumentation and rhythms (*In a Silent Way*, 1969). After retiring for six years due to ill health, he resumed performing at the 1981 Kool Jazz Festival, New York City.

Davis, Raymond (1914–) Physicist, born in Washington, District of Columbia, USA. He studied at the University of Maryland and at Yale, later joining the University of Pennsylvania. He shared the 2002 Nobel Prize for Physics for his pioneering contributions to astrophysics, in particular for the detection of cosmic neutrinos.

Davis, Sammy, Jr (1925–90) Singer, actor, and dancer, born in New York City, USA. He began his career tap-dancing in vaudeville with his father, and went on to solo performing and recording success in the 1950s and 1960s. In 1956 he starred on Broadway in *Mr Wonderful*, and in 1964 in *Golden Boy*. His films include *Porgy and Bess* (1959), *Robin and the Seven Hoods* with fellow 'rat-pack' members Frank Sinatra and Dean Martin (1964), *Sweet Charity* (1968), and *Taps* (1980). He continued to entertain and record until the early 1980s.

Davis, Steve (1957–) Snooker player, born in London, UK. He dominated snooker in the 1980s, winning the world championship six times: 1981, 1983–4, and 1987–9. His first major honour was the Coral UK Championship in Preston (1980), thereafter winning every major honour the game had to offer. In Oldham, during the Lada Classic (1982), he became the first man to compile a televised maximum 147 break. In the late 1980s, he topped the rankings every year. In 1997 he won the Benson & Hedges Masters, the most important non-ranking tournament.

Davis, Stuart (1894–1964) Painter and graphic artist, born in Philadelphia, Pennsylvania, USA. He studied art with Robert Henri in New York City (1910–13), and worked with John Sloan as an illustrator for the left wing journal, *The Masses* (1913–16). The Armory Show in 1913 converted him to avant-garde French art, especially Cubism. His imitation collages such as 'Lucky Strike' (1921, Museum of Modern Art, New York) anticipated Pop Art by 35 years.

Davis, William Morris (1850–1934) Geomorphologist, born in Philadelphia, Pennsylvania, USA. He studied at Harvard, where he became an instructor in physical geography (1878), assistant professor (1885), and professor of geology (1899–1912) until his retirement. He was responsible for introducing professional geography into the USA, and formulated the cycle of erosion.

Davis Cup An annual tennis competition for international male teams, first held in 1900, named after the US public official, Dwight Filley Davis (1879–1945), who donated the trophy. It was held on a challenge basis up to 1971, but since then has been an elimination tournament.

Davis Strait Sea passage between Greenland and Baffin I, connecting Atlantic and Arctic Oceans; c.650 km/400 mi long by 290 km/180 mi wide at its narrowest point; route by which the Labrador current brings icebergs from the Arctic into the Atlantic; visited by British navigator John Davis in 1587.

Davitt, Michael [davit] (1846–1906) Founder of the Irish Land League, born in Straid, Co Mayo,W Ireland. Before becoming a journalist, he worked in a cotton mill, where he lost an arm in an accident. In 1866 he joined the Fenian Movement, and was arrested in 1870 for sending guns to Ireland from the USA, and sentenced to 15 years penal servitude. Released in 1877, he began an anti-landlord crusade which culminated in the Land League (1879). During a further period of imprisonment, he was elected an MP (1882), but disqualifed from taking his seat. A strong Home Ruler and opponent of Parnell, he was twice more an MP (1892–3, 1895–9).

Davos [davohs], Romansch **Tavau** 46°54N 9°52E, pop (2000e) 11 100. Fashionable summer and winter resort town in Graubünden canton, E Switzerland; in a high valley crossed by the R Landwasser, surrounded by forest-covered mountains, SE of Chur; altitude, 1560 m/5118 ft; railway; noted health resort and winter sports centre; Parsenn ski-run nearby; International Ice Hockey Tournament (Dec).

Davy, Sir Humphry (1778–1829) Chemist, born in Penzance, Cornwall, SW England, UK. In 1795 he was apprenticed to a

Penzance surgeon, and in 1797 took up chemistry. He investigated the respiration of gases, and discovered the anaesthetic effect of laughing gas. In 1801 he became a lecturer at the Royal Institution. His fame chiefly rests on his discovery that chemical compounds could be decomposed into their elements using electricity. In this way he discovered potassium, sodium, barium, strontium, calcium, and magnesium. In 1815 he invented the miner's safety lamp. In 1812 he was knighted, made a baronet in 1818, and in 1820 became president of the Royal Society.

Dawes, Charles G(ates) (1865–1951) US statesman and financier, born in Marietta, Ohio, USA. He was head of the Commission which drew up the *Dawes Plan* (1924) for German reparation payments to Europe after World War 1, for which he shared the Nobel Peace Prize in 1925. He was Republican vice-president of the USA under Coolidge (1925–9).

Dawes Plan A report on Germany's economic problems issued in 1924 by a committee presided over by US banker Charles Dawes. The plan laid down a schedule of annual German payments of reparations, outlined the reorganization of the German Reichsbank, and recommended a large foreign loan for Germany. German nationalists rejected it as economically too restricting. French and Belgian forces occupying the industrial Ruhr (to ensure payment of reparations) withdrew in 1925. A further report, which reduced reparations, was drawn up in 1929 by an international commission chaired by US financier Owen Young (1874–1962).

Dawkins, (Clinton) Richard (1941–) British zoologist, born in Nairobi, Kenya. His family returned to England in 1949, where he studied zoology at Oxford. He taught at the University of California, Berkeley (1967–70) then returned to Oxford. His work on animal behaviour and genetics emphasizes that apparently selfish behaviour is designed to ensure survival of the gene, apparently above that of the carrier (*The Selfish Gene*, 1976), and this and wider views on behaviour and evolution have been developed in *The Blind Watchmaker* (1986), *River out of Eden* (1995), *Climbing Mount Improbable* (1996), and other works. He introduced the concept of a cultural analogue of the gene, the *meme*, to capture the notion that some ideas seem to take on a life of their own within society, even affecting the course of evolution. One of the most successful popularizers of his subject, he became Charles Simonyi professor of public understanding of science at Oxford in 1995. He remains a controversial media figure, known as much for his aggressive atheism as for his scientific views on evolution.

dawn redwood A deciduous conifer (*Metasequoia glyptostroboides*) confined to a small area of C China; a so-called 'living fossil', formerly more widespread. It was first described as a fossil species in 1941, four years before its discovery as a living plant. (Family: Taxodiaceae.)

Day, Sir Robin (1923–2000) Journalist and broadcaster, born in London, UK. After service in the Royal Artillery (1943–7), he studied law at Oxford (1947–51) and was called to the bar in 1952. He became a freelance broadcaster in 1954, working first at ITN (1955–9), then joining the BBC's *Panorama*, which he presented from 1967 to 1972. He brought an acerbic freshness to interviewing techniques, and proved a formidable inquisitor of political figures. His radio work includes *It's Your Line* (1970–6) and *The World at One* (1979–87), while his television credits include *Question Time* (1979–89). Among his publications is *...But With Respect – Memorable Interviews* (1993). He was knighted in 1981.

day The elapsed time for the Earth to rotate once, relative to a reference point in the sky. The **sidereal day** is the interval of time between successive passages of the vernal equinox across the same meridian; it is 23 h, 56 min, 4·091 s of mean solar time. The **solar day** is the elapsed time between two successive transits of the mean Sun. The sidereal day measured against the stars is about 4 min less than the solar day, because of the effect of the Earth's orbital motion around the Sun.

Daya Bay or **Ta-ya Bay** Site of China's largest nuclear power project, in Guangdong province, S China; 50 km/30 mi from Hong Kong; designed to supply Hong Kong and Guangdong province with power.

Dayak or **Dyak** The Malayo-Polynesian-speaking indigenous inhabitants of Borneo and Sarawak, including the Bahau, Ngaju, Land Dayak, and Iban, or Sea Dayak. They mostly live along rivers in small village communities in longhouses, cultivating rice, hunting, and fishing.

Dayan, Moshe [diyan] (1915–81) Israeli general and statesman, born in Deganya, Palestine. During the 1930s he joined the illegal Jewish defence organization, Haganah, and was imprisoned by the British (1939–41), then released to fight with the Allies in World War 2 (when he lost his left eye, thereafter wearing his distinctive black eye patch). He became chief-of-staff (1953–8), joined the Knesset as a Labour member in 1959, but left the Labour Party in 1966 to set up the Rafi Party with Ben-Gurion. He won acclaim as defence minister in 1967 when Israeli forces defeated Egypt, Jordan, and Syria in the Six Day War, and he himself became a symbol of Israeli dash and courage. As foreign minister, he participated in negotiations over a peace treaty with Egypt (1977). He resigned from the Begin government in 1979, and launched a new centre party in 1981.

Day-Lewis, C(ecil) (1904–72) Poet, born in Ballintubber, Co Kildare, E Ireland. He studied at Oxford, and became a teacher. During the 1930s he was known as a leading left-wing writer, but in 1939 he broke away from Communism. He was professor of poetry at Oxford (1951–6), and wrote detective stories under the pseudonym of **Nicholas Blake**. His *Collected Poems* appeared in 1954, and his autobiographical *The Buried Day* in 1960. He was created poet laureate in 1968.

Day-Lewis, Daniel (1958–) Film actor, born in London, UK, the son of C Day-Lewis. He trained at the Bristol Old Vic and, after several small roles on stage and television, became well known for *My Beautiful Launderette* (1985) and *Room With A View* (1985). He won awards for his portrayal of handicapped Irish writer Christy Brown in *My Left Foot* (1989, Oscar, BAFTA). Later films include *The Last of the Mohicans* (1992), *In the Name of the Father* (1993), *The Crucible* (1996), and *Gangs of New York* (2002, BAFTA; Oscar nomination). Major theatre performances include *Romeo and Juliet* (1983) and *Hamlet* (1989).

Daylight Saving Time A means of making fuller use of the hours of daylight over the summer months, usually by putting clocks forward one hour so that daylight continues longer into the evening. This idea was first proposed by Benjamin Franklin, and later by William Willett, an English builder. Adopted during World War 1 by Germany in 1917, it was retained after the war by the UK, where it is known as (British) **Summer Time**. In the USA it was enacted in a federal regulation of 1966, but states were given the choice of whether to ignore it (and some have done so). Many countries now have some form of daylight saving time.

day lily A perennial forming large clumps, native to Asia, especially Japan; leaves narrow, pointed; flowers on stalks up to 1 m/3·3 ft or more, funnel-shaped, six perianth-segments, up to 10 cm/4 in long, orange or yellow. (Genus: *Hemerocallis*, 20 species. Family: Liliaceae.)

Dayton 39°45N 84°12W, pop (2000e) 166 200. Seat of Montgomery Co, W Ohio, USA; at the confluence of the Stillwater and Miami rivers, 75 km/47 mi N of Cincinnati; founded, 1796; two universities (1850, 1964); railway; airfield; aviation and aeronautical research centre; Carillon Historical Park; Dayton Airshow (Jul).

Da Yunhe *Grand Canal*

Dazu [dahdzoo] 29°47N 106°30E, pop (2000e) 945 400. City in Sichuan province, SWC China; 160 km/100 mi NW of Chongqing; important Buddhist archaeological site, containing over 50 000 stone carvings (9th–13th-c); Bei Shan (North Hill) nearby, site of first Buddhist shrine in China (892), with over 10 000 figures; 15 km/9 mi NE, Baoding Shan, with 10 000 figures sculpted between 1179 and 1249, including the Sleeping Buddha (over 30 m/100 ft) and the Yuan Jue (Total Awakening) Grotto.

dBase IV® A widely used computer package for personal computers which allows users to design and implement their own database. Most of the features of a relational database management system are available.

D-Day The term used for a secret date on which a military operation is to begin. Terms such as *D-plus-3* (three days after initial attack) are used to plan the sequence of such operations. The most famous D-day is 6 June 1944, when the Allies launched the greatest amphibious operation in history (code-named 'Overlord'), and invaded German-occupied Europe. By the end of D-Day, 130 000 troops had been landed on five beach-heads along an 80 km/50 mi stretch of the coast of Normandy, at a cost of 10 000 Allied casualties. On D-day-plus-14, two vast steel-and-concrete artificial harbours (code-named 'Mulberry') were towed across the English Channel, to provide the main harbour for the campaign.

DDT A chemical mixture, largely consisting of *d*ichloro*d*iphenyl*t*richloroethane. One of the earliest successful insecticides, it has now been largely abandoned both because new strains of insects have developed immunity to it and because its decomposition products are harmful to other organisms, and are not readily decomposed to harmless materials in nature.

deacon (Gr *diakonos*, 'servant') An official of the Christian Church appointed to assist the minister or priest in administrative, pastoral, and financial affairs. The office developed into a third order of ministry after bishops and priests. In the late 20th-c, ecumenical factors revived interest in an order of deacons (the **diaconate**). In many churches, deaconesses are a separate order of parish assistants.

deadly nightshade A stout, large-leaved perennial (*Atropa belladonna*) up to 1·5 m/5 ft high, native to limestone and chalk areas of Europe, W Asia, and N Africa; dull flowers 2·5–3 cm/1–1¼ in, solitary in leaf-axils; tubular, 5-lobed corolla, brownish-violet; berry 1·5–2 cm/0·6–0·8 in diameter, shiny black and cupped by the green sepals. All parts of the plant are narcotic and highly poisonous because of the presence of the alkaloids atropine, hyoscyamine, and solanine. (Family: Solanaceae.)

dead man's fingers A soft coral that forms erect, branching colonies up to 20 cm/8 in high; polyps embedded in a body packed with calcareous slender spikes (*spicules*); with polyps retracted, branches of the colony can resemble human fingers. (Phylum: Cnidaria. Order: Alcyonacea.)

dead-nettle An annual or perennial, found almost everywhere, except in the tropics; stem square, leaves wrinkled, in opposite pairs; flowers 2-lipped, the upper hooded, in whorls at the nodes; mainly pollinated by bees. Several large-flowered or variegated species are cultivated for ornament; others are common weeds, including the **white dead-nettle** (*Lamium album*), a white flowered perennial, and **purple dead-nettle** (*Lamium purpureum*), a pinkish-purple flowered annual. When not in flower, some species, especially white dead-nettle, resemble true nettles but lack stinging hairs, hence the name. (Genus: *Lamium*, c.50 species. Family: Labiatae.)

dead room *anechoic chamber*

Dead Sea, ancient **Lacus Asphaltites**, Hebrew **Bahrat Lut** (Sea of Lot), Old Testament **Salt Sea, Sea of the Plain, East Sea** Inland lake in the Great Rift Valley on the Jordan–Israel border; lowest point on Earth, 400 m/1312 ft below sea-level; fed by Jordan R (N), but no outlet; one of the most saline lakes in the world, containing magnesium, sodium, potassium, and calcium salts; potash and magnesium bromide exploited since 1921; sea level falling because water from the R Jordan used for irrigation and home supply; there are plans for a direct link with the Mediterranean to stabilize sea levels; tourism.

Dead Sea Scrolls Parchment scrolls found accidentally in 1947 and 1952–5 concealed in pottery jars in 11 caves near Qumran on the Dead Sea. Many represent books of the Old Testament, 1000 years older than previously known copies. Written mainly in Hebrew and Aramaic, they are thought to represent the library of an ascetic Jewish sect, the Essenes, concealed when their settlement was overrun by the Roman army in AD 68.

deafness Inability or reduced capacity to hear external sounds. **Conductive deafness** is caused by blockage of the entry of sound to the external canal of the ear (eg through wax in ear), or by abnormalities of the eardrum (tympanic membrane) or bones (ossicles) in the middle ear (eg through middle-ear infection). All sounds irrespective of their pitch are heard with difficulty, and if they are sufficiently loud or amplified they may become clearly heard. **Sensorineural deafness** results from a disturbance of the cochlea, auditory nerve, or neuronal pathways in the brain. Loss of hearing tends to be patchy, affecting only certain frequencies, and amplified or loud sounds are distorted. Causes include certain drugs and lengthy exposure to industrial noise, and it may also develop as a normal part of ageing.

Deák, Francis [dayak] (1803–76) Hungarian statesman, born in Zala (formerly Söjtör), W Hungary. He practised as an advocate, entered the National Diet in 1832, and played the part of a moderate, becoming in 1848 minister of justice. Hailed in 1861 as leader in the Diet, by his efforts Hungary's constitution was restored in 1867 and the dual monarchy of Austria–Hungary established.

Deakin, Alfred (1856–1919) Australian statesman and prime minister (1903–4, 1905–8, 1909–10), born in Melbourne, Victoria, SE Australia. He became minister of public works and water supply, and solicitor general of Victoria; then, under the Commonwealth, attorney general (1901) and prime minister. One of the architects of federation, he established the industrial arbitration system and the first protective tariff, outlined defence policies, advocated the White Australia policy, and introduced the Commonwealth Literary Fund.

Dean, Christopher *Torvill and Dean*

Dean, Dixie, popular name of **William Ralph Dean** (1907–80) Footballer and record goal-scorer, born in Birkenhead, Merseyside, NW England, UK. He turned professional with Tranmere Rovers at the age of 16, then joined Everton in 1925, and scored 349 goals in 399 games. In 1938 he played for Notts County for one season before injury ended his career. He still holds the remarkable scoring record of 60 League goals in one season.

Dean, Howard (1948–) US politician and physician, born in New York City, New York, USA. He studied at Yale University (1971) and Albert Einstein College of Medicine (1978), then set up in private practice with his wife, Dr Judith Steinberg Dean. Entering politics as a Democrat, he served in the Vermont House of Representatives (1982–6), becoming lieutenant governor (1986–91) and governor (1991–2002). Late in 2003 he emerged as a front-runner in the race to secure the Democrat nomination in the 2004 US presidential election, but lost out to John Kerry.

Dean, James (Byron) (1931–55) Film actor, born in Marion, Indiana, USA. He started acting at the University of California, Los Angeles, in 1952 moving to New York City, where he eventually obtained a part in *See the Jaguar* on Broadway. He gained overnight success in the film *East of Eden* (1955). He made only two more films, *Rebel Without a Cause* (1955) and *Giant* (1956), before his death in a car crash. In just over a year he became the personification of contemporary American youth, and a cult figure, and for many years after his death he remained a symbol of youthful rebellion and self-assertion.

dean (ultimately from Lat *decem*, 'ten') Originally, in a monastery, a monk in charge of 10 novices. Later, the term denoted a senior clergyman (after the bishop) in a cathedral chapter or diocese. In lay terms, it is used for a head of a university or college faculty.

Deane, Sir William (Patrick) (1931–) Governor-general of Australia (1996–2001), born in St Kilda, Melbourne, Victoria, SE Australia. He studied arts and law at the University of Sydney, Trinity College Dublin, and the Hague Academy of International Law. On his return to Australia, he was called to the

Sydney bar, became a QC, and was made a judge in the Supreme Court of New South Wales (1977), the Federal Court Bench (1977), and the Australian High Court (1982). He replaced Bill Hayden as governor-general. While he was expected to be a non-activist figurehead, he was in fact outspoken on a number of issues, including the issue of reconciliation with Australian's indigenous population.

Dearie, Blossom (1926–) Singer, pianist, and songwriter, born in East Durham, New York, USA. She sang with Woody Herman and other swing bands, and in 1958 became a nightclub singer accompanying herself on piano. Early recordings on Verve emphasized ballads, but on her own label, Daffodil, since 1974 she has added satirical songs such as 'I'm Hip' and 'Bruce', and a lengthening list of her own songs, including 'Inside a Silent Tear' and 'I Like You, You're Nice'. Her memorable nightclub performances are, at her insistence, early evening soirées in front of silent, non-smoking, non-eating audiences, with a single spotlight on her at the piano.

death The exact definition of death is controversial, and varies among legal systems, although it can be regarded as the cessation of all vital cellular activity. It is no longer enough to rely solely on criteria such as the absence of heartbeat or respiration, since medical science can sometimes revive people who have temporarily lost these functions. This matter is of particular importance when faced with uncertainty over the state of a person who has been on a life-support system for a long time without showing any change. The decision is made in some countries by applying the criteria for brain death. In developed countries, the commonest causes of death are coronary heart disease and cancer. In developing countries, infectious causes of death, such as malaria, tuberculosis, and AIDS are common. Death rates in a society closely reflect standards of sanitation, and are also determined by levels of poverty, unemployment, housing, education, and the quality of health services.

death cap A deadly poisonous, mushroom-like fungus; cap pale greenish or white, with white gills on underside; common on the ground in broad-leaved woodland in late summer and autumn. (Order: Agaricales. Family: Amanitaceae.)

'death of God' theology A style of theology popular especially in the USA in the 1960s. It sought to assert the rationality of the Christian faith and belief in the uniqueness of Christ, without belief in a transcendent God. Hegel, Nietzsche, and Bonhoeffer were claimed as intellectual forerunners.

death's-head moth A large, nocturnal hawk-moth; wingspan up to 12 cm/4¾ in; forewings dark with yellow markings; hindwings ochre-yellow with black bands; black thorax with yellow skull-like marking; feeds on honey and sap exuding from trees; caterpillar feeds on plants, pupates in the ground. (Order: Lepidoptera. Family: Sphingidae.)

Death Valley SE California, USA; ancient rift valley lake bed beside the Nevada border; a deep and arid desert basin; one of the hottest places in the world; contains the lowest point in North America (the Badwater River, altitude −86 m/−282 ft); 225 km/140 mi long; 6–26 km/3¾–16 mi wide; set in a National Monument, area 8400 sq km/3250 sq mi; highest point Telescope Peak (3367 m/11 046 ft); less than 50 mm/2 in rainfall per year; summer temperatures reach 74°C (ground) and 57°C (air); numerous salt and alkali flats, colourful rock formations, desert plants, small animal life, and footprints of prehistoric animals; named in 1849 by a party of gold prospectors, some of whom died while trying to cross it; major source of borax in 19th-c; Scott's Castle, built by the American adventurer Walter Scott.

deathwatch beetle A small, brownish beetle, 5–9 mm/⅛–⅓ in long; lives in decaying trees, but now found mostly in house timbers; larvae, fleshy with tiny legs, bore into wood; adults tap on wood at mating time (Apr–May); larvae leave large holes in timber when they emerge. (Order: Coleoptera. Family: Anobiidae.)

Deayton, (Gordon) Angus [deeton] (1956–) Writer and broadcaster, born in Caterham, Surrey, S England, UK. Educated at Oxford, he contributed widely to revues and radio shows as a writer and performer, joining Rowan Atkinson in his stage show (1986–90), and becoming well known for his role as Victor Meldrew's long-suffering neighbour in BBC television's *One Foot in the Grave* (from 1989), receiving the Newcomer of the Year TV Comedy Award in 1991. He became best known on television as the host of *Have I Got News for You* (1990–2002), and as writer/presenter of *In Search of Happiness* (1995). His books include *The Uncyclopaedia of Rock* (1987) and *In Search of Happiness* (1995).

de Beauvoir, Simone [duh bohvwah(r)] (1908–86) Existentialist writer and novelist, born in Paris, France. She studied philosophy with Sartre at the Sorbonne, where she became professor (1941–3). Closely associated with his literary activities after World War 2, she remained his companion until his death (1980). Her own works provide existentialism with an essentially feminine sensibility, notably *Le Deuxième sexe* (1949, The Second Sex) on women's rights, which became a classic of feminist literature, and *Les Mandarins* (1954, Prix Goncourt), describing existentialist circles in post-war Paris. However, her most enduring contribution to literature may be her memoirs. These include *Mémoires d'une jeune fille rangée* (1963, Memories of a dutiful Daughter). With Sartre she founded the monthly review, *Les Temps modernes* in 1945.

debenture [debencher] A loan raised by a company, usually with a fixed interest rate and possibly a definite redemption date. Debenture holders have no control over the company as long as their interest is paid, but if it is not they can take over control. They rank first among owners in the event of liquidation. **Convertible debentures** carry a right to exchange them for equity at some future date.

de Bono, Edward (Francis Charles Publius) [duh bohnoh] (1933–) Psychologist and writer, born in Malta. He studied medicine at the Royal University of Malta, then went as a Rhodes Scholar to Oxford, where he read psychology, physiology, and medicine. He was a lecturer in medicine at Cambridge (1976–83), and is now involved with a number of organizations to promote the skills of thinking which break out of the trammels of the traditional (*lateral thinking*). These include the Cognitive Research Trust, Cambridge (director since 1971), and the Supranational Independent Thinking Organization (secretary-general since 1983). His books include *The Use of Lateral Thinking* (1967), *Teaching Thinking* (1976), *I Am Right, You Are Wrong* (1990), and *Edward de Bono's Textbook of Wisdom* (1996).

Debrecen [debretsen] 47°33N 21°42E, pop (2000e) 207 000. Capital of Hajdú-Bihar county, E Hungary; economic and cultural centre of the Great Plain; third largest city in Hungary; Kossuth proclaimed independence in the great church, 1849; railway; three universities (1868, 1912, 1951); commercial centre for agricultural region; tobacco, pharmaceuticals, agricultural machinery.

Debrett's Peerage A reference guide to the titled aristocracy of Great Britain, named after John Debrett (c.1752–1822). Peers and baronets are listed separately since baronets are not strictly peers. Debrett's also offers information on forms of address, precedence, the wearing of decorations, and etiquette.

Debreu, Gerard [debroe] (1921–) Economist, born in Calais, NW France. He studied at the University of Paris, went to the USA in 1950 as a researcher with the Cowles Foundation at Chicago University, and was a professor at Yale (1955–61), then professor of mathematics and economics at the University of California, Berkeley (from 1962). He became a US citizen in 1975. He worked on the equilibrium between prices, production, and consumer demand in a free-market economy – an approach first articulated by Adam Smith in 1776. For this work Debreu received the Nobel Prize for Economics in 1983.

de Broglie *Broglie, duc de*

Debs, Eugene V(ictor) (1855–1926) US politician, born in Terre Haute, Indiana, USA. He worked as a locomotive fireman, and in 1893 became president of the American Railroad Union, in 1894 leading a successful national strike for higher wages. He helped to establish the Socialist Party of America, was imprisoned for labour agitation, and between 1900 and 1920 stood five times as socialist candidate for president. His pacifism brought him imprisonment (1918–21).

debt Borrowing by individuals, companies, or governments. Interest is normally payable. This may be at fixed rates, or index-linked to a price index, or at 'floating rates', ie linked to a fixed margin above some market rate such as LIBOR (London Inter-Bank Offered Rate). Companies with high debts are 'highly geared', or 'highly leveraged', and face financial difficulties if their profits fall or interest rates rise. Many less-developed countries and members of the former Soviet bloc have had difficulty in servicing their debts, and foreign lenders in recent years have had to 'roll over' (ie extend the duration of loans beyond the period originally agreed) or write off much of the debt. Individuals in debt through consumer credit or via mortgages on their house also face difficulties if interest rates rise, or if their incomes fall through unemployment.

debugging *bug* (computing)

Deburau, Jean-Baptiste Gaspard [debüroh], originally **Jan Kaspar Dvorak** (1796–1846) Mime artist, born in Kolín, C Czech Republic, into a family of acrobats. He joined the Théâtre des Funambules in Paris (1816), and developed the character of Pierrot into a pale-faced hero and archetypal lover. His work, which culminated in the famous mime-play *L'Enfant prodigue*, popularized mime in France in the 19th-c, and the vogue for it spread to Britain. He has since become a legendary figure of the French theatre, featuring in novels and as a character in plays, and in the film *Les Enfants du Paradis* by Marcel Carné, in which Jean-Louis Barrault played Deburau.

Debussy, Claude (Achille) [debüsee] (1862–1918) Composer, born in St Germain-en-Laye, NC France. Educated at the Paris Conservatoire (1873–84), he studied piano under Antoine-François Marmontel, and in 1884 won the Prix de Rome. His early successes were the *Prélude à l'après-midi d'un faune* (1894, Prelude to the Afternoon of a Faun), and his piano pieces, *Images* and *Préludes*, in which he experimented with novel techniques and effects, producing the pictures in sound which led to his work being described as 'musical Impressionism'. He extended this new idiom to orchestral music in *La Mer* (1905, The Sea) and other pieces.

Debye, Peter (Joseph William) [duhbly], originally **Petrus Josephus Wilhelmus Debije** (1884–1966) Physicist and chemist, born in Maastricht, The Netherlands. He studied at Munich (where he later lectured), and was professor successively at Zürich, Utrecht, Göttingen, and Leipzig, and director of the Kaiser Wilhelm Institute for Physics, Berlin (1935–40). In 1936 he was awarded the Nobel Prize for Chemistry. In 1940 he went to the USA as professor of chemistry at Cornell. He was specially noted for his work on molecular structure, and also for his method of X-ray diffraction analysis using powdered crystals.

decadence A state of cultural decline – often in reaction to the rule of morality and order – where intellectual and moral licence is reflected in artistic sophistication and excess. Themes are morbid and perverse; treatment is sensational and self-indulgent. In modern times, it is used of the late 19th-c symbolist movement in France, especially in French poetry. Notable figures who expressed this aesthetic spirit were Rimbaud, Verlaine, and (in England) Rossetti, Swinburne, Aubrey Beardsley, and Oscar Wilde. The 1890s in England and France provide an example.

Decadents Specifically, a group of French writers in the late 1880s whose journal *La Décadent* appeared briefly at that time: the poets Baudelaire, Verlaine, Rimbaud, and Mallarmé, and the novelist Huysmans. More generally, any writers exhibiting decadent tendencies, such as Poe in the USA in the 1840s; the poet Swinburne, the playwright Oscar Wilde, and the artist Aubrey Beardsley in England in the 1890s; and d'Annunzio in Italy, also during the 1890s.

Decalogue *Ten Commandments*

Decameron (Gr 'ten days') A series of narrative poems written by Boccaccio over a period of many years, but assembled in their definitive form in the period 1349–51. The 'frame' within which the story is set relates how 10 Florentines, taking refuge from the plague in 1348, relate one tale each for 10 days, so that there are 100 tales in all. This device and the stories themselves (many of which were traditional) were widely influential in late mediaeval Europe, for example on Chaucer's *Canterbury Tales*.

Decapoda [dekapoda] A large order of mostly marine crustaceans characterized by three pairs of thoracic legs modified as pincers (*maxillipeds*) for feeding, and five pairs of walking legs; horny covering (*carapace*) fused along back to form gill chamber above leg bases; contains c.10 000 living species, including crabs, lobsters, and shrimps. (Class: Malacostraca.)

decathlon A multi-event track-and-field discipline for men, consisting of 10 events, held over two consecutive days. The events, in order, are: (first day) 100 m, long jump, shot, high jump, and 400 m, and (second day) 110 m hurdles, discus, pole vault, javelin, and 1500 m. Points are awarded in each event based on individual performance. The world record of 9026 points was set by Roman Sebrle of the Czech Republic, at Götzis in Austria in 2001.

Decatur, Stephen [deekayter] (1779–1820) US naval commander, born in Sinepuxent, Maryland, USA. He became a midshipman (1798), and joined the Tripoli Squadron as a first lieutenant in 1801. He led a daring raid into the harbour of Tripoli and burned the captured USS *Philadelphia* (1804). He held various commands in home waters (1805–12) and served on the court martial that suspended Captain James Barron (1808). He led the USS *United States* to victory over HMS *Macedonian* (1812). In 1815 he surrendered the *President* after fighting against a much larger British naval force. He commanded the squadron that ended corsair raids from Algiers, Tunis, and Tripoli (1815) and returned home to give a famous toast, 'Our country! In her intercourse with foreign nations may she always be in the right; but our country, right or wrong'. He was killed in a duel with Barron.

decay rate *mean life*

Deccan [dekan], Sanskrit **Dakshin** Eastward sloping plateau occupying most of CS India, S of the Vindhya Mts; bounded by the Eastern Ghats and the Western Ghats; average altitude 600 m/2000 ft; includes most of Karnataka, S Andhra Pradesh, SE Maharashtra and NW Tamil Nadu states; major towns include Hyderabad, Bangalore, Pune (Poona); noted for cotton; Carnatic plains area was the arena for the British struggle against the French for control of India during the 18th-c.

Decembrists A group of progressive-minded Russian army officers who attempted a coup against the autocratic government of Nicholas I (12 Dec 1825). A few Guards regiments in St Petersburg refused to take the oath of allegiance to the emperor, and marched to the Senate House with a petition of civil rights. There they were met by artillery fire and their ranks decimated. Five of their leaders were executed, and over 100 conspirators exiled to Siberia. The Decembrists' revolt profoundly affected Russia, leading to increased police terrorism, exile in Siberia, and the spread of revolutionary societies among the young intellectuals. They were later regarded as martyrs and founders of the 19th-c Russian revolutionary movement.

decibel Unit of sound level intensity; symbol db; named after Alexander Graham Bell; defined as $10\log_{10}(I/I_o)$, where I is the sound level intensity in question and I_o is defined as 10^{-12}W/m^2, roughly equal to the faintest audible sound; a decibel is a tenth of a **bel**.

deciduous plants Plants which shed their leaves before the onset of harsh seasons, during which they remain dormant. Leaf fall prevents excessive water loss during drought, or when water is locked up as ice, and minimizes frost damage.

decimal system The number system in common use, in which the place values of the digits in a number correspond to multiples of powers of 10. Thus the number 'two hundred and thirty four' is $2 \times 10^2 + 3 \times 10^1 + 4$, so is written 234. Decimal fractions are fractions whose denominators are powers of 10, such as 23/100, usually written 0·23.

decision theory A set of principles designed to enable an agent to make rational choices of self-interest in situations of uncertainty where there are various options, each of whose probable consequences must be assessed. It is used most often in economics and management studies.

Declaration of Independence The document adopted by the Continental Congress in 1776 to proclaim the separation of the 13 colonies in America from Britain. Written mainly by Thomas Jefferson, it announced the right of revolution and detailed the Americans' reasons for the break. The date of its official adoption, July 4, is celebrated as a national holiday.

Declaration of Rights An English statute which ended the brief interregnum after James II quit the throne in December 1688, establishing William III and Mary II as joint monarchs. One of the fundamental instruments of constitutional law, the Bill effectively ensured that monarchs must operate with the consent of parliament, and must not suspend or dispense with laws passed by that body. It also stated that no Roman Catholic could ever be sovereign of Britain. It was supplemented in 1701 by the Act of Settlement.

Declaration of the Rights of Man and Citizen A fundamental document of French constitutional history, drafted by Emmanuel Sieyes and embodied in the French constitution of 1791. The declaration was made by the French National Assembly (27 Aug 1789), proclaiming liberty of conscience, of property, and of the press, and freedom from arbitrary imprisonment. It finally ended the privileged system of the *ancien régime*. Its framers were much influenced by the American Declaration of Independence and by the *philosophes* of the Enlightenment.

declarative programming A way of writing programs for computers in which the relationships between the variables of the program are declared, and the outcome of the program is determined by evaluating those relationships.

declension In linguistics, the scheme of inflections for case contrasts in the noun, seen in a well-developed form in inflected languages, such as Greek or Latin. A language may have several declensions classified according to the particular vowels or consonants which figure in the case forms; for example, in Latin there are many nouns where the *a* vowel is the main feature, as can be seen in *puella* ('girl'), where the cases in the singular are *puella* (nominative, vocative, ablative), *puellam* (accusative), and *puellae* (genitive, dative).

declination A co-ordinate which together with right ascension specifies the location of celestial objects on the sky, or celestial sphere. Analogous to latitude, it is measured in degrees, positive to the N of the celestial equator and negative to the S.

decomposition The breaking down of the complex organic molecules of dead plant and animal matter into simple organic and inorganic molecules which may be recycled as nutrients for primary producers. In natural systems, most decomposition is carried out by bacteria and fungi.

decompression sickness An occupational disease which occurs when individuals who have been working under higher than atmospheric pressure, such as in underwater exploration, return to normal atmospheric pressure too quickly. In these circumstances, nitrogen comes out of solution in the blood and tissues and forms tiny bubbles. These cause damage to the tissues, especially if they lodge in small blood vessels and cut off the blood supply. Permanent brain damage or death can occur. Less severe cases result in dizziness and pain in the muscles and joints (the *bends*). Treatment is to return victims to high atmospheric pressure, and then expose them very gradually to normal atmospheric pressure.

deconstruction An approach to literary criticism, also known as **post-structuralism**, which takes the insights of structuralism to their logical conclusion (or point of a-logical inconclusiveness) by emphasizing not only the arbitrariness but also the radical instability existing between sign and referent, and therefore the impossibility of 'meaning' in any simple sense. Jacques Derrida demonstrated in several books how language must fail in its attempt to relate by reference to a world 'out there' beyond our discourse, and how that discourse itself may/must be broken open (or 'deconstructed') in order to expose the self-protecting fallacies of our 'logocentric' or word-centred conception of reality.

Decorated Style The form of English Gothic architecture prevalent in the late 13th-c and 14th-c, characterized by a maximum of surface decoration, usually in the form of stylized leaves and the double S-shaped curve known as an *ogee*. Good examples are Wells Cathedral (1290–c.1340) and the Lady Chapel and Octagon at Ely (1321–53).

decoration A badge of honour bestowed to reward civil and military achievements. In the UK, many decorative orders are of feudal origin; in some other European countries the abolition of the monarchy has meant the lapse of their chivalric orders also. Newer states, for instance in Africa, have created orders modelled after the European ones.

Decoration Day *Memorial Day*

decorative arts The design and ornamentation of objects, usually with some practical use and outside the field of 'fine art' (painting, sculpture, and architecture); nowadays more exactly called the **applied arts**. Metalwork, ceramics, glass, textiles, and woodwork have all been wrought and decorated to a degree which transcends their functional purpose, and gives them an important role in the development of mainstream artistic styles. The distinction with fine art is often almost non-existent, as in the case of ceramic sculpture and tapestry hangings.

Decroux, Etienne-Marcel [duhkroo] (1898–1991) French actor and mime. A pupil and collaborator of Charles Dullin (1885–1949), he was the first to develop a systematic language of physical expression, which led to the 20th-c revival of mime. In 1940 he opened a school in Paris, and from 1941 onwards toured extensively, both teaching and performing. His pupils and followers included Barrault and Marceau. He became a teacher of mime at the Théâtre Sarah Bernhardt and then worked at the Cabaret Fontaine des Quatre Saisons, both in Paris. He was the author of *Paroles sur le Mime* (1963).

Dedication, Feast of *Hanukkah*

deduction In logic, any inference whose conclusion follows validly and necessarily from its premisses. The premisses may or may not be true: 'London and Chicago are planets; therefore London is a planet' is a valid form of argument; whereas 'Either London or Mars is a planet, therefore Mars is a planet' is invalid.

de Duve, Christian (René) [duh düv] (1917–) Biochemist, born in Thames Ditton, Surrey, SE England, UK. He graduated in medicine at Louvain in 1941, held a chair of biochemistry there from 1951, and held a similar post concurrently at Rockefeller University, New York City, from 1962. He had a major part in discovering the lysosomes which contain the enzymes within animal and plant cells, and afterwards in studying their activity and the diseases linked with their disfunction. He shared the Nobel Prize for Physiology or Medicine in 1974.

Dee, River, Welsh **Afon Dyfrdwy** River in N Wales and adjoining parts of Cheshire, NWC England, UK; rises on Dduallt mountain, in the Snowdonia region, and flows past Llangollen and Chester to an estuary lying W of the Wirral peninsula; length 110 km/70 mi.

Dee, John (1527–1608) Alchemist, geographer, and mathematician, born in London, UK. He studied at Cambridge and on the European mainland, where he travelled widely. He brought back many astronomical instruments, earned the reputation of a sorcerer, and was astrologer to the court of Elizabeth I. He gave advice to those seeking routes to the New World and Far East, and helped write the first English translation of Euclid's works.

Dee, Jack (1962–) British comedian and actor. After various jobs he began his stage career in 1986 as a stand-up comedian at London's Comedy Store. He became known for his deadpan humour, and since 1990 has toured extensively with his one-man show. Television credits include five series of his own show for Channel 4, two series of *Jack Dee's Happy Hour* (BBC 2000–1), and appearances in several dramas. In 2001 television viewers voted him winner of Comic Relief's special fund-raising series *Celebrity Big Brother*.

deed *covenant* 1

deep-freezing Freezing to −20°C or below in either a chest freezer or cabinet freezer. The ability of a freezer cabinet to maintain a sufficiently low temperature for prolonged food preservation is shown on the cabinet by a series of stars; deep-freezers will allow 3 months storage, a level which is symbolized by four stars. Some foods, such as raw beef, fresh vegetables, and fruit, may be stored for up to a year.

Deeping, (George) Warwick (1877–1950) Novelist, born in Southend, Essex, SE England, UK. He trained as a doctor, but after a year gave up his practice to devote himself to writing. His early novels were mainly historical, and it was not until after World War 1 that he gained recognition with his best-seller, *Sorrell and Son* (1925).

deep scattering layer A layer in the sea which reflects sound signals. During World War 2 it was discovered that sonar signals were scattered by a mysterious layer which moved up and down in the water. This was later found to be caused by organisms in the water column. Much of the phenomenon is produced by the air bladders of fishes, but animals as small as microscopic zooplankton may also contribute to it. The layer has been observed to move down towards greater depths during the day and towards the surface at night – a movement known as *vertical migration*.

deep sea diving The descent to the sea bed by divers for relatively long periods to carry out exploration, salvage, or construction work. The airtight diving suit was invented by Augustus Siebe in 1837. Modern diving suits have fibreglass helmets with viewports, and weighted boots for stability. Divers breath air, or an oxygen/helium mixture which is pumped to them. Armoured diving suits allow divers to work comfortably down to 700 m/2300 ft at normal atmospheric pressures. Divers always dive in 'buddy' pairs, keeping watch over and for each other. Communication between the pairs of divers and the people on the surface is vital. A diving bell is used for longer term underwater work such as maintenance of oil rig platform structures.

Deep Space Network (DSN) A NASA tracking and telecommunications system used to operate interplanetary spacecraft. Stations are located at three widely spaced locations around the world (Goldstone, California; Canberra, Australia; Madrid, Spain) to provide a continuous communications capability in all parts of the Solar System. Each station operates one 70-m/230-ft diameter radio antenna and two 34-m/112-ft antennas, capable of two-way communications with spacecraft to beyond Neptune's orbit. It is operated by NASA's Jet Propulsion Laboratory.

deer A type of hoofed mammal of families Cervidae (**true deer**, 36 species), Moschidae (**musk deer**), and Tragulidae (**mouse deer**); an artiodactyl; only true deer have antlers; male musk deer and mouse deer have long prominent canine teeth; true deer found worldwide except Africa and Australasia; usually found in or near woodland; male called a *stag* or *buck*, female a *hind* or *doe*, young a *fawn* or *kid* (names depend on species).

deerhound A breed of dog, developed in Scotland from Mediterranean ancestors; tall, slim; very long legs, long tail; shaggy grey coat; head small with short soft ears; also known as the **Scottish deerhound**, **staghound**, or **buckhound**.

deerlet *chevrotain*

deer mouse A mouse native to North America; grey or brown with white underparts; ears large; used widely in science laboratories; also known as **white-footed mouse** or **deer-footed mouse**. Its agility reminded early observers of a deer (Genus: *Peromyscus*, 49 species.)

deësis [dayeesis] In art, the representation of Christ enthroned in majesty flanked by the Virgin and St John. It is the central motif of certain Byzantine altarpieces.

defaecation / defecation The expulsion of faeces from the bowel. Distension of the rectum by faeces leads to the reflex contraction of its musculature, and the relaxation of the involuntary internal anal sphincter, accompanied by the desire to defaecate. This is accomplished voluntarily by contraction of the abdominal muscles (straining) and relaxation of the external anal sphincter.

defamation The publication or communication of a false statement which tends to injure reputation or lower a person in the view of the community. In England, Wales, and the USA, it takes the form of either defamation in permanent form (libel) or in non-permanent form (slander); Scottish law does not distinguish between the two terms, recognizing only defamation. Both are actionable at civil law, and in certain jurisdictions libel can exist as a criminal offence. In England and Wales, truth is a defence; in the USA, the plaintiff generally must prove not only that the statement was untrue, but was also made with reckless disregard as to its truth.

defecation *defaecation*

defence / defense mechanism A pattern of feeling and thinking which controls sensations of guilt, anxiety, and internal conflict, and which inhibits unacceptable impulses. Examples include repression and denial. It is a normal process which usually occurs unconsciously, but if excessive in any particular form has been considered pathological. First described by Sigmund Freud, it was later elaborated by Anna Freud and others.

Defence of the Realm Act A British Act introduced in 1914 at the beginning of World War 1 to give the government greater controls over the activities of its citizens. The most important control related to restrictions on press reporting and other forms of censorship. The restrictions were increased as the war progressed.

defendant In law, the person who is called on to answer proceedings brought against him or her by some other person, called the **plaintiff**. In criminal cases the defendant is the accused; in civil cases, the person who is sued. The term **defender** is used in Scotland to denote the party against whom a civil action is brought.

Defender of the Faith (Lat *fidei defensor*) A title conferred on Henry VIII of England by Pope Leo X as a reward for the king's written opposition to the teachings of Martin Luther. After the Reformation, the title was confirmed by parliament, and is still used by British sovereigns. The initials *F.D.* appeared on British coinage from the reign of George I.

defibrillation *cardiac resuscitation*

deficiency diseases A wide range of medical disorders caused by insufficient dietary intake of essential substances, either carbohydrates and proteins, or vitamins and minerals. An example is kwashiorkor, a nutritional disorder of young children caused by an inadequate intake of protein.

deficit financing A situation when government spending exceeds tax receipts, and the government is borrowing or printing money. This may be deliberate, to stimulate a depressed economy, or it may be the result of bad luck or incompetence, when the government is unable to collect taxes or there is an unforeseen need for extra spending, such as in wartime or to deal with natural catastrophes. Whether it is deliberate or unplanned, large-scale deficit financing is believed to stimulate inflation.

deflation A government economic policy designed to reduce inflationary pressures. Steps taken include higher interest and tax rates, and a tighter money supply.

Defoe, Daniel [defoh] (1660–1731) Writer, born in London, UK. The son of a butcher, he was educated at a dissenting academy, travelled widely in Europe, and set up in the hosiery trade. In 1688 he joined William III's army, and strenuously supported the King's party. In 1702 his satire *The Shortest Way with the Dissenters* raised much anger with Dissenters and High-Churchmen alike, and he was imprisoned at Newgate for seditious libel, where he continued his pamphleteering. On his release in 1704 he started *The Review*, writing it single-handed, three times a week, until 1713. During this time, his political conduct became highly equivocal; he supported, rejected, then supported again the Tory minister, Harley. After the accession of George I (1714) he returned to the writing of fiction, and achieved lasting fame with *Robinson Crusoe* (1719–20). His other major works include *A Journal of the Plague Year*, *Moll Flanders* (both 1722), and *Roxana* (1724).

defoliant Any preparation which removes or kills the leaves of a plant.

De Forest, Lee [di **for**ist] (1873–1961) Inventor, born in Council Bluffs, Iowa, USA. He studied at Yale and Chicago universities, and became a pioneer of radio, introducing the grid into the thermionic valve, by which feeble radio signals could be amplified. He invented the Audion and the idea of cascading valves to obtain greater amplification, essential for successful radio transmission and reception. He also did much early work on sound reproduction for films. He was widely honoured as 'the father of radio' and 'the grandfather of television'.

deforestation The removal of forest areas, either to make use of the wood or to clear the land for agricultural, industrial, or urban purposes. In W Europe the first major phase occurred about 5000 years ago with the spread of agriculture in the Neolithic period. Today, huge areas of forest, most of it tropical, are being cleared. Much of the tree felling is done by multinational companies which either sell the timber for export or use the cleared land for agriculture. Deforestation on a large scale may contribute to regional and global imbalances. Forests play a major role in carbon storage; with their removal, excessive carbon dioxide in the atmosphere may contribute to global warming.

Degas, (Hilaire Germain) Edgar [popularly **day**gah, Fr duh**gahs**] (1834–1917) Artist, born in Paris, France. After studying at the Ecole des Beaux-Arts, he went to Italy, where he was influenced by the Renaissance painters. On his return to Paris he associated with the Impressionists and took part in most of their exhibitions from 1874 to 1886. He was also influenced by Japanese woodcuts and by photography. Among his best-known works are 'Dancer Lacing her Shoe' (c.1878, Paris) and 'Jockeys in the Rain' (1879, Glasgow). Later, because of failing sight, he concentrated on sculpture.

de Gasperi, Alcide *Gasperi, Alcide de*

de Gaulle, Charles (André Joseph Marie) [duh **gohl**] (1890–1970) French general and first president of the Fifth Republic (1958–69), born in Lille, N France. He fought in World War 1, and became a strong advocate of mechanized warfare, but his efforts to modernize the French Army made little progress. With the fall of France (Jun 1940), he fled to England to raise the standard of the 'Free French', and entered Paris in the vanguard of one of the earliest liberation forces (Aug 1944). He became head of the provisional government, then withdrew to the political sidelines. Following the troubles in North Africa he became prime minister (1958), and emerged as the one man able to inspire confidence after the post-war procession of indecisive leaders. In late 1958 the Fourth Republic was dissolved and a new constitution drawn up, designed to strengthen the powers of the president. The Fifth Republic thus came into being, with de Gaulle as president. He practised a high-handed yet extremely successful foreign policy, repeatedly surviving political crises by the lavish use of the referendum. Independence was granted to all French African colonies (1959–60), and Algeria became independent (1962). He developed an independent French nuclear deterrent and withdrew French support for NATO, signed a historic reconciliation treaty with West Germany, and blocked Britain's entry into the European Economic Community. In the student uprising of May–June 1968, he fled Paris when the industrial workers staged what became the most sustained strike in France's history. He was forced to liberalize the higher education system and make economic concessions to the workers. In 1969 he resigned after the defeat of his referendum proposals for Senate and regional reforms. He then retired to Colombey-les-Deux-Eglises.

degaussing [dee**gow**sing] The neutralizing of an object's magnetic field using current-carrying coils to produce an opposing magnetic field of equal strength. The process is applied to ships, to protect them from magnetically activated mines.

degree (education) The award given at the conclusion of a course in higher education. Most countries use the terms *Bachelor* to denote a first degree, *Master* to signify a higher degree at postgraduate level, and *Doctor* for those who have successfully undertaken a significant piece of original research. The doctorate was originally intended as the licence to teach in higher education.

degree (mathematics) One 360th part of a complete revolution, usually symbolized by °. $90° = 1$ right angle. $180° = \pi$ rad; $90° = 100$ grad.

de Havilland, Sir Geoffrey [duh **hav**iland] (1882–1965) Aircraft designer, born in Haslemere, Surrey, SE England, UK. He built his first plane in 1908 and became director of the firm bearing his name, producing many famous aircraft during and between the two world wars, including the Tiger Moth, the Mosquito, and the Vampire jet. He established a height record for light aircraft in 1928, won the King's Cup air race at the age of 51, and was knighted in 1944.

De Havilland, Olivia (Mary) (1916–) Actress, born in Tokyo, Japan. Brought up in the USA, she made her stage debut in 1933, and joined Warner Brothers (1935–42). She received Best Supporting Actress nominations for her performances in *Gone With the Wind* (1939) and *Hold Back The Dawn* (1941). She won Oscars for *To Each His Own* (1946) and *The Heiress* (1949). She later played many television roles, and published an autobiography, *Every Frenchman Has One* (1963).

dehydration Literally, 'loss of water'; but in medicine, the process of salt depletion as well as water loss. Pure water loss occurs in those who do not or cannot drink water, and results in great thirst and, when severe, mental confusion, and coma. Loss of salt-containing fluids occurs after severe vomiting, diarrhoea, excessive sweating, burns, or excessive urination (as in untreated diabetes mellitus). It particularly affects the circulation, with a rise in pulse rate and falling blood pressure, followed by circulatory collapse and shock.

Deighton, Len [**day**tn], popular name of **Leonard Cyril Deighton** (1929–) Thriller writer, born in London, UK. He became, variously, an art student, a railway platemaker, and an air-steward. His first novel, *The Ipcress File* (1962), was written when he was 33, and became a best seller, as have almost all his books. A leading author of spy novels, notable titles are *Funeral in Berlin* (1964), *Only When I Larf* (1968) and the trilogy *Berlin Game* (1984), *Mexico Set* (1985), and *London Match* (1986). Later works include another trilogy, *Faith* (1994), *Hope* (1995), and *Charity* (1997).

Deimos [**diy**mos] One of the two natural satellites of Mars, discovered in 1877; distance from the planet 23 460 km/14 580 mi; diameter c.15 km/9 mi; orbital period 30 h 17 min. Like Phobos, it has a dark, cratered surface; both are believed to be captured asteroids.

deindustrialization The process by which a smaller proportion of output and employment is in the industrial sector, and an increasing proportion is in services. This has been proceeding for several decades in most advanced countries, where the service sector now makes up the majority of the economy. Deindustrialization in the 20th-c followed a period of industrialization in the 19th-c, when resources shifted out of primary production in agriculture and mining and into industry. The main reason for deindustrialization is improvements in industrial efficiency, which have led to large increases in real incomes. Consumers and governments have chosen to spend a high proportion of this extra income on services, including education, medical care, banking and insurance, entertainment, and tourism.

deism [dayizm] Originally, belief in the existence of a god or gods; today, belief in the existence of a supreme being who is the ground and source of reality but who does not intervene or take an active interest in the natural and historical order. It also designates a largely British 17th-c and 18th-c movement of religious thought emphasizing natural religion as opposed to revealed religion, and seeking to establish reasonable grounds for belief in the existence of God; represented by, among others, Lord Herbert of Cherbury (1583–1648), Matthew Tindal (1657–1733), and Anthony Collins (1676–1729).

Dekker, Thomas (c.1570–c.1641) Playwright, born in London, UK. He was a prolific writer, but only a few of his plays were printed and most of the others are now lost. His best-known works are the comedy, *The Shoemaker's Holiday* (1600), and *The Honest Whore* (1604; part II, 1630). He wrote several plays in collaboration with other Elizabethan playwrights, and was also well known as a writer of prose pamphlets giving a lively account of London life. His writings are marked by his sympathy for the poor and oppressed. During the 1630s he dropped out of notice, and nothing is known of his last years.

de Klerk, F(rederick) W(illem) [duh klairk] (1936–) South African statesman and president (1989–94), born in Johannesburg, NE South Africa. He studied at Potchestroom University, and established a legal practice in Vereeniging. He served in the National Party cabinets under Vorster and P W Botha, and in 1989, when he was minister of education, succeeded Botha as leader in a 'palace coup', becoming president when Botha resigned. He won a general election, though with a reduced number of seats, and set about the dismantling of apartheid. Nelson Mandela was released in February 1990; the state of emergency was lifted; the principal apartheid laws were repealed; constitutional talks were instituted; and victory in a whites-only referendum enabled de Klerk to press on with his reforms. International sanctions were lifted, and the world resumed sporting links with South Africa. However communal violence continued, particularly between the African National Congress and the Zulu Inkatha Freedom Party; and the Goldstone Commission, appointed by de Klerk, discovered that whites in the police and armed forces were responsible for fomenting some of this inter-black violence. The culmination of the process was the signing of a new constitutional agreement with Mandela in late 1993, and in the same year he and Mandela were jointly awarded the Nobel Peace Prize. De Klerk later served as vice-president (1994–6) in the Mandela administration, and announced his retirement from politics in August 1997.

de Kooning, Willem or **William** [duh kooning] (1904–97) Painter, born in Rotterdam, The Netherlands. He studied at Rotterdam, and emigrated to the USA in 1926. By the 1950s he had emerged as a leader of the abstract expressionist movement, especially as seen in action painting. Among his best-known works is his controversial series 'Woman I–VI' (1952–3, New York City), with its violent, aggressive images. In his later years, he worked increasingly with clay sculptures.

Delacroix, (Ferdinand Victor) Eugène [duhlakrwah] (1798–1863) Painter, and leader of the Romantic movement, born in Charenton, NE France. He exhibited his 'Dante and Virgil in Hell' at the Paris Institute in 1822, following this with 'The Massacre at Chios' (1823, Louvre). These pictures, with their loose drawing and vivid colouring, aroused a storm of criticism. In his later work he moved even further away from traditional treatment in his canvases of historical and dramatic scenes, often violent or macabre in subject, such as 'Liberty Guiding the People' (1831, Louvre).

de la Mare, Walter (John) [mair] (1873–1956) Writer, born in Charlton, Kent, SE England, UK. He studied at London, worked for an oil company (1890–1908), then devoted himself to writing. His first work, *Songs of Childhood* (1902), was under the pseudonym of **Walter Ramal**. He wrote several volumes of poetry, novels, and short stories, including the prose romance *Henry Brocken* (1904), the poetic collection *The Listeners* (1912), and his fantastic novel *Memoirs of a Midget* (1921).

Delaney, Shelagh [delaynee] (1939–) Playwright, born in Salford, Greater Manchester, NW England, UK. She left school at 16 and began writing her first and best known play, *A Taste of Honey* (1958) a year later. Later works failed to achieve equal acclaim, though she produced notable screenplays for *Charlie Bubbles* (1968) and *Dance with a Stranger* (1985).

de la Renta, Oscar (1932–) Fashion designer, born in Santo Domingo, Dominican Republic. After studying art in Santo Domingo and Madrid, he worked at Balenciaga's couture house in Madrid. He joined the house of Lanvin-Castille in Paris in 1961, but after two years went to Elizabeth Arden in New York City. In 1965 he started his own company. He has a reputation for opulent, ornately trimmed clothes, particularly evening dresses, but he also designs day wear and accessories.

de la Roche, Mazo [rosh] (1885–1961) Novelist, born in Newmarket, Ontario, SE Canada. She wrote *Jalna* (1927), the first of a series of novels about the Whiteoak family. *Whiteoaks* (1929) was dramatized with considerable success. She also wrote children's stories and travel books.

Delaroche, (Hippolyte) Paul [duhlarosh] (1797–1856) Painter, born in Paris, France. He studied under Gros, from whom he absorbed the technique of the large historical subject painting, as seen in his 'Death of Queen Elizabeth' (1828), and 'Execution of Lady Jane Grey' (1834, National Gallery, London). His major work was the series of murals for the Ecole des Beaux-Arts, where he became professor of painting (1833).

de la Tour, Georges *La Tour, Georges de*

de la Tour, Maurice Quentin *La Tour, Maurice Quentin de*

Delaunay, Robert [duhlohnay] (1885–1941) Painter, born in Paris, France. At first a stage designer, he turned to painting in 1905. He was associated with *Der Blaue Reiter* (1911–12), but is principally known as the co-founder of Orphism. He painted many pictures of Paris (particularly of the Eiffel Tower), and his research into colour orchestration as applied to abstract art was influential.

Delaware pop (2000e) 783 600; area 5296 sq km/2045 sq mi. State in E USA, divided into three counties; the 'First State', 'Diamond State', or 'Blue Hen State'; the original Swedish settlers were supplanted (1655) by the Dutch, who were in turn supplanted by the British (1664); part of Pennsylvania until 1776; one of the original states and first to ratify the Federal Constitution, 1787; capital, Dover; other chief city, Wilmington; bounded E by Delaware Bay and the Atlantic Ocean; the Delaware R forms part of the border with New Jersey; highest point Ebright Road (135 m/443 ft); the second smallest state; poultry, soybeans, corn, dairy products; mainly an industrial state, centred on Wilmington; chemicals, transportation equipment, processed food, plastics, metals; several large corporations based in Wilmington, taking advantage of the state's taxation laws.

Delaware River River in E USA; rises in the Catskill Mts, New York, and empties into Delaware Bay; length 450 km/280 mi; marks part of the state frontiers of Pennsylvania, New York, and New Jersey; navigable to Trenton.

de la Warr, Thomas West, 12th Baron [waw(r)] (1577–1618) English soldier and colonist. After serving under the Earl of Essex, and suffering a brief imprisonment for involvement in Essex's revolt, he became a member of the Virginia Company; he was appointed the first governor of Virginia in 1610. Returning to England in 1611, he wrote the *Relation* about Virginia. He died on a return voyage to Virginia. The state of Delaware is named after him.

Delbrück, Max [delbrük] (1906–81) Biophysicist, born in Berlin, Germany. He studied physics at Göttingen, and worked with Bohr at Copenhagen before turning to chemistry at the Kaiser Wilhelm Institute in Berlin, and to biology from 1937 (at the California Institute of Technology). He did much to create bacterial and bacteriophage genetics, and to inspire early work in biophysics and molecular biology. He exchanged research information with Alfred Day Hershey and Salvador Luria, and with them shared the Nobel Prize for Physiology or Medicine in 1969. He became a US citizen in 1945.

Delesclüze, (Louis) Charles [duhlayklüz] (1809–71) French radical Republican and journalist, born in Dreux, NC France. His revolutionary politics drove him from France to journalism in Belgium (1835), but the February Revolution (1848) brought him back to Paris. His writing made him popular, but brought him imprisonment (1849–53), and he was transported until 1859. He played a prominent part in the Paris Commune, and died on the last barricade.

Delft 52°01N 4°22E, pop (2000e) 94 000. Ancient city and municipality in W South Holland province, W Netherlands, on the R Schie; famous for linen-weaving (14th-c), pottery and porcelain (16th-c); William the Silent assassinated here, 1584; railway; technical university (1863); vehicles, machines, pharmaceuticals, yeast, alcohol, consumer products, electrical engineering, building materials, paper, cardboard, porcelain (Delftware); birthplace of Vermeer; Nieuwe Kerk (1396–1496), Italian Renaissance town hall, Prisenhof.

Delftware The Dutch and English version of faience, named after the town of Delft where it was made in large quantities in the 17th-c. Typically blue and white, much of its decoration was copied from Chinese and Japanese porcelain.

Delhi [delee], Hindi **Dilli**, formerly **Shahjahanabad** 28°38N 77°17E, pop (2001e) 13 783 000. Capital of India and administrative centre of Delhi union territory, NC India, 1190 km/ 739 mi NE of Mumbai; second largest city in India; **Old Delhi**, enclosed within the walls built by Shah Jahan in 1638, on R Yamuna; Mughal architecture and thronged bazaars contrast with formal architecture and wide boulevards of **New Delhi** to the S, largely designed by Lutyens; New Delhi the administrative centre of India since 1912; largest commercial centre in India; airport (Palam); railway junction; metro system (first phase opened in 2002, scheduled for completion in 2005; second phase, 2110); university (1922); chemicals, machine tools, clothing, footwear, drinks, food processing, plastics, bicycles, radios, televisions; traditional crafts include jewellery, papier mâché, textiles, ivory carving; Red Fort, containing imperial palace of Shah Jahan (17th-c); Jama Masijid, largest mosque in India (1644–58); Rajghat, where Gandhi was cremated (1948).

Delhi Sultanate The principal N Indian Muslim kingdom between the 13th-c and 16th-c, in which Sultan Iltutmish (1211–36) made his permanent capital at Delhi. It became an imperial power under the Khalji dynasty (1290–1320), but its power was much reduced under the Saiyid and Lodi dynasties, and the Sultanate was destroyed by Babur at Panipat in 1526.

Delian League [deelian] The association of Greek city-states under Athenian leadership that was formed after the Persian Wars (478–477 BC) for the continuing defence of the Aegean area against the Persians. It was so called because the treasury of the League was initially on the island of Delos.

Delian problem *duplication of the cube*

Delibes, (Clément Philibert) Léo [duhleeb] (1836–91) Composer, born in St Germain du Val, W France. He became second director at the Opéra, Paris (1864) and a Conservatoire professor (1881). He wrote light operas, of which *Lakmé* had the greatest success, but he is chiefly remembered for the ballet *Coppélia* (1870).

Delilah [deliyla] Biblical character, who at the instigation of the Philistines enticed Samson to reveal the secret of his great strength – his uncut hair, according to his Nazirite vow of separation. She contrived to cut his hair to weaken him (*Judges* 16).

DeLillo, Don [deleeloh] (1936–) Writer, born in New York City, New York, USA. He was briefly a New York advertising copywriter before becoming a professional fiction writer. Starting with his first novel, *Americana* (1971), his social satires are known for their precise language and pervasive sense of anomie, and have earned him a reputation as a writer's writer. His books include *Ratner's Star* (1976), *White Noise* (1985, American Book Award), *Libra* (1988), *Underworld* (1997), and *Cosmopolis* (2003).

deliquescence [delikwesens] In chemistry, the state of dissolving gradually after taking up water from the atmosphere. Some salts, such as calcium chloride, will absorb enough water from a damp atmosphere to dissolve in the water absorbed. A **hygroscopic** substance absorbs water from its surroundings; a **deliquescent** substance absorbs water from its surroundings, then dissolves in that water.

delirium An acute and reversible alteration of attention and consciousness associated with impaired memory and impaired orientation, usually the result of organic causes. It may incorporate hallucinatory and delusional experiences, as well as restlessness and irritability. In earlier usage, it was a general term referring to madness of any form.

delirium tremens A form of delirium which occurs following withdrawal of alcohol from alcoholics. Hallucinations often take the form of a sensation of insects crawling on the skin, or visions of Lilliputian individuals or objects. It is usually associated with other features of alcoholic brain damage, notably tremor of the hands and arms.

Delius, Frederick [deelius] (1862–1934) Composer, born in Bradford, West Yorkshire, N England, UK, of German–Scandinavian descent. He followed a commercial career until he was 20, when he went to Florida as an orange planter, studying music in his spare time. He entered Leipzig Conservatory in 1886, and became a friend of Grieg. After 1890 he lived almost entirely in France, composing prolifically. He wrote six operas, including *A Village Romeo and Juliet* (1901), and a variety of choral and orchestral works, such as *Appalachia* (1902) and *On Hearing the First Cuckoo in Spring* (1912). In 1924 he became paralysed and blind, but with the assistance of **Eric Fenby** (1906–97), his amanuensis from 1928, he continued to compose.

Deller, Alfred (George) (1912–79) Countertenor, born in Margate, Kent, SE England, UK. A church chorister from the age of 11, he began a full-time musical career in 1947. He made many recordings of early English songs, notably those of Dowland and Purcell, and in 1950 formed the *Deller Consort*, devoted to the authentic performance of early music. In 1963 he founded the Stour Music Festival.

Del Mar, Norman (René) (1919–94) Conductor and horn player, born in London, UK. He studied at the Royal College of Music, and became assistant conductor of the Royal Philharmonic Orchestra (1947–8), principal conductor of the English Opera Group (1948–56), and conductor of the BBC Scottish Symphony Orchestra (1960–5). His son, **Jonathan Del Mar** (1951–), also became a conductor.

Delon, Alain [delõ] (1935–) Film actor, born in Paris, France. He became known following his success as one of the lead roles in a thriller adapted from a Patricia Highsmith novel, *Purple Moon* (1960). Later films include *The Leopard* (1962), *The Assassination of Trotsky* (1972), *Swann in Love* (1984), *The Day and the Night* (1997), and *Half a Chance* (1998).

de Lorris, Guillaume [duh loris] *Guillaume de Lorris*

Delors, Jacques [duhlaw(r)] (1925–) French and European statesman, born in Paris, France. He served as social affairs adviser to Jacques Chaban-Delmas (1969–72). He joined the Socialist Party in 1973, represented it in the European Parliament from 1979, and served as minister of economy and finance in the administration of President Mitterrand (1981–4). He became President of the European Commission in 1985, and was elected to a second 4-year term in 1988, extended until 1995 despite difficulties ratifying the Maastricht Treaty. He oversaw significant budgetary reforms and the move towards a free Community market in 1992, with increased powers residing in Brussels. He was president of the International Commission on Education for the Twenty-first Century (1993–6) established by UNESCO.

de los Angeles, Victoria *Angeles, Victoria de los*

Delphi [delfiy], Gr **Dhelfoí**, formerly **Pytho** 38°29N 22°30E. Village and ancient site in Fokis department, Greece, on the slopes of Mt Parnassos, 176 km/109 mi from Athens; altitude 520–620 m/1706–2034 ft; renowned throughout the ancient Greek world as the sanctuary of Apollo and the seat of his oracle; remains of the temple and precincts were excavated in the 19th-c.

Delphi, Oracle of [**del**fee, **del**fiy] The oracular shrine of Apollo at Delphi in C Greece. It was the most prestigious oracle in the Graeco-Roman world, for centuries being consulted by states about public policy and by individuals about private matters. On the payment of a fee, enquirers put their questions to Apollo's medium, a priestess called the Pythia. Her ecstatic responses (oracles) were notorious for their ambiguity.

delphinium A tall perennial, native to the N hemisphere; leaves palmately lobed or finely divided; flowers blue, rarely pink or white, each with a conical spur and borne in long showy spikes. A popular garden ornamental, it contains poisonous alkaloids including delphinin. (Genus: *Delphinium*, 250 species. Family: Ranunculaceae.)

Delphinus [del**fiy**nus] (Lat 'dolphin') A small N constellation.

Delphi technique [**del**fiy] A forcasting technique used in business planning. Experts are invited to give their opinion on the likehood of occurrence of a specific event on or by a specific date. The consensus view is taken as a forecast.

delta A fan-shaped body of alluvium enclosed within the bifurcating channels at the mouth of a river. It is formed when a river deposits sediment as its speed decreases, and the coastal processes of erosion are not sufficiently strong to carry the material away. Deltas may take many forms, depending on the environmental factors at the river mouth, but in all cases the coarse sediment is deposited first, with progressively finer material carried further out from the shore. Deltas may form large fertile plains, but are subject to frequent flooding. Among the largest deltas are those of the Nile, the Ganges–Brahmaputra and the Mississippi rivers.

Deluge *Flood, the*

Delvaux, Paul [del**voh**] (1897–1994) Surrealist painter, born in Antheit, SC Belgium. He lived mainly in Brussels, where he studied. Influenced by Chirico and Magritte, he produced a series of paintings depicting nude and semi-nude girls in dreamlike settings, such as 'The Call of the Night'. He was professor of painting at Brussels (1950–62).

de Man, Paul [man] (1919–83) Cultural theorist, born in Belgium. Controversy has surrounded his writings for collaborationist journals during World War 2. After the war he emigrated to the USA, and taught at several universities, including Yale, where he became a leading exponent of the critical method known as *deconstruction*. His most important essays were published in *Blindness and Insight* (1971) and *Allegories of Reading* (1979).

demand In economics, the quantity of goods (products) or services demanded at a particular price (**market demand**). The demand function for a good relates the quantity demanded to various factors. These include the good's own price; quantity demanded normally goes down when price rises. Demand also depends on the prices of other goods which are substitutes or complements for the good, on consumers' incomes, and on other variables including new technologies, the weather, and changes in fashion.

dementia A decline in intellectual capacity as a result of an alteration of brain functioning which leads to impaired social or occupational abilities. It is commonly due to cerebrovascular disease and the ageing process, in which brain cells are destroyed and brain size is markedly reduced. Features include loss of memory, alteration of personality, impaired judgment, and poor impulse control. There is disorientation in time and place, and a failure to recognize friends and relatives. The term is one of many used previously as synonymous with madness.

Demeter [dee**mee**ter] The Greek goddess of agriculture, especially corn, so that a basket or an ear of corn is her symbol. She is the mother of Persephone, for whom she searched through the world, and is also connected with the Mysteries at Eleusis.

de Meung, Jean *Jean de Meung*

De Mille, Agnes [duh **mil**] (1905–93) Dancer, choreographer, and writer, born in New York City, USA, the niece of film director Cecil B De Mille. She studied at the University of California, went to London, and danced with Marie Rambert's company. *Three Virgins and a Devil* (1941) marked her breakthrough into choreography, and she went on to choreograph for musicals such as *Oklahoma!* (1943) and *Carousel* (1945). She was also known for her wit and eloquent public speaking, and her contribution to television and film. Her publications include the autobiographical *Dance to the Piper* (1952) and *Martha* (1991), her tribute to Martha Graham.

De Mille, Cecil B(lount) [duh **mil**] (1881–1959) Film producer and director, born in Ashfield, Massachusetts, USA. He was an actor and writer before making the first US feature film in Hollywood, *The Squaw Man* (1913). He made a reputation for box-office spectacles with such films as *The Ten Commandments* (1923, remade in Cinema-Scope, 1957), *The Plainsman* (1937), and *The Greatest Show on Earth* (1952). He also organized the first commercial passenger airline service in the USA (1917).

Demme, Jonathan (1944–) Film director, born in Long Island, New York, USA. He has directed pop videos, documentaries, and television episodes, making his cinematic directorial debut with *Caged Heat* (1974). He won a Best Director Oscar for the psychological thriller *Silence of the Lambs* (1991). Later films include *Cousin Bobby* (1992), *Philadelphia* (1993), and *Beloved* (1998).

democracy From Greek *demos* ('people') and *kratia* ('authority'), hence 'rule by the people'; contrasted with rule by the few (**oligarchy**) or by one (**monarchy** or **tyranny**); also known as a **liberal democracy**. Since the Greeks first introduced *demokratia* in many city states in the 5th-c BC, there has been disagreement about what constitutes the essential elements of democracy. One debate concerns who should compose 'the people', and only in the 20th-c did this notion come to be viewed as covering the total adult citizenship. Another relates to how the people should rule, particularly in relation to the increasing size of states, which has resulted in a shift from direct democracy to systems of representation. Today it is widely accepted that because the people are too numerous and scattered to come together in assemblies, decision-making has to be handed over to a small group of representatives. Elections, including the right to choose among different groups of representatives offering different doctrines and party programmes, have therefore become seen as essential to democracy. Further necessary conditions are the legal equality of citizens, and the free flow of information to ensure that citizens are in an equal and informed position to choose and hold accountable their rulers. Some radicals argue that economic equality is also necessary, but moves towards economic democracy have been limited.

Democratic Labor Party (DLP) An Australian political party, formed in 1957 from anti-communist groups which had formerly been part of the Australian Labor Party (ALP). The DLP was largely centred in Victoria, and drew most of its support from parts of the Catholic section of Australian society. At its height, in the late 1950s and through the 1960s, its importance lay in its ability to prevent the ALP from winning national government. Its policies were strongly anti-communist and pro-defence, and incorporated elements of Catholic teaching on social matters. No DLP representative has been elected to the national parliament since 1974.

Democratic Party One of the two major parties in contemporary US politics. It was originally composed in the late 18th-c of those opposed to the adoption of the US Constitution, and was called the **Democratic Republican Party** until 1828. The Party's first presidential candidate was Thomas Jefferson; and in the early 1800s it dominated its opponent, the Federalist Party. The Party was split over slavery and secession during the Civil War (1861–5), its dominant position being taken over by the Republican Party. After the war the Party stood for state rights, limited government, and white supremacy until the beginning of the 20th-c. Under William Jennings Bryan (1860–1925) and Woodrow Wilson it became more committed to government intervention in the economy. After faltering in the 1920s, it returned to a majority position in 1932, when Roosevelt introduced his 'New Deal', and added large urban areas and ethnic, racial, and religious support to its conservative Southern base. It also became associated with a more liberal stance of social reform and minority rights, especially in the 1960s. From 1968 onward it experienced difficulty in winning the presidency, with Jimmy Carter's success in 1976 the only break in Republican domination for two decades. The presidency of Bill Clinton brought the Democrats national electoral victories in 1992 and 1996, but they lost their half-century long control of the House of Representatives in 1994. The party made gains in the 1998 elections, but tensions persist between its liberal and conservative wings. In 2001 they regained a working majority and assumed control of the House of Representatives, but lost it to the Republicans in the mid-term elections in 2002.

Democritus [demokritus] (c.460–370 BC) Greek philosopher, born in Abdera, Thrace. He travelled in the East, and was by far the most learned thinker of his time. He wrote many physical, mathematical, ethical, and musical works, but only fragments survive. His *atomic system* assumes an infinite multitude of everlasting atoms, from whose random combinations springs an infinite number of successive world-orders in which there is law but not design. This system, derived from Leucippus, was developed by Epicurus and Lucretius.

demography A branch of sociology which studies the population patterns of the past, present, and future. Demography has been very important in estimating future trends in population growth in order to calculate the pressures on global resources.

demoiselle [demwazel] A crane (*Anthropoides virgo*), native to S Europe, Asia, and N Africa (migrates further S in winter); mainly white with dark chest and throat; ornamental feathers on head. (Family: Gruidae.)

demonology An outmoded branch of theology relating to the Devil and demons, elaborated from the later Middle Ages particularly in association with belief in witches and their power to do harm. The best known and most influential work of demonology is the *Malleus maleficarum* (Hammer of the Witches) by the Dominicans Kramer and Sprenger, published at Cologne in 1484. This was the main source of the idea that witches were agents of the Devil.

De Morgan, Augustus (1806–71) Mathematician, born in Madura, N India. He studied at Cambridge, and became the first professor of mathematics at University College London (1828). He helped to develop the notion of different kinds of algebra, and collaborated with Boole in the development of symbolic logic.

Demosthenes [demostheneez] (c.383–322 BC) The greatest of the Greek orators, the son of a rich Athenian arms manufacturer. After studying rhetoric and legal procedure, he took up the law as a profession, becoming first a speech-writer, then an assistant to prosecutors in public (state) trials. In c.354 BC he entered politics, but did not gain prominence until 351 BC, when he delivered the first of a long series of passionate speeches (the 'First Philippic') advocating all-out resistance to Philip of Macedon. Swayed by his oratory, the Athenians did eventually go to war (340 BC), only to be thoroughly defeated at Chaeronea (338 BC). Put on trial by the peace party of Aeschines, he fully vindicated himself in his oratorical masterpiece, *On the Crown*. He was exiled for embezzlement in 325 BC, and committed suicide after the failure of the Athenian revolt from Macedon following Alexander's death.

demotic script [demotik] An ancient Egyptian form of writing, derived from hieroglyphic script, and used for everyday purposes. The term is also applied to any 'common' style of speech or writing, as opposed to the official or formal system used by a community.

Dempsey, Jack, popular name of **William Harrison Dempsey**, nickname **the Manassa Mauler** (1895–1983) World heavyweight champion boxer, born in Manassa, Colorado, USA. He worked in copper mines before taking to the ring as 'Kid Blackie' in 1914. In 1919 he defeated Jess Willard to win the world heavyweight title, which he lost to Gene Tunney in 1926. After several years fighting exhibitions, Dempsey retired from the ring in 1940, and became a successful restaurateur on Broadway in New York City.

Demuth, Charles [demooth] (1883–1935) Painter and book illustrator, born in Lancaster, Pennsylvania, USA. He studied at the Pennsylvania Academy of the Fine Arts, then went to Paris (1912–14), where he saw the work of the early Cubists and took back their ideas to America. From 1919 he was a major exponent of 'Precisionism', with its hard outlines and semi-abstract treatment of industrial or urban scenery, as seen in 'My Egypt' (1927), a view of grain elevators.

demythologizing A programme of interpretation of the Bible, systematized by Rudolf Bultmann. He attempted to understand the so-called 'mythical' language of Biblical times, which presupposed a pre-scientific world-view, by interpreting it 'existentially' (ie in categories of the existentialist philosopher, Heidegger) making it meaningful to the modern scientifically-minded world.

Denali, Mount *McKinley, Mount*

Denbighshire [denbeesheer], Welsh **Sir Ddinbych** pop (2001e) 93 100; area 844 sq km / 326 sq mi. County (unitary authority from 1996) in NC Wales, UK; drained by R Clwyd; administrative centre, Ruthin; other chief towns, Rhyl, Prestatyn, Denbigh, St Asaph; tourism on coast; St Asaph cathedral (founded 573); music festival at St Asaph (Sep); international eisteddfod at Llangollen (Jul).

dendrite *neurone*

dendrochronology The construction of archaeological chronologies from annual tree-ring sequences. Rings vary in width and structure from year to year, depending on the prevailing climatic conditions; overlapping patterns observed in preserved timbers can therefore be matched and linked to form an accurate and absolute chronology extending back unbroken from the present day. Notable sequences derived from the long-lived Californian bristlecone pine (*Pinus aristata*, to c.6700 BC) and Irish bog oaks (to c.5300 BC) have proved a crucial check on radiocarbon dates.

Deneb *Cygnus*

Deneuve, Cathérine [duhnoev], originally **Cathérine Dorléac** (1943–) Actress, born in Paris, France. She made her film debut in *Les Collégiennes* (1956), and became well known through the unexpected popularity of the musical *Les Parapluies de Cherbourg* (1964, The Umbrellas of Cherbourg). Her films include *Repulsion* (1965), *Belle de Jour* (1967), *Le Sauvage* (1975), *Le Dernier Métro* (1980, The Last Metro), *Place Vendôme* (1999), and *Dancer in the Dark* (2000). She was married to the photographer David Bailey (1965–70), and had a child by director Roger Vadim (1963), and another by actor Marcello Mastroianni (1972).

dengue [denggee] A serious disease caused by a virus, transmitted by mosquitoes. Originally confined to the tropics, it is spreading to other areas of the world as the mosquito migrates. Some people develop classic dengue with fever, headache, joint pain, weakness, and skin rashes, followed by lassitude and depression. It usually resolves in a few weeks. Others develop the haemorrhagic form of the disease. They also suffer vomiting, abdominal pain, and circulatory collapse, and there is a high mortality.

Deng Xiaoping [duhng syowping] or **Teng Hsiao-p'ing** (1904–97) Leader of the Chinese Communist Party, after 1978 the dominant figure in Chinese politics, born in Sichuan province, C China. He studied in France, where he joined the Communist Party, and in the Soviet Union, and became associated with Mao Zedong during the period of the Jiangxi Soviet (1928–34). In 1954 he became secretary-general of the Chinese Communist Party, but reacted strongly against the excesses of the Great

Denmark

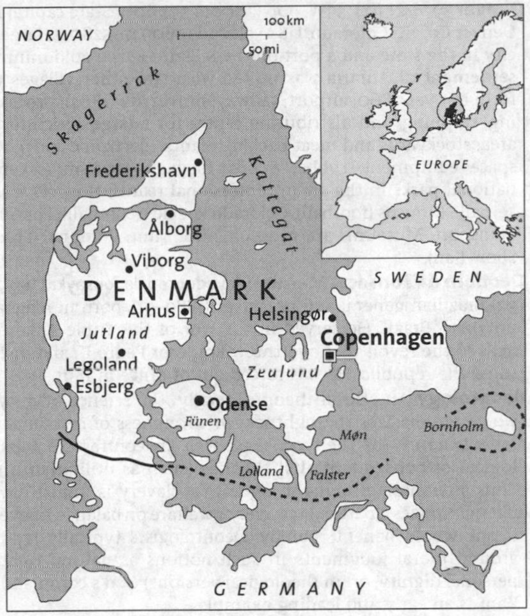

Dan **Danmark**, official name **Kingdom of Denmark**, Dan **Kongeriget Danmark**
Local name Danmark
Timezone GMT +1
Area 43 076 km²/16 627 sq mi (excluding Greenland and Faroe Islands)
Population total (2002e) 5 377 000
Status Kingdom
Capital Copenhagen
Language Danish (official)
Ethnic groups Danish (97%), Turkish (0·5%), other Scandinavian (0·4%)
Religions Evangelical Lutheran (97%), Roman Catholic (0·5%), Jewish (0·1%)
Physical features Consists of most of the Jutland peninsula, several islands in the Baltic Sea, and some of the N Frisian Is in the North Sea; coastline 3400 km/2100 mi; uniformly low-lying; no large rivers and few lakes; shoreline indented by many lagoons and fjords, largest is Lim Fjord.
Climate Modified by Gulf Stream; cold and cloudy winters, warm and sunny summers; average annual temperatures range from 0·5°C (Jan) to 17°C (Jul); average annual rainfall 800 mm/32 in.
Currency 1 Danish Krone (Dkr) = 100 øre
Economy Lack of raw materials has resulted in development of processing industries; intensive agriculture; wide range of food processing; machinery, textiles, furniture, electronics; dairy products.
GDP (2002e) $155·3 bn, per capita $28 900
Human Development Index (2002) 0·926
History Part of Viking kingdoms, 8th–10th-c; Danish Empire under Canute, 11th-c; joined with Sweden and Norway under Queen Margrethe of Denmark, 1389; Sweden separated from union in 16th-c, followed by Norway; 1814; Schleswig-Holstein lost to Germany, 1864; N Schleswig returned after plebiscite, 1920; occupied by Germany during World War 2; Iceland independent 1944; Greenland and Faroe Is remain dependencies; constitutional monarchy since 1849; unicameral system adopted, 1953; legislative power lies with the Monarch and the Diet jointly.
Head of State (Monarch)
1863–1906 Christian IX
1906–12 Frederik VIII
1912–47 Christian X
1947–72 Frederk IX
1972– Margrethe II
Head of Government
1975–82 Anker Jorgensen
1982–93 Poul Schlüter
1993–2001 Poul Nyrop Rasmussen
2001– Anders Fogh Rasmussen

Leap Forward (1958–9). When Mao launched the Cultural Revolution (1966), Deng was criticized and purged along with Liu Shaoqi, but retained the confidence of Premier Zhou Enlai and was restored to power in 1974. Again dismissed in 1976, after the death of Mao he was restored once more to power, and from 1978 had taken China through a rapid course of pragmatic reforms. His prestige was severely damaged by his role in the repression of the mass protests on Tiananmen Square in 1989.

Denham, Sir John [denam] (1615–69) Poet, born in Dublin, Ireland. He studied at London and Oxford, succeeded to his father's estate, and at the outbreak of the Civil War was high sheriff of Surrey. His best-known works were the tragedy, *The Sophy* (1641), and his descriptive poem, *Cooper's Hill* (1642). At the Restoration he was appointed surveyor-general of works, and in 1661 created a Knight of the Bath.

denier [denier] A unit of weight in textiles, measuring the fineness of yarn in such materials as silk, rayon, or nylon. It is equal to the weight in grams of 9000 m of the yarn. Materials of 15 denier would be finer than the material of 20 denier. It is now being replaced by the *tex*.

denim A popular clothing fabric made originally by filling indigo-dyed warp yarns with undyed cotton weft to give a twill structure. The indigo slowly leaches out of the fabric, causing a characteristic lightening of the blue colour. The fabric is hard-wearing, and was used for working clothes, but from the 1950s acquired a fashionable cult status.

De Niro, Robert [duh neeroh] (1943–) Actor and director, born in New York City, USA. A student of acting with Stella Adler (1902–92) and Lee Strasberg, he worked off-Broadway, making his film debut in 1965. He received Oscars for his supporting role in *The Godfather, Part II* (1974), and for his portrayal of boxer Jake La Motta in *Raging Bull* (1980). His many films include *Taxi Driver* (1976), *The Deerhunter* (1978), *Midnight Run* (1988), *Awakenings* (1990), *Mary Shelley's Frankenstein* (1994), *Sleepers* (1996), and *The Score* (2001). He made his directorial debut with *A Bronx Tale* (1993), in which he also starred. He has also developed his own production company, Tribeca Films. In 2003 the American Film Institute honoured him with a Lifetime Achievement Award.

Denis or **Denys, St** [denis], Fr [duhnee] (3rd-c) Traditional apostle of France, and the first Bishop of Paris, born possibly in Rome. He was sent from Rome c.250 to preach the Gospel to the Gauls. He was martyred at Paris under the Roman Emperor Valerian (reigned 253–60). Feast day 9 October.

Denis, Maurice [duhnee] (1870–1943) Artist and art theorist, born in Grandville, W France. One of the original group of Symbolist painters, *Les Nabis*, he wrote several influential critical works, and in 1919 helped to found the Studios of Sacred Art, devoted to the revival of religious painting. Perhaps his most famous picture is 'Hommage à Cézanne' (1900, Paris).

Denmark *see panel*

Denning (of Whitchurch), Alfred Thompson Denning, Baron (1899–1999) British judge, born in Whitchurch, Hampshire, S England, UK. He studied at Oxford, was called to the bar in 1923, became a KC in 1938, and a judge of the High Court of Justice in 1944. In 1963 he led the inquiry into the circumstances of John Profumo's resignation as secretary of state for war. As Master of the Rolls (1962–82) he was responsible for many often controversial decisions. He was knighted in 1944, and made a life peer in 1957. His clear judgments and opinions protecting the individual against the 'big battalions' made him one of the most popular judges of the 20th-c, although some of his opinions, particularly in later years, aroused controversy.

denotation *connotation*

density (physics) The mass of a substance divided by its volume; symbol ρ, units kg/m^3. The density of water is 1000 kg/m^3. An object placed in a liquid more dense than itself will float, whereas an object more dense than the liquid will sink. Density is measured using a hydrometer.

dentistry The treatment and prevention of diseases of the mouth and teeth; with medicine and nursing, one of the major health professions. Dentistry was studied at the Chinese Imperial Medical College from 620, and toothbrushes and toothpaste were known by Song times (10th–13th-c). In the West, it was first practised by barber surgeons. Surgeon dentists first formed a separate guild in France in the reign of Louis XIV, and were required to pass a prescribed examination. In the UK, dental hospitals were built to serve the poor, but formal dental schools were not founded until 1840 in the USA and 1860 in the UK. They were originally privately funded and staffed. Today the practice of dentistry is well-controlled, and its practitioners are licensed under a number of authorities in different countries following specifically dental-oriented training. In Russia, dentists are first trained as physicians and then in operative dentistry, and are called **stomatologists**. In the UK, the right to practise is granted by a General Dental Council, which controls professional and ethical standards. The great majority of dentists in the USA and Europe (but not Russia) are in private dental practice, and in the UK hold contracts with the state, which funds some of the costs. In some countries, **dental hygienists** provide services such as X-rays, scaling of teeth, and dental health education. In the UK, dental assistants and auxiliaries work closely with the dentist, assisting in clinical work, as well as discharging secretarial and receptionist duties.

The trend in dental practice has moved from the repair of individual teeth, or their wholesale removal for the relief of pain, to that of conservation and the prevention of disease (**conservative dentistry**). Hospital dental care for larger and specialist procedures is available in the UK as part of the National Health Service. Apart from general dentistry, several special branches of the subject have developed. **Periodontics** is concerned with the prevention, diagnosis, and treatment of disorders of tissues that surround and support the teeth. The most common disorder is infection of the gums, causing *pyorrhea*, which when severe may lead to loss of teeth. It is believed that bacteria cause the deposition of *plaque*, a hard material that adheres to teeth and promotes gum damage. Scaling of teeth and hygiene tends to prevent these complications. **Orthodontics** is concerned with correcting the malposition of teeth, usually arising from faults in dental development; it includes repair of difficulties in chewing and the treatment of dento-facial deformities. The provision of artificial *prostheses* attempts to restore oral function after the loss of teeth or of tissue; it includes the use of fixed and removable prostheses (**prosthodontics**). **Oral surgery** is concerned with the repair of injury to the jaws by disease or by trauma; it includes the diagnosis and treatment of infections, tumours and cysts, and congenital defects such as cleft palate. The diagnosis of the nature of such conditions is a branch of pathology.

denudation The process of removing the surface of the land by the agents of weathering and erosion, ultimately to form a stable flat landscape. While tectonic processes within the Earth form fold mountains and volcanoes, surface processes continuously remove material and carry it down to the seas and oceans.

Denver 39°44N 104°59W, pop (2000e) 554 600; State capital in Denver Co, NC Colorado, USA; altitude 1609 m/5280 ft; largest city in the state and a port on the S Platte R; the gold-mining settlement of Auraria was united with two other villages to form Denver, 1860; airport; railway; university (1864); processing, shipping, and distributing centre for a large agricultural area; stockyards and meat packing plants; electronic and aerospace equipment, rubber goods, luggage; tourism (several national parks in the area); professional teams, Nuggets (basketball), Broncos (football), Colorado Rockies (baseball); Fornery Transport Museum, art museum, US Mint; National Stock Show (Jan).

Deodoro da Fonseca, Manuel [dayodooroo da fonsayka] (1827–92) Brazilian general and president (1889–91), born in Alagoas province, Brazil. He served in the War of the Triple Alliance, headed the revolt that overthrew Emperor Pedro II, and instituted the republic. He was forced out of office in 1891.

deontology An ethical theory (literally 'the science of duty') which emphasizes the rightness or wrongness of certain acts independently of their consequences, in contrast to **teleological** or **consequentialist** theories (such as utilitarianism). Thus a deontologist might argue that slavery is unjust even if it maximizes a particular society's welfare on balance, or even if one would benefit thereby. Deontologists typically try to ground moral judgments in such notions as natural rights, personal dignity, or (in theological versions) God's commands. Kant is an early and leading example.

deoxyribonucleic acid *DNA*

deoxyribose [deeoksiriybohs] $C_5H_{10}O_4$. A 5-carbon sugar, particularly important for its role in the genetic material DNA. Two of the atoms (OH, HO) are connected to phosphate groups in DNA.

depaato [depahtoh] A Japanese department store. Tokyo's first such store, Mitsukoshi ('the Harrods of Japan'), opened in 1904, and now has many branches in major cities. The stores present high standards of service, contain roof gardens and restaurants, and present cultural exhibitions and other attractions.

De Palma, Brian (1940–) Film director, born in Newark, New Jersey, USA. He won a number of prizes directing short films before making his feature-length debut with *The Wedding Party* (1966). He enjoyed commercial success with *Carrie* (1976) and *The Untouchables* (1987), later films including *Bonfire of the Vanities* (1990), *Carlito's Way* (1993), *Mission Impossible* (1996), *Snake Eyes* (1998), and *Mission to Mars* (2000).

Dépardieu, Gérard [daypah(r)dyoe] (1948–) Actor and director, born in Châteauroux, C France. An unruly child, he was encouraged to enter dramatics as a therapy and made his film debut in *Le Beatnik et le minet* (1965). He continued in occasional film roles while appearing on stage and television, including the series *L'Inconnu* (1974). His films include *Le Dernier Métro* (1980), *Danton* (1982), and *Jean de Florette* (1986). Among later films are *Cyrano de Bergerac* (1990), *Green Card* (1990), *Germinal* (1992), *The Man in the Iron Mask* (1998), and *Astérix and Obélix* (1999). He also directed himself in *Le Tartuffe* (1984). He was awarded the Legion of Honour in 1996.

depersonalization A sensation in which the individual feels unreal and not in the living world. It includes feelings of part of the body changing in size or not belonging to the self, or a sense of looking at oneself from the outside. It can be a normal phenomenon, as when associated with extreme fatigue, and appears frequently as a symptom in a variety of psychiatric disorders.

depilatory [depilatree] A chemical used to remove unwanted hair on the skin, including alkalis, metallic sulphides, and mercaptans. They act by disrupting the chemical structure of the hair protein.

Depp, Johnny, popular name of **John Christopher Depp II** (1963–) Actor, born in Owensboro, Kentucky, USA. He dropped out of high school and played with several rock bands before turning to acting. He made his feature film debut in *A Nightmare on Elm Street* (1984) and appeared in the television series *21 Jump Street* (1987). Often playing unconventional roles, his later films include *Edward Scissorhands* (1990), *Donnie Brasco* (1997), and *Pirates of the Caribbean* (2003).

depreciation An accountancy term measuring the loss of value of an asset due to age, wear and tear, and obsolescence. **Straight-line depreciation** assumes that the asset loses value evenly over its life, by the same amount each year. **Reducing balance depreciation** assumes that an asset loses a constant proportion of its remaining value each year until it is finally scrapped, when the rest disappears.

depression (economics) An economic situation where demand is slack, order-books are low, firms dispense with staff, and profits are poor or absent. The **Great Depression** of the early 1930s (often referred to as the *slump*), which began in the USA, saw many bankruptcies and many millions of people out of work. A less severe form is a *recession*.

depression (meteorology) A meteorological term for a low pressure system at high and mid-latitudes; also known as a **cyclone** at low latitudes. The system generally passes through a number of well-defined stages, each of which is accompanied by characteristic weather patterns, although not all depressions follow the idealized cycle. A depression is initiated when a wave develops on a *front* (a boundary between cold and warm air masses). Pressure falls at the crest of the wave. A *warm front* is the leading edge of the depression, followed by the *cold front*, with a warm sector between the two fronts. As the cold front travels faster than the warm front, it catches up, to produce an *occluded front*. When this happens, pressure rises and the depression loses velocity. Surface winds travel anticlockwise around a depression in the N hemisphere, and clockwise in the S hemisphere. Depressions are typically 1000–2000 km/600–1250 mi across, but are temporary features with an average lifespan of 4–7 days. They form regularly in a number of regions (eg along the polar front of the N Pacific and N Atlantic Oceans, and in the Mediterranean). The most intense depressions usually form in winter. Their formation is associated with Rossby waves.

depression (psychiatry) A mental condition or state in which there are feelings of low mood, despondence, self-criticism, and low esteem. It may be associated with a change (up or down) in appetite for sleep, food, or sex. The term has been used in a variety of ways: in lay use, it may mean little more than common sadness; in psychiatric use, it may refer to specific conditions, such as melancholia or manic-depressive illness, or be a factor in a wide range of disorders. It can be measured by a variety of rating scales, and there are certain biological markers thought to distinguish between depressed and non-depressed individuals. There is a wide variety of treatments that can be used for this condition, including behavioural and psychoanalytic forms of psychotherapy, pharmacological treatments and, in certain situations, electroconvulsive therapy.

Depression, the *Great Depression*

depth charge A munition used by surface warships as a means of destroying submarines, typically an explosive-packed container dropped over the stern of a warship, armed by a fuse primed to detonate when it senses the water-pressure at a predetermined depth. From the middle of World War 2 the depth charge was supplanted by weapons which threw the explosive munition ahead of the anti-submarine warship. From the late 1950s, nuclear depth charges with explosive radii greater than one kilometre have been in service with nuclear-equipped navies. These require a device such as a missile or pilotless aircraft to take them a safe distance away from the launching warship.

depth psychology A group of psychological treatments which emphasize unconscious mental processes as the cause of neurotic illnesses; opposed to behavioural forms of psychology. In psychoanalytic forms of depth psychology, Freudian concepts of id, ego, and superego would be considered, whereas in analytical psychology described by Jung, the collective unconsciousness is considered paramount.

de Quincey, Thomas [duh kwinsee] (1785–1859) Writer and critic, born in Manchester, Greater Manchester, NW England, UK. Educated at Manchester Grammar School, he ran away, and wandered in Wales and London. He then spent a short time at Oxford, where he became addicted to opium. On a visit to Bath, he met Coleridge, and through him Southey and Wordsworth; and in 1809 went to live near them in Grasmere. There he set up as an author, largely writing magazine articles. His *Confessions of an English Opium-Eater*, written in sonorous prose, appeared as a serial in 1821, and brought him instant fame. In 1828 he moved to Edinburgh, and for 20 years wrote for various magazines.

Derain, André [duhrĩ] (1880–1954) Artist, born in Chatou, NC France. He is most famous for his Fauvist pictures (1904–8), when he was associated with Vlaminck and Matisse. Later landscape pictures show a Romantic Realism influenced by Cézanne. He also designed for the theatre (notably the Diaghilev ballet) and illustrated several books.

Derby [dah(r)bee] 52°55N 1°30W, pop (2001e) 221 700. City and unitary authority (from 1997) in Derbyshire, C England, UK; on the R Derwent, 56 km/35 mi NE of Birmingham; chartered in 1637; railway; first silk mill (1719); porcelain centre in 18th-c (Derby ware); aero engines, railway engineering; lawnmowers, sugar refining, textiles, chemicals, plastics, china; Cathedral of All Saints (1525), old silk mill industrial museum; football league team, Derby County (Rams).

Derby, Edward Geoffrey Smith Stanley, 14th Earl of [dah(r)bee] (1799–1869) British statesman and prime minister (1852, 1858–9, 1866-8), born at Knowsley Hall, Lancashire, NW England, UK. He studied at Oxford, entered parliament as a Whig in 1828, and became chief-secretary for Ireland (1830), and colonial secretary (1833), when he carried the Act for the emancipation of West Indian slaves. In 1834 he withdrew from the Party, and soon after joined the Conservatives (subsequently party leader, 1846–68). He entered the House of Lords as a baronet in 1844, retired from the cabinet in 1845, when Peel decided to repeal the Corn Laws, and in 1846 headed the Protectionists in the Lords. In 1851 he succeeded his father as Earl of Derby. Premier on three occasions, his third administration passed the Reform Bill (1867).

Derby, the *Classics*

Derby china Porcelain made in Derby at three factories operating c.1750–1848, 1848–1935, and 1877 to the present, the last becoming Royal Crown Derby in 1890. William Duesbury (1725–86), proprietor from 1756, purchased the Chelsea factory in 1770 and ran it with Derby until 1784. Derby was renowned for its enamelled and 'biscuit' figures, finely painted vases and tableware, including colourful 'Japan' patterns popular in the 19th-c and 20th-c.

Derbyshire [dah(r)bisheer] pop (2001e) 734 600; area 2631 sq km/1016 sq mi. County of C England, UK; rises to The Peak at 636 m/2086 ft; drained by Derwent, Dove, Wye, and Trent Rivers; county town, Matlock; chief towns include Derby (new unitary authority from 1997), Chesterfield, Glossop; the Derwent Valley Mills is a world heritage site; sheep and dairy farming, coal, textiles, iron smelting, engineering.

Dere Street *Roman roads*

Dergue [derg] The regime which ruled Ethiopia from the revolution in 1974 to 1991, under the leadership of Haile Mariam Mengistu. The word means 'Committee', from the Committee of the Armed Forces which overthrew the Emperor Haile Selassie. Wracked by civil war and the Eritrean secessionist movement, the Dergue and Mengistu were overthrown by the Ethiopian People's Revolutionary Democratic Front in 1990.

derivation A major process of word formation. In derivational modification, new words are formed which often belong to a different word class from the base form, as with *truth* (noun), *truth-ful* (adjective), *false* (adjective), *false-hood* (noun). This contrasts with **inflection**, a process of modification where the word class of the form is never altered, but its grammatical status is changed (eg singular to plural, present tense to past tense), as in *girl/girls*, *talk/talked*.

derivatives Securities whose value depends on the prices of other securities. For example, a financial institution may borrow, promising repayment proportional to some index of security prices, such as the FT–SE share price index, or may sell an option giving the other party the right but not the obligation to buy or sell a given share or currency at a fixed price on some future date. New forms of derivatives are continually being invented. Because the future prices of securities are unknown, dealing in derivatives can be extremely risky, especially in the case of new types where there is no relevant experience on which to assess the risks being taken. The treatment of derivatives poses severe problems for the authorities regulating financial markets, and for the accountancy profession in considering how contingent obligations arising from derivatives should be reported in company accounts.

Dermaptera [dermaptera] *earwig*

dermatitis [dermatiytis] The commonest skin disorder, involving an allergic reaction in the skin; also known as **eczema**. It may be provoked by chemical and physical irritants (eg detergents, watch straps), or ingested food and drugs. There is a hereditary element, in that affected individuals often have a family history of dermatitis and other allergic disorders such as hay fever and asthma. The initial reaction in the skin is an increase in blood supply, which causes redness of the affected part (*erythema*). This is followed by blisters which rupture, giving rise to the 'weeping' phase of the disorder. Repair then takes place with the overgrowth of keratin, which causes thickening of the superficial layers of the skin, and which may become chronic.

dermatology The scientific study of the structure and function of the skin and of its diseases. It is a specialized branch of medical practice.

Derrida, Jacques [derida] (1930–) French philosopher-linguist, born in Algeria. He studied in Paris, and teaches at the Ecole Normale Supérieure there. His critique of the referentiality of language and the objectivity of structures founded the school of criticism called *deconstruction*. He advocated that the reader should look at how a text was put together in order to reveal its hidden meanings and the assumptions of the author. Among his highly influential works are *De la Grammatologie* (1967, Of Grammatology), *L'écriture et la différence* (1967, Writing and Difference), and *La dissémination* (1972, Dissemination). His essay *Apories* appeared in 1996. The award of an honorary degree by Cambridge University in 1992 was publicly contested, prompting attacks on and defences of his work.

Derry (city), official name **Londonderry** (but **Derry City Council** since 1984) 55°00N 7°19W, pop (2000e) 77 600. City in Derry district, County Derry, NW Northern Ireland, UK; on a hill above the R Foyle, 8 km/5 mi above its mouth into Lough Foyle; monastery founded by St Columba, c.546; James I proclaimed the city to be part of the Corporation of London, 1613; renamed London-Derry, and settled by a Protestant colony; resisted a siege by James II for 105 days, 1689; railway; textiles, chemicals, engineering, ceramics; old town walls and gates, St Columba's Cathedral (Protestant, 1628–33), St Columba's Church (Catholic, 1873), Guildhall (1912).

Derry (county), official name **Londonderry**, Ir **Doire** pop (2000e) 227 300; area 2067 sq km/798 sq mi. County in N Northern Ireland, UK, divided into four districts (Coleraine, Derry, Limavady, Magherafelt); the name is also used for one of these districts, pop (2000e) 102 000, and its administrative centre; bounded N by Lough Foyle and the Atlantic Ocean, SE by Lough Neagh, and NW by the Republic of Ireland; hilly, with part of the Sperrin Mts rising in the S; county town, Derry; other chief towns, Coleraine, Portstewart; seed potatoes, flax, dairy produce, fishing, textiles, light engineering.

dervish A member of an Islamic ascetic or mystical fraternity. Since the founding of the Qadiriya order in the 12th-c, numerous orders with lodges situated across the Muslim world have been established, each with its own ethos and rituals. One of the most famous orders is the Mevlevi, or **whirling dervishes** of Turkey who practice trans-inducing ecstatic dances.

DES An abbreviation of **diethylstilboestrol/diethylstilbestrol** – a synthetic oestrogen for the treatment of menopausal symptoms and prostate cancer. When first introduced, it was used to prevent spontaneous abortion – a use found to cause genital cancer during puberty in daughters born from these pregnancies. Paradoxically, it is now used as the 'morning-after' pill. It has also been used to promote the growth of domestic animals, but residues can remain in animals after slaughter, and its use is banned in some countries.

Desai, Anita [desiy], *née* **Mazumdar** (1937–) Novelist, born in Mussoorie, N India. She studied at Delhi University, and her works include novels for adults and children and short stories. *Clear Light of Day* (1980) and *In Custody* (1980) were both short-listed for the Booker Prize, and *The Village by the Sea* won the Guardian Award for children's fiction in 1982. Later novels include *Baumgartner's Bombay* (1988), *Journey to Ithaca* (1995), and *Fasting, Feasting* (1999), which was short-listed for the Booker Prize. Her short stories, *Diamond Dust*, appeared in 2000.

Desai, Morarji (Ranchhodji) [daysiy] (1896–1995) Indian statesman and prime minister (1977–9), born in Gujarat, W India. He studied at Bombay University, became a civil servant, and entered politics in 1930. After various ministerial posts, he was a candidate for the premiership in 1964 and 1966, but was defeated by Indira Gandhi. He became deputy prime minister in 1969 to lead the Opposition Congress Party. Detained during the state of emergency (1975–7), he was then appointed leader of the newly-formed Janata Party, and elected premier. The Janata government was, however, characterized by internal strife, and he was forced to resign.

desalination The removal of salt from sea-water or brine to produce water that is potable, industrially or agriculturally usable, or suitable for ships' boilers. Distillation is the oldest process and, in revised efficient forms, still one of the most widely used. Membrane processes are useful with weak brackish water, the brine being forced under pressure against a membrane to produce a reverse osmosis, fresh water passing through to leave increasingly salt water behind. Electrodialysis and the freezing out of ice are also sometimes useful. About half of the world's desalinated water is produced in the Middle East, the rest in Africa, Asia, Australia, and the USA.

Desalvo, Albert [desalvoh] (?–1973) Convicted US sex offender. After his arrest in late 1964 for sex attacks on women in their homes, he confessed to a psychiatrist that he was the Boston Strangler who had murdered 13 women between 1962 and 1964 in Boston, MA. He was never tried for the murders, because under Massachusetts law a doctor who receives information from a suspect cannot use it as evidence. Sentenced to life imprisonment for his other crimes, he was found stabbed to death in his cell in Walpole Prison, MA.

descant A melody sung or played above another well-known one, such as a hymn tune. The term (often as **discant**) is also used for a type of mediaeval polyphony, and to distinguish the highest-pitched member of a family of instruments (eg the descant recorder).

Descartes, René [daykah(r)t], Lat **Renatius Cartesius** (1596–1650) Rationalist philosopher and mathematician, born in La Haye, WC France. Trained at the Jesuit College at La Flèche, he remained a Catholic throughout his life, but soon became dissatisfied with scholasticism. While serving in the Bavarian army in 1619, he conceived it to be his task to refound human knowledge on a basis secure from scepticism. He expounded the major features of his project in his most famous work, the *Meditationes de prima philosophia* (1641, Meditations on First Philosophy). He began his enquiry by claiming that one can doubt all one's sense experiences, even the deliverances of reason, but that one cannot doubt one's own existence as a think-

Largest Deserts

Name/location	Area* km²	sq mi
Sahara, N Africa	8 600 000	3 320 000
Arabian, SW Asia	2 330 000	900 000
Gobi, Mongolia/NE China	1 166 000	450 000
Patagonian, Argentina	673 000	260 000
Great Basin, SW USA	492 000	190 000
Chihuahuan, Mexico	450 000	175 000
Great Sandy, NW Australia	450 000	175 000
Great Victoria, SW Australia	325 000	125 000
Sonoran, SW USA	310 000	120 000
Kyzyl-Kum, Kazakhstan/Uzbekistan	300 000	115 000
Takla Makan, N China	270 000	105 000
Kalahari, SW Africa	260 000	100 000
Kara-Kum, Turkmenistan	260 000	100 000
Kavir, Iran	260 000	100 000
Syrian, Saudi Arabia/Jordan/Syria/Iraq	260 000	100 000
Nubian, Sudan	260 000	100 000
Thar, India/Pakistan	200 000	77 000
Ust'-Urt, Kazakhstan/Uzbekistan	160 000	62 000
Bet-Pak-Dala, Kazakhstan	155 000	60 000
Simpson, C Australia	145 000	56 000
Dzungaria, China	142 000	55 000
Atacama, Chile	140 000	54 000
Namib, SE Africa	134 000	52 000
Sturt, SE Australia	130 000	50 000
Bolson de Mapimi, Mexico	130 000	50 000
Ordos, China	130 000	50 000
Alashan, China	116 000	45 000

*Desert areas are very approximate, because clear physical boundaries may not occur.

ing being: *cogito, ergo sum* ('I think, therefore I am'). From this basis he argued that God must exist and cannot be a deceiver; therefore, his beliefs based on ordinary sense experience are correct. He also argued that mind and body are distinct substances, believing that this dualism made possible human freedom and immortality. His *Discours de la méthode pour bien conduire sa raison, et chercher la vérité dans les sciences* (1637, Discourse on the Method for Rightly Conducting One's Reason and Searching for Truth in the Sciences) contained appendices in which he virtually founded co-ordinate or analytic geometry, and made major contributions to optics. In 1649 he moved to Stockholm to teach Queen Christina of Sweden but could not cope with the rigours of the regime and climate, and died of pneumonia the next year.

descent In anthropology, the tracing of an individual's ancestry in the male line only (*patrilineally*), in the female line only (*matrilineally*), or through both males and females. Descent may be traced for various purposes, most commonly in order to regulate inheritance, or succession to office, or to define rights to the membership of groups. Some social groups may be defined by common descent. Anthropologists call such groups *lineages* or *clans*.

deschooling The notion proposed by Ivan Illich in his book *Deschooling Society* (1973) that formal schooling should be abolished. Children and adults should learn from each other outside the structure of an institutionalized education system.

desensitization An experimental treatment designed to prevent allergic reactions in sensitive individuals. It involves small repeated subcutaneous injections of the allergen believed to be responsible for the reaction. This is believed to train the body not to respond to the allergen. The basis of the treatment is that the antibody produced in response to the injections coats tissue cells, and blocks the access of a later dose of the offending allergen to which the individual was sensitive.

desert An arid and empty region of the Earth, characterized by little or no vegetation, and meagre and intermittent rainfall, high evaporation rates, and low humidity and cloud cover. Low-latitude deserts such as the Sahara are hot and dry, caused by high pressure air masses which prevent precipitation. Mid-latitude deserts such as the Gobi are cold and dry, and are related to mountain barriers which seal off moist maritime winds. Polar deserts of the Arctic and Antarctic are permanently covered by snow and ice. Approximately one third of the Earth's land surface is desert. (*see panel*)

desert fox *fennec fox*

desertification The environmental degradation of arid and semi-arid areas through overcultivation, overgrazing, deforestation, and bad irrigation practices. Changing climatic patterns are also implicated. The land loses its fertility, and is no longer able to support its population. The problem is worsened in many regions by climatic instability (particularly drought), by rapidly-growing populations, and by cash cropping, which reduces the area available for the production of food crops for the local population. In the 1970s and 1980s, desertification occurred at one time or another in most of the Sahel.

Desert Orchid English racehorse. He won the National Hunt Horse of the Year Award a record four times. Out of 70 career races he had 34 wins, 11 seconds, and 8 thirds. Wins include the Cheltenham Gold Cup (1989), King George VI Chase (1986, 1988, 1989, 1990), Racing Post Chase (1990), Cheltenham Gold Cup (1989), Whitbread Gold Cup (1988), and Irish Grand National (1990). He retired in 1991.

desert rat *jerboa*

Desert Rats Members of the 7th British Armoured Division, which in 1940 took as its badge the jerboa or desert rat, noted for remarkable leaps. The media applied the name generally to all British servicemen in the North Africa campaign, and it was readily adopted by those not entitled to wear the jerboa shoulder-flash.

Desert Shield / Storm *Gulf War* (Jan–Feb 1991)

de Sica, Vittorio [seeka] (1901–74) Actor and film director, born in Sora, C Italy. He studied in Naples and Rome, established himself as a romantic star of Italian stage and screen in the 1930s, and became a director in 1940. He achieved international success in the neo-Realist style with *Sciuscià* (1946, Shoeshine), *Ladri di biciclette* (1948, Bicycle Thieves), and *Miracolo a Milano* (1951, Miracle in Milan). His subsequent work was more smoothly sophisticated, but *Il giardino dei Finzi-Continis* (1970, The Garden of the Finzi-Continis) provided a late triumph.

Desiderio da Settignano [dezideryoh da setinyahnoh] (c.1428–61) Sculptor, born in Settignano, NC Italy. He worked in the early Renaissance style, influenced by Donatello and Della Robbia, producing many notable portrait busts of women and children.

design, argument from One of the traditional arguments for the existence of God; also known as the **teleological argument**. The essential claim is that the complexity and efficiency of the design of complex organisms can be explained only by the existence of a Designer. Expounded in its best-known forms by Aquinas and British theologian William Paley (1743–1805), the argument was especially popular in the 18th–19th-c, but lost appeal with the development of Darwinian evolutionary theory.

designer drugs Synthetic drugs, usually similar to amphetamines, which are not controlled by law in the USA; they are so called because they are specifically designed by chemists to be slightly different structurally to drugs that are controlled by law (which are 'named', and thus illegal), yet still chemically so close to them that they have similar biological effects. These 'legal' drugs are produced covertly and sold on the streets to illicit drug users. The normal dangers of drug abuse are increased by the possibility of contamination. In the early

1980s, such contamination (l-methyl-4-phenyl-1,2,3,6-tetrahydropyridine, or *MPTP*) was found to induce permanent symptoms of Parkinson's disease in young users.

desk-top publishing The preparation of typeset output using a microcomputer with appropriate software for the line-by-line composition and editing of text, the creation of illustrations, the compilation and editing of structured pages, and the typographical articulation. The software usually handles hyphenation and justification automatically. The image of typeset text and illustrations can then be output on paper through a compatible dot-matrix printer, laser printer, or phototypesetter. 'Publishing' in this now familiar turn of phrase is a misnomer: 'typesetting' or 'text composition' would be more appropriate. Well known DTP packages are Aldus® PageMaker®, Quark XPress®, and Ventura Publisher®.

desman An insectivore of the mole family (2 species), native to the Pyrenees and W Asia; red-brown; long mobile snout; webbed hind feet; long tail flattened from side to side; lives in streams and pools; eats aquatic animals.

Des Moines [dimoyn] 41°35N 93°37W, pop (2000e) 198 700. Capital of state in Polk Co, C Iowa, USA; at the junction of the Racoon and Des Moines Rivers; developed around a fort established in 1843; city status, 1857; state capital in 1881; largest city in the state; airport; railway; university (1881); important industrial, commercial, and transportation centre in the heart of Iowa's Corn Belt; agricultural processing, machinery, printing and publishing; the Capitol, Des Moines Art Centre, Centre of Science and Industry.

Desmond, Gerald Fitzgerald, 15th Earl of (c.1538–83) Irish Catholic nobleman, who (1579–80) rebelled against Queen Elizabeth I, sacked Youghal by night, and was proclaimed a traitor. He was eventually killed in a cabin in the Kerry mountains.

Desmond, Paul, originally **Paul Breitenfeld** (1924–77) Jazz alto saxophonist, born in San Francisco, California, USA. As soon as he joined Dave Brubeck's quartet in 1951, that band became one of the greatest international successes in jazz history. Two styles have seldom been so diametrically opposed and yet so complementary. Brubeck, the sober, dedicated organizer, played rollicking, noisy piano, and Desmond, the carefree, free-living bachelor, superimposed spindly, delicate melodies. Renowned for his wit, he published one humorous piece, 'How Many of You Are There in the Quartet?' (*Punch*, 1973), and no more. His tune 'Take Five' (recorded with Brubeck in 1959) is one of the great popular and critical successes of modern jazz. He left Brubeck in 1967, with occasional reunions, and kept as busy as he wished as a freelancer.

Desmoulins, (Lucie Simplice) Camille (Benoist) [daymooli] (1760–94) French revolutionary and journalist, born in Guise, N France. He studied law in Paris, but owing to a stutter never practised. He nonetheless was an effective crowd orator, and played a dramatic part in the storming of the Bastille. He was also an influential pamphleteer. A member of the Cordeliers' Club from its foundation, he was elected to the National Convention and voted for the death of the king. He actively attacked the Girondists, but by the end of 1793 argued for moderation, thus incurring the hostility of Robespierre. He was arrested and guillotined.

de Soto, Hernando or **Fernando** [duh **soh**toh] (c.1496–1542) Spanish explorer, born in Jerez de los Caballeros, SW Spain. In 1539 he entered Florida and crossed the Mississippi (1541), but died of a fever on its banks.

Despatie, Alexandre [dayspatee] (1985–) Diver, born in Laval, Québec, SE Canada. He first rose to prominence by winning the gold medal in the 10 m platform event at the 1998 Commonwealth Games at Kuala Lumpur aged 13 years, becoming the youngest champion in the Games history. In 1999 in the Junior World Championships he was first in the 1 m springboard and the 3 m springboard events, a feat he repeated at the 2002 Commonwealth Games at Manchester, England.

Desprez, Josquin *Josquin Desprez*

Dessalines, Jean Jacques [desaleen] (c.1758–1806) Emperor of Haiti (1804–6), born a slave probably in Grande Rivière du Nord, N Haiti (formerly St Domingue. In the slave insurrection of 1791 he was second only to Toussaint L'Ouverture. After compelling the French to leave Haiti (1803), he was created governor and crowned emperor as Jacques I, but his despotic behaviour alienated his adherents and he was assassinated.

De Stijl [duh shteel] A group of Dutch artists and architects formed in 1917, strongly influenced by Cubism, Dutch Calvinism, and theosophy. Its members included Theo van Doesburg, J J P Oud, Piet Mondrian, and Gerrit Rietveld. The group advocated a new, wholly abstract aesthetic style composed solely of straight lines, primary colours, and black and white, typified by the paintings of Mondrian. The group formally ended in 1931, but had a great and lasting influence on 20th-c art, architecture, and design.

Destri, Jimmy *Blondie*

destroyer A small fast warship designed in the late 19th-c to destroy enemy torpedo boats. It has undergone much development and adopted many other roles: submarine hunting, evacuation, invasion, assault support, and convoy escort, as well as providing a battleship screen in both world wars. Modern destroyers are usually guided-missile carriers and pack immense fire power compared to their ancestors. They are more akin to World War 2 cruisers in size.

detached retina *retina*

detective story A story turning on the committing of a crime (usually a murder) and the discovery by a detective of the culprit. It is this element of mystery which makes it distinct from the crime novel. Although Voltaire's *Zadig* (1747) and Godwin's *Caleb Williams* (1794) contain precursive elements, the first true detective stories were Poe's *Murders in the Rue Morgue* (1841) and *The Purloined Letter* (1845), featuring the detective Dupin. These were followed by Emile Gaboriau's full-length detective novels, and then Wilkie Collins's *The Moonstone* (1868). The popularity of the genre was assured after the introduction of Sherlock Holmes by Conan Doyle (in *A Study in Scarlet*, 1887), and the next 50 years were a golden age, with authors such as Austin Freeman, A E W Mason, E C Bentley (*Trent's Last Case*, 1913), and G K Chesterton (The *Father Brown Stories*, appearing 1911–35). Maurice Leblanc created a French rival to Holmes in Arsène Lupin. The US had its private-eye school, with the creations of Dashiell Hammett and Raymond Chandler, with their moralistic 'police procedural' stories. Between the wars, Agatha Christie (Poirot), Dorothy L Sayers (Peter Wimsey), and Georges Simenon (Maigret) wrote to the same classic formula, which still survives in such writers as Dick Francis, Ruth Rendell, and P D James, though more cynical crime and spy fiction is now in fashion.

detente [daytawnt] An attempt to lower the tension between states as a means of reducing the possibility of war and of achieving peaceful coexistence between different social and political systems. A prominent feature of relations between the USA and USSR in the 1970s, it led to several agreements over arms (SALT) and security and co-operation (Helsinki). In the early 1980s, there was a cooling towards detente on the part of the USA, on the grounds that too many concessions had been made and that the USSR did not adhere to the spirit of such agreements; but there was a considerable improvement in relations in the later part of the decade, and the concept was overtaken by events, following the break-up of the Soviet Union in 1990.

detention centre *young offender institution*

detergent A material which lowers the surface tension of water, and makes it mix better with oils and fats. Most detergents contain molecules or ions with a combination of polar (water-seeking) and non-polar (oil-seeking) parts, which serve to bind oil and water together. Soaps are examples of (an)ionic detergents, containing a charged (water-seeking) group bonded to an alkyl (fat-seeking) group. Commercial washing powders, although called detergents, actually contain a relatively small amount of detergent; they mainly contain binders and water-softening agents.

determinant In mathematics, a number determined by the elements of a square matrix. For a 2 × 2 matrix

$$\begin{bmatrix} a & b \\ c & d \end{bmatrix},$$

the determinant

$$\begin{vmatrix} a & b \\ c & d \end{vmatrix}$$

is defined as $ad - bc$. If the matrix is represented by **A**, the determinant of **A** is written det **A** or |**A**|. The determinant of a 3 × 3 matrix

$$\begin{bmatrix} a & b & c \\ d & e & f \\ g & h & j \end{bmatrix}$$

is defined as

$$a\begin{bmatrix} e & f \\ h & j \end{bmatrix} - b\begin{bmatrix} d & f \\ g & j \end{bmatrix} + c\begin{bmatrix} d & e \\ g & h \end{bmatrix}.$$

The determinant of an $n \times n$ matrix can be similarly defined in terms of determinants of $(n-1) \times (n-1)$ matrices. Alternative definitions have been developed for $n \times n$ determinants.

determinism **Causal determinism** is the philosophical thesis that every event has a cause, so that, given the laws of nature and the relevant previous history of the world, the event could not have failed to occur, and could in principle have been predicted. Philosophers have disagreed about whether causal determinism is compatible with free will or is undermined by quantum theory. **Logical determinism** is the stronger thesis, that the laws of nature alone necessitate every event; it is contradictory to conceive of anything being different from what it is. **Theological determinism**, held by Calvin and others, maintains that God predestines everything in creation.

deterrence A concept that has developed in strategic military thinking since the 1930s, following the emergence of long-range weapons of mass destruction. It is based on the threat of effective military or economic counter-action as a means of discouraging acts of aggression. The deterrence can also be extended to protect a state's allies. **Graduated deterrence** refers to a strategy of having a range of counter-actions demonstrating a state's abilities to respond to a number of hostile actions, depending on their severity. It is argued by some that this can lead to an escalation of conflict, while others suggest that it is less likely to inflame the situation. **Mutual deterrence**, most commonly associated with the nuclear weapons of the two superpowers, is a situation in which each side is deterred from attacking the other because of the unacceptably high levels of destruction that would result. (This threat is known as *Mutually Assured Destruction* and has the highly appropriate acronym *MAD*.) There is considerable debate over the effectiveness of deterrence in different circumstances.

detonator A sensitive explosive (eg mercuric fulminate, lead azide) used in a small quantity to initiate the function of larger quantities of principal explosive. By extension, the term is used for any device containing a detonating explosive actuated by heat, percussion, friction, or electricity.

Detroit [deetroyt] 42°20N 83°03W, pop (2000e) 951 300. Seat of Wayne Co, SE Michigan, USA; port on the Detroit R, W of L St Clair; tenth largest city in the USA; founded by the French as a fur-trading outpost, 1701; became the trading and political centre for the Great Lakes region; surrendered to the British during the Seven Years' War, 1760; handed over to the USA, 1796; much of the city rebuilt after a fire in 1805; capital of state, 1837–47; airport; railway; two universities (1877, 1933); the nation's leading manufacturer of cars and trucks (one-third of the country's cars assembled in and around the city); aeroplanes, machinery, metal products, chemicals, food products, printing and publishing; in the early 1980s recession caused high unemployment and a fall in population; professional teams, Tigers (baseball), Pistons (basketball), Red Wings (ice hockey), Lions (football); Science Centre, Historical Museum, Institute of Arts, Motown Museum, Belle Isle; Freedom Festival (Jul).

Dettori, Frankie [detoree], popular name of **Lanfranco Dettori** (1970–) British flat race jockey, born in Milan, Italy. He left school at 13 to became a stableboy and apprentice, a year later continuing in the UK, where a family friend was a Newmarket trainer. A champion apprentice in 1990, his later achievements include the Queen Elizabeth II Stakes (1990), French Derby (1992), Irish Derby (1994), Prix de l'Arc de Triomphe (1995, 2001), and the English Classic races The Oaks (1994, 1995, 2002), St Leger (1995, 1996), Two Thousand Guineas (1996, 1999), and One Thousand Guineas (1998, 2002). He was champion jockey for two successive seasons (1994–5), and in 1996 was winner of all seven races on one card at Ascot. He narrowly escaped death in a light aircraft crash at Newmarket in 2000. In 2003 he won the Hong Kong Cup, the final race in the World Racing Series, and was named top jockey of the series.

Deucalion [dyoo**kay**lion] In Greek mythology, a son of Prometheus. When Zeus flooded the world, Deucalion and his wife Pyrrha built an 'ark' which grounded on the top of Parnassus. As the only survivors, they asked how the human race was to be restored; an oracle told them 'to throw their mother's bones over their shoulders'. They correctly interpreted this oracle, and threw stones which turned into human beings.

deus ex machina [**day**us eks **mak**ina] (Lat 'god from the machine') A device used mainly by classical dramatists to resolve by supernatural intervention (the god descending from above the stage) all the problems which have arisen during the course of a play. The returning Duke may be said to function as a *deus ex machina* in the last scene of Shakespeare's *Measure for Measure*.

deuterium A heavy isotope of hydrogen, in which the nucleus comprises a proton and a neutron rather than a proton alone (as for common hydrogen); symbol *D* or ^2H. It forms 0·015% of naturally occurring hydrogen. Water made with deuterium is called *heavy water*, with a density of 1·1 g/cm³, and is used in some nuclear reactors. Deuterium is also important in nuclear fusion.

Deuteronomistic History The theory that the Biblical narratives from Deuteronomy to 2 Kings were essentially the work of a historian or historians in the mid 6th-c BC, though scholars differ about the date and the nature of the activity, with some accepting only a Deuteronomistic 'revision' of earlier narratives during the exilic period. It portrayed Israel's fate in terms of her leaders' compliance or disregard for Israel's Law and her true prophets.

Deuteronomy, Book of [dyooter**on**omee] The fifth and last book of the Pentateuch, in the Hebrew Bible/Old Testament. Its title means 'a repetition of the law' (from the Septuagint's mistaken rendering into Greek of *Deut* 17.18, where the Hebrew means 'a copy of the law'). It was traditionally attributed to Moses, but many date it much later, c.7th-c BC. It surveys Israel's wilderness experiences, and presents an extensive code of religious laws and duties.

Deutsch, David [doych] (1953–) British theoretical physicist, born in Haifa, NW Israel. Educated at Cambridge and Oxford universities, in 1978 he took up a position at the University of Texas at Austin, and in 1985 returned to Oxford. His reseach interests include quantum information processing, quantum non-locality, the quantum theory of time travel, and the foundations of quantum mechanics and probability. He pioneered the theory of quantum computation.

de Valera, Eamon [deva**lay**ra] (1882–1975) Irish statesman, prime minister (1932–48, 1951–4, 1957–9), and president (1959–73), born in New York City, USA. Brought up on a farm in Co Limerick, he became a teacher in Dublin, and was active in various Republican movements. A commandant in the 1916 rising, he was arrested and narrowly escaped the firing squad. He became an MP in 1917, and leader of Sinn Féin (1917–26). He was elected president of Dáil Eireann, and in 1926 became leader of Fianna Fáil, his newly-formed Republican opposition party, which won the 1932 elections. In spite of his colourful early career, his leadership was moderate, and he opposed extremism and religious intolerance.

devaluation A fall in the amount of foreign currency which can be obtained per unit of a country's own currency. For example, if the £ has been selling for $1·60 and falls to $1·40, it is devalued. Devaluation makes a country's exports cheaper abroad and its imports dearer at home, as long as domestic prices do not change. This tends to improve the balance of payments. Rises in import costs tend to create domestic inflation, however, so that the initial competitive advantage obtained does not last. Under the Bretton Woods system, countries tried to avoid devaluation, though sterling was devalued in 1949 and again in 1967. After 1973 most countries allowed their currencies to 'float', exchange rates being determined by the market. From 1979 to 1999 the EC tried to limit the range of exchange rate variations through the Exchange Rate Mechanism. Britain joined this in 1990, but was forced to leave the ERM and devalue in September 1992. From 1999 devaluation against each others' currencies was no longer possible for countries using the Euro, though the Euro varies in value relative to other currencies.

Devanagari [devanagahree] A range of alphabets used for Indian languages, consisting of a set of consonantal letter-symbols. Vowels are represented by a system of diacritics which can occur above, below, preceding, or following the consonant-letters.

developing countries A label which includes most of the countries of Africa, Asia, and Latin America. Many are predominantly agricultural economies, though Brazil, India, and Pakistan have a well-developed industrial base, and others have rich mineral wealth. They are characterized by very low income per capita (by Western standards), and therefore low savings. Development has often been held back by rapid population growth, crop failure, drought, war, and insufficient demand (at a reasonable price) for their commodities, crops, and goods. In addition to many bilateral aid agreements, there are the aid programmes of the international agencies, such as the United Nations, Commonwealth Development Corporation, Alliance for Progress, and USAid. There are also many privately-funded charities with aid programmes. Western banks have lent large sums to the developing nations, and overdue debt servicing has proved to be a problem.

development The photographic process by which the latent image formed by exposure to light is made visible. It generally involves reducing the exposed silver compounds in the sensitive material to black metallic silver. In colour photography, couplers may be used to form a coloured dye image at the same time.

developmental psychology A branch of psychology which examines the biological, social, and intellectual development of people from before birth throughout the life-course. Most attention has been paid to young children, in whom shifts in understanding appear more obvious. While some psychologists study individual patterns of development, most focus upon the *developmental function* – the changes which are common to all people at various 'stages' of life.

development economics The branch of economics concerned with less developed countries. Its main difference from economics as applied to advanced economies is a need to attend more to problems such as lack of infrastructure – power systems, transport and communications, clean water supply, etc. There are also problems with low educational standards, population pressure, poor agricultural practices and soil erosion, underdeveloped financial institutions, and excessive reliance on single export products, making foreign exchange rates receipts very unreliable.

Devi, Phoolan [devee], known as **Dasyu Sundari** ('Beautiful Bandit') (1957–2001) Bandit and folk hero, born to a low-caste family in India. After a childhood of abuse and humiliation, she was kidnapped by bandits in Uttar Pradesh, then joined the gang, becoming the mistress of one of its leaders. Following a period of capture and further abuse, she escaped to become one of India's most notorious criminals, while at the same time attracting a national reputation among oppressed people. After negotiating with the authorities, she surrendered in 1983 in a much publicized ceremony. Released from prison in 1994, she became a Buddhist convert, and in 1995 launched a new political party in support of the lower castes, winning a seat in the federal Parliament. She portrayed her criminal career as a struggle between low-caste Hindus like herself and the high castes. Mala Sen's story of her life, *India's Bandit Queen* (1991) was the basis of the film *Bandit Queen* (1995), whose accuracy she repudiated. She was assassinated at her Delhi home.

deviance Any behaviour which is regarded as contrary to 'normal' or expected standards of social behaviour, which may or may not be contrary to the law. Within criminology, **deviance theory** claims that what is deviant is 'in the eye of the beholder' because no act is in itself inherently or obviously criminal. Behaviour is judged according to the context in which it occurs; the same action regarded as deviant in one situation may be acceptable in another. Conceptions of deviance therefore vary from one culture to another.

Devil A supernatural evil agent thought to influence human behaviour, in many religious beliefs; when referring to a specific character in the Judaeo-Christian tradition, the chief of the evil spirits or fallen angels; also known as **Satan**. *Devil* is a rare term in the Hebrew Scriptures (where *Satan* is more common), but more frequent in the New Testament, where the Devil is sometimes represented as a serpent (*Rev* 12.9) or as a tempter (*Matt* 4.1). In religious literature the Devil appears in many different guises, human or animal, and with many different names (eg *Beelzebul, Belial, ahuras, jinn*). Exorcism of individuals possessed by demons is long attested in the Judaeo-Christian tradition, but cults of devil-worship (or Satanism) involving witchcraft, black magic, and the occult have persisted despite opposition throughout most of Christian history.

devil ray Any of the giant rays widespread in surface waters of tropical and warm temperate seas; pectoral fins forming large triangular wings; body width up to 6 m/20 ft; sides of head prolonged as fleshy 'horns'; tail whip-like; young are born live; feed on plankton and small fishes. (Genera: *Mobula, Manta*. Family: Mobulidae.)

devil's coach horse A large, black rove beetle; body slender, 20–30 mm/$^{3}/_{4}$–$1^{1}/_{4}$ in long; wing cases short, hindwings present; produces acrid-smelling chemical when threatened; commonly found in woods; predaceous on insects, snails, and worms. (Order: Coleoptera. Family: Staphylinidae.)

Devil's Island *Salut, Iles du*

Devil's Tower The first US national monument, in NE Wyoming, USA; a natural tower of volcanic rock with a flat top, 263 m/863 ft high; used as the setting for the film *Close Encounters of the Third Kind*.

Devine, George (Alexander Cassidy) (1910–65) Actor and theatre director, born in Hendon, NW Greater London, UK. With Michel Saint-Denis and others he founded the London Theatre Studio (1936–9) in an attempt to reform British theatre training. After the War, he continued this work at the Old Vic Centre (1947–52), and directed the Young Vic touring company. In 1956 he became artistic director of the newly formed English Stage Company at the Royal Court Theatre, and for the rest of his career was instrumental in the development and success of this 'writer's theatre'. The *George Devine Award*, inaugurated in 1966, gives encouragement to young theatre practitioners.

devise *property*

Devlin (of West Wick), Patrick Arthur Devlin, Baron (1905–92) British judge. He studied at Cambridge, was called to the bar in 1929, became a KC in 1945, and a High Court judge in 1948. An eminent barrister, he was knighted in 1948 and created a life peer in 1961. He was made a Lord Justice of Appeal in 1960 and a Lord of Appeal in Ordinary in 1961, before retiring in 1964. Following the publication of the Wolfenden Report in 1957, he participated in a lengthy philosophical debate over whether the law could or should enforce moral principles upon society in general. Among his many publications are *Trial by Jury* (1956) and *The Judge* (1979).

devolution The delegation of authority from a country's legislature or government to a subordinate elected institution on a more limited geographical basis. Devolution is distinguished from **federalism**, where the powers of the central government and the federal bodies are set out in the constitution. Under devolution, the subordinate body receives its power from the government, which retains some right of oversight. The idea is to provide for more self-government and to bring decision-making closer to the people, but such democratic arguments are countered by the view that allowing for differences in decisions within the state poses a threat to the state's unity.

Devolution, War of A conflict prompted by Louis XIV of France in pursuit of his wife's legal claims to the Spanish Netherlands. According to the laws of devolution of the provinces of Brabant and Hainault, females of a first marriage took precedence over males of a second with regard to property inheritance. To uphold the claims of Queen Maria Theresa, the elder daughter of Philip IV of Spain, Louis' armies overran Flanders, prompting the Dutch, England, and Sweden to negotiate the Triple Alliance (1668); to this France responded with the invasion of Franche-Comté. The war ended with a secret treaty of compromise between Louis and the Emperor Leopold (1668).

Devon pop (2001e) 704 500; area 6711 sq km/2591 sq mi. County of SW England, UK; bounded NW by the Bristol Channel and Atlantic and S by the English Channel; rises to Dartmoor in SW and Exmoor in NE; drained by the Exe, Dart, Torridge, and Taw Rivers; county town, Exeter; chief towns include Plymouth, Torquay, Barnstaple; Plymouth and Torbay new unitary authorities from 1998; tourism, especially on coast; livestock, dairy products (notable for clotted cream), cider; naval base at Plymouth.

Devonian period A geological period of the Palaeozoic era extending from 408 to 360 million years ago. It contains the oldest widespread continental deposits in Europe (Old Red Sandstone) as well as extensive marine sediments containing fossils of armoured fish, corals, ammonites, and molluscs.

de Vries, Hugo (Marie) [vrees] (1848–1935) Botanist, born in Haarlem, The Netherlands. He was professor at Amsterdam (1878–1918), where he carried out research into the nature of mutation in plant-breeding. His conclusions paralleled those of Mendel, whose work he discovered in 1900.

De Vries, Peter [vrees] (1910–93) Novelist and short-story writer, born in Chicago, Illinois, USA. He studied at Calvin College and Northwestern University, and in 1943 became a regular staff contributor to the *New Yorker*, where he developed the comic manner later displayed in such novels as *The Tunnel of Love* (1954) and *The Mackerel Plaza* (1958). His upbringing in the Dutch Reformed Calvinist faith provided the background of his later, serious novel about a child's terminal illness, *The Blood of the Lamb* (1961).

dew The deposit of moisture on vegetation and ground surfaces. It occurs at night when terrestrial radiation cools the Earth's surface, and the layer of air closest to the ground, to below the dew point temperature, resulting in condensation.

Dewar, Sir James [dyooer] (1842–1923) Chemist and physicist, born in Kincardine, Fife, E Scotland, UK. He studied chemistry at Edinburgh, and in 1875 became professor at Cambridge. Two years later he also became professor at the Royal Institution, London, where he lived, lectured, and pursued a wide range of experimental research; he visited Cambridge rarely. In the 1870s he invented the *Dewar flask* (or thermos flask), using it in his studies of low temperatures and gas liquefaction (1892). With Frederick Abel (1827–1902) he invented cordite, for long the British standard military propellent.

Dewar, Donald (Campbell) (1937–2000) British statesman, born in Glasgow, W Scotland, UK. He studied at Glasgow, and practised law before entering parliament as Labour MP for Aberdeen South (1966–70) and then Glasgow Garscaddon (1978–2000). He served as opposition spokesman on Scottish affairs (1981–92) and then social security (1992–5) before becoming Labour chief whip (1995–7). In 1997 he became secretary-of-state for Scotland in the newly elected Blair government (until 1999) and was responsible for pushing through the legislation that established the new Scottish Parliament. Elected as the MSP for Glasgow Anniesland, he became Scotland's inaugural first minister (1999–2000).

Dewar flask An insulated vessel with double, internally-silvered walls, the inner space being made into a vacuum; heat losses by convection and radiation are thus reduced to a minimum. Devised by James Dewar, it was first used for liquefied gases in 1892, and later developed industrial and domestic uses for maintaining liquids at constant high or low temperatures. Everyday names include **vacuum flask** and the trade name **Thermos flask**.

de Wet, Christiaan (Rudolf) [wet] (1854–1922) Afrikaner statesman and general, born in Smithfield district, Orange Free State, C South Africa. He became conspicuous in the Transvaal War of 1880–1, and in the war of 1899–1902 was the most audacious of all the Boer commanders. In 1907 he became minister of agriculture of the Orange River Colony, and in 1914 joined the South African insurrection, but was captured. Sentenced to six years' imprisonment, he was released in 1915.

Dewey, John (1859–1952) Philosopher and educator, born in Burlington, Vermont, USA. He studied at Vermont and Johns Hopkins universities, taught at Michigan (1884) and Chicago (1894), and became professor of philosophy at Columbia University in 1904. He was a leading exponent of pragmatism, in the tradition of Peirce and William James. His philosophy of education, which stressed development of the person, understanding of the environment, and learning through experience, was extremely influential. His writings include (on philosophy) *The Quest for Certainty* (1929) and (on education) *The School and Society* (1899) and *The Child and the Curriculum* (1902).

Dewey decimal system A library classification system in widespread international use, devised in 1873 by US librarian Melvil Dewey (1851–1931). It recognizes 10 main classes of subject-matter, each class containing 100 numbers, with decimal subdivisions for unlimited supplementary classes. For example, class 600 is Applied Sciences, Medicine, Technology; 612 is Physiology, Human and Comparative, and 612.1 is Blood and Circulation. The system is regularly revised. (*see p.450*)

de Witt, Jan [wit] (1625–72) Dutch statesman, the grand pensionary (chief minister) of the United Provinces of the Netherlands (1653–72), born in Dordrecht, The Netherlands. As leader of the Republican Party, he sought to abolish the office of stadtholder, and to limit the power of the House of Orange. However, when France invaded the Netherlands in 1672, William of Orange was made stadtholder and commander of the Dutch forces. De Witt's brother, Cornelius, was accused of conspiracy and imprisoned. De Witt went to see him in prison at The Hague, where they were killed by an infuriated mob.

dew point temperature The temperature at which a parcel of air would become saturated with water vapour if it were cooled without a change in pressure of moisture content. When moist air is cooled to below this temperature, condensation in the form of dew or hoar frost occurs.

dextrin A complex sugar, a mixture of glucose polymers, obtained from starch which has been broken down enzymatically or by gentle heat. Dextrins are used as thickening agents in foods, as well as adhesives and glazes in paper and textiles. However, their main use is to improve the palatability of starchy foods, and to reduce the osmotic load on the stomach in convalescent drinks.

dextrorotatory *optical activity*

dextrose *glucose*

Dezhnev, Cape [dyezhnyof] 66°08N 169°40W. Northeasternmost point of Asia, NE Siberian Russia; at E end of the Chukchi

The Dewey Decimal System

000 Generalities
010 Bibliographies and catalogues
020 Library science
030 General encyclopedic works
040 (Unassigned)
050 General periodicals
060 General organizations
070 Newspapers and journalism
080 General collections
090 Manuscripts and book rarities
100 Philosophy and related
110 Ontology and methodology
120 Knowledge, cause, purpose, man
130 Pseudo- and parapsychology
140 Specific philosophic viewpoints
150 Psychology
160 Logic
170 Ethics (moral philosophy)
190 Modern Western philosophy
200 Religion
210 Natural religion
220 Bible
230 Christian doctrinal theology
240 Christian moral and devotional theology
250 Christian pastoral, parochial etc
260 Christian social and ecclesiastical theology
270 History and geography of Christian Church
280 Christian denominations and sects
290 Other religions and comparative religion
300 The social sciences
310 Statistical method and statistics
320 Political science
330 Economics
340 Law
350 Public administration
360 Welfare and association
370 Education
380 Commerce
390 Customs and folklore
400 Language
410 Linguistics and non-verbal language
420 English and Anglo-Saxon
430 Germanic languages
440 French, Provençal, Catalan
450 Italian, Romanian, etc
460 Spanish and Portuguese
470 Italic languages
480 Classical and Greek
490 Other languages
500 Pure sciences
510 Mathematics
520 Astronomy and allied sciences
530 Physics
540 Chemistry and allied sciences
550 Earth sciences
560 Paleontology
570 Anthropological and biological sciences
580 Botanical sciences
590 Zoological sciences
600 Technology (applied science)
610 Medical sciences
620 Engineering and allied operations
630 Agriculture and agricultural industries
640 Domestic arts and sciences
650 Business and related enterprises
660 Chemical technology, etc
670 Manufactures
680 Assembled and final products
690 Buildings
700 The arts
710 Civic and landscape art
720 Architecture
730 Sculpture and the plastic arts
740 Drawing and decorative arts
750 Painting and paintings
760 Graphic arts
770 Photography and photographs
780 Music
790 Recreation (recreational arts)
800 Literature and rhetoric
810 American literature in English
820 English and Anglo-Saxon literature
830 Germanic languages literature
840 French, Provençal, Catalan literature
850 Italian and Romanian literature
860 Spanish and Portuguese literature
870 Italic languages literature
880 Classical and Greek literature
890 Literature of other languages
900 General geography and history, etc
910 General geography
920 General biography and genealogy
930 General history of ancient world
940 General history of modern Europe
950 General history of modern Asia
960 General history of modern Africa
970 General history of North America
980 General history of South America
990 General history of rest of world

Peninsula, projecting into the Bering Sea; named after the Russian navigator who discovered it in 1648.

Dhaka [daka], former spelling **Dacca** 23°42N 90°22E, pop (2000e) 7 137 000. Capital city of Bangladesh, in Dhaka region, W of the R Meghna, on a channel of the R Dhaleswari; former French, Dutch, and English trading post; capital of Mughal province of East Bengal (1608–1704); capital of British province of East Bengal and Assam (1905–12); small university town before 1947; major expansion since becoming capital of East Pakistan (1947), with large-scale immigration and growth of industry; centre of the world's greatest jute-growing region; university of Dhaka (1921), Bangladesh University of Engineering and Technology (1961); airport; railway; trade in jute, rice, oilseed, sugar, tea; textiles, chemicals, matches, soap, glass, shoes, printing, engineering, boatbuilding; Suhrawardy Uddyan (city park), Central Shahid Minar monument; known as 'the city of mosques' (over 1000); Sadarghat market; Langalband 12 km/7 mi SE, a sacred Hindu site.

dharma [dah(r)ma] In Hinduism, a Sanskrit word with various levels of meaning. Basically, it is the universal law that applies to the universe, human society, and the individual. As the moral law, it is both a general code of ethics applicable to all, and a moral law specific to an individual's station in life. In Buddhism (Pali, *dhamma*) the word also has several levels of meaning, referring to the teaching of the Buddha taught in every age by every Buddha, not merely in the sense of doctrine, but including righteous living.

dhole [dohl] A member of the dog family (*Cuon alpinus*), native to S and SE Asia; red-brown, with white underneath; black tip to tail; inhabits woodland or open country; hunts large mammals in packs; runs prey to exhaustion; also known as **Asiatic wild dog** or **Indian wild dog**.

diabetes insipidus [diyabeeteez insipidus] An uncommon disorder in which a large volume of dilute urine is produced daily, independently of the volume of fluid ingested. It is caused by the absence or inadequate production of anti-diuretic hormone by the pituitary gland, or by conditions (eg potassium depletion) which reduce the sensitivity of the kidneys to its action. As a result, the kidneys fail to reabsorb water and concentrate the urine. This leads to intense thirst and results in dehydration if water intake cannot be sustained.

diabetes mellitus [diyabeeteez melitus] A common metabolic disorder in which the pancreas fails to produce insulin in the amounts needed to control sugar metabolism. The blood sugar level rises above normal values (*hyperglycemia*) and spills over into the urine, causing large volumes to be produced (*polyuria*). In **Type I** diabetes, the deficiency of insulin is primary, caused by auto-immune damage to the pancreas; onset tends to be in childhood, and insulin injections are normally required to control blood sugar levels. **Type II** diabetes is due to reduced tissue responsiveness to the action of insulin, so that cells do not take up sugar; it tends to affect older adults, and can often be managed with a careful diet or drugs that reduce blood-sugar levels, although insulin injections are sometimes necessary. Diabetes is a leading cause of death and disability in developed countries, as a result of the complications that develop over a long period. Chronically elevated blood-sugar levels damage the eyes, nerves, kidneys, and blood vessels leading to blindness, neuropathies, kidney failure, and atherosclerosis, with heart attack and stroke. High levels also predispose to infection by micro-organisms. Complications can be minimized by careful management of blood sugar, often requiring insulin injections under the skin several times a day.

diablotin [diyablotin] *oilbird*

diachrony [diyakronee] The historical dimension of language development, studying the structural changes in sounds, grammar, and meaning that occur in languages over periods of time. It contrasts with **synchrony** [**sing**kronee], the study of a language as it is at a given time, without reference to its historical development. This distinction, introduced by Swiss linguist Ferdinand de Saussure, formed one of the most important conceptual developments in 20th-c linguistics.

diagenesis [diyajenesis] The physical and chemical processes whereby an unconsolidated sediment is changed to a solid rock. It includes compaction and partial dewatering, followed by cementation and low temperature re-equilibration to a more stable chemical and textural state. It excludes metamorphism.

Diaghilev, Sergei Pavlovich [deeagilef] (1872–1929) Ballet impresario, born in Novgorod, W Russia. He obtained a law degree, but was preoccupied with the arts. In 1898 he became editor of *Mir Iskousstva* (World of Art), and during the next few years arranged exhibitions and concerts of Russian art and music. His company, the Ballets Russes, was founded in Paris in 1909, and revolutionized the world of dance, making music and scenery an integral part of the performance. Many of the great dancers, composers, and painters of his period contributed to the success of the troupe. He also encouraged several major choreographers (eg Fokine, Nijinsky, Balanchine), and gave them opportunities for artistic collaboration.

diagnosis In medicine, the determination by a medical practitioner of the nature of a disease in a patient. A diagnosis is reached by first taking a history of the patient's current symptoms, previous complaints, illnesses in the family, and social circumstances; then by conducting a physical examination to look for signs of disease; and finally by using additional investigations such as blood tests and X-rays.

dialect *dialectology*

dialectic A philosophical term, originally (for Socrates) a conversational mode of argument through question and answer. It is used in different, more technical senses by Plato, Aristotle, Kant, Hegel, and Marx.

dialectical materialism A central doctrine of Marxism, which combines Hegel's idea of dialectic with a thoroughgoing materialism directly opposed to idealism. Its claims are that quantitative changes in matter yield qualitative changes (eg the emergence of mind); that nature is a unity of contradictory opposites; and that the result of one opposite (*thesis*) clashing with another (*antithesis*) is a resolution (*synthesis*) that preserves and transcends the opposites.

dialectical psychology Psychological theory and/or research informed by Hegelian or Marxist notions of tension, co-action, and change. It was promoted principally by Soviet psychologists, following Vygotsky, and places particular emphasis on the influence exerted by social processes on the individual's development.

dialectology The study of varieties of a language (**dialects**) which are regionally or socially distinctive. Dialects are marked by having distinctive words, grammatical structures, and pronunciations. They are studied by wide-ranging questionnaires which gather information about the same linguistic features over the whole geographical area of a language. The result is a **dialect atlas**, which shows dialect areas and boundaries. Dialects which are socially distinctive identify social groups within a community, with reference to such factors as age, sex, occupation, and ethnic background.

dialysis [diyalisis] A means of separating dissolved substances (solutes) of different molecular weights by using the differences in their rates of diffusion across thin layers of certain materials (eg cellulose, peritoneal membranes). Artificial kidney machines (**dialysers**) perform **haemodialysis**, whereby waste products (such as urea or excess salts) are removed from the patient's blood, while blood cells and protein are retained. The system can also be used to provide the patient with nutrients (eg glucose). It causes anaemia, but this can be treated with erythropoietin.

diamagnetism A magnetic effect, measurable in many materials (eg water, copper), in which individual atomic magnetic moments induced within the material align in opposition to an applied magnetic field. The material is repelled by the source of the magnetic field; for sufficiently strong fields objects can be floated above magnets (diamagnetic levitation). Diamagnetism is characterized by negative magnetic susceptibility.

diaminoethanetetra-acetic acid *EDTA*

Diamond, Neil (Leslie) (1941–) Singer and songwriter, born in New York City, USA. He began writing songs while studying at New York University. He wrote the hits 'I'm A Believer' (1966) and 'A Little Bit Me, A Little Bit You' (1967) for the Monkees, and had his own first Number 1 hit with 'Cracklin' Rose' (1970). His albums include *Touching You, Touching Me* (1970), *Jonathon Livingston Seagull* (1974), and *Headed for the Future* (1986). His songs have been taken up by many recording artists, including The Hollies, Elvis Presley, and UB40.

diamond A naturally occurring form of crystalline carbon formed at high pressures and temperatures deep in the Earth's crust. It is found in volcanic pipes, called *kimberlites*, and in alluvial deposits. Major mines are near Kimberley, South Africa. Diamond is the hardest natural substance known, and is the most precious of gemstones. Diamonds may be clear and transparent or of many hues, including yellow, green, and blue, depending on the presence of trace amounts of impurities. **Black diamonds**, generally of poorer quality, are used for industrial purposes.

diamondback North American rattlesnake with bold diamond-shaped markings along back; also known as **diamondback rattlesnake**; two species: the **Eastern diamondback rattlesnake** (*Crotalus adamanteus*), the most venomous snake in North America (bite can kill in one hour); and the **Western diamondback rattlesnake** (*Crotalus atrox*).

diamondbird A small woodland bird native to Australia, also known as **pardalote**; short tail and bill; eats insects; nests in holes. Some migrate within Australia, moving N for the winter. They are placed in the **flowerpecker** family, but their affinity is uncertain. (Genus: *Pardalotus*, 5 or 8 species; experts disagree. Family: Dicaeidae.)

diamorphine *heroin*

Diana [diyana] Roman goddess, associated with the Moon, virginity, and hunting. She was considered to be equivalent to the Greek Artemis, whose cult was primarily at Ephesus; hence the cult of 'Diana of the Ephesians', who was a fertility-goddess.

Diana, Princess of Wales, formerly **Lady Diana (Frances) Spencer** (1961–97) Former wife of Charles, Prince of Wales, and youngest daughter of the 8th Earl Spencer, born at Sandringham, Norfolk, E England, UK. She was educated in Norfolk, and at West Heath School, Sevenoaks, Kent. She became Lady Diana Spencer when her father succeeded to the earldom in 1975, and worked as a kindergarten teacher in Pimlico before marrying the Prince of Wales to great popular acclaim in 1981. They had two sons, **Prince William (Arthur Philip Louis)** (1982–) and **Prince Henry (Charles Albert David)** (1984–), known as **Prince Harry**. Seriously interested in social concerns, she became a popular public figure in her own right, and was honorary president of many charities, particularly those caring for the homeless, deprived and sick children, and people suffering from AIDS. Through her visit to Angola, she raised public awareness of the Red Cross campaign for a world ban on landmines. The royal couple were legally separated in 1992, and divorced in 1996. She continued to travel and work with a range of good causes, both in Britain and abroad, while receiving unprecedented worldwide media attention, with newspapers competing to report on her family situation and on her (real or imaginary) personal relationships; and it was while trying to escape the pursuit of paparazzi in Paris that she died in a car accident in August 1997. Thousands of people flocked to London for her funeral, which took place amid an unprecedented level of public mourning. A British inquest into her death was opened in 2004.

diaphragm (anatomy) A sheet of muscle and tendons separating the thoracic and abdominal cavities. The convex thoracic surface is lined by the *pleura*; the abdominal surface by the *peritoneum*. There are major openings for the passage of structures between the two cavities, such as the aorta, inferior vena cava, and oesophagus. The diaphragm is the principle muscle of respiration, and is also an important muscle used in expulsive acts: coughing, vomiting, micturition, defaecation, and childbirth.

diaphragm (photography) An opening, usually circular, and generally adjustable in diameter or area, which controls the amount of light passing through a lens into an optical system, such as a camera.

diarrhoea / diarrhea [diyareea] The frequent passage of semiformed or liquid motions. Acute diarrhoea usually results from inflammation of the bowel, chemical irritants in food, or infection by micro-organisms (eg dysentery). Chronic or recurring diarrhoea occurs in several chronic diseases of the small or large intestine (eg colitis). Important consequences are loss of body water and salts, which may lead to dehydration.

Diaspora [diyaspora] (Gr 'scattering', Heb *golah* or *galut* 'exile') The Jews scattered in the world outside Palestine from either voluntary or compulsory resettlements, such as the Assyrian and Babylonian deportations in the 8th-c and 6th-c BC, or later dispersions in the Graeco-Roman period; also known as the **Dispersion**. The Babylonian Talmud and the Septuagint were important literary products of those Jews that had settled 'abroad'.

diastole [diyastolee] The interval between successive contractions of the chambers of the heart. During these periods, the chambers fill with blood flowing from the veins into the atria (**atrial diastole**), and from the atria into the ventricles (**ventricular diastole**).

diastrophism [diyastrofizm] The deformation of large masses of the Earth's crust to form mountain ranges, ocean basins, and continents.

diathermy [diyathermee] The application of heat to muscles or joints for the relief of pain. The heat is produced by means of high-frequency electric current, high-frequency electromagnetic short-wave radiation, or ultrasound.

diatom [diyatm] A microscopic, single-celled green alga common in marine and freshwater habitats; possesses an often ornate, external shell (*frustule*) containing silica, and consisting of two separate valves; commonly reproduces by splitting in two (binary fission); green colour derived from chlorophyll pigments. (Class: Bacillarophyceae.)

diatonicism An attribute of a piece or section of music built, exclusively or predominantly, from notes belonging to a particular major or minor scale (*diatonic* notes). For example, the note F sharp is diatonic in the key (scale) of D major, but chromatic in the key of C major.

Diaz or **Dias, Bartolomeu** [deeas], Span also [deeath], Port [deeazh] (c.1450–1500) Navigator and explorer, probably born in Portugal. In 1487 John II gave him two vessels to follow up the discoveries already made on the W coast of Africa. Driven by a violent storm, he sailed round the Cape of Good Hope, and discovered Algoa Bay. The discontent of his crew compelled him to return (1488). He also travelled with Vasco da Gama in 1497, and with Cabral in 1500, during whose expedition he was lost in a storm.

Diaz, Cameron [deeas] (1972–) Film actress, born in San Diego, CA, USA. She left home at 16 and for the next five years travelled abroad before returning to America. Her big break into the cinema came in 1994, when she auditioned for a small part in *The Mask* and was offered the lead. She then worked in a series of low-budget films, but was propelled into international stardom with *My Best Friend's Wedding* (1997) and *There's Something About Mary* (1998). Later films include *Gangs of New York* (2002) and *Charlie's Angels: Full Throttle* (2003).

Díaz, (José de la Cruz) Porfirio [deeas] (1830–1915) President of Mexico (1876–80, 1884–1911), born in Oaxaca, S Mexico. He fought against the French occupation of Mexico (1862–7). Defeated in the presidential election of 1875, he seized power, and served as president for 30 years, until the revolution of Francisco Madero (1873–1913) forced him to resign (1911) and flee into exile. His regime did much to stimulate material progress in Mexico.

diazepam *benzodiazepines*

diazo process *photocopying*

dibbuk or **dybbuk** [dibuhk] In Jewish tradition, an evil spirit, or the restless soul of a dead sinner, that enters the body of a living person and controls his or her behaviour until exorcized by a religious rite.

Dibdin, Charles (1745–1814) Composer, writer, and theatre manager, born in Southampton, Hampshire, S England, UK. He early attracted notice by his singing, and began a stage career in 1762. In 1789 he started his popular series of one-man musical entertainments. He wrote over 1000 songs (such as 'Poor Jack' and 'Tom Bowling') and many stage works, musical pieces, and novels.

Dibdin, Michael (John) (1947–) Novelist, born in Chichester, West Sussex, England, UK. He studied at the universities of Sussex and Alberta, launching his career as an author with *The Last Sherlock Holmes Story* (1978). In 1988 he won the Crime Writer's Award, the Gold Dagger, for *Ratking*. Later books include *Dirty Tricks* (1991), *Cosi Fan Tutti* (1996), *And Then You Die* (2001), and *Medusa* (2003).

DiCaprio, Leonardo (1974–) Film actor, born in Los Angeles. He began his acting career in television at the age of 14, moved into films, and became known after his Oscar-nominated role for Best Supporting Actor in *What's Eating Gilbert Grape?* (1993). Later films include *Romeo and Juliet* (1996), *Marvin's Room* (1996), *Titanic* (1997), *The Man in the Iron Mask* (1998), *The Beach* (2000), and *Gangs of New York* (2002).

dice A six-sided cube, each side generally numbered between 1 and 6, with opposing faces totalling 7; the older singular form, **die**, is now rare. It is used in games of chance and in many children's games, such as snakes-and-ladders. Other forms of dice include **poker dice**, which contain the pictures of the six highest value cards (9 to Ace); poker hands have to be formed as a result of a random throw. A popular form of dice as a casino game is *craps*.

dichotic listening [diykotik] An experimental technique used in psychology and psycholinguistics to determine which side of the brain is dominant in its ability to process particular kinds of sound. It can be tested by feeding different stimuli into both ears at the same time, and identifying the brain's involvement by the accuracy with which the input to the ear is reported by the subject. Generally, people have a right-ear advantage for linguistic signals, and a left-ear one for others, such as music.

Dickens, Charles (John Huffam) (1812–70) Novelist, born in Landport, Hampshire, S England, UK, the son of a clerk in the navy pay office. Painful childhood memories, notably his father's imprisonment in a debtors' prison, and his own work in a warehouse in Southwark, were a formative influence on his writings. In 1814 he moved to London, then to Chatham, where he received some schooling. He found a menial post with a solicitor, then took up journalism, becoming a reporter at Doctors' Commons, and at 22 joined a London newspaper. He published various papers in the *Monthly Magazine*, following this up with sketches and papers for the *Evening Chronicle*. In 1836 his *Sketches by Boz* and *Pickwick Papers* were published; and that year he married Catherine, the daughter of his friend George Hogarth. They had 10 children, but were separated in 1858. Dickens worked relentlessly, producing several successful novels which created a Shakespearean gallery of characters (including Fagin, Scrooge, Uriah Heep, Little Nell) and also campaigned against many of the social evils of his time. The novels first appeared in monthly instalments, notably *Oliver Twist* (1837–9), *Nicholas Nickleby* (1838–9), and *The Old Curiosity Shop* (1840–1). Thereafter a great part of his life was spent abroad. His later novels include *David Copperfield* (1849–50),

Bleak House (1852–3), *A Tale of Two Cities* (1859), *Great Expectations* (1860–1), and the unfinished *The Mystery of Edwin Drood* (1870). In addition, he gave talks and readings, and wrote many pamphlets, plays, and letters. His novels have provided the basis for many successful adaptations in the theatre, in the cinema, on radio, and on television.

Dickey, James (Lafayette) (1923–97) Poet and writer, born in Atlanta, Georgia, USA. He served in World War 2 before entering Vanderbilt University (1949–50). *The Stone* (1960) was his first published book of poems. He travelled widely and taught at a succession of universities, later becoming poetry consultant to the Library of Congress (1966–8). In addition to his poetic works, he is known for his novel *Deliverance* (1970), for which he also wrote the film screenplay (1972).

Dickinson, Emily (Elizabeth) (1830–86) Poet, born in Amherst, Massachusetts, USA. At the age of 23 she withdrew from all social contacts, and lived a secluded life at Amherst, writing in secret over 1000 poems. Hardly any of her work was published before her death, when her sister Lavinia brought out three volumes (1890–6). Her writing, intensely personal and often spiritual, shows great originality both in thought and in form, and has had considerable influence on modern poetry, especially in the USA.

dicotyledons [diykotileednz] One of the two major divisions of the flowering plants, often referred to simply as **dicots**; contrasted with **monocotyledons**. The seed embryo has two cotyledons, and the primary root of the seedling persists, forming a taproot. Dicots usually have broad leaves with reticulate veination and floral parts in fours, fives, or multiples thereof. The vascular bundles form a ring within the stem, and a cambium layer is present, capable of producing secondary vascular tissue and thus woody stems. About 250 different families of dicots are currently recognized. (Subclass: Dicotyledonae.)

Dictation Test A method used by Australian governments (1902–58) to exclude certain classes of intending immigrant. Based on the example of Natal (1897), immigrants received a test in a European language, usually one with which they were unfamiliar. Non-Europeans were the main target, but it was also used with those considered politically undesirable; the most celebrated case was the anti-fascist, Egon Kisch (1885–1948), who was tested in Gaelic (1934).

dictator In strict terms, an absolute ruler, especially one who has seized power unconstitutionally, and who enjoys authority by virtue of some personal characteristic, ie an **autocrat**. In practice, a dictatorship often refers to rule by several people, who are not subject to re-election and who are authoritarian in character, such as a military dictatorship. Personal dictatorships are now very rare. Not all involve arbitrary rule or despotism, and some dictators take account of popular wishes ('benevolent dictatorships').

dictionary A work of reference, traditionally in the form of a book, and now often available as a computational database, giving linguistic information about the words of a language, arranged in alphabetical order under headwords (or *catchwords*). Dictionaries may be *bilingual* or *multilingual*, giving only lists of word correspondences between the languages, or they may provide information about the senses, pronunciation, and grammatical status of the headwords, and illustrate the idiomatic usages into which they can enter. *Monolingual* dictionaries generally present these facts in varying degrees of detail (depending on the size of the dictionary), expanding on the range of meanings and uses of a word. A *historical* dictionary, such as the *Oxford English Dictionary*, provides an account of changes in word forms and meanings, based on usage citations. Some dictionaries (especially those falling within the US and European – particularly French and German – traditions) add encyclopedic data, in the form of pictures, tables, and facts about people and places, or provide special features, such as notes on usage or closely related words (*synonym essays*). *Etymological* dictionaries give information on the historical derivation of the headwords, and on the changes in meaning which they have undergone over time. The term is also applied to short-entry reference books, encyclopedic rather than lexicological in character, which deal only with biography, geography, or other specific subjects. The process of compiling dictionaries, and the study of the issues involved, is known as **lexicography**.

Dicynodon [diysiynodon] A plant-eating fossil reptile known from the late Permian period; skull mammal-like, with single opening behind orbit for insertion of jaw muscles; jaws with horny plates for cutting and crushing vegetation; upper canine tusks prominent. (Order: Therapsida.)

Didache [didakhay] (Gr 'teaching') The short title for 'The Teaching of the Lord through the Twelve Apostles', dated near the beginning of the 2nd-c AD. It consists of a short manual of Christian moral teaching and church order, overlapping somewhat with the canonical Gospels, but also important for its description of early Christian ministry and sacramental practices.

Diderot, Denis [deederoh] (1713–84) Writer and philosopher, born in Langres, NE France. Trained by the Jesuits, he became a tutor and bookseller's hack (1733–44), before beginning as a writer. Always controversial, his *Pensées philosophiques* (1746, Philosophical Thoughts) was burned by the Parliament of Paris for its anti-Christian ideas, and he was imprisoned for his *Lettre sur les aveugles* (1749, trans Essay on Blindness). For 20 years he worked tirelessly as editor of an expanded French version of Chambers's *Cyclopaedia* (1751–76), known as the *Encyclopédie*, a major work of the age of the Enlightenment. A prolific and versatile writer, he published novels, plays, satires, essays, and letters.

didgeridoo, also spelled **didjeridoo** or **didjeridu** A primitive trumpet of the Australian aborigines, made from a hollow eucalyptus branch about 120–150 cm/4–5 ft long. It is used, with a wide variety of playing techniques, to accompany singing and dancing.

Dido [diydoh] In the *Aeneid*, the daughter of the King of Tyre, who founded Carthage. Aeneas was diverted to Africa by storms, and told her his story. They fell in love, but when Aeneas deserted her she committed suicide by throwing herself upon a pyre.

Didrikson, Babe, nickname of **Mildred Ella Zaharias**, *née* **Didrikson** (1914–56) Golfer and athlete, born in Port Arthur, Texas, USA. A great all-round athlete, she was in the All-American basketball team (1930–2), then turned to athletics and won two gold medals at the 1932 Olympics; she also broke the world record in the high jump, but was disqualified for using the new Western Roll technique. Excelling also in swimming, tennis, and rifle-shooting, she turned to golf, and won the US National Women's Amateur Championship (1946), then 17 championships including the British Ladies' Amateur Championship (1947). In 1948 she turned professional, and won the US Women's Open three times (1948, 1950, 1954). She married George Zaharias, a noted wrestler.

Diefenbaker, John G(eorge) [deefenbayker] (1895–1979) Canadian statesman and prime minister (1957–63), born in Neustadt, Ontario, SE Canada. He studied at the University of Saskatchewan, and was called to the bar in 1919. In 1940 he entered the Canadian Federal House of Commons, becoming leader of the Progressive Conservatives (1956), and was elected prime minister after 22 years of Liberal rule. His government introduced important agricultural reforms, and extended the federal franchise to Canada's native peoples. He remained active in national politics until his death.

dieffenbachia *dumb cane*

dielectric A non-conducting material whose molecules align or polarize under the influence of applied electric fields. The degree is indicated by the **dielectric constant**, the ratio of the charge stored by a capacitor with dielectric material between the plates to that stored by a capacitor having a vacuum between the plates. Dielectrics are an essential constituent of capacitors.

dielectric constant *permittivity*

Diemen, Antony Van *Tasman, Abel Janszoon*

diencephalon [diyensefalon] The midline part of the forebrain which lies deep between the cerebral hemispheres, consisting of several component parts (the thalamus, metathalamus, epithalamus, and hypothalamus). The *thalamus* is the largest part, whose diverse functions include various motor, sensory, intellectual, and emotional responses. Each *metathalamus* consists of two major parts concerned with certain auditory and visual processes. The *epithalamus* is a strip of tissue connecting the two thalami; projecting from it is the pineal gland. It contains the third ventricle of the brain.

Dieppe [dyep] 49°55N 1°05E, pop (2000e) 38 300. Seaport in Seine-Maritime department, NW France; below high chalk cliffs on the R Arques, where it meets the English Channel, N of Rouen; scene of heavy fighting in World War 2; ferry links with Newhaven.

Dieri [diree] Aboriginal community of the L Eyre region of South Australia. The Dieri lived in one of the harshest deserts of Australia, where summer temperatures reach 50°C. After 1860, they were drawn into European-controlled cattle stations (ranches) and missions. Following the decline of employment opportunities in the cattle industry and on the Alice Springs railway during the 1970s, many Dieri moved to the S cities of Adelaide and Port Augusta.

Diesel, Rudolf (Christian Carl) [deezl] (1858–1913) Engineer, born in Paris, France. He studied at the Munich Polytechnic, and joined the refrigeration firm Linde in Paris in 1880. He moved to the Berlin branch in 1890, and continued his search for an efficient internal combustion engine. He patented a design in 1892 and, subsidized by the Krupp company, constructed a 'rational heat motor', demonstrating the first compression-ignition engine in 1897. He spent most of his life at his factory at Augsburg. He was lost overboard from the steamer *Dresden* while on his way to London.

diesel engine An internal combustion engine, working upon the diesel cycle, which ignites its fuel/air mixture by heating it to combustion point through compression. Because of this, the diesel engine is classed as a compression-ignition engine.

diet The combination of foods which provide the necessary nutrients for the body. Diets may be rated in quality depending on the balance of nutrients consumed, and not primarily on the type of food eaten. Often a 'diet' is used to imply a restriction of calories for slimming: strictly speaking this is a 'low-calorie' diet, just as there are low-fat diets, low-salt diets, or high-fibre diets. The link between diet and disease was first noted in China in the 14th-c.

Diet, Imperial The *Reichstag* or assembly of the Holy Roman Empire, mediaeval in origin, representing the separate estates of electors, princes, and free cities, and consisting of three bodies (curias), summoned at the will of the Emperor. Although its powers and procedures had expanded considerably by the late 15th-c, its authority was undermined by the religious divisions of the Reformation and the separate ambitions of the German princes after Westphalia (1648). Failing to develop as a supreme legislature, it became increasingly little more than a permanent congress of ambassadors during the last century and a half of its existence (1663–1806).

dietary fibre The part of the diet made up of plant material that is indigestible by humans; also known as **roughage**. Fibre is an important component of the diet. It absorbs water and helps to bulk out the gut contents, thereby increasing the rate of passage through the intestines; people who do not consume sufficient fibre tend to become constipated. It is found in a variety of foodstuffs including bran cereal, beans, and vegetables.

dietetics The clinical management of a patient through dietary intervention, as practised professionally by **dietitians**. The two problems most commonly treated by dietitians are obesity and diabetes.

diethylstilboestrol *DES*

Diet of Worms *Worms, Diet of*

Dietrich, Marlene [deetrikh], originally **Maria Magdalene von Losch** (1904–92) Film actress, born in Berlin, Germany. She studied acting under Max Reinhardt, the innovative theatrical director. She became famous in Josef von Sternberg's film *Der blaue Engel* (1930, The Blue Angel), and developed a glamorous and sensual film personality in such Hollywood films as *Morocco* (1930) and *Blond Venus* (1932), all directed by von Sternberg. During World War 2, she often appeared in shows for Allied troops, and continued to make films after the War, such as *Judgment at Nuremberg* (1961). She also became an international cabaret star. Increasingly reclusive, she refused to be photographed for the 1984 documentary *Marlene*, with a voice-over interview by Maximilian Schell. She wrote an autobiography, *Ich bin, Gott sei Dank, Berlinerin* (1987, I Am, Thank God, a Berliner).

differential calculus A system of mathematical rules which considers small increments of a variable x, and the corresponding change in $f(x)$, to find the rate at which $f(x)$ is changing. The early development of calculus was associated with Isaac Newton, whose *Method of Fluxions* was written in 1671 but not published until 1736, and independently with Gottfried Leibniz, who gave the first published accounts of it in 1684 and 1686. The method is of wide utility in the physical and other sciences to capture the way objects or quantities change. It was given rigorous foundations free of appeal to geometry or dynamics only in the 19th-c after the cumulative efforts of Cauchy, Weierstrass, Dedekind, and others.

Differential GPS *Global Positioning System*

diffraction An interference effect, a property of waves, responsible for the spreading of waves issuing from a small aperture (eg sound waves from a public address loudspeaker). Diffraction causes the waves to 'bend round' objects, which in light produces shadows surrounded by tiny light and dark bands (**diffraction fringes**). Atoms in crystals cause the diffraction of incident X-rays, electrons, or neutrons to give patterns which allow the determination of crystal structure. A **diffraction grating** corresponds to many hundreds of slits per centimetre, and provides a useful way of dividing a light beam into component colours. Diffraction represents the ultimate limit of the resolving power of optical instruments.

diffusion (anthropology) The spread of one or several cultural traits from one group to another. Diffusionism, which dominated 19th-c German anthropology, is the notion that cultural similarities are a result of diffusion, and in its extreme form, that all cultures have a common origin.

diffusion (photography) The scattering of light by a translucent medium; in studio lighting, a sheet of metal gauze, tracing paper, or etched plastic placed in front of a lamp to give softer and less directional illumination. Diffusion discs or nets of very fine fabric can also be placed in front of a camera lens to reduce the sharpness of the image.

diffusion (science) In physics and chemistry, the movement of atoms or particles through bulk material via their random collisions. For example, ions diffuse through solids, and atoms of a gas introduced into a volume of still air will become evenly distributed through it by diffusion. Molecules diffuse at rates inversely proportional to their molecular weights.

Digby, Sir Kenelm (1603–65) Diplomat, scientist, and writer, born in Gayhurst, Buckinghamshire, SC England, UK. He was brought up a Catholic, studied at Oxford, but left to travel abroad. In Madrid he met Prince Charles (1623), and on returning to England was knighted and entered his service. During the Civil War he was imprisoned by the parliament (1642–3), and had his estates confiscated. After the Restoration, he was chancellor to Queen Henrietta Maria until 1664.

digestion The physiological process of animals in which complex foodstuffs are broken down by enzymes into simpler components (monosaccharides, amino acids, fatty acids, and other substances) which can be absorbed into the body and used by body cells. In certain animals (eg protozoa, porifera), digestion is entirely intracellular: food is taken up and digested, simple molecules are formed, and waste products eliminated all by a single cell. Many animals (eg vertebrates, arthropods) depend entirely on extracellular digestion, in which enzyme-rich fluids are secreted into the cavity of the alimentary canal, where digestion takes place. In some animals (eg coelenterates, lamellibranchs), digestion occurs both within and outside the cell.

Diggers A radical group in England formed during the Commonwealth, led by Gerrard Winstanley (1609–72), preaching and practising agrarian communism on common and waste land. An offshoot of the Puritan extremists, the Levellers' philosophy and aims were set down in Winstanley's *New Law of Righteousness* (1649). In his *Law of Freedom* (1652) he extended his thesis that English law and institutions should be modified to bring social and economic equality to all, through common ownership of the land. From April 1649 they established the Digger community at St George's Hill, Surrey, followed by colonies in nine other S and Midland counties. The movement was suppressed and its communities dispersed in 1650 by the local authorities.

digger wasp A hunting wasp that stings and paralyses prey for use in provisioning its nest. In the primitive family Ampulicidae, females typically catch the prey before preparing a nest in a shallow scrape in soil. In the family Sphecidae, they dig nests in soil or wood, place the prey in a cell, and lay eggs in each cell. Adults feed on nectar or honeydew. (Order: Hymenoptera.)

digital Descriptive of any method of representing information (numbers, strings of characters, sounds, pictures) by a sequence of electronic pulses of fixed duration. The existence of a voltage denotes a '1' and the absence denotes a '0'. This allows all numbers to be represented by their binary equivalents. Other forms of information are first represented as a set of numbers and then those numbers are coded in digital electronic form. Digital representation is used for storing information (in computers and on tape and disk) and for transmitting information (over telephone lines or by broadcasting). Digital representation is preferred because it is less vulnerable to noise, easy to compress, and easy to encrypt, preventing unauthorized capture of the information.

digital computer A programmable machine which operates using binary digital data. The basic operations carried out in a digital computer are simple arithmetic or logical operations, but in combination and when carried out at high speed these provide a very powerful facility. Digital computers, both large and small, contain (i) a *central processing unit (CPU)* which controls and co-ordinates all the functions of the computer, and performs the arithmetic and logical operations; (ii) a *memory*, which holds data and program instructions; and (iii) various *input/output devices*, which allow communication to and from the outside world. These units are interconnected by various complex sets of interconnections, called *busses*, which carry data, and control information and memory addresses. Although the basic structure is common to almost all digital computers, they vary in size from small hand-held computers to mainframe computer systems occupying very large rooms.

digitalis [dijitahlis] An extract of *Digitalis purpurea* (the foxglove) which has been used for the treatment of heart failure and oedema ('dropsy') for at least 800 years. The extract contains cardiac glycosides as active ingredients. Purified cardiac glycosides (eg digoxin) are today's first-line treatment for heart failure. All are toxic at doses only slightly higher than therapeutic doses.

digital media The use of digital recording to store media on computers and allow them to be processed by computer software. Different standards have been developed for the compression and storage of images, audio recordings, and video recordings: **GIF** (**Graphics Interchange Format**) is a standard for the storage of still images; **JPEG** (**Joint Photographic Experts Group**) is a standard for the compression and storage of continuous tone still images; **MIDI** (**Musical Instrument Digital Interface**) is a format for representing the output from musical instruments which can be processed by a MIDI synthesizer, whether a computer or a sound reproduction system; **MPEG** (**Motion Picture Experts Group**) is a standard for compressing video (including audio) sequences; **MPEG-1** is used for the storage of movies on CD-ROM; **MPEG-2** is for long-distance video transmission over digital communication lines; **WAV** (**Windows Waveform**) is a format for recording sound digitally. **MIME** (**Multipurpose Internet Mail Extension**) is a protocol for sending image, audio, and video sequences across the Internet; it can handle images in GIF and JPEG formats, and video in MPEG format.

digital recording A technique of sound recording, developed in the 1970s, in which a series of coded pulses replaces the waveform analogues of earlier methods. The advantages of digital recording are that tape noise, pitch fluctuations, and distortion are virtually eliminated. Digitally-recorded master tapes have been widely used in the production of conventional long-playing discs, but the full advantages of the technique can be realized only when the signal is fed directly from a decoder into an amplifier, as happens in the case of the compact disk and digital audio tape. Developments in the 1990s include *digital audio broadcasting*, a high-quality transmission system for radio; the *digital compact cassette*, a format for tape cassettes; and the *digital video disk* (*DVD*; originally, *digital versatile disk*), a disk similar to a compact disk, but double-sided and multi-layered, thus vastly increasing storage capacity. Digital recording has been instrumental in allowing computers to process all kinds of media, such as images, audio sequences, and video sequences.

digital techniques In audio and video transmission and recording, the conversion of a continuously varying analogue signal, for example representing acoustic sound waves or image brightness, into a series of coded numerical values. The original signal is sampled at regular intervals, sufficiently frequent to represent its detailed variation, and the instantaneous value at each interval allocated to one of a series of discrete numerical quantities. These are conveniently expressed in binary terms and processed in groups ('words') of simple on/off signals ('bits'), which are much less liable to distortion and loss in handling than the continuous analogue. At the receiver the digital signal is converted to analogue for final presentation as picture or sound. For the fine detail of scanned television images a very high sampling rate is necessary, 13·5 million times a second (13·5 mHz), with words of 8 bits providing 256 levels of brightness; with sound, a lower sampling rate of 48 kHz can be used, but a much extended intensity scale of 20-bit words (1 048 576 levels) is required.

digital-to-analog conversion, also spelled **analogue** The process of converting digital numbers produced by a computer into an electrical signal such as a corresponding voltage or current; usually carried out by electronic circuits or discrete integrated circuits called **digital-to-analog (D/A) converters**. In many applications the electrical signal is fed into a transducer, which converts the electrical signal into another form of energy such as heat or sound. D/A converters and A/D converters are common in computer-controlled machinery.

diglossia A situation in which a language community uses distinct varieties for specific social functions. The varieties are generally distinguished as *high* (used for education, religion, and other public functions, and the one accorded highest prestige) and *low* (used for family interaction, talk with servants, joke-telling, and other everyday functions). Arabic, Modern Greek, and Swiss German are examples of diglossic languages.

dihydroxybutanedioic acid *tartaric acid*

Dijon [deezhõ], ancient **Dibio** 47°20N 5°00E, pop (2000e) 153 000. Industrial and commercial city and capital of Côte d'Or department, E France; at confluence of rivers Ouche and Ruzon; railway; bishopric; university (1722); historic capital of Burgundy; famous for its restaurants and its mustard; cars, foundries, foodstuffs, centre of wine trade; Palais des Ducs de Bourgogne, Gothic Church of Notre-Dame, Church of St Michel,

Palais de Justice (16th–17th-c), Cathedral of St-Benigne, remains of 14th-c Chartreuse de Champmol (now a hospital).

dik-dik A dwarf antelope, native to Africa; small (height, up to 40 cm/16 in); large ears, elongate nose; male with short straight horns and pronounced secretory gland in front of eye. (Genus: *Madoqua*, 3 species.)

dikkop [dikop] *thick-knee*

dilatation and curettage (D and C) [dilatayshn, kyooretij] A gynaecological operation to investigate the cause of menstrual disorders and possible carcinoma of the uterus. A special type of scoop (*curette*) is passed through the dilated cervix into the uterine cavity, the inner surface of which is scraped. Tissue lining the cavity is removed and examined microscopically.

dill An aromatic annual (*Anethum graveolens*), growing to 60 cm/2 ft, native to India and SW Asia; leaves feathery, finely divided into narrow linear lobes; flowers yellow, in umbels up to 15 cm/6 in across; fruit ellipsoid, strongly compressed, dark brown with a paler wing. It is cultivated as a culinary herb; the leaves and the seeds are used as flavouring. (Family: Umbelliferae.)

Dillane, Stephen, originally **Stephen Delaney** (1958–) Actor, born in London. After training at Bristol Old Vic Theatre School, and work in repertory, he joined the Royal National Theatre, and won the Richard Burton Shakespeare Globe Award in 1995 for the title role in *Hamlet* at the Gielgud Theatre, London. In 1999 he won the Evening Standard Theatre Award for Best Actor in *The Real Thing*, and after its transfer to Broadway the Tony Award for Best Actor (2000). He has appeared in television and films, including *Anna Karenina* (2000), and *Welcome to Sarajevo* (1997).

Dillinger, John (Herbert) [dilinjer] (1903–34) Gangster, born in Indianapolis, Indiana, USA. The most famous of all US bank robbers, he specialized in armed robberies, terrorizing Indiana and neighbouring states (1933–4). After escaping from Crown Point county jail, where he was held on a murder charge, he was shot dead by FBI agents in Chicago. Some researchers have claimed that another man, not Dillinger, was killed by the FBI, as a hoax by his allies, and that he escaped.

Dillon, Matt (1964–) Film actor, born in Larchmont, New York, USA. At the age of 15 he was cast in *Over The Edge* (1979), but his first major film role was in Francis Ford Coppola's *The Outsiders* (1983). Later films include *Kansas* (1988), *Beautiful Girls* (1996), *Wild Things* (1998), and *There's Something About Mary* (1998). In 2002 he directed and starred in *City of Ghosts*.

Dilthey, Wilhelm [diltiy] (1833–1911) Philosopher, born in Biebrich, WC Germany. He studied at Heidelberg and Berlin, then taught at Basel, Kiel, Wrocław, Poland (formerly Breslau, Prussia), and finally Berlin (1882–1911), where he was professor of philosophy. He was much influenced by Kant, and is himself a key figure in the idealist tradition in modern social thought. Using some of Hegel's writings as a point of departure, he argued that human knowledge can only be understood as involving the knower's life lived in a historically conditioned culture. He developed a theory of hermeneutics for the interpretation of historical texts, and favoured biography as the best historical method. His ideas exerted considerable influence on Heidegger.

Dilwara Temples A group of five Jain temples near Mt Abu, Rajasthan, India. Built during the 11th–13th-c, they are renowned for the profusion and delicacy of their sculpture.

DiMaggio, Joe [dimajioh], popular name of **Joseph (Paul) DiMaggio**, nicknames **Joltin' Joe** and **the Yankee Clipper** (1914–99) Baseball player, born in Martinez, California, USA. He spent his entire career with the New York Yankees (1936–51). An outstanding fielder, he also holds the record for hitting safely in 56 consecutive games (1941). His second wife was the film star, Marilyn Monroe. His death was a cue for national mourning.

Dimbleby, David (1938–) Broadcaster, born in London, UK, the son of Richard Dimbleby. He studied at Oxford, joined the BBC as a reporter (1960–1), and became a leading presenter and interviewer on BBC television current-affairs programmes, such as *Panorama* (1974–77, 1980–2, 1989–) and *Election and Results* (1979, 1983, 1987, 1992, 1997). He is also chairman of the BBC's *Question Time* (from 1994).

Dimbleby, Jonathan (1944–) Broadcaster, writer, and journalist, the son of Richard Dimbleby, born in London, UK. He studied at University College London, and became a reporter for the BBC (1969–71). Well known as a presenter of television current-affairs documentaries (1972–88), he hosted *On the Record* for BBC-TV (1988–93), and regularly fronts programmes on major national events, such as the general election. In 1997 he presented the BBC television series *The Last Governor* about Chris Patten's governorship of Hong Kong. His controversial 'official' biography of the Prince of Wales appeared in 1994.

Dimbleby, Richard (Frederick) (1913–65) Broadcaster, born in Richmond on Thames, SW Greater London, UK. He was educated at Mill Hill School, near London, and worked on the editorial staff of various newpapers before joining the BBC in 1931. He became the Corporation's first foreign correspondent, its first war correspondent, and was the first radio man to go into Berlin and Belsen at the end of World War 2. In the post-war era he established himself as a magisterial TV anchorman on *Panorama* and a commentator on major events, especially royal occasions and major funerals (such as President Kennedy and Winston Churchill).

dim-dip The control of motor car headlights, enabling the light's beam to be altered in direction. On approaching an oncoming vehicle, to avoid dazzling its driver, a car's headlights can be altered by means of a switch operated by the driver. Main (far-reaching) beam becomes a dipped beam (local lighting directed to the side) by lighting a different filament in either the same or a separate lamp.

dimensional analysis The analysis of mathematical expressions representing physical theorems in terms of dimensions, using M for mass, L for length, T for time. For example, velocity has dimensions $[v] = LT^{-1}$, force $[F] = MLT^{-2}$, where square brackets denote dimensions. Both sides of an equation must have the same dimensions, as must all terms separated by addition and subtraction signs. It is a powerful technique for deriving new relations between quantities and for checking results.

dimer [diymer] A compound formed when two units (**monomers**), react together, either by addition or by condensation.

dimethylpropane *pentane*

dimethylsulphoxide [diymeethiylsuhlfoksiyd] CH_3SOCH_3, known as **DMSO**, melting point 18°C, boiling point 189°C. A colourless substance, an important solvent for many compounds, but not alkanes.

diminished responsibility A limited defence to a charge of murder which reduces the crime to one of manslaughter (England and Wales) or culpable homicide (Scotland), thereby avoiding the mandatory sentence of life imprisonment. It relates to a state of mind, whether as a result of illness, injury, or any other cause, which substantially impairs a person's mental responsibility and which, while not amounting to insanity, borders on it.

diminishing returns, law of A prediction in economics that, as more capital and labour is put into a factory, the resulting increases in output will eventually start to get smaller. Ultimately the average output per unit of labour or capital will also fall.

Dinaric Alps [dinarik], Serbo-Croatian **Dinara Planina**, Ital **Alpi Dinariche** Mountain range following the Adriatic coast of Croatia and NW Albania; linked to the main Alpine system via the Julian Alps; rises to 2522 m/8274 ft at Durmitor; limestone ranges in the Karst region (NW).

d'Indy, (Paul Marie Théodore) Vincent [dãdee] (1851–1931) Composer, born in Paris, France. He studied law there from a sense of family duty, but at the same time developed an interest in musical composition under the guidance of César Franck. He helped to found the Schola Cantorum in 1894, and taught there and at the Conservatoire until his death. His works include several operas and orchestral pieces, notably *Symphonie sur un chant montagnard français* (1886, Symphony on a French Mountaineering Song).

Dinesen, Isak *Blixen, Karen*

Ding Ling, also spelled **Ting Ling**, pseudonym of **Jiang Bingzhi** (1904–86) Novelist and short-story writer, born in Linli Co, SEC China. A radical feminist, she studied at Beijing University, joined the League of Left-Wing Writers in 1930, and became editor of its official journal. She joined the Communist Party in 1932, but her outspoken comments on male chauvinism and discrimination led to her being disciplined by the Party leaders, until her novel, *The Sun Shines Over the Sanggan River* (1948), about land-reform, restored her to favour. In 1958, however, she was 'purged', and sent to raise chickens in the Heilongjiang reclamation area. She was imprisoned (1970–5) during the Cultural Revolution, but rehabilitated by the Party in 1979.

dingo An Australian subspecies of domestic dog (*Canis familiaris dingo*), descended from dogs introduced thousands of years ago with aboriginal settlers; tawny yellow; cannot bark; eats kangaroos (and now rabbits and sheep); persecuted as a pest.

Dinka E Sudanic-speaking transhumant cattle herders of the Upper Nile in the Sudan Republic, occupying a vast area of low-lying and often swampy country. Without centralized political authority, they comprise many subgroups recognizing only the authority of religious chiefs.

dinoflagellate [diynoh**fla**jeluht] A microscopic, single-celled organism classified either as an alga (Class: Dinophyceae) or as a flagellate protozoan (Phylum: Mastigophora); sometimes containing chlorophyll pigment for photosynthesis; characterized by two whip-like organelles (*flagella*), one lying in a groove around the cell; most species enclosed in a rigid shell (*test*) encrusted with silica.

dinosaur A member of a group of reptiles (Subclass: Archosauria) that dominated life on land for 140 million years from the late Triassic period until their extinction at the end of the Cretaceous period, 64 million years ago. Dinosaurs are distinguished from other reptiles by the way they stood with their limbs held vertically beneath the body, rather than sticking out sideways. This posture allowed them a much more efficient locomotion than the sprawling gait of a typical reptile. There are over 800 known species of dinosaurs, all sharing the specialized kind of hip joint that allowed this upright posture. They fall into two contrasting groups: the **reptile-hipped dinosaurs** (Order: Saurischia), and the **bird-hipped dinosaurs** (Order: Ornithischia). The saurischian dinosaurs include the more primitive **theropod** groups, which comprised the carnivores such as *Tyrannosaurus*, which were exclusively two-legged, and the enormous **sauropods** such as *Apatosaurus* and *Diplodocus*, which were four-legged and predominantly plant-eating. The ornithischians included ankylosaurs, ceratopsians, hadrosaurs, stegosaurs, and *Iguanodon*. Many dinosaurs attained great size. *Diplodocus* reached a length of 28 m/90 ft but weighed only 10 tonnes, whereas *Apatosaurus* was shorter at 25 m/80 ft, but weighed 30 tonnes. Even larger dinosaurs, up to 30 m/100 ft long, are being discovered. These giants were slow-moving (3–4 kph/2–2½ mph) and probably lived in herds. Heavily built flesh-eaters, such as *Allosaurus*, could walk at 8 kph/5 mph. The largest flesh-eater, *Tyrannosaurus*, was a relatively slow-moving scavenger capable of moving at little more than 4 kph/2½ mph. These large dinosaurs were probably warm-blooded. Dinosaurs laid eggs, often on a nest mound of mud, and there is evidence that hadrosaurs showed parental care, protecting their young in a nursery based around the nest. Dinosaurs all became extinct suddenly, at the end of the Cretaceous period. The reason for the extinction is unknown, but a combination of climatic changes and competition from mammals in the changing conditions seems most probable. A widely promulgated theory is that the climatic changes came about as the result of a meteoritic impact. The modern descendants of dinosaurs, the birds, continue to flourish.

Dinosaur Provincial Park A provincial park in Alberta, SW Canada; a world heritage site. The park is noted as a region of severe erosion and fossil deposits; in the early 20th-c the fossil remains of some 60 different species of dinosaur were discovered here.

Dio Cassius [diyoh **ka**sius], also found as **Dion Cassius** and **Cassius Dio Cocceianus** (c.150–c.235) Roman senator and prominent man of affairs, from Bithynia in Asia Minor, who wrote a comprehensive history of Rome in Greek, extending from the foundation of the city down to his own day (229). Large parts still survive, either in full or an abbreviated form, and are an invaluable source, particularly for historians of the early Roman empire.

Diocletian [diyo**klee**shn], in full **Gaius Aurelius Valerius Diocletianus** (245–316) Roman emperor (284–305), a Dalmatian of humble birth, born in Diocles. He rose through the ranks of the army to become the greatest of the soldier emperors of the 3rd-c. He saw the answer to the empire's problems in a division of power at the top and a re-organization of the provincial structure below. In 286 the empire was split in two, with Diocletian retaining the East, and Maximian, a loyal friend, taking the West. Further refinement followed in 293 when, under the famous tetrarchy, the empire was divided into four. Towards the end of his reign he initiated a fierce persecution of Christians throughout the empire. He abdicated in 305.

diode An electronic valve having two electrodes (an anode and a cathode); invented in 1904 by British physicist John Ambrose Fleming. It permits current flow in only one direction, and is thus widely used as a rectifier, changing alternating current (AC) into direct current (DC).

Diogenes Laërtius [diy**o**jeneez **lair**tius] (3rd-c) Greek writer, born in Laërte, Cilicia. He is remembered for his *Lives, Teachings and Sayings of the Great Philosophers*, in 10 books, a compilation of excerpts.

Diogenes of Sinope [diy**o**jeneez] (c.410–c.320 BC) Cynic philosopher, born in Sinope, Pontus. He moved to Athens and became a student of Antisthenes, with whom he founded the Cynic sect. The Cynics preached an austere asceticism and self-sufficiency, and Diogenes became legendary for his ostentatious disregard of domestic comforts and social niceties. His unconventional behaviour (eg looking with a lantern in daylight for an honest man) was intended to portray the ideal of a life lived according to nature. He was said to have lived in a tub ('like a dog', the origin of the term *Cynic*).

Diomedes [diyoh**mee**deez] or **Diomede** A Greek hero who fought in the Trojan War, even taking on the gods in battle; also a wise counsellor, the partner of Odysseus in various schemes. In the mediaeval version of the story, he became the lover of Cressida.

Dion Chrysostom [diyon **kri**sostom], also found as **Dio Chrysostomus** (c.40–c.112) Greek rhetorician and philosopher, born in Prusa, Bithynia. He went to Rome under Vespasian, but was banished by Domitian. He then visited, in the disguise of a beggar, Thrace, Mysia, and Scythia. On Nerva's accession (96) he returned to Rome, and lived in great honour under him and Trajan. About 80 orations or treatises on politics and philosophy are extant.

Dione [diy**oh**nee] The fourth natural satellite of Saturn, discovered by Giovanni Domenico Cassini in 1684; distance from the planet 377 000 km/234 000 mi; diameter 1120 km/700 mi; orbital period 2·737 days; heavily cratered. The small satellite, Helene, moves along the same orbit.

Dionne, Cécile, Yvonne, Annette, Emilie, and **Marie** [deeon] (1934–) Quintuplets, born near Callander, Ontario, SE Canada. Successfully delivered to their French-Canadian parents, Oliva and Elzire Dionne, they were the first documented set of quintuplets to survive beyond a few days. During their childhood they became international celebrities appearing in feature films and advertising. Emilie died in 1954, Marie in 1970, and Yvonne in 2001.

Dionysia [diyonizia] Festivals in honour of Dionysus, the Greek god of fertility, ecstasy, inspiration, drama, and wine. At Athens, the Great Dionysia was the main occasion for dramatic contests.

Dionysius of Halicarnassus [diyoniysius] (1st-c BC) Influential Greek critic, historian, and rhetorician, from Halicarnassus in Asia Minor, who lived and worked in Rome at the time of Augustus. Much of his writing survives, including about half of his masterpiece, *Early Roman History*. Extending from earliest times to the outbreak of the First Punic War (264 BC), it is a mine of information about early Roman society.

Dionysius the Areopagite [diyoniysius, ariopagiyt] (1st-c) Greek Church leader, one of the few Athenians converted by the apostle Paul (*Acts* 17.34). Tradition makes him the first Bishop of Athens and a martyr. The Greek writings bearing his name were probably written by an Alexandrian. They are first mentioned in 533, from which time they were generally accepted as genuine, and had a great influence on the development of theology.

Dionysius the Elder [diyoniysius] (c.431–367 BC) Tyrant of Syracuse (405–367 BC) and ruler of half of Sicily, whose influence extended over most of S Italy. His reign was dominated by intermittent warfare with the Carthaginians, his chief rivals for power in Sicily. A patron of the arts, he invited Plato to his court, and even won a prize himself for tragedy at one of the great Athenian dramatic festivals.

Dionysius the Younger [diyoniysius] (c.397–? BC) Tyrant of Syracuse (367–357/6 BC, 347/6–344 BC), the son and successor of Dionysius the Elder. Groomed by Plato as a potential philosopher-king, he turned out to be a rake and an oppressor. Twice overthrown, he ended his days in exile at Corinth.

Dionysius Thrax [diyoniysius thrayks] (1st–2nd-c) Greek grammarian, a native of Alexandria, who taught at Rhodes and at Rome. His *Technē grammatikē* is the basis of all European works on grammar.

Dionysus or **Dionysos** [diyoniysus] In Greek mythology, the god of wild and uncontrolled ecstasy; later, more specifically, the god of wine, associated with music and dramatic festivals. He was the son of Zeus and Semele; his foreign cult arrived in Greece from Thrace. He was accompanied by a procession of maenads and satyrs, which was said to have reached India.

Diophantine equations Equations that are indeterminate themselves, but have solutions in the set of integers. Thus $3x + 4y = 11$ has solutions of the form $x = 1 - 4\lambda$, $y = 2 + 3\lambda$, where λ is an integer.

Diophantus [diyofantus] (c.200–c.284) Greek mathematician, who flourished in Alexandria c.250. Of his three known works, only six books of *Arithmetica*, the earliest extant treatise on algebra, have survived. His name was later given to that part of algebra which treats of the finding of particular rational values for general expressions under a surd form (*Diophantine analysis*).

dioptre / diopter [diyopter] In optics, the power of a lens; symbol *dpt*; defined as 1 divided by focal length in metres; used mostly in optometry.

Dior, Christian [deeaw(r)] (1905–57) Fashion designer, born in Granville, W France. He was the founder of the international fashion house of that name, and first began to design clothes in 1935. After working for Piguet and Lelong in Paris, he founded his own Paris house in 1945, and achieved worldwide fame with his long-skirted 'New Look' (1947). His later designs included the 'H' line and the 'A' line.

diorite [diyoriyt] A coarse-grained intermediate igneous rock composed mainly of plagioclase feldspar and ferromagnesian minerals, with up to 10% quartz.

Diouf, Elhadji Ousseynou (1981–) Footballer, born in Dakar, Senegal. A striker, he moved from Rennes to Lens at the start of the 2000–1 season. Senegal qualified for the 2002 FIFA World Cup finals by edging out rivals Morocco on goal difference, nine of Senegal's 14 goals being scored by Diouf, including two hat-tricks. The Senegalese fans have dubbed him 'Serial Killer' because of his prolific goal-scoring. Named in the 2002 FIFA All-Star team of the tournament, he joined Liverpool FC at the start of the 2002–3 season.

dioxan(e) [diyoksan, diyoksayn] $C_4H_8O_2$, 1,4-dioxacyclohexane, boiling point 101°C. A colourless liquid, used as a solvent for fats and waxes.

dioxin (**tetrachlorodibenzo-*p*-dioxin**, or **TCDD**) A highly toxic contaminant of the chlorphenoxy group of herbicides whose level is currently regulated at 0·1 parts per million or less. It causes a severe form of skin eruption (*chloracne*), and in laboratory animals causes cancer and damages the fetuses of mothers exposed to it. Dioxin seems to be less toxic in humans than in animals. The jungle defoliant Agent Orange used in Vietnam contained high levels of dioxin as a contaminant. Many violent explosions have occurred during the manufacture of chlorophenoxy herbicides, causing the release of dioxin, including the Monsanto plant in West Virginia, USA (1949) and in Seveso, Italy (1976). In 1999 it was revealed that 1500 times the legal limit of dioxin had contaminated a batch of fat sold to animal feed manufacturers, prompting widespread withdrawal of meat products across Europe.

dip and strike Geological terms to describe the disposition of rock layers. *Dip* is the angle at which a bed of rock is inclined to the horizontal plane, measured in the direction where the slope is the greatest. It is perpendicular to the *strike*, which is the direction of the intersection of the horizontal with the inclined plane.

diphtheria A disease caused by *Corynebacterium diphtheriae*. The bacterium infects the nose and throat, and occasionally wounds on the skin. The illness is severe and potentially lethal. Infection of the throat and larynx results in considerable swelling of the tissues, which may obstruct the airways. Toxin secreted by the bacteria may seriously damage the heart and nerves leading to heart failure, muscle paralysis, blindness, or brain damage. The bacteria are spread by direct contact, and the disease is most common among people living in overcrowded conditions. In the West, better standards of living and the use of a vaccine have led to a dramatic fall in incidence.

diphthong A vowel in which there is a change in auditory quality during a single syllable, as in *my*, *how*. The term is also used for a sequence of two written vowels within the same syllable, eg *fear*, *weight*.

Diplodocus [diplodokus] A semi-aquatic, long necked dinosaur; body length up to 28 m/92 ft, including an extremely long, whip-like tail; plant-eating, feeding around swamps and lakes; four-legged, limbs pillar-like, hindlimbs longer than forelimbs; known from the Upper Jurassic period of North America and Europe. (Order: Saurischia.)

diplomatics The study of legal and administrative documents, to determine their authenticity. The evidence is gathered by an analysis of the writing styles of scribes at different periods in history, the linguistic features characteristic of a period or of an individual scribe, and the nature of the writing materials used.

diplomatic service The body of public servants who are official representatives of their country in another country; also those who provide support to them. In many countries the diplomatic service has more prestige than the home civil service.

diplopia *double vision*

Diplopoda [diplopoda] *millipede*

Dipnoi [dipnoy] A subclass of bony fishes, comprising the lungfishes.

dipole [diypohl] A separation of charge. Diatomic molecules have dipoles when the atoms have different electronegativities, the more electronegative atom having a partial negative charge. In polyatomic molecules, dipoles add as vectors, so the bent molecule H_2O has a dipole, but the linear CO_2 (O=C=O) does not.

dipper A starling-like bird, native to mountains of Eurasia and the W New World; inhabits fast-flowing streams; not obviously modified for aquatic lifestyle, but swims underwater using wings; eats small aquatic animals. (Genus: *Cinclus*, 4 species. Family: Cinclidae.)

Diprotodon [dIyprohtodon] A heavily built, fossil marsupial known from the Pleistocene epoch of Australia; large, up to 2 m/6½ ft tall at the shoulder; front legs short; walked with entire sole of foot in contact with ground; plant-eating, with one pair of forward-pointing lower incisors. (Order: Diprotodonta.)

Diptera [diptera] *fly*

diptych [diptik] A picture consisting of two panels, hinged like the pages of a book. Small portable devotional pictures and altarpieces sometimes took this form in the late Middle Ages.

Dirac, Paul A(drien) M(aurice) [dirak] (1902–84) Physicist, born in Bristol, SW England, UK. He studied engineering at Bristol and physics at Cambridge, where he became professor of mathematics (1932–69). His main research was in the field of quantum mechanics, especially the incorporation of special relativity and development of the theory of electron spin. His proposal of the existence of 'anti-matter' – subatomic particles of opposite charge to those normally found – was confirmed by Anderson in 1932. He shared the Nobel Prize for Physics in 1933. He moved to the USA in 1968, and in 1971 became professor of physics at Florida State University, Tallahassee.

Dirac equation The basic equation of relativistic quantum mechanics; stated by Paul Dirac in 1928. It expresses the behaviour of electron waves in a way consistent with special relativity, requiring that electrons have spin ½, and predicting the existence of an antiparticle partner to the electron (the positron).

direct action Activity taken by a group which is intended to achieve some reform or to promote a particular cause. As the term 'direct' implies, the action is not pursued through the formal government and political channels. Instead, action is carried out on a broader front by individuals and influential groups, and is designed, among other things, to build support and influence opinion among members of society. It is most commonly associated with radical politics. Contemporary examples include Greenpeace and the various groups involved in animal rights and genetically modified crops.

direct current *alternating current*

directed energy weapons A technology under investigation for military purposes, using energy sources such as laser beams, particle beams, plasma beams, and microwave beams, all of which travel at the speed of light. Such weapons, potentially capable of shooting down missiles in space, are regarded as a vital component of the US Strategic Defense Initiative.

direct injection engine An engine working on the diesel cycle where fuel is injected directly into the combustion chamber formed in the cylinder between the top of the piston and the bottom of the cylinder head. This single *undivided* combustion chamber volume contrasts with a *divided* chamber combustion system, where the initial mixing of fuel and air takes place in one chamber, and combustion in a smaller connected chamber.

direction finder A device which determines the direction of an incoming radio signal, and which thus can be used as a navigation aid (eg the radiocompass used in ships and planes). A loop antenna is rotated until the maximum strength signal is received, giving the line of transmission of that signal. This operation is then repeated from a different position, thus enabling a navigator to pinpoint the position of the transmitting station. A receiving position can also be determined, by taking measurements from two transmitters.

Directoire Style A French style of furniture, and women's clothes, strictly belonging to the years 1795–9, but generally used to describe the furniture fashionable between the outbreak of the French Revolution and the introduction of the Empire Style. It was a restrained Neoclassical style strongly influenced by antique Greek art.

director The person who has the primary responsibility for making a theatrical production, cinema film, or television programme. The director approves the script, decides on the production team and artists, and controls the actors' performances through rehearsals. The director's visualization is also the basis for the designer. In films, when shooting is complete, it is the director's concept that the editor must realize in assembling picture and sound. In television, directors have similar responsibilities, but often work during shooting from the studio control suite, giving direct instructions to the floor manager and camera operators in the studio.

Director of Public Prosecutions *Crown Prosecution Service*

Directory The government of the First Republic of France (1795–9), established in the Thermidorian reaction to the Reign of Terror, with two legislative houses and a Council of five executive Directors. Its limited franchise and narrow social base added to the difficulties of rampant inflation. After political conspiracies from Left and Right, it was overthrown by the coup of 18 Brumaire (9–10 Nov 1799), bringing Napoleon to power.

dirigible A cigar-shaped, steerable, rigid-framed, fabric-covered airship. It is fitted with horizontal engines driving propellers which provide the forward thrust.

disaccharide [dIysakariyd] A carbohydrate consisting of two simple sugars joined together, condensed with the elimination of water. The most abundant in nature are *sucrose* (table sugar) which combines one glucose and one fructose molecule, and *lactose*, the sugar of milk, which is a combination of glucose and galactose. Fructose, glucose, and galactose are single-unit sugars, classed as **monosaccharides**.

disarmament Arms control which seeks to promote international security by a reduction in armed forces and/or weapons. The levels are set by agreement, and then opened up for inspection and enforcement by the other side or an independent inspectorate. General (ie applies to all countries) and comprehensive (ie applies to all categories of forces and weapons) disarmament was first attempted in 1927 and 1934 by the League of Nations, and by the United Nations in the 1950s, but such moves have not been successful. Disarmament is therefore limited to agreements between two or a few countries, and restricted to particular classes of weapons and troop levels. Problems arise in determining equivalences between different types of weapons held by different countries, and in verifying arms reduction treaties, especially in respect of nuclear weapons, largely because weapons can be re-assembled. There is also the possibility of nuclear disarmament involving no agreement with other countries, used as a means of encouraging others to follow. Such *unilateral* action may also be taken for moral reasons and as a means of diminishing the chances of being attacked, particularly in relation to nuclear and chemical weapons.

discant *descant*

Disciples of Christ *Churches of Christ*

disco dance A popular form of dance mainly for young people, originating in the late 1960s; the main feature of the accompanying music, which is played very loudly, is a heavy, rhythmic beat. Characteristically, people dance alone yet together in darkened discotheques and clubs. There are definite fashions such as the new romantic style, soul, punk, break dancing, robotics, and gothic style. It takes account of black music, particularly rapping, and heavy rock. The 1980s and 1990s saw the development of *rave* culture, in which large numbers of young people gathered in nightclubs or warehouses for disco dancing.

Discomycetes [diskohmIyseeteez] *cup fungus*

discounted cash flow (DCF) A notion used in business to assess if a capital expenditure proposal will generate an adequate return on the investment (ie sufficient profit). It is useful where projects are expected to last several years, recognizing the 'time value' of money – a given sum received next year is better than the same sum received in three years' time. The expected sums of cash flowing in and out are discounted back to their present value, using a discount rate which may be the rate at which a firm can borrow, adjusted for risk, or the return on the best available alternative project. If the present discounted value exceeds the initial cost of the project, then the investment is expected to be profitable.

discount house 1 In the UK, financial institutions which buy short-dated government stock (Treasury Bills) with money borrowed from commercial banks for very short periods. The difference between the borrowing rate and the lending rate provides the discount house with its profit.

2 A US term for a retail store which sells goods at a lower (**discounted**) price than is standard practice. When the use of the house is available only to members of a particular group (eg a trade union), it is a **closed-door discount house**. Such stores have also developed in other consumer countries, though not always with this label.

discourse analysis The systematic study of stretches of language, whether in speech or writing, to discover the regularities which govern them. An example is the use of grammatical criteria to link certain sequences of text, creating cohesion, as in the use of pronouns *He* and *it* in the sequence *John went to the play last night. He didn't think much of it*. This approach is usually distinguished from **conversation analysis**, the study of the sequential structure of real-life conversations, to understand the strategies used to link different strands and themes, and the ways in which people interact.

Discovery programme A NASA programme of Solar System exploration missions of relatively low cost and payload mass similar in nature to the astrophysics Explorers. **Discovery 1** Mars Pathfinder, launched Dec 1996, landed Jul 1997. **Discovery 2** NEAR (Near Earth Asteroid Rendevous mission), renamed NEAR-Shoemaker, launched Feb 1996, encountered 433 Eros Feb 2000. **Discovery 3** Lunar Prospector, launched Jan 1998, low polar orbits of Moon then controlled impact, Jul 1999. **Discovery 4** Stardust, launched Feb 1999 with encounter in Jan 2004, sample return from Comet Wild-2 [pronounced: vilt] planned for Jan 2006. **Discovery 5** Genesis, launched Aug 2001, solar wind sample return planned for 2004. **Discovery 6** Contour, tour of three comet nuclei launched Jul 2002, but lost soon after. **Discovery 7** Deep Impact, to rendezvous with comet P/Tempel 1, Jan 2004–Aug 2005. **Discovery 8** Messenger, to orbit Mercury, scheduled 2004–8;. **Discovery 9** Dawn, to visit the two oldest and most massive asteroids in the Solar System, 4 Vesta and 1 Ceres, 2006–2010 (for Vesta) and 2014 (for Ceres). **Discovery 10** Kepler survey, to look for planets around stars, launch scheduled for 2007.

discriminant A mathematical expression which shows whether a quadratic equation has real distinct roots, equal roots, or no real roots. The discriminant of the quadratic equation $ax^2 + bx + c = 0$ is $b^2 - 4ac$. If $b^2 - 4ac > 0$, the quadratic has real distinct roots; if $b^2 - 4ax = 0$, it has equal roots; and if $b^2 - 4ac < 0$, it has no real roots. The roots are then expressed in terms of complex numbers.

discus throw An athletics field event using a circular disc of wood with metal plates, weighing 2 kg/4·4 lb for men and 1 kg/2·2 lb for women. The competitor throws the discus with one hand from within the confines of a circle 2·5 m/8·2 ft in diameter, with the aim of achieving a greater distance than anyone else. In competition, six throws are allowed. The current world record for men is 74·08 m/243 ft, achieved by Jürgen Schult (1960–) of Germany in 1986 at Neubrandenburg, Germany; for women it is 76·80 m/252 ft, achieved by Gabriele Reinsch (1963–) of Germany in 1988 at Neubrandenburg, Germany.

disease frequency The analysis of disease in terms of (1) **morbidity** (the frequency of illness and disability) and **mortality** (the frequency of death), and (2) **prevalence** (the proportion of a particular group with the condition at any one moment) and **incidence** (the proportion of a particular group developing the condition over a specific period of time).

diseconomies *externalities*

disequilibrium A situation in which the plans made by various individuals and firms are mutually inconsistent. Firms may, for example, be planning to sell more carpets than customers are planning to buy. Inconsistent plans cannot all be carried out, and as a result some will be changed. An accumulation of unsold carpets will cause firms either to cut production or reduce prices. Because of continual changes in climate and techniques, geographical discoveries and political upsets, disequilibrium is usually widespread in the world economy. Disequilibrium leads to change, which may or may not lead to a new situation of equilibrium in which plans are consistent. *Comparative statics* is the part of economics which considers what would constitute a new equilibrium after any change. *Dynamics* is the part of economics which considers the process of change, and examines whether this will lead to an equilibrium.

dish In telecommunications using microwaves, an antenna having a concave reflecting surface which acts as a secondary radiator to concentrate the signal on the main pick-up element. In television broadcasting by satellite, the main transmission dish is 2–3 m/6–10 ft in diameter, but for domestic reception 30 cm/12 in may be sufficient.

disinfectant A material toxic to bacteria. Phenol (carbolic acid) was one of the earliest used, but is also toxic and corrosive to humans. Phenol derivatives are, however, used in chemical toilets.

disintermediation The practice of companies borrowing directly from the public rather than from financial intermediaries such as banks. This has the advantage of saving the administrative costs and profit margins of financial intermediaries. Disintermediation is used mainly by large firms, with good reputations and names which are household words. It suits relatively rich investors, who can afford to make loans to several firms to spread their risks. Smaller firms and poorer investors mostly prefer to deal with financial intermediaries, which enable investors to spread their holdings among a number of ultimate borrowers while avoiding the administrative costs of numerous small transactions.

disk *magnetic disk*

disk operating system *DOS*

dislocation (medicine) The displacement of a bone from its joint with another bone by force. Ligaments within or around the affected joint (*capsule*) binding adjacent bones together are torn or otherwise damaged. The result is pain, swelling, and deformity over the joint. Most dislocations can be restored manually.

dislocation (physics) *crystal defects*

Disney, Walt(er Elias) (1901–66) Artist, motion-picture animator, and film producer, born in Chicago, Illinois, USA. The son of a carpenter and schoolteacher, he studied cartoon drawing with a correspondence course. During World War 1 he worked as a lorry driver for the American Red Cross in France and Germany. After the war, he worked as a commercial artist before setting up a small studio with the artist U B Iwerks, in which he produced animated cartoons, his most famous character being Mickey Mouse (1928, with Disney providing the original voice). Among his early successes were the *Silly Symphonies* (from 1929) and the first full-length coloured cartoon film, *Snow White and the Seven Dwarfs* (1937). This was followed by *Pinocchio* (1940), *Dumbo* (1941), and *Fantasia* (1940), the first successful attempt to realize music in images. In 1948 he began his series of coloured nature films, including *The Living Desert* (1953). He also produced several swashbuckling colour films for young people, such as *Treasure Island* (1950) and *Robin Hood* (1952), and family films such as *Mary Poppins* (1964). In 1929 Walt and his brother Roy founded the **Walt Disney Company**, a US corporation that became the best-known distributor of child and adult entertainment in the 20th-c. In 1955 the company opened the **Disneyland** amusement park, one of the world's most famous, in Anaheim, California. A second and larger amusement complex, **Walt Disney World**, was opened near Orlando, Florida, in 1971. In 1983 an unrelated Japanese corporation opened **Tokyo Disneyland** near Tokyo. In 1992 the Disney Company itself completed the building of Euro Disneyland at Marne-la-Vallée, France, and in 1996 the Disney corporation acquired Capital Cities/ABC Inc., which owned the ABC television network. In 1995 the Disney corporation made cinematographic history with *Toy Story*, the first full-length computer-animated cartoon film. In 2003, worldwide celebrations marking the 75th birthday of cartoon legend Mickey Mouse were led by the Disney Company.

disorientation Confusion about time, place, or person. People who are disoriented may not know the date and time, where they are, or how to get from one point to another. They may forget their own name or other personal details.

Dispersion *Diaspora*

dispersion The spreading out of some quantity. Examples include the spread by diffusion and convection of ink introduced into water, or the separation of light into component colours upon passing through a prism.

displacement activity In biology, the performance of a particular behaviour pattern out of its normal context, as a result of the inability of an animal to respond instinctively to a stimulus. For example, a bird in an aggressive situation, in which there are simultaneous tendencies to attack and to flee, may preen its feathers as a displacement activity.

display A behaviour pattern or signal given by an animal, conveying a particular kind of information. It is often a stereotyped and genetically controlled pattern associated with courtship, in which physical characters (eg antlers, plumage) are used as a means of attracting a mate.

Disraeli, Benjamin, 1st Earl of Beaconsfield [dizraylee, bekuhnsfeeld] (1804–81) British statesman and twice prime minister (1868, 1874–80), born in London, UK, the eldest son of an Anglicized Jew, baptized in 1817. He made his early reputation as a novelist, publishing his first novel, *Vivian Grey*, in 1826. He is better known for his two political novels, *Coningsby* (1844) and *Sybil* (1846), which date from his period as a Romantic Tory, critical of industrial developments. He became leader of the 'Young England' movement which espoused these values, and came to prominence as a critic of Peel's free trade policies, especially the repeal of the Corn Laws (1845–6). Leader in the Commons of the Conservatives, after the Peelites left the Party, he was Chancellor of the Exchequer in Derby's minority governments of 1852 and 1858–9. While chancellor in the government of 1866–8, he piloted the 1867 Reform Bill through the Commons. He became prime minister on Derby's resignation in 1868, but was defeated soon afterwards in the general election. His second administration was notable both for diplomacy and social reform, though much of the latter only consolidated legislation begun under Gladstone. During his administration, Britain became half-owner of the Suez Canal (1875), and the queen assumed the title Empress of India (1876). His skilful diplomacy at the Congress of Berlin (1878) contributed to the preservation of European peace after conflict between the Russians and the Turks in the Balkans. Defeated in 1880 by Gladstone and the Liberals, he then effectively retired.

Dissenters Christians who separate themselves from the established Church or general religious belief of a country. In a wider sense, it is applied to those who dissent from the very principle of an established or national Church.

dissidents People who oppose the particular regime under which they live, often through peaceful means, and who as a result suffer discrimination and harassment from the authorities. Dissidents may, for example, lose their jobs or be banished to certain areas of the country. They tend to take a moral rather than an overtly political stance in their opposition.

dissociation In chemistry, separation into two or more parts; used especially of acids to describe their ionization in water. Stronger acids dissociate more completely than weak acids. **Association** is the combination of two or more particles; often used of interactions in solution.

dissolve A transition effect in motion pictures or video in which the whole image of a scene gradually disappears as it is replaced by the following scene. It is also termed a **lap dissolve**, as the pictures are overlapped, or a **mix**.

dissonance A psycho-acoustic phenomenon explicable on several levels. In terms of pure sound, two or more notes whose soundwaves peak out of phase (producing a discernible rapid 'beat') may be described as *dissonant*. The phenomenon may also be viewed as a conjunction of two or more notes producing a 'painful', 'harsh', or merely 'unpleasant' effect, or as a chord requiring resolution. This view is more subjective, and the degree of acceptable dissonance has varied at different periods of music history. The concept is nevertheless basic to the harmonic theory of most Western music up to the 20th-c, and many would argue that it is rooted in immutable laws about the nature of sound.

distalgesic [distaljeezik] The trade name of co-proximol, a compound of dextropropoxyphene hydrochloride and paracetamol, which is used to treat pain. Dextropropoxyphene is a morphine-like drug, but is less potent.

distance education Teaching people, usually at home or in their place of work, by means of correspondence units, radio, cassettes, telephone, television, microcomputer, electronic mail, or satellite, rather than through face-to-face contact. Often, though not always, a tutor may be involved to give advice or mark written work, either at a distance or through occasional meetings. Distance education has been particularly popular in sparsely populated areas, or for people not able to attend courses in schools and colleges. Institutions such as the British Open University and Open College have made extensive use of it.

distemper A viral disease of the dog (**canine distemper**) and ferret families, which may also spread to the seal family. It is a life-threatening disease, characterized by attacks of catarrh and severe neurological signs, such as fits. Vaccination is very effective.

distillation (chemistry) The chemical procedure of evaporating a liquid from one container and recondensing it into another container; first recorded in 8th-c China. In the purification of water, dissolved gases will vaporize and not recondense, while solids will not evaporate. Liquids of varying volatility can be separated. In particular, distillation of a mixture of water and ethanol will produce a vapour rich in ethanol (which is recondensed), and leave a residue rich in water and dissolved solids.

Distinguished Flying Cross (DFC) In the UK, a decoration instituted in 1918, awarded to officers and warrant-officers in the RAF for acts of gallantry performed while actually flying on active service. The ribbon is violet and white (equal diagonal stripes).

Distinguished Service Cross (DSC) In the UK, a decoration instituted in 1901 as the Conspicuous Service Cross, and renamed in 1914, awarded to warrant officers and officers below the rank of captain in the Royal Navy for acts of gallantry or devotion to duty, these ranks not being eligible for the DSO. The ribbon has equal stripes: black, white, black.

Distinguished Service Order (DSO) A military award in the UK, founded in 1886, which recognizes special service by officers of the army, navy, merchant navy, and airforce. The ribbon is red edged with blue.

distortion (lens) *aberrations* 1

distribution coefficient In chemistry, the ratio of the solubility of a solute in one solvent to that in another solvent which does not form a homogeneous mixture with the first; also known as the **partition coefficient**. Thus, a solute can be essentially removed from one solvent by several extractions with a second.

distributive operation In mathematics, an operation whose properties can be illustrated by the relation between multiplication and addition. Multiplication is said to be distributive over addition in the set of real numbers, for $a \times (b + c) = (a \times b) + (a \times c)$; but addition is not distributive over multiplication in the set of real numbers, for $a + (b \times c) \neq (a + b) \times (a + c)$. In general, an operation * is distributive over another operation # for all elements in a set S if $a*(b\#c) = a*b\#a*c$, for all a,b,c in S.

district attorney In the USA, the state or county prosecutor, who acts on information supplied by the police or a member of the public, and decides whether to initiate a prosecution; also called a **public prosecutor**, when employed by local government; an **attorney general**, when employed by the state; and a **US attorney**, when working federally. Although federal prosecutors have an interest in certain crimes, the district attorney is responsible for the majority of criminal prosecutions in the USA.

district council In the UK, the tier of local government below that of a county or region. There is a notable imprecision in the use of the term, both across countries and over time, with considerable variation in the area and population covered by a district.

district court The lowest criminal court in Scotland, since 1975, dealing with minor summary cases presided over by non-legally qualified justices of the peace, assisted by a legally qualified clerk, or in some cases, by a stipendiary magistrate. In the USA, district courts are the lowest federal courts, and deal with the majority of both criminal and civil cases arising out of federal rather than state legislation. In Canada, district courts are courts of first instance for more serious criminal offences, and have appellate jurisdiction over the magistrates' courts.

District of Columbia pop (2000e) 572 100; area 174 sq km/ 67 sq mi. Federal district in E USA, co-extensive with the city of Washington; established 1790–1 from land taken from Maryland and Virginia.

dittany An aromatic herb (*Dictamnus albus*), native to Europe; leaves pinnate with 9–13 leaflets; flowers 4-petalled, purple or white. It gives off a highly inflammable volatile oil, which in hot conditions can ignite and burn without harming the plant; hence its alternative name, **burning bush**. (Family: Rutaceae.)

diuretics [diyuretiks] Drugs which increase the production of urine, used in the treatment of fluid retention, heart failure, and high blood pressure. Certain other substances also have a diuretic effect, such as coffee.

diurnal tide A tidal cycle with one high and one low tide per lunar day (12 h 50 min). Also known as **daily tides**, they are common in the Gulf of Mexico and along parts of the coast of China.

diver A large diving bird native to N waters of the N hemisphere; eats mainly fish; only comes ashore to breed; plumage with fine contrasting patterns, usually black and white; also known in the USA as the **loon**. (Genus: *Gavia*, 5 species. Family: Gaviidae.)

divergence (linguistics) *convergence* (linguistics)

diversification The tendency of firms to seek to make a variety of products and sell them in a variety of markets. Diversification has two main advantages. It reduces risk, since with many products and markets it is less likely that they will all do badly at the same time than if activity was highly concentrated on a few products or markets. It also allows for economies of scope, whereby equipment, know-how, or workers already needed for one purpose can be used for another at little extra cost. However, if diversification is carried too far, a firm may move into areas where it realizes too late that it lacks the technical or management skills needed to cope with the problems that will arise. Similar arguments for and against diversification apply to a country's choice of export products and trading partners.

diverticulosis A disorder of the large bowel that affects older people. Small pouches form in the lining of the bowel that penetrate the muscle coat of the gut at points of weakness. Many patients suffer no symptoms, but the pouches are prone to inflammation (**diverticulitis**). This results in abdominal pain and may lead to complications including bleeding, abscesses, and narrowing or obstruction of the colonic canal. A high fibre diet helps to prevent the condition by helping the movement of bowel contents.

divertimento A light musical composition. Mozart and his contemporaries wrote divertimentos in five or more movements for an ensemble of soloists.

dividend An allocation of the profits of an enterprise to its shareholders. Companies may pay out all profits as dividends, retain a proportion, or pay out nothing. There is no legal obligation to pay; the distribution depends on the level of profits and the company's financial needs. **Dividend cover** is the profit per share divided by the dividend per share; this shows the proportion of profit distributed. **Dividend yield** is the dividend per share divided by the current share price; this equates with the interest payable on other savings. Dividends are also sometimes paid, out of reserves accumulated from past profits, when there have been no profits, but management is confident about the future, and wishes to retain the confidence of the public and shareholders.

divination A term applied to several traditional methods of attempting to acquire information by alleged paranormal means. The information to be interpreted is conveyed by some physical source, such as dowsing or palm reading. Divinatory practices are found in many cultures, both past and present.

Divine Right of Kings The concept of the divinely-ordained authority of monarchs, widely held in the mediaeval and early modern periods in part as a reaction to papal intrusions into secular affairs. It is often associated with the absolutism of Louis XIV of France and the assertions of the Stuarts, Charles I being executed for refusing to accept parliamentary control of his policies.

diving Any method of descending under water. The most common form in competition is jumping from an elevated board into a swimming pool. The board can be rigid or sprung, and competitors perform a variety of twists and somersaults. Marks are gained for style, and for successfully completing the dive, based on the level of difficulty of each attempt. Springboard events take place from a board 3 m (9 ft 10 in) above the water; platform diving is from a rigid board 10 m (30 ft 5 in) above the water.

diving beetle A large, shiny beetle found in aquatic habitats as adults and larvae; adult up to 38 mm/1½ in long; traps air beneath wing cases for breathing under water; hindlegs paddle-like; predator of insect larvae, molluscs, and small fishes. (Order: Coleoptera. Family: Dytiscidae.)

diving duck A duck which obtains food by diving beneath the water surface. There are two groups: the inland species favours shallow lakes, and eats vegetation; the marine species (**sea ducks**) dives deeper, and eats fish and invertebrates. The name is sometimes restricted to ducks of genera *Aythya* and *Netta*.

Divisional Court A court in England and Wales presided over by at least two judges from one of the divisions of the High Court. One of its functions is to hear certain appeals; another is to exercise supervisory jurisdiction over inferior bodies. Divisional courts are distinct from the Divisions of the High Court.

Divisionism In painting, a technique (sometimes called **Pointillism**) whereby small patches or spots of pure colour are placed close together so that they mix not on the palette or canvas, but in the eye of the beholder. It was developed systematically by some of the French Postimpressionists, notably Seurat, and designated **Neoimpressionism** by the French critic Félix Fénéon (1861–1944).

division of labour The system by which production is carried out by co-operation between individuals who each perform different functions. This has two main advantages over a system in which individuals are self-sufficient. First, individuals differ in their natural abilities: some are strong, some are intelligent, some have quick reactions, and others are patient; each type can be allocated tasks suited to their abilities. Second, specialization on a limited range of tasks makes it worthwhile providing specific training for them, and experience allows expertise to develop. The disadvantage of too minute division

Djibouti

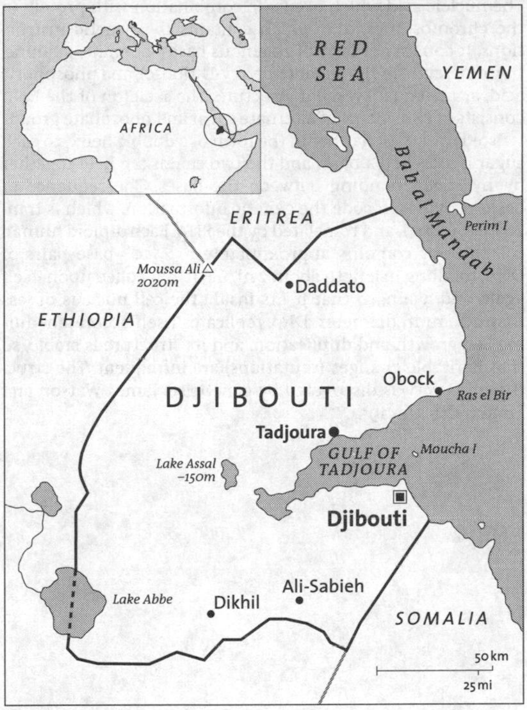

☐ International Airport

[jibootee], official name **Republic of Djibouti**, Arabic **Jumhouriya Djibouti**

Local name Jumhouriyya Djibouti

Timezone GMT +3

Area 23 200 km²/8958 sq mi

Population total (2002e) 473 000

Status Republic

Date of independence 1977

Capital Djibouti

Language Arabic (official)

Ethnic groups Somali (47%), Afar (20%), Arab (mostly Yemeni) (6%), European (4%), other refugees (10%)

Religions Muslim (94%), Christian (Roman Catholic 4%, Protestant 1%, Orthodox 1%)

Physical features Located in NE Africa; series of plateaux dropping down from mountains to flat, low-lying, rocky desert; fertile coastal strip around the Gulf of Tadjoura; highest point, Moussa Ali, rising to 2020 m/6627 ft in the N.

Climate Semi-arid climate, with hot season (May–Sep); very high temperatures on coastal plain all year round; average temperatures 26°C (Jan), 36°C (Jul); slightly lower humidity and temperatures in interior highlands; low rainfall; average annual rainfall 130 mm/5 in.

Currency 1 Djibouti Franc (DF, DjFr) = 100 centimes

Economy Crop-based agriculture possible only with irrigation; livestock-raising among nomadic population; some fishing on coast; port of Djibouti provides an important transit point for Red Sea trade, particularly for Ethiopia; small industrial sector.

GDP (2002e) $619 mn, per capita $1300

Human Development Index (2002) 0·445

History French colonial interest in mid-19th-c; annexed by France as French Somaliland, 1896; French Overseas Territory, following World War 2; French Territory of the Afars and the Issas, 1967; independence, 1977. Political parties combined in 1979 to form People's Progress Assembly (RPP) as single ruling party; overwhelming majority voted in favour of a multi-party constitution, 1992; governed by a President, a Legislative Chamber, an executive Prime Minister, and a Council.

Head of State
1977–99 Hassan Gouled Aptidon
1999– Ismail Omar Guelleh

Head of Government
1977–8 Abdallah Mohammed Kamil
1978–2001 Barkat Gourad Hamadou
2001– Dileila Mohamed Dileila

of labour is that people may lack flexibility if it is necessary to change the type of work they do, and may lack motivation because they cannot see how their job fits in to the overall scheme.

divorce The termination by court order of a valid marriage, the criteria for which vary greatly between countries and jurisdictions. English and Scottish courts now recognize only one ground for divorce: the irretrievable breakdown of marriage. In England and Wales, the Family Law Act (1996) which reformed the law on divorce, is being implemented gradually. Its aim is to remove the acrimony of divorce proceedings by banishing the idea of fault. No divorce will be made until the welfare of the children and financial arrangements have been settled. Either or both parties file a *statement of marital breakdown*, after which a period of between 9 and 15 months follows, with the emphasis on reconciliation. If this fails, the applicant applies for a *Divorce Order*, replacing the old decrees nisi and absolute. Most US jurisdictions recognize no-fault divorce based on incompatibility, irreconcilable differences, living separate and apart for a fixed time (usually 1–3 years), or mutual consent to divorce; however, the grounds for divorce vary considerably. The number of divorces has increased steadily since the 1960s.

Diwali [deewahlee] The Hindu festival of lights, held in October or November (Asvina K 15) in honour of Lakshmi, goddess of wealth and luck, and Rama, an incarnation of the god Vishnu; lamps are lit and gifts exchanged. Sikhs associate Diwali with the sixth Guru's release from prison. Diwali is also a Jain religious festival.

Dix, Dorothea (Lynde) (1802–87) Reformer and nurse, born in Hampden, Maine, USA. She became a teacher, and in 1821 established her own school in Boston, running it successfully until 1834, when a tubercular illness forced her to give it up. She then dedicated herself to the study of conditions in insane asylums, prisons, and almshouses, travelling over 10 000 mi on her investigations (1842–5), and initiating several reforms. In 1861 she became superintendent of women nurses for the federal government, overseeing the recruitment, training, and placement of some 2000 women who cared for the Union war-wounded. After the war she resumed her work among the insane, and travelled widely in Europe and Japan.

Dixieland A style of jazz associated with the 'classic' New Orleans school, and especially with white musicians who based their music on that of the Original Dixieland Jazz Band in the early 1920s.

Djakarta *Jakarta*

Djem, el- [el jem] The world's most intact example of a Roman amphitheatre, situated in the present-day village of el-Djem in W Tunisia; a world heritage monument. It is one of the few surviving relics of the ancient city of Thysdrus, and had a capacity for 35 000 people.

Djemila [jemila] The former Roman garrison of Cuicul in N Algeria; a world heritage site. Founded in the late 1st-c AD, the settlement spread and flourished in the 3rd–4th-c, but

DNA or deoxyribonucleic acid

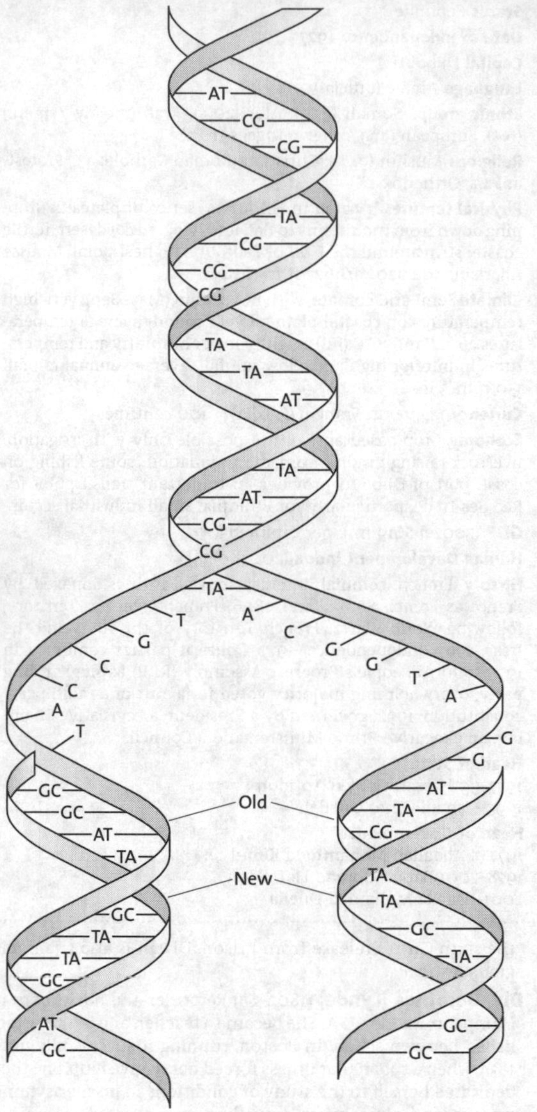

The nucleic acid which occurs in combination with protein in the chromosomes, and which contains the genetic instructions. It consists of four nitrogenous bases (adenine, guanine, thymine, cytosine), a sugar (2-deoxy-D-ribose), and phosphoric acid, arranged in a regular structure. The skeleton of the DNA consists of two chains of alternate sugar and phosphate groups twisted round each other in the form of a double helix; to each sugar is attached a base; and the two chains are held together by hydrogen bonding between the bases. The sequence of bases provides in code the genetic information, which is transcribed, edited, and translated by the RNA. Each diploid human cell nucleus contains approximately 6×10^9 base pairs of DNA, totalling in length about 2 m/6·6 ft, but coiled upon itself again and again, so that it fits inside the cell nucleus of less than 10 μm in diameter. DNA replicates itself accurately during cell growth and duplication, and its structure is stable, so that heritable changes (mutations) are infrequent. The structure of DNA was discovered by geneticists James Watson and Francis Crick in 1953.

had declined by the 6th-c. The ruins include temples, forums, thermal baths, and Christian basilicas.

Djibouti (city) [jibootee] 11°36N 43°08E, pop (2000e) 380 600. Free-port capital of Djibouti, NE Africa; on a coral peninsula 565 km/351 mi NE of Addis Ababa (Ethiopia); NE terminus of railway from Addis Ababa; built 1886–1900 in Arab style; official port of Ethiopia, 1897 (trade declining in recent years); airport; commercial port trade, fishing, tourism.

Djibouti (country) *p.463*

Djilas, Milovan [jeelas] (1911–95) Yugoslav politician and writer, born in Montenegro, Republic of Yugoslavia. Originally a friend of Tito, he rose in the government as a result of his wartime exploits as a partisan. He was later discredited and imprisoned as a result of outspoken criticism of the Communist system as practised in Yugoslavia, but was released from prison under amnesty at the end of 1966. His books include *The New Class* (1957) and *Conversations with Stalin* (1962), as well as a number of novels, short stories, and political memoirs.

DNA or **deoxyribonucleic acid** *see panel*

DNA profiling A biochemical process used both to determine paternity and to identify criminals from human material left at the scene of a crime; developed in 1984 by Alec Jeffreys (1950–) of Leicester University, UK. An individual's DNA profile is argued to be as distinctive as fingerprints, with the statistical possibility of two people (other than identical twins) having the same genetic makeup being very remote (in some estimations, as little as 1 in 738 trillion). DNA is found in blood as well as in many other body fluids and tissue, including semen, vaginal fluid, hair, skin, and fingernails. The process involves isolating DNA patterns using enzymes to break up the sample before passing an electric current through the material and exposing it to X-ray film, eventually producing an *autorad*, or DNA profile. Autorads can thus be compared to show whether a suspect in a crime is the actual offender or to show the genetic relationship between two or more people. Although some questions have been raised concerning the reliability of the procedure (eg relating to human error in the retrieval of tissue samples), DNA profiling is now regularly used by the police and the prosecution in criminal cases, as well as by courts in paternity actions and the Home Office in immigration disputes.

Dnepr, River [dneeper], Eng **Dnieper**, ancient **Borysthenes** River in W Russia; rises in the S Valdayskaya Vozvyshennost range, flows S and W past Smolensk, then makes a wide bend through the Ukraine to enter the Black Sea at Kherson; length, c.2200 km/1400 mi; third longest river in Europe; water from the Kakhovka reservoir irrigates large areas of the lower Dnepr basin and the plain of N Crimea.

Dnepropetrovsk [duhnyepropyetrofsk], formerly **Ekaterinoslav** (to 1926) 48°29N 35°00E, pop (2000e) 1 168 000. Port capital of Dnepropetrovskaya oblast, Ukraine, on R Dnepr; founded in 1783 on the site of a Cossack village; airport; railway; university (1918); iron and steel, machines, chemicals, foodstuffs; cathedral (1830–5).

Dnestr, River *Dniester, River*

Dniester, River [dneester], also **Dnestr**, Pol **Dniestr** River in Ukraine and Moldova, rising in the Carpathian Mts; flows generally SE to enter the Dnestrovskiy Liman, a N inlet of the Black Sea, SW of Odessa; length, 1400 km/870 mi; freezes over (Dec–Mar); formed the USSR–Romanian border, 1918–40.

Dobell, Sir William [dohbel] (1899–1970) Portrait painter, born in Newcastle, New South Wales, SE Australia. He studied at the Julian Ashton Art School in Sydney, and at the Slade School of Art, London. Returning to Sydney, he worked during World War 2 in a camouflage unit with other artists. His controversial portrait of Joshua Smith won the Archibald Prize in 1944. Later work included a portrait of the then prime minister of Australia, Sir Robert Menzies. He left all his estate to establish the art foundation which bears his name.

Doberman(n) pinscher [dohberman pinsher] A breed of dog, developed c.1900 by a German dog-catcher, Herr Dobermann, who crossbred stray dogs, intending to produce the meanest, most vicious dog possible; subsequently crossbred with greyhounds and terriers, and now less vicious; popular guard dogs; large, lean; short brown or black and tan coat; long neck and muzzle; pendulous ears.

dobsonfly A large, soft-bodied insect; adult wingspan up to 16 cm/6¼ in, but flight clumsy and fluttering; found near streams; larvae voracious predators, found in streams and under stones. (Order: Megaloptera. Family: Corydalidae, c.200 species.)

Docetism [dositizm] The belief, arising in early Christianity, that the natural body of Jesus Christ was only apparent (Gr *dokeo*, 'appear, seem') and not real, thereby stressing the divinity of Christ and denying any real physical suffering on his part. It was especially prevalent amongst 2nd-c gnostics, but was also perhaps a problem encountered in 2 *John* 7.

dock (botany) A perennial N temperate herb with strong roots; leaves large, oval, oblong or spear-shaped; flowers tiny, in long, loose, branched inflorescences, three sepals, three petals; fruit a 3-sided nut enclosed in papery, often reddish valves. Some species are persistent weeds. (Genus: *Rumex*, c.200 species. Family: Polygonaceae.)

dock (shipping) A basin in which ships may load cargo, take stores, or be repaired, with or without gates depending on the tidal range. Exceptionally the term has been applied to a straight length of quay side, such as the New Docks (1934) at Southampton, UK. A **dry dock** (or **graving dock**) is one in which the ship can be placed on blocks as the water is pumped out, so that work can be performed on the underwater part of the hull.

Docklands An area of E London, UK along the R Thames, formerly of great poverty, which attracted new housing and office developments in the 1980s. It includes the Canary Wharf tower, the tallest building in Europe. There is a new Docklands airport, and a railway connecting the area with the City (the Docklands Light Railway).

Doctors Without Borders *Médecins Sans Frontières*

Doctor Who A science-fiction series first broadcast on BBC television in 1963. Ten actors have portrayed the character of the Doctor: in the television series these were William Hartnell (1963–6), Patrick Troughton (1966–9), Jon Pertwee (1970–4), Tom Baker (1974–81), Peter Davison (1982–4), Colin Baker (1984–6), and Sylvester McCoy (1987–9). In addition, Peter Cushing appeared as the Doctor in two films for television in 1965 and 1966, and Richard Hurndall took the role of the first Doctor in a special production, *The Five Doctors* (1983), after the death of Hartnell. The series came to an end in 1989, but a further feature film was released in 1996, starring Paul McGann, and a new television series starring Christopher Eccleston is planned for 2005. There is a worldwide cult following, the fans being known as **Whovians**.

document description language A methodology which enables documents to be handled in a consistent way when being electronically processed, through the use of special codes (*tags*). The first widely used system, **HTML** (**HyperText Mark-up Language**), made use of tags indicating which kind of document element (eg main heading, sub-heading, figure caption) a particular section of text happens to be. A browser uses the tags in order to be able to decide how to present the document to the user. **HTTP** (**HyperText Transfer Protocol**) is a protocol for locating documents stored on the World Wide Web and transferring the documents over the Internet from the Web site to the browser. **XML** (**Extensible Mark-up Language**) is a development of HTML which allows much more varied elements (eg video sequences) to be built into Web documents for transfer over the Internet.

dodder A parasitic annual reduced to a reddish, thread-like stem bearing clusters of tiny white or pink flowers; native to temperate and tropical regions. The germinating seed produces a short-lived root and a twining stem which moves in search of a host. When contact is made, the root atrophies, further contact with the soil being unnecessary. The parasite stem produces haustoria which penetrate that of the host, drawing off water and nutrients. A wide variety of host plants are attacked, including crop plants such as hops and flax, which can be severely damaged. (Genus: *Cuscuta*, 170 species. Family: Convolvulaceae.)

Dodecanese [dohdekaneez], Gr **Sporádhes** area 2000 sq km/1000 sq mi. Group of 12 main islands and several islets in the SE Aegean Sea, Greece, off SW coast of Turkey; part of Greece since 1947; chief islands include Cos, Patmos, and Rhodes, the largest island, ancient sites include the Asklepieion on Cos, the Acropolis of Rhodes, and the Acropolis of Lindos; several major tourist centres.

Dodgson, Charles Lutwidge *Carroll, Lewis*

dodo An extinct bird related to pigeons; native to high forests in Mascarene I, E of Madagascar; turkey-like with large bill and rudimentary wings. The probable dates of extinction were: the **common dodo** (*Raphus cucullatus = Didus ineptus*) from Mauritius, 1665–70; the **Rodriguez solitaire** (*Pezophaps solitaria*), c.1761; and the **Réunion solitaire** (*Ornithaptera solitaria*), 1715–20. The **white dodo** (*Victoriornis imperialis*), supposedly from Réunion I, is not generally accepted as a valid species. (Family: Raphidae, 3 species.)

Dodoma [dohdohma] 6°10S 35°40E, pop (2000e) 270 000. Capital of Tanzania, E Africa; altitude 1120 m/3674 ft; replaced Dar es Salaam as capital in 1974, after a 10-year transfer plan; administration, trade in live and stuffed birds.

Doe, Samuel (1951–90) Liberian soldier and president (1985–90), born in Tuzin, Grand Gedeh Co, Liberia. He joined the army in 1969 and became a sergeant in 1975. In 1980 he led an assault on the presidential palace in which President William Tolbert was killed, thus ending the rule of the Americo-Liberians who had been in office since the 19th-c. Other members and associates of the deposed government were publicly executed. He became commander-in-chief of the armed forces, head of state as chairman of the military People's Redemption Council (1981), and was narrowly elected president in 1985 in a promised return to civilian government. Following the outbreak of civil war in 1990, he was captured, tortured, and murdered.

Doenitz or **Dönitz, Karl** [**doe**nits] (1891–1980) German naval commander, born in Grünau, NE Germany. He entered the submarine service of the German Navy in 1916, and became a staunch advocate of U-boat warfare. He planned Hitler's U-boat fleet, was made its commander in 1936, and in 1943 became commander-in-chief of the German navy. Becoming führer on the death of Hitler, he was responsible for the final surrender to the Allies, and in 1946 was sentenced to 10 years' imprisonment for war crimes.

dog A carnivorous mammal (*Canis familiaris*), probably evolved from the wolf; first animal to be domesticated; c.400 modern domestic breeds (though classifications vary, with some recognizing far fewer breeds), sometimes classed as *working*, *sporting*, *hound*, *terrier*, *non-sporting*, and *toy*. The name is also used for some mammals of other families (eg the *prairie dog*). The male of several mammal species is called a *dog*, the female a *bitch*, and the young a *pup*. (Family: Canidae, 1 species.)

dog daisy *ox-eye daisy*

Doge's Palace [dohzh] The residence of the former Doges of Venice. Although parts of the structure date from the 12th-c, the loggias and marble facade of the present-day building are Renaissance additions. It is the repository of many art treasures.

dogfish Small, bottom-living shark found from Norway to the Mediterranean, and common around British coasts; length to 75 cm/30 in, skin very rough; sold in shops as **rock eel**, **rock salmon**, or **huss**. The name is also used for several other small species of sharks.

Dogger Bank A large sandbank forming the shallowest part of the North Sea, c.17–37 m/ 55–120 ft deep, 250 km/155 mi N of the Norfolk coast, England. It is an important breeding ground for North Sea fish.

Dogme [**dog**muh] A set of rules for the making of feature films. Formulated in the mid-1990s by four Danish film directors, **Lars von Trier** (1956–), **Thomas Vinterberg** (1969–), **Kristian Levring** (1957–), and **Søren Kragh-Jacobsen** (1947–) in a document entitled *Dogme 95*, it set out a 'vow of chastity', made up of 10 sections which prescribe strict methods of film-making that run counter to modern cinematic practices. Its methods include filming only in real time, always on location (rather than in a studio), using a hand-held camera and natural light, doing without all superficial action (for example, gratuitous sex or violence), using the 35 mm format, doing without a musical score, creating the sound at the same time as the images (that is, without subsequent dubbing), shooting the film where the story takes place, using no flashbacks, props, or make-up, and not crediting the director on screen. Dogme films include *Festen* (1998, The Celebration, Vinterberg), *Idioterne* (1998, The Idiots, von Trier), and *The King is Alive* (2000, Levring).

dog's mercury A perennial (*Mercurialis perennis*), native to Europe and Asia, 15–40 cm/6–15 in, with creeping rhizomes; leaves opposite, elliptical, toothed; flowers tiny, greenish, with three sepals, males forming long drooping spikes, female in clusters; very early-flowering herb, often dominating woodland floors. (Family: Euphorbiaceae.)

Dog Star *Sirius*

dog's tooth violet A perennial (*Erythronium dens-canis*), 10–15 cm/4–6 in, producing corms, native to woods in Europe and Asia; not a violet; leaves oval, bluish, marbled with brownish-purple; flowers 5 cm/2 in diameter, red-purple or white, solitary, drooping, six perianth-segments curled back to form a Turk's cap; also called **trout lily**. (Family: Liliaceae.)

dog violet A species of violet with short, non-creeping stems and bluish-violet flowers (*Viola riviniana*), native to Europe; in contrast to the related **sweet violet**, it is devoid of scent. (Family: Violaceae.)

dogwood A deciduous shrub or small tree (*Cornus sanguinea*), growing to 6 m/20 ft, native to Europe, SW Asia, and North America; leaves oval, in opposite pairs, turning purple in autumn, veins prominent; flowers small, numerous, in flat-topped clusters; petal-like bracts, white, pink, red; berries black. Related ornamental species from China and North America have crimson young stems. (Family: Cornaceae.)

Doha [**doh**ha], Arabic **ad-Dawhah** 25°25N 51°32E, pop (2000e) 281 000. Seaport capital of Qatar, on the E coast of the Qatar Peninsula, in the Persian Gulf; reclamation of West Bay has created New Doha; chief commercial and communications centre; airport; university; oil refining, shipping, engineering, foodstuffs, refrigeration plant, construction materials; old Turkish fort (1850).

Doherty, Peter (Charles) [**do**kertee] (1940–) Immunologist, born in Brisbane, Queensland, NE Australia. He studied veterinary science at the universities of Queensland and Edinburgh, and with Zinkernagel carried out research into the immune system, using laboratory mice, at the John Curtin School of Medical Research at the Australian National University, Canberra, in the 1970s. In 1988 he moved to the St Jude Children's Research Hospital at the University of Tennessee. He shared the Nobel Prize for Physiology or Medicine in 1996 for his contribution to the discovery of how the immune system recognizes virus-infected cells – research which was first reported in 1974. He also shared the Paul Erlich Prize (1983) and the Albert Lasker Medical Research Award (1995) for this research.

Dohnányi, Ernst von [**doh**nanyee], Hung **Ernő** (1877–1960) Composer and pianist, born in Pozsony, Hungary (now Bratislava, Slovak Republic). He studied at Budapest, travelled widely as a pianist, and taught at Berlin (1908–15). He had some success with his opera *The Tower of Voivod* (1922), but is best known for his piano compositions, especially *Variations on a Nursery Song* (1913), for piano and orchestra. He was musical director of Hungarian radio (1931), and in 1948 left Hungary as an exile, living in Argentina and (from 1949) the USA, where he was composer in residence at Florida State University.

Doisy, Edward (Adelbert) [**doy**zee] (1893–1986) Biochemist, born in Hume, Illinois, USA. He studied at Harvard, and was director of the department of biochemistry at St Mary's Hospital, St Louis (1924–65). In collaboration with US embryologist **Edgar Allen** (1892–1943) he conducted research on reproduction and hormones. In 1939 he isolated two forms of the coagulant agent vitamin K, and shared the Nobel Prize for Physiology or Medicine in 1943.

Dolby system The first effective and still the most widely used noise reduction system, devised originally for professional tape recording (**Dolby A**) by Dr Ray Dolby (1933–) in the mid-1960s. He adapted the circuitry to a simpler form (**Dolby B**) widely incorporated in cassette tape players. **Dolby C** followed in the 1980s, giving noise reduction of up to 20 dB and over a wider frequency range. The removal of background hiss, which originated in the granular nature of the tape coating, is achieved by artificially raising the quiet signals most affected and restoring them to their original levels on replay, simultaneously reducing hiss by c.10 dB.

Dolci, Danilo [**dohl**chee] (1924–97) Social worker, 'the Gandhi of Sicily', born in Trieste, NE Italy. He qualified as an architect, but decided to fight poverty in Sicily, building schools and community centres in the poorest areas, helped by social workers from many European countries. Opposition to his work led to his imprisonment on two occasions. Although not a Communist, he was awarded the Lenin Peace Prize in 1956.

Doldrums Traditionally a zone of cloudy, calm conditions, with light westerly winds associated with the low atmospheric pressure of the intertropical convergence zone in oceanic areas. The region is bounded to the N by the NE trade winds, and to the S by the SE trade winds; however, satellite observations have shown that the region is one of easterly winds, and that it is discontinuous. Formerly, sailing ships would often get becalmed in the Doldrums. This word has since passed into general usage to express listless despondency.

Dole, Bob, popular name of **Robert Joseph Dole** (1923–) US Republican politician, born in Russell, Kansas, USA, he studied at Kansas and Washburn Municipal Universities. A senator for Kansas, and for several years the minority leader in the Senate, he sought the Republican nomination for the presidency in 1980 and 1988. He became majority leader in the Senate in 1994, following Republican gains in the 1994 elections. He resigned in 1996 to campaign for the presidency, but was defeated by Bill Clinton. He is married to Elizabeth Dole.

Dole, Elizabeth, *née* **Hanford**, popularly known as **Liddy Dole** (1936–) US politician, born in Salisbury, North Carolina, USA. After graduating from Harvard Law School, she entered government service. When she married Senator Robert Dole in 1975, she became a Republican. Following periods with Ronald Reagan as Secretary of Transportation (1983–7), and with George Bush as Secretary of Labor (1989–90), she became president of the American Red Cross in 1990. Her effective campaigning for her husband's presidential bid in 1996 made her a potential candidate in 2000, and early in 1999 she left the Red Cross to campaign for the Republican nomination (withdrawing in October). She won a Senate seat in the mid-term elections in 2002.

dolerite [**dol**eriyt] A medium-grained basic igneous rock, dark-green in colour and composed mainly of plagioclase feldspar and pyroxene crystals. It is the common rock of dykes and sills throughout the world.

dollar ($) A unit of currency in the USA, Canada, Australia, New Zealand, and certain other countries. The US dollar is the world's most important currency. Much international trade is conducted in it, and prices of goods and commodities are often quoted in it (notably, the price of oil). Also, over half the official reserves of countries are held in US dollars. US domestic economic policy affects the value of the dollar which, in turn, affects the economies of other nations.

Dollfuss, Engelbert [**dol**foos] (1892–1934) Austrian statesman and chancellor (1932–4), born in Texing, C Austria. He studied at Vienna and Berlin, and became leader of the Christian Socialist Party. As chancellor, he suspended parliamentary government, drove the Socialists into revolt, and militarily crushed them (Feb 1934). In July 1934, an attempted Nazi putsch in Vienna culminated in his assassination.

dolly A mobile platform for a film or video camera and its operator, allowing forward and sideways movement of the point of view during the action of the scene in addition to the pan and tilt of the camera itself. A **dolly shot** is a scene planned to make use of such camera movement.

dolmen *chambered tomb*

Dolmetsch, (Eugène) Arnold (1858–1940) Musician, born in Le Mans, NW France. He is known for the revival of interest in early music and musical instruments, especially the recorder. He established workshops at his home in Haslemere, Surrey, and promoted festivals on early music there from 1925, the Arnold Dolmetsch Foundation dating from 1928. He became a British citizen in 1931. After his death, his family continued and expanded the Haslemere musical tradition, under the direction of his youngest son, Carl.

Dolmetsch, Carl (1911–97) Musician, born in Fontenay-sous-Bois, NC France, the son of Arnold Dolmetsch. He became an expert in early instruments, like his father, studying the violin, and playing all the instruments in the viol family. He proved to be a recorder virtuoso, for nearly 60 years working in partnership with his accompanist, **Joseph Saxby** (who also died in 1997), and became musical director of the Society of Recorder Players (1937–97). He took over the direction of the Haslemere Festival on his father's death in 1940, introduced workshops for children in 1948, and began an international summer school in 1970.

dolomite [**dol**omiyt] A mineral formed from calcium magnesium carbonate $(Ca,Mg)CO_3$. The term is also applied to sedimentary carbonate rocks with more than 50% dolomite. It is usually formed by the alteration of calcite $(CaCO_3)$.

Dolomites [**dol**omiyts], Ital **Alpi Dolomitiche** Alpine mountain range in NE Italy; limestone formation of jagged outlines and isolated peaks, rising to 3342 m/10 964 ft at Marmolada; wooded upper slopes and upland meadows, lower levels arable land and pasture; major area for walking, climbing, winter sports, and health resorts; centres include Cortina d'Ampezzo and San Martino di Castrozza.

dolphin A small, toothed whale. The name is usually used for species with a long slender snout (or 'beak') and streamlined body (though in some dolphins the beak is almost absent). Species with less streamlined bodies and blunt snouts are usually called **porpoises** (especially in genera *Phocoena*, *Phocoenoides*, and *Neophocoena*); worldwide. The name is also used for **fresh water** (or **river**) **dolphins** (family: Platanistidae, 6 species from S Asia and South America), which have a very long beak used for probing in mud for food. Dolphins have become popular display animals in recent years (especially in **dolphinariums**), on account of their ready playfulness, graceful swimming, acrobatic ability, and evident intelligence. (Family: Delphinidae, c.28 species.)

dolphinarium *aquarium*

dolphinfish Large, predatory, marine fish widespread in tropical and temperate seas; feeds at surface on fish and crustaceans; length up to 1·5 m/5 ft, greenish-blue above, underside silver; prized as sport fish and also exploited commercially in some areas. (Genus: *Coryphaena*. Family: Coryphaenidae.)

Dom 46°06N 7°52E. Highest mountain entirely in Switzerland, rising to 4545 m/14 911 ft NE of Zermatt in the Pennine Alps.

Domagk, Gerhard (Johannes Paul) [**doh**mak] (1895–1964) Biochemist, born in Lagow, Germany. He studied at Kiel, and taught at Greifswald and Münster, before becoming director of the I G Farbenindustrie Laboratory for Experimental Pathology and Bacteriology in 1927. He discovered the chemotherapeutic properties of sulphanilamide, and thus ushered in a new age in chemotherapy. In 1939, on instruction from the German government, he refused the Nobel Prize for Physiology or Medicine.

domain name system The system which enables recognizable names (such as *bbc.co.uk*) to be associated with Internet locations (Internet Protocol numbers) that serve as routing addresses on the Internet. It is a directory organized in a hierarchy of levels, with each level separated by a dot. The **top-level domain** is the name which occurs at the top of the Internet domain-name hierarchy – the rightmost element of a domain name. Examples include country codes (eg *uk* in *bbc.co.uk*) or non-geographical generic codes (eg *org* in *www.icann.org*). Most US addresses, for historical reasons, do not end in a country code. Within countries, regional administrators control what **second-level domains** are recognized. These relate to different types of activity, such as *co* for commercial enterprises and *ac* for academic establishments.

dome Any curved termination to a building which is circular in plan; also called a **cupola**. The classic Renaissance dome is a slightly pointed hemisphere, as in St Peter's, Rome. Other shapes range from the flatter dish of the Pantheon in Rome to the bulging onion of St Mark's, Venice. The word also describes the whole architectural ensemble, including the cylindrical area (*drum*) below and the *lantern* above the actual dome itself.

Domenichino [domeni**kee**noh], originally **Domenico Zampieri** (1581–1641) Painter, born in Bologna, N Italy. He trained under Ludovico Carracci and Denis Calvaert, and joined the Bolognese artists in Rome. His masterpiece is 'The Last Communion of St Jerome' (1614) in the Vatican.

Dome of the Rock A masterpiece of Islamic architecture completed in AD 691 on Mt Moriah, Jerusalem. The shrine, which is built on an octagonal plan and surmounted by a gilded wooden cupola, encloses the holy rock where, according to tradition, Mohammed ascended to heaven and Abraham prepared to sacrifice Isaac.

Domesday Book [**doomz**day] The great survey of England S of the Ribble and Tees rivers (London and Winchester excepted), compiled in 1086 on the orders of William the Conqueror;

Dominica

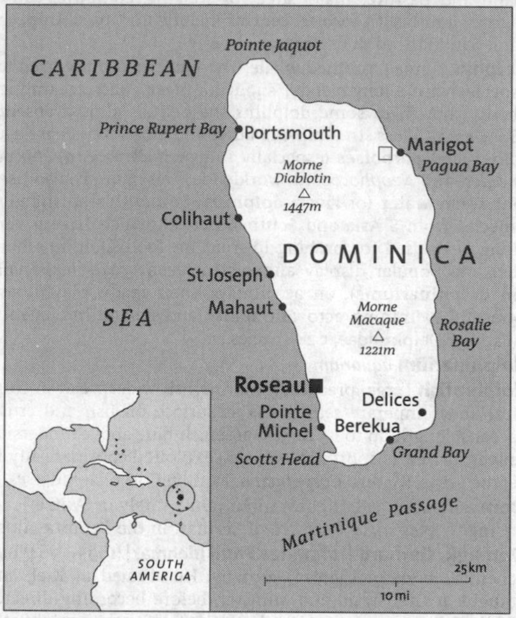

☐ International Airport

[domineeka], Fr **Dominique**, official name **Commonwealth of Dominica**

Local name Dominica

Timezone GMT −4

Area 751 km²/290 sq mi

Population total (2002e) 71 700

Status Independent republic within the Commonwealth

Date of independence 1978

Capital Roseau

Languages English (official), with French widely spoken

Ethnic groups African or mixed African-European descent (97%), Amerindian (2%)

Religions Christian (Roman Catholic 77%, Protestant 16%)

Physical features Island in the Windward group of the West Indies; c.50 km/30 mi long and 26 km/16 mi wide; rises to 1447 m/4747 ft at Morne Diablotin; volcanic origin; central ridge, with several rivers; 67% of land area forested.

Climate Warm and humid tropical climate; temperatures ranging 25·6–32·2°C; rainy season (Jun–Oct); heavy rainfall, varies from 1750 mm/70 in average on the coast, to 6250 mm/246 in inland.

Currency 1 East Caribbean Dollar (EC$) = 100 cents

Economy Agriculture; tourism; coconut-based products, cigars, citrus fruits (notably limes), bananas, coconuts, bay oil.

GDP (2002e) $380 mn, per capita $5400

Human Development Index (2002) 0·779

History Visited by Columbus, 1493; colonization attempts by French and British in 18th-c; British Crown Colony from 1805; part of Federation of the West Indies, 1958–62; independent republic within the Commonwealth, 1978; governed by a House of Assembly, President, Prime Minister, and Cabinet.

Head of State
1998–2003 Vernon Shaw
2003– Nicholas Liverpool

Head of Government
2000 Rosie Douglas
2000–4 Pierre Charles
2004– Roosevelt Skerrit

sometimes spelled **Doomsday Book** (though the *dome* refers to houses, not to doom). Information is arranged by county and, within each county, according to tenure by major landholders; each manor is described according to value and resources. Domesday is one of the greatest administrative achievements of the Middle Ages, yet its central purpose remains unclear. Most probably, it was to assist the royal exploitation of crown lands and feudal rights, and to provide the new nobility with a formal record and confirmation of their lands, thus putting a final seal on the Norman occupation.

domestic fowl A bird kept worldwide for its meat or eggs, also known as the **chicken** or **hen**; descended from one or more species of wild jungle fowl, probably the **red jungle fowl** (*Gallus gallus*); domesticated over 5000 years ago. Modern breeds are grouped as **Mediterranean** or **Asian**.

dominance (genetics) A term applied by Mendel in 1866 to describe the situation in which one allele manifests its effect and obscures that of the other. For example, a mother who is of blood group A and has a blood group O child must be carrying both A and O blood group genes. The presence of her O gene is impossible to detect by testing the gene product (though it can be detected by testing the DNA), since the A gene is dominant.

Domingo, Plácido [dominggoh] (1941–) Tenor, born in Madrid, Spain. He moved to Mexico with his family, and studied piano and conducting at the National Conservatory of Music, Mexico City. In 1959 he made his debut as a baritone, took his first tenor role in 1960, and became a member of the Israeli National Opera (1962–5). He first sang in New York City in 1966, at La Scala in 1969, and at Covent Garden in 1971. His vocal technique and acting ability have made him one of the world's leading lyric–dramatic tenors, notably in works by Puccini and Verdi. He has made numerous recordings and film versions of operas. He received an honorary knighthood in 2002.

Dominic, St (c.1170–1221) Founder of the Order of Friars Preachers, born in Calaruega, Old Castile. He studied at Palencia, where he acquired such a name for piety and learning that he was made a canon in 1193. He led a life of rigorous asceticism, and devoted himself to missionary work, notably among the Albigenses of S France. His preaching order was approved by Pope Honorius III in 1216. By the time of his death, his order occupied 60 houses, and had spread as far as England, where from their dress the friars were called Black Friars. He was canonized in 1234 by Gregory IX. Feast day 8 August.

Dominica *see panel*

Dominican Republic *p.469*

Dominicans A religious order, officially ***Ordo Praedicatorum*** (Lat 'Order of Preachers'), abbreviated **OP**; also known as the **Friars Preachers**, **Black Friars**, or **Jacobins**. It was founded by St Dominic in 1215 in Italy to provide defenders of the Roman Catholic Faith. The order exercises individual and corporate poverty, but is devoted mainly to preaching and teaching. It has a fine record of learning (eg Thomas Aquinas, Albertus Magnus), and also of missionary activity, with houses in every part of the Christian world. There is also a second order (of nuns), and a third or tertiary order (of members not enclosed).

Dominion Day *Canada Day*

Domino, Fats, originally **Antoine Domino** (1928–) Singer, pianist, and composer, born in New Orleans, Louisiana, USA. His cheerful boogie-woogie piano style, with strong backbeat and a bluesy feel, helped popularize rock-and-roll in the 1950s and early 1960s. His songs include 'Blueberry Hill', 'Ain't That a Shame', 'Blue Monday', and 'I'm Walkin'.

dominoes An indoor game which involves the matching of a series of marked blocks. It can be played in various forms by any number of players from two upwards (ideally, four). The dominoes are either wooden or plastic rectangular blocks, with the face of each block divided into two halves, each half containing a number of spots. No two dominoes have the same markings on them. In a double-six set of dominoes, every combination between 6–6 and 0–0 is marked on the 28 dominoes. The object of the basic game is to lay out a sequence (or 'line') of

Dominican Republic

☐ International Airport

Span **República Dominicana**
Local name República Dominicana
Timezone GMT −4
Area 48 442 km²/18 699 sq mi
Population total (2002e) 8 833 000

Status Republic
Date of independence 1844
Capital Santo Domingo
Language Spanish (official)
Ethnic groups Spanish, or mixed Spanish and African descent
Religions Roman Catholic (92%), other (mostly Evangelical Protestant and followers of voodoo) (8%)
Physical features Crossed NW–SE by Cordillera Central, with many peaks over 3000 m/10 000 ft; Pico Duarte, 3175 m/10 416 ft is highest peak in the Caribbean; wide coastal plain in E; main rivers include Yaque del Sur, Yaque del Norte, Yuna (E).
Climate Tropical maritime climate with rainy season (May–Nov); Santo Domingo, average temperature 23·9°C (Jan), 27·2°C (Jul); annual rainfall 1400 mm/55 in; hurricanes (Jul–Nov).
Currency 1 Dominican Peso (RD$, DR$) = 100 centavos
Economy Mainly agriculture, especially sugar, cocoa; tourism expanding with new resort complexes on N coast.
GDP (2002e) $53·78 bn, per capita $6300
Human Development Index (2002) 0·727
History Visited by Columbus, 1492; Spanish colony, 16th–17th-c; E province of Santo Domingo remained Spanish after partition of Hispaniola, 1697; taken over by Haiti on several occasions; independence from Haiti, 1844, as Dominican Republic; occupied by USA, 1916–24, 1965; comprises 26 provinces and a National District which contains the capital; governed by a President and National Congress (Senate and Chamber of Deputies).
Head of State/Government
1965–6 Héctor García Godoy Cáceres
1966–78 Joaquín Videla Balaguer
1978–82 Antonio Guzmán Fernández
1982–6 Salvador Jorge Blanco
1986–96 Joaquín Videla Balaguer Ricardo
1996–2000 Leonel Fernandez Reyna
2000– Hipólito Mejía

dominoes, each player in turn having to put down a domino of the same value as the one left at either end of the line by a previous player.

domino theory A political theory first used by President Eisenhower in 1954, reflecting the view that, as neighbouring states are so interdependent, the collapse of one will spread to the others. The theory particularly relates to military collapse, but also covers insurgence, and is used to justify intervention in a country not immediately threatened, but whose neighbour is. It was an important element in the US policy of intervention in SE Asia in the 1960s and 1970s, and in Central America in the 1980s.

Domitian [domishn], in full **Titus Flavius Domitianus** (51–96) Roman emperor (81–96), the younger son of Vespasian, and the last of the Flavian emperors. An able but autocratic ruler, he thoroughly alienated the ruling class by his rapacity and tyrannical ways. Becoming paranoid about opposition after the armed revolt of Saturninus, the Governor of Upper Germany (89), he unleashed a reign of terror in Rome which lasted until his own assassination.

Don, River River in SW European Russia, rising SE of Tula; flows generally S then sweeps round in a wide bend to enter the Sea of Azov; length, 1958 km/1217 mi; linked to the R Volga (E) by canal; accessible to seagoing vessels as far as Rostov-na-Donu; notable fisheries, especially on the lower course.

Donat, Robert [dohnat] (1905–58) Actor, born in Manchester, Greater Manchester, NW England, UK. He worked on the stage in the 1920s, and had many leading film roles over the next 20 years, including *The Thirty-nine Steps* (1935), *Good-bye, Mr Chips* (1939, Oscar), *The Young Mr Pitt* (1942), and *The Winslow Boy* (1948). Ill health limited his later career, and his final appearance was in *The Inn of the Sixth Happiness* (1958), shortly before his death.

Donatello [donateloh], originally **Donato di Betto Bardi** (c.1386–1466) The greatest of the early Tuscan sculptors, born in Florence, NC Italy. He may be regarded as the founder of modern sculpture, as the first producer since classical times of statues complete and independent in themselves, and not mere adjuncts of their architectural surroundings. Among his works are the marble statues of saints Mark and George for the exterior of Or San Michele; and the tomb of Pope John XXIII in the Baptistery.

Donatists [donatists] African Christian schismatics named after Donatus (4th-c), elected as rival to the Bishop of Carthage. The movement was rigorist and puritan, supported rebaptism, and declared invalid the sacraments celebrated by priests suspected of collaboration in times of persecution. It flourished in Africa in the 4th-c and 5th-c, and despite condemnation by Augustine, the Roman emperor, and the Catholic Church (411), continued until the 7th–8th-c.

Donatus, Aelius [donaytus] (c.300–c.399) Latin grammarian and rhetorician, who taught in Rome AD c.360. His treatises on Latin grammar were in the Middle Ages the only textbooks used in schools, so that *Donat* in W Europe came to mean a 'grammar book'. He also wrote commentaries on Terence and Virgil.

Donau, River *Danube, River*

Doncaster, ancient **Danum** 53°32N 1°07W, urban area pop (2001e) 286 900. Town in South Yorkshire, N England, UK; on R Don, 27 km/17 mi NE of Sheffield; founded as a fort 1st-c AD, later an important Roman station on road from Lincoln to York; railway; coal, nylon, rope, machinery, railway engineering; South Yorkshire industrial museum; St Leger Stakes, the oldest horse-race in England (Sep); football league team, Doncaster Rovers.

D1 and D2 formats Videotape recording systems using digital rather than analogue techniques. The **D1 format** was introduced by Sony in 1987, using separate component tracks for luminance and chrominance on ¾ in/19 mm tape at a speed of 28·69 cm/s. In contrast, the **D2 system**, developed by Ampex in 1988, records a composite signal on ¾ in metal particle tape at a more economical speed of 13·17 cm/s; three sizes of cassette are available, giving playing time of 32, 94, and 208 minutes.

Donegal [donigawl, donigol], Ir **Dún na nGall** pop (2000e) 130 000; area 4830 sq km/1865 sq mi. County in Ulster province, N Ireland; bounded W and N by the Atlantic Ocean and E by N Ireland; watered by Finn and Foyle Rivers; Blue Stack Mts (W), Derry Eagh (NW), and Slieve Snaght (N) rising to 752 m/2467 ft at Errigal; capital, Lifford; tweed manufacture, agriculture, livestock; deposits of uranium; Station I on L Derg an important place of pilgrimage, associated with St Patrick.

Donegan, Lonnie, originally **Anthony Donegan** (1931–2002) Singer and guitarist, born in Glasgow, W Scotland, UK. While playing in traditional jazz bands he introduced 'skiffle' sessions between jazz sets, playing American folk music with a strong rhythm section. During the 1950s he had success both in Britain and the USA with such songs as 'Rock Island Line' (which launched a skiffle craze), 'Gamblin' Man', and 'Cumberland Gap', as well as such comic novelties as 'My Old Man's a Dustman'. He was a widely acknowledged influence on later British guitar-based rock and pop music from the Beatles onwards.

Donetsk [donyetsk], formerly **Stalino** (to 1961), **Yuzovka** (to 1924) 48°00N 37°50E, pop (2000e) 1 101 000. Industrial capital city of Donetskaya oblast, Ukraine; on the R Kalmius, in the Donbas coal basin; founded, 1870; airport; railway; university (1965); coal, metallurgy, engineering, machines, chemicals, foodstuffs; natural gas piped from Stavropol.

Dönitz, Karl *Doenitz, Karl*

Donizetti, (Domenico) Gaetano (Maria) [donizetee] (1797–1848) Composer, born in Bergamo, N Italy. He studied music at Bergamo and Bologna, and produced his first opera in 1818 at Venice. The work which carried his fame beyond Italy was *Anna Bolena* (1830), and he had several other successes, notably *Lucia di Lammermoor* (1835). Stricken by paralysis, he became mentally ill.

Don Juan [hwan] A legendary figure probably derived from Spanish literature sources. He is a philanderer who has no heart, and whose career is terminated by divine intervention. This comes in the shape of a stone statue, who insists on being Juan's guest and who carries him off to Hell. Mozart's opera *Don Giovanni* keeps to the traditional story, but more recently Spanish authors have offered psychological explanations of Juan's behaviour.

donkey *ass; mule* (zoology)

Donleavy, J(ames) P(atrick) (1926–) Writer, born in New York City, USA. He served in the US Navy during World War 2, then studied microbiology at Dublin, and became a friend of Brendan Behan. His first novel, *The Ginger Man* (1955) was hailed as a comic masterpiece. Among his other works are *A Singular Man* (1963), *The Beastly Beatitudes of Balthazar B* (1968), *The Onion Eaters* (1971), *Leila* (1983), *Are you Listening, Rabbi Low?* (1987), and *That Darcy, That Dancer, That Gentleman* (1990). Later novels include *The Lady Who Liked Clean Rest Rooms* (1997) and *Wrong Information is Being Given Out at Princeton* (1997). He has been an Irish citizen since 1967, and published *J P Donleavy's Ireland* in 1986.

Donne, John [duhn] (?1572–1631) Poet and priest, born in London, UK. Of Welsh extraction, he was educated at Oxford and Cambridge, studied law in London, and in 1598 became secretary to Thomas Egerton (1540–1617), keeper of the Great Seal. His career prospects were excellent, but his secret marriage to the Lord Keeper's niece had him dismissed and cast into prison. Originally a Roman Catholic, he then joined the established Church, eventually taking Orders in the Anglican church. He was made Dean of St Paul's, where his sermons were extremely popular. Donne is regarded as the foremost of the metaphysical poets, capable of describing human relationships and a person's relationship with God in religious or philosophical language that is charged with a dramatic intensity of emotion. His creative years fall into three periods. The first (1590–1601) was a time of passion and cynicism, as seen in his *Elegies* and *Songs and Sonnets*. The second, from his marriage to his ordination, was a period of anguished meditation and flattery of the great, as seen in his *Anniversaries* and funeral poems. His third period includes sonnets and hymns, and shows that in transferring his allegiance from the world to God he retained his earlier passion.

Donoghue, Steve [donuhyoo], popular name of **Stephen Donoghue** (1884–1945) Jockey, born in Warrington, Cheshire, NWC England, UK. He won the Derby six times, including a record three consecutive wins (1921–3). Champion jockey in 10 successive years (1914–23), he won a total of 14 classics.

Donovan, Terence (1936–96) Photographer, born in London, UK. After leaving secondary school at the age of 11, he took a course at the London School of Engraving and Lithography before joining the photographic studio of John French. In 1959 he set up on his own, and became well known for his monochrome, documentary-style, street-fashion photographs characterizing the London of the swinging '60s.

Doohan, Mick [dooan], popular name of **Michael Doohan** (1965–) Motor-cyclist, born in Brisbane, Queensland, NE Australia. He first raced in 1984, and won his first Grand Prix in 1990, achieving a total of 54 Grand Prix wins. He survived a serious crash in 1992, and retired from riding after another in 1999. He won five successive 500cc world championships (1994–8), and set a new record for the number of wins in a season (12) in 1997.

Doolittle, Hilda, pseudonym **H D** (1886–1961) Poet, born in Bethlehem, Pennsylvania, USA. She lived in London from 1911, and became an exponent of Imagism. She wrote several books of poetry, beginning with *Sea Garden* (1916) and *Hymen* (1921), and also several prose works and translations. In 1913 she married **Richard Aldington**, and after their divorce (1937) settled near L Geneva.

Doomsday Book *Domesday Book*

dopa [dopa] $C_9H_{11}NO_4$, dihydroxyphenylalanine. A catechol derivative from plants, which can form strong complexes with many metals; also called **L-dopa** or **levodopa** (the L- being an indication of the absolute configuration of the molecule: see **amino acid**). It is used in the treatment of Parkinson's disease, reducing symptoms in more than two-thirds of patients. Shortly after its introduction in the late 1960s some reports stated that it increased male libido in a minority of patients. Although this probably related to the clinical improvement of the patients rather than the drug itself, L-dopa was exploited briefly (and wrongly) as an aphrodisiac.

dopamine [dopameen] A chemical compound (*catecholamine*) widely distributed in the brain and peripheral nervous system, a substance from which noradrenaline and adrenaline are formed, and a central nervous system transmitter. It is a hormone which inhibits the secretion of prolactin, and promotes the release of growth hormone from the front lobe of the pituitary gland. Dopamine is a base for the synthesis of two other neurotransmitters: adrenaline and noradrenaline. Abnormal levels of dopamine in some parts of the brain are associated with particular diseases, eg, an excess is associated with schizophrenia and a deficiency with Parkinson's disease.

doping In chemistry, adding a controlled amount of an impurity, which can radically change the properties of a substance. For example, the addition of minute quantities of aluminium or phosphorus to silicon will increase its semiconducting properties greatly.

Doppler, Christian Johann (1803–53) Physicist, born in Salzburg, C Austria. He studied at Vienna, where he became professor of physics (1851), and is best known for his explanation of the perceived frequency variation of sound and light waves because of the relative motion of the source and the detector (the *Doppler effect*).

Doppler effect or **shift** The change in wavelength observed when the separation between a wave source and an observer is changing; named after Christian Doppler. The wavelength increases as the source and observer move apart, and decreases as they come closer. The increasing separation of the Earth and distant stars is demonstrated by the Doppler redshift of star light. The changing tone of passing motor vehicles represents the Doppler shift in sound waves.

Dorado [**dorahdoh**] (Span 'gilded') A S constellation which includes the Large Magellanic Cloud; also known as 'swordfish' or 'goldfish'.

dor beetle A large, blackish beetle; adult length up to 24 mm/1 in; wing cases furrowed; antennae clubbed; lays eggs in tunnels beneath cattle and horse dung; larvae white and fleshy, feed on dung.

dorcas gazelle A gazelle (*Gazella dorcas*), native to N Africa and S Asia; light brown with white underparts; dark smudge along flank and along side of face; short backward-curving horns ringed with ridges; also known as **jebeer**.

Dorchester, ancient **Durnovaria** 50°43N 2°26W, pop (2000e) 15 800. County town of Dorset, S England, UK; on the R Frome, 12 km/7 mi N of Weymouth; the Roman ramparts became known as 'The Walks' in the 18th-c; mint established here by King Athelstan; Judge Jeffreys' Bloody Assizes held here (1685); model for Casterbridge in Hardy's novels; railway; brewing; Dorset county museum, Dorset military museum, Maiden Castle prehistoric fort (3 km/1¾ mi S); Thomas Hardy festival (Aug).

Dordogne Eng [**daw(r)doyn**], Fr [**dawrdon**], ancient **Durenius** area 9224 sq km/3597 sq mi; Department of SW France in the Aquitaine region; capital, Périgueux; popular tourist area.

Dordogne, River Eng [**daw(r)doyn**], Fr [**dawrdon**], ancient **Duranius** River in SW France, rising in the Auvergne hills; formed by confluence of Dor and Dogne Rivers; flows SW and W to meet R Garonne at Bec d'Ambes, where it forms the Gironde estuary; length 472 km/293 mi; vineyards along valley slopes; source of hydroelectricity.

Dordrecht [**daw(r)drekht**], also **Dordt** or **Dort** 51°48N 4°39E, pop (2000e) 117 000. River port and industrial city in S South Holland province, W Netherlands, 19 km/12 mi SE of Rotterdam; founded, 1008; Synod of Dort (meeting of the Reformed churches), 1618–19; railway; shipbuilding, engineering, chemicals; Grote Kerk (14th–16th-c).

Doré, (Paul) Gustave [**doray**] (1832–83) Painter and book illustrator, born in Strasbourg, NE France. He first made his mark by his illustrations to books by Rabelais (1854) and Balzac, notably the latter's *Contes drolatiques* (1865). These were followed by illustrated editions of Dante, the Bible, Milton, and other works.

Dorians [**dawrianz**] A sub-group of Hellenic peoples, thought to have migrated into Greece around 1100 BC. Dorian settlements there included Argos, Corinth, and Sparta; later Dorian foundations include Halicarnassus and Syracuse.

Doric order The earliest of the five main orders of classical architecture, characterized by a fluted shaft and plain capital. It is subdivided into **Greek Doric** and **Roman Doric**, the former having no base, as used for the Parthenon, Athens (447–438 BC).

dormancy In biology, a state of relative metabolic inactivity in a plant or animal, such as is seen both in winter (*hibernation*) and summer (*aestivation*). The notion is particularly used for the state in which viable seeds and buds fail to germinate even under favourable conditions.

dormouse A mouse-like rodent of family Gliridae (10 species); native to Africa, Europe, and C Asia; intermediate between squirrels and true mice; most resemble mice, with long bushy tails. The name is also used for the **desert dormouse** of family Seleviniidae, and for **oriental dormice** of family Muridae (subfamily: Platacanthomyinae, 2 species).

Dornier, Claude [**daw(r)nyer**] (1884–1969) Aircraft engineer, born in Kempten, S Germany. He studied at Munich Technical College, and began work (1910) at the Zeppelin factory at Friedrichshafen. In 1911 he designed the first all-metal plane, and with the backing of Zeppelin opened an aircraft division at Friedrichshafen and Altenrhein, where he made seaplanes and flying-boats, including the famous 12-engined Do X (1929). The Dornier 17 twin-engined bomber was a standard Luftwaffe type in World War 2.

Dors, Diana, originally **Diana Fluck** (1931–84) Actress, born in Swindon, Wiltshire, S England, UK. A student at the Royal Academy of Dramatic Art, she made her film debut in *The Shop at Sly Corner* (1946). Promoted as a sex symbol, she was cast in various low-budget comedies, and despite an effective dramatic performance in *Yield to the Night* (1956) was usually seen in blowsy supporting assignments. Her accomplished stage work in *Three Months Gone* (1970) brought her a selection of good character parts, as in *The Amazing Mr. Blunden* (1972). She retained her personal popularity, performing in cabaret and as a television agony aunt. She returned to the screen in *Steaming* (1984) immediately prior to her death.

Dorset pop (2000e) 682 800; area 2654 sq km/1025 sq mi. County of S England, UK; bounded S by the English Channel; extensive heathlands and chalk down, drained by the Frome and Stour Rivers; county town, Dorchester; chief towns include Bournemouth, Poole (both new unitary authorities from 1997), Weymouth; tourism, livestock, quarrying; setting for many of Hardy's novels.

Dorsey, Tommy [**daw(r)see**], popular name of **Thomas Dorsey** (1905–56) Trombonist and bandleader, born in Shenandoah, Pennsylvania, USA. Renowned for his sweet-toned instrumental style, his work hovered between jazz and dance music. His big bands were sometimes co-led by his brother **Jimmy Dorsey** (1904–57, alto saxophone, clarinet). The Dorsey Brothers Orchestra existed from 1932 to 1935, reforming again in 1953 until Tommy's death. Both brothers were in great demand as session musicians in the late 1920s, with the expansion of radio in the USA, and their fame was revived through a regular television show in the 1950s.

Dortmund [**daw(r)tmund**] 51°32N 7°28E, pop (2000e) 619 000. Industrial, mining, and commercial city in Arnsberg district, W Germany; river port in the Ruhr valley, connected to the North Sea by the Dortmund–Ems Canal (272 km/169 mi); one of Germany's largest inland harbours; railway; university (1966); iron and steel, engineering, machinery, non-alcoholic drinks, textiles, brewing; sporting centre.

DOS [**dos**] Acronym for **Disk Operating System**, referring to the computer program – part of the operating system – which oversees the communication of data between the computer processor and its magnetic disks, as well as the management of files and programs on the disks.

dose equivalent *radioactivity units*

Dos Passos, John (Roderigo) (1896–1970) Novelist and war correspondent, born in Chicago, Illinois, USA. He studied at Harvard, and was an ambulance driver in the later years of World War 1, out of which came his antiwar novel, *Three Soldiers* (1921). He then worked in Europe and elsewhere as a newspaper correspondent. His best-known work is the trilogy on US life, *U.S.A.* (1930–6).

Dostoevsky or **Dostoyevsky, Fyodor (Mikhailovich)** [**dostoyefskee**] (1821–81) Novelist, born in Moscow, Russia. He became a military engineer, but turned to literature, publishing *Bednye lyudi* (Poor Folk) in 1846. Joining revolutionary circles in St Petersburg, he was condemned to death (1849), reprieved at the last moment, and sent to hard labour in Siberia. Out of this experience came his harrowing novel, *The House of the Dead* (1862). In 1859 he returned to St Petersburg, where he wrote his masterpiece, *Prestupleniye i nakazaniye* (1866, Crime and Punishment), one of the most powerful realistic works of fiction. Other important books are *Idiot* (1868–9, The Idiot) and *Bratya Karamazovy* (1879–80, The Brothers Karamazov). His work is characterized by scenes of confrontation in which the most profound religious, metaphysical, and moral problems are explored. Domestic trials, financial troubles (caused by gambling debts), and ill health (epilepsy) clouded his later life. He lived for a time in W Europe (1867–71), then returned to work as a journalist in St Petersburg.

dot-matrix printer A type of impact printer, where characters are formed by the selection of sets of dots from a rectangular matrix. It is widely used with microcomputer systems, being relatively fast and inexpensive, but it can be noisy. Today the dot-matrix printer has been largely replaced by the ink-jet printer.

dotterel A species of plover, native to mountainous areas of Europe and Asia (*Eudromias morinellus*). The name is also used for two species of plover from South America, and six species of plover from Australia and New Zealand. (Family: Charadriidae.)

Dou or **Douw, Gerard** [dow] (1613–75) Painter, born in Leyden, The Netherlands. He studied under Rembrandt (1628–31), and at first mainly occupied himself with portraiture, but soon turned to genre painting. His 200 works include his own portrait, his wife's, and his celebrated 'Dropsical Woman' (1663), in the Louvre.

Douai [dooay] 50°22N 3°04E, pop (2001e) 42 600. Town in Nord department, N France; on the R Scarpe; probably a 4th-c Roman fortress; belonged to the counts of Flanders in the Middle Ages, received charter, 1228; prosperous cloth trade declined; town passed to the dukes of Burgundy (1384), then to the Spanish Habsburgs (1477); seized by Louis XIV (1667), restored to France by the Peace of Utrecht (1713); town hall (15th-c), Palace of Justice (part 16th-c), St Peter's Church (16th-c); Roman Catholic college for English priests founded here (1568) by William Allen for the translation of the Reims–Douai Bible; coal, iron, engineering, bell founding.

Douai Bible [dooay] An early English translation of the Bible by Roman Catholic scholars. The New Testament was first published at Reims in 1582; the Old Testament in 1609. It is sometimes called the **Reims–Douai** translation (the English college at Douai having moved to Reims in 1578).

Douala or **Duala** [dooala] 4°04N 9°43E, pop (2000e) 1 878 000. Seaport capital of Littoral province, Cameroon, W Africa; on R Wouri estuary, 25 km/15 mi from Gulf of Guinea coast; capital of German Cameroon, as Kamerunstadt, 1885–1901; present name, 1907; capital of French Cameroon, 1940–6; airport; railway; many import-export companies; trade in minerals, agricultural products, foodstuffs; centre for petroleum exploration; aluminium smelting, paper, pulp, textiles, flour milling, metal work, chemicals, brewing, food processing; Pagoda of King Manga Bell.

double bass The largest and lowest in pitch of the orchestral string instruments. There are two basic types: the first, belonging to the viol family, has sloping shoulders and a flat back; the other, belonging to the violin family, has squarer shoulders and a slightly rounded (sometimes also flat) back. Both types have four strings, tuned in fourths: sometimes a fifth, lower string is added. There are similarly two types of bow: the German (or viol) type, held underhand, and the French type, held like a cello bow. The strings are often plucked, almost invariably so in jazz and dance music.

double coconut *coco de mer*

double exposure The intentional combination of two or more images separately exposed on a single photographic record, either in the camera or by subsequent printing. The images may be superimposed so that one is seen through the other, or appear without overlapping by the use of masks or mattes to reserve specific areas. It is widely used for artistic effects and in trick photography.

double glazing Two layers of glass separated by an air space to give improved thermal and/or acoustic insulation. The two layers are either permanently sealed with a partial vacuum inside, or openable for occasional ventilation. The former provides significantly better insulation.

double jeopardy The legal doctrine (included in the Fifth Amendment to the US constitution) that no person can be convicted twice for the same crime, or for different crimes arising from the same set of facts unless the crimes involve substantially different wrongs. It also holds that no person having been acquitted of an offence should be subjected to a second trial for the same offence.

double refraction *birefringence*

Doublespeak Awards Mock awards made annually by the National Council of Teachers of English in the USA to those public figures who have used language that is distorted, unfactual, deceptive, evasive, or euphemistic, usually in an attempt to conceal the real implications of policies advocated. An example is 'collateral damage', referring to civilians killed in war.

double star A pair of stars that appear close together in our sky when viewed through a telescope. Some pairs are stars at very different distances that merely coincide from our vantage point. If the stars are close enough to be linked through their gravitational attractions, they constitute a binary star.

double vision A weakness or paralysis of one or more of the muscles which move one or other of the eyes, resulting in a failure of the eyes to move together in parallel; also known as **diplopia**. As a result, light from a single object does not fall on comparable parts of the two retinae, and the object appears as two images.

Douglas 54°09N 4°29W, pop (2000e) 23 700. Seaport capital of the Isle of Man; on the E coast, 80 km/50 mi W of Barrow-in-Furness; railway; tourism, brewing, light engineering; House of Keys, Manx National Museum, Castle Mona (1804), Tower of Refuge on Conister rock (1832), casino, steam railway.

Douglas, Gawain or **Gavin** (c.1474–1522) Poet and bishop, born in Tantallon Castle, East Lothian, E Scotland, UK. He studied at St Andrews for the priesthood, became Dean of St Giles, Edinburgh (1501), and Bishop of Dunkeld (1515). His works include *The Palace of Honour* (c.1501) and a translation of the *Aeneid* (finished c.1513), the first to be published in English. After the death of James IV of Scotland at Flodden, he became involved in political intrigues, and in 1521 was forced to flee to London.

Douglas, Kirk, originally **Issur Danielovitch Demsky** (1916–) Film actor, born in Amsterdam, New York, USA. He made his Broadway debut in 1941, served in the US Navy, and embarked on a screen career in 1946. His films include *Champion* (1949), *The Bad and the Beautiful* (1952), *Lust for Life* (1956), and *Spartacus* (1960), and from the 1970s he also worked as a director. His son, Michael Douglas, also became an actor.

Douglas, Michael (Kirk) (1944–) US film actor and producer, born in New Brunswick, New Jersey, USA, the son of Kirk Douglas. He studied at the University of California, and achieved recognition in the television police series *The Streets of San Francisco* (1972–5), but left to co-produce *One Flew Over the Cuckoo's Nest* (1975), which won five Academy Awards, including one for Best Picture. He starred in and produced *Romancing the Stone* (1984), and won a Best Actor Oscar for his performance in *Wall Street* (1987). Other acting roles include *Fatal Attraction* (1987), *The American President* (1995), and *A Perfect Murder* (1998). Later films include *Traffic* (2000), in which he co-starred with wife Catherine Zeta-Jones (married 2000), and *The In-Laws* (2003). In 2004 he was honoured with a Golden Globe Lifetime Achievement Award.

Douglas, Norman (George) (1868–1952) Travel writer, novelist, and essayist, born in Thüringen, Austria. Educated in England and Germany, he spent much of his life in continental Europe. His first book, *Unprofessional Tales* (1901), appeared under the pseudonym **Normyx**. *Siren Land* (1911), an exotic account of his travels in S Italy, was followed by *Old Calabria* (1915), *Fountains of the Sun* (1912), *Alone* (1921), and *Together* (1923). The most famous of his novels is *South Wind*, a celebration of hedonism on the island of Nepenthe (Capri). An autobiography, *Looking Back*, appeared in 1933. A friend of the cookery writer Elizabeth David, he published *Venus in the Kitchen* (1952), a collection of aphrodisiac recipes.

Douglas, Stephen A(rnold) (1813–61) US lawyer and statesman, born in Brandon, Vermont, USA. He became attorney general of Illinois in 1834, a member of the legislature in 1835, secretary of state in 1840, and judge of the Supreme Court in 1841. He was returned to Congress in 1843, and to the US Senate in 1847. His policy was to 'make the United States an ocean-bound republic'. In the question of slavery he maintained that each territory should decide whether it should be a free or a slave state. In 1860 he was nominated for the presidency, but was defeated by Lincoln.

Douglas, Tommy, popular name of **Thomas Clement Douglas** (1904–86) Baptist minister and Canadian politician. As premier of Saskatchewan (1944–61), he led the first Socialist government elected in Canada, and was later leader of the federal New Democratic Party for 10 years. He helped establish Democratic Socialism in the mainstream of Canadian politics, and with the introduction of medicare in Saskatchewan is recognized as the Canadian 'father of socialized medicine'.

Douglas-Home, Sir Alec *Home of the Hirsel*

Douglass, Frederick (c.1817–95) Abolitionist and journalist, born in slavery at Tuckahoe, Maryland, USA. He escaped in 1838, and in 1841 emerged as a major anti-slavery force, and also supported the cause of women's rights. After a 2-year lecturing tour in Britain and Ireland, he returned to the USA with enough money to be able to purchase his freedom. He later became US minister to Haiti.

Doukhobors or **Dukhabors** [**doo**kobaw(r)z] A religious sect originating in Russia c.1740. It teaches that God is manifested in the human soul, which is eternal, and which at death passes into another body (*metempsychosis*). Frequently in conflict with the authorities, especially for refusing military service, the adherents were persecuted until 1898, when they were allowed to emigrate. Most settled in Canada.

Doulton An English firm which began making chimney-pots and large architectural ornaments at Lambeth in London in the first half of the 19th-c. From c.1862 they became leading makers of art pottery and in 1877 expanded to Burslem. The firm was renowned for ornamental stoneware and earthenware, figures, decorative panels, and tiles, while still manufacturing large quantities of sanitary ware.

Dounreay [doon**ray**] Former nuclear research station, Caithness, Highland, N Scotland, UK; on the coast of the Pentland Firth, 13 km/8 mi W of Thurso; site of world's first experimental fast-breeder nuclear reactor.

Douro, River [**daw**ru], Eng [**door**oh], Span **Río Duero** [**dwe**ro], ancient **Durius** River of Spain and Portugal; rises in NC Spain, and flows 609 km/378 mi W to the Portuguese border, which it follows for 107 km/66 mi; turns W across N Portugal, emptying into the Atlantic near Oporto; used extensively for irrigation and hydroelectric power; five dams are operated jointly by Spain and Portugal; length 895 km/556 mi; navigable 200 km/124 mi to Barca de Alva; vineyards in the upper Douro valley produce port and table wines.

douroucouli [doorookoo**lee**] A nocturnal New World monkey (*Aotus trivirgatus*); long tail, large eyes, spherical head; cannot see in colour; moves silently; the only nocturnal monkey; may be kept as a pet to control mice and insects; also known as **night monkey**, **night ape**, or **owl monkey**.

dove (ornithology) A bird of the pigeon family. Usually the large-bodied species with rounded tails are called **pigeons**; the smaller-bodied one with longer slender tails are called **doves**. However, this distinction is not applied consistently.

dove (politics) In US foreign policy, someone who prefers to use diplomacy instead of reliance on military power to settle international problems. The term was first used in the period of the Kennedy and Johnson presidencies. Today it is probably used to describe anyone who takes a relatively soft line in foreign policy matters. A **hawk** represents the opposite position, favouring a tougher line. Doves are seen as being left-leaning, while hawks are right-wing.

Dover (UK), Fr **Douvres**, ancient **Dubris Portus** 51°08N 1°19E, pop (2001e) 104 500. Seaport in Kent, SE England, UK; principal cross-Channel port, the shortest link with France (35 km/21¾ mi); the largest of the Cinque Ports; railway; Dover Castle (13th–14th-c); 13th-c St Edmund's Chapel, the smallest chapel in England; Roman painted house (2nd-c AD).

Dover (USA) 39°10N 75°32W, pop (2000e) 32 100. Capital of state in Kent Co, C Delaware, USA; founded, 1683; state capital, 1777; city status, 1929; railway; university; trade in fruit and vegetables; air force base; Old Dover Days (May).

dove tree *handkerchief tree*

Dowding, Hugh (Caswell Tremenheere) Dowding, Baron (1882–1970) British air chief marshal of World War 2, born in Moffat, Dumfries and Galloway, SW Scotland, UK. He served in the Royal Artillery and the Royal Flying Corps in World War 1. As commander-in-chief of Fighter Command (1936–40), he organized the air defence of Britain, which resulted in the victorious Battle of Britain (1940). He retired in 1942, and was created a peer in 1943.

Dowell, Sir Anthony (1943–) Dancer and director, born in London, UK. He studied at the Sadler's Wells and Royal Ballet Schools, and joined the Royal Ballet company in 1961, becoming one of the premier male ballet dancers of the period, noted for his lightness and elegance in classical roles. He was principal dancer of the American Ballet Theatre (1978–80), and became artistic director of the Royal Ballet (1986–2001). He was knighted in 1995.

Dow Jones Index [dow] A statistic showing the state of the New York Stock Exchange, computed on working days by Dow Jones and Co. It enables a measurement to be made of changes in the price of shares of 30 leading US corporations, and is the primary indicator of share price movements in the USA.

Dowland, John (1563–1626) Composer, lutenist, and songwriter, born possibly in Westminster, London, UK. He studied at Oxford, and having failed to become a court musician to Queen Elizabeth I, entered the service of the Duke of Brunswick (1594), and subsequently went to Italy. He returned to England in 1596, where he wrote his first book of 'ayres'. In 1598 he became lutenist to Christian IV of Denmark, producing further collections of music. In London he composed *Lachrimae* (1605, Tears), which contains some of the finest instrumental consort music of the period.

Down, Ir **An Dun** pop (2000e) 404 000; area 2448 sq km/945 sq mi. County in SE Northern Ireland, UK, divided into six districts (Ards, Banbridge, Castlereagh, Down, Newry and Mourne, North Down); the name is also used for one of these districts, pop (2000e) 64 000, and its administrative centre; bounded N by Belfast Lough, S by Carlingford Lough, and E by the Irish Sea; coastline indented (N–S) by Strangford Lough, Dundrum Bay, and Carlingford Lough; Mourne Mts in the S; rises to 852 m/2795 ft at Slieve Donard; county town, Downpatrick; other chief towns, Newry, Bangor, Newtownards; oats, potatoes, vegetables, stock-rearing, linen.

Downing Street A street off Whitehall in C London, UK. Of the original terraced houses only numbers 10 (since 1735 the prime minister's official residence), 11 (used by the Chancellor of the Exchequer), and 12 (used by the party whip) remain. One side of the street has been replaced by the Foreign Office building.

Downing Street declaration A joint agreement between the British and Irish governments, made in 1993, intended to provide the basis of a peace initiative in Northern Ireland. The declaration was made by British and Irish prime ministers John Major and Albert Reynolds, and recommended closer co-operation over Northern Ireland affairs, taking further the initiatives of the 1985 Anglo-Irish agreement.

Downpatrick, Ir **Dun Padraig** 54°20N 5°43W, pop (2000e) 11 000. Town in Down district, County Down, SE Northern Ireland, UK, near the S end of Strangford Lough; a major centre of pilgrimage; St Patrick is said to have landed here in 432 and to have founded a church c.440; reputed burial place of Saints Patrick, Columbus, and Bridget of Kildare; textiles, agricultural trade; St Patrick's Cathedral (1798–1812), remains of Inch Abbey (c.1187) nearby.

Downs Low-lying chalk hill ranges rising in Dorset and Hampshire and extending into Surrey, Kent, and East and West Sussex, S England, UK; North Downs extend from the chalk cliffs of Dover in the E, through Kent and into Surrey; separated from the South Downs by the Weald; South Downs stretch W to Beachy Head, running parallel to the S coast; North Downs rise to 294 m/964 ft at Leith Hill, South Downs to 264 m/866 ft at Butser Hill.

downsizing A term, used by organizations employing computers extensively, which describes the process of changing from the use of very large computers centrally to the use of networks of computer workstations. These workstations are distributed around the organization, possibly as personal computers in individual offices.

Down's syndrome A common congenital abnormality especially liable to affect babies born to mothers over 40 years. Affected individuals have high cheek-bones, a flattened nose, and slanted eyes with a prominent fold over the inner part of either eye. The hands are short and broad with a single palmar crease. There are varying degrees of mental handicap and there may be associated malformations of the heart. The defect stems from a failure of one chromosome of a reproductive germ cell, usually female, to split in the normal way. Instead of a healthy ovum with 23 chromosomes, an ovum with 24 chromosomes is produced (chromosome 21 is duplicated). When this ovum is fertilized, the developing embryo possesses an extra chromosome. The condition is named after English physician J L H Down (1828–96), and is sometimes referred to as **mongolism**.

dowsing A technique in which a held rod, pendulum, or other indicator moves when it is brought near to a certain substance. This technique has been employed to search for a wide variety of substances, including water, oil, and mineral deposits, and maps have been constructed of old field boundaries. Although there are records of its use in Ancient Egypt, the medical applications of dowsing date only from the 1920s when a French priest, the Abbé Mermet, used a pendulum for diagnosis and to select suitable herbal remedies. The dowsing process always involves a human being, and it has been suggested that detecting the object of dowsing is a supersensory phenomenon, and that the use of an indicator is entirely incidental.

Doyle, Sir Arthur Conan (1859–1930) Writer, the creator of Sherlock Holmes, born in Edinburgh, EC Scotland, UK. He studied medicine at Edinburgh, but poverty as a medical practitioner made him turn to writing. His first book, *A Study in Scarlet* (1887), introduced the super-observant, deductive Sherlock Holmes, his good-natured question-raising friend, Dr Watson, and the whole apparatus of detection mythology associated with Baker Street, Holmes's fictitious home. After *The Adventures of Sherlock Holmes* was serialized in the *Strand Magazine* (1891–3), the author tired of his popular creation, and tried to kill off his hero, but was compelled in 1903 to revive him. Conan Doyle himself set greater stock by his historical romances, such as *The White Company* (1890). He served as a physician in the Boer War (1899–1902), and his pamphlet, *The War in South Africa* (1902), earned him a knighthood (1902). He also wrote on spiritualism, to which he became a convert in later life.

Doyle, Roddy (1958–) Novelist, born in Dublin, Ireland. He studied at University College, Dublin, then taught English and geography at a local school, and began writing in his spare time. His first success came with *The Commitments* (1987), the first of the internationally acclaimed Barrytown trilogy, which he completed with *The Snapper* (1990) and *The Van* (1991). Later novels include *Paddy Clarke Ha Ha Ha* (1993, Booker Prize), *The Woman Who Walked into Doors* (1996), *A Star Called Henry* (1999), and *Rory and Ita* (2002).

D'Oyly Carte, Richard **[doylee kah(r)t]** (1844–1901) Theatrical impresario, born in London, UK. After working in his father's musical instrument-making business he became a concert agent, and from 1875 produced the first operettas by 'Gilbert and Sullivan', with whom he formed a partnership. In 1881 he built the Savoy Theatre in London, the first to be lit by electricity. Another theatre building, a Royal English Opera House (1887), failed. After his death the D'Oyly Carte company continued to perform Gilbert and Sullivan in traditional style for many years.

DRA (Driver Reminder Appliance) *train protection systems*

Drabble, Margaret (1939–) Novelist and critic, born in Sheffield, South Yorkshire, N England, UK. She studied at Cambridge. She has written biographies of Arnold Bennett (1974) and Angus Wilson (1994). Her novels include *A Summer Bird-Cage* (1962), *The Ice Age* (1977), *The Radiant Way* (1987), *The Witch of Exmoor* (1996), *The Peppered Moth* (2001), and *The Seven Sisters* (2002). She was the editor of the 5th edition of the *Oxford Companion to English Literature* (1985). Her elder sister is the novelist A S Byatt. She married her second husband, biographer Michael Holroyd, in 1982.

Draco (astronomy) **[draykoh]** (Lat 'dragon') The eighth-largest constellation, a sinuous zone of the N sky near the celestial pole.

Draco (law-giver) **[draykoh]** (7th-c BC) Athenian law-giver. Archon at Athens in 621 BC, he revised the laws of Athens with admirable impartiality; but the severity of his penalty – death for almost every offence – made the strict execution of his code unpopular (hence 'draconian'), and it was superseded by that of Solon (594 BC). Only his ruling on homicide remained.

draco (zoology) *flying lizard*

draft *conscription*

drag A force which impedes the motion of an object through a fluid. It results from both the friction between the object and the fluid flowing over it (**viscous** or **frictional drag**), and the pressure differences caused by the flow around the object (**form** or **profile drag**). Drag experienced by an object in an air stream is called *air resistance*.

dragger A framework attached to a ship, made in an emergency from anything that will float, to stop the ship from drifting down wind too rapidly. More commonly known as a **sea anchor**, it is made fast to a hawser and paid out over the bow.

draghunting *foxhunting*

dragonet Any of a small family of fishes, widespread in coastal waters of tropical to warm temperate seas; includes European *Callionymus lyra* found from Norway to the Mediterranean, living on or in sand and shingle sediments; length up to 30 cm/1 ft, body rather flattened, pelvic fins broad, dorsal fin striped blue and yellow in male; gill openings small on top of head, eyes prominent. (Family: Callionymidae.)

dragon-fish Deep-water fish with slender, snake-like body; length up to 40 cm/16 in; short head with very long mouth, bearing fang-like jaw teeth; light organs present in rows along underside of body, behind eye, and on long chin barbel that serves as lure to attract prey. (Family: Stomiatidae.)

dragonfly A large, long-bodied insect with two pairs of slender wings held horizontally at rest; large compound eyes enable adults to catch insects in flight; larvae aquatic, broad-bodied, predatory. (Order: Odonata. Suborder: Anisoptera.)

dragon-tree An evergreen tree (*Dracaena draco*), native to the Canary Is and Madeira; short, thick branches, bearing clusters of greyish or bluish sword-shaped leaves at the tips; flowers small, greenish-white; berries orange. Red resin exuded by the trunk is known as **dragon's blood**, used in varnish. (Family: Agavaceae.)

drag racing A specialized form of motor racing which is a test of acceleration. Large-engined 'vehicles' with big rear wheels and small front ones race normally two at a time on a 400 m/440 yd straight track, from a standing start. Parachutes are fitted to the machines to help with braking. The sport developed in California in the 1930s, and is now very popular in the USA. Speeds of over 400 kph/250 mph are not uncommon.

Drake, Sir Francis (c.1540–96) Elizabethan seaman, born at Crowndale Farm, near Tavistock, Devon, SW England, UK. In 1567 he commanded the *Judith* in his kinsman John Hawkyns's ill-fated expedition to the West Indies, and returned there several times to recover the losses sustained from the Spaniards, his exploits gaining him great popularity in England. In 1577 he set out with five ships for the Pacific, through the Straits of Magellan, but after his fleet was battered by storm and fire, he alone continued in the *Golden Hind*. He then struck out across the Pacific, reached the Pelew Is, and returned to England via the Cape of Good Hope in 1580. The following year, the queen visited his ship and knighted him. In 1585 he sailed with 25 ships against the Spanish Indies, bringing home tobacco, potatoes, and the dispirited Virginian colonists. In the battle against the Spanish Armada, which raged for a week in the Channel (1588), his seamanship and courage brought him further distinction. In 1595 he sailed again to the West Indies, but died of dysentery off Porto Bello.

Drakensberg Mountains [draknzberg], Zulu **Kwathlamba** or **Quathlamba** Mountain range in South Africa, extending NE–SW; highest peak, near KwaZulu Natal–Lesotho frontier, Thabana Ntlenyana (3482 m/11 424 ft).

drama (Gr 'action') A representation of human action by actors impersonating characters on stage. One of the oldest literary forms, developing in different directions out of religious ritual, its origins are reflected in the frequent use of music, dance, and chorus. Drama was divided by Aristotle into tragedy and comedy, a distinction valid for classical times, with the strict separation of styles. But with the development of drama in the mediaeval and modern world, these categories have proved inadequate. Dr Johnson said Shakespeare's own plays were 'neither comedies nor tragedies, but compositions of a distinct kind', and defended the hybrid tragi-comedy against purist critics because it 'exhibits the true state of sublunary nature'. The drama genre has indeed served as a forum for the testing of old and new feelings and ideas, and competing perceptions of truth; with sentimentality, heroism, and high ideals cast against cynicism, self-indulgence, and practicality. In the 20th-c, Brecht advocated an epic drama which stands outside Aristotelian categories and assumptions. Meanwhile, film and television have allowed unprecedented developments in drama, at formal, technical, and ideological levels.

dramatherapy The use of drama as a creative medium to help in clarifying and alleviating personal and social problems. As a practice it fuses both artistic and therapeutic skills.

draughts A popular board game played on a standard chessboard containing 64 squares of alternate colours (normally black and white); known as **checkers** in the USA. Played by two players, each has 12 small, flat, round counters (known as *pieces*), one set normally being black, the other white. The pieces are lined on alternate squares on the first three rows at either side of the board. The object is to remove your opponent's pieces from the board by jumping over them onto a vacant diagonal square. Only forward moves are allowed until the back line of the opposing 'territory' is reached, when that piece becomes a *king* and can move forward or backward. Pieces cannot be moved between squares of different colours. Draughts is believed to have been played in ancient Egypt; the first book about the game was published in Spain in 1547.

Dravidian languages [dravidian] A group of more than 20 languages, spoken mainly in S India. The principal ones are Telugu, Tamil, Kannada, and Malayalam, which together have over 150 million speakers within the S states. The origin of this group of languages is obscure, but there is general agreement that they were once spoken throughout India, and were displaced from the N by the advance of the Indo-Aryan branch of Indo-European.

Drayton, Michael (1563–1631) Poet, born in Hartshill, Warwickshire, C England, UK. His earliest work was *The Harmony of the Church* (1591), a metrical rendering of scriptural passages, which gave offence to the authorities, and was condemned to be destroyed. His best-known works are *England's Heroical Epistles* (1597), *Poly-Olbion* (1612–22), an ambitious description of the English countryside, and the celebrated sonnet 'Since there's no help, come let us kiss and part', from the sequence *Idea* (1619).

Dr Barnardo's Homes *Barnardo, Thomas John*

dreaming Sensory perceptions experienced during sleep; specifically during the period of sleep associated with rapid movement of the eyes (*REM sleep*). Perceptions are usually visual, but sound, smell, taste, and touch can also be experienced. They may occur in a random fashion, or be guided by the emotional responses and subconscious thoughts of the dreamer.

Dreamtime or **The Dreaming** In the mythology of the Australian Aborigines, one of the names for the time of the Ancestors, who created the world and are still alive in the sacred places. This time continues to exist, and it may be possible to find it through dreams.

dredger A vessel designed to remove spoil from the seabed in order to maintain or increase the depth in a harbour or approaches. Dredgers are also used to obtain sand and gravel from the seabed for constructional purposes.

Dred Scott decision A ruling by the US Supreme Court in 1857 which made slavery legal in all US territories. Dred Scott was a slave who had been taken by his master from Missouri (a slave state) to Illinois and Wisconsin (both free areas). After returning to Missouri, Scott sued for his freedom on the grounds that by living in a free state he had altered his status. The Missouri Supreme Court overruled a decision by a lower court which had considered Scott to be free, and was eventually supported in its view by the Supreme Court. The decision increased anti-slavery feeling in the North, and was an important element in the polarization of opinions which led to the American Civil War.

Dreiser, Theodore (Herman Albert) [driyzer] (1871–1945) Writer, born in Terre Haute, Indiana, USA. He became a journalist in Chicago, St Louis, and New York City. His first novel *Sister Carrie* (1900), starkly realistic, was criticized for obscenity, and he did not write another until 1911, when *Jennie Gerhardt* won acclaim. *An American Tragedy* (1925), based on a famous murder case, brought him success. In 1939 he moved to Hollywood.

Dresden [drezdn] 51°02N 13°45E, pop (2000e) 512 000. Capital of Dresden county, E Germany; on R Elbe, SE of Berlin, close to the Czech frontier; former capital of Saxony; almost totally destroyed by bombing in 1945, now rebuilt; airport; railway; technical university (1828); Dresden china now manufactured in Meissen; motor vehicles, electronics, pharmaceuticals, food processing, optical instruments, market gardening.

dressage [dresahzh] An equestrian discipline which is a test of the horse's obedience skills, consisting of a series of movements at the walk, trot, and canter. Dressage can have its own competition or form part of a *three-day event*.

Dreyer, John (Louis Emil) [drayer] (1852–1926) Astronomer, born in Copenhagen, Denmark. He worked at Birr Castle, Ireland, then became director of Armagh Observatory. He produced the standard catalogue on star clusters, nebulas, and galaxies, the *New General Catalogue* (NGC), which is still in use today.

Dreyfus, Alfred [drayfuhs] (1859–1935) French Jewish army officer, born in Mulhouse, NE France. An artillery captain on the General Staff, he was falsely charged with delivering defence secrets to the Germans (1894). He was court-martialled and transported to Devil's I, French Guiana. The efforts of his wife and friends to prove him innocent provoked a vigorous response from militarists and anti-Semites, and deeply divided the French intellectual and political world. After the case was tried again (1899), he was found guilty but pardoned, and in 1906 the verdict was reversed. Proof of his innocence came when German military documents were uncovered in 1930.

Dreyfuss, Richard [drayfus] (1947–) US film actor, born in New York City, USA. After working on Broadway and in repertory, he gained attention with his roles in *Dillinger* (1973) and *American Graffiti* (1973). He became well known following his performances in *Jaws* (1975), *Close Encounters of the Third Kind* (1977), and *The Goodbye Girl* (1977, Oscar). Later films include *Down* *and Out in Beverly Hills* (1986), *Stakeout* (1987), *Always* (1989), *Postcards from the Edge* (1990), *The American President* (1995), and *Krippendorf's Tribe* (1998).

drift A geological term for glacial or glaciofluvial sedimentary deposits, generally unsorted and unstratified, with a wide range of particle sizes from boulders to clay.

drift chamber *proportional counter*

drill A baboon (*Mandrillus leucophaeus*), native to W African forests; resembles the mandrill, but smaller, with a black face. Drills live to the N of the Sanaga R in Cameroon; mandrills live to the S.

Drinkwater, John (1882–1937) Poet, playwright, and critic, born in London, UK. He was an insurance clerk who achieved an immediate success with his play *Abraham Lincoln* (1918), following this with *Mary Stuart* (1921) and other historical dramas. His first volume of poems appeared in 1923, and he also wrote several critical studies. He was one of the founders of the Pilgrim Players, and became manager of the Birmingham Repertory Theatre.

driver ant A tropical ant; colonies large, with millions of individuals and a single, permanently wingless queen; workers forage in groups; colony nomadic, changing nest site frequently; living workers form walls of bivouac nest to protect queen and brood. (Order: Hymenoptera. Family: Formicidae.)

Drogheda [drouhduh], Ir **Droichead Átha** 53°43N 6°21W, pop (2000e) 25 000. Industrial seaport town in Louth county, NE Leinster, E Ireland; on R Boyne, N of Dublin; Irish parliaments met here until 1494; massacre of garrison by Oliver Cromwell, 1649; railway; brewing, textiles, chemicals; Neolithic passage graves, 7 km/4 mi W; remains of 5th-c monastery at Monasterboice, 8 km/5 mi N; Battle of the Boyne field (1690) 6 km/3¾ mi SW.

Drogheda, Statutes of *Poynings' Law*

dromedary A camel formerly wild in Arabia (*Camelus dromedarius*), now known only in domestication; comprises 90% of the world's camels; found in hot deserts from N Africa to SW Asia (introduced elsewhere); also known as the **Arabian camel** or **one-humped camel**. Originally it was a fast light Arabian camel bred for riding and racing, but the name is now used for all single-humped camels.

drone The male of colonial ants, bees, and wasps, whose only function is to mate with fertile females. It plays no part in brood maintenance. (Order: Hymenoptera.)

drongo A bird native to the Old World tropics; plumage usually glossy black; long forked tail; inhabits woodland; eats mainly insects; fearless in chasing other birds, including hawks. (Family: Dicruridae, 20 species.)

Dronning Maud Land *Queen Maud Land*

dropwort An erect perennial (*Filipendula vulgaris*), growing to 80 cm/30 in, native to Europe, W Asia, and N Africa; roots tuberous; leaves pinnate, with pairs of small leaflets lying between 8–20 pairs of large leaflets; flowers 6-petalled, sepals reflexed, cream tinged with purple, forming an irregular terminal mass; carpels straight. (Family; Rosaceae.)

Drosophila [drosofila] A genus of brownish-yellow fruit flies with typically red eyes. They lay eggs near fermenting fruit, on which the larvae feed. There are c.2600 species, some of which are economically important pests of fruit. The chromosome structure and genetics of *Drosophila* species have been studied extensively. (Order: Diptera. Family: Drosophilidae.)

Droste-Hülshoff, Annette Elisabeth, Freiin (Baroness) **von** [drostuh hülshohf] (1797–1848) Poet, born near Münster, W Germany. Commonly regarded as Germany's greatest woman writer, she led a retired life on her family estate. Her poetry is mainly on religious themes and on the Westphalian countryside. She also wrote a novella, *Die Judenbuche* (1842, The Jew's Beech Tree). Her works were published posthumously in 1851.

drought An extended period of dry weather, generally associated with a blocking anticyclone in which evapotranspiration exceeds precipitation, causing soil moisture deficits. Some regions, especially arid and semi-arid areas, are particularly prone to droughts, which can result in food shortages and human suffering. In the Sahel region on the S edge of the Sahara Desert, rainfall 1968–1972 was only 50% of the 1931–60 average, and was accompanied by major famine. Other areas prone to drought include the W and mid-W USA, parts of Australia and S Africa, but it can occur in any place where there is a low rainfall, including Britain.

drug addiction or **drug dependence** A state whereby an addict habitually takes a drug, the compulsion being fuelled by a continuous need to experience the psychic effect of the particular drug or to avoid the pain and discomfort of its absence. Frequently, long-term addicts need to increase the dose of the drug they are taking to feel the same effect (**drug tolerance**) and often develop anti-social habits, such as theft, to pay for their addiction (if it is to an illegal drug). Addictive drugs include narcotics (eg heroin, cocaine), many types of sedative and tranquillizer, and nicotine.

drug resistance A state in which a patient does not respond to a therapeutic drug. Bacteria may acquire resistance through gene mutation to a particular antibiotic by its overuse or misuse; for example, the first class of antibiotics, the sulphonamides, fell out of use when many common strains of bacteria became resistant. Development of resistance to a range of modern antibiotics, combined with poor living conditions in many inner cities, has led to predictions of new epidemics of infectious diseases such as tuberculosis in the West, which may no longer be curable. Cancer cells may also acquire resistance to drugs which had previously been effective, requiring a change in the course of treatment. Resistance to malarial drugs is a major problem in tropical countries, where malaria causes a million deaths per year. Similarly, insects and other pests acquire resistance to agents (eg DDT) which previously controlled them.

Druids A religious sect among the ancient Celts of pre-Christian Britain and Gaul. They acted as priests, teachers, and judges, taught the immortality of the soul and a doctrine of reincarnation, and it is also thought that they offered human sacrifice. They studied ancient verse and natural philosophy, and were expert in astronomy. The Druids were suppressed in Gaul by the Romans under Tiberius, and probably a little later in Britain. In Ireland they lost their priestly function after the coming of Christianity, and survived as poets and historians.

drum A musical instrument consisting of a membrane of skin or plastic (rarely of other materials) stretched over a hollow resonator or frame, usually of wood or metal. Drums are normally played by striking the membrane with a stick or with the hands, and may be classified according to their shape (eg conical, cylindrical, 'hourglass', kettledrums) and whether they have a single membrane or are double-headed. The kettledrum is one of the few that can be tuned to a definite pitch. Drums are known from Neolithic times, and are found worldwide. Used for a variety of functions in civil and religious ritual, and for communication over distances ('drum-languages'), their powers gave them a special (often sacred) place in early societies.

drumfish Any of a large family of marine and estuarine fishes that have the ability to produce sounds by resonating the swimbladder; many species live in muddy estuarine habitats, and thus have a well-developed sensory apparatus; also known as **croakers**. (Family: Sciaenidae.)

Drumheller pop (2000e) 7300. A city NE of Calgary, Alberta, Canada, located in the Alberta 'Badlands'. Formerly a colliery town, it has been home since 1985 to the Royal Tyrell Museum of Paleontology.

drumlins Small, streamlined, ice-moulded hills made of till, produced by the pressure of moving ice over glacial deposits. They often occur in groups producing a 'basket of eggs' topography. The shape indicates ice flow direction, with their long axis parallel to the ice flow, and their blunter ends pointing towards the ice source.

Drummond (of Hawthornden), William (1585–1649) Poet, born at Hawthornden, near Edinburgh, EC Scotland, UK. He studied law at Bourges and Paris, then became laird of Hawthornden, where he devoted his life to poetry, writing many for Mary Cunningham of Barns, who died on the eve of their marriage (1615), and mechanical experiments. He was the first Scottish poet to write in a form of English not from Scotland. His chief collection, *Poems*, appeared in 1616. His prose works include several royalist pamphlets.

drupe A fleshy fruit in which each of one or more seeds is enclosed by a stony layer.

Druze [drooz] One of the dominant religious communities of Mount Lebanon. The Druze trace their origins to the 11th-c exodus of the followers of Fatimid caliph al-Hakim (996–1021), who left Egypt for Lebanon to avoid persecution for their heterodox views. A sect separate from Islamic orthodoxy, the community is divided between an elite of initiates and the majority who are not initiated. In the 19th-c many Druze moved from Lebanon to the highlands of S Syria, an area known as Jabal Druze. A third community is in Israel. They number c.500 000.

dryad [driyad] In Greek mythology, a being originally connected with oak-trees, but more usually referring to a wood-nymph, living in or among the trees. Dryads were usually friendly, but could frighten travellers.

dry cleaning The cleaning of textiles using organic solvents rather than water. Soil (solid dirt) is held on to fabrics by oil and grease, which are removed by detergents during washing. In dry cleaning, the oil/grease is dissolved by the solvent, and the solid dirt falls away easily.

Dryden, John (1631–1700) Poet, dramatist, and critic, born in Aldwinkle, Northamptonshire, C England, UK. He studied at Cambridge, where he held republican sympathies, and went to London in 1657. In 1658, he wrote *Heroic Stanzas* in homage to Oliver Cromwell. On the restoration of Charles II, he published *Astraea Redux* (1660) in praise of the new monarch. He wrote several plays and satires for the court, his first successful play, written in heroic couplets, being *The Indian Emperor* (1665). After 1676, he began to write in blank verse, producing his best play, *All for Love* (1678). In 1668 Charles II appointed him poet laureate and in 1670 historiographer royal. A loyal Tory, he was called to defend the king's party in a series of verse-satires, notably *Absalom and Achitophel* (1681), which did much to turn the tide against the Whigs, and *The Spanish Friar*, which attacked the Roman Catholic Church. To this era also belong the didactic poem *Religio laici* (1682), which argues the case for Anglicanism. On the accession of James II, a Catholic, Dryden was converted to Catholicism, and his next play, *The Hind and the Panther* (1687), celebrated his new-found faith. He composed the libretti for the operas *Albion and Albanus* (1685) and *King Arthur* (1691) in honour of Charles II and James II respectively. His political reward was a place as controller of customs in the port of London. On the accession of William III (1688), a Protestant, Dryden forfeited his laureateship for refusing to take the oath of allegiance to the king. He also wrote a number of important critical works, many in his late years.

dry dock *dock* (shipping)

dry ice *carbon; sublimation* (chemistry)

Dryopithecus [driyopithekus] A fossil ape abundant in Africa and the Mediterranean region during the Miocene epoch; about the size of a rhesus monkey; walked on all fours; brain gibbon-like; jaw projecting moderately; canine teeth prominent; includes *Proconsul*. (Superfamily: Hominoidea. Family: Pongidae.)

drypoint A method of intaglio printing whereby the metal plate is incised by direct pressure using a steel point. The greatest master was Rembrandt, who often combined drypoint with straightforward etching.

dry rot A serious type of timber decay caused by the fungus *Serpula lacrymans*; infected wood shows a surface growth of white filaments (mycelium); fruiting bodies leathery, bearing rust-coloured spores; common on structural timbers of buildings in damp, poorly ventilated conditions. (Subdivision: Basidiomycetes.)

Drysdale, Russell (1912–81) Painter, born in Bognor Regis, West Sussex, S England, UK. His family settled in Melbourne in 1923, and he studied at the George Bell Art School, Melbourne, in London, and in Paris, where he was influenced by Surrealism. His powerful scenes of the outback were a major contribution to modern art in Australia. He was knighted in 1969, and became a Companion of the Order of Australia in 1980.

DTP *desk-top publishing*

Duala *Douala*

dualism In philosophy, a theory which asserts the existence of two fundamental categories into which everything divides. Examples include Plato's distinction between temporal things and timeless forms, and Descartes' distinction between mind and matter. The notion contrasts with monism and pluralism.

Duarte, Pico [dwah(r)tee], formerly **Monte Trujillo** Mountain in the Cordillera Central of the Dominican Republic, West Indies; height 3175 m/10 416 ft; highest peak in the Caribbean.

Dubai or **Dubayy** [doobiy] pop (2000e) 601 700; area 3900 sq km/1505 sq mi. Second largest of the United Arab Emirates, NE of Abu Dhabi; capital, Dubai, pop (2000e) 427 300; chief town, Mina Jebel Ali, a free trade zone; oil discovered in 1966; natural gas, petrochemicals, desalination, cables, aluminium smelting, steel.

du Barry, Marie Jeanne Gomard de Vaubernier, comtesse (Countess), *née* **Bécu** (c.1743–93) The favourite mistress of Louis XV, born in Vaucouleurs, NE France. Brought up in a Paris convent, she won the notice of Louis XV (1768), and married **Comte Guillaume du Barry** before becoming official royal mistress. Her influence reigned supreme until the death of Louis in 1774, when she was dismissed from court. She lived on her estates until the Revolution when, accused of being a counter-revolutionary, she was tried by the Tribunal of Paris and guillotined.

dubbing The combination of several separate sound recordings into the final composite sound track for a motion picture or video production; sometimes known as **mixing**. The term also refers to the operation of replacing spoken dialogue of a completed sound track by its equivalent in another language, producing a **dubbed** version.

Dubček, Alexander [dubchek] (1921–92) Czechoslovakian statesman, born in Uhrovek, W Slovak Republic. He joined the Communist Party in 1939, fought as a Slovak patriot against the Nazis (1944–5), and rose to become first secretary in the Party (1968). He introduced a series of far-reaching economic and political reforms, including abolition of censorship and increased freedom of speech (the 'Prague Spring'). His liberalization policy led to the occupation of Czechoslovakia by Warsaw Pact forces (Aug 1968), and in 1969 he was replaced by Husak. He became president of the Federal Assembly, but was then expelled from the Presidium, and deprived of Party membership in 1970. In 1989, following a popular uprising, and the resignation of the Communist government, he was elected chairman of the Czechoslovak Federal Assembly, but retired from political life soon after.

Dublin (city), Ir **Baile Átha Cliath**, ancient **Eblana** 53°20N 6°15W, pop (2000e) 485 000 (county borough), 972 000 (including suburbs). County borough and capital of Ireland; at mouth of R Liffey where it meets the Irish Sea; on site of Viking settlement; first Sinn Féin parliament met here, 1919; airport; railway; ferries to Liverpool and to Holyhead (from both Dublin and Dun Laoghaire); two universities (1591, 1908); two cathedrals; trading port, brewing, distilling, textiles, chemicals, food processing; natural gas pipeline from Kinsale; King's Inns, national museum, national gallery, Leinster House, Dublin Castle, Abbey Theatre; literary associations with Oscar Wilde, W B Yeats, George Bernard Shaw, Jonathan Swift, and James Joyce.

Dublin (county), Ir **Baile Átha Cliath** pop (2000e) 1 038 000; area 922 sq km/356 sq mi. County in Leinster province, E Ireland; bisected W–E by R Liffey and the Grand Canal; Wicklow Mts to the S, and Irish Sea to the W; capital, Dublin; agriculture, livestock, Dublin trade and industries.

Du Bois, W(illiam) E(dward) B(urghardt) [doo **boyz**] (1868–1963) Historian, sociologist, and equal rights campaigner, born into a small black community in Great Barrington, Massachusetts, USA. He studied at Fisk, Harvard, and Berlin universities, and in his writings explored the history and lives of African-Americans. In politics he campaigned for full equality, opposing the tactics of Booker T Washington. He helped found the National Association for the Advancement of Colored People, and in his old age lived in Ghana, where he died.

Dubrovnik [doobrovnik], Ital **Ragusa** 42°40N 18°07E, pop (2000e) 69 500. Port on the Dalmatia coast of Croatia; capital of Dalmatia; earthquake damage, 1979; badly damaged during siege by the Federal Army in the civil war, 1991; airport; car ferries to Italy and Greece; silk, leather, dairy products, liqueurs, tourism; mediaeval town walls surrounding the old town, a world heritage site; cathedral, Rector's palace; Dubrovnik Summer Festival (Jul–Aug).

Dubuffet, Jean [dübüfay] (1901–85) Artist, born in Le Havre, NW France. He studied at the Académie Julian in Paris, and invented the concept of Art Brut, pioneering the use of rubbish (eg discarded newspapers, broken glass, rough plaster daubed and scratched like an old wall) to create images. He is regarded as a forerunner of the Pop Art and Dada-like fashions of the 1960s.

du Cange, Charles du Fresne, seigneur (Lord) [dü kãzh] (1610–88) Scholar, born in Amiens, N France. He became a parliamentary advocate, and a prolific writer and editor. He is best known for his glossaries of the Middle Ages, published in 1678 and 1688.

Duccio di Buoninsegna [doochioh dee bwoninsenya] (c.1260–c.1320) Painter, founder of the Sienese school, born in Siena, C Italy. In his work the Gothic tradition in Italian art is seen in its most highly developed state. His masterpiece is the 'Maestà' for the altar of Siena cathedral (1311), from which came the 'Annunciation' and 'Transfiguration' in the National Gallery, London.

Duchamp, Marcel [düshã] (1887–1968) Painter, born in Blainville, NE France. He was associated with several modern movements, including Cubism and Futurism, and shocked his generation with such works as 'Nude Descending a Staircase' (1912, Philadelphia). He was one of the pioneers of Dadaism. In 1915 he left Paris for New York City, where he laboured eight years on an abstract glass construction bizarrely entitled 'The Bride Stripped Bare by Her Bachelors, Even' (1915–23, Philadelphia). He became a US citizen in 1955.

Duchovny, David (1960–) Actor, born in New York City, USA. He studied at Princeton and Yale, became an actor, and took a range of parts in low-budget films, becoming known in his role as Jake, the narrator in the *Red Shoe Diaries* (1992–7). He achieved star success when he was given the role of Fox Mulder in the cult television series *The X-Files* (1993–2002), for which he received a Golden Globe Best Actor award in 1997. His feature films include *Working Girl* (1988), *Beethoven* (1992), *The X-Files: Fight the Future* (1998), and *Full Frontal* (2003).

Duchy of Cornwall The oldest of English duchies, instituted by Edward III in 1337 to provide support for his eldest son, Edward, the Black Prince. Since 1503 the eldest son of the sovereign has inherited the dukedom; it consists of lands (totalling c.52 000 ha/130 000 acres) in Cornwall, Devon, Somerset, and S London, including the Oval cricket ground. The present Prince of Wales pays one quarter of the revenue into the Treasury.

Duchy of Lancaster A duchy created in 1267 from estates originally given by Henry III to his son Edmund in 1265. It was attached to the Crown in 1399 when the last Duke of Lancaster became Henry IV. The duchy lands consist of some 21 000 ha/52 000 acres of farmland and moorland, mostly in Yorkshire, N England, UK; the revenue is paid direct into the Monarch's private allowance (the Privy Purse), so the duchy functions as a department of state. It is controlled by the Chancellor of the Duchy of Lancaster, a political appointment generally held by a member of the cabinet.

duck A smallish bird (the larger species are called **geese** or **swans**), primarily aquatic, with full webbing between the three front toes; relatively long neck; blunt flattened bill; male has penis (rare in birds). (Family: Anatidae.)

duck-billed platypus A mammal native to E Australia (*Ornithorhynchus anatinus*); length, up to 75 cm/30 in; thick brown fur, soft duck-like bill, short legs with webbed feet, short flattened tail which stores fat; pouch inside each cheek where food is 'chewed' by horny ridges; male with venomous 'spur' on hind leg; inhabits muddy fresh-water; eats aquatic invertebrates (especially insect larvae); also known as **platypus** or **duck-bill**. (Family: Ornithorhynchidae.)

duck hawk *peregrine falcon*

duckweed A tiny floating or submerged herb found in fresh water everywhere. It consists of a flat or convex green thallus a few millimetres across, with a groove concealing the flowers on the margin, and roots on the underside. (Genus: *Lemna*, 15 species. Family: Lemnaceae.)

ductile material *plastic deformation*

ductless glands *endocrine glands*

Dudley 52°30N 2°05W, pop (2001e) 305 200. Metropolitan borough in West Midlands, C England, UK; created in 1974 incorporating Dudley, Halesowen, and Stourbridge; 12 km/7 mi W of Birmingham; known as the capital of the Black Country in 19th-c; railway; castle (13th-c), Church of St Thomas the Apostle (1817–19); engineering, cables, chains.

due process A legal principle which states that no one should be deprived of life, liberty, or property except by proper legal proceeding. The principle is enshrined in the 39th clause of Magna Carta (1215) which provides that 'no freeman shall be arrested or imprisoned or deprived of his freehold or outlawed or banished or in any way ruined, nor will we (ie the monarch) take or order action against him, except by the lawful judgment of his equals and according to the law of the land'. The notion of due process is also embodied in the Fifth and Fourteenth Amendments of the US Constitution, and in Articles 5 and 6 of the European Convention on Human Rights.

Dufay, Guillaume [düfiy] (c.1400–74) Composer, probably born in Cambrai, N France. By 1420 he was in Italy and sang in the papal choir (1428–33, 1435–7). He was later a canon at Cambrai (1439–50, 1458–74), and also employed for lengthy periods at the courts of Ferrara and Savoy. During a year spent in Florence he wrote one of his most famous motets *Nuper rosarum flores*, for the dedication of the dome of Florence Cathedral (1436). He also wrote Masses and a large number of secular songs.

Dufourspitze [doofoorshpitsuh], Ital **Punta Dufour** 45°57N 7°53E. Mountain peak in Switzerland; highest peak of the Monte Rosa group of the Pennine Alps, on the Italian–Swiss border; second highest Alpine peak; height 4634 m/15 203 ft.

Dufy, Raoul [düfee] (1877–1953) Artist and designer, born in Le Havre, NW France. He studied at the Ecole des Beaux-Arts, and was much influenced by Fauvism, which he later abandoned. From 1907 to 1918 he produced many fabric designs and engraved book illustrations, and in 1919 went to the Riviera, where he began a long series of swift calligraphic sketches of seascapes, regattas, and racecourse scenes.

dugong [doogong] A marine mammal (*Dugong dugon*), native to tropical coasts of the Old World; streamlined, with a short broad head; male with short tusks hidden beneath fleshy cheeks; front legs are flippers; hind legs absent; tail with pointed horizontal blades (like the tail of a whale); inhabits shallow waters; eats underwater plants. (Family: Dugongidae. Order: Sirenia.)

Duhamel, Georges [dooamel] (1884–1966) Novelist, poet, and man of letters, born in Paris, France. He studied medicine and became an army surgeon, which provided the background for such works as *Civilisation* (1918, Prix Goncourt). His best-known works are his novel cycles *Salavin* (1920–32) and *Chronique des Pasquier* (1933–44, The Pasquier Chronicles).

Dühem, Pierre (Maurice Marie) [düem] (1861–1916) Philosopher of science and physicist, born in Paris, France. He studied at the Ecole Normale Supérieure, held teaching positions at Lille, and Rennes, and became professor of physics at Bordeaux (1895). His early scientific work was in thermodynamics, and many of his ideas were well in advance of their time. He made important contributions to the history of science, in particular reviving an interest in mediaeval science. His chief works are *La Théorie physique* (1906, Physical Theory) and *Sauver les phénomènes* (1908, Saving the Phenomena).

duiker [diyker] A small African antelope; both sexes with arched back and short horns separated by a tuft of long hairs; two types: the **common** (**grey**, **savanna**, or **bush**) **duiker** (*Sylvicapra grimmia*), and the **forest duiker** (genus: *Cephalophus*, 16 species). The name is Afrikaans for 'diver', because they dive into undergrowth when disturbed.

Duisburg [düsboork] 51°27N 6°42E, pop (2000e) 552 000. Industrial and commercial city in Düsseldorf district, W Germany; river port on W edge of R Ruhr, at confluence of Ruhr and Rhine; largest inland port in Europe; badly bombed in World War 2; railway; university (1972); steel, copper, zinc, heavy equipment, plastics, oil refining, brewing, river craft; home of Gerhard Mercator; international rowing regattas at Wedau sports park.

Duisenberg, Willem (Frederik) [dowsenberkh] (1935–) Banker and politician, born in Heerenveen, The Netherlands. He studied economics at Groningen (1965), worked for the International Monetary Fund (1965–9), became director of The Netherlands Bank (1969–70), and professor of macro-economics at the University of Amsterdam. He served as finance minister in the Den Uyl cabinet (Partij van de Arbeid – Labour) (1973–7) and from 1977 as director of the RABO Bank. In 1998–2003 he was appointed first president of the European Central Bank.

Dukas, Paul (Abraham) [dükah] (1865–1935) Composer, born in Paris, France. Some of his music is classical in approach, but he tended mainly towards Impressionism. His best-known work is the symphonic poem *L'Apprenti sorcier* (1897, The Sorcerer's Apprentice). He also wrote several orchestral and piano pieces, and was professor of composition at the Paris Conservatoire from 1927 until his death.

duke In the UK, a nobleman of the highest order. A royal duke is a son of the sovereign who has been given a dukedom, such as Queen Elizabeth's son Andrew, Duke of York. Philip, Duke of Edinburgh is a royal duke, but not a duke of the blood royal, since he is not a descendant of a British sovereign in the male line.

Dukeries, the Area of NW Nottinghamshire, C England, UK; includes Sherwood Forest and the parks of former ducal seats at Clumber, Thoresby, Welbeck, and Worksop.

Dukhabors *Doukhobors*

dulcimer A type of zither, consisting of a wooden soundbox, usually trapeziform, strung with a variable number of metal strings which pass over (or through) one or more bridges held in place by the pressure of the strings themselves. It is played with hammers of various types, and has been widespread in different forms throughout the world since the 15th-c or even longer.

Dulles, John Foster [duhlez] (1888–1959) US Republican secretary of state (1953–9), born in Washington, District of Columbia, USA. He studied at Princeton and the Sorbonne, and became a lawyer. During World War 2 he advocated a world governmental organization, and in 1945 advised at the Charter Conference of the UN, thereafter becoming US delegate to the General Assembly. As US secretary of state he opened a vigorous diplomacy of personal conferences with statesmen in other countries. He resigned in 1959, and was awarded the Medal of Freedom shortly before his death. Dulles airport, in Washington, is named after him.

Dulong, Pierre Louis [dülõ] (1785–1838) Chemist, born in Rouen, NW France. He trained in medicine and science at Paris, and later became director of its Ecole Polytechnique. His name is now most linked with the **Dulong–Petit law** (1819), devised in association with Alexis Thérèse Petit (1791–1820), which relates the specific heat capacity of a solid element to its relative atomic mass, and which for over a century was a valuable route for finding approximate atomic weights.

Duluth [duhlooth] 46°47N 92°07W, pop (2000e) 86 900. Seat of St Louis Co, NE Minnesota, USA, at the W end of L Superior; established in the 1850s; airfield; railway; major lake port handling grain and iron ore (busiest freshwater port in the USA); steel, cement, metal products, electrical equipment; Aerial Lift Bridge and Leif Erikson Park; Grandma's Marathon (Jun).

duma A political assembly in pre-revolutionary Russia, such as the mediaeval 'Boyars'. Municipal dumas (town councils) similar to the rural *zemstvos* were introduced as part of local government reforms in 1870. After the 1905 revolution the State Duma, a quasi-parliamentary body, was established with limited constitutional powers. Four State Dumas were elected between 1906 and the 1917 revolution, when the institution was abolished. The Duma is also the name given to the present-day Federal Assembly, the lower house of the Russian legislature, according to the 1993 constitution. It comprises 450 members elected by popular vote.

Dumas, Alexandre [dümah], known as **Dumas *père*** ('father') (1802–70) Novelist and playwright, born in Villers-Cotterêts, NE France. He moved to Paris in 1823, where he obtained a clerkship, and began to write. At 27 he became famous with his play *Henri III* (1829). After several other plays, some in collaboration, he turned to travelogues and historical novels. He gained enduring success as a storyteller, his purpose being to put the history of France into novels. Among his best-known works are *Le Comte de Monte Cristo* (1844–5, The Count of Monte Cristo), *Les Trois Mousquetaires* (1845, The Three Musketeers), and *La Tulipe noire* (1850, The Black Tulip). He spent two years in exile in Brussels (1855–7), and helped Garibaldi in Italy (1860–4). In 2002, his body was reburied in the crypt of the Panthéon in Paris. His son, **Alexandre Dumas** (1824–95), often known as **Dumas *fils***, was also a writer, whose best-known work was *La Dame aux camélias* (1848); it was adapted for the opera *La traviata* by Verdi (1853).

du Maurier, Dame Daphne [dü mohryay] (1907–89) Novelist, born in London, UK, the grand-daughter of George du Maurier. She wrote several successful period romances and adventure stories, including *Jamaica Inn* (1936), *Rebecca* (1938), and *The Flight of the Falcon* (1965). She also published plays, short stories, and literary reminiscences. She was made a dame in 1969.

du Maurier, George (Louis Palmella Busson) [dü mohryay] (1834–96) Artist and illustrator, born in Paris, France. He studied chemistry in London (1851), but on returning to Paris adopted art as a profession. In 1860 he went back to London, where he gained a reputation as a designer and book illustrator. Finally he joined the staff of *Punch*, and became widely known as a gentle, graceful satirist of fashionable life. He wrote and illustrated three novels, notably *Trilby* (1894).

Dumbarton 55°57N 4°34W, pop (2000e) 23 500. Administrative centre of West Dunbartonshire, W Scotland, UK; at confluence of Leven and Clyde Rivers, 22 km/14 mi NW of Glasgow; railway; distilling, electronics; Dumbarton castle.

dumb cane An evergreen perennial, native to tropical America; leaves large, narrowly oval with long stalks, often yellow or white variegated; flowers in a spadix surrounded by a large spathe. If eaten, the bitter sap causes swelling of the tongue and throat, hence the name. (Genus: *Dieffenbachia*, 30 species. Family: Araceae.)

Dumfries [duhmfrees] 55°04N 3°37W, pop (2000e) 31 000. Market town and administrative centre of Dumfries and Galloway, SW Scotland, UK; on R Nith, 97 km/60 mi SE of Glasgow; railway; light engineering, textiles; Burns's House and Mausoleum, Old Bridge House (1662), Devorgilla's Bridge; Dumfries and Galloway arts festival (May).

Dumfries and Galloway pop (2000e) 149 500; area 6370 sq km/2459 sq mi. Local government council in SW Scotland, UK; bounded SE by England, S by the Solway Firth, Wigtown Bay, and Luce Bay; Rinns of Galloway peninsula (W); drained by the Cree, Dee, Nith, and Annan Rivers; capital, Dumfries; other chief towns, Kirkcudbright, Stranraer; sheep and cattle, agriculture, forestry, tourism; Stranraer linked by ferry to Larne in N Ireland; Ruthwell Cross, Glen Trool National Park, Galloway Hills.

Du Mont, Allen B(alcom) [doomont] (1901–65) Electronics engineer, born in New York City, USA. Working in the laboratories of the Westinghouse Lamp Company he developed methods for the mass production of radio valves, and also invented the radio set's 'magic eye' tuning indicator. He established his own company in 1931, improved the cathode-ray tube and used it in the oscilloscope he developed, and in 1937 began production of the first fully electronic TV receivers using cathode-ray tubes.

Dumont D'Urville, Jules Sébastien César [dümõ dürveey] (1790–1842) Navigator, born in Condé-sur-Noireau, N France. He entered the navy in 1807, and commanded expeditions to survey the South Pacific (1826–9) and the Antarctic (1837–40), discovering Joinville I and Adélie Land. A French Antarctic station is named after him.

Dumouriez, Charles François (du Périer) [dümooryay] (1739–1823) French general, born in Cambrai, N France. In 1792 he defeated the Prussians at Valmy and the Austrians at Jemappes, but in 1793 lost to the Austrians at Neerwinden. His leanings towards the monarchy caused him to be denounced by the revolutionaries, and to save his head he went over to the Austrians. He later settled in England.

dumping A situation when goods are sold in a foreign country at a price which local producers regard as unfairly low. This may mean selling at below cost of production plus transport, or below the price at which goods are sold in the exporting country plus transport costs, or simply at a price with which domestic producers cannot compete. In the short term, dumping benefits consumers in the importing country. In the long term, dumping could harm consumers if it enabled the dumpers to drive out domestic firms and then raise their prices to monopoly levels. This is unlikely if there are several competing exporters. Many countries have laws to allow 'anti-dumping' duties to be imposed on foreign suppliers accused of dumping. Such duties protect domestic producers, but are harmful to consumers and usually to the country as a whole.

Dunant, (Jean) Henri [dünã] (1828–1910) Philanthropist, born in Geneva, SW Switzerland. He inspired the foundation of the International Red Cross after seeing the plight of the wounded on the battlefield of Solferino. His efforts helped to bring about the conference at Geneva (1863) from which came the Geneva Convention (1864), and in 1901 he shared the first Nobel Peace Prize.

Dunaway, Faye (1941–) Film actress, born in Bascom, Florida, USA. She made her Broadway debut in *A Man for All Seasons* (1962), but it was an off-Broadway success in the play *Hogan's Goat* (1965) which led her to a television debut, a personal contract with Otto Preminger, and a film debut in *The Happening* (1966). Her first starring role was in *Bonnie and Clyde* (1967). Later films include *Chinatown* (1974, Oscar nomination), *Don Juan DeMarco* (1995), *Network* (1976, Oscar), the television production of *Rebecca* (1997), *The Messenger: The Story of Joan of Arc* (1999), and *The Thomas Crown Affair* (1999).

Dunbar, William [duhnbah(r)] (c.1460–c.1520) Poet, probably born in East Lothian, E Scotland, UK. He studied at St Andrews, is believed to have become a Franciscan novice, and travelled widely, before leaving the order and entering the diplomatic service. He was a courtier of James IV, who gave him a pension in 1500. He is the best known of the *makaris* (Scottish 'maker' or 'poet'), a group of Scottish courtly poets who flourished c.1425–1550. His poems include *The Thrissil and the Rois* and *Lament for the Makaris*, and several satires, such as *The Dance of the Sevin Deadly Synnis*. His name disappears from the records after 1513.

Dunblane [duhnblayn] Town near Stirling, Perthshire, Scotland, UK, the scene in March 1996 when 16 children and their teacher were killed by gunman Thomas Hamilton, who then killed himself. One of the consequences was a major national movement directed towards the stricter control of firearms, as well as various measures aimed at improving school security.

Duncan I *Macbeth*

Duncan, Andrew (1744–1828) Physician, born near St Andrews, Fife, E Scotland, UK. He studied medicine at Edinburgh, and in 1773 started the publication 'Medical and Philosophical Commentaries', which was the only journal of its kind in Britain at that time. In 1792 he prompted the Royal College of Physicians in Edinburgh to establish a lunatic asylum, which came to fruition in 1807.

Duncan, Isadora, originally **Angela Duncan** (1877–1927) Dancer and choreographer, born in San Francisco, California, USA. She travelled widely in Europe, performing her own choreography, and founding schools in several cities, such as Berlin, Salzburg, and Vienna. She was one of the pioneers of modern dance, basing her work on Greek-derived notions of beauty and harmony, but using everday movements of running, skipping, and walking. Her unconventional views on marriage and women's liberation gave rise to scandal. She was killed in a car accident in Nice.

Duncan Smith, Iain (1954–) British politician, born in Edinburgh, EC Scotland, UK. He was educated at HMS *Conway*, Anglesey, studied at the University of Perugia, Italy, and trained at Sandhurst Military Academy. A former member of the Scots Guards, he joined the Conservative Party in 1981 and was elected MP for Chingford in 1992, rising to be shadow secretary-of-state for social security (1997–99) and defence (1999–2001). A die-hard Eurosceptic, he defeated Kenneth Clarke in the contest for leadership of the Conservative Party in 2001, the first such leader to be elected by ordinary party members. In October 2003 he lost a vote of confidence in his leadership following a ballot of Conservative MPs, and was replaced by Michael Howard.

Dundalk [duhndolk], Ir **Dun Dealgan** 54°01N 6°25W, pop (2000e) 30 000. Capital of Louth county, Leinster, NE Ireland; on R Castletown near its mouth on Dundalk Bay; railway; brewing, cigarettes, food processing, textiles, printing, chemicals, livestock trade; Dun Dealgan mound 3 km/1¾ mi W (birthplace of Cuchulain); Maytime theatre festival.

Dundee 56°28N 3°00W, pop (2000e) 170 700. Port and (since 1996) local council (Dundee City), E Scotland, UK; on N side of the Firth of Tay, 29 km/18 mi E of Perth; royal burgh since 12th-c; airfield; railway; university (1881); jute, textiles, paper, confectionery, oil-related industries, electronics; Barrack Street natural history museum, Caird Hall (1914–23), Broughty Castle Museum, Claypotts Castle (1569–88), Maggie Centre (2003).

Dundee, John Graham of Claverhouse, 1st Viscount, known as **Bloody Claverse** or **Bonnie Dundee** (c.1649–89) Scottish soldier, born of a noble family. In 1672 he entered the Prince of Orange's horse-guards, and at the Battle of Seneff saved William's life. He returned to Scotland in 1677, and defeated the Covenanters at Bothwell Brig (1679). He was made a privy councillor in 1683, and became Viscount Dundee (1688). Joined by the Jacobite clans, he raised the standard for James II against William and Mary, but died from a musket wound after his successful battle against Mackay at the Pass of Killiecrankie.

Dunedin [duhneedin] 45°52S 170°30E, pop (2000e) 119 000. City in Otago, SE South Island, New Zealand; on the E coast at the S end of Otago peninsula; seaport at Port Chalmers, 13 km/8 mi NE; founded by Scottish settlers, 1848; airfield; railway; university (1869); wool, footwear, clothing, agricultural machinery, trade in wool, meat, fruit, and dairy produce; Scottish influence in buildings, parks, and statues; two cathedrals, Octagon, Burns statue, municipal chambers (1878–80), Fortune Theatre (1869), Knox Church (1876), Early Settlers' Museum, Hocken Library.

Dunfermline [dunfermlin] 56°04N 3°29W, pop (2000e) 51 900. City in Fife, E Scotland, UK; 27 km/17 mi NW of Edinburgh; royal burgh since 1588; ancient residence of Scottish kings and the burial place of several, including Robert the Bruce; birthplace of Charles I and Andrew Carnegie; railway; textiles, clothing, metal products, electronics; Dunfermline Abbey and Palace (11th-c foundation).

Dungannon [duhnganon], Ir **Dun Geanainn** 54°31N 6°46W, pop (2000e) 10 100. Market town in Dungannon district, Tyrone, SC Northern Ireland, UK, 56 km/35 mi SW of Belfast; administrative centre of the district of Dungannon, pop (2000e) 50 000; former stronghold of the Earls of Tyrone; textiles (linen), engineering, food processing; High Cross of Arboe (9th-c) nearby; prehistoric stone circles with grave mounds (c.1800 BC) at Beaghmore.

dung beetle A shiny, dark coloured beetle; lives under dung, on fungi, and in other rotting materials; digs vertical holes beneath dung, placing a single egg on a plug of dung. The adults and larvae produce sound by vibration (*stridulation*). (Order: Coleoptera. Family: Geotrupidae.)

Dungeness Head [duhnjnes] 50°55N 0°58E. Point on the S coast of Kent, S England, UK, projecting into the English Channel SE of Lydd; nearby is Dungeness nuclear power station, with gas-cooled, graphite-moderated reactors (operational 1965), and an advanced gas-cooled reactor (1983).

Dunkirk [duhnkerk], Fr **Dunkerque**, Flemish **Duinekerke** 51°02N 2°23E, pop (2000e) 74 300. Seaport in Nord department, NW France, at the entrance to the Straits of Dover; third largest port of France, with extensive docks and quays; ferry connections to Dover and Harwich; during World War 2, the retreating British Expeditionary Force was rescued from the beaches near the town; railway; shipbuilding, oil refining, fishing equipment, cotton spinning.

Dun Laoghaire [doonlaee], Eng **Dunleary** [duhnleeree], formerly **Kingstown** 53°17N 6°08W, pop (2000e) 56 000. Borough in Dublin county, Leinster, E Ireland; on Irish Sea, S of Dublin; fishing port, resort town, yachting centre, dormitory town for Dublin; named Kingstown when George IV landed here in 1821; railway; ferries to Holyhead.

dunlin A small wading bird (*Calidris alpina*), native to the N hemisphere; mottled brown plumage with pale underside; slender probing bill; inhabits shoreline or open areas near water; forms large flocks. (Family: Scolopacidae.)

Dunlop, (Ernest) Edward, nickname **Weary** (1907–93) Army surgeon, born in Wangaratta, Victoria, SE Australia. An accomplished sportsman, he graduated from Melbourne University, enlisted in the Australian Army Medical Corps in 1939, and in 1942, as a prisoner-of-war, was forced by the Japanese to work on the Burma–Siam Railway. Revered by his fellow prisoners, he ministered to the sick under appalling conditions, and was hailed as the 'Christ of the Burma Road'. After the war he continued his work as a surgeon, and fostered Australian–Asian relations. Named Australian of the Year in 1977, by the time he died he was a national hero, and his ashes were scattered over the Burma railway by prime minister Paul Keating in 1994.

Dunlop, Joey, popular name of **(William) Joseph Dunlop** (1952–2000) Motor-cyclist, an outstanding rider at Isle of Man TT races, born in Ballymoney, NE Northern Ireland, UK. Between 1977 and 1995 he won a record 15 races (one more than Mike Hailwood), including the Senior Tourist Trophy (TT) in 1985 and 1987–8. He won the Formula One TT for the sixth successive season in 1988, and was Formula One world champion 1982–6. He was killed in a road race in Estonia.

Dunlop, John Boyd (1840–1921) Inventor, born in Dreghorn, North Ayrshire, W Scotland, UK. He was a flourishing veterinary surgeon near Belfast, when in 1888 he obtained patents on a pneumatic tyre (invented in 1845 by Robert William Thomson) for bicycles. His company, formed in 1889, became known as the Dunlop Rubber Co in 1900.

Dunmore, Helen (1952–) Poet and novelist, born in Yorkshire, England, UK. She studied at the University of York and began writing poetry, her collections including *The Apple Fall* (1983), *The Raw Garden* (1988), and *Secrets* (1994). Her children's novels include *Going to Egypt* (1992) and *Fatal Error* (1996), and among her books for adults are *Zennor in Darkness* (1993), *Talking to the Dead* (1996), and *With Your Crooked Heart* (2000). In 1996 she won the inaugural Orange Prize for women fiction writers for her novel *A Spell of Winter*. Later novels include *Mourning Ruby* (2003).

Dunmow flitch A side of bacon offered as a prize to any married couple, if the husband could in honesty swear that for a year and a day he had not quarrelled with his wife, nor wished himself unmarried. Instituted at Little Dunmow, Essex, in the 13th-c or earlier, the custom continued into the 18th-c, and has been revived in modern times.

Dunn, Douglas (Eaglesham) (1942–) Poet, born in Renfrewshire, W Scotland, UK. His early work, including *Terry Street* (1969) and *Love or Nothing* (1974), was noted for its registration of urban experience. Later volumes, such as *Barbarians* (1979), *Elegies* (1985), and *Northlight* (1988) have more emotional and more intellectual appeal. *New Selected Poems 1964-2000* appeared in 2003. His short story collections include *Secret Villages* (1985) and *Boyfriends and Girlfriends* (1995).

Dunne, Finley Peter (1867–1936) Journalist and humorist, born in Chicago, Illinois, USA. As **Mr Dooley**, he became widely known from 1900 as the exponent of American-Irish humorous satire on current personages and events. Many of his essays were republished in book form, such as *Mr Dooley in Peace and War* (1898).

Dunnet Head 58°41N 3°22W. Cape in NE Highland, NE Scotland, UK; at W end of Pentland Firth, 13 km/8 mi NE of Thurso; northernmost point of the British mainland.

Dunning, John, 1st Baron Ashburton (1731–83) British statesman and lawyer, born in Ashburton, Devon, SW England, UK. He studied for the bar, and became an MP in 1768. A critic of the administration of Lord North, he is best remembered for passing the 1780 resolution – in reality against North rather than George III – that 'the influence of the crown has increased, is increasing, and ought to be diminished'. He entered the cabinet as Chancellor of the Duchy of Lancaster in Rockingham's administration (1782), and was created a baronet in the same year.

dunnock A small, grey-brown, ground-feeding bird with short slender bill (*Prunella modularis*); native to Europe and W Asia (N Africa in winter); inhabits woodland, scrubland, and gardens; eats invertebrates; also known as **(European) hedge sparrow** or **hedge accentor**. (Family: Prunellidae.)

Dunois, Jean d'Orléans, comte (Count) [dünwah], known as **the Bastard of Orléans** (1403–68) French general in the Hundred Years' War, born in Paris, France, the natural son of Louis, Duke of Orléans (1372–1407). He defeated the English at Montargis (1427), defended Orléans with a small force until its relief by Joan of Arc (1429), then inflicted further defeats on the English, forcing them out of Paris, and by 1453 from Normandy and Guyenne.

Duns Scotus, Johannes [duhnz skohtus], known as **Doctor Subtilis** (Lat 'the Subtle Doctor') (c.1265–1308) Mediaeval philosopher and theologian, probably born in Maxton, Scottish Borders, SE Scotland, UK. He became a Franciscan, studied at Oxford, and lectured there. His works are chiefly commentaries on the Bible, Aristotle, and the *Sentences* of Peter Lombard. A critic of preceding scholasticism, his dialectical skill gained him his nickname; but his defence of the papacy led to his ideas being ridiculed at the Reformation (hence the word *dunce*).

Dunstable [duhnstabl] 51°53N 0°32W, pop (2000e) 50 300. Town in Bedfordshire, SC England, UK; at N end of the Chiltern hills, 7 km/4 mi W of Luton; at the junction of the Roman Watling Street and the earlier Icknield Way; engineering, paper; Whipsnade Zoo nearby; London Gliding Club headquarters on Dunstable Downs.

Dunstable, John [duhnstabl] (?–1453) The most important English composer of the 15th-c, whose influence on his continental contemporaries was considerable. He wrote motets, Masses, and secular songs, including the three-part 'O rosa bella'. He was also skilled in mathematics and astronomy.

Dunstan, St (c.909–88) Abbot, born near Glastonbury, Somerset, SW England, UK. Educated at the abbey of Glastonbury, he became a monk there, and was appointed abbot in 945. He began a great work of reformation, making the abbey a centre of religious teaching. An adviser to King Edmund, he later became Bishop of Worcester (957) and of London (959), then (under King Edgar) Archbishop of Canterbury (960). Feast day 19 May.

Dunwoody, Richard (Thomas), nickname **the Prince** (1964–) Jockey, born in Belfast, Northern Ireland, UK. Champion jockey in 1993–5, he was Grand National winning rider in 1986 and 1994. He rode at least 100 winners in Britain every season from 1989–90. In 1999, he rode home his 1679th winner, setting a National Hunt record, and retired at the end of that year.

duodenal ulcer [dyoo-ohdeenl] A peptic ulcer occurring on the first part of the duodenum.

duodenum [dyoo-ohdeenm] A region of the alimentary canal in vertebrates, important in digestion. In humans it is the C-shaped first part of the small intestine, continuous with the stomach at the pylorus, and continuing as the jejunum. It receives secretions from the liver (bile) and the pancreas (digestive enzymes) via ducts which pierce its wall, and itself secretes important enzymes and hormones concerned with digestion. It provides a large area for the absorption of digestive products.

Duparc, (Marie Eugène) Henri (Fouques-) [düpah(r)k] (1848–1933) Composer, born in Paris, France. He studied under César Franck, and is remembered for his songs which, though only 15 in number, rank among the world's greatest. His self-criticism led him to destroy much of his writing and correspondence, and he wrote little after 1890.

duplication of the cube A classical problem in mathematics, which requires one to build a cube double the volume of a given cube, using ruler and compasses only to construct the length of an edge of the cube. It is sometimes called the **Delian problem**, as it was originally set by the oracle of Delos in the 5th-c BC. The Delians were instructed that, in order to rid themselves of a plague, they must double the altar of their god – its shape being a perfect cube. The problem exercised many mathematicians, but only in the 19th-c was it proved to be impossible. Modern proofs use the technique of group theory.

Du Pont [doo pont] Franco-American industrial family; in full, **du Pont de Nemours**. Their firm has a long history of manufacturing gunpowder, fibres, plastics, and chemicals, and played an important economic role in 19th-c Delaware. Among notable members have been Pierre Samuel (1739–1817), Eleuthere Irenée (1771–1834), Henry (1812–89), Lammot (1880–1952), and Pierre Samuel (1870–1954).

du Pré, Jacqueline [doo pray] (1945–87) Cellist, born in Oxford, Oxfordshire, SC England, UK. She made her debut at the age of 16 and quickly established an international reputation. In 1967 she married the pianist Daniel Barenboim, with whom she gave many recitals. Her career as a player ended in 1973, when she developed multiple sclerosis, but thereafter she continued as a teacher.

Dupré, Marcel [düpray] (1886–1971) Organist, born in Rouen, NW France. He won the Prix de Rome for composition in 1914, and became renowned throughout Europe for his organ recitals. The composer of many chorales and an organ concerto, he also wrote on improvisation, and directed the Conservatoires at Fontainebleau (1947–54) and Paris (1954–6).

Dura-Europos [doora yoorohpos] In Roman times, a major caravan city on the middle Euphrates, and a flourishing frontier town until its sack by the Sassanids in AD 256. The wall paintings from its 3rd-c synagogue form an important link between Hellenistic and early Christian art.

Duralumin [dyuralyumin] The trade name for an alloy of aluminium (over 90%) with copper (about 4%) and minor amounts of magnesium and manganese. It is used in the aircraft industry.

Durand, J(ean) N(icolas) L(ouis) [dürã] (1760–1834) Architect, theorist, and educator, born in Paris, France. He studied architecture at Paris, built little, but had a great influence on contemporary Neoclassical architecture through his teaching at the Ecole Polytechnique (1795–1830) and his *Recueil et parallèle des édifices en tout genre* (1800, Collection and Comparison of Buildings of All Types).

Durango [dooranggoh], also **Victoria de Durango** 24°01N 104°40W, pop (2000e) 448 000. Capital of Durango state, NWC Mexico; 903 km/561 mi NW of Mexico City; altitude 1889 m/6197 ft; founded, 1563; railway; university (1957); timber, iron ore, textiles, farming; cathedral (1695); famous for its iron-water spring.

Duras, Marguerite [düra], pseudonym of **Marguerite Donnadieu** (1914–96) Novelist, born in Gia Dinh, S Vietnam. She was educated in Indo-China, and went to France in 1932. Her reputation was made by the novels she wrote in the 1950s, such as *Un Barrage contre le Pacifique* (1950, trans The Sea Wall), *Le Marin de Gibraltar* (1952, The Sailor from Gibraltar), and *Le Square* (1955). She achieved a wider celebrity with the screenplay for Alain Resnais' film *Hiroshima Mon Amour* (1959, Hiroshima, My Love). Her autobiographical novel *L'Amant* (1984, The Lover, Prix Goncourt) was made into a successful film (1992).

Durban or **Port Natal** 29°53S 31°00E, pop (2000e) 860 000. Seaport in KwaZulu Natal province, South Africa; situated on Indian Ocean coast, 485 km/300 mi SE of Johannesburg; population includes many Indians, descendants of those brought to South African sugar plantations in the 1860s; South Africa's third largest city; mission settlement founded here, 1834; airport; railway; university (1960); shipbuilding, oil refining, chemicals, fertilizers, food processing, textiles, tourism; museum and art gallery, oldest Hindu temple in South Africa.

Dürer, Albrecht [dyoorer], Ger [dürer] (1471–1528) Painter and engraver, born in Nuremberg, SC Germany. He studied under Michael Wolgemut (1434–1519), travelled widely (1490–4), and in 1497 set up his own studio, producing many paintings. In 1498 he published his first great series of designs on wood, the illustrations of the Apocalypse. He was much employed by Emperor Maximilian I, in whose honour he drew the 'Triumphal Car' and (with others) the 'Triumphal Arch', the largest known woodcut (9 sq m/100 sq ft).

duress Violence or threats of violence against a person for the purpose of causing that person to act in a particular way, such as to commit a crime, which may amount to a defence or a mitigating factor. Scotland has a similar defence called *coercion*. The developing area of **economic duress** refers to a situation where a contract may be entered into or, more usually, altered as a result of improper pressure or threats. Such contracts may be set aside in appropriate cases, but more than ordinary commercial pressure must be involved. Duress is not a defence to murder or attempted murder, but it may be a defence to aiding and abetting a murder.

Durey, Louis [düray] (1888–1979) Composer, born in Paris, France. In 1916, under the influence of Erik Satie, he became one of the group of young French composers known as *Les Six*, but broke with them in 1921. He wrote large orchestral and choral works, but is chiefly known for his songs and chamber music.

Durga Puja *Navaratri*

Durham (city) [duhruhm] 54°47N 1°34W, pop (2001e) 87 700. City and administrative centre of County Durham, NE England, UK; on the R Wear; founded in the 10th-c by monks who had fled from Lindisfarne; university (1832); railway; textiles, clothing, coal mining, engineering, carpets; Norman cathedral (1093) and castle (11th-c) designated a world heritage site; Gulbenkian Museum, Durham Light Infantry museum; Durham Rowing Regatta (Jun); miners' gala (Jul).

Durham (county) [duhruhm] pop (2001e) 493 500; area 2436 sq km/941 sq mi. County in NE England, UK; bounded E by the North Sea, rising to the Pennines in the W; drained by the Tees, Derwent, and Wear Rivers; county town, Durham; chief towns include Darlington (new unitary authority from 1997),

Chester-le-Street, Bishop Auckland; coal, engineering, chemicals, agriculture.

Durham Report A government report of 1839 recommending the union of Upper and Lower Canada into a single political structure; produced by Lord Durham, governor-general and high commissioner to British North America, it called for the assimilation of the French-Canadians into English–Canadian economic and linguistic culture, and for an executive council responsible to an elected assembly.

durian An evergreen tree (*Durio zibethinus*) native to Malaysia; pink or white flowers growing directly from trunk and main branches; fruit a large spiny capsule, with delicate-tasting but evil-smelling flesh considered to be a delicacy. (Family: Bombacaceae.)

Durkheim, Emile [derkhiym] (1858–1917) Sociologist, born in Epinal, E France, generally regarded as one of the founders of sociology. He studied at Paris, and became a teacher, then taught at the University of Bordeaux (1887) and at the Sorbonne. His writings include *Les Règles de la méthode sociologique* (1894, The Rules of Sociological Method) and a definitive study of suicide (1897). He is perhaps best known for his concept of 'collective representations', the social power of ideas stemming from their development through the interaction of many minds.

Durmitor [doormitaw(r)] 43°08N 19°01E. Highest mountain in Montenegro; in the Dinaric Alps, rising to 2522 m/8274 ft; in a national park, which is a world heritage site.

Durrell, Gerald (Malcolm) [duhrel] (1925–95) British zoologist, traveller, writer, and broadcaster, born in Jamshedpur, E India, the brother of Lawrence Durrell. He was a student keeper at Whipsnade Zoo (1945–6), then went on several animal collecting expeditions to Cameroon, Guyana, and other countries. His popular animal stories and reminiscences include *My Family and Other Animals* (1956), *A Zoo in My Luggage* (1960), *Birds, Beasts and Relatives* (1969), *Catch me a Colobus* (1972), *The Mockery Bird* (1981), *Marrying Off Mother* (1991), and *The Aye-Aye and I* (1992). His television work includes *The Amateur Naturalist* (1983) and *Ourselves and Other Animals* (1987). He founded the Jersey Zoological Park in 1958, and was founder chairman of Wildlife Preservation Trust International in 1972.

Durrell, Lawrence (George) [duhrel] (1912–90) British novelist and poet, born in Darjeeling, NE India. He studied at Canterbury, and eloped with his future wife to Paris, where he met Henry Miller and began to write novels. He taught English in Athens, then served in the Foreign Office in Cairo, Athens, and Belgrade, settling in Cyprus (1953). He first made his name with *Prospero's Cell* (1945), followed by the cosmopolitan multi-love story comprising the 'Alexandria Quartet' (1957–60): *Justine*, *Balthazar*, *Mountolive*, and *Clea*. A series of five novels commenced in 1974 with *Monsieur*, followed by *Livia* (1978), *Constance* (1982), *Sebastian* (1983), and *Quinx* (1985). He also wrote several books of poems, short stories, and travel books.

Dürrenmatt or **Duerrenmatt, Friedrich** [dürenmat] (1921–90) Writer, born in Konolfingen, WC Switzerland. He studied at Bern and Zürich, and turned from painting to writing. His plays, mostly grotesque and written with black humour, include *Die Ehe des Herrn Mississippi* (1952, The Marriage of Mr Mississippi), which established his international reputation, *Die Physiker* (1962, The Physicists), and *Die Frist* (1977, The Appointed Time). He also wrote novels, short stories, critical essays, and works for radio.

Durrës [dooruhs], formerly **Durazzo**, Turkish **Draj** 41°18N 19°28E, pop (2000e) 97 500. Seaport and capital of Durrës district, W Albania; on the Adriatic Sea, 30 km/19 mi W of Tiranë; Albania's principal port; railway; founded as Epidamnos (627 BC) and renamed Dyrrhachium (229 BC); occupied by Italians and Austrians in World War 1, when capital of Albania (1912–21); population largely of Muslim origin; shipbuilding, metalworking, foodstuffs, tobacco, leatherwork, rubber, fishing, tourism; a seaside health resort; former royal villa and the remains of Byzantine–Venetian fortifications.

durum A wheat (*Triticum durum*) with a high protein content, whose flour is used to make pasta. The flour is harder than that produced by other varieties of wheat, used in bread-making.

Duse, Eleonora [doozay] (1859–1924) Actress, born near Venice, NE Italy. The daughter of strolling players, she rose to fame in Italy, then triumphed throughout the European capitals (1892–3), mainly acting in plays by contemporary French playwrights, Ibsen, and the works of her lover, Gabriele d'Annunzio. Her histrionic genius ranks 'The Duse' as one of the world's greatest actresses. She retired through ill health in 1909, but returned to the stage in 1921, and died during a US tour. She was noted for the beauty and expressiveness of her gestures, her lithe grace, and the intensity of her emotional playing.

Dushanbe [dyooshambe], formerly **Kishlak** (to 1925), **Diushambe** (to 1929), **Stalinabad** (1929–61) 38°38N 68°51E, pop (2000e) 743 000. Capital city of Tajikistan, on the R Dushanbe; airfield; railway; university (1948); electrical engineering, metalworking, machines, textiles, silk, foodstuffs.

Düsseldorf [düseldaw(r)f] 51°13N 6°47E, pop (2000e) 594 000. Industrial capital of Düsseldorf district and Nordrhein-Westfalen province, W Germany; on the lower Rhine, 34 km/21 mi NW of Cologne; city status, 1288; railway; university (1965); administrative centre of North Rhine–Westphalia province's heavy industry; iron and steel, aluminium, machinery, oil refining, chemicals, textiles, glassware, plastics, electronics, paper; birthplace of Heinrich Heine; Schloss Benrath (18th-c), art academy (1767), opera house, theatre; fashion centre, congresses, trade fairs.

Dust Bowl The semi-arid area of the US prairie states from Kansas to Texas, which suffers from dust storms. In the 1930s, after several years of good crop yield overcultivation, strong winds and dry weather resulted in major dust storms and soil erosion.

Dutch A member of the W Germanic family of languages, spoken by c.20 million in The Netherlands, Belgium, Suriname, and the Antilles. It is the official language of The Netherlands, and is also spoken in Belgium, where it is called **Flemish**; both dialects are officially referred to as **Nederlands**.

Dutch art The art of the mainly Protestant Dutch Republic (the United Provinces), one of the glories of 17th-c European civilization. The greatest achievements were in painting (Hals, Rembrandt, Steen, Ruysdael, Vermeer) which combined the realistic vision and fine craftsmanship inherited from the early Netherlandish tradition (van Eyck, Bosch) with a new feeling for light and space derived from Renaissance Italy. By the late 16th-c, Haarlem (where Hals worked) was the main centre for painting, while Utrecht saw the latest Italian style of Caravaggio being developed by Terbrughghen and Honthorst. Amsterdam, where Rembrandt worked from 1632, was the prosperous centre of the European art market. There was little call for religious subjects, so painters specialized in genre scenes, portraits, landscapes, or still lifes.

Dutch elm disease A disease affecting all species of elm (genus: *Ulmus*) caused by the fungus *Ceratocystis ulmi*; symptoms include wilting, yellowing of foliage, and eventually death; transmitted from tree to tree by elm-bark beetle. (Order: Eurotiales.)

Dutchman's breeches *bleeding heart*

Dutchman's pipe A perennial climber with twining stems and kidney-shaped leaves (*Aristolochia macrophylla*), native to North America; flowers shaped like a tobacco pipe with a flaring mouth. It is a carrion flower with a typical mottled colouring and scent of decay, which attracts flies to act as pollinators. (Family: Aristolochiaceae.)

Dutch New Guinea *Irian Jaya*

Dutch Reformed Church The largest Protestant Church in Holland, stemming from the Calvinist Reformation in the 16th c. Its leaders and scholars have been influential in Dutch life, in former Dutch colonies, and also in Reformed theology. The Dutch Reformed Church in South Africa (totally separated from the Church in Holland) was the official Church of dominant white Afrikaans-speaking nationals, accused in 1982 by the other Reformed Churches of justifying both theologically and practically the policy of apartheid.

Dutch Wars Three wars between England and the Dutch Republic (1652–4, 1664–7, 1672–4) concerned with issues of world trade and the colonies. The first followed the Navigation Acts, in which England sought to increase its trade; the second involved the colonies in Africa and North America, resulting in the British seizure of the Dutch colony of New Netherland (later New York and New Jersey); and the third resulted from English support of the French in the Treaty of Dover (1670). The wars brought on the decline of Dutch power, and signalled the growing predominance of the English.

Dutch West India Company The organization of Dutch merchants responsible for the settlement of New Netherland, now New York. The Company was established in 1621, and was dissolved in 1674. It was later reorganized as a trading venture.

Dutrochet, René Joachim Henri [dütrohshay] (1776–1847) Physiologist, born in Néon, EC France. He qualified in medicine at Paris, and became physician to Joseph Bonaparte of Spain. He was the first to study and to name osmosis.

Duval, Claude [düval] (1643–70) Highwayman, born in Domfront, NW France. He moved to England at the Restoration (1660) in the service of the Duke of Richmond. Taking soon to the road, he pursued a successful career as a robber, gaining a popular reputation, especially for his daring and gallantry towards the women he robbed. He was captured drunk, and hanged at Tyburn, London.

Duvalier, François [doovalyay], known as **Papa Doc** (1907–71) Haitian politician and president (1957–71), born in Port-au-Prince, Haiti. He trained as a doctor (which gave him his byname) at the University of Haiti, where he worked until 1943. He became director of the National Public Health Service (1946) and minister of health and labour (1948). He organized opposition to the military government of Paul Magloire (1950–6), promoted black nationalism, and was elected president. He held power from 1957 until his death, ruling in an increasingly arbitrary fashion. His regime saw the creation of the dreaded civilian militia known as the Tonton Macoute, and the exile of many people. He became president for life in 1964, and was succeeded in this post by his son, **Jean-Claude Duvalier** (1951–), known as **Baby Doc**, whose regime lasted until 1986.

Duvall, Robert [dooval] (1931–) Actor, born in San Diego, California, USA. He began as a stage actor and made his film debut in *To Kill a Mockingbird* (1963). He earned Oscar nominations for *The Godfather* (1972), *Apocalypse Now* (1979), and *The Great Santini* (1980), before winning the award for *Tender Mercies* (1983). Later films include *Falling Down* (1993), *The Apostle* (1997), and *Secondhand Lions* (2003).

Dvořák, Antonín (Leopold) [dvaw(r)zhak] (1841–1904) Composer, born near Prague (Czech Republic, formerly, Austrian Empire). He was sent to the organ school in Prague in 1857, and began to earn his living from the viola. In 1877 Brahms introduced his music to Vienna, and was a great influence on him. His work, basically classical in structure, but with colourful Slavonic motifs, won increasing recognition, culminating in European acclaim for his *Stabat mater* (1880). By then he had written six symphonies and much chamber and piano music, and in 1891 he was offered the directorship of the New York Conservatory. In the USA he wrote his ninth symphony, the ever-popular 'From the New World'. In 1895 he returned to Prague.

dwarf buffalo *African buffalo; anoa*

dwarfism A disorder of slowed growth in children. It may be due to a variety of factors, including genetic effects (eg achondroplasia) and hormone imbalances, especially deficiencies of thyroid and growth hormones, but also increased secretion of testosterone, which causes premature closure of the growing ends of bone, arresting their linear growth. It may also be due to nutritional deficiencies such as malnutrition or rickets, or generalized chronic illness.

dwarf star Strictly, any star in which the source of energy is the nuclear burning of hydrogen in its core to helium, and therefore lying on the main sequence of stellar evolution. Our Sun, 109 times the diameter of Earth, is a dwarf star. However, the term is also used for white dwarfs, which are not on the main sequence.

Dyak *Dayak*

dyarchy [diyah(r)kee] A system where political authority is divided; associated with constitutional reforms introduced by the British into India in 1919. Under the reforms, some departments of provincial government were under Indian control, while others including finance and security remained under British control. The reforms did not extend to central government.

dyeing The process of permanently changing the colour of a material. This ancient art has developed into a high-technology industry for the coloration of textiles, leather, and other goods. Dyes are usually applied by soaking the material in a solution, which is fixed onto the material by heating.

dye laser A laser in which the lasing medium is a liquid organic dye. It can be made to produce laser light of virtually any frequency, either by altering slightly the chemical composition of the dye, or by including a tuning device within the laser cavity that exploits the unusually broad absorption and emission spectrum of dyes.

dyer's broom or **dyer's greenweed** A variable shrub (*Genista tinctoria*) growing to 2 m/6½ ft, with slender branches, native to Europe and Asia Minor; leaves oblong to lance-shaped; pea-flowers numerous, yellow, borne in long, leafy, terminal inflorescences. The leaves and flowers have been used since Roman times to produce a yellow dye, or mixed with woad to give green. (Family: Leguminosae.)

dyer's rocket *weld*

dyestuff Strongly coloured substances, generally complex organic molecules, which are absorbed by textile materials. Natural dyestuffs of animal and plant origins have now been largely superseded by synthetic dyes. Their uses extend beyond textiles into many areas, including cosmetics, foodstuffs, paper, wood, and biomedical science. Indigo and cochineal are two of the best-known natural dyes, both still in use today. The synthetic *vat* dyes produce strong, bright colours of the highest fastness, and are often used on cotton furnishing fabrics.

Dyfed [duhvid] pop (2000e) 357 500; area 5768 sq km/2227 sq mi. Former county in SW Wales, UK; created in 1974, and replaced in 1996 by Cardiganshire, Carmarthenshire, and Pembrokeshire counties.

Dyke Greg(ory) (1947–) Broadcasting executive, born in London. At first a newspaper journalist, he studied politics at York (1971–4), then became a reporter and producer at LWT. He was editor-in-chief at TVam (1983–4) then director of programmes at TVS (1984–7) and LWT (1987–91), becoming managing director and group chief executive of LWT in 1990. He was chairman and chief executive at Pearson Television (1995–9) before taking over from John Birt at the BBC in 2000. He resigned in 2004 after the Hutton Report severely criticised the BBC.

dyke (geography) A ditch or natural watercourse. The term is also used to describe a long ridge or embankment constructed to prevent flooding, such as those in the Netherlands made to hold back the sea. Low-lying areas of flat land such as the Fens and Broads have many dykes.

dyke (geology) A sheet-like igneous body cross-cutting the bedding planes of country rock, injected under pressure while molten. **Radial** dyke swarms may be associated with doming because of a large igneous intrusion, and **parallel** dyke systems occur as a result of tension at mid-ocean ridges. Usually composed of basic igneous rock (typically dolerite), they vary in thickness from centimetres to tens of metres, and up to hundreds of kilometres in length.

Dylan, Bob [dilan], pseudonym of **Robert Zimmerman** (1941–) Singer, musician, and songwriter, born in Duluth, Minnesota,

USA. He rose to fame in the early 1960s, revitalizing the folk tradition of Woody Guthrie, with its social and political concerns. Opposition to war, the nuclear bomb, and racial and social injustice were the themes of his most famous songs, such as 'Blowin' in the Wind' (1963) and 'The Times They are a-Changin' (1963). In 1965 he outraged folk purists by playing and recording with electrified instruments backed by a rock band; but the results, on the albums *Bringing It All Back Home* (1965), *Highway 61 Revisited* (1965), and *Blonde on Blonde* (1966), revolutionized rock-music lyrics, with a stark and often surreal imagery that was to influence the Beatles and many others. Among his later albums, *John Wesley Harding* (1968), *Blood on the Tracks* (1974), *Desire* (1975), *Street Legal* (1978), and *Love and Theft* (2001) were exceptional achievements.

dynamics (economics) *disequilibrium*

dynamics (mechanics) In mechanics, the study of the properties of the motion of objects, and the relation of this motion to the forces causing it. It is more general than kinematics, which is the study of the motion of objects without attention to forces.

dynamite Once a specific name, now a general term for industrial high explosives consisting of nitroglycerine absorbed on some porous or granular non-explosive substance (such as the *kieselguhr* porous earth of Nobel's first invention) to minimize its vulnerability to shock.

dyne *force*

dysarthria [disah(r)thria] A speech disorder caused by a weakness or paralysis of the vocal organs, due to damage or disease of the nerves that supply them. The voice is indistinct, strained, and imprecise. The effects can range from mild to severe – from a slight slurring to total unintelligibility; its more severe forms are sometimes referred to as **anarthria**.

dysbiosis [disbiyohsis] A disturbance in the bacterial flora of the alimentary canal with resulting gut dysfunction, which may result in diarrhoea, malabsorption, or the absorbing of toxins from the gut with a wide range of symptoms. This condition is probably very common, and up to 50% of the population may be affected at some time. Effective treatment usually requires dietary manipulation to discourage the growth of pathogenic organisms, and it may also be possible to recolonize the gut with 'friendly' bacteria, available in the form of 'probiotics' such as *Lactobacillus acidophilus*.

dysentery [disentree] Intestinal infection leading to profuse diarrhoea, with the passage of blood and mucus in the stool. **Bacillary dysentery** is caused by *Shigella*; the disease is usually mild and short-lived. **Amoebic/amebic dysentery** is caused by a protozoan, *Entamoeba histolytica*, and is more serious, there is more severe and persistent diarrhoea, and the involvement of the liver, with the formation of amoebic abscesses within its substance. Both types are worldwide in distribution, and occur wherever standards of sanitation and hygiene are inadequate.

dysgraphia A disorder affecting a person's ability to write and spell; also called **agraphia**. In adults, it is often associated with damage to the language areas of the brain, for example following a stroke or tumour. The writing may contain badly formed lines and letter shapes, and letters may be misplaced, omitted, or repeated. In particular, several types of spelling disability have been noted, and many patients have related problems of reading.

dyslexia Reading disability, in people with apparently adequate intellectual and perceptual abilities and adequate educational opportunities; sometimes called **alexia**. **Developmental dyslexia** is the term applied to people who have experienced difficulty in learning to read. **Acquired dyslexia** describes those who could once read, but who have lost this ability as a result of brain damage. Further distinctions can be drawn. **Deep** or **phonological dyslexics** can read real words, but have great difficulty with unfamiliar words or nonsense. **Surface dyslexics** can read words showing a regular correspondence between letters and sounds (eg *cat*), but not words where this correspondence is irregular (eg *yacht*). There is no single theory which explains dyslexia, and the nature of the problem has been a source of some dispute. Nevertheless it is common for several members of a family to exhibit similar difficulties with reading and writing, and various educational programmes have been developed for helping sufferers to cope.

dysmenorrhoea / dysmenorrhea [dismenoreea] Discomfort or pain in the lower abdomen associated with menstruation. It is a common, usually mild (but sometimes very painful) complaint, which lasts 12–24 hours from the start of bleeding. In younger women it usually has no obvious cause and tends to resolve with time. In older women, it may be due to pathological causes such as pelvic inflammatory disease, benign tumours of the uterus (*fibroids*), or the presence of uterine tissue outside the uterine cavity (*endometriosis*).

Dyson, Freeman (John) (1923–) Physicist, born in Crowthorne, Bracknell Forest, S England, UK. He studied at Cambridge, and became professor of physics at Cornell University (1951–3), then at the Institute of Advanced Study, Princeton (1953–94). He is well known for his research in quantum theory, especially quantum electrodynamics and the stability of matter, and for contributions to public debate on scientific issues. In 2000 he received the Templeton Prize for Progress in Religion.

dyspareunia [disparoonia] Discomfort or pain experienced by women during sexual intercourse. The most frequent cause is insufficient vaginal lubrication, often as a result of insufficient foreplay prior to sexual intercourse. It may also result from spasm of the vaginal muscle, vulvar infections, or more deeply-sited pelvic disorders.

dyspepsia *indigestion*

dysphasia *aphasia*

dysphonia [disfohnia] A speech disorder in which the voice has an abnormal quality; known as **aphonia** when the voice is completely absent. Voice pitch, loudness, and timbre may be so inefficient that speech can be largely unintelligible; but even when the speech can be understood, the voice quality interferes with communication by drawing attention to itself (eg by being noticeably hoarse or nasal). The condition may arise from physical or psychological causes.

dysplasia A malformation of bone or other body tissue. Cells divide more quickly than normal and do not mature properly, thereby affecting their function. It is a normal finding in damaged tissue while it is repairing. It may also occur in any part of the body for genetic reasons or as a result of adverse environmental stimuli. In some parts of the body (eg the cervix) the dysplastic cells are a precursor of malignancy.

dyspraxia *apraxia*

Dzaoudzi [dzoodzee] 12°47S 45°12E; pop (2000e) 12 000; area 6·7 sq km/2·6 sq mi. Capital and second largest commune of Mayotte, on La Petite Terre I; airport; fishing, agricultural trade.

Dzerzhinsk [dzerzhinsk], formerly **Chernorech** (to 1919), **Rastiapino** (1919–29) 56°15N 43°30E, pop (2000e) 285 000. City in Gorkovskaya oblast, W European Russia; on R Oka, 32 km/20 mi W of Nizhni Novgorod; renamed in honour of Felix Dzerzhinsky, first chairman of the political police organization, Cheka, in 1917; railway; chemicals, construction materials, furniture, textiles, foodstuffs.

dzo *yak*

e

eagle A large-bodied bird of prey that kills its own food (smaller birds of prey – buzzards, falcons, hawks, harriers, or kites). **True** or **booted eagles** have fully feathered, not partly bare, legs. (Family: Accipitridae, 30 species.)

eagle owl An owl native to the Old World; the genus includes the largest of all owls (0·7 m/2·3 ft). It has eyelashes, which are an unusual feature in owls. (Genus: *Bubo*, 11 species. Family: Strigidae.)

Eakins, Thomas [eekinz] (1844–1916) Painter, born in Philadelphia, Pennsylvania, USA. He studied in Paris under Jean Léon Gérôme (1824–1904), and became known for his portraits and genre pictures, especially of sporting scenes. His best-known work is his realistic depiction of a surgical operation, 'The Gross Clinic' (1875, Philadelphia), which was controversially received on account of its detail. He became an influential teacher at the Pennsylvania Academy of Fine Arts in 1879, but his insistence on the use of nude models was controversial, and forced his resignation in 1886. He was also accomplished in photography, sculpture, and other arts.

Ealing Studios, popular name of **Associated Talking Pictures, Ltd** An English motion-picture studio based at Ealing, Greater London, UK. Founded in 1929 by the film producers Basil Dean and Reginald Baker with the financial support of the Courtauld family, the company produced musical comedies and feature films during the 1930s. In World War 2 it created propaganda films for the British Ministry of Information. In the decade after the war, the studio became internationally renowned for a series of satirical 'Ealing Comedies', including *Kind Hearts and Coronets* (1949) and *The Ladykillers* (1955). In 1944 the major portion of stock in the company was sold to the Rank Organization, Ltd, and the studio ceased production in 1955 when it was sold to the British Broadcasting Corporation.

ear *p.487*

ear candles Hollow candles lined with silver foil which are inserted into the external auditory canal and, when lit, produce local heat which stimulates the circulation and local energy points. Herbal extracts in the candle release vapours which circulate in the outer ear, and there is also a mild suction from the rising heat. This is an effective way of softening and extracting ear wax, but there is no evidence for the other beneficial effects claimed.

Earhart, Amelia [ay(r)hah(r)t] (1897–1937) Aviator, born in Atchison, Kansas, USA. She was the first woman to fly the Atlantic, as a passenger, and followed this by a solo flight in 1932. In 1935 she flew solo from Hawaii to California. In 1937 she set out to fly round the world, but her plane was lost over the Pacific.

earl In the UK, a member of the third most senior order of noblemen, and the most ancient title, dating from before the Norman Conquest (Old Norse *jarl*). The wife of an earl is a **countess**.

Earl Marshal In the UK, the hereditary post held by the Howard Dukes of Norfolk. One of the great officers of state, the Earl Marshal is head of the College of Arms and is also responsible for organizing state ceremonies.

Early Christian art *Christian art*

Early English Style The form of English Gothic architecture prevalent during the 13th-c, characterized by pointed arches, rib vaults, and a greater stress on the horizontals than is found in French Gothic architecture. Good examples are the chancel of Lincoln cathedral (c.1192) and Salisbury cathedral (c.1220–70).

EAROM [eeayrom] Acronym for **Electrically Alterable Read-Only Memory**, a type of integrated circuit read-only memory, where the data can be altered electronically while the EAROM remains in circuit. It generally requires rather complicated circuitry, and is not widely used.

Earp, Wyatt (Berry Stapp) [erp] (1848–1929) Gambler, gunfighter, and lawman, born in Monmouth, Illinois, USA. He drifted through the West working at a variety of jobs from confidence trickster to assistant marshal. During his stay in Tombstone, AZ, he befriended Doc Holliday, who joined with the Earp brothers against the Clanton gang in the famous gunfight at the OK Corral (26 Oct 1881). Earp collaborated in the writing of his biography *Wyatt Earp, Frontier Marshal* (1931), published after his death. The book portrayed him as a heroic frontiersman of the Wild West.

Earth The third planet from the Sun, having the following characteristics: mass 5·97 × 10^{24}kg; orbital period 365·26 days; radius (equatorial) 6378 km/3963 mi; obliquity 23°27'; mean density 5·52 g/cm^3; orbital eccentricity 0·017; equatorial gravity 978 cm/s^2; mean distance from the Sun 149·6 × 10^6 km/93 × 10^6 mi; rotational period 23 h 56 min 4 s. It has one large natural satellite, the Moon. There is an oxygen/nitrogen-rich atmosphere, liquid water oceans filling lowland regions between continents, and permanent water ice caps at each pole. It is unique in the Solar System in being able to support life, for which there is fossil evidence in rocks dating from 3·5 thousand million years ago; human population over 6000 million (1999). The interior of the planet is differentiated into zones: an iron/nickel-rich molten *core* (radius c.3500 km/2175 mi) an iron–magnesium silicate *mantle* (c.85% by volume of the Earth); and a *crust* of lighter metal silicates (relatively thin, c.6 km/3½ mi thick under the oceans to c.50 km/30 mi under the continents). The boundary between core and mantle is called the *Gutenberg discontinuity*; that between mantle and crust is the *Mohorovicic* (or *Moho*) *discontinuity*. The interior is hot as a result of energy released through the continuing decay of a small proportion of long-lived radioactive isotopes of potassium, thorium, and uranium. Temperatures in the upper mantle cause partial melting at depths of c.100 km/60 mi. Large sections (*plates*) of the uppermost mantle and crust (the *lithosphere*) move slowly and horizontally relative to one another over the more fluid and partially molten zone (the *asthenosphere*), which extends to a depth of c.250 km/155 mi. The evolution of the Earth's crust is dominated by such motions (*plate tectonics*): the spreading, subduction, and collision of lithospheric plates creates most of the major planetary scale features that have shaped Earth as a planet – volcanism, rifting, mountain building, and continental wandering. The effects of asteroidal impacts are erased/disguised by the rapid rate at which the Earth's surface is reshaped and eroded. Such impacts would have been a dominant process in the earliest evolution of the Earth, and still occur periodically. A complex atmospheric circulation is driven primarily by the non-uniform solar heating of the planet and by its rapid

ear

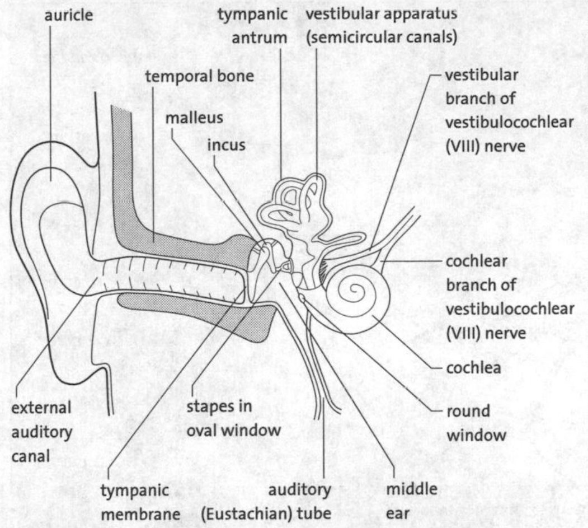

A compound organ concerned with hearing and balance, situated on the side or (in some animals) the top of the head. The **external ear** consists of the *pinna* (commonly referred to as 'the ear') and the *external acoustic meatus* (or *auditory canal*), a tube leading to the eardrum (*tympanic membrane*). In many animals (eg dogs, horses), the pinna can be moved to scan the environment to locate sounds. The **middle ear** (*tympanic cavity*) is an air-filled space, separated from the external ear by the tympanic membrane, and from the internal ear by the oval and round windows. It is continuous with the nasopharynx via the auditory (Eustachian) tube, and contains the auditory *ossicles* (the *malleus*, *incus*, and *stapes*) and two small muscles which act to damp down their vibrations. The **internal ear** consists of a number of parts, but can be divided into that concerned with hearing (the *cochlea*) and that concerned with assessing head position and its movements (the *vestibular apparatus*). The round window is filled with a fibrous membrane which allows movement of the fluid (*perilymph*) within the cochlea, when compressed by the stapes. Sound waves directed down the external auditory canal cause the tympanic membrane to vibrate; movements of the malleus are conveyed to the oval window (via the incus and stapes), where the vibrations are transmitted to the basilar membrane of the cochlea. The *vestibulocochlear nerve* (the VIIIth cranial nerve) conveys information from both parts of the internal ear to the brain. Blockage of the auditory tube leads to the loss of pressure in the middle ear (due to the absorption of air), increased concavity of the tympanic membrane, and progressive deafness. When the blockage is associated with infection of the middle ear, the accumulation of fluid causes the tympanic membrane to bulge towards the external auditory canal, again leading to increasing deafness.

rotation; and there is evidence of repeated climatic changes throughout the geological record.

Earth art *Earthworks*

earthnut A slender perennial (*Conopodium majus*) growing to 60 cm/2 ft, native to Europe; irregular-shaped tubers up to 3·5 cm/$1\frac{1}{2}$ in across, which supposedly resemble nuts; leaves deeply divided into narrow linear segments, soon withering; flowers white or pinkish, in flat-topped umbels 3–6 cm/$1\frac{1}{4}$–$2\frac{1}{2}$ in across; also called **pignut**. The dark brown tubers are edible, cooked or raw. (Family: Umbelliferae.)

earth pig *aardvark*

earthquake *p.488*

earth sciences A general term for the study of the Earth and its atmosphere, encompassing geology and its subdisciplines as well as oceanography, glaciology, meteorology, and the origin of the Earth and the Solar System.

earthshine A phenomenon observable close to new Moon, when the entire disc of the Moon is often bathed in a faint light. The cause is sunlight reflected from the Earth.

earthstar A ground-living fungus with a globular fruiting body; when ripe, outer layer splits into rays, and peels back into a star-shaped structure. (Order: Lycoperdales. Genus: *Geastrum*.)

Earth Summit The name given to the **United Nations Conference on Environment and Development (UNCED)** held in Rio de Janeiro in June 1992. 178 governments were represented at the conference, which brought together more heads of state (114) than had any previous conference on any topic. In addition to government representatives, over 500 interest groups also attended the conference, which attracted a total of 30 000 people to the city. The objective of the conference was to find ways of minimizing the damage done to the environment by the processes associated with economic development. Five agreements were signed, each by most of the governmental participants. The *Framework Convention on Climate Change* introduced measures designed to reduce the threat of global warming. The *Convention on Biological Diversity* put forward proposals aimed at preserving the Earth's biological diversity through the protection of species and ecosystems. *Agenda 21* was an action plan, aimed at introducing sustainable development, which it is hoped would guide government policies throughout the world over the forthcoming decades. The *Rio Declaration* included 27 principles which it was believed should guide action on development and the environment. Finally, the *Forest Principles* emphasized the right of states to exploit their own forest resources while advocating general principles of sustainable forest management. The outcomes of the conference constituted a compromise between the demands of those promoting environmental protection and those advocating continued economic development. It is generally believed that those outcomes favoured development over environment, and the success or otherwise of the conference regarding environmental protection remains to be judged. In particular, the non-governmental organizations meeting in Rio expressed their scepticism about the likelihood of positive international government action. Follow up conferences were held in New York in 1997 (Rio + 5), attended by 185 countries, and in Johannesburg in 2002 (**UN World Summit on Sustainable Development**, Rio + 10).

Earthworks or **Land Art** A modern art movement which started in the late 1960s, in which holes are dug, stones arranged in patterns, etc.; the results are often photographed. Thus in 1968 the US artist Walter de Maria (1935–) chalked two parallel white lines in the Nevada desert and exhibited photographs of them, entitled 'Mile Long Drawing'.

earthworm A terrestrial segmented worm found in soil, feeding mainly on decomposing organic matter; head simple, without sensory appendages; body cylindrical, length up to 4 m/ 13 ft; hermaphrodite; when breeding, develops a saddle (*clitellum*) which secretes material for use during mating and in production of egg cocoon. (Phylum: Annelida. Class: Oligochaeta.)

earwig A slender insect with large pincers at rear end of body, used for courtship, defence, grooming, or predation; forewings small and hard; hindwings membranous; c.1500 species, most abundant in tropics. (Order: Dermaptera.)

easement In English law, a right of use over the land of another. The easement must normally benefit the adjoining land, no matter who is the owner; and will be extinguished if both properties (the *dominant* and *servient tenements*) are subsequently owned and occupied by one person. A private right of way may exist as an easement, though a person may instead have permission to cross land by virtue of a licence. Easements may be expressly or impliedly granted. They may also be

earthquake

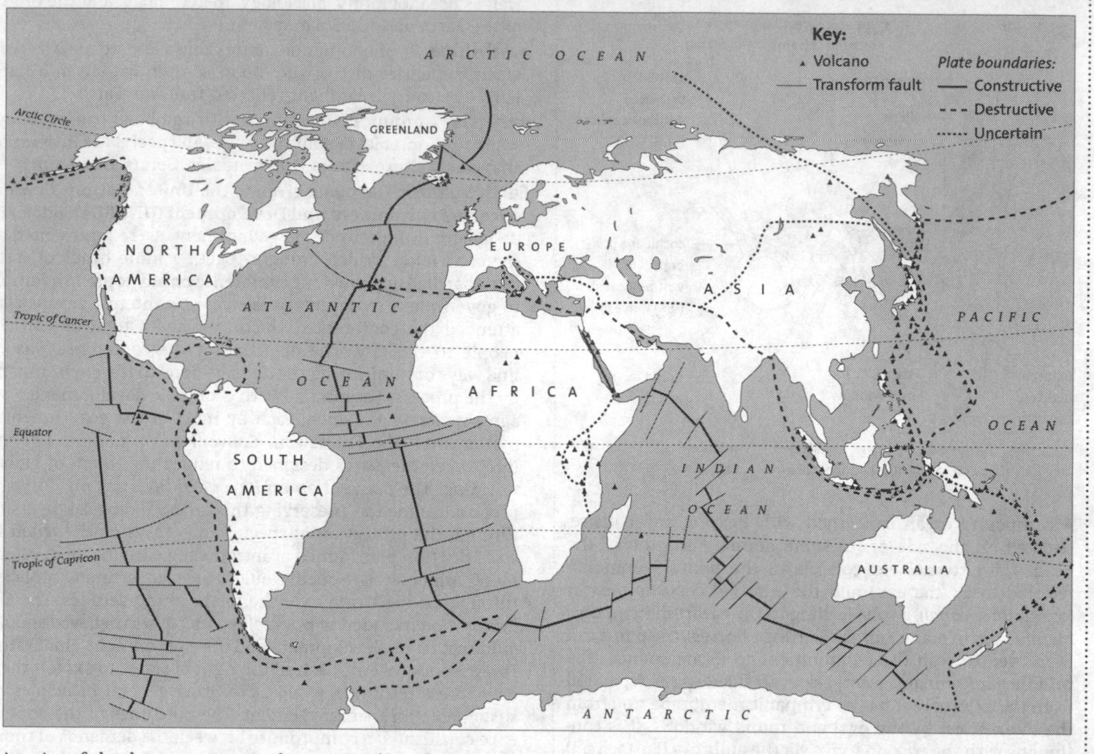

A series of shock waves generated at a point (*focus*) within the Earth, and caused by the movement of rocks on a fault plane releasing stored strain energy. The point on the surface of the Earth above the focus is the *epicentre*. Major earthquakes are associated with the edges of plates that make up the Earth's crust, and along mid-oceanic ridges where new crust is forming. The greatest concentration of earthquakes is in a belt around the Pacific Ocean (the 'ring of fire'), and along a zone from the Mediterranean E to the Himalayas and China. The magnitude of an earthquake is measured on the Richter scale. Major earthquakes, such as in San Francisco in 1906 and Japan in 1923, can cause much damage to property and loss of life.

acquired through long use (*prescription*). Further examples include easement of light, the support of buildings, and the taking of water. An **easement of necessity** is implied when access to land acquired by someone is impossible without a right of way over adjoining land retained by a vendor or lessor. Certain matters may not be the subject of an easement, such as an unspoilt view, though in this particular case a restrictive covenant against building may achieve the desired effect.

East Asian dance The classical dance forms of China, Korea, and Japan, historically linked for more than 2000 years. Traditionally, dance was intermingled with music and drama to create a stylized and symbolic artform, and performances lasted from eight to ten hours. The music that accompanies the dance may be instrumental or vocal; melodies appropriate to the scene, mood, action, or character are selected from a standard musical repertoire. Musical accompaniment is traditionally provided by varying types of *samisen* or three-stringed lutes, and flutes. The dancers themselves may play a musical instrument to express their feelings. East Asian dancers, imbued with the Confucian philosophy of moderation that is conducive to harmony, move in slow, stylized, and often geometric patterns, scarcely raising their feet in the air. Arm and hand movements are important. Dancers portray human or mythological archetypes, especially in masked dances. Among the major traditional dance forms in East Asia today are unmasked dances (the folk and art dances in each country), masked dances (eg Korean *kiak* masked dances), masked dance theatre (eg *Noh* in Japan), danced processions (eg *gyodo* in Japan), dance opera (Peking and other forms of Chinese opera), puppet theatre (eg *bunraku* in Japan), shadow theatre, and dialogue plays with dance (eg *Kabuki* and *Kyogen* in Japan).

East Bank Region in Jordan, E of the R Jordan; comprises the governorates of Amman, al-Balqa, Irbid, al-Karak, and Maan; corresponds roughly to the former Amirate of Transjordan.

East Berlin *Berlin*

Eastbourne 50°46N 0°17E, pop (2001e) 89 700. Coastal town in East Sussex, SE England, UK; on the English Channel, 30 km/19 mi E of Brighton; fashionable 18th-c resort; railway; Lamb Inn (13th-c), Pilgrims Inn (14th-c); Saxon parish church of St Mary; art gallery; tourism; international tennis tournament (Jun).

East End An area of London, UK, situated N of the R Thames and E of Shoreditch and Tower Bridge. With the increasing importance of London as a port in the 19th-c it became a densely-populated industrial area. Although it was heavily bombed during World War 2 and has since been hit by recession, the Dockland Development scheme has recently sought to bring industry and finance into the area.

Easter The chief festival of the Christian Church, commemorating the resurrection of Christ after his crucifixion. It is observed in the Western Churches on a Sunday between 22 March and 25 April inclusive, depending on the date of the first full moon after the vernal equinox; the Orthodox Church has a different method of calculating the date. The name Easter perhaps derives from Eostre, the name of an Anglo-Saxon goddess. Easter customs such as egg-rolling are probably of pagan origin.

Easter Island [paskwa], Span **Isla de Pascua** 27°05S 109°20W; pop (2000e) 2800; area 166 sq km/64 sq mi; maximum length

24 km/15 mi; maximum width 12 km/7 mi. Chilean island just S of the Tropic of Capricorn and 3790 km/2355 mi W of Chile; triangular, with an extinct volcano at each corner; rises to 652 m/2139 ft at Terevaka; undulating grass and tree-covered hills with numerous caves and rocky outcrops; a third covered by Rapa-Nui National Park, established in 1968; rainy season (Feb–Aug); first European discovery by Dutch admiral Jacob Roggeveen on Easter Sunday, 1722; islanders largely of Polynesian origin; capital, Hanga Roa; airport; famous for its *moai* stone statues depicting the human head and trunk of local ancestors; nearly 1000 carved from the slopes of Rano Raraku, where the largest (19 m/62 ft) still lies; remains of the ceremonial city of Orongo on Rano Kau.

Eastern Cape One of the nine new provinces established by the South African constitution of 1994, in SE South Africa, incorporating the former Transkei and Ciskei homelands, and formerly part of Cape Provinces; capital, Bisho; pop (2000e) 6 170 000; area 170 616 sq km/65 858 sq mi; chief languages, Xhosa (85%), Afrikaans, English; second poorest province; automotive industry at Port Elizabeth; agriculture, forestry, tourism (coastal amenities and nature reserves).

Eastern Orthodox Church *Orthodox Church*

Eastern Woodlands Indians A North American Indian group living in the forested region along the Atlantic seaboard from Canada to below S Carolina, and stretching W just beyond the Mississippi R. Algonkin-, Iroquoian-, and Siouan-speaking, they lived by hunting, fishing, and gathering, with some farming of maize, squash, and beans in those areas with a long-enough growing-season (towards the S). They were gradually pushed W and N towards the Great Plains and Canada; others were placed on reservations, some of which still exist in upstate New York and New England.

Easter Rising, also **Easter Rebellion** (24–29 Apr 1916) A rebellion in Dublin of Irish nationalists, whose aims were to establish an Irish Republic. It was organized by two revolutionary groups: the Irish Republican Brotherhood led by Patrick Pearse, and the socialist 'citizen armies' organized by James Connolly. It was preceded by centuries of discontent under British rule, marked by a number of unsuccessful, sporadic revolts. Immediately preceding it was the suspension by the British government of the Home Rule Bill (1914), which had promised some political autonomy. The focal point of the rebellion was the seizing of the General Post Office. The rising was put down and several leaders, including Pearse, Connolly, and Thomas MacDonagh (1878–1916), were executed. De Valera, who later became prime minister and president of Ireland, was sentenced to death, but he was jailed until his release in 1920. The extent of the reprisals, rather than the uprising itself, increased support for the nationalist cause in Ireland. Events following the uprising led to the establishment of dominion status for the Free State in 1921. On Easter Monday, 1949, the Irish Republic was established.

East Germany *Germany*

East India Company, British A British trading monopoly, established in India in 1600, which later became involved in politics, eventually wielding supreme power through a Board of Control responsible to the British parliament. Its first 'factory' (trading station) was at Surat (1612), with others at Madras (1639), Bombay (1688), and Calcutta (1690). A rival company was chartered in 1698, but the two companies merged in 1708. During the 18th-c it received competition from other European countries, in particular France. The company benefited territorially from local Indian disputes and Mughal weakness, gaining control of Bengal (1757), and receiving the right to collect revenue from the Mughal emperor (1765). Financial indiscipline among company servants led to the 1773 Regulating Act and Pitt's 1784 India Act, which established a Board of Control responsible to parliament. Thereafter it gradually lost independence. Its monopoly was broken in 1813, and its powers handed over to the British Crown in 1858 following the Indian Mutiny. It ceased to exist as a legal entity in 1873.

East India Company, Dutch The *Vereenigde Oostindische Compagnie*, a trading company founded in 1602 to protect trade in the Indian Ocean, Indonesia, Japan, and other parts of the East, and to assist in the war against Spain. It established 'factories' (trading stations) on the Indian peninsula, but made little political/cultural contact there, though it did exercise political control in Ceylon. Much larger than the British East India Company, it was at the height of its prosperity during the 17th-c and was dissolved in 1799.

East India Company, French The *Compagnie des Indes Orientales*, a commercial/political organization founded in 1664 which directed French colonial activities in India. It established major trading stations at Chandernagore, Pondicherry, and Mahé, and competed for power with the British during the 18th-c. Its governor, Dupleix, captured Madras (1746), but was defeated during the Seven Years' War (1756–63). The Company lost government support and ceased to exist during the French Revolution.

Eastman, George (1854–1932) Inventor and philanthropist, born in Waterville, New York, USA. He turned from banking to photography, producing a successful roll-film (1884), and the 'Kodak' box camera (1888). In 1889 he manufactured the transparent celluloid film used by Edison and others in experiments which made possible the moving-picture industry.

East Sea, also known as **Sea of Japan** area 978 000 sq km/378 000 sq mi. Arm of the Pacific Ocean, bounded by S and N Korea (SW), Russia (N and W), and the islands of Japan (E and S); NE-flowing warm current keeps coastal conditions ice-free as far N as Vladivostok (Russia).

East Sussex *Sussex, East*

East Timor *p.490*

Eastwood, Clint (1930–) Film actor and director, born in San Francisco, California, USA. He began acting in television Westerns, especially the *Rawhide* series (1959–65), and became an international star with three Italian-made 'spaghetti' Westerns, beginning with *A Fistful of Dollars* (1964). In the USA his box-office status was confirmed with several violent crime thrillers, such as *Dirty Harry* (1971), and from that time he began to combine acting performances with directing, beginning with *Play Misty for Me* (1971) and continuing with *Bronco Billy* (1980), *Heartbreak Ridge* (1986), and *Bird* (1987), among many others. In 1992 he directed the highly successful film *Unforgiven* which received two Oscars (best picture, best director), and later directed and starred in *Absolute Power* (1997), *True Crime* (1998), and *Blood Work* (2002). In 2003 he directed *Mystic River*, for which he also composed the soundtrack. He was elected Mayor of Carmel-by-the-Sea, CA (1986–8).

eau de Cologne mint *mint*

Ebadi, Shirin [ebahdee] (1947–) Lawyer and human rights activist, born in Iran. She studied at Tehran University and became the first female judge in Iran, serving as president of the Tehran City Court from 1975. Forced to resign in 1979 with the advent of the Islamic republic, she went on to set up her own law practice, taking on politically sensitive cases. Her campaigns for greater rights for Iranian women and children, and for the reform of family laws in Iran through changes in divorce and inheritance legislation, have made her a key figure in the reformist movement. She has frequently clashed with the authorities and had brief spells in jail. In 2003 she was awarded the Nobel Peace Prize for her efforts for democracy and human rights.

Ebbinghaus, Hermann [aybinghows] (1850–1909) Experimental psychologist, born in Barmen, W Germany. He taught at Berlin, and became professor at Wrocław, Poland (formerly Breslau, Prussia) (1894–1905), then at Halle. He is best remembered for *Über das Gedächtnis* (1885, On Memory), which first applied experimental methods to memory research, and which introduced the nonsense syllable as a standard stimulus for such work.

EBCDIC code [ebseedik] Acronym for **Extended Binary Coded Decimal Interchange Code**, a binary code used by IBM for information exchange: 256 different characters are defined

East Timor, Democratic Republic of

Local name Port **Timor Leste**, Tetum **Timor Loro Sae**
Timezone GMT + 8
Area 14 874 sq km/5743 sq mi
Population total (2002e) 738 000
Status Republic
Date of Independence 2002
Capital Dili
Languages Tetum and Portuguese (official), Indonesian and English widely spoken
Ethnic groups Tetum
Religion Roman Catholic (91·4 %), traditional animist beliefs
Physical features Occupies E half of the mountainous island of Timor and the enclave of Ocussi (Ambeno) in West Timor, SE Asia, in the Sunda Group, NW of Australia; W half of the island belongs to Indonesia (part of East Nusa Tengarra province); highest peak, Tata Mailau (2950 m/9679 ft); many rivers flowing from the mountains through the coastal plains.
Climate Hot with monsoon rains falling between December and March; average daily temperatures 32°C (Oct–Dec), 21°C (Jan–Sep)
Currency 1 US dollar = 100 cents
Economy 90% of the population live off the land, with one in three households living below the poverty line; coffee is the main export crop, also coconuts, cloves, cacao, and marble; offshore gas and oil to be exploited from 2004.
GDP (2001e) $440 mn, per capita $500
History Former Portuguese colony of East Timor declared itself independent as the Democratic Republic of East Timor, 1975; invaded by Indonesian forces and annexed, the claim not recognized by the UN; administered by Indonesia as the province of Timor Timur; considerable local unrest (1989–90), and mounting international concern over civilian deaths; independence movement (Fretilin) largely suppressed by 1993; UN-sponsored talks, 1993; ongoing conflict, mid-1990s; President Habibie grants referendum, 1999, resulting in 78·5% vote in favour of independence, immediately followed by widespread violence and destruction of property by pro-Jakarta militia groups, and major refugee movements; growing threat to the UN presence in Dili led to arrival of UN-sponsored, Australian-led intervention force; administered by the UN since 1999, with a transitional administration, 2000; elections for an 88-member Constituent Assembly, 2001; Council of Ministers of the Second Transitional Government, 2001; presidential elections (Apr), followed by full independence, May 2002; UN Mission of Support in East Timor (Unmiset) to remain in place until 2004; parliamentary system of government with a largely ceremonial president. *(see map p.767)*
Head of State
2002– Xanana Gusmao
Head of Government
2001– Mari Alkatiri

using an 8-bit code. The characters include all the alphanumeric, punctuation, and non-printing control characters, as well as a considerable number of special characters.

Ebionites [ebioniyts] Literally, 'poor men'; a Judaeo-Christian sect of the early Christian era, opposed by Irenaeus in the late 2nd-c AD. They were apparently ascetic, and continued to observe rigorously the Jewish Law. They also believed that Jesus was the Messiah, a virtuous man anointed by the Spirit, but not truly 'divine'.

Ebla An important Syrian city-state of the third millennium BC, lying S of Carchemish. It traded with Anatolia, Assyria, and Sumeria, and exacted tribute from such places as Mari.

Ebola A virus, first isolated in 1976 in Africa, belonging to the *Filoviridae* family, which causes severe and often fatal haemorrhagic fevers in humans and non-human primates. It is classified as a biosafety level 4 agent because of its extreme pathogenicity and the lack of a protective vaccine or anti-viral drug. Little is known of its natural history and its host is still unidentified.

ebonite *vulcanite*

ebony An evergreen or deciduous tree, native to tropical and subtropical regions, but mainly concentrated in lowland rainforest; leaves alternate, entire, often forming flattened sprays; flowers unisexual, solitary or in small clusters in leaf axils, urn-shaped with 3–5 spreading lobes, white, yellow, or reddish; fruit a berry seated on a persistent calyx. In most species the white outer wood is soft, but the black heartwood, the ebony of commerce, is very hard. Several species are cultivated, both for their superior timber and for the edible fruits (*persimmons*). (Genus: *Diospyros*, 500 species. Family: Ebenaceace.)

Ebro, River [ebroh], ancient **Iberius** Longest river flowing entirely in Spain; rises in the Cordillera Cantabrica and flows SE to enter the Mediterranean at Cape Tortosa; three major reservoirs on its course; used for hydroelectricity and irrigation; length, 910 km/565 mi.

Eccles, Sir John (Carew) (1903–97) Physiologist, born in Melbourne, Victoria, SE Australia. He studied at Melbourne and Oxford, became director of the Kanematsu Institute of Pathology at Sydney (1937), and was professor of physiology at Otago University (1944–51), then at Canberra (1951–66). In 1968 he moved to the State University of New York at Buffalo. A specialist in neurophysiology, he was knighted in 1958, and shared the 1963 Nobel Prize for Physiology or Medicine for work on the functioning of nervous impulses.

Ecclesiastes, Book of [ekleeziasteez] A Biblical work, specifically attributed to 'The Preacher, the son of David, King of Jerusalem', who has traditionally been identified as Solomon, although the work is usually now dated in the post-exilic period of Israel's history. It is largely philosophical in its reflections on the meaning of life, declaring that 'all is vanity'. The title is derived from the Greek rendering of the Hebrew Koheleth: 'the preacher, one who speaks or teaches in an assembly'.

Ecclesiasticus, Book of [ekleeziastikus] (Lat 'the Church (Book)') Part of the Old Testament Apocrypha or Catholic deuterocanonical writings, originally attributed to a Jewish scribe c.180 BC, but later translated into Greek by his grandson; also called **The Wisdom of Jesus, the Son of Sirach**, or just **Sirach** or **Ben Sira**. It consists largely of collections of proverbs and exhortations; praises wisdom, attempting to link it with a Torah-centred way of life; and ends with a historical survey in praise of Israel's famous leaders.

ecclesiology [ekleeziolojee] The theological study of the nature of the Christian Church. The term can also signify the science of church construction and decoration.

ECG *electrocardiography*

echidna [ekidna] An Australasian mammal; coat with spines; minute tail; long claws used for digging; long narrow snout and sticky tongue; eats ants and termites, or larger insects and earthworms; young develop in pouch. (Family: Tachyglossidae, 2 species.)

Echidna [ekidna] In Greek mythology, a fabulous creature, half-woman and half-snake, who was the mother of various monsters.

echinoderm [ekiynoderm] A spiny-skinned marine invertebrate characterized by its typically 5-radial (*pentamerous*) symmetry; body enclosed by a variety of calcareous plates, ossicles, and spines; water vascular system operates numerous tubular feet used in feeding, locomotion, and respiration; includes starfishes, brittle stars, sea lilies, sea urchins, and sea cucumbers, as well as a diverse range of fossils. (Phylum: Echinodermata.)

Echinoidea [ekinoydia] *sea urchin*

Echiura [ekiyoora] *spoonworm*

Echo In Greek mythology, a nymph of whom several stories are told. Either she was beloved by Pan, and was torn to pieces, only her voice surviving; or she was punished by Hera so that she could only repeat the last words of another speaker. She loved Narcissus, who rejected her, so that she wasted away to a voice.

echolalia The automatic repetition of the last words or phrases uttered by someone else. The effect is most commonly seen in dementia, but is also found in childhood psychiatric disorders and in schizophrenia.

echolocation The perception of objects by means of reflected sound waves, typically high-frequency sounds. The process is used by some animals, such as bats and whales, for orientation and prey location.

echo-sounding Bouncing sound waves off the sea-floor to determine the depth of water in the oceans. Echo-sounding is based on the simple principle of measuring the time an acoustic signal takes to travel to the sea floor, be reflected as an echo, and travel back to the sea surface. If the speed of sound in sea water is known, the depth to the sea floor can be calculated. In practice, a device known as a *precision depth recorder* (PDR) is used to print a visual trace of the water depth and provide a picture of the sea-floor topography.

Eck, Johann Mayer von (1486–1543) Roman Catholic theologian, born in Egg, N Switzerland. He became professor of theology at Ingolstadt (1510), and was the ruling spirit of that university until his death. After his Leipzig disputation with Luther, he wrote on papal authority, and went to Rome in 1520, returning with the bull which declared Luther a heretic.

Eckhart, Johannes [ekhah(r)t], also spelled **Eckart** or **Eckehart**, known as **Meister Eckhart** ('Master Eckhart') (c.1260–c.1327) Theologian and mystic, born in Hocheim, WC Germany. He entered the Dominican order, studied and taught in Paris, and became Dominican provincial in Saxony (1303–11). From 1312 he preached at Strasbourg, Frankfurt, and Cologne. His teaching was a mystic pantheism, influential on later religious mysticism and speculative philosophy. In 1325 he was arraigned for heresy by the Archbishop of Cologne, and two years after his death his writings were condemned by Pope John XXII.

eclampsia [eklampsia] Convulsions arising during pregnancy in association with pre-eclampsia. It is a rare disorder, but is dangerous to both the mother and fetus.

eclipse The total or partial disappearance from view of an astronomical object when it passes directly behind, or into the shadow of, another object. In the case of our Sun, a **solar eclipse** can occur only at new Moon, when the Moon is directly between the Earth and the Sun. Although the Moon is much nearer the Earth than the Sun, a coincidence of nature makes both appear nearly the same size in our sky. A **total eclipse**, when the whole disc is obscured, lasts a maximum of 7·5 min, often less; during such an eclipse, the chromosphere and corona are seen. A **partial eclipse** of much longer duration occurs before, after, and to each side of the path of totality. Sometimes the apparent size of the lunar disc is just too small for a total eclipse, and an **annular eclipse** results, in which a bright ring of sunlight surrounds the Moon. A **lunar eclipse** occurs when the Moon passes into the shadow of the Earth, which can happen only at full moon. Then the Moon is a dim coppery hue. Moons and satellites of other bodies in the Solar System are eclipsed when they pass through the shadow of their primary bodies. In binary star systems it is also possible for one star to eclipse another (an *eclipsing binary star*).

ecliptic That great circle which is the projection of the Earth's orbit onto the celestial sphere, and therefore is the apparent path of the Sun across our sky. Positions of the planets as viewed from Earth are generally very close to the ecliptic.

eclogue [eklog] A short dramatic poem, originally with a pastoral setting and theme. Of classical derivation (notably in Theocritus and Virgil), the form was popular in the 16th–17th-c (as Spenser's *Shepheardes Calendar*, 1579), satirized in the 18th-c (eg Gay, Swift), and was adapted to more general purposes by some 20th-c poets (eg Auden, MacNeice).

Eco, Umberto [aykoh] (1932–) Novelist and critic, born in Alessandria, N Italy. He studied at Turin University, has taught semiotics at the University of Bologne for many years, and published several important works on the subject. His novel *Il nome della rosa* (1980, The Name of the Rose), an intellectual detective story, achieved instant fame, and attracted much critical attention; it was filmed in 1986. Later novels are *Foucault's Pendulum* (trans, 1988), *L'isola del giorno prima* (1995, The Island of the Day Before), and *Baudolino* (2002).

ecoanarchy *Greens*

ecology The study of the interaction of living organisms with their physical, biological, and chemical environment. Because of the complexity of ecosystems, ecological studies of individual ecosystems or parts of ecosystems are often made, from which links between different systems can be established. In this way, ecologists attempt to explain the workings of larger ecosystems. Important ecological concepts have had considerable influence in conservation; an example is *carrying capacity*, which relates the available resources of an area to the number of users that can be sustained by these resources. Some ecologists question the role of people in the environment: is humanity dependent on, or independent of, nature? The ecological movement of the 1960s onwards has argued that people must live within the limitations of the Earth's finite supply of resources, and that humanity is very much dependent on its environment. Ecology is therefore seen as a social as well as a scientific subject, providing a link between physical and human environments.

e-commerce The trend, by business and administration, to use data communications to link their computer systems directly to those of their suppliers and customers, also called **electronic commerce**. This allows many transactions to take place without any human involvement, particularly the ordering of materials from suppliers on a just-in-time basis. The term is increasingly used for the marketing of goods and services directly to individual customers through the Internet. Because of the value of the commercial transactions taking place, data communications need to be highly secure, using sophisticated techniques for encryption and authentication.

econometrics A branch of economics which seeks to test and measure economic relationships through mathematical and statistical methods for the purposes of assessing and choosing among alternative policies. It is widely used in economic forecasting. Econometrics now provides the standard of proof across the full range of applied microeconomics, which studies everything from household spending and investment by firms to the organization of industries, labour markets, and the effects of public policy. In 2000 the economists James Heckman and Daniel McFadden were jointly awarded the Nobel Prize for Economics for their contribution to the field of econometrics.

Economic and Social Council *United Nations*

Economic Community of West African States (ECOWAS) An organization formed in 1975 by 15 W African signatories to the Treaty of Lagos: Benin, Gambia, Ghana, Guinea, Guinea-Bissau, Côte d'Ivoire (Ivory Coast), Liberia, Mali, Mauritania, Niger, Nigeria, Senegal, Sierra Leone, Togo, and Upper Volta (now Burkina Faso); Cape Verde joined in 1977. Its principal objectives are the ending of restrictions on trade, the establishment of a common customs tariff, the harmonization of economic and industrial policies, and the elimination of differences in the level of development of member states.

economic history The study of the economies and forms of wealth-creation in past societies. Such work tended to appear as subordinate parts of predominantly political accounts, especially in Britain, until the early 20th-c, but departments of economic history began to appear in universities in the inter-war period. Most of the subject was empirically based, but after c.1950 more attention was paid to prevalent economic theory, especially in the wake of Keynesian analyses, as a means of directing historical enquiry. Sub-specialisms include agricultural history and business history.

economics The study of the allocation of scarce resources among competing ends, the creation and distribution of wealth, and national income. The first major economist was

Adam Smith, and the economic theory of the classical school (*equilibrium*) dominated thinking until the 1930s. The main change in thinking at that time was the result of work by J M Keynes, whose economic theories attempted to solve the problems of depression and economic stagnation. After 1945, the main aim of economic policy was to maintain high employment levels. Inflationary pressures were a test of Keynesian economics: monetarist theories were popular in the 1970s as an attempt to reduce inflation, but these are now believed to have contributed to the high levels of unemployment seen in the early 1980s. Two main aspects are often recognized. **Microeconomics** is the study of the economic problems of firms and individuals, and the way individual elements in an economy behave (such as specific products, commodities, or consumers). **Macroeconomics** is the study of the country as a whole, including such matters as trade, monetary policy, prices, national income, output, exchange rates, growth, and forecasting (*econometrics*). Particular concerns are how to manage an economy to achieve high growth, low inflation, and high employment; and, for individual firms, to predict those economic factors which will affect them in the future, thus enabling them to improve their own planning.

economies of scale The economic theory that, the larger the enterprise, the more profitable will be its operations because there will be lower unit cost, higher productivity, stronger buying power (therefore materials will be bought cheaper), and better plant utilization. However, there are also *dis-economies of scale*: control becomes more difficult, and bureaucratic systems increase costs. The theory is often used to support an argument for merging two companies; but it does not always work out in practice.

ecosocialism A branch of socialism of relatively recent origin which wishes to see socialist practice linked with concern for environmental and ecological matters. In particular, it represents the view that resources other than labour should also be used in a socially useful manner, and reacts against increases in economic growth and high technology production for their own sake.

ecosystem An ecological concept which helps to explain the relationships and interactions between one or more living organisms and their physical, biological, and chemical environment (eg a pond and its associated plants, fish, insects, birds, and mammals). The concept is helpful in describing interactions at any level, from the individual plant in its community to planet Earth. The study of ecosystems is commonly based on transfers of energy along a food chain by examining four elements: *abiotic* or inorganic and dead organic substances (eg inorganic compounds in soil and water); green plants or *producers*, which fix energy from the Sun by photosynthesis and use inorganic material from the soil or atmosphere to manufacture complex organic substances; *consumers* (eg birds, insects, mammals) which use the energy fixed by plants; and *decomposers* (eg bacteria, fungi), which break down dead organisms, releasing nutrients back to the environment for use by the producers. In most natural ecosystems, several food chains interact to form complex food or energy webs. An ecosystem is a convenient model which does not, however, convey the complexity of the interactions which actually take place.

ecotourism *tourist industry*

ecstasy A designer drug which is supposedly mildly hallucinogenic; also called **MDMA** (methylenedioxymethamphetamine), 'E' or 'Adam'. It is reported to heighten the tactile senses of touch and skin sensations, and thereby act as an aphrodisiac. It has been responsible for several deaths because it causes the body to overheat.

ectopic pregnancy [ek**to**pik] The implantation of a fertilized ovum in a site other than within the uterus. The most common abnormal site is within the uterine tube. The main predisposing factor is pelvic inflammatory disease due to *chlamydia trachomatis*. There are two possible outcomes. Either the embryo dies and is reabsorbed, or alternatively the pregnancy ruptures into the abdominal cavity. This presents as a surgical emergency with severe pain and vaginal bleeding, and requires an urgent operation to remove the embryo.

ectoplasm A viscous substance said to exude from the body of a medium during a seance, and from which materializations sometimes supposedly form. This alleged phenomenon was primarily produced by mediums in the late Victorian era. It is the subject of much controversy, as some mediums were discovered to simulate such effects fraudulently, by such means as regurgitation of a previously swallowed substance (such as a piece of cloth).

ECU *European Monetary System*

Ecuador *p.493*

ecumenism [ekyoo**men**izm] (Gr *oikoumene*, 'the inhabited world') A movement seeking visible unity of divided churches and denominations within Christianity. The 4th-c and 5th-c 'Ecumenical Councils' had claimed to represent the Church in the whole world. A dramatic increase of interest in ecumenism and the reuniting of Churches followed the Edinburgh Missionary Conference (1910), and led to the formation in 1948 of the World Council of Churches. Assemblies are held every seven years, the decisions of which guide but do not bind member Churches. The movement encourages dialogue between Churches of different denominations, unions where possible (as in the Churches of N and S India), joint acts of worship, and joint service in the community.

eczema *dermatitis*

edaphology [eeda**fol**ojee] The study of soil as a medium for growth of living organisms. The word is from Greek *edaphos* 'ground, soil'.

Edda (Old Norse 'great-grandmother') The name of two separate collections of Old Norse literature. The **Elder Edda**, long handed down by oral tradition, dating from the 9th-c to the 12th-c, consists of heroic and mythological poems. It comprises mythological poems featuring Germanic gods and goddesses and heroic lays based on early Germanic history. The **Younger** or **Prose Edda** was written (mainly in prose) in the early 13th-c by the Icelandic poet Snorri Sturluson. It contains a discussion of skaldic poetry, giving rules and examples, and a poem in honour of the king and earl of Norway.

Eddington, Sir Arthur S(tanley) (1882–1944) Astronomer, born in Kendal, Cumbria, NW England, UK. He studied at Manchester and Cambridge, where he became professor of astronomy (1913) and director of the Cambridge Observatories, working mainly on the internal structure of stars. In 1919 his observations of star positions during a total solar eclipse gave the first direct confirmation of Einstein's general theory of relativity. He became a renowned popularizer of science, notably in *The Nature of the Physical World* (1928). He was knighted in 1930.

Eddy, Mary Baker, married name **Glover** (1821–1910) Founder of the Christian Science Church, born in Bow, New Hampshire, USA. Brought up a Congregationalist, she had little formal education, because of ill health. In 1866 she received severe injuries after a fall, but read about the palsied man in Matthew's Gospel, and claimed to have risen from her bed similarly healed. Thereafter she devoted herself to developing her spiritual discovery. She set out her beliefs in *Science and Health with Key to the Scriptures* (1875), founded the Christian Science Association in 1876, organized the Church of Christ, Scientist, at Boston in 1879, and founded the *Christian Science Monitor* in 1908.

eddy currents Circulating electrical currents induced in bulk conducting material, rather than circuits, by changing magnetic fields or by the motion of the material in a magnetic field. They are a consequence of electromagnetic induction. The heating effect due to eddy currents in the core material of transformers and motors is a source of power wastage.

Ede, James Chuter, Baron Chuter-Ede of Epsom [eed] (1882–1965) British statesman, born in Epsom, Surrey, SE England, UK. He studied at Cambridge, and became a teacher (1905–14) and local councillor (1920–7), before entering parliament briefly in 1923. He became home secretary in the 1945 Labour govern-

Ecuador

□ International Airport

[ekwadaw(r)], official name **Republic of Ecuador**, Span **República del Ecuador**

Local name Ecuador

Timezone GMT −5

Area 270 699 km^2/104 490 sq mi (including the Galápagos Islands, 7812 km^2/3015 sq mi)

Population total (2002e) 13 095 000

Status Republic

Date of independence 1830

Capital Quito

Languages Spanish (official), with Quechua also spoken

Ethnic groups Quechua (50%), Mestizo (40%), white (8·5%), other Amerindian (5%)

Religions Roman Catholic (94%), other (6%)

Physical features Located in NW South America; includes the Galápagos Is, Ecuadorian island group on the equator 970 km/600 mi W of South American mainland; coastal plain in the W, descending from rolling hills (N) to broad lowland basin; Andean uplands in C rising to snow-capped peaks which include Cotopaxi, 5896 m/19 343 ft; forested alluvial plains in the E, dissected by rivers flowing from the Andes towards the Amazon (source of the Amazon located in Peru).

Climate Hot and humid, wet equatorial climate on coast; rain throughout year (especially Dec–Apr); average annual rainfall 1115 mm/44 in; average annual temperatures in Quito, 15°C (Jan), 14°C (Jul).

Currency 1 US dollar (adopted September 2000)

Economy Agriculture (employs c.35% of population); beans, cereals, livestock; bananas, coffee, fishing (especially shrimps); petrochemicals, steel, cement, pharmaceuticals; oil piped from the Oriente basin in E to refineries at Esmeraldas.

GDP (2002e) $42·65 bn, per capita $3200

Human Development Index (2002) 0·732

History Formerly part of Inca Empire; taken by Spanish, 1534; within Viceroyalty of New Granada; independent, 1822; joined with Panama, Colombia, and Venezuela to form Gran Colombia; left union, to become independent republic, 1830; highly unstable political history; constitution, 1978; comprises 21 provinces, including the Galápagos Is, each administered by a governor; governed by a President and a unicameral National Congress.

Head of State/Government

1966 Clemente Yerovi Indaburu
1966–8 Otto Arosemena Gómez
1968–72 José María Velasco Ibarra
1972–6 Guillermo Rodríguez Lara
1976–9 *Military junta*
1979–81 Jaime Roldós Aguilera
1981–4 Oswaldo Hurtado Larrea
1984–8 León Febres Cordero Rivadeneira
1988–92 Rodrigo Borja Cevallos
1992–6 Sixto Durán Ballén
1996–7 Abdala Bucaram
1997 Rosalia Arteaga *acting*
1997–8 Fabián Alarcón Rivera
1998–2000 Jamil Mahuad Witt
2000–2 Gustavo Noboa Bejarano
2002– Lucio Gutiérrez

ment, and Leader of the House of Commons in 1951. A humanitarian reformer, he was responsible for the Criminal Justice Act of 1948. He became a life peer in 1964.

Edelman, Gerald (Maurice) [aydlman] (1929–) Biochemist, born in New York City, USA. He studied at Pennsylvania and Rockefeller universities, and became professor of biochemistry at Rockefeller in 1966. His special interest was in the chemical structure and mode of action of the antibodies which form part of a vertebrate animal's defence against infection. He shared the Nobel Prize for Physiology or Medicine in 1972.

edelweiss [aydlviys] A perennial (*Leontopodium alpinum*) growing to 20 cm/8 in, native to the mountains of SE Europe; leaves narrowly lance- or spoon-shaped, with a dense covering of white woolly hairs pressed flat against the surface; flower-heads yellowish-white, arranged in a flat-topped cluster surrounded by pointed, spreading, star-like, woolly bracts. It is a well-known alpine plant with romantic associations, protected by law in many districts. (Family: Compositae.)

edema *oedema*

Eden, Sir (Robert) Anthony, 1st Earl of Avon [eedn] (1897–1977) British statesman and prime minister (1955–7), born at Windlestone Hall, Durham, NE England, UK. He studied at Oxford, and served in World War 1 (MC, 1917). He became a Conservative MP in 1923, and was foreign under-secretary (1931), Lord Privy Seal (1933) and foreign secretary (1935), resigning in 1938 over differences with Chamberlain. In World War 2 he was first dominions secretary, then secretary of state for war, and foreign secretary (1940–5). Again foreign secretary (1951–5), he was involved with the negotiations in Korea and Indo-China, and the 1954 Geneva Summit Conference. He succeeded Churchill as prime minister, and in 1956 ordered British forces (in collaboration with the French and Israelis) to occupy the Suez Canal Zone. His action was condemned by the UN and caused a bitter controversy in Britain which did not subside when he ordered a withdrawal. In failing health, he abruptly resigned in 1957. He was created an earl in 1961.

Eden, Garden of Biblical place associated with **Paradise**, where Adam and Eve lived prior to their sin and expulsion (*Gen* 2, 3). 'Eden' may mean 'delight' (Heb) or simply and more probably 'a plain' (Sumerian). It is also used in Ezekiel as a symbol for the future restitution of Israel after the exile.

Eden Project A sustainable garden development created as a tourist attraction near St Austell, Cornwall, SW England, UK. Opened in 2001, the project's aim is to 'promote the understanding and responsible management of the vital relationship between plants, people and resources, leading towards a sustainable future for all'. Sited in the crater of a disused clay pit are two bubble-shaped geodesic domes known as *biomes*. One is designed to recreate a tropical rainforest climate, while the other controls a warm temperate climate. They house a spectacular and diverse collection of plants from around the world, as well as locally-grown specimens. A dry-tropics biome is planned to open in 2005.

Edentata [eedntahta] (Lat 'with no teeth') An order of mammals characterized by having extra contacts between some of the bones in the spine, and by having no front teeth; comprises anteaters, sloths, and armadillos; anteaters have no teeth; sloths and armadillos have simple molar teeth.

Ederle, Gertrude (Caroline) [ayderlee] (1905–2003) The first woman to swim the English channel, born in New York City, USA. She won a gold medal at the 1924 Olympic Games as a member of the US 400 m relay team, and two bronze medals. On 6 August 1926 she swam the Channel from Cap Gris Nez to Kingsdown in 14 h 31 min, very nearly two hours faster than the existing men's record. She became deaf in her late thirties and took up teaching deaf children how to swim.

Edgar or **Eadgar** (943–75) King of all England (from 959), the younger son of Edmund I (reigned 939–46). He was chosen as King of Mercia and Northumbria when his brother Eadwig (?–959) was deposed there in 957, and King of all England after the death of Eadwig, who still controlled Wessex and Kent. He encouraged the English monastic revival as a means of enhancing his prestige and power. In c.973 he introduced a uniform currency based on new silver pennies, whose design was subsequently altered every few years by periodic recoinages.

Edgar, David (Burman) (1948–) Playwright and teacher, born in Birmingham, West Midlands, C England, UK. He studied drama at Manchester University, and was a journalist before turning to the stage, writing numerous agitprop plays during 1971–4. With *Destiny* (1976) he began to portray current political issues in a more complex theatrical language. His plays include *Saigon Rose* (1976), an eight-hour adaptation of *Nicholas Nickleby* for the Royal Shakespeare Company (1980), *The Shape of the Table* (1990), and *Pentecost* (1995). He also writes for television and radio.

Edgar the Ætheling ('Prince') [athuhling] (c.1050–1125) Anglo-Saxon prince, the son of Edward the Ætheling and grandson of Edmund Ironside. Though chosen as king by some influential Englishmen after the battle of Hastings, he was never crowned. He submitted to William the Conquerer (1066), but then rebelled and fled to Scotland (1068). He was finally reconciled with William in 1074. He joined Robert Curthose, to fight against Henry I for the English crown, but was taken prisoner at the Battle of Tinchebrai (1106), and lived in obscurity after his release.

Edgar Awards Annual awards given by the Mystery Writers of America for the best in mystery fiction and non-fiction published the previous year. The awards began in 1954 and are named in honour of Edgar Allan Poe. Categories include Best Novel, Best Fact Crime, Best Juvenile, and the Grand Master Award.

Edgeworth, Maria (1767–1849) Writer, born in Blackbourton, Oxfordshire, SC England, UK. Her work influenced Walter Scott, whom she visited on several occasions. She is best known for her children's stories, and her novels of Irish life, such as *Castle Rackrent* (1800) and *The Absentee* (1812).

ED glass Special optical glass containing fluorite, used in photographic lenses with the property of anomalous or extra-low dispersion (ED) of light. Optical glass disperses white light into a spectrum, so colour photographs would be blurred unless the lens is designed to bring two colours (wavelengths) such as red and blue to a common focus (*achromatic* correction). A small residual spectrum is left uncorrected, but this can be reduced by ED glass. Lens performance is significantly improved and more compact designs are possible.

Edinburgh [edinbruh] 55°57N 3°13W, pop (2000e) 445 400. Capital of Scotland; in EC Scotland, UK, between Pentland Hills and S shore of Firth of Forth; port facilities at Leith; castle built by Malcolm Canmore (11th-c); charter granted by Robert Bruce, 1392; capital of Scotland, 1482; in the 1760s, New Town area designed by James Craig (1744–95), but the business centre remained in the Old Town; Nor' Loch separating old and new towns was drained and laid out as gardens (Princes Street Gardens); new local council status in 1996 (as City of Edinburgh); airport; railway; Edinburgh University (1583); Heriot-Watt University (1966); Napier University (1992, formerly Polytechnic); commercial, business, legal, and cultural centre; brewing, distilling, finance, tourism, printing, publishing, trade in grain; Edinburgh Castle (oldest part, St Margaret's Chapel, 12th-c); Royal Mile from castle to Palace of Holyroodhouse, official residence of the Queen in Scotland; Holyrood Park, containing Arthur's Seat, extinct volcano; Scott Monument (1844), 61 m/200 ft high; observatory on Calton Hill, with unfinished reproduction of the Parthenon; Royal Observatory on Blackford Hill; Gladstone's Land (6-storey tenement, 1620), house of John Knox (15th-c), St Giles Cathedral (15th-c), National Gallery of Scotland, Scottish National Gallery of Modern Art, Scottish National Portrait Gallery, Royal Museum of Scotland, Museum of Childhood, Wax Museum, Royal Botanic Garden, zoo, Meadowbank Stadium sports complex, artificial ski slope; folk festival (Mar), Royal Highland Agricultural Show (Jun), Military Tattoo (Aug); International, Fringe, Jazz, Book, and Film Festivals, and Highland Games (Aug–Sep).

Edinburgh, Prince Philip, Duke of [edinbruh] (1921–) The husband of Queen Elizabeth II of the United Kingdom, the son of Prince Andrew of Greece and Princess Alice of Battenberg, born in Corfu, Greece. He studied at Cheam, Gordonstoun, and Dartmouth, and entered the Royal Navy in 1939 as Lieutenant Philip Mountbatten. He became a naturalized British subject in 1947, when he was married to the **Princess Elizabeth** (20 Nov). Seriously interested in science and the technology of industry, as well as in youth adventure training, he is also a keen sportsman, yachtsman, qualified airman, and conservationist. In 1956 he began the Duke of Edinburgh Award scheme to foster the leisure activities of young people.

Edinburgh Festival [edinbruh] An international festival of the arts, particularly music and drama, that takes place in August/September every year in Edinburgh, UK. It was established in 1947. As well as the Festival proper, the 'Fringe' offers a lively and ever-growing selection of 'alternative' events.

Edison, Thomas (Alva) (1847–1931) Inventor and physicist, born in Milan, Ohio, USA. He began as a railroad newsboy, and after purchasing some old type published the *Grand Trunk Herald*, the first newspaper printed in a train. He became a telegraph operator and developed the Edison Universal Stock Printer, which enabled him to set up as a manufacturer of printing telegraphs (1871). He quit manufacturing for research in 1876 and invented the phonograph (1877), the carbon-filament light bulb (1879), and motion picture equipment. He discovered thermionic emission (1883), which became the basis for the electronic valve. Altogether he held patents for over 1000 inventions.

editing 1 The physical cutting and joining of the first prints of a motion picture film negative ('rush prints'), each scene and take having been identified and synchronized with the corresponding magnetic sound by the clapper board at the head end. Material is studied on an editing table, with separate paths for picture and sound, the picture being shown on a small screen. Selected frames are marked with grease pencil, and the cut sections joined with transparent adhesive tape to build up the work print. When this is finally approved by the director, it acts as the guide for assembling the corresponding original picture negative. In videotape editing, the original is not cut. Scenes are assembled by re-recording selected sections on to another tape, a standard time-code giving precise identification of the chosen points. Time-codes are now increasingly used in film editing also.

2 The preparation of a book for publication. A *commissioning editor* (or *sponsoring editor*) commissions books and assesses submitted typescripts. A *copy-editor, subeditor*, or *desk editor* checks the text for accuracy, consistency and conformation to house style, marks it with instructions for the typesetter, and may recommend changes in content and structure to the author. The work of the editor may also involve correcting typesetters' proofs, checking for libellous statements, and obtaining permission to use copyright material.

Edmonton 53°34N 113°25W, pop (2000e) 691 000. Capital of Alberta province, Canada, on banks of N Saskatchewan R; most northerly large city in North America; Fort Edmonton built by Hudson's Bay Company, 40 km/25 mi below present site, 1795; destroyed by Indians, 1807, and rebuilt on new site, 1819; reached by railway, 1891; chosen as capital, 1905; rapid growth after discovery of oil nearby, 1947; University of Alberta (1906) and Athabasca University (1972); airport; airfield; petrochemicals, retail and trade centre; ice hockey team, Edmonton Oilers; football team, Edmonton Eskimos; Legislative Building, George McDougall Memorial Shrine and Museum (1871); Klondike Days display, including the Sourdough Raft Race (Jul).

Edmund I (921–46) King of the English (939–46), the half-brother of Athelstan. On Edmund's accession, Scandinavian forces from Northumbria, reinforced by levies from Ireland, quickly overran the E Midlands. He re-established his control over the S Danelaw (942) and Northumbria (944) and, until his murder by an exile, ruled a reunited England.

Edmund II, known as **Edmund Ironside** (c.980–1016) King of the English for a few months in 1016, the son of Ethelred the Unready. He was chosen king by Londoners on his father's death (Apr 1016), while Canute was elected at Southampton by the Witan. Edmund hastily levied an army, defeated Canute, and attempted to raise the siege of London, but was routed at Ashingdon, or possibly Ashdon, Essex (Oct 1016). He agreed to a partition of the country, but died a few weeks later, leaving Canute as sole ruler.

Edmund, St, originally **Edmund Rich** (1170–1240) Clergyman, born in Abingdon, Oxfordshire, SC England, UK. He studied and taught at Oxford and Paris, became famous as a preacher, and was commissioned by the pope to preach the Sixth Crusade throughout England (c.1227). As Archbishop of Canterbury (1234), he became the spokesman of the national party against Henry III, defending Church rights and speaking out against the king's continental policies. Revered for his gentleness, austerity, and purity, he was canonized in 1247; feast day 16 November.

Edomites [eedomiyts] According to the Bible (*Gen* 36), the descendants of Esau who settled in the mountainous area S of the Dead Sea to the Gulf of Aqabah; in Greek, **Idumeans**. They often appear as enemies of Israel, having been conquered by David, but retaking parts of Judah and becoming a kingdom in the 8th-c BC. They participated in the overthrow of Judah in 587 BC by the Babylonians, but were eventually conquered by John Hyrcanus in the late 2nd-c BC, forcing their integration into the Jewish people. Herod I (the Great) was of Edomite descent.

EDTA $C_{10}H_{16}N_2O_8$, *diaminoethanetetra-acetic acid* (the abbreviation is from an older form of the name). One of the most versatile of the complexing agents; up to six of its O and N atoms can co-ordinate to a metal ion at one time. It is used to remove small traces of metal ions from solutions.

education What takes place when human beings learn something, often from others but sometimes for themselves. It may happen during the day in specially constructed buildings with qualified teachers following structured, approved courses based on books, equipment, or activities, or more informally away from institutions in homes, streets, or meeting places. It is not confined to traditional school subjects such as mathematics or history, though these will usually constitute an important part of it, nor is it offered only by paid teachers, for parents and elder brothers and sisters may well play a central part in it. Increasingly, education is seen as something which should develop the whole person, not just as a narrow academic training. Thus in a vast variety of locations around the world, from lavishly equipped buildings with the latest laboratory equipment to simple huts in poorer countries, children and adults are learning the basic skills of reading, writing, and arithmetic, developing qualities which will be valuable in adult life whether at home or work, and in many cases taking retraining courses because the job for which they originally prepared has been transformed.

There is considerable variety in educational provision. In some countries the curriculum is prescribed from the centre, with content, books, and even teaching styles laid down in the capital city; in others, with a less centralized curriculum, such decisions are delegated to regional or even individual school level. Most countries operate a primary phase for children up to 11 or 12, a secondary stage for those up to 15, 16, 17, or 18, and then further and higher education for anyone wishing to study beyond the minimum school-leaving age.

Education Act, 1944 Legislation that transformed British education, laying down the framework for the post-war English free secondary education system. In England, pupils were sent to grammar, secondary modern, or technical school. Selection was based on their ability as defined by the '11-plus' examination, which was introduced in the 1950s and lost favour when the non-selective comprehensive system came to dominate state education. The Act was the result of efforts by R A Butler as President of the Board of Education. The Scottish Education Act (1945) and the Northern Ireland Education Act (1947) made similar provisions for primary, secondary, and higher education.

educational drama The use of drama within an educational system, both as a means of learning and as a subject in its own right. Often more emphasis is placed on improvisation and exploration than on performance skills – on drama as process rather than on theatre as product.

educational psychology A branch of psychology developed in the early 20th-c to apply the findings of psychology to the understanding of learning. It was greatly influenced by the psychometric movement, which resulted in the traditional role of the educational psychologist often being limited to one of testing children and placing 'backward' ones into special education. With the decline in popularity of IQ tests and of segregated education, the profession has turned its attention increasingly to the task of assisting teachers in programmes designed to help individual children, and in advising schools about their function as organizations.

Edward, Lake, Democratic Republic of Congo **Lake Rutanzige** area 4000 sq km/1500 sq mi. Lake in EC Africa, in the W Rift Valley on the frontier between the Democratic Republic of Congo and Uganda; length, c.80 km/50 mi; width, 50 km/30 mi; altitude, 912 m/2992 ft; receives the Rutshuru R; Semliki R flows N into L Albert; European discovery by Henry Stanley in 1889; named after the Prince of Wales (later Edward VII).

Edward I (1239–1307) King of England (1272–1307), the elder son of Henry III and Eleanor of Provence, born in London. He married **Eleanor of Castile** (1254) and later **Margaret of France**, the sister of Philip IV (1299). In the Baron's War (1263–7), he at first supported Simon de Montfort, but rejoined his father, and defeated de Montfort at Evesham (1265). He then won renown as a crusader to the Holy Land in the Eighth Crusade (1270–2), and did not return to England until 1274, two years after his father's death. In two devastating campaigns (1276–7, 1282–3) he annexed N and W Wales, and ensured the permanence of his conquests by building magnificent castles. He re-asserted English claims to the overlordship of Scotland when the line of succession failed, and decided in favour of John Balliol (c.1250–1315) as king (1292). But Edward's insistence on full rights of suzerainty provoked the Scottish magnates to force Balliol to repudiate Edward and ally with France (1295), thus beginning the Scottish Wars of Independence. Despite prolonged campaigning and victories such as Falkirk (1298), he could not subdue Scotland as he had done Wales. He died while leading his army against Robert Bruce.

Edward II (1284–1327) King of England from 1307, the fourth son of Edward I and Eleanor of Castile, born in Caernarfon, Gwynedd, NW Wales, UK. In 1301 he was created Prince of Wales, the first English heir-apparent to bear that title, and in 1308 married **Isabella**, the daughter of Philip IV of France. Throughout his reign, Edward mismanaged the barons, who sought to rid the country of royal favourites (such as **Piers de Gaveston**) and restore their rightful place in government. The Ordinances of 1311 restricted the royal prerogative in matters such as appointments to the king's household. Edward was humiliated by reverses in Scotland, where he was decisively defeated by Robert Bruce in the Battle of Bannockburn (1314). The Ordinances were formally annulled (1322), but the king's new favourites, the Despensers, were acquisitive and unpopular, and earned the particular enmity of Queen Isabella. With her lover, Roger Mortimer Earl of March (c.1287–1330), she toppled the Despensers (1326) and imprisoned Edward in Kenilworth Castle. He renounced the throne in favour of his eldest son (1327), who succeeded as Edward III, and was then murdered in Berkeley Castle, near Gloucester.

Edward III, known as **Edward of Windsor** (1312–77) King of England from 1327, born in Windsor, S England, UK, the elder son of Edward II and Isabella of France. He married Philippa of Hainault in 1328, and their eldest child Edward, later called the Black Prince, was born in 1330. By banishing Queen Isabella from court, and executing her lover, Roger Mortimer Earl of March (c.1287–1330), he assumed full control of the government (1330), and began to restore the monarchy's authority and prestige. He supported the attempts of Edward Balliol (c.1250–1315) to wrest the Scots throne from David II, and his victory at Halidon Hill (1333) forced David to seek refuge in France until 1341. In 1337, after Philip VI had declared Guyenne forfeit, he revived his hereditary claim to the French crown through Isabella, the daughter of Philip IV, thus beginning the Hundred Years' War. Renowned for his valour and military skill, he destroyed the French navy at the Battle of Sluys (1340), and won another major victory at Crécy (1346). David II was captured two months later at the Battle of Neville's Cross, near Durham, and remained a prisoner until 1357.

Edward IV (1442–83) King of England (1461–70, 1471–83), the eldest son of Richard, Duke of York, born in Rouen, NW France. His father claimed the throne as the lineal descendant of Edward III's third and fifth sons (respectively Lionel, Duke of Clarence, and Edmund, Duke of York), against the Lancastrian King Henry VI (the lineal descendant of Edward III's fourth son, John of Gaunt). Richard was killed at the Battle of Wakefield (1460), but Edward entered London in 1461, was recognized as king on Henry VI's deposition, and with the support of his cousin, Richard Neville, Earl of Warwick, decisively defeated the Lancastrians at Towton. He threw off his dependence on Warwick, and secretly married **Elizabeth Woodville** (1464). Warwick forced him into exile in Holland (Oct 1470), and Henry VI regained the throne. Edward returned to England (Mar 1471), was restored to kingship (11 Apr), then defeated and killed Warwick at the Battle of Barnet (14 Apr), and destroyed the remaining Lancastrian forces at Tewkesbury (4 May). Henry VI was murdered soon afterwards, and Edward remained secure for the rest of his reign.

Edward V (1470–83) King of England (Apr–Jun 1483), born in London, the son of Edward IV and Elizabeth Woodville. Shortly after his accession, he and his younger brother, Richard, Duke of York, were imprisoned in the Tower by their uncle Richard, Duke of Gloucester, who usurped the throne as Richard III. The two princes were never heard of again, and were most probably murdered (Aug 1483) on their uncle's orders. In 1674 a wooden chest containing the bones of two children was discovered in the Tower, and these were interred in Westminster Abbey as their presumed remains.

Edward VI (1537–53) King of England (1547–53), born in London, UK, the son of Henry VIII by his third queen, Jane Seymour. During his reign, power was first in the hands of his uncle, the Duke of Somerset, and after his execution in 1552, of John Dudley, Duke of Northumberland. Edward became a devout Protestant, and under the Protectors the English Reformation flourished. He died of tuberculosis in London, having agreed to the succession of Lady Jane Grey (overthrown after nine days by Mary I).

Edward VII (1841–1910) King of the United Kingdom (1901–10), born in London, UK, the eldest son of Queen Victoria. Educated privately, and at Edinburgh, Oxford, and Cambridge, in 1863 he married **Alexandra**, the eldest daughter of Christian IX of Denmark. They had three sons and three daughters: **Albert Victor** (1864–92), Duke of Clarence; **George** (1865–1936); **Louise** (1867–1931), Princess Royal; **Victoria** (1868–1935); **Maud** (1869–1938), who married Haaken VII of Norway; and **Alexander** (born and died 1871). As Prince of Wales, his behaviour led him into several social scandals, and the queen excluded him from affairs of state. As king, he carried out several visits to Contintental capitals which strove to allay international animosities.

Edward VIII (1894–1972) King of the United Kingdom (Jan–Dec 1936), born in Richmond, SW Greater London, UK, the eldest son of George V. He studied at Osborne, Dartmouth, and Oxford, joined the navy and (in World War 1) the army, travelled much, and achieved considerable popularity. He succeeded his father in 1936, but abdicated (11 Dec) in the face of opposition to his proposed marriage to **Wallis Simpson**, an American who had been twice divorced. He was then given the title of Duke of Windsor, and the marriage took place in France in 1937. They lived in Paris, apart from a period in the Bahamas (1940–5), where Edward was governor. He died in Paris and was buried at Windsor Castle. His wife, the **Duchess of Windsor** (1896–1986) was born Bessie Wallis Warfield at Blue Ridge Summit, Pennsylvania. She married (1916–27) Lieutenant E W Spencer of the US Navy, then (1927–36) Ernest Simpson, a US-born Englishman. Well known in London society, she met the Prince of Wales at a country house party. After her husband's death, she lived in seclusion, and was in ill health for many years before she died, also in Paris. She was buried beside her husband at Windsor Castle. In recent years claims have been made that he was a Nazi sympathizer.

Edward (Antony Richard Louis), Prince (1964–) Prince of the United Kingdom, the third son of Queen Elizabeth II. He studied at Gordonstoun School, Scotland, then spent several months as a house tutor in New Zealand at Wanganui School. After graduating from Cambridge with a degree in history, he joined the Royal Marines in 1986, but left the following year and began a career in the theatre, beginning as a production assistant with Andrew Lloyd Webber's Really Useful Theatre Company. In 1993 he formed his own company, Ardent Productions. He was made Earl of Wessex and Viscount Severn in honour of his marriage to Sophie Rhys-Jones (1965–) in 1999. Their daughter, Louise Alice Elizabeth Mary Mountbatten-Windsor, Lady Louise Windsor, was born in 2003.

Edward the Black Prince (1330–76) Prince of England, born in Woodstock, Oxfordshire, SC England, UK, the eldest son of Edward III. He was created Earl of Chester (1333), Duke of Cornwall (1337), and Prince of Wales (1343). In 1346, though still a boy, he fought at Crécy, and is said to have won his popular title (first cited in a 16th-c work) from his black armour. He won several victories in the Hundred Years' War, including Poitiers (1356). He had two sons: **Edward** (1356–70) and **Richard**, the future Richard II. In 1362 he was created Prince of Acquitane, and lived there until a revolt forced him to return to England (1371). A great soldier, he was a failure as an administrator.

Edward the Confessor, St (c.1003–66) King of England (1042–66), the elder son of Ethelred the Unready and Emma of Normandy, and the last Anglo-Saxon king before the Conquest.

After living in exile in Normandy, he joined the household of his half-brother Hardicanute in 1041, then succeeded him on the throne. He married **Edith**, the only daughter of the powerful Earl Godwinson of Wessex in 1045. Until 1052 he maintained his position against the Godwin family by building up Norman favourites, and in 1051 very probably recognized Duke William of Normandy (later William I) as his heir. But the Godwins regained their ascendancy, and on his deathbed in London, Edward (who remained childless) named Harold Godwinson (Harold II) to succeed. The Norman Conquest followed soon after. Edward's reputation for holiness began in his lifetime, and he rebuilt Westminster Abbey in the Romanesque style. His cult grew in popularity, and he was canonized in 1161; feast day 13 October.

Edward the Elder (c.870–924) King of Wessex (from 899), the elder son of Alfred the Great. He built on his father's successes and established himself as the strongest ruler in Britain. By one of the most decisive military campaigns of the whole Anglo-Saxon period, he conquered and annexed to Wessex the S Danelaw (910–18). He also assumed control of Mercia (918). Although he exercised no direct power in the North, all the chief rulers beyond the R Humber, including the King of the Scots, formally recognized his overlordship in 920.

Edward the Martyr, St (c.963–78) King of England (975–8). During his reign there was a reaction against the policies in support of monasticism espoused by his father, Edgar. He was murdered by supporters of his stepmother, Elfrida, and canonized in 1001; feast day 18 March.

Edwardes, Sir Michael (Owen) (1930–) British business executive, born in South Africa. He studied at Rhodes University, and joined the Chloride Group of companies in Africa in 1951. He first worked in Britain in 1966, as commercial director then as general manager of Chloride's smallest subsidiary, Alkaline Batteries. He developed a reputation for rescuing ailing companies, and in 1977 was challenged to rescue British Leyland from commercial collapse, which he succeeded in doing over the next five years. He was knighted in 1979.

Edwards, Blake, originally **William Blake McEdwards** (1922–) Director and writer born in Tulsa, Oklahoma, USA. A former actor and radio scriptwriter, he made his film directorial debut in 1955 with *Bring Your Smile Along*. He is best known for *Breakfast at Tiffanys* (1961), and his series of *Pink Panther* films (1964–78) starring Peter Sellers. He also produced, directed, and occasionally wrote for the television series *Peter Gunn*. Other films include *Operation Petticoat* (1959), *S.O.B.* (1981), and *Switch* (1991). He is married to the actress Julie Andrews.

Edwards, Huw (1961–) Television journalist and presenter, born in Llangennech, near Llanelli, Carmarthenshire, SW Wales, UK. He studied French at the University of Wales in Cardiff, and in 1984 entered the BBC's News trainee scheme. In 1985 he joined the television newsroom in BBC Wales, becoming their parliamentary correspondent (1986), and then became chief political correspondent for BBC News 24 (1988). He has presented the Six O Clock News (1999–2002) and the Ten O Clock News (2003–), as well as several general-interest programmes. A Welsh speaker, he presented *The Story of Welsh* (2003).

Edwards, Jonathan (1703–58) Theologian and metaphysician, born in East Windsor, Connecticut, USA. He studied at Yale, was ordained in 1727, and ministered at the Congregationalist Church in Northampton, MA. He was successful for many years, but his extreme Calvinistic orthodoxy led to controversy, and he was dismissed in 1750. He then worked as a missionary with the Housatonnuck Indians until 1757, when he became president of the University College of New Jersey (later, Princeton), but died soon after his installation. His works, which include *Freedom of the Will* (1754), led to the religious revival known as the 'Great Awakening'.

Edwards, Jonathan (1966–) Triple jump athlete, born in London, UK. He studied physics at Durham University, and joined the Gateshead Athletics Club. His sporting achievements include silver medals at the Commonwealth Games (1990, 1994), Commonwealth Games gold (2002), Olympic silver (1996), Olympic gold (2000), European Championship title (1998), and two World Championship gold medals (1995, 2001). He holds six of the best jumps of all time, including the world record of 18·29 m set at the 1995 Athletics World Championships in Gothenburg, Sweden. In 2003, he became England's representative on the board of new communications regulator Ofcom, his role to oversee standards of taste and decency on television. Later that year, he announced his retirement from athletics.

Edwin, St (584–633) King of Northumbria from 616, brought up in North Wales. Under him, Northumbria became united. He pushed his power W as far as Anglesey and Man, obtained the overlordship of East Anglia, and (by a victory over the West Saxons) that of all England, save Kent. He was converted to Christianity, and baptized with his nobles in 627. He fell in battle with the Mercians and Welsh at Hatfield Chase, and was afterwards canonized; feast day 12 October.

EEC *European Economic Community*

EEG *electroencephalography*

eel Any of numerous marine and freshwater fishes with an elongate cylindrical body form; median fins continuous, pelvics absent, and pectorals present or absent; adults live in fresh water, returning to sea to spawn; common European eel (*Anguilla anguilla*. Family: Anguillidae) an important food fish; larval stage called a *leptocephalus*. The name is also used for c.20 families of shallow water and deep-sea fishes that have similar long narrow bodies.

eel grass A grass-like marine plant found in shallow waters around all but tropical coasts; adapted to withstand salt water, it grows completely submerged. It is a major source of food for migrating brent geese. (Genus: *Zostera*, 12 species. Family: Zosteraceae.)

eelpout Slender-bodied fish (*Zoarces viviparous*) with broad head, long dorsal and anal fins, well-developed pectorals, abundant in European coastal waters; length up to 50 cm/20 in; young born fully-formed. The name is also used generally for members of the family Zoarcidae, and as an alternative name for the burbot, *Lota lota*. (Family: Zoarcidae.)

eelworm *nematode*

Efate [efatee], Fr **Vaté**, Eng **Sandwich Island** 17°40S 168°23E; pop (2000e) 39 200; area 985 sq km/380 sq mi. Volcanic island, Vanuatu, SW Pacific; length, 42 km/26 mi; width, 23 km/14 mi; capital, Vila.

EFTA *European Free Trade Association*

egalitarianism A political philosophy which places a high value on equality among members of society, and advocates the removal of barriers to it. It is based on the view that all people are fundamentally equal, and that certain social and political institutions produce inequalities, such as in wealth and income, education, legal rights, and political power. Egalitarianism was one of the tenets of the French Revolution, and is associated with radical and socialist politics.

Egas Moniz, António (Caetano de Abreu Freire) [moneezh] (1874–1955) Neurosurgeon and diplomat, born in Avença, W Portugal. Professor of neurology at Coimbra (1902) and Lisbon (1911–44), he was also a deputy in the Portuguese parliament (1903–17) and foreign minister (1918), and led the Portuguese delegation to the Paris Peace Conference (1918). He is best remembered as the founder of modern psychosurgery, and he shared the 1949 Nobel Prize for Physiology or Medicine for the development of prefrontal lobotomy as a radical treatment for some mental disorders. He also developed the technique of angiography (the X-ray visualization of blood vessels in the brain by injecting an opaque dye into the circulation), used to diagnose brain tumours.

Egbert, in Anglo-Saxon **Ecgberht** or **Ecgbryht** (?–839) King of Wessex (802–39). After his victory in 825 over the Mercians at Ellendun (now Wroughton) in Wiltshire, S England, UK, the areas of Essex, Kent, Surrey, and Sussex submitted to him; in 828 he was recognized as overlord of England, but his conquest of Mercia itself (829) was soon reversed. He extended his control over Cornwall, defeating an alliance between the Vikings and Britons at Hingston Down (838). These successes gave him mastery over S England from Kent to Land's End, and established Wessex as the strongest Anglo-Saxon kingdom.

egg The mature female reproductive cell (*ovum*) in animals and plants; also the fertilized ovum in egg-laying animals, such as birds and insects, after it has been laid. This type of egg is covered by egg membranes, including the hard shell, which prevent it from drying out or being damaged. The eggs produced by domestic poultry (especially hens) are widely used as food. The hen's egg contains all the nutrients needed for a single cell to develop into a day-old chick; it is thus a highly nutritious food – except for vitamin C, which the chick does not need, and minerals such as calcium, which are present in the shell. The yolk is rich in cholesterol, which has led some people for health reasons to restrict their egg intake. In 1987 an increase in food-poisoning cases due to *Salmonella* bacteria led to government investigations in both the UK and USA, and advice that eggs should be thoroughly cooked before being eaten. In the UK, the consequences of a statement on the matter by the junior health minister, Edwina Currie, in 1988 led to public controversy over the extent of the problem, and her eventual resignation.

egg-plant *aubergine*

eggs and bacon *bird's-foot trefoil*

eglantine A species of rose (*Rosa eglanteria*) with aromatic, sweet-smelling foliage; also called **sweet briar**. (Family: Rosaceae.)

Egmont, Mount, Maori **Taranaki** 39°18S 174°05E. Symmetrical volcanic peak, W North Island, New Zealand, S of New Plymouth; height, 2518 m/8261 ft; in a national park, area 335 sq km/129 sq mi, established in 1900.

ego In psychiatry, that aspect of the personality which deals with the practical aspects of the external world. This was one component of Freud's description of the psychic structure which comprises the *id*, the *ego*, and the *superego*. The id represents the most primitive aspect of the personality: basic biological drives (eg hunger, sex, anger, and elimination) and instincts striving for pleasure. The superego represents the conscience and values an individual acquires from parents and society. The ego represents a middle ground in which a compromise between forces maximizing pleasure and those minimizing displeasure are reconciled.

egocentrism In Piagetian psychology, the apparent inability to understand another's viewpoint. Piaget argued that young children are egocentric, acting as if others see the world from the same perspective and share their interests and feelings. However, research has shown that young children are not wholly egocentric.

egoism The thesis that people always do or should promote their own self-interest and that enlightened self-interest is the basis of conventional morality. A notable proponent was Thomas Hobbes.

egret The name used for a number of heron species. It is not applied consistently; some species are called *egret* by some observers, and *heron* by others.

Egypt *p.499*

Egyptian An extinct Afro-Asiatic language, which survives in inscriptions and papyrus manuscripts. In the 2nd-c AD, it evolved into **Coptic**, which is still used as a language of devotion by the Monophysite Christians in Egypt.

Egyptian architecture The architecture of ancient Egypt, characterized by the use of stone on a massive scale and most commonly associated with funereal pyramids, the earliest large example being the stepped 68 m/200 ft-high monument at Saqqara (2650–2600 BC). Regular pyramids came later, including those at Giza (2600–2480 BC). Egyptian temples, such as that of Amon at Karnak (c.1570–1085 BC), are equally monumental, using natural rock formations, battered walls, pillared halls, colonnades, and ramps. Other unique Egyptian features are the obelisk, a monolithic tapering shaft of stone, and the pylon, a truncated pyramidical tower. Domestic architecture, by contrast, was intended to be more temporary, and was built of clay and even papyrus.

Egyptian art The art which flourished under the Pharaohs from c.3000 BC until the conquest of Egypt by Alexander the Great (332 BC). Largely funerary in character, it reflected a rigidly conservative society and religion, and style remained static. Tombs were decorated with wall paintings and reliefs, and contained portrait statues of the dead, together with household utensils, including fine work in metal, ivory, terracotta, etc for use in the next world. Human figures were invariably painted with profile head, single large front-view eye, frontal shoulders, and side-view legs. Statues such as the sphinxes similarly combined profile and front view in a way reflecting the shape of the original block. Mummy-cases were often richly decorated.

Egyptian cobra *asp*

Egyptian history, Ancient The history of ancient Egypt stretches roughly from 3100 BC, when a unified kingdom embracing lower and upper Egypt was first created, to 332 BC, when Alexander the Great brought the rule of the pharaohs to an end. In the intervening millennia, Egypt experienced alternate phases of strong, centralized government and periods of near anarchy, when competing dynasties and warlords fought for power. The periods marked by strong government at home and expansionist policies abroad are called the Old, Middle and New Kingdoms. The chaotic phases go by the name of Intermediate Periods (I–III). In the so-called Late Period, the centuries immediately before Alexander's conquest, Egypt lacked central authority, and the country was easy prey for the great expansionist powers of the Middle East – Assyria conquered her in 671 BC and Persia in 525 BC. (*see panel p.500*)

Egyptian mongoose *ichneumon* (mammal)

Egyptian religion The religion of ancient Egypt, covering the period from c.3100–30 BC. It emerged from the worship of tribal deities represented as totemic animals. These developed into animal-headed local and state gods, many of which represented forces in the natural world which needed to be entreated through worship and sacrifice. For example, the hawk was sacred to the Sun-god Re and the Sky-god Horus; the Ibis to the Moon-god Toth; and the ram to Khnum. In the 14th-c, Akhenaton made an unsuccessful attempt to establish Aten, the Sun's disk, as the sole national deity. Immortality was secured through the rite of mummification.

Ehrenburg, Ilya Grigoryevich [airenberg] (1891–1967) Writer, born in Kiev, Ukraine. He worked for many years in Paris as a journalist, returning at intervals to the USSR. He wrote poetry, short stories, travel books, essays, and several novels, notably *Padeniye Parizha* (1941, The Fall of Paris) and *Burya* (1948, The Storm), both of which won Stalin Prizes.

Ehrlich, Paul [airleekh] (1854–1915) Bacteriologist, born of Jewish family in Strzelin, SW Poland. After studying at Leipzig, he carried out research at Berlin, becoming a pioneer in haematology, immunology, and chemotherapy. In 1910 he discovered a cure for syphilis (Salvarsan), and propounded the side-chain theory in immunology. He shared the 1908 Nobel Prize for Physiology or Medicine.

EI *exposure index*

Eichmann, (Karl) Adolf [iykhman] (1906–62) Nazi war criminal, born in Solingen, W Germany. He was raised in Austria and joined the Austrian Nazi Party in 1932, becoming a member of the SS. He became the SS's 'Jewish expert', acquiring an exhaustive amount of knowledge on Jewish culture, and was put in charge of administering the 'final solution (*Endlösung*) of the Jewish problem' – the intended systematic deportation and extermination of Europe's 11 million Jews. With sustained efficiency, he was instrumental in organizing the round-up of around 6 million Jews from the occupied areas of Europe and their subsequent transportation to labour or death camps, and masterminding the feasibility of their extermination there. Captured by US forces in 1945, he escaped from prison

Egypt

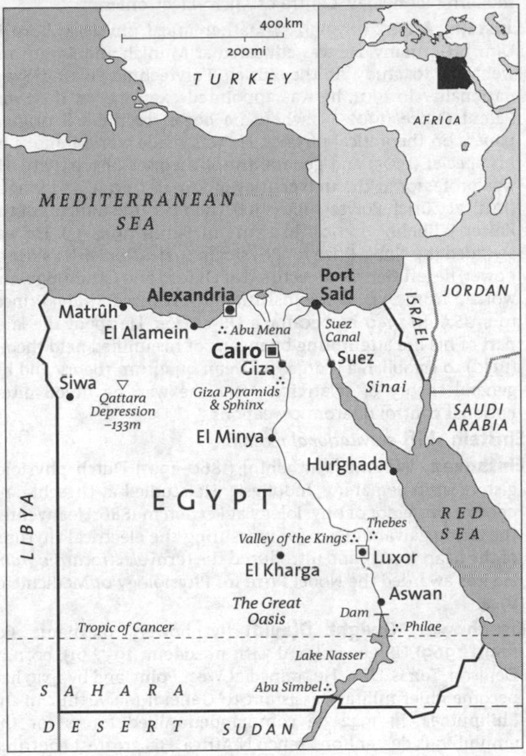

□ International Airport ∴ World heritage site — — Border in dispute

official name **Arab Republic of Egypt**, Arabic **Jumhuriyah Misr Al-Arabiya**

Local name Misr

Timezone GMT +2

Area 1 001 449 km^2/386 559 sq mi

Population total (2002e) 66 341 000

Status Republic

Date of independence 1922

Capital Cairo

Language Arabic (official)

Ethnic group Population mainly of E Hamitic origin (90%)

Religions Sunni Muslim (c.90%), minority largely Coptic Christian (c.10%)

Physical features R Nile flows N from Sudan, dammed S of Aswan, creating L Nasser; huge delta N of Cairo, 250 km/150 mi across and 160 km/100 mi N–S; narrow Eastern Desert, sparsely inhabited, between Nile and Red Sea; broad Western Desert, covering over two-thirds of the country; Sinai Peninsula (S), desert region with mountains rising to 2637 m/8651 ft at Gebel Katherîna, Egypt's highest point; 90% of population lives on Nile floodplain (c.3% of country's area).

Climate Mainly desert climate, except for 80 km/50 mi wide Mediterranean coastal fringe; very hot on coast where dust-laden khamsin wind blows N from Sahara (Mar–Jun); Alexandria, average maximum daily temperatures 18–30°C; elsewhere rainfall less than 50 mm/2 in.

Currency 1 Egyptian Pound (E£, LE) = 100 piastres

Economy Agriculture on floodplain of R Nile accounts for about a third of national income; building of Aswan High Dam extended irrigated cultivation; a major tourist area.

GDP (2002e) $289·8 bn, per capita $4000

Human Development Index (2002) 0·642

History Neolithic cultures on R Nile from c.6000 BC; Pharaoh dynasties from c.3100 BC; Egyptian power greatest during the New Empire period, 1576–1085 BC; became Persian province, 6th-c BC; conquered by Alexander the Great, 4th-c BC; Ptolemaic Pharaohs ruled Egypt until 30 BC; conquered by Arabs, AD 672; Suez Canal constructed in 1869; revolt in 1879 put down by British in 1882; British protectorate from 1914; declared independence, 1922; King Farouk deposed by Nasser, 1952; Egypt declared a republic, 1953; attack on Israel followed by Israeli invasion, 1967; Suez Canal remained blocked, 1967–75; changed name to Arab Republic of Egypt, 1971; Yom Kippur War against Israel, 1973; Camp David peace conference with Israel, 1978; Israel returned disputed Taba Strip, 1989; participated in Gulf War with US-led coalition, 1991; governed by a People's National Assembly, President, Prime Minister, and Council of Ministers.

Monarch
1922–36 Fouad I
1936–7 Farouk *Trusteeship*
1937–52 Farouk I

Head of State
1952–4 Mohammed Najib
1954–70 Gamal Abdel Nasser
1970–81 Mohammed Anwar el-Sadat
1981– Mohammed Hosni Mubarak

Head of Government
1980–1 Mohammed Anwar el-Sadat
1981–2 Mohammed Hosni Mubarak
1982–4 Fouad Monyi ed-Din
1984 Kamal Hassan Ali
1985–6 Ali Lotfi
1986–96 Atef Sidqi
1996–9 Kamal Ahmed Ganzouri
1999– Atef Ebeid

some months later, having kept his identity hidden, and in 1950 reached Argentina. After efforts by Jewish concentration camp survivor Simon Wiesenthal (1908–) to bring him to justice, he was traced and kidnapped by Israeli agents, taken to Israel in 1960, tried, convicted of crimes against humanity, and executed. The Eichmann trial was seen on television by millions, and became an important milestone in revealing the details of the Holocaust.

Eid-al-Adha; Eid-al-Fitr *Id al-Adha; Id al-Fitr*

eider [iyder] Any of four species of sea duck native to the northern N hemisphere; also known as **eider duck**. The female lines her nest with the soft downy feathers from her breast; these are collected commercially as **eiderdown**. (Subfamily: Anatinae, tribe: Somateriini.)

eidophor [iydofaw(r)] A large-screen projection television system in which a scanning electron beam modulated by the video signal distorts the surface of an oil layer in a vacuum tube to refract the beam of light from a xenon lamp. Colour requires a triple-tube unit with the light divided by dichroic filters and recombined in projection.

Eiffel, (Alexandre) Gustave [efel] (1832–1923) Civil engineer, born in Dijon, E France. He designed several notable bridges and viaducts, before working on his most famous project, the *Eiffel Tower*. He also designed the steel framework of the Statue of Liberty, NY, and built the first aerodynamics laboratory, near Paris. In 1893 he was imprisoned for two years and fined for breach of trust in connection with the Panama Canal.

Eiffel Tower [iyfl] A famous city landmark in Paris, France, designed by Gustave Eiffel and erected (1887–9) in the Champs-de-Mars for the Paris Exhibition of 1889. The tower consists of an open-lattice framework supporting three tiered

Dynasties of Rulers: Ancient Egypt

dynasty	*period*	*date* BC
I	early dynastic period	c.3100–2890
II		c.2890–2686
III	old kingdom	c.2686–2613
IV		c.2613–2494
V		c.2494–2345
VI		c.2345–2181
VII	first intermediate period	c.2181–2173
VIII		c.2173–2160
IX		c.2160–2130
X		c.2130–2040
XI		c.2133–1991
XII	middle kingdom	1991–1786
XIII		1786–1633
XIV	second intermediate period	1786–c.1603
XV		1674–1567
XVI		c.1684–1567
XVII		c.1660–1567
XVIII	new kingdom	1567–1320
XIX		1320–1200
XX		1200–1085
XXI	third intermediate period	1085–945
XXII		945–730
XXIII		8172–730
XXIV		720–715
XXV		751–668
XXVI	late period	664–525
XXVII		525–404
XXVIII		404–399
XXIX		399–380
XXX		380–343
XXXI		343–332

platforms. At 300 m/984 ft high, it was the tallest building in the world until 1930.

Eiger [iyger] 46°34N 8°01E. Mountain peak with three ridges in the Bernese Alps, SC Switzerland; its N face is one of the most formidable climbs in the Alps; height, 3970 m/13 025 ft; first ascent by Charles Barrington in 1858; N face first climbed in 1938.

Eigg [eg] Island in Highland, W Scotland, UK; S of Skye, 11 km/7 mi from mainland (E); area 67 sq km/26 sq mi; reserve managed by Scottish Wildlife Trust; rises to 394 m/1291 ft at Sgurr of Eigg; historically associated with the Clan Macdonald; ferry connections to Mallaig; cattle, crofting, fishing.

Eight, the *Ashcan School*

Eightfold Path The fourth of Buddha's Four Noble Truths, prescribing the way to enlightenment. The Path involves right understanding, right aspiration, right speech, right conduct, right means of livelihood, right endeavour, right mindfulness, and right contemplation.

Eighth Route Army *Red Army* (China)

Eijkman, Christiaan [iykman] (1858–1930) Physician and pathologist, born in Nijkerk, The Netherlands. He studied at Amsterdam, and became professor of public health and forensic medicine at Utrecht (1898–1928). Investigating the disease beriberi in Java, his observations of dietary deficiency led to the discovery of vitamins. He shared the 1929 Nobel Prize for Physiology or Medicine.

Eilat or **Elat** [aylat] 29°33N 34°57E, pop (2000e) 34 000. Seaport in Southern district, S Israel, on N shore of the Gulf of Aqaba; founded in 1949; airfield; terminus of oil pipeline from Ashkelon; nature reserve with underwater observatory.

Eindhoven [iynthohvn] 51°26N 5°30E, pop (2000e) 203 000. Modern industrial city in SE North Brabant province, S Netherlands; on the R Dommel, 88 km/55 mi SE of Rotterdam; airport; railway; technical university (1956); electronics, engineering, trucks, tractors, engines, military vehicles, glassware, synthetic fibres, paper, textiles, tobacco; Philips Evoluon museum of modern technology, Centre of Micro-Electronics.

Einstein, Albert (1879–1955) Mathematical physicist, born in Ulm, S Germany. He was educated at Munich and Aarau, and went on to study at the Zürich Polytechnic. Taking Swiss nationality in 1901, he was appointed examiner at the Swiss Patent Office (1902–9), where he began to publish original papers on theoretical physics. He was made world famous by his special (1905) and general (1916) theories of relativity. He was professor at the universities of Zürich (1909), and Prague (1911), at Zürich Polytechnic (1912), then became director of the Kaiser Wilhelm Physical Institute in Berlin (1914–33). He was awarded the Nobel Prize for Physics in 1921. After Hitler's rise to power, he left Germany, lectured at Oxford and Cambridge, and worked from 1934 at the Institute of Advanced Study, Princeton, USA. In 1940 he became a US citizen. He spent the later part of his life attempting by means of his unified field theory (1950) to establish a merger between quantum theory and his general theory of relativity. After the war, he urged international control of atomic weapons.

Einstein shift *gravitational redshift*

Einthoven, Willem [aynthohfn] (1860–1927) Dutch physiologist, born in Semarang, Indonesia. He studied at Utrecht, and became professor of physiology at Leyden in 1886. He invented the string galvanometer for measuring the electrical rhythms of the heart (1903), and introduced the term *electrocardiogram*. He was awarded the Nobel Prize for Physiology or Medicine in 1924.

Eisenhower, Dwight D(avid) [iyznhower], nickname **Ike** (1890–1969) US general and 34th president (1953–61), born in Denison, Texas, USA. He trained at West Point, and by 1939 had become chief military assistant to General MacArthur in the Philippines. In 1942 he commanded Allied forces for the amphibious descent on French N Africa. His greatest contribution to the war effort was his talent for the smooth co-ordination of Allied staff, and this led to his selection as Supreme Commander for the 1944 cross-channel invasion of the continental mainland, which he resolutely launched despite capricious weather conditions. In 1950 he was made the Supreme Commander of the Combined Land Forces in Nato, and in 1952 the popularity which he had gained in Europe swept him to victory in the presidential elections, standing as a Republican, and he was re-elected in 1956. During his presidency the US government was preoccupied with foreign policy, and pursued a campaign against Communism, but was also actively involved in the civil rights movement.

Eisenstein, Sergey (Mikhaylovich) [iyznstiyn] (1898–1948) Film director and artist, born in Riga, Latvia. He launched into films from theatrical scene painting, and became a major influence on the development of the cinema, noted for his method of rapid editing of sharply contrasting sequences of shots (*montage*) to suggest a symbolic meaning. His films are also noticeable for the substitution of the group or crowd for the traditional hero, for the use of non-professional performers, and for his skilful cutting and recutting to achieve mounting Impressionistic effects, as in the Odessa steps sequence of the silent film *Potemkin* (1925). Later films included *Alexander Nevski* (1938) and *Ivan the Terrible*, both with music by Prokofiev. Filmed in the Mosfilm studios in Kazakhstan in 1944–6, part I of *Ivan* was released in 1945, but part II was not shown until 1957, and part III remained incomplete. His theoretical film writings have been published as *Film Form*, *The Film Sense*, *Notes of a Film Director*, and *Immortal Memories*. His expressive, often erotic drawings have done much to enhance his reputation as a graphic artist.

eisteddfod [iystethvod] A Welsh gathering of 12th-c origin for competitions in music and literature, the earlier *eisteddfodau* [iystethvodiy] being concerned with the testing of bards in their art. At the annual National Eisteddfod, held in August (entirely in Welsh) alternately in N and S Wales, the central event is the chairing of the bard for a poem in free verse, a tradition that dates from 1867. Since 1937, the event has also included the presentation of the prose medal. The **International Music Eisteddfod**, held each July at Llangollen, is a cultural event which attracts the participation of many nations.

Ekaterinburg *Yekaterinburg*

ekistics [ekistiks] (Gr *ekos* 'habitat') The science which analyses the nature, origin, and evolution of human settlements. It can be divided into **ekistic geography**, **ekistic economics**, and **social ekistics**.

Ekwensi, Cyprian (Odiatu Duaka) [ekwensee] (1923–) Writer, born in Minna, C Nigeria. He studied at Ibadan University College and the Chelsea School of Pharmacy in London. Early works include the novellas *When Love Whispers* (1947), *The Leopard's Claw* (1950), and *People of the City* (1954, revised 1969). His most successful novel was *Jagua Nana* (1961), about a group of vibrant characters who forsake their rural origins for the attractions of city life. His experiences of civil war are chronicled in *Survive the Peace* (1976) and *Divided We Stand* (1980). He has also written numerous folk-tales and stories for children. He was awarded the Dag Hammarskjöld International Prize in Literature in 1968.

El Alamein, Battle of (23 Oct–4 Nov 1942) A World War 2 battle, named after a village on Egypt's Mediterranean coast. It ended in the victory of the British Eighth Army commanded by Montgomery over Rommel's Afrika Korps. It proved to be the turning point in the war in Africa.

Elam [eelam] The name given in antiquity to what is now SW Iran. Its main city was Susa, and at its zenith in the 13th-c BC it ruled an empire stretching from Babylonia in the W to Persepolis in the E.

eland [eeland] An African spiral-horned antelope; cattle-like, with narrow face and straight horns; the largest antelope (shoulder height, up to 1·8 m/6 ft); easily tamed; two species: the **common** (or **Cape**) **eland** (*Taurotragus oryx*) and the **giant** (or **derby**) **eland** (*Taurotragus derbianus*).

Elara [eelara] The seventh natural satellite of Jupiter, discovered in 1905; distance from the planet 11 740 000 km/7 295 000 mi; diameter 80 km/50 mi.

elastic hysteresis [histereesis] A property of some materials (eg rubber), where the strain due to a given stress is larger when the stress is decreasing than when it is increasing. A graph of stress versus strain, while stress is gradually applied then removed, produces a loop with the area proportional to the energy dissipated in the material. A large loop area means the substance makes a good shock absorber.

elasticity (economics) A measure of the ratio of the proportional change in one variable to the proportional change in another. **Price elasticity** compares the proportional change in quantity supplied or demanded to a proportional change in price. If this ratio is high, supply or demand is **elastic**; if it is small, supply or demand is **inelastic**. **Cross-elasticity** of supply or demand compares the proportional change in the quantity supplied or demanded to the proportional change in the price of a related good. **Income elasticity** of demand compares the proportional change in quantity bought at any given price to proportional change in income. If this ratio is low, a good is a necessity; if high, a luxury. **Elasticity of substitution** compares the proportional change in relative quantities of goods supplied or demanded to proportional change in their relative price. Economists find elasticity measures useful because, as they look only at proportional changes, they are not affected by the choice of units used to measure either prices or quantities.

elasticity (physics) In solids, the property that a stressed material will return to its original size and shape when the stress is removed. It usually corresponds to a direct proportionality between stress and strain. In a metal bar, for example, up to a strain of about 1%, doubling the tension along the bar's length causes double the extension.

elastic modulus *Young's modulus*

elastic rebound theory *isostasy*

elastomers [eelastomerz] Materials, usually synthetic, having elastic properties (ie capable of recovery from severe deformation). Examples include natural rubber and polyisoprene.

Elat *Eilat*

E layer *Heaviside layer*

Elba, Gr **Aithalia**, Lat **Ilva** pop (2000e) 11 000; area 223 sq km/86 sq mi. Italian island in the Ligurian Sea, between the N Italian coast and Corsica, separated from the mainland by the 10 km/6 mi-wide Strait of Piombino; length 27 km/17 mi; width 18·5 km/11½ mi; chief town, Portoferraio; iron working, fisheries, fruit, wine, tourism; Napoleon lived here after his abdication (1814–15).

Elbe, River [elbuh], Czech **Labe**, ancient **Albis** River in the Czech Republic and Germany; rises on S slopes of the Riesengebirge, Czech Republic; flows N and NW to enter the North Sea at Cuxhaven, Germany; length 1158 km/720 mi; connected by canals with R Oder and Baltic Sea; navigable to beyond the Czech border.

Elbert, Mount 39°05N 106°27W. Mountain in Lake Co, C Colorado, USA; the highest peak in the Rocky Mts (4399 m/14 432 ft).

elbow The region of the upper limb between the arm and forearm; specifically, the joint between the humerus and the radius and ulna. It enables angulation of the upper limb, so allowing the hand to reach the mouth (as in eating and drinking). Banging the medial side of the elbow (the 'funny bone') against a solid object may cause pain and a tingling sensation over the hand; when this happens, the ulnar nerve has been compressed between the object and the humerus.

Elbrus, Mount [elbruhs] 43°21N 42°29E. Highest peak of the Caucasus range, S European Russia; height 5642 m/18 510 ft; highest peak in Europe; formed by two extinct volcanic cones; its glaciers give rise to the Kuban, Malka, and Baksan Rivers.

El Cid *Cid, El*

elder (botany) A deciduous shrub (*Sambucus nigra*), growing to 10 m/30 ft, very widespread; bark furrowed, corky; leaves opposite, pinnate, leaflets toothed; flowers creamy, in large, flat-topped clusters 10–20 cm/4–8 in across; berries purplish-black. The flowers and berries are used in wines and preserves, but all other parts of the plant are poisonous. (Family: Caprifoliaceae.)

elder (religion) One who by reason of age or distinction is entrusted with shared authority and leadership in a community. In the ancient Biblical world, the elders of Israel exercised both religious and civil influence from the tribal period onwards; and city elders were active at a local level. Jewish synagogues were also governed by elders, but the title is reserved for scholars in the Mishnaic period. In the New Testament, elders were church officials (Gr *presbuteroi*, 'presbyters') with a collective authority for general oversight of a congregation, and are sometimes even called 'bishops' (Gr *episkopoi*; *Acts* 20.28, *Titus* 1.5–7) but not yet in the monarchical sense. In Reformed Churches, elders are officers ordained to 'rule' along with the minister (a 'teaching' elder), to exercise discipline, and to oversee the life of a congregation and its individual members.

El Dorado [el dorahdoh] (Span 'the gilded one') A powerful early colonial Spanish-American legend of a ruler coated in gold, believed to exist in New Granada (now Colombia); by extension, a land of fabulous wealth. Raleigh organized two expeditions (1595 and 1617) in search of El Dorado.

Eleanor of Aquitaine (c.1122–1204) Queen consort of Louis VII of France (1137–52) and, after the annulment of this marriage (on the ostensible plea of consanguinity), of Henry Duke of Normandy and Count of Anjou. When he became the Angevin king, Henry II of England (1154–89), the lands they claimed stretched from Scotland to the Mediterranean. She was imprisoned (1174–89) for supporting the rebellion of her sons against the king, two of whom became kings as Richard I (in 1189) and John (1199).

Eleanor of Castile [kasteel] (1246–90) Queen consort of Edward I of England (1254–90), the daughter of Ferdinand III. She bore her husband 13 children, accompanied Edward to the Crusades (1270–3), and is said to have saved his life by sucking the poison from a wound. She died at Hadby, Nottinghamshire, and the *Eleanor Crosses* at Northampton, Geddington, and Waltham Cross are the survivors of the 12 erected by Edward at the halting places of her cortège. The last stopping place was Charing Cross, London, where a replica now stands. She was buried at Westminster Abbey.

Eleatics [eliatiks] A group of presocratic Greek philosophers in the 5th-c BC, from Elea in S Italy. In contrast to the more empirical Milesians, Parmenides, Melissus, and Zeno initiated a metaphysical tradition based on deductive argument, which greatly influenced Plato and subsequent philosophers.

elections *franchise* (politics)

elective mutism An emotionally determined selectivity in speaking, which in severe cases results in no speech at all. It is often associated with anxiety or withdrawal.

electoral college A body made up of people who are responsible for electing a person to some office. These people can hold a particular office themselves (as in the case of the College of Cardinals who elect the pope) or be elected from a wider electorate. The most famous electoral college is the one that elects the president of the USA. It is made up of electors from each state pledged to cast their vote for the particular candidate for whom the wider electorate in their state has voted (though they are not legally bound to do so when the time for electing arrives).

electors Members of the electoral college that chose Holy Roman Emperors. By the 13th-c, membership was limited to seven – the Duke of Saxony, King of Bohemia, Count Palatine of the Rhine, Margrave of Brandenburg, and Archbishops of Cologne, Mainz, and Trier. The Golden Bull (1356) of Emperor Charles IV permanently granted the right of election to the seven.

Electra [elektra] In Greek tragedies, but not in Homer, the daughter of Agamemnon and Clytemnestra, who assisted her brother Orestes when he arrived in Argos to avenge his father, and who later married his friend Pylades. Her personality is developed in different ways by the playwrights.

Electra complex *Oedipus complex*

electrical and magnetic properties of matter Electrical and magnetic effects exhibited by matter, due to the charged components of atoms, and the electrical forces binding atoms together into bulk matter. Magnetic effects arise because of the motion of electrical charges. Light is affected as it passes through matter because of its electromagnetic nature.

electrical conduction The transport of electrical charge through some substance. Only metals conduct electricity well; conduction is by means of the free electrons in the electron gas characteristic of metal structure. Ionic and covalently bound solids are insulators; but ionic solids such as salt (sodium chloride) conduct when dissolved in water, as the electrically charged ions become free to move. In *semiconductors*, the low electrical conductivity is due to a small number of electrons acquiring sufficient energy to become released into the body of the material in a way similar to conduction electrons in metals. The spaces vacated by the electrons (*holes*) behave as positively charged particles, and also contribute to conduction. Conduction in semi-conductors may be altered by 'doping' – the introduction of impurities to provide more holes and electrons.

electrical engineering A branch of engineering which studies the practical applications of electricity and electronics. Until the 1940s electrical engineering was a small part of the general field of engineering, confined to communications, lighting, and the generation and transmission of electrical power. As progress was made in the area of electrical and electronic communications, it developed into a separate field, now dealing with the production, distribution, control, and use of electricity in all its forms. Production aspects include the design of generators run by water power (hydroelectricity), coal, oil, and nuclear fuels. Distribution and control concern the delivery of electricity to the consumer: transmission systems need to be designed which are safe and efficient. Any devices which use electricity fall within the field, such as radio, radar, lighting, motors, power generators, and transmission systems. **Electronic engineering** developed as a subdivision of electrical engineering, and is now primarily concerned with automation, missile control systems, satellites, spacecraft, and communication systems.

electrical power The rate of transfer of energy in electrical circuits; symbol P, units W (watt). An example is the rate of heat lost from a circuit due to resistive heating ($P = I^2R$ for current I and resistance R). An electric light of power 60 W running for 1 hour consumes as much energy as a 30 W light running for 2 hours.

electric-arc furnace An electric furnace used particularly in steel making, where a very high temperature is generated in the 'arc' or discharge between two electrodes, the current passing through material evaporated from the electrodes. In the original process devised in 1870 by Siemens, the arc was struck beneath the crucible, heating the metal indirectly. Later, in the type invented by French metallurgist Paul Heroult (1863–1914), the arc was struck between electrodes and the metal itself. In the type devised in 1898 by Italian metallurgist Enrico Stassano, the arc is struck between electrodes above the metal, heating being by radiation.

electric car A motor car designed to be propelled by an electric motor. Although electric traction has been used extensively in delivery vehicles such as milk floats (UK) and in golf carts (USA), it has not been possible for the electric car to compete with the traditionally driven internal-combustion-engined car because of the size and weight of batteries needed. Although much research has gone into the improvement of batteries and alternative battery technology, the electric car is still not competitive with the internal combustion engine for power, weight, and size.

electric charge *charge*

electric conductance *electrical conduction; resistance*

electric dipole moment Symbol p, units C.m (coulomb.metre), a vector quantity; for charges $+q$ and $-q$ separated by distance l (a *dipole*), the electric dipole moment is $p = ql$. A dipole placed in an electric field experiences a twisting force, proportional to p, which attempts to line up the dipole with field direction. Some molecules may have electric dipole moments if the centre of negative charge is displaced from that of positive charge. This displacement may be brought about by the applied field to give an induced dipole moment, or may be present permanently due to the structure of the molecule, in which case the molecule is described as *polar*. Water molecules are polar; for water, $p = 10^{-29}$ C.m approximately.

electric eel Large freshwater fish (*Electrophorus electricus*) found in shallow streams of the Orinoco and Amazon basins of South America; body cylindrical at front, becoming compressed posteriorly, length up to 2·4 m/8 ft; long anal fin; dorsal, tail, and pelvic fins absent; produces powerful electric shocks to stun prey, as defence, and for navigation in turbid waters. (Family: Electrophoridae.)

electric field The region of electric influence surrounding positive or negative electric charges; symbol E, units V/m (volts per metre); a vector quantity, with field direction specified as the direction of motion of a positive charge placed in the field. For a force F on a test charge of q coulombs, the field is given as $E = F/q$, ie the electric field is the electric force per unit charge. It may be represented using field lines.

electric grid In the UK, the system of distributing electricity, across the country and internationally, using a network of cables to provide supplies matching peak and lesser demands with maximum economy. The largest pylons carry the primary supplies at 400 000 or 275 000 volts; smaller ones carry secondary supplies at 132 000 and 66 000 volts. Most carry alternating current, which is easily transformed to different voltages, but the trans-Channel link with France carries direct current supplies, to allow easier matching of differences in frequency or phase.

electricity Phenomena associated with electrical charges and currents, and the study of such phenomena. Between collections of positive and negative charges there exists a potential difference. If a conducting path exists between the two charge groups, charges will flow from one to the other, constituting an electric current. Electric charge which builds up on an insulator and is thus unable to flow is termed **static electricity**.

electric ray Any of a family of sluggish, bottom-living marine rays, widespread in tropical to temperate seas; body disc rounded, skin smooth, tail robust; well-developed electric organs produce strong shocks to stun prey; also called **torpedo rays**; includes large N Atlantic species, *Torpedo nobiliana*; length up to 1·8 m/6 ft. (Family: Torpedinidae.)

electric resistance *resistance*

electrocardiography The investigation of the electrical activity of the heart. The electric voltages accompanying heartbeats can be recorded from the surface of the skin in the form of an electrocardiogram (**ECG** or **EKG**). Electrodes are attached to the skin of the limbs and chest, and the voltages between various pairs of electrodes are recorded on sensitive portable electronic machines. The interpretation of the printout requires skill, but electrocardiography is one of the commonest medical investigations, providing diagnostic information about all aspects of heart disease and also about other illnesses.

electrochemistry The study of chemical change in a solution, resulting from the uptake of electrical energy from an external circuit or its supply to a circuit. Storage batteries (*accumulators*) illustrate this process, as they charge and discharge respectively. In all cases, changes in the oxidation states of elements occur, and energy is converted between chemical and electrical forms.

electroconvulsive therapy (ECT) A treatment for patients with severe psychiatric disorders, in which a convulsion is produced by passing a low-level electric current through the brain of an anaesthetized patient. The technique is mainly used in severe depression and schizophrenia not treatable by any other means.

electrocution Death or severe injury from contact with electric current. High-voltage electric shock induces spasm of the skeletal muscles and rapid irregular contractions (*fibrillation*) of the heart, which stops pumping. Lesser voltages induce burns. It is not always accidental: electrocution is used as a method of capital punishment in some countries (eg in some US states).

electrodynamics The study of the motion of electric charges caused by electric and magnetic fields.

electroencephalography [electrohensefalografee] The investigation of the electrical activity of the brain, using electrodes applied to the scalp, and usually recorded as a tracing on paper (an electroencephalogram, or **EEG**). The EEG changes with the mental activity of the subject, and characteristic patterns of electrical activity (eg for sleep, coma, epileptic seizure) can be recognized. The *alpha rhythm* (c.10 Hz) appears with relaxation and eye closure. The *delta rhythm* (1–4 Hz) appears in deep sleep.

electrolaryngography A technique for recording the vibrations of the vocal cords electronically. Electrodes are attached to the neck on each side of the thyroid cartilage, and the vocal cord activity is displayed as traces on a screen. The rise and fall of the fundamental frequency of the vibrations (corresponding largely to the intonation of the voice) can be clearly seen. The technique was developed in the 1970s, and is now widely used in speech science in relation to both normal and abnormal use of the voice.

electrolysis The splitting of a compound into simpler forms by the input of electrical energy. When water is electrolysed between inert electrodes, the following two half-reactions take place: cathode (reduction) $2e^- + 2H_2O \rightarrow H_2 + 2OH^-$
anode (oxidation) $H_2O \rightarrow \frac{1}{2}O_2 + 2H^+ + 2e^-$

electrolyte A system, usually a solution, in which electrochemical reactions occur. It must be sufficiently conducting to allow current to pass – an effect which is often achieved by using a high concentration of electrochemically inert ions.

electromagnet *magnet*

electromagnetic induction The production of electromotive force (emf) – loosely, a voltage – in a conductor, either by moving the conductor in a magnetic field or by changing the field around the conductor. The emf induced in a circuit equals the rate of change of magnetic flux through it, multiplied by −1 (Faraday's law, 1831). Induction is crucial to the operation of transformers, generators, and motors.

electromagnetic pump A device for pumping conducting fluids. Current is applied to the fluid at right angles to the flow direction. A magnetic field is applied at right angles to both flow direction and electric current. Electromagnetic force acts on the fluid, in the same way that a current-carrying wire placed in a magnetic field experiences a force. The device is used to pump liquid metals.

electromagnetic radiation Oscillating electric and magnetic fields which propagate together through empty space as a radiated wave; velocity *c*, the velocity of light. They include radio waves, light, and X-rays. No ether is required for the propagation of electromagnetic waves, which exhibit particle-like properties, more noticeable for higher frequencies, consistent with quantum theory.

electromagnetism *p.504*

electromotive force The work done by some source in separating electrical charges to produce a potential difference capable of driving current round a circuit; often abbreviated **emf**. The term 'force' is a misnomer; generally, emf is a property of the source, whereas potential difference depends on both source and current flow. A source of emf transfers energy to the circuit by doing work in raising potential. For example, a battery is a source of emf in which chemical energy moves charges to the terminals, making one positive, the other negative. The emf is work done on the charges to bring about this separation: an emf of one volt means that the battery expends one joule of energy to bring about the separation of one coulomb of charge.

electromyography The study of the muscular contractions which take place during speech. Muscles produce tiny amounts of electrical activity when they contract. The activity is recorded by applying electrodes to the individual muscles of the vocal tract, and displaying the signals on a screen or on paper.

electron A fundamental particle, denoted e^-, where the minus sign indicates that the charge is negative; charge of $-1{\cdot}602 \times 10^{-19}$C; mass $9{\cdot}110 \times 10^{-31}$ kg or 0·511 MeV, approximately 1/1836 that of the proton; spin ½ fermion; stable against decay; no known size, assumed point-like; no known substructure; a carrier of negative charge in matter, including electrical currents in conductors. Electrons together with the positively-charged nucleus form atoms. They were discovered by J J Thomson in 1897 through studying cathode rays (now called electron beams) in electric and magnetic fields. The charge was determined by Robert Millikan in 1913. Wave-like properties are exhibited in electron diffraction. The electron is associated with weak nuclear force, as in radioactive beta decay, where the beta particle is the electron.

electron capture A radioactive decay in which an atomic electron combines with a proton in the nucleus to form a neutron (which remains in the nucleus) and a neutrino. Nucleon number remains unchanged; proton number is reduced by one. For example, the decay of fluorine to oxygen, ${}_9F^{17} + e^-$ gives ${}_8O^{17} + \nu$.

electron diffraction An interference effect involving electrons from an incoming beam scattering from different layers of atoms in a solid, giving distinctive intensity patterns which can be used to determine the solid's structure. It is especially

electromagnetism

The electromagnetic spectrum

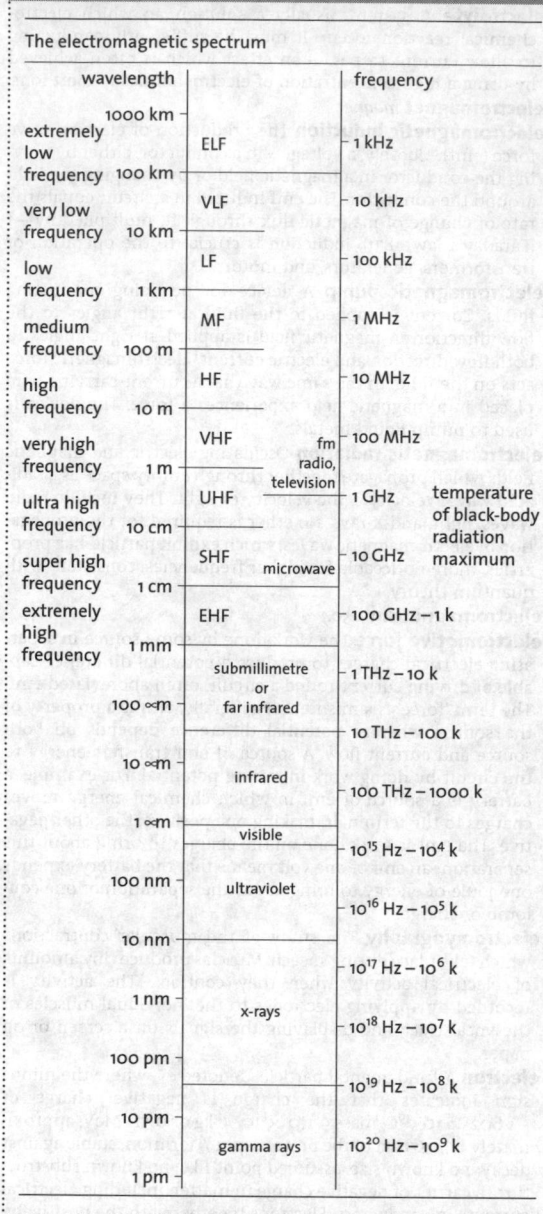

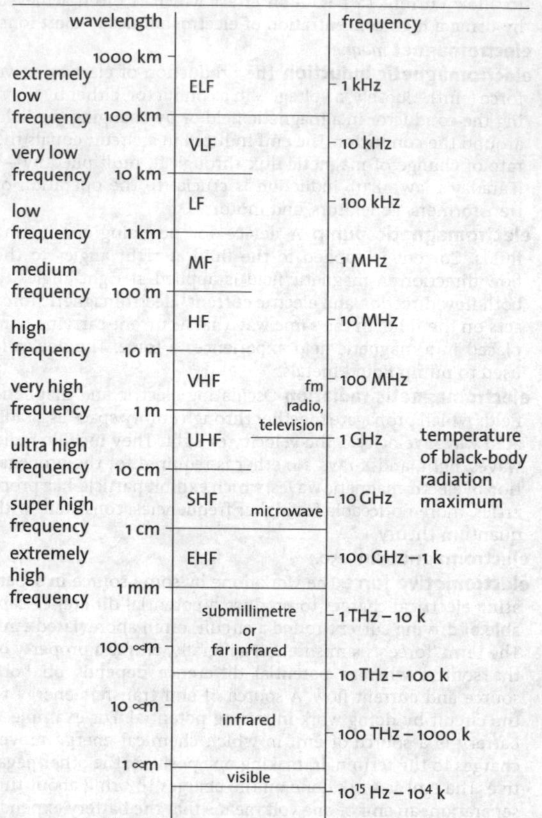

Phenomena involving both electric and magnetic fields, and the study of such phenomena. The first indication of a link between electricity and magnetism was shown by Hans Christian Ørsted, who demonstrated that an electrical current caused the deflection of a compass needle (1819). This established that magnetic effects are produced by a moving electrical charge. Ørsted's observation was interpreted by Michael Faraday in terms of lines of magnetic influence circulating around the wire. Ampère deduced an expression for the magnetic force between two current-carrying wires to give the original form of what is now called Ampère's law (1827). Faraday demonstrated that switching off a current in a circuit produced a momentary current in a nearby circuit, and that moving a magnet close to a circuit also produced momentary currents (1831). This established that electrical charge can be made to flow by changing magnetic fields, the basis of electromagnetic induction (expressed as Faraday's law). Similar work was performed by Joseph Henry (1829). The first generator was built by Faraday in 1831.

The unification of electricity and magnetism into a single theory of electromagnetism is due to James Clerk Maxwell, who first expressed the laws of Faraday and Ampère in their modern form as two of the four Maxwell's equations. Using his equations of electromagnetism, Maxwell postulated that light is electromagnetic disturbance with velocity

$$c = \frac{1}{\sqrt{\varepsilon_0 \mu_0}},$$

where ε_0 and μ_0 are the permittivity and permeability of empty space, respectively (1864). Heinrich Hertz used oscillating electrical circuits to produce radio waves which travelled at the velocity of light (1887), thereby providing experimental support for Maxwell's work. The expression of the velocity of light in terms of fundamental constants suggested to Einstein that it should always be the same for all observers. This conclusion is central to his theory of special relativity (1905), which in turn explains more fully the relationship between electric and magnetic effects. While an observer stationary with respect to an electric charge will see it as a source of electric field only, a second observer moving relative to the first will see the same charge as a source of both electric and magnetic fields in a way dictated by special relativity.

useful for surface studies, since electrons (being charged) do not penetrate far into the material. The original observation of electron diffraction was made in 1927 by US physicists Clinton Davisson (1881–1958) and Lester Germer (1896–1971), and was crucial in establishing the dual wave-particle nature of electrons.

electronegativity A qualitative measure of the tendency to hold electrons, or to form the negative end of a dipole in a bond to other atoms. It is roughly proportional to the sum of the ionization energy and the electron affinity for an atom. A rough scale of values (suggested by Linus Pauling) is: F, 4; O, 3·5; Cl, 3·2; N,Br, 3; S,I, 2·7; C, 2·5; other non-metals 2–2·2; metals 1·0–1·8.

electron gas *electronic structure of solids*

electron gun A device for producing electron beams. A heated cathode produces electrons by thermionic emission. These are attracted away by a nearby positively-charged grid, which regulates the number of electrons and hence beam brightness. Electric fields then accelerate and focus the beam. It is an essential component of television tubes, electron microscopes, and cathode ray tubes.

electronic cash *smart card*

electronic cinematography The production of entertainment programmes for the cinema by video methods, from initial shooting up to final editing and conforming. Only the completed master videotape is transferred to film for release printing.

electronic commerce *e-commerce*

electronic data interchange (EDI) A set of standards which have been established between different computer users to enable data created by one to be sent to another in an understandable form. For example, department stores use EDI to transmit orders to suppliers.

electronic flash A photographic light source which produces a very brief but powerful discharge of light when a capacitor is discharged through an evacuated tube containing a trace of xenon gas. The flash tube is non-conducting until a separate trigger capacitor controlled by contacts in the camera shutter is discharged through a third electrode around the flash tube. This action ionizes the xenon gas, which then becomes conducting for the main discharge. A typical unit has a flash duration of 1/1000 second. The light output may be continuously varied by a thyristor device for automatic exposure control by monitoring the brightness of the illuminated subject with a photocell. Flash duration may be reduced down to 1/50 000 second.

electronic funds transfer at point of sale (EFTPOS) A facility available alongside the till in many retail organizations to permit the shop to transfer the cost of the purchase from the customer's bank account to the shop's bank account electronically.

electronic games Games programmed and controlled by a small microprocessor. Most electronic games are connected to a visual display unit and are known as **video games**. Multi-coloured visual effects and varying sounds are incorporated. Many games are based on war themes or ideas related to 'Star Wars'. Most sports are simulated in various forms, and many popular board games (eg Monopoly, Scrabble, Trivial Pursuit) are available in electronic form. Games are operated either by using a computer keyboard or a joystick plugged into the home computer. Larger versions of games are produced for use in purpose-built amusement arcades and other places of public enjoyment. The first video game appeared in the USA in the early 1970s; it was called *Pong*, and was a simple form of table tennis.

electronic mail or **e-mail** The use of computer systems to transfer messages between users. Messages are usually stored centrally until acknowledged by the recipient. Electronic mail facilities are provided by most large computer systems for their users, and are also available on a national and international basis.

electronic music Music in which the sound is generated by electronic instruments (especially synthesizers), processed by means of tape recorders heard through loudspeakers. Influential studios include those at Cologne (West German Radio), Brussels (Studio de Musique Électronique), Paris (Institut de Recherche et de Coordination Acoustique/Musique), and the Columbia–Princeton Center in New York City.

electronic photography Exposure of a single picture in a special video camera (a *still video camera*, or *SVC*), which records the image in either an analogue or digital way on a rotating 50 mm floppy magnetic disk or solid state memory card. This has the capacity for up to 25 individual shots, which are available for immediate display on a video screen or as a paper printout within 90 seconds. The definition of the image is much below that of a photograph, but the instant replay and the capacity for electronic manipulation, including transmission by telephone landline, are important in special applications.

electronic publishing The issuing to identified users of selected, edited, textual and illustrative material taken from an electronic database. The data may be communicated on-line to the customer's computer, or transferred to a portable medium such as magnetic tape or disk or CD-ROM disk. The term is used generally to cover all publishing except print on paper (though some electronic journals are issued also in conventional printed form).

electronics The scientific study and application of the movement of electrons. The field developed out of 19th-c experiments with electricity, which resulted in the invention of thermionic valves and their subsequent replacement by transistors, introduced at Bell Laboratories in 1948. Transistors facilitated the miniaturization of electronic components, as did the silicon chip and the integrated circuit. The social impact of electronics is far-reaching, including the development of television, computerized office systems, video games, personal computers, pacemakers, and spacecraft.

electronic structure of solids Atoms in a solid bind in one of three ways. In *ionic solids*, such as salt (sodium chloride), an exchange of electrons gives an ionic bond between charged ions. In *covalent solids*, such as carbon and silicon, covalent bonds form between neighbouring atoms by electron sharing. In both these types, electrons are localized and the solid is an insulator. In *metals*, atoms each donate one or more electrons to a sea of nearly free electrons (the *free electron gas*) in which the array of positively-charged metal ions is immersed. Free electron gas results in good electrical and thermal conductivity. The type of bonding in solids is reflected in all physical and mechanical properties.

electron microscope A microscope using a beam of electrons instead of light, and magnetic or electrostatic fields as lenses. If considered as a wave system, the electron beam has a much higher frequency than visible light, and so provides a much higher resolution. In the **transmission electron microscope**, the direct passage of the beam through the specimen produces an image on a fluorescent screen. The specimen must be very thin, but the resolution is high: c.0·2–0·5 nm. In the **scanning electron microscope**, the specimen is scanned by the beam, which produces secondary electron emission. The consequent current produced can be amplified and the signal fed to a cathode ray screen to give the image. The specimen can be thicker, and an image of some depth produced, but resolution is limited to c.10–20 nm. The **scanning tunnelling microscope**, invented by Gerd Binnig and Heinrich Rohrer in 1982 (Nobel Prize for Physics, 1986), has a resolution of a few Ångströms and can image down to atomic scales. In this technique, electrons migrate between the sample surface and the microscope tip via the process of quantum tunnelling.

electron spin resonance *paramagnetic resonance*

electron volt A unit of energy common in atomic, nuclear, and particle physics; symbol eV; equals the change in energy of an electron moving through a potential difference of 1 volt; $1 \text{ eV} = 1{\cdot}602 \times 10^{-19}$ J (joule, SI unit); commonly used as keV (10^3 eV), MeV (10^6 eV), and GeV (10^9 eV).

electro-optic effects Optical effects induced by electric fields applied to a substance through which light passes. Transparent materials (eg water, benzene) become birefringent when placed in an electric field (the *Kerr effect*, discovered in 1875 by British physicist John Kerr (1824–1907)). This is exploited in the Kerr cell, which is used as a high frequency shutter (up to 10^{10} Hz) in laser switching. The *Pockels effect* (discovered by Friedrich Pockels (1865–1913) in 1893) is a birefringence also caused by electric fields, but distinct from the Kerr effect, being present only in certain crystals with particular symmetry properties. It is exploited in the Pockels cell for high speed shutters and beam modulators.

electropalatography The study of the way the tongue makes contact with the palate during speech. An artificial palate containing electrodes is inserted in the subject's mouth. When the tongue makes contact with the electrodes, impulses are transmitted to a monitoring device. As the subject speaks, the changing pattern of contacts can be displayed as lights on a screen or as printed dots on computer paper.

electrophile An entity with a deficiency of electrons which tends to react at a negatively charged centre. Most electrophiles are cations.

electrophone Any musical instrument in which the sound is generated by mechanical or electronic oscillators (eg a synthesizer) or in which acoustically generated vibrations require electrical amplification before they can be heard (eg the electric guitar). Electrophones form a fifth main category of instruments, additional to the four included in the standard classification of Hornbostel and Sachs (1914).

electrophoresis [elektroforeesis] The migration of charged particles under the influence of an electric field, usually in solution. Cations will move towards the negative pole, and anions towards the positive. It is possible to separate amino acids this way by adjusting the pH of the solution so that some are cations and others anions.

electroplating The depositing of a metal, most usually silver or nickel, on another metal by electrolysis. The object to be plated is made the cathode; the metal to be deposited is derived from the anode. The plating may be intended for decoration, or to provide resistance to corrosion.

electro-pollution High and low frequency electromagnetic emissions (EMF) produced by such equipment as microwave ovens, computer terminals, and high voltage cables. Exposure to the EMF field may have adverse long-term effects on health and lead to such problems as headaches, impaired concentration, stress-induced disorders, and possibly cancer. Now that the biological hazards of electromagnetism are recognized, specialist advice is available to protect against these effects.

electroscope A device for detecting the presence of an electric charge and estimating its amount. The simplest form consists of two thin gold leaves which repel each other when charged, the degree of divergence indicating the amount of the charge. It is used indirectly for the measurement of ionizing radiation, indicating the rate of leakage of the charge produced by the passage of radiation around the leaves.

electrosleep *shock therapy*

electrostatic generator A device for producing a large electric charge, usually by the repetition of an induction process and the successive accumulation of the charge produced. An important 19th-c type was the Wimshurst machine (1878), devised by British engineer James Wimshurst (1832–1903). Modern, very high voltage machines are versions of the Van de Graaff belt-operated generator (1929).

electrostatics The study of fields and potentials due to stationary electric charges. Electrostatic forces bind electrons to the nucleus in atoms.

electrostatic separation The separation of fine particles from each other or from a gaseous medium by means of an applied electric field. The process is used for separating the components of a mixture (eg the valuable content of an ore from unwanted mineral substances), or for removing the solid content of an effluent gas (**electrostatic precipitation**).

elegy In classical times, any poem in elegiac metre (a couplet consisting of one hexameter and one pentameter), such as those written (in Greek) by Archilochus (7th-c BC), and (in Latin) by Propertius. In modern literatures, it is a poem of mourning or lament, such as Milton's *Lycidas* (1637) or Shelley's *Adonais* (1821), often incorporating serious general reflections on life, as in Gray's *Elegy Written in a Country Churchyard* (1751) or Whitman's 'When Lilacs Last in the Dooryard Bloom'd' (1861).

elementary particle physics *particle physics*

elements (chemistry) *chemical elements*

elephant A large mammal of family Elephantidae; the only living members of order Proboscidea (many extinct forms); almost naked grey skin; massive forehead; small eyes; upper incisor teeth form 'tusks'; snout elongated as a muscular grasping 'trunk'; ears large and movable (used to radiate heat). There are two living species. The **African elephant** is the largest living land animal (height up to 3·8 m/12½ ft), with three subspecies: the **savanna** (or **bush**) **elephant**, **Cape elephant**, and **forest elephant** (*Loxodonta africana*). The **Asian elephant** has four subspecies: **Indian elephant**, **Ceylon elephant**, **Sumatran elephant**, and **Malaysian elephant** (*Elephas maximus*). The African is larger, with larger ears, a triangular lip on the top and bottom of the trunk tip (not just on the top), and obvious tusks in the female.

Elephanta Caves A group of Hindu cave-temples located on Elephanta I off the W coast of Maharashtra, India; a world heritage site. The temples, which were excavated in the 8th–9th-c, are noted for their sculptures, in particular the 'Trimurti', an enormous bust of Shiva, Vishnu, and Brahma.

elephant bird An enormous bird, known from the Pleistocene and Holocene epochs; fossil remains found on Madagascar; flightless, stood up to 3 m/10 ft tall, and laid eggs more than 30 cm/1 ft long. (Family: Aepyornithidae.)

elephantiasis [elifantiyasis] A gross swelling of one or both legs, scrotum, and occasionally arms as a result of blockage of the lymphatic channels by filariasis. The condition is found only in the tropics.

elephant seal A huge true seal; adult male up to 6 m/20 ft long, weight 3700 kg/8150 lb; swollen pendulous snout (more pronounced during breeding season); two species: the **sea elephant** or **southern elephant seal** from the sub-Antarctic (*Mirounga leonina*), and the **northern elephant seal** from the NE Pacific (*Mirounga angustirostris*.) (Family: Phocidae.)

elephant's-ear *begonia*

Eleusinian Mysteries [elyoosinian] The secret initiation ceremonies connected with the worship of the corn-goddess Demeter and her daughter Persephone, held annually at Eleusis near Athens in ancient times. In origin agricultural fertility rites, they later came to have a moral dimension. Initiation, preceded by ritual purification, was believed to secure happiness in the after-life for those who had led a blameless life.

Eleusis [elyoosis] Ancient settlement founded c.2000 BC on a hillside near Athens, Greece. During the Mycenaean period it developed into a large fortified settlement, mostly due to its strategic position. During this time the cult of Demeter was introduced as a deity connected to nature and the growing of cereals, and successive temples dedicated to her were built on the east side of the hill. The Eleusinian Mysteries in honour of Demeter were established as one of the most important Athenian festivals. With the spread of Christianity and the invasion of the Ostrogoths, the sanctuary was abandoned. Excavations of the site began at the end of the 19th-c and notable finds are housed in the Museum of Eleusis (1889).

elevator (chiefly American English) or **lift** (chiefly British English) A device which carries people or objects from one level to another in a building with several floors. The elevator car is moved by a system of cables and pulleys, which link the car to a counterweight, the power usually being generated by electricity (earlier lifting systems had used a variety of methods, such as animal, steam, and water power). The invention of the elevator fostered the development of the skyscraper in modern cities. Following the invention of a safety device by Otis in 1852, the first (steam-powered) passenger elevator was introduced in New York City in 1857. Later improvements have included increased speeds, noise reduction, safety features (such as lighting and alarm systems), the automatic operation of groups of elevators, and two-deck cars (serving two levels simultaneously).

eleven-plus examination In the UK, a test taken by pupils towards the end of their primary education, in areas where there are selective secondary schools, to determine which school they shall attend. In much of Britain the eleven-plus declined, though did not disappear, with the spread of comprehensive schools in the 1960s and 1970s.

Elgar, Sir Edward (1857–1934) Composer, born in Broad Heath, Hereford and Worcester, WC England, UK. He was largely self-taught, and in his youth worked as a violinist before becoming conductor of the Worcester Glee Club and the County Asylum Band, and organist of St George's Roman Catholic Church, Worcester. After his marriage to **Caroline Alice Roberts** (1889) he went to London, but in 1891 settled in Malvern, devoting himself to composition. The *Enigma Variations* (1899) and the oratorio *The Dream of Gerontius* (1900) made him the leading figure in English music. After the Elgar Festival (London, 1904) he was knighted. His further works included oratorios, symphonies, concertos, and incidental music. From 1924 he was Master of the King's Musick.

Elgin Marbles [elgin] Marble sculptures of the mid-5th-c BC from the Parthenon of Athens. Acquired in 1801–3 by Thomas Bruce, 7th Earl of Elgin (1766–1841), in circumstances of doubtful legality while Greece was under Turkish rule, they were shipped to England, and in 1816 purchased by the government for the British Museum, where they remain on display. In the 1980s in particular, the question of their return to Greece became a heated political issue there.

El Greco *Greco, El*

Elijah [eliyja] (9th-c BC) Hebrew prophet, whose activities are portrayed in four Bible stories (1 *Kings* 17-19, 21; 2 *Kings* 1-2). He was prominent in opposing the worship of Baal in Israel under King Ahab and Jezebel, and by virtue of his loyalty to God was depicted as ascending directly into heaven.

elimination reaction A chemical reaction characterized by the removal of part of a molecule to leave a smaller one. In the following example, bromine is eliminated from dibromoethane to give ethylene:

$CH_2Br–CH_2Br + Zn \rightarrow CH_2=CH_2 + ZnBr_2$.

elint The practice of '*el*ectronic *int*elligence' gathering, in which one finds out the performance factors of hostile weapons systems by interpreting their electronic emissions. The term is also now used to cover any intelligence gathered by electronic means.

Elion, Gertrude (Belle) (1918–99) Chemist, born in New York City, USA. She graduated from Hunter College, New York (1937) and New York University (1941), then joined the Burroughs Wellcome laboratory (1944). In 1951, working with George Hitchings, she made and tested 6-mercaptopurine (6MP) which proved useful in cancer treatment, especially childhood leukaemia. Other work included drugs for the treatment of malaria, gout, viral herpes, and auto-immune disorders. In 1988 they shared, with James Black, the Nobel Prize for Physiology or Medicine, and in 1991 she was awarded the US National Medal of Science.

Eliot, George, pseudonym of **Mary Ann Evans** or **Marian Evans** (1819–80) Novelist, born at Arbury Farm, Astley, Warwickshire, C England, UK. She took charge of the family household when her mother died (1836), and was educated in private schools and by tutors. After the death of her father (1849) she travelled in Europe, then settled in London, and began to write for the *Westminster Review*. She became assistant editor, and the centre of a literary circle, one of whose members was G H Lewes (1817–78), with whom she lived until his death. Her first story appeared in 1857. Her major novels were *Adam Bede* (1859), *The Mill on the Floss* (1860), *Silas Marner* (1861), *Middlemarch* (1871–2), and *Daniel Deronda* (1876). After Lewes's death, she married an old friend, **John Cross**, in 1880, but died soon after.

Eliot, T(homas) S(tearns) (1888–1965) Poet, critic, and playwright, born in St Louis, Missouri, USA. He studied at Harvard and Paris, then obtained a travelling scholarship to Oxford, and was persuaded to stay in England by Ezra Pound, to whom he had shown his poems. His marriage (1915) to **Vivian Haigh Wood** settled him in England. He worked as a teacher and in a bank before becoming a director of Faber publishers (1925–65). The enthusiastic support of Pound led to his first book of poetry, *Prufrock and Other Observations* (1917), and he was introduced by Bertrand Russell into the Bloomsbury Circle. He then published *The Waste Land* (1922) and *The Hollow Men* (1925), and edited the quarterly review, *The Criterion*, from its beginning to its demise (1922–39). In 1927 he became a British subject, and was baptized and confirmed, adhering to the Anglo-Catholic movement within the Church of England. There followed several other works, including his major poetic achievement, *Four Quartets* (1944), and a series of verse dramas, notably *Murder in the Cathedral* (1935) and *The Cocktail Party* (1950). His poetry, together with his critical works, helped to reshape the literature of the 20th-c. His first wife died in 1947 after a long mental illness, and in 1957 he married **Valerie Fletcher**. He also wrote much literary and social criticism, dealing with individual authors as well as general themes, wherein he could be highly provocative. In 1948 he was awarded the Nobel Prize for Literature.

Elisabethville *Lubumbashi*

Elisha [eliysha] (second half of 9th-c BC) Hebrew prophet in succession to Elijah; his activities are portrayed in 1 *Kings* 19 and 2 *Kings* 2. He was active in Israel under several kings from Ahab to Jehoash, was credited with miraculous signs, counselled kings, and attempted to guide the nation against her external enemies, especially the Syrians.

Elizabeth I, known as **the Virgin Queen** and later **Good Queen Bess** (1533–1603) Queen of England and Ireland (1558–1603), the daughter of Henry VIII by his second wife, Anne Boleyn, born in Greenwich, London, UK. On the death of Edward VI (1553) she sided with her half-sister Mary against Lady Jane Grey and the Duke of Northumberland, but her identification with Protestantism made Mary suspicious, and she was imprisoned for her alleged part in the rebellion of Wyatt (1554). Ascending the throne on Mary's death, she steered a skilful course in foreign affairs with the two leading Catholic powers of Spain and France, and presided over the judicious settlement of the Church of England (1559). She made peace with France and Scotland, and strengthened her position by secretly helping Protestants in these countries. From 1594 to 1603 her severe policies in Ireland led to a series of rebellions. She sent Robert Devereux, 2nd Earl of Essex, to restore order, but he failed ignominiously. The countryside was devastated, and the eventual victory in 1603 of the English under Charles Blount, Lord Mountjoy, led to the extension of the Anglican Church's power over Ireland.

Following Mary, Queen of Scots' flight to England (1568) and imprisonment, Elizabeth became a target of successive conspiracies hatched by English Catholics. After the Babington plot was discovered (1586), she was reluctantly persuaded to approve Mary's execution (1587). In response to papal excommunication and Jesuit missions, she approved anti-Catholic legislation, while trying to control the Puritan wing of the Anglican Church. When Philip of Spain attempted an invasion of England, sending his 'invincible armada' (1588), her fleet under Howard of Effingham managed to repel the attack, and the weather completed its destruction. Elizabeth had a number of favourites, but she never married, and died childless. Of all her relationships, only that with Robert Dudley, Earl of Leicester, touched her deeply. A strong-willed, astute, yet capricious woman who faced growing parliamentary turbulence, she was nevertheless popular with her subjects. Her reign was crowned with the maritime exploits of Hawkyns, Drake, and Raleigh, the artistic genius of Shakespeare, Marlowe, and Spenser, and the musical works of Tallis and Byrd. Historians differ over her reign. Some say it anticipated the rise of the power of parliament that culminated in the Civil Wars of 1642–9, and that she had been forced by Parliament in 1559 to accept a more radical religious settlement than she would have preferred. Others emphasize the queen and her counsellors' relationship to policy-making, and the social dynamics of the political process. More recently, gender has been a factor – that she was able to capitalize on people's expectations of her behaviour as a woman and turn this to her own political advantage.

Elizabeth II (1926–) Queen of the United Kingdom (1952–) and head of the Commonwealth, born in London, UK, the daughter of George VI. Formerly Princess Elizabeth Alexandra Mary, she was proclaimed queen on 6 February 1952, and crowned on 2 June 1953. Her husband was created Duke of Edinburgh on the eve of their wedding (20 Nov 1947), and styled Prince Philip in 1957. They have three sons, **Charles Philip Arthur George** (14 Nov 1948), **Andrew Albert Christian Edward** (19 Feb 1960), and **Edward Anthony Richard Louis** (10 Mar 1964), and a daughter **Anne Elizabeth Alice Louise** (15 Aug 1950). Elizabeth's long and mainly peaceful reign has been marked by vast changes in her people's lives, in her country's power, how Britain is viewed abroad, and how the monarchy is regarded and portrayed. When Elizabeth became queen, post-war Britain still had a substantial empire, dominions, and dependencies, most of which achieved independence in the 1950s–1960s. Her reign has seen a revolution in social behaviour and attitudes, and increased prosperity. The 1990s in particular were a problematic period for the royal family. The Windsor Castle fire and the divorces of Prince Charles from Diana, Princess of Wales, and of Prince Andrew from Sarah, Duchess of York, were followed by Diana's death in a car crash in Paris in 1997. This particular tragedy brought to a head the debate about the monarchy's role and continued formality. Overall, however, Elizabeth II has provided the nation's main symbol of continuity, and her many visits to Commonwealth and other countries have won her wide respect.

Elizabeth (Queen Mother), originally **Lady Elizabeth Bowes-Lyon** (1900–2002) Queen-consort of Great Britain, born in St Paul's Walden Bury, Hertfordshire, SE England, UK. Her father became 14th Earl of Strathmore in 1904. Much of her childhood was spent at Glamis Castle in Scotland, where she helped the nursing staff in World War 1. In 1920 she met the **Duke of York**, the second son of George V; they were married in April 1923. **Princess Elizabeth** (later Queen Elizabeth II) was born in 1926 and **Princess Margaret** in 1930. She was a strong support to her husband, during the period of Edward VIII's abdication in 1936, and after her husband came to the throne as King George VI, she scored striking personal success in royal visits to Paris (1938) and to Canada and the USA (1939). She was with the king when Buckingham Palace was bombed in 1940, travelling with him to visit heavily damaged towns throughout the war. After George VI's death (1952), the Queen Mother continued to undertake public duties, flying thousands of miles each year and becoming a widely loved figure. In 1978 she became Lord Warden of the Cinque Ports, the first woman to hold the office. Even after her 100th birthday, which prompted a nation-wide celebration, she continued to attend public events. Her death generated a wave of popular emotion, with 200 000 queuing many hours to walk past her coffin in Westminster Hall, and a million lining the route of her funeral, and the nation marked her death with a level of ceremony not seen in the UK for half a century.

Elizabethan Style A form of early English Renaissance architecture named after Queen Elizabeth I and dating from her reign (1558–1603), characterized by symmetrical facades combined with Netherland decoration and over-sized windows. Plans are often E- or H-shaped; a good example is Longleat, Wiltshire (c.1568 onwards).

Elizabeth Petrovna [petrovna] (1709–62) Empress (tsaritsa) of Russia (1741–62), the daughter of Peter the Great and Catherine I, born in Kolomenskoye, near Moscow. She was passed over for the succession in 1727, 1730, and 1740, but finally became empress on the deposition of Ivan VI. She was guided by favourites throughout her reign. A war with Sweden was brought to a successful conclusion, and her animosity towards Frederick the Great led her to take part in the War of the Austrian Succession and in the Seven Years' War.

elk The largest of the true deer (*Alces alces*) (shoulder height, 2·4 m/8 ft); widespread in temperate N hemisphere; usually solitary; long snout, with broad overhanging top lip; throat with loose flap of skin (called the 'bell'); antlers broad, dish-like, with marginal projections; also known in North America as **moose**.

elkhound A spitz breed of dog, used in Scandinavia (especially Norway) to hunt elk; medium-sized, broad, solid body with thick grey coat; also known as **Norwegian elkhound** or **elk**.

Ellesmere Island [elzmeer] Arctic island in Northwest Territories, Canada; separated from Greenland by the Nares Strait; area 196 236 sq km/75 747 sq mi; barren and mountainous, large ice-cap (SE), fjord coastline; several small settlements; Cape Columbia, northernmost point in Canada.

Ellice Islands *Tuvalu*

Ellington, Duke, popular name of **Edward Kennedy Ellington** (1899–1974) Composer, arranger, bandleader, and pianist, born in Washington, District of Columbia, USA. He was an itinerant piano player in dance bands in Washington and New York City until 1924, when he became leader of the house band at the Kentucky Club and then (1927–31) at the Cotton Club. He developed a unique sound for his musicians by blending instruments ingeniously into startling harmonies. Among his early successes were 'Black and Tan Fantasy' (1927), 'Creole Love Call' (1927), and 'Mood Indigo' (1930). After a European tour in 1933, he worked on extended concert pieces, beginning with 'Reminiscin' in Tempo' (1935), and initiated a series of annual concerts at Carnegie Hall (1943–50). His creative peak is generally said to be 1939–42, with such recordings as 'Warm Valley', 'Cotton Tail', and 'Take the A Train'. Later works included suites such as 'Such Sweet Thunder' (1957) and 'Gutelas Suite' (1971), film scores, ballets, and a series of 'sacred concerts' (1968–74) performed in cathedrals around the world. His autobiography, *Music Is My Mistress,* was published in 1973. He led his band until a couple of months before his death from cancer, when it was taken over by his son, **Mercer Ellington** (1919–96).

Elliott, Herb, popular name of **Herbert James Elliott** (1938–) Athlete, born in Perth, Western Australia. Winner of the gold medal in the 1500 m at the 1960 Olympics in Rome, his time of 3 min 35·6 s for that event was unbeaten for seven years. He was never beaten on level terms over a mile or 1500 m, and he ran the sub-4-minute mile 17 times. He was noted for the rigour and severity of his training schedule.

Elliott, John Dorman (1941–) Businessman, born in Melbourne, Victoria, SE Australia. He studied at Melbourne University, and in 1972 formed a consortium to acquire Henry Jones (IXL) Ltd. A series of mergers and takeovers followed, first with Elder, Smith & Co, then with Carlton and United Brewers, to form Elders IXL, later Foster's Brewing Group. He was managing director from 1981, then chairman and chief executive (1985–90) and deputy chairman (1990–2). He was president of the Liberal Party of Australia (1987–90), and rumours of his entry into politics have been constant. He became known as 'the last of the beer barons' when he was faced with bankruptcy proceedings in 1992.

ellipse In mathematics, the locus of a point which moves so that the sum of its distances from two fixed points (or *foci*) is constant. It can also be defined as a section of a double cone, or as the locus of a point which moves so that the distance from the focus is proportional to its distance from a fixed line (the *directrix*), the constant of proportion being less than 1. The Cartesian equation of an ellipse can be put in the form $x^2/a^2 + y^2/b^2 = 1$. The polar equation of an ellipse with the focus as pole and the major axis as base line is $r = l/(1 + e \cos \theta)$. The planets move around the Sun in ellipses, and the shape is much used in art and architecture.

elliptic geometry *geometries, non-Euclidean*

Ellis, Alice Thomas, originally **Anna Margaret Haycraft**, née **Lindholm** (1932–) Novelist, born in Liverpool, Merseyside, NW England, UK. She studied at the Liverpool College of Art. A writer of cookery books under her original name, it was *The Sin Eater* (1977), which established her reputation as a novelist. *The 27th Kingdom* (1982) is often considered her most successful novel. Other books include *Pillars of Gold* (1992), *Cat Among the Pigeons* (1994), *Fairy Tale* (1996), *Valentine's Day* (2000), a religious book, *Serpent on the Rock* (1994), and an autobiography, *A Welsh Childhood* (1990).

Ellis, (Henry) Havelock (1859–1939) Physician and writer on sex, born in Croydon, S Greater London, UK. He travelled widely in Australia and South America before studying medicine in London. His interest in human biology and his personal experiences led him to compile the seven-volume *Studies in the Psychology of Sex* (1897–1928), the first detached treatment of the subject, which was highly controversial at the time.

Ellis Island A small island (27·5 acres) in New York Bay, USA; named after New Jersey merchant Samuel Ellis, who owned it in the 18th-c. It served as the main immigration centre to the USA from 1892 to 1943, with c.2000 immigrants a day arriving there in the peak years of the early 20th-c. It was sometimes called 'the isle of tears', as not all would-be immigrants were permitted to enter, and families were often separated. It became part of the Statue of Liberty National Monument in 1965. Sovereignty of the island changed from New York to New Jersey, following a US Supreme Court decision in 1998.

Ellison, Ralph (Waldo) (1914–94) Writer, born in Oklahoma City, Oklahoma, USA. He studied as a musician at the Tuskegee Institute, AL, then joined the Federal Writers' Project in New York City. His major work was the novel *Invisible Man* (1952), a semi-autobiographical account of a young black intellectual's search for identity and authentic consciousness, set mainly in the New York City slums. He also published two volumes of essays, *Shadow and Act* (1964) and *Going to the Territory* (1986). His last work, the short story *Flying Home*, was published posthumously in 1996.

Ellora Caves *Kailasa Temple*

elm A deciduous N temperate tree; leaves ovoid, doubly toothed, asymmetric at base; flowers tiny, appearing before leaves; seed oval, with broad papery wing. In recent years the North American elm populations have been devastated by a virulent form of **Dutch elm disease**, so named for the work on resistant strains carried out in The Netherlands. In the mid-1960s it spread to Europe and particularly the UK, killing millions of trees, mainly of species such as **English elm** (*Ulmus procera*), which often reproduce by suckers, giving genetically similar populations. Species such as **Wytch elm** (*Ulmus glabra*), which reproduce by seed, are thought to have some resistance. (Genus: *Ulmus*, 45 species. Family: Ulmaceae.)

elm bark beetle A small brown beetle with pitted wing cases; adults excavate a vertical, shaft-like egg chamber beneath the bark of the elm tree; larvae tunnel away from the chamber, horizontally at first. It carries the fungus that causes Dutch elm disease. (Order: Coleoptera. Family: Scolytidae.)

El Niño [neenyoh] (Span 'the Child') An anomalous seasonal ocean current along the coast of Peru, often occurring around Christmas (hence its name). It carries warm, low salinity, nutrient-depleted tropical surface waters along the coast of N Peru, bringing a stop to the normal upwelling of cooler nutrient-rich water which supports abundant growth of marine plankton, fish, and sea birds. Severe El Niños can result in the collapse of the food chain, causing massive mortality to marine life. The resulting decay of dead organisms can produce enough hydrogen sulphide gas in surface waters to stain the hulls of ships, and has given rise to the other name for El Niño, the **Callao Painter**, after the Peruvian port of Callao. Once thought to be produced by changes in local wind conditions affecting the ocean, it is now known to be part of a much larger phenomenon related to changes in atmospheric pressure in the S Pacific, called the *southern oscillation*. Referred to as **ENSO** events, for **El Niño – Southern Oscillation**, the phenomenon may recur every 2–10 years, and has been blamed for such wide-ranging effects as droughts in N Australia, rising sea level and severe storm damage along the W coast of the Americas, torrential rainfall along the coast of Ecuador and Peru, more frequent tropical cyclones, and severe winters in Europe and North America. Its effects were proving to be especially noticeable during 1997, with some locations experiencing dramatic climatic change (eg a major increase of rainfall on Christmas I). There is a complementary effect, known as **La Niña**, a cooling of the Pacific water, in intervening years.

elocution The study and practice of excellence in the manner and style of vocal delivery. Dating from classical Greek and Roman times, it includes far more than training in effective pronunciation: grammatical structure, choice of vocabulary, and stylistic construction must all be taken into account in order to achieve the greatest effect in using the voice.

Elohim [elohheem] (Heb 'gods') A divine name for the God of Israel, the plural form here being purged of its polytheistic meaning, and used as a plural of majesty. There are over 2500 occurrences in the Hebrew Bible, making it one of the most common divine names therein, but it could still be applied to other gods, angels, or even figures such as Moses.

elongation The angular distance between the Sun and a planet as viewed from Earth. The two inner planets, Mercury and Venus, have maximum elongations of 28° and 47° respectively. The small value for Mercury means that it is never far from the Sun, and is thus a most elusive object to spot.

El Paso [el pasoh] 31°45N 106°29W, pop (2000e) 563 600. Seat of El Paso Co, W Texas, USA; port on the Rio Grande opposite Ciudad Juarez, Mexico; founded, 1827; airfield; railway; university (1913); cattle, cotton, vegetables; refined petroleum, copper, foods, clothing, machinery; tourism; part transferred to Mexico in 1963, after the settlement of the Chamizal border dispute.

El Salvador *p.510*

Elsinore [elsinaw(r)], Danish **Helsingør** 56°03N 12°38E; pop (2000e) 58 200. Seaport on The Sound, NE Zealand, Denmark, opposite Helsingborg, Sweden; railway; shipbuilding, engineering; site of Kronborg Castle, a world heritage site, famous as the scene of Shakespeare's *Hamlet*.

El Tajín [el taheen] An ancient Meso-American city near Papantla, N Veracruz, Mexico, flourishing in c.600–900 but abandoned after 1100. About 9·5 sq km/3¾ sq mi in area, it has a 60 ha/150 acre ceremonial centre with 12 ballcourts – more than any other site. The 18-m/60-ft high Pyramid of the Niches (c.600) has 365 external niches, each reputed to have contained an idol for one day of the year.

Eluard, Paul [elwah(r)], pseudonym of **Eugène Grindel** (1895–1952) Poet, born in Saint-Denis, NC France. He was one of the founders of the Surrealist movement in literature. His first collection of poetry was *Capitale de la douleur* (1926, Capital of Sorrow). Many of his works reflect the major events of the century, such as the World Wars, the Resistance, and the aspirations of the Communist Party, which he joined in 1942.

Elvström, Paul [elvstroem] (1928–) Yachtsman, born in Gentofte, Copenhagen. He is the only yachtsman to win four individual Olympic gold medals: in the Firefly class in 1948, and in the Finn class in 1952, 1956, and 1960. He was also the first to win the same event at four consecutive Olympics. He came fourth in the Tornado class at the 1984 Olympics, his seventh Games, with his daughter, **Trine** (1962–).

Elway, John (1960–) Player of American football, born in Port Angeles, Washington, DC, USA. He attended Stanford University, then spent his entire career with Denver Broncos, leading them to the NFL quarterback record 148 victories and throwing for 51 475 yds, the second highest total in NFL history. He won the Most Valuable Player award in 1999.

Ely [eelee] 52°24N 0°16E, pop (2000e) 10 500. Small city in E Cambridgeshire, EC England, UK; in fertile, wheat-growing fens, on R Ouse, 23 km/14 mi NE of Cambridge; railway; paper, agriculture, engineering, plastics, tourism; 12th-c cathedral (octagonal tower), King's School (1543); Isle of Ely (higher ground surrounded by fens) the location of Hereward the Wake's defence against the Normans.

Elyot, Sir Thomas, also spelled **Eliot** (c.1490–1546) Writer and diplomat, born in Wiltshire, S England, UK. In 1523 he became clerk of the king's council, was ambassador to Emperor Charles V in 1531–2, and became MP for Cambridge in 1542. His chief work, *The Boke Named the Gouernour* (1531), is the earliest English treatise on moral philosophy. He was a strong supporter of the use of English (as opposed to Latin and Greek) in scholarly work and added many new words to the language, including *encyclopaedia* (1539). He was knighted in 1530.

Elysée, Palais de l' [pale duh layleezay], Eng **Elysée Palace** Since 1873 the official residence of the French president, situated on the Rue du Faubourg Sainte-Honoré in Paris. It was built in 1718 for the Compte d'Evreux and, although it was used as a dance-

El Salvador

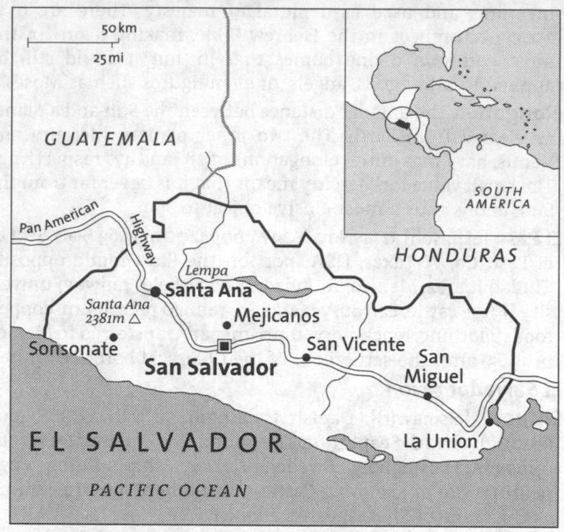

☐ International Airport

official name **Republic of El Salvador**, Span **República de El Salvador**

Local name El Salvador

Timezone GMT -6

Area 21 476 km^2/8290 sq mi

Population total (2002e) 6 354 000

Status Republic

Date of independence 1841

Capital San Salvador

Language Spanish (official)

Ethnic groups Spanish-Indian (89%), Indian (mostly Pipil) (5%)

Religions Roman Catholic (93%), other (mostly Evangelical Protestant) (7%)

Physical features Smallest of Central America republics; two volcanic ranges run E–W; narrow coastal belt in S, rises to mountains in N; highest point, Santa Ana, 2381 m/7812 ft; many volcanic lakes; earthquakes common.

Climate Varies greatly with altitude; hot tropical on coastal lowlands; single rainy season (May–Oct); temperate uplands; average annual temperature at San Salvador 23°C (Jul), 22°C (Jan); average annual rainfall 1775 mm/70 in.

Currency 1 Colón (ES∅) = 100 centavos

Economy Largely based on agriculture; main crops coffee and cotton; sugar, maize, balsam (world's main source); chemicals, rubber, rubber goods, oil products.

GDP (2002e) $29·41 bn, per capita $4600

Human Development Index (2002) 0·706

History Originally part of the Aztec kingdom; conquest by Spanish, 1526; independence from Spain, 1821; member of the Central American Federation until its dissolution in 1839; independent republic, 1841; war with Honduras, 1965, 1969; considerable political unrest in 1970s and 80s, with guerrilla activity directed against the US-supported government; civil war, 1979–91; peace plan agreed, 1991; governed by a President, and Council of Ministers; unicameral Legislative Assembly.

Head of State/Government

1962–7 Julio Adalberto Rivera
1967–72 Fidel Sánchez Hernández
1972–7 Arturo Armando Molina
1977–9 Carlos Humberto Romero
1979–82 Military juntas
1982–4 *Government of National Unanimity* (Alvaro Magaña)
1984–9 José Napoleón Duarte
1989–94 Alfredo Cristiani Burkard
1994–9 Armando Calderón Sol
1999– Francisco Flores

hall for a period during the Revolution, it later became the home of Napoleon I and Napoleon III.

Elysium [elizium] or **Elysian fields** In Greek and Roman mythology, the happy fields, often located on the borders of the Underworld, where the good remain after death in perfect happiness. It is sometimes confused with the pre-Greek Islands of the Blessed, where heroes are said to live immortally.

ema *rhea* (ornithology)

e-mail *electronic mail*

Emancipation Proclamation (1 Jan 1863) A document issued by President Lincoln during the American Civil War, declaring the freedom of all slaves in areas then in arms against the US government; it did not free slaves in areas not in rebellion. He had issued a preliminary proclamation on 22 September 1862.

Emanuel or **Manuel I,** known as **the Great** or **the Fortunate** (1469–1521) King of Portugal (1495–1521), born in Alcochete, W Portugal. He consolidated royal power, and his reign, which was marred by his persecution of the Jews, was the Golden Age of Portugal. He prepared the code of laws which bears his name, and made his court a centre of chivalry, art, and science. He sponsored the voyages of Vasco da Gama, Cabral, and others, which helped to make Portugal the first naval power of Europe and a world centre of commerce. He promoted a religious crusade against the Turks, and expelled all of Portugal's Jews in 1497–8.

embargo An order obstructing or impeding the movement of ships of a foreign power, which can entail preventing them from either leaving or entering a port. In the past, embargoes were associated with anticipating the outbreak of war, but their use is limited today. The term is also employed to describe any attempt to suspend trading with another country, and the imposition of a time and date before which a piece of news cannot be broadcast or published.

Ember Days In the Christian Church, the Wednesday, Friday, and Saturday of the weeks (Ember Weeks) following the first Sunday in Lent, Whitsunday, Holy Cross Day (14 Sep) and St Lucy's Day (13 Dec); formerly observed as special times of fasting and abstinence.

embezzlement The dishonest taking or fraudulent use of money or other property entrusted to an employee (or *agent*) by his or her employer (or *principal*). It is a form of theft, the separate offence of embezzlement having been abolished in England and Wales by the Theft Act (1968). Many US penal codes, likewise, subsume this offence under theft. However, in Scottish law it is distinguished from both theft and fraud.

emblematic staging A style of theatre which uses single scenic images, often three-dimensional and free-standing, to symbolize or indicate an idea or location relevant to the action. A raised throne under a golden canopy might represent Heaven, while a dragon's head with gaping jaws would locate Hell. A number of such images can be portrayed simultaneously, and the acting area close to each image is determined by it, while the rest of the stage conveys no specific scenic connotations.

embolism [embolizm] An obstruction of a blood vessel by the accumulation and adhesion of any undissolved material (such as a blood clot) carried to the site in the bloodstream. It is usually identified according to the vessel involved (cerebral, coronary, pulmonary) or the undissolved material (air, fat). Embolisms are most commonly due to blood clots that break off from areas of thrombosis, often veins in the leg. Fat embolisms may arise as a complication of orthopaedic surgery or severe fractures. Air embolisms may occur in the course of surgery, following an injury, or during intravenous infusions undertaken without satisfactory precautions.

embrasure A recess in a building for a window. It also refers to the splayed opening between any two upstanding parts of a parapet or crenellated wall.

embroidery The ornamentation of fabrics with decorative stitching – an art which dates from very early times (as shown in Egyptian tomb paintings), when the designs were sewn onto a base fabric by hand. It was highly developed in the Middle and Far East, and in India, for rich garments and furnishings. In Europe, church vestments provided consistently sumptuous examples. Embroidery skills were part of the needleworking ability required by most women, and applied to the making of clothes, linens, and soft furnishings; one of the most famous examples is the 11th-c Bayeux tapestry. While hand-embroidery survives as a craft, many of today's goods are embroidered using computer-controlled sewing machines, capable of reproducing complex multi-coloured patterns.

embryo [embrioh] In flowering plants, the young plant developed from an ovum and contained within the seed; in animals, the developing young, typically derived from a sexually fertilized ovum, contained either within the egg membranes or inside the maternal body. The embryonic phase commences with the division of the fertilized egg (*zygote*), and ends with the hatching or birth of the young animal.

embryology The study of the development of animals from the first division of the fertilized egg, through the differentiation and formation of the organ systems, to the ultimate hatching or birth of the young animal.

emerald A gem variety of beryl, coloured green by minor amounts of chromium oxide. The finest crystals are from Colombia.

Emerson, Ralph Waldo (1803–82) Poet and essayist, born in Boston, Massachusetts, USA. He studied at Harvard, and became a teacher, then (1829) pastor of a Unitarian Church in Boston, but his controversial views caused his resignation. In 1833 he travelled to Europe, and visited Thomas Carlyle, thereafter corresponding with him for 38 years. In 1834 he moved to Concord, MA, where he wrote his prose rhapsody, *Nature* (1836), and many poems and essays, notably *The Conduct of Life* (1860). He was a transcendentalist in philosophy, a rationalist in religion, and a bold advocate of spiritual individualism.

emery A natural mixture of crystalline corundum with iron oxides, occurring as dark granules. Very hard, it is used as an abrasive.

emigration *migration* 1

Emin, Tracey (1963–) Multimedia artist, born in London, UK. She gained attention with her controversial entry for the 1999 Turner Prize, 'My Bed'. The exhibit, a dishevelled bed with soiled sheets and debris, was later bought by art collector Charles Saatchi. In 2001 her solo exhibition, 'You Forgot to Kiss My Soul', opened at the White Cube Gallery in London. It included sculptures, embroidered blankets, drawings, photographs, a video, and some work in neon.

emir or **amir** (Arabic 'commander') A senior Muslim title, often used by a provincial governor or military commander; subordinate to the caliph, though in some provinces emirs were in practice largely independent. Important emirates included those of Afghanistan (1747–1926), Bahrain (Al-Khalifa dynasty from 1783), Kuwait (Al Sabah dynasty from 1756), Lebanon (1516–1842, then Turkish rule), Qatar (Al-Thani dynasty from 1868), and Saudi Arabia (Al-Saud dynasty of Najd, from c.1720). The title was finally abolished along with the caliphate in 1924. In the United Arab Emirates, the rulers are not called emirs, but sheikhs; emirate was introduced into the name of the federation because the term sheikhdom was already in use in the region for a township-level administrative unit.

Emmet, Robert (1778–1803) Irish patriot, born in Dublin, Ireland. He left Trinity College, Dublin, to join the United Irishmen, and travelled on the European mainland for the Irish cause, at one point meeting Napoleon. In 1803 he plotted an insurrection against the English, but it proved a failure. He was captured and hanged in Dublin.

Emmy A series of annual awards presented by the American Academy of Television Arts and Sciences since 1949; the television equivalent of the Oscar. It recognizes a very wide range of categories of achievement in such fields as acting, writing, direction, series production, and technical skills. It established a Television Hall of Fame in 1983.

emotion A psychological state involving the arousal of a person's feelings, seen especially in contrast with cognitive states, which describe their rational thoughts and beliefs. The psychological study of the emotions has been dominated by attempts to understand their relationship with concomitant cognitive and physiological states. An influential theory, originally espoused by William James, proposes that emotions are attributions of bodily states; for example, a stimulus arouses fear because it raises heart-rate.

Empedocles [empedokleez] (c.490–c.430 BC) Greek philosopher and poet, born in Acragas, Sicily, who by tradition was also a doctor, statesman, and soothsayer. In his poem, *On Nature*, he agreed with Parmenides that there could be no absolute coming to exist or ceasing to exist; all change in the world is the result of two contrary cosmic forces, Love and Strife, mixing and separating four everlasting elements, Earth, Water, Air, and Fire. The doctrine of four elements became central to Western thought for 2000 years through its adoption by Aristotle.

emperor moth A large, broad-winged moth; wings grey or grey-brown with conspicuous eye-spots on forewings and hindwings; caterpillar green, with hairy warts on each segment, found from May to August; hibernates as pupa in a brown cocoon. (Order: Lepidoptera. Family: Saturniidae.)

emperor penguin The largest of penguins (*Aptenodytes forsteri*), 1·2 m/4 ft tall; never comes to true land; inhabits seas around Antarctica; may dive to depths of 268 m/879 ft; breeds on pack ice at beginning of winter; single egg incubated on the male's feet for 64 days during bitter polar blizzards.

emphysema [emfiseema] A disorder of the lungs in which there is destruction of the elastic fibres that normally cause lung tissue to recoil during expiration. As a result, the lungs become progressively more distended and overfilled with air. The small air tubes (*bronchioles*) become dilated, and the small sacs where gaseous exchange place (*alveoli*) are destroyed and replaced by air-filled cavities (*bullae*). The chest slowly becomes barrel-shaped, and shortness of breath can become severe. The condition is common in heavy cigarette-smokers in whom inhaled cigarette products activate enzymes that digest the elastic tissue. The destruction of tissues also promotes secondary infection.

Empire Day *Commonwealth Day*

Empire State Building An office block in Manhattan, New York City, USA, designed by the firm of Shreve, Lamb & Harman, built 1930–1. At 449 m/1472 ft high (including a 68 m/222 ft high television mast added in 1951) it was the tallest building in the world until 1970.

Empire Style The style of decoration associated with Napoleon I's court after he became Emperor in 1804. It is massive, and heavily ornamented with classicizing motifs, particularly Egyptian sphinxes, winged lions, and caryatids. These are cast in ormolu, and gilded or elaborately carved on the furniture (eg the chaise-longue). The style was also seen in costume (eg high-waisted 'Grecian' dresses for women). The equivalent style in Britain was **Regency**.

empirical formula *chemical formula*

empiricism A philosophical tradition which maintains that all or most knowledge is based on experience and is ultimately derived from the senses; it is usually contrasted with **rationalism**, and with theories which emphasize the importance of innate or *a priori* knowledge. Empiricists such as Locke, Hume, and Mill take the natural sciences as their paradigms of knowledge; rationalists take logic or mathematics.

employers' association or **trade association** A society of companies in the same line of business, whose purpose is to discuss matters of common interest, carry out research, make representations to government on industrial matters, and negotiate with trade unions for industry-wide standards and wages. The companies must not collude on prices in ways contrary to the Restrictive Trade Practices and Competition Acts in the UK and the Anti-trust Laws in the USA.

employment exchange A UK government-run agency to help out-of-work people find a job; originally called a **labour exchange**, and later known as a **job centre**. Employers seeking workers send particulars to the local job centre; these are matched with the skills and qualifications of the persons registered.

Empress Dowager *Cixi*

Empson, Sir William (1906–84) Poet and critic, born in Howden, near Hull, NE England, UK. He studied at Cambridge, and became professor of English literature at Tokyo (1931–4) and Beijing (1937–9, 1947–53), working in the interim with the BBC's Far Eastern Service. From 1953 to 1971 he was professor of English literature at Sheffield University. He wrote several major critical works, notably *Seven Types of Ambiguity* (1930), and his *Collected Poems* were published in 1955. *The Complete Poems of William Empson* (ed. John Haffenden) appeared in 2000. He was knighted in 1979.

empyema [empiyeema] A collection of pus between the two layers of membranes which cover the lung (the *pleura*). It is most commonly due to the spread of infection from pneumonia in the lungs.

Ems, River, Dutch **Eems**, ancient **Amisia** German river, rises N of Paderborn; meanders 400 km/250 mi W and N to the North Sea, forming a 32 km/20 mi-long estuary; length 328 km/204 mi; navigable length 238 km/148 mi; linked to the Ruhr via the Dortmund–Ems Canal.

Ems telegram A despatch (13 Jul 1870) from the Prussian king William I to his chancellor, Bismarck, describing the refusal of the king to accept French conditions over the disputed candidature to the Spanish throne. Altered and published by Bismarck, it helped achieve his aim of provoking Napoleon III of France into declaring war on Prussia. The consequences were the downfall of the French and the creation of the German Second Empire.

emu A flightless bird native to Australia (*Dromaius novaehollandiae*); the second largest living bird (after the ostrich), 1·9 m/6¼ ft tall; inhabits dry plains and woodland; eats fruit, shoots, flowers, and insects; runs at nearly 50 kph/30 mph; swims well; related to the cassowary. (Family: Dromaiidae.)

emulsifiers Chemical substances which help liquids to mix with each other, forming an emulsion. For example, oil and water, which do not normally mix, can be combined into a single phase using an emulsifier, as in margarine and mayonnaise. Emulsifiers also allow gas to be trapped in liquids, as when cream is beaten. Emulsifying agents include locust bean gum, agar, and lecithin.

emulsion A suspension of one liquid in another, particularly of an oil in water. All emulsions eventually separate, 'stable' emulsions merely separating more slowly than 'unstable' ones.

emu wren A small, brightly coloured bird native to Australia, also known as the **Australian wren** or **wren-warbler**; tail often long and held erect (resembling true wrens); forages on ground or lower branches of vegetation; inhabits scrub or dense grass; eats insects. (Genus: *Stipiturus*, 3 species. Family: Maluridae.)

enamel A decorative medium for producing a highly glazed surface on metal. The common base is a soft glass flux, which is painted over the metal. Colours (which are generally inorganic or mineral materials, such as metal oxides) are added, in desired patterns or pictorially. The whole is then fired in a furnace. Similar techniques are carried out industrially to produce enamelled containers or body work for machinery (eg bowls, ovens, refrigerators).

enamelling The use of brightly coloured substances similar to glass which are fired on to metalwork or ceramics as decoration. The techniques used on metalwork are champlevé, cloisonné, basse taille, and painting. Painted enamels of the highest quality on copper were produced in Limoges in the 16th-c, and the same technique was widely used in Europe in the 18th-c for snuff boxes and other small items. Enamel decoration on ceramics is applied on top of the fired glaze, and receives one or more firings at a lower temperature.

enantiomer [enantiohmer] *chirality*

Enceladus [enseladus] The second natural satellite of Saturn, discovered in 1789; distance from the planet 238 000 km/148 000 mi; diameter 500 km/310 mi; orbital period 1·370 days.

encephalitis [ensefaliytis] Inflammation of the brain, usually caused by a viral infection, but other micro-organisms (including syphilis and malaria) may also be responsible. The clinical features are fever, headache, drowsiness, and confusion, as well as hallucinations, paralysis, and abnormal movements.

Encke's comet [engkuh] A comet discovered in 1786, and studied by German astronomer Johann Franz Encke (1791–1865) in 1819, which has the shortest period of any known comet, just 3·3 years. It has been recorded at more than 50 apparitions. Encke's name became attached to this comet because he investigated non-gravitational forces which make it orbit 2·5 hours faster than expected.

enclosure In the UK, the name given to the process whereby land previously part of large open fields or waste was fenced off and held in private ownership. Much land was enclosed for pasture during the 16th-c when sheep-farming became more profitable. This reduced the amount of labouring work available on the land, and contributed to increasing social tension. Most land was enclosed by agreement of proprietors. However, between c.1760 and c.1820, when corn farming was highly profitable, many parishes were enclosed by private Act of Parliament. This parliamentary enclosure, though costly to implement, usually brought rewards to proprietors in terms of more intensive arable cultivation, greater productivity, and higher rentals. Parliamentary enclosure was controversial, many contemporaries arguing that it destroyed customary tenurial rights and disadvantaged the rural poor. Historical controversy about the effects of parliamentary closure remains unresolved, the loss of customary rights and damage to the interests of small landowners needing to be balanced against increased work opportunities at a time of rapid population growth.

encopresis *enuresis*

encounter group A form of group therapy in which the leader facilitates the acquisition of insight and sensitivity to others, using such techniques as bodily contact and the sharing of emotional experiences. Also known as *T-* ('training') *groups*, sessions vary greatly in length and type, and can have both positive and negative effects on members.

encyclical, papal [ensiklikl] Originally, a letter sent to all the churches in a particular area. The term is now restricted to official letters of instruction, usually doctrinal or pastoral in nature, issued by a pope to the whole Roman Catholic Church.

Encyclopaedists / Encyclopedists A collective term for the distinguished editors (Diderot and d'Alembert) and contributors (notably Voltaire, Montesquieu, Condorcet, Helvetius, and Rousseau) to the *Encyclopèdie*, a major work of social and political reference published in France (1751–76), associated with the French Enlightenment. It was a complete review of the arts and sciences of the day, explaining the new sciences of physics and cosmology and supporting the new philosophy of humanism. A decree of 1752 suppressed the first volumes, and in 1759 it was placed on the Index (of books forbidden to Roman Catholic readers). It had immense influence on the liberalism of the 19th-c.

encyclopedia / encyclopaedia A comprehensive reference work containing entries on a single subject, a set of related subjects, or all branches of knowledge. Such works may be single or multi-volume publications, with or without illustrations.

The entries may be grouped thematically or alphabetically, and involve the use of such editorial aids as cross-references and pronunciation guides. Encyclopedic treatments date from classical Greek and Roman times, but the most notable developments took place in 18th-c Britain and France, with Ephraim Chambers' *Cyclopaedia* (1728), the 35-volume *Encyclopédie* of Diderot and his associates (1751–76), and the first edition of the *Encyclopaedia Britannica* (1768–71).

endangered species Plant and animal species which are in danger of becoming extinct. Their classification as endangered species is made by the International Union for the Conservation of Nature and Natural Resources. The danger of extinction generally comes from habitat loss and disturbance caused by human activity, overexploitation, and in many cases pollution. For example, disturbance threatens the pupping beaches of the endangered Hawaiian Monk Seal (*Monachus schauinslandi*), causing increased juvenile mortality. The category also includes species which are possibly now extinct, but which have definitely been seen in the wild within the past 50 years.

Ender, Kornelia (1958–) Swimmer, born in Bitterfeld, EC Germany. Representing East Germany, she won three Olympic silver medals in 1972, aged 13, and between 1973 and 1976 broke 23 world records (the most by a woman under modern conditions). At the 1973 and 1975 World Championships she won 10 medals, including a record eight golds. In 1976 she became the first woman to win four gold medals at one Olympic Games: the 100 m and 200 m freestyle, the 100 m butterfly, and the 4 × 100 m medley relay.

Enders, John (Franklin) (1897–1985) Microbiologist, born in West Hartford, Connecticut, USA. He studied literature at Harvard, but then switched to bacteriology. He researched tuberculosis and pneumococcal infections before studying viral diseases, and in 1946 helped set up a laboratory for poliomyelitis research at Boston. He shared with Frederick Robbins and Thomas Weller the 1954 Nobel Prize for Physiology or Medicine for the cultivation of polio viruses in human tissue cells, thus greatly advancing virology and making possible the development of a polio vaccine by Salk. In 1962 he developed an effective vaccine against measles.

endive An annual or biennial (*Cichorium endivia*) growing to 120 cm/4 ft, native to S Europe; basal leaves lobed, upper leaves lance-shaped, clasping the stem at their base; flower-heads blue, in clusters of 2–5. Closely related to chicory, it is widely grown as a salad plant, cultivated varieties having many different, often crisped leaf forms. (Family: Compositae.)

Endo, Shusaku (1923–96) Novelist and short story writer, born in Toyko, Japan. He graduated in French literature from Keio University, then studied for several years in Lyon. Widely regarded as the leading writer in Japan, he was elected to the Nihon Geijutsuin, the Japanese Arts Academy, in 1981. His books include (trans titles) *Silence* (1966), *The Sea and Poison* (1972), *Wonderful Fool* (1974), *Volcano* (1978), *When I Whistle* (1979), and *Stained Glass Elegies* (1984).

endocarditis Infection and inflammation of the lining of the heart, particularly of the heart valves. Bacteria circulating in the blood colonize and multiply on the heart valves and initiate an inflammatory process; the inflamed valves become thickened and misshapen and are unable to open and close properly; normal control of blood flow through the heart is lost. Clinical features include fever, fatigue, and shortness of breath. Auscultation of the heart may reveal abnormal sounds (murmurs) due to altered blood flow through the valves. Severe infections result in heart failure. Treatment with antibiotics is required to eradicate the infection, and replacement of the valves may be necessary if they have been permanently damaged.

endocrine glands [endokriyn] Ductless glands, present in some invertebrates (certain molluscs, arthropods) and all vertebrates, which synthesize and secrete chemical messengers (hormones) into the blood stream, or lymph for transport to target cells. In vertebrates they collectively form a major communication system (the **endocrine system**) which with the nervous system regulates and co-ordinates body functions. This system classically comprises the pituitary, thyroid, parathyroid, and adrenal (suprarenal) glands, the pancreas (the islets of Langerhans), and the gonads; however, other regions (hypothalamus, kidneys, gastro-intestinal tract, thymus, and pineal gland) have endocrine function. Disorders of the endocrine glands are numerous, and may result in disturbances of growth and development, metabolism, and reproduction. The study of the structure, function, and disorders of the endocrine glands is **endocrinology**.

endogamy and **exogamy** The broad social rules that define who are to be regarded as legitimate marriage partners in society. **Endogamy** allows marriage between members of one's own group or lineage; **exogamy** allows marriage only between members of different groups, to encourage transfer of members and their resources (eg via dowries) between lineages.

endogenous opioids *opioid peptides*

endometriosis A common disorder in which the cells that normally line the uterine cavity (*endometrium*) grow in other sites of the body, usually elsewhere in the pelvis, such as on the ovaries, rectum, and bladder. The cause is unknown, but it is possible that endometrial cells migrate up through the uterine tubes and implant in the pelvis (*retrograde-menstruation*). The endometrial cells outside the uterus respond to the same hormonal signals as those within it: they proliferate and swell every month, then slough off during the next menstrual period. This provokes an inflammatory reaction on other pelvic organs, which can lead to scarring and damage, and on the uterus can lead to the formation of blood-filled cysts (*chocolate cysts*). The main clinical features are heavy periods and pelvic pain, and the condition can lead to infertility. Treatment may be with drugs to mimic a state of pregnancy, preventing proliferation of endometrial cells, or surgery to remove scarring and cysts.

endorphins [endaw(r)finz] Natural substances present throughout the body which have similar (but more controlled) effects to morphine and other narcotics; also called **enkephalins**. Since narcotics have such potent effects, it was long suspected that natural counterparts might exist in the body. British neuroscientist John Hughes (1942–) and British pharmacologist Hans Walter Kosterlitz (1903–96) succeeded in isolating and purifying endorphins in 1975. The substances are believed to act as neurotransmitters.

endoscopy [endoskopee] The introduction of an instrument into a body aperture or duct for direct visual inspection and biopsy. It is carried out with a flexible glass fibre **endoscope**, which can pass narrow channels and bends more easily than the rigid instruments used formerly. Examples include *bronchoscopy* (bronchi), *gastroscopy* (stomach), *colonoscopy* (colon), *cystoscopy* (bladder), *jejunoscopy* (jejunum), and *peritoneoscopy* (peritoneum). Powerful light sources and fibre optics make modern endoscopes very efficient, and some incorporate extra devices (eg laser beams) intended to carry out actual operations deep inside the body.

endothelium *epithelium*

Endymion [endimion] In Greek mythology, a handsome shepherd of Mt Latmos, who was loved by the Moon-goddess Selene. Zeus put him to sleep, while Selene looked after his flocks, and visited him every night. He was also said, as King of Elis, to have founded the Olympic Games.

energy An abstract calculable quantity associated with all physical processes and objects, whose total value is found always to be conserved; symbol *E*, units J (joule); one of the most important concepts in physics. It is an additive, scalar quantity, which may be transferred but never destroyed, and so provides a useful book-keeping device for the analysis of processes. It is sometimes called the capacity for doing work. Although many terms are used to describe energy (eg thermal energy, kinetic energy), they refer to the same energy, but indicate its different manifestations. For example, a battery driving a propeller immersed in water converts chemical energy to electrical

England

□ International Airport

Lat **Anglia** (UK)

Area 130 357 km²/50 318 sq mi

Population total (2001e) 49 138 800

Status Constituent part of the United Kingdom

Capital London

Languages English, with c.100 minority languages

Ethnic groups & Religions (*see* **United Kingdom**)

Physical features Largest area within the United Kingdom, forming the S part of the island of Great Britain; since 1974 divided into 46 counties; includes the Isles of Scilly, Lundy, and the Isle of Wight; largely undulating lowland, rising (S) to the Mendips, Cotswolds, Chilterns, and North Downs, (N) to the N–S ridge of the Pennines, and (NW) to the Cumbria Mts; drained E by the Tyne, Tees, Humber, Ouse, and Thames Rivers, and W by the Eden, Ribble, Mersey, and Severn Rivers; Lake District (NW) includes Derwent Water, Ullswater, Windermere and Bassenthwaite; linked to Europe by ferry and hovercraft, and (from 1994) by the Channel Tunnel.

Economy North Sea oil and gas, coal, tin, china clay, salt, potash, lead ore, iron ore; vehicles, heavy engineering, petrochemicals, pharmaceuticals, textiles, food processing, electronics, telecommunications, publishing, brewing, fishing, livestock, agriculture, horticulture, pottery and tourism.

History (*see* **United Kingdom**)

Counties of England

County / Area (km² / sq mi) / Population total (2000e) / Admin Centre

Avon / 1345 / 520 / 989 800 / Bristol
Bedfordshire / 1235 / 477 / 555 500 / Bedford
Berkshire / 1259 / 486 / 781 700 / Reading
Buckinghamshire / 1883 / 727 / 671 700 / Aylesbury
Cambridgeshire / 3409 / 1316 / 711 000 / Cambridge
Cheshire / 2328 / 899 / 979 700 / Chester
Cleveland / 583 / 225 / 567 600 / Middlesbrough
Cornwall / 3564 / 1376 / 484 800 / Truro
Cumbria / 6810 / 2629 / 497 900 / Carlisle
Derbyshire / 2631 / 1016 / 968 600 / Matlock
Devon / 6711 / 2591 / 1 074 600 / Exeter
Dorset / 2654 / 1025 / 682 800 / Dorchester
Durham / 2436 / 941 / 617 100 / Durham
Essex / 3672 / 1418 / 1 600 000 / Chelmsford
Gloucestershire / 2643 / 1020 / 553 500 / Gloucester
Greater London / 1579 / 610 / 7 077 000 / no central authority
Greater Manchester 1287 / 497 / 2 607 000 / no central authority
Hampshire / 3777 / 1458 / 1 623 000 / Winchester
Hereford and Worcester / 3926 / 1516 / 712 000 / Worcester
Hertfordshire / 1634 / 631 / 1 022 000 / Hertford
Humberside / 3512 / 1356 / 904 000 / Beverley
Isle of Wight / 381 / 147 / 124 200 / Newport
Kent / 3731 / 1441 / 1 558 000 / Maidstone
Lancashire / 3063 / 1183 / 1 440 000 / Preston
Leicestershire / 2553 / 986 / 926 300 / Leicester
Lincolnshire / 5915 / 2284 / 621 200 / Lincoln
Merseyside° / 652 / 252 / 1 447 000 / Liverpool
Norfolk / 5368 / 2073 / 781 700 / Norwich
Northamptonshire / 2367 / 914 / 607 000 / Northampton
Northumberland / 5032 / 1943 / 312 100 / Morpeth
Nottinghamshire / 2164 / 836 / 1 051 000 / Nottingham
Oxfordshire / 2608 / 1007 / 613 100 / Oxford
Shropshire / 3490 / 1347 / 421 200 / Shrewsbury
Somerset / 3451 / 1332 / 489 900 / Taunton
Staffordshire / 2716 / 1049 / 1 069 000 / Stafford
Suffolk / 3797 / 1466 / 637 300 / Ipswich
Surrey / 1679 / 648 / 1 057 000 / Kingston/Thames
Sussex, East / 1795 / 693 / 743 100 / Lewes
Sussex, West / 1989 / 768 / 721 100 / Chichester
Tyne and Wear° / 540 / 208 / 1 160 000 / Newcastle/Tyne
Warwickshire / 1981 / 765 / 506 000 / Warwick
West Midlands° / 899 / 347 / 2 657 000 / Birmingham
Wiltshire / 3481 / 1344 / 608 000 / Trowbridge
Yorkshire, North / 8309 / 3208 / 738 300 / Northallerton
Yorkshire, South / 1560 / 602 / 1 325 000 / Barnsley
Yorkshire, West° / 2039 / 787 / 2 141 000 / Wakefield

New counties in 1974 were formed as follows:
Avon: parts of Somerset and Gloucestershire
Cleveland: parts of Durham and Yorkshire
Cumbria: Cumberland, Westmoreland, parts of Lancashire and Yorkshire
Greater London: London and most of Middlesex
Greater Manchester: parts of Lancashire, Cheshire, and Yorkshire
Hereford and Worcester: Hereford, most of Worcestershire
Humberside: parts of Yorkshire and Lincolnshire
Merseyside: parts of Lancashire and Cheshire
West Midlands: parts of Staffordshire, Warwickshire, and Worcestershire
Tyne and Wear: parts of Northumberland and Durham
° The councils of these metropolitan councils were abolished in 1986.

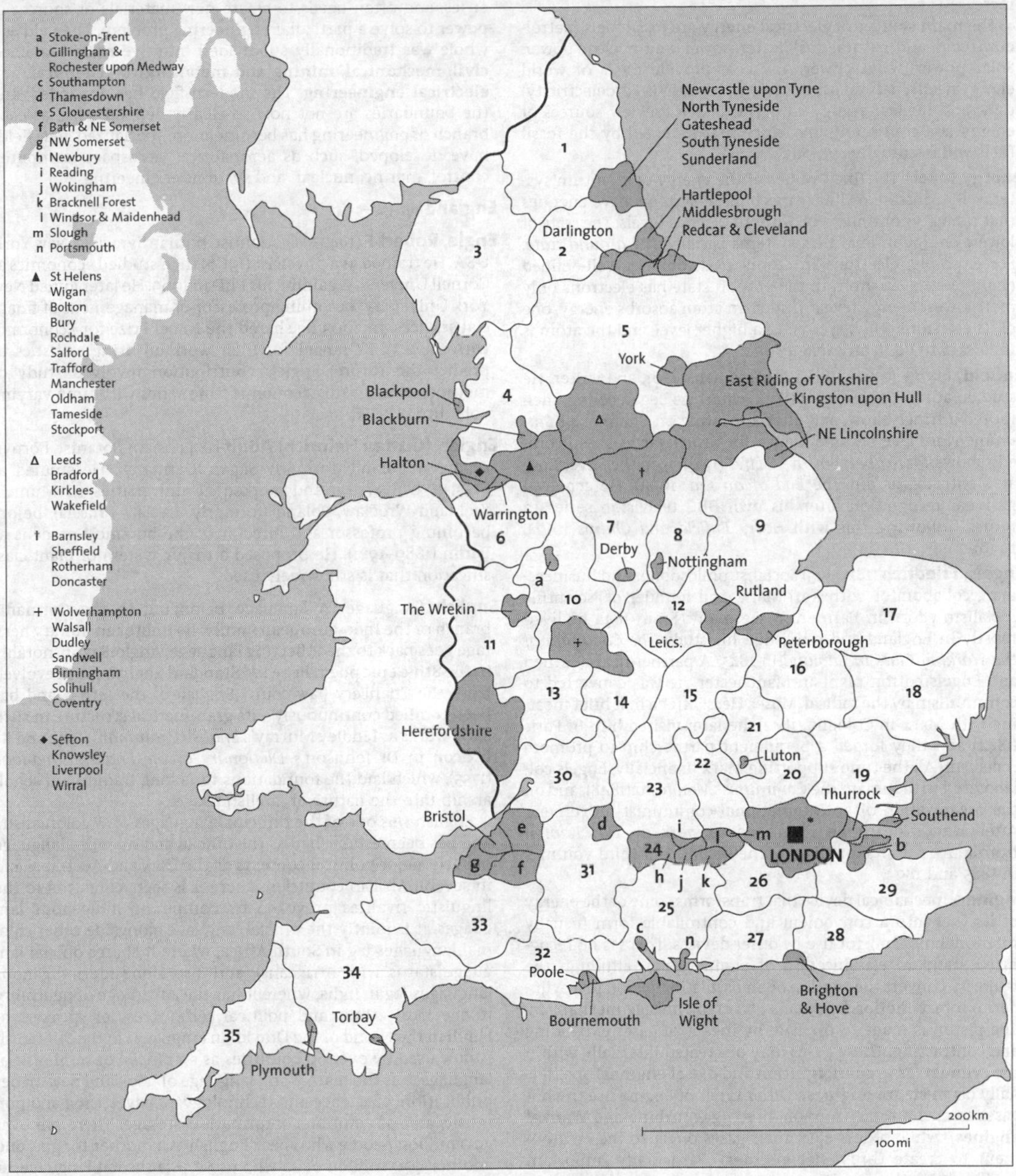

Two-tier authority areas

1 NORTHUMBERLAND
2 DURHAM
3 CUMBRIA
4 LANCASHIRE
5 NORTH YORKSHIRE
6 CHESHIRE
7 DERBYSHIRE
8 NOTTINGHAMSHIRE
9 LINCOLNSHIRE
10 STAFFORDSHIRE
11 SHROPSHIRE
12 LEICESTERSHIRE
13 WORCESTERSHIRE
14 WARWICKSHIRE
15 NORTHAMPTONSHIRE
16 CAMBRIDGESHIRE
17 NORFOLK
18 SUFFOLK
19 ESSEX
20 HERTFORDSHIRE
21 BEDFORDSHIRE
22 BUCKINGHAMSHIRE
23 OXFORDSHIRE
24 BERKSHIRE
25 HAMPSHIRE
26 SURREY
27 WEST SUSSEX
28 EAST SUSSEX
29 KENT
30 GLOUCESTERSHIRE
31 WILTSHIRE
32 DORSET
33 SOMERSET
34 DEVON
35 CORNWALL & ISLES OF SCILLY

***Unitary authorities of London**

City of London
Barking & Dagenham
Barnet
Bexley
Brent
Bromley
Camden
Croydon
Ealing
Enfield
Greenwich
Hackney
Hammersmith & Fulham
Haringey
Harrow
Havering
Hillingdon
Hounslow
Islington
Kensington & Chelsea
Kingston-upon-Thames
Lambeth
Lewisham
Merton
Newham
Redbridge upon Thames
Southwark
Sutton
Tower Hamlets
Waltham Forest
Wandsworth
Westminster

Unitary authority areas

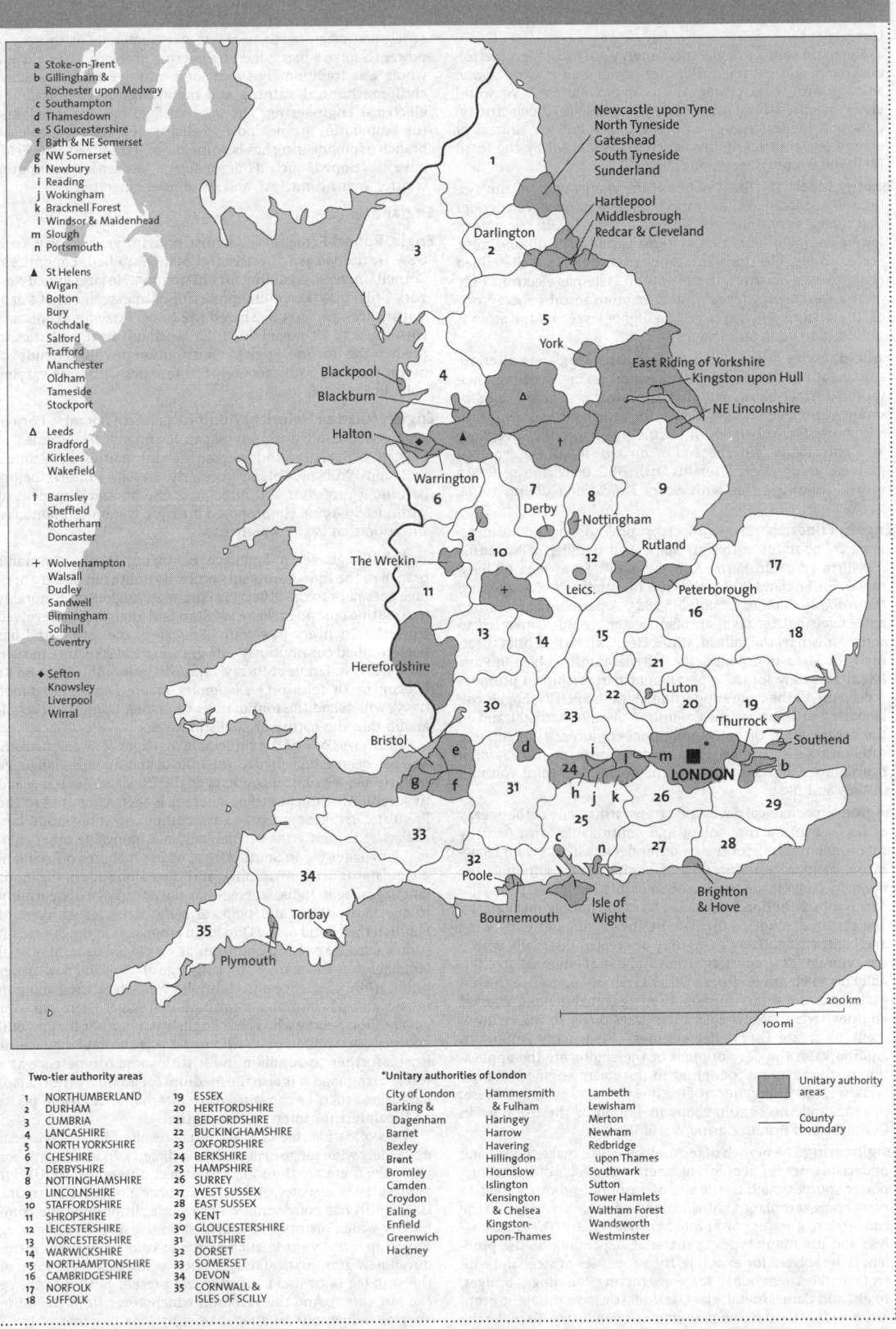

County boundary

energy, which is converted to mechanical energy in the propeller, and finally to heat energy as the water temperature is increased.

The main sources of electrical energy are fossil fuels (petroleum, coal, and natural gas), water power, and nuclear power. Solar power, wind power, and coal provide c.75% of world energy needs; natural gas c.20%; water power (hydroelectricity) c.2%; and nuclear energy c.1%. The search for new sources of energy is a continuing one, since that provided by the fossil fuels will eventually run out.

energy levels The fixed values of the energy of quantum systems. By contrast, ordinary mechanical systems have energies that can vary continuously, without discrete levels. The state of lowest energy in quantum systems is called the *ground state*. For example, electrons in atoms exist only in well-defined energy levels; an atom in the ground state has electrons only in its lowest energy levels. If such an atom absorbs energy, one of its electrons will be raised to a higher level, and the atom is then said to be in an *excited state*.

Enfield, Harry (1961–) British comedian, actor, and writer. He studied at the University of York, where he began acting, then toured a fringe show, and after appearing on Channel 4's *Saturday Night Live* became known for his character-based comedy shows. *Sir Norbert Smith – a Life?* (1989) won the Silver Rose at Montreux, as did *The End of an Era* (1994). He achieved national recognition after his own BBC television series in 1991–2, following this with *Harry Enfield and Chums* (1994, 1996).

Engels, Friedrich (1820–95) Socialist philosopher and businessman, collaborator with Karl Marx, and founder of 'scientific socialism', born in Barmen, W Germany. From 1842 he lived mostly in England and published his study *The Condition of the Working Class in England* in 1845. A partner in the Ermen and Engels cotton plant in Manchester, he was converted to communism by the radical, Moses Hess. After a first brief meeting with Marx in Cologne (1842), he later visited him in Paris (1844) and they forged a permanent partnership to promote socialism. All the time supporting Marx financially, Engels collaborated with him on the *Communist Manifesto* (1848), and on the organization of an international communist movement. After Marx's death he continued to work on *Das Kapital* from Marx's drafts, publishing the second and third volumes in 1885 and 1894.

engine A mechanical device that transforms some of the energy of its fuel into a convenient and controllable form (usually rotational motion), for use by other devices. There is no recognized standard classification of engine types, although the majority convert the motion of an oscillating piston in a cylinder to rotary motion by means of a crank linkage mechanism. The piston is made to oscillate by means of gases expanding and contracting. These gases may be created internally within the cylinder (as in **spark ignition** and **diesel engines**) or externally (as in **steam engines**). Other types of engine use the hot gases to create rotary motion direct (**gas turbine** and **Wankel engines**), while others eject their gases direct to the environment to create thrust (**jet engines**). Particularly important landmarks in the development of the engine are the application of the separate condenser to the steam engine by James Watt in 1764, the invention of the diesel engine by Rudolf Diesel in 1892, and the simultaneous invention of the turbo-jet in Germany and Britain during World War 2.

engineering The branch of technology which makes power and materials work for people. Engineers study ways of harnessing power sources, such as the use of gasoline and other fuels to power cars, aeroplanes, ships, trains, and space vehicles, and the conversion of water power into hydroelectricity. They also analyse and use many types of material, depending on the problem to be solved; for example, the properties of steel and concrete make them ideal for constructing buildings, bridges, roads, and dams; metal, glass, and plastic have different properties widely used in the manufacturing industry. To make the best use of what is available, the engineer has to keep constantly up to date with advances in materials and their properties, and often needs to create new materials or sources of power to solve a particular engineering problem. The field as a whole was traditionally subdivided into five main branches: **civil**, **mechanical**, **mining and metallurgical**, **chemical**, and **electrical engineering**. The modern field has expanded, and the boundaries are not now so clearly defined. Also, as each branch of engineering has become more specialized, new fields have developed, such as aeronautical, aerospace, computer, control, marine, nuclear, and systems engineering.

England *pp.514–5*

Engle, Robert F (1942–) Economist, born in Syracuse, New York, USA. He trained as a physicist (1966) then studied economics at Cornell University, gaining his PhD in 1969. He later joined New York University, becoming professor of management of financial services. In 2003 he shared the Nobel Prize for Economics with Clive W J Granger for their work on using statistics to predict the future. Engle's contribution involved study of methods of analyzing economic time series with time-varying volatility (ARCH).

Engler, (Gustav Heinrich) Adolf (1844–1930) Botanist, born in Zagań, W Poland (formerly Sagan, Germany). He studied at Breslau University, and worked at universities in Munich, Kiel, and Wrocław, Poland (formerly Breslau, Prussia), before becoming professor and director of the botanical gardens at Berlin (1889–1921). He proposed a major system of plant classification that is still widely used.

English (language) A language belonging to the Germanic branch of the Indo-European family. Its unbroken literary heritage goes back to the inflecting language, Anglo-Saxon, notably in the 8th-c epic poem *Beowulf*. Standard English prose evolved from the Chancery (law-court) English of the 14th-c, and has been codified continuously – its grammatical structure in such early works as Lindley Murray's *English Grammar* (1794), and its lexicon in Dr Johnson's *Dictionary of the English Language* (1755), which laid the foundations for a long tradition of scholarship into the nature of English usage.

English was one of the principal languages of W colonialism, and has been established as the official and majority language in such major political contexts as the USA and Australia, and in several African countries, where it is seen as neutral to the linguistic rivalries provoked by competing indigenous languages. It is jointly the official language alongside other colonial languages (eg in South Africa, where it shares official language status with Afrikaans), and also alongside indigenous languages (eg in India, where it has the advantage of neutrality to the local ethnic and political self-interest of speakers of Hindi in the N, and of the Dravidian languages in the S). English is now used by over 60 countries as an official or semi-official language. It is the main world language of book and newspaper publication, of science and technology, of advertising and pop music, and of computer information storage. There are over 400 million people who speak English as a mother-tongue, and another 400 million or so who use it as a second language; at least a further 500 million use it with some competence as a foreign language. It is also the medium for auxiliary (restricted) languages, such as those used by international airline pilots and seafarers for intercommunication.

The worldwide role of English has resulted in its having an extremely wide range of accents and dialects. In vocabulary, for example, there are thousands of dialect differences, eg UK *lift* alongside US *elevator*, Australian *cobber* alongside UK *mate*. US English has gone some way towards simplifying the complexity which history has endowed on the spelling system, eg replacing *-our* by *-or* in such words as *color*. It has also introduced new grammatical usages, such as the past tense form of the verb (eg *I just ate*) instead of the present perfect form (eg *I've just eaten*). And the variation which arises from the influence of indigenous languages in situations like that of India introduces a new and dramatic dimension into English language dialectology which is largely unmeasured as yet.

English art The art associated with England, since prehistoric times influenced by the commercial and cultural links with both the Mediterranean and N Europe. Thus the classical style was introduced by the Roman occupation, but Anglo-Saxon invaders in the 5th-c reaffirmed the priority of abstract pattern-making and animal ornament. The Norman conquest in the 11th-c ushered in one of the greatest periods of English art, attested by cathedrals such as Durham and Ely. The glories of mediaeval art ended at the Reformation (c.1530). A new wave of classical Italian influence in architecture and decoration, as well as the Baroque style of van Dyck in painting, set the standard for the Georgian period and the 'Rule of Taste' (17th–18th-c). The 19th-c saw the major achievements of Turner and Constable in romantic landscape painting. Perhaps the outstanding 20th-c figure was the sculptor Henry Moore.

English Channel, Fr **La Manche**, Lat **Mare Britannicum** Arm of the Atlantic Ocean, bounded N by England and S by France; formed with the rise in sea level after the last glacial period; connected to North Sea by Straits of Dover (E), 34 km/21 mi wide; 565 km/350 mi long by 240 km/150 mi wide at its widest point (Lyme Bay–Golfe de St-Malo); crossings by ferry and hovercraft, linking Dover to Dunkirk and Boulogne, Folkestone to Calais and Boulogne, Plymouth to Roscoff, and Portsmouth to Le Havre, Cherbourg, and St-Malo via Channel Is; one of world's busiest shipping lanes; tunnel opened, 1994; first aeroplane crossing by Bleriot, 1909; first swum by Matthew Webb, 1875; main islands, I of Wight, Channel Is.

English Civil War (1642–8) The country's greatest internal conflict, between supporters of Parliament and supporters of Charles I, caused by Parliamentary opposition to royal policies. Although the King left London in March 1642, open hostilities between Royalists and Parliamentarians did not immediately break out. The prospect of compromise was bleak, but both sides, fearing the consequences of civil strife, moved slowly towards the use of armed force. Charles finally issued commissions of array (Jun 1642), and raised his standard two months later at Nottingham. The first major engagement took place at Edgehill in October. It was a draw, but Royalist forces then threatened London, the key Parliamentary stronghold. Royalist strategy in 1643 centred upon taking the capital by a three-pronged attack from armies in the N, the SW and the Thames valley. By autumn the N and the W (apart from a garrison in Gloucester) were in their hands, although Parliament held back the tide in the (drawn) first Battle of Newbury. The crucial event of 1643 was Parliament's alliance with the Scots in the Solemn League and Covenant, which strengthened its hand militarily and threatened the king's forces on a new front.

In 1644 Parliament, assisted by the Scots, became a formidable foe. This was clear in July when its forces, aided by Scottish invaders, inflicted a serious defeat upon the Royalists at Marston Moor. The battle marked the emergence as a military leader of Oliver Cromwell, whose intervention was decisive. It also signalled the virtual eclipse of Royalism as a miltary force in the N of England. The king's forces in the W, however, were another matter. In 1643 they were victorious over the Earl of Essex in the Battle of Lostwithiel, and in the second Battle of Newbury they were successful against the combined forces of Essex, the Earl of Manchester, and Sir William Waller. But 1645 saw Parliament's cause advance in the Midlands and the W, with important victories at Naseby and Langport. The next year brought to an end the first civil war. Charles surrendered to the Scots at Newark in May, and his stronghold of Oxford fell in June. He was taken into Parliamentary custody (Jan 1647) when the Scots left for home, and in June was seized by the army.

From June 1646 to April 1648 there was an uneasy peace and attempts at compromise. Negotiations between the king and Parliament had begun as early as 1645, but they achieved little. The main sticking points were religion, particularly Parliament's disestablishment of the Church, and the king's prerogative rights, many of which had been abolished by Parliament. The climax came (Aug 1647) when the army presented the king with the Heads of Proposals, calling for religious toleration, and parliamentary control of the armed forces. Charles made a secret alliance with the Scots, promising to establish Presbyterianism in England (which Parliament had failed to do); they invaded England (Apr 1648), and were repulsed only after the Battle of Preston (Aug). Bitterly fought, the second war earned Charles the epithet 'that man of blood' and, ultimately, his execution (30 Jan 1649). Possibly 100 000 died in the two wars – 1 in 10 of adult males.

English cocker spaniel A small, active, friendly spaniel; shoulder height, 45 cm/18 in; long ears set low on head; tail docked short when young; gave rise to the *American cocker spaniel.*

English foxhound *foxhound*

English Heritage In the UK, a body directly responsible for over 350 buildings and monuments formerly in the care of the Department of the Environment, and for protecting and preserving England's collection of 12 500 designated monuments and over 300 000 'listed' buildings. The Historic Buildings and Monuments Board for Scotland, and *Cadw* (Welsh 'heritage'), have similar functions.

English history The study of England's past. Many accounts of English history exist, from the Venerable Bede's 7th-c account of the Christianization of England onwards. The systematic, professional study of English history, however, dates from the second half of the 19th-c. With notable exceptions, early studies were predominantly political and constitutional, tracing the development of forms of government in England and the rise of the country to imperial greatness. Much of this writing was heavily coloured by a concern to emphasize those aspects of England's past which seemed to presage later achievements. It was also concerned with the story of England's development *per se*; the histories of Ireland, Scotland, and Wales tended to be casually incorporated. Much 'British' history was overwhelmingly 'English'.

With professionalization came specialization. It became normal to divide English history into recognizable periods for detailed research. These were generally associated with dynasties or major political events. The traditional divisions, often used also for university and school examinations, were Anglo-Saxon (vaguely and misleadingly running from the collapse of Roman rule in the 5th-c to the Norman Conquest in 1066); Norman (1066–1154); Plantagenet (1154–1485); Tudor (1485–1603); Stuart (1603–1714); Hanoverian (1714–1815, although the dynasty proper continued until the death of Queen Victoria in 1901); and Nineteenth Century (1815–1914). In the 20th-c, studies of English history paid greater attention to non-political themes, with consequential fracturing and elision of traditional chronologies. In the inter-war period, the study of the creation, increase, and distribution of resources developed into a distinct discipline called *economic history*. Much work since the late 1950s has been directed towards the primary study of social groups, their organization and movements, rather than national leaders. Some of this work drew heavily upon the methodology and insights of social science. More recently still, attempts have been made to fuse social and political history to produce more rounded explanations of the forces making for change. Much has been done by gifted amateurs and those for whom the study of English history, while undeniably a skilled craft, was more a means of relaxation than of livelihood. Winston Churchill's much-read *History of the English Speaking Peoples* (1956–8) is a prime example in this latter category, while folk history studies and much-used modern techniques, such as oral history, aerial archaeology, and film archives have been developed by non-professionals and professionals alike.

English literature The earliest texts written in English are chronicles dating from the 7th-c, but literature begins with the heroic poems and fragments of the next century, written in Old English; the most famous is *Beowulf*. After the Norman conquest, the language and culture underwent fundamental changes, and Middle English (11th–14th-c) offers a range of lyrical, courtly, realistic, and satirical poems, the most celebrated by Chaucer (notably *The Canterbury Tales*, c.1400) as well as significant prose works (eg Malory's *Morte d'Arthur*, 1470). Poets such as Wyatt and Surrey brought the Renaissance to England, and the late 16th-c produced important works such as Sidney's *Arcadia* (1590) and Spenser's *Faerie Queene* (1590–6). The sonnet sequence was also popular; but the theatre attracted the most adventurous talents of this time, and the plays of Marlowe, Ben Jonson, Webster and others proved immensely popular. The dramatic works of Shakespeare, unprecedented in their variety, profundity, originality, and poetic power, make this one of the most remarkable ages of English, and indeed of world literature. The 'metaphysical' poets Donne, Herbert, and Marvell also broke new ground; and the way was prepared for Milton, whose *Paradise Lost* (1667) is the greatest English epic poem.

The Restoration period (from 1660) provided a brief resurgence of a distinctive if decadent drama; but by now prose was beginning to assert itself as the dominant medium, and Bunyan's *Pilgrim's Progress* (1678) became the most popular book in English after the Bible. Dryden, the first official poet laureate, wrote great topical satires as well as plays and criticism: he was matched by Pope, master of the heroic couplet (*The Dunciad* 1728–42), and by Swift, whose *Gulliver's Travels* (1726) and other prose satires created public delight and consternation. These typify the English Augustan age. The immense erudition and labour of Dr Johnson (*Dictionary*, 1755) helped to ratify these classical writers; but by the end of the 18th-c the new mood of Romanticism was established (Wordsworth and Coleridge's *Lyrical Ballads*, 1798). The lyrics of Keats, Shelley, and Clare, the visionary works of Blake, and the immensely popular poems of Byron represent another period of great achievement, to be built on by Browning and popular laureate Tennyson, whose poems incorporated much dramatic and novelistic material.

The novel asserted itself in the 18th-century, with writers such as Defoe, Richardson, Fielding, Smollett, and Sterne. By the 19th-c it is clearly the dominant literary form – Scott made his fortune after switching from verse narrative to novels. Dickens, Thackeray, and Hardy wrote for the nation; and novelists such as Jane Austen, Emily and Charlotte Bronte, Mrs Gaskell, and George Eliot claimed a new territory for the woman writer. In the 20th-c, the novel became the vehicle of much literary experiment (Joyce *Ulysses*, 1921; Virginia Woolf *Mrs Dalloway*, 1925; Beckett's Trilogy, 1951–3) while still surviving in its traditional form as the 'one bright book of life' (D H Lawrence), not least with Nobel laureate William Golding. English poetry in the 20th-c was likewise profoundly marked by new techniques and attitudes associated with modernism, brought to Europe by Americans (T S Eliot, Ezra Pound); but the native lyric persisted from Hardy through to Philip Larkin, and the poems of Ted Hughes and the Irishman Seamus Heaney have offered a new and powerful synthesis of traditional materials. English drama has enjoyed a rebirth since the 1950s (with Osborne, Beckett, Pinter, Stoppard, Bennett), reflected in the fruitful exploitation by many writers of the new media of film, radio, and television. Another significant feature has been the prominence of women novelists such as Iris Murdoch, A S Byatt, Sarah Maitland, and Margaret Drabble. Much important work was also produced in the 20th-c and is being produced today by people writing in English from other cultures.

English National Ballet A classical ballet company which tours nationally and internationally from its studio base in Westminster, London, UK. Founded in 1950 by the Polish-born impresario Julian Braunsweg as the London Festival Ballet, the company changed its name to the English National Ballet in 1988. It is one of the world's leading exponents of contemporary dance, under its artistic director, Derek Deane.

English National Opera Opera company founded in 1931 by Lilian Baylis as the Vic-Wells Opera, named after the Old Vic and Sadler's Wells theatres that she also managed. The company moved to its present location at the London Coliseum in 1968 and was renamed English National Opera in 1974. All performances are in English, and the company aims to reach a wide audience through its programme of educational activities, fostering of new talent, and affordable prices.

English Nature A British governmental agency, set up by the Environmental Protection Act (1990), and responsible for the conservation of England's wildlife and natural features. It manages National and Marine Nature Reserves, selects and schedules Sites of Special Scientific Interest and Ramsar sites (Wetlands of International Scientific Importance). It also undertakes research on conservation issues. English Nature continues the work of its predecessor, the Nature Conservancy Council, and works closely with the Scottish Natural Heritage and Countryside Council for Wales. These three agencies work together through the Joint Nature Conservation Committee.

English pointer A breed of dog, developed in England; large, taller at shoulder than at rear end; muzzle long, deep and concave on top; tail tapering, carried almost horizontally; coat short; also known as **pointer**.

English setter A large breed of dog, developed in England; taller at shoulder than at rear end; muzzle deep; coat long, white with dark markings.

English sheepdog *Old English sheepdog*

English sparrow *house sparrow*

English-Speaking Union A charity founded by Sir Evelyn Wrench (1882–1966) in 1918 with the purpose of 'improving understanding about people, international issues, and culture through the bond the English language provides'. Based in London, in 2004 the Union had branches in 51 countries, two-thirds in the UK and the USA.

English springer spaniel *springer spaniel*

English Stage Company An organization and registered charity established under George Devine in 1956 to encourage new playwrights and to promote, maintain, improve, and advance education and the encouragement of the arts in the theatre. It has had a lasting effect on post-war British theatre through its insistence on the value and importance of the contemporary writer. Its base is the Royal Court Theatre in London.

engraving A process of printmaking by the intaglio method; also the resulting print. The term is often used less precisely to mean any process whereby a design is printed on paper. **Reproductive engraving** simply reproduces an already existing work of art and has been superseded by photography; an **original engraving** is a work of art in its own right.

enhanced radiation weapon *neutron bomb*

enkephalins *opioid peptides*

enlightened despots European rulers of the 18th-c, influenced by the French and German Enlightenment. They aimed at increasing the ruler's power within a more efficient state-system at the expense of the Church, nobility, and estates. Some, such as Joseph II of Austria, Frederick II of Prussia, Catherine the Great of Russia, and Charles III of Spain, instituted social reforms to improve the general welfare of the population.

Enlightenment or **Age of Reason** (Ger *Aufklärung*) A European literary and philosophical movement of the 18th-c, rooted in the 17th-c Scientific Revolution and the ideas of Kant, Locke, and Newton. Its basic belief was the superiority of reason as a guide to all knowledge and human concerns; from this flowed the idea of progress and a challenging of traditional Christianity. It is important to distinguish between the national differences that it adopted, in particular the materialism of the French *Encyclopedists* (d'Alembert, Diderot, Voltaire), the Scottish interest in political economy (Hume, Smith, Stuart) and the more cultural concerns of the Germans (Goethe, Herder, Lessing, Schiller). A similar invigorating freedom of ideas affected writers as far apart as Sweden and Russia, while the Yiddish literature of E Europe also experienced a new dynamism through the *maskilim* (purveyors of the Enlightenment movement). The French Revolution marked the end of the Age of Enlightenment, its proponents having been an important catalyst for change.

Enlil The Mesopotamian god of the wind, son of Anu the sky-god, king of the gods before the creation of Marduk.

Enniskillen [iniskilin], also **Inniskilling**, Ir **Inis Ceithleann** 54°21N 7°38W, pop (2000e) 11 500. Town in Fermanagh district, County Fermanagh, SW Northern Ireland, UK, on an island in the R Erne; English families were settled here after Tyrone's rebellion; scene of a victory of William III over James II, 1689; became an important Protestant stronghold; scene of an IRA bombing at the Remembrance Day service in 1987, killing 11 people; airfield; tourism, watersports, engineering, food processing; castle ruins (15th–16th-c), cathedral (Protestant, 17th–18th-c).

Ennius, Quintus [enius] (c.239–169 BC) Latin epic poet and playwright, born in Rudiae, Italy. He is said to have served in the Punic Wars, and returned to Rome with Cato the Elder, where he taught Greek, and attained the rank of Roman citizen. He introduced the hexameter into Latin; but only fragments of his many writings survive.

Enoch [eenok] Biblical character, the son of Jared, and the father of Methuselah. He was depicted as extraordinarily devout, and therefore as translated directly into heaven without dying (*Gen* 5.24). In the Graeco-Roman era his name became attached to Jewish apocalyptic writings allegedly describing his visions and journeys through the heavens (1, 2, and 3 *Enoch*).

enosis [enohsis] A political movement in Cyprus for union with Greece, reflecting the demands of Cypriots opposed to foreign rule, and closely associated with the leadership of the Greek Orthodox Church. There was an enosis rising in 1931, and since then there has been serious conflict, at times amounting to civil war, between the Greek and Turkish populations. Now independent, Cyprus has never achieved union with Greece because of Turkish opposition.

Enright, D(ennis) J(oseph) (1920–2002) Writer, born in Leamington, Warwickshire, C England, UK. He studied at Cambridge and at Alexandria, Egypt. Many years teaching in universities abroad are recalled in *Memoirs of a Mendicant Professor* (1969). He wrote five novels, and much criticism, but is best known for his poetry. A dozen volumes since 1953, including *Some Men Are Brothers* (1960), *Unlawful Assembly* (1968), and *A Faust Book* (1979) are represented in his *Collected Poems* (1987). Later collections include *Old Men and Comets* (1993) and *Collected Poems 1948-1998* (1998).

Ensor, James (Sydney) Ensor, Baron (1860–1949) Painter, born in Ostend, W Belgium. He became known for his bizarre and fantastic images, using masks, skeletons, and other ghostly effects as symbols of the evils of society. His paintings aroused much controversy when they were first shown, as in his best-known work, 'Entry of Christ into Brussels' (1888, Brussels). He was made a baron in 1929.

entablature [entablachoor] The horizontal element supported by the orders of classical architecture. It consists of an architrave, frieze, and cornice.

Entebbe [entebay] 0°05N 32°29E, pop (2000e) 32 000. Town in S Uganda, E Africa; on N shore of L Victoria, 25 km/15 mi SW of Kampala; founded, 1893; former capital of Uganda, 1894–1962; airport; railway; scene in 1976 of a dramatic rescue by Israeli forces of Israelis whose plane had been hijacked by a group of Palestinian terrorists.

entellus [entelus] A langur native to S Asia (*Presbytis entellus*), and traditionally sacred in India; sandy brown, with a black face; long tail; inhabits diverse regions; also known as **entellus langur** or **hanuman monkey**.

Entente Cordiale [ontawnt kaw(r)dial] A term first used in the 1840s to describe a close relationship between the UK and France; then given to a series of agreements in 1904 between the two countries, dealing with a range of issues, in particular establishing the predominant role of the UK in Egypt, and France's interests in Morocco and Algiers.

enteric fever *typhoid fever*

enterprise zones Parts of a country designated by the government as areas where business start-up schemes will get favourable financial help; for example, no taxes might be payable for 10 years. They are usually located in inner-city areas with high unemployment levels. Over 20 such zones exist in the USA, and a similar number in the UK. Schemes of this kind are in operation in many European countries.

enthalpy [enthalpee] An energy quantity appearing frequently in thermodynamics; symbol H, units J (joule); defined as $H = U + pV$, where U is internal energy, p is pressure, and V is volume. For example, for a gas at constant pressure, the total heat that must be added to raise the temperature of the gas is the sum of the increase in internal energy of the gas plus the work done in expanding against surrounding pressure, so the total heat equals the increase in H. There is no absolute zero of enthalpy, so only changes in enthalpy can be measured.

entity–attribute–relationship model (**EAR model** or **ER model**) A method of representing data in a computer database in which any uniquely identifiable entity type is given a table, and the relationships between entities are contained in separate tables. For example, in a library the two entity types could be books and borrowers, and the relationship links a borrower to a book. The attributes for a borrower are borrower number, name, address, etc, and for a book are title, author, ISBN number, etc.

entomology The branch of biology dealing with all aspects of the study of insects. Insects are the most diverse group of organisms on Earth, and their importance has led to the development of several specialized areas of entomology. Many insects are beneficial to humans, such as those responsible for the pollination of crop plants, but others are harmful, by feeding on the crops or their stored products, or by transmitting fungal, bacterial, and viral diseases to the plants. They can cause enormous economic losses. The development of insecticides and alternative techniques for controlling pest insects forms the basis of **applied economic entomology**. **Medical entomology** is a specialized field dealing with the study of insect carriers of numerous diseases (eg typhus, malaria, sleeping sickness) and with the methods of controlling them. Insects have also been used as tools in scientific studies, and many significant discoveries have been made, for example in genetic research using the fruit fly *Drosophila*.

entresol *mezzanine*

entropy [entropee] In thermodynamics, a numerical measure of disorder; symbol S, units J/K (joules per kelvin). As a system becomes increasingly disordered, its entropy increases. For example, the entropy of a system comprising a drop of ink and a tank of water increases when the drop of ink is added to the water and disperses through it, since dispersed ink is highly disordered. Entropy can never decrease, which in the ink-in-water example amounts to the observation that the particles of ink never spontaneously gather themselves back into a single drop.

Formally, an increase in entropy is equal to the quantity of heat added to a system divided by its temperature (in kelvin) at a constant temperature. For instance the increase in entropy of 1 kg of ice melting to water at 273 K (0°C) is 1223 J/K. Freezing water to ice decreases the entropy of the water, but at the expense of increasing the entropy of the whole system, such as the refrigerator and room containing it. Entropy expresses a direction in time for processes which might otherwise appear to be reversible on grounds of energy conservation alone. Only for reversible processes in which no heat is added or removed is entropy constant. The second law of thermodynamics states that for all processes entropy is either constant or increases.

E-number A code number on food labels, used by food manufacturers in member states of the European Union, which identifies most materials added to the food (*E = European*). Among food additives, four categories (preservatives, colourants, antioxidants, and emulsifiers) each have code numbers. For example, E102 is the colourant tartrazine, E210 the preservative benzoic acid, and E420 the emulsifier guar gum.

enuresis [enyureesis] A condition typified by involuntary voiding of urine. The behaviour is abnormal in relation to the individual's mental age, and is not due to organic causes. The involuntary passage of faeces, also not a result of organic illness, is known as **encopresis**.

Enver Pasha (1881–1922) Turkish soldier and politician, born in Istanbul. A leader in the revolution of Young Turks in 1908, he later became minister of war (1914). He fled to Russia in 1918 after the Turkish surrender, and was killed in an insurrection in Turkestan.

environment The conditions and influences of the place in which an organism lives. The large number of different types of environment (eg urban environment, tropical rainforest environment) makes it impossible to formulate a single definition. In general, the **physical environment** describes the characteristics of a landscape (eg climate, geology) which have not been changed markedly by human impact, whereas the **geographical environment** includes the physical environment together with any human modifications (eg agricultural systems, industrialization, urbanization). The relationship between living organisms and their environment forms part of the subject of *ecology*. Concern that large parts of the physical environment are suffering from misuse and overexploitation is central to conservation, and the environmental movement which promotes conservation has gained considerable momentum in recent decades as new threats (eg acid rain, soil erosion, ozone depletion) are widely recognized.

Environment Agency The body established by the Environment Act (1995) of England and Wales to enforce and regulate pollution controls. It is also responsible for certain other functions connected with the environment, such as controlling effluent and sewage sludge in agriculture, land drainage, and coastal defence. The corresponding body in Scotland is the **Scottish Environment Protection Agency**, which in addition to these responsibilities, controls air pollution. The **European Environment Agency** collects and monitors information about the quality of the environment, but it has no clear powers of enforcement. In the USA, the **Environmental Protection Agency**, sometimes referred to as **USEPA**, is the federal agency responsible for the environment.

environmental archaeology The study of past environments and ecological interaction over time between human and contemporary animal and plant communities. The basic raw materials consist of animal bones and teeth; preserved pollen and plants; snails, fish, and insect remains; and soils and sediments.

environmentalism A term which has several meanings according to the perspective of the user. Its broadest meaning is a concern with all environmental matters: a recognition of increasing environmental degradation brought about by mismanagement of the Earth's resources (eg the burning of fossil fuels), and therefore the need for conservation. More narrowly, its use can be applied to the ideology which rejects the 'technocentric' view of the environment, that all environmental problems can be solved through the use of technology and without a reduction in economic growth. Environmentalism adopts an 'ecocentric' approach. This advocates that environmental problems cannot be solved without a shift away from policies of economic growth at any price; therefore economic growth is not seen as a central social issue. There is the recognition that the Earth's resources are finite, and that higher priority should be given to non-material values. Little confidence is placed in the ability of science to solve environmental problems.

Environmentally Sensitive Areas (ESAs) A European Community scheme introduced in 1985 to protect areas of ecological and landscape importance from drainage and loss caused by agricultural change. Payments can be made for farming in ways which help to conserve landscape and wildlife habitats, and so resist pressures to intensify production. Examples include the Broads and the Breckland in East Anglia, UK.

Environmental Protection Agency A US government agency established in 1970. Its job is to determine, regulate, and enforce environmental pollution controls, such as legislation governing the use of pesticides.

environmental studies Those aspects of biology, ecology, and geography which are related to an understanding of the environment: its physical and human components. It is sometimes used synonymously with *ecology*, though environmental studies are more wide-ranging.

enzyme A specialized protein molecule produced by a living cell, which acts as a biological catalyst for biochemical reactions. Each enzyme is specific to a particular reaction or group of similar reactions. The molecule undergoing a reaction (the *substrate*) binds on to an active site on the enzyme to form a short-lived compound molecule, thereby greatly increasing the rate of the reaction. Enzyme activity is strongly influenced by substrate concentration, acidity (pH), temperature, and the presence of other substances (*co-factors*). The names of enzymes typically end in *-ase*, and are derived from the substrates on which they act; for example, lipase is an enzyme that breaks down lipid (fat).

Eocene epoch [eeohseen] The second of the five geological epochs of the Tertiary period, lasting from 55 to 38 million years ago. It was characterized by a warmer climate and the appearance of modern flora and fauna.

Eohippus [eeohhipus] Hyracotherium

EOKA [ayohka] Acronym for **Ethniki Organosis Kipriakou Agonos** ('National Organization of Cypriot Struggle'), a Greek Cypriot underground movement seeking to end British rule and achieve *enosis*, the union of Cyprus with Greece. Founded in 1955 by a Greek army officer, Colonel George Grivas, with the support of Archbishop Makarios III, it pursued a campaign of anti-British violence which climaxed in 1956–7. EOKA declined and was later disbanded following Makarios's acceptance of Cypriot independence rather than *enosis* (1958). In 1971–4 it was unsuccessfully resurrected as EOKA B.

Eos [eeohs] In Greek mythology, the goddess of the dawn, daughter of Helios, mother of Memnon. She abducted various mortals. When she took Tithonus, Zeus granted her request that he should be made immortal, but she forgot to ask for perpetual youth, so he grew older and older, finally shrinking to no more than a voice or, possibly, the cicada.

Epaminondas [epaminondas] (c.418–362 BC) Theban general and statesman, whose victory at Leuctra (371 BC) broke the military power of Sparta and made Thebes the most powerful state in Greece. His death at the Battle of Mantinea abruptly brought this supremacy to an end.

ephedrine [efedrin, efedreen] A drug with similar actions to adrenaline, used as a nasal decongestant. Earlier, it was also used in the treatment of asthma and low blood pressure.

ephemera A term formerly used to refer to short-lived insects (eg the mayfly), latterly extended to apply to the minor printed documents of everyday life (tickets, handbills, labels, advertising material, etc) produced specifically for short-term use. The conservation and study of printed ephemera has increased in recent years. The Ephemera Society, founded in London in 1975, now has offshoots in the USA, Canada, Australia, and a number of European countries. Study collections are held in several libraries, among them notably the Bodleian, Oxford, and the American Antiquarian Society, Worcester, MA.

ephemeral An annual plant with a very short life-cycle, usually producing several generations in a single season. Many weed species are ephemeral, as are desert plants which experience very short favourable seasons.

ephemeris [efemeris] (pl **ephemerides** [efemerideez]) A table giving the computed positions and brightness of an orbiting celestial object such as a planet or comet. It is calculated from the object's orbital elements, which include the orbit period, inclination, eccentricity, and positional direction of the object at the moment when the orbit crosses the equatorial plane of the primary body. The name is also used for a book, published annually, which lists all predictable astronomical phenomena for the coming year, such as planetary, lunar, and eclipse data.

ephemeris time [efemeris] A fundamental measure of time used between 1958 and 1984, defined by reference to the position of the Sun in 1900, and the length of the tropical year. It was used as an invariable measure of time until replaced by terrestrial dynamical time in 1984.

Ephemeroptera [efemeroptera] *mayfly*

Ephesians, Letter to the [efeezhnz] New Testament writing attributed to Paul, but of disputed authorship, and with no specific addressees in the best manuscripts (which lack the words 'in Ephesus' in *Eph* 1.1); many similarities can be detected with the Letter to the Colossians. It sets out God's purposes in establishing the Church and uniting both Jews and Gentiles in it, and concludes with exhortations directed at the Church.

Ephesus [efesus], Turkish **Efes** 37°5N 27°9E. Ancient city of Lydia and important Greek city-state on the W coast of Asia Minor; at the mouth of R Bayindir, near the Aegean coast; centre of the cult of Cybele (an Anatolian fertility goddess) and worship of Artemis/Diana, whose temple was one of the Seven Wonders of the Ancient World; in Roman times, principal city of the province of Asia, and seat of the Roman governor; visited by St Paul; ruins excavated, 19th–20th-c; resort village of Kuşadasi 12 km/7 mi S on the Aegean coast; museum at Selçuk; camel wrestling festival (Jan); 7 km/4 mi from Selçuk is the Mereymana chapel where the Virgin Mary is believed to have spent the last days of her life.

Ephraim, tribe of [eefrayim] One of the 12 tribes of ancient Israel, said to be descended from Joseph's younger son, who was adopted and blessed by Jacob. It was apparently a powerful tribe in ancient Israel, whose territory included the C hill country of Palestine, stretching to Bethel in the S and almost to Shechem in the N.

epic A heroic poem; a long narrative of wars and adventures where larger-than-life characters perform deeds of great public and national significance. The earlier epic poems, in the oral tradition, reach back into myth and legend, where men and gods moved on the same scene; among these are the Sumerian epic *Gilgamesh* (c.3000 BC), the Homeric epics *Iliad* and *Odyssey* (c.1000 BC), and the Indian *Mahabharata* and *Ramayana* (c.500 BC): also the N European epics such as the Old English *Beowulf* (8th-c) and the 13th-c German *Nibelungenlied*. The term **secondary epic** refers to works written in conscious imitation of these primary epic models, such as Virgil's *Aeneid* (30–19 BC), Tasso's *Gerusalemme Liberata* (1581), and Milton's *Paradise Lost* (1667). The poetic and mythological aspects are generally missing when modern works are described as 'epic'. The novel has been presented as an 'epic poem in prose', and some works of significant scale such as Melville's *Moby Dick* (1851) and Tolstoy's *War and Peace* (1863–9) may be so described. Brecht also proposed an 'epic theatre'. Although some films have achieved epic status, the form and the term have generally been travestied in the cinema.

epicalyx An additional whorl of flower parts attached outside the sepals or calyx, which they resemble in both form and function. It is characteristic of some plants, such as members of the Rosaceae.

epicentre *earthquake*

Epictetus [epikteetus] (c.50–c.130) Stoic philosopher, born in Hierapolis. At first a Roman slave, on being freed he devoted himself to philosophy. He was banished by Emperor Domitian along with other philosophers in AD 90, and settled at Nikopolis in Epirus. He wrote no works; the *Enchiridion* is a collection of maxims dictated to a disciple.

Epicurus [epikyoorus] (c.341–270 BC) Greek philosopher, born in Samos, Greece. He visited Athens when he was 18, then opened a school at Mitylene (310 BC), and taught there and at Lampsacus. In 305 BC he returned to Athens, where he established a successful school of philosophy, leading a life of great temperance and simplicity. He divided philosophy into three parts: logic; physics, where he developed the atomistic ideas of Democritus; and ethics, where he held that pleasure is the chief good, by which he meant freedom from pain and anxiety, not (as the term *epicurean* has since come to mean) one who indulges sensual pleasures without stint. He is said to have written 300 volumes on many subjects, but only a few letters and other fragments have survived.

Epidauros Small town located 32 km/20 mi from Nafplion, on the Saronic Gulf in the N Peloponnese. In ancient Greece it was an important commercial centre, but is today famed for its 4th-CBC temple of Asclepius, the god of healing, and for the amphitheatre (350BC) carved out of a hillside where the annual summer Epidauros Festival is now held. The National Theatre of Greece and visiting companies perform the works of the ancient Greek playwrights.

Epidaurus [epidawrus] A Greek city-state situated in the E Peloponnese. It was famous in antiquity for its sanctuary to Asclepius, the god of healing, and for its magnificent open theatre, which is still used today.

epidemiology The study of the distribution and causes of disease in populations. In the 19th-c, the major causes of death were infections. Study of the occurrence of outbreaks in relation to the social conditions prevailing at the time led to effective measures for their control. For example, epidemics of cholera were traced to polluted water, and of puerperal fever to the contaminated hands of medical attendants. In the 20th-c the emphasis changed with the changing pattern of disease and the increased sophistication of epidemiological methods. Scientific techniques such as cohort studies and case-controlled studies are used to establish the links between environmental and lifestyle factors and disease. Thus, the link between cancer of the lung and smoking was established, and information about the relative occurrence of coronary heart disease in different countries and of cancers of different types obtained. It is likely that advances in this field of activity will assist in the prevention of these and many other complaints.

epidermis [epidermis] The outermost layer of a plant or animal. In plants and many invertebrates, the epidermis is a single cell thick. In vertebrates it is many cells thick, and in terrestrial vertebrates it is formed from dead, hardened cells.

epididymis [epididimis] *testis*

epidural anaesthesia [epidyooral] The injection of a local anaesthetic into the epidural space located within the vertebral canal outside the dura (a membrane covering the spinal cord). The anaesthetic blocks the nerve roots emerging from the spinal cord on their way to organs, muscle, and skin. It is often used in surgical procedures on the lower half of the body, and in normal or abnormal childbirth.

epiglottis A pear-shaped sheet of elastic fibrocartilage, broad above (where it lies immediately behind the tongue) and narrow below (where it attaches to the back of the thyroid cartilage), and covered on both surfaces by mucous membrane. The back surface contains taste buds and mucous glands. It moves on swallowing, and partly covers the opening into the larynx. In some mammals it extends above the soft palate into the nasopharynx, making this directly continuous with the larynx, and enabling respiration to occur while swallowing.

Epigoni [epigonee] In Greek mythology, the 'next generation' of heroes. After the failure of the Seven Champions to take Thebes, their sons made another expedition and succeeded; this was shortly before the Trojan War.

epigram Originally, an inscription on a statue; hence, any short, pithy poem. The Latin poet Martial wrote over a thousand. Coleridge's definition is also an example: 'What is an epigram? A dwarfish whole,/Its body brevity, and wit its soul'. Some other famous epigrammatists have been Lord Chesterfield, Byron, George Bernard Shaw, Oscar Wilde, and Ogden Nash.

epigraphy [epigrafee] The study of ancient inscriptions, variously inscribed on memorial stones, clay pots and tablets, marble, wood, wax, and other hard surfaces, and using a wide variety of techniques (eg carving, embossing, painting). The field provides insights into the early development of writing systems, as seen in the carvings on the Egyptian pyramids, the oracle bones from Shang China, and the memorial inscriptions on Ogam stones in the Celtic-speaking parts of the British Is.

epilepsy [e**pi**lepsee] A transient seizure or fit usually associated with a short-lived disturbance of consciousness. It stems from a synchronous high-voltage electrical discharge from groups of neurones in the brain. The disorder takes several forms, which include loss of consciousness with generalized convulsions (**grand mal**), short periods of loss of consciousness in which patients simply stop what they are doing and look blank ('absence' or 'drop attacks', or **petit mal**), seizures with involuntary movements of only part of the body, such as a limb (**Jacksonian epilepsy**), and short-lived sensations of smell and smacking of the lips (**temporal lobe epilepsy**). The majority of cases do not have an obvious cause, but in some individuals seizures follow organic damage to the brain (eg from trauma or tumour), or metabolic disturbances (eg diabetes and kidney failure). Electroencephalography is used in the diagnosis.

Epimetheus [epi**mee**thius] The 11th natural satellite of Saturn, discovered in 1980; distance from the planet 151 000 km/ 94 000 mi; diameter 140 km/90 mi.

epinephrine [epi**ne**frin] *adrenaline*

epipelagic environments [epipe**lay**jik] The shallowest pelagic zone in the ocean, usually defined as extending from the surface to a depth of about 200 m/750 ft. It includes the *euphotic* (or *photic*) zone, the surface layer with light penetration sufficient to support photosynthesis by marine plants. The clearer the water, the greater the depth of this zone: in the clearest waters, it may extend to the base of the epipelagic zone; in the neritic realm, it is usually shallower, around 50 m/150 ft, because of the increased turbidity of the water.

Epiphany A Christian festival (6 Jan) which commemorates the showing of the infant Jesus to the Magi (*Matt* 2), the manifestation of Jesus's divinity at his baptism (*Matt* 3), and his first miracle at Cana (*John* 2). Its eve is Twelfth Night. In some countries, gifts are exchanged at Epiphany rather than at Christmas.

epiphenomenalism A theory which maintains that mental phenomena are distinct from and caused by physical phenomena. They are the incidental effects of physical events, and so exert no causal influence on the physical world. Thus T H Huxley characterized mind as 'the steam above the factory'.

epiphyte A plant not rooted in the soil, but growing above ground level, usually on other plants. It uses such hosts for support only, and should not be confused with **parasites**, which also obtain food from their hosts. Epiphytes have aerial roots which help to attach them to their supports, and to trap organic debris, providing nutrients. They also absorb water, either as rain or directly from the air, and may be green and capable of photosynthesis. In some, the leaves may form a water reservoir in the centre of the rosette. Epiphytes are especially common in tropical rainforests, where the adoption of this lifestyle allows them to grow in the light, which is otherwise shut out by the dense canopy. Orchids and bromeliads are particularly prominent here; elsewhere, mosses and lichens are the most frequent epiphytes.

episcopacy [e**pis**kopasee] (Gr *episkopos*, 'bishop', 'superintendent') A hierarchical (as opposed to consistorial) system of Church government, with bishops occupying the dominant role and authority. In the Roman Catholic, Orthodox, and Anglican communions, those consecrated bishops are the chief ecclesiastical officers of a diocese, normally with a cathedral as the mother church, and have the power to ordain priests and confirm baptized members of the Church. They are responsible for the general oversight of the clergy and the spiritual life of a diocese. They are often claimed to be the direct successors of the first 12 Apostles, but not in the Lutheran and other Reformation Churches which recognize the office of bishop.

Episcopal Church, Protestant The Anglican Church in the USA, formally established in 1784 after the War of Independence when Samuel Seabury (1729–86) was consecrated the first Bishop of Connecticut (by the bishops of the Episcopal Church of Scotland). It is an active missionary Church, especially in the Far East and South America. Traditionally, it has allowed more lay participation in the government of the Church than has the Church of England.

epistemology The branch of philosophy dealing with the theory of knowledge – its sources, limits, kinds, and reliability. These central issues divide such major schools as empiricists, rationalists, and sceptics.

epistolary novel A novel in letters – one whose narrative is conducted by an exchange of letters between the characters. Richardson's *Clarissa* (1748) popularized the form, and influenced Laclos' *Les Liaisons dangereuses* (1782, Dangerous Liaisons). Interesting possibilities and complications arise due to the shifting point of view and the absence of an omniscient narrator. Mark Harris's *Wake Up, Stupid* (1959) and John Barth's *Letters* (1979) are interesting modern examples. Among famous examples of epistolary novels in which all the letters are written by one person are Goethe's *Sorrows of Young Werther* (1774) and Hölderlin's *Hyperion* (1797).

epithelium [epi**thee**lium] A layer of cells lining the internal surface of a hollow organ, and covering the external surface of the body; the internal lining may also be known as **endothelium**. Its function varies in different regions of the body (eg protection, secretion, absorption). Several types have been identified according to the shape and disposition of the individual cells (*columnar, cuboidal, squamous*), their arrangement (*stratified, pseudostratified*), or the presence of hairlike processes on their free surface (*ciliated*). **Transitional epithelium** is a type characteristically found lining hollow organs subject to large mechanical changes arising from contraction and distension (such as the bladder). In closed body cavities (eg pericardial, peritoneal, pleural) the epithelium provides a smooth, moist surface which facilitates movement.

epoch In geology, an arbitrary unit of time used as a subdivision of a *period*.

epoxy resin [i**pok**see **rez**in] A cross-linked polymer formed by the addition of two or more compounds, one of which is the epoxide epichlorohydrin; the choice of the others controls the setting conditions – often only a few minutes at room temperature. All of the monomers have low molecular weight, are fluid, and are easily mixed, but the product resins are hard, and there are no by-products, making them useful as adhesives and embedding materials.

EPROM [**ee**prom] Acronym for **electrically programmable read-only memory**, a type of integrated circuit read-only memory which can be reused by removing the chip from the computer, erasing its contents, electrically writing new data into it, and replacing it in the computer. EPROMs are more widely used than the related EAROMs.

Epsom salts *magnesium*

Epstein, Sir Jacob [**ep**stiyn] (1880–1959) Sculptor, born in New York City, USA. He studied at the Ecole des Beaux-Arts in Paris, moving to London, UK, in 1905, and becoming a British subject. Several of his symbolic sculptures, such as 'Ecce homo' (1934), resulted in accusations of indecency and blasphemy. He was an outstanding modeller of bronze portrait heads of celebrities and children. In the 1950s, his last two large works, 'Christ in Majesty' (in aluminium; Llandaff Cathedral) and 'St Michael and the Devil' (in bronze; Coventry Cathedral), won more immediate acclaim. He was knighted in 1954.

equal area map projection A map projection in which all areas are portrayed at the same scale, eg Lambert's cylindrical equal area projection. This is only possible through a distortion of shape at high latitudes. Consequently this projection is rarely used for areas polewards of 40° N and S of the Equator.

Equal Opportunities Commission A body set up in England and Wales under the Sex Discrimination Act (1975) to work towards the elimination of discrimination on the grounds of sex or marital status and to promote equality of opportunity

Equatorial Guinea

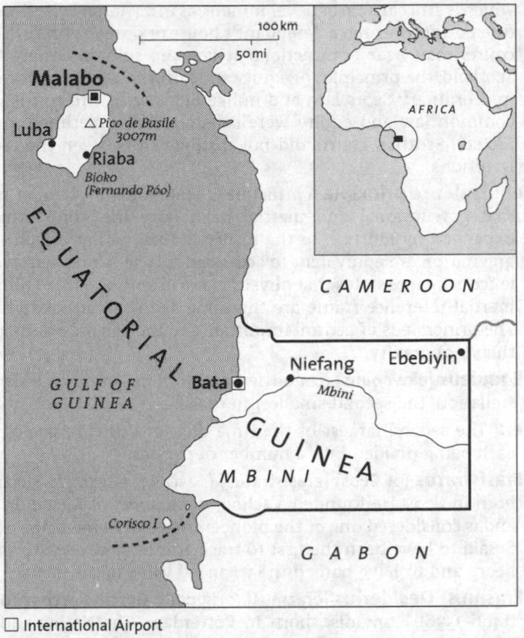

[ginee], official name **Republic of Equatorial Guinea**, Span **República de Guinea Ecuatorial**

Local name Guinea Ecuatorial

Timezone GMT +1

Area 26 016 km²/10 042 sq mi (mainland area) 28 051 km²/10 828 sq mi (total area)

Population total (2002e) 498 000

Status Republic

Date of independence 1968

Capital Malabo

Language Spanish (official)

Ethnic groups Mainland population, mainly Fang (83%), Bubi (10%), Ndowe (4%), Annobonés (2%), Bujeba (1%)

Religions Roman Catholic (80%), traditional beliefs (5%)

Physical features Located in WC Africa; comprises the mainland area (Río Muni) and several islands in the Gulf of Guinea; mainland rises sharply from a narrow coast of mangrove swamps towards the heavily forested African plateau; Bioko, fertile volcanic island in NW, contains Guinea's highest point, Pico de Basilé, 3007 m/9865 ft.

Climate Hot and humid equatorial climate; average maximum daily temperature, 29–32°C; average annual rainfall c.2000 mm/80 in.

Currency 1 CFA Franc (CFA Fr) = 100 centimes

Economy Largely based on agriculture; cocoa, coffee, timber, bananas, cassava, palm oil, sweet potatoes.

GDP (2002e) $1·27 bn, per capita $2700

Human Development Index (2002) 0·679

History First visited by Europeans in 15th-c; island of Fernando Póo claimed by Portugal, 1494–1788; occupied by Britain, 1781–1843; rights to the area acquired by Spain, 1844; independence, 1968; military coup, 1975; governed by Supreme Military Council headed by a President; new constitution, 1991; first multi-party elections held, 1993.

Head of State

1968–79 Francisco Macias Nguema

1979– Teodoro Obiang Nguema Mbasogo

Head of Government

1993–6 Silvestre Siale Bileka

1996–2001 Angel Serafin Seriche Dougan

2001– Candido Muatetema Rivas

between men and women generally. The Commission also reviews the working of the Sex Discrimination Acts and Equal Pay Act (1970). It consists of between 8 and 15 commissioners.

equations The statement that one mathematical expression is equal to another. An equation may always be true (eg $2 + 2 = 4$; $x + y = y + x$, $(x - 1)(x + 1) = x^2 - 1$), when it is called an *identity*, usually written ¡, or it may be true only for some values of the unknowns. Equations may contain more than one unknown quantity. Those containing only one unknown are classified by the *degree* of that unknown. Equations of degree one, called **linear equations**, are of the form $ax = b$, and have the solution $x = b/a$, given $a \neq 0$. Equations of degree two, **quadratic equations**, are of the form $ax^2 + bx + c = 0$, and $a \neq 0$ and have solutions $x = [-b \pm \sqrt{(b^2 - 4ac)}]/2a$; these solutions are in the set of real numbers if the discriminant of the equation $(b^2 - 4ac)$ is greater than or equal to zero. A method for solving general equations of degree three, **cubic equations**, was given in the 16th-c by the Italian mathematician Nicola of Brescia (nicknamed Tartaglia). Cardan, and his pupil Ferrari, later published a method for solving the general equations of degrees three and four. For centuries, mathematicians tried to find a general solution to equations of degree five, but in 1824 N H Abel proved that no such solution could be found.

A **polynomial** equation contains the sum of multiples of powers of a variable, say x; for example $a_0x^n + a_1x^{n-1} + a_2x^{n-2}... = 0$, where $a_0 \neq 0$; n, the highest power of the unknown, is called the degree of the polynomial. Equations are also used in analytical geometry to describe curves. For example, the equation $x^2 + y^2 = 1$ describes the circle, centre the origin, radius 1. In recent years the development of computers has stimulated the discovery of methods of finding successive approximations to the solutions of equations, especially non-algebraic equations, such as $x = e^{-kx}$.

Equator The great circle on the Earth's surface, halfway between the Poles, dividing the Earth into the N and S hemispheres; known as the **terrestrial equator**. Its own latitude is 0°, and from here latitude is measured in degrees N and degrees S. The **celestial equator** is the great circle in the sky in the same plane as the terrestrial equator. When the Sun is on it, day and night are everywhere equal (hence it is also called the *equinoctial line* or *circle*).

Equatorial Guinea *see panel*

equestrianism The skill of horsemanship. As a sport it can fall into one of four categories; **show jumping**, **dressage**, **three-day eventing** (also known as **horse trials**), and **carriage driving**. The governing body is the International Equestrian Federation.

equilibrium (economics) The state of a system in which opposing forces are balanced, so that there is no tendency to change. The term is used in economics in a variety of ways. In microeconomics, equilibrium is used to describe a situation where supply and demand for a good are equal, price being adjusted to bring this about. In macroeconomics equilibrium describes a situation where aggregate supply and demand are equal, the level of real activity being adjusted to bring this about. In game theory, an equilibrium strategy is a rule for choosing actions which seems best to any one agent, given that agent's beliefs about the rules being followed by other agents. In each case equilibrium may not be satisfactory, but will tend not to change unless circumstances alter.

equilibrium (mechanics) A state of balance. In mechanics, if several forces act simultaneously on an object such that it suffers no net force, these forces are said to be in equilibrium. An object or system in equilibrium is unchanging until acted upon by some outside force.

equine colic Spasm of the bowel in horses, resulting in very severe pain. Affected animals are rapidly incapacitated, and if left untreated shock and circulatory collapse can lead to death. Affected individuals may sit down (in the 'dog-sitting position'), roll about, and become very restless. They may get up and down continuously, or lie on their side exhausted. Characteristically they will look round at their flank as they become more agitated. The condition is associated with severe stress, sudden changes of husbandry (especially dietary variations), and intestinal disease. There may be impaction or obstruction of the gut, or dilation due to an accumulation of gas. Watery diarrhoea may accompany colic, leading to marked dehydration, or there may be no faeces at all. Mild cases can recover rapidly, but most require urgent treatment.

equine flu An infectious disease of horses, seen mostly in racing stables or other establishments where such animals are concentrated. A number of viruses are involved. They are similar to, but distinct from, human A-type influenza. The most prominent sign is a persistent dry cough with some degree of fever. Most cases recover within 7–21 days with adequate treatment and nursing. Reliable vaccines are now available for short-term protection.

equine laminitis An inflammation of the internal structures of the hoof, causing very severe pain. There are various degrees of severity depending on the extent of the circulatory and bone disorders. All four feet may be affected. The condition is usually associated with injury, overeating, overweight, stress, and poor foot maintenance. Some cases may be a result of toxaemia or pituitary disease. All but the mildest of cases need urgent veterinary treatment as well as remedial shoeing. Laminitis occurs in most hoofed species, and is of considerable economic importance in cattle, apart from the obvious welfare aspects of the condition.

equine viral arteritis A widespread virus infection of horses, characterized by fever, abortion, coughing, nasal discharge, severe conjunctivitis, and swelling of the legs and lower abdomen. The disease is unusual in being transmitted by both respiratory and venereal routes.

equinox **1** Either of the two points on the celestial sphere where the ecliptic intersects the celestial equator. Physically these are the points at which the Sun, in its annual motion, appears to cross the celestial equator – the **vernal equinox** as it crosses from S to N, and the **autumnal equinox** as it crosses from N to S. The vernal equinox is the zero point in celestial co-ordinate systems.
2 Either of the two instants of time at which the Sun crosses the celestial equator, being about 21 March (vernal) and 23 September (autumnal).

equisetum *horsetail*

equity (economics) The capital of a company, belonging to the shareholders (who are legally the owners). It consists of issued share capital (the money received from the sale of shares); profits retained (traditionally known as *reserves*); share premiums (excess receipts from the sale of shares over their nominal value); and revaluation reserves (sums resulting from the increase in the value of assets since their purchase). In the event of winding up the company, this sum is divided among the shareholders. The shares themselves are called **equities**.

equity (law) A source of English and, later, US law, originally developed by the Lord Chancellor and later by the Court of Chancery. It arose from the right of litigants to petition the monarch. In time these petitions were handled by the Lord Chancellor. Originally flexible and administered according to fairness, as opposed to the sometimes harsh rules of common law, equity developed into a fixed set of rules, its court being notorious for delay. While the Court of Chancery was abolished under the Judicature Acts (1873–5), much equitable work falls within the current jurisdiction of the Chancery Division. Trust law and equitable remedies (such as the injunction) are examples. Equity is now a set of fundamental legal principles which is still capable of development, as in an *Anton Piller Order* (the power to search a defendant's house or property). Most US courts may hear both actions at law and suits in equity. In Scotland, the principles of equity and fairness were interwoven into ordinary Scots law, and unlike England (where courts of common law and equity were separate and sometimes conflicted), Scottish courts did not distinguish between the two traditions.

equivalence principle A principle arising from the observation that gravitational and inertial mass have the same value, expanded by Einstein to the principle that, locally, effects of gravitation are equivalent to acceleration. The (strong) equivalence principle states that physical laws in any local free-falling inertial reference frame are the same as in special relativity. The principle is of central importance to the general relativity theory of gravity.

Equuleus [ekw**oo**lius] (Lat 'little horse') An insignificant N constellation, the second-smallest in the sky.

era The second largest of the time divisions used in geology, each being divided into a number of periods.

Erasistratus (of Ceos) [eras**is**tratus] (c.250 BC) Greek physician, born in Ceos. He founded a school of anatomy at Alexandria, and is considered one of the pioneers of modern medicine. He is said to have been the first to trace arteries and veins to the heart, and to have named the tricuspid valve in the heart.

Erasmus, Desiderius [er**az**mus], originally **Gerrit Gerritszoon** (1466–1536) Humanist, born in Rotterdam, The Netherlands. After six years in an Augustinian monastery, he became private secretary to the Bishop of Cambrai, and a priest (1492). He went to Paris, where he lived as a teacher, then moved to England in 1498, and became professor of divinity and of Greek at Cambridge. Here he wrote his satire, *Encomium moriae* (1509, The Praise of Folly). After 1514 he lived alternately in Basel and England, then in Louvain (1517–21). His masterpiece, *Colloquia*, appeared in 1519, an audacious handling of Church abuses. He also made the first translation of the Greek New Testament into English (1516) and edited the works of St Jerome (1519). In 1521 he left Louvain, and lived mainly in Basel, where he was engaged in continual controversy, but enjoyed great fame and respect in his later years.

Erastianism [er**as**tianizm] An understanding of the Christian Church which gives the state the right to intervene in and control Church affairs. This tendency is associated with Thomas Erastus (1524–83), who, in 16th-c Heidelberg, had argued against Calvinists for the rights of the state in Church affairs, and against the Church's practice of excommunication. It is also evident in the teaching of the Anglican, Richard Hooker; and in the rights of the British Crown in electing bishops in the Church of England.

Erato [eratoh] In Greek mythology, the Muse responsible for lyric poetry and hymns.

Eratosthenes [era**tos**theneez] (c.276–c.194 BC) Greek astronomer and scholar, born in Cyrene. He became chief librarian at Alexandria, and is remembered for the first scientific calculation of the Earth's circumference, which was correct to within 80 km/50 mi.

Erechtheum [erekh**thee**um] The latest building on the Athenian Acropolis, named (by Pausanias in the 2nd-c AD) after the legendary king Erechtheus of Athens. It is a symmetrical, two-part Ionic marble temple dedicated to Athena and Poseidon-Erechtheus, and built during the Peloponnesian War (c.420–407 BC). The six caryatids of the porch (one now among the Elgin marbles) are particularly noteworthy.

Erechtheus [erekthyoos] In Greek mythology, an early king of Athens, born from the Earth and nurtured by Athena. He sacrificed his daughter Chthonia to secure victory over the Eleusinians, but was killed by Poseidon. The Erechtheum, a temple on the Acropolis, is probably on the site of his palace.

Eretria [eretrla] In antiquity, a Greek city-state situated on the island of Euboea off the coast of Attica. It was sacked in the first Persian War for the help it had given to the Ionian cities of Asia Minor in their revolt (499 BC) against Persia.

erg *energy; heat; work*

ergonomics The study of work, including the design of the work situation, the analysis and training of work skills, the effects of physical and psychological environments, work-stress, errors, and accidents. **Human engineering** and **human factors** are equivalent terms. Ergonomic investigations commonly involve collaboration between anatomists, physiologists, psychologists, and engineers. Large amounts of data are collected on the capabilities of the human body in terms of strength and size. The systematic study of work developed from the early 20th-c introduction of mass production, and the use of time and motion study for job analysis and improvement. The subject has applications in such areas as factory design, power station layouts, and the design of vehicle instruments. Recommendations are made about noise and pollution limits, operating times, and lighting conditions. With increasing automation, the requirements for work skills have shifted from eye-hand co-ordination towards information-monitoring and decision-making. Whereas much of pre-1970 ergonomics was concerned with 'man–machine interaction' (MMI), contemporary ergonomics is more concerned with 'human–computer interaction' (HCI). The subject owes much to the early work of US engineer Frederick W Taylor (1856–1915) and the US husband-and-wife team of Frank and Lillian Gilbreth (1868–1924 and 1868–1972).

ergot [ergot] A fungal disease of grasses caused by *Claviceps purpurea*; forms hard black fruiting bodies (*sclerotia*) in flower-heads of infected grasses, including cereal crops; sclerotia contain chemicals (alkaloids) which can cause severe poisoning if ingested. (Class: Pyrenomycetes.)

ergotism [ergotizm] A condition which results from eating bread made from rye heavily infected with the fungus *Claviceps purpurea*, which contains ergot alkaloids. These substances constrict blood vessels, so that victims develop burning sensations in the limbs, gangrene, and convulsions. It also induces abortion in pregnant women. Ergotism is now rare, but epidemics occurred well into the 19th-c. Outbreaks caused great fear, and were referred to as *St Anthony's fire*, in the belief that a visit to the tomb of this saint would bring a cure.

Erhard, Ludwig [airhah(r)t] (1897–1977) German statesman, economist, and Christian Democratic chancellor (1963–6), born in Fürth, SEC Germany. Professor of economics at Munich, in 1949 he was elected to the Federal Parliament at Bonn, and made Chancellor of the Exchequer in the Adenauer administration. He was the pioneer of the West German 'economic miracle' of recovery from wartime devastation. He succeeded Adenauer as chancellor, but economic difficulties forced his resignation.

erica *heath*

Ericsson, John (1803–89) Inventor, born in Långbanshyttan, SC Sweden. He was a Swedish army engineer before he moved to England (1826), where he invented the first successful screw-propeller (1836). In 1839 he went to the USA, becoming a US citizen in 1848. He designed the warship *Princeton*, the first steamer with engines and boilers entirely below the water-line, and in 1861 built the ironclad *Monitor* and other vessels. His inventions revolutionized the construction of warships. He is also known to have investigated solar-power as an energy source.

Eridanus [eridanus] (name of a river) A long and rambling S constellation, sixth-largest in the sky. Its brightest star is Achernar, which is the ninth brightest in our sky. Distance: 44 parsec.

Eridu [ayridoo] The oldest of the Sumerian city-states, lying SW of Ur. Excavations of the site have revealed a continuous series of temples starting in the sixth millennium BC and ending in the third with the great ziggurat.

Erie, Lake [eeree] Fourth largest of the Great Lakes, North America, on frontier between Canada and USA; 388 km/241 mi long, 48–92 km/30–57 mi wide; area 25 667 sq km/9907 sq mi; Detroit R inlet from L Huron (W), via L St Clair; Niagara R (E) outlet to L Ontario; Welland Ship Canal bypasses Niagara Falls; generally closed by ice during winter months (Dec–Mar); major (US) ports include Buffalo, Cleveland, Detroit; islands include Bass, Kelleys, Pelee; British defeated at Battle of Lake Erie, 1813.

Erie Canal [eeree] An artificial waterway extending 580 km/360 mi between Albany and Buffalo, New York State. Constructed 1817–25, it greatly accelerated the development of the mid-West and of New York by providing a water route from the Hudson R to L Erie. Although improved rail transport in the late 19th-c spelled its decline, it is still a significant element in the New York State Barge Canal System.

Erigena, John Scotus [erijena], also known as **John the Scot** (c.810–c.877) Philosopher and theologian, born in Scotia (now Ireland), who stands outside the mainstream of mediaeval thought. He taught at the Court of Charles I, the Bald, in France, then supported Hincmar in the predestination controversy with his *De praedestinatione* (851, On Predestination), which the Council of Valence condemned as *pultes Scotorum* ('Irishman's porridge'). He also translated into Latin and provided commentaries on the Greek writings of the theologians of the Eastern Church. His major work, *De divisione naturae* (c.865, On the Division of Nature), tried to fuse Christian and Neoplatonic doctrines, but his work was later condemned for its pantheistic tendencies.

Eriksson, Sven Goran (1948–) Footballer and football manager, born in Torsby, W Sweden. A knee injury in 1975 playing for the Swedish second division side Karlskoga brought his career as a player to an end. After a period coaching the third division Swedish side Degers, he joined IFK Gothenburg in 1980 and with them won the Swedish championship, two domestic titles, and the 1982 UEFA Cup. He had two periods with the Portuguese side Benfica (1982–84, 1989–91) guiding them to the 1990 European Cup final and the 1991 league title. He coached the Italian teams AS Roma (1984–86), winning with them the Italian Cup title in 1986, Fiorentina (1987–98), Sampdoria (1991–96), and Lazio (1997–2001) taking them to their first European trophy, the Cup Winners' Cup in 1999 and the Italian league and cup double in 1999 2000. In 2001 he became manager of the England football team.

Erik the Red, originally **Erik Thorvaldsson** (10th-c) Norwegian sailor who explored the Greenland coast and founded the Norse colonies there (985). His son **Leif Eriksson** landed in 'Vinland', often identified as America (1000). Both men are the subject of Icelandic sagas.

Erinyes [ereenyeez] In Greek mythology, spirits of vengeance, depicted as carrying torches and covered with snakes; also known as the **Furies**. They are best thought of as personified curses, avengers of crime 'within the kindred' (outsiders could be pursued by the blood-feud). Their names are Alecto 'never-ceasing', Megaira 'grudger', and Tisiphone 'avenger of blood'.

Eris [eris] In Greek mythology, the daughter of Night and the sister of Ares. A late story tells how she was present at the wedding of Peleus and Thetis and threw a golden apple 'for the fairest'; this brought Hera, Athene, and Aphrodite into contention, and was the first cause of the Trojan War. The name means 'strife' in Greek.

Eritrea *p.526*

ERM *European Monetary System (EMS)*

ermine *stoat*

Ermine Street *Roman roads*

Ernst, Max(imillian) (1891–1976) Painter, born in Brühl, near Cologne, W Germany. After studying philosophy at Bonn, he turned to painting. In 1919 he founded at Cologne the German Dada group, and later became part of the Surrealist movement in Paris. He settled in the USA in 1941, but returned to France in 1953. His use of the subconscious as inspiration can be seen in 'Oedipus Rex' (1921) and 'Polish Rider' (1954).

Eritrea

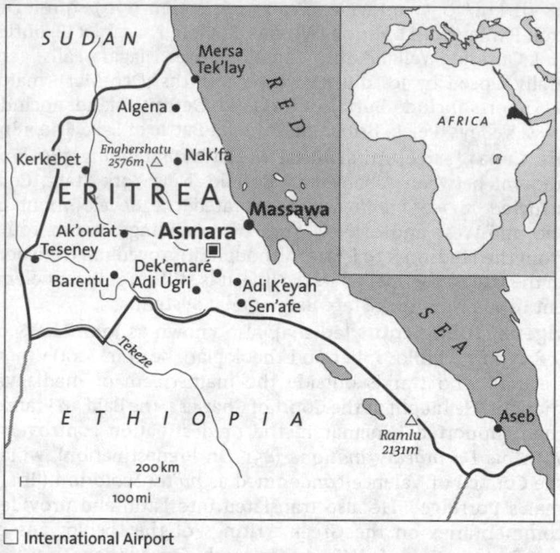

[eritraya], Amharic **Ertra**

Local name Ertra

Timezone GMT+3

Area 93 700 km²/36 200 sq ml

Population total (2002e) 3 981 000

Status Republic

Date of independence 1993

Capital Asmara

Language Tigrinya, Tigray, Amharic

Ethnic groups Tigray, Amhara

Religions Islam (50%), Coptic Christianity (50%)

Physical features Ethiopian plateau drops to low plains; E plain includes the Danakil Depression, descending to 116 m/381 ft below sea level.

Climate Tropical climate, varied by altitude; annual temperature at Asmara, 16°C, at Mitsiwa (on coast) 30°C; hot, semi-arid NE and SE lowlands receive less than 500 mm/20 in rainfall annually; severe droughts have caused widespread famine.

Currency Ethiopian birr replaced (1997) by the nakfa

Economy Largely devoted to agriculture, but badly affected by drought, and heavily dependent on irrigation and foreign aid; textiles, leather, salt, food production.

GNP (2002e) $3·3 bn, per capita $700

Human Development Index (2002) 0·421

History Federated as part of Ethiopia, 1952; province of Ethiopia, 1962, which led to political unrest; civil war in the 1970s, with separatists making major gains; Soviet- and Cuban-backed government forces regained most areas after 1978 offensive; fall of President Mengistu (1991) led to new status as an autonomous region, with a provisional government established by the Eritrean People's Liberation Front; referendum followed by the declaration of independence, 1993; transitional government for 4 years, consisting of a National Assembly, which elects the president, and State Council; escalating conflict with Ethiopia over disputed border territory, 1999–2000; Permanent Court of Arbitration at The Hague issued a border ruling, 2002.

Head of State

1993– Issais Afewerki

Eros (astronomy) **[eeros]** Asteroid 433, discovered in 1898 by Carl Gustav Witt at the Urania Observatory, Copenhagen. It passed within 23 million km/14 million mi of Earth in 1975. It is highly elongated in shape, about 30 × 14 km/18 × 8 mi across. The Near Earth Asteroid Rendevous (NEAR) spacecraft encountered and photographed it in December 1998.

Eros (mythology) **[erohs]**, commonly **[eeros]** Originally, in Homer, simply an abstract force of 'erotic desire'; but in Greek mythology, the son of Aphrodite and Ares. He is first depicted on vases as a handsome athlete, then as a boy with wings and arrows, and finally, in the Hellenistic period, as a chubby baby.

erosion In geology, the alteration of landforms through the removal and transport of material by water, wind, glacial movement, gravity, or living organisms. Rivers are the most effective agents of erosion, forming the pattern of hills and valleys, while wave action forms the coastlines. Erosion can have serious economic effects by removing the topsoil.

Erse *Irish*

Ershad, Hussain Muhammad [air**shad**] (1929–) Bangladeshi soldier, chief martial law administrator, and president (1983–90). Appointed army chief-of-staff by President Ziaur Rahman in 1978, he repeatedly demanded that the armed forces should be involved in the country's administration. In 1982 he led a bloodless military coup, becoming president the following year. He resigned at the end of 1990, was arrested on charges of plundering the nation, and sentenced to 10 years' imprisonment in 1991. He was released in 1997.

Erté [er**tay**], originally **Romain de Tirtoff** (1892-1990) Fashion designer, born in St Petersburg, NW Russia. He went to Paris, where he became a dress and theatrical-costume designer. He worked for the *Folies-Bergère* (1919–30), and designed the costumes for the American musical revues *The Ziegfeld Follies* and *George White's Scandals*. In the 1960s he produced lithographs and sheet-metal sculptures. His autobiography, *Things I Remember*, was published in 1976.

erysipelas [erisipelas] An infectious skin disease caused by haemolytic strains of *Streptococcus*. The bacterium is spread from person to person by direct contact, and enters through small breaks in the skin. The skin becomes reddened and swollen, resembling the texture of an orange, and the infected area spreads rapidly. Patients are extremely unwell, with a high fever. Treatment is with penicillin.

erythrocytes [erithrosiyts] Haemoglobin-containing blood cells present in most vertebrates, whose primary function is the transport of oxygen and carbon dioxide in the blood; also known as **red blood cells**. They are manufactured in bone marrow, usually as large, round, bi-concave, nucleated cells. With maturation of the cells their diameter decreases, haemoglobin is accumulated, and (in mammals) the nucleus is lost before the cells enter the circulation.

erythropoietin [erithroh**poy**itin] A type of hormone (a polypeptide) present in vertebrates, secreted mainly by the kidneys, but also by other organs (eg the liver). It stimulates the proliferation and maturation of red blood cells (*erythrocytes*) in red bone marrow. The enhanced secretion of erythropoietin follows oxygen deficiency in some (as yet unknown) kidney cells, which results in compensatory increases in circulating erythrocytes and blood oxygen.

ESA *European Space Agency*

Esaki, Leo [esahkee], originally **Esaki Reiona** (1925–) Physicist, born in Osaka, C Japan. He studied physics at Tokyo, and in 1957, working for the Sony Corporation, developed the *Esaki diode* (or tunnel diode), a semiconductor device with widespread uses in electronic computers and microwave systems. In 1960 he moved to the IBM Research Center in New York City, where he pioneered quantum well devices and superlattices. He shared the Nobel Prize for Physics in 1973.

Esarhaddon [eesah(r)hadn] (?–669 BC) King of Assyria (680–669 BC), the son of Sennacherib and father of Assurbanipal. He is best known for his conquest of Egypt (671 BC).

Esau [eesaw] Biblical character, the elder son of Isaac. He was depicted as his father's favourite son, but was deprived of Isaac's blessing and his birthright by his cunning brother Jacob (*Gen* 27). The story was used to explain why Esau's descendants, the Edomites, were thereafter hostile to Jacob's descendants, the Israelites.

Esbjerg [aysbyer] 55°28N 8°28E, pop (2000e) 85 000. Seaport on W coast of Ribe county, SW Jutland, Denmark; railway; ferry link with UK and Faroe Is; base for North Sea oil and gas exploration; fishing, trade in agricultural produce; the most important Danish North Sea port.

escalator A moving staircase, used to transport people or goods from one level to another, found mainly in large department stores and in railway stations and airports. Introduced in the USA, the Reno Inclined Elevator was patented by Jesse W Reno in 1892 and installed at the Old Iron Pier on Coney Island in 1896. Escalator steps are mounted on an endless belt, lying flat at the top and bottom to enable people to get on and off, and there is a moving handrail. Modern escalators are usually inclined at an angle of 30°, and travel at a rate of up to 35 m/120 ft per minute. The treads pass through a metal comb at the top and bottom of the escalator, which helps to remove objects. A moving ramp, which transports people or goods horizontally, or at a slight incline, is known as a **travelator**.

escape velocity Spacecraft velocity at which the energy of a craft is sufficient to overcome the gravitational attraction of the parent body, and will thus not return to that body. Earth escape velocity is c.11 km/s (7 mi/s) (root 2 × circular orbit velocity); Sun escape velocity is about 42 km/s (26 mi/s), reached by Voyagers 1 and 2 after Jupiter flyby, when velocity was increased by gravity assist.

Escaut, River *Schelde, River*

eschatology [eskatolojee] The Christian doctrine concerning 'the last things' – the final consummation of God's purposes in creation, and the final destiny of individual souls or spirits and of humanity in general. The expected imminent return of Christ to establish the Kingdom of God was not realized, in early Christianity, which led to alternative, often symbolic, representations of 'the last things'. The notion is sometimes represented as a present spiritual condition rather than as a future cosmic event. Others believe that the Kingdom of God has been inaugurated by the coming of Christ, and then give varying accounts of its future fulfilment. Some continue to adhere to the early belief in the literal 'second-coming' of Christ. In Islam eschatology refers to the final days prior to the end of the world, and to the final destiny of human beings. There are variations in detail, but common is the theme of a period of great tribulation, followed by a millennium and a final judgment.

Escherichia [esherikia] A genus of rod-shaped bacteria that occur in the intestinal tract of animals, including humans, and are common in soil and aquatic habitats. They can cause bacterial dysentery. The only species, *Escherichia coli*, has been intensively studied by microbiologists. (Kingdom: Monera. Family: Enterobacteriaceae.)

Escoffier, (Georges) Auguste [eskofyay] (c.1847–1935) Chef, born in Villeneuve-Loubet, SE France. He became *chef de cuisine* to the general staff of the Rhine army in the Franco-Prussian war (1871) and of the Grand Hotel, Monte Carlo, before coming to the Savoy, London, and finally to the Carlton. The inventor of *Pêche Melba* and *tournedos Rossini* for the singer and composer respectively, and other dishes, he wrote several books on culinary art.

Escorial, El [eskorial] A palace-monastery built (1563–84) for Philip II in New Castile, C Spain; a world heritage site. The granite edifice, constructed by Juan Bautista de Toledo and his successor Juan de Herrara, is renowned for its austere grandeur. It houses a substantial library (founded by Philip II) and an art gallery which includes works by El Greco, Velazquez, and Titian.

Esdras, Books of [ezdras] 1 The **First Book of Esdras**, known also as **3 Esdras** (in the Vulgate), part of the Old Testament Apocrypha; an appendix to the Catholic Bible. It reproduces much of 2 *Chron* 35–6, Ezra, and *Nehem* 7–8, covering two centuries from the reign of Josiah to Ezra's reforms after the exile, with an additional story about three young men of Darius's bodyguard.

2 The **Second Book of Esdras**, known also as **4 Esdras** (in the Vulgate) or **4 Ezra**, sometimes considered part of the Old Testament Apocrypha; also an appendix to the Catholic Bible. It depicts seven apocalyptic visions, ostensibly to Ezra (also called Salathiel), which address the problem of why God has permitted Israel's sufferings and describe the destruction facing the world. Dated probably late 1st-c; chapters 1–2 and 15–16 may be two later Christian additions, today sometimes called 5 Ezra and 6 Ezra, respectively.

Esfahan [esfahahn], ancient **Isfahan**, **Aspadana** 32°40N 51°38E, pop (2000e) 1 383 000. Capital city of Esfahan district, WC Iran; on R Zaindeh, 336 km/209 mi S of Tehran; third largest city in Iran; airport; railway; university (1950); steel, carpets, hand-printed textiles, metalwork; Lutfullah mosque, 17th-c royal mosque, Ali Kapu gate, Chihil Satun, Jolfa cathedral.

esker [esker] A long, narrow hill of gravel and sand which may wind for long distances along a valley floor, probably formed by water flowing in tunnels underneath glaciers.

Eskimo or (in Canada) **Inuit** Eskimo–Aleut-speaking peoples of North America, Russia, and Greenland, living along the N edge of the continent, from Alaskan and E Asian shores in the W to Greenland and Labrador in the E, mostly S of the Arctic Circle. They are closely related to the Aleut. Their ancestors came from Asia, crossing over the Bering Straits when Alaska and Siberia were connected by a strip of land, 10–15 000 years ago, and gradually expanded across the continent. Despite geographical separation, the way of life in different Eskimo groups was very similar, determined largely by climatic considerations – living on the coast during the winter months, and moving inland for the brief summers to hunt land and sea game, and to fish. As a consequence of later contact with Europeans in the 18th-c, the Eskimos' way of life was radically altered, from hunting for food to hunting for furs, which they exchanged for European manufactured goods. By the late 20th-c, many had been settled in villages, and while some continued to hunt and fish, most had at least seasonal employment in the wage economies of the countries where they lived, mainly as labourers in the mining and oil industries. In Russia, Eskimos were organized into hunting collectives. The combined populations of Eskimos and Aleuts in Russia is c.1300, with 33 000 in Alaska, 24 000 in Canada, and 43 000 in Greenland.

eskimo dog *husky*

esophagus *oesophagus*

ESP *extrasensory perception*

esparto A tufted perennial grass (*Stipa tenacissima*), native to N Africa, and naturalized elsewhere, consisting of spikelets with long, feathery bristles in narrow panicles. The leaves are used to make paper. (Family: Gramineae.)

Esperanto The best known of the world's artificial languages, invented by Ludwig Lazarus Zamenhof in 1887, designed to overcome problems of international communication. It has 5 vowels and 23 consonants, a mainly W European lexicon, and shows Slavonic influence on syntax and spelling. Precise estimates of numbers and levels of speaker fluency are difficult to obtain: there are anywhere between 1 and 15 million speakers. Newspapers and journals are published in Esperanto, together with the Bible and the Qur'an. It is used for broadcasting, and is taught as a school subject in several countries.

ESPRIT [espree] An abbreviation for the **European Strategic Programme for Research and Development in Information Technology**, a programme of research funded by the European Commission as part of the Framework Programme. It aims to develop the European computer industry by supporting joint pre-competitive research projects across institutions in the member countries of the European Union.

Essen 51°28N 6°59E, pop (2000e) 647 000. Industrial city in Düsseldorf district, W Germany; 29 km/18 mi NE of Düsseldorf, between Emscher and Ruhr Rivers; badly bombed in World War 2; bishopric; railway; headquarters of many large industrial corporations; important centre of retail trade; mining, iron and steel, engineering, locomotives, electronics, glass, chemicals, plastics, brewing, machine tools, shipbuilding, textiles; the Zollverein coal mine industrial complex is a world heritage site; Minster (9th–14th-c), Werden Abbey church; Baldeney Festival (summer).

Essenes [eseenz] A Jewish sect renowned in antiquity for its asceticism, communistic lifestyle, and skill in predicting the future. The famous Dead Sea Scrolls are believed to have belonged to a local Essene community.

essential amino acids *amino acids*

essential fatty acids *carboxylic acids*

essentialism The philosophical doctrine, articulated by Aristotle and others, that all things have a nature or essence – a cluster of properties which define them, and without which they would cease to exist or be the things they are. For example, being a mammal is an essential property of a cow; in contrast, being brown is an *accidental* property, something which could be different.

essential oil A natural volatile oil produced by plants, giving a distinctive aromatic scent to the foliage. Mostly terpenoids, they help to reduce water loss by evaporating and forming a barrier around the leaf surface; the oil glands can often be seen as shining coloured dots scattered over the foliage or flowers. Common in plants from hot dry habitats, both the quality and quantity of oil is to some extent dependent on the amount of sunshine received.

Essequibo, River [esekeeboh] Largest river in Guyana, South America, draining over half the country; rises in the Guiana Highlands on the Brazilian border; flows c.970 km/600 mi N to meet the Atlantic at a 32 km/20 mi-wide delta, NW of Georgetown; navigable for large vessels for some miles past Bartica (c.80 km/50 mi); course interrupted by many rapids and falls.

Essex pop (2001e) 1 310 900; area 3672 sq km/1418 sq mi. County of SE England, UK; NE of London; bounded E by the North Sea and S by the Thames estuary; county town, Chelmsford; major towns include Harwich (ferry port), Colchester, Southend; Southend and Thurrock new unitary authorities from 1998; agriculture (especially grain), oysters, electronics, motor vehicles, tourism.

Essex, Robert Devereux, 2nd Earl of (1566–1601) English soldier and courtier to Elizabeth I, born in Netherwood, Hereford and Worcester, WC England, UK. He served in The Netherlands (1585–6), and distinguished himself at Zutphen. At court, he quickly rose in the favour of Elizabeth, despite his clandestine marriage in 1590 with Sir Philip Sidney's widow. In 1591 he commanded the forces sent to help Henry IV of France, and took part in the sacking of Cadiz (1595). He became a privy councillor (1593) and earl marshal (1597). However, he alienated the Queen's advisers, and there were constant quarrels with Elizabeth (notably the occasion when he turned his back on her, and she boxed his ears). His six months' lord-lieutenancy of Ireland (1599) proved a failure, and he was imprisoned and deprived of his dignities. He attempted to raise the City of London, was found guilty of high treason, and was beheaded in the Tower.

Estado Novo [estahdoo nohvoo] (Port 'new state') The name given by President Getúlio Vargas to his authoritarian regime in Brazil (1937–45). The term was copied from the Estado Novo established in Portugal by Dr Salazar.

estate duty A tax formerly levied in the UK on the estate of a deceased person, based on the total value of the estate; small estates were exempt, and the levels of tax were varied from time to time. It has now been replaced by the **inheritance tax**. The USA has a federal **estate tax** and a related **gift tax**.

ester A compound obtained by the condensation of an alcohol with an acid, as in the following example:

$$\underset{\text{(alcohol)}}{\underset{\text{ethanol}}{CH_3CH_2OH}} + \underset{\text{(acid)}}{\underset{\text{acetic acid}}{CH_3COOH}} \rightarrow \underset{\text{(ester)}}{\underset{\text{ethyl acetate}}{CH_3COOCH_2CH_3}} + \underset{\text{water}}{H_2O}.$$

Esters are named as if they were salts, the first part being derived from the alcohol, and the second part from the acid. Most simple esters have characteristic fruity odours: ethyl acetate has the odour of pears, and is also an important solvent. Vegetable and animal fats and oils are mainly esters of glycerol.

Esther, Book of A book of the Hebrew Bible/Old Testament, telling the popular story of how Esther, a cousin and foster daughter of the Jew, Mordecai, became the wife of the Persian king Ahasuerus (Xerxes I) and prevented the extermination of Jews by the order of Haman, a king's officer. The event is said to be the source of the Jewish feast of Purim. The **Additions to the Book of Esther** are several enhancements found in the Septuagint but not in the Hebrew Bible. They are part of the Old Testament Apocrypha, and appear as *Esther* 11–16 in the Catholic Bible. These chapters consist of Mordecai's dream and its interpretation, the prayers of Mordecai and Esther, and edicts issued by the king. They may supply a specifically religious perspective which the Book of Esther lacks.

Esthetic movement *Aesthetic Movement*

Estigarribia, José Félix [esteegareebia] (1888–1940) Paraguayan general and war hero, born in Caraguatay, Paraguay. He won fame as a brilliant commander in the Chaco War (1932–5), on the strength of which he became president (1939–40). He died in a plane crash near Asunción.

Estonia *p.529*

Estremadura [ishtremadoora], Lat **Extrema Durii** ('farthest land on the Douro') area 3249 sq km/1254 sq mi. Region and former province of WC Portugal; chief town, Lisbon; wines, fruit, olives, wheat, maize, vegetables; sheep and goats in upland areas (N); thermal springs; the political and cultural centre of Portugal, as well as a popular tourist region.

estrildid finch *finch*

estrogens *oestrogens*

estuary A partly enclosed coastal water body connected with the open ocean and filled with sea water significantly diluted by fresh water run-off from land. Estuaries are among the most biologically productive areas on Earth. The addition of nutrient material from land via surface run-off is trapped by estuarine circulation patterns and continuously recycled by organisms.

Esztergom [estergom], Ger **Gran**, ancient **Strigonium** 47°47N 18°44E, pop (2000e) 29 100. River-port town in Komáron county, N Hungary; on R Danube, NW of Budapest; fortress in Roman times; capital, 10th-c; seat of primate, 1198; railway; school of forestry; coal, lignite, wine, machinery; birthplace of St Stephen, Hungary's first king; 19th-c Basilica (largest church in Hungary); thermal springs nearby.

ETA (Basque, *Euzkadi Ta Azkatasuna* 'Homeland and Liberty') Basque separatist organization whose goal is Basque self-determination. Founded in 1959, it split off from its parent Partido Nacionalista Vasco (PNV), fragmenting further in 1966 to produce a more violent Marxist-Leninist wing, which conducted bomb attacks and assassinations. The Franco government responded with a brutal policy of assaults and torture, but the post-Franco government granted partial Basque autonomy and pardoned ETA members. Increased violence in the 1960s and 1970s was furthered by close links with the IRA and Libya. In 1978 ETA's political wing, *Herri Batasuna*, was founded. In the 1990s it continued terrorist activities despite declaring a ceasefire in 1994. In 1998 the murder of a hostage taken by ETA, a town councillor, caused widespread outrage. ETA announced a truce, followed by a resumption of direct talks with the Spanish government (1999). ETA offered new terms for negotiation, including the key demand for a referendum in the Basque region, but these were turned down, and further bombings have since taken place. The Basque separatist party Batasuna was outlawed in March 2003.

etching A form of intaglio printing invented in the early 16th-c, whereby the design on a copper plate is bitten with acid, rather than cut directly with the engraving tool (*burin*). The greatest master of the technique was Rembrandt.

Eteocles [etiokleez] In Greek legend, the elder of Oedipus's two sons, both of whom he cursed. Eteocles became king of Thebes

Estonia

☐ International Airport

[estohnia], official name **Republic of Estonia**, Estonian **Eesti Vabariik**, Russ **Estonskaya**

Local name Eesti

Timezone GMT +2

Area 45 100 km²/17 409 sq mi

Population total (2002e) 1 359 000

Status Republic

Date of independence 1991

Capital Tallinn

Languages Estonian (official), also Russian

Ethnic groups Estonian (65%), Russian (28%), Ukrainian (3%), Belorussian (2%)

Religions Evangelical Lutheran, with Orthodox minority

Physical features Consists of mainland area and c.800 islands (including the Baltic island of Saaremaa); S covered with morainal hills, C with elongated glacial hills usually arrayed in the direction of glacial movement; most lakes and rivers drain either E into Lake Peipus, N into the Gulf of Finland; a few W into Gulf of Riga.

Climate Mild climate. Average annual temperatures −6°C (Jan) and 17°C (Jul); average annual rainfall 650 mm/26 in.

Currency 1 Kroon = 100 cents

Economy Major industries: agricultural machinery, electric motors; agricultural produce of grain, vegetables; livestock.

GDP (2002e) $15·52 bn, per capita $11 000

Human Development Index (2002) 0·826

History Ceded to Russia, 1721; independence, 1918; proclaimed a Soviet Socialist Republic, 1940; occupied by Germany in World War 2; resurgence of nationalist movement in the 1980s; declared independence, 1991; 105-member Parliament; 495-member Congress of Estonia.

Head of State
1991–2 Arnold Rüütel
1992–2001 Lennart Meri
2001– Arnold Rüütel

Head of Government
1997–9 Mart Siimann
1999–2002 Mart Laar
2002–3 Siim Kallas
2003– Juhan Parts

after his father's death, and refused to share power with his brother Polynices. Seven Champions attacked the city, and Eteocles was killed by Polynices.

ethanal *acetaldehyde*

ethane [eethayn, ethayn] C_2H_6, boiling point −89°C. The second member of the alkane series; an odourless gas, used for refrigeration, which forms explosive mixtures with air. The molecular shape, joined tetrahedra, is characteristic of the whole alkane series.

ethanedioic acid *oxalic acid*

ethanoic acid [ethanohik] *acetic acid*

ethanol CH_3CH_2OH, boiling point 78°C, also called **ethyl alcohol**, **grain alcohol**, and simply **alcohol**. It is a colourless liquid with a characteristic odour, mainly prepared by the fermentation of sugars. An important solvent, disinfectant, and preservative, it is mainly known for its intoxicating properties in beverages.

ethanoyl *acetyl*

Ethelbert or **Æthelbert** [ethelbert] (c.552–616) King of Kent (c.560–616), the first English king to adopt Christianity. During his long reign, Kent achieved hegemony over England S of the Humber. He received with kindness the Christian mission from Rome led by St Augustine, which landed in Thanet in 596, and allowed them to settle at Canterbury, and he himself was baptized with his court. He was also responsible for the first written code of English laws.

Etheldreda or **Æthelthryth, St** [etheldreeda], also known as **St Audrey** (c.630–679) Anglo-Saxon nun, the founder of a monastery at Ely, and revered as a virgin saint, although twice married. The daughter of King Anna of East Anglia, she was widowed after three years of her first marriage, which was said never to have been consummated. In 660 she married **Ecgfrith**, future king of Northumbria, but refused to consummate it. Instead she took the veil and withdrew to the double monastery at Coldingham founded by her aunt, Æbbe, and in 673 founded a double monastery herself on the Isle of Ely, of which she was appointed abbess. Feast day 23 June.

Ethelred I [ethelred], also spelled **Æthelred** (c.830–71) King of Wessex (865–71), the elder brother of Alfred the Great. During his reign, the Danes launched their main invasion of England and established their kingdom (866). He died soon after his victory over the invaders at Ashdown, in the former county of Berkshire.

Ethelred II [ethelred], known as **Ethelred the Unready**, also spelled **Æthelred** (c.968–1016) King of England (978–1016), the son of Edgar. He was aged about 10 when the murder of his half-brother, Edward the Martyr, placed him on the throne. In 1002 he confirmed an alliance with Normandy by marrying as his second wife Duke Richard's daughter **Emma** – the first dynastic link between the two countries. Renewed attacks by the Vikings on England began as raids in the 980s, and in 1013 Sweyn Forkbeard secured mastery over the whole country, forcing Ethelred into exile in Normandy. After Sweyn's death (1014), he returned to oppose Canute, but the unity of English resistance was broken when his son, Edmund Ironside, rebelled. He died in London. 'Unready' is a mistranslation of *Unraed*, not recorded as his nickname until after the Norman Conquest; it means 'ill-advised' and is a pun on his given name, Ethelred (literally, 'good counsel').

Ethelred, St *Ailred of Rievaulx, St*

Ethelwulf, also spelled **Æthelwulf** (d.858) Anglo-Saxon king of England (839–56), the son of the West Saxon king, Egbert. In 835 the Danes had begun large-scale raids on the English coast, and in 851 he fought a victorious battle against the Danish army at Aclea in Surrey. He married his daughter to the Mercian King Burgred in 853. In 856 he was deposed by rivals on his return from Rome, but continued to rule Kent until his death. Four of his sons became kings of Wessex, including Alfred the Great (r.871–99).

ethene *ethylene*

ether [eether] **1** An organic compound containing an oxygen atom bonded to two alkyl groups. Ethers are relatively unreactive compounds. The best known is **ethyl ether** (CH_3CH_2–O–CH_2CH_3), a volatile liquid, boiling point 35°C, used as an anaesthetic.

2 A substance once believed to pervade all space, thought necessary as the medium of propagation of light. The Michelson–Morley experiment was important in demonstrating the absence of ether, which is no longer required by the modern theory of light.

Etherege, Sir George [etherij] (1635–92) Restoration playwright, probably born in Maidenhead, Windsor and Maidenhead, S England, UK. His three plays, *The Comical Revenge; or, Love in a Tub* (1664); *She Would if She Could* (1668); and *The Man of Mode; or, Sir Fopling Flutter* (1676), were highly popular in their day, and introduced the comedy of manners to the English theatre.

Ethernet A model of a local area network in which the workstations of the network are linked by coaxial cable. If any network station wishes to communicate with another, it sends an addressed message along the cable; this is then recognized and picked up only by the workstation to which it is addressed. There is also a model of local area network, called a **'thin' ethernet**, which uses telephone wires but transmits data more slowly than in the standard **'thick' ethernet**. More recently, versions of Ethernet, using unshielded twisted pair (UTP) cables linked to a central hub and operating at 100 Mbps (Megabauds per second), have been developed.

ethics The branch of philosophy dealing with the concepts and principles of morality, and including such theoretical questions as the source and foundation of morality, the status and justification of moral rules, the relationship between moral and other human objectives, and the nature of responsibility. Ethics has various subfields of application, such as medical ethics and business ethics, and its meaning shades into the more everyday, descriptive sense of 'a set of standards'.

Ethiopia *p.531*

Ethiopian Churches Separatist African churches which have broken away from parent missionary bodies, and which seek to select those aspects of Christianity deemed appropriate to African cultural and social needs. They take their inspiration from the Donatist and Coptic Churches, and have appeared in W, C, and S Africa. Some have been apolitical, but many have become a focus for political discontent.

Ethiopianism A form of nationalist and spiritual movement founded among US and West Indian blacks which looks towards Africa (Ethiopia being used as a synonym for Africa) as their place of origin. The movement was influenced by the black activists of the 1930s, particularly **Marcus Garvey** (1887–1940) who attempted to 'reclaim' Africa for the black race. It is connected with messianism and the independent black Churches that broke away from established Christianity.

ethnic cleansing The systematic removal of a racial, political, religious, or cultural group from a geographical area. Ethnic cleansing differs from **genocide** in that the objective is not to exterminate all members of the group; however, mass murder, either organized or on an ad hoc basis, has often been part of the process of ethnic cleansing. The term became widely applied to the activities of various governments in the Balkans during the break-up of former Yugoslavia following the death of Tito, and has been criticized for sanitizing a social evil that tends to accompany most civil wars.

ethnic group A segment of a population within a society who share common descent (actual or putative), attitudes and behaviour, and cultural and physical characteristics, and who perceive themselves as a distinct group.

ethnicity A term which may be confused with 'race', but which refers to a shared cultural identity that has a range of distinctive behavioural and possibly linguistic features, passed on through socialization from one generation to another. There are never clear boundaries, cultural or geographic, that mark the limits of ethnic groups, even though many regard ethnicity as though it were naturally determined. Ethnic differences have been a source of political unrest, often associated with religious or clan differences.

ethnic relations The interactions between different ethnic groups within a society. The main forms are *assimilation*, where ethnic groups adopt common cultural patterns, and eventually merge; *domination*, where one ethnic group controls the other(s), establishing its culture as the main one; and *consociationalism*, as in Switzerland, where groups retain distinct cultures and identity, but are more or less equal.

ethnocentrism A limited or parochial perspective which evaluates other societies and their cultures according to one's own cultural expectations. It implies a very restricted understanding of foreign cultures, and a notion that one's own is not only different, but 'better'. Ethnocentric comments are often heard emanating from disdainful but narrow-minded tourists.

ethnography A detailed description of the culture of a particular society, based on fieldwork by ethnographers or anthropologists, using the method of participant observation. In Europe, the subject is often referred to as **ethnology**.

ethnography of communication The study of the correlations between language and ethnic types and behaviour. It includes a wide range of cultural activities, such as speech-making, conventions of greeting and leave-taking, religious rituals, and marriage ceremonies. More generally, it includes the study of the social variables which lead to culturally-based misunderstandings between the participants in a discourse.

ethnohistory A historical discipline which emerged from anthropology, principally concerned with the reconstruction of the histories of non-literate peoples using oral techniques. It has enjoyed some remarkable successes, in that the past of peoples formerly thought not to have a history in the conventional sense have offered insights for the history of the human race as a whole. The term is now unfashionable, implying a distinction no longer accepted by many historians.

ethnolinguistics The study of the relationship between language and culture. It is concerned with all aspects of language, including its structure and usage, which have any connection with culture and society.

ethnomethodology The sociological theory developed out of the work of the US sociologist Harold Garfinkel (1917–) and others in the 1960s. It studies the methods people use to accomplish successful social interaction, and is derived from earlier phenomenological and symbolic interactionist theories.

ethnomusicology The scientific study of folk and national music, especially that of non-Western countries, in its anthropological, cultural, and social contexts. Studies of some remote or exotic musical cultures were made in the 18th–19th-c, but because ethnomusicology deals with oral traditions, it was not until sound recording became easily available that the discipline could establish itself widely and on a scientific basis.

ethnoscience A branch of social/cultural anthropology which investigates folk beliefs or ideologies that correspond to such fields of Western science as medicine, astronomy, and zoology.

ethology [eetholojee] The study of animal behaviour from the viewpoint of zoology and ecology. It considers the fine details of individual species behaviour in relation to properties of the natural environment to which the species has adapted (its *ecological niche*). The data are derived from direct observation and

Ethiopia

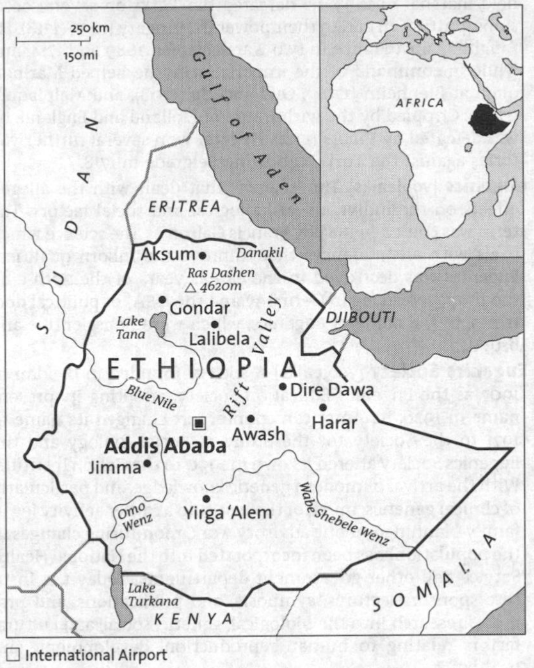

[eethiohpia], official name **Federal Democratic Republic of Ethiopia**, formerly **Abyssinia**, Amharic **Hebretesebawit Ityopia**

Local name Ityopiya

Timezone GMT +3

Area 1 251 282 km²/483 123 sq mi

Population total (2002e) 67 673 000

Status Republic

Capital Addis Ababa

Language Amharic (official)

Ethnic groups Oromo (40%), Amhara and Tigray (32%)

Religions Muslim (45%), Ethiopian Orthodox (37%), traditional beliefs (11%)

Physical features Located in NE Africa; dominated by mountainous C plateau, mean elevation 1800–2400 m/ 6–8000 ft; split diagonally by the Great Rift Valley; highest point, Ras Dashan Mt, 4620 m/15 157 ft; crossed E–W by Blue Nile; Danakil Depression (NE) dips to 116 m/381 ft below sea level.

Climate Tropical climate, moderated by higher altitudes; distinct wet season (Apr–Sep); hot, semi-arid NE and SE lowlands receive less than 500 mm/20 in of rainfall annually; severe droughts in 1980s caused widespread famine, deaths, and resettlement; serious famine in 2003.

Currency 1 Ethiopian Birr (Br) = 100 cents

Economy One of the world's poorest countries; over 80% of population employed in agriculture, especially subsistence farming; production severely affected by drought; distribution of foreign aid hindered by internal civil war and poor local organization.

GDP (2002e) $48·53 bn, per capita $700

Human Development Index (2002) 0·327

History Oldest independent country in sub-Saharan Africa; first Christian country in Africa; Italian presence in north from 1885; defeat of Italians at Adowa (1896), but northern region (Eritrea) ceded to them in peace treaty; independence of Abyssinia (former name of Ethiopia) recognized by League of Nations, 1923; Haile Selassie became Emperor in 1930, and began programme of modernization and reform; Italian invasion, 1935; annexation as Italian East Africa, 1936–41; Italians forced from Ethiopia by the Allies, and Haile Selassie returned to power in 1941; military coup, 1974; ongoing conflict with Somalia over Ogaden region; internal conflict with regional separatist Eritrean and Tigrean forces; transfer of power to People's Democratic Republic, 1987; government overthrown by separatist forces, 1991; Council of Representatives formed; multi-party elections, 1994; new constitution, 1994, recognizing a federal government of nine states, and providing for regional autonomy (allowing the right of secession); new Council of People's Representatives formed, 1995; escalating conflict with Eritrea over disputed border territory, 1999–2000; Permanent Court of Arbitration at The Hague issued a border ruling, 2002.

Monarch
1889–1911 Menelik II
1911–16 Lej Iyasu (Joshua)
1916–28 Zawditu
1928–74 Haile Selassie (Emperor from 1930)

Provisional Military Administrative Council Chairman
1974–7 Teferi Benti
1977–87 Mengistu Haile Mariam
People's Democratic Republic

Head of State
1987–91 Mengistu Haile Mariam
1991–5 Meles Zenawi
1995–2001 Negaso Gidada
2001– Woldegiorgis Girma

Head of Government
1991–5 Tamirat Layne
1995– Meles Zenawi

monitoring (eg by radio-tracking) of animals under natural or quasi-natural conditions. It assumes that most aspects of feeding, prey–predator interaction, and reproductive, competitive, and social behaviour are explicable in terms of (1) the past evolutionary selection pressures influencing the species' genetic endowment, and (2) the physiological or environmental conditions typically present during the natural development of species members.

ethyl [eethiyl, ethil] C_2H_5–. A functional group derived from ethane. Adding it to a name usually indicates its substitution for hydrogen in that compound.

ethyl alcohol *ethanol*

ethylene [ethileen] CH_2=CH_2, IUPAC **ethene**, boiling point −104°C. A colourless gas, the first member of the alkene series. It is a very important industrial chemical, which polymerizes to **polyethylene**. Small traces hasten the ripening of fruit.

ethyne [eethiyn] *acetylene*

Etna, Mount [etna], in Sicily **Mongibello** 37°45N 15°00E. Isolated volcanic mountain in Catania province, E Sicily, Italy, 29 km/18 mi NW of Catania; height 3390 m/11 122 ft; Europe's largest active volcano; first recorded eruption 700 BC; recent major eruptions, 1949, 1971, 1986, 1992, 2001; over 200 subsidiary cones, notably Monti Rossi (948 m/3110 ft); fertile lower slopes, with citrus, olives, vines; forest and macchia higher up, and a desert zone of lava and ashes; snow-covered nine months of the year; solar power station *Eurhelios* on S slope, with average annual sunshine 3000 hours.

Eton *Windsor* (UK)

Etruria [etrooria] The heartland of the Etruscan people, roughly corresponding to modern Tuscany. In antiquity, it was defined as the area between the Arno, Tiber, Apennines, and Tyrrhenian Sea.

Etruscan art The art which flourished 7th–2nd-c BC in what is now Tuscany, containing a mixture of native Italian, Greek, and oriental elements. It can be seen in many lively and colourful wall-paintings in tombs, sculptured sarcophagi, pottery, and decorative metalwork.

Etruscans [etr**uh**sknz] A people of obscure origin who sprang to prominence in WC Italy in the 8th-c BC. At the height of their power their influence extended from the Po valley to Campania, taking in Rome itself. Although they succumbed to the Romans politically in the 3rd-c BC, culturally their influence remained strong. In religion, civil engineering, and urban planning the Romans owed much to them. Their lavishly equipped tombs show that they were particularly skilled in metal work (they had iron in 1000 BC), and heavily engaged in trade with the Greek world.

Etty, William (1787–1849) Painter, born in York, N Yorkshire, UK. He studied at the Royal Academy Schools, then with Lawrence, and in 1822–3 went to Italy, where he was deeply influenced by the Venetian masters. He depicted Classical and historical subjects, and became renowned for his nudes.

etymology The study of the origins of the form and meaning of words and their history; a branch of historical linguistics. The 'parent' of a later word form is known as its *etymon*. Words can be mistakenly analysed in relation to some similarity of form or meaning with other words, to give a **folk etymology**, as when asparagus is referred to as 'sparrow-grass'. The **etymological fallacy** maintains that the 'real' meaning of a word is an earlier or 'original' one, as when *villain* is said to mean 'farm labourer', because it had this meaning several hundred years ago.

Euboea [yoob**ee**a], Gr **Évvoia**, Ital **Negropon** pop (2000e) 218 000; area 3655 sq km/1411 sq mi. Second largest Greek island, in the Aegean Sea, separated from the mainland by a narrow channel; length 144 km/89 mi; rises to 1744 m/5722 ft; capital, Chalcis; chief towns Istiaia, Kimi, and Karistos; olives, grapes, cereals, sheep, goats; several tourist resorts on coast.

eucalyptus *gum tree*

eucaryote or **eukaryote** [yookar**ioh**t] An organism in which cells have an organized nucleus, surrounded by a nuclear envelope, with paired chromosomes containing DNA that are recognizable during mitosis and meiosis. It includes all animals, plants, fungi, and many micro-organisms.

Eucharist (Gr *eucharistia*, 'thanksgiving') For most Christian denominations, a sacrament and the central act of worship, sometimes called the **Mass** (Roman Catholic), **Holy Communion**, or **Lord's Supper** (Protestant). It is based on the example of Jesus at the Last Supper, when he identified the bread which he broke and the wine which he poured with his body and blood (*1 Cor* 11.23–5; *Matt* 26.26–8; *Mark* 14.22–4; *Luke* 22.17–20), and generally consists of the consecration of bread and wine by the priest or minister and distribution among the worshippers (*communion*). Theological interpretations vary from the literal transformation of the elements into the body and blood of Christ, re-enacting his sacrifice on the Cross, through different interpretations such as transubstantiation and consubstantiation, to symbolism representing the real presence of Christ and a simple memorial meal.

euchromatin [yookr**oh**matin] *heterochromatin*

Euclid [y**oo**klid], Gr **Eucleides** (4th–3rd-c BC) Greek mathematician who taught in Alexandria c.300 BC, and who was probably the founder of its mathematical school. His chief extant work is the 13-volume *Elements*, which became the most widely known mathematical book of Classical antiquity, and is still much used in geometry. The approach which obeys his axioms became known as *Euclidean geometry*.

Eudoxos of Cnidus [yood**o**ksus, n**iy**duhs] (c.408 BC–c.353 BC) Greek geometer and astronomer, born in Cnidus, Asia Minor. In geometry he established principles that laid the foundation for Euclid, then applied the subject to the study of the Moon and planets. He introduced an ingenious system of 27 nested spheres in an attempt to explain planetary motion.

Eugene of Savoy, Prince, in full **François Eugène de Savoie Carignan** (1663–1736) Austrian general, born in Paris, France. He was refused a commission by Louis XIV of France, and entered the service of the Emperor Leopold against the Turks. Made field marshal in 1693, he defeated the Turks on several occasions, putting an end to their power in Hungary (1699–1718). He fought against France in two wars between 1689 and 1714, and while in command of the imperial army he helped Marlborough at Blenheim (1704), Oudenaarde (1708), and Malplaquet (1709). Crippled by the withdrawal of Holland and England, he was defeated by Villars (1712). He later won several further victories against the Turks, capturing Belgrade in 1718.

eugenics [yooj**e**niks] The 'science' that dealt with the alleged effects on the individual of biological and social factors. The term was coined in 1883 by Francis Galton as 'the science which deals with all influences that improve the inborn qualities'. Eugenics was destroyed in the earlier years of the 20th-c by the propagation (eg in Germany and the USA) of political doctrines, in the name of eugenics, which were nonscientific and brutal.

Eugenics Society [yooj**e**niks] A society founded in London in 1907 as the Eugenics Education Society, adopting its present name in 1926. Its American counterpart changed its name in 1971 to the Society for the Study of Social Biology and the Eugenics Society altered its own in 1990 to the Galton Institute. With the arrival of modern genetic knowledge, and particularly of clinical genetics, much of the Institute's earlier activity (eg in family planning, genetic advisory work, monitoring changes in the population) has been incorporated into the National Health Service and other government departments. Today the Institute sponsors lectures, symposia, and publications, and promotes research into the biological, genetic, social, and cultural factors relating to human reproduction, development, and health.

Eugénie, Empress *Napoleon III*

Euglena [yoogl**ee**na] A genus of freshwater, single-celled micro-organisms with a whip-like flagellum at their front end used for swimming; usually contains chlorophyll in chloroplasts, and classified as a green alga (class: Chlorophyceae); sometimes lacks chlorophyll, and classified as a protozoan flagellate (phylum: Mastigophora); feeds by ingestion of organic material.

eukaryote *eucaryote*

Eulenspiegel, Till [**oy**lenshpeegl] A legendary 14th-c peasant prankster from Brunswick, NC Germany. Through his practical jokes, which often consisted of taking figuratively-expressed commands literally, he revenged himself on townspeople and those in authority. He was celebrated in popular texts from the 15th-c onwards all over Europe, and in modern times is the subject of a tone poem by Richard Strauss (1894).

Euler, Leonhard [**oy**ler] (1707–83) Mathematician, born in Basel, N Switzerland. He studied mathematics there under Jean Bernoulli, and became professor of physics (1731) and then of mathematics (1733) at the St Petersburg Academy of Sciences. In 1738 he lost the sight of one eye. In 1741 he moved to Berlin as director of mathematics and physics in the Berlin Academy, but returned to St Petersburg in 1766, soon afterwards losing the sight of his other eye. He was a giant figure in 18th-c mathematics, publishing over 800 different books and papers, on every aspect of pure and applied mathematics, physics and astronomy. His *Introductio in analysin infinitorum* (1748) and later treatises on differential and integral calculus and algebra remained standard textbooks for a century and his notations, such as e and π have been used ever since. For the princess of Anhalt-Dessau he wrote *Lettres à une princesse d'Allemagne* (1768–72), giving a clear non-technical outline of the main physical theories of the time. He had a prodigious memory, which enabled him to continue mathematical work and to compute complex calculations in his head when he was totally blind. He is without equal in the use of algorithms to solve problems. Several important notions in mathematics are named after him. **Euler's constant** (usually denoted by γ) is the limit, as $n \rightarrow \infty$, of $1 + \frac{1}{2} + \frac{1}{3} + \frac{1}{4} ... 1/n - \log_e n$, approximately 0·577.

Euler's function (denoted by $\phi(n)$) refers to the number of integers in the set 1,2,3,...$n-1$ which are prime to n; thus $\phi(9) = 6$, since 6 of the integers 1,2,3,...8 are prime to 9. **Euler's formula for polyhedra** states that if a polyhedron has v vertices, f faces, and e edges, $v + f - e = 2$ for all polyhedra; thus a cube has 8 vertices, 12 edges, and 6 faces, and $8 + 6 - 12 = 2$. In any triangle, the centre O of the circumcircle, the orthocentre H, and the centroid G lie on a straight line, called the **Euler Line**, and $OG : GH = 1 : 2$.

Euler, Ulf (Svante) von [oyler] (1905–83) Physiologist, born in Stockholm, Sweden. He studied at the Karolinska Institute in Stockholm, and spent his whole career there (1930–71). He found the first prostaglandin in 1935, and in 1970 shared the Nobel Prize for Physiology or Medicine for his isolation and identification of noradrenaline (norepinephrine), the neurotransmitter for the sympathetic nervous system. He was a member of the Nobel Committee for Physiology or Medicine from 1953, and president of the Nobel Foundation (1965–75).

Euler–Lagrange equations [oyler lagrãzh] A set of equations relating the velocity, time, and space dependence of a lagrangian; also known as **Lagrange's equations**; named after Leonhard Euler and Joseph-Louis Lagrange. Given the lagrangian for some mechanical system, then the Euler–Lagrange equations give the equations of motion for that system. They are central to advanced mechanics.

Eumenides [yoomenideez] A euphemistic name given to the Erinyes after being domesticated at Athens in Aeschylus's play of the same name. The name means 'the kindly ones'.

Eumycota [yoomiysuhta] *Ascomycetes; Basidiomycetes; fungus*

Eupen [uhpen] 50°38N 6°02E, pop (2000e) 17 500. Town in E Liège province, E Belgium; principal town in German-speaking Belgium; popular health resort (Kneipp water-cure) and holiday centre; largest artificial lake in Belgium; railway; textiles, artificial fibres, tourism, cables and wires; St Nicholas Church (1727); carnival (Nov).

euphonium A musical instrument of the tuba family, much used in brass bands and occasionally in orchestral music.

euphorbia *spurge*

euphotic zone *epipelagic environments*

Euphrates, River [yoofrayteez], Arabic **Al-Furat**, Turkish **Firat** Longest river in W Asia; length 2735 km/1700 mi; formed in EC Turkey by the confluence of the Kara (W Euphrates) and Murat; flows generally S to the Syrian border, then SE into Iraq; unites with the Tigris NW of Basra to form the Shatt al-Arab, which flows for 192 km/119 mi to enter the Persian Gulf; upper course flows swiftly through deep canyons; used extensively for irrigation in Syria; canals link with R Tigris; remains of several ancient cities (eg Babylon, Erech, Larsa, Borsippa) along present or former banks.

EURATOM [yooratm] Acronym for **European Atomic Energy Community**, one of the bodies set up during the general movement towards Europeanization in the 1950s. It was originally established as an independent body by the Treaty of Rome (1957), but was brought into the EEC with the European Iron and Steel Community in 1962. Its objectives are the promotion of peaceful uses of atomic energy, particularly nuclear power for electricity. A single European market for nuclear materials has operated since 1959.

Eureka Stockade [yureeka] In Australian history, an armed clash between goldminers and a combined police and military force at the Eureka Stockade, Ballarat, Victoria, (1854), which cost the lives of 30 miners and 5 soldiers, with many others wounded. The miners had objected to the expensive mining licence imposed by the government. Public opinion swung behind the miners, reforms to the goldfields were carried out, and the government was forced to back down.

eurhythmics [yurithmiks] A system of musical training devised by Jaques-Dalcroze, designed to develop a quick response to changing rhythms by fitting bodily movements to pieces of music.

Euripides [yuripideez] (c.480–406 BC) Greek tragic playwright, born in Athens, Greece. He abandoned painting for literature, writing about 80 dramas, of which 19 survive, such as *Alcestis* (438 BC), *Medea* (431 BC), *Orestes* (408 BC), and *Electra* (417 BC). *The Bacchae* (c.405 BC) and *Iphigenia in Aulis* (c.414–412 BC) were put on the Athenian stage only after the author's death, when his work became very popular. He died at the court of Archelaus, King of Macedonia.

Euro [yooroh], symbol <**E**> The common currency unit used in 12 countries of the European Union (from 1 Jan 1999 in Belgium, Germany, Spain, France, Ireland, Italy, Luxembourg, Netherlands, Austria, Portugal, Finland, and from 1 Jan 2001 in Greece), and also from 1999 in Andorra, Monaco, San Marino, and the Vatican. Euro notes and coins entered general circulation on 1 Jan 2002, at which point each country had a period of time to phase out its old currency, replacing it with Euro currency to be used throughout the Euro area ('Eurozone'). Notes are in units of 5, 10, 20, 50, 100, 200, and 500. In the business world, all payment and accounting systems began to use the Euro on 1 January 1999, each national currency unit being irrevocably fixed in relation to it; for example, the exchange rate with the Deutschmark was set at 1·95583, and in the UK 1 Euro was worth approximately 70p. The 2002 launch was celebrated with ceremonies and special events throughout the Eurozone. Thanks to elaborate forward planning, the changeover generally proceeded without difficulty, though problems of availability of the new currency affected a few areas for a while (notably, in Italy).

Eurocommunism An attempt by W European communist parties to fashion a programme and organization more appropriate to liberal democracies and market economies. The Italian communist party was at the forefront, and achieved the most in reform. Such refashioning of Marxism–Leninism has not led to a resurgence of communism, however, and did not receive support from the Soviet communist party. The term has lost most of its currency following the collapse of the East European Communist systems.

Eurocurrency *Euromoney*

Eurodollar US dollars held in banks in Europe. Considerable sums are involved, resulting from such major concerns as the oil industry, where trade is conducted in dollars. They may be borrowed by companies, as Eurodollar loans, and are particularly useful when international trade is planned.

Eurofighter The name given to the standardized air-to-air and ground-attack aircraft with which it is planned to equip several European air forces. A major multi-national collaborative development programme involved Germany, Italy, Spain, and the UK. Revised planning and production schedules delayed the plane's availability until 2003. It was named *Eurofighter Typhoon* in 1998. The four partner nations had (in 2003) ordered 620 of the aircraft, and several other orders were pending.

Euromoney or **Eurocurrency** Convertible currencies such as pounds sterling, French and Swiss francs, Deutschmarks, and US dollars held in banks outside the country of origin. They can be borrowed by commercial undertakings for trade.

Europa (astronomy) [yurohpa] The second natural satellite of Jupiter, discovered by Galileo in 1610 and named by the German astronomer Simon Marius (1573–1624) shortly thereafter; distance from the planet 671 000 km/417 000 mi; diameter 3140 km/1950 mi; orbital period 3·551 days. It has a crust of frozen water possibly no more than 150 km/90 mi thick, crisscrossed by dark curvilinear cracks (typically 20–40 km/15–25 mi wide and thousands of km long), which may be due to the tidal effects of Jupiter's gravity. There may be liquid water under the surface ice. Europa was closely observed in 1979 by the US Voyager 1 and 2 spacecraft.

Europa (mythology) [yurohpa] or **Europe** [yoorohpee] In Greek mythology, the daughter of Agenor, king of Tyre, who was abducted by Zeus in the shape of a bull; he then swam with her on his back to Crete. Her children were Minos and Rhadamanthus.

Europa Nostra [yurohpa nostra] (Lat 'our Europe') An international federation established in 1963 for the preservation of historic sites, buildings, and monuments. It represents more than 200 organizations from 20 countries.

Europe Second smallest continent, forming an extensive peninsula of the Eurasian land-mass, occupying c.7% of the Earth's surface; bounded N and NE by the Arctic Ocean, NW and W by the Atlantic Ocean, S by the Mediterranean Sea, and E by Asia beyond the Ural Mts; supports over 25% of the world's population; major rivers include the Danube, Rhine, Rhône, Loire, and Tagus; major mountain systems include the Alps, rising to 4807 m/15 771 ft at Mont Blanc, and the Pyrenees, rising to 3404 m/11 168 ft at Pico de Aneto. (*see pp.535–6*)

European Atomic Energy Community *EURATOM*

European Bank for Reconstruction and Development A bank founded in 1990 to assist the economic reconstruction of C and E Europe. It has 59 members and has its headquarters in London.

European Central Bank (ECB) A bank established in Frankfurt (am Main) on 1 June 1998 to oversee the introduction and development of the Euro, and to set interest rates (3 per cent, at the outset). The Bank reports to the European Parliament on a yearly basis. The ECB and the national central banks together form the **European System of Central Banks** (ESCB), which govern the conduct of the single monetary policy, and whose primary objective is to maintain price stability.

European Coal and Steel Community (ECSC) The first European economic institution, set up in 1952 under the terms of the Treaty of Paris (1951). It worked to remove customs duties and quota restrictions in coal, iron ore, and scrap, and aimed to ensure that competition in these commodities was fair. Its founding members were France, West Germany, Italy, Belgium, The Netherlands, and Luxembourg. It subsequently came to include Denmark, Ireland, and the UK (1973), Greece (1981), and Portugal and Spain (1986). The former East Germany was admitted as part of reunified Germany in 1990. Austria, Finland, Norway, and Sweden became members in 1995. Its headquarters are in Brussels, Belgluim.

European Commission The administrative and executive bureaucracy of the European Union (EU), carrying out both political and administrative tasks. Its functions are to uphold the European ideal, propose new policy initiatives, and ensure that existing policies are implemented. In a narrow sense it comprises 20 commissioners directly nominated by the member states; the UK, France, Germany, Italy, and Spain each nominate two commissioners, the rest one each. They serve a 5-year term, are responsible for a specific area of work, and are supported by a bureaucracy employing c.15 000 people. The Commission decides by majority vote, and is collectively responsible to the European Parliament, which can remove it on a censure motion carried by a two-thirds majority. The President of the Commission is chosen by the EU heads of state and must be approved by the European Parliament. The Commission was originally intended, as a truly supranational institution, to be the main source of direction and decision-making within the EU, but in practice this role has fallen to the Council of Ministers. In 1999, following the publication of a report severely criticizing maladministration within the EU's bureaucracy, the entire Commission resigned and a new Commission was appointed under Romano Prodi. A strict code of conduct for commissioners was adopted.

European Community (EC), formerly **European Communities** The name generally used in 1967–93 to refer to the organization which then became the European Union. It was a community of Western European states initially created to achieve economic integration, but with the longer-term goal of political integration also in mind. It grew out of the European Coal and Steel Community which was established in 1952 under the Treaty of Paris by Belgium, France, Italy, Luxembourg, The Netherlands, and West Germany. The treaty created common institutions for regulating these industries under a common framework of law, thereby producing the first breach in the principle of national sovereignty. In 1957, under the two Treaties of Rome, the same six states established the European Economic Community (essentially a customs union), and also the European Atomic Energy Community (EURATOM). In 1967 the executive bodies of the three Communities were merged to form the 'European Community'. A further nine members later joined the Community: Denmark, Ireland, and the UK (1973), Greece (1981), Portugal and Spain (1986), and Austria, Finland, and Sweden (1995). Several other countries are seeking to become members. In 1993, the area covered by the EC became a single market, which was extended to incorporate the seven countries of the European Free Trade Association in 1994 (as the European Economic Area). In 1993, the EC member states concluded the process of ratifying the Maastricht Treaty on European Union. This treaty was designed to strengthen the degree of co-operation within the Community and to enhance political integration (at this point the term 'European Community' was formally adopted for the activities of the three former Communities). The Community (now the European Union) is governed by a series of institutions: the European Council, the Council of Ministers, the European Commission, the European Parliament, the European Court of Justice, and the Court of Auditors.

European Convention on Human Rights A convention which sets out the main rights and fundamental freedoms to be protected, contained in the Universal Declaration of Human Rights: the right to life, to a fair trial, and to freedom of thought, conscience, religion, and education. The Convention was originally formulated by the Council of Europe in 1950, and came into force in 1953. It set up the European Commission on Human Rights, and is applied by the European Court of Human Rights in Strasbourg. The Commission may only investigate a complaint if all possible remedies in the national courts have been tried. It attempts to reach a friendly settlement of any breach of the Convention, but failing this the breach may be referred to the European Court of Human Rights, whose judgments have acquired the force of law in most W European countries. Although the Court's judgments cannot be directly enforced, it has never been openly defied by a government, and its decisions have prompted changes in domestic laws, such as telephone tapping in the UK and France.

European Council The summit-level body which brings together (normally two or three times a year) the heads of state and/or government of the member states of the European Union together with the president of the European Commission (who is not a member). Meeting originally on an informal basis, it was constituted formally in 1974, and takes the main decisions in the European Union, for instance on such issues as institutional reform and the admission of new members. The European Council became an official part of the European Community's structure in 1987.

European court dance A dance tradition based on 16th-c and 17th-c aristocratic dances such as the pavane, galliard, and courante performed at masques. Later the minuet, gigue, gavotte, bourrée, sarabande, and hornpipe were popular in the ballrooms of the middle classes. These dance forms were the forerunners of the quadrille and lancers performed in most ballrooms across Europe, its colonies, and the USA. The 19th-c saw the introduction of the waltz and the polka.

European Court of Human Rights (ECHR) A judicial court established by the European Convention on Human Rights, based in Strasbourg, France. It was founded in 1950 to safeguard the rights of free expression and to protect against discrimination. In countries that recognize the Convention within their own legal systems, verdicts in domestic courts concerning discrimination are not binding, and cases can be referred to the ECHR by reference to the Convention. Changes in UK legislation have occurred as a result of ECHR rulings, such as the

Europe

Denmark Strait
Arctic Circle
ICELAND
Barents Sea
White Sea
Nov
Zem
Norwegian Sea
Faeroe Islands (to Denmark)
ATLANTIC OCEAN
NORWAY
SWEDEN
FINLAND
Gulf of Bothnia
Lake Onega
Lake Ladoga
Shetland Islands
Orkney Islands
Outer Hebrides
Aland
Vänern
Vättern
SCOTLAND
NORTHERN IRELAND
REPUBLIC OF IRELAND
Isle of Man (to UK)
UNITED KINGDOM
North Sea
DENMARK
Gotland
Baltic Sea
ESTONIA
LATVIA
Western Dvina
LITHUANIA
RUSS. FED. (Kaliningrad)
WALES
ENGLAND
Thames
NETH.
Elbe
Oder
Vistula
BELARUS
Channel Islands (to UK)
English Channel
BELGIUM
GERMANY
POLAND
LUXEMBOURG
Rhine
Seine
Loire
CZECH REPUBLIC
UKRAINE
Bay of Biscay
FRANCE
Danube
SLOVAKIA
Dniester
MOLDOVA
Dnieper
Sea of Azov
SWITZERLAND
Alps
AUSTRIA
LIECHTENSTEIN
HUNGARY
SLOVENIA
Rhône
Po
CROATIA
ROMANIA
PORTUGAL
Duero
Ebro
Pyrenees
Tagus
ANDORRA
MONACO
SAN MARINO
BOS. & HERZ.
Adriatic Sea
SPAIN
Corsica
SERBIA & MONTENEGRO
BULGARIA
Black
VATICAN CITY
ITALY
Mallorca
Menorca
Elvissa
Balearic Islands
Sardinia
MACEDONIA
Gibraltar (to UK)
Ceuta (to Spain)
Melilla (to Spain)
Tyrrhenian Sea
ALBANIA
Turkey
Aegean Sea
GREECE
Mediterranean Sea
Sicily
Ionian Sea
MALTA
Crete

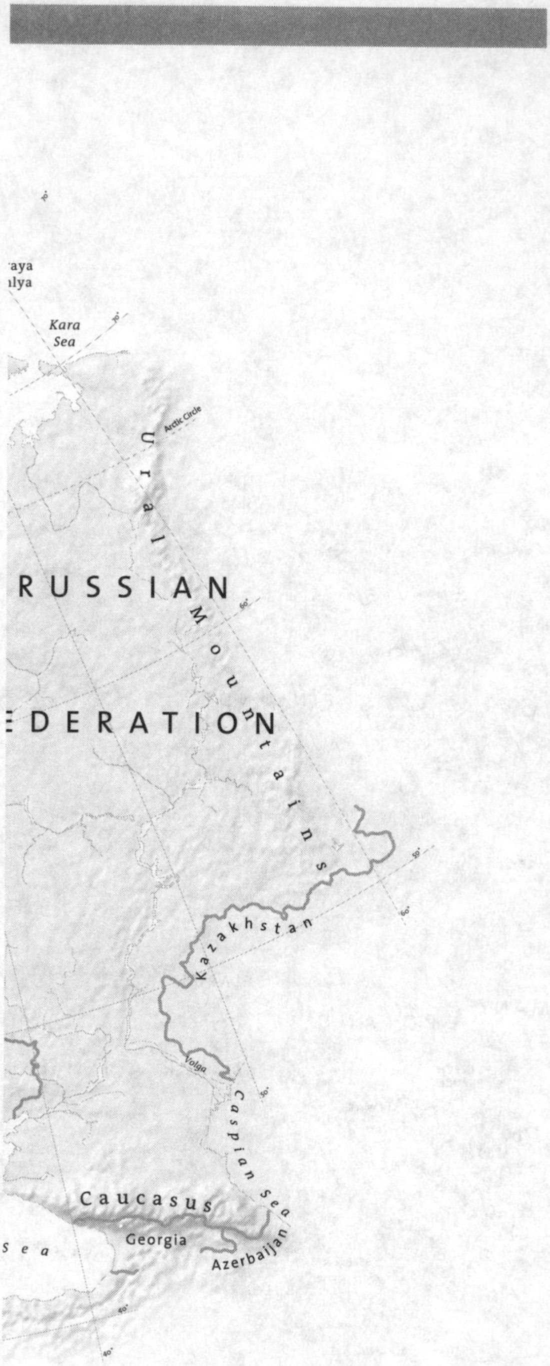

Contempt of Court Act 1981, the Interception of Communications Act 1985, and the Mental Health (Amendment) Act 1982. The Convention was incorporated into English law in October 2000 by the Human Rights Act (1998). This may have significant repercussions on, for example, UK laws on employment and civil rights laws.

European Court of Justice *Court of Justice of the European Communities*

European Currency Unit (ECU) *European Monetary System*

European Defence Community A supranational community which was to ensure the security of its members against aggression, and produce a more coherent grouping than the North Atlantic Treaty Organization. A treaty was signed in May 1952 by the six members of the European Coal and Steel Community (other W European countries could join) but was never ratified by the French parliament, and the project was abandoned.

European Economic Area (EEA) A trading bloc linking the European Union and the European Free Trade Association (with the exception of Switzerland and Liechtenstein), introduced as one of the economic agreements of the Maastricht Treaty in January 1994. Its 372 million members make it the world's biggest free-trade area.

European Economic Community (EEC) A grouping of European states established in 1958 after the Treaties of Rome (1957), referred to as the **Common Market**. Essentially a customs union with a common external tariff and a common market with the removal of internal trade barriers, its founder members were France, West Germany, Italy, Belgium, Luxembourg and the Netherlands. Denmark, Ireland and the UK joined in 1973. A common agricultural policy was established in 1962, consisting of a system of guaranteed prices that would offer protection against imports from markets outside the EEC. (From 1979 onwards these subsidies were gradually eliminated and replaced by fixed-level agricultural prices.) Common policies were introduced for fisheries, regional development, industrial intervention, and economic and social affairs. The four principle institutions of the EEC were the European Commission, the Council of Ministers, the Court of Justice, and the European Assembly (later to become the European Parliament). At the level of the European Commission, the EEC merged in 1967 with the European Atomic Energy Community (EURATOM) and the European Coal and Steel Community (ECSC), and was thereafter unofficially known as the European Community (EC), though this title was not adopted until 1993.

European Environment Agency *Environment Agency*

European Free Trade Association (EFTA) An association originally of seven W European states who were not members of the European Economic Community (EEC), intended as a counter to the EEC; it was established in 1959 under the Stockholm Convention. The members (Austria, Denmark, Norway, Portugal, Sweden, Switzerland, and the UK) agreed to eliminate over a period of time trade restrictions between them, without having to bring into line individual tariffs and trade policies with other countries. Agriculture was excluded from the agreement, although individual arrangements were permitted. Finland joined in 1985. Both the UK (1973) and Portugal (1986) left to join the EEC, but there was a free trade agreement between the remaining EFTA countries and the European Community, and considerable trade between the two groupings, and they united as the European Economic Area in 1994.

European Laboratory for Particle Physics (CERN) The principal European centre for experimental research in particle physics, located in Geneva. Supported by most European countries, CERN was founded in 1954 by the Conseil Européen pour la Recherche Nucléaire (from which the acronym is derived) for fundamental research into the structure of matter and the interactions governing it. CERN houses particle accelerators that are among the largest scientific instruments in the world. In these devices, elementary particles are accelerated to very high energies and then smashed together. CERN is home to such facilities as the SPS (super proton synchroton) and LEAR

(Low Energy Antiproton). The particle accelerator LEP (Large Electron-Positron Collider) is installed in an underground tunnel 27 km (17 mi) in circumference. DELPHI, one of the four LEP detectors, is a horizontal cylinder about 10 m (33 ft) in diameter, 10 m long, and weighing about 3000 tonnes. The LEP will also house the Large Hadron Collider (LHC), a proton–proton collider to be completed c.2005. Since its inception, visiting particle physicists and other scientists from over 70 nations, supported by around 3000 permanent staff, have undertaken wide-ranging research. The W and Z particles were discovered at CERN, and the Word Wide Web was invented there.

European Monetary Institute An institution established in Frankfurt in January 1994 within the framework of the Maastricht Treaty, as a precursor to a European central bank – the second stage towards economic and monetary union. Its aims were to strengthen central bank co-operation and monetary policy co-ordination, and to prepare for the establishment of the European System of Central Banks for the conduct of a single monetary policy and the creation of a single currency. The Institute was liquidated following the establishment of the European Central Bank in 1998.

European Monetary System (EMS) A financial system set up in 1979 by member states of the European Economic Community with the immediate aim of stabilizing exchange rates and the ultimate aim of achieving Economic and Monetary Union (EMU), with a single European currency. A **European Currency Unit (ECU)** was created, but only as a unit of account; later named the **Euro**. Central banks were to consult on exchange rates, and to assist each other in stabilizing them both bilaterally and through a European Monetary Cooperation Fund. Members could join an **Exchange Rate Mechanism (ERM)**, which limited fluctuations in the exchange rates between its members. The first stage of formal EMU was established in 1990, when the Committee of Governors of the Central Banks of the EEC member states was given additional responsibilities to engage in the required preparatory work. The second stage was the replacement of this body by the European Monetary Institute (1 Jan 1994), whose activities included the introduction of a new Exchange Rate Mechanism (ERM II), adopted in mid-1997. The third stage, the adoption of the Euro by those member states which satisfied the entry conditions laid down by the EU Council, began on 1 January 1999. A new European Central Bank was set up (1 Jun 1998) to control monetary policy in the third stage.

European Parliament The representative assembly of the European Union (EU). Created in 1952 as the Common Assembly, its title as the European Parliament was formalized by the 1987 Single European Act. Despite its name, it has few legislative powers, but it does have the right to be consulted by the Council of Ministers, to dismiss the Commission (a right so far never used, but effective as a threat), and to reject or amend the European Union's budget (exercised increasingly frequently). The more forceful role played by the Parliament in recent years reflects the fact that it has been directly and democratically elected since 1979. European-wide elections for the 626 seats are held every five years. Seats are distributed among the EU members on their respective populations, and members do not sit in national blocs. Until the Maastricht Treaty (1991), its legislative powers were largely advisory. Among its new powers are the joint decision-making on accession of new EU member's treaties, and association agreements with non-EU countries, as well as the authority to investigate the maladministration of European law. The bulk of the Parliament's administration is located in Luxembourg; its plenary sessions are normally held in Strasbourg, and most of its committees meet in Brussels, where the European Union is based and the Councils meet.

European Recovery Program *Marshall Plan*

European Southern Observatory (ESO) An agency of eight member states founded in 1962 to operate a European astronomical observatory in the S hemisphere. It is a world-class observatory with a number of optical telescopes, including the 3·6 m aperture at La Silla, Chile (2430 m/7972 ft), and a share in a sub-millimetre telescope. Construction is under way on Cerro Paranal, Chile (2635 m/8645 ft) of an array of four 8·2 m aperture telescopes which can be combined to form an effective 16 m telescope (Very Large Telescope, or VLT). The first telescope came into operation in 1998, and the fourth was completed in 2000; they have been given names in a local indigenous language, Mapuche: Antu (Sun), Kueyen (Moon), Melipal (Southern Cross), and Yepun (Venus). The European headquarters is at Garching, Munich, Germany; this also houses the Space Telescope European Co-ordinating Facility.

European Space Agency (ESA) A consortium space agency of 13 European countries (Belgium, Denmark, Germany, France, Ireland, Italy, the Netherlands, Spain, Sweden, Switzerland, UK (founding nations) together with Austria and Norway, and associate member Finland) to promote space research, technology, and applications for exclusively peaceful purposes; Canada also participates in some programmes. It was created in 1975 as an amalgamation of two predecessors – the European Space Research Organization (ESRO) and the European Launcher Development Organization (ELDO). Its headquarters is in Paris, where programme plans originate. Projects are managed from the European Space Research and Technology Centre (ESTEC) in Noordwijk, The Netherlands, which is also the centre for space technology development. Orbital spacecraft operations are managed by the European Space Operations Centre (ESOC) in Darmstadt, Germany. Launches use the Ariane family of vehicles from a launch centre in Kourou, French Guiana.

European Steel and Coal Community *European Community*

European System of Central Banks *European Central Bank*

European Union (EU), formerly known as the **European Community (EC)** An organization of European nations committed to increasing economic integration and political, judicial and social co-operation among its member states. Its founder members of 1958 – Belgium, France, West Germany, Italy, Luxembourg, and The Netherlands – were joined by the UK, Denmark, and the Republic of Ireland (1973), Greece (1981), and Spain and Portugal (1986). East Germany was incorporated on German reunification in 1990, and Austria, Finland and Sweden joined in 1995. In 1993 the 12 European Community members, in accordance with the Maastricht Treaty on European Union (1991), agreed to extend their co-operation in matters of justice, home affairs, and a common foreign and security policy. The UK government was unwilling to agree to all the proposals adopted by the other countries (notably over the single European currency and a common social policy), and a compromise providing opt-out clauses for the UK was devised; of these, only the opt-out concerning the single currency remains. The Union has adopted the principle of subsidiarity or delegation of authority to competent or local institutions wherever possible. The designation *European Union* in place of *European Community* was formally introduced in late 1993. Negotiations have been continuing since 1998/9 towards a 2004 joining date for Cyprus, Czech Republic, Estonia, Hungary, Latvia, Lithuania, Malta, Poland, Slovakia, and Slovenia, and towards 2007 with Bulgaria and Romania, with Turkey a longer-term pospect. The EU's first military operation took place in March 2003, when it took over NATO's role in Macedonia.

Europort *Rotterdam*

Eurostar International high-speed passenger train service between London (Waterloo) and Continental Europe via the Channel Tunnel. Direct services in 1999 include Paris (and Disneyland), Brussels, Calais, and Lille, as well as Bourg St-Maurice and Moutier in the French Alps. Operated jointly by Eurostar (UK) Ltd, the French Railways (SNCF) and Belgium Railways (SNCB), it commenced operations in 1994. By 1999 there were 31 trains in the fleet, 392 m/1286 ft in length, each containing 766 passenger seats, and capable of speeds of 300 kph/186 mph. On 30 July 2003, a Eurostar train broke the UK rail speed record, reaching 335 kph/208 mph on the 70 km/

43·5nbsp;mi first section of a planned high-speed track from the Channel Tunnel to London's St Pancras Station.

Eurovision Song Contest An annual contest organized by television companies throughout Europe (and Israel) to choose a winning pop song from among those entered by the participating countries. The first was held at Lugano, Switzerland, in 1956; since then it has been customary for the winning country to host the following year's contest.

Eurozone Those 12 countries within the European Union that have adopted the € as their common currency. In 2002 Euro notes and coins entered general circulation in Belgium, Germany, Spain, France, Ireland, Italy, Luxembourg, Netherlands, Austria, Portugal, Finland, and Greece, with each country taking a short period of time to phase out its old currency.

Eurydice [yooridisee] In Greek mythology, a dryad, the wife of Orpheus. After her death, Orpheus went down to the Underworld and persuaded Hades to let her go by the power of his music. The condition was that she should follow him, and that he should not look at her until they reached the light. Not hearing her footsteps, he looked back, and she disappeared.

eurypterid [yooripterid] An extinct, aquatic water scorpion; large, up to 3 m/10 ft in length; resembling a scorpion with a stout body bearing fangs anteriorly and a long, slender tail; known from the Ordovician period to the end of the Palaeozoic era. (Phylum: Arthropoda. Class: Eurypterida.)

Eusebio [yoosaybioo], in full **Eusebio Ferreira da Silva**, nickname **the Black Pearl** (1942–) Footballer, born in Lourenço Marques, S Mozambique. He was largely responsible for Portugal's rise in international football in the 1960s. He made his international debut in 1961, and played for his country 77 times. At club level he played for Benfica, winning 15 Portuguese League and Cup-winner's medals. He appeared in four European Cup finals, winning just once, in 1962. He retired in 1978 after a brief spell playing in the USA, and was later appointed coach to Benfica.

Eusebius of Caesarea [yooseebius] (c.264–340) Historian of the early Church, probably born in Palestine. He became Bishop of Caesarea c.313, and in the Council of Nicaea held a moderate position between the views of Arius and Athanasius. His great work, the *Ecclesiastical History*, is a record of the chief events in the Christian Church until 324.

Euskadi Ta Askatasuma *Basques*

Eustachian tube [yustayshn] *auditory tube*

eustasy [yoostasee] Worldwide changes in sea-level caused by the advance or recession of the polar ice caps, which caused a gradual rise in the sea-level during the 20th-c. Eustatic changes are distinct from localized variations in sea-level due to Earth movements, such as are seen in the Aegean Sea.

Euston Road School A group of English painters working 1937–9 in London, including William Coldstream (1908–87), Victor Pasmore (1908–98), Graham Bell (1910–43), and Claude Rogers (1909–79). They rejected abstraction and surrealism, and practised a quiet naturalism concentrating on domestic subjects.

Euterpe [yooterpee] In Greek mythology, one of the Muses, usually associated with flute-playing.

euthanasia The painless ending of life, usually as an act of mercy to relieve chronic pain or suffering. It has been advocated by pressure groups such as Exit (UK) and the Hemlock Society (USA), and by some physicians as a dignified death for the elderly who have lost the will or desire to live. Since the 1980s, several cases of *doctor-assisted suicide* (the death of a terminally ill patient, through taking lethal drugs provided by a doctor), and associated notions such as *medicide* (*medically assisted suicide*), have been given publicity, and fuelled the medical ethical debate. During the 1990s, several US states made these practices illegal. In 1996 Australia's Northern Territory legalized euthanasia, but the law was repealed after nine months. The Netherlands made doctor-assisted death legal in 2002, followed by Belgium, the first countries to sanction the practice.

eutrophication The enrichment of lake waters through the discharge of run-off carrying excessive fertilizers from agricultural land, and human waste from settlements. The inflow of phosphate and nitrogen-rich waters can result in the loss of lake flora and fauna, as once-clear waters become turbid with microscopic algae. These are better able to live in the enriched conditions, and cause oxygen depletion for other flora and fauna.

Evangelical Alliance A religious movement, founded in 1846 – the formal expression of an international evangelical community embracing a variety of conservative evangelical churches and independent agencies. They are united by the common purpose of winning the world for Christ. In the USA it has been succeeded by the National Council of Churches of Christ in the United States of America.

evangelicalism Since the Reformation, a term which has been applied to the Protestant Churches because of their principles of justification through faith alone and the supreme authority accorded to scripture. Subsequently, it has been applied more narrowly to Protestant Churches emphasizing intense personal conversion ('born-again Christianity') and commitment in their experience of justification and biblical authority. The term is not restricted to Protestantism, and has been a feature of Christianity throughout its history.

Evangelical United Brethren Church A Christian denomination established in the USA in 1946 through the merger of the Church of the United Brethren in Christ and the Evangelical Church. Both Churches were similar in belief and practice, emphasizing the authority of scripture, justification, and regeneration. In 1968 it merged with the Methodist Church to form the United Methodist Church.

evangelist (Gr *evangel*, 'good news') One who preaches the gospel of Jesus Christ. The New Testament suggests that some Christians have special gifts of evangelizing. Although evangelizing is now understood to be the task of the whole Church, the term has been more recently applied to popular preachers on radio, television, and at missionary rallies.

Evans, Sir Arthur (John) (1851–1941) Archaeologist, born in Nash Mills, Hertfordshire, SE England, UK. He was curator of the Ashmolean Museum, Oxford (1884–1908), where he developed an interest in the ancient coins and seals of Crete. Between 1899 and 1935 he excavated the city of Knossos, discovering the remains of the civilization which in 1904 he named *Minoan* after Minos, the Cretan king of Greek legend. He was knighted in 1911.

Evans, Bill, popular name of **William Evans** (1929–80) Jazz pianist, born in Plainfield, New Jersey, USA. He studied music at Southeastern Louisiana College and at Mannes School of Music, New York City, playing when he could. Musicians admired his intricate, ruminative style, but he made no impression on fans until he joined Miles Davis's great sextet in 1958. He stayed only six months but played on some brilliant recordings, including the classic 'Kind of Blue' (1959). In 1960, he led a trio at the Village Vanguard, and found critical and popular success. For the rest of his career, he recorded prolifically, partly to support a heroin habit, but nevertheless with great acclaim, winning three Grammy Awards and numerous prizes. Among his best works are *At the Village Vanguard* (1961), *Know What I Mean* (1961), *Intermodulation* (1966), and *Alone Again* (1977). In the period covered by these records, he was a dominant stylist in jazz, and a major influence.

Evans, Chris (1966–) Disc-jockey and television presenter, born in Warrington, Cheshire, NWC England, UK. He left school at 16 and began presenting a night-time show on Piccadilly Radio in Manchester, later joining BBC's local London station, GLR. For television's Channel 4 he launched *The Big Breakfast* and hosted *Don't Forget Your Toothbrush* and *TFI Friday*. He presented breakfast shows for Radio 1 and later Virgin, having set up his own company, Ginger Productions, which he later sold to the Scottish Media Group (2000). In 1998 he was honoured with a Sony gold award for his contribution to the radio industry. He was dismissed by Virgin Radio in 2001 for breach of contract.

Evans, Dame Edith (Mary) (1888–1976) Actress, born in London, UK. She earned a great reputation for her versatility, with many notable appearances in the plays of Shakespeare and Shaw. Her most famous role was as Lady Bracknell in Wilde's *The Importance of Being Earnest*. During World War 2 she entertained the troops at home and abroad, and in 1946 was created a dame. In 1948, she made her first film appearance in *The Queen of Spades*, and she continued to be active on both stage and screen into her eighties.

Evans, Gareth (John) (1944–) Australian statesman, born in Melbourne, Victoria, SE Australia. He studied at the universities of Melbourne and Oxford, taught law at Melbourne University (1971–6), and was a commissioner for the Australian Law Reform Commission, before becoming Labor Party senator for Victoria in 1978. He was attorney general (1983–4), then served in a range of portfolios, including transport and communications, and became minister for foreign affairs and trade in 1988, and later deputy leader of the opposition and shadow treasurer (1996–8). He was one of the chief architects of the Cambodian peace plan which culminated with general elections in 1993.

Evans, Sir Geraint (Llewellyn) (1922–92) Baritone, born in Pontypridd, Rhondda Cynon Taff, S Wales, UK. He studied in London and on the European mainland, making his operatic debut at Covent Garden in 1948. He soon earned international fame, particularly in comic roles such as Mozart's Leporello, Verdi's Falstaff, and Wagner's Beckmesser. He was knighted in 1971, and retired from the operatic stage in 1984.

Evans, Gil, popular name of **Ian Ernest Gilmore Green** (1912–88) Jazz pianist, composer, and arranger, born in Toronto, Ontario, SE Canada. He was principal arranger for the Claude Thornhill Orchestra (1944–8), which led to a collaboration with trumpeter Miles Davis that lasted until 1960. He was one of the first modern jazz arrangers to use electronics and rock influences successfully in combination with the swing and bebop idioms.

Evans, Oliver (1755–1819) Inventor, born in Newport, Delaware, USA. He improved flour mills, introducing the first automated continuous production line (1784), and invented the first high-pressure steam engine (1790). His amphibious steam dredging machine (1804) is considered the first US steam land carriage.

Evans, Timothy John *Christie, John*

Evans, Walker (1903–75) Photographer, born in St Louis, Missouri, USA. In 1933 he started as an architectural photographer, but from 1935 began to record social deprivation in the Southern states for the US government Farm Security Administration, the two themes being combined in his *American Photographs* (1938). He was associate editor of *Fortune* (1945–65), and professor of graphic design at Yale (1965–74). His work with the writer James Agee to document the lives of the share-croppers of the Deep South, eventually published as *Let Us Now Praise Famous Men* (1941), is considered to be one of the best writer–photographer collaborations.

evaporation The passing from a liquid phase to a gas phase; in particular, the process by which water is lost from the Earth's surface to the atmosphere as water vapour. It is an important part of the exchange of energy within the Earth–atmosphere system which produces atmospheric motions, and therefore climate (the *global energy cascade*). Rates of evaporation depend on such factors as solar radiation, the temperature difference between the evaporating surface and the overlying air, humidity, and wind.

evaporite deposits Mineral deposits formed by the precipitation of dissolved salts (most commonly rock salt, NaCl and gypsum, $CaSO_4 \cdot 2H_2O$) from water.

evapotranspiration The transfer of water vapour to the atmosphere from vegetation and soil surfaces through evaporation and transpiration. Rates of evapotranspiration are determined by factors such as wind velocity, water availability, vapour pressure gradient, and energy availability. *Actual* evapotranspiration is the observed rate, and differs from *potential* evapotranspiration, which is what would occur if there were no limiting factors such as supply of moisture.

Evatt, Elizabeth (Andreas) (1933–) Reformist lawyer, born in Sydney, New South Wales, SE Australia. She studied at Sydney and Harvard universities, and was the youngest law student ever accepted to the Sydney University Law School, and the first woman to win the university law medal. She became deputy president of the Australian Conciliation and Arbitration Commission (1973–89), chaired the Royal Commission on Human Relationships (1974–7), was first Chief Judge of the Family Court of Australia (1976–88), and was president of the Law Reform Commission (1988–93). She was a member of the UN Committee on the Elimination of Discrimination Against Women (1984–92), and was elected to the UN Human Rights Committee (1993–2000).

Eve *Adam and Eve*

Eve, Trevor (1951–) Actor and producer, born in Birmingham, West Midlands, C England, UK. He studied at Kingston College of Art and the Royal Academy of Dramatic Art in London. In 1980 he became well known for his role as Eddie Shoestring in the television series *Shoestring*, and later TV appearances include *Jamaica Inn* (1985), *A Doll's House* (1991), *The Politician's Wife* (1995), *David Copperfield* (1999), and *Waking the Dead* (2001). He works regularly in the theatre, has appeared in feature films, and is also a television producer.

Evelyn, John [evelin, eevlin] (1620–1706) Diarist and writer, born in Wotton, Surrey, SE England, UK. He studied at Oxford and London, and travelled abroad during the Civil War. He was much at court after the Restoration, acted on public committees, and became one of the Commissioners of the Privy Seal (1685–7) and treasurer of Greenwich Hospital (1695–1703). With Robert Boyle, he was a founder-member of the Royal Society (1662). His main literary work is his *Diary*, a detailed sourcebook on the social, political, and religious life of 17th-c England.

even functions In mathematics, functions such that $f(x) = f(-x)$. The graph of an even function is symmetrical about the y-axis, eg $y = x^2$, $y = \cos x$. By contrast, an **odd function** has the property $f(-x) = -f(x)$, eg $y = x^3$, $y = \sin x$.

evening primrose The name given to several very similar species of erect, robust biennials, native to North America, but cultivated and naturalized in many other countries; leaves lance-shaped to oval; flowers large, several cm in diameter, broadly funnel-shaped with four narrow sepals and four overlapping yellow (sometimes red or white) petals, usually fragrant and opening at night. The oil from *Oenothera biennis* and *Oenothera lamarkiana* is claimed to be beneficial in several disorders, including multiple sclerosis, premenstrual tension, heart disease, and skin disorders. These claims have not yet been proven. (Genus: *Oenothera*, 80 species. Family: Onagraceae.)

Evenki [evengkee] *Altaic*

event horizon *black hole*

Everest, Mount [evuhrest], Nepali **Sagarmatha**, Chin **Qomolangma Feng** 27°59N 95°26W. Mountain peak in the Himalayas of C Asia, on the border between Nepal and the Tibet region of China; height (1999 calculation) 8850 m/29 035 ft; highest mountain in the world; named after Sir George Everest (1790–1866), surveyor-general of India; following attempts in 1921 and 1922, Mallory and Irvine, members of the 1924 British Expedition, climbed beyond 8534 m/27 998 ft but failed to return; summit first reached via the Southeast Ridge on 29 May 1953 by Sir Edmund Hillary and Sherpa Tenzing Norgay of Nepal in a British expedition under Col John Hunt; the summit was reached via the West Ridge by a US team in 1963, the Southwest face by a British team in 1975, and the North Wall by a Japanese team in 1980; claimed by China, in 1952 the Chinese banned the name Everest in favour of Qomolangma Feng ('sacred mother of waters').

everglade kite *snail kite*

Everglades S Florida, USA; swampy, subtropical region, length c.160 km/100 mi, width 80–120 km/50–75 mi, area c.12 950 sq km/5000 sq mi; covers most of the Florida peninsula S of L Okeechobee; consists of saw grass savannahs and water dotted by clumps of reeds; in an area of heavy rainfall only a few metres above sea-level; drainage and reclamation schemes have made a large amount of land productive, mostly in citrus fruits and sugar; Seminole Indians fled to the area in 1842, during the Seminole War; Everglades National Park (area 5668 sq km/2188 sq mi) in the S includes much of Florida Bay, with its many keys; a world heritage site.

evergreen plants Plants which retain their leaves throughout the year. They either grow in climates which have no adverse seasons or have leaves adapted to withstand cold and drought. The leaves are shed and replaced gradually, so that the plant always bears foliage.

Everly Brothers, The [eve(r)lee] American duo **Don Everly** (1937– , guitar, vocals), and **Phil Everly** (1939– , guitar, vocals). They had their first major hit with 'Bye Bye Love' (1957), and the style – close harmonies over acoustic guitars and a rock n' roll beat – became their trademark. Other hit records include 'Wake Up Little Susie' (1957) and 'Cathy's Clown' (1960). Their unique sound had a profound influence on The Beatles, and Simon and Garfunkel, as well as the *California sound* rock groups. They split up in 1973 because of personal problems, but after ten years of estrangement they reformed in 1983 with a sell-out concert in the Royal Albert Hall, London.

Evert (Lloyd), Chris(tine Marie) [evert] (1954–) Tennis player, born in Fort Lauderdale, Florida, USA. She won her first Wimbledon title in 1974 at age 19, and later won in 1976 and 1981. She also won the US singles title in 1975–80 and 1982, the French Open in 1974–5, 1979–80, and 1984, and the Australian Open in 1982 and 1984. She married British tennis player **John Lloyd** (marriage dissolved, 1987), and in 1988 US skier **Andy Mill**. She retired from professional tennis in 1989 and was elected to the International Tennis Hall of Fame in 1995.

Evesham [eevshm] 52°06N 1°56W, pop (2000e) 17 300. Town in Worcestershire, WC England, UK; in the Vale of Evesham in a fruit- and vegetable-growing area; railway; foodstuffs, engineering.

evidence Oral statements, documents, materials, or other facts, including forensic information, which when produced in a court or tribunal are used to prove or disprove certain other facts under dispute and ultimately the case itself. Not all evidence is admissible in court, and sometimes quite complicated rules determine what evidence is permissible. Some forms of evidence, such as hearsay evidence, may be permitted in civil cases while being inadmissible in criminal cases. In general, criminal courts require sufficient evidence to prove the matter beyond reasonable doubt, while civil cases need only be proved to the standard of balance of probabilities. Jurisdictions differ over whether children, convicted persons, experts, relatives of the accused, and certain other types of person are permitted to give evidence, and over the rights of a witness to give or withhold evidence. **Circumstantial evidence** is evidence not based on a witness's direct observation of a point at issue. In England and Wales, the law generally does not distinguish between direct and circumstantial evidence. In some circumstances, tape recordings and video evidence may be admissable in court.

evidence-based medicine The use by physicians of the current best scientific evidence in making decisions about the medical care of patients. Often there are gaps between an individual doctor's practice and the latest research about particular conditions, often because the research is not easily available. Increasingly, systems are being developed, including powerful electronic databases, to enable physicians to identify up-to-date information on the causes, diagnosis, and treatment of diseases, and help them make decisions about how best to manage their patients.

Evita *Perón, Eva*

evolution Any gradual directional change; now most commonly used to refer to the cumulative changes in the characteristics of populations of organisms from generation to generation. Evolution occurs by the fixation of changes (*mutations*) in the structure of the genetic material, and the passing on of these changes from ancestor to descendant. It is well demonstrated over geological time by the sequence of organisms preserved in the fossil record. There are two opposing schools of thought regarding the pattern and tempo of evolution. The **gradualist** school is based on a model of evolution in which species change gradually through time by slow directional change within a lineage, producing a long graded series of differing forms. The **punctuated equilibria** school is based on a model in which species are relatively stable and long-lived in geological time, and that new species appear during outbursts of rapid speciation, followed by the differential success of certain of the newly formed species.

evolutionary humanism A form of humanism which holds that modern science and knowledge have emancipated people from bondage to supernaturalistic and dogmatic religion. In this view, the universe has no special human meaning or purpose. Humankind is part of an evolutionary process, and the application of science and human reason are its only resources in creating a more human world.

evolutionism A widely held 19th-c belief that organisms – individuals, races, and even societies – were intrinsically bound to improve themselves, that changes were progressive, and that acquired characters could be transmitted genetically.

Evora [evura], ancient **Ebora** or **Liberalitas Julia** 38°33N 7°57W, pop (2000e) 38 600. Ancient walled market town and capital of Évora district, S Portugal, 105 km/65 mi SE of Lisbon; a world heritage site; airfield; railway; agricultural trade, cork; cathedral (1186), archbishop's palace, Roman Temple of Diana, Church of the Lóios (15th-c), old university (1551); São João fair (Jun).

Evreux [ayvroe] 49°00N 1°08E, pop (2000e) 53 800. Capital of Eure department, NW France, in fertile Iton valley; railway; textiles, rubber goods, chemicals; cathedral (begun 11th-c), Bishop's Palace (15th-c), former Benedictine abbey church of St-Taurin.

Ewald, Johannes [ivahl] (1743–81) Poet and playwright, born in Copenhagen, Denmark. After serving as a soldier, he devoted himself to poetry. He is best known for his prose tragedy, *Rolf Krage* (1770) and his mythological play *Balders Död* (1773, The Death of Baldur). The national song of Denmark comes from his operetta, *Fiskerne* (1779, The Fishermen).

Ewe [evay, ayway] A cluster of Kwa-speaking agricultural peoples of Togo, Ghana, and Benin; the coastal people also fish. They share common traditions of origin – from Oyo, in W Nigeria – and formed alliances in times of war, but they never constituted a centralized state.

ewe *sheep*

examination A method of testing the knowledge, understanding, or skills of candidates for qualifications or positions. Chinese written competitive civil service examinations originated in the 2nd-c BC; oral examinations date from the 12th-c. By the 8th-c, written examinations were being used for six specialized degrees, including medicine (10 papers). Examinations were found in the Arab world until the 10th-c, and were known in Europe (in oral form) until the 13th-c. Europe's first written examinations were in 1702 (at Cambridge). Written examinations for the British civil service began in 1870. Examinations are now employed at all levels worldwide, and have significant educational and social impact.

Excalibur [ekskaliber] In Arthurian legend, the name of King Arthur's sword, which was given to him by the Lady of the Lake. As he lay dying he instructed Sir Bedivere to throw it back into the lake, where a hand drew it under. In another account, he acquires the sword by pulling it from a stone, thus proving he was the rightful king.

exchange controls Government measures aimed at restricting the movement of currency between countries. They are frequently used by developing nations, but also from time to time by Western nations when their reserves are low. Restrictions on the export of currency were lifted in the UK in 1979, after years of gradual easement of controls.

exchange rates The price at which a currency may be bought in terms of a unit of another currency. Until the 1970s, rates were fixed from time to time; today, most are *floating* (ie the rate is determined by the ongoing supply and demand for the currency).

excise tax A tax levied on many goods and services by governments as a way of raising revenues; often called **duty**. Best known are the duties on tobacco, alcoholic drinks, and fuel, Value Added Tax, and Sales Tax. In the USA, such taxes may be levied at three levels – federal, state, and local.

excited state *energy levels*

exciton In insulating and semiconductor crystals, a quantized ripple in electron energy that moves about the crystal transferring energy but not charge. A type of quasi-particle, it is important in understanding optical reflection and transmission properties.

exclusionary rule In the USA, a criminal procedure rule which prevents certain kinds of evidence from being used against a defendant in court: evidence seized in violation of the Fourth Amendment right against unreasonable search and seizure, the Fifth Amendment privilege against self-incrimination, and the Sixth Amendment right to counsel. It was adopted by the US Supreme Court in federal cases in *Weeks* v. *US* (1914) and extended to the states in *Mapp* v. *Ohio* (1961). This case signalled a new era, begun under Chief Justice Earl Warren, of applying provisions of the Bill of Rights to the states to the same extent as they apply to the federal government. The purpose of the exclusionary rule is to deter police misconduct, but it has proved controversial, as obviously guilty defendants have been released on what many view as 'technicalities'. This has given rise to exceptions such as *good faith of the police* (eg where a non-critical detail on a search warrant has been incorrectly filled out), based on the reasoning that there is no deliberate police misconduct to be deterred. England and Wales have no exclusionary rule as such, but judges must exclude confessions obtained through oppression, threat, or force, and have discretion to exclude evidence that is considered oppressive or unfair, including illegally obtained evidence.

exclusion principle *Pauli exclusion principle*

executive information system (EIS) A computer program or suite of computer programs designed to provide executives with the information they need to take decisions. It differs from a **management information system** (MIS) in that, for example, in a retail store the MIS would supply the store manager with information about how various brands were selling and thus allow the manager to determine a pricing policy, whereas an EIS would allow an executive director at head office to define exactly what information should be presented and arrange for that information to be made available in whatever form the executive may have asked for it.

executor(s) The individual(s) named in the will by a deceased person as being responsible for ensuring that his or her wishes are carried out. These duties include paying any debts from the estate, and ensuring that any balance is distributed amongst the beneficiaries according to the instructions in the will. Where a person dies without making a will, or where a named executor refuses to accept the appointment, a court may appoint someone else to administer the estate. Executors and administrators are sometimes referred to as *personal representatives*.

exemption clause or **exclusion clause** A term in a contract, commonly found in insurance policies, whereby one party seeks to exclude or (in the case of a **limitation clause**) limit liability in respect of obligations arising under the contract. In England and Wales the Office of Fair Trading runs an unfair terms unit to monitor such clauses and to enforce the regulations.

Exeter, ancient **Isca Dumnoniorum** 50°43N 3°31W, pop (2001e) 111 100. County town of Devon, SW England, UK; on the R Exe, 70 km/43 mi NE of Plymouth; founded by the Romans 1st-c AD; stone wall erected in 3rd-c against Saxons and (later) Danes; port status partially restored by the construction of England's first ship canal (1560); W headquarters of Royalist forces during Civil War; university (1955); railway; airfield; agricultural trade, textiles, leather goods, metal products, pharmaceuticals, wood products, tourism; 12th-c cathedral (damaged by bombing in World War 2), 12th-c Guildhall, maritime museum; football league team, Exeter City (Grecians).

existentialism A philosophical movement, closely associated with Kierkegaard, Camus, Sartre, and Heidegger. Usually contrasted with empiricist or rationalist traditions, its most salient theses are that there is no ultimate purpose or order in the world; that the world is vaguely hostile; that persons choose and cannot avoid choosing their character and goals, by self-creating 'leaps', and have the obligation only to be 'authentic'; and that truths about the world and our situation are revealed most clearly in moments of unfocused psychological anxiety or dread. These themes greatly influenced continental literature, psychoanalysis, and theology in the 20th-c.

Exmoor National park in Somerset and Devon, SW England, UK; area 686 sq km/265 sq mi; established in 1954; occupies coastline between Minehead and Combe Martin Bay; highest point, Dunkery Beacon, 520 m/1707 ft; Brendon Hills (E); known for its ponies; major tourist area.

Exmoor pony The oldest British breed of horse; a small pony developed on Exmoor, Devon; height, 11·2–12·3 hands/1·2–1·3 m/3 ft 10 in–4 ft 3 in; very hardy; broad chest, deep body, stiff springy coat; brown with cream muzzle; broad nostrils, eyes slightly protruding.

Exmouth [**eksmuhth**] 50°37N 3°25W, pop (2000e) 34 200. Resort town in Devon, SW England, UK; on the R Exe, 15 km/9 mi SE of Exeter; centre for recreational sailing; railway; engineering.

exobiology The study of extraterrestrial life. Techniques include the monitoring of radio waves emitted by other star systems, and the use of space-probe experiments designed to detect life forms, or the presence of the molecules required for life to develop.

Exodus, Book of The second book of the Pentateuch in the Hebrew Bible/Old Testament. It narrates stories about the deliverance of the Jews from slavery in Egypt under the leadership of Moses, and about the giving of the Law to Israel through a revelation to Moses on Mt Sinai. It also provides instructions for building the wilderness tabernacle.

exogamy *marriage*

exon *intron*

exoplanet A planet orbiting a star outside the Solar System; short for **extrasolar planet**. The first such planet, orbiting 51 Pegasi, was discovered by Michael Mayor and Didier Queloz of Geneva in 1995. Others were announced in 1996 in 70 Virginis, 47 Utsaa Rajoris, and 55 Cancri, and several more have since been discovered.

exosphere The outer shell in the atmosphere (at c.400 km/250 mi) from which light gases can escape.

expanded town A British solution to the problems of city growth. Following the designation of *new towns*, a number of towns were chosen for expansion under the 1953 Expanded Towns Act. Cities with surplus population could negotiate with these towns to take the 'overspill' population. For example, the market towns of Haverhill, Suffolk, and Huntingdon and St Neots, Cambridgeshire, expanded to take the overspill from Greater London. Financial aid was available from central government for the provision of amenities, such as waterways and mains sewerage, in the expanding towns.

expanding universe *'big bang'*

experimental psychology The name given to a branch of psychology which relies on experimentation to address research problems. First used to indicate the emergence of a distinct scientific discipline of psychology at the end of the

19th-c, the term came to refer to the study of mental phenomena by experimental methods in contrast to sheer speculation ('armchair psychology'). It is now used for an approach which relies principally on laboratory experiments.

experimenter effect An effect on a subject's performance wrongly attributed to the manipulation of an experimental condition (*variable*) which can be shown to be due to the influence of the experimenter. A well-known example is the *Hawthorne effect*. Improvement in the performance of workers at the Hawthorne factory of the Western Electric Company in the USA was assumed to be an effect of specific changes made in working conditions (eg in the level of illumination), whereas it was eventually established that the workers were responding to the interest shown towards them by the investigators.

expert system A computer system which can perform at least some of the functions of the relevant human expert. Expert systems have been developed for use in areas, such as medical diagnosis and geological prospecting, which require a large amount of organized knowledge plus deductive skills.

Explorer 1 The first US space satellite (launched 31 Jan 1958); a joint effort of the US Army's Ballistic Missile Agency, later to become NASA's George C Marshall Space Flight Center, and the California Institute of Technology's Jet Propulsion Laboratory, later to become NASA's leading centre for planetary exploration. The simple 14-kg/31-lb spacecraft was launched on a Redstone (Jupiter C) rocket vehicle from Cape Canaveral, and instrumented with basic radiation counters built at the University of Iowa. It discovered belts of energetic charged particles trapped in the Earth's magnetic field, which were named after Iowa's James Van Allen. 'Explorer' later became the generic name of a series of relatively simple Earth orbital space physics and astronomy missions carried out by NASA.

explosives Substances capable of undergoing a rapid chemical change to produce hot gases which occupy a much greater volume, and therefore exert a sudden very high pressure. Many types of reaction may proceed explosively, but most military and industrial explosives consist largely of nitrated carbon compounds. (The chief exception is the oldest explosive, gunpowder.) They are distinguished as **propellants** and **high explosives**. Propellants burn rapidly but smoothly, so as to exert a great but steady pressure on a projectile in the barrel of a gun. High explosives change so fast as to produce a violent and disruptive shock in adjacent material. Industrial explosives generally contain some inert moderator to provide control (eg dynamite).

exponent In mathematics, the index or power to which a number has been raised. For example, in the expression x^4, 4 is the exponent.

exponential function In mathematics, a function in which the variable is in the exponent, eg 2^x. The most important exponential function is $y = e^x$ which has the property that $dy/dx = y$ for all values of x. So the rate of growth of e^x is proportional to its size: the larger it is, the faster it grows – hence the popular usage of *exponential* to refer to any process of runaway growth. In its more general form $y = Ae^{kx}$, this function models many physical situations, such as laws of growth and decay, and the discharge of condensors. Radioactive substances obey an exponential decay law, given by $y = Ae^{-kx}$, $k > 0$. The **exponential series** is

$$e^x = 1 + \frac{x}{1!} + \frac{x^2}{2!} + \frac{x^3}{3!} + \frac{x^4}{4!} + \ldots .$$

The trigonometric functions can also be defined in terms of exponentials,

$$\sin x \frac{1}{2i}(e^{ix} + e^{-ix})$$

$$\cos x = \frac{1}{2}(e^{ix} + e^{-ix})$$

and Euler established the remarkable result: $e^{i + 1 = 0}$.

exposure (photography) The controlled presentation of a photosensitive surface to light in order to record an image. For a given sensitivity, exposure level is determined by the intensity of the light and the exposure duration, and must be correctly set to ensure satisfactory reproduction of tone and colour. In still cameras this is done by a suitable combination of lens aperture and shutter speed, but in motion picture and video cameras the exposure time is normally fixed, and level is set by the lens aperture. An **exposure meter** is an instrument for measuring light, either incident on the subject or reflected from it, giving a scale reading (light value) from which lens aperture and shutter setting may be determined for a given photographic material. Modern still cameras embody a meter for reflected light, measuring through the lens, coupled for automatic exposure setting; while in video cameras a signal from the electronically scanned image automatically controls lens aperture.

exposure (physics) A measure of exposure to ionizing radiation, based on the amount of ionization produced in dry air by X-rays or gamma rays; symbol X, units R (röntgen). The modern notions of *absorbed dose* and *dose equivalent* are generally more useful.

exposure index (EI) A number in an arithmetical sequence used to specify the sensitivity of photographic film in actual use. This number may differ from the film speed printed on the box using the ISO, ASA, or DIN speed systems. It can represent a preferred film speed rating, or one that is necessary when a filter is used or when the film is uprated for 'push processing' to increase the effective film speed.

Expressionism A movement in art, architecture, and literature which aims to communicate the internal emotional realities of a situation, rather than its external 'realistic' aspect; the term was first used in Germany in 1911, but the roots of the movement can be traced to van Gogh and Gauguin in the 1880s. Their influence was felt by the Norwegian Edvard Munch, and the Belgian James Ensor, but the full flowering of Expressionism occurred in Germany from c.1905 until suppressed by Hitler. In this approach, traditional ideas of beauty and proportion are disregarded, so that artists can express their feelings more strongly by means of distortion, jarring colours, and exaggerated linear rhythms. The movement was also influential in literature, especially in German theatre after World War 1. The use of dislocation and distortion in fiction and poetry (eg in the writing of Kafka and Joyce) has also been described as Expressionist.

expressivity The degree of manifestation of a gene in those individuals in whom its presence is detectable. The gene for tuberose sclerosis, for example, in one individual may cause epilepsy, mental retardation, and a skin rash, but in another only the skin condition. Such cases are said to be of variable expressivity.

extended family *family*

Extensible Mark-up Language *document description language*

extensive farming Farming with relatively low input levels, especially of fertilizers, sprays, and pharmaceuticals. Lower yields per hectare may be compensated for by larger areas per farm and per farmer; so acceptable income levels may still be achieved. Examples of extensive farming include upland sheep and cattle farming in the UK, and prairie farming in North America.

externalities The effects of economic processes on people other than those conducting them. External *diseconomies* are effects harmful to others, such as traffic congestion or environmental pollution. External *economies* are effects beneficial to others, such as the sight of pleasant private buildings or gardens visible to the public. Externalities may arise from both productive and consumer activities. Because external economies and diseconomies have serious effects on other people's welfare, governments attempt to influence them through direct controls, and via taxes and subsidies. Cost–benefit analysis attempts to measure the overall costs and benefits of activities, including externalities as well as direct effects on those conducting them. Because externalities are not traded in markets, putting a value on them can be controversial.

eye

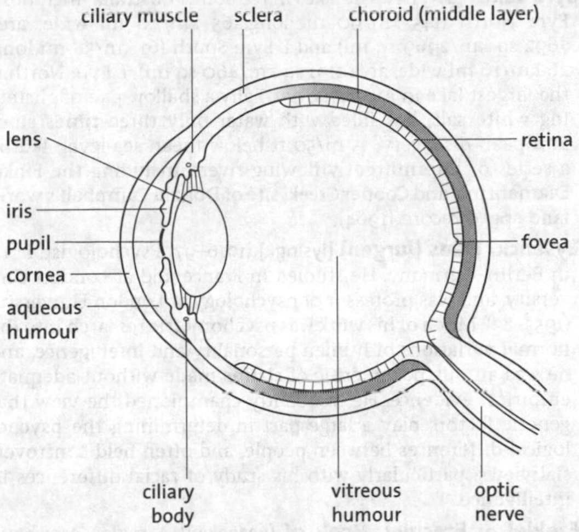

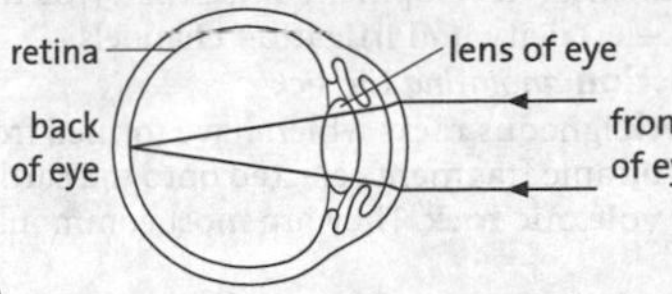

Normal eye
The image is in focus on the retina without a correcting lens in front

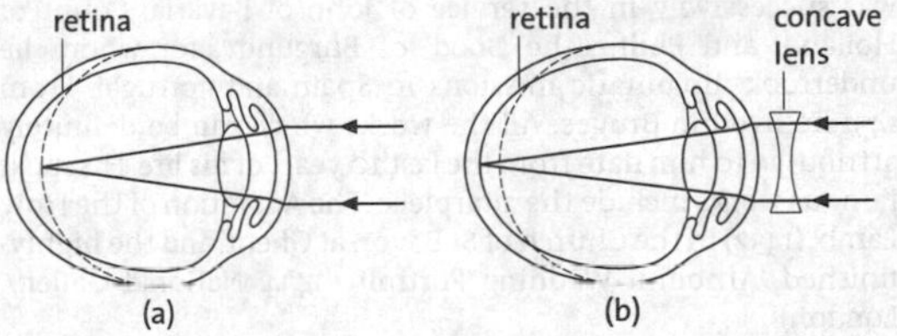

Short-sighted eye
(a) The eye is too long and the image is not in focus on the retina
(b) The use of a concave lens brings the image into focus

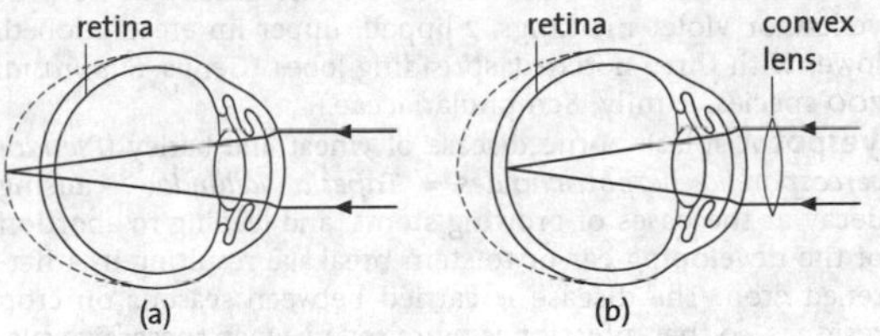

Long-sighted eye
(a) The eye is too short and the image is not in focus on the retina
(b) The use of a convex lens brings the image into focus

A specialized receptor organ responding to light stimuli. Various forms exist, such as the stigmata of certain protozoa, the ocelli of annelids, and the compound eye of insects. In land-based vertebrates, such as humans, the eyeball is composed of two parts: the transparent *corneal* part at the front, and the opaque *scleral* part at the back. Three concentric coats form the wall of the eyeball: an outer *fibrous* coat, consisting of the cornea and sclera; a middle *vascular* coat, consisting of the choroid, ciliary body, and iris; and an inner *nervous* coat (the *retina*). The coats surround and partly divide the contents of the eyeball. The *vitreous body* (a jelly-like substance containing a meshwork of fine fibres) lies between the lens and the retina. The space between the lens and the cornea contains a watery fluid (the *aqueous humour*), and is further partly divided by the iris into front and rear chambers. The *lens* is transparent and biconvex, lying between the iris and the vitreous body; changes in its convexity alter its focal length (the greater the convexity, the shorter the focal length), and are brought about by the action of the ciliary muscles. The lens is soft and elastic in the fetus, but becomes hardened and flatter with increasing age, making focusing on close objects more difficult (*presbyopia*); it may also become opaque in the elderly (*cataract*). Light entering the eye is refracted by the cornea, and passes through the lens, which focuses it to form an inverted image on the retina. This image is coded by the retina and sent to the visual areas of the cerebral cortex for interpretation, thus enabling the original pattern of light stimuli to be 'seen'. The amount of light entering the eye is determined by the size of the pupil, which in turn is determined by the degree of contraction of the iris. If the image from distant objects is focused in front of the retina, the condition is known as *myopia*, with vision being better for near objects ('short-sightedness'). If the image is focused beyond the retina, the condition is known as *hypermetropia*, with vision being better for distant objects ('long-sightedness'). Glasses using concave lenses are used to correct short sight; a convex lens is used for long sight.

extinction The disappearance of a species from a particular habitat (*local* extinction), or the total elimination of a species worldwide. Animal species are categorized as extinct if they have not been definitely located in the wild for the past 50 years.

extracellular fluid (ECF) The fluid which surrounds the cells of the body. In humans the adult volume is c.14 l/25 UK pt/30 US pt, and consists of blood plasma, the interstitial fluid of tissues, and transcellular fluids. Its principal components (apart from water) are sodium, chloride and bicarbonate ions, and proteins. The concept that the body's cells are protected from a continuously changing and often hostile external environment by their own internal environment, a fluid of constant volume and composition, was introduced by French physiologist, Claude Bernard (1813–78). Although the basic concept still holds, extracellular fluid is no longer considered to be constant, but to vary within very narrow limits.

extradition The removal of a person by a state in which that person is currently located to the territory of another state where the person has been convicted of a crime, or is said to have committed a crime. The process is normally conducted through extradition treaties, which specify the cases and the procedures under which extradition will take place. Treaties are normally restricted to more important crimes, but exclude political crimes.

Extranet *Intranet*

extrapolation *interpolation*

extrasensory perception (ESP) One of the two major categories of allegedly paranormal phenomena of interest to parapsychologists (the other being *psychokinesis*). Extrasensory perception is defined as the apparent gaining of information about an object or event (mental or physical; past, present, or future) by means other than those currently understood by the physical sciences. Clairvoyance, telepathy, and precognition are specific types of extrasensory perception.

extraversion *introversion / extraversion*

Extremadura [ekstraymadoora] or **Estremadura** [aystraymadoora] pop (2000e) 1 064 000; area 41 602 sq km/16 058 sq mi. Autonomous region of W Spain on the Portuguese frontier; crossed by the Tagus and Guadiana Rivers, bounded (N) by the Sierra de Gata and Sierra de Gredos (rising to 2592 m/ 8504 ft); merino sheep, pigs, vines, figs, olives, almonds; considerable industrial development since the 1970s through the use of hydroelectricity and irrigation channels.

extreme unction *anointing the sick*

extrusive rock Igneous rocks which have formed from molten magma, or volcanic fragments ejected onto the Earth's surface; also termed **volcanic rock**. They are most commonly basalt or pyroclasts.

Eyck, Jan van [iyk] (c.1389–1441) Painter, born near Maastricht, The Netherlands. The greatest Flemish artist of the 15th-c, he was successively in the service of John of Bavaria, Count of Holland, and Philip 'the Good' of Burgundy, for whom he undertook diplomatic missions in Spain and Portugal. From 1431 he lived in Bruges. All the works which can be definitely attributed to him date from the last 10 years of his life. His most famous works include the altarpiece 'The Adoration of the Holy Lamb' (1432) in the Church of St Bavon at Ghent, and the highly-finished 'Arnolfini Wedding Portrait' (1434, National Gallery, London).

eye *p.543*

eyebright A small annual or perennial, native to most temperate regions; all hemiparasitic, mainly on grasses; leaves opposite or alternate, toothed or lobed; flowers usually white with yellow or violet markings, 2-lipped, upper lip erect, 2-lobed, lower with three notched, spreading lobes. (Genus: *Euphrasia*, 200 species. Family: Scrophulariaceae.)

eyespot A splash-borne disease of wheat and barley (*Pseudocercosporella herpotrichoides = Tapesia yallundae*), causing decay at the bases of growing stems, and leading to abortion of the developing ear or to stem breakage resulting in a flattened crop. The disease is carried between seasons on crop residues, so that infection is more severe when successive susceptible crops are grown on the same field. It may be controlled by fungicidal spray or by crop rotation. Some varieties show resistance. (Order: Ascomycetes.)

Eyre, Sir Richard (Charles Hastings) [air] (1943–) Theatre, film, and television director, born in Barnstaple, Devon, SW England, UK. He studied at Cambridge, and became associate director of the Lyceum Theatre, Edinburgh (1967–70), then director of productions (1970–2). He was artistic director of the Nottingham Playhouse (1973–8), then producer of the BBC Television *Play for Today* series (1978–81). Associate director of the National Theatre, London (1981–8), he became artistic director (1988–97). Films for television include *Tumbledown* (1988, BAFTA for best single drama), *The Absence of War* (1995), and *King Lear* (1998). In 1998 he received the Laurence Olivier Award for best director. He was knighted in 1997.

Eyre Lakes [ayr] Dry salt lakes in NE South Australia; includes L Eyre North (145 km/90 mi long, 65 km/40 mi wide, area 7692 sq km/2969 sq mi) and L Eyre South (61 km/38 mi long, 26 km/16 mi wide, area 1191 sq km/460 sq mi); L Eyre North is the largest lake in Australia, normally a shallow pan of glistening white salt; has filled with water only three times since European discovery; 15 m/50 ft below mean sea-level; fed by a series of intermittently flowing rivers, including the Finke, Diamantina, and Cooper Creek; site of Donald Campbell's world land speed record (1964).

Eysenck, Hans (Jurgen) [iysingk] (1916–97) Psychologist, born in Berlin, Germany. He studied in France and at London University, and was professor of psychology at London University (1955–83). Much of his work was psychometric research into the normal variations of human personality and intelligence, and he was an outspoken critic of claims made without adequate empirical evidence. He frequently championed the view that genetic factors play a large part in determining the psychological differences between people, and often held controversial views, particularly with his study of racial differences in intelligence.

Ezekiel or **Ezechiel, Book of** [eezeekiel] A major prophetic work in the Hebrew Bible/Old Testament, attributed to Ezekiel, a 6th-c BC priest amongst the Jews exiled in Babylonian territories after 597 BC. The prophecies in Chapters 1–24 warn of the impending destruction of Jerusalem (587 BC); Chapters 25–32 present oracles condemning foreign nations; and Chapters 33–48 promise hope for a restoration of Israel. The collection of these prophecies may have been the work of a later editor.

Ezra, Book of [ezra] Part of the Hebrew Bible/Old Testament, and originally probably part of a historical work including Chronicles and Nehemiah. It describes stages in the return to Palestine of exiled Jews from 538 BC onwards, the attempts to rebuild the Temple and city of Jerusalem, and the story of Ezra's mission under Artaxerxes I or II to restore adherence to the Jewish law amongst Palestinian Jews.

Ezra the Scribe [ezra] (5th–4th-c BC) Religious leader who lived in Babylon during the reign of King Ataxerxes (I or II). He reorganized the Jewish community in Jerusalem, and renovated its religious cult. He may have brought part of the Mosaic law (the Pentateuch) with him. An Old Testament book bears his name, as well as the apocryphal works of 1 and 2 Esdras (the Greek equivalent of *Ezra*).

f

Fabergé, Peter Carl [faberzhay], originally **Karl Gustavovich Fabergé** (1846–1920) Goldsmith and jeweller, born in St Petersburg, NW Russia. Educated in several countries, in 1870 he inherited his father's establishment in St Petersburg, moving from the design and manufacture of conventional jewellery to the creation of more elaborate and fantastic objects, most famous of which are probably the celebrated imperial Easter eggs, first commissioned by Alexander III for his tsarina in 1884. He died in exile in Lausanne, after his business had been destroyed by the events of the Russian revolution.

Fabian Society A socialist group established in 1884 which took its name from the Roman general Fabius Cunctator, noted for his cautious military tactics. It adopts a gradualist approach to social reform, and sometimes 'Fabian' is applied to people who are not members of the Society but who believe in reformist socialism. The Society was traditionally a small select group of intellectuals, but has a close association with the British Labour Party, and has been a source of socialist ideas and arguments which are frequently promulgated through the Society's extensive publication activities. In 2004, it had over 6800 members, including over 200 MPs, and 64 local societies. About 1000 members are Young Fabians (under 31).

Fabius Maximus, Quintus [faybius maksimus], known as **Fabius Cunctator** (Lat 'the delayer') (c.260–203 BC) Roman general, statesman, and hero of the Second Punic War, whose refusal to engage Hannibal in set battle earned him his nickname. Originally a term of abuse, it became an honorific title after 216 BC, when Rome's massive and unnecessary defeat at the Battle of Cannae proved that his cautious tactics had been right.

fable (Lat *fabula* 'story') A brief fictitious story about animals or plants that teaches a moral, which may be interpreted as referring to human behaviour. The mode, both in verse and in prose, has been popular at all times; famous examples include Aesop's *Fables* (6th-c BC), the *Fables* of La Fontaine (late 17th-c), and George Orwell's *Animal Farm* (1945). In many fables, the moral is summed up at the end in the form of a proverb.

fabliau [fablioh] A short narrative poem popular in 12th–14th-c France, and also appearing in English (eg Chaucer's *Miller's Tale*). The subjects were usually bawdy, misogynist, and anticlerical.

Fabriano, Gentile da [fabriahnoh] (c.1370–c.1427) Painter, born in Fabriano, EC Italy. He worked chiefly in Venice and Brescia until 1419, and thereafter in Rome, Florence, and Siena. He painted religious subjects, notably 'The Adoration of the Magi' (1423, Florence), but few of his paintings have survived.

Fabricius, Hieronymus [fabreetsius], also known as **Girolamo Fabrici** (1537–1619) Anatomist, born in Acquapendente, C Italy. He studied under Fallopius at Padua, becoming his successor as professor of anatomy there in 1562. He made the first detailed description of the valves of the veins, the placenta, and the larynx. William Harvey was one of his pupils.

fabrics *batik; coated fabrics; denim; felt; non-woven fabrics; tweed; twill*

Fabritius, Carel [fabreetsius] (c.1624–54) Painter, born in Beemster, The Netherlands. He studied under Rembrandt, and from c.1650 lived mainly in Delft, where he was killed in an explosion. Vermeer was much influenced by Fabritius's sensitive experiments in composition and the painting of light as in the tiny 'View of Delft' (1652, National Gallery, London).

facade [fasahd] The exterior face or elevation of a building. Every building has a facade, simply by virtue of having an outside; but the term is particularly associated with consciously designed, overtly formal, aesthetic qualities. The term derives from Italian *facciata*, for the front of a building.

facilities management The process of efficient planning, integration, and operation of the different elements which make up a work environment. This environment may be anything from a small office to a major institution, and the facilities may include everything from day-to-day activities of catering, cleaning, and security to long-term planning considerations of office lay-out, refurbishment, and ergonomics. Many industries are these days adopting the strategy of inviting an outside organization to manage their environment as a whole or in part (eg the management of their computing facilities), rather than using their own staff, and the field of facilities management is now becoming a speciality in its own right.

facsimile machine *fax*

factor analysis A set of techniques popular in psychometric research to reduce data to manageable form. Given a set of correlations between various measures (eg responses to items on a questionnaire), factor analysis identifies a small number of factors (weighted combinations of the observed measures) which best account for the correlations. Such factors are statistical: giving them a psychological interpretation is sometimes difficult and contentious.

factor VIII One of a series of enzymes present in the blood which controls the clotting process. Sufferers from classical haemophilia lack this factor, and their blood therefore lacks the capacity to clot. They are treated by intravenous administration of factor VIII that has been separated from fresh blood. This process carries the risk of transferring infections such as AIDS from the blood donor. In future, haemophiliacs may be cured by gene therapy, which would enable them to make factor VIII themselves. A rarer form of haemophilia results from the absence of factor IX (the Christmas factor, named after the first patient studied in detail with this deficiency), which can similarly be replaced.

factoring The purchase of goods for resale without further processing. **Debt factoring** is the purchase of debts due from a company's customers with the view to collecting them. When payment is problematical the debt will be bought at a discount.

Factory Acts Legislation passed in Britain from 1802 onwards to regulate employment in factories. The early Acts were generally concerned to limit the hours of work of women and children. The 1833 Factory Act prohibited children under nine from working in textile mills, and was the first to appoint factory inspectors. A maximum 10-hour working day in mines and industries for women and older children was agreed in 1847. A Factory Act of 1874 raised the age of children in employment to 10, this being further raised to 12 in 1901 and 14 in 1920.

factory farming An intensive form of livestock production, usually carried out indoors with strict control over the environment and feeding regimes; also known as **battery farming**. It accelerates growth: a battery chick reaches maturity in 42 days (normally 84). Currently the predominant production technique for eggs, poultry meat, and pig meat, it is opposed by many environmentalists who object to the frequent use of prophylactics and antibiotics, and to the use of hormones to enhance the efficiency of production.

Fadeyev, Aleksandr Aleksandrovich [fad**ay**ef] (1901–56) Novelist, born in Kimry, near Tver, W Russia. He became a Communist in 1918, and fought in Siberia. Deeply influenced by Tolstoy, his works include *Molodaya gvardiya* (1946, The Young Guard). As general secretary of the Soviet Writers' Union (1946–55) he mercilessly exposed any literary 'deviationism' from the Party line, but after becoming a target himself he committed suicide in Moscow.

faeces / feces [**fee**seez] Material discharged from the alimentary canal, consisting mainly of the undigested remains of ingested matter, bacteria, and water. In humans the colour is due to pigment formed in the intestine by bacterial decomposition of bilirubins. The odour is the result of the formation of certain amines by intestinal bacteria.

Faeroe or **Faroe Islands** [**fair**oh], Danish **Faerøerne** 62°00N 7°00W; pop (2000e) 40 200; area 1400 sq km/540 sq mi Group of 22 sparsely vegetated volcanic islands in the N Atlantic between Iceland and the Shetland Is; 17 inhabited; settled by Norse, 8th-c; part of Norway, 11th-c; passed to Denmark, 1380; self-governing region of Denmark since 1948; parliament (*Lagting*), restored in 1852, consists of 34 members; capital, Tórshavn; largest islands, Strømø, Østerø; inhabitants speak a Germanic language, Faroese; fish, crafts, sheep, potatoes.

Fahd (ibn Abd al-Aziz) (1923–) Ruler of Saudi Arabia (1982–), born in Riyadh, Saudi Arabia. Effectively ruler since the assassination of his older half-brother **Faisal** in 1975, he became king on the death of his other half-brother, **Khaled**.

Fahrenheit, Gabriel (Daniel) [**fa**renhiyt] (1686–1736) Physicist, born in Gdańsk, N Poland (formerly Danzig, Germany). He invented the alcohol thermometer in 1709, following this with a mercury thermometer in 1714. He spent most of his life in The Netherlands.

Fahrenheit temperature [**fa**renhiyt] A scale which takes the freezing point of water as 32°F and the boiling point at sea level as 212°F; symbol °F; introduced by Gabriel Fahrenheit, based originally on the temperature of an ice and salt solution, and human body temperature.

faience [fiy**ahns**] Earthenware decorated with an opaque glaze containing oxide of tin. The name derives from the Italian town of Faenza, but is usually applied to wares from France and Germany. English and Dutch Delftware and Italian maiolica employ exactly the same technique.

fainting A brief episode of loss of consciousness, usually sudden in onset; also known as **syncope** [**sing**kuhpee]. It is caused either by the reduction of blood supply to the brain or by changes in its electrical activity. Less commonly, low blood sugar may be responsible. Reduced cerebral blood flow may result from the pooling of blood in the lower limbs due to prolonged standing or overactivity of the vagus nerve in response to emotional stimuli, which also slows the heart beat (a *vasovagal attack*). Myocardial infarction, severe valvular disease, and disturbances in rhythm which reduce the output of blood may also be responsible.

Fairbanks 64°50N 147°50W, pop (2000e) 30 200. City in North Star Borough, C Alaska; terminus of the Alaska railway and highway; founded in 1902 after the discovery of gold; university (1922); mining, oilfield services; temperature averages −24°C in January.

Fairbanks, Douglas, (Elton), Snr, originally **Douglas Elton Ulman** (1883–1939) Film actor, born in Denver, Colorado, USA. He first appeared in stage plays in 1901, but in 1915 went into films and made a speciality of swashbuckling hero parts, as in *The Three Musketeers* (1921), *Robin Hood* (1922), and *The Thief of Baghdad* (1924), in which he did all his own stunts. He was a founder of United Pictures. In 1920 he married **Mary Pickford** (divorced, 1935).

Fairfax (of Cameron), Thomas Fairfax, 3rd Baron (1612–71) English parliamentary general, born in Denton, North Yorkshire, N England, UK. In the Civil War, he distinguished himself at Marston Moor (1644), and in 1645 was given command of the New Model Army, defeating Charles I at Naseby. Cromwell replaced him in 1650 for refusing to march against the Scots, who had proclaimed Charles II king, and he then withdrew into private life. In 1660 he was head of the commission sent to The Hague to arrange for the king's return.

fairies Supernatural beings that appear in folklore under many names and in a variety of (more or less human-derived) shapes, with multifarious characteristics and tendencies. Some are noble or royal and of human size, like Shakespeare's Oberon and Titania, and have their own realm (fairyland); most are diminutive and inhabit the human world. The **brownies** of English tradition are almost wholly benevolent, helping with house and farm work; **pixies** and **elves** are tiny and mischievous; **goblins** ugly and malicious. Some fairies, such as **gnomes**, Irish **leprechauns**, and Scandinavian **trolls**, traditionally guard treasure. Others, such as the vindictive Arabic **jinn**, inhabit stones and trees and other natural objects. Fairies also steal human children and mates. The fact that fairyland is often underground suggests an association with the spirits of the dead.

fairy bluebird A bird native to SE Asia (India to Philippines); shiny blue and black plumage; inhabits high forest canopy; eats mainly fruit, especially figs; sheds feathers easily when handled. (Genus: *Irena*, 2 species. Family: Irenidae.)

fairy penguin The smallest of all penguins (*Eudyptula minor*), height 40 cm/15 in; inhabits shallow waters around S Australia and New Zealand; also known as **little blue penguin**; nests in a burrow. (Family: Spheniscidae.)

fairy shrimp A slender and delicate aquatic crustacean that typically swims on its back, beating its leaf-like legs; contains c.180 species, found in ephemeral freshwater pools and inland saline lakes all over the world. (Class: Branchiopoda. Order: Anostraca.)

fairy tales Traditional stories mainly for children, deriving from folk tales, and usually involving magic and fairies or other supernatural creatures. One of the oldest collections is *The Arabian Nights' Entertainments* or *A Thousand and One Nights*, compiled c.1450 but not translated into European languages until the 18th–19th-c. This includes the tales of 'Aladdin', 'Sinbad the Sailor', and 'Ali Baba and the Forty Thieves'. The first published collections of European tales were by Perrault (1697) and the Brothers Grimm (1812). These included such favourites as 'Cinderella', 'The Sleeping Beauty', 'Little Red Riding Hood', and 'The Goose Girl'.

fairy wren *wren*

Faisal II [**fiy**sl], also spelled **Faysal** (1935–58) King of Iraq (1939–58), born in Baghdad, Iraq, the great-grandson of Hussein ibn Ali. He succeeded his father, King Ghazi, who was killed in an accident, and after an education at Harrow school in England, was installed as king. In February 1958 he concluded with his cousin King Hussein of Jordan a federation of the two countries in opposition to the United Arab Republic of Egypt and Syria. In July that year, he and his entire household were assassinated during a military coup, and Iraq became a republic.

Faisal (ibn Abd al-Aziz) [**fiy**zl], also spelled **Faysal** (1904–75) King of Saudi Arabia (1964–75), born in Riyadh, Saudi Arabia. Appointed Viceroy of Hejaz in 1926, he became minister for foreign affairs in 1930, crown prince in 1953, and succeeded his half-brother Saud as king. He was assassinated in the royal palace in Riyadh by his nephew Faisal ibn Musaid.

Faisalabad [**fiy**salabad], formerly **Lyallpur** (to 1979) 31°25N 73°09E, pop (2000e) 1 776 000. City in Punjab province, Pakistan; W of Lahore, in an important cotton and wheat-growing region; railway; grain, textiles, flour, soap, chemicals, textile machinery.

faith healing The alleviation of physical and mental ailments by the prayer of a healer relying on a higher source (usually, the power of God) working in response to faith. Known in several religions, the practice is now a major feature of Christian pentecostal and charismatic movements, often accompanied by the laying on of the healer's hands, usually in the context of worship. Critics assert that, even when apparently effective, it is difficult to ascribe healing to the action of the higher source, because so little is currently understood by medical science about the effects of psychological attitudes upon the body's biochemistry.

Fajans, Kasimir [fahyans] (1887–1975) Physical chemist, born in Warsaw, Poland. He studied at Heidelberg and Munich, and moved to the USA in 1936, teaching at the University of Michigan thereafter. He became a US citizen in 1942. His early work was on radioactive elements, but he is now best known for *Fajans' rules* which predict the degree of covalent or ionic character in the bonds between atoms in a compound.

falabella The smallest breed of horse in the world; height, 7 hands/0·7 m/2 ft 4 in; developed by the Falabella family in Argentina; descended from a small thoroughbred and Shetland ponies; now kept mainly as a pet.

Falange [falanj], Span [falankhay] A Spanish fascist movement, founded in 1933 by José Antonio Primo de Rivera (1903–36). It merged in 1934 with the *Juntas de Ofensiva Nacional-Sindicalista* (JONS) to form the *Falange Española de las JONS*, and participated in the right-wing rising of July 1936 and the subsequent Civil War. It was fused by Franco in 1937 with other rightist forces to form the single party of Nationalist Spain.

falcon Any bird of prey of the family Falconidae (c.60 species); worldwide; includes the carrion-feeding **caracara**, the **forest falcon** (large eyes, acute hearing, hunts in near-darkness), and the **true falcon** (a fast-flying predator which usually kills its prey in flight). True falcons include kestrels, hobbies and the merlin.

Falcone, Giovanni [falkohnay] (1939–92) Judge, born in Palermo, Sicily, S Italy. In 1978 he was appointed to Palermo where he began a campaign against the Mafia, leading to the successful prosecution of 338 top members in 1987. He became director-general of the criminal affairs division in the Justice Ministry in Rome, and several attempts were made on his life. He was killed when a one-ton bomb exploded under his car.

falconry A sport in which birds of prey are trained to hunt animals and other birds; also known as **hawking**. Two kinds of falcon are used. *Long-winged* birds, such as the peregrine, are used in open country, swooping on their prey from a great height and with devastating speed. The *short-winged* birds, or *accipiters*, perch on the falconer's gloved fist or tree branch until they see their prey, and then rely on speed. The birds are hooded until such time as they are ready to 'work'.

Faldo, Nick [faldoh], popular name of **Nicholas Alexander Faldo** (1959–) Golfer, born in Welwyn Garden City, Hertfordshire, SE England, UK. He had early successes in winning the Professional Golf Association championships in 1978, 1980, and 1981, and in 1987 won the Open Championship at Muirfield, UK, in appalling conditions, winning again in 1990 and 1992. In 1989 he won the US Masters, successfully defended his title in 1990, and won it again in 1996. His 23 Ryder Cup wins (1977–97) are a record. In 2003 he was honoured with the inaugural Professional Golfers' Association Recognition Award for outstanding services to golf.

Falkenlust *Augustusburg*

Falkland Islands *see panel*

Falkland Islands

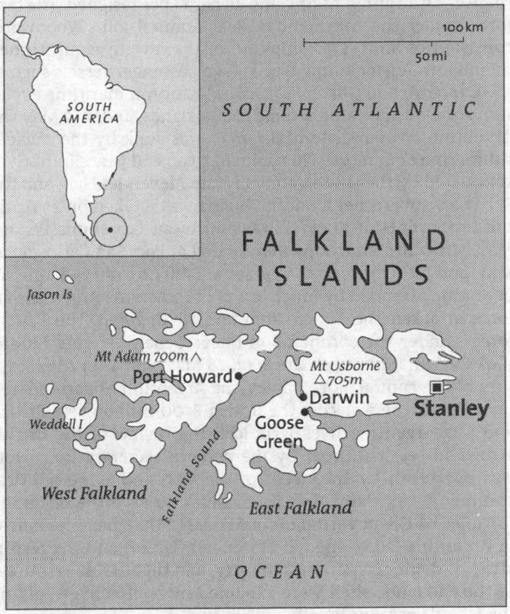

☐ International Airport

Span **Islas Malvinas** (UK British Overseas Territory)

Timezone GMT −4

Area c.12 200 km²/4700 sq mi

Population total (2000e) 2000

Capital Stanley (on East Falkland)

Physical features Located in the S Atlantic, c.650 km/400 mi NE of the Magellan Strait; consists of East Falkland and West Falkland, separated by the Falkland Sound, with over 200 small islands; hilly terrain, rising to 705 m/2313 ft at Mt Usborne (East Falkland) and 700 m/2297 ft at Mt Adam (West Falkland).

Climate Cold, strong westerly winds; low rainfall; narrow temperature range 19°C (Jan), 2°C (Jul); average annual rainfall 635 mm/25 in.

Currency 1 Falkland Pound = 100 pence

Economy Agriculture; oats, sheep; service industries to the continuing military presence in the islands.

History Seen by several early navigators, including Capt John Strong in 1689–90, who named the islands; French settlement, 1764; British base established, 1765; French yielded their settlement to the Spanish, 1767; occupied in the name of the Republic of Buenos Aires, 1820; Britain asserted possession, became a British Crown Colony, 1833; formal annexation, 1908 and 1917; the whole island claimed since independence by Argentina; Falklands War, precipitated by the Argentine invasion of the islands in April 1982, led to the dispatch of the British Task Force and the return of the islands to British rule in June 1982; external affairs and defence are the responsibility of the British government, which appoints civil and military commissioners; internal affairs are governed by executive and legislative councils.

Falklands War (Apr–Jun 1982) A war between Britain and Argentina, precipitated by the Argentine invasion of the Falkland Is, known to Argentinians as the **Malvinas**. Britain had ruled the islands continuously since 1833, but Argentina claimed them by inheritance from the Spanish Empire and through their proximity to her shores. The British had been conducting talks with Argentina on sovereignty over the Falklands, involving either a leaseback arrangement or a joint administration. When these talks broke down, the Argentinian government of General Galtieri issued a warning to the British. The British government announced the withdrawal of HMS *Endurance* from the S Atlantic, and on 19 March scrap merchants landed on South Georgia, ostensibly to demolish a whaling station, but they also raised the Argentine flag.

On the night of 1–2 April the full-scale invasion of the Falklands began. The 70 Royal Marines on the islands were overwhelmed, and the Governor, Mr Rex Hunt, was deported to

Uruguay. The British immediately began to fit out a task force to retake the islands, and the Foreign Office team of Lord Carrington, Humphrey Atkins, and Richard Luce resigned. The task force, under the command of Rear Admiral John Woodward, consisted of almost 70 ships; 40 of them were requisitioned merchantmen, including well-known passenger vessels such as the *Canberra* and *Queen Elizabeth 2*. A 200-mi maritime exclusion zone was declared around the Falklands, and on 2 May the Argentine cruiser *General Belgrano* was sunk by the nuclear submarine *Conqueror*. This brought to an end peace initiatives conducted by the US secretary of state Alexander Haig and the Peruvian government. South Georgia was retaken on 25 April; the destroyer HMS *Sheffield* was sunk by an Exocet missile on 4 May; 5000 British troops were landed at Port San Carlos on 21 May; and more troops were landed at Bluff Cove on 6–8 June, an operation attended by much loss of life when the Argentine air force attacked the *Sir Tristram* and *Sir Galahad*. The British forces, under the command of Major General Jeremy Moore, took Darwin and Goose Green on 28 May, and after the recapture of the capital, Port Stanley, the Argentinians surrendered on 14 June. The war cost the British £700 million; 254 British and 750 Argentine lives were lost; the review of the British armed forces instituted by the defence secretary John Nott was overtaken by the needs of the war; and some political commentators claim that it did much to save the declining fortunes of the government of Margaret Thatcher. The defeat of Argentina led to the fall of General Galtieri and the restoration of democracy in that country; and the marine resources of the Falklands shelf were exploited more effectively, giving the islands economic self-sufficiency.

Falla, Manuel de [falya] (1876–1946) Composer, born in Cadiz, SW Spain. He won prizes in 1905 as a pianist and for his first opera, then moved to Paris (1907–14), where he published his first piano compositions. On returning to Madrid, his works became known for their colourful national Spanish idiom. He is best known for his ballet, *The Three-Cornered Hat* (1919). With the outbreak of the Spanish Civil War, he settled in Argentina.

fallacy In logic, an invalid inference. 'All cats are mammals, Fido is a mammal; therefore Fido is a cat' is a fallacy, easily confused with the valid 'All cats are mammals, Fido is a cat; therefore Fido is a mammal'. An argument can of course be valid but have a false conclusion, or be invalid and have a true one. In everyday speech the word *fallacy* is used much more generally to denote a mistake or error.

Fallopian tubes *uterine tubes*

Fallopius, Gabriel [falohpius], Ital **Gabriello Fallopio** (1523–62) Anatomist, born in Modena, N Italy. He studied at Ferrara, then became professor of anatomy at Pisa (1548) and Padua (1551). He made several discoveries relating to bones and to the organs of reproduction. The *Fallopian tubes* connecting the ovary with the uterus are named after him.

fallout *radioactive fallout*

fallow deer A true deer (*Dama dama*) native to Mediterranean countries (introduced elsewhere); in summer, pale brown with white spots; in winter, grey without spots; antlers long, usually flattened with marginal projections; young male developing antlers for the first time called a **pricket**.

false acacia A deciduous tree (*Robinia pseudacacia*) growing to 25 m/80 ft, native to E and C North America; leaves pinnate with 3–10 pairs of oval leaflets, silvery-haired when young; pea-flowers fragrant, white tinged with yellow, in many-flowered pendulous clusters up to 20 cm/8 in long; also called **locust tree**. Often planted as an ornamental, both in North America and Europe, it provides hard and very durable timber. (Family: Leguminosae.)

false bulrush *reedmace*

false cypress An evergreen conifer, native to North America, Japan, and Formosa; similar to cypress, but with foliage in flattened sprays. As well as producing timber, most species have numerous ornamental forms. (Genus: *Chamaecyparis*, 6 species. Family: Cupressaceae.)

Faltskog, Agnetha *Abba*

Falun Gong (Chin 'law of the wheel') A spiritual sect established in China by Li Hongzhi (1951–), now claiming 100 million adherents worldwide. It offers a mixture of Buddhist meditation, physical exercise, Taoist philosophy, martial arts, and pantheistic mysticism. The sect's beliefs are laid down in its core text, *Zhuan Falun*, written by Li. Its followers have no political agenda, but wish to be officially accepted and allowed to practise their beliefs in peace. The sect first came to public notice in 1992 when a centre was opened in Beijing. In 1999, fearing a threat to the state's authority, the Chinese government banned Falun Gong's activities and publications. Following large-scale demonstrations of passive resistance by the sect, the government began its nationwide persecution through mass arrests, imprisonment, charges of treason, and dismissal from work. The sect's leader, Li, lives in exile in the USA, with the Chinese government demanding his extradition.

Falwell, Jerry L [fawlwel] (1933–) Religious leader, born in Lynchburg, Virginia, USA. After studying at Baptist Bible College, MO, he was ordained a minister. In 1956, he founded Thomas Road Baptist Church, Lynchburg, which became the basis of an extensive evangelical campaign. He was also responsible for founding The Moral Majority, Inc, and Liberty University. He has published widely, and broadcasts regularly to large audiences.

Famagusta [famagoosta], Gr **Ammokhostos**, Turkish **Magusa** 35°07N 33°57E, pop (2000e) 21 300. Capital town of Famagusta district, E Cyprus, on Famagusta Bay; occupies site of ancient Arsinoë (3rd-c BC); strongly fortified by Venetians (15th–16th-c); chief port of Cyprus until 1974 Turkish invasion; now under Turkish occupation; declared by Cyprus government closed to shipping and an illegal port of entry; old town wall; 14th-c citadel; ruins of Church of St George of the Latins (late 13th-c); cathedral of St Nicholas (early 14th-c French Gothic).

family An ambiguous term, referring to both the group formed by a co-resident husband, wife, and children (which sociologists term the **nuclear family**) or to a wider category of relatives, including non-resident grandparents, uncles, aunts, cousins, etc (the **extended family**). The nuclear family was once regarded as the key domestic institution of modern Western societies, but marriage has become somewhat less common, and the divorce rate has greatly increased, so that in societies such as contemporary England and the USA the majority of the population no longer lives within a nuclear family group. According to some estimates, only c.20% of all households are made up of nuclear families, the rest being constituted by single parents, foster, childless, or extended families, or simply individuals living alone. For different reasons, the same may have been true in many European peasant communities and in the early industrial cities. In many parts of the world, and in Europe in the pre-industrial period, the nuclear family was commonly part of a larger domestic group including some other relatives, and also employees, apprentices, etc. Anthropologists have been particularly interested in the circle of kin beyond the nuclear family, and have demonstrated that kinship groupings wider than the nuclear family may have crucial social functions.

family of languages A set of 'daughter' languages which derive from the same 'parent' language, and which are thus genetically related. They can be represented by a **family tree**, as with the Indo-European languages, in which Celtic, Germanic, and Romance languages are all interrelated. They will show systematic correspondences in pronunciation. For example, words with *p* in Latin are often *f* in English, as in *pater/father*, *piscis/fish*. There are c.2000 million speakers of Indo-European languages. The next most populous family is Sino-Tibetan, with over 1000 millions; others include Niger-Congo (260 millions), Afro-Asiatic (230 millions), and Austronesian (200 millions).

family planning *contraception*

family reconstitution A technique developed by historical demographers since the 1960s, which uses parish registers and civil register entries of births, marriages, and deaths to reconstruct a family's fertility, nuptiality, and mortality patterns. These micro-studies of families and local communities permit wider estimates of changes in age-specific fertility and mortality to be made.

family therapy A type of psychiatric treatment, developed in the USA, in which the whole family rather than the individual patient is the focus of therapy. An attempt is made to change the structure and functioning of the unit as well as to improve relationships within it, which then indirectly helps the patient. The main development of this technique took place in the 1960s as a form of psychotherapy. It has subsequently had a number of different schools with distinctive styles of treatment.

family tree *genealogy*

famine A period of food scarcity which may lead to malnutrition and death through starvation. The causes of famines are complex; they may result from natural causes, such as failure of a harvest following lack of rainfall and drought, or from combinations of political and economic circumstances such as war. Famine may also occur in a region where food is not completely scarce, but is unavailable to a sector of the population. This was the case in the Welo province famine of Ethiopia (1972–4), where food was available in the markets but at prices above those which could be afforded by local people.

fandango A Spanish dance for two people in triple time, usually accompanied by guitars and castanets and alternating with sung couplets. It was known from c.1700 as a popular dance at roadside inns, and later became fashionable in aristocratic ballrooms. A striking feature is the introduction of abrupt pauses when the music stops and the dancers freeze in position until the music begins again.

Fanfani, Amintore [fanfahnee] (1908–99) Italian statesman and prime minister (1954, 1958–9, 1960–3, 1982–3), born in Pieve Santo Stefano, NWC Italy. A former professor of political economics, he was prime minister on five occasions. Nominated a life senator in 1972, he became president of the Italian Senate in 1968–73 and 1976–82. He was a member (and former secretary and chairman) of the Christian Democratic Party.

Fangio, Juan Manuel [fanjioh] (1911–95) Motor-racing driver, born in Balcarce, Argentina, of Italian descent. He served his apprenticeship to road racing first as a mechanic, then in South American events with a car he built himself. He first took part in European Grand Prix racing in 1949, and by 1957 had won the World Championship a record five times (1951, 1954–7). He won 24 Grands Prix. After his retirement (1958) he joined Mercedes-Benz in Argentina. He was once held hostage by Castro's revolutionaries in Cuba.

fan palm A dwarf palm (*Chamaerops humilis*), native to dry places in the Mediterranean, often planted as an ornamental; trunk fibre-covered, sometimes extremely short, suckering and forming clumps; leaves fan-shaped. It is the only widespread native palm in Europe. (Family: Palmae.)

Fan Si Pan [fan see pan] 22°19N 103°46E. Highest mountain in Vietnam, rising to 3143 m/10 311 ft SW of Lao Cai, N Vietnam.

fantail The name used for a group of birds of uncertain affinity, native to SE Asia (India to the Philippines, Australia); inhabits forests; eats insects. Some authors classify fantails with flycatchers in the family Muscicapidae; others make a separate family, Rhipiduridae. (Genus: *Rhipidura* contains most of the c.42 species.)

fantasia An instrumental piece in which the composer's imagination is allowed free rein in one direction or another. An element of improvisation is often suggested, but some fantasias (such as Purcell's for strings) are carefully structured.

Fantin-Latour, (Ignace) Henri (Jean Théodore) [fãtĩ latoor] (1836–1904) Painter, pastellist, and lithographer, born in Grenoble, E France. He studied at Paris, and stayed for a while in England. He is best known for his flower studies and portrait groups, such as 'Hommage à Manet' (1870, Louvre). In his later years he specialized in lithography.

fanworm A sedentary marine worm that lives within a tube which it constructs; possesses a crown of tentacles or gills (*branchiae*) around its mouth, used for catching suspended food particles and for respiration; c.800 species, most from shallow seas. (Class: Polychaeta. Order: Sabellida.)

farad SI unit of capacitance; symbol *F*; named after Michael Faraday; defined as the capacitance of a capacitor comprising two parallel plates between which is a potential difference of one volt when the capacitor is charged with one coulomb of electricity; commonly used as μF (**microfarad**, 10^{-6} F) and *pF* (**picofarad**, 10^{-12} F).

Faraday, Michael (1791–1867) Chemist, physicist, and natural philosopher, usually regarded as the greatest of all experimental physicists, born in Newington Butts, Surrey, SE England, UK. Apprenticed to a bookbinder, he devoted his leisure to reading scientific books and joined a weekly club to learn elementary science. In 1813 he was engaged by Davy as his assistant at the Royal Institution, soon became his co-worker, and in 1827 succeeded to Davy's chair of chemistry, a post he held until retirement. His research contributed to an extremely broad area of physical science: he discovered benzene and the laws of electrolysis, invented an electric motor, dynamo and transformer, and was the creator of classical field theory. His major work is the series of *Experimental Researches on Electricity* (1839–55), in which he reports a wide range of discoveries about the nature of electricity. In 1845 he worked on his idea that the forces of electricity, magnetism, light and gravity are connected and was able to show that polarized light is affected by a magnetic field. He failed to get a similar result with an electric field, an effect later discovered (1875) by John Kerr. In 1846 Faraday delivered a lecture that included 'Thoughts on Ray Vibrations' which Maxwell acknowledged as the basis of the electromagnetic theory of light that he presented in 1873. Faraday's popular Christmas lectures for young people, begun in 1826, continue today and are now televised.

faraday The electrical charge on a mole ($6{\cdot}02 \times 10^{23}$) of electrons, $9{\cdot}65 \times 10^4$ coulombs; named after Michael Faraday. This amount of charge is required, for example, to reduce one mole (108 g) of silver ions by the reaction: $Ag^+ + e^- \rightarrow Ag$.

Faraday cage *screening*

Faraday effect The rotation of polarization plane for linearly polarized light passing through some substance in the presence of a strong magnetic field; described by Michael Faraday in 1845, and historically important as a means of demonstrating the link between light and magnetism. It is a type of magneto-optical effect, caused by anisotropy induced by the applied field. It is distinct from optical activity: rotation due to optical activity vanishes if the ray retraces its original path, whereas for the Faraday effect the rotation would be doubled.

Faraday's law *electromagnetic induction*

farandole [farandol] An ancient chain dance originating in Provence, S France, in the Middle Ages. Its participants, linked in a slow, stately line, accompanied themselves with singing or with a flute and drum. They moved sideways or facing forward through streets and around churches or houses, and going under one or more arches made by the raised arms of their companions.

farce A comic dramatic genre, one of the oldest in the history of the theatre, which focuses on both the limitations and liberties of the human body. Throughout a varied history (from Greek and Roman mimes to the Marx Brothers) it has never surrendered its anarchic purpose. Ruthless in pursuit of laughter, farce demands precision plotting and playing, bold stereotyping and mimicry, an aggressive sense of the incongruous, and a forthright recognition of the physical. Its themes never wander far from basic bodily functions. This is as true of the farces of Aristophanes, Labiche, Feydeau, Pinero, or Ben Travers as of their mediaeval precursors (eg the anonymous *Maistre Pierre Pathelin*).

Farel, Guillaume [farel] (1489–1565) Protestant reformer, born in Gap, SE France. He studied at Paris, where he became a convert to Protestantism, and was forced to flee to Switzerland (1524). After being twice compelled to leave Geneva, he returned there in 1534, the town council soon after proclaiming the Reformation. He was responsible for making Calvin stay in Geneva, but the severity of the ecclesiastical discipline which Calvin imposed caused their expulsion from the city (1538). He later returned with Calvin to Geneva, and then went to Neuchâtel (1543), where he died.

Farm Credit Administration (FCA) A system set up in the USA in the 1920s and 1930s to revive agriculture by providing adequate finance, especially mortgages. It was made independent in 1953, and is still in existence.

farmer co-operative A form of organization which enables farmers to work together for mutual benefit. It may involve co-operative production, processing, marketing, or the provision of requisites. It enables farmers to exploit economies of scale without losing financial control over the operation, allows for the sharing of information and knowledge, and provides a mutual support mechanism for farmers, who are often geographically isolated. Control of co-operatives is typically based on one-person one-vote, and returns are strictly in proportion to patronage.

farming *arable / dairy / dryland / extensive / factory / intensive / livestock / organic farming*

Farnaby, Giles [fah(r)nabee] (c.1560–1640) Composer, probably born in Truro, Cornwall, SW England, UK. He was a joiner by trade, but graduated in music at Oxford, and lived for a time near Lincoln. By 1614 he seems to have moved to London. His works include madrigals and settings of the psalms, but he is best remembered for his keyboard music.

Farne Islands or **The Staples** A group of basaltic islets in the North Sea, 3 km/1¾ mi NE of the mainland, Northumberland, NE England, UK; sanctuary for birds and Atlantic seals; St Cuthbert lived and died here; scene of heroic rescue in 1838 by Grace Darling and her father, William Darling (1795–1860), the lighthouse keeper, of survivors of the *Forfarshire*.

Farnese, Alessandro [fah(r)nayzay] (1545–92) Italian general, born in Rome, Italy. He fought in the service of Philip II of Spain, who was his uncle, and distinguished himself against the Turks at Lepanto (1571). As Governor-General of the Spanish Netherlands (1578–92), he captured Antwerp (1585), and compelled Henry IV of France to raise the siege of Paris (1590).

Faro [faru] 37°01N 7°56W, pop (2000e) 31 600. Industrial seaport and capital of Faro district, S Portugal; on S coast, 219 km/136 mi SE of Lisbon; airport; railway; fish, fruit; focal point of Algarve tourism; cathedral, Churches of the Carmo and of Santo Antonio do Alto (1754); Senhora do Carmo fair (Jul), Santa Iria fair (Oct).

Faroe Islands *Faeroe Islands*

Faroese *Germanic languages; Scandinavian languages*

Farouk [farook] (1920–65) Last reigning king of Egypt (1936–52), born in Cairo, Egypt, the son of Fuad I. He was educated in England, and studied at the Royal Military Academy, Woolwich. After World War 2 he turned increasingly to a life of pleasure. The defeat of Egypt by Israel (1948) and continuing British occupation led to increasing unrest, and the Free Officers' coup (1952) forced his abdication and exile, and in 1959 he became a citizen of Monaco. He was succeeded by his infant son as **Fuad II**, but the establishment of a Regency Council was forestalled by the formation of a republic some months later. He died in Rome.

Farquhar, George [fah(r)ker] (c.1678–1707) Playwright, born in Londonderry, Co Londonderry, NW Northern Ireland, UK. He studied at Trinity College, Dublin, and became an actor in a Dublin theatre, but soon left the stage and joined the army. His first comedy, *Love and a Bottle* (1699), proved a success, as were several other plays, notably *The Recruiting Officer* (1706). His best work, *The Beaux' Stratagem* (1707), was written during his last illness.

Farragut, David (Glasgow) [faraguht] (1801–70) US naval commander, born near Knoxville, Tennessee, USA. Entering the navy in 1810, he saw service against the British in 1812, and against pirates in 1820. In the Civil War he led the Union forces that captured New Orleans (1862), and took part in the siege and capture of Vicksburg (1863) and Mobile Bay (1864). He was made an admiral in 1866, but his health prevented him from continuing in active service.

Farrell, James T(homas) (1904–79) Writer of starkly realist novels of American life, born in Chicago, Illinois, USA. His best-known work is the *Studs Lonigan* trilogy (1932–5, filmed 1960), set in the slums of Chicago.

Farr-Jones, Nick, popular name of **Nicholas Campbell Farr-Jones** (1962–) Rugby union player, born in Sydney, New South Wales, SE Australia. A fierce cover defender, he won 63 caps for Australia (1984–93), captaining them 36 times including their victory in the 1991 World Cup. A Sydney solicitor, he later worked and coached in France.

Farrow, Mia (1945–) Film actress, born in Los Angeles, California, USA. She made her stage debut off-Broadway in 1963, and had a 2-year role (as Alison Mackenzie) in the TV soap *Peyton Place*. Her film roles include *Rosemary's Baby* (1968), *The Great Gatsby* (1973), and several Woody Allen films, notably *The Purple Rose of Cairo* (1985), *Hannah and Her Sisters* (1986), and *Husbands and Wives* (1992). Later films include *Widow's Peak* (1994), *Reckless* (1995), and *Miracle at Midnight* (1997). Earlier married to Frank Sinatra (1966–8), her relationship with Woody Allen (with whom she had nine children, five of them adopted) broke up in acrimony in 1992, following her discovery of Allen's affair with their adopted teenage daughter.

Farsi *Iranian languages*

farthing Formerly the coin of the lowest value in British currency, a quarter of an old (pre-decimalization) penny, its value therefore being 1/960th of £1. The farthing is derived from the Anglo-Norman silver penny (*denarius*) divided into four parts on the reverse side, along the lines of a cross. Each penny could be struck in half to make a halfpenny and quartered to make a farthing. The first round farthing coin was struck in 1279, in silver. In 1613 bronze replaced silver as the metal used in the minting of the farthing. It was withdrawn from circulation in 1960.

Fasching [fashing] or **Fastnacht** The period of merrymaking in S Germany and Austria, between Epiphany (6 Jan) and Lent; the equivalent of Carnival in S Europe and of Mardi Gras in the USA.

fasciation The abnormal, flattened growth of a single shoot, which resembles several stems fused together and often bears several inflorescences. Its causes include mechanical damage to meristems, infections by the bacterium *Phytomonas*, and mutation. It is common in such plants as dandelions and plantains. Cock's comb is a mutant which breeds true.

Fasciola [fasiyola] *liver fluke*

fascism A term applied to a variety of vehemently nationalistic and authoritarian movements that reached the peak of their influence in 1930–45. The original fascist movement was founded by Mussolini in Italy (1921), and during the 1930s several such movements grew up in Europe, the most important being the German Nazi Party. The central ideas of fascism are a belief in the supremacy of the chosen national group over other races, and the need to subordinate society to the leadership of a dictator who can pursue national aggrandisement without taking account of different interests. Fascism advocates the abolition of all institutions of democracy, the suppression of sources of opposition such as trade unions, and to varying degrees the mobilization of society under fascist leadership. Fascism is also strongly associated with militaristic and belligerent foreign policy stances. Since World War 2 its appeal has declined, although in some Latin-American countries fascist-type governments have held office, and in Spain General Franco ruled until 1975.

fashion A prevailing style in dress adopted by large numbers of the population. This is a Western phenomenon; in other cultures, styles have altered little over the centuries, until very recent times when 'Westernization' has occurred in some cases. Although many think of 'fashion' as relating only to women's clothing, from the Middle Ages until the 19th-c, it involved men equally. In the latter third of the 20th-c many designers made collections for men as well as women. Until the 20th-c, clothes for the wealthy were made-to-measure, fashions changing quite slowly; the influence was from the top (the court) downwards. However, during the 19th-c a new influence, that of the fashion designer or couturier, began to make itself felt. Charles Worth (1825–95), in Paris and London, not only made clothes for those wealthy clients who could afford his services, he also sold designs to manufacturers who could produce cheaper copies. With the invention around the same time (1850s) of the sewing machine and the paper pattern, followed much later by the development of mass production and artificial fibres, ready-to-wear clothing has gradually become the main source of fashion as we understand it. The French influence, supreme throughout the first half of the 20th-c, is now tempered by the work of designers in London, Milan, Rome, and New York.

Fashoda [fashohda] A settlement (now called Kodok) on the upper White Nile, which was the scene of a major Anglo-French crisis in 1898. French forces under Captain Jean Baptiste Marchand (1863–1934) had reached the Nile after an 18-month journey from Brazzaville. The British, who were in the process of retaking the Sudan, issued an ultimatum, but France was unprepared to go to war, and Marchand was ordered to withdraw. The incident destroyed French ambitions for a transcontinental African empire, and confirmed British mastery of the Nile region.

Fasil Ghebbi [fa**sil** ge**bee**] The royal complex of Emperor Fassilides (1632–67) in Gondar, NW Ethiopia; a world heritage site. Gondar was the permanent capital of Ethiopia in the 17th–18th-c, and today efforts are being made to preserve the castles and monuments of this period.

Fassbinder, Rainer Werner [**fas**binder] (1946–82) Film director, writer, and actor, born in Bad Wörishofen, S Germany. He began his career as an actor in fringe theatre in Munich, founding his own 'anti-theatre' company, a commune of actors which included Hanna Schygulla. His work in cinema began in 1969, and was much influenced by Jean-Luc Godard. He completed over 40 full-length films, largely politically committed criticisms of contemporary Germany, notably *Die bitteren Tränen der Petra von Kant* (1972, The Bitter Tears of Petra von Kant) and *Die Ehe der Maria Braun* (1979, The Marriage of Maria Braun), which won first prize at the 1979 Berlin Film Festival. He also adapted novels such as *Effi Briest* (1974) by Theodor Fontaine, and *Querelle* (1982) by Jean Genet. The most prolific writer-director-actor of the New German Cinema of the 1970s, he died at 36 as a result of alcohol and drug abuse.

Fassett, Kaffe [kayf] (1937–) Fashion designer, born in San Francisco, California, USA. He studied painting at the Museum of Fine Arts in Boston before migrating to England in 1964. Discovering the potential of hand knitting and needlepoint, he formed a design company producing knitting kits for Rowan, needlepoint for Ehrman, and fabrics for the Designers Guild. His television broadcasts and books, such as *Glorious Interiors* (1995), have made his colourful designs popular in Europe and the USA.

Fast, Howard (Melvin) (1914–2003) Writer, born in New York City, New York, USA. As a professional writer after 1932, he became a leading proponent of left-wing views. He was blacklisted for a decade for his Communist Party membership (1944–56), but in 1957 he declared his disenchantment with the Communism of Stalin in *The Naked God*. He wrote novels, children's books, biographies, and plays, but was best known for his historical novels, including *Freedom Road* (1944), *Spartacus* (1952), and *The Immigrants* (1977). His last novel, *Greenwich*, appeared in 2000.

Fastnacht *Fasching*

Fastnet Challenge Race A biennial yacht race from Cowes in the Isle of Wight to Plymouth in the SW of England via the Fastnet rock in the Atlantic Ocean, 6·5 km/4 mi off Cape Clear, Co Cork, SW Ireland. Arguably the toughest race in the British sailing calendar, it was first contested in 1925. Between 1957 and 1999 it formed the final race of the Admiral's Cup competition before it was redesigned as a stand-alone event.

fast reactor *nuclear reactor*

fat **1** A complex mixture of many different triglycerides, each formed when three molecules of fatty acids combine with one of glycerol. It is the major storage fuel of plants and animals. **2** A white or yellowish animal tissue (*adipose tissue*) in which individual cells are swollen with the accumulation of fat forming a single globule within the cytoplasm (**white fat**). The stored triglycerides are an energy source for the organism. White fat acts as a packing and insulating material in many animals (eg subcutaneous tissues in humans), but it can also act as a shock-absorber (eg under the heel, the palm of the hand). Human excess accumulation of body fat (*obesity*) arises when energy intake (diet) exceeds energy output (physical activity). **Brown fat** is darker-coloured fat found in most mammals, particularly those that hibernate and very young individuals. Unlike the single droplet of fat found in white fat cells, the droplets are very small and numerous. Also, unlike white fat cells, they can be stimulated by the sympathetic nervous system into breaking down the fat into heat. This is the means by which young animals can rapidly raise their rates of heat production in response to external cold.

Fatah [fata] *PLO*

fatalism The philosophical doctrine that the future is as unalterable as the past – that what will be will be, no matter what a person may do or not do to affect it. Fatalists are determinists, but not all versions of determinism entail fatalism.

Fatehpur Sikri or **Fathpur Sikri** [fatuh**poor** sik**ree**] A ghost city and architectural masterpiece of the Mughals in Uttar Pradesh, India. Founded as the Imperial capital of Emperor Akbar in 1568, the city was abandoned within two decades because of water shortages.

Fateh Singh, Sant [**fate sing**] (1911–72) Sikh religious leader and campaigner for Sikh rights, born in the Punjab. He was involved in religious and educational activity in Rajasthan, founding many schools and colleges there. In 1942 he joined the Quit India Movement, and was imprisoned for his political activities. During the 1950s he agitated for a Punjabi-speaking autonomous state, which was achieved with the creation of the Indian state of Punjab in 1966.

Fates *Moerae; Parcae*

fat hen An annual (*Chenopodium album*) found in most temperate regions; the whole plant with mealy white covering, flowers minute. Once used as a spinach-like vegetable, the seeds providing flour, nowadays it remains as a common weed of cultivated and waste ground. (Family: Chenopodiaceae.)

Father Christmas *Santa Claus*

Father of the House (of Commons) The honorary and affectionate title given to the longest serving MP in the British parliament. In 2004, this was Tam Dalyell, MP for Linlithgow, Scotland.

Father's Day In some countries, a day on which fathers are honoured. In the USA and the UK, it is held on the third Sunday in June; in Australia, the first Sunday in September.

Fathers of the Church A title usually applied to the leaders of the early Christian Church, recognized as teachers of truths of the faith. They were characterized by orthodoxy of doctrine and personal holiness, and were usually beatified. The study of their writings and thought is known as *patristics*.

Fatima (Portugal) [fatima], also **Fátima** 39°37N 8°38W, pop (2000e) 7700. Pilgrimage town, Santarém district, C Portugal, where three peasant children claimed to have seen 'the

Virgin of the Rosary' in 1917; Basilica (begun 1928, consecrated 1953).

Fatima (religion) (c.605–33) The youngest daughter of the Prophet Mohammed, and wife of the fourth Muslim caliph, Ali; from them the *Fatimids*, the dynasty of Shiite caliphs, who ruled over Egypt and N Africa (909–1171), and later over Syria and Palestine, traced their descent.

fatty acids *carboxylic acids*

Faulkner (of Downpatrick), (Arthur) Brian (Deane) Faulkner, Baron [fawkner] (1921–77) Politician, born at Helen's Bay, Co Down, Northern Ireland. The last Unionist leader to be prime minister of Northern Ireland, he was minister of home affairs (1959–63) at Stormont, and was elected leader of the Parliamentary Unionists in 1971. In an attempt to defeat the IRA, he introduced internment in August 1971; this alienated the Nationalist population while increasing IRA recruitment. In 1973 he entered into Anglo-Irish talks, agreeing to share power with Irish Republicans at an Assembly in Stormont and to take part in a Council of Ireland (the Sunningdale agreement). Faulkner was unable to maintain Unionist unity; in the 1973 election to the new Assembly, the party was split between those who backed the power-sharing policy and those who opposed it. He resigned as leader in 1974, and was created Baron Faulkner of Downpatrick in 1976.

Faulkner, William (Cuthbert) [**fawk**ner], originally **Falkner** (1897–1962) Writer, born in New Albany, Mississippi, USA. He served with the RAF in World War 1, and began his literary career with *Soldier's Pay* (1926), a novel on the aftermath of war. With *The Sound and the Fury* (1929) he began to experiment in literary form and style. *Sartoris* (1929) was the first in a series dealing with the social and racial problems of an imaginary Southern county, Yoknapatawpha. Other major novels include *As I Lay Dying* (1930), *Absalom, Absalom!* (1936), *Intruder in the Dust* (1948), and *The Reivers* (1962). He was awarded the Nobel Prize for Literature in 1949.

fault In geology, a fracture in rock along which displacement has occurred due to stresses in the Earth. Where relative movement is vertical or nearly so, **normal faults** are caused by compression, which in extreme cases may lead to the overthrusting of one body of rock over another, and **reverse faults** are caused by crustal extension. **Tear faults** release compressional stress by sideways displacement, the best known example being the San Andreas Fault in California. Major faults can create significant features of landscape, such as block mountains and rift valleys.

Faure, Edgar (Jean) [fohr], pseudonym of **Edgar Sanday** (1908–88) French writer, statesman, and prime minister (1952, 1955–6) born in Béziers, S France. He trained as a lawyer in Paris, entering politics as a Radical-Socialist. He was minister of finance and economic affairs several times in the 1950s, becoming premier for two short periods. He was later minister of agriculture (1966), education (1968), and social affairs (1969), president of the National Assembly (1973–8), and a member of the European Parliament from 1979. He wrote several detective novels under his pseudonym.

Fauré, Gabriel (Urbain) [fohray] (1845–1924) Composer, born in Pamiers, S France. He became organist (1896) at La Madeleine, Paris, and director of the Conservatoire (1905–20). Though chiefly remembered for his songs, including the evergreen *Après un rêve* (c.1865), he also wrote operas and orchestral pieces, such as *Masques et bergamasques* (1919), and a much-performed *Requiem* (1887–90).

Faust [fowst] or **Faustus** [**fow**stus, **faw**stus] A legendary German scholar of the early 16th-c (derived from a historical magician of that name), who sold his soul to the devil in exchange for knowledge, magical power, love, and prolonged youth. His story inspired Marlowe's *Dr Faustus* (1592), other literary works by Lessing (1784), Goethe (1808, 1832) and Thomas Mann (1947), and musical works including Gounod's opera *Faust* (1859).

Fauvism [**foh**vizm] (Fr *les fauves* 'the wild beasts') A name given by a hostile critic to a group of modern painters (1898–1908) who were experimenting with vivid colours; they included Matisse, Derain, and Vlaminck. Their work was inspired by van Gogh, Gauguin, and Cézanne.

favism A type of anaemia caused by a genetic defect involving a key enzyme in maintaining the integrity of red blood cells. The disease can be exacerbated by certain drugs or by broad beans, and is more likely to be found where broad beans are a common part of the diet.

Favre, Brett [fahvr] (1969–) Player of American football, born in Pass Christian, Mississippi, USA. He set six school passing records while at Southern Mississippi, and was selected by the National Football League Atlanta Falcons in 1991. He later joined the Green Bay Packers as quarterback. He became only the second player to win the NFL's Most Valuable Player Award in consecutive years (1995–6), and shared the award again in 1997, when the Packers won their first Super Bowl in 28 years.

Fawcett, Dame Millicent, *née* **Garrett** (1847–1929) Women's rights campaigner, born in Aldeburgh, Suffolk, E England, UK, the sister of Elizabeth Garrett Anderson. Keenly interested in the higher education of women and the extension of the franchise to her sex, she was made president of the National Union of Women's Suffrage Societies (1897–1919).

Fawkes, Guy (1570–1606) Conspirator and soldier, born in York, North Yorkshire, N England, UK, of Protestant parentage, who became a Catholic at an early age. He was serving with the Spanish army in The Netherlands (1593–1604), and had no share in originating the Gunpowder Plot (1605). He crossed to England at Catesby's invitation and was deputed to fire the gunpowder under the Houses of Parliament. Discovered and arrested on the night of 4–5 November, he revealed under torture on the rack the names of his fellow-conspirators. Exonerating the 'holy fathers' from all share in the plot, he was, together with his fellow-conspirators, in January 1606 hanged, drawn, and quartered opposite the Parliament building, their severed heads being subsequently displayed on poles.

fax The facsimile transmission of documents, diagrams, and photographs over a telephone network, widely available for international communication since 1986, and developed from the earlier inventions of Arthur Korn (telephotography, 1907) and Edouard Belin (the belinograph, 1925). The original is scanned by laser beam and digitally coded for transmission to the receiver, where it is printed out line by line on either thermo-sensitive or plain paper. Reading time is approximately 15 seconds for an A4 sheet of typescript or line diagram; somewhat slower for half-tone illustrations.

Faxian [fahshyan], also spelled **Fa-hsien** (AD c.360–c.430) Buddhist pilgrim, explorer, and diarist. Inspired by the visit of Kumarajiva to China (386) he made a momentous journey through Turkestan, India, and SE Asia (399–414) looking for Buddhist Scriptures. In India he visited every region except the Deccan, learned Sanskrit, and translated the earliest *Life* of Buddha into Chinese. He later wrote his memoirs (AD 416) in Nanjing: *Account of Buddhist Countries* is the oldest known travel book in Chinese literature, and an important source on contemporary C Asia and India. His trip inspired many later visits to India, including that of Xuanzang in the 7th-c.

FBI *Federal Bureau of Investigation*

feather A structure formed from the skin of birds. It may be less than 0·5 mm/$^1/_4$ in long, or more than 1·5 m/5 ft. Birds evolved from reptiles, and feathers are modified scales. The naked region of the central shaft, near the skin of the bird, is called the *calamus*. Beyond this is the *rachis*, bearing many side branches (*barbs*). Each barb also has small side branches (*barbules*). The barbules of adjacent barbs interlock, creating the familiar flattened structure. This flat blade is called the *vane*, or *vexillum*, and the region bearing it is the *pennaceous* part of the feather. At the base of the vane, by the calamus, there may be some wispy barbs. This downy region is the *plumulaceous* part of the feather. The relative proportions of the pennaceous and plumulaceous regions vary between feathers from different parts of the body. Some feathers have no barbs, and the naked shafts resemble simple bristles. 'Down' feathers have flexible and sometimes branched barbs, and the barbules hold the barbs in a three-dimensional shape. This creates a fluffy ball rather than a vane. Down feathers provide insulation; vaned feathers provide smooth aerodynamic surfaces. In many species feathers are important in display, and may be modified in shape and colour.

feather star An unattached sea lily, lacking a stalk in the adult; often brightly coloured, with 40 or more arms; abundant on coral reefs, but also found in deep waters. (Phylum: Echinodermata. Class: Crinoidea.)

February Revolution (France) The revolution in France (22–24 Feb 1848) which campaigned for universal suffrage and the introduction of a socialist government of the people. It resulted in the abdication of King Louis Philippe, the proclamation of a republic, and the establishment of a provisional government. Although not the first of the European revolutions of 1848, it inspired subsequent revolutionary activity in Germany, Austria, and other European states, all of which had collapsed by 1849.

February Revolution (Russia) Popular demonstrations, strikes, and military mutinies in Petrograd, Russia (Feb–Mar 1917), which led to the abdication of Nicholas II and the collapse of the tsarist government. The regime was succeeded by a series of provisional governments composed of liberal and moderate socialist ministers, and by the establishment of the Soviet ('council') of Workers' and Soldiers' Deputies, a situation known as 'dual power'.

feces *faeces*

Fechner, Gustav (Theodor) [fek**h**ner] (1801–87) Physicist, philosopher, anthropologist, and psychologist, born in Gross Sarchen, E Germany. His interest in mind-body relationships led to his book *Elemente der Psychophysik* (1860, Elements of Psychophysics), in which he developed the ideas of Ernst Heinrich Weber on the measurement of sensory thresholds, and laid the foundations for psychophysics. He was also the founder of experimental aesthetics, and his methods were influential in the development of experimental psychology.

Fedayeen [fe**day**een] A label commonly used to describe commandos who operated under the umbrella of the Palestine Liberation Organization. The name is from the Arabic *fidai*, 'one who sacrifices oneself' (for a cause or country).

Federal Bureau of Investigation (FBI) The US organization primarily concerned with internal security or counter-intelligence operations, although it also has responsibility for investigating violations of federal law not remitted by the federal government to any other organization. The FBI is a branch of the Department of Justice.

Federal Constitutional Convention *Constitutional Convention*

federalism A form of territorial political organization which aims to maintain national unity while allowing for regional diversity. This is achieved by distributing different constitutional powers to national and regional governments. Power is not hierarchically distributed, but allocated among independent yet interacting centres; the national government is thus not in a position to dictate to regional governments, as could happen under a system of local government. The key features of federalism usually are: (at least) two tiers of government enjoying their own right of existence under the constitution; separate legislative and executive powers; separate sources of revenue; an umpire (normally the supreme court) to decide upon disputes between the different levels; and a bicameral parliament which provides for representation in regional or state government. Beyond that, federalism can and does take a variety of forms: examples include the USA, Canada, Australia, and Germany.

Federalist Party One of the two political parties that took shape in the USA in the 1790s. The issues behind its formation included President Washington's foreign policy and the domestic policies of secretary of the Treasury Alexander Hamilton. Washington (in office 1789–97) and John Adams (in office 1797–1801) were Federalist presidents, but after Jefferson's victory in the 1800 election the Federalists never held the presidency, and the party slowly faded.

Federal Reserve System (FRS) The USA Central Bank, known as 'The Fed', set up in 1913. It replaced the Independent Treasury System, established in the 1840s. The Fed divides the USA into 12 districts, each with its own Federal Reserve Bank, carries out the normal duties of a central bank, and also manages cheque clearance on behalf of member banks. It is the major regulator of the US money supply and stock market functions. Less than half of the 12 000 banks in the USA are members of the Fed.

Federal Theater Project A US project inaugurated in 1935 by an Act of Congress as part of the Works Projects Administration. It sought to provide employment to theatre professionals during the Depression, and 'free, adult, uncensored theatre' throughout the country. At the height of its activity, it is thought to have operated in 40 states, and employed 10 000 people. This experiment in federal sponsorship was terminated by Congress in June 1939.

Federer, Roger [**fed**erer] (1981–) Tennis player, born in Basel, Switzerland. He won the Wimbledon boys' singles and doubles titles in 1998 and turned professional later that year. At Wimbledon 2001 he caused a sensation by knocking out reigning singles champion Pete Sampras in the fourth round. In 2003 he became the first Swiss man to win a Grand Slam title when he became Wimbledon singles champion. At the beginning of 2004 he had a world ranking of Number 2, and went on to win his second Grand Slam with the Australian Open title.

feedback The process by which information is conveyed to the source of the original output; also, the information itself. The term comes from cybernetics, and is applied both to machines and to animal and human communication, whereby it enables the sender of a message to monitor its reception and make any necessary modification.

Feininger, Lyonel (Charles Adrian) [**fiy**ninger] (1871–1956) Painter, born in New York City, USA. He worked as a political cartoonist, then devoted himself to painting (1907). After World War 1 he taught at the Bauhaus in Weimar and Dessau, and adopted a style reminiscent of Cubism. After the Nazi rise, he returned to the USA, where he helped to found the New Bauhaus in Chicago.

Feldenkrais method [**feld**nkriys] A system of slow exercises developed by nuclear physicist Moshe Feldenkrais. The system was designed to relearn free body movements (ie the way young children move) and to discard acquired restricting movement habits and postures. Feldenkrais emphasized two principles of practice: *awareness through movement*, which is practised during class sessions; and *functional integration*, practised in individual sessions when the teacher makes direct physical corrections of the student's movements. He believed that establishing new patterns of movement in the brain would benefit mental and emotional state.

feldspar or **felspar** An important group of minerals constituting about half of the rocks of the Earth's crust. All are aluminosilicates containing various proportions of potassium, sodium, and calcium (and, rarely, barium). Important minerals of the group are *orthoclase* and *microcline* (both $KAlSi_3O_8$), *albite* ($NaAlSi_3O_8$) and *anorthite* ($CaAl_2Si_2O_8$). Na,Ca feldspars are termed *plagioclase*.

Felidae [**fel**idee] The cat family (37 species); a family of muscular carnivores with camouflaged coloration; round head with powerful jaws, long canine teeth; sharp claws (usually retractable); cannot chew food; eats meat almost exclusively; usually catches own prey; hunts by stalking followed by a pounce or short sprint; species of genus *Panthera* called *big cats*.

feline calici virus / viral rhinotracheitis *cat flu*

feline immunodeficiency virus (FIV) A viral disease related to but quite separate from human immunodeficiency virus (HIV). It does not affect humans. A wide variety of clinical signs is seen in cats, as other organisms overcome the immune system. Chronic inflammation of the mouth associated with a persistent fever can lead to rapid loss of bodyweight. Most clinical signs are not specific enough for a definite diagnosis without a blood test.

feline infectious enteritis (FIE) A serious, often fatal disease of cats and other Felidae; also known as **panleucopenia (FPL)**, and occasionally by the blanket term **cat flu**. It is caused by a virus of the parvovirus group, which is particularly resistant and may persist in the environment. Young cats are very vulnerable and will soon collapse and die when infected. There is a massive drop in the number of white blood cells (*panleucopenia*). Diarrhoea is not always a feature, but dehydration is severe, prostration rapid, and morbidity high. Protection by the use of a vaccine is very effective. Booster vaccinations are essential to maintain immunity.

feline leukaemia virus (FeLV) An infectious disease of cats associated with a virus of the Oncorna group. It is most frequently seen in multi-cat households, or cat concentrations where exposure to the virus is continuous. Tumours of the lymphoid system can follow infection, as well as many other immuno-suppressive conditions. Vaccines are still being developed, but are not yet widely available outside North America. The virus can be eliminated from catteries by the application of blood tests and strict culling. The infection cannot be passed on to humans.

Fellini, Federico [feleenee] (1920–93) Film director, born in Rimini, E Italy. He studied at Bologna, and was a cartoonist, journalist, and scriptwriter before becoming an assistant film director in 1942. His highly individual films, always from his own scripts, include *La strada* (1954, The Road, Oscar), *Le notte di Cabiria* (1956, Nights of Cabiria, Oscar), *Fellini's Roma* (1972), *Amarcord* (1973, I Remember, Oscar), *Otto e mezzo* (1963, 8½), and, his most famous and controversial work, *La dolce vita* (1960, The Sweet Life; Cannes Festival prizewinner), a *succès de scandale* for its cynical evocation of modern Roman high life. In 1943 he married the actress **Giulietta Masina** (1920–94), star of several of his films. Among his later productions are *Città della donna* (1980, City of Women) and *Ginger e Fred* (1986, Ginger and Fred), and *La voce della luna* (1990, Voices of the Moon). He was presented with an Honorary Academy Award in 1993.

felony Originally, at common law, every crime which occasioned the forfeiture of land and goods, usually punishable by death. In modern times, in the USA, a felony is a crime which carries a potential punishment in a state prison of not less than one year. It corresponds roughly to an **indictable offence** in the UK, and is distinguished from a **misdemeanour**. In England and Wales, all distinctions between felony and misdemeanour were abolished in 1967.

felspar *feldspar*

felt A non-woven cloth consisting of loose 'webs' of natural or synthetic fibre, or formed in fabrics by the action of moisture, heat, and repeated pressure; the fibres become locked together by entanglement. Felts have important uses in clothing (eg hats), domestic furnishing (eg floor and table covers), and industry (eg insulators).

feminism A socio-political movement whose objective is equality of rights, status, and power for men and women. It has its roots in early 20th-c struggles for women's political emancipation (the suffragettes), but has been broadened in its political scope by the influence of radical left-wing beliefs, especially Marxism, which has led feminists to challenge both sexism and the capitalist system which is said to encourage patriarchy. Feminists are not necessarily 'anti-men', but against any social system which produces female subordination. There are now several national and international bodies, such as the National Organization of Women (NOW) in the USA. Since the 1960s the movement has been a major influence on the reform of general social attitudes, and there is a pending Equal Rights Amendment to the US Constitution.

feminist criticism Literary criticism written from a feminist standpoint. The main objectives are to re-assess the established 'canon', exposing sexist attitudes in works themselves and their selection; and also to promote the works of neglected women writers. Early influences were Virginia Woolf (eg *A Room of One's Own*, 1929) and Simone de Beauvoir's *Le Deuxième Sexe* (1949, The Second Sex). The field is now large, active, and various.

feminist theology The theological critique of a religious tradition, especially Christianity, which is regarded as being predominantly male-oriented and presented in non-inclusive language. In its reconstruction of traditional theology, emphasis is placed on symbols, models, and images which express the religious, social, and psychological experience of women.

femur [feemer] The long bone of the thigh, having a rounded head, neck, and shaft, and an expanded lower end. It articulates by the head with the pelvis (via the hip joint), the patella, and the tibia (via the knee joint). It is the largest and longest bone in the body, and gives attachment to powerful muscle groups which move the thigh with respect to the trunk, and also the calf with respect to the thigh.

fencing The art of fighting with a sword, one of the oldest sports, which can be traced back to the ancient Egyptians c.1300 BC. Fencing was popular in the Middle Ages, and the rapier was developed by the end of the 16th-c. Modern weapons consist of the *sabre*, *foil*, and *épée*. In competitive fencing, different target areas exist for each weapon, and contestants wear electronically wired clothing to indicate successful hits. Because of its dangers, competitors also wear protective masks.

Fénelon, François de Salignac de la Mothe [faynelõ] (1651–1715) Roman Catholic theologian, born in Fénelon, SW France. Ordained in 1675, in 1689 Louis XIV made him tutor to his grandson, and in this position he wrote several works, notably *Les Aventures de Télémaque* (1699, The Adventures of Telemachus), which received the king's censure for its political undertones. He became Archbishop of Cambrai in 1695. In 1697 he wrote *Explanation of the Sayings of the Saints on the Interior Life* (trans title). The book was condemned by the pope, a decision which Fénelon accepted, and he retired to Cambrai.

feng shui [fung shway] (Chin 'under the canopy of heaven') The study of harmony with nature, based on the principles of I Ching. It was originally used to determine the most auspicious site to place a tomb, so that an ancestor's spirit could be in harmony with heaven and earth. The study of these principles later extended to harmonizing both internal and external environments, and to include the location of buildings, the details of architecture, and even the decoration of rooms and the placement of furniture. Practitioners search for the energy flow through the environment, and use the specific remedies to channel this energy for the good of the people there.

Fenians [feenianz] (Gaelic *Fianna* 'warriors') The short title of the Irish Republican Brotherhood, a nationalist organization founded as the Fenian Brotherhood by John O'Mahony (1816–77) in New York in 1857 and as the Irish Republican Brotherhood by James Stephens (1825–1901) in Ireland in 1858. Its military wing was known as the Irish Republican Army (IRA). The movement quickly espoused violent rebellion as a means of achieving its objective. Fenian invasions of Canada (1866, 1870, 1871) failed. In England, the Fenians attempted to seize Chester Castle; they rescued two of their members in Manchester (1867); and in an unsuccessful bid to rescue Irish prisoners in London the same year, killed 12 people. Several Fenians were executed and hundreds more imprisoned. As a result of the violence, Gladstone tried to solve the problem of Irish discontent through the introduction of Home Rule and the election of several Fenians to Westminster. The movement was superseded in the USA by Clan-na Gael, a secret society headed by John Devoy (1849–1928), and by other organizations supporting Irish republicanism.

Fenn, John B (1917–) Chemist, born in New York City, New York, USA. He studied at Yale University, later joining Virginia Commonwealth University. He shared the 2002 Nobel Prize for Chemistry for the development of soft desorption ionization methods for mass spectrometric analyses of biological macromolecules.

fennec fox A small nocturnal fox (*Vulpes zerda*) native to deserts in N Africa and Kuwait; smallest member of the dog family; thick pale coat, enormous ears; digs long burrows in sand; eats rodents, birds, lizards, insects; also known as **desert fox**.

fennel A strong-smelling, bluish-green biennial or perennial (*Foeniculum vulgare*), growing to 2·5 m/8 ft, native to the Mediterranean region; leaves feathery, much divided into thread-like segments; flowers yellow, in umbels to 8 cm/3 in across; fruit ovoid, ribbed. Cultivated since classical times, the leaves are used as a flavouring. Cultivated forms with swollen bases to the leaf stalks are eaten raw in salads or cooked as a vegetable. (Family: Umbelliferae.)

Fens, the or **the Fen Country** Flat marshy land surrounding the Wash, in Lincolnshire, Norfolk, Suffolk, and Cambridgeshire, E England, UK; extends 112 km/70 mi N–S and 6 km/4 mi E–W; watered by the Witham, Welland, Nene, and Ouse Rivers; remnant of a silted-up North Sea bay; artificially drained since Roman times; major reclamation in 17th-c under 5th Earl of Bedford and his Dutch engineer, Cornelius Vermuyden; in mediaeval times, monasteries built on 'islands' of dry land; market gardening, fruit, vegetables, grazing.

Fenton, James (Martin) (1949–) Poet and essayist, born in Lincoln, Lincolnshire, EC England, UK. Educated at Repton and Magdalen College, Oxford, his first collections of poems, *Terminal Moraine* (1972), won the Eric Gregory Award. He was war correspondent for the *New Statesman*, reporting most notably on the fall of Saigon. Later works of poetry include *Partingtime Hall* (together with John Fuller), *The Memory of War* (1982), and *Out of Danger* (1993). He became professor of poetry at Oxford in 1994.

fenugreek An annual (*Trigonella foenum-graecum*) growing to 50 cm/20 in, a native of SW Asia; leaves have three shallowly toothed leaflets; pea-flowers yellowish-white, solitary or in pairs, stalkless in the upper leaf axils; pod up to 10 cm/4 in long. Grown for fodder, its seeds are edible (used in curries), and it is also employed medicinally. (Family: Leguminosae.)

fer-de-lance [fair duh lahns] (Fr 'spearhead') A New World pit viper; powerful venom; two species: *Bothrops atrox* (**Southern fer-de-lance**) and *Bothrops asper* (**Central American fer-de-lance**), two of the species most responsible for human death by snakebite; also known as **lancehead viper**. Other pit vipers may also be referred to as lanceheads.

Ferdinand I (of the Two Sicilies) (1751–1825) King of Naples, as Ferdinand IV (1759–99, 1799–1806) and of the Two Sicilies (1816–25), born in Naples, SW Italy. He joined England and Austria against France in 1793, and suppressed the French-supported Roman Republic (1799), but in 1801 was forced to make a treaty with Napoleon. In 1806 he took refuge in Sicily, under English protection, being reinstated by the Congress of Vienna (1815). In 1816 he united his two states into the Kingdom of the Two Sicilies and, despite demands for constitutional government, retained a harsh absolutism.

Ferdinand III (of Castile) (1201–52) King of Castile (1217–52) and León (1230–52), the son of Alfonso IX of León and Berengaria of Castile. He permanently united the kingdoms of Castile and León. During his important reign, he campaigned against the Moors, taking Córdoba (1236), Jaén (1246), and Seville (1248), and occupied Murcia, thus completing the reconquest of Spain, except for the kingdom of Granada which became a vassal state. He was succeeded by his son, Alfonso X. Ferdinand was canonized by the Roman Catholic Church in 1671; feast day 30 May.

Ferdinand (of Castile), known as **the Catholic** (1452–1516) King of Castile as Ferdinand V (from 1474), of Aragon and Sicily as Ferdinand II (from 1479), and of Naples as Ferdinand III (from 1503), born in Sos, Aragon, Spain. In 1469 he married **Isabella**, sister of Henry IV of Castile, and ruled jointly with her until her death. He introduced the Inquisition (1478–80), and in 1492, after the defeat of the Moors, expelled the Jews. Under him, Spain gained supremacy following the discovery of America, and in 1503 he took Naples from the French, with the help of the Holy League. After Isabella's death (1504) he was regent of Castile for his insane daughter **Juana**, and in 1512 gained Navarre, thus becoming monarch of all Spain. To him and Isabella, Spain owed her unity and greatness as a nation and the foundation of her imperial influence.

Ferdinand VII, known as **Ferdinand the Desired** (1784–1833) King of Spain (1808–33), born in El Escorial, Spain, the son of Charles IV and Maria Luisa of Parma. He became involved in intrigues against the chief minister and favourite, Manuel de Godoy, and sought the support of Napoleon I. When Godoy let French troops enter Spain, Charles was overthrown by the Revolt of Aranjuez (1808), and abdicated in favour of Ferdinand, who was acclaimed by the people. Napoleon summoned Ferdinand to France and forced him to return the throne to his father. He in turn granted it to Napoleon, who then made his brother, Joseph, king of Spain and held Ferdinand prisoner during the Peninsular War (1808–14). In support of Ferdinand, the Spanish people rose against the French invaders, and the Constitution of Cadiz was proclaimed (1812). Napoleon released Ferdinand, who was restored in 1814. In 1830, Ferdinand's fourth wife, Maria Christina, gave birth to his only child, the future Isabella II.

Ferdinand, Rio (Gavin) (1978–) Footballer, born in London, UK. A defender, he joined West Ham as a schoolboy in 1995 and made his senior debut for the club in 1996. He joined Leeds in 2000 for a record fee of £18 million. He made his England debut in 1997, was a member of the England squad for the FIFA World Cup in 1998 and 2002, and by the end of the 2003 season had won 33 caps. He became the world's most expensive defender when he was bought by Manchester United in 2002 for £30 million. In September 2003 he failed to attend for a routine drugs test, and was charged with misconduct by the Football Association, resulting in a fine and an 8-month suspension (from January 2004).

Ferdusi *Firdausi*

Ferghana [fergana] A strategic point on the ancient Silk Road from China, lying W of the Tian Shan and Tarim Basin (modern Xinjiang) and E of Samarkand. It was conquered by a large Chinese army during the Han period (104–101 BC), thus establishing partial Chinese control over Turkestan. The area, now in Uzbekistan, is famous for its horses.

Ferguson, Sir Alex(ander Chapman) (1941–) Football player and manager, born in Glasgow, W Scotland, UK. A former Queens Park Rangers player, he became a manager, and had success with Aberdeen (1978–86) before taking over at Manchester United (1986–), where his achievements include the FA Cup (1990), the European Cup Winners' Cup (1991), the League and Cup double (1994, 1996, 1999), and the European Cup (1999). In 2003 he received the Manager of the Decade award, presented by the FA Premier League to mark the first 10 years of the Premiership. He was knighted in 1999.

Ferguson, Sarah *Andrew, Duke of York*

Fermanagh [fermana], Ir **Fear Manach** pop (2000e) 54 100; area 1876 sq km/715 sq mi. District and county in SW Northern Ireland, UK; bounded NW, W, S and SE by the Republic of Ireland; hilly in the NE and SW, rising to 667 m/2188 ft at Cuilcagh; Upper and Lower Lough Erne run SE–NW through the centre; county town, Enniskillen; potatoes, livestock, textiles.

Fermat, Pierre de [fermah] (1601–65) Mathematician, born in Beaumont-de-Lomagne, S France. He studied law at Toulouse, where he became a councillor of parliament. His passion was mathematics, most of his work being communicated in letters to friends containing results without proof. His correspondence with Pascal marks the foundation of probability theory. He studied maximum and minimum values of functions in advance of the differential calculus, but is best known for his work in number theory, the proofs of many of his discoveries being first published by Leonhard Euler a hundred years later. His 'last theorem' was the most famous unsolved problem in mathematics until a proof was demonstrated in 1994. In optics, *Fermat's principle* was the first statement of a variational principle in physics: the path taken by a ray of light between two given points is the one in which the light takes the least time compared with any other possible path.

Fermat's last theorem A mathematical theorem proposed by Pierre de Fermat, which states that there are no positive integers *x*, *y*, *z*, and *n* (where *n* is greater than 2), such that $x^n + y^n = z^n$ (compare $x^2 + y^2 = z^2$, where there is an infinite number of integers satisfying this relation). Fermat wrote in the margin of a book 'I have found remarkable proof of this theorem, but the margin is too narrow to contain it'. The theorem was proved by British mathematician Andrew Wiles (1953–) in 1994.

Fermat's principle *see panel*

fermentation A chemical reaction in which an organic compound is broken down through the action of an enzyme. This process is typically carried out using bacteria or yeast to metabolize carbohydrates in the absence of oxygen. The two most common end-products of fermentation are lactic acid and ethanol, but the exact end-product depends on the type of bacteria and the nature of the material used.

Fermi, Enrico [fermee] (1901–54) Nuclear physicist, born in Rome, Italy. He studied at Pisa, Göttingen, and Leyden, and became professor of theoretical physics at Rome in 1927. In 1934 he and his colleagues split a number of nuclei by bombardment with neutrons, for which he was awarded the 1938 Nobel Prize for Physics. He did not return to Italy from his Nobel Prize presentation in Stockholm because the Italian anti-Semitic laws affected his Jewish wife, but became professor at Columbia University (1939). He played a prominent part in developing atomic energy, constructed the first nuclear reactor at Chicago (1942), and was part of the Manhattan project. After the War he joined the newly created Institute of Nuclear Studies at the University of Chicago.

Fermi–Dirac statistics [fermee dirak] In quantum statistical mechanics, the description of collections of many non-interacting fermions. The Fermi–Dirac distribution expresses the partition of energy amongst fermions, used for example in the study of the free electron gas in metals.

fermion Subatomic particle having half integer spin; the particle of matter; named after Enrico Fermi. The Pauli exclusion principle states that no two fermions may occupy the same state. Electrons, protons, and quarks are all fermions.

fern A member of a large group of spore-bearing, vascular plants related to clubmosses and horsetails, and containing some 10 000 species which comprise the class Filicopsida or Filicinae. Like their relatives, they have a long fossil record containing many extinct forms. Ferns appear as early as the Devonian period, but they were especially abundant and diverse during the Carboniferous. The visible plant is the diploid sporophyte, the dominant generation in ferns. It typically has one or more large, often much-divided fronds which are characteristically coiled in a crozier shape when young, unfurling as they grow. The undersides of fertile fronds bear sporangia, which may be grouped into sori forming distinctive patterns; the position, shape, and covering (*indusium*) of each sorus is diagnostically important. When released from the sporangia, the spores germinate to form haploid *prothalli*, the gametophyte generation. In ferns these are very small, often heart-shaped and short-lived; this is the more vulnerable generation, requiring damp habitats and being easily killed by harsh conditions.

Ferns embrace a large number of forms. A few are annuals, but most are perennials with tough rhizomes. The fronds typically form a rosette, but may be produced singly or at intervals along the rhizome. Several species are climbers; some have stout, erect, trunk-like rhizomes; and a few are genuinely arborescent – tree forms with tall, rigid trunks bearing a crown of fronds. A small number of species are aquatic. In these the fronds are very reduced, and have non-wettable hairs to ensure they float. Although more or less cosmopolitan, the majority of species are concentrated in the tropics and in the warmer, more humid parts of the world. (Class: Filicinae.)

Fermat's principle

A principle in physics: light rays travel between two points in such a way that the time taken is a minimum; stated by Pierre de Fermat in 1657. It is a special case of the least-action principle.

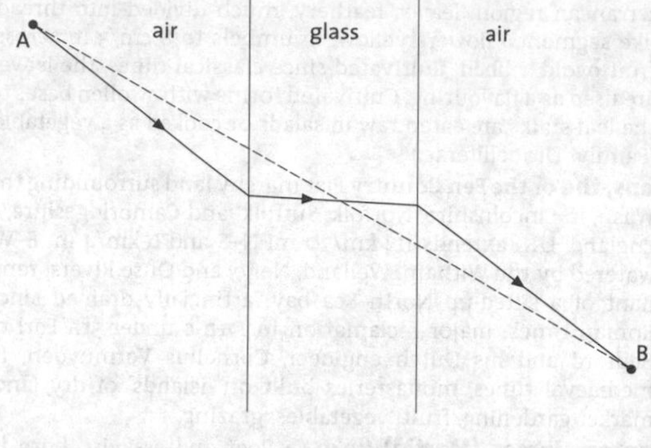

The dotted line shows the shortest path between A and B. A light beam follows the solid line, consistent with the laws of refraction, because the velocity of light in the glass is less than in air. The solid line is the path of least time.

Fernandel [fernãdel], stage name of **Fernand Joseph Désiré Contandin** (1903–71) Film comedian, born in Marseille, S France. He worked in a bank and soap factory before his debut on the stage in 1922, and from 1930 appeared in over a hundred films, interrupted only temporarily by military service and Nazi occupation. He established himself internationally with his moving portrayal of the naive country priest of *The Little World of Don Camillo* (1953), and with his versatile handling of six separate roles in *The Sheep has Five Legs* (1953), which gave full rein to his extraordinary facial mobility.

Fernández de Moratín, Leandro (1760–1828) Poet and playwright, born in Madrid, Spain. Considered the most influential Neoclassical literary figure of the Spanish Enlightenment, he supported the French Encyclopaedists and translated the works of Molière and Shakespeare. His social satires include the plays *La comedia nueva* (1792, The New Comedy) and *El sí de las niñas* (1806, The Maiden's Consent). From 1814 he lived in France, and after his death his remains were taken to Madrid.

Fernando Póo *Bioko*

Ferrar, Nicholas (1592–1637) Anglican clergyman and spiritual mystic, born in London, UK. After studying medicine, and a brief period in politics, he became a deacon in the Church of England (1626). At Little Gidding in Huntingdonshire he founded a small religious community which engaged in constant services and perpetual prayer, while carrying out a range of crafts, such as bookbinding. It was broken up by the Puritans in 1647.

Ferrara [fayrahra] 44°50N 11°38E, pop (2000e) 148 000. Ancient town and capital of Ferrara province, Emilia-Romagna region, N Italy; seat of the Council of Ferrara (1439) and of the 15th-c Renaissance court; ceded to France (1797–1815); part of Kingdom of Sardinia, 1859; archbishopric; railway; university (1391); sugar, hemp, milling, agricultural machinery, chemicals, trade in fruit and wine; birthplace of Savonarola; Castello Estense (14th–16th-c), cathedral (12th–14th-c), Church of San Giorgio 15th-c.

Ferrari, Enzo [ferahree] (1898–1988) Racing-car designer, born in Modena, N Italy. He became a racing driver in 1920 (with Alfa-Romeo), founded the company which bears his name (1929), and was its president until 1977. In 1940 he began designing his own cars. Since 1951, the marque has been a major presence at Grand Prix races.

Ferraro, Geraldine A(nne) [ferahroh], married name **Zacarro** (1935–) US politician, born in Newburgh, New York, USA. She studied at Marymount College, Fordham University, and New York Law School, establishing a successful law practice (1961–74). She was assistant district attorney for the Queens district of New York (1974–8), then worked at the Supreme Court, heading a special bureau for victims of violent crime. She was elected as a Democrat to the US House of Representatives in 1981, where she gained a reputation as an effective, liberal-minded politician. She was selected in 1984 by Walter Mondale to be the first female vice-presidential candidate of a major party. In 1992 and 1998 she ran in the New York senatorial primary, but lost the nomination despite much popular support. In 1993 she was appointed US representative to the UN Human Rights Commission.

ferrate A compound containing iron as part of an anion.

ferret A domesticated form of the European polecat (*Mustela putorius*); yellowish-white with pink eyes; domesticated over 2000 years ago; sent down burrows to chase out rabbits; bred white so it is not mistaken for a rabbit. The name **black-footed ferret** is used for the North American polecat *Mustela nigripes*, formerly thought to be extinct in the wild, but now being re-established through a programme of the US Fish and Wildlife Service.

ferricyanide $Fe(CN)_6^{3-}$, IUPAC **hexacyanoferrate(III)** (red). **Hexacyanoferrate(II)** (yellow), $Fe(CN)_6^{4}$, is called *ferrocyanide*. Both react with more iron ions to form an intense blue precipitate called *Prussian blue*.

Ferrier, Kathleen (1912–53) Contralto singer, born in Higher Walton, Lancashire, NW England, UK. A singing prize at a local music festival led her to undertake serious studies in 1940, and she rapidly won a great reputation. One of her greatest successes was in Mahler's *Das Lied von der Erde* (The Song of the Earth) at the first Edinburgh Festival (1947).

ferrimagnetism The magnetic property of materials for which neighbouring atomic magnetic moments are of different strengths and are aligned antiparallel. It is related to ferromagnetism, but exhibiting much weaker gross magnetic properties. It is observed in ferrites and certain other materials.

ferrites A class of ceramic materials composed of oxides of iron and some other metal such as copper, nickel, or manganese. Of low electrical conductivity, and ferrimagnetic, they are used as core material in high-frequency electrical coils, loudspeaker magnets, and video/audio tape-recorder heads. Ferrous ferrite $Fe(Fe_2O_4)$, or *magnetite*, is the lodestone of antiquity.

ferro-alloys Combinations of elements added to molten steel to impart various properties, such as greater corrosion resistance or strength.

ferrocene [feroseen] $Fe(C_5H_5)_2$, orange solid, melting point 173°C, first prepared in 1951, in which an iron atom is symmetrically bonded to two cyclopentadienyl rings. It was the first of a series of transition metal organometallic compounds called **metallocenes**.

ferroelectrics Crystalline materials (eg barium titanate, $BaTiO_3$) having an overall electric dipole moment, even without an external field present, that can be reversed by the application of an external electric field. The effect is due to displacement between the atoms in the entire lattice, such that the centres of positive and negative charge no longer coincide. Above a certain material-dependent temperature, thermal motion disrupts the lattice ordering, and the ferroelectric property is lost. Thin films of ferroelectric materials offer potential in computer memory chips (ferroelectric memory).

ferromagnetism A property of ferromagnetic substances (eg iron, nickel, cobalt, gadolinium, dysprosium, and many alloys) arising from large-scale alignment between atomic magnetic moments. An applied magnetic field intensity H, supplied by a surrounding electric coil, causes a disproportionately large magnetic flux density B to appear in the bulk material. A field may remain in the material even when the external field has been removed, resulting in permanent magnets. The atoms of many elements have unpaired electrons, giving rise to magnetic moments which typically cause paramagnetism in the bulk material. Ferromagnetism is like paramagnetism, with an extra ingredient causing alignment.

fertility drugs Drugs which treat infertility in women – usually successfully if it is due to a failure to ovulate. Early fertility drugs caused multiple pregnancies, but newer drugs such as clomiphene are not so extreme, though the incidence of twins is 10% of all successful pregnancies. Infertility in males is more difficult to treat.

fertilization The union of two gametes to form a zygote, as occurs during sexual reproduction. The gametes are typically male (a sperm) and female (an egg), and both are haploid (possess a single chromosome set). Fertilization involves the fusion of the two haploid nuclei to form a diploid zygote that develops into a new individual. The process is external in some aquatic animals, such as echinoderms, with both sperm and eggs being released into the water. Most terrestrial organisms, including the higher vertebrates, have internal fertilization, in which union of the gametes occurs inside the female.

fertilizer A substance which provides plant nutrients when added to soil. The term normally refers to inorganic chemicals containing one or more of the basic plant nutrients: nitrogen, phosphorus, or potash. It may also refer to compounds containing trace elements such as boron, cobalt, copper, iron, manganese, molybdenum, and zinc; to lime, which is used to correct acidity; or to a concentrated organic substance such as dried blood and bonemeal. The term is also popularly used in a general sense to include organic materials, such as manure and compost. Fertilizers are added to the soil in granular, crystalline, powder, or liquid forms and may be injected directly into the ground or broadcast on the surface. Nitrogen usually comes in the form of nitrates or ammonium compounds, phosphorus in the form of phosphates, and potash in the form of potassium chloride or sulphate. Since the Second World War the use of inorganic fertilizers has risen in response to the huge increases in grain production. High levels of fertilizer application, especially of nitrogenous compounds, can cause pollution of watercourses and drinking water supplies. In some countries, legal limitations are imposed on the total quantity of fertilizer which may be added to the land during each season.

Fès *Fez*

fescue A tufted grass with inrolled, bristle-like leaves, found almost everywhere; important as pasture grass. Upland species are often viviparous, ie the seeds germinate to form plantlets before being shed from the inflorescence. (Genus: *Festuca*, c.80 species. Family: Gramineae.)

Festival of Britain An event organized in 1951 to mark the centenary of the Great Exhibition held in London in 1851, intended to demonstrate 'the British contribution to civilization, past, present, and future, in the arts, in science and technology, and in industrial design'. The Royal Festival Hall was built for the occasion.

fetch *wave* (oceanography)

fetus / foetus The embryo of a mammal, especially a human, at a stage of development when all the main features of the adult form are recognizable. In humans, this stage is from 8 weeks to birth.

feudalism A modern construct from Lat *feudum* ('fief'), originally coined in 1839, referring to phenomena associated more or less closely with the Middle Ages. In a narrow sense, the word is used to describe the mediaeval military and political order based on reciprocal ties between lords and vassals, in which the main elements were the giving of homage and the tenure of fiefs. Such developments emerged in both Europe and Japan. Though normally associated with political fragmentation, feudalism as here defined could serve as the ally of royal power. The system broke down in the more developed societies in Europe in the 12th-c and 13th-c as towns and individuals achieved independence from their lords, though serfdom survived in some countries (eg Russia) for much longer. Polemicists apply the term to whatever appears backward or reactionary in the modern world.

Feuerbach, Ludwig (Andreas) [**foy**erbakh] (1804–72) Philosopher, born in Landshut, SE Germany. He studied theology at Heidelberg and Berlin, then philosophy at Erlangen. He was a pupil of Hegel, but reacted against his idealism. Feuerbach's most famous work, *Das Wesen des Christentums* (1841, The Essence of Christianity), claims that religion rises from one's alienation from oneself, and the projection of ideal human qualities onto a fictitious supreme 'other'. His naturalistic materialism was a strong influence on Marx and Engels.

Feuillants, Club of the [foeyã] An association of moderate deputies and former members of the Jacobin Club, led by the Marquis de Lafayette (1757–1834), Antoine Barnave (1761–93), and Jean Bailly (1736–93), who aimed at establishing a constitutional monarchy in France during the first stage of the Revolution (1791).

fever A clinical condition when the temperature of the body rises above the upper limit of normal; also known as **pyrexia**. Individuals with a fever are said to be *febrile*. Taking the temperature of a patient has been routine in medical practice for over 100 years. Normal temperature is between 36·6 and 37·7°C, measured with a rectal thermometer. Body temperature depends on a balance between heat production and heat loss, and is regulated by the hypothalamus. Fever is produced when the temperature regulation system is disturbed by chemicals called *pyrogens*, which are released when cells are damaged by certain pathological processes. Fever is most often a result of infection, but some cancers and mycocardial infarction (dead heart tissue) may also be responsible.

feverfew An aromatic perennial (*Tanacetum parthenium*) growing to 60 cm/2 ft, probably native to SE Europe and parts of Asia, and widely introduced elsewhere; leaves yellowish-green, with lobed or toothed leaflets; flower-heads up to 2 cm/¾ in across, long-stalked in loose, flat-topped clusters; spreading outer florets white, inner disc florets yellow. It is grown for ornament and as a medicinal herb, reputed to provide relief from migraines, but it has toxic side-effects. (Family: Compositae.)

Feynman, Richard (Phillips) [**fiyn**man] (1918–88) Physicist, born in Far Rockaway, New York, USA. He worked on the US atomic bomb in World War 2, then became a professor of theoretical physics at Cornell (1945) and the California Institute of Technology (1951). He shared the Nobel Prize for Physics in 1965 for his work on quantum electrodynamics, and is also known for his graphical representation of the behaviour of interacting particles, known as **Feynman diagrams**.

Feynman diagrams [**fiyn**man] Diagrams representing specific terms in calculations in quantum field theory; developed by Richard Feynman in the 1940s. Each line and junction between lines has a precise mathematical equivalent. Such diagrams are extensively used in particle physics calculations, and also in solid-state physics. Any physical process corresponds to an infinite number of diagrams, while actual calculations incorporate only the simplest. The branch of mathematics involved is called *perturbation theory*.

Fez or **Fès** [fez] 34°05N 5°00W, pop (2000e) 653 000. City in Centre-Nord province, NC Morocco, 240 km/150 mi NE of Casablanca; oldest of Morocco's four imperial cities; Old Fez, a world heritage site, founded in 808 by Moulay Idriss II; New Fez founded in 1276 by the Merinade dynasty, includes the Sultan's palace (Dar el Makhzen); modern Fez (Ville Nouvelle) S of the railway; name given to a type of red felt hat worn by many Islamic followers; railway; textiles, carpets, leather, soap, fruit, crafts; major centre of Islamic learning; Karaouine mosque (first built, 9th-c) became famous as a Muslim university.

Fianna Fáil [fiana foyl] (Ir 'Militia of Ireland') An Irish political party founded in 1926 by those opposed to the 1921 Anglo-Irish Treaty. It first came to power under de Valera in 1932, and has been the governing party for most of the period since. In the 1930s it emphasized separation from the British, and has consistently supported the unification of Ireland. In domestic issues its approach is more pragmatic than ideological.

fiber *fibre*

Fibonacci, Leonardo [fibon**ah**chee], also known as **Leonardo Pisano** (c.1170–c.1250) Mathematician, born in Pisa, W Italy. Arguably the most outstanding mathematician of the Middle Ages, he popularized the modern decimal system of numerals, and in his greatest work, the *Liber quadratorum* (1225, The Book of Square Numbers), made an advanced contribution to number theory. He also discovered the **Fibonacci sequence** of integers in which each number is equal to the sum of the preceding two (0,1,1,2,3,5,8...).

fibre / fiber That part of plant carbohydrates which cannot be digested by the normal carbohydrate-digesting enzymes in the small intestine. Fibre consists of the structural carbohydrates of the plant cell wall and some other non-starch polysaccharides. The most abundant fibre in nature, cellulose, is made up of repeating glucose units in long single strands, making it ideal for conversion into the fabric cotton. Other fibre fractions are hemicellulose and pectin. Some fibres are fermented by bacteria in the large bowel, which leads to an increase in stool weight through an increase in faecal bacteria. Other fibres are more resistant to bacterial fermentation, but increase stool weight through their water-binding capacity. A high-fibre diet is also now recommended for diabetics, because of the way dietary fibre can slow down the release of glucose into the blood.

fibre / fiber-distributed data interface (FDDI) A standard protocol for the design and implementation of local area networks. It is based on the use of fibre optics rather than coaxial cable to link the workstations on the network.

fibre-glass / fiber-glass A composite material for the construction of light, generally complex-curved structures, made of glass fibres embedded in a polyester or epoxy resin which can be moulded before setting; more fully described as **glass fibre reinforced plastic**. It is much used for such structures as hulls of boats, tanks for liquids, and occasionally for car bodies. In the USA, *Fibreglas* is a registered trade mark for this material.

fibre optics *optical fibres*

fibres / fibers The fundamental units from which textiles are made. Natural fibres occur naturally in fibrous form, and include wool, cotton, linen, jute, cashmere, and silk. Synthetic fibres are made from polymers using oil as the raw material; examples include nylons, polyesters, and acrylics.

fibroid A benign tumour that develops within or is attached to the uterine wall; also known as a **leiomyoma**. It results from an abnormal overgrowth of the muscle and connective tissue of the uterus. The cause is unknown, but is probably related to oestrogen stimulation, since fibroids tend to enlarge with oestrogen therapy (such as oral contraceptives) and during pregnancy. Fibroids develop from a young age, and are present in a fifth of women over 35. They continue to grow during a woman's reproductive lifetime, and regress after the menopause. Large fibroids produce symptoms of increased menstrual blood loss and abdominal swelling. They can lead to infertility by preventing implantation of an embryo, and can interfere with a pregnancy since the space available for the fetus to grow inside the uterine cavity is reduced. Treatment may involve drugs to shrink a fibroid, or surgery (*myomectomy*) to remove it.

fibrositis [fiybruh**siy**tis] An imprecise lay term referring to aching in the muscles, which may be locally tender. It is usually felt in the neck, shoulders, or back. The underlying nature of the disorder is unknown in the majority of cases.

fibula [**fib**yoola] A long slender bone in the calf, which articulates with the foot (via the ankle joint) and the tibia. It has a head, neck, shaft, and an expanded lower end. It is thought to have no weight-bearing function, but gives attachment to many of the muscles of the calf. Compression on or fracture of the neck of the fibula may lead to nerve damage (the common peroneal nerve) leading to foot drop.

Fichte, Johann Gottlieb [fikhtuh] (1762–1814) Philosopher, born in Rammenau, E Germany. He studied theology and then philosophy at Jena, becoming an ardent disciple of Kant. As professor of philosophy at Jena (1794) he modified the Kantian system in his *Wissenschaftslehre* (1785, Theory of Knowledge) by substituting for the 'thing-in-itself' as the absolute reality, the more subjective *Ego*, the primitive act of consciousness. In 1805 he became professor at Erlangen, where he published the more popular versions of his philosophy. His historical importance is as the author of *Reden an die deutsche Nation* (1807–8, Addresses to the German Nation), in which he invoked a metaphysical German nationalism to resistance against Napoleon. In 1810 the University of Berlin was opened, and Fichte, who had drawn up its constitution, became its first rector.

Fichtelberg [fikhtelberg] Mountain in the Erzgebirge range, S of Chemnitz, on the frontier between Germany and the Czech Republic; height 1214 m/3983 ft; heavily forested.

Fichtelgebirge [fikhtelgebeerguh], Czech **Smrčiny** Horseshoe-shaped mountain range in Bavaria, Germany; highest peak Schneeberg (1051 m/3448 ft); source of rivers Main, Saale, Eger, Naab; largely covered with fir forests; some minerals; links the Erzgebirge and the Bohemian Forest.

Ficino, Marsilio [ficheenoh] (1433–99) Philosopher, born in Figline, NC Italy. A Latin and Greek scholar, Cosimo de' Medici appointed him head of the Platonic Academy in Florence in 1462. He devoted most of his life to translating the works of Plato and his successors into Latin from the original Greek, and trying to reconcile Platonism with Christianity.

fiddler crab A marine crab commonly found on intertidal mud flats in tropical and subtropical regions; adults make burrows in mud, emerging to feed on surface when tide is out; males have a large claw used for signalling during courtship. (Class: Malacostraca. Order: Decapoda.)

FIDE [feeday] *chess*

Fidei Defensor *Defender of the Faith*

fideism The view that the principles of some area of inquiry cannot be established by reason, but must be accepted on faith. Fideism in religion may claim either that the basic tenets of religious belief go beyond what reason can establish or, more radically (with Kierkegaard), that they contradict reason.

Field, Cyrus W(est) (1819–92) Financier, born in Stockbridge, Massachusetts, USA. After a career as a paper manufacturer, he helped to finance the first telegraph cable across the Atlantic (1866), achieved after several attempts. He also organized the New York, Newfoundland, and London Telegraph Co (1854), and the Atlantic Telegraph Co (1856), but suffered heavy financial losses.

Field, John (1782–1837) Composer and pianist, born in Dublin, Ireland. An infant prodigy, he was apprenticed to Clementi, who used him to demonstrate the capabilities of his pianos. In 1804 he settled in Russia as a music teacher, in 1821 moving to Moscow. He wrote mainly for the piano (including seven concertos), and is credited with originating the nocturne. His music influenced Chopin.

field (photography) In television, one complete top-to-bottom traverse of the scanned picture. With interlaced scanning, two such fields of alternate lines are required to build up the complete image or frame.

field emission The emission of electrons from a metal surface caused by the application of an intense electric field. Field emission microscopes guide electrons emitted from a sharp metal point to a screen, forming a highly magnified image of the metal's structure.

fieldfare A thrush native to Europe and Asia (*Turdus pilaris*); found in S Greenland since 1937; brown back, mottled breast, grey head; inhabits woodland and farmland; eats fruit, insects, worms, and slugs.

field hockey *hockey*

Fielding, Helen (1958–) Novelist, born in Yorkshire, N England, UK. She studied at Oxford University, then worked in newspaper and television journalism, producing documentaries in Africa for Comic Relief. This provided her with the inspiration for her first work of fiction, *Cause Celeb* (1994). However, it was her comic novel *Bridget Jones's Diary* (1996, filmed 2001) – originally a weekly newspaper column about the fictional life of a single woman – that brought her enormous success. A sequel *Bridget Jones: The Edge of Reason* appeared in 2000, and *Olivia Joules and the Overactive Imagination* in 2003.

Fielding, Henry (1707–54) Playwright and novelist, born at Sharpham Park, Glastonbury, Somerset, SW England, UK. He studied at Leyden, and began to write theatrical comedies, becoming author/manager of the Little Theatre in the Haymarket (1736). However, the sharpness of his burlesques led to the Licensing Act (1737), which closed his theatre, and resulted in strict control and censorship of the London Theatre. In search of an alternative career, he was called to the bar (1740), but his interests lay in journalism and fiction. On Richardson's publication of *Pamela* (1740), he wrote his famous parody, *Joseph Andrews* (1742). Several other works followed, notably *The History of Tom Jones, A Foundling* (1749), which established his reputation as a founder of the English novel. As a reward for his government journalism, he was made justice of the peace to Westminster, where he helped to form the Bow Street Runners, precursors of the police force.

field ion microscope A sharply pointed metal electrode maintained at a high positive potential relative to a screen. Gas ions form from gas atoms close to the tip, due to the extreme electric field (a form of field emission), and are guided to the screen producing an image of the tip structure. Magnifications of 1·5 million may be achieved, allowing individual atoms to be resolved; useful for studying adsorption at surfaces, and surface reactions in catalysis.

fieldmouse A mouse of genus *Apodemus* (**Old World field mice** or **wood mice**, 13 species) or of genus *Akodon* (**South American field mice** or **grass mice**, 41 species). Old World fieldmice often jump (they may leap 1 m/3¼ ft vertically); South American fieldmice have short legs, and are less athletic.

Field of the Cloth of Gold, the A meeting between Henry VIII and Francis I on a plain in Picardy between Guines and Ardres in 1520, in which France hoped to gain English support against the Emperor Charles V; named after the lavish pavilions of golden cloth erected by the French. The English built a temporary two-storey palace, 320 ft/97 m square, of glass and wood, in which the king and his magnificent retinue were housed. Lavish and spectacular arrangements were made by the French and English for jousting, dancing, and banqueting. Henry, however, later met the emperor, with whom he effected a treaty (1520).

Fields, Dame Gracie, originally **Grace Stansfield** (1898–1979) Singer and variety star, born in Rochdale, Greater Manchester, NW England, UK. She first appeared on stage at the age of 10, made her London debut in 1915, and by 1928 was firmly established in variety. With her sentimental songs and broad Lancashire humour, she won a unique place in the affections of British audiences. Her theme tune, 'Sally', she first sang in 1931. She was created a dame in 1978.

Fields, W C, originally **William Claude Dukenfield** (1879–1946) Actor, born in Philadelphia, Pennsylvania, USA. He ran away from home and became a vaudeville actor and juggler in the early 1900s, touring widely in England, then around the world, including Australia and Hawaii. He appeared in the Ziegfeld Follies, but established his comic persona in silent films such as *Sally of the Sawdust* (1925). His distinctive voice found its full scope with the coming of sound in the cinema, and he was in regular demand during the 1930s.

Fields Medal An award established by the 1924 International Congress of Mathematicians (ICM) in Toronto to honour outstanding mathematical achievement. It was decided to present two gold medals at each future congress (every four years from 1936), and Professor J D Fields donated funds to establish the award. Equivalent to the Nobel Prize, the Fields Medal is restricted to mathematicians up to the age of forty at the year of the ICM and recognizes both existing work and the promise of further achievement. Since 1966 up to four medals may be awarded.

Fiennes, Joseph (Alberic) [fiynz] (1970–) Actor, born in Salisbury, Wiltshire, S England, UK, the brother of Ralph Fiennes. He trained at the Guildhall School of Music and Drama (1993) in London, then had a number of stage roles before joining the Royal Shakespeare Company for two seasons. His first feature film appearance was in *Stealing Beauty* (1996), and he became known after his role as Sir Robert Dudley in *Elizabeth* (1998). Later films include *Shakespeare in Love* (1998), *Enemy at the Gates* (2000), and *Dust* (2001).

Fiennes, Ralph (Nathaniel) [rayf fiynz] (1962–) Actor, born in Suffolk, UK, the brother of Joseph Fiennes. He studied drama at the Royal Academy of Dramatic Art in London before joining the National Theatre (1987) and the Royal Shakespeare Company (1989–90). His film debut was in Emily Bronte's *Wuthering Heights* (1991), and his compelling performance in *Schindler's List* (1993) earned him a Golden Globe Award and an Oscar nomination for Best Supporting Actor. Other films include *The Baby of Macon* (1993), *The English Patient* (1996, Oscar nomination), *Oscar and Lucinda* (1997), *The End of the Affair* (1999), and *Spider* (2002).

Fiennes, Sir Ranulph (Twisleton-Wykeham-) [fiynz] (1944–) Explorer and expedition leader, born in Windsor, S England, UK. Educated at Eton, he served with the Royal Scots Greys and the SAS. He was the leader of several expeditions, from hovercraft on the White Nile (1969) to the Transglobe (1979–82), tracing the Greenwich Meridian across both Poles. With Michael Stroud he completed the first unsupported crossing on foot of the Antarctic in 1993, covering 1350 mi in 95 days. In 2000 he was forced to abandon his 520-mile solo trek to the North Pole because of frostbite. He has published several books recounting his adventures. In 2003, four months after having life-saving heart surgery, he successfully completed the challenge to run seven marathons in seven continents in seven days. With Stroud as his running partner, he began in Santiago, Chile (27 Oct) and flew on to the Falkland Is, Sydney, Singapore, London, and Cairo, finishing in New York (2 Nov).

FIFA [feefa] The abbreviation of **Fédération Internationale de Football Association**, the world governing body of association football, founded in Paris in 1904 with seven members. There are now 150 member countries affiliated. FIFA stages its World Cup tournament every four years.

Fife, also sometimes called **Kingdom of Fife** pop (2000e) 354 500; area 1307 sq km/505 sq mi. Local council in E Scotland, UK; bounded by the Firth of Tay (N), North Sea (E), and the Firth of Forth (S); low-lying region, drained by Eden and Leven Rivers; Lomond Hills in the W; many small fishing ports; oil, gas, and chemical developments in the W at Mossmorran; coal mining (open cast, serving the Longannet power station); interior mainly farmland; capital, Glenrothes; other chief towns, Dunfermline, Cowdenbeath, Cupar, St Andrews (notable golf courses).

fife A small, high-pitched, transverse flute, with six fingerholes and (in modern and some older instruments) metal keys. Fifes have been mainly military instruments, used (like the bugle) for calls and signals, and also, in 'drum and fife' bands, for marching.

Fifteen Rebellion The name given to the first of the Jacobite rebellions against Hanoverian monarchy to restore the Catholic Stuart kings to the British throne. The rising was begun at Braemar (Sep 1715) by the Earl of Mar, proclaiming James Edward Stuart ('the Old Pretender') as king. Jacobite forces were defeated at Preston in November, and the rebellion collapsed early in 1716. Twenty-six officers suffered the death penalty, and about 700 of the rank-and-file were sent to the West Indies to serve as indentured servants. Mar died in exile.

fifth column A popular expression from the early days of World War 2 to describe enemy sympathizers who might provide active help to an invader. The name originally described the rebel sympathizers in Madrid in 1936 during the Spanish Civil War, when four rebel columns were advancing on the city.

fifth force A new force postulated by US physicist Ephraim Fischbach (1942–) and others in 1986, in addition to the four recognized fundamental forces. It is weaker than gravity, and of intermediate range. It is claimed that, due to the fifth force, the apparent gravitational force between objects separated by distances of a few hundred metres depends on the material from which they are made, and varies only approximately as r^{-2}. However, the experimental results were ambiguous, and the theory is no longer taken seriously.

fifth-generation computers *computer generations*

fifty-four forty or fight A slogan used in the 1840s to advocate US seizure of British Columbia, whose N boundary is at 54°40N. The issue was resolved in 1846 by a treaty establishing the present US–Canadian border, at 49°N.

fig A member of a large genus of trees, shrubs, and climbers, mostly native to the tropics; characteristic inflorescence consists of tiny flowers borne on the inner surface of a hollow, fleshy receptacle which forms the fruit after fertilization, symbiotic gall-wasps acting as pollinators. Many species are large evergreen trees, such as the indiarubber tree and the banyan. The **common fig** (*Ficus carica*) is a small deciduous tree with greenish-purple, edible fruits. **Strangler figs** begin as epiphytes, eventually enclosing and strangling the host in a network of aerial roots. (Genus: *Ficus*, 800 species. Family: Moraceae.)

fighting fish Small freshwater fish (*Betta splendens*), native to Thailand; feeds on aquatic insects, especially mosquito larvae; length up to 6 cm/2½ in; eggs laid in bubble nest at surface; renowned for its aggressive behaviour; commonly held in captivity for staged fights. Captive breeding has produced an immense variety of colour and form. (Family: Belontidae.)

Figo, Luis Felipe Madeira Caeiro [feegoh], known as **Figo** (1972–) Footballer, born in Lisbon, Portugal. He made his debut with Lisbon's first team in 1989 aged 16. In 1996 he moved to Barcelona, where coach Johan Cruyff turned the midfielder into a right winger. His honours with Barcelona include the Cup Winners's Cup (1997), consecutive Spanish League titles (1998, 1999), and the Spanish Cup (1997, 1998). He signed a 6-year contract for Real Madrid in 2000 for £40 million. He was named European Footballer of the Year in 2000 and FIFA World Player of the Year in 2001, and was a member of Portugal's World Cup squad for 2002.

figurative art Any form of visual art in which recognizable aspects of the world, especially the human figure, are represented, in however simplified, stylized, or distorted a form, in contrast to abstract or **non-figurative art**.

figurative language Language used in such a way that 'simple' meaning is elaborated and complicated by various rhetorical means, such as metaphor, simile, or alliteration. Although 'plain style' was recommended to the Royal Society in 1667, and has always been the implicit objective of scientists and philosophers, non-figurative (and therefore, supposedly, unambiguous) language is actually difficult to sustain. Language has been described as 'a graveyard of dead metaphors', and all forms of emphasis and parallelism, as well as imagery, may be considered 'figurative'.

figwort A perennial (*Scrophularia nodosa*), native to Europe and Asia; stems square, robust, erect; leaves opposite, toothed; inflorescence tall, branched; flowers with greenish, almost globose tube and five small lobes, the upper two forming a reddish-brown lip, pollinated by wasps. There are many very similar species from temperate regions. (Family: Scrophulariaceae.)

Fiji *p.561*

filariasis [filariyasis] A disease common in tropical areas caused by nematode worms. Larvae are transmitted to uninfected

Fiji

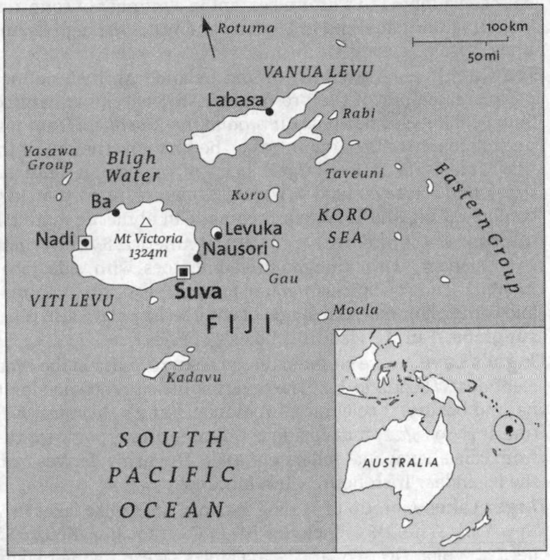

□ International Airport

[feejee], official name **Sovereign Democratic Republic of Fiji**

Local name Viti

Timezone GMT +12

Area 18 333 km^2/7076 sq mi

Population total (2002e) 824 000

Status Republic

Date of independence 1970

Capital Suva (on Viti Levu Island)

Language English (official)

Ethnic groups Indigenous Fijians (44%), Indian (51%)

Religions Native Fijians, mainly Christian (Methodist c.85%, Roman Catholic 12%); Indo-Fijians, mainly Hindu (c.70%) and Muslim (25%)

Physical features Melanesian group of 844 islands and islets in the SW Pacific Ocean; highest peak, Tomaniivi (Mt Victoria) on Viti Levu, 1324 m/4344 ft; most smaller islands consist of limestone, little vegetation; Great Sea Reef stretches 500 km/300 mi along W fringe; dense tropical forest on wet, windward side (SE); mainly treeless on dry, leeward side.

Climate Tropical oceanic climate, high humidity; average annual temperature 27°C, ranging from 35°C (Dec–Apr) to 16°C (Jun–Sep); heavy rainfall; occasional hurricanes.

Currency 1 Fijian Dollar (F$) = 100 cents

Economy Agriculture; sugar cane (accounts for over two-thirds of export earnings); bananas, ginger; gold, silver, limestone, timber; major tourist area.

GDP (2002e) $4·822 bn, per capita $5600

Human Development Index (2002) 0·758

History Visited by Tasman, 1643, and by Cook, 1774; British colony from 1874; independence within the Commonwealth, 1970; 1987 election brought to power an Indian-dominated coalition, which led to military coups (May and Sep), and proclamation of a republic outside the Commonwealth; civilian government restored, Dec 1987; constitution, 1990 and 1997; readmitted to the Commonwealth, 1997; coup, with prime minister and others held as hostages, May–July 2000; suspended from Commonwealth, June 2000; parliamentary elections, 2001; Commonwealth suspension lifted, December 2001; bicameral Parliament of a nominated Senate and an elected House of Representatives.

Republic

Chairman

1987 Sitiveni Rabuka

Head of State

1987–93 Penaia Ganilau
1993–2000 Kamisese Mara
2000– Ratu Josefa Iloilo

Head of Government

1987–92 Kamisese Mara
1992–9 Sitiveni Rabuka
1999–2000 Mahendra Chaudhry
2000 *Military Administration*
2000–1 Laisenia Qarase *Interim*
2001– Laisenia Qarase

human beings by mosquitoes. Adult forms develop within the body, and settle in lymph nodes, very often in the groin. The lymph nodes enlarge and interfere with the flow of lymph, causing gross oedema of the limbs.

filbert A species of hazel (*Corylus maxima*), native to the Balkans, and cultivated elsewhere for its edible nuts, which are completely enclosed in a leafy cup, constricted above the nut to form a neck. (Family: Corylaceae.)

filefish Deep-bodied fish common in shallow tropical and warm temperate waters; body strongly compressed, length up to 25 cm/10 in; dorsal fin spiny; scales finely toothed and rough to touch; valuable food fish in some areas; also called **porky**. (Genus: *Stephanolepis*. Family: Balistidae.)

filibuster To hold up the passage of a bill in the US Senate, by organizing a continuous succession of long speeches in opposition. If more than a third of the senators in a vote on the issue are opposed to closure of the debate, the filibuster cannot be prevented, and the bill is 'talked out'. The term is also more generally applied to any attempt to delay a decision or vote by exercising the right to talk on an issue. Many legislatures have procedures for curtailing such obstructionism.

Filioque [filiohkway] (Lat 'and from the Son') A dogmatic formula expressing the belief that in the operations of God, the Holy Trinity, the Holy Spirit 'proceeds' from the Son as well as from the Father. The term does not appear in the original Nicene–Constantinopolitan Creed, but was inserted by the Western Church, and insistence on its retention was a major source of tension and eventual breach between the Western (Roman Catholic) and Eastern (Orthodox) Churches in 1054. In the late 20th-c, the Western Churches were attempting to reinterpret this doctrine in a sense acceptable to the Orthodox.

Fillmore, Millard (1800–74) US statesman and 13th president (1850–3), born in Summerhill, New York, USA. He educated himself, and became a lawyer. A member of the State Assembly in 1829, he was elected to Congress in 1833, and became comptroller of New York State in 1847. He was vice-president to Zachary Taylor in 1848, becoming president on his death. On the slavery question he was a supporter of 'compromise'.

film A light-sensitive photographic emulsion on a thin flexible transparent support, originally celluloid (cellulose nitrate), but later the less inflammable cellulose triacetate and polyester materials. Film for still cameras is supplied in cut sheets and film packs, but more generally as short rolls in various standard widths coded 110, 126, 127, and 135. Motion picture film is used in long rolls, up to 300 m, in widths 16, 35, and 70 mm, with accurately spaced perforations along the edge for transport and location in the camera and other mechanisms. The amateur movie gauges of 8 mm, Super-8 and 9·5 mm are obsolescent.

film production There are four stages:

(1) **Preparation.** The producer, director, and script writer develop an idea into a story, treatment, or scenario that can be converted into a screenplay. The producer organizes finance resources, and a timetable; the production team and artists are chosen; locations are selected; and sets are designed and constructed in the studio.

(2) **Shooting.** Once photography starts on the studio stage or on location, the director is primarily concerned with the actors and their performance. The visual realization of the director's ideas on film is in the hands of the cameraman, who decides the character and distribution of lighting and selects the camera viewpoints and movement by the camera operator, aided by a focus puller and grips. A clapper-loader assistant is responsible for the film magazines and shot identification. Sound recording is supervised by the floor mixer, with an assistant and engineer, while the boom operator positions the microphone during shooting. The negative exposed each day is developed at the laboratory, and rush prints are returned to the studio for viewing. An assistant editor then assembles the chosen material in script order.

(3) **Post-production.** The period of editing, music recording, adding sound and effects tracks, etc. after photography is complete, up to the premiere. Sometimes post-synchronization, substituting one voice for another, dubbing, and other techniques are added. The ratio of exposed to used film may be anything from 5:1 to 40:1, and it is not uncommon to have several versions of a film available.

(4) **Distribution.** The general release to cinemas, with foreign versions dubbed in other languages, and possibly special versions for markets where certain themes (such as divorce or birth control) are forbidden. Releases may also be made for television broadcasting and for video-cassette or DVD sale and hire in the domestic market.

filmy fern A small fern with creeping rhizomes, commonly found as an epiphyte; fronds pinnate or bi-pinnate, only one cell thick, and translucent except for the veins. These ferns are vulnerable to drying out, and are found only in moist areas outside the tropics. (Genus: *Hymenophyllum*, 25 species. Family: Hymenophyllaceae.)

Filofax The trade name of a 'personal organizer', or portable information and filing system. Paperback-size, loose-leaf, with a flexible binder, filofaxes typically contain a diary, address book, notebook, and information sections (hence 'file of facts'). Their prominence increased through association with the yuppies of the 1980s.

filter 1 A device for removing fine solid particles from a mixture. It usually consists of some woven or felted material (eg paper, textile), and is thus distinct from a **sieve**, which removes coarse particles with a wire mesh or perforated metal. By analogy, the term is also used for any device which separates the components of a wave system (eg sound, light, radio-frequency currents).

2 In photography, a transparent material which modifies the light passing in a specified manner. It is used in front of light sources to alter colour temperature, reduce intensity, or scatter light by diffusion. On camera lenses it changes colour balance or tonal rendering. Other camera filters introduce soft focus, fog effects, or star patterns around bright points.

fin The external membranous process of an aquatic animal, such as a fish or cetacean, used for locomotion and manoeuvring; may be variously modified as suckers and claspers. The **median fins** are called *dorsal*, *anal*, and *caudal* (tail); the paired **lateral fins** are *pectorals* and *pelvics*.

finch Any bird of the family Fringillidae; commonly kept as songbirds; bill internally modified to crush seeds. The name is also applied loosely to any small seed-eating bird with a stout conical bill, such as **estrildid finches** (Family: Estrildidae).

fine A financial penalty paid to the state, following conviction by a court for a criminal offence. Limits are normally set on the levels of fines inferior courts are permitted to levy, and the offender's means are generally taken into account. The court may allow time for payment or payment by instalments. Failure to pay a fine without good cause can lead to imprisonment for default. Fines are the most common form of punishment, and may be imposed in conjunction with some other penalty, such as compensation orders. Fines are often imposed upon companies which are in breach of their statutory obligations. The Swedish system of **day-fines**, first introduced in 1931, which attempts to take account of the offender's financial situation, has been adopted to a limited extent in a number of countries, including Germany, and in England and Wales through its **unit fines** system.

Fine Gael [**feenuh gayl**] (Ir 'United Ireland') An Irish political party created out of the pro-Anglo-Irish Treaty (1921) wing of Sinn Féin. It was known as *Cummann na nGaedheal* from 1923 until it changed its name in 1933. The first government of the Irish Free State, it has largely been in opposition since the 1930s, and has never held power on its own. It supports an Irish confederation, and is largely pragmatic in domestic matters.

finfoot A water-bird, native to Central America, S Africa, and S Asia; slender, with long pointed bill; toes with side lobes; inhabits fresh or brackish water margins; eats small animals and some plant material; angle of wing bears a claw; also called **sungrabe**. (Family: Heliornithidae, 3 species.)

Fingal's Cave A cave situated on the coast of Staffa in the Inner Hebrides, W Scotland, UK. The cavern, which is renowned for its natural beauty, is celebrated in Mendelssohn's *Hebrides Overture*. It is 69 m/227 ft deep and of volcanic origin, being formed from huge hexagonal pillars of basalt. The name derives from the legendary Irish figure, Finn MacCool.

Finger Lakes A group of 11 long, narrow, finger-like lakes in W New York State, USA; includes (W–E) Canandaigua, Keuka, Seneca, Cayuga, Owasco, and Skaneateles lakes; a wine-making centre.

fingerprint An impression made on a surface by the pattern of ridges at the ends of fingers and thumbs. No two people have the same fingerprints, and the technique of fingerprinting has thus long been used by law enforcement agencies as a means of identification. Systems of fingerprint classification have been in use since the end of the 19th-c, based on the general shape of the ridge pattern, its size and position on the finger, the number of ridges in loops and whorls, and other such indicators. Computer systems of classification are also now available. The standard process of fingerprinting (**dactyloscopy**) is one in which the fingers and thumbs are first cleaned, then pressed onto an ink-covered glass surface, then firmly rolled onto a standardized card so as to leave a clear imprint of the full fingertip pattern, so that the ridges may be counted and traced. **Genetic fingerprinting** is a technique based on the fact that no two persons possess the same patterns of DNA; computerized DNA profiles are therefore now often used as a means of identifying criminals.

finger-spelling *dactylology*

finial In Gothic architecture, the decorative termination of a steep triangular form, such as a gable or pinnacle. It is often carved in the form of a *fleur-de-lys*, and can accompany decorative foliage clumps (or *crockets*) running up the sides of the pinnacle below.

Finisterre, Cape [**finistair**] (Span **Cabo**) 42°50N 9°16W. Cape at La Coruña, NW Spain; the most W point on the Spanish mainland; scene of a British naval victory against the French in 1747.

Finland *p.563*

Finland, Gulf of Arm of the Baltic Sea (E), bounded N by Finland, S and E by Russia; c.4600 km/2900 mi long, 16–120 km/10–75 mi wide; shallowness and low salinity result in ice cover (Dec–Mar); main ports, Helsinki, Kotka, Vyborg, St Petersburg, Tallinn.

Finlay, Carlos Juan (1833–1915) Physician, born in Camagüey, Cuba. He first suggested the mosquito as the carrier of yellow fever in 1881, and specified the correct species, now known as *Aëdes aegypti* the following year. Later experiments validated his theory.

Finney, Albert (1936–) Actor, born in Salford, Greater Manchester, NW England, UK. He studied at the Royal Academy of Dramatic Art, London, and has performed a wide variety of roles, from Shakespearean characters to modern working-class individuals, on both stage and screen. It was his definitive portrayal of the working-class rebel in *Saturday Night and Sunday*

Finland

Finn **Suomi**, official name **Republic of Finland**, Finn **Suomen Tasavalta**, Swed **Republiken Finland**

Local name Suomi (Finnish)

Timezone GMT +2

Area 338 145 km²/130 524 sq mi

Population total (2002e) 5 201 000

Status Republic

Date of independence 1917

Capital Helsinki

Languages Finnish and Swedish (official), also Saame (Lappish)

Ethnic groups Finnish (94%), Swedish, Lappish, Russian minorities

Religions Lutheran (90%), Finnish/Greek Orthodox

Physical features Low-lying, glaciated plateau, average height 150 m/500 ft; highest peak Haltiatunturi, 1328 m/4357 ft, on NW border; over 60 000 shallow lakes in SE, providing a system of inland navigation; over a third of the country located N of the Arctic Circle; Archipelago of Saaristomeri (SW), with over 17 000 islands, including Åland Is (Ahvenanmaa) (SW), forest covers 65% of the country, water covers 10%.

Climate Extreme, N of the Arctic Circle: average annual temperatures -30°C (Jan), 27°C (Jul); half annual precipitation falls as snow; sun does not go down beyond the horizon for over 70 days during summer; average temperatures -6°C (Jan), 17°C (Jul) at Helsinki; average annual rainfall 618 mm/24 in.

Currency 1 euro = 100 cents (previous to 2002, 1 Markka (FMk) = 100 penni)

Economy Traditional focus on forestry, farming; rapid economic growth since 1950s; metals, clothing, chemicals; copper, iron-ore mining; wide use of hydroelectric power.

GDP (2002e) $133·8 bn, per capita $25 800

Human Development Index (2002) 0·930

History Ruled by Sweden from 1157 until ceded to Russia in 1809; Grand Duchy of the Russian Czar, 19th-c; independent republic, 1917; parliamentary system created, 1928; invaded by Soviets, 1939–40 (Winter War); lost territory to USSR, including Petsamo and Porkkala peninsula, 1944; signed a friendship treaty with Soviet Union in 1948 (renewed 1955, 1970, 1983), undertaking to resist any attack made on the Soviet Union launched through Finnish territory; Harri Holkeri became Finland's first post-war conservative Prime Minister, 1987; governed by a single-chamber House of Representatives and President assisted by a Council of State; joined the European Union, 1995.

Head of State
1946–56 Juho Kusti Paasikivi
1956–81 Urho Kaleva Kekkonen
1982–94 Mauno Koivisto
1994–2000 Martti Ahtisaarsi
2000– Tarja Halonen

Head of Government
1979–82 Mauno Koivisto
1982–87 Taisto Kalevi Sorsa
1987–91 Harri Holkeri
1991–5 Esko Aho
1995–2003 Paavo Lipponen
2003 Anneli Jaatteenmaki
2003– Matti Vanhanen

Morning (1960) that established him as a star. He directed the film *Charlie Bubbles* (1967), and was associate artistic director of the Royal Court Theatre (1972–5). He has received Oscar nominations for *Tom Jones* (1963), *Murder on the Orient Express* (1974), *The Dresser* (1983), and *Under the Volcano* (1984). Later films include *The Browning Version* (1994) and *Simpatico* (1999). His work for television includes *A Rather English Marriage* (1998), *My Uncle Silas* (2001), and *The Gathering Storm* (2002, Emmy; Golden Globe).

Finn MacCool A legendary Irish hero, the son of Cumhall, and father of Ossian (Oisin). He became leader of the Fenians, and was famous for his generosity.

fiord *fjord*

Fiordland [fyaw(r)dland] area 10 232 sq km/3949 sq mi. National park, SW South Island, New Zealand; largest of New Zealand's national parks, with mountains, lakes and a coastline indented by fjords; established in 1904; a world heritage site.

fir *silver fir*

Firdausi or **Ferd(a)usi** [firdowsee], pseudonym of **Abú al-Qásim Mansúr** (940–c.1020) The greatest of Persian poets, born near Tús, Khorassan. His major work was the epic poem, *Shah Náma* (1010, The Book of Kings), based on actual events from the annals of Persia. One episode from this epic inspired Matthew Arnold's poem, *Sohrab and Rustum* (1853). He also wrote a number of shorter pieces.

firearms A generic description for small arms, from pistols to rifles. The development of such portable weapons began with the first gunpowder-primed, hand-held cannon of the 14th-c, which had to be touched off by a second operator using a flame. The arquebus and later wheel-lock automated and simplified the process of touching off the priming, but still required a flame. The flintlock principle perfected in the 18th-c, which used a spring-loaded lever holding a flint to strike a spark and thus ignite the propellant charge, made pistols and muskets much more wieldy in combat. The percussion lock, using a hammer to set off a self-contained charge in the barrel of the gun, dates from the early 19th-c. The 20th-c saw a wide range of developments, especially in the improved design of rifles and the emergence of firearms with sustained automatic fire. There has also been increasing public concern at the increased use of guns on the streets, especially voiced in the USA, where proposals to restrict the sale of guns have proved controversial.

firebrat A widely-distributed bristletail. It is found as a pest in human dwellings, favouring warm places such as kitchens. (Order: Thysanura. Family: Lepismatidae.)

fireclay Clay with high alumina content that can withstand high temperatures without excessive deformation. It is used for making firebricks and other refractory materials.

firecrest A small bird (*Regulus ignicapillus*) native to Europe, N Africa, and Madeira; head with orange stripe and white 'eyebrows'; inhabits woodland or scrubland; eats insects; Europe's smallest breeding bird. (Family: Regulidae, sometimes placed in Silviidae.)

firedamp Methane found in coal mines. A mixture of methane and air is inflammable or explosive in certain proportions, and has been the cause of many pit disasters. The reduction of the hazard is a major consideration in coal mine operation. One of the best methods of firedamp detection remains the Davy safety lamp.

firefly A small, mostly nocturnal beetle; males with soft wing cases, females larva-like, often wingless; jaws hollow, used to inject digestive juices into prey; larvae found in soil and leaf litter; all stages luminous, but most pronounced in adults; luminous organs near tip of abdomen used to produce mating signals; also known as **glowworms** and **lightning bugs**. (Order: Coleoptera. Family: Lampyridae, c.2000 species.)

Fire of London A devastating fire which started in a baker's shop in Pudding Lane (2 Sep 1666) and, fanned by an E wind, lasted several days. It engulfed c.160 ha/400 acres – four-fifths of the city – destroying 13 000 houses, 89 parish churches including St Paul's, and most public buildings; but casualties were low (no more than 20 died). It was stopped by blowing up buildings in its path. There are eyewitness accounts in the diaries of Pepys and Evelyn. The capital was rebuilt with safer materials. Many new churches were built, including Wren's St Paul's. The fire also helped eradicate the Great Plague of 1664–6.

fire salamander A salamander native to Europe, NW Africa, and SW Asia (*Salamandra salamandra*); black with yellow stripes or spots; broad head; short tail; inhabits damp upland deciduous forest; only adult female enters water (to give birth to live tadpoles). (Family: Salamandridae.)

firethorn A thorny, evergreen shrub (*Pyracantha coccinea*) growing to c.1·5 m/5 ft, occasionally a small tree, native to S Europe; leaves oval, toothed; flowers numerous, 5-petalled, white, in small clusters; berries bright red. An orange fruited form is commonly cultivated for ornament. (Family: Rosaceae.)

firewall A technology which is used by organizations that have linked their enterprise computer systems into the Internet. The firewall prevents users from outside the organization doing anything which would corrupt the system inside. One standard approach uses the firewall to filter out suspicious messages and discard them. Another approach offers a caller a copy of a system so that, if the caller does anything that is malicious, this can be seen before the real system is damaged.

fireweed *rosebay willow-herb*

fireworks Artificial devices, normally used for display purposes, which when ignited produce an array of coloured lights, sparks, and explosions; they were known in China by AD 600. They contain flammable and explosive materials (eg charcoal, sulphur) which react with oxygen-yielding substances (eg nitre, chlorate of potash). Government control is very strict on their manufacture and sale to children. The majority of fireworks in the UK are displayed on 5 November to celebrate Guy Fawkes night, commemorating his attempt to blow up the Houses of Parliament in 1605. Spectacular displays are very popular in the Far East, and also on major public occasions such as Bastille Day in France and US Independence Day. The making of fireworks is called *pyrotechny*.

firmware A concept intermediate between software and hardware, used to describe devices which combine elements of each. A computer program stored in an unalterable form in an integrated circuit such as a read-only memory could be described as firmware, while the same program written on paper or stored on a floppy disk, both of which can be altered, could be described as **software**.

First, Ruth (1925–82) Radical opponent of apartheid, as activist, journalist, writer, and academic, born in Johannesburg, NE South Africa. She joined the Communist Party as a student, and worked for various left-wing newspapers and magazines (1946–60). In 1949 she married **Joe Slovo**; both were arrested and charged with treason in 1956. In 1964 she left South Africa, and subsequently taught at universities in England and Mozambique. In 1982 she was assassinated by a parcel bomb in her office at Maputo, Mozambique.

first aid The treatment and management of a victim at the site of an accident or collapse. In conscious individuals, important steps include the arrest of bleeding by the application of pressure (dressing, plastic bags, or paper) and by laying the victim flat. Injured parts must be handled gently. Unskilled extrication of victims who have suffered neck injury can cause serious damage. Otherwise the individual should be lifted on a flat board or by hands in such a way as to maintain the normal curvature of the spine, which should never be flexed. A simple splint to a leg is obtained by bandaging the injured leg to the uninjured one, or an arm to the trunk. Tea, alcohol, or other fluids should not be given. In unconscious individuals, all of these points should be carried out, but cardiac and respiratory resuscitation should also be given to those whose breathing or heart has stopped.

First Amendment Legislation enacted in 1789 amending the Constitution of the United States to guarantee freedom of worship, of speech, of the press, of assembly, and of petition to the government for redress of grievances. This amendment has been the centre of controversy in recent years in the areas of free speech and religion. The Supreme Court has held that freedom of speech does not include the right to refuse to testify before a Congressional investigating committee.

first cause *cosmological argument*

first fleet In Australian history, the name given to the 11 ships which left Portsmouth, England (1787) carrying the first European settlers to E Australia. The fleet carried officials, 212 marines and their families, and 579 convicts plus provisions. Unusual for the time, all who embarked arrived safely in Australia. The fleet's captain, Arthur Phillip, decided that Botany Bay was unsuitable and proceeded north to Sydney Cove, Port Jackson, where he hoisted the British flag (26 Jan 1788).

first-footing *Hogmanay*

first-generation computers *computer generations*

First Ladies A title applied to the wives of the Presidents of the United States of America. The term seems to have originated during the last quarter of the 19th-c, but came into general use around 1911 after a play written by Charles Nirdlinger, *The First Lady of The Land*, became popular. During the 20th-c, the wives of presidents became more active in pursuing social causes, following the examples of Eleanor Roosevelt (1933–45), Lady Bird Johnson (1963–9), and Betty Ford (1974–7). Jacqueline Kennedy (1961–3) attained the greatest degree of international celebrity for her White House role. Hillary Rodham Clinton (1993–2000) was the most controversial and investigated First Lady in American history. As a result of her professional activities, federal courts have described the work undertaken by the First Lady as making her in legal terms an employee of the federal government. Popular fascination with these women is enormous in the USA, where the president and his family occupy a significant symbolic role in the life of the nation.

First Nations A term used in Canada to describe Canadian aboriginal peoples, introduced in the 1980s as a response to French- and English-Canadian claims to be the 'two founding nations'. They are represented in land claim and constitutional discussions with Ottawa by the Association of First Nations.

first point of Aries The zero point of the celestial co-ordinate system, defined as the intersection of the celestial Equator and ecliptic, or vernal equinox. When Hipparchos used this term, it lay in Aries, but precession of the equinoxes has moved it to the adjacent constellation Pisces.

first-strike capability *strategic capability*

First World *Three Worlds theory*

First World War *World War 1*

Firth, Colin (1960–) Actor, born in Grayshott, Hampshire, UK. He studied drama in London, worked in the West End, and went on to play a series of acclaimed character parts in film and television. He received a BAFTA nomination for his role in the television production of *Tumbledown* (1989), and another for *Pride and Prejudice* (1995), where his brooding performance as the handsome Mr Darcy attracted unprecedented public interest. His films include *The English Patient* (1996), *Fever Pitch* (1997), *Shakespeare in Love* (1998), *Bridget Jones's Diary* (2001), and *Love Actually* (2003).

fiscal drag The effect of inflation on tax revenues. If tax allowances are not kept in line with inflation, individuals pay relatively higher amounts of tax, thus dragging down post tax incomes; consequently the demand for goods and services falls.

fiscal policy The use by government of tax and its own rate of spending to influence demand in the economy. When a government decides to lower taxes or raise public expenditure, the effect is to stimulate economic activity by increasing the demand for goods and services. There is a risk that this may lead to increasing inflation, or an increase in imports, resulting in a trade deficit. In contrast, a tightening of fiscal policy is where taxes are raised or public expenditure is reduced, in order to reduce aggregate demand.

Fischer, Bobby, popular name of **Robert (James) Fischer** (1943–) Chess player, born in Chicago, Illinois, USA. He was world champion in 1972–5, taking the title from Boris Spassky (USSR) in a much-publicized match. He has a ranking of 2785 (on the Elo grading system), the highest ever, making him the greatest of all Grand Masters. He resigned his title shortly before a defence against Anatoly Karpov in 1975, and did not then compete at a major international level until 1992, when he defeated Spassky in a match which generated unprecedented levels of publicity for a chess match.

Fischer, Emil (Hermann) (1852–1919) Organic chemist, born near Cologne, W Germany. He had a dissolute youth, but went on to hold chairs in Würzburg and Berlin. His extensive work included elucidating the chemistry of carbohydrates and the founding of protein chemistry, and he was awarded the Nobel Prize for Chemistry in 1902. He is widely seen as the leading figure in the field of organic chemistry.

Fischer-Dieskau, Dietrich [**fi**sher **dee**skow] (1925–) Baritone, born in Berlin, Germany. He studied under Georg Walter and Hermann Weissenborn, making his professional debut at Freiburg in 1947, and joined the Berlin Municipal Opera as a principal baritone. He became one of the foremost interpreters of German *Lieder*, particularly the song-cycles of Schubert, and has also appeared in a wide range of operatic roles. He performed in the premier of Britten's *A War Requiem* in 1962, as well as in the *Songs and Proverbs of William Blake* (1965) which Britten had composed for him. He has also written several books on music.

Fischer–Tropsch process A method of obtaining hydrocarbons by passing hydrogen and carbon monoxide over a catalyst, either cobalt or iron, at high temperature and pressure. It is named after German chemists Franz Fischer (1877–1948) and Hans Tropsch (1889–1935).

Fischer von Erlach, Johann Bernard [**fi**sher fon **air**lakh] (1656–1723) Architect, born in Graz, SE Austria. He studied in Rome, perhaps under Bernini or his pupil Carlo Fontana, then moved to Vienna, where he became the court architect (1704) and a leading exponent of the Baroque style. He designed many churches and palaces, notably the Karlskirche at Vienna, and the University church at Salzburg. He also wrote a major work on architectural history (1721).

fish Any cold-blooded aquatic vertebrate without legs, but typically possessing paired lateral fins as well as median fins. There is a 2-chambered heart, a series of respiratory gills present throughout life in the sides of the pharynx, and a body usually bearing scales and terminating in a caudal (tail) fin. As a subgroup of the Vertebrata, the fishes are sometimes referred to collectively as Pisces. The primitive **jawless fishes**, the hagfishes and lampreys, are the only living members of a formerly large group, the Agnatha, which have an abundant fossil record. Members of another major group, the Chondrichthyes (800 living species), containing the sharks, rays, and ratfishes, are characterized by a cartilaginous skeleton, and are commonly referred to as the **cartilaginous fishes**. By far the largest extant group are the **bony fishes** (Osteichthyes; 20 000 living species), exhibiting a rich diversity and found in all aquatic habitats – freshwater, estuarine, and marine, from the tropics to polar latitudes, and from high altitude streams to the ocean abyss. Although many fish have the familiar elongate shape, body form shows great variety – strongly compressed from side to side or (in bottom-living species) from top to bottom, asymmetrical with both eyes on the same side (as in the true flatfishes), extremely slender or heavily robust, armoured, spinose, or with reduced tails and huge heads (as in some of the bizarre deep-sea species). Body length ranges from as small as a few centimetres to over 18 m/60 ft in the massive whale shark. Many species have bright coloration, others well-developed camouflage patterns. Light organs are common in those forms living in the darkness of deep oceanic waters. Several species that inhabit turbid shallow waters have well-developed electric organs used for navigation, as defence against predators or for stunning prey. Some fish that live in shallow waters low in oxygen have evolved a capacity for air-breathing, using lungs or other accessory respiratory organs. A few, such as the mudhopper, are well-adapted to living out of water on coastal mud flats. Fish are of immense importance as a source of food, and to the angler and aquarist in pursuit of leisure.

Fishbourne Roman palace near Chichester (**Noviomagus Regnorum**), West Sussex, S England, UK, discovered in 1960. Probably erected in the AD 60s for the British client-king Cogidubnus, a noted Roman collaborator, it continued in use into the 4th-c. Major features are the formal courtyard garden, the monumental entrance and audience hall, the mosaics of the four colonnaded wings, and the site museum.

Fishburne, Larry, popular name of **Laurence John Fishburne III** (1961–) Actor, born in Augusta, Georgia, USA. He made his film debut at age 15 in *Apocalypse Now* and won a Tony Award for his performance in the Broadway play *Two Trains Running*. He had starring roles in the films *School Daze* (1988) and *Boyz N the Hood* (1991). Later films include *Othello* (1995), *The Matrix* (1999), and its sequels *The Matrix Reloaded* and *Matrix Revolutions* (both 2003).

fish eagle *osprey; sea eagle*

Fisher, John, St (1469–1535) Clergyman and humanist, born in Beverley, East Riding of Yorkshire, NE England, UK. He studied at Cambridge, where he became professor of divinity (1503). He zealously promoted the New Learning, and resisted the Lutheran schism. In 1527 he pronounced against the divorce of Henry VIII, refused the oath of succession, and was sent with More to the Tower. In 1535 he was made a cardinal, and soon after was tried and beheaded on Tower Hill. He was canonized in 1935; feast day 22 June.

Fisher (of Lambeth), Geoffrey Fisher, Baron (1887–1972) Archbishop of Canterbury (1945–61), born in Higham-on-the-Hill, Leicestershire, C England, UK. He studied at Oxford, was ordained in 1912, and became headmaster of Repton School (1914–32). He was 45 when he took up his first ecclesiastical appointment, as Bishop of Chester (1932). In 1939 he became Bishop of London, and as archbishop crowned Queen Elizabeth II in Westminster Abbey (1953). He was created a life peer in 1961.

Fisher, Sir R(onald) A(ylmer) (1890–1962) Statistician and geneticist, born in East Finchley, N Greater London, UK. He studied at Cambridge, and became statistician at the Rothamsted agricultural research institute (1919). There he developed his techniques for the design and analysis of experiments where it is not possible to control every element that could affect the outcome. His analysis of variance has become standard practice in medical, biological, and agricultural research. He also worked on genetics and evolution, and studied the genetics of human blood groups, elucidating the Rhesus factor. His book, *The Genetical Theory of Natural Selection* (1929), was a landmark in renewed interest in the study of evolutionary genetics. He became professor of eugenics at University College London (1933–43), and of genetics at Cambridge (1943–57). He was knighted in 1952, and after his retirement in 1957 he moved to Australia.

fisher A mammal, related to the marten, native to North America; length, up to 1 m/3¾ ft; thick brown-black coat; inhabits dense forest; eats small mammals, birds, carrion; also known as **pekan** (*Martes pennanti*). (Family: Mustelidae.)

fisheye lens A distinctive type of lens design that uses a large, curved front element resembling the eye of a fish. A very large angle of view is given, up to 180 or even 220 degrees. This is made possible by abandoning optical correction for curvilinear distortion in the lens, so that the image is characterized by lines that are strongly curved instead of straight. The imagery has a novelty value, as well as scientific applications such as cloud studies of the whole sky.

fish hawk *osprey*

fishing *angling*

fish louse A flattened parasitic crustacean found externally on fishes and occasionally amphibians, mainly in fresh water; usually attaches to host by means of suckers; feeds on blood and mucus by means of a tubular sucking mouth. (Class: Branchiura, c.150 species.)

fish owl A typical owl, adapted to live near water; found in Asia (Genus: *Ketupa*, 4 species) and Africa (Genus: *Scotopelia*, 3 species); plucks fish from water in flight using talons; also eats crayfish, frogs, insects, small mammals; noisier flight than other owls.

fission A method of asexual reproduction by splitting into two (**binary fission**) or more (**multiple fission**) parts, each of which develops into an independent organism. The process is common among single-celled micro-organisms.

fitchet *polecat*

Fitt, Gerry, popular name of **Gerard, Baron Fitt (of Bell's Hill)** (1926–) Northern Ireland politician, born in Belfast, NE Northern Ireland, UK. He was a merchant seaman (1941–53) before entering local politics (1958–81), becoming a Republican Labour MP (1966). He founded and led the Social Democratic and Labour Party (1970–9), until he resigned the leadership to sit as an Independent Socialist. He lost his Westminster seat in 1983 when he received his peerage. He had earlier been a member of the Northern Ireland Executive (1973–5), and was its deputy chief executive in 1974.

fittings *fixture*

Fitzgerald, Edward (1809–83) Scholar and poet, born near Woodbridge, Suffolk, E England, UK. He studied at Cambridge, where he developed close literary friendships with Thackeray, Carlyle, and Tennyson (who dedicated his poem *Tiresias* to him). He published several works anonymously, including translations of six plays by Calderón in 1853. He is best known for his free poetic translation of quatrains from the *Rubáiyát of Omar Khayyám* (1859).

Fitzgerald, Ella (1918–96) Singer, born in Newport News, Virginia, USA. Discovered in 1934 singing in an amateur contest in Harlem, she joined Chick Webb's band and recorded several hits, notably 'A-tisket A-tasket' (1938). Her lucid intonation and broad range made her a top jazz singer. Her series of recordings for Verve (1955–9) in multi-volume 'songbooks' are among the treasures of American popular song. After 1971 her concert schedule was occasionally interrupted because of diabetes, and she had both legs amputated in 1994.

Fitzgerald, F(rancis) Scott (Key) (1896–1940) Novelist, born in St Paul, Minnesota, USA. He captured the spirit of the 1920s ('the jazz age') in *The Great Gatsby* (1925), his best-known book. In 1920 he married **Zelda Sayre** (1900–47), moving in 1924 to the French Riviera, where her subsequent mental breakdown and his alcoholism attracted wide publicity. His other novels include *The Beautiful and the Damned* (1922) and *Tender is the Night* (1934). In 1937 he returned to Hollywood.

Fitzgerald, Garrett (Michael) (1926–) Irish statesman and prime minister (1981–2, 1982–7), born in Dublin, Ireland. He studied at Dublin, where he became a barrister and a lecturer in political economy (1959–73). In 1969 he was elected Fine Gael member of the Irish parliament for Dublin SE, and became minister for foreign affairs (1973–7), and leader of the Fine Gael Party (1977–87).

Fitzgerald, George Francis (1851–1901) Physicist, born in Dublin, Ireland. He was professor of natural philosophy at Dublin (1881–1901). Independently of Lorentz, he concluded that, to a stationary observer, a moving body appears shorter, the degree of forshortening being larger at higher velocities (the *Lorentz–Fitzgerald contraction*), a notion embraced by Einstein as part of his theory of special relativity.

Fitzsimmons, Bob, popular name of **Robert Prometheus Fitzsimmons** (1863–1917) Boxer, born in Helston, Cornwall, SW England, UK. He was brought up in New Zealand, and moved to the USA in 1890, where he won the world middleweight (1891), heavyweight (1897), and light heavyweight championships (1903). He continued fighting until the age of 52. His career record was 40 victories (32 knockouts) and 11 losses.

Fiume *Rijeka*

Five, the A group of 19th-c Russian composers, also known as **the Mighty Handful**, who came together to promote nationalist ideals and styles in music. The group, led by Balakirev, also contained Borodin, Moussorgsky, Rimsky-Korsakov, and César Cui (1835–1918).

Five Civilized Tribes The Muskogean-speaking nations of Indians (Chickasaws, Creeks, Choctaws, Cherokees, Seminoles) who originally inhabited the present SE USA. The Cherokees, in particular, adopted white ways, establishing a republic, and acquiring literacy in their own language and English. Nonetheless, they were removed to beyond the Mississippi R in the 1830s, along the 'trail of tears'.

Five Holy Mountains *Wu Yue*

fives A handball game played by two or four players, derived from the French game *jeu de paume* ('palm [of hand] game'). The first recorded game was at Eton School in 1825; other variations include Rugby and Winchester fives. The origin of the name is uncertain: it may be because the game was played with the five fingers of the hand or because the original scoring system was in multiples of five.

fixative (painting) A liquid preparation sprayed over charcoal drawings, chalks, or pastels to prevent smudging. It is effective with monochromatic work, but less so with pastels, because of the inevitable alteration of colour values brought about when it is applied.

fixing (photography) In photographic processing, the removal of unexposed silver halides remaining in the emulsion after development or bleaching, allowing safe handling in the light and image permanence without staining. A solution of ammonium or sodium thiosulphate (*hypo*) is usually employed.

fixture An object which is regarded for legal purposes as having become part of the land or property. Both the degree and the purpose of annexation are relevant to deciding whether the object has become a fixture or remains a **chattel** (in Scotland, a **movable**). It may be important to define fixtures when land is transferred; for example on a sale of land it is implied, unless otherwise agreed, that fixtures are left for the purchaser (except, for example, some agricultural and trade fixtures). Fixtures can be distinguished from **fittings** by whether the procedure of removal would cause damage.

Fizeau, Armand Hippolyte Louis [feezoh] (1819–96) Physicist, born in Paris, France. In 1849 he was the first to measure the velocity of light by an experiment confined to the Earth's surface, and later collaborated with Léon Foucault. Fizeau also demonstrated the use of the Doppler principle in determining star velocity in the line of sight.

fjord A long, narrow, steep-sided coastal inlet extending far inland and often reaching very great depths. Most are drowned valleys formed by glacial erosion, with subsequent sea-level rise after their retreat. The best-known fjords are in Norway and E Greenland.

flag (botany) A species of iris (*Iris pseudacorus*) with yellow flowers 7·5–10 cm/3–4 in diameter, found in wet, swampy ground in Europe, W Asia, and N Africa. (Family: Iridaceae.)

flag (politics) A piece of cloth, usually with a design, used as an ensign, standard, or signal, or to mark a position, commonly attached at one end to a staff or halyard. Flags have been used since ancient times, and some symbols are universal; a white flag signals a truce; a yellow flag the presence of infectious disease. A nation signifies its mourning by flying its flags at half-mast.

flagellate [**fla**jiluht] A microscopic, single-celled organism that possesses 1, 2, 4, or more thread-like organelles (**flagella**), typically used for swimming; many are parasites of animal hosts; others live in aquatic or even terrestrial habitats. (Phylum: Mastigophora.)

flagellum [fla**je**lum] A thread-like structure found on some bacteria and on or in many eucaryotic organisms. Flagella usually function in locomotion, bacterial flagella rotating and eucaryotic flagella undulating as they beat. In eucaryotic organisms there are two main kinds of flagellum: a smooth whip-like type, and a tinsel type with rows of long hairs along its length.

flageolet [flajio**hlet**] A simple, high-pitched, end-blown flute, made of wood, with six fingerholes; later, often fitted with metal keys and an ivory mouthpiece. It was popular during the 16th–18th-c, and did not become obsolete until about the mid-19th-c. An inferior keyless variety, made of brass, is known as the 'tin whistle', or 'penny whistle'.

Flagstad, Kirsten (1895–1962) Soprano, born in Hamar, E Norway. She studied in Stockholm and Oslo, where she made her operatic debut in 1913. She excelled in Wagnerian roles, and was acclaimed in most of the world's major opera houses. In 1958 she was made director of the Norwegian State Opera.

Flaherty, Robert (Joseph) (1884–1951) Pioneer documentary film-maker, born in Iron Mountain, Michigan, USA. Trained as a mining prospector, he took a movie camera on his expeditions to Hudson Bay in 1913, returning many times to make the silent *Nanook of the North* (1922), a study of Inuit life. He then made further productions in the South Seas: *Moana* (1924) and *Tabu* (1930). For the commercial cinema his films included *Elephant Boy* (1937) and *The Louisiana Story* (1948).

Flamboyant The style of French late Gothic architecture prevalent in the 15th-c, characterized by wavy flame-like tracery. It was especially common in Normandy.

flamboyant tree A showy deciduous tree (*Delonix regia*) growing to 15 m/50 ft, native to Madagascar and widely cultivated for ornament in the tropics and subtropics; leaves large, to 60 cm/2 ft, finely divided, each with up to 1000 individual leaflets; flowers bright scarlet, often appearing before the leaves, with five long stalked petals, one suffused with yellow; pods reddish-brown, up to 60 cm/2 ft long; also called **flame tree**. (Family: Leguminosae.)

flamenco A traditional song and dance of the Rom (gypsies) of Andalusia in S Spain. It evolved over centuries of fusion between Rom, Moorish, Andalusian, and other traditions. *Canto* ('song') is the core of flamenco, whose text and melody, like the flamenco dance, are improvised within traditional conventions of rhythms and chords. The men's dancing involves intricate toe- and heel-clicking steps, while the traditional women's dance is based on graceful body- and hand-movements. Song and dance may be accompanied by finger snapping, hand clapping, and shouting. Castanets, found in other Andalusian dance forms, are not traditional to flamenco.

flame tree *flamboyant tree*

flamingo A large wading bird, native to South America, Africa, S Europe, and W Asia; plumage white or pink (pink colour deriving from pigments in food); inhabits shallow soda or brine lakes; filters minute organisms from water with stout, downwardly angled bill; swims well; forms immense flocks. (Family: Phoenicopteridae, 5 species.)

flamingo flower An evergreen perennial (*Anthurium scherzerianum*) native to Costa Rica; leaves oblong to lance-shaped, leathery; flowers in a slender spadix 5–10 cm/2–4 in long, with a bright scarlet spathe. (Family: Araceae.)

Flaminian Way The second of Rome's major trunk roads, constructed in 220 BC. It ran NE from Rome across the Apennines to Rimini on the Adriatic coast.

Flaminius, Gaius [**fla**minius] (?–217 BC) Roman general and statesman, of plebeian origin. Consul in 223 BC, he distributed the Ager Gallicus tribal lands left uninhabited since 283 BC. He was the first Roman commander to cross the R Po when he defeated the Insubres at the Addua (223 BC). He extended his road, the *Flaminian Way*, from Rome to Ariminum (Rimini) in 220 BC, and built the *Circus Flaminius*. Consul again in 217 BC, he tried to stem Hannibal's invasion of Etruria, but was defeated and killed at L Trasimeno.

Flamsteed, John (1646–1719) The first Astronomer Royal of England (1675–1719), born in Denby, Derbyshire, C England, UK. He studied at Cambridge, and in 1676 instituted reliable observations at Greenwich, near London, providing data from which Newton was later able to verify the gravitational theory.

Flanders, Flemish **Vlaanderen**, Fr **Flandre** Historical region of NW Belgium and NE France; autonomous in early Middle Ages; densely populated industrial area; chief towns Bruges, Ghent, Sint-Niklaas, Aalst, Ronse; traditional textile industry, with linen, silk, cotton processing; intensive farming, especially wheat, sugar-beet, oats, barley, potatoes; scene of heavy fighting in both World Wars.

flash *electronic flash; strobo-flash; zoom flash*

flatfish Any of the bottom-dwelling, mainly shallow-water fishes in which the adult body is strongly compressed laterally and asymmetrical, with both eyes on the same side of the head; nine families (sole, tongue-sole, plaice, halibut, dab, flounder, turbot, brill, topknot); excellent food fishes, very important commercially.

flat foot A condition affecting the normal arches of the foot, which distribute weight of the body over the heel and sole of the forefoot. Loss of the arches strains the ligaments and muscles of the foot, and leads to discomfort on standing. However, many people with flat feet suffer no discomfort.

Flathead A Salish-speaking Indian group living on L Flathead, Montana, USA, the most easterly-based of Plateau Indian groups. They traded in furs with Europeans during the early 19th-c, and under their influence many converted to Christianity.

flathead Bottom-living fish of the Indo-Pacific and tropical Atlantic oceans; body slender, length up to 1 m/3¼ ft, flattened anteriorly with prominent spinose fins; important food fish in some areas. (Genera: *Platycephalus*, *Thysanophrys*. Family: Platycephalidae.)

Flatley, Michael (1958–) Dancer and choreographer, born in Chicago, Illinois, USA. His parents came to the US from Ireland where his grandmother had been an Irish dancing champion in Leinster. At age 11 he began dance lessons and in 1975 became the first American to win the All World Championships in Irish dancing. He shot to fame after the success of his stage routine *Riverdance* at the Eurovision Song Contest in Dublin in 1994, and went on to create, choreograph and star in the show *The Lord of the Dance* (1996). Also a flautist, he played in his later show, *Feet of Flames* (1998), and following a successful world tour, he announced his retirement from the stage (2001).

flat racing *horse racing*

flatworm A flattened, worm-like animal with a definite head but without a true body cavity (*coelom*); digestive system usually lacks an anus; free living flatworms typically feed on small invertebrates; parasitic forms include tapeworms and flukes. (Phylum: Platyhelminthes.)

Flaubert, Gustave [flohbair] (1821–80) Novelist, born in Rouen, NW France. He studied law at Paris, then turned to writing. His masterpiece was *Madame Bovary* (1857), a portrait of a young woman who cannot come to terms with the limitations of provincial life, which was condemned as immoral and its author (unsuccessfully) prosecuted. His other works include *Salammbô* (1862), and *La Tentation de St Antoine* (1874, The Temptation of St Anthony). *Trois contes* (1877, Three Tales) reveals his mastery of the short story, while his genius as a letter writer is apparent in the volumes of his *Correspondance* (1926–33).

flavouring agent Any compound when added to a food to alter its taste, the most widely used being salt and sugar. Monosodium glutamate is an example of a flavour enhancer, bringing out a 'meaty flavour'. Artificial flavours which mimic natural flavours are also commonplace.

flax A slender erect annual (*Linum usitatissimum*), growing to 60 cm/2 ft; leaves narrow; flowers numerous, blue, c.3 cm/1½ in diameter, with five spreading petals; fruit a capsule with numerous seeds. Its origin is unknown, but it is cultivated throughout temperate and subtropical regions for flax fibre obtained from the stems, and for linseed oil from the seeds. (Family: Linaceae.)

Flaxman, John (1755–1826) Sculptor and illustrator, born in York, North Yorkshire, N England, UK. He studied at the Royal Academy, and thereafter was constantly engaged upon sculpture, but his chief source of income was the Wedgwood house, which he furnished with renowned pottery designs. He also studied at Rome (1787–94), where he began his illustrations to the *Iliad* and *Odyssey* (1793), and other works. In 1810 he became professor of sculpture at the Royal Academy.

F layer *Appleton layer*

flea A small, wingless insect that as an adult is a blood-feeding external parasite of warm-blooded animals (mostly mammals, but including some birds); body flattened from side to side, usually hairy; mouthparts specialized for piercing and sucking; hindlegs adapted for jumping; larvae maggot-like, feeding on organic refuse around domicile of host; c.1750 species, many of medical and veterinary importance as carriers of disease. (Order: Siphonaptera.)

fleabane A leafy perennial (*Pulicaria dysenterica*) growing to 60 cm/2 ft, native to marshes and wet places in Europe, N Africa, and Asia Minor; leaves lance-shaped, clasping the stem at the base, wavy-margined, softly hairy; flower-heads up to 3 cm/1·2 in across, golden yellow, daisy-like; fruit with a parachute of hairs. Its dried leaves were formerly burned to repel insects. (Family: Compositae.)

fleawort The name applied to certain species of the genus *Senecio*. **Marsh fleawort** (*Senecio congestus*) is a biennial or perennial with stout hairy stems growing to 2 m/6½ ft; leaves numerous, lance-shaped, wavy-margined; flower-heads numerous, up to 3 cm/1·2 in across, in dense clusters, with c.21 pale yellow outer ray florets; native to C Europe. **Field fleawort** (*Senecio integrifolius*) is a variable perennial growing to 70 cm/27 in; smaller clusters of flower-heads with c.13 bright yellow outer ray florets; native to much of Europe. (Family: Compositae.)

Flecker, (Herman) James Elroy (1884–1915) Poet, born in London, UK. He studied Oriental languages at Cambridge, and entered the consular service. His best-known works are the drama *Hassan* (staged, 1923) and *The Golden Journey to Samarkand* (1913).

Flémalle, Master of *Campin, Robert*

Fleming, Sir Alexander (1881–1955) Bacteriologist, born near Darvel, East Ayrshire, SW Scotland, UK. He studied at St Mary's Hospital, London, where he became professor (1919) after serving in the army during World War 1. He was the first to use antityphoid vaccines on human beings, pioneered the use of Salvarsan against syphilis, and discovered the antiseptic powers of lysozyme. In 1928 he discovered penicillin, for which he shared the Nobel Prize for Physiology or Medicine in 1945. He was elected to the Royal Society in 1943, and was knighted in 1944.

Fleming, Ian (Lancaster) (1908–64) Writer and journalist, born in London, UK, the brother of travel writer and journalist **Peter Fleming** (1907–71). He studied languages at Munich and Geneva universities, worked with Reuters in Moscow (1929–33), then became a banker and stockbroker (1933–9). He served with British Naval Intelligence during World War 2, and was foreign manager of the Kemsley group of newspapers (1945–59), until settling in Jamaica. He achieved worldwide fame and fortune as the creator of 12 sophisticated spy novels, including *Casino Royale* (1953), *From Russia with Love* (1957), *Dr No* (1958), *Goldfinger* (1959), *Thunderball* (1961), and *The Man with the Golden Gun* (1965). Built round the exploits of his amoral hero James Bond '(007)', they provided the basis for a series of highly successful films.

Fleming, Sir John Ambrose (1849–1945) Physicist, born in Lancaster, Lancashire, NW England, UK. He studied at London and Cambridge, and became professor of electrical engineering at University College London (1885–1926). He invented the thermionic valve, and was a pioneer in the application of electricity to lighting and heating on a large scale. He was knighted in 1929.

Fleming and Walloon The two main linguistic and cultural groups of present-day Belgium. Flemings (5·5 million) are based in the N and W, and speak Flemish (Vlaams). The French-speaking Walloons (3 million) live in the S and E. Both groups are predominantly Catholic. Linguistic disputes between the two groups have been a major feature of Belgian politics since the creation of the Kingdom in 1830, but especially since World War 2.

Fleming's rules A set of rules which link the direction of magnetic field, motion, and current using the thumb, first finger, and second finger, held at right angles; named after John Ambrose Fleming. The left hand/right hand correspond to motor/generator respectively.

Flemish *Dutch*

Flemish art The art of the predominantly Catholic S Netherlands, roughly modern Belgium and Luxembourg. Its major achievements were in painting, especially 14th-c manuscript illumination and 15th-c altarpieces and portraits on panel (Campin, van Eyck, van der Weyden, Bouts, Memlinc). The tradition continued in the 16th-c with Bosch and Brueghel, one of the greatest landscape painters, and the Baroque masters Rubens, van Dyck, and Jordaens in the 17th-c. Wars and religious iconoclasm have destroyed much, yet what survives attests to one of the greatest traditions of Western art. Flemish art, unlike Dutch, was always courtly and ecclesiastical in character, yet was largely independent of Italy. In the 20th-c Magritte and Delvaux made a distinct contribution to Surrealism.

Flemming, Walther (1843–1905) Biologist, born in Sachsenberg, WC Germany. He studied medicine at five German universities, and in 1876 became professor of anatomy at Kiel. In 1882 he gave the first modern account of cytology, including the process of cell division, which he named *mitosis*.

Fletcher, John (1579–1625) Playwright, born in Rye, East Sussex, SE England, UK. He came of a literary family, and studied at Cambridge, but little else is known about him apart from his theatrical work. It is difficult to disentangle his own plays from those in which he collaborated with Beaumont, Massinger, Rowley, and Shakespeare. He is best known for his collaboration with Beaumont in such works as *Philaster* (1610), *A King and No King* (1611), and *The Maid's Tragedy* (1611). Collaboration with Shakespeare probably resulted in *Two Noble Kinsmen* and *Henry VIII*.

Fleury, André-Hercule de [floeree] (1653–1743) French clergyman and statesman, born in Lodève, S France. As a young priest he entered court service (1679), became almoner to Louis XIV (1683), Bishop of Fréjus (1698), and in 1715 tutor to the future Louis XV. Replacing the Duc de Bourbon as chief minister (1726), he was made cardinal, and effectively controlled the government of Louis XV until 1743. Through skilful diplomacy he limited French involvement in the War of the Polish Succession (1733–8), restoring the country's prestige as a mediator. His moderation gave France the tranquillity her tangled finances demanded, and he carried out legal and economic reforms which stimulated trade.

Flinders, Matthew (1774–1814) Explorer, born in Donington, Lincolnshire, EC England, UK. He joined the navy in 1789, and became a navigator. In 1795 he sailed to Australia, where he explored the SE coast, and later (1801–3) circumnavigated the country. On his way home he was wrecked off the Great Barrier Reef, then kept prisoner by the French Governor of Mauritius until 1810. The *Flinders R* in Queensland, and the *Flinders Range* in South Australia are named after him.

Flinders Ranges *Lofty–Flinders Ranges, Mount*

flint A type of chert, occurring as grey, rounded nodules in chalk or other limestone. It breaks into sharp-edged flakes and hence was used as a Stone Age tool.

flint glass Heavy crystal glass, containing lead, highly suitable for cutting and engraving. It was first introduced c.1675, and so called because early examples were made with powdered flint instead of the more usual sand. It has a higher refractive index than crown glass (without lead), and thus played an important part in making corrected compound lenses.

Flintshire, Welsh **Sir y Fflint** pop (2001e) 148 600; area 437 sq km/169 sq mi. County (unitary authority from 1996) in NE Wales, UK; drained by R Clwyd; administrative centre, Mold; other chief towns, Flint, Queensferry; tourism, agriculture, light industry; castles at Flint, Hawarden; St Winifred's Well at Holywell; Theatre Clwyd.

FLN Abbreviation of **Front de Libération Nationale**, an organization founded in the early 1950s, which campaigned and fought for Algerian independence from France, under the leadership of Mohammed Ben Bella (1918–). The war with the FLN, supported by the conservative 'pieds-noirs' (French colonialists born in Algiers), led to the collapse of the Fourth French Republic in 1958, and the return to power of de Gaulle. France's inability to defeat the FLN led to the Evian conference in 1962, and complete Algerian independence. The FLN became the governing party of independent Algeria, and until 1991 was the only legal party in the country.

floating rate *exchange rates*

Flodden, Battle of (9 Sep 1513) A victory of the English over the Scots, fought in the Scottish Borders. James IV, allied with France, invaded England in August, but was defeated by English forces under Thomas Howard, Earl of Surrey. Long Scottish spears were no match for the English longbows, and the Scots lost perhaps as many as 10 000 dead, including James IV himself. The battle ended the Scottish threat for a generation.

Flood, Henry (1723–91) Irish statesman. He studied at Dublin and Oxford, and was leader of the Popular Party in the Irish parliament after his election in 1759. In 1775 he became vice-treasurer of Ireland, but was removed in 1781 as a strong nationalist. In 1783 he was returned for Winchester, and in 1785 for Seaford, but he failed to make a great mark at Westminster.

Flood, the In the Bible, the story that in Noah's time God caused a widespread deluge to destroy all people because of their sin (except for the faithful remnant of Noah and his family), this purge providing a new start for humanity (*Gen* 6–8) and the animal world. Similar legends are found also in other ancient near-eastern sources, such as the Babylonian Gilgamesh.

floods (lighting) *luminaires*

floppy disk or **floppy** A flexible plastic disk coated with magnetic material, used as a storage medium for microcomputers. The disks generally have diameters of 3·5 in (7·9 cm), 5·25 in (13·3 cm), or 8 in (20·3 cm), although the latter two are becoming less common, being replaced by 1·5 in (3·8 cm) disks. In use, the disks are rotated at some 300 revolutions per minute and are written to, or read from, by movable magnetic heads. The data is stored on a number of concentric tracks (usually 40 or 80); 5·25 in disks, for example, can store up to 1 megabyte or more of information, the exact amount depending on the particular system. The term has also come to be used by analogy for the rigid 3·5-in/7·9-cm disk.

Flora An ancient Roman goddess of flowers and flowering plants, who appears with the Spring. She was given a temple in 238 BC, and her games were celebrated on 28 April.

Florence, Ital **Firenze** 43°47N 11°15E, pop (2000e) 408 000. Ancient city and capital of Florence province, Tuscany, NC Italy, on R Arno; ancient Etruscan town; major trading centre by 12th-c; cultural and intellectual centre of Italy from the Middle Ages; capital of new Kingdom of Italy, 1865–70; badly damaged by floods, 1966; archbishopric; airport (Pisa, 53 km/33 mi); railway; university (1321); European University Institute (1972); seat of the Accademia della Crusca (1582); metallurgical products, precision engineering, telecommunications, leather, crafts, jewellery, publishing, cosmetics, medicinal products, cultural activities, tourism; city centre a world heritage site; famed for its many religious buildings, palaces and galleries, notably the Baptistery of San Giovanni (c.1000, rebuilt 11th–13th-c), the Duomo (1296); Churches of Santa Croce (begun 1295), Santa Maria Novella (1278–1350), Santa Maria del Carmine (largely rebuilt, 1782), San Lorenzo (393, rebuilt 1425), San Marco (13th-c, since rebuilt), Santissima Annunziata (1250), Or San Michele, (13th–14th-c); Palazzo Vecchio (1298–1314), Palazzo degli Uffizi (1560–74), Palazzo Medici-Riccardi (1444–52), Palazzo Pitti (15th-c and later), Ponte Vecchio (completed 1345); birthplace of Dante and Macchiavelli; religious festivals throughout the year, particularly at Easter; music festival (May); Gioco del Callio 16th-c football (Jun).

Florentine School One of the major centres of European art during the Renaissance period, whose leading figures were chronicled by their fellow-citizen Vasari, in his great *Lives of the Most Excellent Painters, Sculptors and Architects* (1550, enlarged 1568), written partly to glorify Florentine achievements over those of other schools such as the Venetian. The classical revival of the 15th-c began in Florence, as did the rediscovery of perspective; and the first academy of art was founded there in 1563. After c.1500 the leadership in Italian art shifted to Rome and Venice.

floret A very small or reduced flower, usually one of many aggregated together in a head which may itself resemble a single flower, as in members of the daisy family.

Florey (of Adelaide), Sir Howard Walter Florey, Baron [flawree] (1898–1968) Pathologist, born in Adelaide, South Australia. He studied medicine at Adelaide and Oxford, taught at Cambridge and Sheffield, then became professor of pathology at Oxford (1935–62), where he worked with Chain on penicillin, and shared the Nobel Prize for Physiology or Medicine (1945). He was appointed provost of Queen's College, Oxford (1962) and Chancellor of the Australian National University, Canberra (1965). Knighted in 1944, he became a life peer in 1965.

Florida pop (2000e) 15 982 400; area 151 934 sq km/58 664 sq mi. State in SE USA, divided into 67 counties; the 'Sunshine State' or 'Peninsular State'; discovered and settled by the Spanish in the 16th-c; ceded to Britain in 1763, and divided into East and West Florida; given back to Spain after the War of Independence, 1783; West Florida gained by the US in the Louisiana Purchase, 1803; East Florida purchased by the US, 1819; admitted as the 27th state of the Union, 1845; seceded, 1861; slavery abolished, 1865; re-admitted to the Union, 1868; capital, Tallahassee; other chief cities, Jacksonville, Miami, Tampa, St Petersburg, Fort Lauderdale; a long peninsula bounded W by the Gulf of Mexico and E by the Atlantic Ocean; rivers include the St Johns, Caloosahatchee, Apalachicola, Perdido, St Marys; C state has many lakes, notably L Okeechobee (fourth largest lake wholly within the USA); highest point in Walton County (105 m/345 ft); the Florida Keys Islands stretch in a line SW from the S tip of the state, all linked by a series of causeways; the NW is a gently rolling panhandle area, cut by deep swamps along the coast; the S is almost entirely covered by the Everglades; the SE coast is protected from the Atlantic by sandbars and islands, creating shallow lagoons and sandy beaches; a warm sunny climate, but occasional danger of hurricanes (eg widespread damage caused by Hurricane Andrew in 1992); many famous resorts (Palm Beach, Miami Beach); the Everglades National Park, Walt Disney World entertainment park, John F Kennedy Space Center at Cape Canaveral; the nation's greatest producer of citrus fruits; second largest producer of vegetables; sugar cane, tobacco, cattle and dairy products; processed foods, chemicals, electrical equipment, transportation equipment, wood products; phosphate and other minerals; one of the fastest-growing parts of the country; an important area for retirement homes; large Hispanic population (especially from Cuba).

Florida Keys A series of small islands curving approx 240 km/150 mi SW around the tip of the Florida peninsula, USA; about 160 km/100 mi NE of Havana; include (NE to SW) Key Largo, Long Key, Key Vaca, Big Pine Key, Sugarloaf Key and Key West; tropical products (limes, pineapples, etc) in the S; tarpon fishing; tourism; Overseas Highway (1938) runs from the mainland to Key West, 198 km/123 mi long.

florin A type of coin first made in the Italian city of Florence in 1252. Florins became popular for trade during the economic expansion of Europe from the 13th-c to the 15th-c. In 1849, Britain issued its first silver florin, the two-shilling piece, which became the 'old' 10p piece after the coinage was decimalized in 1971. This 10p piece was replaced in 1993.

flotation process The process of separating useful parts of minerals from waste (*gangue*), through the selective attachment of particles of the desired material to bubbles in a froth. The material to be treated is immersed in water and air is blown through. Bubble formation may be promoted by a surface-active or foam-promoting agent.

Flotow, Friedrich, Freiherr von (Baron) [**flohtoh**] (1812–83) Composer, born in Teutendorf, NE Germany. He studied music in Paris, and made his reputation with *Le Naufrage de la Méduse* (1839, The Wreck of the Medusa), *Stradella* (1844), and especially *Martha* (1847). From 1856 to 1863 he was director of the theatre at Schwerin.

flotsam, jetsam, and **lagan** [**laygn**] Three terms used in describing goods or wreckage found in the sea. **Flotsam** refers to anything found floating. **Jetsam** includes anything deliberately jettisoned from a ship, usually for the purposes of lightening it or because it would otherwise be dangerous to the ship. **Lagan** refers to goods on the bottom of the sea, either alone or within the hull of a wrecked vessel.

flounder Common European flatfish (*Platichthys flesus*) found in shallow inshore waters from Norway to the Mediterranean, also penetrating into fresh water in N areas; upper body surface grey-brown with dark patches and orange spots, underside white; length up to 50 cm/20 in; locally important as a food fish. (Family: Pleuronectidae.)

flour The finely ground product of a cereal seed, especially wheat, primarily used to make bread. A wheat seed consists of an outer coat (husk), with the germ (embryo) at one end and a starchy centre (endosperm). When the seed is ground, it forms a wholemeal flour suitable for baking; if the flour is refined to increase the proportion of endosperm, white flour is produced. Wholemeal flour is richer in fibre, and an important constituent of high-fibre diets, which may reduce the risk of some gastro-intestinal diseases.

flowchart A diagrammatic representation of a sequence of events. In the computing context, a **data flowchart** describes the overall operations in a complete data-processing system, such as an accounting system, without giving specific details of the individual computer programs; a **program flowchart** describes the sequence of operations within the program. There are recognized symbols to indicate the various types of operation.

flower The reproductive organ of a flowering plant (*angiosperm*) derived from a leafy shoot of limited growth in which the leaves are modified for specific roles. It typically consists of four distinct *whorls* of parts attached to a receptacle: the sepals (*calyx*), the petals (*corolla*), the stamens (*andrecium*), and the carpels or ovary (*gynecium*). The parts of any whorl may be fused or otherwise highly modified or absent. Structurally, flowers can be divided into two types: **actinomorphic** or radially symmetrical, and **zygomorphic** or bilaterally symmetrical. Both the colour and structure of the flower are closely linked to the method of pollination: brightly-coloured petals, along with any scent or nectar produced by the flower are used to attract pollinators. The colour may be quite specific, so that red is typically a bird-colour, blue and yellow are bee-colours, and dull-purplish flowers are often wasp-pollinated. Flowers which are one colour in the visible spectrum may be another colour in the ultraviolet, visible to many insects. The structure, especially in zygomorphic flowers, may also be geared to particular visitors: flat, open blossoms are visited by a wide range of pollinators, including flies and beetles; more complex blooms may have nectar concealed in long, gullet-like corolla tubes or behind closed lips accessible only to long-tongued bees, moths, or humming-birds. In wind-pollinated flowers, attractive petals are superfluous, and are usually much-reduced or absent. Double or multiple-petalled flowers such as garden roses are rare in nature, being mostly the product of horticultural breeding.

flowering plants One of the two divisions of seed plants, sometimes referred to as the **angiosperms**, the other division being the **gymnosperms**. They are characterized by having the seed enclosed in an ovary which has a specialized extension (the *stigma*) for receiving pollen. The male gametes produced by the pollen undergo double fertilization of the ovum, forming a zygote and a special seed storage tissue (the *endosperm*). Secondary vascular tissue develops from *cambial layers*, and contains cells unique to flowering plants: vessels in the *xylem*, companion cells in the *phloem*. The group includes all plants in which the reproductive organ is a flower, hence the commonly used name. The flowering plants are divided into **monocotyledons** and **dicotyledons** on the basis of cotyledon number, and further subdivided into various major groups such as orders and families, the exact divisions varying with the system in use. Flowering plants are the most advanced vascular plants, and the most common in terms of both numbers and distribution, with an estimated 250 000 species occurring in all parts of the globe. (Class: Angiospermae.)

flowering quince *japonica*

flowering rush A perennial (*Butomus umbellatus*) native to Europe and temperate Asia, growing in or beside water; stems to 1·5 m/5 ft; rhizomatous; leaves grass-like, triangular in cross-section; flowers c.2·5–3 cm/1–1¼ in diameter, pink, 3-petalled, in a terminal umbel. (Family: Butomaceae.)

flowerpecker A name applied loosely to many small woodland birds of the family Dicaeidae; more precisely, the 41 species of the genera *Prionochilus* and *Dicaeum*; found from India to Australia; tongue tube-like; eats nectar and berries, especially mistletoe.

flows *stocks*

flugelhorn [**flooglhaw(r)n**] A musical instrument made of brass, somewhat like a cornet and with a similar compass, but with a slightly larger bell. It is a standard instrument in British brass bands, and is used in jazz, but is rarely found in orchestras.

fluid A substance which flows and is able to fill its container: a liquid, gas, or plasma. Stationary fluids cannot sustain transverse or twisting forces. Their mechanical properties are governed by the laws of fluid mechanics.

fluidics The study of control and detection systems based on fluid movement. Available devices include fluid amplifiers (in which a small flow modifies a large flow), logic circuits, and switches. Fluidic devices contain no moving parts, are robust, and constitute no electrical hazard. An example is the fluidic vortex valve, which uses a controlling stream to alter the principal flow by creating a vortex, and is used in pumping systems in the nuclear industry for radioactive waste, and in mining for abrasive slurries.

fluid mechanics The study of the mechanics of fluids. **Fluid statics** is concerned with the properties of fluids at rest. **Fluid dynamics** considers the properties peculiar to moving fluids. **Hydrostatics** and **hydrodynamics** are the study of stationary and moving incompressible fluids (usually liquids), respectively. **Aerodynamics** is concerned with the flow of gases, especially air. The properties of fluids include *density*, the mass per unit volume, and *compressibility*, which is high for gases but essentially zero for liquids. A fluid also exerts a *pressure* on an object immersed in it, which is the same in all directions. In the absence of gravity, the pressure applied by a fluid is the same on all parts of its container. Objects immersed in fluid experience an upward *buoyancy* force. *Viscosity* measures a fluid's reluctance to flow, more properly its internal friction. The theory of fluids sometimes uses ideal fluids having zero viscosity and compressibility.

The early understanding of fluid pressure (especially atmospheric pressure) was due to Evangelista Torricelli. Pressure applied to a stationary fluid is transmitted undiminished throughout the fluid, and to the walls of the container independent of container shape. This is *Pascal's principle* (after Blaise Pascal, 1653), and forms the basis of hydraulics. The *flow* of fluid is the movement of fluid from one place to another, measured by *flow rate*, which is the mass of fluid passing some point every second. The principal of continuity states that for an incompressible fluid the amount of fluid flowing into some pipe network equals the amount flowing out. Early studies of fluid flow were due to Daniel Bernoulli, who in particular noted the pressure variation in a fluid flowing along a pipe of varying cross section (*Bernoulli's principle*). Modern mathematical theory of fluid flow is based on an approach introduced by Leonhard Euler, who treated a fluid as a continuous substance rather than discrete particles. The theory of viscous fluid flow was developed by British physicist George Stokes (1819–1903).

fluke Either of two groups of parasitic flatworms; **digenetic flukes**, typically parasites of vertebrates as adults, with complex life-cycles involving at least two hosts; **monogenetic flukes**, usually external parasites of fishes with single-host life-cycles. (Phylum: Platyhelminthes. Class: Trematoda.)

fluorescein [floouhreseen] $C_{20}H_{12}O_5$. An anthraquinone dye, red with an intense green fluorescence. Very dilute solutions are used to detect leaks in water systems, and to trace water flow patterns.

fluorescence Light produced by an object excited by means other than heating, where light emission ceases as soon as the energy source is removed. It is a type of luminescence, exploited in dyes and in the coating of fluorescent light tubes.

fluorescent brighteners Colourless substances which are easily absorbed by textiles, and which emit blue or blue/green light when exposed to ultraviolet light. The effect is to counteract the natural yellowness of textiles to maintain clean bright colours. They are an essential component of most detergents.

fluorescent lamp A lamp consisting of a tube, coated inside with fluorescent material (phosphor), filled with mercury vapour, and with an electrode at each end. Light is generated by passing a current between the electrodes through the vapour, producing ultraviolet light that is converted to visible light by phosphor fluorescence. Such lamps are more efficient than filament lamps.

fluoridation of water The production of water containing small amounts of fluorine (1 part per million), whose regular consumption greatly reduces the incidence of caries of the teeth. Water supplies in many regions contain fluorine naturally in sufficient concentrations to increase the resistance of teeth to attack. This has led the authorities to recommend the addition of fluorine to reservoirs deficient in the element. While this is done in many instances, a vociferous minority of the population who object to adding 'chemicals' to water have succeeded in preventing it from becoming universal.

fluoride A compound containing fluorine, especially one containing F^- ions. **Sodium fluoride** (NaF) is commonly added in small amounts to drinking water or dentifrice to supply fluoride ions necessary for strong dental enamel.

fluorine Element 9, composed of molecules F_2, boiling point −187°C. A yellow gas, the first of the halogens, the most electronegative element, oxidation state −1 in nearly all its compounds. It reacts with nearly all substances, including some of the noble gases, and is very corrosive and toxic. It occurs mainly in the mineral *fluorite* (CaF_2), and is obtained by the electrolysis of a mixture of hydrogen fluoride and potassium fluoride.

fluorite or **fluorspar** A common mineral of calcium fluoride (CaF_2), typically blue or purple in colour, and the main source of fluorine. It is found in veins and pockets associated with igneous rocks, and fluoresces in ultraviolet light. It is used as a flux in steel production.

fluorocarbons Compounds of carbon and fluorine, the simplest being CF_4, tetrafluoromethane. The C–F bond is very stable, and saturated fluorocarbons are very unreactive. Tetrafluoroethylene (CF_2=CF_2) forms the very stable polymer PTFE (Teflon®) by addition polymerization.

fluoroscope A medical instrument that projects radiation through the body to form an image of the internal organs on a fluorescent screen. It is used by physicians to assist in diagnosis. Conventional radiographic images are capable of demonstrating greater detail, but fluoroscopy is preferable when a live moving image is required. Similar instruments are used in industry for the examination of materials and mechanical objects.

fluorosis [floo-orohsis] Chronic poisoning by drinking water which contains an excessive amount of fluoride. This happens in several parts of the world (notably India), and results in discoloration of the teeth and a disabling arthritis which chiefly affects the spine. The concentration necessary to produce fluorosis is many times that added to drinking water in reservoirs to prevent dental caries.

fluorspar *fluorite*

Flushing, Dutch **Vlissingen**, Fr **Flessingue** 51°27N 3°35E, pop (2000e) 46 000. Seaport in Zeeland province, W Netherlands, on Walcheren I at the mouth of the Schelde river estuary; scene of Allied landing, 1944; railway; site of a nuclear power station; shipbuilding, machinery, vehicles, leather, fish processing, aluminium, chemicals; 14th-c Grote Kerk.

flute Broadly speaking, a musical instrument in which a column of air is activated by the player blowing across a mouth-hole or (as in the recorder) against a sharp edge (or 'fipple') towards which the breath may be directed through a duct. Flutes may therefore be divided into two categories: **cross-blown** (or transverse) and **end-blown**. The unqualified term 'flute' generally refers to the transverse concert type, known in Britain until c.1900 as the 'German flute'. This is made of wood or (more often now) of metal in three jointed sections, with 13 toneholes, and an elaborate system of keys which allow a fully chromatic compass of three octaves from middle C upwards. The smaller **piccolo** sounds one octave higher.

flutemouth *cornetfish*

fluting or **flutes** Shallow vertical channelling on a building, usually on the shaft of a column or pilaster. It is common in the Doric, Ionic, Corinthian, and Composite orders, but not in the Tuscan.

flux (physics) A term indicating flow, such as a flux of particles flowing past a point, or the flux of some fluid moving from high to low pressure. For electric and magnetic fields, flux indicates the total amount of field flowing from a source through some region.

flux (technology) Any substance used in metallurgical processes to promote the flow of molten metal and waste (*slag*) and to segregate unwanted impurities. Limestone fulfils this purpose in iron smelting. In soldering, rosin is often used.

fluxoid *BCS theory*

fly The common name of many small flying insects. True flies have a single pair of membranous flying wings only; hindwings modified as club-shaped, balancing organs (*halteres*); mouthparts forming a *proboscis* adapted for sucking, occasionally for piercing; feed on nectar, plant and animal secretions, blood, and decomposing matter; larvae maggot-like, lacking true legs, varied in feeding habits; c.150 000 species, many of great medical and veterinary importance as carriers of disease. (Order: Diptera.)

fly agaric [agarik] A toadstool (*Amanita muscaria*) that forms a bright red fruiting body, typically with white patches on cap; common on ground under trees such as birch and pine during autumn; produces hallucinogenic poisons that can be fatal to humans if eaten. (Order: Agaricales.)

flycatcher A name applied to birds of three distinct groups: **New World** or **tyrant flycatchers** (Family: Tyrannidae, 375 species); **Old World flycatchers** (Family: Muscicapidae, 150 species); and **silky flycatchers** (Family: Ptilogonatidae, 4 species). All usually eat insects caught in flight. The name is also used for several birds of other families.

flying buttress *buttress*

flying doctor service The provision of medical services to isolated communities spread over wide areas, based on the use of Air Ambulances. It is particularly well-known in the Australian interior.

Flying Dutchman A ghost ship of disastrous portent, haunting the seas around the Cape of Good Hope; its captain had sworn a blasphemous oath when he failed to round the Cape in a storm, and was condemned to sail those waters forever. The story inspired Wagner's opera *Der Fliegende Holländer* (1843).

flying fish Small, surface-living fish with greatly enlarged pelvic and pectoral fins, and the ability to jump and glide above the water surface; *Exocoetus volitans* (length up to 30 cm/1 ft), is widespread in tropical and warm temperate seas. (Family: Exocoetidae.)

flying fox *bat*

flying lemur *colugo*

flying lizard A SE Asian agamid lizard; able to glide between trees using a semicircular membrane on each side of the body; membrane supported by movable ribs; can be folded back when not in use; also known as **flying dragon**. (Genus: *Draco*, several species.)

flying phalanger A nocturnal squirrel-like marsupial, native to Australia and New Guinea; gliding membrane between front and hind limbs; can glide up to 114 m/374 ft; inhabits woodland; eats plant material and animals. (Family: Petauridae, 4 species.)

flying snake A snake from SE Asia; glides between trees; launches itself into the air, then flattens the body and forms several S-shaped curves; several regions of the body are then broadside to the direction of travel and act like wings; may glide 20 m/65 ft or more. (Genus: *Chrysopelea*, 2 species. Family: Colubridae.)

flying spot scanner A device for reproducing a slide transparency or motion picture film on television by scanning the picture area with a spot of light, usually generated on the screen of a cathode-ray tube. The transmitted light is collected by a photocell or sensor tube to produce the video signal.

flying squirrel A squirrel with a large flap of skin between its front and hind legs; glides between trees (up to 450 m/1475 ft in one leap); active at dawn and dusk; 33 species in Asia (one reaches E Europe, most in SE Asia), and two species in North America.

Flynn, Errol (Leslie Thomson) (1909–59) Actor, born in Hobart, Tasmania, Australia. He moved to England to gain acting experience, joined the Northampton Repertory Company, and after a part in a film was offered a Hollywood contract. His first US film, *Captain Blood* (1935), established him as a hero of historical adventure films, and his good looks and athleticism confirmed him as the greatest Hollywood swashbuckler, in such films as *The Adventures of Robin Hood* (1938) and *The Sea Hawk* (1940). During the 1940s his off-screen reputation for drinking, drug-taking, and womanizing became legendary, and eventually affected his career, which was briefly revived by his acclaimed performance as a drunken wastrel in *The Sun Also Rises* (1957). His autobiography was called *My Wicked, Wicked Ways* (1959).

flywheel A wheel attached to the shaft of an engine, whose distribution of weight enables it to act as a smoothing device for the engine's power output.

f-number A numerical system of indicating the size of the aperture stop in a camera lens, which determines how much light is transmitted to the film and hence the control of exposure in conjunction with shutter speed. The f-number is calculated by dividing the focal length of the lens by the diameter of the clear aperture of the lens as given by the iris diaphragm. A small f-number indicates a large aperture. A lens of focal length 100 mm with apertures of 50 mm and 12·5 mm will have f-numbers of f/2 and f/8 respectively. Increasing the f-number by 'stopping-down' the iris reduces the light transmitted and increases depth of field. The usual range of numbers is from f/1·4 to f/32 in increments that give a progressive halving of transmission by a series such as 1·4, 2, 2·8, 4, 5·6, 8, 11, 16, 22, and 32.

Fo, Dario [foh] (1926–) Playwright, designer, and actor, born in San Giano, N Italy. After working in radio and TV he founded, along with his wife, **Franca Rame**, a radical theatre company in 1959. His populist plays use the comic traditions of farce and slapstick, as well as surreal effects; best known are *Morte accidentale di un anarchico* (1970, Accidental Death of an Anarchist), *Non si paga, non si paga* (1974, Can't Pay, Won't Pay), and *Female Parts* (1981), one-woman plays written with his wife. Later works include *Il Papa e la strega* (1989, The Pope and the Witch) and *Johan Padan a la descoverta de la Americhe* (1992, Johan Padan and the Discovery of America). He was awarded the Nobel Prize for Literature in 1997.

Foale, Michael [fohl] (1957–) Astronaut, born in Louth, Lincolnshire, E England, UK. He studied astrophysics at Cambridge University (1982), then joined the US space programme in Houston, TX and was selected for astronaut training by NASA in 1987. Highlights of his career include a spacewalk outside the Russian space station Mir (1995), four months working aboard Mir (1997), and an eight-day shuttle mission to repair the Hubble Space Telescope (1999). In October 2003 he was chosen to command the International Space Station (ISS), spending 200 days performing routine maintenance and conducting scientific experiments, and thereby clocking up more hours in space than any other US astronaut.

foam A suspension of gas in liquid or of liquid in gas, also called **froth**. It is stabilized by the addition of detergents to the liquid phase. Foams are controlled by adding agents to raise the surface tension of the liquid. They are useful, especially in mineral extraction, as differences in the surface properties of components of an ore can be used to float off part in a foam. They are also used in fire-fighting.

Foch, Ferdinand [fosh] (1851–1929) French marshal, born in Tarbes, S France. He taught at the Ecole de Guerre, proved himself a great strategist at the Marne (1914), Ypres, and other World War 1 battles, and commanded the Allied Armies in 1918.

focus The point of convergence for rays of light passing through a positive lens at which the sharpest real image is formed. The position of a camera lens must be adjusted ('focused') so that this image coincides with the photosensitive surface.

focussing A technique for developing self-awareness in which the mind tunes into the inner self and follows the body's innate wisdom, rather than seeking intellectual solutions to problems. It is decribed as a self-directed process of building up a relationship with one's inner self, and is said to enhance other psychological techniques such as psychotherapy, meditation, and exploring feelings and emotions.

foetus *fetus*

fog A cloud which occurs at ground level, resulting in low visibility. It forms when two air masses with differing temperatures and moisture contents mix together. **Radiation fog** develops on cold, clear nights when terrestrial radiation cools the ground surface, and lowers the temperature of the air close to the ground to below the dew point temperature, causing condensation. **Advective fog** forms when warm, moist air blows over a cold ground surface, is cooled, and condensation results. Fog may also be associated with frontal activity when warm rain falls through cold but saturated air.

Föhn / Foehn wind [foen] A warm, dry wind descending on the leeward side of a mountain. As moist air rises on the windward side, it cools and loses moisture before descending and warming. It may cause a sudden rise in temperature, such as 10°C in a few hours. It is found in the European Alps and other mountainous areas. In the Rockies, North America, it is known as a *chinook* wind, in New Zealand as a *Nor-Wester*, and in Argentina as a *zonda*.

Fokine, Michel [fokeen], originally **Mikhail Mikhaylovich Fokine** (1880–1942) Dancer and choreographer, born in St Petersburg, NW Russia. He worked with Diaghilev's Ballets Russes in Paris from 1909, and in 1923 went to New York City, becoming a US citizen in 1932. He is credited with the creation of modern ballet from the elaborate and ornamental, stylized mode prevalent at the beginning of the 20th-c. He based his choreography on intensely disciplined training, but eliminated rigid tradition, thus enabling a new freedom of movement to come with expressionism. Among the c.70 ballets he created are *The Dying Swan* (1905) solo for Anna Pavlova, *Les Sylphides* (1909), *The Firebird* (1910), and *Petrouchka* (1916).

Fokker, Anthony Herman Gerard (1890–1939) Aircraft engineer, born in Kediri, Java. He built his first plane in 1911, and in 1913 founded the Fokker aircraft factory at Schwerin, Germany, which made warplanes for the German air force in World War 1. After the war he set up a factory in The Netherlands, and later operated also in Britain and the USA, where he became a US citizen.

fold In geology, a bend or flexure in a stratified rock resulting from compressional or gravitational forces. It may exist on many different scales from centimetres to many kilometres. Upward folds are termed *antiforms*; downward folds are *synforms*.

folic acid A B vitamin found in liver and most green vegetables, required for the synthesis and functioning of red cells. A deficiency, which is rare in developed countries, leads to anaemia. Folic acid is often given in association with iron for the routine prevention of anaemia, as in pregnancy.

Folies-Bergère [folee bairzhair] A music hall in Paris, France, opened in 1869. By the end of the 19th-c its stage was dominated by circus acts and semi-nude female performers. It remains famous for its lavish displays.

folium of Descartes One of the simplest curves (and one of the first to be found) with a node, ie a point at which the curve crosses itself. It is represented by the Cartesian equation $x^3 + y^3 = 3axy$.

folklore The traditional songs, tales, proverbs, legends, and beliefs of a people. The term was suggested in 1846 by William John Thoms (1803–85), founder of the folklore journal *Notes and Queries*. Nowadays it often embraces material culture (utensils, arts and crafts, housing, dress) and non-material culture (festivals, dances, customs, and rituals). The field of folklore now overlaps considerably with those of cultural anthropology and popular culture.

folk music Music which is transmitted orally, usually with modifications from generation to generation and from place to place, so that its original form and composer are forgotten. Much folk music exhibits melodic inflections, rhythmic characteristics, or performing styles which link it to a particular country or locality, but it is not unknown for folktunes to cross boundaries, and even seas. Sound recording greatly facilitated the collecting and transcribing of folk music in the 20th-c.

folk tales Traditional stories told orally and found all over the world, known – as far as one can tell – from earliest times. They fall into various categories, such as animal tales, tales involving magic, tales recounting tests, tricks, or reversals of fortune, and tales explaining the origin of customs, topographical features, or the entire cosmos. Folk tales have been extensively collected in modern times, and form the models for printed fairy tales. This process of collection and publication has coincided with the decline of the tale as a living part of folk culture.

follicle-stimulating hormone (FSH) A chemical substance (a glycoprotein gonadotrophin) secreted by the front lobe of the pituitary gland in vertebrates. It has an important role in reproduction: in mammals it stimulates the early maturation of ovarian follicles (in females) and the production of sperm (in males).

Folsom A prehistoric 'kill site' in New Mexico, USA, excavated in 1926: 19 fluted spear points of 9000–8000 BC, found with the skeletons of 23 extinct long-horned bison (*Bison antiquus*), established for the first time the co-existence of humans with Ice Age mammals in the New World and the antiquity of the native American population. Still earlier occupation, c.20 000–5000 BC, is now attested.

Fomalhaut [fomalhoht] A bright S hemisphere star in Piscis Austrinus. Distance: 7·7 parsec. Also called **Alpha Piscis Austrini**, it is the 18th star (excluding the Sun) in order of apparent brightness. A white star, it is used in navigation because of its conspicuous position. Fomalhaut was associated with the Roman goddess Ceres, and her Greek counterpart Demeter.

Fonda, Henry (Jaynes) (1905–82) Actor, born in Grand Island, Nebraska, USA. He studied at the University of Minnesota, and after some success on the Broadway stage, went to Hollywood in 1935. His performances in the *Young Mr Lincoln* (1939), *The Grapes of Wrath* (1940), and *The Oxbow Incident* (1943), established him in the role of the American folk hero, the common man of integrity, and he played many such parts over the next 30 years. His last major appearance was in *On Golden Pond* (1981), for which he was awarded an Oscar.

Fonda, Jane (1937–) Actress and human-rights activist, born in New York City, USA, the daughter of Henry Fonda. After appearances on Broadway and in films in the early 1960s, she married (1965–73) director Roger Vadim, with whom she made *La Ronde* (1964) and *Barbarella* (1968). Later roles widened her dramatic scope: *Klute* (1971, Oscar), *Coming Home* (1978, Oscar), *The China Syndrome* (1979), *On Golden Pond* (1981), *The Morning After* (1986), and *Old Gringo* (1989). She is politically active in anti-nuclear and feminist peace movements, often reflected in her films, and in the 1980s she became involved with women's health and fitness activities.

F_1 hybrid A first-generation hybrid between two plant cultivars, in which the yield or other desirable characters are expressed at a level greater than that in either parent (a condition known as *heterosis*). Such hybrids do not breed true, and must therefore be freshly produced by the breeder in each generation. They were first developed in maize, but are now available in many species.

Fonseca, Manuel Deodoro da *Deodoro da Fonseca, Manuel*

Fontainebleau [fõtenbloh] A magnificent 16th-c chateau built by Italian craftsmen for Francis I on the site of an earlier royal chateau-fortress at Fontainebleau in France; a world heritage site. It was used by Napoleon as his imperial palace.

Fontainebleau School [fontenbloh] A group of artists including Italian Mannerists such as Giovanni Battista Rosso (1495–1540), Niccolo dell' Abbate (c.1512–71) and Francisco Primaticcio (1504–c.70), working for Francis I of France c.1530–60. The main centre was at the royal palace of Fontainebleau.

Fontana, Domenico [fontahna] (1543–1607) Architect, born in Melide, S Switzerland (formerly Italy). He was papal architect in Rome, employed on the Lateran Palace, the Vatican Library, and St Peter's dome. He was afterwards royal architect in Naples.

Fontanne, Lynne, originally **Lillie Louise Fontanne** (1887–1983) Stage actress, born in Woodford, Essex, SE England, UK. A woman of great glamour and sophistication, she was best known for her many collaborations in modern comedies with her husband **Alfred Lunt**. After studying in England with Ellen Terry, she settled permanently in the USA in 1916, when she met Lunt. The couple first appeared as husband and wife in 1924 in *The Guardsman*, and thereafter often performed together in Theatre Guild productions. She received the US Medal of Freedom with her husband in 1964.

Fontenay Abbey [fõtnay] A Cistercian abbey, founded in 1119 by Bernard of Clairvaux at Fontenay in NE France; a world heritage monument. It was abandoned by the order in the 18th-c, but the abbey remains were restored after 1906.

Fonteyn, Margot [fontayn], in full **Dame Margot Fonteyn de Arias**, originally **Margaret Hookham** (1919–91) Ballerina, born in Reigate, Surrey, SE England, UK. She joined the Sadler's Wells Ballet (later the Royal Ballet) in 1934, where she made her first solo appearance in *The Haunted Ballroom*, and became one of the greatest ballerinas of the 20th-c, both in classic roles and in creating new roles for Ashton. A new partnership with Nureyev in the 1960s extended her performing career. She married **Roberto Emilio Arias** (1918–89), then Panamanian ambassador to the Court of St James in London, in 1955, and was created a dame in 1956.

Foochow *Fuzhou*

food Any plant or animal material which is primarily eaten for nutritional purposes. Anything eaten specifically for its therapeutic purposes, real or otherwise, is strictly speaking not a food, even though it may have some nutritive properties. Thus vitamin C supplements, taken to prevent a cold, are being used pharmacologically and not nutritionally.

food allergy A true allergic reaction in which there is accompanying evidence of abnormal immunological response to the food items. A reaction is set up in the body involving immunoglobulins (IgE, IgG, or IgM), which results in the release of substances (*kinins*) causing inflammation and tissue damage. There may be circulating immune complexes present after the food is taken, and the condition is easily diagnosed by the detection of a raised level of immunoglobulin (IgE) and by skin testing to provoke an allergic reaction.

Food and Agriculture Organization (FAO) A specialized agency of the United Nations dealing with agriculture and nutrition. The FAO was set up in 1945 and has its headquarters in Rome. It conducts research and surveys, and publishes statistics, in the areas of agriculture, forestry, and fisheries, and the distribution of their products. It provides technical assistance to improve productivity in the sectors producing and distributing agricultural products, with the aim of preventing famines and improving standards of living in rural areas. It also conducts research in nutrition, and publishes nutritional standards and forecasts of world food needs and supplies.

Food and Drug Administration (FDA) A law enforcement agency in the USA which inspects, tests, and sets safety standards for foodstuffs, medicines, and a wide range of household goods and services that might affect personal health (eg cosmetics, cleaning fluids). It is also involved with the regulations governing associated products (eg labels, packaging, cookers, radiation devices) and locations (eg restaurants and food-stalls).

food chain The sequence of organisms on successive feeding (*trophic*) levels within an ecological community, through which energy is transferred by feeding. Energy enters the food chain mainly during photosynthesis by green plants (*primary producers*), passes to the herbivores (*primary consumers*) when they eat plants, and then to the carnivores (*secondary and tertiary consumers*) when they prey on herbivores. Food chains are interconnected, forming a complex food web.

food fortification The process of adding a nutrient to food. Many breakfast cereals are fortified with iron voluntarily by the manufacturer. Margarine manufacturers are obliged to add vitamins A and D to their product. Food fortification is used by governments to ensure that the intakes of certain nutrients are increased. Thus 'iodized' salt ensures that goitre, an iodine deficiency, is rare.

food labelling The provision of identifying labels on food, which must not only declare the product and manufacturer but also provide data on the product weight, the additives which have been incorporated, and nowadays a brief outline of key nutritional data. Food labelling is readily used on packaged foods. With fresh food such as meat, fish, fruit, and vegetables the label may be adjacent to the product or supplied in leaflet form.

food poisoning An illness that arises from eating food or liquid contaminated with infectious micro-organisms or chemicals that affect the gastro-intestinal tract, causing vomiting and diarrhoea. Infectious causes include *salmonella* and botulism. Non-bacterial food poisoning may be due to eating poisonous mushrooms and shellfish.

food preservation The treatment of food to maintain its quality and prevent deterioration. Food may become available during specific seasons. Preserving perishable food to make it available over a longer period has been an essential component of the technological conquest of nature. Drying removes the water necessary for the growth of spoilage organisms, while bacterial growth can be prevented by acidifying (pickling), salting, heating, canning, freezing, and now by irradiation.

food sensitivity A state of intolerance to a food item, in which there may or may not be evidence of an abnormal immunological reaction. Most food sensitivities are temporary, and the food can be reintroduced into the diet after a period of avoidance, but if subjects are unable to tolerate the substance again they are said to have a **fixed sensitivity**. The various mechanisms involved in food sensitivity reactions include allergic reactions, psychological reactions, pharmacological reactions to either the foodstuff itself or to additives, a direct irritant effect of food on the gut lining (eg wheat), and some enzyme deficiencies in which the body is unable to process the constituents (eg lactase deficiency).

fool's gold *pyrite*

Foot, Michael (Mackintosh) (1913–) British statesman, born in Plymouth, Devon, SW England, UK, the brother of Dingle and Hugh Foot. He studied at Oxford, and joined the staff of the *Tribune* in 1937, becoming editor (1948–52, 1955–60). He was also acting editor of the *Evening Standard* (1942–4) and a political columnist on the *Daily Herald* (1944–64). He became a Labour MP in 1945, and was secretary of state for employment (1974–6), and deputy leader (1976–80) then leader (1980–3) of the Labour Party, resigning after his party's heavy defeat in the general election. He retired from the Commons in 1992. A pacifist, he was a strong supporter of the Campaign for Nuclear Disarmament. A prolific writer, his best-known work is his biography of Aneurin Bevan.

foot The terminal part of the lower limb which makes contact with the ground or other substrate; an instrument of support when standing, and of propulsion and restraint when walking or running. It consists of a number of bony elements (the *tarsal*, *metatarsal*, and *phalangeal* bones), whose size, number, and arrangement differs between species, bound together by ligaments, and supported by tendons and muscles. The tarsal bones articulate with the metatarsals, which in turn articulate with the phalanges. In humans there are seven tarsal bones, five metatarsals, two phalanges in the big toe, and three in the other toes. Many animals use only the toes to make contact with the environment, unlike humans and primates, who use the whole foot. The structural arrangement of the foot (in terms of the bones, muscles, and nerves) is similar to that of the hand. Consequently individuals who have no hands or upper limbs (as in thalidomide defects) can develop the use of the feet to such an extent that they can use them to paint, write, and drive.

foot-and-mouth disease A contagious feverish disease of artiodactyls characterized by blistering inside the mouth and in the cleft of the hooves; also known as **hoof-and-mouth dis-**

ease. It can be caught by humans. In domestic stock, diagnosis (at least in Western countries) would lead to the immediate destruction of the affected herd, as happened with the British outbreak in 2001 (when over 2000 cases were confirmed between Feb and Oct).

football, American *p.576*

football, Association *p.576*

football, Australian Rules *p.577*

football, Canadian A Canadian variant of rugby football. It developed from the 1880s, adapting aspects of 'American' football (which itself had roots in Montreal), and evolving its character independently. It is different from rugby in that (like American football) the ball can be thrown forward, and it involves a 'stop-play' rather than a continuous play format. The field is 110 × 55 yds (100 m × 50 m), with 10-yd (9-m) deep end-zones. The Canadian Football League appeared in 1958 at the end of a long conflict between amateur and professional associations. It presently consists of eight teams, the best of which is annually awarded the Grey Cup.

football, Gaelic A mixture of rugby, soccer, and Australian Rules football. The first game resembling Gaelic football took place in Slane, Ireland, in 1712, between Meath and Louth. Originally played with 21 players per side, it was reduced to 15 in 1913. It is played on a rectangular field 84–100 yd (77–91 m) wide and 140–160 yd (128–146 m) long. At each end is a goal which resembles a set of rugby posts with a soccer-style net attached. The object is to score points by either putting the ball into the goal net, worth three points, or over the crossbar and between the uprights, worth one point.

football, Rugby League A team game played with an oval ball on a rectangular playing area. Rugby League originated when the North of England clubs seceded from the Rugby Football Union in 1895 over its refusal to permit 'broken time' payments for time off work to play rugby. They formed the Northern Rugby Football Union, which became the Rugby Football League in 1922. The Rugby League became openly professional in 1898 and gradually developed into a distinctive game through rule changes such as the reduction of teams from 15 to 13 players and the abolition of the line-out for returning the ball to play. The first World Cup was played in 1954. The means of scoring are the same as in Rugby Union, but with different scoring values: try 4, conversion 2, penalty goal 2, drop goal 1.

football, Rugby Union *p.578*

football hooliganism Hooliganism at football (soccer) matches, regarded as a recent social problem, but found from the beginning of the 20th-c. The Scottish Cup was withheld in 1909 after the fans of Glasgow Celtic and Glasgow Rangers were engaged in a battle which resulted in pay boxes being burned down. A new wave of hooliganism started in the 1960s, and became particularly severe in the mid-1980s, when English 'fans' were involved in several serious incidents at European games, notably, the 1985 riots at the Heysel stadium in Brussels, in which 39 people were killed. After that event, English clubs were banned for a while from playing matches in Europe. Modern hooligans work in organized gangs, and often do not attend 'home' matches but only those involving their club when playing away from home, in an effort to cause aggravation in other towns or countries. More sophisticated methods of policing and crowd control are the main measures being used to combat the problem.

Football League The oldest association football league in the world, formed after a formal meeting at the Royal Hotel, Manchester on 17 April 1888. Twelve clubs became founder members, and Scotsman William McGregor (1847–1911), a Birmingham shop owner, was its first president.

Football War A lightning war fought over several days in July 1969 between Honduras and El Salvador, rapidly halted by international pressure. It was so named because recriminations between the two Central American states had come to a head during the qualifying matches for the 1970 World Cup.

foraminiferan [foraminiferan] An amoeba-like protozoan that secretes an external shell (*test*), typically calcareous and chambered; feeds and moves by means of protoplasmic processes (*pseudopodia*) extruded through shell openings; largely marine; remains can form a sediment on the sea bed known as *foraminiferal ooze*; includes many fossils. (Order: Foraminifera.)

Forbidden City The Imperial Palace in Beijing, the residence of the imperial rulers of China from its construction by 200 000 workmen in 1420 until the fall of the Qing dynasty in 1911. The last Emperor, Puyi, and his retinue resided here until their eviction in 1924. The walled and moated palace complex covers 74 ha/183 acres, and is the best preserved example of mediaeval Chinese architecture. The Imperial Palace Museum was established here in 1925.

force An influence applied to an unrestrained object which results in a change in its motion, causing it to accelerate in some way; symbol *F*, units N (newton); a vector quantity. Force equals mass of object multiplied by acceleration (Newton's second law).

forces of nature In physics, taken to mean gravitation, electromagnetism, weak nuclear force, and strong nuclear force. Examples of their manifestations include the orbit of the Earth round the Sun (gravitation), the force between electrical charges (electromagnetism), radioactive beta-decay (weak nuclear force), and the binding force holding the atomic nucleus together (strong nuclear force). (*see panel p.578*)

Ford, Anna (1943–) British broadcaster. She studied at Manchester University, then worked in further education as a lecturer and tutor. She joined Granada TV as a presenter and reporter (1974–6), then moved to the BBC, where her programmes included *Man Alive* (1976–7) and *Tomorrow's World* (1977–8). She became an ITN newscaster (1978–80), helped to present *TV am* (1980–2), then worked as a freelance broadcaster and writer, and (from 1989) with BBC news and current affairs.

Ford, Elbur *Hibbert, Eleanor*

Ford, Ford Madox, originally **Ford Hermann Hueffer** (1873–1939) Writer and literary critic, born in Merton, Surrey, SE England, UK. He collaborated with Conrad on *The Inheritors* (1901) and *Romance* (1903), wrote *The Good Soldier* (1915) and over 80 other books of fiction and non-fiction, and founded the *English Review* (1908). After World War 1, he changed his name to Ford, and exiled himself to France and the USA, where he edited *The Transatlantic Review* (1924), wrote poetry, a series of war novels, and the tetralogy *Parade's End* (1920s). His appreciation of the works of Joyce, Pound, Cummings, and others, did much to shape the course of 20th-c writing.

Ford, Gerald R(udolph) (1913–) US statesman and 38th president (1974–6), born in Omaha, Nebraska, USA. He studied at Michigan and Yale universities, and served in the US navy during World War 2. He became a Republican member of the US House of Representatives (1949–73), and on the resignation of Spiro Agnew in 1973 was appointed vice-president. He became president in 1974 when Nixon resigned because of the Watergate scandal. The full pardon he granted to Nixon the same year made him unpopular, and this, along with the economic recession of the time, led to his defeat in the 1976 presidential election by Jimmy Carter.

Ford, Harrison (1942–) Actor, born in Chicago, Illinois, USA. He served a long apprenticeship in film and television, interspersed with employment as a carpenter, before achieving stardom in *Star Wars* (1977) and its two sequels. Cast as a resourceful, swashbuckling hero, he found great popularity as the archaeologist adventurer 'Indiana Jones' in a series of films beginning with *Raiders of the Lost Ark* (1981). He enhanced his reputation with testing characterizations in *Witness* (1985, Oscar nomination), *The Mosquito Coast* (1986), *Presumed Innocent* (1990), and *The Fugitive* (1993). Later films include *Clear and Present Danger* (1994), *The Devil's Own* (1997), and *What Lies Beneath* (2000). He received the American Film Institute's Life Achievement Award in 2000.

football, American

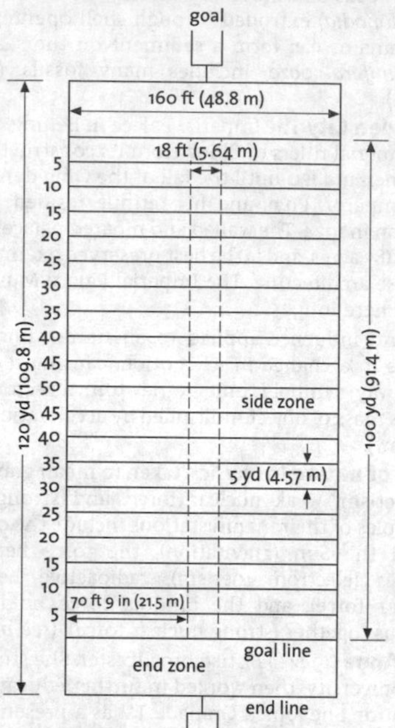

American football

The national fall (autumn) and winter sport in the USA, played between September and January. It resembles rugby, but forward passing of the ball is permitted. It is played on a rectangular field 360 ft (110 m) by 160 ft (49 m), divided into 5-yd (4·6-m) segments which give the field a gridiron effect. The object is to score *touchdowns* - the moving of the ball across the goal line in a running or passing play. This is similar to the *try* in rugby, but progress has to be made upfield by a series of *plays*, and a team must make 10 yd (9·1 m) of ground within four plays, otherwise it loses possession of the ball. Six points are awarded for a touchdown and one point for a *conversion* (kicking the ball between the posts and over the crossbar), as in rugby. A goal kicked from anywhere on the field (a *field goal*) is worth 3 points. Teams consist of more than 40 squad members, but only 11 are allowed on the field for each team at any one time. Special units come on for specific roles. When a team is attacking, the 11 players will be different from those on the field when they are on the defence. The game was first played in US colleges in the mid-19th-c, and the first rules were drawn up at Princeton College in 1867. The professional game in the USA comes under the auspices of the National Football League, which is divided into the American Football Conference (AFC) and National Football Conference (NFC). The leading teams of the two conferences meet in a series of play-off games each January for the Super Bowl (instituted 1966–7).

football, Association

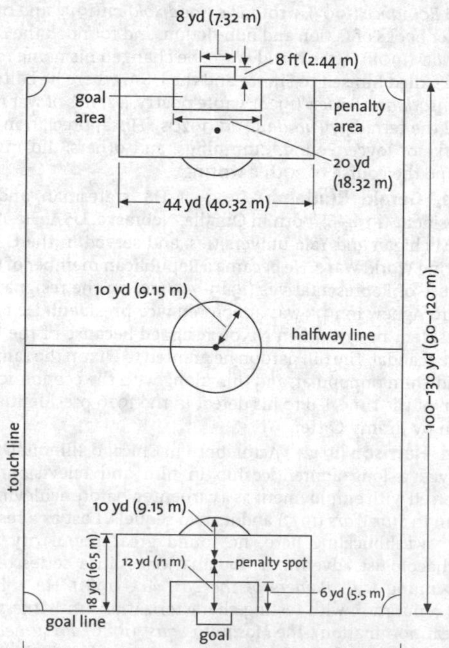

Association football

An 11-a-side team game played on a grass or synthetic pitch (or field) measuring 90–120 m/100–130 yd in length, and 45–90 m/50–100 yd wide. At each end of the field is a goal net measuring 8 yd (7·3 m) wide by 8 ft (2·4 m) high. The object is to move the ball around the field, with the feet or head, until a player is in a position to put the ball into the net and score a goal. The goalkeeper defends the goal, and he is the only person allowed to touch the ball with his hands while it is in play, provided he touches it within his specifically defined area. The ancient Greeks, Chinese, Egyptians and Romans all played a form of football. In the early 19th-c it became an organized game in Britain, and was played in most universities and public schools. Standard rules were drawn up at Cambridge University in 1848, and in 1863 the Football Association was formed. The first FA Cup final was played in 1872. Professionalism increased amongst northern clubs, and the game was legalized in 1885. The Football League was formed in 1888. The world governing body, the Fédération Internationale de Football Association (FIFA), was formed in Paris in 1904. The first World Cup was organized in Uruguay in 1930. The European governing body, the Union of European Football Associations (UEFA), was formed in 1954, and it controls the major European club competitions.

football, Australian Rules

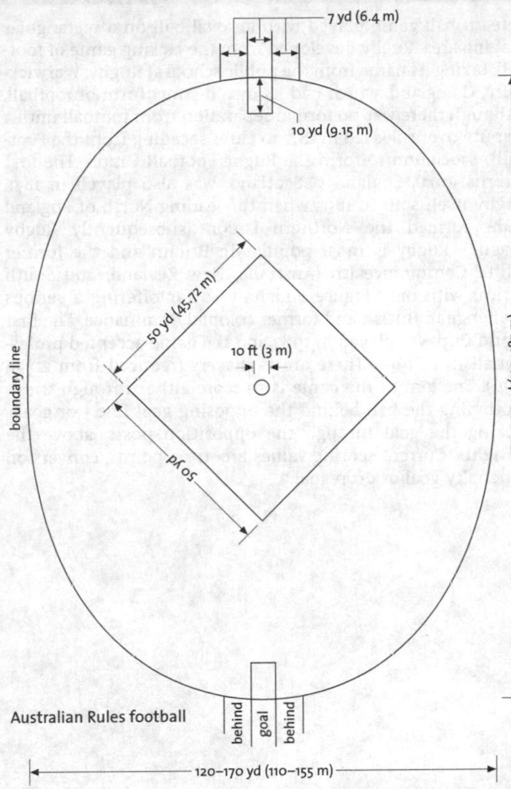

Australian Rules football

A handling and kicking game which is a cross between association football and rugby. Surprisingly, it has few rules. It is played with 18 players per side on an oval field measuring c.165 m/180 yd long by c.137 m/150 yd wide. The object is to score goals by kicking the ball between the opponent's goal posts for six points. Smaller posts are positioned either side of the main goal, and if the ball is kicked through that area then 1 point is scored. The first recorded game was played between Scotch College and Melbourne Grammar School in 1858.

Ford, Henry (1863–1947) Automobile engineer and manufacturer, born in Dearborn, Missouri, USA. He produced his first petrol-driven motor car in 1893, and in 1899 founded a company in Detroit, designing his own cars. In 1903 he started the Ford Motor Company, pioneering the modern 'assembly line' mass-production techniques for his famous Model T (1908–9), 15 million of which were produced up to 1928. He also branched out into aircraft and tractor manufacture. In 1919 he was succeeded by his son **Edsel Bryant Ford** (1893–1943), and in 1945 by his grandson **Henry Ford II** (1917–87), who revitalized the company when it was in difficulties.

Ford, John (c.1586–c.1640) Playwright, born in Ilsington, Devon, SW England, UK. He studied for a while at Oxford and entered the Middle Temple in 1602. He often collaborated with Dekker, Rowley, and Webster. His own plays were greatly influenced by Robert Burton's *Anatomy of Melancholy* (1621), which led him into the stage presentation of the melancholic, the unnatural, and the horrible in such works as *The Lover's Melancholy* (1629) and *'Tis Pity She's a Whore* (1633).

Ford, John, originally **Sean Aloysius O'Fearna** (1895–1973) Film director, born in Cape Elizabeth, Maine, USA. He went to Hollywood in 1913, where he worked as stunt man, actor, and assistant director. His skilful portrayal of US pioneering history reached a peak with *Stagecoach* (1939), *The Informer* (1935, Oscar), and *The Grapes of Wrath* (1940, Oscar). After World War 2 his films included *How Green Was My Valley* (1941, Oscar), *My Darling Clementine* (1946), and *The Quiet Man* (1952, Oscar). He made his last feature film, *Seven Women*, in 1965, and received the first American Film Institute Life Achievement Award in 1973.

Ford Foundation A philanthropic foundation set up in 1936 by Henry Ford and his son, Edsel, as an international charity mainly concerned with food shortages and population control in developing nations. It has also been involved in the arts and humanities, and in public television in the USA.

foreign aid The help given by one nation to another, usually poorer, by means of grants, gifts, special trading deals, cheap loans or credit terms, expertise, or goods. It may be bilateral, or multilateral.

foreign exchange The amount of currency of foreign origin held in a country. It is derived from exporting or from overseas borrowing.

Foreign Legion The elite formation of the French Army, recruited from non-French nationals. *La Légion Etrangère* was first raised in 1831, and has seen action almost wherever French arms have been engaged. Always the subject of romance and adventure, the legion retains its reputation for toughness.

forensic medicine The discipline which relates the practice of medicine to the law. Such areas as the provision of medicines, the supply of drugs of addiction and of human tissues for surgical transplantation, the control of experiments on living animals, the mental health acts, and abortion are all authorized by national and/or (as in the USA) state governments. Forensic medicine concerns itself with the interpretation of these laws, and with their application by individual doctors. In addition, **forensic pathology** includes the study of wounds self-inflicted or caused by others, and with death in which other factors than natural causes might have played a part. It involves the identification of individuals (such as following a mass disaster), the detection of death from poisoning, and analyzing sequences of DNA in body cells in possible criminal cases. The first known book on forensic medicine was Chinese, in the 13th-c.

forensic psychiatry A branch of psychiatry concerned with legal matters, including the soundness of mind of an accused, laws concerning guardianship, the mental health of prisoners, and the protection of society from the criminally insane.

football, Rugby Union

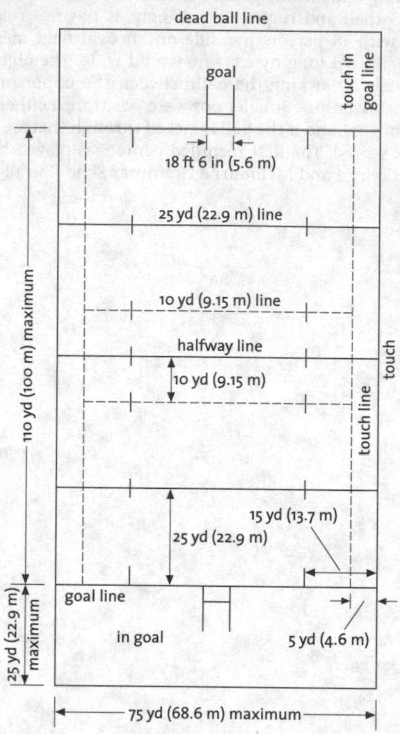

Rugby Union football

A team ball game played with an oval ball on a rectangular playing area. Rugby developed from the kicking game of football, taking its name from the public school at Rugby, Warwickshire, C England, which had its own distinct form of football, although there was no formal separation from football until a dispute over rules led in 1871 to clubs seceding from the Football Association to form the Rugby Football Union. The first international, England v. Scotland, was also played in 1871. Rugby itself split in 1895 when the leading North of England clubs formed the Northern Union (subsequently Rugby League). Rugby is most popular in Britain and the former White Commonwealth (Australia, New Zealand, and South Africa) with only France and Italy so far offering a serious challenge to British and former colonial dominance. The first World Cup was played in 1987 and the game accepted professionalism in 1995. There are 15 players (reduced from 20 in 1876). The aim of the game is to score either through tries - grounding the ball behind the opposing goal line - or goals, kicking the goal through the opposition posts, above the uprights. Current scoring values are: try 5 points, conversion 2, penalty goal or drop goal 3.

foreshortening In art, the representation of forms, especially the human figure, in perspective; for example, a hand stretched out towards the beholder will appear large in proportion to the arm, which will appear very short, or even barely visible. It was a common device in Mannerist and Baroque painting, and the principle behind the famous World War 1 poster 'Your Country Needs You'.

forest buffalo *African buffalo*

Forester, C(ecil) S(cott) (1899–1966) Writer, born in Cairo, Egypt. Chiefly a novelist, he also wrote biographical and travel books. He is known especially for his creation of Horatio Hornblower. He won the James Tait Black Memorial Prize for Literature in 1938 with *Ship of the Line*, and several of his works have been filmed, notably *The African Queen* (1935).

forest falcon *falcon*

forestry The business of growing, harvesting, and marketing trees and of managing the associated wildlife and recreational resources. Foresters grow new timber crops by a process called *artificial reforestation*. The process is called *afforestation* when seedlings are planted on land that was never covered by a forest. About 75 000 seeds per hectare are usually sown to ensure an adequate crop of trees. If seedlings (1–4-year-old trees) are planted, approximately 2000 trees are planted per hectare, using machines. Most countries with forests have state forestry authorities which manage woodlands, conduct research, and market the timber. Wildlife management involves maintaining a balance between the number of animals in a forest and the supply of food, water, and shelter. A number of forests throughout the world have been designated national parks, wildlife reserves, and similar protected areas. However, in spite of the many conservation efforts, there is an increasing threat to the survival both of wild species and their forest habitats.

forgery The act of falsely making, reproducing, altering, or signing a document or instrument with the intention of defrauding others as to its authenticity; also included are disks, tapes, or similar devices in which information is recorded or stored, whether mechanically or electronically. It is essential to the criminal offence of forgery that the false document or device is intended to be used as if it were genuine, as in the cases of wills and bank-notes, though there is no requirement that the intention be successful. In England and Wales it is an offence merely to have some false documents in one's possession, such

Forces Of Nature

	gravity	*electro-magnetism*	*weak nuclear force*	*strong nuclear force*
Range m	infinite	infinite	10^{-18} (subatomic)	10^{-15} (subatomic)
Relative strength	6×10^{-39}	1/137	10^{-5}	1
Examples of application	orbit of Earth around Sun	force between electrical charges	radioactive β-decay	binds atomic nuclei together

as credit cards, money, or passports. In Scotland, forgery by itself is not a crime; the crime is committed when a forged document is 'uttered' or passed off as genuine to the prejudice of another.

forget-me-not An annual or perennial, native to temperate regions; inflorescence coiled, straightening as it elongates; flowers tubular with five spreading lobes, often pink in bud, opening blue, sometimes with a yellow or white eye as a honey guide, or wholly these colours. (Genus: *Myosotis*, 50 species. Family: Boraginaceae.)

forging The shaping of metal from a single piece by hammering into a desired shape or into intimate contact with a shaped die. In **drop forging**, the hammer or die is dropped onto the heated metal to be shaped. In **impact forging**, two dies forcibly approach each other from opposite sides of the metal to be forged. In **roll forging**, a strip is run between cylindrical dies with countersunk depressions.

formaldehyde [faw(r)maldehiyd] HCHO, IUPAC **methanal**, boiling point −21°C. The simplest aldehyde, a gas with a characteristic odour, which polymerizes readily and reversibly to **paraformaldehyde** $(CH_2O)_n$. An aqueous solution, called *formalin*, is used as a disinfectant and preservative. Manufactured by the incomplete oxidation of methanol, it is an ingredient in plastic manufacture of the phenol–formaldehyde type.

Formalists A school of critics in early 20th-c Russia who believed that formal properties were of primary importance in a work of art. Viktor Shklovsky (1893–1984) and Yevgeny Zamyatin (1884–1937) were original members; Roman Jakobson (1896–1982) later exported their ideas, which had considerable influence on the New Criticism.

Forman, Miloš (1932–) Film director, born in Caslav, C Czech Republic. Two feature films, *Lásky jedné plavovlásky* (1965, Loves of a Blonde) and *Hoři, má panenko* (1967, The Firemen's Ball), made in Prague, brought him international recognition. Being abroad at the time of the 1968 Warsaw Pact invasion, he went to the USA, where he became a US citizen. His tragi-comedy of insanity, *One Flew Over the Cuckoo's Nest* (1975), won five Oscar awards, and was successfully followed by his interpretations of stage presentations, *Hair* (1979), *Ragtime* (1980), and *Amadeus* (1983, Oscar). Later films include *The People vs. Larry Flynt* (1996, Oscar nomination) and *Man on the Moon* (1999).

formants The dominant acoustic components which determine the sound quality of particular vowels. They are formed by the air flowing through the vocal tract, and vibrating at different bands of frequencies as it responds to changes in the tract's shape.

Formentera [formentayra] 38°43N 1°26E; pop (2000e) 4390; area 100 sq km/39 sq mi. Island in the Balearic Is, Spain, S of Ibiza; capital, San Francisco; largely formed by two high pine-clad capes (La Mola and Berberia) with a C depression edged by white-sand beaches; tourism; patronal festival (Jul).

formic acid HCOOH, IUPAC **methanoic acid**, boiling point 101°C. A liquid with a pungent odour, the simplest carboxylic acid. It is a moderately strong acid; partially neutralized solutions have a pH of about 4. Formic acid is secreted by some insects, especially red ants, in the sting. It is used in textile and leather manufacture, and as an industrial solvent.

formication A sensation of small insects crawling on or under the skin. It is often seen in drug-induced states, after overdoses, and during withdrawal of (for example) cocaine or alcohol.

Fornax (Lat 'furnace') A faint S constellation.

Forrest, Edwin (1806–72) Actor, born in Philadelphia, Pennsylvania, USA. He made his debut in Philadelphia in 1820. He had successful seasons in London (1836–7), but in 1845 his Macbeth was hissed by the audience, and a resentment which prompted him to hiss Macready in Edinburgh destroyed his reputation in Britain. The hissing of Macready's Macbeth by Forrest's sympathizers in New York City in 1849 led to a riot which cost 22 lives.

Forster, E(dward) M(organ) (1879–1970) Writer, born in London, UK. He studied at Cambridge, and was a member of the Bloomsbury Group. His works include *Where Angels Fear to Tread* (1905), *The Longest Journey* (1907), *A Room with a View* (1908), and *Howard's End* (1910). His masterpiece, *A Passage to India* (1924), paints a picture of society in India under the British Raj and explores the nature of external and internal reality. He also wrote several volumes of essays and short stories. In 1951 he collaborated with Eric Crozier (1914–94) on the libretto of Britten's opera, *Billy Budd*. His novel *Maurice* (written 1913–14), on the theme of homosexuality, was published posthumously in 1971. Film versions of his novels have been very successful.

Forsyth, Bill [faw(r)siyth], popular name of **William David Forsyth** (1947–) Film-maker, born near Glasgow, W Scotland, UK. He entered the film industry in 1963, making his own documentaries, and was one of the original intake at the National Film School in 1971. *That Sinking Feeling*, a comedy using actors from the Glasgow Youth Theatre, was warmly received at the 1979 Edinburgh Festival. He has made several successful comedies, notably *Gregory's Girl* (1981) and *Local Hero* (1983, BAFTA best director), as well as productions for television. He moved to Hollywood in the mid-1980s, directing *Housekeeping* (1987), *Breaking In* (1989), *Being Human* (1993), and *Gregory's Two Girls* (1999).

Forsyth, Bruce [faw(r)siyth], popular name of **Bruce Joseph Forsyth-Johnson** (1928–) Entertainer, born in Edmonton, N Greater London, UK. He trained as a dancer, but is best known as the compère or host on many UK television shows, such as *Sunday Night at the London Palladium* (1958–60) and *The Generation Game* (1971–8, 1992–4). In 1995 he received the Lifetime Achievement Award for Variety.

Forsyth, Frederick [faw(r)siyth] (1938–) Writer of suspense thrillers, born in Ashford, Kent, SE England, UK. Educated at Tonbridge School, Kent, he served in the Royal Air Force and later became a journalist. His reputation rests on three taut thrillers, *The Day of the Jackal* (1971), *The Odessa File* (1972), and *The Dogs of War* (1974). Later novels include *The Fourth Protocol* (1984), *Icon* (1996), and *Avenger* (2003).

Forsythe, William [faw(r)siyth] (1949–) Dancer, choreographer, and artistic director, born in New York City, USA. He trained at the Joffrey Ballet School, and became resident choreographer of the Stuttgart Ballet (1976), and artistic director of Frankfurt Ballet (1984). His controversial, rule-bending works, including *Say Bye Bye* (1980) and *Impressing the Czar* (1988), frequently use spoken text and stage mechanics to enhance the steps. He is known for his challenge to, and remodelling of, the ballet vocabulary for contemporary purposes, making explicit the power and athleticism of the modern dancer.

forsythia A deciduous shrub, suckering and rooting from the tips of arching branches, native to SE Europe and E Asia; leaves oval, toothed, opposite; flowers yellow, with four spreading petals, in clusters appearing before leaves on last season's wood. It is named after Scottish gardener William Forsyth (1737–1804). The commonly planted ornamental is hybrid *Forsythia × intermedia*. (Genus: *Forsythia*, 7 species. Family: Oleaceae.)

Fortaleza [faw(r)talayza] 3°45S 38°35W, pop (2000e) 2 069 000. Port capital of Ceará state, NE Brazil, on the Atlantic coast; airfield; railway; commercial and industrial centre, especially for agriculture; centre for coastal and overseas trade; two universities (1955, 1973); tourist centre in old waterfront prison; modern cathedral; local festival with raft (*jangada*) races (Jul), local Umbanda terreiros (churches) celebrate the festival of Lemanjá on Praia do Futuro, casting offerings into the sea (15 Aug).

Fort-de-France [faw(r) duh frãs], formerly **Fort Royal** 14°36N 61°05W, pop (2000e) 114 000. Capital town of Martinique, Lesser Antilles, E Caribbean; airport; naval base; chief commercial and shipping centre, tourism; cathedral (1895).

Forth, River River in SEC Scotland, UK; formed at Aberfoyle by the confluence of headstreams rising on Ben Lomond; flows generally E, widening into the Firth of Forth estuary (82 km/

51 mi from Alloa to the North Sea, width 2·5 km/1½ mi–28 km/17 mi); crossed by road bridge at Kincardine, and by Forth road and rail bridges at Queensferry; length 186 km/116 mi.

Fort Knox A US army post established in Kentucky in 1917, and noted as the site, since 1937, of the US Bullion Depository.

Fort Lauderdale [**law**derdayl] 26°07N 80°08W, pop (2000e) 152 400. Seat of Broward Co, SE Florida, USA; on the Atlantic Ocean, 40 km/25 mi N of Miami; railway; airport; over 400 km/250 mi of natural and artificial waterways; connected by canal to L Okeechobee; fishing and yachting resort, with one of the largest marinas in the world; electronic products, yachts; Christmas Boat Parade.

FORTRAN [faw(r)tran] Acronym for **FOR**mula **TRAN**slation, a widely used high-level computer programming language developed in the USA from the 1950s onwards for mathematical, engineering, and scientific use.

Fort Sumter The site of the first engagement of the American Civil War (12 Apr 1861), at the mouth of Charleston harbour, South Carolina; named after an officer who fought in the US War of Independence, Thomas Sumter (1734–1832). It was a Federal fort which found itself in Confederate territory, after the secession of the Southern states. When Lincoln refused demands for its evacuation, the fort was attacked, and was soon forced to surrender. Although it was of no strategic value, the loss of the fort was a major factor in arousing public opinion in the North.

Fortuna [faw(r)**too**na] The ancient Roman goddess of Fortune, introduced by King Servius Tullius (578–534 BC). In the Middle Ages she was highly revered as a divine and moral figure, redressing human pride. Her wheel is frequently referred to and depicted, as at St Etienne in Beauvais, where figures can be seen climbing and falling off.

Fortune Theatre Elizabethan playhouse built in 1600 by Philip Henslowe. Located in N London, it was named after the goddess of fortune whose statue stood over the doorway. Established to compete with the newly constructed Globe, the Fortune opened with a performance by the Admiral's Men, who continued to perform there for many years. It was closed by the Puritans in 1642 and demolished in 1661.

Fort William 56°49N 5°07W, pop (2000e) 110 000. Town in Highland, W Scotland, UK; on E side of Loch Linnhe; airfield; railway; aluminium, distilling; Inverlochy castle; Neptune's Staircase (N), eight locks (1805–22) raising the Caledonian Canal by 19·5 m/64 ft; Ben Nevis (SE).

Fort Worth 32°45N 97°18W, pop (2000e) 534 700. Seat of Tarrant Co, NE Texas, USA, on the Trinity R; established as an army post, 1847; cattle town, and still an important livestock market centre; airport at Dallas–Fort Worth; airfield; railway; university (1873); aircraft and aerospace industries, oil refining, pharmaceuticals, textiles, leather goods; Fort Worth Art Center, Amon Carter Museum of Western Art, Greer Island Nature Center; Southwestern Exposition (Jan).

Forty-five Rebellion The Jacobite rebellion of 1745–6 to restore the Catholic Stuart kings to the British throne and displace the Hanoverians. It began in July 1745 when Charles Edward Stuart (Bonnie Prince Charlie, 'the Young Pretender') arrived in Scotland and proclaimed his father ('the Old Pretender') King James III. Support came mainly from the Scottish Highland clans, and there were some early successes. The Jacobite forces reached as far south as Derby, but the rebellion lost support, and was crushingly defeated at Culloden in 1746 by English and German troops led by the Duke of Cumberland. The battle was followed by ruthless slaughter of the Jacobites, earning Cumberland the nickname 'Butcher' and bringing the rebellion to a close.

forty-niners Adventurers who swarmed to California in 1849, after the discovery of gold there the previous year. Their number may have been as high as 100 000.

forum The Roman equivalent of the Greek *agora*; originally the market-place of a town, later its civic centre. Besides shops and stalls, it contained the principal municipal buildings, such as the Council chamber and law courts.

Foscolo, Ugo [**fos**koloh] (1778–1827) Writer, born in Zákinthos, Greece. He studied at Spalato and Venice, and his disappointment when Napoleon ceded Venice to Austria found vent in the *Ultime lettere di Jacopo Ortis* (1802, Last Letters of Jacopo Ortis). After a period in the French army, he returned to Milan, and published his best poem, *Dei sepolcri* (1807, Of the Sepulchres). After 1814 he sought refuge in London, where he supported himself by teaching and writing, but his last years were embittered by poverty and neglect.

Foss, Lukas, originally **Lukas Fuchs** (1922–) Composer, born in Berlin, Germany. He studied in Berlin and Paris, and moved to the USA in 1937. He first attracted attention with his cantata, *The Prairie* (1941), and has since written two symphonies, concertos, chamber music, and operas. He was appointed professor of music at the University of California in 1953, and in 1981 became director of the Milwaukee Symphony Orchestra.

fossa A carnivore, native to Madagascar (*Cryptoprocta ferox*); superficially cat-like with short, thick reddish-brown (occasionally black) coat; long thin tail; inhabits woodland; an efficient predator; eats lemurs, smaller vertebrates, and insects. (Family: Viverridae.)

Fosse Way *Roman roads*

fossil The remains of a once-living organism, usually restricted to organisms that lived prior to the last Ice Age. Fossils typically comprise the bodies or part of the organisms themselves, but also include a variety of trace fossils such as burrows, tracks, impressions, and faeces. Fossils are usually mineralized and found in sedimentary rocks.

fossil fuel Fuels derived from the fossilized remains of plants and animals, such as peat, coal, and crude oil.

Foster, Jodie, originally **Alicia Christian Foster** (1962–) Film actress and director, born in New York City, USA. After a career in television commercials, she became known for her child roles in *Alice Doesn't Live Here Anymore* (1974), *Bugsy Malone* (1976), and *Taxi Driver* (1976). She studied in Los Angeles and at Yale, and then established herself as an adult actress, receiving Best Actress Oscars for her roles in *The Accused* (1988) and *The Silence of the Lambs* (1991). She made her directorial debut with *Little Man Tate* (1991). Later films include *Somersby* (1992), *Nell* (1994), *Home for the Holidays* (1995), which she also directed, *Contact* (1997), *Anna and the King* (1999), and *Panic Room* (2002).

Foster, Stephen (Collins) (1826–64) Songwriter, born in Lawrenceville, now part of Pittsburgh, Pennsylvania, USA. His first songs, such as 'Open Thy Lattice, Love' (1844), were conventional concert songs of the day. When he began writing 'minstrel songs', influenced by itinerant black singers, his melodies and rhythms brightened. Songs such as 'Oh! Susanna' (1848), 'The Old Folks at Home' (1851), and 'Beautiful Dreamer' (1864) sold thousands of song-sheets, and became seminal works of the US songwriting tradition.

Foster, William Z(ebulon) (1881–1961) Writer and communist leader, born in Taunton, Massachusetts, USA. Informally educated, he joined the Communist Party in 1921 and was its chairman until 1957. He wrote a number of books and pamphlets on US and world history and politics.

foster care A form of child care in which children who have been separated (by death, custodial, or other reasons) from their biological parents live with a 'foster family' for varying lengths of time, often many years. Foster parents usually receive some state aid to help support the children. The system was developed in the UK during the late 1940s when many children had become orphaned through World War 2. Fostering is a form of 'social parenting', as is adoption, and is now widespread (eg in the USA).

Foucault, (Jean Bernard) Léon [foo**koh**] (1819–68) Physicist, born in Paris, France. He began by studying medicine, but turned to physics. He determined the velocity of light, and showed that light travels more slowly in water than in air (1850). He invented the gyroscope (1852), and improved the mirrors of reflecting telescopes (1858). In 1851 he demonstrated the rotation of the Earth by using a 67 m/220 ft pendulum hung in the dome of the Panthéon, Paris.

Foucault, Michel [fookoh] (1926–84) Philosopher, born in Poitiers, W France. A student of the Marxist philosopher Louis Althusser, he became professor of the history of systems of thought at the Collège de France (1970). He sought consistently to test cultural assumptions in given historical contexts. His most important writings include *Histoire de la folie* (1961, trans Madness and Civilization), *Les mots et les choses* (1966, trans The Order of Things), *L'Archéologie du savoir* (1969, The Archaeology of Knowledge), and the unfinished *Histoire de la sexualité* (1976–84, The History of Sexuality).

Foucault pendulum [fookoh] A pendulum that is free to swing in any direction, such that the plane of swing gradually rotates as the Earth turns under it; devised by Léon Foucault in 1851. At the North and South Poles, the pendulum would complete one cycle every 24 hours, but would take longer at other latitudes, with no rotation at the Equator – a consequence of the Coriolis force. The pendulum was used by Foucault as proof that the Earth spins.

Fouché, Joseph, duc d'Otrante (Duke of Otranto) [fooshay] (1759–1820) French statesman, born in Nantes, W France. He was elected to the National Convention in 1792 as a Jacobin, and in 1799 became minister of police, a post which he held successfully until 1815. A consummate intriguer, he was banished after the Bourbon restoration, and died in exile in Trieste.

foul marten *polecat*

foumart [foomah(r)t] *polecat*

foundation, philanthropic An organization for distributing private wealth for public benefit. Such endowments have existed since ancient times, and typically supported schools, hospitals, or almshouses. Since the 19th-c huge foundations have been endowed by successful businessmen or corporations: Carnegie's bequests founded a number of such organizations. The Ford Foundation, established in 1936, is the biggest philanthropic trust; others include the Rockefeller Foundation (1913), and the John A Hartford Foundation (1942). Money from these bodies funds education, international activities, health, the arts, social welfare, and religious groups.

founding Casting molten metal in a mould made to a high degree of precision. Mould materials are compounded of sand and clay, packed over a pattern to which the eventual casting is to conform. Pattern making is consequently a highly skilled craft, but much founding is now automatized.

Fountains Abbey A Cistercian monastery founded in 1132 near Ripon, North Yorkshire, N England, UK; a world heritage site. The ground plan of what was once the wealthiest Cistercian house in England can be clearly discerned today. The abbey ruins stand in the magnificent water gardens of Studley Royal, which were laid out in the early 18th-c.

Fouqué, Friedrich Heinrich Karl, Baron de la Motte [fookay] (1777–1843) Romantic writer, born in Brandenburg, EC Germany. He served as a Prussian cavalry officer, devoting himself between campaigns to literary pursuits. He published a long series of romances based on Norse legend and old French poetry, his masterpiece being *Undine* (1811).

Fouquet, Jean [fookay] (c.1420–c.1480) Painter, born in Tours, WC France. He opened a prosperous workshop at Tours, and in 1475 received the official title of king's painter. His most notable illuminations are found in the *Antiquities of the Jews* of Josephus and the *Hours of Etienne Chevalier* at Chantilly.

Fouquet, Nicolas, vicomte de (Viscount of) **Melun et de Vaux, Marquis de Belle-Isle** [fookay] (1615–80) French statesman, born in Paris, France. Mazarin made him *procureur-général* to the parliament of Paris (1650) and superintendent of finance (1653). He became extremely rich, and was ambitious to succeed Mazarin, but Louis XIV himself took up the reins of power on Mazarin's death, and Fouquet was arrested for embezzlement (1661). He was sentenced to life imprisonment in the fortress of Pignerol, where he died.

four-colour process Techniques for the replications of all the colours in the spectrum by printing in only four colours of ink mixed together in varying proportions. The 'original' – colour transparency or photographic print, painting, or other image – is photographed, either by a camera using colour-filters, or by an electronic scanner. Single pieces of film are produced, each corresponding to one of the colours of ink to be used: magenta, yellow, cyan, and black (the usual order of printing).

four-colour theorem A mathematical proposition which states that every map on a plane surface can be coloured using at most four colours. Clearly three colours are not sufficient to distinguish between regions with a common boundary; the difficulty is to prove that all maps, whatever the shape of the regions, can be coloured using at most four colours. First conjectured by Francis Guthrie in 1852, the problem has fascinated many distinguished mathematicians, but the theorem was not proved until 1976, when US mathematicians Kenneth Appel and Wolfgang Haken used computers to carry out the massive reductions required.

Four Corners 37°00N 109°00W. The only place in the USA where the boundaries of four states come together: Colorado, Utah, New Mexico, and Arizona.

four-eyed fish Slender-bodied fish found in turbid shallow coastal waters, estuaries, and freshwater lakes of South and Central America; length up to 30 cm/1 ft; eyes prominent on top of head, divided into distinct upper and lower parts providing simultaneous vision in air and water while swimming along the surface.

Four Freedoms Four basic human rights proclaimed in 1941 at an annual message to Congress by President Roosevelt. They included freedom of speech and worship, and freedom from want and fear.

Four Horsemen of the Apocalypse Symbolic Biblical characters described in *Rev* 6 (also *Zech* 6.1–7), where they signal the beginning of the messianic age. Each comes on a steed of different colour, symbolizing devastations associated with the world's end (black = famine; red = bloodshed, war; pale = pestilence, death), except for the white horse, which has a 'crown' and is sent 'to conquer'.

Fourier, (Jean Baptiste) Joseph, Baron [fooryay] (1768–1830) Mathematician, born in Auxerre, C France. He accompanied Napoleon to Egypt (1798), and on his return (1802) was made prefect of the department of Grenoble, and created baron (1808). He then took up his first interest, applied mathematics, and while working on the flow of heat discovered the equation for it which now bears his name. To solve it, he showed that many functions of a single variable can be expanded in a series of sines of multiples of the variable (the *Fourier series*).

Fourier analysis *wave motion*

Fourneyron, Benoît [foornayrõ] (1802–67) Hydraulic engineer, born in St Etienne, SW France. In 1832 he patented the general design of his hydraulic turbine installations, and eventually built more than 100 of these in different parts of the world.

Four Noble Truths The summary of the central teachings of Buddha. (1) All life involves suffering, and is inevitably sorrowful. (2) The cause of suffering and sorrow is craving or desire arising from ignorance. (3) There is escape from suffering, because craving and desire can end. (4) There is an Eightfold Path leading to the end of suffering and sorrow.

four-stroke engine An engine that works on a practical cycle with one in every four strokes of the piston being the power stroke. This is the type of engine normally used to drive motor cars. The four events are: (1) the drawing of fuel and air into the cylinder; (2) the compression and ignition of the fuel/air mixture; (3) the power stroke; (4) the expelling of exhaust gases.

Fourteen Points A peace programme outlined by US President Wilson to Congress in 1918. The Germans subsequently asked Wilson for an armistice agreement based on their acceptance of these points, which, with two reservations, were accepted by the Allied powers as the basis for a peace settlement.

Fourteenth Amendment The most important amendment to the US Constitution, drawn up shortly after the American Civil War. Adopted in 1868, it extended US citizenship to all persons born or naturalized in the USA (including ex-slaves). It prohibited the states from abridging the privileges and immunities of citizens or depriving any person of life, liberty, or property without due process of law, or denying any person the equal protection of law (thus reversing the Dredd Scott decision). Another clause reduced the representation in Congress of states which denied the vote to blacks. In the late 19th-c the Fourteenth Amendment was used as a device to protect big business from state regulation. In the 20th-c it was the main constitutional instrument of the civil rights movement and of the women's rights movement in the USA. The Fifteenth Amendment, adopted in 1870, provided that the right to vote should not be denied to adult males on grounds of race, colour, or previous condition of servitude. Women, however, were not given the right to vote throughout the USA until 1920.

fourth-generation computers *computer generations*

Fourth of July, July Fourth, or **Independence Day** A public holiday in the USA, commemorating the adoption of the Declaration of Independence (4 Jul 1776).

Fou Ts'ong [foo tsong] (1934–) Concert pianist, born in Shanghai, E China. Internationally acclaimed as an interpreter of Mozart and Chopin, he studied under the Italian pianist and founder of the Shanghai Symphony Orchestra, Mario Paci. He won third prize in the International Chopin Competition in Warsaw (1955). Since 1958 he has made his base in London and performed extensively on the international circuit.

Fowler, H(enry) W(atson) (1858–1933) Lexicographer, born in Tonbridge, Kent, SE England, UK. He studied at Oxford, became a schoolmaster at Sedbergh (1882–99), then went to London as a freelance journalist. In 1903 he joined his tomato-growing brother **F(rank) G(eorge) Fowler** (1871–1918) in Guernsey, and their literary partnership began. Their joint reputation rests on *The King's English* (1906) and the *Concise Oxford Dictionary* (1911). Henry later wrote the *Dictionary of Modern English Usage* (1926), a household work for all who attempt to write good English, even though it is sometimes as mannered as the mannerisms he set out to eradicate.

Fowler, Robbie (1975–) Footballer, born in Liverpool, Merseyside, NW England, UK. He joined Liverpool Football Club in 1990 when aged 16, and made his debut in 1993, scoring the winning goal for his team. His honours include the Coca-Cola (League) Cup (1995) and he has twice been voted the Professional Football Association's Young Player of the Year (1995, 1996). He made his full international debut for England in 1996, and was a member of the Euro 96 squad. Late in 2001 he left Liverpool to join Leeds United Football Club, he then joined Manchester City Football Club in 2003. He was a member of the England squad for the World Cup in 2002.

Fowler, William A(lfred) (1911–95) Astrophysicist, born in Pittsburgh, Pennsylvania, USA. He studied at Ohio State University and the California Institute of Technology. He established a research group working on the application of nuclear physics to all aspects of astronomy, and is one of the founders of the theory of nucleosynthesis, developed in collaboration with Sir Fred Hoyle and others. He shared the Nobel Prize for Physics in 1983.

Fowles, John (Robert) (1926–) Writer, born in Leigh-on-Sea, Essex, SE England, UK. He studied at Oxford, served in the Royal Marines (1945–6), became a teacher, and published his first novel, *The Collector*, in 1963. His writings combine a topographical interest in Devon, a respect for the Victorian novel of social life and personal relationships, and an interest in contemporary developments in the French novel. His books include *The Magus* (1966), *The French Lieutenant's Woman* (1969, filmed with a script by Pinter, 1981), *The Ebony Tower* (1974, televised 1984), *A Maggot* (1985), and *Tessera* (1993). The autobiographical *Daniel Martin* appeared in 1977, and he published a book of essays, *Wormholes* in 1998.

fowl pest The name applied to two diseases of birds, **fowl plague** and **Newcastle disease**; several strains, caused by viruses; usually noticed in poultry, but most birds are vulnerable; attacks nervous, digestive, and respiratory systems; often fatal. It was first recorded in Newcastle-upon-Tyne in 1926.

Fox A North American Algonkin Indian group originally from N Wisconsin. They were mainly sedentary agriculturalists, but they also hunted and fished. Affected by Iroquois expansionism and white settlers, they settled permanently in Iowa in 1842 and are still there, retaining many traditional organizational features.

Fox, Charles James (1749–1806) British statesman and foreign secretary (1782, 1783, 1806), born in London, UK. He studied at Oxford, became a Liberal MP at 19, and two years later was a junior lord of the Admiralty. He supported Lord North, but in 1772 resigned over American policy. He became secretary of state after North's downfall, and in 1783 formed a coalition with him, which held office for a short period in 1783. He supported the French Revolution, and strongly opposed the war with France. After Pitt's death (1806) he was recalled to office, but died soon afterwards.

Fox, George (1624–91) Founder of the Religious Society of Friends (Quakers), born in Fenny Drayton, Leicestershire, C England, UK. Apprenticed to a Nottingham shoemaker, he felt at 19 a divine call to leave his friends, and Bible in hand he wandered about the country, on a small income. The 'inner light' was the central idea of his teaching, and he argued against the formalism of the established Church, and all social conventions. His life is a record of insults, persecutions, imprisonments, and missionary travel to several parts of the world. As a writer he is remembered by his *Journal* (posthumously published), which records the birth of the Quaker movement.

fox A small member of the dog family (21 species), worldwide except SE Asia; usually thin muzzle, large pointed ears, long bushy tail; hunts alone; renowned for its cunning; often nocturnal; lives in a den (burrow or rock crevice).

foxglove A softly hairy biennial (*Digitalis purpurea*) growing to 150 cm/5 ft, native to Europe; rosette leaves up to 30 cm/1 ft, narrowly oval, toothed; tall flower-spike produced in second year; flowers all on one side of the stem, bell-shaped with five very short lobes, drooping, pink to purple, rarely white, usually with dark spots forming honey guide within tube. It is the original source of the heart drug digitalin. (Family: Scrophulariaceae.)

foxglove tree A deciduous tree (*Paulownia tomentosa*) growing to 12 m/40 ft or more, native to China; leaves heart-shaped or with a single large tooth on each side; flowers resembling a foxglove, 6 cm/20 in, tubular with five spreading lobes, purple, yellowish within the tube, in erect clusters. It is a popular ornamental and street tree in Europe. (Family: Bignoniaceae.)

fox-grape *grapevine*

foxhound A domestic dog bred for hunting foxes; large with brown, black, and white coat; soft ears; two breeds: the **English foxhound**, and its larger descendant, the **American foxhound**.

foxhunting A blood sport, which developed in the UK in the late 17th-c, and which since the early 19th-c has been regarded as the pastime of the aristocracy and the wealthy. The foxhunting season lasts from November to April. Famous hunts include the Quorn, Cottesmore and Belvoir, all in the Shire counties in the E Midlands. Each hunt is controlled by a *master of hounds*, and the hounds are controlled by the *huntsman*. Foxhounds are similar in shape and colour to the beagle, but slightly larger. In recent years, animal rights saboteurs have attempted to thwart hunts, and since 1949 (when an anti-foxhunting bill went before parliament) there has been a movement to try to get the sport banned in the UK. In the USA there is a foxless hunt called **draghunting**, in which hunters follow a scent laid across a designated area.

foxtail millet *millet*

fox terrier An active British terrier with a deep chest, pointed muzzle, and soft, folded ears held high; tail usually docked short when young; usually white with black and brown markings; two forms: **wire-haired** and **smooth-haired**.

Foyle, Lough Inlet of the Atlantic, on the N coast of Ireland, bounded W by Donegal (Republic of Ireland) and E by the county of Londonderry (Northern Ireland); mouth 1·5 km/0·9 mi wide; length, 24 km/15 mi; width, 16 km/10 mi; fed by the R Foyle.

fractals Geometrical entities characterized by basic patterns that are repeated at ever decreasing sizes. For example, trees describe an approximate fractal pattern, as the trunk divides into branches which further subdivide into smaller branches which ultimately subdivide into twigs; at each stage of division the pattern is a smaller version of the original. Fractals are not able to fill spaces, and hence are described as having fractional dimensions. They were devised in 1967 by Benoit Mandelbrot, during a study of the length of the coastline of Britain. They are relevant to any system involving self-similarity repeated on diminishing scales, such as in the study of chaos, fork lightning, or the movement of oil through porous rock. They are also used in computer graphics. The most famous fractal is the *Mandelbrot set*, the set of complex numbers that describes the behaviour of points z under the iterative process $f(z) = z^2 + c$ for different values of c. Its fractal nature illustrates the sensitive way in which iterations depend on the choice of c. It also occurs in other iterative processes.

fractionation The separation of the components of a mixture from one another. It is usually carried out chemically by (1) *fractional crystallization*, making use of varying solubilities of the different substances, or (2) *fractional distillation*, making use of differing boiling points.

fractions *numbers*

fracture (medicine) A physical break in the continuity of a bone. Most commonly the result of external force, it occurs occasionally as a consequence of disease, as when cancer affects bone substance (a **pathological fracture**). The break in the bone takes a number of forms, from a hairline transverse fracture with no displacement (a **greenstick fracture**) to a severe fracture in which the bone is shattered into a number of small pieces (**comminuted fracture**). Bones possess a considerable ability to reunite their fragments, and the extent to which the broken pieces remain or can be placed in alignment with the original bone influences the outcome and the treatment. Well-aligned fragments may unite while being kept in place by a simple splint. **Compound fractures** (communicating with the outside) or displaced fractures may need manipulation and the insertion of metal pins to hold the pieces together while they heal.

fracture (physics) The breaking of a material subject to excessive stress. The atomic layers are pulled away from one another. Prior to the fracture, most materials undergo elastic then plastic deformation. The fracture occurs when the applied stress exceeds the tensile strength of the material.

frame relay A technology developed by telephone companies in North America to transfer digitally coded messages over the telephone network at very high speed using fibre-optic cabling. SONET (Sychronous Optical NETwork) is the name given to a fibre-based mesh network employing frame relay to deliver various levels of service, on demand, to a customer. OC-1 offers 51·84 Mbps (megabauds per second) while OC-12 offers 622·08 Mbps (12 × OC-1).

Framework programme A programme of research, funded by the European Commission, designed to improve the level of technical expertise and application within the European Union. It includes the ESPRIT and RACE programmes.

Frampton, Sir George James (1860–1928) Sculptor, born in London, UK. He studied in London and Paris. Among his works are 'Peter Pan' in Kensington Gardens, London, and the Lions at the British Museum. He was knighted in 1908.

franc The former currency unit of many countries, notably France, Belgium, and Switzerland, now replaced by the Euro in EU countries. The name derives from the words on a 14th-c gold coin, *Francorum rex* ('King of the Franks').

France *p.584*

France, Anatole [frãs], pseudonym of **Jacques Anatole François Thibault** (1844–1924) Writer, born in Paris, France. He worked as a publisher's reader, and in 1879 published his first volume of stories. He wrote several graceful, lively novels, which contrast with his later, satirical, sceptical works. The Dreyfus case (1896) stirred him into politics as a champion of internationalism. Among his later novels are *L'Ile des pingouins* (1908, Penguin Island) and *Les Dieux ont soif* (1912, The Gods are Athirst). He was awarded the Nobel Prize for Literature in 1921.

Francesca da Rimini [francheska da **reeminee**] (?–1285) Daughter of Guido da Polenta, Lord of Ravenna, whose tragic love story has often been recounted in literary and artistic works. She was married to **Gianciotto the Lame**, son of Malatesta, Lord of Rimini; but she already loved Paolo, Gianciotto's brother. Gianciotto, surprising the lovers together, killed them both. The story is woven into Dante's *Inferno*.

franchise (economics) A licence to carry out some business activity, using the name, products, and know-how of the franchisor; for example, in fast-food restaurants. The franchisee pays a licence fee and a percentage of the business done to the franchisor, and undertakes to conform to pre-set standards.

franchise (politics) The right to vote. It was only during the 19th-c and 20th-c that the franchise was extended to all citizens in most democratic countries. Various qualifications and rules determine who may be eligible and how the vote may be exercised: in the UK, people over the age of 18 who are registered may vote, providing they are not peers or peeresses in their own right, felons, or lunatics, and have not been convicted of electoral malpractice in the preceding five years. In the USA the right to vote is guaranteed by the US Constitution.

Francis I (1494–1547) King of France (1515–47), born in Cognac, W France. He was Count of Angoulême and Duke of Valois before succeeding Louis XII as king and marrying his daughter, **Claude**. He combined many of the attributes of mediaeval chivalry and the Renaissance prince, the dominant feature of his reign being his rivalry with the Emperor Charles V, which led to a series of wars (1521–6, 1528–9, 1536–8, 1542 4). After establishing his military reputation against the Swiss at Marignano (1515) in his first Italian campaign, he later suffered a number of reverses, including his capture at Pavia (1525) and imprisonment in Madrid. Though he avoided religious fanaticism, he became increasingly hostile to Protestantism after 1534. A patron of the arts and learning, the palace of Fontainbleu was rebuilt during his reign, and the artists Leonardo da Vinci, Benvenuto Cellini, and Andrea de Sarto worked at his court.

Francis II (Emperor) (1768–1835) Last Holy Roman Emperor (1792–1806), the first emperor of Austria (Francis I, 1804–35), and king of Hungary (1792–1830) and Bohemia (1792–1835), born in Florence, NC Italy. Defeated on several occasions by Napoleon (1797, 1801, 1805, 1809), he made a short-lived alliance with him, sealed by the marriage of his daughter, **Marie Louise**, to the French emperor. Later he joined with Russia and Prussia to win the Battle of Leipzig (1813). By the Treaty of Vienna (1815), thanks to Metternich, he recovered several territories (eg Lombardy–Venetia).

Francis of Assisi, St [aseezee], originally **Giovanni Bernardone** (?1181–1226) Founder of the Franciscan Order, born in Assisi, C Italy. In 1205 he left his worldly life, devoting himself to the care of the poor and the sick, and living as a hermit. By 1210 he had a brotherhood of 11 for which he drew up a rule which became the *Franciscan* way of life, in which all property is repudiated. By 1219 the order had 5000 members. He preached widely in Europe and the Holy Land, and on returning to Italy he is said to have received on his body the marks (*stigmata*) of the wounds of Christ (1224). He was canonized in 1228. He is often represented in art among animals and birds, which he called his sisters and brothers. Feast day 4 October.

France

□ International Airport

ancient **Gallia**, official name **Republic of France**, Fr **République Française**

Local name France

Timezone GMT +1

Area 551 000 km²/212 686 sq mi

Population total (2002e) 59 440 000

Status Republic

Capital Paris

Languages French (official), Breton, Occitan and Alsatian are also spoken

Ethnic groups Celtic and Latin origin (91%), Breton, Catalan, and large immigrant population (including Portuguese, Algerian, Moroccan, and Arab minorities)

Religions Roman Catholic (90%), Protestant (4%), Muslim (3%), Jewish (1%)

Physical features Bounded S and E by large mountain ranges, notably (interior) the Massif Central, Jura, and Alps (E), rising to 4807 m/15 771 ft at Mont Blanc, and the Pyrénées (S); chief rivers include Loire (longest at 1020 km/633 mi), Rhône, Seine, Garonne; 60% of land arable.

Climate Mediterranean climate in S, with warm, moist winters and hot, dry summers; average temperatures, 3°C (Jan), 18°C (Jul); continental climate in E; average annual rainfall 786 mm/31 in; searing heatwave in August 2003 caused deaths of many elderly people.

Currency 1 euro = 100 cents (previous to February 2002, 1 French Franc (Fr) = 100 centimes).

Economy Main industries include wine, fruit, cheese; perfume, textiles, clothing; steel, chemicals, machinery, cars, aircraft; natural resources of coal, iron ore, bauxite, timber; tourism important.

GDP (2002e) $1·558 tn, per capita $26 000

Human Development Index (2002) 0·928

History Celtic-speaking Gauls dominant by 5th-c BC; part of Roman Empire, 125 BC to 5th-c AD; feudal monarchy founded by Hugh Capet, 987; Plantagenets of England acquired several territories, 12th-c; lands gradually recovered in Hundred Years' War, 1337–1453, apart from Calais (regained in 1558); Capetian dynasty followed by the Valois, from 1328, and the Bourbons, from 1589; Wars of Religion, 1562–95; monarchy overthrown by the French Revolution, 1789; First Republic declared, 1792; French Revolutionary Wars 1793–99; First Empire, ruled by Napoleon, 1804–14; monarchy restored, 1814–48; Second Republic, 1848–52, and Second Empire, 1852–70, ruled by Louis Napoleon; Third Republic, 1870–1940; great political instability between World Wars, with several governments holding office for short periods; occupied by Germany 1940–4, with pro-German government at Vichy, and Free French in London under de Gaulle; Fourth Republic, 1946; war with Indo-China, 1946–54; conflict in Algeria, 1954–62; Fifth Republic, 1958; governed by a President, an appointed Prime Minster, a Council of Ministers, bicameral National Assembly, and Senate.

Head of State
1958–69 Charles de Gaulle
1969–74 Georges Pompidou
1974–81 Valéry Giscard d'Estaing
1981–95 François Mitterrand
1995– Jacques René Chirac

Head of Government
1958–9 Charles de Gaulle
1959–62 Michel Debré
1962–8 Georges Pompidou
1968–9 Maurice Couve de Murville
1969–72 Jacques Chaban Delmas
1972–4 Pierre Mesmer
1974–6 Jacques René Chirac
1976–81 Raymond Barre

Francis of Sales, St [saylz], Fr [sahl] (1567–1622) Roman Catholic bishop and writer, born in Sales, E France. He studied at Paris and Padua, and became a distinguished preacher, successfully converting the Calvinistic population of Chablais. He became Bishop of Nicopolis (1599) and Bishop of Geneva (1602), where he helped to found a congregation of nuns of the Visitation. He was canonized in 1665; feast day 24 January.

Franciscans Religious orders founded by St Francis of Assisi in the early 13th-c. The first order, of **Friars Minor**, is now divided into three groups: the **Observants** (**OFM**), the **Conventuals** (**OFMConv**), and the **Capuchins** (**OFMCap**). These lead active lives preaching to the poor and needy. The second order is made up of nuns, known as the **Poor Clares** (**PC**). The third order is a lay fraternity. Together, they constitute the largest religious order in the Roman Catholic Church, notable for missionary and social work.

Francis Joseph I, Ger **Franz Josef I** (1830–1916) Emperor of Austria (1848–1916) and king of Hungary (1867–1916), born near Vienna, the grandson of Emperor Francis I. During his reign the aspirations of the various nationalities of the empire were rigorously suppressed. He was defeated by the Prussians in 1866, and established the Dual Monarchy of Austria–Hungary in 1867. His annexation of Bosnia-Herzegovina in 1908 agitated Europe; and his attack on Serbia in 1914 precipitated World War 1.

Francistown 21°11S 27°32E, pop (2000e) 67 300. Independent township in Central district, Botswana, S Africa; altitude 990 m/3248 ft; area 79 sq km/49 sq mi; industrial and commercial centre of Botswana; originally a gold-mining settlement; airfield; railway; textiles, light industry, trade, services.

Francis Xavier, St [zayvier], Span **San Francisco Javier**, known as **the Apostle of the Indies** (1506–52) Roman Catholic mis-

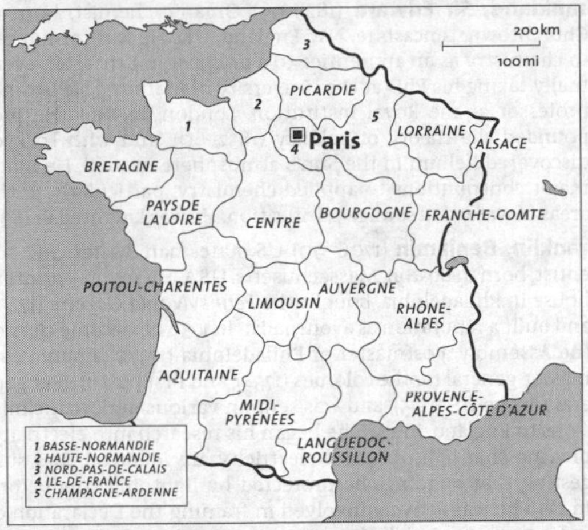

☐ International Airport

1981–4 Pierre Mauroy
1984–6 Laurent Fabius
1986–8 Jacques René Chirac
1988–91 Michel Rocard
1991–2 Edith Cresson
1992–3 Pierre Bérégovoy
1993–5 Edouard Balladur
1995–7 Alain Juppé
1997–2002 Lionel Jospin
2002– Jean-Pierre Raffarin

Internal Collective Territory
Island of Corsica in the Mediterranean Sea: area 8680 km²/ 3350 sq mi; capital, Ajaccio; GMT +1

Overseas departments
Name / Area (km2 / sq mi) / Capital / GMT
Guadeloupe / 1779 / 687 / Basse-Terre / -4
Guiana / 90 909 / 35 091 / Cayenne / -3
Martinique / 1079 / 416 / Fort-de-France / -4
Mayotte / 374 / 144 / Dzaoudzi / +3
Réunion / 2512 / 970 / St Denis / +4
St-Pierre-et-Miquelon / 240 / 93 / St Pierre / -3

Overseas territories
Name / Area (km2 / sq mi) / Capital (chief centre) / GMT
French Polynesia / 3941 / 1521 / Papeete / -6
New Caledonia / 18 575 / 7170 / Nouméa / +11
Southern and Antarctic Territories / 10 100 / 3900 / Port-aux-Français
Wallis and Futuna / 274 / 106 / Matu Utu / +12

sionary who brought Christianity to India and the Far East, born in Navarre, N Spain. He studied in Paris, where he became one of the first seven members of the Jesuit order (1534). He began his missionary work in Goa, India (1542), later travelling to the Malay Is (1545) and Japan (1549). He died of a fever while trying to enter China. He was canonized in 1622, and named patron saint of all missionary work in 1927. Feast day 3 December.

Franck, César (Auguste) [frã̄k, sayzah(r)] (1822–90) Composer, born in Liège, E Belgium. He studied at the Liège Conservatoire and at Paris, where he acquired French nationality, and settled as a teacher and organist, composing in his leisure hours. His reputation rests on a few masterpieces all written after the age of 50, the best known being a violin sonata, a string quartet, a symphony, and the *Variations symphoniques* (1885) for piano and orchestra.

Franco (Bahamonde), Francisco [frangkoh], popular name **el Caudillo** ('the leader') (1892–1975) Spanish general and dictator (1936–75), born in El Ferrol, Galicia, NW Spain. He graduated from Toledo military academy in 1910, acquired extensive combat experience in Morocco, and by 1926 was Spain's youngest general. During the Second Republic (1931–6), he led the repression of the Asturias miners' revolt (1934), and in 1935 served as chief-of-staff. In 1936 he belatedly joined the conspiracy against the Popular Front government (elected Feb 1936) which on 17–18 July launched the rebellion from which the Spanish Civil War (1936–9) resulted. Franco's leadership of the vital Army of Africa, and his close relations with the rebels' Italian and German allies, led to his becoming (Sep 1936) *generalísimo* of the rebel forces and chief of the Nationalist state. Between October 1936 and April 1939 he led the Nationalists to victory, and presided over the construction of an authoritarian regime that endured until his death. During World War 2, he initially stood close to Germany and Italy, opting (1940) for nonbelligerency rather than neutrality, having offered in October 1940 to fight on the side of Hitler, who did not want to expend resources on Spain. He kept Spain out of the war, while making Spanish submarine bases and other facilities available to the Nazis; but from 1943 he shrewdly distanced himself from the Axis. During the 1950s, his anti-Communism made possible a rapprochement with the Western powers. In 1969 he announced that upon his death the monarchy would return in the person of Juan Carlos, grandson of Spain's last ruling king. Within two years of Franco's death, almost every vestige of his dictatorship had disappeared.

Franco-German Treaty of Co-operation A treaty signed (Jan 1963) by President de Gaulle and Chancellor Adenauer signalling a rapprochement and the ending of centuries of conflict. It made provisions for regular summit meetings, and co-operation and consultation in foreign, economic, and cultural affairs. A symbol of the new, post-war order in Europe, the treaty also underpinned the European Economic Community.

francolin A partridge native to Africa and S Asia; large bird with patches of bare skin on head and neck; inhabits forest or scrubland. (Genus: *Francolinus*, 40 species.)

Francome, John [frangkuhm] (1952–) Jockey and trainer, born in Swindon, Wiltshire, S England, UK. In 1970–85 he rode a record 1138 winners over fences. He won the 1978 Cheltenham Gold Cup, the 1981 Champion Hurdle, and twice won the King George VI Chase (1982, 1984). Only the second man to surpass 1000 winners, he was seven times National Hunt champion jockey (1976, 1979, 1981–5). He retired in 1985, and became a trainer, novelist, and television commentator.

Franconia A European duchy which, as its name denotes, was once part of the lands of the Franks. These lands were divided in 843 into three broad divisions, including E Francia (later the kingdom of Germany), with Franconia, between Upper Lotharingia and Thuringia, as one of its constituent duchies.

Franconian Forest, Ger **Frankenwald** Mountain range in Bavaria, Germany; extends 36 km/22 mi between R Rodach (NW) and the Fichtelgebirge (SE); highest peak, the Döbraberg (795 m/2608 ft).

Franco-Prussian War (1870–1) A conflict occasioned by the Hohenzollern candidature for the Spanish throne and the Ems telegram, and caused by the changing balance of power in Europe. It resulted in crushing defeats for France at Sedan and Metz by Moltke's reformed Prussian army, the siege of Paris, and the humiliating Treaty of Frankfurt. Germany gained most of Alsace and part of Lorraine, including Metz, and France had to pay a heavy war indemnity. William I of Prussia was crowned German emperor – confirming the growing strength of Prussia under Bismarck. The war humiliated France and enabled Bismarck to push for German reunification, under Prussian dominance.

frangipani [franjipahnee] A shrub or small tree (*Plumeria rubra*) growing to c.6 m/20 ft, native to tropical America; leaves oval; flowers in large clusters, very fragrant, five petals, white, yellow, or pink. It is widely cultivated in the tropics for the scented flowers which are often placed in Buddhist temples. (Family: Apocynaceae.)

Frank, Anne (1929–45) Jewish diarist and concentration camp victim, born in Frankfurt, WC Germany. Her family fled from the Nazis to The Netherlands in 1933, and after the Nazi occupation of The Netherlands she hid with her family and four others in a sealed-off office flat in Amsterdam from 1942 until they were betrayed in 1944. It is now a museum. She died in Belsen concentration camp. The lively, moving diary she kept during her concealment was published in bowdlerized form by her father, the only Frank survivor, in 1947, dramatized, and filmed, and she became a symbol of past suffering under the Nazis.

Frankenstein A soulless creature made from parts of corpses and animated by supposed scientific means. In Mary Shelley's novel (1818), Frankenstein was the name of the monster's creator, but it has since become transferred to the monster itself. The story readily adapted to the cinema screen: it was made into a film in 1931 by James Whale, with Boris Karloff as the monster, and has since given rise to a whole genre of cinema films.

Frankfort [**frang**kfert] 38°12N 84°52W, pop (2000e) 27 700. Capital of state in Franklin Co, NC Kentucky, USA, on the Kentucky R; founded by Daniel Boone, 1770; state capital, 1792; railway; university; trade and shipping centre for tobacco, livestock and limestone; whisky, automobile parts, shoes, metal items; graves of Daniel and Rebecca Boone; Capital Expo (Jun).

Frankfurt (am Main) [**frang**kfoort, **miyn**] 50°07N 8°40E, pop (2000e) 661 000. Manufacturing and commercial city in Hesse province, WC Germany; port on R Main, 27 km/17 mi N of Darmstadt; most of the German emperors crowned here; meeting place of first German National Assembly (1848–9); international junction for rail, road, and air traffic; university (1914); headquarters of the leading German stock exchange; banking, river craft, precision engineering, chemicals, pharmaceuticals, brewing, metals, machinery, packaging, publishing, oil products, domestic appliances, office machines, telecommunications; birthplace of Goethe; Gothic cathedral (13th–15th-c), the Römer (ancient town hall), Goethe House (rebuilt, 1949); International Frankfurt Fair (Aug), and many other trade fairs; some of Germany's finest health resorts nearby.

Frankfurt (an der Oder) [**frang**kfoort, **oh**der] 52°50N 14°31E, pop (2000e) 91 900. Capital of region in Frankfurt district, WC Germany; 80 km/50 mi E of Berlin, on R Oder, where it follows the frontier with Poland; badly bombed in World War 2; railway; textiles, machinery, furniture, semiconductors.

Frankfurter, Felix (1882–1965) Law teacher and judge, born in Vienna, Austria. He studied at the College of the City of New York and at Harvard, taught at Harvard Law School (1914–39), and served as an associate justice of the US Supreme Court (1939–62). He founded the American Civil Liberties Union, though he advocated judicial restraint in opposing legislative and executive policy.

Frankfurt Parliament An elected assembly convened following the German revolutions of March 1848 to draft a liberal constitution for all of Germany. It represented every state in the German Confederation, but proved to be disunited and powerless. After its offer of the imperial crown to the king of Prussia was repudiated by Austria and rejected by the king himself, the parliament disintegrated.

Frankfurt School The group of philosophers, sociologists, and psychologists who belonged to the Frankfurt Institute for Social Research (1923–69); leading figures included Max Horkheimer, Theodore Adorno, Herbert Marcuse, and more recently Jürgen Habermas. The School developed **critical theory**, an ethical, politically prescriptive critique of society which draws its inspiration from the works of Marx and Freud.

frankincense An evergreen tree or shrub (*Boswellia carteri*) growing to 6 m/20 ft, native to Somaliland; leaves pinnate with oval leaflets, crowded towards the ends of the twigs; flowers white, 5-petalled. Aromatic resin is obtained from cuts in the bark. (Family: Burseraceae.)

Frankland, Sir Edward (1825–99) Organic chemist, born in Churchtown, Lancashire, NW England, UK. He was introduced to chemistry as an apprentice to a druggist in Lancaster, eventually taking his PhD at the University of Marburg. He became professor at the Royal Institution, London, in 1863. He propounded the theory of valency (1852–60), and with Lockyer discovered helium in the Sun's atmosphere in 1868. He made major contributions to applied chemistry, particularly in the areas of water and sewage purification. He was knighted in 1897.

Franklin, Benjamin (1706–90) US statesman, writer, and scientist, born in Boston, Massachusetts, USA. He set up a printing house in Philadelphia, bought the *Pennsylvania Gazette* (1729), and built a reputation as a journalist. In 1736 he became clerk of the Assembly, postmaster of Philadelphia (1737), deputy postmaster-general for the colonies (1754), and first postmaster general for the US (1775), and was sent on various diplomatic missions to England. In 1746 he began his research into electricity, proving that lightning and electricity are identical, and suggesting that buildings be protected by lightning conductors. In 1776 he was actively involved in framing the Declaration of Independence. A skilled negotiator, he successfully won Britain's recognition of US independence (1783). He was US minister in Paris till 1785, then three times President of the Pennsylvania Executive Council. He played a major part in the Federal Constitutional Convention (1787), then retired from public life. His *Autobiography* was begun in 1771, but never completed.

Franklin, Sir John (1786–1847) Arctic explorer, born in Spilsby, Lincolnshire, EC England, UK. He joined the navy at 14, and was present at the Battles of Copenhagen (1801) and Trafalgar (1805). Knighted in 1829, he became Governor of Van Diemen's Land (Tasmania) (1834–45). He then commanded an expedition to discover the Northwest Passage, but his ships were beleaguered by thick ice in the Victoria Strait, and he and his crew died. Their remains, and a record of the expedition, were found several years later. He is credited with the discovery of the Passage, because his ships came within a few miles of known American waters.

Franklin, (Stella Maria Sarah) Miles, pseudonym **Brent of Bin Bin** (1879–1954) Novelist, born in Talbingo, New South Wales, SE Australia. A freelance writer in Sydney and Melbourne, she emigrated in 1906 to the USA, and remained abroad, living in England and America, until 1933. Her best-known novel, *My Brilliant Career* (1901, filmed 1979), was described as 'the very first Australian novel' on account of its original and distinctive Australian character. Its sequel, *My Career Goes Bung*, written soon afterwards, was not published until 1946. Other novels include *Some Everyday Folk – and Dawn* (1909), *Bring the Monkey* (1933), and *All That Swagger* (1936). The annual *Miles Franklin Awards* are now among Australia's most prestigious literary prizes.

Franks Germanic peoples, originally from the lower Rhine region. Clovis led the Salian and Ripuarian Franks and founded a kingdom embracing much of Gaul; Charlemagne, their greatest ruler, attempted to revive the Roman Empire in the West. They gave their name to Francia, which by the 13th-c stood for what is now France, but earlier had diverse territorial connotations, reflecting the vicissitudes of Frankish royal power.

Franks, Tommy, popular name of **Thomas Ray Franks** (1945–) US general, born in Wynnewood, Oklahoma, USA. He studied at the University of Texas (1971) and graduated from military school at Fort Still, OK (1967). From the 1980s, he served in West Germany, commanded in Korea, and was commander of the Third US Army, Fort McPherson, GA. He was promoted to general (2000) and appointed commander-in-chief of the US Central Command (2000–3). He had responsibility for the campaign in Afghanistan to destroy the Taliban regime (2001) and commanded the US-led invasion of Iraq (Mar–Apr 2003).

Franz Josef Land, Russ **Zemlya Frantsa-Iosifa** area 20 700 sq km/8000 sq mi. Archipelago in the Arctic Ocean, N of Novaya Zemlya, NW Russia; over 160 islands of volcanic origin; declared Soviet territory in 1926; most northerly land of the E hemisphere; uninhabited save for a meteorological station on Ostrov Gukera (Hooker I).

Fraser, Lady Antonia, *née* **Pakenham** (1932–) British writer. She studied at Oxford, and as a writer became active in several arts and literary associations, chairing the Society of Authors (1974–5). She is best known for her books about important historical figures, such as *Mary Queen of Scots* (1969, James Tait Black), *Kings and Queens of England* (1975, 1988), and *The Six Wives of Henry VIII* (1992). Other books include *Your Royal Hostage* (1987), *The Gunpowder Plot: Terror and Faith in 1605* (1996), and *Marie Antoinette: The Journey* (2001). She married Harold Pinter in 1980.

Fraser, Dawn (1937–) Swimmer, born in Balmain, Sydney, New South Wales, SE Australia. She is the only swimmer to take the same individual title at three consecutive Olympics, winning the 100 m freestyle in 1956, 1960, and 1964. She also won a gold medal in the 4 × 100 m freestyle relay in 1956, totalling eight Olympic medals, the most by an Australian. She took six Commonwealth Games gold medals, and set 27 world records. In 1962 she became the first woman to break the one-minute barrier for the 100 m. In 1964 she was banned by the Australian association for 10 years (later reduced to four) when she and some colleagues tried to take a souvenir flag from the emperor's palace in Tokyo after winning her third Olympic title. She was however named as 1964 Australian of the Year, and in 1988 was selected as Australia's greatest female athlete. She was elected as an Independent member of the New South Wales Legislative Assembly (1988–91), representing Balmain.

Fraser, (John) Malcolm (1930–) Australian statesman and prime minister (1975–83), born in Melbourne, Victoria, SE Australia. He studied at Melbourne and Oxford, and in 1955 became the youngest MP in the House of Representatives. He was minister for the army (1966–8), defence (1969–71), and education and science (1968–9, 1971–2), and became leader of the Liberal Party in 1975, and prime minister in a Liberal–National coalition. His government was defeated in the 1983 elections, and soon after he resigned his parliamentary seat, becoming a farmer in Nareen, W Victoria. He has also become involved in international affairs, particularly as a member of the Commonwealth Group of Eminent Persons which worked to replace apartheid in South Africa.

Fraser, Simon (1776–1862) Fur trader, born in Bennington, Vermont, USA. He moved to Canada in 1784. He worked as a clerk in the North-West Co, was promoted to partner in 1801, and was sent in 1805 to establish the first trading posts in the Rocky Mountains. Following Mackenzie's route, he opened up a vast area which he called New Caledonia between the plains and the Pacific, and in 1808 followed the Fraser R, named after him, to its mouth. He headed the Red River Department of the North-West Co during conflict with settlers of the rival Hudson's Bay Co, before his retirement in 1818. Simon Fraser University, in British Columbia, is named after him.

Fraser River River in SW Canada, rises in the Rocky Mts, flows NW, S, and W to enter the Strait of Georgia and the Pacific Ocean 16 km/10 mi S of Vancouver; length 1368 km/850 mi; navigable below Yale; Fraser R canyon above Yale; 1858 gold rush along upper reaches led to independent colonial status for the mainland, and the beginnings of permanent non-native settlement; lower river course followed by two major railroads.

Frassinetti, Paula, St, also known as **Paola Frassinetti** (1809–82) Religious foundress, born in Genoa, NW Italy. Her brother was a parish priest in the city, and she assisted him by teaching the local poor children. From this humble beginning, she founded (1834) the Sisters of St Dorothy Congregation, which soon spread across Italy and overseas to the Americas. She was beatified in 1930, and canonized in 1984. Feast day 11 June.

fraternity and sorority In the USA, associations at universities, for men and women respectively, named usually with two or three letters of the Greek alphabet (eg *Kappa Lamda, Sigma Chi*). They are formed mainly for social purposes; membership is by invitation, and is in some cases discriminatory. They are banned in some universities.

fraud A false statement or action made knowingly, recklessly, or without belief in its truth in order to gain a material advantage; the fact that there may have been no intention to cheat anyone is not essential to establish the offence. Any person injured by fraud may bring an action to recover damages in the tort (or delict) of deceit. Any contract induced by fraud can be rescinded or sometimes reformed at the instance of the innocent party on the grounds of fraudulent representation. In England and Wales, fraud is an element in a number of criminal offences, such as obtaining a pecuniary advantage by deception, rather than an offence itself. In the USA, a tort action for deceit requires not only knowledge of falsity or absence of belief in truth, but also the intent that the listener shall act or omit to act in a certain way. The intent to accomplish an ultimate harm to the listener is relevant only regarding punitive damages. In Scotland, the fraudulent statement must have achieved some definite practical result for it to amount to a criminal offence.

Fraunhofer, Joseph von [frownhohfer] (1787–1826) Physicist, born in Straubing, SE Germany. In 1807 he founded an optical institute at Munich, where he improved prisms and telescopes, enabling him to discover the dark lines in the Sun's spectrum which have been named after him. He also pioneered the use of diffraction gratings to examine spectra. In 1823 he became professor and academician at Munich.

Fraunhofer lines [frownhohfer] Sharp, narrow, absorption lines in the spectrum of the Sun, 25 000 of which are now identified. The most prominent lines are due to the presence of calcium, hydrogen, sodium, and magnesium. Most of the absorption occurs in cool layers of the atmosphere, immediately above the incandescent photosphere.

Fray Bentos [friy bentohs] 33°10S 58°20W, pop (2000e) 22 100. River-port capital of Río Negro department, W Uruguay, on R Uruguay; airfield; railway (freight); ferry; meat; former centre of meat packing and canning industry (especially corned beef), plant now closed and made into an industrial museum; international toll bridge (San Martín) across the R Uruguay to Puerto Unzué (Argentina).

Frazer, Sir James George (1854–1941) Social anthropologist, classicist, and folklorist, born in Glasgow, W Scotland, UK. He studied at Glasgow and at Cambridge, where he spent most of his adult life as a fellow of Trinity College. His major work was *The Golden Bough* (1890; rewritten in 12 vols, 1911–15). He became professor of social anthropology at Liverpool in 1907, and was knighted in 1914.

Frears, Stephen Arthur (1941–) Director, born in Leicester, C England, UK. He studied law at Cambridge University and gained his first experience of film production with Karel Reisz and Lindsay Anderson in the 1960s. He won international acclaim with his cult classic, *My Beautiful Launderette* (1985), and later films include *Dangerous Liaisons* (1988), *The Grifters* (1990), and *Dirty Pretty Things* (2002). His work for television includes directing the early television plays by Alan Bennet (1978–9).

Frederick I (Emperor), known as **Frederick Barbarossa** ('Redbeard') (c.1123–90) Holy Roman Emperor, born of the Hohenstaufen family. He succeeded his uncle, Conrad III, in 1152. His reign was a continuous struggle against unruly vassals at home, the city republics of Lombardy, and the papacy. He went on several campaigns in Italy, and though severely defeated at Legnano (1176), he quelled Henry the Lion of Bavaria, and asserted his feudal superiority over Poland, Hungary, Denmark, and Burgundy. He led the Third Crusade against Saladin (1189), and was victorious at Philomelium and Iconium.

Frederick I (of Prussia) (1657–1713) King of Prussia (1701–13), born in Königsberg, Prussia (now Kaliningrad, Russia). He succeeded to the electorate of Brandenburg in 1688 (as Frederick III) and was made the first King of Prussia for his loyalty to Emperor Leopold against the French. He maintained a large court, established a standing army, and was a great patron of the arts and learning.

Frederick II (Emperor) (1194–1250) Holy Roman Emperor, born in Jesi, near Ancona, EC Italy, the grandson of Frederick I. He succeeded Henry VI in 1220, and was the last emperor of the Hohenstaufen line. He was also King of Sicily (1198) and of Germany (1212). He keenly desired to consolidate imperial power in Italy at the expense of the papacy, and devoted himself to organizing his Italian territories, but his plans were frustrated by the Lombard cities and by the popes. Embarking on the Sixth Crusade in 1228, he took possession of Jerusalem, and crowned himself king there (1229). Returning to Italy, he continued his struggles with the papacy until his death.

Frederick II (of Prussia), known as **the Great** (1712–86) King of Prussia (1740–86), born in Berlin, Germany, the son of Frederick William I and Sophia Dorothea, daughter of George I of England. His childhood was spent in rigorous military training and education. In 1733 he married, and lived at Rheinsberg, where he studied music and French literature, and himself wrote and composed. As king, he fought to oppose Austrian ambitions, and earned a great reputation as a military commander in the War of the Austrian Succession (1740–8). He seized Silesia, and defeated the Austrians at Mollwitz (1741) and Chotusitz (1742). The second Silesian War (1744–5) left him with further territories which, by good luck and great effort, he retained after fighting the Seven Years' War (1756–63). In 1772 he shared in the first partition of Poland. Under him, Prussia became a leading European power. An enlightened despot, he believed that a ruler should exercise absolute power; he established full religious toleration, abolished torture, and freed the serfs on his estates. He also built the rococo palace of Sans Souci at Potsdam, composed music, and was the patron of composers and men of letters such as Voltaire. When he died, he had doubled the area of his country, and given it a strong economic foundation.

Frederick IX (of Denmark) (1899–1972) King of Denmark (1947–72), born near Copenhagen, the son of Christian X. He married **Ingrid**, the daughter of King Gustav VI Adolf of Sweden, in 1935, and they had three daughters, **Margrethe** (later Queen Margrethe II), **Benedikte**, and **Anne-Marie**, who married the former King Constantine II of Greece. During World War 2, Frederick encouraged the Danish resistance movement, and was imprisoned by the Germans (1943–5).

Fredericksburg, Battle of In the American Civil War, a fruitless attempt by the Northern army of 113 000 to capture the town of Fredericksburg, Virginia, defended by a Southern army of 75 000.

Frederick William (of Brandenburg), known as **the Great Elector** (1620–88) Elector of Brandenburg (1640–88), born near Berlin, Germany. On his accession, he found the state exhausted by the Thirty Years' War. He therefore made a treaty of neutrality with the Swedes, regulated the finances, sought to re-people the deserted towns, and reorganized the army and administrative system of the Hohenzollern state. He recovered some territory and gained East Pomerania by the Treaty of Westphalia (1648), retrieving the sovereignty of Prussia from Poland (1657). His reforms laid the foundation of future Prussian greatness.

Frederick William III (of Prussia) (1770–1840) King of Prussia (1797–1840), the son of Frederick William II (1744–97), born in Potsdam, EC Germany. At first cautiously neutral towards Napoleon's conquests, he eventually declared war (1806) and was severely defeated at Jena and Auerstadt, with the loss of all territory W of the Elbe. To further Prussia's recovery, he sanctioned the reforms of Hardenburg and Stein, and the military reorganization of Scharnhorst and Gneisenau, sharing in the decisive victory of Leipzig with Alexander I (1813). By the Treaty of Vienna (1815) he recovered his possessions, and thereafter tended to support the forces of conservatism.

Fredericton 45°57N 66°40W, pop (2000e) 52 000. Capital of New Brunswick, Canada, on the St John R; originally settled by Acadians, 1731, as St Anne's Point; renamed 1785 for Prince Frederick, second son of George III; capital, 1787; airfield; railway; university (1783); timber products, plastics, tourism; York-Sunbury Historical Museum, Beaverbrook Art Gallery, Provincial Legislature (1880), Christ Church Cathedral (1853), Old Government House (1828), now headquarters of Royal Canadian Mounted Police.

Fredriksson, Gert (1919–) Swedish canoeist. During 1948–60 he won eight Olympic medals, including six golds, and 13 world titles, all at either kayak singles or pairs. His winning margin of 6·7 sec in the 1948 Olympic singles final was the biggest for any kayak race other than the 10 000 m. When he won his last Olympic gold in 1960, he was aged 40 years 292 days – the oldest canoeing gold medallist.

Freedom Building *World Trade Center*

freedom of the press *press freedom*

free electron gas *electronic structure of solids*

free electron laser A device which produces laser light using a beam of electrons rather than a collection of excited atoms. First demonstrated in 1976, it provides a good source of variable wavelength light. It works by passing a beam of high-speed electrons between a set of magnets with alternating north–south poles. Side-to-side oscillations cause electromagnetic radiation to be emitted, which is produced in a forward direction due to high electron velocity.

free enterprise An economic system in which the initiative for production and consumption decisions lies with individuals or companies. This is contrasted with a *planned economy*, in which the initiative lies with the government. Free enterprise does not imply a total absence of government influence. In any economy, individuals and firms have to operate under rules set by the political authorities – indeed, companies owe their existence to such rules. In 'free market economies' business is subject to numerous rules concerning health and safety, consumer protection, anti-competitive practices, land use control, etc. It is also subject to taxation to pay for the public sector. The rules, however, only operate as constraints on consumer choice and business initiatives, and individuals and firms are free to choose what to consume and produce within these rules.

free fall The motion of objects allowed to fall under the influence of gravity, in which air resistance and variations in gravity with altitude are ignored. The rate of free fall is the same for all objects, regardless of mass or substance, a result deriving from the work of Galileo.

freefalling *skydiving*

Free French French men and women who answered General de Gaulle's appeal, broadcast from London (18 Jun 1940), to reject the impending armistice between France and Germany, and join him in fighting on. He became leader of the Free French forces, and the 2nd French Armoured Division helped liberate Paris (25 Aug 1944). In occupied France there were deep divisions between the French resistance, with its headquarters in London, and the communist-supported Maquis working in isolated cells within France.

freehold Land or property held for use by the owner for an indefinite period of time. This is in contrast to **leasehold**, where the leaseholder has possession only for some finite period (eg 99 years), subject to payment of ground rent, reversion of the property to the ground landlord at the end of the lease, and possibly restrictions on the uses to which the property can be put. In the 19th-c the spacious lands of Australia, Canada, and the USA enabled the governments of these countries to grant substantial holdings cheaply to farmers, who thus became freeholders rather than leaseholders. In the largely agrarian nations of Asia, Africa, and Latin America freeholds remain widespread, and in many countries a few owners still hold most of the land, while the majority of the cultivators have few, if any, rights.

Since the collapse of communism, many former socialist countries (as well as China) have returned to its original owners the freehold on land and property previously appropriated by the state. Elsewhere, safeguards have been introduced piecemeal to protect the leaseholder from exploitation by the freeholder, and the concept of leasehold is under review by governments, notably in Europe.

Freeman, Cathy (1973–) Athlete, born in Mackay, Queensland, NE Australia. At age 17 she won her first gold medal at the 1990 Commonwealth Games as a member of the 4 x 100 m women's relay team, and was named Young Australian of the Year. She won a gold again at the 1994 Commonwealth Games in the 200 m and 400 m events, becoming the first athlete in Commonwealth history to achieve such a feat. Her carrying of both the Aboriginal and Australian flags on her lap of honour endeared her to the public. In 1998 she was again named Australian of the Year. She was chosen to light the Olympic torch in Sydney in 2000, and went on to win gold in the 400 m final. She announced her retirement in 2003.

Freeman, Morgan (1937–) Actor, born in Memphis, Tennessee, USA. The son of a barber and a schoolteacher, he was raised in Chicago and Mississippi. He served in the air force, attended Los Angeles City College, and made his Broadway debut in 1967 in an all-black production of *Hello, Dolly*. His film credits include *Street Smart* (1987, Oscar nomination) and *Glory* (1989), and he received acclaim for his role as Hoke Colburn, the chauffeur in *Driving Miss Daisy* (1989). Later films include *Seven* (1995), *Deep Impact* (1998), and *Bruce Almighty* (2003).

freemasonry A movement claiming great antiquity, whose members (**masons**) are joined together in an association based on brotherly love, faith, and charity. The one essential qualification for membership is a belief in a supreme being. Nonpolitical, open to men of any religion, freemasonry is known for its rituals and signs of recognition that date back to ancient religions and to the practices of the mediaeval craft guild of the stonemasons (in England). During the 17th-c the masons' clubs, or *lodges*, began to be attended by gentlemen who had no connection with the trade. The Grand Lodge of England was founded in 1717, that of Ireland in 1725, and Scotland in 1736; freemasonry spread to the USA, the British colonies, and European countries. Freemasons are now mainly drawn from the professional middle classes. The organization regularly comes under attack for the secrecy with which it carries out its activities.

free port An area near a port or airport where business enterprises may import materials and components free of tax or import duties, as long as the resulting finished articles are exported. It is a means of avoiding problems created by import tariffs and other restrictions, such as high raw material costs, or shortages of key components. An example is Shannon Airport, Ireland (established 1961). The term is also used for a port where goods may be imported without local taxes, as long as they are re-exported. The world's largest ports in this category are Hong Kong and Singapore. The UK set up six free ports in 1984, including Liverpool and Southampton.

free radicals Oxygen molecules with one, two, or three additional electrons produced by oxidative process within the body, and thought to be responsible for tissue damage and disease. Antioxidant vitamins C and E and other micro-nutrients such as ß carotene and selenium are thought to prevent this process and may be protective against a range of disorders, including atherosclerosis and Alzheimer's disease.

free selection In Australian history, the colonial governments' laws passed between 1861 and 1872 to force pastoral occupiers to give way to freehold farming. Anyone could 'select' any land up to 130 ha/320 acres that had not been sold, granted, or dedicated by the Crown. The first law to embody this idea was passed in New South Wales (1861). Although the laws achieved some success, they often failed because of the tactics used by the occupiers ('squatters'), the unsuitability of the land for farming, or the selectors' lack of capital.

freesia A perennial (*Freesia refracta*) growing to 75 cm/30 in, producing corms, native to S Africa; leaves sword-shaped, forming flat fans; flowers up to 5 cm/2 in long, goblet-shaped, creamy white, fragrant, in one-sided sprays. Cultivars may have orange-to-crimson or blue-to-mauve flowers. (Family: Iridaceae.)

Free State, formerly (1910–94) **Orange Free State** pop (2000e) 2 534 000; area 129 437 sq km/49 963 sq mi. One of the nine new provinces established by the South African constitution of 1994, in EC South Africa; capital, Bloemfontein (also, the judicial capital of South Africa); chief languages, Sesotho (56%), Afrikaans, Xhosa; many settlements date from the Great Trek of 1836; claimed by British as the Orange River Sovereignty, 1848; independence, 1854; joined Union of South Africa as Orange Free State, 1910; third largest province in the country; a largely rural province; grain ('the breadbasket of South Africa'), livestock; rich gold deposits; oil, agricultural equipment, fertilizers, wool, clothing, cement, pharmaceuticals, pottery.

freethought A post-Reformation movement which rejected the control of any religious authority over reason in the examination of religious issues. The term was used by the 17th–18th-c deists, such as Anthony Collins (1676–1729). It is represented in the 19th-c by the National Secularist Society (1866) and in the 20th-c and 21st-c by the Secular Society and the Freethinkers of America.

Freetown 8°30N 13°17W, pop (2000e) 722 000. Seaport capital of Sierra Leone; visited by the Portuguese, 15th-c; founded in the 1790s as a foundation for freed slaves; capital of British West Africa, 1808–74; W Africa's oldest university, Fourah Bay, founded as a college in 1827; capital of Sierra Leone, 1961; airport; oil refining, plastics, sugar, cement, footwear, soap, fish processing; trade in platinum, diamonds, gold, chromite, palm kernels, ginger, kola nuts; fort at Bunce I.

free trade An economic doctrine that trade between countries should not be controlled in any way; there should be no tariffs or other barriers. The problems which result from tariffs were identified by Adam Smith in 1776, and the cause of free trade, taken up by Sir Robert Peel, led to the repeal of the Corn Laws in 1846. Since the 19th-c, tariff barriers have become very common, but groups of countries may agree to lower or remove them, forming a **free-trade area**, as in the case of the EU, and the General Agreement on Tariffs and Trade (now the World Trade Organization) has made considerable progress in reducing them worldwide.

Free Trade Agreement A bilateral trade treaty between Canada and the USA, signed and implemented in 1989. Praised for enhancing access to markets, the agreement has also been criticized for compromising subsidized sectors, environmental concerns, state and provincial labour legislation, and English-Canadian concerns for cultural autonomy.

free verse Verse which, while being rhythmical, observes no strict or recurrent metrical pattern or use of rhyme. Much if not most 20th-c verse was written in free verse. It is now the predominant verse form in English. It has some precedents in the poems of Blake, but the pioneers of free verse in English were Whitman, T S Eliot, Pound, and William Carlos Williams. Many poets (such as T S Eliot) have maintained it is more difficult to write well than formal verse.

free will A concept that has generated a famous philosophical problem: is our everyday assumption that we are free agents, able to do or not do this or that at will, compatible with the view that every event has a cause? Free will is generally supposed to be a precondition for moral responsibility, so the question has implications for ethics, for theology, and for the scientific view of the world.

freeze drying *lyophilization*

freezing *deep-freezing*

Frege, (Friedrich Ludwig) Gottlob [frayguh] (1848–1925) Mathematician and logician, born in Wismar, N Germany. He studied at Jena and Göttingen, and became professor of mathematics at Jena (1896). His *Begriffsschrift* (1879, Concept-script) outlined the first complete system of symbolic logic. The technical difficulties involved gave rise to his distinctive philosophical doctrines, forcefully set out in his *Grundlagen der Arithmetik* (1884, The Foundations of Arithmetic). His *Grundgesetze der Arithmetik* (1893–1903, Basic Laws of Arithmetic) contained a postscript acknowledging that Russell had spotted a contradiction in his thinking. Depressed by the poor reception of his ideas, he wrote little after 1903.

Frei (Montalva), Eduardo [fray] (1911–82) Chilean statesman and president (1964–70), born in Santiago, Chile. He studied in Chile, and became one of the leaders of the Social-Christian Falange Party in the late 1930s, and of the new Christian Democratic Party after 1957. His presidency saw an ambitious programme of social reform.

Freire, Paulo (Reglus Neves) [frairay] (1921–97) Philosopher and educator, born in Recife, Brazil. After a short-lived career as a lawyer, he turned to teaching and became the first director of the Department of Cultural Extension at Recife University (1961–4). Regarded as a socialist pedagogue, following the military coup of 1964 he was briefly jailed and then exiled. In Geneva he was appointed special educational adviser for the World Congress of Churches, and on his return to Brazil (1979) was made secretary of education for the city of São Paulo. His works include *Pedagogy of The Oppressed* (1970) and *Pedagogy of Hope* (1994). He was awarded UNESCO's Peace Prize in 1987.

Fremantle [freemantl] 32°07S 115°44E, pop (2000e) 26 300. Seaport city in Western Australia state, Australia, at the mouth of the Swan R, part of Perth metropolitan area; known locally as 'Freo'; founded as a penal colony, 1829; railway terminus; trade in petroleum, iron and steel products, grain, wool, fruit; the Round House (1830), a former jail; maritime museum housing relics from 17th-c Dutch wrecks; a notable sailing club; centre for the 1986–7 America's Cup yacht race, when its historic buildings were restored.

Frémont, John C(harles) [freemont] (1813–90) Explorer, mapmaker, and politician, born in Savannah, Georgia, USA. He began surveying in 1838, and over the next few years mapped much of the territory between the Mississippi and the West coast. Settling in California in 1848, he became the first senator from there in 1850. In 1856 he was the Republican and antislavery candidate for the presidency, but was defeated by James Buchanan; nominated again in 1864, he withdrew in favour of Abraham Lincoln. Appointed an officer in the Union army in 1861, he resigned in 1862. He was then involved in railway development in the West, and became Governor of Arizona (1878–82).

French *Romance languages*

French, Dawn (1957–) Comedy writer and actress, born in Holyhead, Anglesey, NW Wales, UK. After leaving school she won a debating scholarship to study in New York City, then attended the Central School of Speech and Drama in London, where she met Jennifer Saunders. They formed a comedy partnership, moving from clubs to theatre and into television, becoming widely known with *Girls On Top* (1985–6) and *French and Saunders* (from 1987). The series *Murder Most Horrid* was created especially for her, and she has also starred in BBC's *The Vicar of Dibley* (International Emmy, 1998), and with Saunders in *Let Them Eat Cake* (1999). In 2000 she appeared in the film *Maybe Baby*. She is married to comedy performer Lenny Henry.

French, John (Denton Pinkstone), Earl of Ypres (1852–1925) British field marshal (1913), born in Ripple, Kent, SE England, UK. He joined the navy (1866), then the army (1874), and distinguished himself in the Sudan (1884–5) and South Africa (1899–1901). Chief of the Imperial General Staff (1911–14), he held supreme command of the British Expeditionary Force in France (1914–15), but was criticized for indecision, and resigned. He was made a viscount (1915) and earl (1921), and was Lord-Lieutenant of Ireland (1918–21).

French, Marilyn (1929–) Novelist, born in New York City, USA. She studied at Hofstra College, then lectured there and at Harvard. She is best known for her first novel, *The Woman's Room* (1977), hailed as a pioneering feminist text for its angry study of the continuing subjection of women. Later books include *Her Mother's Daughter* (1992), *Our Father* (1994), and *A Season in Hell* (1998).

French and Indian War The last of the 18th-c wars between France and Britain for the control of North America. It was the first phase of what was later the Seven Years' War (1756–63). France accepted final defeat at the Treaty of Paris (1763). One consequence was that the War encouraged the American colonists to seek military independence of the British.

French art The art associated with France can be traced back to remote prehistoric times. It absorbed Greek and Celtic influences from the 6th-c BC onwards, and flourished under Roman rule (the Gallo-Roman period, 120 BC–3rd-c AD). The glories of mediaeval art include architecture, sculpture, and stained-glass at churches and cathedrals, such as Moissac, Vézelay, Souilhac, Saint-Denis, Chartres, Reims, and Notre-Dame in Paris. Italian Renaissance ideas are reflected in 16th-c chateaux of the Loire and the royal residences at Fontainebleau and the Louvre. French classicism flowered under Louis XIV, especially in the paintings of Claude Lorrain and Poussin, and in the architecture of Jacques Lemercier (1585–1654), Mansard, and Louis le Vau (1612–70). In the 18th-c the Rococo style of Watteau and Boucher was superseded by the Neoclassicism of David. Major 19th-c artists include Ingres, Courbet, Manet, and the Impressionists. From the early 19th-c down to c.1940, Paris was the centre of European art, especially painting.

French bean *haricot bean*

French bulldog A breed of dog, developed in France by crossing British bulldogs with local breeds; narrower and taller than the British breed, with smaller head and straighter legs.

French Community A grouping of some former French colonies which under the Constitution of the Fifth Republic (1958) opted to stay closely associated with France. The member states had full internal autonomy, but many matters including currency, defence, and foreign affairs remained the responsibility of the Community, which in effect meant France. Some 12 overseas territories opted to join. Pressures for full independence continued to build up, and in 1960 it became possible to be fully independent within the Community, thus rendering it of no practical relevance.

French Guiana [geeahna], Fr **La Guyane Française** pop (2000e) 173 200; area 90 909 sq km/35 091 sq mi. Overseas department of France in South America, bordering the Atlantic, divided into two arrondissements; bounded W by Suriname, E and S by Brazil; capital Cayenne; timezone GMT −3; mixed Creole, European, and Amerindian population; official language, French; chief religion, Roman Catholicism (87%); unit of currency, the euro; low-lying near the coast; rises S towards the Serra de Tumuc-Hamac, reaching 635 m/2083 ft at Mont Saint Marcel; many rocky islets along the coast, notably Devil's Island; hot and humid tropical climate; rainy season (Dec–Jun); average daily temperatures at Cayenne, 23–33°C; monthly rainfall 551 mm/21·7 in (May), 31 mm/1·2 in (Sep); area settled by French, Dutch, Portuguese, 17th-c; restored to France by Treaty of Paris, 1814; used as penal colony 1798–1935; overseas department of France, 1946; governed by a Commissioner of the Republic (for France), a 19-seat General Council and a 31-seat Regional Council, each headed by a president; head of state is the French President; elects two members to the French National Assembly; chiefly agricultural exports (64%), mostly shrimps, prawns, rice, wood and wood products, from forests covering over 80% of territory; minerals little exploited; some bauxite, kaolin, gold; rum, essence of rosewood; only 0·1% of land under cultivation; rice, maize, manioc, bananas, sugar cane, fruit, vegetables, spices; some cattle, pigs, poultry.

French history The subject is traditionally divided into chronological periods reflecting the development of the French nation-state after the Gallo-Roman, Merovingian, and Carolingian periods. The accepted divisions coincide with dynasties and constitutions: the Capetians (987–1328); the Valois (1328–1589); the Bourbons (1589–1793); the Revolution and First

Empire (1789–1814/15); the Restoration and July Monarchy (1815–48); the Second Republic (1848–52); the Second Empire (1852–70); the Third Republic (1870–1940); the Fourth Republic (1945–58); and the Fifth Republic (1958–). Within this framework certain episodes have evoked considerable controversy, such as the 1789 Revolution, and wartime France and the Vichy regime (1940–4). Political history fell somewhat out of favour with the pre-eminence of the *Annales* school and the present emphasis on social history through local studies, as in the work of French scholar, Emmanuel Le Roy Ladurie (1929–).

French horn *horn*

French literature A literature emerging in the 12th-c from late Latin, which continued to exercise a powerful influence. The earliest vernacular works were the *chansons de geste*, soon followed by courtly romances dealing with both classical and Celtic subjects (Chrétien de Troyes' *Lancelot*, late 12th-c), and the allegorical romance, of which the *Roman de la Rose* (mid-13th-c) is the finest example, its two parts contrasting romance and early realism. François Villon (1431–?) was the most remarkable lyric poet in mediaeval France, to be matched by Ronsard of La Pléiade, while the greatest French writer of the 16th-c was Rabelais, with his inexhaustible masterpieces *Gargantua* and *Pantagruel* (1532–52). The 17th-c was a golden age in French literature, the milieu of court and salon producing not only the three great dramatists Corneille, Racine, and Molière, but the classicists Malherbe and Boileau, the philosopher Descartes, Pascal (*Pensées*, 1660), La Rochefoucauld (*Maximes*, 1665–78), and La Fontaine. It also saw the creation of the Académie Française by Richelieu in 1634. The 18th-c is best characterized by the rationalist satire of Voltaire and the vast *Encyclopédie* (1751–65) written under Diderot. Rousseau heralded the Romantic movement (*Confessions* 1764–70), which was powerfully represented in France by Chateaubriand and Lamartine, Musset, and Vigny, and by the dominating figure of Victor Hugo in verse and prose (*Les Misérables*, 1862). The Realist/Naturalist novel took centre stage in the mid-19th-c, with Balzac, Flaubert (*Madame Bovary*, 1857), and Zola; but the Symbolist poets claimed their due, in Baudelaire, Verlaine, Rimbaud, and Mallarmé.

In the 20th-c, French literature was very diverse, ranging from the intense self-exploration of Proust and Genet and the experiments with the *nouveau roman* of Nathalie Sarraute and Robbe-Grillet to the Catholic revival with Claudel and Maritain and the political *engagement* of Aragon and Sartre. In addition, there is the existentialist fiction of Camus and the absurdist theatre of Ionesco and Beckett; philosophical preoccupations (serious and playful) continue to fascinate the French writer. Meanwhile, Surrealism in all its forms has remained a pervasive influence.

French marigold *African marigold*

French Polynesia [polineezhuh], formerly **French Settlements in Oceania** (to 1958), official name **Territory of French Polynesia**, Fr **Territoire de la Polynésie Française** pop (2000e) 246 000; area 3941 sq km/1521 sq mi. Island territory comprising five scattered archipelagoes in the SE Pacific Ocean, between the Cook Is (W) and the Pitcairn Is (E); capital, Papeete; timezone GMT −6; chief ethnic group, Polynesian; chief religion, Christianity (87%); official language, French and Tahitian, with local languages widely spoken; island groups include the Society Is (including Tahiti and Bora-Bora), Tuamotu Archipelago, Gambier Is, Marquesas Is, and Tubuai Is; mainly volcanic, mountainous, and ringed with coral reefs; some low-lying coral atolls; hot and humid climate (Nov–Apr); tropical storms less frequent than in the W Pacific; French missionary activity, 19th-c; French protectorates introduced from 1843; 'French Oceania' became an Overseas Territory, 1958; administered by a high commissioner and 10-member Council of Ministers, elected by a 30-member Territorial Assembly; economy based on agricultural smallholdings (vegetables, fruit) and plantations (coconut oil, copra); cultured pearls, vanilla, citrus fruits, tourism; maintenance of the French nuclear test base.

French Republican calendar A calendar introduced during the French Revolution by the National Convention to herald the beginning of a new epoch for France and for humanity in general, and to further the anti-clerical campaign for de-christianization. The structure and nomenclature were devised by a committee under the deputy, Fabre d'Eglantine, Year 1 dating from the abolition of the monarchy and the declaration of the Republic (22 Sep 1792). Twelve 30-day months were introduced and divided into three 10-day weeks of *decadi*, eliminating Sundays. They were given names derived from nature, notably the seasons: Vendémiaire, Brumaire, Frimaire, Nivôse, Pluviôse, Ventôse, Germinal, Floréal, Prairial, Messidor, Thermidor, and Fructidor. The system was abolished by Napoleon (1805).

French Revolution A complex upheaval, profoundly affecting every aspect of government and society, and therefore considered a significant turning point in French history. Although its causes have been subject to conflicting interpretation, conventionally the start was the summoning of the Estates General, the Assembly representing the three estates of the realm (spring 1789). Subsequently the National Assembly and its successor, the Constituent Assembly, responded to public pressure, such as the storming of the Bastille (14 Jul 1789), with wide-sweeping political, social, and economic measures (1789–91). These included the abolition of feudal, aristocratic, and clerical privileges, a Declaration of the Rights of Man, the establishment of a constitutional government, the confiscation of church estates, and a reorganization of Church-state relations in the Civil Constitution of the Clergy (1790). Thus the *ancien régime* was effectively dismantled in the name of liberty, equality, and fraternity. Meanwhile the royal family had been removed from Versailles to Paris (Oct 1789), but after their flight to Varennes (Jun 1791) their fate was sealed. A Legislative Assembly was elected, and France was declared a republic (1792). Louis XVI and his queen, Marie Antoinette, were executed (1793). The Revolution then entered more dramatic phases, marked by political extremism and bitter rivalry between Girondins and Jacobins (the latter led by Robespierre). Though the Jacobins seized control of the Committee of Public Safety (Jul 1793) and instituted the dictatorship of the Terror, Robespierre's short-lived triumph ended with his execution (1794). The Convention suppressed the *sans-culottes* with military force before establishing the government of the Directory (1795), which was in turn overthrown by Napoleon Bonaparte in the Brumaire coup (1799). Under the Consulate (1799–1804) and the First Empire (1804–15), many of the ideas of the Revolution, such as popular sovereignty and civil equality, were disseminated in those areas of Europe subjected to French rule. (*see panel p.592*)

French Revolutionary Wars A series of campaigns between France and neighbouring European states hostile to the Revolution and to French hegemony, merging ultimately into the Napoleonic Wars (1799–1815). Starting with France's declaration of war on Emperor Francis II, Prussia, and Sardinia, which precipitated the War of the First Coalition (1792–7), French forces attacked the Rhine, the Netherlands, and Savoy, after checking an initial Austro-Prussian advance at Valmy (1792). France later extended hostilities to Britain, Holland, and Spain (1793); after successfully invading the Netherlands (1794), the French broke the Coalition (1795–6), isolating Britain (1797). A Second Coalition (1798) expelled French forces from Italy and the Rhinelands, before suffering defeat by Napoleon (1799–1800).

French Southern and Antarctic Territories, Fr **Terres Australes et Antarctiques Françaises** French overseas territory, comprising Adélie Land in Antarctica and the islands of Kerguélen, Crozet, Amsterdam, and St Paul in the S Indian Ocean; established, 1955; governed by an administrator and 7-member consultative council which meets twice yearly in Paris.

French Union A term for the political entity of the French Empire introduced by the constitution of the Fourth Republic in 1946. Former colonies were reclassified as departments of France or overseas territories; trust territories became overseas

Events Of The French Revolution 1789–1799

1789	
Mar–May	Election of deputies to the Estates General.
5 May	Opening of the Estates General.
17 Jun	Title of National Assembly adopted by the Third Estate.
Jul	The 'Great Fear'.
14 Jul	Seizing of the Bastille in Paris.
4 Aug	Abolition of the feudal regime.
26 Aug	Declaration of the Rights of Man and Citizen.
Oct	Foundation of the Club des Jacobins.
5–6 Oct	Louis XVI brought to Paris from Versailles.
19 Oct	National Assembly installed in Paris.
1790	
19–23 Jun	Abolition of hereditary nobility and titles.
Jul	Foundation of the Club des Cordeliers.
1791	
20–21 Jun	Flight of the King to Varennes.
16 Jul	Foundation of the Club des Feuillants.
13 Sep	Acceptance of the Constitution by the King.
Oct	Formation of the Legislative Assembly.
1792	
9–10 Aug	Attack on the Tuileries, functions of the King suspended.
12 Aug	King and royal family imprisoned in the Temple.
2–6 Sep	Massacre of nobles and clergy in prisons.
21 Sep	Abolition of the monarchy.
22 Sep	Proclamation of the Republic.
1793	
17 Jan	National Convention votes for the death of the King.
21 Jan	Execution of the King.
1 Feb	Declaration of war against England and Holland.
Mar	Tribunal created in Paris (later called the Revolutionary Tribunal).
6 Apr	Creation of the Committee of Public Safety.
27 Jul	Robespierre elected to the Committee of Public Safety.
5 Sep–27 Jul 1794	Reign of Terror.
11 Sep	Creation of the Revolutionary Army of Paris.
16 Oct	Trial and execution of Marie Antoinette.
24–31 Oct	Trial and execution of the Girondins.
1794	
5 Apr	Execution of the Cordeliers, including Danton.
24 Mar	Execution of the Hebertists.
8 Jun	Inaugural Feast of the Supreme Being and of Nature.
27 Jul (9 Thermidor)	Fall of Robespierre.
19 Nov	Closure of the Club des Jacobins.
1795	
21 Feb	Separation of Church and State.
31 May	Suppression of the Revolutionary Tribunal.
8 Jun	Death of Louis XVII in the Temple.
5 Oct (13 Vendémiaire)	Royalists crushed by Bonaparte.
27 Oct–4 Nov 1799	Institution of the Directory.
9 Nov (18 Brumaire)	Abolition of the Directory.

territories; and former protectorates became associated states. The latter had all become independent when the Union was replaced by the Community in 1958.

French West Indies A geographical label for two French overseas departments, the islands of Martinique and Guadeloupe, and their dependencies, notably the sub-prefectures of St Martin and St Barthélémy (St Barth). The islands have been departments of France since 1946.

Freneau, Philip (Morin) [frenoh] (1752–1832) Sailor and poet, born in New York City, USA. He studied at the College of New Jersey (later Princeton University), commanded a privateer in the American War of Independence, was captured by the British, and wrote *The British Prison Ship* (1781). He wrote many patriotic poems, publishing them in the *National Gazette* (1791–3), which he founded and edited. He is considered the leading US poet of the 18th-c.

Freon *CFCs*

frequency The number of complete cycles per second for a vibrating system or other repetitive motion; symbol f or ν; units Hz, (hertz). For wave motion, it corresponds to the number of complete waves per second. The frequency of tuning C on the piano is 523·25 Hz; the frequency of yellow light 5×10^{14} Hz.

frequency modulation (FM) In wave motion, the altering of frequency in a systematic way, leaving amplitude unchanged. In FM radio, an electrical signal modulates the frequency of a broadcast carrier radio wave by an amount proportional to the signal amplitude. Demodulation takes place in the radio receiver to give a copy of the original signal.

fresco An ancient technique for painting on walls, perfected in the 14th–16th-c in Italy; it is difficult, and is nowadays uncommon. The wall is prepared with layers of plaster, sometimes as many as four, the penultimate (*arricciato*) being marked out with the artist's design (underdrawing or *sinopia*). The final layer of lime-plaster (*intonaco*) is then laid and, while it is still wet (*fresco* means 'fresh' in Italian), the artist works on this with a water-based paint. Just enough intonaco is laid for one day's work (*giornata*). The colours bond into the plaster by chemical action and are therefore very permanent, but they dry lighter, a factor the artist must bear in mind.

Fresno [freznoh] 36°44N 119°47W, pop (2000e) 427 700. Seat of Fresno Co, C California, USA; founded, 1872; city status, 1885; airfield; railway; university; centre of a wine-producing region; grapes, grain, cotton, cattle, agricultural machinery, food processing; often called the world's raisin centre.

Freud, Anna [froyd] (1895–1982) Psychoanalyst, born in Vienna, Austria, the daughter of Sigmund Freud. She chaired the Vienna Psychoanalytic Society, and emigrated with her father to London in 1938, where she organized (1940–5) a residential war nursery for homeless children. She was a founder of child psychoanalysis.

Freud, Sigmund [froyd] (1856–1939) Founder of psychoanalysis, born in Freiburg, Moravia (now Príbor, E Czech Republic), of Jewish parentage. He studied medicine at Vienna, then specialized in neurology, and later in psychopathology. Finding hypnosis inadequate, he substituted the method of 'free association', allowing the patient to express thoughts in a state of relaxed consciousness, and interpreting the data of childhood and dream recollections. He became convinced, despite his own puritan sensibilities, of the fact of infantile sexuality, a theory which isolated him from the medical profession. In 1900 he published his major work, *Die Traumdeutung* (The Interpretation of Dreams), arguing that dreams are disguised manifestations of repressed sexual wishes (in contrast with the widely-held modern view that dreams are simply a biological manifestation of the random firing of brain neurones during a particular state of consciousness). In 1902, he was appointed to a professorship in Vienna, despite previous academic anti-semitism, and began to gather disciples. Out of this grew the Vienna Psychoanalytical Society (1908) and the International Psychoanalytic Association (1910), which included Adler and Jung. It was not until 1930, when he was awarded the Goethe prize, that his work ceased to arouse active opposition from public bodies. In 1933 Hitler banned psychoanalysis, and after Austria had been overrun, Freud and his family were extricated from the hands of the Gestapo and allowed to emigrate. He settled in Hampstead, London, where he died.

Freudian criticism Literary criticism which uses the insights of psychoanalysis, as in Freud's own reading of *Hamlet* in terms of the Oedipus complex (1900); also known as **psychoanalytical criticism**. Such criticism may be 'reductive', although Freud himself cautioned against offering simple psychoanalytic explanations for complex works of art. The early tendency to psychoanalyse characters or, more doubtfully, their creators, has been replaced or at least supplemented by a recognition of the fluidity of the self and a more sophisticated awareness of how language transgresses the boundary of conscious/unconscious. Analysis therefore involves the whole critical discourse, including author, text, and reader.

Frey *Freya*

Freya or **Freyja** [fraya] In Northern mythology, the goddess of love and beauty, especially first love. She and her brother **Frey**, the male fertility god, were the children of Niord and Skadi. To obtain the Brising necklace she betrayed her husband, Odur, and had to wander through the world looking for him.

friar A member of one of the mendicant ('begging') Christian religious orders founded in the Middle Ages. Unlike monks, they are not confined to a single monastery or abbey.

friarbird A bird of the honeyeater family, native to N Australia and the adjacent islands of SE Asia, also known as the **leatherhead**; songbird with head partly or totally naked (hence its common names); eats fruit, insects, and nectar. (Genus: *Philemon*, 17 species. Family: Meliphagidae.)

friar's balsam A resin from the stem of *Styrax benzoin* and *Styrax paralleloneurus* containing aromatic acids (benzoic and cinnamic acids), prepared in an alcoholic solution. It is used as an inhalation in the treatment of chronic bronchitis, and can also be used undiluted as an antiseptic.

Fribourg [freeborg], Ger **Freiburg** [friybork] 46°49N 7°09E, pop (2000e) 36 000. Mediaeval town and capital of Fribourg canton, W Switzerland; on a peninsula in the R Sarine, 27 km/17 mi SW of Bern; founded, 1178; persisted as a Catholic stronghold in the Reformation; bishopric; railway junction; university (1889); foodstuffs, beer, engineering; Cathedral of St Nicholas (13th–15th-c), Church of the Woodcutters (13th-c), town hall (16th-c).

Frick, Henry (Clay) (1849–1919) Industrialist, born in West Overton, Pennsylvania, USA. He had little education, but grasped at post-Civil-War expansion by forming a company to supply the Pittsburgh steel mills with coke, and was a millionaire at 30. He became chairman of the Carnegie Steel Co in 1889, reorganizing it to become the largest steel manufacturer in the world. A hard and ruthless employer, he was shot and stabbed during the steel strike at Homestead, PA, in 1892, but recovered. He broke with Carnegie in 1900, and became director of United States Steel (1901). He built up the distinguished Frick Collection of fine art, which he bequeathed to New York City, and also endowed hospitals, schools, and a large park in Pittsburgh.

Fricker, Peter (Racine) (1920–90) Composer, born in London, UK. He studied at the Royal College of Music, and became musical director of Morley College, London (1952–64), professor of music at the University of California, Santa Barbara (1964–5), then resident composer there. Influenced by Bartók and Schoenberg, he wrote several symphonies, the oratorio *The Vision of Judgement* (1957–8), and other chamber, choral, and keyboard works.

friction A force acting against the direction of motion for two objects in contact sliding across one another. Friction may be sufficient to prevent actual relative motion. It is caused by surface roughness, and by the attraction of the atoms of one surface for those of the other. The **coefficient of friction**, μ, expressed as a number, has only two possible values for a given pair of surfaces, depending on whether the surfaces are moving relative to one another (the *kinetic coefficient of friction*) or are stationary (the *static coefficient of friction*, which is larger). A small coefficient of friction means that the two surfaces slide easily across one another. The force of friction is directly proportional to the applied load, and independent of the apparent area of contact. For surfaces moving relative to one another, dynamic friction is independent of sliding velocity.

Friedan, Betty (Naomi) [freedan], *née* **Goldstein** (1921–) Feminist leader and writer, born in Peoria, Illinois, USA. She studied at Smith College, and became known in 1963 with the publication of her book *The Feminine Mystique*. She was the founder and first president of the National Association for Women in 1966. In *The Second Stage* (1981), she emphasized the importance of both the new and traditional female roles.

Friedman, Milton [freedman] (1912–) Economist, born in New York City, USA. He studied at Chicago and New York universities, and after eight years at the National Bureau of Economic Research (1937–45) became professor of economics at Chicago (1946–83). A leading monetarist, his work includes the permanent income theory of consumption, and the role of money in determining events, particularly the US Great Depression. His ideas have been influential with a number of right-wing governments. He was awarded the Nobel Prize for Economics in 1976. Since 1977, he has been senior research fellow at the Hoover Institution at Stanford University.

Friel, Brian [freel] (1929–) Playwright, born in Killyclogher, Co Tyrone, W Northern Ireland, UK. He was a teacher in Derry, writing short stories and radio plays, before turning to the live theatre with *This Doubtful Paradise* (staged in Belfast in 1959). He gained recognition with *Philadelphia, Here I Come!* (1964), the first of numerous plays – including *The Freedom of the City* (1974), *Faith Healer* (1979), *Translations* (1980), *Dancing at Lughnasa* (1990), *Wonderful Tennessee* (1993), *Molly Sweeney* (1995), and *Give me your Answer, Do!* (1997) – which have made him internationally the best known of contemporary playwrights in Ireland.

friendly society A voluntary mutual-aid organization in the UK which provides financial assistance to members in times of sickness, unemployment, or retirement. The register of Friendly Societies includes some that are several hundred years old. Their operations are governed by the Friendly Society Acts (1974–1984).

Friends *Aniston, Jennifer; Cox, Courtenay; Kudrow, Lisa; LeBlanc, Matt; Perry, Matthew; Schwimmer, David*

Friends, Society of A Christian sect founded by George Fox and others in mid-17th-c England, and formally organized in 1667; members are popularly known as **Quakers**, possibly because of Fox's injunction 'to quake at the word of the Lord'. Persecution led William Penn to establish a Quaker colony (Pennsylvania) in 1682. Belief in the 'inner light', a living contact with the divine Spirit, is the basis of its meetings for worship, where Friends gather in silence until moved by the Spirit to speak. They emphasize simplicity in all things, and are active reformers promoting tolerance, justice, and peace. Today most meetings have programmed orders of worship, though meetings based on silence (unprogrammed) still prevail in the UK and parts of the USA.

Friends of the Earth An international federation of environmental pressure groups with autonomous organizations in member countries. It conducts campaigns on topics such as safe energy, the recycling of waste, acid rain, tropical rainforest destruction, the preservation of endangered species, and transport.

Friese-Greene, William [freez green], originally **William Edward Green** (1855–1921) Photographer and inventor, born in Bristol, SW England, UK. In the 1880s he designed a camera to expose a sequence of photographs for projection by lantern slides as a moving image, and is thus claimed by some as the English inventor of cinematography; but he did not in fact propose perforated strips of film for either photography or projection. His first successful picture, using celluloid film, was shown in public in 1890.

Friesland [freesland], ancient **Frisia** pop (2000e) 630 000; land area 3352 sq km/1294 sq mi. Province in N Netherlands; includes most of the West Frisian Is; capital, Leeuwarden; other chief towns, Harlingen, Sneek; major livestock farming area, specializing in butter and Frisian cattle; extensive land reclamation along North Sea coast.

frieze The middle part of an entablature on a classical building, usually decorated. It may also be the decorative band running along the upper part of an internal wall and below the cornice.

frigate A small warship in World War 2, superior in speed and armament to a corvette, but less powerful and smaller than a destroyer. Its present role is mainly anti-submarine and general-purpose. In days of sail, frigates were used as scouts for the main fleet, being smaller, faster, and less heavily armed than ships of the line.

frigate bird A large bird, native to tropical seas; male with coloured inflatable pouch on throat; steals fish from other birds; unable to take off from level ground, but a good flier, covering long distances. (Genus: *Fregata*, 5 species. Family: Fregatidae.)

Frigg or **Frigga** In Norse mythology, the wife of Odin, and goddess of married love (often confused with Freya).

frigidity A condition in which the female's participation in the sexual act is not accompanied by physiological or psychological arousal, and there is loss of sexual desire. It is sometimes associated with dyspareunia.

frilled lizard An agamid lizard (*Chlamydosaurus kingi*) native to New Guinea and N Australia; slim body; neck with large cape-like frill of brightly coloured skin; frill usually folded, but can be expanded in courtship and to deter predators; inhabits dry woodland; may climb tree or run upright on hind legs when alarmed.

Friml, (Charles) Rudolf [friml] (1879–1972) Composer, born in Prague, Czech Republic. He studied at the Prague Conservatory, and settled in the USA in 1906, where he made his name as a composer of light operas, including *Rose Marie* (1924) and *The Vagabond King* (1925). He became a US citizen in 1925.

Fringe, the Cultural events, particularly theatrical performances, presented around a Festival but not central to it. The term has thus come to be applied to theatre groups working on the margins of the establishment, or to any style of theatre not part of orthodoxy. Fringe productions usually require actors, designers, and directors to work for no money or on a profit-share basis. There are particularly healthy fringe scenes in London, Edinburgh, and New York.

Fringillidae [frinjilidee] A family of small seed-eating birds (approximately 125 species); native to the Americas, Eurasia, and Africa, and introduced in Australasia; also known as **finches**; 9 large primary feathers in wing, 12 large feathers in tail; female builds nest and incubates eggs.

fringing reef *atoll*

Frisbee A brand name for a type of plastic disc approximately the size of a dinner plate, thrown through the air. Most discs are used as a leisure pursuit, but competitions exist. The Frisbee was introduced in the USA in the late 1950s by the Wham-O Manufacturing Company. The name is said to have derived from the defunct Frisbie Baking Company which produced the Mother Frisbie's Pies.

Frisch, Karl von (1886–1982) Ethologist, born in Vienna, Austria. He studied at Munich and Trieste, then taught zoology at several universities, much of his career being spent at Munich, where he founded the Zoological Institute (1932). He was a key figure in developing ethology using field observation of animals combined with ingenious experiments. His 40-year study of the honey bee showed that forager bees communicate information (on the location of food sources) in part by use of coded dances. In 1973 he shared the Nobel Prize for Physiology or Medicine.

Frisch, Max (Rudolf) (1911–91) Playwright and novelist, born in Zürich, N Switzerland. He became a newspaper correspondent and a student of architecture, while developing his literary career. His novels include *Stiller* (1954), a satire on the Swiss way of life, *Homo Faber* (1957), and *Bluebeard* (1983). His plays, modern morality pieces, include *Nun singen sie wieder* (1945, Now They Sing Again), *Andorra* (1962), and *Triptych* (1981).

Frisch, Otto Robert (1904–79) Physicist, born in Vienna, Austria. He studied at Vienna, and in 1945 became head of the nuclear physics division at Harwell. He and Meitner (his aunt) first described 'nuclear fission' in 1939 to explain Hahn's results with uranium and neutrons. He moved to Birmingham in 1939, and worked with Peierls on uranium fission and associated neutron emission, then became involved in the atomic bomb project at Los Alamos, USA. In 1947 he became professor of natural philosophy at Cambridge, UK, and directed the nuclear physics department of the Cavendish Laboratory.

Frisch, Ragnar (Anton Kittil) (1895–1973) Economist, born in Oslo, Norway. A pioneer of econometrics, he created national economic planning decision models, and advised developing countries. In 1969 he shared the first Nobel Prize for Economics.

Frisian *Germanic languages*

Frisian Islands [frizeeuhn] Island chain in the North Sea, extending along the coasts of The Netherlands, Germany, and Denmark, and politically divided between these countries; includes the **North Frisian Is** (Ger **Nordfriesische Inseln**), notably (German) Sylt, Föhr, Nordstrand, Pellworm, Amrum, and (Danish) Rømø, Fanø, Mandø; the German **East Frisian Is** (Ger **Ostfriesische Inseln**), notably Borkum, Juist, Norderney, Langeoog, Spiekeroog, Wangerooge; and the Dutch **West Frisian Is** (Dutch **Friese Eilanden**), notably Texel, Vlieland, Terschelling, Ameland, Schiermonnikoog; tourism, fishing, sheep, cattle, potatoes, oats; several areas of reclaimed land.

fritillary (botany) [fritilaree] A perennial with a small scaly bulb (*Fritillaria meleagris*), native to Europe; stem growing to 50 cm/20 in; leaves grass-like, bluish; flower a broad bell 3–5 cm/1½–2 in, drooping, dull purple rarely white, with a distinctive chequered pattern; cultivated for ornament. It is also called **snake's head** and **guinea flower** from its colour and the drooping habit of the flower. (Family: Liliaceae.)

fritillary (entomology) [fritilaree] A colourful, day-flying butterfly; wings typically yellow-brown with black markings; forelegs reduced, non-functional; eggs ribbed; caterpillars with spines. (Order: Lepidoptera. Family: Nymphalidae.)

Frobisher, Sir Martin [frohbisher] (c.1535–94) Navigator, born in Altofts, West Yorkshire, N England, UK. He made several attempts to find the Northwest Passage to Cathay (1576–8), reaching Labrador and Hudson Bay. *Frobisher Bay* is named after him. In 1585 he commanded a vessel in Drake's expedition to the West Indies, and in 1588 he was knighted for his services against the Armada. He was mortally wounded at the siege of Crozon, near Brest.

Fröding, Gustaf [froeding] (1860–1911) Poet, born near Karlstad, SWC Sweden. He studied at Uppsala, became a schoolmaster and journalist, and suffered several periods of mental illness. Perhaps the greatest Swedish lyric poet, he is often compared with Burns. His use of dialect and folksong rhythm in the portrayal of local characters can be seen in his first collection, *Guitarr och dragharmonika* (1891, Guitar and Concertina).

Froebel, Friedrich (Wilhelm August) [froebl] (1782–1852) Educationist, born in Oberweissbach, C Germany. He studied at Jena, Göttingen, and Berlin, and in 1805 began teaching at Frankfurt. In 1816 he put into practice his educational system, whose aim, to help the child's mind grow naturally and spontaneously, he expounded in *Die Menschenerziehung* (1826, The Education of Man). In 1836 he opened his first kindergarten school at Blankenburg, and spent the rest of his life organizing other such schools, as well as providing educational materials (eg geometrical shapes) for young children, to encourage learning through play.

frog An amphibian of Order: Anura (3500 species), found worldwide except in the Arctic and Antarctic; short body with fewer than 10 vertebrae in the spine; inhabits diverse environments. The smooth wet-skinned species are called **frogs**; the rough dry-skinned species (adapted to drier habitats) are called **toads**. This distinction reflects the different lifestyles of the species; there is no technical difference between the two (and the name *frog* is sometimes used for all species). Anurans of the family Ranidae are sometimes called **true frogs**, those of the family Bufonidae **true toads**.

frogbit A free-floating aquatic plant (*Hydrocharis morsus-ranae*) producing stolons with leaves and roots at nodes, native to Europe and Asia; leaves 3 cm/1¼ in diameter, kidney-shaped; flowers unisexual, c.2 cm/¾ in diameter, white, 3-petalled. It produces winter buds which sink and remain dormant, floating to the surface in the spring. (Family: Hydrocharitaceae.)

frogfish Bizarre, bottom-dwelling fish found amongst rocks and marine growths of warm seas; length up to 20 cm/8 in; body with strong cryptic coloration, skin loose and warty, pectoral fins used for crawling across bottom; filament on front of head acts as lure to attract prey; includes *Antennarius hispidus*, also known as **toadfish**. (Genus: *Antennarius*. Family: Antennariidae.)

froghopper A small, hopping insect that feeds by sucking the sap of plants; also known as **cuckoo-spit insect** and **spittlebug**. The eggs are laid on the plants, and hatch into sedentary larvae which surround themselves with mucus-like 'cuckoo spit' that protects them against drying out and predation. (Order: Homoptera. Family: Cercopidae, c.2500 species.)

frogmouth A large, nocturnal, nightjar-like bird native to Australasia (except New Zealand) and SE Asia; short but very broad bill (hence the name); inhabits forests; eats mainly small animals foraged from ground. (Family: Podargidae, 12 species.)

Fröhlich, Alfred *Babinski, Joseph*

Froissart, Jean [frwasah(r)] (c.1333–c.1404) Historian and poet, born in Valenciennes, N France. He served Philippa of Hainault, the wife of Edward III of England (1361–9), and also travelled widely in Scotland, France, and Italy. Returning to Hainault, he began to compile his *Chronicles*, wrote poems for noble patrons, and became private chaplain to Guy of Châtillon. His *Chronicles*, covering European history from 1325 to 1400, deal in particular with the Hundred Years' War, and were heavily influenced by his devotion to chivalric principles.

Frome [froom] 51°14N 2°20W, pop (2000e) 22 000. Town in Somerset, SW England, UK; on the R Frome, 17 km/10 mi S of Bath; a town of Anglo-Saxon origin with narrow alleys and old stone houses; railway; textiles, plastics, printing, engineering, perry making; Longleat House (1568), 8 km/5 mi NE.

Fromm, Erich (1900–80) Psychoanalyst and social philosopher, born in Frankfurt, WC Germany. He studied at the universities of Frankfurt, Heidelberg, Munich, and the Berlin Institute of Psychoanalysis, and held various university appointments before becoming professor of psychiatry at New York University in 1962. A neo-Freudian, he is known for his investigations into motivation. His works include *Escape from Freedom* (1941) and *The Sane Society* (1955).

Frondes, the [frõd] A series of civil revolts in France during the regency of Anne of Austria, caused by economic grievances and the excessive opportunism of central government, directed by Cardinal Mazarin. The disturbances, named after a contemporary street urchins' game, developed into two phases: the Parlementary Fronde (1648–9), and that of the Princes (1650–3). After the declaration of Louis XIV's majority (1651), the princes' opposition was slowly undermined; royal forces under Turenne recovered Paris (1652) and the provinces (1652–3), ending the most serious threat to the central government during the *ancien régime*.

front A meteorological term for the sharp boundary between two parcels of air of different origin and characteristics, along which a steep horizontal temperature gradient exists. A **warm front** is the leading boundary of warm air, and a **cold front** is the leading boundary of polar or cold air. Each front is associated with its characteristic weather. In a depression, the meeting of the cold front with the warm front results in an **occluded front**.

Front de Libération Nationale *FLN*

Frontenac, Louis de Buade, comte de (Count of) [frõtenak] (1620–98) French-Canadian statesman, born in St Germain-en-Laye, NC France. He served in the army, and in 1672 was appointed governor of the French possessions in North America. He was recalled for misgovernment in 1682, but was sent out again in 1689. He extended the boundaries of New France down the Mississippi, launched attacks on New England villages, repulsed the British siege of Quebec, and broke the power of the Iroquois.

front-line states An informal grouping of seven states bordering South Africa, defined by their position with respect to the apartheid system: Angola, Botswana, Mozambique, Namibia, Tanzania, Zambia, Zimbabwe.

front projection The projection of an image on to an opaque screen to be viewed from the same side as the projector, the normal practice for cinema and audio-visual presentation. In forms of composite cinematography and still photography, a highly directional reflective screen is used to show a background scene against which actors or subjects in the foreground are photographed.

Frost, Sir David (Paradine) (1939–) Broadcaster and businessman, born in Tenterden, Kent, SE England, UK. He studied at Cambridge, participated in the Footlights revues, and edited *Granta* before moving into television in 1961. He presented *That Was the Week That Was* (BBC, 1962–3), an innovative, satirical, and irreverant late-night revue show, and has since hosted many programmes in Britain and America, such as *The Frost Report* (1966–7), *The David Frost Show* (1969–72), *The Guinness Book of World Records* (from 1981), and a range of *Frost Over* ... programmes, dealing with America, Australia, and several other countries. A co-founder of London Weekend Television, in 1983 he was a co-founder, director, and presenter of Britain's TV–AM. His many international honours include the Golden Rose of Montreux (1967) and two Emmy Awards (1970, 1971). He was knighted in 1993.

Frost, Robert (Lee) (1874–1963) Poet, born in San Francisco, California, USA. He studied at Harvard, and became a teacher, cobbler, and New Hampshire farmer before going to Britain (1912–15), where he published *A Boy's Will* (1913) and *North of Boston* (1914), which gave him an international reputation. Back in the USA, he taught at Amherst and Michigan universities. *New Hampshire* (1923) won the Pulitzer Prize, as did his first *Collected Poems* in 1930 and *A Further Range* (1936). A last collection, *In the Clearing*, appeared in 1962. At the time of his death, he was regarded as the unofficial laureate of the USA.

Frost, Sadie, originally **Sadie Liza Vaughn** (1967–) Actress, born in London, UK. She became known for her role as a vampire in *Bram Stoker's Dracula* (1992), and later films include *Splitting Heirs* (1993), *Shopping* (1994), *Captain Jack* (1998), and *Uprising* (2001). She married actor Jude Law in 1997 (divorced 2003) and in 1999 they co-founded a film production company, Natural Nylon, together with other fellow actors including Ewan MacGregor.

frost A meteorological condition which occurs when the air temperature is at or below the freezing point of water, causing condensation. It may cause considerable damage to plants, especially if ground frost is accompanied by air frost.

frostbite The damage of exposed parts of the body by the direct effect of extreme cold. The fingers, nose, and feet are especially vulnerable, and the part may die and become gangrenous.

frottage [frotahzh] A technique used by some modern artists, notably Max Ernst, whereby paper is placed over a textured surface, such as a plank of wood, and rubbed with a pencil or crayon producing an impression. It is often combined with collage.

Froude, James Anthony [frood] (1818–94) Writer and historian, born in Dartington, Devon, SW England, UK. He studied at Oxford, where he became part of the Oxford Movement. His early novels were controversial, notably *The Nemesis of Faith* (1848), and he was forced to resign his post. He then worked as an essayist and editor, and wrote his *History of England* (12 vols, 1856–69). He became Rector of St Andrews in 1869, and professor of modern history at Oxford in 1892.

fructose $C_6H_{12}O_6$. A simple sugar (a monosaccharide) found mainly in fruits in combination with glucose to produce the disaccharide, sucrose (table sugar). Fructose is twice as sweet as glucose, and has been used as a sweetening agent. Fructose consumption does not cause a rise in blood glucose, and so it can be tolerated by diabetics. Fructose intolerance is a very rare hereditary disease.

fruit Strictly, the ripened ovary and seeds of a plant, but more generally used to include any structures closely associated with these, such as a swollen receptacle. A **simple** or **true fruit** develops from a flower with one or several fused carpels; an **aggregate fruit** from a flower with several free carpels; and a **multiple fruit** from several flowers. When structures or tissues other than those of the gynecium are involved, the result is an **accessory** or **false fruit**. Fruits can be divided into two main groups: **dry** and **fleshy**; in the latter, the middle layer of the ovary wall becomes succulent. Further classification is based mainly on carpel or seed number, *dehiscence* (ie whether the fruit splits to release the seeds), and to a lesser extent on derivation of tissues. Dry fruits can be dehiscent or not; fleshy fruits are always indehiscent. Common names such as 'nut' and 'berry' are often wildly inaccurate in describing the actual type of fruit to which they are applied.

The role played in seed dispersal greatly influences the structure of the fruit, which may itself be dispersed as a single unit. Shape may be important for scattering the seeds, as with winged fruits, and in the use of bristles for attaching the fruit to passing animals or for anchoring it in the soil. Corky fruits provide buoyancy in water, while fleshy fruits may attract animals. Some plants produce different types of fruits to take advantage of more than one dispersal agent. A few plants are able to produce fruits without prior pollination and thus fertilization of the flowers, giving seedless fruits, eg banana, cucumber, and some citrus fruits. This trait, called *natural parthenocarpy*, can be commercially desirable, and fruit growers can imitate it by the use of hormones (*induced parthenocarpy*) to produce crops such as seedless tomatoes.

fruit bat *bat*

fruit fly A common name for flies of the families Drosophilidae and Tephritidae; mostly tropical. The latter contains c.4000 species of colourful flies, feeding on sap and fruit. Some are pests of economically important crops such as fruit, cucumber, and celery. (Order: Diptera.)

fruit sugar *fructose*

Frunze [frunzye] *Bishkek*

Fry, Christopher, pseudonym of **Christopher Harris** (1907–) Playwright, born in Bristol, SW England, UK. Educated at Bedford, he was a teacher and actor before becoming director of Tunbridge Wells Repertory Players (1932–6) and of the Playhouse at Oxford (1940). After service in World War 2 he began a series of major plays in free verse, often with undertones of religion and mysticism, including *A Phoenix Too Frequent* (1946) and *The Lady's Not For Burning* (1949). His later works include *Curtmantle* (1962) and *A Yard of Sun* (1970). He also produced highly successful translations of Anouilh and Giraudoux.

Fry, Elizabeth (1780–1845) Quaker prison reformer, born in Norwich, Norfolk, E England, UK. In 1810 she became a preacher in the Society of Friends. After seeing the terrible conditions for women in Newgate prison, she devoted her life to prison reform at home and abroad. She also founded hostels for the homeless, and charitable societies.

Fry, Roger (Eliot) (1866–1934) Art critic, aesthetic philosopher, and painter, born in London, UK. He studied at Cambridge, and is mainly remembered for his support of the Postimpressionist movement in England. He propounded an extreme formal theory of aesthetics, seeing the aesthetic quality of a work of art solely in terms of its formal characteristics. He was director of the Museum of Art in New York City (1905–10). When he returned to London he organized a young artists' collective named the Omega Workshops (1913–19). He became professor of fine art at Cambridge in 1933.

FT–SE Index (Financial Times–Stock Exchange Index), nickname **Footsie** A UK share index which records changes in the prices of shares of 100 leading British companies. It has been in operation since 1982, when it started with a notional value of 1000.

FT30 Index (Financial Times Index) A UK share index which records changes in the prices of shares of 30 leading British companies. It started in 1935 with a notional value of 100.

Fu-chou *Fuzhou*

Fuchs, Klaus (Emil Julius) [fooks] (1912–88) Physicist and atom spy, born in Rüsselsheim, WC Germany. He studied at Kiel and Leipzig, and escaped from Nazi persecution to Britain in 1933. Interned on the outbreak of World War 2, he was released and naturalized in 1942. From 1943 he worked in the USA on the atom bomb, and in 1946 became head of the theoretical physics division at Harwell, UK. In 1950 he was sentenced to 14 years' imprisonment for disclosing nuclear secrets to the Russians. On his release in 1959 he worked at East Germany's Central Institute for Nuclear Research until his retirement in 1979. He remained a committed communist, and received many honours from the East German Communist Party.

Fuchs, Sir Vivian Ernest [fookhs] (1908–99) Antarctic explorer and geologist, born in the Isle of Wight, S England, UK. He studied at Brighton College and Cambridge. After four geological expeditions in East Africa (1929–38), he served in West Africa and Germany during World War 2, then became director of the Falkland Islands Dependencies Survey (1947–50) and later of the British Antarctic Survey (1958–73). He was best known as the leader of the Commonwealth Trans-Antarctic Expedition (1955–8) which completed the first land crossing of Antarctica, from Shackleton Base via the S Pole to Scott Base, taking 99 days for the journey of 3500 km/2000 mi. He was knighted in 1958.

fuchsia [fyooshuh] An evergreen or deciduous shrub, native to Central and South America and New Zealand; leaves lance-shaped to oval, paired or in whorls; flowers pendulous with a long, red 4-lobed tube surrounding a purple bell with projecting stamens and style; numerous cultivars show a wide range of flower colours. It was named in honour of the German physician and herbalist, Leonhard Fuchs (1501–66). (Genus: *Fuchsia*, 100 species. Family: Onagraceae.)

Fucus [fyookuhs] A genus of brown seaweed, found in great abundance in intertidal zones of shores in the N hemisphere; some species have cavities in the blades for buoyancy; commonly known as **wrack**. (Class: Phaeophyceae. Order: Fucales.)

fuel A substance capable of releasing thermal energy in chemical, electrochemical, or nuclear processes. The oldest are combustible natural fuels (such as wood and cow dung). The chief solid **fossil fuels** are fossil vegetable matter in various degrees of carbonization, such as coal, lignite, and peat. **Liquid fuels** include some vegetable oils, but are mainly petroleum products. **Gaseous fuels** mainly comprise manufactured and natural gas. Some use is made of gaseous products arising from the degradation of biological waste. **Fuel cells** operate on an electrochemical reaction which takes place between hydrogen and oxygen. **Nuclear fuels** consist of radioactive isotopes, emitting energy spontaneously by nuclear change. **Rocket fuels** operate by reaction against high speed gases emitted on combustion. Fuels may be used to provide heat for steam generation, for direct combustion or explosion within a machine, for promoting chemical or metallurgical processes, or for environmental heating.

fuel injection A method of introducing the fuel into an engine cylinder. In a diesel engine the fuel is injected at high pressure directly into the combustion chamber. In a petrol engine a special fuel/mixture control unit (increasingly microprocessor controlled) replaces the conventional carburettor, to produce improved running and transient performance. In this system, the petrol is usually injected into the port immediately preceding the inlet valve rather than directly into the cylinder.

Fuentes, Carlos [fwentes] (1928–) Novelist and playwright, born in Mexico City, Mexico. He studied at the University of Mexico and the Institut des Hautes Etudes Internationales in Geneva. He became cultural attaché to the Mexican Embassy in Geneva (1950–2), press secretary to the UN Information Centre, Mexico City, and served as the Mexican ambassador to France (1975–7). His first collection of short-stories was *Los dias enmascarados* (1954, The Masked Days), and his novel *La muerte de Artemio Cruz* (1962, The Death of Artemio Cruz) established him as a major international writer. Other titles include *Terra nostra* (1975), *The Hydra Head* (1979), and selected essays, *Myself with Others* (1988). A further collection of short-stories, *La frontera de cristal*, appeared in 1995. He became professor of Latin-American Studies at Harvard in 1987.

Fugard, Athol (Harold Lanigan) [foogah(r)d] (1932–) Playwright, theatre director, and actor, born in Middleburg, Cape Province, SC South Africa. He studied at Port Elizabeth Technical College and Cape Town University, became director of the Serpent Players in Port Elizabeth (1965), and co-founded the Space Experimental Theatre, Cape Town (1972). His plays, set in contemporary South Africa, met with official opposition, notably *The Blood Knot* (1960) and *Boesman and Lena* (1969). Later works include *Road to Mecca* (1985), *A Place with the Pigs* (1988), *My Children, My Africa!* (1989), and *The Captain's Tiger* (1998). He has also written several film scripts, and a novel *Tsotsi* (1980).

fugu [fugoo] A Japanese globe fish or puffer fish, eaten as a delicacy at special restaurants, cooked or in small slices, raw. Parts of this white fish are poisonous and cause instant death. Only restaurant staff who have passed the official examination and have a special licence are allowed to prepare it.

fugue A musical composition (or part of one) in which a single theme announced by each 'voice' in turn serves to generate the whole, and usually reappears in different keys and sometimes in different guises (inverted, in shorter or longer note-values, etc).

Fujairah, al- [al fujiyra] pop (2000e) 77 600; area 1150 sq km/ 444 sq mi. Member state of the United Arab Emirates, bounded E by the Gulf of Oman; partly mountainous, with a fertile coastal plain and no desert; capital, al-Fujairah; people live mostly in scattered villages, depending on agriculture.

Fuji, Mount [fujee], or **Fujiyama**, also known as **Fuji-san** 35°23N 138°42E. Highest peak in Japan, in Chubu region, C Honshu; 88 km/55 mi WSW of Tokyo; dormant volcano rising to 3776 m/12 388 ft; an isolated peak with an almost perfect cone; crater diameter c.600 m/2000 ft; last eruption, 1707; snow-capped (Oct–May); sacred since ancient times; until the Meiji Restoration of 1868, no woman was allowed to climb it.

Fujiwara Style [fujiwahra] A style of art which flourished in Japan during the late Heian period (9th–12th-c). The aristocratic Fujiwara clan built temples and pagodas, decorated in a delicate, refined manner.

Fukuoka [fukwoka], formerly **Najime** 33°39N 130°21E, pop (2000e) 1 277 000. Port capital of Fukuoka prefecture, NE Kyushu, Japan; port name, Hakata; 145 km/90 mi NNE of Nagasaki; airport; railway; university (1911); institute of technology (1909); food processing, machinery, printing, chemicals, metal goods, shipbuilding; Dazaifu Temman-gu nearby (10th-c shrine, restored 1950).

Fulani [fulahnee], also called **Fulbe** or **Peul** Fula-speaking peoples dispersed across the Sahel zone of W Africa from Senegal to Cameroon. Originally pastoralists, they are today socially very diverse, and in many places are assimilated into the locally dominant culture. Predominantly Muslim, in the 19th-c they initiated several holy wars, and in some areas they established kingdoms. In the early 20th-c they became one of the prototypes of the indirect rule system.

Fulbe [fulbay] *Fulani*

Fulbright, J(ames) William (1905–95) Politician, lawyer, and writer, born in Sumner, Missouri, USA. He studied at Arkansas, Oxford, and George Washington universities, then taught law in Washington and Arkansas. He entered the US House of Representatives as a Democrat in 1943, and the US Senate in 1945. As chairman of the US Senate Committee on Foreign Relations, he became a major critic of the Vietnam War. He lost his Senate seat in 1974. He was also known for introducing the international exchange programme for scholars (*Fulbright scholarships*) in 1945.

Fuller, J(ohn) F(rederick) C(harles) (1878–1966) British general and military thinker, born in Chichester, West Sussex, S England, UK. He served in South Africa, and in World War 1 as a staff officer with the Tank Corps. He planned the breakthrough tank battle of Cambrai in 1917, and proposed the unfulfilled 'Plan 1919', advocating an all-mechanized army. His ideas were discounted, and he retired in 1933 to continue his prophetic if controversial military writings.

Fuller, (Sarah) Margaret (1810–50) Writer, feminist, and revolutionary, born in Cambridgeport, Massachusetts, USA. She entered the Transcendentalist circle that centred on Emerson, and despite a lack of higher education became known as one of its brightest stars. Her *Woman in the Nineteenth Century* (1845) is the earliest major piece of US feminist writing. She died in a shipwreck after taking part in the abortive Italian revolution of 1848.

Fuller, R(ichard) Buckminster (1895–1983) Inventor, designer, poet, and philosopher, born in Milton, Massachusetts, USA. He studied at Harvard, then served in the US Navy (1917–19). He developed the Dymaxion ('dynamic and maximum efficiency') House in 1927, and the Dymaxion streamlined, omnidirectional car in 1932. He also developed the geodesic dome. An enthusiastic educationist, he held a chair at Southern Illinois University (1959–75), and in 1962 became professor of poetry at Harvard. His many books include *Nine Chains to the Moon* (1938) and *Critical Path* (1981).

Fuller, Roy (Broadbent) (1912–91) Poet and novelist, born in Oldham, Lancashire, NW England, UK. He trained as a solicitor, and served in the Royal Navy during World War 2. His first collection, *Poems*, appeared in 1939, and his war-time experiences prompted *The Middle of a War* (1942) and *A Lost Season* (1944). His later poetic works include *Brutus's Orchard* (1957) and *Retreads* (1979). His novels include *Second Curtain* (1953) and *Image of a Society* (1956). He was professor of poetry at

Oxford (1968–73). *New and Collected Poems, 1934–84* were published in 1985, and two volumes of memoirs in 1989 and 1991.

fullerenes A series of molecular allotropes of carbon, of which the best characterized are C_{60} and C_{70}. Named after the designer Buckminster Fuller, C_{60} was first made and its structure proposed in 1985 by the astrophysicists D R Huffman (USA) and W Krätschmer (Germany). It has the form of a regular truncated icosahedron (60 vertices, 90 edges, and 12 pentagonal and 20 hexagonal faces), the shape of a standard soccer ball, also known as 'bucky balls'. C_{70} is somewhat elongated, rather like a rugby or American football. The properties of these compounds and their derivatives are being actively investigated, such as for superconductivity.

Fuller's earth Fine earthy material containing montmorillonite clay; formerly used for cleansing oil and grease from wool (*fulling*), and now used for clarifying vegetable oils by absorbing impurities.

fuller's teasel *teasel*

fulmar A marine tubenosed bird, native to N oceans (*Fulmarus glacialis*) or S oceans (2 species); comes to land only to breed; can eject oily and foul-smelling vomit to deter predators. (Family: Procellariidae.)

fulminate A salt containing the ion CNO^-, also called **isocyanate**. As its name suggests (Lat 'thunder'), it is an explosive; $Hg(CNO)_2$ is used as a detonator.

Fulton, Robert (1765–1815) Engineer, born in Lancaster Co, Pennsylvania, USA. He became a painter of miniature portraits and landscapes, then went to London (1786) and studied mechanical engineering. His inventions include a machine for spinning flax, a dredging machine, and the torpedo, but he is best known for his commercially successful development of the paddle-wheel steamboat which he first demonstrated on the Hudson R in 1807.

fumaric acid [fyoomarik] $C_2H_2(COOH)_2$, IUPAC **trans-butenedioic acid**, melting point 300°C (in a sealed tube). An unsaturated dicarboxylic acid, used in the manufacture of polyester resins. The salts are called *fumarates*, and are often used in preparations of drugs. It is a geometrical isomer of maleic acid.

fumitory A brittle-stemmed annual, sometimes scrambling or climbing, native to the N hemisphere and S Africa; leaves finely divided, bluish; flowers strongly zygomorphic, 2-lipped, with rounded spur. The name is sometimes claimed to mean 'ground smoke', referring to the foliage colour. There are two genera: *Corydalis*, petals lacking dark tips, capsules many-seeded; *Fumaria*, petals dark-tipped, nutlets 1-seeded. (Genus: *Fumaria*, c.50 species. Family: Fumariaceae.)

Funafuti [foonafootee] 8°30S 179°12E, pop (2000e) 3500. Port and capital town of Tuvalu, SW Pacific, on the E side of Funafuti atoll; airfield; US military base; copra.

Funchal [funshal] 32°40N 16°55W, pop (2000e) 109 000. Capital of Madeira, on S coast of Ilha da Madeira; third largest Portuguese city; bishopric; exports Madeira wine, embroidery, fruit, fish, dairy produce, wickerwork; sugar milling, distilling, tobacco products, soap, canning; important port and tourist resort on the transatlantic route from Europe for the Caribbean; cathedral (1485), forts (17th-c), Chapel of Santa Catarina (15th-c), São Lourenço Palace (16th-c), Jardim de São Francisco; Senhora do Monte festival (Aug).

function (mathematics) In mathematics, a relation which associates any one element in one set (the *domain*) with one and only one element in another set (the *range*). For example, the square function $f{:}x \rightarrow x^2$ maps 2 into 4, 3 into 9.

functional group A part of a molecule with characteristic reactions. Important examples include the hydroxyl group, $-OH$, characteristic of alcohols, and the amino group, $-NH_2$, characteristic of amines.

functionalism (art and architecture) The theory, rooted in Greek philosophy, that beauty should be identified with functional efficiency. Occasionally discussed in the 18th-c and 19th-c, it became fashionable in the 1920s and 1930s, especially under Bauhaus influence. In architecture, the form of a building was to be determined by the function it was meant to fulfil – as in the famous definition of a house as a machine for living in.

functionalism (sociology) A theory widely accepted in social anthropology and sociology in the mid-20th-c, according to which particular social institutions, customs, and beliefs all have a part to play in maintaining a social system. The central notion is that a community or society has an enduring structure, its parts fitting together to form a single integrated system. In Britain the leading functionalists were Bronislaw Malinowski and A R Radcliffe-Brown (1881–1955); in the USA, Talcott Parsons (1902–79) and Robert Merton (1910–). It is now generally thought that functionalism offers too static a view of social organization, and understates the conflicts which are likely to be present in the life of any community. The strength of functionalist theory was that it directed attention to the interrelationships between the institutions in a community.

functional programming A method of writing computer programs in which the relationships between variables are stated, rather than instructions to perform operations on the variables. The outcome of running the program is achieved by evaluating the functional relationships. A functional language is an example of a declarative language.

fundamental constants A set of numerical quantities having the same fixed value for all observers. Values of these constants control all physical processes. Planck's constant, the velocity of light, the gravitational constant, Avogadro's constant, the electron charge, the molar gas constant, permittivity, permeability, and certain particle masses are all regarded as fundamental constants.

fundamental forces *forces of nature*

fundamentalism A theological tendency seeking to preserve what are thought to be the essential doctrines ('fundamentals') of a religion. The term was originally used of the conservative US Protestant movement in the 1920s, characterized by a literal interpretation of the Bible, and revived with conservative Christian movements in the late 20th-c. Generally, it is any theological position opposed to liberalism, with important (often violent) manifestations found today in all major religions, notably Islam.

Fundamental Orders In US colonial history, an agreement for self-government adopted by the Connecticut towns of Hartford, Windsor, and Wethersfield, and extended to other towns. It was replaced by a royal charter in 1662.

fundamental particles Those subatomic particles that are thought to be indivisible into smaller particles. They are the **matter particles** (quarks, neutrinos, electrons, muons, and taus) and the **force particles** (gluons, photons, W and Z bosons, and gravitons).

Fundy, Bay of A bay separating the provinces of New Brunswick and Nova Scotia, E Canada. The world's greatest tidal height (16·2 m/53 ft) is used to generate electricity.

Fünen *Fyn*

fungal infection Infection with fungi that cause disease. Examples include *Candida albicans*, the cause of thrush; *Aspergillus*, responsible for respiratory disorders; and *Actinomyces*, which produces fungal swellings in the body (*mycetomas*).

fungicide Any chemical used to control fungi harmful to plants, animals, or foodstuffs. Fungicides are particularly important in controlling rusts in cereals, blight in potatoes, and mildew in fruit. They are also used to control fungi that damage the quality of food in storage or that grow on animals or humans. Commonly used fungicides include mercury- and sulphur-containing compounds.

fungus A primitive plant that obtains its nourishment either *saprophytically*, by secreting enzymes to dissolve insoluble organic food externally before absorption, or *parasitically*, by absorbing food from a host. The body form may be single-celled, but usually consists of a network (*mycelium*) of thread-like strands (*hyphae*) which may produce a compact, fruiting body bearing the reproductive tissues. Cell walls are usually made of chitin, occasionally of cellulose. The true fungi belong to the division Eumycota of the kingdom Plantae, containing all fungi except the slime moulds and their allies. Fungi are sometimes classified as a separate kingdom characterized by their lack of flagella at all stages of the life-cycle; those with flagella are transferred to the kingdom Protoctista. Fungi fulfil a vital ecological role in recycling nutrients. Many are pests of crops or are human pathogens; some are edible or produce useful by-products.

funk A term used for various genres of (mainly black) popular music. The word was originally used for smells, and particularly bodily sexual odour; from the 1950s it described 'hard bop' jazz with a 'soul' feeling, as performed by Julian 'Cannonball' Adderley, Horace Silver, Lee Morgan, and others. Later in the 1960s it was used more generally for soul and rhythm-and-blues music, epitomized by James Brown and by George Clinton's Parliament/Funkadelic bands; and from the 1970s on for a variety of black dance and disco music and its white derivatives.

funnel-web spider A predatory spider that constructs a funnel-shaped web to trap its prey. Some species are venomous. The bite of the Australian funnel-web spider causes severe pain, blindness, and paralysis of the respiratory muscles. (Class: Arachnida. Order: Araneae.)

fur A covering of hairs found today only in mammals, though there is some evidence that extinct flying reptiles had fur. It presumably evolved as a means of controlling heat loss from the body (most modern mammals maintain a constant body temperature).

Furchgott, Robert F (1916–) Pharmacologist, born in Charleston, South Carolina, USA. He worked at the State University of New York Health Science Center, and shared the 1998 Nobel Prize for Physiology or Medicine for his contribution to the discovery of nitric oxide as a signalling molecule in the cardiovascular system.

Furies *Erinyes*

furniture beetle A small, brown beetle; larvae, known as **woodworm**, are C-shaped, white and fleshy with tiny legs, and bore into dead wood as they feed; adults emerge leaving typical woodworm holes. (Order: Coleoptera. Family: Anobiidae.)

Fürstenbund [fürstenbunt] ('League of Princes') A league of German princes founded at Frederick the Great's instigation in the last phase of his conflict with the Austrian Habsburgs. The leading German states (eg Prussia, Saxony, Hanover, Baden, Saxe-Weimar, Palatinate-Zweibrucken) signed an agreement in Berlin (1785) to preserve the status quo, countering the ambitions of Emperor Joseph II.

further education A level of educational provision offered in many countries, often distinguished from **higher education**; known as **adult education** in the USA. Further education is post-school education leading, usually, to qualifications at sub-degree level, though it may not lead to any award at all but simply be taken for its own sake. A great deal is of a vocational nature, and involves study and practical work related to someone's job; but it can also be non-vocational, and take place in informal settings like the home. Higher education, by contrast, takes place in institutions where most or all of the work is at degree level or above.

Furtwängler, (Gustav Heinrich Ernst Martin) Wilhelm [foortvengler] (1886–1954) Conductor, born in Berlin, Germany. He studied in Munich, and in 1922 became conductor of the Gewandhaus concerts in Leipzig and of the Berlin Philharmonic. International tours established his reputation, though his highly subjective interpretations of the German masters aroused controversy. His ambivalent attitude to the Hitler regime cost him some popularity outside Germany, but after the War he quickly re-established himself.

furze *gorse*

Fuseli, Henry [fyoozelee], originally **Johann Heinrich Füssli** (1741–1825) Painter and art critic, born in Zürich, N Switzerland. He went to England in 1763, where he worked as a translator, then studied painting in Italy (1770–8). His 200 paintings include 'The Nightmare' (1781, Detroit) and two series to illustrate Shakespeare's and Milton's works, by which he is chiefly known. He became professor of painting at the Royal Academy in 1799.

fusel oil [fyoozl] Organic material obtained along with ethanol in fermentation, mostly alcohols of higher molecular weight, with 3, 4, or 5 carbon atoms. The presence of a very small proportion of the alcohols contributes to the characteristic flavour of fermented beverages, pleasant or otherwise; larger quantities tend to cause thirst and headaches.

fusion A development of jazz that started in the late 1960s, when jazz artists sought to revitalize the music by drawing on elements from other musical traditions, and particularly rock, soul, and dance music. Miles Davis's albums *In A Silent Way* and *Bitches Brew* (both 1969) were major influences on the genre, followed by ex-Davis musicians in the bands Weather Report, Chick Corea's Return To Forever, and John McLaughlin's Mahavishnu Orchestra, which themselves spawned further groups. At the same time, rock groups like Soft Machine, Chicago, and King Crimson were looking to jazz for fresh inspiration. The term is also used for other blendings of music genres, such as rock and folk, or jazz and classics.

fusional language A type of language in which words contain several features of meaning that cannot be identified in a one-to-one way with the sequence of forms which make up the words; also known as **inflecting** languages. For example, in the Latin *dominus* ('lord'), the suffix *-us* 'fuses' the meanings of 'masculine', 'nominative', and 'singular'.

futhark [fuhthah(r)k] *runes*

futon [futon] A Japanese quilt, equivalent to Western eiderdowns or duvets, traditionally filled with (heavy) cotton padding (now polyester or feathers). Most Japanese sleep on a thick futon on the tatami matting, with another on top in winter. All bedding is kept in a cupboard during the day, leaving the room free for use.

futures In economics, a **futures market** (or *terminal market*) is where commodities are bought and sold for delivery at some future date. Speculators may buy futures in the hope that the price will rise, and thus be able to make a profit by selling on to others. A **futures contract** enables sellers to guard against the risk that the price will fall, and protects buyers from the risk that the price will rise (*hedging*). There is also a market in financial futures: *LIFFE* [liyf], the *London International Financial Futures Exchange*, which deals with foreign exchange, interest rates, and equities. In the USA, futures include US Treasury bills and government-backed mortgages.

Futurism A modern art movement founded by the poet Marinetti in Milan in 1909. Futurism glorified machinery, war, speed, and the modern world generally; artists included Boccioni, Carrà, Balla, and Severini, working in a style derived from Cubism. It had petered out by c.1918.

futurology A controversial area of study which aims to discern the shape of future developments on the basis of analyzing the present and the past. A distinction is made between *projections*, based on collected data and existing trends, and *conjectures*, which are mostly speculative.

Fuzhou, Fu-chou, or **Foochow** [foojoh] 26°09N 119°17E, pop (2000e) 1 564 000, administrative region 5 555 000. Capital of Fujian province, SE China; on N bank of Min Jiang R, founded 202 BC; capital of autonomous state, 10th-c; treaty port, 1842; airfield; railway; steel, fishing, food processing; trade in rice, sugar cane, tea, oranges, fruit; West Lake Park (imperial garden), Twin Pagodas, White Pagoda (904, rebuilt 1548), Ebony Pagoda (941), several temples on Yushan and Wushan hills; 10 km/6 mi outside city is Yongquan Si (Bubbling Spring Temple), containing a tooth of the Buddha.

Fyn [fün], or **Funen**, Ger **Fünen** pop (2000e) 476 300; area 3486 sq km/1346 sq mi. Danish island between S Jutland and Zealand, bounded by the Little Belt (W) and the Great Belt (E); capital, Odense; other towns include Svendborg and Nyborg; second largest island in Denmark; agriculture ('the garden of Denmark'); Viking remains; train ferry from Nyborg to Korsør.

g

gabbro A coarse-grained basic (low in silica) igneous rock composed of calcic plagioclase feldspar, pyroxene, and sometimes olivine.

Gabin, Jean [gabĩ], originally **Jean-Alexis Moncorgé** (1904–76) Actor, born in Paris, France. He started his stage career as a music hall singer and dancer, and played light juvenile leads in films from 1930, but a series of dramatic roles brought him greater depth and international recognition, especially in *Pépé le moko* (1936), *Quai des brumes* (1938, trans Port of Shadows) and *Le Jour se lève* (1939, trans Daybreak). After World War 2 he continued to appear frequently in tough character roles until shortly before his death.

Gabirol, Solomon ben Judah ibn *Avicebron*

Gable, (William) Clark (1901–60) Actor, born in Cadiz, Ohio, USA. He had various industrial jobs before joining a small theatrical stock company. His first leading film role was in *The Painted Desert* (1931). Growing popularity in tough but sympathetic parts soon labelled him 'the King of Hollywood', reaching its peak with his portrayal of Rhett Butler in *Gone With the Wind* (1939). In 1942, after the death of his third wife (Carole Lombard) in an air crash, he joined the US 8th Air Force, and was decorated for bomber missions. His final film was *The Misfits* (1961).

gable The section of wall which conceals the triangular end of a pitched roof. The term is generally used of Gothic architecture. A gable is steeper than its Classical equivalent – the pediment – and is often elaborately shaped, especially in The Netherlands.

Gabo, Naum [gahboh], originally **Naum Neemia Pevsner** (1890–1977) Constructivist sculptor, born in Bryansk, W Russia. He studied at Munich University, and in 1920 helped to form the group of Russian Constructivists, who had considerable influence on 20th-c architecture and design. Forced into exile, he lived in Berlin, Paris, and England, moving to the USA in 1946. Several examples of his geometrical 'constructions in space', mainly made in transparent plastics, are in the Museum of Modern Art, New York City.

Gabon *p.601*

Gaboon viper or **Gabon viper** One of the largest vipers (length, up to 2 m/6½ ft), with the longest fangs of any viper (50 mm/2 in); broad flat head shaped like an arrow-head, with two small 'horns' between nostrils; inhabits African forest; body with bold markings resembling leaves on forest floor; nocturnal; moves little; eats small vertebrates.

Gabor, Dennis [gabaw(r)] (1900–79) Physicist, born in Budapest, Hungary. After obtaining a doctorate in engineering in Berlin (1927) he worked as a research engineer, but left Germany in 1933. In 1948 he joined Imperial College, London, and was appointed professor of applied electron physics (1958–67). He is credited with the invention in 1947 of the technique of holography, a method of photographically recording and reproducing three-dimensional images, for which he was awarded the Nobel Prize for Physics in 1971.

Gaborone [gabuhrohnay] 24°45S 25°55E, pop (2000e) 165 900. Independent township and capital of Botswana, S Africa; altitude 1000 m/3300 ft; area 97 sq km/37 sq mi; WNW of Pretoria (South Africa); capital moved there from Mafeking, 1965; airport; a campus of University of Botswana and Swaziland; light industry, textiles, trade, services.

Gabriel An angel named in both the Old and New Testaments, the only other named angel in the Bible being the archangel Michael (although seven archangels are named in the Jewish apocalyptic work 1 *Enoch*). Gabriel is said to have helped Daniel interpret visions (*Dan* 8, 9). He is also recorded as foretelling the births of John the Baptist and of Jesus (*Luke* 1).

Gabriel, Peter (1950–) Singer and songwriter, born in Surrey, SE England, UK. He co-founded the rock group Genesis, but left to pursue a solo career in 1975. His LP *Peter Gabriel* (1977), the first of four such named albums, was a number 7 hit in the UK. Renowned for the visual effects which accompany his videos, a collection of video hits was released as *CV* (1988), topping the UK music video chart. In 1982 he inaugurated the 'World of Music, Arts and Dance' (WOMAD) festival; and he later wrote the score for *The Last Temptation of Christ* (1988) and music for the inaugural Greenwich Millennium Dome celebration. Other albums include *Us* (1992) and *Up* (2002).

Gabrieli, Andrea [gabrielee] (c.1533–86) Composer, born in Venice, NE Italy. After studying under Lassus he became organist of St Mark's Church. He wrote Masses and other choral works. Several of his organ pieces foreshadow the fugue.

Gad, tribe of One of the 12 tribes of ancient Israel, said to be descended from Jacob's seventh son (the first by Zilpah, Leah's maid). Its territory originally included the valley to the E of the Jordan River, bordered by the tribe of Manasseh in the N.

Gadamer, Hans-Georg [gahdamer] (1900–2002) Philosopher, born in Marburg, WC Germany. A pupil of Heidegger at Freiberg, he became rector at Leipzig and held chairs at Frankfurt (1947) and Heidelberg (1949–68). His major work is *Wahrheit und Methode* (1960, trans Truth and Method). He was known particularly for his theory of hermeneutics, on the nature of understanding and interpretation.

Gaddafi or **Qaddafi, Colonel Muammar** [gadafee] (1942–) Libyan political and military leader, born into a nomadic family. After secondary school he entered the Libyan Military Academy in 1963, and formed the Free Unionist Officers Movement which overthrew King Idris in 1969. He became chairman of the Revolutionary Command Council, promoted himself to colonel (the highest rank in the revolutionary army) and became commander-in-chief of the Libyan armed forces. As *de facto* head of state, he set about eradicating colonialism by expelling foreigners and closing down British and US bases. He developed his own political philosophy, the 'third international theory' which he expounded in his Green Book. A somewhat unpredictable figure, he openly supported violent revolutionaries in other parts of the world while ruthlessly pursuing Libyan dissidents both at home and abroad. He waged a war in Chad, and threatened other neighbours, and in 1986 the US bombed Libya in an attempt to eliminate him. In 1999 he released for trial the alleged perpetrators of the bombing of the American PanAm flight which crashed on Lockerbie, Scotland (1988) and in 2003 agreed to pay compensation to victims' families, following which UN sanctions were lifted. A policy of re-engagement with the wider (non-Arab) world took a further step forward when he renounced Libya's intentions to develop weapons of mass destruction (Dec 2003).

Gabon

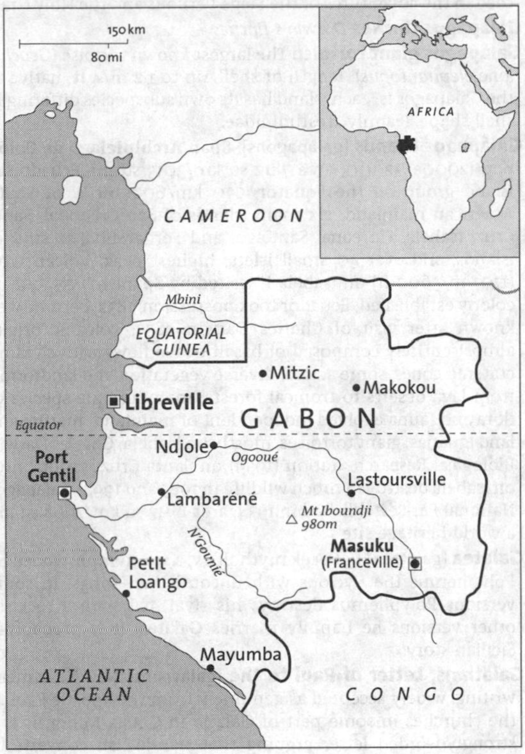

□ International Airport

[gabohn], official name **Gabonese Republic**, Fr **République Gabonaise**

Local name Gabon

Timezone GMT +1

Area 267 667 km²/103 349 sq mi

Population total (2002e) 1 300 000

Status Republic

Date of independence 1960

Capital Libreville

Languages French (official), Fang, Myene, Bateke, and other Bantu dialects spoken

Ethnic groups c.40 Bantu tribes (Fang 30%, Eshira 25%, Bateke and Bapounou 10%) and c.10% expatriate Africans and Europeans

Religions Christian (96%) (Roman Catholic 65%, Protestant 19%, other 12%), traditional beliefs

Physical features Located in W Africa; lies on the equator for 880 km/550 mi W–E; land rises towards the African central plateau, cut by several rivers, notably the Ogooué and N'Gounié; highest point, Mont Ibounoji, 980 m/3215 ft.

Climate Typical equatorial climate: hot, wet, and humid; mean annual temperature 27°C; annual average rainfall 1250–2000 mm/50–80 in inland.

Currency 1 CFA Franc (CFAFr) = 100 centimes

Economy Small area of land under cultivation, but employing 65% of population; coffee, cocoa, palm oil, rubber; timber extraction; rapid economic growth since independence, largely because of offshore oil, natural gas, and minerals; manganese, uranium, iron ore.

GDP (2002e) $8 354 bn, per capita $6500

Human Development Index (2002) 0·637

History Visited by Portuguese, 15th-c; under French control from mid-19th-c; slave ship captured by the French in 1849, the liberated slaves forming the settlement of Libreville; occupied by France, 1885; one of four territories of French Equatorial Africa, 1910; independence, 1960; multi-party elections held, 1990; new constitution, 1991; governed by a President, an appointed Council of Ministers, and a legislative National Assembly.

Head of State
1960–7 Léon M'ba
1967– Omar (Albert-Bernard, to 1973) Bongo

Head of Government
1960–75 *As President*
1975–90 Léon Mébiame (Mébiane)
1990 4 Casimir Oyé M'ba
1994–9 Paulin Obame-Nguema
1999– Jean-François Ntoutoume-Emane

Gaddi, Taddeo [gadee] (c.1300–66) Painter, born in Florence, NC Italy, the son of Gaddo Gaddi. He was Giotto's best pupil and also his godson. His finest work is seen in the frescoes of 'The Life of the Virgin' in the Baroncelli chapel of S Croce. Though the best-known of Giotto's followers, his style deviated from that of his master, whom he does not match in figure painting, but whom he excels in architectural perspective.

Gaddis, William (1922–98) Novelist, born in New York City, USA. He studied at Harvard, then worked as a freelance speech and scriptwriter before making his mark with the novel *The Recognitions* (1955), a complex story using experimental language, which drew acclaim from some quarters and incomprehension from others. A radical satirist, he was one of America's most prominent contemporary novelists; his other works include *JR* (1976), *Carpenter's Gothic* (1985), and *A Frolic of His Own* (1993).

gad fly A robust, biting fly; eyes usually large, often iridescent; females suck blood of cattle and horses, inflicting painful bites; eggs laid in damp or marshy soil; larvae are predators of other insects; some of medical and veterinary importance. (Order: Diptera. Family: Tabanidae, c.2000 species.)

Gadidae [gadiday] The cod family of fishes, a large group comprising about 15 genera and 100 species of marine fish found primarily in continental shelf waters of the cool temperate N hemisphere; only the burbot is freshwater; many are extremely important commercially as food fish, including cod, burbot, haddock, ling, pollack, saithe, torsk, and whiting.

Gadsden Purchase An area in S Arizona and New Mexico bought from Mexico for $10 000 000 as a route for a transcontinental railroad. The purchase, named after US minister to Mexico James Gadsden (1788–1858), defined the present-day US/Mexican border.

gadwall A duck (*Anas strepera*) native to the N hemisphere S of 60°; male grey with black rear end; female brown; feeds at surface; eats weeds and small animals. (Family: Anatidae.)

Gaea, Gaia, or **Ge** [geea, giya, gee] In Greek mythology, 'the Earth' personified, and then the goddess of the whole Earth (not a particular piece of land). She came into being after Chaos, and was the wife of Uranus, producing numerous children. Her Roman equivalent was **Tellus** [telus].

Gaelic *Irish; Scottish Gaelic*

Gaelic football *football, Gaelic*

gaffer The chief electrician in a film or television production crew, working closely with the lighting director. The chargehand electrician working directly under the gaffer is known as the **best boy**.

Gagarin, Yuri (Alekseyevich) [gagahrin] (1934–68) Russian cosmonaut, born in Gagarin (formerly Gzhatsk), W Russia. He joined the Soviet air force in 1957, and in 1961 became the first man to travel in space, completing a circuit of the Earth in the

Vostok spaceship satellite. A Hero of the Soviet Union, he shared the Galabert astronautical Prize with John Glenn in 1963. He was killed in a plane accident while training.

Gage, Thomas (1721–87) British soldier, whose actions helped precipitate the American Revolution, born in Firle, East Sussex, SE England, UK. He accompanied Braddock's ill-fated expedition in Pennsylvania (1754), and the successful campaign in Quebec (1759), and became Military Governor of Montreal in 1760. He was commander-in-chief of the British forces in America (1763–72), and in 1774 Governor of Massachusetts. In April 1775 he sent a force to seize arms from the colonists at Concord, and next day the skirmish at Lexington took place which began the American Revolution. After the Battle of Bunker Hill (Jun 1775) he was relieved by Howe.

Gaia hypothesis [giya] A hypothesis, first proposed by James Lovelock in 1972, which considers the Earth as an intimately linked system of physical, chemical, and biological processes, interacting in a self-regulating way to maintain the conditions necessary for life. This contrasts with the view that the Earth is merely an inanimate habitat, fortuitously having surface conditions that have supported the evolution of plants and animals. Although named after the Greek Earth goddess, it has a scientific rather than a mystical basis.

gaillardia [gaylah(r)dia] An annual or perennial, mostly native to North America, several species being grown in gardens for their cut flowers and long flowering period. Two species are the parents of many garden hybrids: *Gaillardia pulchella*, an annual growing to 30–60 cm/1–2 ft with coarsely toothed, lance-shaped leaves, yellow outer ray florets coloured crimson at the base; and *Gaillardia aristata*, a perennial growing to 70 cm/27 in with yellow and red ray florets. (Genus: *Gaillardia*, 28 species. Family: Compositae.)

Gainsborough, Thomas [gaynzbruh] (1727–88) Landscape and portrait painter, born in Sudbury, Suffolk, E England, UK. In his youth he copied Dutch landscapes, and at 14 was sent to London, where he learnt the art of Rococo decoration. He moved to Bath in 1759, where he established himself with his portrait of Earl Nugent (1760). His best-known paintings include 'The Blue Boy' (c. 1770, San Marino), 'The Harvest Wagon' (1767, Birmingham) and 'The Watering Place' (1777, Tate, London). He moved to London in 1774, painting futher portraits and landscapes, notably 'George III' and 'Queen Charlotte' (1781, Windsor), and 'Cottage Door' (1780, Pasadena).

Gaiseric or **Genseric** [giyserik] (c.390–477) King of the Vandals and Alans (428–77), who led the Vandals in their invasion of Gaul. He crossed from Spain to Numidia (429), captured and sacked Hippo (430), seized Carthage (439), and made it the capital of his new dominions. He built up a large maritime power, and his fleets carried the terror of his name as far as the Peloponnese. He sacked Rome in 455, and defeated fleets sent against him. The greatest of the Vandal kings, he was succeeded by his son Huneric.

Gaitskell, Hugh (Todd Naylor) (1906–63) British statesman, born in London, UK. He studied at Oxford, and became a Socialist during the 1926 General Strike. An MP in 1945, he was minister of fuel and power (1947) and of economic affairs (1950), and Chancellor of the Exchequer (1950–1). In 1955 he was elected Leader of the Opposition by a large majority over Bevan. He bitterly opposed Eden's Suez action (1956), and refused to accept a narrow conference vote for unilateral disarmament (1960). This caused a crisis of leadership in which he was challenged by Harold Wilson (1960), but he retained the loyalty of most Labour MPs.

galactic cluster *open cluster*

galactose A simple sugar (monosaccharide), found in the sugar of milk along with glucose; otherwise, it is rare in nature. Galactosaemia, a genetic defect leading to an inability to metabolize galactose, is very uncommon and requires dietary management.

galago *bushbaby*

Galahad, Sir One of King Arthur's knights, son of Lancelot and Elaine. Distinguished for his purity, he alone was able to succeed in the adventures of the Siege Perilous and the Holy Grail.

Galápagos finches *Darwin's finches*

Galápagos giant tortoise The largest known tortoise (*Geochelone elephantopus*); length of shell, up to 1·2 m/4 ft; native to the Galápagos Is; each island has its own subspecies differing in shell shape. (Family: Testudinidae.)

Galápagos Islands [galapagohs], Span **Archipiélago de Colón** pop (2000e) 12 100; area 7812 sq km/3015 sq mi. Ecuadorian island group on the Equator, 970 km/600 mi W of South American mainland; six main islands of San Cristóbal, Santa Cruz, Isabela, Floreana, Santiago, and Fernandina, 12 smaller islands, and over 40 small islets; highest peak, Volcán Wolf (1707 m/5600 ft) on Isabela I; visited by Spanish, 1535, but no colony established; Ecuador took possession, 1832; became well known after visit of Charles Darwin, 1835; volcanic origin, almost entirely composed of basaltic lava flows with shallow, cratered cones, some active; diverse vegetation and landforms, from lava deserts to tropical forests; many unique species of flora and fauna evolved independent of mainland; marine and land iguanas; giant tortoises, mostly on Isabela; Charles Darwin Biological Research Station (1959) on Santa Cruz; serious fires on Isabela destroyed much wildlife in 1985 and 1994; Galápagos National Park established in 1934; area 6912 sq km/2668 sq mi; a world heritage site.

Galatea [galateea] In Greek mythology, a sea-nymph, wooed by Polyphemus the Cyclops with uncouth love-songs. In some versions Polyphemus destroys his rival Acis with a rock; in other versions he happily marries Galatea. It is probably a Sicilian story.

Galatians, Letter of Paul to the [galayshnz] New Testament writing, widely accepted as genuinely from the apostle Paul to the churches in some part of Galatia in C Asia Minor. It is a strongly-worded letter arguing that non-Jewish converts to Christianity were no longer subject to Jewish practices and laws, and defending Paul's own mission on this basis.

galaxy A huge family of stars held together by their mutual gravitational attractions. Galaxies exist in a great variety of forms, ellipticals predominating, but spirals featuring prominently in popular books on account of their notable shapes. Masses range from a few million suns to 10 million million times as many. The nearest galaxies to the Milky Way are the Magellanic Clouds, some 55 000 parsec away. The furthest seen to date could be 2000 megaparsec or more. Galaxies are the fundamental building blocks of the universe, and are consequently of immense importance in cosmology. There are numerous special types. About one galaxy in a million is a **radio galaxy**, an intense source of cosmic radio waves. A **Seyfert galaxy** has a brilliant nucleus and inconspicuous spiral arms; it is a strong emitter of infrared radiation, and is also detectable as a radio and X-ray source. A **Markarian galaxy** is one with excessive ultraviolet emission, discovered by Armenian astronomer B E Markarian at Byurakan Observatory in the 1970s. Quasars could be a type of extremely luminous galaxy. A galaxy which is either unusually energetic or varies in luminosity is known as an **active galaxy**.

Galaxy The huge star family to which our Sun belongs, seen as the Milky Way. In shape it is basically a bulging flat disc, diameter 35 kiloparsec, thickness 3000 parsec at the centre, and 300 parsec elsewhere. The Sun is 8000 parsec from the nucleus. Within this disc there are star clusters and interstellar matter. A pair of spiral arms merges from the nucleus and is superimposed on the general distribution of stars. The Galaxy as a whole rotates, faster at the centre than further out. The Sun takes 250 million years for one circuit. There are over 100 000 000 000 stars in all, and the Galaxy is 10–15 thousand million years old.

Galbraith, J(ohn) Kenneth [golbrayth] (1908–) Economist and diplomat, born in Iona Station, Ontario, SE Canada. He studied at the universities of Toronto, California, and Cambridge, and became professor of economics at Harvard (1945–75, then emeritus), where he spent his career, except for a short period at Princeton, wartime service in Washington, and two years (1961–3) as US ambassador to India. He was a key adviser to Presidents Kennedy and Johnson, and one of the major intellectual forces in American liberalism, questioning the conventional wisdom of US economic policies and calling for less emphasis on production and more attention to public services. His books include *The Affluent Society* (1958), *The Age of Uncertainty* (1977, also TV series), *A History of Economics* (1987), and *A Journey through Economic Time* (1994).

Galdós, Benito Pérez *Pérez Galdós, Benito*

Galen [gaylen], in full **Claudius Galenus** (c.130–201) Greek physician, born in Pergamum, Mysia. He studied medicine at Pergamum, Smyrna, Corinth, and Alexandria, and later lived in Rome. He wrote at length on medical and philosophical subjects, and gathered up all the medical knowledge of his time, thus becoming the authority used by subsequent Greek and Roman medical writers.

galena [galeena] A lead sulphide (PbS) mineral, with very dense, dark-grey crystals. It is an important source of lead.

Galerius [galeerius], in full **Gaius Galerius Valerius Maximus** (c.250–311) Roman emperor (305–11), born near Serdica, Dacia. He was a Roman soldier of humble extraction who rose from the ranks to become deputy ruler of the E half of the empire under Diocletian (293), and chief ruler after Diocletians's abdication in 305. He was a notorious persecutor of the Christians (303–11) until near the end of his reign, when after an illness he granted them some toleration.

Galicia [galeesha] pop (2000e) 2 745 000; area 29 434 sq km/ 11 361 sq mi. Autonomous region of Spain in the NW corner of the Iberian peninsula extending S to the Portuguese border; crossed by several rivers, reaching the sea in deep fjord-like inlets; a mediaeval kingdom within Castile, 11th-c; ports include Corunna and Vigo; maize, wine, fishing, wolfram, tin; a distinctive cultural and linguistic region; there is a separatist political movement.

Galilean moons The four principal natural satellites of Jupiter, discovered by Galileo in 1610: Io (the innermost), Europa, Ganymede, and Callisto. They are distinct worlds in their own right, in the same size range as the Moon. They lack sensible atmospheres and lie in near circular orbits in Jupiter's equatorial plane. Io and Europa are mainly 'rocky' silicate bodies while Ganymede and Callisto contain an equal component of ice. It is conjectured that the four moons were formed by accretion from the material that collapsed to form Jupiter.

Galilee [galilee], Hebrew **Galil** N region of former Palestine and now of Israel, bounded W by the Mediterranean Sea, N by Lebanon, E by Syria, L Tiberias, and the Jordan valley, and S by the Jezreel plain; chiefly associated in Biblical times with the ministry of Jesus; main centre of Judaism in Palestine after the destruction of Jerusalem (AD 70); scene of fierce fighting during the Arab invasion of Israel, 1948.

Galilee, Sea of *Tiberias, Lake*

Galileo [galilayoh], in full **Galileo Galilei** (1564–1642) Astronomer and mathematician, born in Pisa, W Italy. He entered Pisa University as a medical student in 1581, and became professor of mathematics at Padua (1592–1610), where he improved the refracting telescope (1610), and was the first to use it for astronomy, discovering the four largest satellites of Jupiter. His bold advocacy of the Copernican theory brought severe ecclesiastical censure. He was forced to retract before the Inquisition, and was sentenced to indefinite imprisonment – though the sentence was commuted by the pope, at the request of the Duke of Tuscany. Under house arrest in Florence, he continued his research, though by 1637 he had become totally blind. Among his other discoveries were the law of uniformly accelerated motion towards the Earth, the parabolic path of projectiles, and the law that all bodies have weight. The validity of his scientific work was formally recognized by the Roman Catholic Church in 1993.

Galileo Project A NASA spacecraft mission to Jupiter, launched by the space shuttle in 1989, and designed to study the planet's atmosphere, satellites, and magnetosphere for two years starting in 1995. It was the first mission to make direct measurements from an instrumented probe within Jupiter's atmosphere, and the first to conduct long-term observations of the planet and its magnetosphere and satellites from orbit around Jupiter. It was also the first mission to encounter an asteroid (Gaspra) and to photograph an asteroid's moon (that of Ida). In 1994 Galileo was in a position to obtain images of the far side of Jupiter when more than 20 fragments of Comet Shoemaker-Levy plunged into the night-side atmosphere over a six-day period. The orbiter carried out its planned 23-month, 11-orbit tour of the magnetosphere and the Galilean moons, included 10 close satellite encounters, and then embarked on its extended mission to study the moon Europa over 14 months. Having operated for five years longer than originally planned, the veteran spacecraft burned up in Jupiter's atmosphere in September 2003.

Gall, Franz Joseph [gal] (1758–1828) Anatomist, born in Tiefenbrunn, SW Germany. As a physician in Vienna (1785), he evolved a theory in which a person's talents and qualities were traced to particular areas of the brain. His lectures on phrenology were popular, but suppressed in 1802 as being subversive of religion.

gall An abnormal outgrowth of tissue which can appear on any part of a plant, caused by insects, bacteria, fungi, nematodes, or mites. The precise infecting agent is often, but not always, identifiable from the type of gall. Common examples are oak-apples and the pincushion galls of roses.

Galla *Oromo*

Gallagher, Liam and **Noel** *Oasis*

Gallant, Mavis, *née* **Young** (1922 –) Short-story writer and novelist, born in Montreal, Quebec, SE Canada. Educated bilingually, she has lived mainly in Paris since 1950, contributing regularly to *The New Yorker*. Now recognized as one of Canada's foremost short-story writers, she was not widely read in Canada until publication of *From the Fifteenth District* (1979). Among later works are *Home Truths* (1981), *Overhead in a Balloon* (1985), and *In Transit* (1988). Her novels include *Green Water, Green Sky* (1959) and *A Fairly Good Time* (1970).

Gallaudet College [galuhdet] A college of higher education for the deaf, in Washington, District of Columbia, USA. It was founded by Edward Miner Gallaudet (1837–1917) in 1857, and is financed both privately and publicly.

gall bladder A small muscular sac found near or in the liver of many vertebrates, which acts as a reservoir for the storage and concentration of bile. During digestion food (especially fat) directly stimulates the duodenal mucosa to release the hormone cholecystokinin-pancreozymin (CCK). This induces the gall bladder to contract, and expel bile into the intestine via the biliary duct system.

Galle, Johann Gottfried [gahluh] (1812–1910) Astronomer, born in Pabsthaus, EC Germany. In 1846, at Berlin Observatory, he discovered the planet Neptune, whose existence had been postulated in the calculations of Leverrier.

galleon An elaborate, four-masted, heavily armed 16th-c warship, with a pronounced beak reminiscent of the ram on a galley, hence 'galleon'. The forecastle was relatively small, but the poop was high and ornate.

Galliano, Sir John (Charles) [galiahnoh] (1960–) Fashion designer, born in Gibraltar. His family moved to London when he was six, and he studied at East London College and St Martin's School of Art. He then set up a studio in London, and quickly established himself, receiving the British Fashion Council Designer of the Year Award in 1987. After setting up a studio in Paris in 1994, he again won the British Designer Award (1994, 1995), and after a period with Givenchy became designer-in-chief at Christian Dior in 1996. He received a knighthood in 2001.

galliard *pavane*

Gallicanism A French religious doctrine, emphasizing royal or episcopal authority over matters pertaining to the French church at the expense of papal sovereignty. It emerged during Philip the Fair's struggle with Boniface VIII (1297–1303), and remained a traditional, though controversial force in France, invoked to defend established liberties against Ultramontanism and papal interference.

Gallic Wars The name traditionally given to Julius Caesar's brutal campaigns (58–51 BC) against the Celtic tribes of Gaul (ancient France). They were also the occasion of his two unsuccessful invasions of Britain.

Galliformes [**gali**faw(r)meez] A worldwide order of medium-sized, mainly ground-feeding birds; includes the megapodes, curassows, the hoatzin, and the 'game birds' (pheasants, turkeys, domestic fowl); also known as **gallinaceous birds**.

gallinaceous birds *Galliformes*

gallinule [**gal**inyool] A water-bird of the rail family (c.12 species); native to the Old World and much of South America and Australia; toes often very long for walking on floating vegetation. Renowned oceanic wanderers, the birds may appear thousands of miles from their usual species' location.

Gallipoli [ga**lip**olee], Turkish **Gelibolu** Narrow peninsula extending SW from the coast of Istanbul province, NW Turkey; between the Dardanelles (SE) and the Aegean Sea (W); length c.100 km/60 mi; the scene of fierce fighting in 1915–16.

Gallipoli campaign [ga**lip**olee] A major campaign of World War 1 (1915–16). With stalemate on the Western Front, the British War Council advocated operations against the Turks to secure the Dardanelles and aid Russia. The land campaign began with amphibious assaults on the Gallipoli peninsula (Apr 1915). Australian and New Zealand forces were heavily involved: the beach where they landed is still known as Anzac Cove. Allied casualties were 250 000 out of 480 000 engaged. It was abandoned as a costly failure, with successful evacuations of all remaining troops (Jan 1916).

gallium Ga, element 31. A metal with a remarkable liquid range (melting point 28°C, boiling point 2400°C), relatively rare and found chiefly as an impurity in ores of other elements. In virtually all its compounds, it shows oxidation state +3. It is important mainly as gallium arsenide (GaAs), a compound converting electrical energy into visible light, and used in light-emitting diodes and other electronic devices.

gall midge A minute, delicate fly; eggs and hatching larvae often cause gall-like swellings on host plants; including pests of important crops such as wheat and peas. (Order: Diptera. Family: Cecidomyiidae, c.4000 species.)

Galloway *Dumfries and Galloway*

gallstones Small stones in the gall bladder and its associated ducts. They are found in about 20% of individuals, but give rise to symptoms in only a small proportion of these. Most stones are composed of cholesterol with a little admixture of calcium. Cholesterol stones tend to occur in individuals over 50 years old, and are often attended by infection of the gall bladder (*cholecystitis*); if they obstruct the common bile duct, they cause jaundice. In younger people, small bile pigment stones sometimes form in conditions associated with the breakdown of red blood cells, which liberate haemoglobin (*haemolytic anaemia*). When gallstones cause significant discomfort or jaundice, they are usually removed surgically. In a minority of cases small stones may be dissolved by giving a derivative of bile salts by mouth.

Gallup, George (Horace) (1901–84) Public opinion expert, born in Jefferson, Iowa, USA. He was professor of journalism at Drake and Northwestern universities until 1932, and, after a period directing research for an advertising agency, became professor at the Pulitzer School of Journalism, Columbia University. In 1935 he founded the American Institute of Public Opinion, and evolved the *Gallup polls* for testing the state of public opinion.

gall wasp A very small wasp, each species causing a characteristic gall on its host plant, typically the oak; one or more larvae develops inside each gall. The life-cycle is complex, often involving an alternation between sexual and asexual generations. (Order: Hymenoptera. Family: Cynipidae, c.2000 species.)

Galsworthy, John [**golz**werthee] (1867–1933) Novelist and playwright, born in Kingston Hill, Surrey, SE England, UK. He studied at Oxford, and was called to the bar in 1890, but chose to travel and set up as a writer. From the start he was a moralist and humanitarian, but his novels were also to be documentaries of their time. The six linked novels comprising *The Forsyte Saga* (1906–28), recording the life of the affluent British middle-class before 1914, began a new vogue for 'serial' novels. His plays (31 in all) illustrate his reforming zeal and his interest in social and ethical problems; they include *Strife* (1909), *Justice* (1910), and *The Skin Game* (1920). He was awarded the Order of Merit in 1929 and the Nobel Prize for Literature in 1932.

Galton, Sir Francis [**gawl**tn] (1822–1911) Scientist and explorer, born in Birmingham, West Midlands, C England, UK. He studied at Birmingham, London, and Cambridge, but left the study of medicine to travel in N and S Africa. He is best known for his studies of heredity and intelligence, such as *Hereditary Genius* (1869), which led to the field he called *eugenics*. Several of his ideas are referred to in the work of his cousin, Charles Darwin. Galton was knighted in 1909.

Galton Institute *Eugenics Society*

Galuppi, Baldassare [ga**loo**pee] (1706–85) Light operatic composer, born in the island of Burano, near Venice, NE Italy. He was educated in Venice, where he lived most of his life, apart from visits to London (1741–3) and St Petersburg (1765–8). His comic operas were extremely popular, and he also composed sacred and instrumental music. He is the subject of a well-known poem by Browning, 'A Toccata of Galuppi's'.

Galvani, Luigi [gal**vah**nee] (1737–98) Physiologist, born in Bologna, N Italy. He studied at Bologna, where he became professor of anatomy (1762). Investigating the effects of electrostatic stimuli applied to the muscle fibre of frogs, he discovered (1786) he could also make the muscle twitch by touching the nerve with various metals without a source of electrostatic charge, and greater reaction was obtained when two disimilar metals were used. He attributed the effect to 'animal electricity'. His work inspired his friend Volta, leading to the production of the electrical battery, and also initiated research into electrophysiology. The *galvanometer* is named after him.

galvanizing The application of a zinc coating to iron or steel to protect against atmospheric corrosion. In **hot galvanizing**, the cleaned metal is passed through a flux, then through a bath of molten zinc. The zinc may also be applied electrolytically. Although the term 'galvanizing' derives from Galvani, the process was not devised by him, but by Henry William Crawford in 1837.

galvanometer An instrument for measuring small electrical currents. The **moving coil galvanometer** consists of an indicating needle or mirror attached to a coiled wire suspended in a magnetic field. The coil rotates when a current passes through it. The angle through which it rotates (indicated by the deflection of the needle or by a beam of light reflected from the mirror) is used to measure the current. Other models are **ballistic galvanometers** and **moving-magnet** instruments.

Galway [**gawl**way], Ir **Na Gaillimhe** pop (2000e) 183 000; area 5939 sq km/2293 sq mi. County in Connacht province, W Ireland; largest Gaelic-speaking population in Ireland; farming, tourism, crafts; capital, Galway, pop (2000e) 52 000; port at head of Galway Bay; airfield, university (1849); technical college.

Galway, Sir James [**gawl**way] (1939–) Flautist, born in Belfast, NE Northern Ireland, UK. He studied in London and Paris, and played in various orchestras in London and in the Berlin Philharmonic (1969–75). He became a soloist in 1975, and has since followed a highly successful solo career, playing on a solid gold flute of remarkable tonal range. He published an autobiography in 1978, and was involved in a TV series, *James Galway's Music in Time*, in 1983. He received a knighthood in 2001.

Gama, Vasco da [gahma] (c.1469–1525) Navigator, born in Sines, Alentejo, SW Portugal. He led the expedition which discovered the route to India round the Cape of Good Hope (1497–9), and in 1502–3 led a squadron of ships to Calicut to avenge the murder of a group of Portuguese explorers left there by Cabral. In 1524 he was sent as viceroy to India, but he soon fell ill, and died at Cochin. His body was brought home to Portugal.

Gambetta, Leon (Michel) [gãbeta] (1838–82) French Republican statesman and prime minister (1881–2), born in Cahors, SC France. He was called to the bar in 1859, and elected deputy in 1869. After the surrender of Napoleon III he helped to proclaim the Republic (1870), became minister of the interior in the Government of National Defence, made a spectacular escape from the siege of Paris in a balloon, and for five months was dictator of France. He led the resistance to MacMahon (1877), became president of the Chamber (1879) and briefly prime minister, but fell from office before implementing a programme of radical reform.

Gambia, The *see panel*

Gambia, River, Fr **Gambie** River in W Africa, rising in the Fouta Djallon massif in Guinea; flows c.800 km/500 mi W to the Atlantic Ocean; runs along the length of The Gambia for the last 470 km/290 mi of its course; navigable by ocean-going ships for 200 km/125 mi.

gambling The wagering of either money or material goods of value on the outcome of a chance happening, such as roulette or dice-throwing, or where an element of skill can be used to judge the likelihood of an outcome, such as in horse racing or football. Gambling takes place in some form in every country of the world, from the cockfights of the Philippines to the various forms (roulette, card and dice games, and slot machines) that form the economic basis of the American city of Las Vegas. In America, horse racing and casino gambling are the two most popular pastimes for gamblers, while in Britain, horse racing, greyhound racing, and Association football are most popular. Football gambling takes place predominantly through *pools*, where the gambler tries to predict the score in a range of matches, the most popular aim being to predict eight draws from a choice of 11 games for a relatively small stake.

Gambling is legal only in certain locations. In America, it is legal only in some cities and states; Las Vegas and Reno were granted the first licences in 1931. In Britain, legislation in the early 1960s allowed the opening of bookmaker's shops where 'off-course' bets could be legally laid. Before then, an illegal but thriving trade was lightly policed. All licensed gambling provides revenue for the city, state, or country, and there are firm rules and conditions to ensure fairness to individuals placing the bet. In addition, many places also run lotteries, where purchasing either a pre-set series of random numbers or choosing a set personally can bring the winner a considerable fortune, while providing funds for charitable works. Britain's National Lottery was established in 1994 (renamed Lotto, 2002).

There is no verifiable history of gambling. Archaeologists have discovered marked pieces of bone in some of the world's most ancient sites which resemble modern dice, and it may be presumed that, once language became sophisticated enough, wagers were struck on the outcome of physical feats, hunting expeditions, and even warfare. Records exist of betting on the outcome of competitions at the amphitheatres scattered throughout the Roman Empire and at the ancient Greek Olympics. Evidence of gambling also stems from our knowledge that certain religions (eg Islam) have proscribed it.

Gambon, Sir Michael (John) (1940–) Actor, born in Dublin, Ireland. He joined the National Theatre for its inaugural season in 1963, returning to it in 1978 after appearances in repertory at Birmingham and elsewhere. He played for the Royal Shakespeare Company (1982–3), and has made several television appearances, notably in the title role of Dennis Potter's play *The Singing Detective* (1986, BAFTA) and Stephen Poliakoff's *Perfect Strangers* (2001, BAFTA). His films include *A Dry White Season* (1990), *Mobsters* (1992), *Gosford Park* (2001), and *Open*

Gambia, The

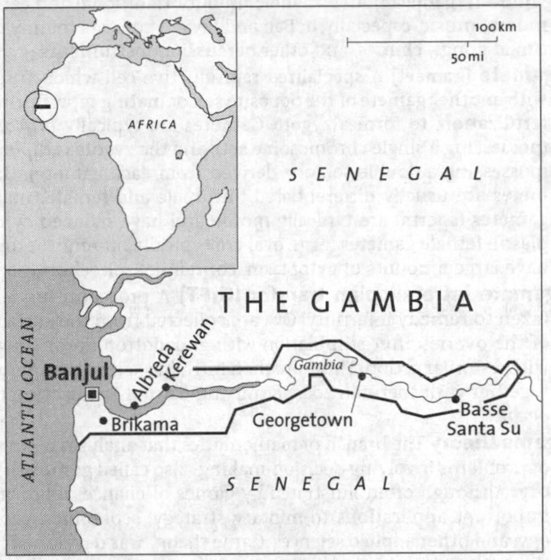

□ International Airport

official name **Republic of the Gambia**

Local name Gambia

Timezone GMT

Area 11 295 km²/4361 sq mi

Population total (2002e) 1 418 000

Status Independent republic within the Commonwealth

Date of independence 1965

Capital Banjul

Languages English (official), also Madinka, Wolof and Fula

Ethnic groups Madinka (40%), Fula (19%), Wolof (15%), Dyola (10%), Sonike (8%)

Religions Muslim (85%), Christian (14%), traditional local beliefs (1%)

Physical features Located in W Africa; surrounded, except for coastline, by Senegal; strip of land 322 km/200 mi E–W along R Gambia; flat country, not rising above 90 m/295 ft; c.25% of land arable.

Climate Tropical climate; average temperatures 23°C (Jan), 27°C (Jul), rising upland to over 40°C; rainy season (Jun–Sep) with high humidity and high night temperatures; rainfall decreasing inland.

Currency 1 Dalasi (D, Di) = 100 butut

Economy Agriculture, especially groundnuts; cotton, rice, millet, sorghum, fruit, vegetables, livestock; groundnut processing, brewing, soft drinks, agricultural machinery assembly, metal working, clothing, tourism.

GDP (2002e) $2·582 bn, per capita $1800

Human Development Index (2002) 0·405

History Visited by Portuguese, 1455; settled by English in 17th-c; independent British Crown Colony from 1843; independent member of Commonwealth, 1965; republic, 1970; joined Confederation of Senegambia, 1982–9; signed treaty of friendship with Senegal, 1991; military coup, 1994; governed by a House of Representatives, President and Cabinet.

Head of State/Government

1965–94 Dawda Kairaba Jawara

1994–6 *Military administration* Yayeh Jameh *Chairman*

1996– Yayeh Jameh

Range (2003). Television films include *Wives and Daughters* (1999) and *Longitude* (2000, BAFTA). He was knighted in 1998.

gamelan [gamelan] An ensemble used for traditional and ceremonial music, especially in Bali and Java. It consists mainly of tuned gongs, chimes, and other percussion instruments.

gamete [gameet] A specialized reproductive cell which fuses with another gamete of the opposite sex or mating type, during fertilization, to form a zygote. Gametes are typically *haploid* (possessing a single chromosome set), and the zygote is *diploid* (possessing a double set, one derived from each gamete). Gametes are usually differentiated into male and female: male gametes (sperm) are typically motile and have reduced cytoplasm; female gametes (eggs, ova) are typically non-motile and have large amounts of cytoplasm, containing mitochondria.

gamete intrafallopian transfer (GIFT) A procedure undertaken to remedy infertility. Ova are collected from the surface of the ovaries after stimulation with gonadotrophin or drugs with a similar action. These are then introduced into the uterus together with spermatozoa, permitting natural fertilization to occur.

game theory The branch of mathematics that analyzes a range of problems involving decision-making; also called **games theory**. Although often illustrated by games of chance, there are important applications to military strategy, economics, ecology, and other applied sciences. Game theory was developed in the 20th-c, principally by French mathematician Emile Borel (1871–1956) and US mathematician John Von Neumann. Games involving one, two, or more players are distinguished, as in patience, chess, and roulette respectively. Game theory analyses the strategies each player uses to maximize the chance of winning, and attempts to predict outcomes.

gametophyte The sexual (ie gamete-producing or *haploid*) generation in the life of a plant. It is the dominant part of the life-cycle in algae and bryophytes; it is the free-living but minor generation in ferns; while in flowering plants it is represented only by the pollen tube and embryo sac. Free-living gametophytes are relatively unspecialized, are prone to dehydration, and are generally confined to damp habitats.

gamma globulins The most abundant fraction of the antibodies in blood serum, produced by the plasma cells of B lymphocytes (derived from bone marrow); also known as **immunoglobulin G (IgG)**. Gamma globulins combine with antigens such as viruses and parasites to kill them by a number of different mechanisms, including enhancement of the inflammatory processes. Newborn infants are protected against infection in early life, partly by gamma globulins received from the mother via the placenta, but mainly by gamma globulins transferred by the mother's milk, particularly that secreted soon after birth (the *colostrum*).

gamma-ray astronomy The study of radiation from celestial sources at wavelengths shorter than 0·01 nm. Gamma-rays have been detected from the gamma-ray background, from a few energetic galaxies and quasars, and from certain highly evolved stars.

gamma rays Electromagnetic radiation of very short wavelength, less than 3×10^{-11} m; particle-like properties; no electric charge; highly penetrating. Emitted in natural radioactivity, it is the result of transitions from high-energy excited states to lower-energy states in atomic nuclei. Cobalt-60 is a common gamma source, with a half-life of 5·26 years.

Gamow, George [gamov], originally **Georgy Antonovich Gamov** (1904–68) Physicist, born in Odessa, S Ukraine. He studied at Leningrad University, where later he was professor of physics (1931–4). He did research at Göttingen, developing a quantum theory for radioactivity, then moved to the USA as professor of physics at George Washington University (1934–55) and at Colorado (1956–68). In 1948, with Ralph Alpher, he developed the 'big bang' theory of the origin of the universe. In molecular biology he hypothesized that patterns within DNA chains formed a genetic code, a proposal shown by the mid-1950s to be correct. He was also a writer, and received acclaim as a popularizer of science, beginning with *Mr Tomkins in Wonderland* (1936).

Gand [gã] *Ghent*

Ganda A Bantu-speaking people of S Uganda, the largest traditional kingdom in the area, founded about the 12th-c. The king, the *kabaka*, was assisted by bureaucratic chiefs. In the 19th-c, most Ganda became Christian, although there is a significant Muslim minority. The kingship was abolished by the Uganda government in 1967. Population c.2 million.

Gandar, Laurence (Owen Vine) (1915–98) Journalist, born in Durban, E South Africa. He studied at Natal University, Pietermaritzburg, and served with South African forces in World War 2. He entered journalism in 1936, and became editor of *The Rand Daily Mail*, Johannesburg, in 1957. His challenges to apartheid, through campaigning journalism and his own articles, transformed the newspaper and set new standards for South African journalism as a whole. Prosecution for publishing reports on jail conditions led to the newspaper's owners sidelining him as editor in 1966. He stayed on as editor-in-chief until 1969, when he became the founding director of the Minority Rights Group in Britain, returning to South Africa in 1972.

Gandhi, (Mohandas Karamchand) [gandee], known as **the Mahatma** (Hindi 'of great soul') (1869–1948) Indian nationalist leader, born in Poorbandar, Kathiawar, W India. He studied law in London, but in 1893 went to South Africa, where he spent 20 years opposing discriminatory legislation against Indians. In 1914 he returned to India, where he supported the Home Rule movement, and became leader of the Indian National Congress, advocating a policy of non-violent non-cooperation to achieve independence. Following his civil disobedience campaign (1919–22), he was jailed for conspiracy (1922–4). In 1930 he led a 320 km/200 mi march to the sea to collect salt in symbolic defiance of the government monopoly. On his release from prison (1931), he attended the London Round Table Conference on Indian constitutional reform. In 1946 he negotiated with the Cabinet Mission which recommended the new constitutional structure. After independence (1947), he tried to stop the Hindu–Muslim conflict in Bengal, a policy which led to his assassination in Delhi by Nathuram Godse, a Hindu fanatic.

Gandhi, Indira (Priyadarshini) [gandee] (1917–84) Indian stateswoman and prime minister (1966–77, 1980–4), born in Allahabad, NE India, the daughter of Jawaharlal Nehru. She studied at Visva-Bharati University (Bengal) and Oxford, and in 1942 married **Feroze Gandhi** (d.1960). She became president of the Indian Congress Party (1959–60), minister of information (1964), and prime minister following the death of Shastri. After her conviction for election malpractices, she declared a state of emergency (1975–7), and was premier again in 1980. She achieved a considerable reputation through her work as a leader of the developing nations, but was unable to stem sectarian violence at home. She was assassinated in New Delhi by Sikh extremist members of her bodyguard.

Gandhi, Rajiv [gandee] (1944–91) Indian statesman and prime minister (1984–9), born in Mumbai (Bombay), W India, the eldest son of Indira Gandhi and the grandson of Nehru. He studied at Cambridge University, and became a pilot with Indian Airlines (1968). Following the death of his brother **Sanjay Gandhi** (1946–80) in an air crash, he was elected to his brother's Amethi parliamentary seat (1981) and appointed a general secretary of the Congress Party (1983). After the assassination of Indira Gandhi (1984), he became prime minister, but resigned after his party was defeated in the 1989 general election. He was assassinated 18 months later while campaigning for the Congress Party. His Italian-born widow, **Sonia**, was elected Congress president in 1998, and was elected to parliament in 1999, becoming leader of the Opposition.

Gandolfini, James [gandolfeenee] (1961–) Actor, born in Westwood, New Jersey, USA. He studied at Rutgers University, NJ and the Actors Studio, New York City. He made his film debut in *A Stranger Among Us* (1992), and later films include *Get Shorty*

(1995), *The Mighty* (1998), and *The Mexican* (2001). He became well known for his role as Tony Soprano in the television series *The Sopranos* (1999–), for which he received Best Actor Golden Globe (1999) and Emmy (2000, 2001, 2003) awards.

Gangdisi Shan [gahngdeesoe] or **Kailas Range** Mountain range in Tibet, N of the Himalayas; rises to 6714 m/22 027 ft at Kangrinboqê Feng peak; a watershed between the inland and Indian Ocean drainage systems.

Ganges, River [ganjeez], Hindi **Ganga** River in N India, formed in the E Himalayas; flows W through the Silwalik Range onto the Ganges Plain; continues SE to Allahabad, then E to Benares; turns E through Bihar, then SE into West Bengal, where it follows the frontier with Bangladesh; joined by the R Brahmaputra NW of Faridpur; as the R Padma it continues SE through Bangladesh, branches into many tributaries, and forms the vast Ganges–Brahmaputra delta in the Bay of Bengal; length 2510 km/1560 mi; important trade artery and irrigation source; the most sacred Hindu river.

ganglion **1** In anatomy, an aggregation of grey (non-myelinated) nervous tissue within the nervous system, constituting the bulk of many invertebrate central nervous systems. In vertebrates, there are some ganglia within the central nervous system (eg the basal ganglia), but the majority occur in the peripheral nervous system, as collections of cell bodies of neurones (eg the spinal ganglia). They are often the site of communication between nerve cells.
2 In clinical medicine, a cyst which forms in relation to a tendon sheath, producing a painless, harmless swelling. It is commonly found over the wrist or back of the hands.

Gang of Four **1** The four Shanghai-based hard-core radical leaders of the Cultural Revolution (1966–76) in China: Zhang Chunqiao, Yao Wenyuan, Wang Hongwen, and Jiang Qing (Mao Zedong's wife). Zhang and Yao were veterans of the Shanghai party machine. All were members of the politburo when they were arrested and disgraced after Mao's death (1976).
2 In British politics, the four politicians who broke away from the Labour Party to found the Social Democratic Party in 1981: Roy Jenkins, William Rodgers, David Owen, and Shirley Williams.

gangrene Death of body tissue which occurs in parts of the body deprived of their blood supply, such as a toe or foot, or internal organ. Without infection, the affected part blackens and shrivels (**dry gangrene**). If it is infected, the affected part becomes swollen and ulcerated and the area of dead tissue spreads, requiring urgent surgery.

ganja *cannabis*

gannet A large marine bird closely related to the booby; native to the N Atlantic, S Africa, Australia, and New Zealand; long blue bill with no external nostrils; bare patches of blackish skin on face; similar habits to boobies. (Family: Sulidae, 3 species.)

Gansu Corridor *Hexi Corridor*

Ganymede (astronomy) [ganimeed] The third natural satellite of Jupiter, discovered by Galileo in 1610; distance from the planet 1 070 000 km/665 000 mi; diameter 5260 km/3270 mi; orbital period 7·155 days. It is the largest moon in the Solar System, and larger than Mercury. The brightest of the Galilean satellites, it seems to have a large rocky core surrounded by a mantle of water and a thick crust of ice. It has many impact craters.

Ganymede (mythology) [ganimeed] In Greek mythology, a beautiful boy, the son of Tros, a Trojan prince. Zeus sent a storm-wind, or (later and more usually) an eagle, who carried Ganymede up to Olympus, where he became the cup-bearer. In return his father was given a stud of exceptional horses.

ganzfeld A type of partial sensory deprivation, in which a person is exposed to unpatterned visual and auditory stimulation. As used in parapsychological research, the ganzfeld technique typically consists of fixing translucent hemispheres over the eyes of a reclining person while a red light is shone upon the face, and masking noises, such as the sound of waves or white noise, are presented via headphones. The ganzfeld is often used in extrasensory perception studies to encourage internally-produced imagery and thoughts.

Gao, Xingjian [gow, shingjian] (1940–) Novelist and playwright, born in Ganzhou, Jiangxi province, E China. He studied French at the Department of Foreign Languages, Beijing (1962), and during the Cultural Revolution (1966–76) he was sent to a re-education camp. His book of collected plays, *The Other Shore* (1986), was banned in China, and the next year he settled in Paris as a political refugee, later taking French citizenship. In 2000 he became the first Chinese writer to receive the Nobel Prize for Literature.

Gao Gang or **Kao Kang** [gow gahng] (c.1902–55) One of the leaders of the Chinese Communist Party, born in Shensi province, China. In the mid-1930s he was in charge of a small independent Communist area at Baoan, Shanxi, where the Long March led by Mao Zedong ended. A close political ally of Mao, he later became chief Party secretary of Manchuria (1949). He set the national pace in economic development, but in 1955 was accused of attempting to set up a 'separate kingdom'. He apparently committed suicide.

Gaoxiong [gowshyung] or **Kao-hsiung** 22°36N 120°17E, pop (2000e) 1 509 000. Special municipality and seaport in SW Taiwan; on the SW coast, facing the Taiwan Strait; largest seaport and second largest city in Taiwan; world's largest ship-breaking centre, and second largest dry dock; occupied by the Japanese, 1895–1945; airport; railway; oil refining, fishing, foodstuffs; Cheng Ching Lake resort, Kenting National Park, Fo Guang Shan (Buddha Torch Mountain), with 25 m/82 ft-tall statue of Buddha on a 12 m/39 ft-high pedestal.

Gaozu (Han dynasty) [gow tsoo], also spelled **Kao-tsu**, originally **Liu Bang** (247–195 BC) First Han dynasty emperor of China. A bandit leader and former prison guard from eastern peasant stock, he seized the throne from the Qin by conquest (202 BC, but he backdated it to 206). He consolidated Qin achievements, building a new capital at Chang-an (modern Xian), re-established suzerainty over the S, and reorganized the empire into 13 provinces. One of only two commoners in Chinese history to found a major dynasty, he showed contempt for the scholar-aristocracy by urinating in their hats. Dying of septicaemia because he despised doctors, he was succeeded by his widow, Empress Lü.

gar Primitive slender-bodied fish confined to fresh and brackish rivers and lakes of North America; length up to 3 m/10 ft, scales rhomboidal, jaws prolonged to form a narrow snout; feeds voraciously on other fishes and crustaceans, caught by rapid striking movements; also called **garpikes**. (Genus: *Lepisosteus*. Family: Lepisosteidae.)

Garamba National park established in 1938 in N Democratic Republic of Congo, on the Sudanese border; area 4480 sq km/1730 sq mi; noted for its unique population of 'white' rhinoceroses; a world heritage site.

garbanzos *chick-pea*

Garbo, Greta, originally **Greta Lovisa Gustafsson** (1905–90) Film actress, born in Stockholm, Sweden. A shop-girl who won a bathing beauty competition at 16, she won a scholarship to the Royal Theatre Dramatic School in Stockholm, and starred in Mauritz Stiller's *Gösta Berling's Saga* (1924); he gave his star the name Garbo, chosen before he met her. She went to the USA in 1925, and her greatest successes, following *Anna Christie* (1930) – her first talking picture – were *Queen Christina* (1933), *Anna Karenina* (1935), *Camille* (1936), and *Ninotchka* (1939). She retired from films in 1941, after the failure of *Two-Faced Woman*. She became a US citizen in 1951, but remained a recluse for the rest of her life.

García Lorca, Federico *Lorca, Federico García*

García Márquez, Gabriel *Márquez, Gabriel García*

Gard, Pont du [põ dü gah(r)] An aqueduct built by the Romans early in the 1st-c AD to carry the water supply of the city of Nîmes in S France. It is c.275 m/900 ft long and towers 55 m/180 ft above the R Gard. Regarded as the finest surviving example of Roman engineering, it is a world heritage site.

Gard, Roger Martin du *Martin du Gard, Roger*

Garda, Lake, ancient **Lacus Benacus** area 370 sq km/143 sq mi. Largest Italian lake, between Lombardy and Venetia; length 52 km/32 mi; width 5–16·5 km/3–10 mi; maximum depth 346 m/1135 ft; N part narrow and fjord-like; fertile Riviera Bresciana on W side; until 1918 N tip belonged to Austria; resort towns include Desenzano, Garda, Sirmione.

Gardel, Carlos [gah(r)del] (1890–1935) Popular singer, born in Toulouse, S France. He was brought up in Buenos Aires, and made his name as a tango singer and later as a film star. Probably the best-known Latin-American singer of the 20th-c, he died in an aircraft accident in Medellín, Colombia.

garden bunting *ortolan*

garden city In the UK, a planned settlement designed to provide a spacious, high-quality, living and working environment. The concept is based on 19th-c ideas of Utopian communities, and was developed by Ebenezer Howard in 1898. Each garden city was planned to a concentric land use pattern, with c.32 000 people and a residential density of 75 per ha/30 per acre. The design featured wide streets and public parks inside the city, with farmland and green belt beyond. The first was built at Letchworth, Hertfordshire, in 1903, followed by Welwyn in 1919. The ideas were developed further in the British 'new towns' of the 1950s, and were also influential in Europe and the USA.

garden cress A slender annual (*Lepidium sativum*), single stem 20–40 cm/8–15 in, with lobed basal leaves and pinnate stem leaves; flowers small, white, cross-shaped; possibly native to W Asia. Long cultivated as a salad plant, it is the cress of mustard-and-cress. (Family: Cruciferae.)

gardenia An evergreen shrub or small tree, native mostly to the Old World tropics, China, and Japan; leaves elliptical, glossy; flowers white, fragrant, petals forming a tube with spreading lobes. It is named after the 18th-c physician and botanist Alexander Garden (1730–91). (Genus: *Gardenia*, 250 species. Family: Rubiaceae.)

garden myrrh *sweet cicely*

Gardiner, Stephen (c.1483–1555) Clergyman, born in Bury St Edmunds, Suffolk, E England, UK. Master of Trinity Hall, Cambridge, he became Wolsey's secretary in 1525. Between 1527 and 1533 he was sent to Rome to further Henry VIII's divorce from Catherine of Aragon, and was made Bishop of Winchester in 1531. He supported the royal supremacy in his *De vera obedientia* (1535), helped to encompass Thomas Cromwell's downfall, and was involved in framing the Six Articles. He was appointed Chancellor of Cambridge in 1540. He opposed doctrinal reformation, and for this he was imprisoned and deprived of his offices on Edward VI's accession. Released and restored by Mary I in 1553, he became an arch-persecutor of Protestants.

Gardner, Ava (Lavinnia), originally **Lucy Johnson** (1922–90) Film actress, born in Smithfield, North Carolina, USA. Signed by MGM as a teenager, she emerged from the ranks of decorative starlets with her portrayal of a ravishing femme fatale in *The Killers* (1946). A green-eyed brunette, once voted the world's most beautiful woman, she remained a leading lady for two decades, her films including *Mogambo* (1953), *The Barefoot Contessa* (1954), and *Night of the Iguana* (1964). In later years she continued to work as a character actress in films and on television. She was married to Mickey Rooney, Artie Shaw, and Frank Sinatra. Her autobiography, *Ava: My Story* (1990), was published posthumously.

Gardner, Erle Stanley (1889–1970) Crime novelist, born in Malden, Massachusetts, USA. After travelling a great deal while young, he settled in California, studied in law offices, and was admitted to the bar, where he became an ingenious lawyer for the defence (1922–38). In the 1940s he set up The Court of Last Resort, an organization to help those unjustly imprisoned. He is best known as the writer of the 'Perry Mason' books, beginning with *The Case of the Velvet Claws* (1933). His books enjoyed enhanced popularity when they were made into a long-running television series. He also wrote a series of detective novels featuring the District Attorney Doug Selby (*The DA...*).

Garfield, James A(bram) (1831–81) US statesman and 20th president (Mar–Sep 1881), born in Orange, Ohio, USA. He was a farmworker, teacher, lay preacher, and lawyer, before being elected to the Ohio State Senate in 1859. He fought in the Civil War until 1863, when he entered Congress and became leader of the Republican Party. After his election as president, he identified himself with the cause of civil service reform, thereby irritating many in his own Party. He was shot at Washington, DC, by a disappointed office-seeker, Charles Guiteau, and died two months later.

garfish *needlefish*

Garfunkel, Art (1942–) Singer and actor, born in Forest Hills, New York, USA. He teamed up with Paul Simon as a teenager, forming a duo called Tom and Jerry, and (as Simon and Garfunkel) issuing their first album, *Wednesday Morning 3 am* in 1964. 'The Sound of Silence' (1965) brought them their first major success as a duo, followed in 1968 by the soundtrack for the film *The Graduate* and the hit album *Bridge Over Troubled Water* (1970). The duo split up following Garfunkel's decision to go into acting. He made his debut in *Catch 22* (1970), and later films included *Carnal Knowledge* (1971) and *Boxing Helena* (1993). He continued to record as a soloist, beginning with the album, *Angel Clare* (1973), and achieved a UK number 1 with 'Bright Eyes' (1979), the theme song from the film *Watership Down*. There have been occasional reunion concerts with Simon.

garganey [gah(r)ganee] A small, slender duck (*Anas querquedula*), native to S Eurasia, W and NE Africa, and Indonesia; male brown with white stripe from eye to back of neck; migrates to tropics for winter; the most numerous duck wintering in Africa. (Family: Anatidae.)

gargoyle In Gothic architecture, a stone rainwater spout carved in the form of a grotesque animal or human face, with its mouth open as if spewing the water. It is usually built so as to project well out from the parapet, thus sending the water away from the building.

Garibaldi, Giuseppe [garibawldee] (1807–82) Italian patriot, born in Nice, SE France. In 1834 he joined Mazzini's 'Young Italy' movement, and was condemned to death for participating in the attempt to seize Genoa, but escaped to South America. Returning to Europe, in 1849 he joined the revolutionary government of Rome, but was again forced to leave Italy. After working in New York, he returned to Italy in 1854 and took up the life of a farmer on the island of Caprera. With the outbreak in 1859 of Italy's war of liberation, he returned to action; with his 'thousand' volunteers he sailed from Genoa (May 1860) and arrived in Sicily, where he assisted Mazzinian rebels to free Sicily from Neapolitan control. Crossing with his army to the mainland, he swiftly overran much of S Italy, and drove King Francis of Naples from his capital (Sep 1860). Thereafter he allowed the conquest of S Italy to be completed by the Sardinians under Victor Emmanuel II. With the Kingdom of Italy a reality, and refusing all personal reward, he retired into private life on Caprera.

Garland, Judy, originally **Frances Gumm** (1922–69) Actress and singer, born in Grand Rapids, Minnesota, USA. She made her first stage appearances in vaudeville with her parents, and became a juvenile film star in *Broadway Melody of 1938*, followed by *The Wizard of Oz* (1939) and *Meet Me in St Louis* (1944), directed by Vincente Minnelli, whom she later married. A demanding series of musical leads coupled with drug problems exhausted her by 1950, and she spent the next four years in variety performances, returning to films with the 1954 remake of *A Star is Born*. Concerts and occasional films continued with public success, but her private life was full of overwhelming difficulties, and she died in London, apparently from an overdose of sleeping pills.

garlic A perennial bulb (*Allium sativum*) up to 60 cm/2 ft; narrow, flat leaves; greenish-to-purple star-shaped flowers mixed with bulbils. Native to Asia, it has been cultivated in the Mediterranean region since ancient times for the strongly flavoured bulbs which are widely used in cooking. Wild relatives are sometimes used as poor substitutes. (Family: Liliaceae.)

garlic mustard A biennial 20–120 cm/8 in–4 ft high (*Alliaria petiolata*), native to Europe and Asia; bright pale-green, heart-shaped leaves; heads of small, white, cross-shaped flowers; The whole plant smells of garlic, especially when crushed. Commonly found along hedgerows, it is sometimes called **hedge garlic**. (Family: Cruciferae.)

Garner, Jay (1938–) US general, born in Florida, USA. He studied at Florida State University (1962) and Shippensburg University, PA. He joined the US Army in 1960, served in Vietnam, and during the 1991 Gulf War supervised the deployment of Patriot missile batteries. After the war he commanded Operation Provide Comfort for the resettlement of Kurdish refugees in N Iraq. In 1994 he became commander of the US Space and Strategic Defense Command, and was assistant chief-of-staff until his retirement in 1997. After the Iraq War (Mar–Apr 2003), he was appointed director of the Office of Reconstruction and Humanitarian Assistance for Iraq.

garnet A group of silicate minerals occurring mainly in metamorphic rocks, but also found in pegmatites. It displays a wide range of composition and colour. Important members and their primary constituents are *pyrope* (Mg, Al), *almandine* (Fe, Al), *grossularite* (Ca, Al), and *andradite* (Ca, Fe). Some varieties are important as gemstones.

Garonne, River [garon], ancient **Garumna** Chief river of SW France, rising in the Val d'Aran, 42 km/26 mi inside the Spanish border; flows from the C Pyrenees NE and NW to the Bec d'Ambes, 32 km/20 mi below Bordeaux, where it meets the R Dordogne to form the Gironde estuary; length 575 km/357 mi; linked to the Mediterranean at Toulouse by the Canal du Midi.

garpike *gar*

Garrett, Lesley (1955–) Soprano, born in Doncaster, South Yorkshire, England, UK. She studied at the Royal Academy of Music and the National Opera Studio, winning the Kathleen Ferrier Memorial Competition in 1979. In 1984 she joined the English National Opera as principal soprano, and made her US debut tour in 1995. Her television work includes two series of *Lesley Garrett Tonight* (BBC 1998, 2000), and among her albums are *Soprano in Red* (1995), *I Will Wait for You* (2000), and *So Deep is the Night* (2003). An autobiography, *Notes From a Small Soprano*, appeared in 2000.

Garrett, Peter (Robert) (1953–) Popular singer and political activist, born in Sydney, New South Wales, SE Australia. He studied at the Australian National University and the University of New South Wales, and became a lawyer. During 1977–2002 he was lead singer with the band Midnight Oil, which has achieved considerable fame in Australia and abroad, many of their songs dealing with issues such as Aboriginal land rights, conservation, and prison reform. He became widely known in 1984 when he stood for parliament, narrowly missing out on becoming a senator for the Nuclear Disarmament Party. He is president (1989–93, 1998–) of the Australian Conservation Foundation, a job he combines with that of a rock-and-roll star. He was awarded the Order of Australia in 2003.

Garrick, David (1717–79) Actor, theatre manager, and playwright, born in Hereford, Hereford and Worcester, WC England, UK. His first play was performed at Drury Lane in 1740, and the following year he won acting fame as Richard III. As an actor, Garrick was opposed to the declamatory and elaborate style fashionable at the time, and developed a more natural way of speaking. As a manager he introduced concealed stage lighting and naturalistically painted backdrops. For 30 years he dominated the English stage, in a wide range of parts, and was joint manager of Drury Lane (1747–76). His own plays include *Miss in her Teens* (1747) and *Bon Ton: or High Life Above Stairs* (1775), as well as adaptations of plays by Shakespeare.

garrigue [gareeg] Evergreen scrubland vegetation found in areas with thin soils and a Mediterranean-type climate; also known as **garigue** or **garriga**. Low, thorny shrubs and stunted oak are characteristic. In places it may result from the degradation of maquis vegetation through mismanagement of the land.

Garrison, William Lloyd (1805–79) Abolitionist, born in Newburyport, Massachusetts, USA. Educated informally, he emerged in 1830 as the foremost anti-slavery voice in the USA. His newspaper *The Liberator* (1831) argued the case for immediate abolition, and his American Anti-Slavery Society (1833) mobilized the energies of thousands of people in the cause.

Garrod, Sir Archibald (Edward) (1857–1936) Physician, born in London, UK. He studied at Oxford, where he went on to hold a chair of medicine (1920–7). His study of inherited human metabolic diseases, described in his *Inborn Errors of Metabolism* (1909), was far ahead of its time: he showed that Mendelian genetics applied to humans, and correctly proposed a connection between an altered gene (a mutation) and a blocked metabolic pathway causing a specific disease. This concept, basic to biochemical genetics, was strangely neglected for 30 years.

garron *Highland pony*

Garter, the Most Noble Order of the (KG) The most ancient order of chivalry in Europe, founded by Edward III of England between 1344 and 1351. The emblem of the order, which is the personal gift of the sovereign, is a gold-edged blue garter, inscribed in gold with *Honi soit qui mal y pense* (Fr 'Shamed be he who thinks evil of it'), traditionally the words spoken by Edward after he picked up the Countess of Salisbury's dropped garter. There are usually 25 knights of the Order under the sovereign.

gas **1** A state of matter in which atoms are disordered and highly mobile, moving randomly with little interaction. Gases are characterized by low densities (typically 1/1000 of a solid), an ability to flow and to fill a container, and high compressibility. All substances will pass into the gas or vapour phase if heated to a high enough temperature. All gases which do not react with one another form a homogeneous mixture in all proportions.
2 A fuel which includes both **manufactured gas**, derived from solid or liquid fossil fuels, and **natural gas**, drawn from existing gaseous subterranean accumulations. The Chinese used natural gas for brine evaporation in the 1st-c BC. In the West, manufactured gas (or **town gas**) was made from the early 19th-c by the distillation of coal. The economics of the coal-gas industry depended to a great extent on its non-gaseous by-products. In the 20th-c, town gas was also made by the chemical conversion of surplus naphtha from the petroleum industry or natural solid fuels other than coal. Natural gas occurs on its own or in association with oil deposits in many locations throughout the world. The main constituent of town gas is hydrogen; that of natural gas is methane. The calorific value of natural gas is about double that of town gas.

Gascoigne, Paul [gaskoyn], nickname **Gazza** (1967–) Footballer, born in Gateshead, Tyne and Wear, NE England, UK. He was an apprentice footballer with Newcastle United before turning professional in 1985. After Tottenham Hotspur signed him in 1988, he established himself as an outstanding player and a flamboyant personality, becoming a member of the England team, and had won 57 caps by the end of his international career. During the 1991 FA Cup Final he sustained a serious knee injury which seemed to threaten his agreed transfer deal to an Italian club, Lazio, for a record £5 million. After a long recovery he moved to Lazio in time for the 1992–3 season, where he continued to be a controversial figure on and off the field. He received a further serious leg injury in 1994, and moved to Rangers from Lazio in 1995. In 1998 he joined Middlesbrough, but was out of the game again in early 2000, after breaking his arm. He then joined a succession of clubs – Everton (2000), Burnley (2002), and Wolverhampton Wanderers (2003).

Gascony [gaskonee], Fr **Gascogne**, Lat **Vasconia** Former province in Aquitaine region, SW France, now occupying the departments of Landes, Gers, Hautes-Pyrénées, and some adjacent areas; bounded S by the Pyrenees and W by the Bay of Biscay; part of the Roman Empire; conquered by the Visigoths, later by the Franks, who made it a duchy; joined to Guienne, 1052; in English hands, 1154–1453.

gas-cooled reactor *nuclear reactor*

gas engine A specially adapted or designed internal combustion engine which uses gas (not in the sense of petrol) as its fuel. In the 19th-c such engines were run off the gas mains, but modern practice stores the gas (usually methane) in pressurized tanks as a liquid.

gas gangrene An infection of muscle and soft tissue by *Clostridium perfringens*. The bacteria infect wounds and secrete a toxin that digests tissues, producing gas bubbles from fermentation. The affected part is blackened and foul smelling, and the infection spreads rapidly, requiring urgent excision or amputation. Rare in peacetime, the infection is the scourge of soldiers on the battlefield.

Gaskell, Elizabeth (Cleghorn), *née* **Stevenson**, known as **Mrs Gaskell** (1810–65) Writer, born in London, UK. In 1832 she married **William Gaskell** (1805–84), a Unitarian minister in Manchester. She did not begin to write until middle age, when she published *Mary Barton* (1848). Her other works include *Cranford* (1853), *Ruth* (1853), *North and South* (1854–5), *Wives and Daughters* (1865, unfinished; televised 2000), and a biography of her friend Charlotte Brontë.

gas laws Boyle's and Charles's Laws together, interrelating pressure, volume, and temperature for a given mass of an ideal gas. These laws may be summarized in a single equation: $pV = nRT$, where p is the pressure exerted by n moles of a gas contained in a volume V at an absolute temperature T. R is a constant, with a value of about 8·3 J $K^{-1}mol^{-1}$, called the *gas constant*.

gasohol A mixture of gasoline with 5/15 % ethanol (ethyl alcohol which must be water-free), useful as a high-octane rating fuel in internal combustion engines. It is economically important in countries with a cheap supply of ethyl alcohol.

gas oil A liquid fuel, the heavier fraction of petroleum distillation. It is used as a heating fuel and in diesel engines.

gasoline *petrol*

Gasperi, Alcide de [gaspayree] (1881–1954) Italian statesman and prime minister (1945–53), born in Trentino, N Italy. He studied at Innsbruck and Vienna, entered parliament in 1911, and was imprisoned by Mussolini as an anti-facist (1927). From 1929 he worked in the Vatican library until he became prime minister of the new republic, heading a succession of coalition cabinets. A founder of the Christian Democratic Party, he was also a strong believer in a United Europe.

Gassendi, Pierre [gasãdee] (1592–1655) Philosopher and scientist, born in Champtercier, SE France. Ordained priest (1616), he became professor of philosophy at Aix (1617) and professor of mathematics at the Collège Royal in Paris (1645). Kepler and Galileo were among his friends. He was a strong advocate of the experimental approach to science, and tried to reconcile an atomic theory of matter (based on the Epicurean model) with Christian doctrine. He is best known for his *Objections* (1642) to Descartes' *Meditations*, but he also wrote on others, including Copernicus. His works include *Institutio astronomica* (1647) and the *Syntagma philosophicum* (Philosophical Treatise), published posthumously in 1658.

gastric juice A mixture of substances secreted by cells and glands within the stomach, consisting of hydrochloric acid (from parietal cells), pepsinogen (from chief cells), mucus, and intrinsic factor (from mucous cells). Excessive secretion of acid and pepsinogen may lead to the formation of ulcers. Inability to produce intrinsic factor results in pernicious anaemia.

gastric ulcer A peptic ulcer arising in the stomach.

gastrin A hormone (a peptide) secreted in the stomach in response to both the presence of protein in the pylorus and increased discharge of the vagus nerve. It stimulates the parietal cells of the stomach to secrete hydrochloric acid, through the mediation of histamine released from cells (*histaminocytes*) close by. It is also present in the duodenum, pituitary gland, and the brain (where it may function as a neurotransmitter).

gastritis [gastr**iy**tis] Inflammation of the stomach lining as a result of irritants, such as alcohol, cigarettes, spicy food, or strongly acid substances such as aspirin. These cause patches of inflammation which sometimes bleed. This leads to upper abdominal pain, nausea, and vomiting, sometimes with blood. Persistent irritation leads to chronic gastritis, with thinning of the lining of the stomach and sometimes ulcers.

gastro-enteritis [gastrohenter**iy**tis] Irritation and inflammation of any part of the gastro-intestinal tract, usually by an infectious micro-organism, characterized by abdominal pain, vomiting, diarrhoea, and severe prostration in some cases. As infants have smaller reserves of water and salt, they are especially vulnerable to losses of body fluids.

gastro-intestinal tract *alimentary canal*

gastropod [**gas**tropod] The snails, slugs, and snail-like molluscs; body consists of a head, muscular foot, and visceral mass largely covered by a calcareous shell, usually spirally coiled; body characterized by torsion during development, so that the anus opens above the head; typically feeds on plant material using a band-like set of rasping teeth (the *radula*); many advanced forms are carnivorous, some are parasitic; includes land and freshwater snails and slugs, as well as a great diversity of marine snails such as the conches, cowries, limpets, sea slugs, whelks, and winkles. (Phylum: Mollusca. Class: Gastropoda.)

gastrotrich [**gas**trotrik] A minute, worm-like animal found in or on bottom sediments and in association with other aquatic organisms in various habitats; body covered in a horny layer (*cuticle*), and may have bristles. (Phylum: Gastrotricha, c.150 species.)

gastrula [**gas**trula] The stage following the blastula in the embryonic development of animals. During this phase (**gastrulation**), cells of the embryo move into their correct position for development into the various organ systems of the adult.

gas turbine An engine that passes the products of the combustion of its fuel/air mixture over the blades of a turbine. The turbine drives an air compressor, which in turn provides the air for the combustion process. The energy of the combustion products not taken up by the compressor can be used to provide a jet of exhaust gases, or drive another turbine.

gas warfare *chemical warfare*

Gates, Bill, popular name of **William Henry Gates** (1955–) Computer engineer and entrepreneur, born in Seattle, Washington, USA. At age 15 he constructed a device to control traffic patterns in Seattle, and in 1975 co-wrote a compiler for BASIC and interested the MITS company in it. He dropped out of Harvard in 1975 to spend his time writing programmes. In 1977, he co-founded Microsoft to develop and produce DOS, his basic operating system for computers. When in 1981 International Business Machines (IBM) adopted DOS for its line of personal computers, his company took a giant step forward; by 1983 he had licensed DOS to more than 100 vendors, making it the dominant operating system. By age 35 he had become one of the wealthiest men in America, and by the late 1990s, the wealthiest. In 1998 the government sued Microsoft for alleged anti-trust violations (*see* **Microsoft** *entry*).

Gates, Horatio (1728–1806) US general, born in Maldon, Essex, SE England, UK. He joined the British army, served in America in the Seven Years War (1756–63), and then settled there. In the War of Independence he sided with his adoptive country, and in 1777 took command of the Northern department, compelling the surrender of the British army at Saratoga, NY. In 1780, he commanded the Army of the South, but was routed by Cornwallis near Camden, SC, and was superseded. He retired to Virginia until 1790, emancipated his slaves, and settled in New York City.

gateway A facility provided between computer networks to enable a network operating according to one protocol to pass messages to a second network working to a different protocol.

Gatling, Richard Jordan (1818–1903) Inventor, born in Maney's Neck, North Carolina, USA. He assisted his father in the construction of cotton-sowing machines, then studied medicine, but never practised. During the American Civil War he turned to the development of firearms, and is best remembered for his invention of the rapid-fire *Gatling gun* (1861–2), a crank-operated revolving multibarrel machine gun. His weapon came to public notice again in 1991, when it was used as the principal weapon platform on US A10 aircraft during the Gulf War.

GATT *General Agreement on Tariffs and Trade*

gaucho [**gow**choh] A nomadic, fiercely independent mestizo horseman of the Argentine pampa, first appearing in the 17th-c. With the advent of ranches, railways, and settled government in the 19th-c, the gaucho vanished, though gaucho skills live on among the rural population of Argentina and Uruguay. An inhabitant of the S states of Brazil is known by a similar name.

Gaudí (I Cornet), Antonio [gow**dee**] (1852–1926) Architect, born in Reus, NE Spain. He studied at the School of Architecture in Barcelona, and became the most famous exponent of Catalan 'modernisme', one of the branches of the Art Nouveau movement. He is best known for the extravagant and ornate church of the Holy Family in Barcelona, which occupied him from 1884 until his death, and which is still unfinished.

Gaudier-Brzeska, Henri [**gohd**yay **bres**ka] (1891–1915) Sculptor, born in St Jean de Braye, C France. He lived in London from 1911, and exhibited with the London Group in 1914 before joining the French army. He was killed in action at Neuville-Saint-Vaast. A pioneering Modernist who drew upon African tribal art, he rapidly developed a highly personal abstract style exemplified in carvings and drawings.

Gaudron, Mary [**god**ron] (1943–) Judge, born in Moree, New South Wales, SE Australia. She studied at St Ursula's College, Armidale, and Sydney University, and became a lawyer. In 1974 she was the youngest ever federal judge when appointed deputy-president of the Arbitration Commission, and in 1981 was the youngest ever NSW solicitor general. Seen as a progressive, in 1987 she became the first woman to be appointed to the High Court of Australia.

gauge theory A type of theory in mechanics in which interactions correspond to special symmetry transformations of the basic equations of the theory. Quantum gauge theories, in which interactions between subatomic particles are related to the preservation of symmetry properties at each point in space and time, are essential to nuclear and particle physics. Quantum electrodynamics, quantum chromodynamics, and the Glashow–Weinberg–Salam theory are all gauge theories. In quantum electrodynamics, the requirement of conservation of electric charge at each point of space and time corresponds to the observed interaction of photons with charged particles.

Gauguin, (Eugène Henri) Paul [goh**gĩ**] (1848–1903) Postimpressionist painter, born in Paris, France. He went to sea at 17, settled in Paris in 1871, married, and became a successful stockbroker who painted as a hobby. By 1876 he had begun to exhibit his own work. He left his family, visited Martinique (1887), and became the leader of a group of painters at Pont Aven, Brittany (1888). From 1891 he lived mainly in Tahiti and the Marquesas Is, using local people as his subjects. He gradually evolved his own style, *Synthétisme*, reflecting his hatred of civilization and the inspiration he found in primitive peoples. Among his best-known works are 'The Vision After the Sermon' (1888, Edinburgh), and the major allegorical work 'D'où venons-nous? Que sommes-nous? Où allons-nous?' (1897–8, Where Do We Come From? What Are We? Where Are We Going?, Boston). He also excelled in wood carvings of pagan idols.

Gaul (Lat *Gallia*) In ancient geography normally used for **Transalpine Gaul**, bounded by the Alps, the Rhine, and the Pyrenees. Julius Caesar completed the Roman conquest in 58–51 BC, the impact of Romanization being felt most in the S, where Roman law remained in use until 1789. With the gradual Roman withdrawal in the 5th-c, Germanic colonies became independent kingdoms. Unity was superficially achieved under Clovis and Charlemagne; later, after many vicissitudes, Gaul – its easternmost territories excluded – developed into the mediaeval kingdom of France. **Cisalpine Gaul** lay S of the Alps and N of the Apennines. Conquered by the Romans in 201–191 BC, it was incorporated into Italy in 42 BC.

Gaulish *Celtic languages*

Gaullists Members of the French political party, the *Rassemblement pour la République* (RPR) whose programmes are based on the doctrine developed by President de Gaulle in 1958–69. Nationalistic in character, Gaullists emphasize the need for strong government, especially in relations with the European Union and foreign powers such as the USA.

Gaultier, Jean-Paul [**goht**yay] (1952–) Fashion designer, born in Paris, France. At the age of eighteen he was designing for the Pierre Cardin fashion house, then joined the couture houses of Jacques Esterel and Jean Patou before producing his own independent collection in 1976. Among his well-known designs were the pointed corsets worn by Madonna during her 1990 Blonde Ambition World Tour. He reached a new audience as co-host of the magazine show *Eurotrash* on British television.

Gaumont, Léon Ernest [goh**mõ**], Eng [**goh**mont] (1864–1946) Cinema inventor, manufacturer, and producer, born in Paris, France. He synchronized a projected film with a phonograph in 1901, and was responsible for the first talking pictures, demonstrated at Paris in 1910. He also introduced an early form of coloured cinematography in 1912.

Gaunt, John of *John of Gaunt*

gaur [**gow**er] A rare wild ox (*Bos gaurus*) native to hill forests of India and SE Asia; largest of wild cattle (shoulder height, 2 m/ 6½ ft); dark brown with white 'stockings'; bony ridge along back behind neck; high, strongly curved horns; also known as **Indian bison** or **seladang**; domesticated form called a **gayal** (or **mithan**).

Gauss, (Johann) Carl Friedrich [gows] (1777–1855) Mathematician, born in Brunswick, NC Germany. A prodigy in mental calculation, he conceived most of his mathematical theories by the age of 17, and was sent to study at Brunswick and Göttingen. He wrote the first modern book on number theory, in which he proved the law of quadratic reciprocity, and discovered the intrinsic differential geometry of surfaces. He also discovered, but did not publish, a theory of elliptic and complex functions, and pioneered the application of mathematics to such areas as gravitation, magnetism, and electricity. In 1807 he became professor of mathematics and director of the observatory at Göttingen, and in 1821 was appointed to conduct the trigonometrical survey of Hanover, for which he invented a heliograph. The unit of magnetic induction has been named after him.

Gauss's law [gows] In electrostatics, the total electric flux through some closed surface is proportional to the total charge enclosed by that surface; stated by Carl Gauss. The constant of proportionality is $1/\varepsilon$, where ε is permittivity. The law is the expression of charge as a source of electric field.

Gauteng [**khow**teng] (Sesotho 'place of gold') One of the nine new provinces established by the South African constitution of 1994, in NC South Africa, occupying the area formerly known as the PWV (Pretoria–Witwatersrand–Vereeniging) triangle; capital, Johannesburg; pop (2000e) 8 118 000; area 18 760 sq km/ 7241 sq mi; chief languages, Afrikaans, Zulu, English; Pretoria is the administrative capital of South Africa; smallest province, most densely populated; commercial, financial, and industrial heartland of South Africa, containing c.70% of the labour force, and producing c.37% of GDP.

Gautier, Théophile [**goht**yay] (1811–72) Writer and critic, born in Tarbes, S France. From painting he turned to literature, and became an extreme Romantic. In 1830 he published his first long poem, 'Albertus', and his celebrated novel *Mademoiselle de*

Maupin appeared in 1835. His most important collection was *Emaux et camées* (1852, Enamels and Cameos).

Gavaskar, Sunil (Manohar) [gavaskah(r)] (1949–) Cricketer, born in Mumbai (Bombay), W India. An opening batsman who scored 774 runs in his first Test series (1970–1), he played 125 Test matches for India, leading them on many occasions, scoring a then record 10 122 runs, and between 1974–5 and 1986–7 played in a record 106 consecutive Test matches. He scored 25 834 runs in first-class cricket at an average of 51·46 per innings. His highest innings was 236 not out against the West Indies in Chennai (Madras) in 1983–4, the highest score made by an Indian batsman in Test cricket.

gavial *gharial*

gavotte [gavot] A French folk dance which originated among the peasants, known as Gavots, of the Pays de Gap region of the former French Province of Dauphiné. It became popular as a court dance during the 17th–18th-c, and was often included in instrumental and orchestral suites of the period. It was in a moderately quick duple or quadruple metre to which pairs of dancers moved in a circle.

Gawain or **Gawayne** [gawayn] One of King Arthur's knights, the son of King Lot of Orkney, whose character varies in different accounts. In the mediaeval *Sir Gawayn and the Grene Knight*, he is a noble hero undergoing a test of faith. In other stories he is a jeering attacker of reputations, especially that of Lancelot.

Gay, John (1685–1732) Poet and playwright, born in Barnstaple, Devon, SW England, UK. He was apprenticed to a London silk mercer, but turned to literature, writing poems, pamphlets, and in 1727 the first series of his popular satirical *Fables*. His greatest success was *The Beggar's Opera* (1728), which achieved an unprecedented theatrical run of 62 performances. He was a friend of Pope and Swift.

gayal [gayal] *gaur*

Gay-Lussac, Joseph Louis [gay luhsak] (1778–1850) Chemist and physicist, born in St Léonard, C France. He studied at the Ecole Polytechnique in Paris, and became assistant to Berthollet (1801). He began a series of investigations into gases, temperature, and the behaviour of vapours. He made hydrogen-filled-balloon ascents to 7000 m/23 000 ft (1804) to study the laws of terrestrial magnetism and to collect samples of air for analysis, which led to his major discovery, the law of combining volumes of gases named after him (1808): volumes of reacting gases bear a simple ratio to one another and to the volumes of the gaseous products. In 1809 he became professor of chemistry at the Polytechnique in Paris, and from 1832 at the Jardin des Plantes.

Gazankulu [gazangkooloo] Former national state or non-independent black homeland in Transvaal province, NE South Africa; achieved self-governing status in 1973; incorporated into Northern Province in the new constitution of 1994.

Gaza Strip pop (2000e) 1 163 000, including c.4000 Jewish settlers; area 202 sq km/78 sq mi. A narrow strip of land bounded NW by the Mediterranean Sea; length, 50 km/30 mi; chief town, Gaza; agricultural economy; formerly part of Egyptian Sinai, after Arab–Israeli War of 1948–9; Israeli-occupied district under military administration containing many Palestinian refugee camps, 1967–94; considerable tension in the area after the beginning of the uprising (*intifada*) in 1988; peace agreement (1993) with PLO assigned it to Palestine.

gazelle An elegant athletic antelope, native to Africa and S Asia; usually pale brown above with white underparts; some species with thick black line along side; face often with weak stripes; when alarmed, moves by 'pronking' (or 'stotting') – a vertical leap using all four legs simultaneously. (Tribe: Antilopini, 18 species.)

gazelle hound *saluki*

GCSE Abbreviation of **General Certificate of Secondary Education**, introduced in England and Wales for the first time in 1988, which merged what had previously been two separate examinations for pupils aged about 16 or older. These earlier examinations were the *General Certificate of Education* (GCE), which was originally aimed at about the top 20% of the ability range, and the *Certificate of Secondary Education* (CSE), which was meant for the next 40%. In practice the situation had become much more complex, with about 90% of pupils taking one or other of the exams, and some schools entering the same pupils for both. A similar examination reform, the *Standard Grade*, had been introduced in Scotland two years earlier.

Gdańsk [gdansk], formerly Ger **Danzig** 54°22N 18°38E, pop (2000e) 469 000. Industrial port and capital of Gdańsk voivodship, N Poland; at the mouth of the Martwa Wisla; held by Prussia, 1793–1919; free city within the Polish tariff area, 1919; annexation by Germany in 1939, precipitating World War 2; Lenin shipyard the scene of much labour unrest in 1980s, in support of Solidarity; part of the *Tri-city* with Sopot and Gdynia; airport; railway; two universities (1945, 1970); maritime research institutes; largest shipyard in Poland; textiles, televisions, fertilizer, oil refining, food processing, cold storage; High Gate, Golden Gate, Bakers' Gate, St George Fraternity Mansion (1487–94), Artus Court, Swan Tower, Royal Granary (1620), national museum, archaeological museum; Churches of the Virgin Mary, St John, St Elizabeth, St Catherine, Holy Trinity; Gdańsk Festival (Aug), Polish film festival (Sep).

GDP *gross domestic product*

Gdynia [gdinya] 54°31N 18°30E, pop (2000e) 254 000. Sea-port city in N Poland, 20 km/12 mi NW of Gdańsk; developed 1924–9 as a major Baltic port and naval base; part of the *Tri-city* with Sopot and Gdańsk; railway; shipbuilding, fishing, oceanographic museum; monument to Polish and Soviet soldiers.

gean [geen] A species of cherry (*Prunus avium*) native to Europe and Asia, forming a tall tree with white flowers and dark, purplish-red, sweet or sour fruit; also called **wild** or **bird cherry**. It is a parent of the sweet cherry of orchards. (Family: Rosaceae.)

gear A device used to transform one rotary motion into another, in terms of speed and direction. The fundamental type of gear is the toothed gear wheel, which can be used in a wide variety of combinations and configurations to produce the desired ratio of output rotation to input rotation.

Gebrselassie, Haile [gabruhselasee, hiylee] (1973–) Athlete, born in Arssi, Ethiopia. The dominant long-distance runner of the 1990s, he was four times world champion (1993, 1995, 1997, 1999) and twice Olympic champion (1996, 2000) at 10 000 m. He broke his first world record in 1994, reducing the 5000 m record to 12 min 56·96 and had set a total of 15 world records by 2000. Undefeated outdoors at distances between 1500 m and 1000 m in 1997 and 1998 seasons, he was International Athletics Federation Athlete of the Year in 1998.

gecko A lizard native to warm regions worldwide; body usually flattened top to bottom; skin soft; eyes large, without movable eyelids; tongue short, often used to lick eyes; many species with flattened toes for walking on vertical surfaces; eats mainly insects; most individuals nocturnal; males are the only lizards with loud calls. (Family: Gekkonidae, 800 species.)

gedankenexperiment *thought experiment*

Geelong [jeelong] 38°10S 144°26E, pop (2000e) 161 000. Port in S Victoria, Australia, on the W side of Corio Bay, part of Port Phillip Bay; Deakin University (1974); railway; aluminium and oil refining, motor vehicles, trade in wheat, wool; many 19th-c villas with beautiful gardens; National Wool Museum; customs house the oldest wooden building in Victoria.

gegenschein [gaygenshiyn] *zodiacal light*

Gehenna [gehena] (Gr form of the Heb *Gehinnom* 'Valley of Hinnom', a ravine SW of Jerusalem) In c.7th-c BC, the site of cultic sacrifices of children to Baal by fire, condemned by Jeremiah (*Jer* 19.4–6); later considered an entrance to the underworld. The name is metaphorically used in both Judaism and the New Testament as a place where the wicked would be tormented (usually by fire) after death (eg *Mark* 9.43).

Gehrig, (Henry) Lou(is) [gerig], nickname **the Iron Horse** (1903–41) Baseball player, born in New York City, USA. He played a record 2130 consecutive games for the New York Yankees (1925–39). An outstanding first-baseman, he ended his career with a batting average of ·340 and hit 493 home runs. His career was cut short by illness – amyotrophic lateral sclerosis, widely known as 'Lou Gehrig's disease' in the USA.

Gehry, Frank O [gairee] (1929–) Architect, born in Toronto, Ontario, Canada. Trained at the University of Southern California and Harvard, he opened his own Los Angeles firm (1962). His work is characterized by sculptural design, 'brutalist' combinations of materials such as corrugated metal and chain-link fencing in residential applications, and undefined interiors. Among his best-known buildings is the Guggenheim Museum, Bilbao (1997). Other projects include the Richard B Fisher Center for Performing Arts at Bard College in the Hudson Valley (2003), and in the UK, the Maggie Centre, a facility for cancer sufferers in Dundee (2003). His awards include the Pritzker Architecture Prize (1989) and the American Academy of Arts and Letters Gold Medal (2002).

Geiger, Hans Wilhelm [giyger] (1882–1945) Physicist, born in Neustadt-an-der-Haardt, SW Germany. He studied at Erlangen, worked under Ernest Rutherford at Manchester (1906–12), investigated beta-ray radioactivity and, with Walther Müller, devised a counter to measure it. He was professor at Kiel (1925) and at Tübingen (1929), and later worked in Berlin.

Geiger counter [giyger] A device for counting atomic particles, named after German physicist Hans Geiger. Gas between electrodes is ionized by the passage of a particle, and so transmits a pulse to a counter.

Geisel, Ernesto [giyzl] (1908–96) Brazilian general and president (1974–9), born in Rio Grande do Sul, Brazil. His military presidency was notable for its policy of 'decompression', which led to the restoration of democracy in 1985.

gel [jel] A colloidal suspension of a solid in a liquid, in which the properties of the solid predominate. An example is gelatine.

gelada baboon [jelada] A baboon native to the mountains of Ethiopia (*Theropithecus gelada*); brown coat (long and thick over head and shoulders); long pale 'whiskers' surround face; top of muzzle ridged; cheeks sunken; tail long; chest with areas of naked scarlet skin.

gelatin(e) [jelatin] A protein formed when collagen (a fibrous protein found in animal bones, skin, and hair) is boiled in water. Its dilute suspension in water sets to a firm colloid. It is used in foods, adhesives, and photographic emulsions.

Geldof, Bob [geldof], popular name of **Robert Frederick Xenon Geldof** (1954–) Rock musician and philanthropist, born in Dublin, Ireland. He studied at Black Rock College, worked in Canada as a pop journalist, then returned home in 1975 to form the successful rock group, the Boomtown Rats (1975–86). Moved by television pictures of widespread suffering in famine-stricken Ethiopia, he established the pop charity 'Band Aid' trust in 1984, which raised £8 million for Africa famine relief through the release of the record 'Do they know it's Christmas?'. In 1985, simultaneous 'Live Aid' charity concerts were held in London and Philadelphia which, transmitted by satellite throughout the world, raised a further £48 million. He was awarded an honorary knighthood in 1986.

gelignite A group of industrial explosives consisting of a gelatinized mixture of nitroglycerine and nitrocellulose. Inert non-explosive material (*extenders*) promote safety in handling.

Gellhorn, Martha (Ellis) (1908–98) Journalist and writer, born in St Louis, Missouri, USA. She studied at Bryn Mawr College, Pennsylvania. In 1936 she met Ernest Hemingway (whom she married in 1940 and divorced in 1946) and the following year became war correspondent for *Collier's Weekly*, covering the Spanish Civil War and wars in Finland, China, and Java. Later she reported from wars in Vietnam (1966), the Middle East (1967), and Central America (1983–5). She is best known for her books of collected journalism and memoirs, which include the acutely observed *Travels with Myself and Others* (1978).

Gell-Mann, Murray [gelman] (1929–) Theoretical physicist, born in New York City, USA. He studied at Yale and the Massachussets Institute of Technology, becoming professor of theoretical physics at the California Institute of Technology in 1956. At 24 he made a major contribution by introducing the concept of *strangeness* into the theory of elemental particles. This allowed new classifications and predictions, outlined by Gell-Mann and Ne'eman in their book *The Eightfold Way* (1964). He proposed the existence of sub-atomic particles, which he named *quarks*, and subsequent research brought widespread acceptance of his hypothesis. He was awarded the Nobel Prize for Physics in 1969. In 1993 he became director of the Santa Fe Institute, New Mexico, and in 1994 published *The Quark and the Jaguar*.

Gemara [gemahra] (Aramaic 'completion') A commentary on the Jewish Mishnah, which together with the Mishnah constitutes the Talmud. It consists largely of scholarly rabbinic discussions that interpret and extend the applications of legal teachings in Rabbi Judah's Mishnah. Distinct versions were produced in Palestine and Babylon.

Gemayel [gemiyel] One of the leading political families of Lebanon's Maronite Christian community. **Sheikh Pierre** (1905–84), educated in Beirut and Paris, founded the Kataeb or Phalangist Party in 1936. Originally a youth group modelled along Spanish and German fascist lines, the Kataeb evolved into a highly organized mass party, with members first elected to the Lebanese parliament in 1960. As head of the party he held various ministerial posts (1960–7) and led the Phalangist militia in the 1975–6 civil war. His younger son **Bashir** (1947–82), a Lebanese army officer, rose through the party and its militia during the civil war. Bashir expanded his popularity and eliminated rivals, until at the age of 34 he was narrowly elected President of Lebanon (Aug 1982). Upon his assassination 20 days later he was succeeded by his elder brother **Amin** (1942–) by a near-unanimous election in parliament. Trained as a lawyer, Amin entered public life in 1970 when elected to parliament as a Phalangist. Politically more moderate than Bashir, in his six years as president he proved ineffectual in resolving the communal conflict stemming from the 1975–89 civil war.

Gemini [jeminiy] (Lat 'twins') A conspicuous N constellation of the zodiac, with a bright pair of stars, **Castor** and **Pollux**, named after the twins of Greek mythology, lying between Taurus and Cancer. Castor is a double star, easily divided through a small telescope; orbital period 470 years; distance: 15·8 parsec. Pollux is a bright orange star, the nearest giant star to Earth; distance: 10·3 parsec.

Gemini North and South Telescopes Large 8·1 m/320 in optical telescope sited on Mauna Kea, Hawaii Island, which became operational in 1999. It is able to achieve very high resolution by the use of adaptive optics, a technique that continually flexes the main mirrors to counteract the defocusing effects of Earth's turbulent atmosphere. The enormous light-collecting power of each giant mirror allows Gemini to see faint objects further away than ever before and is particularly useful for investigating the origins of stars and galaxies. A twin telescope, Gemini South, on the top of Cerro Pachon in the Chilean Andes, was officially opened in January 2002.

Gemini programme [jeminiy] The second-generation US-crewed spacecraft programme, following Mercury and preceding Apollo, using a 2-member crew. It was used to demonstrate the new capabilities of extra-vehicular activity, and extended astronaut endurance to a degree needed to accomplish lunar landing missions. It also perfected the orbital rendezvous and docking technique. There were 10 successful missions between March 1965 and November 1966.

gemma A multicellular unit, usually disc-shaped or filamentous, formed in special structures called **gemmae cups** produced by bryophytes as a means of vegetative reproduction. When dispersed, the gemmae grow into new plants.

gemsbok *oryx*

gemstones A general term for precious or semi-precious stones or minerals valued for their rarity, beauty, and durability; usually cut and polished as jewels. The most highly valued are hard and transparent crystals such as diamond, ruby, emerald, and sapphire.

gender (linguistics) A grammatical concept which expresses such contrasts as masculine/feminine/neuter or animate/inanimate. A distinction is drawn between **natural gender**, which involves reference to the sex of real-world entities, and **grammatical gender**, which is associated with arbitrary word classes, and signals grammatical relationships between words in a sentence. English has natural gender – words such as *he* and *she* are used with reference to male and female entities or personifications. French, on the other hand, also has grammatical gender: a word which is 'feminine' (as shown, for example, by the use of *la* before a noun) does not necessarily refer to a female being.

gender (sociology) The social expression of the basic physiological differences between men and women – social behaviour which is deemed to be appropriate to 'masculine' or 'feminine' roles and which is learned through primary and secondary socialization. Thus, while sex is biological, gender is socially determined. The concept has attracted particular attention since the 1960s, as part of the debate concerning sexism in society.

gene A unit of heredity; a segment of the DNA which contains the instructions for the development of a particular inherited characteristic. When coined by Johannsen (1909) the term referred to a hypothetical entity, and it is only recently with the study of DNA that the structure, size, and location of genes are being established. A gene in the nuclear DNA codes or carries the information for a particular protein (or part of a protein). Genes can exist in several pieces, interrupted by intervening non-coding DNA sequences known as introns. The non-coding sequences are then cut out and the remainder spliced together in transcribing the DNA into the RNA message. The RNS message (mRNA) copy of the gene is then translated in the cytoplasm to give rise to a specific protein.

genealogy The study of family history. It originated as an oral tradition, the ancestry of important members of society (especially sovereigns) being memorized by a priest or bard. Later these lists of ancestors were written down, as in the Bible. Since the 16th-c, records of family descent have been strictly kept in many countries, so that most people in W Europe could trace their ancestry if they wished. A chart showing genealogical descent is a *pedigree*: this may be crucial in establishing a matter of inheritance. In countries where wealth and position were commonly inherited, such as the UK, genealogy has been very important; but even in countries where the legal and social reasons for interest in genealogy are fewer, such as the USA and Australia, many individuals attempt to trace their 'family tree'.

gene bank *plant genetic resources*

gene probe A labelled fragment of single-strand DNA or RNA (labelled with a radioisotope or a fluorescent dye) which can find and hybridize with the DNA or RNA fragments that carry the complementary sequence. Such probes are in increasing use in families where an inherited disorder occurs to detect carriers of the gene responsible.

General Agreement on Tariffs and Trade (GATT) An agency of the United Nations, founded in 1948 to promote international trade. GATT was based in Geneva, and had 125 members in December 1994. It successfully concluded several rounds of negotiations which greatly reduced world tariffs. It was not, however, able to stem the spread of non-tariff barriers to trade, such as voluntary export restraints. The 'Uruguay Round' of negotiations in the early 1990s focused on non-tariff measures which affected trade in agricultural products, trade in services, and intellectual property rights, but agreement on these proved very difficult to reach, with deadlock on certain issues through most of 1994. GATT was succeeded by the World Trade Organization (WTO) in 1995.

General Agreement on Trade in Services (GATS) An international agreement to begin to liberalize trade in services. GATS was set up as part of the Uruguay Round of trade negotiations which led to the creation of the World Trade Organization in 1995. It was intended to start the process of extending to international trade in services the liberalization of trade in goods which had been achieved under the General Agreement on Tariffs and Trade (GATT) since 1948. International trade in services is about a fifth of the value of trade in goods, but has been increasing faster. It is also much more subject to restrictions, partly for protectionist reasons, but also because of concern about problems of regulating foreign providers of services such as insurance. The initial results of GATS have not been great; countries stipulate which sectors are subject to liberalization, and can specify exempt parts of these. Developed countries have nominated about 50% of service sectors, but with many exemptions; less developed countries have been less forthcoming. As with GATT, several rounds of negotiation are likely to be needed to achieve major liberalization of trade in services.

General Assembly (politics) *United Nations*

General Assembly (religion) The highest court, in Churches of Presbyterian order. It normally meets annually and comprises equal numbers of ministers and elders, elected by presbyteries in proportion to their size. It is presided over by a *moderator*, elected annually.

general circulation models Models which seek to explain the atmospheric circulation or wind patterns of the Earth, and also the redistribution of energy and moisture between the tropical and polar regions. Atmospheric circulation is driven by temperature differences between tropical and polar latitudes, and several models have been proposed to explain this phenomenon. One of the simplest recognizes three circulation cells in each hemisphere, based on observations of surface pressure, wind, temperature, and precipitation data. The *Hadley Cell* accounts for the circulation pattern between the Equator and subtropical regions. Heating of the equatorial surface by solar radiation results in rising air and low surface pressure. At high altitudes (upper troposphere and lower stratosphere), this air is carried away from the Equator to a latitude of about 30°, the region of subtropical high pressure systems, where it descends and warms. Surface winds blow out of this high pressure area as trade winds towards the Equator. Mid-latitude surface westerlies also originate in the subtropical high pressure areas and blow towards the low pressure areas centred on a latitude of about 50°. Here the warm air is vertically displaced by cold polar air. Some of the rising air flows back at high altitudes to the subtropical high pressure areas forming the *Ferrel Cell*, and some flows polewards at high altitudes forming the *Polar Cell*. The Coriolis force, resulting from the Earth's rotation, causes deflection of the horizontal surface winds, resulting in the NE and SE trade winds, the westerlies, and polar easterlies. Rising air, associated with low pressure, creates clouds and precipitation; subsiding air creates dry conditions. This model fits observations of surface weather conditions. It is, however, an oversimplification, as shown by satellite observations of upper atmosphere winds, which are in fact westerly (jet streams) and not easterly, as the model predicts.

General Extrasensory Perception (GESP) In parapsychology, acquisition of information from the thoughts or experiences of another (as in telepathy), from the physical environment (as in clairvoyance), and/or from some event yet to occur (as in precognition). In such situations it is impossible to determine theoretically which of these three is responsible for an effect.

General Medical Council (GMC) The statutory body in the UK which controls the professional standing and conduct of members of the medical profession. It is responsible for maintaining the Medical Register of those entitled to practise medicine, and retains the power to erase the name of a doctor because of negligence, malpractice, or breach of medical and professional ethics. It also supervises and maintains standards of undergraduate and immediately postgraduate medical education.

general relativity A theory of gravity deriving almost entirely from Einstein (1916). It supersedes Newton's theory of gravitation, which is reproduced as a weak gravity, low velocity special case, and replaces the Newtonian notion of instantaneous action at a distance with the gravitational field as a distortion of space–time due to the presence of mass. For example, as the Earth moves round the Sun there is distortion of space–time by the Sun's greater mass. An analogy represents space–time as a rubber sheet distorted by a heavy ball representing the Sun; a smaller ball rolling by, representing a planet, will tend to fall into this depression, apparently attracted. General relativity is supported by experiments which measure the bending of starlight due to the presence of the Sun's mass, and also the precession of Mercury's orbit. Other predictions include black holes and gravitational waves. Using general relativity Einstein predicted the impact of the Earth's spin on other rotating objects; this effect, called *frame dragging*, was first reported in 1997 by observing changes in satellite orbits.

General Strike (4–12 May 1926) A national strike in Britain, organized by the Trades Union Congress (TUC) in support of the miners' campaign to resist the imposition by mine owners of wage cuts and longer hours. By April 1926 the dispute between miners and mine owners had intensified and a government subsidy had ended. The strike involved some 3 million workers from the transport, iron, steel, printing, and building industries. The government organized special constables and volunteers to counter the most serious effects of the strike, and issued an anti-strike propaganda journal, *The British Gazette*. The TUC called off the strike after nine days, though the miners' strike continued fruitlessly for three more months. In 1927, the government passed the Trade Disputes and Unions Act to curb the power of the trade unions.

generation, computer *computer generations*

generative grammar A type of grammar, devised by US linguist Noam Chomsky in the 1950s, which explicitly defines the set of grammatical sentences in a language, rather than providing an informal characterization of them. It comprises a formal set of rules which predict the grammatical set from amongst the potentially infinite number of sentences which might occur in any language. Each is assigned a unique structural description, representing the grammatical knowledge (or *competence*) which a native speaker uses. Best known is **transformational grammar**, in which one set of rules assigns a structure to a basal set of sentences, and another 'transforms' those structures into the forms in which they will actually occur in the language.

Genesis, Book of The first book of the Hebrew Bible/Old Testament and of the Pentateuch; traditionally attributed to Moses, but considered by many modern scholars to be composed of several distinct traditions. It presents stories of the creation and of the beginnings of human history (Chapters 1–11), and then focuses on God's dealings with the people destined to become Israel, starting with Abraham and concluding with Jacob's sons.

Genet, Jean [zhuhnay] (1910–86) Writer, born in Paris, France. In his youth he spent many years in reformatories and prisons, and began to write in 1942 while serving a life sentence for theft. His first novel, *Notre-Dame des fleurs* (1944, Our Lady of the Flowers) created a sensation for its portrayal of the criminal world and exaltation of his own amoral values. He later turned from novels to plays, such as *Les Bonnes* (1947, The Maids) and *Les Paravents* (1961, The Screens). In them, he rejects the Western tradition of realism and explores the stylized conventions of Eastern drama. In 1948 he was granted a pardon by the president after a petition by French intellectuals. Sartre's book *Saint Genet* (1952) widened his fame among the French intelligentsia. He wrote little in his later years.

genet or **genette** [**jen**it] An African or European carnivore of the family Viverridae; pale with rows of dark spots and banded tail; rare chestnut-brown **aquatic genet** or **Congo water civet** (*Osbornictis piscivora*); also known as **bush cat**. (Genus: *Genetta*, 10 species.)

gene therapy *somatic gene therapy*

genetically determined disease Disorders which stem directly from abnormalities in chromosomes, each one of which carries many genes, or defects in or absence of single genes. Chromosome abnormalities stem from defects in cell division during reproduction so that the embryo formed at fertilization does not have the expected complement of 46 normal chromosomes. Some of these produce recognizable abnormalities, such as Down's syndrome. Defects of single genes arise from errors or mutations in the DNA code, and are inherited according to Mendel's laws. If the gene is located on one of the sex chromosomes, the disorder will be sex-linked; if it is located on a chromosome not concerned with sex determination, it will not be sex-linked and is said to be *autosomal*. Haemophilia is the best known sex-linked disorder, occurring in males and transmitted by females. Achondroplasia, cystic fibrosis, and Marfan's syndrome are among the more common autosomal disorders. At present there is no way in which these disorders can be treated by direct replacement of the gene.

genetically modified organisms (GMOs) Organisms whose genetic make-up has been altered using genetic engineering technology that does not involve natural methods of reproduction. These transgenic organisms are usually produced for commercial purposes. GMOs can be plants, animals, or other organisms (bacteria, yeast, mammalian cultured cells). Most of the transgenes used contain DNA from several sources (eg a viral enhancer and a plant or animal promoter) attached to the coding region of a bacterial enzyme. Animals can be modified to produce pharmacologically active compounds in their milk, to change the texture of the parts that are eaten, or to add genes to make body parts suitable for transplant into humans (*xenotransplantation*). Bacteria, yeast, and mammalian cultured cells can have genes added to allow them to produce large amounts of specific proteins such as insulin, growth hormone, and blood-clotting factors. Agricultural food crops can be genetically modified by the addition of gene-coding for enzymes that change the metabolic pathways and allow them to be sprayed with otherwise toxic herbicides, or for the production of proteins poisonous to specific pests. Most crops in production at present have been modified to ease agricultural constraints; however, others are in development which are supposed to provide improved nutritional value and taste, or to grow in previously uncultivatable areas. Genetically-modified food crops have caused considerable controversy because the imprecise integration of the transgene into its host genome may cause effects other than those desired, and for which they have not been fully tested. There are also concerns that the GM crop will cross with weedy relatives, making them resistant to herbicides, or that large monoculture crops will cause insects to mutate to become resistant to pesticide transgenes faster than is usual.

genetic code The code in which genetic instructions are written, using an alphabet based on the four bases in DNA and RNA: *adenine*, *cytosine*, *guanine*, and *thymine* (for DNA) or *uracil* (for RNA). Each triplet of bases indicates that a particular kind of amino acid is to be synthesized (see panel for RNA bases). Since there are 20 amino acids and 64 possible triplets, more than one triplet can code for a particular amino acid. The code is non-overlapping; the triplets are read end-to-end in sequence (eg UUU = phenylalanine, UUA = leucine, CCU = proline); and there are three triplets not translated into amino acid, indicating chain termination. The code is universal and applies to all species.

genetic counselling / counseling Advice given to prospective parents concerned at the risk of their future child suffering from a genetic disease. This worry is often due to their having already produced an affected child or to the existence elsewhere in the family of an affected relative. In the UK there are specialist genetic clinics in the National Health Service in almost all regions; clinics are also widely available in North America, Australia, and W Europe, but are not yet common in most countries. The procedure consists of confirmation of the diagnosis in the affected individual; calculation of the risk of occurrence of the disease from the family history and clinical investigation; advice on the risk; discussion of the implications if the child should be affected; and advice on procedures by which the birth of an affected child can be avoided.

genetic engineering The formation of artificial combinations of heritable genetic material which does not involve the use of natural methods of sexual or asexual reproduction. Nucleic acid molecules, produced chemically or biologically outside the cell (eg by recombinant DNA technology), are inserted into a host organism in which they do not naturally occur, but in which they are capable of continued propagation. Genetic engineering has many uses. DNA sequences can be produced in large amounts, and with great purity, so that their structure can be analysed. Biological compounds can be produced industrially (eg human insulin, blood clotting factor, interferon, vaccines, growth hormone). New synthetic capabilities can be incorporated into plants (potentially available for nitrogen fixation). Ultimately it may be possible to repair genes responsible for hereditary disease or insert a normal copy of a gene sequence ('gene therapy').

The implications of genetic engineering have led to public debate, and in most countries there is government control over recombinant DNA work. There is also some public fear that the presence of foreign genetic elements may adversely affect the normal functions of cells. To counter this, safety measures are used to minimize the risk of spread of engineered organisms. Physical containment makes use of microbiological techniques and equipment designed to prevent escape. Biological containment minimizes the chance of a host organism surviving outside the laboratory, usually by using host cells carrying deleterious mutations which permit their growth only under restricted artificial laboratory conditions. However, a great deal of concern has been expressed over the release into the agricultural environment of viable genetically engineered organisms that are capable of reproducing and spreading.

genetics The science of heredity. It originated with the discovery by Gregor Mendel that hereditary characters are determined by factors transmitted without change and in predictable fashion from one generation to the next. The term was coined by British biologist William Bateson in 1907. Genetics occupies a unique position. Its principles and mechanisms extend throughout almost all biology, and it ties together all branches that deal with variation – the molecular structure of cells and tissues, the development of individuals, and the evolution of populations. The mechanisms of genetics are applied to make, in the laboratory, substances formerly obtainable only from organisms (eg vaccines, hormones), and the time may not be far distant when genetic errors responsible for disease may be correctable.

genette *genet*

Geneva [jeneeva], Fr **Genève**, Ger **Genf**, Ital **Ginevra** 46°13N 6°09E, pop (2000e) 175 000. Capital city of Geneva canton, SW Switzerland; on R Rhône at W end of L Geneva; built on the site of a Roman town; free city until end of 13th-c; independent republic until becoming a Swiss canton in 1814; centre of the Reformation under Calvin; former seat of the League of Nations (1920–46); capital of French-speaking Switzerland; airport (Coitrin); railway; university (1559); banking, commerce, administration, precision instruments, chemicals; world capital of high-class watchmaking and jewellery; Old Town on left bank of the Rhône; headquarters of over 200 international organizations (eg International Red Cross, World Health Organization); renowned for its numerous quays and its fountain, Jet d'Eau; St Peter's Cathedral (12th-c); International Motor Show (annual).

Geneva, Lake, Fr **Lac Léman**, Ger **Genfersee**, Lat **Lacus Lemanus** area 581 sq km/224 sq mi. Crescent-shaped lake in SW Switzerland and SE France; largest of the Alpine lakes; height, 371 m/1217 ft; maximum depth, 310 m/1017 ft; maximum width, 14 km/9 mi; on the course of the R Rhône; wine-growing area; chief towns include Morges, Rolle, Lausanne, Vevey; steamer services.

Geneva Accord A peace plan for the Middle East devised by Israeli and Palestinian moderates, launched in Switzerland in December 2003. Under the proposals, the Israeli army would withdraw from the Gaza Strip and most of the West Bank, most Jewish settlements would be dismantled, and an independent Palestinian state would be established. The West Bank's borders would be defined by the 1967 Green Line, but areas of land would be exchanged between Palestine and Israel. East Jerusalem would be the capital of the Palestinian state and West Jerusalem the capital of Israel. Palestine would have sovereignty over most of the Old City, but the Western Wall and the Jewish quarter would remain under Israeli sovereignty. The Palestinians would forego the 'right of return' for Palestinian refugees who fled from what became Israel in 1948. The Palestinians would recognize Israel's existence and right to live in peace, and Israel would recognize the Palestinian state in the same way. A multinational force would oversee implementation of the plan. The Accord did not have the backing of the Israeli or Palestinian governments, and its key compromises (over the division of Jerusalem and the right of return) attracted the opposition of radical groups on both sides. In its emphasis on an immediate political settlement, it differed from the 'road-map' proposed earlier in 2003, which had as its primary phase the establishing of secure conditions under which a settlement would eventually take place.

Geneva Bible An English translation of the Bible, prepared and published in Geneva by Protestant exiles from England; first appeared complete in 1560. It was notable for its notes, for its verse divisions, and in some printings for its small size and legible Roman type. It was especially popular in Scotland, and also in England, even after the Authorized Version (1611).

Geneva Convention An international agreement on the conduct of warfare first framed in 1864 and ratified in 1906. It is chiefly concerned with the protection of wounded and the sanctity of the Red Cross, while prohibiting methods of war (such as the use of 'dumdum' bullets, which expand on impact) that might cause unnecessary suffering. The terms were extended in 1950 and again in 1978 to confirm the prohibition of attacks on non-defended civilians, reprisals against civilians, and the prisoner-of-war rights of guerrilla fighters.

Genghis Khan [jengis kahn], also spelled **Jingis** or **Chingis Khan** ('Very Mighty Ruler'), originally **Temujin** (1162/7–1227) Mongol conqueror, born in Temujin, Mongolia, on the R Onon. He succeeded his father at 13, and struggled for many years against hostile tribes, subjugating the Naimans, conquering Tangut, and receiving the submission of the Turkish Uigurs. In 1206 he changed his name to the one by which he is now known and made his capital at Karakorumand. In 1205–9 he conquered the Xia Xia (Tangut) kingdom in NW China, and 1211–15 the Jin (Jurched) empire in NE China, as well as other empires in Turkestan. At his death, the Mongol empire, which stretched from the Black Sea to the Pacific, was divided between his four sons.

genie *jinni*

genital warts Cauliflower-like lesions on the penis, vulva, and around the anus due to overgrowth of the epidermis. They are caused by infection with a papilloma virus similar to that which causes warts on other parts of the body. They are spread by sexual contact.

Genoa [jenoha], Ital **Genova** 44°24N 8°56E, pop (2000e) 700 000. Largest seaport in Italy and capital of Genoa province, Liguria, NW Italy, on the Gulf of Genoa; larger conurbation extends 35 km/22 mi along the coast; founded as a Roman trading centre; leading Mediterranean port by 13th-c; rebuilt after World War 2, becoming a major Mediterranean port; archbishopric; airport; railway; ferries; university (1471); Academy of Fine Arts (1751); Verdi Institute of Music; shipbuilding, oil refining, chemicals, paper, textiles, animal feedstuffs, detergents, motorbikes, sugar, financial services; birthplace of Columbus, Paganini, Garibaldi; Doge's Palace (13th-c), Church of San Matteo (1278), Cathedral of San Lorenzo (12th–14th-c), Palazzo Reale (begun 1650), Palazzo Rosso (17th-c); religious celebrations (Jun); international ballet festival (Jul).

genocide The crime under international law of the deliberate and systematic destruction of a race of people or an ethnic group by mass murder. The word was coined after events in Europe in 1933–45 and the mass destruction of Jews and Rom (gypsies) by Germany. In 1948 the UN General Assembly adopted a Convention on the Prevention and Punishment of the Crime of Genocide; this confirmed the policy that genocide was a crime under international law as much in peacetime as in war, and was not a matter of private concern for an individual state. This came into effect in 1951. Parties to the Convention undertook to take the necessary measures under their own laws to ensure the effective application of the Convention. Any state may call upon the UN to intervene and take action considered appropriate for the prevention and suppression of genocide. Perpetrators may be tried whether they are rulers, public officials, or private individuals. They may be tried by the state in which the act was committed or by an international tribunal or court whose jurisdiction is accepted by the contracting parties.

genome [jeenohm] The complete genetic information about an organism. In most organisms this is contained in the DNA sequences within chromosomes, while in RNA-based viruses it is the total RNA sequence. Genome sizes have a 100 000 fold range from a few thousand base pairs in simple viruses to 10^{11} base pairs in some plants. Since individual members of an organism may have slightly different genetic constitutions (genotypes), genomes describe the common sequences characteristic of the organism.

genotype The genes carried by an individual member of an organism. The term may refer to the total complement of genes or to particular genes at specified loci in the chromosomes. The interaction of gene products (RNA, protein) with each other and with the environment in which the organism develops gives rise to the **phenotype** – the characteristics that are observed.

genre painting Realistic scenes from everyday life, typically on a small scale, as produced by Dutch 17th-c masters such as Steen and Vermeer; the term may be applied, however, to any period. The genre flourished in 19th-c Britain, largely due to the popularity of the anecdotal scenes of Scottish village life by Wilkie.

Genscher, Hans-Dietrich [gensher] (1927–) German statesman, born in Reideburg, EC Germany. He trained as a lawyer, studying at Halle and Leipzig before coming to the West in 1952. He became secretary-general of the Free Democratic Party (FDP) in 1959 and was elected to the Bundestag in 1965. He was minister of the interior (1969–74) before becoming vice-chancellor and foreign minister (1974–92). In 1974 he became Chairman of the FDP, a post to which he was re-elected (1982–5). He retained his cabinet post after 1982 in the coalition between the FDP and the Christian Democrats. As one of Germany's foremost politicians before and after German reunification in 1990, he was instrumental in the strengthening of the European Union, the negotiation of the Single European Act (1986), and the Treaty of Maastricht (1992). In 1989–90 he worked vigorously for German reunification and became the first foreign minister of the unified Germany.

Genseric *Gaiseric*

Gent *Ghent*

gentian Any of several species, mostly perennials, found almost everywhere, except for Africa; many are low-growing alpines; leaves opposite, entire; flowers usually several cm long, funnel- or bell-shaped, with often long tubes and five spreading lobes, usually deep blue, but also white, yellow, or red. (Genus: *Gentiana*, 400 species. Family: Gentianaceae.)

Gentile, Giovanni [jenteelay] (1875–1944) Philosopher, born in Castelvetrano, Sicily, S Italy. He was professor of philosophy successively at Naples (1898–1906), Palmero (1906–14), Pisa (1914–17), and Rome (1917–44). He became with Croce the leading exponent of 20th-c Italian idealism and collaborated with him in editing the periodical *La Critica* (1903–22), but later quarrelled with his complex distinctions between the theoretical and practical categories of mind, arguing that nothing is real except the pure act of thought. He later became an apologist for fascism and an ideological mouthpiece for Mussolini. He was the fascist minister of public instruction (1922–4), and planned the new *Enciclopedia Italiana* (35 vols, 1929–36), which became the main cultural monument of the regime. He was assassinated by an anti-Fascist Communist in Florence in 1944.

Gentile da Fabriano *Fabriano, Gentile da*

Gentlemen at Arms, Honourable Corps of In the UK, non-combatant troops in attendance upon the sovereign. They provide an escort at coronations, state openings of parliament, receptions, royal garden parties, and during state visits; because of their close proximity to the sovereign, they are known as 'the nearest guard'. Originated as the 'Gentlemen Spears' by Henry VIII in 1509, today the 27 members are chosen from officers in either the Army or the Royal Marines who have received decorations.

genus [jeenuhs] A category in biological classification consisting of one or more closely related and morphologically similar species. The name of the genus (eg *Panthera*) and the species (eg *leo*) together form the scientific name of an organism (eg the lion, *Panthera leo*).

geochemistry A branch of geology concerned with the abundances of elements and their isotopes in the Earth, and the processes that affect their distribution. It also subsumes the study of chemical processes in the evolution of the Earth and the Solar System. Commercial applications include geochemical prospecting, in which the chemical analysis of soils, sediments, and stream waters is used to detect concealed ore deposits.

geochronology The science of dating rocks or geological events in absolute terms (ie in years), usually by radiometric dating. For more recent rocks, varve counting may be applicable to Pleistocene sediments, or tree-ring dating can measure ages back to about 7000 years before the present.

geodesic [geeohdeesik] The extension of the concept of a straight line to curved space, representing the shortest distance between two points. Special cases include straight lines in planes, and great circles on spheres. In general relativity, freely falling bodies move along geodesics in curved space–time.

geodesic dome A structurally stable dome constructed of a grid of straight members connected to each other to form a continuous surface of small triangles. It was invented by Buckminster Fuller in the 1950s. An example is the Climatron in St Louis, MO, built in 1960.

geodesy [jeeodesee] A branch of science concerned with the size and shape of the Earth, its gravitational field, and the location of fixed points. Geodesic surveying, unlike plane surveying, takes into account the Earth's curvature. The shape of the Earth (the *geoid*) is defined as the figure which is perpendicular to the direction of gravity at all points, and approximates to an oblate spheroid, first postulated by Newton on the basis of accurate astronomical observations.

Geoffrey of Monmouth (Gaufridus Monemutensis) (c.1100–54) Welsh chronicler, probably a Benedictine monk, consecrated Bishop of St Asaph in 1152. His *Historia regum Britanniae* (History of the Kings of Britain), composed before 1147, profoundly influenced English literature, introducing the stories of King Lear and Cymbeline, the prophecies of Merlin, and the legend of Arthur in the form known today. The stories have little basis in historical fact. His *Historia* was translated into Anglo-Norman by Gaimar and Wace and into English by Layamon and Robert of Gloucester; it was first printed in 1508 (Paris).

geography The study of the nature of the physical and human environments. It is often divided broadly into **physical geography**, which concerns the Earth's physical environment (the atmosphere, biosphere, hydrosphere, and lithosphere), and **human geography**, the study of people and their activities. In both there is emphasis on *spatial analysis*, the study of location and patterns; on *ecological analysis*, the interaction between the human and physical environments; and on *scale*, as in regional and local studies. Geography encompasses both the physical and social sciences, using and contributing to their methodologies and content. It can be divided into a number of specialist disciplines: for example, **geomorphology**, the scientific study of the origin and development of landforms; **population geography**, concerned with the composition, distribution, growth, and migration of populations; and **resource geography**, the study of the location and exploitation of natural resources. Geography became a separate academic subject in the late 19th-c, though its origins are much older – the first geographical account of China was produced in the 4th-c BC, and a 200-chapter Chinese geographical encyclopedia was published in 993. The nature of the subject has changed considerably in the past 100 years, away from an essentially descriptive and regional study towards a more quantitative and scientific approach.

geological time scale Divisions and subdivisions of geological time, based on the relative ages of rocks determined using the methods of stratigraphy. Correlations between rocks of the same age are made from a study of the sedimentary sequences and the characteristic fossils they contain. The major divisions are termed *eons* (or *aeons*) which are further subdivided into *eras*, *periods*, and *epochs*. With the advent of radiometric dating, absolute ages have been assigned to the time scale. Although the current estimate of the age of the Earth is 4600 million years, evidence of geological events only becomes abundant about 1000 million years later, and the time scale lacks detail until the beginning of the Cambrian period c.590 million years ago (*see pp.619–20*).

geology The science of the Earth as a whole: its origin, structure, composition, processes, and history. The major branches of geology include *mineralogy* (the study of minerals), *petrology* (the study of rocks), *geochemistry* (the study of the chemical evolution of the Earth), *geophysics* (the study of physical processes within the Earth), *structural geology* (the study of the tectonic features produced by large-scale deformation of rocks), *stratigraphy* (the study of the sequences and ages of sedimentary rocks), and *palaeontology* (the study of fossils and evolution of life on the Earth). Geology is applied to the exploration for mineral and oil deposits in the Earth.

geomagnetic field The magnetic field of the Earth which arises from the metallic core, and which may be regarded as produced by a magnetic dipole pointing towards the geomagnetic N and S Poles. The positions of the Poles have varied considerably during geological time, and can be studied by analyzing the direction of the residual magnetism present in rocks. Local variations or anomalies in the magnetic field are due to variations in the nature and structure of the rocks in the crust – a property which may be used to prospect for oil and mineral deposits.

geomancy [geeohmansee] The study of 'earth mysteries', originally a means of divination by scattering earth on a surface and analyzing the resulting patterns. The notion now extends to studying how the Earth's own energy affects daily life. The geomancer's compass, which consists of eight or more rings aligned with natural features such as rivers and mountains, can detect the energy flow through the environment, and be used to assist with the positioning of buildings and other design features.

geometric mean *mean*

geometric sequence A sequence in which the ratio of any one term to the next is constant; sometimes called a **geometric progression**. The terms 1,2,4,8 form a geometric sequence; $1+2+4+8$ is a **geometric series**. If the first term of a geometric sequence is a and the common ratio is r, the nth term is ar^{n-1} and the sum of the terms in the sequence is

$$a = \frac{r^n - 1}{r - 1.}$$

If $r < 1$, this approaches

$$\frac{a}{1-r}$$

as n becomes large.

geometrid moth A moth, small to medium-sized, often with large and cryptically coloured wings; caterpillars often resemble twigs, known as **loopers**, because of their looping mode of progression; c.20 000 species, including many serious pests, such as cankerworm, inch worm, and winter moth. (Order: Lepidoptera. Family: Geometridae.)

geometries, non-Euclidean Geometries developed by varying Euclid's fifth axiom, as stated by the British mathematician John Playfair (1748–1819), 'Through any one point there can be drawn one and only one straight line parallel to a given straight line'. Variations on this took either the form 'Through any one point can be drawn more than one straight line parallel to a given straight line' or 'Through any one point can be drawn no straight line parallel to a given straight line'. The first form was called **hyperbolic geometry**, the second **elliptic geometry**. Mathematicians associated with hyperbolic geometry include Gauss, and Lobachevsky. Early work on elliptic geometry was carried out by Riemann. There are other non-Euclidean geometries. Hyperbolic geometry was the first physically plausible alternative to Euclid's.

geometry The branch of mathematics which studies the properties of shapes and space, originally (as its name suggests) of the Earth. About 2000 BC, the Babylonians were familiar with rules for the area of rectangles, right-angled triangles, and isosceles triangles. They took the circumference C of a circle, diameter d, as $3\frac{1}{8}d$, and the area as $\frac{1}{12}C^2$; they subdivided the circumference of a circle into 360 equal parts; and developed a considerable body of geometrical knowledge. The Egyptians had a similar body of knowledge, but the story that they knew of special cases of Pythagoras's theorem has been disputed. The Greeks from c.300 BC developed geometry on a logical basis, many of the early results being collected in Euclid's *Elements*. Although some of the proofs were probably due to Euclid, the great merit of this work was its skilful selection and arrangement into a logical sequence, showing a statement as a necessary logical consequence of a previous statement, the chain starting with some propositions or axioms. In the past 200 years, abstract geometries have been developed, notably by Gauss and Lobachevsky.

geomorphology A branch of geology (or geography) which studies and interprets landforms and the processes of erosion and deposition which form the surface of the Earth and other planets.

geopathic stress [geeohpathik] A term which covers all forms of naturally occurring environmental stress, but most often applied to the adverse effects which result from electromagnetic fields and other forms of radiation, including radon gas. Environmental factors contributing to geopathic stress may include ley lines, artificial structures such as power lines, and sun spots which disturb the Earth's magnetic field. These factors may have an adverse effect on health, and result in insomnia, depression, rheumatism, hypertension, and even cancer.

geophagy [jeeofajee] *pica*

geophysics A broad branch of geology which deals with the physical properties of Earth materials and the physical processes that determine the structure of the Earth as a whole. Major subjects include seismology, geomagnetism, and meteorology, as well as the study of large-scale processes of heat and mass transfer in the Earth and variations in the Earth's gravitational field. Geophysical surveys measure local variations in magnetic and gravitational field to determine vari-

Geological Time Scale

Eon	*Era*	*Period*	*Epoch*	*Million years ago*	*Geological events*	*Sea life*	*Land life*
Phanerozoic	Cenozoic	Quaternary	Holocene		Glaciers recede. Sea level rises. Climate becomes more equable.	As now.	Forests flourish again. Humans acquire agriculture and technology.
				0·01			
			Pleistocene		Widespread glaciers melt periodically, causing seas to rise and fall.	As now.	Many plant forms perish. Small mammals abundant. Primitive humans established.
				2·0			
		Tertiary	Pliocene		Continents and oceans adopting their present form. Present climatic distribution established. Ice caps develop.	Giant sharks extinct. Many fish varieties.	Some plants and mammals die out. Primates flourish.
				5·1			
			Miocene		Seas recede further. European and Asian land masses join. Heavy rain causes massive erosion. Red Sea opens.	Bony fish common. Giant sharks.	Grasses widespread. Grazing mammals become common.
				24·6			
			Oligocene		Seas recede. Extensive movements of Earth's crust produce new mountains (eg Alpine-Himalayan chain).	Crabs, mussels, and snails evolve.	Forests diminish. Grasses appear. Pachyderms, canines, and felines develop.
				38·0			
			Eocene		Mountain formation continues. Glaciers common in high mountain ranges. Greenland separates. Australia separates.	Whales adapt to sea.	Large tropical jungles. Primitive forms of modern mammals established.
				54·9			
			Palaeocene		Widespread subsidence of land. Seas advance again. Considerable volcanic activity. Europe emerges.	Many reptiles become extinct.	Flowering plants widespread. First primates. Giant reptiles extinct.
				65			
	Mesozoic	Cretaceous	Late		Swamps widespread. Massive alluvial deposition. Continuing limestone formation. S America separates from Africa, India, Africa and Antarctica separate.	Turtles, rays, and now-common fish appear.	Flowering plants established. Dinosaurs become extinct.
			Early	97·5			
				144			
		Jurassic	Malm		Seas advance. Much river formation. High mountains eroded. Limestone formation. N America separates from Africa. Central Atlantic begins to open.	Reptiles dominant.	Early flowers. Dinosaurs dominant. Mammals still primitive. First birds.
			Dogger	163			
			Lias	188			
				213			
		Triassic	Late		Desert conditions widespread. Hot climate slowly becomes warm and wet. Break up of Pangea into supercontinents Gondwana (S) and Laurasia (N).	Ichthyosaurs, flying fish, and crustaceans appear.	Ferns and conifers thrive. First mammals, dinosaurs, and flies.
			Middle	231			
			Early	243			
				248			
	Palaeozoic	Permian	Late		Some sea areas cut off to form lakes. Earth movements form mountains. Glaciation in southern hemisphere.	Some shelled fish become extinct.	Deciduous plants. Reptiles dominant. Many insect varieties.
			Early	258			
				286			
		Carboniferous	Pennsylvanian		Sea-beds rise to form new land areas. Enormous swamps. Partly-rotted vegetation forms coal.	Amphibians and sharks abundant.	Extensive evergreen forests. Reptiles breed on land. Some insects develop wings.
			Mississippian	320			
				360			
		Devonian	Late		Collision of continents causing mountain formation (Appalachians, Caledonides, and Urals). Sea deeper but narrower. Climatic zones forming. Iapetus ocean closed.	Fish abundant. Primitive sharks. First amphibians.	Leafy plants. Some invertebrates adapt to land. First insects.
			Middle	374			
			Early	387			

Eon	Era	Period	Epoch	Million years ago	Geological events	Sea life	Land life
Phanerozoic	Palaeozoic			408			
		Silurian	Pridoli		New mountain ranges form. Sea level varies periodically. Extensive shallow sea over the Sahara.	Large vertebrates.	First leafless land plants.
			Ludlow	414			
			Wenlock	421			
			Llandovery	428			
				438			
		Ordovician	Ashgill		Shore lines still quite variable. Increasing sedimentation. Europe and N America moving together.	First vertebrates. Coral reefs develop.	None.
			Caradoc	448			
			Llandeilo	458			
			Llanvirn	468			
			Arenig	478			
			Tremadoc	488			
				505			
		Cambrian	Merioneth		Much volcanic activity, and long periods of marine sedimentation.	Shelled invertebrates, Trilobites.	None.
			St David's	525			
			Caerfai	540			
				590			
Proterozoic	Precambrian	Vendian			Shallow seas advance and retreat over land areas. Atmosphere uniformly warm.	Seaweed. Algae and invertebrates.	None.
				650			
		Riphean	Late		Intense deformation and metamorphism.	Earliest marine life and fossils.	None.
			Middle	900			
			Early	1 300			
				1 600			
		Early Proterozoic			Shallow shelf seas. Formation of carbonate sediments and 'red beds'.	First appearance of stromatolites.	None.
				2 500			
Archaean		Archaean (Azoic)			Banded iron formations. Formation of the Earth's crust and oceans.	None.	None.
				4 600			

ations in the structure and composition of rocks, and to prospect for oil and mineral reserves.

geopolitics The study of the way geographical factors help to explain the basis of the power of nation states; a combination of political geography and political science. Important characteristics in this mode of analysis include territory, resources, climate, population, social and political culture, and economic activity. Prior to World War 2 it was associated with German nationalism and the Nazi regime.

George I (of Great Britain) (1660–1727) King of Great Britain and Ireland (1714–27), born in Osnabrück, NWC Germany, the great-grandson of James I of England, and proclaimed king on the death of Queen Anne. Elector of Hanover since 1698, he had commanded the imperial forces in the Marlborough wars. He divorced his wife and cousin, the Princess Dorothea of Zell, imprisoning her in the castle of Ahlde, where she died (1726). He took relatively little part in the government of the country. His affections remained with Hanover, and he lived there as much as possible.

George II (of Great Britain) (1683–1760) King of Great Britain and Ireland (1727–60), and Elector of Hanover, born at Herrenhausen, Hanover, NC Germany, the son of George I. In 1705 he married Caroline of Ansbach (1683–1737). Though he involved himself more in the government of the country than his father had, the policy pursued during the first half of the reign was that of Walpole. In the War of the Austrian Succession, he was present at the Battle of Dettingen (1743), the last occasion on which a British sovereign commanded an army in the field. His reign also saw the crushing of Jacobite hopes at the Battle of Culloden (1746), the foundation of British India after the Battle of Plassey (1757), the beginning of the Seven Years' War, and the capture of Quebec (1759).

George II (of Greece) (1890–1947) King of Greece (1922–4, 1935–47), born near Athens, Greece. He first came to the throne after the second deposition of his father, Constantine I. He was himself driven out in 1924, but was restored in late 1935 after a plebiscite. When Greece was overrun by the Germans, he withdrew to Crete, then to Egypt and Britain. After a plebiscite in 1946 in favour of the monarchy, he re-ascended the Greek throne, and died in Athens.

George III (1738–1820) King of Great Britain and Ireland (1760–1820), elector (1760–1815) and king (from 1815) of Hanover, born in London, UK, the eldest son of Frederick Louis, Prince of Wales (1707–51). His father predeceased him, and he thus succeeded his grandfather, George II. Eager to govern as well as reign, he caused considerable friction. With Lord North he shared in the blame for the loss of the American colonies, and popular feeling ran high against him for a time in the 1770s. In 1783 he called Pitt (the Younger) to office, which brought an end to the supremacy of the old Whig families. In 1810 he suffered a recurrence of a mental derangement, most likely caused by the inherited disease porphyria, and the Prince of Wales was made regent.

George IV (1762–1830) King of Great Britain and Hanover (1820–30), born in London, UK, the eldest son of George III. He became prince regent in 1810, because of his father's insanity. Rebelling against a strict upbringing, he went through a marriage ceremony with Mrs Fitzherbert, a Roman Catholic, which was not recognized in English law. The marriage was later declared invalid, and 1795 he married Princess Caroline of Brunswick, whom he tried to divorce when he was king. Her death in 1821 ended a scandal in which the people sympathized with the queen. His reign saw the passage of the Catholic Emancipation Act. He was a leader of taste, fashion, and the arts, and gave his name to the 'Regency' period, now synonymous with elegance and style.

George V (1865–1936) King of the United Kingdom (1910–36), born in London, UK, the second son of Edward VII. He served in the navy, travelled in many parts of the empire, and was created Prince of Wales in 1901. He married Mary of Teck in 1893. His reign saw the Union of South Africa (1910), World War 1, the Irish Free State settlement (1922), and the General Strike (1926).

George VI (1895–1952) King of the United Kingdom (1936–52), born at Sandringham, Norfolk, E England, UK, the second son of George V. He studied at Dartmouth Naval College and Trinity College, Cambridge, and served in the Grand Fleet at the Battle of Jutland (1916). In 1920 he was created Duke of York, and married Lady Elizabeth Bowes-Lyon in 1923. An outstanding tennis player, he played at Wimbledon in the All-England championships in 1926. He ascended the throne in 1936 on the abdication of his elder brother, Edward VIII. During World War 2 he set a personal example coping with wartime restrictions, continued to reside in bomb-damaged Buckingham Palace, visited all theatres of war and delivered many broadcasts, for which he overcame a speech impediment. In 1947 he toured South Africa and substituted the title of Head of the Commonwealth for that of Emperor of India, when that subcontinent was granted independence by the Labour government. Unnoticed by the public, his health was rapidly declining, yet he persevered with his duties, his last great public occasion being the opening of the Festival of Britain in 1951.

George, St (fl. 3rd-c) Patron of chivalry, and guardian saint of England and Portugal. He may have been tortured and put to death by Diocletian at Nicomedia, or he may have suffered (c.303) at Lydda in Palestine, where his alleged tomb is exhibited. His name was early obscured by fable, such as the story of his fight with a dragon to rescue a maiden. Feast day 23 April.

George, David Lloyd *Lloyd George, David*

George, Stefan [gayorguh] (1868–1933) Poet, born in Büdeshein, W Germany. He studied in Paris, Munich, and Berlin, and travelled widely. In Germany he founded a literary group, and edited its journal. His poems show the influence of the French Symbolists, dispensing with punctuation and capitals, and conveying an impression rather than a simple meaning. In *Das neue Reich* (1928, The New Reich) he advocated a new German culture, not in accord with that of the Nazis. He exiled himself in 1933, and died in Switzerland.

George-Brown, Baron, originally **George (Alfred) Brown** (1914–85) British statesman, born in London, UK. He was an official of the Transport and General Workers' Union before becoming an MP in 1945 and minister of works (1951). As Opposition spokesman on defence (1958–61), he supported Gaitskell in opposing unilateral disarmament. Vice-chairman and deputy Leader of the Labour Party (1960–70), he unsuccessfully contested Wilson for Party leadership in 1963. As secretary of state for economic affairs (1964–6), he instigated a prices and incomes policy, and later became foreign secretary (1966–8). Having lost his seat in the 1970 election, he was created a life peer.

George Cross (GC) In the UK, a decoration bestowed on civilians for acts of great heroism or conspicuous bravery, or on members of the armed forces for actions in which purely military honours are not normally granted. (The island of Malta was a recipient in 1942.) Instituted in 1940 and named after George VI, the award, inscribed 'For Gallantry', with a blue ribbon, ranks second after the Victoria Cross.

George Medal (GM) In the UK, the second highest award which may be bestowed on civilians for acts of bravery; instituted in 1940 by George VI. The ribbon is scarlet with five narrow blue stripes.

George Town (Cayman I) 19°20N 81°23W, pop (2000e) 19 400. Seaport and capital of the Cayman Is, W Caribbean, on Grand Cayman I; financial and administrative centre; airport nearby.

George Town (Malaysia) *Pinang* (city)

Georgetown 6°46N 58°10W, pop (2000e) 148 000. Federal and district capital and major port, N Guyana; on right bank of R Demerara; tidal port, protected by sea wall and dykes; founded, 1781; airport; airfield; railway; university (1963); food processing, shrimp fishing, sugar, rice, bauxite; parliament buildings (1839), St George's Anglican Cathedral (1889), Guyana House (1852), Law Courts (1878), city hall (1887), Botanic Gardens.

Georgia (republic) *p.622*

Georgia (USA) pop (2000e) 8 186 500; area 152 571 sq km/ 58 910 sq mi. State in SE USA, divided into 159 counties; the 'Empire State of the South' or the 'Peach State'; discovered by the Spanish; settled as a British colony, 1733; named after George II; the last of the original 13 colonies to be founded; the fourth of the original 13 states (first Southern state) to ratify the Constitution, 1788; seceded from the Union, 1861; suffered much damage in the Civil War (especially during General Sherman's March to the Sea, 1864); slavery abolished 1865; last state to be re-admitted, 1870; capital, Atlanta; other chief cities, Columbus, Savannah, Macon; part of the E border is the Atlantic Ocean; rivers include the Savannah (SE border), the Chattahoochee (part of the W border) and Flint, which join to form the Apalachicola, and the Oconee and Ocmulgee, which join to form the Altamaha; highest point Mt Brasstown Bald (1457 m/ 4780 ft); a low coastal plain in the S, heavily forested; the fertile Piedmont plateau, the Appalachian plateau, and Blue Ridge Mts in the N; many local paper mills in the S; leads the nation in production of pulp; major cotton textile producer; transportation equipment, food products, chemicals; grows nearly half US crop of peanuts; cotton, tobacco, corn, poultry, livestock, soybeans; popular tourist resorts, such as the Golden Isles (off the Atlantic coast) and Okefenokee Swamp.

Georgian poetry A term applied to the poetry of British writers during the reign of George V (1910–36), usually of a pastoral nature and largely traditional. *Georgian Poetry*, a series of five anthologies, was published between 1912 and 1922. The first volume included poems by Rupert Brooke, John Masefield, D H Lawrence, Walter de la Mare, and John Drinkwater. Later volumes included Edmund Blunden, Siegfried Sassoon, Robert Graves, and Isaac Rosenberg.

Georgian Style English architecture of the period 1714–1830. The name is derived from George I, II, III, and IV of that period. The style is characterized by a restrained use of classical elements in low relief on the exterior, and more elaborately decorated interiors, such as those by Robert Adam.

geostrophic wind A wind which blows parallel to isobars, representing the balanced motion between the equal but opposing pressure gradient force and Coriolis force. It is found only in the upper atmosphere, where the frictional force of the Earth's surface is absent.

geosynchronous Earth orbit A spacecraft orbit about the Earth's Equator, where the period of the orbit matches the Earth's day and causes the spacecraft to appear stationary at the longitude in question; orbit altitude is 36 000 km/ 22 500 mi. The orbit is ideally suited for communications satellites, as it permits spacecraft to be in continuous communication with specific ground stations. It is also ideal for meteorological satellites, as it permits spacecraft to have broad coverage of the surface and atmosphere.

geothermal energy Energy extracted in the form of heat from the Earth's crust, arising from a combination of the slow cooling of the Earth since its formation, and heat released from natural radioactive decay. Geologically active regions such as plate margins have higher heat flow values and result in hot springs and geysers. Geothermal energy is commercially exploited for generating electricity in Lardorello in Italy, Warakai in New Zealand, and California, USA.

geranium The name used for two related plant genera: the **cranesbills** (Genus: *Geranium*) and the geraniums of horticulture, the **pelargoniums** (Genus: *Pelargonium*).

Gérard, François (Pascal Simon), Baron [zhayrah(r)] (1770–1837) Painter, born in Rome, Italy. He was brought up in Paris, and became a member of the Revolutionary Tribunal in 1793. His portrait of Isabey the miniaturist (1796) and his 'Cupid and Psyche' (1798), both in the Louvre, established his reputation. He later painted several historical subjects, such as the 'Battle

Georgia

official name **Republic of Georgia**, Georgian **Sakartvelos Respublika**

Local name Georgia

Timezone GMT +4

Area 69 700 km²/26 900 sq mi

Population total (2002e) 4 961 000

Status Republic

Date of independence 1991

Capital Tbilisi

Languages Georgian (official), also Russian

Ethnic groups Georgian (69%), Armenian (9%), Russian (7%), Azerbaijani (5%), Ossetian (3%), Abkhazian (2%)

Religion Georgian Church, independent of the Russian Orthodox Church since 1917

Physical features Mountainous country in C and W Transcaucasia; contains the Greater Caucasus (N) and Lesser Caucasus (S); highest point in the republic, Mt Shkhara, 5203 m/17 070 ft; chief rivers, Kura and Rioni; c.39% of land forested.

Climate Greater Caucasus in N borders temperate and subtropical climatic zones; average temperatures 1–3°C (Jan), 25°C (Jul) in E Transcaucasia; humid, subtropical climate with mild winters in W Mediterranean climate with humid winters, dry summers in N Black Sea region.

Currency (1995) Lari

Economy Kakhetia region famed for its orchards and wines; holiday resorts, spas on the Black Sea; manganese, coal, iron and steel, oil refining; tea, fruits, tung oil, tobacco, vines, silk, textiles, food processing.

GDP (2002e) $16·05 bn, per capita $3200

Human Development Index (2002) 0·748

History Proclaimed a Soviet Socialist Republic, 1921; linked with Armenia and Azerbaijan as Transcaucasian Republic, 1922–36; made a constituent republic within the Soviet Union, 1936; declaration of independence, 1991; quest for regional autonomy led to declaration of secession by S Ossetia, 1991, and declaration of independence by Abkhazia, 1992; did not join Commonwealth of Independent States (CIS), 1991; President Gamsakhurdia overthrown in civil war, 1992, bringing military council to power; Parliament dismissed and powers transferred to a State Council headed by Shevardnadze, 1992; joined Commonwealth of Independent states, 1993; Head of State holds executive power, advised by Cabinet of Ministers; new constitution, 1995; Shevardnadze forced to resign following a people's revolution, replaced by leader of the opposition Mikhail Saakashvili, Nov 2003.

Head of State
1992 *Military Council*
1992–2003 Eduard Shevardnadze
2003–4 Nino Burjanadze *Acting*
2004– Mikhail Saakashvili

Head of Government
1992–3 Tengiz Sigua
1993–5 Otar Patatsia

Minister of State
1992–3 Tengiz Sigua
1993–5 Otar Patatsia
1995–8 Nikoloz Lekishvili
1998–2000 Vazha Lortkipanidze
2000– Gia Arsenishvili

of Austerlitz' (1808, Versailles). He was made court painter and baron by Louis XVIII.

gerbil A type of mouse, native to Africa, Middle East, and C Asia; long hind legs and long furry tail; lives in social groups; inhabits dry open country; digs burrows; eats seeds, roots, etc (some species eat other animals, including reptiles and rodents); one species, the Mongolian gerbil (*Meriones unguiculatus*) is a popular pet; also known as **jird**. (Subfamily: Gerbillinae, 81 species.)

Gere, Richard [geer] (1949–) Actor, born in Philadelphia, Pennsylvania, USA. He studied at the University of Massachusetts, became a pop musician, and went on to gain extensive experience in the theatre, which included the London production of *Grease* (1972). He received acclaim for an off-Broadway appearance in *Killer's Head* (1975), then made his screen debut with a small role in *Report to the Commissioner* (1975). His films include *Yanks* (1979), *American Gigolo* (1980), *An Officer and A Gentleman* (1982), *Pretty Woman* (1990), *Autumn in New York* (2000), and *Chicago* (2002, Golden Globe, Best Actor).

gerenuk [gerenuk] An E African gazelle (*Litocranius walleri*); pale brown; slender, with long neck and small head; male with thick horns (usually curling forward at tips); browses from bushes by standing vertically on hind legs; inhabits dry regions; seldom drinks; also known as **giraffe antelope**.

geriatrics The study of the health needs of the aged and their provision. The numbers of elderly persons have increased in recent years in most Western societies, and continue to do so, making increasing demands on specialized health and social services. There are few diseases specific to old age, but the elderly often suffer from several chronic disorders at the same time. These lead to a number of disabilities which curtail their ability to care for themselves in their own homes, and has given rise to the need for such services as district nurses, home helps, meals on wheels, and health visitors. For those who become unable to live independently in their own homes, institutional accommodation often becomes necessary. The branch of medicine which investigates the process and problems of aging is known as **gerontology**.

Géricault, (Jean Louis André) Théodore [zhayreekoh] (1791–1824) Painter, born in Rouen, NW France. A pupil of Guérin, he was a great admirer of the 17th-c Flemish schools. He painted many unorthodox and realistic scenes, notably 'The Raft of the Medusa' (1819, Louvre), based on a shipwreck which had caused a sensation in France. It was harshly criticized, and he withdrew to England, where he painted racing scenes and landscapes.

Gerlachovska [gerlakofska] or **Gerlachovský Štít**, formerly **Gerlsdorfer Spitze** or **Stalin Peak** Highest peak of the Carpathian range and of the Slovak Republic in the Vysoké Tatry (High Tatra), rising to 2655 m/8711 ft.

German, Sir Edward, originally **Edward German Jones** (1862–1936) Composer, born in Whitchurch, Shropshire, WC England, UK. He studied at the Royal Academy of Music, was made musical director of the Globe Theatre, London (1888), and became known for his incidental music to Shakespeare. He emerged as a light opera composer when he completed Sullivan's *Emerald Isle* (1901) after the composer's death. His own works include *Merrie England* (1902), *Tom Jones* (1907), several symphonies, suites, chamber music, and songs. He was knighted in 1928.

German *Germanic languages; German literature*

German art A term used loosely to cover art in C and E Europe, more narrowly for the region that became Germany in 1871. The tradition began under the Ottonian emperors, 10th–11th-c; great Romanesque basilicas followed at Mainz, Worms, and Speyer; Hildesheim was a centre for bronze sculpture, and manuscript illumination flourished at Reichenau. The Gothic style arrived from France in the 13th-c; 15th-c painting developed partly under Flemish influence; woodcut and line engraving was strong, culminating in the greatest German master, Dürer. The N was affected by the Reformation, but S Germany and Austria saw a flowering of Baroque architecture and decoration in the late 17th-c. Late 18th-c and early 19th-c Germany fully exploited Neoclassicism and Romanticism, as in the landscapes by Caspar David Friedrich (1774–1840). Major 20th-c contributions included Expressionism and the Bauhaus.

German Confederation A C European state system created at the Congress of Vienna (1815) to fill the void left by Napoleon I's destruction (1806) of the Holy Roman Empire. Dominated until after 1848 by Austria, it comprised 39 states: 35 monarchies and four free cities. Its purpose was to guarantee the external and internal peace of Germany and the independence of the member states. It was rendered unstable by the subsequent rising power of Prussia, and was dissolved in 1866 following the Austro–Prussian War (1866). It was replaced by the North German Confederation under Prussian leadership.

germander An annual or perennial, sometimes shrubby, found almost everywhere, most abundant in the Mediterranean region; stems square; leaves in opposite pairs; flowers greenish, pink, or purple with spreading 5-lobed lower lip, upper lip absent. (Genus: *Teucrium*, 300 species. Family: Labiatae.)

Germanic languages A branch of Indo-European comprising the **North Germanic** Scandinavian languages in N Europe, and the **West Germanic** languages English, Frisian, German, and Dutch (with its colonial variant Afrikaans in South Africa) in the W. Scandinavian inscriptions in the runic alphabet date from the 3rd-c AD. Old English and Old High German, precursors of modern English and German, are evidenced from the 8th-c, and the Scandinavian languages from the 12th-c. **East Germanic** languages are extinct, though there are manuscript remains of Gothic. Germanic languages are spoken by over 500 million people as a first language, mainly because of the wide dissemination of English, with c.350 million mother-tongue speakers. There are some 100 million speakers of German, mainly in Germany, but also in Austria, Switzerland, parts of E Europe, the Americas, and S Africa.

Germanic religion The pre-Christian religion of the people bounded by the Rhine, Vistula, and Danube rivers. What little is known of these peoples comes largely from Roman accounts of varying reliability, missionaries, and archaeological finds. There was a pantheon of deities represented in human form, of whom four were particularly important during the Viking Age (9th–11th-c). Odin (Germanic *Wotan*), father of the gods and ruler of Valhalla, was the god of poetry, wisdom and the dead. Thor (Germanic *Donar*), a sky-god, was the god of law and order. Frigg and Freyja were fertility deities. The powers of nature were held to be magical, and were represented as sprites, elves, and trolls.

Germanicus [jermanikus], in full **Gaius Germanicus Caesar** (15 BC–AD 19) The son, father, and brother of Roman emperors (Tiberius, Caligula, and Claudius respectively), and heir apparent himself from AD 14. A man of great charm but mediocre ability, his sudden and suspicious death in Antioch marked a turning point in Tiberius's reign. It crystallized the growing disenchantment with the emperor, and sent his reign on its downward spiral.

germanium [jermaynium] Ge, element 32, melting point 937°C. A metalloid found in composite ores, especially with silver and zinc. It is extracted from other metals as $GeCl_4$, which boils at c.80°C. Ultrapure germanium is used as a semiconductor, and as its properties are markedly changed by doping with arsenic or gallium, its main use is in transistor manufacture.

German literature The Old Saxon poem *Heliand* and the Old High German *Hildebrandslied* date from the 9th-c, but it was not until the 12th-c Minnesingers (troubadours) that the vernacular became established as a medium over Latin. Court epics such as *Tristan und Isolde* and *Parzifal* also appeared at this time. The prose works *Tyll Eulenspiegel* and *Dr Faust* appeared in the 15th-c, to be followed by the Meistersingers ('master singers'), Hans Sachs of Nuremberg being the most celebrated. Luther's German Bible (1522–34) provided an opportunity which was lost to German literature because of the Thirty Years' War (1618–48) – reflected in Grimmelshausen's *Simplicissimus* (1669) – and foreign influence; and it was not until the mid-18th-c that it found a new direction. The classicist Lessing and the nationalist Herder provided inspiration for the *Sturm und Drang* ('Storm and Stress') school, characteristic of German Romanticism. The Schlegel brothers contributed an important element (Wilhelm's translation of Shakespeare appeared 1797–1810), as did the poet Hölderlin, the novelist J-P Richter and the dramatist Schiller; but the greatest writer of the age was Goethe, whose imaginative range transcends any movement or national boundary.

There have been distinguished contributors to the German novel, including Thomas Mann, Herman Hesse, and two Austrians: Herman Broch and Franz Kafka, the latter with his unique haunted fictions. Günter Grass's novel *Die Blechtrommel* (1959, The Tin Drum) is the best-known German work since the war. German drama has been very active, from the Expressionist plays of Wedekind and Schnitzler to the epic theatre of Brecht and the documentary drama of Hochhuth; while poetry produced in Rilke one of its greatest figures.

German measles *rubella*

German reunification (*Die Wende*, 'the change') The reuniting of the Federal Republic of Germany (West Germany) and the German Democratic Republic (East Germany) in the 1990s. Following the widespread and unopposed exodus of East Germans to the West in 1989, the fall of the East German communist government and the collapse of the Berlin Wall, East Germany was formally dissolved in October 1990 and the newly-united country became the Federal Republic of Germany. While it united families, the new government's policy of allowing free access to records compiled by the *Stasi* (the East German State Security Service) revealed the names and details of the many thousands of private citizens who had collaborated with the former state as informers, often against their own families and friends. West Germany and East Germany merged their financial systems in July 1990. Reunification placed a strain on the German economy. Increased taxation was necessary to restore the decaying industries and infrastructure in the East, while heavy subsidies and training in new skills were needed to enable the transition of East Germany from a state-dependent to a market economy. East German labourers frequently commanded lower wages than their West German counterparts, leading to resentment at being perceived as second-class citizens.

German shepherd A breed of large dog developed in Germany in the late 19th-c by crossing spitz breeds with local sheepdogs;

thick coat; long pointed muzzle and ears; trains well; popular with police and military worldwide; also known as an **alsatian**.

German wirehaired pointer A pointer developed in Germany by crossing many other breeds of sporting dog; coat rough, thicker on the eyebrows and ears, and also on the jaws, giving it a short beard.

Germany *pp.625–6*

germination The onset of growth of a seed or spore. It only begins when sufficient warmth, water, and oxygen are available, and any preconditions for breaking dormancy are fulfilled. The young root (*radicle*) emerges first, followed by the young shoot (*plumule*). In **hypogeal germination** the cotyledons remain underground; in **epigeal germination** they are raised above soil level.

germ-line therapy or **transfer** An attempt to insert a gene with 'therapeutic' intention into sex cells. Germ-line genetic manipulation does not have any therapeutic effect for the individual possessing an inherited disease; therefore, many argue that gene-line gene 'transfer' is a more appropriate term. In contrast to somatic cell gene therapy, success in this task alters the inheritance of genetically derived disorders in offspring. The concept has caused a great deal of controversy, because of its potential to be used for character 'enhancement' or alteration, rather than for gene correction purposes, giving rise to fears of a new wave of eugenics. As in the case of gene therapy, the procedure remains experimental.

Geronimo [jeronimoh], Indian name **Goyathlay** (1829–1909) Chiricahua Apache Indian, born along the Gila River in present-day Arizona. The best known of all Apache leaders, he forcibly resisted the internment of 4000 of his people on a reservation at San Carlos (1874), subsequently surrendering then escaping from white control on several occasions. In 1886 the local US commander promised him exile in Florida and a return to Arizona if he surrendered. The promise was not kept, and he and his followers were put to hard labour. In his old age, he became a Christian and a public figure. He dictated his autobiography, *Geronimo: His Own Story*, shortly before his death.

gerontology *geriatrics*

gerrymander A term describing the reorganization of electoral areas so as to give unfair advantage to one or more political parties in forthcoming elections. It was first coined in the USA in 1812 by conflating the name of Elbridge Gerry, Governor of Massachusetts, with *salamander*, the shape of which a new electoral district was said to resemble.

Gershwin, George, originally **Jacob Gershvin** (1898–1937) Composer, born in New York City, USA. He published his first song in 1914, and had his first hit, 'Swanee', in 1919. In 1924 he began collaborating with his brother Ira as lyricist, producing numerous classic songs, such as 'Lady Be Good' (1924) and 'I Got Rhythm' (1930). He also composed extended concert works including *Rhapsody in Blue* (1924), *An American in Paris* (1928), and *Girl Crazy* (1930), importing jazz, blues, and pop-song devices into classical contexts. His masterpiece is generally considered to be the jazz-opera *Porgy and Bess* (1935), with such hit songs as 'Summertime' and 'It Ain't Necessarily So'.

Gershwin, Ira, originally **Israel Gershvin**, pseudonym **Arthur Francis** (1896–1983) Songwriter, born in New York City, USA. His precocious younger brother George was the toast of Broadway, so Ira started writing lyrics under a pseudonym. In 1921, he wrote a hit show *Two Little Girls in Blue* with Vincent Youmans (1898–1946), and by 1924 his successes gave him enough confidence not only to drop the pseudonym but to work with his brother. Among their hits were 'I Got Rhythm' (1930), 'I Got Plenty o' Nothin'' (1935), and 'They Can't Take That Away From Me' (1938). His lyrics were sometimes ostentatious, as when he strung together *'s wonderful ... 's marvelous ... 's what I likes* in ''S Wonderful' (1927), but usually nicely colloquial. After his brother's death, he kept on working, and had such hits as 'My Ship' (1941 with Kurt Weill) and 'Long Ago and Far Away' (1944 with Jerome Kern).

Gerson, Jean de [zhayrsõ], originally **Jean Charlier** (1363–1429) Theologian and mystic, born in Gerson, NE France. He was educated in Paris. As Chancellor of the University of Paris from 1395, he supported the proposal for putting an end to the Great Schism between Rome and Avignon by the resignation of both the contending pontiffs, and participated in the Councils of Pisa (1409) and Constance (1414). His fortunes were marred by the animosity of the Duke of Burgundy after denouncing the murder of the Duke of Orléans. Gerson prudently retired to Germany, returning to France only after the duke's death in 1419.

Gervais, Ricky [zhairvayz] (1962–) Actor, writer, and director, born in Reading, Berkshire, S England, UK. He studied biology at University College, London and had various jobs, including manager of rock group Suede and DJ for a London radio station, before trying comedy. He shot to fame with his role as branch manager David Brent in the BBC television cult show *The Office* (2001–2), a series he co-wrote and co-directed with Stephen Merchant. In 2002 the show won double BAFTA awards for Gervais for best sitcom and best comedy performance, and he repeated this success in 2003.

Gesamtkunstwerk [guhzamtkoonstverk] (Ger 'total work of art') A term sometimes applied to Wagnerian opera, in which music is combined with costume and visual effects to create a total unified work. The idea has roots in early 19th-c German Romanticism.

Gesner, Conrad von (1516–65) Naturalist and physician, born in Zürich, N Switzerland. He studied in Bourges, Paris, and Basel, becoming professor of Greek at Lausanne (1537) and of philosophy then of natural history at Zürich (1541). His *Bibliotheca universalis* (1545–9) contained the titles of all the books then known in Hebrew, Greek and Latin, with criticisms and summaries of each. His *Historia animalium* (1551–8) attempted to bring together all that was known in his time of every animal. He collected over 500 plants undescribed by the ancients, and also wrote on medicine, mineralogy, and philology.

Gestalt psychology [geshtalt] A school of psychological thought characterized by the phrase 'the whole is greater than the sum of its parts' – hence, 'wholistic' or 'holistic'. It is probably most famous for the Gestalt 'laws' of perception, which attempted to describe which properties of visual elements make them appear to 'belong together' as an entity. It was developed by the German psychologists Max Wertheimer (1880–1943), Kurt Koffka, and Wolfgang Köhler.

Gestalt therapy [geshtalt] A humanistic-existential therapy derived from Gestalt psychology, which aims to make individuals 'whole' by increasing their awareness of aspects of their personality which have been denied or disowned. Its most important proponent was German-born US psychiatrist Frederick Perls (1893–1970). It is usually conducted in groups and concentrated in workshops over a short period of time (eg a long weekend). Clients are allowed to speak only in the present tense, and non-verbal behaviour (eg movements, hesitations) is considered as important as verbal. Conflicts are acted out in therapy, as are the thoughts and feelings given to images in dreams. Generally clients are encouraged to be more expressive, spontaneous, and responsive to their own needs.

Gestapo [geshtahpoh] An abbreviation of *Geheime Staatspolizei*, the secret police of the German Third Reich, founded in 1933 by Goering on the basis of the Prussian plain-clothes secret police. It soon extended throughout Germany, and from 1936 came under the control of Himmler, as head of the SS (*Schutsstaffel*). Its purpose was to persecute all political opponents of the Nazis. The SD (*Sicherheitsdienst* – the Security Service) under Reinhard Heydrich supplied the intelligence for Gestapo operations. Suspects were arrested and placed in concentration camps which, although run by the SS, were under Gestapo control. The SD, Gestapo, Criminal Police, and foreign intelligence service together comprised an efficiently run, centralized organization that terrorized occupied Europe and conducted mass murder on an unprecedented scale.

Germany

☐ International Airport

Ger **Deutschland**, official name **Federal Republic of Germany**, Ger **Bundesrepublik Deutschland**

Local name Bundesrepublik Deutschland

Timezone GMT +1

Area 357 868 km²/138 136 sq mi

Population total (2002e) 82 506 000

Status Federal republic

Capital Berlin

Languages German (official)

Ethnic groups German (93%), Turkish (2%), Yugoslav (1%), Italian (1%), other European Community (3%)

Religions Lutheran (55%), Roman Catholic (38%), Muslim (3%)

Physical features Lowland plains rise SW through C uplands and Alpine foothills to the Bavarian Alps; highest peak, the Zugspitze, 2962 m/9718 ft; C uplands include the Rhenish Slate Mts, Black Forest, and Harz Mts; Rhine crosses the country S–N; complex canal system links chief rivers, Elbe, Weser, Danube, Rhine, Main

Climate Oceanic climatic influences strongest in NW, where winters are mild, stormy; elsewhere continental climate; lower winter temperatures in E and S, with considerable snowfall; average annual temperatures -0·5°C (Jan) to 19°C (Jul); average annual rainfall 600–700 mm/23–7 in.

Currency 1 euro = 100 cents (previous to February 2002, 1 Deutsche Mark (DM) = 100 Pfennige).

Economy Economically powerful member of EC (accounts for 30% of European Community output): substantial heavy industry in NW, wine in Rhine and Moselle valleys; increasing tourism, especially in the S; leading manufacturer of vehicles, electrical and electronic goods; much less development in the E, after the period of socialist economy; following unification, a major socio-economic division emerged between W and E, leading to demonstrations in the E provinces, 1991.

GDP (2002e) $2·16 tn, per capita $26 200

Human Development Index (2002) 0·925

History Ancient Germanic tribes united in 8th-c within the Frankish Empire of Charlemagne; elective monarchy after 918 under Otto I, with Holy Roman Empire divided into several hundred states; after Congress of Vienna, 1814–15, a confederation of 39 states under Austria; under Bismarck, Prussia succeeded Austria as the leading German power; union of Germany and foundation of Second Reich, 1871, with King of Prussia as hereditary German Emperor; aggressive foreign policy, eventually leading to World War 1; after German defeat, Second Reich replaced by democratic Weimar Republic; world economic crisis led to collapse of Weimar Republic and rise of National Socialist movement, 1929; Adolph Hitler became dictator of the totalitarian Third Reich, 1933; acts of aggression led to World War 2 and a second defeat for Germany, with collapse of the German political regime; partition of Germany in 1945, with occupation zones given to UK, USA, France, and USSR, who formed a Control Council; USSR withdrew from the Control Council in 1948, dividing Germany into W and E: W Germany controlled by the three remaining powers, UK, USA and France; E administered by USSR.

West Germany (former Federal Republic of Germany) Area 249 535 km²/96 320 sq mi; population total (1990) 62 679 035; including West Berlin; established, 1949; gained full sovereignty, 1954; entered NATO, 1955; founder member of the European Economic Community, 1957; federal system of government, built around 10 provinces (Länder) with considerable powers; two-chamber legislature, consisting of Federal Diet (Bundestag) and Federal Council (Bundesrat).

East Germany (former German Democratic Republic) Area 108 333 km²/41 816 sq mi; population total (1990) 16 433 796; administered by USSR after 1945 partition, and Soviet model of government established, 1949; anti-Soviet demonstrations put down, 1953; recognized by USSR as an independent republic, 1954; flow of refugees to West Germany continued until 1961, largely stopped by the Berlin Wall built along zonal boundary, dividing western sectors of Berlin from eastern; governed by the People's Chamber, a single-chamber parliament (Volkskammer) which elected a Council of State, a Council of Ministers, and a National Defence Council; movement for democratic reform culminated in Nov 1989 in the opening and removal of the Wall and other border crossings to the West, and a more open government policy; first free all-German elections since 1932 held in Mar 1990, paving the way for a currency union with West Germany, Jul 1990, and full political unification, Oct 1990.

United Germany The 10 provinces of West Germany joined by the 5 former East German provinces abolished after World War 2 (Brandenburg, Mecklenburg-West, Pomerania, Saxony, Saxony-Anhalt, Thuringia), along with unified Berlin; West German electoral system adopted in East Germany; first national elections, Dec 1990.

German Democratic Republic (East Germany)

Head of State
1949–60 Wilhelm Pieck

Chairman of the Council of State
1960–73 Walter Ulbricht
1973–6 Willi Stoph
1976–89 Erich Honecker
1989 Egon Krenz
1989–90 Gregor Gysi *General Secretary as Chairman*

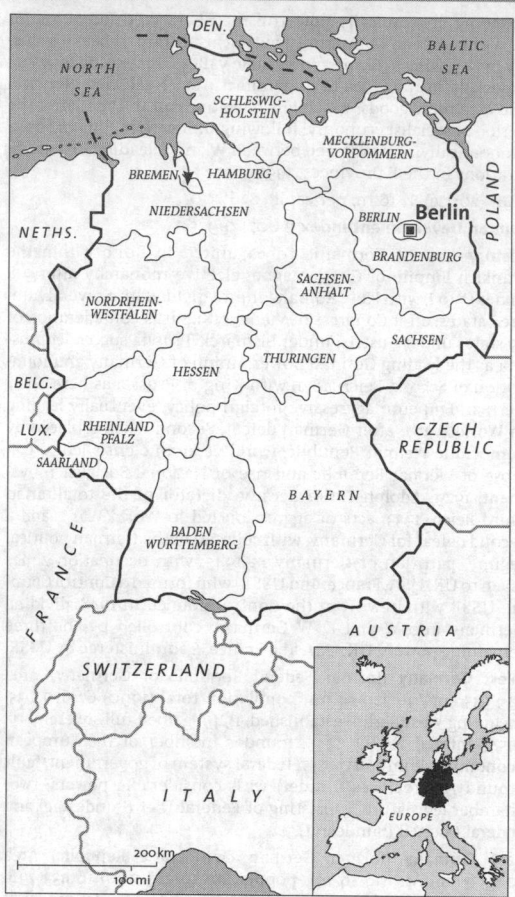

☐ International Airport

Head of Government
1949–64 Otto Grotewohl
1964–73 Willi Stoph
1973–6 Horst Sindermann
1976–89 Willi Stoph
1989–90 Hans Modrow
1990 Lothar de Maizière

German Federal Republic (until 1990 West Germany)

Head of State
1949–59 Theodor Heuss
1959–69 Heinrich Lübke
1969–74 Gustav Heinemann
1974–9 Walter Scheel
1979–84 Karl Carstens
1984–94 Richard von Weizsäcker
1994–9 Roman Herzog
1999– Johannes Rau

Head of Government (Federal Chancellor)
1949–63 Konrad Adenauer
1963–6 Ludwig Erhard
1966–9 Kurt Georg Kiesinger
1969–74 Willy Brandt
1974–82 Helmut Schmidt
1982–98 Helmut Kohl
1998– Gerhard Schröder

gestation period The interval of time from conception to birth in a viviparous animal, during which development of the embryo within the uterus takes place. It is usually relatively constant for any particular species.

Gethsemane [gethsemanee] A place outside Jerusalem near the Mt of Olives where Jesus and his disciples went to pray immediately before his betrayal and arrest (*Mark* 14); described as a 'garden' in *John* 18.1. It is the scene of Jesus's agony over whether to accept martyrdom.

Getty, J(ean) Paul (1892–1976) Oil billionaire and art collector, born in Minneapolis, Minnesota, USA. He studied at the University of California, Berkeley, and at Oxford, entered the oil business in his early twenties, and made a quarter of a million dollars in his first two years. His father (also a successful oil man) died in 1930, leaving him $15 million. He merged his father's interests with his own, and went on to acquire and control more than 100 companies, becoming one of the world's richest men. He founded the J Paul Getty Museum at Malibu, CA, in 1954. His personal wealth was estimated in 1968 at over one billion dollars, and he acquired a huge and extremely valuable art collection. Known for his eccentricity, he was married and divorced five times, and developed a legendary reputation for miserliness, installing a pay-telephone for guests in his English mansion.

Gettysburg, Battle of (Jun–Jul 1863) A major series of engagements in Pennsylvania during the American Civil War between the army of N Virginia (Confederate) and the army of the Potomac (Union), after Robert E Lee, the Southern commander, decided to take the war into the North. Union victory ended any prospect of foreign recognition for the Confederacy.

Gettysburg Address (19 Nov 1863) During the American Civil War, a brief speech (of 272 words) given by President Lincoln at the dedication of a war cemetery in Pennsylvania on the site of the Battle of Gettysburg. Ill-regarded at the time, it is now thought of as one of the masterpieces of American oratory. Its opening lines are familiar still: 'Four score and seven years ago, our Fathers brought forth upon this continent a new nation, conceived in liberty and dedicated to the proposition that all men are created equal'.

Geulincx or **Geulingx, Arnold** [goelingks], pseudonym **Philaretus** (1624–69) Philosopher, born in Antwerp, N Belgium. He taught at the Catholic University of Louvain, but was expelled for his anti-scholasticism in 1658. He then converted to Calvinism, and became professor of philosophy at Leyden in 1665. He was a leading exponent of Descartes' philosophy, and is best known for his doctrine of 'Occasionalism': God himself 'occasions' every mental or physical process, while body and mind operate separately, without causal interaction, like two clocks which are perfectly synchronized. His main works are *Quaestiones quodlibeticae* (1653, Miscellaneous Questions), re-edited by him as *Saturnalia* (1665), *Logica restituta* (1662), and *De virtute* (1665).

geyser [geezer, giyzer] A natural spring which erupts intermittently, throwing up fountains of superheated water and steam from a crack deep in the Earth's crust. Geysers occur in volcanically active areas in New Zealand, Iceland, and the USA.

Geysir [geeser] 64°19N 20°19W. Location in Suðurland, W Iceland, 30 km/19 mi NE of Laugarvatn, E of Reykjavík; water columns of 40–60 m/130–200 ft; gave its name to the word 'geyser'.

Gezhouba Dam [gejohbah] Dam on the Yangtze R, C China, near Yichang; at mouth of Yangtze Gorges; largest water control project in the world.

***g*-factor** In atomic, nuclear, and particle physics, a factor which relates a point-like particle's magnetic moment to its spin; also known as the **Landé *g*-factor**, after US physicist Alfred Landé. For electrons, the *g*-factor is the gyromagnetic ratio in units of $\int^{B}$, the Bohr magnetron. From relativistic quantum mechanics, a point-like electron should have $g = 2$; experiments yield a value about 0·1% larger. Corrections are calculated using quantum electrodynamics, which considers the electron as a bare

Ghana

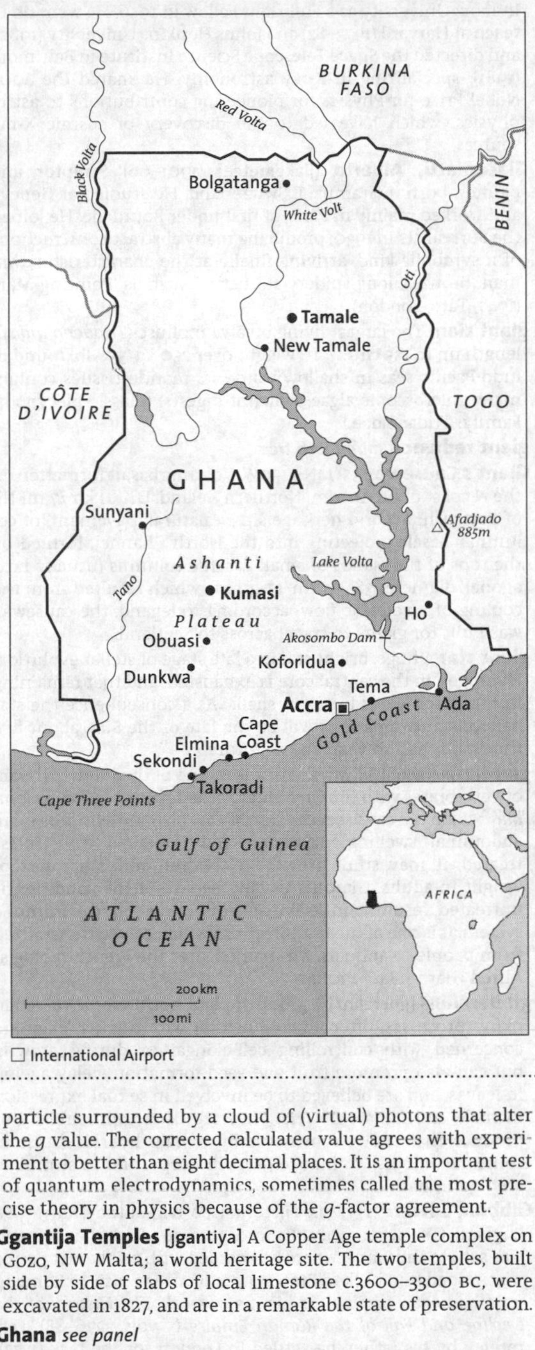

[gahna], official name **Republic of Ghana**

Local name Ghana**Timezone** GMT

Area 238 537 km^2/92 100 sq mi

Population total (2002e) 20 244 000

Status Republic

Date of independence 1960

Capital Accra

Languages English (official), Akan, Ewe, Ga, several minority languages

Ethnic groups c.75 tribal groups, including Akan (44%), Mole-Dagbani (16%), Ewe (13%), and Ga (8%)

Religions Christian (43%), traditional local beliefs (38%), Muslim (12%)

Physical features Located in W Africa; low-lying plains inland, leading to the Ashanti plateau (W) and R Volta basin (E), dammed to form L Volta; mountains (E) rise to 885 m/2903 ft at Mt Afadjado; Ashanti plateau in W and Akwapin Toto Mts in E.

Climate Tropical climate, including a warm dry coastal belt (SE); a hot, humid SW corner; and a hot, dry savannah (N); average temperatures 27°C (Jan), 25°C (Jul) in Accra.

Currency 1 Cedi (c) = 100 pesewas

Economy Agriculture; cocoa (world's leading producer) provides two-thirds of export revenue; tourism; commercial reserves of oil, diamonds, gold, manganese, bauxite, timber.

GDP (2002e) \$41·25 bn, per capita \$2000

Human Development Index (2002) 0·548

History Visited by Europeans in 15th-c; centre of slave trade, 18th-c; modern state created by union of two former British territories, British Gold Coast (Crown Colony, 1874) and British Togoland, merging to form Ghana and declaring independence, 1957; independent republic within the Commonwealth, 1960; constitution provides for a Parliament, executive President, Cabinet, and Council of State; series of military coups (1966, 1972, 1979, 1982) led to the creation of a Provisional National Defence Council, which rules by decree; new multi-party constitution, 1992, allowing for a directly elected executive President and legislature.

Head of State/Government

(Chairman of the Provisional National Defence Council)
1981–92 Jerry John Rawlings

President

1992–2001 Jerry John Rawlings
2001– John Kufuor

particle surrounded by a cloud of (virtual) photons that alter the *g* value. The corrected calculated value agrees with experiment to better than eight decimal places. It is an important test of quantum electrodynamics, sometimes called the most precise theory in physics because of the *g*-factor agreement.

Ggantija Temples [gantiya] A Copper Age temple complex on Gozo, NW Malta; a world heritage site. The two temples, built side by side of slabs of local limestone c.3600–3300 BC, were excavated in 1827, and are in a remarkable state of preservation.

Ghana *see panel*

gharial [gairial] or **gavial** A rare S Asian crocodile-like reptile (*Gavialis gangeticus*) of family Gavialidae; length up to 6·6 m/$21\frac{1}{2}$ ft; very narrow snout; nostrils of male swollen as a bulbous 'pot'; inhabits rivers; eats fish and frogs. The name is also used for the **false gharial** of the family Crocodilidae. The spelling *gavial* was a slip of the pen during early accounts of the gharial.

Ghats [gahts] Two mountain ranges in India; **Eastern Ghats** runs parallel to the Bay of Bengal, forming the E edge of the Deccan Plateau; series of disconnected hill ranges, including the Velikonda, Nallamala, Seshachalam, Palkonda, Melagiri, and Nilgiri Hills; Doda Betta in the Nilgiri Hills reaches 2636 m/8648 ft; **Western Ghats** runs parallel to the Arabian Sea, forming the W boundary of the Deccan plateau; length c.1600 km/1000 mi; two ranges join in the Nilgiri Hills; chief watershed of peninsular India; highest point, Anai Mudi Peak (2695 m/8842 ft) in the Cardamon Hills; subject to heavy rainfall during the SW monsoon; dense tropical forest.

Ghazali, Abu Hamid Mohammed al- [gazahlee] (1058–1111) Islamic philosopher, theologian, and jurist, born in Tus, NE Iran (near modern Meshed). He was appointed professor of philosophy at Nizamiyah College, Baghdad (1091–5), where he exercised great academic and political influence, but later suffered a spiritual crisis which caused him to abandon his position for the ascetic life of a mendicant *sufi* (mystic), spending his time in meditation and spiritual exercises. After a brief return to teaching he retired to Tus to found a monastic community. He was a prolific author, best known for the monumental *The Revival of the Religious Sciences* (trans title).

ghee [gee] An edible fat derived from butter by removing all or most of the water. It is popular in hot climates, where the absence of water improves the keeping quality of the butterfat.

Ghent [gent], Flemish **Gent**, Fr **Gand** 51°02N 3°42E, pop (2000e) 234 200. River port and capital city of East Flanders province, NW Belgium, at the confluence of the Scheldt and Leie Rivers; third largest urban region in Belgium, and second largest port; harbour connected by canal to the North Sea; focus of Flemish nationality; university (1816); railway; spinning and weaving (Flemish linen), chemicals, steel, cars, electrical engineering, publishing, banking; Cathedral of St Bavon (begun 10th-c), town hall (15th–17th-c), House of Free Boatmen (1531), Abbey of St Bavon (642), castle of Gravensteen (1180–1200).

gherkin A variety of cucumber (*Cucumis sativa*) or its very small fruits. (Family: Cucurbitaceae.)

Ghibellines [gibeleenz] The pro-imperial party in Italian cities of the 13th–14th-c, favouring the involvement of the Holy Roman Emperor in Italian politics, even after the decline of the Hohenstaufen state from 1266. They supported the invasion of Emperor Henry VII (c.1270–1313) in 1308, though the power and status of the Empire had much diminished by that date.

Ghiberti, Lorenzo [geebairtee] (1378–1455) Goldsmith, bronze-caster, and sculptor, born in Florence, NC Italy. In 1401 he won the competition to make a pair of bronze gates for the Baptistry of Florence Cathedral. When these were completed (1424), he worked on a further pair of gates, which were finished in 1452.

Ghirardelli, Domingo [zhiradelee], originally **Domenico** (1817–94) Chocolate manufacturer, born in Rapallo, NW Italy, the son of a leading chocolatier. In 1837 he travelled to South America, where he established a chocolate trade, eventually settling in Lima, Peru, and then moved on to San Francisco, where he supplied the 1849 gold rush miners with chocolate. He founded his chocolate company in the city, building it up into one of the largest stores in the W USA. Ghirardelli Square is now a feature of the San Francisco tourist scene, the old store being one of the buildings to survive the 1906 earthquake.

Ghirlandaio, Domenico [geerlandahyoh], originally **Domenico di Tommaso Bigordi** (1449–94) Painter, born in Florence, NC Italy. He was apprenticed to a goldsmith, a metal garland-maker or *ghirlandaio*. His main works were frescoes, in his native city, notably a series illustrating the lives of the Virgin and the Baptist in the choir of Santa Maria Novella (1490).

Ghose, Zulfikar (1935–) Writer, born in Sialkot, NE Pakistan (formerly, India). He and his family moved to England in 1952. He studied at the University of Keele, then married a Brazilian artist, Helena de la Fontaine. In 1969 he moved to the USA, where he taught at the University of Texas. His first novel, *The Contradictions* (1966), was followed by a trilogy, *The Incredible Brazilian*, comprising *The Native* (1972), *The Beautiful Empire* (1975), and *A Different World* (1978). Other works include the novel *The Triple Mirror of the Self* (1992) and a collection of short stories, *Veronica and the Gongora Passion* (1998). *Selected Poems* was published in 1991. Non-fiction works include *The Art of Creating Fiction* (1991) and an autobiography, *Confessions of a Native-Alien* (1965).

Ghost Dance A 19th-c American Indian movement. It began in 1870 among Paiute Indians and spread to other tribes. Under the direction of the prophet Wovoka it reached the Sioux in 1889. It promised deliverance from the Indians' plight, but led to the massacre of US troops at Wounded Knee, SD, in 1890.

ghosts Traditionally, spirits of the dead who return to haunt the living, usually because they have not received the proper funeral rites, or because they have committed or been the victims of an unrighted wrong. For example, the ghost of Hamlet's father appears in Shakespeare's play to indicate that he has been murdered by Claudius, and to prompt Hamlet to avenge him. In modern times, ghosts are now the subject of a popular literary genre, the **ghost story**, and figure also in films. They are sometimes associated with particular places, especially so-called haunted houses; but many people no longer take them seriously.

Giacconi, Riccardo (1931–) Astrophysicist, born in Genoa, Italy. He studied and taught at the University of Milan, then joined Indiana University as a Fulbright Fellow in 1956. He went on to teach at Harvard (1973–82) and Johns Hopkins University (1982), and directed the Space Telescope Science Institute in Baltimore (1981), specializing in X-ray astronomy. He shared the 2002 Nobel Prize for Physics for pioneering contributions to astrophysics, which have led to the discovery of cosmic X-ray sources.

Giacometti, Alberto [jiakometee] (1901–66) Sculptor and painter, born in Stampa, E Switzerland. He studied at Geneva and worked mainly in Paris, at first under Bourdelle. He joined the Surrealists in 1930, producing many abstract constructions of a symbolic kind, arriving finally at the characteristic 'thin man' bronzes, long spidery statuettes, such as 'Pointing Man' (1947, Tate, London).

giant clam The largest living bivalve mollusc (*Tridacna gigas*); length up to 135 cm/2½ ft; weight over 250 kg/550 lb; found in Indo-Pacific seas in shallow water; its mantle tissues contain many microscopic algae, which it digests. (Class: Pelecypoda. Family: Tridacnidae.)

giant redwood *mammoth tree*

Giant's Causeway 55°14N 6°30W. Volcanic basalt formation on the N coast of Co Antrim, Northern Ireland, UK, 11 km/7 mi NE of Portrush; a world heritage site; a natural 'pavement' of columnar basalt projecting into the North Channel, formed by the tops of thousands of small basaltic columns (usually hexagonal, diameter 38–50 cm/15–20 in), which resulted from the cooling of a volcanic flow; according to legend, the causeway was built for giants to travel across to Scotland.

giant star A huge, bright star in a late stage of stellar evolution. Hydrogen in the central core is exhausted, and that remaining in the outer layers burns in shells. As a consequence the star balloons outwards. This will be the fate of the Sun, about five thousand million years in the future.

giardiasis [jeeah(r)diyasis] The infestation of the intestinal tract of vertebrates with the tiny, single-celled parasite *Giardia lamblia*, which can cause severe diarrhoea. The main symptoms are abdominal swelling, diarrhoea, and intestinal gas. Unless treated, it may stunt growth in children and cause loss of weight in adults. Giarditis usually persists if the condition is untreated, resulting in severe anaemia and a reduced immune system. It is one of the few infections which can be transmitted from people to animals. It is named after the French biologist Alfred Giard (1846–1908).

gibberellins [jiberelinz] A group of plant hormones involved in many processes, often in conjunction with auxins. They are concerned with controlling cell-elongation during growth, but can also promote fruit and seed formation, delay ageing in leaves, and are believed to be involved in sexual expression in male and female flowers. They are used commercially to produce male flowers in naturally female hybrids (such as some cucumbers), to induce parthenocarpy, and to stimulate seed germination.

Gibbon, Edward (1737–94) Historian, born in Putney, Surrey, SE England, UK. He studied at Oxford, became a Catholic at 16, and was sent to Lausanne, where he boarded with a Calvinist pastor who wooed him back to Protestantism. After a visit to Rome in 1764 he began to plan for his major work, *The History of the Decline and Fall of the Roman Empire* (5 vols, 1776–88). Left money by his father, he settled in London for the task (1772), in 1774 entering parliament, and becoming commissioner of trade and plantations. After completing his *History*, he spent much of the rest of his life with Lord Sheffield, who published his *Miscellaneous Works* (1796).

Gibbon, Lewis Grassic, pseudonym of **James Leslie Mitchell** (1901–35) Writer, born in Auchterless, Aberdeenshire, NE Scotland, UK. Educated at Stonehaven Academy, he worked as a journalist in Aberdeen, and served in the RAF until 1929. He published the historical novels *Three Go Back* (1932) and *Spartacus* (1933) under his own name, but the three novels *Sunset*

Song (1932), *Cloud Howe* (1933), and *Grey Granite* (1934), which form the trilogy *A Scots Quair* appeared under his pseudonym.

gibbon An ape native to rainforests of SE Asia; acrobatic; slender with small head; thumb small; fingers long; arms as long as body and legs together; arms folded above head when walking; also known as **lesser ape**. (Genus: *Hylobates*, 6 species.)

Gibbons, Grinling (1648–1721) Sculptor and woodcarver, born in Rotterdam, The Netherlands. He moved to England, UK, where he was appointed by Charles II to the Board of Works, and employed in the chapel at Windsor and in St Paul's London. At Chatsworth, Burghley, and other mansions he executed an immense quantity of carved fruit and flowers, cherubs' heads, and other typical Baroque embellishment.

Gibbons, Orlando (1583–1625) Composer, born in Oxford, Oxfordshire, SC England, UK. He studied at Cambridge, and c.1615 was appointed organist of the Chapel Royal, London, and in 1623 of Westminster Abbey. His compositions include services, anthems, and madrigals (notably *The Silver Swan*), and also hymns, fantasies for viols, and music for virginals.

Gibbons, Stella (Dorothea) (1902–89) Writer, born in London, UK. She worked as a journalist, and later began a series of successful novels, as well as writing poetry and short stories. Her *Cold Comfort Farm* (1932), a light-hearted satire on melodramatic rural novels – notably those of Mary Webb (1881–1927), including *Gone to Earth* (1917) and *Precious Bane* (1924) – has established itself as a classic of parody.

Gibbs, James (1682–1754) Architect, born in Aberdeen, NE Scotland, UK. He studied under Carlo Fontana, in Italy. A friend and disciple of Wren, he became in 1713 one of the commissioners for building new churches in London. His designs included St Mary-le-Strand (1717) and St Martin-in-the-Fields (1726), the latter being perhaps his most influential and attractive work. He was also responsible for St Bartholomew's Hospital (1730). His *Book of Architecture* (1728) helped to spread the Palladian style, and influenced the design of many churches of the colonial period in America.

Gibbs, J(osiah) Willard (1839–1903) Mathematician and physicist, born in New Haven, Connecticut, USA. He studied at Yale, becoming the recipient of the first doctorate in engineering awarded in the USA. After studying in Europe for a few years, he returned to Yale in 1869, becoming professor there in 1871. He contributed to the study of thermodynamics, and his most important work, first published as the paper 'On the Equilibrium of Heterogeneous Substances' (1876), established him as a founder of physical chemistry.

Gibraltar [jibrawlter], Span [kheevral**tahr**], Arabic **Jebel Tariq** 36°09N 5°21W; pop (2000e) 29 300; area 6·5 sq km/2·5 sq mi. Narrow rocky peninsula rising steeply from the low-lying coast of SW Spain at the E end of the Strait of Gibraltar; length, c.5 km/3 mi; width 1·2 km/¾ mi, narrowing to the S; gateway between the Atlantic Ocean and the Mediterranean Sea; important strategic point of control for the W Mediterranean; British Crown Colony, playing a key role in Allied naval operations during both World Wars; military base; 8 km/5 mi from Algeciras; official language, English, with Spanish widely spoken; British currency and local banknotes used; timezone GMT +1; airport; car ferries to Tangier; limestone massif, 'The Rock', height 426 m/1398 ft, connected to the Spanish mainland by a sandy plain; extensive limestone caves; home of the Barbary apes, the only native monkeys in Europe; settled by Moors, 711; taken by Spain, 1462; ceded to Britain, 1713; Crown Colony, 1830; British monarch represented by a governor; 18-member House of Assembly; economy largely dependent on the presence of British forces; Royal Naval Dockyard converted to a commercial yard in 1985; transshipment trade, fuel supplies to shipping, tourism; Moorish castle; proposal to end British rule defeated by referendum, 1967; Spanish closure of frontier, 1969–85; Spain continues to claim sovereignty; British–Spanish talks ongoing, with a backdrop of inhabitants' demonstrations against shared sovereignty, 2002; referendum (Nov 2002) resulted in 99 percent rejection of joint sovereignty by Gibraltarians; collapse of talks, 2003.

Gibraltar, Strait of, Arabic **Bab al Zakak**, Lat **Fretum Herculeum** Channel connecting the Mediterranean Sea to the Atlantic Ocean; length, 60 km/37 mi; width between the Rock of Gibraltar and Cape Ceuta (the Pillars of Hercules), 24 km/15 mi; widest point, 40 km/25 mi; narrowest point, 15 km/9 mi.

Gibson, Guy (Penrose) (1918–44) British airman. As a wing-commander in the RAF he led the famous 'dambusters' raid on the Möhne and Eder dams in 1943, an exploit for which he received the VC. He was killed during a later operation.

Gibson, James (Jerome) (1904–79) Psychologist, born in McConnelsville, Ohio, USA. He studied at Princeton and Edinburgh universities, and taught psychology at Smith College (1928–49) and at Cornell (1949–72). During World War 2 he served as director of the Research Unit in Aviation Psychology for the US air force. His influential theory of vision, described in *The Perception of the Visual World* (1950), viewed perception as the direct detection of invariances in the world, requiring neither inference nor the processing of information.

Gibson, Mel, originally **Columcille Gerard Gibson** (1956–) Film actor, born in Peekskill, New York, USA. In 1968 his family emigrated to Australia, where he trained as an actor at the National Institute of Dramatic Art in Sydney, and made several stage appearances before making his film debut in *Summer City* (1977). He became an international star following his leading role in the trio of action-packed *Mad Max* films (1979, 1981, 1985) and the highly successful *Lethal Weapon* series (1987, 1989, 1992, 1998). He displayed different facets of his talent in *Tequila Sunrise* (1988) and *Forever Young* (1992), and gave a well-received interpretation of *Hamlet* (1990). He directed and starred in *Braveheart* (1995, Oscar Best Film, Golden Globe). Later films include *Ransom* (1996), *Payback* (1999), *The Patriot* (2000), and *We Were Soldiers* (2002). *The Passion of the Christ* (2004), which he funded and directed, angered some Jewish groups for its portrayal of the Jews, and aroused controversy for its violent depiction of events.

Gibson, Mike, popular name of **(Cameron) Michael (Henderson) Gibson** (1942–) Rugby union player, born in Belfast, NE Northern Ireland, UK. He played as centre and outside half with the North of Ireland, Cambridge University, Ireland, and the British Lions. When he retired in 1979, his 69 appearances for Ireland were a record for an International Board nation. He toured with the British Lions in 1966, 1968, and 1971, and made 12 international appearances. He is now a Belfast solicitor.

Gibson Desert Central belt of the Western Australian Desert; area c.220 000 sq km/85 000 sq mi; consists of sand dunes, scrub, and salt marshes; includes the salt lakes L Disappointment and L Auld; contains Rudall R national park.

Gide, André (Paul Guillaume) [zheed] (1869–1951) Writer, born in Paris, France. As a young man he symbolized his generation's rebellion against conventional values. He was author of over 50 volumes of fiction, poetry, plays, criticism, biography, belles lettres, and translations. Among his best-known works are *Les Nourritures terrestres* (1897, Fruits of the Earth), *L'Immoraliste* (1902), a short story in which the destruction of others is legitimized, and *Les Faux Monnayeurs* (1926, The Counterfeiters), his translations of *Oedipus* and *Hamlet*, and his *Journal*. He received the Nobel Prize for Literature in 1947.

Gideons International An international organization, which began in Wisconsin in 1898, with the aim of spreading the Christian faith by the free distribution of copies of the Bible to public places, including hotel rooms, hospitals, and military bases. It is named after the Biblical judge, Gideon, who led Israel against the Midianites.

Gielgud, Sir (Arthur) John [geelgud] (1904–2000) Actor and director, born in London, UK. Educated in London, he made his debut in 1921 at the Old Vic Theatre, and established a reputation as Hamlet (1929) and in *The Good Companions* (1931). He became a leading Shakespearian actor, directing several of the Shakespeare Memorial Theatre productions. His many film appearances include his role as Disraeli in *The Prime Minister* (1940), *Arthur* (1970, Oscar), *Prospero's Books* (1991), *Elizabeth*

(1998), and *The Tichborne Claimant* (1999). He was knighted in 1953, and received a special Laurence Olivier Award for his services to the theatre in 1985. He had been president of the International Shakespeare Association since 1976. His books include an autobiography, *An Actor in his Time* (1979), *Backward Glances* (1989), and *Notes from the Gods* (1994). He received the Order of Merit in 1996.

GIF [gif] *digital media*

gift economy A system in which goods of equivalent value are exchanged as tokens of social relationships. The use value of the goods may be minimal, and gifts may consist of specialized items, such as personal ornaments or items of display. Sometimes, as in the North American potlatch, the exchanges become competitive, in a quest for higher status.

gift tax A tax formerly levied in the UK on gifts having a substantial value. Capital transfer tax was in part a gift tax, the aim being to stop the practice of transferring property during a person's lifetime, thus avoiding death duties. In the USA, the tax is levied on the value of the property given away (payable by the donor).

Gigantes [jiyganteez, giganteez] In Greek mythology, the sons of Earth and Tartaros, with snake-like legs; their name means 'the giants'. They made war on the Olympian gods, were defeated, and are buried under various volcanic islands. The **Gigantomachy** ('war of the giants') was the subject of large-scale sculpture, as at Pergamum. A sub-group, the Aloadae, piled Mt Pelion upon Mt Ossa.

Giggs, Ryan (1973–) Footballer, born in Cardiff, S Wales, UK. He made his league debut for Manchester United in 1991, and first played for Wales later that year, becoming the youngest-ever Welsh cap. Twice named the Professional Football Association's Young Player of the Year (1991–2), his honours with Manchester United include the FA Premiership (1993, 1994, 1996, 1997), the FA Cup (1994, 1996), the Rumbelows (League) Cup (1992), and in the 1998–9 season he achieved the treble of FA Cup, Premier League Championship, and European Cup. He won a third consecutive league championship in the 2000–1 season.

Gigli, Beniamino [jeelyee] (1890–1957) Tenor, born in Recanati, EC Italy. He won a scholarship to the Liceo Musicale, Rome, and made his operatic debut in Ponchielli's *La gioconda* in 1914. By 1929 he had won a worldwide reputation as a lyric-dramatic tenor of great vitality, at his best in the works of Verdi and Puccini.

gigue [zheeg] A lively dance, probably of British origin, popular during the 17th–18th-c. The dance was popular with lutenists and became a standard movement in instrumental suites of the period.

gila monster [heela] An American lizard of family Helodermatidae; the only venomous lizard (venom is a nerve poison, but the bite is seldom fatal); length, up to 600 mm/24 in; dark with yellow mottling; bead-like scales; blunt head; fat tail; eats eggs and small vertebrates; two species: **gila monster** (*Heloderma suspectum*) and **Mexican beaded lizard** (*Heloderma horridum*).

Gilbert, Cass (1859–1934) Architect, born in Zanesville, Ohio, USA. He studied at the Massachusetts Institute of Technology. He designed the first tower skyscraper, the 60-storey Woolworth Building in New York City (1912), at that time the tallest building in the world. He also designed the US Customs House in New York City (1907), the Supreme Court Building in Washington, DC (1935), and the campuses of the universities of Minnesota (Minneapolis) and Texas (Austin).

Gilbert, William, also **Gylberde, William** (1544–1603) Physician and physicist, born in Colchester, Essex, SE England, UK. After a period at Cambridge, he was appointed physician to Elizabeth I. He established the magnetic nature of the Earth, and conjectured that terrestrial magnetism and electricity were two allied emanations of a single force. He was the first to use the terms *electricity*, *electric force*, and *electric attraction*. His book, *De magnete* (1600, On the Magnet) is the first major English book in science. The *gilbert*, unit of magnetomotive power, is named after him.

Gilbert, Sir W(illiam) S(chwenck) (1836–1911) Parodist, and librettist of the 'Gilbert and Sullivan' light operas, born in London, UK. He studied at London, became a clerk in the privy-council office (1857–62), and was called to the bar (1864). Failing to attract lucrative briefs, he subsisted on magazine contributions to *Fun*, for which he wrote much humorous verse under his boyhood nickname 'Bab', collected in 1869 as the *Bab Ballads*. He also wrote fairy comedies and serious plays in blank verse. He is remembered for his partnership with Sir Arthur Sullivan, begun in 1871, with whom he wrote 14 popular operas, from *Trial by Jury* (1875) to *The Gondoliers* (1889). The partnership was broken by a quarrel, and on its resolution they wrote little more before Sullivan's death in 1900. He was knighted in 1907.

Gilbert and George Avant-garde artists: **Gilbert Proesch** (1943–) and **George Passmore** (1944–). Gilbert studied at the Academy of Art in Munich, George at Dartington Hall and at the Oxford School of Art. They made their name in the late 1960s as performance artists (the 'singing sculptures'), with faces and hands painted gold, holding their poses for hours at a time. More recently they have concentrated on photopieces, assembled from a number of separately framed photographs which key together to make a single whole.

Gilbert of Sempringham, St (c.1083–1189) Priest, the founder of the Gilbertine Order, born in Sempringham, Lincolnshire, EC England, UK. In 1148 he founded an order of monks and nuns, and lay sisters and brothers. The only mediaeval religious order founded in England, it did not spread beyond England and Scotland, and was dissolved at the Reformation. He was canonized in 1202; feast day 4 February.

Gilbert Islands pop (2000e) 82 000; area 264 sq km/102 sq mi. Main island group of Kiribati, C Pacific Ocean; chain of 17 coral atolls spread over c.680 km/420 mi; mainly 200–300 m/700–1000 ft wide, but 15–100 km/10–60 mi long; most have central lagoons; part of the British colony of Gilbert and Ellice Is until 1977; capital, Tarawa; fishing, farming, copra, phosphate.

Gilchrist, Ellen [gilkrist] (1935–) Writer, born in Vicksburg, Michigan, USA. She studied at Vanderbilt University, Millsap College (Jackson, MI), and the University of Arkansas. She has written poetry, short stories, and novels, and is known especially for her satirical treatment of the upper-class world of the southern states of the USA. Her novels include *The Annunciation* (1983), *I Cannot Get You Close Enough* (1990), and *Net of Jewels* (1993). In 2000 appeared *The Cabal and Other Stories*.

gilding The ancient craft of sticking gold (or other metallic) leaf on to a surface, usually wood. Gilding flourished in the Middle Ages in manuscript illumination and panel painting, and later for picture-frames and furniture.

Giles, Bill, popular name of **William George Giles** (1939–) British weatherman, the head of the Weather Centre at the BBC (1983–2000). He studied at Bristol College of Science and Technology, joining the Meteorological Office in 1959. He became a radio broadcaster in 1972, and moved to television in 1975. His books include *Weather Observations* (1978) and *The Story of Weather* (1990).

Giles, Carl [jiylz] (1916–95) Cartoonist, born in London, UK. He trained as an animator and worked for the film-maker Alexander Korda in 1935. From 1937 he produced his distinctive and popular humorous drawings, first for *Reynolds News*, then (from 1943) for the *Express* newspapers, celebrating the down-to-earth reactions of ordinary British people to great events.

Gilgamesh [gilgamesh] A Babylonian epic poem, partially preserved in different versions, named after its hero, the Sumerian king Gilgamesh (3rd millennium BC). It describes Gilgamesh's legendary adventures, and narrates a story of the Flood that has striking parallels with the Biblical account.

Gill, (Arthur) Eric (Rowton) [gil] (1882–1940) Carver, engraver, and typographer, born in Brighton, East Sussex, SE England, UK. He trained as an architect, but then took up letter-cutting, masonry, and engraving. After his first exhibition (1911) he maintained a steady output of carvings in stone and wood, engravings, and type designs. Among his main works is 'Prospero and Ariel' (1931) above the entrance to Broadcasting House, London.

Gillespie, Dizzy [gilespee], popular name of **John Birks Gillespie** (1917–93) Jazz trumpeter and composer, born in Cheraw, South Carolina, USA. He worked in prominent swing bands (1937–44), including those of Benny Carter and Charlie Barnet. As a band leader, often with Charlie Parker on saxophone, he developed the music known as *bebop*, with dissonant harmonies and polyrhythms, a reaction to swing. His own big band (1946–50) was his masterpiece, affording him scope as both soloist and showman. He was immediately recognizable from the unusual shape of his trumpet, with the bell tilted upwards at an angle of 45° – the result of someone accidentally sitting on it in 1953, but to good effect, for when he played it afterwards he discovered that the new shape improved the sound quality, and he had it incorporated into all his trumpets thereafter. His memoirs *To Be or Not to Bop* (with Al Fraser) appeared in 1979.

Gillette, King C(amp) [jilet] (1855–1932) Inventor of the safety razor, born in Fond du Lac, Wisconsin, USA. Brought up in Chicago, he became a travelling salesman for a hardware company, patented the safety razor in 1895, and founded his razor blade company in 1903. Later he wrote a series of books on industrial welfare and social reform.

Gilliam, Terry [gilyam] (1940–) Artist and film director, born in Minneapolis, Michigan, USA. Originally known for his fantasy animations in the television series 'Monty Python's Flying Circus' (1969–74), he went on to work in film, directing such imaginative adventures as *Jubberwocky* (1977), *The Time Bandits* (1980), *The Adventures of Baron Munchausen* (1988), *The Fisher King* (1991), and *Fear and Loathing in Las Vegas* (1998).

gilliflower *stock*

Gillray, James [gilray] (1757–1815) Caricaturist, born in London, UK. A letter engraver by training, from c.1779 he turned to caricature. He issued about 1500 caricatures of political and social subjects, notably of Napoleon, George III, and leading politicians.

Gilman, Charlotte Anna Perkins, *née* **Perkins**, earlier married name **Stetson** (1860–1935) Feminist and writer, born in Hartford, Connecticut, USA. She studied at Rhode Island School of Design, then moved to California, where she published her first stories. She lectured on women's issues, as well as wider social concerns, and in 1898 wrote *Women and Economics*, now recognized as a feminist landmark. Later books include *The Home* (1903) and *Man-Made World* (1911). In 1902 she married her cousin **George Gilman**, a New York lawyer. She founded, edited, and wrote for the journal *Forerunner* in 1909. She commited suicide on being told that she was suffering from incurable cancer.

gilt-edged securities The name given to UK government loan stock, considered to be a safe investment in terms of its ability to pay interest and capital as and when they fall due. The name derives from the book in which transactions were originally recorded, which was edged in gold.

gin A spirit distilled from grain or malt, and flavoured with juniper berries; the name derives from Dutch *jenever* 'juniper'. Gin was once the true drink of the masses, often referred to as 'mothers' ruin' and associated with 'gin palaces', but its image changed considerably in the 20th-c. **Dutch gin** is drunk neat with beer, while **London** or **dry gin** is usually mixed with tonic.

Ginckell or **Ginkel, Godert de** [gingkel] (1630–1703) Dutch general, born in Utrecht, The Netherlands. He accompanied William III to England in 1688, and fought at the Battle of the Boyne (1690). As commander-in-chief in Ireland, he defeated the remaining rebels, and was created Earl of Athlone (1692). He later led the Dutch troops under Marlborough.

ginger A perennial native to SE Asia (*Zingiber officinale*); stem to 1 m/3¼ ft; rhizomatous; leaves with sheathing stalks, in two rows; yellow and purple flowers, complex, sterile, resembling those of orchids, in long dense spikes with overlapping yellow and green bracts. An important spice since ancient times, it reached Europe by the 1st-c, and England by the 11th-c. The aromatic rhizome contains the essential oil *zingiberene*, used in perfumes as well as food and drink (such as ginger ale). Because the flowers are sterile, propagation is vegetative. (Family: Zingiberaceae.)

Ginger Meggs A famous Australian cartoon character, created in 1921 by J C Bancks in Sydney. Ginger is a boy about 10 years old, living in the suburbs, who stands up against a bully and stupid parents. Syndicated nationally and overseas, he has appeared in book, pantomime, and play form, as well as in a film (1982).

ginger mint *mint*

gingivitis [jinjiviytis] Inflammation of the gums, which become swollen and red, and are prone to bleeding. It is caused by excessive deposits on the teeth of plaque, consisting of food debris, mucus, and bacteria. Plaque irritates the gums, which become prone to infection. The infection can spread to the tissues and bone that support the teeth, ultimately resulting in their loss. Prevention is by good oral hygiene

Gingrich, Newt(on Leroy) [ginggrich] (1943–) US politician, born in Hummelstown, Pennsylvania, USA. He studied at Emory and Tulane universities, then taught history at West Georgia College, and was elected as Republican representative for Georgia in 1979. He became Speaker of the House in 1995 with the promise of enacting a new conservative agenda, but resigned in November 1998 following the poor performance of his party in the mid-term elections. He has also written or co-authored several books, beginning with *Window of Opportunity* (with Marianne Gingrich and David Drake), *Contract with America* (with Dick Armey), *To Renew America*, *Lessons Learned the Hard Way* (1998), and a fiction work, *1945* (with William Fortschen).

ginkgo A deciduous gymnosperm (*Ginkgo biloba*) originally from SW China, but probably no longer existing in the wild; leaves fan-shaped; seed with a fleshy aril covering the edible kernel; also called **maidenhair tree**. It is the sole living survivor of a formerly large and widespread family. (Family: Ginkgoaceae.)

Ginola, David [zhinola] (1967–) Footballer, born in Gassin, near St Tropez, SW France. He played for Paris St Germain, moving to the UK to join Newcastle United (1995), Tottenham Hotspur (1997), Aston Villa (2000), and Everton (2002). He has won 17 caps for France, and in 1994 was voted French Footballer of the Year, but he lost his place in the national team after France failed to qualify in the 1994 World Cup. In 1998 he highlighted the international campaign against land mines by retracing the tour of an Angolan minefield previously undertaken by Princess Diana.

gin rummy *rummy*

Ginsberg, Allen (1926–97) Poet of the 'beat' movement, born in Newark, New Jersey, USA. He studied at Columbia University, where he became friendly with Jack Kerouac, William Burroughs, and others of the movement. *Howl* (1956), his epic poem, was a significant success, and launched him on a high profile career as a public speaker against authoritarianism. Other collections include *Kaddish and Other Poems* (1961), *Reality Sandwiches* (1963), and *Poems All Over The Place: Mostly Seventies* (1978). His *Collected Poems* were published in 1987.

ginseng Either of two species of thick-rooted perennials (*Panax pseudoginseng*, *Panax quinquefolium*), native to North America and Asia; rhizomatous; palmate leaves; 5-petalled, yellowish-green flowers; round, red fruits. The powdered roots are said to have aphrodisiac as well as medicinal and rejuvenative properties. It is popular as a tonic and dietary supplement, and has been recommended for the treatment of tiredness, nervous, kidney, and circulatory problems. Chemical analysis has shown that it contains a series of glycosides (*ginsenosides*) which break down to produce sugars which may have an influence on the immune system, increasing resistance to infection. Other constituents include a range of hormones and vitamins which are said to produce a mild anti-coagulant effect on the blood and to protect tissues against the ageing process. (Family: Araliaceae.)

Ginzburg, Vitaly L (1916–) Physicist, born in Moscow, Russia. He studied at Moscow State University (1938–42), and in 1940 joined the P N Lebedev Physical Institute of the Russian Academy of Sciences in Moscow. In 2003 he shared the Nobel Prize for Physics with Alexei A Abrikosov and Anthony J Leggett for their pioneering contributions to the theory of superconductors and superfluids.

Giordano, Luca [jiaw(r)dahnoh], known as **Fa Presto** ('Make Haste') (1634–1705) Painter, born in Naples, SW Italy. He was able to work with extreme rapidity, hence his nickname, and to imitate the great masters. In 1692 he went to Madrid, at the request of Charles II of Spain, to embellish the Escorial.

Giorgione [jiaw(r)jiohnay], also called **Giorgio da Castelfranco**, originally **Giorgio Barbarelli** (c.1478–1510) Painter, born in Castelfranco, NE Italy. He studied under Giovanni Bellini in Venice, where he painted frescoes, though few have survived. A great innovator, he created the small, intimate easel picture and a new treatment of figures in landscape, 'the landscape of mood'. Among the paintings reliably attributed to him are 'The Tempest' (c.1505, Venice) and 'The Sleeping Venus' (c.1510, Dresden).

Giotto (di Bondone) [jiotoh] (c.1266–1337) Painter and architect, the founder of the Florentine School of painting, born in the village of Vespignano, near Florence, NC Italy. His major work was the fresco cycle, 'The Lives of Christ and the Virgin', in the Arena Chapel, Padua (1305–8). In 1330–3 he was employed by King Robert in Naples, and in 1334 was appointed Master of Works of the cathedral and city of Florence, where amongst other works he designed the Campanile. The fresco cycle on the life of St Francis in the Basilica of St Francis in Assisi is also attributed to him; it was severely damaged in an earthquake in 1997.

Giotto project [jiotoh] The first European interplanetary spacecraft launched in 1985 from Kourou, French Guiana, to intercept Halley's Comet. It encountered the comet successfully (13 Mar 1986) at a distance of 500 km/300 mi from the active nucleus, protected by a dust shield, and obtained TV images of the nucleus, and measurements of gases and dust; it survived the encounter, with potential for flyby of another comet. The final targeting was assisted by optical navigation data provided by the Soviet VEGA project and NASA's Deep Space Network, in a notable example of international space co-operation. It was managed by the European Space Agency's Space Research and Technology Centre. Following the Halley encounter the spacecraft was retargeted to flyby Comet Grigg-Skjellerup in July 1992, where measurements were made by the gas and dust instruments.

Gippsland District of SE Victoria, Australia; mountains in the N drop down to fertile plains in the S; lignite, dairy products, cereals, hops.

Gipsy *Rom*

giraffe An African ruminant mammal (*Giraffa camelopardalis*), the tallest land animal (height, 5·5 m/18 ft); extremely long legs and neck; an artiodactyl; head with 2–5 blunt 'horns'; inhabits savannah and woodland; eats leaves from thorn trees; usually silent; usually pale with large angular brown blotches; nine geographical races with different patterning (*Angolan*, *Kordofan*, *Masai*, *Nubian*, *Reticulated*, *Rothschild*, *Thornicroft*, *South African* (or *Cape*), and *West African*); also known as **camel(e)opard**. (Family: Giraffidae.)

giraffe antelope *gerenuk*

Giralda [heeralda] A bell tower adjacent to Seville Cathedral, in SW Spain. Built (1163–84) as an Islamic minaret, it was converted in the 16th-c after the mosque it served had been displaced by the present cathedral. The tower is 93 m/305 ft high, and takes its name from the *giraldillo* or weathervane which surmounts it.

Giraldus Cambrensis [jiraldus kambrensis], also known as **Gerald of Wales** or **Gerald de Barri** (c.1147–1223) Historian and clergyman, born in Manorbier Castle, Carmarthenshire, SW Wales, UK, the son of Nesta, a Welsh princess. He was elected Bishop of St David's in 1176, but when Henry II refused to confirm his election, he withdrew to lecture at Paris. Later appointed a royal chaplain, in 1185 he accompanied Prince John to Ireland. He wrote an account of Ireland's natural history and inhabitants, following this with *Expugnatio Hibernica* (c.1189, History of the Conquest of Ireland). In 1188 he travelled through Wales to recruit soldiers for the Third Crusade, and wrote up his observations in the *Itinerarium Cambriae* (1191, Itinerary of Wales) and *Cambriae descriptio* (1194, Description of Wales). Gerald recounts his unsuccessful struggles to make the bishopric of St David's independent of Canterbury in his autobiography, *De rebus a se gestis* (c.1204–05, published in English as The Autobiography of Giraldus Cambrensis). His works contain vivid anecdotes about his native Wales, the Christian churches, and the growing universities of Paris and Oxford. He is buried at St David's, Pembrokeshire.

Giraudoux, (Hippolyte) Jean [zheerohdoo] (1882–1944) Writer and diplomat, born in Bellac, C France. He joined the diplomatic service and was for a time head of the French ministry of information during World War 2. He is chiefly remembered for his plays, mainly fantasies based on Greek myths and biblical lore, satirically treated as commentary on modern life. They include *La Guerre de Troie n'aura pas lieu* (1935, trans Tiger at the Gates), *Ondine* (1939), and *La Folle de Chaillot* (1945, The Mad Woman of Chaillot).

Giraut de Bornelh [zheeroh duh baw(r)nel] (c.1140–c.1200) Troubador, born in Excideuil, near Périgeux, France. Dante praises him as one of the great triad (with Arnaud Daniel and Bertrand de Born) in *De vulgari eloquentia*.

Girl Guides *scouting*

girl guide / scout *scouting*

giro [jiyroh] A state-operated low-cost banking system which commenced in the UK in 1968. Now called **Girobank PLC**, it is operated by the Post Office Corporation through its 20 000 post offices, carrying out the normal range of banking services. Similar systems have been operated by post offices in many European countries. Commercial banks have operated a giro system in the UK since 1961, referred to as a **credit-transfer** system.

Girondins [jirondinz], Fr [zhirõdĩ] A group of deputies in the Legislative Assembly (1791–2) and French Convention (1792–5), led by Jean Roland (1734–93), Charles Dumouriez (1739–1823), and Jacques Brissot (1754–93). Sympathetic to the provinces rather than to Paris (their name derived from the Gironde region of SW France), they aroused the hostility of Robespierre and the 'Mountain' in the Convention, many being executed during the Reign of Terror (1793).

Girtin, Thomas [gertin] (1775–1802) Landscape painter, born in London, UK. His landscapes included many on subjects in the N of England and also in France, which he visited in 1802. His works were among the first to exploit water-colour as a true medium, as distinct from a tint for colouring drawings.

Gisborne [gizbaw(r)n] 38°41S 178°02E, pop (2000e) 34 000. Port and resort town in East Coast, North Island, New Zealand, at the head of Poverty Bay; site of Captain Cook's first landing, 1769; airfield; railway; trade in wine, market gardening, farm produce, timber.

Giscard d'Estaing, Valéry [zheeskah(r) daystĩ] (1926–) French statesman and president (1974–81), born in Koblenz, W Germany. He was educated in Paris, and worked for the Resistance during World War 2, after which he entered the Ministry of Finance as a civil servant. In 1955 he became an assistant director of the cabinet, finance minister (1962–6), and launched his own Party (National Federation of Independent Republicans). He returned to the finance ministry in 1969, defeated Mitterrand to become president, and was then beaten by Mitterrand in 1981. Through his attempts at economic reform, he tried to allay social unrest in France during the recession of the early 1980s. In 1988 he was elected President of the Union for

French Democracy, which he had founded in 1978. A lifelong proponent of European unity, he retired from politics in 1996 to set up the Foundation for Democracy.

Gish, Lillian, originally **Lillian de Guiche** (1893–1993) Actress, born in Springfield, Ohio, USA. She started in silent films as an extra under D W Griffith in 1912, and became the girl heroine in all his classics from *The Birth of a Nation* (1915) and *Intolerance* (1916) to *Orphans of the Storm* (1922). After the coming of sound films, she lost interest in the cinema, but continued on the stage, occasionally returning to film and television in character roles, even in the 1970s. Her sister **Dorothy Gish** (1898–1968) was also a film actress, and appeared with her in several films, then went into the theatre for many years. Her later film performances included a role in *The Cardinal* (1963).

Gissing, George (Robert) (1857–1903) Novelist, born in Wakefield, West Yorkshire, N England, UK. He studied at Manchester, was expelled from the university, travelled to the USA, and returned to work as a tutor in London. *Workers in the Dawn* (1880) was the first of over 20 novels largely presenting realistic portraits of poverty and misery, such as *Born in Exile* (1892) and *The Odd Women* (1893). His best-known novel is *New Grub Street* (1891), a bitter study of corruption in the literary world. *The Diary of George Gissing, Novelist* appeared in 1982.

gittern A mediaeval musical instrument resembling a lute, but with a shorter neck which curved smoothly into the body of the instrument. It usually had three or four courses of strings played with a plectrum.

Giuffre, Jimmy [joofree], popular name of **James Peter Giuffre** (1921–) Jazz musician and composer, born in Dallas, Texas, USA. He played clarinet and saxophones with various bands during the 1940s, then for over a decade specialized in the clarinet, developing a distinctive breathy tone. He formed groups of various sizes, early albums including *Ad Lib* (1959), *Jimmy Giuffre With Strings* (1960), and *Free Fall* (1962). He later worked also as a composer, his compositions including several chamber and ballet pieces, and became active in music education.

Giuliani, Rudolph W(illiam) [jooliahni] (1944–) US lawyer, politician, and mayor of New York City, born in New York City, New York, USA. Educated at Manhattan College, Purchase, NY, he received his law degree from New York University, becoming US attorney for the Southern District of New York (1983–9). He spent several years in private law practice, then ran for Mayor of New York City as a Republican in 1993, being re-elected in 1997. His administration was praised for restoring law and order, and making the city a more attractive place to live; however, minorities complained that the police under Giuliani on occasion abused the rights of suspects. Limited to two terms as mayor, he decided to run for the US senate in 2000, but withdrew on health grounds. His popularity soared in the aftermath of the terrorist attack on New York on 11 Sep 2001, and his adept handling of the situation in the city led to calls for his term of office as mayor to be extended, but he stood down. He was awarded an honorary knighthood by the UK in 2002.

Giulio Romano [joolioh romahnoh], originally **Giulio Pippi de' Giannuzzi** (c.1499–1546) Painter and architect, born in Rome, Italy. He assisted Raphael in the execution of several of his later works, and in 1524 went to Mantua, where he drained the marshes and protected the city from floods. He also restored and adorned the Palazzo del Te, the cathedral, and a ducal palace.

Giza [geeza], **al-Giza**, **Gizeh**, or **al-Jizah** 30°36N 32°15E, pop (2000e) 2 667 000. Capital of El Giza governorate, N Egypt; on W bank of R Nile, 5 km/3 mi SW of Cairo; railway; cotton, footwear, brewing, cinema industry; Sphinx, and pyramids of Khufu (Cheops), Khafra, and Mankara, 8 km/5 mi SW.

glaciation The coverage of the surface of the Earth by glaciers, as well as the erosive action produced by the movement of ice over the land surface. The most extensive period of recent glaciation was in the Pleistocene epoch, when polar ice caps repeatedly advanced and retreated, covering up to 30% of the Earth's surface. Glaciation produces erosional landforms resulting from abrasion and deposition. *Periglacial* processes result from frost and snow activity marginal to the ice sheet.

glacier A body of ice originating from recrystallized snow in cirques in mountain areas and flowing slowly downslope by creep under its own weight (**alpine glaciers**). Huge glaciers on continental plateaux are termed **ice sheets**. Glaciers flow until the rate of ice loss at the snout equals the rate of accumulation at the source.

glaciology The scientific study of ice in all its forms, including its crystal structure and physical properties, as well as glaciers and ice sheets in a geological and meteorological context.

gladiators In ancient Rome, heavily armed fighting men who fought duels, often to the death, in public. An import from Etruria, originally their contests were connected with funerary rites. Under the empire, they performed for public entertainment only. They were usually slaves, prisoners of war, or condemned criminals.

gladiolus A perennial with a large fibrous corm, native to Europe, Asia, and Africa; leaves sword-shaped, in flat fans; flower slightly zygomorphic with a short tube and six spreading or hooded perianth-segments in a variety of colours, in one-sided spikes. There are numerous large-flowered cultivars. (Genus: *Gladiolus*, 300 species. Family: Iridaceae.)

Gladstone, W(illiam) E(wart) (1809–98) British statesman and prime minister (1868–74, 1880–5, 1886, 1892–4), born in Liverpool, Merseyside, NW England, UK. He studied at Oxford, and entered parliament in 1832 as a Conservative, working closely with Peel. From 1834 he held various junior posts, becoming President of the Board of Trade (1843–5). A firm supporter of free trade, he was Chancellor of the Exchequer in Aberdeen's coalition (1852–5) and again under Palmerston (1859–66). In 1867 he became leader of the Liberal Party, and soon after served his first term as premier. He disestablished and disendowed the Irish Church, and established a system of national education (1870). Frequently in office until his resignation in 1894, he succeeded in carrying out a scheme of parliamentary reform (the Reform Act, 1884) which went a long way towards universal male suffrage. In his last two ministries he introduced bills for Irish Home Rule, but both were defeated. He is buried in Westminster Abbey. Gladstone's policies followed his strong religious convictions and his liberalism. He resisted imperialist expansion, and his mistrust of socialism was reflected in a belief that government alone cannot solve social problems.

Glåma, Glommen, or **Glomma** [gloma] River in E Norway, rising in Dovrefjell plateau at L Rien; flows S through Øyeren L to Oslo Fjord at Fredrikstad; length 598 km/372 mi; longest river in Norway; brings logs to the sawmills and paper-mills further downstream.

Glamorgan *Mid Glamorgan; South Glamorgan; Vale of Glamorgan; West Glamorgan*

gland A single cell or group of cells secreting specific substances (eg hormones) for use elsewhere in the body. In mammals, most glands are **exocrine**: their secretions are discharged via duct systems into the cavity of a hollow organ (eg the salivary glands), or open directly onto an outer epidermal surface (eg the sweat glands of mammals). Vertebrates and some invertebrates also possess **endocrine glands** (eg the pituitary glands in vertebrates, the thoracic glands in insects), whose secretions are released directly into the blood stream.

glanders or **the glanders** A malignant disease of horses, characterized by a swelling of the glands (especially beneath the jaw) and a mucous discharge from the nostrils; fatal and contagious; may be caught by humans.

glandular fever A generalized and sometimes prolonged infectious disease due to Epstein–Barr virus (EBV), which tends to affect young people. It is transmitted in saliva by coughing, sneezing, or kissing. The blood contains a large number of mononuclear cells, and the condition is technically known as **infectious mononucleosis**. The symptoms include headache, sore throat, and tiredness; the lymph nodes are enlarged and easily felt. The illness may be followed by severe debility lasting several months. There is no specific antiviral remedy.

glare *Polaroid* 1

Glaser, Donald A(rthur) [**glay**zer] (1926–) Physicist, born in Cleveland, Ohio, USA. He studied at the Case (Cleveland) and California institutes of technology. While working at the University of Michigan (1949–59) he developed the 'bubble chamber' for observing the paths of atomic particles, an achievement for which he was awarded the Nobel Prize for Physics in 1960. He became professor of physics (1959) and concurrently of molecular biology (1964) at the University of California, Berkeley.

Glasgow 55°53N 4°15W, pop (2000e) 678 700. City and local council (as City of Glasgow), W Scotland, UK; on R Clyde, 66 km/41 mi W of Edinburgh; largest city in Scotland; expansion in 17th-c, with trade from the Americas; airport; railway; underground; University of Glasgow (1451); Strathclyde University (1964); Glasgow Caledonian University (1992, formerly Glasgow Polytechnic); shipyards, engineering, commerce, whisky blending and bottling, chemicals, textiles, carpets; Kelvingrove art gallery and museum, Hunterian art gallery and museum, the Burrell Collection, Royal Scottish Academy of Music (1847), Museum of Transport, ruins of 15th-c Cathcart castle, cathedral (12th-c), Provand's Lordship (1471), 15th-c Crookston castle, Haggs castle (1585); Mitchell Library (1874); People's Palace (1898); Victorian tenement museum; Mayfest; European City of Culture, 1990.

Glashow–Weinberg–Salam theory A quantum theory of weak interactions, in which weak nuclear force and electromagnetic force are unified; formulated in 1968 by US physicists Sheldon Glashow (1932–) and Steven Weinberg (1933–), and Pakistani physicist Abdus Salam (1926–96). Radioactive decays are viewed as mediated by the W particle. The theory predicts the correct mass for W and Z particles using spontaneous symmetry breaking.

glasnost (Russ 'speaking aloud') A term describing the changes in attitude on the part of leaders of the former Soviet Union after 1985 under Gorbachev, which brought about a greater degree of openness both within Soviet society and in its relations with foreign powers.

Glass, Philip (1937–) Composer, born in Baltimore, Maryland, USA. He studied at the Juilliard School, New York City, and with Nadia Boulanger in Paris, and the Indian musician Ravi Shankar. A proponent of minimalism in music, he is best known for *Einstein on the Beach* (1976), *Satyagraha* (1980), *Akhnaten* (1984), and *The Making of the Representative for Planet 8* (1988). Later works include *The Hydrogen Jukebox* (1990), *Orphee* (1993), and the multimedia opera *Monsters of Grace* (1998). Film scores include *Kundun* (1998) and *The Hours* (2002, Oscar nomination; BAFTA), as well as the music for the 'qatsi' trilogy, a series of three films made in association with Godfrey Reggio: *Koyaanisqatsi: Life out of Balance* (1983), *Powaqqatsi: Life in Transformation* (1988), and *Naqoyqatsi: Life as War* (2002).

glass **1** A non-crystalline solid, typically hard and brittle, in which there is no orderly arrangement of atoms. It is usually formed by the rapid cooling of a viscous liquid, such that the atoms have insufficient time to align into a crystal structure. Glass is sometimes termed a liquid having a viscosity greater than 10^{13} poise. It is not in thermodynamic equilibrium, and may gradually change into crystal form over days or years.
2 The transparent or translucent product of the fusion of lime (calcium oxide), soda (sodium carbonate), and silica (silicon(IV) dioxide). There may be other constituents, yielding a great variety of properties. Boron gives the **borosilicate glass** (Pyrex®) which is stronger and more heat-resistant than common **soda glass**. **Flint glass** contains lead, and is particularly suitable for decoration by cutting and engraving. Having no sharp melting point, glass can be formed by many techniques while hot, most being variants on blowing or moulding. Flat glass used to be made by spinning a flat circle and cutting to size, or by blowing a large cylinder and slitting it. It is now made by drawing a sheet continuously out of a bath of molten glass. The best flat glass is today made by the 'float' process: molten glass flows continuously over a bed of molten tin.

glassfish **1** Small fish widespread in fresh and brackish waters of the Indo-Pacific region; length up to 10 cm/4 in; popular amongst aquarists for its iridescent colours and glass-like transparency. (Genus: *Chanda*. Family: Centropomidae.)
2 Small slender transparent fish of the NW Pacific (*Salangichthys microdon*); important locally as a food fish. (Family: Salangidae.)

glass harmonica *musical glasses*

glass snake A lizard native to North America, Europe, and Asia; snake-like, with no limbs; length, up to 1·3 m/4¼ ft; scales hard and bony; stiff body with groove along each side; tail can be shed to confuse predators, and may break into several pieces (like breaking glass, hence the name); also known as **glass lizard**. (Genus: *Ophisaurus*, several species. Family: Anguidae.)

glasswort An annual herb growing along coasts and in salt marshes more or less everywhere; fleshy, leafless jointed stems resemble spineless miniature cacti with flowers sunk into stems; also called **marsh samphire**. It was burnt to provide soda for early glass making, and was (to a limited extent still is) pickled and eaten as a vegetable. (Genus: *Salicornia*, 35 species. Family: Chenopodiaceae.)

Glastonbury lake village A marshland settlement of the 3rd–1st-c BC near Glastonbury, Somerset, SW England, UK, renowned for its exceptional preservation of timber, wooden utensils, and basketry. Excavations (1892–1907) revealed an artificial island of felled trees, its wooden palisade enclosing c.80 reed-roofed circular huts 5·5–8·5 m/18–28 ft in diameter, their floors made of boards on clay.

Glauber's salt Hydrated sodium sulphate, $Na_2SO_4.10H_2O$. It is named after the German chemist Johann Rudolph Glauber (1604–70), a follower of Paracelsus. It is a mild laxative, an ingredient of many mineral waters, and was once credited with remarkable medicinal properties.

glaucoma [glaw**koh**ma] A rise in the pressure of the aqueous fluid within the eye. High pressures can damage the optic nerve leading to blindness. Acute (*angle closure*) glaucoma arises when drainage of this fluid is blocked because of infection or cataract rupture. There is sudden pain in the affected eye and variable interference with vision, which may develop rapidly into blindness. In other patients the onset is insidious (*open angle glaucoma*); visual loss is slower in its development, and may not be noted until irreversible damage to the optic nerve has occurred. Pressure within the eye can now be measured in most hospitals with a tonometer. Screening for increased pressure is important in the prevention of blindness.

glaze In oil painting, a transparent layer of paint sometimes mixed with varnish laid over dry underpainting. In pottery it is a thin vitreous coating fused to the surface of a pot by firing.

Glazunov, Alexander (Konstantinovich) [**glaz**unof] (1865–1936) Composer, born in St Petersburg, NW Russia. He studied under Rimsky-Korsakov, and was director of the Conservatory at St Petersburg (1906–17), when he was given the title of 'People's Artist of the Republic'. Among his compositions are eight symphonies, and works in every branch except opera. In 1928 he emigrated to Paris.

Glendower, Owen [glen**dow**er], Welsh **Owain Glyndwr** or **Owain ap Gruffudd** (c.1354–c.1416) Welsh chief, born in Powys, E Wales, UK. He claimed descent from Bleddyn ap Cynfyn and from Llewelyn. He studied law at Westminster, and became esquire to the Earl of Arundel. In 1400 (16 Sep) he rebelled against Henry IV, proclaimed himself Prince of Wales, established an independent Welsh parliament, made plans for a university in Wales, and joined the coalition with Harry Percy (Hotspur) (1364–1403), who was defeated at the Battle of Shrewsbury (1403). Aided by the French and Bretons, he captured Harlech and Cardiff (1404), concluded an alliance with France (1405), and summoned a Welsh parliament in the same year. He continued to fight for Welsh independence until his death. His end is unknown.

Glenn, John H(erschel) (1921–) Astronaut, the first American to orbit the Earth, born in Cambridge, Ohio, USA. He studied at the University of Maryland, joined the US Marine Corps (1943), served in the Pacific during World War 2, and later served in Korea. In 1957 he made the first non-stop supersonic flight from Los Angeles to New York City. He became an astronaut in 1959, and in 1962 made a three-orbit flight in the Friendship 7 space capsule. He resigned from the Marine Corps in 1965, was a senator from Ohio (1975–98), and sought the Democratic nomination for the presidency in 1984 and 1988. In 1998 he became the oldest astronaut when, at age 77, he flew as a payload specialist on the space shuttle Discovery. NASA's Lewis Research Center was renamed the Glenn Research Center in 1999.

Glennie, Evelyn (Elizabeth Ann) (1965–) Percussionist, born in Ellon, Aberdeenshire, NE Scotland, UK. Although profoundly deaf, she studied at the Royal Academy of Music, London, winning several prizes, and made her debut recital at the Wigmore Hall in 1986. She has since received international recognition as a percussionist, playing with orchestras all over the world. A composer herself, several pieces have been specially composed for her. She has also worked as a radio and television presenter, and written a volume of autobiography, *Good Vibrations* (1996).

Glenrothes [glen**roth**is] 56°12N 3°11W, pop (2000e) 36 200. Administrative centre of Fife, E Scotland, UK, designated a new town in 1948; airfield; centre for electronic research; timber; plastics, electronics, machinery, paper, food processing.

gliadin [**gli**yadin] A simple protein occurring mainly in wheat. An adverse reaction to this protein is a feature of coeliac disease.

glider An aircraft that flies without the aid of mechanical propulsion. The wings may be fixed or flexible, and if the latter, the machine is known as a **hang glider**. Gliders usually remain aloft by finding rising currents of hot air (*thermals*), and remaining in them. The first piloted glider was designed in 1853 by aviator and inventor Sir George Cayley (1773–1857).

Glinka, Mikhail (Ivanovich) [**gling**ka] (1804–57) Composer, born in Novospasskoye, W Russia. He was a civil servant, but after a visit to Italy began to study music in Berlin. His opera *A Life for the Tsar* (1836, known earlier as *Ivan Susanin*) was followed by *Russlan and Ludmilla* (1842), which pioneered the style of the Russian national school of composers. He left Russia in 1844, and lived in Spain and France, returning home in 1854.

Glittertind or **Glittertinden** [**glit**ertind] 61°40N 8°32E. Highest mountain in Norway, a peak in the Jotunheimen range, SC Norway; height 2470 m/8104 ft.

global economy The view of the whole world as a single market. Globalization means that goods and services, capital, and labour are traded on a worldwide basis, and information and the results of research flow readily between countries. The rise of cheap sea transport and the telegram in the 19th-c, and of cheap air travel, the telephone, and the computer in the 20th-c, together with the rising importance of multinational companies and the general relaxation of controls on trade and international investment, mean that the world has moved some way towards a global economy. It is possible that the rise of the Internet and the start which has been made on liberalizing international trade in services will take this movement further in the 21st-c. The world has, however, a very long way to go before its economy is fully global. In particular, international mobility of labour is tightly restricted, and poor transport and communications in most developing countries mean that only the economies of the richer and more advanced countries are really at all global.

Global Maritime Distress and Safety System (GMDSS) A global search-and-rescue system, based on a combination of satellite and terrestrial radio services, which has changed international distress communications from being primarily based on ship-to-ship procedures to ship-to-shore procedures, using a Rescue Coordination Centre. The system enables automatic distress alerting and locating in cases where a radio operator has no time to send an emergency message, and requires ships to receive broadcasts of maritime safety information. All ships subject to the Safety of Life at Sea (SOLAS) Convention were required to fit GMDSS equipment by 1 February 1999. The system includes several procedures, notably: NAVTEX, an international automated system for distributing maritime navigational warnings, weather forecasts, search-and-rescue notices, and similar information; Inmarsat, several satellites operated by the International Mobile Satellite Organization; Search-and-Rescue Radar Transponders (SARTs); COSPAS–SARSAT, an international satellite-based search-and-rescue system established by Canada, France, the USA, and Russia; and radiotelephone and radiotelex equipment. Mariners are encouraged to use the GMDSS telecommunications equipment for routine purposes, and not just in relation to maritime safety.

Global Positioning System (GPS) A means of determining an exact position on the Earth using a GPS receiver and a system of satellites. Twenty-four satellites make up the American NAVSTAR system, orbiting about 20 000 km above the Earth. Each satellite makes a complete orbit of the Earth every 12 hours. Their positions are carefully calculated so that, from any point on the Earth, four or more of the satellites will be in direct line of sight to the GPS receiver. The GPS receiver picks up signals which are being transmitted continuously from the satellites. Each satellite carries four atomic clocks, so that the transmission time of the signals is known precisely. Using the time difference between the signals being transmitted and received, the GPS calculates the distance to that satellite. It has to lock on to at least three different satellite signals in order to locate itself in three-dimensional space. The **Standard Positioning Service (SPS)** is accurate to about 100 m (325 ft) and the **Precise Positioning Service (PPS)** is accurate to 20 m (65 ft). The **Differential GPS (DGPS)** also uses additional fixed stations on Earth and gives horizontal position accuracy to about 3 m (10 ft). NAVSTAR was begun in the 1970s and all 24 satellites were in operation by 1994.

global warming *greenhouse effect*

globe artichoke A robust perennial (*Cynara scolymus*) growing to 2 m/6½ ft; leaves up to 80 cm/30 in, deeply divided; flower-heads blue, very large, surrounded by distinctive leathery, oval bracts. It is unknown in the wild, but has a long history of cultivation, especially in S Europe. The soft receptacle of the young flower-heads and the fleshy bases to the bracts are eaten as a vegetable, and it is also grown as an ornamental. (Family: Compositae.)

globeflower A perennial (*Trollius europaeus*) growing to 60 cm/2 ft, native to Europe and arctic North America; long-stalked basal leaves palmately 3–5-lobed, stem leaves 3-lobed, all deeply toothed; flowers 2–3 cm/¾–1¼ in diameter, globular, with c.10 incurved, yellow, petaloid sepals. (Family: Ranunculaceae.)

Globe Theatre A theatre completed in 1599 by the Burbage brothers, Cuthbert and Richard, on Bankside in London, UK. It was the largest and most famous Elizabethan theatre and the most closely associated with Shakespeare. Nearly all of Shakespeare's greatest works were performed there. An association between the owner of the land, Sir Nicholas Brend, and the Chamberlain's Men, of which Shakespeare and Richard Burbage were members, gave each a share in the property. In 1613 it was burnt down during a production of Shakespeare's *Henry VIII* and, although subsequently rebuilt, was demolished by the Puritans in 1644. A project to build a working replica of the theatre near the original site was initiated in 1970 under the direction of US actor and film producer Sam Wanamaker (1919–93), and opened in 1996. An exhibition area opened beneath the theatre in 2000. In 1989, part of the foundations of the Globe and Rose theatres were discovered a few metres away and designated a scheduled area.

globigerina [globijeriyna] A type of amoeba-like microscopic organism commonly found in marine plankton; secretes a delicate external shell (*test*), often ornate with spines; dead tests sink, forming a calcareous sediment (**globigerina ooze**), covering large areas of sea floor.

globular cluster A swarm of old stars arranged characteristically as a compact sphere. It contains tens of thousands to millions of stars, formed at the same time, early in the history of our Galaxy. Over 100 are known in our Galaxy.

globulin [globyulin] A simple protein folded into a globular 3-dimensional shape. It is insoluble or only sparingly soluble in water, but soluble in dilute salt solutions. It is found in many animal tissues and in plant seeds, serving a variety of functions.

glockenspiel [glokenshpeel] A musical instrument consisting of tuned metal bars arranged in two rows like a piano keyboard, and played with small hammers held in each hand (in some models an actual keyboard is fitted). Most have a compass of 2½ octaves.

glomerulonephritis [glomerulohnefriytis] An inflammation of the glomeruli, the small clusters of capillaries and tubules in the kidney that are responsible for the initial blood-filtering process. It is caused by foreign antigens invading the body, and combining with antibodies produced by the body in response, so as to form immune complexes. In some cases, the condition is preceded by a recognizable infectious illness. Immune complexes become trapped in the capillaries of the glomeruli, where they initiate an inflammatory process. The resulting damage allows proteins and blood cells to escape into the urine, and impairs salt and water excretion, leading to oedema and hypertension. Some cases resolve spontaneously, but persistent inflammation can cause permanent damage leading to kidney failure.

Glommen / Glomma *Glåma*

Glorious First of June, Battle of the (1794) A naval battle fought off the Isle d'Ouessant (near Brest) between British and French navies. The victory for Admiral Richard Howe resulted in the capture of a third of the French ships, and confirmation of British naval supremacy.

Glorious Revolution or **Bloodless Revolution** The name given to the events (Dec 1688–Feb 1689) during which William landed at Torbay with an army and advanced on London. James II, deserted by John Churchill, later Duke of Malborough, fled from England, effectively abdicating the throne, and William III and Mary II were established by parliament as joint monarchs. The title, coined by Whigs who in the long term benefited most from it, celebrates the bloodlessness of the event, and the assertion of the constitutional importance of parliament.

glory pea *parrot's bill*

glossolalia The practice of 'speaking in tongues' – uttering sounds whose meaning is unknown to the speaker, who is undergoing a religious experience. The phenomenon is related to **xenoglossia**, using a language that the speaker has never known or heard, a power ascribed to the Apostles during the first days of Christianity, as recounted in the Acts of the Apostles. No scientifically attested case of xenoglossia has come to light, but speaking in tongues is nonetheless widely practised by several Christian groups, such as Pentecostalists or charismatic Catholics, and interpreted among its practitioners as a supernatural sign of religious sincerity or conversion.

glottis The narrow part of the larynx at the level of the vocal cords (or vocal folds), which is most directly concerned with the production of sound.

Gloucester [gloster], Lat **Glevum**, Celtic **Caer Glou** 51°53N 2°14W, district pop (2001e) 109 900. County town of Gloucestershire, SWC England, UK; NE of Bristol; connected to R Severn by canal; founded by Romans 1st-c AD; railway; airfield; boatbuilding, trade in timber and grain, engineering; cathedral (13th-c); Bishop Hooper's Lodging; Three Choirs Festival in rotation with Hereford and Worcester (Sep).

Gloucester, Humphrey, Duke of [gloster], known as **the Good Duke Humphrey** (1391–1447) Youngest son of Henry IV, and protector during the minority of Henry VI (1422–9). He greatly increased the difficulties of his brother, Bedford, by his greed, irresponsibility, and factious quarrels with their uncle, Cardinal Beaufort. In 1447 he was arrested for high treason at Bury St Edmunds, and five days later was found dead in bed (apparently from natural causes). His patronage of literature led to his nickname.

Gloucester, Richard (Alexander Walter George), Duke of [gloster] (1944–) British prince, the younger son of Henry, Duke of Gloucester (the third son of George V). In 1972 he married **Birgitte van Deurs** (1946–); they have one son, **Alexander, Earl of Ulster** (1974–), and two daughters, **Lady Davina Windsor** (1977–) and **Lady Rose Windsor** (1980–).

Gloucestershire [glostersheer] pop (2001e) 564 600; area 2643 sq km/1020 sq mi. County in SWC England, UK; bounded W by Monmouthshire in Wales; features include the Cotswold Hills, Forest of Dean; drained by the R Severn; county town, Gloucester; chief towns include Cheltenham, Cirencester; agriculture, fruit, dairy farming, light engineering; South Gloucestershire became a unitary authority in 1996.

glowworm *firefly*

gloxinia A member of a Brazilian genus of plants with large, showy, funnel-shaped flowers in a variety of colours; related to the African violet, and similarly popular as house plants. They are sometimes called **slipper** or **florist's gloxinia** to distinguish them from the genus *Gloxinia*. (Genus: *Siningia*, 20 species. Family: Gesneriaceae.)

Glubb, Sir John Bagot, known as **Glubb Pasha** (1897–1986) British soldier, born in Preston, Lancashire, NW England, UK. He trained at the Royal Military Academy, Woolwich, served in World War 1, and became the first organizer of the native police force in the new state of Iraq (1920). In 1930 he was transferred to British-mandated Transjordan, organizing the Arab Legion's Desert Patrol, and became Legion Commandant (1939). He had immense prestige among the Bedouin, and the Arab Legion fought successfully in the war against Israel (1948–9). He was dismissed from his post in 1956 because of the rise of Arab nationalism. Knighted in 1956, he then became a writer and lecturer.

glucagon [glookagon] A hormone (a polypeptide) found in vertebrates, synthesized in the pancreas by A-cells of the islets of Langerhans. It is secreted in response to low blood glucose concentrations. Its main action is to raise blood glucose levels by promoting the conversion of liver glycogen into glucose. It also stimulates the secretion of insulin, pancreatic somatostatin, and growth hormone.

Gluck, Christoph (Willibald) [glook] (1714–87) Composer, born in Erasbach, Bavaria, SC Germany. He taught music at Prague, then studied in Vienna and Milan. In 1741 he began to write operas, and after collaborating with the librettist Raniero de Calzabigi (1714–95) he produced such works as *Orfeo ed Euridice* (1762) and *Alceste* (1767). In the late 1770s, Paris was divided into those who supported Gluck's French opera style and those supporting the Italian style of Niccolo Piccinni (1728–1800) – the *Gluckists* and *Piccinnists*. Gluck finally conquered with his *Iphigénie en Tauride* (1779), and retired from Paris full of honour.

glucocorticoids [glookohkaw(r)tikoydz] Steroid hormones synthesized and released from the adrenal cortex of vertebrates, important in carbohydrate metabolism and the resistance of the body to stress. In humans they include *cortisol* (*hydrocortisone*), *corticosterone*, and *cortisone*. They are used therapeutically in replacement therapy (eg Addison's disease, a result of glucocorticoid deficiency), and in the suppression of inflammatory and allergic disorders.

glucose $C_6H_{12}O_6$, also called **dextrose**. By far the most common of the six-carbon sugars, the primary product of plant photosynthesis. Starch and cellulose are both condensation polymers of glucose. Maltose, lactose, and sucrose contain at least one glucose residue, and glucose may be obtained from them by acid or enzymatic hydrolysis.

glue *adhesives*

gluon A fundamental particle that carries the strong nuclear force between quarks, and binds them together into other subatomic particles; symbol *g*; mass 0, charge 0, spin 1. There are eight species of gluon distinguished by the colour combinations they carry. Gluons interact with one another; they are never observed directly.

gluten The main protein of wheat, subdivided into two other proteins, **gliadin** and **glutenin**. When mixed with water and kneaded, these proteins become aligned along one plane, imparting an elastic property to the dough. Gas bubbles of carbon dioxide produced by yeast fermentation allow the dough to rise because of entrapment of the gas by gluten. Maize, barley, and oats do not contain gluten and so cannot be used for bread. They tend to be used for flat cereal products such as cookies, biscuits, and tortillas. The small intestine in some people is abnormally sensitive to gliadin, a condition known as *coeliac disease*.

glutton *wolverine*

glycerides [gliseriydz] Esters of glycerol. Glycerol forms three series of ester: mono-, di- and tri-glycerides. Fats are examples of triglycerides.

glycerine *glycerol*

glycerol [gliserol] $OHCH_2–CH(OH)–CH_2OH$, IUPAC **1,2,3-trihydroxypropane**, also known as **glycerine**, boiling point 290°C. A colourless, viscous, and sweet-tasting liquid, obtained from all vegetable and animal fats and oils by hydrolysis, and thus a by-product of soap manufacture. It is used in many medical and cosmetic preparations, and reacts with nitric acid to form nitroglycerine.

glycine [gliyseen] $NH_2–CH_2–COOH$, IUPAC **aminoethanoic acid**, melting point 260°C. A colourless solid, freely soluble in water. It is the simplest of the amino acids, found in almost all proteins, and obtainable from them by acid hydrolysis. It exists in solution as a zwitterion: $^+NH_3–CH_2–COO–$, a hydrogen ion having been shifted from the carboxyl group to the amino group.

glycogen [gliykojen] $(C_6H_{10}O_5)_n$. A polysaccharide found in both plant and animal tissue (eg the liver) as an energy store. It is essentially a condensation polymer of glucose, and very similar to starch.

Glyptodon [gliptodon] An armadillo-like, fossil mammal that grazed the pampas of South America during the Plio-Pleistocene epochs; large, up to 2·5 m/8 ft tall and 3·3 m/11 ft in length; whole body, except underside, enclosed in armoured shell formed of bony plates. (Order: Xenarthra.)

GMDSS *Global Maritime Distress and Safety System*

G-Mex complex Venue for sporting and commercial events in the centre of Manchester, UK; capacity 6000. It was the location of the 1997 World Table Tennis Championships, the 1998 World Veteran Table Tennis Championships, and the gymnastics, judo, and wrestling events at the 2002 Commonwealth Games.

GM food *genetically modified organisms*

gnat **1** An alternative name for the mosquito.
2 A swarming gnat; a type of small, delicate fly. The males fly in dancing swarms low over water or in woodland clearings. Most are predatory, feeding on other insects. (Order: Diptera. Family: Epididae.)

gnatcatcher A name used for many small birds often classified with Old World warblers; native to the New World from Argentina to New England; inhabits broken woodland; eats insects and spiders; builds nests using cobwebs. (Family: Polioptilidae, 10 species.)

Gneisenau, August (Wilhelm Anton), Graf (Count) **Neithardt von** [gniyzuhnow] (1760–1831) Prussian general, born in Schildau, NE Germany. In 1786 he joined the Prussian army, fought at Saalfeld and Jena (1806), helped to reorganize the army after its defeat by Napoleon (1807), and in the war of liberation gave distinguished service at Leipzig (1813). In the Waterloo campaign, as chief of Blücher's staff, he directed the strategy of the Prussian army.

gneiss [niys] A coarse, high-grade metamorphic rock with a banded appearance due to the segregation of light- and dark-coloured minerals.

Gnosticism [nostisizm] (Gr *gnosis*, 'knowledge') A system of belief which became prominent within 2nd-c Christianity, but which may have had earlier, non-Christian roots. Gnostics believed that they were an elect group, saved through acquiring secret revealed knowledge about cosmic origins and the true destiny of the spirit within people; in later forms, this knowledge was imparted by a heavenly redeemer figure. Gnosticism was considered a heresy by the early Church Fathers, particularly for its appeal to secret traditions, its deprecatory view of the Creator God, and its docetic view of Christ.

GNP (gross national product) *gross domestic product*

gnu [noo] *wildebeest*

go The national game of Japan, first played in China c.1500 BC. It is a tactical game, played on a board divided into 324 squares (18 × 18). Each player has a supply of rounded counters or stones (like draughts pieces); one player has black, the other white. They take it in turn to fill up the board with the intention of surrounding the opponent's pieces (army) and capturing them. Some consider it a far more complex game than chess, and a handicapping system exists to enable players of different levels to compete on an equal basis.

Goa [goha] pop (2001e) 1 344 000; area 3496 sq km/1363 sq mi. State in W India; capital, Panaji; conquered by Muslims, 1312; taken by Portugal, 1510; island of Diu taken, 1534; Daman area N Mumbai ceded to Portugal, 1539; Old Goa a prosperous port city in 16th-c; occupied by India, 1961; part of Union territory of Goa, Daman and Diu until 1987; churches and convents are world heritage monuments; burial place of St Francis Xavier.

goat A mammal of family Bovidae; may be classified as an antelope; tail with naked undersurface; both sexes with horns; males with beard; inhabits dry rugged country; browses coarse vegetation; male called a *billy*, female a *nanny*, young a *kid*; six species in genus *Capra*: **wild goat** or **bezoar** (*Capra aegagrus*, the ancestor of the domestic goat, probably domesticated in SW Asia 8–9000 years ago), **ibex**, **Spanish ibex** (also called **Pyrenean ibex**, **Spanish goat**, or **iz(z)ard**), **East Caucasian tur**, **West Caucasian tur**, and **markhor**. The name is also used for the North American **Rocky Mountain goat** (*Oreamnos americanus*).

goat antelope *antelope; Rocky Mountain goat*

goatfish *red mullet*

goat moth A large, nocturnal moth; wings brownish-grey with dark markings; caterpillar smells like a goat; bores ascending tunnels in stems and branches of trees, especially willow; pupates after 3–4 years. (Order: Lepidoptera. Family: Cossidae.)

goatsbeard **1** A variable annual to perennial (*Tragopogon pratensis*), native to Europe and parts of Asia, growing to 80 cm/30 in; also called **Jack-go-to-bed-at-noon** because of the flower-heads' habit of closing up about midday; leaves, grass-like; flower-heads yellow, surrounded by eight or more narrow bracts; fruits with a parachute of feathery interwoven hairs, the fruiting head being similar to a very large dandelion 'clock'. (Family: Compositae.)
2 A perennial (*Aruncus dioicus*) growing to 1 m/3¼ ft or more; native to the temperate N hemisphere; leaves feathery, much divided; flowers tiny, white, 5-petalled, in plume-like inflorescences.

goatsucker The name used in the USA for nightjars with long bristles around the mouth (Subfamily: Caprimulginae). Nightjars without bristles are called **nighthawks** (Subfamily: Chordeilinae.)

go-away bird *turaco*

Gobbi, Tito (1915–84) Baritone, born in Bassano del Grappa, NE Italy. He studied law at Padua, then took up singing in Rome, making his operatic debut in 1935 at Gubbio. He appeared regularly with the Rome Opera from 1938, and soon made an international reputation, especially in Verdian roles such as Falstaff and Don Carlos.

Gobelins, Manufacture nationale des [gohbuhlĩ] A factory on the Left Bank of the R Seine at Paris. It was established in 1440 by Jean Gobelin as a dye works, and in the 17th-c a number of tapestry workshops were brought together here. The quality of the work produced is such that the term *Gobelins* has become synonymous with the art of tapestry making.

Gobi Desert [gohbee] Desert in C Asia; area c.1 295 000 sq km/ 500 000 sq mi, extends c.1600 km/1000 mi E–W across SE Mongolia and N China; on a plateau, altitude 900–1500 m/ 3000–5000 ft; series of shallow, alkaline basins; completely sandy in W; some nomadic Mongolian tribes on grassy margins; many fossil finds, including dinosaur eggs, and prehistoric implements. The downfold of skin across the inner corner of the eye of E Asian people (the *epicanthus*) was possibly an early adaptation to life in the Gobi.

goblin shark Strange-looking shark (*Mitsukurina owstoni*) with a long shovel-like process on front of head, and protruding teeth; body length up to c.3·5 m/11½ ft; known from Atlantic, Pacific and Indian Oceans, primarily from deep water. (Family: Mitsukurinidae.)

goby [gohbee] Any of a large family of mostly small, elongate fishes with stout head, fleshy lips, and large eyes, abundant in coastal waters of tropical to temperate seas; length up to 25 cm/ 10 in, many less than 5 cm/2 in; pelvic fins joined to form single sucker-like fin; 19 genera, including European **black goby** (*Gobius niger*) and **painted goby** (*Pomatoschistus pictus*). (Family: Gobiidae.)

God A supernatural being or power, the object of worship. In some world religions (eg Christianity, Judaism, Islam) there is one God only (*monotheism*), who is transcendent, all-powerful, and related to the cosmos as creator. In other religions (eg Hinduism, Classical Greek and Roman religions, and primitive religions) many gods may be recognized (*polytheism*), with individual gods having particular properties and powers. In the Judaeo-Christian tradition, God, though transcendent and invisible, is believed to have revealed himself in history through the life and response of the people of Israel, and, in the Christian tradition, supremely and finally in the life, death, and resurrection of Jesus of Nazareth, the Christ, all as testified to in the scriptures of the Old and New Testaments. The conviction that Jesus stood in a unique relation to God led to the development in Christian thought of the Trinitarian understanding, whereby the one God is confessed as three persons (Father, Son, and Holy Spirit) of one substance.

In the mainstream Western tradition, influenced by Classical Greek philosophy as well as Christianity, God is conceived as 'being itself' or 'pure actuality' (St Thomas Aquinas), in whom there is no unactualized potentiality or becoming; as absolute, infinite, eternal, immutable, incomprehensible (ie unable to be comprehended by human thought), all-powerful (omnipotent), all-wise (omniscient), all-good (omnibenevolent), and everywhere present (omnipresent). He is also said to be impassible, or incapable of suffering. The fact that the New Testament sums up its understanding of God as 'Love' (1 *John* 4.8), coupled with the apparent fact of evil in the world, has led to various modifications of this traditional Western conception. Thus God is sometimes understood as all-good but finite (and therefore unable to prevent evil); or as di-polar, ie in one aspect absolute and infinite but in another aspect, in so far as he relates to the cosmos, relative and finite (*panentheism* or *process theology*); or as comprising the whole of nature (*pantheism*). Corresponding to particular concepts of God are particular understandings of God's power in relation to human beings and the world of nature. These vary from absolute transcendence, such that God is reponsible for initiating the world process and laying down its laws, thereafter letting it run its course (*deism*) to total immanence, whereby God is understood as a non-transcendent power or spirit within the world motivating human beings. Orthodox Christianity seeks to preserve both the transcendence and immanence of God.

From the time of the ancient Greeks, philosophers have tried to prove the existence of God by reason alone (ie not by divine revelation), and of these attempts the 'ontological' arguments of St Anselm and Descartes, the 'Five Ways' of St Thomas Aquinas, and Kant's moral argument are among the more famous and abiding. While the philosophical consensus seems now to be that none of these arguments is coercive, discussion in the 20th-c of various aspects of individual arguments continued unabated. Attempts to disprove the existence of God or to show concepts of God to be incoherent have been likewise generally unpersuasive.

Godard, Jean-Luc [gohdah(r)] (1930–) Film director, born in Paris, France. Educated in Paris, he was a journalist and film critic before turning director. His first major film *A bout de souffle* (1960, *Breathless*) established him as one of the leaders of *Nouvelle Vague* cinema. He wrote his own film scripts on contemporary and controversial themes, his prolific output including *Vivre sa vie* (1962, trans My Life to Live) and *Weekend* (1968). He then collaborated with other film-makers in the making of politically radical films, but returned to feature films with *Sauve qui peut* (1980, trans Slow Motion), *Detective* (1984), *Je vous salue, Marie* (1985, Hail, Mary), *Nouvelle Vague* (1990), and *For Ever Mozart* (1997).

Goddard, Robert H(utchings) (1882–1945) Physicist and rocketry pioneer, born in Worcester, Massachusetts, USA. He studied at Clark and Princeton universities, becoming professor of physics at Clark (1919–43). He elaborated the theory of rocketry, developing the first successful liquid-fuelled rocket, launched in 1926. In 1929 he launched the first instrumented rocket, and later conducted research for US Navy applications. NASA's Goddard Space Flight Center is named in his honour.

Gödel or **Goedel, Kurt** [goedl] (1906–78) Logician and mathematician, born in Brno, S Czech Republic (formerly Brünn, Moravia). He studied and taught in Vienna, then emigrated to the USA in 1940 and joined the Institute of Advanced Study at Princeton. He became a US citizen in 1948. He stimulated significant work in mathematical logic and propounded one of the most important proofs in modern mathematics: **Gödel's proof**, published in 1931 with reference to Russell's *Principia mathemetica*, showed that any formal logical system adequate for number theory must contain propositions not provable in that system.

Godfrey of Bouillon [booeeyõ] (c.1061–1100) Duke of Lower Lorraine (1089–95), and leader of the First Crusade, born in Baisy, SC Belgium. He served under Emperor Henry IV against Rudolph of Swabia, and in 1084 in the expedition against Rome. He was elected one of the principal commanders of the First Crusade, and later became its chief leader. After the capture of Jerusalem (1099) he was proclaimed king, but he refused the crown, accepting only the title Defender of the Holy Sepulchre.

Godiva, Lady [godiyva] (11th-c) An English lady and religious benefactress, who, according to tradition, rode naked through the market place at Coventry, in order to obtain the remission of a heavy tax imposed by her husband, **Leofric, Earl of Chester** (d.1057), upon the townsfolk (1040). The story first occurs in the *Chronica* of Roger of Wendover (1235). The related story of Peeping Tom, who looked through the closed shutters, did not appear in the legend until the 17th-c.

Godolphin, Sidney Godolphin, 1st Earl of [godolfin] (1645–1712) English statesman, born near Helston, Cornwall, SW England, UK. He entered parliament (1668), visited Holland (1678), and was made head of the Treasury and a baron (1684). He stood by James II when William of Orange landed (1668), and voted for a regency; yet in 1689 William reinstated him as First Commissioner of the Treasury. He was ousted in 1696, but made Lord High Treasurer by Queen Anne (1702), and created an earl (1706). His able management of the finances helped Marlborough in the War of the Spanish Succession (1701–13), but court intrigues led to his dismissal in 1710.

Godoy, Manuel de [gothoy] (1767–1851) Spanish court favourite, and chief minister (1792–1808) under Charles IV, born in

Castuera, WC Spain. An obscure guards officer, he achieved dictatorial power at the age of 25 through the favour of the Queen, Maria Luisa, whose lover he was. His rule represented a corrupt form of 'enlightened despotism'. In 1795 he assumed the title 'Prince of the Peace', following Spain's defeat by Revolutionary France. In 1796 he allied with France against England – a disastrous move which turned Spain into a virtual French satellite, and contributed massively to her losing her American empire. In 1808 he was overthrown by an alliance of aristocrats and the populace, spending the rest of his life exiled in Rome and in Paris.

godparents In Christianity, those who act as sponsors for a child at its baptism or christening and who thereafter assume some sort of moral guardianship over the child. They are usually one or two persons of the same sex and one of the opposite. This duty was taken more seriously in the past, and is now often a simple formality; however, in S Europe and Latin America the institution was and still is used to create extensive and important ties among adults analogous to kinship ties.

God Save the King / Queen The British national anthem, written anonymously in the 18th-c. It is the oldest of all national anthems, and the music has often been used for those of other countries: it is still used for the national anthem of Liechtenstein. In the USA, the melody is used in a popular patriotic song, 'America', or 'My Country 'Tis of Thee'.

Godthåb or **Godthaab** [**got**hop] Eskimo **Nûk** or **Nuuk** 64°11N 51°44W, pop (2000e) 12 900. Capital and largest town of Greenland; on SW coast, on Davis Strait; founded, 1721; ruins of 10th-c Norse settlement nearby; fishing and fish processing, scientific installations, oil and liquid gas storage, reindeer, sheep.

Godunov, Boris (Fyodorovich) [**go**duhnof], Russ [goduh**nof**] (c.1552–1605) Tsar of Russia (1598–1605). Of Tartar stock, he became an intimate friend of Ivan IV (the Terrible), who entrusted to Boris the care of his imbecile elder son, Fyodor. Ivan's younger son, Dmitri, had been banished to the upper Volga, where he died in 1591 – murdered, it was said, at Boris's command. During the reign of Tsar Fyodor (1584–98), Godunov was virtual ruler of the country, with the title of 'the Great Sovereign's brother-in-law', becoming tsar himself on Fyodor's death in 1598. He continued the expansionist policies of Ivan, going to war against both Poland and Sweden. At home, he disposed finally of the Tartar threat, but was embroiled in the last years of his reign in a civil war against a pretender who claimed to be Dmitri, and who was eventually crowned in 1605 after Boris's death. Boris's life is the subject of a drama by Pushkin that was the basis for Moussorgsky's popular opera.

Godwin, also spelled **Godwine** (?–1053) Anglo-Saxon nobleman and warrior, probably son of the South Saxon Wulfnoth, and the father of Harold Godwinsson. He became a favourite of Canute, who made him Earl of Wessex in 1018. In 1042 he helped to raise Edward the Confessor to the throne, and married him to his daughter Edith. He led the struggle against the king's foreign favourites, and Edward revenged himself by confining Edith in a monastery, and banishing Godwin and his sons in 1051. But in 1052 they landed in the S of England and gained so much local support that Edward was forced to grant his demands and reinstate his family. Godwin's son Harold was for a few months Edward's successor.

Godwin, Mary Wollstonecraft *Wollstonecraft*

Godwin, William (1756–1836) Political writer and novelist, born in Wisbech, Cambridgeshire, EC England, UK. His major work of social philosophy was *An Enquiry Concerning Political Justice* (1793), which greatly impressed the English Romantics. His masterpiece was the novel *The Adventures of Caleb Williams* (1794). He married Mary Wollstonecraft in 1797. A bookselling business long involved him in difficulties, and in 1833 he was glad to accept the sinecure post of yeoman usher of the Exchequer.

Godwin-Austen, Mount *K2*

godwit A large sandpiper, native to the N hemisphere but may winter in the S; bill long, very slightly upcurved; probes into sediments for small animals. (Genus: *Limosa*, 4 species.)

Goebbels or **Göbels, (Paul) Joseph** [**goe**blz] (1897–1945) Nazi politician, born in Rheydt, W Germany. A deformed foot absolved him from military service, and he attended several universities. He joined the Nazi Party and founded a new paper for party propaganda, *Der Angriff* ('The Attack'). His brilliantly staged parades and mass meetings helped Hitler to power. He was appointed head of the Ministry of Public Enlightenment and Propaganda (1933), giving him control of the press, radio, and all aspects of culture. A bitter anti-Semite, his gift of mob oratory made him a powerful exponent of the more radical aspects of Nazi philosophy. Wartime conditions greatly expanded his responsibilities and power, and by 1943, while Hitler was running the war, Goebbels became increasingly his public spokesman. He retained Hitler's confidence to the last, and in the Berlin bunker he and his wife committed suicide, after taking the lives of their six children.

Goeppert-Mayer, Maria [**goe**pert **may**er], *née* **Goepert** (1906–72) Physicist, born in Katowice (formerly Kattowitz), S Poland. She studied at Göttingen, then emigrated to the USA, and taught at Johns Hopkins University, where her husband, **Joseph Mayer**, was professor of chemical physics. In World War 2 she was involved in the atomic bomb project, and afterwards worked in Chicago on the theory of atomic nuclei. In 1948 she discovered the 'magic numbers' of subnuclear particles, and from 1950 devised a complete shell theory of nuclear structure. From 1960 she held a chair at the University of California. She shared the Nobel Prize for Physics in 1963.

Goering or **Göring, Hermann (Wilhelm)** [**goe**ring] (1893–1946) Nazi politico-military leader, born in Rosenheim, SE Germany. In the 1914–18 war he fought on the Western Front, then transferred to the air force, and commanded the famous 'Death Squadron'. In 1922 he joined the Nazi Party and was given command of the Hitler storm troopers. He became president of the Reichstag in 1932, and joined the Nazi government in 1933 with responsibility for the Reich's rearmament programme. In 1938 he became Hitler's first deputy. He reorganized the Prussian plain-clothes police as the Gestapo, setting up the concentration camps for political, racial, and religious suspects. From 1940 to 1943 he was responsible for the German economy, and was made Marshal of the Reich, the first and only holder of the rank. As commander-in-chief of the Luftwaffe (air force), he devised the policy of terror bombing of strategic cities such as Rotterdam and Coventry to intimidate civilian populations prior to invasion. He ordered the requisitioning of art treasures from German-occupied countries. Increasingly dependent on narcotics, his prestige began to wane; he was deprived of all authority by Hitler in 1943, and finally dismissed in 1945 after unauthorized attempts to make peace with the Allies. In 1945 he attempted a palace revolution, was condemned to death, but escaped, to be captured by US troops. In 1946 he was sentenced to death at the Nuremberg War Crimes Trial, but hours before his execution he committed suicide.

Goes, Hugo van der *van der Goes, Hugo*

Goethe, Johann Wolfgang von [**goe**tuh] (1749–1832) Poet, dramatist, novelist, and scientist, born in Frankfurt, WC Germany. He studied law at Leipzig and Strasbourg, came under the influence of Herder, and became interested in alchemy, anatomy, and the antiquities. He returned to Frankfurt as a newspaper critic, and captured the spirit of German nationalism with his drama, *Götz von Berlichingen* (1773), following this with his novel *Die Leiden des jungen Werther* (1774, The Sorrows of Young Werther), which reflected the romantic *Sturm und Drang* movement of his time. In 1776 he accepted a post in the court of the Duke of Weimar, where he studied a variety of scientific subjects. He wrote much lyric and ballad poetry at this time, inspired by his relationships with a series of women, culminating in a profound attachment to Charlotte von Stein. Visits to Italy (1786–8, 1790) contributed to a greater preoccupation with poetical form, seen in such plays as *Iphigenie auf Tauris* (1789) and *Torquato Tasso* (1790). His love for classical Italy, coupled with his passion for Christiane Vulpius, whom he married in 1806, was expressed in the poems *Römische Elegien* (1795, Roman Elegies). In his later years he wrote the novel *Wilhelm Meisters Lehrjahre* (1796, Wilhelm Meister's Apprentice Years), continued as *Wilhelm Meisters Wanderjahre* (1821–9, Wilhelm Meister's Journeyman Years), which became the model for the German *Bildungsroman*. His masterpiece is his version of *Faust*, on which he worked for most of his life, published in two parts (1808, 1832).

Gog and Magog [gog, maygog] Biblical names, applied in different ways to depict future foes of the people of God. *Ezek* 38.2–6 predicted that a ruler (Gog) of the land or people from 'the north' (Magog) would battle against Israel in the days before her restoration. *Rev* 20.8 and rabbinic literature treat Gog and Magog as paired figures representing Satan in the final conflict against God's people. In British folklore, the names are given to the survivors of a race of giants annihilated by Brutus, the founder of Britain. Their statues in the Guildhall, London, replace a pair destroyed by World War 2 bombing.

goggle-eye *thick-knee*

Gogol, Nikolai (Vasilievich) [gohgl] (1809–52) Novelist and playwright, born in Sorochintsi, C Ukraine. In 1829 he settled in St Petersburg, and became famous through two masterpieces: *Revizor* (1836, The Inspector General), a satire exposing the corruption and vanity of provincial officials, and a novel, *Myortvye dushi* (1842, Dead Souls). He also wrote several short stories. He lived abroad for many years, mostly in Rome (1836–46), but returned to Russia.

Goiânia [gohyania] 16°43S 49°18W, pop (2000e) 1 227 000. Capital of Goiás state, WC Brazil, SW of Brasília; founded, 1933; replaced old capital, 1937; railway; two universities (1959, 1960); rice, soya, cattle raising, nickel; Parque Mutirama (with planetarium and educational park), racecourse, motor racetrack.

Goidelic [goydelik] *Celtic languages*

goitre / goiter [goyter] Enlargement of the thyroid gland. When associated with hyperthyroidism, it is called a *toxic* goitre; otherwise, it is *non-toxic*.

Gokstad ship [gokstat] A Viking oak-built sailing ship found in 1881 beneath a burial mound at Gokstad, 80 km/50 mi SE of Oslo, Norway. Spectacularly preserved by the surrounding clay, and complete with mast, spars, ropes, blocks, gangplank, and 16 pairs of oars, it measured 23·3 m/76 ft 6 in long, with a 5·2-m/17 ft beam, and was probably 50 years old when buried in the late 9th-c AD. A replica successfully crossed the Atlantic in 1893.

Golan or **Golan Heights** [gohlan], Arabic **al-Jawlan** pop (2000e) 32 000; area 1176 sq km/454 sq mi. Israeli-occupied area of Syria administered as part of Northern district, N Israel, E of the Sea of Galilee; of great strategic importance; occupied by Israel in 1967, and annexed in 1981; several Jewish settlements founded; rises to 1204 m/3950 ft at Mt Avital.

Gold, Thomas (1920–) Astronomer, born in Vienna, Austria. He studied at Cambridge, and worked with Hermann Bondi and Fred Hoyle on the steady-state theory of the origin of the universe (1948). He became professor of astronomy at Harvard (1957), and director of the Center for Radiophysics and Space Research at Cornell (1959–81). In 1968 he suggested that pulsars are rapidly rotating neutron stars, as was later confirmed.

gold Au, element 79, melting point 1064°C. A soft yellow metal of high density (19 g/cm^3), known from ancient times. It is rare and found uncombined in nature. Much of its value is due to its lack of reactivity, its main uses being for decoration and for monetary reserves. It is also used sparingly for electrical contacts. It will react with very strong oxidizing agents, giving compounds showing oxidation states +1 and +3.

Goldbach's conjecture A mathematical conclusion which states that every even integer greater than 2 can be expressed as the sum of two prime numbers; for example, 14 = 3 + 11. This conjecture was first made by Christian Goldbach (1690–1764) in a letter to Leonhard Euler in 1742.

Goldberg, Whoopi, originally **Caryn Johnson** (1955–) Film actress, born in New York City, USA. She gained recognition while on tour with her one-woman show, which was adapted for Broadway and became the critically acclaimed *Whoopi Goldberg Show* (1983). She achieved instant fame with her role in *The Color Purple* (1985), for which she received a Golden Globe Award. Her performance in *Ghost* (1990) won her an Oscar for Best Supporting Actress, becoming only the second African-American woman to win this honour. Later films include *Sister Act* and its sequel (1992, 1994), *Made in America* (1993), *The Associate* (1996), and *Get Bruce* (1999).

Goldblum, Jeff (1952–) Film actor, born in Pittsburgh, Pennsylvania, USA. He began his stage training at the age of seventeen at the New York City's Neighborhood Playhouse, and within a year had made his debut on Broadway in a musical version of *Two Gentlemen of Verona*. His film debut came with a small part in *Death Wish* (1974), and he has since become well known especially for his roles in science-fiction films, including *The Fly* (1986), *Earth Girls Are Easy* (1989), *Jurassic Park* and its sequel (1993, 1997), and *Independence Day* (1996). Later films include *Holy Man* (1998) and *Igby Goes Down* (2003).

Gold Coast (Africa) *Ghana*

Gold Coast (Australia) 27°59S 153°22E, pop (2000e) 174 500. Urban area in Queensland, Australia, S of Brisbane, partly overlapping New South Wales; airfield; railway; Bond University, private (1987); largest resort region in Australia, with restaurants and beaches stretching for 32 km/20 mi; includes Southport, Surfers' Paradise, Broadbeach, Mermaid Beach, Burleigh Heads, Coolangatta; Dreamworld, Sea World, bird sanctuary, air museum.

goldcrest A small woodland bird (*Regulus regulus*), native to Europe and Asia; head with orange or yellow stripe; eats insects; also known as the **golden-crested wren**. Many die during hard winters. (Family: Regulidae, sometimes placed in family Silviidae.)

Golden Bull Any document whose importance was stressed by authentication with a golden seal (Lat *bulla*). Specifically, the term is used for the edict promulgated by Emperor Charles IV in 1356 to define the German constitution. It formally affirmed that election of an emperor was by a college of seven princes, and recognized them as virtually independent rulers.

golden calf An idolatrous image of worship, fashioned by Aaron and the Israelites at Sinai (*Ex* 32), and destroyed by Moses. Two such figures were apparently set up later under Jeroboam I, first king of the N kingdom of Israel, in competition with the worship of God in Jerusalem (1 *Kings* 12).

golden cat A member of the cat family; found mainly in forests; eats deer, domestic animals, and birds; two species: **African golden cat** (*Felis aurata*) from C Africa, solitary, digs a den; **Asian golden cat** (*Felis temmincki*) from SE Asia, hunts in pairs.

golden chain *laburnum*

golden-crested wren *goldcrest*

golden eagle A large eagle (*Aquila chrysaetos*), native to the N hemisphere, probably the most numerous large eagle in the world; inhabits mountains and moorland; eats mainly rabbits, hares, and carrion; catches prey on ground, but attacks from the air; kills with talons; lays two eggs; the first chick to hatch usually kills the second. (Family: Accipitridae.)

goldeneye Either of two species of diving duck, native to the N hemisphere: the **goldeneye** (*Bucephala clangula*) and **Barrow's goldeneye** (*Bucephala islandica*). They inhabit coastal waters, but breed inland. (Family: Anatidae.)

Golden Fleece In Greek mythology, the object of the voyage of the *Argo*. Hermes saved Phrixus from sacrifice by placing him upon a golden ram, which bore him through the air to Colchis, where a dragon guarded the Fleece in a sacred grove. Jason obtained the fleece with Medea's help. The legend may be based on the gold of Colchis.

Golden Gate Bridge A major steel suspension bridge across the Golden Gate, a channel in California, USA, connecting San Francisco Bay with the Pacific; completed in 1937; length of main span 1280 m/4200 ft.

golden hamster *hamster*

Golden Horde A feudal state organized in the 13th-c as part of the Mongol Empire, occupying most of C and S Russia and W Siberia. Its capital was at Sarai on the R Volga. The Russian princes were vassals of the Khan of the Golden Horde, and paid regular tribute. It was finally overthrown by the Grand Princes of Moscow in the late 15th-c and early 16th-c.

golden mole An African insectivore, resembling the golden hamster, but with eyes and ears hidden under shiny fur; nose with leathery pad; front feet with claws for digging; digs burrows or, in desert areas, 'swims' through sand just beneath the surface, leaving a visible ridge. (Family: Chrysochloridae, 18 species.)

Golden Pavilion *Kinkakuji*

golden pheasant A pheasant native to W China and introduced in Britain (*Chrysolophus pictus*); male with a crest of golden feathers; female brown and black; inhabits low vegetation on rocky hillsides (introduced in woodland); eats seeds, shoots, and insects. (Family: Phasianidae.)

golden potto *angwantibo*

golden-rain tree *laburnum; pride of India*

golden ratio In mathematics, a proportion obtained if a point P divides a straight line AB in such manner that $AP : PB = AB : AP$; also known as the **golden section**. It is often denoted by τ.

$$\frac{\tau}{1} = \frac{\tau + 1}{\tau}$$

It was applied to architecture by Vitruvius, and much discussed during the Renaissance. Pietro della Francesca's 'Baptism of Christ' (National Gallery, London) is just one example of a composition set up according to this proportion.

golden retriever A breed of dog, developed in Britain in the late 19th-c; large with long golden or cream coat; solid body, strong legs, long muzzle; calm temperament; popular choice as a guide-dog for blind people.

goldenrod The name applied to several species of *Solidago*. The plant commonly grown in gardens is **Canadian goldenrod** (*Solidago canadensis*), a late-flowering perennial growing to 1·5 m/5 ft, native to North America; leaves lance-shaped, long pointed; flower-heads numerous, tiny, golden-yellow, arranged on more or less horizontally spreading branches in a dense pyramidal panicle. **European goldenrod** (*Solidago virgaurea*) is a smaller perennial, growing to 1 m/3¼ ft, with larger flower-heads up to 1 cm/0·4 in across, borne in leafy clusters. (Genus: *Solidago*. Family: Compositae.)

Golden Rule The name given today to the saying of Jesus about one's duty to others: 'Whatever things you wish that people would do to you, do also yourselves similarly to them' (*Matt* 7.12; *Luke* 6.31). Similar sayings can be traced in earlier Jewish and Greek ethical teaching.

Golden Temple *Harimandir*

goldfinch A bird native to the N hemisphere; one species in the Old World, *Carduelis carduelis*, three in the Americas; inhabits forest, scrubland, or cultivated areas; closely related to the siskin. (Genus: *Carduelis*, 4 species. Family: Fringillidae.)

goldfish Colourful, carp-like, freshwater fish (*Carassius auratus*), native to weedy rivers and lakes of Eurasia, but now very widely distributed as popular ornamental fish; body length up to 30 cm/1 ft, young fish brownish, becoming golden as they mature; mouth lacking barbels; immense variety of forms have been produced through captive breeding. (Family: Cyprinidae.)

Golding, Sir William (Gerald) (1911–93) Novelist, born near Newquay, Cornwall, SW England, UK. He studied at Oxford, became a teacher, served in the navy in World War 2, then returned to teaching until 1961. *Poems* (1934) was followed by his first novel, *Lord of the Flies* (1954), widely considered to be one of the greatest English-language novels of the 20th c. Other books quickly followed, such as *The Inheritors* (1955), *Pincher Martin* (1956), *Free Fall* (1959), and *The Spire* (1964), each confirming Golding's power to create contemporary myth. Later novels include *Darkness Visible* (1979) and the trilogy *Rites of Passage* (1980, Booker), *Close Quarters* (1987), *Fire Down Below* (1989), republished under the general title *To The Ends of the Earth* in 1991. He was awarded the Nobel Prize for Literature in 1983, and knighted in 1988.

Goldman, Emma, known as **Red Emma** (1869–1940) Anarchist, feminist, and birth control advocate, born in Kaunas, C Lithuania. Her family left Russia to avoid anti-Jewish persecution, moving to Germany. She emigrated to the USA in 1885, and was imprisoned in 1893 for inciting a riot in New York City. Imprisoned again during World War 1 for opposing and obstructing the military draft, she was deported to the Soviet Union in 1919, eventually settling in France.

Goldoni, Carlo [goldohnee] (1707–93) Playwright, born in Venice, NE Italy. He studied for the law, and practised intermittently (1731–48), but his real interest was drama. He discovered he had a talent for comedy, and wrote over 250 comic plays in Italian, French, and the Venetian dialect. He was greatly influenced by Molière and the *commedia dell'arte*. His best-known plays are *Il servitore di due padroni* (1746, The Servant of Two Masters), *Il teatro comico* (1750, The Comic Theatre), *La locandiera* (1753, Mine Hostess), *I Rusteghi* (1760, which provided the plot for *The School for Fathers*, produced in London in 1946), *Le baruffe Chiozzotte* (1762, Quarrels at Chioggia), and *Il ventaglio* (1766, The Fan). He also wrote librettos for the comparatively new musical form of *opera buffa*. In 1762 he undertook to write for the Italian theatre in Paris, and was attached to the French court until the revolution. He wrote a number of his last plays in French, including *Le Bourru bienfaisant* (1771, The Beneficent Bear).

gold rush A burst of enthusiasm for sudden wealth among people from all kinds of professions, following the discovery of gold deposits. Major rushes in the USA included California (1849), Colorado (1858–9), Idaho (1861–4), Montana (1863), South Dakota (1875), and Alaska (1896).

Goldsmith, Sir James (Michael) (1933–97) Businessman, publisher, and politician, born in Paris, France. His family left France at the beginning of World War 2, and he was educated in the UK, where after leaving school he built up a range of companies and developed a reputation as a charismatic, risk-taking financier. He lived both in France and the UK, receiving media attention for his flamboyant public and private lives, to which he responded aggressively. In the 1980s he worked chiefly in the USA, then developed environmental and political interests, and was elected a member of the European Parliament for France (1995–7). He was knighted in 1976, and became a controversial figure in the UK when he financed the Referendum Party in the 1997 general election – a campaign he promoted while suffering from the pancreatic cancer from which he died two months later.

Goldsmith, Oliver (1728–74) Playwright, novelist, and poet, born in Kildare, E Ireland. He studied erratically at Dublin, tried law at London then medicine at Edinburgh, drifted to Leyden, and returned penniless in 1756. He practised as a physician in London, held several temporary posts, and took up writing and translating. *The Vicar of Wakefield* (1766) secured his reputation as a novelist, 'The Deserted Village' (1770) as a poet, and *She Stoops to Conquer* (1773) as a dramatist.

gold standard A system in which the price of gold is fixed in each country's currency. This pegs exchange rates within the very narrow band set by the cost of international gold shipments. In theory countries on the gold standard could actually use gold coins as money, but historically the gold exchange standard meant that national banks issued paper currency, with holders exchanging this for gold at fixed prices. An advantage of the gold standard is that if it is regarded as permanent it gives almost fixed exchange rates, which facilitates international trade and credit. The disadvantage is that it deprives countries of control of their own monetary policy, and makes the world money-supply depend on the rate of gold discoveries. Before 1914 the UK and many other countries were on a gold exchange standard. Attempts to restore the system between the Wars collapsed during the great depression in 1931. In the absence of general confidence that it will persist, the gold standard loses its advantages, and it seems unlikely that it will ever be restored.

Goldstone, Richard (1938–) Leading liberal judge and human rights campaigner, born in Boksburg, NE South Africa. He studied at the the University of Witwatersrand, was called to the bar, and practised as a commercial advocate in Johannesburg before being appointed a judge of the Supreme Court of South Africa (1980). He was particularly concerned with the rights of prisoners and prison conditions. He was appointed Chairman of the South African Commission of Inquiry into the Prevention of Public Violence and Intimidation (1990–4), and then served as Chief Prosecutor at the International War Crimes Tribunal at The Hague (1994–6). Since 1994 he has been a Justice of the South African Constitutional Court.

Goldsworthy, Andy (1956–) Artist and sculptor, born in Cheshire, NWC England, UK. He was brought up in Leeds and studied at Bradford College of Art and Preston Polytechnic. He works closely with nature, producing ephemeral works assembled from natural materials, such as stone, wood, foliage and water, which are then photographed. More permanent works include the series of chalk arches made for 'Sculpture at Goodwood' (1995) which are now sited in his studio in Scotland. His Sheepfolds project in Cumbria, to rebuild c.100 traditional drystone sheep corrals, was completed in 2000 and is open to the public.

Goldwater, Barry M(orris) (1909–98) Politician and writer, born in Phoenix, Arizona, USA. He studied at the University of Arizona, then worked in his family's department store. He became a senator for Arizona in 1952, resigning the seat in 1964 to become the Republican nominee for the presidency, but was defeated by Lyndon Johnson. He returned to the US Senate (1969–87), and was one of the architects of the conservative revival within the Republican Party. *The Conscience of a Conservative* (1960) is his most notable book.

Goldwyn, Samuel, originally **Samuel Goldfish** (1882–1974) Film producer, born in Warsaw, Poland. He emigrated to the USA as a child, and helped to found a film company, producing *The Squaw Man* (1913). He founded the Goldwyn Pictures Corporation (1917), Eminent Authors Pictures (1919), and finally Metro-Goldwyn-Mayer (1925), allying himself with United Artists from 1926. His 'film-of-the-book' policy included such films as *Bulldog Drummond* (1929) and *All Quiet on the Western Front* (1930). A colourful personality, many of his remarks have become catch phrases (*Goldwynisms*), such as 'include me out'.

golf A popular pastime and competitive sport, played on a course usually consisting of 18 holes, although some have only 9, 12, or 15. A standard course is usually between 5000 and 7000 yards (c.4500–6500 m). A *hole* consists of three primary areas: the flat starting point where the player hits the ball (the *tee*), a long stretch of mown grass (the *fairway*), and a putting *green* of smooth grass where the hole itself (10·8 cm/4¼ in) is situated. Obstacles, such as areas of sand (*bunkers*) high grass (*rough*), and trees, are placed at various points. The object is to hit a small, rubber-cored ball from a starting point into the hole, which is generally 90–450 m/100–500 yd away. The winner is the player who completes a round with the lowest number of strokes. The expected number of strokes a good player would be expected to play for any given hole is referred to as the *par* for that hole. If the player holes the ball in one stroke below par, this is called a *birdie*; two strokes below is an *eagle*; one shot over par is a *bogey*; an occasional possibility is a *hole in one*. Players may carry up to 14 clubs in their golf bag, each designed for a specific purpose and shot.

The ruling body of the game in Britain is the Royal and Ancient Club at St Andrews, Scotland. Major tournaments include the Open Golf Championship, the US Open, the US Professional Golfers' Association (PGA), and the US Masters. The origins of the game are uncertain, but it is believed that the Dutch first played a similar game with a stick and ball c.1300, known as *kolf* or *colf*. *Gouf* (as it was called) was definitely played in Scotland in the 15th-c, and the world's first club, the Gentlemen Golfers of Edinburgh (later the Honourable Company of Edinburgh Golfers) was formed in 1744.

golf-ball printer A high quality impact printer with a spherical print head used mainly in typewriters. The printhead is removable, allowing different typesets to be used.

Golgi, Camillo [goljee] (1843–1926) Cell biologist, born in Corteno, N Italy. As professor of pathology at Pavia (1876–1918), he discovered the *Golgi bodies* in animal cells which, through their affinity for metallic salts, become readily visible under the microscope. His work opened up a new field of research into the central nervous system, sense organs, muscles, and glands. He shared the 1906 Nobel Prize for Physiology or Medicine.

Golgi body [goljee] A system of flattened, membranous sacs (*vesicles*, or *cisternae*) arranged in parallel stacks about 20–30 nm apart and surrounded by numerous smaller vesicles. Found within almost all eucaryotic cells, Golgi bodies possibly function to package some of the products of cell metabolism.

Golgotha *Calvary*

goliards Wandering scholars and clerks of the 12th–13th-c, who wrote reckless celebrations of women and wine, and satirical verses against the Church. The name may derive from the giant Goliath, a figure of evil and excess.

Goliath [goliyath] Biblical character described (1 *Sam* 17) as a giant from Gath in the Philistine army who entered into single combat with the young David and was slain by a stone from David's sling, resulting in Israel's victory. Some confusion exists over a similar name in 2 *Sam* 21.19 (also 1 *Chron* 20.5).

goliath beetle A very large, brightly-coloured beetle, up to 15 cm/6 in long; adults active in daytime; feeds mostly on fruit and flowers; larvae found in decaying plants. (Order: Coleoptera. Family: Scarabeidae.)

goliath frog A West African frog (*Conraua goliath*), the largest frog in the world (length, up to 36 cm/14 in, not including the legs); lives in deep pools in rivers. Local tradition claims the thigh bones have magical properties and bring good luck. (Family: Ranidae.)

Gollancz, Sir Victor [golangks, golants] (1893–1967) Publisher, writer, and philanthropist, born in London, UK. He studied at Oxford, became a teacher, then entered publishing, founding his own firm in 1928. In 1936 he founded the Left Book Club, which had a great influence on the growth of the Labour Party, and after World War 2 founded the Jewish Society for Human Service, and War on Want (1951). He was knighted in 1965.

Gomateswara, statue of The tallest monolith statue in the world, sculpted in AD 983 at Sravanabelagola, Karnataka, India. The statue, which is 17 m/56 ft high, represents Gomateswara, a Jain holy man, and is the focus of a major Jain festival every 12 years.

Gompers, Samuel [gomperz] (1850–1924) Labour leader, born in London, UK. He went to the USA in 1863, and became a US citizen in 1872. A cigar maker by trade, in 1886 he helped to found the American Federation of Labor, and except for one year was its president until his death. He advocated an emphasis on gains for his members rather than social revolution.

Gomułka, Władysław [gomoolka] (1905–82) Polish Communist leader, born in Krosno, SE Poland. A professional trade unionist, in 1943 he became secretary of the outlawed Communist Party. He was vice-president of the first post-war Polish government (1945–8), but his criticism of the Soviet Union led to his arrest and imprisonment (1951–4). He returned to power as party first secretary in 1956. In 1971, following a political crisis, he resigned office, and spent his remaining years largely in retirement.

gomuti palm *sugar palm*

gonad The organ responsible for the production of reproductive cells (*germ cells* or *gametes*): in males the gonads (*testes*) produce spermatozoa, in females the gonads (*ovaries*) produce ova. In vertebrates the gonads also synthesize and secrete sex hormones (androgens, oestrogens, and progestagens): androgens are most abundant in males; oestrogens and progestagens in females.

gonadotrophin [gonadohtrohfin] A substance having a stimulating effect on the gonads. In vertebrates it includes certain pituitary hormones (follicle-stimulating hormone, luteinizing hormone) and additionally in mammals a placental hormone (chorionic gonadotrophin). Gonadotrophins are responsible for the production of sex hormones and the onset of sexual maturity, and they influence breeding cycles by promoting the maturation of ova and sperm in ovaries and testes respectively. In humans, pregnancy diagnosis depends on the detection of chorionic gonadotrophin in the urine or plasma.

Goncourt brothers [gõkoor] **Edmond de Goncourt** (1822–96) and **Jules de Goncourt** (1830–70) Novelist collaborators, born in Nancy and Paris, France, respectively. They began as artists, in 1849 travelling across France for watercolour sketches. They then collaborated in studies of history and art, and took to writing novels, notably *Germinie Lacerteux* (1865) and *Madame Gervaisais* (1869). They are also remembered for their *Journal*, begun in 1851, a detailed record of French social and literary life which Edmond continued for over 40 years. Edmond also founded in his will the Académie Goncourt to foster fiction, and the Goncourt Prize is awarded annually to the author of an outstanding work of French literature.

Gondar *Fasil Ghebbi*

Gondwanaland *see panel*

gong A percussion instrument: a circular bronze plaque, usually with a turned-down rim, commonly suspended from a frame or bar and struck with a soft beater. The orchestral gong (or **tam-tam**) is of indefinite pitch; other, usually smaller, gongs are tuned to precise pitches.

gong chime A set of tuned bossed gongs, arranged horizontally in rows or in a circle, and played with sticks by one or more players. They appear in the gamelan of Java and Bali and in other ensembles of SE Asia.

Góngora y Argote, Luis de [gongora ee ah(r)gohtay] (1561–1627) Poet, born in Córdoba, S Spain. He studied law, but in 1606 took orders and became a prebendary of Córdoba, and eventually chaplain to Philip III (reigned 1598–1621). His earlier sonnets, romances, and satirical verses are elegant and stylish. His later works, consisting for the most part of longer poems such as *Solidades* and *Polifemo* (both 1613), are written in an elaborate style, which his followers designated *Gongorismo*.

gonorrhoea / gonorrhea [gonuhreea] An acute infection of the genital tract caused by *Neisseria gonorrhoeae*, acquired by sexual intercourse with an infected partner. Males suffer from a discharge from the penis, with pain on urination. The disorder sometimes leads to narrowing of the urethra from scarring. Females may suffer a vaginal discharge, but may have no symptoms. Infection may lead to inflammation and scarring of the uterine tubes. It may also be passed from mother to baby at birth, leading to severe conjunctivitis in the newborn (*ophthalmia neonatorum*). Prevention is by using condoms during sexual intercourse. Treatment is with a single large dose of penicillin.

Gonzaga, Luigi, St [gonzahga], known as **St Aloysius** (1568–91) Jesuit priest, and the patron saint of youth. The eldest son of the Marquis of Castiglione, near Brescia, he renounced his title in order to become a missionary, and entered the Society of Jesus in 1585. When Rome was stricken with plague in 1591, he devoted himself to the care of the sick, but was himself infected and died. He was canonized in 1726, and in 1926 was declared the patron saint of Christian youth by Pope Pius XI. Feast day 21 June.

González, Felipe [gonthahleth] (1942–) Spanish statesman and prime minister (1982–96), born in Seville, SW Spain. He practised as a lawyer, and in 1962 joined the Spanish Socialist Workers' Party (PSOE), then an illegal organization. The Party regained legal status in 1977, three years after he became secretary-general. He persuaded the PSOE to adopt a more moderate policy, and in the 1982 elections they won a substantial majority to become the first left-wing administration since 1936; he was narrowly re-elected in 1993 for a fourth consecutive term of office, and was defeated in the general election of 1996.

Gooch, Graham (Alan) (1953–) Cricketer, born in Leytonstone, E Greater London, UK. He began his career playing for Essex. His Test Match cricket debut in Australia (1975) was a failure, and prompted him to participate in an unofficial tour of South Africa (1982), resulting in his ban from international cricket for three years. A change of fortune brought him the England captaincy (1988–93) and a notable victory over the West Indies in Jamaica (1989). The leading England Test run-scorer, and most-

Gondwanaland

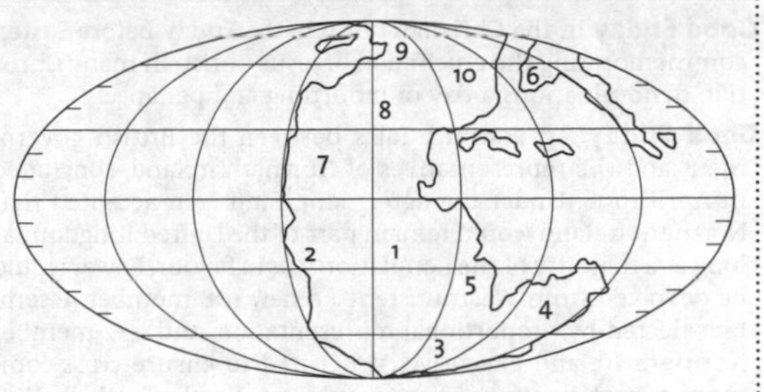

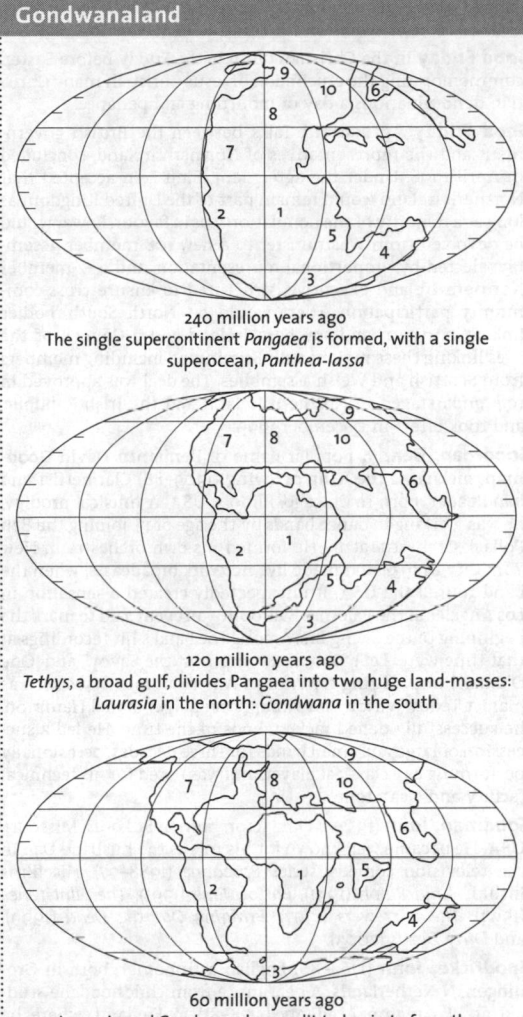

240 million years ago

The single supercontinent *Pangaea* is formed, with a single superocean, *Panthea-lassa*

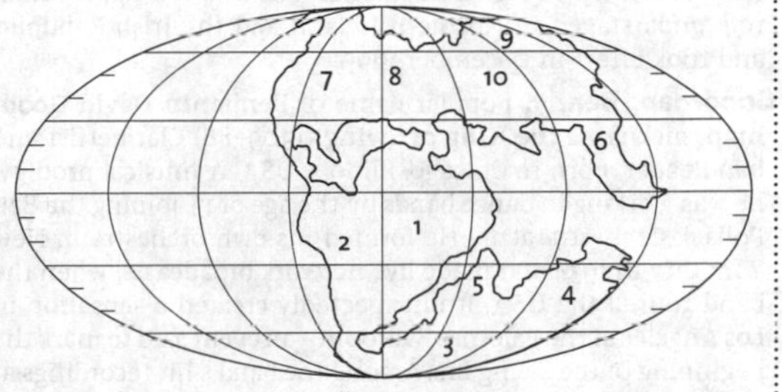

120 million years ago

Tethys, a broad gulf, divides Pangaea into two huge land-masses: *Laurasia* in the north: *Gondwana* in the south

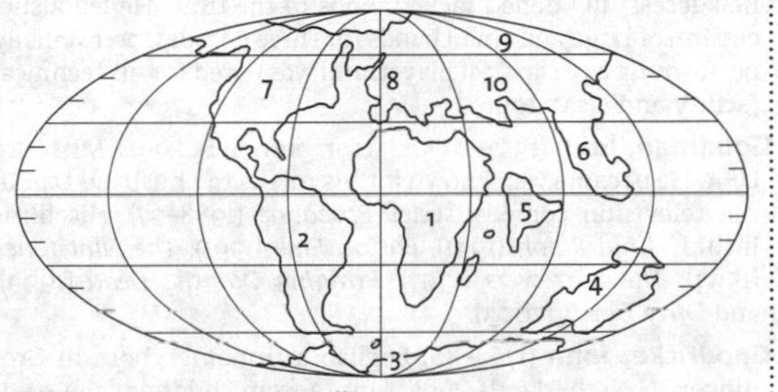

60 million years ago

Laurasia and Gondwana have split to begin to form the continents as we know them today

[gondwahnaland] The name given to the postulated S 'supercontinent' which began to break away from the single land mass Pangaea about 200 million years ago. It included Australia, Africa, Antarctica, India, and South America; the N supercontinent was Laurasia.

capped player, he announced his retirement in January 1995, with 8900 runs scored in 118 Tests, at an average of 42·58.

Good Friday In the Christian Church, the Friday before Easter, commemorating the crucifixion of Jesus Christ; in many Christian denominations a day of mourning and penance.

Good Friday Agreement Talks between the British government and the representatives of Northern Ireland, concluded in April 1998. Under the agreement, Sinn Féin accepted that Northern Ireland would remain part of the United Kingdom as long as a majority of the population was in favour. Power would be devolved from Westminster to a new 108-member Assembly, elected by proportional representation, and a 12-member Northern Ireland executive, structured to ensure cross-community participation. There would be 'North–South' bodies linking northern and southern Ireland and a Council of the Isles linking these regions with Britain, and including members from Scottish and Welsh assemblies. The deal was approved in referenda staged in Northern Ireland and the Irish Republic, and took effect in December 1999.

Goodman, Benny, popular name of **Benjamin David Goodman**, nickname **the King of Swing** (1909–86) Clarinettist and bandleader, born in Chicago, Illinois, USA. A musical prodigy, he was working in dance bands by the age of 13, joining the Ben Pollack Orchestra at 16. He formed his own orchestra in New York City in 1934 and made live network broadcasts; when the band toured the USA, it unexpectedly created a sensation in Los Angeles at the Palomar Ballroom – an event said to mark the beginning of the Swing Era. Among the band's hit recordings at that time were 'Let's Dance', 'Stompin' at the Savoy', and 'One O'Clock Jump'. Hiring top African-American musicians such as pianist Teddy Wilson and vibraphone-player Lionel Hampton, he successfully defied racial taboos of the time. He led a succession of large and small bands for three decades, occasionally performing as a classical player, and was noted for his technical facility and clean tone.

Goodman, John (1952–) Film actor, born in St Louis, Missouri, USA. He became well known for his role as the husband Dan in the television comedy series *Roseanne* (1988–97). His films include *King Ralph* (1991), *Barton Fink* (1991), *The Flintstones* (1994), *The Borrowers* (1997), *Bringing Out the Dead* (1999), and *Dirty Deeds* (2003).

Goodricke, John (1764–86) English astronomer, born in Groningen, N Netherlands. A deaf-mute from childhood, he studied at Warrington Academy (1778–81) in England, where he excelled in mathematics. In 1782 he noticed that the brightness of the star known as Algol varied, and was the first to establish the periodic nature of this variation. He also suggested that the variability of Algol was due to its being eclipsed by a darker companion body, a theory eventually confirmed and which forms the basis of the class of stars known as eclipsing variables.

Goodyear, Charles (1800–60) Inventor, born in New Haven, Connecticut, USA. In 1834 he began research into the properties of rubber. Amid poverty and ridicule he pursued the experiments which ended, in 1844, in the invention of vulcanized rubber. This led to the development of the rubber-manufacturing industry and the production of the well-known tyres named after him. Legal battles over patent infringements left him impoverished, and he died in debt.

Goons, The Four comedians who came together after World War 2 to create the Goon Show, which revolutionized British radio comedy: **Spike Milligan**, **Peter Sellers**, **Harry Secombe**, and **Michael Bentine**. They first performed on radio together in 1951: the show, called *Crazy People*, soon became *The Goon Show*, running for nine years and winning a worldwide band of devotees. The Goons prefigured much of British comedy since the fifties, especially in their imaginative use of sound effects, their mixture of surrealism and slapstick, and their anarchic humour. The members of the group later each developed individual careers in the world of entertainment.

goosander A sea-duck (*Mergus merganser*) native to N areas of the N hemisphere, also known in the USA as the **common merganser**; both sexes with dark head and long red bill; male with dark back; inhabits fresh water. (Family: Anatidae.)

goose A term not applied precisely, but used for large birds with more terrestrial habits than the 'swans' or 'ducks' comprising the rest of the family. The 14 N hemisphere species comprising the **grey geese** (Genus: *Anser*) and **black geese** (Genus: *Branta*) are sometimes called **true geese**. (Family: Anatidae.)

gooseberry A deciduous shrub (*Ribes uva-crispa*) growing to c.1 m/3¼ ft, native to Europe and N Africa; stems and branches spiny; leaves 3–5-lobed; flowers greenish, tinged purple, in ones or twos on drooping axillary stalks; edible berry oval, up to 4 cm/1½ in long, green or reddish, bristly or smooth. It is cultivated for its fruit. (Family: Grossulariaceae.)

goosefish *anglerfish*

goosegrass An annual, sometimes overwintering; a common weed (*Galium aparine*) native to Europe and Asia; 4-angled stems weak and straggling, climbing by means of small reflexed hooks; 6–8 leaves in whorls, margins with hooks; flowers tiny, white, 4-petalled; fruit a burr with two more or less equal globular halves covered in whitish bristles, dispersed by clinging or cleaving to animals; hence the alternative name **cleavers**. (Family: Rubiaceae.)

Goose Green 51°52S 59°00W, pop (2000e) 100. Settlement on East Falkland, Falkland Is; at the head of Choiseul Sound, on the narrow isthmus that joins the N half of East Falkland to Lafonia in the S; second largest settlement in the Falkland Is.

Goossens, Sir Eugène (1893–1962) Composer and conductor, born in London, UK, the son of Eugène Goossens (1867–1958). He studied in Bruges and London, became associate conductor to Sir Thomas Beecham, then worked in the USA (1923–45) as a conductor of orchestras in Rochester (New York) and Cincinnati (Ohio). As conductor of the Sydney Symphony Orchestra and director of the New South Wales Conservatory (1947–56), he became a major influence on Australian music. His compositions include two operas, a ballet, an oratorio, and two symphonies. He was knighted in 1955.

Goossens, Léon (1897–1988) Oboist, born in Liverpool, Merseyside, NW England, UK, the son of Eugène Goossens (1867–1958). He studied at the Royal College of Music, London, and held leading posts in most of the major London orchestras, before devoting himself to solo playing and teaching. He was the brother of the conductor Eugène Goossens; his sisters **Marie Goossens** (1894–1991) and **Sidonie Goossens** (1899–) became well-known harpists.

gopher A name used in North America for many animals which burrow (eg **pocket gophers**, some sousliks, a burrowing tortoise, a burrowing snake, and some salamanders); said to be from the French word *gaufre*, 'honeycomb' – a reference to the burrows.

goral A small goat-antelope (*Nemorhaedus goral*), native to the high mountains of E Asia; thick yellow-grey coat, pale throat; both sexes with short horns; also known as the **common goral**, **red goral**, or **Himalayan chamois**.

Gorbachev, Mikhail Sergeyevich [go(r)bachof] (1931–) Soviet statesman, general secretary of the Communist Party of the Soviet Union (1985–91), and president of the Supreme Soviet of the USSR (1988–91), born in Privolnoye, E Russia. He studied at Moscow State University and Stavropos Agricultural Institute, began work as a machine operator (1946), and joined the Communist Party in 1952. He held a variety of senior posts in the Stavropol city and district Party organization (1956–70), and was elected a deputy to the USSR Supreme Soviet (1970) and a member of the Party Central Committee (1971). He became secretary for agriculture (1979–85), a member of the Politburo in 1980, and, on the death of Chernenko, general secretary of the Central Committee (1985–91). In 1988 he also became chairman of the Presidium of the Supreme Soviet, and in 1990, the first (and last) executive president of the USSR. On becoming party general secretary he launched a radical programme of reform and restructuring (*perestroika*) of the Soviet economic and political system. A greater degree of civil liberty, public debate, journalistic and cultural freedom, and a reappraisal of Soviet history was allowed under the policy of *glasnost* (openness of information). In foreign and defence affairs he reduced military expenditure, pursued a policy of detente and nuclear disarmament with the West, and ended the Soviet military occupation of Afghanistan (1989). He briefly survived a coup in August 1991, but was forced to resign following the abolition of the Communist Party and the dissolution of the Soviet Union in December 1991. Since 1992 he has been president of the International Foundation for Socio-Economic and Political Studies (the Gorbachev Foundation), which he established in 1991. He failed to attract a significant vote in the 1996 presidential elections.

Gorbals, The A district of Glasgow, W Scotland, UK. Originally a village on the S bank of the R Clyde, it developed into a fashionable suburb, but by the end of the 19th-c had become infamous as an area of overcrowding and deprivation. Redevelopment, involving the rehousing of the community in high-rise flats or in new towns, started in 1950, and most of the old buildings were demolished in the next 20 years.

Gorboduc [gaw(r)boduk] A legendary King of Britain, first heard about in Geoffrey of Monmouth's *History*. He was the subject of an early Elizabethan tragedy in Senecan style, written by Norton and Sackville (1561).

Gordian knot In Phrygia, a complicated knot with which the legendary King Gordius had tied up his wagon. An oracle said that whoever succeeded in untying it would rule Asia. Alexander the Great cut it with his sword.

Gordimer, Nadine (1923–) Writer, born in Springs, E South Africa. She has lived in Johannesburg since 1948, and taught in the USA during the early 1970s. In novels such as *A Guest of Honour* (1971, James Tait Black), *The Conservationist* (1974, Booker), *Burger's Daughter* (1979), and *A Sport of Nature* (1987), she adopts a liberal approach to problems of race and repression, both in her native country and in other African states. Later books include *My Son's Story* (1990), *None to Accompany Me* (1994), *The House Gun* (1998), and *The Pickup* (2001). A collection of short stories, *Loot*, appeared in 2003. She was awarded the Nobel Prize for Literature in 1991.

Gordon, Adam Lindsay (1833–70) Poet, born in Fayal in the Azores. He was raised and educated in England. A wild and reckless youth, his father sent him to South Australia, where he became a horsebreaker and amateur steeplechaser. During the next few years he moved several times, published three volumes of poetry without success, suffered a series of mishaps, and finally committed suicide. Much of his best work is collected in *Sea Spray and Smoke Drift* (1867) and *Bush Ballads and Galloping Rhymes* (1870). He is recognized as the first poet to write in an Australian style, and is the only Australian poet honoured in the poets' corner of Westminster Abbey.

Gordon, Charles George (1833–85) British general, born in Woolwich, E Greater London, UK. He trained at Woolwich Academy, joined the Royal Engineers in 1852, and in 1855–6 fought in the Crimean War. In 1860 he went to China, where he crushed the Taiping Rebellion, for which he became known as **Chinese Gordon**. In 1877 he was appointed Governor of the Sudan. He resigned in poor health in 1880, but returned in 1884 to relieve Egyptian garrisons which lay in rebel territory. By tradition (there is some doubt about the actual events), he was besieged at Khartoum for 10 months by the Mahdi's troops, and was killed there two days before a relief force arrived. The incident captured the public imagination, and there are memorials to Gordon in St Paul's Cathedral and elsewhere.

Gordon Riots Anti-Catholic riots in London which caused a breakdown of law and order in parts of the capital for several days in early June 1780. They occurred after Lord George Gordon (1751–93), leader of the Protestant Association (an association formed to secure the repeal of the Catholic Relief Act of 1778), had failed in his attempt to have clauses in the Act (removing restrictions on the activities of priests) lifted. Huge crowds gathered in London, and the demonstration rapidly turned into an orgy of destruction and plunder that lasted a week. The gaols were broken open and probably more than 800 people were killed or injured. Dickens vividly describes the riots in *Barnaby Rudge* (1841).

Gordon setter A breed of dog developed in Britain, slightly larger than the English setter; coat black with small brown patches on underside.

Gore, Al(bert Arnold, Jr) (1948–) US vice-president (1993–2000), born in Washington, District of Columbia, USA. He studied at Harvard and Vanderbilt Universities, worked as a journalist, then became a Democratic congressman (1977–85) and senator (1985–92). He was elected vice-president to Bill Clinton in 1992. He conceded defeat to George W Bush after five weeks of complex legal argument over the voting procedure in the presidential election in 2000.

Górecki, Henryk Mikolaj [goreskee] (1933–) Composer, born in Czernica, near Rybnik, S Poland. He studied in Paris and at the Katowice Conservatory, and in 1975 was elected provost of the State Higher School of Music, but resigned in protest four years later when the government refused to allow Pope John Paul 2 to visit Katowice. His work, usually based on tragic themes and in very slow tempi, was virtually unknown in the West until 1993, when his *Symphony No. 3: Symphony of Sorrowful Songs* (1973), with texts from a 15th-c monastic song, a folk song, and a prayer scratched on a cell wall by a girl imprisoned by the Gestapo, reached number six in the British best-selling album charts, and sold over half a million copies worldwide. Later works include *Miserere* (1981), *Good Night* (1990), and *Kleines Requiem* (1993).

Gorée Island [goray] A small island off the Cape Verde peninsula, Senegal. Throughout the 18th-c and early 19th-c, when Gorée was first a French, and then a British colony, it was a major centre of slave storage before shipping to the Americas. Today it is a museum of slave trade history (House of Slaves), and a world heritage site.

Göreme [goereme] Valley in Cappadocia, C Turkey; noted for its cave dwellings; a world heritage site.

Gorgias [gaw(r)gias] (c.485–c.380 BC) Greek sophist, sceptical philosopher, and rhetorician, born in Leontini, Sicily. He went to Athens as ambassador in 427 BC and, settling in Greece, won wealth and fame as a teacher of eloquence. In his work *On Nature* he argued that nothing exists; even if something did exist, it could not be known; and even if it could be known it could not be communicated; we live in a world of opinion, manipulated by persuasion. Plato's dialogue *Gorgias* is written against him.

Gorgon A terrible monster of Greek mythology. There were three Gorgons, who had snakes in their hair, ugly faces, and huge wings; their staring eyes could turn people to stone. Perseus killed Medusa (the only mortal one), and cut off her head; this was used to rescue Andromeda, and eventually found a place on Athena's aegis. It is the detached head which is frightening; this occurs in art before the Gorgons were invented to explain it.

gorilla An ape (*Gorilla gorilla*) native to the rainforests of WC Africa; the largest primate (height, up to 1·8 m/6 ft); massive muscular body; usually walks on all fours (resting on the knuckles of its hands); ears small; adult male with marked crest; black, except in old males (*silverbacks*), which have a silvery grey torso; two races: the **lowland gorilla** and the shaggier **mountain gorilla**.

Göring, Hermann *Goering, Hermann*

Gorky *Nizhni Novgorod*

Gorky, Arshile, originally **Vosdanig Manoog Adoian** (1905–48) Painter, born in Khorkom Vari, Turkish Armenia. He emigrated in 1920, and studied at the Rhode Island School of Design and in Boston. He combined ideas and images derived from Surrealism and Biomorphic art, and played a key role in the emergence of the New York school of abstract Expressionists in the 1940s.

Gorky, Maxim, pseudonym of **Alexey Maksimovich Peshkov** (1868–1936) Novelist and playwright, born in Nizhni Novgorod, W Russia. He held a variety of menial posts before becoming a writer, producing several Romantic short stories, then social novels and plays, notably the drama *Na dne* (1902, The Lower Depths). At first he modelled his plays on Chekhov. An autobiographical trilogy (1915–23) contains his best writing. Involved in strikes and imprisoned in 1905, he was an exile in Italy until 1914, then engaged in revolutionary propaganda for the new regime. He was the first president of the Soviet Writers' Union, and a supporter of Stalinism. He died in mysterious circumstances, and may have been the victim of an anti-Soviet plot. His birthplace was renamed Gorky in his honour (1929–91).

Gormley, Antony (Mark David) (1950–) Sculptor, born in London, UK. He studied at Cambridge, then attended Goldsmith's School of Art and the Slade School of Fine Art in London. His work has featured in many solo and group exhibitions around the world, and among his awards is the Turner Prize in 1994. Later projects include the giant steel statue 'The Angel of the North' (1998) near Gateshead in Tyneside, and a 29 m/95 ft high metal structure named 'Quantum Leap' (2000) sited outside the Millennium Dome in London. In 2003 he created 'Domain Field', a series of life-size metal skeletons representing human beings' energy fields, exhibited at Tyneside's Baltic Centre.

gorse A spiny shrub (*Ulex europaeus*) growing to 2 m/6½ ft, from Europe and NW Africa; green-stemmed; leaves reduced to rigid needle-like spines, or small scales in mature plants; pea-flowers yellow, fragrant; pod 2-valved, exploding to release the seeds; also called **furze** and **whin**. (Family: Leguminosae.)

Gorsedd [gaw(r)seth] A society of Welsh bards, founded in 1792 by Iolo Morganwg, that takes a major part in the organization of the National Eisteddfod, in particular the bardic ceremony.

Gorton, Sir John Grey (1911–2002) Australian statesman, and prime minister (1968–71), born in Melbourne, Victoria, SE Australia. He studied at Oxford, and in 1940 joined the RAAF, but was seriously wounded, and discharged in 1944. He was a Liberal senator for Victoria (1949–68) and a member of the House of Representatives (1968–75). He served in the governments of Sir Robert Menzies and Harold Holt before becoming prime minister. In 1971 he was defeated on a vote of confidence, and resigned in favour of William McMahon, becoming deputy leader of his Party (until 1975). He was knighted in 1977 and named to the Order of Australia in 1988. In 1993 he announced that he was to wed for the second time, at the age of 82.

goshawk [gos-hawk] A smallish hawk with short rounded wings and a long tail (20 species). The **northern goshawk** (*Accipiter gentilis*) is found in much of the N hemisphere; other species are native to Africa, S and SE Asia, and Australia; inhabits woodland; eats vertebrates or insects. (Family: Accipitridae.)

Gospel (music) Music developed in black churches of the US South from a secular musical style in the early decades of the 20th-c. It was practised both by soloists and choirs, often with instrumental accompaniment, and became known for its infectious rhythms, close harmonies, and lively presentation. Noted solo performers include Sister Rosetta Tharpe and Mahalia Jackson. The style later had a major influence on other musical styles, especially soul music. The term is also associated with the revivalist movement of the late 19th-c, and the *Gospel Hymns* (1875–94) of US evangelists Philip Paul Bliss (1838–76) and Ira David Sankey (1840–1908).

Gospels, apocryphal Several writings from the early Christian era which are often somewhat similar to the canonical gospels in title, form, or content, but which have not been widely accepted as canonical themselves. They include popular infancy stories about Jesus (eg *Infancy Gospel of Thomas*, *Protoevangelium of James*), apocryphal accounts of Jesus's final suffering (*Gospel of Peter*, *Gospel of Nicodemus*), gnostic collections of sayings and stories (*Gospel of Thomas*, *Gospel of Philip*), and Judaeo-Christian works (*Gospel of the Hebrews*). Many are known from citations in the early Church fathers or from recent Nag Hammadi discoveries.

Gospels, canonical Four books of the New Testament, known as the **Gospels according to Matthew, Mark, Luke, and John**; called 'gospels' by the 2nd-c Church (Gr *euangelion*, 'good news'), but not itself a recognized genre in earlier Greek literature. Each portrays a perspective on the ministry and teaching of Jesus of Nazareth, concluding with an account of his arrest, crucifixion, and resurrection. Three of the four (Matthew, Mark, Luke) are sufficiently close in wording and order to suggest a close literary interrelationship, but the precise solution to this relationship is much debated (the *synoptic* problem). John's Gospel is different in character, and raises questions about whether its author knew the other Gospels at all, even though it is frequently dated as the latest because of the extent of theological reflection. None of the writings actually states its author's name.

Gosplan (abbreviation of **Gosudarstvennyi Planovyi Komitet**) The name of the State Planning Commission in the former USSR. Established in 1921 as an advisory council to the government, it supervised various aspects of planning, translating the general economic objectives of the state into specific plans. It assumed a central role in 1928, when the first Five-Year Plan, which called for rapid industrialization and a drastic reduction of the private sector of the economy, was adopted. Its responsibilities varied over the years, as the focus of state policy changed.

Gossaert, Jan [gosah(r)t] *Mabuse, Jan*

Gothenburg [gothenberg], Swed **Göteborg** 57°45N 12°00E, pop (2000e) 450 000. Seaport and capital city of Göteborg och Bohus county, SW Sweden; at the mouth of the R Göta on the Kattegat; second largest city in Sweden; founded, 1619; free port, 1921; railway; ferry services to UK, Denmark, Germany; university (1891), technical university (1829); linked to the Baltic by the Göta Canal; shipbuilding, vehicles, chemicals, ball-bearings; cathedral (1633, restored 1956–7), town hall (1750).

Gothic *black letter writing; Germanic languages*

Gothic architecture A form of architecture, usually religious, prevalent in W Europe from the 12th-c to the late 15th-c. It is characterized by a structural system comprising the pointed arch, rib vault, flying buttress, and a propensity for lofty interiors and maximum window area, with sophisticated stained glass. Various styles were developed.

Gothic art A term first used by Renaissance artists to mean 'barbaric', referring to the non-classical styles of the Middle Ages. Since the 19th-c, it has been in standard use to mean European art roughly of the period 12th–15th-c.

Gothic novel A type of fiction, written in reaction to 18th-c rationalism, which reclaims mystery and licenses extreme emotions. Early Gothic novels were usually set in a gloomy, frightening castle or monastery (hence 'Gothic'), for example in Horace Walpole's *The Castle of Otranto* (1765). Some (eg Mrs Radcliffe's novels) are actually quite innocent, and their supernatural occurrences are explained away; others (eg Lewis's *The Monk*, 1797) make confident forays into the unconscious, exploring sexual fears and impulses and making free use of ghosts and demons. It was parodied by Jane Austen in *Northanger Abbey* (1818), but revived by Poe and 19th-c Irish novelists such as Le Fanu and Bram Stoker. The Gothic horror stories of the 20th-c represented a fresh development for the genre, providing the input for a new medium of expression, the horror film.

Gothic Revival The movement to revive Gothic architecture, prevalent during the late 18th-c and 19th-c, popular in England, France, Germany, and North America. It was associated with the spiritual and social conditions of the Middle Ages, particularly in the writings of Pugin and Ruskin. The style was considered to be especially suitable for churches, such as St Denys-de-l'Estrée (1864–7), architect Viollet-le-Duc, and St Patrick's Cathedral in New York City. It was also extensively applied to a multitude of different building types, including railway stations, hotels, town halls, memorial buildings, and the parliament buildings at London, Budapest, and Ottawa.

Goths Germanic peoples who moved S, possibly from the Baltic area (Gotland), to the lower Vistula valley. They had expanded into the Black Sea region by the 3rd-c, and divided into two confederations, Ostrogoths and Visigoths. Displaced by the Huns, they created two kingdoms in the 5th-c out of the ruins of the Roman Empire in the W.

Gotland, Gottland, or **Gothland** pop (2000e) 60 000; land area 3140 sq km/1212 sq mi. Island county of Sweden, in the Baltic Sea off the SE coast; includes Gotland (the largest island), Fårö, and Karlsö; colonized by Germans, 12th-c; taken by Sweden in 1280, by Denmark in 1361, and again by Sweden in 1645; capital, Visby; cattle, sheep, tourism.

gouache [gooahsh] A type of opaque watercolour paint, also known as 'body colour', or 'poster paint' – familiar to most people from school art lessons. It was used in ancient Egypt, and widely in the Middle Ages, especially in illuminated manuscripts. During the Renaissance, Dürer used a type of gouache for his landscape sketches and studies of animals. Gouache is adaptable, and may be combined with pencil, watercolour, or pen-and-ink.

Gouda 52°01N 4°43E, pop (2001e) 72 800. City in Zuid Holland province, W Netherlands; 23 km/14 mi NE of Rotterdam; at the confluence of the Gouwe and Ijssel rivers; chartered, 1272; railway; Gothic town hall (1449–59), the Weighouse (1668), Grote Kerk (rebuilt 1552); ceramics, candles, clay pipes, dairy products; famous cheese market.

Goujon, Jean [goozhõ] (c.1510–c.68) The foremost French sculptor of the 16th-c, probably born in Normandy, NW France. His finest work is a set of reliefs for the Fountain of the Innocents (1547–9, Louvre). He worked for a while at the Louvre in Paris, but his later career is obscure. He was a Huguenot, but seems to have died before the St Bartholomew massacre (1572).

Gould, Glenn (Herbert) [goold] (1932–82) Pianist, born in Toronto, Ontario, SE Canada. He studied at the Royal Conservatory of Music, Toronto, before making his debut as a soloist with the Toronto Symphony Orchestra. He then performed extensively in the USA and Europe, but left the concert stage after only 10 years, in 1964. He became a renowned recording artist, particularly of works by Bach and Beethoven, and was known for his innovative radio documentaries, television shows, and occasional writings.

Gould, Shane (Elizabeth) (1956–) Swimmer, born in Brisbane, Queensland, NE Australia. She created Olympic history by being the first and only woman to win three individual gold swimming medals in world record time. She won the World Trophy (Helms) Medal in 1971. In 1972 she held every swimming record from 100 m to 1500 m, and in the same year gave the greatest performance of any Australian at a single Olympics in Munich. She retired in 1973, at the age of 17.

Gounod, Charles (François) [goonoh] (1818–93) Composer, born in Paris, France. He studied at the Paris Conservatoire and in Rome, then became organist of the Eglise des Missions Etrangères, Paris, where his earliest compositions, chiefly polyphonic in style, were performed. His major works include the opera, *Le Médecin malgré lui* (1858, trans The Mock Doctor), and his masterpiece, *Faust* (1859). He also published Masses, hymns, and anthems, and was popular as a songwriter.

gourami [gooramee] Deep-bodied freshwater fish (*Osphronemus goramy*) native to rivers and swamps of SE Asia, but now more widespread from India to China through aquaculture; length up to 60 cm/2 ft, with large median fins and very long pelvic fin ray; valuable food fish that survives well out of water. (Family: Osphronemidae.)

gourd Any of several members of the cucumber family, with hard, woody-rinded fruits of various shapes and colours. All are trailing or climbing vines with tendrils, palmately-lobed leaves, funnel-shaped flowers, and round pear- or bottle-shaped fruits. The best known are **ornamental gourds** (*Cucurbita pepo* variety *ovifera*), flowers yellow, native to America, and the **bottle-gourd** or **calabash**. (Family: Cucurbitaceae.)

gout A disorder arising from a raised concentration of uric acid in the blood, which is deposited in the joints and soft tissues leading to recurrent acute attacks of arthritis, classically affecting the big toe, and accumulations of uric acid in the fingers, ear lobes, and kidneys. The cause is unknown, but affected individuals are typically overweight males.

goutweed *ground elder*

Gower, David (Ivon) (1957–) Cricketer, born in Tunbridge Wells, Kent, SE England, UK. He came to the fore chiefly because of the elegance of his left-handed stroke play. He was captain of England (1984–6, 1989), leading them to the Ashes in 1985 with 715 runs, the most by an England captain in a series against Australia. He became the leading Test run-scorer in 1992, with 8231 runs in 117 matches, at an average of 44·25, but he lost this place to Graham Gooch after the final Test against the Australians the following August. He retired in 1993 and became a cricket journalist and television commentator, and was a regular team captain (1995–2003) of BBC television's sports quiz show, *They Think It's All Over*.

Gower, John (c.1325–1408) Mediaeval poet, born in Kent, SE England, UK, a friend of Chaucer. His works include many French ballads, written in his youth, and *Vox clamantis*, in Latin elegiacs (1382–4), describing the rising under Wat Tyler. His best-known work is the long English poem, *Confessio amantis* (c.1383), comprising over 100 stories from various sources on the theme of Christian and courtly love. He became blind in his last years.

Gowers, Sir Ernest (Arthur) (1880–1966) British civil servant, and author of an influential work on English usage. He studied at Cambridge, and was called to the bar in 1906. After a distinguished career in the civil service, he wrote *Plain Words* (1948) and *ABC of Plain Words* (1951) in an attempt to maintain standards of clear English, especially in official prose.

Goya (y Lucientes), Francisco (José) de [gohya] (1746–1828) Artist, born in Fuendetodos, NEC Spain. After travelling in Italy, he returned to Spain to design for the Royal Tapestry factory. In 1798 he produced a series of frescoes, incorporating scenes from contemporary life, in the Church of San Antonio de la Florida, Madrid, and over 80 satirical etchings, 'Los caprichos' (1799, The Caprices). He became famous for his portraits, and in 1799 was made court painter to Charles IV, which led to 'The Family of Charles IV' (1800, Prado) and other works. He settled in France in 1824.

Goyen, Jan van [goyen] *van Goyen, Jan*

Gozo [gohzoh], Maltese **Ghaudex**, ancient **Gaulus** 36°00N 14°13E; pop (2000e) 28 000 (with Comino); area 67 sq km/26 sq mi. Island in the Maltese group, often called 'the Isle of Calypso'; 6 km/4 mi NW of the main island of Malta; coastline, 43 km/27 mi; chief town, Victoria (Rabat); largely given over to agriculture; prehistoric temples, Ta' Pinu church a centre of pilgrimage to the Virgin Mary.

Gozzi, Carlo, conte (Count) [gotzee] (1720–1806) Playwright, born in Venice, NE Italy. After a period in the army, he took up writing in Venice. Among his works are several satirical poems and plays, defending the traditions of the *commedia dell'arte* against the innovations of Goldoni and others. His best-known works include the comedy, *Fiaba dell' amore delle tre melarance* (1761, The Love of the Three Oranges) and *Re Turandot* (1762, made into an opera by Puccini). His brother, **Gasparo Gozzi** (1713–86) was a journal editor and press censor, who also became known for his verse satires.

graben [grahbn] A rift valley, usually of great size, formed when a narrow block of the Earth's crust drops down between two normal faults.

Grable, Betty, originally **Ruth Elizabeth Grable** (1916–73) Actress, born in St Louis, Missouri, USA. She worked as a chorus girl from the age of 13 and made her film debut in the musical *Whoopee!* (1930). She had her first major film role in *Hold 'em Jail* (1932), and became more established with *Pigskin Parade*

(1936), and *Million Dollar Legs* (1939). She was adopted by American GI's during World War 2 as a pin-up girl, with the famous picture in which, dressed in a swimsuit, with her back to the camera and hands on hips, she glances saucily over her right shoulder. She went on to appear on Broadway in *Hello, Dolly* (1965).

Gracchi, (the brothers) [grakee], in full **Tiberius Sempronius Gracchus** (c.168–133 BC) and **Gaius Sempronius Gracchus** (c.159–121 BC) Roman politicians of aristocratic lineage who attempted to solve the major social and economic problems of their day – the growing landlessness of the Roman peasantry and the consequent decline in army recruitment – by forcing through sweeping reforms while they were tribunes of the plebs (133 BC, 123–122 BC). The ruthlessness of their methods provoked such a backlash that on each occasion rioting broke out on the streets of Rome. Tiberius was lynched, and a decade later Gaius was forced to commit suicide.

grace In Christianity, the free and unmerited assistance or favour or energy or saving presence of God in his dealings with humankind through Jesus Christ. The term has been understood in various ways, eg as *prevenient* (leading to sanctification), or *actual* (prompting good actions). Sacraments are recognized as a 'means of grace', but the manner of their operation and the extent to which humans co-operate has been a subject of controversy.

Grace, W(illiam) G(ilbert) (1848–1915) Cricketer, born in Downend, South Gloucester, SWC England, UK. By 1864 he was playing cricket for Gloucester County, and was chosen for the Gentlemen v. the Players at 16. He practised medicine in Bristol, but his main career was cricket. He toured Canada, the USA, and Australia, twice captaining the English team. His career in first-class cricket (1865–1908) as batsman and bowler brought 126 centuries, 54 896 runs, and 2876 wickets.

Graces, the (Gr *Charites*) In Greek mythology, three daughters of Zeus and Hera, embodying beauty and social accomplishments. They are sometimes called **Aglaia**, **Euphrosyne**, and **Thalia**.

grackle A bird of the New World, any of 11 species of the family Icteridae (American blackbirds and orioles). The name is also used for several starlings from SE Asia and Indonesia (family: Sturnidae).

Grade (of Elstree), Lew Grade, Baron, originally **Louis Winogradsky** (1906–98) Theatrical impresario, born near Odessa, S Ukraine, the eldest of three brothers who were to dominate British show-business for over 40 years. He arrived in Britain in 1912, accompanied by his parents and younger brother **Boris Grade**, who became **Baron Bernard Delfont of Stepney** (1909–94). The brothers became dancers, then theatrical agents, along with the youngest brother **Leslie Grade**. Bernard entered theatrical management in 1941, and acquired many properties, notably the London Hippodrome. His many companies embraced theatre, film, television, music, and property interests. From 1958 to 1978 he presented the annual Royal Variety Performance. Lew was an early entrant to the world of commercial television, and became managing director of ATV in 1962. He headed several large film entertainment and communications companies. He was knighted in 1969 and made a life peer in 1976.

gradient A measure of the inclination of a straight line to a fixed straight line. In mathematical terms, the gradient of a straight line, in a rectangular co-ordinate system, is the tangent of the angle made by the straight line and the positive x-axis. The gradient of a curve at a point P is the gradient of the tangent to the curve at the point P.

Graf, Steffi [grahf] (1969–) Tennis player, born in Brühl, near Heidelberg, SW Germany. In 1982 she became the youngest person to receive a World Tennis Association ranking, aged 13, and reached the semi-final of the US Open in 1985. She won the French Open in 1987, and took all four major titles in 1988, as well as the Olympic crown – a unique feat. She beat Natalya Zvereva 6-0 6-0 to win the Australian title, the first shutout in a major final since 1911. She won the Wimbledon title again in 1989, 1991, 1992, 1993, 1995, 1996, and the French Open in 1999. She announced her retirement in 1999.

graffito *sgraffito*

graft (botany) The portion of a woody plant inserted into a slot cut in the stem or rootstock of another plant, so that the vascular tissues combine and growth continues. Successful only between closely related species, grafting is widely used in horticulture to combine desirable but weak-growing varieties with vigorous or disease-resistant ones. Sometimes the rootstock donor breaks out, producing suckers bearing their own flowers among those of the other donor.

graft (medicine) A tissue or organ that can be used for transplantation. An **allograft** (**homograft**) is taken from a member of the same species but one that is genetically dissimilar. An **autograft** is taken from the animal's or the patient's own body or a genetically identical individual (eg an identical twin). A **xenograft** (**heterograft**) is taken from a species different to that of the host.

Graham, Billy, popular name of **William Franklin Graham, Jr** (1918–) Evangelist, born in Charlotte, North Carolina, USA. He attended Florida Bible Institute, was ordained a Southern Baptist minister in 1939, and quickly gained a reputation as a preacher. During the 1950s he conducted a series of highly organized revivalist campaigns in the USA and UK, and later in South America, the former USSR, and W Europe. A charismatic figure, his campaigns continued to attract large audiences into the 1990s. His books include *Peace with God* (1952), *World Aflame* (1965), and *Storm Warning* (1992). He received the Templeton Prize for Progress in Religion in 1982.

Graham, Martha (1894–1991) Dancer, teacher, and choreographer, born in Pittsburgh, Pennsylvania, USA. She first appeared in vaudeville and revue, and started the Martha Graham School of Contemporary Dance in 1927. She was the most famous exponent of modern dance ballet in the USA, emphasizing emotional expression. Her works dealt with frontier life, as in *Appalachian Spring* (1944), Greek myths, as in *Clytemnestra* (1958), and psychological drama, in which her use of angularity of movement was complemented by the Japanese-American artist Isamu Noguchi (1904–88). Her method of dance training has been widely adopted in professional schools.

Graham, Thomas (1805–69) Chemist and physicist, born in Glasgow, W Scotland, UK. He was professor of chemistry at Glasgow (1830–7) and London (1837–55), and Master of the Mint (1855–69). One of the founders of physical chemistry, he formulated the law that the diffusion rate of gases is inversely proportional to the square root of their density (*Graham's law*). He also studied the properties of colloids, and devised dialysis for separating colloids from crystalloids.

Grahame, Kenneth (1859–1932) Writer, born in Edinburgh, EC Scotland, UK. He entered the Bank of England in 1879, became its secretary in 1898, and retired for health reasons in 1908. He wrote several stories for children, the best known being *The Wind in the Willows* (1908), which was dramatized in 1930 by A A Milne as *Toad of Toad Hall*.

Graham Land Mountainous Antarctic peninsula; rises to c.3600 m/11 800 ft at Mt Jackson; Weddell Sea lies to the E.

Graiae [griyee] In Greek mythology, three sisters with the characteristics of extreme old age, who had one eye and one tooth between them. Perseus took the eye and made them tell him the route to the Gorgons, who were their sisters.

Graian Alps [griyan], Fr **Alpes Graian**, Ital **Alpi Graie** N division of the W Alps in SE France and NW Italy, on French–Italian border; extending in an arc from the Alpes Cottiennes at Mont Cenis to the St Bernard Pass and Dora Baltea valley; highest peak, Gran Paradiso/Grand Paradis (4061 m/13 323 ft).

Grail, Holy or **Sangreal** In the Arthurian legends, the dish or chalice used by Christ at the Last Supper. Joseph of Arimathea brought it to Glastonbury. It appeared at Pentecost at King Arthur's table, and the knights set out to find it; this diversion of energy into unworldly matters contributed to the break-up of the Round Table. The grail may have features of Celtic magic cauldrons, but the cult of relics is a better clue to its origins.

grain (agriculture) A single cereal seed or a growing cereal crop. The grain harvest refers to the total bulk of cereals harvested, and includes seed grain for planting the following year, feed grain destined for animal rations, grain used in the production of alcohol, and grain used for human consumption – either direct (eg rice) or in the form of flour products or breakfast cereals.

grain (photography) The clumping of the black metallic silver particles which form a developed photographic image. Their size and distribution can be measured with a micro-densitometer and expressed as a numerical factor termed *granularity*. **Graininess**, the degree to which grain is visible in a picture, is a subjective concept affected by both the image structure and the conditions of viewing.

Grainger, Percy (Aldridge), originally **George Percy Grainger** (1882–1961) Composer and pianist, born in Melbourne, Victoria, SE Australia. A child prodigy on piano, he studied in Melbourne and Frankfurt, and became a travelling virtuoso based in London. After making a sensational US debut (1915) with the piano concerto by his friend Grieg, he remained in the USA for most of the rest of his life. He championed the revival of folk music in such works as 'Molly on the Shore' and 'Shepherd's Hey' (1911), but was also one of the first to compose for electronic instruments. He often returned to Australia, and in 1935 founded the Grainger Museum at Melbourne.

gram *kilogram*

grammar The study of the structure of words (also known as **morphology**), phrases, clauses, and sentences (also known as **syntax**). At word level, the grammarian is concerned with the changes in form that signal such features as case and number (eg *mouse/mice, cat/cats*); at phrase level, with the structure of such units as *the very tall building* ('noun phrases') and *may have been running* ('verb phrases'); at clause and sentence level, with the order of such constituents as subject, verb, and object (*the bear/ate/an apple*) and the relationship between constructions, such as statement and question. Several types of grammar exist. A **prescriptive grammar** lays down conventions of usage regarded by some sections of society as being 'correct', such as 'Never end a sentence with a preposition'. By contrast, a **descriptive grammar** describes actual usage patterns, without making value judgments about their social standing. A **comparative grammar** compares the grammatical features of languages that are genetically related, and a **universal grammar** investigates those grammatical features shared by the structure of all languages.

grammar school In the UK, a selective school choosing usually the most able 15–25% of 11-year-olds on the basis of the eleven-plus examination. The oldest schools date back to mediaeval times, and were originally established to teach Latin. During the 1960s and 1970s many were reorganized, along with local secondary modern schools, and became comprehensive schools. The term is also used in the USA, but referring to an earlier level of schooling – the first six to eight grades of elementary education.

Grammer, Kelsey (1955–) Actor, born on St Thomas, US Virgin Islands. Brought up in New Jersey and Florida, he trained at the Juilliard School, then acted on stage in theatres across the USA. He is best known for his role as Dr Frasier Crane, originally seen in *Cheers* (1982–93) and *Wings*, and then in *Frasier* (1993–2004, 31 Emmies). His feature films include *Down Periscope* (1996) and *The Real Howard Spitz* (1998). In 1995 he published a volume of autobiography, *So Far...* .

Grammy An annual popular music award given by the US National Academy of Recording Arts and Sciences for special achievement in the record industry. Established in 1958, it recognizes a wide range of categories, such as best record, album, song, and new artist, as well as best performance in several pop music genres (eg rock, rhythm and blues, rap, hard rock, metal).

Grammy Award Categories

The 28 Grammy domains listed below are subdivided into 104 categories (as of 2004). General Field, for example, is divided into Record of the Year, Song of the Year, Album of the Year, and Best New Artist.

General Field	World Music
Traditional Pop	Polka
Rock	Children's
Alternative Music	Spoken Word
R&B	Musical Show
Rap	Film/TV/Visual Media
Country	Composing/Arranging
New Age	Package
Jazz	Album Notes
Gospel	Historical
Latin	Production
Blues Folk	Classical
Reggae	Music Video

gramophone An acoustic device for reproducing sounds, stored as acoustically generated, laterally cut grooves in the flat surface of a disc rotated on a turntable beneath a stylus. First demonstrated in 1888 by US inventor Emile Berliner (1851–1929), it progressively displaced the phonograph, as discs could be multiply produced with relative ease, and played longer than most cylinders. However, the term *phonograph* continued to be used in the USA, with *gramophone* becoming the norm in the UK.

Grampian pop (2000e) 548 400; area 8704 sq km/3361 sq mi. Former region in NE Scotland, UK; created in 1975, and replaced in 1996 by Moray and Aberdeenshire councils.

Grampians (Australia) Mountain range in SWC Victoria, Australia, SW spur of the Great Dividing Range; Aboriginal name **Gariwerd**; rises to 1167 m/3829 ft at Mt William.

Grampians (Scotland) or **Grampian Mountains** Mountain system extending SW–NE across Scotland, UK; gentle slopes in the S, steep slopes in the N; rises to 1344 m/4409 ft at Ben Nevis; includes several smaller chains of mountains, such as the Cairngorms; source of the Dee, Don, Spey, Findhorn, Esk, Tay, and Forth Rivers.

grampus A toothed whale; correctly the **grey grampus** or **Risso's dolphin** (*Grampus griseus*), a widespread temperate and tropical deep-water species of short-nosed dolphin which eats squid. The name was formerly used for other species, especially the killer whale. (Family: Delphinidae.)

Gramsci, Antonio [gramshee] (1891–1937) Italian political leader and theoretician, born in Ales, Sardinia, Italy. Brought up in poverty, he studied at Turin University, helped found a left-wing paper, *L'ordine nuovo* (1919, The New Order), and was active in promoting workers' councils in factories. Dissatisfied with moderate, reformist Socialism, he helped to establish the Italian Communist Party (1921), which he represented at the Third International in Moscow (1922), and in 1924 he became leader of the Party in parliament. When Mussolini banned the Party, he was arrested and spent the rest of his life in prison (1926–37), where he completed some 30 notebooks of reflections which were published posthumously (*Lettere del carcere*, 1947, Letters from Prison), and are now regarded as one of the most important political texts of the 20th-c.

Gram's stain An important staining procedure used in the identification of bacteria. The bacteria are stained with basic dyes, such as crystal violet, and then exposed to organic solvents. Some (*Gram-negative* bacteria) lose their colour readily with exposure to organic solvents, whereas others (*Gram-positive* bacteria) retain the dye. The procedure is named after Danish bacteriologist Hans Christian Joachim Gram (1853–1938).

Granada 37°10N 3°35W, pop (2000e) 257 000. Capital of Granada province, Andalusia, S Spain; on R Genil, 434 km/270 mi S of

Madrid; average altitude 720 m/2360 ft; founded by the Moors, 8th-c; capital of the Kingdom of Granada, 1238; last Moorish stronghold in Spain, captured in 1492; archbishopric; airport; railway; university (1531); textiles, paper, soap, tourism; cathedral (16th-c), with tombs of Ferdinand and Isabella; Generalife Palace and the Alhambra, a world heritage site; Conquest Day (Jan), Fiesta of Las Cruces de Mayo (May), international festival of music and dance (Jun–Jul), international sports week (winter), Costa del Sol Rally (Dec).

granadilla Any of several species of passion flower which produce edible fruits. **Purple granadilla** (*Passiflora edulis*) has purple fruits, 5–7·5 cm/2–3 in long. The **giant granadilla** (*Passiflora quadrangularis*) has greenish-yellow fruits, up to 10 cm/4 in long. (Family: Passifloraceae.)

Granados (y Campiña), Enrique [granahthos] (1867–1916) Composer and pianist, born in Lérida, NE Spain. He studied at the Paris Conservatoire, and achieved fame as a pianist and composer of piano music. In 1916 he used his piano suite *Goyescas* (1911) as the basis for an opera with the same title. He was drowned when the *Sussex* was torpedoed by the Germans in the English Channel.

Granby, John Manners, Marquess of (1721–70) British army officer, the eldest son of the Duke of Rutland, whose reputation was made in the Seven Years' War (1756–63) when he led the British cavalry in a major victory over the French at Warburg (1760). He became a popular hero, and in 1763 was appointed Master-General of the Ordnance.

Gran Canaria [gran kanaria], Eng **Grand Canary** 28°00N 15°35W; area 1532 sq km/591 sq mi. Volcanic Atlantic island in the Canary Is; highest point, Pozo de las Nieves (1980 m/6496 ft); steep cliffs in N and W; wide beaches in S, with tourist facilities; chief town, Las Palmas de Gran Canaria; sugar cane, distilling, tobacco, chemicals, light engineering; airport on the E coast.

Gran Chaco [gran chakoh] Lowland plain covering part of N Argentina, W Paraguay, and S Bolivia; consists of Chaco Boreal in the N (250 000 sq km/100 000 sq mi), Chaco Central (130 000 sq km/50 000 sq mi), and Chaco Austral in the S (250 000 sq km/100 000 sq mi); drained chiefly by Paraná, Paraguay, and Pilcomayo rivers; scrub forest and grassland, with a tropical savannah climate and sparse population; cattle raising; tannin, cotton, sunflowers, maize, sorghum; disputed area in the Chaco War between Paraguay and Bolivia (1932–5).

Gran Colombia [grankolombia] (Span 'Greater Colombia') The name given by historians to the union of Venezuela, New Granada, and Quito (Ecuador) formed in 1819 by Simón Bolívar and known by him as Colombia. The union dissolved in 1830; the name Colombia was later adopted by New Granada.

Grand Alliance, War of the (1805–7) A phase in the Napoleonic Wars. A Third Coalition of states (Britain, Austria, Russia, Sweden, and Prussia) was formed to attack France by land and sea. Despite Britain's success at Trafalgar (1805), the coalition was undermined by spectacular French victories at Ulm, Austerlitz (1805), and Jena (1806). The Treaties of Pressburg (1805) and Tilsit (1807) ended hostilities.

Grand Army of the Republic (GAR) An organization of veterans of the Union side in the American Civil War. Established in 1866, the GAR became an important force in post-war politics.

Grand Bahama pop (2000e) 47 400; area 1372 sq km/530 sq mi. Island in the NW Bahamas; fourth largest island in the group; length 120 km/75 mi; chief town Freeport-Lucaya; popular tourist resort; home of the Underwater Explorers' Club; International Bazaar; oil transshipment at South Riding Point.

Grand Banks A major fishing ground in the N Atlantic Ocean, off the coast of Newfoundland, Canada, formed by an extensive submarine plateau on the continental shelf. The plankton-rich shallow waters are an important breeding area for fish.

Grand Canal, Chin **Da Yunhe** Canal in E China, length 1794 km/1115 mi, average width, 30 m/100 ft; world's longest artificial waterway; Sui Emperor Yangdi (r.604–18) linked existing canals into a continuous waterway from Hangzhou (S of the Yangtze) to Kaifeng (Yellow R), with connections to Changan (now Xian) and Beijing. The canal was built rapidly between 604 and 610 by 3·5 million labourers. It was tree-lined, with roads both sides, and could take barges of 800-ton capacity. By the 8th-c over 2 million tons of grain were being transported annually. It fell into disuse in the 12th-c, and was ruined by Yellow R floods in the 13th-c. An improved Canal was built to Beijing in 1295, and the system was further reconstructed in the 15th-c and 16th-c. It was abandoned after 1849.

Grand Canyon Enormous gorge in NW Arizona, USA; 349 km/217 mi long; 8–25 km/5–15 mi wide from rim to rim; maximum depth c.1900 m/6250 ft; the result of large-scale erosion by the Colorado R, exposing hundreds of millions of years of geological formations; parts of the side walls have formed isolated towers ('temples') due to stream erosion (best known are Vishnu Temple, Shiva Temple, Wotan's Throne); located in Grand Canyon National Park (4931 sq km/1903 sq mi); one of the main US tourist attractions.

Grand Canyon of the Snake *Hell's Canyon*

Grand Coulee [koolee] Valley in Douglas County, NE Washington, USA; the **Grand Coulee Dam** is a major gravity dam on the Columbia R, impounding L Franklin D Roosevelt; built 1933–42; height 168 m/550 ft; length 1272 m/4173 ft; can generate 6180 megawatts of hydroelectricity.

Grande Comore *Njazidja*

Grande-Terre [grãd tair] pop (2000e) 209 000; area 585 sq km/226 sq mi. One of the two main islands of the Overseas Department of Guadeloupe, Lesser Antilles, E Caribbean; chief town, Pointe-à-Pitre; of coral formation, rising to only 150 m/500 ft; agriculture, especially sugar cane; tourism.

Grand Guignol [grã geenyol] Short sensational shows, in vogue in Paris in the late 19th-c, which depict violent crimes in a style designed to shock and titillate. Guignol was originally a puppet in the French marionette theatre, the French eqivalent of the British Punch and the German Hanswurst or Kasperle. Performances may still be seen in the small theatres of Montmartre.

grand mal [grã mal] *epilepsy*

Grand National The most famous steeplechase in the world, first held at Maghull near Liverpool in 1836. The race moved to its present course at Aintree in 1839. Racing over 4 mi/855 yd (7·2 km), the competitors have to negotiate 31 difficult fences, including the hazardous Becher's Brook. There is also a greyhound Grand National.

Grand Ole Opry Country-music radio show broadcast from the Grand Ole Opry House theatre in Nashville, Tennessee, USA. Begun in 1925, it is the nation's longest continuously running radio show and the last survivor of the big country music shows of radio's 'golden age'.

Grand Remonstrance The statement of Charles I of England's abuses, and of reforms made by the Long Parliament in 1640–1; passed by 11 votes in the House of Commons (22 Nov 1641), and thereafter published as an appeal for support. The close vote reflected the formation of roughly equal parties of 'royalists' and 'parliamentarians'.

Grand St Bernard 45°53N 7°11E. Alpine mountain pass between Martigny, Switzerland, and Aosta, Italy, on the Italian–Swiss border; in the SW Pennine Alps, E of the Mont Blanc group; usually open only from June until October; construction of the St Bernard Tunnel (5828 m/19 120 ft long) in 1959–63 made the route passable throughout the year; height, 2469 m/8100 ft; hospice run by monks nearby.

grand unified theories (GUTs) A class of speculative theories which seek to express strong nuclear, weak nuclear, and electromagnetic forces in a single theory by combining quantum chromodynamics and the Glashow–Weinberg–Salam theory. The earliest attempts to construct such theories were made in 1974 by US physicists Howard Georgi (1947–) and Sheldon Glashow (1932–), predicting super-heavy particles denoted X and Y of mass approximately 10^{15} that of a proton, the slow decay of protons, and the existence of heavy magnetic monopoles. None of these predictions have been observed.

Granger, Clive W J (1934–) Economist, born in Swansea, SC Wales, UK. He studied at Nottingham University, gaining his PhD in 1959, and later joined the University of California at San Diego, USA. In 2003 he shared the Nobel Prize for Economics with Robert F Engle for their work on using statistics to predict the future. Granger's contribution involved study of methods of analyzing economic time series with common trends (cointegration).

Granger, Stewart, originally **James Lablanche Stewart** (1913–93) Film actor, born in London, UK. He studied at Epson College and at the Webber-Douglas School of Dramatic Art, then worked in repertory companies and as a film extra before being cast as the romantic lead in *So This Is London* (1938). He assumed his professional name in the 1930s, to avoid confusion with actor James Stewart. The success of the film *The Man In Grey* (1943) swept him to star status in Britain. Later films included *King Solomon's Mines* (1950), *Beau Brummell* (1954), *North to Alaska* (1960), and *The Wild Geese* (1977). He became a US citizen in 1956.

Granger movement A US organization of farmers, officially known as **the Patrons of Husbandry**, founded in 1867, which adopted a radical stance towards farmers' problems and big business. The name stems from the title *grange* (or farm) adopted by local units. In the 1870s some states passed a series of laws (popularly known as 'Granger laws') establishing the federal regulation of private utilities. The organization still exists.

granite A coarse-grained, acid (high in silica) igneous rock containing orthoclase feldspar, quartz, and mica (and/or hornblende); pale pink or grey in colour, its durability makes it an important building stone.

Grant, Cary, originally **Archibald Leach** (1904–86) Film actor, born in Bristol, SW England, UK. He went to Hollywood in 1928, played opposite Marlene Dietrich and Mae West, and from the late 1930s developed in leading comedy roles, especially under the direction of Howard Hawks, such as *Bringing Up Baby* (1938) and *His Girl Friday* (1940). He also provided several memorable performances for Hitchcock in *Suspicion* (1941), *Notorious* (1946), *To Catch a Thief* (1955), and *North by North-West* (1959), but during the 1960s his appearances were fewer.

Grant, Duncan (James Corrow) (1885–1978) Painter, born in Rothiemurchus, Highland, N Scotland, UK. He studied at the Westminster and Slade Schools, in Italy, and in Paris, and was associated with Fry's Omega Workshops, and then with the London Group. His works were mainly landscapes, portraits, and still-life, and he also designed textiles, pottery, and stage scenery.

Grant, Hugh (John Mungo) (1960–) Actor, born in London, UK. He studied English at Oxford, then began a career in the theatre. His early films include *Maurice* (1987) and *Bitter Moon* (1992), but he became internationally known following his role in *Four Weddings and a Funeral* (1994, Best Actor Golden Globe). Later films include *Notting Hill* (1999), *Bridget Jones's Diary* (2001), *About a Boy* (2002), and *Love Actually* (2003). He received the Stanley Kubrick Britannia Award for excellence in film in 2003.

Grant, Richard E(sterhuysen) (1957–) Actor, born in Mbabane, Swaziland. He studied drama at Cape Town University before moving to London in 1982. He became known following his role as the down-and-out thespian in *Withnail and I* (1987), and later films include *The Player* (1992), *The Portrait of a Lady* (1996), *Little Vampire* (2000), and *Gosford Park* (2001). Television roles include BBC TV's *The Scarlet Pimpernel* (1998), *Trial and Retribution* (1999), and *A Christmas Carol* (1999). He has also published his diaries, *With Nails* (1997) and a novel, *By Design*.

Grant, Ulysses S(impson) (1822–85) US general and 18th president (1869–77), born in Point Pleasant, Ohio, USA. He trained at West Point, fought in the Mexican War (1846–8), then settled as a farmer in Missouri. On the outbreak of the Civil War (1861), he rejoined the army and rose rapidly, leading Union forces to victory, first in the Mississippi Valley, then in the final campaigns in Virginia. He accepted the Confederate surrender at Appomattox Court House (1865), and was made a full general in 1866. Elected president in 1868 and 1872, he presided over the reconstruction of the South, but his administration was marred by scandal. He wrote two volumes of memoirs (1885–6), which were highly acclaimed as a contribution to military history.

Granth Sahib *Adi Granth*

grant-maintained school A school, established by the 1988 Education Act, which is independent of the local education authority and receives its annual grant directly from the government. In order to 'opt out' of local authority control a majority of parents must vote in favour by secret ballot.

granulation (astronomy) *photosphere*

Granville, Earl *Carteret, John*

Granville-Barker, Harley (1877–1946) Actor, playwright, and producer, born in London, UK. After a career in acting, he entered theatre management at the Court Theatre (1904) and the Savoy (1907). He wrote several plays himself, such as *The Voysey Inheritance* (1905), collaborated in translations, and wrote a famous series of prefaces to Shakespeare's plays (1927–45).

Granz, Norman (1918–2001) Concert impresario and record producer, born in Los Angeles, California, USA. He borrowed money to stage a jazz concert at the Philharmonic Auditorium, and its success led to national and international tours called Jazz at the Philharmonic. His recording companies Clef (1951) and Norgran (1954) originally released his concert recordings. He discovered Oscar Peterson and became his manager, and also managed Ella Fitzgerald. In 1973 he started Pablo Records and quickly established its name by recording Dizzy Gillespie, Count Basie, Duke Ellington, and many others. He was widely recognized as a leading disseminator of jazz music around the world.

grape *grapevine*

grapefruit A citrus fruit (*Citrus paradisi*) 10–15 cm/4–6 in diameter; usually globose with thick, pale, yellow rind; some varieties may be slightly pear-shaped or have thin or pinkish rind. (Family: Rutaceae.)

grape hyacinth A bulb native to Europe and the Mediterranean region; leaves grass-like, semi-cylindrical; flowers in a dense spike-like inflorescence, drooping, urn-shaped with six small lobes; the blue upper flowers often sterile, brighter-coloured, acting as an extra attractant. It is cultivated for ornament. (Genus: *Muscari*, 60 species. Family: Liliaceae.)

grapevine A deciduous woody climber (*Vitis vinifera*), entering cracks and swelling to form a sticky mass which provides support; leaves palmately 3–5-lobed, toothed; flowers numerous, in drooping inflorescences, tiny, green; ripe fruits sweet, yellowish or purple, often with a waxy, white bloom; tendrils negatively phototropic. Probably native to E Asia, many varieties are now cultivated in most temperate regions, especially those with a Mediterranean climate. It is of considerable economic importance as the source of wine. North American species resistant to the insect pest *Phylloxera*, such as **summer-grape** (*Vitis aestivalis*) and **fox-grape** (*Vitis labrusca*), are used as root-stocks for European vines. Dried grapes are sold as currants, raisins, and sultanas. (Family: Vitidaceae.)

graph A diagram illustrating the relationship between two sets of numbers, such as the relationship between the height of a plant in centimetres and the time in days since germination. The sets of numbers may be purely algebraic; for example, described by the equation $y = x - 1$. Although the scales on the axes are usually constant, that is not necessary. Logarithmic graph paper is so calibrated that a logarithmic graph appears as a straight line. Many other kinds of graph paper can be obtained.

graphic design A set of skills and techniques employed in the design of all printed matter. The major skills include typography, photography, illustration, and printmaking. These disciplines, formerly taught and practised more or less in isolation, have been successfully brought together through the dominance of offset lithography as the most popular printing method and the development of allied photographic techniques.

graphics tablet A device by which the movements of a pen over a special surface can be translated into digital input for a computer. This provides a means of converting two-dimensional information, such as maps and drawings, into computer-readable form. It is very widely used in engineering and design applications.

graphic user interface (GUI) The screen interface with a computer's operating software, where graphical components such as icons are used to represent computer files and programs. Users simply click on the icons to activate the program or file. The usual range of graphical components in such an interface normally include *windows*, *icons*, *menus*, and *pointers*, and as a result are sometimes referred to as **WIMP interfaces**.

graphite A mineral form of carbon, found in metamorphic rocks; black, soft, and greasy to the touch. It is a very good electrical conductor and dry lubricant. Mixed with clay, it is used in pencil 'leads'.

graphology **1** The analysis of handwriting as a guide to the character and personality of the writer. It was introduced during the late 19th-c by the French abbot, Jean Hippolyte Michon (1806–81). Graphologists study such factors as the size, angle and connection of letters, line direction, shading of strokes, and layout, and interpret these with reference to a wide range of psychological and physiological states. Scientific evidence of the validity of these techniques is lacking, but they are quite widely practised, and have proved to be of value (eg in personnel selection).
2 In linguistics, the study of the writing system of a language; also the writing system itself. The system is analysed into a set of graphemes, most of which have a more-or-less systematic relationship with its sounds (as with those in *dog*). Other types of grapheme include those which indicate punctuation conventions (?, ", !, etc) and those which refer to whole words (eg &, +, Σ).

graph theory The study of networks – systems of points joined by lines. A famous unsolved problem is the travelling salesman problem: given a number of towns and the roads between them, what is the shortest route that enables a salesman to visit every one? This exemplifies the way problems in graph theory are not amenable to the calculus, and defy even the largest computers when the number of possible routes becomes vast. A more conceptual side concerns graphs of various types, and asks if there is a route visiting each vertex exactly once. Colouring questions ask if each edge and/or each vertex can be coloured with a given set of paints so that no two adjacent edges or vertices have the same colour. The four-colour theorem can be formulated as a question about graphs. It asks: given a map of *n* countries on the sphere and four colours, can each country be so coloured that no two with a common boundary have the same colour? On replacing each country by its capital, and joining capitals by a line if and only if the countries have a common border, it becomes a question about the corresponding graph.

Grappelli, Stéphane [grapelee] (1908–97) Jazz violinist, born in Paris, France. He and Django Reinhardt were the principal soloists in the Quintet of the Hot Club of France (1934–9), the first European jazz band to exert an influence in the USA. Grappelli's suave, piercing violin lines made a perfect foil for Reinhardt's busy guitar. Their partnership ended when Grappelli escaped to England during the Occupation. He returned to Paris in 1948, and continued to make international appearances.

graptolite An extinct marine animal (a hemichordate), mostly found in surface plankton, living in colonies; known from the Cambrian to the Carboniferous periods; individual polyps of colony lived in chitinous tubes arranged in single or double rows along the main axes. (Class: Graptolithina.)

Grasmere 54°28N 3°02W, pop (2000e) 1220. Scenic resort village in Cumbria, NW England, UK; by L Grasmere, 23 km/14 mi N of Kendal; home (Dove Cottage) and burial place of Wordsworth; Church of St Oswald.

Grass, Günter (Wilhelm) (1927–) Writer, born in Gdańsk, N Poland (formerly Danzig, Germany). He was educated at Danzig Volksschule and Gymnasium, the Academy of Art, Düsseldorf, and the State Academy of Fine Arts, Berlin. He served in World War 2 and was held as a prisoner-of-war. *Die Blechtrommel* (1959, The Tin Drum) was the first of the novels that have made him Germany's greatest living novelist, and it caused a furore in Germany because of its depiction of the Nazis. Intellectual and experimental, his books consistently challenge the status quo and question our reading of the past. Important books are *Katz und Maus* (1961, Cat and Mouse), *Hundejahre* (1963, Dog Years), *Örtlich betäubt* (1969, Local Anaesthetic), and *Der Butt* (1977, The Flounder). Later novels include *Kopfgeburten* (1980, Headbirths), *Ein weites Feld* (1995, A Wide Field), and *Crabwalk* (2003). He worked as a ghost-writer for the leader of the Social Democrats, Willy Brandt, and has published a collection of speeches and essays, 'Der Bürger und seine Stimme' (1974, The Citizen and his Vote). He was awarded the Nobel Prize for Literature in 1999.

grass A member of one of the largest flowering plant families, with over 9000 species distributed worldwide, including the Arctic and the Antarctic, where they are the only flowering plants to survive. They are monocotyledons, ranging from tiny annuals to perennials over 30 m/100 ft high. Most are herbaceous; a few are woody shrub- or tree-like in form; but all show great uniformity of structure. A typical grass has fibrous roots and hollow, cylindrical stems which branch at the base to form a tuft, and may also produce rhizomes or stolons, forming a turf. Long, narrow leaves grow singly from the nodes of the stem and have an upper part (the *blade*), and a lower part (the *sheath*), which fits around the stem like a sleeve. The junction of blade and sheath often bears a flap or ring of hairs (the *ligule*), which is diagnostically important. Unlike most other plants which have meristems at the tip of the shoot, those of grasses are at the base of the stem, at or even below ground level. This, together with the basal branching of the stems, is important, allowing the plant to withstand damage to the aerial parts by cutting, grazing, or trampling, with little adverse effect on further growth. Grasses are wind-pollinated, and have specialized and very reduced flowers. The stamens and ovary are enclosed in a series of small bracts or scales, together forming a spikelet. The spikelets are arranged in inflorescences ranging from dense, cylindrical spikes to loose, spreading panicles. Grasses occur in every type of habitat, terrestrial and aquatic, including the sea, and especially in the vast, open prairies, savannah, and steppe, where their ability to survive grazing allows them to dominate other vegetation. They are the most important economic plant group. As well as providing forage for wild and domesticated animals in the form of grazing, hay, and silage, they include grain-bearing species (the *cereals*), which are staple foods for most of the world's population. They also provide sugar, materials for thatching, paper, mats, and even light timber. Minor products include aromatic oils and beads. They have an important role as soil stabilizers, and are used for lawns and verges. A few are ornamentals but, conversely, a number are tenacious weeds. (Family: Gramineae.)

grassfinch A bird found mainly in Australia; usually inhabits open grasslands near water; eats seeds and insects. (Family: Estrildidae, 15 species.)

grasshopper A medium to large, terrestrial insect with hindlimbs adapted for jumping; forewings leathery; hindwings forming membranous fan, or reduced; feeds mostly on plants; many produce sound by rubbing together forewings or hindlimbs, or rubbing forewings against hindlimbs; antennae may be long (as in the family Tettigoniidae) or short (as in the family Acrididae). (Order: Orthoptera.)

grass monkey *vervet monkey*

grass mouse *fieldmouse*

grass owl An owl native to Africa, India, and Australasia; resembles barn owls but legs naked; inhabits grassland; eats small mammals; nests on ground. (Genus: *Tyto*, 3 species. Family: Tytonidae.)

grass snake A harmless snake native to the Old World from Europe to SE Asia, and to North America; lives near water; swims well; eats mainly frogs; anal gland emits foul-smelling secretion when alarmed; often called **water snake** in the USA – a name also used for snakes of other groups. (Genus: *Natrix*, many species. Family: Colubridae.)

grass tree A perennial with a woody trunk up to 4·5 m/15 ft (*Xanthorrhoea hastilis*), crowned with a tuft of narrow, arching leaves over 1 m/3·3 ft long, and a cylindrical spike of small white flowers; native to Australia, and characteristic of vegetation there; also called **blackboy**, from the scorching of the fire-resistant stems by bush-fires. As with several Australian trees, flowering is stimulated by fire. (Family: Xanthorrhoeaceae.)

grasswren *wren*

Grateful Dead, The US improvising rock band led by **Jerry Garcia** (1942–95, guitar, pedal steel guitar), with varying membership through the years since 1967 including **Ron 'Pigpen' McKernan** (1945–73, keyboards, vocals, harmonica), **Phil Lesh** (born Philip Chapman, 1940– , bass, vocals), **Bob Weir** (born Robert Hall, 1947– , guitars, vocals), and **Bill Kreutzmann** (1946– , drums). They were commonly known just as **the Dead**, and their faithful fans as Deadheads. With Garcia's death in 1995 the band split up. Garcia and other members of the band had also formed the country rock group **New Riders of the Purple Sage** in 1970.

Grattan, Henry (1746–1820) Irish statesman, born in Dublin, Ireland. In 1772 he was called to the Irish bar, and in 1775 entered the Irish parliament, where his oratory made him the leading spokesman for the patriotic party. He secured Irish free trade in 1779, and legislative independence in 1782. He was returned for Dublin in 1790, and in 1805 was elected to the House of Commons, where he fought for Catholic Emancipation.

gravel Unconsolidated deposits of rock in the form of pebbles (2–60 mm/0·08–2·5 in in size) laid down by rivers or along seashores. It may be mined for alluvial mineral deposits, but is most commonly used as an aggregate in concrete.

Gravenhage, 's- [skhrahvenhahguh] *Hague, The*

graver *burin*

Graves, Michael (1934–) Architect, born in Indianapolis, Indiana, USA. After training at the University of Cincinnati and at Harvard, he joined the architecture faculty at Princeton (1962) and established an independent practice (1964). His designs for museums, residences, housing, and urban planning projects have put him at the forefront of postmodernist architecture. His works frequently incorporate colour as architectural metaphor, and include the Fargo–Moorehead Cultural Center Bridge (1977). In 2001 he was presented with the Gold Medal of the American Institute of Architects, the AIA's lifetime achievement award.

Graves, Robert (Ranke) (1895–1985) Poet and novelist, born in London, UK. He studied at Oxford, served in the trenches in World War 1, became professor of English at Cairo, and after 1929 lived mainly in Majorca. His best-known novels are *I, Claudius* (Hawthornden and James Tait Black prizes) and its sequel, *Claudius the God* (both 1934), which were adapted for television in 1976. He wrote several autobiographical works, notably *Goodbye to All That* (1929), expressing the disillusion of the post-war generation, and *Occupation Writer* (1950), published critical essays, carried out Greek and Latin translations, and was professor of poetry at Oxford (1961–6). His *Collected Poems* (1975) draws on more than 20 volumes and confirms his status as a major poet of the 20th-c.

Graves' disease *hyperthyroidism*

Gravesend 51°27N 0°24E, pop (2001e) 51 200. Seaport in the local government district of Gravesham, Kent, SE England, UK; on S bank of the R Thames facing Tilbury; pilot station for the Port of London; birthplace of Sir Edwin Arnold, Sir Derek Barton, Thom Gunn, Katharine Hamnett; Pocahontas is buried in St George's churchyard; railway; paper, cement; highest UK temperature since records began, 38·1°C (100·6°F), recorded here, Aug 2003.

Gravettian [gravetian] A European archaeological culture of the Upper Palaeolithic Age, c.26 000–18 000 BC (sometimes referred to as the **Later Aurignacian/Later Perigordian**). It is named after the cave at La Gravette, Dordogne, SW France, notable for its associations with carved Venus figurines.

gravitation The mutually attractive force between two objects due to their masses; expressed by Newton's law of gravitation $F = Gm_1m_2/r^2$, where F is the force between objects of mass m_1 and m_2 separated by distance r, and G is the gravitational constant. The direction of force is along a line joining the two bodies. It is the weakest of all forces, important only on a large scale. The form of Newton's law was verified experimentally by determining the force between heavy spheres placed close together, as in the experiment to measure G by British scientist Henry Cavendish (1798). Newtonian theory is adequate for predictions of planetary motion to high accuracy. The improved theory is general relativity, in which gravitation is viewed as a distortion of space–time. Attempts to produce a gravitation theory consistent with quantum theory have been unsuccessful. **Gravity** refers to the intensity of gravitation at the surface of the Earth or some other celestial body.

gravitational collapse A phenomenon which occurs when the supply of nuclear energy in the core of a star runs out, and the star cools and contracts; a prediction of general relativity. This disturbs the precise balance inside the star between the inward pull of gravity and the star's gas pressure. Once the star radius is less than a critical value (Schwarzschild radius, $R = 2MG/c^2$, value 3 km/2 mi for the Sun), the collapse cannot be reversed by any force now known to physics. Implosion to a black hole seems inevitable.

gravitational constant A fundamental constant, symbol G, value $6{\cdot}673 \times 10^{-11}\text{Nm}^2/\text{kg}^2$, which measures the strength of gravitation. It is a constant of proportionality in Newton's law of gravity, and also appears in equations of general relativity.

gravitational lens A phenomenon resulting from Einstein's general theory of relativity. The theory showed that light follows a curved path when it passes close to massive objects, and thus presented the possibility that galaxies can focus the light of more distant objects along the same line of sight. This lensing effect has been observed around certain massive galaxies and clusters of galaxies.

gravitational radiation Very weak gravity waves produced when a massive body is disturbed or accelerated. The phenomenon is predicted by the general theory of relativity, but not yet observed with certainty.

gravitational redshift A frequency shifting of light to lower frequencies for sources emitting light in a relatively strong gravitational field; also called the **Einstein shift**. It means that light travelling away from a massive body appears at a lower frequency (redshifted) than expected. The redshift of light travelling away from Earth was first measured in 1961 using the Mössbauer effect. Interpreted as the faster running of clocks in regions of weaker gravitational fields, it was demonstrated by comparing atomic clocks flown at high altitude (lower gravitational field) with clocks left on the ground (higher gravitational field); the high altitude clocks ran more quickly. Considered by Einstein a test of general relativity, the effect is now viewed as a test of the equivalence principle.

gravitational waves A prediction of general relativity that changes in some large mass (eg the collapse of a star into a black hole) will produce space–time 'ripples' spreading radially from the source at the speed of light. Such waves will cause distortions in any large object through which they pass. In 1974

Russell Hulse and Joseph Taylor discovered a pulsar orbiting an invisible companion star, the orbit time shortening as predicted for a system losing energy via radiation of gravitational waves; they were awarded the 1993 Nobel Prize for Physics for their work. Gravitational wave detectors on Earth have yet to find direct evidence of such waves.

graviton A hypothetical quantum of gravitation whose role is the mediation of gravitational force between masses; mass 0, spin 2, charge 0. Gravitons are the quanta of gravitational waves, as photons are the quanta of electromagnetic waves; but, unlike photons, gravitons will interact with one another, one reason why quantum gravity is hard to formulate.

gravity *gravitation*

gravity assist The additional increment of velocity acquired by a spacecraft on passing a planet. Through accurate targeting, it can be used to speed up a spacecraft to achieve a trajectory not possible using present launch capabilities. The technique made possible the Mariner 10 mission to Mercury, the Pioneer 11 mission to Saturn, the Voyager mission beyond Jupiter, the VEGA mission to Halley's Comet, and the Galileo and Cassini-Huygens missions to Jupiter and Saturn respectively; in future it may be used to slow down spacecraft at Mercury to allow chemical rocket orbit insertion.

gravure A form of printing, known as **intaglio**, in which the image to be communicated is engraved or etched into the surface of a metal cylinder; after inking, surplus ink is removed from the surface of the cylinder, and the ink retained in the engraved cells is transferred to paper when that is brought into contact with the cylinder. Gravure is a major process in the printing of popular illustrated magazines.

Gray, Asa (1810–88) Botanist, born in Sauquoit, New York, USA. He trained in medicine, but then took up botany, becoming professor of natural history at Harvard (1842–73), and a strong Darwinian. His main works were the *Flora of North America* (1838–42), which he compiled with John Torrey, and the *Manual of the Botany of the Northern United States* (1848), often known simply as *Gray's Manual*.

Gray, Thomas (1716–71) Poet, born in London, UK. He studied at Cambridge, where in 1768 he became professor of history and modern languages. In 1742 he wrote his 'Ode on a Distant Prospect of Eton College', and began his masterpiece, 'Elegy Written in a Country Churchyard' (1751), set at Stoke Poges, Buckinghamshire. In it, he reflects on the obscure destinies of the people buried there and, through them, on the fate of all. He then settled in Cambridge, where he wrote his *Pindaric Odes* (1757). He was a friend of Horace Walpole.

gray In radioactivity, the unit of absorbed dose, ie the energy deposited in an object by radiation, divided by the mass of the object; SI unit; symbol *Gy*; 1 Gy defined as 1 J/kg.

grayling Freshwater fish (*Thymallus thymallus*) widespread in clean swift rivers of N Europe; length up to 50 cm/20 in; body silvery with longitudinal violet stripes; good food fish and popular with anglers. (Family: Thymallidae; sometimes placed in Salmonidae.)

Gray's Inn *Inns of Court*

Graz [grahts] 47°05N 15°22E, pop (2000e) 242 200. Capital of Steiermark state, SE Austria; on the R Mur, at the foot of the Schlossberg (473 m/1552 ft); second largest city in Austria; airport; railway; two universities (1585, 1811); outskirts heavily industrialized; iron, steel, coal, paper, textiles, chemicals, vehicles; opera house, Renaissance Landhaus (1557–65), Landeszeughaus (Provincial Arsenal), Gothic cathedral (15th-c); 28 m/92 ft-high clock tower (1561); Piber Stud Farm, where Lippizaner horses bred for the Spanish Riding School in Vienna, 3·5 km/2 mi NE; Austrian open air museum at Stübing, 15 km/9 mi N; International Autumn Fair (engineering and production display, end Sep); Steirischer Herbst avant-garde festival ('Styrian Autumn', Oct–Nov).

Great Australian Bight Area of the Southern Ocean off the S coast of Australia between Cape Pasley (W) and Port Lincoln (E) (1450 km/900 mi); depth 70 m/230 ft over the continental shelf to c.5600 m/18 400 ft over the Great Bight abyssal plain.

Great Awakening A widespread 18th-c Christian revival movement in North America, which reached its high point in the 1740s in New England. Jonathan Edwards and George Whitefield were among its leaders.

Great Barrier Reef Coral reef in the Coral Sea off the NE coast of Australia, part of the Coral Sea Islands Territory; 50–150 km/30–90 mi offshore and 2000 km/1200 mi long; the largest accumulation of coral known, yielding trepang, pearl-shell, and sponges to divers; the surf is violent and dangerous, but the intervening channel, clustered with atolls, forms a safe, shallow passage connected by several navigable channels with the deeps of the Coral Sea; major tourist area; world heritage site.

Great Basin Vast interior region in W USA, between (W) the Sierra Nevada and the Cascade Range and (E) the Wasatch Range and Colorado Plateau; area c.500 000 sq km/200 000 sq mi; covers parts of Oregon and Idaho, most of Nevada, W Utah, and part of SE California; rugged N–S mountain ranges; semi-arid climate; the few streams (largest are the Humboldt and Carson Rivers) drain into saline lakes or sinks; biggest lakes are the Great Salt, Utah, Sevier, Pyramid, and Walker, remnants of the enormous prehistoric lakes, Bonneville and Lahontan; also several deserts (Great Salt Lake, Mojave, Colorado, Black Rock, Smoke Creek, Death Valley, Carson Sink); Black Rock site of land speed record, 1997; agriculture possible only with irrigation; some minerals and grazing land.

Great Bear Lake Lake in Northwest Territories, NW Canada, on the Arctic Circle; 320 km/200 mi long; 40–177 km/25–110 mi wide; maximum depth 413 m/1356 ft; area 31 153 sq km/12 025 sq mi; drained SW by the Great Bear R; navigable for only four months each year because of ice.

Great Bitter Lake, Arabic **Buheiret Murrat al-Kubra** Lake on Suez Canal between Ismailiya (N) and Suez (S); Little Bitter Lake lies SE.

Great Britain *United Kingdom*

great burnet *burnet*

great circle A circle described on the surface of a sphere with its plane passing through the centre of the sphere. The shortest distance between any two points on a sphere lies along a great circle. On the Earth, lines of longitude lie on great circles.

great crested grebe A large water bird (*Podiceps cristatus*) native to Europe, Asia, Africa S of the Sahara, Australia, and New Zealand; long slender neck and long sharp bill; both sexes with head crest; catches fish by diving from surface. (Family: Podicipedidae.)

Great Dane One of the largest breeds of dog (height, 0·75 m/2½ ft), perfected in Germany from a mastiff-like ancestor; used for hunting; long powerful legs; square head with deep muzzle and pendulous ears; coat short, pale brown with dark flecks.

Great Depression The worldwide slump in output and prices, and the greatly increased levels of unemployment, which developed between 1929 and 1934. It was precipitated by the collapse of the US stock market (the Wall Street crash) in October 1929. This ended American loans to Europe and greatly reduced business confidence worldwide. A major Austrian bank also collapsed, producing destabilization in much of C and E Europe, leading to hyperinflation in Germany and thus contributing to the rise of Hitler and German national socialism.

Great Divide *Continental Divide*

Great Dividing Range Mountain range in Queensland, New South Wales, and Victoria, Australia; extends 3600 km/2200 mi from Cape York Peninsula to the Victoria–South Australia border; includes the McPherson and New England Ranges, the Australian Alps, the Blue Mts and the Grampians; rises to 2228 m/7310 ft at Mt Kosciusko.

Greater Manchester *Manchester, Greater*

Great Exhibition An international exhibition held in Hyde Park, London (May–Oct 1851). Intended as a celebration of 'the Works of Industry of all Nations', in reality it symbolized the industrial supremacy of Britain in the mid-19th-c. Prince Albert helped to organize the Exhibition, for which the Crystal Palace, designed by Joseph Paxton, was constructed.

Great Indian Desert *Thar Desert*

Great Lakes The largest group of freshwater lakes in the world, in C North America, on the Canada–USA border; drained by the St Lawrence R; consists of Lakes Superior, Michigan (the only one entirely in the USA), Huron, Erie, Ontario; sometimes L St Clair is included; water surface c.245 300 sq km/94 700 sq mi, c.87 270 sq km/33 700 sq mi in Canada; connected by navigable straits and canals (St Mary's R and the Soo Canals, Strait of Mackinac, St Clair R and Lake, Detroit R, Niagara R, Welland Canal and the St Lawrence R and Seaway), giving the lakes access to each other and to the Atlantic Ocean; used (May–Dec) for an enormous volume of coal, ore, grain, and other products; water pollution a recent problem.

Great Leap Forward A movement in China, initiated by Mao Zedong in 1958, which aimed at accelerating industrial expansion through mass participation in industrial activities such as iron smelting. Simultaneously, agricultural production was to increase following socialistic reorganization into communes. Both initiatives seriously impaired China's economic well-being.

Great Malvern *Malvern*

Great Northern War (1700–21) A war between Russia and Sweden for the mastery of the Baltic coastal region. Charles XII of Sweden defeated Peter I of Russia's army at Narva in 1700, but failed to pursue his advantage. Peter introduced sweeping military reforms, and later defeated Sweden at the battle of Poltava (1709). The war was finally concluded by the Treaty of Nystadt.

Great Plains Region of C North America; a sloping plateau, generally 650 km/400 mi wide, bordering the E base of the Rocky Mts from Alberta (Canada) to the Llano Estacado in New Mexico and Texas; includes parts of Alberta and Saskatchewan, the E parts of Montana, Wyoming, Colorado, and New Mexico, and the W parts of North Dakota, South Dakota, Nebraska, Kansas, Oklahoma, and Texas; limited rainfall, short grass; large level tracts, with some highlands (Black Hills, South Dakota), badlands (South Dakota), sand hills (Nebraska), and lowlands; drained by the headwaters of the Missouri and by the Platte, Republican, Arkansas, Kansas, and Canadian Rivers; used chiefly for stock grazing and grain growing; mineral resources of oil, natural gas, coal, and lignite; dry farming on unsuitable land and overpasturing led to the dust storms of the drought years of the mid-1930s, creating the **Dust Bowl**, semi-arid regions where wind storms carry off large quantities of topsoil.

Great Red Spot The largest, best-known, and probably longest-lived 'storm' feature of Jupiter's atmosphere; a reddish oval feature in the S hemisphere, about 30 000 km/19 000 mi across, first noted 300 years ago. It was observed in detail by Voyager spacecraft cameras for many days, and determined to be a region high in atmosphere exhibiting a counter-clockwise rotation lasting about six days. Similar but smaller (10 000 km/6000 mi) features were discovered by Voyager at other latitudes – 'white ovals'. Jupiter's clouds are basically white condensates, so the red colour of the Spot and of other Jovian clouds is ascribed to chemicals (eg sulphur, phosphorus) in the atmosphere.

Great Rift Valley *Rift Valley*

Great Salt Lake Large inland salt lake in NW Utah, USA, NW of Salt Lake City; length 120 km/75 mi; width 80 km/50 mi; maximum depth 11 m/36 ft; average depth 4 m/13 ft; fed by the Jordan, Weber, and Bear Rivers; has no outlet and fluctuates greatly in size; includes Antelope I and Fremont I; its water is 20–27% saline; commercial salt extraction; crossed by a railway (completed 1903); a remnant of the enormous prehistoric L Bonneville.

Great Salt Lake Desert Arid region in NW Utah, USA, to the W of the Great Salt L; extends 177 km/110 mi S from the Goose Creek Mts; c.10 000 sq km/4000 sq mi; Bonneville Salt Flats near the Nevada border, where world speed car records were established in the 1930s.

Great Sandy Desert N belt of the Western Australian Desert; consists mostly of sand dune, scrub and salt marsh; area c.450 000 sq km/175 000 sq mi; extends W as far as the Indian Ocean.

Great Slave Lake Lake in W Northwest Territories, C Canada; 480 km/300 mi long; 50–225 km/30–140 mi wide; maximum depth over 600 m/2000 ft; area 28 570 sq km/11 030 sq mi; contains numerous islands; drained W by the Mackenzie R; town of Yellowknife on N shore.

Great Smoky Mountains Mountain range, part of the Appalachians, on the Tennessee–North Carolina state frontier, USA; a national park, protecting the largest tract of red spruce and hardwood in the USA; rises to 2025 m/6644 ft at Clingmans Dome.

Great Society An American political term for the domestic programme of President Johnson (in office 1963–9). It was characterized by strong government programmes intended to secure social justice.

great tit A typical tit, native to Europe, NW Africa, S Asia, and Indonesia (*Parus major*), also known as **tomtit** (a name additionally used for the bluetit); plumage slate grey and yellow with black cap and throat; eats seeds, fruit, buds, and small animals; usually lives in large groups. (Family: Paridae.)

Great Train Robbery *Biggs, Ronald*

Great Trek The movement of parties of Boers (*Voortrekkers*) which made them the masters of large tracts of the interior of S Africa. They began to leave Cape Colony in 1836 in separate trekking groups. Two parties were wiped out by African resistance and malaria when they headed for Delagoa Bay in Mozambique. Some settled in the Transvaal, where they were threatened by the Ndebele. A party in Natal was massacred by the Zulu, an event avenged by the Battle of Blood River in 1838. When the British annexed Natal in 1843, the majority of the Boers returned to the interior. The British made several unsuccessful attempts to resolve the divisions in the area, but when the region was reunited it was largely under Boer control.

Great Victoria Desert or **Victoria Desert** S belt of the Western Australian Desert, N of the Nullarbor Plain; consists of sand dunes and salt marsh; area c.325 000 sq km/125 000 sq mi; contains three national parks.

Great Wall of China (Chin *chang cheng*, 'long wall') The defensive and symbolic frontier stretching 4100 km/2550 mi across N China from the Yellow Sea to the C Asian desert; a world heritage site. Under Qin Shihuangdi, using 300 000 troops, the earliest connected wall was built from 221 BC to repel attacks from the Jung and Ti nomads to the N. It was improved during later dynasties, notably during the Han (202 BC–AD 220), by extension to Yumen in the W and the addition of 25 000 turrets. Considerably later is the conserved stretch of stone-faced wall now seen by visitors at Badeling Pass, N of Beijing, which dates to the Ming dynasty (AD 1368–1644), when the wall was extended by c.1000 km/600 mi, with 15 m/40 ft cannon-towers added. The wall is c.7·6 m/25 ft high and 3·7 m/12 ft broad, made of earth and stone with a facing of bricks.

Great Zimbabwe A group of drystone enclosures near Fort Victoria, SE Zimbabwe, capital of a powerful African chiefdom in the 14th–15th-c, its prosperity based on cattle-herding, gold production, and trade; a world heritage site. The largest valley enclosure, internally subdivided, is 244 m/800 ft long, up to 5 m/16 ft thick and 10 m/33 ft high; it contains c.5150 cu m/6750 cu yd of stonework, and incorporates a 9 m/29 ft drystone tower. The population of the city was c.10–18 000.

grebe An aquatic bird, native to temperate regions or high tropical lakes worldwide; swims underwater using feet; toes lobed and slightly webbed; inhabits fresh or shallow coastal waters. Some species are small and eat invertebrates; others are large and eat fish; fish eaters eat large numbers of their own feathers. (Family: Podicipedidae, 22 species.)

Greco, El [grekoh] (Span 'the Greek'), nickname of **Domenikos Theotokopoulos** (1541–1614) Painter, born in Candia, Crete, Greece. He studied in Italy, probably as a pupil of Titian, and is known to have settled in Toledo, Spain, c.1577. He became a portrait painter whose reputation fluctuated because of the suspicion which greeted his characteristic distortions, such as his elongated, flamelike figures. His most famous painting is probably the 'Burial of Count Orgaz' (1586) in the Church of San Tomé, Toledo. Many of his works are in Toledo, where there is also the Museo del Greco.

Greece *p.657*

Greek architecture The architecture evolved by the Greek city states during the classical period, 7th–4th-c BC, and further developed in the Hellenistic kingdoms 4th–2nd-c BC. It is characterized by the use of stone or marble in post-and-lintel construction that imitated the principles and form of earlier timber buildings. The basic elements are the column, entablature, and pitched roof, with details refined over time to produce a bold yet simple unity of design. Decoration is used to enhance rather than hide structure, and is controlled according to one of three architectural orders: Doric, Ionic, and Corinthian (Tuscan and Composite were not used by the Greeks). The apogee is the Parthenon, Athens (447–438 BC). Greek architecture has had a profound influence upon much of Western architecture for over 2000 years.

Greek art The art associated with classical Greece, which can usefully be divided into four periods: *Geometric* (11th–8th-c BC), known mainly through painted pottery; *Archaic* (late 8th-c–480 BC), when oriental influences were absorbed, and the human figure emerged as a central theme; *Classical* (480–323 BC), the zenith of ancient civilization, when architecture, sculpture, and painting achieved an ideal beauty and sense of proportion that set standards for figurative art for nearly 2500 years; and *Hellenistic* (323–27 BC), which saw technically skilful and dramatic works in a variety of styles, from realism to Baroque. The tradition was prolonged by the Romans.

Greek history Throughout antiquity, Greece was poor and over-populated; this helped to make the Greeks one of the most restless and mobile peoples of the ancient world. In the Dark Ages (c.1000–800 BC) they migrated *en masse* to the shores of Asia Minor. In the Archaic period (c.800–600 BC) they colonized the entire Mediterranean and Black Sea areas, and from 400 BC they served by the thousand as mercenaries overseas. Competition for resources made them quarrelsome at home. *Stasis* – chronic, economically based feuding – was endemic to the Greek city-state (*polis*), and inter-state warfare was the norm rather than the exception. Rarely did they unite to face a common enemy – hence the ease with which they were undermined, first by Philip of Macedon (330s BC), then by Rome (2nd-c BC): Greek history is not the history of a single, unified state; it is the history of individual sub-groups (Dorians, Ionians, Aeolians) and individual city-states (such as Athens, Sparta, Corinth).

Greek Independence, War of (1820–8) The struggle of the Greeks against Turkish rule. Until 1825 Greece fought unaided; thereafter her cause was seconded by Britain, Russia, and later France. In 1830, following Turkey's naval defeat at Navarino (1827) and the Treaty of Adrianople (1829), Greek independence was guaranteed by her allies.

Greek language An Indo-European language, spoken by c.11·5 million people in Greece and nearby areas, in the Greek part of Cyprus, and as an immigrant language in several other countries. The language is known from around the 14th-c BC in the Cretan inscriptions called *Linear B*. **Mycenaean Greek** of this period is distinguished from later **Classical** or **Ancient Greek** of the 8th-c BC and after, when texts came to be written in the Greek alphabet. A later variety, **Koiné** ('common') or **Hellenistic Greek**, was spoken throughout the E Mediterranean from the 4th-c BC for c.800 years. A period of **Byzantine Greek** followed until the 15th-c, after which the language developed into **Modern Greek**, now found in two main varieties: **Dimotiki** ('popular language'), based on the spoken language, widely used in everyday communication; and **Katharévusa** ('pure language'), found in formal written contexts, and more closely reflecting the classical language.

Greek literature The earliest works belong to the oral tradition; the *Iliad* and *Odyssey* of Homer come down from c.8th-c BC. Lyric poetry was written from the 6th-c BC (elegiac by Archilochus, erotic by Sappho), and reached perfection with Pindar. The great moment of Greek drama came in the 5th-c BC, with the verse tragedies of Aeschylus, Sophocles, and Euripides, and the comedies of Aristophanes. Most of these plays are now lost. Simultaneous with these were the historical writings of Herodotos, to be followed within half a century by those of Xenophon; and then the flowering of Greek philosophy with the teachings of Socrates, and the comprehensive works of Plato and Aristotle. During the Hellenistic period (327–37 BC) prose writing continued to flourish, comedy persisted with Menander, while the Ptolemaic court at Alexandria, where Theocritus introduced pastoral poetry, also revived epic and didactic verse. Greek literature survived the Roman dominance into the 2nd-c AD with such writers as Plutarch, Longinus, and Lucian. Modern Greek writers include the poet Constantine Cavafy (1863–1933), the Nobel prizewinner poets Odysseus Elytis (1911–96) and George Seferiades (1900–71), and the novelists Nikos Kazantzakis and Matilde Serao (1856–1927).

Greek–Persian Wars *Persian Wars*

Greek Orthodox Church The self-governing (*autocephalous*) Orthodox Church of Greece. After the schism of 1054, the Orthodox Church in Greece remained under the patriarch of Constantinople, but was declared independent in 1833. The governing body is the Holy Synod, which comprises 67 metropolitan bishops, presided over by the archbishop of all Greece in the head see of Athens. In doctrine, it shares the beliefs of Orthdox Churches, and in worship uses the Byzantine liturgy. There is a strong monastic movement, still maintained in 150 monasteries.

Greek philosophy Western philosophy began with the Greeks, though 'philosophy' originally embraced much of natural science too. Four main periods span over 1000 years. The *Presocratics* (c.600–400 BC) speculated (often very imaginatively) about the natural world – its origins, dynamics, and ultimate constituents. The 5th-c and 4th-c are dominated by *Socrates*, *Plato*, and *Aristotle*, who continue to be hugely influential today and made fundamental contributions to all the main branches of philosophy. *Hellenistic philosophy* (c.323–30 BC) developed more practically-oriented philosophies of life, such as Stoicism and Epicureanism, and survived in the Roman world well into the Christian era. *Neoplatonism* was a revival of Platonism in the 1st-c BC, often synthesized with other traditions, and most fully developed by Plotinus; it remained influential philosophically for over 1000 years, and links ancient to mediaeval philosophy.

Greek religion *p.658*

Greeley, Horace (1811–72) Editor and politician, born in Amherst, New Hampshire, USA. He was editor of the weekly *New Yorker* in 1834, and in 1841 founded the daily New York *Tribune*, of which he was the leading editor until his death, exerting, without concern for popularity, a supreme influence on US opinion. The *Tribune* was at first Whig, then anti-slavery Whig, and finally extreme Republican. He maintained his anti-slavery stance throughout the Civil War. After Lee's surrender he warmly advocated a universal amnesty; but his signing the bail-bond of Jefferson Davis awakened a storm of public indignation. He made a bid in 1872 for the presidency, but died before the election was completed.

Green, Lucinda, *née* **Prior-Palmer** (1953–) Three-day eventer, born in London, UK. She is the only person to win the Badminton Horse Trials six times (1973, 1976–7, 1979, 1983–4), and the

Greece

□ International Airport

ancient **Hellas**, Gr **Ellás**, official name **The Hellenic Republic**, Gr **Elliniki Dimokratia**

Local name Ellás

Timezone GMT +2

Area 131 957 km²/50 935 sq mi

Population total (2002e) 10 994 000

Status Republic

Date of independence 1830

Capital Athens (Athínai)

Languages Greek (official), English and French widely spoken

Ethnic groups Greek (98%), Albanian, Slav, Turkish minorities, and others (2%)

Religions Christian (98%) (Greek Orthodox 97·5%, Roman Catholic 0·4%, Protestant 0·1%), Muslim, Judaism, and others (2%)

Physical features Located in SE Europe, occupying the S part of the Balkan peninsula and numerous islands in the Aegean and Ionian seas; mainland includes the Peloponnese (S), connected via the narrow Isthmus of Corinth; over 1400 islands (only 169 inhabited), including Crete, the largest, 8336 km²/3218 sq mi, Rhodes, Milos, Corfu, Lesbos, Kos; nearly 80% of Greece mountainous or hilly; Pindus Mts run N to S; highest point, Mt Olympus, 2917 m/9570 ft; principal rivers include the Néstos, Strimón, Arakhthos; c.30% of land arable or under permanent cultivation; c.20% forested.

Climate Mediterranean climate for coast and islands, with mild, rainy winters and hot, dry summers; rainfall almost entirely in winter; island of Corfu receives maximum rainfall 1320 mm/52 in; severe winters in mountains; average annual temperatures 9°C (Jan), 28°C (Jul) in Athens.

Currency 1 euro = 100 cents (previous to February 2002, 1 Drachma (Dr) = 100 lepta)

Economy Strong service sector accounts for c.60% of national income; agriculture based on cereals, cotton, tobacco, fruit, figs, raisins, wine, olive oil, vegetables; major tourist area, especially on islands; world's largest shipping fleet (under own and other flags); member of the EC from 1981.

GDP (2002e) $203·3 bn, per capita $19 100

Human Development Index (2002) 0·885

History Prehistoric civilization culminated in the Minoan-Mycenean culture of Crete; Dorians invaded from the N, 12th-c BC; Greek colonies established along N and S Mediterranean and on the Black Sea; many city-states on mainland, notably Sparta and Athens; Persian invasions, 5th-c BC, repelled at Marathon, Salamis, Plataea, Mycale; Greek literature and art flourished, 5th-c BC; conflict between Sparta and Athens (Peloponnesian War) weakened both, and hegemony passed to Thebes, and then Macedon under Philip II, 4th-c BC; his son, Alexander the Great, conquered the Persian Empire; Macedonian power broken by the Romans, 197 BC; part of the Eastern Roman and Byzantine empires; ruled by the Ottoman Turks from 15th-c until 19th-c; national reawakening led to independence as kingdom, 1830; territorial gains after Balkan War and World War 1; absorbed over 1 00 000 refugees after defeat in Asia Minor, 1922; republic established, 1924–35; German occupation, 1941–4; civil war, 1944–9; military coup, 1967; abolition of monarchy, 1969; democracy restored, 1974; governed by a Prime Minister; Cabinet, unicameral Parliament, and President.

Monarch

1935 Georgios Kondylis *Regent*
1935–47 Georgios (George) II
1947–64 Pavlos (Paul) I
1964–7 Konstantinos (Constantine) II
1967–73 *Military junta*
1973 Georgios Papadopoulos *Regent*

Head of State

1973 Georgios Papadopoulos
1973–4 Phaedon Gizikis
1974–5 Michael Stasinopoulos
1975–80 Konstantinos Tsatsos
1980–5 Konstantinos Karamanlis
1985–90 Christos Sartzetaki
1990–5 Konstantinos Karamanlis
1995– Kostas Stephanopoulos

Head of Government

1973–4 Adamantios Androutsopoulos
1974–80 Konstantinos Karamanlis
1980–1 Georgios Rallis
1981–9 Andreas Georgios Papandreou
1989 Tzannis Tzannetakis
1989–90 Xenofon Zolotas
1990–3 Konstantinos Mitsotakis
1993–6 Andreas Papandreou
1996–2004 Kostas Simitis
2004– Kostas Karamanlis

Badminton and Burghley Horse Trials in the same year, on *George* in 1977. She was individual European champion in 1975 and 1977, and the 1982 world champion on *Regal Realm*, when she also won a team gold medal. She married Australian eventer **David Green** in 1981 (marriage dissolved, 1992).

Green (politics) *Greens*

green algae A large and diverse group of alga-like plants characterized by the photosynthetic pigments, chlorophylls *a* and *b*, which give them their green colour; typically storing food as starch in chloroplasts; found predominantly in fresh water; many have motile stages (*zoospores*) that swim using flagella. (Class: Chlorophyceae.)

Greenaway, Kate, popular name of **Catherine Greenaway** (1846–1901) Artist and book-illustrator, born in London, UK. She became well known in the 1880s for her coloured portrayals of child life, in such works as *The Birthday Book* (1880). The *Greenaway Medal* is awarded annually for the best British children's book artist.

Greek religion

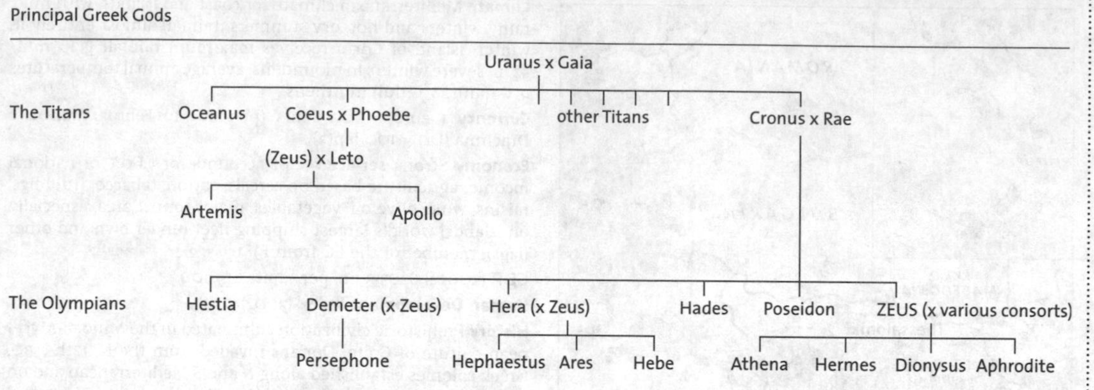

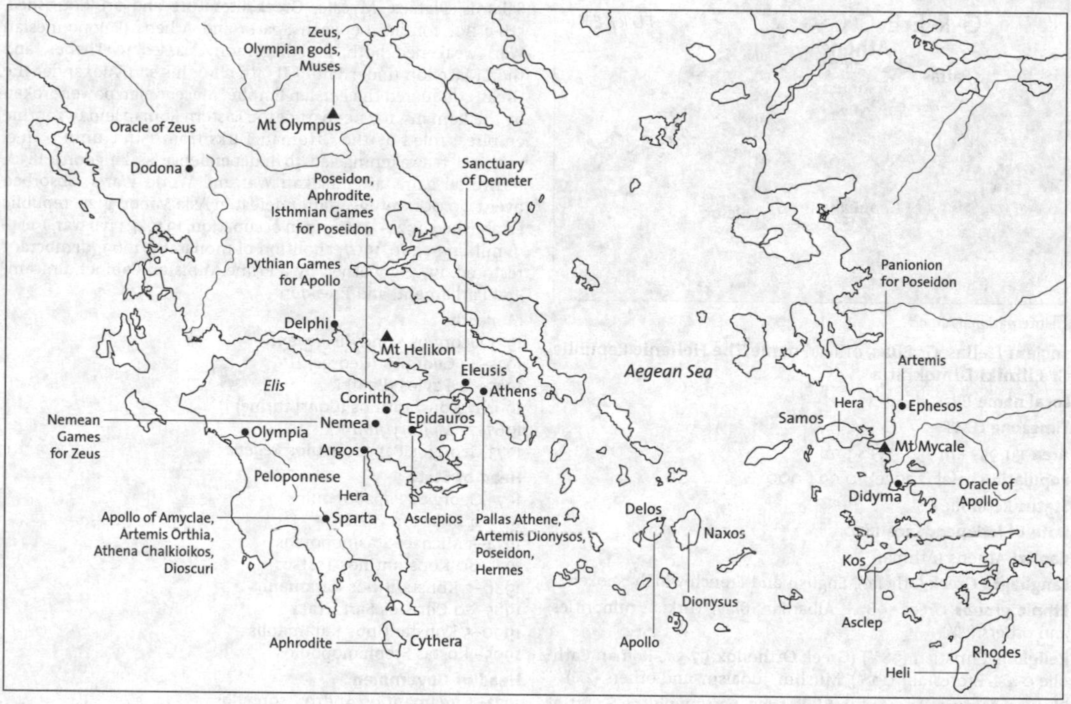

The religion of the Ancient Greeks was polytheistic, as were earlier systems of belief in the Near East. The gods each had a sphere of influence (eg Poseidon over the sea) or an attachment to a locality (eg Athena at Athens); often both. Though mythologists try to systematize the relationships between the gods, it is unwise to take their tidying up too seriously. It is doubtful whether the average Greek knew more than is contained in Homer. Besides the 12 major Olympian gods, there were later introductions of 'Oriental' deities, especially female, such as Cybele and Isis, who acquired great influence. The Homeric gods are very human in their passions and spiteful jealousies; the main difference is that they do not eat human food, and they do not die. They shade into a lower group of demi-gods and heroes, special people whose cults centred on their tombs. In the cults, ritual and sacrifice were important duties, in return for which the suppliant expected benefits. The system had to be seen to work, as in the case of the oracle at Delphi. In the 5th-c the whole basis of religion was challenged by the Sophists, and the weakening of supernatural belief reinforced Greek humanism. Yet, at the same time, the Eleusinian and Orphic mystery cults began to grow; though highly secret, they were concerned with personal survival after death. Finally, after Alexander the Great had himself proclaimed as a god, the way was open to the ruler-cults of the Roman Empire.

Greenaway, Peter (1942–) Film-maker and painter, born in Newport, SE Wales, UK Trained as a painter, he first exhibited at the Lord's Gallery in 1964. Employed at the Central Office of Information (1965–76), he worked as an editor and began making his own short films, gaining a reputation on the international festival circuit with such works as *A Walk Through H* (1978) and *The Falls* (1980), before *The Draughtsman's Contract* (1982) won him critical acclaim and a wider audience. His later works explore such preoccupations as sex, death, decay, and gamesmanship, and include *The Belly of An Architect* (1987), *Drowning By Numbers* (1988), *The Cook, The Thief, His Wife and Her Lover* (1989), *Prospero's Books* (1991), *The Baby of Macon* (1993), and *The Pillow-Book* (1996). *8 ½ Women* appeared in 1999.

green belt In the UK, a planning measure in which areas are designated free from development to prevent urban sprawl encroaching into the countryside, and the merging of neighbouring towns. It surrounds existing major urban areas, not necessarily continuously. It provides open land for recreation, and protects agricultural land. The concept is incorporated into garden cities and new towns.

Greene, Maurice (1974–) Athlete, born in Kansas City, Kansas, USA. Among his achievements are World Championship gold medals for the 100 m in 1997 and 1999 (world record), and for the 200 m in 1999.

Greene, (Henry) Graham (1904–91) Writer, born in Berkhamsted, Hertfordshire, SE England, UK. He studied at Oxford, converted from Anglicanism to Catholicism (1926), and moved to London, where he became a journalist and then a freelance writer. His early novels, beginning with *The Man Within* (1929), and 'entertainments', such as *Stamboul Train* (1932), use the melodramatic technique of the thriller. In his major novels, central religious issues and moral dilemmas emerge, first apparent in *Brighton Rock* (1938), and more explicit in *The Power and the Glory* (1940), *The End of the Affair* (1951), and *A Burnt-Out Case* (1961). He also wrote several plays, film scripts (notably, *The Third Man*, 1949), short stories, and essays, as well as three volumes of autobiography. His plays include *The Complaisant Lover* (1959). His later works include *Dr Fischer of Geneva* (1980), *Monsignor Quixote* (1982), and *The Tenth Man* (1985). He lived in Antibes, France, for many years.

Greene, Nathanael (1742–86) US general, born in Warwick, Rhode Island, USA. In the American Revolution, he fought (1775–6) at Boston, Trenton, the Brandywine, and Germanton, and in 1780 took command of the Southern army, which had just been defeated by Cornwallis. He was defeated by Cornwallis at Guildford Courthouse (1781), but the victory was so costly that Greene was able to recover South Carolina and Georgia, paving the way to American victory in the South. He was considered second only to Washington as a general.

Greene, Robert (1558–92) Playwright, born in Norwich, Norfolk, E England, UK. He studied at Oxford and Cambridge, moved to London, and began to write a stream of plays and romances, his most popular work being the comedy *Friar Bacon and Friar Bungay* (c.1589). He helped to lay the foundations of English drama, and his *Pandosto* (1588) was a source for Shakespeare's *The Winter's Tale*. In his final years, his work grew more serious, and after his death appeared his *A Groat's Worth of Wit bought with a Million of Repentance* (1592), in which he lays bare the wickedness of his former life.

greenfinch A bird of the finch genus, *Carduelis* (4 species), native to S Europe and S Asia; inhabits forest and cultivated areas; eats seeds and insects; closely related to goldfinches. (Family: Fringillidae.)

greenfly A soft-bodied aphid that feeds by sucking plant sap; wingless female has plump, greenish body, winged male darker; secretes honeydew, and may be tended by ants. It has a complex life cycle, with up to 10 generations each year produced asexually. It can be a serious pest when present in large numbers.

Greengard, Paul (1925–) Biochemist, born in New York City, New York, USA. He studied at Johns Hopkins University (1953), and became professor of pharmacology and psychiatry at Yale University School of Medicine (1968–83), and head of the Laboratory of Molecular and Cellular Neuroscience, The Rockefeller University (from 1983). He shared the 2000 Nobel Prize for Physiology or Medicine with Arvid Carlsson and Eric Kandel for their discoveries concerning signal transduction in the nervous system.

Greenham Common The site of a US military base in West Berkshire, S England, UK subjected to continuous picketing during most of the 1980s by the Women's Peace movement, opposed in particular to the siting of Cruise missiles in Britain, and in general to nuclear weaponry. Following the end of the Cold War, the missiles were withdrawn and the base closed down in 1992.

greenheart An evergreen tree (*Nectandra rodiaei*) growing to 18 m/60 ft, native to subtropical South America; leaves alternate, oval, leathery; flowers greenish, bell-shaped, 6-petalled; berries black. (Family: Lauraceae.)

greenhouse effect A planetary atmosphere warming phenomenon, resulting from the absorption of infrared radiation by atmospheric constituents. Radiant energy arrives at the planetary surface mainly as visible light from the Sun, which is then re-emitted by the surface at infrared wavelengths as heat. Carbon dioxide and water vapour in the atmosphere absorb this infrared radiation and behave as a blanket, with the net effect that atmospheric temperatures rise. On Earth, the burning of fossil fuels and large-scale deforestation enhance the effect, so that there is likely to be a gradual increase in mean air temperature of several degrees, with the consequent melting of polar ice and a rise in mean sea level. Experimental models predict global temperature increases of between 1°C and 5°C by 2050, but there are many uncertainties about possible effects. It is also likely that global rainfall patterns will shift away from the sub-tropical areas towards higher latitudes, so disrupting present agricultural patterns. The energy balance between incoming solar radiation and outgoing radiation (both heat and reflected sunlight) takes place at the top of the atmosphere. For Earth, the warming effect is about 35°C at the surface; for Venus, in spite of reflective cloud cover, surface temperatures of over 400°C are reached. It is postulated that early Venus had oceans that were warmed by a carbon dioxide greenhouse effect, leading to the evaporation of water which, in turn, amplified warming and produced a 'runaway' greenhouse effect and the total loss of surface liquid water (later lost to space). (The term 'greenhouse' is misleading, since the mechanism by which glasshouses provide warming is mainly due to the inhibition of convection.)

Greenland *p.660*

Greenland Sea area 1 205 000 sq km/465 000 sq mi. Gulf connecting the Atlantic and Arctic Oceans; bounded W by Greenland, E by Svalbard; cold surface current from the Arctic brings icebergs and fog; depths range from c.180 m/590 ft on the continental shelf to 3535 m/11 598 ft in the abyssal plain.

Greenland shark Very large shark (*Somniosus microcephalus*) widespread in the N Atlantic and Arctic Oceans; length up to 6·5 m/21 ft; weight 1400 kg/3000 lb; greyish brown; feeds on fish, seals, seabirds, and squid; in the past was fished commercially around Greenland. (Family: Dalatiidae.)

Green Line **1** The dividing line between Muslim W Beirut and Christian E Beirut, Lebanon, introduced during the 1975–6 civil war.

2 The dividing line between N (Turkish) and S (Greek) sectors of Nicosia.

green manure A crop which is ploughed into the soil when green to improve its humus content and water-retaining capacity. Mustard and grass can be used in this way, as can shrubs, herbs, and the branches of certain trees.

green monkey *vervet monkey*

green monkey disease A rare but serious virus infection with widespread tissue and organ involvement and high mortality; also known as **Marburg disease**. It occurs in scattered out-

Greenland

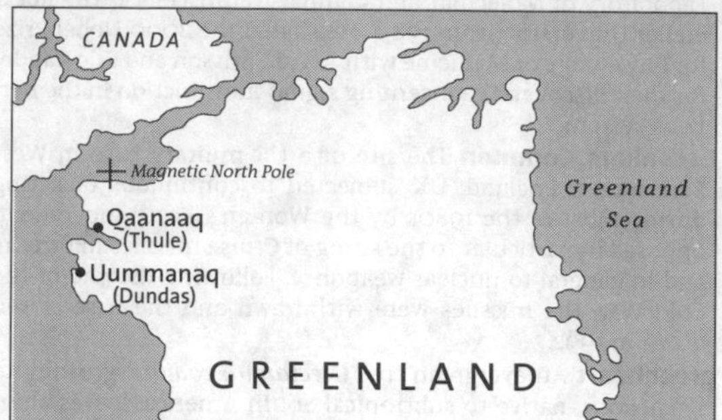

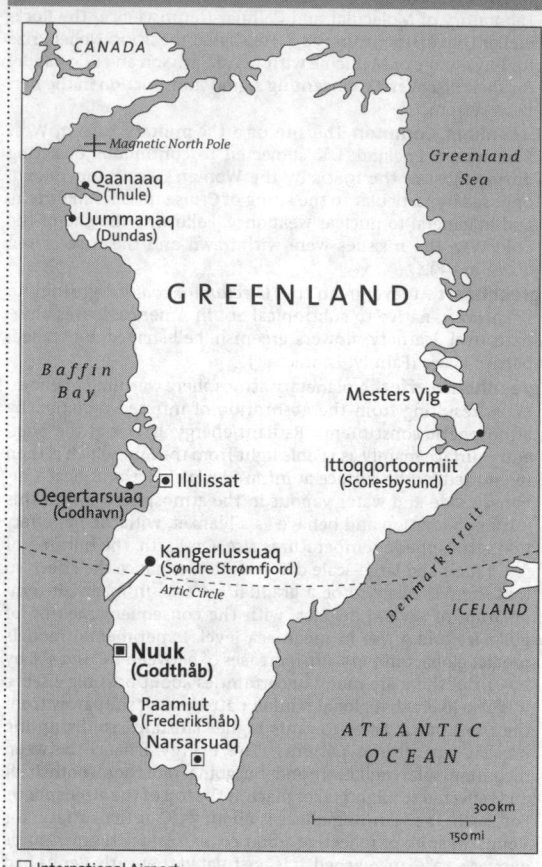

Dan **Grønland**, Eskimo **Kalâtdlit-Nunât**

Local names Kalaalit Nunaat (Greenlandic), Grønland (Danish), Kalâtdlit-Nunât (Inuit)

Timezone GMT 0, -1, -4;

Area 2 175 600 km²/839 800 sq mi

Population total (2000e) 60 000

Status Self-governing province of Denmark

Capital Nuuk (Godthåb)

Languages Danish (official), Inuit

Ethnic groups Largely Inuit (Eskimo), with Danish admixtures

Religions Lutheran, Shamanist

Physical features Located in N Atlantic and Arctic Oceans; largely covered by an ice-cap (up to 4300 m/14 000 ft thick); coastal mountains rise to 3702 m/12 145 ft at Gunnbjørn Fjeld (SE); less than 5% of island is habitable.

Climate Arctic to subarctic.

Currency 1 Danish Krone (Dkr) = 100 óre

Economy Largely dependent on fishing from ice-free SW ports; hunting for seal and fox furs in N and E; reserves of lead, zinc, molybdenum, uranium, coal, cryolite.

GDP (2001e) $1·1 bn, per capita $20 000

History Settled by seal-hunting Eskimos from North America c.2500 BC; Norse settlers in SW, 12th–15th-c AD; explored by Frobisher and Davis, 16th-c; Danish colony from 1721; self-governing province of Denmark, 1979; elected Provincial Council sends two members to the Danish Parliament.

Head of State (Monarch)
1972– Margrethe II

Head of Government
1987–2002 Jonathan Motzfeldt
2002– Hans Enoksen

breaks in Africa. The natural animal reservoir of the disease is unknown.

Green Mountain Boys In the American Revolution, an insurrectional group of settlers, led by Ethan Allen, which created the state of Vermont from territory disputed between New York and New Hampshire. Of many rural insurrections in early America, the Green Mountain Boys was the only one that succeeded. They helped capture the British fort at Ticonderoga, on L Champlain (1775). The cannon taken were important in the successful American siege of occupied Boston.

green paper In the UK, a document published by the government for discussion by interested parties, usually prior to formulating or changing policy. The practice first began in the late 1960s in response to calls for more consultation and open government.

Greenpeace An international environmental pressure group which began in Canada and the USA in 1971, and was set up in the UK in 1976. It campaigns by direct action (non-violent, passive resistance) against commercial whaling and seal culling, the dumping of toxic and radioactive waste at sea, and the testing of nuclear weapons.

green pound The special agricultural exchange rates in the EU, which ensure that currency movements are not reflected in national farm prices. The aim is that the price of each agricultural product should be the same throughout the EU. If ordinary exchange rates were used, prices would be changing continuously as exchange rates vary. Different 'green currency' exchange rates are therefore fixed for different products, and special adjustments are made from time to time to offset the gap between the green exchange rate and the national exchange rate. This is the *Monetary Compensation Amount (MCA)*.

Green Revolution A description for the phenomenal increase in cereal output and cash returns which occurred in some developing countries during the 1960s and 70s. This was made possible by Borlaug's plant breeding research in Mexico, which produced high-yielding dwarf wheat varieties, and by work at the International Rice Research Institute in the Philippines, which did the same for rice varieties. Success with these new varieties depended on a monocultural, integrated production system, with high fertilizer applications, adequate water supplies, fossil fuels, and agrochemical weed and pest controls. It benefited a relatively small number of farmers.

Greens A label applied to members of political parties and social movements which espouse ideologies having as a central tenet a concern over the damaging effect human activity is having on the environment. The first green party (the Values Party) was formed in New Zealand in 1972, to be followed in the UK in 1974 by People. Since then, almost all advanced industrial countries have seen the formation of at least one, and in some cases more than one, green party. The most successful in parliamentary terms has been the German Green Party, which has had members of the Bundestag since 1983 and of the European Parliament since 1984, and which entered government as part of a national coalition in 1998. The most successful in terms of votes was the UK Green Party, which obtained 15% of the national vote in the 1989 European elections. Since then, however, the fortunes of the UK Green Party have declined dramatically. There is also a much larger green movement made up of environmental pressure groups and individuals whose occupations or lifestyles are informed by environmental concerns. This wider movement has grown rapidly since 1987, and has had a significant political impact in many countries, forcing environmental issues onto the political agenda, and promoting legislation and other government measures to enhance environmental protection. Generally, greens attribute the environmental crisis to industrialism, though some (*ecosocialists*) also blame capitalism, some (*ecofeminists*) blame patriarchy, and yet others (*ecoanarchists*) blame the impact on individual behaviour of increasing social and political control.

greenshank A wading bird (*Tringa nebularia*), native to N Europe and N Asia; migrates to Africa, S Asia, Australia, and New Zealand for winter; long pale green legs; long bill slightly upturned; inhabits fresh water, estuaries, and upland moors. (Family: Scolopacidae.)

green tourism *tourist industry*

green turtle The only vegetarian sea turtle (*Chelonia mydas*); worldwide in warm seas; slender head with saw-like jaws; eats mainly sea-grass and sea weeds; turtle soup made from this species; endangered due to overhunting. (Family: Chelonidae.)

Greenwich [grenich], Anglo-Saxon **Grenawic** 51°28N 0°00, pop (2001e) 214 500. Borough of EC Greater London, UK; S of R Thames; site of the original Royal Greenwich Observatory; meridians of longitude reckoned from this point; also the source of world time standard, Greenwich Mean Time (GMT); birthplace of Henry VIII, Elizabeth I, and Mary I; railway; Greenwich Hospital (1694), Royal Naval College, National Maritime Museum, including Inigo Jones' Queen's House (1616–35); clipper *Cutty Sark* and Francis Chichester's *Gypsy Moth IV* at Greenwich Pier; maritime Greenwich made a world heritage site in 1997; Millennium Dome.

Greenwich Mean Time (GMT) [grenich] The basis for world time zones, set by the local time at Greenwich, near London. This is located on the Greenwich Meridian, longitude 0°, from which other time zones are calculated. It was originally established within the UK to regularize railway timetables nationally, and later adopted internationally. It is now known as **coordinated universal time**.

Greenwich Village [grenich] A district of Manhattan, New York City, USA, which became famous during the 20th-c as the quarter of writers, intellectuals, and bohemians. It has recently developed into a more fashionable residential area.

Greenwood, Walter (1903–74) Writer, born in Salford, Greater Manchester, NW England, UK. His best-known novel is *Love on the Dole* (1933), inspired by his experiences of unemployment and depression in the early 1930s. It made a considerable impact as a document of the times, and was subsequently dramatized in 1934 and filmed in 1941.

Greer, Germaine (1939–) Feminist, writer, and lecturer, born in Melbourne, Victoria, SE Australia. She studied at Melbourne, Sydney, and Cambridge universities, and became a lecturer in English at Warwick University (1968–73) and is currently professor of English and Comparative Studies there. Her controversial and highly successful book *The Female Eunuch* (1970) portrayed marriage as a legalized form of slavery for women, and attacked the misrepresentation of female sexuality by male-dominated society. She was director (1979–82) of the Tulsa Center for the Study of Women's Literature, OK, and since 1989 has been special lecturer and unofficial fellow of Newnham College, Cambridge. Later works include *The Change* (1991), *Slip-shod Sibyls* (1995), *The Whole Woman* (1999), which takes stock of the current situation of the feminist movement, and *The Beautiful Boy* (2003).

Gregorian calendar A calendar instituted in 1582 by Pope Gregory XIII, and now used in most of the world. Its distinguishing feature is that a century year is a leap year if, and only if, divisible by 400. This gives a year of 365·2425 days when averaged over 400 years, very close to the actual value 365·2422 days. When introduced, a discrepancy of 10 days had built up, which was eliminated by jumping straight from the 4 to 15 October in Catholic countries. Britain and its colonies (including America) switched in 1752, and also moved New Year's Day from 25 March back to 1 January.

Gregorian chant The monophonic and (in its purest form) unaccompanied chant of the Roman Catholic liturgy. The earliest musical sources date from the late 9th-c and 10th-c, but the compilation of the repertory has been credited to Pope Gregory the Great. Its rhythmic interpretation has been the subject of much controversy, since the sources do not indicate note lengths.

Gregory I, St, known as **the Great** (c.540–604) Pope (590–604), a Father of the Church, born in Rome, Italy. Appointed praetor of Rome, he left this office (c.575), distributed his wealth among the poor, and withdrew into a monastery of Rome. It was here that he saw some Anglo-Saxon youths in the slave market, and was seized with a longing to convert their country to Christianity. As pope, he was a great administrator, reforming all public services and ritual, and systematizing the sacred chants. In his writings the whole dogmatic system of the modern Church is fully developed. He died in Rome, and was canonized on his death; feast day 12 March.

Gregory VII, St, originally **Hildebrand** (c.1020–85) Pope (1073–85), the great representative of the temporal claims of the mediaeval papacy, born near Soana, NW Italy. He became a cardinal in 1049. As pope, he worked to change the secularized condition of the Church, which led to conflict with the German Emperor Henry IV, who declared Gregory deposed in a diet at Worms (1076), but then yielded to him after excommunication. In 1080 Henry resumed hostilities, appointing an antipope (Clement III), and after a siege took possession of Rome (1084). Gregory was freed by Norman troops, but was forced to withdraw to Salerno, where he died. He was canonized in 1606; feast day 25 May.

Gregory XIII, originally **Ugo Buoncompagni** (1502–85) Pope (1572–85), born in Bologna, N Italy. He was professor of law at Bologna for several years, settled at Rome in 1539, was one of the theologians of the Council of Trent, and became a cardinal in 1565. As pope, he displayed great zeal for the promotion of education; many of the colleges in Rome were wholly or in part endowed by him. He also corrected the errors of the Julian calendar, and in 1582 introduced the calendar named after him.

Gregory XI, originally **Pierre-Roger de Beaufort** (1329–78) Pope (1370–8), born in Limoges-Fourche, France. He was the last French pope, and the last of the Avignonese popes when Avignon was the papal seat (1309–77). Made a cardinal (1348) by his uncle, Pope Clement VI, he was elected pope at Avignon (1370) to succeed Urban V. Encouraged by Catherine of Siena, in 1377 he eventually succeeded in returning the papacy to Rome under Pope Urban VI.

Gregory of Nazianzus, St [nazianzus] (c.329–90) Bishop and theologian, born in Cappadocia, Asia Minor. Educated at Caesarea, Alexandria, and Athens, he became a close friend of Basil the Great, and was made Bishop of Sasima, but withdrew to a life of religious study at Nazianzus. Feast day 2 January (W), 25 or 30 January (E).

Gregory of Nyssa, St [nisa] (c.331–95) Christian theologian, born in Caesarea, Asia Minor. He was consecrated Bishop of Nyssa in Cappadocia by his brother Basil the Great (c.371). Deposed in 376 by the Arian Emperor Valens, he regained office in 378 after Valens's death. An outstanding scholarly defender of orthodoxy, he wrote several theological works, sermons, and epistles. Feast day 9 March.

Gregory of Tours, St [toor], originally **Georgius Florentinus** (c.538–c.594) Frankish historian, born in Arverna (now Clermont). His recovery from sickness, through a pilgrimage to the grave of St Martin of Tours, led Gregory to devote himself to the Church, and he was elected Bishop of Tours in 573. His *Historia Francorum* is the chief authority for the history of Gaul in the 6th-c. Feast day 17 November.

Grenada *p.662*

grenade A munition, typically an explosive-packed container with a simple ring-pull fuse, designed for use in close-quarters

Grenada

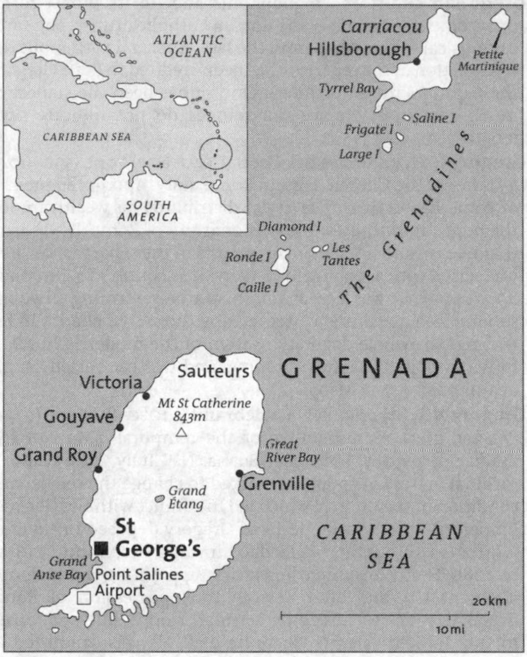

☐ International Airport

[grenayda]

Local name Grenada

Timezone GMT −4

Area 344 km²/133 sq mi

Population total (2002e) 101 900

Status Independent state within the Commonwealth

Date of independence 1974

Capital St George's

Languages English (official), French patois

Ethnic groups African descent (84%), mixed (12%), E Indian (3%) European (1%)

Religions Roman Catholic (64%), Protestant (21%)

Physical features Most southerly of the Windward Is, E Caribbean; comprises the main island of Grenada, 34 km/21 mi long, 19 km/12 mi wide; and the S Grenadines; Grenada volcanic in origin, with a ridge of mountains along its entire length, the highest point, Mt St Catherine, rising to 843 m/2766 ft; many rivers and lakes, including Grand Étang.

Climate Sub-tropical climate; average annual temperature 23°C; wet season (Jun–Dec); annual rainfall varies from 1270 mm/150 in (coast) to 5000 mm/200 in (interior); lies within Caribbean hurricane zone.

Currency 1 East Caribbean Dollar (EC$) = 100 cents

Economy Economy based on agriculture, notably fruit, vegetables, cocoa, nutmegs, bananas, mace; processing of agricultural products and their derivatives.

GDP (2002e) $440 mn, per capita $5000

Human Development Index (2002) 0·747

History Visited by Columbus and named Concepción, 1498; settled by French, mid-17th-c; ceded to Britain, 1763; retaken by France, 1779; ceded again to Britain, 1783; British Crown Colony, 1877; independence, 1974; popular people's revolution, 1979; Prime Minister Maurice Bishop killed during further uprising, 1983; a group of Caribbean countries requested US involvement, and troops invaded the island in Oct 1983, to restore stable government; governed by a Senate, House of Representatives, Prime Minister, and Cabinet.

Head of State
(British monarch represented by Governor-General)
1996– Daniel Charles Williams

Head of Government
1974–9 Eric Matthew Gairy
1979–83 Maurice Bishop
1983–4 Nicholas Brathwaite *Chairman of Interim Council*
1984–9 Herbert Augustus Blaize
1989–90 Ben Jones *Acting*
1990–5 Nicholas Brathwaite
1995 George Brizan
1995– Keith Mitchell

fighting. It may be either thrown by hand or projected from a launcher. Catapulted grenades were documented in China, 1042. Modern varieties include smoke, white phosphorous, shrapnel, delayed fuse, and stun grenades.

grenadier (zoology) *rat-tail*

Grenadines, The [grenadeenz] Group of 600 small islands and islets in the Windward Is, E Caribbean; administered by St Vincent (**N Grenadines**) and Grenada (**S Grenadines**); includes Carriacou, Union, Mustique, Bequia, Canouan, Mayreau; five airfields; some agriculture, tourism.

Grenoble [gruhnobl], ancient **Cularo**, **Gratianopolis** 45°12N 5°42E, pop (2000e) 157 000. Ancient fortified city and capital of Isère department, E France; at confluence of rivers Isère and Drac, in a striking Alpine setting; Mont Blanc to the NE; prospered during French colonial period; railway; bishopric; university (1339); electro-metallurgy, chemicals, plastic products, electrical engineering, nuclear research, glove manufacturing, walnuts; important sports and tourist centre; skiing facilities to the E and SW; World Trade Centre, Industrial Science Park (the Zirst); 12th–13th-c cathedral of Notre-Dame, 13th-c brick church of St André, Palais de Justice (part 15th-c); scene of 1964 Olympic skating championships and 1968 Winter Olympics.

Grenville, Sir Richard (c.1542–91) English naval commander, a cousin of Sir Walter Raleigh. He fought in Hungary and Ireland (1566–9), was knighted c.1577, and in 1585 commanded the seven ships carrying 100 English colonists to Roanoke Island, NC. In 1591, as commander of the *Revenge*, he fought alone against a large Spanish fleet off the Azores, dying of wounds on board a Spanish ship.

Grenville, William Wyndham Grenville, 1st Baron (1759–1834) British statesman, the son of George Grenville. He studied at Oxford, entered parliament in 1782, and became paymaster-general (1783), home secretary (1790), and foreign secretary (1791). He resigned with Pitt in 1801 on the refusal of George III to agree to Catholic Emancipation. In 1806–7 he formed the coalition 'Government of All the Talents', which abolished the slave trade.

Gresham, Sir Thomas [greshm] (1519–79) Financier, born in London, UK. He studied at Cambridge, passed into the Mercers' Company, and in 1551 was employed as 'king's merchant' at Antwerp. He was knighted in 1559, and was for a time ambassador at Brussels. An observation in economics is attributed to him (*Gresham's law*): if there are two coins of equal legal exchange value, and one is suspected to be of lower intrinsic value, the 'bad coin' will tend to drive the other out of circulation, as people will begin to hoard it. He built the Royal Exchange (1566–8), and founded Gresham College.

Gretzky, Wayne, nickname **the Great One** or **the Great Gretzky** (1961–) Ice-hockey player, born in Brantford, Ontario, SE Canada. He joined the Edmonton Oilers in 1979, and scored more goals in a season than any other player (92 in 1981–2), and a record 215 points in 1985–6. Voted the Most Valuable

Player in the National Hockey League for the ninth year in 1989, he is the NHL's all-time leading scorer (894 goals, 1963 assists). A member of four Stanley Cup winning teams with Edmonton, he transferred to the Los Angeles Kings in 1988 for a record $15 million, and in 1993 agreed a $25·5 million contract, making him the NHL's highest-paid player. He played with the New York Rangers from 1997 until his retirement in 1999. His shirt number, 99, was also retired. He was elected to the ice-hockey Hall of Fame in 1999.

Greville, Sir Fulke, 1st Baron Brooke (1554–1628) Poet, born at Beauchamp Court, Warwickshire, C England, UK. He studied at Cambridge, and travelled abroad on diplomatic missions. He wrote several didactic poems, over 100 sonnets, and two tragedies. Knighted in 1597, he was Chancellor of the Exchequer (1614–22), and created baron in 1621. He died after being stabbed by a servant. His life of Sir Philip Sidney appeared in 1652.

Grey, Charles Grey, 2nd Earl (1764–1845) British statesman and prime minister (1830–4), born in Fallodon, Northumberland, NE England, UK. He studied at Cambridge, became a Whig MP in 1786, and was a leading supporter of parliamentary reform in the 1790s. In 1806 he became First Lord of the Admiralty, foreign secretary, and Leader of the House of Commons. In 1807 he succeeded his father as second Earl Grey. In 1830 he formed a government promising peace, retrenchment, and reform, and after considerable difficulties secured the passage of the 1832 Reform Bill. In the new parliament he carried the Act for the abolition of slavery in the colonies, but was forced to resign following disagreement over the Irish question.

Grey, Lady Jane (1537–54) Queen of England for nine days in 1553, born in Bradgate, Leicestershire, the eldest daughter of Henry Grey, Marquess of Dorset, and great-granddaughter of Henry VII. In 1553 the Duke of Northumberland, foreseeing the death of Edward VI, aimed to secure the succession by marrying Jane (against her wish) to his fourth son, Lord Guildford Dudley. Three days after Edward's death (9 Jul), she was named as his successor, but was forced to abdicate in favour of Mary, who had popular support. She was imprisoned, and beheaded on Tower Green.

Grey, Zane, pseudonym of **Pearl Grey** (1872–1939) Novelist, born in Zanesville, Ohio, USA. He first worked as a dentist, but after a trip out West in 1907 began to write Westerns. Best known of his many popular books was *Riders of the Purple Sage* (1912), which sold nearly two million copies. He also wrote on big-game fishing and other outdoor pursuits.

greyhound A breed of dog, now raced for sport, but used thousands of years ago for hunting hares, foxes, and deer; thin with short coat; long legs, tail, and muzzle; the **Italian greyhound** is a miniature breed developed in Italy. Greyhound racing takes place on an enclosed circular or oval track, round which dogs are lured to run by a mechanical hare. The first regular track was at Emeryville, CA, in 1919. Betting takes place at greyhound race meetings.

greylag goose A goose (*Anser anser*) native to Europe and Asia, where it is the most numerous and widespread goose species; plumage mainly grey; inhabits estuaries and flood plains; eats vegetation in water or on land. It is the ancestor of the domestic goose. (Family: Anatidae.)

grey mullet Any of a large family of fish, widespread in tropical and warm temperate seas; body elongate, robust; dorsal profile rather flat; feeds on detritus and small algae from sea bottom; blue-grey above, sides silvery; valuable food fish in some areas; includes the common European thick-lipped mullet, *Chelon labrosus.* (Family: Mugilidae, 4 genera.)

greywacke [graywakuh] A type of impure sandstone, composed of angular grains in a matrix of clay. It is deposited in areas of rapid fluid flow, specifically turbidity currents formed in tectonically active, mountain-building regions.

Gribbin, John Richard (1946–) Astronomer, writer, and broadcaster, born in Maidstone, Kent, SE England, UK. He graduated from Sussex (1967) and Cambridge (1970) universities, becoming staff writer for the journal *Nature* (1970–5) and a member of the Science Policy Research Unit at the University of Sussex (1975–8). His first book, *The Jupiter Effect* (1974) was followed by over 50 others, including *In Search of Schrödinger's Cat* (1984), and biographies of Stephen Hawking and Albert Einstein. In 1993 he became a visiting fellow in astronomy at the University of Sussex, studying the age of the universe.

gribble A small wood-boring crustacean that burrows into boat hulls and other submerged timber, causing extensive damage. (Class: Malacostraca. Order: Isopoda.)

grid reference A unique set of numbers locating any place on a map onto which a grid of numbered squares has been imposed. References in the UK are based on the National Grid. The distance eastwards (*easting*) is always given before the distance northwards (*northing*) when giving a National Grid reference.

Grieg, Edvard (Hagerup) [greeg] (1843–1907) Composer, born in Bergen, SW Norway. He studied at Leipzig, where he was much influenced by Schumann's music, then worked in Copenhagen (1863–7), and developed into a strongly national Norwegian composer. After some years teaching and conducting in Christiania, the success of his incidental music for Ibsen's *Peer Gynt* (1876), and a state pension, enabled him to settle near Bergen. His other major works include the *Piano Concerto in A Minor*, orchestral suites, violin sonatas, and numerous songs and piano pieces.

Grierson, John [greerson] (1898–1972) Producer of documentary films, born in Kilmadock, Stirling, C Scotland, UK. He went to Glasgow University, then studied film art in Chicago, making his name with *Drifters* (1929), a study of North Sea fishermen. Regarded as the founder of the British documentary movement, he moved to the GPO Film Unit in 1933 for his most creative period, during which he produced *Night Mail* (1936). In 1938 he was invited to set up the Canadian Film Board, with which he remained until 1945.

grievous bodily harm *bodily harm*

Griffin, Bernard (1899–1956) Roman Catholic clergyman, born in Birmingham, West Midlands, C England, UK. He studied at the English and Beda Colleges, Rome, became Archbishop of Westminster in 1943, and was made a cardinal in 1946. He toured post-war Europe and America, and in 1950 was papal legate for the centenary celebrations of the reconstitution of the English hierarchy.

griffin or **gryphon** A fabulous beast, originating in Greek tales of the Arimaspians, who hunted the creature for its gold. It had a lion's body, and an eagle's head, wings, and claws. It collected fragments of gold to build its nest, and, instead of an egg, laid an agate.

Griffith, Arthur (1872–1922) Irish nationalist politician, born in Dublin, Ireland. He worked as a compositor, then as a miner and journalist in South Africa (1896–8), before editing the *United Irishman*. In 1905 he founded *Sinn Féin*, editing it until 1915. He was twice imprisoned, became an MP (1918–22), signed the peace treaty with Britain, and was a moderate president of the Dáil Eireann (1922).

Griffith, D(avid) W(ark) (1875–1948) Pioneer film director, born in La Grange, Kentucky, USA. He began with literary ambitions, then turned to film-making, where he experimented with new techniques in photography and production, and brought out two masterpieces, *The Birth of a Nation* (1915) and *Intolerance* (1916). He continued to make films until 1931, but his studio went into artistic decline, and failed in the economic aftermath of the Depression.

Griffith, Melanie (1957–) Actress, born in New York City, USA. The daughter of Hitchcock actress Tippi Hedren, she made her screen debut in *Night Moves* (1975). She appeared in a number of films as a teenager, then after a gap of four years her adult career commenced with *Body Double* (1984). Later films include *Bonfire of the Vanities* (1990), *Born Yesterday* (1993), *Lolita* (1997), *Crazy in Alabama* (1999), and *Tempo* (2003). She married actor Antonio Banderas in 1996.

griffon (ornithology) An Old World vulture, native to S Europe, Africa, and S Asia; head and neck lack long feathers; inhabits open country; eats carcasses of large mammals; usually numerous when present. It can eat a quarter of its own body weight at one meal. (Genus: *Gyps*, 7 species.)

griffon (zoology) A domestic dog, found in two unrelated breeds: **Brussels griffon** or **griffon Bruxellois**, developed to catch rats; small with short muzzle, jutting jaw, small beard; the **wire-haired pointing griffon**, a French pointer and retriever; muscular body, long legs, soft ears; last two-thirds of tail docked.

Grignard, (François Auguste) Victor [greenyah(r)] (1871–1935) Organic chemist, born in Cherbourg, NW France. He studied chemistry at Lyon, and became professor there in 1919. He introduced the use of organo-magnesium compounds (*Grignard reagents*), which form the basis of the most valuable class of organic synthetic reactions, for which he shared the Nobel Prize for Chemistry in 1912.

Grigson, Sophie, popular name of **Hester Sophia Frances Grigson** (1959–) British cookery writer and broadcaster. She studied at the University of Manchester Institute of Science and Technology and became a cookery correspondent for the *Evening Standard* (1986–93), *The Sunday Express* (1988–91), *The Independent* (1993–4), and *The Sunday Times* (1994–6). Her television programmes for Channel 4 include *Grow Your Greens/ Eat Your Greens* (1993) and *Sophie's Meat Course* (1995), and among her books are *Food for Friends*, *Sophie's Table*, and *Sophie Grigson's Country Kitchen* (2004).

Grimaldi, Joseph [grimaldee] (1779–1837) Comic actor, singer, and acrobat, born in London, UK. From 1800 until his retirement through ill health in 1828, he dominated the stage of Sadler's Wells as the figure of 'Clown' in the English harlequinade. Many of his innovations became distinctive characteristics of the pantomime clown, or 'Joey'. His *Memoirs of Joseph Grimaldi* (1838) was edited by Charles Dickens.

Grimes Graves Prehistoric flint mines on the Norfolk Breckland, E England, UK, in use c.3000–2500 BC. Spread over 14 ha/ 35 acres are 300–400 shafts up to 15 m/50 ft deep and 5 m/16 ft wide, with radial shafts at the bottom following the flint seams. Though two-thirds of the site remains unexcavated, ancient production is estimated at 14 000 tonnes – enough to make 28 million flint axes.

Grimké sisters [grimkay] Abolitionists and feminists: **Sarah Moore Grimké** (1792–1873) and **Angelina Emily Grimké** (1805–79), born to a major slaveholding family in Charleston, South Carolina, USA. They rejected their family's way of life and joined the Quakers, who were officially anti-slavery. They moved to Philadelphia and lived quietly, until in 1835 Angelina published a letter in an anti-slavery newspaper, *The Liberator*. They became public figures, and Angelina undertook an unprecedented speaking tour. She resisted efforts to silence her, but gave up public life after her marriage to the abolitionist **Theodore Weld** (1803–95). Sarah lived with the couple thereafter, and the two remained committed to social change.

Grimm brothers Folklorists and philologists: **Jacob Ludwig Carl Grimm** (1785–1863) and **Wilhelm Carl Grimm** (1786–1859), both born in Hanau, WC Germany. After studying at Marburg, Jacob became a clerk in the War Office at Kassel, and in 1808 librarian to Jerome Bonaparte, King of Westphalia. Wilhelm, in poorer health, remained in Kassel, where he became secretary of the elector's library. He was joined there by Jacob in 1816. Between 1812 and 1822 they published the three volumes known as *Grimm's Fairy Tales* (Ger *Kinder und Hausmärchen*). Jacob's *Deutsche Grammatik* (1819, Germanic Grammar, revised 1822–40) is perhaps the greatest philological work of the age; he also formulated *Grimm's law* of sound changes. In 1829 the two removed to Göttingen, where Jacob became professor and librarian, and Wilhelm under-librarian (professor in 1835). In 1841 they both received professorships at Berlin, and in 1854 began work on their historical dictionary, *Deutsches Wörterbuch*.

Grimmelshausen, Hans Jakob Christoffel von [grimels-howzen] (c.1622–76) Writer, born in Gelnhausen, WC Germany. He served on the imperial side in the Thirty Years' War, led a wandering life, then settled in Renchen, near Kehl. In later life he wrote a series of novels, the best of them on the model of the Spanish picaresque romances, such as the *Simplicissimus* series (1669–72).

Grimond (of Firth), Jo(seph) Grimond, Baron [grimuhnd] (1913–93) British politician, born in St Andrews, Fife, E Scotland, UK. He studied at Oxford, was called to the bar in 1937, served in World War 2, and entered parliament in 1950. Elected leader of the Liberal Party (1956–67), he was largely responsible for the modernizing of both the Party and Liberalism, and called for a 'realignment of the left' of British politics. He served again as Party leader for a short period following the resignation of Jeremy Thorpe (1976), retiring from the House of Commons in 1983, when he was created a life peer. He was also Chancellor of the University of Kent (1970–90).

Grimsby, formerly **Great Grimsby** 53°35N 0°05W, pop (2000e) 90 900. Port town in North East Lincolnshire, NE England, UK; on the S side of the R Humber estuary; railway; largest fishing port in England; fertilizers, chemicals, engineering; trade in fish, coal, grain, timber; football league team, Grimsby Town (Mariners).

grip The member of a camera crew in film or TV production who moves equipment and mountings. A **key grip** may also take part in associated set construction.

Griqua [greekwa] People of mixed race who spoke Dutch and established stock-raising, hunting, and trading communities under patriarchal leadership on the frontier of Cape Colony in the late 18th-c and early 19th-c. Their peoples are now integrated into the Cape Coloured community.

Griqualand [greekwaland] Region of Eastern Cape province, South Africa; bounded N by Lesotho; **East Griqualand** joined to Cape Colony in 1879; **West Griqualand**, including the diamond fields of Kimberley, joined in 1880; chief towns include Kokstad and Kimberley.

Gris, Juan [grees], pseudonym of **José Victoriano Gonzàlez** (1887–1927) Painter, born in Madrid, Spain. He studied there, and in 1906 went to Paris, where he associated with Picasso and Matisse and became one of the most logical and consistent exponents of Synthetic Cubism. He settled at Boulogne and in 1923 designed the décor for three Diaghilev productions. He also worked as a book illustrator. In most of his paintings, the composition of the picture dictates the deliberate distortion and re-arrangement of the subjects, as in *Still Life with Dice* (1922).

grisaille [greeziy] A painting executed entirely in shades of grey. This may be done for its own sake, or to look like sculpture as part of a decorative scheme. A reduced grisaille copy of a painting was often made for an engraver to work from. Many Renaissance painters began their pictures with a grisaille underpainting. Mediaeval stained-glass windows, normally richly-coloured, were sometimes executed in grisaille as a sign of austerity (eg by the Cistercians).

Grisham, John (1955–) Novelist, born in Jonesboro, Arkansas, USA. He studied accountancy at Mississippi State University (1975–7), then law at the University of Mississippi (1978–81), after which he practised criminal and civil law. Also interested in politics, he was elected to the Mississippi House of Representatives (1983–90). His first novel, the crime thriller *A Time To Kill* (1989), was followed by a string of best-sellers, many of which have been made into successful films, and include *The Firm* (1991), *The Rainmaker* (1995), and *The Testament* (1999). Later novels include *The Brethren* (2000), *The King of Torts* (2003), and *The Last Juror* (2004).

grison [griysn, grizn] A mammal native to South America; resembles a large weasel, with a coarse coat and colour pattern of a badger; formerly domesticated and used to chase chinchillas out of their holes. (Genus: *Galictis*, 2 species. Family: Mustelidae.)

Grivas, Georgeios (Theodoros) [greevas] (1898–1974) Greek political leader, born in Trikomo, E Cyprus. He commanded a

Greek Army division in the Albanian Campaign of 1940–1, and led a secret organization called 'X' during the German occupation of Greece. In 1955 he became head of the underground campaign against British rule in Cyprus (EOKA), calling himself 'Dighenis' after a legendary Greek hero. In 1959, after the Cyprus settlement, he left Cyprus and was promoted general in the Greek army. In 1971 he returned secretly to Cyprus and, as leader of EOKA-B, directed a terrorist campaign for *enosis* (union with Greece) until his death.

grivet monkey *vervet monkey*

grizzly bear *brown bear*

Groening, Matt [grayning] (1954–) Cartoonist, born in Portland, Oregon, USA. He studied at The Evergreen State College in Olympia, Washington, then moved to Los Angeles (1977), intent on becoming a writer. He joined the staff of the *Los Angeles Reader* and began contributing a comic strip entitled *Life In Hell* (1980), which was later syndicated. *The Simpsons*, a cartoon family featuring dad Homer, mother Marge, and children Bart, Lisa and Maggie, proved so popular that it debuted as a series in 1990, winning an Emmy for Best Animated Series. In 1999 he created the animated series *Futurama*.

Gromyko, Andrei Andreevich [gromeekoh] (1909–89) Soviet statesman and president (1985–8), born near Minsk, Belarus. He studied agriculture and economics, and became a research scientist at the Soviet Academy of Sciences. In 1939 he joined the staff of the Russian embassy in Washington, becoming ambassador in 1943, and after World War 2 was permanent delegate to the UN Security Council (1946–9). As longest-serving foreign minister (1957–85), he was responsible for conducting Soviet relations with the West during the Cold War, presenting an austere and humourless demeanour for which he became notorious in diplomatic circles. He became president in 1985, but retired from office following the 19th Party Conference (1988) and was replaced by Gorbachev.

Groningen [khroningn] 53°13N 6°35E, pop (2000e) 177 000. Capital of Groningen province, N Netherlands; at the confluence of the Drentse Aa (Hoornse Diep) and Winschoter Diep; bishopric; most important city in N Netherlands; connected to its outer port, Delfzijl, by the Eems Canal; airport; railway; university (1614); large market, dealing in cattle, vegetables, fruit, and flowers; headquarters of the Dutch Grain Exchange; shipbuilding, chemicals, electrical equipment, textiles, paper, tobacco, cigarettes, furniture; Martinkerk (13th-c), town hall (1777–1810).

Gropius, Walter (Adolph) [grohpius] (1883–1969) Architect, born in Berlin, Germany. He studied at Munich, and after serving in World War 1 was appointed director of the Grand Ducal group of schools of art in Weimar, which he reorganized to form the Bauhaus, aiming at a new functional interpretation of the applied arts. His revolutionary methods and bold use of unusual building materials were condemned in Weimar, and the Bauhaus was transferred to Dessau in 1925. When Hitler came to power he moved to London (1934–7), designing factories and housing estates, and then to the USA, where he was professor of architecture at Harvard University (1937–52). He became a US citizen in 1944.

grosbeak [grohsbeek] A name applied to birds of several unrelated groups, all with a large, stout bill: the finch family Fringillidae (12–32 species); the weaver family Ploceidae (1 species); and the **cardinal grosbeaks** of the family Emberizidae (14 species).

Gros Morne [groh maw(r)n] National park on the W coast of Newfoundland, Canada, established in 1970; area 2000 sq km/ 775 sq mi; noted for its landscape of forests and fjords, and for its wildlife, which includes caribou, moose, arctic hares, pine martins, seals, and whales; a world heritage site.

Gross, Michael [grohs], nickname **the Albatross** (1964–) Swimmer, born in Frankfurt, WC Germany. An outstanding butterfly and freestyle swimmmer, he uses his great height (6 ft 7 in/ 201 cm) and long arm span to advantage. In 1981–7 he won a record 13 gold medals at the European Championships. He was the world 200 m freestyle and 200 m butterfly champion in 1982 and 1986, and has won three Olympic gold medals: the 100 m butterfly and 200 m freestyle in 1984, and the 200 m butterfly in 1988.

gross domestic product (GDP) A measure of national income, calculated in any of three ways. The *output method* is the total of selling prices less the cost of bought-in materials. The *income method* is the total of wages, rents, dividends, interest, and profits. The *expenditure method* is the national expenditure on goods and services (known as 'GDP at factor cost'). The last method is the one most used by economists in forecasting economic growth. The **gross national product (GNP)** is similarly calculated, but includes residents' income from economic activity overseas and excludes UK incomes accruing to foreign residents.

Grosseteste, Robert [grohstest] (c.1175–1253) Scholar, bishop, and Church reformer, born in Stradbroke, Suffolk, E England, UK. He studied at Oxford and Paris, taught theology at Oxford, then became Bishop of Lincoln in 1235. He undertook the reformation of abuses in the Church, which brought him into conflict both locally and with the papacy.

Grossglockner [grohsglokner] 47°05N 12°44E. Mountain in the Hohe Tauern range, SC Austria; height 3797 m/12 457 ft; highest peak in Austria; first climbed in 1800; feeds the Pasterze glacier; at 2505 m/8218 ft the Grossglocknerstrasse is Austria's highest pass.

Grossmith, George [grohsmith] (1847–1912) Comedian and entertainer, born in London, UK. From 1877 to 1889 he took leading parts in Gilbert and Sullivans's operas, and with his brother, **Weedon Grossmith** (1853–1919), wrote *Diary of a Nobody* in *Punch* (1892). His son, **George Grossmith** (1874–1935) was a well-known musical-comedy actor, songwriter, and manager of the Gaiety Theatre, London.

Grosz, George [grohs] (1893–1959) Artist, born in Berlin, Germany. He studied at Dresden and Berlin, and was associated with the Berlin Dadaists (1917–18). While in Germany he produced a series of bitter, ironic drawings attacking German militarism and the middle classes. He fled to the USA in 1932, and became a US citizen in 1938. He later produced many oil paintings of a symbolic nature.

grotesque In art, a form of decoration derived from antiquity and revived during the Renaissance. Human and animal forms are mixed fancifully with plants and abstract shapes to create a bizarre kind of decorative pattern.

Grotius, Hugo [grohshius], also found as **Huig de Groot** (1583–1645) Jurist and humanist, born in Delft, The Netherlands. He studied at Leyden, practised in The Hague, and in 1613 was appointed pensionary (chief magistrate) of Rotterdam. In 1618 religious and political conflicts led to his imprisonment, but he escaped to Paris in 1621, where Louis XIII for a time gave him a pension. In 1625 he published *De jure belli ac pacis* (On the Law of War and Peace), in which he laid the foundations of international law. His chief innovation was his insistence that nations as well as private individuals are bound by natural law.

Grotowski, Jerzy [grotofskee] (1933–99) Theatre director, teacher, and drama theorist, born in Rzeszów, SE Poland. His work had a major impact on experimental theatre and actor training in the West during the 1960s and 1970s. After studying in Kraków and Moscow, he founded the Theatre of 13 Rows in Opole (1956–64), which moved to Wrocław as the Laboratory Theatre (1965–84). After 1982 he lived and worked in the USA and Italy.

ground beetle An active, terrestrial beetle; adults mostly predatory, found in litter or vegetation; larvae external parasites or predatory, feeding on predigested prey. (Order: Coleoptera. Family: Carabidae, c.30 000 species.)

ground elder A perennial (*Aegopodium podagraria*) native to Europe and temperate Asia and introduced into North America; long creeping underground stems give rise to numerous leafy shoots and stems to 1 m/3¾ ft; leaves divided into toothed oval segments up to 8 cm/3 in long; flowers white, in umbels 2–6 cm/¾–2½ in across. It is a persistent weed of gardens. The young leaves are sometimes eaten like spinach. It is an old remedy for gout, hence its alternative name, **goutweed**. (Family: Umbelliferae.)

groundhog *woodchuck*

Groundhog Day A day (2 Feb) recognized in US popular tradition when the groundhog (or woodchuck), an American marmot, is supposed to appear from hibernation; it is said that if the groundhog sees its shadow, it goes back into hibernation for six more weeks, thereby indicating six weeks of winter weather to come. The tradition derives from similar beliefs in England concerning the weather at Candelmas.

ground ivy A creeping perennial, native to Europe and Asia (*Glechoma hederacea*); stems square; leaves rounded, bluntly toothed, in opposite pairs; flowers in pairs in leaf axils, all facing the same way, 2-lipped, with long tube, violet-blue. It was used for brewing ale before the advent of hops. (Family: Labiatae.)

groundnut *peanut*

ground-roller *roller*

groundsel A very variable annual (*Senecio vulgaris*) growing to 45 cm/18 in, native to Europe, Asia, and N Africa, and widely introduced elsewhere; leaves slightly succulent, oblong with irregular toothed lobes; flower-heads numerous, cylindrical, surrounded by narrow black-tipped bracts; florets yellow; fruit with a parachute of hairs. Flowering all year round, it is a common and often problematic weed of cultivated ground and waste places. (Family: Compositae.)

ground squirrel *souslik*

ground state *energy levels*

groundwater Water which is present in porous rocks such as sandstones and limestones. It may originate from percolated surface waters (*meteoric water*), from water present when the sedimentary rock was originally deposited (*connate water*), or from igneous intrusions (*juvenile water*). The water table is the level below which the rocks are saturated, and springs develop where this reaches the Earth's surface.

Ground Zero The name given to the site of the former World Trade Center in lower Manhattan, New York City, USA, where rescue teams worked to clear the wreckage and debris left after the terrorist attack on 11 September 2001. The term was originally used with reference to the part of the ground situated immediately under an exploding bomb (especially an atomic bomb).

group (chemistry) **1** A column in the periodic table, the elements being related by having the same configuration of valence electrons.

2 *functional group*

group (mathematics) In mathematics, a set of elements S under an operation $*$, if (1) S is closed under $*$; (2) the operation $*$ is associative over S, ie $a*(b*c) = (a*b)*c$ for all a,b,c in S; (3) there is an identity element e in S, ie an element e such that $a*e = e*a = a$ for all a in S; and (4) every element a in S has an inverse, a^{-1} in S, where $a*a^{-1} = a^{-1}*a = e$. If in addition the operation $*$ is commutative, the group is called an **Abelian group**. Examples of groups are the integers under addition; the numbers 1, i, −1, $-i$ under multiplication; and the rotations about a common point, where $*$ is 'first one rotation then another rotation'. The properties of groups are studied by **group theory**.

grouper Large, heavy-bodied fish with mottled cryptic coloration, common around reefs, rocks, and wrecks but also found in open water; prized as a sport fish and food fish; **Indo-Pacific grouper**, *Epinephelus lanceolatus*, may reach 3·7 m/12 ft, weight 270 kg/600 lb. (Family: Serranidae.)

Group of Seven A Canadian group of artists, who established themselves as a Romantic, nationalistic landscape school from 1920. In rebellion against 19th-c naturalism, their Expressionist-tending work initially outraged the art establishment, but they were promoted by Eric Brown, director of the National Gallery of Canada, and eventually became an establishment of their own. Original members were Frank Carmichael, Lawren Harris, A Y Jackson, Frank Johnston, Arthur Lismer, J E H MacDonald, and F H Varley. The painter Tom Thomson was a friend of many of the group, and awakened their interest in painting the Ontario North, but he died in 1917, before the group's official founding. Later members were A J Casson, Edwin Holgate, and L L Fitzgerald.

Group Theatre A New York theatre company founded in 1931, whose importance extends beyond the 23 plays it produced during its nine years of existence. The company was dedicated to the principles of group work and to the social importance of a theatre independent of commercialism. Among the names of those involved in the venture (Clurman, Strasberg, Kazan, Odets, Carnovsky) are many who came to be associated with the best of US theatre for more than a generation.

group therapy The interaction of several individuals on a cognitive and emotional level, as part of a therapeutic programme. It incorporates the sharing of personal experiences and feelings, with the purpose of increasing self-understanding and the treatment of psychological problems. This form of treatment is attributed to US physician Joseph Hersey Pratt (1872–1942). It came into widespread use after World War 2 when it was used in the treatment of shell-shock victims.

groupware Computer programs which are developed especially for the purpose of enabling groups of people either in the same or different locations to work together on a common task. A special case of groupware is the computer conference. Using the techniques of virtual reality, conferences can now be set up with groups in different locations, giving the appearance to each group of all the participants being in the same room.

grouse A plump, ground-dwelling bird of the family Tetraonidae (19 species); inhabits high latitudes of the N hemisphere; camouflaged coloration; short curved bill; nostrils covered by feathers; legs feathered; eats vegetation and insects. Many (possibly millions) are killed annually by hunters. The name is also used for the **sandgrouse** of the family Pteroclididae.

Grove, Sir George (1820–1900) Musicologist, born in London, UK. He practised as a civil engineer, then became secretary to the Society of Arts (1849), and secretary and director of the Crystal Palace Company (1852). His major work was as editor of the *Dictionary of Music and Musicians* (1878–89), and he also edited *Macmillan's Magazine* (1868–83) and contributed to biblical study. He was knighted in 1883 on the opening of the Royal College of Music, of which he was director until 1895.

Grove, Sir William Robert (1811–96) Lawyer and physicist, born in Swansea, SC Wales, UK. He graduated at Oxford in 1835, and became a barrister, then turned to electrochemistry, and taught physics. He returned to the law to improve his income, becoming a judge in 1871. In 1842 he made the first fuel cell, generating electric current from a chemical reaction using gases, and the first filament lamp (1845). He also published early ideas on energy conservation. Since 1991, the Grove Medal has been awarded to acknowledge an individual or company that has made valuable contributions to the development of fuel cell technology.

Groves, Sir Charles (1915–92) Conductor, born in London, UK. He studied at the Royal College of Music, London. He trained the BBC Chorus (1938–42), conducted the BBC Northern (1944–51), the Bournemouth Symphony (1951–61), and the Royal Liverpool Philharmonic (1963–77) orchestras, and was also musical director of the Welsh and English National Operas (1961–3 and 1978–9 respectively), as well as president of the National Youth Orchestra (1977–92). He became musical director of the Leeds Philharmonic Society in 1988. He was noted for his mastery of the Romantic repertoire and for championing living composers. He was knighted in 1973.

growth factors Small peptide factors that are produced by certain cells which, when released, have a growth-promoting effect on other specific types of cell. They may play a role in some cancers. Examples include **epidermal growth factor** (EGF) and **platelet-derived growth factor** (PDGF). Insulin can also act as a growth factor.

growth hormone (GH) A hormone (a polypeptide), secreted by the front lobe of the pituitary gland in vertebrates with jaws, which stimulates body growth through its effects on protein, carbohydrate, and lipid metabolism; also known as **somatotrophin** or **somatotrophic hormone**. It is species-specific in its actions. Its abnormal secretion may result in dwarfism, gigantism, or acromegaly (the abnormal enlargement of the facial features, hands, and feet).

growth ring *annual ring*

Grozny [groznee] 43°21N 45°42E, pop (2003e) 80–160 000 (estimates affected by refugee and militia movements). Capital city of Chechnya, SE European Russia; on a tributary of the R Terek, in the N foothills of the Greater Caucasus; founded as a fortress, 1818; airfield; railway; university (1972); major damage and disruption during war with Russia, 1995; almost totally destroyed in renewed fighting, 1999–2000; oil refining, chemicals, foodstuffs.

Gruner, Elloth [grooner] (1882–1939) Painter, born in Gisborne, New Zealand. Having arrived in Sydney as an infant, he was accepted by Julian Ashton as a pupil in 1894, and later became an assistant at Ashton's Sydney Art School. He won his first Wynne prize, for landscape painting, in 1916, and was to win six more in the next 20 years. Although sometimes criticized for a primness and lack of vitality, his best work captures the special quality of the Australian light, and he is regarded as one of Australia's leading landscape artists.

Grünewald, Matthias [grünevalt], originally **Mathis Gothardt** (?1470–1528) Artist, architect, and engineer, probably born in Würzburg, SC Germany. Very little is known of his life, but he was court painter at Mainz (1508–14) and Brandenburg (1515–25), and in 1516 completed the great Isenheim altarpiece (Colmar Museum).

grunion Slender-bodied fish (*Leuresthes tenuis*) confined to inshore waters of the Californian coast; length up to 18 cm/7 in; body with silvery side-stripe. Communal spawning occurs intertidally on the spring tide, the eggs being buried in moist sand near the high-water mark. (Family: Atherinidae.)

grunt Any of the family Haemulidae (formerly Pomadasyidae, 5 genera) of mainly tropical fishes common in shallow coastal waters and around coral reefs. They are so called because they produce audible sounds by grinding their pharyngeal teeth.

Grus [groos] (Lat 'crane') A S constellation.

Grylloblattaria [grilohblatairia] *rock crawler*

gryphon *griffin*

G-7 (Group of Seven) An economic grouping formed between states in 1975 with the aim of co-ordinating efforts to promote growth and stability in the world economy and to bring the world's key exchange rates into line. It consists of the seven leading industrialized countries: Canada (from 1976), France, Germany, Italy, Japan, UK, and USA. Its annual meetings are attended by the president or prime minister of each member country. The European Union is also now represented, and Russia became a full member in 1998, to make the group G-8. Other groupings include G-10 (comprising 11 countries, the G-7 members plus Belgium, Netherlands, Switzerland and Sweden) and G-24 (whose membership comes from developing countries).

guacharo *oilbird*

Guadalajara [gwadalakhahra] 20°30N 103°20W, pop (2000e) 1 960 000. Capital of Jalisco state, WC Mexico, 535 km/332 mi NW of Mexico City; altitude 1567 m/5141 ft; founded, 1530; second largest city in Mexico; airport; railway; two universities (1792, 1935); textiles, clothing, tanning, soap, glass, pottery, food processing; many colonial buildings, cathedral (1561–1618), government palace (1643), Jalisco state museum, Santa Mónica Church (1718), San Francisco Church (1550), Museo Taller José Clemente Orozco, Hospicio Cabañas (a world heritage site); fiesta (Oct), fiesta of the Virgin of Guadalupe (Dec); scene of a major industrial accident (1992) when a gasline explosion destroyed parts of the central city.

Guadalcanal [gwadalkanal] pop (2000e) 76 000; area 5302 sq km/2047 sq mi. Largest of the Solomon Is, SW Pacific; length, 144 km/89 mi; maximum width, 56 km/35 mi; rises to 2477 m/8126 ft at Mt Makarakomburu; capital, Honiara; airport; copra, rubber, rice, oil palms, gold; scene of the first World War 2 Allied Pacific invasion northward (1942).

Guadalquivir, River [gwadalkiveer] (Span **Río**), ancient **Baetis**, Arabic **Wad-el-kebir** River rising in the Sierra de Cazorla, Andalusia, S Spain; flows W then SW to enter the Atlantic at Sanlúcar de Barrameda; length, 657 km/408 mi; navigable to Seville; reservoirs for irrigation and hydroelectric power.

Guadalupe Hidalgo, Treaty of [gwadaloop hidalgoh] (1848) The agreement that settled the Mexican War, with Mexico yielding all of Texas, Arizona, Nevada, California, and Utah, and parts of New Mexico, Colorado, and Wyoming. The US paid $15 000 000, and assumed Mexican debts worth $3 250 000.

Guadeloupe [gwadeloop] pop (2000e) 425 000; area 1779 sq km/687 sq mi. Overseas department of France, a group of seven islands in the C Lesser Antilles, E Caribbean; capital, Basse-Terre; largest town, Pointe-à-Pitre; timezone GMT −4; 90% black or mulatto population, with several minorities; chief religion, Roman Catholicism; official language, French; unit of currency, the French franc; main islands of Grand-Terre and Basse-Terre make up 80% of total land area and accommodate over 90% of the population; warm and humid climate; average annual temperature, 28°C; visited by Columbus, 1493; occupied by France, 1635; later held by Britain and Sweden; returned to France, 1816; departmental status, 1946; administrative region, 1973; two senators and four deputies sent to the National Assembly in Paris; Commissioner advised by a 43-member General Council and a 41-member elected Regional Council; economy mainly agricultural processing, especially sugar refining and rum distilling; chief crops, sugar cane, bananas, aubergines, sweet potatoes; tourism.

Guam *p.668*

guanaco [gwanahkoh] A wild member of the camel family (*Lama guanicoe*), native to the Andean foothills and surrounding plains; brown with white underparts and grey head; inhabits dry open country; eats mainly grass; can survive without water; possibly ancestor of llama and alpaca.

Guandi [gwahn dee] or **Kuan-ti** In Chinese mythology, Lord Guan, the Chinese god of war and loyalty. He is based on a warrior who died in AD 219, and who was deified in 1594.

Guangxu or **Kuang-hsu** [gooahngsü], reign-title of **Zai Tian**, (also spelled **Tsai-t'ien**) (1871–1908) Ninth emperor of the Qing dynasty (1875–1908), who remained largely under the control of the Empress Dowager Ci-Xi. In 1898, after the defeat of China by Japan (1894–5), he was determined to reform and strengthen China, and threatened to abdicate if not given full authority. He issued a series of reforming edicts; but his attempts to gain power precipitated a coup, after which he was confined to his palace until his mysterious death one day before the death of the Empress Dowager.

Guangzhou [kwangjoh], **Canton**, also **Kwang-chow** or **Kuang-chou** 23°08N 113°20E, pop (2000e) 4 387 000, administrative region 6 552 000. Capital of Guangdong province, S China, on Pearl R delta; founded in 200 BC; forcibly opened to foreign trade after Opium War, 1842; revolutionary centre, 1910–11; rival capital to Beijing, 1917–20, 1921–8; power centre of Sun Yixian; seat of first national Guomindang conference, 1924; occupied by Japan, 1938–45; railway; airport; university (1958); medical college (1953); designated a special economic zone; industrial and foreign trade centre in S China; engineering, textiles, shipbuilding, chemicals, clothes; Yuexiu public park, containing Guangdong Historical Museum and Five Goats Statue; Huaisheng Mosque (627), National Peasant Movement Institute (1924), Mausoleum of the 72 Martyrs, Sun Yatsen Memorial Hall; biannual Chinese Export Commodities Fair.

guanine [gwaneen] $C_5H_5N_5O$. One of the purine bases in DNA, normally paired with cytosine.

Guam

[gwahm] (USA Formal Dependencies)
Local name Guam (*see map p.966*)
Timezone GMT +10
Area 541 km²/209 sq mi
Population total (2000e) 154 600
Status Unincorporated territory of the United States of America
Capital Agaña
Languages Chamorro and English (official), Japanese is also spoken
Ethnic groups Chamorro (47%), Filipino (29%), Caucasian (18%), Micronesian (13%)
Religion Roman Catholic
Physical features Largest and southernmost of the Mariana Islands, covering c.48 km/30 mi in the Pacific Ocean; volcanic island fringed by a coral reef; relatively flat limestone plateau, with narrow coastal plains in N, low rising hills in C and mountains in S; highest point, 406 m/1332 ft at Mt Lamlam.
Climate Tropical maritime climate; average annual temperature 24-30°C; average annual rainfall 2125 mm/84 in; wet season (Jul-Dec); hit by Typhoon Pongsona (Dec 2002).
Currency 1 US Dollar (US$) = 100 cents
Economy Economy highly dependent on government activities; military installations cover 35% of the island; diversifying industrial and commercial projects; oil refining, dairy products, furniture, watches, copra, processed fish; rapidly growing tourist industry.
History Originally settled by Malay-Filipino peoples; Ferdinand Magellan landed on the island, 1521; claimed for Spain, 1565; rebellion against Spanish missionaries, 1670–95; US consulate established, 1855; ceded to US by Spain after defeat in Spanish-American War, 1898; occupied by Japan, 1941–4; unincorporated territory of the US, Organic Act, 1950; elected Governor and a unicameral legislature.

guano [gwahnoh] An accumulation of animal droppings, typically of birds but also of mammals such as bats. Guano deposits build up beneath breeding colonies, and are a rich source of phosphates and nitrates. They are often used as a fertilizer.

Guanyin or **Kuan-yin** [gwahnyin] Popular Chinese Buddhist goddess of mercy, the protector of women and children. She is the equivalent of Avolokiteshvara, the male bodhisattva of compassion in Indian Mahayana Buddhism.

guarana [gwarahna] A woody liane (*Paullinia cupana*) with coiled tendrils, fern-like leaves and clusters of small, 5-petalled flowers; native to tropical America, cultivated in Brazil. The seeds are rich in caffeine, and it is used like cacao to produce a drink called guarana. (Family: Sapindaceae.)

Guaraní [gwaranee] A Tupian-speaking South American Indian group, who lived in Brazil, Paraguay, and Argentina, practising slash-and-burn agriculture, hunting, and fishing. A few scattered groups still live in the forests of Paraguay and Brazil. About a million speak Guaraní, the only Indian language to achieve the status of becoming a country's majority language.

Guaranis, Jesuit Missions of the [gwaranee] Religious settlements established in the 17th–18th-c by Spanish Jesuit missionaries to convert the Guaraní Indians of South America to Christianity. Five of these missions, São Miguel das Missões in Brazil, and San Ignacio Mini, Santa Ana, Nuestra Señora de Loreto, and Santa Maria la Mayour in Argentina, are world heritage sites.

Guardi, Francesco [gwah(r)dee] (1712–93) Painter, born in Venice, NE Italy. A pupil of Canaletto, he was noted for his views of Venice, full of sparkling colour, with an Impressionist's eye for effects of light, as in the 'View of the Church and Piazza of San Marco' (National Gallery, London).

guardian A person who by right or appointment acts on behalf of another, taking care of that person's interests in full (or some cases to a limited or specified degree) as a result of the other's inability, either due to youth or (in some jurisdictions) mental incapacity. In the case of a child, the parents are normally the guardians, having full parental rights and duties. The parents may arrange for the appointment of another person as guardian, in the event of their death. Courts similarly have the power to appoint a guardian for a child where there is no suitable guardian. The guardian automatically assumes full responsibility for the child for the duration of the guardianship order.

Guareschi, Giovanni [gwareskee] (1908–68) Writer and journalist, born in Parma, N Italy. He became editor of the Milan magazine *Bertoldo*, and after World War 2 continued in journalism. He achieved fame with his stories of the village priest, beginning with *The Little World of Don Camillo* (1950). The books were illustrated with his own drawings.

Guarini, (Giovanni) Battista [gwareenee] (1538–1612) Poet, born in Ferrara, NE Italy. He was entrusted by Duke Alfonso II with diplomatic missions to the Pope, the Emperor, Venice, and Poland. His chief work was the pastoral play, *Il pastor fido* (1585, The Faithful Shepherd), which helped to establish the genre of pastoral drama.

Guarini, Guarino [gwareenee], originally **Camillo Guarini** (1642–83) Architect, philosopher, and mathematician, born in Modena, N Italy. A Theatine priest, he studied under Borromini in Rome (1639–47). He designed several churches in Turin, of which the only two survivors are San Lorenzo (1668–80) and Capella della SS Sindone (1668); in both he replaces the traditional dome with a tall basket of ribs pierced by multiple light-tunnels. Other works include the Palazzo Carignano (1679), considered his masterpiece, as well as palaces for Bavaria and Baden, and churches in Paris, Messina, Prague, and Lisbon (known only from his writings). He also published books on mathematics, astronomy, and architecture, and was responsible for the spread of the Baroque style beyond Italy. His influential *Architettura civile* (published posthumously in 1737), concerning the relationship of geometry and architecture, also included a defence of Gothic architecture.

Guarnieri [gwah(r)nyayree], also found as **Giuseppe Guarneri**, known as **Giuseppe del Gesù** (1687–1745) Celebrated violin maker from Cremona, N Italy. His byname came from his practice of signing *IHS* (*Jesu hominum salvator*) after his name on his labels. His instruments are noted for their tonal qualities. He was the nephew of **Andrea Guarnieri** (fl.1628–98) who, with his two sons **Giuseppe Guarnieri** (fl.1690–1730) and **Pietro Guarnieri** (fl.1690–1725), also made quality instruments.

Guatemala *p.669*

Guatemala City or **Guatemala** [gwatuhmahla] 14°38N 90°22W, pop (2000e) 1 389 000. Capital city of Guatemala, on a plateau in the Sierra Madre mountain range; founded to serve as capital, 1776, after Antigua destroyed by earthquake; itself almost totally destroyed by earthquakes in 1917–18, and since rebuilt; altitude 1500 m/4920 ft; airport; railway; University of San Carlos (1680) and four other universities; foodstuffs, textiles, footwear, tyres, cement; cathedral (1782–1815); churches of Santo Domingo and San Francisco; Mayan ruins of Kaminal Juyú to the W.

Guayaquil [gwiyakeel] 2°13S 79°54W, pop (2000e) 1 861 000. Capital of Guayas province, W Ecuador; largest city, major seaport and commercial city, on W bank of R Guayas; founded, 1537; birthplace of Frederick Ashton; airport; railway; four universities (1867, 1958, 1962, 1966); banana trade (world's chief exporter), mining (sand, clay), food processing, textiles, engineering, pharmaceuticals, iron and steel, oil refining, chemicals; racecourse; golf, tennis, and yachting clubs; location of world's first submarine trial; municipal and government palaces, Museo Municipal, Casa de la Cultura, cathedral, San Francisco Church (1603, rebuilt 1968), Santo Domingo Church (1548); Carnival (pre-Lent), New Year's Eve festivities.

Guatemala

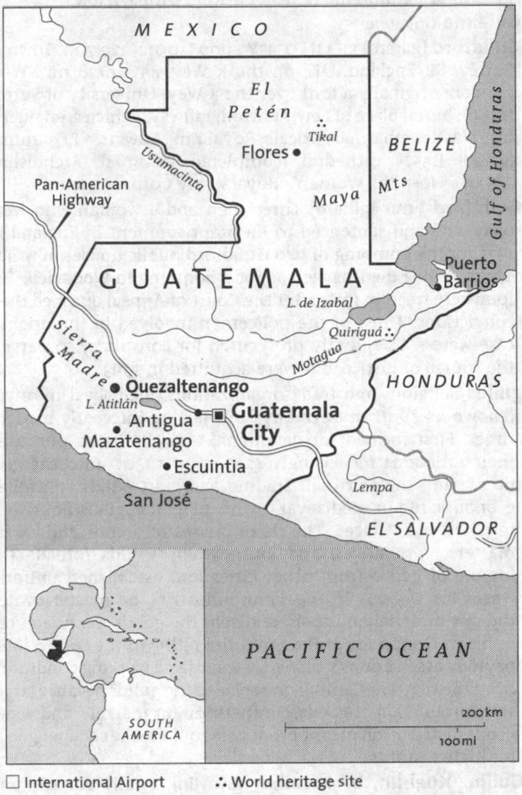

[gwatemahla], official name **Republic of Guatemala**, Span **República de Guatemala**
Local name Guatemala

Timezone GMT –6
Area 108 889 km^2/42 031 sq mi
Population total (2002e) 11 987 000
Status Republic
Date of independence 1838
Capital Guatemala City
Languages Spanish (official), c.40% speak Indian dialects, including Quiche, Cakchiquel, Kekchi
Ethnic groups Indian (41%) and Mestizo
Religions Roman Catholic (75%), Protestant (25%)
Physical features Northernmost of the Central American republics; over two-thirds mountainous, with large forested areas; narrow Pacific coastal plain, rising steeply to highlands of 2500–3000 m/8000–10 000 ft; many volcanoes on S edge of highlands, low undulating tableland of El Petén to the N.
Climate Humid tropical climate on lowlands and coast; average annual temperatures 17°C (Jan), 21°C (Jul) in Guatemala City; rainy season (May–Oct); average annual rainfall 1316 mm/51·8 in; area subject to hurricanes and earthquakes.
Currency 1 Quetzal (Q) = 100 centavos
Economy Agricultural products account for c.65% of exports, chiefly coffee, bananas, cotton, sugar; on higher ground, wheat, maize, beans; on the Pacific coastal plain, cotton, sugar cane, rice, beans.
GDP (2002e) $53·2 bn, per capita $3900
Human Development Index (2002) 0·631
History Mayan and Aztec civilizations before Spanish conquest, 1523–4; independence as part of the Federation of Central America, 1821; independence as the Republic of Guatemala, 1838; 1985 constitution provides for the election of a President (who appoints a Cabinet), and a National Assembly; long-standing claim over Belize resolved in 1991.
Head of State/Government
1991–3 Jorge Serrano Elias
1993–6 Ramiro de Léon Carpio
1996–9 Alvaro Arzú Irigoyen
1999–2003 Alfonso Portillo Cabrera
2003– Oscar Berger

Gucci, Guccio [goochee] (1881–1953) Fashion designer, founder of the Gucci firm, born in Florence, NC Italy. He opened his first shop in Florence in 1920, becoming known for his leather craftsmanship and accessories. His four sons joined the firm, and in 1953 (the year he died) the first overseas shop opened in New York City. His grandson, **Maurizio** (1949–95) oversaw the resurrection of the firm in the 1980s, and became group president in 1989. Following a series of legal and family disputes, the company was sold to the multinational Investcorp in 1993.

gudgeon Small, bottom-dwelling freshwater fish (*Gobio gobio*) widespread in clean gravelly rivers and lakes of Europe; body elongate, cylindrical, length up to 20 cm/8 in; head large, mouth with pair of barbels; greenish-brown with darker patches on back, sides yellowish, underside silver. (Family: Cyprinidae.)

Gudrun [gudrun] In Norse mythology, the wife of Sigurd the Volsung. After his death she married Atli (the legendary Attila) who put her brothers to death; in revenge she served up his sons in a dish, and then destroyed him by fire. In the similar German story she is known as **Kriemhild**.

guelder rose [gelder] A deciduous shrub or small spreading tree (*Viburnum opulus*), growing to 4 m/13 ft, native to Europe and W Asia; leaves with 3–5 irregularly-toothed lobes; flowers 5-petalled, white, in a cluster 4–10 cm/1½–4 in across, the outer flowers sterile and much larger than the inner; fruits berry-like, red, often persisting after the leaves have fallen. A mutant form with only sterile flowers in globular clusters first appeared in Guelderland province, Holland, in the 14th-c. It is much grown as an ornamental under the name **snowball tree**. (Family: Caprifoliaceae.)

Guelph [gwelf] 43°34N 80°16W, pop (2000e) 98 600. Town in SE Ontario, Canada, on the Speed R; 43 km/27 mi NW of Hamilton; founded, 1827; railway; university (1964); agricultural centre; iron, steel, textiles, rubber, chemicals; Church of Our Lady, modelled on Cologne cathedral; waterfowl park, electric railway museum.

Guelphs The pro-papal, anti-imperial party in Italian cities in the 13th–14th-c, opposed to the power of the Holy Roman Emperors, and successful in resisting the authority of the Hohenstaufen family, whose power was eclipsed after 1266. Allied with the papacy, the Guelphs resisted the claims of potential successors, and dominated Florentine politics.

guenon [guhnon] An Old World monkey native to Africa S of the Sahara; round head with beard, and 'whiskers' at side of face; slender, with long hind legs and tail; some species with colourful coats. The name *red guenon* is used for the *patas monkey*; **pygmy guenon** for the *talapoin*. (Genus: *Cercopithecus*, c.17 species.)

Guercino, Il [eel gwercheenoh], nickname of **Giovanni Francesco Barbieri** (1591–1666) Painter of the Bolognese School, born in Cento, N Italy. His major work is the ceiling fresco 'Aurora' at the Villa Ludovisi in Rome for Pope Gregory XV. After 1642 he became the leading painter of Bologna, where he died. His name means 'the squint-eyed'.

guereza *colobus*

Guericke, Otto von [gayrikuh] (1602–86) Physicist, born in Magdeburg, EC Germany. An engineer in the Swedish army, he later defended his home town in the Thirty Years' War, resulting in his election as one of its four burgomasters in 1646. He improved a water pump (1650) so that it would exhaust air from a container, and was able with this air pump to give dramatic demonstrations of pressure reduction (the *Magdeburg hemispheres*). He also made the first recorded electrostatic machine.

Guernica [gairneeka] 43°19N 2°40W, pop (2000e) 16 300. Basque town in Vizcaya province, N Spain; 25 km/15 mi NE of Bilbao, on an inlet of the Bay of Biscay; German planes bombed the town in 1937, during the Spanish Civil War, an event recalled in a famous painting by Picasso (now in Madrid); armaments, metal products, furniture, foodstuffs.

Guernsey [gernzee] pop (2000e) 66 200; area 63 sq km/24 sq mi. Second largest of the Channel Is, NW of Jersey and W of Normandy; rises to c.90 m/300 ft; airport; ferries to the UK and France; forms the Bailiwick of Guernsey with Alderney, Sark, and some smaller islands; chief town, St Peter Port; horticulture, dairy farming (Guernsey cattle), tourism.

Guesclin, Bertrand du [gayklĩ] (c.1320–80) French knight and military leader during the Hundred Years' War, born in La Motte-Broons, NW France. He entered royal service on the eve of Charles V's accession, and on becoming Constable of France (1370) assumed command of the French armies, reconquering Brittany and most of SW France. He died while besieging Châteauneuf-de-Randon in the Auvergne.

Guevara, Che [gayvahra], popular name of **Ernesto Guevara (de la Serna)** (1928–67) Revolutionary leader, born in Rosario, Argentina. He trained as a doctor (1953), then played an important part in the Cuban revolution (1956–9), after which he held government posts under Castro. He left Cuba in 1965 to become a guerrilla leader in South America, and was captured and executed in Bolivia.

Guggenheim, Solomon R(obert) [gugenhiym] (1861–1949) Businessman and art collector, born in Philadelphia, Pennsylvania, USA, the son of financier Meyer Guggenheim (1828–1905). He studied in Zürich, and became a partner in his father's Swiss embroidery import business. He returned to the USA (1889), worked in the family mining industry in Colorado and New Mexico, then moved to the business headquarters in New York City (1895). He was a director of many family companies and a founder of the Yukon Gold Co in Alaska before retiring from business in 1919. With the assistance of Hilla Rebay, he collected important Modernist paintings and established the Solomon R Guggenheim Foundation (1937). This was the source of funds for the temporary Museum of Non-Objective Paintings (1937) and the permanent Solomon R Guggenheim Museum, designed by Frank Lloyd Wright in 1959.

GUI *graphic user interface*

Guiana Highlands [geeahna] Mountainous tableland mainly in S and SE Venezuela, and extending into Brazil and Guyana, South America; forested plateau, covering half of Venezuela; rises to 2875 m/9432 ft at Mt Roraima; vast plateaux separated by deep valleys with major waterfalls; Angel Falls in Venezuela considered to be the highest waterfall in the world.

guided missile A weapon system (ranging in size from a small portable antitank missile to an intercontinental ballistic missile) which has the ability to fly towards its target under its own power. Its progress is directed either by an external source of command or by an internal computer which sends electronic guidance instructions to the missile's control surfaces.

guide dog A dog trained to assist the blind in finding their way, notably in urban traffic and crowded areas. The dogs are selectively bred, and include labradors, often crossed with golden retrievers, and German shepherd dogs.

Guido d'Arezzo [gweedoh daretzoh], also known as **Guido Aretino** (c.990–c.1050) Benedictine monk and musical theorist, probably born in Arezzo, NC Italy. He was a monk at Pomposa, and is supposed to have died as prior of the Camaldolite monastery of Avellana. He contributed much to musical science: the invention of the staff is ascribed to him, and he introduced the system of naming the notes of a scale with syllables.

Guienne *Guyenne*

Guildford [gilferd] 51°14N 0°35W, pop (2001e) 129 700. Town in Surrey, SE England, UK; on the R Wey, 45 km/28 mi SW of London; originally a ford over the R Wey; University of Surrey (1966); burial place of Lewis Carroll; railway; vehicles, engineering, plastics, pharmaceuticals; Royal King Edward VI Grammar School (1557), cathedral (completed in 1964), Archbishop Abbot's Hospital, Women's Royal Army Corps museum.

Guildford Four [gilferd] Three men and a woman who were convicted and sentenced to life imprisonment in England in 1975 for the bombing of two Guildford public houses in which seven people died, as well as for a bombing in Woolwich. The four were freed in 1989 after the Court of Appeal quashed their convictions. Three of the policemen involved in the original case were subsequently prosecuted for conspiracy to pervert the course of justice, but were acquitted in 1993.

guilds Religious and trade organizations, mediaeval in origin (known as *Zünft* in Germany), but lasting into early-modern times. First formed for devotional and charitable purposes, their functions increasingly split from c.1300 into the economic and the spiritual. Trading and craft guilds controlled economic life in mediaeval towns; religious guilds flourished in cities and villages. The three classes of a craft guild were masters, apprentices, and journeymen. Guilds forbade the import of goods from other cities and established uniform wages for workers in the same industry. The master owned the raw material and tools, and sold the goods manufactured in his workshop for profit. From the 14th-c to the 16th-c, journeymen associations won better wages and working conditions from the masters. Capitalism replaced the guilds because large-scale production of goods, competition for markets, and wider goods distribution meant producers could make cheaper goods for higher profits.

Guilin, Kuei-lin, or **Kweilin** [gwaylin] 25°21N 110°11E, pop (2000e) 626 000, administrative region 1 296 000. City in Guangxi Zhuang autonomous region, S China, on W bank of Li R; contains large Muslim population; badly damaged while US air base in World War 2; airfield; railway; grain, fishing, cotton, spun silk, rubber, medicines, machinery, tourism; Reed Flute Cave, with Shuiqinggong (Crystal Palace) Grotto; Zengpiyan Cave (Stone Age village); Seven Star Park, with Forest of Tablets (stelae from the Tang and Ming dynasties); river boat trips.

Guillain Barre syndrome [geean baray] A rare disorder that affects the peripheral nerves and leads to a loss of function of the body that is variable in severity but usually completely reversible. It tends to follow viral infections, particularly of the respiratory tract, and is due to an auto-immune response induced by the infection that attacks nerve cells and destroys the coating around them (*myelin*) that is essential to the transmission of nerve impulses. The most obvious clinical feature is a progressive symmetrical paralysis, but loss of sensation and loss of involuntary regulation of blood pressure and bowel and bladder control also occur. Treatment is to maintain the patient's vital functions during the acute illness; sometimes steroids and plasmapheresis are used to reduce the immune reaction. Most patients survive and begin to recover in a few weeks; even those with total paralysis can recover completely, though some have a residual weakness that persists for years.

Guillaume de Lorris [geeyohm duh loris] (c.1200–?) Poet, born in France – his surname derives from a village near Orléans. He wrote, before 1260, the first part (c.4000 lines) of the encyclopedic *Roman de la Rose* – an allegory presenting love as a garden, the lady as a rose, and the knight as in quest of her favour. The work was widely influential in mediaeval Europe, and was continued a few decades later by Jean de Meung.

Guillaume de Machaut [geeyohm duh mashoh] (c.1300–77) Poet and musician, born possibly in Reims, NE France. He worked successively under the patronage of John of Luxemburg and John II of France. One of the creators of the harmonic art, he wrote a Mass, motets, songs, ballads, and organ music. His poetry greatly influenced Chaucer.

Guillem, Sylvie [gee-em] (1965–) Ballet dancer and choreographer, born in Paris, France. She trained at the Paris Opéra Ballet School (1977–80) and at age 16 joined the company's corps de ballet. Her first solo appearance (1981) was in *Don Quixote*, staged by Rudolf Nureyev, and in 1984 she gained the status of *étoile*. In 1988 she partnered Nureyev to great acclaim in a production of *Giselle* performed with the Royal Ballet in London, and from 1989 became principal guest artist with the company. She has also had success as a choreographer.

Guillemin, Roger C(harles) L(ouis) [geelmin] (1924–) Physiologist, born in Dijon, E France. He studied at Dijon, Lyon, and Montreal universities, joining Baylor University, TX, in 1953, where he became professor and director of neuroendocrinology (1963–70). Since 1970 he has been at the Salk Institute for Biological Studies. He shared the 1977 Nobel Prize for Physiology or Medicine for his work on the isolation of peptide hormones of the hypothalamus.

guillemot [gilimot] An auk with a long pointed bill, also known as **tystie** or (in the USA) **murre**; eats larger fish than other auks; nests in colonies on cliffs. (Genera: *Uria*, 2 species, or *Cepphus*, 4 species. Family: Alcidae.)

Guillotin, Joseph Ignace [geeyohtī] (1738–1814) Physician and revolutionary, born in Saintes, W France. He proposed to the Constituent Assembly, of which he was a deputy, the use of a decapitating instrument as a means of execution. This was adopted in 1791 and named after him (the *guillotine*), though a similar apparatus had been used earlier in Scotland, Germany, and Italy. It was last used in France in 1977.

guillotine In the UK a parliamentary device whereby debate on particularly contentious items of government business can be limited by fixing the times at which various parts must be voted on, so that those opposing the business cannot instigate tactics designed to filibuster. It is used by all governments, usually on major pieces of legislation, and its imposition is itself subject to debate in the House of Commons. It cannot be applied to Private Members' Bills.

Guimarães [geemarīysh] 41°26N 8°19W, pop (2000e) 47 800. Fortified city in Braga district, N Portugal, 16 km/10 mi SE of Braga; first capital of Portugal; textiles, cutlery; birthplace of Afonso I; castle (10th-c), ducal palace, Chapel of São Miguel (1105); Cruzes festival (May), International Folk Festival (Jul).

Guinea *see panel*

Guinea, Gulf of area 1 533 000 sq km/592 000 sq mi. Arm of the Atlantic Ocean, lying in the great bend of the W African coast; bounded (N) by Côte d'Ivoire, Ghana, Togo, Benin and (E) by Nigeria, Cameroon, Equatorial Guinea, Gabon; the Equator lies to the S.

Guinea Bissau *p.672*

guinea corn *sorghum*

guinea flower *fritillary* (botany)

guinea fowl A sturdy, ground-dwelling bird native to Africa; plumage speckled grey; head and neck virtually naked, often

Guinea

[ginee], Fr **Guinée**, formerly **French Guinea**, official name **Republic of Guinea**, Fr **République de Guinée**

Local name Guinée

Timezone GMT

Area 245 857 km^2/94 926 sq mi

Population total (2002e) 7 775 000

Status Republic

Date of independence 1958

Capital Conakry

Languages French (official), Fulani, Malinké, Susu, Kissi, Kpelle

Ethnic groups Fulani (40%), Malinké (25%), Susu (11%), Kissi (6%), Kpelle (5%)

Religions Muslim (75%), traditional beliefs (24%)

Physical features Located in W Africa; coast characterized by mangrove forests, rising to a forested and widely cultivated narrow coastal plain; Fouta Djallon massif beyond, c.900 m/3000 ft; higher peaks near Senegal frontier include Mt Tangue, 1537 m/5043 ft; savannah plains in E; forested Guinea Highlands in S.

Climate Tropical climate; wet season (May–Oct); annual rainfall 4923 mm/194 in at Conakry; average temperature 32°C (dry season) on coast, 23°C (wet season).

Currency 1 Guinean Franc (GFr) = 100 cauris

Economy Agriculture (employs 75% of population); rich in minerals, with a third of the world's bauxite reserves; gold, diamonds; independence brought a fall in production as a result of withdrawal of French expertise and investment.

GDP (2002e) $18·69 bn, per capita $2100

Human Development Index (2002) 0·414

History Part of Mali empire, 16th-c; French protectorate, 1849; governed with Senegal as Rivières du Sud; separate colony, 1893; constituent territory within French West Africa, 1904; overseas territory, 1946; independent republic, 1958; death of Sékou Touré, Guinea's first President (1961–84); coup in 1984 established a Military Committee for National Recovery (CMRN); CMRN replaced by a mixed military and civilian Transitional Committee of National Recovery (CTRN), 1991; governed by a President and Council of Ministers; new constitution, 1990.

Head of State

1961–84 Ahmed Sékou Touré
1984– Lansana Conté

Head of Government

1958–72 Ahmed Sékou Touré
1972–84 Louis Lansana Beavogui
1984–5 Diarra Traore
1985–96 *No Prime Minister*
1996–9 Sidia Toure
1999– Lamine Sidime

Guinea-Bissau

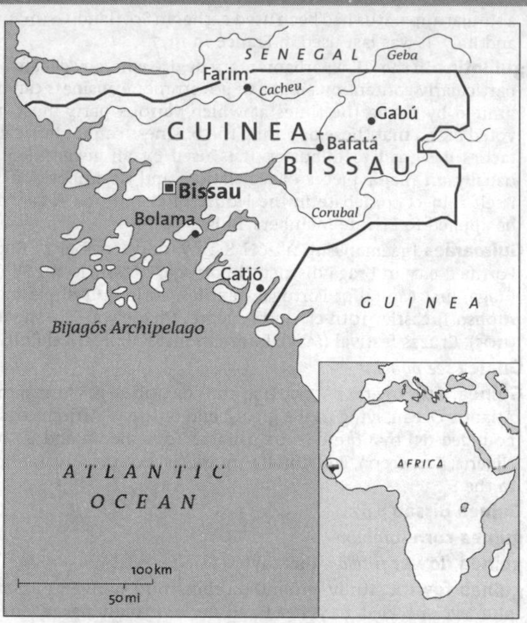

☐ International Airport

[ginee bisow], offical name **Republic of Guinea-Bissau**, Port **Republica da Guiné-Bissau**, formerly **Portuguese Guinea** (to 1974)

Local name Guiné-Bissau

Timezone GMT

Area 36 125 km²/13 948 sq mi

Population total (2002e) 1 345 000

Status Republic

Date of independence 1973

Capital Bissau

Languages Portuguese (official), Criolo, Balante

Ethnic groups Balanta (32%), Fula (22%), Mandyako (14%), Mandingo (13%), Pepel (10%)

Religions Traditional beliefs (54%), Muslim (38%), Christian (5%)

Physical features Located in W Africa; indented coast backed by forested coastal plains; main rivers, Geba and Cacheu; low-lying, with savannah-covered plateaux (S, E), rising to 310 m/1017 ft on the Guinea border; includes the heavily-forested Bijagos archipelago located in the Atlantic Ocean off the shores of the mainland.

Climate Tropical climate, hot and humid; wet season (Jun-Oct); average annual rainfall at Bissau, 1950 mm/76in; average annual temperature 24°C (Jan), 27°C (Jul) in Bissau.

Currency 1 CFA Franc (CFAFr) = 100 centimes

Economy Based on agriculture, especially rice, maize, beans, peanuts, coconuts, palm oil, groundnuts, shrimps, fish, timber; reserves of petroleum, bauxite, phosphate.

GDP (2002e) $901·4 mn, per capita $700

Human Development Index (2002) 0·349

History Visited by the Portuguese in 1446; Portuguese colony, 1879; overseas territory of Portugal, 1952; independence, 1973; military coup, 1980; new constitution, 1984; National Assembly elects Council of State; President of the Council of State also the Head of Government; introduction of a multi-party system, 1991; governed by a president, prime minister, and a 100-seat National People's Assembly; military coup, 2003, President Yalla deposed after repeatedly cancelling elections; military junta led by General Verissimo Correira, transitional government to be formed.

Head of State
1984–99 Joao Bernardo Vieira
1999–2000 Malam Bacai Sanhá
2000–3 Kumba Yalla
2003 General Verissimo Correira Seabre (*military junta*)
2003–4 Henrique Perreira Rosa
2004– General Verissimo Correira Seabre *Interim*

Head of Government
1994–7 Manuel Saturnino da Costa
1997–8 Carlos Correia
1998–2000 Francisco Fadul
2000–1 Caetano N'Tchama
2001 Faustino Imbali
2001–2 Alamara Ntchia Nhasse
2002–3 Mario Pires
2003– Antonio Artur Sanha *Interim*

with coloured or rough, folded skin; top of head may bear crest of feathers or horny projection (*casque*). (Family: Numididae, 7 species.)

guinea pig *cavy*

guineaworm A thread-like parasitic worm, a serious human parasite in Africa and India; larvae live in copepod crustaceans, and are swallowed in untreated drinking water; adult worm develops in musculature of lower limbs, causing ulceration and incapacitation. (Phylum: Nematoda.)

Guinevere [gwiniveer] King Arthur's queen; originally **Guanhamara** in Geoffrey of Monmouth's *History*, and there are other spellings. In later romances, much is made of her affair with Sir Lancelot (an example of courtly love). In Malory's epic poem she survives Arthur's death and enters a nunnery.

Guinness, Sir Alec (1914–2000) Actor, born in London, UK. He had no training as an actor, and began in repertory in 1934. He joined the Old Vic company in 1936, rejoining it in 1946 after serving in the Royal Navy. His famous stage performances include Hamlet (1938) and Macbeth (1966). Among his notable films are the Ealing Studio comedies *Kind Hearts and Coronets* (1949) and *The Lavender Hill Mob* (1951). In 1958 he received an Oscar for his part in the film *The Bridge on the River Kwai*. Later roles include Ben Kenobi in the *Star Wars* series, and Smiley in the television versions of John Le Carré's novels (1979, 1982). He was knighted in 1959 and made a Companion of Honour in 1994.

Guiscard, Robert [geeskah(r)] (c.1015–85) Norman adventurer, the son of Tancred de Hauteville, who campaigned with his brothers against the Byzantine Greeks, and created a duchy comprising S Italy and Sicily. In 1059 the papacy recognized him as Duke of Apulia, Calabria, and Sicily. He ousted the Byzantines from Calbria by 1060, then conquered Bari (1071) and captured Salerno (1076). In 1081 he crossed the Adriatic, seized Corfu, and defeated the Byzantine Emperor, Alexius Comnenus, at Durazzo. He died at Cephalonia, while advancing on Constantinople.

Guise [geez] French ducal house of Lorraine, named after the town of Guise, whose members were prominent as staunch leaders of the Catholic Party during the 16th-c civil wars, through their relationship with the Stuart and Valois royal houses. The first duke was Claude de Lorraine (1496–1550), who served under Francis I in Italy and was given the ducal title in 1528. Henry, the third duke, instigated the murder of Coligny in the massacre of St Bartholomew's Day (1572). On the death of the seventh duke, Francis Joseph (1675) the estates reverted to Mary of Lorraine, on whose death the line became extinct.

guitar In its modern form, a musical instrument with a wooden, 'waisted' body, flat back, fretted neck, and six strings which are plucked (usually by fingers or fingernails) or strummed. Before the late 18th-c, most guitars had four or five courses (a 'course' being one or more strings tuned to a single pitch). Since its earliest days the guitar has been associated with folk and popular music, especially Spanish flamenco, but the 19th-c six-course instrument also attracted an extensive printed repertory from guitarist-composers such as Mauro Giuliani (1781–1829) and Fernando Sor (1778–1839). The elevation of the classical guitar to the status of a recital and concerto instrument owes much to the example and influence of Andrés Segovia.

The **electric guitar**, the sound of which is amplified and fed through a loudspeaker, exists in two types: the semi-acoustic, with a hollow body, and the more common type with a solid body acting not as a resonator but as an anchor for the strings, and a panel to which the electronic pickups and tone and volume controls are attached. The standard instrument has six strings, played with plectrum or fingers; the **bass guitar** has four strings, tuned one octave below the four lowest strings of the standard instrument. Both sizes are widely used in all types of modern popular music.

guitar fish Bottom-dwelling, ray-like fish of families Rhinobatidae or Rhynchobatidae, in which the flattened head, broad pectoral fins, and slender body resembles the shape of a guitar; includes *Rhinobatus rhinobatus*, widespread in NE Atlantic and Mediterranean; length up to 1 m/3¼ ft.

Guitry, Sacha [geetree], originally **Alexandre Georges Guitry** (1885–1957) Actor and playwright, born in St Petersburg, NW Russia, the son of French actor-manager **Lucien Guitry** (1860–1925). He first appeared on stage in Russia with his father's company, and later acted in Paris (1902) and London (1920). He wrote nearly 100 plays, mostly light comedies, many performed in English. He also wrote and directed several films, including *Le Roman d'un tricheur* (1936, trans The Cheat).

Guiyang or **Kuei-yang** [kwayyahng] 26°35N 106°40E, pop (2000e) 1 856 000. Capital of Guizhou province, S China; airfield; railway; steel, machinery, aluminium.

Guizot, François (Pierre Guillaume) [geezoh] (1787–1874) Historian and statesman, born in Nîmes, S France. He studied law in Paris, but in 1812 became professor of modern history at the Sorbonne. A member of the Doctrinaires under Louis XVIII, he was elected to the Chamber (1830), became minister of the interior (1830), and then of public instruction (1832). As the king's chief adviser (1840), he relapsed into reactionary methods of government, and escaped to London with Louis-Philippe in 1848. After 1851 he gave himself up entirely to his historical publications.

Gujarat [goojaraht] pop (2001e) 50 597 000; area 195 984 sq km/75 650 sq mi. State in W India, bounded N by Pakistan, SW, S and SE by the Arabian Sea; independent sultanate, 1401; part of Mongol Empire, 1572; retained its own princely rulers under British control; part of Bombay state, 1947; created in 1960 from the N and W Gujarati-speaking areas of Bombay state; capital, Gandhinagar; governed by a 182-member Legislative Assembly; airfield; six universities; highly industrialized; textiles, electrical engineering, petrochemicals, machine tools, cement, oil refining, fertilizers; cotton, rice, groundnuts; reserves of crude oil and gas; scene of flood disaster in 1983, after bursting of the Fodana Dam; major earthquake in 2001, with 100 000 deaths recorded.

Gujarati [gujarahtee] *Indo-Aryan languages*

Gujranwala [gujrahnvala] 32°06N 74°11E, pop (2000e) 1 069 000. City in NE Punjab province, Pakistan, 67 km/42 mi NW of Lahore; Sikh ruler Ranjit Singh born there, 1780; former Sikh capital; railway; copper and brass handicrafts, grain trade, textiles, ceramics.

Gujrat [gujrat] 32°35N 74°06E, pop (2000e) 209 000. City in Punjab province, E Pakistan, 109 km/68 mi N of Lahore, between the Jhelum and Chenab Rivers; founded, 16th-c; railway; gold and silver crafts, trade in wheat, millet, cotton, rice.

gulag [goolag] Acronym for **Glavnoye Upravleniye Ispravitelno-Trudovykh Lagerey** (Main Administration of Corrective Labour Camps), the Soviet Union's secret police department which administered the system of forced labour for those found guilty of crimes against the state. Forced labour was the 'punishment' of many Soviet dissidents.

Gulbenkian, Calouste (Sarkis) [gulbengkian] (1869–1955) Financier, industrialist, and diplomat, born in Scutari, NW Turkey. He entered his father's oil business in 1888, and became a naturalized British subject in 1902. After a lifetime of oil deals between Europe, the USA, and the Arab countries, he left $70 million and vast art collections to finance an international Gulbenkian Foundation.

Gulf, The *Persian Gulf*

Gulf Co-operation Council (GCC) An organization which encourages co-operation among the Arab states in the Persian Gulf area. It was established in 1981 by Bahrain, Kuwait, Oman, Qatar, Saudi Arabia, and the United Arab Emirates. The relationship with Yemen is under consideration.

Gulf Intracoastal Waterway *Intracoastal Waterway*

Gulf Stream Ocean current named after the Gulf of Mexico; flows past Florida and along the E coast of the USA until deflected near Newfoundland NE across the Atlantic Ocean (the N Atlantic Drift); its warm water has an important moderating effect on the climate of NW Europe.

Gulf War (Jan–Feb 1991) A war caused by the invasion of Kuwait by Iraq (Aug 1990). Iraq failed to comply with a UN resolution calling on it to withdraw, which resulted in the formation of a 29-member coalition, led by the USA, launching an air attack against Iraq (Operation Desert Storm) on 16 January 1991, followed by a ground war (Operation Desert Sabre) on 24 February. Kuwait was liberated two days later, and hostilities were suspended on 28 February (a total of 43 days fighting). Iraq then accepted the UN resolutions. Among notable events of the conflict were the Scud missile attacks on Israel; Iraq's pumping of Kuwaiti oil into the Gulf; and the burning of Kuwaiti oil wells (all capped by Nov 1991).

Gulf War (1980–8) *Iran–Iraq War*

gull A medium or large bird, found worldwide, usually near water; feet webbed; plumage white, grey, and black; wings long and slender; bill long, stout; omnivorous, often scavenging; related to terns and skuas. (Family: Laridae, 44 species.)

gullet *oesophagus*

Gullit, Ruud [khulit, rood] (1962–) Football player and manager, born in Suriname. The son of a former Suriname international, he began his professional career at age 16 with Haarlem, made his debut for Holland in 1981, and gained honours with Dutch teams Feyenoord and PSV Eindhoven. In 1987 he was named European Footballer of the Year, later joining AC Milan for a then world record £7·5 million fee. He captained Holland to win the European Championships (1988), and with AC Milan won the European Cup (1989, 1990). In 1995 he joined Chelsea, and the next year took over as player-manager, leading his team to FA Cup victory (1996–7). He was manager at Newcastle United (1998–9), then returned to Holland.

gum arabic A resin which exudes from the branches of several species of *Acacia*, particularly *Acacia senegal*, a shrub or small tree native to dry areas of Africa, from Senegal to Nigeria. It provides the gum arabic of commerce. The gum is harvested during the dry season, and is used as an adhesive, and in ink and confectionery manufacture. (Family: Leguminosae.)

gumbo *okra*

gums Dense fibrous connective tissue surrounding the roots of the teeth, firmly attached to the underlying bone (the alveolar bone of the jaws). They are covered by a smooth vascular mucous membrane continuous with the lining of the lips and cheeks.

gum tree A member of a genus of evergreen trees, native to and typical of Australia. The leaves are often of two kinds: the *juvenile* are fused in pairs to form discs with the stem passing through the centre; the *adult* are alternate, oval or lance-shaped. The flowers are modified to form woody cups with lids which fall to release numerous, showy stamens. Groups of species can be recognized by their characteristic bark: smooth gum trees, scaly blood-woods, fibrous stringy-barks, and hard iron-barks. They are often dominant forest trees, and a major or sole food for various animals, such as koalas. They are fast growing, the tallest reaching 97 m/318 ft. They provide useful timber and oils, including eucalyptus oil, and are now grown in many parts of the world for timber, ornament, and soil stabilization. (Genus: *Eucalyptus*, 500 species. Family: Myrtaceae.)

gun-cotton *nitrocellulose*

Gundelach, Finn Olav [gundelach] (1925–81) Danish diplomat and European Commissioner, born in Vejle, C Denmark. He studied at Århus, joined the Danish Diplomatic Service, and became ambassador to the European Community in 1967, directing the negotiations for Denmark's entry into the Community (1973), and becoming his country's first European commissioner. In 1977 he was made vice-president of the new European Commission, and was given charge of the Common Agricultural Policy.

gundog *sporting dog*

gun-metal A form of bronze once favoured for the making of weapons. Modern gun-metal, with a composition of c.88% copper, 10% tin, and some zinc, has good anti-corrosion properties within the conditions encountered in valves and other steam fittings.

Gunn, Thom(son William) (1929–) Poet, born in Gravesend, Kent, SE England, UK. After studying at Cambridge, he went to California (1954), where he taught English at Stanford and Berkeley. His often erotic poems are written in an intriguing variety of regular and free forms. Volumes include *Fighting Terms* (1954), *Jack Straw's Castle* (1976), *The Passages of Joy* (1982), *The Man With Night Sweats* (1992), *Shelf Life* (1993), and *Frontiers of Gossip* (1997).

Gunnbjørn Fjeld [goonbyern] 68°50N 29°45W. Highest mountain in Greenland, rising to 3702 m/12 145 ft near the SE coast.

gunnel Small, slender-bodied fish found in inshore and intertidal habitats of the N Atlantic and Pacific Oceans; length up to 30 cm/1 ft; pelvic fins reduced or absent; includes the Atlantic butterfish (*Pholis gunnellus*), common among rocks and kelp. (Family: Pholidae.)

Gunnell, Sally (Janet) (1966–) Athlete, born in Chigwell, Essex, SE England, UK. She gained international recognition with a gold medal for the 100 m hurdles in the 1986 Commonwealth Games. She won the 400 m hurdles in the 1992 Olympics, and was world champion and world record holder for the same event in 1993 with a time of 52·74 s. In 1993–4 she became European Cup, Commonwealth, and World Cup champion in the hurdles. She has written a book about her career, *Running Tall* (1994).

gunpowder The oldest known explosive, a mixture of sulphur, charcoal and saltpetre (nitre, potassium nitrate). Invented in China in the 9th-c, the Chinese had guns by 900, rockets and grenades by 1042, and cannon by 1259. Gunpowder was first used in Europe in 1325. Gunpowder mixtures have a range of properties, depending on formulation and granulation. It was the principal military explosive until late in the 19th-c, and is still valuable in primers, fuses, and pyrotechnics.

Gunpowder Plot A conspiracy by Catholic gentry, led by Robert Catesby, to blow up the English Houses of Parliament. It failed when Guy Fawkes, who placed the explosives, was arrested (5 Nov 1605). The plot failed because one conspirator, Francis Tresham, warned his brother-in-law, Lord Monteagle, not to attend the parliamentary sitting; and Monteagle reported the matter to the government. The scheme reflected Catholic desperation after the failure of previous plots to remove James I in 1603; peace with Spain in 1604, which ended the prospect of foreign support; and new sanctions imposed against recusant Catholics, including an Oath of Allegiance, resulting in 5000 convictions in the spring of 1605 alone.

Gunwinggu An Australian Aboriginal people of W Arnhem Land. During the late 19th-c, many settled at the camp of a buffalo shooter named Paddy Cahill, which became the settlement of Oenpelli. Many Gunwinggu still live in small 'outstations' on Aboriginal land, gaining most of their subsistence by hunting and gathering, and earning cash from the sale of bark paintings in the distinctive 'X-ray' style, which depicts species of fish and vertebrates with organs such as heart and liver inside the body.

Guomindang or **Kuomintang (KMT)** [gwohmindang] The Chinese National People's Party (or Nationalists), founded in 1912 by Sun Yatsen out of the Alliance Party (established in 1905) and espousing his Three People's Principles – nationalism, democracy, and economic reform. Its capital was Guangzhou (Canton) from 1921. Jiang Jieshi led the party from 1925, with the capital in Nanjing (1927–37, 1945–9) and Chongqing during the Japanese occupation (1937–45). After its defeat by the Communists in 1949, it retreated to Taiwan, where it still rules.

guppy Small, freshwater fish (*Poecilia reticulata*) native to South and Central America but now widespread through the aquarium trade; feeds on invertebrates and algae; length up to 3 cm/1¼ in; males with metallic blue-green coloration. Captive breeding has produced a considerable variety of forms and colours. (Family: Poecilidae.)

Gupta Empire [gupta] (320–540) A decentralized state system covering most of N India, with provinces (*desa*) and districts (*pradesa*). It was materially prosperous, especially in urban areas, and is known as India's 'Classical' or 'Golden' Age, when norms of Indian literature, art, architecture, and philosophy were established, and Hinduism underwent revival.

Gur Amir or **Gur Emir** [goor ameer] The mausoleum of Timur, Ulugh Beg, and others of the house of Timur, built in Samarkand (in present-day Uzbekistan) in the 15th-c. The interior of the mausoleum is decorated with turquoise and gold designs, while the exterior is dominated by a splendid ribbed dome. The Gur Amir was restored in 1967.

gurdwara [goordwara] (Sanskrit, 'guru's door') A Sikh temple, or any place where the scripture is installed. In addition to a worship area housing the scripture, it should include a hostel and a place for serving meals.

Gurkhas [gerkuhz] **1** The name of the Nepalese ruling dynasty since 1768.
2 An elite infantry unit of the British army recruited from the hill tribes of Nepal. Their characteristic weapon, the *kukri* fighting knife with its curved blade, has contributed to their fame, in battles from the North West Frontier of India in the 19th-c, via the Western Front in World War 1, to the Burma and Italian campaigns of World War 2. Gurkha infantry also took part in the Falklands War of 1982.

gurnard [gernah(r)d] Any of the bottom-living marine fishes of the family Triglidae, widespread in inshore waters of tropical to temperate seas; also called **sea robins**; length up to 75 cm/30 in; head armoured with bony plates; pectoral fin rays used as feelers or as stilts; many produce audible sounds; includes European **grey gurnard** (*Eutrigla gurnardus*).

Gurney, Edmund (1847–88) Psychical researcher, born in Hersham, Surrey, SE England, UK. He studied at Cambridge, and became one of the founding members of the Society for Psychical Research. He conducted important experimental studies of hypnosis and telepathy, and a statistical survey of hallucinations. His investigation of apparitions, telepathy, and other such phenomena culminated in his classic *Phantasms of the Living* (with F W H Myers and F Podmore, 1886).

Gurney, Ivor (Bertie) (1890–1937) Composer and poet, born in Gloucester, Gloucestershire, SWC England, UK. He studied at the Royal College of Music in London. As a composer he found his voice in 1913/14 with the composition of *Five Elizabethan Songs*. Gassed and shell-shocked in 1917, he published two volumes of poems from hospital: *Severn and Somme* (1917) and *War's Embers* (1919). From 1922 he was confined in an asylum, and died in London. Some 300 songs and 900 poems survive, whose quality is increasingly recognized. In 1982 a major collection of his 300 poems was issued.

guru [gooroo] In Hinduism, a spiritual teacher or guide who gives instruction to a disciple or pupil, who in return is required to render reverence and obedience. In Sikhism, it is identified with the inner voice of God, of which the 10 Gurus were the human vehicles. The term has developed a more general sense in recent years, referring to anyone who comes to be recognized as leader or originator of a cult or idea, not necessarily to do with religion.

Gush Emmunim [gush emuneem] (Heb 'Group of those who keep the faith') A militant Israeli movement set up after the 1973 elections, dedicated to an active settlement policy in territories such as the West Bank, occupied by the Israelis after the 1967 war.

Gustav I, originally **Gustav Eriksson Vasa** (1496–1560) King of Sweden (1523–60), the founder of the Vasa dynasty, born into a gentry family in Lindholmen, E Sweden. In 1518 he was carried off to Denmark as a hostage, but escaped to lead a peasant rising against the occupying Danes, capturing Stockholm (1523) and driving the enemy from Sweden. He was elected king by the Diet and, despite several rebellions, his 40-year rule left Sweden a peaceful realm.

Gustav II Adolf or **Gustavus Adolphus**(1594–1632) King of Sweden (1611–32), born in Stockholm, Sweden, the son of Charles IX. On ascending the throne, he reorganized the government with the assistance of Chancellor Oxenstierna, raised men and money, and recovered his Baltic provinces from Denmark. He ended wars with Russia (1617) and Poland (1629), and carried out major military and economic reforms at home. In 1630 he entered the Thirty Years' War, leading the German Protestants against the Imperialist forces under Wallenstein, and won several victories, notably at Breitenfeld (1631). He was killed during the Swedish victory at Lützen, near Leipzig.

gut *alimentary canal*

Gutenberg, Johannes (Gensfleisch) [gootnberg] (1400–68) Printer, born in Mainz, WC Germany. He is regarded as the European inventor of printing from movable type (Chinese movable type dates from the 1040s). Between 1430 and 1444 he was in Strasbourg, probably working as a goldsmith, and here he may have begun printing. In Mainz again by 1448 he entered into partnership with Johann Fust (c.1400–1466), who financed a printing press. This partnership ended in 1455, when Fust sued him for repayment of the loan, and forced him to give up his machinery, leaving him ruined. Aided by Konrad Humery, he was able to set up another press, but little is known of his work thereafter. His best-known book is the 42-line Bible, often called the *Gutenberg Bible* (c.1455).

Guterson, David (1956–) Writer, born in Seattle, Washington, USA. He was a postgraduate student at the University of Washington. After moving to Bainbridge I in Puget Sound he taught English at a local high school and starting writing for *Sports Illustrative* and *Harpers* magazines. His works include a collection of short stories, *The Country Ahead of Us, The Country Behind* (1996), a best-selling novel, *Snow Falling On Cedars* (1995, PEN/Faulkner Award), and *East of the Mountains* (2000).

Guthrie, Sir (William) Tyrone (1900–71) Theatrical director, born in Tunbridge Wells, Kent, SE England, UK. He studied at Oxford, and became director of the Scottish National Players (1926–8) and the Cambridge Festival Theatre (1929–30). He was responsible for many fine productions of Shakespeare at the Old Vic during the 1930s, and became administrator of the Old Vic and Sadler's Wells (1939–45), and director of the Old Vic (1950–1). He often worked abroad, and founded the Tyrone Guthrie Theatre in Minneapolis, MN, in 1963. He was knighted in 1961.

Guthrie, Woody, popular name of **Woodrow Wilson Guthrie** (1912–67) Folksinger and songwriter, born in Okemah, Oklahoma, USA. He took to the road during the Great Depression, singing for his meals, and wrote hundreds of songs, lauding migrant workers, pacifists, and underdogs of all kinds. His best-known songs are 'So Long, It's Been Good to Know You' and 'This Land is Your Land'. He helped to form the Almanac Singers, a group that advocated public power at workers' rallies. In 1952, he was hospitalized with Huntington's chorea, and died of it 15 years later, by which time a new generation, including Joan Baez and Bob Dylan, had learned his songs and adopted his causes.

Gutland [gootlant] or **Pays Gaumais** Geographical region of S Luxembourg, occupying nearly 70% of the country, part of the fertile uplands of Lorraine; includes important wine-producing area along the R Moselle; city of Luxembourg in C of region.

gutta percha A grey-black substance similar to rubber, but non-elastic, obtained from the latex of *Palaquium*, a genus of tropical trees related to chicle. It has been widely used in dental fillings, electrical insulation, and (especially) golf balls. (Family: Sapotaceae.)

Guy, Thomas [giy] (c.1644–1724) Philanthropist, born in London, UK. He began business in 1668 as a bookseller, and then became a printer of Bibles, amassing a fortune of nearly half a million pounds. In 1707 he built and furnished three wards of St Thomas' Hospital, and in 1721 founded the hospital in Southwark, London, which bears his name.

Guyana *p.676*

Guyenne or **Guienne** [güyen], Lat **Aquitania** A mediaeval duchy, including Gascony, in SW France, bounded W by the Bay of Biscay. The rump of Aquitaine, it remained a possession of the English crown after Normandy and other French territories were lost in 1204–5. The claim of the kings of England to be independent rulers of Guyenne was one of the causes of the Hundred Years' War. It was finally conquered by the French in 1453. The area is now occupied by the departments of Gironde, Dordogne, Lot, Aveyron, Tarn-et-Garonne, and Lot-et-Garonne.

Guy Fawkes Night or **Bonfire Night** The evening of 5 November, the anniversary in the UK of the Gunpowder Plot (1605), celebrated with fireworks and bonfires, on which are often burned effigies of Guy Fawkes known as **guys**.

guyot *seamount*

Guzmán Blanco, Antonio [goosmahn] (1829–99) Venezuelan dictator, born in Carácas, Venezuela. He was vice-president from 1863 to 1868. Driven from office (1868), he headed a revolution which restored him to power (1870), and became dictator, holding the presidency on three occasions (1873–7, 1879–84, 1886–8). He then retired to Paris.

Gwalior [gwaliaw(r)] 26°12N 78°09E, pop (2000e) 814 000. City and former princely state in Madhya Pradesh, C India; founded, 8th-c; famous cultural centre, 15th-c; Mughal city, 15th–16th-c; taken by the British, 1780; railway; commercial centre; fort on Gwalior Rock, with several palaces, temples, and shrines.

Gwent pop (2000e) 456 500; area 1376 sq km/531 sq mi. Former county in SE Wales, UK; created in 1974, and replaced in 1996 by Monmouthshire, Blaenau Gwent, Torfaen, and Newport counties.

Gweru [gwayroo], formerly **Gwelo** 19°25S 29°50E, pop (2000e) 115 500. Capital of Midlands province, Zimbabwe, 155 km/96 mi NE of Bulawayo; airfield; railway; important communications and administrative centre; shoes, glassware, metal alloys, dairy products, batteries.

Gwyn or **Gwynne, Nell,** popular name of **Eleanor Gwyn** (c.1650–87) Mistress of Charles II, possibly born in London, UK. Of humble parentage, she lived precariously as an orange girl before going on the boards at Drury Lane, where she quickly established herself as a comedienne. She had at least one son by the king – Charles Beauclerk, Duke of St Albans – and James Beauclerk is often held to have been a second.

Gwynedd [gwineth] pop (2001e) 116 800; area 3869 sq km/1494 sq mi. County in NW Wales, UK, bounded NW by the Menai Straits and Anglesey, N and W by the Irish Sea; created in 1996; formerly (1974–96) a wider area, including Anglesey, now consists only of Caernarfonshire and Merionethshire; rises to 1085 m/3560 ft at Snowdon in Snowdonia National Park; drained by the R Conwy; bilingual language policy; administrative centre, Caernarfon; other chief towns, Bangor, Pwllheli, Barmouth; livestock, slate quarrying, textiles, electronics, light

Guyana

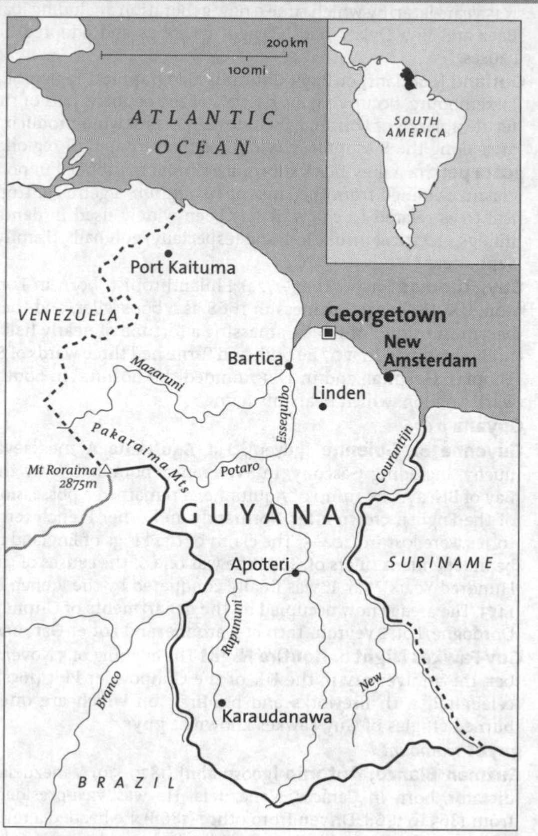

[giyahna], official name **Co-operative Republic of Guyana**, formerly (to 1966) **British Guiana**

Local name Guyana
Timezone GMT −3
Area 214 969 km²/82 978 sq mi
Population total (2002e) 775 000
Status Co-operative republic
Date of independence 1966
Capital Georgetown
Languages English (official), Hindi, Urdu, Amerindian dialects
Ethnic groups E Indian (51%), black (30·5%), Amerindian (5%) (Carib 4%, Arawak 1%)
Religions Christian (42%), Hindu (37%), Muslim (9%)
Physical features Located on N coast of South America; inland forest covers c.83% of land area; highest peak Mt Roraima, rising to 2875 m/9432 ft in the Pakaraima Mts (W); main rivers, Essequibo, Rupununi, and Corantijn, with many rapids and waterfalls in upper courses.
Climate Equatorial climate in the lowlands; hot, wet, with constant high humidity; average annual temperature 26°C (Jan), 27°C (Jul) in Georgetown; two seasons of high rainfall (May–Jul, Nov–Jan); average annual rainfall 2175 mm/87 in.
Currency 1 Guyana Dollar (G$) = 100 cents
Economy High unemployment, influenced by labour unrest, low productivity, and high foreign debt; economy largely based on sugar, rice, bauxite, shrimps, livestock, cotton, molasses, timber.
GDP (2002e) $2·628 bn, per capita $3800
Human Development Index (2002) 0·708
History Sighted by Columbus, 1498; settled by the Dutch, late 16th-c; several areas ceded to Britain, 1814; consolidated as British Guiana, 1831; independence, 1966; cooperative republic within the Commonwealth, 1970; governed by a President who holds executive power and appoints a Prime Minister and National Assembly, elected every five years.
Head of State/Government
1997–9 Janet Jagan
1999– Bharrat Jagdeo
Prime Minister and First Vice-President
1985–92 Hamilton Green
1992–7 Samuel Hinds
1997 Janet Jagan
1997– Samuel Hinds

engineering, tourism; castles at Caernarfon, Conwy, Criccieth, Harlech; Llyn Tegid (Bala), largest Welsh lake.

gymkhana A mixed sports meeting in a public place, especially one involving a range of horse-riding skills for young riders. Gymkhanas originated in India in 1860, where horse and pony races were introduced for British soldiers' entertainment. Over the years athletic events and other competitions (eg model aeroplane flying) have been introduced. In the USA, the term is often used for an obstacle competition for automobiles.

gymnastics A series of physical exercises now used primarily for sporting contests. The ancient Greeks and Romans performed such exercises for health purposes. Modern techniques were developed in Germany towards the end of the 18th-c. In competition, gymnasts perform exercises which are subsequently marked out of a score of 10 by a series of judges. Men compete on the parallel bars, pommel horse, horizontal bar, rings, horse vault, and floor exercise. Women compete on the asymmetrical bars, beam, horse vault, and floor exercise. It has become an important sport in the Olympics.

gymnosperms The commonly used name for one of the two divisions of seed plants, the other being the *flowering plants* (**angiosperms**). They are characterized by having naked seeds (ie not enclosed in an ovary), but the members differ widely from each other, and are now regarded as deriving from several entirely separated ancestral lines. It contains both living (eg conifers) and entirely fossil groups. Early gymnosperms were abundant during the Carboniferous period, forming many of the coal deposits, and becoming the dominant vegetation during the Jurassic and Cretaceous periods, after which many became extinct. Living genera again became widespread, particularly during the last glaciations, and are still found from cold temperate to subtropical regions, and even in the tropics on high mountains; but many genera are now confined to small geographical areas. (Class: Gymnospermae.)

gymnure [jimnyoor] *moonrat*

gynaecology / gynecology [giynikolojee] The study of the functions and disorders of the female organs of reproduction. Disorders of menstruation and of fertility constitute a major part of the discipline. In addition, it includes the investigation and treatment of infections of the reproductive organs, as well as benign and malignant tumours of the cervix, uterus, and ovaries. Liberalization of the laws relating to abortion has increased the need for specialized gynaecological care.

gynaecomastia / gynecomastia [giynikohmastia] Enlargement of the male breast due to overgrowth of its cells. It occurs naturally and transiently in many male adolescents, and also develops if female sex hormones are given to men, and as a consequence of certain drugs.

gynecium / gynoecium *carpel; flower*

Györ [dyür], Ger **Raab**, Lat **Arrabona** 47°41N 17°40E, pop (2000e) 126 000. Industrial city and capital of Györ-Sopron county, NW Hungary; at the junction of the Rába and Repce Rivers and the R

Danube; linked to L Fertö by canal; railway; bishopric; vehicles, steel, machinery, foodstuffs, textiles, distilling, horse breeding; noted for its modern ballet company; Carmelite convent (18th-c), cathedral (12th-c, rebuilt 18th-c), city hall (18th-c).

gypsum A mineral of calcium sulphate ($CaSO_4{\cdot}2H_2O$) found in evaporite deposits as crystals (*selenite*) or fine-grained masses (*alabaster*). When partly dehydrated, it forms *plaster of Paris*, a fine, quick-setting, white powder.

Gypsy *Rom*

gypsy moth A medium-sized tussock moth; rare in Britain but a pest of fruit trees in North America; wings whitish with dark zigzag markings; caterpillar greyish with tufts of brown hair; pupates in a loose cocoon. (Order: Lepidoptera. Family: Lymantridae.)

gyre A large semi-enclosed ocean circulation cell made up of surface currents. As these circulate around the oceans, the currents which make up their limbs receive, store, and give up heat to the atmosphere and adjacent ocean currents, resulting in temperature changes in the surface water. In many cases the heat transported by gyres strongly influences the weather and climate of surrounding land areas.

gyrfalcon [jerfawlkn] The largest of all falcons (*Falco rusticolus*) (length 50–60 cm/20–24 in); native to Arctic regions; inhabits mountains and tundra; plumage white, grey, or dark; hunts close to ground; eats mainly ground-dwelling birds.

gyrocompass A form of gyroscope which is set to maintain a N-seeking orientation as an aid to navigation.

gyromagnetic ratio For spinning particles, the ratio of magnetic moment to particle spin; symbol γ, units $T^{-1}s^{-1}$ (per tesla per second). For protons, $\gamma = 2{\cdot}675 \times 10^8\ T^{-1}s^{-1}$.

gyroscope An instrument consisting of a rapidly spinning wheel so mounted as to use its tendency to maintain a fixed position in space, and to resist any force which tries to change it. The way it will move if a twisting force is applied depends on the extent and orientation of the force and the way the gyroscope is mounted. A free vertically spinning gyroscope (in *gimbals*, two semicircular mountings at right angles, such that the mounted object can turn in any direction) remains vertical as the carrying vehicle tilts, so providing an artificial horizon. A horizontal gyroscope will maintain a certain bearing, and therefore indicate a vessel's heading as it turns. Modern gyroscopes no longer have a spinning wheel. In an **Interferometric Fibre-Optic Gyro**, a laser beam is split into two waves which pass in opposite directions round a fibre-optic coil. If the coil rotates, there will be a difference in intensity of the light when it returns to the detector. The difference is converted into the degree of rotation. In a **ring laser gyro**, laser light is reflected by mirrors in both directions through a closed optical channel. If the gyroscope rotates, the two beams will not arrive exactly in phase at the detector, resulting in an interference fringe pattern. Interpretation of this pattern determines the degree of rotation of the gyroscope.

h

Haakon VII [**haw**kon] (1872–1957) King of Norway (1905–57), born in Charlottenlund, E Denmark. He became king when Norway voted herself independent of Sweden in 1905, dispensed with regal pomp, and emerged as the 'people's king'. During World War 2, he remained active in Norwegian resistance to Nazi occupation from England.

Haarlem *Harlem* (The Netherlands)

Haavelmo, Trygve [**haw**velmoh] (1911–99) Econometrician and economist, born in Skedsmo, SE Norway. In 1947, he became head of a division in the Norwegian ministry of commerce, and in 1948 was appointed professor of political economy and statistics at the University of Oslo. He was awarded the 1989 Nobel Prize for Economics for his contributions to developing the field of econometrics, especially methods to estimate and test quantitative relations.

Habakkuk or **Habacuc, Book of** [**hab**akuk] One of the 12 so-called 'minor' prophetic books of the Hebrew Bible/Old Testament, attributed to the otherwise unknown prophet Habakkuk, possibly of the late 7th-c BC. It consists of two dialogues about why God allows the godless to 'surround' the righteous (Israel), with the response that 'the just shall live by his faith' (*Hab* 2.4; *Rom* 1.17; *Gal* 3.11). The final prayer celebrates God's coming in victory over his enemies.

habeas corpus [**hay**bias **kaw(r)**pus] (Lat 'you must have the body') An ancient and fundamental common-law right that (in the form developed in England and Wales since the 15th-c) requires a person who detains another to appear in court and justify that detention. If there is no good reason for the detention, release is ordered. The writ can be obtained whether the detainee is held by the state or privately. A habeas corpus writ is a means of testing whether a person has been given full legal rights; it does not establish his or her guilt or innocence. In England and Wales it is issued by the Divisional Court of the Queens Bench Division (or, in the vacation, by a High Court judge). In Scotland, the term is not used; however, a petition to the High Court of Justiciary can achieve the same result. The right to bring a writ of habeas corpus is guaranteed in Article 1 Section 9 of the US constitution, and is used to challenge governmental restraint contrary to fundamental or constitutional law.

Haber, Fritz [**hah**ber] (1868–1934) Chemist, born in Wrocław, SW Poland (formerly Breslau, Prussia). He studied in Berlin, Heidelberg, and Zürich. Professor of chemistry at Karlsruhe and Berlin, he became known for his invention of the process for making ammonia from the nitrogen in the air. He was awarded the Nobel Prize for Chemistry in 1918.

Habermas, Jürgen [**hab**ermas] (1929–) Philosopher and social theorist, born in Düsseldorf, W Germany. He studied at Göttingen and Bonn universities, taught at Heidelberg (1962) and Frankfurt (1964), and became director of the Max Planck Institute (1971). He continues the tradition of Marxist social philosophy associated with the Frankfurt School, and a central theme of his work is the possibility of a rational political commitment to socialism in societies in which science and technology are dominant. His books include *Erkenntnis und Interesse* (1968, Knowledge and Human Interests) and *Theorie des kommunikativen Handelns* (1982, Theory of Communicative Action).

Haber–Bosch process [**hah**ber **bosh**] A chemical process developed in the early 20th-c for making ammonia from the nitrogen of the atmosphere. It is one of the most important chemical processes ever devised, because it makes possible the fixation of atmospheric nitrogen and therefore, by conversion of the ammonia to nitric acid, the production of nitrates needed for fertilizers (and explosives). Fritz Haber showed theoretically and experimentally how to maintain the reaction between nitrogen from air and hydrogen from water at suitable temperature and pressure, and with effective catalysts. Carl Bosch showed how to operate the process on an industrial scale. The overall reaction is $3H_2+N_2 \rightarrow 2NH_3$.

Habima (Hebrew, 'scene', 'stage') A theatre company formed in Moscow, after the Revolution, to stage plays in Hebrew. It became one of the studios of the Moscow Art Theatre and toured extensively. The company moved to Palestine in 1931, and in 1953 became Israel's National Theatre. Its repertoire included plays by Asch, Peretz, Katzenelson, and Berkowitz. Ansky's *The Dybbuk* (1922) became a model production. Today the Habima also has its own drama school.

habitat loss The loss of distinctive areas which provide breeding and range territories for plants and wildlife. Destruction and disturbance by human activity is a major threat to wild species. Many areas of wilderness have been modified into artificial landscapes of settlement, agriculture, and industry. There is increased intrusion into remote areas for exploitation of timber, oil, and mineral resources.

habituation The weakening or disappearance of an individual's initial spontaneous reaction to a stimulus (eg alertness, defence, attack) as a result of the stimulus occurring repeatedly without any interesting consequences. Changes in the form or consequences of the stimulus may cause the habituated response to reappear.

Habsburgs One of the principal dynasties of modern Europe, pre-eminent in C Europe from the mediaeval period as sovereign rulers of Austria, from which the family extended its territories and influence to secure the title of Holy Roman Emperor (1452–1806). The zenith of Habsburg power was reached under Charles V (1500–58), who presided over an empire stretching from the Danube to the Caribbean. After Charles's retirement (1556) his inheritance was divided between his son and brother, thus creating the **Spanish Habsburg** line, rulers of Spain until 1700, and the **Austrian Habsburgs**, whose descendants retained the imperial title and ruled the Habsburg possessions in C Europe until 1918.

hacker A computer user who communicates with other remote computers, usually via the telephone network or the Internet. In recent years, the term has acquired a pejorative sense, referring to those who access remote computers without permission, often obtaining access to confidential information of a personal or business nature. Malicious hacking is now illegal within several countries. Computer systems are vulnerable to the infiltration of viruses or 'bugs' which give control of the computers to hackers with malicious intent. This has led to a growing demand for anti-virus programs designed by computer security experts.

Hackman, Gene (1931–) Film actor, born in San Bernardino, California, USA. Having established himself as a theatre performer, he made his film debut in *Mad Dog Coll* (1961), and had small roles in many films before earning a Best Supporting Actor Oscar nomination for his performance in *Bonnie and Clyde* (1967). He won an Oscar for his role as 'Popeye Doyle' in *The French Connection* (1971), and received further Oscar nominations for *Mississippi Burning* (1989), and *Unforgiven* (1992). Later films include *Wyatt Earp* (1994), *Get Shorty* (1995), *Absolute Power* (1997), *Twilight* (1998), and *The Royal Tenenbaums* (2001, Golden Globe).

hackney horse An English breed of horse; height, 14·3–16 hands/1·5–1·6 m/4 ft 11 in–5 ft 4 in; graceful and spirited, with an emphasized strutting step; black or brown with tail held high. There is also a **hackney pony** (**bantam hackney** in USA), bred to pull carriages.

Hadar [hadah(r)] A locality in Afar region, Ethiopia, with important early hominid sites along the Awash R dated 2·8–3·4 million years ago, and providing extensive and highly variable remains of *Australopithecus afarensis*. One locality yielded parts of at least 13 individuals; another the partial skeleton of a small female, nicknamed 'Lucy'.

haddock Bottom-living fish (*Melanogrammus aeglefinus*) widespread in cold N waters of the Atlantic; length up to c.80 cm/32 in; body dark greenish-brown on back, sides silvery grey with dark patch above pectoral fins, underside white, lateral line black; feeds mainly on molluscs, worms, and echinoderms; important food fish, exploited commercially throughout the N Atlantic. Exceptionally high stock in the 1960s and 1970s was followed by a decrease in the 1980s, which led to quotas being imposed for catches under the Common Fisheries Policy in 1983. (Family: Gadidae.)

Hades [haydeez] In Greek mythology, the king of the Underworld, terrible but just; he was responsible for the seizure of Persephone. To the Greeks, Hades was always a person, never a place, but by transference the Underworld – 'the house of Hades' – became known by that name (which means 'the unseen'). It is located below the Earth or in the far West; there the shades or feeble spirits of the dead continue to exist.

Hadith [hadeeth] Sayings attributed to the Prophet Mohammed, prefaced by a chain of authorities through whom the tradition is said to have been transmitted. One of the chief sources of Islamic law, it is second in authority only to the Qur'an.

Hadlee, Sir Richard (John) (1951–) Cricketer, born in Christchurch, New Zealand. He started his first-class career with Canterbury in 1971–2, and made his Test debut in 1973. A right-arm fast bowler, and a left-handed batsman, he also played for Nottinghamshire and Tasmania. New Zealand's best all-round cricketer, he took 431 Test wickets (passing Ian Botham's record of 383) and scored 3124 Test runs. He retired in 1990, when he was knighted.

Hadrian [haydrian], in full **Publius Aelius Hadrianus** (76–138) Roman emperor (117–38), ward, protégé, and successor of the Emperor Trajan, a fellow-Spaniard and relation by marriage. Coming to power in ambiguous circumstances, Hadrian was always unpopular in Rome, and even the object of a serious conspiracy there (118). He spent little of his reign in Rome, but toured the empire, consolidating the frontiers (as in Britain, where he initiated the building of the wall named after him), visiting the provinces, and promoting urban life.

Hadrian IV (Pope) *Adrian IV*

Hadrian's Wall The principal N frontier of the Roman province of Britain. Built AD 122–8 on the orders of the Emperor Hadrian (117–138) and possibly inspired by travellers' accounts of the Great Wall of China, it runs 117 km/73 mi from the Solway Firth to the R Tyne, the wall itself 4·5 m/15 ft high (probably with a 2 m/6 ft timber parapet), its forward defensive ditch c.8·5 m/28 ft wide and 3 m/10 ft deep. Sixteen forts (the best preserved at Housesteads and Chesters) were supplemented by 80 milecastles and numerous signal turrets. Overrun by Picts and N tribes in AD 139 and again in 367, the Wall was finally abandoned c.400–410. It is now a world heritage site.

hadron In particle physics, a collective term for all composite particles which experience strong interactions. All baryons and mesons are hadrons (eg protons and pions).

hadrosaur [hadrosaw(r)] A duck-billed dinosaur; front of snout flattened and expanded to form duck-like bill; dentition specialized, with several rows of teeth; fed on tough plant material; widely distributed during the Cretaceous period; probably organized into social groups, with nurseries for nest protection. (Order: Ornithischia.)

Haeckel, Ernst (Heinrich Philipp August) [haykl] (1834–1919) Naturalist, born in Potsdam, EC Germany. He studied at Würzburg, Berlin, and Vienna, and became professor of zoology at Jena (1862–1909). One of the first to sketch the genealogical tree of animals, he strongly supported Darwin's theories of evolution.

haemangioma [heemanjiohma] A benign tumour of vascular tissues, most commonly affecting the skin and liver. Such tumours are often found on the skin at birth as a result of a local overgrowth of capillaries during fetal development, where they appear as well demarcated red patches (*portwine stains*). Sometimes the capillaries form larger blood-filled sinuses, causing the discoloured area to be swollen and raised from the skin surface (a *strawberry naevus*). They often resolve spontaneously, but may be treated with a laser if they are producing a serious cosmetic defect.

haematemesis / hematemesis [heematuhmeesis] Vomiting of blood or of blood-stained vomitus. It indicates bleeding in the oesophagus, stomach, or upper gastro-intestinal tract, and usually results from ulceration of the lining of the gastro-intestinal tract or tumour growth. Occasionally, enough blood is lost to cause death.

haematite / hematite A mineral iron oxide (Fe_2O_3), the most important ore of iron. It often occurs as dark-brown nodules (*kidney ore*). Powdered haematite is used as a pigment (red ochre).

haematology / hematology [heematolojee] The study of the formation and function of the cells which circulate in the bloodstream and reside in the bone marrow and lymph nodes, and of the abnormalities that cause diseases.

haematuria / hematuria [heematyooria] Passage of blood in the urine. Severe haematuria gives rise to obviously red urine; lesser degrees may be detected only by chemical tests of the urine or by its examination by microscope. It indicates disease somewhere in the urinary tract, including the kidneys, such as infection or urinary stones.

haemodialysis *dialysis; kidney dialysis*

haemoglobin / hemoglobin [heemoglohbin] A widely occurring red-coloured protein, found for example in some protozoa, many invertebrates, vertebrates, certain yeasts, and plants of the family Leguminosae. In vertebrates it is the oxygen-carrying pigment present in red blood cells (*erythrocytes*). When bound to oxygen it appears scarlet, while in the absence of oxygen it is dark-blue. Haemoglobin shows species differences in its structure, molecular weight, and affinity for oxygen. It consists of an iron-containing element (the *haem*) which combines reversibly with oxygen, and polypeptide (*globin*) chains. Variations in the position or type of amino acids in the polypeptide chains give different forms of haemoglobin, which may have different affinities for oxygen (eg human fetal haemoglobin).

haemophilia / hemophilia [heemofilia] An inherited disorder of blood coagulation, in which there is a deficiency of a circulating protein (*factor VIII*) responsible for normal blood clotting. It is caused by the inheritance of an abnormal gene transmitted on the female X chromosome. Mothers with the gene have a 50% chance of passing it to their offspring. Girls are unaffected by the disease, but become carriers of the gene.

Boys develop the condition, and suffer spontaneous haemorrhages from an early age. Bleeding most commonly occurs into the skin and joints, leading to bruises and arthritis. It can also occur from the gastro-intestinal tract or in the brain. Repeated bleeding results in anaemia, and sudden serious haemorrhage can result in shock and death. Treatment is with regular infusions of factor VIII concentrates to replace the defective clotting protein. In the past, this has carried a risk of infection with viruses such as HIV and hepatitis; so blood products are now screened carefully to prevent the transmission of infectious agents. A similar but milder disorder (*Christmas disease*) results from deficiency of another blood-clotting protein, *factor IX*.

haemoptysis / hemoptysis [him**op**tisis] Coughing up blood or bloodstained sputum. It usually indicates underlying lung disease, such as tuberculosis, cancer, or pneumonia, but also occurs in pulmonary embolism and some forms of heart disease.

haemorrhage / hemorrhage [**hem**erij] Loss of blood externally or internally from any size of blood vessel. It is caused by injury to a blood vessel, or by a defect in normal blood clotting, as in haemophilia. Damage to the blood vessel may be the result of trauma, infection, or other disease. Arterial bleeding is pulsatile and appears in spurts; it is usually the most severe, as the arterial blood pressure is higher than that within veins or capillaries. Venous and capillary bleeding often induces a slower ooze of blood from the skin or between planes of tissues. The body is able to compensate for the loss of small amounts of blood. However, prolonged gradual bleeding leads to anaemia, and sudden heavy bleeding may lead to shock and death unless blood transfusion is available.

haemorrhoids / hemorrhoids [**hem**eroydz] A cluster of distended veins at the junction of the rectum and the anal canal, 2–3 cm/¾–1⅛ in above the opening of the anus; also known as **piles**. Usually there is no detectable cause, but they may occur as a result of blockage to the passage of blood draining the intestines, as in cirrhosis of the liver. They are also associated with constipation, and sometimes develop during pregnancy, when the uterus slows the passage of blood draining the pelvic organs. Anaemia may develop from slow but persistent loss of blood. Haemorrhoids, which are very common, can be removed surgically when large and giving discomfort; otherwise they may be treated by injections of a sclerosing solution.

haemostasis / hemostasis [heemo**stay**sis] The spontaneous arrest of bleeding from a damaged vessel, involving a series of interrelated events. The vessel constricts to reduce blood flow and loss. A platelet plug forms to seal the vessel wall and to release *vasoconstrictor* substances, which further reduce blood flow and initiate coagulation. The blood coagulates (soluble plasma protein fibrinogen is converted to insoluble fibrin) by a series of enzymatic reactions involving several factors present in blood and tissues. The resulting meshwork traps blood cells to form a clot, which strengthens the platelet plug formed earlier. Deficiencies or defects in any of these factors can lead to bleeding disorders (eg haemophilia).

Haerbin / Haerhpin *Harbin*

Háfiz or **Háfez,** pseudonym of **Shams-ed-Din Mohammad** (c.1326–c.1390) Lyrical poet, born in Shiraz, SW Iran. He worked as a religious teacher and wrote commentaries on sacred texts. A member of the mystical sect of Sufi philosophers, his short poems (*ghazals*), all on sensuous subjects, such as love, wine, and flowers, contain an esoteric signification to the initiated.

Haganah [haga**hn**a] The Jewish underground militia in Palestine, founded during the period of the British Mandate in the 1920s. After the declaration of the State of Israel in 1948, the Haganah became the official Israeli army, fielding some 100 000 troops during the war of that year.

Hagar [**hay**gah(r)] Biblical character, the maid of Sarah (the wife of Abraham). Due to Sarah's barrenness, Abraham had a son Ishmael by Hagar (*Gen* 16), but Hagar and her son were later expelled into the wilderness by Abraham after Isaac's birth (*Gen* 21).

Hagen [**hah**gn] 51°22N 7°27E, pop (2000e) 222 000. Industrial city in Freiburg district, W Germany; 48 km/30 mi ENE of Düsseldorf; at junction of important traffic routes; railway; household goods, ironworking, accumulators, foodstuffs, textiles, paper; Westphalian Open-Air Museum of Technology.

Hagen, Walter (Charles) [**hay**gn], nickname **the Haig** (1892–1969) Golfer, born in Rochester, New York, USA. The first US-born winner of the (British) Open, he won the title four times (1922, 1924, 1928–9), the US Open twice (1914, 1919), the US Professional Golfers' Association Championship a record five times (1921, 1924–7), and captained the first six US Ryder Cup teams (1927–37). A flamboyant personality who insisted on good manners, he is credited with raising the image and social standing of the game. He published an autobiography, *The Walter Hagen Story* (1956).

hagfish Primitive marine fish lacking true jaws, vertebrae, paired fins, and scales; includes *Myxina glutinosa*, widespread in the N Atlantic and Arctic; body eel-like, covered in copious slime, length up to 60 cm/2 ft; mouth slit-like surrounded by stout barbels; burrows in soft mud, feeding off invertebrates and fish. (Family: Myxinidae, 3 genera.)

Haggai, Book of [**hag**iy] One of the 12 so-called 'minor' prophetic books of the Hebrew Bible/Old Testament, attributed to the prophet Haggai, a contemporary of Zechariah, both of whom supported the rebuilding of the Temple in Jerusalem in c.520 BC after the return from exile. It consists of exhortations to the governor and high priest in Judea to pursue the rebuilding of the Temple, and to purify the Temple cult as preparations for God's new kingdom.

Haggard, Sir H(enry) Rider (1856–1925) Novelist and social historian, born at Bradenham Hall, Norfolk, E England, UK. Educated at Ipswich, he travelled widely in government service in South Africa, before taking up a literary life in England in 1881. The novel *King Solomon's Mines* (1885) immediately acquired the status of a children's classic, and was followed by *She* (1887) and several other stories. He wrote 58 volumes of fiction in all, and seven volumes of economic, political, and social history. He was knighted in 1912.

haggis A traditional Scottish dish comprising the minced heart, liver, and lungs of a sheep, as well as suet, oatmeal, and various seasonings. The ingredients are cooked in a bag made from the *rumen* or forestomach of a sheep.

Hagia Sophia [**hah**gia soh**fee**a], or **Santa Sophia** A masterpiece of Byzantine architecture built (532–7) at Constantinople (now Istanbul). The lavishly-decorated, domed basilica was commissioned by Emperor Justinian I and designed by Anthemius of Tralles and Isidore of Miletus. The Ottoman Turks, who took Constantinople in 1453, converted it into a mosque. Since 1935 it has been a museum.

Hague, The [hayg], Dutch **Den Haag** or **'s-Gravenhage** 52°05N 4°16E, pop (2000e) 466 000. Capital city of South Holland province, W Netherlands, and seat of the Dutch government; 3 km/1¾ mi from the North Sea; third largest city in The Netherlands, part of the Randstad conurbation; meeting-place of the States-General, 1527; centre of European diplomacy from 17th-c; Hague Convention (1907) formulated much of the law governing international warfare; a cultural, administrative, and political city; ministries, embassies, and headquarters of several international organizations, including the International Court of Justice and the Permanent Court of Arbitration; railway; noted for its furniture, pottery, and silverware; textiles, electronic equipment, hardware, furniture, printing, rubber, pharmaceuticals, cigarettes, car parts, food processing; home of many Dutch painters; 13th-c Gothic Hall of the Knights, Palace of Peace (1913), Nieuwe Kerk (1641), royal residence 'House in the Wood' (1647), town hall (16th-c); seaside resort of Scheveningen nearby.

Hague, William (Jefferson) [hayg] (1961–) British politician. He came to notice at an early age, when at 16 he received a standing ovation after addressing the 1977 Tory Party Conference. He studied at Oxford, where he became president of the

Union, joined a firm of management consultants, and was elected an MP in 1989. He acted as parliamentary private secretary to Chancellor of the Exchequer Norman Lamont (1990–3), then became under-secretary (1993–4) and minister of state for social security (1994–5), and minister for Wales (1995–7). He won the leadership of the Conservative Party following John Major's resignation in 1997. He resigned as leader after the general election defeat of 2001.

Hague Agreement A convention of 1899 for the Pacific Settlement of International Disputes. It established a Permanent Court of Arbitration – the forerunner of the World Court.

Hague Peace Conferences Two conferences at The Hague, The Netherlands, in 1899 and 1907. The first met to discuss the limitation of armaments, but the 26 countries represented made little progress. A permanent court of arbitration was set up for states in dispute wishing to use its services. The second produced a series of conventions to try to limit the horrors of war.

Hahn, Otto (1879–1968) Physical chemist, born in Frankfurt, WC Germany. He studied at the University of Marburg, and lectured in Berlin from 1907, becoming director of the Kaiser Wilhelm Institute there in 1927. With Meitner he discovered the radioactive element protactinium (1917), and in 1938 bombarded uranium with neutrons to find the first chemical evidence of nuclear fission products. He was awarded the Nobel Prize for Chemistry in 1944.

Hahnemann, (Christian Friedrich) Samuel [hahnuhman] (1755–1843) Physician and founder of homeopathy, born in Meissen, E Germany. He studied at Leipzig, and for 10 years practised medicine. He observed that a medicine administered to a healthy person produced similar symptoms to those of the illness it was intended to cure, and developed his law of 'similars', around which he built his system of homeopathy. His methods caused him to be prosecuted wherever he tried to settle. In 1811 he published *Reine Arzneimittellehre* (Precept of Pure Drugs), a homeopathic drug catalogue. He taught again in Leipzig (1810–21), but was driven out, retired to Köthen, and in 1835 moved to Paris, where he pursued a very lucrative practice.

Haida [hiyda] A Pacific Northwest Coast American Indian group in Queen Charlotte I, British Columbia, famous for their wood carvings, totem poles, and canoes. They traditionally lived by fishing and hunting, and held potlatch ceremonies, distributing ceremonial goods.

Haidar Ali [hiyder alee], also spelled **Hyder Ali** (1722–82) Muslim ruler of Mysore, born in Budikote, S India. Having conquered Calicut and fought the Marathas, he waged two wars against the British, in the first of which (1767–9) he won several gains. In 1779 he and his son, Tippoo, again attacked the British, initially with great success; but in 1781–2 he was defeated.

Haider, Jörg [hiyder] (1950–) Austrian politician, born in Upper Austria. He studied law at the University of Vienna, and embarked on an academic career as assistant law professor (1977–8). At 29, he entered the national parliament as a representative of the ultra-right wing Freedom Party (FPÖ – *Freiheitspartei Österreich*) in Carinthia, and in 1983 was elected chairman of the Carinthian Freedom Party. From 1986 to 2000 he was leader of the national FPÖ, campaigning against further immigration, and expressing sympathy for the Nazi cause. The FPÖ was returned as Austria's second largest party in the 1999 elections, and in February 2000 he became the junior partner in the coalition government with the conservative People's Party. Protests erupted in Austria against the Freedom Party's presence in the national government, and bilateral European Union sanctions were introduced in 2000 by member states. Shortly afterwards, Haider resigned as leader of the Freedom Party and returned to his base as governor of Carinthia.

Haifa or **Hefa** [hiyfa] 32°49N 34°59E, pop (2000e) 322 000. Industrial centre and seaport in Haifa dist, NW Israel; third largest city in Israel; airfield; railway; university (1963); Technion (Israel Institute of Technology, 1912); oil, agricultural produce, steel, shipbuilding, chemicals, textiles; Bahai Shrine, Persian Gardens, Mt Carmel.

Haig, Alexander (Meigs) [hayg] (1924–) US army officer and statesman, born in Philadelphia, Pennsylvania, USA. He trained at West Point, studied at Georgetown University, and joined the US army in 1947, serving in Korea (1950–1) and in the Vietnam War (1966–7), and becoming a general in 1973. He then retired from the army to become White House chief-of-staff during the last days of the Nixon presidency. Returning to active duty, he was supreme NATO commander before returning again to civilian life, as president of United Technologies Corporation. He served President Reagan as secretary of state in 1981–2, and sought the Republican nomination for the presidency in 1988. He has been chairman of Worldwide Associates Inc since 1984.

Haig (of Bemersyde), Douglas Haig, 1st Earl [hayg] (1861–1928) British field marshal, born in Edinburgh, EC Scotland, UK. He studied at Oxford and Sandhurst Military Academy, obtained a commission in the 7th Hussars, and served in Egypt, South Africa, and India. In 1914 he led the 1st Army Corps in France, and in 1915 became commander of the British Expeditionary Force. He waged a costly and exhausting war of attrition, for which he was much criticized, but led the final successful offensive (Aug 1918). In post-war years he devoted himself to the care of ex-servicemen, organizing the Royal British Legion. His earldom was awarded in 1919.

haiku [hiykoo] A Japanese poetic miniature, consisting of three lines of 5, 7, and 5 syllables. (The classic *tanka* has two further lines of 7 syllables.) This highly concentrated form, best exemplified by the 17th-c work of Matsuo Basho, has proved very popular outside Japan, and influenced among others the Imagists.

hail A form of precipitation comprising small balls or pieces of ice, which may reach up to 50 mm/2 in diameter. It is generally associated with rapidly rising convection currents in low latitudes, or the passage of a cold front in temperate latitudes. Hail storms can cause considerable damage to crops and property.

Haile Selassie I [hiylee selasee], originally **Prince Ras Tafari Makonnen** (1891–1975) Emperor of Ethiopia (1930–6, 1941–74), born near Harer, E Ethiopia. He led the revolution in 1916 against Lij Yasu, and became regent and heir to the throne, westernizing the institutions of his country. He settled in England after the Italian conquest of Abyssinia (1935–6), but in 1941 was restored after British liberation. In the early 1960s he helped to establish the Organization of African Unity. The disastrous famine of 1973 led to economic chaos, industrial strikes, and mutiny among the armed forces, and he was deposed (1974) in favour of the crown prince. Accusations of corruption levelled at him and his family have not destroyed the reverence in which he is held by certain groups, notably the Rastafarians.

Hailey, Arthur (1920–) Popular novelist, born in Luton, Bedfordshire, SC England, UK. He became a naturalized Canadian in 1947. He worked in industry and sales before becoming a freelance writer in 1956. He has written many best-selling blockbusters about disasters, several of which have become highly successful films, such as *Hotel* (1965), *Airport* (1968), and *Wheels* (1971). Later novels include *Strong Medicine* (1984), *The Evening News* (1990), and *Detective* (1997).

Hail Mary (Lat **Ave Maria**) A prayer to the Virgin Mary, also known as the **Angelic Salutation**, used devotionally since the 11th-c in the Roman Catholic Church, and finally officially recognized in 1568. The first two parts are quotations from scripture (*Luke* 1.28, 2), the third part being added later. In its Latin form, it is often sung in Roman Catholic ceremonies, and has received many famous musical settings.

Hailsham, Quintin (McGarel) Hogg, 2nd Viscount [haylsham] (1907–2001) British statesman, born in London, UK. He studied at Oxford, was called to the bar (1932), and became an MP (1938). He succeeded to his title in 1950, and was First Lord of the Admiralty (1956–7), minister of education (1957), Lord President of the Council (1957–9, 1960–4), chairman of the Conservative Party (1957–9), minister for science and technology

(1959–64), and secretary of state for education and science (1964). In 1963 he renounced his peerage and re-entered the House of Commons in an unsuccessful bid to become leader of the Conservative Party. In 1970 he was created a life peer (**Baron Hailsham of Saint Marylebone**) and became Lord Chancellor (1970–4), a post he held again from 1979 until his retirement in 1987.

Hailwood, Mike, popular name of **Stanley Michael Bailey Hailwood**, nickname **the Bike** (1940–81) Motor-cyclist, born in Oxford, Oxfordshire, SC England, UK. He took nine world titles: the 250 cc in 1961 and 1966–7, the 350 cc in 1966–7, and the 500 cc in 1962–5, all using Honda or MV Agusta machines. In addition, he won 14 Isle of Man Tourist Trophy races between 1961 and 1979 (a record that stood until 1995). During the 1960s he also had a career in motor racing, but was unable to match his success on two wheels. His awards included the George Medal. He was killed in a car accident.

Hain, Peter (Gerald) [hayn] (1950–) British politician, born in Nairobi, Kenya. His family moved to the UK in 1966, and he was educated at London and Sussex universities. He was active in the anti-apartheid movement in the UK, and prominent in successful campaigns to prevent tours by South African sports teams. Chairman of the Young Liberals (1971–3) and active in the anti-Nazi League (1977–80), he was a trade union research officer (1976–91) before becoming Labour MP for Neath (1991–), having left the Liberal Party in the early 1980s. He became under-secretary at the Welsh Office in 1997. Following the Welsh Assembly election (1998) he was moved to the Foreign Office, then had a brief spell as energy minister before returning to the Foreign Office as minister for Europe after the 2001 general election. He became secretary of state for Wales in 2002 and Leader of the Commons in 2003. The post of secretary of state for Wales was abolished in 2003 and merged with the Scottish Office as the new Department for Constitutional Affairs.

Hainan Island [hiynan] area 34 000 sq km/13 000 sq mi. Island off S coast of China, formerly a prefecture of Guangdong province; a province since 1987; separated from mainland by Hainan Strait; rises to 1879 m/6165 ft at Wuzhi Shan; airport at Haikou; opened to tourism and foreign trade in 1982; special economic zone, 1984; rubber, coconut, sugar, coffee, cocoa, betel nut, pineapple, fishing; reserves of many minerals, including limestone, marble, quartz, china clay, iron ore; principal cities Haikou, Dongfang, and resort port of Yulin.

Haiphong [hiyfong] 20°50N 106°41E, pop (2000e) 1 730 300. Seaport in N Vietnam; in the Red R delta, 88 km/55 mi SE of Hanoi; founded, 1874; badly bombed in Vietnam War; third largest city in Vietnam; rail link to Kunming, China; plastics, textiles, phosphates, rice.

hair A thread-like structure consisting of dead keratinized cells produced by the epidermis in mammalian skin. The root of the hair below the skin surface is contained in a hair follicle, which is responsible for producing the hair. The covering of hair in mammals helps to maintain constant body temperature by insulating the body. Some hairs, such as whiskers, have a specialized sensory function.

hair diagnosis A hair sample used to measure the level of minerals in the body as a guide to nutritional status, and to detect the presence of harmful substances such as aluminium and lead. It is important that the hair sample is plucked out rather than cut, the best site being the nape of the neck, where the hair grows quickest. The most reliable results are achieved when that part of the hair nearest the skin surface is analysed, since other parts are susceptible to environmental contamination such as shampoos, sprays, and other hairdressings.

hair fibres Animal fibre other than that derived from sheep. Often such fibres are identified with the animal from which they are obtained, eg mohair from the Angora goat.

hair seal *common seal*

hairstreak An inconspicuous butterfly; wings typically blackish-brown, often with coloured patches; wingspan up to 40 mm/1½ in. The name is applied to several different species of the family Lycaenidae. (Order: Lepidoptera.)

hairy frog An African frog (*Trichobatrachus robustus*) of the family Hyperoliidae; lives almost entirely in water. During the breeding season the male has hair-like projections from the skin on the sides of the body and tops of the legs.

Haiti *p.683*

Haitink, Bernard [hiytingk] (1929–) Conductor, born in Amsterdam, The Netherlands. He studied at the Amsterdam Conservatory, and was an orchestral violinist before becoming second conductor of The Netherlands Radio Union (1955). He was later conductor of the Amsterdam Concertgebouw Orchestra (from 1961) and of the London Philharmonic (1967–79), and was appointed musical director at Glyndebourne (1978–88), and Covent Garden (1988–2002), he is also principal guest conductor of the Boston Symphony Orchestra (1995–). He was granted an honorary knighthood in 1977 and was made an honorary Companion of Honour in 2002.

Hajj [haj] Annual pilgrimage to the holy city of Mecca during the Islamic lunar month of Dhu-ul-Hijja. It is one of the Five Pillars of Islam.

hake Commercially important, edible, cod-like fish widely distributed in offshore continental shelf waters of temperate seas; includes the European *Merluccius merluccius*, length up to c.1 m/3¼ ft, head and jaws large, teeth strong; blue-grey on back, underside silvery white; feeds mainly on fish and squid. (Genus: *Merluccius*. Family: Merlucciidae.)

Hakka A people from N China who settled in S China in the 12th–13th-c, but remained unassimilated. During the 18th–19th-c they were involved in feuds over land. Hakka impoverishment contributed to the Taiping Rebellion (1850–64). Many migrated to other areas, including Taiwan, Hong Kong, Indonesia, Malaysia, and Singapore.

Hakluyt, Richard [hakloot] (c.1552–1616) Geographer, born in Hertfordshire, SE England, UK. He studied at Oxford, where he lectured in geography, and was ordained some time before 1580. He wrote widely on exploration and navigation, notably his *Principal Navigations, Voyages, and Discoveries of the English Nation* (1589; 3 vols, 1598–1600). He also introduced the use of globes into English schools. Made a prebendary of Westminster in 1602, he is buried in Westminster Abbey. The *Hakluyt Society* was instituted in 1846.

Halakhah [halakah] The subject matter contained in the Talmudic and Rabbinic literature of Judaism dealing with the laws governing religious or civil practice in the community. It is distinguished from the **Haggadah**, which is not concerned with religious law, and includes such material as parables, fables, sagas, and prayers.

halation The spread of the photographic image of a bright object, caused by light scattered in the emulsion and reflected from the rear surface of the base. In some films, this surface is coated with a thin black 'anti-halation' layer to reduce the effect.

Halcyone or **Alcyone** [halsiyonee] In Greek mythology, **1** A daughter of Aeolus, who married Ceyx, son of the Morning Star. Either for impiety, or because she mourned his death at sea, both were changed into sea-birds – halcyons, or kingfishers – who are fabled to calm the sea.
2 One of the Pleiades.

Haldane, J(ohn) B(urdon) S(anderson) [holdayn] (1892–1964) Biologist and geneticist, born in Oxford, Oxfordshire SC England, UK, the son of John Scott Haldane. He studied at Oxford, became reader in biochemistry at Cambridge (1922–32), and professor of genetics (1933–57) and of biometry (1937–57) at London. He then emigrated to India, adopting Indian nationality, and worked in Kolkata (Calcutta) and Orissa. He wrote widely on his subject, and was well known for his popularizations. He was also chairman of the editorial board of the *Daily Worker* (1940–9), but left the British Communist Party in 1956.

Haldane, John Scott [holdayn] (1860–1936) Physiologist, born in Edinburgh, EC Scotland, UK. A fellow of New College, Oxford,

Haiti

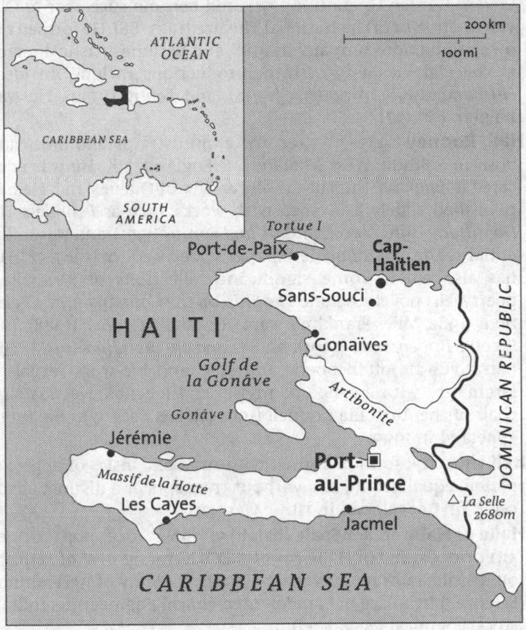

□ International Airport

[haytee], locally [hiytee], also written **Haïti**, official name **Republic of Haiti**, Fr **République d'Haiti**

Local name Haïti

Timezone GMT −5

Area 27 750 km^2/10 712 sq mi

Population total (2002e) 7 064 000

Status Republic

Date of independence 1804

Capital Port-au-Prince

Languages French (official), with Creole French widely spoken

Ethnic groups African descent (95%), European (mulatto) (5%)

Religions Roman Catholic (80%), voodoo

Physical features Consists of two mountainous peninsulas, Massif du Nord (N) and Massif de la Hotte (S), separated by a deep structural depression, the Plaine du Cul-de-Sac; highest peak, La Selle, 2680 m/8793 ft; includes islands of Gonâve (W) and Tortue (N).

Climate Tropical climate; average annual temperatures 25°C (Jan) 29°C (Jul) in Port-au-Prince; wet season (May–Sep); average annual rainfall for N coast and mountains 1475–1950 mm/58–77 in, but only 500 mm/20 in on W side; hurricanes common.

Currency 1 Gourde (G, Gde) = 100 centimes

Economy Based on agriculture; large plantations grow coffee, sugar, sisal, rice, bananas, corn, sorghum, cocoa; sugar refining, textiles, flour milling; cement, bauxite; tourism; light assembly industries.

GDP (2002e) $10·6 bn, per capita $1400

Human Development Index (2002) 0·471

History Visited by Columbus, 1492; created when W third of island ceded to France as Saint-Domingue, 1697, slave rebellion followed by independence as Haiti, 1804; united with Santo Domingo (Dominican Republic), 1822–44; under US occupation, 1915–34; Duvalier family had absolute power, 1957–86; after 1986 coup, new constitution provided for a bicameral National Congress consisting of a Senate and National Assembly; military coup in 1992 forced Jean-Bertrand Aristide to flee the country, and a provisional government created; Marc Bazin resigned as head of an army-backed coalition government, 1993; talks between deposed President Aristide and coup leader Cédras reached deadlock, June 1993; peaceful invasion by US forces to restore democratic government, 1994; Aristide re-elected amid claims of fraudulent procedure, 2000; rebel uprising forced Aristide into exile, March 2004.

Head of State
1992–4 Marc Bazin
1994–6 Jean Bertrand Aristide
1996–2000 René Préval
2001–4 Jean Bertrand Aristide
2004– Boniface Alexandre *Interim*

Head of Government
1994–5 Smarck Michel
1995–6 Claudette Werleigh
1996–7 Rosny Smarth
1997–9 *No prime minister*
1999–2001 Jacques Edouard Aléxis
2001–2 Jean-Marie Chéréstal
2002–4 Yvon Neptune
2004– Gerald Latortue *Interim*

he made a study of the effects of industrial occupations upon human physiology, especially respiration, and served as director of a mining research laboratory at Birmingham.

Hale, George Ellery (1868–1938) Astronomer, born in Chicago, Illinois, USA. He studied at the Massachusetts Institute of Technology, and became director of the Yerkes Observatory, WI (1892–1904), and at Mt Wilson, CA (1904–23), where he initiated the construction of some of the world's largest telescopes, notably the 5 m *Hale reflecting telescope* on Mt Palomar, CA. His research led to the discovery of magnetic fields within sunspots. The Palomar and Mt Wilson observatories were established under his guidance, and operated jointly 1948–80, from 1970 under the name Hale Observatories.

Haleakala Crater [halayakala] or **Kolekole** 20°42N 156°16W. Dormant volcano in E Maui I, Hawaii, USA; rises to 3055 m/10 023 ft; contains the largest inactive crater in the world: area 49 sq km/19 sq mi; depth 600 m/2000 ft, length 12 km/$7^1/_2$ mi, width 3·8 km/2·4 mi, circumference 32 km/20 mi; in Haleakala National Park.

Hale–Bopp The name given to a comet discovered independently by two amateur astronomers, Alan Hale (in Cloudcroft, NM) and Thomas Bopp (in Stanfield, AZ) in 1995, passing closest to the Sun in April 1997. This comet was also identified on a photograph taken with the UK Schmidt Telescope at Siding Springs, Australia, in 1993. With a nucleus some 40 km/25 mi in diameter, it proved to be the biggest and brightest comet in recent times. It will not return for another 2400 years.

Halévy, (Jacques François) Fromental (Elié) [alayvee] (1799–1862) Composer, born in Paris, France. He studied in Paris, and won the Prix de Rome in 1819. His first successful opera was *Clari* (1828), but he is best known for *La Juive* (1835), which established his reputation. Bizet and Gounod studied under him.

Haley, Bill, popular name of **William Haley** (1927–1981) Popular singer and musician, born in Highland Park, Michigan, USA. With his group 'The Comets' he popularized rock-and-roll in the 1950s. His most famous song, 'Rock Around the Clock', was used in the film *Blackboard Jungle* (1955), and caused widespread hysteria among teenager cinemagoers enthralled by the new sound.

half-life In radioactivity, the time taken for a group of atoms to decay to half their original number; symbol $T_{1/2}$, units s (second), also minutes and years. It varies from seconds to thousands of years, depending on the atomic species. The half-life of plutonium-239 is 24 400 years; for helium-6 it is 0·8 seconds. The term also applies to the decay of excited atoms by the emission of light.

half-marathon *marathon*

halibut Largest of the Atlantic flatfishes (*Hippoglossus hippoglossus*), found on sandy and stony bottoms (100–1500 m/300–5000 ft) in cold N waters; length up to 2·5 m/8 ft; eyes on right side, mouth and teeth large; brown to greenish-brown with white underside; edible, commercially important, and prized by sea anglers. (Family: Pleuronectidae.)

Halicarnassus [halikah(r)**na**sus] A Greek city-state founded by the Dorians on the coast of SW Asia Minor; modern Bodrum, Turkey. It was the birth-place of Herodotos, and the site of the Tomb of Mausolus.

Halifax 44°38N 63°35W, pop (2000e) 127 700. Seaport, provincial capital of Nova Scotia, Canada; major transatlantic port and rail terminus; joined to Dartmouth by two suspension bridges; founded in 1749 as a British military and naval base, used in the American Revolution and the War of 1812; naval base and convoy terminal in both World Wars; scene of harbour disasters, 1917, 1945; victims of the *Titanic* disaster buried here, 1912; airport; four universities (1789, 1802, 1818, 1925); shipbuilding, clothing, furniture, food processing, trade in fish and timber; Historic Properties area, including Privateers' Warehouse; Citadel Hill (height 82 m/269 ft), a National Historic Park, cannon fired daily at noon; Maritime Museum of the Atlantic.

Halifax, Charles Montagu, 1st Earl of (1661–1715) English Whig statesman, born in Horton, Northamptonshire, C England, UK. He studied at Cambridge, became MP for Maldon (1688) and a Lord of the Treasury (1692), establishing the National Debt and the Bank of England (1694). As Chancellor of the Exchequer (1694–5), he introduced a new coinage. In 1697 he was First Lord of the Treasury and Leader of the House of Commons, but resigned when the Tories came to power in 1699, and became Baron Halifax. On Queen Anne's death he was made a member of the Council of Regency, and on George I's arrival (1714) became an earl and prime minister. He was also a patron of letters and a poet.

Halifax, George Savile, 1st Marquess of (1633–95) English statesman, born in Thornhill, West Yorkshire, N England, UK. He was created viscount (1668) for his share in the Restoration, and in 1672 was made a marquess and Lord Privy Seal. On the accession of James II (1685) he became president of the Council, but was dismissed soon after. He was one of the three Commissioners appointed to treat with William of Orange after he landed in England (1688). He gave allegiance to William and resumed the office of Lord Privy Seal; but, joining the Opposition, resigned his post in 1689.

halite [**hal**iyt] The mineral form of sodium chloride (NaCl); also known as **rock salt**.

Hall, Ben(jamin) (1837–65) Bushranger, born in New South Wales, SE Australia. After arrest in 1862 in connection with a robbery, then acquittal, he was deserted by his wife and young son. He joined the Gardiner gang to rob a bullion coach, was arrested, but released again. Returning home, he discovered it burned down by the police and all his cattle killed. He was now committed to a life of outlawry, and a series of audacious exploits followed, which engaged the sympathies of the locals. However, after the needless shooting of a constable by one of the gang, he decided to change his ways. He retired to a secluded camp, but was betrayed by a companion and died in a hail of police bullets at the age of 28.

Hall, Sir Peter (Reginald Frederick) (1930–) Theatre, opera, and film director, born in Bury St Edmunds, Suffolk, E England, UK. He studied at Cambridge, where he produced and acted in more than 20 plays. After working in repertory and for the Arts Council, he became artistic director of the Elizabethan Theatre Company (1953), director (1955–6) of the London Arts Theatre, and formed his own company, The International Playwrights' Theatre (1957). After several productions at Stratford, he became director of the Royal Shakespeare Company, and remained as managing director of the company's theatres in Stratford and London until 1968. He was also director of the Covent Garden Opera (1969–71), and became successor to Olivier as director of the National Theatre (1973–88). He formed his own production company in 1988, and became artistic director at the Old Vic in 1997. Later productions include *An Ideal Husband* (1996), *Amadeus* (1998), and *Lenny* (1999). He was knighted in 1977.

Hall, Rodney (1935–) Writer, arts administrator, and musician, born in Solihull, West Midlands, C England, UK. He was educated in England, then at the University of Queensland. He has published widely as a poet, with works such as *Penniless Till Doomsday* (1962) and *Romulus and Remus* (1971), and was influential as *The Australian* newspaper's poetry editor (1967–78). He has also edited some significant collections of Australian poetry. His novels include *The Ship on the Coin* (1972), *Just Relations* (1982, Miles Franklin Award), *Captivity Captive* (1988), *The Second Bridegroom* (1991), and *Island in the Mind* (1997). His narratives are often poetic and epic, and his work reveals a familiarity with a range of myths and legends. He was also chair of the Australia Council (1991–4). His *Return to the Brink* appeared in 1999.

hall church A form of church with nave and aisles of approximately equal height, and without transepts or a distinct chancel. It first developed in 11th-c Germany.

Halle or **Halle an der Saale** [**hal**uh] 51°29N 12°00E, pop (2000e) 310 000. Capital of Halle county, EC Germany; NW of Leipzig, on R Saale; railway; university (1694); Academy of Agricultural Science; birthplace of Handel; mechanical engineering, rolling stock, chemicals, sugar refining.

Hallé, Sir Charles [**hal**ay] (1819–95) Pianist and conductor, born in Hagen, W Germany. He studied at Darmstadt and Paris, where his reputation was established by his concerts of classical music. Driven to England by the Revolution of 1848, he settled in Manchester, where in 1858 he founded his famous orchestra. He was knighted in 1888.

Hall effect The deflection of the carriers of charge in a conductor, caused by an externally applied magnetic field; described in 1879 by US physicist Edwin Hall (1855–1938). A potential difference forms at right angles to both current and field. It may be used to demonstrate the difference in the nature of the charge carriers in metals and semiconductors.

Haller, Albrecht von [**hal**er] (1708–77) Biologist, anatomist, botanist, physiologist, and poet, born in Bern, Switzerland. He studied at Tübingen and Leyden, and was professor of anatomy, surgery, and medicine in the new university of Göttingen (1736–53). Here he carried out biological experiments leading to the publication of *Elementa physiologiae corporis humani* (8 vols, 1757, Physiological Elements of the Human Body), a major contribution to the understanding of the functioning of the body, which opened the door to modern neurology. He also organized a botanical garden, an anatomical theatre, and an obstetrical school, helped to found the Academy of Sciences, and took an active part in the literary movement. In 1753 he resigned and returned to Bern, where he became a magistrate.

Halles, Les [layal] The former wholesale food-markets and, by association, the district in C Paris in which they were situated for over 700 years. In 1969 the markets were moved to the suburbs, and a multilevel shopping complex (**Forum des Halles**) was constructed on the site.

Halley, Edmond [**hal**ee, **haw**lee] (1656–1742) Astronomer and mathematician, born in London, UK. He studied at Oxford, but left without taking a degree to undertake cataloguing the stars of the S hemisphere. He published his catalogue in 1687 and was elected a member of the Royal Society, as well as receiving his degree after intercession by the king. He then began a study of planetary orbits, and correctly predicted the return in 1758 of the comet now named after him. He published studies on magnetic variations (1683), trade winds and monsoons (1686), and sea-charts of magnetic variation (1701). He encouraged Isaac Newton to write his celebrated *Principia* (1687), and paid for the publication out of his own pocket. With his *Breslau Table of Mortality* (1693), he laid the actuarial foundations for life insurance and annuities. In 1720 he became astronomer-royal.

Halley's comet [halee] The most famous of all comets, recorded by Chinese astronomers in 467 BC (and possibly in 611 BC), a spectacular periodic comet orbiting the Sun in a retrograde direction with a period of 76 years. It is named for Edmond Halley, who applied to comets Newton's theory of planetary motions and correctly predicted the return of the bright comet of 1531, 1607, and 1682 in the year 1758, 16 years after his death. Its present-day spectacular appearance is due to the relatively long period and subsequent slow rate at which the volatile content of the nucleus is lost on its relatively close passage (0·59 Astronomical Units) by the Sun. During its 1986 apparition, it was the subject of an intense study by an 'armada' of spacecraft, and by a ground-based International Halley Watch. The spacecraft encounters were at high speed (c.75 km/s), because of the comet's retrograde motion. The images revealed a nucleus of irregular shape, about 16 × 8 km/10 × 5 mi. The very dark surface of the nucleus, and the presence of carbon in the comet dust, indicate that there are significant quantities of organic molecules in the nucleus: water, carbon monoxide, carbon dioxide, methane, and ammonia ices have been inferred from measurements of the emitted gases.

Halliwell, Geri *Spice Girls, The*

hallmarks The official marks struck on all modern and much old English, Scottish, and Irish silver and gold, and since 1975 on platinum. The metal is tested (*assayed*) for standard or quality. Hallmarks date from 1300, when a decree was made that no silver or gold items should leave the smith until they had been assayed and marked with a leopard's head. Each assay office had its own mark.

Hallowe'en The evening of 31 October, when spirits of the dead are supposed to return to their former homes, and witches and demons are thought to be abroad at night. This was the last day of the Celtic and Anglo-Saxon year, and many Hallowe'en customs have their origin in pagan ceremonies. On Hallowe'en, children in some parts of the UK dress up, especially as witches or ghosts, and go from door to door offering short entertainments in return for presents; similarly, in the USA, children go around demanding 'trick or treat' – if no 'treat' or present is forthcoming, a trick or practical joke will be played on the householder.

Hallstatt [halshtat] 47°34N 13°39E, pop (2000e) 1200. Small market town in the Salzkammergut of Oberösterreich state, N Austria; on the SW shore of Hallstätter See, 50 km/30 mi SE of Salzburg; known for the **Hallstatt period**, the first phase of the European Iron Age (8th–4th-c BC), characterized by goods from burial tombs nearby; Hallstatt–Dachstein Salzkammergut cultural landscape, a world heritage site; salt mines; lake procession at Corpus Christi.

hallucination A sensory perception occurring without any stimulation of the sense organ. In its true form the individual is fully awake and the perception is located out of the body. Hallucinations indicate a loss of contact with reality, but they can be a normal phenomenon, such as during grief. This term was introduced in its current form by the French physician Jean Etienne Esquirol (1772–1840).

hallucinogens or **psychotomimetic drugs** Drugs that produce hallucinations, such as angel dust, LSD, magic mushrooms, and mescaline; also called **psychedelic drugs**. Many naturally occurring hallucinogens have been used in ancient medicine and in religious ceremonies. Some are widely used (illegally) for recreational purposes. Their use was particularly prevalent in the 1960s and early 1970s.

Halmahera [halmahera], formerly **Djailolo** area 17 936 sq km/6923 sq mi, pop (2000e) 129 000. Largest island in the Moluccas, Indonesia, on the Equator SW of the Philippines; forested mountain chains, including active volcanoes; taken by the Dutch in 1683; independence, 1949; hunting, fishing, rice, coconuts.

halogens [halojnz] The group of the periodic table with seven valence electrons. It comprises fluorine, chlorine, bromine, iodine, and the artificial element astatine. All are characterized by salts in which they appear as ions with a charge of −1.

Hals, Frans [hals] (c.1580–1666) Portrait and genre painter, probably born in Antwerp, N Belgium. Among his best-known works are 'The Laughing Cavalier' (1624, Wallace Collection, London) and 'Gypsy Girl' (c.1628–30, Louvre), and several portraits of militia groups, notable for their lively facial expressions, and bold use of colour. After 1640, his mood became more contemplative and sombre, as in 'Man in a Slouch Hat' (c.1660–6, Kassel). For most of his life, he lived in Haarlem.

Hal Saflieni [hal saflyenee] A vast prehistoric rock-cut catacomb (*hypogeum*) near Valletta, SE Malta; a world heritage site. The hypogeum, which was in use throughout the Copper Age (c.4000–2500 BC), consists of three levels of painted tomb-chambers dug into a natural hill of soft limestone and linked by halls and corridors. Originally holding the remains of some 7000 individuals, it was discovered in 1902.

Hälsingborg *Helsingborg*

Ham Biblical character, one of Noah's three sons, the brother of Shem and Japheth, and father of Canaan. He is described as helping Noah to build the ark, but after the Flood his son Canaan is cursed by God for Ham's apparent sin of having seen 'the nakedness of his father' Noah (*Gen* 9.22). This curse may be an attempt to explain the later subjugation of the Canaanites to Israel as resulting from Canaanite sexual perversion.

hamadryad (mythology) [hamadriyad] In Greek mythology, a tree-nymph. The hamadryad was offended or died when the tree containing her was harmed.

hamadryad (zoology) [hamadriyad] *king cobra*

hamadryas baboon [hamadriyas] A baboon (*Papio hamadryas*) native to NE Africa and SW Arabia; silver-brown fur (long and thick over male's head and shoulders); naked face; long tail; inhabits rocky hillsides; sacred to ancient Egyptians; also known as **sacred baboon**.

HAMAS (acronym for *Harakat al-Muqawama al-Islamiyya* 'movement of Islamic resistance') An Islamic resistance movement founded in Gaza in 1987 from a faction of the Muslim Brotherhood. Its aims are to carry on a jihad (struggle) against the Israeli 'occupation' of Palestine, largely through suicide bombings and attacks. It refused to recognize peace with Israel and did not join the government of the Palestine National Authority (PNA). Its leader Sheikh Ahmad Yasin was arrested by the Israelis but released in 1997 to Gaza. He was assassinated by Israel in March 2004. The movement appeals to many dispossessed Palestinians, and its members took an active part in the Palestine intifada (1988).

Hamburg [hamberg] 53°33N 10°00E, pop (2000e) 1 703 000; area 755 sq km/291 sq mi (including islands of Neuwerk and Scharhörn). Industrial port, cultural city, and province of Germany; on the R Elbe, 109 km/68 mi from its mouth; largest German port; second largest city of Germany; founded by Charlemagne in the 9th-c; formed alliance with Lübeck in the 12th-c, which led to the Hanseatic League; badly bombed in World War 2; railway; university (1919); commerce, shipbuilding, oil, metalworking, electronics, engineering, aircraft, vehicles, packaging, rubber, cosmetics, chemicals, foodstuffs, brewing, cigarettes; birthplace of Brahms and Mendelssohn; town hall (1886–97), St Michael's Church (1750–62), art gallery, opera house; Hamburger Dom (Nov–Dec), international boat show.

Hamer, Robert (1911–63) Film director, producer, and scriptwriter, born in Kidderminster, Worcestershire, WC England, UK. He studied at Cambridge, and first worked as a clapper-boy for the Gaumont film studio. Later at Ealing Studios he directed many successful films, including *Pink String and Sealing Wax* (1945), *It Always Rains on Sunday* (1947), *Kind Hearts and Coronets* (1949), *Father Brown* (1954), and *School for Scoundrels* (1960).

Hamersley Range Mountain range in NW Western Australia, S of the Fortescue R; extends for 257 km/160 mi; rises to 1244 m/ 4081 ft at Mt Meharry; the great iron-bearing area of Western Australia; contains a national park (6176 sq km/2384 sq mi).

Hamilcar [hamilkah(r)], known as **Hamilcar Barca** ('Lightning') (c.270–228 BC) Carthaginian statesman and general at the time of the First Punic War, the father of Hannibal. Following Carthage's defeat in 241 BC, and the loss of her empire in Sicily and Sardinia to Rome, he set about founding a new Carthaginian empire in Spain. Between 237 BC and his death, he conquered most of the S and E of the peninsula.

Hamilton (Bermuda) 32°18N 64°48W, pop (2000e) 1180. Port, resort, and capital of Bermuda, on Great Bermuda; deep harbour approached by a long intricate channel through Two Rock Passage; modern berthing and container facilities; founded 1612; capital since 1815; tourism; cathedral, Bermuda College.

Hamilton (Canada) 43°15N 79°50W, pop (2000e) 356 600. City in SE Ontario, Canada, at head (W) of L Ontario, 58 km/36 mi SW of Toronto; founded, 1813; site of Battle of Stoney Creek (1813); railway; McMaster University (1887); football team, Hamilton Tiger-Cats; industrial and commercial centre; textiles, iron and steel, vehicles, agricultural machinery, electrical equipment.

Hamilton (New Zealand) 37°46S 175°18E, pop (2000e) 162 000. City in North Island, New Zealand, on R Waikato; New Zealand's largest inland city; airfield; railway; university (1964); noted for horse breeding and agricultural research; dairy farming, market gardening, forest products; Waikato Art Museum; regatta at Turangawaewae Marae (home of the Maori Queen) to the N (Mar).

Hamilton, Alexander (1757–1804) US statesman, born in the West Indian island of Nevis. He studied at King's (now Columbia) College, New York City, and fought in the American Revolution, becoming Washington's aide-de-camp (1777–81). After the war, he studied law, and in 1782 was returned to Congress. He was instrumental in the movement to establish the USA in its present political form. As secretary to the Treasury (1789–95), he restored the country's finances, and was leader of the Federalist Party until his death. His successful effort to thwart the ambition of his rival, Aaron Burr, led to a duel in New Jersey, in which Hamilton was killed.

Hamilton, Emma, Lady, *née* **Emily Lyon** (c.1765–1815) Lord Nelson's mistress, probably born in Ness, Cheshire, NWC England, UK. In 1782 she accepted the protection of Charles Greville, to exchange it in 1786 for that of his uncle, Sir William Hamilton (1730–1803), English ambassador to Naples, whom she married in 1791. She first met Nelson in 1793, and bore him a daughter, **Horatia** (1801–81). After the death of her husband and Nelson, she became bankrupt, and in 1813 was arrested for debt. The next year she fled to Calais, where she died in obscurity.

Hamilton, James Hamilton, 1st Duke of (1606–49) Scottish Royalist commander during the English Civil War. He fought during the Thirty Years' War, leading an army in support of Gustavus Adolphus (1631–2), and later played a conspicuous part in the contest between Charles I and the Covenanters. Created duke in 1643, he led a Scottish army into England (1643), but was defeated by Cromwell at Preston, and beheaded.

hamiltonian The total energy of a mechanical system; symbol H, units J (joule); after Irish mathematician William Hamilton (1805–65). It is equal to the sum of kinetic energy K and potential energy V; $H = K+V$. Mechanics can be formulated using H in a way complementary to that based on lagrangians.

Hammarskjöld, Dag (Hjalmar Agne Carl) [hamershohld] (1905–61) Swedish statesman, and secretary-general of the UN (1953–61), born in Jönköping, S Sweden. After teaching at Stockholm University, he was secretary (1935) then chairman (1941–8) of the Bank of Sweden, and Swedish foreign minister (1951–3). At the UN, he helped to set up the Emergency Force in Sinai and Gaza (1956), and worked for conciliation in the Middle East (1957–8). He was awarded the 1961 Nobel Peace Prize after his death in an air crash near Ndola, Zambia, while engaged in negotiations over the Congo crisis.

hammerhead *hammerkop*

hammerhead shark Large, active shark of inshore tropical and temperate waters, characterized by a flattened head with broad lateral lobes which are thought to aid manoeuvrability; eyes and nostrils widely spaced; includes the **great hammerhead** of tropical Atlantic waters (*Sphyrna mokarran*), length up to 6 m/ 20 ft. (Genus: *Sphyrna*. Family: Sphyrnidae.)

hammerkop A large brown bird (*Scopus umbretta*), native to tropical Africa and SW Arabia, also known as **hamerkop, hammerhead, hammer-headed stork**, or **anvilhead**; feathers on head give a hammer-like profile; lives near water; eats mainly fish, frogs, and tadpoles; common in fishing villages; builds huge unkempt nest of twigs in tree. (Family: Scopidae.)

Hammerstein, Oscar, II [hamerstiyn] (1895–1960) Librettist, born in New York City, USA. He wrote the book and lyrics for many operettas and musical comedies. With composer Jerome Kern he wrote *Show Boat* (1927), a landmark of musical theatre, with such songs as 'Ol' Man River' and 'Only Make Believe'. Later, with composer Richard Rodgers, he wrote some of the greatest musicals, including *Oklahoma!* (1943, Pulitzer), *South Pacific* (1949, Pulitzer), *The King and I* (1951), and *The Sound of Music* (1959). **Oscar Hammerstein I** (1847–1919) was his impresario grandfather.

hammer throw An athletics field event using a metal sphere weighing 16 lb (7·6 kg), thrown from within the confines of a 7 ft (2·13 m) circle. The ball is attached to a chain at the end of which is a triangular frame gripped by the contestant. In competition, six throws are allowed, the object being to attain a greater distance than anyone else. Because of the dangers, the throwing circle is protected by a wire cage. The current world record is 86·74 m/284 ft 7 in, achieved by Yuriy Sedykh (1955–) of Russia, in 1986 at Stuttgart, Germany; for women, it is 76·07 m/249 ft 6·8 in, achieved by Mihaela Melinte of Romania, in 1999 at Rüdlingen, Switzerland.

Hammett, (Samuel) Dashiell (1894–1961) Crime writer, born in St Mary's Co, Maryland, USA. He left school at 14 and took various menial jobs before joining the Pinkerton Detective Agency as an operator. After World War 1 he wrote stories for magazines, developing a style of unsentimental writing which came to be known as 'hard-boiled' fiction. He published two novels, then achieved international fame with his 'private eye' novels *The Maltese Falcon* (1930), made into a classic film starring Humphrey Bogart (1941), and *The Thin Man* (1932), which was also filmed and later made into a television series.

Hammond, Dame Joan (1912–96) Soprano, born in Christchurch, New Zealand. She studied at the Sydney conservatory, and played violin in the Philharmonic Orchestra there, making her operatic debut in 1929. She toured widely, and became noted particularly for her Puccini roles. She was made a dame in 1974.

Hammurabi [hamurahbee] (18th-c BC) Amorite king of Babylon (c.1792–1750 BC), best known for his Code of Laws. He is also famous for his military conquests that made Babylon the greatest power in Mesopotamia.

Hamnett, Katharine (1948–) Fashion designer, born in Gravesend, Kent, SE England, UK. She studied fashion at art school in London, then worked as a freelance designer, setting up her own business in 1979. She draws inspiration for designs from workwear, and also from social movements, such as the peace movement, which she supports.

Hampden, John (1594–1643) English parliamentarian and patriot, born in London, UK. He studied at Oxford, became a lawyer, and in 1621 an MP. His opposition to Charles I's financial measures led to his imprisonment (1627–8), and in 1634 he became famous for refusing to pay Charles's imposed levy for outfitting the navy ('ship money'). A member of both the Short and the Long Parliaments, he was one of the five members whose attempted seizure by Charles (1642) precipitated the Civil War. He fought for the Parliamentary army at Edgehill and Reading, but was killed at Thame.

Hampi The site of the former Hindu capital of Vijayanagar, near the SW Indian village of Hampi. The city was founded in the 14th-c, and remained the centre of a vast and powerful Hindu empire until 1565, when it was sacked. It remains an important religious and tourist centre, and is a world heritage site.

Hampshire pop (2001e) 1 240 000; area 3777 sq km/1458 sq mi. County of S England, UK; bounded S by the Isle of Wight and English Channel; crossed by the North Downs in the NW and W; drained by Test and Itchen Rivers; W of Southampton is the New Forest; county town, Winchester; chief towns, Portsmouth, Southampton (new unitary authorities from 1997); agriculture, livestock, shipbuilding, oil refining, chemicals, pharmaceuticals, electronics, tourism; naval bases at Portsmouth and Gosport.

Hampshire, Susan (1938–) British actress, born in London. She was educated in London, made her stage debut in *Expresso Bongo* (1958), and has since taken leading roles in numerous plays and films. She won Emmy awards for best actress as Fleur in the television series *The Forsyte Saga* (1970), Sarah Churchill in *The First Churchills* (1971), and Becky Sharp in *Vanity Fair* (1973). Later series include *The Grand* (1997–8) and *Monarch of the Glen* (2000–3). She published a volume of autobiography, *Susan's Story* in 1981, in which she writes about her problems with dyslexia, and is also known for her series of *Lucy Jane* books.

Hampton, Christopher (James) (1946–) British playwright, born on Fayal I, in the Azores. He studied at Oxford; his first play, *When Did You Last See My Mother?* (1966), was produced in London and New York while he was still an undergraduate, and led to his appointment as the Royal Court Theatre's first resident playwright. The Court produced more of his plays, including *Total Eclipse* (1968), *The Philanthropist* (1970), *Savages* (1973), set in Brazil, and *Treats* (1976). His finest play is considered to be *Tales From Hollywood* (1982), but his most commercial success has been *Les Liaisons dangereuses* (1985), adapted from the novel by Laclos. Later works include a semi-autobiographical play, *White Chameleon* (1991), *Alice's Adventures Under Ground* (1994), *Carrington* (1995), and *The Talking Cure* (2002).

Hampton Court The royal residence situated by the R Thames near London, UK, built by Cardinal Wolsey, who occupied it until 1529. Thereafter it became the favourite residence of British monarchs for over two centuries. Queen Victoria declared it open to the public in 1851, and its gardens and maze are a major tourist attraction.

Hampton Institute A privately funded, co-educational college established in 1869 by Samuel Chapman (1839–93) in Hampton, Virginia, USA, to provide vocational training for slaves freed after the American Civil War. The foundation received a charter in 1870 and achieved college status in 1929. It is an important centre for studies in black American history.

hamster A small rodent of the sub family Cricetinae (24 species); short tail, large ears; food can be stored in internal cheek pouches; lives in burrows; communicates using very high frequency sound. One species, the **golden hamster** (*Mesocricetus auratus*), is a popular pet. It is thought that all domestic golden hamsters are descended from a family of 13 (mother plus 12 young), dug from their burrow in 1930 at Aleppo, Syria.

Hamsun, Knut [hamsoon], pseudonym of **Knut Pedersen** (1859–1952) Novelist, born in Lom, SC Norway. Raised on the Lofoten Is with little education, he worked at various odd jobs, and twice visited the USA (1882–4, 1886–8), where he worked as a streetcar attendant in Chicago and a farmhand in North Dakota. He sprang to fame with his novel *Sult* (1890, Hunger), followed by *Mysterier* (1892, Mysteries) and the lyrical *Pan* (1894). His masterpiece is considered *Markens grøde* (1917, Growth of the Soil), which was instrumental in his award of the 1920 Nobel Prize for Literature. A recluse during the inter-war years, he lost popularity during World War 2 for his Nazi sympathies, but his reputation has been largely rehabilitated.

Han Term used in China to differentiate the 93% of native Chinese population from the 7% made up of 50 ethnic minorities, including Hakka, Mongols, and Tibetans.

Hancock, Lang(ley) George (1909–92) Australian mining industrialist, born in Perth, Western Australia. In 1934 he leased claims for mining blue asbestos, and developed a processing plant. After making a forced landing in bad weather, he discovered substantial iron ore deposits in the Pilbara region, and concluded mining agreements with a number of companies, thus initiating the growth of Australian extractive industries. He went on to make further discoveries, including Rhodes Ridge, the largest iron ore deposit in the world. He held controversial right-wing views on politics and Aboriginal affairs, and in 1974 formed a secessionist movement in Western Australia with the aim of better political representation. By the late 1980s his personal wealth was estimated to be $A60 million, and the family feuds over the inheritance were much publicized after his death.

Hancock, Tony, popular name of **Anthony John Hancock** (1924–68) Comedian, born in Birmingham, West Midlands, C England, UK. After a brief period as a civil servant, he enlisted in the RAF (1942). Overcoming extreme stage-fright he tried his hand as a stand-up comic with touring shows before making his professional stage debut in *Wings* (1946). Pantomimes, cabaret, and radio appearances in *Educating Archie* (1951) contributed to his growing popularity, and he made his film debut in *Orders is Orders* (1954). He achieved national fame and popularity with the radio, and later TV, series *Hancock's Half Hour* (1954–61). A chronic alcoholic beset by self-doubt and unable to reconcile his ambition with his talent, he spent his final years in a self-destructive round of aborted projects and unsatisfactory performances, and committed suicide while attempting a comeback on Australian television.

hand The terminal part of the upper limb, used to manipulate (motor function) or assess (sensory function) the environment. It is a highly mobile organ, capable of fine discriminative function and manipulation, both of which require a copious blood supply. It is richly endowed with sensory nerve endings, and consists of a number of bony elements (the *carpels*, *metacarpals*, and *phalanges*) whose size and arrangement differ between species, bound together by ligaments and supported by tendons and muscles. In humans the bony elements are the eight carpels, the five metacarpals, the three phalanges in each finger, and the two phalanges in the thumb. In primates (including humans) the thumb is set almost at right angles to the fingers, and is capable of being brought into contact with each finger in turn (*opposition*). Opposition is important in the *precision grip* (eg threading a needle). In the *power grip*, the thumb is used as a buttress to support the object and prevent it from slipping out of the hand (eg holding a power tool). In the *hook grip* only the fingers are used (eg carrying a shopping bag). The fine sensory discriminative ability of the fingers enables the blind to read braille.

handball An indoor and outdoor game first played in Germany c.1890, resembling association football, but played with the hands. The indoor game is played with seven on each side. The outdoor game (known as **field handball**) is played on a field with 11 on each side. In the USA handball is commonly played as a singles or doubles game on a court, in which players alternately strike a two-ounce rubber ball with bare hands or hands covered with soft gloves. This version was first played by the Irish in the 10th-c. An Irish immigrant, Phil Casey, imported the game to Brooklyn c.1882.

Handel, George Frideric (1685–1759) Composer, born in Halle, EC Germany. He was organist of Halle Cathedral at the age of 17, while also studying law, and worked as a violinist and keyboard player in the Hamburg opera orchestra (1703–6). In Italy (1706–10) he established a great reputation as a keyboard virtuoso, and had considerable success as an operatic composer. He was appointed in 1710 to the court of the Elector of Hanover (later George I of Great Britain). In 1720 he worked at the King's

Theatre, London, where he produced a stream of operas, and then developed a new form, the English oratorio, which proved to be highly popular. After a stroke in 1737, he rallied, and afterwards wrote some of his most memorable work, such as *Saul* (1739), *Israel in Egypt* (1739), and *Messiah* (1742). His vast output included over 40 operas, about 20 oratorios, cantatas, sacred music, and orchestral, instrumental, and vocal works. He is buried in Poet's Corner, Westminster Abbey.

handkerchief tree A deciduous tree (*Davidia involucrata*) growing to 18 m/60 ft, often much smaller in cultivation, native to China; leaves ovoid, toothed; flower clusters tiny, protected by two large, white, pendulous bracts, which give the tree its name; also called **dove tree**. It is named after the French missionary Père David (1826–1900), who introduced it to Europe. (Family: Nyssaceae.)

Handley, Tommy, popular name of **Thomas Reginald Handley** (1892–1949) Comedian, born in Liverpool, Merseyside, NW England, UK. He served in World War 1, then worked in variety, and in the infancy of radio became known as a regular broadcaster. In 1939 he achieved nationwide fame through his weekly programme *ITMA* (*It's That Man Again*) which, with its mixture of satire, parody, slapstick, and wit, helped to boost wartime morale, and continued as a prime favourite until brought to an untimely end by his sudden death.

handloom A weaving machine operated by hand. In industrial societies, such looms are now almost exclusively restricted to craft weavers and designers, but in less developed nations (such as several countries of Central and South America), handloom weaving is often of great economic importance.

Hands, Terry, popular name of **Terence David Hands** (1941–) Stage director, born in Aldershot, Hampshire, S England, UK. He studied at Birmingham University, co-founded the Everyman Theatre, Liverpool (1964), then joined the Royal Shakespeare Company in 1966, where he became an associate director (1967–77), joint artistic director with Trevor Nunn (1978–86), and sole artistic director and chief executive (1986–91). He was consultant director at the Comédie Française (1975–7), and has directed Shakespeare at the Burgtheater in Vienna. He took over as director of Theatr Clwyd in 1997.

Handsome Lake (?–1815) Seneca Indian religious leader. His *gaiwiio* or Old Religion blended Christian and Indian themes, and was a response to Indian defeat during the American Revolution. Among its tenets is abstinence from alcohol. Unlike many such religious innovations it did not lead to further military disaster. It is still practised.

handwriting *chirography*

Handy, W(illiam) C(hristopher) (1873–1958) Blues composer, born in Florence, Alabama, USA. He studied at Teachers Agricultural and Mechanical College, Huntsville, AL, became a schoolteacher, then joined a minstrel show as a cornet player. In 1903, despite becoming blind, he formed his own band in Memphis, subsequently moving to Chicago and to New York City, where he formed his own publishing company. He was the first to introduce the 'blues' style to printed music, his most famous work being the 'St Louis Blues' (1914). He wrote *Father of the Blues* (1958).

Han dynasty Major Chinese dynasty (206 BC–AD 220), commonly divided into Early or Western Han (206 BC–AD 8), which had its capital at Changan (modern Xian), and Later or Eastern Han (25–220), with its capital at Luoyang. The dynasty was founded by Liu Bang (r.206–195 BC). A dynastic territorial expansion occurred in the reigns of Wudi (141–86 BC) and Han Yuan (48–33 BC), including the conquest of what is now N Korea, N Vietnam, Kyrgyzstan, Uzbekistan, and Xinjiang. The Han period saw important economic and urban development, and major developments in education, science, technology, astronomy, and public health. During this period Buddhism was introduced to China, and trade links developed with Europe via the Middle East. The Han period was contemporaneous with Rome, and of comparable significance to world history. Much is known from archaeology and contemporary texts.

Hangchow *Hangzhou*

hang glider A person-carrying glider using a delta-shaped flexible wing, developed for NASA in the late 1950s as a gliding parachute. The pilot is suspended by a harness from the light frame holding the wing, and controls the movement of the craft by body movement. Providing the angle of attack is maintained, lift is generated. Later, engines were fitted, wing spans increased, the delta wing configuration was dropped for reasons of efficiency, and the type developed into a form of ultralight aircraft called a **microlight**. A typical microlight has a span of 10 m/33 ft and a speed of 90 kph/55 mph. Although popularized in the mid-1970s, hang gliding was pioneered in the 1890s by Otto Lilienthal in Germany.

hangul *red deer*

Hangzhou or **Hangchow** [hahngjoh], also **Kinsai** 30°18N 120°07E, pop (2000e) 1 645 000, administrative region 6 065 000. Capital of Zhejiang province, E China; on Qiantang R at S end of Grand Canal; grew rapidly as trade and administration centre, from 6th-c, especially after building of Grand Canal (610); capital of several kingdoms and dynasties, 8th–12th-c, especially of S Song (1127–1279); airfield; railway; technical university (1927); university (1959); iron and steel, refining, engineering, hydroelectricity, silk; trade in bamboo, wheat, barley, rice, cotton, sweet potatoes, tea; Spirits' Retreat (Buddhist temple founded in 326).

Hani, Chris [hanee], popular name of **Martin Thembisile Hani** (1942–93) South African political leader, born in Cofimvaba, SE South Africa. His record as guerrilla leader and his charisma made him the most popular African political figure of his generation. He joined the African National Congress (ANC) Youth League at the age of 15, and in 1963 became a member of Umkhonto we Sizwe, the ANC's armed wing. He left the country in 1963, and rose through the ranks of Umkhonto, serving as chief-of-staff between 1987 and 1992. In 1991, he topped the poll for the ANC's National Executive Committee, and was also elected secretary-general of the South African Communist Party. He was shot dead on Easter Saturday by a white right-winger, and his murder triggered massive protests and some rioting.

Hanif Mohammad (1934–) Cricketer, born in Junagadh, W India. One of five Test-playing brothers, he made his first-class debut for Karachi at the age of 16. Noted for his dour play, he took 970 minutes to amass 337 runs against the West Indies in 1957–8, still the slowest innings in Tests, and established a world record score of 499 against Bahawalpur in 1959. He made his Test debut at the age of 17, and played in 55 Tests, scoring 3915 runs. He captained Pakistan 11 times between 1964 and 1967.

haniwa *Kofun*

Hankou / Hankow / Han-k'ou *Wuhan*

Hanks, Tom, popular name of **Thomas J Hanks** (1957–) Film actor, born in Oakland, California, USA. He studied at the California State University, Sacramento, where he worked as stage manager and actor in university productions. He spent three seasons performing the classics with the Great Lakes Shakespeare Festival in Ohio before making his film debut in the thriller *He Knows You're Alone* (1981). After some well received television comedy, he was cast in the film *Splash* (1984), and received an Oscar nomination for his role in *Big* (1988). He gained an Oscar and Golden Globe Award for his character performance as an AIDS victim in *Philadelphia Story* (1993), and another Oscar for *Forrest Gump* (1994). Later films include *Saving Private Ryan* (1998), *The Green Mile* (1999), *Cast Away* (2000, Golden Globe), and *Catch Me If You Can* (2002). He made his directorial debut in 1996 with *That Thing You Do!*, and in 2001 he collaborated with Steven Spielberg on the TV mini-series *Band of Brothers* (Golden Globe; Emmy).

Hanna–Barbera [hana bah(r)bera] Animated cartoonists, in partnership for nearly 50 years. **William (Denby) Hanna** (1910–2001), born in Melrose, New Mexico, USA, was a structural engineer by training. He turned to cartooning in 1930, and became one of the first directors at the new MGM animation studio in 1937, making Rudolph Dirks's *Captain and the Kids*. He then teamed up with **Joseph (Roland) Barbera** (1911–), born in New York City, who initially worked as an accountant, drawing cartoons for magazines in his spare time. He joined MGM as an artist at the same time as Hanna. Together they created the first *Tom and Jerry* cartoon (1939), and produced more than 200 films of the series (1940–57), winning seven Oscars between 1943 and 1952. Working as Hanna-Barbera Productions from 1957, they created numerous television cartoon series using computer animation, including *The Flintstones*, *Yogi Bear*, and *Huckleberry Hound*.

Hannibal [hanibl] (247–182 BC) Carthaginian general and statesman, the son of Hamilcar Barca. As a child, his father made him swear eternal enmity to Rome. He served in Spain under Hamilcar and Hasdrubal (his brother-in-law), and as general brought most of S Spain under his authority (221–219 BC). In the Second Punic War (218–202 BC), he completely wrong-footed the Romans by his bold and unexpected invasion of Italy from the N (with elephants), and thus inflicted a series of heavy defeats on them – at the Ticinus, the R Trebia (218 BC), L Trasimene (217 BC), and Cannae (216 BC). Failure to win over Rome's allies in Italy, plus lack of support from Carthage, severely hampered him, and Rome was still undefeated when he was recalled to Africa in 203 BC to face the invading army of Scipio. Decisively defeated at Zama (202 BC), he turned in the post-war years to political reform; but this raised such opposition that he voluntarily exiled himself, first to Syria, then Crete and finally Bithynia, where he committed suicide to avoid Roman capture.

Hannover *Hanover*

Hanoi [hanoy] 21°01N 105°52E, pop (2000e) 2 398 900. Capital of Vietnam; on Red R, 88 km/55 mi NW of Haiphong; former capital of Vietnamese Empire, 11th–17th-c; capital of French Indo-China, 1887–1946; occupied by the Japanese in World War 2; severely damaged by bombing in Vietnam War; university (1956); centre of industry and transport; textiles, tanning, brewing, engineering, rice milling, coal, food processing, tapioca, sesame, millet, wood products, resins, footwear; many historical sites destroyed by war; surviving sites include Co Loa citadel (3rd-c BC), Temple of Literature (11th-c), Mot Cot Pagoda (11th-c), several museums.

Hanover, Ger **Hannover** 52°23N 9°44E, pop (2000e) 530 000. Commercial and industrial capital city of Lower Saxony province, NC Germany; on R Leine, 56 km/35 mi NW of Brunswick; chartered, 1241; home of the dukes of Brunswick-Lüneburg (later electors of Hanover) in the early 17th-c; Elector George Louis became George I of Great Britain, 1714; badly bombed in World War 2; railway; on the Mittelland Canal; three universities (1831, 1913, 1961); commerce, electronics, vehicles, tyres, metals, cement, pharmaceuticals, brewing, engineering, rubber, foodstuffs; Neoclassical opera house (1845–52), Leine Palace, Gothic Old Town Hall (15th-c); Hanover Trade Fair (Apr), International Aviation Trade Fair (every 2 years).

Hanover, House of A dynasty of British monarchs, encompassing George I (1714–27), George II (1727–60), George III (1760–1820), George IV (1820–30), William IV (1830–7), and Victoria (1837–1901), though only the Georges and William are usually referred to as 'Hanoverians'. The dynasty secured the Protestant succession after the death of Queen Anne, and was descended through the female line from Princess Elizabeth, the sister of Charles I.

Hanoverian One of the oldest German breeds of horse; developed in the 17th-c from **Hanoverian creams** (also known as *Isabellas*); height, 15¾–17 hands/1·6–1·7 m/5 ft 3 in–5 ft 8 in); powerful body, with shortish muscular legs; popular for show-jumping.

Hansard, Luke (1752–1828) British printer, who went from Norwich to London, and entered the office of Hughes, printer to the House of Commons, he became acting manager in 1774, and in 1798 succeeding as sole proprietor of the business. He and his descendants printed the regular parliamentary reports from 1774 to 1889. In 1943 *Hansard* became the official name for the parliamentary reports (since 1909 printed by Her Majesty's Stationery Office, or HMSO).

Hanseatic League A late mediaeval association of 150 N German towns, including Bremen, Hamburg, and Lübeck. Formed in 1241 as a trading alliance, it dominated trade from the Atlantic to the Baltic, and fought successful wars against neighbours between 1350 and 1450. The **Hansa**, as it was also known, declined because of internal divisions, English and Dutch competition, and the growth of princely power.

Hansen, Martin (Jens) Alfred (1909–55) Novelist, born in Stroby, E Denmark. He worked on the land and as a teacher, but after 1945 devoted himself to writing. His early novels deal with social problems in the 1930s, and he later developed a more profound style, notably in his psychological novel *Løgneren* (1950, The Liar) and the metaphysical *Orm og Tyr* (1952, The Serpent and the Bull).

Hansen's disease An ancient chronic infectious disease due to *Mycobacterium leprae* that still affects 20 million people, mainly in tropical Asia and Africa, Central and South America, but also endemic in the Middle East and S Europe; named after Norwegian bacteriologist Armauer Hansen (1841–1912), who discovered the bacillus in 1879. For centuries the disease was known as **leprosy** – a name applied to a variety of skin disorders, and still retaining (along with *leper*) strong negative emotional connations from the era when the basis of this disease was not understood; the trend in modern medical usage is to avoid this stigmatized term. China had specialist leprosy hospitals from the 11th-c. The organisms show a predilection for the skin, peripheral nerves, and upper respiratory tract. Onset of the disease is gradual, with the development of an area of numbness in the skin, followed by nodules on the external surfaces of the limbs, and enlarged nerves that are easily felt. The lining of the mouth and nose develops ulcers, and there are deformities in cartilage and bones. Drug treatment is complex and prolonged, but the condition tends to disappear with improved socio-economic conditions.

Hanson, Pauline (1954–) Politician, born in Brisbane, Queensland, NE Australia. She stood as a Liberal candidate for Oxley in the Queensland parliament in 1966, but backing was withdrawn when she made derogatory remarks about Aborigines. She won the seat as an Independent, and went on to form her own party, One Nation. One of the most controversial figures to emerge in Australian politics in the 1990s, in the 1998 Australian general election her party failed to win a single seat in the House of Representatives. She resigned as leader of One Nation in 2002. In 2003 she was found guilty of electoral fraud and sentenced to three years in jail, but the conviction was quashed on appeal.

Hanukkah or **Chanukah** [hanuka] An annual Jewish festival held in December (begins 25 Kislev), commemorating the rededication of the Temple at Jerusalem after the victory of Judas Maccabaeus over the Syrians in 165 BC (1 Maccabees); also known as the **Feast of Dedication** or **Feast of Lights** (candles being lit on each of the eight days of the festival).

Hanuman [hanuman] The monkey-god of the Ramayana epic, who is the courageous and loyal supporter of Rama. A popular Hindu deity, he is represented as half-human and half-monkey.

hanuman monkey *entellus*

happening A modern art 'event', or performance; often planned but sometimes 'spontaneous'. Happenings (so-called since c.1960) need not take place in a gallery but may occur in the street, or anywhere, and usually involve spectator participation. The event itself, rather than any finished, saleable product, is regarded as the work of art. The genre originated in the USA with artist and art theorist Allan Kaprow (1927–).

Harald III Sigurdsson, nickname **Harald Hardrada** ('the Ruthless') (1015–66) King of Norway (1045–66). The half-brother of Olaf II (St Olaf), he was present at the Battle of Stiklestad in 1030 where St Olaf was killed, and sought refuge in Kiev at the court of Prince Yaroslav the Wise. He fought as a Viking mercenary with the Varangian Guard in Constantinople, and returned to Norway in 1045, shared the throne with his nephew Magnus, and became sole king in 1047. After long and unrelenting wars against Sweyn II of Denmark, he invaded England in 1066 to claim the throne after the death of Edward I, but was defeated and killed by Harold II at Stamford Bridge.

Harappa [harapa] A prehistoric city on the dried-up course of the R Ravi in the Pakistani Punjab, c.800 km/500 mi S of Islamabad, occupied c.2300–1750 BC. Its 20 m/65 ft high mound with a circuit of 5 km/3 mi was discovered in 1826, and excavated from 1921. To the W is a massive, walled citadel of moulded mudbrick; to the E a residential lower city with a rectangular street grid. Its houses were provided with drains, washrooms, and latrines. Its ancient population numbered c.25 000.

Harare [harahray], formerly **Salisbury** (to 1982) 17°43S 31°05E, pop (2000e) 980 700. Capital and largest city of Zimbabwe, 370 km/230 mi NE of Bulawayo; altitude, 1473 m/4833 ft; founded in 1890, and named after Lord Salisbury; airport; railway; university (1970); administration, commerce, packaging, polythene, paints, adhesives, timber, textiles, tobacco; international conference centre; horse-racing and trotting tracks; motor-racing circuit; Queen Victoria Museum, national gallery, national archives, national botanical garden, two cathedrals.

Harbin, also spelled **Haerhpin** or **Haerbin** 45°54N 126°41E, pop (2000e) 3 334 000, administrative region 4 704 000. Capital of Heilongjiang province, NE China; industrial centre on Songhua R; founded, 12th-c; developed as major rail junction; c.500 000 White Russians fled here in 1917; airfield; food processing, machinery, linen, sugar refining, paper; Stalin Park, Harbin Zoo (1954); Harbin Summer Music Festival (Jul).

harbour seal *common seal*

Harburg, Edgar 'Yip', originally **Isidore Hochberg** (1898–1981) Songwriter, born in New York City, USA of Russian Jewish immigrants. He studied at City College and ran an electrical appliance store. When the Depression closed his business in 1929, he began writing song lyrics, and in 1932 incisively captured the mood of the day with the melancholy lament 'Brother, Can You Spare a Dime?' (with music by Jay Gorney). Almost alone among his colleagues, he was politically active in civil rights groups. In his music, his political convictions were realized in a quiet idealism that a better world was in the offing, as in 'April in Paris' (1932, with Vernon Duke), and his masterwork 'Somewhere Over the Rainbow' (1939, with Harold Arlen). He could also write genuinely funny lyrics, as in 'If I Only Had a Brain' and the other clown songs for *The Wizard of Oz* (1939). In 1947, with Burton Lane, he wrote the Broadway musical *Finian's Rainbow* with such hit songs as 'How Are Things in Glocca Morra?' and 'Old Devil Moon'.

Hardanger Plateau [hah(r)danger], or **The Vidda**, Norwegian **Hardangervidda** Extensive mountain plateau in SW Norway, extending 160 km/100 mi between the head of Hardanger Fjord and the Hallingdal valley; average elevation of 1000 m/3500 ft, rising to 1862 m/6109 ft at Hardangerjøkulen; winter sports and tourist area.

hard copy Computer output which is, for example, printed on paper and can therefore be directly read and understood by the user. The contrast is with **soft copy**, which refers to information stored in ways which can be understood only by a machine, such as on a floppy disk or in a computer memory.

hard disk A rigid magnetic storage disk for computer data, such as the Winchester disk. It is generally capable of storing much more data than a similar-sized floppy disk. On larger computers, stacks of removable hard disks are often used, and give very large data storage potential.

Hardicanute [hah(r)dikanoot], also spelled **Harthacnut** (c.1018–42) King of Denmark (1035–42), and the last Danish King of England (1040–2), the only son of Canute and Emma of Normandy. Canute had intended that Hardicanute should succeed him in both Denmark and England simultaneously, but he was unable to secure his English inheritance until his stepbrother, Harold I, died in 1040. Hardicanute's death without children led to the restoration of the Old English royal line in the person of Edward the Confessor, the only surviving son of Emma and Ethelred the Unready.

Hardie, (James) Keir (1856–1915) British politician, born near Holytown, North Lanarkshire, C Scotland, UK. He worked in the mines between the ages of seven and 24, and was victimized as the miners' champion. He became a journalist and the first Labour candidate, entering parliament in 1892. He founded and edited the *Labour Leader*, and was chairman of the Independent Labour Party (founded 1893). Instrumental in the establishment of the Labour Representation Committee, he served as chairman of the Labour Party (1906–8). His strong pacifism led to his becoming isolated within the Party, particularly once World War 1 had broken out.

Harding, Warren G(amaliel) (1865–1923) US statesman and 29th president (1921–3), born in Corsica, Ohio, USA. He studied at Ohio Central College, then became a journalist and a newspaper owner (the *Marion Daily Star*). He gained a seat in the Ohio State Senate (1899) and the lieutenant-governorship (1902), after which he returned to journalism until 1914, when he was elected to the US Senate. Emerging as a power in the Republican Party, he won its nomination and the presidency in 1920, campaigning against US membership of the League of Nations. As president, he delegated much authority to his cabinet chiefs. He fell ill and died of a heart attack during a series of scandals involving corruption among members of his cabinet, the full extent of which was revealed only after his death. He was succeeded by his vice-president, Calvin Coolidge.

hardness A measure of a material's resistance to denting, scratching, and abrasion, related to the yield stress and tensile strength of the material. It is determined using indentation

Hardness Scale

Friedrich Mohs (1773–1839) introduced a simple definition of hardness, according to which one mineral is said to be harder than another if the former scratches the latter. The Mohs scale is based on a series of common minerals, arranged in order of increasing hardness.

Mineral	*Composition*	*Simple hardness test*	*Hardness*
Talc	$Mg_3Si_4O_{10}(OH)_2$	Crushed by finger nail	1
Gypsum	$CaSO_4 \cdot 2H_2O$	Scratched by finger nail	2
Calcite	$CaCo_3$	Scratched by copper coin	3
Fluorite	CaF_2	Scratched by glass	4
Apatite	$Ca_5(PO_4)_3F$	Scratched by penknife	5
Orthoclase (feldspar)	$KAlSi_3O_8$	Scratched by quartz	6
Quartz	SiO_2	Scratched by steel file	7
Topaz	$Al_2SiO_4F_2$	Scratched by corundum	8
Corundum	Al_2O_3	Scratched by diamond	9
Diamond	C		10

tests, which measure the size of a hole formed by a hard indenter driven into the material, as in the Vickers and Brinell tests. It is sometimes classified using the Mohs test of mineral hardness (devised by German mineralogist Friedrich Mohs in 1812), which rates talc as hardness 1 and diamond as hardness 10. (*see panel p.690*)

hardware In computing, a term used, in contrast to **software**, to include all the physical units which make up an electronic or computer system, such as keyboards, magnetic disks, circuits, and visual display units.

Hardy, Godfrey (Harold) (1877–1947) Mathematician, born in Cranleigh, Surrey, SE England, UK. He studied at Cambridge, was professor of geometry at Oxford (1919–30), then returned to Cambridge as professor of pure maths (1931–42). He was an internationally important figure in mathematical analysis, collaborating with John Littlewood (1885–1977) in much of his work in analytic number theory. He was greatly influenced by the work of Srinivasa Ramanujan. His mathematical philosophy was described for the layman in his book *A Mathematician's Apology* (1940). In his one venture into applied maths he developed (concurrently with, but independent of, Wilhelm Weinberg) the **Hardy–Weinberg law** fundamental to population genetics.

Hardy, Oliver *Laurel and Hardy*

Hardy, Thomas (1840–1928) Novelist and poet, born in Upper Bockhampton, Dorset, S England, UK. After schooling in Dorchester, he studied as an architect, and at 22 moved to London, where he began to write poems expressing his love of rural life. Unable to publish his poetry, he turned to the novel, and found success with *Far from the Madding Crowd* (1874). He then took up writing as a profession, and produced a series of novels, notably *The Return of the Native* (1878), *The Mayor of Casterbridge* (1886), *Tess of the D'Urbervilles* (1891), and *Jude the Obscure* (1896). His main works were all tragedies, increasingly pessimistic in tone, and after *Tess* he was dubbed an atheist. He then took up poetry again, writing several volumes of sardonic lyrics, as well as the moving elegies to his first wife **Emma Gifford** (d.1912), and the epic drama, *The Dynasts* (1903–8). Several of his novels have been filmed and televised, notably *Far from the Madding Crowd* (Schlesinger, 1967) and *Tess* (Polanski, 1979).

Hardy–Weinberg law A principle governing allele and genotype frequencies in a stable outbred population; formulated in 1908 by British mathematician Godfrey H Hardy and German physician Wilhelm Weinberg (1862–1937) They pointed out that if there are two alleles, A and a, with frequencies p and q, $p + q = 1$. Furthermore, $p^2 + 2pq + q^2 = 1$, where p^2 is the frequency of AA homozygotes, q^2 the frequency of aa homozygotes, and $2pq$ the frequency of heterozygotes. The equation may be expanded to cover more than two alleles at a locus. Deviations from the Hardy–Weinberg law are found in small or inbred populations. It is frequently used to calculate heterozygote frequencies ($2pq$) for a recessive disorder where the frequency of affected homozygotes (q^2) is accurately known. For example, if the birth incidence of cystic fibrosis is 1 in 2500 ($q^2 = 0{\cdot}0004$), $q = 0{\cdot}02$ and $2pq = 2 \times 0{\cdot}98 \times 0{\cdot}02$ or 0·0392.

hardy plants Plants which are able to withstand frost damage. All perennials and some annuals from cold and cool temperate regions are hardy; most (though not all) tropical and some warm temperate plants are not.

Hare, Sir David (1947–) Playwright and director, born in St Leonard's-on-Sea, East Sussex, SE England, UK. He studied at Cambridge, founded the Portable Theatre (1968), and went on to be resident playwright at the Royal Court (1969–71) and elsewhere. His politically engaged plays include *Slag* (1970), *Teeth 'n Smiles* (1975), *Plenty* (1978), and *Pravda* (1985, with Howard Brenton). He has also written several plays for television, including *Licking Hitler* (1978) and *Dreams of Leaving* (1980), and the films *Wetherby* (1985) and *Strapless* (1989). *The Secret Rapture* (1988) won two awards for best play of the year. Later works include *Amy's View* (1997), *The Judas Kiss* (1998), and *A Breath of Life* (2002). He was knighted in 1998.

Hare, William *Burke, William*

hare A mammal of the genus *Lepus* (11 species); also known as **jackrabbit**. There are several differences from the closely related rabbit: hares give birth to young (*leverets*) with fur, are larger, have black tips to the ears, are more solitary, and do not burrow. (Family: Leporidae. Order: Lagomorpha.)

harebell A slender perennial (*Campanula rotundifolia*) with creeping underground stolons, native to N temperate regions; stems horizontal at base, becoming erect, growing to 40 cm/15 in; lowest leaves heart-shaped, toothed, becoming narrower and entire up the stem; flowers 5-lobed bells c.1·5 cm/0·6 in, blue, rarely white, 1–several, drooping on slender stalks. In Scotland it is known as the **bluebell**. (Family: Campanulaceae.)

Hare Krishna movement [haree krishnah] A religious movement founded in the USA in 1965 by His Divine Grace A C Bhaktivedanta, Swami Prabhupada as the International Society for Krishna Consciousness. The movement promotes human well-being by promoting God consciousness based on the ancient Vedic texts of India. It is one of the best known of the new religious movements coming from the East, largely as a result of saffron-robed young people gathered in town centres chanting the Maha mantra, from which their popular name is derived. In their pursuit of spiritual advancement devotees practise vegetarianism, do not use intoxicants, do not gamble, and are celibate apart from procreation within marriage.

hare lip *cleft lip and palate*

Harewood, George Henry Hubert Lascelles, 7th Earl of [hah(r)wud] (1923–) Elder son of Princess Mary, and cousin of Queen Elizabeth II, born in Harewood, West Yorkshire, N England, UK. He studied at Cambridge, served as captain in the Grenadier Guards in World War 2, and was a prisoner of war. Since the 1950s he has been much involved in the direction of operatic and arts institutions, such as at Covent Garden, Edinburgh, and Leeds.

Hargreaves, James (c.1720–78) Inventor, probably born in Blackburn, Lancashire, NW England, UK. An illiterate weaver and carpenter, c.1764 he invented the spinning jenny (named after his daughter); but his fellow spinners broke into his house and destroyed his frame (1768). He moved to Nottingham, where he erected a spinning mill, and continued to manufacture yarn until his death.

Hargreaves, Roger (1935–88) Children's writer, born in Cleckheaton, West Yorkshire, N England, UK. He began a career in advertising and turned to writing after creating the storybook character 'Mr Tickle' for his son **Adam** in 1971. A hugely popular series of 43 Mr Men books followed, which he also illustrated. In 1981 he began the equally successful series of 30 Little Miss books which were written for his twin daughters. In 2003 Adam wrote and illustrated a further set of books, crediting his father as author.

haricot bean An annual (*Phaseolus vulgaris*) growing to 3 m/10 ft, sometimes climbing, a native of South America; leaves with three broadly oval leaflets; pea-flowers white, yellow, or bluish, in small shortly stalked clusters in the leaf axils; pods up to 20 cm/8 in long, containing edible ellipsoid or kidney-shaped seeds; also called **kidney bean** and **French bean**. Numerous varieties are cultivated as a vegetable, both the young pods and the mature beans being eaten. The whole plants provide fodder for livestock. (Family: Leguminosae.)

Harimandir [harimandeer] or **Golden Temple** The centre of the Sikh religion at Amritsar, Punjab, India. The temple dates from 1766 and stands in a sacred lake. It is faced with copper-gilt plates bearing inscriptions from the Granth Sahib, the holy book of the Sikhs, which is housed within.

Harlem (The Netherlands), Dutch **Haarlem** 52°23N 4°38E, pop (2000e) 157 000. Capital city of North Holland province, W Netherlands; 7 km/4 mi from the North Sea coast, on the R Spaarne; part of the Randstad conurbation; founded, 10th-c;

charter, 1245; sacked by the Spaniards (1573); railway; centre for tulip, hyacinth, and crocus bulbs; chemicals, publishing and printing, shipyards, railway works, machines, food processing; town hall (13th–17th-c), Grote Kerk (1472), Frans Hals museum.

Harlem (USA) District in New York City, USA, largely in N Manhattan Island, centred on 125th St; named (1658) after Haarlem, The Netherlands; a chiefly black residential area, known for its poverty and racial tension; area to the E contains a large Puerto Rican community (**Spanish Harlem**), and several other minority groups also live in the district; centre of a literary movement in the 1920s (the **Harlem Renaissance**).

Harlem Globetrotters An American professional touring basketball team, usually all-black, formed in 1927 by London-born immigrant Abraham Saperstein (1903–66). They developed a comedy routine to add to their skills, and now tour worldwide, giving exhibitions. Their signature tune is 'Sweet Georgia Brown'. The team was inducted into the Basketball Hall of Fame in 2002.

Harlequin Columbine's young lover in the English harlequinade, with a costume of multi-coloured diamond-shaped patches, whose cunning and ingenuity has had a long and varied theatrical history. He originated as Arlecchino, a servant and clown, one of the stock masks of the *commedia dell'arte*.

harlequinade An English theatrical entertainment developed in the 18th-c by the actor John Rich, who specialized in the acrobatic and pantomimic portrayal of Harlequin. Scenes of this character's comic courtship of the servant girl Columbine interspersed the performance of a serious play, which they served to satirize. By the beginning of the 19th-c, these largely silent harlequinades had become a separate form, with spectacular scenic transformations and magical fairy-tale locations, and as such were the immediate precursors of the English pantomime.

harlequin duck A small duck, native to N areas of N hemisphere (*Histrionicus histrionicus*); dark with white stripes and spots; inhabits fast-flowing streams in summer, rough coasts in winter; dives for small animals which it pulls from rocks. (Family: Anatidae.)

Harley, Robert, 1st Earl of Oxford (1661–1724) British statesman, born in London, UK. He became a lawyer, and a Whig MP in 1689. In 1701 he was elected Speaker, and in 1704 became secretary of state. Shortly after, he became sympathetic to the Tories, and from 1708 worked to undermine the power of the Whigs. In 1710 Godolphin was dismissed, and Harley made Chancellor of the Exchequer, head of the government, and (1711) Earl of Oxford and Lord High Treasurer. The principal act of his administration was the Treaty of Utrecht (1713). In 1714 he was dismissed, and after the Hanoverian succession spent two years in prison.

Harlow, Jean, originally **Harlean Carpentier**, nickname **the Blonde Bombshell** (1911–37) Film star, born in Kansas City, Missouri, USA. After a broken childhood, at 16 she moved to Los Angeles, where she became a film extra and worked at the Hal Roach Studios. Signed to a contract by Howard Hughes, she rocketed to fame in *Hell's Angels* (1930), her platinum-blonde hair initiating a craze across the country. Subsequent roles in *Platinum Blonde* (1931), *Red-Headed Woman* (1932), and *Red Dust* (1932), established her as a brazenly sexual screen goddess. Under contract to MGM from 1932, she played opposite the studio's top male stars in *Bombshell* (1933) and other films. Her private life caused many a scandal, and she died of uraemic poisoning at the age of 26 during the shooting of *Saratoga*.

Harman, Harriet (1950–) British stateswoman. She was educated at York University, became a solicitor, and was legal officer for the National Council of Civil Liberties (1978–82). She became a Labour MP in 1982, held shadow ministerial posts for social services (1984, 1985–7), health (1987–92, 1995–6), the Treasury (1992–4), employment (1994–5), and social security (1996–7), and became secretary of state for social security and minister for women (1997–8). She was appointed Solicitor General after the 2001 election.

Harmattan [hah(r)matan] A hot, dry wind which blows from the Sahara desert in W Africa. Dust carried by the Harmattan may be blown across to the Caribbean.

harmonic A pitch sounded by a string or column of air vibrating at a half, a third, a quarter, etc of its length. The timbre of a voice or instrument depends on the prominence or otherwise of these harmonics (or *upper partials*) when the fundamental note is sounded. Harmonics may be sounded independently of the fundamental note, on brass instruments by means of the player's embouchure (tightening or slackening of the lips), and on the harp and instruments of the violin family by lightly touching the vibrating string at an appropriate node.

harmonica A musical instrument, popularly known as the **mouth organ**, in which metal 'reeds' arranged in a row are made to vibrate by the inhalation and exhalation of the player's breath. The standard diatonic model is tuned to a 'gapped' scale (ie one with some notes missing) and is suitable only for simple, unsophisticated melodies. In the chromatic model a slide mechanism brings into play a second set of reeds tuned a semitone higher; virtuosi such as Larry Adler (1914–2001) and Tommy Reilly (1919–) inspired many serious composers to write for it. It was favoured in China from before 600 BC.

harmonic motion *simple harmonic motion*

harmonic series The complex of musical pitches produced when a string or column of air is made to vibrate. The first 16 partials of the note *C* are shown below; the black notes are 'out of tune', ie their pitches cannot be adequately represented on a staff designed to accommodate the notes of the tempered scale.

harmonium A type of reed organ patented in 1842 by French instrument maker A F Debain (1809–77). The name has been widely used for reed organs in general.

harmony The combining of musical notes into chords, and then into sequences of chords, with emphasis on the 'vertical' component of the music rather than on the 'horizontal' fitting together of melodic strands (counterpoint). Harmony is thus generally thought of as accompanying, or 'clothing', one or more lines of melody. It may be *diatonic* (using wholly or mainly the notes of a particular key), *chromatic* (employing many notes foreign to the key), or *atonal* (independent of any reference to a key centre). In a looser sense, the term *harmonious* is often used to mean 'pleasant-sounding', in contrast to *discordant*, but in reality discord has been an essential part of the harmonic theory of all periods of music history.

Harmsworth, Alfred (Charles William), 1st Viscount Northcliffe (1865–1922) Journalist and newspaper magnate, one of the pioneers of mass circulation journalism, born near Dublin, Ireland. Brought up in London, he became editor of *Youth*, and with his brother, Harold, founded *Comic Cuts* (1890), the basis for the Amalgamated Press. In 1894 he absorbed the *London Evening News*, published a number of Sunday magazine papers, and in 1896 revolutionized Fleet Street with his *Daily Mail*, introducing popular journalism to the UK. In 1908, he became proprietor of *The Times*. A baronet in 1904, he was created baron in 1906 and viscount in 1917.

Harmsworth, Harold (Sydney), 1st Viscount Rothermere (1868–1940) Newspaper magnate, born in London, UK. Closely associated with his brother, Alfred, he also founded the Glasgow *Daily Record* and in 1915 the *Sunday Pictorial*. He became air minister (1917–18), and after his brother's death acquired control of the *Daily Mail* and *Sunday Dispatch*. A baronet in 1910, he was created baron in 1914 and viscount in 1919.

Harnack, Adolf (Karl Gustav) von (1851–1930) Protestant Church historian and theologian, born in born in Tartu (formerly Dorpat), E Estonia. He was professor at Leipzig (1876), Giessen (1879), Marburg (1886), and Berlin (1889), where he also became keeper of the Royal (later State) Library (1904–21). His major writings include works on the history of dogma, on early Gospel traditions, and on a reconstruction of the essence of Jesus's teachings.

harness racing A horse race in which the rider is seated in a small two-wheeled cart, known as a *sulky*. The horses either trot or *pace*, and must not gallop. Races are run on an oval dirt track measuring 400–1500 m/½–1 mi in circumference. It was first introduced in Holland in 1554, but popularized in the USA in the mid-19th-c.

Harnick, Sheldon (1924–) Songwriter, born in Chicago, Illinois, USA. He went to New York City as a violinist, and began selling songs to revues. His first real success came when he teamed with composer Jerry Bock (1928–) on *The Body Beautiful* (1958), a musical about boxers. This was followed by *Fiorello* (1959, with Bock), a political satire based loosely on the life of New York Mayor LaGuardia, which was awarded the Pulitzer Prize. His greatest success has been *Fiddler on the Roof* (1964), which includes 'Matchmaker, Matchmaker', 'If I Were a Rich Man', and 'Sunrise, Sunset'.

Harold I, nickname **Harold Harefoot** (c.1016–40) King of England (1037–40), the younger son of Canute and Ælfgifu of Northampton. Canute had intended that Hardicanute, his only son by Emma of Normandy, should succeed him in both Denmark and England. But in view of Hardicanute's absence in Denmark, Harold was accepted in England, first as regent (1035–6), and from 1037 as king.

Harold II (c.1022–66) Last Anglo-Saxon king of England (1066), the second son of Earl Godwin. By 1045 he was Earl of East Anglia, and in 1053 succeeded to his father's earldom of Wessex, becoming the right hand of Edward the Confessor. After Edward's death (Jan 1066), Harold, his nominee, was crowned as king. He defeated his brother Tostig and Harold Hardrada, King of Norway, at Stamford Bridge (Sep 1066), but Duke William of Normandy then invaded England, and defeated him near Hastings (14 Oct 1066), where he died, shot through the eye with an arrow.

Harold III *Harald III Sigurdsson*

harp A musical instrument of great antiquity existing in a wide variety of forms and sizes, its distinguishing characteristic being that its strings run in a plane perpendicular to the resonator. Early types had a single row of strings tuned diatonically; later, one or (as in the Welsh triple harp of the 17th-c) two further rows were added, enabling chromatic notes to be played. The modern concert harp, designed in 1810 by French pianoforte maker Sébastien Erard (1752–1831), has a single row of 46 or 47 strings tuned to the major scale of C♭, and seven pedals by means of which any pitch may be raised by a semitone or a tone.

Harpers Ferry Raid (1859) An attack on the Federal arsenal in Virginia, led by abolitionist John Brown, intending to launch a slave insurrection. The raiders were captured, and Brown was executed amidst great publicity.

Harpies [hah(r)peez] In Greek mythology, fabulous monsters with women's features and bird's wings and claws. They were originally rapacious ghosts or the storm-winds. They plagued Phineus, until chased away by the Argonauts. The name means 'snatchers'.

Harpocrates *Horus*

harpsichord A keyboard instrument known in China from at least the 8th-c, in use in the West from the 15th-c to the early 19th-c, and revived in recent times mainly for performing early music. The keys, when depressed, cause wooden *jacks*, fitted with plectrums of leather or quill (or, in some modern instruments, plastic), to pluck the strings, which extend away from the keyboard and are dampened when the jacks fall into place again.

harpy eagle The world's largest eagle (*Harpia harpyja*), 90 cm/3 ft; inhabits lowland rainforest from Central America to Argentina; rare; black, white, and grey; feet large; eats tree-dwelling mammals (monkeys, sloths, etc), and some birds. (Family: Accipitridae.)

Harrelson, Woody (1961–) Actor, born in Midland, Texas, USA. He studied at Hanover College, went into the theatre, and became well known for his role as the bartender in the popular television series *Cheers* (1983–93). His feature films include *Indecent Proposal* (1993), *Natural Born Killers* (1994), *The People vs. Larry Flynt* (1996, Oscar nomination), *The Hi-Lo Country* (1999), and *Anger Management* (2003). In 1996 he attracted publicity when he was arrested twice as an activist during events drawing attention to endangered forests. He made his British stage debut in *On an Average Day* in 2002.

harrier (ornithology) A medium-sized hawk of worldwide genus *Circus* (10 species); wings and tail long; inhabits marsh, moors, and grassland; eats mainly small mammals and birds; hunts by flying low, following regular search pattern; most nest on ground. The name **brown harrier eagle** is used for the hawk *Circaetus cinereus*; **harrier hawk** is used for two hawks of the genus *Polyboroides* and several falcons of the genus *Micrastur*. (Family: Accipitridae.)

harrier (zoology) A hound used for hunting hares; slightly smaller than a foxhound, with a keen sense of smell.

Harriman, W(illiam) Averell (1891–1986) US statesman and diplomat, born in New York City, USA. He studied at Yale, and became a diplomat, taking up posts as ambassador to the USSR (1943) and to Britain (1946). He was secretary of commerce (1946–8), and special assistant (1950–1) to his close friend, President Truman, helping him to organize NATO. He became Governor of New York (1955–8), ambassador-at-large (1961, 1965–9), and US representative at the Vietnam peace talks in Paris (1968). He negotiated the partial nuclear test-ban treaty between the USA and USSR in 1963, and continued to visit the USSR on behalf of the government, making his last visit there at age 91. His wife, **Pamela C(hurchill) Harriman** (d. 1997) became vice-chairman of the Atlantic Council and then US ambassador to France.

Harris S part of the Lewis with Harris island district, Western Isles, NW Scotland, UK; area c.500 sq km/200 sq mi; ferry links between Tarbert and Uig (Skye) and Lochmaddy (N Uist); tweed manufacture.

Harris, Sir Arthur Travers, nickname **Bomber Harris** (1892–1984) British airman, born in Cheltenham, Gloucestershire, SWC England, UK. He served in the Royal Flying Corps in World War 1, and as commander-in-chief of Bomber Command in World War 2 (1942–5) organized mass bomber raids on industrial Germany. He was knighted in 1942, and created a baronet in 1953.

Harris, Joel Chandler (1848–1908) Humorist and dialect writer, born in Eatonton, Georgia, USA. He was in turn printer, lawyer, and journalist, became apprentice on the *Countryman* weekly, and then joined the staff of the Atlanta *Constitution* (1876–1900). His 'Tar Baby' story (1879), and later *Uncle Remus* stories about 'Brer Rabbit' and 'Brer Fox', made him internationally famous, known especially for his distinctive use of Southern African-American folklore and dialect. He edited *Uncle Remus's Magazine* from 1907.

Harris, Joanne (1964–) Novelist, born in N England, UK. The daughter of an English father and French mother, her childhood was spent living between Barnsley in South Yorkshire, and France. She studied at Cambridge and became a teacher of French at Leeds Grammar School (1989–99). Her first successful novel, *Chocolat* (1999; filmed 2000), was shortlisted for the Whitbread Book Award. Further books include *Blackberry Wine* (2000), *Five Quarters of the Orange* (2001), and *Holy Fools* (2003).

Harris, Rolf (1930–) Entertainer and artist, born in Bassendean, Western Australia. He won a radio 'Amateur Hour' competition at the age of 18, and after graduating from the University of Western Australia, went to London in 1952 where he studied art. While there he performed at the Down Under Club, and in 1954 started working for the BBC children's department. He returned to Perth in 1960 to present a children's television programme, and then had commercial success with his recordings. Returning to Britain, he has since appeared widely on stage and television, and fronted BBC's popular long-running series *Animal Hospital* (1994–2003). In 2003 he celebrated 50 years in television with a concert at the Royal Albert Hall.

Harris, Roy, popular name of **LeRoy Ellsworth Harris** (1898–1979) Composer, born in Lincoln Co, Oklahoma, USA. A truck driver, he turned to music at 24, and after tuition in California won a Guggenheim scholarship, enabling him to study in Paris under Nadia Boulanger. He later held positions in Californian universities as a teacher of composition. His music is ruggedly American in character, as in his symphonic overture *When Johnny Comes Marching Home* (1935). He wrote 16 symphonies, the third being the best known.

Harrisburg 40°16N 76°53W, pop (2000e) 48 900. Capital of state (since 1812) in Dauphin Co, S Pennsylvania, USA, on the Susquehanna R; scene of many important conventions, especially the Harrisburg Convention (1788); site of Camp Curtin, the first Union camp in the Civil War; scene of nuclear power station accident on Three Mile Island (1979); railway; former steel industry giving way to a more diversified economy based on textiles, paper, machinery, food processing, bricks.

Harrison, Benjamin (1833–1901) US statesman and 23rd president (1889–93), born in North Bend, Ohio, USA, the grandson of William Henry Harrison. He studied at Miami University, and in 1854 settled as a lawyer in Indianapolis. During the Civil War (1861–5) he fought in Sherman's Atlanta campaign. He was elected a Republican senator for Indiana in 1880. In 1888 he defeated the incumbent president Cleveland on the issue of the protective tariff. Harrison admitted several new states to the Union during his term. The first Pan-American Conference (1889), held during his presidency, created new commercial and diplomatic ties with the republics in Latin America. He failed to gain re-election in 1892, and returned to his law practice in Indianapolis.

Harrison, George (1943–2001) Singer, musician, and songwriter, born in Liverpool, Merseyside, NW England, UK. He played lead guitar and sang with the Beatles, and developed an interest in Indian music and Eastern religion, receiving instruction on the sitar from Ravi Shankar, and associating with the religious leader, Maharishi Mahesh Yogi. Following the break-up of the Beatles, he made a solo album, *All Things Must Pass* (1970), which included the gospelly hit 'My Sweet Lord', later the subject of an expensive plagiarism suit. Later solo albums included *Living in the Material World* (1973), *Dark Horse* (1974), and *Somewhere in England* (1981), and he joined with other artists in the 'super-group' The Traveling Wilburys (1988–90), and with Starr and McCartney to produce the Beatles anthology (1995). He formed Dark Horse Records in 1974, and a film company, HandMade Films, in 1978, producing a number of feature films, such as *Monty Python's Life of Brian* (1979), *Time Bandits* (1981, also writing the music and lyrics), *A Private Function* (1984), and *Withnail and I* (1987). He also wrote a volume of autobiography, *I Me Mine*. He was severely wounded following a knife attack by an intruder at his Henley home at the end of 1999, and died in 2001 after a long battle against cancer.

Harrison, John (1693–1776) Inventor and horologist, born in Foulby, West Yorkshire, N England, UK. By 1726 he had constructed a clock with compensating apparatus for correcting errors due to variations of climate. In 1713 the British government had offered three prizes for the discovery of a method to determine longitude accurately (only possible with very accurate timepieces). After long perseverance he developed a marine chronometer which, in a voyage to Jamaica (1761–2) determined the longitude within two geographical miles. After further trials, he was awarded the first prize (1765–73).

Harrison, Sir Rex, originally **Reginald Carey Harrison** (1908–90) Actor, born in Huyton-with-Roby, Lancashire, NW England, UK. He reached the London stage by 1930, and had his first leading film role in *Storm in a Teacup* (1937). His charming, somewhat blasé style attracted many star comedy parts, such as in *Blithe Spirit* (1945), *The Constant Husband* (1958), and *My Fair Lady* (1964, Oscar).

Harrison, Tony (1937–) Poet, born in Leeds, West Yorkshire, N England, UK. After studying in Leeds, and teaching in Nigeria and Prague, he became known with *The Loiners* (1970) and the translation *Palladas Poems* (1975). His combination of classical technique and colloquial language has produced powerful effects in the open sequences *Ten Poems from the School of Eloquence* (1976) and *Continuous* (1981), also evident in his vigorous adaptations from French, Greek, and mediaeval drama. Poems on social conflict ('V'. 1985, televised 1987) and the Gulf War ('A Cold Coming', 1991) underline his commitment to public issues, confirmed in *The Gaze of the Gorgon* (1992, Whitbread). Later works include *The Prince's Play* (1996), and he was a contributor to *The Poetry Quartets* (1999).

Harrison, William Henry (1773–1841) US soldier, statesman, and ninth president (1841), born in Charles City Co, Virginia, USA. He fought against the Indians, and when Indiana Territory was formed (1800) he was appointed governor. He tried to avoid further Indian wars, but was compelled to suppress Tecumseh's outbreak, which ended in the Battle of Tippecanoe (1811). In the War of 1812 he defeated the British in the Battle of the Thames (1813). In 1816 he was elected to Congress, became a senator in 1824, and president in 1841, but died of pneumonia a month after his inauguration.

Harrow 51°35N 0°20W, pop (2001e) 207 400. Borough of NW Greater London, UK; it is thought that there was once a temple on top of Harrow on the Hill, and during the Middle Ages 12 individual settlements sprang up around it that now make up the borough; railway; tube station; Harrow School (1572); church of St Mary (1087) on Harrow Hill; largely a suburban commuter community.

Harsanyi, John C(harles) (1920–2000) Economist, born in Budapest, Hungary. He studied mathematics at Budapest, moved to the USA in 1956, and worked at Stanford and Yale universities before moving to the Haas School of Business at the University of California, Berkeley, in 1964. He shared the Nobel Prize for Economics in 1994 for his contribution to the analysis of equilibria in the theory of non-co-operative games.

Harte, Bret, pseudonym of **Francis Brett Hart** (1836–1902) Writer, born in Albany, New York, USA. He went to California in 1854, and wrote about the miners in the *Northern Californian* weekly. He later became a clerk at the US Mint in San Francisco (1864–70), during which time he edited the *Californian* and then the *Overland Monthly*. His collection of articles, *The Luck of Roaring Camp* (1870), brought him world fame, and he was contracted to *The Atlantic Monthly* (1871) to write 12 stories a year. He moved to the East coast, where he was lionized, but his work suffered as a consequence. He was US consul at Krefeld (1878–80) and at Glasgow (1880–5), then lived in London, never returning to the USA.

hartebeest [hah(r)tibeest] An ox-antelope closely related to the topi; pale brown; two species: the **hartebeest** or **kongoni** (*Alcelaphus buselaphus*, 12 subspecies), and **Lichtenstein's hartebeest** (*Alcelaphus lichtensteini*).

Hartford 41°46N 72°41W, pop (2000e) 121 600. Capital of Connecticut, USA; in Hartford Co, on the Connecticut R; founded by Dutch settlers, 1633; city status, 1784; railway; university; aeroplane parts, motor vehicles, electrical equipment, machinery, metal products; world's largest concentration of insurance companies; professional team, Whalers (ice hockey); Old State House, Wadsworth Atheneum, Museum of Connecticut History.

Hartford Convention (1814–15) A gathering at Hartford, Connecticut, of delegates from the New England states to oppose the War of 1812 and to propose changes in the US Constitution. The Treaty of Ghent, ending the war, and US victory at New Orleans discredited both the Convention and the Federalist Party, with which it was associated.

Hartington, Lord *Cavendish, Spencer Compton*

Hartley, L(eslie) P(oles) (1895–1972) Writer, born near Peterborough, Cambridgeshire, EC England, UK. His early short stories, such as *Night Fears* (1924), established his reputation as a master of the macabre. Later he turned to depicting psychological relationships, and made a new success with such novels as *The*

Shrimp and the Anemone (1944), *The Boat* (1950), and *The Go-Between* (1953, filmed by Joseph Losey, 1970).

Hartnell, Sir Norman (1901–78) Fashion designer and court dressmaker, born in London, UK. He studied at Cambridge, then started his own business in 1923, receiving the Royal Warrant in 1940. He was president of the Incorporated Society of London Fashion Designers (1946–56). His work included costumes for leading actresses, wartime 'utility' dresses, the Women's Royal Army Corps uniform, and Princess Elizabeth's wedding and coronation gowns. He was knighted in 1977.

Hartono (Kurniawan), Rudy [hah(r)tohnoh] (1948–) Indonesian badminton player. The winner of a record eight All-England titles (1968–74, 1976), he was also a member of Indonesia's Thomas Cup winning teams in 1970, 1973, 1976, and 1979. He was world champion in 1980.

Hartwell, Leland H, known as **Lee Hartwell** (1939–) Geneticist, born in Los Angeles, California, USA. He studied at the California Institute of Technology and the Massachusetts Institute of Technology, in 1968 joining the University of Washington, where he became professor of genome sciences and adjunct professor of medicine. He became president and director of the Fred Hutchinson Cancer Research Center, Seattle, in 1997. He shared the 2001 Nobel Prize for Physiology or Medicine for his pioneering work in yeast genetics, which contributed to understanding the key regulators of the cell cycle.

haruspices [haruspikayz] In ancient Rome, the practitioners of the Etruscan system of divination, of which inspection of the entrails of sacrificial animals was the main part. Though less prestigious than augurs, haruspices were widely employed, and their art survived well into the Christian era.

Harvard University *Ivy League*

Harvester judgment A landmark decision for the Australian industrial relations system, which introduced the concept of the 'basic wage' that remained a central feature of the national system until 1967, and of the State system until 1967–70. The case was brought by a manufacturer of agricultural harvesters in 1907.

harvestman An extremely long-legged arthropod; typically a predator of small insects, molluscs, or worms; some are scavengers; body compact, carried on four pairs of long legs; female with long egg-laying tube; also called **daddy longlegs**. (Class: Arachnida. Order: Opiliones, c.4500 species.)

harvest-mite A small, predatory mite; tiny, red-coloured, 6-legged larvae often occur in large numbers in damp fields in autumn; feed by sucking blood of small mammals and humans, causing severe itching and rash; larvae known as **chiggers**. (Order: Acari. Family: Thrombidiidae.)

harvest moon The full Moon closest to the autumnal equinox. It rises at almost the same time on successive evenings, seemingly providing light to help the farmers of old get in the harvest.

harvest mouse A mouse of the genus *Reithrodontomys* (**American harvest mouse**, 19 species) from Central and North America; also, **Old World harvest mouse** (*Micromys minutus*) from Europe and Asia, the smallest living rodent (may weigh as little as 5 g/0·2 oz); build spherical nests of dry grass attached to tall grass stems.

Harvey, Caroline *Trollope, Joanna*

Harvey, William (1578–1657) Physician who discovered the circulation of the blood, born in Folkestone, Kent, SE England, UK. He studied at Cambridge and Padua, and settled in London as a physician, holding appointments at St Bartholomew's Hospital (1609–43) and from 1615 at the College of Physicians. He was also appointed physician to James I and Charles I. His celebrated treatise, *De motu cordis et sanguinis in animalibus* (On the Motion of the Heart and Blood in Animals), in which the circulation of the blood was first described, was published in 1628.

Harwich [harich] 51°57N 1°17E, pop (2000e) 20 000. Port in Essex, SE England, UK; on the North Sea coast, 26 km/16 mi E of Colchester; railway; container freight terminal; ferries to Denmark, Germany, Holland; engineering.

Hasdrubal [hazdrubl] The name of several Carthaginian leaders, notably **1** Hamilcar Barca's son-in-law and successor in Spain (died 221 BC), and **2** Hannibal's younger brother, who died in battle with the Romans at the R Metaurus (207 BC).

Hašek, Jaroslav [hashek] (1883–1923) Novelist and short-story writer, born in Prague, Czech Republic. An accomplished practical joker who despised pomposity, he is best known for his novel *The Good Soldier Švejk* (1921–3), a satire on military life and bureaucracy, four volumes of which were completed by his death.

Haselrig, Sir Arthur [hayzlrig], also spelled **Hesilrige** (?–1661) English parliamentarian. In 1640 he sat in the Long and Short Parliaments for his native county, Leicestershire, and was one of the five members whose attempted seizure by Charles I in 1642 precipitated the Civil War. He commanded a parliamentary regiment, and in 1647 became Governor of Newcastle upon Tyne. After the Restoration, he died a prisoner in the Tower.

Hashemites Arab princely family of sharifs, or descendants of the Prophet, who ruled parts of Arabia and the Fertile Crescent in the 20th-c, including the current royal family of Jordan. **Husayn ibn Ali** (c.1852–1931), Sharif of Mecca, won British support for the Arab Revolt (1916–18) against Ottoman rule, and was subsequently recognized as king of the Arabian province of the Hejaz. Of his four sons, three came to occupy Arab thrones. **Ali** (1879–1935) succeeded his father for one year before the Saudi conquest of the Hejaz in 1925; **Faisal** (1884–1933) reigned in Syria until 1920 and thereafter in Iraq (1921–33); and **Abdullah** (1882–1951) ruled in Jordan from 1920 until his assassination in Jerusalem.

hashish *cannabis*

Hashman, Judy, popular name of **Judith Hashman**, *née* **Devlin** (1935–) Badminton player, born in Winnipeg, Manitoba, C Canada. The winner of the singles title at the All-England Championships a record 10 times (1954, 1957–8, 1960–4, 1966–7), she also won seven doubles titles – six with her sister, **Susan Peard** (1940–). She was a member of the US Uber Cup-winning teams in 1957, 1960, and 1963. Her Irish-born father, **Frank Devlin** (1899–1988), won 18 All-England titles.

Hasidim or **Chasidim** [hasideem], also **Hasideans** (Heb 'faithful ones') Originally, those Jews in the 2nd-c BC who resisted Greek and pagan influences on Israel's religion and sought strict adherence to the Jewish law; probably ancestors of the Pharisees. They supported the early Maccabean revolt, but refused to fight for national independence once the legitimate high priesthood had been restored. More recently the name refers to extreme conservative Orthodox Jews deriving from the Hasidism movement.

Hasidism [hasidizm] A popular movement of Jewish mysticism, usually traced to a persecuted sect in the latter half of the 18th-c in Poland, characterized by an ascetic pattern of life, strict observance of the commandments, and loud ecstatic forms of worship and prayer. It was originally opposed to rabbinic authority and traditional Jewish practices, stressing prayer rather than study of the Torah as the means of communicating with God, but as it spread through the Ukraine, E Europe, and eventually W Europe and America, it was finally accepted as a part of Orthodox Judaism. It continues to flourish in the USA, especially in New York City.

Hasmoneans *Maccabees*

Hassan II (1929–99) King of Morocco (1961–99), born in Rabat, Morocco, the eldest son of Sultan Mulay Mohammed Bin Yusuf, who was proclaimed king as Mohammed V in 1957. He was 20th of the Filali line of sharifs, or descendants of the Prophet, who have ruled Morocco since 1631. Having studied in France at Bordeaux University, Crown Prince Hassan served his father as head of the army and, on his accession as king in 1961, also became prime minister. He suspended parliament and established a royal dictatorship in 1965 after riots in Casablanca. Despite constitutional reforms (1970–2), he retained supreme religious and political authority. His forces occupied Spanish (Western) Sahara in 1975, and he mobilized a large army to check the incursion of Polisario guerrillas across his W Saharan frontier (1976–88). Unrest in the larger towns led Hassan to appoint a coalition 'government of national unity' under a civilian prime minister in 1984. He helped form the Arab Maghreb Union in 1989, and was chairman of its Presidential Council in 1991.

Hastert, J(ohn) Dennis [hastert], known as **Denny Hastert** (1942–) US politician, born in Aurora, Illinois, USA. He studied at Wheaton College, Il, and was a high school teacher and coach in Yorkville, IL, until elected to the state legislature in 1980. Six years later he ran successfully for the US House of Representatives. He became Speaker in 1999 with a small working majority of Republicans amid promises of bipartisan co-operation.

Hastings, Warren (1732–1818) British colonial administrator in India, born in Churchill, Oxfordshire, SC England, UK. Educated at Westminster, he joined the East India Company in 1750, and by 1774 was Governor-General of Bengal. Carrying out several reforms, he made the Company's power paramount in many parts of India. However, wars (1778–84) interfered with trade, and damaged his reputation, and on his return to England in 1784 he was charged with corruption. After a seven-year trial, he was acquitted. The Company made provision for his declining years, which he spent as a country gentleman in Daylesford, Gloucestershire.

Hastings, Battle of (14 Oct 1066) The most decisive battle fought on English soil, which led to the successful Norman Conquest of England. The battle was fought at Senlac, inland from Hastings, where the Norman cavalry and crossbowmen overcame the resolute defence of the Anglo-Saxon army fighting on foot and mainly with axes. Harold II's death in battle cleared the way for Duke William of Normandy's coronation. Not until 1092 (the capture of Carlisle) were the Normans masters of all England.

hatchetfish Small, strongly compressed fish, with a deep body resembling a hatchet; two different groups, the deep-sea family Sternoptychidae (2 genera), and the South and Central American freshwater **flying hatchetfishes**, family Gasteropelecidae, which achieve true flight by rapid beats of large pectoral fins.

hatching In art, the technique of shading a drawing with close-set parallel lines. When this is crossed at right angles by another series of lines, the technique is called **cross-hatching**.

Hatfield 51°46N 0°13W, pop (2000e) 33 900. Town in Hertfordshire, SE England, UK; 30 km/19 mi N of London; designated a 'new town' in 1948; railway; University of Hertfordshire (1992, formerly Hatfield Polytechnic); aircraft, engineering.

Hathaway, Anne *Shakespeare, William*

Hathor [hahthaw(r)] The ancient Egyptian goddess of love, together with joyful music and dancing. She is represented by a cow, or has cow-like features, and is often associated with the papyrus plant. She was identified by the Greeks with Aphrodite.

Hatra [hatra] An ancient Parthian fortress city located between the Tigris and Euphrates rivers in N Iraq; a world heritage site. Founded in the 1st-c BC, it flourished as a trading and religious centre for four centuries before being razed by the Persian Sassanids.

Hatshepsut [hatshepsoot] (c.1540–c.1481 BC) Queen of Egypt of the XVIIIth dynasty, the daughter of Thutmose I. She was married to Thutmose II, on whose accession (1516 BC) she became the real ruler. On his death (1503 BC) she acted as regent for his son, Thuthmose III, then had herself crowned as Pharaoh. Maintaining the fiction that she was male, she was represented with the regular pharaonic attributes, including a beard.

Hattersley, Roy (Sydney George), Baron (1932–) British statesman, born in Sheffield, South Yorkshire, N England, UK. He studied at Hull University, and was a journalist and local authority politician before becoming a Labour MP in 1964. A supporter of Britain's membership of the European Economic Community, he was a minister at the Foreign Office (1974–6), then secretary of state for prices and consumer protection in the Callaghan government (1976–9). He has since been Opposition spokesman on the environment and on home affairs, shadow Chancellor, and deputy leader of the Labour Party (1983–92). He is a regular contributor to newspapers and periodicals. He was created a life peer in 1997.

Hattusas [hatusas] or **Hattusha** The ancient capital of the Hittites, now Bogazkoy in C Turkey, 160 km/100 mi E of Ankara. Originally an Assyrian trading colony, the settlement was taken by the Hittites in the 17th-c BC. It was destroyed in 1200 BC by marauders known as the Sea Peoples. The ruins were discovered in 1834, and are now a world heritage site.

Haughey, Charles (James) [hokhee] (1925–) Irish statesman and prime minister (1979–81, 1982, 1987–92), born in Castlebar, Co Mayo, W Ireland. He studied at Dublin, was called to the bar in 1949, and became a Fianna Fáil MP in 1957. From 1961 he held posts in justice, agriculture, and finance, but was dismissed in 1970 after a quarrel with the prime minister, Jack Lynch. He was subsequently tried and acquitted on a charge of conspiracy to import arms illegally. After two years as minister of health and social welfare, he succeeded Lynch as premier in 1979, was in power again for a nine-month period in 1982, and defeated Garrett Fitzgerald in the 1987 election. He resigned after a phone-tapping scandal.

Hauptmann, Gerhart (Johann Robert) [howptman] (1862–1946) Writer, born in Wałbrzych, SW Poland (formerly Obersalzbrunn, Germany). He studied sculpture in Wrocław, Poland (formerly Breslau, Prussia), and Rome before settling in Berlin (1885), where he established a reputation with his first play, *Vor Sonnenaufgang* (1889, trans Before Dawn). He followed this with several other social dramas, such as *Die Weber* (1892, The Weavers). He also wrote several novels, as well as poetry, and was awarded the Nobel Prize for Literature in 1912.

Hausa [howsa] A Chadic-speaking, predominantly Muslim people of Nigeria and Niger; the largest ethnic group in the area. They are intensive farmers, and Hausa traders are found throughout W Africa; they are also famed for their crafts. Most Hausa were conquered by the Fulani in the early 19th-c, and today form the populations of the Muslim emirates of Nigeria. The Hausa language, which has c.25 million mother-tongue speakers, is used as a lingua franca throughout N Nigeria and adjacent territories. It is the only Chadic language to be written, now in a Roman alphabet which has displaced an Arabic one used from the 16th-c.

Hauser, Kaspar [howzer] (c.1812–33) German foundling, a 'wild boy', found in the market place of Nuremberg in May 1828. Though apparently 16 years old, his mind was a blank, and his behaviour that of a little child. He later gave some account of himself, as having lived in a hole, looked after by a man who had brought him to the place where he was found. In 1833 he was discovered with a wound in his side, from which he died. Many have regarded him as an imposter who committed suicide: others, as a person of noble birth who was the victim of a crime. His mysterious life was celebrated in much imaginative literature.

Haussmann, Georges Eugène, Baron [howsman] (1809–91) Financier and town planner, born in Paris, France. He entered public service, and under Napoleon III became prefect of the Seine (1853), improving Paris by widening streets, laying out boulevards and parks, and building bridges. He was made baron and senator, but the heavy burden laid upon the citizens led to his dismissal (1870). He was elected to the Chamber of Deputies in 1881.

haustorium A sucker-like organ inserted by a parasite into the cells of the host, through which food is withdrawn. It is found in fungi and parasitic flowering plants, such as dodder.

hautbois strawberry *strawberry*

Havana [havana], Span **La Habana** 23°07N 82°25W, pop (2000e) 2 263 000. Capital city and province of Cuba, on N coast; founded on this site, 1519; airport; railway; country's chief port on fine natural harbour; university (1721); trade in sugar, cotton, tobacco; cathedral (1704), presidential palace (1920); several old fortresses including La Fuerza (1538), oldest building in Cuba; old city centre a world heritage site; castles of El Morro (1589–1630) and La Punta (late 16th-c); International Conference Centre; carnival in July.

Havana cat A breed of domestic cat, developed in the UK from Siamese cats; green eyes and plain brown coat; a *foreign short-haired* cat, also known as **Havana brown** or **chestnut brown (foreign) short-hair**.

Havel, Václav [havl, vahtslaf] (1936–) Playwright, president of Czechoslovakia (1989–92), and president of the Czech Republic (1993–2003), born in Prague, Czech Republic. He studied at the Prague Academy of Dramatic Art, and began work in the theatre as a stagehand, then became resident writer for the Prague 'Theatre on the Balustrade' (1960–9). He was active in the Prague Spring era of reform which ended with the Warsaw Pact invasion in 1968. In 1977 Havel became co-founder of the Charter 77 human rights initiative. He was under-house arrest in 1978–9, and then imprisoned for four years, his plays only being performed abroad. These include *Zahradni slavnost* (1963, The Garden Party), *Spiklenci* (1970, The Conspirators), and *Temptation* (1987). He was imprisoned again in 1989, but, as one of the leaders of the Civic Forum, a liberal political party, was elected president by direct popular vote in December following the collapse of the hardline Communist Party leadership. He resigned in 1992 in acknowledgement of the dissolution of Czechoslovakia, but was elected the first president of the new Czech Republic in January 1993. He retired at the end of his second term as president. A selection of his speeches and writings from 1990 to 1994, *Towards a Civil Society*, was published in English in 1995.

Hawaii (state) [hawahee] pop (2000e) 1 211 500; area 16 759 sq km/6471 sq mi. Pacific state of the USA, a group of eight major islands (Hawaii, Kahoolawe, Kauai, Lanai, Maui, Molokai, Niihau, Oahu) and numerous islets in the C Pacific Ocean; the 'Aloha State', divided into five counties; reached by the Polynesians over 1000 years ago; discovered by Captain Cook in 1778, and named the Sandwich Is; King Kamehameha I united the islands in 1810, and encouraged trade with the USA; arrival of Christian missionaries, 1820; monarchy overthrown, 1893; a request for annexation to the USA rejected by President Cleveland, then accepted by President McKinley, 1898; became a territory, 1900; surprise attack by Japanese planes on the US naval base at Pearl Harbor, Oahu I (7 Dec 1941) brought the USA into World War 2; remained the chief US Pacific base throughout the war; under martial law until March 1943; admitted to the Union as the 50th state, 1959; capital, Honolulu; islands of volcanic origin, with offshore coral reefs; highest point Mauna Kea, a dormant volcano on Hawaii I (4201 m/13 783 ft), a major astronomical site; Mauna Loa (4169 m/13 678 ft) an active volcano; generally fertile and highly vegetated, although Kahoolawe is arid; food processing, pineapples, sugar cane; coffee, cattle, dairy produce, macadamia nuts; fishing (especially tuna); defence installations at Pearl Harbor; major tourist area; Haleakala and Hawaii Volcanoes National Parks; diverse ethnic population, a large proportion of Japanese descent.

Hawaii (island) [hawahee] pop (2000e) 132 000; area 10 488 sq km/4048 sq mi. Largest island and county of the US state of Hawaii; the 'orchid isle'; chief town, Hilo; Volcanoes National Park; tourism; Hula Festival (Apr).

Hawaiian goose A rare goose, native to the uplands of Hawaii (*Branta sandvicensis*); wings short; feet with reduced webbing; eats fruit and herbs; also known as **nene**. There were less than 50 individuals in 1950, but captive breeding has increased this number to more than 2000. (Family: Anatidae.)

Hawaiian guitar A guitar with a straight body placed across the player's knees. It has metal strings which are stopped with a steel bar, instead of the fingers of the left hand, to produce the characteristic scooping (glissando) sound. It was developed in Hawaii during the second half of the 19th-c. Electric Hawaiian (or 'steel') guitars, sometimes free-standing, have been manufactured since the 1930s.

hawfinch A stout finch (*Coccothraustes coccothraustes*) native to Europe, Asia, and N Africa; golden-brown with black face; bill huge, strong, used for cracking tree fruits; shy, inhabits tree-tops in mature woodland. The name is also used for some birds of the genus *Eophona*. (Family: Fringillidae.)

Haw-Haw, Lord *Joyce, William*

hawk (ornithology) A bird of prey of the family Accipitridae, the name being used especially for smaller members of the family (but not for Old World vultures, which also belong to this family). It includes sparrowhawks, harriers, kites, and buzzards. Larger members are called *eagles*. In the USA, the name is also used for some falcons (Family: Falconidae).

hawk (politics) *dove* (politics)

Hawke, Bob, popular name of **Robert (James Lee) Hawke** (1929–) Australian statesman and prime minister (1983–91), born in Bordertown, South Australia. He studied at the universities of Western Australia and Oxford, and worked for the Australian Council of Trade Unions for over 20 years, before becoming a Labor MP in 1980. His party defeated the Liberals in the 1983 election only one month after adopting him as leader. A popular politician, known for his emotional outbursts, he was a skilled negotiator who won praise for his handling of industrial disputes. In 1990 he became the first Labor prime minister to win a fourth term in office, and the party's longest serving prime minister, but his role was challenged by Paul Keating in 1991, who narrowly defeated him in a leadership ballot. Hawke was largely responsible for his party's electoral successes, but many felt that traditional Labor values were discarded under his leadership.

Hawke (of Towton), Edward Hawke, Baron (1705–81) British admiral, born in London, UK. As a young commander, he fought against the French and Spanish, for which he was knighted (1747). His major victory was against the French at Quiberon Bay (1759), which caused the collapse of their invasion plans. He also became an MP (1747) and First Lord of the Admiralty (1766–71), and was created a baron in 1776.

Hawking, Stephen (William) (1942–) Theoretical physicist, born in Oxford, Oxfordshire, SC England, UK. He studied at Oxford, then spent his career in Cambridge, holding a chair there from 1977. His work has been concerned with cosmology in a variety of aspects, dealing with black holes, singularities, and the 'big bang' theory of the origin of the universe. His popular writing is also notable, especially *A Brief History of Time* (1988). Later books include *Black Holes and Baby Universes* (1993) and *The Universe in a Nutshell* (2002). His achievement is all the more noteworthy because since the 1960s he has suffered from a neuromotor disease, amyotrophic lateral sclerosis, causing extreme physical disability; he communicates with the aid of a computer. He was made a Companion of Honour in 1989.

Hawking radiation A type of radiation predicted in 1974 by Stephen Hawking to emerge continuously from black holes. Of pairs of particles produced by quantum effects in space near a black hole, one is absorbed by the black hole while the other is radiated. The theory predicts that black holes slowly evaporate into photons and other particles, finally expiring in a huge burst of gamma rays.

Hawkins, Coleman (1901–69) Jazz tenor saxophonist, born in St Joseph, Missouri, USA (he claimed 1904 as his birth year). He joined Fletcher Henderson's jazz orchestra in 1923. The performances on romping swing tunes such as 'The Stampede' (1926), and on slow ballads such as 'One Hour' (1929), altered the way the tenor saxophone was played, and popularized the instrument in jazz music. He played widely in Europe (1934–9), and on returning to New York City recorded 'Body and Soul', a jazz landmark.

Hawkins, Sir John *Hawkyns, Sir John*

hawk-moth A medium to large moth, typically with long, triangular wings and an elongate body; fast fliers, capable of hovering flight; proboscis often long, used to suck nectar; most abundant in tropics. (Order: Lepidoptera. Family: Sphingidae, c.1000 species.)

hawk owl A typical owl (*Surnia ulula*), native to N areas of the N hemisphere; short pointed wings; long tail; resembles the hawk when flying and perching; inhabits forests; eats mammals and birds; hunts in daylight. (Family: Strigidae.)

Hawks, Howard (Winchester) (1896–1977) Film director, born in Goshen, Indiana, USA. He studied at Cornell, working as a prop man in Hollywood on vacations. He wrote and directed his first feature, *The Road to Glory* (1926), and was always closely involved with the scripts in his later productions. With the coming of sound films, he had many successes over some 40 years, in such varied genres as airforce dramas (*The Dawn Patrol*, 1930), detection and crime (*The Big Sleep*, 1946), Westerns (*Rio Lobo*, 1970), and comedy (*Man's Favorite Sport?*, 1962).

hawksbill turtle A sea turtle (*Eretmochelys imbricata*), native to tropical oceans; narrow head with hooked 'beak'; back with saw-tooth outline due to overlapping plates of shell; produces the finest quality tortoiseshell; endangered due to overhunting. (Family: Chelonidae.)

Hawksmoor, Nicholas (1661–1736) Architect, born in East Drayton, Nottinghamshire, C England, UK. His most individual contributions are the London churches, St Mary Woolnoth, St George's (Bloomsbury), and Christ Church (Spitalfields), as well as parts of Queen's College and All Souls, Oxford.

hawkweed A widely distributed perennial, mostly occurring in the N hemisphere; leaves entire to deeply toothed, arranged spirally around the stem or often in a basal rosette; flower-heads solitary or in loose clusters, florets usually yellow. Many hawkweeds reproduce from fruits formed without fertilization having occurred, resulting in vast numbers of distinct populations or microspecies, perhaps as many as 20 000. (Genus: *Hieracium*, c.250 species. Family: Compositae.)

Hawkyns or **Hawkins, Sir John** (1532–95) English sailor, born in Plymouth, Devon, SW England, UK. He was the first Englishman to traffic in slaves (1562) between W Africa and the West Indies, but on his third expedition his fleet was destroyed by the Spanish (1567). He became navy treasurer in 1573, and was knighted for his services against the Armada in 1588. In 1595, with his kinsman Drake, he commanded an expedition to the Spanish Main, but died in Puerto Rico.

Hawn, Goldie (Jeanne) [hawn] (1945–) US actress, born in Washington, District of Columbia, USA. She became known through her comedy roles in Rowan and Martin's TV review *Laugh In* (1968–70), then won a Best Supporting Actress award for her first film role in *Cactus Flower* (1969). Later films include *There's A Girl in My Soup* (1970), *Private Benjamin* (1980), which she also produced, *Bird on a Wire* (1990), *Death Becomes Her* (1992), *The First Wives Club* (1996), *Everyone Says I Love You* (1997), and *The Out-of-Towners* (1999).

hawthorn A spiny, deciduous shrub or tree (*Crataegus monogyna*), growing to 18 m/60 ft, native to Europe; leaves oval to rhomboidal, deeply 3–7-lobed; flowers white, in clusters; berries (*haws*) red to maroon, flesh thin over a large stone; also called **quickthorn** and **may**. It is very common and much planted, forming dense stock-proof hedges and attractive park or street trees. (Family: Rosaceae.)

Hawthorne, Nathaniel (1804–64) Novelist and short-story writer, born in Salem, Massachusetts, USA. Educated at Bowdoin College, he shut himself away for 12 years to learn to write fiction. His first novel was amateurish, but later some of the stories gained favourable notice from the London *Athenaeum*, and a volume of them, *Twice-Told Tales*, was published in 1837. His first major success was the novel *The Scarlet Letter* (1850), still the best known of his works. Other books include *The House of the Seven Gables* (1851), *The Snow Image* (1852), and a campaign biography of his old schoolfriend, President Franklin Pierce, on whose inauguration Hawthorne became consul at Liverpool (1853–7). Only belatedly recognized in his own country, he continued to write articles and stories, notably those for the *Atlantic Monthly*, collected as *Our Old Home* (1863).

Hawthorne, Sir Nigel (Barnard) (1929–2001) Actor, born in Coventry, West Midlands, C England, UK and brought up in Cape Town, South Africa. He made his British theatrical debut in 1951, and worked extensively in theatre, including award-winning performances in *Privates On Parade* (1978, SWET and Clarence Derwent awards), *Shadowlands* (1989, Tony) and *The Madness of George III* (1991, Olivier). He played the title role in *King Lear* in the Royal Shakespeare's millennium production. He achieved television fame for his acclaimed role as the suave and calculating civil servant Sir Humphrey Appleby in the series *Yes Minister* (1980) and its sequel *Yes Prime Minister* (1986). His films include *The Madness of King George* (1994, Oscar nomination), *Twelfth Night* (1996), and *Amistad* (1997). In 1997 he was awarded a BAFTA Best Actor award for *The Fragile Heart*. He received a knighthood in 1999.

Hawthorne effect *experimenter effect*

Hay, John (Milton) (1838–1905) US secretary of state (1898–1905) and writer, born in Salem, Indiana, USA. He studied at Brown University, became a lawyer, and was private secretary (1861–5) to President Lincoln. After Lincoln's death, he served as a diplomat in Paris, Vienna, and Madrid. He returned to the USA and to journalism in 1870, going on to write poetry, fiction, and a multi-volume biography of Lincoln. He became assistant secretary of state (1878), ambassador to Britain (1897), and served as secretary of state under Presidents McKinley and Theodore Roosevelt. He is best-remembered for the Open Door Policy towards China (1899).

Hay, Will (1888–1949) Comedian and actor, born in Stockton-on-Tees, NE England, UK. The son of an engineer, he worked as an engineering apprentice before starting in the music halls. He joined Fred Karno's comedy troupe (1914–18), going on to star in several films in the role of an incompetent, seedy schoolmaster. His films include *Good Morning Boys* (1937), *Oh Mr Porter* (1938), *The Ghost of St Michael's* (1941), and *My Learned Friend* (1944). In private life he was a linguist, an amateur astronomer, and a pilot.

Hayden, Bill, popular name of **William George Hayden** (1933–) Australian statesman, born in Brisbane, Queensland, NE Australia. He studied at Queensland University, then served in the state civil service (1950–2) and the police (1952–61), before he joined the Australian Labor Party and entered the federal parliament in 1961. He served under Gough Whitlam and replaced him as Party leader in 1977. In 1983 he surrendered the leadership to the more charismatic Bob Hawke, and was foreign minister in his government (1983–8). As Governor-General of Australia (1989–96), he characteristically refused the customary knighthood which accompanies the post, and was rumoured to be Australia's first republican governor-general. In 1998, he was appointed to the Constitutional Convention which was to discuss whether Australia should become a republic.

Haydn, Franz Joseph [hiydn] (1732–1809) Composer, born in Rohrau, NE Austria. Educated at the Cathedral Choir School of St Stephen's, Vienna, he earned his living initially by playing in street orchestras and teaching. He became musical director (1759–60) for Count von Morzin's court musicians, for whom he wrote his earliest symphonies. He entered the service of the Esterházy family as musical director in 1761, staying with them until 1790. He was given great scope for composition, and among his innovations were the four-movement string quartet and the 'classical' symphony. His output was vast, and he earned a major international reputation. His works include 104 symphonies, about 50 concertos, 84 string quartets, 24 stage works, 12 Masses, orchestral divertimenti, keyboard sonatas, and diverse chamber, choral, instrumental, and vocal pieces.

Hayek, Friedrich A(ugust von) [hiyek] (1899–1992) Economist, born in Vienna, Austria. He studied in Vienna, became director of the Austrian Institute for Economic Research (1927–31), lectured at Vienna (1929–31), and was appointed professor of economic science at London (1931–50), becoming a British citizen in 1938. He was professor of social and moral science at Chicago (1950–62). Strongly opposed to Keynesianism, and often called 'the father of monetarism', he believed that government intervention in a free market leads eventually to inflation, unemployment, recession, or depression. He shared the Nobel Prize for Economics in 1974.

Hayes, Helen, originally **Helen Hayes Brown** (1900–93) Actress, born in Washington, District of Columbia, USA. A successful actress from the age of five, her adult stage productions brought her national popularity, and include *Caesar and Cleopatra* (1925), *The Glass Menagerie* (1956), and *Long Day's Journey into Night* (1971). She received many awards for her work on radio and television, and appeared in several films, including *A Farewell to Arms* (1932), *The Sin of Madelon Claudet* (1931), and *Airport* (1970), winning Oscars for the latter two. The Helen Hayes Theater in New York City was named after her.

Hayes, Rutherford B(irchard) (1822–93) US statesman and 19th president (1877–81), born in Delaware, Ohio, USA. He practised as a lawyer at Cincinnati (1849–61), served with distinction in the Civil War, entered Congress as a Republican (1865–7), and became Governor of Ohio (1868–76). Following a dispute over voting returns in the 1876 election, he was awarded all the contested votes by a commission of congressmen and Supreme Court justices. Under his presidency, the country recovered commercial prosperity after the corruption following the Civil War. His policy included reform of the civil service and the conciliation of the Southern states. He chose to serve only one term of office as president, and devoted himself thereafter to humanitarian causes such as prison reform and educating young blacks.

hay fever An allergic reaction affecting the eyes and nasal passages, resulting in watering of the eyes, nasal congestion, and sneezing. It is usually provoked by exposure to the pollen of grasses in the air, which are present in highest concentrations in late spring or early summer, but the reaction is not confined to any season or to a single stimulus. Other allergens are house dust, spores of fungi, and dander from animals. Symptoms can be reduced by antihistamine drugs.

haymaker *pika*

Haywood, William D(udley), nickname **Big Bill Haywood** (1869–1928) Political activist, born in Salt Lake City, Utah, USA. As a young miner he became actively involved in politics, and went on to become leader of the Industrial Workers of the World (IWW). He became nationally known following his acquittal on a murder charge (1907–8). The IWW lent support to striking industries (1909–13) and achieved notable successes, but Haywood was later arrested on treason and sabotage charges. He jumped bail (1921) and fled to Russia, where he worked for the Russian revolutionary government. His biography, *Bill Haywood's Book* (1929) was published after his death.

Hayworth, Rita, originally **Margarita Carmen Cansino** (1918–87) Film actress, born into a show business family in New York City, USA. Her nightclub appearances as a Spanish dancer led to a succession of small roles in B-pictures. Blossoming into an international beauty after dyeing her hair red, she partnered both Fred Astaire and Gene Kelly in musicals of the 1940s, and found her best-known lead in *Gilda* (1946). A pin-up of US servicemen, her Hollywood career was effectively closed by a scandal involving her romance with Aly Khan (1949), whom she later married. During the 1960s she appeared in character parts, often in Europe, including *The Money Trap* (1966) and *The Wrath of God* (1972). Married five times, she suffered from Alzheimer's disease for several years prior to her death.

hazard A card game for four players in pairs. It is similar to solo, but all cards with a face value of 2 to 8 are discarded, and the joker is added, to make 25 cards.

hazardous substances Generally human-made substances, potentially damaging to health, which when incorrectly disposed of result in contamination and pollution of the environment. They include toxic substances, heavy metal pollutants (eg lead, mercury), and radioactive waste produced in the generation of nuclear power. The disposal of hazardous substances is a source of environmental concern in many countries.

hazel A deciduous shrub or small tree (*Corylus avellana*), native to Europe and Asia Minor; leaves broadly oval, toothed; male catkins long, pendulous; females short, bud-like with prominent red stigmas; edible nut partially enclosed in a ragged green leafy cup. It is cultivated on a small scale, but is common in hedgerows, and is often coppiced. (Family: Corylaceae.)

Hazlitt, William (1778–1830) Essayist, born in Maidstone, Kent, SE England, UK. The son of a Unitarian minister, he took up painting, but was encouraged by Coleridge to write *Principles of Human Action* (1805), and further essays followed. In 1812 he found employment in London as a journalist, and also contributed to the *Edinburgh Review* (1814–20), proving himself to be a deadly controversialist, and a master of epigram, invective, and irony. His best-known essay collections are *Table Talk* (1821) and *The Spirit of the Age* (1825).

H-bomb *hydrogen bomb*

headache An aching sensation over the vault of the skull, temples, or back of the head, usually diffuse and poorly localized. In the majority of instances, the complaint is trivial and responds to simple analgesics, such as aspirin. Very occasionally, headaches herald serious intracranial disease such as haemorrhage, meningitis, or tumour. The brain itself is insensitive to touch, and headaches arise from the stretching or distortion of its covering membranes, from tension arising from the muscles overlying the skull, or from vascular dilatation with increased blood supply, as occurs in generalized fevers or over-indulgence in alcohol.

Head-Smashed-In Bison Jump An important archaeological site in the Porcupine Hills of SW Alberta, Canada. From c.4000 BC until the early 19th-c, indigenous peoples slaughtered vast herds of bison here by stampeding them over the edge of the 'jump', a 10 m/33 ft high cliff. It is now a world heritage site.

Head Start A national project begun in the USA in the early 1960s to help pre-school children from a disadvantaged background prepare for schooling. The main emphasis was on language and social development, but attention was also paid to health care and parent education.

Healey (of Riddlesden), Denis (Winston) Healey, Baron (1917–) British statesman, born in Eltham, Kent, SE England, UK. He studied at Oxford, served in N Africa and Italy (1940–5), then became secretary of the Labour Party's international department, and an MP (1952). He was secretary of state for defence in the Wilson governments of 1964–70, and Chancellor of the Exchequer (1974–9). Unsuccessful in the Labour leadership contests of 1976 and 1980, he became deputy leader (1980–3) and then shadow foreign minister. He resigned from the shadow cabinet in 1987, and retired in 1992, when he was created a life peer. A keen photographer, he published a selection of his work in *Healey's Eye* (1980).

healing Any method by which an illness or injury is cured; specifically, the use of a technique which is not recognized within orthodox medicine and involves no form of physical therapy or manipulation. Techniques such as the 'laying on of hands' are seen as involving the transmission of energy from, or channelling through, a healer and into the sick person. Sometimes prayer, visualization, meditation, or other methods are used by the patient, healer, or both to help focus beneficial thoughts and energy onto the illness. Although touch may be used to transmit healing energies, some healers claim to be able to treat their patients from a distance. Controlled studies have shown the beneficial effects of positive thoughts and healing energies directed at bacteria, plants, cancer cells, and even animals such as mice. There are many anecdotal reports of untreatable illnesses being cured, including those which form part of the sacred literature of most major religions.

health foods An umbrella term for so-called 'whole food', additive-free food, and diet supplements such as minerals, vitamins, trace elements, essential fatty acids, and other nutrients.

Many of these are sold simply as a supplement to diet, but others make specific therapeutic claims that a particular mix of nutrients will have an effect, eg that vitamin B_6 in mega-doses will cure premenstrual tension. Most health-food shops are now actively promoting what is popularly called alternative medicine.

health insurance A way of offsetting the cost of medical treatment. The individual pays an annual fee (premium) to a health insurance company, and when treatment is needed the company pays the bills. This is common practice in the USA, and in the UK before 1948, when the National Health Service was introduced. Today, private health insurance is re-emerging as a major factor in British health care. At the same time, there is pressure in the USA for the adoption of a national health plan.

Health Maintenance Organizations (US) Private health insurance groups that in the last quarter of the 20th-c dominated the way in which Americans under the age of 65 received medical coverage, popularly known as **HMOs**. Begun in the 1960s and authorized by Congress in 1973, HMOs offered an attractive programme of 'managed care' that emphasized cost-cutting, careful review of patient claims and diagnoses, and an emphasis on preventative methods and a healthy lifestyle. Although not subsidized directly, they participate in the Medicare Plan when they enrol senior citizens or government employees, and to that extent are reliant on the federal government for subsidies. In the 1990s these organizations captured an ever-growing share of the health-care market. By the end of the decade, however, they encountered serious problems in providing affordable care to a burgeoning population of needy patients. Many of the large HMOs and managed-care providers experienced huge losses in 1998 amid charges that some companies had engaged in fraud to obtain government payments. Increasing regulations also seemed probable in the wake of consumer complaints of poor coverage and faulty diagnoses. HMOs have become a significant part of the American health-care scene, but face an uncertain future.

Heaney, Seamus (Justin) [heenee, **shay**mus] (1939–) Poet, born on a farm near Castledawson in Co Londonderry, N Northern Ireland, UK. The eldest of nine children, he studied at Belfast, and moved to Dublin in 1976. Early works such as *Death of a Naturalist* (1966) and *Door into the Dark* (1969) established a deep bond between language and the land. Later volumes (*North*, 1975; *Field Work*, 1979; *Station Island*, 1984) extended this to reveal a problematic political dimension, and the more recent *Haw Lantern* (1987, Whitbread) and *Seeing Things* (1991) confirm him as one of the most significant of contemporary English-language poets. His play *The Cure at Troy* (1990) is a version of Sophocles' *Philoctetes*. He became professor of rhetoric and oratory at Harvard in 1985, and professor of poetry at Oxford in 1989. Volumes of selected poems appeared in 1980, 1990, and 1998, and his collection *The Spirit Level* received the Whitbread poetry award in 1996. He was awarded the Nobel Prize for Literature in 1995. His translation of the Anglo-Saxon epic *Beowulf* (1999, Whitbread) into modern English is considered a masterpiece of poetic creativity. In 2002 appeared *Finders Keepers: Selected prose 1971-2001*.

Heard and McDonald Islands area 412 sq km/159 sq mi. Island group in S Indian Ocean, about 4000 km/2500 mi SW of Fremantle, Australia; an Australian external territory comprising Heard I, Shag I, and the McDonald Is; transferred from UK to Australian control in 1947; Heard I (rises to over 2000 m/6500 ft) is actively volcanic, largely ice-covered, and has a weather station; made a world heritage site in 1997.

hearing *auditory perception; cochlea; ear*

hearing aid A device for amplifying sound, used by persons with defective hearing. The earliest type was the *ear-trumpet* – a conical apparatus collecting sound at the wide end and delivering it to the ear-drum at the small end. Modern aids are electronic, consisting of a microphone, amplifier, and earphone, usually compressed into a very small container to fit directly on to the ear. Transmission may be to the ear-drum or by bone conduction.

Hearne, Samuel [hern] (1745–92) Explorer of N Canada, born in London, UK. He served in the Royal Navy, then joined the Hudson's Bay Company, who sent him to Fort Prince of Wales (Churchill) in 1769. He became the first European to travel overland by canoe and sled to the Arctic Ocean by following the Coppermine R north of the Great Slave Lake (1770). In 1774 he set up the first interior trading post for the company at Cumberland House, then became governor of Fort Prince of Wales. He was taken prisoner by the French in 1782, and taken to France, where he was encouraged to publish an account of his travels. Released in 1783, he returned to Canada, but ill health forced him to return to England in 1787.

Hearns, Thomas [hernz], nicknames **Hit Man** and **Motor City Cobra** (1958–) Boxer, born in Memphis, Tennessee, USA. In 1988 he became the first man to win world titles at four and five different weights, and in 1991 the first to win titles at six different weights: he defeated Pipino Cuevas for the welterweight title (WBA, 1980), Wilfred Benitez for the super-welterweight (WBC, 1982), Roberto Duran for the vacant WBA junior-middleweight title (1984), Dennis Andries for the light-heavyweight (WBC, 1987), Juan Roldan for the middleweight (WBC, 1987), James Kinchen for the super-middleweight (WBO, 1988), and Virgil Hill for the light-heavyweight (WBA, 1991). He was fated, however, to be best remembered as the loser in two of the ring's greatest fights – against Sugar Ray Leonard (1980) and Marvin Hagler (1985).

hearsay A complex rule of evidence in common-law countries which prohibits an out-of-court oral or written statement from being used in court to prove the truth of an issue. In general, this means a witness cannot testify about what other persons told him/her or said (or wrote) about an incident, because those persons are not present in court to be subjected to cross-examination and to have their credibility challenged. The rule is still widely followed in the USA, but has been virtually abolished in civil cases in Scotland, and in England and Wales by the Civil Evidence Act (1995). It has many exceptions, generally situations in which the speaker is likely to be truthful, such as confessions, dying declarations, and declarations against self-interest.

Hearst, William Randolph (1863–1951) Newspaper publisher, born in San Francisco, California, USA. He studied at Harvard, then took over the *San Francisco Examiner* in 1887 from his father. He acquired the *New York Morning Journal* (1895), and launched the *Evening Journal* in 1896. He sensationalized journalism by the introduction of banner headlines and lavish illustrations. Believed by many to have initiated the Spanish–American War of 1898 to encourage sales of his newspaper, he also advocated political assassination in an editorial just months before the assassination of President McKinley. A member of the US House of Representatives (1903–7), he failed in attempts to become mayor and governor of New York. His national chain of newspapers and periodicals grew to include the *Chicago Examiner*, *Boston American*, *Cosmopolitan*, and *Harper's Bazaar*. His life inspired the Orson Welles film *Citizen Kane* (1941).

heart *p.701*

heartburn A burning sensation usually felt intermittently within the chest over the lower part of the breastbone. It results from regurgitation of the contents of the stomach into the lower part of the oesophagus, inducing a spasm. In some cases this is due to part of the stomach rising into the opening where the oesophagus passes through the diaphragm (hiatus hernia).

heart disease Disease of the heart and the associated blood vessels; a major cause of death in all countries, though the pattern of individual disorders varies in different parts of the world and in different age groups. For example, coronary heart disease is common in the UK, the USA, and the West as a whole, but less common in Japan or Hong Kong. **Rheumatic heart disease** is now rare in the UK, but common in many parts of

heart

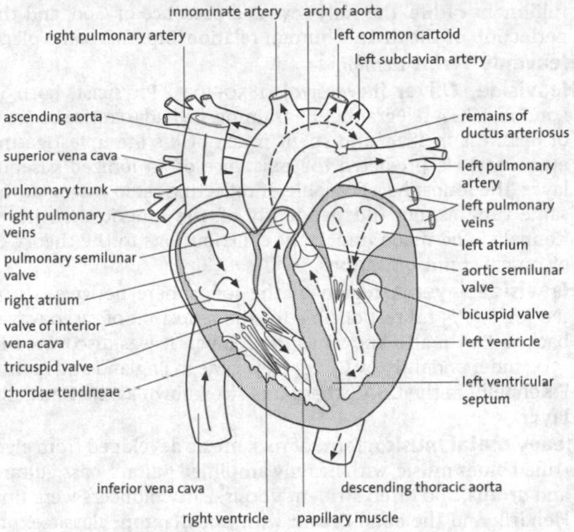

A hollow muscular organ, divided into chambers (right and left *atria*, right and left *ventricles*) and enclosed within a fibrous sac (the *pericardium*) found within the thorax. It lies directly under the sternum, being protected by it and the adjacent ribs. It is the first organ to develop in the embryo (in humans by three weeks). In mammals it is separated into right and left halves concerned with pulmonary and systemic circulation respectively. It consists mainly of cardiac muscle (the *myocardium*) enclosed between two sheets of fibrous and elastic tissue, the *epicardium* and the *endocardium*. The myocardium forms a network of sheets and strands which have a characteristic arrangement in different parts of the heart. The heart also possesses a fibrous skeleton which surrounds and strengthens many of its openings. In humans, the ventricles have a capacity of between 90 and 120 ml. The right atrium receives deoxygenated blood from the body (via the superior and inferior *venae cavae*) and from the heart itself (via the *coronary sinus*) during diastole, and conveys it to the right ventricle via the right atrioventricular opening (guarded by the *tricuspid valve*). The right ventricle expels blood into the *pulmonary trunk* (guarded by the *pulmonary valve*) and thence to the lungs. The left atrium receives oxygenated blood from the lungs and conveys it to the left ventricle via the left atrioventricular opening (guarded by the *mitral valve*). The left ventricle forcibly expels blood into the *aorta* (guarded by the *aortic valve*) and thence to the rest of the body. In the fetus, blood bypasses the non-functioning lungs in two ways. Freshly oxygenated blood returning from the placenta enters the right atrium and passes directly into the left atrium through the *foramen ovale*, an opening in the inter-atrial septum, to be distributed to body tissues via the left ventricle. Deoxygenated blood returning to the right atrium passes into the right ventricle and pulmonary trunk and then into the descending aorta by a communicating channel (the *ductus arteriosus*). After birth, the foramen ovale closes (failure to do so leads to a 'hole in the heart', with the mixing of pulmonary and systemic blood), and the ductus arteriosus becomes obliterated. The conducting system of the mammalian heart consists of a 'pacemaker' (the *sinuatrial node*), a 'relay station' (the *atrioventricular node*), and the *atrioventricular bundle* within the *interventricular septum*. Both nodes are situated in the right atrium. The contractile impulse begins at the sinuatrial node, reaches the atrioventricular node via atrial muscle fibres, and reaches the ventricles via the atrioventricular bundle. Damage to the atrioventricular bundle (by disease or experimentally) causes the ventricles to contract independently and at a slower rate than the atria (known as 'heart block'). The sinuatrial node has the highest degree of inherent rhythmicity, and determines the rate of the heart beat. It is influenced by the autonomic nervous system. The walls of the heart are supplied by the coronary arteries, and drained by the cardiac veins and by *venae cordae minimae* (small veins draining the deeper layers of myocardium). A **heart attack** (*myocardial infarction*) occurs when part of the coronary arterial supply becomes blocked by a blood clot (*thrombus*), leading to the cessation of blood flow and death of the myocardium.

the world, notably India and the Middle East. As the heart is essentially a pump, interference with its function whatever the cause gives rise to the cardinal symptoms of shortness of breath and fluid retention (*oedema*), which may be accompanied by palpitations, chest pain, and fainting.

heart–lung machine An apparatus which takes over the pumping action of the heart, together with the breathing action of the lungs, so that the heart can be stopped and operated upon. Pumps are used to circulate the blood through special plastic tubing and a bubble oxygenator which puts oxygen into the blood and removes carbon dioxide before the blood is returned to the body. The blood is filtered and kept at a suitable temperature during its passage through the machine – if necessary, for several hours.

heartsease A species of violet (*Viola tricolor*), also called **wild pansy**, native to Europe. The flowers are blue, yellow, white, or a combination of these colours. (Family: Violaceae.)

heart urchin A bilaterally symmetrical sea urchin which burrows into soft sediment, maintaining breathing passages to the surface by means of its tube feet; mouth displaced to a front position. (Class: Echinoidea. Order: Spatangoida.)

heartworm A parasite (*Dirofilaria immitis*) which inhabits the heart chambers and major blood vessels, mainly affecting dogs, with some cases occurring in cats. Individuals with heartworm can develop severe chronic bronchitis, pneumonia, and heart changes. Heavy infestation can lead to an early death. The life cycle of the parasite is dependent upon a mosquito. It is usually restricted to hot humid areas such as the S states of the USA and similar climates, though the geographical scope of the parasite may be increasing. Blood tests are available which can recognize the early stages of development, and preventive treatment is normally effective. Surgical treatment may be the only remedy once adult worms have developed.

heat The transfer of energy from one object to another, due solely to their difference in temperatures; symbol *Q*, units J (joule). The quantity of heat sometimes ascribed to an object or process is the total amount of energy transferred in this way.

heat capacity The quantity of heat needed to produce a temperature rise of one kelvin (or 1°C) in some material. Loosely, it measures the ability of a substance to get hot while absorbing energy. **Specific heat capacity** *c* (also called **specific heat**), units J/(kg.K), is the heat capacity per kilogram of material. For water, $c = 4180$ J/(kg.K).

heat engine The name given to a device that transforms disordered heat energy into ordered, useful, mechanical work. This is achieved by taking a working fluid at high temperature and high heat energy, and subjecting it to a thermodynamic cycle involving compression and expansion, during which time heat is expelled at a lower temperature. The differences in heat energy of the working fluid between input and output appear as work. For physical and theoretical understanding, the thermodynamic cycle is usually idealized, and does not take into account such factors as frictional losses. A large number of idealized thermodynamic cycles exist, of which the Carnot, Diesel, Otto and Stirling cycles are particular examples.

Heath, Sir Edward (Richard George), known as **Ted Heath** (1916–) British statesman and prime minister (1970–4), born in Broadstairs, Kent, SE England, UK. He studied at Oxford, served in the Royal Artillery in World War 2, and became an MP in 1950. Following a career in the Whip's office (1951–9), he was minister of labour (1959–60), then Lord Privy Seal (1960–3) and the chief negotiator for Britain's entry into the European Economic Community. Elected Leader of the Conservative Party in 1965, he was Leader of the Opposition until his 1970 victory. After a confrontation with the miners' union in 1973, he narrowly lost the two elections of 1974, and in 1975 was replaced as Leader by Mrs Thatcher. He continued to play an active part in politics, and was Father of the House (of Commons) from 1997 to his retirement in 2001. He is known for his interests in yachting, having won the 1969 Hobart Ocean race and captained the British entry in the Admiral's Cup races of 1971 and 1979. He is also an accomplished musician, giving organ recitals and conducting at charity concerts.

heath A low evergreen shrub or small tree, native to Europe, Asia, N Africa, and especially S Africa; leaves small, narrow to needle-shaped with inrolled margins, in whorls of three or more; flowers often numerous, bell- or urn-shaped, pink, purple, or white. It is often dominant on poor, acid soils of moors and heathland, but some grow on alkaline soils. Many species are grown for ornament. They are also called **ericas**, and are widely known as **heathers**, which is a source of possible confusion with true heather, from which they are easily distinguished by the latter's different leaves and four green sepals. (Genus: *Erica*, c.500 species. Family: Ericaceae.)

heather **1** A small, bushy, evergreen shrub (*Calluna vulgaris*), native to Europe, especially N and W; leaves in pairs, 1–2 mm/0·04–0·08 in, scale-like with backward projecting basal lobes; flowers tiny, in loose spikes, four sepals, four petals, all purple; also called **ling**. Often the dominant plant on acid soils, especially heathland and moors, in Scotland it forms the major food source of endemic red grouse. A rare form with white flowers is considered lucky. (Family: Ericaceae.)
2 *heath*

heat of reaction *chemical energy*

heat storage Any means by which heat can be stored for release later. Domestic electric storage heaters usually contain large, heat-absorbing bricks. They also contain electric coils which are wound through thousands of tiny holes in the bricks. During the night, the electric current switches on the coils in the storage heater and they heat up. In the morning the current switches off, and the bricks slowly give off their heat during the day. Other heat storage systems use the principle that a substance will give off heat as it changes from one state to another (*a phase change*). An example is Glauber's salt, which melts at about 31°C. It is liquefied during the night when electricity is cheap, and gives off its stored heat during the day as it changes back into a solid.

heat stroke A raised body temperature (often above 41°C) which occurs when heat production exceeds heat loss, for example during heavy exercise, feverish illness, or when the environmental temperature is excessive. The clinical features result from the high temperature and from dehydration. There is weakness and vomiting followed by loss of consciousness and kidney failure. Treatment is by urgent cooling of the body, and rehydration. The condition is also known as **sunstroke**, though it may occur with or without exposure to direct sunlight.

heat treatment Subjecting a metal component to a cycle of heating and cooling so as to modify its internal crystalline structure and therefore promote desirable physical and mechanical properties. The form and rate of the cycle is important: for example, the rapid quenching of a heated alloy may preserve at the low temperature the crystalline structure or chemical composition characteristic of the high temperature.

heaven Generally, the dwelling-place of God and the angels, and in traditional Christianity the ultimate eternal destiny of the redeemed, there to reign with Christ in glory. In the Bible, it is usually conceived as high above the Earth. In modern theology, the emphasis is more on the quality, transformation, or fulfilment of life, the fully-revealed presence of God, and the perfection of the divine–human relationship, than on a place.

Heavenly Twins *Gemini*

Heaviside, Oliver [heveesiyd] (1850–1925) Physicist, born in London, UK. A telegrapher by training, he had to retire because of deafness in 1874, and spent much of his life investigating electricity. He predicted the existence of an ionized gaseous layer (the ionosphere) capable of reflecting radio waves, at the same time as, but independently of, the American Arthur E Kennelly, and made important contributions to the theory of electrical communications.

Heaviside layer A region of the ionosphere between c.90–120 km/55–75 mi responsible for the reflection of radio waves back to Earth; also known as the **E layer**. It was discovered in 1902 independently by Oliver Heaviside in England and Arthur E Kennelly in the USA (where it is also known as the **Kennelly layer**).

heavy metal music A form of rock music developed from electrified blues music, with heavily amplified guitars, bass guitars, and drums, and often strident vocals. Early pioneers were Jimi Hendrix and the band Cream with Eric Clapton; classic exponents of the genre included US bands Grand Funk (Railroad), Vanilla Fudge, and Mountain, and the British Led Zeppelin, Deep Purple, and Black Sabbath. These were succeeded by new generations of bands, including AC/DC, Def Leppard, Iron Maiden, and Guns 'n' Roses, whose popularity depended as much on their live appearances at concerts and festival as on recordings.

heavy water *deuterium*

Hebb, Donald (Olding) (1904–85) Psychologist, born in Chester, Nova Scotia, SE Canada. He spent most of his academic career at McGill University, Montreal, where he became an influential theorist concerned with the relation between the brain and behaviour. His most important book *The Organization of Behavior* (1949), was influential in the development of connectionism.

Hebe [heebee] In Greek mythology, the goddess of youth and youthful beauty, daughter of Zeus and Hera. She became cupbearer to the Olympians, and was married to Heracles after he was deified.

Hébert, Jacques René [aybair] (1757–94) French revolutionary extremist who represented the aspirations of the sans-culottes, born in Alençon, NE France. He became a popular political journalist, assumed the pseudonym **le Père Duchesne** after launching a satirical newspaper of that name (1790), and joined both the Cordelier and Jacobin Clubs. He became a member of the Revolutionary Council, playing a major part in the September Massacres and the overthrow of the monarchy. After denouncing the Committee of Public Safety for its failure to help the poor, he tried to incite a popular uprising, but having incurred the suspicion of Danton and Robespierre, he and 17 of his followers (*Hébertists*) were guillotined.

Hebrew A Semitic language which dates from around the 2nd millennium BC. Classical Hebrew is the written language of Judaism, and its modern variety is the official language of the state of Israel. It is spoken by c.4 million people around the world.

Hebrew literature The classical period was from the 10th-c to the 4th-c BC, the time of the composition of the Pentateuch (the five books of Moses) and much more of the Bible, though some of the later books are in Aramaic. The Hebrew Mishna and the Aramaic Gemara form the Talmud, the basis of Jewish law and scholarship. Despite frequent persecution, Hebrew literature survived through the Middle Ages, when many fine *piyytim* or liturgical poems were composed. European (especially Spanish) Judaism produced several important Hebrew writers, such as the poet Judas Ha-Levi (c.1080–1141) and Moses Maimonides (1135–1204). Hebrew literature contributed to the 18th-c enlightenment with Moses Mendelssohn, and to the 19th-c novel with Abraham Mapu's *Ahavat Zion* (1853, The Love of Zion). The 20th-c saw a revival of Hebrew literature with Zionism and the State of Israel, though writers such as I L Peretz (1851–1915), Shmuel Agnon, and Amos Oz (1939–) also wrote in Yiddish.

Hebrews, Letter to the New Testament writing of unknown authorship and recipients, sometimes attributed to Paul, but this attribution was widely doubted even from early times. It emphasizes how Jesus as Son of God is superior to the prophets, the angels, and Moses, and how Jesus acts as the perfect heavenly high priest in the heavenly sanctuary. Whether warning Jewish Christians not to return to Judaism, or challenging proto-gnostic heresies or Gentile cultic practices, the main instructions are against spiritual lethargy and falling back into sin.

Hebrides [hebrideez] Over 500 islands off the W coast of Scotland, UK; divided into the **Inner Hebrides** (notably Skye, Rhum, Eigg, Coll, Mull, Iona, Staffa, Islay, Jura) and **Outer Hebrides** (notably Lewis with Harris, the Uists, Barra), separated by the Minch; farming, fishing, Harris tweed, tourism.

Hebron, Arabic **al-Khalil**, Hebrew **Hevro** 31°32N 35°06E, pop (2000e) 135 000. Capital city of Hebron governorate (Jordan), Israeli-occupied West Bank, W Jordan; 29 km/18 mi SW of Jerusalem; one of the oldest cities in the world, built 1730 BC; a religious centre of Islam; the home of Abraham; shrine of Haram al-Khalil over the Cave of Machpelah.

Hecate [hekatee, hekat] In Greek mythology, the goddess associated with witchcraft, spooks, and magic. Not in Homer, she appears in Hesiod, and seems to represent the powerful mother-goddess of Asia Minor. She is worshipped with offerings at places where three roads cross, and so given three bodies in sculpture.

Heckman, James J (1944–) Economist, born in Chicago, Illinois, USA. He studied economics at Princeton University, and joined the faculty at the University of Chicago (1973), where he became professor of economics. In 2000 he shared the Nobel Prize for Economics with Daniel L McFadden for their work in the field of microeconometrics.

Hector [hektaw] According to Greek legend, the bravest Trojan, who led out their army to battle; the son of Priam, and married to Andromache. Achilles killed him and dragged his body behind his chariot all around the walls of Troy; Priam ransomed the corpse at the end of the *Iliad*.

Hecuba [hekyooba] or **Hecabe** [hekabee] In Greek legend, the wife of Priam, King of Troy, and mother of 18 children, including Hector and Cassandra. After the Greeks took Troy, she saw her sons and her husband killed, and was sent into slavery.

hedge garlic *garlic mustard*

hedgehog An insectivorous mammal native to Europe, Africa, and Asia; body covered with spines; tail short; many species dig burrows; young born with spines hidden beneath the skin; adults coat spines with saliva. In heraldry, the hedgehog is called a **herisson**. (Family: Erinaceidae, 12 species.)

hedge sparrow *dunnock*

hedging *futures*

hedonism 1 An ethical doctrine which maintains that the only intrinsic good is pleasure, and the only intrinsic evil is pain. Different philosophical schools, such as the Cyrenaics, Epicureans, and utilitarians, have gone on to interpret 'pleasure' or 'happiness' in very different ways.
2 A psychological thesis, often enlisted in aid of ethical hedonism, which claims that people are as a matter of fact always motivated to seek pleasure and avoid pain.

Hedren, Tippi, originally **Nathalie Hedren** (1935–) Film actress, born in New Ulm, Michigan, USA. She was discovered by Alfred Hitchcock, who cast her in *The Birds* (1963) and *Marnie* (1964). Later films include *Roar* (1981), which she also produced, *Deadly Spygames* (1989), and *Citizen Ruth* (1996), and she has appeared in several television movies, including *Birds 2: The Land's End* (1994). She now runs an animal preserve near Los Angeles, called The Roar Foundation. She is the mother of actress Melanie Griffith.

Heeger, Alan J (1936–) Physical chemist, born in Sioux City, Iowa, USA. He studied at the University of California, Berkeley, and became professor of physics at the University of California, Santa Barbara (1982). In 2000 he shared the Nobel Prize for Chemistry with Alan MacDiarmid and Hideki Shirakawa for their discovery and development of conductive polymers.

Heenan, John Carmel (1905–75) Roman Catholic Archbishop of Westminster (1963–75), born in Ilford, E Greater London, UK. Educated at Ushaw and the English College, Rome, he was ordained in 1930, became a parish priest in E London, and during World War 2 worked with the BBC, when he was known as the 'Radio Priest'. He became Bishop of Leeds in 1951, Archbishop of Liverpool in 1957, and Archbishop of Westminster in 1963. A convinced ecumenist, he was created a cardinal in 1975.

Hegel, Georg Wilhelm Friedrich [haygl] (1770–1831) Idealist philosopher, born in Stuttgart, SW Germany. He studied theology at Tübingen, and taught at Bern (1793), Frankfurt (1796), and Jena (1801). He edited with Schelling the *Kritische Journal der Philosophie* (1802–3, Critical Journal of Philosophy), in which he outlined his system with its emphasis on reason rather than the Romantic intuitionism of Schelling, which he attacked in his first major work, *Phänomenologie des Geistes* (1807, The Phenomenology of the Mind). While headmaster of a Nuremberg school (1808–16) he wrote his *Wissenschaft der Logik* (1812–16, Science of Logic). He then published his *Enzyklopädie der philosophischen Wissenschaften* (1817, trans Encyclopedia of the Philosophical Sciences), in which he set out his tripartite system of logic, philosophy of nature, and mind. He became professor in Heidelberg (1816) and Berlin (1818). His approach, influenced by Kant, rejects the reality of finite and separate objects and minds in space and time, and establishes an underlying, all embracing unity, the Absolute. The quest for greater unity and truth is achieved by the famous dialectic, positing something (*thesis*), denying it (*antithesis*), and combining the two half-truths in a *synthesis* which contains a greater portion of truth in its complexity. His works exerted considerable influence on subsequent European and American philosophy. Later works include the *Grundlinien der Philosophie des Rechts* (1821, trans Philosophy of Right), which contains his political philosophy and his philosophy of art and history.

Heian period [hiyan] A phase of Japanese history beginning with the establishment of the Imperial capital at Heian (modern Kyoto) in 794. The supremacy established by the Fujiwara nobility during the preceding Nara period continued until 1068, and intermarriage occurred between the Fujiwara and the royal family. The period is notable for architecture, bronze statuary, and literature. Heian remained Japan's capital until 1868.

Heidegger, Martin [hiydeger] (1889–1976) Philosopher, born in Messkirch, SW Germany. He became professor of philosophy at Marburg (1923–8) and Freiburg (1929–45), when he was retired for his connections with the Nazi regime. In his incomplete main work, *Sein und Zeit* (1927, Being and Time), he presents an exhaustive ontological classification of 'being', through the synthesis of the modes of human existence. He disclaimed the title of Existentialist, since he was not only concerned with personal existence and ethical choices but primarily with the ontological problem in general. Nevertheless, he was a key influence in Sartre's Existentialism.

Heidelberg [hiydlberg] 49°23N 8°41E, pop (2000e) 141 000. Industrial city in Karlsruhe district, SWC Germany; 18 km/11 mi SE of Mannheim; centre of German Calvinism during the 16th-c; railway; oldest university in Germany (1386); printing presses, pens, machinery, adhesives, scientific apparatus, cement, plaster, publishing, tourism; castle (1583–1610), Holy Ghost Church (15th-c), town hall (18th-c).

Heidelberg jaw [hiydlberg] A strongly built, chinless jaw found in 1907 at Mauer, near Heidelberg, Germany and, at c.0·5 million years ago, still the oldest human fossil from Europe. It is usually classed as *H. erectus* or, more likely, archaic *H. sapiens*, and may represent an early stage in the differentiation of Neanderthal populations.

Heifetz, Jascha [hiyfets] (1901–87) Violinist, born in Vilnius, E Lithuania. He studied violin from the age of three, at nine entered St Petersburg Conservatory, and at 12 toured Russia, Germany, and Scandinavia. After the Russian Revolution he settled in the USA, becoming a US citizen in 1925. He first appeared in Britain in 1920. Among works commissioned by him from leading composers is Walton's violin concerto.

Heilbrun, Carolyn [hiylbrun], *née* **Gold**, pseudonym **Amanda Cross** (1926–2003) Writer and teacher, born in East Orange, New Jersey, USA. She studied at Wellesley and Columbia University, and taught English at several institutions before joining the faculty at Columbia (1960–93). She published scholarly works, but is best known as a writer of popular mystery novels featuring Kate Fansler, also an urban college professor, as seen in *The Theban Mysteries* (1972), *A Trap for Fools* (1989), and *The Edge of Doom* (2002).

Heilong Jiang *Amur River*

Heimlich manoeuvre [hiymlikh] A first-aid life-saving procedure used to dislodge food or other obstruction from the upper respiratory passage; also known as an **abdominal thrust**. A forceful upward thrust is applied to the upper abdomen above the umbilicus by the clenched fist, and repeated until the difficulty in breathing is relieved. It is often applied by clasping the victim around the waist from the back. It is named after US physician Henry J Heimlich (1920–).

Heine, (Christian Johann) Heinrich [hiynuh] (1797–1856) Poet and essayist, born in Düsseldorf, W Germany, of Jewish parentage. He studied banking and law, and in 1821 began to publish poetry, establishing his reputation with his four-volume *Reisebilder* (1826–7, 1830–1, Pictures of Travel) and *Das Buch der Lieder* (1827, The Book of Songs). In 1825 he became a Christian to secure rights of German citizenship, but this alienated his own people, and his revolutionary opinions made him unemployable in Germany. Going into voluntary exile in Paris after the 1830 revolution, he turned from poetry to politics, and became leader of the cosmopolitan democratic movement, writing widely on French and German culture. Schubert and Schumann set many of his poems to music.

Heinz, H(enry) J(ohn) [hiynts] (1844–1919) Food manufacturer, born in Pittsburgh, Pennsylvania, USA. At age eight he peddled produce from the family garden, at 16 employed others to tend and sell his produce, and in 1876 became co-founder, with his brother and cousin, of F & J Heinz. The business was reorganized as H J Heinz Co in 1888, and he became its president (1905–19). He invented the advertising slogan '57 Varieties' in 1896, promoted the pure food movement in the USA, and was a pioneer in staff welfare work.

Heisenberg, Werner (Karl) [hiyznberg] (1901–76) Theoretical physicist, born in Würzburg, SC Germany. He studied at Munich and Göttingen. After a brief period working with Max Born (1923) and Niels Bohr (1924–7), he became professor of physics at Leipzig (1927–41), director of the Kaiser Wilhelm Institute in Berlin (1941–5), and director of the Max Planck Institute at Göttingen (and from 1958 at Munich). He developed a method of expressing quantum mechanics in matrices (1925), and formulated his revolutionary principle of indeterminacy (the *uncertainty principle*) in 1927. He was awarded the 1932 Nobel Prize for Physics.

Heisenberg uncertainty principle In quantum theory, a fundamental limit on the precision of simultaneous measurements, irrespective of the quality of the measuring equipment used; stated by Werner Heisenberg in 1927. The product of uncertainty in position with uncertainty in momentum exceeds $h/2\pi$, where h is Planck's constant. Hence, the precise measurement of a subatomic particle's position means that the uncertainty in its momentum will be large, and vice versa. A consequence of the wave description of matter, the principle may be interpreted as a result of disturbance to a system due to the act of measuring it. It is sometimes expressed as the product of uncertainty in energy with uncertainty in time exceeding $h/2\pi$.

Hel or **Hela** In Norse mythology, the youngest child of Loki; half her body was living human flesh, the other half decayed. She was assigned by Odin to rule Helheim (the Underworld) and to receive the spirits of the dead who do not die in battle.

Helen In Greek legend, the wife of Menelaus of Sparta, famous for her beauty; her abduction by Paris the Trojan caused the Trojan War. She was the daughter of Zeus and Leda, in mythical accounts. According to Stesichoros, however, Helen stayed in Egypt, while a phantom accompanied Paris to Troy.

Helena, St (c.255–c.330) Mother of the Roman Emperor Constantine (the Great), born in Bithynia, Asia Minor. The wife of Emperor Constantius Chlorus, she early became a Christian, and when Constantine became emperor he made her empress dowager. In 326, according to tradition, she visited Jerusalem, and founded the basilicas on the Mt of Olives and at Bethlehem. Feast day 18 August (W), 21 May (E).

Helene The 12th natural satellite of Saturn, discovered in 1980; distance from the planet 377 000 km/234 000 mi; diameter 36 km/22 mi. It moves along the same orbit as Dione.

Helfgott, David [helfgot] (1947–) Pianist, born in Australia. After many competition successes as a child, in 1966 he obtained a place at the Royal College of Music, London, where he is remembered for his acclaimed performance of Rachmaninov's third piano concerto in 1969. Following a nervous breakdown, he spent the next few years in psychiatric hospitals in England and Australia. Since leaving institutional care in 1975, and especially following his marriage in 1984, he has come to cope with a serious mood disorder which has left him with a rapid and repetitive interactional style of speech, and a distinctive mode of playing which is often accompanied by highly audible vocalization. His life-story was dramatized in the film *Shine* (1995). His world tour in 1997 received a generally cool reception from music critics, but the concerts were given sell-out support and enthusiasm from the public.

helical scan A system of magnetic tape recording in which the tape is wrapped in a partial helix around a drum carrying two or more rotating heads which trace a series of tracks diagonally across its width. The relative head-to-tape velocity, the 'writing speed', is much higher than the rate at which the tape itself advances, so that very high frequencies can be recorded economically. The technique was originally developed for video recording, but later applied to produce compact high quality audio tracks.

Helicon [helikon] The largest mountain in Boeotia. In Greek mythology, it was the sacred hill of the Muses, whose temple was to be found there, together with the fountains of Aganippe and Hippocrene.

helicopter A vertical take-off and landing aircraft whose lift is provided by means of a horizontal, large-diameter set of powered blades which force the air downwards and by reaction create a lifting force upwards. Forward flight is achieved by tilting the plane of the blades in the direction of flight, varying their angle to the horizontal as they rotate.

Heligoland, Ger **Helgoland** 54°09N 7°52E, pop (2000e) 3640. Rocky North Sea island of the North Frisian Is, in Heligoland Bay, Schleswig-Holstein, Germany, 64 km/40 mi NW of Cuxhaven; area 2·1 sq km/0·8 sq mi; captured from Denmark by the UK, 1807; ceded to Germany in exchange for Zanzibar, 1890; German naval base in both World Wars; tourism; centre for the study of birds.

heliocentric system Any theory of our planetary system that has the Sun at the centre. It was proposed by Aristarchus in the 3rd-c BC, and revived with great success by Copernicus in 1543.

Helios [heelios] In Greek mythology, the Sun-god, represented as a charioteer with four horses. In early times Helios was not worshipped, except at Rhodes; in the late classical period, there was an Imperial cult of the Sun, *Sol Invictus*.

Helios project A joint space mission of West Germany and the USA, designed to study the interplanetary medium to as close as 0·3 astronomical units (AU) from the Sun, ie to the inside of Mercury's orbit. Two spacecraft were built by West Germany and launched on Titan III–Centaur vehicles (Dec 1974, Jan 1976). They operated successfully for over 10 years, tracked by West German ground stations and by NASA's Deep Space Network.

heliotrope A small evergreen shrub (*Heliotropium peruvianum*) 0·5–2 m/1½–6½ ft, a native of Peru; leaves lance-shaped to oblong, hairy, puckered; flowers small, tubular, with spreading lobes, white to lilac or violet, in terminal clusters. It is cultivated for its fragrant flowers. (Family: Boraginaceae.)

helium He, element 2, the most inert of the chemical elements, forming no stable compounds; the lightest of the *noble* or *inert* gases. It condenses to a liquid only at −269°C (4 K). Formed by radioactive decay of the heaviest elements, it is obtained mainly as a small fraction of natural gas. Because of its inertness and low density (less than 15% of the density of air), it is used to fill balloons. Liquid helium is used as the ultimate coolant, and was important in the discovery and development of superconductivity.

hell In traditional Christian thought, the eternal abode and place of torment of the damned. It developed out of Hebrew *sheol* and Greek *hades* as the place of the dead. Much contemporary Christian thought rejects the idea of vindictive punishment as incompatible with belief in a loving God. The emphasis accordingly shifts from hell as a place of retribution to a state of being without God.

hellbender A nocturnal salamander (*Cryptobranchus alleganiensis*), native to E and C USA; length, up to 75 cm/30 in; small eyes, broad head, deep narrow tail, loose skin along sides of body; inhabits streams and rivers; eats invertebrates and fish. (Family: Cryptobranchidae.)

hellebore [helibaw(r)] A perennial with glossy divided leaves and large flowers, native to Europe and W Asia; flowers with five green, white, or pinkish-purple petaloid sepals, and up to 20 prominent 2-lipped nectar-secreting glands; highly poisonous, with a burning taste because of the presence of alkaloids. (Genus: *Helleborus*, 20 species. Family: Ranunculaceae.)

helleborine [heliborin] Either of two closely related genera of orchids. *Epipactis* (24 species), from N temperate regions and parts of the tropics, has stalked flowers in which the lower lip (*labellum*) forms a nectar-containing cup with a tongue-like extension. *Cephalanthera* (12 species), from N temperate regions, has stalkless flowers which never open fully. (Family: Orchidaceae.)

Hellen [helen, heleen] In ancient Greek genealogies, the eldest son of Deucalion, and father of Doros, Xuthos, and Aiolos, who were the progenitors of the Dorian, Ionian, and Aeolic branches of the Greek race. The Greeks (or *Hellenes*) were named after him.

Hellenistic Age The period from the death of Alexander the Great (323 BC) to the beginning of the Roman Empire (31 BC), during which a number of Greek or Hellenized dynasties, many descended from Alexander's generals (such as the Ptolemies and Seleucids), ruled the entire area from Greece to the N of India.

Hellenistic philosophy A period of philosophy conventionally defined as running from 323 BC to 30 BC and centred on the philosophical schools in Athens: the Lyceum, the Academy and, most importantly, the new schools of the Stoics and the Epicureans. It is also known as **post-Aristotelian philosophy**.

Hellenists [helenists] A group referred to in the Book of Acts (6.1, 9.29), contrasted with the 'Hebrews', and usually interpreted as Greek-speaking Jewish Christians who were critical of the Temple worship and who prepared for the Christian mission to non-Jews. Stephen may have been one of them. Other interpretations of this group consider them Jews (not Christians) whose mother-tongue was Greek, or even non-Jews (Greeks).

Hellenization In the ancient world, the process by which Greek language and culture were disseminated among non-Greek (usually oriental) peoples. Initially a spontaneous development, from the time of Alexander the Great, it became a deliberate policy: he and his successors planted Greek city-states all over their dominions to produce cultural unification.

Heller, Joseph (1923–99) Novelist, born in New York City, USA. He served in the US Army Air Force in World War 2, and studied at New York, Columbia, and Oxford universities. His wartime experience formed the background for his first book, *Catch 22* (1961), which launched him as a successful novelist. The anti-war plot centred on the view that US airmen on dangerous combat missions must be considered insane, but if they seek to be relieved on grounds of mental derangement, they find themselves ineligible, since such a request proves their sanity. Hence 'Catch 22' has come to signify any logical trap or double bind. A sequel, *Closing Time*, appeared in 1994. His other works include *Something Happened* (1974), *God Knows* (1984), *Picture This* (1988), and the autobiographical *Now and Then: From Coney Island to Here* (1998).

Hellespont *Dardanelles*

Hell's Canyon or **Grand Canyon of the Snake** Gorge on the Snake R where it follows the Oregon–Idaho state border, USA; with a depth of c.2450 m/8030 ft, it is one of the deepest gorges in the world; length 65 km/40 mi.

helmet shell A marine snail known mostly from warm tropical seas; shell typically has a series of external flange-like ribs (*varices*), and is much sought after by collectors; used as raw material for cameos. (Class: Gastropoda. Order: Mesogastropoda.)

Helmholtz, Hermann von (1821–94) Physiologist and physicist, born in Potsdam, EC Germany. He was successively professor of physiology at Königsberg (1849), Bonn (1855), and Heidelberg (1858), and in 1871 became professor of physics in Berlin. He was equally distinguished in physiology, mathematics, and experimental and mathematical physics. His physiological works are principally connected with the eye, the ear, and the nervous system. His work on vision is regarded as fundamental to modern visual science. He invented an ophthalmoscope (1850) independently of Charles Babbage. He is best known for his statement of the law of the conservation of energy, which was more precise and wide-ranging than previous attempts, and well supported with examples of its application.

helminthology The study of parasitic worms (**helminths**), including roundworms, flatworms, and their larval stages.

Helmont, Jan Baptista van (1579–1644) Chemist, born in Brussels, Belgium. He studied medicine, mysticism, and chemistry under the influence of Paracelsus, devoting much study to gases, and invented the term *gas*. He was the first to take the melting-point of ice and the boiling-point of water as standards for temperature. Through his experiments he bridged the gap between alchemy and chemistry.

Héloïse *Abelard, Peter*

Helpmann, Sir Robert (Murray) (1909–86) Dancer, actor, and choreographer, born in Mount Gambier, South Australia, Australia. He made his debut in Adelaide in 1923, studied with Pavlova's touring company in 1929, and in 1931 moved to Britain to study under Ninette de Valois. He was first dancer of the newly founded Sadler's Wells Ballet (1933–50) and its principal choreographer (1943–50), and became known for his dramatic roles in de Valois' works. His ballets include *Hamlet* (1942) and *Miracle in the Gorbals* (1944), he also appeared in many films, choreographing and starring in the legendary *The Red Shoes* (1948). Joint artistic director of the Australian Ballet Company in 1965, he was knighted in 1968.

Helsingborg, Swed **Hälsingborg** 56°03N 12°43E, pop (2000e) 115 000. Seaport and commercial town on W coast of Malmöhus county, SW Sweden; on The Sound opposite Helsingør, Denmark; railway; ferry services to Denmark; shipbuilding, textiles, machinery, copper refining, fertilizers, trade in chemicals, timber, paper; town hall (1897), St Mary's Church (13th-c).

Helsingfors [helsingfaw(r)z] *Helsinki*

Helsingør *Elsinore*

Helsinki [helsingkee], Swed **Helsingfors** 60°08N 25°00E, pop (2000e) 507 000. Seaport, capital of Finland and Uudenmaa province, S Finland; on the Gulf of Finland, on a peninsula surrounded by islands; founded by Gustavus Vasa in 1550; capital, 1812; heavily bombed in World War 2; airport; railway; university (transferred from Turku, 1828); technical university (1908); shipbuilding, textiles, engineering, porcelain, metals, paper, export trade; cathedral (completed 1852), Olympic Stadium, Rock Church (Tempeliaukio), Ateneum Museum, National Museum, open-air museum of country life on nearby island of Seurasaari.

Helsinki Conference (1975) A conference on security and co-operation in Europe, attended by the heads of 35 states, including the USA and USSR, with the objective of forwarding the process of detente through agreements on economic and technological co-operation, security, and disarmament. These were set out in the Final Act within the principles of sovereignty and self-determination.

Helvellyn [helvelin] 54°32N 3°02W. Mountain in the Lake District of Cumbria, NW England, UK; rises to 950 m/3117 ft between Ullswater and Thirlmere; Striding Edge descends to the E.

Helvetii [helwaytiee] Celtic people forced S by Germanic tribesmen in the 2nd-c BC into modern Switzerland. In 58 BC, when renewed Germanic pressure prompted Helvetian migration into Gaul, Julius Caesar drove them back to their Swiss lands. They became allies then subjects of Rome, until c.400. The official names for Switzerland derive from this source: *Helvetia* and *Confederatio Helvetica*.

Helvétius, Claude-Adrien [elvaysyus] (1715–71) Philosopher, born in Paris, France. He trained for a financial career, and in 1738 was appointed to the lucrative office of farmer-general. In 1751 he withdrew from public life to the family estate at Voré, where he spent the rest of his life in philosophy, and as host to the Philosophes, a group of French thinkers, including Diderot and d'Alembert with whom he was later to collaborate on the *Encyclopédie*. In 1758 he published the controversial *De l'esprit* (On the Mind), advancing the view that sensation is the source of all intellectual activity and that self-interest is the motive force of all human action. The book was promptly denounced by the Sorbonne and condemned by the parliament of Paris to be publicly burnt. As a result it was widely read, translated into all the main European languages and, together with his posthumous *De l'homme* (1772, On Man), greatly influenced Bentham and the British utilitarians.

hem- *haem-*

hemichordate A bottom-living, marine invertebrate with gill slits in its pharynx similar to those of primitive vertebrates; includes the acornworms and graptolites. (Phylum: Hemichordata.)

Hemingway, Ernest (Miller) (1899–1961) Novelist and short-story writer, born in Oak Park, Illinois, USA. He worked as a reporter for *The Kansas City Star*, served with an ambulance unit in World War 1, was wounded in 1918, and was decorated for heroism. His first important work was a collection of short stories, *In Our Time* (1925), and success came with his novel, *The Sun Also Rises* (1926), inspired by his experience as one of the 'lost generation' of young expatriates in France and Spain after World War 1. Obsessed with war, big-game hunting, and bullfighting, his works include *A Farewell to Arms* (1929), *Death in the Afternoon* (1932), *For Whom the Bell Tolls* (1940), and *The Old Man and the Sea* (1952, Pulitzer). In 1954 he was awarded the Nobel Prize for Literature. A war correspondent in World War 2, he took part in the D-Day landings (1944), and after the Spanish Civil War lived in Cuba, staying there until the 1960 revolution, when he moved to the USA. Married four times, he was subject to depression, and fearing ill health he took his own life with a shotgun.

hemione *ass*

hemiplegia *paralysis*

hemipode *button quail; plains wanderer*

Hemiptera [hemiptera] A group of insects comprising two orders, the Homoptera and the Heteroptera.

hemispheric specialization *laterality*

hemlock **1** An evergreen conifer native to North America and E Asia; branches drooping; leaves short, narrow, in two ranks; cones ripen after one year, but do not shed seeds until the second year. It yields timber, Canada pitch, and tanning bark. (Genus: *Tsuga*, 15 species. Family: Pinaceae.)
2 A biennial (*Conium maculatum*) growing to 2·5 m/8 ft, native to Europe and temperate Asia, and widely introduced; stem hollow, furrowed, spotted with purple; leaves divided with oblong toothed segments; flowers white, lacking sepals, in umbels 2–5 cm/¾–2 in across; fruit ovoid; a fetid smell. All parts are very poisonous because of the presence of the alkaloid *coniine*, used as a poison since classical times, and reputedly the poison given to Socrates by the Athenian leaders. (Family: Umbelliferae.)

hemo- *haemo-*

hemp *abaca; cannabis*

hen *domestic fowl*

henbane An annual or biennial (*Hyoscyamus niger*), sticky-haired and fetid, native to Europe, W Asia, and N Africa; leaves large, soft, coarsely toothed; flowers 2–3 cm/¾–1¼ in across, borne in a curved inflorescence; calyx tubular; corolla 5-lobed, lurid yellow and purple. It is poisonous, containing various aklaloids, principally hyoscyamnine and scopalomine. Its extracts are still used in modern medicine, mainly as sedatives. (Family: Solanaceae.)

Henbury Crater A meteorite crater at Henbury, Northern Territory, Australia; c.100 km/60 mi SW of Alice Springs.

Henderson, Fletcher (1897–1952) Pianist, arranger, and jazz bandleader, born in Cuthbert, Georgia, USA. He graduated in chemistry from Atlanta University, and moved to New York City in 1920 to continue his studies, but was diverted into a musical career, starting as house pianist for publishing and recording companies. In 1924 he put together a big band for what was supposed to be a temporary engagement, but stayed at the head of the orchestra until the mid-1930s, attracting the finest instrumentalists and arrangers of the time. His own orchestrations, and those of Don Redman, set the standard for the swing era.

Hendrix, Jimi, popular name of **James Marshall Hendrix** (1942–70) Rock guitarist, singer, and songwriter, born in Seattle, Washington, USA. He learned basic blues licks as a sideman for Little Richard and the Isley Brothers. After his 1965 discharge from the army, he explored electronic tricks on his guitar, to which he added stage gimmicks, playing behind his back or with his teeth. Discovered by Chas Chandler (1938–96), who took him to London, he formed the Jimi Hendrix Experience, with **Noel Redding** (1945–) and **Mitch Mitchell** (1947–). The band's first single, 'Hey Joe', was an immediate British success, and his adventurous first album, *Are You Experienced?*, was an unexpected international success which paved the way for other psychedelic and experimental rock acts. He died after taking barbiturates and alcohol.

Hendry, Stephen (Gordon) (1969–) Snooker player, born in Edinburgh, EC Scotland, UK. He became a professional in 1985, won the Scottish championship in 1986, and went on to dominate the game in the 1990s. His wins include seven Embassy world championships (1990, 1992–6, 1999), and he holds the record for the most titles won in a season (9 in 1991–2). In 1997–8 he won his 29th ranking event, beating the career record previously held by Steve Davis, but lost his Number 1 world record ranking position to John Higgins. In 2003 he added the British Open title to his achievements.

Hengduan Shan [huhngdwahn shahn] Mountain range in SW China; series of parallel ranges running N–S; average height, 3–4000 m/10–13 000 ft; rises to 7556 m/24 790 ft at Gongga Shan peak.

Hengist and **Horsa** Brothers, leaders of the first Anglo-Saxon settlers in Britain, said by Bede to have been invited over by Vortigern, the British king, to fight the Picts in about AD 450. According to the *Anglo-Saxon Chronicle*, Horsa was killed in 455, and Hengist ruled in Kent until his death in 488.

Henie, Sonja [henee] (1912–69) Ice-skater, born in Oslo, Norway. The winner of three Olympic gold medals (1928, 1932, 1936), she also won a record 10 individual world titles (1927–36). In 1936 she turned professional and starred in touring ice-shows, then went to Hollywood where she made several films. She became an American citizen in 1941, and became known in the USA for her touring ice carnivals.

Henin-Hardenne, Justine [aynĩ ah(r)den], *née* **Justine Henin** (1982–) Tennis player, born in Liège, Belgium. She won her first WTA Tour event as a professional at Antwerp in 1999. In 2001 she reached the semi-final of the French Open and the final at Wimbledon, and by the end of the year was ranked number seven in the world. In 2003 she won her first two Grand Slam events: the French Open and the US Open. The Australian Open followed in early 2004. At the beginning of 2004 she was ranked world Number 1.

Henley Royal Regatta Rowing races which take place annually on the R Thames at Henley-on-Thames, Oxfordshire, England, UK, inaugurated in 1839. The Diamond Sculls (first contested 1884) and the Grand Challenge Cup are the most coveted events. The course has varied over the years, but is now approximately 2 km 112 m/1 mi 550 yd. It is as much an elegant social occasion for the public as a sporting one.

Henman, Tim(othy) (1974–) Tennis player, born in Oxford, Oxfordshire, SC England, UK. He turned professional in 1993, and his achievements include the British National Championships (singles and men's doubles, 1995–6, singles 1996), an Olympic silver medal in the men's doubles (1996), and the Association of Tennis Professionals Tour title at Sydney (1997). He had become Britain's Number 1 player by early 1997, and reached the quarter-finals at Wimbledon that year. Although he lost this position to Greg Rusedski later in 1997, he regained it during 1998. In 1999 his performance continued to improve, reaching the semi-finals at Wimbledon for the second year in succession, a feat he repeated in 2001 and 2002, when he also rose to fourth in the world rankings, the highest ever for a Briton. He claimed the biggest title of his career with victory in the Paris Masters in 2003. At the beginning of 2004 he had a world ranking of 14.

henna An evergreen shrub (*Lawsonia inermis*) growing to 3 m/10 ft, native to the Old World tropics; leaves opposite, oval to lance-shaped; flowers 4-petalled, white, pink, or red; fruit a 3-chambered capsule. The powdered leaves produce a red dye, used as a cosmetic for skin and hair since ancient times. (Family: Lythraceae.)

Henrietta Maria (1609–69) Queen consort of Charles I of England, born in Paris, France, the youngest child of Henry IV of France. She married Charles in 1625, but her French attendants and Roman Catholic beliefs made her unpopular. In 1642, under the threat of impeachment, she fled to Holland and raised funds for the Royalist cause. A year later she landed at Bridlington, and met Charles near Edgehill. At Exeter she gave birth to Henrietta Anne, and a fortnight later she was compelled to flee to France (1644). She paid two visits to England after the Restoration (1660–1, 1662–5), and spent her last years in France.

Henry I (of England) (1068–1135) King of England (1100–35) and Duke of Normandy (1106–35), the youngest son of William the Conqueror. Under Henry, the Norman empire attained the height of its power. He conquered Normandy from his brother, Robert Curthose, at the Battle of Tinchebrai (1106), maintained his position on the European mainland, and exercised varying degrees of authority over the King of Scots, the Welsh princes, the Duke of Brittany, and the Counts of Flanders, Boulogne, and Ponthieu. His government of England and Normandy became increasingly centralized and interventionist, with the overriding aim of financing warfare and alliances, and consolidating the unity of the two countries as a single cross-Channel state. His only legitimate son, **William Adelin**, was drowned in 1120, and in 1127 he nominated his daughter Empress **Matilda**, widow of Emperor Henry V of Germany, as his heir for both England and Normandy. But Matilda and her second husband, Geoffrey of Anjou, proved unacceptable to the king's leading subjects. After Henry's death at Lyons-la-Forêt, near Rouen, the crown was seized by Stephen, son of his sister, Adela.

Henry II (of England) (1133–89) King of England (1154–89), born in Le Mans, NW France, the son of Empress Matilda, Henry I's daughter and acknowledged heir, by her second husband, Geoffrey of Anjou. Already established as Duke of Normandy (1150) and Count of Anjou (1151), and as Duke of Aquitaine by marriage to Eleanor of Aquitaine (1152), he invaded England in 1153, and was recognized as the lawful successor of the usurper, Stephen. He founded the Angevin or Plantagenet dynasty of English kings, and ruled England as part of a wider Angevin empire. He restored and transformed English governance after the disorders of Stephen's reign. His efforts to restrict clerical independence caused conflict with his former Chancellor Thomas Becket, Archbishop of Canterbury, which was ended only with Becket's murder (1170). He led a major expedition to Ireland (1171), which resulted in its annexation. The most serious challenge to his power came in 1173–4, when his son, the young Henry, encouraged by Eleanor, rebelled in alliance with Louis VII of France, William I of Scotland, and Count Philip of Flanders. All parts of the king's dominions were threatened, but his enemies were defeated. In 1189 he faced futher disloyalty from his family when his sons, John and Richard, allied with Philip II of France, who overran Maine and Touraine. Henry agreed a peace which recognized Richard as his sole heir for the Angevin empire, and he died shortly afterwards.

Henry II (of France) (1519–59) King of France (1547–59), born near Paris, the second son of Francis I. In 1533 he married Catherine de' Medici. Soon after his accession, he began to oppress his Protestant subjects. Through the influence of the Guises he formed an alliance with Scotland, and declared war against England, which ended in 1558 with the taking of Calais. He continued the long-standing war against the Emperor Charles V, gaining Toul, Metz, and Verdun, but suffered reverses in Italy and the Low Countries, which led to the Treaty of Cateau-Cambrésis (1559).

Henry III (of England) (1207–72) King of England (1216–72), the elder son and successor, at the age of nine, of John. He declared an end to his minority in 1227, and in 1232 stripped the justiciar, Hubert de Burgh, of power. His arbitrary assertion of royal rights conflicted with the principles of Magna Carta, and antagonized many nobles. Although he failed to recover Poitou (N Aquitaine) in 1242, he accepted for his son Edmund the Kingdom of Sicily (1254), then occupied by the Hohenstaufens. This forced him to seek the support of the barons who, under the leadership of the king's brother-in-law, Simon de Montfort, imposed far-reaching reforms by the Provisions of Oxford (1258), which gave them a definite say in government. When Henry sought to restore royal power, the barons rebelled and captured the king at Lewes (1264), but were defeated at Evesham (1265). The Dictum of Kenilworth (1266), though favourable to Henry, urged him to observe Magna Carta. Organized resistance ended in 1267, and the rest of the reign was stable. He was succeeded by his elder son, Edward I.

Henry III (of France) (1551–89) King of France (1574–89), born in Fontainebleau, C France, the third son of Henry II. In 1569 he gained victories over the Huguenots, and took an active share in the massacre of St Bartholomew (1572). In 1573 he was elected to the crown of Poland, but two years later succeeded his brother, Charles IX, on the French throne. His reign was a period of almost incessant civil war between Huguenots and Catholics. In 1588 he engineered the assassination of the Duke of Guise, enraging the Catholic League. He joined forces with the Huguenot Henry of Navarre, and while marching on Paris was assassinated by a fanatical priest. The last of the Valois line, he named Henry of Navarre as his successor.

Henry IV (of England), originally **Henry Bolingbroke** (1366–1413) King of England (1399–1413), the first king of the House of Lancaster, the son of John of Gaunt. He was surnamed Bolingbroke from his birthplace in Lincolnshire. In 1397 he supported Richard II against the Duke of Gloucester, and was created Duke of Hereford, but was banished in 1398. After landing at Ravenspur, Yorkshire, Henry induced Richard, now deserted, to abdicate in his favour. During his reign, rebellion and lawlessness were rife, and he was constantly hampered by lack of money. Under Owen Glendower the Welsh maintained their independence, and Henry's attack on Scotland in 1400 ended in his defeat. Henry Percy (Hotspur) and his house then joined with the Scots and the Welsh against him, but they were defeated at Shrewsbury (1403). He was a chronic invalid in his later years.

Henry IV (of France), originally **Henry of Navarre** (1553–1610) The first Bourbon king of France (1589–1610), born in Pau, SW France, the third son of Antoine de Bourbon. Brought up a Calvinist, he led the Huguenot army at the Battle of Jarnac (1569), and became leader of the Protestant Party. He married Marguerite de Valois in 1572. After the massacre of St Bartholomew (1572), he was spared by professing himself a Catholic, and spent three years virtually a prisoner at the French court. In 1576 he escaped, revoked his conversion, and resumed command of the army in continuing opposition to the Guises and the Catholic League. After the murder of Henry III, he succeeded to the throne. In 1593 he became a Catholic again, thereby unifying the country, and by the Edict of Nantes Protestants were granted liberty of conscience. His economic policies, implemented by his minister, Sully, gradually brought new wealth to the country. He was assassinated in Paris by a religious fanatic.

Henry V (of England) (1387–1422) King of England (1413–22), born in Monmouth, Monmouthshire, SE Wales, UK, the eldest son of Henry IV. He fought against Glendower and the Welsh rebels (1402–8), and became Constable of Dover (1409) and Captain of Calais (1410). To this time belong the exaggerated stories of his wild youth. The main effort of his reign was his claim, through his great-grandfather Edward III, to the French crown. In 1415 he invaded France, and won the Battle of Agincourt against great odds. By 1419 Normandy was again under English control, and in 1420 was concluded the 'perpetual peace' of Troyes, under which Henry was recognized as heir to the French throne and Regent of France, and married Charles VI's daughter, Catherine of Valois.

Henry VI (of England) (1421–71) King of England (1422–61, 1470–1), born in Windsor, S England, UK, the only child of Henry V and Catherine of Valois. During Henry's minority, his uncle John, Duke of Bedford, was Regent of France, and another uncle, Humphrey, Duke of Gloucester, was Lord Protector of England. Henry was crowned King of France in Paris in 1431, two years after his coronation in England. But once the Burgundians had made a separate peace with Charles VII (1435), Henry V's French conquests were progressively eroded, and by 1453 the English retained only Calais. Henry had few kingly qualities, and from 1453 suffered from periodic bouts of insanity. Richard, Duke of York, seized power as Lord Protector in 1454, and defeated the king's army at St Albans in 1455, the first battle of the Wars of the Roses. Fighting resumed in 1459, and although York himself was killed at Wakefield (1460), his heir was proclaimed king as Edward IV after Henry's deposition (1461). In 1464 Henry returned from exile in Scotland to lead the Lancastrian cause, but was captured and imprisoned (1465–70). Richard Neville, Earl of Warwick, restored him to the throne (Oct 1470), his nominal rule ending when Edward IV returned to London (Apr 1471). After the Yorkist victory at Tewkesbury (May 1471), where his only son was killed, Henry was murdered in the Tower.

Henry VII (of England) (1457–1509) King of England (1485–1509), born at Pembroke Castle, Pembrokeshire, SW Wales, UK. Henry's claim to the English throne was traced back tenuously through his father, Edmund Tudor, the younger son of Catherine of France and of her clerk to the wardrobe, the Welshman Owen Tudor. Through his mother, Margaret Beaufort, Henry claimed descent from Edward III's son, John of Gaunt, and Katherine Swynford. Known as Duke of Richmond before his accession, he was the founder of the Tudor dynasty. After the Lancastrian defeat at Tewkesbury (1471), Henry was taken to Brittany, where several Yorkist attempts on his life and liberty were frustrated. In 1485 he landed unopposed at Milford Haven, and defeated Richard III at Bosworth. As king, his policy was to restore peace and prosperity to the country, and this was helped by his marriage of reconciliation with Elizabeth of York, daughter of Edward IV. He was also noted for the efficiency of his financial and administrative policies. He firmly dealt with Yorkist plots, such as that led by Perkin Warbeck. Peace was concluded with France, and the marriage of his heir, Prince Arthur, to Catherine of Aragon cemented an alliance with Spain. He was succeeded by his son, Henry VIII.

Henry VIII (of England) (1491–1547) King (1509–47), born in Greenwich, EC Greater London, UK, the second son of Henry VII. Soon after his accession he married **Catherine of Aragon**, his brother Arthur's widow. As a member of the Holy League, he invaded France (1512), winning the Battle of Spurs (1513); and while abroad, the Scots were defeated at Flodden. In 1521 he published a book on the Sacraments refuting Luther, receiving from the pope the title 'Defender of the Faith'. From 1527 he determined to divorce Catherine, whose children, except for Mary, had died in infancy. He tried to put pressure on the pope by humbling the clergy, and in defiance of the Roman Catholic Church was privately married to **Anne Boleyn** (1533). In 1534 it was enacted that his marriage to Catherine was invalid, and that the king was the Supreme Head of the English Church. The policy of Dissolution of the Monasteries then began. In 1536 Catherine died, and Anne Boleyn was executed on the grounds of infidelity. Henry then married **Jane Seymour**, who died leaving a son, afterwards Edward VI. In 1540 **Anne of Cleves** became his fourth wife, in the hope of attaching the Protestant interest of Germany; but dislike of her appearance caused him to divorce her speedily. He then married **Catherine Howard** (1540), who two years later was executed on grounds of infidelity (1542). In 1543 his last marriage was to **Catherine Parr**, who survived him. His later years saw ineffectual and expensive wars with France and Scotland, but a powerful English navy was created. He was succeeded by his son as Edward VI.

Henry the Lion (1129–95) Duke of Saxony (1142–80) and Bavaria (1156–80), the head of the Guelphs. His ambitious designs roused against him a league of princes in 1166, but he retained power through an alliance with Emperor Frederick I Barbarossa. After breaking with Frederick in 1176, he was deprived of most of his lands, and exiled. Ultimately he was reconciled to Frederick's successor, Henry VI. He encouraged commerce, and founded the city of Munich.

Henry the Navigator (1394–1460) Portuguese prince, the third son of John I, King of Portugal, and Philippa, daughter of John of Gaunt, Duke of Lancaster. He set up court at Sagres, Algarve, and erected an observatory and school of scientific navigation. He sponsored many exploratory expeditions along the W African coast, and the way was prepared for the discovery of the sea route to India.

Henry, Joseph (1797–1878) Physicist, born in Albany, New York, USA. In 1832 he became professor of natural philosophy at Princeton, and in 1846 first secretary of the Smithsonian Institution. He discovered electrical induction independently of Michael Faraday, constructed the first electromagnetic motor (1829), demonstrated the oscillatory nature of electric discharges (1842), and introduced a system of weather forecasting. The *henry* unit of inductance is named after him.

Henry, Lenny, popular name of **Lenworth George Henry** (1958–) Comedian and actor, born in Dudley, West Midlands, C England, UK. He won the *New Faces Talent Show* in 1975, joined the children's television show *Tiswas*, was one of *Three of a Kind* (1981–3), and went on to star in his own BBC television comedy series the *Lenny Henry Show* (1984–95) and *Chef* (3 series, from 1992). He also hosts the annual BBC *Comic Relief* telethon. He appeared in the film *True Identity* (1991). He has also written a volume of autobiography, *The Quest for the Big Woof* (1991) and a book for children (1995). He is married to Dawn French.

Henry, O, pseudonym of **William Sydney Porter** (1862–1910) Writer, master of the short story, born in Greensboro, North Carolina, USA. Brought up during the post-Civil War depression in the South, he held various jobs before becoming a teller in the First National Bank. Jailed for embezzlement (1898), he started writing short stories in prison under his pseudonym. In 1902 after his release, he moved to New York City, and produced the first of his many volumes, *Cabbages and Kings*, in 1904. His stories provide a romantic and humorous treatment of everyday life, and are noted for their use of coincidence and trick endings. Other collections include *The Voice of the City* (1908), *Whirligigs* (1910), and *Waifs and Strays* (1917, posthumously). Despite enormous success, his life was marred by debts, ill health, and alcoholism.

Henry, Patrick (1736–99) American revolutionary and statesman, born in Studley, Virginia, USA. After training as a lawyer, he entered the colonial Virginia House of Burgesses, where his oratorical skills won him fame. He was outspoken in his opposition to British policy towards the colonies, particularly on the subject of the Stamp Act (1765), and he made the first speech in the Continental Congress (1774). In 1776 he became governor of independent Virginia, and was four times re-elected. The words 'give me liberty or give me death' are often attributed to him, but are probably apocryphal.

Henry, Thierry (Daniel) [onree] (1977–) Footballer, born in Les Ulis, Paris, France. He was admitted to France's football academy, Clairefontaine, at the age of 13, and within four years was playing for the French first division side AS Monaco (1994–9). He spent six months with Juventus before signing for Arsenal in 1999. A regular in the French national team, he played during their 1998 World Cup win and spearheaded the attack in their triumphant Euro 2000 championship. He was voted Young Footballer of the Year in France in 1996. In early 2003 he scored his 100th goal for Arsenal, and later that year was voted the Professional Football Association Player of the Year and the Football Writers' Association Player of the Year.

Henry, William (1774–1836) Chemist, born in Manchester, Greater Manchester, NW England, UK. He studied medicine at Edinburgh, and practised in Manchester, but soon devoted himself to chemistry. He formulated the law named after him, that the amount of gas absorbed by a liquid varies directly as the pressure of the gas above the liquid, provided no chemical action takes place. A childhood injury led to continuing pain, and he committed suicide.

henry SI unit of inductance; symbol *H*; named after Joseph Henry; defined as the inductance of a closed circuit in which a current changing at the rate of 1 ampere per second produces an electromotive force (emf) of 1 volt.

Henry Moore Institute Exhibition centre in Leeds, West Yorkshire, N England, UK, supported by the Henry Moore Sculpture Trust (established in 1988). Formerly a group of Victorian merchants' offices and warehouses, the building is now devoted to the exhibition, study, and promotion of sculpture.

Henry's law In chemistry, a law formulated by William Henry: the solubility of a gas in a liquid at any given temperature is proportional to the pressure of the gas on the liquid. This has wide application, including the production of carbonated beverages, and in 'the bends', a condition in deep-sea divers where nitrogen, having dissolved in the blood at high pressure, is released with sometimes fatal consequences when the diver returns to the low pressure of the surface.

Henryson, Robert [henrison] (c.1425–1508) Scottish mediaeval poet. He is usually designated a schoolmaster of Dunfermline, and he was certainly a notary in 1478. His works include *The Testament of Cresseid; Robene and Makyne*, the earliest Scottish specimen of pastoral poetry; and a metrical version of 13 *Morall Fabels of Esope*, often viewed as his masterpiece.

Henslowe, Philip (c.1550–1616) Theatre manager, born in Lindfield, West Sussex, S England, UK. Originally a dyer and starch-maker, in 1587 he rebuilt the Rose Theatre on Bankside, London, and afterwards managed the theatre at Newington Butts and The Swan on Bankside. From 1591 until his death he was in partnership with Edward Alleyn, founder of Dulwich College, who married his stepdaughter. Henslowe's business diary (1598–1609) contains invaluable information about the stage of Shakespeare's day.

Henson, Jim, popular name of **James Maury Henson** (1936–90) Puppeteer, born in Greenville, Mississippi, USA. He lived near Washington, DC, working on a local television station as a puppeteer while studying at Maryland University. His 'Muppets' (Marionettes/puppets) first appeared on a five-minute programme entitled 'Sam and His Friends'. Other commercial and short appearances led to nationwide popularity on the children's television workshop, *Sesame Street* from 1969. Kermit the Frog, Miss Piggy, and friends went on to gain phenomenal success in *The Muppet Show* (1976–81), which reached an estimated 235 million viewers in more than 100 countries, appearing also in a string of films and on a Grammy-winning album (1979). The recipient of numerous Emmy awards, he continued to make television programmes combining live action and increasingly sophisticated puppetry, including *Fraggle Rock* (from 1983) and *The Storyteller* (from 1987).

Henze, Hans Werner [hentsuh] (1926–) Composer, born in Gütersloh, WC Germany. He studied at Heidelberg and Paris, and was influenced by Schoenberg, exploring beyond the more conventional uses of the 12-tone system. His more recent works, which include operas, ballets, symphonies, and chamber music, often reflect his left-wing political views. He settled in Italy in 1953, and has taken master classes in composition at the Salzburg Mozarteum since 1961.

heparin [heparin] A chemical substance (a polysaccharide) found in the mast cells of the liver, lungs, and intestinal mucosa, which prevents blood clotting. Its physiological importance is controversial, but its extracted and purified form is used as an anti-coagulant drug in medicine (eg in the prevention of thrombosis).

hepatitis *infectious hepatitis*

Hepburn, Audrey, originally **Eda van Heemstra** (1929–93) Actress and film star, born in Brussels, Belgium. She trained as a ballet dancer in Amsterdam, and at the Marie Rambert school in London, making her film and stage debuts in London in 1948. Noticed by the French writer Colette, she was given the lead in the Broadway production of her novel, *Gigi* (1951), and went on to win international acclaim for *Roman Holiday* (1953, Oscar), in which she starred with Gregory Peck. One of the most enchanting stars of the 1950s and 60s, her popular film roles included *Sabrina* (1954), *The Nun's Story* (1959), *Breakfast at Tiffany's* (1961), all Oscar nominations, and *My Fair Lady* (1964). Contrasting roles included *Two for the Road* (1967), and as the blind girl terrorized in *Wait Until Dark* (1967, Oscar nomination). She travelled extensively as a goodwill ambassador for UNICEF.

Hepburn, Katharine (Houghton) (1907–2003) Actress, born in Hartford, Connecticut, USA. She studied at Bryn Mawr College, PA, made her professional stage debut in 1928 in Baltimore, and from 1932 attained international fame as a strong character actress. Among many of her outstanding films was *Woman of the Year* (1942), which saw the beginning of a 25-year professional and personal relationship with co-star Spencer Tracy. She won Oscars for *Morning Glory* (1933), *Guess Who's Coming* *to Dinner?* (1967), *The Lion in Winter* (1968), and *On Golden Pond* (1981), and is also remembered for her role in *The African Queen* (1952). On Broadway she played Shakespearean roles in the 1950s, and enjoyed enormous success in the stage musical *Coco* (1969). In 1991 she published *Me: Stories of My Life*.

Hephaestus [hefeestus] In Greek mythology, a god of fire, associated with volcanic sites; then of the smithy and metalwork. Because of his marvellous creations, such as the shield of Achilles, he was worshipped as the god of craftsmen. He was the son of Hera, who was annoyed at his lameness and threw him out of heaven; he landed on Lemnos.

heptane C_7H_{16}. An alkane hydrocarbon with seven carbon atoms. There are nine structural isomers, most of which occur in the gasoline fraction of petroleum. The straight-chain compound, boiling point 98°C, n-heptane, $CH_3CH_2CH_2CH_2CH_2$-CH_2CH_3, is particularly bad for causing 'knocking' in petrol engines.

heptathlon A multi-event track-and-field competition discipline for women, consisting of seven events held over two consecutive days; (first day) 100 m hurdles, shot put, high jump, 200 m; (second day) long jump, javelin, and 800 m. It replaced the pentathlon in 1981.The world record of 7291 points was set by Jacqueline Joyner-Kersee (1962–) of the USA, at Seoul, South Korea, in 1988.

Hepworth, Dame (Jocelyn) Barbara (1903–75) Sculptor, born in Wakefield, West Yorkshire, N England, UK. She studied at the Leeds School of Art (where she befriended Henry Moore, a fellow student), the Royal College of Art, and in Italy. She married, first, the sculptor **John Skeaping** (1901–80), then (1933) the painter Ben Nicholson, who had a strong influence on her work. She was one of the foremost nonfigurative sculptors of her time, notable for the strength and formal discipline of her carving (as in *Contrapuntal Forms*, exhibited at the Festival of Britain, 1951). Her representational paintings and drawings are of equal power. She was made a dame in 1965.

Hera [heera] In Greek mythology, the daughter of Cronus and wife of Zeus, but a most independent and powerful goddess, probably illustrating the survival of pre-Hellenic cults of the mother-goddess. She was associated with Argos and hostile to Troy. The name means 'lady', and is the feminine form of Hero.

Heracles [herakleez], Lat **Hercules** A Greek hero, depicted as a strong man with lion-skin and club, and often represented as a comic on stage. He undertook Twelve Labours for Eurystheus of Argos: (1) to kill the Nemean Lion, (2) to kill the Hydra of Lerna, (3) to capture the Hind of Ceryneia, (4) to capture the Boar of Erymanthus, (5) to clean the Stables of Augeas, (6) to shoot the Birds of Stymphalus, (7) to capture the Cretan Bull, (8) to capture the Horses of Diomedes, (9) to steal the Girdle of the Amazon, (10) to capture the oxen of the giant Geryon, (11) to fetch the Apples of the Hesperides, (12) to capture Cerberus, the guardian of Hades. His wife Deianira killed him by mistake with a shirt smeared with the poison of Nessus; after immolation on a pyre he was received into Olympus, and became the subject of a cult. His name means 'Hera's glory'.

Heraclitus or **Heracleitos** [herakliytus] (?–460 BC) Greek philosopher, born in Ephesus. He became known as 'the obscure' and 'the riddler' because of his oracular style. Although only fragments of his writings survive, he seems to have thought that all things are composed of opposites (eg hot/cold, wet/dry). Because the opposites are constantly at strife with one another, all things are in perpetual change. Yet the change is governed by *logos* (Greek: reason), a principle of order and intelligibility. Fire is the ultimate constituent of the world, and the fire of the human soul is thus linked to the cosmic fire which virtuous souls eventually join.

Heraklion [heraklion], Gr **Iráklion**, Ital **Candia** 35°20N 25°08E, pop (2000e) 275 000. Administrative centre and capital town of Crete region (since 1971), S Greece; on N coast of Crete I; airfield; ferries to Piraeus; commercial harbour; leather, soap, tourism, agricultural trade; Church of St Titos; Cathedral of St Minas (19th-c); old city within Venetian walls (begun 1538), archaeological museum; Navy Week (Jun–Jul).

heraldry The granting and designing of pictorial devices (*arms*) originally used on the shields of knights in armour to identify them in battle. In the early 12th-c these devices became hereditary in Europe through the male line of descent, though with occasional modifications. The science of describing such devices is **blazonry**. Arms are regarded as insignia of honour, and their unauthorized display is subject to legal sanction in most European countries. It is regulated by the College of Arms in England and by the Court of the Lord Lyon King of Arms in Scotland (whose heraldic rules are by no means the same as England's).

Herat 34°20N 62°10E, pop (2001e) 161 700. Capital of Herat province, W Afghanistan, close to the Hari Rud; lies on the old trade route from Persia to India and caravan route from China to C Asia and Europe; birthplace of Ustad Kamal al-Din Bihzad; became part of a united Afghanistan (1881); Great Mosque (12th-c); textiles, carpets, weaving; market for dried fruits, nuts, wool.

herb A plant with a distinctive smell or taste, used to enhance the flavour and aroma of food. Herbs are usually grown in temperate climates (whereas spices are usually tropical). Some are often used for their medicinal properties, hence the speciality of the **herbalist**. In the USA the word is usually pronounced [erb], to distinguish it from herb [herb] referring to non-woody plants in general.

herbaceous plant Any non-woody plant which dies at the end of the growing season; often referred to simply as **herb**. Herbaceous perennials die back to ground level, but survive as underground organs such as bulbs or tubers, sending up new growth in the spring.

herbalism The use of herbs to prevent and cure illness; also called **herbal medicine** or **phytotherapy**. The treatment is based upon a holistic assessment of the patient, and uses whole plants, or parts of plants, rather than separating and purifying the active constituents. Plant derivatives may be highly active and concentrated in various parts of the plant. The season of the year and the time of day may affect the best time for gathering. These preparations are difficult to standardize, since they are complicated mixtures which may have hundreds of constituents. Nevertheless a computerized data bank is now available, and a pharmacopoeia has been produced by the British Herbal Medical Association. In some countries (eg Germany) most phytotherapists are medically qualified.

herb Bennet *avens*

Herbert (of Cherbury), Edward Herbert, Baron (1583–1648) English soldier, statesman, and philosopher, born in Eyton, Shropshire, WC England, UK, the brother of George Herbert. He studied at Oxford, was knighted at James I's coronation, became a member of the Privy Council, and was ambassador to France (1619). He is regarded as the founder of English deism. His main works are *De veritate* (1624, On Truth), *De religione Gentilium* (published 1663, On the Religion of the Gentiles), and his *Autobiography* (published 1764).

Herbert, George (1593–1633) Clergyman and poet, born at Montgomery Castle, Powys, E Wales, UK. He studied at Cambridge, where he was public orator (1619), and became an MP before entering the Church (1630), serving as parish priest of Bemerton, Wiltshire. Nearly all his surviving poems in English (he also wrote in Greek and Latin) were collected in *The Temple* (1633), and his chief prose work, *A Priest to the Temple*, was published in *Remains* (1652). He is now accepted as one of the greatest English metaphysical poets.

Herbert, Zbigniew [hairbairt, zhbignev] (1924–98) Poet, born in Lviv, W Ukraine (formerly Lwow, Poland). His first collection was *Struna swiatla* (1956, Chords of Light). Later volumes include *Studium przedmiotu* (1961, Study of the Object), *Pan Cogito* (1974, Mr Cogito), and *Raport z oblezonego miasta* (1983, Report from a Besieged City). He had also written plays which have been broadcast in Poland and abroad.

herbicide A chemical compound which kills weeds. **Nonselective herbicides** may be used to kill all vegetation before cultivation and planting begin. Once the crop has emerged, **selective herbicides** are used. These target the troublesome weeds and leave other weeds and the growing crop unharmed. There are no 'organic' herbicides. Organic systems rely on planned rotations, competitive crops, mulching, and mechanical means of weed control.

herbivore [herbivaw(r)] An animal that feeds on vegetation – a label used especially of the large plant-eating mammals, such as the ungulates. Its teeth are typically adapted for grinding plants, and its gut is adapted for digesting cellulose. Unlike *Carnivora*, which is a defined order of mammals, *Herbivora* is a descriptive term, encompassing many unrelated forms.

herb Paris A perennial growing to 40 cm/15 in (*Paris quadrifolia*), native to woodland in Europe and Asia; rhizomatous; four or more leaves in a single whorl near top of stem; flower 2·5–3·5 cm/1–1½ in, green, solitary, terminal, four sepals, four thread-like petals; berry black. (Family: Liliaceae.)

herb Robert An annual or biennial species of cranesbill (*Geranium robertianum*), growing to 50 cm/20 in; leaves with red stalks, palmately divided into deeply toothed lobes; flowers c.1 cm/0·4 in diameter, pink; fruit beaked; native to temperate Europe, Asia, and N Africa, and introduced elsewhere. (Family: Geraniaceae.)

Herculaneum [herkyulaynium] In Roman times, a prosperous town situated near Mt Vesuvius in SW Italy. It was destroyed completely in the volcanic eruption of AD 79 (now a world heritage site).

Hercules (astronomy) [herkyuleez] A constellation in the N sky, fifth-largest of all, but hard to recognize because its stars are faint. It contains the largest and brightest globular cluster in the N sky, M13.

Hercules (mythology) [herkyuleez] *Heracles*

hercules beetle A dark, shiny beetle, one of the largest in the world; males up to 17 cm/7 in long, females smaller; adults nocturnal. It belongs to the rhinoceros beetle group, in which the males have a slender, recurved horn on their heads. (Order: Coleoptera. Family: Scarabeidae.)

hercules emperor moth One of the largest known insects, with a wingspan up to 27 cm/10½ in; found in New Guinea and N Australia.

Herder, Johann Gottfried von (1744–1803) Critic and poet, born in Mohrungen, Germany. He studied at Königsberg, and there made the acquaintance of Kant. He was a teacher and pastor in Riga (1764–9), and met Goethe in Strasbourg (1769). He was appointed court preacher at Bückeburg (1770), and first preacher in Weimar (1776). His love for the songs of the people, for unsophisticated human nature, found expression in *Volkslieder* (1778–9, Folk Songs), a treatise on the influence of poetry on manners (1778), in oriental mythological tales, in parables and legends, in his version of the *Cid* (1805), and in several other works. The supreme importance of the historical method is recognized in a work on the origin of language (1772), and especially in his masterpiece, *Ideen zur Geschichte der Menschheit* (1784–91, Outlines of a Philosophy of the History of Man), which is remarkable for its anticipations of evolutionary theories. He is best remembered for the influence he exerted on Goethe and the growing German Romanticism.

hereditary diseases *genetically determined diseases*

heredity *genetics*

Hereford [hereferd] 52°04N 2°43W, pop (2000e) 51 500. Administrative centre of Herefordshire (unitary authority from 1998), WC England, UK; on the R Wye at the centre of a rich farming region; railway; foodstuffs, engineering, cattle (Herefords), hops, cider; 11th-c Cathedral of St Mary and St Ethelbert, with the largest chained library in the world and the *Mappa Mundi*, a mediaeval map of the world; Three Choirs Festival in rotation with Gloucester and Worcester (Sep); football league team, Hereford United.

Hereford and Worcester [hereferd, wuster] pop (2001e) 717 000; area 3926 sq km/1516 sq mi. County of WC England, UK; created 1974 from former counties of Herefordshire and Worcestershire; Herefordshire unitary authority from 1998; bounded W and SW by Wales; drained by the Severn, Wye, and Teme Rivers; Malvern Hills rise SW of Worcester; county town, Worcester; chief towns include Hereford, Kidderminster, Malvern, Evesham; horticulture (hops, soft fruit, vegetables), especially in Vale of Evesham; cattle (Herefords), cider production, high technology, food processing.

heresy False doctrine, or the formal denial of doctrine defined as part of a particular faith. If consciously adhered to, heresy entails excommunication, and in certain countries has been punishable as a crime. Total heresy or the rejection of all faith is termed **apostasy**.

Hereward, known as **Hereward the Wake** (?–c.1080) Anglo-Saxon thegn who returned from exile to lead the last organized Anglo-Saxon resistance against the Norman invaders. In 1070 he sacked Peterborough with the aid of a Danish fleet. He held the Isle of Ely against William the Conqueror for nearly a year (1070–1), then disappeared from history, and entered mediaeval outlaw legend as a celebrated opponent of the forces of injustice.

Hergé [herzhay], Fr [airzhay], pseudonym of **Georges Rémi** (1907–83) Strip cartoonist, the creator of 'Tin-Tin' the boy detective, born in Etterbeek, C Belgium. He drew his first strip, *Totor*, for a boy scouts' weekly in 1926. He created the *Tin-Tin* strip for the children's supplement of the newspaper *Le Vingtième Siècle*, using the pseudonym Hergé, a phonetic version of his initials, RG.

herm *term*

Herman, Woody, popular name of **Woodrow Charles Herman** (1913–87) Bandleader, alto saxophonist, and jazz clarinettist, born in Milwaukee, Wisconsin, USA. He was a member of the band led by Isham Jones, but when this broke up (1936) he took certain key members as the nucleus of his own first band, the Woodchoppers, which became noted for the way it blended saxophones (the 'Woodchopper's Ball' became his theme tune). The Herman Orchestra (or 'Herd') was one of the very few big bands to survive intact beyond the 1950s, continuing to tour throughout the 1970s and 80s, and nurturing the talents of scores of fine jazz players.

Hermandszoon, Jakob *Arminius, Jacobus*

hermaphrodite An animal or plant having both male and female reproductive organs. The male organs may mature before the female (*protandrous*), after the female (*protogynous*), or simultaneously (*synchronous*). Species in which both sets of organs mature simultaneously often have mechanisms that prevent self-fertilization.

Hermaphroditus [hermafrodiytus] In Greek mythology, a minor god with bisexual characteristics, the son of Hermes and Aphrodite. The nymph Salmacis, unloved by him, prayed to be united with him; this was granted by combining them in one body.

hermeneutics [hermenyootiks] **1** The theory of the interpretation and understanding of texts. Though its origins lie in ancient Greek philosophy, hermeneutics received fresh impetus in 18th-c discussions of the problems of biblical interpretation posed by the development of historical-critical method. Schleiermacher shifted attention from the formulation of rules of interpretation to the question of how it is possible to understand the written discourse of different cultures and ages. The discussion was carried further by Dilthey and, in the 20th-c, by Heidegger and especially Gadamer. During this time the discussion expanded to embrace all aspects of the understanding of texts and entered many fields, including literary theory, the social sciences, social philosophy, and aesthetics.

2 In psychology, the term has been applied to psychological methods which go beyond mere experimentation in an attempt to understand the reason behind human actions.

Hermes (astronomy) [**hermeez**] An asteroid which came within 760 000 km/475 000 mi of Earth in 1937, at that time a record. It was only a few km in diameter, and was lost to view within a few days.

Hermes (mythology) [**hermeez**] In Greek mythology, the ambassador of the gods, the son of Zeus and Maia; depicted with herald's staff (the *caduceus*), and winged sandals. He is variously associated with stones, commerce, roads, cookery, and thieving; also arts such as oratory. He was the inventor of the lyre, and, as **Hermes Psychopompos**, the guide of souls.

hermetic A term used to describe obscure and difficult poetry, as of the Symbolist school. The allusion is to the mythical Hermes Trismegistus (the Egyptian god Thoth), the supposed author of mystic doctrines actually composed in the Neoplatonic tradition c.3rd-c AD. Hermeticism was influential in the Renaissance, after the translation of these texts by Marsilio Ficino (1433–99). More broadly, the term denotes poetry in which the language and imagery are subjective, and where the suggestive power of the sound of words is as important as the words themselves.

Hermitage A major art gallery in St Petersburg, Russia, built in the 18th–19th-c to house the art collection of the tsars, and opened to the public in 1852. The complex now includes the Winter Palace, built for Tsarina Elizabeth Petrovna by Bartolomeo Rastrelli (1754–62). After the deposition of the tsar, this became the headquarters of Kerensky's provisional government, but was stormed by the Bolsheviks (Nov 1917). It now contains over 3 million works of art, and almost 400 rooms.

hermit crab A crab-like crustacean which uses an empty snail shell as a portable refuge covering its soft abdomen; body typically asymmetrical to fit inside spiral shells; it changes shells as it grows; common in shallow coastal waters. (Class: Malacostraca. Order: Decapoda.)

hernia The protrusion of tissue from its natural site through an adjacent orifice or tissue space. Examples are *inguinal*, *femoral*, and *umbilical* herniae, in which abdominal contents such as intestines push through weak sites in the abdominal wall; the herniae emerge as externally protruding masses in the groin, over the upper thigh, and at the navel, respectively. Umbilical herniae are common in babies, and resolve within one to two years. The blood supply of a hernia may be imperilled and lead to death of part of the contents, such as a length of intestine; this is a dangerous complication, and demands urgent surgical attention. Internal herniation also occurs, for example, when part of the stomach enters the lower chest through an aperture in the diaphragm. This is a common defect, which gives rise to heartburn in a minority of cases.

Hero of Alexandria (1st-c) Greek mathematician and inventor. He devised many machines, among them a fire engine, a water organ, coin-operated devices, and the *aeolipile*, the earliest known steam engine. He showed that the angle of incidence in optics is equal to the angle of reflection, and devised the formula for expressing the area of a triangle in terms of its sides.

Hero and Leander [**heeroh, leeander**] A Greek legend first found in the Roman poet, Ovid. Two lovers lived on opposite sides of the Hellespont; Hero was the priestess of Aphrodite at Sestos, and Leander, who lived at Abydos, swam across each night guided by her light. When this was extinguished in a storm, he was drowned, and Hero committed suicide by throwing herself into the sea.

Herod [**herod**], known as **the Great** (c.73–4 BC) King of Judea, the younger son of the Idumaean chieftain, Antipater. He owed his initial appointment as Governor of Galilee (47 BC) to Julius Caesar, his elevation to the kingship of Judea (40 BC) to Marcus Antonius, and his retention in that post after Actium (31 BC) to Octavian, later Augustus. Judea was annexed by Rome in 6 BC. Besides being a loyal and efficient Roman client king, who ruthlessly kept all his subjects in check, he was also an able and far-sighted administrator who did much to develop the economic potential of his kingdom, founding cities, and promoting agricultural projects. Life at court was marked by constant and often bloody infighting between his sister, his various wives, and their many offspring. Undoubtedly he was cruel, and this is reflected in the Gospel account of the Massacre of the Innocents.

Herod Agrippa I [**herod agripa**] (10 BC–AD 44) King of Judaea (41–4), the grandson of Herod the Great. Reared at the court of the Emperor Augustus, Agrippa's early contacts with the imperial family stood him in good stead later on. Caligula gave him two-thirds of the former kingdom of Herod the Great, while Claudius added the remaining third, the Judaean heartland (41). Loved by the Jews, despite being a Roman appointee, and an active Hellenizer, he was no friend to the Christians, executing St James and imprisoning St Peter.

Herod Agrippa II [**herod agripa**] (c.27–c.93) King of Chalcis (49/50–53), ruler of the Ituraean principality (53–c.93), the son of Herod Agrippa I. He was not permitted by Rome to succeed to his father's Judaean kingdom in 44, but was given various minor territories to the N, mostly Arab. A supporter of Rome in the Jewish War (66–70), he was rewarded for it afterwards with grants of land in Judaea and public honours in Rome. It was before him that St Paul made his defence and was found innocent.

Herod Antipas [**herod antipas**] (?–AD 39) The son of Herod the Great and ruler (tetrarch) of Galilee and Peraea (4–39), after Herod's death. An able client of the Romans, he enjoyed an especially good relationship with the Emperor Tiberius, but fell foul of his successor, Caligula, largely through the machinations of his nephew, Herod Agrippa. In the Christian tradition he looms large as the capricious murderer of John the Baptist.

Herodotos or **Herodotus** [**herodotus**] (c.485–425 BC) Greek historian, born in Halicarnassus, Asia Minor. He travelled widely in Asia Minor and the Middle East, and in 443 BC joined the colony of Thurii, from where he visited Sicily and Lower Italy. On his travels, he collected material for his great narrative history, which gave a record of the wars between the Greeks and the Persians. Cicero called him 'the father of history'.

heroic couplet A pair of rhymed 10-syllable lines, usually in iambic pentameter. First found in Old French, then Chaucer, it was used by Spenser, Shakespeare, Jonson, Donne, Walker, Denham, and Oldham. Thereafter it became the staple of Augustan satiric poetry (Dryden and Pope), and is often revived on account of its pointedness and economy: 'A fop her passion, but her prize a sot;/ Alive, ridiculous, and dead, forgot' (Pope). In the 19th-c Byron, Keats, Shelley, Browning, Swinburne, and William Morris all made use of it. In the 20th-c Nabokov used the heroic couplet in his anti-novel, *Pale Fire* (1962).

heroin or **diamorphine** A derivative of morphine developed in 1896, and originally launched as a non-addictive narcotic. It was soon found to be extremely addictive. Because of its extreme potency it is used to ease the severe pain that can accompany terminal illness, but even this medical use is banned in the USA. It is widely abused.

heron A wading bird related to the bittern; worldwide (mainly tropical); flies with neck retracted, not extended; some feathers ('powder-down') break down to form a powder used in preening. There are three main groups: **day herons** or 'typical herons' (including egrets), **night herons**, and **tiger herons**. (Family: Ardeidae, 64 species.)

Herophilus [**herofilus**] (c.335–c.280 BC) Greek anatomist, founder of the school of anatomy in Alexandria, born in Chalcedon. He was the first to dissect the human body to compare it with that of other animals. He described the brain, liver, spleen, sexual organs, and nervous system, dividing the latter into sensory and motor.

herpes labialis *cold sore*

herpes simplex [**herpeez simpleks**] A viral infection which causes a rash, followed by the appearance of small blisters containing fluid, which ulcerate and may become infected. There are two types of the virus. **Type 1** affects the lips and mouth. **Type 2** affects the genital region, and is sexually transmitted.

Recurrent attacks are common, between which the virus lies dormant.

herpesvirus [herpeezviyruhs] A spheroidal virus, contained within an outer envelope c.150 nm in diameter. It stores genetic information in a double strand of deoxyribonucleic acid. Herpesviruses are associated with a variety of systemic diseases which often remain latent for long periods between outbreaks. It includes the causative agent of chickenpox.

herpes zoster *shingles*

Herrick, Robert (1591–1674) Poet, born in London, UK. He studied at Cambridge, was ordained in 1623, and worked in Devon, until deprived of his living as a royalist in 1647. His writing, both secular and religious, is mainly collected in *Hesperides* (1648), and includes such well-known lyrics as 'Cherry ripe'. He resumed his living after the Restoration.

herring Surface-living, marine fish (*Clupea harengus*) abundant in the N Atlantic and Arctic, ranging S to Portugal (E) and Cape Hatteras (W); body length up to 40 cm/16 in; colour deep blue on back, underside silvery white; feeds on plankton, especially crustaceans; prey to many larger fish, seabirds, and marine mammals; supports important commercial fisheries, being sold fresh, smoked as kippers or bloaters, or preserved in salt or vinegar; first-year herring sold as whitebait; the name is also used for several other herring-like species. A combination of over-fishing and natural causes led to a collapse of stock in the North Sea in 1965–77, culminating in closure of the North Sea fishery in 1978–82. This coincided with a depletion of stock throughout the N Atlantic. During the 1980s, stock recovered significantly, but during the 1990s, there was increasing international concern over reduced stocks, and controversy over fishing quotas. (Family: Clupeidae.)

herring gull A large gull common in the N hemisphere (*Larus argentatus*); legs usually pink (sometimes yellow); head white; bill yellow with red spot below tip; considered a pest and controlled in some areas. (Family: Laridae.)

Herriot, James, pseudonym of **James Alfred Wight** (1916–95) Veterinary surgeon and writer, born in Glasgow, W Scotland, UK. Beginning in the 1970s, he brought the vet's world to the notice of the public with a number of best-selling books, such as *It Shouldn't Happen to a Vet* and *Vet in a Spin*, as well as several compilations and children's books. Feature films and television series made his work known all over the world, especially the television series *All Creatures Great and Small* (1977–80). The stories prompted a thriving tourist industry based on 'Herriot country', and transformed the public image of his profession, making veterinary medicine one of the most competitive university subjects. In 1992 he was the first recipient of the Chiron Award, created by the British Veterinary Association for exceptional service to the profession.

Herschel, Sir (Frederick) William [hershl], originally **Friedrich Wilhelm Herschel** (1738–1822) Astronomer, born in Hanover, NC Germany. He moved to England to escape the French occupation of Hanover (1757), became a music teacher (1766), then took up astronomy and the construction of ever more powerful reflecting telescopes. He discovered the planet Uranus in 1781, and became famous overnight, being appointed private astronomer to George III. He continued his research at Slough, S England, assisted by his sister Caroline and his son John, adding greatly to knowledge of the Solar System, of the Milky Way, and of the nebulae. He found two satellites of Saturn, extensively observed double stars, and produced a notable star catalogue. He was knighted in 1816. His house in Bath has been restored as a museum.

Hertford [hah(r)tferd] 51°48N 0°05W, pop (2000e) 23 500. County town in Hertfordshire, SE England, UK; on R Lea, 32 km/20 mi N of London; railway; plastics, brewing, engineering, printing; Hertford Castle (12th-c); Waltham Abbey (20 km/12 mi SE).

Hertfordshire [hah(r)tferdsheer] pop (2001e) 1 034 000; area 1634 sq km/631 sq mi. County of SE England, UK; N of Greater London; drained by the Colne and Lea Rivers and the Grand Union Canal; county town, Hertford; chief towns include St Albans, Harpenden, Welwyn Garden City; wheat, cattle, horticulture, brewing, paper, printing, electronics, pharmaceuticals, aerospace.

Hertz, Heinrich (Rudolf) (1857–1894) Physicist, born in Hamburg, N Germany. He studied under Kirchhoff and Helmholtz in Berlin, and became professor at Bonn in 1889. His main work was on electromagnetic waves (1887), and he was the first to broadcast and receive radio waves. The unit of frequency is named after him.

hertz SI unit of frequency; symbol *Hz*; named after Heinrich Hertz; defined as the number of complete cycles per second; applicable to all wave and periodic phenomena.

Hertzog, J(ames) B(arry) M(unnik) [hertzokh] (1866–1942) South African statesman and prime minister (1924–39), born in Wellington, Cape Colony, SW South Africa. He studied law at Stellenbosch and Amsterdam, became a Boer general (1899–1902), and was minister of justice (1910) in the first Union government. He founded the Nationalist Party in 1914, advocating complete South African independence, and in World War 1 opposed co-operation with Britain. As premier, in coalition with Labour (1924–9), and with Smuts in a United Party (1933–9), he renounced his earlier secessionism, but on the outbreak of World War 2 declared for neutrality, was defeated, lost office, and in 1940 retired.

Herzl, Theodor [hertsl] (1860–1904) Zionist leader, born in Budapest, Hungary. He trained as a lawyer in Vienna, then became a journalist and playwright. After reporting the Dreyfus trial (1894), he was converted to Zionism, and in the pamphlet *Der Judenstaat* (1896, The Jewish State) he called for a world council to discuss the question of a homeland for the Jews, convened the first Zionist Congress at Basel (1897), and became the first president of the World Zionist Organization.

Herzog, Werner [hertzog], originally **Werner Stipetic** (1942–) Film director, screenwriter, and producer, born in Sachrang, SE Germany. He made numerous shorts in the 1960s, and became recognized as a leading member of the New Cinema in Germany with his features *Aguirre, der Zorn Gottes* (1973, Aguirre, Wrath of God) and the story of Kaspar Hauser (1975). His treatment of *Nosferatu, the Vampyre* (1979) reflected the German silent film Expressionists of the 1920s, but his general themes are metaphysical in character, often with remoteness in time or location, as in *Where the Green Ants Dream* (1984). Later films include *Scream of Stone* (1991) and *My Best Fiend* (1999).

Hertzsprung–Russell diagram *p.714*

Heselrig, Sir Arthur *Haselrig, Arthur*

Heseltine, Michael (Ray Dibdin), Lord [heseltiyn] (1933–) British statesman, born in Swansea, SC Wales, UK. He studied at Oxford, and built up a publishing business before becoming an MP in 1966. After holding several junior posts, he was appointed secretary of state for the environment (1979–83), then defence secretary (1983–6). He resigned from the government in dramatic fashion by walking out of a cabinet meeting over the issue of the takeover of Westland helicopters. He stood unsuccessfully as a candidate in the leadership contest following Mrs Thatcher's resignation (1990). His posts under John Major included environment secretary (1990–2), President of the Board of Trade (1992–5), and first secretary and deputy prime minister (1995–7). He was made a Companion of Honour in 1997, and he received a peerage in 2001.

Hesiod [heesiod] (fl.8th-c BC) Poet, born in Ascra, Greece, at the foot of Mt Helicon. One of the earliest known Greek poets, he is best known for two works. *Works and Days* exalts honest labour and denounces corrupt and unjust judges. *Theogony* contains advice as to the days, lucky or unlucky, for the farmer's work. His poetry is didactic. *Works and Days* gives an invaluable picture of the Greek village community in the 8th-c BC, and the *Theogony* is of importance to the comparative mythologist.

Hesperides [hesperideez] In Greek mythology, the daughters of the evening star (**Hesper**), who guard the Golden Apples together with the dragon, Ladon. They sing as they circle the

Hertzsprung–Russell diagram

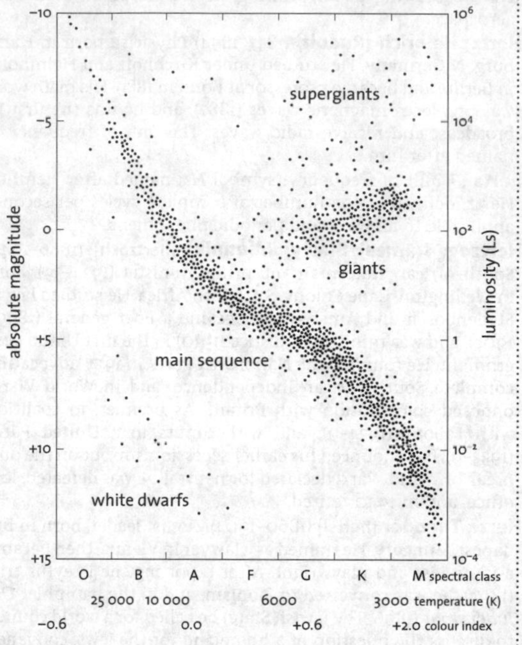

[**hert**shprung] The graphical representation of the correlation between the spectrum and luminosity for a sample of stars, discovered independently by Danish astronomer Ejnar Hertzsprung (1873–1967) and US astronomer Henry Norris Russell (1877–1957). The diagram achieves its astrophysical significance when the plotted points are restricted to a particular sample (such as all the members of a star cluster) or a particular type (such as one class of variable star). It then effectively graphs surface temperature against luminosity. In the diagram, normal stars that are burning hydrogen form a broad band known as the *main sequence*. Evolved stars clump together as red giants. Almost defunct stars are grouped as white dwarfs. The theory of stellar evolution explains the main features of the diagram.

tree, which was given by Gaia to Hera as a wedding-present. When Heracles had to fetch the apples, he either killed the dragon, or sent it to sleep, or, more usually, persuaded Atlas to get them for him while he took over Atlas's function of holding up the sky.

Hess, Dame Myra (1890–1965) Pianist, born in London, UK. She studied at the Royal Academy of Music, and was an immediate success on her first public appearance in 1907. During World War 2 she organized the lunchtime concerts in the National Gallery, for which she became a dame in 1941.

Hess, (Walter Richard) Rudolf (1894–1987) German politician, Hitler's deputy as Nazi Party leader, born in Alexandria, N Egypt. Educated at Bad Godesberg, he fought in World War 1, then studied at Munich. He joined the Nazi Party in 1920, and became Hitler's close friend and (in 1934) deputy. In 1941, on the eve of Germany's attack on Russia, he flew alone to Scotland to plead the cause of a negotiated Anglo-German peace. He was temporarily imprisoned in the Tower of London, then placed under psychiatric care near Aldershot. At the Nuremberg Trials (1946) he was sentenced to life imprisonment, and remained in Spandau prison, Berlin (after 1966, as the only prisoner) until his death.

Hess, Walter Rudolf (1881–1973) Physiologist, born in Frauenfeld, N Switzerland. As professor of physiology at Zürich (1917–51) he did much important research on the nervous system, and developed methods of stimulating localized areas of the brain by means of needle electrodes. He shared the 1949 Nobel Prize for Physiology or Medicine.

Hesse [**he**suh], Ger **Hessen** pop (2000e) 5 891 000; area 21 114 sq km/8151 sq mi. A state formed in 1945 from the former Prussian province of Hesse-Nassau; wine produced along Rhine valley; capital, Wiesbaden; chief towns, Frankfurt (am Main), Kassel, Darmstadt.

Hesse, Hermann [**he**suh] (1877–1962) Novelist and poet, born in Calw, SW Germany. He was a bookseller and antiquarian in Basel (1895–1902), and published his first novel in 1904. His works include *Rosshalde* (1914), *Siddhartha* (1922), *Steppenwolf* (1927), and *Das Glasperlenspiel* (1945, The Glass Bead Game). He was awarded the Nobel Prize for Literature in 1946. From 1911 he lived in Switzerland. His psychological and mystical concerns made him something of a cult figure after his death.

Hestia [**hes**tia] Greek goddess of the hearth, the daughter of Cronus and Rhea. She has two functions: looking after the family fire, and the public cult of the communal hearth.

Heston, Charlton, originally **John Charles Carter** (1923–) Actor, born in Evanston, Illinois, USA. He made his film debut in an amateur production of *Peer Gynt* (1941) and, after air force war service and further theatre experience, his Broadway debut in *Antony and Cleopatra* (1947). In Hollywood from 1950, he portrayed historic or heroic roles in such epics as *The Ten Commandments* (1956), *Ben Hur* (1959, Oscar) and *El Cid* (1961). He displayed his potential as a character actor in *Touch of Evil* (1958), *The War Lord* (1965), and *Will Penny* (1967). Frequently returning to the stage, he also directs for film and television, including *Antony and Cleopatra* (1972, film) and *A Man for All Seasons* (1988, television). Later film appearances include *True Lies* (1994) and *Any Given Sunday* (1999). He has played a prominent role in US arts, theatre, and film organizations, and became president of the US National Rifle Association in 1998. He received the inaugural Charlton Heston Prize in 2003, awarded by the American Film Institute to honour acting talent.

heterochromatin [heterohkrohmatin] Originally identified as those parts of the chromosome showing an excessive degree of condensation and compaction and heavier staining properties during the process of nuclear division, as distinct from **euchromatin**, which shows lower condensation and lighter staining. This is especially evident during chromosome condensation in cell division. Heterochromatin is particularly abundant around the centromeric regions of chromosomes, which are deficient in coding genes and rich in repetitive DNA sequences. Heterochromatin is now generally used to describe any region of condensed, transcriptionally inactive chromatin.

Heteroptera [hetero**p**tera] A large order of insects comprising the true bugs; body typically depressed, forewings usually leathery at base and membranous at tip; mouthparts modified for piercing and sucking; feeding on plants, fungi, or as predators; life-cycle without pupal stage; c.35 000 species, including many crop pests and disease carriers. (Class: Insecta.)

heterosexism A belief which regards attraction to the opposite sex as the only legitimate form of sexual expression. That such a term has appeared indicates the strength of the debate over what is to be regarded as 'normal' or 'acceptable' sexuality.

heterosis [hetero**h**sis] *F*, *hybrid*

Heuneberg, the [**hoy**nuhberg] A prehistoric hillfort of the Hallstatt Iron Age on a spur overlooking the R Danube near Binzwagen, Württemberg, S Germany. Of five building periods covering the 7th-c to the late 5th-c BC, the second (early 6th-c) is notable for its spectacular defensive wall of unbaked clay bricks, 3–4 m/10–13 ft high with square bastions, clearly constructed under Greek influence.

heuristic Any set of rules whose application to a complex problem will tend to yield satisfactory if not optimal results (in contrast to an algorithm). 'Control the centre of the board' is a heuristic for playing chess.

Heuss, Theodor [hoys] (1884–1963) First president of the Federal Republic of Germany (1949–59), born in Brackenheim, SW Germany. He studied at Munich and Berlin, became editor of the political magazine *Hilfe* (1905–12), professor at the Berlin College of Political Science (1920–33), and an MP (1924–8, 1930–2). A prolific author and journalist, he wrote two books denouncing Hitler, and when the latter came to power in 1933, he was dismissed from his chair and his books publicly burned. In 1946 he became a founder member of the Free Democratic Party, and helped to draft the new federal constitution.

Hewish, Antony (1924–) Radio astronomer, born in Fowey, Cornwall, SW England, UK. He studied at Cambridge and spent his career there, becoming professor of radio astronomy (1971–89). In 1967 he began studies, using a radio telescope of novel design, on the scintillation ('twinkling') of quasars (a class of radio stars). This led him and his student Susan Jocelyn (Burnell) Bell (1943–) to discover the first radio stars emitting radio signals in regular pulses; named as pulsars, many others have since been discovered. Hewish shared the Nobel Prize for Physics in 1974 with his former teacher, Sir Martin Ryle.

Hewitt, Patricia (Hope) (1948–) British stateswoman, born in Canberra, Australia. Educated in Canberra, Cambridge, and Oxford, she worked in a number of voluntary organizations before becoming general secretary of the National Council for Civil Liberties (1974–83). She was policy co-ordinator and press secretary to the Labour leader Neil Kinnock (1988–9) before becoming deputy director of the Institute for Public Policy Research (1989–94). Elected as Labour MP for Leicester West in 1997, she became minister for trade and industry (1997–8), then economic secretary to the Treasury (1998–9), and information technology minister (1999–2001). In 2001 she became trade and industry secretary and minister for women.

Hewitt, Lleyton (1981–) Tennis player, born in Adelaide, South Australia. He turned professional in 1998, and made his Davis Cup debut in 1999. He won the Queen's Club Championship three years in succession (2000–2), the US Open singles title (2001), and the ATP Tour World Championships (2001, 2002), becoming the youngest man to conclude a year (2001) as the world Number 1 ranked player. In 2002 he won the Wimbledon singles title. At the beginning of 2004 he had a world ranking of Number 16.

Hewson, John (1946–) Australian politician and economist, born in Sydney, New South Wales, SE Australia. He studied at the University of Sydney and Johns Hopkins University, USA, worked as a consultant to the International Monetary Fund and to a range of business and industrial concerns, and became professor of economics at the University of New South Wales (1978–87). He entered federal politics in 1987, and was shadow minister for finance (1988–9) and shadow treasurer (1989–90), becoming leader of the Liberal Party in 1990 when Andrew Peacock lost the federal election. He was a strong advocate of neoclassical economics. In 1993, to the surprise of many, the Liberal Party lost their fifth successive federal election. Hewson was replaced as leader in 1994, and served as shadow minister for industry in 1994–5.

hexachlorophene [heksaklorofeen] $C_{13}H_6Cl_6O_2$. A white powder with antiseptic properties, widely used in toilet preparations.

hexadecanoic acid *palmitic acid*

hexadecimal coding A number notation using the number base 16. The 16 individual characters are 0–9, and A–F inclusive, representing decimal 10 to decimal 15 respectively. The notation is widely used in computer applications, where it provides a convenient means of representing binary numbers.

hexane C_6H_{14}. An alkane hydrocarbon with six carbon atoms. There are five structural isomers. The straight-chain compound, n-hexane, $CH_3CH_2CH_2CH_2CH_2CH_3$, has boiling point 69°C.

hexanedioic acid *adipic acid*

Hexi Corridor [huhshee], also **Gansu** or **Kansu Corridor** Natural corridor from C China through Gansu province to Xinjiang Uighur autonomous region; length c.1200 km/750 mi; a major part of the ancient Silk Road; scene of numerous battles, from 3rd-c BC.

Heyer, Georgette [hayer] (1902–74) Writer, born in London, UK. She studied at Westminster College, London, married in 1925, and travelled in East Africa and Yugoslavia until 1929. Her early work includes historical novels, and fictional studies of real figures in crisis, such as William I. An outstanding authority on the Regency period, she had success with *Regency Buck* (1935), and later novels. She also wrote modern comedy detective novels, such as *Death in the Stocks* (1935), and historical thrillers.

Heyerdahl, Thor [hiyerdahl] (1914–2002) Anthropologist, born in Larvik, S Norway. After studying at Oslo, he served with the free Norwegian forces in World War 2. In 1947 he set out to prove, by sailing a balsa raft (the *Kon-Tiki*) from Peru to Tuamotu I in the S Pacific, that the Peruvian Indians could have settled in Polynesia. His success in the venture, and his archaeological expedition to Easter I, won him popular fame and several awards. In 1970 he sailed from Morocco to the West Indies in a papyrus boat, *Ra II*, and made the journey from Iraq to Djibouti in a reed boat, the *Tigris*, in 1977–8. Among his many publications are *The Maldive Mystery* (1986), *Pyramids of Tucume* (1995, jointly), and *Green was the Earth on the Seventh Day* (1996).

Heyhoe Flint, Rachel [hayhoh flint] (1939–) British cricketer. She studied at Dartford College of Physical Education and became a PE teacher. A member of the Women's England Cricket Team (1960–83, captain 1966–77), she captained England to victory in the first women's World Cup in 1973. In the 1976 Test against Australia, she scored 179, a world record for England and the world's fourth highest score by a woman in tests. She also played for the England women's hockey team as goalkeeper in 1964. She later became a journalist and public relations consultant.

Heysel stadium [hayzl] A football stadium in Brussels, Belgium; scene of a tragedy during the European Champions' Cup Final between Liverpool and Juventus (Turin) in 1985, when a wall and safety fence collapsed during a riot, killing 39 and injuring over 200. After that event, English football clubs were not allowed to play matches in Europe for several years – a ban which began to be lifted in 1990.

Heywood, Thomas (c.1574–1641) Playwright and poet, born in Lincolnshire, EC England, UK. He studied at Cambridge, was writing plays by 1596, and by 1633 had shared in the composition of 220 plays, and written 24 of his own, notably his domestic tragedy, *A Woman Killed with Kindness* (1607). He also wrote many pageants, tracts, treatises, and translations.

Hezekiah [hezekiya] Biblical character, King of Judah in the late 8th-c BC (precise dating much disputed), renowned for his religious reforms, including the re-establishment of Temple worship in Jerusalem (2 *Chron* 29–32), and for his political attempts to obtain independence from Assyrian domination (2 *Kings* 18–20; *Isa* 36–9).

hiatus hernia [hiyaytus] A protrusion of the upper part of the stomach into the chest through the hole in the diaphragm that allows the oesophagus to pass into the abdomen. It is a common condition, and most individuals affected are untroubled. However, it predisposes to a reflux of acid from the stomach into the oesophagus, which lacks a protective lining and becomes inflamed. The result is heartburn, felt as a burning pain in the lower chest.

Hiawatha [hiyawotha], Indian name **Heowenta** (16th-c) Legendary Mohawk leader, born in present-day New York State, USA. Although he is known only through Iroquois mythology and legend, it is now generally accepted that he was a real person who was influential in founding the Five Nations League, or Long House – an alliance of five (later six) Iroquois tribes that ended inter-tribal feuding from c.1550, or earlier, to

1775. Longfellow used Hiawatha's name for the hero of his poem (1855), but set the action in Minnesota, and used only elements of the legendary Hiawatha and other Indian stories for his essentially Romantic tale.

Hibbert, Eleanor (Alice Burford) (1906–93) Novelist, born in London, UK. She was a prolific writer of romantic novels, writing under several pseudonyms. She began with **Eleanor Burford** (*Daughter of Anna*, 1941), and under the name of **Jean Plaidy** wrote over 40 historical novels, beginning with *Together They Ride* (1945). Her other pseudonyms were **Elbur Ford**, beginning with *The Flesh and the Devil* (1950), **Kathleen Kellow** (*Danse Macabre*, 1952), **Ellalice Tate** (*Queen of Diamonds*, 1958), **Victoria Holt** (*Mistress of Mellyn*, 1961), and **Philippa Carr** (*The Miracle at St Bruno's*, 1972).

hibernation A strategy for passing the cold winter period in a torpid or resting state, found in mammals and some other animals. Metabolism is reduced, and the animal enters a deep sleep, surviving on food reserves stored in its body during a favourable summer period. The similar strategy for surviving a hot, dry summer is known as **aestivation**.

hibiscus An annual, perennial, or shrub native to warm regions; flowers often very large and showy, 5-petalled, the stamens united into a central column. It is best known as a decorative plant with many species grown as ornamentals, but some also provide useful fibres and edible fruits. (Genus: *Hibiscus*, species 300. Family: Malvaceae.)

hiccup / hiccough An involuntary contraction of the diaphragm causing an intake of air which is halted by spasm (closure) of the glottis, thereby producing a sharp, characteristic, inspiratory sound. Its cause is unknown, but there are many folk-remedies, such as drinking vinegar, or drinking from the 'wrong side of the glass'. The standard medical treatment is the administration of chlorpromazine.

Hickock, Wild Bill *Calamity Jane*

hickory A tall deciduous tree, sometimes with shaggy bark, native to E Asia and E North America; leaves pinnately divided into finely toothed leaflets; flowers small, green, lacking petals; males in catkins, females in clusters; nut 4-valved, edible. (Genus: *Carya*, 25 species. Family: Juglandaceae.)

Hicks, Sir John Richard (1904–89) Economist, born in Leamington Spa, Warwickshire, C England, UK. He studied at Oxford, taught at the London School of Economics (1926–35), and was professor of political economy at Manchester (1938–46) and Oxford (1952–65). He wrote a classic book on the conflict between business-cycle theory and equilibrium theory (*Value and Capital*, 1939), and other works include *A Theory of Economic History* (1969) and *Causality in Economics* (1979). He shared the 1972 Nobel Prize for Economics.

Hidatsa [hidatsa] American Plains Indians, speaking a Siouan language, living in villages along the Missouri R in the 18th-c; an offshoot group were the Siouan Crow. They later joined with the Mandan and Arikara (the 'Three Affiliated Tribes') to defend themselves against the Dakota. In 1868 they were settled by the US government on Fort Berthold Reservation in N Dakota.

hidden curriculum A term developed by sociologists of education to describe the unwritten, informal code of conduct to which children are expected to conform in the classroom. Children are said to be rewarded not only for learning their subject curriculum but appearing to do so with enthusiasm, alertness, and deference to and respect for authority. In this way education imparts not only formal knowledge but an understanding of how to act 'properly' in wider society.

Hideyoshi, Toyotomi [hideyoshee] (1536–98) The second of the three great historical unifiers of Japan, between Nobunaga and Ieyasu Tokugawa, sometimes called 'the Napoleon of Japan'. Unusually, he was of peasant origin, an ordinary soldier who rose to become Nobunaga's foremost general. Between Nobunaga's death (1582) and 1590 he established his overlordship of Japan, being appointed regent in 1585. His law forbade all except samurai to carry swords (1588), and he banned Christianity for political reasons (1597). His armies invaded Korea (1592–8), but withdrew after his death at Fushimi Castle, Kyoto.

hieroglyphics *see panel*

hi-fi *high fidelity sound system*

Higgins, Alex(ander Gordon), nickname **Hurricane Higgins** (1949–) Snooker player, born in Belfast, NE Northern Ireland, UK. He had a tempestuous career after becoming the youngest world champion in 1972, at age 23. A former trainee jockey, he became a professional snooker player in 1971, and won the world title at the first attempt. He won the title for a second time in 1982, and though less successful thereafter he has remained a favourite with snooker fans despite (or because of) his confrontations with the authorities.

Higgins, John (1975–) Snooker player, born in Wishaw, Lanarkshire, Scotland. He turned professional in 1992, and became known in 1994–5 when he was the first teenager to win three ranking events in a season. His wins include the German Open (1995, 1997), the British Open (1995, 1998), the European Open (1997), and Liverpool Victoria United Kingdom Championship (2000). His win in the Embassy World Championship (1998) gave him the Number 1 ranking position (previously held by Stephen Hendry), which he retained in 1999. When competing in the British Open tournament in 2003, he made history as the first player to compile maximum 147 breaks in successive matches.

Higgs particle In particle physics, a yet to be discovered particle implicated in the process of mass generation; named after British physicist Peter Higgs (1929–). It is assumed to be very heavy, and to have charge 0. Spontaneous symmetry breaking arises when the symmetry of the lowest energy state of a system is less than that of the interaction governing the system. The Higgs mechanism is the manifestation of symmetry breaking in quantum field theory, and shows how the breakdown of

hieroglyphics

The study of the symbols of ancient Egyptian writing; also, the symbols themselves. The characters were originally pictograms, and were named **hieroglyphs** (from the Greek 'sacred carving') because of their frequent use in religious contexts, such as temple and tomb inscriptions. The symbols are usually written from right to left, and were developed to represent three kinds of information: some are ideograms, representing objects or concepts in the real world; others stand for a consonant or consonant sequence; and a third type has no phonetic value, but serves to disambiguate a hieroglyph with more than one meaning.

symmetry leads to massive particles where field theory alone predicts massless particles. Weinberg and Salam used the Higgs mechanism to predict masses for the W and Z particles in the theory of weak and electromagnetic interactions. A by-product of the acquisition of mass by these particles is the Higgs particle. Finding the Higgs particle, or **Higgs boson**, remains one of the great outstanding challenges of particle physics. However, in 2001 a CERN study concluded that the particle might not exist.

High Commissioner In the UK, a person carrying out the same duties and possessing the same rank as an ambassador, representing one Commonwealth country in another Commonwealth country. The High Commission is the Commissioner's residence and houses the administrative organization.

High Court (of Justice) A court in England and Wales established by the Judicature Acts (1873–5), and principally a trial court for civil cases. It hears appeals on points of law from magistrates' courts in both civil and criminal cases, and also undertakes judicial review. The court has three divisions: Queens Bench Division, Chancery Division, and Family Division. In Scotland, the **High Court of Justiciary** is the supreme criminal court, presided over by Scotland's senior judge, the Lord Justice-General. It is both a trial court for serious criminal matters and the final appellate court in criminal matters. There is no appeal to the House of Lords.

high-definition television (HDTV) Any television system using substantially more scanning lines than the 500–600 of established broadcast standards, with improved picture quality in a wide-screen format. In the 1980s, the Japanese NHK proposed a completely new system, Hi-Vision, as a worldwide standard, using 1125 lines at 60 fields per second (60 Hz). However, the need to provide transmissions having some compatibility with existing receivers led to alternative approaches, such as the Eureka project in Europe (related to PAL, using 1250 lines/50 Hz) and several proposals in the USA (with NTSC compatibility, such as Advanced Compatible TV, using 1050 lines/60 Hz).

high energy physics *particle physics*

higher education *further education*

high fidelity sound system An assembly of sound reproduction components capable of regenerating an original musical performance to the highest attainable quality across the whole range of audible frequencies (20–20 000 Hz) and amplitudes; also known as **hi-fi**. It was a concept which emerged after World War 2, made possible by a combination of several factors. A new record material (vinylite) facilitated the introduction of the long-playing record at the end of the 1940s; stereophonic recording was patented in 1931, though not marketed significantly until 1958; and transistors after 1948 gradually replaced thermionic valve circuitry. Digital recording, noise reduction, FM radio, and the compact disk were later embellishments.

high jump An athletics field event in which competitors attempt to leap over a bar set at a predetermined height without knocking the bar over. The height of the bar is gradually increased, and competitors are allowed three attempts to clear each new height; they are eliminated if they fail. The person clearing the greatest height, or (if two or more tie) the person with the fewest misses at the lower heights, is the winner. The current world record for men is 2·45 m/8 ft½ in, achieved by Javier Sotomayor (1967–) of Cuba in 1993 at Salamanca, Spain; for women, it is 2·09 m/6 ft 10¼ in, achieved by Stefka Kostadinova (1965–) of Bulgaria in 1987 at Rome.

Highland pop (2000e) 213 100; area 25 391 sq km/9804 sq mi. Council in N Scotland, UK; bounded N and E by the North Sea, W by the Minch and Little Minch; includes Inner Hebrides; sparsely inhabited region of great scenic beauty; Grampian, Monadhliath, and Cairngorm Mts; crossed by numerous rivers, mountain ranges and lochs (notably Linnhe, Lochy, Oich, Ness, route of the Caledonian Canal); rises to 1344 m/4409 ft in Ben Nevis (SW); capital, Inverness; other chief towns, Wick, Dingwall, Thurso, Nairn; forestry, livestock, oil, winter skiing, fishing, fish farming, game hunting; Eas Coul Aulin (NW), highest waterfall in UK (drop of 200 m/650 ft); John o' Groats (extreme NE); Glencoe in SE, site of 1692 massacre.

Highland Games Athletic meetings held in Scotland; the first Games were organized by the St Fillans (Perthshire) Highland Society in 1819. A range of athletic events takes place, in addition to specifically Scottish events, such as tossing the caber. There may also be highland dancing and bagpipe-playing competitions. The most famous meeting is the Braemar Gathering.

Highland pony A Scottish breed of horse; two types: **Western Isles** (two divisions: height 12·2–13·2 hands/1·2–1·3 m/4 ft–4 ft 4 in, and height 13·2–14·2 hands/1·3–1·4 m/4 ft 4 in–4 ft 8 in), and the more powerful **garron** or **Mainland** (height, 14·2 hands/1·5 m/4 ft 10 in); formerly used for stalking deer. The garron has Arab blood, and is the largest of British pony breeds.

high-level language A computer language in which every instruction or statement is equivalent to several machine-code instructions (ie those instructions which can be directly understood by the computer). High-level languages, such as BASIC, FORTRAN, and PASCAL, are written using notations which are relatively easy for the user to understand. A program written in high-level language can in general be run on any computer where an interpreter or a compiler for the language is provided.

high pressure physics The study of the effects of increased pressure on matter. Most properties of matter are affected by pressure. For example, some insulators become metallic conductors or even superconductors (eg sulphur), iron loses its strong magnetic properties, and typically gases turn to liquid. Pressures of more than a million times atmospheric pressure can be achieved, for example using a diamond anvil cell.

high school The common form of secondary school in the USA for 15–19-year-olds, following the **junior high school** phase for 11–15-year-olds. The schools are non-selective, and the successful completion of this phase of education results in graduation, with the award of the high-school diploma.

Highsmith, Patricia (1921–95) Writer of detective fiction, born in Fort Worth, Texas, USA. She studied at Barnard College and Columbia University, New York City. Her first novel, *Strangers on a Train* (1949), became famous as a source of Hitchcock's 1951 film of that name, but her best novels are generally held to be those describing the criminal adventures of her psychotic hero, Tom Ripley, beginning with *The Talented Mr Ripley* (1956, filmed 1999). Other titles included *Ripley Under Ground* (1971), *Found in the Street* (1986), and *Ripley Under Water* (1991).

high-speed anti-radiation missile (HARM) A guided missile developed initially by the US Navy following experience in the air combat over Vietnam. HARMs are equipped with a 'homing head' designed to pick up, lock onto, and cause the missile to fly towards enemy ground-based radar transmitters. The missile's high speed means that the hostile radar should not have time to switch off before the HARM arrives and destroys it.

high-speed photography The photographic recording of transient phenomena with very short periods of exposure. Electronic flash can be as brief as one-millionth of a second, and non-mechanical shutters (such as the polarizing Kerr cell) can operate 200 times faster. In an indirect system, an instantaneous video image is stored on the screen of a cathode ray tube for photography over a longer period. In cinematography the limit for mechanical intermittent film movement is about 600 pictures per second, but rotating prism optics and continuously moving film can expose at a rate of 10 000 frames a second for a very short burst.

hi-hat cymbals A pair of cymbals mounted on a stand, and operated by a foot-pedal which brings the upper cymbal into contact with the fixed, lower one. Also known as 'Chinese cymbals', they have been used since 1927 in dance bands, and in jazz and pop groups.

Hijra [hijra], formerly also spelled **Hegira** The migration of the Prophet Mohammed from Mecca to Medina in 622. The departure marks the beginning of the Muslim era.

Hilary (of Poitiers), St (c.315–c.368) Clergyman, one of the Doctors of the Church, born of pagan parents in Limonum (Poitiers), W France. He did not become a Christian until he was advanced in life. About 350 he was elected Bishop of Poitiers, and immediately rose to the first place as an opponent of Arianism. His principal work is that on the Trinity, but his three addresses to Emperor Constantius II are remarkable for the boldness of their language. His feast day marks the beginning of a term at Oxford and Durham universities, and English law sittings, to which his name is consequently applied. Feast day 13 January.

Hilbert, David (1862–1943) Mathematician, born in Königsberg, Prussia (now Kaliningrad, Russia). He studied at Königsberg and became professor there (1893). He moved to Göttingen in 1895, where he critically examined the foundations of geometry. He made important contributions to the theory of numbers, the theory of invariants and algebraic geometry, and the application of integral equations to physical problems. He later extended his axiomatic approach to geometry to an attempt to base all mathematics on finitely many axioms – an approach shown to be inadequate by Gödel in 1931. At the International Congress of Mathematicians in 1900 he listed 23 problems which he regarded as important for contemporary mathematics; the solutions of many of these have led to interesting advances, while others are still unsolved.

Hildebrand, St *Gregory VII*

Hildesheim [hildes-hiym] 52°09N 9°55E, pop (2000e) 108 000. Port in Hanover district, NC Germany; 29 km/18 mi SE of Hanover; founded, 1300; railway; linked to the Mittelland Canal; iron, machinery, hardware, carpets, electronics; St Michael's Church (11th-c) and Romanesque cathedral (1054–79), world heritage sites.

Hill, Benny, popular name of **Alfred Hawthorne Hill** (1925–92) Comedian, born in Southampton, Hampshire, S England, UK. An enthusiastic performer in school shows, he was a milkman, drummer, and driver before finding employment as an assistant stage manager. During World War 2 he appeared in *Stars in Battledress*, and later followed the traditional comic's route of working-men's clubs, revues, and end-of-the-pier shows. An early convert to the potential of television, he appeared in *Hi There* (1949), and was named TV personality of the year in 1954. He gained national popularity with the saucy *The Benny Hill Show* (1957–66), and spent over two decades writing and performing in top-rated television specials that were seen around the world.

Hill, Damon (Graham Devereux) (1960–) Motor-racing driver, born in Hampstead, London, UK, the son of Graham Hill. He joined the Williams Formula One team as a test driver in 1991, and drove for Brabham in his first Grand Prix at Silverstone in 1992. He won over 20 grands prix in the next four years, succeeding Nigel Mansell on the Williams team. He took third place in the world championship in 1993, was runner-up in 1994, and won in 1996. The next season he joined the TWR Arrows Yamaha team, and in 1998 drove for the Benson & Hedges Jordan Mugen Honda team. He retired from Formula One racing in 1999.

Hill, Geoffrey (William) (1932–) Poet, born in Bromsgrove, Hereford and Worcester, WC England, UK. He studied at Oxford, taught at the universities of Leeds (1954–80) and Cambridge (1981–8), and became professor at Boston, MA, in 1988. His first volume *For the Unfallen* (1959) introduced a serious and astringent voice, which has commanded increasing authority with *King Log* (1968), *Mercian Hymns* (1971), and *Tenebrae* (1978). His religious preoccupation is fully revealed in *The Mystery of the Charity of Charles Péguy* (1983), and later works include *New and Collected Poems 1952–1992* (1994), *Canaan* (1996), and *The Triumph of Love* (1998). Among his critical works is *Illuminating the Shadows: Mythic Powers of Film* (1992).

Hill, (Norman) Graham (1929–75) Motor-racing driver, born in London, UK. He won 14 races from a record 176 starts (since surpassed) between 1958 and 1975, and was world champion in 1962 (in a BRM) and in 1968 (Lotus). He won the Monaco Grand Prix five times (1963–5, 1968–9). In 1975 he started his own racing team, Embassy Racing, but was killed when the plane he was piloting crashed near Hendon, N London. His son, Damon, also went into motor-racing.

Hill, Octavia (1838–1912) Housing reformer and founder of the National Trust, born in London, UK. She worked among the London poor, and in 1864, supported by Ruskin, commenced her project to improve the homes of people in the slums – methods which were imitated in Europe and the USA. In 1869 she helped to found the Charity Organization Society. A leader of the open-space movement, she was a co-founder in 1895 of the National Trust for Places of Historic Interest or Natural Beauty.

Hill, Sir Rowland (1795–1879) Educator, inventor, and postal reformer, the originator of penny postage, born in Kidderminster, Hereford and Worcester, WC England, UK. He became a teacher, and helped to found the Society for the Diffusion of Useful Knowledge (1826). He invented a rotary printing press (1833). In his *Post-office Reform: its Importance and Practicability* (1837), he advocated a low and uniform rate of postage, to be prepaid by adhesive stamps, and in 1840 a uniform penny rate was introduced. He became secretary to the Post Office (1854), and was knighted in 1860.

Hillary, Sir Edmund (Percival) (1919–) Mountaineer and explorer, and later writer and lecturer, born in Auckland, New Zealand. As a member of John Hunt's Everest expedition he attained, with Tenzing Norgay, the summit of Mt Everest in 1953, for which he was knighted. As part of the Commonwealth Trans-Antarctic Expedition (1955–8) led by Sir Vivian Fuchs, he and a New Zealand expeditionary party reached the South Pole in 1958. He subsequently established a medical and educational charity, the Himalayan Trust, for the Sherpa peoples of Nepal, which since 1961 has built many schools and two hospitals. His autobiography, *Nothing Venture, Nothing Win*, appeared in 1975. He was appointed New Zealand High Commissioner to India in 1984. On 29 May 2003, he was granted honorary citizenship of Nepal to mark the 50th anniversary of the first ascent of Mt Everest.

Hillel [hilel], known as **Hillel Hazaken** (the Elder), or **Hillel Habavli** ('the Babylonian') (1st-c BC–1st-c AD) One of the most respected Jewish teachers of his time, probably born in Babylonia. He immigrated to Palestine at about age 40. He founded a school of followers bearing his name, which was frequently in debate with (and often presented more tolerant attitudes than) the contemporary followers of Shammai. Noted for his use of seven rules in expounding Scripture, his views were influential for later rabbinic Judaism.

Hillery, Patrick (John) (1923–) Irish statesman and president (1976–90), born in Miltown Malbay, Co Clare, W Ireland. He studied at Dublin. Following his election as an MP (1951), he held ministerial posts in education (1959–65), industry and commerce (1965–6), and labour (1966–9), then became foreign minister (1969–72). Before becoming president, he served as European Commissioner for social affairs (1973–6).

Hilliard, Nicholas (1547–1619) Court goldsmith and miniaturist, born in Exeter, Devon, SW England, UK. He worked for Elizabeth I and James I, and founded the English school of miniature painting.

hill mynah A bird of the starling family (*Gracula religiosa*), native to India and SE Asia; inhabits forest; eats fruit, insects, nectar, and occasionally lizards; black with yellow wattles on head; lives in small groups; nests in hole in tree trunk. It is a common cage bird because it mimics the human voice; in the wild it does not mimic sounds.

Hillsborough Football stadium in Sheffield, England, the scene of the worst disaster in British sporting history, when 95 Liverpool fans died and 400 people were injured at the FA Cup semi-final match between Liverpool and Nottingham Forest (15 Apr 1989). The tragedy occurred when police opened a main gate into the terraced area to relieve pressures caused by a build-up of people at the entrance allocated to Liverpool fans. This caused a flood into the packed terraces, and people were crushed at the perimeter fences.

Hilton, Conrad (Nicholson) (1887–1979) Hotelier, born in San Antonio, New Mexico, USA. He became a partner in his father's general store, expanding the business after his father's death, and buying the Mobley Hotel in Cisco. This led to the purchase of other hotels in Texas, and by 1939 he was buying or starting up hotels further afield. The Hilton Hotels Corporation was formed in 1946, becoming the Hilton International Company (1948), one of the world's largest hotel organizations, diversifying in the 1950s to include car-rental and credit-card operations.

Hilton, James (1900–54) Novelist, born in Leigh, Lancashire, NW England, UK. He studied at Cambridge, and quickly established himself as a writer, his first novel, *Catherine Herself*, being published in 1920. His success was dual, for many of his novels were filmed, notably *Lost Horizon* (1933, Hawthornden Prize), and *Goodbye Mr Chips* (1934). He settled in the USA in 1935.

Hilversum 52°14N 5°10E, pop (2000e) 89 000. City in SE North Holland province, W Netherlands; famous for its radio and television stations; fashionable residential and commuter district of Amsterdam; railway; textiles, leatherwork, printing, electrical engineering, pharmaceuticals.

Himalayan cat A domestic cat, known as **Himalayan** in the USA and **colourpoint** in the UK; a *long-haired* cat, with a pale coat, and dark face, legs, and tail; breeds named after the dark colour (eg *blue point Himalayan* or *blue colourpoint*).

Himalayan chamois *goral*

Himalayas [himahlyaz, himalayaz] Gigantic wall of mountains in C Asia, N of the Indus and Brahmaputra Rivers; a series of parallel ranges, generally rising towards the N; length over 2400 km/1500 mi, from the Pamirs (NW) to the borders of Assam and China (E); three main ranges, the Outer, Middle, and Inner Himalayas, which become five ranges in Kashmir – the Lesser and the Great Himalayas, the Zāskār Range, the Ladākh Range, and the Karakorams; Mt Everest rises to 8848 m/29 028 ft on the Nepal–Tibet border; other major peaks include K2 in the Karakorams (8611 m/28 251 ft), Kangchenjunga (8586 m/28 169 ft), Makalu (8475 m/27 805 ft), Dhaulagiri (8167 m/26 794 ft), Nanga Parbat (8126 m/26 660 ft), and Annapurna (8091 m/26 545 ft); in Hindu mythology the mountains are highly revered.

Himalia [himahlia] The sixth natural satellite of Jupiter, discovered in 1904; distance from the planet 11 480 000 km/7 134 000 mi; diameter c.186 km/116 mi.

Himmler, Heinrich (1900–45) German Nazi leader and chief of police, born in Munich, SE Germany. He began life as a poultry farmer, joined the Nazi Party in 1925, and in 1929 was made head of the SS (*Schutzstaffel*, protective force), which he developed from Hitler's personal bodyguard into a powerful Party weapon. With the help of Reinhard Heydrich (1904–42), deputy-chief of the Gestapo, he founded the SD (security service) in 1932. In 1936 he became chief of all the police services, including the Gestapo, and initiated the systematic liquidation of Jews. As head of the Reich administration from 1939 he extended his field of repression to all German-occupied Europe. In 1943 he became minister of the interior, and in 1944 commander-in-chief of the home forces. He ruthlessly put down the conspiracy against Hitler in the July Plot (1944), but a few months later was himself secretly negotiating German surrender to the Allies. Hitler expelled him from the Party, and Himmler attempted to escape. He was captured by the Allies (1945), and committed suicide in Lüneburg.

Hinault, Bernard [eenoh] (1954–) Cyclist, born in Yffignac, W France. In 1985 he joined Eddy Merckx and Jacques Anquetil as a five-times winner of the Tour de France. He was French pursuit champion in 1974, and turned professional in 1977. In 1982 he won the Tours of Italy and France, and overcame knee surgery in 1983 to win his fifth Tour de France. He retired at 32, and became technical adviser to the Tour de France.

Hindemith, Paul [hinduhmit] (1895–1963) Composer, born in Hanau, WC Germany. He studied at Frankfurt, then played violin in the Rebner Quartet and the Opera Orchestra (1915–23), which he often conducted. His works include operas, concertos, and a wide range of instrumental pieces. He also pioneered *Gebrauchsmusik*, pieces written with specific aims, such as for newsreels and community singing. His music was banned by the Nazis in 1934, and he moved to Turkey, the UK, and the USA. In 1941 he was appointed professor at Yale and in 1953 at Zürich.

Hindenburg, Paul (Ludwig Hans Anton von Beneckendorff und) von [hindenberg] (1847–1934) German general and president (1925–34), born in Poznan, WC Poland (formerly Posen, Prussia). He studied at Wahlstatt and Berlin, fought in the Franco–Prussian War (1870–1), rose to the rank of general (1903), and retired in 1911. Recalled at the outbreak of World War 1, he won victories over the Russians (1914–15), but was forced to direct the German retreat on the Western Front (to the *Hindenburg line*). A national hero, he became the second president of the German Republic in 1925. He was re-elected in 1932, and in 1933 appointed Hitler as chancellor.

Hindenburg [hindnberg] A famous airship, of rigid-frame construction, built by the German government in 1936, capable of carrying 72 passengers in a style matching the ocean liners of the day. After 63 successful flights, most of which were across the Atlantic, the *Hindenburg* caught fire in May 1937 while coming in to moor at Lakehurst, NJ. The fire was probably due to hydrogen leaks being ignited by atmospheric electricity.

Hindi *Indo-Aryan languages*

Hindley, Myra *Brady, Ian*

Hinduism [hinduizm] The Western term for a religious tradition developed during the first millennium and intertwined with the history and social system of India. Hinduism does not trace its origins to a particular founder, has no prophets, no set creed, and no particular institutional structure. It emphasizes the right way of living (*dharma*) rather than a set of doctrines, and thus embraces diverse religious beliefs and practices. There are significant variations between different regions of India, and even from village to village. There are differences in the deities worshipped, the scriptures used, and the festivals observed. Hindus may be theists or non-theists, revere one or more gods or goddesses, or no god at all, and represent the ultimate in personal (eg Brahma) or impersonal (eg Brahman) terms.

Common to most forms of Hinduism is the idea of reincarnation or transmigration. The term *samsara* refers to the process of birth and rebirth continuing for life after life. The particular form and condition (pleasant or unpleasant) of rebirth are the result of *karma*, the law by which the consequences of actions within one life are carried over into the next and influence its character. The ultimate spiritual goal of Hindus is *mohsha*, or release from the cycle of samsara.

There is a rich and varied religious literature, and no specific text is regarded as uniquely authoritative. The earliest extant writings come from the Vedic period (c.1200–500 BC), and are known collectively as the Veda. Later (c.500 BC–AD 500) came the religious law books (*dharma sutras* and *dharma shastras*) which codified the classes of society (*varna*) and the four stages of life (*ashrama*), and were the bases of the Indian caste system. To this were added the great epics, the Ramayana and the Mahabharata. The latter includes one of the most influential Hindu scriptures, the Bhagavadgita.

There have been many developments in Hindu religious thought. In particular, Shankara (9th-c) formulated the *Advaita* (non-dual) position that the human soul and God are of the same substance. Ramanuja (12th-c) established the system of *Vishishtadvaita* (differentiated non-duality) which, while accepting that the human soul and God are of the same essence, holds that the soul retains its self-consciousness and, therefore, remains in an eternal relationship with God. This provided the impetus for the later theistic schools of Hindu thought.

Brahma, Vishnu, and Shiva are the chief gods of Hinduism, and together form a triad (the *Trimurti*). There are numerous lesser deities, including the goddesses Maya and Lakshmi. Hinduism is concerned with the realization of religious values in every part of life, yet there is a great emphasis upon the performance of complex and demanding rituals under the supervision of Brahman priests and teachers. There are three categories of worship: temple, domestic, and congregational. Pilgrimage to local and regional sites is common, and there is an annual cycle of local, regional and all-Indian festivals. The cow is considered a sacred animal, and killing it is forbidden. There were over 830 million Hindus in 2004.

Hindu Kush [hindoo kush], ancient **Paropamisus** Mountain range in C Asia, an extension of the Himalayan system, covering c.800 km/500 mi; world's second highest range; runs SW, rising to 7690 m/25 229 ft in Tirich Mir; four subsidiary ridges; peaks permanently snow-covered, little vegetation; crossed by several passes; the Salang Tunnel is the main break in the system, allowing Kabul to be linked to the N area and Tajikistan; Alexander the Great and Tamerlane followed these passes in their invasions of India.

Hines, Earl (Kenneth) [hiynz], nickname **Fatha** ('Father') **Hines** (1903–83) Jazz pianist and bandleader, born in Duquesne, Pennsylvania, USA. He worked under such leaders as Erskine Tate and Carroll Dickerson, then in association with trumpeter Louis Armstrong (1927–9), with whom he made several recordings now considered jazz classics, notably 'Weather Bird' and 'West End Blues'. Hines formed his own band in 1928, expanding it to a large orchestra resident at the Grand Terrace Ballroom, Chicago. His economical, linear approach to solo improvisation, known as 'trumpet-style piano', had great influence on succeeding jazz pianists. As the Swing Era ended, he faded into obscurity. In 1965, he took part in a New York concert and was rediscovered, making many recordings and playing all over the world.

Hingis, Martina [hingis] (1981–) Tennis player, born in Kosice, SE Slovak Republic. She was brought up in Switzerland and, playing for that country, in 1997 became the youngest singles Grand Slam tournament winner of the 20th-c after her victory in the Australian Open, and the youngest-ever world number one when she replaced the injured Steffi Graf. Winner of the 1996 and 1998 Wimbledon doubles title, she won the singles title in 1997 at the age of 16, and that same year won the US and Australian titles, retaining the latter in 1998 and 1999. Her doubles titles include the Australian Open, 1997, 1998, and 1999, the US Open, 1998, and the French, 1998 and 2000. Injury forced her retirement in 2003.

hinny *mule* (zoology)

Hinshelwood, Sir Cyril Norman (1897–1967) Chemist, born in London, UK. He studied at Oxford, and was professor there from 1937. He did valuable work on the effect of drugs on bacterial cells, and investigated chemical reaction kinetics, for which he shared the Nobel Prize for Chemistry in 1956. A considerable linguist and Classical scholar, he had the unique distinction of being president of both the Royal Society (from 1955) and the Classical Association (in 1960). He was knighted in 1948.

Hinton (of Bankside), Christopher Hinton, Baron (1901–83) Nuclear engineer, born in Tisbury, Wiltshire, S England, UK. He studied at Cambridge, after winning a scholarship while an apprentice in a railway workshop. From 1946, as deputy director of atomic energy production, he constructed the world's first large-scale commercial atomic power station at Calder Hall, Cumbria, opened in 1956 (ceased operation in 2003). He was knighted in 1951, and created a life peer in 1965.

hip The outer rounded region at the side of the upper thigh – in anatomical terms, the joint between the head of the femur and the pelvis, and the point of articulation of the lower limb with the trunk. It possesses great strength and stability, at the expense of limitation of movement. The circumference of the trunk at the level of the hip is an important measurement in the fitting of clothes.

hip-hop A US black popular music culture first developed in New York in the 1970s. The music may be created by disco DJs 'scratching' – manipulating dance-music records on the turntable to produce new sounds and rhythms – or, more recently, by 'sampling' – selecting and mixing digital samples from recordings by other artists. It relies on hard and heavy percussion, often from electronic drum machines, and this can provide a backing for improvised rap lyrics. Hip-hop culture also encompasses break-dancing and 'body-popping', street graffiti, and baggy-clothes fashion.

Hipparchos / Hipparchus [hipah(r)kus] (2nd-c BC) Astronomer, born in Nicaea, Rhodes. He carried out observations at Rhodes, discovered the precession of the equinoxes and the eccentricity of the Sun's path, determined the length of the solar year (to within seven minutes), estimated the distances of the Sun and Moon from the Earth, and drew up a catalogue of 850 stars. He also fixed the geographical position of places by latitude and longitude, and invented trigonometry.

Hipparcos [hipah(r)kos] A satellite launched in 1989 by the European Space Agency to measure positions, brightness, distances, and motions of the stars far more accurately than possible through telescopes on Earth, where the unsteadiness of the atmosphere interferes with observations. The Hipparcos catalogue, containing data for over 100 000 stars, was published in 1997.

Hipparion A fossil horse that originated in North America about 15 million years ago, and spread extensively over grasslands of the Old World; became extinct in the Pleistocene epoch; cheek teeth with complex enamel patterns; lateral toes very reduced. (Family: Equidae.)

hippeastrum [hipeeastruhm] *amaryllis*

Hippocrates [hipokrateez] (c.460–c.377 BC) Physician, known as 'the father of medicine', and associated with the medical profession's **Hippocratic oath**, born on the island of Cos, Greece. The most celebrated physician of antiquity, he gathered together all that was sound in the previous history of medicine. A collection of 70 works, the *Hippocratic corpus*, has been ascribed to him, but very few were written by him, it being more likely that they formed a library at a medical school.

Hippocratic oath An ethical code attributed to Hippocrates. Parts of it are still used in medical schools throughout the world to encourage young graduates to aspire to conduct that befits those who care for sick people. An extract is as follows: 'Whatsoever house I enter, there will I go for the benefit of the sick, refraining from all wrongdoing... Whatsoever things I see or hear in my attendance on the sick which ought not to be voiced abroad, I will keep silence thereon.'

Hippolytus [hipolitus] A Greek hero, son of Theseus and Hippolyta. Theseus's new wife, Phaedra, made advances to Hippolytus, which were refused; so she falsely accused Hippolytus of rape. Theseus invoked a curse, Poseidon sent a frightening sea-monster, and Hippolytus was thrown from his chariot and killed.

hippopotamus (Gr 'river horse') A mammal of family Hippopotamidae; an artiodactyl, found in two species: **hippopotamus** (*Hippopotamus amphibius*) of tropical African rivers; body large, barrel-shaped; naked skin dehydrates easily; spends day in water, emerges at night; skin exudes red droplets which protect from sunburn (and possibly infection); large oblong head; nostrils, ears, and eyes level with water surface when swimming; four webbed toes on each foot; can submerge for five minutes; also, the **pygmy hippopotamus** (*Choeropsis liberiensis*) from W Africa; inhabits swamps and forests; shoulder height, 75 cm/30 in; less aquatic than *Hippopotamus amphibius*; also known as **hippo**.

hippotigris *zebra*

hire purchase (UK) / **installment credit** (US) A legal agreement to buy an article by means of small regular payments, meanwhile having use of the article. The item is not owned by the buyer until the final payment has been made. Payment may include an element of interest as well as part of the cost of the article.

Hirohito [hirohheetoh] *Showa Tenno*

Hiroshige, Ando [hirohsheegay] (1797–1858) Painter, born in Edo (modern Tokyo), Japan. He is celebrated for his impressive landscape colour prints. His 'Fifty-three Stages of the Tokaido' had a great influence on Western Impressionist painters, but heralded the decline of *ukiyo-e* (wood block print design) art.

Hiroshima [hirosheema, hiroshima] 34°23N 132°27E, pop (2000e) 1 094 000. Capital of Hiroshima prefecture, S Honshu I, Japan; on the S coast, on R Ota delta; founded as a castle, 1594; military headquarters in the Sino-Japanese War (1894–5) and the Russo–Japanese War (1904–5); atomic bomb dropped here (6 Aug 1945), c.150 000 killed or wounded, 75% of the buildings destroyed or severely damaged; town rapidly rebuilt; airport; railway; university (1949); machinery, cars, chemicals, textiles, food processing; Peace Memorial Park, containing the Cenotaph, Eternal Flame, Fountain of Prayer, Peace Memorial Museum, shell of the Industrial Exhibition Hall (only major building to survive the holocaust, now known as the Atom Dome); Rijô Castle (rebuilt, 1958); Peace Festival (6 Aug).

Hirst, Damien (1965–) Avant-garde artist, born in Bristol, SW England, UK. He studied art at Goldsmith's College, London, produced several paintings and mixed-medium sculptures, then became known for his works which made use of parts or all of dead animals, preserved in formalin, such as 'Mother and Child Divided' – four tanks contained the severed halves of a cow and calf. Considerable controversy surrounded the show he organized in London for young artists in 1994, at which one of his works, 'Away from the Flock', consisting of a dead lamb suspended within a tank, became the focus of attention when another artist poured ink into the tank. At the centre of debate over the nature and role of art, he became an established figure after being awarded the Turner Prize in 1995. Later works include 'Amazing Revelations' (2003), a collage of thousands of butterfly wings, part of his exhibition *Romance in the Age of Uncertainty*.

Hislop, Ian (1960–) British writer, editor, and broadcaster. He studied at Oxford, became a television scriptwriter for *Spitting Image* (1984–9), a columnist for *The Listener* (1985–9), and long-standing editor of the satirical magazine *Private Eye* (1986–). Presenter of *The Canterbury Tales* series for Channel 4 (1996), he is also a team captain of the BBC's popular *Have I Got News For You* (1991–), and has co-written a number of plays for television. His TV comedy sitcom series, *My Dad's the Prime Minister*, appeared in 2003.

Hispanic American Any person resident in the USA who comes from, or whose parents came from, Spanish-speaking countries in Central and South America, including the Caribbean. They are now thought to number c.35 million, but the figures are highly inaccurate because there are many illegal immigrants. Hispanic Americans are Roman Catholics, and the second-largest (after black Americans), poorest, and fastest-growing ethnic group in the country. The main groups are Mexican Americans, Puerto Ricans, and Cubans. There are (according to the 2000 census) about 20·6 million Mexican Americans, concentrated in California, Texas, and other parts of the SW. Called *Chicanos*, they migrated to the USA to find work, and the majority hold poorly-paid unskilled jobs. They are racially *mestizo*, descended from Europeans and Indians. The Puerto Ricans (3·4 millions), of mixed European, Indian, and black ancestry, are the poorest of the Hispanic ethnic groups, with many unemployed; they live mostly in New York City (where they are the largest ethnic minority) and the NE. By contrast, most of the 1 242 000 Cubans are well-off middle-class white political refugees who fled from Castro's Cuba, and now live in Miami, Florida, which is today a predominantly Spanish speaking city. In New York City, the largest number of recent Hispanic arrivals have been from the Dominican Republic.

Hispaniola [hispanyohla], formerly **Santo Domingo** Second largest island of the Greater Antilles, E Caribbean; between Cuba (W) and Puerto Rico (E); W third occupied by Haiti, remainder by the Dominican Republic; predominantly mountainous, traversed NW–SE by several forested ranges, notably the Cordillera Central, where the highest peak in the West Indies rises to 3175 m/10 416 ft at Pico Duarte; named by Columbus **La Isla Española** in 1492.

Hiss, Alger [aljer] (1904–96) US State Department official, born in Baltimore, Maryland, USA. He studied at Johns Hopkins University and Harvard Law School, and reached high office in the State Department. He stood trial twice (1949, 1950) on a charge of perjury, having denied before a Congressional Committee that he had passed secret state documents to Whittaker Chambers, in 1938 an agent for an international Communist spy ring. The case aroused great controversy, but he was convicted at his second trial, and sentenced to five years' imprisonment. He did not return to public life after his release. The justice of his conviction continues to be disputed, but revelations from American intelligence intercepts point to his guilt.

histamine [histameen] A local hormone derived from the amino acid *histidine*, found in virtually all mammalian tissues, and particularly abundant in the skin, lungs, and gut, in association with mast cells. It is released by antigen–antibody reactions, and after skin damage by heat, venom, or toxins. Its actions include the dilation and increased leakiness of blood vessels, and the stimulation of gastric acid secretion.

histochemistry The chemistry of living biological tissue. It is particularly significant in the study of immune response, such as in organ transplant surgery.

histology The microscopic study of the tissues of living organisms. Particular use is made of staining techniques to differentiate between cell types and between parts of cells.

histopathology The microscopic examination of diseased tissues to determine the nature of the condition. Small pieces of tissue taken at autopsy or by biopsy are placed in a fixative solution, cut into thin slices, and then stained with chemicals that colour the cell membrane, cytoplasm, and nucleus, rendering them more easily visible. Characteristic changes are found in the presence of cell death (*necrosis*), inflammation, malignancy, scarring, and other disease processes. The extent to which the normal structure of the tissue is replaced and disrupted can also be seen.

historical demography A recent technique for the study of population movements in the past. It involves the systematic collection of data from parish and civil registers, from which estimates of birth rates, death rates, and marriage rates can be more reliably made. Historical demographers, using the technique of family reconstitution, have advanced empirically-grounded hypotheses about the long-term factors which underlie differential rates of population growth and decline. The technique has embraced both wide-ranging hypotheses and detailed community studies.

historical materialism The perception of history informed by Marxist theories, concentrating on material factors as the primary agents of change. In most guises, such explanations stress the crucial importance of economic factors. Orthodox Marxist histories are rooted in studies of interaction, identified by Marx, between the 'economic base' and the 'political superstructure'. In recent years, uniform interpretations of this type have been in retreat, with Marxist historians offering broader interpretations of materialism which encompass cultural factors and social interaction. Critics of historical materialism argue that its emphasis on economic causation oversimplifies and distorts the complex of factors making for change.

historicism Either of two rather different theories about historical understanding. (1) The view that ideas and systems of thought can be understood only from within the historical contexts that produced them. (2) The view that there are general laws of historical development which permit long-term social forecasts.

historiography The study of the writing and interpretation of historical events and conditions, and their effect on human societies. New standards of research based on primary evidence subjected to critical evalution were pioneered by the German historians Barthold Georg Niebuhr and Leopold von Ranke (1795–1886). This 'scientific history' led to a systematic collection and cataloguing of sources (eg *Monumenta Germaniae Historicae*, 1825–1925). Another form of scientific history, the positive belief in underlying general laws, was pioneered by the French historian Auguste Comte and echoed in Karl Marx's theory of dialectical materialism, which presented the general law that change comes through class struggle. Historiography was developed further in the French journal *Annales d'histoire économique et sociale* launched in 1929 by Lucien Febvre (1878–1956) and Marc Bloch (1836–1944), and refined in the work of Fernand Braudel (1902–83). In their search for 'total history', these scholars sought an understanding of the structures within which people act, and of 'mentalities', drawing on psychology and other sciences. With the development of computers, quantitative and statistical techniques have become important to economic, demographic, and social historiographers. The study of the role of women and of gender has also added an important dimension to mainstream historiography.

history The study of the past. The subject is traditionally divided into ancient, mediaeval, and modern periods, and often classified according to countries or regions (eg British, European, African). There is also a dimension of classification according to subject-matter, recognizing such domains as political, ecclesiastical, social, and economic history, and overlapping with the interests of other academic disciplines. Recent years have also seen the emergence of new perspectives, such as comparative history and oral history, and new emphases in methodology, such as the focus on the role of techniques of investigation in establishing historical 'facts'.

History Classic (**Shu Jing** or **Shu Ching**) A set of 60 Chinese documents, mainly later Zhou period (6th–3rd-c BC) and substantially rewritten, including such details as the building of Luoyang, royal and military speeches, and condemnations of alcohol. Over a dozen may be pre-600 BC.

Hitchcock, Sir Alfred (Joseph) (1899–1980) Film director, born in London, UK. The son of a London poultry dealer, he studied engineering at London, and began in films as a junior technician in 1920. He directed his first film in 1925, and rose to become an unexcelled master of suspense, internationally recognized for his intricate plots, insight into human psychology, and novel camera techniques. His British films included *The Thirty-Nine Steps* (1935) and *The Lady Vanishes* (1938). In 1939 he left England for Hollywood where his first US film, *Rebecca* (1940), won an Oscar. Later films included *Psycho* (1960), *The Birds* (1963), and *Frenzy* (1972). From the 1940s onwards, Hitchcock usually made a fleeting appearance in a bit part in each of his films. He was knighted in 1980.

Hitchings, George (Herbert) (1905–98) Chemist, born in Hoquiam, Washington USA. He studied at the University of Washington and at Harvard, where he taught for a while before moving to Western Reserve University (1939). From 1942 he worked at the Burroughs Wellcome Research Laboratories in Tuckahoe, New York, being joined by Gertrude Elion in a major programme of drug development, notably 6-mercaptopurine (6MP) for the treatment of childhood leukaemia, and later other drugs for use in relation to a wide range of diseases, auto-immune disorders, and tissue transplantation. In 1988 they shared, with James Black, the Nobel Prize for Physiology or Medicine.

Hitler, Adolf, popular name **der Führer** ('the Leader') (1889–1945) German dictator, born in Braunau, Upper Austria, the son of a minor customs official, originally called **Schicklgruber**. One of history's most brutal leaders, he converted Germany, a defeated nation, into a fully remilitarized society, and launched World War 2. With anti-Semitism and racism the cornerstone of his ideology and policies, he conquered and dominated most of Europe over five years, and ordered the deaths of millions of Jews and others whom he considered inferior (*Untermenschen*).

He studied at Linz and Steyr, and attended an art school in Munich, but failed to pass into the Vienna Academy. He lived in Vienna (1904–13), doing a variety of menial jobs. In 1913 he emigrated to Munich, where he found employment as a draughtsman. In 1914 he served in a Bavarian regiment, became a corporal, and was wounded in the last stages of the war, twice winning the Iron Cross for bravery. In 1919 he joined a small political party which in 1920 he renamed as the National Socialist German Workers' (or NAZI) Party. In 1923, with other extreme right-wing factions, he attempted to overthrow the Bavarian government in an abortive uprising, the 'Munich beer-hall putsch'. He was imprisoned for nine months in Landsberg jail, during which time he dictated his political testament, *Mein Kampf* (1925, My Struggle), to Rudolf Hess. He expanded his party greatly in the late 1920s, and though he was unsuccessful in the presidential elections of 1932 against Hindenburg, he was made chancellor by Hindenburg in 1933. He then suspended the constitution, silenced all opposition, exploited successfully the burning of the *Reichstag* building, and brought the Nazi Party to power, having several of his opponents within his own party (the SA) murdered by his bodyguard, the SS, in the Night of the Long Knives (1934). In contravention of the Versailles Treaty, he rearmed the country (1935), established the Rome–Berlin 'axis' with Mussolini (1936), created 'Greater Germany' by the Anschluss with Austria (1938), and absorbed the German-populated Sudeten region of Czechoslovakia, in which Britain and France acquiesced at Munich (1938). He then demanded from Poland the return of Danzig and free access to East Prussia, which, when Poland refused, precipitated World War 2 (3 Sep 1939).

His domestic policy was one of total Nazification, enforced by the Secret State Police (*Gestapo*). He established concentration camps for political opponents and Jews, over 6 million of whom were murdered in the course of World War 2. He concluded the Nazi Soviet non-aggression pact (1939), but broke this when he invaded the Soviet Union in 1941. With his early war successes, he increasingly ignored the advice of military experts, and the tide turned in 1942 after the defeats at El Alamein, Stalingrad, and Kursk. He survived the explosion of the bomb placed at his feet by Colonel Stauffenberg (Jul 1944), and purged the army of all suspects. When Germany was invaded, he retired to his *Bunker*, an air-raid shelter under the Chancellory building in Berlin. With the Russians only a few hundred yards away, he went through a marriage ceremony with his mistress, Eva Braun, in the presence of the Goebbels family, who then poisoned themselves. All available evidence suggests that he and his wife committed suicide and had their bodies cremated (30 Apr 1945).

Hitler used tremendous forcefulness, charisma, oratory, and his ability to appeal to people's baser instincts to manipulate them. He rose at a time of defeat and disillusionment. His 'Thousand-Year Reich' lasted 12 years and three months.

Hittites A people of uncertain origin who became prominent in C Asia Minor in the first part of the second millennium BC, probably related to their possession of iron; they spoke an Indo-European language known as Hittite. At their zenith (1450–1200 BC), their Empire covered most of Anatolia and parts of N Syria (eg Carchemish). It was destroyed by marauding invaders, known as the Sea Peoples, around 1200 BC.

HIV Abbreviation of **human immunodeficiency virus**; a retrovirus that can cause the breakdown of the human immune system known as *acquired immunodeficiency syndrome* (AIDS).

hives *urticaria*

Hizbullah or **Hizbollah** [hizbulah] (Arabic "party of God') The largest of the Shiite Islamic fundamentalist parties in Lebanon. Under Iranian sponsorship, Hizbullah has called for the creation of an Islamic republic in Lebanon. The group was associated in particular with the kidnapping of Westerners in the mid-1980s to advance its political aims. Some of the hostages were executed by their captors, though most were released after several years in captivity. Hizbullah has been in conflict with Israeli forces in the south of Lebanon since the 1982 invasion by Israel. Supporters of the party won eight seats in the parliamentary elections of 1992, six in 1996, and eight in 2000.

HLA *human leucocyte antigens*

Hoad, Lew(is Alan) [hohd] (1934–94) Tennis player, born in Sydney, New South Wales, SE Australia. With his doubles partner, Ken Rosewall (1934–), he had a meteoric rise to fame, winning the Wimbledon doubles title and a Davis Cup challenge match against the USA before he was 20 years old. He defeated Rosewall in the Wimbledon final of 1956, and won again the following year, but thereafter turned professional and was ineligible by the rules of the time to compete for the game's major honours.

Hoare–Laval Pact [haw(r) laval] An agreement concluded in 1935 by the British foreign secretary Samuel Hoare (1880–1958) and the French prime minister Pierre Laval (1883–1945) aimed at the settlement of a dispute between Italy and Abyssinia. The terms included ceding large parts of Abyssinia (Ethiopia) to Italy. A public outcry in Britain against the pact led to its repudiation by Britain and to Hoare's resignation.

hoarhound *horehound*

hoatzin [hohatsin] An unusual South American bird (*Opisthocomus hoazin*), found on wooded banks of the Amazon and Orinoco; large wings and tail; small head with untidy crest; eats fruit and leaves; flies weakly; uses wings for balance on branches; juveniles have two hooked claws at the bend of each wing to assist climbing. (Family: Opisthocomidae.)

Hobart [hohbah(r)t] 42°54S 147°18E, pop (2000e) 200 600. Seaport and state capital in SE Tasmania, Australia; on the Derwent R at the foot of Mt Wellington; fine natural harbour; founded as a penal colony, 1804; state capital, 1812; city status, 1842; airport; railway; University of Tasmania (1890); textiles, zinc, paper, food processing; Hobart Theatre Royal.

Hobbema, Meindert [hobema], originally **Meyndert Lubbertsz(oon)** (1638–1709) Landscape painter, probably born in Amsterdam, The Netherlands. He studied under Ruysdael, but lacked his master's genius and range, contenting himself with florid, placid, and charming watermill scenes. Nevertheless his masterpiece, 'The Avenue, Middelharnis' (1689, National Gallery, London) is a striking exception, and has greatly influenced modern landscape artists.

Hobbes, Thomas (1588–1679) Political philosopher, born in Malmesbury, Wiltshire, S England, UK. He studied at Oxford, and began a long tutorial association with the Cavendish family, through which he travelled widely and became acquainted with such leading intellectuals of the day as Bacon, Ben Jonson, Galileo, Descartes, and Gassendi. After studying Euclidean geometry, he thought to extend its method into a comprehensive science of man and society. Obsessed by the civil disorders of his time, he wrote several works on government, including *Elements of Law* (completed in 1640) and *De cive* (1642). In 1646 he became mathematical tutor to the Prince of Wales at the exiled English court in Paris, where he wrote his masterpiece, *Leviathan* (1651), presenting his mature thoughts on metaphysics, psychology, and political philosophy. He was a thoroughgoing materialist, and argued that human beings are wholly selfish; enlightened self-interest explains the social contract in which we surrender the right of aggression to the sovereign state. In 1652 he returned to England, submitted to Cromwell, and settled in London. After the Restoration, he was given a pension, but continued to be a highly controversial figure. His last works, written in his 80s, were an autobiography in Latin verse (1672) and verse translations of the *Iliad* (1675) and *Odyssey* (1676).

hobbits The name for the reluctant heroes, living in holes in the ground, found in the works of Tolkien. He described them as 'little people, half our height with brown hair on the feet'. Among their number are Bilbo and Frodo Baggins. Tolkien said he was providing England with a mythology, as 'it had no stories of its own'. In the 1960s a cult developed, with peace-loving people sporting badges saying 'Frodo lives'.

Hobbs, Jack, popular name of **Sir John Berry Hobbs** (1882–1963) Cricketer, born in Cambridge, Cambridgeshire, EC England, UK. He played in county cricket for Cambridgeshire (1904) and Surrey (1905–34), and for England (1908–30), when he and **Herbert Sutcliffe** (1894–1978) established themselves as an unrivalled pair of opening batsmen. He made 5410 runs in 61 Test matches (average 56·94), and a record number of 197 centuries and 61 237 runs in first-class cricket. He was the first English cricketer to be knighted, in 1953.

hobby A small falcon native to the Old World; usually hunts at dusk; eats insects or birds caught in flight. (Genus: *Falco*, 4 species. Family: Falconidae.)

hobby-horse A horse made of wood, wicker, and cloth, sometimes with a real horse's head or skull, and donned by a man in traditional rituals and dances in many parts of Europe. Hobby-horse customs are associated with fertility and general well-being, and the mock animals are probably group emblems or totems.

Hobday, Sir Frederick (George Thomas) (1870–1939) British veterinarian. He was principal of the Royal Veterinary College, London (1927–37), and responsible for the 'Farthing Fund' to raise £250 000 for the new College building, opened by George VI in 1937. He is said to have performed **Hobday's operation** (stripping part of the larynx as a remedy for laryngeal hemiplegia) on more than 4000 horses.

Hobday, Peter (1937–) British journalist and broadcaster. Educated at Leicester University, he spent a year with a local newspaper in Wolverhampton, then joined the BBC, working in both radio and television. He became known for his contributions to such programmes as BBC2's *The Money Programme* (1979–81) and *Newsnight* (1980–2), and Radio 4's *Today* (from 1981).

Hobsbawm, Eric (John Ernest) (1917–) Historian, born in Alexandria, N Egypt. The son of Jewish parents – an English-born father and Viennese mother – his early years were spent in Vienna and Berlin before moving to London (1933). He studied at Cambridge and became a lecturer at Birkbeck College, University of London (1947), and later professor of Economic and Social History there (1970–82, emeritus 1982). His many works include *Labour's Turning Point* (1948), *The Age of Revolution* (1962), *The Age of Capital* (1975), and *Age of Extremes: the Short Twentieth Century* (1994).

Hochdorf [hokhdaw(r)f] An exceptional prehistoric chariot-burial of c.550–500 BC near Ludwigsburg, SW Germany, intact when excavated in 1978–9. Beneath a 60 m/200 ft diameter barrow lay a timber-lined tomb 5 m/16 ft square, containing a decorated 2·75 m/9 ft-long bronze couch, a cauldron (both imports from Italy), drinking horns, dishes, textiles, weapons, gold jewellery and clothing decorations, a chariot, and horse-trappings.

Hochhuth, Rolf [hokhhoot] (1931–) Playwright, born in Eschwege, C Germany. He studied at Heidelberg and Munich. His play *Der Stellvertreter* (1963, The Representative), focusing on the role of the Pope in World War 2, excited controversy and introduced the fashion for 'documentary drama'. Later plays have touched on other sensitive issues: *Soldaten* (1967, Soldiers) on the war morality of the Allies, and *Juristen* (1980, trans The Legal Profession) on collaboration with the Nazis.

Ho Chi-Minh [hoh chee min], originally **Nguyen That Thanh** (1892–1969) Vietnamese statesman, prime minister (1954–5), and president (1954–69), born in Kim-Lien, North Vietnam.

From 1912 he visited London and the USA, and lived in France from 1918, where he was a founder member of the Communist Party. From 1922 he was often in Moscow. He led the Viet Minh independence movement in 1941, and directed the successful military operations against the French (1946–54), becoming President of North Vietnam. He was a leading force in the war between North and South Vietnam during the 1960s.

Ho Chi Minh City [hoh chee min], formerly **Saigon** (to 1976) 10°46N 106°43E, pop (2000e) 4 568 900. Largest city in Vietnam; on R Saigon, 54 km/34 mi from the South China Sea; former capital of French Indochina, 1887–1902; former capital of South Vietnam; occupied by the USA in Vietnam War; jointly administered with Cholon city; airport; chief industrial centre of Vietnam; shipbuilding, metalwork, textiles, rubber products, soap, brewing, food processing, bamboo, fruit, vegetables.

hockey *see panel*

Hockney, David (1937–) Artist, born in Bradford, West Yorkshire, N England, UK. He studied at Bradford School of Art and the Royal College of Art, London, and was associated with the Pop Art movement from his earliest work. He taught at the University of California, Los Angeles (1965–7), and it was a visit to California that inspired his 'swimming pool' paintings, prompted by his fascination with the representation of water. His later work, often portraits, has become more representational. He has also worked in printmaking and photography, and designed sets and costumes.

Hoddinott, Alun (1929–) Composer, born in Bargoed, Caerphilly, S Wales, UK. He studied in Cardiff, and taught at the College of Music and Drama there before joining the music staff at University College, Cardiff in 1959, becoming professor (1967–87, now emeritus). In 1967 he was co-founder of the Cardiff Festival, serving as artistic director (1967–89) and president (1990–). He is a prolific composer of operas, symphonies, concertos, and a large corpus of choral and chamber works.

Hoddle, Glenn (1957–) Football manager and player, born in Hayes, NW Greater London, UK. He made his professional debut with Tottenham Hotspur (1976), moved to AS Monaco (1986), and returned to England as player/manager of Swindon Town (1991–3), continuing this dual role at Chelsea (1993–6). He replaced Terry Venables as England's manager in 1996, but after a controversial newspaper interview in 1999 that offended the disabled community, the Football Association relieved him of his duties. He became manager of Southampton in 2000, then returned to Tottenham as manager (2001–3).

Hodges, Johnny (1906–70) Jazz alto and soprano saxophonist, born in Cambridge, Massachusetts, USA. He joined Duke Ellington's orchestra in 1928, and became an indispensable colour in Ellington's sound palette, staying with him until 1951 and, after leading his own band with moderate success, rejoining in 1955 until his death. Ellington wrote numerous showpieces for Hodges, one of the most distinctive instrumental voices in jazz, such as 'Sophisticated Lady' (1933), 'The Star-Crossed Lovers' (1957), and 'Blues for New Orleans' (1970). Despite their musical intimacy that lasted for 38 years, Hodges and Ellington were not close. At performances when Hodges had been drinking heavily, Ellington often called for three or four of his featured numbers in a row; and Hodges stopped playing soprano saxophone forever, a sound Ellington loved, because Ellington refused him a raise in 1940.

Hodgkin, Sir Alan (Lloyd) (1914–98) Physiologist, born in Banbury, North Oxfordshire, SC England, UK. He studied at Cambridge, worked on the development of radar (1939–45), was a lecturer at Cambridge (1945–52), becoming Royal Society research professor (1952–69), and professor of biophysics at Cambridge (1970–81). With his former student Andrew Huxley he researched the passage of impulses in nerve fibres, for which they shared the 1963 Nobel Prize for Physiology or Medicine.

Hodgkin, Dorothy Mary, *née* **Crowfoot** (1910–94) Chemist, born in Cairo, Egypt. She studied at Oxford and Cambridge, became a research fellow at Somerville College, Oxford (1936–77), and research professor at the Royal Society (1960–77). A crystallographer of distinction, she was awarded the Nobel Prize for Chemistry in 1964 for her discoveries, by the use of X-ray techniques, of the structure of certain molecules, including penicillin, vitamin B^{12}, and insulin.

Hodgkin, Thomas (1798–1866) Physician and pathologist, born in London, UK. He studied at Edinburgh, held various posts at Guy's Hospital, and described the glandular disease lymphadenoma, which is named after him (**Hodgkin's disease**). He died while travelling in Palestine, and is buried in Jaffa.

Hodgkin's disease An uncommon disease of unknown cause in which there is malignant proliferation of lymphoid tissue throughout the body; also called **Hodgkin's lymphoma**. Uncontrolled multiplication of lymphoid cells produces specific large, multinucleated cells known as *Reed–Sternberg cells*, which can be isolated from affected tissue. Presentation is with one or more painless enlarged lymph nodes, often appearing as a lump in the neck, armpit, or groin, and accompanied by fatigue, fever, and sweating. Treatment is with radiotherapy to affected areas. Prognosis depends on the extent of the disease.

hockey

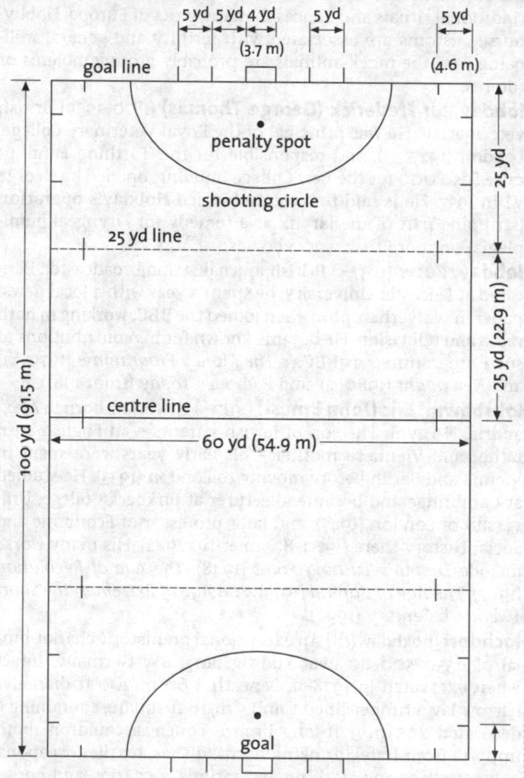

A stick-and-ball game played by two teams, each of 11 players; also known as **field hockey**, especially in the USA. The object is to move the ball around the field with the stick until a player is in a position to strike the ball into the opposing side's goal. The playing area is 100 yd (91 m) long and 60 yd (54 m) wide. A game lasts 70 minutes, split into two 35-minute halves. A similar game to hockey was played by the ancient Greeks c.2500 BC. Modern hockey dates from 1875, when the English Hockey Association was formed in London. Indoor hockey is increasingly popular during the winter months.

Hoff, Jacobus Henricus van't (1852–1911) Chemist, a founder of physical chemistry and stereochemistry, born in Rotterdam, The Netherlands. He studied at Leyden, and became professor of chemistry at Amsterdam (1877), Leipzig (1887), and Berlin (1895). He postulated the asymmetrical nature of bonds formed with carbon atoms, was the first to apply thermodynamics to chemical reactions, discovered that osmotic pressure varies directly with the absolute temperature, and investigated the formation of double salts. He was awarded the first Nobel Prize for Chemistry in 1901.

Hoffman, Dustin (1937–) Actor, born in Los Angeles, California, USA. A student at the Pasadena Playhouse, he pursued a career on stage and television in New York City, making his Broadway debut in 1961. His first leading film role was *The Graduate* (1967), and this was followed by a number of similar 'anti-hero' roles: *Midnight Cowboy* (1969), *Little Big Man* (1970), and *Marathon Man* (1976). He found wider scope in *All the President's Men* (1976), *Kramer v. Kramer* (1979, Oscar), and *Tootsie* (1982). He returned to Broadway in *Death of a Salesman* (1984), winning an Emmy for its television reprise (1985). His later films include *Rain Man* (1988, Oscar), *Billy Bathgate* (1991), *Outbreak* (1995), *A Walk on the Moon* (1999), *Personal Injuries* (2000), and *Moonlight Mile* (2002).

Hoffnung, Gerard (1925–59) Cartoonist and musician, born in Berlin, Germany, but raised in England. Educated at Highgate School of Arts, he taught art at Stamford School (1945) and Harrow (1948). His first cartoon was published in *Lilliput* magazine while he was still at school (1941). He was staff cartoonist on the London *Evening News* (1947) and after a brief time in New York (1950) returned in 1951 to freelance for *Punch* and others. His interest in music led to his creation of the Hoffnung Music Festivals at the Royal Festival Hall, in which his caricatures came to life and sound. They were also animated by Halas-Batchelor in the television series, *Tales From Hoffnung* (1965).

Hofmannsthal, Hugo von [hofmanztahl] (1874–1929) Poet and playwright, born in Vienna, Austria. He early attracted attention by his symbolic, neo-Romantic poems, then wrote several plays, notably *Electra* (1903), the morality play *Jedermann* (1912, Everyman), and the comedy, *Der Schwierige* (1921, The Difficult Man). He also collaborated with Richard Strauss, for whom he wrote the libretti for *Der Rosenkavalier* (1911) and *Die Frau ohne Schatten* (1919). With Strauss and Max Reinhardt, he founded the Salzburg Festival after World War 1.

Hofmeister, Wilhelm (Friedrich Benedikt) [hohfmiyster] (1824–77) Botanist, born in Leipzig, EC Germany. Although he was completely self-taught, he was appointed professor of botany at Heidelberg (1863), and in 1872 at Tübingen. He did fundamental work on plant embryology, and pioneered the science of comparative plant morphology.

hog *pig*

Hogan, Ben(jamin William), nickname **The Hawk** (1912–97) Golfer, born in Dublin, Texas, USA. A professional at various country clubs, he fought his way to the top despite financial difficulties, and in 1948 became the first man in 26 years to win all three US major titles. He had a near-fatal car accident in 1949, but amazed everyone by his determination to continue playing, and despite pain from his injuries he returned to win a further three major titles in 1953. He won the US Open four times (1948, 1950–1, 1953) before retiring in 1970 with a grand total of 63 US Professional Golf Association tour victories. A film on his life, *Follow the Sun*, starring Glenn Ford, was made in 1951, and he wrote an influential manual on the game in 1957.

Hogan, Paul (1941–) Comedian and actor, born in Lightning Ridge, New South Wales, SE Australia. When he appeared on a television talent show as a comedian, his original style proved so popular that he was given his own programme, *The Paul Hogan Show*, which ran for nine years. International fame followed with the successful films *Crocodile Dundee* (1986, Golden Globe) and *Crocodile Dundee II* (1988). His series of television advertisements for the Australian Tourist Board did much to promote his country, and he has become something of a national folk hero. His 1990 film *Almost an Angel* was less successful, but in 1993 he listed his next film, *Lightning Ridge*, on the Australian Stock Exchange to raise funds – a unique and successful venture. Later films include *Crocodile Dundee in Los Angeles* (2001).

Hogarth, William [hohgah(r)th] (1697–1764) Painter and engraver, born in London, UK. By 1720 he had his own business as an engraver, and by the late 1720s as a portrait painter. Tiring of conventional art forms, he began his 'modern moral subjects', such as 'A Rake's Progress' (1733–5), and his masterpiece, the 'Marriage à la Mode' (1743–5, Tate, London). His crowded canvases are full of revealing details and pointed subplots. In 1743 he visited Paris, and followed this with several prints of low life, such as the 'Industry and Idleness' series (1747).

hog cholera *swine fever*

hogfish Deep-bodied, bottom-living fish, *Lachnolaimus maximus*, belonging to the wrasse family Labridae, found in the warmer waters of the W North Atlantic; length up to 90 cm/3 ft; excellent food fish, but now scarce in some areas.

Hogg, James, known as **the Ettrick Shepherd** (1770–1835) Writer, born near Ettrick, Scottish Borders, SE Scotland, UK. He tended sheep in his youth, and after only a spasmodic education he became a writer of ballads, which achieved some success thanks to the patronage of Walter Scott. He eventually settled in Edinburgh, and wrote several works in verse and prose, notably *The Private Memoirs and Confessions of a Justified Sinner* (1824).

Hogg, Quintin *Hailsham, Viscount*

Hoggar Mountains *Ahaggar Mountains*

Hogmanay [hogmanay, hogmanay] The name in Scotland for New Year's Eve, the last day of the year. One custom associated with Hogmanay, although it does not take place until after midnight, is *first-footing*, the first-foot being the first person to enter a house on New Year's Day. Traditionally the first-foot should be tall, dark-haired, and male, and should carry gifts of food, drink, and fuel.

hogweed A very variable robust biennial (*Heracleum sphondylium*), growing to 3 m/10 ft, native to N temperate regions; leaves up to 30 cm/12 in, divided into oval or lance-shaped segments, often lobed or toothed; flowers white or pinkish in umbels 5–15 cm/2–6 in across; fruit flattened, broadly winged; also called **keck** or **cow parsnip**. The closely related **giant hogweed** (*Heracleum mantegazzianum*) is distinguished by its greater size, growing to 5 m/16 ft tall; stems red-spotted, umbels up to 50 cm/20 in across; native to SW Asia. Sometimes grown for ornament, it can cause painful skin irritations if touched in bright sunlight. (Family: Umbelliferae.)

Hohenstaufen [hohenshtowfn] A German dynasty named after the castle of Staufen in Swabia. Dukes of Swabia from 1079, they ruled as German kings or king-emperors (1138–1254), and as kings of Sicily (1194–1266). The greatest member of the family was Emperor Frederick I Barbarossa.

Hohenzollerns [hohentzolernz] A German ruling dynasty of Brandenburg–Prussia (1415–1918) and Imperial Germany (1871–1918). Originating in Swabia in the 9th-c, one branch of the family became Burgraves of Nuremberg; a descendant, Frederick VIII, was rewarded by the Holy Roman Emperor with the title of Elector of Brandenburg (1415). After the Thirty Years' War, the Hohenzollerns pursued a consistent policy of state expansion and consolidation, generating a long-standing rivalry with the Habsburgs (1740–1871), from which Bismarck ensured the Hohenzollerns emerged successfully with the imperial title (1871). World War 1 ruined Hohenzollern militarism, and forced the abdication of the last emperor, William II (1918).

Hohokam [hohhokam] The prehistoric inhabitants of the S Arizona desert c.300 BC–AD 1400, ancestors of the modern Pima and Papago Indians. From AD c.500, they adopted maize cultivation, the Mesoamerican ballgame, and the ceremonial use of platform mounds, under Mayan influence. From c.1000, sophisticated irrigation engineering and intensive agriculture allowed a population spread over c.26 000 sq km/10 000 sq mi, stimulating the development of an extended trade network. Hohokam jewellery of this period is notable.

Hokan languages [hohkn] A group of about 30 North American Indian languages, spoken by small numbers, but forming a bridge between the indigenous languages of North and South America. The only language with more than 20 000 speakers is Tlapanek.

Hokkaido [hokaeedoh], formerly **Yezo** or **Ezo** pop (2000e) 5 811 000; area 83 513 sq km/32 236 sq mi. Northernmost and second largest island of the Japanese archipelago; bounded by the East Sea (Sea of Japan) (W), Pacific Ocean (E), and Sea of Okhotsk (NE); separated from Honshu I (S) by the Tsugaru-kaikyo Strait, from Sakhalin I (N) by the La Pérouse (Soya-kaikyo) Strait; 418 km/260 mi N–S, 450 km/280 mi E–W, with an irregularly shaped peninsula SW; largely mountainous, with active and inactive volcanic cones (C); numerous hot springs (SW); rises to 2290 m/7513 ft at Mt Asahi-dake; originally populated by the Ainu; capital, Sapporo; potato, corn, soya beans, rice, rye, sugar beet, grazing, forestry, fishing; iron, gold, chrome, oil, natural gas; winter sports resort.

Hokusai, Katsushika [hokusiy] (1760–1849) Artist and wood engraver, born in Edo (modern Tokyo), Japan. He early abandoned traditional styles of engraving for the coloured woodcut designs of the *ukiyo-e* school. His 10 volumes of the *Mangwa* (1814–19, Sketches at Random) depict most facets of Japanese life. He is best known for his 'Hundred Views of Mount Fuji' (1835), many of which are widely known through reproductions in Western homes today. His work greatly influenced the French Impressionists.

Holbein, Hans [holbiyn], known as **the Younger** (1497–1543) Painter, born in Augsburg, S Germany, the son of **Hans Holbein the Elder** (c.1460–1524). He studied under his father, worked in Zürich and Lucerne, and from c.1516 was in Basel, where he settled in 1520. His early religious pictures include the celebrated 'Dead Christ' (1521). The 'Dance of Death' woodcuts were designed in 1523–6 (published in 1538). He went to France (1524) and then to England (1526), where he finally settled in 1532. Here there was no demand for religious art, and he painted portraits almost exclusively, notably of Sir Thomas More (to whom he had been introduced by Erasmus), Henry VIII (whose service he entered in 1537), and Henry's wives.

Holberg, Ludvig, Baron (1684–1754) Poet, playwright, and philosopher, born in Bergen, SW Norway. He was professor at Copenhagen of metaphysics (1717), eloquence (1720), and history (1730). His first notable works were satirical poems, among them *Peder Paars* (1719–20), the earliest classic in Danish. After 1724 he turned to history, producing a history of Denmark, and other works. In 1741 appeared another classic, the satirical comic romance *Nicolai Klimii iter subterraneum* (Niels Klim's Subterranean Journey). He became a baron in 1747.

Holden The brand name of the first mass-produced car designed and built for Australian conditions; previously, most motor vehicles had been imported. Holdens were first produced in 1948 by General Motors-Holden Ltd, which was the leading Australian car manufacturer until 1982.

Hölderlin, (Johann Christian) Friedrich [hoelderlin] (1770–1843) Poet, born in Lauffen, SE Germany. He studied theology at Tübingen and philosophy at Jena, and trained as a Lutheran minister, then became a family tutor in Frankfurt. He began to publish, with the help of Schiller, notably the philosophical novel, *Hyperion* (1797–9). He became increasingly schizophrenic, spent a period in an asylum (1806–7), and lived in Tübingen until his death. Today ranked among the greatest of German poets, his supple, condensed lyricism emphasizes the regeneration of humanity.

holding company A company which effectively controls another by owning at least half of the nominal value of its ordinary share capital or controlling the composition of its board of directors. The owned company is thereby a *subsidiary* of the holding company.

Holi [hohlee] A Hindu spring festival of obscure origin, occurring in February or March (Phalguna S 15), characterized by boisterous revelry, including the throwing of coloured water over people. Sikhs also celebrate Holi, with sports competitions.

Holiday, Billie, originally **Eleanora Fagan**, nickname **Lady Day** (1915–59) Jazz singer, born in Philadelphia, Pennsylvania, USA. She began recording in 1933, and her wistful voice and remarkable jazz interpretation of popular songs led to work with Benny Goodman and Teddy Wilson. In the late 1930s she worked with the big bands of Count Basie and Artie Shaw, singing such memorable ballads as 'Easy Living' (1937) and 'Yesterdays' (1939), and her recordings have been a major influence on later pop and jazz singers. By the late 1940s she was falling victim to drug and alcohol addiction, and losing her voice, though not her technique. Her autobiography *Lady Sings the Blues* (1956, actually written by William Dufty) was filmed in 1972. She died while under house arrest in a New York City hospital.

Holinshed, Raphael [holinshed] (?–c.1580) English chronicler, born apparently of a Cheshire family. He went to London early in Elizabeth I's reign, and became a translator. He compiled *The Chronicles of England, Scotland, and Ireland* (1577). Expanded and reissued under the editorship of John Hooker, alias Vowell, in 1586, it was a major source for many of Shakespeare's plays.

holism A thesis which maintains that some wholes are more than the sum of their parts; the wholes could be biological organisms, societies, art works, or networks of scientific theories. Methodological holism claims that there are large-scale laws of societal behaviour which do not reduce to laws of individual behaviour.

holistic medicine An approach to medical treatment based on the theory that living creatures and the non-living environment function together as a single integrated whole (*holism*); first propounded by Jan Christian Smuts in *Holism and Evolution* (1926). Implicit in this view is that, when individual components of a system are put together to produce a larger functional unit, qualities develop which are not predictable from the behaviour of the individual components. The holistic approach to medicine insists on the study not only of individual disease but also of the response of people to their disease – physically, psychologically, and socially. A treatment plan must meet the unique needs of each individual, and all aspects of an illness are taken into account, such as the effects of the illness on personal relations, the family, work, and the patient's emotional well being. Holistic treatment prefers to encourage the patient's own capacity for self-healing, rather than having recourse to surgical or drug remedies, and emphasizes education and self-care, including proper diet and exercise.

Holland *Netherlands, The*

Holles (of Ifield), Denzil Holles, Baron [holis] (1599–1680) English statesman, born in Houghton, Nottinghamshire, C England, UK. He entered parliament in 1624, and in 1642 was one of the five members whom Charles I tried to arrest. In the Civil War, he advocated peace, was accused of treason, and fled to Normandy. In 1660 he was spokesman of the commission delegated to recall Charles II at Breda, and in 1661 was created a baron.

Holloway, Stanley (1890–1982) Entertainer, born in London, UK. He had various occupations before making his London stage debut in *Kissing Time* (1920) and first film appearance in *The Rotters* (1921). He was an original member of The Co-Optimists revue group (1921–30). Popular on radio and in pantomime, he created the monologue characters of Sam Small and the Ramsbottom family, and he was a genial comedy actor in such Ealing film classics as *Passport to Pimlico* (1948), *The Lavender Hill Mob* (1951), and *The Titfield Thunderbolt* (1952). He is perhaps best known for his role of Alfred Dolittle in *My Fair Lady* on Broadway (1956–8) and later on film (1964). He published an autobiography, *Wiv a Little Bit of Luck* (1969).

Hollows, Fred(erick) Cossom (1929–93) Ophthalmologist, born in Dunedin, New Zealand. He studied in New Zealand

and in Britain, and became associate professor at the University of New South Wales and chairman of ophthalmology at Prince of Wales Hospital, Sydney. He was famed for his contribution to the prevention and treatment of blinding eye infections, especially trachoma, among Australian Aborigines, Eritreans, and Vietnamese. In Eritrea he trained doctors to perform simple eye surgery, and helped establish a factory to manufacture plastic intra-ocular lenses. He planned similar projects for Vietnam, Bangladesh, Burma, and Nepal. In 1991 he was named Australian of the Year, and in 1993 won the Rotary International Award for Human Understanding.

Holly, Buddy, popular name of **Charles Hardin Holley** (1936–59) Rock singer, songwriter, and guitarist, born in Lubbock, Texas, USA. Originally from a country-and-western background, he was also influenced by hill-billy, Mexican, and African-American music. He was the first to add drums and a rhythm-and-blues beat to the basic country style, and his band, The Crickets, was among the first to use the now standard rock-and-roll line-up of two guitars, bass, and drums. He left The Crickets in 1958, and was killed when a plane carrying him between concerts crashed. At the time he had released only three US albums. He became an important cult figure, much of his material being released posthumously. His most popular records include 'That'll Be The Day', 'Not Fade Away', 'Peggy Sue', and 'Oh Boy'.

holly An evergreen tree or shrub (*Ilex aquifolia*) growing to 10 m/30 ft, native to Europe; bark silvery-grey; leaves leathery, glossy above with wavy, spiny margins; flowers 4-petalled, white, followed by red berries, males and females on separate trees. It is widely cultivated for ornament, especially at Christmas time; many cultivars have variegated leaves or yellow berries. (Family: Aquifoliaceae.)

hollyhock A biennial or perennial (*Althaea rosea*), native to China, and a popular garden plant; stem growing to 3 m/10 ft in second year; leaves 30 cm/12 in across, rounded and shallowly-lobed; flowers 6–7 cm/$2\frac{1}{2}$–$2\frac{3}{4}$ in diameter in a wide range of colours, forming a long spike. (Family: Malvaceae.)

Hollywood A suburb of Los Angeles, California, USA, which after 1912 developed into the centre of film production in the USA. Its studios dominated the world motion picture market from the 1920s, and it is still a major centre for the production of visual entertainment in both film and television.

Holmes, Larry, nickname **the Easton Assassin** (1949–) Boxer, born in Cuthbert, Georgia, USA. He beat Ken Norton for the World Boxing Council heavyweight title in 1978, retained it 16 times, gave it up in 1984, was named International Boxing Federation champion that year, and held the title until 1985, when he finally lost to Michael Spinks in his 49th contest, just one short of Rocky Marciano's record. He lost the return contest with Spinks, and in 1988 challenged Mike Tyson for the title, but was defeated in four rounds. He retired after winning 48 of his 51 contests, 34 by a knockout, then launched a comeback in 1991, but lost a title challenge to Evander Holyfield in 1992 when well into his forties.

Holmes, Oliver Wendell, Jr, nickname **the Great Dissenter** (1841–1935) Judge, born in Boston, Massachusetts, USA, the son of writer **Oliver Wendell Holmes** (1809–94). He studied at Harvard Law School, then served in the Union army as captain in the Civil War. From 1867 he practised law in Boston, edited Kent's *Commentaries* (1873), became editor of the *American Law Review* (1870–8), and was appointed professor of law at Harvard (1873–82). He made his reputation with a fundamental book on *The Common Law* (1881). He then became associate justice (1882) and chief justice (1899–1902) of the Supreme Court of Massachusetts, and associate justice of the US Supreme Court (1902–32). He was one of the great judicial figures of his time, and many of his judgments on common law and equity, as well as his dissent on the interpretation of the Fourteenth Amendment, have become famous.

HOLMES Abbreviation for **Home Office Large Major Enquiry System**, a computer system introduced for crime detection in the UK in the 1980s, as a result of the problems experienced by the police in the Yorkshire Ripper enquiry. It gives the police immediate access to large databases containing information about crimes, thus saving time and reducing the risk of human error in carrying out investigations.

Holmes a Court, (Michael) Robert Hamilton [hohmz uh kaw(r)t] (1937–90) Entrepreneur, born in South Africa. He studied in South Africa, New Zealand, and at the University of Western Australia, Perth, and became a lawyer. He acquired his first company in 1970, and went on to establish the Bell Group, where he demonstrated his skill in managing takeovers, even making money out of unsuccessful takeover bids such as those for the Ansett Transport Group and Elders. The Bell Group owned the Herald and Weekly Times newspaper group, among numerous other interests, and in 1984 stunned the business world by bidding for BHP, Australia's largest company. The Bell Group was debilitated after the 1987 stock-market crash, but by 1990, when he died, Holmes a Court's private company was recovering well, consolidating his position as one of the wealthiest people in Australia. He had a significant collection of Australian art and was involved in horse breeding and racing. His widow **Janet Holmes a Court** (1944–) became chair of the $400 million family company Heytesbury Holdings after her husband's sudden death.

Holocaust The attempt by Nazi Germany, under Hitler, to systematically destroy European Jews. From the inception of the Nazi regime in 1933 Jews were deprived of civil rights, persecuted, physically attacked, imprisoned, and murdered. With the gradual conquest of Europe by Germany, the death toll increased, and a meeting at Wannsee (Jan 1942) made plans for the so-called 'final solution'. Goering, Himmler, Reinhard Heydrich (1904–42), and Eichmann were the principal architects. Jews were driven from their homes, and transported to concentration camps, slave-labour camps, and extermination camps. There they were herded into gas chambers and their bodies burned in crematoria. Mass shootings had already occurred in Russia and other Eastern European countries, carried out by action squads (*Einsatzgruppen*). By the end of the war in 1945, more than 6 million Jews had been murdered out of a total Jewish population of 8 million in those countries occupied by the Nazis. Of these the largest number, 3 million, were from Poland. Other minorities (gypsies, political and religious opponents, the handicapped, and homosexuals) were also subject to Nazi atrocities. The major consequence was the acceleration of the establishment of the state of Israel.

Holocene epoch [holoseen] The most recent of the two geological epochs of the Quaternary period, from 10 000 years ago to the present time.

holography A method of lensless photography which gives true 3-dimensional images; invented by Dennis Gabor in 1948. Modern holograms are made using laser light. The light beam is divided into two parts: one falls directly onto photographic film; the other is reflected onto the film via the object. An interference pattern forms, which is recorded on the film; there is no actual picture in the usual sense. The processed film is the hologram. The image is viewed by illuminating the hologram using laser light; it may be viewed using ordinary light, but the image is multi-coloured. Holograms have many uses – for example, as a security device on credit cards, and some bank notes.

holophrase [holofrayz] A one-word utterance, characteristic of the usage of very young children in the process of language acquisition, eg *naughty*, *gone*. It takes the place of what would be a full sentence in older speech.

holoplankton *plankton*

Holothuroidea [holothuhroydia] *sea cucumber*

Holst, Gustav (Theodore) (1874–1934) Composer, born of Swedish origin in Cheltenham, Gloucestershire, SWC England, UK. He studied at the Royal College of Music, London, but neuritis in his hand prevented him from becoming a concert pianist. From 1905 he taught music at St Paul's School, Hammersmith, and from 1907 at Morley College. He emerged as a major composer with the seven-movement suite *The Planets* (1914–16), and gave up most of his teaching in 1925. Among his other major works are *The Hymn of Jesus* (1917), his comic operas *The Perfect Fool* (1922) and *At the Boar's Head* (1924), and his orchestral tone poem, *Egdon Heath* (1927).

Holt, Harold (Edward) (1908–67) Australian politician and prime minister (1966–7), born in Sydney, New South Wales, SE Australia. He studied law at Melbourne University, joined the United Australia Party, which was to be replaced by the Liberal Party of Australia, and entered the House of Representatives in 1935. He became deputy leader of his Party in 1956, and leader and prime minister when Robert Menzies retired in 1966. During the Vietnam War he strongly supported the USA with the slogan 'all the way with LBJ'. He died in office while swimming at Portsea, near Melbourne.

Holt, Victoria *Hibbert, Eleanor*

Holub, Miroslav [holoob] (1923–98) Poet, born in Plzen, W Czech Republic. He studied medicine in Prague, specializing in immunology, and worked at the Max Planck Institute in Freiburg (1968–9). His collections include *Kam tece krev* (1963, Where the Blood Flows), *Udalosti* (1971, Events), and *Naopal* (1982, On the Contrary).

Holyfield, Evander [holeefeeld] (1962–) Boxer, born in Atlanta, Georgia, USA. He became the World Boxing Association (WBA) heavyweight champion in 1996 and the International Boxing Federation heavyweight champion in 1998. He was undisputed heavyweight champion of the world in 1990–2. He lost the WBA crown to John Ruiz in 2001.

Holy Ghost *Holy Spirit*

Holyhead [holeehed], Welsh **Caergybi** 53°19N 4°38W, pop (2000e) 12 900. Port and largest town on the island of Anglesey, NW Wales, UK; on N coast of Holy I; railway; ferry to Dun Laoghaire and Dublin, Ireland; aluminium, marine engineering, light industry, tourism, yachting; Holyhead Mountain (Mynydd Twr), 216 m/710 ft; breakwater (1845–73), 2·4 km/1½ mi long; St Cybi's Church (founded 6th-c) within 3rd-c Roman walls; Ucheldre Centre; summer Leisure Island Festival (Jul); Arts Festival (Jun/Oct).

Holy Innocents' Day A Christian festival (28 Dec) which commemorates the killing of the male children around Bethlehem by Herod (*Matt* 2).

Holy Island *Holyhead; Lindisfarne*

Holy League The name given to a number of European alliances formed during the 15th-c, 16th-c, and 17th-c. The Holy League of 1495 was forged between the Hapsburg Emperor Maximilian I, Pope Alexander VI, Spain, Venice, Milan, and ultimately England to protect Italy from French ascendancy. The League of 1511–13 was organized by Pope Julius II, and included Henry VIII of England, Spain, Venice, the Hapsburg Empire, and Switzerland. The Holy League of 1526 was formed against the Emperor Charles V of Spain by France, the Papacy, England, Venice, and Milan. In 1571 an alliance was formed between Venice, Spain, and the Papacy to counter Turkish supremacy in the E Mediterranean. The League's fleet commanded by Don John of Austria smashed the Turks at Lepanto in the same year, before disagreements divided the Allies; by 1573 Spain continued the struggle alone. The French Holy League of 1576, also known as the Catholic League, was led by the Guise faction during the French Wars of Religion. Henry III ordered its dissolution in 1577, but it was revived in 1584 to play a major part in the War of the Three Henrys (1585–9). The Holy League of 1609 was a military alliance of the German Catholic princes, formed at the start of the Jülich Succession (1606–14). During most of the Thirty Years War (1618–38) its forces served the imperial cause. In 1683 a Holy League was formed against Ottoman Turkey following the Imperial repossession of Vienna, consisting of Poland, the Hapsburg Empire, Venice, and the Papacy. Pope Innocent XI planned further crusades in Hungary, Greece, and Moldavia; the latter failed (1686), but after several years' fighting (1683–99) the League recovered most of Hungary for the Hapsburgs.

Holyoake, George (Jacob) (1817–1906) Social reformer, born in Birmingham, West Midlands, C England, UK. He taught mathematics, lectured on Owen's socialist system, edited the *Reasoner*, and promoted the bill legalizing secular affirmations. He was the last person imprisoned in England on a charge of atheism (1842). He wrote histories of the co-operative movement and of secularism.

Holy of Holies The innermost and most sacred part of the Jewish tabernacle, and later of the Jerusalem Temple, cubic in shape, which contained the Ark of the Covenant. Only the High Priest was permitted to enter, and only once yearly on the Day of Atonement (Yom Kippur).

Holy Orders *Orders, Holy*

Holy Roman Empire The revived mediaeval title of the Roman Empire, dating from the 9th-c, when the papacy granted the title to Charlemagne, King of the Franks. It was later bestowed upon German princely families, including the Hohenstaufens, Luxemburgs, and Habsburgs. After Charlemagne, imperial power was greatest under the Hohenstaufens in the 12th–13th-c: the full title 'Holy Roman Empire' (*sacrum Romanum imperium*) was used from the reign of Frederick I (**'Barbarossa'**); and Frederick II came close to uniting diverse imperial territories that covered much of C Europe and Italy. From the 14th-c, the Empire's power declined with the rise of princely power and city-states. In 1806 the imperial crown was surrendered to Napoleon. It was not revived after his downfall.

Holyroodhouse, Palace of [holeeroodhows] The official residence in Scotland of the reigning monarch. Built in the 16th-c at Edinburgh, the palace was reconstructed in the 1670s by the architect Sir William Bruce (d.1710).

Holy Shroud or **Shroud of Turin** A relic, alleged to be the burial-sheet of Jesus Christ, known since the 14th-c, and preserved in the Cathedral at Turin since 1578. It portrays an image (clearer when shown using a photographic negative) of the front and back of a man's body, with markings that seem to correspond to the stigmata of Jesus. Controversy over its authenticity resulted in the use of independent radiocarbon-dating tests by three research centres in 1988, using a tiny piece of the fabric. The results indicated a late provenance for the shroud, but controversy over the methods used continued in the 1990s. The question of how the body image was produced remains open.

Holy Spirit A term used to denote the presence or power of God, often imbued with personal or quasi-personal characteristics; in Christian thought considered the third person of the Trinity, alongside the Father and the Son. Doctrinal differences exist, though, between Western churches which regard the Spirit as 'proceeding from' both the Father and the Son, and Eastern Christianity which accepts procession from the Father only. In the Bible the Spirit was often the vehicle of God's revelatory activity, inspiring the prophets, but it was also depicted as an agent in creation. In the New Testament, the Spirit is described as descending upon Jesus 'as a dove' at his baptism (*Mark* 1.10), as glorifying Jesus after his death (*John* 16.12–15), and even as 'the Spirit of Christ' in *Rom* 8.9. In Acts, the Church received the Spirit at Pentecost, from which time it continued to direct the Church's missionary activities. Paul not only considered the 'gifts of the Spirit' as empowering various ministries in the Church, but also as associated with the ecstatic practices of speaking in tongues and prophesying (*1 Cor* 12–14), which continue to feature prominently in Pentecostal churches.

Holy Week In the Christian Church, the week before Easter, beginning on Palm Sunday. It includes Maundy Thursday and Good Friday.

Holywell [holeewel], Welsh **Treffynnon** 53°17N 3°13W, pop (2000e) 12 400. Town in Flintshire, NE Wales, UK; 6 km/4 mi NW of Flint; woollens, rayon, chemicals; 'the Welsh Lourdes', place of pilgrimage since the 7th-c, where St Winefride (Gwenfrewi) was beheaded; 15th-c St Winefride's Chapel; pilgrimages (Jun, Nov).

Home of the Hirsel, Baron [hyoom], formerly **Sir Alec Douglas-Home**, originally **Alexander Frederick Douglas-Home, 14th Earl of Home** (1903–95) British statesman and prime minister (1963–4), born in London, UK. He studied at Oxford, became a Conservative MP in 1931, and was Chamberlain's secretary during the negotiations with Hitler and beyond (1937–40). He became minister of state at the Scottish Office (1951–5), succeeded to the peerage as 14th Earl (1951), and was Commonwealth Relations secretary (1955–60) and foreign secretary (1960–3). After Macmillan's resignation, he astonished everyone by emerging as premier. He made history by renouncing his peerage and fighting a by-election, during which, although premier, he was technically a member of neither House. After the 1964 defeat by the Labour Party, he was leader of the Opposition until replaced in 1965 by Edward Heath, in whose 1970–4 government he was foreign secretary. In 1974 he was made a life peer.

home counties Those counties which border London, UK, and into which the city has expanded. These are Essex, Kent, Surrey, Buckinghamshire, Hertfordshire, and the former counties of Middlesex and Berkshire.

Home Guard A home defence militia, raised during the summer of 1940, when the German armies seemed poised to complete the conquest of W Europe by invading the UK. At first called the Local Defence Volunteers, the name was changed at Prime Minister Winston Churchill's urging to the more evocative title of 'Home Guard'. The force was finally disbanded in 1945.

Homelands *apartheid; South Africa*

homeobox In genetics, a sequence of c.180 nucleotides which codes for a 60-amino-acid region in proteins involved in the regulation of transcription. Originally discovered in *Drosophila*, homeoboxes have now been found in the genes of all higher eucaryotic species. They appear to provide the type of positional information necessary for orderly development in the embryo. There is evidence that the positioning of homeobox genes along the chromosome is, in some cases, linearly related to their expression in development; ie genes are arranged in the order in which they are expressed both spatially and temporally in the organism.

homeopathy A practice of medicine devised by German physician Samuel Hahnemann in the early 19th-c with the principles of (1) like cures like; and (2) drug activity is enhanced by dilution. Thus a drug which in large doses would induce particular symptoms in a healthy individual is used after a series of dilutions to treat a sick individual suffering similar symptoms. There is no scientific evidence that the theory of homeopathy is correct. Homeopathic medicines are prescribed individually by the study of the whole person according to their basic temperament and responses, and its approach is gaining popularity following the public example of several famous personalities, such as members of the British Royal Family, who have endorsed this form of treatment.

homeostasis / homoeostasis [hohmiohstaysis] A term initially used to describe the stability or steady state of the extracellular fluid apparent in healthy individuals. Nowadays it is often used to describe the ways in which this stability is achieved, not only in humans but also in other animals. Disturbance of the volume, composition, and temperature (in warm-blooded animals) of extracellular fluid may result in ill-health and possibly death. Consequently much of physiology is concerned with the study of the mechanisms which operate to ensure that this fluid is maintained within precise limits at all times. For example, body temperature in warm-blooded mammals is maintained by active metabolic mechanisms such as shivering, if it falls too low, or panting, if it rises too high.

Homer, Greek **Homēros** (c.8th-c BC) Greek poet, to whom are attributed the great epics, the *Iliad*, the story of the siege of Troy, and the *Odyssey*, the tale of Ulysses's wanderings. The place of his birth is doubtful, probably a Greek colony on the coast of Asia Minor, and his date, once put as far back as 1200 BC, from the style of the poems attributed to him, is now thought to be much later. Arguments have long raged over whether his works are in fact by the same hand, or have their origins in the lays of Homer and his followers (*Homeridae*), and there seems little doubt that the works were originally based on current ballads which were much modified and extended. Like much orally transmitted poetry, they are characterized by much use of repeated phrases, lines, epithets, and even paragraphs. Of the true Homer, nothing is positively known. The so-called *Homeric hymns* are certainly of a later age.

Homer, Winslow (1836–1910) Painter, born in Boston, Massachusetts, USA. After an apprenticeship to a lithographer (1855–7), he began his career as an illustrator for such magazines as *Harper's Weekly* (1859–67), making drawings of routine life at the front during the Civil War. He spent two years (1881–3) at Tynemouth, Tyne and Wear, and began painting maritime scenes. On his return to the USA he continued to depict the sea, living at Prouts Neck, an isolated fishing village on the E seaboard, where he spent the rest of his life. His highly original work is often regarded as a reflection of the American pioneering spirit.

home rule The handing down of certain legislative powers and administrative functions, previously exercised by a higher authority, to an elected body within a geographically defined area; usually put forward as an alternative to separatism. It was illustrated by the government of Northern Ireland until 1972 when Stormont, the Northern Ireland Parliament, was abolished. Since the early 1970s in the UK, for political movements such as the Scottish National Party and Irish republicans, home rule has tended to become synonymous with separatism.

Homestead Act (1862) A US law allowing a grant of 160 acres of public land to settlers, conditional on their staying five years, the making of improvements to the property, and the payment of fees. Homesteaders had to be US citizens or intending citizens, and either heads of families or over 21, but could be of either sex.

homicide The unlawful killing of one human being by another. The term varies in its application among different jurisdictions. In England and Wales, for example, unlawful homicide includes the crimes of murder, manslaughter, and infanticide. The victim must be an independent human being (and not, for example, a fetus which is not viable). In certain circumstances homicide may be lawful, such as in self-defence, or killing an enemy in battle during war, or possibly in the defence of property or in properly conducted surgery, but the action taken has to be reasonable in all the circumstances. In both Scotland and the USA, homicide involves causing the death of another either by an act or by an intentional or negligent omission when there is a legal duty to act. Criminal homicide usually includes murder (first and second degree), manslaughter, and negligent homicide. In Scotland, the term **culpable homicide** is used instead of *manslaughter* for deaths which result from assaults or acts of criminal negligence.

homing overlay device Part of a US experiment to achieve a practical ballistic missile defence using space-based systems. A 'layer' of defences would be established outside the atmosphere to intercept incoming nuclear warheads.

hominid A member of the primate family Hominidae, containing humans, their immediate ancestors, and close extinct relatives. Two genera are usually recognized: *Australopithecus* and *Homo*. Hominid defining features include truncal erectness, bipedality, and rotary chewing; brain expansion and face and jaw reduction were later developments. Anatomical and molecular evidence indicate that the hominid and African ape lineages separated c.6–8 million years ago. The earliest definite hominid fossils are c.5·5 million years old, although most finds are <4 million years. Humans have greater reasoning ability than other species, and have developed language and a wide use of tools. Unlike most species, they no longer have an intimate biological relationship with one particular habitat, but can use their powers of reason and technology to control the environment, allowing them to occupy virtually all habitats. Worldwide population passed 6000 million in 1999.

Homo [**ho**moh] (Lat 'man') A genus of the family Hominidae, order Primates. *Homo* features include a medium-large brain (500–2000 cm^3), a high brain:body ratio, bipedal gait, upright posture, and adaptable hands with a precision grip based on thumb–index finger opposition. The genus probably evolved in Africa c.2 million years ago (mya) from *Australopithecus*. Environmental change (increased seasonality, grassland expansion, forest contraction) may have promoted the evolution of *Homo* species by favouring co-operative behaviour in food-gathering and sharing, the making and use of tools involving hand–eye co-ordination, improved communication, and a progressively extended period of infant care and childhood learning. There are four named species of *Homo*, three extinct. *Homo habilis* known from Olduvai Gorge in Tanzania, L Turkana (Rudolf) in Kenya, Sterkfontein in South Africa, and possibly elsewhere, is dated c.2–1·5 mya. It had a lightly built braincase (capacity 500–700 cm^3), projecting face and jaws, relatively large front teeth, but small narrow cheek teeth. Body size was 25–40 kg/55–88 lb with long, powerfully-muscled arms and hands suggesting climbing ability, and short hindlimbs. *Homo rudolfensis*, known only from sites around L Turkana dated 1·9–1·7 mya, was probably bigger-bodied than *H. habilis*, with more modern limb proportions. It was bigger-brained (750–900 cm^3), with a broader, flatter face and larger cheek teeth. *Homo erectus*, also known from sites around L Turkana dated at 1·8–1·6 mya, had strongly built but otherwise largely modern bodily proportions. The skull was also strongly built, with a retreating frontal, flat, thick-walled vault (800–1200 cm^3 capacity), big face and jaws, but only moderate-sized teeth. The evolutionary relationships of *H. habilis*, *H. rudolfensis*, and *H. erectus* are unclear, but since they overlap in time and space they do not form a single evolutionary sequence. On balance, *H. rudolfensis* and *H. erectus* appear more closely related to each other than either is to *H. habilis*, which may be an advanced 'human-like' *Australopithecus* rather than true *Homo*. More evidence is needed to clarify these and other issues. Crude pebble tools and modified bones are known for the same sites as the early *Homo* species, but it is not clear which were tool-making – perhaps all three were. *H. habilis* and *H. rudolfensis* disappear around 1·7–1·5 mya, but *H. erectus* persists for c.1·5 my down to c.300 000 years ago. There are increasing fossil finds in Africa c.1·5–0·6 mya, together with better-made tools (hand axes) and larger sites with more animal bones, suggesting skilled hunting. By 700 000 years ago *H. erectus* had expanded beyond Africa, with finds in Java and China, where evidence of fire indicates ability to exploit a range of habitats and climates. *Homo sapiens*, our own species, evolved from *H. erectus* through archaic, big-faced forms such as Neanderthal Man (Europe, Middle East) and equivalents in Africa and Asia, to fully modern man *H. sapiens sapiens*, which is first known from Africa c.100–120 000 years ago, and shortly afterwards in the Middle East. This subspecies has a relatively light build, a large rounded braincase (12 000–2000 cm^3 – average 1400 cm^3), a high forehead, flat and lightly-built face and jaws, slight or no brow ridges, small crowded teeth, and a definite chin. The earliest fossils (Africa, Middle East) have tools no different from those of archaic *H. sapiens* but later specimens (40 000 years ago) are found with more complex, specialized tool kits which include bone, ivory, and antler as well as stone artefacts, and fine engraving, carving, and cave art. These innovations reflect more complex behaviour patterns that enabled *H. sapiens sapiens* to colonize all continents save Antarctica by the final Pleistocene (10 000 years ago). Subsequent developments include agriculture, domestication, and civilization, and more recently industrialization and explosive population growth.

homoiothermy [homoy**oh**thermee] The regulation of internal body temperature at a relatively constant level, independent of fluctuations in ambient temperature. Higher vertebrates, such as mammals and birds, are warm-blooded (**homoiothermic**), and typically have insulated body coverings to aid temperature regulation.

homology The relationship between equivalent structures and traits in living organisms, derived from the same part of the embryo but existing in different states in related organisms. The forelimb of a horse, the wing of a bird, and the human arm are all homologous structures, as they are derived from the same part of the embryo, even though they differ in appearance.

Homoptera [homo**p**tera] A large order of insects comprising c.45 000 species, including the cicadas, plant hoppers, froghoppers, leaf hoppers, psyllids, whiteflies, aphids, scale insects, and mealybugs; hindlegs often adapted for jumping; feeding on plants, with modified mouthparts for piercing and sucking.

homosexuality A form of sexuality in which the sexual attraction is between members of the same sex. There are both clinical (eg Freudian psycho-medical) and sociological theories to account for homosexuality. Most sociological theories see any form of sexuality as a social construction rather than as displaying any specific, pre-given biological process. Homosexuality has been a subject of considerable political controversy in the West, especially since the formation of the Gay Liberation Movement and the onset of the AIDS virus.

Homs or **Hims**, ancient **Emesa** 34°44N 36°43E, pop (2000e) 665 000. Industrial capital city of Hims governorate, WC Syria; on R Orontes, 160 km/100 mi N of Damascus; road and rail junction; commercial centre in well-irrigated area; oil refining, sugar refining, textiles, cement, metals, silk, rayon, fertilizers, refrigeration plant; Crusader fortress.

Honduras *p.731*

Honecker, Erich [**hon**eker] (1912–94) East German statesman and head of state (1976–89), born in Neunkirchen, W Germany. Active in the Communist youth movement from an early age, he was involved in underground resistance to Hitler, and was imprisoned for 10 years. Released by Soviet forces, he became the first chairman of the Free German Youth in the German Democratic Republic (1946–55). He first entered the Politburo in 1958, was elected Party chief in 1971, and became head of state from 1976 to 1989, when he was dismissed as a consequence of the anti-Communist revolution. Charges were brought against him in the new united Germany that he had ordered the killings along the Berlin Wall and GDR Border, but he was allowed to leave for Chile in 1993 on grounds of illness.

Honegger, Arthur [**on**eger] (1892–1955) Composer, born in Le Havre, NW France, of Swiss parentage. He studied in Zürich and at the Paris Conservatoire, and after World War 1 became one of the group of Parisian composers known as *Les Six*. His dramatic oratorio *King David* established his reputation in 1921, and *Pacific 231* (1923), his musical picture of a locomotive, won considerable popularity. His other works include five symphonies.

honesty A roughly hairy biennial (*Lunaria annua*) 30–100 cm/12–40 in, native to SE Europe; leaves heart-shaped; flowers cross-shaped, reddish-purple, rarely white; capsules 3–4·5 cm/1¼–1¾ in, flat, oval, with a persistent, silvery, central dividing wall (septum). It is often grown in gardens, especially for the old fruiting stems with persistent septa, and is used in dried decorations. (Family: Cruciferae.)

honey A substance prepared by bees from nectar found in blossoms. Because of its palatability and its relative rarity, honey has always been a highly prized food. Its intimate association with nature (meadows and bees, milk and honey) has led to claims of specific health effects for honey, which are not justified. Nectar is sucrose, and this disaccharide is broken down by the bee to yield an equal quantity of the monosaccharides of glucose and fructose (*invert sugar*). The protein, mineral, and vitamin content of honey is negligible. The colour and flavour of honey varies with the flora on which bees feed.

honey ant An ant that stores honeydew in specialized workers, called **repletes**. The abdomen of the replete becomes distended, and it hangs from the ceiling of underground cham-

Honduras

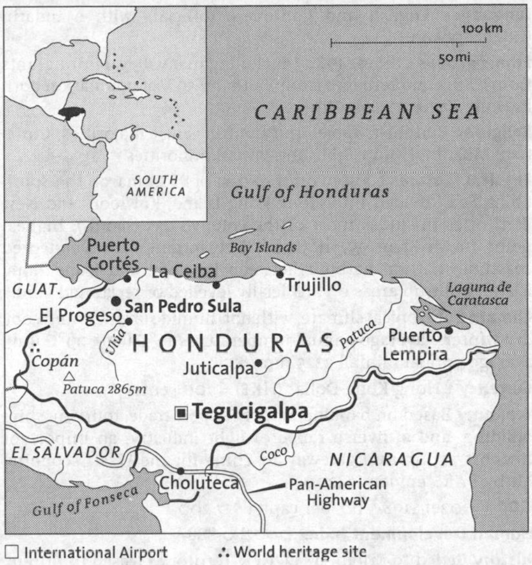

[hondyooras], official name **Republic of Honduras**, Span **República de Honduras**

Local name Honduras

Timezone GMT −6

Area 112 088 km²/43 266 sq mi

Population total (2002e) 6 561 000

Status Republic

Date of independence 1821

Capital Tegucigalpa

Languages Spanish (official), a number of Indian dialects also spoken by aboriginal population

Ethnic groups Spanish-Indian origin (90%), Indian (7%), black (2%)

Religions Roman Catholic (85%), Protestant (mainly Fundamentalist, Moravian, and Methodist) (10%)

Physical features Coastal lands (S) separated from Caribbean coastlands by mountains running NW–SE; S plateau rises to 2849 m/9347 ft at Cerro de las Minas; includes Bay Is in the Caribbean Sea and nearly 300 islands in the Gulf of Fonseca.

Climate Tropical climate in coastal areas, temperate in C and W; average annual temperatures 19°C (Jan), 23°C (Jul) in Tegucigalpa; two wet seasons in upland areas (May–Jul, Sep–Oct); country devastated by hurricane Mitch in 1998.

Currency 1 Lempira (L, La) = 100 centavos

Economy Agriculture (provides a third of national income), forestry, mining, cattle raising; bananas, coffee, beef, cotton, tobacco, sugar; exports of silver, lead and zinc; offshore oil exploration in the Caribbean.

GDP (2002e) $16·29 bn, per capita $2500

Human Development Index (2002) 0·638

History Centre of Mayan culture, 4th–9th-c; settled by the Spanish in early 16th-c, and became province of Guatemala; independence from Spain, 1821; joined Federation of Central America; independence, 1838; several military coups in 1970s; since 1980, a democratic constitutional republic, governed by a President and National Assembly.

Head of State/Government

1982–6 Roberto Suazo Córdova
1986–90 José Azcona Hoyo
1990–4 Rafael Callejas
1994–7 Carlos Roberto Reina
1997–2001 Carlos Roberto Flores Facussé
2001– Ricardo Maduro

bers, acting as a food store. (Order: Hymenoptera. Family: Formicidae.)

honey badger *ratel*

honey bear *kinkajou; sun bear*

honeybee The European honeybee (*Apis mellifera*) and three other species of the genus *Apis*. It is a bee that forms true perennial societies, typically consisting of one queen, several hundred drones, and 50 000 to 80 000 workers. The queen daily lays up to 3000 eggs, one per wax cell on the honeycomb. The drones fertilize new queens during nuptial flights. The workers forage, clean the hive, feed larvae, and perform all other duties. Colonies do not hibernate, but survive over winter on stored honey and pollen. (Order: Hymenoptera. Family: Apidae.)

honeycreeper A name used for two distinct groups of birds inhabiting woodland and eating insects, fruit, and nectar: the **Hawaiian honeycreeper** (Family; Drepanididae, c.17 living species), and some **tanagers** (Family: Thraupidae, 16 species) native to Central and South America.

honeyeater An Australasian bird specialized to eat nectar; tongue long with brush-like tip; also eats fruit and insects; inhabits trees and bushes; lives in small groups; shows great variation in bill shape and lifestyle. (Family: Meliphagidae, 167 species.)

honey fungus A mushroom-shaped fungus (*Armillaria mellea*) which produces creamy white spores on gills on underside of cap; destructive parasite of trees, shrubs, and other plants. (Order: Agaricales.)

honey guide Markings, usually patterns of lines or dots, on the petals of a flower which help guide pollinators to the nectar within.

honeyguide A small brownish bird native to Africa and S or SE Asia; inhabits evergreen forest; eats insects (especially bees) and beeswax; some said to lead animals to bees' nests; lays eggs in nests of other birds. (Family: Indicatoridae, c.13 species.)

honey locust A deciduous tree (*Gleditsia triacanthos*) growing to 45 m/150 ft, a native of North America; trunk and branches covered with stout, often branched spines; leaves divided into oblong leaflets; flowers fragrant, greenish, and inconspicuous, arranged in catkin-like inflorescences; pods up to 4·5 cm/1¾ in long, dark brown, twisted. It is sometimes planted for hedging, and as an ornamental or street tree. (Family: Leguminosae.)

honey possum A marsupial (*Tarsipes rostratus*), native to SW Australia; superficially shrew-like, with a long clasping tail and long narrow snout; tongue brush-like at tip; inhabits heathlands; eats nectar and pollen; also known as **honey mouse**. (Family: Tarsipedidae.)

honeysuckle A member of a large genus mainly comprising shrubs, with a few well-known species of woody climbers with twining stems, deciduous or evergreen; native to the N hemisphere, and widely grown as ornamentals; leaves opposite, members of a pair often joined around the stem; flowers tubular, 2-lipped, often fragrant, in the axils of leaves; berries red, blue, or black. The **common honeysuckle** or **woodbine** is pollinated by night-flying moths, and produces sweet scent at night. (Genus: *Lonicera*, 200 species. Family: Caprifoliaceae.)

Hong Kong *p.732*

Hong Kong Island area 75 sq km/29 sq mi. Island within Hong Kong region, bounded on all sides by the South China Sea; contains the city of Hong Kong; highest point, Victoria Peak (554 m/1818 ft).

Hongwu [hongwoo], also spelled **Hung-wu**, originally **Zhu Yuanzhang** (1328–98) First emperor of the Chinese Ming dyn-

Hong Kong

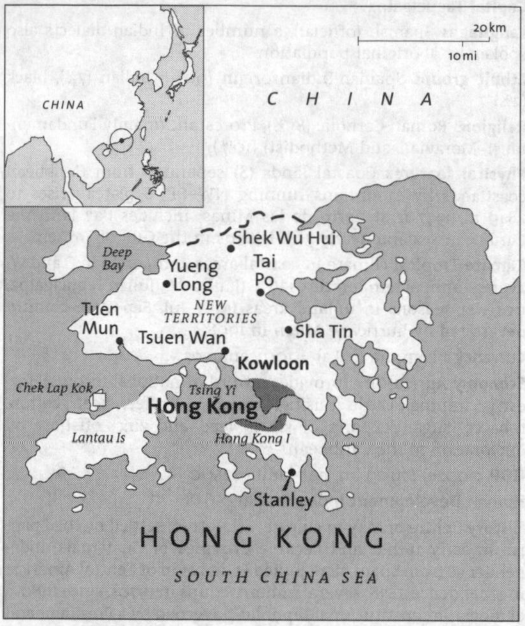

Chin **Hsiang Kang** (Special administrative region of China)

Timezone GMT +8

Area 1066 km²/412 sq mi

Population total (2000e) 6 967 000

Capital Hong Kong

Languages English and Cantonese (official), with Mandarin widely spoken

Ethnic groups Chinese (98%), including many illegal immigrants from China and refugees from Vietnam; 59% of population born in Hong Kong, 37% in China

Religions Buddhist, Taoist and Confuncianist majorities, Christian, Muslim, Hindu, Sikh, and Jewish minorities

Physical features Located off the coast of SE China, on the South China Sea; divided into Hong Kong Island, Kowloon, and New Territories (includes most of the colony's 235 islands); highest point, Tai Mo Shan, 957 m/3140 ft; hilly terrain, sharply indented coastline; natural harbour between Kowloon and Hong Kong Island; built-up areas on artificially levelled or reclaimed land.

Climate Subtropical climate, with hot, humid summers and cool, dry winters; average annual temperatures 16°C (Jan), 29°C (Jul); average annual rainfall 2225 mm/88 in.

Currency 1 Hong Kong Dollar (HK$) = 100 cents

Economy Based on banking, import-export trade, tourism, shipbuilding, and a diverse range of light industry; an important freeport acting as a gateway to China for the West; economy hit by SARS epidemic (2003).

GDP (2002e) $198·5 bn, per capita $27 200

Human Development Index (2002) 0·888

History Ceded to Britain, 1842; New Territories leased to Britain, 1898; occupied by the Japanese in World War 2; British Crown Colony, Governor represented the British Crown, advised by an Executive Council; in 1997, Britain's 99-year lease of the New Territories expired, whereupon Hong Kong was restored to China; China has designated Hong Kong a special administrative region from 1997; it will remain a freeport, foreign markets will be retained, and the Hong Kong dollar will remain as official currency; new Chief Executive appointed (first incumbent, Tung Chee-hwa), with new membership of advisory councils; however, anxiety over the colony's political future remains.

Chief Executive

1997– Tung Chee-hwa

asty (1368–1644), known posthumously as **Taizu**. His rise has few world history parallels. Born into a poor Nanjing family and orphaned at 16, he was in turn Buddhist novice, beggar, White Lotus secret society member, and Red Turban rebel. Setting up his own organization, he seized Nanjing (1356), overran the Yangtze basin, took Beijing, overthrew the Yuan dynasty (1368), established a Ming ('brilliant') dynasty at Nanjing, and took the reign name **Hongwu** ('vast military power'). He then drove the Mongols out of China, Korea, Manchuria, and beyond the Tien Shan. He bloodily suppressed secret societies and subversives, set up a special police with torture prisons, and concentrated all power in his own hands. Grotesque in appearance with a snout-like face, he was known as 'pig emperor': puns about it were risky.

Honiara [hohniahra] 9°28S 159°57E, pop (2000e) 46 000. Port and capital town of the Solomon Is, SW Pacific, on R Mataniko, NW coast of Guadalcanal I; airport; developed after World War 2 around the site of US military headquarters; coconuts, fishing, timber.

Honolulu [honolooloo] 21°19N 157°52W, pop (2000e) 371 700. State capital in Honolulu Co, Hawaii, USA; largest city in the state, and a port on Mamala Bay, Oahu I; a noted tourist resort, with the famous beach at Waikiki; harbour entered by William Brown, an English captain, 1794; capital of the Kingdom of Hawaii, 1845; US naval base at Pearl Harbor, attacked by the Japanese (7 Dec 1941); airport; three universities; sugar processing, fruit canning; headquarters of US Pacific Fleet; Bishop Museum, Pearl Harbor, Iolani Palace (the only royal palace in the USA), Aloha Tower, Diamond Head Crater; King Kamehameha Day (Jun), Aloha Week (Sep).

Honorius, Flavius [onawrius] (384–423) Roman Emperor of the West (393–423), the younger son of Theodosius I. A young and feeble ruler, he abandoned Britain to the barbarians, and cowered in Ravenna while Alaric and the Goths besieged and sacked Rome (408–10). From 395 to 408, power was effectively in the hands of Stilicho.

honours list In the UK, the military and civil awards suggested by the prime minister and approved by the sovereign at New Year and on the sovereign's official birthday in June. The recipients are people who have, broadly, rendered conspicuous service to the nation, and range from public servants and captains of industry through voluntary workers to distinguished participants in the fields of sport, entertainment, and the arts.

Honshu [honshoo] pop (2000e) 102 151 000; area 231 119 sq km/ 89 212 sq mi. Largest of the four main islands of Japan; bounded W by the East Sea (Sea of Japan), E by the Pacific Ocean; separated from Hokkaido I (N) by the Tsugaru-kaikyo Strait, from Shikoku I (S) by the Seto Naikai Sea, and from Kyushu I (SW) by the Shin-Kanmon-Kaikyo Tunnels and Suo-nada Sea; c.1290 km/800 mi long, 48–240 km/30–150 mi wide; broadest in the C, rising to the Japan Alps; highest peak, Mt Fuji (3776 m/ 12 388 ft); Lake Biwa (W), largest lake in Japan; coastal lowlands include most of the population, and several major cities; earthquakes common; rice, tea, cotton, fruit, silk; oil, zinc, copper; wide range of industries centred on cities.

Honthorst, Gerrit van [honthaw(r)st] (1590–1656) Painter, born in Utrecht, The Netherlands. He moved to Italy (c.1610), returning to Holland in 1620, and twice visited England (1620, 1628), where he painted portraits of the royal family. He was fond of painting candle-lit interiors. His brother **William van Hont-**

horst (1604–66), historical and portrait painter, worked for the court of Berlin (1650–64).

Hooch or **Hoogh, Pieter de** [hohkh] (c.1629–c.1684) Painter, born in Rotterdam, The Netherlands. By 1654 he was living in Delft, and probably came under the influence of Carel Fabritius and his pupil, Vermeer. 'Courtyard of a House in Delft' (1658, National Gallery, London) and the 'Card Players' (royal collection) are among the outstanding examples of the Dutch school of the 17th-c, with their characteristically serene domestic interior or courtyard scenes, warm colouring, and delicate light effects.

Hood (of Whitley), Samuel Hood, 1st Viscount (1724–1816) British admiral, born in Thorncombe, Dorset, S England, UK. He joined the navy in 1741, and fought during the American Revolution, when he defeated the French in the West Indies (1782), for which he was made a baron in the Irish peerage. In 1784 he became an MP, and in 1788 a Lord of the Admiralty. In 1793, he directed the occupation of Toulon and the operations in the Gulf of Lyon. He was created a viscount in 1796.

Hood, Thomas (1799–1845) Poet and humorist, born in London, UK. He achieved recognition when, with **John Hamilton Reynolds** (1794–1852), he published *Odes and Addresses to Great People* (1825). In his *Whims and Oddities* (1826) he showed his graphic talent in 'picture-puns', of which he seems to have been the inventor. In 1844 he started his own *Hood's Monthly Magazine*.

hooded crow *carrion crow*

hooded seal A true seal, native to the N Atlantic and adjoining seas (*Cystophora cristata*); grey with irregular black patches; adult male with enlarged nasal cavity which inflates, forming enormous bulbous 'hood' on top of head; lives around drifting ice; young called *bluebacks*.

hoof-and-mouth disease *foot-and-mouth disease*

Hooft, Pieter [hohft] (1581–1647) Poet, playwright, and historian, born in Amsterdam, The Netherlands. He wrote lyrical verse early in his career, then plays (*Granida*, 1605; *Baeto*, 1626), and finally turned to the writing of history with his unfinished *Nederlandsze Historien 1555–85* (1642–54), important also for the establishment of the Dutch language.

Hooke, Robert (1635–1703) Chemist and physicist, born in Freshwater, Isle of Wight, S England, UK. He studied at Oxford, became curator of experiments to the Royal Society (1662), and in 1677 was appointed its secretary. He formulated the law governing elasticity (**Hooke's law**), and invented the balance spring for watches. The Gregorian telescope and microscope are materially his inventions, with which he made important observations, many of which were published in his *Micrographia* (1665).

Hooker, John Lee (1917–2001) Musician, born in Clarksdale, Missouri, USA. A blues singer and guitarist, he began his career in Detroit in 1948 with the release of 'Boogie Chillun', the biggest of his several hit records. He toured continually, appearing with many of the leading figures in rock. He also appeared in the films *The Blues Brothers* (1980) and *The Color Purple* (1985). He was inducted into the Rock 'n' Roll Hall of Fame in 1991.

Hooker, Richard (1554–1600) Anglican theologian, born in Heavitree, Devon, SW England, UK. He studied at Oxford, was ordained in 1581, and became rector of a parish near Tring. After engaging in doctrinal controversy, he resolved to set forth the basis of Church government, and in 1591 accepted the living of Boscombe near Salisbury, where he began his eight volume work *Of the Laws of Ecclesiastical Polity* (1594, 1597, 1648, 1662). It is mainly to this work that Anglican theology owes its tone and direction.

Hooke's law In physics, a law expressing the proportionality of strain to the stress causing it; stated by Robert Hooke. It is valid for small stresses only. When applied to springs, a small extension x of the spring exerts a proportional restoring force, $F = -kx$, where k is a constant, a measure of the spring's stiffness.

Hook of Holland, Dutch **Hoek van Holland** Cape on the SW coast of South Holland province, SW Netherlands; N of the mouth of the Nieuwe Maas R; also the name of a port 27 km/ 17 mi NW of Rotterdam; ferry links with Harwich, UK.

hookworm infestation An important cause of anaemia and ill health in tropical countries or warm environments, caused by nematode worms that become hooked on to the lining of the small intestine and suck blood. The adult worms lay eggs which are passed out in the stool and hatch into larvae. The disease is acquired when these larvae penetrate the skin of people working in wet land.

Hoon, Geoffrey (1953–) British statesman, born in Derby, Derbyshire, C England, UK. He studied at Nottingham and Cambridge universities and worked as a lecturer at Leeds University and in Kentucky before becoming a barrister. He joined the Labour Party in 1977, became an MEP (1984–94), and was elected MP for Ashfield in 1992. An able politician, he quickly rose through the ranks gaining posts within the Lord Chancellor's Department (1998) and the Foreign Office (1999), and in 1999 was appointed defence secretary. His department faced a challenging period during Britain's involvement in the Iraq War (2003).

hoopoe A ground-dwelling bird (*Upupa epops*) native to Africa and S Eurasia; pink body; black and white wings and tail; large crest; long curved bill; inhabits woodland edges; eats worms and insects. (Family: Upupidae.) The name is also used for **wood-hoopoes** (Family: Phoeniculidae) and **hoopoe larks** (Family: Alaudidae).

Hoover, Herbert (Clark) (1874–1964) US statesman and 31st president (1929–33), born in West Branch, Iowa, USA. He studied at Stanford, then worked abroad as an engineer. During and after World War 1 he was associated with the relief of distress in Europe. In 1921 he became secretary of commerce, and in 1928 received the Republican Party's presidential nomination. As president, his opposition to direct governmental assistance for the unemployed after the world slump of 1929 made him unpopular, and he was beaten by Roosevelt in 1932. He assisted Truman with the various American–European economic relief programmes which followed World War 2. The *Hoover Dam* is named after him.

Hoover, J(ohn) Edgar (1895–1972) US public servant, born in Washington, District of Columbia, USA. He studied law at George Washington University in 1917, after taking evening classes. He entered the Justice Department, becoming special assistant to the attorney general in 1919, and assistant director of the Federal Bureau of Investigation (FBI) in 1921. He became FBI director in 1924, and remained in charge until his death, remodelling it to make it more efficient, and campaigning against city gangster rackets in the inter-war years, and against Communist sympathizers in the post-war period. He was later criticized for abusing his position by engaging in vendettas against liberal activists. It is generally accepted that he retained his position as FBI director over 48 years as a result of his knowledge of the private and political activities of the presidents under whom he served. Ironically, since his death many details of his own unconventional lifestyle have emerged.

Hoover Dam, formerly **Boulder Dam** (1936–47) 36°01N 114°45W. One of the world's major dams, on the Colorado R, Arizona, USA, impounding L Mead; built 1931–6; height 221 m/ 726 ft; length 379 m/1244 ft; can generate 1345 megawatts of hydroelectricity; named after President Hoover.

hop A perennial climber (*Humulus lupulus*) native to Europe and W Asia; stems 3–6 m/10–20 ft, twining clockwise with small hooks to aid support; male and female flowers on separate plants; males tiny, 5-petalled; females forming papery cones in fruit. It was used in brewing from the 13th-c (*hops*), but not cultivated on a large scale until the 16th-c. Only the fruiting heads are used to flavour and preserve beer. (Family: Cannabidaceae.)

Hope, A(lec) D(erwent) (1907–2000) Poet and critic, born in Cooma, New South Wales, SE Australia. He studied at Sydney and Oxford, and became professor of literature at the Australian National University. His works include *The Wandering Islands* (1955) and *Poems* (1960). His *Collected Poems* (1972) is one of the major books of Australian verse, and later works include the play *Ladies from the Sea* (1987) and *Orpheus* (1991). He wrote according to strict metrical rules and eschewed modernism.

Hope, Anthony, pseudonym of **Sir Anthony Hope Hawkins** (1863–1933) Writer, born in London, UK. He studied at Oxford, and in 1887 was called to the bar; but after the success of his 'Ruritanian' romance *The Prisoner of Zenda* (1894) he turned entirely to writing. He was knighted in 1918.

Hope, Bob, originally **Leslie Townes Hope** (1903–2003) Comedian, born in London, UK. He emigrated with his parents to the USA in 1907. After some years on the stage as a dancer and comedian, he made his first film appearance in *The Big Broadcast of 1938* singing 'Thanks for the Memory', which became his signature tune. In partnership with Bing Crosby and Dorothy Lamour, he appeared in the highly successful *Road to ...* comedies (1940–52), and in many others until the early 1970s. During World War 2 and the Korean and Vietnam Wars he spent much time entertaining the troops in the field. For these activities and for his continued contributions to the industry he was given a special Academy Award on five occasions, and he received an honorary knighthood in 1998. His 100th birthday was marked with various celebrations across America.

Hope, Christopher (1944–) Writer, born in Johannesburg, South Africa. His novels include *Kruger's Alp* (1984, Whitbread Prize), *Serenity House* (1992, shortlisted for the Booker Prize), *Darkest England* (1996), and *Signs of the Heart* (1999). Among his non-fiction works are *White Boy Running* (1988) and *Moscow! Moscow!* (1990).

Hopewell The native American culture of C USA c.100 BC–AD 400, its focus the Scioto R valley of S Ohio. Though socially and agriculturally unsophisticated, it is notable for its geometric ceremonial earthworks – at Newark, Ohio, covering 6·4 sq km/ 2·5 sq mi – and richly furnished burial mounds averaging 30 m/ 100 ft in diameter and 12 m/40 ft in height. The enclosure at Hopewell itself, excavated in the 1890s, included the largest such mound in the USA.

Hopi [**hoh**pee] A Shoshonean-speaking Pueblo Indian group living in Arizona, USA, c.15000 (2000 census). They farmed corn and other crops and became famous for their basketry and pottery. Peaceful (Hopi means 'peaceful ones') and democratic, they lived in houses of stone and adobe. Today many work in cities, but several features of their traditional life survive.

Hopkins, Sir (Philip) Anthony (1937–) Actor and director, born in Port Talbot, SC Wales, UK. He trained at the Royal Academy of Dramatic Art, London, and made his stage debut in *The Quare Fellow* (1960) at Manchester. A member of the National Theatre, he appeared there in numerous plays, including *Pravda* (1985), *King Lear* (1986), and *Antony and Cleopatra* (1987). He made his film debut in 1967, and appeared in *The Lion in Winter* (1968), *The Elephant Man* (1980), *84 Charing Cross Road* (1987), and numerous other films, all acclaimed, but none so widely as his compelling performance as serial murderer Hannibal Lecter in Jonathan Demme's *The Silence of the Lambs* (1991, Oscar, BAFTA). Later films include *Shadowlands* (1994), *Legends of the Fall* (1995), *Mission Impossible 2* (2000), and *The Human Stain* (2003). He made his directorial debut with *August* (1996), a loose version of Chekhov's *Uncle Vanya* (1899) transposed to Wales. Among real historical characters he has portrayed are the disgraced American president in *Nixon* (1995), the Spanish painter in *Surviving Picasso* (1996), and President John Quincy Adams in the Steven Spielberg film *Amistad* (1997). On television he won a BAFTA for *War and Peace* (1972), and Emmies for *The Lindbergh Kidnapping Case* (1976) and *The Bunker* (1981). He won a further BAFTA for *The Remains of the Day* (1994). He was knighted in 1993, and became a US citizen in 2000.

Hopkins, Sir Frederick (Gowland) (1861–1947) Biochemist, born in Eastbourne, East Sussex, SE England, UK. Professor at Cambridge from 1914, he was a pioneer in the study of accessory food factors, now called vitamins. He was knighted in 1925, and shared the 1929 Nobel Prize for Physiology or Medicine.

Hopkins, Gerard Manley (1844–89) Poet, born in Stratford, E London, UK. He studied at Oxford where, influenced by the Oxford Movement, he became a Catholic in 1866. He studied for the priesthood with the Jesuits in North Wales, absorbing the language and poetry of the region; he was ordained in 1877, and became professor of Greek at Dublin (1884). There he wrote his profoundly tragic 'Dark Sonnets', which express his sense of exile, spiritual aridity, and artistic frustration. None of his poems was published in his lifetime. His friend and literary executor, Robert Bridges, published an edition in 1918, which was given a very mixed reception, notably to Hopkins' skilful experiments with 'sprung rhythm'; but a new and expanded edition in 1930 established him as a major poet in the English language, and his work became influential. His best-known poems include 'The Wreck of the *Deutschland*' and 'The Windhover'.

Hopkins, Harry L(loyd) (1890–1946) US administrator, born in Sioux City, Iowa, USA. He was Federal emergency relief administrator in the depression of 1933, and under Franklin D Roosevelt headed the 'New Deal' projects in the Works Progress Administration (1935–8). He became secretary of commerce (1938–40), and supervised the lend-lease programme in 1941. As Roosevelt's closest confidante and special assistant, he undertook several important missions to Europe during World War 2, and helped to set up the Potsdam Conference (1945).

Horace, in full **Quintus Horatius Flaccus** (65–8 BC) Latin poet and satirist, born near Venusia, Italy. The son of a freed slave, he was educated in Rome and Athens. While in Athens he joined Brutus, and fought at Philippi. Back in Italy, he joined the civil service, but had to write verses to avoid poverty. His earliest works were chiefly satires and lampoons, and through the influence of Virgil he came under the patronage of Maecenas, a minister of Octavianus. Given a farm in the Sabine Hills, he devoted himself to writing, and became the unrivalled lyric poet of his time. He produced his greatest work, the three books of *Odes*, in 19 BC.

Horae [**haw**riy] In Greek mythology, 'the seasons', implying the right or fitting time for something to happen. They are therefore given various names either connected with fertility or (as in Hesiod) justice, being called Eunomia 'good government', Dike 'right', and Irene 'peace'.

Horatti and Curiatii [hor**ah**tiee, kyooriahtiee] An early Roman legend used to justify appeals. Under Tullus Hostilius there was war between Rome and Alba. Two groups of three brothers were selected from Rome (the Horatii) and Alba (the Curiatii) to fight, the winners to decide the battle. All were killed except one Horatius. When his sister, who was betrothed to a Curiatius, abused him, he murdered her, but was acquitted after appealing to the Roman people.

Hordern, Sir Michael (Murray) (1911–95) Actor, born in Berkhamsted, Hertfordshire, SE England, UK. He studied at Brighton College, and made his professional debut in 1937 after a spell in amateur dramatics. Despite being a popular actor for 20 years, he only became a major London star with his appearance in John Mortimer's *The Dock Brief*. A formidable classical actor, he appeared as Malvolio at The Old Vic (1954), as Jonathan Miller's King Lear (1960), and as Prospero in *The Tempest* (1978, Stratford). His outstanding performances in modern roles included Tom Stoppard's *Jumpers* (1972) and Howard Barker's *Stripwell* (1975). He made numerous film and television appearances, notably in the television adaptation of John Mortimer's *Paradise Postponed* (1986). He was knighted in 1983.

Horeb, Mount *Sinai, Mount*

horehound or **hoarhound** A perennial occurring in two species, native to Europe, Asia, and N Africa, both related to mint; stems square; leaves wrinkled, in opposite pairs; flowers 2-lipped, in whorls. **Black horehound** (*Ballota nigra*) is a fetid plant with hooded, purple flowers. **White horehound** (*Marrubium vulgare*) is a white-hairy plant, the flowers white with a centrally cleft upper lip, used as a medicinal herb for cough remedies. (Family: Labiatae.)

horizon The plane lying 90° from the observer's zenith. The plane of the horizon intersects the celestial sphere in a great circle termed the **astronomical horizon**.

horizontal integration A business situation where a company achieves growth by buying up, or merging with, other companies in the same line of business. This has the effect of reducing competition, and can lead to economies of scale.

Horkheimer, Max [haw(r)khiymer] (1895–1973) Philosopher and social theorist, born in Stuttgart, SW Germany. He studied at Frankfurt, where he was director of the Institute for Social Research (1930–3) (the 'Frankfurt school'). He moved with the school to New York City when the Nazis came to power, and returned to Frankfurt in 1950 as professor at the university. He published a series of influential articles in the 1930s, collected in two volumes under the title *Kritische Theorie* (1968), which expound the basic principles of the school in their critique of industrial civilization. His other major works include *Dialektik der Aufklärung* (1947, Dialectic of Enlightenment), with Adorno, and *Eclipse of Reason* (1947).

hormone replacement therapy (HRT) The use of synthetic oestrogen and progesterone, taken orally in combination, to replace natural female hormones when the body has stopped producing them, usually after the menopause. It is commonly taken to relieve symptoms of the menopause such as hot flushes, night sweats, poor sleep, and vaginal dryness; it also has the beneficial effect of reducing osteoporosis. Potential side effects include thrombosis, vaginal bleeding, and an increased risk of breast cancer.

hormones Chemical messengers synthesized and secreted in small amounts into blood or lymph vessels by the endocrine glands of vertebrates and some invertebrates (eg certain molluscs and arthropods), which affect the functioning of the body's cells and organs. Their usual chemical classification is into *amines* (eg noradrenaline, thyroxine), *peptides* (eg oxytocin), *proteins* (eg insulin), and *steroids* (eg aldosterone, testosterone). They are usually carried by the blood to bind to specific protein receptors within or on target cells some distance away. Hormone-receptor binding triggers a series of events within the cell, culminating in a cellular response (such as contraction or secretion). Some disorders (eg diabetes insipidus, insulin resistance) are due to the absence or abnormality of receptor sites.

Hormuz, Strait of [haw(r)mooz] Passage linking the Persian Gulf to the Arabian Sea; between the S coast of Iran and the Musandam Peninsula of Oman; 50–80 km/30–50 mi wide; a strategic route controlling ocean traffic to the oil terminals of the Gulf; Qeshm I separated from Iran by Clarence Strait; major point of international tension in the Iran–Iraq and Gulf Wars.

horn A musical instrument made from metal (usually brass) tubing, with a conical bore, coiled and twisted several times and ending in a wide bell; the narrow end is fitted with a small, funnel-shaped mouthpiece. It was traditionally associated with hunting. Until the 19th-c the orchestral horn (or **French horn**) was largely restricted to the notes of the harmonic series, the fundamental pitch of which could be varied by fitting 'crooks' (pieces of tubing) to alter the instrument's overall length. Since about 1840 valves have performed the same function more easily. The tubing of the modern horn is about 3·6 m/12 ft in length; it has four valves and is a transposing instrument pitched in F. The **double horn** can be switched from F to B♭.

hornbeam A deciduous tree (*Carpinus betulus*) growing to 30 m/100 ft, native to Europe and Asia Minor; leaves ovoid, double-toothed; flowers tiny in pendulous male and female catkins; nutlets each with a 3-lobed wing-like bract which aids dispersal. It is often the dominant tree in coppices. (Family: Corylaceae.)

hornbill A large bird native to tropical Africa, S Asia, and Australasian islands; bill large, often brightly coloured, topped with large ornamental outgrowth; plumage black, brown, and white; inhabits forest or savannah; eats fruit or small animals. (Family: Bucerotidae, 45 species.)

hornblende A common variety of the amphibole group of ferromagnesian silicate minerals; a hydrated calcium magnesium iron aluminosilicate that is dark green or black in colour. It is widely found in granite and other igneous rocks.

Horne, Donald (Richmond) (1921–) Writer, academic, and arts administrator, born in New South Wales, SE Australia. He became associate professor of political science at the University of New South Wales in 1964 (emeritus, 1987). His best-known book is *The Lucky Country* (1964), the title of which has become a common Australian expression, used without the ironic sense originally intended. Other books include *A History of the Australian People* (1985), *The Lucky Country Revisited* (1987), and *Ideas for the Nation* (1989). He was editor of *The Bulletin* (1967–72), chairman of the Australia Council (1985–90), Chancellor of the University of Canberra, and chairman of the Ideas for Australia programme since 1991. A leading member of the Australian Republican Movement, he has written *The Coming Republic* (1992) and *The Public Culture* (1994), which analyses societies and nation-states.

Horne, Lena (1917–) Singer and actress, born in Brooklyn, New York, USA. Raised by her actress mother, by the age of 16 she was dancing at Harlem's Cotton Club, becoming a popular singer with bands such as those of Noble Sissle and Teddy Wilson. She performed in the musical *Blackbirds of 1939*, and went into film, becoming the first African-American to be signed to a long-term contract (although her scenes were sometimes excised for distribution in the South). The title song of *Stormy Weather* (1943) became her signature. She was blacklisted in the early 1950s for little more than her friendship with Paul Robeson and her outspokenness about discrimination, but she performed in the musical *Jamaica* (1957) and later made several other films. She toured Europe and the USA as a nightclub singer, spoke out increasingly against racism, and published her autobiography, *Lena* (1965).

Horne, Marilyn (Bernice) (1934–) Mezzo-soprano opera singer, born in Bradford, Pennsylvania, USA. She studied at the University of Southern California, and made her opera debut in *The Bartered Bride* in Los Angeles in 1954. She is noted for her efforts to revive interest in the lesser-known operas of Rossini and Handel.

horned lizard An iguana native to North and Central America; body covered with sharp spines, especially around the neck; usually inhabits dry sandy areas; as a defence may squirt blood from its eyes; not known to shed tail; also called **horned toad** or **horny toad**. (Genus: *Phrynosoma*, 14 species.)

horned poppy A deep-rooted perennial (*Glaucium flavum*) producing yellow latex; chiefly coastal and native to Europe, the Mediterranean region, and W Asia; leaves lobed, slightly fleshy, bluish; flowers 6–9 cm/2½–3½ in diameter, yellow, 4-petalled; fruit a long, slender capsule with 2-lobed, horn-like stigma. (Family: Papaveraceae.)

horned toad A SE Asian frog of the family Pelobatidae (76 species); head often with spiky extensions of skin resembling horns; adults usually live on dry land. The name is also sometimes used for the horned lizard, and also for some South American frogs of genus *Ceratophrys* (Family: Leptodactylidae).

horned viper A nocturnal viper native to N Africa and Arabia (*Cerastes cerastes*); a horn-like scale above each eye; spends day buried in sand. The name is also used for the European sand viper (*Vipera ammodytes*), with a small horn on its nose.

hornet The largest social wasp; a fierce predator, up to 35 mm/1½ in long; yellow and black coloration; nests often built in old trees, containing several horizontal combs; colonies with up to 4000 individuals. (Order: Hymenoptera. Family: Vespidae.)

Horne-Tooke, John *Tooke, John Horne*

Horney, Karen, *née* **Danielsen** (1885–1952) Psychiatrist and psychoanalyst, born near Hamburg, N Germany. While still a medical student in Germany, she married a fellow student and they had three children. Her personal life was already under great strain by 1915, and she underwent Freudian analysis with Karl Abraham. She began to take on patients for analysis in 1919, and was affiliated to the Berlin Psychoanalytic Clinic and Institute until 1932, when she joined the Chicago Institute for Psychoanalysis. During the 1920s she began to publish papers that took issue with orthodox Freudianism, particularly in relation to women's particular psychosexuality, and in the 1930s developed theories about the importance of sociocultural factors in human development which, at the time, were considered heretical by many Freudians. In 1934 she moved to New York City, fell out with the orthodox Freudians there, and with other prominent psychoanalysts formed (1941) the Association for the Advancement of Psychoanalysis. Her influential books include *Our Inner Conflicts* (1945) and *Neurosis and Human Growth* (1950).

hornpipe An energetic dance of British origin, popular in the 16th–19th-c. Although the best-known example is the 'Sailors' Hornpipe', the dance was not associated particularly with the navy. Originally performed in triple time, a simple duple time form of the dance was later developed. In Irish ceilidhs the hornpipe continues to be danced to the accompaniment of fiddles, pipes, or flutes.

horntail A large woodwasp; body typically long, cylindrical, without distinct waist; coloured black, banded with yellow or red; egg-laying tube large, used for wood boring; eggs laid in wood, larvae burrow deep into tree timber. (Order: Hymenoptera. Family: Siricidae.)

hornwort **1** A plant (a bryophyte) belonging to the class Anthoceratae, resembling and related to thallose liverworts, but with a long-lived, green sporophyte capable of surviving after the gametophyte dies.

2 A submerged aquatic perennial without roots; stems growing to 1 m/3¼ ft; leaves regularly forked, in whorls, the old ones translucent, stiff and horn-like; one flower at each node, tiny, unisexual, lacking petals; fruits warty and sometimes spiny; very widespread in fresh water. (Genus: *Ceratophyllum*, 10 species. Family: Ceratophyllaceae.)

horny devil *moloch* (zoology)

Horologium [horolo**h**jium] (Lat 'clock') A faint S constellation contrived in the 1750s by French astronomer Nicolas Lacaille.

Horowitz, Vladimir [**ho**rovits] (1904–89) Pianist, born in Kiev, Ukraine. He studied in Kiev, made his concert debut when he was 17, and toured widely before settling in the USA and becoming a US citizen. There were long periods of retirement from concert life, but in 1986 he played again in Russia.

Horrocks, Sir Brian (Gwynne) (1895–1985) British general, born in Ranikhet, NE India. He trained at Sandhurst Military Academy, joined the army in 1914, and served in France and Russia. In 1942 he commanded the 9th Armoured Division and then the 13th and 10th Corps in N Africa, where he helped to defeat Rommel. Wounded at Tunis, he headed the 30th Corps during the Allied invasion (1944). He became well known as a military journalist and broadcaster after the war.

Horsa *Hengist and Horsa*

horse A hoofed mammal with many domestic breeds. Modern breeds are thought to have developed from three wild ancestral types: the heavy **forest** type, and the lighter **steppe** and **plateau** types. Modern breeds may be classed as *coldbloods* (strong heavy horses suitable for work, supposedly descended from forest types), *hotbloods* (fast athletic horses such as the *Arab*, supposedly descended from steppe and plateau types), or *warmbloods* (produced by interbreeding the other two), but these groups are not well defined. Technically any horse up to 14·2 hands/1·5 m/58 in high at the shoulder is termed a *pony*; taller than this it is a *horse* (in a narrow sense). An *entire* (ie not castrated) male horse aged 1–4 years is called a *colt*; older than 4 years it is a *stallion*; a castrated male is a *gelding*. A female of 1–4 years is a *filly*; older than 4 years it is a *mare*. A horse less than one year old is a *foal* (*colt foal* or *filly foal*). The name *horse* is also used for any member of the family Equidae (including asses and zebras). The domestication of the horse was crucial in world history, both for agrarian and military purposes; for example, superior cavalry enabled the rapid expansion of the Huns. Fundamental, also, was the Chinese invention of the breast strap, collar harnesses (5th–6th-c AD), and stirrup (before 300). (Order: Perissodactyla. Family: Equidae, 1 species: *Equus caballus*.)

horse antelope *antelope; roan antelope*

horse bean *broad bean*

horse chestnut A large, spreading, deciduous tree (*Aesculus hippocastanum*) growing to 25 m/80 ft, native to the Balkans, and a widely planted park tree; leaves palmate with 5–7 leaflets each 8–20 cm/3–8 in, widest above the middle, toothed; flowers 2 cm/¾ in, 4-petalled, white with yellow and pink spots, in pyramidal spikes; nuts (*conkers*) brown, shiny, two in a leathery, prickly capsule. The red-flowered trees commonly seen in parks are *Aesculus carnea*, a hybrid of garden origin. (Family: Hippocastanaceae.)

horse fly A biting fly with large, often iridescent eyes; mouthparts form a piercing proboscis in females, used to suck mammalian blood, inflicting painful bites; eggs laid in damp soil; larvae are predators of other insects. (Order: Diptera. Family: Tabanidae, c.2000 species.)

Horse Guards An elite regiment of the British Army, first raised in 1661, known as the Royal Horse Guards, whose nickname was 'the Blues'. Amalgamated in 1969 with the Royal Dragoon Guards, 'the Blues and Royals' form, with the Life Guards, the British Sovereign's *Household Cavalry*.

horsehair worm An extremely elongate, unsegmented worm; feeds as an internal parasite of arthropods when juvenile, emerging into aquatic habitats as a non-feeding adult; adults are a short-lived reproductive stage. (Phylum: Nematomorpha.)

Horsehead nebula A famous dark nebula in the constellation Orion, resembling the silhouette of a horse's head.

Horse Latitudes Two belts of ocean calm at 30° N and S of the Equator, where conditions of high atmospheric pressure exist almost permanently; Trade Winds constantly blow from these belts towards the Doldrums.

horsepower Unit of power; symbol *hp*; equal to 745·7 W (watt, SI unit); almost obsolete, but still used in engineering to describe the power of machinery; equal to 1·0139 metric horsepower.

horse racing The racing of horses against one another, each ridden by a jockey. The ancient Egyptians took part in horse races c.1200 BC, and the sport was part of the Ancient Olympic Games. Racing was popularized in England in the 12th-c, and many monarchs have supported the sport, which has thereby become known as 'the sport of kings'. The first recorded meeting at England's oldest course, Chester, was on 9 February 1540. In North America, the first horse-racing trophy was offered in 1665 for a race at Long Island. Most of the famous races (the *Classics*) were instituted in the following 200 years, such as the Derby in 1780 (England), the Prix du Jockey Club in 1836 (France), the Melbourne Cup in 1861 (Australia), and the Belmont Stakes in 1867 (USA).

Racing comes in two categories: **flat racing** and **national hunt racing**. **Flat racing** is a straightforward race on a flat surface (grass or dirt) over a predetermined distance which can be anything between 5 furlongs (1 km) and 2½ mi (4 km). **National hunt racing** involves the horses negotiating fences which can be either movable hurdles or fixed fences. These races (eg the Grand National) are longer than flat races, and can be anything up to 4½ mi (6·5 km) in length. Bets are usually placed on the horses likely to come first (a *win*), second (a *place*), or third (a *show*), with professional bookmaking emerging in the 19th-c (along with a host of illegal or semi-legal activities), and the Totalizator concept in the 1920s. Horse racing is now big business, with more frequent meetings, larger prizes, and (through media coverage) greater public awareness.

horse-radish A perennial (*Armoracia rusticana*), probably native to S Europe, but long cultivated for the pungent seasoning prepared from the roots, and widely naturalized; fleshy, cylindrical roots; coarse, oblong leaves; white, cross-shaped flowers. (Family: Cruciferae.)

horseshoe bat A bat of the family Rhinolophidae (genus: *Rhinolophus*, 68 species), worldwide except for the New World; nose shaped like a horseshoe with an upward pointing flap (*nose leaf*). *Rhinonicteris aurantius* (family: Hipposideridae) is called the **golden horseshoe bat**.

horseshoe crab A bottom-living, marine arthropod related to the arachnids (subphylum: Chelicerata) not to the true crabs (subphylum: Crustacea); body divided into a *prosoma*, covered by a horseshoe-shaped carapace, and an *opisthosoma*, carrying six pairs of legs and five pairs of gills; also known as **king crabs**. (Class: Merostomata. Order: Xiphosura.)

horsetail A primitive, spore-bearing perennial related to ferns and clubmosses; creeping rhizomes; annual, distinctively jointed stem; whorl of scale-like leaves around each joint; cone-like strobilus at the tip. It is found everywhere, except for Australasia, and the only living genus of a large and formerly widespread group, the Sphenopsida, dominant during the Carboniferous period. All extant species are herbaceous, but many fossil species were arborescent. (Genus: *Equisetum*, 23 species. Family: Equisetaceae.)

horst An uplifted block of the Earth's crust, usually of great size, bounded by two normal faults. It is often elongated in shape, and may form block mountains.

Horthy (de Nagybánya), Miklós [**haw(r)tee**] (1868–1957) Hungarian statesman and regent (1920–44), born in Kenderes, Hungary. He commanded the Austro-Hungarian fleet (1918), and was minister of war in the counter-revolutionary 'White government' (1919), opposing Bela Kun's Communist regime, which he suppressed (1920). He became regent, presiding over a resolutely conservative, authoritarian regime. In World War 2 he supported the Axis Powers until Hungary was overrun by the Germans in 1944. He was imprisoned by the Germans, released by the Allies in 1945, and went to live in Estoril, Portugal.

horticulture The business of growing fruit, vegetables, flowers, and shrubs for pleasure or for commercial marketing; also practised widely as a hobby and an art form. It is usually associated with the intensive production of high-value crops, and often involves the use of irrigation in drier areas, and glass or polythene protection in cooler areas. Glass or polythene houses may be heated to allow all-year-round production, and polythene tunnels are becoming increasingly popular as a means of bringing on early crops. Horticultural research studies ways of improving cultivation and controlling plant disease and pests, as well as the breeding of plants to produce new varieties that are especially beautiful, hardy, or productive.

Hortobagy [**haw(r)tobady**] area 520 sq km/201 sq mi. National park in NEC Hungary; established in 1973; noted for its wild birds, plants and stock breeding; contains a nine-arched bridge, the longest stone bridge in Hungary.

Horus [**hawrus**] An ancient Egyptian sky-god in the shape of a man with a hawk's head; also depicted as the child of Isis, when he is often called **Harpocrates**. He is associated with the divinity of the Pharaoh, who is the 'living Horus' ruling Egypt.

Horvitz, H Robert (1947–) Microbiologist, born in Chicago, Illinois, USA. He studied at Harvard University, later joining the Massachusetts Institute of Technology. He shared the 2002 Nobel Prize for Physiology or Medicine for discoveries concerning the genetic regulation of organ development and programmed cell death.

Horyuji [**horioojee**] A Buddhist complex built near Nara, Japan, for Prince Shotoku in 647, and rebuilt after a fire in 670. It comprises 45 buildings, of which 17 (especially the Golden Hall and the Pagoda – the world's oldest wooden buildings) are national treasures, and house many magnificent works of art. Fire in 1949 damaged valuable frescoes.

Hosea, Book of, also spelled **Osee** [**hohzeea**] The first of the 12 so-called 'minor' prophetic writings of the Hebrew Bible/Old Testament; attributed to the prophet Hosea, who was active in the N kingdom of Israel c.750–725 BC, during a period of Assyrian military invasions. The work warns of judgment for Israel's defection to the Canaanite Baal cult, but affirms God's love in seeking to restore Israel. Many of these prophecies are presented as corresponding to Hosea's own experiences with his unfaithful wife Gomer.

Hoskins, Bob, popular name of **Robert William Hoskins** (1942–) Actor and director, born in Bury St Edmunds, Suffolk, E England, UK. He left school at 15 and sampled numerous occupations before choosing acting and making his debut in *Romeo and Juliet* (1969) at Stoke-on-Trent. His stage performances include *Richard III* (1971), *The Iceman Cometh* (1976), and *Guys and Dolls* (1981). He achieved widespread public recognition with Dennis Potter's television series *Pennies From Heaven* (1978), as the menacing hoodlum in the film *The Long Good Friday* (1980), and the minder in *Mona Lisa* (1986, BAFTA best actor). After several years as a reliable and much-employed supporting actor in films he acquired international stardom with his award-winning performance in *Who Framed Roger Rabbit* (1988). He wrote and directed *The Raggedy Rawney* (1987), an anti-war saga about gypsies. Later films include *Hook* (1991), *Nixon* (1995), in which he played J Edgar Hoover, *The Secret Agent* (1996), *Felicia's Journey* (1999), and *Last Orders* (2001).

hospice A type of hospital normally reserved for the treatment of the terminally ill, usually catering for specific age groups, typically children or the elderly. The term was originally used to describe a hostel or refuge attached to a monastery. It is also frequently used to refer to programmes which provide home care.

hospital An institution in which certain kinds of illness are investigated and treated. The first documented hospital was Chinese, in 491. In the European Middle Ages the well-to-do were all treated at home, while the sick poor were cared for in a hospital attached to the local poor house. This pattern of care persisted into the 18th-c, when voluntary hospitals were built throughout the UK, and physicians and surgeons from the locality attended to the inmates without remuneration. With the advance of scientific medicine and the development of increasingly elaborate and specialized investigative and therapeutic procedures, all sections of the population whose medical needs might benefit from admission to hospital are now treated in hospital. In most developed countries today, hospitals are run as either private charities or public (state) institutions, with 'teaching hospitals' closely related to the research departments of neighbouring universities. Most hospitals not only cater for emergencies of all types and for those whose illnesses develop acutely and unexpectedly (the *acute hospital*), but they contain specialized departments for non-emergency work and for numerous branches of medicine, such as cardiology and neurology. Other hospitals have become exclusively specialized, and cater for the needs of single categories of ill health, such as psychiatric, orthopaedic, maternity, paediatric, and geriatric hospitals. An additional important role is the provision of out-patient departments providing consultative services for the patients of general practitioners who are under care in their own home. In the 1990s, in the UK, hospitals were allowed to opt out of local health authority control, forming themselves into *hospital trusts* (or *NHS trusts*), the others remaining as *directly-managed units* (*DMUs*).

Hospitallers Members (priests or brother knights subject to monastic vows) of the Order of the Hospital of St John of Jerusalem, originally a purely charitable organization established in Jerusalem with Muslim permission to care for sick pilgrims to the Holy Land. The warrior element developed and became predominant, and from the 12th-c they played a prominent role in the Crusades as an international religious-military order. They adopted a black habit bearing a white eight-pointed (Maltese) cross. After the loss of Acre in 1291, they transferred their headquarters to Limassol, Cyprus (1292), then Rhodes (1309), but were expelled by the Ottoman Turks in 1523. They moved to Malta (1530), which they held until dislodged by Napoleon I in 1798. The Sovereign Order is now based in Rome.

hosta A perennial native to China and Japan; striking leaves up to 45 cm/18 in long, lance-shaped to broadly oval, often variegated or bluish; flowers tubular, violet, or white, in spike-like inflorescences; also known as **plantain lily**. (Genus: *Hosta*, 10 species. Family: Liliaceae.)

hot-air balloon *balloon*

hot rock *geothermal energy*

hot spring A spring of hot or warm groundwater which emerges at the Earth's surface and which often contains dissolved minerals and sulphurous gases. Such springs are often used as health spas. Very hot springs emerge as geysers, and may be used as sources of geothermal energy.

Hotspur, Harry *Percy*

Hottentot fig A sprawling perennial native to S Africa (*Carpobrotus edulis*); pairs of thick, succulent, three-sided leaves; yellow or pink daisy-like flowers; fruits juicy, edible. Related to the Livingstone daisy, it is planted in many countries as a coastal sandbinder, and often naturalized. (Family: Aizoaceae.)

Hottentots *Khoisan*

Hotter, Hans (1909–2003) Baritone, born in Offenbach-am-Main, WC Germany. He studied in Munich and, after working as an organist and choirmaster, made his debut as an opera singer in 1930. In 1940 he settled in Munich, but sang frequently in Vienna and Bayreuth, becoming one of the leading Wagnerian baritones of his day. He retired from opera in 1972, but continued to do recital work until 1991.

Houdini, Harry [hoodeenee], originally **Erich Weiss** (1874–1926) Magician and escape artist, born in Budapest, Hungary. His family emigrated to the USA while he was still a child, where he became a trapeze performer, then gained an international reputation as an escape artist. He took his name from Jean Eugène Robert Houdin, a great French magician of the 19th-c. He could escape from any kind of bonds or container, from prison cells to padlocked underwater boxes. His most sensational feat consisted of escaping from an airtight tank that was filled with water. A vigorous campaigner against fraudulent mediums, he became president of the Society of American Magicians.

Houdon, Jean Antoine [oodō] (1741–1828) Classical sculptor, born in Versailles, NC France. He won the *Prix de Rome* in 1761, spent 10 years in Rome, and there executed the colossal figure of 'St Bruno' in Santa Maria degli Angeli. In 1785 he visited America to execute a marble statue of Washington (Richmond, VA). His most famous busts are those of Diderot, Voltaire (foyer of the Théâtre Français, Paris), Napoleon, Catherine the Great, and Rousseau (Louvre). He was appointed professor at the Ecole des Beaux-Arts in 1805.

hound A category of domestic dog; name is applied to breeds developed for hunting, especially those which track by scent; sometimes used for any hunting dog, including those which track by sight (eg greyhounds, borzois).

Hounsfield, Sir Godfrey (Newbold) (1919–) Physicist, born in Newark, Nottinghamshire, C England, UK. He studied in London, and joined Electrical and Musical Industries (EMI) in 1951. Independently of Allan Cormack, he developed the method of X-ray computer-assisted tomography (CAT), the first body scanners being made by EMI in the early 1970s. He continued to work on new medical imaging methods, and shared the Nobel Prize for Physiology or Medicine in 1979. He was knighted in 1981.

Houphouët-Boigny, Felix [oofway bwīnyee] (1905–93) African statesman, the first president of Côte d'Ivoire (Ivory Coast) (1960–93), born in Yamoussoukro, SC Côte d'Ivoire. He became a doctor, and the leading African politician of French West Africa. He was a member of the French Constituent Assembly (1945–6) and of the National Assembly (1946–59), and held several ministerial posts. He became president when the country was granted independence, was re-elected at every subsequent election, and commenced his seventh term of office in 1990.

housefly A small, darkish fly; females lay masses of 100–150 eggs on decaying organic matter or dung; white, worm-like maggots mature in a few days; adults feed on decomposed matter. It is a pest and carrier of diseases. (Order: Diptera. Family: Muscidae.)

Household Cavalry *Horse Guards*

houseleek A succulent, mat-forming perennial, native to the mountains of S Europe; leaves thick, fleshy, in dense rosettes to 14 cm/5½ in diameter, sometimes with a cobweb of hairs, often bluish or tinged dull red; inflorescences curved, branched, on thick stalks; flowers starry, with 6–18 narrow petals, often pink, purplish, or yellow. It was formerly planted to help keep roofs weatherproof. (Genus: *Sempervivum*, 25 species. Family: Crassulaceae.)

housemaid's knee A painful inflammation of the liquid-filled pouch (*bursa*) in front of the knee joint, provoked by trauma or excessive kneeling. It is so called because of its former frequent occurrence as an occupational hazard.

house music Popular dance music that spread from south Chicago, USA, in the early 1980s. Its instrumentation is often no more than a synthesizer and drum machine; the music is loud and repetitive, with a heavy beat and baseline, insistent riffs, and 'sampled' extracts from more imaginative recordings. Perhaps the best known (and best selling) example is 'Pump Up The Jam' from Technotronic (real name Jo Bogaert).

House of Commons *Commons, House of*

House of Lords *Lords, House of*

House of Representatives In the USA, one of the two chambers of the bicameral legislature, in which, under the constitution, federal legislative power is vested. The 435 members of the House are elected from single member constituencies of approximately the same population size, although each state has at least one representative. All revenue bills must originate in the House.

Houses of Parliament The Palace of Westminster in London, UK. The first royal palace of this name was built for King Canute in the first half of the 11th-c, and remained the main residence of the kings of England and the headquarters of the court – administrative, judicial, and parliamentary – until Henry VIII abandoned it for Whitehall Palace in 1512. Although the Lords were accommodated in the palace, the Commons had for three centuries no permanent meeting place of their own, and had to make do with makeshift accommodation in the chapter house, the refectory, or any other vacant chamber of Westminister Abbey. During the Reformation the royal chapel of St Stephen was secularized, and for over two centuries became the meeting place for the Commons. In 1834 almost all of the palace except Westminster Hall, the cloisters, and the Jewel House were destroyed by fire. By 1860 the two new, purpose-built Houses of Parliament and St Stephen's clock tower (Big Ben) had been completed, designed by the architects Charles Barry and Augustus Pugin in the Victorian perpendicular Gothic style. In 1940–1, large parts of the palace were destroyed by German incendiary bombs. Sir Giles Gilbert Scott (1880–1960) was commissioned to rebuild (1945–50) the palace in the Victorian style, retaining Barry's general plan but scaling down Pugin's ornate Gothic decoration.

house sparrow A small, brown and grey, ground-feeding bird (*Passer domesticus*), native to Europe, Asia, and N Africa, and introduced worldwide; usually near habitation; eats almost anything; nests in holes; also known as the **English sparrow**. (Family: Ploceidae.)

Housman, A(lfred) E(dward) (1859–1936) Scholar and poet, born near Bromsgrove, Hereford and Worcester, WC England, UK, the brother of writer Laurence Housman (1865–1959). He studied at Oxford, failed his degree, and entered the Patent Office, but his contributions to learned journals enabled him to return to academic life, and he became professor of Latin at London (1892), then at Cambridge (1911). He is best known for his own poetry, notably *A Shropshire Lad* (1896) and *Last Poems* (1922). He saw himself chiefly as a Latinist, and devoted much of his life to an annotated edition (1903–30) of Manilius.

Houston [hyoostn] 29°46N 95°22W, pop (2000e) 1 953 600. Seat of Harris Co, SE Texas, USA; port on the Houston Ship Channel (1914), near Galveston Bay; fourth largest city and third busiest port in the USA; settled, 1836; capital of the Republic of Texas, 1837–9, 1842–5; airports (Intercontinental, Hobby); railway; five universities; industrial, commercial, financial, and cultural centre; deep-water channel enables ocean-going vessels to reach the city; major oil centre with huge refineries and the largest petrochemical complex in the world; corporate headquarters of numerous energy companies; base for several space and science research firms; at nearby Clear Lake City is NASA's Lyndon B Johnson Space Center; steel, shipbuilding, brewing, paper, rice, cotton; professional teams, Astros (baseball), Rockets (basketball), Oilers (football); National Space Hall of Fame, San Jacinto battleground, Astroworld, Sam Houston Historical Park, the battleship *Texas*.

Houston, Sam(uel) [hyoostn] (1793–1863) US soldier and statesman, born in Lexington, Virginia, USA. In his teens he lived for three years among the Cherokee Indians, learning their customs and language. He enlisted in the army in 1813, but resigned in 1818 and studied law. In 1823 he was elected a member of Congress, and in 1827 became Governor of Tennessee. As commander-in-chief in the Texan War, he defeated the Mexicans on the San Jacinto in 1836, and achieved Texan independence. He was elected president of the republic, re-elected in 1841, and on the annexation of Texas (1845) returned to the US Senate. Elected Governor of Texas in 1859, he opposed secession, was deposed in 1861, and retired to private life. Houston, TX, is named after him.

Houston, Whitney (1963–) Singer and film actress, born in Newark, New Jersey, USA. Daughter of gospel singer **Cissy Houston** (c.1930–), she began singing in the local gospel choir, and became a backing singer for Chaka Khan, Lou Rawls, and others. The album *Whitney Houston* (1985) won a Grammy award and included her first US number 1 hit single 'Saving All My Love For You'. Her second album, *Whitney* (1987), entered the UK chart and became the first album by a female artist to debut at number 1. Later albums include *My Love is Your Love* (1999) and *One Wish – The Holiday Album* (2003). In 1988 she broke a US chart record with seven consecutive number 1 hits, overtaking the previous record of six achieved by The Beatles and The Bee Gees. Her films include *The Bodyguard* (1992) and *The Preacher's Wife* (1996).

hovercraft *air cushion vehicle*

hoverfly A medium to large fly often found hovering over flowers; adults resemble wasps, feeding on pollen and nectar; larvae diverse in habits, may be plant feeders, predators of aphids and insect larvae, or scavengers. (Order: Diptera. Family: Syrphidae, over 5000 species.)

Howard, Catherine (?–1542) Fifth wife of Henry VIII, a granddaughter of the 2nd Duke of Norfolk. She was married to the king in the same month as he divorced Anne of Cleves (July 1540). However, after Henry learned of Catherine's alleged premarital affairs (1541), she was arrested for treason, and beheaded, together with her cousin Lady Jane Rochford, in the Tower of London. All persons supposed privy to her conduct, as well as several relatives and servants, were imprisoned and suffered the fortfeiture of their property and possessions.

Howard, Charles, 1st Earl of Nottingham (1536–1624) Lord High Admiral, a cousin of Elizabeth I, who commanded the English fleet against the Spanish Armada (1588). He succeeded to his father's title of Lord of Effingham in 1573, and became Lord High Admiral in 1585. For his role alongside Essex in the Cadiz expedition (1596) he was created an earl, and in 1601 he quelled Essex's rising.

Howard, Sir Ebenezer (1850–1928) Founder of the garden city movement, born in London, UK. He emigrated to Nebraska in 1872, but returned to England in 1877 and became a parliamentary shorthand-writer. His *Tomorrow* (1898) envisaged self-contained communities with both rural and urban amenities and green belts, and led to the formation in 1899 of the Garden City Association and to the laying out of Letchworth (1903) and Welwyn Garden City (1919) in Hertfordshire. He was knighted in 1927.

Howard, Elizabeth Jane (1923–) Novelist, born in London, UK. She trained as an actress at the London Mask Theatre School, then worked as a model and later as an editor and book critic. Her first novel, *The Beautiful Visit* (1950), an examination of the subtleties of relationships, won the John Llewellyn Rhys Memorial Prize. The *Cazalet Chronicles*, a quartet comprising *The Light Years* (1990), *Marking Time* (1991), *Confusion* (1993), and *Casting Off* (1995), traces the fortunes of a middle-class family in World War 2. She has been married three times, to Peter Scott, James Douglas-Henry and, most famously, Kingsley Amis.

Howard, John (1726–90) Prison reformer, born in London, UK. While travelling in Europe he was captured by the French, and spent some time in prison at Brest. In 1773 he became high sheriff for Bedfordshire, and began a series of tours in which he investigated the condition of prisons and prisoners. As a result, two acts were passed in 1774, one providing for fixed salaries to jailers, and the other enforcing cleanliness. He died of typhus, contracted while visiting a military hospital in Kherson, Russia. The Howard League for Penal Reform, founded in 1866, is named after him.

Howard, John (Winston) (1939–) Australian statesman and prime minister (1996–), born in Sydney, New South Wales, SE Australia. Educated at Sydney University, he became a solicitor, and was elected Liberal MP for Bennelong, New South Wales, in 1974. He held ministerial posts in business and trade before becoming Federal Treasurer (1977–83) and deputy-leader (1983–5) then leader of the Liberal Party in Opposition (1985–9, 1995–6). He became prime minister following his party's general election victory in 1996, and remained as head of a Liberal–National Party coalition following the 1998 election. He won a third time in 2001.

Howard, Leslie, originally **Leslie Howard Stainer** (1893–1943) Actor, born in London, UK. He made his film debut in 1914, and turned to the theatre after being invalided home from the Western Front. During the 1930s he had many leading film roles, including *The Scarlet Pimpernel* (1935), *Pygmalion* (1938, co-director), and as Ashley Wilkes in *Gone with the Wind* (1939). He appeared in several British wartime productions, such as *The First of the Few* (1942), and is thought to have been killed when a special mission flight from Lisbon to London was shot down.

Howard, Michael (1941–) British statesman, born in Gorseinon, near Swansea, SC Wales, UK. Brought up in Llanelli, Carmarthenshire, he studied at Cambridge, where he was president of the Union, and was called to the bar in 1964. He was elected an MP in 1983, and after several junior posts became minister for local government (1987–8), minister for water and planning (1988–90), secretary-of-state for employment (1990–2) and the environment (1992–3), and home secretary (1993–7). He emerged as a contender for the leadership of the Conservative Party following John Major's resignation in 1997, but withdrew after the first ballot and became shadow foreign secretary (1997–9). He was appointed shadow chancellor (2001–3), and in 2003 was elected unopposed as party leader.

Howard, Ron(ald William) (1954–) Actor, director, and producer, born in Duncan, Oklahoma, USA. Born into a show business family, he began appearing regularly on stage, television, and in films from an early age. Among his best-known TV series are *The Andy Griffith Show* (1960–8) and *Happy Days* (1973–80). He made his directorial debut with *Grand Theft Auto* (1977), and later successes include *Cocoon* (1985), *Apollo 13* (1995), and *A Beautiful Mind* (2002, Oscar best director; Golden Globe best film).

Howard, Thomas, 3rd Duke of Norfolk, Earl of Surrey (1473–1554) English statesman, the son of Thomas Howard, 2nd Duke of Norfolk (1443–1524), and brother-in-law of Henry VII. Howard was Lord High Admiral (1513), and helped defeat the Scots at Flodden Field (1513). He became Lord Lieutenant of Ireland (1520). He was uncle to Anne Boleyn, but as Lord Steward presided over her trial for adultery (1536). He lost influence at court when another niece, Catherine Howard, was beheaded for adultery in 1542. Throughout the reign of Edward VI he was imprisoned on suspicion of the treason for which Henry VIII had executed his eldest son, Henry Howard, Earl of Surrey, in 1547. He was released on the accession of Mary I in 1553.

Howard, Trevor (Wallace) (1916–88) Actor, born in Cliftonville, Kent, SE England, UK. He trained in London and had a successful stage career until joining the army at the beginning of World War 2. Invalided out in 1944, he turned to films, and sprang to stardom with *Brief Encounter* (1945), followed by *The Third Man* (1949) and *Outcast of the Islands* (1951). His versatile and often eccentric characterizations were regularly in demand for both film and television, with later appearances in *Gandhi* and *The Missionary* (both 1982), *Dust* (1985), and *White Mischief* (1987).

Howard League for Penal Reform A charity dedicated to the cause of penal reform, named after John Howard; formed by the amalgamation of the Howard Association with the Prison Reform League in 1921. Internationally, it urges the UN to promote the standard minimum rules for the treatment of prisoners, and campaigns for the abolition of corporal and capital punishment.

Howe, Elias (1819–67) Inventor, born in Spencer, Massachusetts, USA. He worked as a mechanic in Lowell and Boston, where he constructed and patented (1846) the first sewing machine. After an unsuccessful visit to England to introduce his invention, he returned to Boston, where he found his patent had been infringed. Harassed by poverty, he entered on a seven years' war of litigation to protect his rights, was ultimately successful (1854), and amassed a fortune.

Howe (of Aberavon), (Richard Edward) Geoffrey Howe, Baron (1926–) British statesman, born in Port Talbot, SC Wales, UK. He studied at Cambridge, was called to the bar in 1952 and became a Conservative MP in 1964. Knighted in 1970, he became solicitor general (1970–2), minister for trade and consumer affairs (1972–4), Chancellor of the Exchequer (1979–1983), and foreign secretary (1983–9). In 1989 he was made deputy prime minister, Lord President of the Council, and Leader of the House of Commons, but resigned from the government (Nov 1990) in opposition to Mrs Thatcher's hostility towards European monetary union. He was created a life peer in 1992, and a Companion of Honour in 1996.

Howe, Richard Howe, 1st Earl (1726–99) British admiral, born in London, UK, the brother of William Howe. He entered the navy at 13, and distinguished himself in the Seven Years' War (1756–63). He became a Lord of the Admiralty (1763), Treasurer of the Navy (1765), First Lord of the Admiralty (1783), viscount (1782), and earl (1788). In 1776 he was made commander of the British fleet during the American War of Independence. In 1778 he defended the American coast against a superior French force, and in the French Revolutionary Wars defeated the French at 'the Glorious First of June' (1794).

Howe, William Howe, 5th Viscount (1729–1814) British soldier who commanded the army in North America during the American Revolution, the brother of Richard Howe. He joined the army in 1746, and served under Wolfe at Louisburg (1758) and Quebec, where he led the famous advance to the Heights of Abraham. He became an MP in 1758. In the American War of Independence his victories included Bunker Hill (1775), the Brandywine (1777), and the capture of New York City (1776). He returned to England, and succeeded to the viscountcy on the death of his brother in 1799.

Howerd, Frankie, originally **Francis Alex Howard** (1922–92) Comedian and actor, born in London, UK. He made his debut at the Stage Door Canteen, Piccadilly, London, in 1946, and appeared in revues in London during the 1950s, including *Out of This World* (1950), *Pardon My French* (1953), and *Way Out In Piccadilly* (1960). He occasionally acted in plays, and gave a notable performance in Sondheim's musical, *A Funny Thing Happened on the Way to the Forum*, in 1963. He appeared regularly on television and in films, his most famous role being that of a Roman slave in the television series *Up Pompeii* (1970–1), a series drenched in sexual innuendo. His films include *The Ladykillers* (1956), *Carry On Doctor* (1968), *Up Pompeii* (1971), and *Up the Chastity Belt* (1972). His brand of humour became increasingly appreciated in the 1980s, and he presented several successful television series, including *Frankie Howerd on Campus* (1990).

howitzer An artillery piece in which the shell is projected at a high angle of trajectory, typically at low muzzle velocity, to fall on to its target as plunging fire.

howler monkey A New World monkey; thick coarse coat and naked face; long 'beard' covers throat, which produces a very loud call; sometimes swings from branches using only its long tail. (Genus: *Alouatta*, 6 species.)

howling jackass *kookaburra*

Hoxha, Enver, also spelled **Hodja** [**hoj**a] (1908–85) Albanian prime minister (1946–54) and Communist Party secretary (1954–85), born in Gjirokastër, S Albania. He founded and led the Albanian Communist Party (1941) in the fight for national independence. In 1946 he deposed King Zog (who had fled in 1939), and became head of state.

hoxsey A cancer treatment developed by John Hoxsey in the 1840s, based on the use of a secret herb which is prepared in the form of an infusion, ointment, or powder. The herb was said to have cured a cancerous growth on a horse's leg. Hoxsey had watched the animal seeking out and eating the plant, and reasoned that there must be natural anti-cancer properties to which the horse was instinctively drawn. He founded a clinic based on the use of this plant, and also on other herbs, together with diet, immunotherapy, and live cell therapy for the treatment of all forms of malignancy.

Hoyle, Edmond (1672–1769) Writer on card games, called 'the father of whist', who lived in London, UK. His popular *Short Treatise on Whist* (1742) ran into many editions, and was ultimately incorporated with his manuals on backgammon, brag, quadrille, piquet, and chess into an omnibus volume (1748).

Hoyle, Sir Fred(erick) (1915–2001) Astronomer, mathematician, astrophysicist, and science fiction writer, born in Bingley, West Yorkshire, N England, UK. He studied at Cambridge, where he taught applied mathematics, became professor of astronomy (1958–72), and founded a world-famous Institute of Theoretical Astronomy. His work on the origin of chemical elements is particularly important. He was a leading proponent of steady-state cosmology, of the notion that viruses come from outer space, and a believer in an extraterrestrial origin for life on Earth. His scientific works include *Nature of the Universe* (1952), *Frontiers of Astronomy* (1955), and he collaborated on *A Different Approach to Cosmology* (1999). His science fiction writing includes *The Black Cloud* (1957), *A for Andromeda* (1962, with J Elliot), and *The Molecule Men* (1971, with G Hoyle). His other writing includes stories for children, space serials for television, and two volumes of autobiography, *The Small World of Fred Hoyle* (1966) and *Home is Where the Wind Blows* (1994). He was knighted in 1972.

Hradčany Castle [**rad**chanee] Since 1918, the official residence of the Czech president in Prague. The Přemysl dynasty founded a stronghold and royal residence on the site in the late 9th-c.

This was destroyed by fire in 1303, and the present citadel, which incorporates both Gothic and Renaissance architecture, was built from 1344 onwards. The complex includes St Vitus' Cathedral and the royal palace as well as other churches, palaces, museums, and galleries. Hradčany Castle was the scene of the so-called 'Defenestration of Prague' (1618), when two councillors of the Catholic emperor Matthias were thrown out of the window by Protestant Czech nobles – an event which triggered the Thirty Years' War.

HRT *hormone replacement therapy*

Hsia dynasty *Xia dynasty*

Hsia-men *Xiamen*

Hsi-ning *Xining*

HTLV An abbreviation of **Human T-cell Leukaemia/lymphoma Virus**, a virus that causes aggressive forms of leukaemia and lymphoma and a disease called *tropical spastic paraparesis*, a severe progressive disorder of the nerves that produces paralysis. The infection is spread by sexual intercourse or by inoculation with contaminated needles, and is widespread in the Far East, Africa, and South America.

HTML *document description language*

HTTP *document description language*

H2 blockers, also called **H2 (histamine-2)** A family of drugs which act as receptor antagonists. H2 blockers revolutionized the treatment of gastric ulcers because they can heal an ulcer in around six weeks and obviate the need for surgery. They work by stopping the local hormone histamine from stimulating acid secretion into the stomach. The first H2 blocker to be used clinically was cimetidine, also known as Tagamet in the UK. Cimetidine was launched in 1976, and quickly became one of the most prescribed drugs. It was developed by Sir James Black, whose 1988 Nobel Prize for Physiology or Medicine was partly awarded because of this work.

Hu Jintao (1942–) Chinese politician. He trained as an engineer, and rose to prominence as head of the Chinese Communist Party's youth league, becoming party secretary in Guizhou (1984) and Xizang (Tibet) (1988), where he pursued a hardline policy, crushing anti-Chinese demonstrations at Lhasa in 1989. A member of the Politburo standing committee in 1992, he was appointed vice-president in 1998, being seen as an eventual successor to Jiang Zemin.

Hua Guofeng [hwah gwohfeng], also spelled **Hua Kuo-feng** (1920–) Chinese statesman and prime minister (1976–80), born in Jiaocheng, Shanxi province, NE China. He was vice-governor of Hunan (1958–67), but came under attack during the Cultural Revolution. A member of the Central Committee of the Party from 1969, and of the Politburo from 1973, he became deputy prime minister and minister of public security (1975–6), and in 1976 was made prime minister and chairman of the Central Committee. Under him China adopted a more pragmatic domestic and foreign policy, with emphasis on industrial and educational expansion, and closer relations with Western and Third World countries. He resigned as chairman in 1981.

Huangguoshu Falls [hwahnggwohshoo] Waterfall in W Guizhou province, SC China; largest waterfall in China, 84 m/275 ft wide, 67 m/220 ft high; on Bai Shui R; at the side is Waterfall Cave, 100 m/325 ft-long cavern set in the cliff face.

Huang He; Huang Ho *Yellow River*

Huangtu Gaoyuan *Loess Region*

Huari [wahree] An ancient Andean city near Ayacucho, the capital (AD c.650–800) of a powerful pre-Inca state, controlling all Peru N of Cuzco. At its peak c.700, the 1·5 sq km/0·6 sq mi core contained 70–80 walled rectangular compounds, housing an estimated 20 000–30 000 people.

Huascarán [waskaran] area 3400 sq km/1312 sq mi. National park in W Peru; a world heritage site; consists of the Cordillera Blanca, part of the Andean Cordillera Occidental; established in 1975; rises to 6768 m/22 205 ft in Nevado de Huascarán, highest peak in Peru.

Hubbard, L(afayette) Ron(ald) (1911–86) Writer, founder of Dianetics® healing technology and of the Scientology® applied religious philosophy, born in Tilden, Nebraska, USA. During the 1930s he became a prolific writer of novels and short stories in several different genres. His most famous work, *Dianetics: the Modern Science of Mental Health* (1950), became an instant best seller, and the basic text of the Scientology movement. Later books include the science-fiction novel *Battlefield Earth* (1982) and the 10-volume *Mission Earth* series (from 1985).

Hubble, Edwin (Powell) (1889–1953) Astronomer, born in Marshfield, Missouri, USA. He studied mathematics and astronomy at Chicago University, then law at Oxford. He joined the Kentucky bar in 1913, but left to make astronomy his career. He worked at the Mt Wilson Observatory from 1919, studying nebulae, and in 1924 discovered that there were other galaxies apart from our own. While carrying out studies to classify these galaxies, he discovered in 1929 that the universe is expanding, establishing a ratio between the galaxies' speed of movement and their distance, **Hubble's constant**. **Hubble's law** states that the recession velocity of a distant galaxy is directly proportional to its distance from the observer.

Hubble constant The figure that specifies the rate at which the universe is expanding, from which the time elapsed since the 'big bang' can be estimated. To derive the Hubble constant, both the speed of recession of galaxies and their distances must be known. Speeds can be deduced from the redshift in their light, but distances are more difficult to ascertain. Improved distance measurements, aided by the Hubble Space Telescope, give a value of around 60 km/sec per million parsecs for Hubble's constant. At this rate of expansion, the universe would have taken about 16 billion years to reach its present size. In practice, the expansion was probably faster in the past, and a revision announced in 1999 suggested that the true age of the universe is closer to 12 billion years, similar to the age of the oldest stars in our Galaxy.

Hubble Space Telescope An orbiting observatory, a joint project of the European Space Agency and NASA, launched in 1990 with a 2·4 m (94 in) aperture telescope; named after Edwin Hubble. It was expected to image objects more sharply than telescopes on Earth, and detect fainter sources. However, following the launch, a defect was discovered in the main mirror, which limited its performance. A space shuttle mission added optics to correct the defect and carried out other repairs in 1993. Further new equipment was installed by astronauts on servicing missions in 1997 and 2002, but in 2004 NASA announced that no futher servicing would take place.

huckleberry An evergreen or deciduous shrub which varies from mat-forming to erect, native to the New World; leaves small, oval; flowers urn- or bell-shaped; berries black, edible. In the UK, the name huckleberry is sometimes used for the bilberry. (Genus: *Gaylussacia*, 49 species. Family: Ericaceae.)

Huddersfield 53°39N 1°47W, urban area pop (2000e) 220 200. Town in West Yorkshire, N England, UK; on the R Colne, 17 km/10 mi S of Bradford; railway; University of Huddersfield (1992, formerly Polytechnic); woollen and worsted textiles, textile machinery, clothing, dyes, carpets; football league team, Huddersfield Town (Terriers).

Huddleston, (Ernest Urban) Trevor (1913–98) Anglican missionary. He studied at Oxford, and was ordained in 1937. He entered the Community of the Resurrection, and in 1943 went to Johannesburg, where he ultimately became provincial of the Order (1949–55). After working in England (1956–60), he became Bishop of Masasi, Tanzania (1960–8), Bishop Suffragan of Stepney until 1978, then Bishop of Mauritius and Archbishop of the Indian Ocean. After his retirement, he returned to London, and became president of the Anti-Apartheid Movement (1981–94).

Hudson, Henry (?–1611) English navigator, who explored the NE coast of North America, making claims for both the English and the Dutch. Nothing is known about his early life. He sailed in search of a passage across the Pole (1607), reached Novaya Zemlya (1608), entered the river which was named after him (1609), and (1610) travelled through the strait and bay which now bear his name. He resolved to winter there, but food ran short, the men mutinied, and he and eight others were cast adrift to die.

Hudson Bay area c.1 232 250 sq km/476 000 sq mi. Inland sea in Northwest Territories, Canada; connected to the Arctic Ocean via the Foxe Basin and Channel, and to the Atlantic Ocean by the 800 km/500 mi-long Hudson Strait; maximum length c.1600 km/1000 mi, including James Bay (S); maximum width c.1000 km/650 mi; slowly becoming shallower; generally ice-clogged (but open to navigation mid-July–Oct); rocky E shore, fringed by small islands; explored by Henry Hudson (1610) during his search for the North-West Passage.

Hudson River River rising in the Adirondack Mts, New York State, USA; flows 560 km/350 mi S past New York City to the Atlantic Ocean; navigable for large craft as far as Albany; tidal for 240 km/150 mi; explored in 1609 by Henry Hudson.

Hudson River School A group of 19th-c US landscape painters, including Thomas Cole (1801–48) and Thomas Doughty (1793–1856). The Hudson R valley and Catskill Mts provided favourite subjects.

Hudson's Bay Company A London-based corporation which was granted a Royal Charter to trade (principally in furs) in most of N and W Canada (Rupert's Land) in 1670. It annexed its main competitor, the North West Company, in 1821, and developed trade in otter pelts along the coast of British Columbia. Rupert's Land was purchased by the Canadian Government in 1869. The firm still exists as a commercial company, based in Winnipeg, Manitoba, dealing in such areas as real estate and chain store merchandising.

Hué [hway] 16°28N 107°35E, pop (2000e) 310 300. Town in Binh Tri Thien province, C Vietnam; near the mouth of R Hué, 8 km/5 mi from the South China Sea; ancient town, part of the Chinese Empire; former capital of Annam and of the Vietnamese Empire; many historical sites destroyed in Vietnam War; railway; university (1957); commerce, rice, timber, textiles.

Hueffer, Ford Hermann *Ford, Ford Madox*

Huelva [welva], Lat **Onuba** 37°18N 6°57W, pop (2000e) 143 000. Port and capital of Huelva province, Andalusia, SW Spain; in the delta of the Odiel and Tinto Rivers, 632 km/393 mi SW of Madrid; bishopric; railway; shipbuilding, fishing, canning, chemicals, oil refining, trade in ores, wine; New World fiesta (Aug), patronal fair of Our Lady La Cinta (Sep).

Huggins, Sir William (1824–1910) Astronomer, born in London, UK. He built an observatory near London (1855), where he invented the stellar spectroscope, which had a major influence on the study of the physical constitution of stars, planets, comets, and nebulae. He discovered that comets emit the light of luminescent carbon gas (1868), and determined the amount of heat that reaches the Earth from some of the stars. He was knighted in 1897.

Hugh Capet *Capet, Hugh*

Hughes, Howard (Robard) (1905–76) Millionaire businessman, film producer, film director, and aviator, born in Houston, Texas, USA. He studied at the California Institute of Technology, inheriting his father's machine tool company in 1923. In 1926 he ventured into films, producing *Hell's Angels* (1930), *Scarface* (1932), and *The Outlaw* (1941). He also founded his own aircraft company, designing, building, and flying aircraft, and broke several world air speed records (1935–8). His most famous aircraft, the 'Spruce Goose', was an oversized wooden sea-plane designed to carry 750 passengers, which was completed in 1947, but flew only once over a distance of one mile. Throughout his life he shunned publicity, and after severe injuries in an air crash (1946), his eccentricity increased, eventually becoming a recluse while still controlling his vast business interests from sealed-off hotel suites, and giving rise to endless rumour and speculation. In 1971 an 'authorized' biography was announced, but the authors were imprisoned for fraud, and the mystery surrounding him continued until his death.

Hughes, Owain Arwel (1942–) Conductor, born in Cardiff, S Wales, UK. He studied at University College, Cardiff, and the Royal College of Music, London, and became associate conductor of the BBC Welsh Symphony Orchestra (1980–6) and the Philharmonia Orchestra, London (1985–90), musical director of the Huddersfield Choral Society (1980–6), and founding artistic director and conductor of the Annual Welsh Proms (1986–). In 1992 he was the creator and musical director of The World Choir (10 000 male voices), and since 1995 has been principal conductor of the Aalborg Symphony Orchestra, Denmark. He continues to work as a guest conductor for European orchestras.

Hughes, Richard (Arthur Warren) (1900–76) Writer, born in Weybridge, Surrey, SE England, UK. He studied at Oxford, co-founded and directed the Portmadoc Players (1922–5), and was vice-president of the Welsh National Theatre (1924–36). He wrote the first radio drama, *Danger*, for the BBC (1924), and a collection of poems *Confessio juvenis* (1925). He travelled widely in Europe, America, and the West Indies, and eventually settled in Wales in 1934. He co-authored *The Administration of War Production* (1956), one of the official war histories, but he is best known for *A High Wind in Jamaica* (1929, entitled *The Innocent Voyage* in the USA). His books take a wide-ranging view of developments in 20th-c society. *The Fox in the Attic* (1961) was the first of a projected series of novels about the rise of fascism in Germany (1933–45), but only one other book, *The Wooden Shepherdess* (1977), was completed. He also wrote several children's stories (eg *The Spider's Palace*, 1931).

Hughes, Robert (Studley Forrest) (1938–) Art critic and writer, born in Sydney, New South Wales, SE Australia. He studied at the University of Sydney, decided to become an art critic rather than an artist, and was art critic of the *Sydney Observer* (1958–9) and *Nation* (1960–4). Since 1970 he has been senior art critic for *Time* magazine. He was awarded the Frank Jewett Mather Award for Distinguished Art Criticism in 1982 and 1985. He has written many important books on a wide range of subjects, including *The Art of Australia* (1966) and *The Shock of the New* (1980) – a guide to 20th-c art based on the BBC television series. Later works include *The Fatal Shore* (1987), a history of convict transportation to Australia, *The Culture Complaint* (1993), a polemical discussion about 'political correctness' in the USA, and the television series *American Visions* (1996, published 1997), a history of American art. His *Nothing if not Critical* (1999) contains essays on art and artists.

Hughes, Ted, popular name of **Edward (James) Hughes** (1930–98) Poet, born in Mytholmroyd, West Yorkshire, N England, UK. He studied at Cambridge, where he read English for two years, then switched to archaeology and anthropology for his final year. After various sporadic jobs, he became a teacher, then went to the USA (1957-9). Best known for his very distinctive animal poems, his first collections were *The Hawk in the Rain* (1957) and *Lupercal* (1960). His mythopoeic imagination is attested in such later volumes as *Cave Birds* (1978) and *River* (1983), and in a startling critical work, *Shakespeare and the Goddess of Complete Being* (1992). He married the US poet, Sylvia Plath, in 1956, but the marriage deteriorated, and he left her in 1962. After her suicide, a few months later, he destroyed the final volume of her journal, to avoid her children seeing it – an action which brought criticism as Plath's reputation grew, and he became increasingly reclusive. He was nonetheless responsible for bringing her work before a wider public, editing her collected poems in 1981. *Selected Poems, 1957–81* was published in 1982, and he became British poet laureate in 1984. Later works include *Rain Charm for the Duchy* (1992) and *Tales from Ovid* (1997, Whitbread). He wrote a great deal for children, beginning with *Meet My Folks* (1961) and *Earth Owl* (1963). His story *The Iron Man* (1968, *The Iron Giant* in the USA) received a complementary volume, *The Iron Woman*, in 1993. *Birthday Letters* (1998, Whitbread), a series of poems about his relationship with Plath, written over 25 years, appeared unexpectedly. He was awarded the Order of Merit shortly before his death.

Hughes, Thomas (1822–96) Writer, born in Uffington, Oxfordshire, SC England, UK. He studied at Oxford, was called to the bar (1848), and became a county court judge (1882). A Liberal MP (1865–74), closely associated with the Christian Socialists, he helped to found the Working Men's College (1854), of which he became principal (1872–83). He is primarily remembered as the author of the public school classic, *Tom Brown's Schooldays* (1857), based on his school experiences at Rugby under the headmastership of Arnold.

Hughes, William Morris, known as **Billy** (1862–1952) Australian statesman and prime minister (1915–23), born in London, UK. He went to Australia in 1884, entered the New South Wales and Commonwealth parliaments, and became federal prime minister. He was the major proponent of conscription in World War 1, and as Nationalist prime minister represented Australia at the Versailles conference. A founder of the United Australian Party in the early 1930s, he served in successive cabinets until 1941, and remained an MP until his death.

HUGO [hyoogoh] Acronym for **Human Genome Organization**, set up in 1989 as the first international group co-ordinating activities within the human genome project. Its role is to organize workshops, facilitate access to databases, disseminate information, and act as a broker for specialized funding. Its legal headquarters is in Geneva, while its administrative headquarters is currently in London.

Hugo, Victor (Marie) (1802–85) Writer, born in Besançon, NE France. Educated in Paris and Madrid, he wrote his first play at the age of 14, and went on to become the most prolific French writer of the 19th-c. His early works include *Odes et Ballades* (1822, 1826), and *Hernani* (1830), the first of the 'five-act lyrics' which compose his drama. The 1830s saw several plays, such as *Marion Delorme* (1831), books of poetry, notably *Les Feuilles d'automne* (1831, Autumn Leaves), and novels, of which the most popular is *Notre Dame de Paris* (1831, trans The Hunchback of Notre Dame). He was elected to the Legislative Assembly, and joined the democratic republicans; but in 1851, after the coup, he fled into exile in Brussels, and in 1852 moved to the Channel Is. There he wrote several major works, notably his books of poems *Les Châtiments* (1853, Punishments) and *Les Contemplations* (1856), and his panoramic novel of social history, *Les Misérables* (1862). He returned to Paris in 1870, was made a senator in 1876, and upon his death was given a national funeral.

Huguenots [hyoogenohz] French Calvinist Protestants whose political rivalry with Catholics (eg the House of Guise, which had possession of the French throne) led to the French Wars of Religion (1562–98). Their leader, Henry of Navarre, succeeded to the throne (1589), granting them important concessions on his conversion to Catholicism (Edict of Nantes, 1598); these were later revoked by Louis XIV (1685), resulting in persecution and emigration. In 1572, thousands of Huguenots were slaughtered in Paris in the St Bartholomew's Day massacre, which had been royally sanctioned. In Louis XVI's reign, the edict was recalled. One million Huguenots left France. Many settled in Britain, where they have played a vital role in education, law, social reform, and industry (such as Courtaulds).

huia [hooya] A bird native to forests in New Zealand (*Heteralocha acutirostris*); probably extinct; black with long white-tipped tail; yellow wattle on each cheek; weak flier; female with long, slender, down-curved bill; male with shorter, straighter bill; ate insects and fruit. (Family: Callaeidae.)

Huitzilopochtli [witsilopochtlee] Aztec god of the Sun and of war; there were human sacrifices before his image. He has been identified with the Toltec Quetzalcoatl, whom he replaced after the Aztec conquest.

Hull (Canada) 45°26N 75°45W, pop (2000e) 67 900. City in SW Quebec, Canada, on the Ottawa R, across from Ottawa; founded in 1801 by settlers from the USA; railway; timber, paper milling, textiles, meat packing, cement; Federal Government offices, Canadian Museum of Civilization.

Hull (UK), properly **Kingston-upon-Hull** 53°45N 0°20W, pop (2001e) 243 500. Seaport and unitary authority (from 1996), NE England, UK; at the junction of the Hull and Humber Rivers, 35 km/22 mi from the North Sea and 330 km/205 mi N of London; city status granted 1897; a major UK container port; university (1954); University of Humberside (1992, formerly Polytechnic); railway; ferry service to Rotterdam, Zeebrugge; Humber Bridge, completed 1981; chemicals, paper, pharmaceuticals, iron and steel, fishing, service industries; William Wilberforce house; football league team, Hull City (Tigers); The Deep aquarium centre.

Hull, Clark L(eonard) (1884–1952) Psychologist, born in Akron, New York, USA. He studied at Michigan and Wisconsin universities, then taught at Wisconsin and (from 1929) in the Institute of Human Relations at Yale, where he conducted experimental research into behaviour and learning processes. Much of his work was based on reinforcement theory, as seen in such books as *Principles of Behavior* (1943). He developed a rigorous mathematical theory of the learning process that attempted to reduce learned behaviour to a few simple axiomatic principles.

Hull, Cordell (1871–1955) US statesman, born in Overton Co, Tennessee, USA. He studied at Cumberland University, Tenessee, qualified as an attorney, then entered politics, becoming a member of the US House of Representatives (1907–21, 1923–31). Under Franklin Roosevelt he became secretary of state in 1933, and served for the longest term in that office until he retired in 1944, having attended most of the great wartime conferences. He was a strong advocate of maximum aid to the Allies. One of the architects of 'bipartisanship', he received the Nobel Peace Prize in 1945.

Hull House A settlement house founded (1889) in Chicago by the social reformer Jane Addams and her associates. Set up primarily as a welfare agency for needy families, it also assisted immigrants to learn English and become American citizens. Originally housed in a single building (Hull Mansion), the settlement later expanded to become one of the largest institutions of its kind in the USA and was designated a national historic landmark in 1967.

Hulme, Keri (Ann Ruhi) [hyoom] (1947–) Writer, born in Otautahi, Christchurch, New Zealand. From a novelist with a moderate measure of local recognition, she acquired international renown in 1985 when her story *The Bone People* (1984) was awarded the Booker Prize. Maori themes figure prominently in her work, which also reflects a desire to live in close affinity to the natural environment. Later books include *The Windeater* (1987) and *Bait* (1992).

human capital The knowledge and experience which make some people more productive than others. These may be acquired through formal training, either academic or provided by employers, or through on-the-job training by working in association with more experienced colleagues. Most professionals obtain their human capital through both methods. Human capital resembles physical capital in that it involves costs in time, money, and effort to create it. It differs from physical capital in that in a society free from slavery it cannot be bought or sold, but only hired or used in self-employment. The wages and salaries of those earning more than minimum wages, and much of the profits of the self-employed, can be regarded as the rewards of human capital. Having more or less human capital is believed to be the principal cause of the large differences in income levels between rich and poor countries.

human engineering *ergonomics*

human genome project An ambitious plan launched in 1985 to determine the exact sequence of all 3×10^9 base pairs in the human genome. The project is loosely co-ordinated by a number of national and international organizations, including HUGO. There is a suggestion that it makes more sense to concentrate initially on the human genes which are transcribed into RNA or transcribed and translated into protein, and whose function can be determined. The remaining 95% of the human genome could then be sequenced at a later date. An announcement that 90% of the code had been deciphered was made in June 2000, and published in February 2001. Almost a third of the code had been worked out at the Sanger Centre, Cambridge, UK under the direction of John Sulston (1943–), who joined the project in 1992, using a sequencing technique developed by Frederick Sanger in 1977. His team completed the first sequence of a human chromosome in 1999. During the 1990s the project found itself engaged in controversy, when a private research institute was set up in 1992 by US geneticist Craig Venter (1946–), followed in 1998 by a commercial venture (Celera Genomics), which aimed to be the first to complete the decipherment using a different technique (*expressed sequence tags*). Following a period of (at times bitter) argument over the issues of public accessibility to the information, ownership (especially patenting), and commercial exploitation, the parties co-operated in the public announcement and agreed to parallel publication. A surprisingly low number of genes (less than 40 000) have been revealed. Many legal, social, and ethical questions remain; but it was universally agreed that the announcement was a highly significant moment in the growth of scientific understanding.

human immuno-deficiency virus *AIDS*

humanism Historically, a movement that arose with the Italian Renaissance, in the writings of Ficino, Pico, and later Erasmus and More. The humanists drew on classical literature (particularly that of Greece) and emphasized the centrality of human achievements and potential, in opposition to many of the claims of dogmatic theology and science.

human leucocyte antigens (HLA) [l(y)ookuhsiyt antijenz] Antigens originally discovered on the surface of human white blood cells (leucocytes), and now known to be present on all nucleated cells, platelets, and human lymphocytes. Over 100 different antigens exist, with most people possessing their own individual complement. They are inherited from both parents, and only identical twins have the same HLA patterns. Their importance first lay in their influence in predicting the outcome in organ transplantation, but there are strong associations between HLA and susceptibility to certain diseases, notably auto-immune diseases.

human rights A concept deriving from the doctrine of natural rights, which holds that individuals, by virtue of their humanity, possess fundamental rights beyond those prescribed in law. First formally incorporated into the US Declaration of Independence (1776), a Declaration of the Rights of Man and the Citizen was adopted by the French National Assembly (1789). Most written constitutions contain a bill of rights. Although having no legal standing, the UN's General Assembly adopted a Universal Declaration of Human Rights in 1948, detailing individual and social rights and freedoms, followed in 1953 by the European Convention on Human Rights. The European Court of Human Rights was established within this framework.

Human T-cell Leukaemia/lymphoma Virus *HTLV*

Humayun (1507–56) Second Mughal emperor of India (1530–56), the son and successor of Babar. He was opposed by Sher Shah in Bihar who overran Bengal (1537), routed Humayan at Chausa (1539) and defeated him at Kanauj (1540). Humayan fled to Sind and found refuge with Shah Tahmasp of Persia (1544). After the death of Sher Shah's son, Humayan invaded India with Persian support (1555) and restored Mughal authority. He died soon after, and was succeeded as emperor by his son, Akbar.

Humber, River River estuary in NE England, UK; estuary of Ouse and Trent Rivers; runs 64 km/40 mi E and SE; entrance dominated by Spurn Head; Hull on N shore, Immingham and Grimsby on S; Humber Bridge, 1981.

Humber Bridge Single-span suspension bridge, built (1973–81) across the R Humber, E England, UK; length of main span 1410 m/4626 ft; total length 2220 m/7283 ft; second-longest suspension bridge (after Akashi-Kaikyo) in the world.

Humberside pop (2000e) 904 000; area 3512 sq km/1356 sq mi. Former county of NE England, UK; created in 1974 from parts of Lincolnshire and Yorkshire; replaced in 1996 by unitary authorities of East Riding of Yorkshire, Hull, North Lincolnshire, and North East Lincolnshire.

Humboldt, (Friedrich Wilhelm Heinrich) Alexander, Freiherr (Baron) **von** [humbohlt] (1769–1859) Naturalist and geographer, born in Berlin, Germany. He studied at Frankfurt, Berlin, Göttingen, and Freiberg, then in 1799 spent five years with **Aimé Bonpland** (1773–1858) exploring South America. He worked mainly in France until 1827, then explored Central Asia. From 1830 he was employed in political service. His major work, *Kosmos* (1845–62), endeavours to provide a comprehensive physical picture of the universe. The ocean current off the W coast of South America is named after him.

Humboldt, (Karl) Wilhelm von [humbohlt] (1767–1835) German statesman and philologist, born in Potsdam, EC Germany. After travelling in Europe, he became a diplomat, and for some years devoted himself to literature. He became Prussian minister at Rome (1801), first minister of public instruction (1808), and minister in Vienna (1810). He was the first to study Basque scientifically, and he also worked on the languages of the East and of the South Sea Is.

Hume, (George) Basil, Cardinal [hyoom] (1923–99) Roman Catholic Benedictine monk and cardinal. He studied at Ampleforth, Oxford, and Freibourg, and was ordained in 1950. He became Magister Scholarum of the English Benedictine Congregation (1957–63), and in 1963 Abbot of Ampleforth, where he remained until created Archbishop of Westminster and a cardinal in 1976. He was the first Catholic bishop to be appointed to the Order of Merit, in 1999. His books include *Searching for God* (1977), *Towards a Civilisation of Love* (1988), and *Basil in Blunderland* (1997).

Hume, David [hyoom] (1711–76) Philosopher and historian, born in Edinburgh, EC Scotland, UK. A leading figure in the Scottish Enlightenment, he studied at Edinburgh, took up law, and in 1734 went to La Flèche in Anjou, where he wrote his masterpiece, *A Treatise of Human Nature* (1739–40), consolidating and extending the empiricist legacy of Locke and Berkeley. His views became widely known only when he wrote two volumes of *Essays Moral and Political* (1741–2), and the abridgement of the *Treatise* entitled *Enquiry concerning Human Understanding*, which provoked Kant and the idealists to counter Hume's empiricism and scepticism. He wrote the posthumously published *Dialogues concerning Natural Religion* in the 1750s. His atheism thwarted his applications for professorships at Edinburgh and Glasgow, and he became a tutor, secretary, and keeper of the Advocates' Library in Edinburgh, where he published his popular *Political Discourses* (1752), and his six-volume *History of England* (1754–62). In 1763–5 he was secretary to the ambassador in Paris and cut a figure in French society, returning to London in 1766 and to Edinburgh in 1768.

Hume, Joseph (1777–1855) British radical politician, born in Montrose, Angus, E Scotland, UK. He studied medicine at Edinburgh University, and in 1797 became assistant surgeon under the East India Company. After returning to England (1808), he sat in parliament (1812, 1819–55), where his arguments for reform included the legalizing of trade unions, freedom of trade with India, and the abolition of army flogging, naval impressment, and imprisonment for debt.

Hume, John (1937–) Northern Ireland politician, born in Londonderry, Co Londonderry, NW Northern Ireland, UK. He studied at the National University of Ireland, and was a founder member of the Credit Union Party, forerunner to the Social Democratic Labour Party (SDLP). He sat in the Northern Ireland parliament (1969–72) and Assembly (1972–3), and became widely respected as a moderate, non-violent member of the Catholic community. He became SDLP leader in 1979, and in the same year was elected to the European Parliament. He has represented Foyle in the House of Commons since 1983. In 1993 he and Sinn Féin leader Gerry Adams entered into a series of discussions known as the **Hume–Adams peace initiative**. He shared the 1998 Nobel Peace Prize with David Trimble, and that year was elected to the new Northern Ireland Assembly. He stepped down as leader of the SDLP in 2001. In 2002 he was awarded the Gandhi Peace Prize.

humidity The amount of water vapour in a sample of air, usually expressed as relative or absolute humidity. **Absolute humidity** is the total mass of water in a given volume of air, expressed in grams per cubic centimetre. A sample of air of a given temperature and pressure can hold a certain amount of water, above which point (known as the *dew point*) saturation occurs. Warmer air is able to hold more water vapour than cold air and so, for the same pressure, has a higher absolute humidity.

hummingbird A small bird restricted to the New World; often brightly coloured; possibly related to swifts; feeds on nectar from plants and small insects caught in flight; fast wing-beat and modification of wing structure allows hovering; important pollinator for some flowers. (Family: Trochilidae, 320 species.)

humpback whale A baleen whale of the rorqual family (*Megaptera novaeangliae*), found worldwide; dark back and pale undersurface; wide tail and very long slender flippers; jaws and flippers with many rough knobs; have complex 'songs' unique to each population; may 'breach' (leap vertically from water).

humped cattle *zebu*

Humperdinck, Engelbert (1854–1921) Composer, born in Siegburg, W Germany. He studied music at Cologne, Frankfurt, Munich, and Berlin, and travelled widely as a teacher. He composed several operas, one of which, *Hänsel und Gretel* (1893), was highly successful.

Humperdinck, Engelbert, popular name of **Arnold George Dorsey** (1936–) Singer, born to British parents in Chennai (Madras), SE India and brought up in Leicester, Leicestershire, C England. He started singing aged 17 at a working-man' club in Leicester, and following national service he resumed his singing career under the stage name **Gerry Dorsey**, but with little success. In 1965 he changed his name and had his first hit single 'Release Me' (1967). He had further hits with 'There Goes My Everything' (1967) and 'The Last Waltz' (1967). After the 1970s his career as a cabaret artist blossomed in America.

Humphrey, Doris (1895–1958) Dancer, choreographer, and teacher, born in Oak Park, Illinois, USA. She studied a range of dance forms before joining Ruth Saint Denis to learn an early form of modern dance. In 1928 she formed her own group with Charles Weidman (1901–75), and toured with performances of her own choreography. Her dances were often concerned with form and based on musical structures, such as *With My Red Fires* (1935–6) and *Day on Earth* (1947). She also wrote the key text on dance composition in modern dance, *The Art of Making Dances* (1959).

Humphrey, Hubert H(oratio) (1911–78) US politician, born in Wallace, South Dakota, USA. He studied at Minnesota and Louisiana universities, entered politics as Mayor of Minneapolis in 1945, and was elected senator in 1948. He built up a strong reputation as a liberal, particularly on the civil rights issue, but, as vice-president from 1964 under Johnson, alienated many supporters by defending the policy of continuing the war in Vietnam. Although he won the Democratic presidential nomination in 1968, a substantial minority of Democrats opposed him, and he narrowly lost the election to Nixon.

Humphries, (John) Barry (1934–) Comic performer and satirical writer, born in Melbourne, Victoria, SE Australia. He studied at Melbourne University, and made his theatrical debut at the Union Theatre, Melbourne (1953–4). In Britain from 1959, he made his London debut in *The Demon Barber* (1959) and subsequently appeared in *Oliver!* (1960, 1963, 1968, 1997). He created the Barry McKenzie comic strip in *Private Eye* (1964–73) and wrote the screenplay for *The Adventures of Barry McKenzie* (1972), in which he also appeared. His many one-man stage shows include *A Nice Night's Entertainment* (1962) and *Back With a Vengeance* (1987–9). He is best known for his characters Sir Les Patterson and 'housewife megastar' Dame Edna Everage, who have frequently appeared on television and in film. He has written several books, including an autobiography, *More Please* (1992). He was voted Television Personality of the Year in 1990.

Humphrys, John (Desmond) (1943–) Television journalist and presenter, born in Cardiff, S Wales, UK. He was educated at Cardiff High School and began his career with the *Western Mail*. In 1966 he joined the BBC as a reporter and became foreign correspondent in the USA and South Africa (1970–80), diplomatic correspondent (1980–1), and presenter on the Nine O'Clock News (1981–6). He joined the *Today* programme on Radio 4 (1987), and began to present *On the Record* for BBC 1 (1993). In 2003 he became host of the revived classic TV quiz show *Mastermind*. His contribution to the industry has been honoured with the 2001 Media Society Award and the 2003 Sony Radio Award, and in 2003 he was inducted into the newly established Radio Hall of Fame.

Humpty Doo 12°37S 131°14E, pop (2000e) 1500. Town in Northern Territory, Australia; site of Graeme Gow's Reptile Park, a collection of Australia's most venomous snakes and reptiles; bird sanctuary.

humus Decomposed organic matter, usually present in the topsoil layers. It improves soil structure, making cultivation easier, and gives the soil a characteristically dark colour.

hundred An old subdivision of a shire, sometimes containing about 100 hides (c.12 000 acres), which had its own court, and formed a unit of local administration in the government of England from at least the 10th-c to the 19th-c, especially for tax-collection and maintaining public order. In the Danelaw, the corresponding unit was the **wapentake**.

Hundred Days (Mar–Jun 1815) The period between Napoleon I's escape from Elba and his defeat at the Battle of Waterloo, during which he returned to Paris and tried to reconstitute the Empire. He was finally exiled to St Helena.

Hundred Days of Reform A reform movement in China in 1898, which lasted for just over 100 days, during which period Kang Youwei and his supporters succeeded in securing the Guangxu emperor's approval of radical reforms affecting the constitution, administration, army, and education. All were rescinded on the intervention of the Empress Dowager Ci-Xi. Six leading reformers were executed, and Kang fled abroad.

Hundred Flowers A campaign in China (1956–7) which encouraged freedom of expression under the slogan 'Let a hundred flowers bloom and a hundred schools of thought contend', in art and literature as well as political debate. By June 1957 a clampdown was imposed on the violent criticism of the Communist Party, and the Anti-Rightist Campaign was launched.

Hundred Years' War A series of wars between England and France dated by convention 1337–1453. They formed part of a longer contest which began when England was linked with Normandy (1066), then with Anjou and Aquitaine (1154). In the 13th-c, the Capetians redoubled their efforts to rule all France. But when Edward III claimed the French throne, from 1340 styling himself 'King of England and France', traditional rivalries exploded into a dynastic struggle. In 1417 the English turned from raiding to territorial conquest, a task ultimately beyond their resources. Eviction from Guyenne (1453) reduced England's French territories to Calais (lost 1558) and the Channel Is, but the title of King of France was abandoned only in 1801.

Hungarian uprising (Oct–Nov 1956) National insurgency in Budapest following Khrushchev's denunciation of Stalin at the 20th Soviet Communist Party Congress. Rioting students and workers overthrew Stalin's statues and demanded radical reform. Hungarian soldiers joined the uprising. When the new prime minister, Imre Nagy, announced plans for Hungary's withdrawal from the Warsaw Pact, Soviet and Hungarian troops and tanks crushed the uprising. Many were killed, thousands fled abroad, and Nagy and other prominent figures were secretly executed.

Hungary *p.746*

Hunniford, Gloria (1940–) British broadcaster, born in Northern Ireland, UK. She started singing at the age of nine, releasing four records, and during the 1960s became involved in several shows on radio and television, including a weekly broadcast to

Hungary

☐ International Airport

Hung **Magyarország**, official name **Republic of Hungary**, Hung **Magyar Köztársaság**

Local name Magyarország

Timezone GMT +1

Area 93 033 km²/35 912 sq mi

Population total (2002e) 10 162 000

Status Republic

Date of independence 1918

Capital Budapest

Language Hungarian (Magyar) (official)

Ethnic groups Magyar (92%), German (2%), Slovak (1%), Romanian and Yugoslav minorities

Religions Roman Catholic (67%), Calvinist (20%), Lutheran (5%)

Physical features Drained by the R Danube (flows N–S) and its tributaries; crossed (W) by a low spur of the Alps; highest peak, Kékestetö, 1014 m/3327 ft; frequent flooding, especially in the Great Plains (E); 54% of land arable; 18% forested.

Climate Fairly extreme continental climate, due to landlocked position; average annual temperature 0°C (Jan), 21°C (Jul) in Budapest; wettest in spring and early summer; average annual rainfall 600 mm/23·6 in; cold winters; R Danube sometimes frozen over for long periods; frequent fogs.

Currency 1 Forint (Ft) = 100 fillér

Economy Large-scale nationalization as part of centralized planning strategy of the new republic, 1946–9; greater independence to individual factories and farms, from 1968; grain, potatoes, sugar beet, fruit, wine; coal, bauxite, lignite; metallurgy, engineering, chemicals, textiles, food processing.

GDP (2002e) $134 bn, per capita $13 300

Human Development Index (2002) 0·835

History Kingdom formed under St Stephen I, 11th-c; conquered by Turks, 1526; part of Habsburg Empire, 17th-c; Austria and Hungary reconstituted as a dual monarchy, 1867; republic, 1918; communist revolt led by Béla Kun, 1919; monarchical constitution restored, 1920; new republic with communist government, 1949; uprising crushed by Soviet forces, 1956; during 1989, pressure for political change towards a multi-party system; multi-party elections in 1990 saw an end to communist rule; governed by a National Assembly which elects a Presidential Council and Council of Ministers.

Head of State
1987–8 Károly Németh
1988–9 Brunó Ferenc Straub
1989–90 Mátyás Szűrös
1990–2000 Arpád Göncz
2000– Ferenc Madl

Head of Government
1987–8 Károly Grosz
1988–90 Miklós Németh
1990–3 József Antall
1993–4 Peter Boross
1994–8 Gyula Horn
1998–2002 Viktor Orban
2002– Peter Medgyessy

British forces in Germany (1969–81). She became widely known with her daily radio programme for BBC's Radio 2 (1982–95), while participating in a wide range of shows, including London Weekend Television's *Sunday Sunday* (1982–91) and BBC's *Gloria Live* (1990–3). The recipient of several broadcasting personality awards, she has also written an autobiography, *Gloria* (1994), and a cookbook (1995).

Huns An Asiatic people, probably the 'Xiongnu' ('Hsiung-nu') invaded by the Chinese Han dynasty who, forced W by the Chinese, overran the Gothic tribes of S Russia, and precipitated the great Germanic migration into the Roman Empire. (It has therefore been argued that, through the Huns, Chinese expansionism helped cause the fall of Rome.) Pastoral nomads famed for their horsemanship, they were feared for their brutality throughout the Empire. They invaded SE Europe in c.AD 370, and conquered the Ostrogoths. In 376 they drove the Visigoths into Roman territory, and in the early 4th-c they advanced W, driving the Alans, Vandals, and others west into Gaul, Italy, and finally Spain. United under Attila, they laid waste parts of Gaul, the Balkans, and Italy (451–2), but were then forced to retreat, and Hunnic dominance was soon eclipsed.

Hunt, (R) Tim(othy) (1943–) Biochemist, born in London, UK. He studied at the University of Cambridge, then at the Albert Einstein College of Medicine, New York, and at the Department of Biochemistry, University of Cambridge. In 1990 he joined the Cell Cycle Control Laboratory at the Imperial Cancer Research Fund in London. He shared the 2001 Nobel Prize for Physiology or Medicine for his contributions to understanding the key regulators of the cell cycle.

Hunt, Henry, known as **Orator Hunt** (1773–1835) Radical agitator, born in Upavon, Wiltshire, S England, UK. He was a well-to-do farmer who in 1800 became a staunch radical, and spent the rest of his life advocating the repeal of the Corn Laws, democracy, and parliamentary reform. In 1819, on the occasion of the Peterloo massacre, he delivered a speech which cost him three years' imprisonment. He became an MP in 1831.

Hunt, (William) Holman (1827–1910) Painter, born in London, UK. He studied at the Royal Academy, shared a studio with Rossetti, and helped inaugurate the Pre-Raphaelite Brotherhood, which aimed at detailed and uncompromising truth to nature. His first public success was 'The Light of the World' (1854, Keble College, Oxford). The influence of several visits to the East appeared in 'The Scapegoat' (1856) and 'The Finding of Christ in the Temple' (1860). His *Pre-Raphaelitism and the Pre-Raphaelite Brotherhood* (1905) is a valuable record of the movement.

Hunt (of Llanfair Waterdine), (Henry Cecil) John Hunt, Baron (1910–98) Mountaineer, born in Marlborough, Wiltshire,

S England, UK. A British army officer, he saw military and mountaineering service in India and Europe, and in 1953 led the first successful expedition to Mt Everest. He also led the British party in the British–Soviet Caucasian mountaineering expedition (1958). He was knighted in 1953, and made a life peer in 1966.

Hunt, (James Henry) Leigh (1784–1859) Poet and essayist, born in Southgate, N Greater London, UK. Educated at Christ's Hospital, from 1808 he edited with his brother *The Examiner*, which became a focus of Liberal opinion and attracted leading men of letters, including Byron, Shelley, and Lamb. After travelling with Shelley to Italy, and associating with Byron, he returned to England in 1825. His *Autobiography* (1850) is a valuable picture of the times.

hunter–gatherers Populations living entirely, or almost so, by hunting animals and gathering food; also called **foragers** or **band societies**, as they are typically organized in bands. Typically the men hunt and women forage. In 10 000 BC the entire world population consisted of hunters and gatherers; today they are fewer than 0·001%, including the Pygmies, Khoisan, and Hadza in Africa, Australian Aborigines, and scattered groups in Malaysia, India, and the Philippines. Some pastoral and agricultural groups also engage in part-time hunting and gathering.

Hunterston 55°42N 4°51W. Port facility in South Ayrshire, W Scotland, UK; gas-cooled nuclear reactors came into commercial operation in 1964, and advanced gas-cooled reactors in 1976–7; iron ore and coal trade.

Huntingdon 52°20N 1°12W, pop (2000e) 21 300, with Godmanchester. Town in Cambridgeshire, EC England, UK; on Great Ouse R, 24 km/15 mi NW of Cambridge; birthplace of Oliver Cromwell; railway; engineering, plastics, furniture, transport equipment; 13th-c Hinchingbrooke House, 13th-c Church of St Mary the Virgin, Cromwell Museum, Buckden Palace (8 km/5 mi SW).

Huntingdon, Selina Hastings, Countess of, *née* **Shirley** (1707–91) Methodist leader, born in Staunton Harold, Leicestershire, C England, UK. In 1728 she married the Earl of Huntingdon, but was widowed in 1746. Joining the Methodists in 1739, she made Whitefield her chaplain, and assumed a leadership among his followers, who became known as 'the Countess of Huntingdon's Connexion.' She built a training school for ministers, and many chapels.

Huntingdonshire Former county of EC England, UK; part of Cambridgeshire since 1974.

Huntington's chorea [koreea] An inherited degenerative disorder of the brain, presenting in early adult life, in which slowly developing dementia is associated with uncontrolled jerking or slow writhing movements. There is no effective treatment. It is named after US physician George Sumner Huntington (1850–1916).

Huntsville 34°44N 86°35W, pop (2000e) 158 200. Seat of Madison Co, N Alabama, USA; railway; university; major US space research centre; tyres, glass, agricultural equipment, electrical goods; Alabama Space and Rocket Center (NASA), world's largest space museum.

Hunyady, János [hoonyodi] (c.1387–1456) Hungarian statesman and warrior, apparently a Wallach by birth, who was knighted and in 1409 presented by Emperor Sigismund with the Castle of Hunyad in Transylvania. His life was one unbroken crusade against the Turks, whom he defeated in several campaigns, notably in the storming of Belgrade (1456). During the minority of Ladislaus V he acted as Governor of the Kingdom (1446–53). One of his sons, Matthias, became King of Hungary.

Hupa [hoopa] Athapascan-speaking Pacific Coast Indians of NW California, USA. They lived in villages along Trinity R, and hunted, trapped, gathered, and fished. They were renowned for their basketry, but, unlike groups further N, did not make fine wood carvings.

Huppert, Isabelle [üpair] (1953–) Actress, born in Paris, France. She first worked in the theatre, then made her mark in such films as *La Dentellière* (1977, The Lace-maker) and *Violette Nozière* (1978). For her role in *La Pianiste* (2001, The Pianist) she won the Palme d'Or for Best Actress at the Cannes Film Festival.

Hurd (of Westwell), Douglas (Richard), Baron [herd] (1930–) British statesman, born in Marlborough, Wiltshire, S England, UK. He studied at Cambridge, and followed a career in the Diplomatic Corps (1952–66) before moving to work in the Conservative Research Department (1966–70). A Conservative MP from 1974, he became Northern Ireland secretary (1984), home secretary (1985), and foreign secretary (1989–95). He stood unsuccessfully as a candidate in the leadership contest following Mrs Thatcher's resignation (1990). He was made a Companion of Honour in 1996, and received a life peerage in 1997. His writing includes political memoirs as well as novels.

hurdling 1 An athletics event which involves foot racing while clearing obstacles (**hurdles**) en route. Race distances are 100 m and 400 m for women, 110 m and 400 m for men. The height of a hurdle varies according to the type of race: 2¾ ft (84 cm) for the 100 m; 3 ft (91·4 cm) for the 400 m; and 3½ ft (106·7 cm) for the 110 m. Hurdles are also included in the steeplechase. The current world record for men (110 m) is 12·91 s, achieved by Colin Jackson (Great Britain), in 1993 at Stuttgart, Germany, and (400 m) 46·78 s, achieved by Kevin Young (USA) in 1992 at the Barcelona Olympics; for women (100 m) it is 12·21 s, achieved by Yordanka Donkova (Bulgaria) in 1988 at Stara Zagora, Bulgaria, and (400 m) 52·61 s, achieved by Kim Batten (USA) in 1995 at Gothenburg, Sweden.
2 A form of horse race in which the horses have to clear hurdles. It is not as testing as the steeplechase.

hurdy-gurdy A mechanically bowed string instrument known since mediaeval times, especially among folk musicians. The player turns a handle which causes a wooden wheel, coated with resin, to rotate and to sound a number of accompanimental drone strings. Melodies are played on a simple keyboard, operated by the other hand.

hurling or **hurley** An Irish 15-a-side team field game played with curved sticks and a ball. The object is to hit the ball with the stick into your opponent's goal: under the crossbar scores 3 points; above the crossbar but between the posts scores 1 point. It has been played since 1800 BC, and was standardized in 1884 following the formation of the Gaelic Athletic Association. The All-Ireland Championships have taken place since 1887 and played on the first Sunday in September each year.

Huron [hyooron] Iroquoian-speaking North American Indians, who settled in large towns and farming villages in Quebec and Ontario in the 16th-c. They supplied furs to French traders, competing with tribes of the Iroquois League. Defeated by the Iroquois in 1648–50, many were driven to the W, and eventually settled on land in Ohio and Michigan. They were finally driven by whites to Oklahoma.

Huron, Lake [hyooron] Second largest of the Great Lakes, North America, on the US–Canadian frontier; 330 km/205 mi long; 294 km/183 mi wide; maximum depth 229 m/751 ft; area 59 570 sq km/22 994 sq mi, 60% in Canada; linked to L Superior (NW) via St Marys R and Sault Ste Marie Canals, and to L Michigan (W) via the Straits of Mackinac; empties into L Erie (E) via the St Clair R, L St Clair, and the Detroit R; contains Georgian Bay (NE) and Saginaw Bay (SW); ports include Bay City, Alpena, Cheboygan (all in Michigan), and Midland (Ontario); generally ice-bound in winter months (Dec–Apr); probably the first of the Great Lakes to be visited by Europeans, c.1612.

Hurrians An ancient, non-Semitic, non-Indo-European people first detected in the Caucasus area in the latter part of the third millennium BC. From there they migrated in great numbers to N Mesopotamia, Syria, and E Anatolia, where in the next millennium they greatly influenced the Hittites.

hurricane An intense, often devastating, tropical storm which occurs as a vortex spiralling around a low pressure system. Wind speeds are very high (above 34 m/s/75 mph), but the centre (*eye*) of the storm is characterized by calm weather. Hurricanes originate over tropical oceans, usually between

July and October, and move in a W or NW direction (SW in the S hemisphere), losing energy as they reach land. They are also known as **typhoons** in the western N Pacific and **cyclones** in the Bay of Bengal. Each year they are named in alphabetical sequence as they occur (excluding rare letters, such as Q and X), to avoid confusion when more than one storm is being followed at the same time. Different sets of names are used in the central Pacific, eastern Pacific, and the Atlantic Basin. In the Atlantic, for example, the names are English, Spanish, and French, and occur in a six-year cycle. Originally female names were used, but male names were introduced for the first time in 1978. Names are sometimes retired, if their storms are exceptionally damaging (such as David in 1979 and Bob in 1991). From mid-2000, typhoons have been named using the languages of the Pacific rim (eg Cambodian *damrey*, 'elephant', Korean *kriogi* 'wild goose').

Hurt, John (1940–) Actor, born in Chesterfield, Derbyshire, C England, UK. He trained at the Royal Academy of Dramatic Art and made his stage debut in 1962 at the Arts Theatre, London. He won an Emmy Award for playing the part of Quentin Crisp in the television play *The Naked Civil Servant* (1975), and BAFTA awards for *Midnight Express* (1978) and *The Elephant Man* (1980). Later TV work includes *Bait* (2002) and *The Alan Clark Diaries* (2004). Other films include *Alien* (1978), *Rob Roy* (1995), *You're Dead* (1999), and *Captain Corelli's Mandolin* (2001). His theatre work includes Samuel Beckett's solo play *Krapp's Last Tape* (2000).

Hurt, William (1950–) Actor, born in Washington, District of Columbia, USA. He studied at the Juilliard School in New York City, acted in a succession of off-Broadway productions, then worked in television before making his cinema debut in *Altered States* (1980). He won a Best Actor Oscar for *Kiss of The Spider-woman* (1985), and Oscar nominations for *Children Of A Lesser God* (1986) and *Broadcast News* (1987). Frequently returning to the stage between films, he won an Obie and Theatre World Award for *My Life* (1977), a Tony nomination for Best Supporting Actor in *Hurlyburly* (1984-5), and the 1988 Spencer Tracy Award. Later films include *Trial By Jury* (1993), *Jane Eyre* (1996), and *Dark City* (1998).

Hu Shih [hoo shee] (1891–1962) Liberal scholar and reformer, born in Chiki, Anhwei, E China. He studied at Cornell and Columbia universities, where he became a disciple of the philosopher, John Dewey. He became professor of philosophy at Beijing University (1917–49), where he led the gradualist New Culture movement from 1919, urging the re-examination of China's culture and increased personal liberty, and opposing the increasingly rigid Marxism of Chen Duxiu and Li Dazhao. He wrote extensively on Chinese philosophy, and is also known for his championing of *pai-hua*, the new Chinese vernacular that would make literature accessible to the masses. He served the Nationalist government as ambassador to the USA (1938–42) and the UN (1957), and was president of the Academica Sinaica on Taiwan (1958–62).

husky A domestic dog, one of several spitz breeds traditionally used in the Arctic as a beast of burden (especially to pull sledges); powerful body with thick double-layered insulating coat; also known as **eskimo dog**.

Huss or **Hus, John** (c.1369–1415) Bohemian religious reformer, born in Husinec, SW Czech Republic, from which his name derives. In 1398 he lectured on theology at Prague, where he was influenced by the writings of Wycliffe. In 1408 he continued to preach in defiance of a papal bull, and was excommunicated (1411). After writing his main work, *De ecclesia* (1413, On the Church), he was called before a General Council at Constance, and burned after refusing to recant. The anger of his followers in Bohemia led to the Hussite Wars, which lasted until the middle of the 15th-c.

hussar monkey *patas monkey*

hussars Light cavalry, regiments of which were formed in many national armies from the late 18th-c onwards. They were modelled on an idealized 'Hungarian' style of horseman-warrior, with an exotic uniform typically trimmed with braid and knots, and an elaborate fur helmet.

Hussein (ibn Talal) [husayn] (1935–99) King of Jordan (1952–99), born in Amman, Jordan, a member of the Hashemite dynasty. He studied at Alexandria, Harrow, and Sandhurst Military Academy. He steered a middle course in the face of the political upheavals inside and outside his country, favouring the Western powers, particularly Britain, while supporting Arab nationalism. In 1967 Jordan joined Egypt and Syria in their war against Israel. Thereafter, the PLO made increasingly frequent raids into Israel from Jordan, their power developing to such an extent that he ordered the Jordanian army to move against them, and after a short civil war (Black September, 1970), the PLO leadership fled abroad. His decision to cut links with the West Bank (1988) prompted the PLO to establish a government in exile. Alone among the Arab Middle-East States he was forced by domestic pressure to give verbal support to Iraq during the Gulf War (1990–1), and for a time lost Western aid for Jordan. In 1994 he signed an official peace with Israel. He was married four times; his second wife, Toni Gardiner, was an Englishwoman, by whom he had a son, Abdullah, in 1962, whom he named his heir in 1999. (Until that time his brother Hassan had been Crown Prince.)

Hussein, Nasser [husayn] (1968–) Cricketer, born in Madras, India. A batsman, he joined Essex in 1987 and made his England debut in 1990. He achieved a career-best 207 runs against Australia at Edgbaston in 1997, and during 1998–9, he was England's most successful batsman in the Ashes series defeat in Australia. Appointed England captain in 1999, he led his country to its first series victory over the West Indies on home soil since 1969. Following a captaincy of mixed fortunes, he announced his retirement as one-day captain in 2003, and later stepped down as Test captain.

Hussein, Saddam [husayn], also spelled **Sadam Husain** (1937–) President of Iraq (1979–2003), born in Takrit, NC Iraq. He joined the Arab Baath Socialist Party in 1957, and was sentenced to death in 1959 for the attempted assassination of President Kassem, but escaped to Egypt. He played a prominent part in the 1968 revolution, became vice-president of the ruling Revolutionary Command Council (1969), and sole president in 1979. His disastrous attack on Iran in 1980 led to a war of attrition which ended in 1988, during which he quelled a Kurdish uprising by the widespread use of chemical weapons. He invaded Kuwait in 1990, but was forced to withdraw when he was defeated by a coalition of Arab and Western forces in Operation Desert Storm (1991). Iraq then suffered international isolation and economic sanctions. His breaching of the peace terms led to further military strikes during the next decade, but he continued to resist UN and US pressure for a programme of weapons inspection within Iraq. World opinion was divided in 2002 following President Bush's threat of war as part of a renewed campaign to remove him from office. UN weapons experts resumed inspections, 2002–3, but Iraq's apparent failure to comply with UN resolutions to eliminate its weapons of mass destruction led to a US-led military invasion in March 2003. He was deposed the following month, but his whereabouts in the immediate aftermath of the war were unknown. In December 2003 he was captured by US forces on a farm in the town of Al-Dawr, near Tikrit, and held as a prisoner-of-war.

Husserl, Edmund (Gustav Albrecht) [huserl] (1859–1938) Philosopher, founder of the school of phenomenology, born in Prossnitz, EC Czech Republic. He studied mathematics at Berlin and psychology at Vienna, and taught at Halle (1887), Göttingen (1901), and Freiburg (1916). His two-volume *Logische Untersuchungen* (1900–1, Logical Investigations) defended the view of philosophy as an *a priori* discipline, unlike psychology, and in his *Ideen zu einer reinen Phänomenologischen Philosophie* (1913, trans Ideas: General Introduction to Pure Phenomenology) he presented a programme for the systematic investigation of consciousness and its objects. His approach greatly influenced philosophers in Germany and the USA, particularly Heidegger, and gave rise to *Gestalt* psychology.

Hussites Followers of John Huss, who in the early 15th-c constituted a movement for the reform of the Church in Bohemia (Czech Republic). They anticipated the 16th-c Reformation by demanding the moral reform of the clergy, free preaching of the Word of God, and the availability of the Eucharist for all believers in two species or kinds (ie bread and wine).

Huston, John (Marcellus) [hyoostn] (1906–87) Film director, born in Nevada, Missouri, USA. He moved to Hollywood in 1930 as a script writer, and in 1941 was given the direction of *The Maltese Falcon*, following this with a series of films for the US army. After the War, several films, such as *The Treasure of the Sierra Madre* (1948, Oscar), *The Asphalt Jungle* (1950), and *The African Queen* (1951), established him as a leading director of action drama, and his imaginative use of colour was given full expression in such films as *Moulin Rouge* (1952) and *Moby Dick* (1956). In 1982 he made the musical, *Annie*.

Hutchinson, Anne, *née* **Marbury** (1591–1643) Religious leader and American pioneer, born in Alford, Lincolnshire, EC England, UK. In 1634 she emigrated with her husband to Boston, MA, where she was intensely committed to the Puritan movement and began to organize religious discussion meetings which rapidly took on a political tone. These meetings were suppressed in 1637, and she was expelled from the province after being tried for heresy and sedition. With some friends she acquired territory from the Narragansett Indians of Rhode Island, and set up a democracy (1638). After her husband's death (1642), she removed to a new settlement in what is now Pelham Bay in New York State, where she and most of her family were killed by Indians.

hutia [hooteea] A cavy-like rodent, native to the Caribbean Is; resembles a large rat (weight, up to 7 kg/15½ lb); inhabits woodland; eats vegetation and lizards; related to the coypu. (Family: Capromyidae, 12 living species, and nearly 20 recently extinct.)

Hutton, James (1726–97) Geologist, born in Edinburgh, EC Scotland, UK. He studied medicine there, at Paris, and at Leyden. In 1754 he devoted himself to agriculture and chemistry in Berwickshire, which led him to mineralogy and geology; in 1768 he moved to Edinburgh. The *Huttonian theory*, emphasizing the igneous origin of many rocks and deprecating the assumption of causes other than those we see still at work, was expounded in *A Theory of the Earth* (1795), which forms the basis of modern geology.

Hutton, Len, popular name of **Sir Leonard Hutton** (1916–90) Cricketer, born in Fulneck, West Yorkshire, N England, UK. He was the inspiration of England after World War 2, and skipper of the team which regained the Ashes in 1953. England's first professional captain, he never captained his county, Yorkshire. Playing for England against Australia at the Oval in 1938, he scored a world record 364 runs. Between 1937 and 1955 he scored 6971 Test runs in 79 matches (average 56·67), and during his first-class career (1934–60) scored 40 140 runs (average 55·51), including 129 centuries. He was knighted in 1954.

Hutu and Tutsi Bantu-speaking peoples of the republics of Burundi and Rwanda, EC Africa, speaking the same language and having a common culture. The Hutu, mostly peasant farmers, comprise more than 80% of the total population in both countries. They were subjugated by the Tutsi, warrior–pastoralists of Nilo-Hamitic stock, who migrated S in the 14th–15th-c. The Tutsi dominated Rwanda until 1961, when Belgian colonial rulers helped the Hutu to seize power and form the first independent government, and 10 000 Tutsi were killed. In Burundi, the Hutu led an unsuccessful revolt against the Tutsi in 1971, in which over 100 000 Hutu were massacred by the army, and 120 000 fled to Tanzania. In April 1994, following the shooting down of an aircraft carrying President Habyarimana, Hutu militias sought revenge on the Tutsi minority. About a million people were killed in subsequent months. Following successes by the Tutsi-led Rwanda Patriotic Front, over the next year some 2 million refugees (mainly Hutu) fled to neighbouring countries. Conflict continued in 2002 against a backdrop of international concern, but a ceasefire was announced in December.

Huxley, Aldous (Leonard) (1894–1963) Novelist and essayist, born in Godalming, Surrey, SE England, UK, the grandson of T H Huxley. He studied at Oxford, lived mainly in Italy in the 1920s, (where he met and befriended D H Lawrence) and moved to California in 1937. His early writing included poetry, short stories, and literary journalism, but his reputation was made with his satirical novels *Crome Yellow* (1921) and *Antic Hay* (1923). Later novels include *Point Counter Point* (1928) and, his best-known work, *Brave New World* (1932), where he warns of the dangers of dehumanization in a scientific age. His later writing became more mystical in character, as in *Eyeless in Gaza* (1936) and *Time Must Have a Stop* (1944), while *Island* (1962) is an optimistic Utopia.

Huxley, Sir Andrew Fielding (1917–) Physiologist, born in London, UK, a grandson of T H Huxley, and half-brother of Aldous and Julian Huxley. He studied at Cambridge, then taught there in the department of physiology (1941–60). He helped to provide a physico-chemical explanation for nerve transmission, and outlined a theory of muscular contraction. He was professor of physiology at London (1960–9) and a Royal Society Research Professor (1969–83). He shared the Nobel Prize for Physiology or Medicine in 1963, and was knighted in 1974.

Huxley, Elspeth (Josceline) (1907–97) Novelist and essayist, born in London, UK. She wrote much about life in Kenya, where she lived as a child. Her best-known novel, *The Flame Trees of Thika* (1959), was about her childhood, as was *The Mottled Lizard* (1962) and *Love Among the Daughters* (1968). She also wrote detective novels, such as *Death of an Aryan* (1939, also known as *The African Poison Murders*). In 1993 she published a biography of the ornithologist Peter Scott, *Peter Scott: Painter and Naturalist*. She was married to Gervas Huxley (1894–1971), grandson of the biologist T H Huxley.

Huxley, Sir Julian (Sorell) (1887–1975) Biologist, born in London, UK, the grandson of T H Huxley. He studied at Oxford, became professor of zoology at London (1925–7) and at the Royal Institution (1926–9), and was secretary to the Zoological Society of London (1935–42). He applied his scientific knowledge to political and social problems, formulating a pragmatic ethical theory based on the principle of natural selection. He was the first director-general of UNESCO (1946–8), and was knighted in 1958.

Huxley, T(homas) H(enry) (1825–95) Biologist, born in London, UK. He studied medicine at London, worked as a naval surgeon, and developed his interest in natural history during a visit to the Australian coast. In 1854 he was appointed professor of natural history at the Royal School of Mines, and became the foremost expounder of Darwinism, to which he added an anthropological perspective in *Man's Place in Nature* (1863). He also studied fossils, influenced the teaching of science in schools, and wrote essays on theology and philosophy from an 'agnostic' viewpoint, a term he introduced.

Hu Yaobang [hoo yowbang] (1915–89) Chinese politician, born in Hunan province, SEC China. He took part in the Long March (1934–6), and held a number of posts under Deng Xiaoping before becoming head of the Communist Youth League (1952–67). He was purged during the Cultural Revolution (1966–9), then briefly rehabilitated (1975–6), but did not return to high office until 1978, when, through his patron Deng, he joined the Communist Party's Politburo. From head of the secretariat he was promoted to Party leader in 1981, but dismissed in 1987 for his relaxed handling of a wave of student unrest. Popularly revered as a liberal reformer, his death triggered an unprecedented wave of pro-democracy demonstrations.

Huygens, Christiaan [hoygenz] (1629–95) Physicist and astronomer, born in The Hague, The Netherlands. He studied at Leyden and Breda, discovered the ring and fourth satellite of Saturn (1655), and made the first pendulum clock (1657). In optics he propounded the wave theory of light, and discovered polarization. He lived in Paris, a member of the Royal Academy of Sciences (1666–81), but as a Protestant felt it prudent to return to The Hague.

Huygens' principle [**hoy**genz] In wave theory, a construction technique for deducing the shape of an evolving wavefront; devised by Christiaan Huygens in 1678. Each point of the wavefront is taken to be the source of secondary waves spreading in all directions. The new wavefront is the surface tangent to these wavelets. The principle is applicable to all waves, especially in optics.

Huysmans, Joris Karl [**hoys**mahnz] (1848–1907) Novelist of Dutch origin, born in Paris, France. His books reflect many aspects of the spiritual and intellectual life of late 19th-c France. His best-known works are *À rebours* (1884, Against the Grain), a study of aesthetic decadence (which influenced Oscar Wilde); the controversial *Là-bas* (1891, Down There), which dealt with devil-worship; and *En route* (1892), an account of his return to Catholicism.

Hvannadalshnjúkur [hwanadalshnyookur] 64°02N 16°35W. Highest mountain in Iceland, rising to 2119 m/6952 ft in SE Iceland at S edge of Vatnajökull glacier.

hyacinth A bulb native to the Mediterranean region and Africa; leaves narrow or approximately strap-shaped; flowers bell-shaped, held horizontally or drooping in spikes. Rather variable in size and flower density, large florists' hyacinths are fragrant cultivars with a wide range of colours. (Genus: *Hyacinthus*, 30 species. Family: Liliaceae.)

Hyades [**hi**yadeez] A bright open cluster of several hundred stars 46 parsec distant. It makes a V-shaped group for the bull's face in the zodiacal constellation Taurus.

hyaena *hyena*

hybrid An individual animal or plant resulting from cross-breeding between genetically dissimilar parents. It is typically used for the offspring of mating between parents of different species or subspecies, such as the mule (produced by cross-breeding an ass and a horse). Hybrids are often sterile.

hybrid computer A combination of a digital and an analog computer. It was widely used in the 1960s and 1970s especially in the field of numerical control. Since then the digital computer has taken over many of the roles previously assigned to analog computers.

hydatid disease [**hiy**datid] A disease acquired by ingesting eggs of the dog tapeworm (*Echinococcus*) following the handling of dogs infected through eating contaminated food, usually sheep-meat. The eggs hatch in the intestine, and the larvae enter the blood stream, producing large cysts in many organs, notably the liver, lungs, spleen, and brain. Fluid within the cyst, if released, may cause an anaphylactic reaction.

Hyde, Douglas, Ir **Dubhighlas de Hide** (1860–1949) Writer, philologist, and first president of Ireland (1937–45), born in Frenchpark, Co Roscommon, WC Ireland. He studied at Trinity College, Dublin, and was the founder and first president (1893–1915) of the Gaelic League. Professor of Irish in the National University (1909–32), he wrote *A Literary History of Ireland* (1899), as well as poems, plays, works on history and folklore, in Irish and English.

Hyde Park A royal park covering 255 ha/630 acres in C London, UK. It was first opened to the public during the reign of James I, and became a popular place for riding for members of fashionable society until the end of World War 1. The Albert Memorial, Speaker's Corner, and Marble Arch are situated in the park.

Hyderabad (India) [**hiy**drabad] 17°22N 78°26E, pop (2000e) 3 529 000. Capital of Andhra Pradesh, S India; on R Musi, 611 km/380 mi SE of Mumbai; founded in 1589 as capital of the Kingdom of Golconda; former capital of Hyderabad state; joined with India, 1948; Muslim stronghold in S India; airfield; railway; four universities (1918, 1964, 1972, 1974); commercial centre; vehicle parts, cigarettes, textiles, pharmaceuticals; ruins of Golconda fort, tombs of the Qutb Shahi kings, mosque modelled on the Great Mosque of Mecca, Charminar (1591).

Hyderabad (Pakistan) [**hiy**drabad], also **Haidarabad** 25°23N 68°24E, pop (2000e) 1 300 000. City in Sind province, SE Pakistan; 164 km/102 mi NE of Karachi, on the E bank of the R Indus, c.190 km/120 mi N of its mouth; provincial capital from 1768 until captured by the British in 1843; airfield; railway; university (1947); gold and silver embroidery, enamelware, pottery, shoes, glass, furniture.

Hyder Ali *Haidar Ali*

Hydra (Greece) [**hiy**dra], Gr **Ídhra** pop (2000e) 3960; area 50 sq km/20 sq mi. Island in the Aegean Sea, Greece, off the E coast of the Peloponnese; linked by ferry to Piraeus; chief town, Hydra, pop (2000e) 2460; popular resort island.

Hydra (astronomy) [**hiy**dra] (Lat 'sea serpent') The largest and longest constellation in the sky, extending from the celestial equator into the S hemisphere, but with no particularly bright stars.

Hydra (mythology) [**hiy**dra] In Greek mythology, a many-headed monster, the child of Typhon and Echnida, which lived in a swamp at Lerna. As the heads grew again when struck off, Heracles could kill it only with the assistance of Iolaos, who cauterized the places where the heads grew. The name means 'water-snake'.

Hydra (zoology) [**hiy**dra] A genus of solitary, freshwater coelenterates; stalk-like body attached at the base; apical mouth surrounded by tentacles; catches prey using stinging cells on tentacles; typical green colour derived from green algal cells contained in body; reproduces mostly by budding. (Phylum: Cnidaria. Class: Hydrozoa.)

hydrangea [hiy**dray**nja] An evergreen or deciduous shrub, or a climber with aerial roots, native to Asia, and North/South America; leaves oval, in opposite pairs; flowers in heads, often composed of small fertile and large sterile flowers. Two forms of the shrub *Hydrangea macrophylla* are popular ornamentals: **lacecaps** have heads with large, sterile flowers surrounding the fertile ones; **hortensias** or **mop-heads** have heads composed entirely of large, sterile flowers. Both forms produce blue flowers on acid soils, pink on alkaline soils. (Genus: *Hydrangea*, 80 species. Family: Hydrangaceae.)

hydrate A compound containing water, usually one in which the water is present as 'water of crystallization', such as in gypsum ($CaSO_4.2H_2O$), a hydrate of calcium sulphate. However, the water may have been incorporated into a molecule, as with chloral hydrate ($CCl_3CH(OH)_2$) from chloral (CCl_3CHO).

hydration A reaction of a substance with water to form an adduct. For example, the hydration of ethylene ($CH_2{=}CH_2$) gives ethanol ($CH_3{-}CH_2OH$). Often, the product of the reaction is a hydrate.

hydraulic machinery Machines operated by pressure, transmitted through a pipe, by a liquid such as water or oil. Cars have hydraulic brakes in which the braking force is transmitted from the pedal to the brakes by a liquid under pressure. The hydraulic press and hydraulic ram use the same principle.

hydraulics The study of systems using liquids, whether stationary or moving, for the transmission of force; often, water or oil is the transmitting fluid. Any machine which uses, controls, or conserves a liquid makes use of the principles of hydraulics. The applications include such fields as irrigation, domestic water supply, hydroelectric power, and the design of dams, canals, and pipes. Most motor vehicles have hydraulic braking systems. The hydraulic press relies on applying a small force f to a small area a, to produce a pressure $p = f/a$. By Pascal's principle this pressure is transmitted through pipes to a larger area A to give force F available to perform work, such that $F/A = p$. The produced and applied forces are in the ratio $F/f = A/a$, so the hydraulic press is a force transmitter and multiplier.

hydraulis An early type of organ, devised by the Greek inventor Ctesibius in the 3rd-c BC, in which water was used to maintain a constant pressure of air to the pipes. It is considered to be an ancestor of the modern pipe organ.

hydride Any compound of hydrogen. Three types are usually distinguished: (1) **covalent hydrides**, molecular compounds formed with other non-metals, such as hydrogen chloride (HCl), water (H_2O), and ammonia (NH_3); (2) **metallic hydrides**, with properties of alloys, formed with most transition elements; and (3) **saline hydrides**, ionic compounds formed with alkali and alkaline earth elements, where hydrogen is present as the hydride ion, H^-, eg sodium hydride (NaH).

hydrobiology The branch of biology dealing with the study of life in aquatic habitats, especially those in fresh water. Its core is formed by the study of planktonic plants and animals, and of their relationship to the major physical and chemical features of the water column.

hydrocarbons Compounds containing only carbon and hydrogen. Many hundreds of such compounds are known, and most occur in coal, petroleum, or natural gas. There are two main subdivisions: **aliphatic hydrocarbons**, of which methane (CH_4) is the simplest, and **aromatic hydrocarbons**, based on benzene. Aliphatic compounds are further divided into alkanes, alkenes, and alkynes.

hydrocephalus [hiydrohsefaluhs] The abnormal accumulation of cerebrospinal fluid within the ventricular system inside the brain. It arises because of an abnormal rate of fluid formation or an obstruction to its flow out of the brain, as a result of a variety of disorders including congenital defects, brain tumours, brain haemorrhage, or infections of the central nervous system (eg meningitis). It leads to distension of the brain and, in infants, enlargement of the skull.

hydrochloric acid An aqueous solution of hydrogen chloride (HCl), a strong acid, fully dissociated into H^+ and Cl^- ions. It is the only common strong acid that is not an oxidizing agent, and is widely used as a general acid. Gastric juice in the human stomach is 2% hydrochloric acid.

hydrocortisone *corticosteroids; cortisol*

hydrocyanic acid [hiydrohsiyanik] Hydrogen cyanide (HCN), or its aqueous solution; also known as **prussic acid**. Pure hydrogen cyanide is an exceedingly poisonous liquid, boiling at 26°C, and having an odour of almonds. It is a very weak acid; partially neutralized solutions have $pH > 9$, and solutions of cyanide salts contain substantial concentrations of it. It is a potent fumigant, and an important reagent in organic syntheses.

hydrodynamics *fluid mechanics*

hydroelectric power (HEP) Electricity generated using the potential energy of water. It is a renewable energy source with considerable potential worldwide, although it accounts for only a small proportion of the world's energy needs. It is especially important in countries with scarce oil, coal, or gas reserves. A major source of energy in countries such as Norway, Switzerland, and Sweden, it is also important in developing countries. Many power stations are driven by water held back by large dams in order to even out seasonal fluctuations in discharge and assure steady flow through turbines, such as the Kariba Dam on the Zambezi R and the Hoover Dam on the Colorado R. The world's largest HEP scheme, at Itaipú on the Parana R (built 1975–91), supplies 25% of Brazil's electricity needs and nearly 80% of those of Paraguay.

hydrofluoric acid Hydrogen fluoride (HF), or its aqueous solution. Although extremely corrosive, it is only a moderately strong acid, partially neutralized solutions having a pH of about 3. The acid etches glass by the reaction: $4HF + SiO_2 \rightarrow SiF_4 + 2H_2O$, as the silicon fluoride formed is volatile.

hydrofoil A vessel able to reduce its effective displacement by raising itself clear of the water on attaining a certain speed. Foils are fitted at a depth greater than the draft of the hull. Successful trials were first held in Italy in 1906, but 50 years elapsed before the Italians put it to commercial use. Hydrofoils are used extensively for inland water transport in Russia, and have been used for many years in the Channel Is and Southampton Water. Speeds of around 40 knots are common in commercial service.

hydrogen H, element 1, the lightest of the chemical elements, the commonest isotope having only one proton and one electron in an atom. Its stable form is a gas with diatomic molecules (H_2). Although it makes up more than 90% of the atoms in the universe, it is much less common on Earth, does not occur free, and mainly occurs combined with oxygen in water and with carbon in hydrocarbons. It is of great industrial importance, and is prepared in large quantities by various means, such as the action of steam on hot carbon. It forms compounds with most elements, generally showing oxidation numbers of ±1.

hydrogenation The addition of hydrogen to a compound, also often called **reduction**. One of the most important hydrogenation reactions is that at a hydrocarbon double bond, for example the conversion of ethylene to ethane: $CH_2{=}CH_2 + H_2 \rightarrow CH_3{-}CH_3$. This reaction is particularly important in the saturation of fats and in petroleum refining.

hydrogen bomb The popular name (often shortened to **H-bomb**) for thermonuclear weapons which achieve their destructive effects through the intense release of heat and blast produced when the nuclei of hydrogen isotope materials used in the construction of the weapon are fused together in a nuclear reaction. The reaction is triggered by the detonation of an atomic bomb used as the weapon's core. Unlike atomic weapons, whose yield is limited by the critical mass of fissile material at their core being finite, the yield of thermonuclear weapons is limited only by the amount of hydrogen isotope 'fuel' the weapon contains. The biggest weapon ever tested (by the Soviets in 1961) yielded the equivalent explosive force of 60 million tons (60 megatons) of TNT chemical explosive. The hydrogen bomb was first developed in the USA, the principle theoretical work being performed by Edward Teller at Los Alamos laboratories. The first successful test was made at Enewetak Atoll in November 1952. The USSR first tested a thermonuclear device in August 1953.

hydrogen bond A very strong intermolecular attraction between the electrons of one electronegative atom and the nucleus of a hydrogen atom bonded to another. The strongest hydrogen bonds involve fluorine atoms, but those involving oxygen are much more common, and are important in explaining the properties of water and ice. Hydrogen bonds may also be formed within molecules, and are the main force giving shape to a protein molecule.

hydrography The science of charting the water-covered areas of the Earth, including the determination of water area, coastline, and depth, as well as the flow characteristics of rivers, lakes, and seas. It also includes the location of shoals and wrecks, and the use of navigational aids.

hydrology The science concerned with the occurrence and distribution of water on or near the Earth's surface, in oceans and in the atmosphere, particularly in relation to the interaction of water with the environment and fresh water as a resource. It involves the study of the **hydrological cycle**: water from the oceans evaporates; moist air moves onto continents, condenses, and precipitates; it then eventually migrates back into the sea by run-off or groundwater movement, or back into the atmosphere by evaporation from open water or transpiration from plants. **Applied hydrology** covers topics such as irrigation schemes, dam design, drainage, flood control, hydroelectric power, and the management of all resources depending on variations in the supply and flow of water.

hydrolysis [hiydrolisis] The splitting of a molecule by the action of water. It is applied particularly to the conversion of an ester into an alcohol and an acid (eg fats into glycerol and fatty acids), and to the reversal of condensation polymerization, converting proteins into amino acids and polysaccharides into sugars. It is also used to describe the conversion of a salt of an acid or base back into that acid or base.

hydrophilic [hiydrofilik] In chemistry, water-seeking; a property of compounds with polar groups and most ionic compounds. It is opposed to **hydrophobic**, water-avoiding, a property of non-polar covalent compounds, especially hydrocarbons (eg oils).

hydrophobia *rabies*

hydrophobic *hydrophilic*

hydroponics The growing of plants in nutrient solutions, without soil. The method is especially used in the production of high-quality tomatoes and cucumbers, under glass. In *water culture*, plants are suspended with their roots submerged in water that contains plant nutrients, and are mechanically supported from above. In *aggregate culture* the roots can be placed in such materials as coarse sand, gravel, peat, or vermiculite.

hydrostatics *fluid mechanics*

hydrotherapy *hyperthermia*

hydrothermal deposit A deposition of minerals from the hot, hydrous fluids within the Earth's crust associated with igneous activity. Many of the world's most important ore minerals form in hydrothermal vein deposits.

hydrothermal vents Sea floor hot springs found along the rift valleys of oceanic ridge systems and certain other sea-floor volcanic fissures. In some cases metal sulphides and oxides precipitate from the very hot (350°C) hydrothermal solutions as they surface at the sea floor and build edifices up to 10 m/30 ft in height, known as 'smokers'. High concentrations of hydrogen sulphide are present in the hydrothermal waters and support large populations of sulphide-oxidizing bacteria. These bacteria are the base of a diverse benthic food-chain restricted to the hydrothermal vents, and one of the few food-chains on Earth that do not depend on solar radiation as their ultimate energy source.

hydroxide The ion OH^- or a compound containing it. The only metal hydroxides soluble in water are those of the alkali metals and, to a lesser extent, calcium, strontium, and barium. These are strong bases, giving solutions with a high pH.

hydroxybenzene *phenol*

hydroxybutanedioic acid *malic acid*

hydroxypropanoic acid *lactic acid*

Hydrozoa [hiydrozoha] A class of mainly marine coelenterates in which the life-cycle involves alternation between attached polyp and planktonic medusa phases; polyps mostly in colonies, often with an external skeleton that may be calcified, as in the corals. (Phylum: Cnidaria.)

Hydrus [hiydrus] (Lat 'water snake') An inconspicuous constellation of the S hemisphere.

hyena or **hyaena** [hiyeena] A nocturnal carnivorous mammal; stocky, dog-like, with short back legs; large head with strong jaws; inhabits plains in SW Asia and Africa; eats carrion, insects, and fruit; also hunts mammals; related more to mongooses and cats than to dogs. (Family: Hyaenidae, 3 species.)

Hyères, Iles d' [eel dyair], or **Les Iles d'Or** Island group in the Mediterranean Sea, SE France, SE of Toulon; chief islands are (E–W) Levant (occupied partly by the French Navy, partly by a nudist colony), Port-Cros (nature reserve), and the fortified island of Porquerolles.

Hygeia [hiygeea] In Greek mythology, a minor deity, the daughter of Asclepius; the name is a personification of the word for 'health'.

hygrometer [hiygrometer] A meteorological instrument used for measuring the relative humidity of the air. A **hygrograph** gives a continuous record of relative humidity.

hygroscopic *deliquescence*

Hyksos [hiksos] The so-called 'shepherd kings' of ancient Egypt, who founded the XVth dynasty there c.1670 BC. Originally desert nomads from Palestine, the Egyptians themselves called them 'the princes from foreign parts'.

Hymen [hiymen] In ancient Greece and Rome, the cry of 'O Hymen Hymenaei' at weddings (later a marriage song) led to the invention of a being called Hymen or Hymenaeus, who was assumed to have been happily married, and therefore suitable for invocation as a god of marriage. He is depicted as a youth with a torch.

Hymenoptera [hiymenoptera] A diverse order of insects containing about 130 000 species, including the sawflies, horntails, wasps, bees, and ants; adults typically with two pairs of membranous wings; mouthparts adapted for chewing, or sucking nectar; social organization exhibited by many species; egg-laying tube (*ovipositor*) often modified for stinging.

hymn A song of praise to God, usually with a non-Biblical text in verses and sung congregationally with accompaniment on the organ or other instruments. In ancient times, however, hymns were sung in honour of heroic or notable people, and the Latin hymns of the early Christian church were sung without harmony or accompaniment.

Hypatia [hiypateea] (c.375–415) Neoplatonist philosopher, the daughter of Theon, an astronomer and mathematician of Alexandria. Her learning, wisdom, beauty, and high character made her the most influential teacher in Alexandria, her philosophy being an attempt to combine Neoplatonism with Aristotelianism. Associated by many Christians with paganism, she was murdered by a fanatical mob at Alexandria.

hyperactivity The combination of overactive, poorly controlled behaviour with inattention and lack of concentration for a particular task. This condition is most frequently seen in children, and may have its origin in organic brain injury. It has also been observed in autistic children, anxiety states, hyperthyroidism, catatonic schizophrenic patients, and following the epidemic of encephalitis which occurred shortly after World War 1.

hyperbola In mathematics, the locus of a point which moves so that the difference of its distances from two fixed points (*foci*) is constant. A hyperbola can also be defined as a section of a double cone or as the locus of a point which moves so that its distance from a focus is proportional to its distance from a fixed line (a *directrix*), the constant of proportion being greater than 1. Some of the comets move in hyperbolae, and the curve is much used in architecture.

hyperbole Exaggeration, used often for comic or rhetorical effect, as throughout the writings of Rabelais, or in the mouth of Shakespeare's Falstaff. It was common in Jacobean drama and is an essential feature of burlesque. Charles Dickens used it skilfully, as have other writers of comic fiction and satire. It is the staple of the tabloid press, and also of ordinary conversation ('I'm dying for a drink').

hyperbolic geometry *geometries, non-Euclidean*

Hyperboreans In Greek mythology, an unvisited people of fabled virtue and prosperity, living in the land 'beyond the North Wind'; in Herodotos they worship Apollo and still send offerings to Delos. This could refer to a lost Greek colony in what is now Romania, or even to the Swedes at the end of the trans-European amber route.

hypercube (computing) An arrangement of computers in the form of a cube. Communications links between the computers enable them to carry out tasks in parallel.

hypercube (mathematics) *p.753*

hyperglycemia / hyperglycaemia [hiypergliyseemia] A level of blood sugar above the upper limit of the normal range (> 160 mg/100 ml).

Hyperion (astronomy) [hiypeerion] The seventh natural satellite of Saturn, discovered in 1848; distance from the planet 1 481 000 km/920 000 mi; diameter 400 km/250 mi; orbital period 21·277 days.

Hyperion (mythology) [hiypeerion] In Greek mythology, a Titan, son of Uranus and Gaia, and father of Eos (the Dawn), Helios (the Sun), and Selene (the Moon); later, as in Shakespeare and Keats, identified with the Sun.

hypermedia A form of document which can be held on a computer, consisting of elements of text, audio and video sequences, and computer programs, linked together in such a way that users can move from one element to another and back again. The computer programs can be activated from within the document and may modify the document. When these operations are carried out within a database consisting solely of texts, the domain is known as **hypertext**.

hypermetropia *eye*

Hyperrealism *Photorealism*

hypersensitivity *allergy*

hypercube

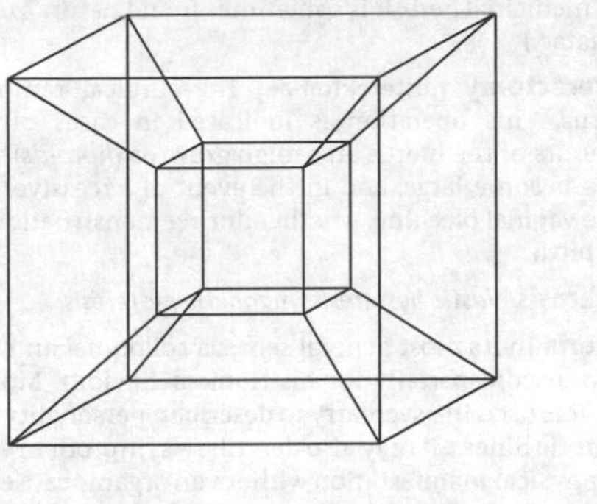

In mathematics, the four-dimensional analogue of a cube. A cube has four square faces meeting at each vertex; a hypercube has 4 cubes meeting at each vertex. It is (fairly) hard to draw a cube on paper, as this requires representing a 3-dimensional solid in 2 dimensions; to draw a hypercube requires using 2 dimensions to represent a 4-dimensional solid. Each cube is face to face with each of six others, and four cubes meet at each vertex. There is one large cube, one small cube, and six others distorted by 'perspective' to look like truncated pyramids.

hypertension A condition in which both systolic and diastolic blood pressure (BP) rise above normal levels. **Malignant hypertension** is a severe degree of high BP in which the diastolic pressure is above 130 mmHg, and an immediate threat to life. All levels of BP above normal damage blood vessels throughout the body; the greater the increase, the greater the damage. The vessels most vulnerable are those of the brain, eyes, heart, and kidneys. As a result, individuals may develop a stroke, poor vision, coronary heart disease, and kidney failure. In the majority of cases the cause of high BP is unknown, but obesity and smoking contribute. In a few cases the condition is attributable to hormonal disturbances, such as Cushing's syndrome, or to kidney disease.

hypertext *document description language; hypermedia*

HyperText Mark-up Language / Transfer Protocol *document description language*

hyperthermia The use of artificial fever for the treatment of disease. The fever can be induced by heat, hydrotherapy (water-treatment, in the form of steam or hot bath immersion), diathermy, and the injection of foreign protein. Since fever is one of the body's natural reactions to the presence of infection or other disease, it is reasoned that a high body temperature may have beneficial effects. The aim of treatment is to achieve a central core temperature of 40°C for a period of up to 60 min, and this has been shown to increase cell membrane permeability, enhance some immunological responses, and induce the death of heat-sensitive cells (including micro-organisms). This form of treatment may be dangerous for children and the elderly, who have poor temperature-regulating mechanisms, and for patients who have cardiovascular disease. Where the technique is not contra-indicated, it has been applied to the treatment of a wide variety of conditions, including cancer and AIDS.

hyperthyroidism Oversecretion of thyroid hormones, leading to an increase in the body's metabolic rate; It may be due to a benign tumour (adenoma) of the thyroid gland, or to an aberrant immunoglobulin that stimulates the thyroid gland to overactivity: also known as **Graves' disease** after Irish physician Robert James Graves (1796–1853). The thyroid gland may appear enlarged and nodular. Patients develop a warm skin with tremor of the hands; there is intolerance to warm weather, a voracious appetite, and weight loss; a rapid heart rate with palpitations is common, and can lead to heart failure in older individuals. A curious complication is protrusion of the eyes with weakness of some of the muscles which move them. Treatment is by drugs which block the synthesis of the thyroid hormone, or by partial destruction of the gland using radioactive iodine or surgery.

hypnosis A temporary trance-like state induced by suggestion, in which a variety of phenomena (eg increased suggestibility and alterations in memory) can be induced in response to verbal or other stimuli. A hypnotic trance is not in any way related to sleep, but there is a constriction of responses by the hypnotized subject. As a treatment technique it is unreliable; spectacular achievements can be obtained in some patients, while for many total failure of benefit is recorded. It has been used as a technique for limiting addictive behaviour (eg cigarette smoking) and for relieving anxiety (eg wedding nerves). The technique was first used by Mesmer in France, and the term *hypnosis* was coined by the British surgeon James Braid (1795–1860).

hypnotics Drugs that promote drowsiness and sleep. They include benzodiazepines and barbiturates. Low doses of hypnotics are sometimes used as sedatives.

hypo Popular name for sodium thiosulphate, incorrectly known as 'hyposulphite'. It is used as a fixing solution in photographic processing.

hypochondria A preoccupation with physical health and excessive anxiety about illness. The hypochondriac interprets common physical symptoms as being due to a serious disease, for example headache is believed to be due to a brain tumour. The fear of disease can interfere with daily life, often leading to medical examinations, but persists despite medical reassurance.

hypoglycemia / hypoglycaemia [hiypohgliyseemia] A blood sugar level below the lower limit of normal. It is rare except in diabetics who have mistakenly administered themselves with too much insulin. It initially produces weakness, sweating, and confusion, which may be followed by fainting and coma. Blood sugar can be restored by giving sugar by mouth or by intravenous injection.

hyponym [hiypohnim] *synonym*

hypophysis [hiypofisis] *pituitary gland*

hypothalamus [hiypohthalamus] A region of the vertebrate brain, situated below the thalamus, which has an important regulatory role regarding the internal environment (eg the control of food intake, water balance, body temperature in mammals, and the release of hormones from the pituitary gland). It is also involved in the control of emotions by the limbic system.

hypothermia [hiypohthermia] A deep body temperature of 35°C or less, measured clinically by a rectal thermometer. It occurs after immersion in cold water, exposure to low environmental temperatures, and following prolonged unconsciousness or immobilization, especially in alcohol poisoning, hypothyroidism, or after strokes or heart attacks. Infants and the elderly are particularly vulnerable. The initial response to falling body temperature is shivering. Thereafter, the muscle of the heart is affected, leading to a slowed heart rate, falling blood pressure, and cardiac arrhythmias. Mental function is also affected, leading to confusion, loss of memory, and ultimately loss of consciousness and death. Treatment is by gradual rewarming. Controlled low temperatures have also proved to be helpful in the management of some clinical conditions.

hypothyroidism [hiypohthiyroydizm] Reduced function of the thyroid gland, with a fall in the secretion of thyroid hormones. It may occur from a primary failure of secretion by the thyroid gland, probably as a result of an auto-immune process, or secondarily to pituitary disease. Body metabolism falls, and patients develop an increased dislike of cold weather; physical and mental activity slows down.

hypsometer An instrument for measuring altitude by observing the effect on boiling point of a liquid. Boiling point, being dependent on pressure, decreases with increasing altitude.

Hyracotherium [hiyrako**thee**rium] The first fossil horse, known from the early Eocene epoch of North America, Europe, and Asia; small, short-faced, lamb-sized mammals; four hoofed toes on forelimbs, three on hind limbs; formerly known as *Eohippus*. (Family: Equidae.)

hyrax [**hiy**raks] A mammal, native to Africa and Arabia, related to the elephant and aardvark; superficially resembles a large guinea pig, with pointed muzzle and round ears; three types: *rock*, *bush*, and *tree* hyraxes; the only members of the order Hyracoidea; also known as **daman**, **dassie**, **rock rabbit**, or (in Bible) **cony**. (Family: Procaviidae, 11 species.)

Hyrcanus I, John [heer**kay**nus] (2nd-c BC) High priest of Israel, and perhaps also a king subject to Syrian control (c.134–104 BC), the son of the high priest Simon, and in the line of Hasmonean priestly rulers. He consolidated his own hold over Israel, destroyed the Samaritan temple on Mt Gerizim, and forced the Idumeans (residents of S Judea) to adopt Judaism. Eventually he supported the Sadduceans against the Pharisees, who opposed his combination of political and religious leadership.

hyssop [**hi**sop] A small, shrubby perennial (*Hyssopus officinalis*) growing up to 60 cm/2 ft, native to S Europe and W Asia; leaves narrow, in opposite pairs; flowers 2-lipped, violet-blue, in whorls forming long, loose 1-sided spikes. Originally cultivated as a medicinal herb, it is sometimes found naturalized. (Family: Labiatae.)

hysterectomy [hister**ek**tomee] The surgical removal of the uterus. This operation is indicated in cases of malignant tumours of the uterus, in benign growths (*fibroids*) when these have become large, and in the event of excessive, uncontrollable vaginal bleeding, whether during menstruation or following birth.

hysteresis *elastic hysteresis; magnetic hysteresis*

hysteria In its most general sense, a colloquial and derogatory term, used especially for histrionic behaviour. More specifically, it is used in psychiatry to describe a personality profile or a neurotic illness. It may also describe a symptom in which there is a physical manifestation without an organic cause to account for the physiological dysfunction. Hysteria is additionally used to describe a group of states of altered consciousness – a situation where patients may suddenly wander away from what they were doing and subsequently have amnesia for that period. In psychoanalytic use, the term also applies to a psychopathological pattern in which the predominant defence mechanism is repression.

i

Iacocca, Lee [yakocha], popular name of **Lido Anthony Iacocca** (1924–) Businessman, born in Allentown, Pennsylvania, USA. He worked for the Ford Motor Company (1946–78), at first in sales, rising to become president in 1970. In 1978 he joined Chrysler Corporation as president and chief executive officer when the company was in serious financial difficulties, and steered the company back to profitability. He published a best-selling autobiography (with William Kovak), *Iacocca* (1985), and a sequel, *Talking Straight* (1989).

***Alabama* claims** (1869–72) A US/British diplomatic dispute, arising from damage inflicted during the American Civil War by Confederate naval vessels (one named *Alabama*) built in Britain. It was resolved in 1872 by an international tribunal (Italy, Switzerland, Brazil), with an indemnity to the USA of $15 500 500.

iamb [iyam] A metrical foot consisting of one unstressed and one stressed syllable, as in the word 'release'. It is the most common measure in English verse because it fits the prevailing natural pattern of English words and phrases: 'And leaves the world to darkness, and to me' (Gray). In Greek and Latin verse, iambs consist of one short syllable followed by one long syllable, and are found mainly in dramatic dialogue. The term derives from a Greek word of unknown origin.

Iapetus (astronomy) [iyapitus] The eighth natural satellite of Saturn, discovered in 1671 by Giovanni Domenico Cassini; distance from the planet 3 560 000 km/2 212 000 mi; diameter 1460 km/910 mi; orbital period 79·33 days.

Iapetus (mythology) [iyapitus] In Greek mythology, one of the Titans, the father of Prometheus, Epimetheus, Atlas, and Menoetius; the grandfather of Deucalion. The close resemblance to Japhet may indicate borrowing from near Eastern sources.

iatrogenic disease [iyatrohjenik] A disorder that arises as a result of intervention by a physician, usually due to the treatment of another disease. It includes adverse and unwanted effects of drug treatment, and complications of surgery.

IAU *International Astronomical Union*

Ibadan [ibadan] 7°23N 3°56E, pop (2000e) 1 578 000. Capital of Oyo state, Nigeria, 113 km/70 mi NE of Lagos; founded in the 1830s; British control, 1896; airfield; railway; regarded as the intellectual centre of the country; university (1948); metals, chemicals, brewing, vehicles, electronics, trade in cotton and cocoa; zoo.

Ibáñez, Vicente Blasco *Blasco Ibáñez, Vicente*

Ibárruri (Gómez), Dolores [eebaruree], known as **la Pasionaria** ('The Passionflower') (1895–1989) Spanish politician and orator, born of a Catholic mining family in Gallarta, N Spain. She became a member of the Central Committee of the Spanish Communist Party (1930), served as Spanish delegate to the Third International (1933, 1935), and was elected deputy to the Spanish Cortes (1936). With the outbreak of the Civil War (1936), she became the Republic's most emotional and effective propagandist. After the war she took refuge in the USSR, becoming president of the Spanish Communist Party in exile. In 1977 she returned to Spain as Communist deputy for Asturias.

Iberian Peninsula [iybeerian] area c.593 000 sq km/229 000 sq mi. The region of Europe SW of the Pyrenees, including Portugal and Spain; the name is probably derived from *Iberus*, the Roman name for the R Ebro; Iberia is an ancient name for Spain.

Iberians A group of iron-age peoples inhabiting the S and E periphery of present-day Spain (Andalusia, Valencia, Aragon, and Catalonia), and extending N into present-day France as far as the Rhône valley.

Ibert, Jacques (François Antoine) [eebair] (1890–1962) Composer, born in Paris, France. He studied in Paris, won the Prix de Rome in 1919, and became director of the French Academy in Rome (1937–55) and of the Opéra-Comique in Paris. His works include seven operas, ballets, cantatas, and chamber music, the orchestral *Divertissement* (1930), based upon his incidental music for Labiche's play, *The Italian Straw Hat*, and the *Escales* (1922) suite.

ibex A wild goat with high sweeping curved horns; horns round in cross-section and ringed with ridges; two species: **ibex** (*Capra ibex*) from the mountains of Europe, N Africa, and S Asia; **Spanish ibex** (*Capra pyrenaica*) from the Pyrenees.

Ibibio [ibibeeoh] A cluster of Kwa-speaking peoples of SE Nigeria, including the Efik, Oran, and Ibibio proper. Agriculturalists, they export palm oil and kernels, and are renowned for their wood carvings. They are also well known for their secret societies (*ekpo*).

ibis A wading bird native to tropical and warm temperate regions; related to spoonbills; long curved bill; face naked; eats small water creatures and insects. The **wood-ibis** (*Mycteria ibis*) of S Africa is a stork, not an ibis. (Family: Threskiornithidae, c.23 species.)

Ibiza [ibeetha] or **Iviza** [eeveetha], ancient **Ebusus** pop (2000e) 71 000; area 572 sq km/221 sq mi. Third largest island in the Mediterranean Balearic Is, 88 km/55 mi SW of Majorca, surrounded by islets; a major tourist island; car ferries to Alicante, Valencia, Palma de Mallorca, Barcelona, Genoa; capital, Ibiza, pop (2000e) 30 000, founded by the Carthaginians, 645 BC; almonds, figs, olives, apricots; Roman Portus Magnus, now San Antonio Abad, with its chapel-catacomb of Santa Ines, a national monument.

Iblis [iblis] The Islamic name for the archangel Lucifer, who rebelled against God and was banished from heaven to become the Devil, the tempter.

IBM *International Business Machines*

Ibn Gabirol *Avicebrón*

Ibn Saud, Abdul Aziz [ibn sahood], in full **Abdul Aziz ibn Abd al-Rahman Al Saud** (1880–1953) The first king of Saudi Arabia (1932–53), born in Riyadh, Saudi Arabia. He followed his family into exile in 1890 and was brought up in Kuwait. A leader of the Wahabis, a fundamentalist Muslim sect, he succeeded his father in 1901, and set out to reconquer former Saudi territory from the Rashidi rulers, an aim which he achieved with British recognition in 1927. He changed his title from Sultan of Nejd to King of Hejaz and Nejd in 1927, and in 1932 to King of Saudi Arabia. After the discovery of oil (1938), he granted substantial concessions to British and US oil companies. His son, **Saud** (1902–69) had been prime minister for three months when he succeeded his father (1953). In 1964 he was peacefully deposed by the council of ministers, and his brother **Faisal**

ice hockey

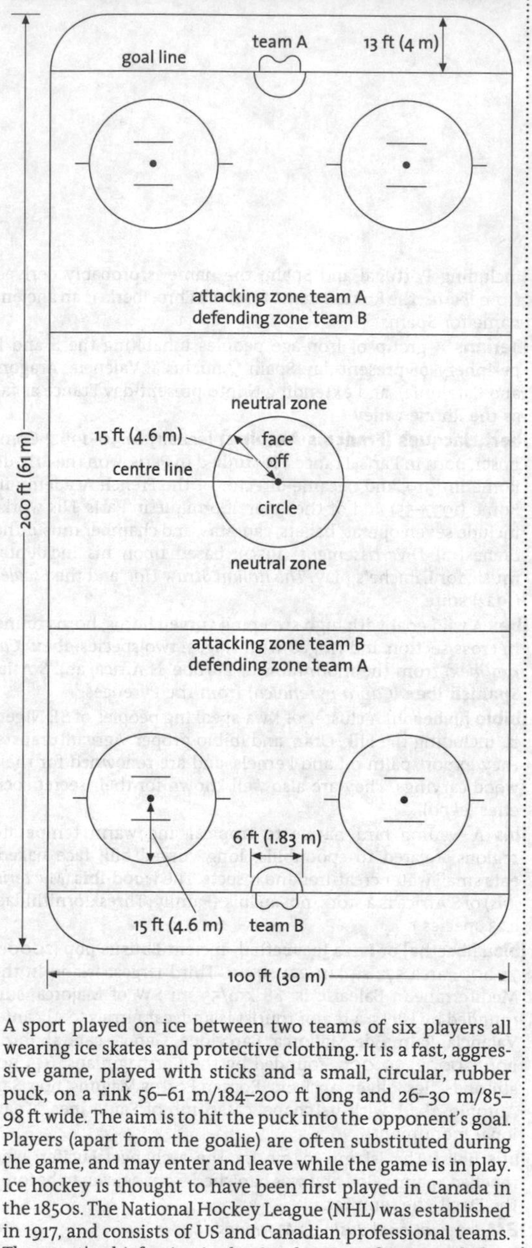

A sport played on ice between two teams of six players all wearing ice skates and protective clothing. It is a fast, aggressive game, played with sticks and a small, circular, rubber puck, on a rink 56–61 m/184–200 ft long and 26–30 m/85–98 ft wide. The aim is to hit the puck into the opponent's goal. Players (apart from the goalie) are often substituted during the game, and may enter and leave while the game is in play. Ice hockey is thought to have been first played in Canada in the 1850s. The National Hockey League (NHL) was established in 1917, and consists of US and Canadian professional teams. The sport's chief prize is the Stanley Cup, first awarded in 1893 in Canada, and later presented by the NHL. The governing body is the International Ice Hockey Federation, founded in 1908.

became king and absolute ruler of Saudi Arabia until his assassination in 1975.

Ibo *Igbo*

Ibsen, Henrik (Johan) (1828–1906) Playwright and poet, born in Skien, S Norway. He worked at theatres in Bergen and Christiania (Oslo), and wrote several conventional dramas before his first major play, *Kongsemnerne* (1857, The Pretenders). His theatre having gone bankrupt, and angry at Norway's aloofness in the struggle of Denmark with Germany, he went into voluntary exile to Rome, Dresden, and Munich (1864–92). His international reputation began with *Brand* and *Peer Gynt* (1866–7). He regarded his historical drama, *Kejser og Galilaeer* (1873, Emperor and Galilean) as his masterpiece, but his fame rests more on the social plays which followed, notably *Et Dukkehjem* (1879, A Doll's House) and *Gengangere* (1881, Ghosts), which was controversially received. In his last phase he turned more to Symbolism, as in *Vildanden* (1884, The Wild Duck), *Rosmersholm* (1886), and *Bygmester Solness* (1892, trans The Master-Builder). The realism of *Hedda Gabler* (1890) was a solitary escape from Symbolism. He suffered a stroke in 1900 which ended his literary career.

Icaria [ikaria], Gr **Ikaría** area 255 sq km/98 sq mi. Greek island in the Aegean Sea, SW of Samos; named after the legendary Icarus; medicinal springs at Thermai; Ayios Kyrikos is a popular resort.

Icarus (astronomy) [**ikarus**] Asteroid no.1566, discovered in 1949, diameter 1·5 km/0·9 mi. It has an orbital period of 1·12 years and occasionally passes close to the Earth.

Icarus (mythology) [**ikarus**] In Greek mythology, the son of Daedalus. His father made him wings to escape from Crete, but he flew too near the Sun; the wax holding the wings melted; and he fell into the Aegean at a point now known as the Icarian Sea.

ICBM *intercontinental ballistic missile*

ice The common solid form of water, stable below 0°C. Unlike most solids, it is less dense than its liquid, this being explained by the fact that the strong hydrogen bonds formed hold the molecules in a relatively open network. An even more open network occurs when ice forms around noble gas atoms or hydrocarbon molecules. Such clathrates may be important reservoirs of natural gas. Their formation is also used in desalination processes.

Ice Age A period of time in the Earth's history when ice sheets and glaciers advanced from polar regions to cover areas previously of temperate climate. Several ice ages are evident in the geological record, the most recent ('the Ice Age') being from c.1 million years ago and lasting until c.10 000 years ago, when the ice retreated to its present polar extent.

iceberg A floating mass of ice, detached from ice sheets or glaciers, drifting on ocean currents for up to several years and for many hundreds of kilometres before melting. With only a fraction of their mass above water level they are a danger to shipping, particularly in the N Atlantic, where they originate in Greenland. Antarctic icebergs are characteristically huge and tabular and many tens of kilometres in size.

icebreaker A vessel designed to clear waterways of ice by propelling itself onto the surface of the ice, breaking it with the weight of the fore part of its hull, which is specially shaped and strengthened for this purpose. Icebreakers are commonly employed in Russia, the Baltic, and Canada.

icefish Sedentary, bottom-living fish (*Chaenocephalus aceratus*) found in icy antarctic waters around South Georgia; blood pale in colour, lacking haemoglobin; body length up to 60 cm/2 ft. (Family: Channichthyidae.)

ice hockey *see panel*

Iceland *p.757*

Icelandic *Germanic / Scandinavian languages; Icelandic literature*

Icelandic literature The Icelandic sagas, for centuries transmitted orally, were written down by Christian scribes, beginning with the 11th-c skaldic poetry, and followed in the next century by the documentary *Landnámabók* (Book of Settlements). In the 13th-c appeared the great Icelandic sagas, masterpieces of mediaeval prose; among them *Egils Saga* and *Njals Saga*. Humanism made its mark in the 16th–17th-c, and the Enlightenment found a voice in Eggert Olafsson (1726–68). Romantic poetry and the novel were represented in the 19th-c by Jonas Hallgrímsson (1807–45) and Jón Thoroddsen (1828–68). In the 20th-c, writers such as Einar Benediktsson (1864–1940), Gunnar Gunnarsson (1889–1975), and Halldór Laxness (Nobel Prize, 1955) continued to make Icelandic literature known abroad.

Iceland spar *calcite*

Iceland

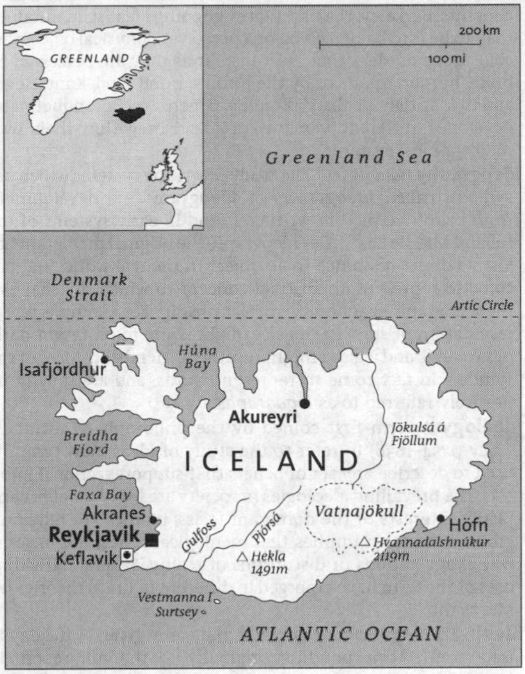

☐ International Airport

Icelandic **Ísland**, official name **Republic of Iceland**, Icelandic **Lýdhveldidh Ísland**

Local name Ísland

Timezone GMT

Area 103 000 km²/40 000 sq mi

Population total (2002e) 288 000

Status Republic

Date of independence 1944

Capital Reykjavík

Language Icelandic (official)

Ethnic groups Homogeneous (96%), with European minorities

Religions Protestant (95%) (Evangelical Lutheran 93%, other Lutheran 2%), Roman Catholic (1%), non-religious (1%)

Physical features Several active volcanoes, including Hekla, 1491 m/4920 ft; Helgafell, 215 m/706 ft; and Surtsey, 174 m/570 ft; famous for its geysers; many towns heated by subterranean hot water; heavily indented coastline with many long fjords; high ridges rise to 2119 m/6952 ft at Hvannadalshnjúkur (SE); several large snowfields and glaciers.

Climate Changeable; summers cool and cloudy, mild winters; average annual temperature 1°C (Jan), 11°C (Jul); Reykjavík generally ice-free throughout year; average monthly rainfall reaches 94 mm/3·7 in (Oct).

Currency 1 Krónur (1Kr, 1SK) = 100 aurar

Economy Based on inshore and deep-water fishing (75% of national income); stock and dairy farming, potatoes, greenhouse vegetables; aluminium, diatomite; tourism.

GDP (2002e) $8·444 bn, per capita $30 200

Human Development Index (2002) 0·936

History Settled by the Norse, 9th-c; world's oldest Parliament (Althing), 10th-c; union with Norway, 1262; union with Denmark, 1380; independent kingdom in personal union with Denmark, 1918; independent republic, 1944; extension of the fishing limit around Iceland in 1958 and 1975 precipitated the 'Cod War' disputes with the UK; ceased whaling in 1992 but resumed in 2003; governed by a bicameral Parliament (Althing), President, Prime Minister, and Cabinet.

Head of State
1944–52 Sveinn Björnsson
1952–68 Asgeir Asgeirsson
1968–80 Kristján Eldjárn
1980–96 Vigdís Finnbogadóttir
1996– Olafur Ragnar Grimsson

Head of Government
1980–3 Gunnar Thoroddsen
1983–7 Steingrímur Hermannsson
1987–8 Thorstein Pálsson
1988–91 Steingrímur Hermannsson
1991– Davíd Oddsson

Iceni [ikaynee] An ancient British tribe occupying what is now Norfolk and NW Suffolk. They rebelled in AD 47 and again in 60, when their queen, Boudicca, led them and other tribes in a major revolt that nearly brought about the collapse of the Roman administration in Britain.

ice plant An annual lying flat on the ground (*Mesembryanthemum crystallinum*), with broad succulent leaves and white, daisy-like flowers. The whole plant is covered with glistening papillae, resembling ice crystals. Native to S Africa, and introduced elsewhere, it was formerly a source of soda ash (commercial sodium carbonate), obtained by burning the plants. (Family: Aizoaceae.)

ice skating **1 Figure skating**, artistic dancing on ice. Competitions are held for individual, pairs, and ice dancing. The first known skating club was formed mid-18th-c in London, and the first artificial rink was opened at Baker Street in 1876. **2 Speed skating**, in which one competitor races against another on an oval ice track over distances of 500–10 000 m (550–11 000 yds).

I-ching [ee ching] *Book of Changes*

Ichkeul [ishkoel] area 108 sq km/42 sq mi. National park in Tunisia, established in 1978, now a world heritage site.

ichneumon (entomology) [iknyoomn] A slender, parasitic wasp; females often have elongate egg-laying tube; eggs typically deposited on larvae or pupae of other insects and spiders; larvae feed on these as parasites during their development. (Order: Hymenoptera. Family: Ichneumonidae.)

ichneumon (mammal) [iknyoomn] The largest living mongoose (*Herpestes ichneumon*) (length, 1 m/3¾ ft), native to Africa and the Middle East (introduced in S Europe); also known as **Egyptian mongoose** or **Pharaoh's rat**.

ichthyosaur [ikthiosaw(r)] An aquatic reptile with streamlined body for fast swimming; tail typically large, paddle-like; eyes large, usually surrounded by bony plates; teeth small, fed mainly on cephalopods and fish; bore live young; known mainly from the Jurassic period. (Subclass: Ichthyopterygia.)

Icknield Way [ikneeld] A Neolithic track linking Salisbury Plain in SE England, UK to the E coast. The Romans gravelled it and used it as a secondary road.

Ickx, Jacky [iks] (1945–) Motor-racing driver, born in Brussels, Belgium. He won eight races from 116 starts in Formula One. Outstanding at endurance racing, he won 34 world sports car championship races, and was world champion in 1982–3 (both Porsche). He won the Le Mans 24-hour race a record six times, in 1969 (with Oliver), 1975 (with Bell), 1976 (with van Lennep), 1977 (with Barth and Haywood), and 1981–2 (both with Bell).

icon (art and religion) (Gr *eikon*, 'image') A representation of Christ, the Virgin Mary, angels, saints, or even events of sacred history, used since the 5th-c for veneration and an aid to devotion, particularly in the Greek and Russian Orthodox Churches. They are typically in Byzantine style, flat, and painted in oils on wood, often with an elaborately decorated gold or silver [illegible]. They are believed to be the channel of blessing from God.

icon (computing) In computing, a small image or symbol used in graphic user interfaces to represent an item such as a program or a disk drive. Commands can be given to the computer using a mouse to point at an icon, thereby selecting the task related to the icon that needs to be performed.

iconoclasm [iykonoklazm] (Gr 'image breaking') The extreme rejection of the veneration of images. The practice was justified as an interpretation of the second of the Ten Commandments (*Ex* 20.4), and was supported by the pope and the Roman emperor in the 8th-c, and again by certain Reformers in the 16th-c.

iconography The branch of art history which, faced with a picture, or any kind of image, takes as its central question: who or what is represented? Originally it was concerned with the identification of portraits; thus van Dyck's *Iconography* (1645) is a set of engraved portraits. Since the pioneer work of Mrs Anna Jameson (1794–1860) and Adolphe Didron (1806–67) in the mid-19th-c it has been extended to cover the whole science of subject-matter and symbolism, especially under the influence of Aby Warburg (1866–1929) and his followers.

iconology A term used by the Italian writer Cesare Ripa (c.1560–before 1625) as the title of his collection of personifications (eg 'Deceit' with serpent's tail, 1593). Nowadays it is used for the historical study of the meaning of works of art in a broad sense – religious, social, political – following German art historian Erwin Panofsky (1892–1968), whose seminal article 'Iconography and Iconology' was published in 1939; but modern usage is often imprecise.

Ictinos or **Ictinus** [iktiynus] (5th-c BC) Greek architect. With **Callicrates** he designed the Parthenon (447–438 BC). He was also architect of the Temple of the Mysteries at Eleusis and the Temple of Apollo Epicurius at Bassae.

id *ego*

Idaho [iyda-hoh] pop (2000e) 1 294 000; area 216 422 sq km/ 83 564 sq mi. State in NW USA, divided into 44 counties; the 'Gem State'; first European exploration by Lewis and Clark, 1805; held jointly by Britain and the USA until 1846; discovery of gold (1860) led to an influx of settlers; Territory of Idaho established, 1863; admitted to the Union as the 43rd state, 1890; capital, Boise; other chief cities, Pocatello and Idaho Falls; bounded N by Canada (British Columbia); rivers include the Snake (forms part of W border) and Salmon; the Bitterroot Range lies along much of the Montana border; in the C and N are the Sawtooth Mts, Salmon River Mts, and Clearwater Mts; highest point Borah Peak (3860 m/12 664 ft); largely rugged, mountainous country, with nearly half the state (mostly N) under national forest; the Snake R Plain is one of the largest irrigated areas in the USA; river dams also generate hydroelectric power; mainly an agricultural state; cattle, wheat, potatoes, hay, sugar-beets, dairy produce; wood products, processed foods, chemicals; silver and antimony mined; contains one of the deepest gorges in the world, on the Snake R (Hell's Canyon).

Id al-Adha [eed al adha] The Muslim 'Feast of Sacrifice', celebrating the faith of Abraham, who was willing to sacrifice his son at Allah's request; sheep and goats are killed as a reminder of the sheep Allah provided as a substitute for the boy, and the meat is shared with the poor.

Id al-Fitr [eed al feeter] A Muslim festival, the 'Feast of Breaking Fast', occurring on the first day after Ramadan, and celebrated with festive meals, the wearing of new clothes, and giving gifts to charity.

ide *orfe*

ideal gas A model gas in which atoms do not interact with one another, approximated well by noble gases such as helium and neon, and other gases at low pressures; also called a **perfect gas**. More exactly, an ideal gas is one for which the equation of state is $pV = nRT$, where p is pressure, V volume, n number of moles of gas, T temperature, and R the molar gas constant having the value 8·314 $J.mol^{-1}K^{-1}$.

idealism In philosophy, the theory that the material world is in some sense created by the mind and does not exist independently of it; the only things which fully exist are minds and their contents. Berkeley, the first thoroughgoing idealist, maintained that 'to be is to be perceived or a perceiver'; physical objects are collections of ideas that exist insofar as they are perceived by finite, human minds or by the infinite mind, God. Kant, Hegel, and the 'British Idealists' (Bradley, Green, and Bosanquet) later developed different versions of idealism within their own philosophical systems.

ideography [idiografee] The study of writing systems which use symbols called **ideographs** or **ideograms** – a development from primitive picture writing, found in early systems of the Far and Middle East. In an ideograph, the original pictogram has lost its direct reference to an object in the real world, and has come to represent an abstract concept to which the shape of the ideograph bears no clear relationship. For example, a representation of stars in the sky might come to represent darkness or evil, and a hand might represent friendship. Most of the symbols in fact come to represent words, and are thus more precisely referred to as *logographs*.

ideology A term first coined by the philosopher Destutt de Tracy (1754–1836) to refer to the study of ideas; now typically used to describe any set of beliefs that support sectional interests. The prevailing ideologies in society are likely to reflect and justify interests of the dominant (class, political, or religious) groups. The term implies that ideological beliefs are in some way exaggerations or distortions of reality. Several individual uses of the term have emerged in different political theories (eg Marxism).

ides [iydz] In the Roman calendar, the name given to the day in mid-month corresponding originally to the full moon. In March, May, July, and October this was the 15th, and in all other months the 13th.

idiolect [idiohlekt] The total linguistic system of an individual, in a given language, at any specific time. Dialects are made up of more-or-less similar idiolects. It is unlikely that any two people have identical idiolects: different preferences in usage, grammar, vocabulary, and pronunciation will serve to keep them apart.

idiophone Any musical instrument whose sound proceeds from the body of the instrument itself, without the action of vibrating strings, membranes, loudspeakers, or columns of air. Idiophones form one of the main categories in the standard classification of Hornbostel and Sachs (1914).

Idomeneus [iydomenyus] According to Homer, the leader of the Cretans who assisted the Greeks at Troy; a descendant of Minos. Being caught in a storm at sea, he vowed to sacrifice the first thing he met on his safe return. This was his own son; and after carrying out the sacrifice he was driven into exile.

Idriess, Ion Llewellyn [idruhs] (1889–1979) Writer, born in Sydney, New South Wales, SE Australia. After various occupations, which later helped to provide colour for his works, he became a writer. *Lasseter's Last Ride* (1931) was his first success. In the next 40 years he wrote almost one book each year, of which the best known are *Flynn of the Inland* (1932, about Rev John Flynn, founder of the Flying Doctor Service), *The Desert Column* (1932, based on his experiences with the Australian Light Horse during World War 1), *The Cattle King* (1936, the life of Sir Sidney Kidman), and *Onward Australia* (1944).

Idumeans *Edomites*

Ieper *Ypres*

Ife [eefay] A Yoruba ceremonial and trading centre in SW Nigeria, occupied from the 11th-c AD, from which the Yoruba dispersed to found their kingdoms. It is noted for its naturalistic figures in brass and terracotta, possibly dating from the late 14th/early 15th-c. The related Benin tradition may also derive from Ife.

Igbo or **Ibo** [eeboh] A people of E Nigeria, a collection of many small and traditionally autonomous communities, with a common culture; the Igbo language is a member of the Kwa branch of the Niger–Congo family. Principally agriculturalists, with some export crops, they dominated the long-distance trade in Nigeria, and produced the earliest bronze art in the region. They established the short-lived state of Biafra (1960–70), and genocide of Igbo living in other parts of Nigeria occurred during this period.

Ignarro, Louis J (1941–) Pharmacologist, born in New York City, USA. He studied at Columbia and Minnesota universities, later working at Tulane University (1979–85), and at the University of California, Los Angeles. He shared the 1998 Nobel Prize for Physiology or Medicine for his contribution to the discovery of nitric oxide as a signalling molecule in the cardiovascular system.

Ignatius (of Antioch), St [ignayshus] (c.35–c.107) One of the apostolic Fathers of the Church, reputedly a disciple of St John, the second Bishop of Antioch. According to Eusebius, he died a martyr in Rome. The *Ignatian Epistles*, whose authenticity was long controversial, were written on his way to Rome after being arrested. They provide valuable information on the nature of the early Church. Feast day 17 October.

Ignatius de Loyola, St *Loyola, Ignatius of, St*

igneous rock Rocks that have formed by crystallization of magma originating within or below the Earth's crust. Two main classifications exist. In terms of chemical composition, there are *acid* rocks, with more than 66% total silica (SiO_2); *basic* rocks with less than 55% total silica; and intermediate rocks. In terms of crystal size and mode of occurrence, *plutonic* rocks form deep in the Earth and are coarse-grained (eg granite); *volcanic* rocks form on the Earth's surface and are fine-grained (eg basalt); and *hypabyssal* rocks form at relatively shallow depths (eg dolerite).

ignis fatuus [ignis fatyoouhs] Flickering lights sometimes seen at night in marshy areas, and thought to be due to the spontaneous combustion of marsh gas (methane) generated by decaying vegetation. It is commonly termed **will-o'-the-wisp** or **Jack-o'-lantern**.

Iguaçu [igwasoo], Brazil **Iguaçu**, Argentina & Paraguay **Iguazú** National park close to the borders of Argentina, Brazil and Paraguay; area 1950 sq km/750 sq mi; noted for its spectacular scenery, particularly the 82 m/269 ft-high Iguaçu Falls; 275 falls over a frontage of 2470 m/8104 ft; a world heritage site.

iguana [igwahna] A lizard, native to the New World, Madagascar, Fiji, and Tonga; active during the day; often has crest of tooth-like projections along back; tongue thick and fleshy, not long and forked. (Family: Iguanidae, 650 species.)

Iguanodon [igwahnodon] A heavily built two-legged dinosaur; up to 8 m/26 ft in length; plant-eating, with a cropping, horny beak present at the front of both jaws; probably lived in herds; known mainly from the Lower Cretaceous period of Europe. (Order: Ornithischia.)

Iguvine tablets [igyuviyn] A set of seven inscribed bronze tablets, relating to the period c.400–90 BC, discovered in 1444 near Iguvium (modern Gubbio), Italy. They contain rules for the ceremonies of a brotherhood of priests, with a wealth of information about the cults of Roman gods and goddesses, including Jupiter and Pomona.

idée fixe [eeday feeks] A short theme associated with a particular person, object, or idea, which recurs (sometimes in altered form) in different movements or sections of a musical work. The term is used particularly with reference to the *Symphonie fantastique* and other works by Berlioz.

Ijsselmeer or **Ysselmeer** [eselmair] area 1240 sq km/480 sq mi. Shallow lake in NW Netherlands, formed from the S part of the Zuider Zee inlet by the construction of the Afsluitdijk Sea Dam (1932); fresh water fed by the Ijssel R; large areas have been reclaimed as polder land.

Ikaría *Icaria*

ikebana [eekaybahna] The formal Japanese style of flower arrangement, which selects a few blooms or leaves and places them in a very careful relationship to one another. It was a popular pastime in W Europe in the second half of the 20th-c.

Illampu, Nevado de [eelyampoo], also **Mount Sorata** 15°51S 68°30W. Highest mountain in the Andean Cordillera Oriental, in the Cordillera de la Paz; consists of two peaks, Illampu (6485 m/21 276 ft) and Ancohuma (6388 m/20 958 ft).

Illinois [ilinoy] pop (2000e) 12 419 300; area 145 928 sq km/56 345 sq mi. State in NC USA, divided into 102 counties; the 'Prairie State'; 21st state admitted to the Union, 1818; explored by Jolliet and Marquette in 1673 and settled by the French, who established Fort St Louis, 1692; included in French Louisiana, it was ceded to the British in 1763 and by the British to the USA in 1783; capital, Springfield; other chief cities, Chicago (the leading city of the Midwest), Rockford, Peoria; the Mississippi R forms the W border, the Ohio R follows the Kentucky border, the Wabash R forms the lower part of the Indiana border, and the Illinois R flows SW across the state to meet the Mississippi R; direct link to the Atlantic through the Great Lakes and the St Lawrence Seaway; highest point is Charles Mound (376 m/1234 ft); mostly flat prairie producing corn, soybeans, wheat; grazing pigs and cattle; coal mining; diverse manufacturing, especially in the Chicago area; Lincoln began his political career here.

illiteracy *literacy*

illuminance In photometry, the incident luminous flux per unit area, ie the amount of visible light available to provide illumination per square metre; symbol E, units lx (lux); also called **illumination**. It decreases with the square of the distance from the source. The human eye can detect down to 10^{-9} lx.

illumination *illuminance*

illusion A true sensory stimulus which is misinterpreted. For example, the sound of a dripping tap may be thought to be malevolent voices, or flickering shadows in a dark room might be interpreted as ferocious animals.

illusionism In art, the use of perspective, foreshortening, light and shade, and other devices to deceive the eye. Ancient Roman wall-paintings (such as at Pompeii), Renaissance stage-scenery, and Baroque ceiling-decoration are notable examples.

Illyria [iliria] In antiquity, the E seaboard of the Adriatic and its mountainous hinterland. It was roughly the equivalent of the W half of former Yugoslavia and NW Albania; its inland boundaries were never precisely defined.

ilmenite [ilmeniyt] A black oxide mineral, iron titanate ($FeTiO_3$), found in basic igneous rocks and beach sand deposits. It is the major ore of titanium.

ILO *International Labour Organization*

Ilyushin, Sergey Vladimirovich [ilyooshin] (1894–1977) Aircraft designer, born in Dilialevo, Russia. After working as an aviation mechanic, he graduated in engineering, and in 1931 took charge of the design of both military and civil aircraft, including the Il-4 long-range bomber, which was important in World War 2. Afterwards his passenger aircraft became the basic Soviet carriers.

imagery Figurative language; the illustration and emphasis of an idea by analogies and parallels of different kinds, to make it more concrete and objective. Images may be explicit in the form of a simile ('As cold as any stone') or implicit in the form of a metaphor ('You blocks, you stones, you worse than senseless things'). They may be incidental, or form part of a system of imagery running through a work; organized images may also function as symbols. Imagery is often thought of as mainly visual, but this is far from being the case: images often invoke the other senses (smell, taste, touch, hearing) individually or combined (*synaesthesia*), and may operate even on an abstract, intellectual level. Imagery is a recognized grace of poetry, but also plays an important part in much prose writing.

imaginary number *numbers*

Imagism An early Anglo-American 20th-c poetic movement which sought to return (and confine) poetry to its essential ingredient, the image, which 'presents an intellectual and emotional complex in an instant of time' (Ezra Pound). Other ingredients included a preference for free verse over metric forms, a stress on economy and exactness, the use of the language of common speech, and a sophisticated, erudite quality. In 1914 Ezra Pound edited the anthology *Des Imagistes* which contained poetry by D H Lawrence, James Joyce, William Carlos Williams, Amy Lowell, and himself. Imagist poetry as such may lack interest through such reduction, but the movement has been widely influential.

imam [imahm] **1** A religious leader and teacher of a Sunni Muslim community, who leads worship in the mosque.
2 A title given to the founders or great leaders of important Muslim communities or schools.
3 A charismatic leader among Shiite Muslims, who believe that in every generation there is an imam who is an infallible source of spiritual and secular guidance. The line of imams ended in the 9th-c, and since then the ayatollahs serve as the collective caretakers of the office until the return of the expected imam.

IMAX [iymaks] A large-screen cinematograph system, developed in Canada in 1968, using a frame 70 × 46 mm on 70 mm film running horizontally. This is projected on a screen typically 18–23 m/60–75 ft wide and 14–18 m/45–60 ft high, which is viewed by an audience seated comparatively close so that the picture fills their field of vision. Sound from six magnetic tracks is reproduced from speakers around the auditorium. OMNIMAX was a further development in 1972, using wide-angle lenses for projection on a domed screen c.23 m/75 ft in diameter.

Imhotep [imhohtep] (fl.27th-c BC) Egyptian physician and adviser to King Zoser (3rd dynasty). He was probably the architect of the so-called Step Pyramid at Sakkara, near Cairo. In time, he came to be revered as a sage, and during the Saite period (500 BC) he was worshipped as the life-giving son of Ptah, god of Memphis. The Greeks identified him with their own god of healing, Asclepius, because of his reputed knowledge of medicine. Many bronze figures of him have been discovered.

Immaculate Conception The belief that the Virgin Mary from the moment of her conception was free from sin. After many centuries' history, this was promulgated as a dogma of the Roman Catholic Church by Pope Pius IX in 1854. It was always rejected by Protestants as unbiblical, and, since 1854, has been rejected by the Orthodox Church.

Immanuel or **Emmanuel** [imanyuel] (Heb 'God with us') In the Hebrew Bible, a name which appears only in *Isaiah* (7.14, 8.8 (10)), where the birth of a son of this name to a young woman is a sign to King Ahaz of Judah's security against her N enemies. The text of *Isa* 7.14 is cited in *Matt* 1.23 as a prophecy of the birth of Jesus the Messiah, one to be born of a young woman (or virgin), whose name is to be called Immanuel.

immigration *migration 1*

immortelle The name applied to various species of the daisy family (*Compositae*), cultivated for the papery flower-heads which retain their colour and are often used dried in flower arrangements. Commonly grown species include *Helichrysum bracteatum*, a perennial growing to 120 cm/4 ft, native to Australia, but often grown as an annual; flower heads surrounded by large shining papery bracts in yellow, orange, purple, or white.

immunity (medicine) The reaction of the body to material that it perceives to be 'not-self'. The term was originally used to describe the body's ability to resist the development of disease in the event of exposure to a disease-causing micro-organism. It now also includes the body's response to other foreign proteins such as transplants and allergens. Naturally occurring or **innate immunity** protects individuals from infections with which they have not had previous contact; it is a non-specific response to any material perceived as 'not-self'. Cells in the blood and tissues surround and destroy foreign proteins using chemicals (eg interferon, lysozyme) and by engulfing them (phagocytosis). Natural immunity may be suppressed by chronic illnesses such as diabetes. **Acquired** or **adaptive immunity** is a specific response mediated by lymphocytes and antibodies. These cells have the ability to recognize and remember foreign proteins; they act directly against them and help the innate immune system. In the event of re-exposure to an infection, the adaptive immune system dramatically increases the level of the body's response. The HIV virus interferes with this process.

immunity (law) A state of freedom from certain legal rules and their consequences. Diplomatic immunity is a provision of the Vienna Convention on Diplomatic Relations (1961), an international treaty, which states that diplomatic agents will have immunity (ie, no liability for prosecution) from all criminal jurisdiction of the receiving state and immunity from certain civil jurisdiction, although they may be subject to exclusion in such cases. Technical and service staff have criminal immunity, but civil immunity is limited to their official acts. The ambassador may waive immunity. Foreign sovereigns and the governments of foreign states generally have immunity from jurisdiction of municipal courts in other courts. In England and Wales, the sovereign is personally immune from legal proceedings. Members of parliament are immune from defamation proceedings upon words spoken in debate, as are judges from words spoken in court. In 1999 a legal ruling in Britain pronounced certain crimes such as torture to be of international concern and as such to forfeit immunity, thus opening the way for the extradition of the Chilean former head-of-state, General Pinochet, then resident in the UK, to be tried or extradited for crimes against humanity committed in his country during his term of office.

immunization The artificial introduction into the body of immunity against infectious micro-organisms. *Passive immunization* involves administering antibodies against the infectious agent, derived from the blood of another individual who has recovered from the disease. This gives rapid but short-lived protection, as the antibodies are broken down within a few weeks. It may be given to people who have already been exposed to the micro-organism to prevent them developing the disease. *Active immunization* (*vaccination*) involves administering proteins (*antigens*) belonging to the infectious agent itself. This stimulates the body to mount an effective immune response to the micro-organism if it threatens in the future.

immunoglobulin *antibodies*

immunology Originally the study of the biological responses of a living organism to its invasion by living bacteria, viruses, or parasites, and its defence against these. It now also includes the study of the body's reaction to other foreign substances, particularly proteins, such as those in transplanted organs, and of how the body recognizes such proteins as being foreign.

immunosuppression The suppression of the immune response of the body to the presence of foreign protein. It may occur as a result of diseases of the immune system, such as leukaemia and AIDS, or other chronic diseases such as diabetes. It may also be induced deliberately by drugs or radiation, either to prevent rejection of transplants, or as a side effect of the treatment of some diseases, especially cancers. Several groups of drugs are immunosuppressive: these include alkylating drugs, which are toxic to dividing cells; antimetabolites, which reduce the power of cells of the immune system to manufacture antibodies; and corticosteroids. Immunosuppression renders patients vulnerable to infections in general, and also to micro-organisms which are not commonly the cause of disease in normal individuals (*opportunistic* infections).

impact printer A printer which relies on the character being pressed onto the paper via an inked ribbon. Examples include dot matrix, daisy-wheel, golfball, and line printers.

impala [impahla] An African grazing antelope (*Aepyceros melampus*); golden brown, paler on underside; tuft of dark hairs on each heel; dark stripe each side of tail; male with lyre-shaped horns ringed with ridges; lives in groups at edge of open woodland.

impasto [impastoh] Oil paint applied with a heavily loaded brush so that it stands up on the surface of the picture. Traditionally, artists worked with a mixture of smooth underpainting, thinly-executed shadows, and thick (impasted) lights, plus transparent glazing.

impatiens [impayshienz] A member of a large genus of annuals and perennials, native to Europe, Asia, most of Africa, and North America; translucent, watery stems; leaves alternate or opposite, oval, toothed; flowers hanging horizontally from a slender stalk, showy, zygomorphic and complex, appearing to have either five flat petals and a slender curved spur, or 2-lipped with a funnel-shaped tube and spur; fruit a capsule exploding audibly and scattering seeds. Hybrids between *Impatiens holstii* and *Impatiens sultanii*, with mostly red, pink, or white flowers, are popular ornamentals known as **busy Lizzie**. (Genus: *Impatiens*, 500–600 species. Family: Balsaminaceae.)

impeachment A legal process for removing undesirable persons from public office. Originating in mediaeval England, it was revived in the 17th-c during the conflict between the monarch and parliament. Normally it is the legislature that can move to impeach a public official, although there are usually simpler mechanisms (eg parliamentary votes) for removing persons from office, whatever the reason for their failure to maintain support. In the USA, presidents may be impeached by the House of Representatives and tried by the Senate. It is generally agreed that impeachment is a cumbersome method because of the problem of defining unacceptable behaviour and crimes. The move to impeach US President Nixon did, however, force his resignation. The previous move to impeach President Andrew Johnson in 1868 on suspect political grounds failed, as did that to impeach President Clinton in 1999.

impedance In alternating current circuits, a measure of the restriction of current flow (in much the same way as resistance is used for direct current circuits); defined as voltage divided by current; symbol Z, units Ω (ohm). A complex quantity, with a real part equal to resistance, it depends on the inductance and capacitance of the circuit components.

Imperial Conferences *Colonial and Imperial Conferences*

imperialism The extension of the power of the state through the acquisition, normally by force, of other territories, which are then subject to rule by the superior power; also called **colonialism**. Many suggest that the motivation behind imperialism is economic, through the exploitation of cheap labour and resources, and the opening up of new markets. Others suggest that non-economic factors are involved, including nationalism, racism and the pursuit of international power. The main era of imperialism was the 1880s to 1914, when many European powers sought to gain territories in Africa and Asia. Imperialism of the form associated with the establishment of European empires has in large measure disappeared, but the term is now often applied to any attempts by developed countries to interfere in underdeveloped countries. There is also increasing interest in the idea of *neo-colonialism*, where certain countries are subjugated by the economic power of developed countries, rather than through direct rule.

Imperial War Museum The Museum of British and Commonwealth military operations since 1914, founded in London as a memorial to those who died in World War 1. It was housed in the Crystal Palace until 1924, when it was moved to the former Imperial Institute and then to the Royal Bethlehem Hospital. A new branch, the Imperial War Museum North, opened in Manchester in 2002. Its theme is war and conflict in the 20th and 21st centuries.

impetigo [impetiygoh] A superficial infection of the skin common in children, usually due to *Staphylococcus aureus*. Infection affects the face, hands, and knees, and is characterized by reddened areas followed by transient blisters which break and then develop crusts.

impotence Inability in males to engage in sexual intercourse because of failure to achieve an erection. A minority of cases of impotence are from a number of organic diseases; these include inadequate secretion of sex hormones by the pituitary gland or the testes; conditions such as diabetes, in which there is damage to the sympathetic nerve supply to the blood vessels of the penis; and in other severe debilitating diseases. Insufficient bloodflow, failure of neurotransmitters, and the side-effects of medication may also be factors. More commonly a number of psychological causes are responsible. These include factors such as the strength of the sexual drive, attitudes to sex held by either of the partners, and the marital, family and social relationships.

Impressionism (art) A modern art movement which started in France in the 1860s – though the genre was anticipated in Ming China by the landscapist Shen Zhou (1427–1509). The name, coined by a hostile critic, was taken from Claude Monet's picture, 'Impression: sunrise' (1872). The Impressionists, who included Pissarro, Sisley, and Renoir, rejected the dark tones of 19th-c studio painting, set up their easels out-of-doors, and tried to capture the brilliant effects of sunlight on water, trees and fields, and pretty girls. Impressionist pictures are typically bright and cheerful, avoiding the sort of social realism favoured earlier by Gustave Courbet (1819–77), and others, and have been enormously popular with art-lovers and collectors.

Impressionism (literature) A term taken from painting to signify the conveying of a subjective impression of the world rather than its objective appearance. In literature the term is rather imprecise, and to some extent overlaps with Expressionism. It relates primarily to the practice of the Symbolist poets and the psychological or stream-of-consciousness novel, drawing attention to the blurred outlines, shifting categories, and uncertain truth-values of the relativized modern world. Examples are to be found in the writings of James Joyce, Virginia Woolf, and Marcel Proust.

Impressionism (music) A style of harmony and instrumentation which, on analogy with the Impressionist school of painting, blurs the edges of tonality, shuns the primary instrumental colours of the Romantics, and generally aims for veiled suggestion and understatement. The term has been used (sometimes indiscriminately) with reference to music by Debussy and some of his French contemporaries.

imprinting (behaviour) The process whereby animals rapidly learn the appearance, sound, or smell of significant individual members of their own species (eg parent, offspring) or important subcategories (eg suitable mates, potential competitors) through being exposed to them, often during a restricted period of life. Imprinting to parent or offspring usually results in attachment/following behaviour.

imprinting (genetics) The specific silencing of some DNA regions from a parent during meiosis and the formation of sperm or egg. In the resulting offspring the genes in these areas will not be able to be active. Disease can occur where a DNA deletion from the non-imprinted parent is matched by imprinting on the corresponding chromosome from the other parent. Examples of diseases caused by imprinting are Angelman and Prader-Willi syndromes. It is not fully understood why imprinting takes place.

improvisation The performance of music without following a predetermined score; an important constituent of music for many centuries. In the Baroque period, a keyboard continuo player was expected to improvise an accompaniment from a figured base, while the reputations of singers and instrumentalists depended greatly on their ability to introduce suitable ornaments and embellishments, especially into slow pieces. In the classical concerto, the cadenza provided a major formal context for brilliant soloistic improvisation, but most of the major composers of the 18th–19th-c, including Bach, Mozart, Beethoven, and Liszt, were renowned for their abilities in improvising entire pieces. Since then the art of improvising on a given theme has survived mainly in organ lofts and in jazz, where both individual and ensemble improvisations have always played an important role.

Imran Khan, in full **Ahmad Khan Niazi Imran** (1952–) Cricketer, born in Lahore, NE Pakistan. He studied at Oxford, playing in his first Test at 18 while at the university. One of the greatest all rounders, he was a fast bowler, adaptable batsman, and astute captain who inspired Pakistan's rise to prominence in world cricket. After leading Pakistan to the 1992 World Cup, he retired with a total of 3807 runs and 362 wickets in Test matches. He also played for Sussex and Worcester. He married, with much attendant publicity, in 1995, and has since been developing a career in politics forming his own party, Pakistan Tehrik-i-Insaaf (Pakistan Justice Movement).

Incahuasi, Cerro [seroh eengkawasee] 27°03S 68°20W. Andean volcano on the Chile–Argentina border; 200 km/124 mi NE of Copiapó (Chile); height 6709 m/22 011 ft.

incandescent lamp A lamp which produces visible light from a heated source or filament. Examples include arc lamps, gas lights, and filament electric light bulbs. A filament light bulb produces light from a tungsten wire heated to over 2000°C by an electric current.

Incarnation (Lat 'the putting on of flesh') In Christianity, the union between the divine and human natures in the one Jesus Christ; the 'Word' of God becoming 'flesh' (*John* 1.14). The term is also appropriate to other religions (eg Hinduism) in which a life-spirit is given a material form.

Incas or **Inka** Originally a small group of Quechua-speaking Indians living in the Cuzco Basin of the C Andean highlands; during the 15th-c, one of the world's major civilizations, and the largest PreColumbian state in the New World, with an estimated population of 5–10 million. Inca was originally the name of their leader. In the 11th-c, they established their capital at Cuzco, the Sacred City of the Sun, where they built huge stone temples and fortresses, and covered their buildings in sheets of gold. During the 15th-c, they brought together much of the Andean area, stretching along the entire W length of South America, from near the present Ecuador–Columbia border to SC Chile, and occupied much of the Andean regions of Bolivia as well.

The Incas succeeded in creating an organizational structure that could hold a vast area together, and were able to extract from it the resources necessary to support armies of conquest and a sizeable state apparatus. They used former rulers as regional administrators (provided they were loyal) but these were denied any independence, and Inca culture, language (Quechua), and the cult of the Sun were forcibly imposed. The Inca emperor was a despotic ruler of a highly stratified society, a quasi-religious figure, and a direct descendant of the Sun-god Inti. Underneath him, a noble class ran the empire. The Incas were not innovative; they merely expanded and intensified existing practices, such as in agriculture. They had a system of more than 15 000 km of roads, and hundreds of way stations and administrative centres that provided an essential infrastructure for communication, conquest, and control. They also had impressive storage facilities, such as the food warehouses at the administrative city of Huanuco Pampa in C Peru.

In 1523, Spanish invaders under Pizarro encountered the Incas. They captured the emperor Atahualpa, whom they later murdered, and took control of the empire, and by the 1570s Indian power was totally destroyed. The present descendants of the Incas, 3 million Quechua-speaking peasants of the Andes, comprise 45% of Peru's population. Their preferred spelling of the traditional name is *Inka*.

Ince, Paul (1967–) Footballer, born in Ilford, E Greater London, UK. A midfielder, he played for West Ham, Manchester United, and Inter Milan, signing for Liverpool in 1997, Middlesbrough in 1999, and Wolverhampton Wanderers in 2002. A member of the Euro 2000 team, he has won 53 caps playing for England.

incendiary bomb A bomb which causes its destructive effects by burning fiercely and igniting the structures on which it lands. The earliest were deployed in Ming China (14th–17th-c). It was used with great effect during World War 2 in 'firestorm' bombing raids on German, Japanese, and British cities. It is a popular weapon with W European terrorists, with the aim of causing maximum superficial damage.

incense A mixture of gums and spices which gives off a fragrant odour when burnt. It is widely used in many religious rites, and its smoke is often regarded as symbolic of prayer. Its use in Christianity cannot be traced before c.500. Its use in the Churches of the East is more widespread than in those of the West.

incense cedar An evergreen conifer native to North America (*Calocedrus decurrens*); related and similar to arbor vitae, but its foliage is not aromatic. Conical with spreading branches in the wild, cultivated forms are dwarf or, more commonly, very narrowly columnar. (Family: Cupressaceae.)

incest Sexual relations with close kin. In Western society, it refers to sex in the nuclear family other than between man and wife, but the precise specification of when a relationship is too close to allow sexual relations varies between cultures and over time. The forbidding of sexual intercourse – and marriage – between kin who are regarded as too closely related, is known as an **incest taboo**.

Inch'ŏn [inchon], also **Jinsen** or **Chemulpo** 37°30N 126°38E, pop (2000e) 1 996 000. Special city of W Korea with provincial status; W of Seoul, on the coast of the Yellow Sea; scene of battle between Japanese and Russian navies, 1904; UN forces landed there during Korean War, 1950; major port for Seoul, to which it is linked by subway; university (1954); fishing; Songdo leisure resort (S); Inch'ŏn Munhak Stadium (2001).

inch worm *looper*

incidence (of disease) *disease frequency*

incitement To instigate or encourage another person to commit a crime or offence – itself a crime at common law. If the offence is actually committed, the inciter is as guilty as the perpetrator, and where the crime or offence is either impossible to commit or the inciter does not persuade the other to commit the crime, the inciter may be guilty of attempted incitement. While there can be incitement to commit any crime, certain specific offences of incitement exist: in Britain, for example, incitement to racial hatred and incitement to dissaffection (ie to undermine a member of the military's loyalty to the Crown).

incomes policy *prices and incomes policy*

income tax A major source of government revenue, levied on personal incomes. Income below some lower limit is usually exempt, and the tax rate levied on further slices of income varies, at rates fixed from time to time in the budget. There may also be a range of special tax allowances, such as for charitable covenants. In the UK, income tax is collected 'at source', by deduction from wages through 'Pay As You Earn' by employers, and deducted from dividends by companies. Income tax is levied in many other countries, with a very wide range of tax rates and systems of allowances. In the USA, income tax was introduced by Constitutional amendment in 1913; some states and cities also have income taxes.

incontinence The involuntary loss of urine or faeces, which tends to occur when intra-abdominal pressure is increased, such as during coughing. It is common in children, particularly in the form of bedwetting at night (*nocturnal eneuresis*). It also affects the elderly due to a loss of tone in the muscular rings (*sphincters*) that control the passage of urine and faeces from the bladder and bowel; these muscles may also be damaged by childbirth. Treatment may involve muscle strengthening exercises, dietary changes, drugs, or surgery.

incubator (neonatal) A chamber, used for small, premature, or unwell newborn babies, designed to provide a sterile environment with a constant temperature. The chamber provides access for medical care and may be used in conjunction with other instruments and machines, such as a ventilator in the case of respiratory distress syndrome.

incubator bird *megapode*

incubus [ingkyubus] A malevolent male spirit supposed in mediaeval and later demonology to have intercourse with women in their sleep. Witches and demons could be the offspring of such unions. The equivalent female spirit was a **succubus**.

Independence Day *Fourth of July*

Independence Hall A building in Independence National Historical Park, Philadelphia, Pennsylvania, USA, where the Declaration of Independence was proclaimed (1776); a world heritage site. The Liberty Bell, rung at the proclamation, is kept here.

Independent Labour Party (ILP) A British political party formed in 1893 with the objective of sending working men to parliament. It was socialist in aim, but wished to gain the support of working people whether they were socialist or not. One of its leading figures was Keir Hardie. Many of its leaders played a major part in founding the Labour Representation Committee (1900), which became the Labour Party in 1906. It was affiliated to the Labour Party but put up its own candidates, and was disaffiliated in 1932. It continued to have a few members of parliament up to 1946. In 1975, the ILP returned to the Labour Party as a publishing body and pressure group, and also changed its name to Independent Labour Publications.

independent schools Schools in the UK which are not dependent on either the government or local authorities for their income, but derive it principally from the fees paid by parents. Many are run by independent trusts.

Independent Treasury System *Federal Reserve System*

index (bibliography) *indexing*

index (mathematics) A notation which simplifies the writing of products, eg $2 \times 2 \times 2 \times 2$ is written 2^4, where 4 is the index (or *exponent*); it can be extended to give meaning to fractional, negative, and other indices. When numbers are written in index form, eg $16 = 2^4$, certain **laws of indices** exist. These are $a^m \times a^n = a^{m+n}$; $a^m \div a^n = a^{m-n}$; $(a^m)^n = a^{mn}$; $a^0 = 1$; $a^{-n} = 1/a^n$; $a^1/q = \sqrt[q]{a}$; $a^n/q = \sqrt[q]{a^n}$.

indexation A system under which contracts provide for regular revision of prices, wages, pensions, or rents in line with some chosen index of prices. The argument for indexation is that it offers stability of real incomes in times of inflation to workers or pensioners, and avoids the need for repeated ad hoc renegotiation of wages, etc. The disadvantage of widespread indexation is that if the various revisions are staggered over time, as seems inevitable, this gives rise to a wage–price spiral, making inflation extremely difficult to stop once it has started. There is also a political economy argument: without indexation, many people lose through inflation, and there is thus a great deal of political support for policies to control it. If most people are protected against inflation, in a political equilibrium there will be more inflation, which will injure the minority who are not protected by having their incomes indexed. Many countries have adopted some degree of indexation; in the UK, for example, pensions and other benefits are updated annually in line with the Retail Price Index.

index fund An investment fund where shares are bought in all the companies listed in the main stock exchange index, then held. In this way the portfolio of shares will always equal movements in the stock market. The strategy is attractive where there is a fear of underperforming the market. It is more popular in the USA than in the UK.

indexing The compiling of systematic guides to the location of words, names, and concepts in books and other publications. An index consists of a list of entries, each of which comprises a heading, together with any qualifying phrase and/or sub heading(s), and at least one page reference or cross-reference ('see..'). Several procedures are available, such as 'letter-by-letter' indexing (in which *seabird* would appear before *sea horse*) and 'word-by-word' indexing (in which *sea horse* would appear before *seabird*). Computer data processing systems usually offer users a range of indexing options handling numerical as well as alphabetical data. The basic principles and mechanics of indexing, including the use of computers, have been codified and can readily be learned. However, individual judgment and sensitivity remain essential for producing an index that is effective and a pleasure to use.

Index Librorum Prohibitorum [indeks librawrum prohhibitawrum] (Lat 'index of forbidden books') A list of books which members of the Roman Catholic Church were forbidden to read. It originated with the Gelasian Decree (496), and was frequently revised, the last revision being published in 1948. Although the Roman Catholic Church still claims the right to prevent its members reading material harmful to their faith or morals, it was decided in 1966 to publish no further editions.

index number A statistical device used mainly in economic and financial practice for tracking changes in some activity over time. Most start from a base of 100.

India *pp.764–5*

Indian, American *American Indians*

Indiana [indiana] pop (2000e) 6 081 00; area 93 716 sq km/36 185 sq mi. State in EC USA, S of L Michigan, divided into 92 counties; the 'Hoosier State'; 19th state to join the Union, 1816; visited by La Salle in 1679 and 1681; occupied by the French, who ceded the state to the British in 1763; scene of many major Indian battles; capital, Indianapolis; chief towns, Fort Wayne, South Bend, Gary, Evansville; ports on L Michigan; hilly in the S, fertile plains in the C, and flat glaciated land in the N; grain, soybeans, pigs, cattle; bituminous coal, limestone, steel and iron, chemicals, motor vehicles, electrical goods.

Indianapolis [indianapolis] 39°46N 86°09W, pop (2000e) 782 000. Capital of state in Marion Co, C Indiana, USA, on the White R; founded, 1820; state capital, 1825; airport; railway; university (1855); major medical centre at Indiana–Purdue Universities campus (1969); aircraft, motor vehicles, electronics, telephones, machinery, chemical and metal products; professional teams, Indiana Pacers (basketball), Colts (football); state museum, museum of art, City Market Internationale, Motor Speedway (where the world-famous 'Indianapolis 500' motor race is held).

Indian architecture The architecture of the Indian sub-continent, which varies greatly according to time, location, and religion. Before the 16th-c, the earliest examples are Buddhist cave temples and stupas. Hindu temples are characterized by an elaborate use of carved decoration, and can be sub divided into three geographical types: Northern, Chalukyan, and Dravidian. The formation of the Mughal dynasty in 1526 preceded the construction of the great Islamic monuments, such as the city of Fatehpur-Sikri (1568–75), built on a monumental scale with great attention to rich and intricate detail. The extension of the British Empire into India led to the introduction of Western architectural forms, including the idiosyncratic classicism used by Edwin Lutyens for New Delhi (1913–31). The most notable 20th-c buildings are in the new regional capital of Chandigarh, designed in the 1950s by Le Corbusier. In recent years, a more basic and suitable modern architecture for Indian conditions has been promoted by Indian architects themselves, including Charles Correa.

Indian art The art associated with the Indian sub-continent. Visual art, especially sculpture, has flourished here since prehistoric times, but the historical tradition of Indian art really begins in the 3rd-c BC during the reign of Asoka (264–223 BC). Buddhist *stupas* (earth mounds) were adorned with relief sculpture from the 1st-c AD. Figurative sculpture at Ganhara (2nd–6th-c AD) reflected Hellenistic influence from Egypt and Syria. Richly-coloured Buddhist wall-paintings occur at Ajanta. The Gupta period (4th–5th-c AD) is considered the 'classical' period of Indian civilization, especially in literature, but much of the visual art has vanished. Islamic influence increased, reaching its zenith under the Mughal emperors in the 17th-c.

Indian bean tree A domed deciduous tree (*Catalpa bignioides*) growing to 20 m/65 ft, native to SE USA and widely planted as a street tree and ornamental; leaves opposite, 7–22 cm/2¾–8½ in, more or less heart-shaped; flowers 5 cm/2 in, bell-shaped with five spreading, frilled lobes, white with purple and yellow spots;

India

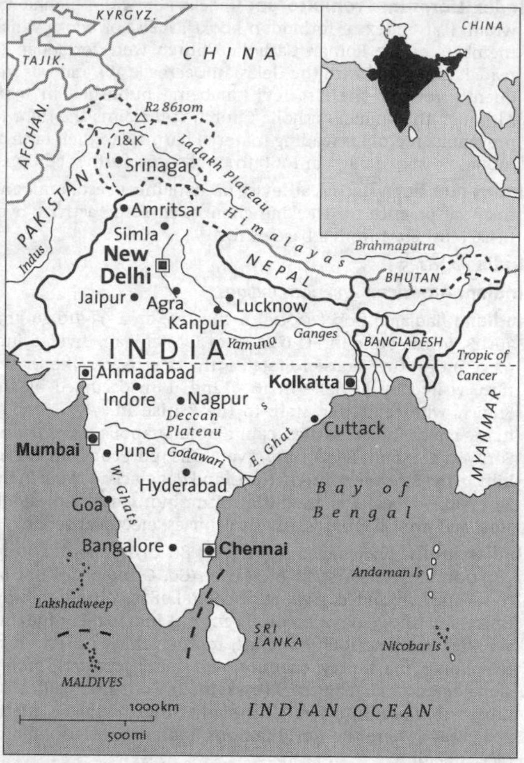

☐ International Airport - - - Disputed boundary J&K Jammu & Kashmir
- - - India/Pakistan line of control

Hindi **Bharat**, official name **Republic of India** Local name Bhārat (Hindi)

Timezone GMT +5·5

Area 3 166 829 km^2/1 222 396 sq mi

Population total (2002e) 1 047 671 200

Status Republic

Date of independence 1947

Capital New Delhi

Languages Hindi and English (official); others include Urdu, Panjabi, Gujarati, Marathi, Bengali, Oriya, Kashmiri, Assamese, Kannada, Malayalam, Sindhi, Tamil and Telugu

Ethnic groups Indo-Aryan (72%), Dravidian (25%), with Mongoloid and other minorities

Religions Hindu (83%), Muslim (11%), Christian (2%), Sikh (2%), Buddhist (1%)

Physical features Seventh largest country in the world, located in S Asia; includes Andaman and Nicobar Is in the Bay of Bengal, and Laccadive Is in the Indian Ocean; folded mountain ridges and valleys in N, highest peaks over 7000 m/23 000 ft; C river plains of the Ganges, Yamuna, Ghaghari, and Brahmaputra to the S - control measures needed to prevent flooding; Thar Desert in NW bordered by semi-desert areas; Deccan Plateau in the S peninsula, with hills and wide valleys, bounded by the Western and Eastern Ghats; the coastal plains are important areas of rice cultivation.

Climate Dominated by the Asiatic monsoon; rains come from the SW (Jun–Oct); rainfall decreases E–W on the N plains, with desert conditions in extreme W; tropical in S even in cool season; average annual temperature 14°C (Jan), 31°C (Jul) in New Delhi; average annual rainfall 640 mm/25in; cyclones and storms on SE coast (especially Oct–Dec).

Currency 1 Indian Rupee (Re, Rs) = 100 paisa

Economy Agriculture employs over two-thirds of the labour force; tea, rice, wheat, coffee, sugar cane, cotton, jute, oil seed, maize, pulses, milk; floods and drought cause major problems; considerable increase in industrial production since independ-

fruit a long pendulous capsule resembling a bean pod. (Family: Bignoniaceae.)

Indian corn *maize*

Indian dance An ancient dance tradition based on Hindu thought, but showing Arab and Mughal influences. Shiva is the god who symbolizes eternal movement. Dance forms can be divided into classical and folk. Classical dance forms are of religious or court origin, while folk forms are social and based in village life. Indian classical dance is traditionally learned through attachment to a guru, the dances ranging in style from highly controlled forms of religious temple worship to the performance of violent legends based on mythical characters, which may last for a whole night. Religious or mythical themes rely on the poetic language of codified hand gestures (*mudras*) and facial expressions. They are accompanied by traditional instruments such as the tabla and sitar, and by voices, often in rhythmic counterpoint to the dance.

Indian languages *Devanagari; Dravidian languages; Indo-Aryan*

Indian literature A label which includes the literatures of numerous languages, principally Classical Sanskrit, Tamil, Hindi, Urdu, and Bengali. The oldest works are in Sanskrit. These include the texts of the Veda ('sacred love') in four collections which date back to the first millennium BC: *Rigveda*, *Atharvarvedra*, *Yagurvedra*, and *Samavedra*; and also the great Hindu epics *Mahabharata* and *Ramayana*. Later Sanskrit literature featured ritual Tantras, philosophical poems, and scholarly lyrics. A vernacular literature in Prakrit also developed in modern times. The early Tamil anthologies, *Ettutogaiad* and *Pattuppattu*, contain romantic and heroic verse from the 1st–4th-c AD; later Tamil literature was influenced by other Indian traditions, and then in the 19th–20th-c by European forms. A similar underlying pattern may be observed in Bengali literature, documented from 1400, which contains translations of Sanskrit epics, and later shows successive Muslim, Christian, and English influences. Distinguished individual writers are the 19th-c novelist Bakim Chandra Chatterji and the poet and Nobel recipient Rabindranath Tagore.

By contrast with Classical Sanskrit writings, the literatures of both Hindi and Urdu are essentially populist and reformist. Hindi has a tradition of poetry going back to the Rajasthani bards of c.1400, and includes 16th-c devotional poetry and (later) erotic literature such as the *Kesav Das*; there is also a modern vernacular. But the vernacular initiative passed in the 17th-c to Urdu, enriched by Persian models and material, and favoured by the Muslim nobility. Poets such as the satirist Saudi (d.1781), and the *ghazal* love poets Mir (d.1810) and Ghalib (d.1869), were matched in the 20th-c by the mystical poet Mohammed Iqbal; and modern Urdu literature flourishes in all forms in Pakistan.

Indian Mutiny (1857–9) A serious uprising against British rule, triggered by the belief among Indian troops in British service that new cartridges had been greased with animal fat – something which would have been abhorrent to both Hindus and Muslims. At the same time there was resentment among the old governing class over the reduction in their power, and Western innovations. The mutiny at Meerut (10 May 1857) spread throughout N India; Delhi quickly fell; and Kanpur and Lucknow garrisons were beseiged. The British finally regained full control in mid-1858. The immediate result was the transfer of government from the East India Company to the British Crown (1858), but the long-term result was a legacy of bitterness on both sides. The element of national consciousness present ence; iron, steel, oil products, chemicals, fertilizers, chromite, barytes, oil, natural gas; tourism.

GDP (2002e) $2·664 tn, per capita $2600

Human Development Index (2002) 0·577

History Indus civilization emerged c.2500 BC, destroyed in 1500 BC by the Aryans, who developed the Brahmanic caste system; Mauryan Emperor Asoka unified most of India, and established Buddhism as the state religion, 3rd-c BC; spread of Hinduism, 2nd-c BC; Muslim influences during 7th-8th-c AD, with sultanate established at Delhi; Mughal Empire established by Babur in 1526 and extended by Akbar and Aurangzeb; Portuguese, French, Dutch, and British footholds in India, 18th-c; conflict between France and Britain, 1746–63; development of British interests represented by the East India Company; British power established after the Indian Mutiny crushed, 1857; movement for independence from the late 19th-c; Government of India Act of 1919 allowed election of Indian ministers to share power with appointed British governors; a further Act in 1935 allowed election of independent provincial governments; passive-resistance campaigns of Mohandas Gandhi from 1920s; independence granted in 1947, on condition that a Muslim state be established (Pakistan); Indian states later reorganized on a linguistic basis; Pakistan-India war over disputed territory in Kashmir and Jammu, 1948; federal democratic republic within the Commonwealth, 1950; Hindu-Muslim hostility, notably in 1978, and further India-Pakistan conflict in 1965 and 1971; separatist movements continue, especially relating to Sikh interests in the Punjab; suppression of militant Sikh movement in 1984 led to assassination of Indira Gandhi; Rajiv Gandhi assassinated, 1991; ongoing tension with Pakistan over Kashmir, with some fighting, 2001, escalating into a major crisis, mid-2002; ceasefire announced (Nov 2003) and diplomatic ties resumed; each of the 27 states administered by a governor appointed by the President; each state has an Assembly; the President, advised by a Council of Ministers, appoints a Prime Minister; Parliament comprises the President, an Upper House, and a House of the People.

Head of State
1950–62 Rajendra Prasad
1962–7 Sarvepalli Radhakrishnan
1967–9 Zakir Husain
1969 Varahagiri Venkatagiri *Acting*
1969 Mohammed Hidayatullah *Acting*
1969–74 Varahagiri Venkatagiri
1974–7 Fakhruddin Ali Ahmed
1977 B D Jatti *Acting*
1977–82 Neelam Sanjiva Reddy
1982–7 Giani Zail Singh
1987–92 Ramaswami Venkataraman
1992–7 Shankar Dayal Sharma
1997–2002 K(ocheril) R(aman) Narayanan
2002– Avul Pakir Jaunilabdeen Abdul Kalam

Head of Government
1947–64 Jawaharlal Nehru
1964 Gulzari Lal Nanda *Acting*
1964–6 Lal Bahadur Shastri
1966 Gulzari Lal Nanda *Acting*
1966–77 Indira Gandhi
1977–9 Morarji Ranchhodji Desai
1979–80 Charan Singh
1980–4 Indira Gandhi
1984–9 Rajiv Gandhi
1989–90 Vishwanath Pratap Singh
1990–1 Chandra Shekhar
1991–6 P V Narasimha Rao
1996 Atal Bihari Vajpayee
1996–7 Deve Gowda
1997–8 Inder Kumar Gujral
1998– Atal Bihari Vajpayee

made the episode a source of inspiration for later Indian nationalists.

Indian National Congress A broad-based political organization, founded in 1885, which spearheaded the nationalist movement for independence from Britain under the leadership of charismatic figures such as M K Gandhi and Jawaharlal Nehru. It has been the dominant political party in India since 1947.

Indian Ocean, ancient **Erythræan Sea** area 73 426 000 sq km/ 28 350 000 sq mi. Third largest ocean in the world, bounded W by Africa, N by Asia, E by Australia and the Malay archipelago, and S by the Southern Ocean; width c.6400 km/4000 mi at the Equator; maximum depth of 7125 m/23 375 ft in the Java Trench; linked to the Mediterranean by the Suez Canal; floor divided into E and W sections by the Mid-Oceanic Ridge; rift valley runs along ridge axis, centre of sea-floor spreading; main island groups, Andaman, Nicobar, Chagos, Seychelles; largest islands, Madagascar and Sri Lanka.

Indian philosophy Philosophical inquiry in India goes back to the late Vedic age when, with a shift in focus from ritual to knowledge, two directions emerged. One was the ritually based *Mimamsa*, incorporating the injunctions of the Veda and concerned with its exegesis as a system of ritual and with its language; the other was the gnostic *Vedanta*, with its ontology of unity. Buddhism reacted to this unity by postulating a completely pluralistic ontology, replacing the idea of any stable entity such as 'self' by the idea of a flux of momentary cognitions, and thereby laid the foundation for a philosophical controversy which stimulated Indian thought for 1500 years. The study of the Veda also triggered a remarkable eminence in linguistics and the philosophy of language, firmly anchored in the grammar of Panini (c.500 BC) and alive to this day. Eminent also were the philosophical schools of Shaivism, which reached a high point with Abhinavagupta (flourished c.975–1025). In addition to Mimamsa and Vedanta, four other 'systems' (*darshana*, 'seeing; point of view') are found. The dualistic *Samkhya* (the theoretical basis for the system of Yoga) was the earliest attempt at a systematic philosophy. *Nyaya* and *Vaisheshika* were primarily concerned with logic and with the question of being and what there is, and also with epistemology and language. The schools then merged, and gave rise to the extremely sophisticated *Navyanyaya* or 'Neo-logic'. Consolidated by Gangesha in the 14th-c, this flourished for several centuries, particularly in Mithila and Bengal.

Indian Territory Land set aside in the USA as a 'permanent' home for native Americans removed from the area E of the Mississippi R between 1825 and 1840. Originally it included most of Oklahoma and parts of Kansas and Arkansas, but by the end of the 19th-c most of it had been opened to whites.

Indian theatre / theater The theatrical traditions of the Indian sub-continent, with an ancient history and diverse regional forms. A semblance of order is given by the traditional division into *Margi* ('belonging to the path'), equivalent to 'classical', illustrated in Sanskrit theatre, and *Desi* ('place' or 'region'), equivalent to 'folk', illustrated in Chau. However it is clear that many of its most distinctive styles (eg Kathakali and Yakshagana) lie between these two categories.

Indian Wars (1622–1890) The process of invasion and conquest by which white people settled the present USA. The Europeans set out to remake the New World in the image of the old, if possible by persuasion, if necessary by force. The result was the destruction of the Indians' population, cultures, and economies.

The whites' two greatest allies were disease and their own culture, as represented by artifacts as diverse as the bottle and the Bible. The total hemispheric drop in native population was from roughly 90 million at first contact to a low of about 9 million. Microbes to which the Indians had no natural resistance were the prime cause. Faced with such a disaster, their culture collapsed as well, and its place was taken by European ways. Most Europeans believed this was as it should be. Thus the first Puritan settlers, knowing that an epidemic had just swept through Massachusetts, took it as God's way of clearing the region for them.

The main effect of actual warfare was to remove the remaining Indians from the land and to destroy their political structures. It was not always easy. The woodland tribes of the E kept the Dutch, English, and French at bay from the early 17th-c to the late 18th-c, retreating only a few hundred miles inland before the American Revolution. But after independence they faced a powerful, single-mindedly expansionist state. Now bereft of potential allies, the Indians quickly lost whatever the whites wanted.

The list of specific Indian wars is endless, beginning with a bloody attack by the Powhatan Confederacy on white Virginians in 1622 and ending with the massacre at Wounded Knee in 1890; but four main phases can be distinguished.

(1) In the 17th-c, the coastal tribes confronted the earliest invaders. Specific conflicts included the 'massacres' (as whites called them) of 1622 and 1644, which brought many white deaths, the war of Bacon's Rebellion (1676) in Virginia, and the Pequot War (1636) and King Philip's War (1675–6) in New England.

(2) From 1689 to 1763 Indian warfare was bound up with the great struggle between France and Britain for control of the continent. King William's War (1689–97), Queen Anne's War (1702–13), the War of Jenkins' Ear (1739–42), King George's War (1740–8), and the great French and Indian War (1754–63) were the white colonists' names for specific conflicts. The English, eventually victorious, enjoyed the support of the Iroquois Confederacy of W New York, important both for their internal strength and for their control of the Mohawk Valley and Lake Ontario plain, which formed the only natural break in the Appalachian Mountains.

(3) Whichever side a tribe chose during the American Revolution, it made no difference, for the new United States implemented a policy of almost total Indian removal E of the Mississippi. Despite resistance in the Ohio Valley (Fallen Timbers in 1794 and Tippecanoe in 1811), and from the 'Five Civilized Tribes' of the South, the cause was hopeless. The Seminoles of Florida, whose number included many escaped black slaves, were most successful, accepting final defeat only in 1842.

(4) The last phase imposed white control on the trans-Mississippi plains and on the deserts of the SW. This was the era of the most famous tribes (Cheyenne, Sioux, Apaches), Indian leaders (Black Kettle, Sitting Bull, Cochise) Indian fighters (Sheridan, Terry, Custer), and events (Sand Creek 1864, the Washita 1868, the Little Bighorn 1876). By this time the few remaining Indians were facing the full might of an industrial civilization. The plains wars were sometimes spectacular, but there was no question of long-term Indian victory.

Throughout the wars, the Indians fought at material and numerical disadvantage. They were disadvantaged as well by their own concept of what warfare was about, for they understood it in wholly different terms from their foes. Finally, they were handicapped by their own lack of unity. Specific Indian tribes approached each war in terms of their own friendships and enmities. That gave some, such as the Iroquois, great power to shape their own futures. But only on a very few occasions, such as King Philip's War, Pontiac's Conspiracy (1763), Tecumseh's War (1811), and the victory over Custer at Little Bighorn did Indians surmount tribal boundaries and act together.

indiarubber tree An evergreen tree (*Ficus elastica*) with elliptical, leathery, very glossy leaves, native to India and SE Asia. It is a relative of the edible fig. A source of rubber, sometimes used as a shade tree, young specimens are sold as house plants under the name **rubber plants**. (Family: Moraceae.)

indictment [indiytment] A document specifying the particulars of an offence of which a person is accused. More than one offence may be involved; these are listed as separate 'counts' or 'charges' within the one document. **Indictable offences** in England and Wales are generally those triable before a judge and jury in the Crown Court, such as murder. In Scotland, such offences are tried in the High Court or the Sheriff Court with a jury, and are termed *solemn proceedings*. However, in some jurisdictions some less serious indictable offences, such as theft, may be tried on a summary basis in a lower court or without a jury. The Fifth Amendment to the US constitution guarantees the right to indictment by a Grand Jury for 'capital or infamous crimes'; this applies only to federal cases, and many states have abolished Grand Juries, allowing prosecutors to proceed with 'informations' in felony cases, and 'complaints' in misdemeanours.

indigestion Upper abdominal pain or discomfort related to eating; also known as **dyspepsia**. It is an extremely common complaint that may be precipitated by overeating, or by particular foods such as spices, fried foods, or alcohol. The majority of sufferers have no demonstrable organic disease, but may suffer from stress or anxiety. The condition is usually relieved by taking antacids. A number of organic diseases, notably peptic ulceration, are responsible in a minority of cases.

indigo A dye obtained from a species of *Indigofera*, particularly anil (*Indigofera anil*), a tropical American shrub, and *Indigo tinctoria*, a shrubby perennial growing to 2·5 m/8 ft; leaves pinnate; pea-flowers red, in short clusters. It was formerly cultivated in India and Sumatra, but is now little grown, since the demand for natural indigo virtually ceased following the introduction of aniline dyes. At first widely used on wool, silk, and cotton, it is now mainly used to dye the warp yarns of denim. (Family: Leguminosae.)

indigo bird / finch *whydah*

indirect rule A form of colonial rule especially characteristic of British rule in Africa during the inter-war years. In general terms it involved the use of existing political structures, leaders, and local organs of authority. Thus local political elites enjoyed considerable autonomy, although they still had to keep in accord with the interests of the colonial power. It was adopted on grounds of its cheapness and to allow for independent cultural development, but was increasingly criticized for its failure to introduce a modernizing role into colonial administration, and was gradually given up after 1945.

individualism Any thesis which maintains that wholes of a certain type (organisms, societies) can be fully understood and explained in terms of the properties and relations of their individual parts. Methodological individualism is the thesis that the workings of societies can be explained entirely by reference to the activities of the individuals in them; the contrary thesis is **holism**.

Individual Retirement Account *pension*

Indo-Aryan languages The easternmost branch of the Indo-European languages, comprising some 500 languages spoken by 500 million people in N and C India. Its subgroupings are exemplified by Panjabi (or Punjabi, c.73 million) in the NW; Gujarati (c.43 million) and Marathi (c.65 million) in the W and SW; Hindi and Urdu (together, 240 million) in the mid-N; and Bengali and Assamese (together, c.93 million) in the E. (Figures are for first-language speakers.) The pairs Hindi/Urdu and Bengali/Assamese are mutually intelligible, and distinguished from each other only on socio-political grounds. Romani also belongs to this family.

Indo-China *Cambodia; Laos; Vietnam*

Indo-European languages The family of languages which developed in Europe and S Asia, and which gave the modern languages of W Europe (eg the Germanic, Romance, and Celtic languages) as well as many in the Baltic states, Russia, and N India. The parent language of the family has been labelled

Proto-Indo-European (PIE); there is no documentary evidence for it, but it is thought to have been spoken before 3000 BC. The forms of PIE have been reconstructed on the basis of correspondences of sound between the forms of the related languages. The key relationships were discovered in the 19th-c, when it was shown that the main European languages and Sanskrit (the oldest language of the Indian sub-continent) were derived from the same parent language.

Indo-Iranian languages The E branch of the Indo-European family of languages. It comprises the Iranian and Indo-Aryan subgroups.

Indonesia *see panel*

Indonesian *Bahasa Indonesia*

Indo-Pacific languages A hypothesized group of languages, centred on Papua New Guinea, located in the middle of the geographical area of the Austronesian group, but independent of it linguistically. There seem to be about 3·5 million speakers, but little is known of the languages, and many tribes have not been contacted. The isolation of some of these tribes means that they are able to maintain independent languages with in some cases as few as 100 speakers. The grouping is highly speculative, linking the Papuan languages (themselves genetically diverse) with Andamanese and the extinct languages of Tasmania.

Indra In Hinduism, the Vedic king of the gods, to whom many of the prayers of the Rig Veda are addressed.

Indonesia

☐ International Airport

[indohneezha], official name **Republic of Indonesia**, Bahasa Indonesia **Republik Indonesia**, formerly **Netherlands Indies, Dutch East Indies, Netherlands East Indies, United States of Indonesia**

Local name Indonesia

Timezone GMT +7 to +9

Area 1 906 200 km²/735 800 sq mi

Population total (2002e) 211 023 000

Status Republic

Date of independence 1945

Capital Jakarta

Languages Bahasa Indonesia (official), English, Dutch, and Javanese widely spoken

Ethnic groups Madurese (40%), Javanese (33%), Sudanese (15%), Bahasa Indonesian (12%)

Religions Muslim (88%), Christian (9%) (Roman Catholic 6%, Protestant 2%), Hindu (2%), Buddhist (1%)

Physical features World's largest island group of 13 677 islands and islets, of which c.6000 are inhabited; five main islands: Sumatra, Java, Kalimantan (two-thirds of Borneo I), Sulawesi, Irian Jaya (W half of New Guinea I); characterized by mountainous volcanic landscape and equatorial rainforest; many volcanic peaks - over 100 on Java, 15 active.

Climate Hot and humid equatorial climate; dry season (Jun–Sep), rainy season (Dec–Mar); average annual temperature 26°C (Jan), 27°C (Jul) in Jakarta; average annual rainfall 1775 mm/69 in.

Currency 1 Indonesian Rupiah (Rp) = 100 sen

Economy Mainly agrarian, notably rice; oil, natural gas, and petroleum products from Borneo and Sumatra account for nearly 60% of national income; small manufacturing industry.

GDP (2002e) $714·2 bn, per capita $3100

Human Development Index (2002) 0·684

History Settled in early times by Hindus and Buddhists, whose power lasted until the 14th-c; Islam introduced, 14th–15th-c; Portuguese settlers, early 16th-c; Dutch East India Company established, 1602; Japanese occupation in World War 2; independence proclaimed with Sukarno as President, 1945; changed name from Netherlands East Indies to the Republic of the United States of Indonesia, 1949; federal system replaced by unified control, 1950, and the unitary Republic of Indonesia proclaimed (W New Guinea remained under Dutch control until 1963 and is now called Irian Jaya); military coup, 1966; governed by a President elected by a 700-member People's Consultative Assembly, and advised by a Cabinet and several advisory agencies; separatist movements in Irian Jaya, East Timor, and Aceh; referendum in East Timor in favour of independence (Sep 1999), with subsequent violence by anti-independence militias, and arrival of a UN-sponsored force; independence achieved, May 2002; terrorist bomb in Kuta, Bali, killed 202 people (Oct 2002); military offensive launched in Aceh after failed peace talks with rebel Free Aceh Movement (GAM), May 2003.

Republic of Indonesia

Head of State/Government

1949–66 (Achmed) Sukarno
1966–98 (T N J) Suharto
1998–9 Bacharuddin Jusuf Habibie
1999–2001 Abdurrahman Wahid
2001– Megawati Sukarnoputri

indri or **indris** A leaping lemur (*Indri indri*), the largest living primitive primate (body length, 70 cm/27½ in); very short tail; dark with white legs and hindquarters; fluffy round ears; has a very loud, far-reaching cry; inhabits tree tops; eats leaves. The name **woolly indri** is used for the **woolly lemur** or **avahi** (*Avahi laniger*).

Indricotherium [indrikotheerium] The largest land mammal that ever lived; known from the Oligocene epoch of C Asia; a gigantic, hornless rhinoceros standing 5·5 m/18 ft at the shoulder; probably weighing 30 tonnes; fed by browsing on vegetation. (Order: Perissodactyla.)

inductance A measure of a coil's ability to produce a voltage in another coil (**mutual inductance**, *M*) or in itself (**self inductance**, *L*) via changing magnetic fields; units H (henry). It is equal to the ratio of electromotive force produced to rate of change of current.

induction (embryology) The action of natural stimuli that cause unspecialized tissue to develop into specialized tissue. In the earliest embryonic stage immediately after the zygote starts dividing, the cells of the embryo are unspecialized, and have the potential to develop into any cell type. As development proceeds, certain cells (*inducers*) influence neighbouring cells to develop along a determined course into a particular type of cell.

induction (logic) An inference from particular, observed instances to a general law or conclusion. The premisses of a sound induction may give good reason for believing the conclusion ('The Sun has always risen in the past, therefore it will rise tomorrow') but do not logically entail the conclusion, as they do in a valid deduction.

induction (obstetrics) The initiation of childbirth by artificial means. A common technique is the injection of the hormone oxytocin, which causes contractions of the uterus.

induction (physics) *electromagnetic induction*

indulgences In Roman Catholicism, grants of remission of sin to the living, following repentance and forgiveness; also, to the dead in purgatory. They were based on the Church's treasury of merit, accumulated through the good works of Jesus Christ and the saints. Abuses in the Middle Ages, leading to the 'buying and selling' of places in heaven, finally occasioned Martin Luther's '95 Theses', which launched the Reformation. Little reference is made to them today.

Indurain, Miguel [induhran] (1964–) Racing cyclist, born in Villava, N Spain. A talented basketball player, he chose cycling as his career and turned professional in 1982. In 1991 he won the first of five successive Tours de France races (1991–5) becoming the first to achieve this distinction, and in 1996 won an Olympic Gold in the time trial. He retired in 1997.

Indus (astronomy) (Lat 'Indian') An inconspicuous constellation of the S hemisphere.

Indus, River, Sanskrit **Sindhu** River of Asia, the longest of the Himalayan rivers (3000 km/1900 mi); rises in the Kalias Range in Xizang region (Tibet); flows NW through Tibet, Jammu, and Kashmir, then S into Pakistan; within Pakistan the flow is generally SSW in a broad braided channel, to enter the Arabian Sea SE of Karachi in a level, muddy delta supporting little cultivation; navigable for small vessels as far as Hyderabad; barrage at Sukkur supplies an extensive irrigation system and power project; relics of Indus Civilization (flourished 4000–2000 BC) excavated at Mohenjo-daro and Harappa.

indusium *sorus*

industrial action The activities of trade unions, or groups of workers or employers, to bring pressure on the others when negotiations and/or arbitration have failed to settle industrial disputes. Action by workers can include go-slows or 'working to rule', overtime bans, or strike action. Strikes may be accompanied by picketing to persuade other workers to join the strike, or to persuade other people not to make deliveries to or purchases from the firm. Industrial action by employers may involve lockouts.

industrial democracy A situation in companies where employees have a say in determining corporate policies. Examples include works councils, and employee representatives on the board of directors.

industrial design A term used increasingly nowadays to refer to the design of anything made by machine, from Coke bottles to Volkswagens. Early industrial design included Wedgwood pottery and Sheffield plate.

industrial disease *occupational diseases*

industrial espionage The illicit acquisition of information about a company's activities. Such information may concern formulae, designs, personnel, or business plans. Methods include theft of documents, telephone tapping, and computer hacking, with or without collusion by corrupt employees.

industrial relations The dealings and relationships between the management and the workforce of a business, particularly one where trade unions are present and collective bargaining is normal; also known as **labour** or **employee relations**. The main topics covered include pay, hours and conditions of work, holidays, security of employment, and disciplinary and grievance procedures. Some of these are affected by legislation, but the law usually leaves scope for disagreement. Disputes may be resolved by negotiation, or by arbitration; if both of these fail, industrial action may be taken by either side.

Industrial Revolution A term usually associated with the accelerated pace of economic change, the associated technical and mechanical innovations, and the emergence of mass markets for manufactured goods. It began in Britain in the last quarter of the 18th-c with the mechanization of the cotton and woollen industries of Lancashire, C Scotland, and the West Riding of Yorkshire. After the harnessing of steam power, cotton and woollen factories were increasingly concentrated in towns, and there were hugely increased rates of urbanization. A rapid population increase, stimulated by greater economic opportunities for early marriage, is also associated with this type of economic growth. The mechanization of heavier industries (iron and steel) was slower, but sustained the Industrial Revolution in its second phase from c.1830. In the second half of the 19th-c, Britain's early industrial lead was increasingly challenged by Germany and the United States. The use of machines was central to the new economics, making possible the division of labour, which greatly increased productivity. Marx believed that industrialization, in separating the workers from their products, made them alienated and less than human. However, he still believed in the uprecedented power of technological advance, condemning 'the idiocy of rural life'. Other economic historians have highlighted the importance of technological invention and commercial enterprise.

industrial textiles Textiles used for industrial purposes, as found in the manufacture of conveyor belts, filter cloths, geotextiles, and ropes. Some 30% of all textile products are categorized as industrial.

Industrial Workers of the World (IWW) US revolutionary labour organization, founded in Chicago in 1905, its members informally known as **Wobblies**. In the following two decades it provided a powerful voice in opposition to capitalism and in favour of worker control of industrial production. Its tactics, which involved strikes, sabotage, and violence, brought it considerable publicity, but the prosecution and conviction of several of its leaders caused the movement to decay during the 1920s. Among its leaders were William D Haywood and Eugene V Debs.

industry A group of business enterprises which produce or supply goods or services. Industries can be classified into several types. **Primary industries** are those based on the use of the earth for cultivation (eg agriculture, forestry, fishing) or the extraction of raw materials (eg mining, quarrying). **Secondary industries** (or **manufacturing industries**) are those which process raw materials into consumer products and components; they are often divided into **heavy industries**, involving the large-scale use of plant, machinery, personnel, and output (eg iron and steel, machinery, cement) and **light industries**, involving production on a much smaller scale (eg textiles, electronics, food processing). Under the heading of manufacturing industries are also included those industries which are involved with the production of electricity. **Tertiary industries** (or **service industries**) are those which do not produce goods, but provide support for other areas of the economy (eg banking, law, defence, insurance) or are concerned with quality of life (eg tourism, entertainment, education).

Indus Valley Civilization The earliest known S Asian civilization, flourishing c.2300–1750 BC across 1·1 million sq km/½ million sq mi around the R Indus in Pakistan. Over 100 sites have been identified with important urban centres at Mohenjo-daro and Harappa (Pakistan), and Kalibangan and Lothal (W India). There were uniform principles of urban planning, with streets set out in a grid pattern and public drainage systems. Weights and measures were standardized, and there was widespread trade with W Asia. A common writing system was used, which remains undeciphered. Great granaries on citadel mounts suggest the existence of priest-kings or a priestly oligarchy. There is no firm explanation for the decline of the civilization.

inert gases *noble gases*

inertia The reluctance of a massive object to change its motion. Inherent to mass, it is present in the absence of gravity. Newton's first law is sometimes called the **law of inertia**, and is equivalent to ascribing the property of inertia to objects.

inertial guidance An automatic navigation system used in guided missiles, aeroplanes, and submarines, which depends on the tendency of an object to continue in a straight line (*inertia*). Any changes in the direction and magnitude of motion of the vehicle are sensed, compared to an onboard computer programme of the expected motion, and corrected automatically.

infallibility In the Roman Catholic Church, the claim that statements on matters of faith or morals, made by a pope speaking *ex cathedra* (Lat 'from the throne'), or by a General Council if confirmed by the pope, are guaranteed the assistance of the Holy Spirit (ie free from error). The claim is rejected by Protestants, for whom only God and the word of God are infallible.

Infante / Infanta [infantay, infanta] In Spain and Portugal, the title given to the sons and daughters of the sovereign.

infanticide The putting to death of the newborn with the consent of the parent, family, or community. In England and Wales, the term is also used where a mother wilfully causes the death of her child. The child must be under 1 year old, and at the time of the mother's act or omission the mother must have been disturbed in her mind as a result of the stress of the birth. The difficulty of obtaining jury convictions for murder in these situations led to the introduction of this crime in the Infanticide Act (1938). Most cases of infanticide are dealt with by probation or discharge. In the USA, the offence is usually subsumed under the general homicide statute, and in Scotland it is usually tried as culpable homicide.

infantile paralysis *poliomyelitis*

infant mortality rate The number of deaths per year of infants in the first year of life (age 0–1) in relation to the total number of live births. It is used as a measure of community health since, when standards of hygiene, sanitation, and nutrition are low, many infants die of gastro-enteritis and respiratory infections. Deaths during the first week of life are also influenced by prenatal and intranatal factors, congenital defects, prematurity, and birth injury. This is reflected in the **perinatal mortality rate**, defined as the number of deaths, including stillbirths, during the first week of life in relation to the total number of live births and stillbirths occurring in the same year. The most important determinant of the perinatal mortality rate is low birth weight, which is associated with poor nutrition, poverty, multiple pregnancy, and smoking during pregnancy. It is also influenced by the standards of antenatal and obstetric care, and by the facilities available to care for small and premature babies. Both rates have fallen steadily in developed countries over the last hundred years because of increasing socio-economic status, improvements in the standards of community health, and technological advances in medical care.

infant school A UK school taking children from the age of 5 up to 7 or 8. In areas with middle schools, such schools are sometimes known as **first schools**.

infection The invasion of the body by micro-organisms that are capable of multiplying there and producing illness. Such organisms are called *pathogenic*. However, some pathogenic organisms can exist on the skin or in other parts of the body without causing illness; in these circumstances the individual is said to be a 'carrier' of the organism. An infection begins by the entry of an organism at a specific site, such as the tonsils, skin, urinary, and respiratory tracts. This is followed by a short interval in which the person feels well (the *incubation period*), during which the micro-organisms multiply. They may cause disease locally or disperse throughout the body causing disease in other tissues and organs, such as in cystitis (the bladder), pneumonia (the lungs), and hepatitis (the liver).

infectious hepatitis [hepatiytis] Inflammation of the liver, which may be caused by several different viruses. The best known are hepatitis A, B, and C. **Hepatitis A** infection is acquired by ingesting contaminated food or water. It causes an acute illness with fever, nausea, fatigue, and jaundice. Although it may be debilitating for several months, and may be fatal in older people, it causes no long-term effects. **Hepatitis B** and **C** infections are acquired from contaminated blood or body fluids either directly (eg from a needle) or during sexual intercourse. They can cause an acute illness similar to hepatitis A, but can also cause serious long-term liver damage, resulting in cirrhosis and liver cancer.

inference In logic, a sequence of steps leading from a set of premisses to a conclusion. Rules of inference are rules for the construction of good and valid arguments.

inferiority complex A fundamental sense of inadequacy and insecurity out of proportion to real circumstances. An example may be of short individuals who have a driven need to assert themselves in social situations to overcome their sensitivity about their height.

infertility The inability of a couple to conceive, affecting about 10% of couples, with a wide range of causes affecting both partners. In the female, failure of ovulation is common, and ovaries may be stimulated to produce ova by giving gonadotrophic hormones or by drugs which simulate their action in the body. Infection of the cervix, obstruction of the uterine (Fallopian) tubes, and abnormalities in the uterus are also recognized factors. In the male, factors include the absence or inadequate production of sperm, and the clumping of sperm (*agglutination*) with impaired mobility due in some individuals to sperm antibodies in the male serum.

infinity In mathematics, a number greater than any other number. The symbol ∞ was first used for infinity by the English mathematician John Wallis (1616–1703). Cantor and other mathematicians in the 19th-c and 20th-c showed the complexity of the concept of infinity, arising out of their work on set theory, investigating, for example, how the cardinal number of the set of all points in an infinite straight line compares with the cardinal number of the set of all points in an infinite plane. Cantor's introduction of an endless hierarchy of infinite sets of different sizes admitted paradoxes that were resolved by the axiomatic approach of German mathematician Ernst Zermelo (1871–1953) and others, but the whole enterprise was strongly rejected by Dutch mathematician Jan Brouwer (1881–1966) and other intuitionists as exceeding the capacity of the human mind. Later developments have shown how infinitely large and infinitely small numbers can be introduced into the calculus.

infix *affix*

inflammation The body's reaction to injury, whether caused by a physical or chemical insult, an infectious agent, or an auto-immune process. In the acute stage there is an increased blood flow to the damaged part, due to chemical substances which dilate the small blood vessels. Certain types of white blood cells (*neutrophil polymorphs* and monocytes) are attracted to the site, and these engulf and digest damaged tissue and any infectious micro-organisms (*phagocytosis*). The reaction is accompanied by pain, heat, swelling, redness, and loss of function of the affected part. If the defence is successful, the tissues reorganize and repair themselves; if not, the inflammation may become chronic or an abscess may develop.

inflation An economic situation of widespread and persistent increases in prices and wages. Common measures of inflation are the Retail Price Index, which covers a wide range of consumer goods, and the gross domestic product deflator, an index of all goods prices. Inflation is believed to be bad for both equity and efficiency. If interest rates do not rise, inflation injures savers; if interest rates do rise, the need for high payments early in the life of loans makes borrowing for business or for house ownership very risky. Economists differ over the cause of inflation: the main models blame excess demand and excessive rises in the money supply. Cost inflation, in which each price or wage rate rises because others have risen, or are expected to rise, does not explain how inflation starts, but does explain why it is so persistent once it has started. Under very rapid inflation, or **hyperinflation** (eg Germany in the 1920s and early 1930s, or some Latin-American countries in the 1970s and 1980s), money becomes useless and the economy is forced back to barter, with great losses of efficiency. Governments have often tried to cure inflation, frequently incurring unemployment in the process, without much success.

inflationary universe A theory proposed in 1980 by US physicist Alan Guth (1947–) and others which posits a mechanism for the extraordinary expansion of the early universe from a diameter of 10^{-26} m to 10 cm in 10^{-32} sec. Such expansion is thought necessary to understand the uniformity and density of the universe. A variant on the 'big bang' model of the universe, it relies on the phase transition in the earliest epochs of the universe.

inflecting language *fusional language*

inflection *derivation; fusional language*

inflexion, point of In mathematics, the point at which a curve changes the nature of its concavity, either from being concave upwards to concave downwards, or vice-versa. If the equation of the curve is given in Cartesian co-ordinates x and y, $d^2y/dx^2 = 0$ is a necessary, but not sufficient, condition for an inflexion point.

inflorescence The arrangement of more than one flower on the stem, together with any associated structures, such as bracts. Development is triggered by changes in light duration or temperature, and is probably controlled by hormones. The vegetative growth of the plant may cease with production of the inflorescence, or may continue afterwards; this is of significance in some crop plants where yield, ripening, and harvesting techniques are important. The type of inflorescence is often significant as a diagnostic character in recognizing plant families. Basic types are distinguished by the different branching patterns and by the positions of the oldest and youngest flowers. In **cymose inflorescences**, the meristem of the main axis differentiates into a flower with new growth coming from a lateral branch (*monochasia*) or branches (*dichasia*) which in turn are terminated by a flower. In **racemose** [**ra**simohz] **inflorescences**, the main axis continues to grow, flowers being formed below the tip.

influenza or **flu** A disease caused by the influenza virus. It causes an acute respiratory illness with cough and congested airways, as well as headache, fever, and muscle pain. The virus spreads rapidly through the air or by direct contact, and tends to cause epidemics and pandemics. There is a significant mortality, mainly affecting infants, the elderly and the debilitated. In 1918, an influenza outbreak killed 25 million people worldwide. Vaccination is not always effective, because the virus develops different strains with varying antigenic properties. The name is derived from *influentia coeli*, a mediaeval name for the disease, thought to be due to the influence of the sky. It was described by Chinese doctors in the 12th-c.

information engineering *information technology*

information processing A psychological approach in which the performance of an organism is described in terms of the elementary operations or computations it performs on *input* information (the *stimulus*) to produce *output* information (the *response*). It is often associated with cognitive psychology.

information retrieval The act of tracing information contained in databases. Applicable in principle to any search for information, the term has been associated since the 1960s with the online technique of scanning and interrogating large computer files for specific data. This may take the form of bibliographic references, full-length documents, or constantly updated information (eg share prices). The use of computers makes the process not only quick and relatively cheap, but also thorough and reliable.

information superhighway *Internet*

information technology A term commonly used to cover the range of technologies relevant to the transfer of information (knowledge, data, text, drawings, audio recordings, video sequences, etc), in particular to computers, digital electronics, and telecommunications. Technological developments during the 1970s and 1980s, such as very large scale integration, and satellite and optical-based communication methods, have been responsible for enormous scientific and commercial growth in this area. The related field of **information engineering** deals with the analysis and design of new computer-based systems, along with the development of associated support software.

information theory The mathematical theory of information, deriving from the work of the US mathematicians Claude E Shannon and Warren Weaver, in particular *The Mathematical Theory of Communication* (1949), and from the theory of probability. It is concerned with defining and measuring the amount of information in a message, with the encoding and decoding of information, and with the transmission capacity of a channel of communication. The basic notion is that the less predictable something is, the more information it contains. For example, the letter *z* carries a lot more information than *e* (in English, less so in German), when it occurs in a message. In contrast, the *u* after *q* carries no information at all, since it is wholly predictable, and thus technically redundant.

The theory also deals with the problem of *noise* (random interference) in the channel, which can impair the reception and decoding of a signal. To reduce the risk of errors which may arise, and thereby to increase efficiency, a signal should contain a degree of redundancy. For example, the final digit of the number identifying books (the ISBN) provides information to check that the rest of the number is valid. Information theory has been influential in generating models for understanding communication processes and in the design of codes for the transmission of information, especially by computers. It is not, however, concerned with the content, meaning, or importance of that information or any other communication.

Infrared Astronomical Satellite (IRAS) project The first mission to survey the universe in the thermal infrared region of the electromagnetic spectrum, where the 'signature' of relatively cool materials in space can be observed. Launched in January 1983, it operated successfully for 300 days until the helium was exhausted, achieving an all-sky survey. It catalogued 250 000 IR sources, identified stars apparently in the process of forming, and discovered six comets and their long dust tails. It was a collaborative project of the UK, The Netherlands, and the USA.

infrared astronomy The study of celestial objects by their radiation in the wavelength range 1000 nm–1 mm. Absorption by water vapour in our atmosphere poses severe difficulties, some of which are overcome at high-altitude observatories such as

Mauna Kea in Hawaii at 4 000 m/13 000 ft, or by using cryogenically cooled telescopes on spacecraft. Many objects emit most of their radiation in the infrared. This type of astronomy has increased in importance with the availability of imaging detector arrays to photograph objects of infrared wavelengths.

infrared photography Photography which uses wavelengths beyond visible red light. Black-and-white film has medical and forensic application; for example, it is used for camouflage detection, since chlorophyll in green living foliage reflects infrared strongly, unlike visually matching pigments. Multilayer colour film including an infrared sensitive emulsion gives a false colour rendering in which natural vegetation appears red or magenta; this is used in aerial surveying.

infrared radiation Electromagnetic radiation of a wavelength a little longer than light, between 10^{-3} m and $7{\cdot}8 \times 10^{-7}$ m; discovered by William Herschel in 1800. Emitted by oscillating and rotating molecules and atoms, and invisible to the naked eye, it is perceived by us as 'radiant heat'. Infrared detectors are used in night and smoke vision systems (for fire fighting), intruder alarms, weather forecasting, and missile guidance systems.

infrared transmission A technique for using an infrared laser beam as a device for data communications. It is usually used between buildings which are close together but involve crossing public thoroughfares, where it would be difficult to lay cables. It is most commonly associated with a remote control linking to a video recorder, television, or hi-fi.

infrasound Sound having a frequency of less than 20 Hz. Such waves cannot be heard by humans, but may be felt. Infrasonic waves are produced by explosions and by an unsteady airflow past an object. The study of infrasound is **infrasonics**.

infrastructure The network of factors which enables a country's economy or an industrial operation to function effectively. They include such matters as transport, power, communication systems, housing, and education.

Inge, William Ralph [ing], known as **the Gloomy Dean** (1860–1954) Clergyman and theologian, born in Crayke, North Yorkshire, N England, UK. He studied at Cambridge, taught at Eton, and was vicar of All Saints, Kensington, before being appointed professor of divinity at Cambridge (1907). He was Dean of St Paul's (1911–34), earning his byname from the pessimism displayed in his sermons and newspaper articles.

Ingenhousz, Jan [eengg*enhows] (1730–99) Physician and plant physiologist, born in Breda, The Netherlands. He practised as a doctor in England, then became physician to Empress Maria Theresa. He improved methods of generating static electricity (1766), and was the first to make quantitative measurements of heat conduction in metals. He is best known as the discoverer of photosynthesis (1779).

Ingham, Sir Bernard [ingam] (1932–) Journalist, born in Hebden Bridge, West Yorkshire, N England, UK. He studied at Hebden Bridge Grammar School, then embarked on a career as a journalist, joining the *Hebden Bridge Times* (1948–52), *The Yorkshire Post* and *Yorkshire Evening Post* (1952–62), and *The Guardian* (1962–7). He was a government press adviser (1976) and under-secretary in the Department of Energy (1978–9), becoming nationally known after his appointment as chief press secretary to prime minister Margaret Thatcher (1979–90). He was knighted in 1990.

Ingrams, Richard (Reid) (1937–) Writer and journalist, born in Westcliffe-on-Sea, Essex, SE England, UK. He was educated at Shrewsbury School and University College, Oxford. In 1962 he founded, together with Peter Cook and Willie Rushton (1937–96), the satirical magazine *Private Eye*, whose editor he remained until 1986. In 1992 he founded *The Oldie*, a lively magazine for older readers. He was television critic for *The Spectator* and became a columnist for the *Observer* in 1988. Other writings include the satirical *Dear Bill: the Collected Letters of Denis Thatcher* (1980), *You Might As Well Be Dead* (1986), and a biography of Malcolm Muggeridge (1995).

Ingres, Jean Auguste Dominique [ĩgruh] (1780–1867) Painter, the leading exponent of the Classical tradition in France in the 19th-c, born in Montauban, S France. He studied in Paris under David in 1796, and at the Ecole des Beaux-Arts; in 1801 he won the Prix de Rome. He then lived in Rome (1806–20), where he began many of his famous nudes, including 'Baigneuse' (1808, Louvre) and 'La Source' (1807, completed 1856, Musée d'Orsay). He became professor at the Ecole des Beaux-Arts, Paris, and director of the French Academy in Rome. He was made a senator in 1862.

inheritance tax A UK tax started in 1986 which replaced capital transfer tax. It is levied on the value of a deceased person's 'estate', and includes property, land, investments, and other valuable assets. Small estates are not liable to tax. Similar taxes are imposed in several countries, and can be traced back to Roman times. In the USA, such taxes are collected by the individual states, with an estate tax being imposed federally, based on the amount left, not owned; there is also a gift tax, to prevent evasion.

initialism *acronym*

Initial Teaching Alphabet *i.t.a.*

initiation rites Ceremonies effecting a transition from one social condition or role to another, especially from childhood to adulthood; also known as **rites of passage** or **passage rites**. The chief rites involve birth, admission into a social group (eg baptism, circumcision), coming of age, weddings, and funerals. The French ethnographer Arnold van Gennep (1873–1957) considered rites of passage to be any transition via ritual from one status to another (including such rites as coronation and ordination). In his analysis he emphasized the three stages of all such rituals: removing individuals from their old social status (*rites of separation*), transforming them in subsequent rites (*rites of transition*), and returning them in their 'reborn' social position back into the community (*rites of aggregation*).

injection The administration by a syringe of a drug or other pharmacological preparation in solution or suspension through a needle inserted into the skin (*intradermal*), underneath the skin (*subcutaneous*), into the muscle tissue (*intramuscular*), or into a vein (*intravenous*).

injection engine *fuel injection*

injection moulding A process used in the manufacture of plastics. Raw plastic, usually in granular form, is heated until soft enough to squeeze through a nozzle into a mould of the shape of the desired article. With thermoplastics, the mould is cold. With thermosetting resins, the mould is kept hot to promote the setting reactions. This type of manufacture is highly automated.

injunction A court order in equity instructing a defendant to refrain from committing some act or course of action (**prohibitory injunction**), or, less commonly (but found for example in the USA), to carry out some act (**mandatory injunction**), such as an order to demolish a building that the defendant has built in breach of a covenant. The term **interdict** forbidding a particular act is used in Scots law. It is a remedy; for example, a prohibitory injunction might be granted to stop a continuing nuisance. Interim injunctions may be granted where there is a degree of urgency until a full hearing can be arranged, and they are normally intended to preserve the status quo.

ink A substance, usually coloured, used for writing, drawing, or printing; known in China before 1100 BC. At its simplest, it is a solution of a pigment or dye in a liquid (eg soot in water). The production of the many kinds of inks required for commercial, educational, and cultural purposes has now become a sophisticated chemical–industrial process.

Inka *Incas*

Inkatha [inkahta] A Zulu-based political organization, founded in South Africa in 1928, and now led by Chief Buthelezi; in full, **Inkatha yeNkululeku yeSizwe**. *Inkatha* refers to the woven headring worn by the Zulu to support loads; *yeNkululeku yeSizwe* means 'freedom for the nation'. Its disagreements with the politics of the African National Congress and its fear that the

ANC was being privileged in constitutional talks in the mid-1990s led to violent conflict between members of the two organizations, despite efforts for reconciliation between Buthelezi and Mandela.

inkcap A mushroom-like fungus with spore masses that appear dark brown or black; gills on cap liquefy by self-digestion as the spores mature; resulting black fluid can be boiled, strained, and used as ink. (Order: Agaricales. Family: Coprinaceae.)

ink-jet printer A type of fast and relatively quiet printer which produces characters or graphics by squirting very fine jets of rapid-drying ink onto paper. The principle of the ink-jet has been used to build relatively cheap high-quality colour printers

INLA *Irish National Liberation Army*

inlaying A method of decorating furniture and other wooden objects by cutting away part of the surface of the solid material, and replacing it with a thin sheet of wood in another contrasting colour. Occasionally slivers of ivory, bone or shell are used in this way.

innateness hypothesis A controversial claim that the speed and efficiency with which children acquire language can be explained only by attributing to them a genetic predisposition for this particular task. They are thought to be born with an innate knowledge of at least some of the universal features of language structure, which they are able to apply to the facts of a particular language as they are exposed to them. The hypothesis was proposed by US linguist Noam Chomsky in the 1960s, and became a tenet of generative linguistic theory.

Inner Mongolia, Chin **Nei Mongol** pop (2000e) 23 921 000; area 450 000 sq km/173 700 sq mi. Autonomous region in N China, bordered N by Mongolia and Russia; part of S border formed by Great Wall of China; two-thirds grasslands, remainder desert; Greater Khingan range (NE) rises to over 1000 m/3000 ft; Hedao Plain, fertile area N of Yellow R; several deserts further S; capital, Hohhot; principal town, Baotou; horse breeding, cattle and sheep rearing, forestry, iron and steel, coal mining; wheat now grown in irrigated areas.

Inner Temple *Inns of Court*

Innis, (Emile Alfredo) Roy (1934–) Civil rights activist, born in St Croix, US Virgin Isles. Moving to New York City at 14, he dropped out of high school to join the army, then worked in a New York research laboratory (1963–7). He joined the Congress of Racial Equality in 1963, advocating black separatism and community school boards, and became CORE national president in 1968. He promoted community development corporations, founded several African-American business groups, and was co-editor of the *Manhattan Tribune*. Dogged by charges from associates of being too dictatorial, he often took positions that put him at odds with other prominent African-Americans.

Innocent III, originally **Lotario de' Conti di Segni** (1160–1216) Pope (1198–1216), born in Anagni, C Italy. His pontificate is regarded as the high point of the temporal and spiritual supremacy of the Roman see. He proclaimed the Fourth Crusade (1202–4) to recover the Holy Places, judged between rival emperors in Germany, and had Otto IV deposed. He laid England under an interdict, and excommunicated King John for refusing to recognize Stephen Langton as Archbishop of Canterbury. Under him the fourth Lateran Council was held in 1215.

Innocents' Day *Holy Innocents' Day*

Innsbruck [inzbruk] 47°17N 11°25E, pop (2000e) 119 600. Capital of Tirol state, W Austria; in the valley of the R Inn, surrounded by mountains; a mediaeval old town, with narrow and irregular streets and tall houses in late Gothic style; a great tourist attraction, noted for its mountaineering course and tobogganing, and a popular winter skiing centre; 1964 and 1976 Winter Olympic Games held here; Alpine zoo; university (1914–23); glass, textiles; Goldenes Dach ('golden roof', 1494–6); cathedral (1717–22); Hofburg (15th–16th-c palace), Hofkirche (Court Church, 1553–63), Altes Landhaus (1725–8); Innsbruck Summer (Jul–Aug), Festival of Early Music (Aug), Innsbruck Autumn Fair (Sep), biennial Alpine Folk Music Competition alternates with biennial Youth Music Festival (Oct).

Inns of Court Voluntary unincorporated societies having the exclusive right to confer the rank of barrister in England, Wales, and Northern Ireland. For England and Wales, four sets of buildings (Inns) have existed in London since the 14th-c: the Inner Temple, the Middle Temple, Lincoln's Inn, and Gray's Inn. The Inn of Court of Northern Ireland was established in Belfast in 1926. Each Inn is governed by its Benchers (Masters of the Bench), who mainly comprise judges and Queen's or King's Counsels.

inoculation *immunization*

Inönü, Ismet [inoenü], originally **Mustafa Ismet** (1884–1973) Turkish soldier, prime minister (1923–37, 1961–5), and president (1938–50), born in Izmir, W Turkey. He fought in World War 1, then became Atatürk's chief-of-staff in the war against the Greeks (1919–22), defeating them twice at Inönü. As the first premier of the new republic, he introduced many political reforms, and was elected president in 1938 on Atatürk's death. He maintained the neutrality of Turkey in World War 2. After the war he aligned Turkey with the Western Allies. From 1950 he was leader of the Opposition, and became premier again in 1961, resigning in 1965. He failed to win re-election in 1969 and was discredited by his support of the military regime that seized power in 1971. He resigned as party chairman in 1972, but remained a senator until his death.

inorganic chemistry That branch of chemistry which deals with the structures, properties, and reactions of the elements other than carbon, and their compounds.

inositol A component of phytic acid in cereal and other vegetable foods. Some species (eg mice) require inositol for growth; humans do not, though large amounts are present in the body, especially in the brain.

input–output analysis In economics, an analysis showing flows of goods and services between industries. It assists economists in understanding how different sectors of the economy are interrelated. Much of the original work in this area was carried out by Wassily Leontief.

inquilinism [ingkwilinizm] An association between two different species, in which one (the **inquiline**) lives within another (the *host*) without causing harm. The term is also used for the relationship in which a species lives inside the burrow, nest, or other domicile of a host species.

Inquisition A tribunal for the prosecution of heresy, originally of the mediaeval Christian Church. Pope Gregory IX (13th-c) gave special responsiblity to papal inquisitors to counter the threat to political and religious unity from heretical groups. The activities of the inquisitors were later characterized by extremes of torture and punishment, most notoriously in the case of the **Spanish Inquisition**, which survived until the 19th-c.

inquisitorial system *prosecution*

INRI The first letters of the Latin wording of the inscription placed on Jesus's cross at Pilate's command (*John* 19.19–20): *Iesus Nazarenus, Rex Iudaeorum* ('Jesus of Nazareth, the king of the Jews').

insect An arthropod belonging to the largest and most diverse class of living organisms, the Insecta; c.1 million recognized species, grouped into 28 orders, estimated as representing a small fraction of the total world fauna; head typically bears a pair of feelers (*antennae*) and a pair of compound eyes; each of three thoracic segments bears a pair of legs, the last two also typically bear a pair of wings each; genital openings located at rear end of abdomen; known as fossils from the Devonian period. Insects exhibit varied habits, and are of vital importance as pollinators of plants, as pests, and as carriers of diseases.

insecticide A substance which kills insects. Most commonly these are synthetic organic compounds, applied as sprays by farmers, but they may also be applied in granular or powder forms. There is current concern about these substances entering the food chain and having a detrimental impact on wildlife, and perhaps on humans. DDT was one of the most widely used insecticides in the post-war period; it is now banned in many countries, because of its persistence in the food chain. An alternative development has been through the use of a bacteria species, *bacillus thuringensis*, or *B.t*, which produces a natural insecticide toxic to a broad range of insect pests.

insectivore The most primitive of placental mammals, native to Africa, Europe, Asia, and North America; small with narrow pointed snout; most are solitary, nocturnal; eats insects and other invertebrates. (Order: Insectivora, 345 species.)

insectivorous plant *carnivorous plant*

insider dealing (UK) or **insider trading** (US) A business situation where an individual takes advantage of information about a company before it is made public, in order to make a profit (or avoid a loss) by dealing in the company's stocks or shares. It is illegal in most countries. In the UK it has been so since 1980, but there were few prosecutions until the Financial Services Act (1986) was passed, which gave the Department of Trade and Industry power to investigate and prosecute. In the USA it is regulated by the Security and Exchange Commission. However, it is not always easy to prove that such activities have taken place.

insolation The amount of solar radiation (both diffuse and direct) which reaches the Earth. Insolation varies with latitude and season: it is consistently high at the Equator, and high at the Poles during the polar summer, but zero in winter. The amount of solar radiation which reaches the outer limit of the Earth's atmosphere is the *solar constant*, and is only a small proportion of the Sun's energy. Of the solar constant, 53% is lost before reaching the Earth's surface by scattering, absorption, and reflectance by clouds and dust.

insomnia Unsatisfactory sleep, whether in quantity or in quality. It may be a component of a variety of physical or mental disorders. There may be difficulty in either initiating or maintaining sleep, a preoccupation about sleep, and interference with social and occupational functioning as a result of sleep disruption.

installment credit *hire purchase*

instinct An unlearned tendency to behave in a particular way. Instinctive behaviours are those actions or reactions to specific stimuli, shown in similar form by all normally developed members of a species (or sex or age-group thereof), no specific life experience being necessary for their emergence. The distinctive courtship-displays of several species are an illustration.

Institute of Space and Astronautical Science (ISAS) of Japan An agency for space science research in Japan; established in 1981 by re-organizing the University of Tokyo's Institute of Space and Aeronautical Science. It is responsible for developing science spacecraft and launch vehicles (space applications programmes are the responsibility of the National Space Development Agency). Launches are made from Kagoshima Space Centre on Kyushu I at the S tip of Japan.

instrumentalism In philosophy, the thesis associated with the pragmatists William James and Dewey, that propositions and theories are tools in the process of enquiry and can be regarded only as more or less effective or ineffective, not true or false.

instrumental learning In psychology, an elementary learning process. An individual comes to perform a certain action more/less frequently or intensely than before, by virtue of that action having produced positive/negative consequences.

insulation *thermal insulation*

insulator A material or covering which prevents or reduces the transmission of electricity, heat, or sound. All electrical devices are insulated for protection from the passage of electricity. Thermal insulators keep things hot, cold, or maintain an even temperature. Sound insulators act as mufflers.

insulin [insyulin] A protein of vertebrates, secreted by B-cells of the islets of Langerhans (in the pancreas) in response to increases in blood glucose concentration (eg after a meal). It has widespread effects in the body, but its main action is to lower blood glucose concentration by accelerating its uptake by most tissues (except the brain), and promoting its conversion into glycogen and fat. Insulin-like substances are present in some invertebrates, but their significance is not known.

insurance A system of guarding an individual or institution against the possibility of an event occurring which will cause some harm – usually financial. The insured pays a fee (the *premium*) to an insurance company. The size of the premium (calculated by actuaries) depends on the size of the risk at stake, the number of premiums to be received, and the risk (or chance) of the event occurring. It is possible to obtain cover against most events. There are four main classes of insurance: marine, fire, life, and accident. An **insurance broker** is an agent for anyone who wishes to be insured, by finding others who are willing to underwrite the risk. Their commission is termed *brokerage*.

intaglio [intahlioh] **1** A technique of printmaking. The design is incised into a metal plate, ink is forced into the cut lines and wiped off the rest of the surface; damp paper is laid on top; and both plate and paper are rolled through a press. This differs from other types of printing, in which the ink lies on the raised surface of the plate or block.
2 A type of engraved gem in which the design is cut into the stone, instead of standing up in relief as in a *cameo*.

integers *numbers*

integral calculus *see panel*

integral tripack Material for colour photography with three separate emulsion coatings on one base, also termed **monopack**. In negative and reversal films the upper layer is sensitive to blue light, the middle to green, and the bottom to red. While processing after exposure, dye images are formed in each layer in colours complementary to their original sensitivity.

integrated circuit A single chip of semiconductor, such as silicon, in which a large number of individual electronic components are assembled. Integrated circuits are smaller, lighter, and faster than conventional circuits. They use less power, are cheaper, and last longer. The circuit is usually made from pure silicon, doped with impurities – the type of impurity determining the job of that part of the chip: transistors, diodes,

integral calculus

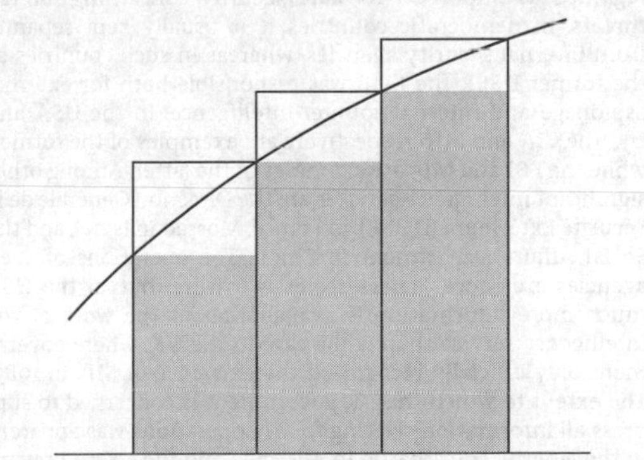

A system of mathematical rules, often defined as the inverse of differentiation, but developed on its own by Riemann and others, that finds areas as the limits of sums. The region between a curve representing a function $f(x)$ and the x-axis is divided into n strips of equal width, each of which has an area less than that of one rectangle and greater than that of another rectangle. As n increases, the sums of the areas of the larger rectangles and of the smaller rectangles approach the same limit (assuming $f(x)$ is integrable); this is the **integral** over that interval. A later variant, developed by Frenchman Henri Lebesgue (1875–1941), is easier to use in pure and applied mathematics, but is not so widely applicable, and other generalizations of the integral concept have been developed.

or resistors. When an integrated circuit fails, the whole chip is replaced, so making maintenance easier. Microelectronics using integrated circuits have made the development of sophisticated electronic watches and pocket calculators possible. Even smaller integrated circuits are being built using nanotechnology to manipulate and exactly position individual atoms.

integrated optics The study of minute optical devices linked by light guides into single units containing several components. Such an integrated optical circuit might contain semiconductor lasers, modulators, and switches, all fabricated on a single chip. It may offer improved information-handling capacity, low weight, and high protection against interference, compared to conventional electronic chips. Currently experimental, its first likely applications will be in telecommunications.

Integrated Services Digital Network (ISDN) A service provided by the Posts, Telegraph and Telephones Authorities, which allows voice and data communications to be effected on the same line. This enables voice messaging to be carried out in the same way as data transmission. Facilities are available also for transmitting television pictures of medium quality.

integration *civil rights*

intelligence The ability to respond adaptively to novel situations. Psychologists attempt to measure this ability by constructing tests which appear related to intelligence, and extensively using these tests on a target population, so enabling them to assess the mental age of any individual. (For a given score on a particular test, mental age is the average age of those members of the tested population having this score.) **IQ** (**intelligence quotient**) equals mental age divided by actual (chronological) age. It is usual to distinguish **fluid intelligence** (mental flexibility) from **crystallized intelligence** (knowledge). Statistical techniques such as factor analysis can be used to identify various subcategories of ability, particularly **verbal** and **nonverbal intelligence**. A general intelligence factor derived by these methods is sometimes called *Spearman's g*.

intelligence service A state agency which gathers information regarded as important to state security concerning foreign threats. In democratic countries it is usually kept separate from internal security agencies, whereas in such countries as the former USSR the KGB was responsible both for external espionage and internal counter-intelligence. In the USA and UK, the CIA and MI6 respectively are examples of the former, while the FBI and MI5 are examples of the latter. Among other significant intelligence services are the Direction Générale de la Sécurité Extérieure (DGSE), in France, Mossad in Israel, and the Social Affairs Department in China. The operations of such agencies are more or less secret in nature, but in the USA much more information is available about the work of the intelligence service than is the case in the UK, where government only officially recognized the existence of MI5 in 1989. The extent to which the UK government is concerned to suppress all information relating to MI5 operations was apparent in the lengthy court battle in Australia and the UK to prevent publication, or reporting in the media, of the book *Spycatcher*. This was written by Peter Wright, a former intelligence officer, who alleged misconduct and 'misuse' of the law by MI5, in particular as it related to a 'plot' to destabilize the Wilson government of the 1970s. The government's claim that former members of the security forces are bound by a lifelong duty of confidentiality was upheld by a House of Lords judgment in 1988, but the Lords rejected the claim that other parties receiving confidential information from a Crown servant in all circumstances were so bound. MI5 was placed on an official footing for the first time by the 1989 Security Services Act. In 1991 the first woman to head MI5 was appointed (Stella Rimington, 1935–). This was also the first time that the name of the head of the service had been made public. Following the end of the Cold War the emphasis has changed to economic intelligence and industrial espionage, and the fight against domestic and international terrorism.

intelligent agent *cyberintelligence*

intelligent building / home A building in which all areas of the building have been linked by cable capable of providing voice, video, and data communications. These communications could be used, for example, to provide continuous monitoring of the building, to ensure that the temperature, lighting, and environment always obey preset parameters. An **intelligent home** is one in which domestic appliances, meters, and alarms are linked to a central computer for the purposes of remote monitoring and control.

intensive care The continuous monitoring of several vital bodily functions in very seriously ill patients or in premature infants. The variables most commonly assessed (depending on the nature of the illness) are pulse rate, systemic arterial blood pressure, pulmonary artery blood pressure, heart output, central venous pressure, respiratory rate, body temperature, the levels of oxygen, carbon dioxide, sugar, and acidity in the blood, and the electrical activity of the heart. These are usually measured and recorded electronically. Close supervision is required to detect dangerous deviations from normal, and to fine-tune life-support systems such as assisted ventilation machines, artificial kidneys, and pumps supplying fluids and powerful drugs.

intensive farming Farming with relatively high input levels, especially of fertilizers, sprays, and pharmaceuticals. It produces higher yields per hectare, which may compensate for limited farm size and allow the small farmer to make an acceptable income. Intensive farming relies on the use of farm machinery (eg automatic feeders and milking machines) to do the work of labourers, and on chemicals to control plant and animal diseases and to stimulate growth and productivity. Genetic selection and breeding, together with feedstuff containing artificial growth hormones and inorganic plant nutrients, ensure that today's intensively farmed animals and lands are more productive than at any time in history. Some practices have been condemned as being cruel to animals, and some scientists now advocate the banning of antibiotics in high doses on the grounds that resistant strains of bacteria in animals might transfer their resistance to bacteria that infect humans.

intent / intention At law, the desire to produce a given result, or the knowledge or belief that a given result is substantially certain to result from one's conduct. In civil law, a person is generally presumed to intend the natural and probable consequence of his or her acts; for example, in the tort of battery, the defendant must have intended to touch another person (ie it was not an accident) but not necessarily to have harmed the person, although the defendant will normally be liable for any harm that occurs. Intent is an essential element of most crimes (*mens rea*), though it must often be inferred from the actions of the defendant. A general intent to commit the particular harmful act is usually all that is required; knowledge that the act is unlawful is not necessary. Some crimes require a specific intent, eg murder requires more than the act of killing another person – an intent to kill or to cause grievous bodily harm, or 'malice aforethought' in the USA, must also be present. Criminal negligence, usually defined as reckless disregard for the safety of others, can sometimes replace intent. Intent, in England and Wales, is distinguished from *motive*. Motive is what prompts a person to act, or to fail to do so, whereas intent refers to the state of mind with which the act is done or omitted.

intentionality In philosophy, the characteristic of being directed to or being about something, which seems fundamentally to distinguish mental phenomena from physical phenomena. Beliefs, hopes, desires, and fears all point outside themselves to some object or content. The term was coined by the scholastics in the Middle Ages, revived by Brentano in the 19th-c, and is much invoked in current discussions within cognitive science and psychology.

interactive computing A mode of computing in which the user communicates directly with the computer and receives a fairly rapid response. Almost all microcomputers work in an interactive mode, as can most larger computers.

interactive video A closed-circuit recorded video system in which the display responds to the instructions of the viewer. Applications range from simple press-button or touch-screen question-and-answer interactions to complex branched learning programmes.

Inter-American Development Bank An international bank set up in 1959 to finance economic development projects in South and Central America. The main subscribers are the USA, Argentina, Brazil, Mexico, and Venezuela.

intercellular fluid *interstitial fluid*

intercontinental ballistic missile (ICBM) A very large, long-range nuclear-armed missile developed by the USA and the former Soviet Union from the late 1950s onwards. ICBMs are based in silos spread out over a wide land mass. They are capable of delivering a load of independently-targeted nuclear warheads (MIRVs) on the enemy heartland some 30 minutes after launch.

interest The amount of money charged by a person or institution that lends a sum to a borrower. The sum lent, on which interest is calculated, is known as the *principal*. The lender will be paid a percentage of the principal as interest on the loan, the rate of interest depending on the amount of the principal, the length of time the loan is outstanding, and the risk involved. Interest rates in general vary according to the state of the economy. Economists regard interest as the price of money, the rate rising and falling as the demand for money rises and falls. The **interest rate** is the percentage payable; for example, an 8% interest rate on £100 gives the lender £8 interest at the end of a year. The **annual percentage rate** (**APR**) shows the actual rate of interest payable on borrowings, especially hire-purchase agreements, where interest has to be paid more often than once a year. In **simple interest**, the interest gained in a given year is paid to the lender, so that the principal available does not change from year to year. In **compound interest**, the interest gained in a given year is not paid to the lender, but is added to the principal, which thereby increases year by year.

interest group *pressure group*

interference In physics, the result of two or more waves of similar frequency passing through the same point simultaneously. It is usual to consider simplified interference (*superposition*), in which the net result of waves overlapping is described by the simple addition of the original waves. An interference pattern is determined by the relative phases of the constituent waves. Beats and diffraction are interference effects. Interference is a property of all types of waves, including light. However, light beams arriving at a point from two ordinary light bulbs do not appear to produce such patterns. This arises from the mixture of colours in such light, as well as from incoherence (ie if a maximum of one wave corresponds to the maximum of another at one moment, such a relationship will not exist moments later). Light waves arriving from two independent bulbs are incoherent. Although at any one instant interference occurs, no stable pattern is formed. To observe interference in light, it is necessary to use light of a single colour from a single source, with the beam divided into two parts which are then brought together at a screen. Using such an arrangement, and passing a beam through two narrow parallel slits to divide it, Thomas Young observed such interference, and concluded that light was a wave (1804). Lasers provide an ideal light source. Interference is exploited in interferometers, including certain telescopes, compact disk players, phased-array radar, and holography.

interferometer A device which relies on monitoring the interference pattern formed by combining two wave beams, usually light, derived from a single source. Changes to one beam, for example by passing it through some gas, produce changes in the interference pattern. The technique is used in the study of gas flow, in wind tunnels, and in plasma physics. The laser ring gyroscope is a type of interferometer. Interferometers capable of measuring displacements as small as 10^{-18} m form the heart of gravitational wave detectors; signals from several radio telescopes can be combined in interferometric mode to give images having a resolution controlled by the distance between individual telescopes. In 1995 Cambridge astronomers led by John Baldwin created the first images from combined outputs at optical telescopes.

interferons A class of protein molecules produced by body cells that are part of the body's defences against infection, notably by viruses. Their mode of action remains obscure. They are extremely potent substances, but cells need to be exposed to them for several hours before resistance to a virus develops. Interferons appear to inhibit the multiplication of viruses within cells, and to stimulate the immune system to combat infection. Some interferons, produced by genetic engineering technology, have been tested as drugs for viral infection and some cancers, but new trials suggest therapy with interferon genes may be safer and more effective, at least in cancer. When interferon genes are transferred to a patient's own cells, these cells can make interferon locally, specifically targetted to cancer cells. The potential of interferons in medical practice however remains uncertain.

intergalactic medium A general term for the material isolated in space far from any galaxy. Theoretical considerations suggest that an enormous quantity of undetected material exists, far exceeding the contribution from visible galaxies.

Intergovernmental Maritime Consultative *United Nations*

Intergovernmental Panel on Climatic Change A panel established by the World Meteorological Organization and the UN Environment Programme in 1988 to assess the scientific information relating to climatic change, such as emissions of greenhouse gases and ensuing alterations to the Earth's climate. It also assesses environmental and socio-economic impacts of climatic change, and formulates response strategies. Comprised of more than 400 scientists from 25 countries, the panel first reported in 1990. It concludes that emissions of gases from human activity are enhancing the greenhouse effect, and predicted (on the basis of one scenario) a possible global warming of 0·3°C per decade during the 21st-c.

inter-industry trade *intra-industry trade*

interior design The design of the interior of a building, usually concerned with decoration, furniture, and fittings rather than the permanent fabric, and carried out only after all other work has been completed. The work of the Renaissance artists such as Raphael and Michaelangelo, of the 18th-c Robert Adam, and of the 19th-c Arts and Crafts Movement might all be called interior design, but the term is usually restricted to the modern profession.

Interleaf® A desk-top publishing package which provides the facilities needed by more sophisticated publishing operations.

Intermediate Nuclear Force Treaty A treaty signed (Dec 1987) in Washington by US President Reagan, and USSR General Secretary Gorbachev, involving the elimination of 1286 missiles from Europe and Asia, and over 2000 warheads. It was noted for its inclusion of the most comprehensive and stringent verification procedures ever seen in an arms control treaty, including short notice on-site verification, and was regarded as a major break in the arms race and a step forward in arms control.

intermedin *melanocyte-stimulating hormone*

intermezzo An instrumental piece, especially for piano, in a lyrical style and in no prescribed form. The title has been used by Brahms and other 19th–20th-c composers. Earlier it was used for short, comic interludes performed on stage between the acts of a serious opera; Pergolesi's *La serva padrona* (1733) is a famous example.

internal combustion engine An engine (such as a diesel or petrol engine) which burns its fuel/air mixture within the engine as part of its operating cycle. This cycle may be *two stroke* (one power stroke for every two strokes of the piston) or *four stroke* (one power stroke for every four strokes of the piston).

internal energy In thermodynamics, the difference between the heat supplied to a system and the work done by that system on its surroundings; symbol *U*, units J (joule). In general, adding heat to a system will increase its internal energy, corresponding to an increase in the system's temperature.

internal focusing An optical arrangement to focus a lens on a nearby subject by moving an element or group of elements axially inside the lens, instead of moving the whole lens away from the film plane to focus. This internal focusing arrangement has the advantages of keeping the lens compact and non-rotating during focusing, and gives an improved performance for close-up photography.

International An abbreviation of **International Working Men's Association**, the name given to attempts to establish international co-operative organizations of socialist, communist, and revolutionary groups. The **First International** was created in London in September 1864 with Marx playing a significant role in its development. The **Second International** was formed in Paris in 1889, and still survives as a forum for reformist socialist parties. The **Third International** (Comintern) was founded by Lenin, and represented communist parties until abolished in 1943. There was a brief attempt in the 1930s by Trotsky to launch a **Fourth International**.

International Amateur Athletic Federation (IAAF) The supreme governing body which controls athletics worldwide. Founded in Stockholm in July 1912 with 17 members, this had risen to 211 by 2004. In 2001 the IAAF voted to drop the word 'amateur' from its name after 89 years – while leaving the acronym unchanged. The IAAF is responsible for ratifying world records.

International Astronomical Union (IAU) The organization responsible for co-ordinating international co-operation and standardization in astronomy, founded in 1919, with its secretariat in Paris. There were sixty-seven participating countries and over 9000 individual members in 2004. The IAU is the sole internationally recognized authority for naming celestial bodies and their surface features.

International Atomic Energy Agency (IAEA) An international agency which promotes research and development into the peaceful uses of nuclear energy, and oversees a system of safeguards and controls governing the misuse of nuclear materials for military purposes. Founded in 1957, and based in Vienna, in 2004 it had 137 member countries.

International Baccalaureate An award taken by 18-year-old school leavers, and accepted in most countries as a qualification for entry to higher education. Particularly popular in international schools or with students whose parents have to work abroad, the examination covers a spread of subjects including languages, mathematics, science, humanities, and the arts.

International Bank for Reconstruction and Development (IBRD) A bank, generally known as the **World Bank**, founded in 1945, to help raise standards of living in the developing countries. It is affiliated to the United Nations, and based in Washington, DC. By the early 21st-c, agriculture and rural development had become the most important lending area. Industry, water-supply, and sewage systems, as well as education, are also major lending areas.

International Bill of Rights *Universal Declaration of Human Rights*

International Brigades In the Spanish Civil War (1936–9), foreign volunteer forces recruited by the Comintern and by individual communist parties to assist the Spanish Republic. Almost 60 000 volunteers, mostly workers and refugees from Fascism, plus its French, British, and American opponents, fought in Spain between October 1936 and the brigades' withdrawal in October 1938. They played a particularly important role in the defence of Madrid (1936–7). They also contributed to the capture of Belchite and Teruel. The volunteers lost almost 10 000, out of a total of 59 380 men.

International Bureau for American Republics *Pan-American Union*

International Business Machines Inc (IBM) A US computer manufacturing and sales company, for many years the most successful in the world. Although initially concerned with mainframe computers, it launched the IBM personal computer in 1983. Their machines, now including other personal computers of the same design (**IBM compatible** computers), occupy c.85% of the personal computer market. Although still a major provider of computer hardware, IBM has now diversified into **facilities management**, providing total support (both development and operations) for an organization's computing needs.

International Campaign to Ban Landmines (ICBL) A campaign, launched in 1991, with the aim of banning antipersonnel landmines. There are thought to be over 100 million such mines scattered over large areas on several continents, a deadly legacy of conflicts in Afghanistan, Cambodia, Angola, Iraq, Vietnam, and the former Yugoslavia. Around 20 000 people annually, many of them children, are killed or disfigured by mines. Many rural dwellers returning to farm lands have to clear the areas of mines. The campaign is coordinated by a steering committee of 16 organizations, and brings together over 1,300 non-governmental organizations in over 75 countries. The campaign and its coordinator, Jody Williams, shared the Nobel Peace Prize in 1997. A treaty signed by 133 countries, and ratified by 58, to ban the use, production, stockpiling, and transfer of landmines, became international law in March 1999.

International Cometary Explorer (ICE) project The first space mission to encounter a comet, flying through the dust and ion tails of the periodic Comet Giacobini-Zinner (11 Sep 1985). Originally launched in 1978 as the International Sun–Earth Explorer to monitor solar wind at Earth–Sun Lagrangian point L1, it was retargeted to the comet in 1983 by means of a series of propulsive manoeuvres, multiple Earth swing-bys, and a final close lunar flyby which added the gravitational energy needed to place the spacecraft on a comet-intercept trajectory. It made the first measurements of the interaction of a comet with the solar wind, and demonstrated an ability to survive a high speed 21 km/s (13 mi/s) encounter with cometary dust. It was managed by NASA's Goddard Space Flight Center.

International Confederation of Free Trade Unions (ICFTU) An association of some 233 trade union federations from 152 countries and territories (in 2004) on all five continents, with a membership of over 158 million, located in Brussels. It was founded in 1949 after withdrawing from the World Federation of Trade Unions because of differences with the communist unions. Its aim is collaboration between free and democratic trade unions throughout the world. It organizes and directs campaigns on issues such as workers' rights, the eradication of child labour, the promotion of equal rights for working women, and the environment.

International Court of Justice A court established by the United Nations Organization for the purpose of hearing international legal disputes; known widely as the 'World Court'. Nation states must consent to the jurisdiction of the court with regard to contentious proceedings. The court sits at The Hague, The Netherlands, and is presided over by 15 judges. Disputes are decided in accordance with international law, customs, or conventions, or, if the parties agree, on the basis of a 'fair solution'. The court's judgments may be enforced by the United Nations Security Council.

international date line *Date Line*

International Development Association (IDA) An organization affiliated to, but distinct from, the International Bank for Reconstruction and Development, based in Washington, DC. It was set up in 1960 to provide help to the world's 50 poorest countries by giving them aid on very easy terms.

International Finance Corporation (IFC) An institution for lending to the private sector in developing countries, affiliated to the World Bank. The IFC was founded in 1956 to supplement the work of the World Bank or International Bank for Reconstruction and Development (IBRD), which lent only to the state sector or with state guarantees. It was believed that development would be faster if the private sector invested more in developing countries, and that this could be encouraged by an international institution. Like the IBRD, the IFC is based in Washington. It borrows from the IBRD, and both lends its own money to the private sector in developing countries, and guarantees loans from private investors. It can also hold some equity in projects it finances.

International Gothic A style of art which flourished in W Europe c.1375–c.1425, characterized by jewel-like colour, graceful shapes, and realistically-observed details. The style was seen especially in miniature paintings, drawings, and tapestries, often representing secular themes from courtly life.

International Labour Organization (ILO) An autonomous agency associated with the League of Nations, founded in 1919, which became a specialized agency of the United Nations in 1946; it had 180 members in 2004. A tripartite body representing governments, employers, and workers, it is concerned with industrial relations and the pay, employment, and working conditions of workers.

international law The law that governs relationships between nation states. It is based principally on custom and treaties; there is no worldwide international legislature, and thus the enforcement and interpretation of international law may pose problems. Although there is an International Court, it may only adjudicate with the consent of the parties. Alternative use of sanctions may well be unsatisfactory if the injured state is less powerful than the wrongdoer. The United Nations Security Council has a limited power to impose sanctions on behalf of member states. International law is also known as **public international law**, as distinct from **private international law** which regulates, in cases involving citizens of two or more countries, which country's courts and laws should be applied.

International Monetary Fund (IMF) A financial agency affiliated to the United Nations, and located in Washington, DC. It was formed in 1945 to promote international monetary co-operation, trade and exchange rate stability, and economic growth and high levels of employment, and to give temporary financial and technical assistance to states in need. It had 184 members in 2004.

international monetary system A financial system which enables international trade to function effectively. Until 1914, the pound sterling was the currency in which most world trade was conducted. By 1945, the US dollar had taken over the role. The Bretton Woods Agreement established exchange rates for most major currencies which linked the dollar to the price of gold. By 1973 this system was working less well, and was abandoned in favour of a system of floating exchange rates. Governments intervened from time to time to control the exchange rates of their currencies by, for example, raising or lowering interest rates. The EU nations then moved towards a linked currency system, with several countries eventually adopting the Euro. Some countries have convertible currencies, in that they can be bought and sold freely and exchanged for one another. The developing nations often restrict movement of their currency and the export of foreign exchange. The 'money markets' of London, New York, and Tokyo are the major centres for the sale and purchase of convertible currencies.

International Olympic Committee (IOC) The multi-sport organizational body responsible for the summer and winter Olympics, held every four years. It was formed in 1894 by Pierre de Fredi, Baron de Coubertin. Member countries of the IOC are allowed two delegates on the organization's ruling body. In 1998-9, its international image was tarnished when it was revealed that cities bidding to host the Olympics had offered delegates incentives that breached IOC regulations.

International Organization for Standardization A non-governmental organization established in 1947 for the preparation of international standards for materials, products, and codes of practice; its headquarters are in Geneva, Switzerland. It coordinates the activities of over 130 regional standardization organizations.

International Packet Switching Service (IPSS) A service provided by the Posts, Telegraph and Telephones Authorities which allows a computer to send a packet of data to another computer anywhere in the world, without a dedicated physical wire communication being established between the two. The sender is charged only for the number of packets and their destination, and not for the length of time that the sender and receiver are linked together.

International Save the Children Alliance *Save the Children Fund*

International Space Station (ISS) A multinational space station planned to orbit Earth at an altitude of 400 km/250 mi with an inclination of 51·6°. Begun as a NASA project in the 1980s, the ISS has evolved into an international programme led by the USA and also involving Russia, Canada, Japan, Brazil, and the 11 nations of the European Space Agency. On planned completion in 2004, the ISS will have a mass of about 450 000 kg/1 000 000 lb and will measure 107 m/356 ft across and 88 m/290 ft in length. Power is provided by solar electric panels covering about 0·4 ha/1 acre. About 160 US and Russian spacewalks are required over five years to construct and maintain the ISS. Thirty-six launches of the Shuttle and nine launches of Russian vehicles will be required. The six laboratories of the ISS will be used for research in space medicine, gravitational biology, and microgravity sciences such as crystal growth, materials science, and combustion science. The first two station modules were assembled in orbit in late 1998 and the first 3-person crew to live aboard the ISS was launched in late 2000. The construction phase was preceded by the Shuttle-Mir programme. In April 2001 the station welcomed its first 'space tourist', retired American businessman, Dennis Tito.

International Standard Book Numbering (ISBN) A system of 10-digit numbers allocated to books on publication. Internationally adopted in 1971, it simplifies identification and ordering, since each book has its own individual number printed on the reverse of the title page and on the back cover.

International Style **1** A term sometimes used by art historians to refer to the more or less homogeneous Gothic style which flourished throughout Europe c.1400.

2 A term first used in the USA to describe a new style of architecture developed in the 1920s, principally in Europe; also known as the **Modern Movement**. It is characterized by geometric shapes, an absence of decoration and historical references, white rendered walls, flat roofs, large expanses of glass, pilotis, and asymmetrical compositions. It was at first particularly concerned with low-income, standardized housing projects.

International Telecommunication Union (ITU) An agency of the United Nations, which since 1947 has promoted worldwide co-operation in all aspects of telecommunications, such as the regulation of global telecom networks and radio frequencies. The ITU organizes internal conferences and manages its own publications and databases. Originally founded in Paris in 1865, it acquired its present name in 1934, and is now headquartered in Geneva, Switzerland.

International UN Agencies *United Nations*

International Union for the Conservation of Nature and Natural Resources (IUCN) An international organization which exists to promote sustainable use and conservation of natural resources. Founded in 1948, and based in Switzerland, by 2004 the members made up a global network of 1010 institutions and organizations in over 140 countries. Its Commissions consist of more than 10 000 conservation experts from over 180 countries. It publishes Red Data books which list endangered species of plants and wildlife, and administers the Convention on International Trade in Endangered Species.

International Union of Pure and Applied Chemistry *IUPAC*

International Working Men's Association *International*

International Youth Hostel Association An organization found in some 50 countries which provides simple, low-cost accommodation for those wishing to travel. In many youth hostels the guests cook their own meals and help with the cleaning; in some countries there is a maximum age limit for guests.

Internet An association of computer networks with common standards which enable messages to be sent from any host on one network to any host on any other. It developed in the 1970s in the USA as an experimental network designed to support military research, and steadily grew to include federal, regional, campus, and other users. Growth has been particularly rapid since 1990. It is now the world's largest computer network, with over 100 million hosts connected by 2000, providing an increasing range of services and enabling unprecedented numbers of people to be in touch with each other through electronic mail, discussion groups, and the provision of digital 'pages' on every conceivable topic. The **World Wide Web** is an Internet facility designed for multimedia use, in which individuals or organizations make available 'pages' of information to other users anywhere in the world, generally at no cost, but in the case of certain commercial operations (such as an encyclopedia or electronic journal) through subscription. Functional information, such as electronic shopping, business data, advertisements, and bulletins, can be found alongside creative works, such as novels, poems, and scripts, with the availability of movies, TV programmes, and other kinds of entertainment being actively progressed. Some commentators have likened the Internet to an amalgam of television, telephone, and conventional publishing, and the term **cyberspace** has been coined to capture the notion of a world of information present or possible in digital form (the **information superhighway**). During the 1990s, alongside claims that the Internet provides fresh opportunities for self-publishing, creativity, and freedom of speech, there has been increasing concern about the safeguarding of rights of privacy and intellectual property (copyright), the application of existing laws to the Internet (in such domains as pornography and libel), the extent to which the content of some of the new 'virtual communities' can or should be regulated, and the impact that the growing numbers of Internet communities ('cyburbia') will have on individuals and on society as a whole. The potential of the Internet is also currently limited by relatively slow data-transmission speeds, and by the problems of information management and retrieval posed by the existence of such a vast amount of information.

Internet Service Provider (ISP) An organization which offers access to the Internet to individuals who do not belong to an organization (such as a university or a large company) which is connected directly. A home PC can be linked to the ISP via a modem and the public telephone network; the ISP then provides the additional connection to the Internet. Most ISPs also offer many value-added services, such as mailboxes and Web pages.

interplanetary matter Material in the Solar System other than the planets and their satellites. It includes streams of charged particles from the solar wind, dust, meteorites, and comets.

Interpol [interpol] Originally the telegraphic address, adopted in 1946, of the **International Criminal Police Organization** (earlier, **Commission**), initiated by Prince Albert I of Monaco in 1914. The address became widely used as a name, and was formally incorporated into the organization's title in 1956 as **ICPO–Interpol**. It is an international organization which exists to promote international co-operation in law enforcement. Member states are linked by a sophisticated, secure messaging system, and have direct access to specially designed international law enforcement databases, to assist national police forces with international enquiries. Interpol manages and stores information on behalf of its members, and also provides criminal analysis services from its own global viewpoint. A key factor in international co-operation is understanding the different legal frameworks within which national police forces work; Interpol works to promote harmonization in this area, and offers model legislation on such topics as extradition. Based in Lyon, France, it had 181 members in 2004.

interpolation In mathematics, estimating an intermediate value of a variable between two known values of that variable; for example, if $f(1)$ and $f(2)$ are known, estimating $f(1{\cdot}1)$. **Linear interpolation** is the form used most frequently, which assumes that the function $f(x)$ is linear. Then if $x_0 < x_0 + h < x_1$,

$$f(x_0 + h) = \frac{f(x_1) - f(x_0)}{x_1 - x_0}.$$

If $x_1 - x_0$ is small, this is likely to be a good approximation. **Extrapolation** is estimating a value of a variable *outside* the interval between two known values; for example, if $f(1)$ and $f(2)$ are known, estimating $f(2{\cdot}1)$. This is often not justified mathematically, but may be necessary in making projections for the future.

interpreter A computer program which reads source code written in a high-level computer language, one statement at a time, and carries out the computer instructions implied by that statement immediately. It differs in this respect from a *compiler*, which checks and translates the entire source code into a set of equivalent machine-code instructions (the object code).

intersection (mathematics) *set*

intersexuality Abnormal sexual development, either because of anomalies in the normal complement of sex chromosomes (XX in the female and XY in the male) or as a result of faults in the development of gonads in the early embryo. Thus babies may be born whose sex is in doubt, while in other cases intersex or ambiguous sexual states may be suspected only at puberty. Detailed chromosomal studies, the estimation of sex hormone secretions, and biopsy of sex glands may be needed to disentangle what is a complex but rare problem.

interstellar molecule More than 100 species of molecule are found within the gas nebulae of the interstellar medium, particularly in cold dense clouds. The most common include CO, H_2O, NH_3, HCHO, CH_4, and CH_3OH.

interstitial cells *Leydig cells*

interstitial cell-stimulating hormone *luteinizing hormone*

interstitial fluid [interstishl] That part of the extracellular fluid which lies outside the vascular system and surrounds the tissue cells of animals; also known as **tissue fluid** and **intercellular fluid**. It is similar in composition to blood plasma, except for a relatively low protein content (due to the low permeability of capillaries to plasma proteins).

intertidal zone *benthic environments*

intertropical convergence zone (ITCZ) A discontinuous zone of low pressure around the Equator, on which the NE and SE trade winds converge. The converging air rises, lowering the atmospheric pressure, and convective clouds form, associated with heavy precipitation. The ITCZ coincides approximately with the heat equator, and shifts N and S with the seasons, through about 5° of latitude. The zone is weakly defined over the oceans, particularly in the areas known as the Doldrums.

interval In mathematics, all numbers between two fixed numbers a and b form an **open interval**, written (a,b). If the numbers a and b are themselves included in the interval, this is called a **closed interval** $[a,b]$. a and b are the *limits* of the interval. An open interval is represented on the number-line with the end-circles unshaded; a closed interval has shaded end-circles.

intestacy The situation where a person dies without a valid will. In the case of a **partial intestacy**, the will does not provide for the disposal of the entire estate. In the USA, statute laws govern the rules of intestate succession, ie, the distribution of the deceased's property. In England and Wales, the statutory rules which govern succession on an intestacy provide that any surviving spouse is given the larger share of the estate.

intestine A tube of muscular membrane extending from the pyloric opening of the stomach to the anus, generally divided into the **small intestine** (*duodenum*, *jejunum*, and *ileum*), the **large intestine** (*caecum*, *appendix*, and the *ascending*, *transverse*, *descending*, and *sigmoid colon*), and the **rectum**. Most digestion and absorption of digestive products, vitamins, and fluids (both ingested and secreted from the gastro-intestinal tract) occurs in the small intestine, while the large intestine absorbs electrolytes and water from the fluid that enters it, as well as synthesizing vitamin K and some B complex vitamins, and forming the faeces ready for expulsion from the body. The rectum lies in contact with the pelvic surface of the sacrum, and pierces the pelvic diaphragm to become the anal canal, which opens at the anus. The length of the small intestine is c.6 m/20 ft, and of the large intestine is c.1 m/5 ft, but there is considerable variation. Medical problems affecting the intestine include coeliac disease, colic, colitis, diverticulosis, dysentery, hernia, and irritable bowel syndrome.

Intifada [intifahda] A Palestinian uprising which erupted in December 1987 in the Gaza Strip and quickly spread to the West Bank. The uprising reflected frustrations with two decades of Israeli military occupation, the expansion of Israeli settlement in the Occupied Territories of Gaza and the West Bank, and the failure of the PLO and the Arab states to change the status quo. The tactic of rock-throwing mass demonstrations provoked an armed response from Israeli forces which claimed nearly 1000 Palestinian lives. However, the Intifada is credited with breaking the political deadlock. The peace talks initiated by the 1991 Madrid Conference are seen as one consequence of the uprising, as are the signing of the 1993 peace accord and the formation in 1994 of a limited self-governing Palestinian presence in Gaza and Jericho. The term *intifada* has since been used to refer to the 1991 Shiite uprisings in S Iraq against Saddam Hussein's rule, and is now used to mean any mass uprising against oppressive rule.

Intimisme [ĩnteemeezm] A modern art movement that flourished from c.1890 in France. Vuillard's quiet little paintings and lithographs of Montmartre, and Bonnard's more colourful nudes and family scenes typify the movement.

Intolerable Acts (1774) The American name for laws passed by parliament to punish Massachusetts for the Boston Tea Party (1773). They were the Boston Port Act, the Massachusetts Government Act, the Administration of Justice Act, and a Quartering Act.

intonaco *fresco*

intonation The melody of an utterance, brought about by the distinctive use of pitch patterns in sentences. It has several functions, notably the marking of grammatical structure (eg statements with a falling pitch, and questions with a rising pitch), and the expression of speaker attitudes (eg surprise, sympathy, irony).

intoxilyzer *breathalyzer*

intracellular fluid The fluid contained within cells. In humans the total adult volume is about 28 l/49 UK pt/59 US pt. Its composition varies from tissue to tissue depending on their functions. Its principal components (apart from water) are potassium ions, organic phosphates, and proteins.

Intracoastal Waterway A shipping route extending 5000 km/3100 mi along the E coast of the USA from Massachusetts to Florida (the **Atlantic Intracoastal Waterway**) and from Apalachee Bay, Florida, to Brownsville, Texas (the **Gulf Intracoastal Waterway**). The waterway is composed of natural water routes, such as bays and rivers, linked by canals. It is used by both commercial and pleasure craft.

intra-industry trade Trade where countries import and export goods produced by the same industries. *Intra-industry trade* is contrasted with *inter-industry trade*, where countries export the products of some industrial sectors and import those of different sectors. Inter-industry trade is thus trade between countries whose economic structure is different; intra-industry trade is between countries whose economic structure is similar. The point of intra-industry trade in both final goods and intermediate products is to enable countries to combine economies of scale in production with a wide choice of products for consumers. Exactly how much intra-industy trade there is depends on how wide or narrow a definition of industry is used, but on a wide definition about half of world trade is now intra-industry, mainly between industrial countries.

Intranet The use of Internet technology to provide an organization with an internal communications network. A development of the mid-1990s, such networks can either be linked to the global Internet, or be completely isolated from it. An Intranet system which permits links to selected outside organizations is an *Extranet*.

intra-ocular lens implantation A perspex lens introduced into the front chamber of the eye following surgical removal of a cataract. The power of the lens chosen is calculated from the curvature of the cornea and the length of the eye.

intra-uterine device *contraception*

intravenous feeding Nutrients given to a patient through a tube which enters the bloodstream directly via a vein; also known as **parenteral nutrition**. All nutrients used are of basic structure, ie glucose and not starch; amino acids and not protein.

Intrepid *Stephenson, William*

intron A non-coding sequence that occurs within a gene, separating two parts of the coding sequence; also known as an **intervening sequence**. Most genes have one or more introns. The initial transcript synthesized from a gene (known as the *primary transcript*) is a contiguous sequence of coding (**exons**) and non-coding (introns) RNA. The introns are removed and the exons joined together by a process known as *splicing*, to form messenger RNA (mRNA) which now possesses an uninterrupted protein reading frame or sequence. The mRNA is transported to the cytoplasm of the cell, where the genetic information it contains is translated into a protein.

introversion / extraversion Psychological terms formerly used as two categories of personality (**introvert**, **extravert**). The distinction is now considered to be a dimension with high levels of extraversion and introversion at the extremes. Strongly extraverted individuals are sociable, excitement-seeking, and carefree. They are often aggressive, may lose their temper quickly, and be unreliable. Strongly introverted individuals are quiet, reserved, and have few friends. They dislike excitement, are reliable, serious-minded, and like a well-ordered life. These behavioural differences are thought to have a biological basis in cortical and subcortical arousal systems.

intrusive rock Igneous rock formed by the emplacement and crystallization of magma formed at depth into higher levels of the Earth's crust. Igneous intrusions form a variety of rock masses.

intuitionism 1 In ethics, the view that we apprehend moral truths directly by a special faculty analogous to sense-perception. More generally, this is supposed to be an aspect of the faculty by which we apprehend all *a priori* truths.
2 In mathematics, the theory associated with Dutch mathematician L(uitzen) E(gbertus) J(an) Brouwer (1881–1966), equating truth with what can be proven. His approach attacked the logical foundations of mathematics, proposing instead a view of the subject as a set of mental constructs governed by self-evident laws. His work was seen as a major contribution to topology.

Inuit *Eskimo*

Invalides, Hôtel des [ohtel dayzãvaleed] A hospital for the care of old and disabled soldiers, founded in Paris by Louis XIV and built in 1671–6. The main building, which now houses fewer than 100 soldiers and is mainly given over to a museum, was designed by Libéral Bruant (c.1635–97). In the courtyard stands Hardouin-Mansart's St Louis Church, where Napoleon's tomb has rested since 1840.

Invar (trademark) [**invah(r)**] An alloy containing 65% iron with 35% nickel. It has very low thermal expansion, and hence is used in surveying rods and pendulum bars.

Inverness 57°27N 4°15W, pop (2000e) 43 500. Capital of Highland, NE Scotland, UK; at mouth of R Ness, 181 km/112 mi NW of Edinburgh; city status, 2000; airfield; railway; NE terminus of the Caledonian Canal; electronics, distilling, boatbuilding, textiles, tourism; Inverness museum and art gallery, castle (Victorian); battle site of Culloden Moor (1746), 8 km/5 mi E; Highland games (Jul).

inversion temperature *Joule–Thompson effect*

invertebrate A multicellular animal that lacks a vertebral column. It includes the vast majority (over 97%) of all animal species.

invert sugar *sucrose*

Investiture Controversy (1075–1122) A conflict between reforming popes and lay rulers, notably the German emperor, over the leadership of Christian society. It was named after the royal practice of investing a newly appointed bishop or abbot with a ring and pastoral staff, the symbols of his spiritual office. This was condemned in 1075 by Pope Gregory VII as epitomizing secular domination of the Church.

investment A term used in economics in two different, though related, senses: the acquisition of financial assets with a view to income or capital gains; and the creation of productive assets, which may be 'fixed investment' (ie buildings and equipment) or stocks and work in progress. The two activities may be connected, as when a company issues shares and uses the money to build a new factory. They may however be unconnected, as when an investor puts money in a bank which uses it to make consumer loans, or a firm builds a new works out of retained profits, without issuing any new shares. In ordinary speech the term *investment* is even more widely used: people 'invest' in works of art and antiques, and even in football pools.

investment bank A US bank handling new share issues, often in a syndicate with others. It may buy all the shares on offer and then resell them to the general public, in effect underwriting the issue. It is similar in function to a British merchant bank.

investment company or **investment trust** A company which holds a portfolio of shares in a range of other companies, aimed at obtaining a reasonable dividend yield, growth, and with less risk (ie a *balanced portfolio*). Such a company is of value to investors without experience or time who wish to invest in the stock market.

invisibles The export and import of services; opposed to goods, which are known as **visibles**. Invisible exports include tourism, shipping, air freight, banking, insurance, and other financial services. They are a major contributor to a country's balance of payments; total world trade in invisibles is believed to be equal to a quarter of visible trade in goods.

***in vitro* fertilization** *test-tube baby*

Inyangani, Mount [**inyangahnee**] 18°18S 32°54E. Highest peak in Zimbabwe; rises to 2592 m/8504 ft near the Mozambique frontier.

Io (astronomy) [**iyoh**] The first natural satellite of Jupiter, discovered by Galileo in 1610; distance from the planet 422 000 km/262 000 mi; diameter 3630 km/2260 mi; orbital period 1·769 days. It is the most volcanically active object in the Solar System, being in a state of continuous eruption; fountains of gases and fine particles have been observed by Voyager to reach altitudes of 280 km/175 mi. The volcanic features are found across the entire body, including hot regions that may be lava lakes.

Io (mythology) [**iyoh**] In Greek mythology, the daughter of Inachos of Argos. She was beloved by Zeus, who turned her into a heifer to save her from Hera's jealousy. Hera kept her under the gaze of Argus; but she escaped with Hermes's help. She was then punished with a gad-fly which drove her through the world until she arrived in Egypt. There Zeus changed her back into human shape, and she gave birth to Epaphos, ancestor of many peoples.

iodine I, element 53, melting point 114°C. A violet solid, made up of diatonic molecules I_2, with a sharp odour; a halogen, not found free in nature, but as an impurity in sodium nitrate deposits, and concentrated in kelp and other seaweeds. It is an essential element in biological systems, and lack of it causes goitre in humans. A dilute solution of iodine in ethanol (**tincture of iodine**) is a traditional household antiseptic. Its compounds show oxidation numbers of −1, +1, +3, +5, and +7.

iodoform [**iyohdofaw(r)m**] CHI_3, triiodomethane, melting point 119°C. A yellow solid with a peculiar odour, used as a mild antiseptic.

ion An atom which has lost one or more electrons (a *positive* ion) or which has gained one or more electrons (a *negative* ion). Atoms with a net positive charge are called **cations**; those with a net negative charge, **anions**. The type and magnitude of a charge is indicated by a superscript sign; for example, the positively charged sodium ion is identified as Na^+, and the negatively charged chloride ion as Cl^-. The formation of ions is called **ionization**: they may be formed by firing light or electrons on to atoms, or by passing an electric spark through gas. Ions are present in all animal and plant cells, where they are involved in many important and diverse roles, including the activation of enzymes, osmotic balance, muscle contraction, and nerve impulse conduction.

Iona [**iyohna**] A remote island off Mull, W Scotland, UK, the site of a monastery established in AD 563 by the Irish missionary St Columba and 12 companions to convert the inhabitants of N Britain to Christianity. The monastery flourished until the onset of Viking attacks (c.800), then declined until c.1200, when a Benedictine abbey was founded on the site.

ion engine An engine designed to propel spacecraft or manoeuvre satellites by means of the reaction caused by the discharge of charged particles (*ions*). These particles are accelerated within the engine by means of electrostatic fields. The continuous discharge of ions produces a charge of opposite polarity in the vehicle, which must be removed. This is usually accomplished by discharging separately charged negative and positive beams and recombining them behind the vehicle. The engine has an energy source, such as a nuclear reactor, and a conversion system that converts the reactor's heat into electricity. The electricity is then used to convert a propellant (such as argon) into an ionized state, and then to accelerate it.

Ionesco, Eugène [**yoneskoh**] (1912–94) Playwright, born in Slatina, S Romania. He studied in Bucharest and Paris, where he settled before World War 2. After the success of *La Cantatrice chauve* (1950, trans The Bald Prima Donna), he became a prolific writer of one-act plays which came to be seen as typical examples of the Theatre of the Absurd, such as *Les Chaises* (1952, The Chairs) and *Rhinocéros* (1960). His later, full-length plays centre around a constant, semi-autobiographical figure, Bérenger, who, isolated from the rest of humanity, faces as best he can the cruelties of life. Ionesco's *Notes and Counternotes* (1962) expresses his ideas on theatre and on writing plays. After 1970, his writing was mainly non-theatrical, including essays, children's stories, and a novel.

Ionia [**iyohnia**] In antiquity, the C part of the W coast of Asia Minor, the birthplace of Greek philosophy and science. The name came from the extensive occupation of the area by Ionian Greeks around the beginning of the first millennium BC.

Ionian Islands [**iyohnian**], Gr **Ioníai Nísoi** or **Eptánisos** pop (2000e) 200 000; area 2307 sq km/890 sq mi. Region and island group of W Greece, from the Albanian frontier to the Peloponnese; a chain of about 40 islands, including Corfu, Cephalonia, and Zacynthus; under British control, 1815–64; mountainous with fertile plains and valleys; wine, olives, fruit, tourism.

Ionian Sea [**iyohnian**] Part of the Mediterranean Sea, lying W of the Greek islands and S of Italy; separated from the Adriatic Sea by the Strait of Otranto; connected to the Aegean Sea by the Sea of Crete.

ionic *chemical bond*

Ionic order [iyonik] One of the five main orders of classical architecture; lighter and more elegant than the Doric, with slim, usually fluted shafts and spiral scrolls known as *volutes* on the capitals. It originated in Ionia in the 6th-c BC.

ionization *ion*

ionization energy The energy required to remove an electron from an atom in the gas phase. This is characteristic of an atom, and is relatively low for alkali metals (eg 500 kJ mol^{-1} for sodium) and relatively high for halogens (eg 1680 kJ mol^{-1} for fluorine).

ionizer [iyoniyzer] An electrical apparatus which generates a negative electrical charge that is taken up by airborne particles, including smoke and dust; these are then attracted to earth, thus clearing the air. The electrical activity from appliances such as heaters, computers, and televisions tends to destroy negative charges, leaving the atmosphere with a relative positive charge which is thought to contribute to respiratory problems, headaches, allergies, and depression. The manufacturers of ionizers claim beneficial effects on health, with improvements in alertness, concentration, and productivity.

ionosphere The region of the Earth's upper atmosphere from c.50–500 km/30–300 mi in height where short-wave radiation from the Sun is absorbed and partly ionizes the gas molecules or atoms, removing their outer electrons and leaving them positively charged. The ionized layers reflect short-wavelength radio waves, and so make long-distance radio communication possible. The ionosphere is layered according to the concentration of free electrons: the lowest layers, termed D and E (also called the *Heaviside* or *Kennelly layer*) result from molecular ionization, and the upper layer F (the *Appleton layer*) from atomic ionization. The thicknesses of the layers vary with latitude, season, time of day, and solar activity.

ion plating Coating a metal surface by exposing it to ions of a metal, generated by discharge or thermionically. The ions are directed to the metal by making it the cathode in a low pressure discharge circuit. Non-conductors may also be ion-plated by siting them in a shielded region of ion transfer. The special value of the process is its ability to coat intricate and convoluted surfaces uniformly and firmly.

ion trap A device for confining ions slowed by laser cooling to a region typically less than a centimetre across. It relies on a system of electric and magnetic fields. Ions may be trapped singly or in clusters, thus enabling the study of their properties, such as energy levels, lifetimes, and reactions. A Penning trap uses a fixed electric field and uniform magnetic field; a Paul trap relies on time-varying electric fields but no magnetic field.

Ios [eeos] 36°43N 25°17E; area 108 sq km/42 sq mi. Island of the Cyclades, Greece, in the Aegean Sea, SSW of Naxos; linked by boat to Piraeus, Paros, and Santorini; Homer is said to have died here; port of Ormos Iou on the W coast.

Iowa [iyohwa] pop (2000e) 2 926 300; area 145 747 sq km/ 56 275 sq mi. State in NC USA, divided into 99 counties; the 'Hawkeye State'; 29th state admitted to the Union, 1846; became part of USA with the Louisiana Purchase, 1803; became a state, 1846; capital moved from Iowa City to Des Moines, 1857; other chief cities, Cedar Rapids, Davenport, Sioux City; Mississippi R follows the E border; Des Moines R flows SE before emptying into the Mississippi; Big Sioux R forms the border with South Dakota, emptying into the Missouri R, which then follows the Nebraska state border; highest point is Ocheyedan Mound (511 m/1677 ft); almost entirely prairie-land (95%) with rich soil; chief crops corn and soybeans; over half the corn grown used for feeding pigs and cattle; leads the nation in corn and pig production; industry dominated by food processing and machinery manufacture; also chemicals, electrical equipment.

Ipatieff, Vladimir Nikolayevich [eepatyef] (1867–1952) Chemist, born in Moscow, Russia. An officer in the Russian army, he was professor of chemistry at the Artillery Academy in St Petersburg (1898–1906). He synthesized isoprene, the basic unit of natural rubber, and made contributions to the catalytic chemistry of unsaturated carbons, of great value to the petrochemical industry. During World War 1 he directed Russia's chemical industry. He emigrated to the USA in 1930, and became professor at Northwestern University (1931–5), where he developed a process for making high-octane petrol.

ipecacuanha [ipikakyooahna] A perennial (*Cephaelis ipecacuanha*) with roots thickened to resemble a string of beads, native to Brazil; stems sprawling; leaves oval; flowers small, white, in heads. The roots provide the drug ipecacuanha, used to induce vomiting and to treat dysentery. (Family: Rubiaceae.)

Iphigeneia [iyfijeniya] According to Greek legend, the daughter of Agamemnon and Clytemnestra. She was about to be sacrificed at Aulis as the fleet could not sail to Troy, because the winds were against it. At the last moment she was saved by Artemis, who made her a priestess in the country of the Tauri (the Crimea). Finally her brother Orestes saved her.

Ipswich, Anglo-Saxon **Gipeswic** 52°04N 1°10E, pop (2001e) 117 100. Port and county town in Suffolk, E England, UK; at the head of the R Orwell estuary, 106 km/66 mi NE of London; a major wool port in the 16th-c; birthplace of Cardinal Wolsey; home of Thomas Gainsborough; railway; engineering, brewing, food processing, agricultural machinery, electrical equipment, textiles, tobacco products, fertilizers, plastics; Churches of St Mary-le-Tower and St Margaret, Ipswich museum; music festival at Aldeburgh (32 km/20 mi NE); football league team, Ipswich Town.

IQ *intelligence*

Iqbal, Sir Mohammed [ikbal] (1876–1938) Poet and philosopher, born in Sialkot, NE Pakistan. He studied at Lahore, Cambridge (where he read law and philosophy), and Munich. On his return to India, he achieved fame through his poetry, whose compelling mysticism and nationalism caused him to be regarded almost as a prophet by Muslims. His efforts to establish a separate Muslim state eventually led to the formation of Pakistan. He was knighted in 1923.

Iquique [eekeekay] 20°13S 70°09W, pop (2000e) 171 700. Port capital of Tarapacá region, N Chile; free port, S of Arica; founded in 16th-c; partly destroyed by earthquake, 1877; scene of naval battle in War of the Pacific (1879); airfield; railway; trade in fishmeal, fish oil, tinned fish, salt, nitrates; naval museum, Palacio Astoreca (1904); La Fiesta de Tirana (religious festival) 70 km/40 mi E (Jul).

Iquitos [eekeetohs] 3°51S 73°13W, pop (2000e) 314 000. Capital of Loreto department, NE Peru; fast-developing city on the W bank of the Amazon, 3700 km/2300 mi from its mouth; limit of navigation for ocean vessels; access only by air and river; university (1962); chief town of Peru's jungle region; rubber, nuts, timber; centre for oil exploration in Peruvian Amazonia.

IRA Abbreviation of **Irish Republican Army**, an anti-British paramilitary force established in 1919 by Irish nationalists to combat British and Protestant Irish forces in Ireland. It opposed the Anglo-Irish Treaty of 1921 because Ireland was a dominion and the six counties of the North of Ireland were part of the UK, but it was suppressed by the Irish government in the 1922 rising, and remained largely inactive until the late 1960s. In 1969, a major split in its ranks led to the formation of the **Provisional IRA** alongside the **Official IRA**, and a serious schism between the two sides in the early 1970s. The Official IRA was virtually inactive after 1972, and generally supported political action to achieve Irish unity. The Provisionals became the dominant republican force, responsible for shootings and bombings in the N of Ireland, Britain, and W Europe. Targets were mainly British security and military personnel and establishments, although there were many sectarian killings of Protestant paramilitary opponents, and bombings of economic targets on mainland Britain. At any time during the period of 'The Troubles' its total membership was reputed to be c.500. The organization announced a ceasefire (1994), but this was withdrawn (1996) following dissatisfaction with political progress, and a new campaign began, with bombs causing severe damage in Docklands, London, and Manchester, UK. The ceasefire was resumed in 1997, and Sinn Féin, the political wing of the IRA, entered into talks with the new Blair government. These led to the Good Friday Agreement of 1998, when the IRA accepted that Northern Ireland would remain part of the UK in return for a Northern Ireland Assembly and executive, structured to ensure cross-community participation. Under the mediation of former US senator George Mitchell and the British minister for Northern Ireland, Peter Mandelson, the Unionists dropped their demand that decommissioning of arms must precede Sinn Féin's participation in government, and the new Northern Ireland Assembly came into effect in December 1999, with former IRA activists assuming power-sharing roles (suspended Feb–May 2000, because of a lack of progress on arms decommissioning). Since 1997, new dissident organizations opposed to the peace process have emerged (the **Real IRA**, the **Continuity IRA**), with an ongoing programme of violence. In 2001 the IRA announced that it would begin the process of arms decommissioning, a move that was perceived as a breakthrough in paving the way for a new beginning in the peace process.

Iran *see panel*

Iran–Contra scandal or **Irangate** A political scandal in 1986 that grew out of the Reagan administration's efforts to obtain the release of US captives held in the Middle East by the covert supply of arms to the government of Iran, which was believed to have influence with the captors; popularly known as **Irangate**. In an additional complication, officials (notably, Colonel Oliver North) tried to use the proceeds of arms sales to Iran as a means of financing support for the anti-government Contra rebels in Nicaragua, despite official prohibition by Congress, and without the knowledge of the president. In addition to questions surrounding violations of the law, the affair raised issues concerning executive incompetence, which a Congressional Committee reported on in 1988.

Irangate *Iran–Contra scandal*

Iranian languages A branch of the E Indo-European language family, spoken in the region of present-day Iran and Afghanistan. Old Persian, and Avestan, in which the sacred texts of the

Iran

[iran], formerly **Persia** (to 1935), official name **Islamic Republic of Iran**, Farsi **Jumhuri-e-Eslami-e-Iran**

Local name Īrān

Timezone GMT + 3·5

Area 1 648 000 km²/636 128 sq mi

Population total (2002e) 65 457 000

Status Islamic Republic

Date of independence 1925

Capital Tehran

Languages Farsi (Persian) (official), several minority languages including Kurdish, Baluchi, Luri, and Turkic (including Afshari, Shahsavani, and Turkish)

Ethnic groups Persian (63%), Turkic (18%), other Iranian (13%), Kurdish (3%), Arab, and other Semitic (3%)

Religions Muslim (Shi'ite 93%, Sunni 5%), Zoroastrian (2%), Jewish, Baha'i, and Christian (1%)

Physical features Largely composed of a vast arid C plateau, average elevation 1200 m/4000 ft; bounded N by the Elburz Mts, rising to 5670 m/18 602 ft at Mt Damavand; Zagros Mts in W and S.

Climate Mainly a desert climate, hot and humid on Persian Gulf; average annual temperatures 2·2°C (Jan), 29·4°C (Jul) in Tehran; average annual rainfall 246 mm/9·7 in; frequent earthquakes; preserved medieval city of Bam in SE destroyed in earthquake, 2003.

Currency 1 Iranian Rial (RIs, RI) = 100 dinars

Economy World's fourth largest oil producer, but production severely disrupted by 1978 revolution, and Gulf War, 1991; agriculture and forestry (employs a third of population); natural gas, iron ore, copper, coal, salt; textiles, sugar refining, petrochemicals; traditional handicrafts (especially carpets).

GDP (2002e) $458·3 bn, per capita $6800

Human Development Index (2002) 0·721

History Early centre of civilization, dynasties including the Achaemenids and Sassanids; ruled by Arabs, Turks, and Mongols until the Sasavid dynasty in the 16th–18th-c, and the Qajar dynasty in the 19th–20th-c; military coup, 1921, with independence under Reza Shah Pahlavi, 1925; changed name from Persia to Iran, 1935; protests against Shah's regime in 1970s led to revolution, 1978; exile of Shah, and proclamation of Islamic Republic under Ayatollah Khomeini, 1979; Islamic Cultural Revolution under Khomeini saw a return to strict observance of Muslim principles and traditions; occupation of US Embassy in Tehran, 1979–81; Gulf War following invasion of Iraq, 1980–8; overall authority exercised by appointed spiritual leader: post of Prime Minister abolished, 1989; governed by a President and a Consultative Assembly (Majlis).

Shah
1896–1907 Muzaffar-ud-Din
1907–9 Mohammed Ali
1909–25 Ahmad Mirza
1925–41 Reza Khan
1941–79 Mohammed Reza Pahlavi

Republic

Leader of the Islamic Revolution
1979–89 Ayatollah Khomeini
1989– Ayatollah Sayed Ali Khamenei

Head of State/Government
1980–1 Abolhassan Bani-Sadr
1981 Mohammed Ali Rajai
1981–9 Seyed Ali Khamenei
1989–97 Ali Akbar Hashemi Rafsanjani
1997– Sayed Mohammad Khatami

Zoroastrians was written, are recorded from the 6th-c BC. Modern Iranian languages, of which Persian (Farsi) is one of the major examples, are spoken by over 60 million people.

Iranian Revolution One of the great revolutions of modern history which, like the French or Russian, confronted the West with a disruptive new political order. The consequence of widespread discontent at rapid socio-economic change and the authoritarian rule of the shah, the revolution took the exiled religious scholar Ayatollah Khomeini as its figurehead. A cycle of demonstrations was initiated when six theology students in Qom were killed by security forces (Jan 1978), which culminated in the massacre of hundreds of protestors in Tehran's Juleh Square (Sep 1978). Unable to regain control without yet more violent repression, the shah went into exile (Jan 1979). On 1 February Khomeini returned to Iran to lead the revolution and the establishment of the Islamic Republic.

Iran–Iraq War (1980–8) A war between Iran and Iraq, which began as an Iraqi attempt under the aggressive leadership of Saddam Hussein to overthrow the new Islamic republic of Iran under Ayatollah Khomeini. The secular Baath regime in Baghdad claimed it feared Iranian attempts to export its revolution. The surprise Iraqi invasion was soon halted, and the war deteriorated into a series of costly and futile battles. Both sides reluctantly accepted a UN ceasefire in July 1988. There was no victor, but one million casualties, great economic hardship, and widespread destruction.

Iraq *see panel*

Iraq War (Mar–Apr 2003) A war between Iraq and US-led coalition forces, brought about by Iraq's apparent continued failure

Iraq

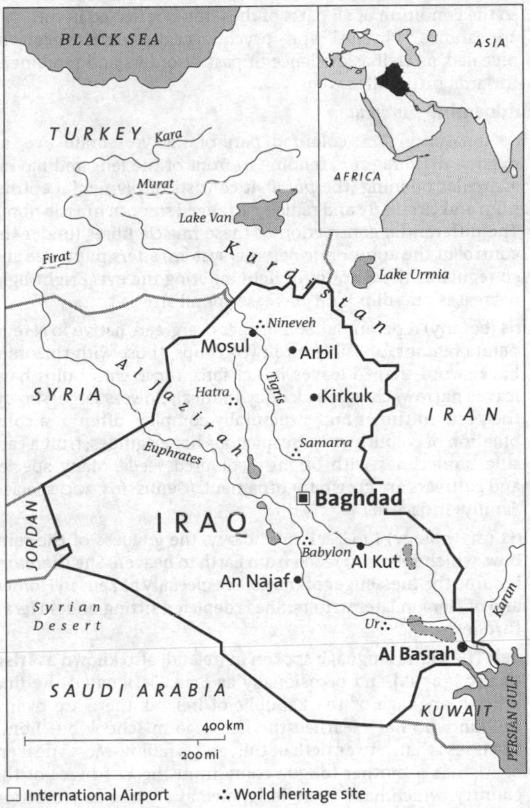

[irak], official name **Republic of Iraq**, Arabic **al-Jumhuriya al-Iraquia**

Local name Al-'Īrāq

Timezone GMT +3

Area 434 925 km²/167 881 sq mi

Population total (2002e) 24 002 000

Status Republic

Date of independence 1932

Capital Baghdad

Languages Arabic (official), also English, Kurdish, Persian, Turkish, and Assyrian spoken

Ethnic groups Arab (79%), Kurd (largely in NE) (16%), Persian (3%), Turkish (2%)

Religions Muslim (95%) (Shi'ite 63%, Sunni 32%), Christian (3%)

Physical features Comprises the vast alluvial tract of the Tigris-Euphrates lowland (ancient Mesopotamia); Tharthar and Euphrates rivers, divided by al-Jazirah plain, flow over dense swampland and join to form the navigable Shatt al-Arab; mountains (NE) rise to over 3000 m/9800 ft; desert in other areas.

Climate Mainly arid climate; summers very hot and dry; winters often cold; average annual temperature 10°C (Jan), 35°C (Jul) in Baghdad; average annual rainfall 140 mm/5·5 in.

Currency 1 Iraqi Dinar (ID) = 1000 fils

Economy World's second largest producer of oil, but production severely disrupted during both Gulf Wars (several oil installations destroyed); natural gas, oil refining, petrochemicals, cement, textiles; dates, cotton, winter wheat, rice, sheep, cattle.

GDP (2002e) $58 bn, per capita $2400

History Part of the Ottoman Empire from 16th-c until World War I; captured by British forces, 1916; British-mandated territory, 1921; independence under Hashemite dynasty, 1932; monarchy replaced by military rule, and Iraq declared a republic, 1958; since 1960s, Kurdish nationalists in NE fighting to establish a separate state; invasion of Iran in 1980, led to the Iran-Iraq War, lasting until a ceasefire in 1988; invasion and annexation of Kuwait in Aug 1990 led to the 1991 Gulf War (Jan–Feb): UN imposed a no-fly zone over S Iraq to protect the Shi'ites, and a security zone in N Iraq to protect Kurdish refugees, 1992; ongoing confrontation with UN (1997–8) over access of weapons inspectors to sensitive sites, leading to US/UK air-strikes (Operation Desert Fox) from 1998; UN weapons experts resumed inspections, 2002–3, but with increasing dissatisfaction from US-led coalition over Iraq's apparent failure to comply with UN resolution to eliminate its weapons of mass destruction; build-up of US-led military forces in the Gulf leading to invasion by coalition forces (Mar 2003) begins Iraq War; Saddam Hussein's regime toppled, Apr 2003; capture of Saddam Hussein (Dec 2003); attacks on occupying forces in Iraq ongoing, 2003–4; Iraqi Governing Council established to oversee task of drawing up new Iraqi constitution and set date for elections; interim constitution signed, March 2004.

Monarch

1921–33 Faisal I
1933–9 Ghazi I
1939–58 Faisal II (Abdul Illah Regent 1939–53)

Republic

Commander of the National Forces

1958–63 Abdul Karim Qassem

Head of Council of State

1958–63 Mohammed Najib ar-Rubai

Head of State/Government

1963–6 Abdus Salaam Mohammed Arif
1966–8 Abdur Rahman Mohammed Arif
1968–79 Said Ahmad Hassan al Bakr
1979–2003 Sadam Hussein at-Takriti
2003– *Interim administration*

to comply with UN Security Council Resolution 1441 to disarm itself of weapons of mass destruction. UN weapons inspectors, headed by Hans Blix, urged that more time be given for inspections to be carried out, but US President George W Bush, supported by UK Prime Minister Tony Blair, set a deadline for Iraqi cooperation (19 Mar). No positive response was received from Iraqi leader, Saddam Hussein, and the conflict began with air missile strikes on the capital, Baghdad (20 Mar), launched from warships in The Gulf in a 'shock and awe' campaign. Armoured columns of troops entered Iraq from Kuwait, and the strategically important port of Umm Qasr was surrounded. Troops from the US 3rd Infantry Regiment took control of the international airport near Baghdad and later entered the city (5 Apr). British troops advanced towards Basra in the S and surrounded the city for several days. On entering (6 Apr) they met limited resistance, but widescale looting by Iraqi civilians became a major problem. A large US force advanced through Kurdish N Iraq to secure the oilfields around Kirkuk and Mosul. The campaign was notable for its live global television coverage, which included the historic moment (9 Apr) when Saddam Hussein's giant statue in Baghdad was toppled by a US tank. The search then began for the senior officials of Saddam's regime, some of whom were captured in subsequent weeks. President Bush appointed US diplomat Paul Bremer to the task of restoring civil order and forming an interim administration in Iraq. In December 2003, Saddam was captured by US forces on a farm in the town of Al-Dawr, near Tikrit, and held as a prisoner-of-war. Plans to restore power to an Iraqi government were scheduled for mid-2004.

Ireland (republic) *p.785*

Ireland (island), Lat **Hibernia** Island on W fringe of Europe, separated from Great Britain by the Irish Sea; maximum length 486 km/302 mi, maximum width 275 km/171 mi; since 1921, divided politically into the independent 26 counties of the **Republic of Ireland** (area 70 282 sq km/27 129 sq mi; pop (2000e) 3 647 000), and **Northern Ireland**, part of the UK, containing six of the nine counties of the ancient province of Ulster (area 14 120 sq km/5450 sq mi; pop (2000e) 1 664 000); known poetically as **Erin**, derived from Strabo's name for the island, **Ierne**; 6th–13th-c, often known as **Scotia**; the name is also in widespread use for the Republic of Ireland.

Ireland, John (Nicholson) (1879–1962) Composer, born in Bowdon, Greater Manchester, NW England, UK. He studied under Charles Stanford at the Royal College of Music, London, where he later became a teacher of composition. He established his reputation with his Violin Sonata in A (1917), and between the wars was a prominent member of the English musical renaissance. He is best known for his picturesque orchestral pieces *The Forgotten Rite* (1913) and *Mai-dun* (1921), the piano concerto (1930), and *These Things Shall Be* (1937) for chorus and orchestra.

Irenaeus, St [irenayus] (c.130–c.200) One of the Christian Fathers of the Greek Church, probably born near Smyrna. A priest of the Graeco–Gaulish Church of Lyon, he became bishop there in 177. A successful missionary bishop, he is chiefly known for his opposition to Gnosticism, his theological writing, and his attempts to prevent a rupture between Eastern and Western Churches over the computing of Easter. Feast day 28 June (W), 23 August (E).

Irene (mythology) [iyreenee] In Greek mythology, a personification of 'peace'; one of the Horae, or 'seasons'.

Ireton, Henry [iy(r)tn] (1611–51) English soldier, born in Attenborough, Nottinghamshire, C England, UK. He studied at Cambridge, and in the Civil War fought for parliament, serving at Edgehill, Naseby, and the siege of Bristol. Cromwell's son-in-law from 1646, he was one of the most implacable enemies of the king, and signed the warrant for his execution. He accompanied Cromwell to Ireland, and in 1650 became lord deputy. He died of the plague during the siege of Limerick.

Irgun (Zvai Leumi) [irgun zviy loomee] (Heb 'National Military Organization') A Jewish resistance group in Palestine, founded in 1937, whose aim was the establishment of the State of Israel by any means. Led by Menachem Begin, it was responsible for the hanging of British soldiers and the massacre of the villagers of Deir Yassin in 1948, when its members numbered about 5000. It was the nucleus for the Herut Party in Israel.

Irian Jaya [irian jiyah], officially **Papua** (from 2002), formerly **West Papua**, **West Irian**, earlier **Dutch New Guinea** pop (2000e) 1 928 000; area 421 981 sq km/162 885 sq mi. Autonomous province of Indonesia, comprising the W half of New Guinea and adjacent islands; mountainous and forested; Pegunungan Maoke range rises to 5029 m/16 499 ft at Jaya Peak; part of Indonesia, 1963; bicameral council introduced, 2002; ongoing separatist Free Papua Movement (OPM); capital, Jayapura; copra, maize, groundnuts, tuna, pepper, gold, oil, coal, phosphate.

iridology [iridolojee] The detailed study of the visible parts of the eye, especially the iris, which is used as a diagnostic aid in conjunction with many forms of therapy, including acupuncture, herbal medicine, and homeopathy. Iridologists claim that, since the nervous system comes to the body surface in the eyes, so the condition of all parts of the body is reflected in the eye's appearance. Physical and psychological problems can be revealed, as well as evidence of past disorders and tendencies towards future illness.

iridosmine *osmiridium*

iris (anatomy) The coloured part of the vertebrate eye, an opaque diaphragm extending in front of the lens and having a circular opening (the *pupil*). It consists of pigmental epithelium and circularly and radially arranged smooth muscle fibres. The differential contraction of these muscle fibres (under the control of the autonomic nervous system) alters pupil size and so regulates the amount of light entering the eye. Bright light decreases and dim light increases pupil size.

iris (botany) A perennial, sometimes evergreen, native to N temperate regions, divisible into two groups; those with rhizomes have sword-shaped leaves in flat fans; those with bulbs have leaves narrow, channelled, or cylindrical; flowers large, showy, the parts in threes and structurally complex, often in a combination of colours with conspicuous honey guides; fruit a capsule, sometimes with brightly coloured seeds. Many species and cultivars are grown for ornament. (Genus: *Iris*, 300 species. Family: Iridaceae.)

Iris (mythology) In Greek mythology, the goddess of the rainbow, which seems to reach from Earth to heaven. She therefore became the messenger of the gods, especially of Zeus in Homer, and of Hera in later writers. She is depicted sitting under Hera's throne.

Irish The Celtic language spoken in Ireland; also known as **Irish Gaelic** [gaylik] and occasionally as **Erse**. Designated the first official language of the Republic of Ireland, there are over a million who have learned the language in school, but home use is less than a twentieth of this, and is falling. Most speakers of Irish as a mother-tongue come from the W fringes of the country, which have been designated as an area of protection for the language, the *Gaeltacht*. Irish is taught in the schools, and language planning has introduced a standard grammar and simplified spelling system.

Irish Civil War Conflict in Ireland following the Easter Rising of 1916. In 1920 the Government of Ireland Act provided for two Irish parliaments, one (Stormont) for the six counties of Ulster in the N, and one for the remaining 26 counties of Ireland. The Anglo-Irish Treaty (1921) suspended part of the 1920 Act: while Northern Ireland remained part of the United Kingdom, the 26 counties gained separate dominion status as the Irish Free State. The Treaty split the IRA and Sinn Féin between Michael Collins, who had negotiated the Treaty, and the opposing faction led by Eamon de Valera, which felt that the Treaty had fallen short of a fully independent Irish republic. Anti-Treaty forces used the guerilla tactics the IRA had deployed successfully against the British, bombing bridges, roads, and railways. Leading treaty supporters were assassinated, including Collins.

Ireland

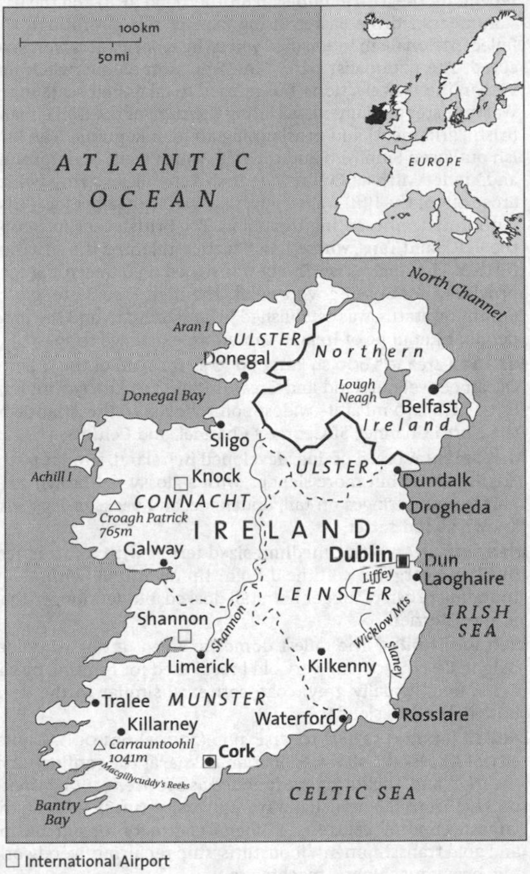

(republic), Ir **Eire** [ayruh], official name also **Republic of Ireland**

Local name Éire (Gaelic)

Timezone GMT

Area 70 282 km^2/27 129 sq mi

Population total (2002e) 3 926 000

Status Republic (occupying S, C, and NW Ireland; bounded NE by Northern Ireland, part of the UK)

Capital Dublin

Languages Irish Gaelic and English (official)

Ethnic groups Celtic (94%), small English minority

Religions Roman Catholic (95%), Anglican (Church of Ireland) (3%), Presbyterian (1%)

Physical features Mountainous landscapes in W, part of Caledonian system of Scandinavia and Scotland with quartzite peaks weathered into conical mountains such as Croagh Patrick, 765 m/ 2510 ft; landscape of ridges and valleys in SW, rising towards Macgillycuddy's Reek Mts; lowlands in E drained by slow-moving rivers such as the Shannon (S), Liffey (E), and Slaney (SE).

Climate Mild and equable climate. Average annual temperature 5°C (Jan), 15°C (Jul); rainfall heaviest in W, often over 3000 mm/ 20 in.

Currency 1 euro = 100 cents (previous to February 2002, 1 Irish Pound/Punt (1£, IR£) = 100 new pence)

Economy Primarily agriculture (two-thirds of country covered by improved agricultural land); forestry developed since 1950s; fishing; food, drink, tobacco, textiles; recent growth in light engineering; synthetic fibres, electronics, pharmaceuticals; several peat-fired power stations; Kinsale natural-gas field near Cork; major tourist area; member of the EC, 1973.

GDP (2002e) $113·7 bn, per capita $29 300

Human Development Index (2002) 0·925

History Occupied by Goidelic-speaking Celts during the Iron Age; conversion to Christianity by St Patrick, 5th-c; SE attacked by Vikings, c.800; Henry II of England declared himself lord of Ireland, 1171, but English influence restricted to area round Dublin (the Pale); Henry VIII took the title 'King of Ireland', 1542; Catholic rebellion during English Civil War suppressed by Oliver Cromwell, 1649–50; supporters of deposed Catholic King James II defeated by William III at Battle of the Boyne, 1690; struggle for Irish freedom developed in 18th-19th-c, including such revolutionary movements as Wolfe Tone's United Irishmen, 1796–8, and later Young Ireland, 1848, and the Fenians, 1866–7; Act of Union, 1801; Catholic Relief Act enabling Catholics to sit in Parliament, 1829; population reduced by half during famine, 1846; Land Acts, 1870–1903, attacking Irish poverty; Home Rule Bills introduced by Gladstone, 1886, 1893; third Home Rule Bill passed in 1914, but never came into effect because of World War I; armed rebellion, 1916; republic proclaimed by Sinn Féin, 1919; partition proposed by Britain, 1920; treaty signed, giving dominion status, 1921; right of Northern Ireland to opt out was exercised, and frontier agreed, 1925; renamed Éire, 1937; left Commonwealth, 1949; Anglo-Irish Agreement signed, 1985; a President (Uachtarán na h'Éireann) elected for seven years; a Prime Minister (Taoiseach); the National Parliament (Oireachtas) includes a House of Representatives (Dail Éireann) and a Senate (Seanad Éireann).

Head of State

1976–90 Patrick J Hillery
1990–7 Mary Robinson
1997– Mary McAleese

Head of Government

1987–92 Charles Haughey
1992–4 Albert Reynolds
1994–7 John Bruton
1997– (Patrick) Bertie Ahern

Counties of Ireland

County / Area (km^2 / sq mi) / Population total (2000e) / Admin centre
Carlow / 896 / 346 / 41 000 / Carlow
Cavan / 1891 / 730 / 53 000 / Cavan
Clare / 3188 / 1231 / 92 000 / Ennis
Cork / 7459 / 2880 / 415 000 / Cork
Donegal / 4830 / 1865 / 130 000 / Lifford
Dublin / 922 / 356 / 1 038 000 / Dublin
Galway / 5939 / 2293 / 183 000 / Galway
Kerry / 4701 / 1815 / 123 000 / Tralee
Kildare / 1694 / 654 / 124 000 / Naas
Kilkenny / 2062 / 796 / 75 000 / Kilkenny
Laoighis (Leix) / 1720 / 664 / 53 000 / Portlaoise
Leitrim / 1526 / 589 / 24 000 / Carrick
Limerick / 2686 / 1037 / 164 000 / Limerick
Longford / 1044 / 403 / 31 000 / Longford
Louth / 821 / 317 / 92 000 / Dundalk
Mayo / 5398 / 2084 / 112 000 / Castlebar
Meath / 2339 / 903 / 107 000 / Trim
Monaghan / 1290 / 498 / 52 000 / Monaghan
Offaly / 1997 / 771 / 59 000 / Tullamore
Roscommon / 2463 / 951 / 53 000 / Roscommon
Sligo / 1795 / 693 / 55 000 / Sligo
Tipperary / 4254 / 1642 / 134 500 / Clonmel
Waterford / 1869 / 710 / 92 000 / Waterford
Westmeath / 1764 / 681 / 63 000 / Mullingar
Wexford / 2352 / 908 / 103 000 / Wexford
Wicklow / 2025 / 782 / 98 000 / Wicklow

De Valera called for a ceasefire on 24 April 1923. In 1949 the 26 counties attained full independence as the Republic of Ireland.

Irish elk A giant fossil deer that ranged through open woodland from Ireland to Siberia and China during the Pleistocene epoch; enormous, palmate antlers of stags could span 3·7 m/12 ft, used to establish dominance over herd. (Genus: *Megaloceros*.)

Irish Famine, also known as the **Great Hunger** The widespread starvation of Irish peasantry which followed the effects of potato blight in 1845–7, due to the destruction of the crop by a fungus, *Phytophthora infestans*. Because of starvation and emigration (to Britain and the USA), the population of Ireland fell by almost 25 per cent between 1845 and 1851. The British government's reaction was slow, so that it failed to deal with the crisis. The famine hastened the repeal of the Corn Laws by Robert Peel in 1846. When Russell's subsequent administration made loans for relief available, many thousands of people converged on the towns, leading to epidemics of typhoid, cholera and dysentery. Out of a total loss to the population of over two million people, one million died from starvation and disease; the rest attempted emigration.

Irish Home Rule Legislative independence of Ireland from Britain. It was sought by various Irish groups from the 1860s, such as the Home Rule League, which won 56 seats in the 1874 election. Parnell's unified party linked home rule to land reform, and in 1885 won 86 seats. Gladstone tried to resolve what was called the 'Irish question' with a Home Rule Bill, which was defeated in 1886. His Second Home Rule Bill was thrown out of the Unionist-dominated Lords (1892). Asquith's Third Home Rule Bill became law in January 1913, but the Lords delayed its implementation. Complicating the issue was partition for Ulster, whose Protestant majority wanted to remain within the UK. After the Easter Rising in Dublin in 1916, Sinn Féin became the main Irish movement against British rule. In 1920, at the height of the Irish Civil War, Lloyd George passed legislation to create a home rule parliament in Belfast (for the six counties), and in Dublin (for the other 26 counties). The Anglo-Irish Treaty (1921) established an independent Irish Free State in December 1922.

Irish literature A literature with two distinct traditions; the native Irish Gaelic, and the Anglo-Irish. Irish remained oral later than any other European literature. Not only the early, short prose sagas (such as the famous *Tain Bo Cuailnge* (The Cattle-Raid of Cooley)) but also mediaeval lyrics and still later odes and panegyrics were kept alive by recitation. Political persecution also drove Irish literature underground. The Gaelic League (1893) promised an Irish revival, but conditions have never proved favourable. Meanwhile, many celebrated Anglo-Irish writers (eg Swift, Sterne, Burke, Wilde, Shaw) wrote entirely within the English tradition. But with the Irish revival, the poet Yeats and the dramatists Synge and O'Casey drew inspiration from Irish sources; and the novels of the self-exiled James Joyce are all set in Dublin. This re-rooting in Ireland is also evident in several contemporary Irish writers, such as the poet Seamus Heaney and the playwright Brian Friel, and in the work of another celebrated self-exile, Samuel Beckett, who wrote in both English and French.

Irish National Liberation Army (INLA) The military wing of the Irish Republican Socialist Party, a small paramilitary group which committed few terrorist attacks, but was noted for the ruthless nature of those it does carry out. Probably created by former members of the Official IRA disenchanted with the 1972 ceasefire, it was responsible for the killing of the Conservative MP Airey Neave (Mar 1979). It suffered internal feuds in the 1980s. A ceasefire was announced in August 1998.

Irish Republican Army *IRA*

Irish Republican Socialist Party A political party formed in 1974 largely as a breakaway group from the official Sinn Féin, who disagreed with its political strategy and the 1972 ceasefire. Its most prominent member was Bernadette McAliskey (1947–). It was involved in a feud with the Official IRA in the 1970s, and subsequently moved closer to the Provisional Sinn Féin.

Irish Revolution The struggle for Irish independence against English rule. Following centuries of sporadic uprisings and rebellions, the Irish Republican Brotherhood (IRB) and the Irish Volunteers led the Easter Rising (24 Apr 1916). Although this failed, nationalism intensified when the rebel leaders were executed. The nationalist party Sinn Féin won an overwhelming vote in the 1918 elections, but refused to take their seats in the Westminster parliament, declaring themselves the Dáil Éireann (Irish Parliament) and proclaiming an Irish Republic. The British outlawed Sinn Féin and the Dáil, which went underground and, under Michael Collins, the Irish Republican Army (which arose out of the IRB) waged guerrilla warfare against local Irish authorities representing the union. The British sent in troops, the Black and Tans, whose harsh tactics inflamed the situation further. The Anglo-Irish Treaty was signed on 6 December 1921, providing some self-government; the Irish Free State, giving dominion status, was established in January 1922; and the independent Republic of Ireland came into existence in 1949.

Irish Sea area 103 600 sq km/39 990 sq mi. Arm of the Atlantic Ocean between Ireland and Great Britain; 210 km/130 mi long by 225 km/140 mi at its widest point; linked to the Atlantic by the North Channel, St George's Channel, and Celtic Sea.

Irish setter A breed of dog, developed in Ireland, similar to the English setter but more slender, with a glossy red-brown coat; hair forming fringes on tail, underside, and backs of legs; also known as **red setter**.

Irish terrier An active medium-sized terrier with a coarse red-dish-tan coat; ears soft, held high; tip of muzzle with a surrounding brush of longer hair; tail docked, but left longer than in most terriers.

Irish wolfhound The tallest domestic breed of dog (shoulder height, 80 cm/30½ in); very old breed, used for hunting by the Celts; long (usually grey) coat; soft ears; similar to the deerhound, but less slender.

Irkutsk [irkutsk] 52°18N 104°15E, pop (2000e) 635 000. Capital city of Irkutskaya oblast, S Siberian Russia; at the confluence of the Irkut and Angara Rivers; founded as a fortress, 1661; airport; on the Trans-Siberian Railway; university (1918); one of the largest economic centres of E Siberia; centre for fur-purchasing and gold transshipment; foodstuffs, ship repairing, woodworking, heavy machinery, machine tools.

iron Fe (from Lat *ferrum*), element 26, a metal with density of 7·8 g/cm^3, melting point 1535°C. It is the fourth most common element in the Earth's crust, not found uncombined except in some meteorites. Learning to recover (*smelt*) it from its ores (mainly the oxide Fe_2O_3) was a major step in human civilization. The first to have iron were the Hittites (13th-c BC) and the Etruscans (1000 BC). Cast iron is first documented in China (512 BC), with bellows used in the process, and cupola furnaces are recorded in 28 BC. China produced 125 000 tons of iron a year by 1100. The Mongol seizure of Chinese iron capacity enabled them to defeat Russia (1240) and seize Baghdad (1258). The first European cast iron dates from 1380. Smelting is still done largely by reduction using carbon. Most iron is used as metal, usually alloyed with some quantities of other elements, especially carbon and silicon. Steel is iron alloyed with other metals, mainly vanadium, chromium, manganese, and nickel. In its compounds, iron shows both +2 and +3 oxidation states, and is an essential element in biology, particularly as part of haemoglobin.

Iron Age *Three Age System*

iron-bark *gum tree*

Ironbridge A historic industrial town in the Severn R gorge, WC England, UK, 21 km/13 mi SE of Shrewsbury, Shropshire, the birthplace of England's Industrial Revolution. In 1709 Abraham Darby (1678–1717), a Bristol ironmaster, was the first to smelt iron, with coke replacing traditional charcoal, nearby at Coalbrookdale, and in 1778–9 Europe's first iron bridge was cast and erected here; 196 ft (59·8 m) long, its centre span 100 ft (30·5 m) and its rise 45 ft (13·7 m), the weight precisely recorded as 378·5 tons (384·6 tonnes). Since 1968 it has been the focus of a successful open-air museum on the model of Colonial Williamsburg. Ironbridge Gorge is a world heritage site.

ironclad A 19th-c term for warships which were either protected by iron plates or built entirely of iron, and more recently of steel. The first ironclad was the French frigate *La Gloire* of 1859, followed one year later by Britain's HMS *Warrior*.

Iron Cross A military decoration (an iron cross edged with silver) instituted in Prussia in 1813 and reinstated in 1870 for the Franco-Prussian War and as a German medal in 1914 and 1939 for the two World Wars. The ribbon is black, white, and gold.

iron curtain A term used to describe the separation of certain E and C European countries from the rest of Europe by the political and military domination of the Soviet Union. The term was first used by Nazi propaganda minister Goebbels in 1945 and quoted in translation by the British press. It became widely known after Churchill used it in a speech in Fulton, USA, in 1946. It became redundant following the collapse of the Soviet system in Eastern Europe.

iron lung *respirator*

Irons, Jeremy (John) [iyonz] (1948–) Actor, born in Cowes, Isle of Wight, S England, UK. A student with the Bristol Old Vic, he made his London stage debut as John the Baptist in the rock musical *Godspell* (1971–2), and joined the Royal Shakepeare Company. In 1984 he won a Tony award for Best Actor in *The Real Thing*. His role as Charles Ryder in the acclaimed television series *Brideshead Revisited* (1981) made him a household name. His film debut came in *Nijinsky* (1980), and he won a Best Actor Oscar for his performance in *Reversal of Fortune* (1990). Other films include *The Mission* (1985), *Stealing Beauty* (1996), and *The Night of the Iguana* (2001).

Ironside, William Edmund Ironside, Baron (1880–1959) British field marshal, born in Ironside, Aberdeenshire, NE Scotland, UK. He served as a secret agent disguised as a railwayman in the Boer War, held several staff-appointments in World War 1, and commanded the Archangel expedition against the Bolsheviks (1918). He was Chief of the Imperial General Staff at the outbreak of World War 2, and placed in command of the home defence forces (1940). The *Ironsides*, fast light-armoured vehicles, were named after him. He was made a peer in 1941.

irony One of the most complex forms of literary expression, more a habit of mind than a rhetorical figure, requiring continual alertness on the part of the reader for proper interpretation. Irony is not simply saying one thing and implying the opposite; the name for this crude form is *sarcasm*. Irony invites the reader to consider several shades of meaning simultaneously, some of which are elided or cancelled out in the process. The meaning of irony lies precisely in the tension between single statement and multiple meaning. It was suggested by Kierkegaard that the finest irony is undecipherable as such – which comes close to the position of the Romantic ironist, who writes with a keen sense of the double sidedness of truth and the irreducible ambiguity of language itself. This conception is also referred to as *cosmic* or *philosophical* irony.

Iroquois [irokwoy] A North American Indian people concentrated in the Great Lakes area, speaking Iroquoian languages of the Hokan–Siouan family, c.80 000 (2000 census). Mostly settled in villages in longhouses, the women farmed, and the men hunted, fished, traded, and defended the communities from attack. They fought many wars with their neighbours, enslaving captives or absorbing them into the community.

Iroquois Confederacy [irokwoy] A confederation of Iroquois groups during the 17th–18th-c in upper New York State: the Mohawk, Oneida, Onondaga, Cayuga, and Seneca, later joined by the Tuscarora; also known as the **Iroquois League** or the 'Six Nations'. United largely for defence and for control of the fur trade, they defeated most of their Indian rivals, and prevented the settlement of Europeans in the NE. The League broke up during the American Revolution, but later reconstituted itself.

irradiance *radiometry*

irrational numbers *numbers*

Irrawaddy, River *Ayeyarwady, River*

Irredentists In the new nations of 19th–20th-c Europe, supporters of the acquisition, by negotiation or more usually conquest, of 'unredeemed' territory. The term is most commonly applied to those Italians who, after 1870, sought 'redemption' of Italian-speaking lands still under Austrian rule, and to those Greeks who sought to incorporate Greek-speaking, Turkish-controlled areas into the new Greek kingdom.

irrigation The application of water to soil and crops by artificial methods, first recorded in China, 560 BC. The water used for irrigation is taken from lakes, rivers, streams, and wells. In some desert areas all the moisture requirements for plant growth may be provided through irrigation, with water being supplied via a complex canal and irrigation channel network. In other areas irrigation is used to achieve optimal growth and high quality produce, especially in the horticulture sector. In dry areas water may be applied by flooding or through inter-row channels. More general application techniques include rain guns, sprinklers, and (more expensively) drip lines, which provide water to plants and trees on an individual basis. This latter system also facilitates the application of nutrients and other chemicals, along with the water in the irrigation lines.

irritable bowel syndrome A common condition involving abdominal discomfort and altered bowel habit. Not serious, it may be related to an increased spontaneous movement of the intestines, though there is almost certainly a psychological element; there are no obvious abnormal findings and it is exacerbated by emotional stress. Changes in diet, such as increased dietary fibre, may help to reduce symptoms, and measures to reduce anxiety may also be successful.

Irtysh, River [irtish] Chief tributary of the R Ob in Kazakhstan and Russia; rises in N China on the W slopes of the Mongolian Altai Mts; flows W to enter L Zaysan, then generally NW to join the R Ob at Khanty Mansiysk; length, 4248 km/2640 mi; hydroelectric power stations serve the non-ferrous mineral industry.

Irvine (of Lairg), Alexander Andrew Mackay Irvine, Baron (1940–) British judge. He studied at Glasgow University and Christ's College, Cambridge, and became a lecturer at the London School of Economics (1965–9). He was called to the bar in 1967, and became a QC (1978) and a deputy judge in the High Court (1987). Appointed shadow Lord Chancellor (1992–7), he then served as Lord Chancellor (1997–2003). He was made a life peer in 1987.

Irvine, Andy [ervin], popular name of **Andrew (Robertson) Irvine** (1951–) Rugby union player, born in Edinburgh, EC Scotland, UK. He studied at George Heriot's School and Glasgow University, and his club rugby was played with Heriot's Former Pupils. An outstanding fullback, he won 51 caps for Scotland (1972–82), scored more points in South Africa than any touring Lion had previously done, and was the first player in the world to score more than 300 points in international rugby. He toured with the Lions in 1974, 1977, and 1980.

Irving, David (1938–) Historian, born in Essex, SE England, UK. He studied at University College London, then worked at various jobs in Europe. His Holocaust revisionist agenda began with his best-selling 1977 book, *Hitler's War*, and was followed by a number of publications including *Goebbels; Mastermind of the Third Reich* (1996). In them he denied the exterminationist nature of German anti-Semitism. In 2000 he sued the publisher, Penguin Books Ltd, and the American historian, Deborah Lipstadt, for libel and falsification of history in her book, *Denying the Holocaust: the Growing Assault on Truth and Memory* (1993), but the verdict went against him.

Irving, Sir Henry, originally **John Henry Brodribb** (1838–1905) Actor and theatre manager, born in Keinton-Mandeville, Somerset, SW England, UK. He went on stage in 1865, appeared in Sunderland, Edinburgh, Manchester, and Liverpool, and in 1866 made his London debut at the St James's Theatre. He transferred to the Lyceum (1871), where he achieved fame overnight with his appearance in *The Bells*, and gained a reputation as the greatest English actor of his time. In 1878 he began a theatrical partnership with Ellen Terry which lasted until 1902. He became the first actor to receive a knighthood (1895).

Irving, John (Winslow) (1942–) Writer, born in Exeter, New Hampshire, USA. He studied at the universities of New Hampshire (1965 BA), Iowa (1967 MFA), Pittsburgh (1961–2), and Vienna (Austria) (1963–4), and went on to teach at Mount Holyoke (1967–72), the University of Iowa (1972–5), and at Bread Loaf Writers Conference, Middlebury, VT. His first three novels received little attention, but he made his name with *The World According To Garp* (1978, filmed 1982). He is considered an inventive writer who combined elements of tragedy and antic comedy. He is also widely praised for several later novels, including *The Hotel New Hampshire* (1981, filmed 1984), *The Cider House Rules* (1985, filmed 1999, Oscar), *A Prayer for Owen Meany* (1989), *A Widow for One Year* (1998), and *The Fourth Hand* (2002). In 1999 appeared *My Movie Business: A Memoir*.

Irving, Washington, pseudonym **Geoffrey Crayon** (1783–1859) Man of letters, born in New York City, USA. He studied law, travelled through Europe, was admitted to the bar in 1806, and began writing in 1807. Under his pseudonym he wrote *The Sketch Book* (1819–20), a miscellany, containing in different styles such items as 'Rip Van Winkle' and 'The Legend of Sleepy Hollow'. He lived in Europe (1815–32), and his stay in Spain (1826–9) produced *Columbus* (1828), *The Companions of Columbus* (1831), and *Conquest of Granada* (1829). He was later appointed US ambassador to Spain (1842–6).

Isaac [iyzak] Biblical character, the son of Abraham by Sarah, through whose line of descent God's promises to Abraham were seen to continue. He was nearly sacrificed by Abraham at God's command (*Gen* 22). He fathered Esau and Jacob by his wife Rebecca, but was deceived into passing his blessing on to his younger son Jacob.

Isabella I (of Castile), also known as **Isabella the Catholic** (1451–1504) Queen of Castile (1474–1504), born in Madrigal de las Altas Torres, WC Spain, the daughter of John II, King of Castile and León. In 1469 she married Ferdinand V of Aragon, with whom she ruled jointly from 1479. During her reign, the Inquisition was introduced (1478), the reconquest of Granada completed (1482–92), and the Jews expelled (1492). She sponsored the voyage of Christopher Columbus to the New World.

Isabella of France (1292–1358) Queen of England, the consort of Edward II, and daughter of Philip IV of France. She married Edward in 1308 at Boulogne, but then became the mistress of Roger Mortimer, Earl of March, with whom she overthrew and murdered the king (1327). Her son, Edward III, had Mortimer executed in 1330, and Isabella was sent into retirement, eventually to join an order of nuns.

Isaiah [iyziya], Heb **Jeshaiah** (8th-c BC) The first in order of the major Old Testament prophets, the son of Amoz. A citizen of Jerusalem, he began to prophesy c.747 BC, and exercised his office until at least the close of the century. According to tradition, he was martyred.

Isaiah or **Isaias, Book of** [iyziya] A major prophetic work in the Hebrew Bible/Old Testament, ostensibly from the prophet Isaiah, active in Judah and Jerusalem in the latter half of the 8th-c BC during a period of Assyrian threats. Many scholars doubt the unity of the contents, with Chapters 40–55 considered a much later exilic work looking forward to Judah's restoration and called **Deutero-Isaiah** ('Second Isaiah') and Chapters 56–66 either as part of Deutero-Isaiah or as a distinct **Trito-Isaiah** ('Third Isaiah').

Isaias *Isaiah, Book of*

ISBN *International Standard Book Numbering*

ischaemic / ischemic heart disease *coronary heart disease*

Isherwood, Christopher (William Bradshaw) (1904–86) Novelist, born in Disley, Cheshire, NWC England, UK. He studied at Repton, Cambridge, and London, and taught English in Germany (1930–3). His best-known novels, *Mr Norris Changes Trains* (1935) and *Goodbye to Berlin* (1939), were based on his experiences in the decadence of post-slump, pre-Hitler Berlin, and later inspired *Cabaret* (musical, 1966; filmed, 1972). In collaboration with Auden, a school friend, he wrote three prose-verse plays with political overtones. He also travelled in China with Auden in 1938, and wrote *Journey to a War* (1939). In 1939 he emigrated to California to work as a scriptwriter, and became a US citizen in 1946. There he developed his interest in Hinduism, producing several works on the Vedanta and translations of Hindu texts. Later novels include *Prater Violet* (1945), *The World in the Evening* (1954), and *A Meeting by the River* (1967).

Ishiguro, Kazuo [ishigooroh] (1954–) Novelist, born in Nagasaki, Japan. He came to Britain to study at the University of Kent before joining Malcolm Bradbury's creative writing course at the University of East Anglia. His third novel, *The Remains of the Day* (1989, filmed 1993), won the Booker Prize and established his reputation. Later books (all written in English) include *The Unconsoled* (1995) and *When We Were Orphans* (2000).

Ishmael [ishmayel] Biblical character, the son of Abraham by Hagar, his wife's maid. He was expelled into the desert with his mother from Abraham's household after the birth of Isaac. He is purported to have fathered 12 princes, and is considered the ancestor of the Bedouin tribes of the Palestinian deserts (the *Ishmaelites*). Mohammed considered Ishmael and Abraham as ancestors of the Arabs, and as associated with the construction of the Kaba at Mecca.

Ishtar [ishtah(r)] Originally a Mesopotamian mother-goddess of love and war; also known as **Astarte**; later the goddess of love, identified with the planet Venus. She travelled to the Underworld to rescue her consort Tammuz, an event commemorated in annual ceremonies.

Isidore of Seville, St [izidaw(r), sevil] (c.560–636) Ecclesiastic, encyclopedist, and historian, born either in Seville or Carthagena, Spain. Archbishop of Seville in c.600, his episcopate was notable for the Councils at Seville (618 or 619) and Toledo (633). A voluminous writer, his most influential work was the encyclopedia *Etymologies*. He was canonized in 1598; feast day 4 April.

isinglass [iyzinglahs] A pure gelatin found in fish. Its particular use, for which other gelatins are not suitable, is in the clarification of fermented beverages, presumably due to its fibrous structure. The name is also applied to a form of mica, with similar appearance.

Isis [iysis] Ancient Egyptian goddess, wife of Osiris and mother of Horus, sometimes portrayed with horns and the Sun's disc. In Hellenistic and Roman times, she was a central figure in mystery religions, and was associated with magical beliefs.

Islam [izlahm] The Arabic word for 'submission' to the will of God (Allah), the name of the religion originating in Arabia during the 7th-c through the Prophet Mohammed. Followers of Islam are known as Muslims, or Moslems, and their religion embraces every aspect of life. They believe that individuals, societies, and governments should all be obedient to the will of God as it is set forth in the Qur'an, which they regard as the Word of God revealed to his Messenger, Mohammed. The Qur'an teaches that God is one and has no partners. He is the Creator of all things, and holds absolute power over them. All persons should commit themselves to lives of grateful and praise-giving obedience to God, for on the Day of Resurrection they will be judged. Those who have obeyed God's commandments will dwell for ever in paradise, but those who have sinned against God and not repented will be condemned eternally to the fires of hell. Since the beginning of creation God has sent prophets, including Moses and Jesus, to provide the guidance necessary for the attainment of eternal reward, a succession culminating in the revelation to Mohammed of the perfect word of God.

There are five essential religious duties known as the **Pillars of Islam**. (1) The *shahada* (profession of faith) is the sincere recitation of the twofold creed: 'There is no god but God' and 'Mohammed is the Messenger of God'. (2) The *salat* (formal prayer) must be performed at five points in the day (varying with time of sunrise and sunset) while facing towards the holy city of Mecca. (3) Alms-giving through the payment of *zakat* ('purification') is the duty of sharing one's wealth out of gratitude for God's favour, according to the uses laid down in the Qur'an. (4) There is a duty to fast (*saum*) during the month of Ramadan. (5) The *Hajj* or pilgrimage to Mecca is to be performed if at all possible at least once during one's lifetime. *Sharia* is the sacred law of Islam, and applies to all aspects of life, not just religious practices. It describes the Islamic way of life, and prescribes the way for a Muslim to fulfil the commands of God and reach heaven. There is an annual cycle of festivals, including the Feast of the Sacrifice (*Id al-Adha*), commemorating Abraham's willingness to sacrifice Isaac, which comes at the end of the Hajj pilgrimage, and the *Id al-Fitr*, marking the end of the month of fasting in Ramadan. There is no organized priesthood, but great respect is accorded to descendants of Mohammed, and other publicly acknowledged holy men, scholars, and teachers, such as mullahs and ayatollahs.

There are two basic groups within Islam. *Sunni Muslims* are in the majority, and they believe that correct religious guidance derives from the practice or *sunna* of the Prophet. They recognize the first four caliphs as Mohammed's legitimate successors. The *Shiites* comprise the largest minority group, and they believe that correct religious guidance obtains from members of the family of the Prophet, on which basis they recognize only the line of Ali, the fourth caliph and nephew and son-in-law of Mohammed as the Prophet's legitimate successors. While the Sunnis have through history believed that just government could be established on the basis of correct Islamic practice, the Shiites believe government to be inherently unjust, particularly since the last recognized member of the line of Ali, the Twelfth Imam, became hidden from view in AD 873. There are a number of sub-sects of Islam, and in 2004 there were over 1200 million Muslims throughout the world.

Islamabad [islamabad] 33°40N 73°08E, pop (2000e) 329 000. Capital city of Pakistan, on the R Jhelum; a modern planned city, built since 1961; head of navigation for larger vessels in the Vale of Kashmir; two universities (1965, 1974); centre of agricultural region; shrine of Bari Imam; museum of folk and traditional heritage.

Islamic architecture An architectural form at first deriving from converted Christian or pagan buildings, its distinctive features appearing after the 8th-c, such as the horseshoe arch, masonry tunnel vaults, rich carved surface decoration, mosaics, and paint. Minarets, attached to mosques and used to call followers to prayer, were developed during the Arab Umayyad dynasty.

Islamic art An essentially ornamental and abstract style of art, in contrast to the Christian emphasis on figurative art, created largely in the service of the Islamic religion. It began in the 7th-c and spread W to Spain and E to India and China.

Islamic law *Sharia*

Islamic philosophy The Arabic term, *falsafah*, indicates the Greek origins of this science in Islamic culture. A major translation movement centred in Baghdad during the 9th-c, and introduced to Muslims an eclectic body of Greek knowledge, embracing not only the ideas of Plato, Aristotle, and Pythagoras but also of Galen, Plotinus, and Proclus, as well as doctrines of hermetic origin. The complexity of this inheritance is found in the earliest thinkers, Kindi (d.c.870), al-Farabi (d.950), and Ibn Sina (Avicenna) (d.1037), whose works are a synthesis of Neoplatonic metaphysics, natural science, and mysticism. They assumed, moreover, an essential harmony between Plato and Aristotle. The philosophers' labours met a cool reception, as Sunni Muslim legal and theological thought was becoming consolidated during this same period. Questions were debated pertaining to God's knowledge of particulars as against universals, the spiritual rather than material nature of punishment and reward in the afterlife, and whether creation was an emanation from the First Principle instead of *ex nihilo* – philosophers holding to the first of these positions, theologians to the latter. The famous jurist-theologian-philosopher, al-Ghazali (d.1111) condemned these particular philosophical views as unbelief, though his position was in turn refuted by Ibn Rushd (Averroës). Muslim philosophers also made contributions to the fields of logic, psychology, and ethics. While philosophy retreated in formal Sunni thought after Ibn Rushd, it nevertheless has continued to be important in Shia Muslim circles and in the mystical traditions influenced by Ibn Arabi (d.1240) and Suhrawardi (d.1234).

island A piece of land totally surrounded by water, in an ocean, sea, or lake. It may be formed by: (1) remnants of former high land cut off from the mainland by a rise in sea level, or by subsidence, as with the islands of the Aegean, and the Western Is of Scotland; (2) volcanic eruptions on the ocean floor, as with the Hawaiian Is and Iceland; (3) deposition of sediment, as with the Frisian Is; and (4) coral islands.

island arc Oceanic islands occurring in arc-shaped chains, such as the Aleutians, Mariana, Lesser Antilles, S Sandwich, and Tonga-Kermadec Is. They usually contain active volcanoes, and are adjacent to deep ocean trenches. The theory of plate tectonics maintains that island arcs are formed by volcanism generated as the rigid plates making up the Earth's surface are recycled into the Earth's interior beneath the trenches.

Isle of Man *Man, Isle of*

Isle of Wight *Wight, Isle of*

Ismailis [izmayeeleez] Adherents of a secret Islamic sect, one of the main branches of the Shiites; also known as the **Seveners**. It developed from an underground movement (c.9th-c), reaching political power under the Fatimids in Egypt and N Africa in the 10th–12th-c. It distinguished between inner and outer aspects of religion, was critical of Islamic law, and believed that in the eventual new age of the Seventh Imam, a kind of universal religion would emerge that was independent of the laws of all organized religions. Thus it welcomed adherents of other religions, but retained its own secret traditions and rites. Today, the Khojas are the largest Ismaili sect, numbering c.20 million. Their line of imams continues to the present, in the person of the Aga Khan.

Ismailiya or **Ismailia** [izmiyleea] 30°36N 32°15E, pop (2000e) 268 100. Capital of Ismailiya governorate, NE Egypt; on W bank of Suez Canal by L Timsah, 72 km/45 mi NW of Suez; founded in 1863 as a base for constructing the Canal; railway; market gardening in irrigated area.

Ismail Pasha [ismaeel] (1830–95) Khedive of Egypt, born in Cairo, Egypt, the second son of Ibrahim Pasha. Educated at St Cyr, France, he worked briefly for the Ottoman Sultan in Istanbul, and was granted the title of khedive (viceroy) in 1866. His massive development programme included the building of the Suez Canal, which was opened in splendour in 1869. The accumulation of a large foreign debt led to European intervention; he was deposed under European pressure by the Ottoman sultan in 1879, and replaced by his eldest son, Tewfik.

isobar **1** In meteorology, a line on a weather map joining places of equal barometric pressure. Because of variations in barometric pressure with altitude, recordings from different elevations are corrected and adjusted to pressure at sea level. The closer the lines are together, the stronger the pressure gradient force, and therefore the stronger the winds.
2 In thermodynamics, a line of constant pressure on a graph, depicting the relationship between volume and temperature.

Isocrates [iysokrateez] (436–338 BC) Greek orator and prose writer, born in Athens, Greece. In his youth, he joined the circle of Socrates, but abandoned philosophy for speech writing. He then became an influential teacher of oratory (c.390 BC), and presented rhetoric as an essential foundation of education.

isocynate *fulminate*

isoelectronic Having the same number of electrons. Examples of isoelectronic ions and atoms are O^{2-}, F^-, Ne, Na^+, and Mg^{2+}, each with 10 electrons; the molecules N_2O and CO_2 are also isoelectronic, with 22 electrons.

isohyet [iysohhiyet] A line on a weather map joining places receiving equal amounts of rainfall.

isolating language *analytic language*

isolationism A foreign policy strategy of withdrawing from international affairs as long as the country's interests are not affected. It is a means of avoiding involvement in international conflicts, and implies neutrality in most cases. It was practised by the USA, which kept out of the League of Nations, World War 1, and World War 2 until attacked by the Japanese, and has long been associated with Switzerland.

isolation unit A location designed to accommodate either highly infective patients or those susceptible to infection from others. Entry and exit to the unit is tightly controlled to prevent contaminated materials moving into or out of the room. Persons entering or leaving the room are required to wear sterile protective gowns. Airflow to and from the room is controlled to avoid contamination by airborne micro-organisms.

isoline [iysohliyn] A line on a map which joins places of equal value; also known as an **isopleth**. For example, on a temperature map, places recording the same temperature are joined by an isotherm.

isomers [iysohmerz] Substances having the same molecular formula but with the atoms arranged differently. The main types are: (1) **structural isomers**, such as ethanol (CH_3CH_2OH) and methyl ether (CH_3OCH_3), with different connectivities, (2) **geometrical isomers**, such as maleic and fumaric acid, where two different arrangements arise because of restricted rotation about a bond, and (3) **optical isomers**, such as the two forms of lactic acid, where the isomers are non-superimposable mirror images of one another.

isometrics [iysohmetriks] A form of physical exercise in which muscles are contracted, but not allowed to move the associated joints. Muscles are used in this way when exerting force on a closed door or fixed bar. Isometric exercises are often undertaken to strengthen muscles not much used in everyday movements.

isopentane *pentane*

isopleth *isoline*

Isopoda [iysopoda] A diverse order of crustaceans characterized by a flattened body and seven similar pairs of thoracic legs; typically bottom-living in aquatic habitats, sometimes parasitic on fishes and crustaceans; some, the woodlice, are highly successful in terrestrial habitats. (Class: Malacostraca.)

isoprene [iysohpreen] C_5H_8, IUPAC **2-methylbuta-1,3-diene**, a liquid, boiling point 34°C. Natural rubber may be considered an addition polymer of isoprene. It is also the basic structural unit of terpene molecules.

isopropyl *propyl*

Isoptera [iysoptera] *termite*

ISO speed rating The sensitivity to light of photographic material expressed on a numerical scale defined by the International Standards Organization (ISO). It replaces both the former systems established by the American Standards Association (ASA) and a Deutsche Industrie Norm (DIN). A film speed is expressed in the form ISO 200/24°. The first set of digits refer to an arithmetical film speed, the second to a logarithmic system. For a film of half this sensitivity, the rating would be 100/21°, while a doubling would be 400/27°.

isospin In particle and nuclear physics, a vector quantum number conserved in strong interactions only, useful in determining allowed reactions and classifying particles; sometimes called **isotopic spin**. For example, neutrons and protons both have an isospin vector of length ½ unit that points up for protons and down for neutrons. The strong nuclear force is independent of the orientation of this vector, reflecting the fact that the strong force is independent of electric charge. It is modelled on the spin quantum number.

isostasy [iysostasee] A theory describing the state of mass balance in the Earth's crust which can be considered as less dense blocks floating on the denser semi-molten mantle. Thus high mountains must be regions where the crust is thickest, with deep roots extending into the mantle. Also, continents uplift (*elastic rebound*) when material is removed by erosion or an overburden of ice is melted away, as at the end of an ice age.

isotherm 1 In meteorology, a line on a weather map joining places of equal temperature.
2 In thermodynamics, a line of constant temperature on a graph, depicting the relationship between volume and pressure.

isothermal process In thermodynamics, a process in which the temperature is constant while the system changes. Examples include melting and boiling.

isotopes Species of the same element that are chemically identical, having the same proton number, but of different atomic masses due to a differing number of neutrons in the nucleus. All elements have isotopes. Many elements occur naturally as a mixture of isotopes.

isotope separation The separation of an isotopic mixture into its component isotopes. The charged ions of isotopes are deflected in electric and magnetic fields by differing amounts, depending on their mass – an effect exploited in the mass spectrometer. The rate of diffusion of a gas of isotopic mixture depends on the isotope mass, exploited in gaseous uranium hexafluoride for the enrichment of nuclear fuel.

isotopic spin *isospin*

isotropic A term used to describe a material or feature whose properties are the same in all directions. For example, metals are isotropic, since their properties (eg conductivity and tensile strength) are the same throughout. The term contrasts with **anisotropic**, where the properties are not the same in all directions. An example is wood, which is stronger along the grain than across it. Anisotropy in certain crystals causes birefringence.

ISP *Internet Service Provider*

Israel *p.791*

Israel, tribes of In the Bible, a confederacy of 12 tribes generally traced to Jacob's 12 sons – six by Leah (Reuben, Simeon, Levi, Judah, Issachar, Zebulun), two by Rachel (Joseph, Benjamin), two by Rachel's maid Bilhah (Dan, Naphtali), and two by Leah's maid Zilpah (Gad, Asher); the name *Israel* had been given to Jacob (*Gen* 32.28) after the story of his wrestling with a divine being. During the settlement of Canaan and the Transjordan, the tribes were allocated portions of land (*Josh* 13–19); but the Levites, a priestly class, had no allocation and possibly were never a 'tribe' as such, and Joseph's 'tribe' was actually two tribes, traced to his two sons Ephraim and Manasseh (*Gen* 48). The number of tribes was thereby maintained as 'twelve'. Once the monarchy was established in Israel (c.10th-c BC), the tribal confederation effectively ended, although it still played a role in Jewish religious thought.

Issachar, tribe of [isakah(r)] One of the 12 tribes of ancient Israel, said to be descended from Issachar, one of Jacob's sons by his wife Leah. Its territory included the central plain of Jezreel between Mt Tabor and Mt Gilboa.

issuing house A merchant bank which specializes in the issue of shares and bonds on the stock market. Over 50 banks belong to the Issuing Houses Association in the UK.

Istanbul [istanbul], or **Stamboul**, formerly **Byzantium** (c.660 BC–AD 330), **Constantinople** (330–1930) 41°02N 28°57E, pop (2000e) 7 862 000. Capital city of Istanbul province, NW Turkey, on the Golden Horn and on both sides of the Bosporus; the only city in the world situated on two continents; chief city and seaport of Turkey; commercial and financial centre; damaged in terrorist bomb attacks, 2003; the part corresponding to historic Constantinople is on the European side; founded and renamed by Constantine I in AD 330 on the site of ancient Byzantium, becoming the new capital of the Roman Empire; remains of ancient Constantinople are a world heritage site; see of the patriarch of the Greek Orthodox Church and of the Armenian Church; airport; railway (once noted as the E terminus of the Orient Express, and still an important rail junc-

Israel

□ International Airport - - - Palestinian National Authority

Heb **Yisrael**, official name **State of Israel**, Heb **Medinat Yisrael**

Local names Yisra'el (Hebrew), Isrā'īl (Arabic)

Timezone GMT +2

Area 20 770 km²/8017 sq mi (within boundaries defined by 1949 armistice agreements)

Population total (2002e) 6 394 000 (excluding E Jerusalem and Israeli settlers in occupied territories)

Status Republic

Date of independence 1948

Capital Jerusalem

Languages Hebrew and Arabic (official), also European languages spoken

Ethnic groups Jewish (83%), Arab (11%)

Religions Jewish (85%), Muslim (11%), Christian and others (4%)

Physical features Extends 420 km/261 mi N–S; width varies from 20 km/12 mi to 116 km/72 mi; mountainous interior, rising to 1208 m/3963 ft at Mt Meron; mountains near Galilee (Lake Tiberius) and Samaria in the West Bank, dropping E to below sea-level in the Jordan-Red Sea rift valley; R Jordan forms part of E border; Dead Sea, between Israel and Jordan, 400 m/1286 ft below sea level, is the largest lake and has no outlet; Negev desert (S) occupies c.60% of the country's area.

Climate Mediterranean climate in N and C, with hot, dry summers and warm, wet winters; average annual temperature 9°C (Jan), 23°C (Jul) in Jerusalem; rainfall 528 mm/21 in.

Currency 1 New Israeli Shekel (NIS) = 100 agorot

Economy Over 90% of exports are industrial products; major tourist area, primarily to the religious centres; copper, potash, phosphates, citrus fruits, cotton, sugar beet, bananas, beef and dairy products; a world leader in agrotechnology, with areas of intensive cultivation; the kibbutz system produces c.40% of food output, but in recent years has turned increasingly towards industry.

GDP (2002e) $117·4 bn, per capita $19 500

Human Development Index (2002) 0·896

History Zionist movement founded by Theodor Herzl, end of 19th-c; thousands of Jews returned to Palestine, then part of the Ottoman Empire; Britain given League of Nations mandate to govern Palestine and establish Jewish national home there, 1922; British evacuated Palestine, and Israel proclaimed independence, 1948; invasion by Arab nations, resulting in armistice, 1949; Israel gained control of the Gaza Strip, Sinai Peninsula (as far as the Suez Canal), West Bank of the R Jordan (including E sector of Jerusalem), and the Golan Heights in Syria, during the Six-Day War, 1967; Camp David conference between Egypt and Israel, 1978; Israeli withdrawal from Sinai, 1979; invasion of Lebanon, forcing the PLO to leave Beirut, 1982–5; renewed tension with uprising of Arabs in occupied territories (the Intifada), 1988; peace agreement with PLO, and planned recognition of Palestine, 1993; withdrawal from Gaza and Jericho, 1994; conflict with Jordan formally ended, 1994; assassination of Yitzhak Rabin, 1995; Arafat elected President in first Palestine general election, Jan 1996; withdrawal from S Lebanon, 2000; escalating reprisal attacks on Palestinian targets, 2001; siege of Bethlehem, 2002; conflict ongoing, 2003–4; Geneva Accord peace plan launched, December 2003; a parliamentary democracy, with a Prime Minister, a Cabinet, and a unicameral Parliament (Knesset); President elected for a maximum of two five-year terms.

Head of State
1948–52 Chaim Weizmann
1952–63 Itzhak Ben-Zvi
1963–73 Zalman Shazar
1973–8 Ephraim Katzair
1978–83 Yitzhak Navon
1983–93 Chaim Herzog
1993–2000 Ezer Weizmann
2000 Avraham Burg *Interim*
2000– Moshe Katzav

Head of Government
1948–53 David Ben-Gurion
1954–5 Moshe Sharett
1955–63 David Ben-Gurion
1963–9 Levi Eshkol
1969–74 Golda Meir
1974–7 Itzhak Rabin
1977–83 Menachem Begin
1983–4 Yitzhak Shamir
1984–6 Shimon Peres
1986–92 Yitzhak Shamir
1992–5 Itzhak Rabin
1995–6 Shimon Peres
1996–9 Binyamin Netanyahu
1999–2001 Ehud Barak
2001– Ariel Sharon

tion); five universities (1453, 1773, 1863, 1883, 1911); suspension bridges (first in 1973) link European and Asian sections; commerce, textiles, shipbuilding, food processing, leather, tobacco, cement, glass; a major tourist area; Topkapi Palace (15th-c), Hagia Sophia Basilica (6th-c), Blue Mosque of Sultan Ahmet (17th-c), Mosque of Sulaiman the Magnificent (16th-c), Roman cisterns, covered bazaar; International Culture and Art Festival (Jun–Jul).

Isthmian Games In ancient Greece, one of the main Pan-Hellenic contests, held every other year near the Isthmus of Corinth. They were in honour of the god Poseidon, and consisted of athletic contests, horse racing, and poetical and musical competitions.

Istria [eestria], Serbo-Croatian **Istra** area 3160 sq km/1220 sq mi. Peninsula at the N end of the Adriatic Sea, Croatia; occupied by Croats, Slovenes, and Italians; formerly part of the Italian province of Venezia Giulia; ceded to Yugoslavia, 1947 (apart from Trieste); chief town, Pula; tourist area.

i.t.a. Abbreviation of **Initial Teaching Alphabet**, devised in 1959 by UK educationist Sir (Isaac) James Pitman (1901–85) to assist children in the early stages of reading. It is a lower-case system of 44 symbols in which each symbol represents a phoneme, giving a closer correlation between symbol and sound than in traditional English orthography, which it was intended not to replace, but to supplement. At its peak, i.t.a. was being used in many schools in Britain and abroad, but is rarely used today.

Itaipú Dam [eetiypoo] A major earth- and rock-fill gravity buttress dam on the R Paraná at the Brazil-Paraguay frontier; completed in 1991; height 189 m/620 ft. It has the capacity to generate 12 600 megawatts of hydroelectricity, and is claimed to be the largest hydroelectric complex in the world.

Italian *Italian literature; Romance languages*

Italian art The central tradition in European art, and the most powerful source of stylistic influences from the late Middle Ages to the 18th-c, affecting all other culture. Mediaeval Italy saw classical motifs re-used for Christian subjects, while antique figure sculpture dominated styles and standards for 1500 years. The succession of great masters begins with Giotto in the early 14th-c and continues unbroken down to Canova (died 1822). Italy was never unified during that time, and Florentine art developed very differently from that of Venice, Rome, or Bologna.

Italian literature After some allegorical romances written under French influence in the 13th-c and the spread of love lyrics performed by troubadours, Italian literature came to precocious maturity the next century with the work of Dante (*Divina commedia*, c.1300), Petrarch, and Boccaccio (*Decameron*, 1348–58). These great poets and humanists had imitators but no real successors until the Renaissance. Then, the courts of Florence and Naples produced many spirited writers, while at Ferrara Boiardo wrote the *Orlando innamorato* (1486), Ariosto provided a more famous sequel, the *Orlando furioso* (1516), and Tasso wrote the heroic epic *Gerusalemme liberata* (1581). Machiavelli's cynical treatise *Il principe* (1532, The Prince) and Aretino's licentious *Letters* (published 1609) are also an index of the times. A further long period of relative decline was punctuated by the scientific and philosophical works of Galileo and Vico, and Goldoni's comedies. The Romantic movement brought the anguished lyrics of Leopardi, and Manzoni's historical novel *I promessi sposi* (1825–7, The Betrothed). The Realist novel took root in Sicily with Giovanni Verga (1840–1922) and in Sardinia with Grazia Deledda (1875–1936; Nobel Prize, 1926). After *Six Characters in Search of an Author* (1921), Luigi Pirandello conducted a single-handed revival of the Italian theatre, which has been followed up by the radical plays of Dario Fo (eg *The Accidental Death of an Anarchist*). Significant 20th-c Italian novelists included Italo Svevo, Alberto Moravia, Ignazio Silone, and Italo Calvino; while the poets Quasimodo and Montale have both received a Nobel Prize.

Italian millet *millet*

Italian Wars A series of conflicts lasting from 1494 to 1559 (Treaty of Cateau-Cambrésis) between the French Valois monarchs and the Habsburgs for the control of Italy. Both houses laid claim to the throne of the Kingdom of Naples, but after seven phases of warfare, involving a host of different monarchs and states, Spain emerged victorious.

Italic languages The early languages spoken in the area of modern Italy. The major language of the group was *Latin*, the language of Rome and the surrounding provinces, evidenced in inscriptions from the 6th-c BC, and in literature from the 3rd-c BC; it is used now only in formulaic contexts of religion, and in public (usually governmental) declamations. The modern Romance languages ultimately belong to the Italic family.

italic script A sloping style of handwriting introduced by Aldus Manutius of Venice in c.1500, which was later introduced into printing. Today, it has a wide range of functions, including the identification of foreign words, quoted forms, book titles, emphatic utterance, and special emotional effects.

Italy *p.793*

ITAR-TASS The Russian state central information agency, with headquarters in Moscow. The successor to TASS, the Soviet news agency, it was renamed in 1992. The present name comprises two acronyms, ITAR: **Informationoe Telegrafnoe Agentsvo Rossi** (Information Telegraph Agency of Russia) and TASS: **Telegrafnoe Agentsvo Sovetskovo Soyuza** (Telegraph Agency of the Soviet Union). ITAR-TASS is today one of the world's largest news agencies.

itch An irritating sensation in the skin, also known as **pruritus** [prooriytuhs], which may be extremely distressing. It may occur in one area as the result of a local irritant or skin disease (eg lice, scabies, dermatitis, psoriasis). It may also be a generalized symptom of an underlying disorder (eg lymphoma, jaundice). Occasionally the complaint is the result of a psychoneurosis.

itch mite A parasitic mite (Sarcoptes scabiei) found in humans; causes itching by burrowing into the horny layer of skin; females lay eggs in burrows; larvae and nymphs also feed on skin; also known as **scabies**. (Order: Acari.)

Ito, Hirobumi [eetoh] (1841–1909) Japanese statesman and premier (1885–8, 1892–6, 1898, 1900–1), born in Choshu province, S Japan. He visited Europe and the USA on several occasions, drafted the Meiji constitution (1889), and played a major role in abolishing Japanese feudalism and building up the modern state. He was assassinated at Harbin by a supporter of Korean independence.

Itúrbide, Agustín de [eetoorbithay] (1783–1824) Mexican general, born in Morelia, C Mexico. He became prominent in the movement for Mexican independence, and made himself emperor as Agustin I (1822–3). He was forced to abdicate, travelled in Europe, and was executed on his return to Mexico.

IUD *contraception*

IUPAC [yoopak] Acronym for **International Union of Pure and Applied Chemistry**, best known as the more-or-less acknowledged authority on chemical nomenclature. Its system, which requires frequent change, attempts to provide clear rules for naming compounds unambiguously.

Iuppiter *Jupiter* (mythology)

Ivan III, known as **the Great** (1440-1505) Grand Prince of Moscow (1462–1505), born in Moscow, Russia. He succeeded in ending his city's subjection to the Tartars, and gained control over several Russian principalities. In 1472 he assumed the title of 'Sovereign of all Russia', and adopted the emblem of the two-headed eagle of the Byzantine Empire.

Ivan IV, known as **the Terrible** (1530–84) Grand prince of Moscow (1533–84), born near Moscow, the first to assume the title of 'tsar' (Lat *Caesar*) in 1547. He subdued Kazan (1552) and Astrakhan (1556), made the first inroads into Siberia (1581–3), and established commercial links with England (1550). In 1564 the treachery of some of his counsellors caused him to see treachery everywhere, and he embarked on a reign of terror, directed principally at the feudal aristocracy (boyars) and the church. He nonetheless did much for Russian commerce, and printing was introduced into Russia during his reign.

Ivanisevic, Goran [ivaneesevich] (1971–) Tennis player, born in Split, W Croatia. He turned professional in 1988 and won his first tour title in Stuttgart in 1990. Ranked number two in the world in 1992, he won a bronze medal at the Barcelona Olympics. He lost the Wimbledon final that year to Andre Agassiz, and was a losing finalist twice more (1994, 1998). In 2001 he had a disappointing season dogged by injury and fell to 129 in the rankings, but he entered Wimbledon on a wild card, and went

Italy

☐ International Airport ∴ World heritage site

Ital **Italia**, official name **Italian Republic**, Ital **Repubblica Italiana**

Local name Italia

Timezone GMT +1

Area 301 255 km²/116 314 sq mi

Population total (2002e) 57 988 000

Status Republic

Capital Rome

Languages Italian (official), with German spoken in the Trentino-Alto Adige, French in Valle d'Aosta, and Slovene in Trieste-Gorizia

Ethnic groups Homogeneous (98%), with German-Italian, French-Italian, and Slovene-Italian minorities

Religions Roman Catholic (83%), non-religious (14%)

Physical features Comprises the boot-shaped peninsula extending south into the Mediterranean Sea, as well as Sicily, Sardinia, and some smaller islands; Italian peninsula extends c.960 km/600 mi SE from the Lombardy plains; Apennines rise to peaks above 2900 m/9000 ft; Alps form a border in N; broad, fertile Lombardo-Venetian plain in basin of R Po; several lakes at foot of the Alps, including Maggiore, Como, Garda; flat and marshy on Adriatic coast (N); coastal mountains descend steeply to the Ligurian Sea on the Riviera (W); Mt Vesuvius, 1289 m/4230 ft, and Vulcano, 502 m/1650 ft, are active volcanoes; island of Sicily separated from the mainland by the 4 km/2·5 mi wide Strait of Messina; the island includes the volcanic cone of Mt Etna, 3390 m/11 122 ft.

Climate Warm and temperate in S; hot and sunny summers, short cold winters; average annual temperatures 7°C (Jan), 25°C (Jul); average annual rainfall 657 mm/ 26 in; cold, wet, often snowy in higher peninsular areas; Mediterranean climate in coastal regions; Adriatic coast colder than the W coast, and receives less rainfall.

Currency 1 euro = 100 cents (previous to February 2002, 1 Italian Lira (L, Lit) = 100 centesimi).

Economy Industry largely concentrated in N; machinery, iron and steel; tourism; poorer agricultural region in S; Po valley a major agricultural region, with wheat, maize, sugar, potatoes, rice, beef, dairy farming; foothills of the Alps produce apples, peaches, walnuts, wine; further S, citrus fruits, vines, olives, tobacco.

GDP (2002e) $1·455 tn, per capita $25 100

Human Development Index (2002) 0·913

History Inhabited by the Etruscans (N), Latins (C), and Greeks (S) in pre-Roman times; most regions part of the Roman Empire by 3rd-c BC; invaded by barbarian tribes, 4th-c AD; last Roman emperor deposed, 476; ruled by the Lombards and by the Franks under Charlemagne, crowned Emperor of the Romans, 800; part of the Holy Roman Empire under Otto, 962; conflict between popes and emperors throughout Middle Ages; dispute between Guelphs and Ghibellines, 12th-c; divided among five powers, 14th–15th-c (Kingdom of Naples, Duchy of Milan, republics of Florence and Venice, the papacy); major contribution to European culture through the Renaissance; numerous republics set up after the French Revolution; Napoleon crowned King of Italy, 1804; upsurge of liberalism and nationalism (Risorgimento) in 19th-c; unification achieved under Victor Emmanuel II of Sardinia, aided by Cavour and Garibaldi, by 1870; fought alongside Allies in World War I; Fascist movement brought Mussolini to power, 1922; conquest of Abyssinia, 1935–6, and Albania, 1939; alliance with Hitler in World War 2 led to the end of the Italian Empire; institution of monarchy abolished and became a democratic republic, 1946; parliament consists of a Chamber of Deputies and a Senate; the President of the Republic is Head of State and appoints a Prime Minister; continued political instability, with some 50 governments in power since the formation of the republic.

Head of State

1946–8 Enrico de Nicola
1948–55 Luigi Einaudi
1955–62 Giovanni Gronchi
1962–4 Antonio Segni
1964–71 Giuseppe Saragat
1971–8 Giovanni Leone
1978–85 Alessandro Pertini
1985–92 Francesco Cossiga
1992–9 Oscar Luigi Scalfaro
1999– Carlo Ciampi

Head of Government

1970–2 Emilio Colombo
1972–4 Giulio Andreotti
1974–6 Aldo Moro
1976–8 Giulio Andreotti
1979–80 Francesco Cossiga
1980–1 Arnaldo Forlani
1981–2 Giovanni Spadolini
1982–3 Amintore Fanfani
1983–7 Bettino Craxi
1987 Amintore Fanfani
1987–8 Giovanni Goria
1988–9 Ciriaco de Mita
1989–92 Giulio Andreotti
1992–3 Giuliano Amato
1993–4 Carlo Azeglio Ciampi
1994–5 Sylvio Berlusconi
1995–6 Lamberto Dini
1996–8 Romano Prodi
1998–2000 Massimo D'Alema
2000–1 Giuliano Amato
2001– Silvio Berlusconi

on to win the title in a dramatic 5-set final against Pat Rafter of Australia.

Ivanovo [eevahnovo], formerly **Ivanovo-Voznesensk** (1871–1932) 57°00N 41°00E, pop (2000e) 480 000. Capital city of Ivanovskaya oblast, C European Russia; on R Uvod, 318 km/198 mi NW of Moscow; founded, 1871; noted for its revolutionary activities in the 1880s, 1905, and 1917; railway; historic centre of Russia's cotton-milling; textiles, machines, chemicals, wood products, foodstuffs.

Ivanovo churches [ivahnovo] A series of cells, chapels, and churches cut out of the rock face on the banks of the Rusenski Lom R, near the village of Ivanovo in NE Bulgaria. The complex, which is now a world heritage site, was constructed by monks during the 13th-c and 14th-c.

Ives, Charles E(dward) (1874–1954) Composer, born in Danbury, Connecticut, USA. He studied music at Yale, and worked in insurance until 1930, when he retired due to ill health. His music is firmly based in the American tradition, but at the same time he experimented with dissonances, polytonal harmonies, and conflicting rhythms, anticipating modern European trends. He composed four symphonies, chamber music (including the well-known 2nd piano sonata, the *Concord Sonata*), and many songs. In 1947 he was awarded the Pulitzer Prize for his third symphony (composed in 1904).

Iviza *Ibiza*

Ivor Novello Awards British awards given annually since 1955 for the best songs, and musical scores in various categories. There is also an award for services to popular music.

Ivory, James (Francis) (1928–) Film director, born in Berkeley, California, USA. As a student at the University of Southern California, he directed a short subject, *Four in the Morning* (1953), and was then commissioned by the Asia Society to go to India to make a documentary (1960). There, in partnership with a local producer, Ismail Merchant, he formed Merchant-Ivory Productions in 1961, which became one of the most enduring and productive of independent film associations. International success came with *Shakespeare Wallah* (1965), which he wrote with Ruth Jhabvala, and other films dealing with the clash of cultural sensibilities in India. Basing their company in the USA from the early 1970s, the Ivory–Merchant team enjoyed its greatest success with relatively pure adaptations of literary works, such as *The Europeans* (1979), *The Bostonians* (1984), *A Room With a View* (1987), and *Howard's End* (1992, BAFTA best film). He also wrote *Bombay Talkie* (1970), and wrote and produced *A Soldier's Daughter Never Cries* (1998). In 2002 they were awarded a BAFTA Fellowship for outstanding contributions to world cinema.

ivory Pieces of walrus and elephant tusk, regarded as precious material by many societies throughout the world. Carved ivory ornaments, jewellery and religious objects were produced in China from about the 15th-c BC, and later by the Greeks and Romans in Europe. Most of the finest small-scale sculptures to survive from the mediaeval period are carved from ivory, and it continued to be widely used for luxury goods until modern concern for wildlife conservation strictly curtailed its supply.

Ivory Coast *Côte d'Ivoire*

ivy An evergreen woody climber (*Hedera helix*), growing to 30 m/100 ft, native to Europe and W Asia; adhesive aerial roots; leaves dark green often with pale veins; those of juvenile, climbing shoots palmately 3–5-lobed; those of mature, non-climbing shoots, oval, entire; flowers greenish-yellow, 5-petalled, petals 3–4 mm/0·12–0·16 in, in rounded umbels produced on non-climbing shoots; fruits berry-like, black, ribbed, poisonous. (Family: Araliaceae.)

Ivy League A group of long-established and prestigious colleges in NE USA. The league was formally established in 1956 to oversee inter-collegiate sports. It includes the universities of Harvard (Cambridge, MA, founded 1636), Yale (New Haven, CT, founded 1701), Pennsylvania (Philadelphia, PA, founded 1740), Princeton (Princeton, NJ, founded 1746), Columbia (New York City, NY, founded 1754), Brown (Providence, RI, founded 1764), Dartmouth College (Hanover, NH, founded 1769), and Cornell (Ithaca, NY, founded 1865).

Iwo Jima [eewoh jeema] area c.21 sq km/8 sq mi. The most important and largest of the Volcano Is; in the W Pacific Ocean, 1222 km/759 mi S of Tokyo; 8 km/5 mi long; maximum width 4 km/2½ mi; rises to 161 m/528 ft at Suribachi-yama, an extinct volcano; coastguard station (N); scene of major battle of World War 2 (1944–5), when the heavily fortified Japanese air base was taken in a 3-month campaign; returned to Japan, 1968; no permanent population; sugar, sulphur.

Ixion [ikseeon] In Greek mythology, a king of Thessaly, the first murderer; also the father of the Centaurs. For attempting to rape Hera he was bound to a wheel of fire, usually located in the underworld.

Ixtaccihuatl [eestaseewatl], Aztec **Iztaccihuatl** 19°11N 98°38W. Dormant volcano in C Mexico; rises to 5286 m/17 342 ft, 56 km/35 mi SE of Mexico City; irregular-shaped, snow-capped volcano with three summits; situated in Ixtaccihuatl-Popocatépetl National Park, area 260 sq km/100 sq mi, established in 1935.

Izabal, Lake [eesaval] (Span **Lago de**) Lake in Izabal department, E Guatemala; drains into an inlet of the Caribbean Sea, via the R Dulce; area 1000 sq km/400 sq mi; length 48 km/30 mi; width 24 km/15 mi; the largest lake in the country, serving as an important commercial waterway.

Izanagi no Mikoto and **Izanami no Mikoto** Respectively, male and female Japanese gods. In the creation myth these were the first beings, who created islands in the water and the other gods.

iz(z)ard [izah(r)d] *goat*

Izhevsk [izhefsk], formerly **Ustinov** (1985–7) 56°49N 53°11E, pop (2000e) 690 000. Capital city of Udmurtia, Russia; founded, 1760; city status, 1918; capital of Udmurtia, 1921; renamed in honour of Soviet armaments politician, Dmitri Fedorovich Ustinov (1908–84); airfield; railway; university; cultural and educational centre; metalworking, machine building, motorcycles, paper, foodstuffs.

Izmir [eezmeer], formerly **Smyrna** 38°25N 27°10E, pop (2000e) 2 115 000. Seaport capital of Izmir province, W Turkey, on an inlet of the Aegean Sea; third largest city in Turkey; severely damaged by earthquakes, 1928, 1939; airfield; railway; two universities (1955, 1982); brewing, electronics, packaging, foodstuffs, steel, engines, cement, plastics, paper; largest poultry and egg farm in the Middle East; Kadifekale fortress (4th-c BC), Roman remains; annual international fair (Aug–Sep).

Iznik ware Pottery made at Iznik (formerly Nicaea) in NW Anatolia during the Ottoman period. The body, containing a mixture of ground glass (*frit*), silica, and white clay, was coated with a white paste, painted, and clear glazed. From c.1480 to 1530 the decoration was predominantly blue and strongly influenced by Chinese porcelain. Later a polychrome palette developed, which after c.1560 included sealing-wax red. Dishes, tankards, bottles, mosque lamps, and tiles were exuberantly decorated with flowers and foliage, arabesques and palmettes, geometrical patterns, ships, and more rarely animals or human figures. The potteries declined in the 17th-c.

Izzard, Eddie [izah(r)d] (1962–) British comedian, actor, and writer, born in Aden, SW Yemen. His family moved to Northern Ireland, then South Wales, and he studied at the University of Sheffield, where he presented his first shows. He worked in street theatre and comedy clubs before devising a theatre act as a stand-up comic, and becoming nationally known through live videos of his major shows at the Ambassadors (1993) and the Albery (1995) in London. He was voted best live stand-up comic in 1993, and in 2000 he won two Emmy awards for *Eddie Izzard: Dressed to Kill*. Other shows include *One Word Improv* (1997), *Glorious* (1997), and *Sexie* (2003). He also wrote the television sitcom, *The Cows* (1996), and made film appearances in *The Secret Agent* (1996), *Circus* (2000), and *Revengers Tragedy* (2002). In 2003 he starred in the television drama, *40*, for Channel 4.

j

jabiru [jabiroo] A name used for several species of stork; especially *Jabiru mycteria* of Central and South America; also the **saddle-bill stork** (*Ephippiorhyncus senegalensis*) from S Africa, and the **black-necked stork** (*Ephippiorhyncus asiaticus*) from India to N Australia. (Family: Ciconiidae.)

Jabneh [jabne], or **Jamnia** An ancient city on the coastal plain W of Jerusalem and S of modern Tel Aviv, referred to occasionally in writings of the Biblical and Maccabean periods. It achieved special prominence in early Judaism after the fall of Jerusalem (AD 70), when Rabban Johanan ben Zakkai asked the Roman Emperor for the city, and re-established the Sanhedrin council there for a time. Famous Jewish scholars gathered there to lay the foundations for the Mishnah and engage in study of the Torah.

jacamar [jakamah(r)] A bird native to the New World tropics; long bill and tail; iridescent plumage; inhabits forests; eats insects caught in flight; nests on ground in burrow. (Family: Galbulidae, 15 species.)

jacana [jakana], Port **jaçaná** [jasanah] A bird native to the tropics worldwide; inhabits fresh water lakes and ponds; eats small aquatic animals and plants; resembles rails, but not related; toes extremely long; walks on floating vegetation; also known as **lily-trotter** or **lotus bird**. (Family: Jacanidae, 8 species.)

jacaranda A small deciduous tree (*Jacaranda mimosifolia*) growing to 12 m/40 ft; leaves pinnately divided into segments, which in turn are pinnately divided into numerous small, oval leaflets; inflorescences pyramidal; flowers drooping, funnel-shaped, blue. Native to Argentina, it has been widely planted in warm regions as an ornamental and street tree. (Family: Bignoniaceae.)

jacinth [jasinth] A rare red, orange, or yellow gemstone variety of the mineral zircon.

jackal A member of the dog family, resembling a large fox in appearance and habits; three African species: the **black-backed jackal** (*Canis mesomelas*), **side-striped jackal** (*Canis adustus*), and **simien(ian) jackal** (*Canis simensis*); also, the **golden jackal** (*Canis aureus*) from N Africa to SE Asia.

jackass *kookaburra*

jackdaw Either of two species of bird of the genus *Corvus*: the omnivorous jackdaw (*Corvus monedula*) from N Africa, Europe, and W Asia; and the insect-eating **daurian jackdaw** (*Corvus dauuricus*), from E Asia. Both nest in holes. (Family: Corvidae.)

Jack-go-to-bed-at-noon *goatsbeard* 1

Jacklin, Tony, popular name of **Anthony Jacklin** (1944–) Golfer, born in Scunthorpe, North Lincolnshire, EC England, UK. He won the 1969 Open at Royal Lytham (the first British winner for 18 years), and in 1970 won the US Open at Hazeltine, MN (the first British winner for 50 years). He turned professional in 1962, and won the Jacksonville Open in 1968, the first Briton to win on the US Tour. A former Ryder Cup player (1967–80), he was appointed non-playing captain of the European team (1983–9), and became director of golf at the San Roque club. He retired from the professional tournament circuit in 1999, and was elected to the World Golf Hall of Fame in 2002.

jackrabbit *hare*

Jack Russell A small terrier, developed in Britain by Rev John Russell (1795–1883); sent into foxes' burrows; originally fox-like in size, but white (to avoid confusion with the fox); now smaller, with shorter legs; often dark.

Jackson 32°18N 90°12W, pop (2000e) 184 300. Capital of state in Hinds Co, C Mississippi, USA, on the Pearl R; largest city in the state; established as a trading post (Le Fleur's Bluff), 1792; state capital, 1822; named after President Andrew Jackson; much of the city destroyed by Sherman's forces during the Civil War, 1863; airfield; railway; university; oil, natural gas, food processing, timber, metal and glass products; many civil rights demonstrations in the 1960s; 'Casey' Jones buried here; Dixie Livestock Show (Feb).

Jackson, Andrew, nickname **Old Hickory** (1767–1845) US statesman and seventh president (1829–37), born in Waxhaw, South Carolina, USA. His parents left Carrickfergus in Nothern Ireland in 1765 and settled in the Carolinas. He trained as a lawyer, and became a member of Congress for Tennessee (1796), a senator (1797), and a judge of its Supreme Court (1798–1804). In the War of 1812 against Britain, he was given command of the South, and his first military fame came from action against Creek Indians. His victory over the British at New Orleans (1815) further enhanced his reputation. His election as president was the result of a campaign in which he gained the support of the mass of voters – a new development in US politics which came to be called 'Jacksonian democracy'.

Jackson, Betty (1949–) Fashion designer, born in Backup, Lancashire, NW England, UK. She studied at the Birmingham College of Art, and became a freelance fashion illustrator (1971–3), design assistant (1973–5), and chief designer with Quorum (1975–81). In 1985 she was British Designer of the Year, and the same year won the British Fashion Council award. She is design director of Betty Jackson Ltd.

Jackson, Colin (Ray) (1967–) Athlete, born in Cardiff, S Wales, UK. His achievements in the 110 m hurdles include World Championship gold medals (1993, 1999), silver medals (1987, 1997), and Olympic silver (1988). He also held the European Championship title four times (1990, 1994, 1998, 2002). In the Commonwealth Games he won gold (1990, 1994) and silver medals (1986, 2002). He retired in 2003.

Jackson, Glenda (1936–) Actress and politician, born in Birkenhead, Merseyside, NW England, UK. She trained at the Royal Academy of Dramatic Art in London, and became a leading member of the Royal Shakespeare Company before appearing in films in 1967, winning Oscars for *Women in Love* (1969) and *A Touch of Class* (1973). She continued to portray complex characterizations on stage and screen, such as the poet Stevie Smith, whom she played first in the theatre and then in the film *Stevie* (1979), and made several television appearances. Later films include *Beyond Therapy* (1985), *Business as Usual* (1986), and *The Rainbow* (1989). A director of British Artists in 1983, she became a Labour MP in 1992 after which she devoted herself full-time to politics. In 1997 she was appointed Transport minister in the new Labour government. In 1999 she resigned from government to run as Labour candidate for the post of Lord Mayor of London, but was not selected by the party.

Jackson, Helen (Maria) Hunt, *née* **Fiske** (1830–85) Writer, born in Amherst, Massachusetts, USA. She turned to writing after the deaths of her first husband and two sons, remarried (1875), and settled in Colorado. A campaigner for American Indian rights, she highlighted the injustices of government policy in her book *A Century of Dishonor* (1881). She was appointed to a Federal Commission to investigate the Indian question, and the experience provided material for her successful novel *Ramona* (1884), which aroused social awareness but was acclaimed mainly for its nostalgic portrayal of old California.

Jackson, Jesse (Louis) (1941–) Clergyman and politician, born in Greenville, North Carolina, USA. He studied at the University of Illinois and Chicago Theological Seminary, and was ordained a Baptist minister in 1968. He was an active participant in the Civil Rights movement, and organized Operation PUSH (People United to Save Humanity) in 1971. In 1984 and 1988 he sought the Democratic nomination for the presidency, winning considerable support, and becoming the first African-American to mount a serious candidacy for the office. Active in a wide variety of public domains, and frequently controversial, he remained one of the more striking figures in American public life in the late 20th-c. In 2001 he decided to withdraw temporarily from public life following revelations of an extramarital affair.

Jackson, Mahalia (1911–72) Gospel singer, born in New Orleans, Louisiana, USA. The daughter of a clergyman, she sang in his choir as a child, later moving to Chicago, where she performed religious songs in Baptist churches. Her strong religious background and the influence of contemporary blues music were unmistakeably evident in her singing style. Two notably successful records were 'Move On Up a Little Higher' and 'Silent Night'. She appeared in the film *Jazz on a Summer's Day* (1958), singing Gospel music.

Jackson, Michael (1958–) Pop singer and dancer, born in Gary, Indiana, USA. With his brothers, Jackie, Tito, Marlon, and Jermaine in the pop group The Jackson Five, later The Jacksons, he knew stardom from the age of 11. Between 1972 and 1975 he had six solo hits on the Motown record label. In 1977 he played the scarecrow in *The Wiz*, a black remake of the film *The Wizard of Oz*. His first major solo album was *Off The Wall* (1979), and he consolidated his career with *Thriller* (1982), which sold over 35 million copies and established him as a pop superstar. He repeated this success with his album *Bad* (1987), and in 1988 wrote an autobiography *Moonwalk*, filmed as *Moonwalker*. Deals in 1991 for handling his album *Dangerous* were the most lucrative in pop history. *HIStory* appeared in 1995 and *Number Ones* in 2003. He developed a reclusive lifestyle in adulthood, though he continues to tour widely. Worldwide publicity surrounded him in 1993, when allegations about his sexual life caused the cancellation of an international tour on health grounds. In 2003 he was arrested on child molestation charges and released on $3m bail. He married Lisa Marie Presley, daughter of Elvis, in 1994 (divorced, 1996), and later in 1996 nurse Debbie Rowe (divorced, 1999).

Jackson, Thomas Jonathan, nickname **Stonewall Jackson** (1824–63) Confederate general in the American Civil War, born in Clarksburg, West Virginia, USA. In 1851 he became a professor at the Viriginia Military Institute. During the War, he took command of the Confederate troops at Harper's Ferry on the secession of Virginia, and commanded a brigade at Bull Run, where his firm stand gained him his nickname. He showed tactical superiority in the campaign of the Shenandoah Valley (1862), and gained several victories, notably at Cedar Run, Manassas, and Harper's Ferry. He was accidentally killed by his own troops at Chancellorsville.

Jack the Ripper Unidentified English murderer, who between August and November 1888 murdered and mutilated at least seven prostitutes in the East End of London. The murderer was never discovered. The affair roused much public disquiet, provoked a violent press campaign against the CID and the home secretary, and resulted in some reform of police methods. Speculation about the murderer's identity was still continuing in the 1990s, fuelled by the publication of his alleged diary in 1993.

Jacob Biblical character, the son of Isaac, and patriarch of the nation Israel. He supplanted his elder brother Esau, obtaining his father Isaac's special blessing and thus being seen as the inheritor of God's promises. He was re-named *Israel* (perhaps meaning 'God strives' or 'he who strives with God') after his struggle with a divine being. By his wives Leah and Rachel and their maids he fathered 12 sons, to whom Jewish tradition traced the 12 tribes of Israel.

Jacobean Style A form of English Renaissance architecture, named after James I and dating from his reign (1603–25). Very close to Elizabethan Style, it is characterized by a symmetry of facades, large windows and, in the case of manor houses such as Hatfield (1608–12), E- or H-shaped plans.

Jacobi, Sir Derek (George) [jakohbee] (1938–) Actor, born in London, UK. He studied at Cambridge, made his professional debut in *One Way Pendulum* at Birmingham Repertory Theatre (1961), and joined the National Theatre's inaugural company playing Laertes in *Hamlet* (1963). He was with the Prospect Theatre (1972–8), made his New York debut in *The Suicide* (1980), and joined the Royal Shakespeare Company in 1982. He has made several film and television appearances, of which the most popular was the title role in the television drama serial *I, Claudius* (1977). He gave a highly acclaimed performance in Hugh Whitmore's *Breaking the Code* (1986–7), and appeared in films such as *Dead Again* (1991), *Hamlet* (1996), *Gladiator* (2000), and *Revengers Tragedy* (2002), but his main work continues to be in the theatre. He was knighted in 1994, and 1995–7 was associate director of the Chichester Festival Theatre.

Jacobins (French history) [jakobinz] A radical political group in the French Revolution, originally the Club Breton in Versailles, but renamed after transferring to the premises of the Dominican or 'Jacobin' fathers in Paris (1789). After successive purges, the club became the instrument of the Reign of Terror under Robespierre's dictatorship (1793–4), the name being associated thereafter with left-wing extremism.

Jacobins (religion) *Dominicans*

Jacobites Those who supported the claim of the Catholic James II, and his successors, to the British throne. The Jacobites launched two rebellions, in 1715 and 1745, against the Protestant Hanoverian succession, and in the period 1714–60 some British Tory politicians had Jacobite sympathies.

Jacobsen, Arne [yahkobsen] (1902–71) Architect and designer, born in Copenhagen, Denmark. He studied at the Royal Danish Academy, where he later became professor of architecture (1956). He won a House of the Future competition in 1929 and became a leading exponent of Modernism. He designed many private houses in the Bellavista resort near Copenhagen; his main public buildings were the SAS skyscraper in Copenhagen (1955) and St Catherine's College, Oxford (1964). He also designed cutlery and textiles, and classic furniture, especially the 'Egg' and 'Swan' chairs for his Royal Hotel in Copenhagen.

Jacobson, Dan (1929–) Novelist and short-story writer, born in Johannesberg, South Africa. He studied at the University of Witwatersrand in Johannesburg, then spent some time on a kibbutz in Israel before settling in Britain in 1958. He began writing in the 1950s, with *The Trap* (1955), later novels including *The Beginners* (1966), *The Wonder-Worker* (1973), *Her Story* (1987), and *Heshel's Kingdom* (1999). A volume of autobiography, *Time and Time Again*, appeared in 1985.

Jacopo della Quercia [yakohpoh dela kwairchia] (c.1374–1438) Sculptor, born in Siena, C Italy. His greatest works include the city's fountain (the 'Fonte Gaia', executed 1414–19) and the reliefs on the portal of San Petronia, Bologna.

Jacopone da Todi [yakopohnay da tohdee], originally **Iacopo di Iacobello dei Benedetti** (c.1236–1306) Religious poet, born in Todi, C Italy. He practised as an advocate, was converted in 1268, became a Franciscan in 1278, and was imprisoned (1298–1303) for satirizing Pope Boniface VIII. To him is ascribed the authorship of the *Stabat Mater* and other Latin hymns, and he wrote *laudi spirituali* ('spiritual praises'), important in the development of Italian drama.

Jacquard, Joseph Marie [zhakah(r)] (1752–1834) Silk-weaver, born in Lyon, SC France. His invention (1801–8) of the *Jacquard loom*, controlled by punched cards, enabled an ordinary workman to produce the most beautiful patterns in a style previously accomplished only with patience, skill, and labour. But though Napoleon rewarded him with a small pension and the Légion d'Honneur, the silk weavers were long opposed to his machine. At his death his machine was in almost universal use, and his punched card system was adopted in the 20th-c as a control and data input system for many office machines and early digital computers.

Jacquerie [zhakuhree] (1358) A serious peasant rebellion in NE France, noted for its savagery. Started by mercenaries following the English victory at Poitiers (1356), it degenerated (May 1358) into bitter violence between the oppressed peasantry, aggrieved Parisians, and their noble overlords; the latter massacred the insurgents indiscriminately at Meaux and Clermont-en-Beauvaisis (Jun 1358).

jade A semi-precious stone, either of two distinct mineral species: the relatively rare *jadeite* (a green pyroxene) which is often translucent, and *nephrite* (a variety of amphibole) which has a waxy lustre. Commonly green or white in colour, it is often used in ornamental carvings. Nephrite was in use for ritual objects in China by the 3rd millennium BC, the rarer jadeite in Europe for axes in the later 4th/3rd millennium. Though worked in Mexico from c.1500 BC, New World jadeite reached the West only after the Spanish Conquest (AD 1519), and China even later, c.1780. In traditional China, jade was believed to preserve corpses; complete funerary suits have been found in 2nd-c BC tombs.

jaeger *skua*

Jaffa *Tel Aviv–Yafo*

Jagger, Mick, popular name of **Sir Michael Phillip Jagger** (1943–) Singer, born in Dartford, Kent, SE England, UK. He attended the London School of Economics, but left to form his own rock group, The Rolling Stones, together with Keith Richard, Bill Wyman, Charlie Watts, and Brian Jones. Following their debut in London (1962), the group released its first single, 'Come On' (1963). Jagger's unconvential behaviour on stage, and the group's uninhibited lifestyles, cultivated a rebellious image which appealed to a generation of teenagers during the 1960s. He wrote and sang many of their hit singles including 'The Last Time' (1965), 'I Can't Get No Satisfaction' (1965), and various albums. He released two solo albums, *She's the Boss* (1985) and *Primitive Cool* (1987). Still popular after three decades, the group released the *Steel Wheels* album (1988), went on tour (1989), and were still in the charts in the 1990s with such albums as *Bridges to Babylon* (1997). In 2001 Jagger released a further solo album, *Goddess in the Doorway*. His film appearances include *Performance* (1968), *Ned Kelly* (1969), and *Freejack* (1992). He was knighted in 2002.

Jagiellons [yagyelonz] The ruling dynasty of Poland–Lithuania, Bohemia, and Hungary, which dominated EC Europe from the Baltic to the Danube in the 15th–16th-c. Founded when Jagiello, Grand Duke of Lithuania, became King of Poland (1386–1434), it flourished under his acquisitive successors until Sigismund II Augustus (r.1548–72) died without heirs.

jaguar A big cat (*Panthera onca*), found from S USA to N Argentina; coat with rings of dark blotches surrounding dark spots; some individuals almost black; inhabits woodland and savannah near water; swims and climbs well; eats peccaries, capybaras, other mammals, birds, fish, turtles.

jaguarundi or **jaguarondi** [jagwarundee] A member of the cat family (*Felis yagouaroundi*), found from S USA to Paraguay; short legs; long body; grey or reddish-brown (red form formerly called **Eyra cat**); inhabits woodland margins; eats birds and small mammals; once trained by Mayans to control rodents. It is an unusual cat, in that it may chase prey for up to 1·6 km/1 mi, and sometimes eats fruit.

jai alai *pelota*

Jainism [jiynizm] An indigenous religion of India which regards Vardhamana Mahavira (599–527 BC), said to be the last Tirthankara, as its founder. Jains believe that salvation consists in conquering material existence through adherence to a strict ascetic discipline, thus freeing the 'soul' from the working of karma for eternal all-knowing bliss. Liberation requires detachment from worldly existence, an essential part of which is the practice of *Ahimsa*, non-injury to living beings. The ascetic ideal is central to both monastic and lay Jainism, although final renunciation is possible only within the former. They numbered over 4·3 million in 2004.

Jaipur [jiypoor] 26°53N 75°50E, pop (2000e) 1 708 000. Capital of Rajasthan state, NW India, SW of Delhi; founded, 1727; railway; university (1947); textiles, metallurgy, stone carving, jewellery; Maharaja's palace, Sawai Man Singh Museum, Hawa Mahal (1739), Jantar Mantar observatory (1726); known as the 'pink city' since 1875, when Sawai Ram Singh had all the buildings of the bazaar painted pink.

Jakarta or **Djakarta** [jakah(r)ta], formerly **Batavia** 6°08S 106°45E, pop (2000e) 10 069 000. Seaport capital of Indonesia; on NW coast of Java, at mouth of R Liwung on Jakarta Bay; largest Indonesian city; developed as a trading post, 15th-c; headquarters of Dutch East India Company, 17th-c; capital of Indonesia, 1949; airport; railway; 11 universities (1950–60); timber, textiles, shipbuilding, paper, iron, rubber, tin, oil, coffee, palm oil, tea; Istiqlal Mosque; 90 m/295 ft high national monument; Taman Mini provincial exhibition.

Jaki, Stanley L (1924–) Catholic priest and physicist, born in Györ, Hungary. He entered the Benedictine Order in 1942, and in 1947 went to Rome, where he studied at the Pontifical Institute of San Anselmo. He was ordained in 1948. During 1954–8 he studied physics, and after 1965 was professor of astrophysics at Seton Hall University, NJ. Noted as a leading writer on interdisciplinary studies in the areas of science and theology, he is the recipient of the Lecomte du Nouy Prize (1970) and the Templeton Prize for Progress in Religion (1987).

Jakobson, Roman (Osipovich) [yahkobson] (1896–1982) Linguist, born in Moscow, Russia. The founder of the Moscow Linguistic Circle (which generated Russian formalism), he moved in 1920 to Czechoslovakia (starting the Prague Linguistic Circle), and finally in 1941 to the USA, where he taught at Harvard and the Massachusetts Institute of Technology until his death. His many books and papers on language have had a great influence on linguistic and literary thought.

Jalalabad [jalalabad] 34°26N 76°25E, pop (2001e) 100 000. Capital of Nangarhar province, E Afghanistan; on Kabul R, near Khyber Pass, linked by road to Kabul; founded c.1570 by Akbar the Great; nearest Afghan city of importance to the Pakistan border; in Afghan Wars, British troops held the city (1842) against an Afghan siege; in the 1990s, a Taliban stronghold with many guerilla training camps, some believed run by Osama bin Laden; camps targeted in US-led attack in campaign against the Taliban, Oct 2001; university and medical school; airfield; leading trading centre with India and Pakistan; sugarcane, rice, oranges; sugar-refining and paper-making industries.

jalap A perennial climber (*Ipomaea purga*) with tuberous roots and twining annual stems; leaves heart-shaped-triangular; flowers funnel-shaped, pinkish-purple; native to Mexico. The resinous roots yield a purgative drug. (Family: Convolvulaceae.)

Jamaica *p.798*

Jamal, Ahmad, originally **Fritz Jones** (1930–) Jazz pianist, born in Pittsburgh, Pennsylvania, USA. In 1952 he became the house pianist at the Lounge of the Pershing Hotel in Chicago with a guitarist and bassist, and his distinctive style, characterized by melodic understatement, harmonic inventiveness, and rhythmic lightness, attracted a small but fervent audience, among them Miles Davis. In 1956–9, Jamal's trio consisted of Israel Crosby on bass and Vernell Fournier on drums. A live recording

Jamaica

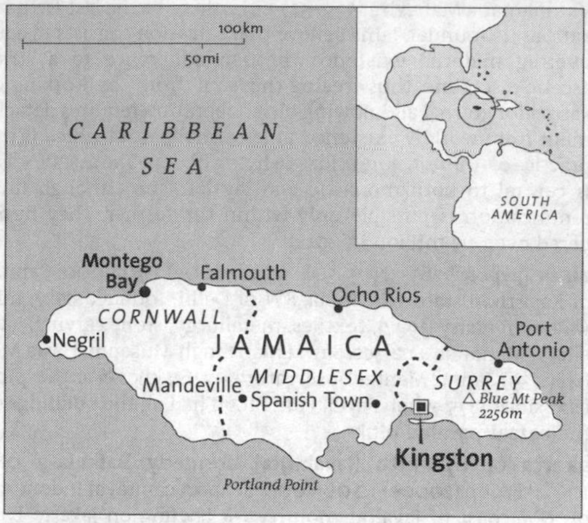

☐ International Airport

Local name Jamaica

Timezone GMT −5

Area 10 957 km²/4229 sq mi

Population total (2002e) 2 630 000

Status Independent state within the Commonwealth

Date of independence 1962

Capital Kingston

Languages English (official), with Jamaican Creole widely spoken

Ethnic groups African (76%), Afro-European (15%), East Indian and Afro-Indian (3%), white (3%), Chinese and Afro-Chinese (1%)

Religions Christian (Protestant 56%, Roman Catholic 5%), non-religious (17%)

Physical features Third largest island in the Caribbean; maximum length, 234 km/145 mi; width, 35–82 km/22–51 mi; mountainous and rugged, particularly in the E, where the Blue Mt Peak rises to 2256m/7401 ft; over 100 small rivers, several used for hydroelectric power.

Climate Humid, tropical climate at sea-level; more temperate at higher altitudes; average annual temperature 24°C (Jan), 27°C (Jul); mean annual rainfall 1980 mm/70 in; virtually no rainfall on S and SW plain; lies within the hurricane belt.

Currency 1 Jamaican Dollar (J$) = 100 cents

Economy Plantation agriculture (still employs about a third of workforce); sugar, bananas, citrus fruits, coffee, cocoa, ginger, coconuts; bauxite (world's second largest producer); cement, fertilizer, textiles, rum, chemical products; tourism.

GDP (2002e) $10·08 bn, per capita $3800

Human Development Index (2002) 0·742

History Visited by Columbus in 1494; settled by Spanish, 1509; West African slave labour imported for work on sugar plantations from 1640; British occupation, 1655; self-government, 1944; independence, 1962; Governor-General appoints Prime Minister and Cabinet; bicameral Parliament consists of a House of Representatives and a Senate.

Head of State
(British monarch represented by Governor-General)
1973–91 Sir Florizel Glasspole
1991– Sir Howard Cooke

Head of Government
1989–1992 Michael Norman Manley
1992– Percival Patterson

of 'But Not For Me' at the Pershing Lounge in 1958 stayed on the national best-selling lists for 108 weeks.

jamb The vertical moulding immediately surrounding a door, window, or other aperture, not including any column or pilaster. If sunk into a wall, as in Gothic architecture, it is also called a **reveal** or **splay**. The Classical door or window frame, projecting from the wall, can also be called an **architrave**.

James I (of England) (1566–1625) The first Stuart king of England (1603–25), also king of Scotland (1567–1625) as James VI, born in Edinburgh, EC Scotland, UK, the son of Mary, Queen of Scots, and Henry, Lord Darnley. On his mother's forced abdication, he was proclaimed king, and brought up by several regents. When he began to govern for himself, he ruled through his favourites, which caused a rebellion and a period of imprisonment. In 1589 he married **Anne of Denmark**. Hating Puritanism, he managed in 1600 to establish bishops in Scotland. On Elizabeth's death, he ascended the English throne as great-grandson of James IV's English wife, Margaret Tudor. At first well received, his favouritism again brought him unpopularity.

James II (of England) (1633–1701) King of England and Ireland (1685–8), also king of Scotland, as James VII, born in London, UK, the second son of Charles I. Nine months before his father's execution, he escaped to Holland. At the Restoration (1660) he was made Lord High Admiral of England, and commanded the fleet in the Dutch Wars; but after becoming a convert to Catholicism he was forced to resign his post. The national ferment occasioned by the Popish Plot (1678) became so formidable that he had to retire to the European mainland, and several unsuccessful attempts were made to exclude him from the succession. During his reign his actions in favour of Catholicism raised general indignation, and William, Prince of Orange, his son-in-law and nephew, was formally asked by leading clerics and landowners to invade (1688). Deserted by ministers and troops, James escaped to France, where he was warmly received by Louis XIV. He made an ineffectual attempt to regain his throne in Ireland, which ended in the Battle of the Boyne (1690), and remained at St Germain until his death.

James IV (1473–1513) King of Scots (1488–1513), the eldest son of James III. He became active in government at his accession, at the age of 15, and gradually exerted his authority over the nobility. In 1503 he married Margaret Tudor, the elder daughter of Henry VII – an alliance which led ultimately to the union of the crowns. However, he adhered to the French alliance when Henry VIII joined the League against France, and was induced to invade England by the French. He was defeated and killed, along with the flower of his nobility, at the Battle of Flodden, Northumberland.

James V (1512–42) King of Scots (1513–42), the son of James IV. An infant at his father's death, he grew up amid the struggle between the pro-French and pro-English factions in his country. In 1536 he visited France, marrying **Magdeleine**, the daughter of Francis I (1537), and after her death, **Mary of Guise** (1538). War with England followed from the French alliance (1542), and after attempting to invade England he was routed at Solway Moss. He retired to Falkland Palace, Fife, where he died soon after the birth of his daughter Mary (later, Mary, Queen of Scots).

James, St ('brother' of Jesus), also known as **St James the Just** (1st-c) Listed with Joseph, Simon, and Judas (*Matt* 13.55) as a 'brother' of Jesus of Nazareth, and identified as the foremost leader of the Christian community in Jerusalem (*Gal* 1.19, 2.9; *Acts* 15.13). He is not included in lists of the disciples of Jesus, and should not be confused with James, the son of Alphaeus, or James, the son of Zebedee, but he did apparently witness the resurrected Christ (1 *Cor* 15.7). He showed Jewish sympathies over the question of whether Christians must adhere to the Jewish law. According to Josephus, he was martyred by stoning (c.62). Feast day 1 May.

James, St (son of Alphaeus), also known as **St James the Less** (1st-c) One of the 12 apostles (*Mark* 3.18). He may be the James whose mother Mary is referred to at the crucifixion of Jesus (*Mark* 16.1, 15.40). Feast day 3 May.

James, St (son of Zebedee), also known as **St James the Great** (1st-c) One of Jesus's 12 apostles, often listed with John (his brother) and Peter as part of an inner group closest to Jesus. They were fishermen, among the first called by Jesus, and were with him at his Transfiguration and at Gethsemane. He and his brother John were also called *Boanerges* ('sons of thunder'). According to *Acts* 12.2, he was martyred under Herod Agrippa I (c.44). Feast day 25 July.

James, Clive (Vivian Leopold) (1939–) Writer, satirist, broadcaster, and critic, born in Sydney, New South Wales, SE Australia. He studied at the universities of Sydney and Cambridge, and became television critic for the English newspaper *The Observer*. He has published several books of comment and criticism, including *The Metropolitan Critic* (1974) and *Snake-charmers in Texas* (1988). Other writing includes volumes of verse, such as *Other Passports: Poems 1958–85* (1986), three volumes of autobiography, *Unreliable Memoirs* (1980, 1985, 1990), and the novel *The Silver Castle* (1996). His television programmes have been a combination of chat, humour, and commentary, and include *Saturday Night Clive*, as well as a series of 'documentaries' set in cities around the world, such as *Clive James Live in Japan* (1987).

James, Harry (Hagg) (1916–83) Jazz trumpeter and bandleader, born in Albany, Georgia, USA. He played with Benny Goodman before forming and leading his own band in 1938, and enjoyed success through the 1940s and 1950s; vocalists with the band included Frank Sinatra and Dick Haymes. His many hits included 'One O'Clock Jump' and 'You Made Me Love You'. He married the film actress Betty Grable in 1943.

James, Henry (1843–1916) Novelist, born in New York City, USA. After a roving youth in America and Europe, he began in 1865 to write literary reviews and short stories. His work as a novelist falls into three periods. In the first he is mainly concerned with the impact of American life on the older European civilization, as in *Roderick Hudson* (1875), *Portrait of a Lady* (1881), and *The Bostonians* (1886). From 1876 he made his home in England, chiefly in London and in Rye, East Sussex. His second period is devoted to purely English subjects, such as *The Tragic Muse* (1890), *What Maisie Knew* (1897), and *The Awkward Age* (1899). He reverts to Anglo-American attitudes in his last period, which includes *The Wings of a Dove* (1902) and his masterpiece, *The Ambassadors* (1903). The acknowledged master of the psychological novel, he was a major influence on 20th-c writing.

James, Jesse (Woodson) (1847–82) Wild West outlaw, born in Centerville, Missouri, USA. After fighting with a guerrilla group in the Civil War, he and his brother **Frank James** (1843–1915) led numerous bank, train, and stagecoach robberies in and around Missouri, before Jesse was murdered for a reward by Robert Ford, a gang member. Frank gave himself up soon after, stood trial, was released, and lived the rest of his life on the family farm.

James, Dame Naomi (Christine) (1949–) Yachtswoman and writer, born in New Zealand. After attending school in Rotorua, she worked as a hair stylist (1966–71) and language teacher (1972–4), before joining the crew of a charter yacht (1975–7). She became the first woman to sail solo around the world, and first woman solo around Cape Horn (Sep 1977–Jun 1978) on her yacht *Express Crusader*. In 1980 she entered the Observer Transatlantic Race on *Kriter Lady*, winning the Ladies Prize and achieving the women's record for a single-handed Atlantic crossing. Among her books are *Woman Alone* (1978), *At Sea on Land* (1981), and *Courage at Sea* (1987).

James, P D, pseudonym of **Phyllis Dorothy White, Baroness James of Holland Park** (1920–) Detective-story writer, born in Oxford, Oxfordshire, SC England, UK. Educated at Cambridge High School, she worked as a National Health Service administrator (1949–68) and at the Home Office (1968–9), first in the Police Department, then in the children's division of the Criminal Department. The experience provided the backgrounds of several of her novels, such as *Shroud for a Nightingale* (1971), *Death of an Expert Witness* (1977), *A Taste for Death* (1986), *Original Sin* (1994), and *A Certain Justice* (1997). The futuristic novel *The Children of Men* (1992) represents a new departure. Later books include *Time to be in Earnest* (1999) and *The Murder Room* (2003). She was made a baroness in 1991.

James, William (1842–1910) Philosopher and psychologist, born in New York City, USA, the brother of Henry James. He studied in New York and in Europe, and received a medical degree from Harvard (1869), where he began teaching anatomy and physiology (1873), then philosophy (1879). His books include *The Principles of Psychology* (1890), *The Will to Believe and Other Essays in Popular Philosophy* (1897), and *The Varieties of Religious Experience* (1902). He was a leader of philosophical pragmatism, and helped found the American Society for Psychical Research, publishing numerous papers on the subject.

James, Letter of New Testament writing attributed to 'James', who was considered in early tradition to be James the brother of Jesus, but who today is sometimes considered an unknown late 1st-c author, in view of the apparent distance from Pauline theology and the polemic in the writing. The letter's recipients are described only as 'the 12 tribes in the Dispersion'. It emphasizes a variety of ethical teachings, but was sometimes criticized (most notably by Luther) for lacking a distinctively Christian message and for its un-Pauline emphasis on 'works' rather than 'faith'. It is the first of the Catholic (or General) Epistles, which also include the letters of Peter, John, and Jude.

Jameson Raid An expedition against the South African Republic (Dec 1895–Jan 1896), which was supposed to link up with a revolt by white workers on the Rand and topple the government of President Kruger. Leander Starr Jameson (1853–1917), administrator for the South Africa Company at Fort Salisbury, led a detachment of British South Africa Police into the Transvaal, but they were easily defeated and arrested. The German kaiser, Wilhelm II, sent a telegram of congratulation to Kruger, and the incident caused a major government crisis in Britain as well as precipitating the resignation of Cecil Rhodes as Cape premier and contributing to the tensions that led to the Boer War.

James Tait Black Memorial Prize Annual literary prize awarded in two categories: best work of fiction and best biography first published in Britain in the previous 12 months. The award was established in memory of a partner at A & C Black Publishers Ltd (founded 1807 in Edinburgh by Adam Black), and is administered by the University of Edinburgh, Department of English Literature. The prize is £3000 for each category.

Jamestown (St Helena) 15°56S 5°44W, pop (2000e) 1500. Seaport capital and only town on the British island of St Helena in the S Atlantic; passenger and cargo services to the UK and S Africa.

Jamestown (USA) A deserted 25 ha/62 acre town, 24 km/15 mi inland from Chesapeake Bay, VA, the site of the first successful British settlement in America. Excavated archaeologically 1934–56, it was founded in 1607 by 105 settlers as James Fort, but after 1699 was superseded as the capital of Virginia by Williamsburg, and abandoned. It is now a National Historical Park, with replicas of original buildings and facilities.

Jammu–Kashmir [jamoo kashmeer] pop (2001e) 10 069 900; area 101 283 sq km/39 095 sq mi. State in the extreme N of India; bounded N by the July 1972 Line of Control (LoC) separating territory claimed by both India and Pakistan, W by Pakistan, E by China; crossed by several mountains and rivers; part of the Mughal Empire, 1586; Afghan rule, 1786; annexed to the Sikh Punjab, 1819; Kashmir asked for agreements with both India and Pakistan at independence, 1947; attacked by Pakistan, and acceded to India; further hostilities, 1965, 1972, 1999, 2002; separatist violence escalated in March 2003; ceasefire agreed along the LoC, November 2003; summer capital, Srinagar; winter capital, Jammu; governed by a 36-member Legislative Council and a 76-member Legislative Assembly; rice, wheat, maize, fruit, forestry, crafts; manufacturing industry largely in Jammu; horticulture widespread in Kashmir.

Jamnia *Jabneh*

Jamuna, River *Brahmaputra, River*

Janáček, Leoš [yanachek] (1854–1928) Composer, born in Hukvaldy, E Czech Republic (formerly Moravia, Austrian Empire). He became choirmaster in Brno, where he eventually settled after studying at Prague and Leipzig, and became professor of composition (1919). Devoted to the Czech folksong tradition, he wrote several operas, a Mass, instrumental chamber pieces, and song cycles.

Jane, Frederick Thomas (1865–1916) Writer, journalist, and artist, born in Upottery, Devon, SW England, UK. He worked first as an artist, then as a naval correspondent on various periodicals. He founded and edited *Jane's Fighting Ships* (1898) and *All the World's Aircraft* (1909), the annuals by which his name is still best known.

JANET *Joint Academic Network*

janissaries [janisareez] An elite force of Turkish soldiers established in the 14th-c. Throughout their history they mutinied several times, and were finally suppressed after a revolt in Constantinople in 1826.

Jan Mayen [yahn miyen], formerly Eng **Hudson's Tutches** area 380 sq km/147 sq mi. Norwegian volcanic island in the Arctic Ocean, 480 km/298 mi E of Greenland, 576 km/358 mi NE of Iceland; length 53 km/33 mi; highest point, Beerenberg (2277 m/7470 ft); discovered by Henry Hudson in 1608; annexed to Norway, 1929; radio and meteorological stations.

Jansen, Cornelius (Otto) [jansen], Dutch [yahnsen] (1585–1638) Theologian, founder of the reform movement known as Jansenism, born in Acquoi, The Netherlands. He studied at Utrecht, Louvain, and Paris, became professor of theology at Louvain (1630), and Bishop of Ypres (1636), where he died just after completing his four-volume work, *Augustinus* (published 1640). This sought to prove that the teaching of St Augustine on grace, free will, and predestination was opposed to the teaching of the Jesuit schools. The book was condemned by Pope Urban VIII in 1642, but the controversy raged in France for nearly a century, when a large number of **Jansenists** emigrated to Holland.

Jansky, Karl (Guthe) [yanskee] (1905–50) Radio engineer, born in Norman, Oklahoma, USA. He studied at the University of Wisconsin and joined Bell Telephone Laboratories in 1928. His fundamental discovery (1932) was of radio waves from outer space, while working on interference suffered by radio reception. This discovery allowed the development of radio astronomy during the 1950s. The unit of radio emission strength, the *jansky*, is named after him.

jansky [yanskee] A unit used in radio astronomy to measure the power received at the telescope from a cosmic radio source. 1 jansky (Jy) = 10^{-26}Wm^{-2}Hz^{-1}sr^{-1}. It is named after the American discoverer of cosmic radio emission, Karl Jansky.

Januarius, St [janyuahrius], Ital **San Gennaro** (?–c.305) Christian martyr, Bishop of Benevento, believed to have been a victim of the persecution under Diocletian. Two phials kept in Naples cathedral are said to contain his dried blood, believed to liquefy on his feast day and on certain other occasions throughout the year. Feast day 19 September.

Janus (astronomy) [jaynuhs] The 10th natural satellite of Saturn, discovered in 1966; distance from the planet 151 000 km/94 000 m; diameter 200 km/120 mi.

Janus (mythology) [jaynuhs] An ancient Roman divinity who guards the 'gate' or the door; there is no Greek equivalent. Because one goes out to begin an action, Janus became the god of beginnings; he is the first god named in a list, and the god of the first month (January). He is always depicted in art with two faces, one at the back of the head.

Japan *p.801*

Japanese The language of Japan, spoken by c.122 million in Japan, and a further 2 million elsewhere, mainly in the USA and Brazil. The relationship of Japanese to other languages is uncertain, though it is thought to resemble the Altaic family more than others. It is not related to Chinese, though it has written records from the 8th-c in Chinese characters (*kanji*), still used in one of the Japanese writing systems.

Japanese architecture The architecture of Japan, largely deriving from China, based on the column and wooden frames with non-structural wood and paper infill. Unique characteristics are delicate and intricate naturalistic decorations; dominant, projecting roofs of various materials; and an ordered disposition of columns, posts, cornice brackets, and cornice rafters. The earliest surviving buildings are religious, such as the Horyuji Buddhist monastery (7th-c AD). Many castles were built, 16th–17th-c. Houses are usually of one-storey design based on a rectangular plan. The arrival of Frank Lloyd Wright and Antonin Raymond at the beginning of the 20th-c marked the start of an increasing Westernization of Japanese architecture, culminating in the Corbusier-influenced Olympia Sports Stadium, Tokyo (1963–4), architect Kenzo Tange (1913–), and the Metabolist work of Kisho Kurokawa and Arata Isozaki since the 1960s.

Japanese art The art associated with Japan, which has always depended upon the techniques and styles of China, but is distinguished by its enthusiasm for surface pattern, its emphasis on technical virtuosity, and its fondness for strong colours. Its most characteristic achievements have been in the fields of colour-prints (the names of Utamaro, Hokusai, and Hiroshige are familiar in the West), painted scrolls, pottery, lacquer, and decorative metalwork. Buddhism reached Japan in the 6th-c AD, bringing with it Korean craftsmen under whose influence a great school of religious sculpture emerged, while Zen, another import from China, deeply affected painting.

Japanese cedar An evergreen conifer native to Japan (*Cryptomeria japonica*); narrowly conical, leaves scale-like but long-pointed, spirally arranged; cone scales with spines. It is an important forest tree in Japan, and also widely used in gardens and temples. Elsewhere, it is much planted for timber. (Family: Taxodiaceae.)

Japanese deer *sika*

Japanese literature After some centuries of oral literature, the earliest surviving Japanese work is the *Kojiki*, a story of the creation of the world and of the Japanese race, which dates from AD 712; closely followed by the *Nihon Shoki* (720, Chronicles of Japan). Emancipation from Chinese influence was illustrated by the significant 8th-c anthology of poetry, the *Man'yoshu* (Collection of the Myriad Leaves), whereas another anthology from the same period, the *Kaifuso*, was written by courtiers in Chinese. The 10th-c collection *Kokin-shu*, using the newly developed *kana* script, stands comparison with the *Man'yoshu*. Murasaki Shikibu's early 11th-c *Monogatari* (Tale of Genji) and Sei Shonagon's *Pillow Book* are among the masterpieces of Japanese literature, their realism followed up by the tradition of the *zuihitsu* or occasional journal which was written (often by women) for the next two centuries. Buddhism influenced the 12th-c *Ujishui* tales, and the wars of that time are also reflected in many gloomy and introspective narratives. The same atmosphere pervades the next important anthology of poetry, the *Shin Kokin Shu* (1205), and also the celebrated Noh plays of the 14th–15th-c, with their high stylization and conscious artifice.

After a period of destructive wars, the 17th-c witnessed a literary revival linked to the new mercantile class, whose values are reflected in the novels of Ihara Saikaku (1642–93). Matsuo Basho perfected and popularized the *haiku*, and Chikamatsu Monzaemon (1653–1725) introduced the Kabuki plays, often using puppets. Western influence transformed Japanese literature from the mid-19th-c. Mori Ogai (1863–1922) had lived in Germany, and Natsume Sozeki (1867–1916) in England: they revalued the novel, which quickly achieved decadence with Nagai Kafu (1879–1959) and Tanizaki Jur'ichiro (1886–1965). Proletarian literature emerged in the 1920s and 1930s, and new, freer verse forms were introduced. But the prevalent nihilism of 20th-c Japanese literature may be reflected in the suicides of

Japan

☐ International Airport

Jap **Nippon** or **Nihon**

Local name Nihon (Nippon)

Timezone GMT +9

Area 377 728 km^2/145 803 sq mi

Population total (2002e) 127 347 000

Status Monarchy

Capital Tokyo

Language Japanese (official)

Ethnic groups Japanese (99%), with Korean minorities

Religions Shintoist (40%), Buddhist (39%), Christian (4%)

Physical features Island state comprising four large islands (Hokkaido, Honshu, Kyushu, Shikoku) and several small islands; consists mainly of steep mountains with many volcanoes; Hokkaido (N) central range runs N–S, rising to over 2000 m/6500 ft, falling to coastal uplands and plains; Honshu, the largest island, comprises parallel arcs of mountains bounded by narrow coastal plains, and includes Mt Fuji, 3776 m/12 388 ft; heavily populated Kanto plain in E; Shikoku and Kyushu (SW) consist of clusters of low cones and rolling hills, mostly 1000–2000 m/3000–6000 ft; Ryukyu chain of volcanic islands to the S, largest Okinawa; frequent earthquakes notably in Kanto (1923), Kobe (1995).

Climate Oceanic climate, influenced by the Asian monsoon; heavy winter rainfall on W coasts of Honshu and in Hokkaido; short, warm summers in N, and severe winters, with heavy snow; variable winter weather throughout Japan, especially in N and W; typhoons in summer and early autumn; mild and almost subtropical winters in S Honshu, Shikoku, and Kyushu; average annual temperatures 5°C (Jan), 25°C (Jul) in Tokyo.

Currency 1 Yen (Ë, Y) = 100 sen

Economy Limited natural resources (less than 20% of land under cultivation); intensive crop production (principally of rice); timber, fishing, engineering, shipbuilding, textiles, chemicals; major industrial developments since 1960s, especially in computing, electronics, and vehicles.

GDP (2002e) $3·651 tn, per capita $28 700

Human Development Index (2002) 0·933

History Originally occupied by the Ainu; developed into small states, 4th-c; culture strongly influenced by China, 7th–9th-c; ruled by feudal shoguns until power passed to the emperor, 1867; limited contact with the West until the Meiji Restoration, 1868; successful war with China, 1894–5; gained Formosa (Taiwan) and S Manchuria; formed alliance with Britain, 1902; war with Russia, 1904–5; Russia ceded southern half of Sakhalin; Korea annexed, 1910; joined allies in World War 1, 1914; received German Pacific islands as mandates, 1919; war with China; occupied Manchuria, 1931–2; renewed fighting, 1937; entered World War 2 with surprise attack on the US fleet at Pearl Harbor, Hawaii, 1941; occupied British and Dutch possessions in SE Asia, 1941–2; pushed back during 1943–5; atomic bombs dropped on Hiroshima and Nagasaki by allied forces in 1945, ending World War 2 with Japanese surrender; allied control commission took power, and Formosa and Manchuria returned to China; Emperor Hirohito became figurehead ruler, 1946; full sovereignty regained, 1952; joined United Nations, 1958; strong economic growth in 1960s; regained Bonin, Okinawa, and Volcano Islands, 1972; a constitutional monarchy with Emperor as Head of State; government consists of a Prime Minister, Cabinet, and bicameral Diet (Kokkai), with a House of Representatives and a House of Councillors; co-location (with South Korea) of the FIFA 2002 World Cup.

Head of State (Emperor)
1867–1912 Mutsuhito (Meiji)
1912–26 Yoshihito (Taisho)
1926–89 Hirohito (Showa)
1989– Akihito (Heisei)

Head of Government (Prime Minister)
1945 Naruhiko Higashikuni
1945–6 Kijuro Shidehara
1946–7 Shigeru Yoshida
1947–8 Tetsu Katayama
1948 Hitoshi Ashida
1948–54 Shigeru Yoshida
1954–6 Ichiro Hatoyama
1956–7 Tanzan Ishibashi
1957–60 Nobusuke Kishi
1960–4 Hayato Ikeda
1964–72 Eisaku Sato
1972–4 Kakuei Tanaka
1974–6 Takeo Miki
1976–8 Takeo Fukuda
1978–80 Masayoshi Ohira
1980–2 Zenko Suzuki
1982–7 Yasuhiro Nakasone
1987–9 Noburu Takeshita
1989 Sasuke Uno
1989–91 Toshiki Kaifu
1991–3 Kiichi Miyazawa
1993–4 Morihiro Hosokawa
1994–4 Tsutomu Hata
1994–5 Tomiichi Murayama
1995–8 Ryutaro Hashimoto
1998–2000 Keizo Obuchi
2000–1 Yoshiro Mori
2001– Junichiro Koizumi

several leading writers, including Akutugawa Ryunosuke (in 1927), Mishima Yukio (in 1970), and the Nobel Prize Winner for Literature in 1968, Kawabata Yasunari (in 1972). In the last decade of the 20th-c, Japanese creative writing once again found an international readership, with Oe Kenzaburo awarded the Nobel Prize for Literature in 1994. Among the younger generation of acclaimed writers is Ishiguro Kazuo who, although born in Japan of Japanese parentage, has chosen to write through the medium of English. His best-known novel, *The Remains of the Day* (1989), was filmed in 1993.

Japanese music The feudalism that isolated Japan from the rest of the world from the late 12th-c to the late 19th-c allowed a slow but unhindered development of traditional musical genres. The most important were: the accompanied chants of the Shinto and Buddhist religious ceremonies; *gagaku*, the traditional court music played by ensembles of string, wind, and percussion instruments; and music for the Noh and Kabuki theatres. There was also a rich repertory of music for individual instruments such as the koto, shamisen, and shakuhachi (a bamboo flute). Since the Meiji Restoration (1868), traditional music has been preserved mainly as a museum culture, while Western pop and art music have increasingly taken its place in the everyday experience of the urban Japanese.

Japanese quince *japonica*

Japanese tosa *mastiff*

japanning A European substitution for Oriental lacquer, produced with layers of copal varnish. Instructions for decorating furniture were published by John Stalker and George Parker in the *Treatise of Japaning and Varnishing* (1688). Japanned tinwares were produced commercially in Pontypool and Usk in the late 18th-c, and copied in Birmingham in the 19th-c.

Japan, Sea of *East Sea*

Japheth [**jay**feth] Biblical character, one of the sons of Noah who survived the Flood, the brother of Shem and Ham. He is portrayed as the ancestor of peoples in the area of Asia Minor and the Aegean (*Gen* 10).

Japonaiserie A term used for the imitation of Japanese motifs, patterns, and compositions by European artists from the mid-19th-c to the early 20th-c. Whistler and van Gogh were among those inspired, in particular by coloured woodcuts.

japonica [ja**pon**ika] A deciduous, sometimes spiny shrub (*Chaenomeles speciosa*), native to E Asia; leaves oval to oblong with small teeth; flowers 5-petalled, bowl-shaped, usually scarlet, produced on old wood; also known as **flowering quince** or **Japanese quince**. It is cultivated for ornament. (Family: Rosaceae.)

Jaques-Dalcroze, Emile [zhak dal**krohz**] (1865–1950) Music teacher and composer, born in Vienna, Austria. He studied composition, and became professor of harmony at Geneva, where he originated eurhythmics, a method of expressing the rhythmical aspects of music by physical movement, which had great influence on the development of 20th-c dance. He was head of a school of eurhythmic instruction in Geneva (1914–50), where his pupils included Mary Wigman and Hanya Holm (1893–1992).

Jarash [**ja**rash], ancient **Gerasa** 32°10N 35°50E. Village in Irbid governorate, East Bank, NW Jordan; 35 km/22 mi N of Amman; site of old city of Gerasa; paved streets and colonnades, temples, theatres, baths, and a triumphal arch.

Jardine, Al(an) *Beach Boys, The*

Jardine, Douglas (Robert) [**jah(r)**din] (1900–58) Cricketer, born in Mumbai (Bombay), W India. He was captain of England during the controversial 'bodyline' tour of Australia (1932–3), where he employed Harold Larwood to bowl extremely fast at the batsman's body, the first use of intimidatory bowling in the game. The event almost caused England and Australia to sever diplomatic relations. He wrote a defence of his tactics in *In Quest of the Ashes* (1933).

Jarrell, Randall (1914–65) Poet and critic, born in Nashville, Tennessee, USA. He studied at Vanderbilt University, and taught English literature and creative writing at the University of North Carolina (1947–65). He wrote an early campus novel, *Pictures from an Institution* (1954), and published several volumes of criticism. A dozen volumes from *Blood for a Stranger* (1942) to *The Lost World* (1966) feature in his *Complete Poems* (1971).

Jarrow March (Oct 1936) A march to London by unemployed workers in the Co Durham shipbuilding and mining town and port, to put the unemployed case. Jarrow was among the municipal boroughs worst affected by the Depression, and the march took place at a time when the economy was recovering in much of the rest of the country. It alerted the more prosperous South and Midlands to the desperate problems of depressed areas.

Jarry, Alfred [zha**ree**] (1873–1907) Writer, born in Laval, NW France. Educated at Rennes, his satirical play, *Ubu-Roi*, was first written when he was 15; later rewritten as a marionette play, it was given its first live stage performance in 1896. Now considered the founding play of the avant-garde theatre, it was a seminal influence on French Surrealism and on the Theatre of the Absurd. Many of the marionette elements in the play became common currency in the works of playwrights such as Genet and Ionesco and directors such as Brecht and Roger Planchon (1931–). Seen as a vehicle for subversion against authoritarian society, the play was banned in the Soviet Union and its satellite states during the 1960s. Jarry went on to write short stories, poems, and other plays in a Surrealist style, inventing an anarchic logic of the absurd which he called *pataphysique* and developing the farcical prototype of the anti-hero of the 20th-c. He ended his life destitute and alcoholic.

Jaruzelski, General Wojciech (Witold) [yaru**zel**skee] (1923–) Polish general, prime minister (1981–5), head of state (1985–90), and president (1989–90), born near Lublin, E Poland. He became chief of general staff (1965), minister of defence (1968), a member of the Politburo (1971), and prime minister after the resignation of Pinkowski in 1981. Later that year, in an attempt to ease the country's economic problems and to counteract the increasing political influence of the free trade union Solidarity, he declared a state of martial law, which was lifted in 1982. He became president, but in 1990 bowed to pressure to resign as an anachronism from the former Communist regime.

jasmine A slender shrub or woody climber, sometimes evergreen; flowers tubular with spreading lobes; fruit a berry. **Winter jasmine** (*Jasminum nudiflorum*), an evergreen shrub native to China, has leaves with three leaflets, and bright yellow flowers in winter. **Summer jasmine** (*Jasminum officinale*), a deciduous climber native to Asia, has pinnate leaves, and fragrant white flowers in summer. (Genus: *Jasminum*, 300 species. Family: Oleaceae.)

Jason [**jay**sn] In Greek legend, the son of Aeson, King of Iolcos. When Pelias usurped the kingdom, Jason was taken away and educated by Chiron. He returned to the city wearing only one sandal, so fulfilling a prophecy which endangered Pelias. He was therefore sent on the quest of the Golden Fleece, leading the Argonauts to Colchis; there he obtained the fleece with Medea's assistance. Later he deserted her for Glauke, and died sitting under the wreck of the *Argo*, whose stern-post fell on him.

Jason, David (1940–) Actor, born in Edmonton, N Greater London, UK. He made his professional debut with the Bromley Repertory in 1965, and then appeared regularly in theatre, but became best known as a television actor. His many series include *Open All Hours* (1976, 1981–5), *Only Fools and Horses* (several series), *A Bit of a Do* (1988–9), *The Darling Buds of May* (1990–3), and *A Touch of Frost* (1992–). In 1999 he appeared in BBC's *All the King's Men*. He received BAFTAs for best actor (1988), best light entertainment performer (1990), and best comedy actor (1997), and a National Television special recognition award (1996). In 2003 he received a BAFTA Fellowship, the highest award in British television.

jasper A red variety of chalcedony.

Jaspers, Karl (Theodor) [**yas**perz] (1883–1969) Philosopher, born in Oldenburg, NW Germany. He studied medicine at Berlin, Göttingen, and Heidelberg, where he undertook research in a psychiatric clinic (1909–15), published a textbook on psychopathology (*Allgemeine Psychopathologie*, 1913) and was professor of psychology (1916–20). From 1921 he was professor of philosophy at Heidelberg, until dismissed by the Nazis in 1937. His work was banned but he stayed in Germany, and was awarded the Goethe Prize in 1947 for his uncompromising stand. In 1948 he settled in Basel as a Swiss citizen, and was appointed professor. Among his many works are *Philosophie* (3 vols, 1932), considered his most important writing, and *Die Atombombe und die Zukunft des Menschen* (1958, trans The Future of Mankind), in which he talks of the possibility of a world political union under which all could live and communicate in peace and freedom.

Jataka [**jah**taka] Stories of the Buddha's previous births, contained in the Buddhist Sutra literature.

jaundice A condition in which there is a rise in the amount of bile pigments (bilirubin and biliverdin) in the blood. These stain the skin and other tissues, including the whites of the eyes, a greenish-yellow colour. Jaundice arises as a result of (1) excessive breakdown of the blood pigment, haemoglobin (**haemolytic jaundice**), when abnormally large amounts of bile pigments are produced, saturating the capacity of the liver to excrete them, (2) severe liver disease, when the liver's capacity to eliminate bile pigments from the blood to the intestine is reduced, and pigments accumulate in the body, and (3) obstruction to the passage of bile pigments out of the liver through the common bile duct, such as a gallstone.

Jaurès, (Auguste Marie Joseph) Jean [zhohres] (1859–1914) Socialist leader, writer, and orator, born in Castres, S France. He lectured on philosophy at Toulouse, became a deputy (1885), co-founded the Socialist paper *L'Humanité* (1904), and was the main figure in the founding of the French Socialist Party. He was assassinated in Paris while advocating reconciliation with Germany.

Java (country), Indonesian **Jawa** pop (2000e) 128 516 000; area 132 187 sq km/51 024 sq mi. Island of Indonesia, in the Greater Sunda group, SE of Sumatra and S of Borneo; one of the most densely populated islands in the world; major cities include Jakarta, Bandung, Surabaya; mountainous, rising to 3676 m/12 060 ft at Semeru; covered with dense rainforest; 115 volcanic peaks, 15 still active; tobacco, rubber, tea, textiles, timber, rice, maize, sugar; noted for its batik method of cloth decoration.

JAVA (computing) Trade-name of a programming language devised to create networking applications that will run on any computer, whatever operating system the computer uses. The name derives from Java coffee, whose strong, rich properties were thought by its devisers to be just as applicable to their new language. It has proved to be of special value to people wanting to manipulate data on pages of the World Wide Web. A tag naming a short program (*applet*) is embedded in a Web page and when that page is accessed by a user, either over the Internet or corporate intranet, the applet automatically downloads from the server and runs on the user's machine.

Java Man The first known fossil of *Homo erectus*, found in Java in 1891 by the Dutch anatomist Eugène Dubois (1858–1940). It was long known by the name he gave it: *Pithecanthropus erectus*. Subsequent discoveries (1920s to the present) show specimens to date from ?0·8–0·3 million years ago (mya), with evidence of long-term trends for increased brain size and tooth reduction. Java was probably first colonized by *H. erectus* during a glacial period (c.0·9 mya) when low sea level exposed the Sunda shelf, joining Java with mainland Asia. Thereafter it was periodically isolated again during subsequent glacials (low sea levels).

Javanese The largest ethnic group of Java, Indonesia. Their language (Javanese), a member of the Austronesian family, is spoken throughout Java and in parts of Indonesia, and has a literary tradition dating from the 8th-c; but its use in writing is diminishing because of pressure from the standard language, Bahasa Indonesia. The people are Muslim with some Hindu traditions retained from an earlier period.

Javanese music Music and dance are of prime importance in the cultural life of Java. Ensemble music predominates, the most important being the classical gamelan, composed mainly of percussion instruments. The larger gamelans, some of them of great antiquity, are divided into two sets of instruments, each with its own tuning system (*slendro* and *pelog*). The music they play, although highly sophisticated and rhythmically complex, is mainly anonymous and was transmitted orally until the late 19th-c. Since then some systems of skeletal notation have been introduced.

Java Sea Area 430 000 sq km/165 000 sq mi. Sea of SE Asia, bounded N by Borneo, S by Java, and W by Sumatra linked to the Celebes Sea by the Makassar Strait.

javelin throw An athletics field event consisting of throwing a javelin (a long, lightweight, spear-like implement). The javelin consists of three parts; the pointed metal head, the shaft, and the grip. The men's javelin is 2·6–2·7 m/8·6–8·10 ft in length, and weighs 800 g/1 lb 12 oz; the women's javelin is 2·2–2·3 m/7 ft 3 in in length, and weighs at least 600 g/1·5 lb. With the javelin in one hand, the competitor runs to a specified mark and throws it; for the throw to count, the metal head must touch the ground before any other part. The first mark made by the head is the point used for measuring the distance achieved. Each competitor is allowed six throws. The current world record for men is 98·48 m/324 ft, achieved by Jan Zelezny (1966–) of the Czech Republic, in 1996 at Jena, Germany; for women it is 71·54 m/234 ft 8·40 in, achieved by Osleidys Menendez (1979–) of Cuba, in 2001 at Réthymnon, Greece.

jaw The upper and lower bones surrounding the mouth, which contain the teeth. The upper jaw (**maxilla**) is usually firmly fixed to the face, while the lower jaw (**mandible**) moves against it. The jaws move against each other during the chewing and grinding of food. The mandible also moves during speech.

Jawlensky, Alexey von [yav**len**skee] (1864–1941) Painter, born in Kuslovo, Russia. He studied at St Petersburg Academy and in Munich, and developed his own brightly-coloured Fauvist style by c.1905. After c.1913 he came under Cubist influence, and painted simpler, more geometrical arrangements using more subdued colours.

Jay, John (1745–1829) US statesman and jurist, born in New York City, USA. He studied at King's College (now Columbia University), New York City, and was admitted to the bar (1768). Elected to the Continental Congress (1774–7), he became president of Congress in 1778, secretary for foreign affairs (1784–9), and Chief Justice of the Supreme Court (1789–95). In 1794 he negotiated *Jay's Treaty* with Britain, in an attempt to avoid war. It was unpopular with the US public, and instrumental in the formation of the Democratic-Republicans as an Opposition party. He retired in 1801, after a period as Governor of New York.

jay A name used for many birds, usually of the crow family (Corvidae, 42 species), especially the **common jay** (*Garrulus glandiarus*) from N areas of the Old World. The **blue jay** of India (not that of North America) is a roller (Family: Coraciidae). **Jay-thrushes** are babblers (Family: Timaliidae).

Jayawardene, Junius Richard [jayawah(r)**de**nay] (1906–96) Sri Lankan statesman, prime minister (1977–8), and president (1978–89), born in Colombo, W Sri Lanka. He studied law in Colombo, and became a member of the State Council (1943) and the House of Representatives (1947). He was honorary secretary of the Ceylon National Congress (1940–7), minister of finance (1947–53), and vice-president of the United National Party. He led his Party in Opposition, both as deputy leader (1960–5) and Leader (1970–7), before becoming prime minister and president.

Jay's Treaty (1794) An agreement between the USA and Britain to end the British occupation of NW military posts on US territory, and to alter the terms of US commerce with Britain and its colonies. Negotiated by John Jay, it was very unpopular with the US public, and was instrumental in the formation of the Democratic-Republicans as an opposition party.

jazz A type of music developed from ragtime and blues in the S states of the USA during the second decade of the 20th-c. It originated among black musicians, who were much influenced by African-inspired works songs and spirituals, but was soon taken up by whites also and spread throughout the USA and abroad, influencing such composers of 'serious' music as Milhaud, Ravel, Stravinsky, and Walton. What constitutes jazz is notoriously difficult to define, but prominent features of the earliest New Orleans jazz included *syncopation* (strongly accented rhythms which conflict with the basic pulse of the music), collective *improvisation*, and the exploitation of unusual timbres and extreme ranges in an ensemble which consisted typically of clarinet, trumpet (or cornet), trombone, piano, double bass (played pizzicato), guitar, and drums. At least one of these elements is usually present in later jazz, which has developed many different styles.

jazz dance A North American form of vernacular dancing performed to the rhythms of jazz. It is a style that swings, owing its origins to African and Caribbean forms of dance, blended with European influences. It is a popular dance style, used in musical shows on Broadway and in the UK (eg *Cats*, 1982). Jazz dance emphasizes fast, accurate footwork with the feet parallel, and exaggerated movements of individual body parts.

j-curve In economics, the shape of the curve showing the balance of trade statistics for a period following a currency devaluation. A devaluation should eventually improve the balance of trade, as exports become cheaper abroad (which encourages sales) and imports become dearer at home (which discourages purchases). As the various quantity reponses take time, the initial effect of devaluation may be little change in trade volumes and a fall in relative export prices, which worsens the trade balance for a few months, after which the balance improves.

Jean de Meung [zhā duh mõe], or **Jean Clopinel** (c.1250–1305) Poet and satirist, born in Meung-sur-Loire, C France. He flourished in Paris in the reign of Philip IV. He translated many books into French, but his great work is his lengthy continuation (18 000 lines) of the *Roman de la Rose* by Guillaume de Lorris, in which he replaced allegory with satirical pictures of actual life, and an encyclopedic discussion of contemporary learning.

Jeans, Sir James (Hopwood) [jeenz] (1877–1946) Astrophysicist and popularizer of science, born in Ormskirk, Lancashire, NW England, UK. He taught at Cambridge (1904–5, 1910–12) and Princeton (1905–9), where he was professor of applied mathematics, then became a research associate at Mt Wilson Observatory, Pasadena until 1944. He made important contributions to the theory of gases, quantum theory, and stellar evolution, and became widely known for his popular exposition of physical and astronomical theories. He was knighted in 1928.

jebeer *dorcas gazelle*

Jedda or **Jeddah** 21°29N 39°16E, pop (2000e) 2 278 000. Seaport in Mecca province, WC Saudi Arabia; on the E shore of the Red Sea, 64 km/40 mi W of Mecca; Saudi Arabia's commercial capital and largest port; port of entry on pilgrimage route to Mecca; W section stands on land reclaimed from the Red Sea; airport; university (1967); shipping, steel, cement, oil refining; walled city.

jeep The name given to a general purpose (GP) light vehicle developed in World War 2 for the United States Army. It became particularly renowned for its exceptional sturdiness and capability for operating on rough terrain, because of its high clearance and four-wheel drive. After the War, its easy availability, alongside its technical features, laid down the standard against which later specialized rough-terrain working vehicles (eg the Land Rover) developed. With the boom in leisure in the 1970s, there arose a market for non-working rough-terrain vehicles in the USA, and thence worldwide, which led to the manufacture of such types as the Range Rover.

Jefferson, Thomas (1743–1826) US statesman and third president (1801–9), born in Shadwell, Virginia, USA. He studied at the College of William and Mary, became a lawyer (1767), joined the revolutionary party, and took a prominent part in the first Continental Congress (1774), drafting the Declaration of Independence (1776). He was Governor of Virginia (1779–81), minister in France (1785), and secretary of state (1789). Vice-president under Adams (1797–1801), he then became president. Events of his administration included the war with Tripoli, the Louisiana Purchase (1803), and the prohibition of the slave trade. He retired in 1809, but continued to advise as an elder statesman. He was highly accomplished in architecture, science, the humanities, and education.

Jefferson City 38°34N 92°10W, pop (2000e) 39 600. Capital of state in Cole Co, C Missouri, USA, on the Missouri R; city status, 1839; railway; university (1866); government services, agricultural trade.

Jeffreys (of Wem), George Jeffreys, Baron, known as **Judge Jeffreys** (1648–89) Judge, born in Acton, Wrexham, NE Wales, UK. Called to the bar in 1668, he rose rapidly, was knighted (1677), and became recorder of London (1678). He was active in the Popish Plot prosecutions, became Chief Justice of Chester (1680), baronet (1681), and Chief Justice of the King's Bench (1683). In every state trial he proved a willing tool of the Crown, and was raised to the peerage by James II (1685). His journey to the West Country to try the followers of Monmouth earned his court the name of 'the Bloody Assizes' for its severity. His sentencing of the 80-year-old Alice Lisle to be burnt for treason caused widespread revulsion. He was Lord Chancellor (1685–8), but on James's flight was imprisoned in the Tower, where he died.

Jeffries, John (1744–1819) Balloonist and physician, born in Boston, Massachusetts, USA. A loyalist during the American Revolution, he settled in England and made the first balloon crossing of the English Channel with the French aeronaut Blanchard in 1785.

Jehovah [jehohva] Term used since the 11th-c as a form of the Hebrew name for Israel's God, **Yahweh**. It is formed from a combination of the Latinized consonants of the Hebrew word *YHWH* with the vowels of the Hebrew word *Adonai* ('Master, Lord').

Jehovah's Witnesses A millenarian movement organized in the USA in 1884 under Charles Taze Russell (1852–1916). They adopted the name Jehovah's Witnesses in 1931; previously they were called 'Millennial Dawnists' and 'International Bible Students'. They have their own translation of the Bible, which they interpret literally. They believe in the imminent second coming of Christ, avoid worldly involvement, and refuse to obey any law which they see as a contradiction of the law of God – refusing, for example, to take oaths, enter military service, or receive blood transfusions. They publish *The Watchtower*, meet in Kingdom Halls, and all 'witness' through regular house-to-house preaching. They numbered some 6 million in 2004, and are now an international movement.

Jellicoe, John Rushworth Jellicoe, 1st Earl [jelikoh] (1859–1935) British admiral, born in Southampton, Hampshire, S England, UK. He became Third Sea Lord (1908), and was commander-in-chief at the outbreak of World War 1. His main engagement was the Battle of Jutland (1916), for which he was much criticized at the time, although it is now accepted he rendered the German high seas fleet ineffective for the remainder of the war. Promoted to First Sea Lord, he organized the defences against German submarines, and was made Admiral of the Fleet (1919). He later became Governor-General of New Zealand (1920–4), and was created an earl in 1925.

jellyfish A typically bell-shaped, marine coelenterate with a ring of marginal tentacles containing stinging cells and a central mouth on undersurface of bell; body displays a 4-part radial symmetry; endodermal gastric tentacles present in gut; represents the medusa phase of the coelenterate life-cycle, the polyp phase being reduced or absent. (Phylum: Cnidaria. Class; Scyphozoa.)

Jena [yayna] 50 56N 11 35E, pop (2000e) 105 300 Town in Jena district, Gera, EC Germany, on R Saale; first planetarium built here, 9th-c; defeat of Prussians by Napoleon, 1806; railway; university (1588); chemicals, precision instruments.

Jenkins, David (Edward) (1925–) Theologian and clergyman, born in Bromley, S Greater London, UK. He studied at Oxford, and was a lecturer in Birmingham and Oxford before being appointed director of *Humanum* studies at the World Council of Churches, Geneva (1969–73). He then became director of the William Temple Foundation, Manchester (1973–8), and professor of theology at Leeds (1979–84). He was appointed Bishop of Durham (1984–94), amidst controversy over his interpretation of the Virgin Birth and the Resurrection. He has published several books, including his recent trilogy, *God, Miracle and the Church of England* (1987), *God, Politics and the Future* (1988), and *God, Jesus and Life in the Spirit* (1988).

Jenkins (of Hillhead), Roy (Harris) Jenkins, Baron (1920–2003) British statesman, born in Abersychan, Torfaen, SE Wales, UK. He studied at Oxford, became a Labour MP in 1948, and was minister of aviation (1964–5), home secretary (1965–7), Chancellor of the Exchequer (1967–70), deputy leader of the Opposition (1970–2), and again home secretary (1974–6). He resigned as an MP in 1976 to take up the presidency of the European Commission (1977–81). Upon his return to Britain, he co-founded the Social Democratic Party (1981), and became its first leader, standing down after the 1983 election in favour of David Owen. Defeated in the 1987 election, he was given a life peerage and also became Chancellor of Oxford University. In 1997 he was appointed to chair the Independent Commission on the Voting System, which was charged with finding the most appropriate proportional alternative to the UK's 'first-past-the-post' electoral system.

Jenkins' Ear, War of A war between Britain and Spain starting in 1739, and soon merging into the wider War of the Austrian Succession (1740–8). Some of the violent anti-Spanish indignation in Britain that provoked the war was due to Captain Robert Jenkins, who claimed to have had an ear cut off by Spanish coastguards in the Caribbean.

Jenner, Edward (1749–1823) Physician, the discoverer of the vaccination for smallpox, born in Berkeley, Gloucestershire, SWC England, UK. After an apprenticeship with a local surgeon, he studied under John Hunter (1728–93) in London, then returned to practise in Berkeley (1773), while remaining a firm friend of Hunter. Having observed how an infection of the mild disease cowpox prevented later attacks of smallpox, in 1796 he inoculated a child with cowpox, then two months later with smallpox, and the child failed to develop the disease. His discovery was violently opposed at first, but within five years vaccination was being practised throughout the civilized world.

Jennings, Elizabeth (Joan Cecil) (1926–2001) Poet and writer, born in Boston, Lincolnshire, EC England, UK. She studied at St Anne's College, Oxford. A Roman Catholic, her verse is intensely personal, with themes of childhood, age, religion, and art. Her first published work was *Poems* (1953), followed by *A Way of Looking* (1955, Somerset Maugham Award). Following a nervous breakdown she retired to Oxford, where she produced *Collected Poems 1967* (1967), *The Animals' Arrival* (1969), *Lucidities* (1970), and *Relationships* (1972). Her *Selected Poems* appeared in 1980. She also published poems for children.

Jennings, Pat(rick) (1945–) Footballer, born in Newry, Co Down, SE Northern Ireland, UK. Britain's most capped footballer, he played for Northern Ireland 119 times. He started his career with Newry Town before joining Watford, moved to Tottenham Hotspur in 1974, and became their regular goalkeeper for over 10 years before joining Arsenal in 1977. He made a total of 747 Football League appearances, and won several cup-winner's medals. He retired in 1986.

Jennings, Waylon (1937–2002) Country-rock singer and songwriter, born in Littlefield, Texas, USA. In the 1970s he and Willie Nelson championed the 'outlaw movement' of country music, breaking away from the commercialism of Nashville; their *Wanted! The Outlaws* (1976) was the first country album to sell a million copies. Jennings continued to enjoy steady success with records and performances through the 1980s and 1990s, and appeared in several films.

Jepson, Willis (Linn) (1867–1946) Botanist, born near Vacaville, California, USA. He spent his career at the University of California, Berkeley (1899–1937), and his works include the classic *A Manual of the Flowering Plants of California* (1925). An outspoken conservationist, he founded the California Botanical Society (1913) and the Save the Redwoods League (1918). A genus of flowering plants, *Jepsonia*, is named after him.

jerboa A mouse-like rodent; moves by jumping (may leap 3 m/10 ft); hind legs at least four times as long as front legs; ears large; long tail, with long hairs at tip; eats seeds, plants, or insects; does not drink; also known as **desert rat**. (Family: Dipodidae, 31 species.)

Jeremiah or **Jeremias, Book of** [jeremiya] A major prophetic work of the Hebrew Bible/Old Testament, attributed to the prophet Jeremiah, who was active in Judah c.627–587 BC and who died apparently after fleeing to Egypt from Jerusalem. The work is notable for its record of the prophet's inner struggles, persecution, and despair. Warnings of disaster for Judah's immorality and idolatry are tempered only briefly by support for King Josiah's reforms; the warnings anticipate the fall of Jerusalem (587 BC) and the Babylonian Captivity of the Jews. The present book probably results from a complex history of transmission.

Jeremiah, Letter of [jeremiya] In the Roman Catholic Bible, Chapter 6 of the Book of Baruch; for Protestants, a separate work in the Old Testament Apocrypha. It is ostensibly a letter from the prophet Jeremiah to Jewish captives in Babylon (c.597 BC) warning them against idolatry. Today it is often considered to derive from the later Hellenistic period, possibly in Maccabean times.

Jeremais *Jeremiah, Book of*

Jerez (de la Frontera) [hereth], also **Xeres** 36°41N 6°07W, pop (2000e) 185 000. Picturesque town a few miles inland from Cádiz, Andalusia, S Spain, giving its name to *sherry*; airport; noted centre for sherry, wine, and brandy; horse breeding; Fiesta of the Horse (May), wine festival (Sep).

Jericho [jerikoh], Arabic **Eriha**, Heb **Yeriho** 31°51N 35°27E, pop (2000e) 29 000. Oasis town in Jerusalem governorate, Israeli-occupied West Bank, W Jordan, 38 km/24 mi NE of Jerusalem; focus of the state of Palestine (area 62 sq km/24 sq mi), following Israeli–PLO peace agreement, 1993; 95% Sunni Muslim, 5% Christian; farming, tourism; site of the world's earliest known town, continuously occupied c.9000–1850 BC; a tell (mound), area 4–5 ha/10–12 acres, encircled by a 3 m/10 ft-thick wall, and provided with a solid defensive tower still standing 8·5 m/28 ft high; 20th-c excavations revealed 20 successive settlement layers; scene of famous siege during the Israelite conquest of Canaan, when it is said that the walls fell down at the shout of the army under Joshua; Mount of the Temptation (NW); ruins of palace of Qirbat al-Mafyar (724).

Jerome, St [jerohm], originally **Eusebius Hieronymus** (c.342–420) Christian ascetic and scholar, born in Stridon, W Croatia. After living for a while as a hermit, he was ordained in 379, and became secretary to Pope Damasus (reigned 366–84). He moved to Bethlehem in 386, where he wrote many letters and treatises, and commentaries on the Bible. He is chiefly known for making the first translation of the Bible from Hebrew into Latin (the Vulgate). Feast day 30 September.

Jerome, Jerome K(lapka) [jerohm] (1859–1927) Humorous writer, novelist, and playwright, born in Walsall, Staffordshire, C England, UK. Brought up in London, he was successively a clerk, schoolmaster, reporter, actor, and journalist, then became joint editor of *The Idler* (1892) and started his own weekly, *To-Day*. His novel *Three Men in a Boat* (1889) became a humorous classic.

Jersey pop (2000e) 90 000; area 116 sq km/45 sq mi. Largest of the Channel Is, lying W of Normandy; chief languages, English with some Norman-French; airport; ferries to UK and France; capital, St Helier; noted for its dairy farming (Jersey cattle) and potatoes; tourism; Jersey Zoological Park founded by Gerald Durrell in 1959; underground German headquarters from World War 2.

Jerusalem, Hebrew **Yerushalayim** 31°47N 35°15E, pop (2000e) 686 000. Capital city of Jerusalem district and the State of Israel; a holy city of Christians, Jews, and Muslims, on the E slope of the Judean range; the old city is a world heritage site, surrounded by a fortified wall and divided into four quarters (Armenian, Muslim, Christian, Jewish); ancient holy city, frequently referred to in Biblical sources; part of Roman Empire (1st-c BC); under Muslim rule until conquered by Crusaders, and Kingdom of Jerusalem established, 1099; retaken by Saladin, 1187; ruled by Ayyubids and Mamluks from Cairo until conquered by the Ottomans in 1516 (ruled until 1917); capital of Palestine (1922–48); divided between Israel and Jordan by 1949 armistice; declared capital of Israel, 1950, but lacks international recognition; E Jerusalem annexed after Six-Day War, 1967; airfield; railway; Hebrew University (1925); government services, tourism, light industry; citadel (24 BC), 12th-c Cathedral of St James, Temple Mount, El Aqsa Mosque (705–15), Dome of the Rock (685–705), Western Wall, Antonia Fortress (37–4 BC), Church of the Holy Sepulchre (1099), Garden of Gethsemane, Tomb of the Kings, Mount of Olives.

Jerusalem artichoke A large perennial growing to 2·8 m/9·2 ft (*Helianthus tuberosus*), a native of North America; numerous underground stolons have potato-like tubers at their tips, persisting through the winter; leaves lance-shaped, coarsely toothed; flower-heads 4–8 cm/1½–3 in across, yellow, surrounded by dark green pointed bracts. Introduced to Europe in the 16th-c, it has been cultivated for its edible tubers (Jerusalem artichokes) containing inulin, a source of the sugar fructose. (Family: Compositae.)

Jespersen, (Jens) Otto (Harry) [yespersen] (1860–1943) Philologist, born in Randers, N Denmark. He studied at Copenhagen, and became professor of English language and literature there (1893–1925), where he revolutionized the teaching of languages. His *Sprogundervisning* (1901, trans How to Teach a Foreign Language) became perhaps the best-known statement of what is now called the 'direct method'. His other books include *Growth and Structure of the English Language* (1905), *A Modern English Grammar on Historical Principles* (1909), and *Philosophy of Grammar* (1924). He also invented an international language, 'Novial', with its own grammar and lexicon.

Jesuit Estates Act An act of 1888 introduced by the Quebec government of Honoré Mercier, following arbitration by Pope Leo XIII, which assessed the value of Crown Lands in Canada claimed by the Jesuits, and assigned a financial settlement to the Order and the Catholic Church of more than $300 000. The act stimulated discontent and protest among the Orangemen in Canada.

Jesuits A religious order, the **Society of Jesus (SJ)**, founded in 1534 by Ignatius de Loyola. A non-contemplative order, it demands strict obedience, compliance with Ignatius's Spiritual Exercises, and special loyalty to the pope. Its aim is missionary in the broadest sense, ministering to society in many ways, especially in education, where it has founded several colleges and universities throughout the world. Jesuits have been leading apologists for the Roman Catholic Church, particularly at the time of the Counter-Reformation.

Jesus Christ (c.6 /5 BC–AD c.30 /33) The central figure of the Christian faith, whose nature as 'Son of God' and whose redemptive work are traditionally considered fundamental beliefs for adherents of Christianity. 'Christ' became attached to the name 'Jesus' in Christian circles in view of the conviction that he was the Jewish Messiah ('Christ').

Jesus of Nazareth is described as the son of Mary and Joseph, and is credited with a miraculous conception by the Spirit of God in the Gospels of Matthew and Luke. He was apparently born in Bethlehem c.6–5 BC (before the death of Herod the Great in 4 BC), but began his ministry in Nazareth. After having been baptized by John the Baptist in the Jordan (perhaps AD 28–29, *Luke* 3.1), he gathered a group of 12 close followers or apostles, the number perhaps being symbolic of the 12 tribes of Israel and indicative of an aim to reform the Jewish religion of his day.

The main records of his ministry are the New Testament Gospels, which show him proclaiming the coming of the kingdom of God, and in particular the acceptance of the oppressed and the poor into the kingdom. He was apparently active in the villages and country of Galilee rather than in towns and cities, and was credited in the Gospel records with many miraculous healings, exorcisms, and some 'nature' miracles, such as the calming of the storm. These records also depict conflicts with the Pharisees over his exercise of an independent 'prophetic' authority, and especially over his pronouncing forgiveness of sins; but his arrest by the Jewish priestly hierarchy appears to have resulted more directly from his action against the Temple in Jerusalem. The duration of his public ministry is uncertain, but it is from John's Gospel that one gets the impression of a 3-year period of teaching. He was executed by crucifixion under the order of Pontius Pilate, the Roman procurator, at the prompting of the Jewish authorities, and also perhaps because of the unrest Jesus's activities were causing. The date of death is uncertain, but is usually considered to be in 30 or 33. Accounts of his resurrection from the dead are preserved in the Gospels, Pauline writings, and Acts of the Apostles; Acts also refers to his subsequent ascension into heaven.

The New Testament Gospels as sources for the life of Jesus have been subject to considerable historical questioning in modern Biblical criticism, partly in view of the differences amongst the Gospel accounts themselves (with the differences between John's Gospel and the other three often casting doubt on the former). Form criticism has drawn attention to the influences affecting the Jesus-traditions in the period before the Gospels were written, and when traditions were being transmitted mainly in small units by word of mouth. Redaction criticism has, in addition, drawn attention to the creative role of the Gospel writers. Some scholars have been pessimistic about efforts to reconstruct the life of Jesus at all from our Gospel sources, and have distinguished between the 'Jesus of history' and the 'Christ of faith', with only the latter being theologically significant for faith. More recent scholars have often attached greater importance to the historical Jesus for Christian faith, and in particular efforts have been made to present a credible hypothesis about the historical Jesus in terms of the social, political, and cultural situation in Palestine in the early 1st-c. Limited references to Jesus can also be found in works of the Jewish historian Josephus and the Roman historians Tacitus and Suetonius; and other noncanonical Christian traditions circulated about Jesus, many of which are late and probably spurious.

jet A resinous, hard, black variety of lignite, formed from wood buried on the sea floor. It is often polished, and used in jewellery.

jet engine An engine that accelerates a fluid into its surrounding environment to form a fast-moving jet. The reaction felt by the engine to this expulsion is the *thrust force*, which acts in the opposite direction to the jet. This reactive thrust force is the propulsion force of the engine. Although by definition a rocket motor and a ship's propeller produce thrust in this way, the term is usually taken to apply to air-breathing engines such as turbojets and ramjets.

jetfoil A hydrofoil with a waterjet form of propulsion. Water is sucked in from the sea and expelled at great pressure through the after foils. Jetfoil craft have operated a successful ferry service across the English Channel, though the service was withdrawn for economic reasons.

jet lag Unpleasant mental and bodily sensations of fatigue, inability to concentrate, and impaired judgment, induced by rapid air travel through several time-zones. The condition is due to a disturbance in biological circadian rhythms, and usually subsides within a few days.

jet stream A narrow band of high velocity, westerly winds found at or just below the top of the troposphere at c.9000–15 000 m/30 000–50 000 ft. Maximum velocities are 100–150 mph (c.45–70 m/s), but may increase to 300 mph (c.135 m/s) in winter. Jet streams are found in both hemispheres.

Jew *Judaism*

Jewish philosophy Judaism, like Christianity and Islam, represents a constructive synthesis of biblical monotheism and Greek philosophical thought. The Hebrew Bible, though nowhere presenting a systematic philosophy, is rich in reflections on metaphysics, physics, and ethics, and the earliest Greek references to the Jews described them as a race of philosophers. Jews responded by rewriting the Bible in the language of Greek thought. Later, Jewish thinkers reacted to the rise of Islamic religious philosophy by writing (in Arabic) about the relationship of rational knowledge to tradition based on revelation. Arabic Jewish authors such as Avicebrón and Maimonides were influential not only in Jewish and Muslim circles but also, through Latin translations, on Christian scholasticism. By the 17th-c the centre of gravity of Jewish thought had moved to Christian W Europe, and after the 18th-c Enlightenment and later political emancipation, Jews engaged fully in Western philosophical thought, while remaining preoccupied with the old questions concerning the relationship between revelation and reason. A straight line leads from the mediaeval Arabic writers to Spinoza and Mendelssohn, and on to Hermann Cohen (1842–1918), a founder of neo-Kantianism who developed an original synthesis of Judaism and idealism. The most influential 20th-c Jewish religious thinkers, Leo Baeck (1873–1956), Martin Buber, and Franz Rosenzweig (1886–1929) were all disciples of Cohen. Nowadays, outside the philosophy of religion, it is hard to discern a specific Jewish contribution, as Jewish philosophers share the presuppositions and methods of philosophy at large.

jew's harp A simple musical instrument held between the player's lips and teeth. A flexible metal tongue is set in motion with the hand, and the pitch and timbre of its vibrations are controlled by the mouth. The origin of the name itself is unknown.

Jhabvala, Ruth [jabvahla], *née* **Prawer** (1927–) Writer, born in Cologne, W Germany, of Polish parents. Her parents emigrated to Britain in 1939. She studied at London University, married a visiting Indian architect, and lived in Delhi (1951–75). Most of her fiction relates to India, taking the viewpoint of an outsider looking in. Significant novels include *To Whom She Will* (1955), *The Householder* (1960), and *Heat and Dust* (1975, Booker). Later novels include *Poet and Dancer* (1993) and *Shards of Memory* (1995), and in 2000 appeared *Out of India: Selected Stories*. In association with the film makers James Ivory and Ismail Merchant, she has written several accomplished screenplays, among them *Shakespeare Wallah* (1965, with James Ivory) and *A Room with a View* (1986, Oscar).

Jhelum, River [jayluhm] River in Asia, the most westerly of the five rivers of the Punjab, Pakistan; rises in the Himalayas, flows NW through the Vale of Kashmir, then W and generally S to meet the R Chenab SW of Jhang Maghiana; length 725 km/ 450 mi; source of many canals and irrigation systems of the Punjab plain.

Jiang Jieshi [jiang jieshee], or **Chiang Kai-shek** [chang kiy shek] (1887–1975) Revolutionary leader of 20th-c China, the effective head of the Nationalist Republic (1928–49), and head thereafter of the emigré Nationalist Party regime in Taiwan, born into a merchant family in Zhejiang. He interrupted his military education in Japan to return to China and join the Nationalist revolution. In 1918 he joined the separatist revolutionary government of Sun Yixian (Sun Yatsen) in Canton, where he was appointed commandant of the new Whampoa Military Academy. After Sun's death (1925), he launched an expedition against the warlords and the Beijing government, entering Beijing in 1928, but fixed the Nationalist capital at Nanjing (Nanking). He proclaimed loyalty to Sun's principles, which he built into his Confucianist New Life Movement (1934). Marriage to Sun's US-educated sister-in-law (1927) involved Jiang with international businessmen, and he also became a Methodist. During the ensuing decade the Nationalist Party steadily lost support to the Communists. When Japan launched a campaign to conquer China (1937), the Nationalists were able to provide strong resistance, which continued throughout World War 2, thereby making an important contribution to the Allied victory. Defeated by the Communist forces, Jiang was forced to retreat to Taiwan (1949), where he presided over the beginnings of Taiwan's 'economic miracle', and where, under US military protection, he maintained unyielding hostility to the new People's Republic. His son, **Jiang Jingguo** (Chiang Ching-kuo, 1918–88), became prime minister in 1971 and president in 1978.

Jiang Jingguo [jiang jinggwoh], also spelled **Chiang Ching-kuo** (1918–) Taiwanese prime minister (1972–8) and president (1978–87), born in Chekiang Province, China. The son of Jiang Jieshi, he studied in the Soviet Union during the early 1930s, returning to China with a Russian wife in 1937. After the defeat of Japan in 1945 he held a number of government posts before fleeing with his father and the defeated Kuomintang forces to Taiwan in 1949. He was defence minister (1965–72) before becoming prime minister, and succeeded to the post of Party leader on his father's death in 1975. State president in 1978, in his later years he instituted a progressive programme of political liberalization, which was continued by his successor, Lee Teng-hui.

Jiang Qing [jiang ching], also spelled **Chiang Ch'ing** (1914–91) Chinese politician, born in Zhucheng, Shandong Province, E China. She studied at Qingdao University, and was an actress in Shanghai when she went to the Chinese Communist Party headquarters at Yenan to study Marxist–Leninist theory (1936), and met the Communist leader, Mao Zedong; she became his third wife in 1939. In the 1960s she began her attacks on bourgeois influences in the arts and literature, and became one of the leaders of the 'Cultural Revolution' (1966–76). She was elected to the Politburo (1969), but after Mao's death (1976) was arrested with three others – the 'Gang of Four' – imprisoned, expelled from the Communist Party, and tried in 1980 on a charge of subverting the government and wrongly arresting, detaining, and torturing numbers of innocent people. She was sentenced to death, though the sentence was later commuted.

Jiang Zemin (1926–) Chinese president (1993–), born in Yangzhou, Jiangsu Province, E China. An electrical engineer, he became commercial counsellor at the Chinese embassy in Moscow (1950–6) and during the 1960s and 1970s held a number of posts in the ministries of heavy industry and power. He was elected to the Chinese Communist Party's (CCP) central committee in 1982, and appointed Mayor of Shanghai in 1985. A cautious reformer, loyal to the Party, he was inducted into the Politburo in 1987, and following the Tiananmen Square pro-democracy massacre and the dismissal of Zhao Ziyang, was elected Party leader (1989), and chairman of the Central Military Commission (1990). He has pledged to maintain China's 'open door' economic strategy, and has developed a reputation as a pragmatic politician.

Jiddah *Jedda*

jig A dance of Great Britain and Ireland. The **Irish jig** involves rapid, intricate footwork, a rigidly-held body, and vigorous leaps. The French *gigue* is probably derived from it. Several different types are recorded from the 16th-c to the 19th-c. Jig music is usually in 6/8 time, with some varieties (the **hop** or **slip jig**) in 9/8 time.

jihad [jeehad] (Arabic 'struggle') The term used in Islam for 'holy war'. According to the Qur'an, Muslims have a duty to oppose those who reject Islam, by armed struggle if necessary, and jihad has been invoked to justify both the expansion and defence of Islam. Islamic states pledged a jihad against Israel in the Mecca declaration of 1981, though not necessarily by military attack.

Jilong [jeelung], also **Keelung** or **Chi-lung**, formerly Span **Santissima Trinidad** 25°06N 121°34E, pop (2000e) 385 000. Independent municipality and second largest seaport in Taiwan; on N coast of Taiwan I, overlooking the East China Sea; occupied by the Spanish and Dutch, 17th-c; destroyed by earthquake, 1867; occupied by the Japanese, 1895–1945; naval base; shipbuilding, fishing, chemicals, coal.

Jim Crow Laws A nickname for statutes enacted by Southern states and municipalities in the USA, beginning in the 1880s, to keep black people in a segregated condition. The term is believed to be derived from a character in a minstrel show.

The court ruling in 1896 in *Plessy* v. *Ferguson* that separate facilities for whites and blacks were constitutional encouraged the enactment of further discriminatory laws, and wiped out the gains made by black Americans during the Reconstruction period of 1865–77. They were abolished in the mid-20th-c as a result of popular protest, Supreme Court decisions, and federal policies.

Jiménez, Juan Ramón [himayneth] (1881–1958) Lyric poet, born in Moguer, SW Spain. He made his birthplace famous by his delightful story of the young poet and his donkey, *Platero y yo* (1914, Platero and I), one of the classics of modern Spanish literature. He abandoned law studies and settled in Madrid, where he began to write poetry, such as *Sonetos espirituales* (1916, Spiritual Sonnets). In 1936 he left Spain because of the Civil War, and settled in Florida. In his last period he emerged as a major poet, and was awarded the Nobel Prize for Literature in 1956.

jimson weed *thorn apple*

Ji'nan [jeenahn], **Tsinan**, or **Chi-nan**, nickname **City of Springs** 36°41N 117°00E, pop (2000e) 2 680 000, administrative region 5 901 000. Capital of Shandong province, E China; founded in 8th-c BC; commercial centre in the Tang dynasty (618–907); airfield; railway; metallurgy, chemicals, textiles, paper, flour; wheat, corn, cotton, tobacco, peanuts, fruit; over 100 natural springs at Daming L; dam on Yellow R for flood control and irrigation.

Jindyworobak [jindeeworobak] An Australian nationalist literary movement of the 1930s. Influenced by D H Lawrence and the Australian writer P R Stephensen (1901–65), the movement drew inspiration from Aboriginal legends. It produced some notable poets, such as Ian Mudie (1911–70) and Roland Robinson (1912–92).

Jinghis Khan *Genghis Khan*

Jinja [jinja] 0°27N 33°14E, pop (2000e) 71 000. City in Busoga province, Uganda; on the N shore of L Victoria at the outflow of the Victoria Nile River, 80 km/50 mi E of Kampala; power station at Owen Falls; second largest city in Uganda; airfield; railway; textiles, metal products, grain milling, petrol depot.

jinja [jinja] A Shinto shrine or sanctuary. It may be a small roadside shrine, a larger building surrounded by smaller buildings, or a large group of temple buildings surrounded by a wooded area. Its central feature is the *honden*, the main dwelling of the deity, containing a single chamber in which is housed the sacred symbol.

Jinnah, Muhammad Ali [jina] (1876–1948) Muslim politician and founder of Pakistan, born in Karachi, SE Pakistan (formerly India). He studied in Bombay and London, was called to the bar in 1897, and practised in Bombay. He became a member of the Indian National Congress (1906) and the Muslim League (1913), and supported Hindu–Muslim unity until 1930, when he resigned from the Congress in opposition to Gandhi's policy of civil disobedience. His advocacy of a separate state for Muslims led to the creation of Pakistan in 1947, and he became its first governor-general.

jinni (plural **jinn**), or **genie** In Arab mythology a supernatural creature that could take human or animal form and then interfered, often vengefully, in human affairs. Jinn can inhabit stones, trees, fire and air. They are frequently mentioned in the Qur'an and in the collection of oriental tales called *The Arabian Nights*.

jird *gerbil*

Jizo [jeezoh] (Jap polite form *ojizosan*; Sanskrit *Ksitigarbha Bodhisattva*) In Japan, the Buddhist patron deity of children. Wayside stone *jizo* are common in town and country. Sometimes decked out with colourful clothing, they are offered flowers.

Joachim of Fiore or **Joachim of Floris** [johakim] (c.1135–1202) Mystic, born in Calabria, S Italy. In 1177 he became abbot of the Cistercian monastery of Corazzo, and later founded a stricter Order, the *Ordo Florensis*, which was absorbed by the Cistercians in 1505. He is known for his mystical interpretation of history, recognizing three ages of increasing spirituality: the Age of the Father (the Old Testament), the Age of the Son (the New Testament and the period to 1260), and the Age of the Spirit, a period of perfect liberty, which would emerge thereafter.

Joad, C(yril) E(dwin) M(itchinson) [johd] (1891–1953) Controversialist and popularizer of philosophy, born in Durham, Co Durham, NE England, UK. He studied at Oxford, became a civil servant (1914–30), then joined the philosophy department at Birkbeck College, London. He wrote 47 highly personal books, notably *Guide to Philosophy* (1936), and was a fashionable atheist until his last work, *Recovery of Belief* (1952). He is also remembered for his highly successful BBC Brains Trust intervention, 'It all depends what you mean by ...'.

Joan, Pope (9th-c) Fictitious personage long believed to have been, as John VII, pope (855–8). One legend claims she was born at Mainz, and elected pope while in male disguise. Her reign is said to have ended abruptly when she died on giving birth to a child during a papal procession.

Joan of Arc, St, Fr **Jeanne d'Arc**, known as **the Maid of Orléans** (c.1412–31) Traditionally recognized patriot and martyr, who halted the English ascendancy in France during the Hundred Years' War, born into a peasant family in Domrémy, NE France. At the age of 13 she heard the voices of Sts Michael, Catherine, and Margaret bidding her rescue France from English domination. She was taken to the Dauphin, and eventually allowed to lead the army assembled for the relief of Orléans. Clad in a suit of white armour and flying her own standard, she entered Orléans (1429), forced the English to retire, and took the Dauphin to be crowned Charles VII at Reims. She then set out to relieve Compiègne, but was captured and sold to the English by John of Luxembourg. Put on trial (1431) for heresy and sorcery, she was found guilty by an English-constituted court, and burned. She was canonized in 1920. Recent historical evidence has challenged the traditional account, with the contention that Joan of Arc has been confused with Jehanne, the illegitimate daughter of Queen Isabeau of France and Louis, duc d'Orléans, brother of the king. Feast day 30 May.

Job, Book of [johb] A major book of the wisdom literature of the Hebrew Bible/Old Testament, named after its hero and probably drawing on old popular traditions, but in its present form showing evidence of several additions. It is composed of narrative and speeches in which the poet tackles the question of the meaning of undeserved suffering and of faith; despite the advice of his friends, Job persists in his struggles until presented with the inscrutable majesty of God directly.

Jocasta [johkasta] In Greek legend, the wife of King Laius of Thebes and mother of Oedipus, later unwittingly becoming the wife of her son; she is called **Epikaste** in Homer. She bore Oedipus four children – Eteocles, Polynices, Antigone, and Ismene – and killed herself when she discovered her incest.

Jochum, Eugen [yokhuhm] (1902–87) Conductor, born in Babenhausen, S Germany. He studied in Augsburg (1914–22) and Munich (1922-4), and became musical director of the Hamburg Staatsoper and conductor of the Hamburg Philharmonic Orchestra (1934–49). In 1949 he returned to Munich, where he conducted the Bavarian Radio Symphony Orchestra.

Jockey Club The controlling body for horse racing in Britain, founded c.1750 at the Star and Garter Coffee House, Pall Mall, London. In 1968 the Jockey Club and National Hunt Committee amalgamated.

Jodl, Alfred [yohdl] (1890–1946) German general, born in Aachen, W Germany. An artillery subaltern in World War 1, he became general of artillery in 1940, the planning genius of the German High Command and Hitler's chief adviser. He was found guilty of war crimes at Nuremberg (1946), and executed.

Jodrell Bank 53°13N 2°21W. Observatory station in Macclesfield district, Cheshire, NWC England, UK; 5 km/3 mi NE of Holmes Chapel; leading radio astronomy centre.

Joel, Billy (1949–) Singer, songwriter, and pianist, born in Long Island, New York, USA. He played with various bands before beginning his solo career in 1971. He earned a gold disk with the album *Piano Man* (1974), and one of his most popular singles, 'Uptown Girl' (1983), topped the UK charts for five weeks. Later albums include *Stormfront* (1989) and *River of Dreams* (1993).

Joel, Book of One of the 12 so-called 'minor' prophetic writings of the Hebrew Bible/Old Testament, attributed to Joel, of whom nothing is known, but who is today usually assigned to the post-exilic period (c.400–350 BC), a prophet with a strong interest in priesthood and the Jerusalem Temple cult. It contains a notable reference to a locust plague, warning Judah of a devastating coming judgment and of the final 'Day of the Lord' when Israel's enemies will be destroyed.

Joffre, Joseph Jacques Césaire [zhofruh] (1852–1931) French general, born in Rivesaltes, S France. He entered the army in 1870, and rose to be French chief-of-staff (1914) and commander-in-chief (1915), carrying out a policy of attrition against the German invaders of France. He was made a marshal of France (1916) and president of the Allied War Council (1917).

Johanan ben Zakkai, Rabban [yohhanan ben zakiy] (1st-c) Prominent Jewish teacher and leader of the reformulation of Judaism after the fall of Jerusalem (AD 70), who helped to found rabbinic Judaism. His early career was apparently in Galilee, although there are also traditions of his legal disputes with the Sadducees in Jerusalem before its fall. Afterwards he was instrumental in reconstituting the Sanhedrin council in Jabneh.

Johannesburg [johhanizberg], Afrikaans [yohhanuhsberkh], abbreviated **Jo'burg** 26°10S 28°02E, pop (2000e) 1 837 000 (metropolitan area). Largest city in South Africa, and capital of Gauteng province; 50 km/31 mi SSW of Pretoria; altitude 1665 m/5462 ft; founded in 1886 after the discovery of gold in the Witwatersrand; airport; railway; two universities (1922, 1966); commerce (stock exchange), chemicals, textiles, clothing, leather products, engineering, diamond cutting, gold mining; art gallery, civic centre, several museums.

Johannsen, Wilhelm Ludvig [johhansen] (1857–1927) Botanist and geneticist, born in Copenhagen, Denmark. He studied in Copenhagen, Germany, and Finland, and worked at the Institute of Agriculture in Copenhagen before becoming professor of agriculture at the university there (1905). His pioneering experiments with princess beans laid the foundation for later developments in the genetics of quantitative characters. The terms *gene*, *phenotype*, and *genotype* are due to him.

Johanson, Donald (Carl) [johhanson] (1943–) Palaeoanthropologist, born in Chicago, Illinois, USA. A graduate of Chicago University, he worked at the Cleveland Museum of Natural History, where he became curator in 1974. His spectacular finds of fossil hominids 3–4 million years old at Hadar in the Afar triangle of Ethiopia (1972–7) generated worldwide interest. They include 'Lucy', a unique female specimen that is half complete, and the so-called 'First Family', a scattered group containing the remains of 13 individuals. Since 1981 he has been director of the Institute of Human Origins, Berkeley, CA, and from 1986 began conducting fieldwork in Olduvai Gorge, Tanzania.

John (of England), also known as **John Lackland** (1167–1216) King of England (1199–1216), the youngest son of Henry II, born in Oxford, Oxfordshire, SC England, UK, and one of the least popular monarchs in English history. He tried to seize the crown during Richard I's captivity in Germany (1193–4), but was forgiven and nominated successor by Richard, who thus set aside the rights of Arthur, the son of John's elder brother Geoffrey. Arthur's claims were supported by Philip II of France, and, after Arthur was murdered on John's orders (1203), Philip marched against him with superior forces, conquering all but a portion of Aquitaine (1204–5). In 1206 John refused to receive Stephen Langton as Archbishop of Canterbury, and in 1208 his kingdom was placed under papal interdict. He was then excommunicated (1209), and finally conceded (1213). His oppressive government, and failure to recover Normandy, provoked baronial opposition, which led to demands for constitutional reform. The barons met the king at Runnymede, and forced him to grant the Great Charter (Magna Carta) (Jun 1215), the basis of the English constitution. His repudiation of the Charter precipitated the first Barons' War (1215–17).

John II, known as **John the Good** (1319–64) King of France (1350–64), the son of Philip VI, born near Le Mans, NW France. In 1356 he was taken prisoner by Edward the Black Prince at the Battle of Poitiers, and brought to England. After the treaty of Brétigny (1360) he returned home, leaving his second son, the Duke of Anjou, as a hostage. When the duke broke his parole and escaped (1363), John chivalrously returned to London, and died there.

John, St, also known as **John, son of Zebedee** and **John the Evangelist** (1st-c) One of the 12 apostles, the son of Zebedee, and the younger brother of James, a Galilean fisherman. He was one of the inner circle of disciples who were with Jesus at the Transfiguration and Gethsemane. Acts and Galatians also name him as one of the 'pillars' of the early Jerusalem Church. Some traditions represent him as having been slain by the Jews or Herod Agrippa I; but from the 2nd-c he was said to have spent his closing years at Ephesus, dying there at an advanced age, after having written the Apocalypse, the Gospel, and the three Epistles which bear his name (though his authorship of these works has been disputed by modern scholars). Feast day 27 December.

John XXII, originally **Jacques Duèse** (c.1249–1334) Pope (1316–34), one of the most celebrated of the popes of Avignon, born in Cahors, SC France. He intervened in the contest for the imperial crown between Louis of Bavaria and Frederick of Austria, supporting the latter. A long contest ensued both in Germany and Italy between the Guelph (papal) party and the Ghibelline (imperial) party. In 1327 Louis entered Italy, was crowned emperor at Rome, and deposed the pope, setting up an antipope (1328). Although Guelphic predominance at Rome was later restored, John died at Avignon.

John XXIII, originally **Angelo Giuseppe Roncalli** (1881–1963) Pope (1958–63), born in Sotto il Monte, N Italy. He was ordained in 1904, served as a chaplain in World War 1, and was subsequently apostolic delegate to Bulgaria, Turkey, and Greece. Patriarch of Venice in 1953, he was elected pope in 1958 on the 12th ballot. He convened the Second Vatican Council (1962–5) to renew the religious life of the Church and to modernize its teachings, disciplines, and organization, with the aim of eventual unity of all Christians. His beatification was announced in 2000.

John, Augustus (Edwin) (1878–1961) Painter, born in Tenby, Pembrokeshire, SW Wales, UK. He studied in London and Paris, and made an early reputation with his etchings (1900–14). His favourite themes were gypsies, fishing folk, and naturally regal women, as in 'Lyric Fantasy' (1913); and he painted portraits of several political and artistic contemporary figures, such as Shaw, Hardy, and Dylan Thomas.

John, Sir Elton, originally **Reginald Kenneth Dwight** (1947–) Rock singer and pianist, born in Pinner, NW Greater London, UK. He played the piano by ear from age four, and studied at the Royal Academy of Music at 11. From 1967, he and Bernie Taupin began writing songs such as 'Rocket Man' (1972), 'Honky Cat' (1972), and 'Goodbye Yellow Brick Road' (1973). Their publisher pressed John to perform them, for which he obscured his short, plump, myopic physique in a clownish garb that included huge glasses, sequinned and fringed jump suits, and ermine boots. A top pop star of the 1970s, he later became chairman (1976–90) and then honorary life president (from 1990) of the Watford Football Club and a stock-market speculator. Despite health problems in 1993 brought about by his stressful lifestyle he continues to perform live across the world. His recording of 'Candle in the Wind '97', sung at the funeral of Princess Diana, became the largest-selling single in history within a month of its release. He was knighted in 1998.

John, Otto [yohn] (1909–97) West German ex-security chief, the defendant in a major post-war treason case. In 1944 he was part of the plot against Hitler, after which he escaped to Britain. In 1950 he was appointed to the West German Office for the protection of the constitution. In 1954 he mysteriously disappeared from West Berlin, and later broadcast for the East German Communists. In 1956 he returned to the West, was arrested, tried, and imprisoned. His defence was that he had been drugged, driven to the Communist sector, held prisoner, and forced to make broadcasts until he managed to escape. Released in 1958, he continued to protest his innocence.

John of Austria, Don, Span **Don Juan** (1547–78) Spanish soldier, the illegitimate son of Emperor Charles V, born in Regensburg, SE Germany. He defeated the Moors in Granada (1570) and the Turks at Lepanto (1571). In 1573 he took Tunis, and was then sent to Milan and (1576) to Holland as viceroy. He planned to marry Mary, Queen of Scots, but died of typhoid at Namur.

John of Damascus, St, also called **St John Damascene** (c.675–c.749) Theologian and hymn writer of the Eastern Church, born in Damascus. He was educated by the Italian monk, Cosmas, and defended the use of images in church worship during the iconoclastic controversy. His later years were spent in a monastery near Jerusalem, where he was ordained. Feast day 4 December.

John of Gaunt (1340–99) Duke of Lancaster, born in Ghent, NW Belgium, the fourth son of Edward III, and ancestor of Henry IV, V, VI, and VII. In 1359 he married his cousin, **Blanche of Lancaster**, and was created duke in 1362. After her death (1369), he married **Constance**, the daughter of Pedro (Peter) the Cruel of Castile, and assumed the title of King of Castile, though he failed by his expeditions to oust his rival, Henry of Trastámara. In England he became highly influential as a peacemaker during the troubled reign of Richard II. He was made Duke of Aquitaine by Richard (1390), and sent on several embassies to France. On his second wife's death (1394) he married his mistress, **Catherine Swynford**, by whom he had three sons; from the eldest descended Henry VII.

John of Leyden (1509–36) Anabaptist leader, born in Leyden, The Netherlands. He worked as a tailor, merchant, and innkeeper, and became noted as an orator. Turning Anabaptist, he went to Münster, became head of the movement, and set up a 'kingdom of Zion', with polygamy and community of goods. In 1535 the city was taken by the Bishop of Münster, and John and his accomplices were executed.

John of Nepomuk, St (c.1330–93) Patron saint of Bohemia, born in Nepomuk, SWC Czech Republic. He studied at Prague, and became confessor to Sophia, the wife of Wenceslaus IV (ruled 1378–1419). For refusing to betray the confession of the queen, he was tortured and drowned. He was canonized in 1729; feast day 16 May.

John of the Cross, St, originally **Juan de Yepes y Álvarez** (1542–91) Christian mystic and poet, the founder with St Teresa of the Discalced Carmelites, born in Fontiveros, WC Spain. He became a Carmelite monk in 1563, and was ordained in 1567. Imprisoned at Toledo (1577), he wrote a number of poems, such as *Canto espiritual* (Spiritual Canticle), which are highly regarded in Spanish mystical literature. After escaping, he became vicar-provincial of Andalusia (1585–7), and died in seclusion at the monastery of Úbeda. He was canonized in 1726; feast day 14 December.

John the Baptist, St (1st-c) Prophetic and ascetic figure referred to in the New Testament Gospels and in Josephus's *Antiquities*, the son of a priest named Zechariah; roughly contemporary with Jesus of Nazareth. A story of his birth to Elizabeth, the cousin of Mary the mother of Jesus, is recorded in *Luke* 1. He baptized Jesus and others at the R Jordan, but his baptism seemed mainly to symbolize a warning of the coming judgment of God and the consequent need for repentance. He was executed by Herod Antipas, but the circumstances differ in the accounts of Josephus and the Gospels. He is treated in the New Testament as the forerunner of Christ, and sometimes as a returned Elijah (*Matt* 11.13–14). Feast day 24 June.

John, Gospel according to New Testament book, known also as the **Fourth Gospel**, distinct from the other three ('synoptic') gospels because of its unique theological reflections on Jesus as the Son of God and the divine Word come from God, and its records of Jesus's sayings and deeds. It is strictly anonymous, although *John* 21.24 associates it with 'the disciple whom Jesus loved', traditionally held to be John the son of Zebedee but often disputed today.

John, Letters of Three relatively short New Testament writings, the latter two of which have the form of letters from 'the Elder', but the first of which lacks direct references to its writer or recipients. They were traditionally considered the work of the author of the Fourth Gospel, but today they are often assigned to a later stage of the 'Johannine community'. *1* and *2 John* confront the problem of a schism within this Christian community, apparently over false teachings about the importance of the humanity (as opposed to divinity) of Jesus and about the significance of sin for Christians. *3 John* appears to be a private letter addressing problems with a local church leader called Diotrephes.

John Birch Society A moderately sized, extreme right-wing pressure group in the USA which promotes conservative ideas and policies, and is strongly patriotic and anti-communist. Founded in 1958, the name derives from a US missionary and intelligence officer, killed by Chinese Communists on 25 August 1945, who was seen by the Society as the first hero of the Cold War.

John Bull A personification of the typical Englishman, or of England itself, first depicted in *The History of John Bull* by Arbuthnot. In many political cartoons of the 18th-c and 19th-c, he is drawn as a short stocky figure, often wearing a waistcoat showing the British flag.

John Henry The hero of an American ballad, who pits himself against a steam drill, and succeeds in crushing more rock than the machine, but dies from the effort. He is known as 'the black Paul Bunyan'.

John o'Groats [jonuhgrohts] Locality in NE Highland, NE Scotland, UK; on Pentland Firth, 23 km/14 mi N of Wick; often mistakenly thought to be the northernmost point on mainland UK; 'from Land's End to John o'Groats', a common phrase for the length of Britain (970 km/603 mi apart); no remains of the octagonal house said to have been built here by Dutchman John de Groot, who settled in Scotland in the 16th-c.

John Paul I, originally **Albino Luciani** (1912–78) Pope (Aug–Sep 1978), born in Forno di Canale, NE Italy. He studied at the Gregorian University in Rome, and was ordained in 1935. He became a parish priest and teacher in Belluno, vicar-general of the diocese of Vittorio Veneto (1954), a bishop (1958), patriarch of Venice (1969), and a cardinal (1973). He was the first pope to use a double name (from his two immediate predecessors, John XXIII and Paul VI). He died only 33 days later, the shortest pontificate of modern times.

John Paul II, originally **Karol Jozef Wojtyła** (1920–) Pope (1978–), born in Wadowice, S Poland, the first non-Italian pope in 450 years. He studied in Poland, was ordained in 1946, and became professor of moral theology at Lublin and Kraków. Archbishop and Metropolitan of Kraków (1964–78), he was created cardinal in 1967. Noted for his energy and analytical ability, his pontificate has seen many foreign visits, in which he has preached to huge audiences. In 1981 he survived an assassination attempt, when he was shot in St Peter's square by a Turkish national, Mehmet Ali Agca, the motives for which have remained unclear. A champion of economic justice and an outspoken defender of the Church in Communist countries, he has been uncompromising on moral issues. Although in failing health, he joined in the celebrations for his silver jubilee in 2003.

Johns, Jasper (1930–) Painter, sculptor, and printmaker, born in Augusta, Georgia, USA. He studied at the University of South Carolina, became a painter in New York City in 1952, and was attracted by the Dadaist ideas of Marcel Duchamp. Because conventional art critics placed so much emphasis on 'self expression' and 'originality', he chose to paint flags, targets, maps, and other pre-existing images in a style deliberately clumsy and banal. He was one of the creators of Pop Art.

Johns, W(illiam) E(arl) (1893–1968) Writer, author of the 'Biggles' stories, born in Hertford, Hertfordshire, SE England, UK. He trained as a surveyor before serving in the Norfolk Yeomanry (1914). He transferred to the Royal Flying Corps, and was shot down and imprisoned; he then escaped, but was recaptured. He retired from the Royal Air Force in 1930, and edited *Popular Flying*, where he first wrote his stories featuring Captain James Bigglesworth ('Biggles'). He went on to write over 70 novels, many of which are still in print.

Johnson, Amy (1903–41) Pioneer aviator, born in Hull, NE England, UK. She flew solo from England to Australia (1930), to Japan via Siberia (1931), and to Cape Town (1932), making new records in each case. A pilot in Air Transport Auxiliary in World War 2, she was drowned after bailing out over the Thames estuary.

Johnson, Andrew (1808–75) US statesman and 17th president (1865–9), born in Raleigh, North Carolina, USA. With little formal schooling, he became alderman and mayor in Greenville, TN, and a member of the Legislature (1835), State Senate (1841), and Congress (1843). He was made Governor of Tennessee in 1853, and a senator in 1857. During the Civil War he became military governor of Tennessee (1862), US vice-president (1865), and president on Lincoln's assassination (1865). A Democrat, his conciliatory policies were opposed by Congress, who wished to keep the Southern states under military government. He vetoed the congressional measures, was impeached, brought to trial, and acquitted.

Johnson, Dame Celia (1908–82) Actress, born in Richmond, SW Greater London, UK. Well-established on the stage, she had leading roles in Noel Coward's wartime films *In Which We Serve* (1942) and *This Happy Breed* (1944), and is best remembered for her performance in *Brief Encounter* (1945). Her later film appearances were infrequent, among them *The Prime of Miss Jean Brodie* (1968), but she continued in the theatre and on television until very shortly before her death.

Johnson, Eyvind (1900–76) Writer, born near Boden, NE Sweden. After minimal schooling, and a number of years in mainly manual occupations, he spent most of the 1920s in Paris and Berlin, and began to write. His four-part *Romanen om Olof* (1934–7, The Story of Olof) is the finest of the many working-class autobiographical novels written in Sweden in the 1930s. He was much involved in anti-Nazi causes, and produced a number of novels, especially the *Krilon* series (1941–3), castigating totalitarianism. The same humanitarian values are evident in his later historical novels, particularly *Strändernas svall* (1946, trans Return to Ithaca), and *Hans nådes tid* (1960, trans The Days of his Grace). He shared the 1974 Nobel Prize for Literature with his fellow Swede, Harry Martinson.

Johnson, James P(rice) (1894–1955) Jazz pianist and composer, born in New Brunswick, New Jersey, USA. He was given rudimentary piano instruction by his mother, and while still at school played ragtime with other performers. In 1912 he began a series of piano-playing jobs in cabarets, movie-houses, and dance-halls, eventually becoming the most accomplished player in the post-ragtime 'stride' style. A prolific performer in the 1920s and during the traditional jazz revival of the 1940s, he wrote more than 200 songs (including 'The Charleston') as well as several stage shows, and was a strong influence on such later pianists as Fats Waller and Art Tatum.

Johnson, James Weldon (1871–1938) Writer and diplomat, born in Jacksonville, Florida, USA. He practised at the bar there (1897–1901), and in 1906 was US consul at Puerto Cabello, Venezuela, and at Corinto, Nicaragua (1909–12). He was secretary of the National Association for the Advancement of Colored People (1916–30), and from 1930 was professor of creative literature at Fisk University. He wrote extensively on African-American problems, and compiled collections of African-American poetry.

Johnson, Lyndon B(aines), also known as **LBJ** (1908–73) US statesman and 36th president (1963–9), born in Stonewall, Texas, USA. He studied at Southwest Texas State Teachers College, and became a teacher and congressman's secretary before being elected a Democrat representative in 1937. He became a senator in 1948, and an effective leader of the Democratic majority. Vice-president under Kennedy in 1960, he was made president after Kennedy's assassination, and was returned to the post in 1964 with a huge majority. His administration passed the Civil Rights Act (1964) and the Voting Rights Act (1965), which helped the position of African-Americans in US society. However, the escalation of the war in Vietnam led to active protest and growing unpopularity, and after 1969 he retired from active politics.

Johnson, Magic, popular name of **Earvin Johnson** (1959–) Basketball player, born in Lansing, Missouri, USA. Named the National Basketball Association's Most Valuable Player in 1979, he was a member of NBA championship teams in 1980, 1982, 1985, 1987, and 1988, and played 12 years as a guard for the Los Angeles Lakers (1980–91). He retired from the NBA in 1992 when he tested positive for the HIV virus, but returned to play for the Lakers in 1996. His autobiography was called, simply, *Magic* (1983). In 1992 his book *What You Can Do to Avoid AIDS* generated controversy when two of the largest US retailers refused to carry it. He was inducted into the Basketball Hall of Fame in 2002.

Johnson, Michael (1967–) Track athlete, born in Dallas, Texas, USA. He attended Baylor University, TX. Four-times world champion at 400 m (1993, 1995, 1997, 1999), he achieved the 200 m/400 m double at the 1995 championships, and an unprecedented male double of 200 m and 400 m gold medals at the 1996 (Atlanta) Olympics.

Johnson, Pamela Hansford (1912–81) Writer, born in London, UK. Best known for her portrayal of her native post-war London, her books include *An Avenue of Stone* (1947), *The Unspeakable Skipton* (1958), *A Bonfire* (1981), and several works of non-fiction, such as her study of the Moors murders, *On Iniquity* (1967). In 1950 she married the novelist C P Snow.

Johnson, Philip C(ortelyou) (1906–) Architect and theorist, born in Cleveland, OH. A graduate of Harvard, he also studied under Marcel Breuer, and became a proponent of the International Style. He designed his own home, the Glass House, New Canaan, CT (1949–50), on principles of space unification derived from Ludwig Mies van der Rohe, with whom he designed the Seagram Building skyscraper, New York City (1945). Further works include the New York State Theater, Lincoln Center (1964), and the American Telephone and Telegraph Company building (1978–84).

Johnson, Samuel, known as **Dr Johnson** (1709–84) Lexicographer, critic, and poet, born in Lichfield, Staffordshire, C England, UK. The son of a bookseller, he studied at Lichfield and Oxford, but left because of poverty before taking a degree, and became a teacher. In 1737 he went to London, and worked as a journalist. From 1747 he worked for eight years on his *Dictionary of the English Language*, started the moralistic periodical, *The Rambler* (1750), and wrote his philosophical romance of Abyssinia, *Rasselas* (1759). In 1762 he was given a crown pension, which enabled him to figure as arbiter of letters and social personality, notably in the Literary Club, of which he was a founder member (1764). In 1765 he produced his edition of Shakespeare, from 1772 engaged in political pamphleteering, in 1773 went with Boswell on a tour of Scotland, and later wrote *Lives of the Most Eminent English Poets* (1779–81). His reputation as a man and conversationalist outweighs his literary reputation, and for the picture of Johnson in society we are indebted above all to Boswell.

Johnson, Uwe (1934–84) Writer, born in Kammin, Pomerania (now part of Poland). He studied at Rostock and Leipzig, and left East for West Germany after completing his first novel, *Mutmassungen über Jakob* (Speculations about Jakob) in 1959. His second and third novels, *Das dritte Buch über Achim* (1961, The Third Book about Achim), and *Zwei Ansichten* (1965, Two Views), develop the theme of the relation between the two Germanies.

He later moved to university posts in the USA, and then to England, but published no fiction after 1965.

Johnson, Virginia E *Masters and Johnson*

Johnston, Bruce *Beach Boys, The*

Johnston Islands 16°45N 169°32W; pop (2000e) 327; area 2·5 sq km/1 sq mi. Coral atoll enclosing four islets in the C Pacific Ocean, 1150 km/715 mi SW of Honolulu; discovered, 1807; claimed by Hawaii, 1858; taken over by US Navy, 1934; now used as a store for poisonous gas; airfield.

Johor or **Johore** [johaw(r)] pop (2000e) 2 622 000; area 18 985 sq km/7328 sq mi. State in S Peninsular Malaysia, occupying the entire S tip of the peninsula; bounded W by the Strait of Malacca, E by the S China Sea; separated from Singapore by the Johor Strait; capital, Johor Baharu; tin, bauxite, rubber, oil palms, pineapples, pepper, timber.

Johor Baharu [johaw(r) bahroo] 1°29N 103°44E, pop (2000e) 377 000. Capital of Johor state, S Peninsular Malaysia, 365 km/227 mi SE of Kuala Lumpur; connected to Singapore by causeway; trading centre, tourism; Grand Palace (19th-c), Abu Bakar mosque, Johor Safariworld (SE Asia's only safari park), Fiesta Village.

joint The region of contact between bones of the body. Some bones articulate at movable joints, others at only slightly movable joints, and others at immovable joints. The shape of the articular surfaces, and the structure and arrangement of the ligaments that unite the bones at the joint, principally determine the amount of movement which may occur. Three distinct classes of joint are recognized. **Fibrous joints** allow almost no movement, because the two bones are held firmly together by fibrous tissue. These include *sutures*, (allowing virtually no movement, eg between the skull bones), *gomphases* (allowing minimal movement, eg between the roots of the teeth and the alveolar bone), and *syndesmoses* (where the fibrous tissue may be much greater, allowing some movement, as between the lower end of the adult tibia and fibula). **Cartilaginous joints** unite the two bones by a continuous plate of hyaline cartilage, with or without an intervening fibrocartilaginous disc. They include the joints which occur in the median plane of the body, such as those between the bodies of the vertebrae. **Synovial joints** are specialized to allow generally free movement, and constitute the majority of permanent joints in the limbs. Several types can be identified according to the shape of their articulating surfaces, which in turn determines the type of movement possible at the joint: *plane* joints (eg between the carpel bones), *saddle* joints (eg the carpo-metacarpal joint of the thumb), *hinge* joints (eg the elbow joint), *pivot* joints (eg the superior radio-ulnar joint), and *ball-and-socket* joints (eg the hip joint).

Joint Academic Network (JANET) A computer network provided in the UK to link computer centres in higher education and research establishments, providing electronic mail, file transfer, and the ability for a user at one computer centre to log into the facilities at another. A particular use of JANET allows researchers at many universities to scan the library catalogues of other universities in order to locate books. Gateways are provided from JANET to BITNET, Internet, and USENET.

Joint European Torus (JET) A research facility in nuclear fusion comprising a large doughnut-shaped experimental fusion reactor called a tokamak, which became operational in 1983 at Abingdon, Oxfordshire. It is funded by 15 European countries and EURATOM. It stands c.9 m/30 ft high, and weighs c.3000 tonnes. In 1997 JET achieved a record of 16 MW peak fusion power, with a ratio of power out to power in of 65%.

Joinville, Jean, sieur de (Lord of) [zhwĩveel] (c.1224–1317) Historian, born in Joinville, NE France. He became seneschal to the Count of Champagne and King of Navarre, took part in the unfortunate Seventh Crusade (1248–54) of Louis IX, returned with him to France, and lived partly at court, partly on his estates. While imprisoned at Acre with Louis, he composed a Christian manual, his *Credo* (1250). Throughout the Crusade he took notes of events and wrote down his impressions which he fashioned, at the age of almost 80, into his delightful *Histoire de Saint Louis* (1309).

Jolie, Angelina [johlee], in full **Angelina Jolie Voight** (1975–) Actress, born in Los Angeles, California, USA, the daughter of actor Jon Voight. At age 11 she attended the Lee Strasberg Theater Institute and later studied at New York University. She gained her first film lead role in *Hackers* (1995), and later films include *Gia* (1998, Best Actress Golden Globe), *The Bone Collector* (1999), *Girl, Interrrupted* (1999, Golden Globe; Best Supporting Actress Oscar), and *Lara Croft: Tomb Raider* (2001, sequel 2003).

Joliot-Curie, (Jean) Frédéric [zholyoh küree], originally **Jean Frédéric Joliot** (1900–58) Physical chemist, born in Paris, France. He studied at the Sorbonne, where in 1925 he became assistant to Marie Curie, and in 1926 married her daughter Irène, with whom he shared the 1935 Nobel Prize for Chemistry. Professor at the Collège de France (1937), he became a strong supporter of the Resistance movement during World War 2, and a member of the Communist Party. After the liberation he became high commissioner for atomic energy (1946–50), a position from which he was dismissed for his political activities. President of the Communist-sponsored World Peace Council, he was awarded the Stalin Peace Prize in 1951.

Joliot-Curie, Irène [zholioh kyooree], *née* **Curie** (1897–1956) Physical chemist, born in Paris, France, the daughter of Pierre and Marie Curie. She studied at the Collège Sévigné, and worked as her mother's assistant at the Institut du Radium in Paris. There she met her future husband Frédéric Joliot, with whom she discovered artificial radioactivity in 1934, a major step on the road to nuclear energy. A strong Socialist and an outspoken anti-Fascist, she was under-secretary of state for scientific research in the Popular Front government (1936). She became director of the Institut du Radium (1946–50), and shared with her husband the Nobel Prize for Chemistry in 1935.

Jolson, Al [johlson], originally **Asa Yoelson** (1886–1950) Actor and singer, born in Srednike (now Seredzius), Lithuania. Brought to the USA in 1893, he made his stage debut in 1899, and with his brother toured with circus and minstrel shows. His sentimental songs, such as 'Mammy', 'Sonny Boy', and 'Swanee', delivered on one knee, arms outstretched, brought tears to the eyes of vaudeville audiences in the 1920s. He called himself 'the World's Greatest Entertainer'. In 1927, he starred in *The Jazz Singer*, the first motion picture with sound. Years after his popularity waned, his career revived briefly with the release of the films *The Jolson Story* (1946) and *Jolson Sings Again* (1949).

Jomon [johmon] A broad term used to describe Mesolithic and Neolithic Japan (c.8000–300 BC) and all archaeological remains of the period. It may represent several cultures. Over 10 000 sites are known, with five main chronological periods. The name derives from the twisted-cord-decorated (*jomon*) pottery excavated from the Omori shell mounds near Tokyo in 1877.

Jonah or **Jonas, Book of** One of the 12 so-called 'minor' prophetic writings of the Hebrew Bible/Old Testament, unusual for its narrative about the reluctance of the prophet himself in preaching to the city of Nineveh. It includes the famous legend of Jonah's being swallowed by and saved from a 'great fish'. Although the story is set in the mid-8th-c BC, the work is probably post-exilic; it emphasizes Israel's role in addressing the heathen nations, and thus implicitly opposes Jewish exclusivism.

Jonas *Jonah, Book of*

Jonathan (c.11th-c BC) Biblical character, the son and heir of Saul (the first king of Israel) and loyal friend of David. He is portrayed in 1 Samuel as a cunning soldier, but he faced conflicting loyalties when he continued his friendship with David in spite of Saul's mounting hostility to David. David succeeded Saul as King of Israel, since Jonathan was killed in the Battle of Gilboa against the Philistines.

Jones, Bobby, popular name of **Robert (Tyre) Jones** (1902–71) Golfer, born in Atlanta, Georgia, USA. A practising lawyer, he was an amateur golfer throughout his career, winning the (British) Open three times (1926–7, 1930) and the US Open four times (1923, 1926, 1929–30). He also won the US Amateur title five times and the British Amateur title once. In 1930 he took the Amateur and Open titles of both countries, the game's greatest Grand Slam. He was responsible for the founding of the US Masters at Augusta, GA.

Jones, Daniel (1881–1967) Phonetician, born in London, UK. He was called to the bar in 1907, when he was also appointed lecturer in phonetics at University College London (professor 1921–49). He collaborated with others in compiling Cantonese (1912), Sechuana (1916), and Sinhalese (1919) phonetic readers. He wrote *An Outline of English Phonetics* (1916), and compiled an *English Pronouncing Dictionary* (1917, 15th edn 1997). His other works included *The Phoneme* (1950), and *Cardinal Vowels* (1956). He was secretary (1928–49) then president (1950–67) of the International Phonetic Association.

Jones, (Alfred) Ernest (1879–1958) Psychoanalyst, born in Llwchwy, S Wales, UK. He studied at University College, Cardiff, and qualified as a physician in London. Medical journalism and neurological research brought him into contact with the work of Sigmund Freud. He introduced psychoanalysis into Britain and North America, founded the British Psycho-Analytical Society (1913), as well as the *International Journal of Psycho-Analysis*, which he edited (1920–33). He was professor of psychiatry at Toronto (1909–12) and director of the London Clinic for Psycho-Analysis. Among his numerous works and translations is a psychoanalytical study of *Hamlet and Oedipus*, and an authoritative biography of Freud (1953–7).

Jones, Henry, pseudonym **Cavendish** (1831–99) Physician and writer, born in London, UK. He studied at King's College and St Bartholomew's Hospital, practised as a surgeon (1852–69), and began writing about whist, publishing *Principles of Whist* (1862), and became whist editor of *The Field* magazine (1862). He wrote manuals on many other games, and helped found the All-England Croquet Club (1870). His pseudonym derives from the name of the first whist club he went to in London.

Jones, Inigo (1573–1652) The first of the great English architects, born in London, UK. He studied landscape painting in Italy, and from Venice introduced the Palladian style into England. In 1606 James I employed him in arranging the masques of Ben Jonson, and he introduced the proscenium arch and movable scenery to the English stage. In 1615 he became surveyor-general of the royal buildings. He designed the Queen's House at Greenwich (1616–35), the Banqueting House in Whitehall (1619–22), and laid out Covent Garden and Lincoln's Inn Fields, all in London.

Jones, Jack, popular name of **James (Larkin) Jones** (1913–93) Trade unionist, born in Liverpool, Merseyside, NW England, UK. He was general secretary of the Transport and General Workers Union (1969–78), favouring the decentralization of trade union power to the local branches, and had some influence on the Labour government's policies of 1974–6. Made a Companion of Honour in 1978, his autobiography, *Union Man*, was published in 1986.

Jones, John Paul, originally **John Paul** (1747–92) American naval officer, born in Kirkbean, Dumfries and Galloway, SW Scotland, UK. He made voyages to America, and assumed the name of Jones after escaping from a mutinous crew. In the American War of Independence he was commissioned as a senior lieutenant. In 1778 he cruised into British waters in the *Ranger*, and made a daring descent on the Solway Firth in Scotland. In 1779, as commodore of a French squadron displaying American colours, he threatened Leith, and off Flamborough Head won a hard-fought engagement on the *Bonhomme Richard* against the British Frigate *Serapis*. In 1788 he entered Russian service, and as rear-admiral of the Black Sea fleet fought in the Russo-Turkish war of 1788–9.

Jones, Marion (1975–) Track and field athlete, born in Los Angeles, California, USA. A sprinter and jumper, she won the 100 m World Championship in 10·83 sec in 1997. The International Athletics Federation Woman Athlete of the Year in 1998, she headed the rankings for 100 m, 200 m and long jump (the first woman to do this since 1943), was US champion in all three, and was unbeaten in 34 consecutive competitions before losing the World Cup long jump to Heike Drechsler. She became the first woman in history to win five athletics medals at a single Olympic Games, a feat she accomplished at Sydney in 2000.

Jones, Mary Harris, known as **Mother Jones** (1830–1930) US labour agitator, born in Co Cork, S Ireland. She migrated to the USA via Canada, lost her family to an epidemic in 1867, and her home to the Chicago fire of 1871, and thereafter devoted herself to the cause of labour. Homeless after 1880, she travelled to areas of labour strife, especially in the coal industry, and was imprisoned in West Virginia on a charge of conspiracy to murder in 1912, at the age of 82. Freed by a new governor, she returned to labour agitation, which she continued almost until her death.

Jones, Robert Edmond (1887–1954) Scene designer, born in Milton, New Hampshire, USA. He studied at Harvard, went to Berlin to learn from Max Reinhardt, then returned to the USA to design for a Broadway production of *The Man Who Married A Dumb Wife* by Anatole France. His symbolic use of primary colours and light frame construction, a radical departure in 1915 from the prevailing norms of realism, ushered in a career that was to revolutionize stagecraft in the USA. His simplified designs sought to engage the audience's imagination rather than copy reality and, together with his theoretical work, had an enduring influence.

Jones, Tom, originally **Thomas Jones Woodward** (1940–) Singer, born in Pontypridd, Rhondda Cynon Taff, S Wales, UK. He began singing as a child, later performing in working-men's clubs, and became known following his hit single, 'It's Not Unusual' (1965), which made UK number 1 and US number 10. His version of 'Green Green Grass of Home' (1966) was his biggest selling single, other hits including 'What's New Pussycat?' (1965), 'Delilah' (1968), 'Love Me Tonight' (1969), and 'She's a Lady' (1971). His recording career was revived in the late 1980s, with further hits including 'A Boy From Nowhere' (1987), and Prince's 'Kiss' (1988). Later albums include *Reload* (1999) and *Mr Jones* (2002). In 2003 he received a Brit Award for Outstanding Contribution to Music.

Jones, Sir William (1746–94) Orientalist, born in London, UK. He studied at Oxford, was called to the bar (1774), became a judge in the Supreme Court in Bengal (1783), and was knighted. He devoted himself to Sanskrit, whose resemblance to Latin and Greek he pointed out in 1787, thus motivating the era of comparative philology.

Jones* v. *Clinton (1997) A unanimous US Supreme Court decision that a sitting president may be subject to civil lawsuits during his term of office. The case arose out of the civil rights lawsuit of Paula Corbin Jones (1966–), who alleged that President Bill Clinton had made a sexual advance to her in 1991 and then penalized her for her unwillingness to participate in sex with him. President Clinton and his lawyers contended that he should not have to respond to Jones's charges while he was in the White House. While praised at the time for its assertion that the president was not above the law, subsequent events leading up to the Monica Lewinsky scandal provoked criticism of the Court's decision for a failure to realize the extent to which litigation could adversely impact a sitting president.

Jongkind, Johan Barthold [yongkint] (1819–91) Painter, born in Lattrop, The Netherlands. He studied at The Hague, but moved to Paris in 1846, establishing close links with French art. He was a friend of Eugène Boudin, and exhibited with the Barbizon painters. An important precursor of Impressionism, he influenced the young Monet.

Jönköping [yoenchoeping] 57°45N 14°10E, pop (2000e) 117 000. Industrial town and capital of Jönköping county, S Sweden; at S end of L Vättern; charter, 1284; railway; focus point for agriculture and forestry; textiles, machinery, paper.

Jonson, Ben(jamin) (1572–1637) Playwright and poet, born in London, UK. Educated at Westminster School, he worked as a bricklayer, did military service in Flanders, and joined Henslowe's company of players, where he killed a fellow player in a duel. His *Every Man in His Humour*, with Shakespeare in the cast, was performed in 1598. After some less successful works, including two Roman tragedies, he wrote his four chief plays: *Volpone* (1606), *The Silent Woman* (1609), *The Alchemist* (1610), and *Bartholomew Fair* (1614). In collaboration with Inigo Jones, he produced several masques before 1625, when the death of James I ended his period of court favour. A major influence on 17th-c poets (known as 'the tribe, or sons, of Ben'), he was appointed poet laureate in 1617.

Jooss, Kurt [johs] (1901–79) Dancer, choreographer, teacher, and director, born in Wasseralfingen, SWC Germany. He studied ballet before meeting Laban, with whom he then worked. He was appointed director of the dance department at the Essen Folkwang School in 1927, from which the dance theatre company developed. His best-known work, *The Green Table*, was created in 1932. He left Germany in 1933 for England, where he formed a new group, Ballets Jooss, and toured extensively. He returned to Essen in 1949, and retired in 1969, but his works continue to be mounted by his daughter **Anna Markard** (1931–).

Joplin, Scott (1868–1917) Pianist and composer, born in Texarkana, Arkansas, USA. Largely self-taught, he became a professional musician in his teens, but later studied music at George Smith College, Sedalia. He gained fame as a pianist in Chicago and St Louis in the 1890s, but he longed for recognition as a serious composer. His 'Maple Leaf Rag' (1899) made ragtime music a national craze, and was the first of his several popular rags. Ragtime experienced a revival in the 1970s, and Joplin's music (especially 'The Entertainer', featured in the film *The Sting*) became more widely known.

Jordaens, Jakob [yawdahns] (1593–1678) Painter, born in Antwerp, N Belgium. He became a member of an Antwerp guild in 1616 and from 1630 came under the influence of Rubens, who obtained for him the patronage of the kings of Spain and Sweden. He painted several altarpieces, and became known for his scenes of merry peasant life, such as 'The King Drinks' (1638, Brussels). After Rubens' death he was considered the greatest painter in Antwerp.

Jordan *p.815*

Jordan, River River in the Middle East; rises in several headstreams in the Anti-Lebanon mountains on the Lebanon–Syria border; flows over 320 km/200 mi S through L Tiberias and El Ghor to the Dead Sea; N half of the river forms part of the Israel–Jordan and Israel–Syria borders; S half separates the East Bank of Jordan from the Israeli-occupied West Bank; baptism of Jesus Christ took place in its waters.

Jordan, (Marie-Ennemond) Camille [zhawdã] (1838–1922) Mathematician, born in Lyon, SC France. He became professor at the Ecole Polytechnique (1876–1912) and at the Collège de France. He pioneered group theory, wrote on the theory of linear differential equations, and on the theory of functions, which he applied to the curve which bears his name. His work brought full understanding of the importance of the pioneering work done by Evariste Galois (1811–32).

Jordan, Dorothea, *née* **Bland** (1762–1816) Actress, born near Waterford, W Ireland. She made her debut in Dublin in 1777, and appeared with great success at Drury Lane in 1785. For nearly 30 years she kept her hold on the public, mainly in comic tomboy roles. Between 1790 and 1811 she was involved with the Duke of Clarence, afterwards William IV, by whom she had 10 of her 15 children. In 1814 she retired to Saint-Cloud, France.

Jordan, Michael (Jeffrey), nickname **Air Jordan** (1963–) Basketball player, born in New York City, USA. He played with the Chicago Bulls from 1984, and was named as the National Basketball Association's Most Valuable Player in 1988, 1991, 1992, 1996, and 1997. A member of the USA Olympic gold medal-winning team in 1984 and 1992, he holds the record for most points in an NBA play-off game (63), against Boston in 1986, and scored over 50 points in a game on 34 occasions. He earned his nickname for his remarkable athleticism. One of the world's most idolized sportsmen, he announced his retirement in 1993, turned to baseball, but returned to the Chicago Bulls in 1995. In addition to his MVP award in 1996, he also took the NBA scoring title for the eighth time to break Wilt Chamberlain's record, and won it again in 1997. In 1998 he won his sixth NBA title with the Chicago Bulls. Appearances in television commercials led to his role in the Warner Bros part-animated film *Space Jam* (1996). He retired in 1999, but made a comeback with the Washington Wizards in 2001, finally retiring in 2003.

Jordan, (Ernst) Pascual (1902–80) Physicist, born in Hanover, NC Germany. He was professor of theoretical physics at the universities of Rostock (1928–44), Berlin (1944–51), and Hamburg (after 1951). In the late 1920s he founded quantum mechanics (with Max Born and Werner Heisenberg) and quantum electrodynamics (with Wolfgang Pauli and Eugene Wigner). He also discovered an important class of non-associative algebras known as **Jordan algebras**.

Jordan, Vernon E(ulion), Jr (1935–) Attorney and civil rights leader, born in Atlanta, Georgia, USA. He studied at the Howard University Law School, Washington, DC, worked in the South during the civil rights movement of the 1960s, and became president of the National Urban League (1971–81). In 1980 he suffered serious wounds from a racially-motivated sniper attack. After his recovery, he became an influential Washington lobbyist with strong ties to the Democratic Party and President Clinton. Jordan's efforts to find a job for Monica Lewinsky in 1997–8 brought him directly into the obstruction of justice charges in the impeachment proceedings against the president.

Joseph II (1741–90) Holy Roman Emperor (1765–90), born in Vienna, Austria, the son of Francis I and Maria Theresa. Until his mother's death (1780) he was co-regent, and his power was limited to the command of the army and the direction of foreign affairs. A sincere enlightened despot, he was known as 'the revolutionary emperor' for his programme of modernization. He was determined to assert Habsburg leadership, but some of his ambitious plans were thwarted variously by the diplomatic obstruction of France, Prussia, the United Provinces, and Britain, by war (with Prussia in 1778–9 and Turkey in 1788), and by insurrection (in The Netherlands in 1787, Hungary in 1789, and the Tyrol in 1790).

Joseph, St (1st-c BC) Husband of the Virgin Mary, a carpenter in Nazareth, who last appeared in the Gospel history when Jesus Christ was 12 years old (*Luke* 2.43). He is never mentioned during Jesus's ministry, and must be assumed to have already died. Feast day 19 March.

Joseph Biblical character, the subject of many stories (*Gen* 37–50); the 11th son of Jacob, but the first by his wife Rachel. He is depicted as Jacob's favourite son (marked by the gift of a multi-coloured coat) who was sold into slavery by his jealous brothers, yet who by prudence and wisdom rose from being a servant to high office in Pharaoh's court, with special responsibility for distributing grain supplies during a time of famine. Eventually he is portrayed as reconciled with his brothers, who came to Egypt to escape the famine. His sons, Ephraim and Manasseh, were blessed by Jacob, and became ancestors of two of the tribes of Israel.

Joseph (of Portsoken), Keith (Sinjohn) Joseph, Baron (1918–94) British statesman, born in London, UK. He studied at Oxford, was called to the bar (1946) then became a Conservative MP (1956). A former secretary of state for social services (1970–4) and industry (1979–81), he held the education and science portfolio (1981–6). He was given an overall responsibility for Conservative policy and research in 1975, and with Margaret

Jordan

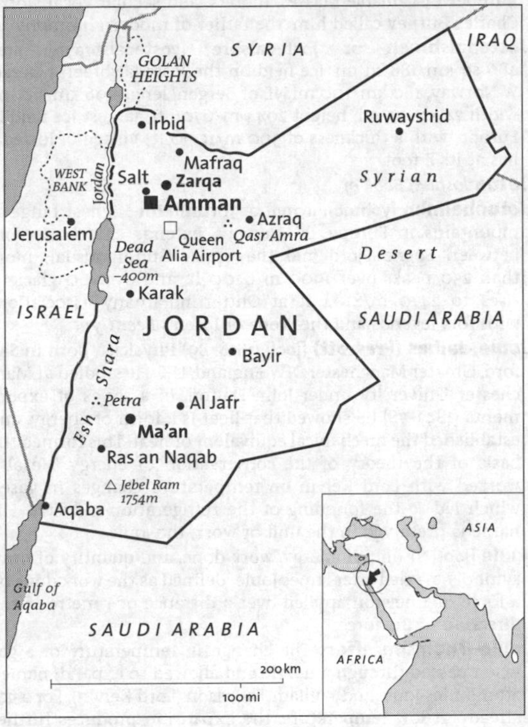

official name **Hashemite Kingdom of Jordan**, Arabic **Al-Mamlaka al-Urduniya al-Hashemiyah**

Local name al'Urdun

Timezone GMT +2

Area 89 544 km²/34 564 sq mi

Population total (2002e) 5 260 000

Status Hashemite kingdom

Date of independence 1946

Capital Amman

Language Arabic (official)

Ethnic groups Arab (99%), Circassian, Armenian, Turkish, Kurd minorities

Religions Muslim (Sunni 95%), Christian (including Roman Catholic, Anglican, Coptic, Greek Orthodox, and Evangelical Lutheran) (5%)

Physical features Located in Middle East. Divided N–S by Red Sea-Jordan rift valley, much lying below sea level; lowest point, −400 m/−1312 ft at the Dead Sea; highest point, Jebel Ram, 1754 m/5754 ft; land levels out to the Syrian desert (E); c.90% of Jordan is desert.

Climate Mediterranean; hot, dry summers, cool, wet winters; desert area uniformly hot, sunny; rainfall below 200 mm/8 in; average annual temperatures 7·5°C (Jan), 24·9°C (Jul) in Amman.

Currency 1 Jordanian Dinar = 1000 fils

Economy Oil, cement, potash, phosphate (world's third largest exporter), light manufacturing; cereals, vegetables, citrus fruits, olives.

GDP (2002e) $22·63 bn, per capita $4300

Human Development Index (2002) 0·717

History Part of Roman Empire; Arab control, 7th-c; part of Turkish Empire, 16th-c until World War 1; area divided into Palestine (W of R Jordan) and Transjordan (E of R Jordan), administered by Britain; independence as Hashimite Kingdom of Jordan, 1946; British mandate over Palestine ended, 1948, with newly-created Israel fighting to control West Bank area; armistice in 1949 left Jordan in control of West Bank; Israeli control of West Bank after Six-Day War, 1967, civil war, following attempts by Jordanian army to expel Palestinian guerrillas from West Bank, 1970–1; claims to the West Bank ceded to the Palestine Liberation Organization, 1974; links with the West Bank cut, and PLO established a government in exile, 1988; martial law formally abolished by King Hussein in 1992, and ban on political parties lifted; conflict with Israel formally ended, 1994; Monarch is Head of State and appoints a Prime Minister, who selects a Council of Ministers; Parliament consists of a Senate and a House of Representatives.

Head of State (Monarch)
1949–51 Abdullah I
1951–2 Talal I
1952–99 Hussein I
1999– Abdullah II

Head of Government
1989–91 Mudar Badran
1991 Taher al-Masri
1991–3 Sharif Zaid bin Shaker
1993–6 Abdul Salam Majali
1996–7 Abdul Karim Kabariti
1997–8 Abdul Salam Majali
1998–9 Fayez Tarawneh
1999–2000 Abdul-Raouf Rawabdeh
2000–3 Ali Abu al-Ragheb
2003– Faisal al-Fayez

Thatcher founded the Centre for Policy Studies. He became a life peer in 1987.

Joseph, Père, known as **l'Eminence grise** ('Grey Eminence'), originally **François Joseph le Clerc du Tremblay** (1577–1638) French diplomat and mystic, born in Paris, France. He became a Capuchin monk in 1599, and Cardinal Richelieu's secretary in 1611. His nickname derives from his contact with Richelieu (the 'Red Eminence'), for whom he went on several important diplomatic missions, especially during the Thirty Years' War.

Joseph of Arimathea, St [arimatheea] (1st-c) In the New Testament a rich Israelite, a secret disciple of Jesus, and a councillor in Jerusalem. He went to Pontius Pilate and begged the body of Jesus, burying it in his own rock-hewn tomb (*Mark* 15.42–7). He is frequently referred to in later Christian literature, such as the Gospel of Nicodemus. According to legend, he was sent by Philip (the apostle) to Glastonbury, England, where he is recognized as patron. He was also said to have been given the Holy Grail by Christ, when in prison. Feast day 17 March (W), 31 July (E).

Joseph, tribes of Although Joseph was the 11th son of Jacob, his descendants were not usually described as 'the tribe of Joseph', one of the 12 tribes of Israel, but were represented by two tribes – Manasseh and Ephraim, Joseph's two sons who were blessed by Jacob (*Gen* 48–9). It is uncertain whether a single 'tribe of Joseph' ever existed, since reference is often to 'the *tribes* of Joseph'.

Joséphine de Beauharnais, *née* **Marie Josèphe Rose Tascher de la Pagerie** (1763–1814) First wife of Napoleon Bonaparte, and French empress, born in Trois-Ilets, Martinique. In 1779 she married the **Vicomte de Beauharnais** who was executed during the French Revolution (1794). Two children were born of the marriage, Eugène (later viceroy of Italy) and Hortense (later queen of Holland). She married Napoleon (1796), and accompanied him on his Italian campaign, but soon returned to Paris. At Malmaison, and afterwards at the Luxembourg and the Tuileries, she attracted round her the most brilliant society of France, and contributed considerably to the establishment of her husband's power. The marriage, being childless, was annulled in 1809 because of her alleged sterility, but she retained the title of empress and lived in retirement at Malmaison.

Josephson, Brian (David) (1940–) Physicist, born in Cardiff, S Wales, UK. He studied at Cambridge, was elected a fellow of Trinity College (1962), and became professor of physics from 1974. While a research student (1962) he deduced theoretically what is now called the *Josephson effect* at the junction of two superconductors, and for which he shared the 1973 Nobel Prize for Physics. His subsequent research interests include paranormal phenomena and the theory of intelligence.

Josephson constant The international standard of voltage measurement; symbol K_J, defined as $2e/h$, where e is the electron charge and h is Planck's constant; based on the Josephson effect (discovered by Brian Josephson); K_J is measured experimentally; an internationally agreed exact value of K^{J-90} = 483 597·9 GHz/V (gigahertz per volt) became the basis of the standard for voltage measurement in 1990.

Josephson junction A thin layer of insulating oxide material between two superconducting electrodes, used mainly in measuring magnetic fields; devised by Brian Josephson. At sufficiently low temperatures, electron-pairs pass through the insulating portion by quantum tunnelling. A magnetic field applied to the junction modifies the current through the oxide layer, allowing the junction to operate as a high-speed switch, potentially useful in computers.

Josephus, Flavius [johseefus], originally **Joseph ben Matthias** (c.37–?) Jewish historian and soldier, born in Jerusalem, who commanded a Galilean force during the Jewish Revolt against Rome in 66. He cunningly gained favour upon surrendering to the Romans, and went to Rome, where he produced several writings on Jewish history and religion, including *History of the Jewish War* (75–9) and *Antiquities of the Jews* (93).

Joshua, Heb **Yehoshua** In the Old Testament, the son of Nun, of the tribe of Ephraim, who during the 40 years' wanderings of the Israelites acted as 'minister' or personal attendant of Moses, and upon Moses' death was appointed to lead the people into Canaan. The Book of Joshua is a narrative of the conquest and settlement of Canaan under his leadership.

Joshua or **Josue, Book of** A book of the Hebrew Bible/Old Testament named after its main hero, Joshua (originally Hoshea, but renamed by Moses). It continues the stories of the Pentateuch, beginning with the death of Moses, and presents narratives of how Israel under the leadership of Joshua conquered the land W of the Jordan from the Canaanites after 40 years of wandering in the desert. It ends with the death of Joshua after the conquest and the apportionment of the land among the tribes of Israel. The author is anonymous, and the present form of the work seems to be composed of several distinct strands of tradition.

Josiah [johsiya] (7th-c BC) Biblical character, king of Judah (c.639–609 BC), a favourite of the Deuteronomistic historians because of his religious reforms (2 *Kings* 22–3, 2 *Chron* 34–5), allegedly based on the discovery of 'the book of the law' in the 18th year of his reign. He is credited with destroying pagan cults and attempting to centralize worship in Jerusalem and the Temple. He died in battle against the Egyptians at Megiddo.

Jospin, Lionel [zhospĩ] (1937–) Prime minister of France (1997–2002), born in Meudon, France. He studied in Paris at the Institute of Political Studies and the National School of Administration, became first secretary for foreign affairs and also taught economics at the University of Paris. Elected to the National Assembly in 1981, he became first secretary of the Socialist Party (1981–8), then held posts in education (1988–92) and foreign affairs (1992–7), before being elected prime minister. He also stood as a presidential candidate in 1995 and 2002, after which he announced his retirement from politics.

Josquin des Prez or **Prés** [zhoskĩ day pray] (c.1440–1521) Composer, probably born in Condé, NE France. Possibly a pupil of Jean d'Okeghem, he was composer to the Sforza family in Milan and Rome, Louis XII of France, and the Duke of Ferrara. From 1504 he was provost in Condé. A master of polyphony, he left a number of valuable Masses, motets, and secular vocal works. Charles Burney called him 'the father of modern harmony'.

Jostedalsbreen or **Jostedalsbre** [yostedalsbrayn] area 486 sq km/188 sq mi. Ice field on the Jostedalsbreen plateau, W Norway, 160 km/100 mi NE of Bergen; length 96 km/60 mi; width 24 km/15 mi; height 2044 m/6706 ft; largest ice field in Europe, with a thickness of 300 m/1000 ft; village of Jostedal lies at its E foot.

Josue *Joshua, Book of*

Jotunheimen [yohtoonhiymn] or **Jotunheim** Highest range of mountains in Europe, SC Norway; extends c.112 km/70 mi between Sogne Fjord and the upper Gudbrandsdal; more than 250 peaks over 1900 m/6200 ft, and over 60 glaciers; rises to 2470 m/8104 ft at Glittertind; many associations with folk legends and the scene of Ibsen's *Peer Gynt*.

Joule, James (Prescott) [jool] (1818–89) Physicist, born in Salford, Greater Manchester, NW England, UK. He studied at Manchester University under John Dalton. In a series of experiments (1843–78) he showed that heat is a form of energy, and established the mechanical equivalent of heat. This formed the basis of the theory of the conservation of energy. He also worked with Lord Kelvin on temperature changes in gases, which led to the founding of the refrigeration industry. His name is preserved in the unit of work, the *joule*.

joule [jool] SI unit of energy, work done, and quantity of heat; symbol J; named after James Joule; defined as the work done by a force of 1 newton applied over a distance of 1 metre in the direction of the force.

Joule–Thomson effect The change in temperature of a gas when passed through a nozzle and allowed to expand; named after James Joule and William Thomson (Lord Kelvin). For a gas already at low temperature, the expansion produces further cooling, a property exploited in the liquification of oxygen and nitrogen. For a gas above a certain temperature (the inversion temperature for that gas), the effect causes warming. Oxygen and nitrogen have inversion temperatures of 620°C and 348°C respectively.

journalism The practice and profession of producing material of current interest for the press, broadcasting, and the Internet. Originally limited to the written word (**print journalism**), but now extended to the spoken word on radio and television (**broadcast journalism**) and pictures (**photojournalism**), the term applies to the collecting, working up, and editing of material, especially news. Journalism has its own trade unions, professional associations, codes of conduct, awards, and training schemes. Its laudable claim to 'Fourth Estate' status is often compromised by its collusion with those with power in society, invasions of personal privacy, and **chequebook journalism** ('revelations' bought at great expense).

Jouvet, Louis [zhoovay] (1887–1951) Actor and theatre/film director, born in Crozon, NW France. He studied as a pharmacist but took to the stage, touring the USA with Jacques Copeau's company (1918–19). He became stage-manager (1922) and director (1924) of the Comédie des Champs Elysées. He was the first to recognize Giraudoux, all but one of whose plays he produced. In 1934 his company transferred to the Théâtre de l'Athénée, and he became professor at the Paris Conservatoire.

Jovian [johvian], in full **Flavius Claudius Jovianus** (c.331–64) Roman emperor (363–4), appointed by the army in Mesopotamia on Julian's death in battle. He was immediately forced to make a humiliating peace with Shapur II, ceding great tracts of Roman territory to Sassanian Persia, and agreeing to pay a subsidy.

Jowell, Tessa (Jane Helen Douglas) (1947–) British stateswoman, born in London. Educated at Aberdeen, Edinburgh, and London, she became a Labour councillor in Camden (1971–86) where she chaired the social services committee. Before becoming Labour MP for Dulwich and West Norwood in 1992, she was active in the voluntary sector, being deputy director of MIND (1974–86), director of community care special project, Birmingham (1986–90), and director of Rowntree Foundation projects (1990–92). Following a number of shadow posts, she became minister for public health in 1997, and employment minster. She was appointed secretary of state for culture, media and sport (2001–).

Joyce, James (Augustine Aloysius) (1882–1941) Writer, born in Dublin, Ireland. He studied in University College, Dublin, went in 1902 to Paris to study medicine, then took up voice training for a concert career. Back in Dublin, he published a few stories but, unable to make a living by his pen, left for Pola to tutor in English. He started the short-lived Volta Cinema Theatre in 1909, and left Dublin in 1910. He later went to Zürich (1915), where he formed a company of English players, settled in Paris (1920–40), where he married Nora Barnacle in 1931, then returned to Zürich, where he died. His early work includes the short stories, *Dubliners* (1914), and *A Portrait of the Artist as a Young Man* (1916). His best-known book, *Ulysses*, based on one day in Dublin (16 Jun 1904), was published in Paris by Silvia Beach in 1922, but was banned in the UK and USA until 1934. *Work in Progress* began to appear in 1927, and finally emerged as *Finnegans Wake* (1939), which presents the story of a Dublin tavern-keeper, Chimpden Earwicker. His work revolutionized the novel form, partly through the abandonment of ordinary plot for 'stream of consciousness', but more fundamentally through his unprecedented exploration of language and linguistic experimentation.

Joyce, William, nickname **Lord Haw Haw** (1906–46) British Nazi propagandist, born in New York City, USA. As a child he lived in Ireland, and in 1922 his family emigrated to England. He founded the fascist British National Socialist Party and fled to Germany before war broke out. Throughout World War 2 he broadcast from Radio Hamburg propaganda against Britain, gaining his nickname from his upper-class drawl. He was captured by the British at Flensburg, convicted of treason, and executed in London.

joystick A computer peripheral, similar to a mouse, which controls the movement of a cursor on a visual display terminal. Like the joystick of an aeroplane, it can indicate movement in any direction.

JPEG [jaypeg] *digital media*

Juan Carlos I [hwan kah(r)los] (1938–) King of Spain (1975–), born in Rome, Italy, the son of **Don Juan de Borbón y Battenberg, Count of Barcelona** (1908–93), and the grandson of Spain's last ruling monarch, Alfonso XIII. He studied in Switzerland and from 1948 in Spain (by agreement between his father and General Franco). He earned commissions in the army, navy, and air force (1955–9), and studied at the University of Madrid (1959–61). In 1962 he married **Princess Sophia of Greece** (1938–), and they have three children. In 1969 Franco named him as his eventual successor, and he was proclaimed king on Franco's death in 1975. Instead of upholding the Franco dictatorship (as had been intended), he decisively presided over Spain's democratization, helping to defeat a military coup (1981) and assuming the role of a constitutional monarch.

Juan Fernández Islands [hwan fernandez] Group of three Chilean islands in the Pacific Ocean, 640 km/398 mi W of mainland; Robinson Crusoe (formerly Más a Tierra), Alejandro Selkirk, (formerly Más Afuera), Santa Clara; total area 181 sq km/70 sq mi; Alexander Selkirk shipwrecked on Robinson Crusoe (1704–9) (basis of Defoe novel, *Robinson Crusoe*); cave on beach open to visitors.

Juárez, Benito Pablo [hwahres] (1806–72) Mexican national hero and president (1861–72), born of Indian parents in San Pablo Guelatao, S Mexico. His ideas for reform forced him to live in exile (1853–5), but he then joined the new Liberal government. During the civil war of 1857–60, he assumed the presidency, and was elected to that office on the Liberal victory (1861). The French invasion under Maximilian forced him to the far N, from where he directed resistance until the defeat of Maximilian, in 1867.

Jubilees, Book of An account purporting to be an extended revelation to Moses during his 40 days on Mt Sinai, a book of the Old Testament Pseudepigrapha, perhaps from the mid-2nd-c BC. Its name is derived from the division of time into 'jubilees' (49 years, representing 7 weeks of years), but it has also been called the *Little Genesis* or the *Testament of Moses*. It retells *Gen* 1 to *Ex* 12 (the Creation to the Passover), amplifying the account and emphasizing separation from non-Jews, loyalty to the Jewish religious law, and the importance of secret traditions for readers of its own times.

Judah, Kingdom of [jooda] An ancient Jewish state which incorporated the tribal areas of Judah and Benjamin, established when the united monarchy split into the kingdoms of Judah (in the S) and Israel (in the N) in the late 10th-c BC after the reign of Solomon. Each kingdom had separate kings, with Jerusalem being in the kingdom of Judah. Both Judah and Jerusalem fell to the Babylonians in 587 BC.

Judah, tribe of [jooda] One of the 12 tribes of ancient Israel, said to be descended from Jacob's fourth son by his wife Leah. Its territory originally extended S of Jerusalem, bounded on the W by the Mediterranean and on the E by the Dead Sea, but later it was restricted.

Judaism The religion of the Jews, central to which is the belief in one God, the transcendent creator of the world who delivered the Israelites out of their bondage in Egypt, revealed his law (*Torah*) to them, and chose them to be a light to all humankind. The Hebrew Bible is the primary source of Judaism. Next in importance is the *Talmud*, which consists of the *Mishnah* (the codification of the oral Torah) and a collection of extensive early rabbinical commentary. Various later commentaries and the standard code of Jewish law and ritual (*Halakhah*) produced in the late Middle Ages have been important in shaping Jewish practice and thought.

However varied their communities, all Jews see themselves as members of a community whose origins lie in the patriarchal period. This past lives on in its rituals, and there is a marked preference for expressing beliefs and attitudes more through ritual than through abstract doctrine. The family is the basic unit of Jewish ritual, though the synagogue has come to play an increasingly important role. The Sabbath, which begins at sunset on Friday and ends at sunset on Saturday, is the central religious observance. The synagogue is the centre for community worship and study. Its main feature is the 'ark' (a cupboard) containing the hand-written scrolls of the Pentateuch. The rabbi is primarily a teacher and spiritual guide. There is an annual cycle of religious festivals and days of fasting. The first of these is Rosh Hashanah, New Year's Day; the holiest day in the Jewish year is Yom Kippur, the Day of Atonement. Other annual festivals include Hanukkah and Pesach, the family festival of Passover.

Modern Judaism is rooted in rabbinic Judaism, and its historical development has been diverse. Today most Jews are the descendants of either the *Ashkenazim* or the *Sephardim*, each with their marked cultural differences. There are also several religious branches of Judaism. *Orthodox* Judaism (19th-c) seeks to preserve traditional Judaism. *Reform* Judaism (19th-c) represents an attempt to interpret Judaism in the light of modern scholarship and knowledge – a process carried further by *Liberal* Judaism. *Conservative* Judaism attempts to modify orthodoxy through an emphasis on the positive historical elements of Jewish tradition. Anti-Semitic prejudice and periods of persecution have been a feature of the Christian culture of Europe, and increased with the rise of European nationalism, culminating in the Nazi Holocaust. Its effect has been incalculable, giving urgency to the Zionist movement for the creation of a Jewish homeland, and is pivotal in all relations between Jews and non-Jews today. In 2004 there were some 14.5 million Jews.

Judas Iscariot [iskaryot] (1st-c) One of the 12 apostles of Jesus, usually appearing last in the lists in the synoptic Gospels (*Mark* 3.19), identified as the one who betrayed Jesus for 30 pieces of silver by helping to arrange for his arrest at Gethsemane by the

Jewish authorities (*Mark* 14.43–6). Other traditions indicate his role as treasurer (*John* 13.29) and his later repentance and suicide (*Matt* 27.3–10, *Acts* 1.16–19). The meaning of *Iscariot* is unclear: it may mean 'man of Keriot' or 'man of falsehood'. The Latin word *sicarius* referred to a curved dagger; and the *sicarii* were a Zealot sect of politically motivated assassins.

Judas tree A deciduous tree (*Cercis siliquastrum*) growing to 10 m/30 ft, native to the Mediterranean region, and often planted as an ornamental; leaves suborbicular, heart-shaped at the base; pea-flowers pink, usually appearing before the leaves; pods up to 10 cm/4 in long. By tradition, this is the tree from which Judas Iscariot hanged himself. (Family: Leguminosae.)

Jude, St or **Thaddeus** (1st-c) One of the 12 Apostles. He is called 'Judas (son) of James' (*Luke* 6.16, *Acts* 1.13), and appears to correspond to the **Thaddeus** mentioned in Mark 3.18 and Matthew 10.3, perhaps to avoid confusion with Judas Iscariot. He is traditionally thought to have preached and healed in Mesopotamia and Persia. Some scholars have considered him the author of the Letter of Jude, who is there described as 'Judas, a servant of Jesus Christ and brother of James', but this identification is disputed. He is traditionally thought to have been martyred in Persia with St Simon, whose feast is held on the same day. Feast day 28 October (W), 19 June or 21 August (E).

Jude, Letter of A brief New Testament writing, considered one of the 'catholic' or 'general' letters, attributed to Jude the brother of James and thus of Jesus of Nazareth, but believed by some today to originate from very late in the 1st-c AD. The work strongly warns an unspecified readership about false teachers, who are portrayed as immoral, intemperate, and divisive, and who perhaps represented libertine, gnostic views. The canonicity of the letter was long disputed in the early Church.

Judea [joodeea] Roman–Greek name for S Palestine, area now occupied by SW Israel and W Jordan; southernmost of the Roman divisions of Palestine; rises to 1020 m/3346 ft in the S near Hebron; chief town, Jerusalem; following 1948–9 war, W region became part of Israel, and E region part of Jordan; since 1967, West Bank and E Jerusalem occupied by Israel.

Judea–Samaria *West Bank*

judge A public officer with authority to adjudicate in both civil and criminal disputes; in some jurisdictions (eg the USA) this authority is limited to a single branch of law (eg administrative law judges). In the UK, judges are appointed by the sovereign on the advice of the prime minister in the cases of the offices of the Lord President and the Lord Justice-Clerk, the Court of Appeal and House of Lords; on the advice of the Lord Chancellor in the case of High Court and circuit judges; and on the advice of the secretary of state for Scotland in the case of the Court of Session and the High Court of Justiciary. Judges are appointed in the main from the ranks of experienced barristers or advocates, though in England and Wales experienced solicitors with the necessary advocacy qualification may be appointed as circuit judges, and in Scotland as sheriffs. Senior judges (other than the Lord Chancellor, a government minister) can be removed only on an address presented by both Houses of Parliament and agreed by the monarch; this rule is intended to secure the independence of the judiciary. Circuit judges (as magistrates) can be removed by the Lord Chancellor for incapacity or misbehaviour. In the USA, state and local judges are often appointed subject to election or confirmation by the public after a fixed time. Federal judges are appointed for life.

Judges, Book of A book of the Hebrew Bible/Old Testament, with 'judges' referring to the tribal heroes (such as Deborah, Gideon, and Samson) whose acts of leadership are described. It relates to the unstable period between the initial conquest of Palestine by the Israelites and the establishment of the monarchy over Israel, and it attempts to draw moral lessons from the contrasting examples of good and bad leadership. Its stories probably underwent editing at several stages of Israel's history.

judicial review A legal means of obtaining remedies in a higher court against inferior courts, tribunals, and administrative bodies. In England and Wales, the High Court may make various orders, including *certiorari* (which quashes a decision), *mandamus* (to compel a duty to be carried out), and *prohibition* (to stop an intended action). Damages may also be awarded. The increasing use of wide powers of discretion by administrators has led to a corresponding increase in the number and importance of judicial reviews as a means of controlling them in favour of the individual. Judicial review is concerned not with the actual decision complained of, but with the manner of the decision-making process. Grounds for such review are illegality, irrationality, or procedural impropriety. The US Supreme Court uses this power to review Acts of Congress and State legislatures in terms of their constitutionality.

Judith, Book of Book of the Old Testament Apocrypha (or deuterocanonical writings recognized by the Catholic Church), possibly dating from the Maccabean period (mid-2nd-c BC). It tells the story of how Judith, an attractive and pious Jewish widow, saved the city of Bethulia from siege by the Assyrian army (ostensibly c.6th-c BC) by beheading Holofernes, its general, in his tent once she had beguiled and intoxicated him.

judo An unarmed combat sport, developed in Japan, and useful in self-defence. The present-day sport was devised by Dr Jigoro Kano (1860–1938), headmaster of two leading Japanese schools, who founded the Kodokan school in 1882. Contestants wear a *judogi* (loose fitting suit) and compete on a mat to break their falls. They are graded in their ability from 5th to 1st *Kyu*, and then 1st *Dan* to the highest, 12th *Dan*. Only Kano has been awarded the 12th *Dan*. Different coloured belts indicate a fighter's grade.

Jugendstil *Art Nouveau*

Juggernaut [juhgernawt] (Sanskrit 'protector of the world') A Hindu deity equated with Vishnu. His temple is at Puri in E India, and is noted for its annual festival. The modern English sense of a massive, irresistible force (and its application to a large, heavy vehicle) is related to the belief that devotees of the god threw themselves beneath the wheels of the cart bearing his image during the festival procession.

Jugoslavia *Yugoslavia*

jugular veins Blood vessels draining the structures of the head and neck. The **internal jugular vein** returns blood from the brain, face, and much of the neck (particularly the deeper structures). It begins at an opening in the base of the skull (the *jugular foramen*) and ends by joining the subclavian vein (returning blood from the upper limb) to form the brachiocephalic vein. The **external jugular vein** returns blood from the scalp and superficial aspects of the neck. The **anterior jugular veins** are found close to the midline at the front of the neck, and drain into the external jugular vein.

Jugurtha [jugoortha] (c.160–104 BC) King of Numidia (118–105 BC), after whom the **Jugurthine War** (112–104 BC) is named. Rome's difficulty in defeating him provided Marius with a launching pad for his career, and led to important reforms in the Roman army. Jugurtha's surrender to Marius's deputy, Sulla, ended the war, but was the starting point of the deadly feud between Marius and Sulla which plunged Rome into civil war 20 years later.

Juilliard School [jooliah(r)d] Music conservatory at Lincoln Center, New York City, USA. Founded by Frank Damrosch in 1905 as the Institute of Musical Art, it is now named after US financier Augustus D Juilliard, following a bequest made upon his death in 1919. Numerous famous musicians have trained there, and it is home to the renowned Juilliard String Quartet.

jujitsu The Japanese art of offence and self-defence without weapons, used by the Samurai. Jujitsu forms the basis of many modern forms of other combat sports, such as judo, aikido, and karate. It is thought to have been introduced into Japan by a Chinese monk, Chen Yuan-ping, at the turn of the 17th-c.

jujube [joojoob] A deciduous shrub (*Ziziphus jujuba*) growing to 9 m/30 ft, native to the E Mediterranean region; characteristic zig-zag stem and paired spines, one hooked, one straight; leaves oval; flowers yellow; olive-like fruits black. It is cultivated for its edible fruits. (Family: Rhamnaceae.)

juku [jukoo] A Japanese crammer's school. Educational qualifications are crucial in Japan for getting such jobs as in a large company, or a government office. Applicants must be university graduates. Starting at primary school, many pupils have extra classes in the evenings and/or at weekends to prepare them for a series of entrance examinations, from secondary education to university.

Julia The name of numerous ladies of the Julian family (*gens*), notably: **1** the wife of Marius and aunt of Julius Caesar; **2** the daughter of Augustus by his first wife Scribonia (39 BC–AD 14), banished for adultery in 2 BC; **3** the daughter of **2** and Agrippa (c.19 BC–AD 28); her disgrace and banishment somehow involved the poet Ovid.

Julian, in full **Flavius Claudius Julianus**, known as **Julian the Apostate** (332–63) Roman emperor (361–3), the son of a half-brother of Constantine the Great. Appointed deputy emperor in the West by his cousin, Constantius II (355), he served with great distinction on the Rhine, and was proclaimed emperor by his adoring troops in 360. As emperor, he publicly proclaimed himself a pagan (hence his nickname) and initiated a vigorous policy of reviving the old pagan cults, though without persecuting Christians. He was killed in battle against the Sassanid Persians.

Julian or **Juliana of Norwich** (c.1342–1413) English mystic who probably lived in isolation outside St Julian's Church, Norwich, E England, UK. Her work, *Sixteen Revelations of Divine Love*, based on a series of visions she received in 1373, has been a lasting influence on theologians stressing the power of the love of God. Her assurance that everything is held in being by the love of God, so that 'all shall be well', and her characterization of the Trinity as Father, Mother, and Lord, has particularly appealed to the contemporary Church.

Juliana, in full **Juliana Louise Emma Marie Wilhelmina** (1909–2004) Queen of The Netherlands (1948–80), born in The Hague. She studied at Leyden, became a lawyer, and in 1937 married Prince Bernhard zur Lippe-Biesterfeld; they had four daughters. On the German invasion of Holland (1940), Juliana escaped to Britain and later resided in Canada. She returned to Holland in 1945, and became queen on the abdication of her mother, Wilhelmina. She herself abdicated in favour of her eldest daughter, Beatrix.

Julian Alps, Slovenian **Julijske Alpe** Mountain range in Slovenia and NE Italy; a SE extension of the Alpine system, bounded to the N by the Karawanken Alps; rises to 2863 m/9393 ft at Triglav, the highest peak in Slovenia.

Julian calendar A calendar established in 46 BC by Julius Caesar, further modified in AD 8, when leap years were correctly implemented, then used in Catholic Europe until 1582, when it was replaced by the Gregorian calendar. Since 153 BC, the year had slipped by 3 months, relative to the seasons, because of manipulations by political opportunists (to shorten officials' terms of office). Caesar ended this confusion, inserting an extra 67 days into 43 BC, and decreeing a year of 365 days, with an extra day every fourth year, initially by using February 24 twice. The Julian year is 11 min longer than the tropical year, and by the 15th-c its 11 March was falling 10 days later than the true equinox.

Julian date The number of days that have elapsed since 1200 GMT on 1 January 4713 BC. This consecutive numbering of days gives a calendar independent of month and year used for analysing periodic phenomena, especially in astronomy. The Julian day beginning at noon on 1 January 2000 was 2 451 544. Devised in 1582 by the Dutch philologist and historian Joseph Justus Scaliger (1540–1609), it has no connection with the Julian calendar.

Julunggul *Rainbow Snake*

July Days (2–5 Jul 1917) Anti-government demonstrations in Petrograd marking a decisive stage in the Russian Revolution. Demonstrators demanded Russia's withdrawal from World War 1, the overthrow of the provisional government, and the transfer of 'All power to the soviets'. Lenin judged the time for a proletarian-socialist revolution to be premature, and urged restraint.

July Revolution (1830) A three-day revolt in Paris which ended the Bourbon Restoration, forcing the abdication of the reactionary Charles X (r.1824–30). It resulted in the establishment of a more liberal regime dominated by the wealthy bourgeoisie, the so-called *July Monarchy*, under the Orleanist, Louis Philippe, 'King of the French'.

Jumblat, Kemal (1919–77) Lebanese Socialist statesman and hereditary Druze chieftain, born in the Chouf Mts, Lebanon. He founded the Progressive Socialist Party in 1949, held several cabinet posts (1961–4), and was minister of the interior (1969–70). The Syrian intervention on the side of the Christians in 1976 was a response to the increasing power of his authority in partnership with the Palestinians. He was assassinated in an ambush outside the village of Baaklu in the Chouf Mts. His son **Walid Jumblat** became leader of the Druze after his death.

Jumna, River *Yamuna, River*

jumping bean A seed of *Sebastiania pringlei*, a Mexican shrub of the spurge family Euphorbiaceae. It provides food for the larva of the small moth *Carpocapsa solitaris*, which occupies the seed. Warmth intensifies movement of the larva, causing the 'bean' to jump or jerk erratically.

jumping hare *springhaas*

jumping mouse A mouse-like rodent, native to North America (3 species) and China (1 species); long rear legs; may leap 3 m/10 ft; does not dig burrows; may hibernate for nine months; eats seeds and insects. (Family: Zapodidae, 4 species.)

jumping plant louse *psyllid*

Juneau [joonoh] 58°18N 134°25W, pop (2000e) 30 700. Seaport capital of state in SE Alaska, USA, on Gastineau Channel; developed as a gold-rush town after 1880; airport; trade centre, with an ice-free harbour; salmon and halibut fishing, lumbering, tourism; House of Wickersham; Salmon Derby (Aug).

June Days (1848) A violent episode in the French Revolution of 1848, when working-class radicals resisted the dissolution of the National Workshops in Paris. They were crushed by the National Guard and troops of the Republican government under the direction of General Louis Eugène Cavaignac (1802–57), thus exacerbating class divisions in France for generations.

June War *Arab–Israeli Wars*

Jung, Carl (Gustav) [yung] (1875–1961) Psychiatrist, born in Kesswil, NE Switzerland. He studied medicine at Basel, and worked at the Burghölzli mental clinic in Zürich (1900–9). He met Freud in Vienna in 1907, became his leading collaborator, and was president of the International Psychoanalytic Association (1911–14). He became increasingly critical of Freud's approach, and *Wandlungen und Symbole der Libido* (1911–12, trans The Psychology of the Unconscious) caused a break in 1913. He then developed his own theories, which he called 'analytical psychology' to distinguish them from Freud's psychoanalysis and Adler's individual psychology. Jung's approach included a description of psychological types ('extraversion/introversion'); the exploration of the 'collective unconscious'; and the concept of the psyche as a 'self-regulating system' expressing itself in the process of 'individuation'. He held chairs at Basel and Zürich.

Jungfrau [yungfrow] 46°33N 7°58E. Mountain peak in the Bernese Alps, SC Switzerland; height 4158 m/13 642 ft; mountain railway to near the summit; first ascended in 1811.

jungle fowl A pheasant native to India and SE Asia; gregarious; inhabits forest and scrub; eats grain, shoots, berries, and insects; ancestral to the domestic fowl. The name is also used in Australia for the megapode *Megapodius freycinet*. (Genus: *Gallus*, 4 species.)

Juninho [zhooneenyo], popular name of **Osvaldo Giroldo Jr** (1973–) Footballer, born in Brazil. A midfielder, he joined Middlesbrough in 1995 from São Paulo, moving to Atletico Madrid in 1997, was briefly on loan to Middlesbrough during the 1999–2000 season, and joined Brazilian team Vasco da Gama in 2000. A broken leg kept him out of the game for several months in early 1998. He scored on his international debut for Brazil (1995) and was a member of the 2002 Brazilian World Cup winning team. He was back at Middlesbrough for a third time in 2002. His honours include Footballer of the Year in 1994.

junior high school *high school*

juniper An evergreen coniferous tree or shrub native to most of the N hemisphere; leaves of two kinds, needle- or scale-like, in some species on the same tree; cones fleshy, berry-like. The timber is durable; the foliage yields an oil used in perfume; and the berries are used to flavour gin. (Genus: *Juniperus*, 60 species. Family: Cupressaceae.)

junk bonds The debt of firms whose creditors are doubtful whether they will be paid, on time or at all. The debt of any one such firm is very risky, so cautious lenders regard it as junk and refuse to hold it. However, such bonds pay high rates of interest, and lenders can hold a mixture of the debts of many different borrowers, of whom only a proportion can be expected to default. Thus while junk bonds always present a risk, the rewards may be sufficient to induce less risk-averse lenders to take it.

Junkers [**yung**kerz] Prussian aristocrats whose power rested on their large estates, situated predominantly to the E of the R Elbe, and on their traditional role as army officers and civil servants. Their position came increasingly under threat in late 19th-c Germany as a result of industrialization, but they jealously safeguarded their privileges and power.

Juno (astronomy) The third asteroid to be discovered, in 1804. Its diameter is 248 km/154 mi.

Juno (mythology) In Roman mythology, the supreme goddess, and the wife of Jupiter. Originally an ancient Italian deity associated with the Moon and the life of women, she was later identified with Hera.

Jupiter (astronomy) The fifth planet from the Sun, and the innermost of the giant outer planets. It contains two-thirds of the matter in the Solar System, apart from the Sun. It has been observed in close-up by five space probes: Pioneer 10 and 11, Voyagers 1 and 2, and Galileo. Its basic characteristics are: mass $1{\cdot}90 \times 10^{27}$ kg; equatorial radius 71 492 km/44 423 mi; polar radius 66 854 km/41 541 mi; mean density 1·33 g/cm^3; rotational period 9 h 55 min 41 s; orbital period 11·9 years; inclination of equator to orbit 3·1°; mean distance from the Sun 5·203 AU. It is made primarily of hydrogen (82%) and helium (17%), and believed to have an innermost core of terrestrial composition of 5–10 Earth masses, a large outer core of hydrogen and helium in a metallic phase, a liquid hydrogen/helium mantle, and a deep gaseous atmosphere. The planet has a significant internal source of heat, and radiates twice as much heat from inside as it receives from the Sun.

The face of the planet is covered by clouds, organized into bands, called *belts* and *zones*. Zones are light, and cold (−130°C) because they are high in the atmosphere; belts are darker and warmer clouds (−40°C) at a lower elevation; and a third, warmer level of clouds has also been observed (20°C). The uppermost clouds are inferred to be solid ammonia, the middle clouds ammonium hydrosulphide, and the lowest clouds water. The rotation period in the equatorial region is 5 min faster than that of the rest of the planet – a differential which contributes to the formation of a richly coloured banded structure in the cloudy atmosphere. Complex currents and vortices are observed within the bands, including a long-lived atmospheric storm called the *Great Red Spot*. The known Jovian moons (Mar 2004) number 63, including the four large satellites discovered by Galileo (1610), which are distinct worlds in themselves and lie in near-circular orbits in an equatorial plane. A dark ring of dust around the planet was discovered by Voyager, between 100 000 and 215 000 km from the centre of the planet, consisting of material from the surface of Jupiter's four innermost moons.

Jupiter (mythology) or **Iuppiter** The chief Roman god, equivalent to Greek Zeus, originally a sky-god with the attributes of thunder and the thunderbolt. He is sometimes given additional names (eg **Jupiter Optimus Maximus**). Roman generals visited his temple to do him honour.

Jura Mountains [**joo**ra] Limestone mountain range in E France and W Switzerland, on Franco-Swiss border, forming a plateau 250 km/155 mi long by 50 km/31 mi wide; highest point in France, Crêt de la Neige (1718 m/5636 ft), in Switzerland, Mt Tendre (1682 m/5518 ft); forested slopes, with poor pasture; caving, winter sports.

Jurassic period [jura**sik**] A geological period of the Mesozoic era extending from c.213 to 144 million years ago; characterized by large reptiles on land, sea, and air, with shallow seas rich in marine life (eg ammonites), and the appearance of the first birds; mammals still primitive.

jurisdiction **1** The legal competence of a particular court to hear a certain type or class of case.

2 The geographical area covered by a particular court or legal system, or the types of cases which it has power to hear; this is not necessarily the same area as that of the national political unit. For example, in the UK, the jurisdiction of England and Wales is separate from that of Scotland. The English courts have jurisdiction over England, Wales, Berwick-upon-Tweed, and those parts of the sea included in *territorial waters*. In the USA, the individual states constitute separate jurisdictions; US courts must have both subject matter and territorial jurisdiction to competently hear a case. *Venue* is the proper place for a trial, which is normally where a crime was committed or where a court has jurisdiction to try an offence. Traditionally, venue was laid in the county where an offence was committed, but many exceptions to this rule have developed. In civil law, the idea of venue has been abolished in England and Wales, and the place of trial is fixed at the hearing of the summons for directions, and can be 'altered by order'.

jurisprudence The science or philosophy of law. As with philosophy generally, jurisprudence has concerned itself not only with what is, but what ought to be, with inevitably an ideological dimension. It has some claim to be regarded as a science of law, in that it seeks to ascertain regularities in human behaviour: judicial behaviourists claim good success rates in predicting the outcome of legal decision-making.

jury A group of lay persons of varying numbers who decide, on the basis of evidence, matters of fact in criminal and civil cases. They are usually 12 in number, although in Scotland 15 jurors sit in criminal trials. In the USA certain juries also have a role in deciding whether a person should be prosecuted for a particular crime; these juries, known as **Grand Juries**, have up to 23 people sitting on them. In the UK jurors are chosen from the electoral role and must be aged between 18 and 65. In the USA great effort is taken to ensure that jurors are selected randomly from the general population; however, in certain cases a 'special jury' may be selected to try matters of unusual importance or intricacy. In the USA there is a constitutional right to trial by jury in criminal matters where the penalty is six months or more, and also in most civil matters. In the UK serious criminal matters are tried before a jury, but juries are little used in civil cases (though certain cases such as defamation are heard before a jury in England and Wales). Also in England and Wales, an accused person has a right in certain cases to trial by jury; in Scotland no such right exists, the mode of trial being the decision of the procurator fiscal. In England and Wales a majority verdict (10–2) is now permitted, and many US States allow majority verdicts. In Scotland, jurors have in addition to guilty or not guilty, a third verdict of not proven, and all that is required is a simple majority of 8 to 7. Certain people are ineligible for jury service (eg members of the Judiciary and the mentally ill) or may be excused (eg MPs, doctors), or disqualified (eg if previously convicted of certain types of offence). In most jurisdictions both the prosecution and the defence are permitted to challenge a juror's suitabilty to sit in a case. A certain number of 'peremptory challenges' are allowed without reason, and usually a limitless number of challenges 'for cause', such as the juror being related to the victim or the accused. In England and Wales, the judge directs the jury on questions of law, but must leave them to decide all questions of fact; however there must be a direction to acquit in criminal cases, unless the jury are convinced that the accused is guilty 'beyond reasonable doubt'. In certain parts of the world (eg Europe), juries have largely died out, and many countries including Italy, France, and Germany have abandoned the institution altogether.

Jussieu [zhüsyoe] The name of a family of French botanists, notably **Bernard de Jussieu** (c.1699–1777), who created the botanical garden at Trianon for Louis XV, and adopted a system which has become the basis of modern natural botanical classification. His brother **Antoine de Jussieu** (1686–1758) was a physician and professor at the Jardin des Plantes, Paris. His nephew, **Antoine Laurent** (1748–1836), was also professor at the Jardin, and elaborated his uncle's system in *Genera plantarum* (1778–89).

justice of the peace (JP) A judicial appointment, also known as a **magistrate**. In England and Wales, JPs are appointed and may be removed by the Lord Chancellor, or in Scotland by the secretary of state for Scotland. Their principal function is to preside in the magistrates' courts (England and Wales) or the district courts (Scotland), administering immediate (or *summary*) justice in a large number of the less serious criminal cases, and in certain circumstances committing the most serious cases for further trial elsewhere. They have a number of other powers, such as administering oaths, signing warrants of arrest, and search warrants. Each magistrate exercises his or her functions for a particular commission area. JPs are not necessarily legally qualified – most are not – though the absence of a legal qualification is not quite as surprising as it seems, as most cases involve disputes about the facts and not the law. A legally qualified clerk or assessor is present and advises on the law. When trying cases, a JP in Scotland may sit alone, but in England and Wales sits with at least one other colleague. Magistrates now receive basic training, but no salary. In the USA, JPs are usually elected but sometimes appointed; in recent years, the tendency has been for their powers and functions to be transferred to other courts. American JPs also have an important role in the performing of marriages.

justiciar [juhstisiah(r)] In mediaeval times, the chief administrative and judicial officer of the English crown, who also acted as vice-regent during the king's absences overseas. The history of the office can be followed from Bishop Roger of Salisbury (d.1139) to 1234 and then, after a long break (1234–58), to 1265, when it finally lapsed.

Justin (Martyr), St (c.100–c.165) One of the Fathers of the Church, born in Sichem, Samaria. He was converted to Christianity, studied Stoic and Platonic philosophy, and founded a school of Christian philosophy at Rome, where he wrote two *Apologies* on Christian belief (150–60). He is said to have been martyred at Rome. Feast day 1 June.

Justinian [justinian], in full **Flavius Petrus Sabbatius Justinianus** (c.482–565) Roman emperor (527–65), the protégé of his uncle, the Byzantine emperor, Justin (reigned 518–27). At first co-emperor with Justin, on his death he became sole ruler. Along with his wife Theodora, he presided over the most brilliant period in the history of the late Roman empire. Through his generals, Belisarius and Narses, he recovered N Africa, Spain, and Italy, and carried out a major codification of the Roman law (begun 529).

Justinian Code The Emperor Justinian's great codification of Roman law, carried out under the direction of Tribonian and published in four sections in the AD 530s. Also known as the *Corpus juris civilis*, it is regarded as the pinnacle of Roman Law.

Just in Time system *Kanban system*

jute An annual (*Corchorus capsularis*) growing to 3·5 m/11½ ft, a relative of the lime tree, and native to S Asia; leaves ovoid; flowers in axils of leaves, yellow. The stems, soaked and beaten to separate the fibres, are used in hessian and sacking. (Family: Tiliaceae.)

Jutes A Germanic people whose original homeland was the N part of the Danish peninsula (Jutland). The tradition preserved by Bede, that Jutes participated in the 5th-c Germanic invasions of Britain and settled in Kent, SE England and the Isle of Wight, S England, UK, is confirmed by archaeological evidence. Their name is preserved in Jutland and Juteborg.

Jutland, Battle of (1916) A sea battle of World War 1, in which Admiral Jellicoe led the British Grand Fleet from Scapa Flow and intercepted the German High Seas Fleet off the W coast of Jutland, Denmark. Though the battle itself was inconclusive, German naval chiefs withdrew their fleet to port for the rest of the war, and turned to unrestricted submarine warfare as a means of challenging British command of the seas.

Juvenal, in full **Decimus Junius Juvenalis** (c.55–c.130) Satirist, born in Aquinum, Italy. He served as tribune in the army, in Britain and in Egypt. He is best known for his 16 brilliant satires in verse (c.100–c.127), dealing with life in Roman times under Domitian and his successors. Written from the viewpoint of an angry Stoic moralist, they range from the exposures of unnatural vices, the misery of poverty, and the extravagance of the ruling classes, to the precarious makeshift life of their hangers-on. His influence on English poetry is best seen in Johnson's poems 'London' and 'The Vanity of Human Wishes', while Dryden's versions of five of Juvenal's satires are among the best of his works.

juvenile court A court specifically concerned with the interests of children and young persons, where the emphasis is on rehabilitation and treatment rather than punishment. South Australia is believed to be the first state to have introduced a juvenile court system, in the late 19th-c, after which the idea spread rapidly throughout the USA, Canada, and parts of Europe (but not Scandinavia, which developed its own non-court-based system). Some juvenile courts (such as those existing in England and Wales between 1908 and 1990) deal both with those children who have committed offences and with those who are believed to be in need of care and protection as a result of acts committed against them, while others (such as the English youth courts) deal solely with young offenders. Juvenile courts in Scotland were abolished in 1971 and were replaced by a lay tribunal system, entitled the Children's Hearings System, more akin to Scandinavian models of juvenile justice.

juvenile delinquency The anti-social behaviour of young people which may or may not be criminal. Theories explaining juvenile delinquency abound in criminology and sociology. Many account for such youthful misconduct in terms of playfulness, rebelliousness, frustration, or as a form of working-class rebellion against the inequities and frustrations of capitalism. Criminal statistics indicate that some groups tend towards greater delinquency than others; this may, however, reflect the fact that certain groups (eg young blacks in Europe) receive a greater amount of attention and even hostility from law enforcement agencies.

juvenilia The very early works of writers who later become well-known. Jane Austen's *Minor Works* (published 1932) contain extensive entertaining examples, as do the Brontë sisters' Gondal writings, surviving in miniature bound books, and Byron's *Hours of Idleness* (first called *Juvenilia*) published in 1807 when Byron was 19.

Juventud, Isla de la [yooventtood, eelya] ('isle of youth'), formerly **Isle of Pines** pop (2000e) 67 000; area 2199 sq km/849 sq mi. Province of Cuba, an island 97 km/60 mi off SW coast; capital, Nueva Gerona; formerly used as a penal colony; new name in 1958, to recognize young people's contribution to development; rises to 416 m/1365 ft at Sierra de Canada; fine beaches on S coast; tourism; grapefruit, mangoes, oranges.

Kaba, Kaaba, or **Kabah** [kaba] The most sacred site in Islam, situated within the precincts of the Great Mosque at Mecca, Saudi Arabia. It is a small cube-shaped building, unadorned except for the sacred Black Stone, a meteorite, set into the E corner of its walls. Earlier shrines on this spot were important centres of pilgrimage even in pre-Islamic times, but in AD 630 Mohammed stripped the Kaba of its pagan decorations and it became the spiritual centre of Islam. The stone, or *qibla*, is the focus-point to which Muslims turn when they pray.

Kabbalah [kabahla] (Heb 'tradition') Jewish religious teachings originally transmitted orally, predominantly mystic in nature, and ostensibly consisting of secret doctrines. It developed along two lines – the 'practical', centring on prayer, meditation, and acts of piety; and the 'speculative' or 'theoretical', centring on the discovery of mysteries hidden in the Jewish Scriptures by special methods of interpretation.

Kabuki [kabookee] A state-controlled city entertainment in Japan, popular from 1650 to 1850. A 4-part play in numerous acts, lasting all day, was presented in a manner which allowed great actors to ad-lib, and the audience to talk and picnic in carnival spirit. The spectacular resources of Kabuki are nowadays employed only to present selected highlights from the traditional repertoire.

Kabul [kahbul] 34°30N 69°10E, pop (2000e) 2 375 000. Capital city of Afghanistan, and capital of Kabul province, E Afghanistan; on R Kabul in a high mountain valley, commanding the approaches to the Khyber Pass; capital of Mughal Empire (1504–1738); modern state capital, 1773; captured in 1839 and 1879 by the British during the Afghan Wars; target of US-led military bombardment in October 2001 in response to the Taliban government's refusal to give up Osama bin Laden, chief suspect behind the terrorist attacks on New York and Washington on 11 September 2001; university (1931); airport; wool, cloth, sugar-beet, plastics, leather goods, furniture, glass, soap, heavy industry; power production increased 25% in 1984 by the opening of a gas turbine plant.

Kabyle [kabeel] A Berber people of Algeria. Organized into different castes with serfs, they speak Kabyle, an Afro-Asiatic language, and are predominantly Muslims. They live in villages, grow grains and olives, and herd goats.

Kádár, János [kahda(r)] (1912–89) Hungarian statesman, premier (1956–8, 1961–5) and first secretary (1956–88), born in Kapoly, WC Hungary. He joined the (illegal) Communist Party in 1931, and was arrested several times. He became a member of the Central Committee (1942) and the Politburo (1945), and minister of the interior (1949), but was arrested for anti-Stalinist views (1951–3). When the anti-Soviet uprising broke out in 1956, he was a member of the 'national' government of Imre Nagy, but then formed a puppet government which repressed the uprising. He resigned in 1958, becoming premier again in 1961. His long reign as Party secretary ended in 1988, when he stepped down as leader, and was given the new titular post of Party president. He was removed from this position shortly before his death.

Kaddish [kadeesh] (Aramaic 'holy') An ancient Jewish congregation prayer, mostly in Aramaic, which marks the closing parts of daily public worship, praising the name of God and seeking the coming of the kingdom of God. There are variations in its use, but it is mostly recited while standing and facing Jerusalem. It has affinities with the Christian formulation of the Lord's Prayer.

kaffir corn *sorghum*

Kafka, Franz [kafka] (1883–1924) Novelist, born in Prague, Czech Republic, of German Jewish parents. He studied law, became an official in an insurance company (1907–23), moved to Berlin, but soon after succumbed to tuberculosis. His short stories and essays, such as *Die Verwandlung* (1915, The Metamorphosis), appeared in his lifetime, but his three unfinished novels were published posthumously (against his wishes) by his friend Max Brod: *Der Prozess* (1925, The Trial), *Das Schloss* (1926, The Castle), and *Amerika* (1927). He has influenced many authors with his vision of society (often called 'Kafkaesque') as a pointless, schizophrenically rational organization, with tortuous bureaucratic and totalitarian procedures, psychological labyrinths, and masochistic fantasies, into which the bewildered individual has strayed.

kagu [kahgoo] A ground-dwelling bird (*Rhynochetos jubatus*) native to New Caledonia; slate grey with short tail, pointed bill, and long erectile crest on head; virtually flightless; inhabits forests; eats worms, insects, and snails; once abundant, but now endangered. (Family: Rhynochetidae.)

Kahn, Oliver (1969–) Footballer, born in Karlsruhe, SW Germany. He made his debut for the Bundesliga (German Football League) in 1990, joining Bayern Munich for the 1994–5 season for €2·5 million, a record fee for a goalkeeper at the time. In 2000 he was voted German Footballer of the Year and Best European goalkeeper. In the 2002 World Cup finals in Korea/Japan, he was named in the All-Star Team of the tournament, and went on to win the Lev Yashin Award for Best Goalkeeper and the Golden Ball Award for the best player, the first goalkeeper to win the award.

Kahneman, Daniel Economist, born in Tel Aviv, Israel. He studied at the Hebrew University, Jerusalem and the University of California at Berkeley, later joining Princeton University. He holds dual citizenship, of Israel and the USA. He shared the 2002 Nobel Prize for Economics for having integrated insights from psychological research into economic science, especially concerning human judgment and decision-making under uncertainty.

Kaieteur Falls [kiyuhtoor] Waterfall in C Guyana, on the R Potaro; nearly five times the height of Niagara, with a sheer drop of 226 m/742 ft from a sandstone tableland c.100 m/350 ft wide into a wide basin where the water drops a further 22 m/72 ft; discovered in 1870; set in the 116 sq km/45 sq mi Kaieteur National Park, established in 1929.

Kaifeng or **K'ai-feng** [kiyfeng] 34°48N 114°21E, pop (2000e) 572 000. City in Henan province, NEC China; on Yellow R, at N end of Grand Canal; as Bianjing, capital of N Song dynasty (960–1127); major cultural centre, 10th–12th-c; centre of Chinese Zoroastrianism, 6th–12th-c; centre of Chinese Judaism, 12th–15th-c; conquered by Jin (1127) and Mongols (1245); railway; medical college; agricultural machinery, food processing, chemicals, silk, zinc, electrical products; museum; Old Music Terrace (8th-c), Dragon Pavilion (10th-c).

Kai-hsiung *Gaoxiong*

Kaikoura Ranges [kiykohra] Mountain ranges in NE South Island, New Zealand; two parallel ranges, the Inland Kaikoura and the Seaward Kaikoura; length 40 km/25 mi, separated by the Clarence R; highest peak, Mt Tapuaenuku (2885 m/9465 ft) in the Inland Kaikoura.

Kailasa Temple [kiylasa] The most famous of the 34 Hindu, Buddhist, and Jain cave temples and monasteries at Ellora, Maharashtra, India. The edifice, which was built in the 8th-c, represents Shiva's Himalayan home of Mt Kailasa, and is renowned for its sculptures and friezes.

Kailas Range *Gangdisi Shan*

Kairouan [kayrwan] 35°42N 10°01E, pop (2000e) 94 000. Capital of Kairouan governorate, NE Tunisia, 130 km/81 mi S of Tunis; founded in 671; capital of the Aglabite dynasty, 9th-c; carpets, crafts; an important Muslim holy city; Great Mosque, the oldest in the Maghreb; carpet museum; archaeological site of Reqqada nearby.

Kaiser [kiyzer] (Lat *caesar*) The title assumed (Dec 1870) by the Prussian king, William (Wilhelm) I, following the unification of Germany and the creation of the German Second Empire. He was succeeded on his death in 1888 by his son Frederick (Friedrich) III, who survived him by only three months, and then by his grandson William (Wilhelm) II, who ruled until his enforced abdication in 1918.

Kaiser, Georg [kiyzer] (1878–1945) Playwright, born in Magdeburg, EC Germany. He worked in Buenos Aires as a clerk, returned to Germany in ill health, and began to write plays which established him as a leader of the Expressionist movement, such as *Von Morgens bis Mitternachts* (1916, From Morn to Midnight), *Gas I* (1918), and *Gas II* (1920). His work was banned by the Nazis, and he left Germany in 1938.

Kakadu [kakadoo] National park in Arnhem Land, Northern Territory, Australia; a world heritage site; bordered N by the Van Diemen Gulf; includes the Jim Jim and Twin Falls; Aboriginal rock paintings found here, 18 000 years old; area 6144 sq km/2372 sq mi; home of the Aboriginal Mirrar people.

kakapo [kahkapoh] A flightless, ground-dwelling parrot (*Strigops habroptilus*), native to New Zealand, also known as an **owl parrot**; face with owl-like array of radiating feathers; nocturnal; inhabits mountain forest; eats fruit, shoots, moss, and fungi; seriously endangered. (Family: Psittacidae.)

kakee *persimmon*

Kakiemon porcelain [kakee-emon] Japanese porcelain made in Arita from the 1670s or 1680s, and named after the Kakiemon family of potters. It has a milky-white body with sparse, often asymmetrically placed decoration of plants, animals, and occasionally humans, painted overglaze in blue, green, orange-red, pale yellow, and black enamels, sometimes enhanced by gilding. It was exported to Europe and imitated by 18th-c factories such as Meissen, Chantilly, Chelsea, and Worcester.

Kakopetria [kakohpetria] 34°59N 32°54E. Summer resort town in Nicosia district, Cyprus; tomb of Archbishop Makarios III; nearby are the Byzantine churches of Lagoudhera and Stavros tou Ayiasmatos.

kala-azar [kahla azah(r)] *leishmaniasis*

Kalahari [kalahahree] Desert region of Africa, in SW Botswana, SE Namibia and N Cape Province, South Africa; between Orange and Zambezi Rivers; area c.260 000 sq km/100 000 sq mi; elevation generally 850–1000 m/2800–3280 ft; mainly covered with grass and woodland; bare sand in extreme SW, where annual rainfall below 200 mm/8 in; higher rainfall in the N, with savannah woodland; annual average rainfall over whole area, 150–500 mm/6–20 in; frosts common in dry season; sparsely inhabited by nomads; game reserve in S.

kalanchoe [kalankohee] A succulent herb or shrub, native mainly to tropical Africa and Madagascar; rather variable in appearance, but often with leaves blotched or marked with brown. In many species, the leaf-margins bear plantlets which drop off and grow into new plants. (Genus: *Kalanchoe*, 125 species. Family: Crassulaceae.)

kale A very hardy mutant of cabbage (*Brassica olerace*, variety *acephala*) with dense heads of plain or curled, green or purple leaves. It is widely grown as a vegetable and fodder crop. The leaves are sometimes called *borecole*. (Family: Crucifereae.)

Kalevala [kahlevahla] The name given to a compilation of Finnish legends, published by Elias Lönnrot in 1835, and now regarded as the Finnish national epic. The poem is in a trochaic metre, imitated by Longfellow in *Hiawatha*.

Kalgoorlie [kalgoorlee], or **Kalgoorlie–Boulder** 30°49S 121°29E, pop (2000e) 27 600. Gold-mining town in Western Australia, 550 km/340 mi E of Perth; gold discovered here, 1893; 60% of Australia's gold mined in the suburb of Boulder; Kalgoorlie and Boulder amalgamated, 1966; between them lies the 'Golden Mile', a square mile of ground, rich in gold; airfield; railway; a Flying Doctor centre; located in the middle of infertile desert, water has to be piped in from Mundaring Weir near Perth.

Kali [kahlee] The Hindu goddess of destruction, who is also represented as the Great Mother, the giver of life. She is the consort of Shiva.

Kalidaśa [kalidahsa] (c.5th-c) Indian poet and dramatist, best known through his drama *Abhijnana-Sakuntala* (The Recognition of Sakuntala). Also attributed to him are two other plays, two epic poems, and a lyric poem.

Kalimantan [kalimantan] pop (2000e) 9 529 000. Group of four provinces in the Indonesian part of Borneo: **Kalimantan Barat**, **West Kalimantan**, or **West Borneo**, pop (2000e) 3 806 000, area 146 760 sq km/56 649 sq mi, capital, Pontianak; **Kalimantan Selatan**, **South Kalimantan**, or **South Borneo**, pop (2000e) 3 053 000, area 37 660 sq km/14 537 sq mi, capital, Banjarmasin; **Kalimantan Tengah**, **Central Kalimantan**, or **Central Borneo**, pop (2000e) 465 000, area 152 600 sq km/58 904 sq mi, capital, Palangkaraya; **Kalimantan Timur**, **East Kalimantan**, or **East Borneo**, pop (2000e) 2 205 000, area 202 440 sq km/78 142 sq mi, capital, Samarinda; coffee, copra, pepper, coal, timber, rubber, diamonds, gold; an active guerrilla separatist movement; ethnic unrest in 1997.

Kalinin, Mikhail Ivanovich [kaleenin] (1875–1946) Soviet statesman, born in Tver, W Russia. He was the formal head of state after the 1917 Revolution and during the years of Stalin's dictatorship (1919–46). A peasant and metal-worker, he entered politics as a champion of the peasant class, and won great popularity. He became president of the Soviet Central Executive Committee (1919–38), and of the presidium of the Supreme Soviet (1938–46). His birthplace was renamed Kalinin after him (until 1991).

Kaliningrad [kaliningrad], formerly **Königsberg, Prussia** 54°40N 20°30E, pop (2001e) 424 800. Capital of Kaliningrad region, W Russia; on the R Pregel at the point where it flows into the Vistula Lagoon, an inlet of the Baltic Sea; founded (1255) as a fortress of the Teutonic Knights; renamed (1946) after E Prussia was ceded to Russia; a major ice-free Baltic seaport and naval base; important industrial, fishing, and commercial centre; birthplace of Frederick I, Immanuel Kant, Regiomontanus; university (1967); railway; airfield; cathedral; Institute of Oceanography; botanical and zoological gardens; shipbuilding, machinery, wood-pulp, chemicals, agricultural products.

Kalmar or **Calmar** 56°39N 16°20E, pop (2000e) 59 000. Capital town of Kalmar county, SE Sweden; on the Kalmar Sound, opposite Öland I; site of the Union of Kalmar; railway; glass, foodstuffs, shipbuilding, engineering, vehicles; castle (11th-c).

Kalmar Union The dynastic union of Denmark, Norway, and Sweden achieved at Kalmar, Sweden, where in 1397 Eric of Pomerania was crowned king of all three kingdoms. In 1523 Sweden broke away from the Union, which was dominated by Denmark, but Norway was united with Denmark until 1814.

Kaluza–Klein theory [kalooza kliyn] A 5-dimensional theory, a variant of general relativity, which attempts the unification of gravitation and electromagnetism; after Polish physicist Theodor Kaluza (in 1921) and Swedish physicist Oskar Klein (in 1926). It was revived in the 1980s with further dimensions added to incorporate nuclear interactions. The extra dimensions are assumed to be of a size tending to the Planck length, hence unobservable. The theory has no experimental support.

Kama [kahma] The Hindu god of love; also, one of the four ends of life in Hindu tradition. In this view, the pursuit of love or pleasure, both sensual and aesthetic, is necessary for life, but should be regulated by considerations of dharma.

Kamakura shogunate [kamakoora] (1185–1333) The first Japanese shogunate, when the head of the Minamoto family, Minamoto Yoritoko (1147–99) took the title *shogun* ('generalissimo') and established a governmental system which was to prevail for nearly 700 years. He established his headquarters at Kamakura, a fishing village S of modern Tokyo, and laid the foundations of the Japanese military feudal system, with land fiefs and vassalage. Zen Buddhism, the secular True Pure Land Buddhism, and the nationalistic Lotus Buddhist sect were all established in the Kamakura period. Chinese-style architecture was favoured, huge bronze Buddhas were made, and important court poetry was produced.

Kamchatka [kamchatka] area 270 033 sq km/104 233 sq mi. Large peninsula in Kamchatskaya oblast, E Siberian Russia, separating the Sea of Okhotsk (W) from the Bering Sea (E); extends c.1200 km/750 mi S from the Koryakskiy Khrebet range to Cape Lopatka; width, 130–480 km/80–300 mi; volcanic C range, with several cones still active; highest peak, Klyuchevskaya Sopka (4750 m/15 584 ft); abundant hot springs; chief population centre, Petropavlovsk-Kamchatskiy.

Kamenev, Lev Borisovich [kamyaynef], originally **Lev Borisovich Rosenfeld** (1883–1936) Soviet politician, born in Moscow, Russia. He was an active revolutionary from 1901, and was exiled to Siberia in 1915. Liberated during the revolution (1917), he became a member of the Communist Central Committee. Expelled as a Trotskyite in 1927, he was readmitted next year but again expelled in 1932. He was shot after being arrested with Zinoviev for conspiring against Stalin.

Kamerlingh-Onnes, Heike [kamerling awnes] (1853–1926) Physicist, born in Groningen, The Netherlands. He studied at Heidelberg and Groningen, and became professor of physics at Leyden. He was the first to produce liquid helium, and worked in low-temperature physics, discovering the phenomenon of superconductivity. He was awarded the 1913 Nobel Prize for Physics.

kamikaze [kamikahzee] (Jap 'divine wind') A term identifying the volunteer suicide pilots of the Japanese Imperial Navy, who guided their explosive-packed aircraft onto enemy ships in World War 2. They emerged in the last year of the Pacific War, when 1465 pilots died in the battle for Okinawa, destroying 26 US warships and damaging 164. Other kamikaze tactics (eg using boats and submarines) were also employed. Death for the Emperor was always a great honour.

Kamloops 50°39N 120°24W, pop (2000e) 66 500. City in S British Columbia, SW Canada; at the confluence of the N and S Thompson Rivers; European settlement with the arrival of fur traders, 1811; expanded with gold rushes, 1858–63; arrival of the Canadian Pacific Railway, 1885; University College of the Cariboo (1970); cattle ranching, farming, forest industries, copper refining, tourism, outdoor recreation; Gold Rush museum; indoor rodeo (Apr), Indian Days Festival (Jul).

Kammersee [kamerzay] *Attersee*

Kampala [kampahla] 0°19N 32°35E, pop (2000e) 739 000. Capital of Uganda, close to the N shore of L Victoria; founded, late 19th-c; capital, 1963; airport at Entebbe; railway; Makerere University (1922); banking, administration, fruit and vegetable trade, tea blending and packing, brewing, textiles, coffee, petrol depot; two cathedrals.

Kampong Saom *Kompong Som*

Kampuchea *Cambodia*

kana *syllabary*

Kananga [kanangga], formerly **Luluabourg** (to 1966) 5°53S 22°26E, pop (2000e) 462 300. Capital of Kasai Occidental region, WC Democratic Republic of Congo, on R Lulua; scene of a mutiny by Congo Free State troops, 1895; airfield; railway; commerce, agricultural trade, diamonds.

Kanarese *Kannada*

Kanban system A Japanese manufacturing system, also called the 'Just in Time' system (*Kanban*, 'signboard'). First introduced at the Toyota Motor Co after World War 2, its aim is efficient manufacturing without large warehouses. Parts are supplied to the production line 'just in time'. *Kanban* cards show when boxes need refilling by parts makers. The idea has been extremely successful, and has since spread to the West.

Kanchenjunga *Kangchenjunga*

Kandahar [kandahah(r)] 31°36N 65°47E, pop (2000e) 409 200. Capital of Kandahar province, S Afghanistan; on the ancient trade routes of C Asia, and fought over by India and Persia; capital of Afghanistan 1748–73; occupied by the British (1839–42, 1879–81) during the Afghan Wars; Taliban stronghold attacked by US-led military forces in October 2001 in response to the Taliban government's refusal to give up Osama bin Laden, chief suspect behind the terrorist attacks on New York and Washington, 11 Sep 2001; airfield; woollen cloth, silk, felt; market for sheep, wool, grain, tobacco, fresh and dried fruits.

Kandel, Eric (1929–) Neurophysiologist, born in Vienna, Austria. He went to the USA with his family in 1939, and studied at Harvard and New York University School of Medicine. In the 1970s he joined the Center for Neurobiology and Behaviour at Columbia University. He shared the 2000 Nobel Prize for Physiology or Medicine with Arvid Carlsson and Paul Greengard for their discoveries concerning signal transduction in the nervous system.

Kandinsky, Wasily [kandinskee] or **Vasily Vasilyevich** (1866–1944) Painter, born in Moscow, Russia. He spent his childhood in Italy, and his early work was carried out in Paris. In Russia (1914–21) he founded the Russian Academy and became head of the Museum of Modern Art. In 1922 he was in charge of the Weimar Bauhaus. He moved to Paris in 1933, and became a naturalized French citizen in 1939. He had a great influence on young European artists, and was a leader of the *Blaue Reiter* group.

Kandy [kandee], known as **City of the Five Hills** 7°17N 80°40E, pop (2000e) 116 000. Capital of Kandy district, Sri Lanka, looped by the R Mahaweli, 116 km/72 mi NE of Colombo; royal city until 1815; commercial centre for tea-growing area; focal point of the Buddhist Sinhalese culture; Dalada Maligawa (Temple of the Tooth), where the eye tooth of Buddha is enshrined; Peradeniya Botanical Gardens; Esala Perahera religious festival (Jul–Aug).

Kanem A mediaeval Sudanic state based to the N of L Chad, and dominating the E trade across the Sahara to Fezzan. It had its origins in the 9th-c, embraced Islam in the 11th-c, conquered Fezzan in the 13th-c, and controlled trade to Egypt and the Red Sea. It declined as a result of dynastic quarrels, but its power was recreated at Bornu in the 16th-c.

kangaroo A marsupial, usually with long hind legs used for hopping, short front legs, and a long stiff tail (held against the ground as a prop when stationary; held horizontally to counterbalance the weight of the front of the body when hopping); young (a *joey*) develops in a pouch on the mother's abdomen; large species tend to be called *kangaroos*, smaller species *wallabies*; inhabits grassland or woodland; some species climb trees. (Family: Macropodidae, 50 species.)

kangaroo paw An evergreen perennial native to SW Australia; c.1 m/3¼ ft high; leaves sword-shaped, sheathing at the base; flowers in branched inflorescence, zygomorphic, often brightly coloured; the woolly, curved tube ending in 6 claw-like lobes resembling a paw. (Genus: *Anigozanthus*, 10 species. Family: Haemadoraceae.)

kangaroo rat A squirrel-like rodent, native to North America; hind legs longer than front legs; long tail with long hairs at tip; moves by hopping. (Genus: *Dipodomys*, 22 species. Family: Heteromyidae.)

Kangchenjunga or **Kanchenjunga, Mount** [kanchenjungga], Tibetan **Gangchhendzönga**, Nepali **Kumbhkaran Lungur** 27°42N 88°09E. Mountain on the border between Nepal and the Sikkim state of India, in the Himalayan range; third highest mountain in the world; five peaks, the highest at 8586 m/ 28 169 ft; Zemu glacier on the E slope; scaled by the Charles Evans British Expedition in 1955, which turned back a few metres from the summit at the request of the Sikkim authorities, for whom the mountain is sacred.

Kang de *Puyi*

KaNgwane [kahngwahnay] Former national state or non-independent black homeland in Natal province, South Africa; self-governing status, 1971; incorporated into KwaZulu Natal following the South African constitution of 1994.

Kangxi [kangshee], also spelled **K'ang-hsi**, originally **Xuanye** (1654–1722) Fifth emperor of the Manchurian Qing dynasty, and the second to rule China. He succeeded at the age of eight, and ruled personally at 16, cultivating the image of an ideal Confucian ruler, and stressing traditional morality. He organized the compilation of a Ming history, a 50 000-character dictionary, and (1726) a 5000-volume encyclopedia. He adopted the Western calendar, and permitted an East India Company trading post (1699). A pro-Ming revolt was crushed in the SE (1673–81), and he conquered Outer Mongolia (1696), Taiwan (1683), W Mongolia, and Turkestan (from 1715), and established a Tibetan protectorate (1720). A man of wide personal interests, he published three volumes of essays.

Kang Youwei [kang yooway], also spelled **K'ang Yu-wei** (1858–1927) Philosopher and historian, the leader of the Hundred Days of Reform in China (1898). Impressed by British administration, he saw equality as a product of Confucianism. In 1898 he organized thousands of young scholars to demand drastic national reforms. The young Emperor Zaitian summoned him to implement reforms as the first step to creating a constitutional monarchy, but the movement was ended when Dowager Empress Ci-Xi seized the emperor, executed six of the young reformers, and punished all who had supported them. Kang escaped to Japan with foreign help, returning to China in 1914.

kanji [kanjee] A character in Chinese writing, as used in Japan. Schoolchildren learn the Ministry of Education's basic 1850 Chinese characters; 46 hiragana (originally simplified phonetic characters, since the 9th-c used as convenient signs for Japanese syllables); 46 katakana (further syllable symbols, often used for foreign words); and romaji (the Roman alphabet). Many kanji are simpler than the Chinese originals, and are pronounced differently.

Kankan [kankan] 10°22N 9°11W, pop (2000e) 122 000. Capital of Haute-Guinée region, E Guinea, on the R Milo; second largest town in Guinea; railway terminus; commercial and transportation centre; light industry, crafts; national police school.

Kannada [kanada] A Dravidian language of S India; also known as **Kanarese**, spoken mainly in the state of Karnataka. It has about 25 million speakers, and has written records from the 5th-c.

Kano [kahnoh] 12°00N 8°31E, pop (2000e) 853 000. Capital of Kano state, N Nigeria, 1130 km/700 mi NE of Lagos; ancient Hausa settlement; modern city founded in the 19th-c, becoming a major terminus of trans-Saharan trade; city walls nearly 18 km/11 mi long, 12 m/40 ft thick at the base, and up to 12 m/ 40 ft high; airport; railway; university (1975); food processing, brewing, textiles, leather, groundnuts, cattle, glass, metals, chemicals.

Kanpur [kahnpoor], formerly **Cawnpore** 26°35N 80°20E, pop (2000e) 2 300 000. City in Uttar Pradesh, N India; on R Ganges, 185 km/115 mi NW of Allahabad; ceded to the British, 1801; entire British garrison massacred during the Indian Mutiny, 1857; airfield; railway; university (1966); major trade and industrial centre; chemicals, jute, textiles, food products, chemicals.

Kansas [kanzas] pop (2000e) 2 688 400; area 213 089 sq km/ 82 277 sq mi. State in C USA, divided into 105 counties; the 'Sunflower State'; part of the Louisiana Purchase, 1803; virtual civil war in 1854–6 over whether it should be a free or slave state; 34th state admitted to the Union (as a free state), 1861; capital, Topeka; other chief cities, Wichita and Kansas City; the Missouri R forms part of the E state border; the Republican and Smoky Hill Rivers join to form the Kansas R, which meets the Missouri at Kansas City; the Arkansas R also crosses the state; highest point Mt Sunflower (1227 m/4025 ft); land rises steadily from prairies (E) to semi-arid high plains (W); suffered severe land erosion in the 1930s (part of the Dust Bowl); nation's leading wheat producer; sorghum, corn, hay; major cattle state; aircraft, chemicals, processed foods, machinery; petroleum, natural gas, helium.

Kansas City (Kansas) [kanzas] 39°07N 94°38W, pop (2000e) 146 900. Seat of Wyandotte Co, E Kansas, USA; port at the junction of the Kansas and Missouri Rivers, adjacent to Kansas City, MO, with which it shares many functions; settled by Wyandotte Indians, 1843; sold to the US government, 1855; railway; together with its sister city, a major commercial and industrial centre; market for surrounding agricultural region; stockyards, grain elevators; automobiles, metal products, processed foods, machinery, petroleum; Agricultural Hall of Fame.

Kansas City (Missouri) [kanzas] 39°06N 94°35W, pop (2000e) 456 000. River port city in Jackson Co, W Missouri, USA; on the S bank of the Missouri R, adjacent to its sister city, Kansas City, KS, with which it shares many functions; town of Kansas established, 1838; city status, 1853; present name, 1889; airport; railway; university (1929); automobiles and parts, metal products, electronics, processed foods, machinery, oil refineries, railway shops; large stockyards and grain elevators; the nation's leading winter-wheat market; jazz centre in the 1930s–40s; professional teams (representing the two Kansas Cities), Royals (baseball), Chiefs (football); Nelson Art Gallery, Atkins Museum of Fine Arts.

Kansu Corridor *Hexi Corridor*

Kant, Immanuel [kant] (1724–1804) Philosopher, born in Königsberg, Prussia (now Kaliningrad, Russia). He spent his entire life there, studying at the university, and becoming professor of logic and metaphysics in 1770. His early publications were in the natural sciences, particularly astronomy and geophysics, and he published prolifically on a great range of subjects throughout his life. His main work, now a philosophical classic, is the *Kritik der reinen Vernunft* (1781, Critique of Pure Reason), in which he provided a response to the empiricism of Hume. His views on ethics are set out in the *Grundlagen zur Metaphysik der Sitten* (1785, Foundations of the Metaphysics of Morals) and the *Kritik der praktischen Vernunft* (1788, Critique of Practical Reason), in which he elaborates on the Categorical Imperative as the supreme principle of morality. In his third and last Critique, the *Kritik der Urteilskraft* (1790, Critique of Judgment), he argued that aesthetic judgments, although universal, do not depend on any property (such as beauty or sublimity) of the object. He also wrote on politics, and his *Perpetual Peace* (1795) advocates a world system of free states. He exerted tremendous influence on subsequent philosophy, especially the idealism of Fichte, Hegel, and Schelling.

Kanto earthquake The worst Japanese earthquake of modern times, occurring in E Japan in 1923. There were many fires spread by strong winds, and about 100 000 people were killed. Old Tokyo and Yokohama were destroyed.

Kantorovich, Leonid Vitaliyevich [kantorohvich] (1912–86) Economist and mathematician, born in St Petersburg, NW Russia. He studied there, receiving his doctorate at the age of 18. He was a professor at Leningrad State University (1934–60), director of the mathematical economics laboratory at the Moscow Institute of National Economic Management (1971–6), and from 1976 directed the Institute of System Studies at the Moscow Academy of Sciences. He is credited with the development of linear programming, which had been used for optimal economic planning of resources on both the micro and macro level. He shared the 1975 Nobel Prize for Economics.

Kanuri [kanuree] A Nilo-Saharan-speaking people of Bornu, NE Nigeria, and SE Niger. Well-known as traders, they formed the empire of Bornu, at its zenith during the 16th-c. Muslim since the 11th-c, they have a highly stratified social organization.

Kao Kang *Gao Gang*

kaolin [kayolin] A pure clay formed by the decomposition of feldspar in granite, and composed chiefly of the mineral *kaolinite*, a hydrous aluminium silicate; also known as **china clay**. It is used in the manufacture of fine porcelain, and as a filler in paper making and paints. It was also used therapeutically in China from before the 17th-c.

Kapil Dev, Nihanj (1959–) Cricketer, born in Chandigarh, Punjab, N India. An all-rounder, he made his first-class debut for Haryana at the age of 16, and played county cricket in England for Northants and Worcester. He led India to victory in the 1983 World Cup, and set a competition record score of 175 not out against Zimbabwe. In 1983 he became the youngest player (at 24 years 68 days) to perform a Test double of 2000 runs and 200 wickets (surpassing Ian Botham). In 1994 he broke Sir Richard Hadlee's record of 431 Test wickets by taking 432 wickets in his 130th Test match. He was named as India's Wisden Cricketer of the Century.

Kapitza, Pyotr Leonidovich [kapitza] (1894–1984) Physicist, born in Kronstadt, NW Russia. He studied at St Petersburg (then Petrograd), and taught there until 1921. He then studied under Rutherford at Cambridge, where he became assistant director of magnetic research at the Cavendish Laboratory (1924–32). He was elected fellow of the Royal Society in 1929. He returned to Russia for a conference, but was prevented from leaving again, and was appointed director of the Institute of Physical Problems. He was dismissed in 1946 for refusing to work on the atomic bomb, but reinstated in 1955. He is known for his work on high-intensity magnetism, low temperature, and the liquefaction of hydrogen and helium. He shared the Nobel Prize for Physics in 1978.

kapok tree [kaypok] One of various members of the baobab family, with fruits containing seeds embedded in cotton-like fibres, used as filling for cushions, etc. The principal species are the **silk-cotton tree** (*Ceiba pentandra*) from tropical America, but cultivated in W Africa, and the **cotton tree** (*Bombax ceiba*) from India and Ceylon. (Family: Bombacaceae.)

Kapoor, Anish [kapoor] (1954–) Artist and sculptor, born in Mumbai (Bombay), W India. He moved to London in 1973, where he studied at the Hornsey College of Art and the Chelsea School of Art, and became a teacher at Wolverhampton Polytechnic (1979) and artist in residence at the Walker Art Gallery, Liverpool (1982). He has exhibited at major venues around the world, and his awards include the Premio Duemila Venice Biennale (1990) and the Turner Prize (1991). In late 2003 he won a competition to create the centrepiece for a planned memorial garden to British victims of the 11 September terrorist attacks in New York City.

Karachi [karahchee] 24°51N 67°02E, pop (2000e) 8 345 000. Provincial capital of Sind province, SE Pakistan; on the Arabian Sea coast, NW of the mouths of the Indus; Pakistan's principal seaport; founded, 18th-c; under British rule from 1843; former capital, 1947–59; airport; railway; university (1951); trade in cotton, grain, skins, wool; chemicals, textiles, plastics, shipbuilding; tomb of Quaid-i-Azam, Mohammad Ali Jinnah, founder of Pakistan; national museum.

Karadžić, Radovan [karajich] (1945–) Militant leader of the Bosnian Serbs within Bosnia and Herzegovina, born in the village of Petnijca in Montenegro, former Yugoslavia. He graduated in psychiatry from the University of Sarajevo, and worked in local hospitals. In the 1990s' upsurge of nationalism, he founded and became president of the Serbian Democratic Party. When Bosnia and Herzegovina declared independence, Bosnia's Serbs, led by Karadžić, sought union with Serbia. By the end of 1992, Serbs had seized almost two-thirds of Bosnia and Herzegovina, and he declared himself president of the self-styled 'Serb Republic'. A period of purges followed, during which over 3 million people were dispossessed. He accepted the Dayton peace accord (1995) under considerable Serb pressure. In the face of international efforts to bring him before the UN war crimes tribunal in The Hague, he formally resigned his presidency (1996), though retaining political power. In 1997 the breakaway Bosnian Serb republic held elections which deprived his front organization of power in the republic. He went into hiding, avoiding efforts to bring him to trial at The Hague.

Karageorge, Turkish **Karadjordje** ('Black George'), also **Czerny George**, nickname of **George Petrović** (1766–1817) Leader of the Serbians in their struggle for independence and founder of the dynasty of Karadjordjević, born in Viševac, Serbia, the son of peasants. His nickname arose from his dark complexion. He led a revolt against Ottoman Turkey, and in 1808 was elected governor and recognized as Prince of Serbia by the sultan, Selim III (ruled 1789–1807). When Turkey regained control of Serbia in 1813, Karageorge was exiled. When he tried to return, he was murdered at the instigation of his rival, Prince Milosch Obrenović (ruled 1815–39).

Karajan, Herbert von [kara-yan] (1908–89) Conductor, born in Salzburg, C Austria. He studied there and in Vienna, and conducted at the Städtisches Theater, Ulm (1928–33), at Aachen (1934–8), and at the Berlin Staatsoper (1938–42). After the war he was banned from working by the Russian occupation authorities until 1947, having been a member of the Nazi Party (1933–42), but in 1955 he was made principal conductor of the Berlin Philharmonic, and it is with this orchestra that he was mainly associated until his resignation in 1989. He also conducted frequently elswhere, and was artistic director of the Salzburg Festival (1956–60) and of the Salzburg Easter Festival (from 1967).

karakul [karakl] A breed of sheep native to Asia; also known as **caracul**. The name is also used for the skin of a young lamb of this breed, and for cloth which resembles this fur.

Kara-Kum [kara **koom**], Russ **Peski Karakumy** area c.300 000 sq km/120 000 sq mi. Extensive desert in Turkmenistan, between the Caspian Sea (W) and the R Amudarya (N and E); crossed (SE) by the Trans-Caspian railway.

Karamanlis, Konstantinos [karamanlees], also spelled **Caramanlis** (1907–98) Greek statesman, prime minister (1955–63, 1974–80), and president (1980–5, 1990–5), born in Próti, Greece. A former lawyer, he was elected to parliament in 1935, became minister of public works (1952), then prime minister, and formed his own party, the National Radical Union. During his administration, Greece signed a Treaty of Alliance with Cyprus and Turkey. After his party's election defeat in 1963, he left politics and lived abroad, but returned to become premier again in 1974, when he supervised the restoration of civilian rule after the collapse of the military government. He then served as president.

karat *carat*

karate [karahtay] A martial art of unarmed combat, with strong philosophical undertones, dating from the 17th-c, and developed in Japan in the 20th-c; its name was adopted in the 1930s. The aim is to be in total control of the muscular power of the body, so that it can be used with great force and accuracy at any instant. Experts may show their mental and physical training by performing such acts of strength as breaking various thicknesses of wood; but in fighting an opponent, blows do not actually make physical contact. Levels of prowess are symbolized by coloured belts, as in other martial arts.

Karawanken Alps [karavangkn], Serbo-Croatian **Karavanke** Mountain range of the E Alps on the border between Slovenia and Austria, mostly in the Austrian state of Kärnten; an extension of the Carnic Alps; highest peak, Hochstuhl (2238 m/ 7342 ft); road from Klagenfurt to Ljubljana via the Loibl Tunnel.

Karelia [kareelia], Russ **Karelskaya** pop (2000e) 796 000; area 172 400 sq km/66 560 sq mi. Constituent republic of Russia; bounded W by Finland and E by the White Sea; in mediaeval times, an independent state with strong Finnish associations; under Swedish domination, 17th-c; annexed by Russia, 1721; constituted as a Soviet Socialist Republic, 1923; many lakes and rivers; heavily forested; mining, timber, cereals, fishing.

Karen Sino-Tibetan-speaking, ethnically-diverse groups of S Myanmar (Burma). With Burmese independence (1948), fighting broke out between government and groups identifying themselves as Karen, wanting autonomy. Sometimes divided into White Karen and Red Karen, they have united in common opposition to Burmese control. In the late 1980s many fled to refugee camps in Thailand.

Kariba Dam A major concrete arch dam on the Zambezi R at the Zambia–Zimbabwe border, impounding L Kariba; completed in 1959; height 128 m/420 ft; length 579 m/1900 ft. It has the capacity to generate 705 megawatts of hydroelectricity.

Karloff, Boris, originally **William Henry Pratt** (1887–1969) Film star, born in London, UK. He studied at London University, then went to Canada and the USA, aiming for a diplomatic career, and became involved in acting. He spent 10 years in repertory companies, went to Hollywood, and after several silent films made his name as the monster in *Frankenstein* (1931). Apart from a notable performance in a World War 1 story, *The Lost Patrol* (1934), his career was mostly spent in popular horror films, though his performances frequently transcended the crudity of the genre, bringing, as in *Frankenstein*, a depth and pathos to the characterization. He continued to appear in films, on television, and on the stage until his death.

Karlovy Vary **[kah(r)lovee varee]**, Ger **Karlsbad** 50°14N 12°53E, pop (2000e) 60 200. Town in Západočeský region, Czech Republic; on R Ohre, W of Prague; airport; railway; kaolin, glass, footwear, mineral water; famous health resort with hot alkaline springs.

Karlsbad *Karlovy Vary*

Karlsruhe **[kah(r)lzroouh]** 49°03N 8°23E, pop (2000e) 284 000. Capital of Karlsruhe district, SW Germany; port on R Rhine, 56 km/35 mi S of Mannheim; former capital of Baden; birthplace of Karl Benz; railway; university (1825); oil refining, machine tools, chemicals, tyres, machinery, defence equipment, rubber products, dairy produce; palace (1752–85).

karma **[kah(r)ma]** (Sanskrit 'action' or 'work') In Indian tradition, the principle that a person's actions have consequences meriting reward or punishment. Karma is the moral law of cause and effect by which the sum of a person's actions are carried foward from one life to the next, leading to an improvement or deterioration in that person's fate.

Karnataka **[kah(r)nataka]**, formerly **Mysore** pop (2001e) 52 734 000; area 191 773 sq km/74 024 sq mi. State in SW India; bounded W by the Arabian Sea; formed as Mysore under the States Reorganization Act of 1956, bringing the Kannada-speaking population of five states together; official language, Kannada; renamed Karnataka, 1973; crossed by numerous rivers; bicameral legislature comprises a 63-member Legislative Council and an elected 225-member Legislative Assembly; capital, Bangalore; rice, groundnuts, silk, cotton, coffee, sandalwood, bamboo; gold, silver, iron ore, manganese, limestone, chromite; iron and steel, engineering, electronics, chemicals, textiles, cement, sugar, paper.

Karnische Alpen *Carnic Alps*

Karoo **[karoo]** Dry steppe country in South Africa, from the Orange R down to the Cape; Karoo National Park covers 180 sq km/70 sq mi of the arid region called the Great Karoo; established in 1979.

Kárpathos **[kah(r)pathos]**, Ital **Scarpanto**, ancient **Carpathus** pop (2000e) 5040; area 301 sq km/116 sq mi. Mountainous, elongated island of the Dodecanese group, E Greece, in the Aegean Sea, between Rhodes and the E end of Crete; length 48 km/30 mi; rises to 1216 m/3989 ft; capital, Pigadhia, numerous bathing beaches.

Karpov, Anatoly Yevgenyevich **[kah(r)pof]** (1951–) Chess player and world champion (1975–85), born in Zlatoust, W Russia. Trained by former world champion Mikhail Botvinnik, he won the world junior championship (1969). He became world champion by default after Bobby Fischer refused to defend his title (1975), and successfully defended his title until losing to Kasparov in a controversial match (1985). He defeated Jan Timman of The Netherlands in an official world championship match in 1993, though publicity for this event and his victory suffered as a result of the independent championship match being played at the same time between Kasparov and Nigel Short. He successfully defended the FIDE title in 1996 and 1998, but lost it in 1999 when he refused to accept the tournament format.

Karski, Jan, original surname **Kozielecki** (1914–2000) Polish resistance hero, born in Lodz, C Poland. A Roman Catholic, he graduated from Lvov (Lwow) University in 1935, worked in diplomatic posts until 1939, then joined the army. Taken prisoner first by the Soviets then by the Germans, he escaped and became a government courier. After discovery by German intelligence, he emigrated to the USA in 1942, where he wrote the best-selling *Story of a Secret State* (1944). He became a US citizen, a professor at Georgetown University, and a lecturer for the Pentagon and State Department. While in Poland, he secretly toured the Warsaw Ghetto and a concentration camp, gathering evidence of Nazi atrocities against Polish Jews, and was the first to present documented proof of Hitler's extermination policy to Allied leaders in Britain and the USA. Embittered by the Allies' failure to take decisive action, he refused to speak about his activities in the post-war years, but his story became known in 1979, after the writer Elie Wiesel made contact with him, and he was the subject of a biography by E T Wood & S M Jankowski, *One Man Tried to Stop the Holocaust* (1994). He was made an honorary citizen of Israel in 1994.

Karst, Slovenian **Kras**, Ital **Carso** Barren, stony limestone plateau in the Dinaric Alps of SW Slovenia; extending c.80 km/50 mi from the R Isonzo (NW) to the Kvarner Gulf (SE); notable caves at Postojna; the name has come to be used in geography to describe limestone topography of this kind.

karst region A distinctive landscape associated with limestone regions, and characterized by the complete absence of surface drainage and its replacement by a drainage system through vertical cracks, underground channels, and planes of weakness in the rock. Sink holes, labyrinths of passages, caves with stalactites and stalagmites, and underground lakes are typical features. The name derives from an area along the Adriatic coast, where this landscape is found.

karting Motor racing of small four-wheeled vehicles, usually with single-cylinder and two-stroke engines. They are raced in categories dependent on engine size. Karts can have either bodyless tubular frames or, in top-class competitions, sophisticated streamlined bodies.

karyology **[kariolojee]** The branch of cytology dealing with the study of nuclei inside cells, especially with the structure of chromosomes. It includes the determination of numbers and sizes of chromosomes, the identification of sex chromosomes, the study of chromosome banding using staining techniques, and the study of the nucleic acids involved.

Karzai, Hamid (1957–) Afghan head of state (2001–), born in Kandahar, Afghanistan. A Pashtun, and son of a powerful chief of the Popolzai tribe, he studied politics at the University of Simla, India. In 1983 during the war with the Soviet Union he channelled money, weapons, and supplies to the Mujahideen fighters in Afghanistan. When the Soviets left, he served as deputy foreign minister in the Mujahideen administration (1992), but quickly became disenchanted with them and sided with the Taliban. By 1994 he had become increasingly disillusioned with the movement, refused the post of ambassador to the UN in 1996, and went into exile in Pakistan, where he began organizing resistance against the Taliban. He travelled repeatedly to the USA to lobby for support, and secretly returned to Afghanistan to recruit anti-Taliban fighters in October 2001. At the UN Bonn conference on Afghanistan (Dec 2001), he was named leader of the interim government, and became head of state in 2002.

Kashmir *Jammu–Kashmir*

Kasparov, Gary (Kimovich) [kaspahrof] (1963–) Chess player, born in Baku, Azerbaijan. When he beat Anatoly Karpov for the world title (Nov 1985), he became the youngest world champion, at the age of 22 years 210 days. He has successfully defended his title, and is the highest-ranked active player, with a ranking of 2783 (in 2003). His 1984–5 match with Karpov was the longest in the history of chess. Long-term friction between him and the international chess organization, FIDE, resulted in his establishing the Grandmasters' Association in 1987, and arranging a World Championship match in 1993 without FIDE involvement, in which he defeated Nigel Short of Britain. In 1996 he competed against Deep Blue, the world's best chess-playing computer, winning four of the six games, but in a rematch the following year he was decisively beaten by the machine. He lost his title to Vladimir Kramnik in 2000. His autobiography, *Child of Change* (a reference to Gorbachev's policy of glasnost), appeared in 1987.

Kassel or **Cassel** 51°19N 9°32E, pop (2000e) 201 000. Cultural, economic, and administrative centre of Kassel district, C Germany; on the R Fulda, 114 km/71 mi NW of Erfurt; an important traffic junction; badly bombed in World War 2; railway; university (1971); mineral salts, dairy products, natural gas and oil, locomotives, vehicles, machinery, cloth, optical and geodetic instruments; Wilhelmshöhe (health resort), Gallery of Old Masters in the Schloss Wilhelmshöhe, Schloss Wilhelmsthal (11 km/7 mi NW); Kurkonzerte in Wilhelmshöhe Park (May–Sep), modern art exhibition (Jul–Sep).

Kästner, Erich [kestner] (1899–1974) Writer, born in Dresden, E Germany. He was a teacher and journalist, then turned to writing poetry and novels. He is best known for his children's books, which include *Emil und die Detektive* (1928, Emil and the Detectives). After World War 2, he became magazine editor of *Die Neue Zeitung*, and founded a paper for children.

katabatic wind A local downslope wind which develops in a valley. At night, surface air over mountain ridges cools faster than air above the valley floor. Thus, colder and denser air flows from high elevations to valley bottoms. Downslope winds also flow from mountainous areas to adjacent lowlands: the chinook wind of the Rockies and the Föhn wind of the European Alps are warm katabatic winds; the Mistral of the Rhône Valley, France, is a cold katabatic wind.

Katanga [katangga] The southernmost province of Democratic Republic of Congo, rich in minerals. In 1960, when the Congo (Zaire) achieved independence from Belgium, Katanga (known as Shaba, 1971–97) attempted to secede under the leadership of Moise Tshombe (1919–69). In the ensuing chaos the government of Patrice Lumumba was overthrown. Lumumba was assassinated in 1961, and the unitary state was later recreated under the military leadership of President Mobutu.

Kathak [katak] A major form of Indian classical dance, developed in NW India from the 15th-c to the 18th-c, more relaxed in performance than the older forms such as Bharata Natyam. It is often secular rather than religious, using a dramatic story-telling form that may include improvisation. Musical accompaniment is provided by drums, bowed and stringed instruments, and the human voice. It is strongly rhythmic and uses swift, intricate foot movements.

Kathakali [katakahli] Epic theatre from the SW coastal region of India in which troupes of actors, in stylized make-up and costume, enact dramas based on the Ramayana and Mahabharata, using music, song, dance, and an elaborate system of hand symbols equivalent to speech.

Katherine Gorge National park in Northern Territory, Australia; spectacular gorges on the Katherine R, up to 60 m/200 ft high; many Aboriginal rock drawings; area 1800 sq km/700 sq mi.

Kathmandu or **Katmandu** [katmandoo], formerly **Kantipur** 27°42N 85°19E, pop (2000e) 587 000. Capital and principal city of Nepal; 121 km/75 mi from the Indian frontier in the Kathmandu Valley, altitude 1373 m/4504 ft; on the ancient pilgrim and trade route from India to Tibet, China, and Mongolia; built in its present form, 723; Gurkha capital, 1768; British seat of administration, 18th-c; university (1959); commercial centre, religious centre, tourism; Machendra Nath Temple, Hanuman Dhoka Palace, Kasthamanadap temple, Swayambhunath (Buddhist shrine), Pashupatinath Temple (centre of an annual pilgrimage), natural history museum; the Vale of Kathmandu is a world heritage site.

Katowice [katoveetse], Ger **Kattowitz** 50°15N 19°01E, pop (2000e) 370 000. Capital of Katowice voivodship, S Poland; centre of the Upper Silesian Industrial Region; airport; railway; two universities (1945, 1968); coal mining, iron and steel, zinc works, chemicals, optics, fertilizer; Kościuszko Park, cathedral; drama festival (Nov).

katydid [kaytidid] A large, grasshopper-like insect in which sound communication is well-developed; characterized by a sword-shaped egg-laying tube; mostly plant feeders. (Order: Orthoptera. Family: Tettigoniidae, c.5000 species.)

Katyn massacre [katin] A massacre of 14 000 Polish army officers in May 1940 in the Katyn forest near Smolensk, Belarus. The officers were shot and buried, and their mass graves were discovered by German occupying forces in 1943. Soviet authorities persistently denied responsibility for the massacre, blaming it on the Germans. In 1989 the Soviet–Polish historical commission (set up in 1987 to establish the truth) reported that the crime was most probably committed by the Soviet security service (NKVD).

Katz, Sir Bernard (1911–2003) Biophysicist, born in Leipzig, EC Germany. He studied at Leipzig and London, carried out research in London (1935–9) and Sydney (1939–42), and became professor of biophysics at London (1952–78), then an honorary research fellow. Knighted in 1969, in 1970 he shared the Nobel Prize for Physiology or Medicine for his studies on how transmitter substances are released from nerve terminals.

Kauai [kowiy], formerly **Kaieiewaho** pop (2000e) 58 500; area 1692 sq km/653 sq mi. Island of the US state of Hawaii; forms Kauai county with Niihau I; chief town, Lihue; sugar; tourism.

Kaufman, George S(imon) [kowfman] (1889–1961) Playwright and director, born in Pittsburgh, Pennsylvania, USA. In collaboration with Moss Hart he wrote *You Can't Take It With You* (1938, Pulitzer) and *The Man Who Came to Dinner* (1939). Other works include *The Solid Gold Cadillac* (with Howard Teichmann, 1953) and many musicals, some of which have been filmed. He directed much of his work.

Kaufman, Philip [kawfman] (1936–) Film director and screenwriter, born in Chicago, Illinois, USA. As an independent filmmaker he wrote, produced, and directed his first film, *Goldstein* (1964), in collaboration with Benjamin Manaster. He also worked closely with his wife Rose, co-writer on *The Wanderers* (1979) and *Henry and June* (1990), and his son Peter, who produced *Rising Sun* (1993). He wrote the story for *The Outlaw Josey Wales* (1975) and *Raiders of the Lost Ark* (1981). Other films include *Invasion of the Body Snatchers* (1978), *The Unbearable Lightness of Being* (1988), and *China: The Wild East* (1995).

Kaunas [kownas], formerly **Kovno** (to 1917) 54°52N 23°55E, pop (2000e) 431 000. Ancient town and river port in Lithuania; on the R Neman at its confluence with the R Vilnya; capital of independent Lithuania, 1918; airfield; railway; chemicals, radio engineering, machines, clothing, foodstuffs, woodworking; ancient centre of artistic trades; castle (13th–17th-c), Massalski Palace (17th-c), Vytautas church (1400).

Kaunda, Kenneth (David) [kaoonda] (1924–) Zambian statesman and president (1964–91), born in Lubwa, N Zambia. He became a teacher in Zambia and Tanganyika (Tanzania), then joined the African National Congress, becoming its secretary-general, and in 1958 founding a development of this organization, the Zambian African National Congress. He was subsequently imprisoned, and the movement banned. Elected president of the United National Independent Party (1960), he played a leading part in his country's independence negotiations, and became the first president of the country. After a failed military coup in 1990, he agreed to multi-party elections in 1991; but lost the presidency to Frederick Chiluba, leader of the Movement for Multi-Party Democracy. Following a failed coup attempt in the country in 1997, in which he denied his involvement, he was placed under house arrest and barred from political activities.

Kaunitz(-Rietberg), Wenzel Anton, Fürst von (Prince of) [**kow**nits **reet**berg] (1711–94) Austrian statesman and chancellor (1753–92), born in Vienna, Austria. He distinguished himself at the Congress of Aix-la-Chapelle (1748), and as Austrian ambassador at the French court (1750–2). As chancellor, he instigated the Diplomatic Revolution, and directed Austrian politics for almost 40 years under Maria Theresa and Joseph II. He was a liberal patron of arts and sciences.

kauri gum A commercially important resin obtained from kauri pine, used mainly in paint and in the manufacture of linoleum. **Copal** is the name for the fossilized gum often found in large quantities on the sites of ancient forests, said to be superior to fresh gum.

kauri pine An evergreen conifer related to araucaria, native to SE Asia and Australasia. It is the source of an important resin as well as timber. One species, *Agathis australis*, is an important forest tree in New Zealand. (Genus: *Agathis*, 20 species. Family: Araucariaceae.)

kava A Polynesian beverage made by fermenting chewed or grated, peeled roots of *Piper methysticum*, a relative of black pepper. The drink is narcotic and sedative as well as intoxicating.

Kawasaki [kawasakee] 35°32N 139°41E, pop (2000e) 1 192 000. Capital of Kanagawa prefecture, Kanto region, E Honshu, Japan; S of Tokyo, on W shore of Tokyo-wan Bay; railway; iron, steel, oil industry, electronics, shipbuilding, machinery, chemicals, textiles.

Kay, John (1704–c.1764) Inventor, born near Bury, Greater Manchester, NW England, UK. He took charge of his father's woollen mill, made many improvements to the machinery, and obtained a patent for a device for twisting and cording mohair and worsted (1730). In 1733 he patented his flying shuttle, one of the most important inventions in the history of textile machinery. The new shuttle was eagerly adopted by weavers, but they were reluctant to pay the royalties due to him, and the cost of court actions against defaulters nearly ruined him. After his house was ransacked by a mob of textile workers, who feared that his machines would destroy their livelihood, he left England for France (1753), where he is believed to have died a pauper.

kayak [**kiy**ak] A small double-ended craft of Eskimo design, similar to a canoe, but enclosed except for a very small cockpit. It is made effectively watertight by a detachable spray deck attached to the body of the paddler. It is usually propelled with a double-ended paddle.

Kaye, Danny, originally **David Daniel Kaminski** (1913–87) Comic actor and entertainer, born in New York City, USA. A singer and dancer at school and summer camps, he toured extensively in the 1930s, and made his film debut in 1937. His first feature film, *Up in Arms* (1944), was an instant success, and launched him on a career as an international star, noted for his mimicry and tongue-twisting speciality songs. His best-loved films include *The Secret Life of Walter Mitty* (1946), *Hans Christian Andersen* (1952), and *The Court Jester* (1956). As a straight dramatic actor his most accomplished performance was as a concentration camp survivor in the television film *Skokie* (1981). Well known for his fundraising activities for UNICEF, he received a special Academy Award in 1955.

Kazakh or **Kazak** [kazak] A Turkic-speaking Mongoloid people of Kazakhstan and adjacent areas in China. Traditionally nomadic pastoralists, in the 19th-c many settled and grew crops. After the Russian Revolution (1917), wealthy Kazakh herders fled to Xinjiang (China) and Afghanistan. Apart from one group, the remaining nomads were forced onto collective cattle farms; in China, many are still nomadic.

Kazakhstan *p.830*

Kazan [kazan] 55°45N 49°10E, pop (2000e) 1 100 000. River-port capital of Tatarstan, E European Russia; on the R Volga at its confluence with the R Kazanka; founded, 13th-c; airport; railway; university (1804); important industrial and cultural centre of the Volga region; chemicals, engineering, instruments, machines, fur, leather, foodstuffs; Cathedral of the Annunciation (19th-c), Governor's Palace (1845–8).

Kazan, Elia [kazan], originally **Elia Kazanjoglous** (1909–2003) Stage and film director, born in Istanbul, NW Turkey. His family went to the USA in 1913, and he studied at Williams College and Yale, then acted in minor roles on Broadway and in Hollywood before becoming a director of plays and films. With Lee Strasberg, he founded the Actors Studio in 1947. Many of his films have a social or political theme, such as *Gentleman's Agreement* (1948, Oscar) and *On the Waterfront* (1954, Oscar). Other notable films include *A Streetcar Named Desire* (1951), *East of Eden* (1955), and *America, America* (1964). His last film was *The Last Tycoon* (1976). He published his autobiography, *My Life*, in 1988, and *Beyond the Aegean* appeared in 1994. A lifetime achievement award at the 1999 Oscars ceremony was given a mixed response, with opponents recalling that Kazan had given the names of Communists in the film industry to the Un-American Activities Committee in the 1950s.

Kazanlak tomb A 4th-c BC Thracian tomb located near Kazanlak, Bulgaria; a world heritage site. The tomb is noted for the frescoes which decorate the burial chamber and vaulted corridor within. It was discovered in 1944.

Kazantzakis, Nikos [kazanzakis] (1883–1957) Writer, born in Heraklion, Crete, Greece. He studied law at Athens, spent some years travelling in Europe and Asia, and published his first novel in 1929. He is best known for the novel *Vios kai politia tou Alexi Zormpa* (1946, trans Zorba the Greek, filmed 1964) and the epic autobiographical narrative poem, *Odissia* (1938, trans The Odyssey, a Modern Sequel).

Kaziranga [kazirangga] National park on the S bank of the Brahmaputra R in Assam, India; area 430 sq km/166 sq mi; established in 1908 to protect the great Indian rhino and the swamp deer; a world heritage site.

kazoo or **bazouka** A child's musical instrument, consisting of a short metal tube flattened at one end, with a hole in the top covered by a disc of membrane. This imparts a buzzing edge to the tone when the player sings or hums into the flattened end. A similar effect may be obtained with a piece of paper round the edge of a comb.

kea A large, stocky, dull-coloured parrot (*Nestor notabilis*) native to S New Zealand; male with long upper bill; inhabits forest or open country; eats fruit, leaves, insects, or carrion; scavenges on refuse dumps; nests in hole. (Family: Psittacidae.)

Kean, Edmund (c.1789–1833) Actor, born in London, UK. He became a strolling player, and after 10 years in the provinces made his first appearance at Drury Lane as Shylock (1814). A period of great success followed as a tragic actor, but because of his irregularities he gradually forfeited public approval, his reputation being finally ruined when he was successfully sued for adultery in 1825. He reintroduced a naturalistic style of acting that relied on movement and the beauty of the language, rather than the exaggerated, melodramatic delivery then in fashion.

Keane, Roy (Maurice) (1971–) Footballer, born in Cork, Ireland. An all-round midfielder, he left Ireland in 1990 to join Nottingham, moving to Manchester United in 1993 for £3·75 million, a record between British clubs at that time. He became captain in 1997 following the retirement of Eric Cantona. He won his first cap for the Republic of Ireland in 1991 and by 2002 had won 58 caps. In 2000 he was voted The Football Writers' and the Professional Footballers Association's Player of the Year. He was named captain of Ireland at the start of the 2002 FIFA World Cup campaign, but after a disagreement he left the squad

Kazakhstan

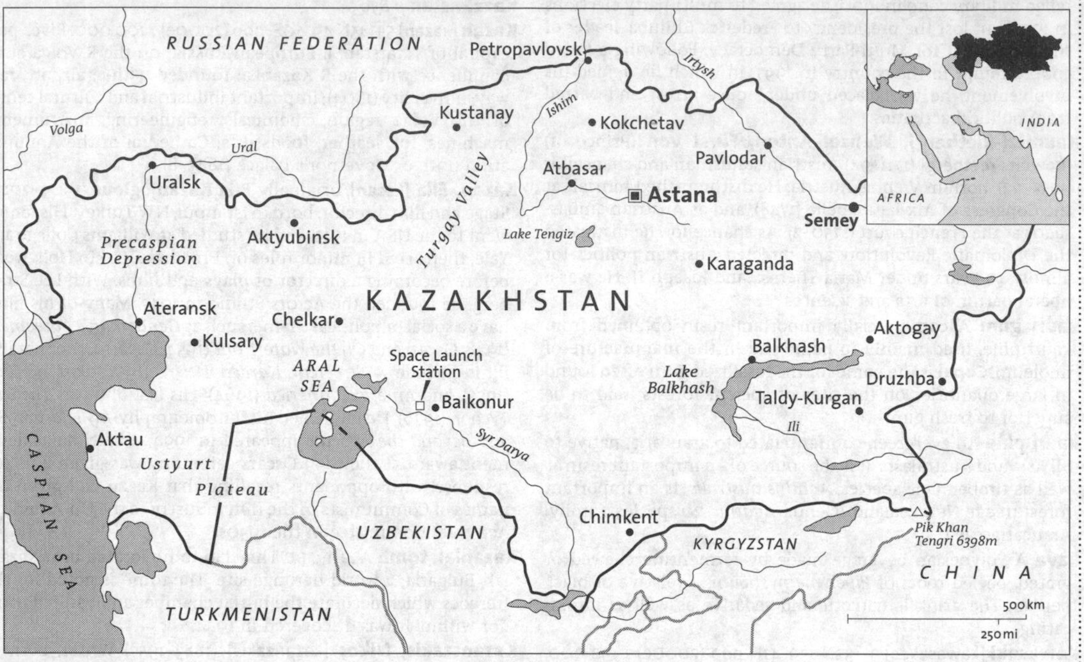

[kazakstahn], official name **Republic of Kazakhstan**, Kazakh **Qazaqstan Respublikasï**, Russ **Kazakhskaya**

Local name Kazakstan

Timezone GMT +5/6

Area 2 717 300 km²/1 048 878 sq mi

Population total (2002e) 14 888 000

Status Republic

Date of independence 1991

Capital Astana (from 1998), formerly Almaty (Alma-Ata)

Languages Kazakh (official), Russian, German

Ethnic groups Kazakh (40%), Russian (37%), German (6%), Ukrainian (5%)

Religions Muslim (Sunni), Christian (Russian Orthodox, Protestant)

Physical features Bounded E by China and W by Caspian Sea; second largest republic in former USSR; mountain ranges in E and SE; steppeland (N) gives way to desert (S); lowest elevation near E shore of the Caspian Sea, 132 m/433 ft below sea-level; main rivers, Irtysh, Syr Darya, Ural, Ili; largest lake, L Balkhash; space launch centre at Tyuratam, near Baikonur.

Climate Continental; hot summers, extreme winters; wide range of temperatures, from -17°C in N and C ranges, to -3°C in S (Jan), 20°C in N, 29°C in S (Jul); strong, dry winds common in NW.

Currency (1992) 1 tenge = 100 kopecks

Economy Coal, iron ore, bauxite, copper, nickel, oil; oil refining, metallurgy, heavy engineering, chemicals, leatherwork, footwear, food processing; cotton, fruit, grain, sheep.

GDP (2002e) $120 bn, per capita $7200

Human Development Index (2002) 0·750

History Under the control of the Mongols, 13th-c; gradually under Russian rule, 1730–1853; became constituent republic of USSR, 1936; independence movement, 1990–1; independence declared in 1991, and joined Commonwealth of Independent States; governed by a President, Prime Minister, and Supreme Soviet.

Head of State
1991– Nursultan A Nazarbayev

Head of Government
1991–4 Sergei Tereshchenko
1994–7 Kazhageldin Akezhan Magzhan Ulu
1997–9 Nurlan Balgimbayev
1999–2002 Kasymzhomart Tokayev
2002–3 Imangali Tasmagambetov
2003– Daniyal Akhmetov

before the start of the tournament and announced his retirement from international football (a decision revised in 2004).

Keating, Paul (John) (1944–) Australian statesman and prime minister (1991–6), born in Sydney, New South Wales, SE Australia. He managed a rock-and-roll band before entering the federal parliament as a member of the House of Representatives in 1969. He was minister for Northern Australia in the Whitlam Government in 1975, and president of the New South Wales Labor Party (1979–83). As Treasurer (1983–91), he was the main architect of the government's economic policies, particularly the deregulation of financial markets. Elected leader by his party in 1991, he managed to win a general election in 1993 that was seen as unwinnable. An outspoken republican, he retired from parliament following the election defeat of 1996. In 1997 he declined the award of Companion to the Order of Australia – the first living former prime minister not to accept the honour. He continues to speak on political issues.

Keating, Tom (1918–84) Art restorer and celebrated forger of paintings, born in London, UK. The scandal about his fakes of the works of the great masters broke in 1976, when an art expert suggested that a work by Samuel Palmer, which sold at an auction for £9400, was not genuine. Keating admitted that a series of nine pictures, bearing imitations of Samuel Palmer's signature, were in fact drawn by himself, and estimated that there were some 2500 of his fakes in circulation. In 1979 he was put on trial at the Old Bailey for forgery, but charges were eventually dropped because of his deteriorating health. Keating became a popular public celebrity, making a television series, and writing (with Geraldine and Frank Norman) a book, *The Fake's Progress*.

Keaton, Buster, popular name of **Joseph Francis Keaton** (1895–1966) Film comedian, born in Piqua, Kansas, USA. He joined his parents' vaudeville act 'The Three Keatons' at the age of 3, developing great acrobatic skill. In 1917 he went to Hollywood, where he made his film debut. Renowned for his inimitable deadpan expression, he starred in and directed such silent classics as *Our Hospitality* (1923), *The Navigator* (1924), and *The General* (1927). His reputation went into eclipse with the advent of talking films until the 1950s, when many of his silent masterpieces were re-released. He also began to appear in character roles in several films, such as *Sunset Boulevard* (1950) and *Limelight* (1952). He received a special Academy Award in 1959.

Keaton, Diane [**kee**ton] (1946–) Film actress and director, born in Los Angeles, California, USA. She played opposite Woody Allen in the Broadway production of *Play It Again, Sam* (1969), then went on to star in several of his films, such as *Annie Hall* (1977, Oscar) *Manhattan* (1979), and *Manhattan Murder Mystery* (1993). Other films include *The Godfather* (1972), *Reds* (1981), *Baby Boom* (1987), *First Wives Club* (1996), *Marvin's Room* (1996, Oscar nomination), and *Something's Gotta Give* (2003). Her first major film as a director was *Unstrung Heroes* (1995), and she directed and acted in *Hanging Up* (2000).

Keaton, Michael (1951–) Actor, born in Caraopolis, Pennsylvania, USA. He started with Chicago's Second City improvisational group, then went to Los Angeles and appeared in a few film comedies. His breakthrough came with the film *Mr Mom* (1983), and five years later, after *Beetlejuice* (1988) and *Clean and Sober* (1988), he was named Best Actor by national film critics. Other films include *Batman* (1989), *Batman Returns* (1992), *Much Ado About Nothing* (1993), *Multiplicity* (1996), *Jack Frost* (1998), and *A Shot at Glory* (2000).

Keats, John (1795–1821) Poet, born in London, UK. Educated at Enfield, he was apprenticed to a surgeon and became a dresser at Guy's Hospital, London. Leigh Hunt introduced him to other young Romantics, including Shelley, and published his first sonnets in the *Examiner* (1816). His first book of poems was published in 1817. His long mythological poem *Endymion* (1818) was attacked by the critics as the writing of an ignorant apothecary, but he was nonetheless able to write *Lamia and Other Poems* (1820), a landmark in English poetry, which contains 'The Eve of St Agnes' and 'Lamia', and his major odes. Seriously ill with tuberculosis, he sailed for Italy, and died in Rome. He was buried in the Protestant cemetery in Rome, where his friend David Severn designed a monument for him. His *Letters* (1848) are among the most celebrated in the language, and he is regarded as one of the principal figures of the Romantic movement.

Keble, John [**kee**bl] (1792–1866) Anglican clergyman and poet, born in Fairford, Gloucestershire, SWC England, UK. He studied at Oxford, was ordained in 1816, and became a college tutor (1818–23) and professor of poetry (1831–41). In 1827 his book of poems on the liturgical calendar, *The Christian Year*, was widely circulated. His sermon on 'National apostasy' (1833) began the Oxford Movement, encouraging a return to High Church ideals, and his circle issued the 90 *Tracts for the Times*. In 1835 he moved to the Hampshire living of Hursely, where he remained until his death. Keble College, Oxford, was erected in his memory.

Kebnekaise [**keb**nekiysuh] 67°55N 18°35E. Peak in the Kjölen Mts, NW Sweden; height 2111 m/6926 ft; highest peak in Sweden; several glaciers.

keck *cow parsley; hogweed*

Kedah [**kay**dah] pop (2000e) 1 758 000; area 9425 sq km/ 3638 sq mi. State in NW Peninsular Malaysia; bounded E by Thailand and W by the Strait of Malacca; governed by Thailand from early 19th-c until 1909, when it came under British rule; capital, Alor Setar; rice, rubber, tin, tungsten.

Keeler, Christine (1942–) Former model and showgirl, raised in Wraysbury, Windsor and Maidenhead, S England, UK. She was involved in an affair with a Soviet naval attaché, Ivanov, and the Conservative cabinet minister, John Profumo, which led to Profumo's resignation from politics (1963), the prosecution of her patron Stephen Ward (d.1963) for living off the immoral earnings of Keeler and Mandy Rice Davies, and Ward's eventual suicide. Keeler served a prison sentence for related offences. In the late 1980s, her autobiography, and the film *Scandal* (1989), in which she collaborated, revived interest in the events and raised doubts about the validity of the charges made against her and Ward.

Keeling Islands *Cocos Islands*

Keelung *Jilong*

keeshond [**kays**hond] A small, sturdy spitz breed of dog from The Netherlands; grey with dark tinges; head dark with pale rings around eyes; coat very thick, especially around neck; tail tightly curled; formerly used as a guard dog, especially on barges.

kefir [**ke**feer] A fermented milk originating in the Caucasus. Traditionally made from camel's milk, it is now made from cow's milk, and can be mild, medium, or strong, depending on the degree of fermentation.

Keflavik [**kef**lavik, **kye**plaveek] 64°01N 22°35W, pop (2000e) 8100. Fishing port in Suðurland region, SW Iceland; 48 km/ 30 mi SW of Reykjavík; important trade centre since the 16th-c; first modern freezing plant started in 1929; airport.

Keillor, Garrison [**kee**ler], pseudonym of **Gary Edward Keillor** (1942–) Humorous writer and radio performer, born in Anoka, Minnesota, USA. He studied at Minnesota University, became a radio announcer, then began writing for *The New Yorker*. In 1974 he first hosted the live radio show, 'A Prairie Home Companion', delivering a weekly monologue set in the quiet, fictional mid-western town of Lake Wobegon, 'where all the women are strong, all the men are good looking, and all the children are above average'. When the show closed in 1987 he was celebrated for his wry, deliberate, hypnotic storytelling. His books include *Happy To Be Here* (1981), the best-selling *Lake Wobegon Days* (1985), *Leaving Home* (1987), *We Are Still Married* (1989), and *WLT: A Radio Romance* (1992). In 1999 appeared *Me: by Jimmy (Big Boy) Valente*.

Keitel, Wilhelm [**kiy**tl] (1882–1946) German field marshal, born in Helmscherode, C Germany. He joined the army in 1901, and became an artillery staff officer in World War 1. An ardent Nazi, he was made chief of the Supreme Command of the Armed Forces (1938). In 1940 he signed the Compiègne armistice with France, and in 1945 was one of the German signatories of surrender in Berlin. He was convicted of war crimes at Nuremberg, and executed.

Kékes, Mount [**kay**kesh] Mountain in N Hungary; highest peak in the Matra Mts and in Hungary, rising to 1014 m/3327 ft.

Kekulé von Stradonitz, (Friedrich) August [**kay**kuhlay fon sh**tra**donits] (1829–1896) Chemist, born in Darmstadt, WC Germany. He studied at Giessen and Paris, where he met and was influenced by the work of Charles Gerhardt (1816–56). He became professor at Ghent (1858) and at Bonn (1865), and made a major contribution to organic chemistry by developing structural theories, in particular the cyclic structure of benzene.

Kelantan [**ke**lantan] pop (2000e) 1 519 000; area 14 796 sq km/ 5711 sq mi. State in NE Peninsular Malaysia; bounded N by Thailand and E by the South China Sea; drained by the R Kelantan and its tributaries; governed by Thailand from early 19th-c until 1909, when it came under British rule; capital, Kota Baharu; rice, rubber, copra, tin.

Keldysh, Mstislav (Vsevoldvich) (1911–78) Mathematician and space programme leader, born in Riga, Latvia. He studied at Moscow, and conducted aeronautical research at Zhukovskii Aero-Hydrodynamics Institute (from 1934) and at Steklow Mathematics Institute (from 1939). He was a leading figure in the development of the theory of rocketry and in the emergence of the USSR in space exploration.

Keller, Helen (Adams) (1880–1968) Writer and lecturer, born in Tuscumbia, Alabama, USA. She became blind and deaf at 19 months, and was taught to speak, read, and write when she was seven years old by Anne Mansfield Sullivan (later Mrs Macy), known as 'Teacher' to Keller and 'the Miracle Worker' among the general public. Sullivan remained Keller's interpreter and companion until her death in 1936. Keller received communications by lipreading, braille, and finger-spelling using a manual alphabet, and she expressed herself through finger-spelling, typewriting, and speech. She graduated from Radcliffe College (1904), and as an adult lectured and published widely on her own experiences and on political, social, and educational issues. Her autobiography, *The Story of My Life* (1902), was dramatized by William Gibson in *The Miracle Worker* (1959, Pulitzer, filmed 1962).

Kelley, Florence (1859–1932) Feminist and social reformer, born in Philadelphia, Pennsylvania, USA. She studied at Cornell, and Zürich where she translated Engels and was converted to socialism, and in 1891 joined Jane Addams's Hull House Settlement in Chicago. She became the first woman factory inspector in Illinois, successfully fighting to reduce working hours and improve methods and conditions of production. Gaining a law degree from Northwestern University (1895), she moved to New York City in 1899, becoming general secretary of the National Consumers' League, and in 1910 was one of the founders of the National Association for the Advancement of Colored People. She helped establish the Women's International League for Peace and Freedom (1919).

Kellogg–Briand Pact A proposal made in 1927 by French foreign minister Aristide Briand (1862–1932) to US secretary of state Frank B Kellogg (1856–1937) that the two countries should sign a pact renouncing war as an instrument of national policy. At Kellogg's suggestion, a Paris conference in 1928 formally condemned recourse to war, and the pact was subsequently signed by 65 states (the **Pact of Paris**). However, there was no machinery for punishing aggressors.

Kellow, Kathleen *Hibbert, Eleanor*

Kells *Ceanannus Mór*

Kelly, David (Christopher) (1944–2003) British microbiologist and consultant on arms control, born in the Rhondda Valley, S Wales, UK. He studied at Oxford, and specialized in biological pesticides, joining the chemical research centre at Porton Down, Wiltshire, where he became head of microbiology (1984). He was the Ministry of Defence's chief scientific officer and senior adviser to the proliferation and arms control secretariat, and was also senior adviser on biological warfare for the UN in Iraq (1994–9). In 2003 he became a key figure in the row between the government and the BBC over claims that Downing Street 'sexed up' a dossier on Iraq's weapons capability. Having been identified by the press, he became the centre of media attention, and he committed suicide soon after. The circumstances surrounding his death became the subject of an enquiry chaired by Lord Hutton later that year. The Hutton Report (Jan 2004) criticised the BBC, said that Dr Kelly had broken the rules governing civil servants talking to journalists, and attached no blame to the government for the naming of Dr Kelly.

Kelly, Gene, popular name of **Eugene Curran Kelly** (1912–96) Modern dancer and actor, born in Pittsburgh, Pennsylvania, USA. A dance instructor with a degree in economics from the University of Pittsburgh, he travelled to New York City, and found employment in the chorus of *Leave it to Me* (1938). His stage success in *Pal Joey* (1939) led to a Hollywood debut in *For Me and My Girl* (1942), followed by a long series of musicals in which he was often co-director and choreographer, such as *An American in Paris* (1951) and *Singin' in the Rain* (1952). In 1951 he received a special Academy Award, and from the 1960s worked mostly as a director, notably of *Hello, Dolly!* (1969). He received an American Film Institute Life Achievement Award in 1985.

Kelly, Grace (Patricia), married name **Grimaldi, Princess Grace of Monaco** (1929–82) Film actress and princess, born in Philadelphia, Pennsylvania, USA. After studying at the American Academy of Dramatic Art, she acted in television and on Broadway, and made her film debut in 1951. Her short but highly successful film career as a coolly elegant beauty included such classics as the Western *High Noon* (1952), *Rear Window* (1954), *The Country Girl* (1954, Oscar), *To Catch a Thief* (1955), and *High Society* (1956). In 1956 she married Prince Rainier III of Monaco, and retired from the screen. She was killed in a car accident.

Kelly, Jude, professional name of **Judith Pamela Kelly** (1954–) Theatre director, born in Liverpool, NW England, UK. After graduating from Birmingham University in 1975 she worked as an actress with Michael Bogdanov's Leicester Phoenix Theatre. She began her directing career in 1976 when she founded the Solent People's Theatre, later becoming artistic director of the Battersea Arts Centre, assistant director at the Royal Shakespeare Company (1986), and artistic director of the West Yorkshire Playhouse (1988–2002). She then set up METAL in West Hampstead, London, a centre for research and experiment in the arts.

Kelly, Ned, popular name of **Edward Kelly** (1855–80) Outlaw, born in Beveridge, Victoria, SE Australia. After shooting a policeman who was attempting to arrest his brother, Dan, he fled to the outback, where he was joined by his brother and two others, and formed the Kelly gang. They carried out a series of daring robberies (1878–80) which, coupled with Ned's home-made armour, made them into legendary figures. After a siege at Glenrowan township, he was arrested, taken to Melbourne, and hanged.

Kelman, James (1946–) Novelist and short-story writer, born in Glasgow, W Scotland, UK. He published his first book of short stories in 1983, and his first novel, *The Busconductor Hines*, in 1984. Regarded as one of the major talents in contemporary Scottish fiction, he won the Booker Prize in 1994 for *How Late It Was, How Late*. Later works include *The Good Times: Stories* (1998), a novel *Translated Accounts* (2001), and collected essays *And the Judges Said...* (2002).

keloid [keeloyd] The overgrowth of scar tissue (fibroblasts and collagen) in response to a surgical or accidental wound of the skin. It appears as a raised, warm, reddened, tender lump along the line of the wound. It is more common in people of African descent, and is sometimes induced deliberately as a form of body art.

kelp A large brown seaweed common in lower inter-tidal and sub-tidal zones in colder seas; life-cycle involves alternation between a filamentous form (*gametophyte*) and a large robust form (*sporophyte*) differentiated into a holdfast, narrow stalk (*stipe*) and a flattened blade. (Division: Phaeophyceae. Order: Laminariales.)

kelpie A breed of dog developed in Australia as a sheepdog from imported Scottish sheepdogs; medium size with thick, coarse coat and bushy tail; muzzle pointed; ears erect; also called **Australian kelpie**.

Kelvin (of Largs), William Thomson, 1st Baron (1824–1907) Mathematician and physicist, born in Belfast, NE Northern Ireland, UK. He studied at Glasgow and Cambridge, and became professor of natural philosophy at Glasgow (1846). He designed several kinds of electrometer, and his sounding apparatus and compass were widely adopted. In pure science, he carried out fundamental research into thermodynamics, helping to develop the law of the conservation of energy, and the absolute temperature scale (now given in kelvin). He also presented the dynamical theory of heat, developed theorems for the mathematical analysis of electricity and magnetism, and investigated hydrodynamics, particularly wave-motion and vortex-motion. He was created a peer in 1892.

kelvin Base SI unit of thermodynamic temperature; symbol *K*; defined as the fraction 1/273·16 of the thermodynamic temperature of the triple point of water; named after Lord Kelvin; always written *K*, not °*K*.

Kemble The name of a famous British acting family of the 18th-c. The founding member was **Roger** (1721–1802), a travelling manager, whose children were **John Philip** (1757–1823), **Stephen** (1758–1822), **Charles** (1775–1854), and **Sarah** (1775–1831). Charles' daughter, **Frances Ann**, known as **Fanny** (1809–93), became one of the leading actresses of the 19th-c.

Kemi, River [kemee], Finn **Kemijoki**, Swed **Kemiä** River in Lappi province, N Finland, rising near the Russian border; flows S then W to meet the Gulf of Bothnia at Kemi; length 480 km/ 300 mi; longest river in Finland.

Kempe, Margery [kemp], *née* **Brunham** (c.1373–c.1440) Writer of one of the earliest autobiographies in English, the daughter of a Mayor of Lynn. She was the wife of a burgess in Lynn and the mother of 14 children. After a period of insanity she experienced a conversion, and undertook numerous pilgrimages. Between 1432 and 1436 she dictated her spiritual autobiography, *The Book of Margery Kempe*, which recounts her persecution by devils and men, repeated accusations of Lollardism, and her journeys to Jerusalem, Rome, and Germany. Her book is valuable as a source of contemporary expression.

Kempe, Rudolf [kempuh] (1910–76) Conductor, born near Dresden, E Germany. He studied at the Musikhochschule in Dresden, and played the oboe in orchestras at Dortmund and Leipzig before making his debut as a conductor in 1935. He then worked at Leipzig and, after the war, at Dresden and Munich. He later appeared frequently at Covent Garden, London, and was principal conductor of the Royal Philharmonic Orchestra (1961–75), then of the BBC Symphony Orchestra until his death.

Kempe, William [kemp] (c.1550–c.1603) Comic actor and dancer, who was famous in the Elizabethan theatre, and a member of the Lord Chamberlain's Men at the time they decided to build the Globe theatre (1598–9). In 1594 he was summoned, together with Richard Burbage and William Shakespeare, to act before Queen Elizabeth at Greenwich. The original Dogberry in *Much Ado About Nothing*, he spent the latter part of his life abroad. For some unknown reason he left London and morris-danced his way to Norwich, publishing an account of his feat in *Nine Daies Wonder* (1600).

Kempis, Thomas à [kempis], originally **Thomas Hemerken** (1379–1471) Religious writer, whose name derives from his birthplace, Kempen, in W Germany. He entered the Augustinian convent of Agnietenberg near Zwolle (1400), was ordained in 1413, chosen sub-prior in 1429, and died as superior. His many writings include the influential devotional work *Imitatio Christi* (c.1415–24, The Imitation of Christ).

Kenai bear *brown bear*

kendo The Japanese martial art of sword fighting, now practised with *shiani*, or bamboo swords. The earliest reference to the art is in AD 789. The object is to land two scoring blows on the opponent's target area. **Kendokas** (participants) wear traditional dress of the Samurai period, including face-masks and aprons, and are graded according to ability from 6th to 1st *Kyu*, and then from 1st to 10th *Dan*.

Kendrew, Sir John (Cowdery) (1917–97) Biochemist, born in Oxford, Oxfordshire, SC England, UK. He studied at Bristol and Cambridge, where he became a fellow (1947–75), and carried out research into the chemistry of blood. He was co-founder (with Max Perutz) and deputy chairman of the Medical Research Council unit for molecular biology at Cambridge (1946–75). He discovered the structure of the muscle protein myoglobin (1957), and was awarded the 1962 Nobel Prize for Chemistry jointly with Perutz. He was director of the European Molecular Biology Laboratory at Heidelberg (1975–82), and president of St John's College, Oxford (1981–7). He was knighted in 1974.

Keneally, Thomas (Michael) [keneelee] (1935–) Writer, born in Kempsey, New South Wales, SE Australia. Educated at Strathfield, Sydney, he studied for the priesthood, but left before ordination, becoming a teacher and then a full-time writer. His novels are frequently historical, and include *Gossip from the Forest* (1975), about the armistice negotiations in 1918, and *Schindler's Ark* (1982, Booker, filmed as *Schindler's List* in 1993 by Steven Spielberg), the story of an industrialist who saved the lives of Polish Jews during the early 1940s. He is a prolific writer whose later novels include *Towards Asmara* (1989), *Flying Hero Class* (1991), *A River Town* (1995), *The Great Shame* (1999), and *The Tyrant's Novel* (2003). *Memoirs from a Young Republic* (1993) expresses his passionate support for the Australian republican cause.

Kennedy, A(lison) L(ouise) (1965–) Novelist and short-story writer, born in Dundee, E Scotland, UK. She studied at Warwick University. Regarded as an important and original Scottish voice, her first collection of short stories was the prize-winning *Night Geometry and the Garscadden Trains* (1990). Her first novel was *Looking for the Posssible Dance* (1994, Somerset Maugham Award), followed by *So I Am Glad* (1995, Encore Award) and *Everything You Need* (1999). Her non-fiction works include *The Life and Death of Colonel Blimp – BFI Film Classics* (1997) and *On Bullfighting* (2000).

Kennedy, Charles (1959 –) British politician, born in Inverness, Highland, N Scotland, UK. He studied at the universities of Glasgow and Indiana, USA, then worked as a journalist before being elected Social Democratic MP for Ross, Cromarty and Skye (1983–) and becoming the youngest MP in the Commons. A supporter of merger with the Liberal Party, he was elected president of the new Liberal Democrat Party in 1990, and leader upon Paddy Ashdown's resignation in 1999.

Kennedy, Edward M(oore) (1932–) US politician, born in Brookline, Massachusetts, USA, the youngest son of Joseph Kennedy. He studied at Harvard and at Virginia University Law School, was called to the bar in 1959, and elected a Democratic senator for his brother John F Kennedy's Massachusetts seat in 1962. In 1969 he became the youngest-ever majority whip in the US Senate, but his involvement the same year in a car accident at Chappaquidick in which a woman companion (Mary Jo Kopechne) was drowned, dogged his subsequent political career, and caused his withdrawal as a presidential candidate in 1979.

Kennedy, Jackie *Onassis, Jacqueline Kennedy*

Kennedy, John F(itzgerald), also known as **JFK** (1917–63) US statesman and 35th president (1961–3), born in Brookline, Massachusetts, USA, son of Joseph Kennedy. He studied at Harvard, and served as a torpedo boat commander in the Pacific in World War 2. His *Profiles in Courage* (1956) won the Pulitzer Prize. Elected Democratic representative (1947) and senator (1952) for Massachusetts, in 1960 he became the first Catholic, and the youngest person, to be elected president. His 'new frontier' in social legislation involved a federal desegregation policy in schools and universities, along with Civil Rights reform. He displayed firmness and moderation in foreign policy. In October 1962, at the risk of nuclear war, he induced the Soviet Union to withdraw its missiles from Cuba, and achieved a partial nuclear test ban treaty with the Soviet Union in 1963. On 22 November, he was assassinated by rifle fire while being driven in an open car with his wife Jackie through Dallas, TX. The alleged assassin, Lee Harvey Oswald, was himself shot and killed at point-blank range by Jack Ruby two days later, while under heavy police escort on a jail transfer.

Kennedy, Joseph P(atrick) (1888–1969) Multimillionaire businessman, born in Boston, Massachusetts, USA, the father of John F, Robert, and Edward Kennedy. The grandson of an Irish Catholic immigrant, he studied at Harvard, then made a large fortune in the 1920s. During the 1930s he was a strong supporter of Roosevelt and the 'New Deal', and became ambassador to Britain (1938–40). After World War 2 he concentrated on fulfilling his ambitions of a political dynasty through his sons. He had married in 1914 Rose Fitzgerald, daughter of a local politician, John F Fitzgerald, also of Irish immigrant descent. They had nine children, at whose political disposal he placed his fortune. The eldest son, **Joseph Patrick** (1915–44), was killed in a flying accident; the others achieved international political fame.

Kennedy, Nigel (Paul), professional name (from 1997) **Kennedy** (1956–) British violinist. He studied at the Yehudi Menuhin School, London, and the Juilliard School, New York City. He made his debut as a concert soloist in 1977, and has since played with many of the world's major orchestras, and alongside jazz violinist Stéphane Grappelli. He is noted for his unconventional style of dress, as well as for his remarkable playing ability. His recording of Vivaldi's *Four Seasons* held the Number 1 spot in the UK Classical Chart for over a year (1989–90).

Kennedy, Robert F(rancis) (1925–68) US politician, born in Brookline, Massachusetts, USA, the third son of Joseph Kennedy. He studied at Harvard and at Virginia University Law School, served at sea (1944–6) in World War 2, was admitted to the bar (1951), and served on the Senate Select Committee on Improper Activities (1957–9), when he prosecuted several top union leaders. An efficient manager of his brother John F Kennedy's presidential campaign, he was an energetic attorney general (1961–4), notable in his dealings with civil rights problems. He became senator for New York in 1965. After winning the Californian Democratic presidential primary election, he was shot at a hotel in Los Angeles. His assassin, Sirhan Sirhan, a 24-year-old Jordanian-born immigrant, was sentenced to the gas chamber in 1969, but was not executed.

Kennedy Space Center, John F US space centre situated on Merrit I and Cape Canaveral (known as Cape Kennedy 1963–73) off the E coast of Florida, USA. Since the late 1950s Cape Canaveral has been used as the principal launch site for the US space programme.

kennel cough An infection of the upper respiratory tract in dogs, resulting in a characteristic, harsh, non-productive cough. The disease is highly infectious and especially prevalent in boarding kennels, dog homes/pounds, and similar concentrations of unrelated animals during the summer months. The condition is usually self-limiting, though treatment is usually necessary to avoid complications. Bacteria (*Bordetella bronchiseptica*) and various viruses (of the Herpes-, Adeno-, and Parainfluenza groups) are the main agents involved. Modern vaccines give a reasonable measure of protection. Evidence of up-to-date vaccination is usually required by boarding establishments before accepting dogs at risk.

Kennelly, Arthur E(dwin) [**ken**elee] (1861–1939) Engineer, born in Mumbai (Bombay), W India. He went to the USA in 1887, and worked as assistant to Edison. In 1894 he founded a consultancy firm in Philadelphia, where he developed new mathematical analyses of electrical circuits, and in 1902 discovered the ionized layer in the atmosphere, sometimes named after him.

Kenneth I, known as **Kenneth MacAlpin** (?–858) King of the Scots of Dal Riata (from 841) and King of the Picts (from c.843). He combined the territories of both peoples in a united kingdom of Scotia (Scotland N of the Forth–Clyde line).

Kensington and Chelsea 51°30N 0°12W, pop (2001e) 158 900. Borough of C Greater London, UK; N of R Thames; Kensington granted the designation 'Royal Borough' by Edward VII in 1901; railway; Kensington Palace, Kensington Gardens, Chelsea Royal Hospital, Victoria and Albert Museum, Science Museum, British Museum (Natural History); Nottingham House (birthplace of Queen Victoria); Crufts dog show (Feb), Chelsea antiques fair (Mar, Sep), Ideal Home Exhibition (Mar), Chelsea Flower Show (May), Royal Tournament (Jul), Smithfield agricultural show (Dec).

Kent pop (2001e) 1 329 700; area 3730 sq km/1440 sq mi. County in SE England, UK; bounded N by the R Thames estuary and E by the English Channel; rises to 251 m/823 ft in the North Downs; The Weald in the SW; drained by Thames, Medway, and Stour Rivers; high chalk cliffs, especially at Dover; county town, Maidstone; principal cross-Channel ports, Dover, Folkestone, Ramsgate, Sheerness; Medway a unitary authority from 1998; tourism, fruit and hops ('the Garden of England'), cattle and sheep, grain, vegetables, cement, paper, shipbuilding, fishing, electronics, pharmaceuticals, oil.

Kent, Edward (George Nicholas Paul Patrick), Duke of (1935–) British prince, the eldest son of **George, Duke of Kent**. He was commissioned in the army in 1955, and in 1961 married **Katharine Worsley** (1933–). He retired from the army in 1976. They have three children: **George Philip Nicholas Windsor, the Earl of St Andrews** (1962–), **Helen Marina Lucy, Lady Helen Windsor** (1964–), and **Nicholas Charles Edward Jonathan, Lord Nicholas Windsor** (1970–). George, Earl of St Andrews married **Sylvana Tomaselli** (1957–) and they have one son, **Edward, Lord Downpatrick** (1988–), and two daughters, **Marina Charlotte Windsor** (1992–) and **Amelia Windsor** (1995–). Lady Helen Windsor married Timothy Taylor to become Lady Helen Taylor; they have two sons, **Columbus George Donald Taylor** (1994–) and **Cassius Edward Taylor** (1996–), and a daughter, **Eloise** (2003–).

Kent, Prince Michael of (1942–) British prince, the younger brother of Edward, Duke of Kent. He married in 1978 **Baroness Marie-Christine Von Reibniz**, and their children are **Frederick Michael George David Louis, Lord Frederick Windsor** (1979–) and **Gabriella Marina Alexandra Ophelia, Lady Gabriella (Ella) Windsor** (1981–).

Kent, William (1685–1748) Painter, landscape gardener, and architect, born in Bridlington, East Riding of Yorkshire, NE England, UK. He studied in Rome, and became the principal exponent of the Palladian style of architecture in England. His buildings include the Horse Guards block in Whitehall, the Royal Mews in Trafalgar Square and the Treasury Buildings. An example of his gardens is at Stowe House in Buckinghamshire, and his artistry is visible in the Gothic screens at Westminster Hall and Gloucester Cathedral, and the interiors of Burlington House and Chiswick House in London.

Kentucky pop (2000e) 4 041 800; area 104 658 sq km/ 40 410 sq mi. State in EC USA, divided into 120 counties; the 'Bluegrass State'; part of the territory ceded by the French (1763); explored by Daniel Boone from 1769; the first permanent British settlement at Boonesborough, 1775; included in US territory by the Treaty of Paris, 1783; originally part of Virginia; admitted to the Union as the 15th state, 1792; capital, Frankfort; other chief cities, Louisville and Lexington; rivers include the Mississippi (part of the SW border), Ohio (part of the NW and N border), Tennessee, Cumberland, Kentucky, and Big Sandy with its tributary, the Tug Fork (part of the E border); Cumberland Mts in the SE; highest point Mt Black (1263 m/4144 ft); the C plain is known as Bluegrass country; to the W and E are rough uplands with vast coal reserves; in the SW corner are floodplains bounded by the Ohio, Mississippi, and Tennessee Rivers; famous for the distilling of bourbon whiskey (still the country's leading producer), and for its thoroughbred racehorses; tobacco, cattle, dairy produce, soybeans; machinery, electrical equipment, processed foods, chemicals, fabricated metals; the nation's leading coal producer; petroleum, natural gas; Mammoth Cave National Park; Kentucky Derby held annually at Louisville.

Kentucky and Virginia Resolutions (1798) Declarations by two state legislatures that the Alien and Sedition laws violated the US Constitution. They were written by Thomas Jefferson (Kentucky) and James Madison (Virginia).

Kenya, Mount 0°10S 37°18E. Extinct volcano cone in C Kenya; 112 km/70 mi NNE of Nairobi; second highest mountain in Africa; comprises three peaks of Batian (5199 m/17 057 ft), Nelion (5188 m/17 021 ft), and Lenana (4985 m/16 355 ft); many lakes and glaciers; summit of Kilimanjaro often visible 323 km/ 200 mi away, one of the longest confirmed lines of sight on Earth; national park of 588 sq km/227 sq mi established in 1949, a world heritage site.

Kenya *p.835*

Kenya African National Union (KANU) The party which led Kenya to independence in 1963. It was founded in 1960 as a successor to the Kikuyu Central Association of 1929 and the

Kenya

[kenya], formerly [keenya], official name **Republic of Kenya**
Local name Kenya
Timezone GMT +3
Area 580 367 km^2/224 081 sq mi
Population total (2002e) 31 139 000
Status Republic
Date of independence 1963
Capital Nairobi
Languages English and Swahili (official), with many local languages spoken
Ethnic groups Kikuyu (21%), Luhya (13%), Luo (11%), Kamba (11%), Kalejin (6%) Kisii (6%), Meru (6%)
Religions Christian (66%) (Roman Catholic 28%, Protestant 38%), local beliefs (26%), Muslim (6%)
Physical features Crossed by the Equator; SW plateau rises to 600–3000 m/2000–10 000 ft, includes Mt Kenya, 5200 m/ 17 058 ft; Great Rift Valley (W) runs N–S; dry, arid semi-desert in the N, generally under 600 m/2000 ft; rivers include Tana and Athi; L Turkana in NW.
Climate Tropical climate on coast, with high temperatures and humidity; average annual temperature 18°C (Jan), 16°C (Jul) in Nairobi; average annual rainfall 958 mm/38 in; national disaster declared (May 2003) following prolonged heavy rains and flooding, particularly in the W.
Currency 1 Kenyan shilling (KSh) = 100 cents
Economy Agriculture (accounts for c.35% of national income); coffee, tea, cashew nuts, rice, wheat, maize, sugar cane; textiles, chemicals, cement, oil refining, tobacco, rubber; reserves of soda ash, salt, limestone, lead, gemstones, silver, gold; 14 national parks attract large numbers of tourists.
GDP (2002e) $32·89 bn, per capita $1100
Human Development Index (2002) 0·513
History Very early fossil hominids found in the region by anthropologists; coast settled by Arabs, 7th-c; Portuguese control, 16th–17th-c; British control as East African Protectorate, 1895; British colony, 1920; independence movement led to Mau Mau rebellion, 1952–60; independence within the Commonwealth, 1963; declared Republic of Kenya, 1964; first leader, Jomo Kenyatta; multi-party elections, 1992, gave Arap Moi a fourth term of office; result condemned by opposition parties; Moi defeated (Dec 2002) after 24 years rule; governed by a president elected for a 5-year term, with a unicameral National Assembly of 224 members; all UK flights temporarily suspended (May–Jul 2003) after Kenyan security alert.
Head of State/Government
1978–2003 Daniel Arap Moi
2003– Mwai Kibaki

Kenya African Union of 1947. The **Kenya African Democratic Union** (KADU) was a rival body which represented mainly non-Kikuyu groups. KANU won the first Kenyan election, with President Kenyatta becoming the leader of independent Kenya, although he tried to bring KADU into a coalition.

Kenyatta, Jomo [kenyata], originally **Kamau Ngengi** (c.1889–1978) Kenyan statesman and president (1964–78), born in Mitumi, Kenya. Educated at a Scots mission school, he studied at London, and became president of the Pan-African Federation. In the late 1940s his Kenya African Union advocated total independence in a unitary state. He was charged with leading the Mau Mau terrorist organization (a charge he denied), and was sentenced to seven years' hard labour in 1952, then exiled. In 1960, while still in detention, he was elected president of the new Kenya African National Union Party. He became an MP in 1961, prime minister in 1963, and President of the Republic of Kenya in 1964. He adopted moderate social and economic policies, and succeeded in conciliating many members of the Kenyan white community.

Kenzo, in full **Kenzo Takada** (1940–) Fashion designer, born in Kyoto, C Japan. After studying art and graduating in Japan, he worked there for a time, but produced freelance collections in Paris from 1964. He started a shop called Jungle Jap in 1970, and is known for his innovative ideas and use of traditional designs. He creates clothes with both oriental and Western influences, and is a trendsetter in the field of knitwear.

Keoladeo National park in Rajasthan, India, also known as **Bharatpur**; area 29 sq km/11 sq mi provides breeding grounds for thousands of migrating birds from Siberia and China, including herons, storks, and cranes; a world heritage site.

Kepler, Johannes (1571–1630) Astronomer, born in Weil-der-Stadt, SW Germany. He studied at Tübingen, and in 1593 was appointed professor of mathematics at Graz. In c.1596 he commenced a correspondence with Tycho Brahe, who was then in Prague, and from 1600–1 worked with him, showing that planetary motions were far simpler than had been imagined. He announced his first and second laws of planetary motion in *Astronomia nova* (1609, New Astronomy), which formed the groundwork of Isaac Newton's discoveries. His third law was promulgated in *Harmonice mundi* (1619, Harmony of the World). He succeeded Brahe as court astronomer to Emperor Rudolf II, and in 1628 became astrologer to Albrecht von Wallenstein at Zagan in Silesia.

Kepler's laws of planetary motion Fundamental laws deduced by Kepler from Tycho Brahe's data, which clarified the spatial organization of the solar system. (1) Each planet travels an elliptical orbit with the Sun at one focus. (2) For a given planet radius, the vector to the Sun sweeps equal areas in equal times. (3) For any two planets, the squares of the periods are proportional to the cubes of the distances from the Sun. Newton derived these from first principles using gravitational theory.

Kerala [kerala] pop (2001e) 31 838 600; area 39 000 sq km/ 15 000 sq mi. State in S India, bounded W along the Malabar coast by the Arabian Sea; capital, Trivandrum; governed by a 140-member unicameral legislature; crossed by several rivers; created out of the former state of Travancore–Cochin under the 1956 States Reorganization Act; rice, tapioca, coconut, oilseeds, sugar cane, pepper, rubber, tea, coffee; teak, sandalwood, ebony, blackwood; textiles, ceramics, fertilizer, chemicals, glass, electrical goods, paper; ivory carving, weaving, copper and brass ware, furniture.

keratin [keratin] A tough, fibrous protein synthesized by the outer layer of the skin (*epidermis*) of vertebrates. It is the major component of hair, nails, claws, horns, feathers, scales, and the dead outer layers of cells of skin.

keratosis [keratohsis] Small dark scaly lesions on exposed parts of the skin, commonly found in individuals over 60 years of age and in younger white-skinned residents in sunny climates. A minority become malignant tumours (skin cancer).

Kerensky, Alexander Fyodorovich [kerenskee] (1881–1970) Russian Socialist, born in Simbirsk, W Russia. He studied law in St Petersburg, and took a leading part in the 1917 revolution, becoming minister of justice (Mar), minister of war (May), and premier (Jul) in the provisional government. Being on the right wing of Socialism, Kerensky suppressed the Bolshevik party whose leader, Lenin, escaped to Finland; Trotsky was arrested. Kerensky could not prevent economic and military deterioration, however, enabling renewed disruption by the Bolsheviks. He crushed the military revolt (Aug) led by Kornilov, the Russian army commander, but was deposed (Oct) by the Bolsheviks, and fled to France. In 1940 he went to Australia, and in 1946 to the USA, and wrote several books on the Russian revolution.

Kérkira *Corfu*

Kerkuane Carthagian town in N Tunisia, founded in the 5th-c BC and abandoned c.140 BC after the destruction of Carthage; a world heritage site. It was a small settlement of identical houses, each with its own private bath. A necropolis was discovered nearby in 1968.

kermes [kermiz] A scale insect that feeds mainly on oaks; some species produce galls; lays up to 5000 eggs in protected brood chambers; c.70 species in the N hemisphere. A red dye can be extracted from dried bodies of the insect. (Order: Homoptera. Family: Kermesidae.)

Kermode, Sir (John) Frank [kermohd] (1919–) Literary critic, born in the Isle of Man, UK. He studied at Liverpool University, served in the navy during World War 2, then taught at Durham and Reading universities, before holding professorial posts at Manchester (1958–65), Bristol (1965–7), University College London (1967–74), and Cambridge (1974–82), where he was a fellow of King's College (to 1987). His works (which negotiate the boundaries of literary scholarship, theory, and the reader's experience) include *Romantic Image* (1957), *The Sense of an Ending* (1967), *Forms of Attention* (1985), *Uses of Error* (1991), and *Shakespeare's Language* (2000). He was knighted in 1991.

Kern, Jerome (David) (1885–1945) Songwriter and composer, born in New York City, USA. After studying at the New York College of Music, and briefly in London and Heidelberg, he worked as a rehearsal pianist. His first complete score for a musical play, *The Red Petticoat*, was in 1912, followed by a string of successful Broadway shows. His greatest musical was *Show Boat* (1928, book and lyrics by Hammerstein). *Roberta* (1933) included three of his finest songs: 'Smoke Gets in Your Eyes', 'Yesterdays', and 'The Touch of Your Hand'. Other notable songs are 'The Way You Look Tonight' and 'A Fine Romance'.

kerosene or **paraffin** A petroleum distillation product, with larger molecules and consequently less volatility than the fraction used for gasoline (petrol). Formerly used widely as a fuel for domestic lighting, it is now an important source of domestic heating, and is the main fuel for jet engines. An early source, developed in the mid-19th-c and still exploited commercially, was oil-bearing shale.

Kerouac, Jack [kerooak], popular name of **Jean Louis Libris Kerouac** (1922–69) Writer, born in Lowell, Massachusetts, USA. Discharged from the navy with a personality problem, he served as a merchant seaman, then took a variety of jobs before publishing his first novel, *The Town and the City* (1950). It was written in a conventional style which he abandoned in *On the Road* (1957), a formless, spontaneous work, expressing the youthful discontent of the 'Beat generation', which he was the first to name. Later works, all in this vein, and all autobiographical in character, include *The Subterraneans* (1958) and *Big Sur* (1962).

Kerr, John [kair] (1824–1907) Physicist, born in Ardrossan, North Ayrshire, W Scotland, UK. He studied at Glasgow, where he was an assistant to Lord Kelvin. He then became a lecturer in mathematics at a teachers' training college, where he carried out research on light passing through electromagnetic fields, and discovered the effect that is now named after him.

Kerr, Sir John (Robert) [kair] (1914–91) Lawyer and administrator, born in Sydney, New South Wales, SE Australia. He studied at the University of Sydney, was admitted to the bar in 1938, and became a QC in 1953. He was made Chief Justice of New South Wales in 1972, and was appointed Governor-General of Australia in 1974. In 1975, his actions as governor-general made Australian constitutional history: the Coalition opposition had refused to pass the Labor government's budget bill unless a general election was called. To resolve this impasse he exercised the regal 'reserve powers' and sacked the elected prime minister, Gough Whitlam, asking leader of the Liberal opposition, Malcolm Fraser, to form a caretaker government and call a general election. Stepping down as governor-general in 1977, he was named Australian ambassador to UNESCO in 1978, but the ensuing controversy forced him to resign without taking up the appointment.

Kerr cell *electro-optic effects*

Kerry, Ir **Chiarraighe** pop (2000e) 123 000; area 4701 sq km/ 1815 sq mi. County in Munster province, SW Ireland; bounded W by Atlantic Ocean; rises to Slieve Mish Mts on N side of Dingle Bay and Macgillycuddy's Reeks on S side; watered by Feale and Blackwater Rivers; capital, Tralee; chief towns include Killarney (notable lakeland area) and Listowel; tourism, fishing, textiles.

Kerry, John (Forbes) (1943–) US politician, born in Denver, Colorado, USA. He studied at Yale University, and then served with the US Navy in the Vietnam War winning several awards for bravery in combat. He embarked on a career in law and worked as a prosecutor in Massachusetts before going into politics. In 1982 he was voted lieutenant governor for Massachusetts, and became senator in 1984, being successfully re-elected for a fourth term in 2002. In early 2004 he emerged as the front-runner in the race to secure the Democrat nomination in the US presidential election later that year.

Kertész, Imre [kertesh] (1929–) Writer, born in Budapest, Hungary. Of Jewish descent, in 1944 he was deported to Auschwitz and then Buchenwald, where he was liberated in 1945. He became a translator of German authors and an independent writer. His first novel, *Sorstalanság* (1975, trans Fateless, 1992), based on his experiences in the concentration camps, was followed by *A kudarc* (1988, trans Fiasco) and *Kaddis a meg nem születetett gyermekért* (1990, trans Kaddish for a Child not Born, 1997). Collections of essays include *A holocaust mint kultúra* (1993, trans title The Holocaust as Culture), *A gondolatnyi csend, amíg kivégzóoztag újratölt* (1998, Moments of Silence while the Execution Squad Reloads), and *A számuzött nyelv* (2001, The Exiled Language). He was awarded the 2002 Nobel Prize for Literature for writing that upholds the fragile experience of the individual against the barbaric arbitrariness of history.

kerygma [kerigma] (Gr 'proclamation', 'that which is announced', often referring to the content of a priestly or prophetic proclamation) In the New Testament it often refers to the Apostles' announcement of the saving nature of Jesus's death and resurrection (1 *Cor* 15.3–5), so that Jesus becomes not just the proclaimer of salvation but that which is proclaimed.

Kesey, Ken (Elton) [keezee] (1935–2001) Writer, born in La Junta, Colorado, USA. He worked as a ward attendant in a mental hospital, an experience he used to telling effect in *One Flew Over the Cuckoo's Nest* (1962). Filmed in 1975 by Milos Forman, it won five Oscars. After the failure of *Sometimes a Great Notion* (1966), he relinquished 'literature' for 'life'. He served a prison sentence for marijuana possession, and formed the 'Merry Pranksters', whose weird exploits are described at length in Tom Wolfe's *The Electric Kool-Aid Acid Test* (1967). The stories, essays, and poems in *Demon Box* (1986) are also partly autobiographical. A later novel, *Sailor Song*, appeared in 1993, and *Last Go Round* in 1994.

Kesselring, Albert [keslring] (1885–1960) German air commander in World War 2, born in Markstedt, Germany. He led the *Luftwaffe* attacks on France and (unsuccessfully) on Britain, in 1943 was made commander-in-chief in Italy, and in 1945 in the West. Condemned to death as a war criminal in 1947, he had his sentence commuted to life imprisonment, but was released in 1952.

kestrel A falcon of the worldwide genus *Falco* (13 species), especially *Falco tinnunculus*; inhabits open country and cultivation, occasionally forest; eats insects and small vertebrates; catches prey on ground after hovering. (Family: Falconidae.)

ketch A two-masted fore-and-aft-rigged sailing vessel. The shorter (after-) mast, called the *mizzen*, is placed in position forward of the rudder post. By contrast, in a **yawl**, this mast is placed aft of the rudder post.

ketones [keetohnz] IUPAC **alkanones**. Organic compounds containing a carbonyl (C=O) group bonded to two other carbon atoms. The simplest example is acetone (CH_3COCH_3).

Kettering, Charles F(ranklin) (1876–1958) Inventor, born in Loudonville, Ohio, USA. He developed the first electric cash register (1904), and went on to become co-founder of Dayton Engineering Laboratories (Delco). His notable early invention was the electric starter, which revolutionized the automotive industry. Among his many achievements were advances in aircraft design, fuels, and diesel engines, and he invented the refrigerant known as Freon™. His lifelong interest in science culminated in the building of the Sloan-Kettering Institute for Cancer Research, and the C F Kettering Foundation.

Ketterle, Wolfgang [keterlay] (1957–) Physicist, born in Heidelberg, SWC Germany. He studied at universities in Munich and at the Max-Planck Institute for Quantum Optics, later joining the Massachusetts Institute of Technology. He shared the 2001 Nobel Prize for Physics for the achievement of Bose–Einstein condensation in dilute gases of alkali atoms, and for early fundamental studies of the properties of the condensates.

kettledrum *timpani*

Kevorkian, Jack [kuhvaw(r)kian], media nickname **Dr Death** (1928–) Physician, born in Pontiac, Michigan, USA. He graduated in medicine at the University of Michigan in 1952, served in the Korean War, then began to specialize in pathology. He became known for his conviction that medical experimentation on condemned prisoners be legalized, and in the late 1980s moved into the area of euthanasia. Known to participate in the facilitation of deaths since 1990, he had twice been charged with murder and several times with assisting suicide, but found not guilty. In 1998 he became internationally known when a video showing the death of one of his clients was shown on national television, a strategy he had chosen to bring the public debate on euthanasia to a head. In 1999 he was convicted of second degree murder and delivery of a controlled substance and imprisoned.

Kew Gardens The Royal Botanical Gardens at Kew, Surrey, SE England, UK. The gardens, which were inherited by George III from his mother, expanded and flourished under the direction of Sir Joseph Banks (1743–1820). Its architecture was strongly influenced by Chinese taste. In 1841 it was given to the nation. Now occupying 120 ha/300 acres, it is the premier botanical institution in the world and was designated a world heritage site in 2003.

key *tonality*

keyboard instrument A musical instrument in which the different pitches are controlled by means of a keyboard, ie a succession of levers arranged (for acoustical, historical, or practical reasons) in two rows. The front row produces the notes of the diatonic C major scale, the rear the pitches in between; played in order from left to right, they produce an ascending 12-note chromatic scale. In modern keyboards the front keys are white, the rear ones black; in some earlier instruments the colours are reversed, while in the case of the organ pedalboard there is usually no colour differentiation. Keyboards are integral to many aerophones (eg the accordion), chordophones, (eg the piano), and electrophones (eg the synthesizer). The term **keyboards** is also often used as a collective term for all the electronic keyboard instruments (electric pianos, electronic organs, and synthesizers) in a pop group.

key grip *grip*

Keynes (of Tilton), John Maynard Keynes, Baron [kaynz] (1883–1946) Economist, the founder of macroeconomics, whose theories have influenced governments on both sides of the Atlantic, born in Cambridge, Cambridgeshire, EC England, UK. He studied at Cambridge, became one of the 'Bloomsbury group', and lectured in economics. In both World Wars he was an adviser to the Treasury, and his views on a planned economy influenced Roosevelt's 'New Deal' administration. The unemployment crises inspired his two great works, *A Treatise on Money* (1930) and the revolutionary *General Theory of Employment, Interest and Money* (1936). He took a leading part in negotiations leading to the foundation of the International Monetary Fund and his views underpinned the foundation of the welfare state in Britain. A keen patron of the arts, he helped to found the Vic–Wells ballet and the Arts Theatre, Cambridge. He married the ballerina Lydia Lopokova. He was created a peer in 1942.

Keynesian [kaynzian] A follower and exponent of the economic concepts propounded by economist J M Keynes in the 1930s. The 'Keynesian revolution' is so-called because it radically changed the view of how economies should be managed, particularly in relation to the notion of full employment. Prior to Keynes, the classical school of economics believed that economies would tend towards full employment equilibrium. Keynesian thinking challenged this, with a view based on the experience of Western economies after World War 1, that economies could be in equilibrium at less than full employment. Unless demand in the economy is stimulated, growth and therefore full employment are not possible. Keynesian theories were subject to critical appraisal in the 1960s and 1970s by Monetarists. Many argue that the fundamental theory holds good, but does not fully address endemic economic problems, such as inflation.

Keystone US film production company of silent films (1912–19), founded by Mack Sennett, and specializing in knockabout comedy shorts. Particularly famous were those featuring the **Keystone Kops** troupe.

keystone The distortion of a projected image in which the vertical sides of a rectangle converge. The effect is caused by the optical axis of projection not meeting the screen at right angles.

KGB Abbreviation of **Komitet Gosudarstvennoy Bezopasnosti** ('Committee for State Security'), after 1953 one of the Soviet Union's two secret police organizations with joint responsibility for internal and external order and security. Its tasks included the surveillance of key members of the Communist Party, the administration, and the military; the monitoring and regulation of dissidents; and espionage and subversion abroad. It underwent radical reform following glasnost and the failed 1991 coup in the USSR, and is now known as the Ministry of State Security.

Khajuraho [kajirahhoh] A group of 20 Hindu temples in Madhya Pradesh, India; a world heritage site. The temples were constructed, mainly of sandstone, in 950–1050. The sculptures which embellish their internal and external walls are considered masterpieces of erotic art.

Khaled ibn Abdul Aziz *Saud, al-*

Khama, Sir Seretse [kahma] (1921–80) Botswana statesman and president (1966–80), born in Serowe, E Botswana (formerly Bechuanaland). He studied at Oxford, became a lawyer, and after marrying an Englishwoman, Ruth Williams, in 1948, was banned from the chieftainship and the territory of the Bamangwato. Allowed to return as a private citizen in 1956, he became active in politics, and was restored to the chieftainship in 1963. He became the first prime minister of Bechuanaland (1965), and the first president of Botswana. He was knighted in 1966.

Khamsin [kamsin] A hot, dry dust-laden SE wind which blows from desert areas in N Africa and Arabia. The word means '50', as it regularly blows for a 50-day period.

Khan, Jahangir (1963–) Squash rackets player, born in Karachi, SE Pakistan. A member of a prolific squash-playing family, he won three world amateur titles (1979, 1983, 1985), a record six World Open titles (1981–5, 1988), and eight consecutive British Open titles (1982–9). He was undefeated from April 1981 to November 1986, when he lost to Ross Norman (Australia) in the World Open final.

Khan, Mohammad Ayub *Ayub Khan, Mohammad*

Kharga, El [kah(r)ga] or **al-Kharijah** 25°27N 30°32E. Capital of Al-Wadi Al-Jadid governorate, SC Egypt; in the Great Oasis, Egypt's largest oasis; railway; dates, figs, olives; ruins of Temple of Hibis (now a Christian necropolis, c.500 BC) and Nadura (Christian convent, AD c.150).

Kharkov [khah(r)kof], Ukrainian **Kharkiv** 50°00N 36°15E, pop (2000e) 1 596 000. Capital city of Kharkovskaya oblast, Ukraine, on tributaries of the R Severskiy Donets; founded as a fortress, 1655–6; badly damaged in World War 2; airport; railway junction; university (1805); Donets Basic coalfield nearby; heavy engineering, machines, metalworking, foodstuffs, building materials; Pokrovskii cathedral (1689), Uspenskii cathedral (1821–41).

Khartoum [kah(r)toom] or **El Khartûm** 15°33N 32°35E, pop (2000e) 764 000. Capital of Sudan, near the junction of the White Nile and the Blue Nile Rivers, 1600 km/1000 mi S of Cairo (Egypt); founded, 1820s; garrison town in 19th-c; scene of the British defeat by the Mahdi, in which General Gordon was killed, 1885; city regained by Lord Kitchener, 1898; airport; railway; university (1955); major communications and trade centre; headquarters of the Bank for African Development; regarded as the economic link between the Arab countries (N) and the African countries (S); commerce, food processing, textiles, glass; oil pipeline runs NE to Port Sudan; three cathedrals, mosques, Sudan National Museum.

khat [kaht] A shrub (*Catha edulis*) growing in E Asia and the SW part of the Arabian peninsula, whose leaves are chewed for their stimulant effect. The active principle is *cathinone*, whose properties are similar to amphetamine.

Khatami, (Hojjatoleslam Seyed) Mohammed [katamee] (1943–) President of Iran (1997–), born in Ardakan, Yazd, Iran. He studied at Qom, Isfahan, and Tehran, and was active in the protest movement that led to the removal of the Shah of Iran. Following the revolution, he became head of the Hamburg Islamic Centre in Germany before being elected to the first Iranian parliament in 1980. He served twice as minister for culture and Islamic guidance (1982, 1989–92) and held a number of military-related posts during the war with Iraq. Appointed as cultural adviser to the president (1992–6), he went on to win almost 70 per cent of the votes in the 1997 presidential election.

Khatchaturian, Aram [kachatooryan] (1903–78) Composer, born in Tiflis, Georgia. He was a student of folksong, and an authority on oriental music. His compositions include symphonies, concertos, choral works, and ballet music. An excerpt from his ballet music *Spartacus* topped the popular music charts when used as the theme music for the TV series *The Onedin Line* in the 1970s.

khedive [kedeev] An ancient Persian title acquired from the Ottoman Sultan by the autonomous Viceroy of Egypt, Ismail, in 1867. It was used until Egypt became a British protectorate (1914).

Khmer [kmair] An Austro-Asiatic language, spoken by over 7 million people; also known as **Cambodian**. It is the official language of Cambodia. Inscriptions date from the 6th–7th-c.

Khmer Empire [kmair] Buddhist kingdom/empire in SE Asia, founded in the 6th-c, with its capital at Angkor Thom from 802. By the 12th-c it included S Laos, much of Thailand, and Cambodia. Vast funerary temples were erected at Angkor Wat (early 12th-c). Cambodia was invaded by the Mongols (1284) and the newly established Siamese kingdom (after 1350). Angkor was abandoned in 1431, and the Khmer Empire had collapsed by 1460.

Khmer Rouge [kmair **roozh**] A Cambodian communist guerrilla force. It gained control in 1975 and, led by Pol Pot, set about a drastic transformation of 'Democratic Kampuchea', involving mass forced evacuation from the towns to the countryside, the creation of agricultural co-operatives, and the execution of thousands of 'bourgeois elements'. More than 90% of Cambodia's traditional artists, performers, and scholars were murdered. In 1979, Vietnam invaded, and the Khmer Rouge withdrew to the Thai border region. Following the Vietnamese withdrawal in 1989, they mounted a major offensive, especially in the W and S provinces. The Paris Conference on Cambodia brought about a ceasefire (1991) and an international peace plan launched by the UN, which led to elections in 1993. However, the Khmer Rouge refused to take part in the elections or to become part of the new political system, and tension remained, with continued fighting between government troops and guerrillas. The organization was banned in 1994. In addition to Pol Pot, senior Khmer Rouge personnel included the deputy leader Ieng Sary (1930–), guerrilla commander Son Sen (1930–), and the leader of Khmer Rouge delegations at international conferences, Khieu Samphan (1931–).

Khoisan [koysan] A collective term for the San (Bushmen) and Khoi (Hottentot) peoples of S Africa. The San were formerly hunter-gatherers, with a simple material culture but a rich oral literature and accomplished rock art. They once populated most of EC and S Africa, but today are marginalized in the Kalahari Desert of Botswana. Many now work for African or white cattle-farmers. The Khoi were traditionally pastoralists, and today are represented only by groups of mixed ancestry in Namibia. They were devastated by a smallpox epidemic in 1713, and their culture collapsed. There are no evident racial differences between the groups.

Khomeini, Ayatollah Ruhollah [homaynee] (1900–89) Iranian political and religious leader, born in Khomeyn, WC Iran. A Shiite Muslim who was bitterly opposed to the pro-Western regime of Shah Mohammed Reza Pahlavi, he was exiled to Turkey and Iraq in 1964, and from Iraq to France in 1978. He returned to Iran amid great popular acclaim in 1979 after the collapse of the Shah's government, and became virtual head of state. Under his leadership, Iran underwent a turbulent 'Islamic Revolution' in which a return was made to the strict observance of Muslim principles and traditions. In 1979, a new Islamic constitution was sanctioned, into which was incorporated his leadership concept of the *Vilayet-i faqih* (Trusteeship of the Jurisconsult). This supreme religious and political position was recognized as belonging to Khomeini, as was the title *Rabhar* (Leader).

Khorana, Har Gobind [korahna] (1922–) Molecular biologist, born in Raipur, C India. He studied at Punjab, Liverpool, Zürich, and Cambridge universities, and moved to Vancouver in 1952. His work on nucleotide synthesis at Wisconsin (1960–70) was a major contribution to the elucidation of the genetic code, and in 1970 he synthesized the first artificial gene. In 1971 he moved to the Massachusetts Institute of Technology. He shared the Nobel Prize for Physiology or Medicine in 1968.

Khrushchev, Nikita Sergeyevich [khrush**chof**, **khrush**chof] (1894–1971) Soviet statesman, first secretary of the Soviet Communist Party (1953–64), and prime minister (1958–64), born in Kalinovka, Ukraine. Joining the Bolshevik Party in 1918, he fought in the Russian civil war and rose rapidly in the Party organization. In 1939 he was made a full member of the Politburo and of the Presidium of the Supreme Soviet. In 1953, six months after the death of Stalin, he became first secretary of the Communist Party of the Soviet Union, and three years later, at the 20th Party Congress, denounced Stalinism and the 'personality cult'. Among the events of his administration were the Poznań riots and Hungarian uprising (1956), and the failed attempt to install missiles in Cuba (1962). He nevertheless was the first Soviet leader to enjoy good relations with the West, notably the USA, and agreed to the establishment of a 'hot line' of communication between the Kremlin and the White House. He was deposed in 1964, replaced by Brezhnev and Kosygin, and went into retirement.

Khubilai Khan *Kublai Khan*

Khyber Pass [**kiy**ber] A defile through the Safed Koh mountain range on the frontier between Pakistan and Afghanistan. A route favoured through history by both traders and invaders, it is 45 km/28 mi long, and reaches heights of 1280 m/3518 ft. The present road was built by the British during the Afghan Wars, when the Pass was the scene of several clashes.

kiang [kiang] *ass*

kibbutz, plural **kibbutzim** (Heb 'gathering', 'collective') A Jewish co-operative settlement in Israel which is mainly self-supporting in terms of food supplies and many other goods. A kibbutz may support itself through agricultural, industrial, or entrepreneurial means. The first kibbutz, Deganya, was founded in 1910; its land was held in the name of the Jewish people by the Jewish National Fund. Kibbutzim spread in the 1950s as part of Israeli attempts at self-sufficiency, and now number c.300. One of their distinctive features was the collective responsibility members took for child rearing: rather than being cared for in nuclear family units, the young were looked after by the elder children. Moreover, great stress was placed on the system of job rotation which was used to prevent the consolidation of a social hierarchy based on the occupancy of certain social positions. Since c.1970, however, the movement to include children within the nuclear family has grown, and is now the norm.

Kidd, William, known as **Captain Kidd** (c.1645–1701) Privateer and pirate, probably born in Greenock, Inverclyde, WC Scotland, UK. He established himself as a sea captain in New York (1690), saw much privateering service, and gained a high reputation for courage. In 1696 he was commissioned to suppress piracy, and reached Madagascar, but then turned pirate himself. After a 2-years' cruise he returned to the West Indies, ventured to Boston, and was arrested. He was convicted of piracy and murder, and hanged in London. The unsubstantiated legends about his buried treasure have often been referred to in literature, especially in Edgar Allen Poe's *The Gold Bug* (1843) and Robert Louis Stevenson's *Treasure Island* (1883).

Kiddush [**ki**dush] (Heb 'sanctification') A prayer usually recited by the head of the family over a cup of wine at the start of a meal in the home on the eve of a Sabbath or festival; sometimes used also in synagogues to consecrate the Sabbath or a festival. In addition, a 'minor' Kiddush is often said over a beverage or bread before the first meal on the following morning of such events.

Kidman, Nicole (1967–) Film actress, born in Honolulu, Hawaii, USA. At age four she moved with her parents to Sydney, Australia. As a schoolgirl she attended a local theatre group and, encouraged by director Jane Campion, made a notable film debut in *Bush Christmas* (1983). Her US breakthrough came with *Dead Calm* (1989), and success followed with *Billy Bathgate* (1991), *To Die For* (1995), and *Eyes Wide Shut* (1999), in which she co-starred with husband Tom Cruise (divorced, 2001). Later films include *Moulin Rouge* (2000, Golden Globe), *The Hours* (2002, Golden Globe; BAFTA; Oscar), and *Cold Mountain* (2003).

kidney bean *haricot bean*

kidney dialysis The artificial control of blood electrolyte levels and the removal of waste products from the body when the kidneys are not functioning in patients with kidney failure. Two methods are available. *Haemodialysis* involves removing blood from the patient through a specially created vein in the forearm and circulating it through a machine where diffusion of solutes occurs between the blood and a dialysis solution; the process takes about four hours three times a week at a special centre. *Peritoneal dialysis* is performed by introducing dialysis solution into the abdominal cavity through a catheter, to allow diffusion of solutes to occur across the membrane lining the cavity, before waste products and excess water are drained out of the abdomen; four exchanges each day are required, but the procedure can be carried out at home.

kidney failure Deterioration of the ability of the kidneys to regulate the water and electrolyte content of the body and to excrete the end products of protein metabolism (urea and creatinine). Urine output is much reduced, leading to oedema, and the blood of some electrolytes (especially potassium) rises, which can be fatal. There are many causes, including poor kidney perfusion (eg in shock), certain infections and drugs (especially when they produce glomerulonephritis), diabetes, and hypertension. Kidney failure may arise acutely and be completely reversible, or it may be chronic and progressive, in which case dialysis is required to maintain the body's water and electrolyte balance.

kidney machine *dialysis*

kidneys The urine-producing organs of vertebrates. In humans the symmetrical, bean-shaped kidneys are situated on the upper part of the rear abdominal wall, one each side of the vertebral column. The ureter conveys urine to the bladder. Each kidney has a suprarenal (adrenal) gland immediately above, weighs about 130 gm/4·6 oz, is enclosed by connective tissue, and is supported by fat. Each consists of approximately 1 million *nephrons* (the functional units) and supporting tissue. The nephrons eliminate unwanted substances from the blood, but retain important body constituents (eg glucose, sodium, and potassium), so maintaining the volume and composition of body fluids within normal limits. The kidneys also produce important agents (eg renin, erythropoietin, prostaglandins), which are transported in the blood to their target organs. Medical problems affecting the kidneys include glomerulonephritis, kidney failure, pyelonephritis, urinary stones, and uraemia.

Kiel [keel] 54°02N 10°08E, pop (2000e) 251 000. Port and capital of Schleswig-Holstein province, N Germany; at S end of the Kieler Förde, an arm of the Baltic Sea; Kiel Canal (1877–95), 98 km/61 mi between North Sea and Baltic Sea; badly bombed in World War 2; railway; university (1665); ferry service to Scandinavia; naval base; shipbuilding, engineering, precision instruments, fish processing, oil, railway vehicles, telephone systems, marine electronics, armaments; Schloss (13th-c); Kiel Week, sailing regattas and cultural events (Jun).

Kielder Water [**keel**der] Reservoir in Northumberland, NE England, UK; one of the largest artificial lakes in Europe, supplying water to the industrial NE; built 1974–82 by damming R North Tyne; first regional water grid system in UK; planting of nearby **Kielder Forest** begun in 1922; area with other Border forests, 650 sq km/250 sq mi; largest area of planted forest in Europe.

Kierkegaard, Søren (Aabye) [**keer**kuhgaw(r)d] (1813–55) Philosopher and theologian, a major influence on 20th-c existentialism, born in Copenhagen. He studied theology, philosophy, and literature at Copenhagen, and came to criticize purely speculative systems of thought, such as Hegel's, as irrelevant to existence-making choices. For Hegel's rationalism, Kierkegaard substituted the disjunction *Enten-Eller* (1843, Either/Or). In *Afsluttende Uvidenskabelig Efterskrift* (1846, Concluding Unscientific Postscript), he attacked all philosophical system building, and formulated the thesis that subjectivity is truth. Other works include (trans titles) *The Concept of Irony* (1841), *Fear and Trembling* (1843), and *The Sickness unto Death* (1849).

Kiesinger, Kurt Georg [keesinger] (1904–88) German statesman and chancellor (1966–9), born in Ebingen, SW Germany. He studied at Berlin and Tübingen, practised as a lawyer (1935–40), and served during World War 2 at the Foreign Office on radio propaganda. Interned after the war until 1947, he was exonerated of Nazi crimes. In 1949 he became a Conservative member of the *Bundestag*, and succeeded Erhard as chancellor. Long a convinced supporter of Adenauer's plans for European unity, he formed with Brandt a government combining the Christian Democratic Union and the Social Democrats, until in 1969 he was succeeded as chancellor by Brandt.

Kiev [kee-ef], Ukrainian **Kiyiv**, also **Kiyev** 50°28N 30°29E, pop (2000e) 2 587 000. Capital city of Ukraine, on R Dnepr; earliest centre of Slavonic culture and learning; founded, 6th–7th-c; capital of mediaeval Kievan Russia, 9th-c; conquered by Mongols, 1240; capital of Ukraine SSR, 1934; besieged and occupied by Germany in World War 2; airport; railway; university (1834); major industrial, cultural, and scientific centre; chemicals, clothing, knitwear, leatherwork, footwear, instruments; opera and ballet companies, St Sofia cathedral (1037), Zabrovsky Gate (1746), Monastery of the Caves (1051), All Saints Church (17th-c), Vydubetsky Monastery (1070–7).

Kikuyu [kikooyoo] A Bantu-speaking agricultural people of the C highlands of Kenya, and the country's largest ethnic group. During the 1950s they were involved in the Mau Mau uprising against European colonialists; after Kenya's independence (1963) they provided many of the country's political leaders.

Kilby, Jack St Clair (1923–) Electrical engineer, born in Jefferson City, Missouri, USA. He studied electrical engineering at the University of Illinois and the University of Wisconsin. Working for Texas Instruments (1958–70), he invented the monolithic integrated circuit (1958) and later the first hand-held calculator. In 2000 he shared the Nobel Prize for Physics for his invention of the integrated circuit.

Kildare [kildair], Ir **Cill Dara** pop (2000e) 124 000; area 1694 sq km/654 sq mi. County in Leinster province, E Ireland; watered by Liffey and Barrow Rivers; low-lying C plain known as the Curragh; capital, Naas; other chief towns, Kildare, Athy, Droichead Nua; farming, cattle, horse breeding; national stud at Tully, racecourse at the Curragh.

Kilimanjaro, Mount [kilimanjahroh] (Chagga 'glittering mountain') 3°02S 37°20E. Mountain on the frontier between Tanzania and Kenya, E Africa; height 5895 m/19 340 ft; highest point on the African continent; glaciated double-peaked massif of volcanic origin, capped by the dormant cone of Kibo peak and the jagged extinct Mawenzi peak; first climbed in 1889; Kilimanjaro National Park is a world heritage site.

Kilkenny (city) [kilkenee], Ir **Cill Choinnigh** 52°39N 7°15W, pop (2000e) 18 000. Capital of Kilkenny county, Leinster, SE Ireland, on R Nore; railway; clothing, footwear, brewing; Kilkenny College and design workshops; cathedrals, town hall (Tholsel), 18th-c Kilkenny Castle, Bishop Rothe's house; Kilkenny Arts Week (Aug).

Kilkenny (county) [kilkenee], Ir **Cill Choinnigh** pop (2000e) 75 000; area 2062 sq km/796 sq mi. County in Leinster province, SE Ireland; fertile county watered by R Nore; Slieve Ardagh Hills rise W; capital, Kilkenny; agriculture, livestock.

Killarney [kilah(r)nee] Ir **Cill Airne** 52°03N 9°30W, pop (2000e) 10 000. Resort town in Kerry county, Munster, SW Ireland; centre of scenic lakeland area; railway; engineering, container cranes, hosiery; pan-Celtic week with Celtavision Song Contest (May); Killarney regatta (Jul); Kerry boating carnival (Sep).

killer whale A toothed whale (*Orcinus orca*), found worldwide in cool coastal waters; length, 9–10 m/30–33 ft; black with white underparts; white patches on head; dorsal fin narrow and vertical (tallest in males); eats marine mammals, birds, fish, and squid (groups may attack baleen whales). The name is also used for the **false killer whale** (*Pseudorca crassidens*) and the **pygmy killer whale** (*Feresa attenuata*). (Family: Delphinidae.)

killifish Small, colourful, carp-like freshwater fish widespread in tropical and warm temperate regions; jaws bearing small teeth; lacks bony linkage between swim bladder and inner ear; popular as an aquarium fish; also called **top minnows**. (Family: Cyprodontidae.)

Killy, Jean-Claude [keelee] (1943–) Alpine skier, born in Val d'Isère, E France. He won the downhill and combined gold medals at the world championship in Chile in 1966; and in 1968, when the Winter Olympics were held almost on his own ground at Grenoble, he won three gold medals for slalom, giant slalom, and downhill. He turned professional immediately afterwards and pursued a highly profitable career as an endorser and later manufacturer of winter sports equipment.

kiln An oven for baking clay for bricks or pottery, or the clay and lime for cement, usually constructed of fireclay or resistant alloys. The term is also used for ovens operating at low temperatures for the drying of hops or grain.

kilobyte *byte*

kilocalorie *calorie*

kilogram Base SI unit of mass; symbol *kg*; defined as equal to the international prototype of the kilogram, a platinum–iridium bar kept at the International Bureau of Weights and Measures at Sèvres, near Paris; commonly used as **gram** (*g*, 1/1000 kg) and **tonne** (*t*, 1000 kg); 1 kg = 2·205 pounds.

kilohm *ohm*

kilometre *metre* (physics)

kiloparsec *parsec*

kiloton (TNT) A measure of explosive power; symbol *kT*; one kiloton equivalent to the explosive power of 1000 tons of TNT; used to describe the destructive power of nuclear weapons, which range from 10 kT to thousands of kT; one **megaton**, MT, equals 1000 kT.

kilowatt *watt*

kilowatt-hour The total energy consumed by a device of power 1 kilowatt operating for 1 hour; symbol *kWh*; equal to $3{\cdot}6 \times 10^6$ J (joule, SI unit); standard unit for the electricity supply industry.

Kilvert, (Robert) Francis (1840–79) Clergyman and diarist, born in Hardenhuish, Wiltshire, S England, UK. He was a curate at Clyro in Radnorshire and then vicar of Bredwardine on the Wye until his early death from appendicitis. His notebooks (1870–9), giving a vivid and affectionate picture of rural life in the Welsh marches, were discovered in 1937 and published as *Kilvert's Diary*, in three volumes (1938–40).

Kim, Dae-jung [day-jung] (1925–) South Korean president (1997–2003), born in Ha Eui (S Cholla Province), South Korea. Leaving school after his secondary education in Mokpo (he was later to attend Kyunghee University), he made a fortune in shipping. Much of this was spent during the 1950s in an unsuccessful attempt to enter politics. After overcoming difficulties in his private life, he was finally elected to the National Assembly in 1962. He ran for president in 1971, 1987, and 1992 before finally being elected in 1997. An opponent of South Korea's military governments, he was sentenced to death in 1980 before being reprieved after the intervention of US President Reagan. He was awarded the Nobel Peace Prize in 2000 for his groundbreaking efforts to achieve reconciliation with North Korea.

Kimberley 28°45S 24°46E, pop (2000e) 195 000. City in Northern Cape province, South Africa, 450 km/280 mi SW of Johannesburg; major diamond-mining centre since its foundation, 1871; under siege in the Boer War (1899–1900); airfield; railway; diamonds, metal products, furniture, clothing, cement; the Big Hole (formerly Kimberley Mine), 800 m/2625 ft deep and 500 m/1640 ft across, said to be the biggest artificial hole on Earth; two cathedrals, Bantu Gallery.

Kimberley, Siege of (1899–1900) One of the three sieges of the second Boer War, in which Boer forces attempted to pen up their British opponents and secure control of vital lines of communication. The siege lasted from the middle of October

1899 until February 1900, when the town was relieved by General French.

Kim Il-sung [kim ilsung], originally **Kim Song-ju** (1912–94) North Korean soldier, statesman, prime minister (1948–72), and president (1972–94), born near Pyongyang, Korea. He founded the Korean People's Revolutionary Army in 1932, and led a long struggle against the Japanese. He proclaimed the Republic in 1948, and became effective head of state. He was re-elected president in 1982 and 1986, established a unique personality cult wedded to an isolationist, Stalinist political-economic system, and named his son, **Kim Jong-il** (1942–), as his successor.

kimono [kimohnoh] Japanese traditional costume, today mostly worn for special occasions, such as weddings and the tea ceremony. It is not worn to work except by Buddhist priests, waitresses in traditional style restaurants, and a few others. Plain colours are for men; bright for girls and young women. The *obi* (waist sash) for women is frequently of an expensive material.

Kinabalu, Mount [kinabahloo] (Malay **Gunong**) 6°03N 116°32E. Mountain in Sabah state, E Malaysia, in the Crocker Range; highest peak in SE Asia, 4094 m/13 432 ft; within the Kinabalu National Park. The park is a world heritage site.

kinaesthesis / kinesthesis [kinuhstheesis] Perceived sensations of position and movement of body and limbs, and of the force exerted by muscles. The sense organs responsible are in the skin and joints and, more importantly, in the muscles themselves. The term *proprioception* has a somewhat wider application: it includes information about posture and movement not consciously perceived, as well as the senses of balance, rotation, and linear acceleration vertically and horizontally, resulting from stimulation of the vestibular organs of the inner ear.

kindergarten A nursery school for children under the age at which they must legally attend school. In many countries the kindergarten is organized on informal lines, with the emphasis on social development as well as on preparation for formal schooling. Provision of preschool education varies from near universal availability to very low. In the USA, kindergartens are part of the public school system.

kinematics *dynamics*

kine pox *cow pox*

kinescoping [kineeskohping] A US term for the recording of a television or video programme on cinematograph film.

kinesics [kiyneeziks] The study of visual body language as communication. Kinesics is concerned partly with the conventional movements and gestures that convey deliberate messages, and also with the way facial expressions, body movements, and posture provide patterns of involuntary clues to the emotional state of the person observed, and to the nature of social interaction. It particularly studies the way winks, eyebrow movements, smiles, waving, finger gestures, and other movements of the face and limbs vary in meaning between different cultures.

kinesiology [kiyneeziolojee] A system of diagnosis and treatment which uses assessment of a patient's muscle responses to manual pressure to detect and locate blockage and imbalance of energy flow; developed by US chiropracter George Goodheart. Diagnosis is based on the belief that each group of muscles is related to other distant parts of the body, and generally follows the principles of traditional Chinese medicine. The kinesiology channels are identical to the 12 classical acupuncture meridians; and treatment is given by massaging 'pressure points' to enhance blood, lymphatic, and energy flow to the muscles. The diagnostic application of kinesiology is for allergy testing, when food, chemicals, or other possible allergens placed in the hand or on the tongue are said to induce detectable effects upon the body's muscle power and electrical field.

kinetic To do with motion; in chemistry, to do with the speed at which reactions reach equilibrium. Mixtures which reach equilibrium quickly are called *labile*; those which react slowly *inert*.

kinetic art A term applied to certain types of modern art, especially sculptures, which move. For example, the hanging mobiles of the US sculptor Alexander Calder (1898–1976), all the parts of which revolve separately to create changing patterns in space, usually rely on air currents, but some kinetic works are connected to a motor.

kinetic energy Energy associated with an object's motion; a scalar quantity; symbol K, units J (joule). For an object of mass m moving with velocity v, kinetic energy $K = mv^2/2$. A change in kinetic energy is work done to the object by a force.

kinetic energy weapons Weapons which achieve their destructive effect by the sheer force of their impact; distinguished, in the terminology of modern warfare, from those which do damage by blast and heat (**chemical energy** or **explosive** weapons) on arrival at the target. An arrow fired from a bow or a bullet fired from a gun is a kinetic energy weapon, as is a solid-shot anti-tank round, fired at high velocity from a gun barrel.

kinetic theory of gases A classical theory of gases in which a gas is assumed to comprise large numbers of identical particles which undergo elastic collisions and obey Newtonian mechanics. The statistical application of the laws of mechanics gives the relationships between the bulk thermodynamic properties of a gas and the motion of gas particles.

King, Billie Jean, *née* **Moffat** (1943–) Tennis player, born in Long Beach, California, USA. She won the women's doubles title at Wimbledon in 1961 (with Karen Hantze Susman) at her first attempt, and between 1961 and 1979 won a record 20 Wimbledon titles, including the singles in 1966–8, 1972–3, and 1975. She also won 13 US titles (including four singles), four French titles (one singles), and two Australian titles (one singles). She was the first president of the Women's Tennis Association in 1974. In 1987 she was elected to the International Tennis Hall of Fame.

King, Cecil (Harmsworth) (1901–87) Newspaper proprietor, born in Totteridge, Hertfordshire, SE England, UK, the nephew of the Harmsworth brothers. He joined the *Daily Mirror* in 1926, and became chairman of Daily Mirror Newspapers Ltd and Sunday Pictorial Newspapers Ltd (1951–63), and chairman of the International Publishing Corporation and Reed Paper Group (1963–8).

King, Francis (Henry) (1923–) Novelist and short-story writer, born in Adelboden, WC Switzerland. He studied at Shrewsbury and Oxford, after a childhood spent partly in India, and worked for the British Council in Finland, Greece, Egypt, and Japan (1945–64). His novels include *The Dividing Stream* (1951, Somerset Maugham Award), *The Needle* (1975), *Act of Darkness* (1983), *Visiting Cards* (1990), *The Ant Colony* (1991), and *Ash on an Old Man's Sleeve* (1996). His volumes of short stories include *The Japanese Umbrella* (1964) and *Hard Feelings* (1976), and he has also written poetry and travel books.

King, Larry, originally **Lawrence Harvey Zeiger** (1933–) Talk-show host, born in New York City, USA. After leaving school, he joined a Florida radio station, and in the 1960s hosted local talk-shows. He joined CNN in 1985, taking *Larry King Live* to the top of the ratings by 1992, widely watched for its commentary and debate on contemporary events. He has made many specials, and written several books, starting with *Tell It to the King* (1988) and including *The Best of Larry King Live* (1995).

King, Martin Luther, Jr (1929–68) Clergyman and civil rights campaigner, born in Atlanta, Georgia, USA, the son of a Baptist pastor. He studied at Morehouse College, Atlanta, Crozer Theological Seminary, PA, and Boston University, and became a leader of the black Civil Rights movement, known for his policy of passive resistance and his acclaimed oratorical skills. In 1964 he received the Kennedy Peace Prize and the Nobel Peace Prize. His greatest success came in challenging the segregation laws of the South. After 1965, he turned his attention to social conditions in the North, which he found less tractable. He was assassinated in Memphis, TN; his assassin, James Earl Ray, was apprehended in London, and in 1969 was sentenced in

Memphis to 99 years. A national holiday in King's honour has been recognized in many states since 1986.

King, Stephen (Edwin) (1947–) Novelist, born in Portland, Maine, USA. He graduated from the University of Maine in 1970, and became an English teacher (1971–3), turning to full-time writing after the success of his first novel, *Carrie* (1974). He has become known for his vivid treatment of horrific and supernatural themes, later books (many of which have been filmed) including *Salem's Lot* (1975), *The Shining* (1976), *It* (1986), and *Bag of Bones* (1998). He has also written collections of short stories, such as *Hearts in Atlantis* (1999), and other novels under the name of Richard Bachman.

King, W(illiam) L(yon) Mackenzie (1874–1950) Canadian statesman and prime minster (1921–6, 1926–30, 1935–48), born in Kitchener (formerly Berlin), Ontario, SE Canada. He studied law at Toronto University, and economics at Chicago and Harvard. He became an MP (1908), minister of labour (1909–11), and Liberal leader (1919). As premier, he introduced legislation for the resolution of industrial disputes through third-party arbitration, and helped to craft new Imperial relationships between Britain and the Commonwealth (1926–30). His view that the dominions should be autonomous communities within the British empire resulted in the Statute of Westminster (1931). He resigned from office in 1948.

King Charles spaniel A breed of dog developed in Britain, receiving its name for its popularity under King Charles II; small active spaniel with short legs, long low-set ears, and large round frontal eyes; in original paintings, with a long face and flat skull; by 19th-c bred to a completely flat face, undershot jaw, and domed skull; this breed in the USA also called **English Toy Spaniel**; during 1920s, breeders worked to restore the original appearance, eventually producing the **Cavalier King Charles spaniel**, recognized by the Kennel Club in 1945.

king cobra The world's largest venomous snake (*Ophiophagus hannah*), native to India and SE Asia; (length, up to 5·5 m/18 ft); inhabits forests, especially near water; eats snakes (including venomous species) and monitor lizards; female builds nest on ground and coils on top to incubate eggs; also known as **hamadryad**.

king crab *horseshoe crab*

kingcup A perennial (*Caltha palustris*) growing in wet marshy places throughout the N hemisphere; leaves glossy, kidney-shaped; flowers cup-shaped, golden-yellow, up to 5 cm/2 in across; also called **marsh marigold**. (Family: Ranunculaceae.)

kingdom (biology) The highest category into which organisms are classified. Traditionally two kingdoms have been recognized – *Plantae* (plants) and *Animalia* (animals) – but increasing knowledge of micro-organisms has made it difficult to fit them into this system. Modern systems recognize five kingdoms: *Monera* (comprising the procaryotes such as bacteria and blue-green algae), *Protoctista* (comprising the eucaryotic protozoans and some flagellated algae and fungi), *Fungi* (the eucaryotic fungi that lack flagella at all stages of their life-cycle), *Plantae*, and *Animalia*.

kingfisher A bird found almost worldwide (especially Old World tropics); short-tailed, with large head; bill usually long, straight; bright blue-green back; occupies diverse habitats, usually (but not necessarily) near water. Some species eat only fish; most eat insects and small vertebrates. (Family: Alcedinidae, c.85 species.)

King James Bible *Authorized Version of the Bible*

Kingman, Sir John (Frank Charles) (1939–) British academic. He studied at Cambridge, where he became a fellow of Pembroke College, and taught mathematics. He was professor at the University of Sussex (1966–9) and at Oxford (1969–85), before becoming Vice-Chancellor of the University of Bristol in 1985. His name became widely known as chairman of the Committee of Inquiry into the Teaching of the English Language (1987–8), which produced the *Kingman Report*, a major influence on changing practices in English language teaching in British schools in the 1990s. He was knighted in 1985.

King Philip's War (1675–6) An attempt by the Indians of C New England to stop further white expansion. It was led by Metacom (Philip), chief of the Wampanoags, who tried to build an inter-tribe coalition. The Indians lost, and were killed or enslaved.

Kings, Books of A pair of books of the Hebrew Bible/Old Testament, consisting of a compilation of stories about the kings and prophets of Judah and Israel from the enthronement of Solomon to the fall of the kingdom of Israel in c.721 BC, and the final collapse of Judah and Jerusalem in c.587/6 BC. It is part of the Deuteronomistic History, probably once connected to the books of Samuel, and in some Catholic versions entitled 3 and 4 *Kings*. It is strongly critical of idolatry, apostasy, and religious fragmentation away from the Jerusalem Temple cult.

king's evil *scrofula*

Kingsley, Sir Ben, originally **Krishna Bhanji** (1943–) Actor, born in Snainton, North Yorkshire, N England, UK, to Kenyan Asian parents. Educated in Manchester he had no formal training in the theatre, beginning his acting career in regional repertory and with a group touring schools. He joined the Royal Shakespeare Company (1970–80, 1985–6), and emerged there as a leading actor. He is best known for his title role in the film *Gandhi* (1980), for which he won many awards, including an Oscar and BAFTA. Other films include *Schindler's List* (1993), *Death and the Maiden* (1995), *Twelfth Night* (1996), *The Triumph of Love* (2001), and *House of Sand and Fog* (2003). Notable stage performances include the première of Harold Pinter's *Betrayal* (1982) and Peter Hall's 1997 production of *Waiting for Godot* at the Old Vic, London. He received a knighthood in 2001.

Kingsley, Charles (1819–75) Writer, born in Holne, Devon, SW England, UK. He studied at Cambridge, was ordained in 1842, and lived as curate and rector of Eversley, Hampshire. A 'Christian Socialist', he was much involved in schemes for the improvement of working-class life, and his social novels, such as *Alton Locke* (1850), had great influence at the time. His best-known works are *Westward Ho!* (1855), *Hereward the Wake* (1866), and his children's book, *The Water Babies* (1863). In 1860 he was appointed professor of modern history at Cambridge, and in 1873 chaplain to the queen.

Kingston (Canada) 44°14N 76°30W, pop (2000e) 63 400. City in SE Ontario, Canada; at the NE end of L Ontario, where it joins the St Lawrence R; site of former fort (Fort Frontenac); founded in 1784 by United Empire Loyalists; Canadian naval base in War of 1812; capital of United Canada, 1841–4; railway; Royal Military College (1876); Queen's University (1841); textiles, chemicals, mining machinery, aluminium products, food processing; Pump House Steam Museum, Fort Henry.

Kingston (Jamaica) 17°58N 76°48W, pop (2000e) 690 000 (metropolitan area). Capital city and commercial centre of Jamaica; on N side of a landlocked harbour, SE coast; founded, 1693; capital, 1870; airport; railway; Institute of Jamaica (1879); University of the West Indies (1948); agricultural trade, cement manufacture; St Peter's Church (1725), coin and note museum, national gallery, Hope Botanical Gardens, Tuff Gong International studio built by reggae star Bob Marley.

Kingston-upon-Hull *Hull* (UK)

Kingston-upon-Thames [temz] 51°25N 0°17W, pop (2001e) 140 400. Borough of SW Greater London, UK, on R Thames; said to have been the coronation place of Anglo-Saxon kings; railway; Kingston University (1992, formerly Polytechnic); chemicals, plastics, paint, light engineering.

Kingstown 13°12N 61°14W, pop (2000e) 21 300. Capital and main port of St Vincent, Windward Is, on SW coast; airfield; bananas, copra, arrowroot, cotton; beach resorts nearby; botanical gardens (1763), St George's Cathedral, courthouse.

King William's War (1689–97) The first of the great wars between France and England for the control of North America. Known in Europe as the **War of the League of Augsburg**, it was settled by the Treaty of Ryswick (1697).

kinkajou [kingkajoo] A nocturnal mammal (*Potos flavus*) native to Central and South America; superficially monkey-like, with a round head, small rounded ears, short face, large eyes, and long clasping tail; eats mainly fruit; also known as **honey bear** or **potto**. (Family: Procyonidae.)

Kinkakuji [kinkakujee] or **Golden Pavilion** A three-tiered gilded pavilion built in 1394 by Ashikaga Yoshimitsu (1358–1408) in a lakeside setting at Kyoto, Japan. The present building dates from 1955; it is a faithful reconstruction of the original which was burnt down.

Kinmei [kinmay] (?–571) Yamato period ruler in Japan. His linking of the Yamato ruling clan (*uji*) with the Soga *uji* through marriage led to the later ascendancy of Shotoku (early 7th-c). In Kinmei's reign (540–71), Buddhism was introduced.

Kinnock, Neil (Gordon) (1942–) British politician, born in Tredegar, Blaenau Gwent, SE Wales, UK. He studied at Cardiff, became a Labour MP in 1970, joined the Labour Party's National Executive Committee (1978), and was chief Opposition spokesman on education (1979–83). A skilful orator, he was elected party leader following Michael Foot in 1983, and resigned as Leader of the Opposition after the 1992 general election. He became a European Commissioner (with responsibility for transport) in 1994. Following the mass resignation of the Commission in 1999, he was appointed vice-president for administrative reform under the new president, Romano Prodi.

kinnor A musical instrument of the ancient Hebrews – a type of lyre plucked with the fingers or a plectrum. The word is also the modern Hebrew name for the violin.

Kinsey, Alfred (Charles) (1894–1956) Sexologist and zoologist, born in Hoboken, New Jersey, USA. He studied at Bowdoin College, ME, and at Harvard, becoming professor of zoology at Indiana University from 1920. In 1942 he was the founder-director of the Institute for Sex Research, Bloomington, for the scientific study of human sexual behaviour. He published two controversial studies, *Sexual Behavior in the Human Male* (1948, the so-called 'Kinsey Report') and *Sexual Behavior in the Human Female* (1953).

Kinshasa [kinshasa], formerly Belgian **Léopoldville** (to 1964) 4°18S 15°18E, pop (2000e) 4 221 600. River-port capital of Democratic Republic of Congo; on the R Congo opposite Brazzaville; founded by Stanley, 1887; capital of Belgian colony, 1926; US troops stationed here during World War 2; airport; railway; university (1954); commerce, food processing, textiles, chemicals, brewing.

kinship Relationships between people which follow upon descent from a common ancestor. In every human society common descent (*consanguinity*) is thought to mark off a special category of kin, relationships with whom are different in kind from relationships with non-kin. Further significant distinctions may be made between relatives traced through the father and through the mother, between closer and more distant kin, and between kin of different generations. In small-scale, non-industrial societies, kinship relationships may provide the primary basis for association. Systems vary considerably in terms of residence patterns, marriage laws, and inheritance.

Kinski, Klaus, originally **Nikolaus Gunther Nakszynski** (1926–91) Film actor, born in Sopot, N Poland. In the 1930s his family moved to Germany, where he joined the army in 1942. Soon captured, he spent the rest of the War in a British concentration camp, where he first went on stage. He later played many minor parts in films such as spaghetti Westerns (including Clint Eastwood's *For a Few Dollars More*), then became known for his leading roles in the films of Werner Herzog, such as *Aguirre, the Wrath of God* (1972) and *Fitzcarraldo* (1982). He was also acclaimed for his role in *Nosferatu, the Vampyre* (1979), a remake of the Dracula story.

Kintai Bridge [kintiy] 'Bridge of the Brocade Sash', famous for the grace of its five arches. Built at Iwakuni, Japan, in 1673, the original wood, bronze, and iron structure was swept away in 1950. The present bridge is a replica.

Kintyre [kintiy(r)] Peninsula in Argyll and Bute, SWC Scotland, UK; bounded by the North Channel and the Atlantic Ocean (W) and the Firth of Clyde (E); runs S to the **Mull of Kintyre** from a narrow isthmus; 64 km/40 mi long; average width 13 km/8 mi; chief town, Campbeltown.

Kipling, (Joseph) Rudyard (1865–1936) Writer, born of British parents in Mumbai (Bombay), W India. Educated at boarding school in England, UK, he returned in 1882 to India, where he worked as a journalist. His satirical verses and short stories, such as *Plain Tales From the Hills* (1888) and *Soldiers Three* (1892), won him a reputation in England, to which he returned in 1889 and settled in London. His verse collections *Barrack Room Ballads* (1892) and *The Seven Seas* (1896) were highly successful, as were the two *Jungle Books* (1894–5), which have become classic animal stories. *Kim* appeared in 1901, and the classic *Just So Stories* in 1902. Later works include *Puck of Pook's Hill* (1906) and the autobiographical *Something of Myself* (1937). He was awarded the Nobel Prize for Literature in 1907.

Kipping, Frederick (Stanley) (1863–1949) Chemist, born in Manchester, Greater Manchester, NW England, UK. He studied at Manchester and in Germany, and worked in Nottingham (1897–1936) as professor of chemistry. He is now best known as the founder of silicone chemistry, although the technical uses for silicones were developed by others from 1940 onwards.

Kirchhoff, Gustav (Robert) [keerkhhohf] (1824–87) Physicist, born in Königsberg, Prussia (now Kaliningrad, Russia). After lecturing at Berlin (1847), he became professor of physics at Wrocław, Poland (formerly Breslau, Prussia) (1850)) and Heidelberg (1854), and of mathematical physics at Berlin (1875). He formulated the laws involved in the mathematical analysis of an electrical network (*Kirchhoff's laws*, 1845). He also investigated heat, and with Bunsen helped to develop the prism spectrometer and the technique of spectrum analysis, used in the discovery of caesium and rubidium (1859).

Kirchhoff's laws [keerkhhohf] Laws applying to direct current theory, stated by German physicist Gustav Kirchhoff in 1846. At any point where three or more components join, the total current into the junction is zero; and, for a closed circuit loop, the sum of all potential differences around the loop is zero. Useful in circuit analysis, the laws are the direct consequences of charge and energy conservation.

Kirchner, Ernst Ludwig [keerkhner] (1880–1938) Artist, born in Aschaffenburg, SWC Germany. He studied architecture at Dresden, then turned to painting, and became the leading spirit in the formation of *Die Brücke* ('The Bridge', 1905–13), the first group of German Expressionists. Many of his works were confiscated as degenerate by the Nazis in 1937, and he committed suicide in 1938.

Kirghizia *Kyrgyzstan*

Kiribati *p.844*

Kiritimati [krismas], Eng **Christmas Island** 2°00N 157°30W, pop (2000e) 3000; area 390 sq km/150 sq mi. Largest atoll in the world, one of the Line Is, Kiribati, C Pacific Ocean, 2000 km/1250 mi S of Honolulu; indented on the E by the Bay of Wrecks; visited by Captain Cook, 1777; annexed by the British, 1888; used as an air base; nuclear testing site in late 1950s; coconut plantations.

Kirkpatrick, Jeane (Duane Jordan) (1926–) US stateswoman and academic, born in Duncan, Oklahoma, USA. She studied at Columbia and Paris universities, then became a research analyst for the state department (1951–3). She concentrated on a career as an academic, at Trinity College and Georgetown University, Washington, DC, becoming Georgetown's professor of government in 1978. Noted for her anti-Communist defence stance and advocacy of a new Latin-American and Pacific-orientated diplomatic strategy, she was appointed permanent representative to the UN by President Reagan (1981–5).

Kirkwall 58°59N 2°58W, pop (2000e) 6800. Port capital of Orkney, N Scotland, UK; on island of Mainland, between Wide Firth (N) and Scapa Flow (S); airport; fishing, textiles, tourism, oil; Earl Patrick's palace (1607), St Magnus Cathedral (1137–1200), Tankerness House (1574), museum of Orkney life.

Kirlian photography A technique in which a very high voltage (30 000–50 000 volts) creates a high intensity electric field

Kiribati

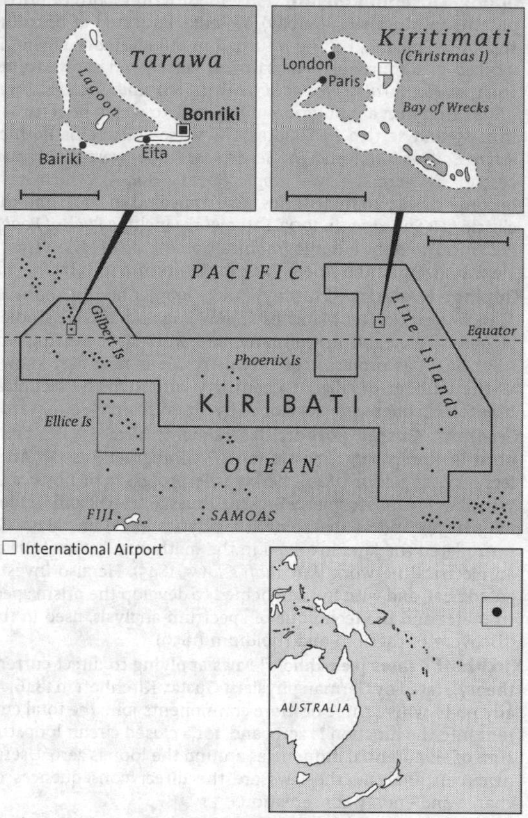

[kiribas], formerly **Gilbert Islands**, official name **Republic of Kiribati**
Local name Kiribati

Timezone GMT −12
Area 717 km²/277 sq mi
Population total (2002e) 90 600
Status Republic
Date of independence 1979
Capital Bairiki (on Tarawa Atoll)
Languages English (official) and Gilbertese
Ethnic groups Micronesian, small Polynesian and non-Pacific minorities
Religions Roman Catholic (54%), Kiribati Protestant (39%), Baha'i (2%), Seventh-day Adventist (2%), Mormon (2%)
Physical features Group of 33 low-lying islands scattered over c.3 000 000 km²/1 200 000 sq mi of the C Pacific Ocean; comprises the Gilbert Is Group, Phoenix Is, and 8 of the 11 Line Islands, including Christmas I; islands seldom rise to more than 4 m/13 ft and usually consist of a reef enclosing a lagoon.
Climate Maritime equatorial climate in central islands, tropical further N and S; periodic drought in some islands; wet season (Nov–Apr); subject to typhoons; average annual temperatures 28°C (Jan), 27°C (July) in Tarawa; average annual rainfall 1977 mm/78 in.
Currency 1 Australian Dollar ($A) = 100 cents
Economy 50% of land under permanent cultivation; main exports include fish, particularly tuna; phosphates; copra, coconuts, bananas, pandanus, breadfruit, papaya; sea fishing.
GDP (2001e) $79 mn, per capita $800
History Gilbert and Ellice Is proclaimed a British protectorate, 1892; became a Crown Colony, 1916; occupied by Japan during World War II, but driven out by US forces; Ellice Is severed links with Gilbert Is to form separate dependency of Tuvalu, 1975; Gilbert Is independence as Kiribati, 1979; a sovereign and democratic republic, with a President and an elected House of Assembly.
Head of State/Government
1979–91 Ieremia T Tabai
1991–4 Teatao Teannaki
1994–2003 Teburoro Tito
2003– Anote Tong

which can be recorded on a photographic plate as a form of electrical interference. The phenomenon was discovered by Russian engineer Semyon Kirlian and his wife Valentina during the 1950s. Materials which are good conductors give an image of the surface of the object; poor conductors show detail of their inner structure. Dead objects have a constant image, whereas living objects show a constantly changing pattern, which in human beings is said to correspond to the aura and to reflect the physical and psychological state of the subject. There is now research interest into the electrical interference patterns associated with normal and diseased tissue, including cancer cells. Computer evaluation of these patterns may, in the future, form the basis of a new system of tissue diagnosis.

Kirov, Sergey Mironovich [kirof] (1886–1934) Russian revolutionary and politician, born in Urzhum, W Russia. Educated at Kazan, he played an active part in the October Revolution and Civil War, and during the 1920s held a number of leading provincial Party posts. In 1934 he became a full member of the Politburo, and at the 17th Party Congress was elected a secretary of the Central Committee. Later that year he was assassinated at his Leningrad headquarters, possibly at the instigation of Stalin, and his death served as the pretext for a widespread campaign of reprisals.

Kirov Ballet, officially, the **Mariinsky Theatre of Opera and Ballet** One of the two major ballet companies of Russia, based in St Petersburg. Originally the **Imperial Russian Ballet**, it was founded in 1738 as an academy to train dancers for the imperial court. In the late 19th-c the company moved to the Mariinsky Theatre, whose name it adopted. From 1867 to 1903 Petipa was principal ballet master, staging elaborate performances for the aristocracy and court. The company experienced hardship during the early Soviet years, but under the tutelage of Agrippina Vaganova (1879–1951) its strict tradition of classical elegance and beauty was maintained. In 1935 the company was renamed the Kirov Ballet. It enjoyed world-wide acclaim during its first visit, in 1961, to the West, marred by the subsequent defection of its leading dancers, Nureyev, Baryshnikov, and Natalia Makarova (1940–). In 1991 the company was renamed the *Kirov–Mariinsky Ballet*. Valery Gergiev (1953–) became artistic and executive director in 1996.

Kisalföld [keesholfuld], Eng **Little Plain** Flat, lowland geographical region in NW Hungary; bounded by the R Danube, the Hungarian Alps and the Transdanubian Central Mountain Range.

Kisangani [keesangahnee], formerly **Stanleyville** (to 1966) 0°33N 25°14E, pop (2000e) 426 600. Capital of Haut-Zaïre region, NC Democratic Republic of Congo; on the R Congo, 1250 km/775 mi NE of Kinshasa; founded by Stanley, 1882; airport; university (1963); agricultural trade, textiles, brewing, furniture.

Kishinev [kishinyof], Romanian **Chisinau** 47°00N 28°50E, pop (2000e) 763 000. Capital city of Moldova; on the R Byk; founded in 1420 as a monastery town; railway; airfield; university (1945); solar research and development, machine building, tobacco, textiles, foodstuffs; Cathedral of the Nativity (1836).

Kissinger, Henry (Alfred) [**kis**injer] (1923–) US secretary of state (1973–6) and academic, born in Fürth, SC Germany. His family emigrated to the USA in 1938 to escape the Nazi persecution of the Jews. He studied at Harvard, and after war service worked for a number of public agencies before joining the Harvard faculty (1962–71). He became President Nixon's adviser on national security affairs in 1969, was the main US figure in the negotiations to end the Vietnam War (for which he shared the 1973 Nobel Peace Prize), and became secretary of state under Nixon and Ford. His 'shuttle diplomacy' was aimed at bringing about peace between Israel and the Arab states, and resulted in a notable improvement in Israeli–Egyptian relations. After leaving public office (1977), he became professor of diplomacy at Georgetown, and established Kissinger Associates, a consulting firm. His book *Diplomacy* was published in 1994.

Kistna, River *Krishna, River*

kit A small violin, usually with four strings and a narrow body, in use from the 16th-c to the 19th-c, especially (though not exclusively) by dancing masters.

Kita-Kyushu [keeta **kyu**shoo] 33°52N 130°49E, pop (2000e) 1 044 000. City in Fukuoka prefecture, N Kyushu, Japan; comprises former towns of Tobata, Kokura, Moji, Wakamatsu, and Yawata; airport; railway; Japan's leading centre for chemicals and heavy industry.

Kitano, Takeshi [kit**ah**noh] (1947–) Actor, comedian, director, and writer, born in Tokyo, Japan. After completing his studies at Meiji University in 1965, he had various jobs until 1972, then worked in comedy shows. He made his film debut in *Danpu Wataridori* (1981), and first received international attention for his role in *Merry Christmas Mr Lawrence* (1983). Later films include *Johnny Mnemonic* (1995) and *Gonin* (1995). He made his directorial debut in 1989 with the thriller *Violent Cop*. He appears regularly on Japanese television and is a prolific writer of both books and magazine columns.

Kit-Cat Club A political and literary club that flourished in London during 1700–20. Its membership comprised leading Whig politicians, writers, and painters, and included Robert Walpole, Joseph Addison, William Congreve, Richard Steele, John Vanbrugh, and artist Godfrey Kneller – who painted portraits of the members.

kit-cat portrait A life-size half-length portrait painted on a canvas 36 × 28 in (c.90 × 70 cm). The term derives from Kneller's series of portraits painted c.1700–17 of the members of the Kit-Cat Club in London (now in the National Portrait Gallery).

Kitchener (of Khartoum and of Broome), (Horatio) Herbert Kitchener, 1st Earl (1850–1916) British field marshal, born near Ballylongford, Co Kerry, SW Ireland. He joined the Royal Engineers in 1871, and served in Palestine (1874), Cyprus (1878), and the Sudan (1883). By the final rout of the Khalifa at Omdurman (1898), he won back the Sudan for Egypt, and was made a peer. Successively chief-of-staff and commander-in-chief in South Africa (1900–2), he brought the Boer War to an end, and was made viscount. He then became commander-in-chief in India (1902–9), consul-general in Egypt (1911), and secretary for war (1914), for which he organized manpower on a vast scale ('Kitchener armies'). He was lost with HMS *Hampshire*, mined off the Orkney Is.

kite (ornithology) A hawk of the subfamily Milvinae (**true kites**) or subfamily Elaninae (**white-tailed kites**), found worldwide; the most varied and diverse group of hawks; eats insects, snails, and small vertebrates, or scavenges. (Family: Accipitridae, c.27 species.)

kite (recreation) A frame covered with a light fabric or paper, flown on a long string. It was first documented in China (AD 549) in relation to military communications. Kites spread to Europe via the Arabs, and were first used in Italy in 1589. They continue to be popular as a leisure activity, and have practical applications in meteorology and surveying.

kithara A musical instrument of classical antiquity, resembling a lyre. It had a wooden resonator (usually rectangular) from which two arms (usually hollow) extended upwards, and were connected by a crossbar from which between 3 and 11 strings were stretched to the base of the resonator. These strings were plucked with a plectrum. The lyre, a smaller instrument, had a resonator of tortoise-shell.

Kitt, Eartha (Mae) (c.1928–) Entertainer and singer, born in North, South Carolina, USA. She studied at the New York School of the Performing Arts, making her debut in 1945. She toured throughout Europe, and was cast by Orson Welles in his production of *Dr Faustus* (1951). Her vocal vibrancy, fiery personality, and cat-like singing voice made her a top international cabaret attraction and recording artiste. Since her debut in *Casbah* (1948), her film appearances have included *St Louis Blues* (1957) and the documentary *All By Myself* (1982). On television from 1953, she received the Golden Rose of Montreux for *Kaskade* (1962), and was appropriately cast as Catwoman in the series *Batman* (1966). Later theatre work has included *Follies* (1988–9) and a one-woman show.

kittiwake Either of two species of marine bird of the genus *Rissa*: the **black-legged kittiwake** (*Rissa tridactyla*) from N areas of the N oceans; and the **red-legged kittiwake** (*Rissa brevirostris*) from the Bering Sea. They spend much time at sea, and nest on cliffs in large numbers. (Family: Laridae.)

Kitt Peak National Observatory An observatory near Tucson, Arizona, USA, site of the largest collection of optical telescopes in the world. The largest is the 4-m/158-in Mayall reflector (1973). Kitt Peak is part of the National Optical Astronomy Observatories, which also includes the Cerro Tololo Inter-American Observatory in Chile, operating a similar 4-m reflector to that at Kitt Peak, and the National Solar Observatory, which has instruments on Kitt Peak including the McMath-Pierce solar telescope, the world's largest telescope for observing the Sun.

Kitwe [**keet**way] 12°48S 28°14E, pop (2000e) 633 200. Modern mining city in Copperbelt province, Zambia; extended in 1970 to include several townships; railway; copper, electrical equipment, paint, fibreglass, food processing, iron foundry, furniture, clothing, plastics; Mindolo Ecumenical Centre.

Kitzbühel [**kitz**büel] 47°27N 12°23E, pop (2000e) 8500. Winter sports resort and capital of Kitzbühel district, Tirol, C Austria, in the Kitzbüheler Alps, on the route to the Thurn Pass; mining of copper and silver in the 16th–17th-c; railway; health resort, tourism, casino; Kitzbühel District Fair (May), summer concerts.

kiva [**kee**va] A subterranean circular room c.5–14 m/16–46 ft in diameter and 2·5 m/8 ft high, with a ceiling hatch and access ladder, used by the prehistoric Anasazi Indians of the American SW for meetings, rituals, storytelling, weaving, and crafts. Inside is a firepit and *sipapu*, a small hole in the floor symbolizing the point at which the ancestral Anasazi emerged from the underworld.

Kivi, Aleksis [**kee**vee], pseudonym of **Alexis Stenvall** (1834–72) Playwright and novelist, born in Nurmijärvi, S Finland. He wrote penetratingly of Finnish peasant life, notably in *Seitseman Veljesta* (1870, Seven Brothers), and is now recognized as one of his country's greatest writers. He died insane, poverty-stricken, and unrecognized.

Kivu, Lake [**kee**voo] area 4750 sq km/1800 sq mi. Lake in EC Africa; highest lake in the Albertine Rift, on the frontier between Democratic Republic of Congo and Rwanda; length, c.95 km/60 mi; width, 50 km/30 mi; altitude, 1460 m/4790 ft; drains into L Tanganyika via the Ruzizi R; contains Idiwi I (S); European discovery by German explorer Count von Gotzen.

Kiwanis International *service club*

kiwi A flightless nocturnal bird, native to New Zealand; small eyes; acute sense of smell (rare in birds); long curved bill with nostrils at tip; strong legs; tail and wings not visible through thick, shaggy plumage; usually inhabits woodland; eats worms, other invertebrates, and berries; nests in burrow. Its egg is the largest, relative to body size, of any bird (25% of the female's weight). (Genus: *Apteryx*, 3 species. Family: Apterygidae.)

kiwi fruit A woody climber (*Actinidia chinensis*), native to China, and also called **Chinese gooseberry**, but cultivated on a commercial scale in New Zealand, hence the better-known name; leaves rough, oval to heart-shaped; flowers creamy, 6-petalled, in axillary clusters; fruit oblong-oval, furry with reddish-green hairs, flesh green, sweet, with surrounding black seeds. (Family: Actinidiaceae.)

Kizil Irmak [kuzul irmak] (Turkish 'red river'), ancient **Halys** Longest river of Turkey; rises in the Kizil Dağ, NC Turkey, and flows in a wide arc SW then generally N to enter the Black Sea N of Bafra; length 1355 km/842 mi; important source of hydroelectric power.

Kjölen Mountains [kyoeluhn] or **Kolen Mountains** Mountain range along the boundary between NE Norway and NW Sweden; rises to 2111 m/6926 ft at Kebnekaise, Sweden's highest peak; source of many rivers flowing SE to the Gulf of Bothnia.

Klammer, Franz (1953–) Alpine skier, born in Mooswald, S Austria. He was the Olympic downhill champion in 1976, and the World Cup downhill champion five times (1975–8, 1983). In 1974–84 he won a record 25 World Cup downhill races.

Klaproth, Martin Heinrich [klaproht] (1743–1817) Chemist, born in Wernigerode, C Germany. He learnt chemistry as an apprentice to an apothecary, and did much to develop analytical chemistry. He was able to deduce, but not isolate, the elements uranium (1786), zirconium (1789), strontium, and titanium. He was appointed the first professor of chemistry in the new University of Berlin (1810).

Klaus, Václav [klows, vatslav] (1941–) Czech politician, prime minister (1992–7), and president (2003–), born in Prague, Czech Republic. Educated at the Prague School of Economics and Cornell University, he lost his post at the Czech Academy of Sciences after the Warsaw Pact invasion in 1968. Employed in the State Bank until 1986, he then returned to the Czech Academy as a member of the Prognostic Institute. A leading figure in the Civil Forum movement during November 1989, he became minister of finance in the Government of National Accord, a position to which he was re-elected after the first free elections. In 1991 he became deputy prime minister and then prime minister of the Czech Republic. In 1997 he resigned after allegations of financial scandals. However, he won re-election as leader of his centre-right Civic Democratic Party in December 1997.

Klee, Paul [klay] (1879–1940) Artist, born in Münchenbuchsee, near Bern, Switzerland. He studied at Munich and settled there, becoming a member of the *Blaue Reiter* group (1911–12). He then taught at the Bauhaus (1920–32), and after returning to Bern (1933) many of his works were confiscated in Germany. His early work consists of bright watercolours, but after 1919 he worked in oils, producing small-scale, mainly abstract pictures, as in his 'Twittering Machine' (1922, New York).

Klein, Calvin (Richard) [kliyn] (1942–) Fashion designer, born in New York City, USA. He graduated from New York's Fashion Institute of Technology in 1962, gained experience in New York, and set up his own firm in 1968. He quickly achieved recognition, and became known for understatement and the simple but sophisticated style of his clothes, including designer jeans.

Klein, Lawrence (Robert) [kliyn] (1920–) Economist, born in Omaha, Nebraska, USA. He studied at the University of California, Berkeley, and the Massachusetts Institute of Technology, and became professor at the universities of Chicago (1944–7), Michigan (1949–54), and Pennsylvania (1958–91, now emeritus). He is best known for his development of several models (the Brookings and Wharton models of the US economy, and the Project LINK model of the global economy) used to plan and forecast the performance of many variables in the economy. He was economic adviser to President Carter (1976–81), and was awarded the 1980 Nobel Prize for Economics for his work on forecasting business fluctuations and portraying economic interrelationships.

Klein, Melanie [kliyn] (1882–1960) Austrian child psychoanalyst. She studied under Sigmund Freud, and opened a practice in London. She was the first to use the content and style of children's play to understand their mental processes, a technique now widely used to help troubled children.

Kleist, (Bernd) Heinrich (Wilhelm) von [kliyst] (1777–1811) Playwright and poet, born in Frankfurt an der Oder, E Germany. He left the army in 1799 to study, and soon devoted himself to literature. He eloquently expresses the conflict of reason and emotion, heroism and cowardice, dreaming and action. His best plays are still popular, notably *Prinz Friedrich von Homburg* (1821) and his finest tale, *Michael Kohlhaas* (1810–11). He committed suicide in 1811.

Klemperer, Otto (1885–1973) Conductor, born in Wrocław, SW Poland (formerly Breslau, Prussia). He studied at Frankfurt and Berlin, first appeared as a conductor in 1906, made a name as a champion of modern music, and was appointed director of the Kroll Opera in Berlin (1927–31). Nazism drove him to the USA, where he became director of the Los Angeles Symphony Orchestra (1933–9). In his later years, he concentrated mainly on the German classical and Romantic composers, and was particularly known for his interpretation of Beethoven. He also composed six symphonies, a Mass, and Lieder.

Klimt, Gustav (1862–1918) Painter, born in Vienna, Austria. The leading master of the Vienna *Sezession*, he began with a firm of decorators, painting nondescript murals for museums and theatres, but in 1900–3 he painted some murals for the University of Vienna in a new and shocking Symbolist style which caused great controversy. His portraits combine realistically painted heads with flat abstract backgrounds.

Kline, Kevin [kliyn] (1947–) Film actor, born in St Louis, Missouri, USA. He studied music at Indiana University, then switched to drama, training at the Juilliard School in New York City. On Broadway he won Tonies for two hit musicals, *On the Twentieth Century* (1978) and *The Pirates of Penzance* (1980). Though known for his dramatic abilities, it was his comic role in *A Fish Called Wanda* (1988) that earned him an Oscar as Best Supporting Actor. Later films include *Chaplin* (1992), *French Kiss* (1995), *Looking for Richard* (1996), and *Wild, Wild West* (1999).

Klinger, Friedrich Maximilian von (1752–1831) Playwright and writer, born in Frankfurt, WC Germany. He was a poet with a touring theatre company before joining the Russian army as an officer (1780–1811), and became curator of Dorpat University (1803–17). The *Sturm-und-Drang* school was named after one of his tragedies, *Der Wirrwarr, oder Sturm und Drang* (1776, Confusion, or Storm and Stress). He wrote several other plays and some novels.

Klinsmann, Jürgen (1964–) Footballer, born in Göppingen, W Germany. He began his career in 1982 with second division club Stuttgart Kickers, later joining Vfb Stuttgart. In 1988 he became top scorer of the Bundesliga and was voted German Player of the Year. Among later clubs are Inter Milan, Monaco, and Bayern Munich. He also had two successful spells with English Premier side Tottenham Hotspur (1994–5, 1997–8), and was voted English Player of the Year in 1995. International honours include captaining Germany to win the European Championship (1996), and victory in the 1990 World Cup in Italy. He also played in the 1994 finals, scoring five goals, although Germany were knocked out in the quarter-finals. He announced he would retire after the 1998 World Cup, where he scored three goals as Germany once again bowed out in the quarter-finals. During his career he gained 108 caps and scored 47 goals.

Klippel, Robert Edward (1920–2001) Sculptor, born in Sydney, New South Wales, SE Australia. He served in the Royal Australian Navy (1939–45), and later studied, worked, and exhibited in London and Paris. He spent the years 1957–63 in New York City. He was professor of sculpture at the University of Minneapolis (1966–7), after which he returned to Sydney. His sculptures are intricate and complex, often made of metal 'found objects' welded together (hence the name 'junk sculpture'), although he did also work with wood, plaster, and bronze. He was Australia's senior and best-known sculptor.

klipspringer A dwarf antelope (*Oreotragus oreotragus*) native to Africa S of the Sahara; thick yellow-grey speckled coat; black feet; stands on points of small peg-like hooves; short vertical horns; rounded ears with dark radiating lines; inhabits rock outcrops in scrubland.

Klitzing *von Klitzing*

Klondike gold rush A flood of prospectors (largely US) when gold was discovered in Canada's Yukon Territory in 1896. The rush lasted for five years, generated an estimated $50 million in gold, established the town of Dawson, and invigorated the economies of British Columbia, Alberta, Alaska, and Washington State.

Klopstock, Friedrich Gottlieb (1724–1803) Poet, born in Quedlinburg, C Germany. Inspired by Virgil and Milton, he began *Der Messias* (The Messiah) as a student at Jena (1745), completing it in 1773. He lived in Copenhagen (1751–71), then moved to Hamburg. Regarded in his own time as a great religious poet, he helped to inaugurate the golden age of German literature, especially by his lyrics and odes.

Klosters [klohsterz] 46°54N 9°54E, pop (2000e) 3800. Alpine winter skiing resort in Graubünden canton, E Switzerland; on R Landquart, NE of Davos, with which it shares snowfields; comprises the villages of Platz, Dörfli, and Brücke; Kloster Pass (12 km/7 mi E) leads to Austria; children's ski school.

Kluane National park in SW Yukon territory, Canada; contains part of the St Elias Mts, rising to 5950 m/19 521 ft at Mt Logan; area 22 015 sq km/8498 sq mi; established in 1972; along with the Wrangell–St Elias park, forms the world's largest nature reserve, on both sides of the US/Canadian border; a world heritage site.

klystron A device for amplifying microwave beams, in which energy is transferred to the microwave beam via its modulation of an electron beam passing through resonance cavities. It is used in particle accelerators and radar, and may also be used as a producer of microwaves.

knapweed The name for many species of *Centaurea*, mostly perennials; characterized by the hard, rounded flower-heads surrounded by many closely overlapping bracts which often terminate in a fringed papery border with comb-like teeth; florets purple or yellow. (Genus: *Centaurea*. Family: Compositae.)

knee Commonly used to refer to the region around the kneecap (*patella*); more specifically, in anatomy, the largest joint in the human body, being the articulation between the femoral projections (*condyles*) and the tibial plateaux, and including the joint between the patella and the femur. It allows a wide range of movement, yet still retains a high degree of stability, because of the presence and arrangement of the ligaments of the joint. It contains the medial and lateral *menisci* (pieces of fibrous tissue between the femur and tibia), which help compensate for the differences in shape between the surfaces, aid in joint lubrication, and assist in weight-bearing.

Kneller, Sir Godfrey [kneler], originally **Gottfried Kniller** (1646–1723) Portrait painter, born in Lübeck, N Germany. He studied at Amsterdam and in Italy, went to London (1676), and was appointed court painter (1680). He was knighted (1692), and in 1715 made a baronet. His best-known works are his 48 portraits of the Whig 'Kit-Cat Club' (1700–17, National Portrait Gallery, London), and of nine sovereigns.

Knesset [kneset] The Israeli parliament and state legislature. It is a unicameral body of 120 members elected under a system of proportional representation. Its term of office is four years, and the country's president is elected by the Knesset for five years.

Kngwarreye, Emily Kame [nuhwaray] (c.1910–96) Artist, born in Alhalkere, Northern Territory, Australia. The pre-eminent artist of the internationally renowned Utopia group of artists, she first became known by exhibiting with Utopia Women's Batik (1977–88), a group which used non-traditional batik techniques. She began painting in her seventies, working mainly with acrylic paints, and her works now feature in major public and private collections throughout Australia and the USA. A non-English speaking elder of the Alhalkere people, her innovative style is based on Amnatyerre ceremonial body designs and symbols and Dreaming maps, over which she applied her own distinct images. She is known as much for being an Aboriginal artist as a contemporary abstract painter.

Knievel, Evel [kneevel, eevel], professional name of **Robert Craig Knievel** (1938–) Motorcycle stunt performer, born in Butte, Montana, USA. He began carrying out motorcycle stunts as a teenager, and after a succession of jobs, from hockey player to safecracker, formed Evel Knievel's Motorcycle Devils in 1965, becoming internationally known for his spectacular and dangerous performances. He later managed the stunt career of his son, **Robbie Knievel**.

Knight, Dame Laura, *née* **Johnson** (1877–1970) Artist, born in Long Eaton, Derbyshire, C England, UK. Trained at Nottingham, she produced a long series of oil paintings of the ballet, the circus, and gypsy life, in a lively and forceful style, and also executed a number of watercolour landscapes. She was made a dame in 1929.

knight In the UK, a title of honour granted as a reward for services, permitting the use of *Sir* with one's name; originally (in the Middle Ages) men who formed an elite cavalry (Fr *Chevalier*, Ger *Ritter*). The ideal of knighthood involved the maintenance of personal honour, religious devotion, and loyalty to one's lord. This ideal was most nearly achieved at the time of the Crusades (11th–13th-c).

knight bachelor (KB) In the UK, the lowest, but most ancient, form of knighthood, originating in the reign of Henry III. A KB is not a member of any order of chivalry.

Knights Hospitallers / of Jerusalem / of Malta / of Rhodes *Hospitallers*

Knights of Labor (1878–93) A US industrial union that tried to organize all workers in support of a large-scale political and social programme, regardless of age, race, and sex. The knights reached a membership of 700 000 in 1886, but then declined.

Knights Templars *Templars*

knitting An ancient craft used for making fabric by linking together loops of yarn using two, three, or four hand-held needles. The first knitting machine was invented in England by William Lee (c.1550–c.1610). Machines are now used to produce complex knitted garments and fabrics of many kinds, but they cannot create all the intricate designs that are commonly produced by skilled hand knitters. The manufacture of knitted fabrics in tubular form is known as *circular knitting*; such fabrics are often used in underwear and sportswear.

knocking An audible shuddering sound produced by an engine, because of the uneven burning of its air/fuel mixture. A high-compression ratio spark ignition engine gives good fuel consumption for a given power output. However, a high-compression ratio also interferes with the fuel's combustion process, leading to uneven ignition, unsteady combustion, and eventually damage. Diesel engines tend to have knocking characteristics opposite to those of a spark ignition engine. To overcome these problems, antiknocking fuels are used.

Knossos [knosos] An Aegean Bronze Age town at Kephala, NC Crete, noted for the sophistication of its art and architecture. Flourishing c.1900–1400 BC, the settlement covered c.50 ha/125 acres, its mansions and houses linked by paved roads and dominated by the 19 000 sq m/4·7 acre Minoan palace discovered in 1899, and later partly reconstructed by Sir Arthur Evans. The traditional association with Minos, the labyrinth of Theseus, and the Minotaur has no historical basis.

knot (ornithology) Either of two species of sandpiper; the widespread **knot** or **red knot** (*Calidris canutus*); and the **eastern knot** or **great knot** (*Calidris tenuirostris*) from E regions of the Old World.

knot (physics) A unit of speed equivalent to one nautical mile (1·85 km) per hour. It is used especially of ships, aircraft, and winds.

knotgrass A spreading annual (*Polygonum aviculare*), a very widespread weed; each node of the stem enclosed in a silvery sheath; leaves small, elliptical, with small pink or white flowers in the axils. (Family: Polygonaceae.)

knowledge-based system A computer system which operates on knowledge, organized as a set of rules, rather than on data. It is used to mirror human decision-making processes, such as medical diagnosis or actuarial assessments. The collection of rules on which the system operates is called a **knowledge base**.

Knowles, William S (1917–) Chemist, born in the USA. He studied at Columbia University, later joining the Monsato Co in St Louis. He shared the 2001 Nobel Prize for Chemistry for work on chirally catalysed hydrogenation reactions.

Know-Nothing movement (1856) The popular name for the anti-immigrant American Party in 19th-c USA. It was so called from the response members were instructed to give to questioning: 'I know nothing'.

Knox, John (c.1513–72) Protestant reformer, born near Haddington, East Lothian, E Scotland, UK. A Catholic priest, he acted as a notary in Haddington (1540–3), and in 1544 was influenced by George Wishart to work for the Lutheran reformation. After Wishart was burned (1546), Knox joined the reformers defending the castle of St Andrews, and became a minister. After the castle fell to the French, he was kept a prisoner until 1549, then became chaplain to Edward VI, and was consulted over the Second Book of Common Prayer. On Mary's accession (1553), he fled to Dieppe, then to Geneva, where he was much influenced by Calvin. He returned to Scotland in 1555 to preach, and again in 1559, where he won a strong party in favour of reform, and founded the Church of Scotland (1560). He played a lasting part in the composition of *The Scots Confession, The First Book of Discipline*, and *The Book of Common Order*.

Knox, Ronald (Arbuthnott) (1888–1957) Theologian and essayist, born in Birmingham, West Midlands, C England, UK. He studied at Oxford, where he became a lecturer (1910), but resigned in 1917 on being converted to Catholicism. He was then ordained, and appointed Catholic chaplain to the university (1926–39). He wrote an influential translation of the Bible, and several works of apologetics, as well as detective novels. His autobiography, *A Spiritual Aeneid*, appeared in 1918.

Knox-Johnston, Robin, popular name of **Sir William Robert Patrick Knox-Johnston** (1939–) British yachtsman, the first person to circumnavigate the world non-stop and single-handed, 14 June 1968–22 April 1969. He is also holder of the British Sailing Trans Atlantic Record (1986: 10 days, 14 h, 9 min), and he co-skippered *Enza* achieving the world's fastest circumnavigation under sail (1994: 74 days, 22 h, 17 min, 22 s). His books include *World of My Own* (1969), *The Columbus Venture* (1991), and *Beyond Jules Verne* (1995). He was knighted in 1995.

koala [kohahla] E Australian marsupial (*Phascolarctos cinereus*); thick soft grey or grey-brown fur with white chest; round head with small eyes, erect fluffy ears, large dark nose pad; tail not obvious; first two fingers oppose other three when climbing; female with pouch opening backwards; eats leaves (mainly of eucalyptus trees); also known (incorrectly) as a **koala bear**. (Family: Phascolarctidae.)

koatimundi *coati*

kob A grazing antelope native to C Africa (*Kobus kob*, 10 subspecies); reddish-brown (male may be black) with white throat and black marks on legs; female without horns; male with thick neck and lyre-shaped horns ringed with ridges.

Kobe [kohbay] 34°40N 135°12E, pop (2000e) 1 500 000. Port capital of Hyogo prefecture, C Honshu, Japan, W of Osaka; Japan's leading international commercial port; continuing land reclamation on seaward side of the city; railway; 15 universities; badly damaged by earthquake, January 1995; food industry, machinery, electronics, shipbuilding, iron and steel, chemicals, saké; harbour and naval museum, Museum of Namban Art, Minatogawa Shrine; Port Island; Kobe Wing Stadium (2001); Nankosai Festival of Minatogawa Shrine (May).

Koblenz [kohblents], Eng **Coblenz**, ancient **Confluentes** 50°21N 7°36E, pop (2000e) 113 000. Capital of Koblenz district, W Germany; at confluence of Mosel and Rhine Rivers, 80 km/50 mi SE of Cologne; seat of Frankish kings, 6th-c; badly bombed in World War 2; largest garrison town in former West Germany; railway; major centre of Rhine wine trade; hygienic tissues, furniture, pianos, clothing; birthplace of Metternich; St Castor's church (836), fortress of Ehrenbreitstein.

Koch, (Heinrich Hermann) Robert [kokh, rohbert] (1843–1910) Bacteriologist, born in Clausthal-Zellerfeld, C Germany. He studied at Göttingen, became a physician and surgeon, and settled in Wollstein. He discovered the tuberculosis bacillus (1882), and led a German expedition to Egypt and India, where he discovered the cholera bacillus (1883). He became professor and director of the Hygienic Institute at Berlin (1885), and director of the new Institute for Infectious Diseases (1891). The major figure in medical bacteriology, he was awarded the 1905 Nobel Prize for Physiology or Medicine.

Köchel, Ludwig Ritter von [koekhel] (1800–77) Musicologist, born in Stein, N Austria. A botanist by training, he compiled the famous catalogue of Mozart's works, arranging them in chronological order, and giving them the 'K' numbers now commonly used to identify them.

Kocher, Emil [kokher] (1841–1917) Swiss surgeon. He worked at Bern University, and won the 1909 Nobel Prize for Physiology or Medicine for his work on the physiology, pathology, and surgery of the thyroid gland.

Kodály, Zoltán [kohdiy] (1882–1967) Composer, born in C Kecskemét, Hungary. He studied at the Budapest Conservatory, where he became professor. Among his best-known works are his *Háry János* suite (1926), and several choral compositions, especially his *Psalmus Hungaricus* (1923) and *Te Deum* (1936). He also published editions of folk songs with Bartók.

Kodiak bear *brown bear*

Kodiak Island 57°20N 153°40W, pop (2002e) 12 000. Island in the Gulf of Alaska, USA; 160 km/100 mi long; scene of the first settlement in Alaska (by the Russians, 1784); till 1804 the centre for Russian interests in the USA and of the fur trade; dairying, cattle and sheep raising, fur trapping, fishing, farming, tourism; home of the Kodiak brown bear (grizzly), the largest living carnivore; Kodiak National Wildlife Refuge (1941); Baranof Museum (Alaska's oldest wooden structure).

Koechlin, Pat *Smythe, Pat*

koedoe *kudu*

Koestler, Arthur [kestler] (1905–83) Writer and journalist, born in Budapest, Hungary. He studied science at Vienna, embraced the cause of Zionism, and became a journalist and editor, and a British citizen. His masterpiece is the political novel, *Darkness at Noon* (1940). His non-fiction books and essays deal with politics, scientific creativity, and parapsychology, notably *The Act of Creation* (1964), and he wrote several autobiographical volumes. He and his wife were active members of the Voluntary Euthanasia Society and, after he developed a terminal illness, they committed suicide. He endowed a chair of parapsychology at Edinburgh University.

Koffka, Kurt (1886–1941) Psychologist, born in Berlin, Germany. At the University of Giessen (1911–24) he helped to conduct experiments in perception, which led to the founding of the *Gestalt* school of psychology. In 1927 he moved to the USA, becoming professor of psychology at Smith College.

Kofun [kohfuhn] The burial-mounds characteristic of early historic Japan, which have given their name to the archaeological period AD c.300–710. The most spectacular, keyhole-shaped and moated like that of the Emperor Suinin in the Nara Basin, measure over 400 m/1300 ft in length. Large hollow clay *haniwa* models of heavily armed warriors were often placed on top or inside.

Koheleth *Ecclesiastes, Book of*

Koh-i-noor [koheenoor] (Persian 'mountain of light') A famous Indian diamond with a history dating back to the 14th-c. It was presented to Queen Victoria in 1850, and is now among the British crown jewels.

Kohl, Helmut (1930–) German statesman and chancellor (1982–98), born in Ludwigshafen-am-Rhein, SW Germany. He studied at Frankfurt and Heidelberg, became a lawyer, and joined the Christian Democrats. In 1976 he moved to Bonn as a member of the Federal Parliament, became Leader of the Opposition, and his party's candidate for the chancellorship. After the collapse of the Schmidt coalition in 1982, Kohl was installed as interim chancellor, and in the elections of 1983 formed a government which has since adopted a central course between political extremes. After the collapse of East Germany in 1989, he played a key role in German reunification and was elected chancellor of the united Germany in 1990. He is a strong supporter of a united Europe. In 1998 German unemployment was at its highest since World War 2, and Kohl lost power to Schröder, ending the longest period of chancellorship since Kaiser Wilhelm's rule. He resigned his leadership of the CDU, and in 1999 his reputation suffered when he admitted accepting illicit contributions to the CDU's party finances.

Köhler, Wolfgang [**koe**ler] (1887–1967) Psychologist, born in Tallinn, Estonia. He studied at Berlin, lectured at Frankfurt (1911), and participated in experiments which led to the formation of the school of *Gestalt* psychology. Professor of psychology at Berlin in 1921, he emigrated to the USA in 1935, where he taught at Swarthmore College, PA, until 1955, and at Dartmouth College, New Hampshire, from 1958.

kohlrabi [**kohl**rabee] A variety of cabbage (*Brassica oleracea*, variety *caulorapa*) with a very short, swollen, green or purple stem resembling a turnip. It is eaten as a vegetable. (Family: Cruciferae.)

Kohn, Walter [kohn] (1923–) Chemist, born in Vienna. He graduated from Harvard in 1948, and taught at Carnegie Mellon and at the University of California, San Diego (1960–79) and Santa Barbara (1979–91), where he was the founding director of the Institute of Theoretical Physics. He shared the 1998 Nobel Prize for Chemistry for his contribution to methods that can be used for theoretical studies of the properties of molecules and the chemical processes in which they are involved – specifically, for his development of the density-functional theory.

Kok, Willem, known as **Wim Kok** (1938–) Trade Union official, politician, and Dutch prime minister (1994–2002), born in Bergambacht, The Netherlands. He studied at Breukelen, and in 1961 joined the building trade union of the NNV (Netherlands Association of Trade Unions). In 1985 he entered parliament, representing the PvdA (Partij van de Arbeid) from 1986. He served as finance minister and vice-premier (1989–94) and became prime minister of a PvdA, D66 (Democraten '66), and VVD (Volkspartij voor Vrijheid en Democratie) cabinet in 1994. In 2002 he resigned with his entire cabinet in the light of an offical report criticising the Dutch peace keeping forces and the UN for failing to prevent the 1995 massacre in Srebrenica.

Kokoschka, Oskar [ko**kosh**ka] (1886–1980) Artist and writer, born in Pöchlarn, NC Austria. He studied at Vienna, and taught at the Dresden Academy of Art (1919–24). He travelled widely, and painted many Expressionist landscapes in Europe. In 1938 he fled to England, and became naturalized in 1947. From 1953 he lived in Switzerland.

kola or **cola** An evergreen tree native to tropical Africa. The woody fruits contain glossy nuts high in caffeine, which is released when the nuts are chewed. It is not cultivated, but the nuts of several species are much used in trade, and are an important part of local diet in W Africa. (Genus: *Cola*, 125 species. Family: Sterculiaceae.)

Kola Peninsula [**ko**la], Russ **Kol'skiy Poluostrov** Peninsula in Murmanskaya oblast, NW European Russia, forming the NE extension of Scandinavia; length, 400 km/250 mi; width, 240 km/150 mi; separates the Barents Sea (N) from the White Sea (S); numerous rivers and small lakes; NE is tundra-covered while the SW is forested; road and rail transport confined to the W; rich mineral deposits.

Kolbe, St Maximilian (Maria) [**kol**buh] (1894–1941) Franciscan priest, born near Łódź, C Poland. He joined the Franciscans in 1907, and studied at the Gregorian University in Rome. In 1917 he founded a devotional association, the Militia of Mary Immaculate, was ordained in 1918, and became director of a religious centre and publishing company. He was arrested by the Gestapo in 1939, and again in 1941, and imprisoned in Auschwitz, where he gave his life in exchange for one of the condemned prisoners, Franciszek Gajowniczek. He was canonized in 1982. Feast day 14 August.

Kolchak, Alexander Vasilevich (1874–1920) Russian admiral and leader of counter-revolutionary (White) forces during the Russian Civil War, born in the Crimea. He fought in the Russo–Japanese War (1904–5), and in 1916 became commander of the Black Sea Fleet. After the 1917 Revolution he established an anti-Bolshevik government in Siberia, and proclaimed himself 'Supreme Ruler' of Russia. He was captured and shot by Red Army forces in Irkutsk.

Kolekole *Haleakala Crater*

Kolen Mountains *Kjölen Mountains*

Kolkatta *Calcutta*

Kolmogorov, Andrey Nikolayevich [kol**mo**gorof] (1903–87) Mathematician, born in Tambov, W Russia. He studied at Moscow University, where he became professor in 1931. He worked on the theory of functions of a real variable, functional analysis, mathematical logic, and topology. He also worked in applied mathematics on the theory of turbulence, information theory, and cybernetics. He is particularly remembered for his creation of the axiomatic theory of probability in his book *Grundbegriffe der Wahrscheinlichkeitsrechnung* (1933, Foundations of the Theory of Probability), and for his work with mathematician Alexander Khinchin (1894–1959) on Markov processes.

Köln *Cologne*

Kolyma [ko**li**ma] A gold-producing area around the valley of the R Kolyma which leads to the Arctic Ocean. Used in Stalin's time as a forced labour camp, it is estimated that up to 4 million people died there as a result of the conditions.

Kolyma, River [ko**li**ma] River in Russia, rising in the SE Khrebet Cherskogo, N of the Sea of Okhotsk; flows generally N and NE to enter the E Siberian Sea, forming a delta W of Ambarchik; length, 2513 km/1562 mi.

Komodo [ko**moh**doh] Small island in Nusa Tenggara Timur province, Indonesia; part of the Lesser Sunda Is; national park established in 1980, area 375 sq km/145 sq mi; home of the Komodo dragon.

Komodo dragon A rare SE Asian monitor lizard (*Varanus komodoensis*), native to the islands of Komodo, Flores, Pintja, and Padar (Indonesia); the world's largest lizard (length, up to 3 m/10 ft); climbs and swims well; inhabits grassland; often kills pigs and deer; capable of killing an adult water buffalo; occasionally attacks and kills people; also known as **Komodo lizard** or **ora**.

Kompong Som or **Kampong Saom** 10°38N 103°30E. Seaport in S Cambodia, on Gulf of Thailand; a new city, completed in 1960; chief deepwater port and commercial centre of Cambodia; airfield; railway; oil refining, tractors, fish processing, agricultural trade.

Komsomol [**kom**somol] The All-Union Leninist Communist League of Youth, founded in 1918, incorporating almost all persons between the ages of 14 and 28. Its purpose being the socialization of youth in the thought and ways of the Communist Party, it served as a recruiting ground for party membership. It was disbanded in 1991.

Konev, Ivan Stepanovich [**kon**yef] (1897–1973) Soviet military commander and marshal of the Soviet Union (1944), born in Lodeyno, Russia. He was drafted into the Tsarist army in 1916, and joined the Red Army in 1918. During World War 2 he commanded several different fronts against the Germans. He then became commander-in-chief, ground forces (1946–50), first

Korea, North

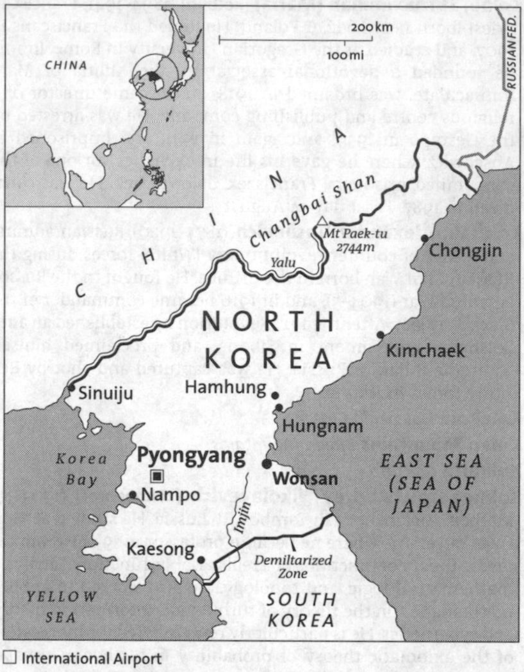

official name **Democratic People's Republic of Korea**, Korean **Choson Minjujuui In'min Konghwaguk**

Local name Ch-oson Minjujuŭi In'min Konghwaguk

Timezone GMT +9

Area 122 098 km²/47 130 sq mi

Population total (2002e) 22 224 000

Status Democratic people's republic

Date of independence 1948

Capital Pyongyang

Language Korean (official)

Ethnic groups Korean (99·8%), Chinese (0·2%)

Religions Atheist or non-religious (68%), Buddhist (2%), Christian (1%)

Physical features Located in E Asia, in the N half of the Korean peninsula; separated from South Korea to the S by a demilitarized zone of 1262 km²/487 sq mi; volcanic peak of Mount Paek-tu rises 2744 m/9003 ft in NE; Yalu river valley marks Korean-Chinese border in NW; fertile Chaeryong and Pyongyang plains in SW; 74% of land forested, 18% arable.

Climate Temperate; warm summers, severely cold winters; often rivers freeze for up to 3–4 months in winter; average annual temperatures -8°C (Jan), 24°C (Jul); average annual rainfall 916 mm/26 in.

Currency 1 Won (NKW) = 100 chon

Economy Agriculture (employs c.48% of workforce, generally on large-scale collective farms); rice, maize, vegetables, livestock, wheat, barley, beans, tobacco; timber, fishing; severely affected during the Korean War, but rapid recovery with Soviet and Chinese aid; machine building, mining, chemicals, textiles.

GDP (2002e) $22·26 bn, per capita $1000

History (*see* Korea, South history); formally annexed by Japan, 1910; N area occupied by Soviet troops following invasion by US and Russian troops and the dividing of the country into N and S, 1945; Democratic People's Republic of Korea declared, 1948; Korean War, 1950–3; demilitarized zone established, 1953; friendship and mutual-assistance treaty signed with China, 1961; unsuccessful reunification talks in 1980; non-aggression agreement signed with S Korea, 1991; became a member of UN, 1991; death of Kim Il-sung, 1994; withdrawal from the 1970 Nuclear Non-Proliferation Treaty (Jan 2003); governed by a President and a Supreme People's Assembly; first road link to be opened between North and South Korea since the Korean War inaugurated (Feb 2003).

Head of State
1957–72 Choi Yong-kun
1972–94 Kim Il-sung
1994– Kim Jong-il

Head of Government
1984–6 Kang Song-san
1986–8 Yi Kun-mo
1988–92 Yon Hyong-muk
1992–7 Kang Song-san
1997–2003 Hong Song-nam
2003– Pak Pong-ju

deputy minister of defence, and commander-in-chief of the Warsaw Pact forces (1956–60).

Kongo An African kingdom situated to the S of the R Congo which by the late 15th-c had a coastline of 250 km/150 mi and reached inland for 400 km/250 mi. It was already involved in trade in ivory, copper, and slaves when the Portuguese arrived in the area in 1482. Some of its kings accepted Christianity, but it was disrupted by the stepping up of the slave trade, and declined during the 18th-c when the Portuguese turned their attention to S Angola.

kongoni *hartebeest*

Konstanz *Constance*

Kon Tiki [kon teekee] A balsa-wood raft built in 1947 by Thor Heyerdahl. He and five others sailed 6000 km/3800 mi from South America to Polynesia in the 13·7 m/45 ft-long raft to prove his theories on the migration of early man. The vessel is now preserved in an Oslo museum.

Konya [konya], ancient **Iconium** 37°51N 32°30E, pop (2000e) 618 000. Holy city and capital of Konya province, SC Turkey, 260 km/162 mi S of Ankara; visited by St Paul; order of the Whirling Dervishes founded here by Islamic mystical poet, Jalal al-Din Rumi, known as Mevlana ('our lord'); airfield; railway; trade centre of a rich agricultural and livestock-raising region; carpets, textiles, leather; notable Seljuk architecture; annual ceremony of the dance to commemorate the death of Mevlana (Dec).

kookaburra Either of two species of bird of the kingfisher family: the **laughing kookaburra** or **laughing jackass** (*Dacelo novaeguinae*) from Australia; and the **blue-winged kookaburra** or **howling jackass** (*Dacelo leachii*) from Australia and New Guinea. They inhabit dry forest and savannah, eat insects and small vertebrates, and have loud laugh-like cries. (Family: Alcedinidae.)

Koopmans, Tjalling C(harles) (1910–85) Economist, born in 's Graveland, The Netherlands. He studied at Utrecht and Leyden, worked at the League of Nations in Geneva (1936–40), then emigrated to the USA (1940) and worked for a shipping firm, devising a system to optimize transport costs. He became a US citizen in 1946. He was professor of economics at Chicago (1948–55) and Yale (1955–81), and shared the 1975 Nobel Prize for Economics for his contributions to the theory of optimal allocation of resources.

Kópavogur [kopavogur] 64°06N 21°56W, pop (2000e) 17 600. Second largest town in Iceland, in Suðurland region, SW Iceland; developed since 1945 to house people working in Reykjavík.

kopje *tor*

Koran *Qur'an*

Korea, South

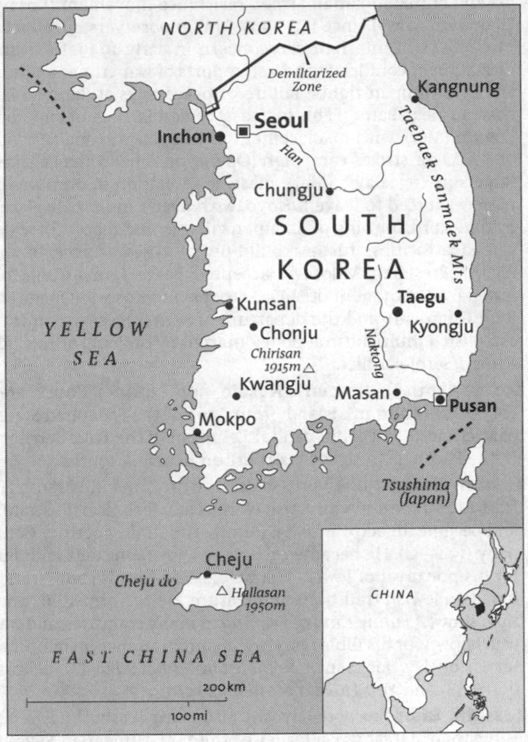

□ International Airport

or **Korea,** official name **Republic of Korea**, Korean **Tae Han Minguk**

Local name Taehan-Min'guk

Timezone GMT +9

Area 98 913 km²/38 180 sq mi

Population total (2002e) 47 640 000

Status Republic

Date of independence 1948

Capital Seoul

Language Korean (official)

Ethnic groups Korean (99·9%), Chinese (0·1%)

Religions Buddhist (18%), Christian (Protestant 41%, Roman Catholic 3%), Confucianist (1%)

Physical features Occupies the S half of the Korean peninsula; bordered N by North Korea, from which it is separated by a demilitarized zone at 38°N; Taebaek Sanmaek Mt range runs N–S along the E coast; descends to broad, undulating coastal lowlands; rivers include Naktong and Han; c.3000 islands off the W and S coasts; largest island is Cheju do, which contains Korea's highest peak, Hallasan, 1950 m/6398 ft.

Climate Extreme continental climate, cold winters, hot summers; average annual temperatures -5°C (Jan), 25°C (Jul); average annual rainfall 1250 mm/49 in.

Currency 1 Won (W) = 100 chon

Economy Light consumer goods, with a shift towards heavy industries; petrochemicals, textiles, electrical machinery, steel, ships, fish; one of the world's largest deposits of tungsten; only a fifth of land suitable for cultivation; rice, wheat, barley, grain, pulses, tobacco.

GDP (2002e) $941·5 bn, per capita $19 600

Human Development Index (2002) 0·882

History Originally split into three rival kingdoms, united in 668 by the Silla dynasty; succeeded by the Koryo dynasty, 935; Yi dynasty, 1392–1910; independence recognized by China, 1895; annexation by Japan, 1910; entered by Russia (from N) and USA (from S) to enforce the Japanese surrender, dividing the country in N and S at the 38th parallel, 1945; declared Republic of Korea, 1948; North Korean forces invaded, 1950; UN forces assisted South Korea in stopping the advance, 1950–3; military coup, 1961; assassination of Park Chung Hee, 1979; non-aggression pact signed with N Korea, 1991; governed by a President, a State Council, and a National Assembly; co-location (with Japan) of the 2002 FIFA World Cup; first road link between North and South Korea since the Korean War inaugurated (Feb 2003).

Head of State
1993–98 Kim Young-sam
1998–2003 Kim Dae Jung
2003–4 Roh Moo-hyun *suspended*
2004– Koh Kun *Acting*

Head of Government
1997–8 Koh Kun
1998–2000 Kim Jong-pil
2000 Park Tae-joon
2000–2 Lee Han-dong
2002–3 Kim Suk-soo
2003– Koh Kun

Korda, Sir Alexander, originally **Sándor Laszlo Korda** (1893–1956) Film producer, born in Puszta, E Hungary. He began as a journalist in Budapest, became a film producer there, and then in Vienna, Berlin, and Hollywood, where he directed for First National. He moved to the UK, and in 1932 founded London Film Productions and Denham studios. His films include *The Private Life of Henry VIII* (1932), *The Third Man* (1949), and *Richard III* (1956). He was knighted in 1942, the first film-maker to be so honoured.

Kordestan *Kurdistan*

Korea, North *p.850*

Korea, South *see panel*

Korean A language of uncertain origin, showing resemblances to the Altaic family and to Japanese. It is spoken by over 50 million people in N and S Korea (where it is the official language), China, Japan, and Russia.

Korean War (1950–3) A war between Communist and non-Communist forces in Korea, which had been partitioned along the 38th parallel in 1945 after Japan's defeat. US troops occupied South Korea after World War 2. The Communist North invaded the South in 1950 after a series of border clashes, and a United Nations force intervened, under MacArthur's command, driving the invaders back to the Chinese frontier. China then entered the war, and together with the North Koreans occupied Seoul (1951). The UN forces counter-attacked, and by 1953, when an armistice was signed, had retaken all territory S of the 38th parallel.

Koresh, David [koresh] (1960–93) Cult leader, born in Texas, USA. He was the charismatic leader of a heavily armed group of Branch Davidians (a sect which had split away from the Seventh Day Adventist Church in 1959) who were put under siege by federal agents at a ranch in Mount Carmel, Waco, TX, between February and April 1993. The siege ended after a devastating fire in which Koresh and many of his followers were killed.

Kórinthos *Corinth*

Kornberg, Arthur (1918–) Biochemist, born in New York City, USA. A graduate in medicine from Rochester University, he was director of enzyme research at the National Institutes of Health (1947–52) and head of the department of microbiology at Washington University (1953–9). He discovered the DNA enzyme polymerase, for which he shared the 1959 Nobel Prize for Physiology or Medicine. In 1959 he was appointed professor at Stanford University, and became the first to synthesize viral DNA (1967).

Korolyov, Sergey (Pavlovich) [**ko**rolyof], also spelled **Korolev** (1907–66) Aircraft engineer and rocket designer, born in Zhitomir, WC Ukraine. Educated at Moscow Higher Technical School, in 1931 he formed the Moscow Group for Investigating Jet Propulsion, which launched the Soviet Union's first liquid-propelled rocket in 1933. By 1949 he was engaged in high-altitude-sounding flights employing rockets. As chief designer of Soviet spacecraft, he directed the Soviet Union's space programme, launching the first artificial satellite (1957), the first manned space flight (1961), the *Vostok* and *Voskhod* manned spacecraft, and the *Cosmos* series of satellites.

Koror [**koh**raw(r)] 7°21N 134°31E, pop (2000e) 12 900. Capital town of Belau, W Pacific Ocean, on Koror I; airport on neighbouring island of Babeldoab; tuna, copra, boatbuilding; Belau National Museum.

korrigum *topi*

Kós *Cos*

Kosciusko, Mount [koseeuhs**koh**] 36°28S 148°17E. Highest mountain in Australia (2228 m/7310 ft); in the Snowy Mts of the Australian Alps, New South Wales; within a national park (6458 sq km/2493 sq mi); a popular winter sports area.

Kościuszko or **Kościusko, Thaddeusz (Andrzej) Bonaventura** [kosh**chooshkoh**] (1746–1817) Polish general and patriot, born near Slonim, SW Belarus (formerly Lithuania). Although a captain in the Polish army, he volunteered his services to Benjamin Franklin during the American Revolution, arrived in Philadelphia in 1776, and was commissioned a colonel in the engineers. He fought in several campaigns, and was promoted brigadier-general in 1783. He then returned to Poland (1784), and achieved fame for his defence of Dubienka against the Russians (1792), and in 1794 became head of the national movement. His defeat of the Russians at Raclawice was followed by a rising in Warsaw. He established a provisional government, but was defeated at Maciejowice (1794) and taken prisoner until 1796. In 1816 he settled in Soleure, Switzerland. His will directed that the 500 acres in Ohio granted him by the US Congress (1797) be sold and the money used to free slaves; instead it was used to found the Colored School of Newark, NJ, one of the earliest schools for African-Americans in the USA.

Köseg [**ker**shag] 47°14N 16°37E, pop (2000e) 11 700. Historic town in Vas county, W Hungary; at the foot of the Alps, close to the Austrian frontier; highest town in Hungary; Jurisich Square, castle with Jurisich Miklós Museum.

kosher [**koh**sher] Food fulfilling the requirements of Jewish Law, including the manner of preparation. In orthodox Judaism, only certain animals, which must be ritually slaughtered, may be eaten.

Koshiba, Masatoshi (1926–) Physicist, born in Toyohashi, C Honshu, Japan. He studied at the University of Rochester, later joining the International Center for Elementary Particle Physics in Tokyo. He shared the 2002 Nobel Prize for Physics for his pioneering contributions to astrophysics, in particular for the detection of cosmic neutrinos.

Košice [**ko**shitsuh], Ger **Kaschau**, Hung **Kassa** 48°43N 21°14E, pop (2000e) 240 000. Industrial capital of Východoslovenský region, Slovak Republic; on R Hornád; formerly part of Hungary; airport; railway; technical university (1952); iron and steel, textiles, chemicals, tobacco, brewing; 13th-c St Elizabeth Cathedral.

Kosovo [**ko**suhvuh] (Serbian), **Kosova** (Albanian) pop (2002e) 2 400 000; area 10 887 sq km/4200 sq mi. Province of S Serbia; capital, Pristina; 90% of population Albanian (Kosovars, mostly Muslim); agricultural region; central part of Serbian kingdom, 11th–14th-c; Kosovo Polje the site of a famous battle between Serbs and Turks (1389); under Ottoman rule, 14th-c–1912; annexed by Serbia, 1912; incorporated into Kingdom of Serbs, Croats, and Slovenes, 1918 (Yugoslavia from 1929); part of Greater Albania under Italian occupation, 1941–3; autonomous province of Serbia to 1989; declared independence in 1990, with president and parliament elected in 1992, but implementation disallowed by Serbian authorities; conflict between Serbia and ethnic Albanian armed resistance movement (Kosovo Liberation Army) since late 1997; NATO observers introduced, 1998; focus of international concern in early 1999, following escalation of conflict, with fresh reports of war crimes and violations of human rights; failure of peace talks at Rambouillet chateau near Paris (Feb); increase of Serbian incursions into Kosovo (Mar), with displacement of Kosovar Albanians; onset of NATO air-strikes campaign (Operation Allied Force) against targets in Yugoslavia (Mar); massive escalation in numbers of refugees forced to leave Kosovo, with over a million displaced by mid-April, burning of Albanian villages, and reports of widespread atrocities; further build-up of NATO forces in the region; President Milosevic accepted peace terms (Jun), followed by deployment of NATO troops into Kosovo (Operation Joint Guardian), and the departure of Serb forces; attempts to establish a multicultural policy marred by ongoing ethnic (Albanian/Serb) conflict.

Kosrae [**koz**ray], formerly **Kusaie** pop (2000e) 8900; area 100 sq km/40 sq mi. Island group, one of the Federated States of Micronesia, W Pacific; capital, Lelu; part of the Trust Territory of the Pacific Is until 1977; airport on Kosrae I; tourism.

Kossoff, David (1919–) British actor, writer, and illustrator. He trained as a commercial artist, worked as a technical illustrator, and became an actor in 1943, joining the BBC Repertory Company (1945–51). He became especially known on stage and film for his portrayal of Jewish characters, and for his short stories based on Jewish traditions and culture. He performed his one-man show, *A Funny Kind of Evening* in many countries, and was well known for his Bible story-telling programmes on radio and television. His books include *Bible Stories Retold by David Kossoff* (1968) and *You Have a Minute, Lord?* (1977).

Kossuth, Lajos [**ko**sooth, **lo**yosh], also Hung [koshut] (1802–94) Hungarian statesman, a leader of the 1848 Hungarian Revolution, born in Monok, N Hungary. He practised law, and became a political journalist, for which he was imprisoned (1837–40). In 1847, he became Leader of the Opposition in the Diet, and in 1848 demanded an independent government for Hungary. At the head of the Committee of National Defence, he was appointed provisional governor of Hungary (1849), but internal dissensions led to his resignation, and he fled to Turkey, and then to England.

Kosygin, Alexey Nikolayevich [ko**see**gin] (1904–80) Russian statesman and premier (1964–80), born in St Petersburg, NW Russia. Educated in Leningrad, he joined the army in 1919, and the Communist Party in 1927. Elected to the Supreme Soviet (1938), he held a variety of industrial posts, becoming a member of the Central Committee (1939–60) and the Politburo (1946–52). Chairman of the State Economic Planning Commission (1959–60), and first deputy prime minister (with Mikoyan) from 1960, he succeeded Khrushchev as chairman of the Council of Ministers in 1964. He resigned in 1980 because of ill health.

koto A Japanese zither, about 1·85 m/6 ft long, with 13 silk strings stretched across movable bridges which allow a variety of tunings. It is placed on the floor; the player sits cross-legged or kneels before it, and plucks the strings with three plectra on the right hand, using the left to control the pitch by pressing on the strings.

Kotor [**ko**tuh(r)] A region of both natural and culturo-historical interest, located on the Gulf of Kotor on the Montenegrin coast; a world heritage site. The area is noted for its plant and marine life, and for its historic settlements, which have played a decisive role in the cultural and artistic development of the Balkans.

Kotzebue, August (Friedrich Ferdinand) von [**kot**zebyoo] (1761–1819) Playwright, born in Weimar, C Germany. He worked in government service in Russia, and wrote about 200 poetic dramas, notably *Menschenhass und Reue* (1789–90, trans The Stranger), as well as tales, satires, and historical works. While on a mission for Emperor Alexander I, he was assassinated Mannheim by a radical student as an alleged spy.

Koulouri *Salamis* (Greece)

koumiss or **kumiss** A fermented drink obtained from ass's or mare's milk. Originally made by nomadic peoples of C Asia (eg the Tartars), it has been used both as medicine and beverage.

Kourou [kooroo] 5°09N 52°39W, pop (2000e) 9300. Port in French Guiana, 56 km/35 mi W of Cayenne; stretches c.30 km/20 mi along coast; bisected by R Kouron; main French Space Centre (Centre Spatial Guyanais), used for European Space Agency's Ariane programme; tourism.

Koussevitsky, Serge [koosevitskee], originally **Sergei Alexandrovich Koussevitsky** (1874–1951) Conductor, composer, and double-bass player, born in Vishni-Volotchok, W Russia. He founded his own orchestra in Moscow in 1909, and after the revolution was director of the State Symphony Orchestra in Petrograd (St Petersburg). He left Russia in 1920, worked in Paris, and settled in Boston in 1924, remaining conductor of its symphony orchestra for 25 years. He became a US citizen in 1941. A champion of new music, he commissioned and premiered many works which became 20th-c classics. He founded the Berkshire Symphonic Festivals (1934) and the Berkshire Music Centre (1940) at Tanglewood, MA.

Kowloon [kowloon], also **Jiulong** area 11 sq km/4 sq mi. Peninsula and region of Hong Kong; one of the most densely populated areas in the world (28 500 people per sq km in 1981); railway link to Guangzhou (Canton); site of Hong Kong's airport, to the E; Victoria Harbour lies between the peninsula and Hong Kong I.

Kozhikode [kohzhuhkohd], formerly **Calicut** 11°15N 75°43E, pop (2000e) 941 000. Port city in Kerala, SW India; on the Malabar Coast of the Arabian Sea, 530 sq km/329 sq mi; SW of Chennai (Madras); trade centre since the 14th-c; Vasco da Gama's first Indian port of call, 1498; railway; university (1968); textiles, trade in timber, spices, tea, coffee, cashew nuts; gave its name to calico cotton.

Kraepelin, Emil [kraypelin] (1856–1926) Psychiatrist, born in Neustrelitz, NE Germany. He studied at Würzburg, and did further study under Wundt, whose techniques he later used for research on the effects of alcohol. Professor at Dorpat, Heidelberg, and Munich, he was a pioneer in the psychological study of serious mental diseases (psychoses), which he divided into two groups, manic-depressive and dementia praecox. He compiled a classification of disorders *Compendium der Psychiatrie* (1883, Compendium of Psychiatry), which he continued to revise throughout his life, and which was very influential at the beginning of the 20th-c.

Krafft-Ebing, Richard, Freiherr von (Baron) [kraft ebing] (1840–1902) Psychiatrist, born in Mannheim, SWC Germany. He studied in Germany and Switzerland, and was professor at Strasbourg and Vienna. Much of his work was on forensic psychiatry and on sexual aberrations. He is best known for *Psychopathia sexualis* (1886).

kraft process A paper pulp-making process, which uses sodium hydroxide and sodium sulphate instead of sulphite. The pulp is stronger and less crude than that made by the sulphite process. The name derives from Swedish *kraft* 'strong'.

krait [kriyt] A venomous Asian snake of genus *Bungarus* (several species); related to the cobra, but smaller and lacks a 'hood'; causes many deaths each year in India. The name is also used for sea snakes of genus *Laticauda*.

Krajina [krajina] Serbian enclave in SW Croatia; proclaimed autonomy as Serbian Autonomous Region (SAR), 1990; administrative base, Knin; unilaterally declared status as republic, 1991; united with SARs of Slavonia, Baranja & Western Srem (Croatia), and Bosanska Krajina (Bosnia and Herzegovina), 1991; conflict between Croats and Serbs for possession of strategic Maslenica bridge brought serious structural damage to Peruca dam, and extensive flooding of R Cetina, 1993; retaken by Croatia, 1995; commanding officer of the republic Mile Mrksic indicted by UN war crimes tribunal, 2002.

Krakatoa [krakatoha] Volcanic island in the Sunda Strait between Java and Sumatra. Active for the last million years, it erupted catastrophically in 1883. Activity began on 20 May 1883 culminating in an explosion on 27 August which ejected ash to a height of 80 km/50 mi and which was heard 3200 km/2000 mi away in Australia; several tsunamis were generated and responsible for the deaths of 36 000 people in the coastal areas of Java and Sumatra. The eruption left a small island 816 m/2677 ft high and a sea basin 275 m/900 ft deep. Further small eruptions have continued, including that of 26 January 1928, when an ash cone rose above the sea to form **Anak Krakatoa** ('Child of Krakatoa').

Kraków or **Cracow** [krakuf], Ger **Krakau**, ancient **Cracovia** 50°04N 19°57E, pop (2000e) 757 000. Industrial capital of Kraków voivodship, S Poland, on R Vistula; third largest city in Poland; capital, 1305–1609; airport; railway; Jagiellonian University, one of the oldest in Europe (1364); technical university (1945); includes Nowa Huta industrial centre, 10 km/6 mi E; pig iron, metallurgy, chemicals, food processing, clothing, printing; cathedral (14th-c), royal castle, city museum; Churches of St Andrew, SS Peter and Paul, St Barbara, the Virgin Mary; Market Square (14th-c), a world heritage site; Kraków Days (Jun).

Kramer, Dame Leonie (Judith) [kraymer] (1924–) Academic, writer, and administrator, born in Melbourne, Victoria, SE Australia. She studied at Melbourne and Oxford universities, was professor of Australian literature at Sydney (1968–89) then emeritus professor, and in 1991 became chancellor of the university. She has held positions on a number of influential bodies, including the board of the Australian Broadcasting Commission (since 1947, chairman 1981–3) and the Universities Council (1977–86), and became a director of the Australian and New Zealand Banking Group (1983). She is a prominent member of the group 'Australians for Constitutional Monarchy', founded in 1992 in response to growing republican sentiment. She was created a dame in 1983.

Krasnoyarsk [krasnoyah(r)sk] 56°08N 93°00E, pop (2000e) 918 000. Fast-growing river-port capital of Krasnoyarskiy kray, W Siberian Russia, on the R Yenisey; founded as a fortress, 1628; grew rapidly after discovery of gold in the area, 19th-c; airport; on the Trans-Siberian Railway; university (1969); heavy machinery, grain harvesters, electrical goods, steel, aluminium.

Kray brothers Convicted British murderers, twin brothers who ran a criminal Mafia-style operation in the East End of London, UK in the 1960s: **Ronald Kray** (1933–95) and **Reginald Kray** (1933–2000). Their gang collected protection money, organized illegal gambling and drinking clubs, and participated in gang warfare. An early attempt to convict them of murder failed. Their activities became increasingly violent, and in the late 1960s Ronnie Kray shot dead a member of a rival gang, and Reggie stabbed another to death because he had threatened his brother. The twins were tried at the Old Bailey in 1969, found guilty, and were sentenced to life imprisonment of not less than 30 years. A campaign to free them in 1987 failed.

Krebs, Sir Hans (Adolf) (1900–81) Physiologist, born in Hildesheim, NC Germany. He began his research at Freiburg, but was forced to emigrate to England in 1933, where he continued his work at Cambridge, then at Sheffield (1935–54) and Oxford (1954–67). He shared the Nobel Prize for Physiology or Medicine in 1953 for his work on the nature of metabolic processes, the way living creatures obtain energy from food. He was knighted in 1958.

Krebs cycle A sequence of biochemical reactions in biological systems which results in the release of large amounts of energy; named after Hans Adolf Krebs, and also called the **citric acid cycle**. It is the final pathway for the oxidation of the fuel molecules, ie carbohydrates, fats, and proteins.

Kreisler, Fritz [kriysler] (1875–1962) Violinist, born in Vienna, Austria. He began studies at the Vienna Conservatory at the age of seven, later moving to the Paris Conservatoire. He also studied medicine in Vienna, art in Paris and Rome, and became an army officer. From 1889 he became one of the most successful violin virtuosos of his day, and composed violin pieces, a string quartet, and an operetta, *Apple Blossoms* (1919), which was a Broadway success. He became a US citizen in 1943.

Kremlin The mediaeval citadel of a Russian town, generally used with reference to the Kremlin at Moscow, which occupies a wedge-shaped 36 ha/90 acre site by the Moscow R. The Moscow Kremlin was built of wood in the 12th-c, subsequently rebuilt in brick in the 14th-c, and altered and embellished so that its palaces and cathedrals reflect a variety of architectural styles. It was the residence of the tsars until 1712, and in 1918 became the political and administrative headquarters of the USSR.

Kreutzer, Rodolphe [kroytzer] (1766–1831) Violinist, born in Versailles, NC France. He studied with his father, and from 1784 until 1810 was one of the leading concert violinists in Europe. He also taught at the Paris Conservatoire (1793–1826), conducted at the Opera (from 1817), and composed. He became friendly with Beethoven, who dedicated a sonata to him.

krill A typically oceanic, shrimp-like crustacean, length up to 50 mm/2 in; gills exposed beneath margins of its hard covering (*carapace*); feeds on minute plant plankton; often migrates to surface, massing into vast aggregations that form the main food source of baleen whales. (Class: Malacostraca. Order: Euphausiacea.)

Krishna [krishna] According to Hindu tradition, the eighth incarnation, in human form, of the deity Vishnu. A great hero and ruler, the Mahabharata tells the story of his youthful amorous adventures, which is understood to symbolize the intimacy between the devotee and God. His story reaches its climax when, disguised as a charioteer in an eve-of-battle dialogue with Arjuna, he delivers the great moral discourse of the Bhagavadgita.

Krishna or **Kistna, River** [krishna] River in S India; rises in the Western Ghats, 65 km/40 mi E of the Arabian sea; length 1300 km/800 mi; flows generally SE through Maharashtra and Andhra Pradesh to enter the Bay of Bengal; its source is sacred to Hindus.

Krishna Menon, V(engalil) K(rishnan) [krishna menon] (1896–1974) Indian politician and diplomat, born in Kozhikode (formerly Calicut), Malabar, SW India. He studied at Chennai (Madras) and London, and became a history teacher and a barrister. In 1929 he was secretary of the India League and the mouthpiece of Indian nationalism in Britain. He was India's first high commissioner in London (1947), and the leader of the Indian delegation to the UN (1952). As defence minister (1957–62), he came into conflict with Pakistan over Kashmir.

Krishnamurti, Jiddu [krishnamoortee] (1895–1986) Theosophist, born in Chennai (Madras), SE India. He was educated in England by Annie Besant, who in 1925 proclaimed him the Messiah. Later he rejected this persona, dissolved The World Order of the Star in the East (founded by Dr Besant), and travelled the world teaching and advocating a way of life and thought unconditioned by the narrowness of nationality, race, and religion. He set up the Krishnamurti Foundation, and wrote several books on philosophy and religion.

Kristiansen, Ingrid, *née* **Christensen** (1956–) Athlete, born in Trondheim, C Norway. A former cross-country skiing champion, and then an outstanding long-distance runner, she is the only person to hold world best times for the 5000 m, 10 000 m, and marathon, which she achieved in 1985–6. In 1986 she knocked 45·68 s off the world 10 000 m record, and easily won the European title. She has won most of the world's major marathons, including Boston, Chicago, and London, and was the world cross-country champion in 1988.

Kristianstad [kristyanstad] 56°02N 14°10E, pop (2000e) 75 000. Seaport and capital of Kristianstad county, S Sweden, on R Helge; founded by Denmark, 1614; ceded to Sweden, 1658; taken by the Danes, 1676–8; earliest example of Renaissance town-planning in N Europe; engineering, textiles, sugar.

Kroemer, Herbert [kroemer] (1928–) Physicist, born in Germany. He studied theoretical physics at the University of Göttingen (1952), and after research work in Germany and the USA he joined the University of California, Santa Barbara (1976). In 2000 he shared the Nobel Prize for Physics for his groundbreaking work in the development of semiconductor heterostructures.

Kropotkin, Pyotr Alexeyevich, Knyaz (Prince) [kropotkin] (1842–1921) Revolutionary and geographer, born in Moscow, Russia. The son of a prince, he was educated at the Corps of Pages, St Petersburg. He became an army officer and was stationed in Siberia (1862–7), where he made zoological and geographical studies that won him recognition in scientific circles. In 1871 he renounced his title and devoted himself to a life as a revolutionary. Arrested and imprisoned (1874), he escaped to Switzerland in 1876. Expelled from Switzerland in 1881, he went to France, and was condemned in 1883 to five years' imprisonment for anarchism. Released in 1886, he settled in England until the revolution of 1917 took him back to Russia. He wrote of an anarchy where mutual support and trust in a harmonious society is the central theme, not the lawlessness and chaos more usually associated with the term.

Kroto, Harold [krohtoh] (1939–) Chemist, born in Wisbech, Cambridgeshire, EC England, UK. He studied at the University of Sheffield, moving to the University of Sussex in 1967. He shared the Nobel Prize for Chemistry in 1996 for his contribution to the discovery of fullerenes (1985).

Kru A Kwa-speaking people of Liberia and Côte d'Ivoire, famous as fishermen and stevedores throughout W Africa from Senegal to Cameroon. Land shortages have forced many into cities, and the largest settlement of Kru is now in Monrovia, Liberia.

Kruger, Paul [krooger], in full **Stephanus Johannes Paulus Kruger**, nickname **Oom** ('Uncle') **Paul** (1825–1904) President of the Transvaal (1883–1902), born in Colesberg, Cape Colony, SC South Africa. With his fellow-Boers he trekked to Natal, the Orange Free State, and the Transvaal, and won such a reputation for cleverness, coolness, and courage that in the first Boer War (1881) he was appointed head of the provisional government. In 1883 he was elected President of the Transvaal and held the post until the Boers submitted to British control in 1902. After the discovery of gold on the Rand, he strove to protect the Boer state, refusing civil rights to the 'Uitlanders', and resisting British power by seeking alternative railway outlets as well as capital and arms from the Germans and the Dutch. During the second Boer War (1899–1902), after weeks as a fugitive, he left for Europe, urging the Boers to fight on. He died in Switzerland.

Kruger National Park A game reserve in South Africa. Founded in 1898 as the Sabi Game Reserve, in 1926 it was renamed in honour of Paul Kruger. The sanctuary covers about 20 700 sq km/8000 sq mi, and is one of the largest national parks in the world.

Krugerrand A gold coin of the Republic of South Africa, 1 ounce in weight, named after the Boer statesman Paul Kruger (the *rand* being the unit of South African currency). Krugerrands are minted for issue overseas, and are bought for investment. They are not part of the everyday currency of South Africa.

Krupp, Gustav, originally **Gustav von Bohlen und Halbach** (1870–1950) Industrialist, born in The Hague, The Netherlands. He was a Prussian diplomat when he was chosen by Wilhelm II as a suitable husband for **Bertha Krupp** (1886–1957), heiress to the Krupp industrial empire. They married in 1906 and by special imperial edict he was allowed to adopt the name Krupp. He took over the firm, gained the monopoly of German arms manufacture during World War 1, and manufactured the long-range gun for the shelling of Paris, nicknamed 'Big Bertha'. He turned to agricultural machinery and steam engines after the war, gave financial support to Hitler, and connived in secret rearmament, contrary to the Versailles Treaty, after the latter's rise to power in 1933. Hitler's *Lex-Krupp* (1943) confirmed exclusive family ownership for the firm. After World War 2, the Krupp empire was split up by the Allies, but Gustav was too senile to stand trial as a war criminal at Nuremberg.

krypton Kr, element 36, the fourth of the noble gases. It liquefies at −150°C, and makes up about 0·0001% of the atmosphere. It forms few compounds, the most stable being a fluoride, KrF_4.

K2 or **Mount Godwin-Austen** Second highest mountain in the world and highest in the Karakoram range, NE Pakistan; height 8611 m/28 250 ft; named for English topographer Henry Godwin-Austen (1834–1923); the second peak to be measured in this range (hence, K2).

Kuala Lumpur [kwahla lumpoor] 3°08N 101°42E, pop (2000e) 1 534 000. Capital of Malaysia, E Peninsular Malaysia; large Chinese and Indian population; former capital of Selangor; capital of Federated Malay States, 1895; designated a Federal Territory, 1974; airport; railway; university (1962); technical university (1954); commercial centre; trade in rubber, tin; Petronas Twin Towers (1996), in 2000 tallest building in the world (451·9 m/1483 ft); national mosque, Sri Mahamariamman (Hindu temple, 1873), national museum, national museum of art, Selangor Turf Club, Mimaland recreational complex; annual Malaysian golf tournament.

Kubelík, Rafael (Jeronym) [kubelik] (1914–96) Conductor and composer, born in Býchory, C Czech Republic. He studied at Prague Conservatory, and conducted the Czech Philharmonic Orchestra (1936–9, 1942–8). He left Czechoslovakia and settled first in England (1948), then in Switzerland, where he became a citizen in 1973. He was conductor of the Chicago Symphony Orchestra (1950–3) and the Bavarian Radio Orchestra (1961–79), conducted at Covent Garden (1955–8), and was musical director of the New York Metropolitan Opera (1973–4). He has composed five operas, symphonies, concertos, and other works.

Kubitschek (de Oliveira), Juscelino [kubshek] (1902–76) Brazilian statesman and president (1956–61), born in Diamantina, Minas Gerais, Brazil. He studied medicine at Belo Horizonte, Paris, and Berlin. His government sponsored rapid economic growth, and the dramatic building of a new capital, Brasília.

Kublai Khan [koobliy kahn] (1214–94) Mongol emperor of China (1279–94), the grandson of Genghis Khan. He was acclaimed Great Khan in 1260, with suzerainty from the Pacific to the Black Sea. An energetic prince, he suppressed his rivals, adopted the Chinese mode of civilization, encouraged mathematicians and men of letters, and made Buddhism the state religion. He established himself at Cambaluc (modern Beijing), the first foreigner ever to rule in China, and ruled an empire which extended as far as the R Danube. Recognizing China's importance, he made it a separate realm within the Mongol Empire. The splendour of his court was legendary.

Kubrick, Stanley [koobrik] (1928–99) Screen writer, film producer, and director, born in New York City, USA. He started as a staff photographer with *Look* magazine, before making his directorial debut in documentaries in 1950. He moved to features, and after directing *Spartacus* (1960), went to the UK, where he made a series of unusual features in several film genres: *Lolita* (1962), black comedy in *Dr Strangelove* (1964), psychedelic science fiction in *2001: a Space Odyssey* (1965), urban violence in *A Clockwork Orange*, scripted by Anthony Burgess (1971, withdrawn from circulation in Britain at the director's request, but released there in 2000), a period piece in *Barry Lyndon* (1975), and a horror film, *The Shining* (1980). Later productions were infrequent, but included the Vietnam saga, *Full Metal Jacket* (1987) and *Eyes Wide Shut* (1999). His screenplay for an epic film, *Napoleon*, was published on the Internet in 2000, and later withdrawn by the executors of the Kubrick estate.

Kudelka, James [kudelka] (1955–) Ballet dancer, choreographer, and director, born in Newmarket, Ontario, SE Canada. He graduated from the National Ballet School in Toronto in 1972, then joined the National Ballet of Canada. He moved to Les Grands Ballets Canadiens in Montreal in 1981 as principal dancer, and became resident choreographer there (1984–90). Artist in residence at the National Ballet of Canada from 1992, he took over as director in 1996.

Kudrow, Lisa [kudroh] (1963–) Actress, born in Encino, California, USA. She studied biology at Vassar College, then took up acting, becoming a member of the Groundlings, a Los Angeles improvisational comedy group. After a range of small parts in television, she became known for her role as Ursula in *Mad About You* (1992), then achieved a major success as Phoebe Buffay (Ursula's 'twin sister') in the acclaimed television series *Friends* (1994–2004). Her feature films include *Romy and Michelle's High School Reunion* (1997), *The Opposite of Sex* (1998), and *Analyze This* (1999).

kudu or **koedoe** [koodoo] A spiral-horned antelope native to Africa; greyish-brown with thin vertical white lines; female horns small or absent; male horn length up to 1·6 m/5¼ ft; inhabits dense undergrowth; two species: the **greater** and the **lesser kudu**. (Genus: *Tragelaphus*.)

Kuei-yang *Guiyang*

Kuhn, Thomas (Samuel) [koon] (1922–96) Philosopher and historian of science, born in Cincinnati, Ohio, USA. He studied physics at Harvard and worked as a physicist, but then became interested in the historical development of science. He is chiefly known through his book, *The Structure of Scientific Revolutions* (1962), which challenged the idea of cumulative, unidirectional scientific progress. His theory of 'paradigms', as sets of related concepts which compete for acceptance in times of rapid scientific change or revolution, has been influential in many fields of enquiry. He held positions at Harvard, Boston, Berkeley (1958–64), Princeton (1964–79), and the Massachusetts Institute of Technology (from 1979).

Kuiper, Gerard (Peter) [kiyper] (1905–73) Astronomer, born in Harenkarspel, The Netherlands. He studied at Leyden, moved to the USA in 1933, and became a US citizen in 1937. He took an appointment at the Lick Observatory, CA, then taught at Harvard (1935–6), and joined the Yerkes Observatory before moving to the McDonald Observatory, TX, in 1939. He discovered two new satellites: Miranda, the fifth satellite of Uranus; and Nereid, the second satellite of Neptune (1948–9). His study of the planetary atmospheres detected carbon dioxide on Mars and methane on Titan, the largest Saturnian satellite. He was involved with the early US space flights, including the Ranger and Mariner missions.

Kuiper Belt [kiyper] A region in the Solar System beyond the planet Neptune where a swarm of icy asteroids orbits the Sun. Its existence was predicted in 1951 by Dutch-born US astronomer Gerard Kuiper; the first was found in 1992. A billion of these objects a few hundred kilometres in diameter and smaller could exist. The Kuiper Belt is thought to be the source of most comets with orbital periods shorter than a century or two. About a thousand times the Earth' distance from the Sun, the Kuiper Belt probably merges with the Oort cloud of comets.

Ku Klux Klan The name of successive terrorist organizations in the USA, thought to derive from Greek *kyklos* 'circle'. The first was founded after the Civil War (1861–5) to oppose Reconstruction and the new rights being granted to blacks: the members, disguised in robes and hoods, terrorized blacks and their sympathizers in the country areas of the South. It faded after Federal measures were passed against it, but was re-established in a stronger and wider-based form after World War 1. This time its targets were Catholics, foreigners, Jews, and organized labour, as well as blacks. It gained great political power, but the movement ended by 1944. It was revived by the fear of communism in the 1950s, then by opposition to the civil rights movements in the 1960s. Much violence was unleashed in the South before strong measures from the federal government (under President Johnson) imposed some control. The organization is still sporadically active in various parts of the USA.

kulaks The most progressive and wealthy stratum of the late 19th-c and early 20th-c Russian peasantry. (*Kulak* is Russian for 'fist', as they often employed hired hands as bullies.) The kulaks developed after the emancipation of the serfs, and engaged in capitalist farming and entrepreneurial activities. During the collectivization of agriculture in the 1930s, Stalin 'liquidated' the kulaks as a class – a process known as *dekulakization*. They were sent *en masse* to Siberia. As it was not easy to tell kulaks from other peasants, millions of people not classed as kulak died.

kulan [koolan] *ass*

Kulturkampf [kultoorkampf] In the German Second Empire, a 'cultural conflict' between the Prussian state, headed by Bismarck, and the Roman Catholic Church. It was inspired by Bismarck's suspicion of Catholics' extra-German loyalties, and involved discriminatory legislation against the Church's position within Prussia. Most intense during 1870–8, Bismarck subsequently repealed many of the anti-clerical laws in the hope of regaining Catholic support in the Reichstag. The Kulturkampf gradually subsided following the election of Pope Leo XIII (1878), and effectively ended by 1886.

Kumasi [koomahsee], known as **Garden City**, **City of the Golden Stool** 6°45N 1°35W, pop (2000e) 537 000. Capital of Ashanti region, SC Ghana, 180 km/112 mi NW of Accra; second largest city in Ghana; centre of the Ashanti kingdom since the 17th-c; centre of Ghanaian transport network; airfield; railway; university (1951); National Cultural Centre, including zoo, art gallery, open-air theatre; nearby Bonwire, woodcarving and cloth centre; large market centre for cocoa-growing region.

kumquat or **cumquat** [kuhmkwot] A spiny evergreen shrub related to and closely resembling citrus, native to E and SE Asia, and cultivated elsewhere; fruits look and taste like tiny oranges, and are often candied. (Genus: *Fortunella*, 6 species. Family: Rutaceae.)

Kun, Béla (1886–c.1939) Hungarian political leader and revolutionary, born in Szilágycseh, S Hungary. He was a journalist, soldier, and prisoner in Russia, and in 1918 founded the Hungarian Communist Party. In March 1919 he organized a Communist revolution in Budapest, and set up a Soviet republic which succeeded Karolyi's government. It failed to gain popular support, and he was forced to flee for his life in August of that year. After escaping to Vienna he returned to Russia. Some historians believe that he was killed in a Stalinist purge.

Kundera, Milan [kundaira] (1929–) Novelist, born in Brno, S Czech Republic. He studied in Prague, and lectured in cinematographic studies there until he lost his post after the Russian invasion of 1968. His first novel, *Zert* (1967, The Joke), was a satire on Czechoslovakian-style Stalinism. In 1975 he fled to Paris, where he has lived ever since, taking French nationality in 1981. He came to prominence in the West with *Kniha smichu a zapomneni* (1979, The Book of Laughter and Forgetting). *Nesnesitelna lehkost byti* (The Unbearable Lightness of Being) appeared in 1984, and was filmed in 1987. *Immortality* (1991) is set in his adoptive France. Later novels include *Testaments Betrayed* (1995) , *Identity* (1998), and *La Ignorancia* (2001).

Küng, Hans (1928–) Roman Catholic theologian, born in Sursee, NC Switzerland. A professor at Tübingen (1960–96), he has written extensively for fellow theologians and for lay people. His questioning of received interpretations of Catholic doctrine, as in *Justification* (1965), *The Church* (1967), and *Infallible? An Inquiry* (1971), and his presentations of the Christian faith, as in *On Being a Christian* (1977), *Does God Exist?* (1980), and *Eternal Life?* (1984), aroused controversy both in Germany and with the Vatican authorities, who withdrew his licence to teach as a Catholic theologian in 1979. He defended himself in *Why I Am Still a Christian* (1987). Later works include *Yes to a Global Ethic* (1996).

kung fu A form of Chinese unarmed combat dating from the 6th-c, when it was practised at the Shaolin Temple. There are many forms; the best known is *wing chun*, popularized by the actor Bruce Lee (1940/1–73) in several films.

Kunlun Shan [kunlun shahn] or **K'un-lun Shan** Mountain range in W China; extends 2500 km/1500 mi along border of Xinjiang province and Tibet (Xizang); divides E to form the Altun Shan and Hoh Xil Shan ranges; rises to 7723 m/25 338 ft at Muz Tagh peak.

Kunming or **K'un-ming** 25°04N 102°41E, pop (2000e) 1 797 000, administrative region 4 053 000. Capital of Yunnan province, S China, on Yunnan plateau; altitude 1894 m/6214 ft; major market and transport centre from 279 BC; spring-like weather and scenery ('City of Eternal Spring'); airfield; railway; university (1934); agricultural university; minerals, engineering, metallurgy, food processing, chemicals, textiles; Qiongzhu Si (Bamboo Temple), 11 km/7 mi W; Stone Forest, 126 km/78 mi SE.

Kuomintang *Guomindang*

Kurchatov, Igor (Vasilevich) [koorchatof] (1903–60) Physicist, born in Sim, W Russia. He graduated from the Crimean University in Simferopol and went to the Physico-Technical Institute, Leningrad (St Petersburg) where he became director of nuclear physics (1938). He carried out important studies of neutron reactions, and was the leading figure in the building of Russia's first atomic (1949) and thermonuclear (1953) bombs, and the world's first industrial nuclear power plant (1954). He became a member of the Supreme Soviet in 1949.

Kurdistan or **Kordestan** [koordistahn] pop (2000e) 1 312 000; area 24 998 sq km/9649 sq mi. Province in NW Iran, bounded W by Iraq; capital, Sanandaj; inhabited by Kurds, who also occupy parts of NE Iraq, SE Turkey, and NE Syria; in 1920 a Kurdish autonomous state was agreed at the Treaty of Sèvres, but the terms were never carried out; new Kurdish Council formed after elections, 1992, not recognized by central government.

Kurds A W Iranian-speaking ethnic group settled in neighbouring mountainous areas of Turkey, Iraq, Iran, Syria, and the former Soviet Union, an area which they themselves call **Kurdistan**, and numbering 25 million. They were originally pastoral nomads with some agriculture, but the creation of national boundaries after World War 1 restricted their seasonal migrations, and most are now urbanized. They have been Sunni Muslims since the 7th-c AD. The Kurds form the world's largest ethnic group without their own state, and their aim is to achieve independence or autonomy within their national area. Internal rivalries and political divisions have forestalled any united attempt to gain independence. In addition, their host countries have suppressed Kurdish independence movements. Turkey has been particularly severe in repressing them and has pursued Kurdish fighters into Iraq. They suffered religious persecution in Iran, especially after the Iranian revolution of 1979. In Iraq, the Kurds' failure to achieve autonomous status for Kurdistan during the 1970s, despite promises by the Baathist government, resulted in vicious hostilities between Kurds and government forces. Following the Gulf War (Jan–Feb 1991), there was an Iraqi offensive against Kurdish rebels. Many sought refuge in Turkey and Iran, while UN troops tried to maintain safe havens in Iraq. It is only Anglo–US surveillance flights over N Iraq that have prevented further Iraqi attacks. In Turkey, an armed separatist movement, the Kurdistan Workers' Party (PKK), has been active since the mid-1980s. Its leader, Abdullah Ocalan, was captured in Kenya (Feb 1999) and imprisoned in Turkey, triggering widespread international protests by Kurdish supporters.

Kurgan culture The semi-nomadic population of the S Russian steppes in the fourth millennium BC, characterized archaeologically by burials sprinkled with red ochre beneath a burial mound or *kurgan*. They were long held responsible for the dissemination across Europe from c.3000 BC of the Indo-European family of languages, a view which continues to attract controversy.

Kuril Islands [kureel], Russ **Kurilskiye Ostrova** area 15 600 sq km/6000 sq mi. Archipelago off the N Japanese coast, between the N Pacific Ocean (E) and the Sea of Okhotsk (W); extends c.1200 km/750 mi from the S tip of Kamchatka Peninsula to the NE coast of Hokkaido I, Japan; rises to 2339 m/7674 ft; over 50 islands, actively volcanic, with hot springs; visited in 1634 by the Dutch; divided between Russia and Japan, 18th-c; all ceded to Japan, 1875; occupied by Soviet troops, 1945; part of the USSR, 1947; claimed by Japan.

Kuwait

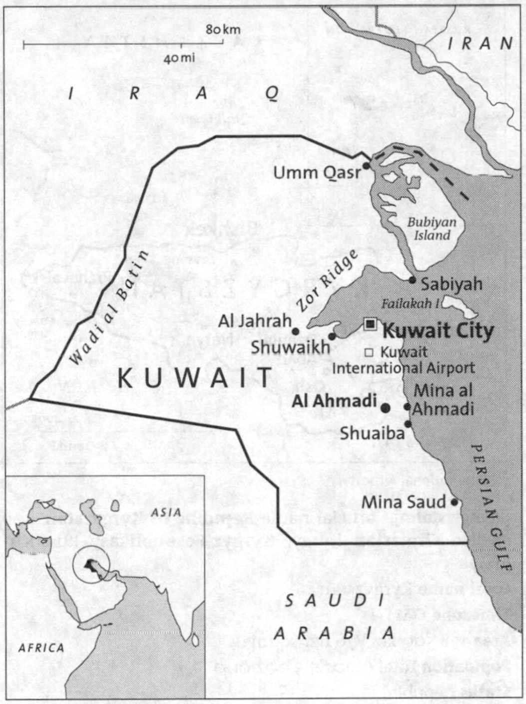

□ International Airport

[koowayt], official name **State of Kuwait**, Arabic **Dowlat al-Kuwait**

Local name Dowlat al-Kuwait (Arabic)

Timezone GMT +3

Area 17 818 km²/6878 sq mi

Population total (2002e) 2 253 000

Status Independent state

Date of independence 1961

Capital Kuwait City

Language Arabic (official)

Ethnic groups Kuwaiti (52%), non-Kuwaiti Arab (45%), Asian (3%)

Religions Muslim (90%), Christian (8%), Hindu (2%)

Physical features Consists of mainland and nine offshore islands; terrain flat or gently undulating, rising SW to 271 m/889 ft; Wadi al Batin on W border with Iraq; low ridges in NE generally stony with sparse vegetation.

Climate Hot and dry climate; summer temperatures very high, often above 45°C (Jul–Aug); humidity often over 90%; sandstorms common all year; average annual temperature 14°C (Jan) to 37°C (Jul) in Kuwait City; average annual rainfall 111 mm/4 in.

Currency 1 Kuwaiti Dinar (KD) = 1000 fils

Economy Oil discovered, 1938, providing 95% of government revenue; active programme of economic diversification; petrochemicals, fertilizers, construction materials, asbestos, batteries; agriculture gradually expanding; dates, citrus fruits, timber, livestock.

GDP (2002e) $36·85 bn, per capita $17 500

Human Development Index (2002) 0·813

History Port founded in 18th-c; British protectorate, 1914; full independence from Britain, 1961; invasion and annexation by Iraq (Aug 1990), leading to Gulf War (Jan–Feb 1991), with severe damage to Kuwait City; Kuwait liberated with the aid of UN forces in 1991, and government returned from exile; large refugee emigration; major post-war problems, including burning of Kuwaiti oil wells by Iraq and pollution of Gulf waters by oil; Emir is Head of State, governing through an appointed Prime Minister and a Council of Ministers.

Head of State (Emir)
1965–77 Sabah III al-Salim
1978– Jabir al-Ahmad al-Jabir

Head of Government (Prime Minister)
1965–78 Jabir al-Ahmed al-Jabir
1978–2003 Saad al-Abdallah al-Salim Al Sabah
2003– Sabah al-Ahmad al-Jabir al-Sabah

Kurosawa, Akira [kurohsahwa] (1910–98) Film director, born in Tokyo, Japan. He began as a painter, and joined a cinema studio in 1936, making his first feature film (*Sanshiro Sugata*) in 1943. He was renowned for his adaptation of the techniques of the Noh theatre to film-making, in such films as *Rashomon* (1950), which won the Venice Film Festival Prize, and *Shichinin No Samurai* (1954, The Seven Samurai). Also characteristic were his literary adaptations, such as *Kumonosu-Jo* (1957, The Throne of Blood, from *Macbeth*) and *Donzoko* (1957, The Lower Depths, from Gorky). Later films included *Kagemusha* (1980, Palme d'Or, BAFTA best director), *Ran* (1985, from *King Lear*), *Dreams* (1990), and *Madadayo* (1993).

kuru [kuroo] A prion disease endemic to the Fore peoples of Papua New Guinea in the early part of the 20th-c. It involves progressive degeneration of the central nervous system, leading to dementia, inco-ordination, and paralysis. Abnormal protein deposits known as **kuru plaques** are present in the brain. It is thought to be transmitted by cannibalistic funerary rites, involving eating the brains of the deceased. Changes in these practices have led to a marked reduction in incidence.

Kurzweil, Raymond C [kertzviyl] (1948–) Computer scientist, a pioneer of reading technology, born in New York City, USA. Since the 1970s he has led the development of the first optical character recognition device, the first text-to-speech synthesizer, the first flat-bed scanner, the first orchestral music synthesizer, and a large vocabulary automatic speech recognizer. He has formed then sold-on a number of successful companies including Kurwzeil Music Systems (1982–90), Kurzweil Applied Intelligence (1982–97), and Kurzweil Educational Systems (1996–98). In a joint venture with the American Board of Family Practice in 1997 he formed the Medical Learning Company based on his Medical Synthesizer System. He received the major prize for inventors, the Lemelson-MIT Award, in 2001.

Kush An independent kingdom on the Nile which emerged from the Egyptian province of Nubia in the 11th-c BC, with its capital at Napata. In the 8th-c BC Kush conquered Egypt and established the XXVth dynasty, which ruled until the Assyrian conquest in 671–666 BC. The Kush kings became Egyptianized, but after their withdrawal from Egypt in the 7th-c BC they moved to the more southerly capital of Meroe, where there were good supplies of iron ore and timber. It became an important centre of iron smelting, and large slag heaps can still be seen there.

Kutab Minar *Qutb Minar*

Kutch, Rann of [kuch], also spelled **Kachch**, or **Cutch** area 9000 sq km/3500 sq mi. Region of salt marsh in the Indian state of Gujarat and Sind province, Pakistan; bounded W by the Arabian Sea and N by the Thar Desert; once a shallow arm of the Arabian Sea; great accumulations of salt on the surface when dry; inundated during SW monsoon; scene of Indo-Pakistani fighting in 1965.

Kuti, Fela Anikulapo [kootee], born **Fela Ransome Kuti** (1938–97) Singer, musician, composer, and dissident, born in Abeokuta, SW Nigeria. The pioneer of 'Afro-beat', he successfully took his music to Europe and America, and in Nigeria used it as a form of political protest and championing African identity. He was a frequent target for government repression, including imprisonment. His saxophonist son **Femi Kuti** continues the family tradition of music combined with political activism.

Kutiyattam [kootiyahtam] An Indian theatrical tradition found in Kerala, and believed to be a surviving example of the style of Sanskrit theatre.

Kutuzov, Mikhail Ilarionovich, Knyaz (Prince) [kutoozof] (1745–1813) Russian field marshal, born in St Petersburg, NW Russia. He distinguished himself in the Turkish wars, and in 1805 commanded against the French, but was defeated at Austerlitz. In 1812, as commander-in-chief, he fought Napoleon obstinately at Borodino, and later obtained a major victory over Davout and Ney at Smolensk.

Kuwait *p.857*

Kuwait City, Arabic **al-Kuwayt**, formerly **Qurein** 29°20N 48°00E, pop (2000e) 45 000. Capital city of Kuwait, on S shore of Kuwait Bay, at head of Persian Gulf; developed in the late 1940s after discovery of oil; suburban port of Shuwaikh, SW; airport; ferry service to Failaka I; university (1966); centre for communications, banking, investment centre; shipbuilding; severely damaged during the Gulf War (1991).

Kuybyshev [kooibishef] *Samara*

Kuznets, Simon (Smith) (1901–85) Economist and statistician, born in Kharkov, E Ukraine. He emigrated to the USA in 1922, studied at Columbia, and investigated business cycles for the National Bureau of Economic Research from 1927. He was professor of economics at Pennsylvania (1930–54), Johns Hopkins (1954–60), and Harvard (1960–71). In his work he combined a concern for facts and measurement with creative and original ideas on economic growth and social change, such as the 20-year **Kuznets cycle** of economic growth. His major publication was *National Income and its Composition, 1919–1938* (2 vols, 1941). He was awarded the Nobel Prize for Economics in 1971.

Kuznets Basin [kuznets] Basin of the Tom R in Kemerovo oblast, Russia; stretches from Tomsk SE to Novokuznetsk; a major industrial zone, with rich deposits of coal and iron ore.

Kuznetsov, Alexander Vasilievich [kuznetsof] (1929–79) Writer, born in Kiev, Ukraine. He published short stories as early as 1946, but first came to public notice in the USSR with the short novel *Prodolzheniye legendy* (1957, The Continuation of a Legend). He is best known for *Babi Yar* (1966), a novel about the massacre of Ukrainian Jews by the German SS in 1941. Both novels were heavily censored before publication, and he defected to England in 1969, changing his name to **A Anatoli**.

Kwakiutl [kwakiootl] A N Pacific Coast American Indian group living on the coast of British Columbia as fishermen and traders. They were famed for their woodwork, frequently painted in bright colours, including masks, totem poles, war canoes, whale hunting vessels, and decorative boxes. Art is still produced, much of it for the tourist trade. They also had elaborate dances and ceremonies, including the recently revived potlatch.

KwaNdebele [kwahndebelay] Former national state or non-independent black homeland in Transvaal province, NE South Africa; situated NE of Johannesburg and E of Pretoria; self-governing status, 1981; incorporated into Mpumalanga following the South African constitution of 1994.

Kwang-chow *Guangzhou*

kwashiorkor [kwashiaw(r)ker] A nutritional disorder of young children, stemming from an inadequate intake of protein in the diet, usually with an adequate calorie intake. In Africa, it frequently begins after weaning. Failure to thrive, apathy, oedema, anaemia, and diarrhoea are characteristic.

KwaZulu Natal [kwahzooloo natahl] pop (2000e) 8 071 000; area 91 481 sq km/35 312 sq mi. One of the nine new provinces established by the South African constitution of 1994, in E South Africa, on the Indian Ocean; comprises former areas of Natal and KwaZulu; Natal, annexed to Cape Colony, 1844; separate colony, 1856; joined Union of South Africa, 1910; KwaZulu, former national state or non-independent black homeland; self-governing status, 1971; provincial status, 1994; capital, alternating between Ulundi and Pietermaritzburg; Durban, business port and second largest city in South Africa; chief languages, Zulu (80%), English, Afrikaans; 'the garden province'; sugar cane, citrus, grain, vegetables, dairying; chemicals, paper, food processing, iron and steel, oil refining, explosives, fertilizers, meat canning; tourism (coastal resources and game reserves).

Kyrgyzstan

□ International Airport

[keergizstahn], official name **Republic of Kyrgyzstan**, also spelled **Kirgizstan**, Kyrgyz **Kyrgyz Respublikasy**, Russ **Kirgiziya**

Local name Kyrgyzstan

Timezone GMT +5

Area 198 500 km²/76 621 sq mi

Population total (2002e) 5 002 000

Status Republic

Date of independence 1991

Capital Bishkek (formerly Frunze)

Language Russian, Kirgiz (official)

Ethnic groups Kyrgyz (52%), Russian (21%), other (27%)

Religion Sunni Muslim (chief religion)

Physical features Located in C Asia, bounded SE and E by China; largely occupied by the Tien Shan Mts; highest point within the republic at Pik Pobedy, 7439 m/24 406 ft; chief river, the Naryn. Largest lake, L Issyk-Kul.

Climate Typical desert climate in N, W, and SE; hot, dry summers in valleys; mean annual temperature -18°C (Jan), 28°C (Jul).

Currency 1 Kyrgyzstani som (KGS) = 100 tyiyn

Economy Metallurgy; machines; coal; natural gas; textiles, food processing, gold; wheat, cotton, tobacco, animal husbandry.

GDP (2002e) $13·88 bn, per capita $2900

Human Development Index (2002) 0·712

History Part of an independent Turkestan republic, 1917–24; proclaimed a constituent republic of the USSR, 1936; declaration of independence, 1991, and joined Commonwealth of Independent States; governed by a president, prime minister, and Supreme Soviet.

Head of State

1991– Askaar Akayev

Head of Government

1999–2000 Amangeldy Muraliev

2000–2 Kurmanbek Saliyevich Bakiyev

2002– Nikolai Tanayev

Kweilin; Kuei-lin *Guilin*

Kyd or **Kid, Thomas** (1558–94) Playwright, born in London, UK. He was probably educated at the Merchant Taylors' School, and brought up as a scrivener under his father. His tragedies early brought him reputation, especially *The Spanish Tragedy* (c.1589). He has been credited with a share in several plays, and may have written an earlier version (now lost) of *Hamlet*. Imprisoned in 1593 on a charge of atheism, he died in poverty.

Kyoga, Lake [keeohga] area 4427 sq km/1709 sq mi. Lake in C Uganda, N of Kampala; the Victoria Nile R passes through from L Victoria.

Kyogen [kyohgen] Comic plays often performed between Japanese Noh plays.

Kyoto [kyohtoh] 35°02N 135°45E, pop (2000e) 1 491 000. Capital of Kyoto prefecture, C Honshu, Japan; SW of Lake Biwa; founded, 8th-c; capital of Japan, 794–1868, and one of the Tokugawa Shogunate power centres from 1603; railway; 22 universities, including university of industrial arts and textiles (1949); electrical goods, machinery, silk, crafts; over 2000 temples and shrines; Nijo-jo Castle (1603), containing the Imperial Palace; Kinkakuji, the Golden Pavilion (1394), Ryoanji temple (1450, later rebuilt), Zen gardens, Daitokuji monastery (14th-c), Kiyomizudera temple (8th-c), Sanjusangen do (12th-c); Mikayo Odori cherry blossom dance (Apr), Kamogawa Odori (May, Oct), Aoi (hollyhock) Matsuri processions (May); Mifune Matsuri boat festival (May), Gion Matsuri parade (Jul), Jidai Matsuri parade (Oct).

Kyoto Protocol An addendum to the 1992 Rio Earth Summit agreement on climate change, initiated when delegates from the world's industrialized nations met in Kyoto in December 1997 and agreed to reduce their combined emissions by about 5 per cent between 1990 and 2012. Despite fears that the Protocol would not survive, progress was made at a meeting in Bonn in July 2001 when 178 countries agreed to a compromise involving lower targets (of around 2 per cent), enabling the process of ratification to proceed. Among the contentious issues was the question of how far countries could use 'carbon sinks' (forest vegetation which can absorb carbon) to meet pollution reduction targets. The USA refused to accept the Protocol and withdrew in 2001, thereby attracting much international criticism. By December 2002 the Protocol had been ratified by 100 countries, but in December 2003 Russia refused to ratify it in its present form, putting its future in serious doubt.

Kyrgyzstan *p.858*

Kyushu [kyushoo] pop (2000e) 13 597 000; area 42 143 sq km/16 267 sq mi. Island region in Japan; southernmost and most densely populated of the four main islands; four volcanic ranges, rising to 1935 m/6348 ft at Mt Miyanoura-dake on Yaku-shima I (S); subtropical climate; heavily forested apart from the NW, which is an extensive rice-growing area; major industrial towns include Fukuoka, Kita-Kyushu, Oita, Kagoshima, Nagasaki; many spas; rice, grain, sweet potatoes, fruit, silk, timber, fishing, porcelain.

Kyzyl-Kum [kizil kum], Russ **Peski Kyzylkum** area 300 000 sq km/115 000 sq mi. Extensive desert in Kazakhstan and Uzbekistan, between the Amudarya (W) and Syr-Darya (E) Rivers; extends SE from the Aral Sea; rises to 922 m/3025 ft in the C; partially covered with sand dunes.

La (in place name) *also under initial letter of the following word*

Laban, Rudolf von [**lay**bn] (1879–1958) Dancer, choreographer, dance theorist, and notator, born in Bratislava, Slovak Republic. He studied ballet, acting, and painting in Paris, and from 1910 founded numerous European schools, theatres, and institutions. He was ballet director of Berlin State Opera (1930–4), and created dances for the Berlin Olympic Games in 1936. In Manchester he established the Art of Movement Studio in 1948, now known as the Laban Centre and part of Goldsmiths College, London University. As the leader of the C European dance movement he was instrumental in the development of modern dance as a theatre form. His system of dance notation, *Labanotation*, was published as *Kinetographie Laban* in 1928.

labelled compound A compound containing a larger amount than usual of a particular isotope of an element. These may be radioactive isotopes, or stable isotopes detectable by spectroscopy. Widely used isotopes include deuterium and ^{13}C.

labelling theory The view, developed primarily during the 1950s and 1960s in American criminology, that certain people and their behaviour come to be 'labelled' by law enforcement agencies as in some way 'deviant' or 'criminal'. Labelling theorists argue that one must look at those doing the labelling – the law-makers and community at large – and not just the law-breakers.

Labiche, Eugène [la**beesh**] (1815–88) Playwright, born in Paris, France. He was the author of over 100 comedies, farces, and vaudevilles, including *Frisette* (1846), which was the original of *Cox and Box* (1847), by British dramatist **John Maddison Morton** (1811–91), and *Le Voyage de Monsieur Perrichon* (1860).

labile [**lay**biyl] *kinetic*

Labor Day *Labour Day*

labor union *trade union*

labour / labor A three-stage process by which a pregnant woman expels her baby and other products of conception from the uterus through the vagina. The first stage consists of uterine muscle contractions with progressive relaxation and dilatation of the cervix, so creating a passage to the vagina. The second stage consists of the descent of the baby through the widely dilated cervix and the vagina; the expulsive process is reinforced by the mother's voluntary efforts. The third stage consists of the expulsion of the placenta, or afterbirth. Labour pains are due to the muscular contractions.

Labour / Labor Day A day of celebration, public demonstrations, and parades by trade unions and labour organizations, held in many countries on 1 May or the first Monday in May; in the USA, Canada, and Bermuda it is the first Monday in September, and in New Zealand the fourth Monday of October.

Labour Party (UK) A socialist/social democratic political party in Britain, originally formed in 1900 as the Labour Representation Committee to represent trade unions and socialist societies as a distinct group in Parliament. In 1906, 26 MPs were elected, and the name was changed to the Labour Party. In 1922 it overtook the Liberals as the main opposition party, and the first minority Labour government was elected in 1924, lasting 11 months. Following a period as a member of the wartime coalition government, the first majority Labour government (1945–51) established the welfare state and carried out a significant nationalization programme. Since then Labour have been in office in 1964–70, 1974–9, 1997–2001, and 2001– . The breakaway Social Democratic Party of the 1980s hurt the Party's electoral chances throughout that decade. Outside Parliament, the annual conference and the National Executive Committee sit at the apex of policy-making, although their influence was traditionally greater in opposition than in government. Since the mid-1990s, policy-making has been overwhelmingly dominated by the leadership of the party, with policy formulated through a commission chaired by the party leader and then discussed by 45 forums involving party members. The annual conference has increasingly become stage-managed to resemble that of the Conservatives. In 1995, Tony Blair persuaded the party to abandon Clause 4, Labour's constitutional commitment to socialism through public ownership. The leader and deputy leader are elected annually when in opposition by an electoral college composed of trade unions, constituency parties, and the Parliamentary Labour Party. There is no election when the party is in government. The party has been little influenced by Marxism, unlike the corresponding parties in Europe, and the 'modernizing' undertaken by recent leaders has, in the eyes of some commentators, effectively removed the party from the socialist camp.

labour / labor relations *industrial relations*

labour / labor theory of value An economic theory that the relative prices of goods (their values) are determined by the relative quantity of labour put into them. This view was first propounded by Ricardo in 1817, and was the foundation of the economic works by Karl Marx. The theory is nowadays not thought to be satisfactory; other factors enter the costs of goods, and labour itself commands wages which vary widely between occupations and countries.

Labrador area 285 000 sq km/110 000 sq mi. Mainland part of Newfoundland, Canada; bounded E by the Labrador Sea; separated from Newfoundland by the Strait of Belle Isle; mainly a barren plateau, part of Canadian Shield; heavily indented E coast; many lakes; fishing, iron ore, hydroelectric power; interior region awarded to Newfoundland, 1927, disputed by Quebec.

Labrador retriever A breed of dog, developed in Britain from imported Newfoundland dogs and local breeds; large, with muscular legs and body; long tail and muzzle; short, pendulous ears; thick fawn or black (occasionally brown) coat; also known as **labrador**.

Labrador Sea Arm of the Atlantic Ocean between Newfoundland and Greenland; depths fall from the continental shelves below 3200 m/10 500 ft towards the Mid-Oceanic Canyon; cold SE-flowing Labrador Current brings icebergs, while warm NW-flowing W Greenland Current helps modify the climate of the SW shore of Greenland.

La Bruyère, Jean de [broo**yair**] (1645–96) Writer, born in Paris, France. His only well-known work, *Caractères*, (1688, Characters), consists of two parts: a translation of Theophrastus, and a masterpiece of French literature in the form of a collection of maxims, reflections, and character portraits of the time. He was chosen to aid Jacques Bossuet in educating the dauphin, and also became tutor to the Duc de Bourbon, grandson of the great Condé.

laburnum A deciduous tree (*Laburnum anagyroides*) growing to 7 m/23 ft, native to S and C Europe, and commonly planted as an ornamental; leaves divided into three leaflets; pea-flowers yellow, numerous, in pendent leafy clusters; pods up to 6 cm/ 2½ in long, hairy when young; seeds black; also called **golden rain** or **golden chain**. All parts but especially the seeds are extremely poisonous. Garden plants are often the hybrid *Laburnum* × *watereri*. (Family: Leguminosae.)

Lacaille, Nicolas Louis de [lakiy] (1713–62) Astronomer, born in Rumigny, NE France. From 1750 to 1754 he led an expedition to the Cape of Good Hope, where he was the first to measure the arc of the meridian in South Africa, compiled a catalogue of nearly 10 000 S stars, *Coelum Australe Stelliferum* (1763, Star Catalogue of the Southern Sky), and introduced 14 new S constellations.

Laccadive Islands *Lakshadweep Islands*

lace An ornamental fabric in which a large number of separate threads are twisted together into a decorative network. Lace is often used for the edges of items of clothing or furnishing, such as collars, cuffs, tablecloths, and altar cloths, but whole garments or covers (eg curtains) can be made in this way. Hand-made lace is still widely produced, but machines have been used for making lace since 1808.

lacecap *hydrangea*

Lacedaemon [lasedeemon] The official name in antiquity for the Spartan state. It comprised the districts of Laconia and Messenia.

Lacerta [laserta] (Lat 'lizard') A smallish, faint N constellation. It includes the object BL Lacertae, the prototype of a class of quasar-like objects.

lacewing A medium to large insect possessing two pairs of similar, membranous wings, each with a lacework of veins; adults and larvae predatory, with simple, biting mouthparts; feed mainly on sap-sucking insects; pupation typically occurs inside a silk cocoon. (Order: Neuroptera.)

laches [lachiz] *limitation of actions*

Lachesis *Moerae*

Lachlan River [laklan] River in New South Wales, Australia; rises in the Great Dividing Range, N of Canberra; flows 1484 km/ 922 mi to join the Murrumbidgee R.

lac insect A bug that lives in clusters on twigs of trees; females legless, with reduced antennae; body enclosed in a protective shell of resinous secretion from which shellac is made. (Order: Homoptera. Family: Kerridae.)

Laclos, Pierre (Ambroise François) Choderlos de [lakloh] (1741–1803) Novelist and soldier, born in Amiens, N France. He spent nearly all his life in the army, but saw no active service until he was 60, and ended his career as a general. His one masterpiece, *Les Liaisons dangereuses* (1782, Dangerous Acquaintances), a novel in epistolary form, became an immediate sensation for its cynical analysis of personal and sexual relationships. It has been successfully adapted for the theatre and several films.

Laconia [lakohnia] In ancient Greece, the SE portion of the Peloponnese, of which Sparta was the principal settlement.

lacquer A hard waterproof substance made from the resin of the *Rhus vernicifera* tree. An ancient Chinese invention, it can be coloured, polished, carved, and used to decorate wooden vessels and furniture. Chinese black, gold, green, red, and silver lacquers were popular in late 17th-c Europe.

lacquer tree A deciduous tree (*Rhus vernicifera*) growing to c.9 m/30 ft, native to China and Japan; leaves pinnate, leaflets oval; flowers tiny, 5-petalled, yellowish, in drooping clusters; also called **varnish tree**. A resin obtained from cuts in the stem is a major constituent of Chinese and Japanese lacquer. (Family: Anacardiaceae.)

Lacroix, Christian [lakrwah] (1951–) Fashion designer, born in Arles, SE France. He studied Classics in Montpellier, specializing in French and Italian painting and the history of costume. After working at Hermès and with Guy Paulin, he joined Jean Patou, who showed his first collection in 1982. In 1987 he left Patou and, with other partners, opened the House of Lacroix in Paris. He is known for his ornate and frivolous designs. He now has shops in a number of countries, including China and Russia.

lacrosse A stick-and-ball field game derived from the North American Indian game of *baggataway*. Because the stick resembled a bishop's crozier, French settlers called the game *La Crosse*. Played since the 15th-c, the game spread to Europe in the early part of the 19th-c, and to Britain in 1867. It is especially popular in Canada and the USA, where it is widely represented in colleges. It is a team game played with 10 on each side (at international level women have 12 per side) on a field measuring 100–110 m/110–120 yd by 55–75 m/60–85 yd. The object is to score goals by throwing the ball into the goal using the lacrosse stick, or *crosse*. The crosse is at least 0·9 m/3 ft in length with a triangular net attached to the end in which to catch the ball.

lactation The process of suckling a newborn infant. During pregnancy, milk-producing glands in the breasts proliferate, and at birth hormones from the pituitary gland stimulate the secretion of milk, which is further augmented when the infant suckles.

lactic acid CH_3–CH(OH)–COOH, IUPAC **2-hydroxypropanoic acid**. An acid which takes its name from milk, in which it is formed on souring. It is an important stage in the breakdown of carbohydrates during respiration. It has two enantiomeric forms, both found in nature.

lactone A ring compound formed by internal ester formation in a compound containing both an acid and an alcohol function.

lactose $C_{12}H_{22}O_{11}$. A sugar occurring in the milk of all mammals. It is a disaccharide, a combination of glucose and galactose, and only slightly sweet-tasting.

lactose intolerance A condition arising from inadequate amounts of lactase in the lining of the intestine, an enzyme that is responsible for digesting lactose, a protein found in milk. It leads to abdominal distension, cramps, and diarrhoea. The disorder is common and not serious. Symptoms can be relieved by avoiding milk products.

ladies' fingers *okra*

Ladoga, Lake, Russ **Ozero Ladozhskoye**, Finnish **Laatokka** area 17 700 sq km/6800 sq mi. Largest lake in Europe, in European Russia, close to the Finnish border; length 219 km/136 mi; maximum depth 230 m/755 ft; over 90% of the outflow via the R Neva into the Gulf of Finland; c.660 islands; navigation difficult in winter because of ice and storms; extensive network of canals.

ladybird A rounded, convex beetle usually red, black, or yellow with a pattern of spots or lines; adults and larvae typically active predators, feeding mostly on aphids and other plant pests (often introduced as a control in agriculture); also known as a **ladybug**. If provoked, some exhibit active bleeding of a sticky, irritating fluid from knee joints and spines. (Order: Coleoptera. Family: Coccinellidae.)

ladybug *ladybird*

Lady chapel A chapel dedicated to the Virgin Mary. It is usually built behind the main altar, and forms an extension to the main building.

Lady Day *Annunciation*

lady's mantle A dome-shaped perennial, native to N temperate regions and tropical mountains; leaves palmate, lobes often shallow, softly hairy; flowers in clusters, small, numerous, green or yellowish; epicalyx four lobes, four sepals, petals absent. (Genus: *Alchemilla*, 250 species. Family: Rosaceae.)

Ladysmith, Siege of (1899–1900) One of the three sieges of the second Boer War, in which Boer forces attempted to pen up their British opponents, and around which many of the actions of the war took place. An attempt to relieve the town was frustrated at the Battle of Spion Kop (Jan 1900), but General Sir Redvers Buller (1839–1908) succeeded in raising the siege on 28 February 1900.

lady's slipper A N temperate orchid in which the lower lip (*labellum*) of the flower is sac-like; also called **moccasin flower**. Insects visiting the flower enter the labellum, but can leave only via a hole at the base, squeezing past both stigma and anthers, and thus pollinating the flower. (Genus: *Cypripedium*, 35 species. Family: Orchidaceae.)

lady's smock *cuckoo flower*

Laënnec, René (Théophile Hyacinthe) [laynek] (1781–1826) Physician, born in Quimper, NW France. An army doctor from 1799, in 1816 he became chief physician to the Hôpital Necker where he invented the stethoscope (1816), with which he studied patients' lung and heart sounds for a three-year period. He published the classic *Traité de l'auscultation mèdiate* (1819, On Mediate Auscultation), and is sometimes called 'the father of thoracic medicine'.

Laetoli [liytohlee] Fossil site in Tanzania, 50 km/30 mi S of Olduvai Gorge. It is renowned for the discovery by Mary Leakey in 1978 of three trails of hominid footprints fossilized in volcanic ash which showed unequivocally that our ancestors already walked upright 3·6 million years ago.

laetrile [laytriyl] The trade name of the drug *Amygdalin* (bitter almond), which can be extracted from some fruit stones (eg apricot). Formerly known as vitamin B_{17}, it was recommended as a cancer cure and as a prophylactic agent for those at high risk of developing cancer. It was never recognized as effective by orthodox medical opinion, and was banned from use as being potentially dangerous, since it was shown to be metabolized to cyanide in the body.

Lafayette, Marie Joseph (Paul Yves Roch Gilbert Motier), marquis de [lafiyet] (1757–1834) French soldier and politician, born in Chavaniac, Auvergne, C France. He fought in America against the British during the War of Independence (1777–9, 1780–2), and became a hero and friend of Washington. In the National Assembly of 1789 he presented a draft of the declaration of the Rights of Man, based on the US Declaration of Independence. During the French Revolution he was hated by the Jacobins for his moderation. He won the first victories of the Revolutionary Wars, but as Jacobin opposition increased he rode over the frontier to Liège, and was imprisoned by the Austrians until Napoleon obtained his release in 1797. During the Restoration he sat in the Chamber of Deputies (1818–24), became a radical leader of the Opposition (1825–30), and commanded the National Guard in the 1830 Revolution.

La Fayette, Marie Madeleine (Pioche de la Vergne), comtesse de (Countess of) [lafiyet], known as **Madame de La Fayette** (1634–93) Novelist and reformer of French romance-writing, born in Paris, France. She married the Comte de La Fayette in 1655, and played a leading part at the French court. When she was 33 she formed a liaison with La Rochefoucauld which lasted until his death in 1680. Her novels are *Zaïde* (1670) and, recognized as a masterpiece, *La Princesse de Clèves* (1678), which gives a vivid picture of the court life of her day.

La Fontaine, Jean de [fonten] (1621–95) Poet, born in Château-Thierry, NE France. He assisted his father, a superintendent of forests, then moved to Paris, and devoted himself to writing. His major works of verse include *Contes et nouvelles en vers* (1664, Tales and Novels in Verse) and *Les Amours de Psyché et de Cupidon* (1669, The Loves of Cupid and Psyche). He is best known for the *Fables choisies mises en vers* (12 vols, 1668–94), in translation usually called 'La Fontaine's Fables', which he uses as a starting point for his observations of human nature. In 1684 he presented a *Discours en vers* on his reception by the Academy.

lager *beer*

Lagerfeld, Karl [lahgervelt] (1939–) Fashion designer, born in Hamburg, N Germany. He was design director at Chanel, and updated the Chanel look. Known for his high quality ready-to-wear clothing, he showed the first collection under his own label in 1984. He received the Council of Fashion Designers of America Lifetime Achievement Award in 2002.

Lagerkvist, Pär (Fabian) [lahgerkvist] (1891–1974) Writer, poet, and playwright, born in Växjö, S Sweden. He was the most significant figure in Swedish literature in the first half of the 20th-c, and was awarded the Nobel Prize for Literature (1951) for his novel *Barabbas*. His first best seller was the novel *Dvärgen* (1944, The Dwarf), and *The Marriage Feast* (1973) contains English translations of his short stories.

Lagerlöf, Selma (Ottiliana Lovisa) [lahgerloef] (1858–1940) Novelist, born in Mårbacka, S Sweden. She was the first woman and the first Swedish writer to receive the Nobel Prize for Literature (1909), and became the first female member of the Swedish Academy (1914). She sprang to fame with her novel *Gösta Berlings saga* (1891, The Story of Gösta Berling), based on the traditions and legends of her native Värmland. She also wrote the children's classic, *Nils Holgerssons underbara resa genom Sverige* (1906–7, trans The Wonderful Adventures of Nils).

lagomorph [lagoma(r)wf] An order of mammals comprising rabbits, hares, and pikas; virtually worldwide (not native to Australasia, but now introduced); related to rodents; long soft fur, long ears, short tails, fully furred feet, slit-like nostrils which can be closed; eat coarse plant material; also eat some of their own faeces to ensure that nourishment is extracted from the food. (Order: Lagomorpha, 58 species.)

lagoon A shallow body of sea water separated from the open sea by island barriers. Coastal lagoons occur in regions where little surface run-off enters the sea. Organic reefs may also form lagoons, as is the case at coral atolls and barrier reefs.

Lagos [laygos] 6°27N 3°28E, pop (2000e) 1 642 000. Chief port and former capital (to 1982) of Nigeria, 120 km/75 mi SW of Ibadan; on Lagos I (8 km/5 mi long and 1·6 km/1 mi wide), connected to the mainland by two bridges; port facilities at Apapa and Tin Can I; settled c.1700; slave trade centre until the mid-19th-c; occupied by the British, 1851; colony of Lagos, 1862; part of the S Nigeria protectorate, 1906; capital of Nigeria, 1960–82; airport; university (1962); tanker terminal; metals, chemicals, fish, gas, brewing, tourism; national museum, palace, racecourse.

Lagrange, Joseph Louis, comte de l'Empire (Count of the Empire) [lagrãzh], originally **Giuseppe Luigi Lagrangia** (1736–1813) Mathematician and astronomer, born in Turin, NW Italy. In 1766 he became director of the Berlin Academy, and published papers on many aspects of number theory, mechanics, the stability of the Solar System, and algebraic equations. His major work was the *Mécanique analytique* (1788, Analytical Mechanics), and he was appointed professor of mathematics at the Ecole Polytechnique, heading the committee reforming the metric system (1795). He was made a senator and a count by Napoleon. The **Lagrangian point** in astronomy, the **Lagrangian function** in mechanics, and several notions in mathematics are all named after him.

Lagrange's equations *Euler–Lagrange equations*

lagrangian [lagronjian] The difference between kinetic energy K and potential energy V; symbol L, units J (joule); $L = K - V$; after Joseph Lagrange. It is the fundamental expression of the properties of a mechanical system, from which equations of motion can be derived using Euler–Lagrange equations.

lagrangian points [lagronjian] Five points in the plane of revolution of two bodies (eg Earth and the Moon, the Sun and Jupiter) where gravitational forces balance so as to allow a small third body to remain in equilibrium. For example, the Trojan asteroids are found in stable orbits at L-4 and L-5 points, forming an equilateral triangle with the Sun and Jupiter.

La Guardia, Fiorello H(enry) [la gah(r)dia] (1882–1947) US politician and lawyer, born in New York City, USA. He became deputy attorney general (1915–17), sat in Congress (1917–21, 1923–33) as a Republican, and held three terms of office as Mayor of New York City (1933–45). One of the city's airports is named after him.

Laguna, La [lagoona] 28°29N 16°19W, pop (2000e) 111 000. Second largest town and former capital of Tenerife I, Canary Is; bishopric; university (1701); textiles, brandy, leather, tobacco; cathedral (16th-c), Church of the Conception (1502).

Lahore [lahaw(r)] 31°34N 74°22E, pop (2000e) 4 777 000. City in Punjab province, Pakistan, between the Ravi and the Sutlej

Rivers, 1030 km/640 mi from Karachi; second largest city in Pakistan; taken in 1849 by the British, who made it the capital of Punjab; railway; two universities (1882, 1961); trade and communications centre; textiles, carpets, footwear, electrical goods, railway engineering, metal goods; considered the cultural capital of Pakistan; museum, Badshahi Mosque, Wazir Khan Mosque, Shalimar Gardens, royal fort of Akbar; a world heritage site.

laissez-faire [laysay fair] (Fr 'let do') An economic doctrine advocating that commerce and trade should be permitted to operate free of controls of any kind. It was a popular view in the mid-19th-c. The term was originally employed by the French physiocrats in the 18th-c, who maintained that society should be governed according to an inherent natural order and that the soil is the only source of wealth and proper object of taxation. It was subsequently taken up by classical economists such as Adam Smith to signify minimum government intervention in the economic system and maximum scope for market forces.

Laius [liyus] In Greek legend, a king of Thebes, son of Labdacus and father of Oedipus; he married Jocasta, and was warned by an oracle that their son would destroy him. This happened when Oedipus, assumed to be dead, returned from Corinth and accidentally killed Laius during a quarrel on the road.

lake A body of water surrounded by land, and lying in a hollow which may be caused by Earth movement, as in rift valleys, or by glaciation, volcanic craters, or the collapse of the roof of limestone caves. Saltwater lakes may be parts of seas or oceans cut off by Earth movement, or formed in areas of low rainfall where mineral salts can accumulate due to evaporation.

Lake District Part of Cumbria, NW England, UK; area of c.1800 sq km/700 sq mi noted for its scenery; a system of glaciated valleys and ribbon lakes; lakes include Windermere, Derwent Water, Ullswater, Bassenthwaite, Thirlmere, Buttermere, and Coniston Water; L Windermere, largest lake in England; mountains include Scafell (highest peak in England), Skiddaw, Helvellyn; chief towns include Keswick, Windermere, Ambleside, Grasmere; area associated with Wordsworth, Coleridge, Southey, Ruskin; national park, established in 1951, protects 866 sq km/334 sq mi; walking, climbing, water sports; farming, quarrying, forestry.

lake dwellings *Glastonbury lake village; Swiss lake dwellings*

Lakeland terrier A medium-sized terrier developed in the English Lake District to hunt foxes; coarse coat, very thick on the legs, forehead, and muzzle.

Lake Placid 44°18N 74°01W, pop (2000e) 2600. Resort in Essex county, N New York State, USA; in the Adirondack Mts, 65 km/40 mi SW of Plattsburg on Mirror Lake; scene of Winter Olympic events (1932, 1980).

Lake poets A phrase used for the poets who took up residence in the English Lake district in the early 19th-c. Wordsworth and Coleridge were the best known.

Laker, Sir Freddie, popular name of **Sir Frederick Alfred Laker** (1922–) Business entrepreneur, born in Kent, SE England, UK. Best known as chairman and managing director of Laker Airways (1966–82), he started his career in aviation with Short Brothers, was a member of the Air Transport Auxiliary (1941–6), and a manager with British United Airways (1960–5). In 1966 he headed the successful Laker Airways Ltd, but was severely set back by the failure of the 'Skytrain' fares-buster project (1982). Since 1992 he has been chairman and managing director of Laker Airways (Bahamas) Ltd. He was knighted in 1978.

Laker, Jim, popular name of **James Charles Laker** (1922–86) Cricketer and broadcaster, born in Bradford, West Yorkshire, N England, UK. He was a member of the Surrey county side which won seven consecutive championships between 1952 and 1958. His off-spinners (along with the bowling of Tony Lock (1929–95)) were a large factor in England's domination of international cricket in the late 1950s. His great season was 1956, when he took 19 of the 20 Australian wickets in the Test Match at Old Trafford. He took 193 wickets in 46 Test matches and during his career (1946–64) took 1944 wickets (average 18·41). In later years he became a television commentator.

Largest Lakes

Name/location	Area* km²	sq mi
Caspian Sea, Iran/Russia	371 000	143 200[1]
Superior, USA/Canada	82 260	31 760[2]
Victoria, E Africa	62 940	24 300
Aral Sea, Kazakhstan	62 000	24 180[1]
Huron, USA/Canada	59 580	23 000[2]
Michigan, USA	58 020	22 400
Tanganyika, E Africa	32 000	12 350
Baikal, Russia	31 500	12 160
Great Bear, Canada	31 330	12 100
Great Slave, Canada	28 570	11 030
Erie, USA/Canada	25 710	10 030[2]
Winnipeg, Canada	24 390	9 420
Malawi/Nyasa, E Africa	22 490	8 680
Balkhash, Kazakhstan	17 000–22 000	6 500–8 500[1]
Ontario, Canada/USA	19 270	7 440[2]
Ladoga, Russia	18 130	7 000
Chad, W Africa	10 000–26 000	4 000–10 000
Maracaibo, Venezuela	13 010	5 020[3]
Patos, Brazil	10 140	3 920[3]
Onega, Russia	9 800	3 800
Rudolf, Kenya	9 100	3 500
Eyre, Australia	8 800	3 400[3]
Titicaca, Peru/Bolivia	8 300	3 200

[1]Salt lakes
[2]Average of areas given by Canada and USA
[3]Salt lagoons
*Areas are given to the nearest 10 km²/sq mi. The Caspian and Aral Seas, being entirely surrounded by land, are classified as lakes. Pollution is reducing the size of many lakes, notably the Aral Sea, which may now be less than half its original size.

Lakshadweep Islands [lahkshadweep], formerly **Laccadive Islands** (to 1973) pop (2001e) 60 600; area 32 sq km/12 sq mi. Union territory of India, comprising 10 inhabited and 17 uninhabited coral islands in the Arabian Sea 300 km/190 mi off the Malabar Coast of Kerala; Amindivi Is (N), Laccadive (Cannanore) Is (S); Minicoy I further S; ruled by British, 1792; ceded to India, 1956; centre of administration on Kavaratti I; population mainly Muslim; coconuts, coir, bananas, fishing, tourism.

Lakshmi [lakshmee] The Hindu goddess of prosperity and good fortune, the consort of Vishnu, sometimes called 'the lotus-goddess'. She is associated with Diwali, the autumn festival of lights.

Lalibela churches [lalibela] A group of 11 churches in the holy city of Lalibela, C Ethiopia; a world heritage monument. The buildings, which date from c.13th-c BC, are remarkable for the ingenuity and artistry of their execution. Each is hewn from a single rock, hollowed and sculpted to look as if it were constructed from separate stones.

Lalić, Susan (Kathryn) [lalich] (1965–) British chess player. She first represented England when aged 14, and her achievements include the national girls under-18 championship (1983), the British Ladies Championships (1986, 1990–2, 1998), and the Commonwealth Ladies Championships (1988–92). She gained the woman international master title in 1985, and is the first British-born woman to achieve the woman grandmaster title (1988).

Lalique, René [laleek] (1860–1945) Jeweller and designer, born in Ay, NE France. He studied in Paris and London, and founded his own jewellery firm in Paris in 1885. His glass designs, decorated with relief figures, animals, and flowers, were an important contribution to the Art Nouveau and Art Deco movements.

Lally, Thomas Arthur, comte de (Count of) (1702–66) French general, son of an Irish Jacobite, born in Romans, SE France. He accompanied Prince Charles Edward to Scotland in 1745, and in 1756 became commander-in-chief in the French East Indies. Active against the British in the Seven Years' War, he was defeated, and capitulated in 1761. On returning to France, he was accused of treachery, and was executed in Paris. In 1778 a royal decree declared the condemnation unjust.

Lamaism [**lah**maizm] The religion of Tibet, a form of Mahayana Buddhism. Buddhism entered Tibet in the 7th-c, where it was opposed by the traditional Bon religion. It was not until the next century, when the Indian missionary Padmasambhava combined elements of both religions, that Lamaism developed. Later the reformer Tsong Kha Pa (1357–1419) founded a school called the Gelu, and its heads acquired the title of Dalai Lama, eventually becoming the spiritual and temporal rulers of Tibet, a position they held until 1959. Upon the death of a reigning Lama, a search is conducted to find an infant who is his reincarnation.

Lamarck, Jean Baptiste (Pierre Antoine) de Monet, Chevalier de [lamah(r)**k**] (1744–1829) Naturalist and pre-Darwinian evolutionist, born in Bazentin, N France. He was an army officer and worked in a bank before developing his interests in medicine and botany, in 1773 publishing the successful *Flore française* (French Flora). In 1774 he became keeper of the royal garden, and in 1793 was made professor of invertebrate zoology at the Museum of Natural History, Paris. His major works were *Philosophie zoologique* (1809), in which he postulated that acquired characters can be inherited by future generations, and *Histoire des animaux sans vertèbres* (1815–22, Natural History of Invertebrate Animals).

Lamartine, Alphonse (Marie Louis) de [lamah(r)**teen**] (1790–1869) Poet, statesman, and historian, born in Mâcon, EC France. His best-known work was his first volume of lyrical poems, *Méditations poétiques* (1820, Poetic Meditations). He became a diplomat at Naples and Florence, a member of the provisional government in the 1848 revolution, and acted as minister of foreign affairs, finally devoting himself to literature. Among his later works are the *Histoire des Girondins* (1847, 8 vols, History of the Girondists), and histories of the French restoration, the 1848 Revolution, and other events of his lifetime.

Lamb, Charles, pseudonym **Elia** (1775–1834) Essayist and poet, born in London, UK. He studied at Christ's Hospital, and worked as a clerk for the East India Company (1792–1825). He achieved success through joint publication with his sister, **Mary** (1764–1847), of *Tales from Shakespear* (1807), and they followed this by other works for children. In 1796 his mother was killed by his sister Mary in a fit of insanity. He himself was for a short time mentally deranged (1795–6), but continued to look after his sister at his house in Islington until his death. In 1818 he published his collected verse and prose, and was invited to join the staff of the new *London Magazine*. This led to his best-known works, the series of essays under his pseudonym, the *Essays of Elia* (1823–33).

Lamb, Henry (1883–1960) Painter, born in Adelaide, South Australia. He studied at Manchester University Medical School and at Guy's Hospital before taking up painting. He exhibited with the Camden Town Group, and was an official war artist (1940–4). His best-known work is the portrait of Lytton Strachey (1914, Tate, London).

lamb *sheep*

Lambert, Constant (1905–51) Composer, conductor, and critic, born in London, UK. He studied at the Royal College of Music, London, became conductor of the Sadler's Wells Ballet (1928–47), and was also known as a concert conductor and music critic, notably in *Music Ho!* (1934). His best-known composition is the choral work in jazz idiom, *The Rio Grande* (1927). Other works include the ballets *Pomona* (1927) and *Horoscope* (1938), and the cantata *Summer's Last Will and Testament* (1936).

Lambert, Johann Heinrich (1728–77) Mathematician, born in Mülhausen, Alsace, NE France. Largely self-educated, he worked as a secretary and tutor, and in 1764 moved to Berlin, where Frederick the Great became his patron. He was among the first to appreciate the nature of the Milky Way, and in an inconclusive attempt to give a rigorous proof of Euclid's parallel postulate he established several theorems in non-Euclidean geometry. He also demonstrated that pi is an irrational number (1768). The first to show how to measure scientifically the intensity of light (1760), the unit of light intensity is now named after him.

Lambert, John (1619–84) English general, born in Calton, North Yorkshire, N England, UK. He studied law, then joined the parliamentary army in the English Civil War, commanding the cavalry at Marston Moor (1644). He helped to install Oliver Cromwell as protector, but opposed the movement to declare him king, and headed the Cabal which overthrew Richard Cromwell in 1659. Considered the leader of the 'fifth monarchy', or extreme republican party, he suppressed the Royalist insurrection of August 1659, and virtually governed the country with his officers as the 'committee of safety'. At the Restoration (1661) he was tried, and imprisoned on Drake's I, Plymouth, until his death.

Lambeth Conferences Gatherings of bishops of the Anglican Communion throughout the world at the personal invitation of the Archbishop of Canterbury for consultations, but without legislative powers. The first conference was held at the instigation of the Provincial Synod of the Church of Canada in 1867 at Lambeth Palace, the London house of the Archbishop of Canterbury, and although the interval between conferences has varied, it is normally convened every 10 years. Recent meetings have lasted about a month, and have considered not only internal Anglican matters (such as the ordination of women) and theological issues, but also social issues (such as race relations and human rights).

lamellibranch [lamelibrangk] *bivalve*

Lamentations (of Jeremiah) A book of the Hebrew Bible/Old Testament, probably dated shortly after the Babylonian conquest of Jerusalem (c.587/586 BC), attributed in tradition to the prophet Jeremiah, but not of the same style as the Book of Jeremiah. It consists of five poems lamenting the destruction of Jerusalem, expressing the distress of its people, and petitioning God for its restoration. The first four poems are acrostics, the stanzas beginning with successive letters of the Hebrew alphabet.

Lamian War [**lay**mian] (323–322 BC) The unsuccessful revolt of the Greek states from Macedon after the death of Alexander the Great.

Laminaria [laminairia] *kelp*

Lammas [**la**mas] In the UK, a former church festival (1 Aug); its name derives from Old English *hlaf-maesse* 'loaf-mass', the festival originally being held in thanksgiving for the harvest, with the consecration of loaves made of flour from the newly harvested wheat. It is a quarter-day in Scotland.

lammergeier [**la**mergiyer] An Old World vulture (*Gypaetus barbatus*), native to S Europe, Africa, India, and Tibet; also known as the **bearded vulture**; grey back; reddish head and underparts; white chest, on which it rubs reddish iron oxide dust; dark 'beard' of stiff feathers; inhabits mountains; eats carrion, especially bones, which it breaks by dropping them from the air onto rocks. (Family: Accipitridae.)

Lamont (of Lerwick), Norman Lamont, Baron [**la**mont] (1942–) British politician, born in Lerwick, Shetland Is, NE Scotland, UK. He studied at Cambridge, worked for the Conservative Research Department, then became a merchant banker and journalist, before entering parliament in 1972. Always a staunch supporter of Margaret Thatcher, she appointed him financial secretary to the Treasury (1986) and promoted him to the cabinet (1989). In 1990 he managed John Major's successful campaign for the Conservative Party leadership and was made Chancellor of the Exchequer. However, following his replacement in the 1993 cabinet reshuffle, he attacked Major's policies. He was given a life peerage in 1998.

Lampedusa, Giuseppe Tomasi, duca di (Duke of) **Palma** [lampedooza] (1896–1957) Novelist, born in Palermo, Sicily, S Italy. His memorial, his only novel, *Il gattopardo* (1958, The Leopard), was rejected by publishers throughout his life, and published posthumously. It was rapturously received then vilified by the Italian literary establishment, but has subsequently come to be regarded as a masterpiece.

lamprey Primitive, jawless fish (*Petromyzon marinus*) found in marine and adjacent fresh waters of the N Atlantic; length up to 90 cm/36 in; mouth sucker-like with rasping teeth; adults feed on body fluids of other fish; may be a serious pest to local fisheries. (Family: Petromyzonidae.)

lamp shell An unsegmented, marine invertebrate possessing a bivalve shell and a long stalk (*pedicel*); typically found attached to a substrate or in a burrow in sediment; feeds using an array of tentacles (the *lophophore*) around the mouth; contains c.350 living species found from the intertidal zone to deep sea; over 12 000 fossil species described. (Phylum: Brachiopoda.)

LAN *local area network*

Lanai [laniy] pop (2000e) 3200; area 365 sq km/140 sq mi. Island of the US state of Hawaii; part of Maui county; chief town, Lanai City; pineapples.

Lancashire pop (2001e) 1 135 000; area 3063 sq km/1182 sq mi. County of NW England, UK; bounded W by the Irish Sea; Pennines in the E; drained by the Lune and Ribble Rivers; county town, Preston; other chief towns include Blackpool, Blackburn (both unitary authorities from 1998), Lancaster, Burnley; ports at Heysham, Fleetwood; world centre for cotton manufacture in 19th-c; textiles, footwear, fishing, mining, tourism, aerospace, electronics; Forest of Bowland.

Lancaster (UK) 54°03N 2°48W, pop (2001e) 133 900. Town in Lancashire, NW England, UK; on R Lune, 32 km/20 mi N of Preston; chartered 1193; city status 1937; port trade declined with river silting; university (1964); railway; paper, textiles, plastics, chemicals; 12th-c castle, on site of Roman fort; Priory Church of St Mary (15th-c).

Lancaster (USA) *Lincoln* (USA)

Lancaster, Burt(on Stephen) (1913–94) Film actor, born in New York City, USA. A former circus acrobat, he performed in army shows before making his name in Hollywood. Cast in a succession of tough-guy roles, he increasingly found opportunities to show his dramatic abilities, notably in *From Here to Eternity* (1953), *Elmer Gantry* (1960, Oscar), and *Birdman of Alcatraz* (1962). Later films include *Atlantic City* (1980, BAFTA best actor), *Local Hero* (1983), and *Field of Dreams* (1989).

Lancaster, Sir Osbert (1908–86) Cartoonist, writer, and theatrical designer, born in London, UK. He studied at Oxford and the Slade School of Art, London. His lifelong passion was architecture, and he worked on *Architectural Review* (1932), writing and illustrating humorous articles. He began drawing pocket-sized front-page cartoons for the *Daily Express* in 1939, creating Lady Maudie Littlehampton and friends. He was knighted in 1975. His autobiography, *All Done From Memory*, was published in 1953.

Lancaster, Duchy of *Duchy of Lancaster*

Lancaster, House of The younger branch of the Plantagenet dynasty, founded by Edmund 'Crouchback', the younger son of Henry III and first Earl of Lancaster (1267–96), whence came three kings of England: Henry IV (1399–1413); Henry V (1413–22); and Henry VI (1422–61, 1470–1).

Lancaster House Agreement An agreement which ended the war in Zimbabwe and created a new constitution under which the country would be given independence in April 1980. An election, held under British supervision, was won by the Zimbabwe African National Union under the leadership of Robert Mugabe.

lancehead viper *fer-de-lance*

lancelet *amphioxus*

Lancelot, Sir or **Launcelot du Lac** The most famous of King Arthur's knights, though he is a relatively late addition to the legend. He was the son of King Ban of Benwick, the courtly lover of Guinevere, and the father of Galahad by Elaine. In spite of his near-perfection as a knight, he was unable to achieve the Grail adventure; he arrived too late to help Arthur in the last battle.

lancet A sharp pointed arch in a building, mainly used in Early English architecture of the 13th-c. It may also refer to a tall and narrow pointed-arch window of the same period.

Lanchester, Frederick William (1868–1946) Automobile and aeronautics pioneer, born in London, UK. He built the first experimental motor car in Britain (1895), and founded the Lanchester Engine Co in 1899. He was also consultant to Daimler, and in 1907–8 published an important two-volume work on aerodynamics, which had considerable influence on other pioneers.

Lanchow *Lanzhou*

Land, Edwin (Herbert) (1909–91) Inventor and physicist, born in Bridgeport, Connecticut, USA. He studied at Harvard, and co-founded laboratories at Boston in 1932, where he produced the light-polarizing filter material 'Polaroid' (1936). His well-known 'Land Polaroid' camera (1947) was a self-developing system of instant photography.

Land Acts, Irish A succession of British Acts passed in 1870, 1881, 1903, and 1909 with the objective of relieving agrarian distress in Ireland under British rule. Gladstone's Land Act of 1870 protected the tenant from arbitrary eviction and provided some compensation for improvements. The Land Act of 1881 recognized the three 'Fs' – fair rent, fixity of tenure, and freedom of sale. The Wyndham Act of 1903 and the Amended Land Purchase Act of 1909 provided loans to tenants and gave bonuses to landlords who sold. A compulsory law transferred all remaining land to Irish tenants soon after the establishment (1922) of the Irish Free State.

Land Art *Earthworks*

Landau, Lev Davidovich [landow], known as **Dev Landau** (1908–68) Physicist, born in Baku, Azerbaijan. He studied at Leningrad University, and with Niels Bohr in Copenhagen, and became professor of physics at Moscow (1937). He received the Nobel Prize for Physics in 1962 for his work on theories of condensed matter, particularly superfluidity and superconductivity in helium.

land crab A true crab that has colonized the land; breathes by means of gills, protected from drying out by a chamber formed from the margins of its hard covering (*carapace*); feeds on fallen fruit, carrion, and other detritus; returns to sea to spawn and for early larval development. (Class: Malacostraca. Order: Decapoda.)

Landé *g*-factor *g-factor*

Landers, Ann, pseudonym of **Esther Pauline Friedman Lederer** (1918–2002) Journalist, born in Sioux City, Iowa, USA. In 1955 she inherited her job as a Chicago-based advice columnist from a previous 'Ann Landers', creating an international institution. She earned a devoted following for her guidance to the perplexed, weathering her own 1975 divorce along the way. She also won many public service awards for her open discussions of medical issues.

landing craft Small warships configured for the landing of troops and vehicles on hostile shorelines. They are typically flat-bottomed boats with a bow ramp from which infantry and armour can go directly into the assault.

Land League An association formed in Ireland in 1879 by Michael Davitt to agitate for greater tenant rights, in particular the '3 Fs': *fair rents*, to be fixed by arbitration if necessary; *fixity of tenure* while rents were paid; and *freedom* for tenants to sell rights of occupancy. Gladstone conceded the essence of these demands in the 1881 Land Act.

Landor, Walter Savage (1775–1864) Writer, born in Warwick, Warwickshire, C England, UK. He was sent down from both Rugby School and Trinity College, Oxford, but despite this and his difficult character, he became an outstanding classicist. He published *Poems* in 1795, *Citation and Examination of William Shakespeare* (1834), and *Hellenics* (1847). His best-known work is the prose dialogue *Imaginary Conversations* (1824–9).

Landowska, Wanda (Louise) [landofska] (1877–1959) Harpsichordist and music teacher, born in Warsaw, Poland. After studying at Warsaw Conservatory, she became a prominent concert pianist in Europe, was appointed professor of the harpsichord at the Berlin Hochschule (1912), and in 1927 estabished a school for the study of old music near Paris. She emigrated to the USA in 1940, and settled in Connecticut in 1949. She composed and wrote prolifically, her best-known work being *La Musique ancienne* (1908).

landrace A type of domestic pig; long, pale body with large pendulous ears; bred mainly for bacon; three varieties: *Scandinavian* (reared indoors) and the hardier *British lop* (or *long white national lop-eared*) and *Welsh*.

landrail *corncrake*

land registration A legal procedure in which ownership of land (*title*) is officially registered. In England and Wales, for example, this is with the **Land Registry**. Registration is now compulsory in all areas on transfer, though there is no compulsion on existing owners to register. It simplifies the procedure whereby land is transferred from vendor to purchaser. The registered proprietor (the owner) proves his or her title by reference to the appropriate entry on the register. Instead of traditional title deeds, there is a land certificate issued by the registry, and title is, in a sense, guaranteed by the state. In the USA, all states have recording systems for instruments affecting the title to land. Recording is generally not a condition of conveying between parties, but time of recording in relation to other claimants is often decisive in proving valid title.

landscape gardening The art of laying out gardens and estates for aesthetic or spiritual effect. A variety of techniques (including terracing, the use of artificial mounds, still and running water, walls, and trees), disseminated mainly from the Near and Middle East, have in different combinations and with different emphases developed into several distinct styles. In Japan the naturalistic use of trees and water evolved into a highly stylized and religiously significant arrangement of natural elements. In 18th-c Europe, formal landscaping (best characterized by the work of Le Nôtre, who made heavy use of symmetry, topiary, and artificial ornament) gave way to an artfully informal naturalism, seen particularly in the work of Kent, Repton, Olmsted, and Capability Brown.

landscape painting The representation of natural scenery in art. Trees, rivers, mountains, etc have featured in the backgrounds of pictures since ancient times, but the depiction of unified landscape for its own sake, frequently with a moral dimension, dates only from the 16th-c in Europe, though 600 years earlier in China.

Landseer, Sir Edwin (Henry) (1802–73) Artist, born in London, UK. Trained by his father to sketch animals from life, he exhibited at the Royal Academy at the age of 13. Dogs and deer were his main subjects, often with the Highlands of Scotland as a backdrop. His paintings include 'Rout of Comus' (1843), and 'Monarch of the Glen' (1851), and he modelled the four bronze lions at the foot of Nelson's Monument in Trafalgar Square (unveiled in 1867). He was knighted in 1850.

Land's End, ancient **Bolerium** 50°03N 5°44W. A granite headland in Cornwall, SW England, UK; the W extremity of England; Longships lighthouse lies offshore.

Landsteiner, Karl [landstiyner] (1868–1943) Pathologist, born in Vienna, Austria. A research assistant at the Pathological Institute, Vienna, he became professor of pathological anatomy from 1909. He worked in the Rockefeller Institute for Medical Research, New York City (1922–43), and received the 1930 Nobel Prize for Physiology or Medicine for his discovery of the human ABO blood-group system (1901) and type AB (1902). In 1940 he also discovered the Rhesus (Rh) system.

Lane, Sir Allen, originally **Allen Lane Williams** (1902–70) Publisher, born in Bristol, SW England, UK. He studied at Bristol, and was apprenticed in 1919 to The Bodley Head publishing house. He resigned as managing director in 1935 in order to form Penguin Books Ltd, where he began by reprinting novels in paper covers at sixpence each, a revolutionary step in the publishing trade. This expanded to other series such as non-fictional Pelicans and children's Puffins. He was knighted in 1952.

Lang, Fritz (1890–1976) Film director, born in Vienna, Austria. He studied at the College of Technical Sciences and the Academy of Graphic Arts in Vienna, and intended to paint, but turned to the cinema after working with a film company in Berlin. His early films include *Dr Mabuse, der Spieler* (1922, Dr Mabuse, the Gambler), the first of three Mabuse films (the others in 1932 and 1960), and the futuristic *Metropolis* (1926), with its nightmare vision of urban living. When Hitler came to power in 1933, Goebbels offered Lang the post of head of the German film industry. Lang refused, and the same night fled to Paris, and later to the USA. Among his many films of this period, *Fury* (1936) was acclaimed as a masterpiece. Later films include *You Only Live Once* (1937) and *The Big Heat* (1953). He largely abandoned film-making after 1956.

Langdon, Harry (Philmore) (1884–1944) Comedian, born in Council Bluffs, Iowa, USA. As a child he appeared in amateur shows, and joined *Dr Belcher's Kickapoo Indian Medicine Show* in 1897. He made his film debut in the serial *The Master Mystery* (1918), and was signed by Mack Sennett for a series of short comedies. He moved on to features and the very popular trio of *Tramp Tramp Tramp* (1926), *The Strong Man* (1926), and *Long Pants* (1927). He is remembered for his character as a baby-faced innocent, handicapped by indecisiveness and bemused by the wider world. His attempts at directing failed, but he continued to work in films until the 1940s.

Lange, David (Russell) [longee] (1942–) New Zealand politician and prime minister (1984–9), born in Otahuhu, Auckland, New Zealand. After qualifying in law at Auckland University, he worked for the underprivileged in Auckland. Elected to the House of Representatives in 1977, he rose rapidly to become leader of the Labour Party in 1983. His non-nuclear defence policy won him the 1984 general election, and made him New Zealand's youngest prime minister of the 20th-c. He and his party were re-elected in 1987, but he resigned in 1989. He was made a Companion of Honour in 1990.

Langland, William, also spelled **Langley** (c.1332–c.1400) Poet, probably born in Ledbury, Hereford and Worcester, WC England, UK. Little is known about his life, but he is thought to have been a clerk and a minor cleric who lived many years in London in poverty. He is credited with the authorship of the great mediaeval alliterative poem on the theme of spiritual pilgrimage, *Piers Plowman* (written over an uncertain period from c.1360). The poem is written in colloquial, simple English, using familiar symbols and images, while reiterating mediaeval Christian doctrine.

Langley, Samuel (Pierpont) (1834–1906) Astronomer and aeronautical pioneer, born in Roxbury (now part of Boston), Massachusetts, USA. He practised as a civil engineer and architect in Chicago and St Louis, and in 1867 became professor of astronomy at Western University, PA. He invented the bolometer for measuring the Sun's radiant heat, and was the first to build a heavier-than-air flying machine – a steam-powered model aircraft (it flew for 1280 m/4200 ft, weighing 9·7 kg/26 lb).

Langmuir, Irving [langmyoor] (1881–1957) Physical chemist, born in New York City, USA. He studied at Columbia and Göttingen universities, and was attached to the General Electric Company (1909–50), becoming associate director of the research laboratory in 1932. He received the Nobel Prize for Chemistry in 1932 for his work on solid and liquid surfaces. His many inventions include the gas-filled tungsten lamp and atomic hydrogen welding.

Langobards *Lombards*

Langton, Stephen (c.1150–1228) Theologian, probably born in Lincolnshire, EC England, UK. He studied at the University of Paris, was made a cardinal by Pope Innocent III in 1206, and became Archbishop of Canterbury in 1207. His appointment was resisted by King John, and Langton was kept out of the see until 1213, living mostly at Pontigny. He sided warmly with the barons against John, and his name is the first of the subscribing witnesses of Magna Carta.

Langtry, Lillie, popular name of **Emilie Charlotte Langtry**, *née* **Le Breton**, nickname **the Jersey Lily** (1853–1929) Actress, born in Jersey, Channel Is. One of the most noted beauties of her time, she married Edward Langtry in 1874, and was the first society woman to appear on stage. Her beauty brought her to the attention of the Prince of Wales, later Edward VII, and she became his mistress. She managed the Imperial Theatre, which was never successful. Widowed in 1897, she married in 1899 **Hugo Gerald de Bathe**, and became well known as a racehorse owner.

language **1** A species-specific communicative ability, restricted to humans, which involves the use of sounds, grammar, and vocabulary, according to a system of rules. Though other animals can communicate vocally and by gesture, they are restricted to a particular set of messages, genetically given, which cannot be creatively varied.

2 An individual manifestation of **1**, found within a particular community. The concept of 'a language' is not always easy to define, since it is not solely a linguistic matter. Even the apparently common-sense requirement that speakers of 'the same' language should be able to understand one another (that their dialects should be mutually intelligible) does not always obtain. In most of W Europe, the situation is straightforward, because language boundaries tend to coincide with the boundaries of nation-states, and the languages of France, Germany, Italy, etc are not mutually intelligible. But in Scandinavia, political autonomy in Norway and Sweden has led to Norwegian and Swedish being called separate 'languages', despite the fact that they are largely mutually intelligible. In China, the opposite situation obtains: varieties which occur are called 'dialects' of the Chinese language, despite the fact that several are not mutually intelligible. This comes about because they all use the same writing system, which is seen as a unifying factor. The designation of 'language' status is therefore dependent on a wide variety of social, linguistic, and political considerations, and as a result, estimates of the number of living languages in the world (usually ranging between 5000 and 7000) are inevitably uncertain, and should be accepted with caution.

language isolates Languages which have no certain historical or structural affiliation with any other languages, such as Basque. Languages may be so classified simply because too little is known about them. There are some well-documented instances, however, which defy classification.

language laboratory A room made up of banks of booths, each one containing a cassette recorder for a student's use, connected to a central console. At the console, a language instructor monitors the performance of students as they listen to taped exercises and record their responses to them. The system is useful for administering repetition exercises, pronunciation drills, and tests of a student's mastery at all levels of language. Its great advantage is that the students are each able to advance at their own pace. Modern laboratories are now often equipped with video recorders and various kinds of computational aids.

Languedoc [lãguhdok] Former province between the R Rhône, Mediterranean, and Guyenne and Gascogne, S France; Cévennes Mts in the E; name derived from the local variety of language, *langue d'oc* (Provençal); centre of wine production.

langur [langgoor] An Old World monkey, native to S and SE Asia; prominent dark 'eyebrows'; slender hand with short thumb; long tail; inhabits forests; eats leaves; two genera: **langur** or **leaf monkey** (*Presbytis*, 15 species) and **snub-nosed langur** (*Pygathrix*, 4 species). The latter name (along with **pig-tailed langur**) is also used for a relative of the proboscis monkey (*Nasalis concolor*).

Lanier, Sidney [laneer] (1842–81) Poet, born in Macon, Georgia, USA. After a variety of jobs, he became a lecturer in English literature at Johns Hopkins University (1879). He believed in a scientific approach towards poetry-writing, breaking away from traditional metrical techniques and making it more akin to musical composition (he was also a musician), illustrated in later poems such as 'Corn' (1875) and 'The Symphony' (1875). He also wrote a novel and several critical studies.

lanner falcon A large falcon (*Falco biarmicus*) native to S Europe and Africa; inhabits desert and open country; eats mainly birds. (Family: Falconidae.)

lanolin [lanolin] A waxy material occurring naturally in wool. It is a mixture of esters of cholesterol with stearic, palmitic, and oleic acids. It forms strong emulsions with water, and is used in toilet preparations and ointments.

Lansbury, George (1859–1940) British politician, born near Lowestoft, Suffolk, E England, UK. Active as a radical since boyhood, he became a convinced socialist in 1890, and a Labour MP in 1910, resigning in 1912 to stand in support of women's suffrage. He was defeated and not re-elected until 1922. He founded and edited the *Daily Herald* (1912–22), and became commissioner of works (1929), and leader of the Labour Party (1931–5).

L'Anse aux Meadows [lahnsee medohz] An isolated Norse settlement of nine turf-built houses on Epaves Bay, Newfoundland, Canada, discovered in 1961 by Helge and Anne Ingstad. Dated by radiocarbon to AD c.970–1000, the settlement proves that the Vikings reached North America in pre-Columbian times. It has been designated a national park and a world heritage site.

Lansing 42°44N 84°33W, pop (2000e) 119 100. Capital of state in Ingham Co, SC Michigan, USA, on the Grand R; railway; car and truck manufacturing centre; machinery and fabricated metals.

lanternfish Any of the small deep-sea fishes of family Myctophidae (6 genera), widely abundant in the world's oceans, typically at depths of 500–1000 m/1600–3300 ft, but may migrate to the surface at night; length up to 15 cm/6 in; head blunt, eyes large, body with numerous light organs in characteristic patterns.

lanthanides [lanthaniydz] or **rare earth elements** Elements with atomic numbers from 58–72 inclusive. They have very similar chemistry, mainly forming compounds in which they show oxidation state +3. They usually occur together in mixed oxides in nature, and are separated only with difficulty.

Lanza, Mario, originally **Alfredo Arnold Cocozza** (1921–59) Tenor, born in Philadelphia, Pennsylvania, USA. Discovered while working in the family's grocery business, he auditioned for Serge Koussevitzky in 1942, and appeared that summer at Tanglewood. His career was interrupted by service in World War 2, and afterwards he went on to Hollywood to appear in several musicals, including his most famous role in *The Great Caruso* (1951).

Lanzhou [lahnjoh], **Lan-chou**, or **Lanchow** 36°01N 103°19E, pop (2000e) 1 803 000, administrative region 2 926 000. Capital of Gansu province, NC China, on the upper Yellow R; airfield; railway; university (1946); centre for China's atomic energy industry since 1960; trade in wheat, millet, tobacco, sorghum, melons; oil refining, metallurgy, light engineering, textiles; Gansu Province Museum.

Laocoon [layokohon] In Greek mythology, a Trojan prince, a priest of Apollo, who objected to the plan to bring the Wooden Horse into Troy. Two serpents came out of the sea and killed him, together with his two sons.

Laoighis, Laois [layish], or **Leix** [layks], formerly **Queen's County** pop (2000e) 53 000; area 1720 sq km/664 sq mi. County in Leinster province, SC Ireland; watered by R Nore; Slieve Bloom Mts rise in NW; capital, Portlaoighise; agriculture, livestock; huge tracts of peat used to fuel power stations.

Laos *see panel*

Lao She [lau shoe], also known as **Shu Ching-chün** (1899–1966) Writer, born in Beijing, China. He lectured in Britain, USA, and China, and was influenced by Western writers including Dickens and Swift. His earlier work on humorous stories was later replaced by social concerns. His major novel *Rickshaw Boy* (1937) sympathetically recounted rickshawmen's lives in the early 20th-c and exposed the dismal existence of republican China's masses. *Cat City* (influenced by *Gulliver's Travels*) was a satirical allegory on the state of China. After 1949 he wrote several plays acceptable to Communist orthodoxy, and *Rickshaw Boy* has been filmed (1984) and serialized on Chinese television.

Laozi [lautsee], also spelled **Lao-tzu** or **Lao-tse** ('Old Master') (?6th-c BC) The legendary founder of Chinese Taoism (Daoism). Nothing is known of his life: the oldest biography (c.100 BC) claims he held official rank. He was first mentioned by Zhuangzi. Taoist tradition attributes their classic text, the *Daodejing* (*Tao Te Ching*) to Laozi, but it was written in the 3rd-c BC. By the 2nd-c AD, Taoists claimed he had lived more than once and had travelled to India, where he became the Buddha. (Later he was claimed to have founded Manichaeism.) The Tang emperors (618–906) claimed descent from him.

La Paz [la pas] 16°30S 68°10W, pop (2000e) 1 244 000. Regional capital and government capital of Bolivia, La Paz department, W Bolivia; highest capital in the world, altitude 3636 m/11 929 ft in centre; Mt Illimani (6402 m/21 004 ft) towers above the city to the SE; founded by Spanish, 1548; airport (Kennedy International, referred to as El Alto); railway; university (1826); copper, wool, alpaca; cathedral, Presidential Palace (Palacio Quemado), National Congress, National Art Museum, Monastery of San Francisco; skiing nearby at world's highest ski run, Mt Chacaltaya.

lap dissolve *dissolve*

lapis lazuli [lapis lazyuliy, lazyulee] A deep-blue ornamental stone, principally lazurite (a silicate of sodium and aluminium), found in metamorphosed limestones. It was formerly the source of the blue pigment ultramarine, now made synthetically.

Lapita people [lapeeta] Austronesian-speaking voyagers, ancestors of the Polynesians. Some of them, after moving southwards through Melanesia, travelled E from Vanuatu to the then uninhabited groups of Fiji and Tonga about 1500 BC. Evidence of their movements is mostly provided by archaeological remains, especially pottery.

Lapiths [lapiths] In Greek mythology, a people of Thessaly, mentioned in several legends. Perithous, King of the Lapiths, invited the Centaurs to his wedding with Hippodameia. A terrible fight took place between the two groups, in which the Centaurs were defeated.

Laplace, Pierre Simon, Marquis de [laplas], also known as **Comte de** (Count of) **Laplace** (1749–1827) Mathematician and

Laos

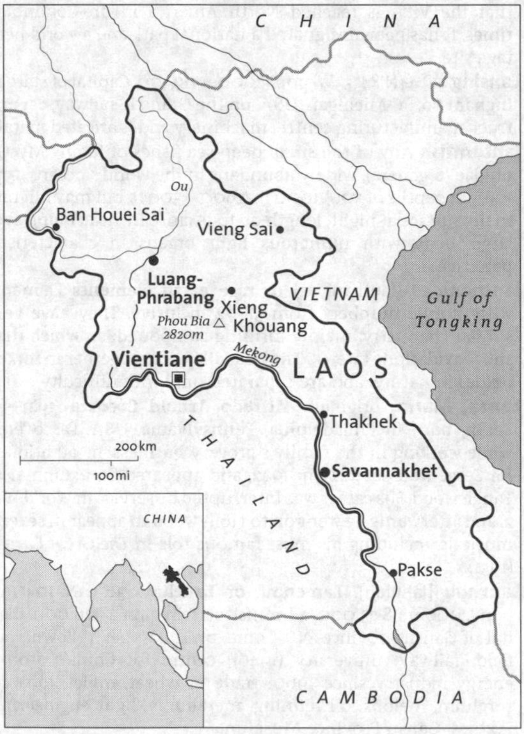

☐ International Airport

[lows], official name **Lao People's Democratic Republic**, Lao **Sathalanalat Paxathipatai Paxaxôn Lao**

Local name Lao

Timezone GMT +7

Area 236 800 km^2/91 405 sq mi

Population total (2002e) 5 777 000

Status Republic

Date of independence 1949

Capital Vientiane

Languages Lao (official), French, and tribal languages

Ethnic groups Laotian (60%), hill tribes (35%)

Religions Buddhist (58%), animist (largely the Lao-Theung) (34%), Christian (2%)

Physical features Landlocked country on the Indo-Chinese peninsula; dense jungle and rugged mountains (E), rising to 2751 m/9025 ft on Vietnamese border, and 2820 m/9252 ft at Phou Bia on the Xieng Khouang plateau; Mekong R flows NW–SE, fertile Mekong floodplains in W. 4% of land arable, 58% forested.

Climate Monsoonal climate; average annual rainfall 1715 mm/67·5 in; (heaviest, May–Sep); average annual temperature 14°C (Jan), 34°C (Jul) in Vientiane.

Currency (1992) 1 Kip (Kp) = 100 at

Economy Agricultural economy suffered severely in the civil war; rice, coffee, tobacco, cotton, spices, opium; tin, iron ore, potash; forestry (1991 logging ban to halt deforestation), rubber, cigarettes, matches; textiles.

GDP (2002e) $10·4 bn, per capita $1800

Human Development Index (2002) 0·485

History Visited by Europeans, 17th-c; formed French Indo-Chinese Union with Cambodia and Vietnam, 1887; French protectorate, 1893; occupied by Japanese in World War 2; independence from France, 1949; civil war, 1953–75, between the Lao government, supported by the USA, and the communist-led Patriotic Front (Pathet Lao), supported by North Vietnam; monarchy abolished and communist republic established, 1975; draft constitution approved, 1991 provides for a directly elected National Assembly and executive President.

Head of State
1991–2 Kaysone Phomvihane
1992–8 Nouhak Phoumsavan
1998– Khamtay Siphandon

Head of Government
1991–8 Khamtay Siphandon
1998–2001 Sisavat Keobounphanh
2001– Boungnang Vorachith

astronomer, born in Beaumont-en-Auge, NW France. He studied at Caen, and became professor of mathematics at the Ecole Militaire, Paris. He applied his mathematical knowledge to physical astronomy, particularly the stability of orbits in the Solar System. His five-volume *Mécanique céleste* (1799–1825, Celestial Mechanics) is a landmark in applied mathematics. In his study of the gravitational attraction of spheroids, he formulated the fundamental differential equation in physics which now bears his name. He entered the Senate in 1799, and was made a peer in 1815.

Lapland, Swed **Lappland**, Finn **Lapin Lääni** pop (2000e) 207 000, area 98 938 sq km/38 190 sq mi. Province of N Finland, bounded W by Sweden, NW by Norway, and E by Russia; mainly within Arctic Circle; largely tundra (N), forest (S), and mountains (W); occupies c.30% of total area of Finland; Mt Haltia on frontier with Norway; provincial capital, Rovaniemi; considerable emigration to the S in recent years; chromium, iron mining; farming, fishing, trapping. The area generally called Lapland also includes large parts of Norway, Sweden, and Russia.

La Plata [la **plah**ta] 34°52S 57°55W, pop (2000e) 610 200. Port and capital of Buenos Aires province; on the R Plate, SE of Buenos Aires; founded in 1882; three universities (1884, 1965, 1968); named **Eva Perón** (1946–55); railway; main outlet for produce from the pampas; trade in refrigerated meat, grain, oil; oil refining (pipeline to Buenos Aires); museum of natural history; zoological gardens; observatory; Garden of Peace, with each country in the world represented by one flower.

Lapp A people living in the sparsely populated N areas of Finland, Sweden, Norway, and Russia, mostly within the Arctic Circle, with more than half in Norway. They speak Lapp, a Uralic language, although most are bilingual and some speak only the national language of the country. They have probably been in the area for 2000 years, but originally were more widely dispersed. Most are fishermen, while others farm, breed reindeer, are foresters, and work in factories.

laptop computer A small lightweight computer, usually powered by internal batteries, which can easily be carried around and used comfortably on the user's lap. They became generally available in the mid-1980s.

lapwing A plover, especially the **common lapwing** (*Vanellus vanellus*); inhabits grassland, cultivation, water edges, and swamps. (Genus: *Vanellus*, 10 species. Family: Charadriidae.)

Lara, Brian (1969–) Cricketer, born in Cantaro, NW Trinidad, West Indies. He came to prominence in the 1994 season, when he broke several cricketing records, scoring seven centuries in eight successive innings, and breaking the world Test record with 375 for the West Indies against England. Six weeks later he became the first batsman to score over 500 runs in one innings in first-class cricket, playing for Warwickshire against Durham. After a slump in form, he burst back to life with three successive centuries against Australia in 1999. He has captained the West Indies three times (1999, 2003–4). He broke the World Test record again in April 2004, scoring 400 for West Indies against England.

larch A deciduous conifer native to colder parts of the N hemisphere; long shoots rough-textured with persistent bases of fallen leaves; short shoots with tufts of needles. It tolerates intense cold, but needs full light to grow well. Often dominant in N forests, it is widely planted for timber. (Genus: *Larix*, 10–12 species. Family: Pinaceae.)

lard A fat produced from pigs, widely used in cooking and baking, and also in the preparation of certain perfumes and ointments. **Lard oil** is used as a lubricant and in soap manufacture.

Lardner, Ring(gold Wilmer) (1885–1933) Writer, born in Niles, Michigan, USA. He studied at the Armour Institute of Technology, Chicago, then worked as a reporter on the *South Bend Times* (1905). He became a specialist sportswriter for several important Chicago papers, and published successful collections of stories, such as *You Know Me, Al* (1916) and *How to Write Short Stories* (1924). Between then and 1929 he wrote prolifically in a number of genres, including novels, plays, poetry, and an autobiography, *The Story of a Wonder Man* (1927). Regarded as a gifted satirist, several biographies were published during the 1970s.

Lares [**lah**reez] Minor Roman deities. Normally associated with the household was the guardian of the hearth (*lar familiaris*), but there were also guardians of crossroads (*lares viales*) and of the State (*lares praestites*).

lark A small, dull-coloured songbird, found mainly in the Old World, especially Africa; inhabits open country; eats seeds and insects; nests on ground. The name is also used for the **lark quail** (Family: Turnicidae); the **meadowlark** (Family: Icteridae); and the **mudlark** (Family: Grallinidae). (Family: Alaudidae, 75 species.)

Larkin, Philip (Arthur) (1922–85) Poet, librarian, and jazz critic, born in Coventry, West Midlands, C England, UK. He studied at Oxford – an experience on which he based his first novel, *Jill* (1946). *A Girl in Winter* (1947) was his only other novel. His early poems appeared in the anthology, *Poetry from Oxford in Wartime* (1944), and in a collection *The North Ship* (1945). *XX Poems* was published privately in 1950. He became librarian at the University of Hull in 1955, and further collections appeared at regular intervals, including *The Less Deceived* (1955), *The Whitsun Weddings* (1964) and *High Windows* (1974). *Collected Poems* was published posthumously (1988) and became a best seller. His articles on jazz were collected in *All What Jazz?* (1970), and his essays in *Required Writing* (1983). His *Letters*, many of them addressed to his friend Kingsley Amis, were published in 1992, and the first biography of his life in 1993.

lark quail *quail*

larkspur An annual native to the N hemisphere; related and very similar to delphiniums, and sometimes included in that genus, but generally smaller; flowers blue, pink, or white, borne in short spikes. (Genus: *Consolida*, 40 species. Family: Ranunculaceae.)

Larnaca [**lah(r)**naka], Gr **Larnax**, Turkish **Larnaka**, **Iskele** 34°55N 33°36E, pop (2000e) 68 400. Port and capital town of Larnaca district, S Cyprus, on Larnaca Bay; SW of Dhekelia British base; airport; old Turkish fort (1625), now a museum.

La Rochefoucauld, François, duc de (Duke of) [la rosh**foo**koh] (1613–80) Classical writer, born in Paris, France. He devoted himself to the cause of the queen, Marie de' Medicis, in opposition to Richelieu, and became entangled in a series of love adventures (including one with Marie La Fayette) and political intrigues, and was forced to live in exile (1639–42). Involved in the wars of the Frondes, he was wounded at the siege of Paris, and retired to the country after being wounded again in 1652. His *Mémoires*, written in retirement, was published in 1664, but as it gave wide offence he denied its authorship. He is best known for his *Réflexions, ou sentences et maximes morales* (first edition, 1665), commonly known as the *Maximes*, making him the leading exponent of the French literary term *maxime* ('maxim'). It remains a masterpiece of French literature.

Larousse, Pierre (Athanase) [la**roos**] (1817–75) Publisher and lexicographer, born in Toucy, C France. He studied at Versailles, became a teacher, and began his linguistic research in Paris in 1840. He wrote several grammars, dictionaries, and other textbooks, notably his *Grand dictionnaire universel du XIXe siècle* (15 vols, 1865–76, Great Universal Dictionary of the Nineteenth Century).

larva A general term for a stage in an animal's development between hatching and the attainment of the adult form, or maturity. Larval stages are often typical of the group, such as the caterpillar larva of butterflies, the nauplius larva of crustaceans, and the cercaria larva of digenetic flukes. Larvae often occupy a different habitat from the adults, and serve as a dispersal stage in the life cycle.

laryngitis [larin**jiy**tis] Acute or chronic inflammation of the larynx, with swelling of the vocal cords. It often accompanies infection elsewhere in the respiratory tract, such as common cold or bronchitis.

larynx That part of the air passage lying in humans between the trachea below and the laryngopharynx above, situated in the middle of the front of the neck; also called the 'voice box', because it contains the *vocal folds* or *cords*, responsible for the production of sounds. It consists of a framework of cartilages joined together by a number of ligaments and capable of movement with respect to each other. It is attached by muscles to the hyoid bone, and so moves upwards on swallowing. The prominent hard projection in the front of the neck, especially in males (the *Adam's apple*), is part of the thyroid cartilage. The larynx acts as a valve to prevent the passage of food and liquids into the airways below (failure to do so results in choking, and the expulsion of the offending material). It may also be modified to control the expulsion of air from the lungs (by changing the size of the glottis) and to change the pitch of the sound (by altering the length and tension of the vocal folds). The deeper voices of males (which develop at puberty) result from their having a larger larynx and longer vocal folds than females.

Las (in place names) *also under initial letter of the following word*

La-sa *Lhasa*

La Salle, René Robert Cavelier, sieur de (Lord of) [la sal] (1643–87) Explorer of North America, born in Rouen, NW France. He settled as a trader near Montreal, and descended the Ohio and Mississippi to the sea (1682), claiming Louisiana for France and naming it after Louis XIV. In 1684 he led an expedition to the Gulf of Mexico, but spent two fruitless years looking for the Mississippi Delta. His followers mutinied, and he was murdered.

La Scala [la skahla], or **Teatro Alla Scala** (Ital 'theatre at the stairway') The world's most famous opera house, built (1776–8) on the site of the Church of Santa Maria della Scala in Milan, N Italy. It was severely damaged by bombing in World War 2, and reopened in 1947.

Las Campanas Observatory An astronomical observatory on Cerro Las Campanas, Chile. Instruments include the 2·5 m/100 in du Pont reflector and the 1 m/39 in Swope reflector, both owned by the Carnegie Institution of Washington. The first of two 6·5 m/256 in telescopes, called Magellan, was completed in 2000 (named after Walter Baade); the second (named after Landon Clay) was completed in 2002.

Las Casas, Bartolomé de [las kahsas], known as **the Apostle of the Indians** (1474–1566) Missionary, born in Seville, SW Spain. He sailed in the third voyage of Columbus (1502) to Hispaniola, was ordained (1512), and travelled to Cuba (1513). His desire to protect the natives from slavery led him to visit the Spanish court on several occasions. Appointed Bishop of Chiapa, he was received (1544) with hostility by the colonists, returned to Spain, and resigned his see (1547). His most important work is the unfinished *Historia de las Indias* (1875–6).

Lascaux [laskoh] A small, richly-decorated Palaeolithic cave of c.15 000 BC near Montignac, Dordogne, SW France, renowned for its naturalistic mural paintings and engravings of animals – cows, bulls, horses, bison, ibex, musk-ox, and reindeer. Found by schoolboys in 1940 and opened to the public in 1947, it was closed permanently in 1963 when humidity changes threatened the paintings. A replica was opened nearby in 1984.

Las Cruces [las krooses] 32°19N 106°47W, pop (2000e) 74 300. Seat of Dona Ana Co, S New Mexico, USA, on the Rio Grande; founded, 1848; railway; university (1888); White Sands Missile Range nearby, a major military and NASA testing site; name commemorates massacre of 40 travellers by Apache Indians in 1830; Enchilada Fiesta (Oct).

laser A device which produces light, infrared, or ultraviolet radiation with special properties, for example using a system of excited atoms; the name is an acronym of *light amplification by the stimulated emission of radiation*. The first laser was built in 1960 in the USA by physicist Theodore Maiman, following theoretical work by Charles Townes and Arthur Schawlow. In Russia similar independent work was carried out by Nikolai Basov (1922–2001) and Alexander Prokhorov (1916–2002). Atoms absorb energy in well-defined amounts, raising electrons to excited states; the electrons are said to move from one energy level to a level of higher energy. Usually an electron returns to its original level after less than 10^{-8} seconds, releasing energy as a photon of light. If another photon, of energy similar to that of the photon about to be released, strikes the excited atom, then photon production is more rapid; this is called *stimulated emission* (after Einstein, 1917). The result is two photons identical in phase moving in the same direction. Should these photons themselves interact with more excited atoms, eventually a cascade of identical photons will be produced, all moving in one direction. Laser action depends on the choice of special atomic systems for which an energy supply is able to raise large numbers of atoms to excited states, ready to emit photons when stimulated. Mirrors at either end of the laser reflect light end-to-end inside the laser to maintain its action. At one end, the mirror is partially transparent, allowing a portion of the light to escape to produce a laser beam. Typically, energy is supplied to the laser by electrical discharge or a powerful light source. Laser light is monochromatic (all one colour), coherent (in step), produced as a beam which does not spread, and travels large distances undiminished in intensity. The light is produced either as a continuous beam or as pulses. Intensities of up to 10^{20}W/m^2, and pulses of less than 10^{-14}sec, are possible. The many uses of lasers include supermarket bar code scanners, welding, surveying, phototherapy in medicine, eye surgery, hologram production, and directed energy weapons.

laser cooling A technique for reducing the velocity of atoms or ions by bombardment with laser light; used in atom and ion traps. When a laser photon strikes an oncoming atom, the photon is absorbed and subsequently re-emitted in some random direction, reducing the atom's velocity. Many such cycles allow atom velocity to be reduced from hundreds to tens of metres per second in a thousandth of a second. The atoms absorb laser photons only while moving towards the laser, because the laser is tuned to match the Doppler-shifted absorption frequency of an oncoming atom. For extreme cooling, the laser beams that slow atoms down are sometimes termed 'optical molasses'.

laser mass spectrometer A mass spectrometer which uses a laser to convert a sample for analysis into a form which can pass through the analyzing system. Mass spectrometry needs a pure and uncontaminated source of matter propelled to the system, which deflects different components of the sample in slightly different directions. Lasers can be used particularly for the non-destructive evaporation of the sample, providing a highly localized action on the specimen without disturbing the mounting or medium.

laser printer A type of printer which uses a small laser to generate characters. It generally operates using xerographic principles, and is capable of producing very high quality typescript and graphics. Early laser printers were relatively expensive, but decreasing costs are establishing them as an economic means of fast, quiet printing. Colour laser printers are now available at a price acceptable to a small business.

laser scanning **1** Causing a laser beam to scan, ie move in such a way as to point in all directions in succession. The direction of the beam may need to be varied for some uses (eg *ladar*, or laser radar). This can be done by electro-acoustic methods (using the vibration of a medium at or near the source), or by electro-optical methods (such as electrically modifying the effect on a polarized beam of some transparent cell in its path).
2 Scanning with a laser. A digital recording (yielding an eventual sound or visual signal), consisting of pits in a metallized plastic disk, is moved past a laser beam. The response of the beam is received by a photodetector, analysed, and reproduced aurally or visually.

laser typesetter A form of typesetting used by printers in which the characters are drawn by a computer-controlled laser onto a bromide film. The bromide film is then used to etch a lithographic plate from which the required documents are printed.

Lashley, Karl S(pencer) (1890–1958) Psychologist, born in Davis, Virginia, USA. He studied at Johns Hopkins University, and became professor at the universities of Minnesota (1920–9), Chicago (1929–35), and Harvard (1935–55). In 1942 he also became director of the Yerkes Laboratory for primate biology at Orange Park, FL. He made valuable contributions to the study of localization of brain function, and is often called 'the father of neuropsychology'.

Lasker, Emanuel (1868–1941) Chess player and mathematician, born in Berlinchen, NE Germany. He won the world championship in 1894, retaining it until 1921, when he was defeated by Capablanca. He studied mathematics at Erlangen University, and formulated a theorem of vector spaces which is known by his name. He left Germany in 1933, and finally settled in the USA, continuing to play chess until his late 60s.

Laski, Harold J(oseph) (1893–1950) Political scientist and socialist, born in Manchester, Greater Manchester, NW England, UK. He studied at Oxford, and lectured at several US universities before joining the London School of Economics (1920), becoming professor of political science in 1926. He was chairman of the Labour Party (1945–6). His political philosophy was a modified Marxism which he expounded in his many books, including *Authority in the Modern State* (1919), *A Grammar of Politics* (1925), and *The American Presidency* (1940).

Laski, Marghanita (1915–88) Novelist and critic, born in Manchester, Greater Manchester, NW England, UK, the niece of Harold Laski. She studied at Oxford, and her first novel, *Love on the Supertax*, appeared in 1944. She wrote extensively for newspapers and reviews, and published a number of critical works. Her later novels include *Little Boy Lost* (1949) and *The Victorian Chaise-longue* (1953).

Las Palmas (de Gran Canaria) [**pal**mas] pop (2000e) 760 000; area 4072 sq km/1572 sq mi. Spanish province in the Canary Is, comprising the islands of Gran Canaria, Lanzarote, and Fuerteventura; tourism, shipyards, mineral water, cement, livestock, textiles, fruit and vegetables, metal products, food processing; capital, Las Palmas (de Gran Canaria), pop (2000e) 347 000, resort and seaport (Puerto de la Luz); airport; tourism, trade in sugar, tomatoes, bananas; Columbus's House, cathedral, hermitage of San Telmo, Church of San Francisco; Los Reyes Magos (Jan), Winter Festival (Feb–Mar), Festival of Spain (Apr–May).

Lassa fever An infectious disease caused by a virus confined at the present time to sub-Saharan W Africa. It is highly contagious, and causes fever, vomiting, chest pain, and haemorrhage. It carries a high mortality.

Lassus, Orlandus, also known as **Orlando di Lasso** (c.1532–94) Musician and composer, born in Mons, S Belgium. He travelled widely, visiting Italy, England, and France. In 1570 he was ennobled by Maximilian II, and received the knighthood of the Golden Spur (1574). He wrote over 2000 compositions, secular pieces as well as church music, his best-known work being *Psalmi Davidis poenitentiales* (1584).

Last Supper In the New Testament Gospels, the last meal of Jesus with his disciples on the eve of his arrest and crucifixion. In the three synoptic gospels, this is considered a Passover meal, and is significant for Jesus's words over the bread and cup of wine, where he declares 'This is my body' and 'This is my blood of the covenant which is poured out for many' (*Mark* 14.22–4). John's gospel dates the meal before the Passover day, and gives no record of these words but includes the story of the footwashing of the disciples. The event is commemorated in the early Church's celebration of the Lord's Supper (1 *Cor* 11), and subsequently in the sacrament of Holy Communion.

Las Vegas [las **vay**gas] (Span 'the meadows') 36°10N 115°09W, pop (2000e) 478 400. Seat of Clark Co, SE Nevada, USA; largest city in the state; named after the natural meadows which served as camping sites on early trails to the W; settled by Mormons, 1855–7; purchased by a railway company, 1903; city status, 1911; airport; railway; university (1957); noted for its gaming casinos and 24-hour entertainment; commercial centre for a mining and ranching area; printing and publishing, chemicals, glass products; Mormon Fort, Liberace Museum.

La Tène [la **ten**] A prehistoric site on the shores of L Neuchâtel, W Switzerland, with rich votive deposits of decorated weapons and brooches excavated from 1858. Its name is commonly used to describe the later European Iron Age that succeeded Hallstatt culture c.500 BC and survived until the coming of the Romans. Hillforts, increasing trade and warfare, the development of towns and coinage, and a vigorous curvilinear art style are characteristic features of the period.

latent heat Heat absorbed or released when a substance undergoes a change of state at a constant temperature, such as solid to liquid (*latent heat of fusion*) or liquid to gas (*latent heat of vaporization*); symbol L, units J (joule). For ice at 0°C, the latent heat of fusion is $3{\cdot}35 \times 10^5$ J/kg; for water, heat of vaporization at 100°C is $2{\cdot}26 \times 10^6$ J/kg.

latent image The invisible image formed in a photographic emulsion by its exposure to light. It is made visible by development when the light-affected silver halide grains are converted to black metallic silver.

laterality or **lateralization** A characteristic of the human brain, in which the left and right cerebral hemispheres are specialized for different functions; also known as **hemispheric specialization**. In the majority of both right- and left-handed people, the left hemisphere is specialized for language functions: speaking, understanding, reading, and writing. The right hemisphere is specialized for the perception of complex patterns, both visual (eg faces) and tactile. Normally, the two hemispheres work together, sending information from one to the other by way of complex brain connections.

lateral thinking *de Bono, Edward*

Lateran Church of St John The oldest of the four patriarchal basilicas of Rome, the episcopal seat of the pope as Bishop of Rome. Until the 14th-c, when it was destroyed by fire, it was the centre of the Roman Catholic world. The present building dates from the 16th-c.

Lateran Councils A series of councils of the Church held at the Lateran Palace, Rome, between the 7th-c and the 18th-c. Those held in 1123, 1139, 1179, and especially 1215 are the most significant. The Fourth or Great Council defined the doctrine of the Eucharist (*transubstantiation*), and represents the culmination of mediaeval papal legislation.

Lateran Treaty (1929) An agreement between the Italian fascist state and the papacy, ending a church-state conflict dating from 1870. Italy recognized the sovereignty of Vatican City, and Catholicism as the country's only religion; the papacy recognized the Italian state, and accepted the loss of other papal territories as irreversible. The treaty was confirmed in the Italian constitution of 1948.

laterite Tropical soil in which seasonal fluctuations of groundwater have concentrated aluminium and iron oxide, forming a thick, hard, reddish layer. It is often used as roadstone.

latex A milky fluid found in special cells or ducts (*lactifers*) and present in many different plants. It is usually white, but can be colourless, yellow, orange, or red, and contains various substances in solution or suspension, such as starch, sugars, alkaloids, and rubber. In some cases it may be involved with nutrition of the plant or represent waste products, but the exact function is unknown.

lathe A common machine tool used to shape workpieces of various materials. These are held in the jaws of the lathe's chuck, and rotated under power. The tools for boring, threading, cutting, or facing the workpiece are brought into contact with it either manually or under machine control.

lathyrism A permanent paralysis, caused by excessive intake of a vetch crop (*Lathyrus sativus*). The crop is sown together with wheat in many parts of Africa and Asia, so that if dry weather prevents wheat growth, the vetch will provide an alternative harvest.

Latimer, Hugh (c.1485–1555) Protestant martyr, born in Thurcaston, Leicestershire, C England, UK. In 1510 he was elected a fellow of Clare College, Cambridge, and in 1522 was appointed a university preacher, soon becoming noted for his reformed doctrines. He was made rector of West Kington in Wiltshire, and in 1535 was consecrated as Bishop of Worcester. Twice during Henry VIII's reign he was sent to the Tower, in 1532 and 1546, and under Mary I he was examined at Oxford (1554) and committed to jail. The next year he was found guilty of heresy, and was burned with Ridley opposite Balliol College.

Latin *Italic / Romance languages; Latin literature*

Latin America The 18 Spanish-speaking republics of the W hemisphere, together with Portuguese-speaking Brazil (the largest Latin-American country) and French-speaking Haiti. The name first came into use in France just before 1860.

Latin-American Free Trade Association (LAFTA) An economic association of Latin-American countries set up by the Treaty of Montevideo in 1960; its members are Argentina, Bolivia, Brazil, Chile, Colombia, Ecuador, Mexico, Paraguay, Peru, Uruguay, and Venezuela. It aimed at eliminating tariffs and other trade barriers by gradual reduction over a 12-year period. Progress was made, but not as fast as had been hoped, due to the varying levels of economic development exhibited by the member countries. In the late 1970s negotiations were begun to establish a new framework for economic integration. In 1980 the **Latin-American Integration Association** (LAIA) was formed, adopting an alternative to the concept of a free-trade area, in that it opted for the establishment of bilateral preference agreements that would take into account the varying stages of economic development of the member countries. Cuba was admitted in 1986 with observer status.

Latin-American literature There were some remarkable writers in both Spanish and Portuguese from the South American continent in the late 19th-c, including the poet and novelist Machado de Assiz (1839–1908) in Brazil, the poet José Hernández (1834–86) in Argentina, and the early modernist Rubén Darío in Nicaragua. But it was in the 20th-c that Latin-American literature commanded world attention. This was first achieved in poetry. Major writers include the Chilean Gabriela Mistral and the immensely popular Pablo Neruda, who both received the Nobel Prize; the Peruvian exile Cesar Vallejo (1882–1938), the Mexican Octavio Paz, and the Nicaraguan Sergio Ramírez. After World War 2 it was the sophisticated short fictions of Jorge Luis Borges that captured the imagination, and exercised a powerful influence. The 'magic realism' of later novelists has been attributed to the volatile politics of the region. Among the best known are the Argentinian Julio Cortázar (1914–84; eg *Hopscotch*, 1963), the Columbian García Márquez (eg *A Hundred Years of Solitude*, 1967), and the Mexican Carlos Fuentes (eg *The Death of Artemio Cruz*, 1962). The Brazilian Jorge Amado wrote, in exile, from a more explicit ideological position: and the Peruvian Mario Vargas Llosa is likewise deeply involved in politics.

Latin literature Oratory was respected from the earliest days of republican Rome (from 500 BC), and hymns and songs graced popular festivals; but Latin literature emerged in the pre-Classical period (250–85 BC), when many experiments were made on Greek models. The most significant writers of this time were the comic dramatists Plautus and Terence, the poet Ennius, who introduced the hexameter, and the satirist Lucilius (180–102 BC), of whose works only fragments survive. During the last century BC, the greater sophistication of poets such as Catullus and Lucretius heralded the Golden Age of Latin literature, which was fulfilled by the refinement of Latin prose in the oratory of Cicero, and the historical and philosophical writings of Caesar and Sallust (86–34 BC). The 45 years of the Augustan Age, from Actium (31 BC) to the death of Augustus (AD 14), witnessed a remarkable output of poetry: the odes and epistles (as well as the satires) of Horace, the *Georgics* and the posthumous *Aeneid* of Virgil, the love poetry and the *Metamorphoses* of Ovid, and the elegies of Propertius and Tibullus. The prose writings of Livy, the greatest Roman historian, also form part of this peak of achievement. After a barren period, the death of Nero (AD 68) brought Martial's brilliant epigrams and the more sober work of the elder Pliny and Quintilian. Classical Latin literature concludes with the writers of the 'Silver Age' under Trajan and Hadrian (98–138). These include the greatest Roman satirist, Juvenal; the historian Tacitus; the master of the private letter, the younger Pliny; and the biographer Suetonius.

Latinus [latiynus] In legends of early Rome, the ancestor and eponymous King of the Latins. He was either descended from Circe (according to Hesiod) or from Faunus (according to Virgil). In the *Aeneid*, Latinus gives his daughter Lavinia to Aeneas.

latitude and longitude Two dimensions used in mapping. The **latitude** of a point on the Earth's surface is the angular distance, N or S from the Equator (at latitude 0°); the Poles are at latitude 90°; lines (*parallels*) of latitude are parallel circles running E–W joining points of equal latitude. The distance between 1° of latitude varies slightly, because the Earth is not a perfect sphere. At the Equator, it is 110·551 km/68·694 mi; at latitude 45° it is 111·130 km/69·053 mi; and near the Poles it is 111·698 km/69·406 mi. Important lines of latitude are the

latitude and longitude

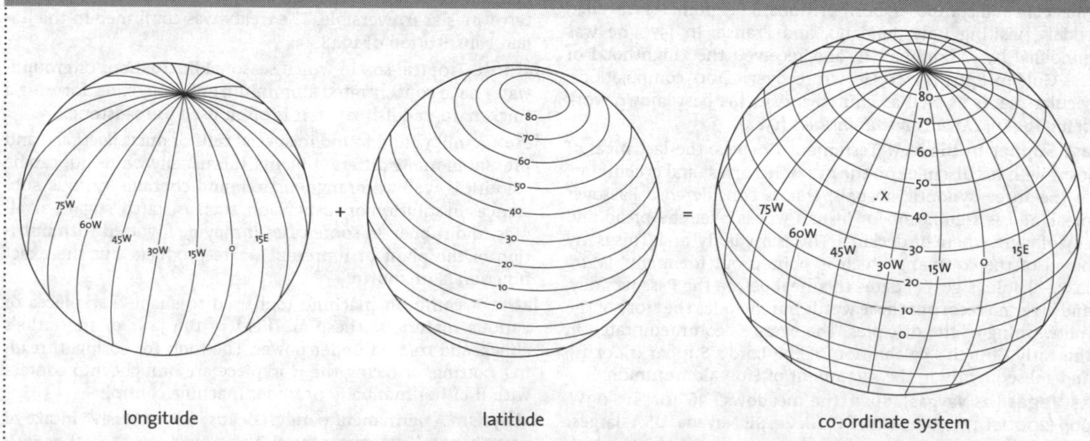

Lines of longitude and latitude on the Earth's surface, measured in degrees °, minutes ′, and seconds ″. The point x would have the following co-ordinate locations: 44°10′10″N, 39°25′40″W.

Latvia

official name **Republic of Latvia**, Latvian **Latviya**, Russ **Latviskaya**

Local name Latvija (Latvian)

Timezone GMT +2

Area 64 600 km²/24 900 sq mi

Population total (2002e) 2 331 000

Status Republic

Date of independence 1991

Capital Riga

Language Latvian (official)

Ethnic groups Latvian (52%), Russian (34%), Belorussian (5%), Ukrainian (4%), Polish (2%), Lithuanian (1%)

Religions Predominantly Evangelical Lutheran, with Orthodox and Roman Catholic minorities

Physical features Flat, glaciated region; highest point, central Vidzeme (Livonia) elevation, 312 m/1024 ft; over 40% forested; coastline ranges over 472 km/293 mi; wooded lowland, marshes, lakes; NW coast indented by the Gulf of Riga; chief river, Daugava.

Climate Mild climate, with high humidity; only c.30–40 days of sunshine annually; summers cool and rainy; average mean temperature -2°C (Jan), 17°C (Jul); average annual rainfall 700–800 mm/28–31 in.

Currency (1991) 1 Latvian Lat (LVL) = 100 santims

Economy Machine-building, metalworking, electrical engineering, electronics, chemicals, furniture, food processing, fishing, timber, paper and woollen goods, meat and dairy products.

GDP (2002e) $20·99 bn, per capita $8900

Human Development Index (2002) 0·800

History Incorporated into Russia, 1721; independent state, 1918–40; proclaimed a Soviet Socialist Republic, 1940; occupied by Germany in World War 2; USSR regained control, 1944; coalition government elected, 1989; declared independence, 1991; governed by a President, Prime Minister and Congress of Latvia.

Head of State
1991–3 Anatolijs Gorbunovs
1993–9 Guntis Ulmanis
1999– Vaira Vike-Freiberga

Head of Government
1997–8 Guntar Krasts
1998–9 Vilis Kristopans
1999–2000 Andris Skele
2000–2 Andris Berzins
2002– Einars Repse

Tropic of Cancer (23·5°N), Tropic of Capricorn (23·5°S), the Arctic Circle (66·5°N), and the Antarctic Circle (66·5°S). Lines (*meridians*) of **longitude** are great circles running N–S and meeting at the Poles; the longitude is measured as an angular distance from the Greenwich meridian defined as 0° up to 180°E or W. At the Equator, the distance between lines of longitude 1° apart is 111·32 km/69·172 mi. This is reduced to 78·848 km/48·995 mi at latitude 45°, and is zero at the Poles.

Latium [layshium] In antiquity, the area SE of Rome between the Apennine Mts and the sea. It was the territory of the Latini, Latin-speaking peoples of whom the Romans are the most famous. Densely populated in early Roman times, by the imperial period it had become the recreation area of the Roman rich, who filled it with luxurious villas.

La Tour, Georges de (1593–1652) Artist, born in Vic-sur-Seille, NE France. From 1620 he worked at Lunéville and achieved a high reputation. The Duke of Lorraine became his patron, and later Louis XIII accepted a painting by him, liking it so much he had all works by other masters removed from his chambers. La Tour was entirely forgotten until his rediscovery in 1915. He specialized in candle-lit scenes, mostly of religious subjects, such as 'St Joseph the Carpenter' (1645, Louvre).

La Tour, Maurice Quentin de [latoor], also spelled **Latour** (1704–88) Pastellist and portrait painter, born in St Quentin, N France. He settled in Paris, where he became immensely popular, and was made portraitist to Louis XV (1750–73). His best works include portraits of Madame de Pompadour, Voltaire, and Rousseau.

Látrabjarg [lowtrabyark] 65°30N 24°32W. Westernmost point of Iceland, and one of the highest cliff faces in the world; in Vestfirðir region, W Iceland; British trawler *Dhoon* ran aground below the cliff in 1947, the entire crew being saved by men lowered down the cliff on ropes in one of the world's greatest rescue achievements.

Latrobe, Benjamin (Henry) [latrohb] (1764–1820) Architect and civil engineer, born in Fulneck, West Yorkshire, N England, UK. He trained in England with Cockerell, enjoying a successful practice there before emigrating to the USA (1795), where he introduced the Greek Revival style and was surveyor of public buildings in Washington, DC (1803–17). As an engineer he designed waterworks for the city of Philadelphia (1801), worked on the Washington navy yard, and joined with Robert Fulton in a scheme to build steamboats (1813–15). His most notable work is the Basilica of the Assumption of the Blessed Virgin Mary, Baltimore (begun 1805).

Latter-Day Saints (LDS) *Mormons*

lattice energy The energy required to convert one mole of an ionic solid to gaseous ions. Its value can be estimated reasonably for many compounds, and used to calculate other energies.

Latvia *see panel*

Latvian *Baltic languages*

Latynina, Larisa Semyonovna [lateenina] (1934–) Gymnast born in Kherson, S Ukraine. She studied at the Kiev State Institute of Physical Culture, competed in three Olympic Games (1956, 1960, 1964), and was the first woman athlete to win nine gold medals. During her 13-year career she won 24 Olympic, World, and European titles. She retired in 1966.

Laud, William [lawd] (1573–1645) Clergyman and Archbishop of Canterbury, born in Reading, S England, UK. He studied at

Oxford, and was ordained in 1601. His learning and industry brought him many patrons, and he rapidly received preferment, becoming King's Chaplain (1611), Bishop of St David's (1621), Bishop of Bath and Wells and a privy councillor (1626), Bishop of London (1628), and Archbishop of Canterbury (1633). With Strafford and Charles I, he worked for absolutism in Church and state. In Scotland, his attempt (1635–7) to anglicize the Church led to the Bishops' Wars. In 1640 the Long Parliament impeached him. He was found guilty, and executed on Tower Hill.

Lauda, Niki [lowda], popular name of **Nikolas Andreas Lauda** (1949–) Motor-racing driver, born in Vienna, Austria. He was world champion racing driver in 1975, 1977 and 1984. In 1976 he suffered horrific burns and injuries in the German Grand Prix at the Nürburg Ring. Despite a series of operations, he remained a contender for the 1976 Japanese Grand Prix, but finally declined to race because of adverse weather conditions. He then refuted rumours that he had lost his nerve by winning again in 1977. Going on to drive for Brabham involved a two-year absence from Grand Prix racing. He crowned his come-back with McLaren by winning his third and last Grand Prix championship in 1984. He retired in 1985 and became the proprietor of Lauda-Air.

laudanum [lawdanum] A preparation of opium introduced by Paracelsus in the early 16th-c. Addiction to laudanum was socially acceptable until the early 19th-c, when the invention of the hypodermic syringe and needle made narcotic addiction more serious.

Lauder, Estée [lawder], *née* **Mentzer** (c.1910–2004) Businesswoman, born in New York City, USA. From a poor immigrant family, she worked her way up in the cosmetics industry by selling a face cream made by her uncle. She co-founded Estée Lauder Inc with her husband **Joseph Lauder** in 1946, and had great success with the fragrance 'Youth Dew' in the 1950s. She was named one of 100 women of achievement by *Harper's Bazaar* in 1967, and one of the Top Ten outstanding women in business in 1970. Her autobiography, *Estée: a Success Story*, appeared in 1985. She retired in 1995 and the role of head of the family business passed to her daughter-in-law, Evelyn Lauder (1937–).

Lauder, Sir Harry (MacLennan) [lawder] (1870–1950) Singer, born in Edinburgh, EC Scotland, UK. He started his career on the music-hall stage as an Irish comedian, but made his name as a singer of Scots songs, many of which were of his own composition, such as 'Roamin' in the Gloamin''. He was knighted in 1919 for his work in organizing entertainments for the troops during World War 1. Some of his biggest successes were in London's famous music halls, but he was also popular abroad, especially in the USA and Commonwealth countries, which he toured extensively after 1907. He wrote volumes of memoirs, the best known of which is *Roamin' in the Gloamin'* (1928).

Lauderdale, John Maitland, Duke of [lawderdayl] (1616–82) Scottish statesman, born in Lethington, East Lothian, E Scotland, UK. He was an ardent supporter of the Covenanters (1638), and in 1643 became a Scottish Commissioner at Westminster, succeeding his father as second Earl of Lauderdale in 1645. He was taken prisoner at Worcester in 1651, and spent nine years in the Tower, at Windsor, and at Portland. At the Restoration, he became Scottish secretary of state. A member of the Privy Council, he had a seat in the so-called Cabal ministry, and was created a duke in 1672.

laughing gas *nitrous oxide*

laughing jackass / kookaburra *kookaburra*

Laughlin, Robert B (1950–) Physicist, born in Vesalia, California, USA. He graduated from MIT in 1979, joining Stanford University, and shared the 1998 Nobel Prize for Physics for his contribution to the discovery of a new form of quantum fluid with fractionally charged excitations.

Laughton, Charles [lawtn] (1899–1962) Film and stage actor, born in Scarborough, North Yorkshire, N England, UK. He trained at the Royal Academy of Dramatic Art, London, and first appeared on stage in London in 1926. This was followed by successes in *The Cherry Orchard*, *A Man with Red Hair*, and *Payment Deferred*. He appeared with the Old Vic Company in 1933, played in and produced Shaw's *Don Juan in Hell* and *Major Barbara*, and as a Shakespearean actor gave fine performances in *Macbeth*, *Measure for Measure*, and *King Lear*. He began to act in films in 1932 and among his memorable roles are *The Private Life of Henry VIII* (1932, Oscar), Mr Barrett in *The Barretts of Wimpole Street* (1934), Captain Bligh in *Mutiny on the Bounty* (1935), and Quasimodo in *The Hunchback of Notre Dame* (1939). He was married to the actress **Elsa Lanchester** (1902–86), and became a US citizen in 1950.

Launceston [lonsestn] 41°25S 147°07E, pop (2000e) 73 200 (Greater Launceston). City in Tasmania, Australia, at the confluence of the N Esk, S Esk, and Tamar Rivers; second largest city in Tasmania; airfield; railway; timber, engineering, textiles, brewing; Cataract Gorge (with suspension bridge and chairlift).

launch opportunity The dates between which launches can take place to insert an interplanetary spacecraft on a minimum energy transfer orbit to a planet; typically 10 to 20 days in duration. Launches are not practicable at other times because of launch vehicle performance limitations. Because Earth and the target planet are both orbiting the Sun, launch opportunities occur at intervals that repeat cyclically: for the other outer planets, they occur about every 12–13 months, for Mars every 26 months, for Venus every 19 months, and for Mercury also every 19 months (but due to the 7° inclination of Mercury's orbit to the ecliptic, practical opportunities are every 36 months).

launch vehicle A rocket-propelled vehicle used to carry aloft spacecraft from the Earth's surface, generally consisting of several 'stages' which separate sequentially as fuel in each is consumed. The thrust is provided by the controlled explosive burning of liquid fuels (eg kerosene and oxygen, hydrogen and oxygen) or solid propellants (typically a synthetic rubber fuel mixed with an oxidizer powder). The technique derived from weapon delivery systems developed during and after World War 2, and was pioneered by Konstantin Tsiolkovsky in the USSR, Robert Goddard in the USA, and Wernher von Braun in Germany.

launch window The time during a given day when a spacecraft may be launched on its desired trajectory. It can last from minutes to more than an hour, depending on the mission and, for interplanetary launches, on an exact date within the launch opportunity. There are two windows during each 24-hour period, one of which may be impractical because of other factors, such as launch safety for night launches.

Laurasia The name given to the N 'supercontinent' comprising present-day North America, Europe, and Asia, excluding India, which began to break away from the single land mass Pangaea about 200 million years ago. The S supercontinent was Gondwanaland.

laurel A name applied to various unrelated trees and shrubs which have glossy, leathery, evergreen leaves, but mainly to members of the large family Lauraceae in which the tissues contain numerous oil cavities and are aromatic.

Laurel and Hardy Comedians who formed the first Hollywood film comedy team. The 'thin one', **Stan Laurel** (1890–1965), originally **Arthur Stanley Jefferson**, was born in Ulverston, Lancashire, NW England, UK. He began in a British touring company, went to the USA in 1910, and worked in silent films from 1917. The 'fat one', **Oliver Hardy** (1892–1957), born near Atlanta GA, left college to join a troupe of minstrels before drifting into the film industry. They came together in 1926. They made many full-length feature films, but their best efforts are generally thought to be their early (1927–31) shorts. Their contrasting personalities, general clumsiness, and disaster-packed predicaments made them a universally popular comedy duo.

Lauren, Ralph [loren], originally **Ralph Lifschitz** (1939–) Fashion designer, born in New York City, USA. He attended night school for business studies and worked as a salesman in Bloomingdale's. In 1967 he joined Beau Brummel Neckwear and created the Polo range for men, later including womenswear. He is famous for his American styles, such as the 'prairie look' and 'frontier fashions'.

Laurentian Shield *Canadian Shield*

Laurier, Sir Wilfrid [loryay] (1841–1919) Canadian statesman and prime minister (1896–1911), born in St Lin, Quebec, SE Canada. He became a lawyer, a journalist, and a member of the Quebec Legislative Assembly. He entered federal politics in 1874, and became minister of inland revenue (1877), leader of the Liberal Party (1887–1919), and the first French-Canadian to be prime minister of Canada (1896). A firm supporter of self-government for Canada, in his home policy he was an advocate of compromise and free trade with the USA.

laurustinus [loruhstiynuhs] A dense evergreen shrub or small tree (*Viburnum tinus*), growing to 7 m/23 ft, native to S Europe; leaves oval, shiny; flowers 5-petalled, white, in clusters 4–9 cm/ $1\frac{1}{2}$–$3\frac{1}{2}$ in across; fruit berry-like, dark, metallic blue. It is grown for ornament, but often fails to fruit in cooler regions. (Family: Caprifoliaceae.)

Lausanne [lohzan] 46°32N 6°39E, pop (2000e) 129 000. Tourist resort, convention centre, and capital of Vaud canton, W Switzerland; seat of the Federal Supreme Court; on N shore of L Geneva, 51 km/32 mi NE of Geneva; railway junction; university (1891); clothing, confectionery, printing, leather; seat of the International Olympic Committee; Mon Repos Park, with Olympic Museum; cathedral (1275), town hall (17th-c), Bishop's Palace; Fête of Lausanne (Jun), biennial Festival of Tapestry (ancient and modern).

Lauterbur, Paul C [lowterboor] (1929–) Chemist, born in Sidney, Ohio, USA. He studied at Case Institute of Technology, Cleveland (1951) and the University of Pittsburgh (1962), and became professor of chemistry at New York University, Stony Brook (1969–85). He was then appointed director of the Biomedical Magnetic Resonance Laboratory at the University of Illinois, Urbana-Champaign. In 2003 he shared the Nobel Prize for Physiology or Medicine for discoveries concerning magnetic resonance imaging.

Lautréamont, comte de (Count of) [lohtrayamõ], pseudonym of **Isidore Ducasse** (1846–70) Poet, born in Montevideo, Uruguay. He went to France as an adolescent, and published the sequence of prose poems *Les Chants de Maldoror* (1868, The Songs of Maldoror). *Poésies* was published in 1870, the year he died in Paris. His work was a significant influence on the Surrealists and other Modernist writers.

lava Hot molten rock erupted onto the Earth's surface from a volcano. On solidification it forms volcanic igneous rocks such as rhyolite, andesite, or basalt. Lava temperature and viscosity depends on its chemical composition, with the more silica-rich lava being cooler (around 900°C) and more viscous than basic lavas (temperature up to 1100°C), which flow more freely, forming volcanoes with gentle slopes.

Laval, Pierre (1883–1945) French statesman and prime minister (1931–2, 1935–6, 1942–4), born in Châteldon, C France. He became a lawyer, deputy (1914), and senator (1926), before serving as premier. From a position on the left, he moved rightwards during the late 1930s, and in the Vichy government was Pétain's deputy (1940), then his rival. As prime minister, he openly collaborated with the Germans. Fleeing after the liberation to Germany and Spain, he was brought back, charged with treason, and executed in Paris.

lavallier *microphone*

La Vallière, Louise-Françoise de La Baume le Blanc, duchesse de (Duchess of) [la valyair] (1644–1710) Mistress of Louis XIV, born in Tours, WC France. Brought to court by her mother, she became the king's mistress in 1661 and bore him four children. When the Marquise de Montespan superseded her, she was publicly humiliated, then compensated by being made a duchess (1667). After one escape attempt, she retired to a Carmelite nunnery in Paris (1674), where she lived in penitence for 36 years.

lavender A small aromatic shrub, native mainly to Mediterranean regions and Atlantic islands, typical of dry scrub; young stems square; leaves narrow, sometimes deeply lobed, greyish, in opposite pairs; flowers 2-lipped, lavender or mauve, in dense spikes. It is widely cultivated for ornament, and as the source of oil of lavender for the perfume industry and for potpourri. (Genus: *Lavandula*, 28 species. Family: Labiatae.)

La Venta An Olmec ceremonial centre in Tabasco province, Mexico, occupied c.900–400 BC, but now destroyed by oil operations. Supported by an estimated hinterland population of c.18 000, its linear complex of platforms, plazas, and 34 m/ 112 ft high Great Pyramid covered 5 sq km/2 sq mi. Of particular note are its carved stone pillars, pavements, colossal heads, and votive figurines of basalt, serpentine, and jade, now displayed at Parque La Venta, near the original site.

Laver, Rod(ney George) [layver], nickname **the Rockhampton Rocket** (1938–) Tennis player, born in Rockhampton, Queensland, NE Australia. An aggressive left-handed player, he first won the Wimbledon singles title in 1961, and again in 1962 in the course of a Grand Slam of all the major titles (British, US, French, and Australian). He turned professional in 1962 and won the world singles title five times between 1964 and 1970. In 1968, when Wimbledon went open, he took the title, and won again in the course of another Grand Slam the following year. The first professional to make more than $1 million, he won more money than anyone else until 1978.

Lavoisier, Antoine Laurent [lavwazyay] (1743–94) Chemist, born in Paris, France. To finance his investigations, in 1768 he accepted the office of farmer-general of taxes, and became director of the government powder mills in 1776. In 1788 he showed that air is a mixture of gases which he called *oxygen* and *nitrogen*, thus disproving the earlier theory of phlogiston. His major work is the *Traité élémentaire de chimie* (1789), containing the ideas which set chemistry on its modern path. He also devised the modern method of naming chemical compounds, and was a member of the commission which devised the metric system. Politically a liberal, and despite his many reforms, he was guillotined in Paris on a contrived charge of counter-revolutionary activity. He is now recognized as the founder of modern chemistry.

Law, (Andrew) Bonar [law, boner] (1858–1923) British statesman and prime minister (1922–3), born in New Brunswick, E Canada. He studied in Canada and Glasgow, was an iron merchant in Glasgow, became a Unionist MP in 1900, and in 1911 succeeded Balfour as Unionist leader. He acted as colonial secretary (1915-16), a member of the war cabinet, Chancellor of the Exchequer (1916-18), Lord Privy Seal (1919), and from 1916 Leader of the House of Commons. He retired in 1921 through ill health, but returned to serve as premier for several months in 1922–3.

Law, (David) Jude (1972–) Actor, born in London, UK. He joined the National Youth Music Theatre and went on to gain a role in the Granada TV soap opera *Families*. He later performed with the Royal Shakespeare Company and Royal National Theatre. His feature films include *Wilde* (1997), *The Talented Mr Ripley* (1999), *AI: Artificial Intelligence* (2001), and *Cold Mountain* (2003). He was married to actress Sadie Frost (1997–2003).

Law, William (1686–1761) Clergyman, born in Kingscliffe, Northamptonshire, C England, UK. He studied at Emmanuel College, Cambridge, where he became a fellow (1711), and was ordained, but was forced to resign on refusing to take the oath of allegiance to George I. He wrote several treatises on Christian ethics and mysticism, notably the *Serious Call to a Devout and Holy Life* (1729), which influenced the Wesleys.

law Specifically, a rule of conduct laid down by a controlling authority; generally, the whole body of such rules, recognized and enforced by society in the courts by sanctions. Laws are made by the body recognized as having the constitutional authority to make them, ie in most countries, the legislature. In common law systems, the courts are particularly influential in developing the law; although they may be said to interpret the law, the growth in case decisions can be regarded as effectively creating or developing the law, even though (as in the UK) parliament is sovereign (subject to the jurisdiction of the European Parliament). In states with a written constitution, such as the USA, the Supreme Court may have the power to declare particular laws, practices, or decisions as unconstitutional, ie inconsistent with the provisions of the constitution.

Law Advocate *attorney general*

Law Commission A body established by the Law Commissions Act (1965) for England and Wales (with a separate commission for Scotland), appointed from the judiciary and from practising and academic lawyers. Its function is to examine the law with a view to its systematic development, reform, and codification, and to suggest the removal of obsolete and anomalous rules. While influential, it has no power to change the law.

Lawler, Ray(mond Evenor) (1921–) Playwright, producer, and actor, born in Melbourne, Victoria, SE Australia. He was a factory-hand at the age of 13, and had several jobs before joining the National Theatre Company in Melbourne. He gained an international reputation from his first major piece of writing, *Summer of the Seventeenth Doll*, a play of the outback, which he produced in 1956, with himself in the leading role. *Kid Stakes* (1975) and *Other Times* (1977) completed the *Doll* trilogy. His work was influential in introducing greater realism into Australian drama.

Lawrence D(avid) H(erbert Richard) (1885–1930) Novelist, poet, and essayist, born in Eastwood, Nottinghamshire, C England, UK. The son of a miner, he studied at University College, Nottingham, and became a schoolmaster, but illness, and the moderate success of his first novel, *The White Peacock* (1911), made him leave teaching and turn to writing. In 1912 he eloped with **Frieda Weekley** (*née* von Richthofen), the wife of Lawrence's professor at Nottingham. They travelled in Germany, Austria, and Italy (1912–13), and married in 1914 after her divorce. Meanwhile Lawrence had secured his success with *Sons and Lovers* (1913). They returned to England at the outbreak of World War 1. In 1915 he published *The Rainbow*, and was prosecuted for obscenity. He left England in 1919, and after three years' residence in Italy, where he produced *Women in Love* (1920), he settled in Mexico, returning to Italy in 1925. He died in Vence, near Nice, of tuberculosis. His novel *Lady Chatterley's Lover* (expurgated edition, 1928; unexpurgated, Paris, 1929) was published privately in Florence, and copies were confiscated in England the next year; it was not published in the UK in unexpurgated form until after a sensational obscenity trial in 1960. Some of his most original writing occurs in his poems, notably *Birds, Beasts and Flowers* (1923), and in his *Letters* (7 vols, 1979–93). His other major novels include *Aaron's Rod* (1922), *Kangaroo* (1923), and *The Plumed Serpent* (1926), and his collected poems were published in 1928. Many films have been made from his fiction, notably by Ken Russell.

Lawrence, Ernest (Orlando) (1901–58) Physicist, born in Canton, South Dakota, USA. He studied at South Dakota, Minnesota, and Yale universities, and in 1931 constructed the first cyclotron for the acceleration of protons, later used to create new radioactive isotopes. He was professor at Berkeley, CA, from 1930, and in 1936 was appointed first director of the radiation laboratory there. He was awarded the Nobel Prize for Physics in 1939.

Lawrence, Stephen (1974–93) Teenage victim of racist murder, born in Plumstead, S London, UK. In 1993 Stephen, a black student, was murdered in Eltham, SE London, by a group of white youths. At the inquest, the five suspected of the crime claimed their right to silence and refused to answer questions in the witness box. Lawrence's parents complained that the police were not doing enough to find their son's killers, and after criminal charges against the accused had been dropped by the police 'for lack of sufficient evidence', they themselves brought a private prosecution, which collapsed for the same reason. In 1999 an official inquiry concluded that the police investigations had been marred by incompetence and institutional racism.

Lawrence, T(homas) E(dward), known as **Lawrence of Arabia** (1888–1935) Soldier, Arabist, and writer, born in Tremadoc, Gwynedd, NW Wales, UK. He studied at Oxford, and became a junior member of the British Museum archaeological team at Carchemish, on the Euphrates (1911–14). In 1916 he was appointed the British liaison officer to the Arab Revolt against the Turks, led by Feisal, the son of the Sherif of Mecca, and was present at the taking of Aqaba in 1917 and of Damascus in 1918. He was an adviser to Feisal at the Paris Peace Conference and a member of the Middle East Department at the Colonial Office (1921). He was a delegate to the Peace Conference, and later became adviser on Arab affairs to the Colonial Office (1921–2). His exploits received so much publicity that he became a legendary figure, and he attempted to escape his fame by enlisting in the ranks of the RAF as an aircraftman under the assumed name of **John Hume Ross**. When his identity was discovered, he joined the Royal Tank Corps in 1923 as **T E Shaw**, transferring back to the RAF in 1925. He was discharged in 1935, and was killed in a motor-cycling accident near his Dorset home. His major works were *The Seven Pillars of Wisdom* (for private circulation, 1926), *Revolt in the Desert* (1927), *Crusader Castles* (1936), *Oriental Assembly* (1929), and *The Mint* (1936).

Law Society The professional body for solicitors in England and Wales; a separate Law Society exists for Scotland and another for Northern Ireland. The Law Societies have disciplinary powers relating to solicitors' conduct, and prescribe the rules governing their admission to practice. More generally, the Societies promote the interests of the profession as a whole, as seen in their attempts to secure greater rights for their members to be heard in the courts (*rights of audience*). In England and Wales the Law Society is also responsible for examining intending solicitors, and organizes training through the College of Law and recognized universities.

Lawson, Henry (1867–1922) Poet, born in Grenfell, New South Wales, SE Australia, the son of Louisa Lawson. After his parents' separation, he moved to Sydney with his mother and began writing verse, including such bush ballads as 'Andy's Gone with the Cattle' and 'Roaring Days', and his stories, published by *The Bulletin* from 1888, were immensely popular. In 1895 his collection of prose *While the Billy Boils* was published. His work has received little critical acclaim, although his authentic dramatization of the hardship and comradeship of bush life is recognized. For many he is seen as the national poet. He was given a state funeral when he died.

Lawson, Louisa (1848–1920) Suffragist and social reformer, born in Mudgee, New South Wales, SE Australia, and educated to primary level there. She married Norwegian immigrant Niels Larsen (who later anglicized his name) and lived on many New South Wales goldfields throughout their marriage. They separated after 17 years together, and she moved to Sydney, surrounding herself with radical thinkers and social reformers. In 1888 she founded *Dawn*, Australia's first feminist journal, which elevated women's affairs and promoted women's suffrage. Known also for her famous son, Henry, whom she set on the path of writing, she ended her days in Gladesville Hospital for the Insane.

Lawson (of Blaby), Nigel, Baron (1932–) British statesman, born in London, UK. He studied at Oxford, then worked for various newspapers, including *The Financial Times* and the *Daily Telegraph*, where he was city editor, and also for television (1956–72), and during this time edited the *Spectator* (1966–70). Elected to parliament in 1974, when the Conservatives returned to office he became financial secretary to the Treasury (1979–81), energy secretary (1981-3), and Chancellor of the Exchequer (1983-9). During his time at the Exchequer, Britain saw lower direct taxes, but high interest rates and record trade deficits. He was created a life peer in 1992.

Lawson, Nigella (1960–) Journalist and cookery writer, born in London, England, UK. The daughter of politician Nigel Lawson, she studied at Oxford (1979) and entered journalism, becoming deputy literary editor of *The Sunday Times*. Working as a freelance writer, she began a restaurant column in *The Spectator* and later wrote the food column for *Vogue*. Her first book *How to Eat* (1998) was the basis for her Channel 4 television series, *Nigella Bites*, with an accompanying book (2001). Other bestsellers include *How to be a Domestic Goddess* (2000), which received the Guild of Food Writers Award, and *Forever Summer* (2002). Her second husband is Charles Saatchi (married 2003).

Lawson cypress A species of false cypress (*Chamaecyparis lawsoniana*), identifiable by the parsley-like scent of its bruised foliage; extremely variable in height, shape, branching, and colour; native to SW Oregon and NW California, but one of the most widely cultivated conifers with c.200 named cultivars. (Family: Cupressaceae.)

laxative A drug which causes emptying of the bowels; also known as a **purgative**. Laxatives are overused for the treatment of constipation, which is usually cured by a high fibre diet. Except when medically recommended, authorities believe, they do more harm than good. Examples include castor oil and diphenylmethane.

Laxness, Halldór (Gujónsson Kiljan) (1902–98) Novelist, born in Reykjavík, Iceland. He travelled in Europe and the USA after World War 1, and became a Catholic before going to Canada and the USA (1927–30), where he was converted to Socialism. His major works include *Salka Valka* (1934), a story of Icelandic fishing folk, and the epic *Sjálfstaet Folk* (1934–5, Independent People). He also wrote a number of plays, and adapted some of his own novels for the stage. He was awarded the Nobel Prize for Literature in 1955.

Layamon [layamon] (13th-c) Poet and priest, thought to have lived at Areley Kings, Hereford and Worcester, WC England, UK. He wrote (c.1200) an alliterative verse chronicle, *Brut*, a mythical history of England from the landing of Brutus to the final Saxon victory in 689. His source was Wace's *Brut d'Angleterre*, and *Brut* was important in English versification as the first considerable poem written in Middle English. It is also notable for giving for the first time in English the story of Arthur, as well as those of Lear and Cymbeline.

layering A means of propagating plants by burying a stem in the soil while it is still attached to the plant. The buried portion forms roots, and eventually a separate plant.

lay-planning or **laying up** A technique in industrial garment-making which permits the simultaneous cutting of many garment pieces, achieved by laying a number of fabric pieces on top of each other. Lay planning is done to ensure economy of fabric use. By carefully arranging the pattern pieces on the fabric, the minimum quantity of fabric is used.

Lazarists A religious order, founded in France at the priory of St Lazare, Paris, in 1625 by St Vincent de Paul; properly known as the **Congregation of the Mission** (**CM**); also called the **Vincentians**. Originally missionaries to rural districts and educators of the clergy, they now have foundations worldwide.

L-dopa or **levodopa** A drug used very effectively in the treatment of Parkinson's disease, reducing symptoms in more than two-thirds of patients. Shortly after its introduction in the late 1960s some reports stated that it increased male libido in a minority of patients. Although this probably related to the clinical improvement of the patients rather than the drug itself, L-dopa was exploited briefly (and wrongly) as an aphrodisiac.

Leach, Bernard (Howell) (1887–1979) Studio potter, born in Hong Kong. He studied at the Slade School of Art, London, and went to Japan at the age of 21. There he took up pottery, becoming the sole pupil of Ogata Kenzan (1911–19). He returned to England in 1920, where with Shoji Hamada (1894–1978) he established the Leach pottery at St Ives in Cornwall, where he made earthenware and stoneware. He played a crucial role in promoting handmade pottery which could be appreciated as art. From 1932, he taught at Dartington Hall, Devon. His written works include *A Potter's Book* (1940) and *A Potter's Work* (1967). He was made a Companion of Honour in 1973.

Leach, Johnny, popular name of **John Leach** (1922–) Table tennis player, born in Romford, Essex, SE England, UK. He won the world singles title in 1949 and 1951, and was a member of England's winning Swaythling Cup team in 1953. During 12 years as an England international (1947–59), he represented his country 152 times. He became England's non-playing captain upon retirement, and team manager in 1968, retiring in 1970 to concentrate on his sports goods firm.

Leacock, Stephen (Butler) (1869–1944) Writer and humorist, born in Swanmore, Hampshire, S England, UK. He studied at Toronto, Canada, becoming head of the economics department at McGill University, Montreal (1908). He wrote several books on his subject, including *The Economic Prosperity of the British Empire* (1931), but it is as a humorist that he became widely known. Among his popular works are *Literary Lapses* (1910), *Winsome Winnie* (1920), and *The Garden of Folly* (1924). *The Boy I Left Behind Me*, an unfinished autobiography, was published in 1946. Also in 1946, the Leacock Society decided to present an annual silver medal to the best book of humour published in Canada, known as The Stephen Leacock Medal.

lead Pb (from Lat *plumbum*) element 82, a soft, dense (11·5 g/cm^3) metal, melting point 328°C. Its main natural source is the sulphide (PbS). Its good corrosion resistance and easy workability led to its early use in plumbing and for containers for corrosive liquids. These uses had considerable toxic effects, as lead is slowly oxidized in the presence of air and water. It is used in quantity for the production of accumulators (storage batteries).

Leadbelly, nickname of **Huddie William Ledbetter** (c.1889–1949) Folk-blues musician, born in Mooringsport, Louisiana, USA. In his early life he experienced poverty and violence as he drifted through the South. He was imprisoned for murder (1918), pardoned after six years, then imprisoned again for attempted murder (1930). The folklorists John and Alan Lomax secured his release in 1934, and organized a concert tour and recording contract. His songs highlighted the plight of African-Americans during the Depression. He died penniless, although a number of his songs became standards, notably 'Goodnight, Irene'.

lead poisoning A disorder of children acquired by swallowing or inhaling lead, which is present in the environment in paint, car exhaust fumes, and air and water contaminated with industrial waste. High levels of lead in the blood result in brain, liver, and kidney damage, and lead is deposited in the bones, affecting their growth. There is mounting evidence that even low levels of lead can impair childhood development and lower IQ.

leaf The main photosynthetic organ of green plants, divided into a blade (*lamina*) and a stalk (*petiole*). The lamina is usually broad and thin, to present maximum surface area to sunlight and allow easy diffusion of gases and water vapour to and from the leaf. It is composed of several distinct layers of tissues: the *epidermis* protects the inner tissues – the *palisade layer*, which is the primary site of photosynthesis, and the spongy *mesophyll*, which has large air spaces and is the primary site of gas exchange. A network of vascular tissue, the *veins*, transports water and sap to and from the leaf. The epidermis secretes a waxy cuticle, mostly impervious to water and gases which enter and leave via pores (*stomata*) concentrated in the lower surface of the leaf. The main source of water loss for a plant is due to transpiration via the leaves. This is minimized by the waxy cuticle, and by the opening and closing of the stomata in response to changes in humidity. Other modifications to reduce water-loss are found particularly in plants from dry or cold regions, including reduction in leaf size, inrolled margins to protect stomata, and regular shedding of leaves during unfavourable seasons. Some plants have replaced their leaves entirely with less vulnerable photosynthetic organs, such as green stems. Leaves range from a few mm to 20 m/65 ft in length, exhibit a great variety of shapes, and may be entire, toothed, lobed, or completely divided into separate *leaflets*. These characters and the arrangement of the leaves on the stem are diagnostic for many plant groups. Leaves may also have specialized functions, such as water-storage in succulents, traps in carnivorous plants, and tendrils in climbers.

leaf beetle A robust, often brightly coloured beetle; most are surface feeders on plant leaves; larvae grub-like, feeding on leaves, or are root and stem borers; species include the Colorado potato beetle. (Order: Coleoptera. Family: Chrysomelidae, c.35 000 species.)

leafcutter ant A fungus-feeding ant; foraging workers cut leaves to provide the basic material for a fungus garden inside their soil nest; workers harvest fungus to feed larvae; mostly found in the New World tropics. (Order: Hymenoptera. Family: Formicidae, c.200 species.)

leafcutter bee A solitary bee that cuts pieces of leaf to line or close its nest. It can be an important pollinator of plants, such as alfalfa. (Order: Hymenoptera. Family: Megachilidae.)

leaf hopper A small, hopping insect that feeds by sucking sap or cell contents of plants; causes damage by direct feeding, by toxic secretions, and by transmitting viral diseases; includes many serious pests affecting economically important crops. (Order: Homoptera. Family: Cicadellidae, c.20 000 species.)

leaf insect A large, flattened insect with broad, flattened extensions on its legs, giving its entire body a leaf-like appearance. About 50 species are found mainly in SE Asia and New Guinea. (Order: Phasmoptera. Family: Phyllidae.)

leaf miner An insect larva that eats its way through leaf tissues between upper and lower surfaces of the leaf, leaving spaces (*mines*) behind; most have flattened bodies and wedge-like heads; leaf miners are mostly the larvae of flies, moths, and beetles.

leaf monkey *langur*

League of Nations An international organization whose constitution was drafted at the Paris Peace Conference in 1919, and incorporated into the peace treaties. The main aims were to preserve international peace and security by the prevention or speedy settlement of disputes and the promotion of disarmament through open diplomacy. It operated through a Council, which met several times a year, and an annual Assembly, which met at its Geneva headquarters. The USA refused to join, but there were 53 members by 1923, including the UK, France, Italy, and Japan. Germany joined in 1926, and Russia in 1934, but Germany and Japan withdrew in 1933, and Italy in 1936. It became increasingly ineffective in the later 1930s through the refusal of member nations to put international interests before national ones. The League was powerless in the face of Italian, German, and Japanese expansionism. After World War 2 it was replaced by the United Nations which, unlike the League of Nations, has a peace-keeping force and military observer groups built into its charter.

League of Rights An Australian populist right-wing organization, founded in 1960 by Eric Butler (1916–), who had been engaged in similar activities since 1934. The League, which operates on the fringe of conservative politics, supports God, the Queen, the Commonwealth of Nations, apartheid, and private enterprise. It opposes fluoridation of water supplies, communism, bureaucracy, and Asian immigration.

Leakey, L(ouis) S(eymour) B(azett) [leekee] (1903–72) Archaeologist and physical anthropologist, born in Kabete, WC Kenya. He studied at Cambridge, took part in several archaeological expeditions in East Africa, and became curator of the Coryndon Memorial Museum at Nairobi (1945–61). His great discoveries took place in East Africa, where in 1959, he and his wife, **Mary Leakey** (1913–96), unearthed the skull of *Zinjanthropus*. In 1964 they found remains of *Homo habilis*, and in 1967 discovered *Kenyapithecus africanus*. He also unearthed evidence of human habitation in California more than 50 000 years old. Their son, **Richard Leakey** (1944–), has continued to make further important finds in the area.

Lean, Sir David (1908–91) Film director, born in Croydon, S Greater London, UK. Beginning as a clapperboard boy, he gradually progressed to become film editor for *Gaumont Sound News* (1930) and *British Movietone News* (1931–2), before moving on to fictional features. His co-direction with Noel Coward of *In Which We Serve* (1942), led to a full-scale directorial career, including *Blithe Spirit* (1945), *Brief Encounter* (1945), *Great Expectations* (1946), and *Oliver Twist* (1948). He won Oscars for *Bridge on the River Kwai* (1957) and *Lawrence of Arabia* (1962). In 1965 he made *Dr Zhivago*, followed by *Ryan's Daughter* (1970), and *A Passage to India* (1984). In 1990 he was the first non-American recipient of the American Film Institute Life Achievement Award.

Leander *Hero and Leander*

Leaning Tower, Ital **Torre Pendente** Marble belltower in Pisa, W Italy, 54 m/177 ft high, begun in 1173, completed in 1372. The ground beneath the tower began to sink after three storeys had been built, and the tower was 5·2 m/17 ft out of line in 1997. Closed to visitors in 1990, a programme of strengthening work stopped the process of tilting by 2000, and it was re-opened in December 2001.

leap year In the Gregorian calendar, a year of 366 days, with a day added to the month of February. Any year whose date is a number exactly divisible by four is a leap year, except years ending in 00, which must be divisible by 400 to be leap years. The extra day is added every 4 years to allow for the difference between a year of 365 days and the actual time it takes the Earth to circle the Sun (approximately 365¼ days). The system was introduced to the Western Julian calendar in its final form in AD 8, and modified by the Gregorian calendar of 1582.

Lear A legendary king of Britain, first recorded in Geoffrey of Monmouth, though his name resembles that of the Celtic god of the sea. The son of Bladud, he reigned for 60 years. In his old age two of his daughters, Goneril and Regan, conspired against him, but the third daughter, Cordelia, saved him and became queen after his death. (The story is changed by Shakespeare, so that she dies before his eyes.) Leicester is named after him.

Lear, Edward (1812–88) Artist and writer, born in London, UK. The youngest of 21 children, he suffered from epilepsy and depression. Employed by the Zoological Society of London and the British Museum as an artist, and later by the 13th Earl of Derby, he travelled widely in Europe, making landscape sketches and oil paintings which he published in several travel books, including *Sketches of Rome* (1842) and *Illustrated Excursions in Italy* (1846). He entertained children with nonsense limericks and verse, illustrated by his own sketches, and published as *A Book of Nonsense* (1846). His other humour includes *Nonsense Songs, Stories, Botany, and Alphabets* (1870), *More Nonsense Rhymes* (1871), and *Laughable Lyrics* (1876). Since his death, his reputation as a landscape artist has risen steadily.

learning The acquisition of knowledge and/or behavioural tendencies as a result of specific experiences in an individual's life. It is distinguished from behavioural changes due to motivation (an individual's varying physiological state, needs, desires) or maturation (the growth and development of body structures and functions, such as the appearance of sexual responsiveness at puberty). Imprinting, habituation, and conditioning are examples of very general widespread types of learning. Psychological **learning theories** aim to discover the general laws and properties of such simple, universal processes. Some cases of learning, however, are thought to involve more unusual special-purpose systems, such as song-learning by many birds, and language acquisition by children.

lease A legal arrangement, also known as a **tenancy**, whereby the **lessor** (or landlord) grants the **lessee** (or tenant) the right to occupy and use land or property for a defined period of time, usually on payment of rent. The period may be fixed (eg 10 years) or periodic (eg weekly). If the lessee or tenant does not have exclusive possession, there may be a *licence*. The term is also used widely in connection with the rental of property other than land.

leaseback An economic operation where a business sells an asset (such as property), the buyer renting (ie leasing) the asset back to the business. The firm continues to have use of the asset, but also has cash from the proceeds of the sale which it can use in other ways.

leasehold *freehold*

least-action principle A fundamental principle in mechanics which states that a mechanical system evolves in such a way that its action is as small as possible. The principle allows the derivation of Euler–Lagrange equations. Fermat's principle is a special case applicable to optics. The Feynman path integral is the quantum analogue.

leather Animal skin rendered durable and resistant to wear and degeneration by tanning. The skin is limed to remove hair, cleaned of flesh, and then soaked in solutions of extracts of bark, galls, or other vegetable products which contain tannins (tannic acids widely distributed in nature) or chrome salts. It is finished mechanically according to use. The properties of leather are due to its fibrous and porous structure, and to its resistance to deterioration on repeated wetting and drying. *Morocco* leather is a goat skin, repeatedly polished. *Chamois* leather was originally from the chamois deer, but most is now from other skins split and tanned for softness. Synthetic materials with a porous structure resembling leather are now made.

leatherback turtle A sea turtle (*Dermochelys coriacea*), worldwide in warm seas; the largest turtle (length, over 1·5 m/5 ft); no shell (adult has only small bony plates embedded in leathery skin); seven ridges along back; long front limbs (over 2·5 m/8 ft tip to tip); no claws; weak jaws; eats jellyfish; also known as **leathery turtle**. (Family: Dermochelyidae.)

leatherhead *friarbird*

leatherjacket *cranefly*

Leavis, F(rank) R(aymond) [leevis] (1895–1978) Literary critic, born in Cambridge, Cambridgeshire, EC England, UK. He studied at Cambridge, returning after service in World War 1 to become a lecturer in English at Emmanuel College (1925), and later a fellow of Downing College (1936–52). He edited the journal *Scrutiny* (1932–53), and wrote several major critical works, notably *New Bearings in English Poetry* (1932), *The Great Tradition* (1948), and *The Common Pursuit* (1952). Throughout his work, much of it shared with his wife **Queenie Dorothy Leavis** (1906–91), he stresses the moral value of literary study, and his re-assessments of such major figures as Joseph Conrad and D H Lawrence were to prove extremely influential.

Leavitt, Henrietta Swan (1868–1921) Astronomer, born in Lancaster, Massachusetts, USA. She studied at Radcliffe College, and became a volunteer research assistant at Harvard College Observatory. By 1902 she was head of the department of photographic photometry, where her major work was the discovery of the period–luminosity relationship of Cepheid variable stars (1912). This work proved invaluable in establishing the distance scale of the universe.

Lebanese Civil War A war sparked by the killing of 27 Palestinians in a bus passing through a Christian neighbourhood in April 1975. Its roots lay in a distribution of government office by sectarian community which many believed gave Christians a disproportionate share of political power. In its first phase alone (1975–6) 30 000 died before an Arab peace-keeping force separated the combatants. The war passed through a number of phases, drawing in most of Lebanon's diverse sectarian communities and its neighbours, notably Syria and Israel. It was marked by the fragmentation of the country and the division of the capital city Beirut into a Christian E and a Muslim W half, over which the central government had no control (particularly after the collapse of the Lebanese army). Notable events of the war include the Israeli invasion and siege of Beirut (1982), the massacre of defenceless Palestinian non-combatants at Sabra and Shatila refugee camps (1982), the suicide bombings which claimed 241 US and 58 French marines (1983), the hijacking of a TWA airliner (1985), and the taking of Western hostages. A framework for reconciliation was agreed in 1989 by Lebanese parliamentarians meeting in the Saudi Arabian city of Taif, which was haltingly put into practice.

Lebanon *p.880*

Lebanon Mountains, Arabic **Jebel Liban** Mountain range in Lebanon; extending c.160 km/100 mi NE–SW parallel to the Mediterranean coast; separated from the Anti-Lebanon range to the E by the fertile Beqaa valley; rises to 3087 m/10 128 ft at Qornet es-Saouda; grapes, olives, apples on lower slopes.

Lebed, Alexander (Ivanovich) [ljebed] (1950–2002) General and politician, born in Novocherkassk, SW Russia. He served in Afghanistan (1981–2) and the Caucasus (1988–90), and became commander of the 14th Army in Moldova in 1992. After retiring from the army in 1995, he entered politics, coming to international attention during the 1996 presidential elections, when he unexpectedly finished third, with 15% of the vote. He then gave his support to Yeltsin, and was appointed National Security Advisor in the new Yeltsin administration. He acted as chief negotiator in the Chechen conflict later in 1996. After what many observers saw as a power struggle within the Kremlin, Yeltsin dismissed him. He then formed the Russian Popular Republican Party, and announced the continuation of his presidential aspirations. In 1998, he was elected Governor of Krasnoyarsk as part of this strategy. He died from injuries sustained in a helicopter crash.

Lebensraum [laybnsrowm] (Ger 'living space') A slogan adopted by German nationalists (especially Nazis) in the 1920s and 1930s to justify the need for German territorial expansion into E Europe. They argued that Germany was overpopulated, and needed more agriculturally productive land to guarantee future food supplies for an expanded German population. The slogan *Drang nach Osten* ('drive towards the East') was used to convey the same message.

LeBlanc, Matt (1967–) Actor, born in Newton, Massachusetts, USA. After leaving school, he took several television commercial parts in New York City, then (1988) trained as an actor. He went to Hollywood, where he played a range of television roles before achieving success as Joey Tribbiani in the acclaimed series *Friends* (1994–2004). His feature films include *Lookin' Italian* (1994), *Lost in Space* (1998), and *Charlie's Angels: Full Throttle* (2003).

Lebowa [leboha] Former national state or non-independent black homeland in N Transvaal province, NE South Africa; situated NE of Pretoria; self-governing status, 1972; incorporated into Northern Province in the South African constitution of 1994.

Le Brun, Charles [luh brõe] (1619–90) Painter and designer, born in Paris, France. He studied in Rome for four years under Poussin and Vouet, and for nearly 40 years (1647–83) exercised a despotic influence over French art and artists. He is usually considered to be the founder of the French school of painting. He helped to found the Academy of Painting and Sculpture in 1648, and was the first director of the Gobelins tapestry works in 1662. From 1668 to 1683 he was employed by Louis XIV in the decoration of Versailles.

Le Carré, John [luh karay], pseudonym of **David John Moore Cornwell** (1931–) Novelist, born in Poole, Dorset, S England, UK. He studied at Bern and Oxford universities, taught French and German for two years at Eton, then went into the British Foreign Service as second secretary in Bonn, and consul in Hamburg. He resigned in 1964 to become a full-time writer. His first published novel, *Call for the Dead* (1961, filmed as *The Deadly Affair*, 1967), introduced his 'anti-hero' George Smiley, who appears in most of his stories. His many popular works include *The Spy Who Came in from the Cold* (1963, Somerset Maugham Award, later filmed), *Tinker, Tailor, Soldier, Spy* (1974, televised 1979), *The Honourable Schoolboy* (1977, James Tait Black), *Smiley's People* (1980, televised 1982), *The Little Drummer Girl* (1983, filmed 1985), *The Russia House* (1989, filmed 1991), *The Tailor of Panama* (1996), and *Absolute Friends* (2003).

Lechtal Alps [lekhtal], Ger **Lechtaler Alpen** Mountain range of the E Alps in Tirol state, W Austria; rises to 3036 m/9960 ft at

Lebanon

Fr **Liban**, official name **Republic of Lebanon**, Arabic **Al-Jumhouriya al-Lubnaniya**

Local names al-Lubnān (Arab), Liban (French)

Timezone GMT +2

Area 10 452 km^2/4034 sq mi

Population total (2002e) 3 678 000

Status Republic

Date of independence 1943

Capital Beirut

Languages Arabic (official), French, English, and Armenian also spoken

Ethnic groups Arab (93%), with several minorities

Religions Muslim (c.75%), Christian (c.25%), also many religious sects including Armenian, Greek, Roman Catholic, Alawite, Druze, and Jewish

Physical features Narrow coastal plain rises gradually E to the lebanon Mts (Jebel Liban) reaching 3087 m/10 128 ft at Qornet es Saouda; arid E slopes fall abruptly to the fertile Beqaa plateau, average elevation 1000 m/3300 ft; Anti-Lebanon range (Jebel esh Sharqi) in the E; R Litani flows S between the two ranges.

Climate Mediterranean climate, varying with altitude; hot, dry summers, warm, moist winters; average annual temperatures 13°C (Jan), 27°C (Jul); average annual rainfall 920 mm/36 in; much drier and cooler in the Bekaa valley.

Currency 1 Lebanese Pound/Livre (LL, £L) = 100 piastres

Economy Commercial and financial centre of the Middle East until the civil war, which severely damaged economic infrastructure and reduced industrial and agricultural production; oil refining, textiles, chemicals, food processing; citrus fruits, apples, grapes, bananas, sugar beet, olives, wheat; tourism has virtually collapsed, but began to revive in the mid-1990s.

GDP (2002e) $17·61 bn, per capita $4800

Human Development Index (2002) 0·755

History Part of the Ottoman Empire from 16th-c; after the massacre of (Catholic) Maronites by (Muslim) Druzes in 1860, Maronite area around Jabal Lubnan granted special autonomous status; Greater Lebanon, based on this area, created in 1920 under French mandate; Muslim coastal regions incorporated, despite great opposition; constitutional republic, 1926; independence, 1943; Palestinian resistance units established in Lebanon by late 1960s despite government opposition, including the Palestine Liberation Organization (PLO); several militia groups developed in the mid-1970s; following terrorist attacks, Israel invaded S Lebanon, 1978 and 1982; heavy Israeli bombardment of Beirut forced the withdrawal of Palestinian forces, 1982; unilateral withdrawal of Israeli and Syrian forces from Lebanon brought clashes between the Druze (backed by Syria) and Christian Lebanese militia; ceasefire announced in late 1982, broken many times; Syrian troops entered Beirut, 1988 in an attempt to restore order; release of Western hostages taken by militant groups began in 1990; timetable for militia disarmament introduced, 1991; Israeli withdrawal from South Lebanon border area, May 2000; constitution provides for a Council of Ministers, a President (a Maronite Christian), Prime Minister (a Sunni Muslim), a Cabinet, and a Parliament, equally divided between Christians and Muslims.

Head of State

1970–6 Suleiman Frenjieh
1976–82 Elias Sarkis
1982 Bachir Gemayel
1982–8 Amin Gemayel
1988–9 *No President*
1989 Rene Muawad
1989–98 Elias Hrawi
1998– Emile Lahoud

Head of Government

1970–3 Saeb Salam
1973 Amin al-Hafez
1973–4 Takieddine Solh
1974–5 Rashid Solh
1975 Noureddin Rifai
1975–6 Rashid Karami
1976–80 Selim al-Hoss
1980 Takieddine Solh
1980–4 Chafiq al-Wazan
1984–8 Rashid Karami
1988–90 Michel Aoun/Selim al-Hoss
1990 Selim al-Hoss
1990–2 Umar Karami
1992 Rashid al-Solh
1992–8 Rafiq al-Hariri
1998–2000 Selim al-Hoss
2000– Rafiq al-Hariri

Parseierspitze; numerous lakes, including the Spullersee; the Arlberg (W) is a major skiing area.

lecithin [lesuhthin] *choline*

Leconte de Lisle, Charles Marie René [luhkõt duh leel] (1818–94) French poet, born in Saint-Paul, La Réunion. After travels in India and the East he settled in Paris. He collaborated on the fouriériste review, *La Democratie pacifique*, from which he distanced himself, disappointed by the failure of the 1848 revolution. He wrote various collections of poetry which he eventually arranged to form *Poèmes antiques* (1852), *Poèmes barbares* (1862–78), *Poèmes tragiques* (1886), and *Derniers poèmes* (published 1895). He was a member of the anti-Romantic school called Parnassians, and succeeded Victor Hugo in the Académie Française in 1886.

Le Corbusier [luh kaw(r)büsyay], pseudonym of **Charles Edouard Jeanneret** (1887–1965) Architect and artist, born in La Chaux-de-Fonds, W Switzerland. He left school at age 13 to learn the trade of engraving watch faces. Encouraged by a local art teacher he taught himself architecture, travelling throughout Europe to observe architectural styles. Settling in Paris in 1917, he met Amédée Ozenfant (1886–1966), who introduced him to Purism, and with whom he collaborated in writing several articles under his pseudonym (the name of a relative on his father's side). He developed a theory of the interrelation between modern machine forms and architectural techniques, and his first building, based on the technique of the *Modulor* (a system using units whose proportions were those of the human figure), was the *Unité d'habitation* ('living unit'), Marseille (1945–50). Some of his buildings are raised on stilts or *piloti*, an innovation he first used in the Swiss Pavilion at the Cité Universitaire at Paris. His main interest was large urban projects and city-planning, and although many of his designs were rejected, they influenced other architects throughout the world. Other examples of his work are Chandigarh, the new capital of the Punjab; the Swiss Dormitory in the Cité Universitaire in Paris; and the Exposition Pavilion in Zürich.

LED *light-emitting diode*

Leda (astronomy) [**lee**da] The 13th natural satellite of Jupiter, discovered in 1974; distance from the planet 11 100 000 km/ 6 900 000 mi; diameter 16 km/10 mi.

Leda (mythology) [**lee**da] In Greek mythology, the wife of Tyndareus, and mother, either by him or Zeus, of Castor and Pollux, Helen, and Clytemnestra. A frequent subject in art is Zeus courting Leda in the form of a swan; Helen was believed to have been hatched from an egg, preserved at Sparta into historic times.

Lederberg, Joshua [**lay**derberg] (1925–) Biologist and geneticist, born in Montclair, New Jersey, USA. He studied biology at Columbia and became professor at Wisconsin (1947–59), Stanford (1959–78), and president of Rockefeller University (1978–90). With Edward Tatum (1909–75) he demonstrated that bacteria can reproduce by a sexual process, thus founding the science of bacterial genetics. He also discovered the process allowing the possibility of genetic engineering. He shared the Nobel Prize for Physiology or Medicine in 1958.

Ledoux, Claude Nicolas [luh**doo**] (1736–1806) Architect, born in Dormans-sur-Marne, NE France. As architect to Louis XVI, his major works include the Château at Louveciennes for Madame du Barry (1771–3), and the Saltworks at Arc-et-Senans (1775–80). In 1785 he was employed by the Fermes-Général to erect 60 tax buildings around Paris, though only a few were built.

LED printer A form of computer printer, similar to a xerographic printer, where the ionization of the drum is carried out using a row of light-emitting diodes (LEDs) rather than a laser beam.

Lee, Ann, known as **Mother Ann** (1736–84) Religious mystic, born in Manchester, Greater Manchester, NW England, UK. In 1758 she joined the 'Shaking Quakers', or 'Shakers', who saw in her the second coming of Christ. Imprisoned in 1770 for street-preaching, she emigrated with her followers to the USA in 1774, and in 1776 founded the parent Shaker settlement.

Lee, Ang (1954–) Film director, producer, and screenwriter, born in Taipei, Taiwan. He attended the National Taiwan College of Arts (1975), then went to the USA, where he studied at the University of Illinois and New York University. He made his directorial debut in 1992 with *Pushing Hands*, and earned Academy Award nominations for his next two films, *The Wedding Banquet* (1993) and *Eat Drink Man Woman* (1994). Later films include *Sense and Sensibility* (1995, Best Picture Oscar nomination), *The Ice Storm* (1997), *Crouching Tiger, Hidden Dragon* (2000, four Oscars, four BAFTA Awards, Best Director Golden Globe), and *Hulk* (2003).

Lee, Christopher (1922–) Film actor, born in London, UK. His gaunt appearance and sinister image led to acclaimed performances in *Dracula* (1958) and its sequels, as well as in a range of other horror movies. Later films include *The Three Musketeers* and its sequel (1973, 1989), *Gremlins 2* (1990), *Funny Man* (1994), *The Stupids* (1996), and he played the role of Saruman the wizard in parts one and two of the *Lord of the Rings* trilogy (2001–2). Recent television work includes *Gormenghast* (2000).

Lee, David M(orris) (1931–) Physicist, born in Rye, New York, USA. He studied at Yale, then worked at Cornell University, where he, along with Robert Richardson and Douglas Osheroff, in 1972 discovered the superfluidity of helium-3. They shared the Nobel Prize for Physics in 1996.

Lee (of Ashridge), Jennie Lee, Baroness (1904–88) British stateswoman, born in Lochgelly, Fife, E Scotland, UK. She studied at Edinburgh University and, as a Labour MP for North Lanark at the age of 24, became the youngest member of the House of Commons. A dedicated Socialist, she married Aneurin Bevan (1934). Appointed Britain's first arts minister in 1964, she doubled government funding for the arts, and was instrumental in setting up the Open University. In 1970 she retired from the House of Commons to be made a life peer. She published two autobiographies, *Tomorrow Is a New Day* (1939) and *My Life with Nye* (1980).

Lee, (Nelle) Harper (1926–) Writer, born in Monroeville, Alabama, USA. She attended Huntington College (1944–5), studied law at the University of Alabama (1945–9), and attended Oxford University for one year. She was an airline reservation clerk in New York City during the 1950s before returning to Monroeville. Her first and only novel, *To Kill a Mockingbird* (1960), received critical acclaim and was made into a highly successful film in 1962.

Lee, Laurie (1914–97) Writer, born in Stroud, Gloucestershire, SWC England, UK. He was educated at the village school at Slad, where the family had moved, and worked as a scriptwriter for documentary films during the 1940s. His poetic works included *The Sun My Monument* (1944) and *My Many-Coated Man* (1955). His books *Cider With Rosie* (1959), *As I Walked Out One Midsummer Morning* (1969), and *I Can't Stay Long* (1975) are widely acclaimed for their evocation of a rural childhood and of life in the many countries he had visited. His last book, *A Moment of War* (1991), recalls his experiences during the Spanish Civil War.

Lee, Robert E(dward) (1807–70) Confederate general, born in Stratford, Virginia, USA. He trained at West Point, and in the Mexican War became chief engineer of the central army in Mexico (1846). He commanded the US Military Academy (1852–5), was a cavalry officer on the Texan border (1855–9), and in 1861 was made commander-in-chief of the Virginia forces. He was in charge of the defences at Richmond, and defeated Federal forces in the Seven Days' Battles (1862). His strategy in opposing General Pope, his invasion of Maryland and Pennsylvania, and other achievements are central to the history of the war. In 1865, he surrendered his army to General Grant at Appomattox Courthouse. After the war, he became President of Washington College at Lexington.

Lee, Spike, popular name of **Shelton Jackson Lee** (1957–) Filmmaker, born in Atlanta, Georgia, USA. At New York University's Institute of Film and Television he gained artistic recognition and a student Oscar for his graduation film, *Joe's Bed-Study Barbershop: We Cut Heads* (1982). *She's Gotta Have It* (1986) established him internationally. Other films, centred around African-American culture, include *Mo' Better Blues* (1990), *Get on the Bus* (1996), *Summer of Sam* (1998), and *25th Hour* (2003). He received a BAFTA special achievement award in 2002.

Lee, Tsung Dao (1926–) Physicist, born in Shanghai, E China. He studied at Zhejiang University, won a scholarship to Chicago University in 1946, became a lecturer at the University of California, and from 1956 was professor at Columbia University, as well as a member of the Institute for Advanced Study (1960–3). With Chen Ning Yang he realized that parity, until then considered a fundamental physical symmetry principle, was violated in weak nuclear interactions. They shared the Nobel Prize for Physics in 1957.

leech A specialized ringed worm related to the earthworms; body highly contractile, usually with a sucker at each end; many are blood-feeders on vertebrate hosts, others are predators of invertebrates; found in aquatic and damp terrestrial habitats. One species was used in early medicine for 'bleeding' patients suffering from various illnesses. (Phylum: Annelida. Subclass: Hirudinea.)

leechee *litchi*

Leeds 53°50N 1°35W, urban area pop (2001e) 715 400. City in West Yorkshire, N England, UK; on the R Aire, 315 km/196 mi NW of London; ford across the R Aire in Roman times; in the 18th-c became an important centre of cloth manufacture; birthplace of Lord Darnley (Temple Newsam); incorporated by Charles I in 1626; canals link to Liverpool, Goole; railway (important early freight and passenger centre); university (1904); Leeds Metropolitan University (1992, formerly Leeds Polytechnic); textiles, clothing, leather, chemicals, furniture, plastics, paper, electrical equipment; Civic Hall (1933), Town Hall (1858), art gallery, Churches of St John (1634) and St Peter (1841), Kirkstall Abbey (1147); Leeds Music Festival (every 3 years, Apr); International Pianoforte Competition (every 3 years, Sep); film festival; football league team, Leeds United (Peacocks).

leek A perennial with strap-shaped, sheathing leaves in two rows, and white flowers sometimes mixed with bulbils. Its origin is unknown, but it is probably derived from the wild leek of Europe (*Allium ampeloprasum*), and is now cultivated as a vegetable (*Allium porrum*). (Family: Liliaceae.)

Leeuwarden [layvah(r)dn], Frisian **Liouwert** 53°12N 5°48E, pop (2000e) 90 000. Capital city of Friesland province, N Netherlands, on the R Ee; railway; canal junction; economic and cultural capital of Friesland; major cattle market; dairy products, flour milling, glass, tourism; former centre for gold and silverware; Grote Kerk (13th–16th-c), Frisian museum.

Leeuwenhoek, Antonie van [layvenhook] (1632–1723) Microscopist, born in Delft, The Netherlands. A clerk in an Amsterdam cloth warehouse until 1650, he returned to Delft, where he made a series of discoveries in relation to the circulation of the blood. He also first detected the fibres of the crystalline lens, the fibrils and striping of muscle, the structure of ivory and hair, the scales of the epidermis, and the distinctive characters of rotifer micro-organisms.

Leeward Islands (Caribbean), Span **Islas de Sotavento** Island group of the Lesser Antilles in the Caribbean Sea, N of the Windward Is; from the Virgin Is (N) to Dominica (S); sheltered from the NE prevailing winds; the name was formerly used by the Spanish to include the Greater Antilles; also formerly the name of a British colony comprising Anguilla, Antigua and Barbuda, British Virgin Is, Montserrat, St Kitts and Nevis.

Leeward Islands (French Polynesia), Fr **Iles sous le Vent** pop (2000e) 29 200; area 507 sq km/196 sq mi. Island group of the Society Is, French Polynesia; comprises the volcanic islands of Huahine, Raiatea, Tahaa, Bora-Bora, and Maupiti, with four small uninhabited atolls; chief town, Uturoa (Raiatea); copra, vanilla, pearls.

Le Fanu, (Joseph) Sheridan [lefuhnyoo] (1814–73) Writer and journalist, born in Dublin, Ireland. He studied at Trinity College, Dublin, and was called to the bar in 1839, but soon abandoned law for journalism. He began writing for the *Dublin University Magazine*, of which he became editor and proprietor (1869), and later bought three Dublin newspapers. Of his 14 novels, the best-known are *The House by the Churchyard* (1863) and *Uncle Silas* (1864). He also wrote short stories, mainly of the supernatural, such as *In a Glass Darkly* (1872).

Lefkosia *Nicosia*

Left Bank The S bank of the R Seine in Paris, an area occupied by numerous educational establishments, including the University of Paris (now scattered across the city) and the Ecole des Beaux-Arts. As a result, it is noted as a haunt of writers and intellectuals.

left wing A place on the political continuum, ranging from left to right, traditionally occupied by those with radical, reforming, and progressive attitudes towards social change and the political order. Its origins lie in the seating of members of the French National Assembly of 1789, when the reactionaries placed themselves on the right, the moderates in the centre, and the democrats and extremists on the left. What counts as 'left' varies with time and place: classical liberal views, for instance, generally count as 'right' in parliamentary democracies, whereas 'left' is seen by communist rulers as any demand for greater direct popular participation in government than is permitted by the party bureaucracy. Trotskyists, Maoists, anarchists, and others were often labelled as 'left' deviants whose aims threatened to bring about a disintegration of 'socialist' society.

leg A term commonly used to refer to the whole of the lower limb, primarily used for support and movement; more precisely, in anatomy, the region between the knee and ankle joints, distinguished from the *thigh* (between the hip and knee joints) and the *foot* (beyond the ankle joint). It articulates with the trunk via the *pelvic girdle* (the hip bones and sacrum). The bones are the *femur* in the thigh, the *tibia* and *fibula* in the leg, and the *tarsals*, *metatarsals*, and *phalanges* in the foot. The muscles on the front of the thigh and leg cause flexion at the hip, and extension at the knee and ankle joints and of the toes; those on the back of the thigh and leg cause opposite movements. The muscles within the foot also move the toes.

legacy *property*

Legacy In Australia, an organization (called at first the Remembrance Club) founded in 1922 by Major-General Sir John Gellibrand. It cares for the families of servicemen who have died as a result of war.

Legal Aid A statutory scheme in the UK which provides for the payment out of public funds of legal costs to those with limited financial means for advice; assistance and mediation in family matters from solicitors and, if necessary, barristers or advocates; and the costs of litigation including appeals, with representation at civil and criminal trials and at certain tribunals. Civil legal aid is administered by the relevant Legal Aid Board; help is means tested, and a contribution may be required depending on the person's disposable income. There must also be a reasonable chance of success. A person seeking criminal legal aid applies to the court, and this may grant such aid if the person's financial circumstances require it and if, in certain cases, it is in the interests of justice to do so by making a **Legal Aid Order**. In serious offences, Legal Aid is granted by the relevant Legal Aid Board. Once criminal legal aid is granted, no contribution from the applicant is required. In the USA, there is a constitutional right in criminal cases to be represented by a lawyer appointed by the court, often called the *public defender*, where someone has insufficient means to pay privately. This right extends to all cases where the possible sentence is a jail term and also to juvenile delinquency proceedings. The Legal Services Corporation provides financial assistance for legal help in non-criminal proceedings for those unable to afford such help. Similar schemes exist in many other countries.

legal tender Forms of money that a creditor is bound to accept in settlement of a debt. Some money, such as coin or small denomination notes, may be legal tender only for amounts up to a limit. Other money, such as large denomination notes, is not legal tender for smaller amounts, as nobody is legally required to give change. The point of having a definition of legal tender is to avoid uncertainty as to when a debtor has offered payment. In the past, under the UK Truck Acts, for the protection of employees it was required that they be paid in legal tender. The vast majority of actual transactions in a modern economy are in fact carried out by the use of cheques, credit or debit cards, or electronic transfer, none of which are legal tender. This, however, is for convenience and at the recipient's discretion; nobody is legally obliged to accept a cheque.

legend A vague term, either referring to stories of ancient heroes, saints, or ordinary men and women which have been handed down by oral or written tradition; or simply to fairy stories. It is usually, but not always, distinguished from *myth*, which deals with gods; and opposed to *history*, which is subject to critical judgment. Nevertheless, because ancient peoples were not given to fiction, in the modern sense of the term, a legend often contains a kernel of truth.

Legendre, Adrien-Marie [luhzhãdr] (1752–1833) Mathematician, born in Paris, France. He studied at the Collège Mazarin, became professor of mathematics at the Ecole Militaire (1775–80), a member of the Académie des Sciences (1783), and professor at the Ecole Normale (1795). He made major contributions to number theory and elliptical functions, but due to the jealousy of his colleague Laplace, he received little recognition or reward for his work.

Léger, Fernand [layzhay] (1881–1955) Painter, born in Argentan, NW France. He studied in Paris, and helped to form the Cubist movement, but later developed his own 'aesthetic of the machine' as seen in 'Contrast of Forms' (1913, Philadelphia). He also designed theatre sets, taught at Yale University, and painted murals for the UN building in New York (1952). He collaborated on the first 'art-film', *Le Ballet mécanique*, in 1923, and there is a museum dedicated to his work at Biot on the Côte d'Azur.

Leggett, Anthony J (1938–) Physicist, born in London, England, UK. He studied at Oxford University (1964), then worked at the University of Illinois as a research associate (1964–5, 1967). In 1983 he returned to Illinois and joined the faculty at Urbana-Champaign. Recognized as a world leader in the theory of low-temperature physics, he shared the 2003 Nobel Prize for Physics for his pioneering work on superfluidity.

Leghorn *Livorno*

leghorn A small breed of domestic fowl; named after Legorno (now Livorno) in Italy.

legion The principal unit of the Roman army. It was made up of 10 cohorts, each one of which was divided into six centuries.

Légion d'Honneur [layzhõ donoe(r)] (Legion of Honour) In France, a reward for civil and military service created by Napoleon I in 1802. The president of the Republic is grand master, and the five grades are grand cross, grand officer, commander, officer, and chevalier. The ribbon is scarlet.

legionella [leejuhnela] A bacterium that occurs naturally in freshwater habitats, living and multiplying inside amoebae. It can become infective to humans and, when inhaled, can cause legionnaire's disease.

legionnaire's disease A serious form of pneumonia caused by *Legionella pneumophilia*. The bacteria live in warm water and are transmitted by water droplets from contaminated shower heads, humidifiers, and particularly from hot-water systems. When the cooling towers of air-conditioning plants are affected, larger numbers of people tend to be involved. The disease is so named because the first outbreak in 1976 affected members of the American Legion in Philadelphia.

Legion of Mary An organization founded in Ireland in 1921 to enable lay members of the Roman Catholic Church to engage in apostolic (missionary and charitable) work within the community. It was inspired by writings devoted to the Virgin Mary by St Louis Marie Grignon de Montfort (1673–1716).

legislature The institution recognized as having the power to pass laws. In the UK the legislature is the Monarch-in-Parliament, comprising the monarch, the House of Lords, and the House of Commons. The role of the monarch in this respect is now purely formal. In the USA, the President has a qualified and limited power of veto over bills from Congress which is comprised of the House of Representatives and the Senate. Additionally, each state has its own legislature for enacting state laws.

legitimacy The legal status of a child at birth. A child is legitimate if born when its parents are validly married to each other, and the child is the biological issue of the couple, though most jurisdictions presume legitimacy where the child is born to a married woman living with her husband who is not impotent. A person born illegitimate may be legitimized by the subsequent marriage of his or her parents. In addition, an adopted child is regarded as the legitimate child of adoptive parents, as is a child born to a wife who has been artificially inseminated, provided that the husband has consented to this procedure. In practice there is now little legal difference between legitimate and illegitimate children.

legitimate theatre / theater Serious drama rather than variety; originally a term for the productions mounted by the patent theatres in London, as opposed to those put on at the 'illegitimate' theatres such as musical comedy, revue, music hall, and opera, where to circumvent legislation plays had to contain music, dance, mime, or some 'non-dramatic' element. It arose in the 18th-c when only two London theatres, Covent Garden and Drury Lane, were licensed to perform plays in the strict sense of the word.

legume A dry, 1–many-seeded fruit of the pea family (*Leguminosae*). When ripe it splits into two valves, each bearing alternate seeds. The splitting may be explosive, or the valves may twist to help scatter the seeds. Many kinds are eaten as vegetables.

Lehár, Franz [luhhah(r)] (1870–1948) Composer, born in Komárom, NW Hungary. He studied at the Prague Conservatory, became a conductor in Vienna and wrote a violin concerto, but is best known for his operettas, including *The Count of Luxembourg* (1909), *The Land of Smiles* (1929), and his internationally acclaimed *The Merry Widow* (1905).

Le Havre [luh hahvr], formerly **Le Havre-de-Grace** 49°30N 0°06E, pop (2000e) 205 000. Commercial seaport in Seine-Maritime department, NW France; on the English Channel, on N side of R Seine estuary, 176 km/109 mi NW of Paris; naval base under Napoleon I; Allied base in World War 1; largely rebuilt since heavy damage in World War 2; chief French port for transatlantic passenger liners; ferry service to UK; machinery, cars; trade in tropical goods, oil (pipeline to Paris); mediaeval town of Harfleur to the E; Church of St Joseph.

Lehmann, Lilli [layman] (1848–1929) Soprano, born in Würzburg, SC Germany. She was taught singing by her mother, and made her debut at Prague in 1865. She sang in Danzig, Lepzig, London, New York City, and elsewhere, and took part in the first performance of Wagner's *Ring* (1876) at Bayreuth.

Lehmann, Lotte [layman] (1888–1976) Soprano, born in Perleberg, NEC Germany (no relation to Lilli Lehmann). She studied in Berlin, made her debut in Hamburg in 1910, and sang at the Vienna Staatsoper (1914–38). She also appeared frequently at Covent Garden and at the New York Metropolitan, and was noted particularly for her performances in operas by Richard Strauss, including two premieres. She took US nationality, and in 1951 retired to Santa Barbara.

Leibniz, Gottfried Wilhelm [liybnits] (1646–1716) Philosopher and mathematician, born in Leipzig, EC Germany. He studied there and at Altdorf, spent time in Paris and London, and in 1676 became librarian to the Duke of Brunswick at Hanover. He also travelled in Austria and Italy, and went in 1700 to persuade Frederick I of Prussia to found the Prussian Academy of Sciences in Berlin, of which he became the first president. A man of remarkable breadth of knowledge, he made original contributions to optics, mechanics, statistics, logic, and probability theory. He conceived the idea of calculating machines, and of a universal language. He wrote on history, law, and political theory, and his philosophy was the foundation of 18th-c Rationalism. He was involved in a controversy with Isaac Newton over whether he or Newton was the inventor of integral and differential calculus; the Royal Society formally declared for Newton in 1711, but the matter was never really resolved. Unpopular with George of Hanover, he was left behind in 1714 when the Elector moved his court to London (as George I). He died in Hanover two years later, without real recognition and with almost all his work unpublished. Probably his greatest influence (eg on Bertrand Russell) was as a mathematician and a pioneer of modern symbolic logic.

Leicester [lester], Lat **Ratae Coritanorum** 52°38N 1°05W, pop (2001e) 279 900. City and county town of Leicestershire, C England, UK; unitary authority from 1997; 160 km/100 mi N of London; an important royal residence in mediaeval times; charter granted by Elizabeth I (1589); university (1957); De Montfort University (1992, formerly Leicester Polytechnic); railway; hosiery, knitwear, footwear, engineering; many Roman remains; 14th-c Cathedral of St Martin, Churches of St Margaret, St Mary de Castro, and St Nicholas; 17th-c Guildhall, Belgrave Hall museum; football league team, Leicester City.

Leicester, Robert Dudley, Earl of [lester], also known as **Baron Denbigh** and **Sir Robert Dudley** (c.1532–88) Nobleman, the favourite and possibly the lover of Elizabeth I. He became Master of the Horse, Knight of the Garter, a privy councillor, baron, and finally Earl of Leicester (1564). In 1550 he married Amye Robsart and was supposed by some to have brought about her murder in 1560. He was high steward of Cambridge University (1562) and chancellor of Oxford University (1564). He continued to receive favour from Elizabeth in spite of his unpopularity at court and a secret marriage in 1573 to the Dowager Lady Sheffield. In 1575 he entertained Elizabeth with masques at Kenilworth Castle, and in 1577 took part in Drake's expedition. In 1578 he bigamously married the widow of Walter, Earl of Essex, yet Elizabeth was only temporarily offended. In 1585 he commanded the expedition to the Low Countries, but was recalled in 1587 for alleged conspiracy with the Prince of Orange. He was nonetheless appointed in 1588 to command the forces against the Spanish Armada but died before he could set sail.

Leicester (of Holkham), Thomas William Coke, Earl of [lester, holkam] (1752–1842) Agriculturist, born in London, UK. He was educated at Eton, and became one of the first agriculturists of England. He improved the Suffolk breed of pigs, bred Southdown sheep and Devon cattle, and first grew wheat (instead of rye) in W Norfolk. People visited his estate from all over the world, and special meetings were held at sheep clipping time – called *Coke's Clippings* – the last of which took place in 1821, lasting three days and attracting 7000 visitors. He became MP for Norfolk at 21, holding the seat for 57 years. A protectionist, he campaigned for independence of the American Colonies.

Leicestershire [lestersheer] pop (2001e) 609 600; area 2553 sq km/986 sq mi. County of C England, UK; Leicester and Rutland new unitary authorities from 1997; drained by the R Soar; administrative centre, Leicester; chief towns include Market Harborough, Loughborough; agriculture, livestock, cheese (Stilton), coal mining, limestone, engineering, hosiery, footwear; Charnwood Forest, Vale of Belvoir.

Leiden *Leyden*

Leif Eriksson [layv erikson] (fl.1000) Icelandic explorer, the son of Erik the Red, the first European to reach America. He introduced Christianity to Greenland, and c.1000 discovered land which he named *Vinland* after the vines he found growing there. It is still uncertain where Vinland actually is and whether he was indeed the first to find it. Two Icelandic sagas, *Eiríks Saga* and *Groenlendinga Saga*, tell the story of the Norse discovery and attempted colonization of North America, 500 years before Christopher Columbus arrived in the area.

Leigh, Mike [lee] (1943–) Playwright and theatre director, born in Salford, Greater Manchester, NW England, UK. He has scripted a distinctive genre based on actors' improvizations around given themes. His most successful work for the theatre has had a second life on film, as in *Bleak Moments* (1970), and on television, as in *Abigail's Party* (1977). Later films include *Life is Sweet* (1990), *Naked* (1993), *Topsy Turvy* (1999), and *All or Nothing* (2002). *Secrets and Lies* (1996) won the 1996 Cannes Palme d'Or and received Oscar nominations for best director and best screenplay.

Leigh, Vivien [lee], originally **Vivian Hartley** (1913–67) Actress, born in Darjeeling, NE India. She had a convent education, then studied at the Royal Academy of Dramatic Art, London. She became an overnight sensation in the comedy *The Mask of Virtue* (1935). She married Laurence Olivier in 1940, and appeared opposite him in numerous classical plays, including *Romeo and Juliet* and *Antony and Cleopatra*. She is best remembered for her Oscar-winning performance as Scarlett O'Hara in the film *Gone With the Wind* (1939). Other major starring roles followed, notably in *Lady Hamilton* (1941), *Anna Karenina* (1948), and *A Streetcar Named Desire* (1951, Oscar). Manic depression and ill health marred her career and her marriage, and she was divorced from Olivier in 1961.

Leinster [lenster] pop (2000e) 1 884 000; area 19 633 sq km/7578 sq mi. Province in E Ireland; comprises the counties of Louth, Meath, Westmeath, Longford, Offaly, Kildare, Dublin, Laoighis, Wicklow, Carlow, Kilkenny, and Wexford; capital, Dublin.

leiomyoma *fibroid*

Leipzig [liypzig], ancient **Lipsia** 51°20N 12°23E, pop (2000e) 528 000. Capital of Leipzig county, E Germany; second largest city of former East Germany; airport; railway; Karl Marx University (1409); college of technology; commercial centre, mechanical engineering, machine tools, furs, printing and publishing; St Thomas's Church, museum of fine art, Battle of the Nations monument, Renaissance town hall, Lenin Memorial, Dimitrov museum; Documentary and Short Film Week; centre for education and music (associations with Bach and Mendelssohn); annual trade fairs.

Leipzig, Battle of [liypzig] (1813) The overwhelming defeat of Napoleon's forces by the armies of the Fourth Coalition, also called the **Battle of the Nations**. Heavily outnumbered by the Allied force of Austrians, Prussians, Russians, and Swedes, Napoleon tried to withdraw, but his troops were badly mauled; he effectively surrendered French control E of the Rhine.

leishmaniasis [leeshmaniyasis] A group of conditions caused by the protozoan *Leishmania*, conveyed by sandflies, occurring on the Mediterranean shores, Africa, and S Asia; also known as **kala-azar**. The *skin form* of the disease occurs as pimples (*papules*) at the site of the bite, which enlarge and ulcerate. The *visceral form* is a generalized febrile disease affecting the liver, spleen, and lymph nodes.

leitmotif [liytmohteef] A short musical motif associated with a character, object, or attribute, which returns at appropriate places in an opera or oratorio. The use of the device is particularly associated with Wagner.

Leitrim [leetrim], Ir **Liathdroma** pop (2000e) 24 000; area 1526 sq km/589 sq mi. County in Connacht province, Ireland, stretching SE from Donegal Bay; bounded NE by N Ireland; capital, Carrick-on-Shannon; coarse angling on R Shannon and L Allen; cattle, sheep, potatoes, oats; considerable land drainage in recent times.

Lely, Sir Peter [leelee], originally **Pieter van der Faes** (1618–80) Painter, born in Soest, The Netherlands. He studied in Haarlem before settling in London in 1641 as a portrait painter. He was patronized by Charles I and Cromwell, and in 1661 was appointed court painter to Charles II, for whom he changed his style of painting. His 'Windsor Beauties' series is collected at Hampton Court, and the 13 Greenwich portraits, 'Admirals' are among his best works. He was knighted in 1679.

Lemaître, Georges (Edouard) [luhmaytruh] (1894–1966) Astrophysicist, born in Charleroi, S Belgium. A civil engineer, army officer, and ordained priest, he studied physics at Cambridge and the Massachusetts Institute of Technology. He became professor of the theory of relativity at Louvain (1927), where he did research on cosmic rays and the three-body problem, and proposed (1927) the 'big bang' theory of the origin of the universe, later developed by Gamow and others.

Léman, Lac *Geneva, Lake*

Le Mans [luh mã], ancient **Oppidum Suindinum** 48°00N 0°10E, pop (2000e) 152 000. Commercial city and capital of Sarthe department, NW France; on R Sarthe, 187 km/116 mi SW of Paris; ancient capital of Maine; fortified by the Romans, 3rd–4th-c; railway junction; centre of commerce and agricultural trade; motor vehicles; cathedral (11th–15th-c), Notre-Dame-de-la-Coutore (11th-c); annual 24-hour motor race (Jun).

Lemieux, Mario [luhmyoe] (1965–) Ice hockey player, born in Montreal, Quebec, SE Canada. A member of the Pittsburgh Penguins from 1984, in 834 National Hockey League matches he scored 683 goals and 966 assists. He was All-Star MVP in 1985, 1988, and 1990, and Hart MVP in 1988, 1993, and 1996. He retired in 1997, but returned in 1999 after buying the Pittsburgh team.

lemma *theorem*

lemming A mouse-like rodent of the tribe: Lemmini (9 species); large powerful head, long fur, short tail; prone to large fluctuations in numbers. The **Norway lemming** (*Lemmus lemmus*) undergoes a population 'explosion' every 3–4 years. When this happens there is a mass migration, thought to be a response to overcrowding (not food shortage). The direction of migration appears random, and sometimes groups reaching large bodies of water, including the sea, will swim offshore and drown in large numbers. There is no basis for the popular belief that lemmings march suicidally into the sea.

Lemnos [leemnos], Gr **Límnos** pop (2000e) 17 000; area 476 sq km/184 sq mi. Greek island in the N Aegean Sea, off the NW coast of Turkey; length 40 km/25 mi; rises to 430 m/1411 ft; airfield; capital, Kastron; several Neolithic remains.

lemon A citrus fruit (*Citrus limoni*) 6–12·5 cm/2$\frac{1}{2}$–4$\frac{3}{4}$ in diameter; ovoid, with thick, bright yellow rind and sour pulp. (Family: Rutaceae.)

lemon sole Common European flatfish (*Microstomus kitt*) found in shelf waters from N Norway to the Bay of Biscay; body oval, length up to 65 cm/26 in; mouth small; brown with a mosaic of yellow and green patches; feeds mainly on polychaetes; valuable food fish taken by trawl and nets (seines). (Family: Pleuronectidae.)

lemon thyme *thyme*

lemon verbena [verbeena] A deciduous shrub native to Chile (*Lippia citriodora*); lemon-scented foliage; heads of small, 2-lipped, purplish flowers. (Family: Verbenaceae.)

lemur [leemer] A primitive primate from Madagascar; large eyes and pointed snout; most species with long tail; 27 species in three families: **lemur** (*Lemuridae*), **mouse** (or **dwarf**) **lemur** (*Cheirogaleidae*), and **leaping lemur** (*Indriidae*).

Le Nain [nã] A family of French painters: three brothers, **Antoine** (c.1588–1648), **Louis** (c.1593–1648), and **Mathieu** (c.1607–77). All were born in Laon, but worked in Paris from c.1630, and all were foundation members of the Académie in 1648. Louis is considered the best, with his large genre-scenes and groups of peasants painted in beautiful greyish greens and browns. 'The Forge' (Louvre) may have been painted by Louis and Mathieu together, for the brothers seem occasionally to have collaborated.

Lena, River [lyena] River in Siberian Russia; rises in the Baykalskiy Khrebet, and flows generally NE and N to enter the Laptev Sea in a wide swampy delta, NW of Tiksi; length, 4400 km/2700 mi; coal, oil, gold nearby.

Lenclos, Ninon de [lãkloh], popular name of **Anne de Lenclos** (1620–1705) Courtesan, born in Paris, France. Her salon attracted the aristocracy as well as leading literary and political figures, and the most respectable women sent their children to her to acquire taste, style, and manners. Her lovers included the great Condé, and the Duc de La Rochefoucauld. She bore two sons, one of whom, brought up in ignorance of his mother, conceived a passion for her; when informed of their relationship, he committed suicide.

lender of last resort An institution, usually a central bank, willing and able to lend to banks unable to borrow money elsewhere to meet their liabilities. The point of having a lender of last resort is to avoid financial collapse during a general financial panic, in which everybody tries to hold cash and refuses to lend. If any bank is in financial trouble, the lender of last resort has to decide whether or not to rescue it. The benefit of assisting any one bank in difficulties is that one default is liable to provoke a general panic. The disadvantage is that if the troubled bank's problems arise through irresponsible lending to risky firms, bailing it out will encourage similar conduct by it and others in the future. This policy dilemma is particularly acute when the problem bank is too large to fail.

Lendl, Ivan [lendl] (1960–) Tennis player, born in Ostrava, NE Czech Republic. He became a US citizen in 1992. He dominated male tennis in the 1980s, winning the singles title at the US Open (1985–7), French Open (1984, 1986–7), and Australian Open (1989, 1990), and becoming the Masters champion (1986–7) and the World Championship Tennis champion (1982, 1985). He won 94 singles titles, but failed to win at Wimbledon. He was forced to retire in December 1994 because of a spinal condition.

Lend-Lease Agreement The means by which the USA lent or leased war supplies and arms to Britain and other countries during World War 2. The Act was passed by Congress in March 1941, when British reserves were almost exhausted. Up to the end of August 1945, the UK received about £5000 million worth of materials.

L'Enfant, Pierre Charles [lãfã] (1754–1825) Architect and city planner, born in Paris, France. He trained as an artist at the Royal Academy of Painting and Sculpture, Paris, moving to America in 1777 to fight the British in the Revolutionary War. In New York City after 1786, he designed ceremonial and monumental works introducing symbolic and allegorical European decorative motifs to America. At Washington's invitation, in 1791 he submitted a plan for the new federal capital in the District of Columbia, which became an influential model of urban planning.

Leng, Virginia (Helen Antoinette), *née* **Holgate** (1955–) Equestrian rider, born in Malta. The European junior champion in 1973, she won the team gold at the senior championship in 1981, 1985, and 1987, and individual titles in 1985 (on *Priceless*), 1987 (on *Night Cap*), and 1989 (on *Master Craftsman*). She won the World Championship team gold in 1982 and 1986, and the individual title in 1986 on *Priceless*. She also won at Badminton (1985, 1989, 1993) and at Burghley (1983–86, 1989).

Lenglen, Suzanne [lãlã] (1899–1938) Tennis player, born in Compiègne, N France. She was the woman champion of France (1920–3, 1925–6), and her Wimbledon championships were the women's singles and doubles (1919–23, 1925), and the mixed doubles (1920, 1922, 1925). In 1920 she was Olympic champion. She became a professional in 1926, toured the USA, and retired in 1927 to found the Lenglen School of Tennis in Paris.

length contraction *Lorentz contraction*

Lenin, Peak, Russ **Lenina, Pik**, formerly **Mt Kaufmann** 39°21N 73°01E. Highest peak in the Alayskiy Khrebet, and second highest in Russia; height, 7134 m/23 405 ft; first climbed in 1928.

Lenin, Vladimir Ilyich, originally **Vladimir Ilyich Ulyanov** (1870–1924) Marxist revolutionary, born in Simbirsk, W Russia. He studied at Kazan and St Petersburg, where he graduated in law. From 1897 to 1900 he was exiled to Siberia for participating in underground revolutionary activities. At the Second Congress of the Russian Social Democratic Labour Party (1903), he caused the split between the Bolshevik and Menshevik factions. Following the February 1917 revolution, he returned to Petrograd (St Petersburg) from Zürich, and urged the seizure of political power by the proletariat under the slogan 'All Power to the Soviets'. In October 1917 he led the Bolshevik revolution and became head of the first Soviet government. He aimed, above all, to maintain the Revolution and to pit the power of the new Soviet regime against domestic and foreign enemies. With Trotsky, he brought it successfully through the ensuing Civil War (1918–21), after which he introduced the New Economic Policy, restoring a market economy and some of the pluralism that characterized the early years of the Soviet government. His critics in the Party saw it as a 'compromise with capitalism' and a retreat from strictly Socialist planning. On his death, his body was embalmed and placed in a mausoleum near the Moscow Kremlin. In 1924 Petrograd was renamed Leningrad in his honour, but since the collapse of Communism the city is once more St Petersburg; similarly, Simbirsk was renamed Ulyanovsk during that period. Some historians regard Lenin's early ideas as similar to those of Stalin. However, he is still regarded by many as one of history's greatest revolutionaries, whose practical strategies achieved the revolutionary's main goals – the seizure and maintenance of power.

Leningrad *St Petersburg*

Leninism *Marxism-Leninism*

Lenin Library *Russian State Library*

Lenin Mausoleum The tomb of Lenin, designed by Aleksey V Shchusev and built in 1930 in Red Square, Moscow. The granite building contains the Soviet leader's burial vault, where his embalmed body may be viewed by the public.

Lennon, John (Winston) (1940–80) Pop star, composer, songwriter, and recording artist, born in Liverpool, Merseyside, NW England, UK. He was the Beatles rhythm guitarist, keyboard player, and vocalist, and a partner in the Lennon–McCartney song-writing team. He married Japanese artist **Yoko Ono** (1933–) – his second marriage – in 1969. Together they invented a form of peace protest by staying in bed while being filmed and interviewed, and the single recorded under the name of The Plastic Ono Band, 'Give Peace a Chance' (1969), became the 'national anthem' for pacifists. He had five more chart singles between 1971–4, but only 'Imagine' (1971) had any immediate impact. On the birth of his son, **Sean** (1975–), he retired from music to become a house-husband. Five years later he recorded '(Just Like) Starting Over', but he was shot and killed by a deranged fan just before its release. His death affected millions of people, record sales soared, and he continues to be admired by new generations of fans.

Leno, Dan [leenoh], originally **George Galvin** (1860–1904) Comedian and music-hall star, born in London, UK. He began his career as an entertainer at the age of four, and by 18 had become a champion clog-dancer. Ten years later he joined the Augustus Harris management at Drury Lane, where he starred for many years in the annual pantomime, particularly successful in comic women's roles, such as Widow Twankey and Cinderella's stepmother. A thin, small man, his foil was the huge, bulky Herbert Campbell. Leno was the first music hall performer to give a command performance (for Edward VII), in 1901.

Le Nôtre, André [luh nohtr] (1613–1700) Landscape architect, born in Paris, France. The creator of French landscape-gardening, he designed many celebrated European gardens, including those at Versailles and Fontainebleau, and St James's Park and Kensington Gardens in London.

lens A transparent optical element comprising two refracting surfaces, at least one of which is curved; parallel light rays passing through the lens may converge (and focus at a point) or diverge, depending on the lens shape. Lenses are characterized by their *focal length* (the distance at which the image of a distant object is most sharply defined) and their *aperture* or *f-number* (the light transmission). They are widely used in optical instruments, binoculars, projectors, and cameras, and are usually made of glass, sometimes of plastic.

Lent In the Christian Church, the weeks before Easter, observed as a period of prayer, penance, and abstinence in commemoration of Christ's 40-day fast in the wilderness (*Matt* 4.2); in the Western Churches, Lent begins on Ash Wednesday, 40 days before Easter; in the Eastern Churches, it begins eight weeks before Easter, but excludes Saturdays and Sundays.

lenticel A small pore in a stem or root, with a similar role to that of stomata in leaves, allowing the passage of gases to and from tissues.

lentil An annual growing to c.40 cm/15 in (*Lens culinaris*); leaves pinnate with 3–8 pairs of oblong leaflets, and terminating in a tendril; pea-flowers white, veined with lilac, borne 1–3 on a long stalk; pods rectangular with 1–2 disc-shaped seeds. It is of unknown origin, but has been cultivated since ancient times as a food plant. Its seeds (lentils) are rich in protein. (Family: Leguminosae.)

lentivirus [lentiviyruhs] A virus which resembles other members of the retrovirus family, Retroviridae, both chemically and morphologically, but does not induce tumour formation. Many lentiviruses have been linked to the causation of chronic diseases, such as arthritis, progressive pneumonia, and slow neurological diseases.

Lenya, Lotte [laynya], originally **Karoline Wilhelmine Blamauer** (1900–81) Actress and cabaret singer, born in Vienna, Austria. She studied drama and ballet at Zürich, lived in Berlin from 1920, and came to represent the spirit of that decadent era. In 1926 she married Kurt Weill, starring in many of his works, including *The Little Mahagonny* (1927) and *The Threepenny Opera* (1928, filmed 1931). They fled to Paris in 1933, then to New York City, where she made many stage appearances, and after Weill's death she became the public custodian of his legacy. Later stage appearances included *Brecht on Brecht* (1962) and *Mother Courage* (1972), and her rare film roles included *From Russia with Love* (1963) and *Semi-Tough* (1977).

Lenz's law [lentz] A law in physics: in electromagnetic induction, any induced current always flows in a direction so as to oppose its source; formulated in 1833 by German physicist Heinrich Lenz (1804–65). Were this not so, perpetual motion machines could be built. The law is responsible for speed self-regulation in electric motors.

Leo III, known as **Leo the Isaurian** (c.680–741) Byzantine emperor from 717, born in Syria, his byname coming from the region of his birth. He reorganized the army and financial system, and in 718 repelled a formidable attack by the Saracens. In 726 he issued an edict prohibiting the use of images in public worship. In Italy the controversy raised by the edict rent the empire for over a century. In 728 the exarchate of Ravenna was lost, and the E provinces became the prey of the Saracens, over whom he won a great victory in Phrygia.

Leo I, St, known as **the Great** (c.390–461) Pope (440–61), probably born in Tuscany. One of the most eminent of the Latin Fathers, he summoned the Council of Chalcedon (451), where the intention of his 'Dogmatical Letter', defining the doctrine of the Incarnation, was accepted. He also made treaties with the Huns and Vandals in defence of Rome, and consolidated the primacy of the Roman see. Feast day 10 November (W), 18 February (E).

Leo III, St (c.750–816) Pope (795–816), born in Rome, Italy. In 799, opposition to his election forced him to flee from Rome to the protection of Charlemagne. After returning safely, he crowned Charlemagne Emperor of the West (800), thus initiating the Holy Roman Empire. He was canonized in 1673. Feast day 12 June.

Leo X, originally **Giovanni de' Medici** (1475–1521) Pope (1513–21), born in Florence, NC Italy. It is as a patron of learning and art that he is best remembered. He founded a Greek college in Rome and established a Greek press. His vast project for the rebuilding of St Peter's, and his permitting the preaching of an indulgence in order to raise funds, provoked Luther's Reformation.

Leo (Lat 'lion') A N constellation of the zodiac, lying between Cancer and Virgo. Easy to recognize (the lion's head looks like a sickle), its brightest star is Regulus, 23·6 parsec distance. **Leo Minor** ('little lion') is a hard-to-see constellation N of Leo.

León (Mexico) [layon] 21°06N 101°41W, pop (2000e) 1 050 000. City in Guanajuato state, SC Mexico; 200 km/124 mi N of Morelia; altitude, 1804 m/5919 ft; railway; commercial centre, shoes, leather work, including decorated saddles.

León (Spain) [layon] 42°38N 5°34W, pop (2000e) 146 000. Capital of León province, Castilla-León, NW Spain; at the junction of the Torio and Bernesga Rivers, 333 km/207 mi NW of Madrid; bishopric; capital of a mediaeval kingdom; railway; anthracite, glass, leather, iron, timber; cathedral (13th–14th-c), town walls, San Isidore, Monastery of St Mark; Fiestas of St John and St Peter (Jun), Foro and Oferta pageant in the cathedral (Aug).

Leonard, 'Sugar' Ray (1956–) US boxer, born in Wilmington, Delaware, USA. He won the 1976 Olympic welterweight gold and became WBC world welterweight champion in 1979, adding the WBA light middleweight crown in 1981. He is one of only two boxers to have been world champion at five weights. His bouts with Roberto Duran rank among the most memorable in ring history.

Leonardo da Vinci [leeonah(r)doh da veenchee] (1452–1519) Painter, sculptor, architect, and engineer, born in Vinci, NC Italy. About 1470 he entered the studio of Andrea del Verrocchio, and in 1482 settled in Milan, where he painted his 'Last Supper' (1498) on the refectory wall of Santa Maria delle Grazie. In 1500 he entered the service of Cesare Borgia in Florence as architect and engineer, and with Michelangelo decorated the Sala del Consiglio in the Palazzo della Signoria with historical compositions. About 1504 he completed his most celebrated easel picture, 'Mona Lisa' (Louvre). In 1506 he was employed by Louis XII of France, and in 1516 was given a pension by Francis I. Very few of his paintings have survived. His notebooks contain original remarks on most of the sciences, including biology, physiology, hydrodynamics, and aeronautics.

Leoncavallo, Ruggero [leeonkavaloh] (1857–1919) Composer, born in Naples, SW Italy. He studied at Naples Conservatory, and earned his living as a pianist and giving singing lessons. His only major success was the opera *I Pagliacci* (1892). His *La Bohème* suffered by comparison with Puccini's on the same theme.

Leonidas [leeonidas] (?–480 BC) King of Sparta (c.491–480 BC), and Greek hero. In 480 BC his small command resisted the vast army of Xerxes, King of Persia, at Thermopylae. After two days he dismissed his troops, and with only his 300-strong Spartan royal guard, fought to the last man. The legend that Spartans never surrender emanated from his heroism.

Leonids [leeuhnidz] A meteor shower due around 17 November each year that is spectacular at 33-year intervals, when thousands can be seen per hour. Particularly spectacular sightings occurred in 1966 and 2001.

Leontief, Wassily [layontyef, vasilee] (1906–99) Economist, born in St Petersburg, NW Russia. He studied at Leningrad (St Petersburg) and Berlin universities, taught at Harvard (1931–75), and became director of the Institute of Economic Analysis at New York University (1975–84). He was awarded the 1973 Nobel Prize for Economics for developing the input–output method of economic analysis, used in more than 50 industrialized countries for planning and forecasting.

leopard A member of the cat family (*Panthera pardus*), found from Siberia to Africa; solitary; inhabits diverse habitats; reddish- or yellowish-brown with small empty rings of dark blotches; black individuals (**black panthers**) sometimes found in dense forests; eats mainly small grazing mammals and monkeys; stores carcasses in trees.

leopard cat A member of the cat family (*Felis bengalensis*), native to E Asia and offshore islands (the most common wild cat in SE Asia); pale with dark bars and spots; inhabits woodland; eats small mammals, birds, reptiles, fish; swims well.

Leopardi, Giacomo, conte (Count) [layohpah(r)dee] (1798–1837) Poet and scholar, born in Recanati, EC Italy. He was a gifted, congenitally handicapped (hunch-backed) child who by the age of 16 had read all the Latin and Greek classics, and outstripped any tutor found for him. Most of his afflicted life was lived in hopeless despondency and unrequited love, and this became the basis of his superb lyric poetry and prose. Among his most noted works are those collected under the title *I canti* (1831).

leopard seal An Antarctic true seal (*Hydrurga leptonyx*); slim with pointed head; dark grey above, pale beneath with dark spots; lives along edge of pack ice; eats mainly penguins (may shake them, literally, out of their skins); also eats other seals, fish, and carrion; only seal in which female is larger than male; also known as **sea leopard**.

Leopold I (Emperor) (1640–1705) Holy Roman Emperor (1658–1705), born in Vienna, Austria, the second son of Ferdinand III and the Infanta Maria Anna. He was elected to the crowns of Hungary (1655) and Bohemia (1656), and succeeded to the imperial title in 1658. In 1666 he married his niece, **Margaret Theresa**, the second daughter of Philip IV of Spain, and after her death (1673) he took a second Habsburg bride, **Claudia Felicitas**, before his third marriage (1676) to **Eleonore of Palatinate-Neuberg**, by whom he had two sons, the future emperors Joseph I and Charles VI. Committed to the defence of the power and unity of the House of Habsburg, he faced constant threats from the Ottoman Turks and the King of France, as well as the hostility of the Hungarian nobility. Treaties of neutrality (1667, 1671) between Leopold and Louis XIV of France gave way to military conflict over the Rhine frontier (1674–9, 1686–97), and to substantiate the rights of his son, Charles, against the French claimant, he took the empire into the Grand Alliance (1701). He died during the War of the Spanish Succession (1701–13) and the Hungarian revolt of Rákóczi (1703–11).

Leopold I (of Belgium) (1790–1865) First king of Belgium (1831–65), born in Coburg, EC Germany, the son of Francis, Duke of Saxe-Coburg, and uncle of Queen Victoria. In 1816 he married **Charlotte**, daughter of the future George IV of England, and lived in England after her death in 1817. He declined the crown of Greece (1830), but in 1831 he was elected King of the Belgians. His second marriage, to **Marie Louise of Orléans**, daughter of Louis-Philippe, ensured French support for his new kingdom against the Dutch, and he was an influential force in European diplomacy and in domestic reform.

Leopold II (of Belgium) (1835–1909) King of Belgium (1865–1909), born in Brussels, Belgium, the eldest son of Leopold I. He married **Maria Henrietta**, daughter of the Austrian Archduke Joseph in 1853. In 1885 he became king of the newly-independent Congo Free State, which became a Belgian colony in 1908. He proceeded to amass great personal wealth from its rubber and ivory trade at enormous cost of Congolese lives. His mistreatment of the Congo native population became an international scandal (1904), and he was forced (1908) to hand over the territory to his parliament. He strengthened his country by military reforms, and under him Belgium developed commercially and industrially.

Leopold III (1901–83) King of Belgium (1934–51), born in Brussels, Belgium. He was the son of Albert I, and he married **Princess Astrid of Sweden** in 1926. He is especially known for his brave decision in 1940 to prolong the resistance of the Belgian army to the German invasion for a further two days, thus enabling the British evacuation at Dunkirk to succeed. (At the time, his action was vilified as treachery by French prime minister Reynaud, a misinterpretation which remained publicly uncorrected by Churchill, with the result that criticism of Leopold's action continued to be made for several decades.) He remained a prisoner in his own palace at Laeken until 1944, and afterwards in Austria. On returning to Belgium in 1950, he was finally forced to abdicate in favour of his son, Baudouin.

Léopoldville *Kinshasa*

Lepanto, Battle of [lepantoh] (1571) The defeat of the Turkish navy in the Gulf of Corinth, ending the Turks' long-standing domination of the E Mediterranean. It was inflicted by the Christian forces of Spain and the Italian states in coalition, following the fall of Cyprus to the Turks in 1569.

Le Pen, Jean-Marie [luh pen] (1928–) French politician, born in La Trinité-sur-Mer, Brittany, NW France. He graduated in law at Paris before serving in the 1950s as a paratrooper in Indochina and Algeria, where he lost an eye in a street battle. In 1956 he won a National Assembly seat as a right-wing Poujadist. He was connected with the extremist Organisation de l'Armée Sécrète before forming the National Front in 1972. This party, with its extreme right-wing policies, emerged as a new 'fifth force' in French politics in the 1986 Assembly elections, winning 10% of the national vote. A controversial figure and noted demagogue, he unsuccessfully contested the presidency in 1988 and 1995 (gaining 15% of the vote). Within the party, factions developed regarding tactics, with newer members rejecting Le Pen's direct-action approach. His decision to promote his wife to the top of the candidate's list for the 1999 parliamentary elections led to a split in the party and the establishment of a rival party, the National Front–National Movement. His success in the first round of the 2002 presidential election (gaining 16·86% of the vote), knocked Lionel Jospin of the Socialist Party out of the race and caused widespread demonstrations across France.

Lepenski Vir [lepenskee veer] A small prehistoric settlement of hunter-fisher-gatherers on the banks of the R Danube in the Iron Gates Gorge, Yugoslavia. Seven phases of occupation with 136 buildings of c.6500–5500 BC have been identified since excavations began in 1965. Of outstanding importance are its 53 abstract and representational sandstone sculptures of humans and animals, the earliest monumental sculpture in Europe.

Lepidodendron [lepidodendron] A fossil clubmoss which was widely distributed during the late Palaeozoic era; tall, up to 30 m/100 ft, and dichotomously branched; plants bearing diamond-shaped leaf scars and large cones.

Lepidoptera [lepidoptera] A large order of insects comprising the 165 000 species of butterflies and moths; adults have two pairs of membranous wings covered with scales; forewings and hindwings coupled together; mouthparts typically modified as a slender sucking proboscis; caterpillar larvae usually plant feeders with chewing mouthparts.

Lepidus, Marcus Aemilius [lepidus] (?–13 /12 BC) Roman statesman. He declared for Julius Caesar against Pompey (49 BC), and Caesar made him dictator of Rome and his colleague in the consulate (46 BC). He supported Marcus Antonius, and became one of the triumvirate with Octavian Augustus and Antonius, with Africa for his province (40–39 BC). He thought he could raise Sicily against Octavian, but his soldiers deserted his cause, and he retired from public life.

leprechaun [leprekawn] A fairy of Irish folklore, traditionally a tiny old man in green occupying himself with cobbling, and the possessor of a crock of gold whose whereabouts he could be persuaded to reveal by threats of violence.

leprosy *Hansen's disease*

Leptis Magna or **Lepcis Magna** 32°59N 14°15E. An ancient seaport of N Libya, the site of spectacular Roman remains; now a world heritage site. Founded by the Phoenicians as a trading post perhaps as early as the 7th-c BC, the city's greatest days came in the 3rd-c AD, after one of its citizens, Septimius Severus, became Roman emperor.

lepton In particle physics, a collective term for all those particles of half integer spin (ie fermions) not affected by strong interactions. The leptons are electrons, muons, and taus, and their respective neutrinos.

Lepus [leepus] (Lat 'hare') A constellation in the S sky, easy to see S of Orion.

Lermontov, Mikhail Yuryevich [lermontof] (1814–41) Poet and writer, born in Moscow, Russia. He attended Moscow University and the military cavalry school of St Petersburg. A poem he wrote in 1837 on the death of Pushkin caused his exile to the Caucasus. Reinstated, he was again banished following a duel with the son of the French ambassador. The scenery of the Caucasus inspired his best poetry, such as 'The Novice' and 'The Demon', and his novel, *A Hero of our Time* (1840), is a masterpiece of prose writing. He was killed in another duel at the age of 27, and much of his fame as the leading Romantic poet was posthumous.

Leroux, Gaston (Louis Alfred) [leroo] (1868–1927) Writer, born in Paris, France. He was raised in Normandy, and began to write while studying law in Paris. He qualified for the bar, then became a journalist, while writing short stories, poetry, and eventually novels and plays. His first novel, *The Seeking of the Morning Treasures* (trans, 1903) was followed by a series of detective stories. He moved to Nice in 1908, where he wrote his best-known work, *The Phantom of the Opera*, in 1911. Although it attracted little attention in its early days, it became a hit following a Lon Chaney film in 1924. A prolific author, publishing at least a book a year, Leroux would signal the completion of a manuscript by firing a loaded revolver from his balcony.

Lerwick [lerwik] 60°09N 1°09W, pop (2000e) 8100. Capital of Shetland, N Scotland, UK; on E Mainland, by Bressay Sound; airfield; ferry terminus from Scottish mainland; fishing, oil supply services, woollens; museum; Fort Charlotte (1665), Clickhimin Broch (Iron Age); Up-Helly-Aa festival (Jan).

Lesage, Alain René [luhsahzh], also spelled **Le Sage** (1668–1747) Novelist and playwright, born in Sarzeau, NW France. A poor but well-educated orphan, he studied law in Paris briefly, but married early and sought his fortune in literature. The Abbé de Lionne allowed him a pension and access to a good Spanish library. He became a prolific playwright, sometimes accused of borrowing stories from others. He is best known for the novel *Histoire de Gil Blas de Santillane* (12 vols, 1715–35, The Adventures of Gil Blas of Santillane). As a playwright, his leading work is *Turcaret* (1708).

Le Saux, Graeme [luh soh] (1968–) Footballer, born in Jersey, Channel Is. A left back defender, he played in Jersey, then joined Chelsea, later moving to Blackburn Rovers, and returning to Chelsea in 1997. He joined England in 1995, and though hampered by injuries, he won 36 international caps. He transferred to Southampton for the start of the 2003–4 season.

lesbianism A sexual attraction and expression between women, which may or may not involve the complete exclusion of men as potential sexual partners. As with male homosexuality, lesbianism became increasingly politicized in the latter part of the 20th-c, often linked, though not invariably, with feminism.

Lesbos, Gr **Lesvos** or **Mitilini** pop (2000e) 108 000; area 1630 sq km/629 sq mi. Greek island in the E Aegean Sea, off NW coast of Turkey; third largest island of Greece; length 61 km/38 mi; hilly, rising to 969 m/3179 ft; in classical times, a centre of Greek lyric poetry; chief town, Mitilini; cereals, grapes, olives, fishing, tourism.

Lescot, Pierre [leskoh] (c.1515–78) Architect, born in Paris, France. He studied architecture, mathematics, and painting. One of the greatest classical architects of his time, among his works are the screen of St Germain l'Auxerrois, the Fontaine des Innocents, and the Hôtel de Ligneris. His masterwork was the rebuilding of the Louvre.

Leskovac or **Leskovats** [leskovats] 43°00N 21°57E, pop (2000e) 167 000. Town in SE Serbia, 37 km/23 mi S of Niš; railway; wine trade, soap, furniture, textiles; nearby 6th-c Byzantine ruins of Caračin Grad; international textile fair (Jul).

Lesotho *889*

less developed countries (LDCs) The majority of the world's countries, typically characterized by poverty, low levels of nutrition, health, and literacy, poorly developed industry, transport, and communications, and the export of agricultural products and minerals. The average, however, includes a very wide variety. A number of 'newly industrialized countries', such as Korea and Singapore, have highly developed industries, and trade and living standards near to Western levels. Some major oil producers, while still exporting mainly primary products, have high *per capita* incomes. Many countries, while still on average underdeveloped, have large and growing industrial sectors and are catching up with the world leaders. The most backward LDCs, however, especially in Africa, continue to be poor, and in some cases have descended to famine and anarchy.

Lesseps, Ferdinand (Marie), vicomte de (Viscount of) [leseeps] (1805–94) French diplomat and entrepreneur, born in Versailles, NC France. From 1825 he held various diplomatic posts, and in 1854 began his campaign for the construction of a Suez Canal. The works started in 1859, and were completed in 1869. In 1881 his ambitious scheme for a sea-level Panama Canal commenced, but had to be abandoned in 1888. His company was subsequently charged with breach of trust, and Lesseps, then elderly, was sentenced to five years' imprisonment; but the sentence was reversed, and did little to ruin his esteem.

Lesotho

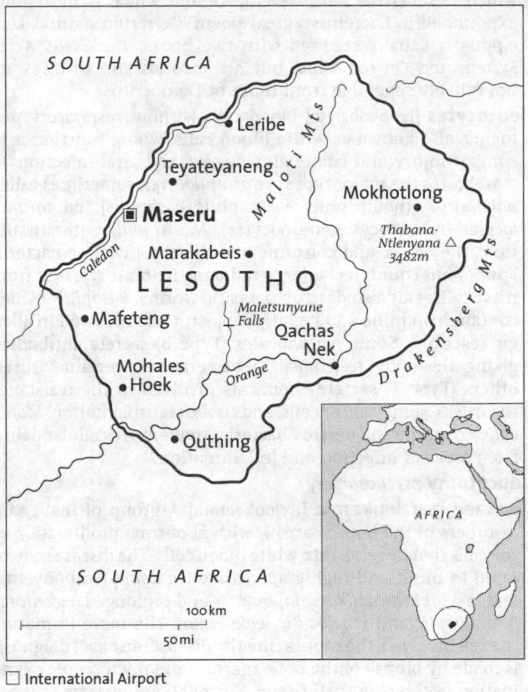

[lesootoo], official name **Kingdom of Lesotho**

Local name Lesotho

Timezone GMT +2

Area 30 355 km²/11 720 sq mi

Population total (2002e) 2 208 000

Status Independent kingdom within the Commonwealth

Date of independence 1960

Capital Maseru

Languages Lesotho (Sesotho) and English (official), Zulu, Afrikaans, French, Xhosa also spoken

Ethnic groups Basotho (99%), Zulu, Tembu, and Fingo tribes, European and Asian minorities

Religions Roman Catholic (44%), Protestant (mostly Lesotho Evangelical) (30%), Anglican (12%), other Christian (8%), traditional beliefs (6%)

Physical features S African kingdom completely bounded by South Africa; Drakensberg Mts in NE and E, highest peak Thabana-Ntlenyana, 3482 m/11 424 ft; serious soil erosion, especially in W; main rivers, the Orange and the Caledon; mountainous land, particularly in SW with the Maloti Mountain range.

Climate Mild, dry winters; warm summer season (Oct–Apr); average annual temperatures 15°C (Jan), 25°C (Jul); average annual rainfall 725 mm/28·5 in (Oct–Apr).

Currency 1 Loti (plural Maloti) (M, LSM) = 100 lisente

Economy Economy based on intensive agriculture and contract labour working in South Africa; wheat, peas, beans, barley, cattle; diamonds, textiles, pharmaceuticals; jewellery, crafts, wool, mohair.

GDP (2002e) $5·106 bn, per capita $2700

Human Development Index (2002) 0·535

History Originally inhabited by hunting and gathering bushmen; Bantu arrived 16th-c, and Basotho nation established; incorporated in Orange Free State, 1854; under British protection as Basutoland, 1869; independence, 1960; declared Kingdom of Lesotho in 1966, as a hereditary monarchy within the Commonwealth; constitution suspended and country ruled by Council of Ministers, 1970–86; Prime Minister deposed by coup and political activity banned, 1986, with Military Council as effective ruling body; King Moshoeshoe dethroned by military council in 1990, and replaced by eldest son; elections (first since 1970) to restore civilian rule, 1993; Moshoeshoe returned to the throne, 1994, but died in a car accident, 1996; status of the monarchy a continuing issue; new electoral system introduced, 2002.

Head of State (Monarch)
1966–90 Moshoeshoe II
1990–4 Letsie III (abdicated)
1994–6 Moshoeshoe II
1996– Letsie III

Head of Government
1966–86 Leabua Jonathan

Chairman of Military Council
1986–91 Justin Metsing Lekhanya
1991–3 Elias Tutsoane Ramaema

Head of Government
1993–4 Ntsu Mokhehle
1994 Hae Phoofolo (Chairman of Transitional Council)
1994–8 Ntsu Mokhehle
1998– Bethuel Pakalitha Mosisili

He wrote *Histoire du canal de Suez* (1875–9, History of the Suez Canal), and a biography.

lesser celandine A perennial species of buttercup (*Ranunculus ficaria*), common in damp woods and meadows throughout Europe and W Asia; leaves heart-shaped, glossy dark-green; flowers with 8–12 golden-yellow petals which turn white as they fade. (Family: Ranunculaceae.)

Less Favoured Areas (LFAs) Areas established in 1975 under a European Community directive to provide assistance to farmers in order to conserve the countryside, protect coastlines, and preserve areas of tourist potential. In the UK, most LFAs are in upland regions, where capital grants are available for such work as land drainage.

Lessing, Doris (May), *née* **Tayler** (1919–) Writer, born in Kermanshah, W Iran. She lived on a farm in Rhodesia, and was married and divorced twice (Lessing is her second husband's name). Her first published novel was *The Grass is Singing* (1950), a study of white civilization in Africa, the theme of many early works. Her experiences of life in working-class London after her arrival in 1949 are described in *In Pursuit of the English* (1960). In 1952 she published the first in a series of the important *Martha Quest* novels, *Children of Violence*, which is semi-autobiographical and, typically, explores political and social undercurrents in contemporary society. Her many other novels include the popular *The Golden Notebook* (1962), and the later books *London Observed* (1992), *Love, Again* (1996), and *Mara and Dann* (1999). Her work also includes several collections of short stories, fantasies, and science fiction. She became a Companion of Honour in 1999.

Lessing, Gotthold (Ephraim) (1729–81) Playwright and man of letters, born in Kamenz, E Germany. After studying theology at Leipzig University, he worked as a translator, then continued his studies at Wittenberg (1751). The first German playwright of lasting importance, he introduced blank verse to German drama, producing his classic tragedy *Miss Sara Sampson* in 1755. While secretary to the Governor of Breslau, he wrote his famous *Laokoon* (1766), a critical treatise defining the limits of poetry and the plastic arts. His *Minna von Barnhelm* (1767) was the first German comedy on the grand scale. In 1769 the Duke of Brunswick appointed Lessing as Wolfenbüttel librarian, and in 1772 he wrote another great tragedy, *Emilia Galotti*, followed by *Nathan der Weise* (1779), a powerful plea for balance and tolerance, making him an eloquent German proponent of the Enlightenment.

Lester, Dick, popular name of **Richard Lester** (1932–) US film director. He studied at the University of Pennsylvania, and first worked as a television director for CBS (1951–4). He came to Britain and gained success with two feature films starring The Beatles, *A Hard Day's Night* (1964) and *Help!* (1965). Later film credits include *Superman II* and its sequel (1980, 1983), *The Return of the Musketeers* (1989), and *Get Back* (1991).

Lethe [leethee] In the Greek and Roman Underworld, the name of a slow-moving river. When the souls of the dead drank from it, they forgot their lives on Earth. The word means 'forgetfulness', ie oblivion.

Leto [leetoh] or **Latona** In Greek mythology, a Titan, the mother by Zeus of the twins Apollo and Artemis. They were born at Delos, because in her jealousy Hera would allow no land to harbour Leto; luckily, at that time Delos was a floating island.

letter *alphabet*

Letterman, David (1947–) Television talk-show host, born in Indianapolis, Indiana, USA. He studied at Ball State University, Indiana, then worked as a TV weatherman and on radio before starting in New York City as a writer. He became well-known following guest-host appearances on the Johnny Carson Show in 1979–80, hosted a late-night show for MBC from 1982, noted for its irreverent manner and zany comic stunts, then in 1993 joined CBS as host of 'Late Night with David Letterman'.

letter of credit A document issued by a bank or other body in which the issuer undertakes to substitute its financial strength for that of the beneficiary, when presented with a draft (bill of exchange) or other demand for payment along with other specified documents. They are especially used abroad, as a means of paying for foreign goods. A *confirmed* letter of credit is one which a party other than the issuer commits itself to honour the demand, either replacing the issuer or providing an additional undertaking. An *irrevocable* letter cannot be amended or cancelled without the agreement of all parties, whereas a *revocable* letter may be.

letterpress A form of printing in which the image to be communicated is placed on a relief surface of metal or wood, and transferred as an inked impression to the printing foundation, usually paper. To be read correctly on the paper, the printing image has to be reversed from left to right. The image to be printed is made up of type and of illustration blocks. In the early 20th-c, the Linotype and Monotype systems automated the process of assembling type by using keyboards that controlled the casting, from molten metal, of complete lines of type or 'slugs' (Linotype) or of individual characters arranged in lines (Monotype). Modern methods can produce flat or curved plates, each producing a whole page or sequence of pages. Letterpress has now been largely superseded by offset lithography.

letters patent In the UK, a document conferring certain privileges on an individual, normally the right to exclusive benefit from an invention. This is usually simply called a **patent**, and the fuller term tends to be used only for the document which confers the privileges of the peerage on a new peer.

lettres de cachet [letruh duh kashay] A royal order of the French kings, sealed with the monarch's private seal, issued for the arrest and imprisonment of individuals during the *ancien régime*. The practice was abolished in the French Revolution (1790).

lettuce An annual or perennial, very widespread but mostly N temperate; leaves often with prickly margins; flower heads small, often in clusters, yellow or blue. The well-known garden lettuce (*Lactuca sativa*) is of uncertain origin, and unknown in the wild, but has a long history of cultivation. It is an important salad plant, its numerous cultivars being divided into two main groups: *cos*, with upright heads of crisp oblong leaves, and the round-headed *cabbage* types, with broadly rounded leaves, often softer-textured and convoluted. (Genus: *Lactuca*, 100 species. Family: Compositae.)

Leucippus [loosipus] (5th-c BC) Philosopher, born in Miletus, Asia Minor. He was the originator of the atomistic cosmology which Democritus later developed, and which is most fully expounded in Lucretius's great poem 'De rerum natura'. Leucippus is usually credited with two books, *The Great World System* and *On the Mind*, but his theories and writings are not reliably separable from those of Democritus.

leucocytes [lyookohsiyts] Blood cells without respiratory pigments, also known as **white blood cells**, whose function is to combat injury and bacterial, parasitic, and viral infection. In vertebrates the major types are *granulocytes*, sometimes called *polymorphs* (neutrophils, eosinophils, basophils) and *agranulocytes* (lymphocytes, monocytes). *Neutrophils* enter tissues from the blood, and consume and destroy invading bacteria. *Eosinophils* counteract allergy-inducing irritants released from mast cells, and also destroy parasitic worms. *Basophils* (which contain histamine and heparin) appear to be involved in allergic reactions. Some *lymphocytes* (Type B) secrete antibodies, giving the body resistance to bacteria and certain viruses; others (Type T) secrete chemicals involved in the resistance to viruses, some cancer cells, and tissue transplantation. *Monocytes* consume and destroy bacteria, and remove cellular debris from areas of infection and inflammation.

leucotomy *psychosurgery*

leukaemia / leukemia [l(y)ookeemia] A group of malignant disorders of the bone marrow, with abnormal proliferation of the cells that develop into white blood cells. The disease may be rapid in onset and highly aggressive (eg *acute lymphoblastic* and *myeloblastic leukaemia*) or slow and prolonged (eg *chronic lymphocytic* and *myelocytic leukaemia*). The more immature the cell involved, the more acute the disease; an exact diagnosis is made by biopsy of the bone marrow and microscopic examination of the abnormal tissue. Normal bone marrow cells are destroyed and replaced, leading to a reduction in the number of circulating red and white blood cells, and platelets. Patients thus become anaemic and vulnerable to infection, and blood clotting is impaired. The cause is unknown, but some cases occur in clusters, and have been associated with ionizing radiation, industrial chemicals such as benzene and toluene, electromagnetic fields, and viruses. Some cases have been treated successfully with bone marrow transplantation.

leukotrienes [lyookohtriynz] A group of five or more local hormones (*paracrines*), formed by an enzyme (lipoxygenase) from the same membrane fatty acid (arachidonic acid) as prostaglandins. They are released by mast cells, neutrophils, and other leucocytes, and are involved in inflammatory and hypersensitivity reactions. They act to produce chemotaxis, bronchiolar constriction, and an increase in blood vessel permeability.

Leuven [loeven], Fr **Louvain**, Ger **Lowen** 50°53N 4°42E, pop (2000e) 87 000. University town in Brabant province, C Belgium, on both banks of the R Dijle; old town, circular in shape, once surrounded by moats; centre of cloth trade in Middle Ages; largely destroyed in World War 1; Catholic University (1425), reorganized into French- and Flemish-speaking divisions since 1970; railway; beer and soft drinks, fertilizers, animal feedstuffs; town hall (1448–63), Church of St Peter (15th–16th-c), Church of St Michael (1650–6), Premonstratensian Abbey of the Park to the SE (1129).

Levant, The [levant] A general name formerly given to the E shores of the Mediterranean Sea, from W Greece to Egypt. The **Levant States** were Syria and Lebanon, during the period of their French mandate (1920–41).

Le Vau or **Levau, Louis** [luh voh] (1612–70) Architect, born in Paris, France. He produced outstanding Baroque designs for the aristocracy, and the Hôtel Lambert, Paris, stands out particularly for the ingenious use of site. His design of Vaux-le-Vicomte (1657–61), with formal landscape by André Le Nôtre, constituted an influential milestone in French architecture, leading to his Baroque masterpiece of Versailles (from 1661, again with Le Nôtre), designed on a palatial scale for court and government.

Levellers A radical political movement during the English Civil War and the Commonwealth. It called for the extension of manhood franchise to all but the poorest, religious toleration, and the abolition of the monarchy and the House of Lords. Led by John Lilburne (c.1614–57), Richard Overton (c.1631–64), and William Walwyn (1600–80), it was supported by 'agitators' in the parliamentary army 1647–9, and defeated at Burford (May 1649).

Leven, Loch [leevn] Largest freshwater loch in lowland Scotland, UK; in Perth and Kinross; drained by R Leven (SE); area 13·7 sq km/5·3 sq mi; famous for its trout fishing and its associations with Mary, Queen of Scots, who abdicated the throne during her imprisonment here in 1567–8; nature reserve; should be distinguished from loch of same name in Lochaber district, Highland council.

Leverhulme (of the Western Isles), William Hesketh Lever, 1st Viscount [leeverhyoom], also known as **Baron Leverhulme of Bolton-Le-Moors** (1851–1925) Soap-maker and philanthropist, born in Bolton, Greater Manchester, NW England, UK. In 1886, with his brother, **James Darcy Lever**, he started the manufacture of soap from vegetable oils instead of tallow. He turned the small soap works into a national business through skilled advertising and continuous consideration for the customer and his staff, founding the model industrial new town of Port Sunlight. He was made a baron in 1917, and a viscount in 1922. Among his many benefactions, he endowed to Liverpool University a school of tropical medicine, and Lancaster House to the nation.

Leverrier, Urbain Jean Joseph [luhveryay] (1811–77) Astronomer, born in St Lô, NW France. In 1836 he became teacher of astronomy at the Polytechnique, and 10 years later gained admission to the Academy. From disturbances in the motions of planets he predicted the existence of an undiscovered planet, and calculated the point in the heavens where, a few days afterwards, Neptune was actually discovered by Galle at Berlin (1846). In 1852 Louis Napoleon made him a senator, and in 1854 he became director of the observatory of Paris.

Levesque, Rene [luhvek] (1922–87) Journalist, and premier of Quebec, SE Canada, born in Campbellton, New Brunswick, Canada. A war correspondent and pioneer on television news, he was elected to the Quebec National Assembly as a Liberal in 1960. He served in three cabinet positions until he resigned in 1968 and founded the Parti Québecois, whose main objective became Quebec sovereignty and the creation of a new form of association with Canada. Levesque was elected premier in 1976, and again in 1981. The Parti Québecois was not able to prevail in a 1980 referendum on sovereignty-association, but passed Bill 101, which formalized the status of French as the official language of Quebec. His government was defeated in 1985.

Levi [leeviy] Biblical character, the third son of Jacob by his wife Leah. It is debated whether his descendants ever formed one of the 12 tribes of Israel descended from Jacob's sons. Although they were called a tribe, no territory was apparently allocated to them (*Josh* 13.14), and they seem to have been a kind of priestly class. Moses is later depicted as a descendant of Levi.

Levi, Primo [layvee] (1919–87) Writer and chemist, born in Turin, NW Italy, to Jewish parents. On completing his schooling he enrolled at Turin University to study chemistry. During the war he joined a small guerrilla force, but he was betrayed and despatched to Auschwitz. He was one of the few to survive, and returned to Italy in 1945. All of his writings attempt to understand the nature of Nazi barbarity and the variety of responses to it evinced by its victims. *Se questo è un Uomo* (1947, If this is a Man), was the first of these. With *La tregua* (1963, The Truce), its sequel, it acquired the status of a classic work on the concentration camps. His best-known book is *The Periodic Table* (1985), a volume of autobiographical reflections, each named after a chemical element. His death was apparently suicide.

Leviathan [leviyathan] A rare Hebrew loan-word of uncertain derivation, apparently used to refer to a kind of sea or river monster (*Psalms* 104.26; also *Isa* 27.1; *Psalms* 74.14). In *Job* 41, it seems nearer a crocodile; but Ugaritic parallels suggest it may have been a mythical supernatural figure, a sea dragon, perhaps symbolic of chaos or evil.

Levi-Montalcini, Rita [layvee montalcheenee] (1909–) Neurophysiologist, born in Rome, Italy. Graduating in medicine at Rome when World War 2 began, she had to go into hiding as a non-Aryan; her early research on the neuro-embryology of the chick was done in her bedroom. In the USA for several years from 1947, she discovered nerve growth factor. She directed the Rome Cell Biology Laboratory until retirement in 1979, and shared the Nobel Prize for Physiology or Medicine in 1986 with Stanley Cohen (1922–).

Levinson, Barry (1942–) Film director and producer, born in Baltimore, Maryland, USA. He was a comic writer for television before Mel Brooks engaged him as a scriptwriter. He made his directorial debut with *Diner* (1982), which earned him an Oscar nomination for Best Screenplay. Other films include the comedy *Good Morning Vietnam* (1987), *Rain Man* (1988, Oscar), and *Bugsy* (1991). He produced, directed, and wrote *Sleepers* (1996), produced *Donnie Brasco* (1997), produced/directed *Sphere* (1997) and *Wag the Dog* (1998), and directed *Liberty Heights* (1999) and *Bandits* (2001).

levirate A marriage custom or law which expects a widow to marry a brother (either real or a close relative classified as such) of her deceased husband. In some instances, the brother stands in proxy for the deceased, and all his children are regarded as children of the dead man, so no new marriage is entered into. A **sororate** is a custom whereby a man has the right to marry his wife's sister, though this normally applies only if the wife is childless or dies young.

Lévi-Strauss, Claude [layvee strows] (1908–) Social anthropologist, born in Brussels, Belgium. A graduate in law and philosophy, he became interested in anthropology while lecturing at São Paulo University, Brazil (1934–9). He subsequently worked in the New School for Social Research in New York City before becoming director of studies at the Ecole Pratiques des Hautes Etudes in Paris (1950–74), and professor of social anthropology at the Collège de France (1959). He has been a major influence on contemporary anthropology, establishing a new method for analysing various collective phenomena such as kinship, ritual, and myth. His major four-volume study, *Mythologiques* (1964–72), studied the systematic ordering behind codes of expression in different cultures.

Levites [leeviyts] Descendants of the Biblical character Levi (one of Jacob's sons), who apparently formed a class of auxiliary ministers dedicated to the care of the Tabernacle and eventually the Jerusalem Temple (*Num* 3.5–10). This role is distinct from that of the Aaronic priesthood itself, but the division between priest and Levite is blurred, and it is arguable that such distinctions arose only in later exilic times.

Leviticus, Book of [levitikus] A book of the Hebrew Bible/Old Testament, the third book of the Pentateuch, the English title referring to the priestly traditions of the Levites. It was probably compiled from earlier materials during the exile, despite the traditional attribution to Moses. It continues from the end of the Book of Exodus, and contains directions about offerings (chapters 1–7), priesthood (8–10), purity laws (11–15), and the Day of Atonement (16), followed by a major section called the 'holiness code' (17–26) and an appendix (27).

levodopa *L-dopa*

levorotatory *optical activity*

Lewes [looz] 50°52N 0°01E, pop (2001e) 92 200. County town of East Sussex, SE England, UK; located on the R Ouse, 13 km/8 mi NE of Brighton; site of the Battle of Lewes (1264); railway; light engineering, brewing, printing; churches of St Anne (12th-c) and St John the Baptist (12th-c–18th-c).

Lewinsky, Monica [luhwinskee] (1973–) Former White House intern, born in San Francisco, California, USA. She graduated from Lewis & Clark College at Oregon, and joined the White House as an intern in 1995, moving to the Pentagon the following year. She became internationally known in January 1998 during the official investigation into claims of sexual harrassment made by Paula Jones against President Clinton (a claim later dismissed, and settled in November). It was alleged that Lewinsky had had an 18-month sexual relationship with the president, and that he had persuaded her to deny the affair in her deposition to lawyers acting for Jones, and then subsequently denied the affair himself, while under oath. The enquiry was fuelled by a series of covert tape recordings of conversations betwen Lewinsky and the president made by her friend Linda Tripp (1950–), a former White House aide. Lewinsky continued to maintain a high national profile into 1999, following Clinton's acquittal.

Lewis, Sir (William) Arthur (1915–91) British economist, born in St Lucia. He was professor of economics at Manchester (1948–58), then became the first president of the University of the West Indies (1959–63). He served as an adviser to several African governments, and became the president of the Caribbean Development Bank, which he helped to establish (1970–4). From 1963 until his retirement in 1983 he held a chair in economics at Princeton. In 1979 he shared the Nobel Prize for Economics for work on economic development in the Third World.

Lewis, (Frederick) Carl(ton) (1961–) Track and field athlete, born in Birmingham, Alabama, USA. An all-round athlete at Houston University (1979–82), he won the world long jump gold medal at the 1981 World Cup, and went on to win three gold medals in the inaugural World Championships in 1983. He emulated Jesse Owens' record by winning four gold medals at the 1984 Olympic Games (100 m, 200 m, 4 × 100 m relay, and long jump), won two more at the 1988 Olympics (100 m, long jump), an unprecedented third consecutive gold medal in the long jump in the 1992 Olympics, and another gold medal for the long jump at the 1996 Games. He was awarded the gold medal for the 100 m in 1988 when Ben Johnson (the winner on the track) was disqualified for drug abuse; but Lewis held the world record in the 100 m for many years.

Lewis, C Day *Day-Lewis, C*

Lewis, C(live) S(taples) (1898–1963) Academic, writer, and Christian apologist, born in Belfast, NE Northern Ireland, UK. Educated privately, he served in World War 1, then studied at Oxford. He taught at Oxford (1925–54), and was professor of Mediaeval and Renaissance English at Cambridge from 1954. His novel *The Screwtape Letters* (1942), is the most well known of more than 40 works on Christian apologetics, and *The Lion, the Witch and the Wardrobe* (1950), was the first in the *Chronicles of Narnia*, which has become a classic children's series. He also wrote science fiction books, such as *Out of the Silent Planet* (1938). His autobiography, *Surprised by Joy* (1955), describes his conversion to Christianity. His brief marriage to **Joy Davidman** (d.1960) was the subject of the play and film, *Shadowlands*.

Lewis, Edward B (1918–) Developmental biologist, born in Wilkes-Barre, Pennsylvania, USA. He studied at the California Institute of Technology, where he carried out his research. He shared the Nobel Prize for Physiology or Medicine in 1995 for his research into how genes control early development of the human embryo. Using the fruit fly, he investigated how genes could control development of body segments into specialized organs.

Lewis, G(ilbert) N(ewton) (1875–1946) Physical chemist, born in Weymouth, Massachusetts, USA. He studied at Nebraska University, Harvard, and in Germany before taking a post as government chemist in the Philippines. He taught at the Massachusetts Institute of Technology (1905–12), then moved to California University (1912–45). He was a pioneer in taking ideas from physics and applying them to chemistry, much of his research focusing on the arrangement of electrons around atomic nuclei.

Lewis, Jerry Lee (1935–) Rock singer, country singer, and pianist, born in Ferriday, Louisiana, USA. After working as a session musician at Sun Studios in Memphis, he was invited to record by the label's founder, Sam Phillips. His 1957 recordings 'Whole Lotta Shakin' and 'Great Balls of Fire' became classics of rock, copied by successive generations of musicians. After he married his 14-year-old cousin, Myra, in 1958 (divorced 1971), he was effectively boycotted by television and the pop radio stations. During the 1960s he concentrated on country music, returning to rock-and-roll only in the 1970s.

Lewis, John L(lewellyn) (1880–1969) Labour leader, born in Lucas, Iowa, USA. He began working as a coal miner in 1897, and entered union politics, becoming president of the United Mine Workers' Union (1920–60). In 1935 he formed a combination of unions, the Congress of Industrial Organizations, of which he was president until 1940. A skilful negotiator, he made the miners' union one of the most powerful in the USA.

Lewis, Lennox (1965–) Heavyweight boxer, born in Stratford, London, UK. He moved to Canada with his mother in 1977 and won the super-heavyweight gold for Canada in the 1988 Olympic Games. He then returned to the UK, beginning his professional career in 1989. Awarded the World Boxing Council (WBC) heavyweight title in 1993, he lost it in 1994 to Oliver McCall, but regained the title from McCall in 1997. In 1999 he drew a unification bout with World Boxing Association champion Evander Holyfield. A rematch was called for after protests over the scoring. Lewis won the rematch but was stripped of the title by a New York court in 2000. In 2001 he lost the WBC and the International Boxing Federation heavyweight titles but regained them the same year, and successfully defended them against Mike Tyson in 2002. He retained the WBC title following a controversial match with Vitali Klitschko in 2003, and announced his retirement in 2004.

Lewis, Martyn (John Dudley) (1945–) British television journalist, presenter, and newsreader. He studied at Trinity College, Dublin, became a presenter with BBC Belfast (1967–8), moved to HTV Wales (1968–70), and joined ITN (1971), becoming newsreader and foreign correspondent on *News at Ten* and *News at 5.45* (1978–86). His work for the BBC includes presenter of the *One O'Clock News* (1986), *Nine O'Clock News* (1987–94), *Six O'Clock News* (1994–9), the *Crimebeat* series (1996, 1997), and he hosted *Today's the Day* (1993–7). His books include *Tears and Smiles – The Hospice Handbook* (1989), *Go For It* (annual, 1993–), and *Reflections on Success* (1997).

Lewis, Meriwether (1774–1809) Explorer, born in Charlotteville, Virginia, USA. He grew up in the wilderness, served in the army, and in 1801 became personal secretary to President Thomas Jefferson. He was invited with his long-time friend William Clark to lead an expedition (1804–6) to explore the lands to the W of the Mississippi, and to keep a detailed journal of his experiences. It was the first overland journey by Americans to the Pacific Coast, and one of the longest transcontinental journeys ever undertaken. He became Governor of Louisiana in 1808, and died in a shooting incident on his way to Washington.

Lewis, M(atthew) G(regory), nickname **Monk Lewis** (1775–1818) Novelist, born in London, UK. He studied at Oxford and Weimar universities, and in 1794 was an attaché to The Hague where he wrote *The Monk* (1796), a Gothic novel which caught the public's attention and inspired his nickname. After the success of his musical drama, *The Castle Spectre* (1798), his concern about the treatment of the slaves on the vast estates he inherited in the West Indies took him there twice, and he subsequently died of yellow fever. His memorable *Journal of a West Indian Proprietor* was published posthumously in 1834.

Lewis, Saunders (1893–1985) Playwright, poet, and Welsh nationalist, born in Cheshire, NWC England, UK. He studied English and French at Liverpool, became a lecturer in Welsh at University College, Swansea, in 1922, and in 1924 published a study on classical Welsh 18th-c poetry, *A School of Welsh Augustans*. He was co-founder of the Welsh Nationalist Party (later Plaid Cymru) in 1925, and became its president in 1926. Imprisoned for an act of arson (1936), he was dismissed from Swansea and made his living by journalism, teaching, and farming until his appointment in 1952 as lecturer (later senior lecturer) in Welsh at University College, Cardiff. He published many essays, plays, poems, novels, and historical and literary criticism, chiefly in Welsh.

Lewis, (Harry) Sinclair (1885–1951) Novelist, born in Sauk Center, Minnesota, USA. He studied at Yale, became a journalist, and wrote several minor works before *Main Street* (1920) appeared, the first of a series of best-selling novels satirizing US small-town life. *Babbitt* (1922) still lends its title as a synonym for the small-town middle-class American. He refused the Pulitzer Prize for *Arrowsmith* (1925), but accepted the Nobel Prize for Literature in 1930, being the first US writer to receive it. Other notable works are *Elmer Gantry* (1927, filmed 1960) and *Dodsworth* (1929).

Lewis, (Percy) Wyndham [windam] (1882–1957) Artist, writer, and critic, born on a yacht in the Bay of Fundy, Nova Scotia, SE Canada. He studied at the Slade School of Art, London, and with Ezra Pound founded *Blast* (1914–15), the magazine of the Vorticist school. His writings include the satirical novel *The Apes of God* (1930), and the multi-volume *The Human Age* (1955–6), as well as literary criticism, such as *Men Without Art* (1934), and autobiographical books, such as *Blasting and Bombardiering* (1937). His paintings include works of abstract art, a series of war pictures, and portraits.

Lewis and Clark Expedition *Clark, William; Lewis, Meriwether*

Lewis with Harris area 2134 sq km/824 sq mi. Island in the Western Isles, NW Scotland, UK; largest and northernmost of the Hebrides; separated from the mainland (W) by the North Minch; Lewis (N) linked to Harris (S) by a narrow isthmus; chief towns, Stornoway, Tarbert; fishing, crofting, tweeds.

lexeme The basic unit in the meaning system of a language. It represents the constant semantic element in a set of related forms (eg *think, thinks, thought, thinking*), independently of the grammatical variations possible in the language. **Lexicology** is the study of a language's vocabulary, investigating the structure of word sets and relationships, and determining the structural similarities and differences between the vocabularies of different languages. Words for colour, kinship terms, and food frequently display cross-linguistic differences. For example, both Welsh and English have words for *brother* and *sister*, but Welsh has terms for male (*cefnder*) and female (*cyfnither*) cousins, where English has only the one word.

lexicography *dictionary*

lexicology *lexeme*

Lexington 42°27N 71°14W, pop (2000e) 30 400. Town in Middlesex Co, NE Massachusetts, USA, 16 km/10 mi NW of Boston; flashpoint of the American War of Independence.

Lexington (Virginia) 37°47N 79°26W, pop (2000e) 6900. Historic town in Rockbridge Co, Virginia, USA; birthplace of Sam Houston, Pat Robertson, Cy Twombly; Washington and Lee university; Virginia Military Institute houses the George C Marshall Museum; Stonewall Jackson House; Virginia Horse Centre.

Lexington and Concord, Battle of (19 Apr 1775) The first armed conflict of the US War of Independence, fought in Massachusetts after British troops tried to seize supplies stored at the village of Concord.

Leyden [liydn], Dutch **Leiden** 52°09N 4°30E, pop (2000e) 118 000. University city in South Holland province, W Netherlands, on the R Oude Rijn; charter, 1266; famous for its weaving, 14th-c; besieged for a year by the Spaniards (1573), relieved when William the Silent ordered the dykes to be cut enabling the Dutch fleet to sail to the city walls; as a reward for their bravery the citizens were given Holland's first university, 1575; hardware, machinery, printing; birthplace of several painters, notably Rembrandt; Gemeenlandshuis van Rijn (1596), Weighhouse (1658), Church of St Pancras (15th-c), Church of St Peter (1315), town hall (17th-c), municipal museum (1869).

Leyden jar [liydn] The earliest device for storing electric charge, named after the University of Leyden, where it was invented in 1746. A glass jar was coated inside and outside with metal foils, which were connected by a rod passing the insulating stopper. The jar was usually charged from an electrostatic generator, and was an early form of capacitor.

Leydig cells [laydig] Endocrine cells found within the vertebrate testis which are necessary for the occurrence of normal spermatogenesis and for the development and maintenance of male secondary sexual characteristics; also called **interstitial cells**. They are situated between the seminiferous tubules. Their main secretion is testosterone, which is a powerful androgen, converted by its target organs to the much more powerful dihydrotestosterone.

leyland cypress An inter-generic hybrid (× *Cupressocyparis leylandii*) of garden origin between the false cypress and the cypress. Its appearance depends on which species is the female parent, but it is always columnar in outline, hardy and vigorous. Clones with grey or green foliage are the most common. First raised in 1888, it is much used nowadays for fast-growing hedges. (Family: Cupressaceae.)

ley lines [lay] Visible lines that connect ancient sites and features (eg burial mounds, standing stones) across the countryside. They have been interpreted as ancient trading tracks, as 'energy lines' which can be detected and mapped by dowsing, and as 'spirit lines' or ghost paths which begin and end in cemeteries.

Lhasa [lahsa], Chin **Lasa**, known as **The Forbidden City** 29°41N 91°10E, pop (2000e) 156 000, administrative region 419 100. Capital of Tibet (Xizang), SW China; altitude 3600 m/11 800 ft; airfield, light industry, crafts; ancient centre of Tibetan Buddhism, with many temples and holy sites; closed to foreigners in 19th-c; Chinese occupation, 1951; many monks fled (including the Dalai Lama), especially after uprising in 1959; Potala Palace (17th-c), including Red Palace, former home of the Dalai Lama; Drepung Monastery (1416), still an active lamasery; Jokhang Temple (6th-c). The Potala Palace and Jokhang Temple monastery are world heritage sites.

Lhasa apso [lahsa apsoh] A toy breed of dog developed in Tibet; small with dense coat of stiff straight hair parted along spine; usually golden (but other colours possible); head with mass of hair covering eyes; ears pendulous.

liability *strict liability*

liane [liahn], or **liana** [liahna] A woody climber growing from the ground to the top of the tree canopy, where it branches out and produces flowers. Many reach considerable heights, especially in tropical forests, where they are abundant.

Libby, Willard (Frank) (1908–80) Chemist, born in Grand Valley, Colorado, USA. He studied and lectured at Berkeley, CA, and was involved in atom bomb research at Columbia (1941–5). He became professor of chemistry at Chicago (1945–54), a member of the US Atomic Energy Commission (1954–9), and professor of chemistry at Los Angeles (1959–76). He received the Nobel Prize for Chemistry in 1960 for his part in the invention of the carbon-14 method of dating.

libel A defamatory statement published in permanent form. In many jurisdictions this is extended to include broadcast by wireless telegraphy (radio, television), and words spoken during the public performance of a play. Also, the libel need not involve words – a sculpture or painting may be libellous, as may conduct (such as hanging someone in effigy). In England and Wales, it is not necessary to prove that a libel has caused actual loss to the defamed person, whether financial or otherwise, for the action to succeed. To decide if something is libellous is to ask whether it is a false statement which discredits someone. Generally, only the rich or those sure of success are able to sue for civil libel, as hearings are in the higher courts. The expression is not used in this technical sense in Scottish law, being subsumed under defamation. There is no universally accepted distinction between libel and slander; in the USA, for example, defamation on radio and television is usually classified as slander.

Liberace [libuhrahchee], also known as **Walter Busterkeys**, originally **Wladziu Valentino Liberace** (1919–87) Entertainer, born in Milwaukee, Wisconsin, USA. He appeared as a soloist with the Chicago Symphony Orchestra at 14, and earned a living under his stage name. Over the years he developed an act of popular piano classics performed with a lavish sense of showmanship. His television series, *The Liberace Show* (1952–7), won him an Emmy as Best Male Personality, and he broke all box-office records at Radio City Music Hall in New York City during 1985. His enduring career rested on his live performances and a flamboyant lifestyle, full of piano-shaped swimming pools, glittering candelabra, and sartorial excess. His books include *The Things I Love* (1976).

Liberal Democrats *Liberal Party* (UK); *Social Democratic Party*

liberalism A political philosophy developed largely in the 18th–19th-c associated with the rise of the new middle classes, challenging the traditional monarchical, aristocratic, or religious views of the state. Liberals sought political power to match economic power, and argued for secular, constitutional, and parliamentary governments. Classical liberalism argues for limited government, and the values traditionally espoused are those of freedom – of the individual, religion, trade and economics (expressed in terms of *laissez faire*), and politics. This tendency was reversed later in the 19th-c with the arrival of 'New Liberalism', committed to social reform and welfare legislation. In the 20th-c, liberalism in most countries was overtaken by socialism as the major radical challenge to conservative parties, and came to occupy a position in the centre ground, finding it difficult to establish a firm electoral base. In some countries (eg the UK), liberals have combined traditional values with a belief in the need for governmental intervention to overcome social injustice, leading to demands for constitutional government, civil rights, and the protection of privacy.

liberalization The process of reducing government controls and moving towards a market economy. This has occurred in countries converting from centrally planning, and in developing countries reacting against highly state-controlled governments. Liberalization takes a variety of forms. Discretionary controls on foreign trade may be replaced by published tariffs, and tariffs may be replaced by currency depreciation. Price controls and rationing may be relaxed or abolished. Compulsory deliveries to the state from farms or factories may be reduced or abolished. Liberalization may be accompanied by institutional changes, such as splitting up monopolies, privatizing state-owned firms, reforming banks, and establishing bankruptcy procedures. The order in which various liberalization measures should be undertaken, and the speed with which they should be introduced, are matters of considerable controversy. In the case of the former planned economies this is not surprising, as there were no precedents to guide them.

Liberal Party (Australia) Australia's largest conservative political party, formed by R G Menzies in 1944 from existing conservative groups. It built up a mass following in the late 1940s, and was victorious in 1949. It stayed in power until 1966, and was then in coalition with the Country Party until 1972 and again in 1975–83. Under Menzies (prime minister, 1949–66), the party followed policies of economic growth and conservative pragmatism, espousing private enterprise. Support surged in the mid-1970s, but in the 1983 elections it was unable to match the resurgent Labor Party. Nevertheless, by 1988 the Liberal Party still had 100 000 members, and remained the main alternative to the Australian Labor Party, achieving success under John Howard in 1996.

Liberal Party (Canada) A Canadian national and provincial political organization that grew out of 19th-c reformism. At the federal level, it was the most successful party in the 20th-c, regaining power in the general election of 1993.

Liberal Party (UK) A British political party, originating in the mid-19th-c, whose electoral appeal was to the new middle classes and working-class elite of skilled artisans. Its first major victory came one year after the 1867 Reform Act. The Liberals and Conservatives were the two major parties until 1922, when the Labour Party overtook the Liberals in popular support, since when their status has declined to a centrist minority party. Espousing the values of individual and economic freedom combined with social justice, it played a significant part in the development of the welfare state. After the formation of the Social Democratic Party (SDP) in 1980, the Liberal Party entered into an electoral 'Alliance', and in 1987 voted to merge with the SDP, subsequently forming the **Social and Liberal Democrats Party**, from 1988 known as the **Liberal Democrats**. A small 'rump' Liberal Party remains.

Liberal Republican Party (1872) An insurgent movement in the US Republican Party. It was opposed to reconstruction policies in the South, and to the notorious corruption in the administration of President Grant (in office 1869–77).

liberation theology A style of theology originating in Latin America in the 1960s, and later becoming popular in many developing countries. Accepting a Marxist analysis of society, it stresses the role and mission of the Church to the poor and oppressed in society, of which Christ is understood as liberator. Its sympathy for revolutionary movements led to clashes with established secular and religious authorities.

Liberia *p.895*

libertarianism **1** The philosophical theory, opposed to determinism, that not all human actions are causally explicable, and that there is therefore both free will and moral responsibility. **2** The political theory that society and the state should place the minimum restraints on individual freedom of action. As an ideology it has been influential chiefly in the USA, where the Libertarian Party has polled over 1 million votes in post-World War 2 elections. Robert Nozik (1938–) in his book *Anarchy, State and Utopia* (1974) offers a defence of the minimal state position.

liberty, equality, fraternity The motto of the French Republic; adopted in June 1793, it remained the official slogan of the state until the Bourbon Restoration (1814). It was re-adopted during the Second Republic (1848–51), and has remained the national slogan from 1875 to the present day, except during the German Occupation (1940–4).

Liberty, Statue of The representation of a woman holding aloft a torch, which stands at the entrance to New York harbour; a world heritage site. The idea for 'Liberty Enlightening the World' was conceived in France; it was designed by the French sculptor Bartholdi, and shipped to New York to be assembled and dedicated in 1886. The statue is 40 m/152 ft high.

Liberty Bell *Independence Hall*

Libra [leebra] (Lat 'scales') An inconspicuous S constellation of the zodiac, lying between Virgo and Scorpius. In Greek times it represented the claws of Scorpius, the scorpion.

librarianship *library science*

library A building or room containing a collection of books, records, photographs, etc, organized to facilitate consultation or borrowing by private individuals or the public; also, the collection itself. Libraries date from the earliest recorded times, being known in several ancient countries of the Middle East, such as Babylonia, Egypt, and Mesopotamia. There were famous libraries at Alexandria, Athens, and Rome. In Christian Europe, libraries were usually attached to monasteries; secular collections emerged during and after the Renaissance, several of which have provided the basis of major modern libraries, such as the Bodleian at Oxford. Libraries can be classified according to their size and importance, and whether they are public or privately owned, are general or specialized in coverage, offer a lending or reference-only service, and permit open or closed access. Other varieties include subscription libraries and mobile libraries (often found in country areas). An international library network now exists.

Library of Congress The US depository and the largest library in the world, founded in 1800 in Washington, District of Columbia, USA. The library provides bibliographical and cataloguing services for libraries throughout the world, but its main function is the provision of reference materials for the

Liberia

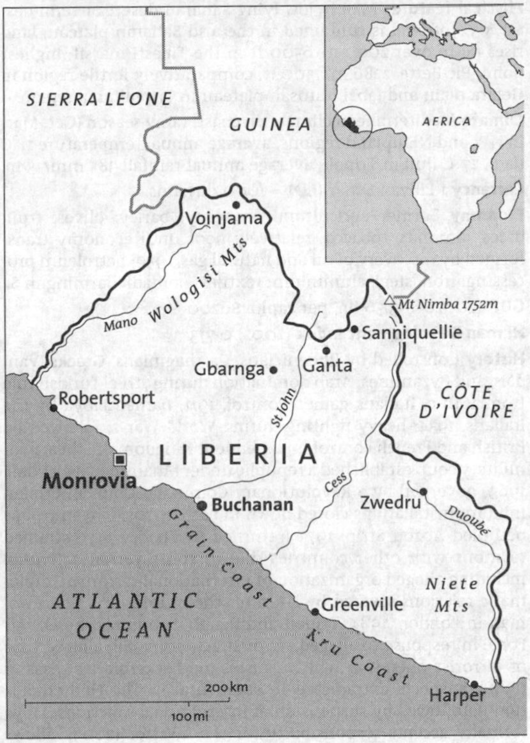

□ International Airport

[liybeeria], official name **Republic of Liberia**

Local name Liberia

Timezone GMT

Area 111 370 km²/43 760 sq mi

Population total (2002e) 3 288 000

Status Republic

Date of independence 1847

Capital Monrovia

Languages English (official) with many dialects/languages of Niger-Congo spoken

Ethnic groups Indigenous tribes (including Kpelle, Bassa, Gio, Kru, Gola, Kissi, Vai, and Bella) (95%), Americo-Liberians (repatriated slaves from the USA) (5%)

Religions Traditional animist beliefs (70%), Muslim (20%), Christian (10%)

Physical features Low coastal belt with lagoons, beaches, and mangrove marshes; land rises inland to mountains, reaching 1752 m/5748 ft at Mt Nimba; rivers include Mano, Moro, St Paul, St John, Cess, Duoubé, Cavalla.

Climate Equatorial climate; high temperatures, abundant rainfall; high humidity during rainy season (Apr–Sep), especially on coast; average annual temperatures 26°C (Jan), 24°C (Jul); average annual rainfall 5138 mm/202 in.

Currency 1 Liberian Dollar (L$) = 100 cents

Economy Based on minerals, especially iron ore; two-thirds of the population rely on subsistence agriculture; rubber, timber, palm oil, rice, cassava, coffee, cocoa, coconuts; large merchant fleet, including the registration of many foreign ships.

GDP (2002e) $3·116 bn, per capita $1000

History Mapped by the Portuguese in 15th-c; created as a result of the activities of several US philanthropic societies, wishing to establish a homeland for former slaves; founded in 1822; constituted as the Free and Independent Republic of Liberia, 1847; military coup and assassination of President, 1980, established a People's Redemption Council, with a chairman and a Cabinet; new constitution in 1986, with an elected Senate and a House of Representatives; civil war, followed by arrival of West African peacekeeping force, 1990; interim Government of National Unity installed; transitional Council of State, 1994; peace accord signed, 1995; elections held, 1997; rebels of the Liberians United for Reconciliation and Democracy (LURD) launched a large-scale offensive in the NW (Feb 2003), later agreeing to government talks, but fighting continued; rebels attack Monrovia (Jul 2003), leading to the exile of President Taylor, arrival of US troops to help Nigerian-led UN peacekeepers, and a new power-sharing government.

Head of State/Government
1986–90 Samuel Kanyon Doe
1990–4 Amos Sawyer *Acting*

Council of State – Chairman
1994–5 David Kpormakor
1995–6 Wilton Sankawulo *Transitional*
1996–7 Ruth Perry

Head of State/Government
1997–2003 Charles Taylor
2003 Moses Blah *Interim*
2003– Gyude Bryant

US Congress. It has holdings of some 18 million books and over 100 million other items.

library program A computer program which carries out a specific function and which can be incorporated into another program doing a more sophisticated task. For example, a library program to print a current debit can be incorporated into a program to print a credit-card customer's statement.

library science The study of all aspects of library functions. It covers such topics as selection and acquisition policy, classification systems, and cataloguing, as well as bibliography and administration. As a discipline in its own right, library science, or **librarianship**, is a late 19th-c development.

libration A slight irregularity in the motion of the Moon which makes it look as if it is oscillating. The phenomenon is useful to observers on Earth, because it lets them see around the *limb*, or outer edge, of the Moon as it runs ahead or behind in its orbit. These librations mean that, over a period of time, 59% of the Moon is visible from Earth.

Libreville [leebruhveel] 0°30N 9°25E, pop (2000e) 448 000. Capital of Gabon, W Africa, at the mouth of R Gabon, 520 km/325 mi NW of Brazzaville; founded in 1849 as a refuge for slaves freed by the French; occupied by the British and Free French, 1940; airport; railway; university (1970); commercial and administrative centre; timber, cement, ceramics, food and drink processing, oil exploration; Cathedral of Sainte-Marie, museum, art gallery; first Central African Games held here, 1976.

Librium *benzodiazepines*

Libya *p.896*

lice *louse*

lichen [liykn, lichn] A type of composite organism formed as an association between a fungus (the *mycobiont*) and an alga or blue-green bacterium (the *phycobiont*). The body (*thallus*) may be encrusting, scale-like, leafy, or even shrubby, according to species. The fungal partner typically belongs to the Ascomycetes. Many lichens are very sensitive to atmospheric pollution and can be used as indicators.

Lichfield 52 42N 1 48W, pop (2000e) 29 300. City in Lichfield district, Staffordshire, C England, UK; railway; cathedral; engineering; birthplace of Elias Ashmole and Samuel Johnson; Johnson museum; Staffordshire regiment museum; Garrick Theatre (2003), annual festival (Jul).

Libya

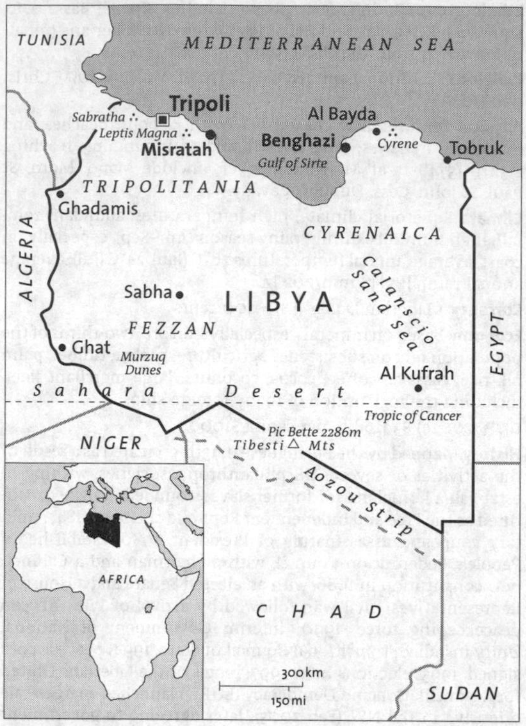

official name **Socialist People's Libyan Arab Jamahiriya**

Local name Lībiyā

Timezone GMT +1

Area 1 758 610 km²/678 823 sq mi

Population total (2002e) 5 369 000

Status Republic

Date of independence 1951

Capital Tripoli

Languages Arabic (official), with English and French widely spoken

Ethnic groups Berber and Arab (97%), Greek, Maltese, Italian, Egyptian, Pakistani, Turk, Indian, and Tunisian minorities (3%)

Religions Sunni Muslim (96%), Christian (Roman Catholic, Anglican, Coptic Orthodox) (3%), Jewish (1%)

Physical features Mainly low-lying Saharan desert or semi-desert; 93% of land is contained in the arid Saharan plateau; land rises (S) to over 2000 m/6500 ft in the Tibesti massif; highest point, Pic Bette, 2286 m/7500 ft; comparatively fertile region in Gefara plain and Jabal Nafusah plateau in Tripolitania region.

Climate Mediterranean climate on coast; rainy season (Oct–Mar) in NW and NE upland regions; average annual temperature 11°C (Jan), 27°C (Jul) in Tripoli; average annual rainfall 385 mm/15 in.

Currency 1 Libyan Dinar (LD) = 1000 dirhams

Economy Former agricultural economy; barley, olives, fruit, dates, almonds, tobacco; relatively poor until economy transformed by discovery of oil and natural gas, 1959; petroleum processing; iron, steel, aluminium; textiles; nomadic farming in S.

GDP (2002e) $33·36 bn, per capita $6200

Human Development Index (2002) 0·773

History Controlled by Phoenicians, Carthaginians, Greeks, Vandals, and Byzantines; Arab domination during 7th-c; Turkish rule from 16th-c; Italians gained control, 1911; named Libya by the Italians, 1934; heavy fighting during World War 2, followed by British and French control; independent Kingdom of Libya, 1951; military coup established a republic under Muammar al-Gaddafi, 1969; governed by a Revolutionary Command Council; foreign military installations closed down in early 1970s; Libyan troops occupied Aozou Strip, 1973 (returned to Chad, 1994); strained relations with other countries due to controversial activities, including alleged organization of international terrorism; diplomatic relations severed by UK after the murder of a policewoman in London, 1984; Tripoli and Benghazi bombed by US Air Force in response to alleged terrorist activity, 1986; alleged base of terrorist operation which caused the Lockerbie air disaster (1988), suspects extradicted to stand trial in The Netherlands (1999), followed by suspension of international sanctions; Libya formally accepts responsibility for the disaster (2003); allows international inspection of nuclear sites (Dec 2003); a socialist state, governed by a chief-of-state, a General People's Committee, and a 750-member General People's Congress.

Monarch
1951–69 Mohammed Idris al-Mahdi al-Senussi

Revolutionary Command Council Chairman
1969–77 Muammar al-Gaddafi (Qaddifi)

General Secretariat

Secretary General (Prime Minister)
1977–9 Muammar al-Gaddafi
1979–84 Abdul Ati al-Ubaidi
1984–6 Mohammed az-Zaruq Rajab
1986–90 Omar al-Muntasir
1990–7 Abu Zaid Omar Dourda
1997–2000 Muhammad Ahmad al-Mangoush
2000–3 Mubarak Abdullah as-Shamikh
2003– Shukri Mohammed Ghanim

Leader of the Revolution (Head of State)
1969– Muammar al-Gaddafi

Lichtenstein, Roy [likhtenstiyn] (1923–97) Painter, born in New York City, USA. He studied at the Art Students' League, New York City (1939), and at Ohio State College, and taught at Ohio State, New York State, and Rutgers universities. From the early 1960s he produced many of the best-known images of American Pop Art, especially frames from comic books complete with speech balloons, enlarged onto canvases and painted in primary colours in a hard-edged style imitated from cheap printing techniques. The huge 'Whaam' (1963, Tate, London) is a typical example.

Lick Observatory The observatory of the University of California, on Mount Hamilton near San Jose, California, USA. Its main telescopes are a 91 cm/36 in refractor (1888), at the base of which the observatory's benefactor James Lick (1796–1876) is buried, and a 3 m/120 in reflector (1959).

licorice *liquorice*

Li Dazhao [lee dajow], also spelled **Li Ta-chao** (1888–1927) One of the founders of the Chinese Communist Party, whose interpretation of Marxism as applied to China had a profound influence on Mao Zedong. Appointed head librarian of Beijing University and professor of history (1918), he had the young Mao as a library assistant, and founded one of the first of the Communist study circles which in 1921 were to form the Communist Party. In 1927, when the Manchurian military leader Chang Tso-lin (1873–1928), then occupying Beijing, raided the Soviet Embassy, Li was captured and executed.

Liddell Hart, Sir Basil (Henry) [lidl hah(r)t] (1895–1970) Military journalist and theorist, born in Paris, France. He studied at Cambridge, served in World War 1, and was wounded as an infantry officer. He joined the Army Education Corps, then became military correspondent for the *Daily Telegraph* (1925–35) and *The Times* (1935–9), advocating the principles of modern mobile warfare. He was knighted in 1966.

Lie, Trygve (Halvdan) [lee, **trig**vuh] (1896–1968) Norwegian statesman and UN secretary-general (1946–52), born in Oslo (formerly Kristiania), Norway. He studied at the University of Kristiania, became a Labour member of the Norwegian parliament and held several posts, before having to flee to Britain (1940), where he was Norway's foreign minister-in-exile until 1945. He was elected the first secretary-general of the UN, but resigned in 1952 as a result of Soviet opposition to his support of UN intervention in the Korean War. He later became minister of industry (1963–4), and minister of commerce and shipping from 1964.

Liebig, Justus, Freiherr von (Baron) [**lee**bikh] (1803–73) Chemist, born in Darmstadt, WC Germany. He studied at Bonn and Erlangen, and in 1822 went to Paris, where he worked with Gay-Lussac. He became professor of chemistry at Giessen (1824) and Munich (1852). He investigated many aspects of organic, animal, and agricultural chemistry, and developed new techniques for carrying out analyses, such as the distillation equipment known as **Liebig's condenser**. He was created baron in 1845.

Liechtenstein *see panel*

Lied [leet] plural **Lieder** A song with German words. In certain contexts the word implies a simple folksong (or a song in folk style), as distinct from the more ambitious and 'arty' *Gesang*, but *Lied* is generally used with reference to the solo songs with piano of the great German Romantic composers.

lie detector An instrument supposed to indicate whether a person to which it is applied is responding truthfully to questions; also known as a **polygraph**. Involuntary physiological reactions detected by electrodes attached to the subject's skin indicate stresses. Its validity is not universally acknowledged nor accepted judicially.

Liège [lyezh], Flemish **Luik**, Ger **Lüttich** 50°38N 5°35E, pop (2000e) 199 000. River port and capital city of Liège province, E Belgium, at confluence of Ourthe and Meuse rivers; bishopric; university (1817); fifth largest city in Belgium; railway; centre of former coal-mining area; blast furnaces, metalworking, civil engineering, textiles, foodstuffs, electronics, chemicals, glassware, arms; Church of St Jacques (11th-c, rebuilt 1513–38), Palace of Justice (1526–40), Gothic St Paul's Cathedral.

Lif [leef] and **Lifthrasir** [**leef**thrahser] In Norse mythology, the mother and father of the new race of human beings after Ragnarok (the last battle). The names presumably mean 'life' and 'strong life'.

Lifar, Serge [lifah(r)] (1905–86) Dancer and choreographer, born in Kiev, Ukraine. He was a student and friend of Diaghilev, whose Ballets Russes company he joined in 1923. He scored his first triumph as a choreographer in Paris with *Créatures de Promethée* (1929), and became the guiding genius behind the Paris Opéra (1929–58). He wrote several works on ballet, including a biography of Diaghilev (1940).

Liechtenstein

□ International Airport

[likhtnshtiyn], official name **Principality of Liechtenstein**, Ger **Fürstentum Liechtenstein**

Local name Liechtenstein

Timezone GMT +1

Area 160 km²/62 sq mi

Population total (2002e) 33 300

Status Independent principality

Date of independence 1719

Capital Vaduz

Language German (official)

Ethnic groups Liechtensteiner (64%), Swiss (16%), Austrian (8%), German (4%)

Religions Roman Catholic (87%), Protestant (9%)

Physical features Alpine principality, located in C Europe; fourth smallest country in the world; land boundary 76 km/47 mi; bounded W by the R Rhine; mean altitude, 450 m/1475 ft; forested mountains rise to 2599 m/8527 ft in the Grauspitz; Samina River flows N.

Climate Mild, equable climate; temperatures range from 15°C (Jan), 20–8°C (Jul); average annual rainfall 1050–1200 mm/41–47 in.

Currency 1 Swiss Franc (SFr, SwF) = 100 centimes

Economy Industrial sector developing since 1950s; export-based, centred on specialized and high-tech production; metal-working, engineering, chemicals, pharmaceuticals; international banking and finance; tourism.

GDP (1999e) $825 mn, per capita $25 000

History Became a sovereign state in 1342; independent principality within Holy Roman Empire, 1719; part of Holy Roman Empire until 1806; adopted Swiss currency, 1921; united with Switzerland in a customs union, 1923; became a member of UN, 1990; joined European Free Trade Association (EFTA), 1991; constitutional monarchy ruled by hereditary princes of the House of Liechtenstein; governed by a Prime Minister, four Councillors, and a unicameral Parliament; referendum for constitutional reforms was approved in 2003, including the granting of extensive new powers to the reigning prince.

Head of State (Monarch)
1858–1929 Johann II
1929–38 Franz von Paula
1938–89 Franz Josef II
1989– Hans Adam II

Head of Government
1928–45 Franz Josef Hoop
1945–62 Alexander Friek
1962–70 Gérard Batliner
1970–4 Alfred J Hilbe
1974–8 Walter Kieber
1978–93 Hans Brunhart
1993 Markus Büchel
1993–2001 Mario Frick
2001– Otmar Hasler

life The state or property of organisms which, by their metabolic processes, use substances from their environment for the purposes of growth, the maintenance of their functional systems, the repair of their own structure, and for reproducing themselves. All life forms on Earth are based on nucleic acids, either deoxyribonucleic acid (DNA) or ribonucleic acid (RNA), which carry their hereditary genetic information. Life on Earth, in the form of simple bacteria, is thought to have originated between about 3·5 and 3·8 thousand million years ago in conditions in which the primordial atmosphere contained the basic constituents of organic matter (methane, ammonia, hydrogen, and water vapour). These underwent a process of chemical evolution using energy from the Sun and electric storms, combining into more and more complex molecules until self-replicating nucleic acids developed.

lifeboat A vessel designed specifically for saving life at sea; also, a craft carried by seagoing vessels to save the lives of personnel in the event of abandoning ship. Lionel Lukin is believed to have been the first to build a lifeboat, in 1786, basing it at Bamburgh Head, Northumberland, UK. In 1890 the first mechanically powered lifeboat was launched, equipped with a steam engine; in 1904 the petrol engine was introduced, and a few years later the diesel. Several countries now run lifeboat services; some are government controlled, and others are voluntary or semi-voluntary. Many are modelled on the British RNLI. Only the Chinese lay claim to pre-dating the British, by organizing a river rescue service as early as 1737. In the USA, lifesaving operations are part of the air-and-sea rescue services of the US Coast Guard.

life cycle The complete series of stages through which an organism passes, from the formation of an individual by the fertilization of gametes produced by one generation, through to maturation and the production of gametes by that individual, and to its eventual death. In vertebrates there is usually a simple life-cycle from fertilization to death, but in lower animals and plants the life-cycle is often complex, involving the alternation of sexually reproducing and asexually reproducing generations which may or may not be similar in appearance.

life imprisonment A sentence involving imprisonment in theory for the remainder of the convicted person's life. In the UK, it is the mandatory sentence for murder, and the maximum sentence for certain other crimes such as manslaughter and rape. In practice, the sentence usually means 15 years, followed by parole for life. A prisoner in England and Wales may be released on licence by the home secretary on the advice of the Parole Board, following consultation with the Lord Chief Justice and, if possible, the trial judge. The Crime (Sentences) Act 1997 provides for compulsory life sentence for an accused convicted for the second time of certain offences. In Scotland, the secretary of state for Scotland has the power to release persons on licence after consultation with the Lord Justice-General. When passing this sentence, the trial judge may recommend a minimum term of imprisonment, although this is not binding on the home secretary or the secretary of state for Scotland. In the USA, life imprisonment usually means 10–30 years, at the end of which the prisoner may become eligible for parole by the Parole Board.

life insurance Insurance designed to provide protection against financial hardship for dependents following the death of the insured person; also (especially in the UK) called **life assurance**. *Whole life policies* run for the whole of a person's life, accumulating a cash value which is paid when the policy matures (or is surrendered), but which is less than the policy's face value. *Endowment policies* run for a specified period of time, and pay the full face value when the policy matures. *Term policies* run for a specified number of years, but when the policy expires there is no cash sum remaining. Premiums may be at regular intervals or made in a lump sum. Policies may be for a fixed money amount or *with profits*, where the amount payable is related to the profits the life company has been able to make by investing the premium.

LIFFE *futures*

Liffey, River [lifee] River in E Ireland, rising in N Wicklow county; flows W, NE, and E through Dublin to meet the Irish Sea at Dublin Bay; length 80 km/50 mi; crossed by the Grand Canal.

lift *elevator*

lifting body A spacecraft designed for controlled atmospheric flight following entry from space. The aerodynamic configuration is designed to withstand entry loads and also to generate significant lift. The NASA space shuttle orbiter is an example.

ligament A tough band of tissue connecting bones (eg across joints) or supporting internal organs (eg peritoneal ligaments). Ligaments are generally composed of inextensible collagen arranged in parallel bundles, but some contain a significant amount of elastic tissue, which allows limited movement to occur. When associated with joints they can vary from the thickenings of the joint capsule to substantial extra- or intracapsular structures, their thickness being directly related to the forces they are required to resist. They act to prevent mechanical disruption at joints, and as sensory organs for the perception of movement and joint position.

ligand [**lig**and] A molecule or ion bonded to another. It is most often used to describe species bonded to the central metal ion in a co-ordination compound.

liger [**liy**ger] A member of the cat family, resulting from the mating of a male lion with a female tiger. The offspring produced when a male tiger mates with a female lion is called a **tigon**.

Ligeti, György (Sándor) [**li**getee] (1923–) Composer, born in Dicsöszent-Márton, Hungary. He studied and later taught at the Budapest Academy of Music. After leaving Hungary in 1956, he worked at the electronics studio in Cologne, then settled in Vienna, where he developed an experimental approach to composition. His first large orchestral work, *Apparitions* (1958–9), made his name widely known. In *Aventures* (1962) he uses his own invented language of speech sounds. He has also written a choral requiem, a cello concerto, and music for piano, harpsichord, organ, and wind and string ensembles.

light The visible portion of the electromagnetic spectrum, corresponding to electromagnetic waves ranging in wavelength from approximately $3{\cdot}9 \times 10^{-7}$ m (violet) to $7{\cdot}8 \times 10^{-7}$ m (red) (corresponding frequencies $7{\cdot}7 \times 10^{14}$ Hz and $3{\cdot}8 \times 10^{14}$ Hz, respectively). Different wavelengths of light are perceived by humans as different colours. *White light* is composed of light of different wavelengths (colours), as may be seen by dispersing the beam through a prism. Light of a single colour is called *monochromatic*, a term sometimes taken to mean a single wavelength (which is in practice unachievable). The best source of monochromatic light is the laser.

Light as an electromagnetic wave was deduced by James Clerk Maxwell: he derived an expression for the velocity of electromagnetic waves, using electric and magnetic quantities only, which equals the velocity of light ($2{\cdot}998 \times 10^{8}$ m/s; approximately 186 000 mi/s). Interactions with matter (in particular, the photoelectric effect) show that light can also be viewed as composed of particles (*photons*) of definite energy; the polarization of light as a wave effect translates into the spin properties of photons. The modern description of light is as particles whose behaviour is governed by wave principles according to the rules of quantum theory. In geometrical optics (eg lens systems), light is thought of as rays, travelling in straight lines, causing shadows for opaque objects; these rays change direction when passing between regions of different refractive index.

Light comes from many sources. Light bulbs produce light from electrically heated filaments; thermal energy causes the motion of atoms and electrons in the filament, producing thermal radiation with a frequency spectrum related to the temperature of the filament; for filament temperatures of a few hundred degrees Celsius, the radiation produced is mostly infrared; for higher temperatures (c.3000°C for household bulbs), light is produced. Mercury arc lamps produce light by electrical discharge (the arc) in mercury vapour. Fluorescent lamps rely on electrical excitation in a gas to produce ultraviolet radiation, which in turn causes the phosphor coating on a glass tube to emit visible light by fluorescence. Electrical discharge in gases (eg neon signs) or the application of heat to substances often produces light having specific spectra; this is related to the atomic structure of the substance, and is explained in terms of quantum theory.

light-emitting diode (LED) A tiny semiconductor diode which emits light when an electric current is passed through it. It is used in electronic calculator displays and digital watch readouts, where the digits are made up from the diodes. The colour of the light emitted depends on the material of the crystal.

lighthouse A tower or other structure erected to give guidance and warning to ships and aircraft by either visible or radio-electrical means. The first man-made lighthouse was the Pharos of Alexandria (3rd-c BC). Early lighthouses were erected on land and burnt mainly wood, coal, or oil. The Eddystone lighthouse built by Henry Winstanley (1644–1703) was the first structure (1699) fully exposed to the open sea, while the masonry tower, built by John Smeaton (1724–94) on the same site in 1756–9, embodied an important new construction principle, using masonry blocks dovetailed together in an interlocking pattern. Modern lighthouses are generally built of concrete and steel, standing on submerged caissons or steel-piled structures similar to those used for offshore oil and gas rigs. Equipment within the lighthouse includes rotating paraboloid mirrors to create a pattern of flashes. Lights are beamed on and off by an electrical code unit using modern lens equipment driven by an electric motor. Most lighthouses are now automated and self-sustaining.

lightning A visible electric discharge in the form of a flash of light which results from charge separation in a thundercloud. There are two parts to the flash: the first is from the cloud to the ground or tall structure; the second is the return stroke from ground to cloud. The reflection of lightning on surrounding clouds, in which the illumination is diffused, is known as **sheet lightning**.

lightning bug *firefly*

lightning conductor A means of protecting buildings and tall structures from lightning strikes; also called a **lightning rod**. It consists of a metal rod or strip, usually made of copper, placed at the highest point of a building. The lower end of the rod is connected to earth by a low-resistance cable. A lightning flash hitting the rod will be given a safe passage along this line of least resistance to the ground.

lightpen A computer input device used in conjunction with a visual display unit (VDU). The pen is held against the screen of the VDU and its exact position can be detected by the computer. It can be used to generate or to alter information on the screen.

Lights, Feast of *Hanukkah*

light valve An optical or mechanical device to control the amount of light transmitted by an optical system. One arrangement is two superimposed linear polarizing filters where one can be rotated, thus varying the light transmitted, right down to zero when the filters are at right angles to each other. Another method found in video projectors uses a liquid crystal display (LCD) to modulate the light beam with an image.

light year The distance travelled through empty space in 1 tropical year by any electromagnetic radiation: $9{\cdot}4607 \times 10^{12}$ km/$5{\cdot}8788 \times 10^{12}$ mi. It is widely used in popular literature, but not normally used by astronomers, who prefer the parsec.

lignite *coal*

lignum vitae [lignum viytee] An evergreen tree (*Guaiacum officinale*) growing to c.10 m/30 ft, native to the West Indies; bark pale, smooth; leaves pinnate with oval leaflets; flowers blue, 5-petalled. It is a source of durable timber. (Family: Zygophyllaceae.)

Ligurian Sea [liygyurian] Arm of the Mediterranean Sea, bounded N and E by NW Italy and S by Corsica and Elba; chief ports include Genoa, Livorno, Bastia.

lilac A deciduous shrub or small tree (*Syringa vulgaris*), native to the Balkans; growing to 3–7 m/10–23 ft, domed and suckering freely; leaves oval to heart-shaped, in opposite pairs; flowers in dense, conical inflorescences, tubular with four spreading lobes, lilac or white, fragrant; fruit a pointed capsule. A widely cultivated garden ornamental, its botanical name should not be confused with the syringa or mock orange of horticulture. (Family: Oleaceae.)

Lilburne, John (c.1614–57) Pamphleteer and extreme Leveller (Puritan), probably born in Greenwich, EC Greater London, UK, but with family origins in Sunderland, Tyne and Wear. In 1638 he imported illegal Puritan literature from Holland, for which he was whipped, and imprisoned until 1640 by the Star Chamber. He was a captain in the Parliamentary army in the Civil War (1642), but resigned in 1645 over the Covenant. He became an indefatigable agitator for the Levellers, demanding greater liberty of conscience and numerous reforms, and was repeatedly imprisoned for his treasonable pamphlets.

Lilienthal, Otto [leelyentahl] (1849–96) Aeronautical inventor and pioneer of gliders, born in Anklam, NE Germany. After graduating from the Berlin Trade Academy, he studied bird flight in order to build heavier-than-air flying machines resembling the birdman designs of Leonardo da Vinci. He made hundreds of short flights in his gliders, but crashed to his death near Berlin.

Li Lisan [lee leesan] (1900–67) Chinese politician, and effective head of the Communist Party (1928–30), born in Hunan province, SEC China. He enforced what has since become known as the 'Li Lisan line', in which the Party's weak and undeveloped military forces were used in futile attempts to capture cities. His authoritarian methods alienated his fellow leaders. He was demoted in 1930, and lived in the Soviet Union until 1945. Thereafter he was employed by the Chinese Communist Party in various minor roles.

Lilith [lilith] In Jewish legend, the first wife of Adam; or, more generally, a demon woman.

Lille [leel], formerly Flemish **Lisle** or **Ryssel**, ancient **Insula** 50°38N 3°03E, pop (2000e) 177 900. Industrial and commercial city and capital of Nord department, N France, near the Belgian frontier, 208 km/129 mi NE of Paris; badly damaged in both World Wars; road and rail junction; university (1560); part of the main industrial centre of N France; textiles, tents, sugar-processing, hygiene goods, foodstuffs, chemicals, engineering, metalworking, printing, brewing; Gothic Church of St-Maurice, 16th-c Church of Ste-Catherine; cathedral (begun, 1854), 16th-c citadel, Palais des Beaux-Arts; international trade fair (Apr).

Lilley, Peter (Bruce) (1943–) British statesman and writer. He studied at Cambridge, and became an investment adviser. He was elected an MP in 1983, then became parliamentary private secretary to Chancellor of the Exchequer Nigel Lawson (1985–7), economic secretary (1987–9) and financial secretary (1989–90) to the Treasury, and secretary-of-state for trade and industry (1990–2) and for social security (1992- -7). He is the author of several books on economic and political affairs. He emerged as a contender for the leadership of the Conservative Party following John Major's resignation in 1997, but withdrew after the first ballot. Under William Hague's leadership, he became deputy leader of the party (1997–9) and shadow chancellor (1997–9).

Lillie, Beatrice (Gladys) (1898–1989) Revue singer, born in Toronto, Ontario, SE Canada. After an unsuccessful start as a drawing-room ballad singer, she found her true talent in 1914 in music hall and the new vogue of 'intimate revue' which came from Paris. She is particularly remembered for her version of Noel Coward's 'Mad Dogs and Englishmen'. During World War 2 she played to the troops, and was decorated by General de Gaulle. After the War she continued to work on the stage and in films, such as *Thoroughly Modern Millie* (1967).

Lilongwe [leelonggway] 13°58N 33°49E, pop (2000e) 319 000. Capital of Malawi, SE Africa, in Central region, on R Lilongwe; altitude 1100 m/3600 ft; capital since 1975; airport; railway; seeds, tobacco, light engineering, clothes, tourism, commerce.

lily A perennial with a bulb formed from swollen, overlapping, scale-like leaves, native to N temperate regions; stem erect, unbranched, with numerous narrow, alternate, or whorled leaves; flowers with six perianth-segments, large, terminal, often hanging; usually trumpet-shaped or with perianth rolled back to resemble a Turk's cap; in a wide range of colours, mostly white, yellow to red, purple, and often spotted; stamens long, protruding. Many species are prized for their beautiful and often fragrant flowers. The name 'lily' is often applied to various other plants. (Genus: *Lilium*, 80 species. Family: Liliaceae.)

lily-of-the-valley A perennial growing to 20 cm/8 in (*Convallaria majalis*), native to Europe and Asia; rhizomatous; leaves elliptical, in pairs, the stalks sheathing; inflorescence slender, 1-sided; flowers drooping, globular bells with six short lobes, white, fragrant; berries red. It is cultivated for ornament, and as a source of perfume. (Family: Liliaceae.)

lily-trotter *jacana*

Lima [leema] 12°06S 77°03W, pop (2000e) 7 721 000. Federal capital of Peru; on both sides of the R Rímac, at the foot of the Cerro San Cristóbal; founded by Pizarro, 1535; chief city of Spanish South America until independence; devastated by earthquake, 1746; airport; railway; 10 universities, including San Marcos (1551); vehicles, textiles, foodstuffs, paper; cathedral (1625), Palacio del Gobierno, archbishop's palace, Santo Domingo Church (1549), San Francisco Church (1674), many museums, including National Museum of Art, Museum of Peruvian Culture, Gold Museum; Parque de las Leyendas; carnival (pre-Lent), Pacific International Fair (Nov alternate years).

Lima bean A twining annual or perennial (*Phaseolus lunatus*), native to tropical South America; leaves with three leaflets; pea-flowers white or yellowish, in long clusters from the axils of the leaves; pods up to 12·5 cm/5 in long, oblong, containing 2–4 flattened, whitish seeds; also called **butter bean**. It is widely grown in the tropics and subtropics for the edible seeds (beans). Cultivars with red, brown, purple, and black seeds are also grown. (Family: Leguminosae.)

Limassol [limasol], Gr **Lemesos**, Turkish **Limasol** 34°41N 33°02E, pop (2000e) 148 000. Port and capital town of Limassol district, S Cyprus; on Akrotiri Bay, NE of Akrotiri; influx of Greek Cypriot refugees since 1974 Turkish invasion has dramatically increased population; airfield; wine-making, export of fruit and vegetables, distilling; castle (14th-c); spring carnival; arts festival (Jul); wine festival (Sep).

Limbaugh, Rush H(udson) [limbaw] (1951–) Conservative talk-radio host and activist, born in Cape Girardeau, Missouri, USA. He worked as a disc jockey and sports publicist before beginning a radio programme in San Diego, CA, at the end of the 1980s, blending political commentary and satire. His growing popularity soon led him to New York City, where he built a national audience for his daytime show. He was given credit for rousing conservative sentiment that contributed to the Republican capture of the House of Representatives in 1994. By the end of the decade, his national influence had somewhat ebbed, but he remained a symbol of how talk radio could reshape American politics.

limb girdle The bones which connect the limb skeleton to the axial skeleton. In the upper limb, the girdle (consisting of the scapula and clavicle) is connected to the axial skeleton only at the sternoclavicular joint. Other connections are muscular, which accounts for the great mobility of the shoulder and upper limb. In the lower limb the three bones of the girdle (the ilium, ischium, and pubis) are fused together to form the hip bone, and connected to the axial skeleton (of the sacrum) by the sacro-iliac joint, which has very limited mobility. Movement between axial skeleton and hip bone is thus very limited, a necessity if the lower limb is to be efficient in support of the body and in locomotion.

limbo In mediaeval Christian theology, the abode of souls excluded from the full blessedness of the divine vision, but not condemned to any other punishment. They included unbaptised infants and Old Testament prophets.

lime (botany) **1** A deciduous N temperate tree; leaves heart-shaped, often sticky with honey-dew caused by aphids; flowers fragrant, white, 5-petalled, in pendulous clusters; fruits rounded, the whole cluster with a wing-like bract which aids in dispersal; also called **linden**. Common lime (*Tilia* × *europaea*) is a hybrid often planted as a street tree. (Genus: *Tilia*, 50 species. Family: Tiliaceae.)
2 A citrus fruit resembling lemon, but smaller and more globose. *Citrus aurantifolia* has sour red fruits. *Citrus limetta*, the sweet lime, with sweeter, greenish fruits, is possibly a mutant of lemon. (Family: Rutaceae.)

lime (chemistry) Mainly calcium oxide or hydroxide, produced by heating limestone above 800°C, expelling carbon dioxide. Some of the calcium may be replaced by magnesium. The dry product is called **quicklime**; the addition of water converts the oxide to hydroxide or 'slaked' lime.

Limerick (city), Ir **Luimneach** 52°40N 8°38W, pop (2000e) 75 000. County borough and river-port capital of Limerick county, Munster, SW Ireland; industrial city at head of Shannon Estuary; founded, 1197; scene of major sieges by Cromwell and William III; railway; teacher training college; trade in farm produce, flour milling, brewing, fishing, lace; Belltable arts centre, St Mary's Cathedral (12th-c), St John's Cathedral (19th-c), remains of city walls, King John's Castle, treaty stone; festival of Irish dancing and Gaelic drama (Mar); Seisiún, traditional Irish entertainment (summer).

Limerick (county), Ir **Luimneach** pop (2000e) 164 000; area 2686 sq km/1037 sq mi. County in Munster province, SW Ireland; bounded N by R Shannon; capital, Limerick; dairy farming, hydroelectric power (Ardnacrusha), lace.

limerick 'The limerick, it would appear, / Is a verse form we owe Edward Lear: / Two long and two short / Lines rhymed, as was taught, / And a fifth just to bring up the rear.' Lear, in fact, popularized the form, which is known from the 11th-c, and usually consists of five predominantly anapaestic lines rhyming aabba. It is especially used with the opening 'There was a ... ' (young man from Dundee, young lady of Cheam, etc).

limestone A sedimentary rock consisting mainly of carbonates, primarily calcite (calcium carbonate, $CaCO_3$) or dolomite ($CaMg(CO_3)_2$), with some sand or clay as impurities. Most limestones are organically formed from the secretions, shells, or skeletons of plants and animals such as corals and molluscs. Inorganic limestones are formed by precipitation from water containing dissolved carbonates. Limestone is of economic importance as a building material, and as a source of lime and cement.

limit In mathematics, a value approached by a variable. The variable may be the sum of a number of terms of a sequence, eg if

$$S_n = 1 + \frac{1}{2} + \frac{1}{4} \cdots \frac{1}{2^n}$$

as n becomes large (ie $n \to \infty$), S approaches the value 2. Or the variable y may be dependent on another variable x, and may approach a limit as x approaches a given value, eg if $y = 2 + 1/x$, y approaches the value 2 as x becomes large. The idea of a limit is fundamental to calculus and other branches of mathematics. The limit, L, of a function $f(x)$ as x approaches a value x_0 is defined, when it exists, by the rule that for every $\varepsilon > 0$, there is a $\delta > 0$ such that

$$[x - x_0] < \delta$$

implies that

$$[f(x) - L] < \varepsilon.$$

This way to define limits was successfully introduced into mathematics in the 1820s by French mathematician Augustin Louis Cauchy (1789–1857) as part of the first adequate attempt to rigorize the calculus.

limitation clause *exemption clause*

limitation of actions Legal rules which require civil actions to be brought within specific time limits; usually referred to as the **statute of limitations**. Periods vary greatly across jurisdictions and types of actions. In the UK, for tort or delict and simple contract, the period is six years from the cause of action, though for personal injuries and death the period is normally three years from the date when the injuries or death occurred. These periods may be extended in some circumstances (eg where the injured person is disabled). For actions relating to land and some contracts made by deed, the period is 12 years. Some jurisdictions impose time limits in certain cases on the prosecution of criminal offences. The defence of *laches* [**la**chiz] may be used where unreasonable delay in bringing an action in equity has caused prejudice to the defendant, even where the applicable limitations period has not yet run.

limner A painter of portraits 'in little', ie in miniature. Nicholas Hilliard's treatise *The Art of Limning* (c.1600) describes the highly specialized techniques required by the limner, following Holbein's approach.

limnology The scientific study of freshwater lakes and ponds, including their equatic ecology, biology, chemistry, and physical characteristics. **Palaeolimnology** is the study of lake sediments to infer past lake conditions.

Limoges [leemohzh], ancient **Augustoritum Lemovicensium**, later **Lemovic** 45°50N 1°15E, pop (2000e) 140 000. Ancient town and capital of Haute-Vienne department, C France; in R Vienne valley, 176 km/109 mi NE of Bordeaux; Gallic tribal capital, destroyed 5th-c; sacked by the English, 1370; road and rail junction; university (1808); meteorological observatory; rapid post-war expansion; famed for manufacture of enamels and porcelain since 18th-c; electrical fittings, shoes; uranium mined near Ambazac; Gothic Cathedral of St-Etienne (begun, 1273); Church of St-Pierre-du-Queyroix (13th-c belfry), Church of St-Michel-des-Lions (14th–16th-c).

limonite [liymoniyt] A general name for a rock rich in hydrous iron oxides, formed by the tropical weathering of iron ore. It is formed in bogs (*bog ore* or *brown ore*).

Limousin or **Limosin, Léonard** [limoozĩ] (c.1505–77) Painter in enamel, born in Limoges, C France. From one of the most famous families of enamellers working in Limoges, he was the most accomplished. He became court painter to Francis I from 1930, and was appointed head of the royal factory at Limoges. He was also well known for his work in oils.

limpet A primitive snail with a simple, flattened, conical shell; lives attached to rocks by its muscular foot; found in the intertidal zone or shallow seas; typically feeds at night, grazing algae off rocks using a band of teeth (*radula*). (Class: Gastropoda. Order: Archaeogastropoda.)

Limpopo *Northern Province*

Limpopo, River [limpohpoh], also **Crocodile River** River in South Africa, Botswana, Zimbabwe, and Mozambique, SE Africa; length c.1600 km/1000 mi; rises in the S Transvaal, N of Johannesburg; follows the Botswana–Transvaal and Transvaal–Zimbabwe borders; enters Mozambique at Pafuri, and flows into the Indian Ocean 130 km/80 mi NE of Maputo; Vasco da Gama named it the Rio do Espiritu Santo in 1497.

linac *linear accelerator*

Linacre, Thomas (c.1460–1524) Physician and scholar, born in Canterbury, Kent, SE England, UK. He studied at Oxford, was elected fellow of All Souls in 1484, and studied to be a physician at Padua. One of the earliest champions of the 'new learning', he taught Greek to Erasmus and Sir Thomas More. About 1500 Henry VII made him tutor to Prince Arthur. As king's physician to Henry VII and Henry VIII, he practised in London. In 1518 he founded the Royal College of Physicians, becoming its first president, and took Catholic orders in 1520.

Lin Biao or **Lin Piao** [lin byow] (1907–71) Chinese military leader, born in Huang-kang, EC China. He trained at Whampoa military academy in 1926, joined the Communists, and became a marshal of the Red Army. He commanded the First Army Corps on the Long March (1934–5), and led the Red Army in Manchuria during the civil war. He was minister of defence from 1959, and in 1968 replaced the disgraced Liu Shaoqi as heir apparent to Mao Zedong. He was one of the promoters of the Cultural Revolution of 1966, and appears to have been a patron of extreme left-wing factions. In 1971, after a political struggle, he was killed in a plane crash in Mongolia, apparently in the course of an attempt to seek refuge in the USSR.

Lincoln (UK) [**ling**kn] 53°14N 0°33W, pop (2001e) 85 600. County town of Lincolnshire, EC England, UK; on the R Witham, 230 km/143 mi N of London and 64 km/40 mi from the North Sea; an important centre of the wool trade in the Middle Ages; railway; pharmaceuticals, vehicles, radios, engineering; parts of 3rd-c Roman wall remain; Lincoln Castle; cathedral (1073), including Wren Library (contains an original Magna Carta manuscript); cycle of mystery plays (Jun–Jul); football league team, Lincoln City (Imps).

Lincoln (USA) [**ling**kn], formerly **Lancaster** (to 1867) 40°49N 96°41W, pop (2000e) 225 600. Capital of state in Lancaster Co, SE Nebraska, USA; state capital in 1867, when it was renamed after President Lincoln; railway; two universities (1867, 1887); trade in grain and livestock; planetarium, art gallery, sculpture garden.

Lincoln, Abraham (1809–65) US statesman and 16th president (1861–5), born in a log cabin to pioneer farmers near Hodgenville, Kentucky, USA. Elected to the Illinois legislature in 1834, he became a lawyer in 1836. A decade later, he was elected to a single term in Congress, where he spoke against the extension of slavery, became a Republican in 1856, and in 1860 was elected president on a platform of hostility to slavery's expansion. When the Civil War began (1861), he defined the issue in terms of national integrity, not anti-slavery, a theme he restated in the Gettysburg Address of 1863. Nonetheless, the same year he proclaimed freedom for all slaves in areas of rebellion. He was re-elected in 1864, and after the final Northern victory he intended to reunite the former warring parties in a manner that provided some civil rights for freed slaves; but on 14 April 1865 he was shot at Ford's Theater, Washington, DC, by a Southern actor, John Wilkes Booth, and died next morning. He is remembered for his considerable political skills, and his self-education and broad vision have come to be a symbol of American democracy.

Lincoln Center for the Performing Arts A group of theatres, recital halls, etc erected to the W of Broadway, New York City, USA. The complex, constructed chiefly in the 1960s, principally comprises the New York State Theater, Avery Fisher Hall, the Metropolitan Opera House, Vivian Beaumont Theater, Alice Tully Hall, the Juilliard School for the Performing Arts, and the Library and Museum of the Performing Arts.

Lincoln Memorial A monument in Washington, District of Columbia, USA, dedicated in 1922 to President Abraham Lincoln. The building, designed on the plan of a Greek temple by Henry Bacon (1866–1924), houses the statue of Lincoln (6 m/19 ft high) by Daniel Chester French (1850–1931).

Lincolnshire [lingknsheer] pop (2001e) 646 600; area 5915 sq km/2284 sq mi. Flat agricultural county in EC England, UK; county town, Lincoln; chief towns include Grantham, Gainsborough, Spalding; North Lincolnshire and North East Lincolnshire unitary authorities from 1996; bounded E by the North Sea; drained by the Welland, Witham, and Trent Rivers; Fens drained in 17th-c; intensive farming, horticulture, tourism.

Lincoln's Inn *Inns of Court*

Lind, James (1716–94) Physician, born in Edinburgh, EC Scotland, UK. He served in the navy as a surgeon's mate, qualified in medicine at Edinburgh, and became physician at the Haslar naval hospital at Gosport. He is remembered for his research into cases of scurvy aboard ship; and his recommendation to the Royal Navy to issue citrus fruits and juices to sailors eradicated the disease. He also instigated delousing procedures, hospital ships, and distillation of seawater for drinking.

Lind, Jenny, originally **Johanna Maria Lind**, known as **the Swedish Nightingale** (1820–87) Soprano, born in Stockholm, Sweden. She trained in Stockholm and Paris, made her debut in Stockholm in 1838, and attained great popularity everywhere. After 1856 she lived in England, and became professor of singing at the Royal College of Music (1883–6).

Lindbergh, Charles A(ugustus) [lindberg] (1902–74) Aviator, born in Detroit, Michigan, USA. He worked as an airmail pilot on the St Louis–Chicago run, then in 1927 made the first non-stop solo transatlantic flight, from New York City to Paris, in the monoplane *Spirit of St Louis*. His book of the same name won the Pulitzer Prize in 1954. In 1932 his infant son was kidnapped and murdered, a sensational crime for which **Bruno Richard Hauptmann** was executed (1936), and the Lindberghs retreated to Europe. He later became an aeronautics consultant. His grandson, Erik Lindbergh, successfully duplicated the 1927 Atlantic solo flight in 2002.

Lindemann, Frederick Alexander *Cherwell, Viscount*

linden *lime* (botany)

Lindgren, Astrid (1907–2002) Children's novelist, born in Vimmerby, SE Sweden. She established her reputation with *Pippi Långstrump* (1945, Pippi Longstocking), and followed this with a succession of other popular characters, later turning to folklore with such titles as *Bröderna Lejonhjärta* (1973, The Brothers Lionheart).

Lindisfarne [lindisfah(r)n] area 10 sq km/3¾ sq mi. An island off the NE coast of England, UK, 15 km/9 mi SE of Berwick-upon-Tweed, renowned for its monastery founded from Iona by St Aidan in AD 634, burnt by Danish Vikings in 793, and ultimately abandoned c.875; also known as **Holy Island**. It was a notable centre of early English Christianity and learning, its most famous bishop being the ascetic St Cuthbert. The Lindisfarne Gospels were illuminated here, probably in the 690s, by Eadfrith (Bishop, 698–721). The island is accessible from the mainland at low water by a causeway.

Lindow Man *bog burials*

Lindrum, Walter (1898–1960) Billiards player, born in Kalgoorlie, Western Australia. Regarded as the world's greatest billiards player, he set the current world record break of 4317 while playing Joe Davis in 1932, at Thurston's Hall, London. He competed in only two world championships (1933–4), and won both. He retired from competitive play in 1950.

Lindsay, Norman (1879–1969) Artist, born in Victoria, SE Australia. One of 10 children, three of his brothers and a sister also became artists. In 1895 he moved to Melbourne to work on a local newspaper with his brother Lionel, and in 1901 they joined the weekly Sydney *Bulletin*, where Norman was chief cartoonist for many years. In 1912 he settled in Springwood in the Blue Mountains region of New South Wales, where he spent most of the rest of his life. His home there is now a gallery and museum housing much of his work. A prolific artist, he produced vigorous drawings, etchings, oil paintings, and watercolours. He also wrote poems, novels, and the children's book *The Magic Pudding* (1918), now regarded as an Australian classic.

lineage *descent*

Linear A A system of writing found throughout Minoan Crete. It was used mainly by administrators in the compilation of inventories.

linear accelerator A particle accelerator comprising a straight vacuum tube along which charged particles are accelerated through a sequence of cylindrical electrodes; also called **linac**. At the Stanford Linear Accelerator Center in the USA is a linear accelerator approximately 3 km/2 mi long.

Linear B A system of writing found on clay tablets at Mycenaean palace sites. Deciphered in the 1950s by Michael Ventris, it is (unlike Linear A) an early form of Greek.

line-engraving A method of intaglio printing, the metal plate being cut with a burin. The technique originated in 15th-c Germany, and the greatest early master was Martin Schongauer (1450–91).

Line Islands pop (2000e) 5900. Coral island group of Kiribati, C and S Pacific Ocean; largest **N Line Is** are Kiritimati (Christmas I) (390 sq km/150 sq mi), Fanning I (34 sq km/13 sq mi), and Washington I (9·6 sq km/3·7 sq mi), inhabited by coconut plantation workers; **S Line Is**, worked for guano in the past, now uninhabited; three of the N group are US territories.

Lineker, Gary (Winston) [lineker] (1960–) Footballer, journalist, and broadcaster, born in Leicester, Leicestershire, C England, UK. He played for Leicester City (1978–85), Everton (1985–6), FC Barcelona (1986–9), Tottenham Hotspur (1982–92), and Grampus 8, Nagoya, Japan (1993–4). He made his England debut in 1984 (captain 1990–2), playing in the 1986 and 1990 World Cups, and also in two European Championships (1988, 1992), and gaining 80 caps. He was voted the Professional Footballers' Association Player of the Year (1986) and the Football Writers' Association Player of the Year (1986, 1992). Retiring in 1994, he became a regular presenter of sports programmes for the BBC, including television's *Match of the Day* (from 1999), and was a team captain (1995–2003) of the sports quiz show, *They Think It's All Over*. He is also a columnist for *The Observer* (1995–), and a familiar figure on television commercials.

linen Yarn and fabrics made from flax fibres, probably the earliest textile made from plants. Linen was made in ancient Egypt, and the Romans brought flax-growing to Britain. Linen fabrics and yarns are fine, strong, and lustrous, and still fashionable, though less widely used today because of their poor easy-care properties.

line printer A type of printer, usually associated with larger computer systems, which prints a complete line of information at a time. It is very fast, especially when compared with printers that print one character at a time. Their principal advantage is speed, and they tend to be economic only in commercial situations where there is a heavy printing load.

ling (botany) *heather*

ling (zoology) Slender-bodied fish (*Molva molva*) of the cod family, abundant in offshore waters of the NE Atlantic from Norway to the Bay of Biscay at depths of 300–400 m/1000–1300 ft; length up to 2 m/6½ ft; mottled brownish-green on back; fished commercially, mainly on lines. (Family: Gadidae.)

lingam [linggam] The principal symbolic representation of the Hindu deity Shiva, a phallic-shaped emblem. The female equivalent is the **yoni**, the shaped image of the female genitalia.

lingua franca [linggwa frangka] An auxiliary language used for routine and often restricted purposes by people who speak different native languages. English and French are frequently used for this purpose in many parts of the world. German is an important lingua franca in E Europe, and Swahili in E Africa. English is an occupational lingua franca in several domains, such as in international air traffic control.

linguistic philosophy A movement within 20th-c English-language analytic philosophy, associated particularly with the later work of Wittgenstein and with Ryle and Austin. The main methodological assumption is that many traditional philosophical problems arise from a misuse of language. The philosopher's task is to solve, or dissolve, these problems by revealing the distinctions available in ordinary language.

linguistics The scientific study of language. The discipline is concerned with such matters as providing systematic descriptions of languages, investigating the properties of language structures as communicative systems, exploring the possibility that there are universals of language structure, and accounting for the historical development of linguistic systems. **Applied linguistics** is the application of linguistics to the study of such language-based fields as foreign language teaching and learning, speech pathology, translation, and dictionary writing. The 19th-c saw the flowering of comparative philology, which studied the historical development of language families. Modern linguistics is generally said to have begun with the posthumous publication of Ferdinand de Saussure's *Cours de Linguistique Générale* (1916, Course in General Linguistics), which introduced the essential distinction between *diachronic* (historical) linguistics, and *synchronic* (descriptive) linguistics, and laid the foundation for the era of **structural linguistics**, which dominated the first half of the 20th-c. Structuralists (notably US linguist Leonard Bloomfield (1887–1949)) stressed the uniqueness of language systems, and the need to base structural descriptions on observed evidence alone. The major development in the second half of the 20th-c was the emergence of generative grammar, originally proposed by linguist Noam Chomsky in *Syntactic Structures* (1957), and since elaborated in a wide range of works. Since the 1960s, several developments of and alternatives to Chomsky's original model have been proposed. Also, many points of contact between linguistics and other academic areas have been explored, leading to the growth of such 'hybrid' fields as *sociolinguistics* and *psycholinguistics*.

linkage Genes carried sufficiently close together on a chromosome as to tend to be transmitted together in inheritance. Several such genes are known as a **linkage group**.

Linklater, Eric (Robert Russell) (1899–1974) Novelist, born in Dounby, Orkney Is, NE Scotland, UK. He studied medicine and English at Aberdeen, served in World War 1, then became a journalist in Mumbai (1925–7), and an English lecturer at Aberdeen. While in the USA (1928–30) he wrote *Poet's Pub* (1929), the first of a series of satirical novels which include *Juan in America* (1931) and *Private Angelo* (1946). Later books include *A Year of Space* (1953) and *Fanfare for a Tin Hat* (1970), which are autobiographical.

Linnaeus, Carolus [linayus], Swed **Carl von Linné** (1707–78) Botanist, born in Råshult, SE Sweden. He studied at Lund and Uppsala, where in 1730 he was appointed a botany assistant. He travelled widely on botanical exploration, and is the founder of modern taxonomic botany. His *Systema naturae fundamenta botanica* (1735), *Genera plantarum* (1737), and *Species plantarum* (1753), expound his influential system of classification, based on plant sex organs, and in which names consist of generic and specific elements, with plants grouped hierarchically into genera, classes, and orders. He practised as a physician in Stockholm, and in 1742 became professor of botany at Uppsala. He was ennobled in 1757.

linnet Any of three species of finch of the genus *Carduelis*, especially the **Eurasian linnet** (*Carduelis cannabina*); native to Europe, N Africa, and W Asia; inhabits open country; eats seeds and insects. (Family: Fringillidae.)

linoleic acid *arachidonic acid*

Linotype *typesetting*

linsang [linsang] A carnivorous mammal of family Viverridae; inhabits forest and builds nest from leaves; three species: the SE Asian **Oriental linsang**, which includes the **banded linsang** (*Prionodon linsang*) and the **spotted linsang** (*Prionodon pardicolor*); and the **African linsang** or *oyan* (*Poiana richardsoni*).

Linz [lints] 48°18N 14°18E, pop (2000e) 211 000. Industrial town and capital of Oberösterreich, N Austria; situated on both banks of the R Danube, centre of a rich agricultural region; extensive port installations; University of Social and Economic Sciences (1966); third largest city in Austria; iron and steel, fertilizers, tobacco, chemicals, pharmaceuticals; many historical buildings, including early 16th-c castle, Martinskirche (oldest preserved church in Austria), Landhaus (former seat of the state assembly); museums, art galleries, theatres, opera house; International Bruckner Festival (Sep–Oct).

lion A member of the cat family (*Panthera leo*), native to Africa and NW India (in prehistoric times was almost worldwide); brown; male with mane of long dark hair; inhabits grassland and open woodland; often territorial; lives in 'prides' averaging 15 individuals; the only cat that hunts in groups; eats mainly large grazing mammals.

Lions Clubs, International Association of *service club*

lipase [lipayz] An enzyme that stimulates the breakdown of triglycerides (esters of fatty acids) into fatty acids and glycerol; for example, pancreatic lipase secreted into the duodenum promotes the breakdown of dietary fats.

Lipchitz, Jacques [lipshitz], originally **Chaim Jacob Lipchitz** (1891–1973) Sculptor, born in Druskininkai, S Lithuania. He studied engineering, then moved to Paris (1909–11), where he started producing Cubist sculpture in 1914. In the 1920s he experimented with abstract forms he called 'transparent sculptures'. Later he developed a more dynamic style which he applied with telling effect to bronze figure and animal compositions. He emigrated to the USA in 1941, by which time he had established an international reputation, and lived in Italy from 1963.

Lipizzaner [lipitsahner] A breed of horse, developed at Lipizza in Austria, now in Slovenia, in the 16th-c from the Andalusian horse; height, 15–16 hands/1·5–1·6 m/5 ft–5 ft 4 in; grey or pale brown; famous as the *white horses of Vienna*, where the stallions are used at the Spanish Riding School.

Li Po [lee poh], also found as **Li Bo** and **Li T'ai Po** (c.700–762) Poet, born in Szechwan Province, China. Possibly of Turkish origin, he grew up in Sichuan, later moving to the Tang court of Xuanzong where he led a dissipated life. He later joined a wandering band calling themselves 'The Eight Immortals of the Wine Cup'. Regarded as the greatest poet of China, he wrote over 1000 imaginative and rhapsodic free-style poems about wine, women, and nature. It is believed that he was drowned while trying to pluck the Moon from a lake.

lipogram [lipohgram] A text composed with the intentional omission of a particular letter of the alphabet throughout. The 5th-c BC Greek poet Tryphiodorus wrote an epic of 24 books, each omitting a different letter of the Greek alphabet.

Lippershey, Hans or **Jan** [lipers-hay], also spelled **Lippersheim** (c.1570–1619) Dutch optician, born in Wesel, W Germany. He is one of several spectacle-makers credited with the discovery that the combination of a convex and a concave lens can make distant objects appear nearer. He is believed to be the inventor of the telescope (1608), but this is unproven. Certainly, in 1608 he offered the government of The Netherlands what we would now call a refracting telescope.

Lippi, Filippino [lipee] (c.1458–1504) Painter, born in Florence, NC Italy. He was the son of Fra Filippo Lippi, and was apprenticed to Botticelli. He completed the frescoes in the Brancacci Chapel, Florence, left unfinished by Masaccio c.1484. Other celebrated series of frescoes were painted by him between 1487 and 1502, the one in the Caraffa Chapel, S Maria sopra Minerva, Rome, being his most influential. 'The Vision of St Bernard' (c.1480–6) is his best-known picture.

Lippi, Fra Filippo [lipee], known as **Lippo** (c.1406–69) Religious painter, born in Florence, NC Italy. In 1424 he became a pupil of Masaccio, who was painting the frescoes in the Brancacci Chapel where Lippi had taken his monastic vows. The style of his master can be seen in his early work, such as in the frescoes, 'The Relaxation of the Carmelite Rule' (c.1432). His greatest work, on the choir walls of Prato Cathedral, was begun in 1452. Between 1452 and 1464 he abducted a nun, **Lucrezia Buti**, and was released from his vows by Pope Pius II in order to marry her. She was the model for many of his fine Madonnas, and the mother of his son, Filippino Lippi. His later works, deeply religious, include the series of 'Nativities'.

Lippmann, Walter (1889–1974) Journalist, born in New York City, USA. He studied at Harvard, was on the editorial staff of the *New York World* until 1931, then became a special writer for the New York *Herald Tribune*. His daily columns became internationally famous, and he won many awards, including the Pulitzer Prize for International Reporting (1962). Among his best-known books is *The Cold War* (1947).

lip reading The act of observing the movements of a speaker's mouth in order to understand what is being said. It is a skill practised mostly by the deaf and hard-of-hearing, but is also used to some degree by those working in factories and other environments where noise is a problem.

liqueur A spirit, usually distilled from grain, mixed with syrup, and with the addition of fruits, herbs, or spices to infuse a strong aroma and taste. Liqueurs have a high alcohol content, and are usually drunk in small quantities after a meal. Examples include Cointreau, Bénédictine, and Chartreuse (France), Cherry Heering (Denmark), Tia Maria (Jamaica), and Drambuie (Scotland).

liquid A dense form of matter which is able to flow but unable to transmit twisting forces; density typically a few per cent less than the corresponding solid. It is virtually incompressible. The atoms are constantly changing position in a random way; there is no ordering of atoms, unlike many solids, except for a slight degree of short-range order. Highly viscous liquids are similar in structure to amorphous solids.

liquidation *bankruptcy*

liquid crystals Organic materials, crystalline in the solid state, which form a partially ordered state (the **liquid crystal state**) upon melting, and become true liquids only after the temperature is raised further. Liquid crystals have directional properties, and so are birefringent. Their optical transparency can be reduced by applying electric fields, a property extensively exploited in displays for watches, calculators, and other electronic devices.

liquidity In business and banking, actual money, or assets that are easily convertible into money. Firms need to be sufficiently liquid to be able to pay off debts, to be able to buy assets when required, and to be covered in case of emergencies. **Liquid assets** are cash, short-term investments, and debtors (ie amounts due from customers). The notion is used in economics in relation to the study of money supply in the economy.

liquidity preference A concept introduced by J M Keynes to explain the demand for money, referring to the percentage of assets held in the form of cash or 'near money' by an individual, bank, or company. The intention is to avoid tying up money in fixed assets, or long-term investments which may not be easily realizable, or which may lose value (such as shares in a company).

liquorice or **licorice** A perennial growing to 1 m/3¾ ft (*Glycyrrhiza glabra*), native to SE Europe and W Asia; creeping rhizomes; leaves pinnate with 9–17 elliptical-oblong leaflets; pea-flowers whitish-violet, in long-stalked, spike-like inflorescences. Often cultivated, its roots are a source of liquorice, used medicinally and as a confectionery ingredient. (Family: Leguminosae.)

Lisbon, Port **Lisboa**, ancient **Olisipo** or **Felicitas Julia** 38°42N 9°10W, pop (2000e) 672 000. Seaport and capital of Portugal, on N bank of R Tagus; largest city in Portugal; settlement in Roman Empire; occupied by Moors, 8th-c; Portuguese capital, 1256; devastated by earthquake, 1755; Chiado shopping district of old town destroyed by fire, 1988; archbishopric; airport; railway; university (1911); steel, textiles, chemicals, shipbuilding, fishing, banking; 16th-c Tower of Belém and Jerônimos Monastery, a world heritage site; cathedral (1150), Church of São Roque, São Jorge Castle, National Museum of Art, botanical garden.

Lisdoonvarna [lishdoon**vah(r)**na] 53°02N 9°17W, pop (2000e) 850. Spa town 37 km/23 mi NW of Ennis, Clare county, Munster, W Ireland; leading sulphur-spring health centre; Lisdoonvarna fair (Oct), with its famous mating game when shy bachelors go in search of a wife; 3-day folk festival (Jul).

LISP [lisp] Acronym for **LISt Processing**, a high-level computer programming language designed for use with non-numeric data. It differs radically from traditional programming languages, and is widely used in artificial intelligence applications.

Lissitsky, El(iezer) [li**sit**skee], also spelled **Lissitzky** (1890–1941) Painter and designer, born in Smolensk, W Russia. He trained in engineering and architecture at Darmstadt, Germany. In 1919 Chagall appointed him professor of architecture and graphic art at the art school in Vitebsk, where he came under the influence of his colleague, Kasimir Malevich. He produced a series of abstract works, called 'Proun' (1919), in which he combined flat rectilinear forms and dramatic architectonic elements.

Lister, Joseph Jackson (1786–1869) Wine merchant and amateur microscopist, born in London, UK. A wine merchant with an interest in optics, he developed a method of building lens systems to greatly reduce chromatic and spherical aberrations. In 1826 **James Smith** (d.1870) built a much improved microscope to Lister's design, and this was used a year later to produce the first competent article on histology. Lister was elected a fellow of the Royal Society in 1832.

Lister (of Lyme Regis), Joseph Lister, Baron (1827–1912) Surgeon, born in Upton, Essex, SE England, UK, the son of Joseph Jackson Lister. He studied at London, and became professor of surgery at Glasgow (1859), Edinburgh (1869), and London (1877). His great work was the introduction (1865) of the use of antiseptic conditions during surgery, which greatly reduced surgical mortality. He was made a baronet in 1883, and a baron in 1897.

Listeria [lis**teer**ia] A genus of typically rod-shaped bacteria, of uncertain taxonomic position; typically motile by means of flagella and exhibiting a tumbling motion. It grows best in the presence of small quantities of oxygen; some strains cause food poisoning.

Liszt, Franz (1811–86) Composer and pianist, born in Raiding, Hungary. He studied and played at Vienna and Paris, touring widely in Europe as a virtuoso pianist. From 1835 to 1839 he lived with the Comtesse d'Agoult, by whom he had three children. He gave concerts throughout Europe, and in 1847 met Princess Carolyne zu Sayn-Wittgenstein with whom he lived until his death. In 1848 he went to Weimar, where he directed the opera and concerts, composed, and taught. His works include 12 symphonic poems, Masses, two symphonies, and a large number of piano pieces. In 1865 he received minor orders in the Catholic Church, and was known as Abbé.

Li Ta-chao *Li Dazhao*

litany A form of prayer used in public or private worship. Supplications or invocations are made by the priest or minister, to which the congregation replies with a fixed formula.

litchi, litchee, leechee, or **lychee** [**ly**chee] An evergreen tree (*Litchi chinensis*) native to China; leaves pinnate; flowers white, starry; edible fruit 2·5–4 cm/1–1½ in long, ovoid with thin, warty, horny, red-brown rind enclosing an ivory, fleshy aril and a single glossy brown seed surrounded by sweet, white pulp. The edible aril tastes like both grapes and melon. (Family: Sapindaceae.)

literacy The ability to read and write in a language. Discussion of the problem of **illiteracy**, both within a country and on a world scale, is complicated by the difficulty of measuring the extent of the problem in individuals. The notion of **functional literacy** was introduced in the 1940s, in an attempt to identify minimal levels of reading/writing efficiency in a society, such as being able to read road signs, shop labels, and newspapers, and to write one's name; but defining even minimal levels is difficult, especially today, with increasing demands being made on people to be literate in a wider range of contexts. Current world estimates suggest that c.900 million adults are illiterate to a greater or lesser extent. In the UK, figures were being cited in the 1980s of c.2 million illiterate people, or 3·5% of the population; in the USA, estimates have varied between 10% and 20%. In some Third World countries, illiteracy may be as high as 80%. National literacy campaigns in several countries have raised public awareness, and standards are slowly rising.

literary agent A person who sells the various rights in a book to publishers and other potential purchasers (eg film companies) on behalf of the author, and represents the author in negotiations. The agent retains a percentage of the author's earnings as commission. Agents may specialize in certain types of book or publisher.

literary criticism The explication and evaluation of works of literature, a task as old as literature itself. Criticism has trad-

Lithuania

□ International Airport

official name **Republic of Lithuania**, Lithuanian **Lietuvos Respublika**

Local name Lietuva

Timezone GMT +2

Area 65 200 km²/25 167 sq mi

Population total(2002e) 3 473 000

Status Republic

Date of independence 1991

Capital Vilnius

Language Lithuanian (official)

Ethnic groups Lithuanian (80%), Russian (9%), Polish (7%), Belorussian (2%)

Religions Roman Catholic, small minority of Evangelical Lutherans and Evangelical Reformists

Physical features Glaciated plains cover much of the area; central lowlands with gentle hills in W and higher terrain in SE; highest point, Jouzapine in the Asmenos Hills, 294 m/964 ft; 25% forested; some 3000 small lakes mostly in E and SE; complex sandy dunes on Kursiu Marios lagoon; chief river, the Nemunas.

Climate Continental climate, affected by maritime weather of W Europe and continental E; Baltic Sea influences a narrow coastal zone; average annual temperatures -5°C (Jan), 16°C (Jul); average annual rainfall 630 mm/25 in.

Currency 1 Litas (Lt) = 100 centas

Economy Electrical engineering, computer hardware, instruments, machine tools, ship building; synthetic fibres, fertilizers, plastics, food processing, oil refining; cattle, pigs, poultry, grain, potatoes, vegetables.

GDP (2002e) $30·08 bn, per capita $8400

Human Development Index (2002) 0·808

History United with Poland, 1385–1795; intensive russification led to revolts in 1905 and 1917; occupied by Germany in both World Wars; proclaimed a republic, 1918; annexed by the USSR, 1940; growth of nationalist movement in the late 1980s; declared independence in 1990, but not recognized until 1991; governed by a President, Prime Minister and Supreme Council; impeachment of President Paksas, 2004.

Head of State
1991–3 Vytautas Landsbergis
1993–8 Algirdas Brazauskas
1998–2003 Valdas Adamkus
2003–4 Rolandas Paksas
2004 Arturas Paulauskas *Acting*

Head of Government
1992–3 Bronislovas Lubys
1993–6 Adolfas Šleževičius
1996 Gediminas Vagnorius
1999 Irena Degutiene *Acting*
1999 Rolandas Paksas
1999 Irena Degutienë *Acting*
1999–2000 Andrius Kubilius
2000–1 Rolandas Paksas
2001 Eugenijus Gentvilas *Acting*
2001– Algirdas-Mykolas Brazauskas

itionally proposed three main questions concerning (1) the truth, (2) the function, and (3) the formal qualities of literature. Addressed by Plato and Aristotle, these set the parameters until Neoclassical times. With the Romantic movement came a new interest in the genesis of a work of literature, subsequently reinforced by Symbolism and psychoanalysis and (from different directions) by Marxist and sociological analysis. The influence of 20th-c linguistics and structuralism gave new impetus to the formal approach, emphasizing the role of the reader in producing meaning within a more broadly defined cultural discourse.

literary prizes Annual awards, accompanied usually by money prizes, given in many countries, including France, the UK, and USA. Best known are the Nobel Prize for Literature (international), the Booker Prize (UK, fiction), the Prix Goncourt (France), the Pulitzer Prize (USA), and the Whitbread Literary Awards (UK, five categories).

literature The collective writings proper to any language or nation. World literature includes all these in translation. The term *literature* is a site of ideological conflict; it may be taken to refer exclusively to those canonical works in the established genres which 'have pleased many and pleased long' (Dr Johnson), or inclusively to the sum total of writings which are read, even the most ephemeral, such as comics and newspapers. Essays, letters, memoirs, historical, biographical and travel writings, occasional verse, etc, will be considered 'literature' depending on the point of view. Fundamental questions are addressed by Jean-Paul Sartre in *What is Literature?* (1948), and by contemporary cultural critics. The term is also used to refer to the body of secondary writings on a given subject, as in 'medical literature', 'ornithological literature'.

litharge [lithah(r)j] Lead(II) oxide (PbO); a bright yellow pigment used in paints.

lithium Li, element 3, melting point 181°C. The lightest of the alkali metals; not common, but found widely in several minerals. These are converted to the chloride (LiCl), from which the element is obtained by electrolysis. Its compounds are used in organic synthesis: lithium aluminium hydride ($LiAlH_4$) is a powerful reducing agent. Its salts, such as Li_2CO_3, have found application as anti-depressants in psychiatry.

lithography A method of printing, invented by Aloys Senefelder in 1796, based on the principle that grease (ie ink) and water do not mix. A flat surface is treated so that the image area alone will attract ink. Ink and water are then applied to the surface; ink adheres to the image area and water to the non-image area. Paper is then brought into contact with the printing surface. In **offset lithography**, the modern form of this printing method, the image to be printed is created photographically and the printing plate is wrapped round a cylinder. When the plate cylinder has been inked and dampened, the image is transferred ('offset') to a rubber 'blanket' cylinder and then transferred again to the printing substrate (normally paper, but also metal and plastic).

lithosphere Part of the Earth, consisting of the crust and the solid outermost layer of the upper mantle, extending to a depth of around 100 km/60 mi.

lithotripsy *urinary stones*

Lithuania *p.905*

Lithuanian *Baltic languages*

litmus A complex vegetable dye traditionally used as a pH indicator. It is red in acid solutions and blue in alkaline ones.

litre Unit of volume; symbol *l*; formerly defined as the volume occupied by a mass of 1 kilogram of water at its maximum density and at standard pressure; according to this definition, 1 litre is approximately equal to 1·000028 cubic decimetres. This definition was abrogated in 1964, and the litre is no longer considered to be a precisely defined unit of volume. Officially the term may be used as a name for the cubic decimetre, but the litre should not be used for high accuracy measurements. The precise unit of volume is the cubic metre, approximately 1000 litres.

Little Bighorn, Battle of the, also known as **Custer's Last Stand** (25 Jun 1876) The engagement in Montana between US cavalry, under Lieutenant-Colonel Custer, and the Sioux and Cheyenne, under Sitting Bull and Crazy Horse. The Indians destroyed Custer's force. Issues behind the battle included Custer's bloody dawn attack on a Cheyenne village at the Washita in 1868, and his sponsorship in 1875 of white invasion of the Black Hills, sacred to the Sioux.

little boatman / captain / corporal *schipperke*

little owl A typical owl of genus *Athene* (2 species), especially the **little owl** (*Athene noctua*), native to C and W Asia, Europe, and Africa, and introduced in New Zealand and the UK; inhabits open country, forest, and towns; eats insects, small mammals, occasionally birds or carrion. The **Rodriguez little owl** (*Athene murivora*) is extinct. (Family: Strigidae.)

Little Richard, popular name of **Richard Wayne Penniman** (1932–) Rock-and-roll singer and pianist, born in Macon, Georgia, USA. Raised as a Seventh-Day Adventist, he sang in church choirs throughout his childhood. Leaving home at 14, he started singing professionally, and became well known on the southern vaudeville circuit. 'Tutti Frutti' (1955) brought him international popularity. Most of his recordings from 1958 to 1964 were of Gospel songs, but he later made a comeback with his album *The Rill Thing* (1970).

Little Rock 34°45N 92°16W, pop (2000e) 183 100. Capital of state in Pulaski Co, C Arkansas, USA; largest city in the state, and a port on the Arkansas R; settled, 1821; railway; university; processing of fish, beef, poultry, bauxite, timber; in 1957 Federal troops were sent to the city to enforce a 1954 US Supreme Court ruling against segregation in schools; Territorial Restoration, old statehouse; Riverfest (May).

Littlewood, (Maudie) Joan (1914–2002) Theatre director, born in London, UK. She trained at the Royal Academy of Dramatic Art, London, and with Ewan MacColl (1915–89) founded in Manchester the Theatre of Action (1934) and the Theatre Union (1936). Out of this pioneering work in left-wing, popular theatre was formed the Theatre Workshop in 1945. She directed the first British production for Brecht's *Mother Courage* in Barnstaple in 1955, in which she played the title role, and after settling at the Theatre Royal, Stratford East, her productions included *The Hostage* (1958) and *Oh! What a Lovely War* (1963). She received a Lifetime Achievement Award from the Directors' Guild in 1995.

littoral zone *benthic environments*

liturgical movement A movement to reform the worship of the Christian Church by promoting more active participation by laity in the liturgy. Beginning in 19th-c France in the Roman Catholic Church, it became influential and effective in the mid-20th-c in other Churches, often through the World Council of Churches and the ecumenical movement.

liturgy (Gr *leitourgia*, 'duty, service') The formal corporate worship of God by a Church. It includes words, music, actions, and symbolic aids, and in Christian form is derived from Jewish ritual. Liturgies exist in a wide variety of prescribed forms, reflecting the needs and attitudes of different religious communities.

Litvinov, Maxim (Maximovich) [litveenof] (1876–1951) Russian politician and diplomat, born in Bialystok, NE Poland. He joined the Russian Social Democratic Party (1898), was exiled to Siberia (1903), but escaped. At the Revolution he was appointed Bolshevik ambassador in London (1917–8). He became deputy people's commissar for foreign affairs in 1921, then commissar (1930–9), achieving US recognition of Soviet Russia (1934). He was dismissed in 1939, but reinstated after the German invasion of Russia, and became ambassador to the USA (1941–3) and vice-minister of foreign affairs (1943–6).

Liupanshui or **Liu-p'an-shui** [liopahnshway] 25°45N 104°40E, pop (2000e) 2 056 000, administrative region 2 566 000. City in Guizhou province, S China; W of Guiyang; railway.

Liu Shaoqi [lyoo showchee], also spelled **Liu Shao-ch'i** (1898–1969) Chinese political leader, born in Ningxiang, Hunan, SEC China. He studied at Changsa and Shanghai, went to Moscow to study, joined the Chinese Communist Party, and became a party labour organizer in Shanghai. He was elected to the Politburo in 1934, joined Mao Zedong as the chief Party theorist on questions of organization (1939), became secretary-general of the Party (1943), vice-chairman (1949), and chairman of the People's Republic of China in 1958. During the Cultural Revolution (1966–9) he was denounced, and banished to Hunan province. He reportedly died in detention, but was posthumously rehabilitated in 1980.

Live Aid *Geldof, Bob*

Lively, Penelope (Margaret), *née* **Low** (1933–) Novelist and children's author, born in Cairo, Egypt. She settled in England, UK and studied at Oxford. Her first books were for children, and include *The Ghost of Thomas Kempe* (1973), *A Stitch in Time* (1976), and *The Revenge of Samuel Stokes* (1981). Her adult novels include *Judgement Day* (1980), *Moon Tiger* (1987, Booker), *Cleopatra's Sister* (1993), *Spiderweb* (1999), and *The Photograph* (2002). In 1997 appeared a collection of short stories, *Beyond the Blue Mountains*.

liver In vertebrates, a large, unpaired gland with digestive functions, situated in the upper part of the right-hand side of the abdominal cavity under cover of the ribs, separated from the thoracic contents by the diaphragm. It is attached by the peritoneum to the abdominal wall and the stomach, and divided into four lobes. The liver performs many important functions. It secretes bile, which is emptied into the duodenum (via the common bile duct), and facilitates the digestion and absorption of fats. It deals with the newly absorbed products of digestion (eg the formation of glycogen or fats from monosaccharides, the release of glucose into the blood stream). It manufactures the anticoagulant heparin and other plasma proteins. It stores glycogen, fat, iron, copper, and the vitamins A, D, E, and K. It detoxifies harmful substances such as drugs and toxins, and consumes and destroys red blood cells. Medical problems affecting the liver include cirrhosis, infectious hepatitis, jaundice, and Reye's syndrome.

liver fluke A leaf-like, parasitic flatworm (*Fasciola hepatica*), with a mouth sucker on its cone-shaped front end; life-cycle complex, involving a snail as intermediate host in which asexual multiplication takes place; final host is a vertebrate, often sheep; can be a serious pest of domesticated animals. (Phylum: Platyhelminthes. Class: Trematoda.)

Liverpool 53°25N 2°55W, pop (2001e) 439 500. Seaport in Merseyside, NW England, UK; on the right bank of the R Mersey estuary, 5 km/3 mi from the Irish Sea and 312 km/194 mi NW of London; founded in the 10th-c, became a borough in 1207 and a city in 1880; port trade developed in the 16th–17th-c; importance enhanced in the 18th-c by the slave trade and the Lancashire cotton industry; major world trading centre and the UK's most important seaport for Atlantic trade; railway; container terminal (1972); linked to Birkenhead under the R Mersey by road and rail tunnels (1934, 1971); ferries to Belfast, Dublin, Isle of Man; John Lennon Airport; university (1903); Liverpool John Moores University (1992, formerly Liverpool Polytechnic); trade in petroleum, grain, ores, non-ferrous metals, sugar, wood, fruit, and cotton; Catholic cathedral, modern design by Frederick Gibberd on earlier classical foundation by Edward Lutyens (consecrated 1967); Anglican cathedral, designed by Giles Gilbert Scott (begun 1904, completed 1980); Royal Liver Building (landmark at Pier Head), St George's Hall, Albert Dock redevelopment, Maritime Museum, Tate in the North (1987), Walker Art Gallery, Merseyside Innovation Centre, Speke Hall; Royal Liverpool Philharmonic Orchestra; home of the Beatles (museum, 1984), and many other pop groups; football league teams, Liverpool (Reds) and Everton (Toffeemen); International Garden Festival held here in 1984; nominated European Capital of Culture for 2008; Grand National steeplechase at Aintree (Apr).

Liverpool, Robert Banks Jenkinson, 2nd Earl of (1770–1828) British prime minister (1812–27), born in London, UK. He studied at Oxford, entered parliament in 1790, and was a member of the India Board (1793–6), Master of the Royal Mint (1799–1801), foreign secretary (1801–4), home secretary (1804–6, 1807–9), and secretary for war and the colonies (1809–12). He succeeded his father as Earl of Liverpool in 1807. As premier, he oversaw the final years of the Napoleonic Wars and the War of 1812–14 with the USA. He resigned after a stroke early in 1827.

Liverpool poets A group of poets writing out of Liverpool after the success of the Beatles in the 1960s, when the city was referred to by Allen Ginsberg as 'the cultural centre of the Universe'. The best known are Adrian Henri (1932–2000), Roger McGough, and Brian Patten (1946–); selections are given in *The Mersey Sound* (1967). A 25th anniversary reading by these three was broadcast by the BBC in 1992.

liverwort A small, spore-bearing, non-vascular plant of the Class Hepaticae, closely related to mosses and hornworts. They are divided into two types, depending on their gametophytic form: **thalloid** liverworts have a flattened, often lobed or branched body (the *thallus*); **foliose** or leafy liverworts have slender, creeping stems with three rows of leaves, of which usually only two develop fully. They have single-celled, root-like rhizoids which anchor the plant to the ground, but do not absorb water. The sporophyte consists of a stalked, star-shaped capsule containing spores and sterile structures (*elaters*). When the spores are mature the stalk elongates, the capsule opens, and the elaters help disperse the spores. Liverworts also reproduce by means of *gemmae*, multicellular discs which are budded off and develop into new plants. Liverworts are found almost everywhere, but are very vulnerable to drying out, and thus restricted to damp, shady habitats.

livery companies In the UK, charitable and professional associations in the City of London, which have developed from the City Craft Guilds of the Middle Ages, originally for religious and social purposes, and later as trade organizations for fixing wages, standards of craftsmanship, etc. They also acted as friendly societies. The 12 'great' companies (nominated in 1514) are the mercers, grocers, drapers, fishmongers, goldsmiths, merchant taylors, skinners, haberdashers, salters, ironmongers, vintners, and clothworkers. Some of these are famous for their educational foundations, still have their halls in the City, and contribute from their funds to charities, especially to education.

livestock farming The farming of domestic animals, especially cattle, sheep, pigs, and poultry primarily for their meat, milk, skins, or wool. Although in many developing countries livestock farming has so far remained an integrated part of the whole farming system (including crops), in the developed world there has been an increased specialization of large-scale livestock farming which is both more capital- and input-intensive and more commercially rewarding.

liveware A term used by computer organizations to refer to the human element of any computer-based system, without which the system would not operate.

Livia Drusilla (58 BC–AD 29) Roman empress, the third wife of the emperor Augustus, whom she married in 39 BC after divorcing her first husband Tiberius Claudius Nero. From her first marriage she had two children: Tiberius and Nero Claudius Drusus. She was influential with Augustus, and conspired maliciously to ensure Tiberius's succession, gaining the nickname 'Ulysses in Petticoats'. Relations with Tiberius after his accession became strained, and when she died he did not execute her will or allow her to be deified.

living fossil A species that has persisted to modern times with little or no detectable change over a long period of time, and typically sharing most of its characters only with otherwise extinct organisms (fossils). The coelacanth discovered off the coast of South Africa in 1939 is a typical example of a living descendant of a group previously thought to be extinct.

Living Newspaper A unit of the US Federal Theater Project, founded in 1935, and the style of documentary theatre it espoused, which dramatized current social and political issues in short immediate sketches. Joseph Losey was a creative exponent of the form. It was closed down in 1939 on political grounds as a result of its unbiased and outspoken productions. The technique was later successfully used in England for adult education and propaganda in the armed forces during World War 2.

living stone A perennial native to S Africa and adapted to very dry, desert conditions. It consists of a single, annual pair of succulent leaves, grossly swollen with water, and more or less fused together; the daisy-like flower appears between the leaves. Each species is associated with a particular kind of rock, and has leaves coloured to resemble that rock and no other – a rare example of plant mimicry. (Genus: *Lithops*, 50 species. Family: Aizoaceae.)

Livingstone, David (1813–73) Missionary and explorer, born in Blantyre, South Lanarkshire, WC Scotland, UK. After studying medicine in London, he was ordained under the London Missionary Society in 1840, and the next year arrived in Cape Town to begin exploration in Africa. In 1852–6 he was the first European to discover L Ngami, and the Victoria Falls (1855) of the Zambezi. He was welcomed home as a hero, and published his *Missionary Travels* (1857). He led an expedition (1858–63) exploring the Zambezi, and discovered Lakes Shirwa and Nyasa. The expedition was recalled, he journeyed as far as Bombay, and returned to England in 1864. He was asked to return to Africa and settle a dispute regarding the sources of the Nile, and in 1867–8 he discovered Lakes Mweru and Bangweulu. On his return to Ujiji after severe illness he was found there by Henry Morton Stanley, sent to look for him by the *New York Herald*. He returned to Bangweulu, but died, and his body was taken for burial in Westminster Abbey.

Livingstone, Ken(neth Robert) (1945–) British politician, born in London. He worked as a laboratory technician before training as a teacher. Elected a member of Lambeth Council in 1971 and then of Camden (1978–82) he was also a member of the Greater London Council (GLC) (1973–86). He was elected leader of the GLC in 1981 and fought a long battle to prevent its abolition by Magaret Thatcher. Following the GLC's demise, he became Labour MP for Brent East in 1987. Always to the left of the party, he was a member of its national executive committee in 1987–9 and was re-elected again in 1997. He was an unsuccessful Labour candidate for the newly established position of Mayor of London in 2000, but nonetheless stood as an independent and was elected. He was subsequently expelled from the Labour Party for five years but readmitted in January 2004.

Livingstone daisy A sprawling annual with succulent leaves and stems (*Dorotheanthus bellidiflorus*) native to arid parts of S Africa; flowers daisy-like, in various colours from yellow and pink to mauve, opening only in full, bright sunlight. It is sometimes referred to by the old botanical name **mesembryanthemum**. (Family: Aizoaceae.)

Living Theater / Theatre A theatre begun by Judith Malina and Julian Beck in 1947 as an Off-Broadway venture. It became one of the best known, most influential, and most-attacked of the radical anti-bourgeois cultural experiments that swept the USA and much of Europe during the 1960s and early 1970s. Influenced by the theories of Artaud, its main feature was a conscious refusal to separate the art of theatre from the art of living. Their ideological and aesthetic radicalism and their techniques of presentation (violently expressive movement and speech) have been imitated by other experimental companies.

Livius *Livy*

Livonian Knights Brothers of the Knighthood of Christ in Livonia, commonly known as the **Sword-Brothers**, founded c.1202 to convert the pagan Latvians; then, from 1237 to its dissolution in 1561, members of the Livonian branch of the Teutonic Knights. By the 14th-c they controlled the E Baltic lands of Courland, Estonia, and Livonia.

Livorno [leevaw(r)noh], Eng **Leghorn** 43°33N 10°18E, pop (2000e) 183 000. Port and capital of Livorno province, W Tuscany, Italy; on the low-lying coast of the Tyrrhenian Sea, 20 km/12 mi SW of Pisa; railway; ferries to Bastia in Corsica; linked with the R Arno by canal; birthplace of Modigliani; shipbuilding, engineering, cement, soap, petrochemicals, straw hats, trade in wine, olive oil, marble; 17th-c cathedral.

Livy [livee], in full **Titus Livius** (c.59 BC–AD 17) Roman historian, born in Patavium, Italy. He settled in Rome sometime before 29 BC, when he began his history of Rome from its foundation to the death of Nero Claudius Drusus (9 BC). This momentous work of 142 books (of which only 35 survive in full) became the foundation of historical writing through to the 18th-c, and placed him at the forefront of Latin writers.

Li Xiannian [lee shanyan] (1905–92) Chinese statesman, born in Hubei province, EC China. He worked as a carpenter before serving with the Kuomintang (Nationalist) forces (1926–7). After joining the Communist Party in 1927 he established the Oyuwan Soviet (people's republic) in Hubei, participated in the Long March (1934–6), and was a military commander in the war against Japan and in the civil war. He was inducted into the Politburo and secretariat in 1956 and 1958, but fell out of favour during the 1966–9 Cultural Revolution. He was rehabilitated, as finance minister, by Zhou Enlai in 1973, and later served as state president under Deng Xiaoping (1983–8).

lizard A reptile, found worldwide except in the coldest regions. Some have no obvious limbs and resemble snakes; but most differ from snakes in having eyelids and an obvious ear opening. Many species can voluntarily break off their tail to distract predators (a new tail grows). Only 2% of species are primarily vegetarian. (Suborder: Sauria or Lacertilia. Order: Squamata, c.3750 species.)

Lizard Point 49°56N 5°13W. Promontory in Cornwall, SW England, UK; the most S point on the UK mainland, near Lizard Town.

Ljubljana [lyooblyahna], Ital **Lubiana**, ancient **Emona** 46°00N 14°30E, pop (2000e) 292 000. Capital of Slovenia; on Sava and Ljubljanica Rivers, 120 km/75 mi WNW of Zagreb; founded, 34 BC; capital of the former Kingdom of Illyria, 1816–49; badly damaged by earthquake, 1895; ceded to Yugoslavia, 1918; airport; railway; university (1595); textiles, paper, chemicals, food processing, electronics; education and convention centre; Tivoli sports park, national museum, castle, cathedral, Ursuline church; Alpe-Adria International Trade Fair (Apr), Ljubljana Festival (Jul–Aug), International Festival of Graphic Art (alternate years Jun–Aug), International Wine Fair (Aug), flower show (Sep), International 'Ski Expo' Fair (Nov).

llama A member of the camel family (*Lama glama*), found in the C Andes; domesticated c.4500 years ago; used mainly as a beast of burden; long flat-backed body with long erect neck and long ears; dense coat; two breeds: *chaku* and *ccara*.

Llandudno [hlandidnoh] 53°19N 3°49W, pop (2001e) 20 000. Seaside resort town in Gwynedd, NW Wales, part of the Aberconwy and Colwyn unitary authority; on a small peninsula terminating in the Great Orme's Head; Great Orme country park with tramway, dry ski slope and toboggan run; railway; promenade; Oriel Mostyn, North Wales Theatre and Conference Centre, Alice in Wonderland Centre; Victorian Extravaganza weekend (May), October Festival; fishing, water sports, tourism.

Llanfairpwllgwyngyll [hlanviyrpulhgwingihl], in full **Llanfairpwllgwyngyllgogerychwyrndrobwllllantysiliogogogoch** ('St Mary's Church in the hollow of the white hazel near a rapid whirlpool and the Church of St Tysilio by the red cave') 53°13N 4°12W. Village in Anglesey, NW Wales, UK; W of Menai Bridge; gained notoriety through the extension of its name (to 58 letters) by a poetic cobbler in the 18th-c, probably to attract visitors; tourism; Marquess of Anglesey's Column (1816); Plas Newydd stately home nearby; first Women's Institute in Britain founded here, 1915.

Llangefni [hlangevnee] 53°16N 4°18W, pop (2000e) 4800. Town in Anglesey, NW Wales, UK, on the R Cefni; administrative centre for the island; market, agricultural implements, livestock; Oriel Môn.

Llangollen [hlangolhen] 52°58N 3°10W, pop (2000e) 3200. Town in Denbighshire, NE Wales, UK; on the R Dee, 15 km/9 mi SW of Wrexham; hide and skin dressing, printing, crafts, agricultural trade, tourism; 14th-c St Collen's Church, 14th-c bridge; Valle Crucis abbey nearby (c.1200), and Eliseg's Pillar (8th–9th-c cross); Plâs Newydd, headquarters of the Welsh National Theatre since 1943; site of annual international musical eisteddfod since 1947.

Llano Estacado [lahnoh estakahdoh] ('staked plain') Vast semi-arid S portion of the Great Plains, in E New Mexico and W Texas, USA; flat, windswept grasslands broken by streams; formerly devoted to cattle raising; natural gas, oil fields, irrigated farming.

llanos [lyahnos] The savannah grasslands of the plains and plateaux of the Orinoco region (Colombia, Venezuela), N South America. Traditionally it was an important livestock farming area, and there have been recent schemes to re-establish cattle ranching following a decline in the early 20th-c.

Llewellyn, Richard [hlooelin], pseudonym of **Richard Dafydd Vivian Llewellyn Lloyd** (1906–83) Writer, born in St David's, Pembrokeshire, SW Wales, UK. He established himself, after service with the regular army and a short spell in the film industry and journalism, as a best-selling novelist with *How Green Was My Valley* (1939), a novel about a Welsh mining village. It was filmed under the direction of **John Ford** in 1941. Later works include *The Flame of Hercules* (1957) and *I Stand on a Quiet Shore* (1982).

Lleyn Peninsula [hleen] Peninsula in Gwynedd, NW Wales, UK; separates Cardigan Bay and Tremadog Bay (S) from Caernarfon Bay (N); chief towns, Pwllheli, Porthmadog; agriculture, tourism.

Llosa, (Jorge) Mario (Pedro) Vargas [hohsa] (1936–) Novelist, born in Arequipa, S Peru. After studying law and literature at home he became a student in Paris and Madrid, building up a reputation as a writer before returning. *The Time of the Hero*, his first novel, published in 1962 and depicting the abuse of power, so outraged the Peruvian authorities that a thousand copies were publicly burned. Subsequent novels include his masterpiece *Aunt Julia and the Scriptwriter* (1977), *The War at the End of the World* (1985), *A Fish in the Water* (1994), and *The Notebooks of Don Rigoberto* (1998), and he is heralded as one of the world's greatest novelists, winning many honours. Critics acclaim *La fiesta del chivo* (2000, The Feast of the Goat) as his finest novel. Set in Trujillo's Dominican Republic, it is based on historical as well as fictional figures, through whom he recreates the stifling atmosphere of moral confusion and servility that personal despotism provokes. He is also a football commentator, and in 1990 ran unsuccessfully for the Peruvian presidency, having declined an offer of the premiership in 1984.

Lloyd, Harold (Clayton) (1893–1971) Film comedian, born in Burchard, Nebraska, USA. Stagestruck from an early age, he started as a film extra in 1913, and subsequently made hundreds of short, silent comedies, adopting from 1917 his character of the unassuming 'nice guy' in horn-rimmed glasses and straw hat. He became one of America's most popular daredevil comedians in films such as *High and Dizzy* (1920) and, most famously, *Safety Last* (1923), in which he dangles perilously from the hands of a high-rise clock face. He enjoyed a remarkable run of hits from *Why Worry?* (1923) to *Speedy* (1928), and received an honorary Academy Award in 1952.

Lloyd, Marie, originally **Matilda Alice Victoria Wood** (1870–1922) Music-hall singer and entertainer, born in London, UK. She made her first appearance at the Royal Eagle Music Hall (later The Grecian) in 1885. Her first great success was with a song called 'The Boy I Love Sits Up in the Gallery', and she became one of the most popular music-hall performers of all time, appearing in music halls in America, South Africa, and Australia. Among her most famous songs was 'My Old Man Said Follow the Van'.

Lloyd-George (of Dwyfor), David Lloyd George, 1st Earl (1863–1945) British Liberal statesman and prime minister (1916-22), born in Manchester, Greater Manchester, NW England, UK. He studied in Wales, became a solicitor and, in 1890, an MP for Caernarfon Boroughs (a seat he was to hold for 55 years). He was President of the Board of Trade (1905–8) and Chancellor of the Exchequer (1905–15). His 'people's budget' of 1909–10 was rejected by the House of Lords, and led to a constitutional crisis and the Parliament Act of 1911, which removed the Lords' power of veto. He became minister of munitions (1915), secretary for war (1916), and coalition prime minister. After World War 1, he continued as head of a coalition government dominated by Conservatives. He negotiated with Sinn Féin, and conceded the Irish Free State (1921) – a measure which brought his downfall. Following the 1931 general election, he led a 'family' group of Independent Liberal MPs. He was made an earl in 1945. A film about his life, directed by Maurice Elvey and starring Norman Page, was made in 1918, but was then mysteriously suppressed and lost. Rediscovered in 1994, it was restored by the Welsh and National Film Archives, and premiered in 1996.

Lloyd's An international market for insurance, based in London. It originated in Edward Lloyd's coffee house in Tower Street in the City of London from 1688. Anyone wishing to insure a ship or its cargo would seek out individuals willing to 'underwrite the risk' – or pay for any losses sustained to the items insured. By the early 1700s Lloyd's became a private club, with its members owning and controlling operations. In 1871 the Lloyd's Act of Parliament was passed, setting a legal framework on its activities. All kinds of insurance are now handled worldwide, with some three-quarters of all business from outside the UK. The members (*underwriters*) of Lloyd's are organized into syndicates, and risks are spread among the members of the syndicate so that no single individual (or 'name') carries too large a risk personally. There is, however, no limit to a member's liability, and large losses made by some syndicates in 1990 and 1991 gave rise to controversy concerning the management of Lloyd's. It has now become possible for limited liability companies to be members of Lloyd's. *Lloyd's List* is London's oldest daily newspaper, providing in particular an information service on shipping matters. *Lloyd's Shipping Index* gives daily information about the worldwide movements of over 20 000 merchant vessels. In 1979 the Lloyd's site was redeveloped and a new building designed by Richard Rogers and Partners, whose externally exposed service ducts and pipes make it one of the most arresting architectural features of the City of London.

Lloyd's Register of Shipping A publication which catalogues information about the construction and characteristics of individual vessels, to help insurance underwriters. Known as the Underwriters' Register, or 'Green Book', it was first published in 1760, but has been published by a separate organization from Lloyd's since 1834. 'A1 at Lloyd's' refers to the top grade of the classification made by the Register, indicating that the vessel is in first-class order.

Lloyd-Webber, Andrew Lloyd Webber, Baron (1948–) Composer, born in London, UK. From a distinguished musical family, he had no conventional musical education. With Tim Rice he wrote *Joseph and the Amazing Technicolour Dreamcoat* (1968), and the rock opera *Jesus Christ Superstar* (staged 1970), the LP of which achieved record-breaking sales. He has since composed the music for many West End hits, including *Evita* (1978), *Cats* (1981), and *Starlight Express* (1984). Other successes have included *The Phantom of the Opera* (1986) and *Aspects of Love* (1989); less successful were *Whistle Down The Wind* (1997), and other recent ventures. With the opening of *Sunset Boulevard* in 1993, he had five musicals concurrently in production in London. He wrote the film scores for *Gumshoe* (1971) and *The Odessa File* (1974), and, in a fresh departure, composed a Requiem Mass in 1985. He was knighted in 1992, and received a life peerage in 1997.

Lloyd Webber, Julian (1951–) Cellist, born in London, UK, the brother of composer Andrew Lloyd Webber. He studied at the Royal College of Music and with Pierre Fournier in Geneva, and in 1972 made his UK debut. He has since performed with all the major British orchestras, appeared internationally, and made many recordings. His books include *The Young Cellist's Repertoire* (1984), *The Great Cello Solos* (1991), and *Cello Song* (1994).

Llull or **Lull, Ramón** [lul], Eng **Raymond Lully**, known as **the Enlightened Doctor** (c.1235–1315) Theologian and mystic, born in Palma, Majorca. He served as a soldier and led a dissolute life, but from 1266 gave himself up to asceticism, became a Franciscan, and went on a spiritual crusade to convert the Mussulmans. His major work is the *Ars magna* (The Great Art), condemned in 1376 for its attempt to link faith and reason, but later viewed more sympathetically. He travelled widely, and was allegedly killed on missionary work in Budia (Bougie), Algeria. His followers, known as *Lullists*, combined religious mysticism with alchemy.

Llullaillaco, Cerro [yooyiyyakoh] 24°43S 68°30W. Snow-capped extinct volcano on the Chile–Argentina border; 300 km/186 mi W of Salta (Argentina); height 6723 m/22 057 ft; Socampa Pass and railway are to the NE.

Llywelyn [hlooelin]

loach Slender-bodied, freshwater fish of the family Cobitidae (7 genera), found in rivers and lakes throughout Europe and Asia; length commonly less than 10 cm/4 in; mouth fringed with barbels; popular amongst aquarists; includes the colourful **collie loach** (*Acanthophthalmus kuhlii*) and **tiger loach** (*Botia macracantha*).

loam An easily worked soil, composed of varying mixtures of sand, clay, and humus. Sandy loams are often favoured by horticulturalists because of their good draining qualities and the possibility of producing crops early in the season.

Lobachevsky, Nikolay Ivanovich [lobachefskee] (1792–1856) Mathematician, born in Nizhni Novgorod, W Russia. He became professor at Kazan in 1816, where he spent the rest of his life. In the 1820s he developed a theory of non-Euclidean geometry in which Euclid's parallel postulate did not hold. A similar theory was discovered almost simultaneously and independently by János Bolyai (1802–60).

lobbying A term originating in the attempts by organized groups to influence elected politicians, administrators, or public opinion through personal contacts in the 'lobbies' of legislative buildings or through the media. Originating in 19th-c USA, contemporary usage has broadened the term to incorporate making demands upon civil servants, state institutions, and influencing public opinion by reasoned argument, public relations campaigns, mass media coverage, or sometimes the offer of favours. Significant in all liberal democracies, many groups now employ paid, professional lobbyists.

lobefish Any of the mainly fossil bony fishes belonging to the Sarcopterygii, but including also the extant lungfishes (Dipnoi) and the coelacanth (Crossopterygii); characteristic fleshy bases to the paired fins.

lobelia [lohbeelia] A member of a large and very diverse genus, ranging from small annuals to shaggy, columnar perennials reaching several metres high; found almost everywhere, but mostly tropical and subtropical, especially in the New World; leaves alternate, simple; flowers twisted through 180°, usually red, blue, or violet, zygomorphic with five fused petals forming a curved, 2-lipped tube. Many are cultivated for ornament. They occupy a wide range of habitats: several are aquatic, while the giant lobelias are restricted to individual mountains of E Africa. Many contain deadly alkaloids; just the scent of the Chilean *Lobelia tupa* is said to cause poisoning. (Genus: *Lobelia*, 200–300 species. Family: Campanulaceae.)

lobotomy *psychosurgery*

lobster A large marine crustacean with a well-developed abdomen and the front pair of legs modified as pincers (*chelipeds*); chelipeds asymmetrical, one for crushing and one for cutting; feeds at night on molluscs and carrion; length up to 60 cm/2 ft; eggs carried in masses stuck to abdominal legs of female; found in holes and crevices in shallow coastal seas; edible, caught commercially using pots or wickerwork traps (*creels*). (Class: Malacostraca. Order: Decapoda.)

lobster claw *parrot's bill*

local area network (LAN) A system which allows communication between computers situated within a well-defined geographical area, and which does not use the public telephone system. By contrast, a **wide area network** or **long distance network** allows computer communication over a large geographical area, generally using the telephone system.

local education authority (LEA) A regional government organization responsible for education in its area. In the UK, this is usually a city or county council. The elected members of the LEA are local politicians; they decide policy, stand for election, and receive no payment other than attendance allowances. It also comprises professional officers, responsible for the day-to-day running of the education system in their area.

local government A set of political institutions constitutionally subordinate to the national, provincial, or federal government, with delegated authority to perform certain functions within territorially defined parts of the state. Sovereign authority remains with the higher levels of government, which may create, dissolve, or change local structures and add to or take away their powers and functions. Some of the services most commonly provided by local government include education, public transport, roads, social services, housing, leisure and recreation, public health, and water. The rationale for local government includes the need for local participation, achieved through direct or indirect elections, and in local authorities' revenue-raising powers. Although considerable discretion may be granted to local authorities in some political systems, conflict with the centre can occur. This is usually centred around the extent of legitimate democratic authority possessed by local government derived from the electoral process, as different views exist about whether local government should be an agent or partner of central government.

Local Group The family of galaxies to which the Milky Way, Magellanic Clouds, and the Andromeda galaxy belong. Its diameter is about 1 megaparsec, and contains 3 large spiral galaxies, plus about 30 much smaller galaxies of irregular, elliptical, and spheroidal shape – about 5×10^{12} solar masses in all.

Locarno Pact [lokah(r)noh] A series of international agreements reached in 1925 at an international conference held at Locarno, Italy, guaranteeing post-1919 frontiers between France, Belgium, and Germany, and the demilitarization of the Rhineland. The treaty was signed by France, Germany, and Belgium, and guaranteed by Britain and Italy. Germany also signed arbitration conventions with France, Belgium, Poland, and Czechoslovakia; and France signed treaties of mutual guarantee with Poland and Czechoslovakia. Stresemann, as German foreign minister, refused to accept Germany's E frontier with Poland and Czechoslovakia as unalterable, but agreed that any realignment of territorial boundaries must come peacefully. In the 'spirit of Locarno' Germany was invited to join the League of Nations. In 1936, denouncing the Locarno Pact, Hitler sent troops into the demilitarized Rhineland; in 1938 he annexed the Sudetenland in contravention of the Pact, and in 1939 he invaded Poland.

locational analysis The study of the spatial patterning of features on the Earth's surface, a major component of human geography in the UK and USA in the 1960s and 1970s. By establishing general models and laws, and continually testing these, locational analysis seeks to explain the factors accounting for the regularity with which spatial arrangements (eg the location of particular types of business) occur.

Lochner, Stefan [lokhner] (c.1400–1451) Religious painter, born in Meersburg am Bodensee, SW Germany. He may have studied in the Netherlands before settling in Cologne c.1440, where he became the principal master of the Cologne school, marking the transition from the Gothic style to Naturalism. His best-known work is the great triptych, 'Adoration of the Kings', in Cologne Cathedral.

Loch Ness Monster *Ness, Loch*

lock (canal) A means of altering the height of a canal waterway while allowing the passage of boats. A **pound lock** has a chamber which can be filled and emptied of water by opening and closing paddles, to bring the level to the upper or the lower height. The lower gates are usually double, pointing upstream so as to be pressed together by the water. The upper gate may be single in small locks, or double in large. The locks on older British canals are small, taking boats 70 ft by 7 ft; canals such as the Panama take very large ocean-going vessels.

lock (security) A device for securing objects, usually doors on houses or safes. It is normally a mechanical device operated by levers and keys, but many are nowadays magnetically or electronically operated, and can be computer controlled. Time locks can be opened only at certain predetermined times of the day.

Locke, John (1632–1704) Philosopher, born in Wrington, Somerset. He studied at Oxford, and in 1667 joined the household of Anthony Ashley Cooper, later first Earl of Shaftesbury, gaining through him a succession of official appointments and meeting the leading intellectuals of the day, including Robert Boyle. In 1672, Locke became secretary of the Board of Trade, lived in France for health reasons (1675–9), then moved to Holland. He returned to England in 1689, and became a commissioner of appeals, retiring in 1691 to Oates, Essex. His major work, the *Essay Concerning Human Understanding* (1690) is a systematic enquiry into the nature and scope of human reason, very much reflecting the scientific temper of the times in seeking to establish that 'all knowledge is founded on and ultimately derives from sense...or sensation'; the work was the starting point of the British empiricist tradition which led from Locke to Berkeley and Hume. His *Two Treatises of Government* (1690) were also influential, and his sanctioning of rebellion in defence of natural rights and constitutional law had a powerful influence on the American and French revolutionaries.

Lockerbie 55°07N 3°22W, pop (2000e) 3040. A town in Dumfries and Galloway, SW Scotland, UK, the scene of Britain's worst air disaster, when a Pan Am Boeing 747 flying from Frankfurt to New York via London crashed on 21 December 1988. There were no survivors. The total death toll was 270, including townspeople killed by plane debris which demolished houses. The explosive device which led to the disaster was incorporated into a radio-cassette player placed in the baggage hold and taken on board at Frankfurt. Efforts to extradite suspected Libyan terrorists to stand trial were finally successful in early 1999, the trial taking place at a Scottish court at Camp Zeist in The Netherlands. In January 2001, one of the two people charged, Abdelbaset ali Mohmed al-Megrahi, was found guilty and jailed for life; an appeal was rejected in March 2002. In August 2003,

Libya formally accepted responsibility for the bombing and agreed to pay compensation to the bereaved families.

lockjaw *tetanus*

lockout An industrial situation in which a company refuses to allow its workforce into the premises. It is an extreme measure, used infrequently in negotiations, especially with trade unions, to persuade the workforce to accept the company's terms of employment.

Lockwood, Margaret (1916–90) English actress, born in Karachi, SE Pakistan (formerly India). She studied at the Royal Academy of Dramatic Art, made her film debut in *Lorna Doone* (1935), and starred in the Alfred Hitchcock film *The Lady Vanishes* (1938). In the late 1940s she was Britain's most popular leading lady, appearing regularly in theatre productions. Later films include *Cast a Dark Shadow* (1955) and *The Slipper and the Rose* (1976).

Lockyer, Sir Joseph Norman (1836–1920) Astronomer, born in Rugby, Warwickshire, C England, UK. As a clerk in the War Office (1857–75) he detected and named *helium* in the Sun's chromosphere (1868), a generation before William Ramsay found it on Earth. He worked in the government science and art department (1875–90), started and edited *Nature* (1869–1920), and was professor of astronomical physics at the Royal College of Science (1908–13). He was knighted in 1897.

locomotive The vehicle that provides the tractive force to haul trucks and carriages on a railway. The locomotive can be powered by a steam engine, an internal combustion engine, an electric motor, or some combination of these power sources. If it is propelled by steam, the steam is generated in a boiler mounted on the locomotive and normally burning coal. If it is propelled by an electric motor, the electricity is taken either from a special rail or from overhead lines. The normal internal combustion engine used for propulsion is the diesel engine, which may drive the locomotive directly through suitable gears, or sometimes in diesel-electric configuration. In the latter case the diesel engine is used to drive a generator whose electricity drives an electric motor, which in turn drives the locomotive and its load. The world's first locomotive was built by Richard Trevithick in 1801, and although some famous locomotives (such as 'Puffing Billy' and 'Locomotion') were used on railways to haul coal after that time, it was not until 1829 that the 'Rocket' won the Rainhill trials and inaugurated the full-time carriage of passengers. A number of British locomotives were exported to the USA from 1829, the first US-built locomotive ('Best Friend of Charleston') being built in 1831. By the mid-19th-c, the steam locomotive had developed into a form which did not change substantially thereafter, although there were many individual variations. The front wheels were small and swivelled, allowing the locomotive to enter a bend, and the main driving wheels were coupled to each other, and driven directly by the steam engine itself. This led to the description of locomotives by their wheel arrangements; for example, 2–6–2 refers to two leading wheels (one on each side), six drive wheels, and two trailing wheels. During the 20th-c the steam locomotive was progressively displaced as the main type of locomotive by diesel, diesel–electric, and electric motive power, the last countries to still use steam locomotives extensively being South Africa and China. In an effort to counter the competition posed by road transport, new types of propulsion are currently under test, such as the use of linear electric motors for propulsion coupled with magnetic levitation. Countries that have investigated or are investigating these new systems include the UK, Germany, and Japan.

locus (genetics) *chromosome*

locust Any of several species of grasshoppers, with a 2-phase life-cycle. At low population density they are solitary in behaviour and show camouflaged coloration, but at high density they become brightly coloured and gregarious. They swarm and migrate, often causing massive destruction of crops and natural vegetation. The main species are the **migratory locust**, the **desert locust**, and the **red locust**. (Order: Orthoptera. Family: Acrididae.)

locust tree *carob; false acacia*

lodestone *magnetite*

Lodge, David (John) (1935–) Novelist and critic, born in London, UK. He studied at University College London, then taught at Birmingham University (1960–87, then honorary professor). Three early realist novels gave place to parodic fictions in pursuit of literature itself, including *Changing Places* (1975) and *Small World* (1984, televised 1988). The real world returns in *Nice Work* (1988, televised 1989), a rewrite of the 19th-c industrial novel. Later books include *Paradise News* (1991), *Therapy* (1995), *Home Truths* (a novella, 1999), and *Thinks* (2001). His critical works include *Language of Fiction* (1966), *The Novelist at the Crossroads* (1971), *Write On* (1986), a collection of essays, *After Bakhtin* (1990), and *The Practice of Writing* (1996).

Lodge, Henry Cabot (1850–1924) US Republican senator, historian, and biographer, born in Boston, Massachusetts, USA. He studied at Harvard, and received the first PhD in political science to be granted there (1876). He became assistant editor of the *North American Review*, but from 1878 his career was mainly political, becoming a member of the US House of Representatives in 1887 and a senator in 1893. He led the opposition to the Treaty of Versailles in 1919, and prevented the USA joining the League of Nations in 1920.

Lodge, Thomas (c.1558–1625) Playwright, romance writer, and poet, probably born in London, UK. He studied at Oxford, then at Lincoln's Inn. Around 1588 he took part in a buccaneering expedition to the Canaries, and wrote the romance, *Rosalynde* (1590), his best-known work, the source of Shakespeare's *As You Like It*. Lodge excelled as a lyric poet of amorous verse and songs; his chief volume of verse, *Phillis*, was issued in 1593. He went on a second freebooting expedition to South America in 1591, and wrote many other works. He is believed to have taken a medical degree at Avignon (1600), and was a physician in Oxford in 1602.

Łódź [wudzh, lodz] 51°49N 19°28E, pop (2000e) 858 000. Industrial capital of Łódź voivodship, C Poland; second largest city in Poland; charter, 500; development since 1820 through the textile industry; railway; two universities (1945); textiles, chemicals, electrical engineering, textile machinery, transformers, radios; film studios; museums of art, archaeology, ethnography, textile industry; botanical gardens; spring festival of arts (May).

loerie *turaco*

Loesser, Frank (Henry) [lerser] (1910–69) Songwriter and composer, born in New York City, USA. He published his first lyric in 1931, and in 1937 went to Hollywood as a contract writer. With a succession of collaborators he turned out several hit songs including 'Baby, It's Cold Outside' (1949). He branched out into writing his own music, soon achieving international fame with the music and lyrics for *Guys and Dolls* (1950). Later musicals included *The Most Happy Fella* (1956) and *How to Succeed in Business Without Really Trying* (1961).

Loess Region [lohis] NC Chinese highlands, intersected by the Yellow R basin; area 400 000 sq km/150 400 sq mi; altitude 800–2000 m/2600–6500 ft; covered with a layer of wind-blown loam and river alluvium (*loess*), generally 100 m/325 ft deep, but much deeper in places; excellent for crops, especially grains, and important in early agrarian history and the origins of civilization; has suffered serious soil erosion; trees and grass now being planted to help conserve soil and water; site of China's oldest anthropoid remains (700 000 years ago) and principal Palaeolithic to Neolithic sites; location of first historical Chinese dynasty (16th-c BC), and the power-centres of all later dynasties until 12th-c AD.

Loewe, Frederick [loh] (1904–88) Composer, born in Berlin, Germany. He went to the USA in 1924, and worked as a composer on a number of Broadway musicals. Those he wrote in collaboration with **Alan J Lerner** (1918–86), including *Briga-*

doon (1947) and *My Fair Lady* (1956), were particularly successful, as also was the film *Gigi* (1958), for which he wrote the score.

Löffler, Friedrich August Johannes [loefler] (1852–1915) Bacteriologist, born in Frankfurt an der Oder, E Germany. He studied medicine at Würzburg, started as a military surgeon, became professor at Greifswald (1888), and from 1913 was director of the Koch Institute for Infectious Diseases in Berlin. He first cultured the diphtheria bacillus (1884), discovered the causal organism of glanders and swine erysipelas (1886), isolated an organism causing food poisoning, and prepared a vaccine against foot-and-mouth disease (1899).

Lofoten Islands [lohfohtn] area 1425 sq km/550 sq mi. Mountainous island group in the Norwegian Sea, off the NW coast of Norway, separated from the mainland by Vest Fjord; major fishing grounds nearby; fish processing.

Lofty–Flinders Ranges, Mount Mountain ranges in South Australia state, Australia; extending 800 km/500 mi N from Cape Jervis to the N end of L Torrens, running roughly N–S; the Mt Lofty Ranges are in the S, comparatively low, rising to Mt Lofty (727 m/2385 ft); Flinders Ranges in the N include a national park (802 sq km/310 sq mi), rising to St Mary Peak (1166 m/3825 ft); unusual basins (notably Wilpena Pound) with multi-coloured rock faces and wild flowers; numerous examples of Aboriginal art, some 10 000 years old; copper, coal, and gold have been mined here; popular tourist area.

Logan, Mount 60°34N 140°24W. Highest mountain in Canada, and second highest in North America; rises to 5950 m/19 521 ft in the St Elias Mts, SW Yukon territory; to the N of the Seward Glacier, in Kluane National Park.

loganberry An accidental hybrid between raspberry and blackberry which arose in the garden of Judge Logan of California, after whom it was named. It is less thorny than the blackberry, and the fruits, which resemble raspberries, are much larger and more tart than either parent. It is widely grown in the USA and UK. (Family: Rosaceae.)

logarithm The power n to which a number a must be raised to equal another number b, ie 'the logarithm to the base a of b': $a^n = b \Rightarrow \log_a b = n$; for example, since $10^2 = 100$, $\log_{10}100 = 2$. From the definition, the *logarithmic function* is the inverse of the exponential function. Properties of the logarithmic function can be deduced from the laws of indices, and include: $\log(ab) = \log a + \log b$, and $\log(a/b) = \log a - \log b$. These properties enabled logarithms to be used extensively as calculating aids before the advent of computers. Logarithms to the base e are called *natural* or *Napierian* logarithms, denoted by ln; logarithms base 10 are denoted by lg.

loggia [lohjia] A gallery in a building, behind an open arcade or colonnade, and facing onto a garden, street, or square. It is sometimes a separate structure.

logic The formal, systematic study of the principles of valid inference and correct reasoning. **Deductive logic** is the study of inferences that are valid (or invalid) in virtue of their structure, not their content. 'If A then B; A; therefore B' is valid whatever the values of A and B; and any inference with that structure is valid. There are two main parts of elemental deductive logic. **Propositional logic** deals with inferences involving simple sentences in the indicative mood joined by such connectives as *not* (negation), *and* (conjunction), *or* (disjunction), and *if...then* (conditional). **Predicate logic** (also known as **quantification theory**) deals with sentences in the indicative mood involving such quantifying terms as *some*, *all*, and *no*. Thus, 'All cats are mammals, and no mammals are worms; therefore no cats are worms' is a (valid) inference in predicate logic. The investigation of deductive inference has also been extended beyond propositional and predicate logic to include: **modal logic**, which treats the notions of necessity and possibility; **epistemic logic**, the logic of knowledge and belief; **many-valued logic**, which allows some sentences to be assigned a designation other than true or false; **tense logic**, which analyses inferences involving such temporal notions as past, present, and future; and **deontic logic** which deals with imperatives, practical reasoning, and expressions of obligation. **Inductive logic** is the study of inferences which are not deductively valid, but are such that the premisses, if true, would increase the likelihood of the truth of the conclusion, and this leads naturally to probability theory and statistics. Aristotle wrote the first systematic treatise on logic, which remained extremely influential for 2000 years, until Boole and others evolved a rigorous mathematical logic in the 19th-c.

logical positivism A philosophical movement beginning with the Vienna Circle in the 1920s and 1930s under the leadership of Moritz Schlick and Rudolf Carnap, and associated in Britain with A J Ayer. The positivists were strongly influenced by the empirical tradition of Hume and others, and contrasted traditional philosophy unfavourably with science and mathematics. Most of metaphysics, and by extension most of ethics and religious discourse was said to be literally meaningless, since its propositions could be verified neither by observation and experiment nor by logical deduction.

logic programming A form of computer programming concerned with the evaluation of rules rather than the issue of instructions to a computer. Languages for logic programming include LISP and PROLOG.

logo [lohgoh, logoh] A visual symbol comprising an image and/or a name designed to identify an organized group (such as an army regiment); an abbreviation of **logotype**. It differs from a **pictogram**, which is a graphic sign showing an entity or an idea (eg a pedestrian crossing at a traffic light) in a direct, representational way. An **ideogram** may be either an abstract or a conventional graphic sign representing a thing or notion (eg a cross against a cigarette, expressing the prohibition of smoking).

logography The study of writing systems in which the symbols (**logographs** or **logograms**) represent whole words, or, in some cases, components of words. A few logographs are found in European languages, such as & ('and'), ÷ ('divided by'), @ ('at'), and £ ('pound'); but Chinese and Japanese are the most famous examples of a logographic writing system. Though originally derived from ideographs, the symbols of these languages now stand for words and syllables, and do not refer directly to concepts or things.

Lohengrin [lohengrin] In Germanic legend, the son of Parsifal. He leaves the temple of the Grail and is carried to Antwerp in a boat drawn by swans. There he saves Princess Elsa of Brabant, and is about to marry her; but she asks forbidden questions about his origin, and he is forced to leave her, the swan-boat taking him back to the Grail temple.

Loire, River [lwah(r)], ancient **Liger** River in E France, rising in the Massif Central; flows N and NW to Orléans, then turns W to empty into the Bay of Biscay by a wide estuary below St-Nazaire; longest river in France; length 1020 km/634 mi; canal link to R Seine; valley known for its vineyards; several important chateaux.

Loki [lohkee] A mischievous Norse god; originally a Giant, he was later accepted into the company of the gods. Although he plays tricks on them, he is also able to save them from danger by his cleverness. However, after contriving the death of Balder, he was tied to a rock where he will stay until Ragnarok.

Lollards A derisive term applied to the followers of the English theologian John Wycliffe (14th-c). The movement, responsible for the translation of the Bible into the vernacular, was suppressed; however, it continued among the enthusiastic but less literate of society, generally anticlerical in attitude, and prepared the way for the Reformation in England.

Lomax, Alan (1915–) Ethnomusicologist, born in Austin, Texas, USA. He studied at Harvard, Texas, and Columbia universities before accompanying his father **John Avery Lomax** (1867–1948), on a tour of prisons in the deep South, where they discovered blues singer Leadbelly, and arranged for his pardon. Alan Lomax devoted his life to the study of folk and blues music. In 1938 he interviewed Jelly Roll Morton, obtaining an oral record of early jazz which appeared first as Lomax's book *Mister Jelly Roll* (1950) and later as a series of recordings. Among his notable publications is *Cantometrics: a Handbook and Training Method* (1976).

Lombard, Peter, known as **Magister Sententiarum** ('Master of Sentences') (c.1100–60) Theologian, born near Novara, N Italy. He studied in Bologna, at Reims, and in Paris, and, after holding a chair of theology there, became Bishop of Paris (1159). He was generally styled 'Master of Sentences', because of his collection of sentences from Augustine and others on points of Christian doctrine, with objections and replies. The theological doctors of Paris in 1300 denounced some of his teachings as heretical, but his work became the standard textbook of Catholic theology until the Reformation.

Lombard League A coalition of N Italian cities, established in 1167 to assert their independence as communes (city-republics) against the German emperor, Frederick I Barbarossa. The League, of which new versions were later formed, set a model for inter-city alliances, and underlined the rising political importance of urban communities in the mediaeval West.

Lombardo, Pietro [lombah(r)doh] (c.1435–1515) Sculptor and architect, born in Carona, N Italy. After working in Padua, and probably Florence, he settled in Venice c.1467, and became the head of the major sculpture workshop of the day. With the assistance of his sons, **Tullio** (c.1455–1532) and **Antonio** (c.1458–c.1516), he was responsible for both the architecture and sculptural decoration of Santa Maria dei Miracoli (1481–9), one of the finest Renaissance buildings in Venice. He also designed many monuments, including the tomb of Dante in Ravenna.

Lombards A Germanic people settled in Hungary – their name deriving from the long beards (*langobardi*) they traditionally wore – who invaded N Italy in AD 568 under their king, Alboin. They founded a new capital at Milan, and in time controlled most of the peninsula except for the S and the area around Ravenna. Their kingdom was annexed by Charlemagne in 774, but the Lombard duchies (Benevento, Spoleto) survived as autonomous entities until the 11th-c.

Lombardy [lombah(r)dee], Ital **Lombardia** pop (2000e) 8 931 000; area 23 835 sq km/9200 sq mi. Region of N Italy; capital, Milan; chief towns, Bergamo, Brescia, Mantua, Pavia, Varese; S Lombardy, highly developed industrial and agricultural region (plain of R Po); tourism important around the Alpine lakes and in the mountains.

Lombardy poplar A form of poplar (*Populus nigra*, cultivar *Italica*) with upswept branches and a distinctive narrow columnar crown; named from plants originating in N Italy, and brought to Britain in the 18th-c. The trees are almost invariably male. They are resistant to air pollution, and are often planted along roads and avenues. (Family: Salicaceae.)

Lombroso, Cesare [lombrohsoh] (1836–1909) Founder of the science of criminology, born in Verona, N Italy. After working as an army surgeon, he became professor of mental diseases at Pavia, director of an asylum at Pesaro, and professor of forensic medicine (1876), psychiatry (1896), and criminal anthropology (1906) at Turin. His theory (now discredited) postulated the existence of a criminal type distinguishable from a normal person by physiological and psychological characteristics.

Lomé [lohmay] 6°10N 1°21E, pop (2000e) 589 000. Seaport capital of Togo; important market centre, noted for its marble, gold, and silver crafts; airport; railway junction; university (1965); oil refining, steel processing, tourism; location of trade conventions in 1970s and 1980s arranged between African, Caribbean, and European Community states.

Lomé Convention A series of conventions governing the European Union's trading relationship with 71 developing countries in Africa, the Caribbean, and the Pacific (the 'ACP countries'). The first convention was signed in 1975, with follow-up conventions every five years (1979, 1984). The 1989 convention was for a 10-year period. The system was replaced by a new treaty, the **Suva Convention**, in 2000, expected to run for 20 years.

Lomond, Loch [lohmond] Largest lake in Scotland, and largest stretch of inland water in the UK; 32 km/20 mi NW of Glasgow; area 70 sq km/27 sq mi; 34 km/21 mi long; narrow in the N, opening out to 8 km/5 mi at the S end; up to 190 m/625 ft deep; hydroelectricity in NW; outlet is R Leven (S); major tourist area; pleasure cruises.

Lomu, Jonah [lohmoo] (1975–) Rugby union player, born in Mangere, New Zealand, of Tongan parents. A brilliant athlete while at school, he played rugby league, then switched to union, being selected for the New Zealand All Blacks in 1994. He became internationally known as a member of the World Cup squad in 1995, when his massive physique (1·95 m/6 ft 5 in; 119 kg/266 lb) made him an awesome opponent. He scored four tries against England in the semi-final at Cape Town. A serious kidney disorder kept him out of the game for over a year, but he returned to international rugby in 1997. He was forced to retire from the game in 2003.

London, Lat **Londinium** (in the 4th-c, **Augusta**) 51°30N 0°10W, pop (2001e) 7 172 000 (Greater London), 3300 (City of London). Capital city of England and the UK; on the R Thames in SE England; **Greater London** consists of 32 boroughs and the City of London, area 1579 sq km/610 sq mi; from 1st–5th-c, a Roman town (AD c.43), situated where the Thames narrowed to its lowest convenient crossing; sacked by Boudicca (c.61); later surrounded by a defensive wall, fragments of which remain (c.350); developed as the leading trade and administrative centre of England; received charter privileges in 1067; mayoralty established in 1191; major building programmes in Middle Ages; extended W, especially in 16th-c; Great Plague (1665), Great Fire (1666), followed by major reconstruction; many squares laid out in 17th–18th-c; in 17th-c developed into a major trade centre and became one of the world's largest cities; severe damage especially to City and East End in World War 2 (the Blitz), with much subsequent rebuilding; administered by London County Council (1888–1963), and by the Greater London Council until 1986, its functions then transferring to the boroughs and other bodies; **City of London**, occupying site of the old mediaeval city N of the Thames, is the financial and business centre, including the Bank of England, Stock Exchange, and Royal Exchange; National Westminster Building (1977) is the tallest building in C London (183 m/600 ft); **City of Westminster** is the administrative and judicial centre, including the Houses of Parliament, Buckingham Palace, and government departments; the **West End** is the main shopping and entertainment centre, around Oxford Street, Piccadilly, and Regent Street; outer boroughs comprise mixed residential and industrial developments; extensive dockland, much now scheduled for redevelopment; headquarters of Port of London Authority; major railway terminuses (Euston, King's Cross, Paddington, St Pancras, Victoria, Waterloo); extensive underground system (known as 'the Tube') run by London Transport Executive; main airports at Heathrow (W) and Gatwick (S), also at London City, Luton (N), and Stansted (E); central bridges across R Thames include Westminster (1750), Blackfriars (1769), Waterloo (1817), and Southwark (1819); markets (Billingsgate, Smithfield; Nine Elms at Vauxhall, replacing Covent Garden, now a tourist centre); parks (Battersea / Hyde / Regent's / St James's Parks, Kensington Gardens); zoological gardens at Regent's Park; leading cultural centre, with many theatres, museums (British / London / Natural History / Science / Victoria and Albert), galleries (National / National Portrait / Tate Galleries, Courtauld Institute), concert halls (Albert / Queen Elizabeth / Royal Festival / Wigmore Halls, Barbican Centre), churches and cathedrals (Saint Paul's / Westminster Cathedrals; Westminster Abbey and St Margaret's Church, a world heritage site); BBC Symphony / London Philharmonic / London Symphony / Royal Philharmonic Orchestras; Royal Shakespeare Company / Opera House (Covent Garden) / Ballet (Sadler's Wells) / Academy of Music / College of Music / Academy of Dramatic Art; centre for radio (Broadcasting House), television, and the press (traditionally at Fleet Street, now largely elsewhere); Central Criminal Court (Old Bailey), Planetarium, Madame Tussaud's; Millennium Dome at Greenwich; London Eye; leading medical centre, with several major hospitals, and Harley Street (private practices); leading educational centre, with several constituent colleges of London University (from 1836), and many other institutions, including City and Brunel Universities (both 1966); University of East London (1992, formerly Polytechnic), London Guildhall University (1992, formerly City of London Polytechnic), Middlesex University (1992, formerly Polytechnic), University of North London (1992, formerly Polytechnic), South Bank University (1992, formerly Polytechnic), Thames Valley University (1992, formerly Polytechnic of West London), University of Westminster (1992, formerly Polytechnic of Central London), University of Greenwich (1992, formerly Thames Polytechnic); Trooping of the Colour on the Queen's official birthday (Jun); procession to the Royal Courts of Justice (Lord Mayor's Show) (Nov); football league teams, Arsenal (Gunners), Charlton Athletic (Valiants), Chelsea (Blues), Crystal Palace (Eagles), Fulham (Cottagers), Leyton Orient ('O's'), Millwall (Lions), Queens Park Rangers ('R's'), Tottenham Hotspur (Spurs), Watford (Hornets), West Ham United (Hammers), Wimbledon (Dons).

London, Jack, pseudonym of **John Griffith Chaney** (1876–1916) Novelist, born in San Francisco, California, USA. Deserted by his father, he educated himself at public libraries, gained admittance to the University of California, but left to seek his fortune in the Klondike gold rush (1897). He returned and made a living by writing prolifically, including the highly successful *The Call of the Wild* (1903), the more serious political novel *The Iron Heel* (1907), and several autobiographical tales, notably *John Barleycorn* (1913).

London Bridge A bridge over the R Thames linking Southwark with the City of London, UK. Early wooden structures were replaced in the 12th-c by a 19-arch stone bridge bearing shops and houses. This was superseded in 1831 by a 5-arch bridge which was dismantled and sold to Lake Havasu City, AZ, in 1968. It was replaced by a concrete structure.

London clubs *club*

Londonderry *Derry* (county)

London Eye An observation wheel, the largest in the world, located on the South Bank of the R Thames, London, UK, opened in 2000 as part of the millennium celebrations; originally called the **Millennium Wheel**. Sponsored by British Airways, it was designed by London architects David Marks and Julia Barfield, and operated by the Tussauds Group; height 135 m/443 ft; weight 1500 tons. Its 32 capsules carry passengers on a 30-minute journey, offering views up to 25 miles.

London Festival Ballet *English National Ballet*

London Group A society of British artists founded in 1913 by Nash, Epstein, Fry, and others; its first president was Harold Gilman (1878–1919). It held regular exhibitions for half a century.

London Missionary Society (LMS) Formed in London in 1795 by evangelical Protestants to undertake missionary work in the Pacific islands. It was particularly successful in Tahiti (1797), the Cook Is (1821), Samoa (1830), and Papua New Guinea (1871). The LMS also came to operate in other parts of the world, including Africa.

London Museum A museum at London Wall in the City of London, UK, created from the former London and Guildhall museums and opened in 1975. It covers the history of London from prehistoric times to the present day.

London plane *plane tree*

London pride A mat-forming perennial (*Saxifraga × umbrosa*) with rosettes of paddle-shaped, blunt-toothed leaves; flowers in sprays on erect stems growing to 30 cm/12 in, white to pinkish with red spots. It is a hybrid of unknown origin, widely grown in gardens. (Family: Saxifragaceae.)

London University A federation of colleges, medical schools, and research institutions established as a university in London, UK in 1836. In addition to the medical schools of the London teaching hospitals, several major institutions form part of the university. (*see panel*)

lone pair In a molecule, a pair of valence electrons which are associated with one atom only. They affect the shape of the molecule, and are often important in the formation of coordination compounds.

LONDON UNIVERSITY

College	*Founded*
Wye College (Ashford) (controlled by London University since 1900)	1447
Royal Veterinary College	1791
Birkbeck College	1823
University College London	1826
King's College London (merged with Queen Elizabeth College and Chelsea College 1985)	1829
School of Pharmacy	1842
Goldsmith's College (controlled by London University since 1904)	1891
London School of Economics and Political Science	1895
Institute of Education (controlled by London University since 1932; school of London University since 1987)	1902
Imperial College of Science Technology and Medicine	1907
School of Oriental and African Studies	1916
Royal Holloway and Bedford New College (Egham) (founded through merger of Bedford College and Royal Holloway College)	1985
Queen Mary and Westfield College (founded through merger of Queen Mary College and Westfield College)	1989

Long, Crawford Williamson (1815–78) Physician, born in Danielsville, Georgia, USA. He was the first to use ether to relieve pain during a surgical procedure, and is considered by many to be the discoverer of anaesthesia. He trained at the University of Pennsylvania and graduated in 1839. On 30 March 1842, he painlessly removed a tumour from the neck of a patient after administering ether by dropping the liquid on a cloth. However, he did not make his work public until 1849, and the delay in reporting his findings prevented him from being recognized as the pioneer anaesthetist for many years. The anniversary of his accomplishment is celebrated in the USA as 'Doctor's Day'.

Long, Huey (Pierce), nickname **Kingfish** (1893–1935) US Democratic politician, born in Winnfield, Louisiana, USA. A lawyer by profession, he became Governor of Louisiana (1928–31) and a US senator (1930–5). He became notorious for his corruption and demagoguery. He secured the wrath of the rich and support of the poor by his intensive 'Share the Wealth' social services and public works programmes, but also squandered public funds on extravagant personal projects, including the construction of a marble and bronze statehouse at Baton Rouge. He was assassinated by Carl Weiss, the son of a political opponent. Despite his flaws, historians regard him as an authentic expression of the popular protest during the Depression.

Long Beach 33°47N 118°11W, pop (2000e) 461 500; City in Los Angeles Co, SW California, USA, on San Pedro Bay; developed rapidly after the discovery of oil, 1921; railway; university (1949); oil refining; diverse manufacturing; tourist centre; a long bathing beach; location for the British cruise liner *Queen Mary*, now a museum-hotel-convention centre; Long Beach Marine Stadium (scene of the 1932 Olympic boating events).

longbow An English bow with a shaft of yew-wood 1·5 m/5 ft long, which could shoot an arrow capable of penetrating plate armour at 400 yd (365 m). It dominated the battlefield for 200 years from 1300, proving decisive at the Battles of Crécy, Poitiers, and Agincourt.

Longchamp *Bois de Boulogne*

long-distance network *local area network*

Longfellow, Henry Wadsworth (1807–82) Poet, born in Portland, Maine, USA. He studied at Bowdoin College in Brunswick, ME, and as a gifted translator was sent to Europe to qualify for a chair of foreign languages. On his return, he was unable to settle, and when offered a professorship at Harvard he accepted it as another opportunity to go abroad. After the early death of his wife in 1835, he returned and became professor of modern languages and literature at Harvard (1836–54). During this period he remarried, and published many works, notably the immensely successful *Ballads and Other Poems* (1841), including 'The Wreck of the Hesperus'. His most popular work, 'The Song of Hiawatha', with its distinctive 'Indian drum' rhythm, was published in 1855, and in 1863 appeared *Tales of a Wayside Inn*, which included the famous 'Paul Revere's Ride'.

Longford (city), Ir **Longphort** 53°44N 7°47W, pop (2000e) 6900. Capital of Longford county, NW Leinster, C Ireland; on R Camlin and a branch of the Royal Canal; former literary centre; railway; St Mel's Cathedral; Tullynally Castle at Castlepollard.

Longford (county), Ir **Longphort** pop (2000e) 31 000; area 1044 sq km/403 sq mi. County in NW Leinster province, C Ireland; drained by R Shannon and its tributaries; crossed by the Royal Canal; hilly in NW; capital, Longford; sheep, cattle, oats, potatoes.

Longhi, Pietro [longgee], originally **Pietro Falca** (1702–85) Painter, born in Venice, NE Italy. He excelled in small-scale satirical pictures of Venetian life. Most of his work is in Venetian public collections, but the National Gallery, London, has three, of which the best known is 'Rhinoceros in an Arena'. His son **Alessandro** (1733–1813) was also a painter, and some of his portraits are now attributed to his father.

Longinus [lonjiynus], also called **Dionysius Longinus** and **Pseudo-Longinus** (fl. 1st-c) Name assigned to the Greek author of the surviving portion of a treatise on excellence in literature, *On the Sublime*, which influenced many Neoclassical writers, such as Dryden and Pope; about a third of the manuscript (in its earliest form, dating from the 10th-c) is lost. Several attempts have been made to identify the author, without success.

Long Island area 3600 sq km/1400 sq mi, length 190 km/118 mi. Island in SE New York State, USA; bounded N by Long Island Sound; separated from the Bronx and Manhattan by the East River, and from Staten I by the Narrows; comprises the boroughs of Brooklyn and Queens, and the New York State counties of Kings (includes Brooklyn), Nassau, Queens, Suffolk; many residential towns and resort beaches; contains John F Kennedy airport; settled by the Dutch in 1623, and by the English c.1640; site of the Battle of Long Island (1776) in the US War of Independence, when British forces under Howe defeated American forces under Washington.

longitude *latitude and longitude*

longitudinal wave *wave motion*

long jump An athletics field event in which the competitors leap for distance into a sandpit after running up to a take-off board. The contestant having the longest fair jump, measured from the farthest edge of the take-off board to the pit, is the winner. A jump from beyond the take-off board is a foul. It is sometimes called the **running broad jump**. The current world record for men is 8·95 m/29 ft 4¼ in, achieved by Mike Powell (1963–) of the USA, in 1991 at Tokyo; for women is 7·52 m/24 ft 8¼ in, achieved by Galina Chistyakova (1962–) of the USSR, in 1988 at St Petersburg, Russia.

Longman, Thomas (1699–1755) Publisher, born in Bristol, SW England, UK. He bought a bookselling business in Paternoster Row, London, in 1724, and shared in publishing such works as Ephraim Chambers's *Cyclopaedia*, and Johnson's *Dictionary*. He was the founder of the British publishing house that still bears his name.

Long March The epic of Chinese communist revolutionary history. In 1934 the Red Army was blockaded in SE China by Jiang Jieshi's forces. In October, Mao Zedong, Zhu De, and Lin Biao broke out with 100 000 troops to lead a 13 000 km/8000 mi evacuation westwards then north. The march ended with the arrival of under 20 000 in Shaanxi, N China, the following October. Though a military disaster, the Long March established Mao's supremacy in the party. Lasting 20 million paces, it later became a key element in communist hagiography.

Long Parliament An English parliament called (Nov 1640) by Charles I after his defeat by the Scots in the second Bishops' War. It was legally in being 1640–60, but did not meet continuously. It attacked prerogative rights and alleged abuses of power by the king and his ministers, and abolished the Court of Star Chamber, the Councils of the North and for Wales, and the Ecclesiastical Court of High Commission (1641), the bishops and the Court of Wards (1646), and the monarchy and the House of Lords (1649). Moderates were eliminated in Pride's Purge (Dec 1648), and the remaining Rump was dismissed by Cromwell in 1653. The Rump was recalled in the death-throes of the Protectorate (May 1659), and all members in December 1659.

long-range navigation system *loran*

longship A vessel used by the Vikings in their voyages of exploration, plunder, and conquest. The largest were 45 m/150 ft in length, made of overlapping wooden planks ('clinker built'), very strong, and propelled by both oars and sail. They usually carried 30 or 40 men, but there was room for more (such as captured Saxon maidens), and the larger vessels may well have carried twice this number.

longshore transport The movement of sediment particles along a beach in response to wave activity. The particles may be transported along the beach face, being rolled up and down at an angle with the waves (*beach drift*). They may also be transported in suspension by the turbulent water in the surf zone as it moves along the beach (the *longshore current*).

long-sightedness *eye*

long-tailed tit A small bird of the long-tailed **titmouse** family (*Aegithalos caudatus*); native to Europe and Asia; black, white, and pink; body shorter than long straight tail; inhabits scrub and woodland; eats seeds, buds, and insects.

Lonsdale, Dame Kathleen, *née* **Yardley** (1903–71) Crystallographer, born in Newbridge, Co Kildare, E Ireland. The family came to Britain in 1908 and she studied physics at Bedford College, London, and spent the next 20 years in the research team of William Bragg based at the Royal Institution. She worked at University College London, as professor of chemistry and head of the department of crystallography (1946–68). From the 1920s she applied X-ray crystal diffraction to determine chemical structures. In 1945 the Royal Society agreed to elect women fellows, and she became the first female FRS. She was created a dame in 1956.

Lonsdale Belt In boxing, a championship belt awarded to a fighter who wins a British title fight. If he wins three fights in one weight division, he is allowed to keep the belt permanently. The wins do not necessarily have to be in succession. It is named after the 5th Earl of Lonsdale, who presented the first belt to the National Sporting Club in 1909. The heavyweight boxer Henry Cooper is the only man to have won three Lonsdale Belts outright.

loofah An annual climbing vine with tendrils (*Luffa cylindrica*), native to the tropics; leaves heart-shaped; flowers yellow, funnel-shaped; fruit marrow-like, up to 30 cm/12 in long, roughly cylindrical. The familiar sponge-like item of bathrooms is the fibrous vascular tissue of the fruit left when the soft parts are removed. (Family: Cucurbitaceae.)

look-and-say A method of teaching reading through whole-word recognition, linking the form with a visual stimulus, and using frequently occurring short words (eg *go, see*) as a prelude to introducing longer words of which they may form component parts. The aim is to teach words as meaningful entities, rather than as sequences of phonic syllables.

loon *diver*

looper The caterpillar larva of a geometrid moth, characterized by its looping locomotion pattern; possesses only one pair of pro-legs and one pair of claspers; body held rigid at rest, resembling a twig; also known as **inch worm**. (Order: Lepidoptera. Family: Geometridae.)

Loos, Adolf [loos] (1870–1933) Architect and writer on design, born in Brno, S Czech Republic. After studying architecture in Dresden, and visiting America (1893–6), he settled in Vienna in 1896. One of the major architects of the Modern Movement, he is particularly remembered for articulating the view that ornament is decadent; his essay *Ornament and Crime* (1908) attacks both revivalist and more recent Art Nouveau ornament. His designs reflect this view, notably the Villa Karma, Clarens, Switzerland (1904–6).

Lope de Vega *Vega, Lope de*

Lopez, Jennifer [lohpez], popularly known as **J-Lo** (1970–) Actress and pop singer, born in the Bronx, New York City, USA. She trained as a dancer and gained a part in the television comedy-sketch series *In Living Color* (1990–3). She went on to co-star in the feature film *Money Train* (1995) and took the title role in *Selena* (1997). Later films include *The Wedding Planner* (2001) and *Maid in Manhattan* (2002). Her albums include *J-Lo* (2001) and *This is Me... Then* (2002).

loquat [lohkwat] A small evergreen tree (*Eriobotrya japonica*) with very hairy twigs, native to China, but widely grown in S Europe; leaves coarse, reddish, hairy beneath; flowers white, fragrant, in terminal clusters; fruits 3–6 cm/$1\frac{1}{4}$–$2\frac{1}{2}$ in, round, yellowish-orange, flesh sweet and edible; one or more seeds. (Family: Rosaceae.)

loran Acronym for **long-range navigation system**. Radio pulses emitted at fixed intervals by pairs of transmitters define a grid pattern, over a very large area, not in two sets of straight lines but in sets of intersecting hyperbolae. The timing of the reception of these paired pulses by an aircraft or ship indicates its position on the network.

Lorca, Federico García [law(r)ka, gah(r)seea] (1898–1936) Poet, born in Fuente Vaqueros, S Spain. A gifted musician, he studied law at Granada, to please his father, but soon turned to the arts, and after publishing a promising book of prose, entered the residence of scholars at Madrid. His *Canciones* (1927, Songs), *Romancero Gitano* (1928, 1935, The Gypsy Ballads), and tragic poems place him among the greatest of 20th-c poets. He also wrote successful prose plays, including the trilogy *Bodas de Sangre* (1933, Blood Wedding), *Yerma* (1934), and *La Casa de Bernarda Alba* (1936, The House of Bernarda Alba). He was assassinated in the Spanish Civil War at Granada.

Lord Chancellor The head of the judiciary of England and Wales, a member of the cabinet, and the Speaker of the House of Lords. The appointment is by the Crown on the advice of the prime minister. As someone who holds prominent positions in all three branches of government, the office is a clear exception to the doctrine of the separation of powers. The Lord Chancellor appoints, and may dismiss, magistrates and circuit judges. In the House of Lords, he generally presides from the woolsack, but may take part in debates and divisions.

Lord Chief Justice The president or head of the Queen's Bench Division of the High Court in England and Wales, and of the Criminal Division of the Court of Appeal. In the judicial hierarchy, the position ranks second only to the Lord Chancellor.

Lord Howe Island 31°33S 159°04E, pop (2000e) 600. Volcanic island in the Pacific Ocean, 702 km/436 mi NE of Sydney; part of New South Wales; area 16·6 sq km/6·4 sq mi; rises to 866 m/2841 ft at Mt Gower; discovered, 1788; a popular resort island; a world heritage site.

Lord-Lieutenant [leftenant] In the UK, the sovereign's permanent representative in a county or county borough of England, Wales, or Northern Ireland, or in a part of one of the Scottish regions. The lordly prefix is by custom only, and the office is now primarily one of honour.

Lord Lyon King of Arms *heraldry*

Lords, House of The non-elected house of the UK legislature. Its membership (formerly 1330, currently c.670) traditionally included both hereditary peers and life peers (including judicial members – the *Lords of Appeal in Ordinary*), as well as the two archbishops and certain bishops of the Church of England. In 1999 it underwent the first stage of what is intended to be a two-stage process of reform (pending the results of a Royal Commission) involving the removal of the hereditary peers. After this stage, the House contained only 92 hereditary peers, elected by and from their number. In addition, 10 hereditary peers were also awarded life peerages to enable them to continue to sit in the interim chamber. The House can no longer veto bills passed by the House of Commons, with the exception of a bill to prolong the duration of a parliament, although it can delay measures. Its functions are mainly deliberative, its authority being based on the expertise of its membership. The House of Lords also constitutes the most senior court in the UK, normally being the final court of appeal in all matters from England, Wales, and Northern Ireland, and in civil cases from Scotland. However, on matters of European law, cases may be referred from the House of Lords to the Court of Justice of the European Communities. Appeals heard by the House are confined to matters of law. Government proposals for the second stage of reform (Nov 2001) were controversially received (especially the proposal that in a new house of 600 members only 120 would be directly elected). Voting in February 2003 failed to achieve parliamentary agreement on the method of constituting a reformed House.

lords-and-ladies A perennial native to Europe and N Africa (*Arum maculatum*), with glossy dark-green arrowhead-shaped leaves and poisonous scarlet berries; also called **cuckoo-pint**. The complex inflorescence consists of a cylindrical spadix the colour of dead meat, which becomes warm and emits a rotting scent to attract flies. These crawl into the bulbous base of the pale green spathe enclosing the male and female flowers, and are trapped by a ring of guard hairs. The flies pollinate the female flowers and collect pollen from the male flowers, but can escape only when the spadix collapses and the hairs wither after pollination. (Family: Araceae.)

Lord's Cricket Ground A cricket ground founded by Thomas Lord (1755–1832) in 1814 in NW London, UK. It is the home of the Marylebone Cricket Club (MCC) and the Middlesex County Cricket Club, and the recognized administrative and spiritual home of national and international cricket. Its cricketing treasures include the Ashes.

Lord's Prayer A popular prayer of Christian worship, derived from *Matt* 6.9–13 and (in different form) *Luke* 11.2–4; also known as the **Pater Noster** ('Our Father'). It is a model for how Jesus's followers are to pray, consisting (in Matthew) of three petitions praising God and seeking his kingdom, followed by four petitions concerning the physical and spiritual needs of followers. The closing doxology ('For thine is the kingdom...') was apparently added later in Church tradition.

Lorelei [loreliy] The name of a precipitous rock on the Rhine, dangerous to boatmen and celebrated for its echo. The story of the siren of the rock whose songs lure sailors to their death originates in Heine's poem *Die Lorelei* (1827).

Loren, Sophia [loren], originally **Sofia Scicolone** (1934–) Actress, born in Rome, Italy. An illegitimate child from a poor home in Naples, she became a teenage beauty queen and model. Her film debut was as an extra. She came under contract to film producer **Carlo Ponti** (1912–), later her husband, and blossomed as an actress. An international career followed and she won an Oscar for *La Ciociara*, (1961, trans Two Women). Frequently appearing with Marcello Mastroianni, her many films include *The Millionairess* (1961) and *Marriage Italian Style* (1964). In 1979 she published *Sophia Loren: Living and Loving* (with A E Hotchner) which was filmed for television as *Sophia Loren: Her Own Story* (1980), in which she played herself and her mother. She received an honorary Academy Award in 1991.

Lorentz, Hendrik Antoon [lohrents] (1853–1928) Physicist, born in Arnhem, The Netherlands. He studied at Leyden and became professor of mathematical physics there (1878), and from 1923 directed research at the Taylor Institute, Haarlem. He clarified the electromagnetic theory of James Clerk Maxwell, and introduced the concept of local time while working on the Michelson–Morley experiment. In 1902 he and Pieter Zeeman were awarded the Nobel Prize for Physics for their work on electromagnetic radiation. Their efforts presaged Einstein's theory of special relativity.

Lorentz contraction [lorents] The apparent contraction of objects in their direction of motion when their velocity is comparable to the velocity of light, as described by special relativity; also called the **length contraction**. Named after Hendrik Lorentz, it is also known as the **Lorentz–FitzGerald contraction**, after Irish physicist George FitzGerald (1851–1901), who made this proposal independently in 1889.

Lorenz, Konrad (Zacharias) [lohrents] (1903–89) Zoologist and ethologist, born in Vienna, Austria. He studied medicine at Vienna, and became professor at the Albertus University in Königsberg, headed the Institute of Comparative Ethology at Altenberg, established a comparative ethology department in the Max Planck Institute, and became its co-director in 1954. The founder of ethology, his studies have led to a deeper understanding of behaviour patterns in animals, notably imprinting in young birds. In his book *On Aggression* (1963) he argued that aggressive behaviour in humans may be modified or channelled, but in other animals it is purely survival motivated. *King Solomon's Ring* (1949) and *Man Meets Dog* (1950) also enjoyed wide popularity. He shared the 1973 Nobel Prize for Physiology or Medicine.

Lorenzetti, Ambrogio [lorenzetee] (c.1280–c.1348) Painter born in Siena, C Italy. Probably taught by his brother Pietro (c.1280–c.1348), he worked in Cortona and Florence, and is best known for his allegorical frescoes in the Palazzo Pubblico at Siena, symbolizing the effects of good and bad government. His 'Annunciation' is also at Siena.

Lorenzo [lorenzoh], known as **il Monaco** ('the Monk'), originally **Piero di Giovanni** (c.1370–c.1425) Painter, born in Siena, C Italy. By 1391 he was a monk in the Camaldolite monastery of S Maria degli Angeli, Florence, and his great altarpiece, 'The Coronation of the Virgin' (1414, now in the Uffizi) was painted for the high altar there. His graceful, linear, Gothic style epitomizes the last phase of mediaeval art before the onset of the Renaissance.

Loreto [loretoh] 43°26N 13°36E, pop (2000e) 10 000. Town in Marche region, E Italy; located on a hill overlooking the Adriatic Sea; famous place of pilgrimage to the sanctuary and Holy House (Santa Casa) of the Virgin Mary; according to legend, the house was brought from Nazareth through the air by angels in 1294 and set on a hill surrounded by laurels; Our Lady of Loreto is designated the patron saint of airmen; silk industries; tourism.

lorikeet *lory*

loris A primitive primate, native to forests in S and SE Asia; no tail; pale face with dark rings around large eyes; slow climbers; three species: **slender loris** (*Loris tardigradus*) with long thin legs; **slow loris** or **cu lan** (*Nycticebus coucang*), and **lesser slow loris** (*Nycticebus pygmaeus*). (Family: Lorisidae.)

Lorrain, Claude *Claude Lorrain*

Lorraine [loren], Ger **Lothringen** pop (2000e) 2 417 000; area 23 547 sq km/9089 sq mi. Region and former province of NE France, comprising departments of Meurthe-et-Moselle, Meuse, Moselle, and Vosges; bordered by the Plaine de Champagne (W), Vosges (E), Ardennes (N), and Monts Faucilles (S); frequent source of Franco-German conflict; duchy since the 10th-c; part of France, 1766; ceded to Germany as part of Alsace-Lorraine, 1871; returned to France after World War 1; chief towns, Metz, Nancy, Luneville, Epinal; corn, fruit, cheese; iron ore, coal, salt; mineral springs.

Lorraine, Cross of [lorayn] A cross with two horizontal crosspieces. The symbol of Joan of Arc, it was adopted by the Free French forces leader (Charles de Gaulle) in 1940.

Lorris, Guillaume de *Guillaume de Lorris*

lory [lawree] A parrot of the subfamily Loriinae (c.60 species), found from SE Asia to Australia; eats mainly pollen and nectar, but also insects and seeds; tongue has brush-like tip. Smaller species are called **lorikeets**. (Family: Psittacidae.)

Los (in place names) *also under initial letter of the following word*

Los Alamos [los alamos] 35°52N 106°19W, pop (2000e) 11 900. Community in Los Alamos Co, N New Mexico, USA; 56 km/35 mi NW of Santa Fe in the Jemez Mts; a nuclear research centre since 1943; the first nuclear weapons were developed here during World War 2; government control ended in 1962.

Los Angeles 34°04N 118°15W, pop (2000e) 3 694 800. Seaport seat of Los Angeles Co, California, USA; founded by the Spanish, 1781; originally called **Nuestra Señora Reina de Los Angeles**; captured from Mexico by the US Navy, 1846; established, 1850; grew after the arrival of the Southern Pacific Railroad and the discovery of oil nearby in 1894; has absorbed several towns, villages, and independent cities; second largest US city; three airports (Los Angeles, Long Beach, Santa Clara); railway; five universities; harbour on San Pedro Bay, 40 km/25 mi S of city centre; major industrial and research centre; military and civil aircraft, machinery, petroleum products, electronic equipment, glass, chemicals, oil refining, fish canning and distributing; high density of road traffic; smog a major problem; major tourist area; professional teams, Dodgers (baseball), Clippers, Lakers (basketball), Raiders, Rams (football), Kings (ice hockey); district of Hollywood a major centre of the US film and television industry; Los Angeles County Museum of Art; 28-storey City Hall; Old Mission Church (c.1818), now a museum; new Cathedral of Our Lady of the Angels (dedicated 2002); La Brea Tar Pits; Hollywood Bowl; Hollywood Wax Museum; Universal Film Studios; Disneyland; scene of summer Olympic Games, 1984.

Losey, Joseph (Walton) [lohsee] (1909–84) Film director, born in La Crosse, Wisconsin, USA. He attended Dartmouth College, NH, and Harvard, and worked first as a show-business reporter before becoming a stage director on Broadway. His early films centred on controversial topics, and when he was blacklisted as a suspected Communist by the McCarthy Committee he left Hollywood for England (1952). Working anonymously at first, he went on to direct a number of successful films, including *The Servant* (1963), *Modesty Blaise* (1966), *Accident* (1967), and *The Go-Between*, which won the Cannes Film Festival in 1971. From the mid-1970s he worked mainly in France, where his last film was *La Truite* (1982, The Trout).

Lossiemouth [loseemowth] 57°43N 3°18W, pop (2000e) 7800. Port town in Moray, NE Scotland, UK; fishing, tourism; air force base nearby (often involved in air-sea rescue); birthplace of Ramsay MacDonald.

lost generation A term applied by Gertrude Stein to a group of US expatriates (including herself) living in Paris in the 1920s, among them Ezra Pound, Ernest Hemingway, and Scott Fitzgerald. Their work reflects the breakdown of order and values after World War 1.

Lost World Name given by novelist Arthur Conan Doyle to an imaginary range of mountains where prehistoric animals survived into the 20th-c; based on Col Percy Fawcett's description of the Serra Ricardo Franco in the Mato Grosso state of W Brazil. Mt Roraima in Venezuela also claims to be Lost World.

Lot Biblical character, portrayed in Genesis as the nephew of Abraham who separated from him and settled in Canaan, near Sodom. Stories describe his rescue from the wickedness of that place by Abraham and two angels. Symbolic of backsliding, Lot's wife is described as looking back during this escape and being turned into 'a pillar of salt'. Lot was named also as the ancestor of the Moabites and Ammonites.

Lotharingia [lotharinggia] Originally, the kingdom of Lothar II (855–69), great-grandson of Charlemagne; subsequently, though disputed with France, two duchies of the kingdom of Germany. Only one, Upper Lotharingia (modern Lorraine), survived the 12th-c, and it was eventually incorporated into France (1766).

Lothian [lohthian] pop (2000e) 755 500; area 1755 sq km/678 sq mi. Former region in E Scotland, UK (1975–96); replaced in 1996 by North Lanarkshire, Falkirk, West Lothian, Midlothian, East Lothian, and City of Edinburgh councils.

Lotophagi *lotus-eaters*

Lots, Feast of *Purim*

lottery A way of raising money through the sale of chances (tickets) and the use of a random procedure to decide the prize-winners. Very large numbers of people take part, producing a correspondingly large sum of money which (after deduction of taxes and organizational expenses) is available for prizes. Many countries now organize state lotteries, which provide an attractive extra source of government income, as well as offering a promise of vast wealth for a few. They have also been used to finance major projects, such as roads, buildings, and universities, as well as projects to do with the arts, the environment, and all forms of charity. The popularity of large lotteries has, at the same time, generated controversy, as stories come to light of families harmed by compulsive gambling or of winners unable to manage their new-found wealth, and there has been considerable opposition to lotteries throughout their history, with many accounts of bribery and corruption. Lotteries in Europe have been known since the 16th-c. Famous lotteries include those of Italy, Ireland (the Irish Hospitals' Sweepstake), and Australia (where a lottery helped finance the Sydney Opera House). Britain's national lottery began in 1994.

Lotto, Lorenzo (c.1480–1556) Religious painter, born in Venice, NE Italy. He worked in Treviso, Bergamo, Venice, and Rome, and became known for his altarpieces and portraits. In 1554 he became a lay brother in the Loreto monastery.

lotus A name given to three different plants. The sacred lotus of Egypt (*Nymphaea lotus*) is a species of waterlily. The sacred lotus of India and China (*Nelumbium nuciferum*), traditionally associated with the Buddha, is also an aquatic plant, but with circular leaves which have the stalks attached in the centre of the blade, and pink and white flowers. The lotus of classical times (*Zizyphus lotus*) is a type of jujube from the Mediterranean region.

lotus bird *jacana*

lotus-eaters or **Lotophagi** [lotofajiy] In Homer and Tennyson, a fabulous people encountered by Odysseus, living on 'a flowery food' which makes those who eat it forget their own country, and wish to live always in a dreamy state. Odysseus had to force his men to move on.

Lotus 123 A popular computer package to enable the user to work on a spreadsheet. It is a registered trade mark of Lotus Development Corporation.

Louangphrabang or **Luang Prabang** [luangprabang] 19°53N 102°10E, pop (2000e) 68 000. Town in W Laos, on R Mekong, at head of navigation; former capital (1946–75); centre of agricultural region; Buddhist pagodas.

loudspeaker or **speaker** A device which converts electrical energy into sound waves. The loudspeaker is fed a current having frequencies and amplitudes proportionate to some original sound waves. It reconverts these signals, radiating a new set of sound waves which reproduce at a listener's ears as nearly as possible the acoustic experience of the original performance. The majority of loudspeakers use the electromagnetic principle. An alternating signal current passes through one or more voice coils set in powerful permanent magnetic fields. The alternating magnetic fields which result cause the coils (and the diaphragm or cone to which each one is fixed) to move to and fro in vibration, and it is this mechanical vibration that regenerates the sound waves.

Louganis, Greg(ory) [looganis] (1960–) Diver, born in El Cajon, California, USA. In the 1983 world championships, his routine won him more than 700 points for his 11 dives, the first man to achieve such a score. He was Olympic champion (1984, 1988, when he became the first man to win golds in both springboard and platform events at successive Games), platform world champion (1978, 1982, 1986), and springboard champion (1982, 1986). In 1984 he won the Sullivan Award as America's best athlete of the year. In 1995 he revealed he had AIDS.

Louis IX, St (1214–70) King of France (1226–70), born in Poissy, near Paris, NC France, the son of Louis VIII. By his victories he compelled Henry III of England to acknowledge French suzerainty in Guienne (1259). He led the Seventh Crusade (1248), but was defeated in Egypt, taken prisoner, and ransomed. After returning to France (1254), he carried out several legal reforms, and fostered learning, the arts, and literature. He embarked on a new Crusade in 1270, and died of plague at Tunis. He was canonized in 1297; feast day 25 August.

Louis XII (1462–1515) King of France (1498–1515), born in Blois, C France, the son of Charles, duc d'Orléans, to whose title he succeeded in 1465. He commanded the French troops at Asti during Charles VIII's invasion of Italy (1494–5), before succeeding him to the French throne (1498), and marrying his widow, Anne of Brittany. He proved a popular ruler, concerned to provide justice and avoid oppressive taxation. His Italian ambitions brought him into diplomatic and military involvement with Ferdinand II of Aragon, who finally outmanoeuvred Louis with the formation of the Holy League (1511). Meanwhile, Louis had foiled the Emperor Maximilian's dynastic designs on Brittany, but paid the price when his forces were driven from Italy (1512), and was then defeated by an Anglo–Imperial alliance at the Battle of Guinegate (1513). To guarantee peace, Louis married Mary Tudor, the sister of Henry VIII (1515), but died in Paris shortly afterwards.

Louis XIII (1601–43) King of France (1610–43), born in Fontainebleau, C France, the eldest son of Henry IV and Marie de Médicis. He succeeded to the throne on the assassination of his father (1610), but was excluded from power, even after he came of age (1614), by the queen regent. She arranged Louis' marriage to Anne of Austria, the daughter of Philip III of Spain (1615). In 1617 Louis took over the reins of government, and exiled Marie de Médicis to Blois (1619–20). By 1624 he was entirely dependent upon the political acumen of Richelieu, who became his chief minister. Various plots to oust the Cardinal were foiled by the king's loyalty to his minister, whose domestic and foreign policies seemed to fulfil the royal ambition for great achievements. Louis' later years were enhanced by French military victories in the Thirty Years' War against the Habsburgs, and by the birth of two sons in 1638 and 1640, including the future Louis XIV.

Louis XIV, known as **le Roi soleil** ('the Sun King') (1638–1715) King of France (1643–1715), born in St Germain-en-Laye, NC France, the son of Louis XIII, whom he succeeded at the age of five. During his minority (1643–51) France was ruled by his mother, Anne of Austria, and her chief minister, Cardinal Mazarin. In 1660 Louis married the Infanta Maria Theresa, the elder daughter of Philip IV of Spain, through whom he was later to claim the Spanish succession for his second grandson. In 1661 he assumed sole responsibility for government, advised by various royal councils. His obsession with France's greatness led him into aggressive foreign and commercial policies, particularly against the Dutch. His patronage of the Catholic Stuarts also led to the hostility of England after 1689; but his major political rivals were the Austrian Habsburgs, particularly Leopold I. From 1665 Louis tried to take possession of the Spanish Netherlands, but later became obsessed with the acquisition of the whole Spanish inheritance. His attempt to create a Franco–Spanish Bourbon bloc led to the formation of the Grand Alliance of England, the United Provinces, and the Habsburg empire, and resulted in the War of the Spanish Succession (1701–13). In later years Louis was beset by other problems. His determination to preserve the unity of the French state and the independence of the French Church led him into conflict with the Jansenists, the Huguenots, and the papacy, with damaging repercussions. His old age was overshadowed by military disaster and the financial ravages of prolonged warfare. Yet Louis was the greatest monarch of his age, who established the parameters of successful absolutism. In addition, his long reign marked the cultural ascendancy of France within

Europe, symbolized by the Palace of Versailles. He was succeeded by his great-grandson as Louis XV.

Louis XV, known as **Louis le Bien-Aimé** ('Louis the Well Beloved') (1710–74) King of France (1715–74), born in Versailles, NC France, the son of Louis, duc de Bourgogne and Marie-Adelaide of Savoy, and the great-grandson of Louis XIV, whom he succeeded at the age of five. His reign coincided with the great age of decorative art in the Rococo mode (dubbed the *Louis XV style*). Until he came of age (1723) he was guided by the regent, Philippe d'Orléans, and then by the Duc de Bourbon, who negotiated a marriage alliance with **Maria Leszczynska**, daughter of the deposed King Stanislas I of Poland. In 1726 Bourbon was replaced by the king's former tutor, the elderly Fleury, who skilfully steered the French state until his death (1744). Thereafter Louis vowed to rule without a First Minister, but allowed the government to drift into the hands of ministerial factions, while indulging in secret diplomatic activity, distinct from official policy, through his own network of agents. This system – *le secret du roi* – brought confusion to French foreign policy in the years prior to the Diplomatic Revolution (1748–56), and obscured the country's interests overseas. Instead, France was drawn into a trio of continental wars during Louis's reign, which culminated in the loss of the French colonies in America and India (1763). In 1771 Louis tried to introduce reforms, but these came too late to staunch the decline in royal authority. He was succeeded by his grandson, Louis XVI.

Louis XVI (1754–93) King of France (1774–93), born in Versailles, NC France, the third son of the dauphin Louis and Maria Josepha of Saxony, and the grandson of Louis XV, whom he succeeded in 1774. He was married in 1770 to the Archduchess Marie Antoinette, daughter of the Habsburg Empress Maria Theresa, to strengthen the Franco-Austrian alliance. He failed to give consistent support to ministers who tried to reform the outmoded financial and social structures of the country, such as Turgot (1774–6) and Necker (1776–81). He allowed France to become involved in the War of American Independence (1778–83), which exacerbated the national debt. Meanwhile, Marie Antoinette's propensity for frivolous conduct and scandal helped to discredit the monarchy. To avert the deepening social and economic crisis, he agreed in 1789 to summon the States General. However, encouraged by the queen, he resisted demands from the National Assembly for sweeping reforms, and in October was brought with his family from Versailles to Paris as hostage to the revolutionary movement. Their attempted flight to Varennes (Jun 1791) branded the royal pair as traitors. Louis reluctantly approved the new constitution (Sep 1791), but his moral authority had collapsed. In August 1792 an insurrection suspended Louis's constitutional position, and in September the monarchy was abolished. He was tried before the National Convention for conspiracy with foreign powers, and was guillotined in Paris.

Louis (Charles) XVII (1785–95) Titular King of France (1793–5), born in Versailles, NC France, the second son of Louis XVI and heir to the throne from June 1789. After the execution of his father (Jan 1793) he remained in the Temple prison in Paris. His death there dealt a blow to the hopes of Royalists and constitutional monarchists. The secrecy surrounding his last months led to rumours of his escape, and produced several claimants to his title.

Louis XVIII, originally **Louis Stanislas Xavier, comte de** (Count of) **Provence** (1755–1824) King of France in name from 1795 and in fact from 1814, born in Versailles, NC France, the younger brother of Louis XVI. He fled from Paris in June 1791, finally taking refuge in England, becoming the focal point for the Royalist cause. On Napoleon's downfall (1814) he re-entered Paris, and promised a Constitutional Charter. His restoration was interrupted by Napoleon's return from Elba, but after Waterloo (1815) he again regained his throne. His reign was marked by the introduction of parliamentary government with a limited franchise.

Louis, Joe [loois], popular name of **Joseph Louis Barrow**, nickname **the Brown Bomber** (1914–81) Boxer, born in Lafayette, Alabama, USA. He was the US amateur light-heavyweight champion in 1934, and turned professional the same year. He beat James J Braddock (1905–74) for the world heavyweight title in 1937, and held the title for a record 12 years, making a record 25 defences. He retired in 1949, but made a comeback in 1950. He lost the world title fight to Ezzard Charles (1921–75), and had his last fight against Rocky Marciano in 1951. In all, he won 67 of his 70 professional fights, 53 by knockouts.

Louisiade Archipelago [looeeziahd] pop (2000e) 25 000; area 1550 sq km/600 sq mi. Mountainous island group in Papua New Guinea, SE of New Guinea; comprises the islands of Tacuta, Rossel, and Misima, with numerous other small islands and coral reefs; named in 1768 after Louis XIV of France; gold has been worked on Tacuta.

Louisiana [loozeeana] pop (2000e) 4 469 000; area 123 673 sq km/47 752 sq mi. State in S USA, divided into 64 parishes (the only state to use this term for its counties); the 'Pelican State'; name (after Louis XIV of France) originally applied to the entire Mississippi R basin, claimed for France by La Salle, 1682; most of the E region ceded to Spain in 1763, then to the USA in 1783; W region acquired by the USA in the Louisiana Purchase, 1803; admitted to the Union as the 18th state, 1812; seceded from the Union, 1861; re-admitted, 1868; experienced an economic revolution in the early 1900s when large deposits of oil and natural gas were discovered, capital, Baton Rouge; other chief cities, New Orleans and Shreveport; bounded S by the Gulf of Mexico; rivers include the Mississippi (large delta area in the S), Red, Sabine, and Pearl; highest point Mt Driskill (162 m/532 ft); vast coastal areas of marsh, lagoon, and fertile delta lands; further inland are plains and low rolling hills; over half the land area forested, supporting a major lumber and paper industry; highly productive in agriculture; soybeans, rice, sugar cane, sweet potatoes, cotton, cattle, dairy products; fishing, particularly for shrimps and oysters; a major source of pelts, especially muskrat; second only to Texas in oil and natural gas production (mainly offshore); oil refineries and petrochemical plants in several cities; leads the nation in salt and sulphur production; foods, clay, glass, transportation equipment; tourism increasing; world famous for the jazz music which grew up in and around New Orleans; special population groups of Creoles (French descent) and Cajuns (descendants of French Acadians driven from Canada by the British in the 18th-c).

Louisiana Purchase (1803) The sale by France to the USA of an area between the Mississippi R and the Rocky Mts for $15 000 000. The purchase gave the USA full control of the Mississippi Valley.

Louis Napoleon *Napoleon III*

Louis period styles A range of classical, Baroque, and Rococo stylistic variations used in the 17th-c and 18th-c, and particularly associated with the reign of Louis XIV of France. They are broadly characterized by lavish and ornate internal decoration and comparatively restrained facades and formal gardens; in the case of the Palais de Versailles (1661–1756), it also involved enormous amounts of labour, materials, and money.

Louis-Philippe [fileep], known as **the Citizen King** (1773–1850) King of the French (1830–48), born in Paris, France, the eldest son of the duc d'Orléans, Philippe Egalité. At the Revolution he entered the National Guard, and with his father renounced his titles to demonstrate his progressive sympathies. He joined the Jacobin Club (1790), and fought in the Army of the North before deserting to the Austrians (1793). He lived in Switzerland (1793–4), the USA, and England (1800–9), and in 1809 moved to Sicily and married **Marie Amélie**, daughter of Ferdinand I of Naples and Sicily. He returned to France in 1814, but fled to England again in the Hundred Days. On the eve of Charles X's abdication (1830) he was elected lieutenant-general of the kingdom, and after the July Revolution was given the title of King of the French. He strengthened his power by steering a middle course with the help of the upper bourgeoisie; but political corruption and industrial and agrarian depression (1846) caused discontent, and united the radicals in a cry for electoral reform. When the Paris mob rose (1848), he abdicated, and escaped to England.

Louisville [looeevil] 38°15N 85°46W, pop (2000e) 256 200. Seat of Jefferson Co, NW Kentucky, USA; port at the Falls of the Ohio R; settled, 1778; named after Louis XVI of France; city status, 1828; largest city in the state; University of Louisville (1798), the oldest municipal US university; a major horse breeding centre; important shipping point for coal; whiskey, cigarettes, machinery, electrical appliances, fabricated metals, foods; JB Speed Art Museum, Kentucky Railway Museum, Kentucky Derby Museum; Kentucky Derby (May) at Churchill Downs.

Lourdes [loordz], Fr [loord] 43°06N 0°00W, pop (2000e) 17 400. Town and important site of Roman Catholic pilgrimage in Hautes-Pyrénées department, S France; Bernadette Soubirous was led by a vision of the Virgin Mary to the springs at the Grotte de Massabielle in 1858; scene of many reputed miraculous cures; Basilica of the Rosary (1885–9), Church of St-Pie-X (completed, 1958).

lourie *turaco*

louse A secondarily wingless insect, parasitic on warm-blooded vertebrates. **Sucking lice** (Order: Anoplura) suck blood of mammals; length up to 6 mm/¼ in; bodies flattened, legs with claws for attaching to host; eyes reduced or absent; c.300 species. They include two varieties of human louse: **head lice** (*Pediculus humanus capitis*) and **body lice** (*Pediculus humanus humanus*), both transmitted by direct contact; lay eggs (*nits*) on hair and clothing; can transmit typhus and other diseases. **Biting lice** (Order: Mallophaga) live mostly on birds, have biting mouthparts for feeding on feathers; c.2700 species, a few found on mammals, feeding on hair.

Louth [lowth], Ir **Lughbhaidh** pop (2000e) 92 000; area 821 sq km/317 sq mi. County in NE Leinster province, Ireland; bounded N by N Ireland and E by Irish Sea; capital, Dundalk; cattle, oats, potatoes.

Loutherbourg, Philip James de [lootherboorg] (1740–1812) Stage designer and illustrator, born in Fulda, C Germany. He studied at Strasbourg, and after working in Paris was hired by Garrick as artistic adviser at the Drury Lane theatre, London (1771–81). His innovations in scene design and particularly in stage lighting laid the foundations for the development of pictorial illusion and the picture-frame concept in stagecraft. He abandoned theatre in 1781 to develop and exhibit his Eidophusikon, a model stage displaying panoramic transformations through the use of transparencies and coloured plates.

Louvain [looṽi] *Leuven*

L'Ouverture, Toussaint *Toussaint L'Ouverture*

Louvois, François Michel le Tellier, marquis de [loovwah] (1641–91) French statesman, and secretary of state for war under Louis XIV, born in Paris, France. He proved an energetic minister in the War of Devolution (1668), reforming and strengthening the army. His work bore fruit in the Dutch War, ending with the Peace of Nijmegen (1678). He was recognized as a brilliant administrator and the king's most influential minister in the years 1683–91.

Louvre [loovr] The national museum of art in Paris, France, and one of the finest art collections in the world. Built for Francis I in 1546, the Louvre was added to by successive French monarchs. The Grande Galerie of the Louvre was officially opened to the public in 1793.

lovage A strong-smelling perennial (*Levisticum officinale*) growing to 2·5 m/8 ft, native to Iran; leaves divided into large oval coarsely toothed leaflets; flowers small, greenish-yellow, in umbels up to 10 cm/4 in across; fruit ellipsoid with narrowly winged ribs. It is often cultivated and used for flavouring. (Family: Umbelliferae.)

Love, Mike *Beach Boys, The*

love apple *tomato*

lovebird A small parrot native to Africa and Madagascar; inhabits woodland, brush, and open country; eats seeds and berries; forms large flocks; female sometimes larger than male; a popular cagebird. They preen one another, hence the name, which is also used for the budgerigar. (Genus: *Agapornis*, nine species. Family: Psittacidae.)

Lovecraft, H(oward) P(hillips) (1890–1937) Science fiction writer and poet, born in Providence, Rhode Island, USA. Educated at local schools, he supported himself by ghost writing. From 1923 he was a regular contributor to *Weird Tales*. His cult following, particularly in America and France, can be traced to the 60 or so horrific 'Cthulhu Mythos' stories. His novellas included *The Case of Charles Dexter Ward* (1928) and *At the Mountains of Madness* (1931).

love-in-a-mist An annual native to Europe and W Asia (*Nigella damascena*); finely divided, feathery leaves and bracts; large, pale blue flowers; a globular, papery capsule. (Family: Ranunculaceae.)

Lovelace, Richard (1618–58) English Cavalier poet. He studied at Oxford, SC England, UK, and in 1642 was imprisoned for presenting to the House of Commons a petition from the royalists of Kent 'for the restoring the king to his rights', and was released on bail. He spent his great estate in Kent in the king's cause, assisted the French in 1646 to capture Dunkirk from the Spaniards, and was flung into jail on returning to England in 1648. In jail he revised his poems, including 'To Althea, from Prison', and in 1649 published his collection of poems, *Lucasta*.

Lovell, Sir (Alfred Charles) Bernard (1913–) Astronomer, born in Oldland Common, Gloucestershire, SWC England, UK. He studied at Bristol, and became professor of radio astronomy at Manchester (1951–80, then emeritus), and director of Jodrell Bank experimental station (now the Nuffield Radio Astronomy Laboratories). He gave the BBC Reith Lectures in 1958, taking for his subject *The Individual and the Universe*. He has written several books on radio astronomy and on its relevance to life and civilization today. His works include *Radio Astronomy* (1951), *The Story of Jodrell Bank* (1968), *Voice of the Universe* (1987), and an autobiography, *Astronomer by Chance* (1990). He was knighted in 1961.

Low, Sir David (Alexander Cecil) (1891–1963) Political cartoonist, born in Dunedin, New Zealand. After working for several newspapers in New Zealand and for the *Bulletin of Sydney*, he joined the *Star* in London, then the *Evening Standard* in 1927, for which he drew some of his most successful cartoons. His work ridiculed all political parties, notably with his character 'Colonel Blimp', whose name has been incorporated into the English language. From 1950 he worked for the *Daily Herald*, and from 1953 with *The (Manchester) Guardian*. He produced volumes of collected cartoons, including *Low and I* (1923), *A Cartoon History of the War* (1941), and *Low's Company* (1952). He was knighted in 1962.

lowan *mallee fowl*

Low Countries A term used to refer to The Netherlands and Belgium. It derives its name from the low-lying coastal plain of both countries.

low Earth orbit (LEO) A spacecraft orbit about the Earth typically used for manned missions and for Earth remote-sensing missions; the minimum altitude above the surface is c.200 km/125 mi to minimize drag effects of the Earth's atmosphere. The inclination of orbit is chosen to allow the ground track of the spacecraft to pass over regions of interest; polar inclination orbits are needed for complete global coverage. Typical orbital periods are c.100 min; circular velocity c.7·8 km/s (4·9 mi/s). Depending on altitude, the orbit may eventually decay, causing the spacecraft to re-enter Earth's atmosphere and burn up; because of the occasional destruction of spacecraft in LEO there is an increasing accumulation of tiny debris particles there, a new hazard to spacecraft.

Lowell, Amy (Lawrence) (1874–1925) Imagist poet, born in Brookline, Massachusetts, USA, the sister of Percival and A Lawrence Lowell. Privately educated, an unconventional member of the great Lowell dynasty, she began to write poetry in her late 20s, producing volumes of free verse which she named 'unrhymed cadence' and 'polyphonic prose', as in *Sword Blades and Poppy Seed* (1914). She also wrote several critical volumes, and a biography of Keats.

Lowell, James Russell (1819–91) Poet, essayist, and diplomat, born in Cambridge, Massachusetts, USA. He studied at Harvard, then published two volumes of poetry, helped to edit *The Pioneer*, and in 1846, at the outbreak of the Mexican War, started work on what was to become *The Biglow Papers* (1848), a poem denouncing the pro-slavery party and the government. In 1855 he was appointed professor of modern languages and literature at Harvard, went to Europe to finish his studies, and edited the *Atlantic Monthly* from 1857. The second series of *Biglow Papers* appeared in 1867. He was later appointed US minister to Spain (1877–80) and Britain (1880–5).

Lowell, Percival (1855–1916) Astronomer, born in Boston, Massachusetts, USA, the brother of Amy and A Lawrence Lowell. He studied at Harvard, and established the Flagstaff (now Lowell) Observatory in Arizona (1894). He is best known for his observations of Mars, which were intended to prove the existence of artificial Martian canals, and for his prediction of the existence of the planet Pluto (discovered by Clyde William Tombaugh in 1930).

Lowell, Robert (Traill Spence), Jr (1917–77) Poet, born in Boston, Massachusetts, USA into the renowned Lowell family. He studied at Harvard, but left to study poetry, criticism, and classics under John Crowe Ransom at Kenyon College, OH. During World War 2 he was a conscientious objector, and served five months of a prison sentence. In 1940 he married the writer Jean Stafford (1915–79), and during their turbulent relationship published his first collection – the self-critical autobiographical *Land of Unlikeness* (1944). His widely acclaimed second volume, *Lord Weary's Castle* (1946), was awarded the Pulitzer Prize in 1947, and he was accorded the status of a major poet. He divorced in 1948, and married twice more. Other confessional volumes followed, including *Life Studies* (1959) and *The Dolphin* (1973).

Lowestoft [**loh**stoft] 52°29N 1°45E, pop (2000e) 65 800. Port town and resort in Suffolk, E England, UK; on North Sea, 62 km/38 mi NE of Ipswich; Lowestoft Ness the most E point in England; railway; transport equipment, fishing and fish processing, radar and electrical equipment, yachting, tourism; Royal Naval Patrol Service Memorial.

low-level language A computer language in which each instruction has a single machine-code equivalent, such as assembly language. Programs written in low-level languages can be run only on computers using the same type of processor.

Lowry, L(aurence) S(tephen) [**low**ree] (1887–1976) Artist, born in Manchester, Greater Manchester, NW England, UK. He worked as a clerk in the city all his life, but studied art in his spare time, and from 1939 produced many pictures of the Lancashire industrial scene which became immensely popular after his death, mainly in brilliant whites and greys, peopled with scurrying stick-like men and women. A major retrospective exhibition of his work was held at the Royal Academy in 1976.

Lowry, (Clarence) Malcolm [**low**ree] (1909–57) Novelist, born in Liscard, Merseyside, NW England, UK. He left school to go to sea and, after an 18-month journey to the East, returned to England, where he studied at Cambridge. His reputation is based on *Under the Volcano* (1947), a novel set in Mexico, where he lived in 1936–7. He also wrote *Ultramarine* (1933), based on his first sea voyage, and several other novels published posthumously, such as *Dark as the Grave Wherein My Friend Is Laid* (1968). He spent most of his writing years in British Columbia, Canada, but died in England, where he lived from 1954.

Lowry Centre [**low**ree] Arts centre situated in the heart of Salford Quays, 2·5 km/1·5 mi from Manchester city centre in NW England, UK; named after artist L S Lowry. Opened in April 2000, the steel and glass structure houses a permanent Lowry exhibition, contemporary art works, theatre, conference room, and restaurants, with further developments planned. It attracted 250 000 visitors in its first year, and in 2001 was named building of the year by the Royal Fine Art Commission Trust.

Loy, Myrna [loy] (1905–93) Film actress, born in Helena, Montana, USA. She began her career as a dancer, moved into silent films, and made her debut in 1925 in *Pretty Ladies*, the next year starring in *Don Juan*. For nearly a decade she played a series of exotic female roles, then developed a bright and witty persona in films throughout the 1930s and 1940s, such as *The Thin Man* (1934), *The Great Ziegfeld* (1936), and *Too Hot to Handle* (1938). She worked with the Red Cross during World War 2, then returned to full-time film-making, and starred in *The Best Years of Our Lives* (1946). Known as the 'Queen of Hollywood', she continued to appear in films until the early 1980s, and received an honorary Oscar in 1991.

Loyalists Refugees from the 13 British American colonies who fled to Britain, New Brunswick, Nova Scotia, Prince Edward Island, and Canada (1783) as a result of the American War of Independence (1765–88). Some 45 000 settled in British North America, including white farmers, pro-British Iroquois, and black ex-slaves.

Loyalty Islands, Fr **Iles Loyauté** pop (2000e) 22 000; area 1981 sq km/765 sq mi. Group of coral islands in the SW Pacific Ocean, 128 km/79 mi E of New Caledonia, comprising Ouvéa, Lifu, Mare, Tiga, and many small islets; dependency of the Territory of New Caledonia; capital, We (Lifu I); coconuts, sandalwood, copra.

Loyang *Luoyang*

Loyola, Ignatius of, St [loy**oh**la], originally **Iñigo López de Recalde** (1491 or 1495–1556) Theologian and founder of the Jesuits, born in his ancestral castle of Loyola in the Basque province Guipúzcao. He became a soldier, was wounded, and while convalescing read the lives of Christ and the saints. In 1522 he went on a pilgrimage to Jerusalem, studied in Alcalá, Salamanca, and Paris, and in 1534 founded with six associates the Society of Jesus. Ordained in 1537, he went to Rome in 1539, where the new order was approved by the Pope. He wrote the influential *Spiritual Exercises*, and was canonized in 1622; feast day 31 July.

Lozi [**loh**zee] or **Barotse** A cluster of Bantu-speaking agricultural and cattle-herding people of W Zambia, formerly Barotseland, living in the floodplain of the upper Zambezi. During the colonial period, they were controlled by indirect rule, so that their kingship and distinctive institutions survived. Population c.325 000.

LSD or **lysergic acid diethylamide** A hallucinogen which was a popular drug of abuse in the 1960s and early 1970s, taken as 'microdots' and known as 'trips', 'tabs', or simply 'acid'. In 1943 the Swiss chemist Albert Hoffmann (1906–) discovered its powerful effect after taking a dose in the course of his work for the Sandoz drug company. At one time LSD was recommended by some psychologists for use during psychotherapy. The cult of LSD-taking was promoted by Dr Timothy Leary (1920–96), who was dismissed from his post as clinical psychologist at Harvard in 1963.

LSI *very large scale integration*

Lü, Empress [lü] (?–180 BC) Consort of the first Han dynasty Chinese emperor, Gaozu, and dowager empress after his death (195 BC). She tried to ensure her own family's succession, but after her death all were murdered, and Wendi, Gaozu's son, acceded.

Luanda [**lwan**da], formerly also **Loanda**, Port **São Paulo de Loanda** 8°50S 13°15E, pop (2000e) 2 460 000. Seaport capital of Angola, on Bay of Bengo, SW Africa; on the R Cuanza estuary 530 km/329 mi SSW of Kinshasa, Democratic Republic of Congo; founded in 1575; the centre of Portuguese administration from 1627; a major slave trading centre with Brazil in 17th–18th-c; university (1962); airport; railway; oil refining, export of minerals and agricultural produce; cathedral, governor's palace, São Miguel fortress.

Luang Prabang *Louangphrabang*

Luba-Lunda Kingdoms A succession of African states occupying territory in what is now Democratic Republic of Congo. They were powerful by the 17th-c, involved in slave and ivory trading with the Portuguese and later with Zanzibar. The Luba states were relatively unstable, but the Lunda Empire seems to have consolidated its power through trade. The central Lunda state did not survive the ending of the Angolan slave trade in the 1840s, and the others fell to European imperialism.

Lubbock, Sir John, 1st Baron Avebury (1834–1913) Archaeologist, biologist, and politician, born in London, UK. He became an MP in 1870, and initiated over a dozen Acts of Parliament, including Bank Holidays ('St Lubbock's Days') in 1871. In science his work was on human prehistory in Europe, and also on social insects, where he devised new methods of study.

Lübeck [lübek] 53°52N 10°40E, pop (2000e) 222 000. Commercial and manufacturing seaport in E Schleswig-Holstein province, N Germany; on R Trave, 56 km/35 mi NE of Hamburg; major city in the Hanseatic League; railway; important Baltic port; machinery, aeronautical and space equipment, steel, ironwork, tiles, foodstuffs, fish canning, shipbuilding; birthplace of Thomas Mann; Holstentor (1477), town hall (13th–15th-c), St Mary's Church (13th–14th-c), Holy Ghost hospital (13th-c), cathedral (1173); noted for its red wine trade and its marzipan; the Hanseatic City is a world heritage site.

Lubitsch, Ernst [loobich] (1892–1947) Film director, born in Berlin, Germany. A teenage actor in Max Reinhardt's theatre company, he then starred as 'Meyer' in a popular slapstick series before beginning his directorial career. He was invited to Hollywood by Mary Pickford, whom he directed in *Rosita* (1923), and stayed on to become an acknowledged master of light, sophisticated sex comedies graced with 'the Lubitsch touch' of elegance, including *Forbidden Paradise* (1924), *Ninotchka* (1939), and *Heaven Can Wait* (1943). He received an honorary Academy Award in 1947.

Lublin [lubleen] 51°18N 22°31E, pop (2000e) 356 000. Capital of Lublin voivodship, E Poland, on a plateau crossed by the R Bystrzyca; a castle town, gaining urban status in 1317; Poland's first Council of Workers' Delegates formed here, 1918; railway; university (1918); food processing, lorries, agricultural machinery; castle, Kraków Gate, cathedral (16th-c), Brigittine convent, Bernardine monastery.

Lublin, Union of [lubleen] (1569) An Act uniting Poland and the Grand Duchy of Lithuania. The Union, separately confirmed by the Polish and Lithuanian assemblies (*sejms*), completed the formal unification of the two states begun in the 14th-c. It established a common political system and currency, and a Commonwealth headed by a king jointly elected by the Polish and Lithuanian aristocracy.

lubricant A substance used to reduce friction between two surfaces moving in contact with each other. It is most often a liquid, such as a mineral or vegetable oil, but it can be a solid, such as a wax and, importantly, graphite. Some conditions call for special lubricants; for example, molybdenum sulphite is useful at high temperatures. Gases (eg air, helium) can be used, the gas being pumped into the bearing to maintain sufficient pressure between the faces.

Lubumbashi [lubumbashee], formerly **Elisabethville** (to 1966) 11°40S 27°28E, pop (2000e) 862 500. Capital of Katanga region, SE Democratic Republic of Congo; on R Lualaba, close to the Zambian frontier; founded, 1910; airport; railway; university (1955); copper mining and smelting, food processing; cathedral.

Lucan [lookn], in full **Marcus Annaeus Lucanus** (39–65) Roman poet, born in Córdoba, S Spain. The nephew of the philosopher Seneca the Younger, he studied in Rome and in Athens, and was recalled to Rome by Emperor Nero, who made him quaestor and augur. In 62 he published the first three books of his epic *Pharsalia* on the civil war between Pompey and Caesar. After the emperor forbade him to write poetry, he joined the conspiracy of Piso against Nero, but was betrayed and compelled to commit suicide.

Lucan, George Charles Bingham, Earl of [lookn] (1800–88) British soldier, born in London, UK. He accompanied the Russians as a volunteer against the Turks in 1828, and succeeded as third earl in 1839. As commander of cavalry in the Crimean War (1853–6), he is best remembered for interpreting an ambiguous order from Lord Raglan as a command directly to charge the Russian heavy artillery during the Battle of Balaclava (1854) – the 'Charge of the Light Brigade', with the loss of 410 of the 608 soldiers involved. In 1855 he was recalled from his command. He later fought at Inkerman, and was promoted field marshal in 1887.

Lucan, Richard John Bingham, 7th Earl of [lookn], known as **Lord Lucan** (1934–?) British aristocrat, and alleged murderer. He disappeared following events on the evening of 7 November 1974, when police found the body of the Lucan family's nanny, Sandra Rivett, in a mail-bag in the basement of Lady Lucan's house. Lady Lucan told police that she had gone downstairs to find the nanny when a man, whom she identified as her estranged husband, had attacked her, claiming that he had mistaken the nanny for her and had killed her. The police failed to trace Lucan, who had amassed large gambling debts and who had fought for and lost custody of his children. In June 1975 the coroner's jury charged Lord Lucan with the murder. Speculation about Lucan's whereabouts and about events that night continues to this day.

Lucas, George (Walton) (1944–) Film director, screenwriter, and producer, born in Modesto, California, USA. A producer of many successful films, including those involving Indiana Jones, he is best known as director/writer of the *Star Wars* series (1977, 1980, 1983), including *Star Wars Episode 1: The Phantom Menace* (1999) and *Star Wars II: Attack of the Clones* (2002). In 1975 he started Industrial Light and Magic, a company that creates special visual and audio effects for film and television. In 1997 the release of digitally enhanced versions of the original three Star Wars films was a huge box-office success. A further episode of the Star Wars series is scheduled for 2005.

Lucas, Robert E, Jr (1939–) Economist, born in Yakima, Washington, USA. He studied at the University of Chicago, taught at Carnegie Mellon University (1963–74), then returned to Chicago. He won the Nobel Prize for Economics in 1995 for developing and applying the hypothesis of rational expectations in macroeconomic analysis. He is known for his *Lucas critique* (1976), showing that shifts in economic policy can produce unexpected outcomes if people adapt their expectations to new policy stances.

Lucas van Leyden [laydn], or **Lucas Jacobsz** (1494–1533) Painter and engraver, born in Leyden, The Netherlands. He practised almost every branch of painting, his most notable works including the triptych of 'The Last Judgement' (1526) and 'Blind Man of Jericho Healed by Christ' (1531). As an engraver he is believed to have been the first to etch on copper rather than iron, and ranks almost with Albrecht Dürer, by whom he was much influenced.

Luce, Clare Boothe, *née* **Boothe** (1903–87) Playwright, editor, and public figure, born in New York City, USA. Privately educated, she became associate editor of *Vogue* (1930), and associate editor and managing editor of *Vanity Fair* (1930–4), and was the author of several Broadway successes including *The Women* (1936) and *Kiss the Boys Goodbye* (1938). She divorced her first husband, and married millionaire publisher Henry Luce in 1935, with whom she became a major influence in the Republican Party. She was US ambassador to Italy (1953–7), and the first woman to receive the Sylvanus Thayer Award for distinguished civil service.

Luce, Henry R(obinson) (1898–1967) Magazine publisher and editor, born in Shandong, E China, to a missionary family. He studied at Yale, and with Briton Hadden founded the weekly news magazine *Time* in 1923. In 1929, when Hadden died, he launched the business magazine *Fortune*, and later the popular picture magazine *Life* (1936). In the 1930s he inaugurated the radio programme 'March of Time', which became cinema newsreels in 1935. His empire made him a millionaire, and he became the most powerful figure in American journalism. He married playwright and editor Clare Boothe in 1935, and together they were a major influence in national politics.

Lucerne [loosern], Ger **Luzern** 47°03N 8°18E, pop (2000e) 62 000. Resort capital of Lucerne canton, C Switzerland, on W shore of L Lucerne, 40 km/25 mi SW of Zürich; developed as a trade centre on the St Gotthard route; railway junction; lake steamers; engineering, tourism; Lion Monument, painted footbridge (16th-c), cathedral (17th-c), town hall (17th-c); International Music Festival (Aug–Sep), folk festivals, winter carnival (Feb–Mar).

Lucerne, Lake, Ger **Vierwaldstätter See** area 114 sq km/44 sq mi. Irregular and indented lake in C Switzerland; fourth largest of the Swiss lakes; length 38 km/24 mi; maximum depth 214 m/702 ft; main arm runs E and SE from Lucerne, then S in a narrower arm, the Urner See; associated with the origins of the Swiss Confederation and the legend of William Tell; resorts on its shores include Weggis, Gersau, Brunnen, Vitznau.

lucerne A bushy perennial (*Medicago sativa*, subspecies *sativa*) growing to 90 cm/3 ft; leaves with three leaflets, broadest and toothed towards the tip; pea-flowers purple or blue, in dense spike-like inflorescences; fruit a spiral pod with 1½–3 coils; also called **alfalfa**. Its origin is unknown, but it is now an important forage crop, widely introduced in temperate regions. (Family: Leguminosae.)

Lucian [looshan] (c.117–c.180) Rhetorician, born in Samosata, Syria. He practised as an advocate in Antioch, travelling widely in Asia Minor, Greece, Italy, and Gaul. He then settled in Athens, where he devoted himself to philosophy, and produced a new form of literature – humorous dialogue. His satires include *Dialogues of the Gods* and *Dialogues of the Dead*. His ironic *True History* describes a journey to the Moon, and inspired a number of imaginary voyages. In his later years, he spent some time attached to the court in Alexandria.

Lucid, Shannon [loosid] (1943–) US astronaut and biochemist. In 1996 she set a new record for the longest US space mission (188 days) in orbit aboard the *Mir* space station. The distance she travelled during that time was equivalent to roughly half the distance between the Earth and the Sun. She became the first woman to be awarded the Congressional Space Medal of Honor.

Lucifer *Devil*

Lucknow [luhknow] 26°50N 81°00E, pop (2000e) 1 869 000. Capital of Uttar Pradesh, NC India; 410 km/255 mi SE of New Delhi, on R Gomati; capital of the Kingdom of Oudh, 1775–1856; capital of the United Provinces, 1877; British garrison besieged for five months during the Indian Mutiny (1857); focal point of the movement for an independent Pakistan; airfield; railway; university (1921); paper, chemicals, railway engineering, carpets, electrical products; Imamabara Mausoleum (1784), British Residency (1800), palaces, royal tombs.

Lucretia [lookreesha] (6th-c BC) Roman heroine, the wife of Lucius Tarquinius Collatinus who, according to legend, was raped by Sextus, the son of Tarquinius Superbus. She incited her father and husband to take an oath of vengeance against the Tarquins, then committed suicide by plunging a knife into her heart. The incident led to the expulsion of the Tarquins from Rome, and the tale has formed the basis of several works, notably Shakespeare's *Rape of Lucrece* and the opera *The Rape of Lucretia* by Benjamin Britten.

Lucretius [lookreeshus], in full **Titus Lucretius Carus** (c.94–c.55BC) Roman poet and philosopher. His major work is the six-volume hexameter poem *De rerum natura* (On the Nature of Things), in which he tried to popularize the philosophical theories of Democritus and Epicurus on the origin of the universe, denouncing religious belief as the one great source of human wickedness and misery. Little is known about his life, but one story recounts that a love potion given to him by his wife Lucilia sent him insane, and that he committed suicide.

Lucullus, Lucius Licinius [lukuhlus] (c.110–57 BC) Roman politican and general, famous for his victories over Mithridates VI, and also for his enormous wealth, luxurious lifestyle, and patronage of the arts. He is believed to have introduced the cherry to Italy from Asia Minor, the scene of his greatest military triumphs and administrative reforms. The term *Lucullan* has since been used as an epithet for luxurious living.

Lucy *Johanson, Donald*

Lud According to Geoffrey of Monmouth, a legendary King of Britain who first walled the principal city, from that time called Kaerlud after him, and eventually London. He is buried near Ludgate, which preserves his name.

Lüda *Dalian*

Luddites The name given to groups of workers, angered by the rapid changes brought about by the Industrial Revolution, who in 1811–12 destroyed newly introduced textile machinery in Nottingham, Yorkshire, and Lancashire, England, UK. Their fear was that the output of the equipment was so much faster than the output of a hand-loom operator that many jobs would be lost. The men involved claimed to be acting under the leadership of a certain 'Ned Ludd' or 'King Ludd', although it is doubtful that such a person ever existed. The movement ended with a mass trial in York in 1813; many were hanged or transported to Australia. The term has since been used to describe any resistance to technological innovation.

Ludendorff, Erich von [ludendaw(r)f] (1865–1937) General, born near Poznan, WC Poland (formerly Posen, Prussia). He became chief-of-staff under Hindenburg, defeated the Russians at Tannenberg (1914), and conducted the 1918 offensives on the Western Front. In 1923 he was a leader in the unsuccessful Hitler putsch at Munich, but was acquitted of treason. He became a Nazi, but from 1925 led a minority party of his own.

Luderitz [lüderits], formerly **Angra Pequena** 26°38S 15°10E, pop (2000e) 11 000. Seaport in SW Namibia, on Luderitz Bay, an inlet of the Atlantic Ocean; Diaz landed here in 1486; first German settlement in SW Africa, 1883; taken by South African forces during World War 1; railway; fishing.

Ludlow 52°22N 2°43W, pop (2000e) 8500. Historic market town in Shropshire, WC England, UK; on R Teme, 38 km/24 mi S of Shrewsbury; developed in the 12th-c around a Norman fortress; clothing, agricultural machinery, precision engineering; 11th-c Ludlow Castle, 12th–14th-c Church of St Lawrence, Reader's House.

Ludwig, Carl F(riedrich) W(ilhelm) [ludveekh] (1816–95) Physiologist, born in Witzenhausen, C Germany. Professor at Leipzig (1865–95), he did pioneer research on glandular secretions, and his invention of the mercurial blood-gas pump revealed the role of oxygen and other gases in the bloodstream. He also invented the kymograph (1847) for recording changes in blood pressure, and was the first to keep animal organs alive in vitro (1856).

Ludwigshafen (am Rhein) [ludviks-hahfen] 49°29N 8°27E, pop (2000e) 167 000. Commercial and manufacturing river port in E Rheinland-Pfalz province, SWC Germany; on W bank of the R Rhine, opposite Mannheim; railway; chemicals, resins, plastics, dyestuffs, pharmaceuticals, fertilizers, consumer goods.

Luftwaffe [luftvahfuh] (Ger 'air-weapon') The correct name for the German Air Force, re-established in 1935 under Göring, in contravention of the Treaty of Versailles. Dominant in the years of German victory in World War 2, the Luftwaffe had all but ceased to exist by 1945, having lost some 100 000 aircraft. The Federal Republic of Germany's air force, also known as the Luftwaffe, was re-established in 1956, and became a critical element in NATO.

Lug [lookh], **Lugh**, or **Lugus** In Irish mythology, the god of the Sun, the divine leader of the Tuatha De Danann, who led his people to victory over the Formorians.

Lugano [loogahnoh] 46°01N 8°57E, pop (2000e) 27 000. Resort town in Ticino canton, S Switzerland, on N shore of L Lugano (area 49 sq km/19 sq mi); on N–S road and rail route over the St

Gotthard Pass; third largest financial centre in Switzerland; clothing, engineering, tourism; town hall (1844), Cathedral of St Lawrence (13th-c).

Lugansk [lugansk], formerly **Voroshilovgrad** (1970–91) 48°35N 39°20E, pop (2000e) 491 000. Capital city of Voroshilovgradskaya oblast, E Ukraine, on a tributary of R Severskiy Donets; founded, 1795; airfield; railway; iron and steel; wool textiles, leatherwork, footwear, mining equipment.

lugeing [loozhing] Travelling across ice on a toboggan sled, usually made of wood with metal runners. The rider sits upright or lies back, as opposed to lying on the stomach in tobogganing. In competitive lugeing, competitors race against the clock on a predetermined run of at least 1000 m/1094 yd. The luge is approximately 1·5 m/5 ft in length, and is steered by the feet and a hand rope. Competitions are held for single- and two-seater luges.

Lugo [loogoh], Lat **Lucus Augusti** 43°02N 7°35W, pop (2000e) 84 000. Capital of Lugo province, Galicia, NW Spain; on R Miño, 511 km/317 mi NW of Madrid; bishopric; railway; electrical equipment, leather, trade in cattle, cheese; hot springs nearby; town walls (world heritage site), cathedral (12th-c); Fiestas of St Froilan (Oct).

lugworm A large annelid worm that burrows in soft inshore or estuarine sediments; feeds on deposited organic matter; breathes using external gills along body; widely used as fishing bait. (Class: Polychaeta. Order: Capitellida.)

Luhya [looya] A cluster of small groups of Bantu-speaking agricultural and trading people of SW Kenya. Each group is traditionally autonomous, forming a national group only during the 1940s in order to be more effective politically. Many now work in the cities.

Luik [loyk] *Liège*

Lukács, Georg or **György** [lookach] (1885–1971) Marxist philosopher and critic, born in Budapest, Hungary. He took a degree in jurisprudence at Budapest (1906), then studied at Berlin and Heidelberg. He became a member of the Hungarian Communist Party in 1918, spent several years in Vienna (1919–29) and Moscow (1933–45), then returned to Budapest to a chair of aesthetics and joined Nagy's short-lived revolutionary government in 1956 as minister of culture. He was arrested and deported to Romania but allowed to return to Budapest in 1957, where he devoted himself to works on Hegel, existentialism, and aesthetics. His major books include *Studies in European Realism* (1948, trans 1950) and *The Destruction of Reason* (1955). His earlier work on Marxism, *History and Class Consciousness* (1923, trans 1971), was repudiated as heretical by the Russian Communist Party and later by Lukács himself.

Luke, St (1st-c) New Testament evangelist, a Gentile Christian, perhaps 'the beloved physician' and companion of St Paul (*Col* 4.14, *Phil* 24), but this is disputed. Church tradition made him a native of Antioch in Syria, and a martyr. He is first named as author of the third Gospel in the 2nd-c, and tradition has ever since ascribed to him both that work and the Acts of the Apostles. Feast day 18 October.

Luke, Gospel according to New Testament writing, one of the four canonical Gospels, and the first part of a two-fold narrative that includes the Acts of the Apostles. It is anonymous, but traditionally considered the work of 'Luke', a Gentile convert, physician, and friend of Paul. The Gospel is noteworthy for its stories of the births of Jesus and John the Baptist (*Luke* 1–2), Jesus's promises to the poor and oppressed, the extensive so-called 'travel narrative' (*Luke* 9–19) containing many popular parables and sayings, and its special accounts of Jesus's passion and resurrection.

Lull, Ramón *Llull, Ramón*

Lully, Jean Baptiste [loolee], originally **Giovanni Battista Lulli** (1632–87) Composer, born in Florence, NC Italy. He came as a boy to Paris, and after much ambitious intriguing was made operatic director by Louis XIV in 1672. With Philippe Quinault (1635–88) as librettist, he composed many operas in which he made the ballet an essential part, including *Phaéton*, *Isis*, and *Acis et Galatée*. He also wrote church music, dance music, and pastorals. He died of blood poisoning after striking his foot with his conducting stick.

Lully, Raymond *Llull, Ramón*

Luluabourg *Kananga*

lumbago [luhmbaygoh] An imprecise term used to indicate pain or discomfort in the back over the lumbar region, without identifying or defining a specific cause.

lumbar puncture The introduction of a needle between the vertebrae in the lower back (the *lumbar* region) into the narrow space lying between the inner two layers of membranes surrounding the spinal cord and its nerve roots. Its purpose is to obtain a sample of cerebrospinal fluid for examination in the diagnosis of infections (eg meningitis) or bleeding (eg subarachnoid haemorrhage).

Lumbini [lumbeenee] Town and centre of pilgrimage in the W Terai of Nepal, 431 km/268 mi SW of Kathmandu; the birthplace of Buddha; world heritage site; preserved here are the broken Ashokan Pillar, the remains of a monastery, and images of Maya Devi (Buddha's mother); the town is being developed with the help of international aid.

lumen [loomin] SI unit of luminous flux; symbol *lm*; defined as the luminous flux emitted from a light source of intensity 1 candela into a solid angle of 1 steradian.

Lumière brothers [lümyair] Chemists, born in Besançon, NE France: **Auguste (Marie Louis) Lumière** (1862–1954) and **Louis (Jean) Lumière** (1864–1948) Manufacturers of photographic materials, in 1893 they developed a cine camera, the *cinématographe*, and showed the first motion pictures using film projection in 1895. They also invented the Autochrome screen plate for colour photography in 1903, producing the first film newsreels, and the first 'movie', *La Sortie des usines Lumière* (1895, trans Workers Leaving the Lumière Factory).

luminaires Artificial light sources used in photography and video. Flood lights give general illumination over a wide area; directional **spot** lights can be adjusted from an intense narrow beam, 'full spot', to a wider 'flood' setting. Hinged flaps, termed 'barndoors', are used to limit the illuminated area.

luminance The component of a video signal which determines the brightness of an image point. It contrasts with *chrominance*, which specifies its colour.

luminescence The emission of light from a substance for reasons other than heating, classified according to energy source. **Photoluminescence** corresponds to a bombardment with light, exploited in zinc sulphide-based paints, which continue to glow after the external light source is removed. **Bioluminescence** is observed for example in fireflies, and results from chemical reactions. Energy is absorbed by atoms of the substance, raising the electrons to an excited state. After a short time, the electrons return to an unexcited state, giving off light. Solids which luminesce are called *phosphors*.

Luminism In art, a term formerly applied to the brilliant, high-key effects of light found in the work of painters such as the Impressionists. Since the 1960s, however, the term has been used for moving patterns of light projected mechanically to create 'light spectacles'. Light has in fact been used as an artistic medium since the 18th-c; a 'colour organ' linked to music was demonstrated in 1734.

luminosity The intrinsic or absolute amount of energy radiated per second from a celestial object. Luminosity is related to the surface area and surface temperature of a star; two stars with the same surface temperatures but different luminosities must differ in size. Stars vary greatly in their observed luminosities, between about 1 million times more and 1 million times less than the Sun. In astronomy, luminosity is measured in *magnitudes*.

luminous flux The total flow of visible light available for illumination from some source, taking into account the source's ability to generate visible light; symbol Φ, unit *lm* (lumen). Luminous flux from a 60 watt incandescent bulb is about

600 lm, and considerably more from a 60 watt fluorescent tube.

luminous intensity The flow of visible light capable of causing illumination, emitted from a source per unit solid angle; symbol *I*, unit cd (candela). It takes account of the fact that although two sources may produce the same total light output, one may produce a single strong beam. It is independent of distance from source. A related quantity is **luminance**, formerly called **brightness**, symbol *L*, units cd/m², the luminous intensity per square metre. The luminance of a clear blue sky is approximately 4000 cd/m².

lumpsucker Heavy-bodied fish (*Cyclopterus lumpus*) widespread in the N Atlantic and Arctic Oceans; length up to 60 cm/2 ft; body rounded, bearing rows of spiny plates and with a large underside sucker; feeds on a variety of invertebrates and small fish; marketed commercially, salted or smoked, in some areas. (Family: Cyclopteridae.)

Lumumba, Patrice (Hemery) [lumumba] (1925–61) Congolese statesman and prime minister (1960), born in Katako Kombé, C Democratic Republic of the Congo (formerly Zaire, and earlier Belgian Congo). He studied at a Protestant mission school, wrote essays and poems, and became an accountant. He was imprisoned for embezzlement, and on his release became active in politics, founding and leading the Congolese National Movement. When the Congo became an independent republic in June 1960 he was made premier. Almost immediately the country was plunged into chaos by warring factions, and after being deposed in September 1960, he was assassinated in 1961, becoming a national hero.

Luna programme A highly successful evolutionary series of Soviet lunar missions carried out between 1959 and 1976. Luna 2 (1959) was the first spacecraft to impact the Moon; Luna 3 (1959) acquired the first pictures of the lunar farside; Luna 9 (1966) achieved the first soft landing, and returned the first TV pictures from the surface; Luna 10 (1966) achieved the first lunar orbit; Luna 16 (1970) achieved the first automated lunar soil sample return to Earth, repeated by Luna 20 (1972) and Luna 24 (1976); and Luna 17 (1970) deployed the first automated surface rover – Lunakhod 1 (repeated by Lunar 20, which deployed Lunakhod 2).

Lunar Orbiter programme A series of US spacecraft, managed by NASA's Langley Research Center, used to survey the Moon at high resolution from a lunar orbit, prior to the crewed Apollo landings. Launched 1966–7, and equipped only with cameras, it provided the database for the selection of Apollo landing sites. Lunar Orbiters 1 to 5 were all successful, providing the principal source of lunar geological mapping coverage for science analysis until the mid-1990s, when the next phase of lunar exploration began with the Clementine and Lunar Prospector missions. Precision tracking mapped the lunar gravity field, discovering mass concentrations ('mascons') under the lunar seas.

Lund 55°42N 13°10E, pop (2000e) 93 000. Ancient city in Malmöhus county, SW Sweden, NE of Malmö; intermittently under Danish rule prior to 1658; bishopric; university (1666); technical institute (1961); railway; paper, textiles, furniture, printing, publishing, sugar; cathedral (1080).

Lunda *Luba-Lunda Kingdoms*

Lundy Island [luhndee] Island in the Bristol Channel, off the NW coast of Devon, SW England, UK; 19 km/12 mi NW of Hartland Point; noted for its interesting flora and birdlife; two lighthouses; area 9·6 sq km/3·7 sq mi; National Trust area, since 1969.

lune In mathematics, a crescent-shaped region bounded by circular arcs. The notion is often associated with the Greek mathematician Hippocrates of Chios (5th-c BC), who proved that the sum of the areas of the lunes on the two shorter sides of a right-angled triangle is equal to the area of the triangle.

Lüneburger Heide [lüneberguh hiyduh] ('Luneburg Heath') A region of moorland and forest lying between the R Aller and R Elbe in W Germany, where Field Marshal Montgomery accepted the capitulation of the German Army (4 May 1945).

lungfish Any of a small group of freshwater fishes, the only living representatives of an order that flourished from the Devonian to Triassic periods; has a pair of lungs on the underside of the gut and connected to the oesophagus, as in higher vertebrates; gills much reduced; includes the African lungfish (Family: Protopteridae), Australian lungfish (Family: Ceratodontidae), and South American lungfish (Family: Lepidosirenidae).

lungs The organs of respiration, where the exchange of oxygen and carbon dioxide between the blood and air takes place. They are present in terrestrial vertebrates (reptiles, birds, mammals) and some fish (eg lungfish). In humans the paired lungs lie free within the *pleural cavities* of the thorax, except for the attachment by their roots to the trachea and the heart by the bronchi and pulmonary blood vessels respectively. Each lung is highly elastic, and appears mottled dark grey because of the accumulation of atmospheric particles (in the newborn they are pink). Each is covered by a thin, moist membrane, the pleura, which secretes a watery fluid that facilitates movement of the lung within the pleural cavity and on the chest wall during breathing. The lungs are divided into a number of lobes, each of which is further subdivided; each lobe receives a *bronchus* (*bronchiole* when the lobules become small) and blood vessels (a branch of the pulmonary artery, a tributary of the pulmonary vein). The subdivisions continue until the respiratory bronchioles divide into a cluster of *atria*, *alveolar sacs* and *alveoli* (thin-walled air-filled spaces surrounded by a capillary bed), where gaseous exchange occurs. At rest, the volume of air passing in and out of the lungs at each breath is about 500 ml: this can increase eight-fold during extreme exertion. Medical problems affecting the lungs include asphyxia, emphysema, empyema, pneumonia, and tuberculosis.

Lungshan [loongshan] A later Neolithic culture on the lower Yellow River in China, first excavated between the wars. Dating from 2000 BC, the village was surrounded by 2 km/1·2 mi of pound earth walls (still 3 m/10 ft high and 10 m/33 ft wide). Houses were sunken and circular, 4 m/13 ft in diameter. Animals were domesticated and rice was cultivated. Pottery was wheel-made, thin, and distinctively burnished black.

lungwort A perennial growing to 30 cm/12 in (*Pulmonaria officinalis*), with creeping rhizome, native to Europe; leaves broadly oval, often spotted with white; flowers 1 cm/0·4 in in diameter, tubular or funnel-shaped, pink or reddish, changing to blue with age. (Family: Boraginaceae.)

Lunt, Alfred (1892–1977) Actor, born in Milwaukee, Wisconsin, USA. He studied at Carroll College, Waukesha, abandoned early plans to be an architect, and made his stage debut in 1912 with the Castle Square Theatre Company in Boston, MA. He met **Lynne Fontanne** in 1916, when they both appeared in *A Young Man's Fancy*. They were married in 1922, and from 1924 became a popular husband-and-wife team, known especially for their performances in Noel Coward's plays, such as *Design for Living* (1933). Broadway's Lunt–Fontanne Theatre, opened in 1958, was named in the couple's honour, and in 1964 they received the US Medal of Freedom.

Luo [loooh] A Nilotic-speaking people of W Kenya. Unlike most other Nilotes, who are traditionally pastoralists, the Luo are mainly farmers and fishers, but many are employed as migrant labourers throughout E Africa. They are the second largest ethnic group in Kenya, and politically a significant opposition to the ruling party.

Luoyang or **Loyang** [lwohyahng] 34°47N 112°26E, pop (2000e) 1 341 000, administrative region 5 874 000. City in Henan province, NC China; capital of ancient China during the E Zhou dynasty (770–256 BC); railway; trade in wheat, sorghum, corn, sesame, peanuts, cotton; mining equipment, glass, construction equipment, light engineering; Wangcheng (Royal Town) Park, Luoyang Museum; 8 km/5 mi NE, Baimasi (White Horse) Temple (founded AD 75); 14 km/9 mi S, Longmen Caves, with c.100 000 images and statues of Buddha (5th–7th-c) is a world heritage site.

Lupercalia [looperkaylia] An ancient festival of purification and fertility. It was held every year in ancient Rome (on 15 Feb) at a cave on the Palatine Hill called the Lupercal.

lupin A member of a large group of annual and perennial herbs or (less commonly) shrubs, native to America and the Mediterranean region; leaves palmately divided with up to 15 narrow leaflets; pea-flowers in long, terminal, often showy spikes, blue, pink, yellow, or white; pods splitting open explosively to release the seeds. Several species are grown for fodder and green manure. Highly prized as ornamentals, garden plants are usually of hybrid origin. Particularly popular are **Russell** hybrids, which come in a wide range of colours, but are often short-lived. (Genus: *Lupinus*, 200 species. Family: Leguminosae.)

Lupus (astronomy) [loopus] (Lat 'wolf') A small but prominent S constellation next to Centaurus, known since Greek times.

lupus erythematosus *systemic lupus erythematosus*

lupus vulgaris [loopus vulgahris] Tuberculosis of the skin, now rare in countries in which pulmonary tuberculosis is well controlled. It causes ulceration and scarring of the skin of the face or neck, and when untreated results in great disfigurement.

lurcher A cross-bred dog formerly kept by poachers for catching rabbits and hares; usually a cross between a greyhound and a collie.

Lusaka [loosaka] 15°26S 28°20E, pop (2000e) 1 150 300. Capital of Zambia; replaced Livingstone as capital of former N Rhodesia, 1935; capital of Zambia, 1964; airport; railway; university (1965); banking, administration, agricultural trade, cement, chemicals, insecticides, clothing, metal and plastic products; cathedral (1957), geological survey museum, national archives, Munda Wanga Gardens, zoo.

Lusatians *Wends*

Lusitania [loositaynia] A Cunard passenger liner of 31 000 tonnes gross, sunk in the Irish Sea in 1915 by a German U-boat, with great loss of life. Her sinking caused worldwide anger. The Germans claimed she was carrying armaments, but this was officially denied by the British.

Lusophone Community, formally the **Comunidad dos Paises de Língua Portuguesa** An organization to facilitate social, cultural, and economic co-operation among Portuguese-speaking countries: Angola, Brazil, Cape Verde, Guinea-Bissau, Mozambique, Portugal, and São Tomé and Principe. It was formally created in 1996.

lute A European musical instrument, descended from the Arabian ud, in use from the Middle Ages to the 18th-c, and revived in modern times for performing early music. It has a large pear-shaped body, a flat soundboard, a wide neck and fingerboard with gut frets, and a pegbox set at a 90° angle to the neck. By the 16th-c there were normally six courses of 'stopped' strings (ie fingered by the left hand to produce different pitches); lower 'open' (ie unstopped) strings were later added. Players pluck the strings with their right hand.

luteinizing hormone (LH) [lyootiniyzing] One of the gonadotrophic hormones (a glycoprotein) secreted by the front lobe of the pituitary gland in vertebrates. In female mammals it is involved in the final maturation of ovarian follicles, the process of ovulation, and the initial formation of the *corpus luteum*. In males, it stimulates the interstitial (Leydig) cells of the testes to secrete testosterone: accordingly, it is also known in males as *interstitial cell-stimulating hormone* (ICSH).

Luther, Martin (1483–1546) Religious reformer, born in Eisleben, EC Germany. He spent three years in an Augustinian monastery, obtained his degree at Erfurt, and was ordained in 1507. His career as a reformer began after a visit to Rome in 1510–11, where he was angered by the sale of indulgences. In 1517 he drew up 95 theses on indulgences, which he nailed on the church door at Wittenberg. Violent controversy followed, and he was summoned to Rome to defend his theses, but did not go. He then began to attack the papal system more boldly, and publicly burned the papal bull issued against him. An order was issued for the destruction of his books; he was summoned to appear before the Diet at Worms, and was put under the ban of the Empire. In 1525 he married a former nun, Katharina von Bora. The drawing up of the Augsburg Confession, where he was represented by Melanchthon, marks the culmination of the German Reformation (1530). His translation of the Bible became a landmark of German literature.

Lutheranism Churches derived from the Reformation of Martin Luther, and the doctrine which they share. Lutheran Churches originally flourished in Germany and Scandinavia, then in other parts of Europe; later, through emigration from Europe, in the USA, and through missionary activity in Africa and Asia. The doctrine is based on the Augsburg Confession (1530), the Apology (1531), Luther's two Catechisms, and the Formula of Concord (1577). It emphasizes justification by faith alone, the importance of scripture, and the priesthood of all believers. Three sacraments are recognized: baptism, Eucharist, and penance. The Lutheran World Federation, a free association of Lutheran Churches, was founded in 1947, and is the largest of the Protestant confessional families.

Luthuli or **Lutuli, Albert (John Mvumbi)** [lutoolee] (c.1899–1967) Resistance leader, born in Zimbabwe (formerly Rhodesia). He studied at an American mission school, and was a teacher before being elected tribal chief of Groutville, KwaZulu Natal. Deposed for anti-apartheid activities, he became president-general of the African National Congress (1952–60), and was a defendant in the Johannesburg treason trial (1956–7). He was awarded the 1960 Nobel Peace Prize for his unswerving opposition to racial violence, and was elected rector of Glasgow University (1962), but severe restrictions imposed by the South African government prevented him from leaving Natal. In 1962 he published *Let My People Go*.

Lutine Bell [looteen] A bell formerly rung at Lloyd's of London insurers' offices to announce the loss of a ship or other news of great importance to the underwriters. With regard to overdue vessels, it was rung once for bad news and twice for good news. The bell belonged to a vessel (HMS *Lutine*), carrying gold bullion, which foundered off the Dutch coast in 1799; the loss of the gold fell upon the underwriters. Nowadays it is rung mainly on ceremonial occasions.

Luton [lootn] 51°53N 0°25W, pop (2001e) 184 400. Industrial town and unitary authority (from 1997) in Bedfordshire, SC England, UK; 45 km/28 mi NW of London; railway; airport; university (1992); engineering, clothing, hats, motor vehicles; 13th–15th-c Church of St Mary; Luton Hoo (3 km/1¾ mi S), within a park laid out by Capability Brown; football league team, Luton Town (Hatters).

Lutosławski, Witold [lootohslavskee] (1913–94) Composer and conductor, born in Warsaw, Poland. He studied at Warsaw Conservatory with Mailiszewski, and his first internationally applauded work was *Concerto for Orchestra* (1954). He travelled and taught widely in W Europe and the USA, being honoured with many awards. From a huge, varied output, his orchestral works stand to the fore, including *Symphonic Variations* (1938), a cello concerto (1970), and a piano concerto (1988).

Lutuli, Albert John *Luthuli, Albert*

Lutyens, Sir Edwin Landseer [lutyenz] (1869–1944) Architect, born in London, UK. He studied at the London Royal College of Art, and became known as a designer of country houses. His best-known projects are the Cenotaph, Whitehall (1919–20), and the laying out of the Indian capital New Delhi, with its spectacular Viceroy's House (1912–30). He was knighted in 1918. His project for a Roman Catholic cathedral in Liverpool was incomplete at his death.

lux SI unit of illuminance; symbol *lx*; defined as 1 lumen of luminous flux incident on 1 square metre.

Luxembourg (city) [luhksmberg] 49°37N 6°08E, pop (2000e) 82 000. Capital of Luxembourg, on the Alzette and Pétrusse Rivers; residence of the Grand Duke of Luxembourg and seat of government; also site of the Court of Justice of the European

Luxembourg

or **Luxemburg**
(country) [**luhksmberg**], official name **Grand Duchy of Luxembourg**, Fr **Grande-Duché de Luxembourg**, Ger **Grossherzogtum Luxemburg**, Letzeburgish **Grousherzogdem Lëtzebuerg**

Local names Letzebuerg (Letzeburgish), Luxembourg (French), Luxemburg (German)

Timezone GMT +1

Area 2586 km²/998 sq mi

Population total (2002e) 447 000

Status Grand Duchy

Date of independence 1867

Capital Luxembourg

Languages French (official), Letzeburgish, German

Ethnic groups Luxemburger (73%), Portuguese (9%), Italian (5%), French (3%), Belgian (3%), German (2%)

Religions Roman Catholic (97%), Protestant (2%), Jewish (1%)

Physical features Divided into the two natural regions of Ardennes (Ösling) (N); forest in N, and Gutland in S, flatter, average height 250 m/820 ft; principal rivers include the Sûre, Our, Moselle.

Climate Mild climate, influenced by warm S wind (Föhn); average annual temperatures 0·7°C (Jan), 18°C (Jul) in Luxembourg; average annual rainfall, 1050–1200 mm/41–7 in.

Currency 1 euro = 100 cents (previous to February 2002, 1 Luxemburgish Franc (LFr) = 100 centimes).

Economy Important international centre based in city of Luxembourg; iron and steel, food processing; chemicals, tyres, metal products; mixed farming, dairy farming; wine; forestry; tourism.

GDP (2002e) $21·94 bn, per capita $48 900

Human Development Index (2002) 0·925

History Made a Grand Duchy by the Congress of Vienna, 1815; granted political autonomy, 1838; recognized as a neutral independent state, 1867; occupied by Germany in both World Wars; joined Benelux economic union, 1948; neutrality abandoned on joining NATO, 1949; a hereditary monarchy with the Grand Duke as Head of State; Parliament consists of Chamber of Deputies and State Council; Head of Government is the Minister of State.

Head of State (Grand Dukes and Duchesses)
1919–64 Charlotte (in exile, 1940–4)
1964–2000 Jean
2000– Henri

Head of Government
1979–84 Pierre Werner
1984–95 Jacques Santer
1995– Jean-Claude Juncker

Communities, the General Secretariat of the European Parliament, the Consultative Committee, the European Investment Bank, the European Monetary Fund, and the Coal and Steel Union; airport; railway; steel, chemicals, textiles, food processing; Musée de l'Etat with the 8th-c Echternach stone; Luxembourg International Trade Fair (May), Schobermesse amusement fair and market (Aug).

Luxembourg or **Luxemburg** *see panel*

Luxembourg, Palais du [pale dü lüksãboorg] Since 1958, the seat of the French Senate in Paris. The palace was built in 1613–14 by Salomon de Brosse (1565–1626) for Henri IV's Florentine widow, Marie de Médicis; its design was based on that of the Pitti Palace. It was altered and enlarged in the 19th-c.

Luxemburg, Rosa (1871–1919) Revolutionary, born in Russian Poland. She became a German citizen in 1895, and emigrated to Zürich in 1889, where she studied law and political economy. With the German politician Karl Liebknecht (1871–1919) she formed the Spartacus League, which later became the German Communist Party. She was arrested by right-wing irregular troops, the *Freikorps*, in Berlin, and brutally murdered during the Spartacus revolt of 1919.

Luxor [luhksaw(r)], Arabic **al-Uqsor**, or **al-Uqsur** 25°41N 32°24E, pop (2000e) 191 800. Winter resort town in Qena governorate, EC Egypt; on E bank of R Nile, 676 km/420 mi S of Cairo; known as Thebes to the Greeks; numerous tombs of pharaohs in Valley of the Kings; Theban ruins, Temple of Luxor (built by Amenhotep III); one of the obelisks was removed to the Place de la Concorde in Paris.

Lu Xun [loo shün], also spelled **Lu-hsün** or **Lu-hsin** (1881–1936) Writer and revolutionary, born in Shaoxing, E China. He studied as a doctor, but by 1913 was professor of Chinese literature at the National Peking University and National Normal University for Women. In 1926 he became professor at Amoy University, and later dean of the College of Arts and Letters at Yixian University, Canton. His career as an author began with his famous short story, 'Diary of a Madman' (1918), followed in 1921 by *The True Story of Ah Q*, his most successful book, translated into many languages. A revolutionary hero, he was posthumously adopted by the Chinese Communists as an exemplar of Socialist Realism. He is regarded by many as the outstanding 20th-c Chinese writer, comparable in status to Gorky. His stories have been filmed in China since the 1950s.

Luzon [loozon] pop (2000e) 35 813 000; area 108 130 sq km/41 738 sq mi. Largest island of the Philippines; bounded W by the South China Sea, E by the Philippine Sea, N by the Luzon Strait; many bays and offshore islets; Cordillera Central rises to 2929 m/9609 ft in the NW at Mt Puog; Sierra Madre in the NE; largest lake, Laguna de Bay; occupied by Japanese in World War 2; chief city, Manila; grain; sugar cane, timber, hemp, chromite, tourism.

Lvov [livof], Pol **Lwow**, Ger **Lemberg**, Ukrainian **Lwiw** 49°50N 24°00E, pop (2000e) 778 000. Capital city of Lvovskaya oblast, W Ukraine; close to the Polish border, near the R Poltva;

founded, 1256; important centre on the Black Sea–Baltic trade route; part of Poland (1340–1772), then given to Austria; ceded to Poland after World War 1; ceded to USSR, 1939; airfield; railway junction; university (1661); oil refining, machines, heavy engineering, clothing, knitwear, pottery, footwear; centre for Ukrainian culture; St Yuri's Uniate Cathedral, Church of the Assumption (16th-c).

Lvov, Prince Georgy Yevgenyevich [lvof] (1861–1925) Russian statesman and social reformer, born in Popovka, W Russia. He studied law at Moscow and worked in the civil service, briefly becoming head of the provisional government in the revolution of 1917. Kerensky succeeded him, and he was arrested by the Bolsheviks, but he escaped and fled, eventually to live in Paris.

Lyallpur *Faisalabad*

lycanthropy [liykanthropee] In popular belief, the assumption by humans of the shapes of other animals, typically the most dangerous beast of the area. In Europe and N Asia it is usually a wolf or bear, in India and other parts of Asia a tiger, and in Africa a leopard. The belief is probably linked to initiation ceremonies in which youths donned animal skins and lived 'wild' for a time.

Lyceum [liyseeum] The school of philosophy founded by Aristotle in 335 BC, in a gymnasium just to the E of the city walls of Athens. Under Aristotle and later heads, such as Theophrastus (322–287 BC) and Strato (287–269 BC), it rivalled the Academy of Plato as a research centre in the ancient world.

lychee *litchi*

lych-gate, also spelled **lich-gate** A roofed gateway to a churchyard, where a coffin would rest to await the arrival of the officiating minister, and the first part of the burial service would then be read. The name derives from the Old English *lic*, 'body'. Remains of lych-gates in England are known from early Anglo-Saxon times, though their wooden construction has meant that few have survived.

Lycia [lisia] Ancient maritime district of SW Anatolia, on the Mediterranean Sea between Caria and Pamphylia, and extending inland to the Taurus Mountains. The Lycians took part in the Sea Peoples' attempt to invade Egypt (c.1231 BC), but nothing more is known of them until the 8th-c BC, when they reappear as a prosperous maritime people belonging to the Lycian League. Lycia was eventually taken by Cyrus's General Harpagus, but later, under the Romans, enjoyed relative freedom until the time of Augustus. It was annexed to Pamphylia (AD 43) and became a separate province after the 4th-c.

Lycra An artificial elastomeric fibre which has the ability to return to its original size and shape even after it has been stretched up to 600 times its starting length. Elastomeric fibres of this type are known generally as Elastene in Europe and as Spandex in America and Canada. Lycra, invented by Du Pont, is a segmented polyurethane fibre which behaves as a single continuous thread but is actually made up of a bundle of tiny filaments. It is this segmented molecular structure which gives Lycra its stretch properties. Lycra is always combined with other fibres in a material. Even a few percent of Lycra added to a fabric can greatly increase and enhance its ability to hold its shape and improve a fabric's movement.

Lycurgus [liykergus] The name of various Greeks, including, in mythology, **1** The King of Thrace who opposed Dionysus and was blinded. **2** The founder of the Spartan constitution, with its military caste-system. (The date when this originated has been much disputed, and is now thought to be c.600 BC, much too late for the legendary Lycurgus to have participated.)

Lydgate, John [lidgayt] (c.1370–c.1451) Monk and poet, born in Lidgate, Suffolk, E England, UK. He may have studied at Oxford and Cambridge. He became a Benedictine monk at Bury St Edmunds, and in 1423 was made prior of Hatfield Broad Oak, Essex. A court poet, his longer moralistic works include *The Troy Book* (1412–20), *The Story of Thebes* (1420), and *Falls of Princes* (1430–8). He also wrote devotional, philosophical, scientific, historical, and occasional poems, as well as allegories, fables, and romances.

Lydia [lideeuh] In antiquity, the area of W Asia Minor lying inland of Ionia. Its capital was Sardis. At the height of its power in the 7th-c and 6th-c BC, it was the centre of an empire which stretched from the Aegean to C Turkey. Conquered by the Persians in 546 BC, it lost its political independence for ever, and was ruled in succession by Persians, Seleucids, Attalids, and Romans.

Lyell, Sir Charles [liyl] (1797–1875) Geologist, born in Kinnordy, Angus, E Scotland, UK. He studied law at Oxford, but turned to geology, becoming professor of geology at King's College, London (1832–3). His *Principles of Geology* (1830–3) taught that the greatest geological changes might have been produced by forces still at work, and *The Geological Evidences of the Antiquity of Man* (1863) startled the public in its unbiased attitude towards Charles Darwin. He discredited the catastrophic view of geology, and finally established the doctrine of uniformitarianism, first propounded by Hutton. He was knighted in 1848, and made a baronet in 1864.

Lyly, John [lilee] (c.1554–1606) Writer, born in the Weald of Kent, SE England, UK. He studied at Oxford and Cambridge, and was MP for a while (1597–1601). He is remembered for the style of his writing, as seen in his two-part prose romance *Euphues* (1578, 1580). This work gave rise to the term *euphuism*, referring to an artificial and extremely elegant language, with much use made of complex similes and antithesis. Among his plays are *The Woman in the Moone* (1597) and *Endimion, the Man in the Moone* (1591). As a dramatist, he is important as the first English writer of high comedy, and for the use of prose as its medium of expression.

Lyme disease An infectious disease caused by the bacteria *Borrelia burgdorferi*, which is transmitted to humans in the bite of ticks that normally infest deer and other wild animals. It was first described in the town of Old Lyme, CT, in 1975 and has since been reported across the USA. A red skin lesion (*erythema migrans*) appears at the site of the tick bite and expands over a few days accompanied by fever, muscle pains, headaches, and inflammation of the joints. The disease can be cured completely with antibiotics, but complications including chronic inflammation of the heart and nervous system can occur if it is not treated early.

lymph A clear, colourless tissue fluid comprising protein, water, and other substances derived from blood, and conveyed in an independent system of thin-walled vessels. It drains from the intercellular spaces of the body tissues back to the vascular system by vessels which empty into the subclavian veins. It contains lymphocytes for destroying infective organisms, and, after a meal, fats (absorbed from the intestine for transport to the vascular system).

lymphadenoma *Hodgkin's disease*

lymphocyte [limfohsiyt] A type of white blood cell (*leucocyte*), present in blood and lymph vessels and in organized lymphoid tissues (ie spleen and lymph nodes). Lymphocytes are classified as bone-marrow-derived B lymphocytes (*B cells*) and thymus-derived T lymphocytes (*T cells*). B lymphocytes mature in bone marrow, and include the substances which form plasma cells, the producers of antibodies. T lymphocytes mature in the thymus from precursor cells that have migrated from bone marrow, and may help (*helper T cells*) or inhibit (*suppressor T cells*) B cells. T lymphocytes also include the precursors of *cytotoxic T cells* which directly kill virus-infected cells without the use of antibodies. The immunodeficiency seen in HIV infection (AIDS) results primarily from a loss of T helper cells as a result of the selective infection of the T cell population by the virus, which leads to their destruction.

lymphogranuloma venereum [limfohgranyoolohma veneerium] A sexually transmitted disease caused by *Chlamydia trachomatis*. Genital ulceration is followed by enlargement of lymph nodes draining the initial site of the infection. It responds to antibiotics.

lymphoid tissue Lymphocyte-containing tissues such as lymph nodes, spleen, thymus, tonsils, and Peyer's patches of the small intestine. It forms part of the body's defence against foreign organisms, such as bacteria, toxins, and viruses.

lymphoma (non-Hodgkin's) [limfohma] The malignant proliferation of lymphoid cells, usually of lymphocytes; the condition merges with lymphocytic leukaemias. Like Hodgkin's disease, the condition presents with painless enlarged lymph nodes; however, non-Hodgkin's lymphomas tend to be more widespread when first diagnosed, and the prognosis is worse.

Lynam, Desmond (Michael) [liynam] (1942–) British sports broadcaster. He studied at Brighton Business College, then worked in insurance before becoming a freelance journalist and local radio reporter. He joined the BBC in 1969 as a sports presenter and commentator, moving to television in 1978, where he became nationally known for his contributions to such programmes as *Grandstand*, *Sportsnight*, and *Match of the Day*. He has also presented *Holiday* (from 1988) and *How Do They Do That?* (from 1994) for BBC television. Several times Sports Presenter of the Year, he received the BAFTA Richard Dimbleby Award in 1995. He joined Independent Television in 1999. His books include accounts of the 1986 Commonwealth Games, the 1988 Olympics, and the 1992 Olympics.

Lynch, Jack, popular name of **John Lynch** (1917–99) Irish statesman and prime minister (1966–73, 1977–9), born in Cork, Co Cork, S Ireland. Following a career in the Department of Justice (1936), he was called to the bar (1945). Elected an MP in 1948, he held ministerial posts in lands (1951), the Gaeltacht (1957), education (1957–9), industry and commerce (1959–65), and finance (1965–6), before becoming prime minister. Perceived as a strong supporter of the Catholic minority in Ulster, he drew criticism from both Ulster and mainland Britain. He lost the premiership in 1973, regaining it four years later, but in 1979 resigned both the post and the leadership of Fianna Fáil. He retired from politics in 1981.

Lyngstad, Anni-Frid *Abba*

Lynx A very faint N constellation near to Ursa Major.

lynx A nocturnal member of the cat family, native to the northern N Hemisphere; plain brown or with dark spots; very short tail; tips of ears tufted; cheeks with long 'whiskers'; inhabits scrubland and coniferous forest; eats birds, rodents, hares, rabbits, young deer; two species: **lynx** (*Felis lynx*), and the rare **Spanish lynx** (*Felis pardina*.)

Lyon [leeõ], Eng also **Lyons**, ancient **Lugdunum** 45°46N 4°50E, pop (2000e) 434 000. Manufacturing and commercial capital of Rhône-Alpes region, SC France; at confluence of Rhône and Saône Rivers; third largest city in France; city centre on peninsula between rivers, linked by many bridges; Roman capital of Gaul, centre of military highway network; airport; road and rail junction; metro; archbishopric; two universities (1875, 1896); business and commercial centre; leading centre of French textile industry, particularly silk production; pharmaceuticals, electrical products, tinned milk, vehicles, armaments, nuclear equipment, chemicals, metallurgy; international exhibition hall (Eurexpo); 17th-c Palais St-Pierre, Church of St-Nizier, Hôtel de Ville (1646–72), 12th–15th-c Cathedral of St-Jean, 19th-c Basilica of Notre-Dame-de-Fourvière (1872–96); Olympic swimming pool and artificial ski piste.

Lyon, John (1962–) Boxer, born in St Helens, Merseyside, NW England, UK. An outstanding amateur boxer, he is the only man to win eight Amateur Boxing Association titles – the light-flyweight title in 1981–4, and the flyweight title in 1986–9. He also won the 1986 Commonwealth Games flyweight title.

Lyons, Sir John (1932–) Linguist, born in Manchester, Greater Manchester, NW England, UK. He studied at Cambridge, taught at London (1957–61) and Cambridge (1961–4), then became professor of linguistics at Edinburgh (1964–76) and Sussex (1976–84), and Master of Trinity Hall, Cambridge (1984–). A specialist in semantics and linguistic theory, his major publications include *Semantics* (2 vols, 1977), *Language, Meaning and Context* (1980), and *Linguistic Semantics* (1995). He was knighted in 1987.

Lyons, Joseph Aloysius (1879–1939) Australian statesman and prime minister (1932–9), born in Stanley, Tasmania, Australia. He studied at Tasmania University, became a teacher, entered politics in 1909 as Labor member in the Tasmanian House of Assembly, held the post of minister of education and railways (1914–16), and was premier (1923–9). In the federal parliament he became postmaster-general, minister of public works, and treasurer. In 1931 he broke away and founded and led an Opposition party, the United Australian Party. As prime minister he saw the country's economic recovery after the years of the Depression.

lyophilization or **freeze drying** The process for the removal of solvent or adherent water from materials (eg blood plasma, foodstuffs, beverage bases) while in a frozen condition. The material is frozen and held under vacuum at a temperature just high enough to allow sublimation (eg evaporation direct from the solid state without passing through a melting phase).

Lyra [liyra] ('harp') A small but obvious N constellation. It includes the fifth-brightest star, Vega, as well as the prototype variable RR Lyrae, and the Ring nebula, a planetary nebula 600 parsec away. Vega, 7·8 parsec distant, was the Pole Star c.14 000 years ago.

lyre A musical instrument of great antiquity, with a resonator, two arms, and a crossbar. Gut strings, from 3 to 12 in number, were stretched from the front of the resonator to the crossbar, and plucked with a plectrum. The tortoise-shell resonator of the classical lyre distinguishes it from the larger kithara, with its wooden rectangular soundbox.

lyrebird Either of two species of a shy, ground-feeding, Australian bird of the genus *Menura*: the **superb lyrebird** (*Menura novaehollandiae*); and **Albert's lyrebird** (*Menura alberti*); long legs; flies poorly but runs well; tail of male shaped like lyre; spectacular display and song; mimics complex sounds; inhabits mountain forest with rock outcrops; eats small invertebrates. (Family: Menuridae.)

Lysenko, Trofim Denisovich [lisengkoh] (1898–1976) Geneticist and agronomist, born in Karlovka, EC Ukraine. He studied in Uman and Kiev, gained a reputation in crop husbandry during the famine of the 1930s and developed a doctrine, compounded of Darwinism and the work of horticulturalist Ivan Michurin (1855–1935), that heredity can be changed by good husbandry. As director of the Institute of Genetics of the Soviet Academy of Sciences (1940–65), he declared the accepted Mendelian theory erroneous, and ruthlessly silenced any Soviet geneticists who opposed him. He was dismissed by Khrushchev in 1965, having gravely hampered scientific and agricultural progress in the USSR.

Lysias [lisias] (c.445–c.380 BC) Greek orator, the son of a rich Syracusan. Educated at Thurii in Italy, he settled in Athens c.440 BC. The Thirty Tyrants in 404 BC stripped him and his brother Polemarchus of their wealth, and killed Polemarchus. The first use to which Lysias put his eloquence was in 'Against Eratosthenes' to prosecute the tyrant chiefly to blame for his brother's murder. He then practised with success as a writer of speeches for litigants. His family home in Athens is portrayed in Plato's *Republic*.

Lysithea [liysitheea] The 10th natural satellite of Jupiter, discovered in 1938; distance from the planet 11 720 000 km/7 283 000 mi; diameter 36 km/22 m.

lysosome [liysosohm] A membrane-bound sac which contains numerous enzymes capable of digesting a wide variety of substrates. Lysosomes are found within cells, and are probably formed by the Golgi body. They are involved in the digestion of food and in the destruction of bacteria in white blood cells.

lysozyme [liysohziym] An enzyme present in tears, saliva, sweat, milk, and nasal and gastric secretions; also known as *muramidase*. It destroys bacterial cell walls by digesting their polysaccharide component.

Lytham St Anne's [litham] 53°45N 3°01W, pop (2000e) 43 500. Resort town in Lancashire, NW England, UK; on the R Ribble estuary, 20 km/12 mi W of Preston; railway; championship golf course; engineering.

Lyttelton, Humphrey [litltuhn] (1921–) Jazz trumpeter and bandleader, born in Windsor, S England, UK. He formed a band in 1948, and became the leading figure in the British revival of traditional jazz. His group expanded to an octet, emulating Ellington's early ensembles, and then modernized even further, to the horror of many fans of traditional jazz. He responded with a satirical book *I Play As I Please* (1954). He retained his stature, and increased the tolerance for more modern jazz styles in Britain. On BBC Radio he has hosted *The Best of Jazz* for many years, and has been chairman of the panel game *I'm Sorry I Haven't a Clue* since 1972.

Lytton (of Knebworth), Edward George Earle Bulwer-Lytton, Baron [litn] (1803–73) Writer and statesman, born in London, UK. He took early to poetry, and in 1820 published *Ismael and other Poems.* At Cambridge (1822–5) he won the Chancellor's Gold Medal for a poem. Writing under the name of Bulwer Lytton, his enormous output, extremely popular during his lifetime, includes the novel *The Last Days of Pompeii* (1834), his play *Money* (1840), and the epic poem 'King Arthur' (1848–9, revised, 1870). MP for St Ives (1831–41), he was created a baronet in 1838, and in 1843 succeeded to the Knebworth estate. He re-entered parliament as member for Hertfordshire in 1852, and in 1858–9 was colonial secretary. In 1866 he was raised to the peerage.

m

Ma, Yo-Yo (1955–) Cellist, born in Paris, France. Coming to New York City with his family at age seven, he enrolled at the Juilliard School, New York City at nine, and after studies at Harvard ascended rapidly to the highest rank of international soloists. He is noted for his warmth of playing, superlative technique, a repertoire stretching from Bach to the moderns, and an energetic stage presence.

Maasai *Masai*

Maastricht [mahstrikht], ancient **Traieclum ad Mosam** or **Traiectum Tungorum** 50°51N 5°42E, pop (2000e) 124 000. Capital city of Limburg province, S Netherlands, on the R Maas; commercial hub of an area extending well into Belgium; railway junction; noted for its vegetable and butter markets; paper, packaging, leatherwork, brewing, printing, ceramics, glass, tourism; St Pietersburg underground gallery; Church of St Servatius (6th-c), Romanesque basilica (10th–11th-c).

Maastricht Treaty [mahstrikht, mahstrikht] An agreement reached in December 1991 at Maastricht, The Netherlands, during a meeting of the heads of state and government of the European Community. It was the conclusion of a series of inter-governmental conferences on European political union and economic/monetary union which had been taking place since December 1990. The summit agreed a treaty framework for European union, incorporating political and economic agreements and setting a timetable for their implementation, and providing for new security/defence co-operation. UK opposition to the inclusion of 'social policy' led to its removal from the agreement. The word 'federal' was also dropped. January 1999 was agreed as the latest date for the introduction of a European currency. The treaty required ratification by the 12 national governments: rejection by Denmark in June 1992 necessitated a revision of the ratification timetable, but by the end of 1992 all countries except Denmark and the UK had ratified, and these did so in mid-1993.

Maazel, Lorin (Varencove) [mahzel] (1930–) Conductor, born to American parents in Neuilly, NC France. Brought to the USA as a child, he was a prodigy as a violinist, pianist, and conductor, conducting the New York Philharmonic at age 12. He studied at the University of Pittsburgh, making his professional debut as a violinist in 1945 and as a conductor in 1953. He directed the Deutsche Oper, Berlin (1965–71), the Cleveland Orchestra (1972–82), the Vienna Staatsoper (1982–4), and the Pittsburgh Symphony Orchestra (1988–96). He is known for his exacting musicianship and intense interpretations of the classical repertoire. In 2002 he conducted the premiere of John Adams' work, *The Transmigration of Souls*, commissioned to commemorate the terrorist attacks of 11 September 2001.

Mabinogion, The [mabinogion] The name widely given to a collection of 12 mediaeval Welsh stories, first translated by English diarist Charlotte Guest (1812–95), and published in three volumes (1838–49). It includes the tales of Branwen, Culhwch and Olwen, Geraint and Enid, Llud and Llefelys, Manawydan, Math, Owain, Peredur, Pwyll, Taliesin, the Dream of Macsen Wledig, and the Dream of Rhonabwy. Four *Mabinogi* are contained in the *Red Book of Hergest*, compiled in the 14th-c and 15th c. They form part of a cycle of legends of ancient Irish and Welsh mythology and later myths of Celtic, Roman, and Christian Britain.

Mabo, Eddie Koiki [mahboh] (1940–92) Traditional leader of the Meriam people of Murray I in Torres Strait, NE Australia. In 1982, with four other Meriam people, he began legal proceedings against the Queensland government, seeking recognition of their traditional ownership of the island and its surrounding seas. He persisted with the case, and in 1992 the High Court of Australia held that the Australian common law recognizes a form of native title, making it a landmark case which overturned the 18th-c notion of *terra nullius*. The victory for Eddie Mabo was posthumous, but the decision was so controversial that his case rapidly became a cause célèbre.

MAC (Multiplex Analogue Components) A system of colour television transmission in which coded signals representing luminance, chrominance, and sound, along with synchronizing data, are sent in succession as separate components during each TV line. The system requires greater bandwidth than normal, but offers enhanced definition and picture quality.

McAdam, John Loudon (1756–1836) Inventor of macadamized roads, born in Ayr, South Ayrshire, SW Scotland, UK. He went to New York City in 1770, where he made a fortune in his uncle's counting house. On his return in 1783 he bought an estate and started experimenting with new methods of road construction. In 1816 he was appointed surveyor to the Bristol Turnpike Trust, re-made the roads there with crushed stone bound with gravel, and raised the carriageway to improve drainage. In 1827 he was made surveyor-general of metropolitan roads in Great Britain, and his *macadam surfaces* were adopted in many other countries.

macadamia nut [makadaymia] An evergreen tree (*Macadamia integrifolia*) growing to c.20 m/65 ft, native to NE Australia, and cultivated in Australia and Hawaii; leaves up to 30 cm/12 in, lance-shaped, widest above middle, rigid and sometimes prickly, in whorls of 3–4; flowers in long, drooping spikes, 2·5 cm/1 in diameter, zygomorphic with four creamy perianth segments; fruits green, splitting to reveal round, edible nut. (Family: Proteaceae.)

Macao [makow], Chin **Aomen**, Port **Macáu** pop (2000e) 445 000; area 16 sq km/6 sq mi. Special administrative region of China, and former overseas province of Portugal; flat, maritime tropical peninsula in SE China and the nearby islands of Taipa and Colôane; on the Pearl R delta, 64 km/40 mi W of Hong Kong; airport; capital, Nome de Deus de Macau; population largely Chinese (99%); official languages, Portuguese, Chinese (Cantonese generally spoken); chief religions, Buddhism, Roman Catholicism; unit of currency, the pataca of 100 avos; ferry links with Hong Kong; occupied by Portugal from 1557, with official consent from 1678; ceded to Portugal, 1887; a Chinese territory under Portuguese administration, 1979; returned to Chinese rule in December 1999; governor appointed by China, with a 23-member Legislative Assembly; licensed gambling since the 19th-c; tourism, textiles, electronics, plastics, toys, banking, fishing; several fortresses, Jaialai Palace; grand prix racing.

macaque [makahk] An Old World monkey, native to S and SE Asia (18 species) and NW Africa (*Barbary ape*); legs and arms of equal length; tail often short; lives in trees or on ground (depending on species); buttocks with naked patches. (Genus: *Macaca*, 19 species.)

macaroni *pasta*

MacArthur, Douglas (1880–1964) US general, born in Little Rock, Arkansas, USA. He trained at West Point, joined the US army engineers, and in World War 1 served with distinction in France. In 1941 he became commanding general of the US armed forces in the Far East, and from Australia directed the recapture of the SW Pacific (1942–5). He formally accepted the Japanese surrender, and commanded the occupation of Japan (1945–51), introducing a new constitution. In 1950 he led the UN forces in the Korean War, defeating the North Korean army, but was relieved of command when he tried to continue the war against China.

MacArthur, Ellen (1977–) Yachtswoman, born in Derbyshire, C England, UK. At age 18 she won the BT/YJA Young Sailor of the Year, and in 1998 was named BT/YJA Yachtsman of the Year. In 2000 she entered the gruelling Vendée Globe yacht race in *Kingfisher* and made history by becoming the fastest woman ever to sail solo around the world in a time of 94 days, 4 hrs, 25 min, 40 s, gaining second place in the race. In 2001 she was named female world sailor of the year by the International Sailing Federation. She won the Route du Rhum solo transatlantic race in record-breaking time of 13 days, 13 hrs, 31 min, 47 s aboard *Kingfisher* in 2002.

Macassar *Makassar Strait; Ujung Padang*

Macaulay, Dame (Emilie) Rose (1881–1958) Novelist, essayist, and poet, born in Rugby, Warwickshire, C England, UK. She read history at Oxford, where she wrote her first book. She won a considerable reputation as a social satirist, with such novels as *Dangerous Ages* (1921). Her best-known novel is *The Towers of Trebizond* (1956). Two posthumous volumes, *Letters to a Friend* (1961–2), describe her return to the Anglican faith. She was made a dame in 1958.

Macaulay (of Rothley), Thomas Babington Macaulay, Baron [muh**kaw**lee] (1800–59) Essayist and historian, born in Rothley Temple, Leicestershire, C England, UK. He was educated privately and at Cambridge, where he became a fellow. Called to the bar in 1826, he had no liking for his profession, and turned to literature. He also became an MP (1830), and established his powers as an orator in the Reform Bill debates. After a period in Bengal (1834–80), he became secretary of war (1839–41), and wrote the highly popular *Lays of Ancient Rome* (1842). His major work, the *History of England from the Accession of James II*, was published between 1848 and 1861, the fifth volume unfinished. He became a peer in 1857.

macaw A large parrot native to the Caribbean, and to Central and tropical South America; inhabits woodland or savannah; eats fruit, seeds, and nuts; nests in holes. (Genera: *Ara, Anodorhynchus, Cyanopsitta*, c.16 species.)

Macbeth (c.1005–57) King of Scots (1040–57). The *mormaer* (provincial ruler) of Moray (c.1031), he became king (1040) after slaying Duncan I in battle near Elgin, and in 1050 went on a pilgrimage to Rome. He was defeated and killed by Duncan's son, Malcolm Canmore, at Lumphanan, Aberdeenshire. Macbeth represented the northern Scots who were opposed to the ties with the Saxons, advocated by Duncan. Shakespeare's version of events comes from the accounts of Holinshed and Boece.

MacBeth, George (Mann) (1932–92) Poet and novelist, born in Shotts, North Lanarkshire, C Scotland, UK. He was educated in Sheffield and at New College, Oxford, and during 1955–76 was a producer for the BBC. A prolific poet, he was associated with the Group (poets which included Philip Hobsbaum (1932–) and Edward Lucie-Smith (1933–)), and the macabre content of the *The Penguin Book of Sick Verse* (1963), which he edited, shows its influence. His first novel, *The Transformation*, appeared in 1975, and he also produced several books for children and many anthologies. He was married three times, his second wife being the novelist Lisa St Aubin de Terán (1953–).

McBride, Willie John, popular name of **William John McBride** (1940–) Rugby union player, born in Toomebridge, Co Antrim, NE Northern Ireland, UK. He played his entire club career with Ballymena. Tall and massively built, he won 63 caps as a lock for Ireland, plus 17 British Lions caps from five tours – both records. After retiring in 1975, he was Irish national coach, manager of the 1983 British Lions team in New Zealand, and a vocal campaigner for contact with South Africa.

MacBride principles A code of conduct for Northern Ireland advocated by Irish statesman Sean MacBride (1904–88), and adopted in 1976, recommending that local firms should aim for balanced community representation in their staff recruitment. The code was created as part of a policy of creating jobs for the Catholic minority in Northern Ireland, and was initially focused on US companies which had branches in the region.

Maccabees [**mak**abeez] An important Jewish family, and those of its party (also known as the **Hasmoneans**) who initially resisted the influences of Greek culture on Israel and its religion during Syrian rule over Palestine. **Judas Maccabeus** (or **ben Mattathias**) led a revolt in 168 BC by attacking a Jewish apostate, and it was continued by his sons through a kind of guerrilla warfare. It resulted eventually in semi-independence from Syrian control, with Jonathan and Simon beginning a Hasmonean dynasty of high priestly rulers which lasted until the rise of Herod the Great under Roman patronage (c.37 BC).

Maccabees or **Machabees, Books of the** [**mak**abeez] Four writings, the first two being part of the Old Testament Apocrypha (or deuterocanonical works of the Roman Catholic canon) and the last two being assigned to the Old Testament Pseudepigrapha. 1 *Mac* is a historical narrative concerned with the victories of Judas Maccabeus and his family in 2nd-c BC Palestine, leading eventually to Jewish semi-independence from Syrian control. 2 *Mac* roughly parallels 1 *Mac* 1–7, but is of less certain historical value. 3 *Mac* narrates stories of Jewish resistance before the Maccabean period, particularly in Egypt under Ptolemy IV Philopater (r.221–204 BC). 4 *Mac* presents vivid descriptions of tortures and martyrdoms during the early years of the Maccabean revolt, formulated to commend certain theological and philosophical ideals.

MacCaig, Norman (Alexander) [muh**kayg**] (1910–96) Poet, born in Edinburgh, EC Scotland, UK. He read Classics at University there, and was a primary school teacher for nearly 40 years. The first fellow in creative writing at Edinburgh University (1967–9), he then lectured in English studies at Stirling University (1970–7). The leading Scottish poet of his generation writing in English, he was awarded the Queen's Gold Medal for Poetry in 1986. His collections of quick, imagistic, and philosophic poems include *Riding Lights* (1955), *A Round of Applause* (1962), *The White Bird* (1973), and *Voice-Over* (1988). His *Collected Poems* were published in 1985 (revised 1990).

McCarroll, Tony *Oasis*

McCarthy, Eugene J(oseph) (1916–) US politician, born in Watkins, Minnesota, USA. He studied at St John's University, MN, and Minnesota University, then taught at St John's (1940–3) before working in military intelligence during World War 2, after which he was elected to the US House of Representatives (1948). He became nationally known when he challenged President Lyndon B Johnson in the race for the Democratic presidential nomination (1968), a decision which ultimately led to Johnson's withdrawal. McCarthy was eventually defeated by Robert F Kennedy. In 1971 he turned to writing, producing works of non-fiction, poetry, and children's stories.

McCarthy, Joseph R(aymond) (1909–57) US Republican politician and inquisitor, born in Grand Chute, Wisconsin, USA. He studied at Marquette University, Milwaukee, became a circuit judge in 1939, and after war service was elected senator (1945). He achieved fame for his unsubstantiated accusations, in the early 1950s, that 250 Communists had infiltrated the State Department, and in 1953 became chairman of the powerful Permanent Subcommittee on Investigations. By hectoring cross-examination and damaging innuendo he arraigned many innocent citizens and officials, overreaching himself when he came into direct conflict with the army. The kind of anti-Communist witchhunt he instigated became known as *McCarthyism*. Formally condemned by the US Senate, he lost most of his remaining Republican support.

McCarthy, Cormac (1933–) Novelist, born in Providence, Rhode Island, USA, and raised in Tennessee. His first work, *The Orchard Keeper*, was published to great acclaim in 1965 (William Faulkner Foundation Award). Most of his early novels, with their dark themes of justice and retribution, are set in Tennessee, and include *Outer Dark* (1968), *Child of God* (1974), and his most autobiographical work, *Suttree* (1979). He moved to Texas in 1982, where he concentrated on deeper philosophical themes of spiritual desolation and loneliness. *Blood Meridian* appeared in 1985, followed by the Border Trilogy, comprising the best-selling *All The Pretty Horses* (1992), *The Crossing* (1994), and *Cities of the Plain* (1999).

McCarthy, Mary (Therese) (1912–89) Writer and critic, born in Seattle, Washington, USA. Orphaned at the age of six, she was brought up by relatives. She studied at Vassar College, NY, then worked as a publisher's editor, theatre critic, and teacher before writing her first novel, *The Company She Keeps* (1942). Other novels include *The Groves of Academe* (1952) and *The Group* (1963). She also published critical works, travel books, and the autobiographical *Memories of a Catholic Girlhood* (1957).

McCartney, Sir (James) Paul [muhkah(r)tnee] (1942–) Musician, songwriter, and composer, born in Liverpool, Merseyside, NW England, UK. The Beatles' bass guitarist, vocalist, and member of the Lennon–McCartney songwriting team, he made his debut as a soloist with the album *McCartney* (1970), heralding the break-up of the group. In 1971 he formed the band Wings (disbanded in 1981) with his wife **Linda** (1942–98). 'Mull of Kintyre' (1977) became the biggest-selling UK single (2·5 million). In 1979 he was declared the most successful composer of all time: by 1978 he had written or co-written 43 songs that sold over a million copies each. Later albums included *Band on the Run* (1973), *Wings Over America* (1977), *Give My Regards To Broad Street* (1984), *Tripping the Live Fantastic* (1990), and *Flaming Pie* (1997), and his music attracted numerous Grammy awards. 'Ebony and Ivory', recorded with Stevie Wonder, was an international hit of the year in 1982. He has performed at concerts all over the world, gaining a place in the Guinness Book of Records for playing before the largest-paid attendance (1990, Rio de Janeiro). He wrote and produced the film/video featuring 'We All Stand Together' (1984), which has become a perennial Christmas favourite. His *Liverpool Oratorio* (written in association with Carl Davis) was performed by the Royal Liverpool Philharmonic Orchestra at Liverpool Cathedral in 1991, and he has since continued to develop his interests as a classical composer, notably in *Standing Stones* (1997). He collaborated with Harrison and Starr in the retrospective Beatles' anthology in 1995. He wrote the books *All You Need Is Love* (1968) and *Paul McCartney In His Own Words* (1976), and wrote, produced, and composed the music for a successful animated film, *Rupert and the Frog Song* (1984, BAFTA). An exhibition of his paintings opened in Liverpool in 2002. Later that year he married Heather Mills (1968–), and their daughter was born in 2003. He was knighted in 1997.

McCartney, Stella (1972–) British fashion designer, the daughter of Paul McCartney. At age 15 she began an apprenticeship working with Christian Lacroix on his first couture collection, and later spent several years training on Savile Row. She then studied at St Martin's College of Art and Design, London, graduating in 1995, and was appointed chief designer at the French couture house Chloé (1997). At the 2000 Vogue Fashion Awards in New York, her father presented her with the Designer of the Year Award. She showed the first collection under her own label in 2001.

macchia [makia] The evergreen scrub vegetation of the Mediterranean region; also known as **maquis**. The vegetation includes spiny shrubs and many aromatic species. In some areas it may result from overcultivation and overgrazing. It is equivalent to the chaparral of North America.

McClellan, George B(rinton) (1826–85) US Union general in the American Civil War, born in Philadelphia, Pennsylvania, USA. He trained at West Point, fought in the Mexican War, then worked on military engineering projects. When the War began, he drove the enemy out of West Virginia, and was called to Washington to reorganize the Army of the Potomac. His Peninsular Campaign in Virginia ended disastrously at Richmond (1862). He forced Lee to retreat at Antietam, but failed to follow up his advantage, and was recalled. In 1864 he opposed Lincoln for the presidency, and in 1877 was elected governor of New Jersey.

McClintock, Barbara (1902–92) Geneticist and biologist, born in Hartford, Connecticut, USA. She studied at Cornell, where she later taught (1927–31). Working at the Cold Spring Harbor Laboratory from the 1940s, she discovered and studied a new class of mutant genes in corn, concluding that the function of some genes is to control other genes, and that they can move on the chromosome to do this. She was awarded the National Medal of Science (1970), the first MacArthur Laureate Award (1981), and received the first unshared Nobel Prize for Physiology or Medicine to be awarded to a woman (1983). A biography which detailed her pioneering work *A Feeling for the Organism* appeared in 1983.

McClung, Nellie (Letitia), *née* **Mooney** (1873–1951) Suffragist, writer, and public speaker, born in Chatsworth, Ontario, SE Canada. Educated in Manitoba, she rose to prominence through the Women's Christian Temperance Union and the suffrage movement, and was elected to the Alberta Legislative Assembly (1921–6).

McClure, Sir Robert (John le Mesurier) [muhkloor] (1807–73) Explorer, born in Wexford, Co Wexford, SE Ireland. He joined the navy in 1824, and served in an expedition to the Arctic in 1836. He was with the Franklin expedition (1848–9), and again in 1850, when he commanded a ship that penetrated E to the coast of Banks Land, where he was icebound for nearly two years. Rescued by another ship which had travelled from the W, he thus became the first person to navigate the Northwest Passage. The McClure Strait is named after him.

McColgan, Liz [muhkolgan], popular name of **Elizabeth McColgan**, *née* **Lynch** (1964–) Athlete, born in Dundee, E Scotland, UK. She studied in Dundee and at the University of Alabama. Her athletic achievements in the 10 000 m include gold medals at the Commonwealth Games (1986, 1990), gold at the World Championships (1991) – a few months after giving birth – and silver at the Olympics (1988). She also won the silver for the 3000 m at the Indoor World Championships (1989), and was winner of the New York Marathon (1991) and the London Marathon (1996). She was voted Sportswriters' Athlete of the Year (1988, 1991) and BBC Sports Personality of the Year (1991).

McCormack, John (Francis) (1884–1945) Tenor, born in Athlone, near Dublin, Ireland. He studied in Milan, made his London debut in 1905, and was engaged by Covent Garden opera for the 1905–6 season, appearing also in oratorio and as a *Lieder* singer. As an Irish nationalist, he did not appear in England during World War 1, but took US citizenship in 1919, and turned to popular sentimental songs. He was raised to the papal peerage as a count in 1928.

McCormick, Cyrus (Hall) (1809–84) Inventor of the reaper, born in Rockbridge Co, Virginia, USA. He continued experiments begun by his father, and produced a successful model in 1831, at the age of 22. He patented his machine in 1834, made his first sale in 1840, and moved to Chicago in 1847, where he manufactured more than six million harvesting machines during his lifetime. His McCormick Harvesting Machine Co became in 1902 the International Harvester Co, with his son **Cyrus Hall, Jr** (1859–1936) as first president and chairman of the board.

McCourt, Frank [muhkaw(r)t] (1930–) Writer and teacher, born in Brooklyn, New York City, USA. His family returned to their native Ireland when he was four, and settled in Limerick. His best-selling memoir, *Angela's Ashes* (1996), chronicles the bitter years of an impoverished childhood up until he left Ireland in 1949. The work won him the 1997 Pulitzer Prize for Biography. A sequel, *Tis: A Memoir* (1999), charts his return to the USA, where he struggles through poverty and lack of education to gain a place at New York University.

McCoy, Tony, properly **Anthony Peter McCoy** (1974–) Jockey, born in Co Antrim, NE Northern Ireland, UK. National Hunt Champion jockey since 1995, he broke Peter Scudamore's previous jumps record of 221 wins in a season by winning 253 (1997–8). In 2002 he broke the record for the number of winners in a season, 269, set on the Flat by Sir Gordon Richards in 1947, finishing with a total of 289 winners. He rode his 1700th winner on Mighty Montefalco at Uttoxeter in 2002 to beat Richard Dunwoody's all-time British winners' record.

McCullers, (Lula) Carson, *née* **Smith** (1917–67) Writer, born in Columbus, Georgia, USA. She studied at Columbia and New York universities. She married and divorced Reeves McCullers twice (1937–41, 1945–8). From the age of 29, paralysis of one side confined her to a wheelchair. Her work reflects the sadness of lonely people, and her first book, *The Heart Is a Lonely Hunter* (1940), about a deaf mute, distinguished her immediately as a novelist of note. She wrote the best and the bulk of her work in a six-year burst through World War 2, including the novella *The Ballad of the Sad Café* (1951), which was dramatized by Edward Albee.

McCullough, Colleen [muhkuhluh] (1937–) Novelist, born in Wellington, New South Wales, SE Australia. She studied in Sydney and London, and pursued a career as a neurophysiologist in Sydney, London, and Yale University Medical School. She then moved to Norfolk I in the South Pacific (1979) and became a best-selling novelist. Her books include *The Thorn Birds* (1977), which sold 20 million copies, *The Grass Crown* (1991), and a Roman trilogy, *Caesar's Women* (1995), *Caesar: A Novel* (1997), and *The October Horse: A Novel About Caesar and Cleopatra* (2002).

MacDiarmid, Alan G [muhkdermid] (1927–) Chemist, born in New Zealand. He went to the USA and studied at the University of Wisconsin (1953) and at Cambridge, UK (1955). He joined the faculty at the University of Pennsylvania (1955) where he became professor of chemistry (1988). In 2000 he shared the Nobel Prize for Chemistry with Alan J Heeger and Hideki Shirakawa for their discovery and development of conductive polymers.

MacDiarmid, Hugh [muhkdermid], pseudonym of **Christopher Murray Grieve** (1892–1978) Poet, born in Langholm, Dumfries and Galloway, SW Scotland, UK. He became a pupil-teacher at Broughton Higher Grade School in Edinburgh before turning to journalism. After World War 1, he married, settled as a journalist in Montrose, and edited anthologies of contemporary Scottish writing. After publishing his outstanding early lyrical verse, *Sangschaw* (1925) and *Penny Wheep* (1926), he established himself as the leader of a vigorous Scottish Renaissance with *A Drunk Man Looks at the Thistle* (1926), full of political, metaphysical, and nationalistic reflections on the Scottish predicament. He became professor of literature at the Royal Scottish Academy (1974), and president of the Poetry Society (1976). He was a founder member of the Scottish Nationalist Party, and an active Communist.

McDonagh, Martin [muhkdona] (1970–) British playwright. Brought up in London by Irish parents, much of his work is set in Ireland. In 1997 his first four plays were running simultaneously in London's West End: *The Leenane Trilogy* (comprising *The Beauty Queen of Leenane*, *A Skull in Connemara*, and *The Lonesome West*) and *The Cripple of Inishmaan*. Later plays include *The Lieutenant of Inishmore* (2001).

Macdonald, Flora (1722–90) Scottish heroine, born in South Uist, Western Isles, W Scotland, UK. After the rebellion of 1745, she conducted the Young Pretender, Charles Edward Stuart, disguised as 'Betty Burke', to safety in Skye. For this she was imprisoned in the Tower of London, but released in 1747. She married in 1750, and in 1774 emigrated to North Carolina, where her husband fought in the War of Independence. When he was captured, Flora returned to Scotland in 1779, and her husband rejoined her there in 1781.

Macdonald, Sir John A(lexander) (1815–91) Canadian statesman and prime minister (1857–8, 1864, 1867–73, 1878–91), born in Glasgow, W Scotland, UK. His family emigrated in 1820, and he was educated in law at Kingston. Entering politics in 1843, he became leader of the Conservative Party, and joint premier in 1856. He was instrumental in bringing about the confederation of Canada, and in 1867 formed the first government of the new Dominion. The 'Pacific scandal' brought down his government in 1874, but he regained the premiership in 1878.

MacDonald, (James) Ramsay (1866–1937) British statesman and prime minister (1924, 1929–31, 1931–5), born in Lossiemouth, Moray, NE Scotland, UK. He had little formal education, worked as a clerk, then joined the Independent Labour Party in 1894, eventually becoming its leader (1911–14, 1922–31). He became an MP in 1906, and was prime minister and foreign secretary of the first British Labour government. He met the financial crisis of 1931 by forming a largely Conservative 'National' government, most of his party opposing; and in 1931 reconstructed it after a general election. Defeated as an MP by Shinwell in 1935, he returned to parliament in 1936, and became Lord President.

McDonald, Sir Trevor (1939–) Television journalist and newscaster, born in Trinidad. He worked in the media in Trinidad in the 1960s, joining the Caribbean section of the World Service in London in 1969. He became a reporter for ITN in 1973, then a sports correspondent (1978), diplomatic correspondent (1980), and diplomatic editor (1987). After doing some newscasting for ITN and Channel Four, he joined ITN's *News at Ten* (1990–9), becoming a nationally known personality. From 1999 he presented the weekly news programme *Tonight With Trevor McDonald*, and also that year received the BAFTA Richard Dimbleby Award for his contribution to factual television. In 2003 he received a National Television Award for special achievement. His books include biographies of cricketers Clive Lloyd (1985) and Viv Richards (1987) and a volume of autobiography, *Fortunate Circumstances* (1993). He was knighted in 1999.

MacDonnell Ranges Mountain ranges in Northern Territory, C Australia; extend 320 km/200 mi W from Alice Springs; rising to 1525 m/5000 ft at Mt Liebig, the highest point in the state.

mace A spice obtained by grinding up the red, net-like aril which surrounds the seed of the nutmeg tree (*Myristica fragrans*). Like nutmeg, mace is poisonous if consumed in large quantities because of the presence of a narcotic.

Macedon [masedon] In antiquity, the territory to the N of Greece abutting on to the NW corner of the Aegean. Regarded by the Greeks as backward, Macedon did not attract much notice until the military and diplomatic genius of Philip II (359–336 BC) transformed her into the most powerful state in the whole of Greece. Under his son, Alexander the Great, the Persian Empire was overthrown; but with Alexander's death (323 BC) decline set in, and eventually Macedon, like the rest of his western empire, fell to the Romans. It became a Roman province in 146 BC.

Macedonia (Greece) [masedohnia], Gr **Makedhonia** pop (2000e) 2 308 000; area 34 177 sq km/13 192 sq mi. N region of Greece, from the Albanian frontier (W) to the R Nestos (E), and from the former Yugoslav frontier (N) to Mt Olympus (S); capital, Thessaloniki; chief towns, Kavalla, Drama, Edhessa, Kastoria; mountainous, with fertile plains; ancient sites include Pella (former capital) and Vergina; livestock, grain, tobacco, olives, grapes.

Macedonia (republic) *p.935*

McEnroe, John (Patrick) [makenroh] (1959–) Tennis player, born in Wiesbaden, WC Germany. He trained at Port Washington Tennis Academy in New York State, and at 18 became the youngest man to reach the Wimbledon semifinals (1977). He

Macedonia

☐ International Airport

[masedohnia], Serbo-Croatian **Makedonija**, also called **Former Yugoslav Republic of Macedonia (FYROM)**

Local name Makedonija

Timezone GMT +2

Area 25 713 km²/9925 sq mi

Population total (2002e) 2 036 000

Status Republic

Date of independence 1991

Capital Skopje

Language Macedonian (status as language or dialect is a political issue with Greece), and Albanian

Ethnic groups Macedonian Slav (66%), Albanian (23%), with Turk (4%), Serb (3%), and other minorities (but minority totals disputed as underestimates by Albanians and Serbs)

Religions Macedonian Orthodox Christian (autocephalous), Muslim

Physical features Landlocked, mountainous region, bordered by Serbia, Bulgaria, Greece, Albania; divided from Greek Macedonia by the Kožuf and Nidže ranges, highest point, Korab, 2764 m/9068 ft; main rivers, Struma and Vardar.

Climate Continental climate; average annual temperatures 0°C (Jan), 24°C (Jul); often heavy winter snowfalls; average annual rainfall 500 mm/20 in.

Currency 1 Macedonian denar = 100 paras

Economy Agriculture; wheat, barley, corn, rice, tobacco; sheep, cattle; mining of minerals, iron ore, lead, zinc, nickel; steel, chemicals, textiles.

GDP (2002e) $10·57 bn, per capita $5100

Human Development Index (2002) 0·772

History Part of Macedonian, Roman, and Byzantine Empires; settled by Slavs, 6th-c; conquered by Bulgars, 7th-c, and by Serbia, 14th-c; incorporated into Serbia after the Balkan Wars; united in 1918, in what later became Yugoslavia, but continuous demands for autonomy persisted; occupied by Bulgaria during World War 2, 1941–44; declaration of independence, 1991; international discussions continue over the name under which the country will be accorded international recognition (the adjacent province of Greece bears the name Macedonia); President Gligorov seriously injured in assassination attempt, 1995; received large numbers of refugees during the Kosovo crisis, 1999; peace agreement signed and NATO task force deployed, 2001; EU took over operations, Mar 2003 (the EU's first military operation); President Trajkovski killed in air crash, 2004; governed by a President, Prime Minister, and Assembly.

Head of State

1991–9 Kiro Gligorov
1999 Savl Klimovski *Interim*
1999–2004 Boris Trajkovski
2004– Ljubco Jordanovski *Acting*

Head of Government

1996–8 Branko Crvenkovski
1998–2002 Ljubco Georgievski
2002– Branko Crvenkovski

won four US Open singles titles (1979–81, 1984) and three Wimbledon singles titles (1981, 1983-4), and was an invaluable member of the US Davis Cup team between 1978 and 1985. He was also Grand Prix winner in 1979 and 1984–5, and World Championship Tennis champion in 1979, 1981, and 1983–4. His skill as a player was often overshadowed by his fierce emotional outbursts on court and frequent wrangling with umpires, which always attracted the attention of the media, and which led to professional censure on several occasions. He married film actress **Tatum O'Neill** (1963–) in 1986, but they separated in 1993. Since 1995 he has been a TV commentator at major tennis tournaments, and more recently host of the TV quiz show *The Chair* (2002). An autobiography, *Serious*, appeared in 2002.

McFadden, Daniel L (1937–) Economist, born in Raleigh, North Carolina, USA. He studied economics at the University of Minnesota (1962), and joined the faculty at the University of California, Berkeley (1963), where he became professor of economics. In 2000 he shared the Nobel Prize for Economics with James J Heckman for their work in the field of microeconometrics.

Macgillycuddy's Reeks [makgilikuhdeez reeks] Mountain range in Kerry county, Munster, SW Ireland, rising to 1041 m/3415 ft at Carrantuohill, highest peak in Ireland.

McGonagall, William [muhgonagl] (1830–1902) Scottish poet and novelist, the son of an immigrant Irish weaver. He spent some of his childhood in the Orkneys, and in Dundee. He did some acting at Dundee's Royal Theatre, and in 1877 began to write poems, the best-known of which is 'The Tay Bridge Disaster' (1880). From then on he travelled in C Scotland, giving readings and selling his poetry in broadsheets, and was lionized by the legal and student fraternity. His poems are uniformly bad, but possess a disarming innocence and a calypso-like disregard for metre which still never fail to entertain.

McGough, Roger [muhgof] (1937–) Poet and performer, born in Liverpool, NW England, UK. He studied at Hull University. He became known as one of the 'Liverpool Poets' together with Adrian Henri (1932–2000) and Brian Patten (1946–). A poet of bizarre irony and wit, he is well-known for his public readings. He established his reputation with the publication of *Frinck, A Day in the Life of, and Summer with Monika* (1967). Other collections of poems include *Gig* (1973), *In the Glassroom* (1976), *Waving at Trains* (1982), and *Everyday Eclipses* (2003). He has also written a book for children, *The Magic Fountain* (1995), and a novel, *Defying Gravity* (1996).

McGovern, George S(tanley) [muhguhvern] (1922–) US politician, born in Avon, South Dakota, USA. During World War 2, he served with distinction in the Army Air Force. He studied at Northwestern University, and became professor of history and government at Dakota Wesleyan University. He was a Democratic member of the US House of Representatives (1956–61), and senator for South Dakota from 1963. He sought the Democratic presidential nomination in 1968, and opposed Nixon in the 1972 presidential election, but was defeated. He tried again for the presidential nomination in 1984, but withdrew.

McGrath, John (Peter) (1935–2002) Playwright and theatre director, born in Birkenhead, Merseyside, NW England, UK. Between 1958 and 1961 he was a television director with the BBC, and wrote scripts for *Z Cars*. He founded the *7:84* Theatre Company in 1971, and was their artistic director until 1988. His many popular political plays include *Fish in the Sea* (1975), *Yobbo Nowt* (1978), and *Swings and Roundabouts* (1981). Later works include: *John Brown's Body* (1990), *Watching for Dolphins* (1991), *The Wicked Old Man* (1992), and *The Last of the MacEachans* (1996).

McGregor, Ewan (1971–) Actor, born in Crieff, Perthshire, Scotland, UK. He studied acting at the Guildhall School of Music and Drama in London. His first important role was in the television series *Lipstick on Your Collar* (1993), and feature film success followed with *Shallow Grave* (1994) and *Trainspotting* (1996). Later films include *Star Wars Episode 1: The Phantom Menace* (1999), *Moulin Rouge* (2000), and *Young Adam* (2003).

McGuffey, William (Holmes) [muhguhfee] (1800–73) Educator, born near Claysville, Pennsylvania, USA. He studied at Washington and Jefferson College (1926) and became professor of languages at Miami University. His later posts include professor of philosophy at Woodward College, Cincinnati (1843–5) and professor of moral philosophy at the University of Virginia (1845–73). He compiled the famous *McGuffey Readers*, six elementary schoolbooks (1836–57) that sold 122 million copies and became standard texts for generations of 19th-c US children.

McGuigan, Paul *Oasis*

McGuigan, Barry [muhgwigan], properly **Finbar Partick McGuigan** (1961–) Boxer, born in Clones, Co Monaghan, NE Ireland. In 1978 as an amateur he won the Irish bantamweight title and Commonwealth Games gold medal. On turning professional he won the British featherweight title in 1983, and in 1985 took the world featherweight championship.

McGuinness, Martin [muhginis] (1950–) Sinn Féin politician, born in Londonderry, Northern Ireland. A militant supporter of the IRA, who served two jail sentences in the Irish Republic, he developed a major role as a political strategist during the Northern Ireland peace process in the 1990s. He became an MP, though not attending at Westminster, and Sinn Féin's senior minister in the Stormont Assembly. He became minister of education in the devolved Assembly in November 1999.

McGwire, Mark [muhgwiyuh] (1963–) Baseball player, born in Pomona, California, USA. A power-hitting first baseman, whose home-run race with Sammy Sosa during the 1998 baseball season transfixed the USA, his final total of 70 homers passed the previous seasonal record of 61 set by Roger Maris in 1961. McGwire was the most consistent hitter of homers since Babe Ruth. He was voted American League Rookie of the Year in 1987, after hitting 49 homers, the most ever by a rookie, for Oakland Athletics. In 1997 he was traded to the St Louis Cardinals, with whom he had his record season. He announced his retirement in 2001.

Mach, Ernst [mahk] (1838–1916) Physicist and philosopher, born in Turas, Austria. He studied at Vienna University, and became professor of mathematics at Graz in 1864, and of physics at Prague (1867) and Vienna (1895). His experimental work has proved of great importance in aeronautical design and the science of projectiles, and his name has been given to a unit of velocity (the **Mach number** – the ratio of speed of object to the speed of sound in the medium in which the object is moving), and to the angle of a shock wave to the direction of motion (the **Mach angle**). His writings greatly influenced Einstein, and laid the foundations of logical positivism.

Machabees *Maccabees, Books of the*

Machado (y Ruiz), Antonio [machahthoh] (1875–1939) Poet and playwright, born in Seville, SW Spain. He studied at the Sorbonne, became a French teacher, and wrote lyrics characterized by a nostalgic melancholy, among them *Soledades, galerías y otros poemas* (1907), and *Campos de Castilla* (1912). With his brother **Manuel** (1874–1947), he also wrote several plays.

Machaut, Guillaume de *Guillaume de Machaut*

Machel, Samora Moïsés [mashel] (1933–86) Leader of the guerrilla campaign against Portuguese rule in Mozambique, and first president of Mozambique (1975–86). He studied at a Catholic mission school, and worked as a hospital nurse, rising to a senior position. He was commander-in-chief of the army of Frente de Libertação de Moçambique (FRELIMO) (1966–70), president of FRELIMO from 1970, and became president of the country at its independence. Although a Marxist, he established warm relations with Western governments, and attempted an accommodation with the South African regime. He was killed in an air crash over South African territory.

Machiavelli, Niccolò (di Bernardo dei) [makiavelee] (1469–1527) Italian statesman, writer, and political theorist, born in Florence, NC Italy. Little is known of his early life, but he travelled on several missions in Europe for the Republic of Florence (1498–1512). On the restoration of the Medici, he was arrested on a charge of conspiracy (1513) and, though pardoned, was obliged to withdraw from public life. He devoted himself to literature, writing historical treatises, poetry, short stories, and comedies. His masterpiece is *Il Principe* (1532, The Prince), whose main theme is that all means may be used in order to maintain authority. It was condemned by the pope, and its viewpoint gave rise to the adjective *machiavellian*. His writings were not published until 1782.

machine An assembly of connected parts arranged to transmit or modify force to perform useful work. All machines are based on six types: (1) lever; (2) wheel and axle; (3) pulley; (4) inclined plane; (5) wedge; and (6) screw. The wheelbarrow, human arm, and crowbar are all levers. Wheel and axles are used to raise loads by pulling a rope attached to the axle. Pulleys work in the same way, but the force and movement of load may be in different directions. Inclined plane and screw are used to move heavy weights with little effort. Wedges exert large sideways forces. The mechanical advantage can be determined for each type.

machine code The fundamental instructions which can be directly understood and acted on by a computer, written in a hexadecimal system. Programmers seldom write directly in machine code; instead they use either the assembly language for the specific computer or one of the many available high-level languages.

machine-gun A gun firing a rifle calibre bullet with an automated ammunition feed and firing cycle, allowing sustained automatic fire with the operator needing to do no more than squeeze the trigger and ensure there is enough ammunition. Multi-barrel weapons such as the Gatling gun appeared in the mid-19th-c, but it was the inventor Hiram Maxim who, in 1883, hit on the principle of using the force of recoil to power the automatic cycle in his water-cooled weapon, to eject the spent cartridge, chamber a new one, close the breech block, and fire. Machine-guns made a huge impact on warfare, their firepower consigning the infantry of 1914–18 to positional trench warfare. But lighter, air-cooled weapons were on the way, using gas bled off from the firing cycle as their operating power source, producing such weapons of World War 2 as the British Bren gun and the German MG 34. Machine-guns are still an important weapon of world armies, although weapons technology has produced lightweight assault rifles, themselves capable of sustained automatic fire.

machine tools A variety of powered machines used in industry to work and shape components made of metal or other material, and operated either manually by skilled operators or under the control of other machines or computers. They include lathes, planes, saws, and milling machines. Finer tolerances and greater repeatability of product is possible with machine tools than with old hand tools, and their development during the Industrial Revolution made mass production and the concept of replaceable parts possible.

Mach number [mahk] Unit of velocity; symbol *Ma*; defined as the ratio of velocity of an object to that of sound in some medium, usually air; named after Ernst Mach; an aircraft travelling at Ma 1 has velocity 331·5 m/s, the velocity of sound in air.

macho *dark matter*

Mach's principle [mahk] In physics, an argument that the acceleration of an object cannot be measured relative to absolute space, but must instead be measured against all matter in the universe. The inertia of an object is determined by all matter around it, and has no meaning in empty space. The argument, propounded by Ernst Mach in 1863, influenced Einstein's development of general relativity.

Machu Picchu [machoo peechoo] 13°07S 72°34W. Ruined Inca city in SC Peru; a world heritage site; on the saddle of a high mountain with terraced slopes falling away to the R Urubamba; comparatively well-preserved because it was never found by the Spaniards; discovered in 1911 by US explorer Hiram Bingham; ruins consist of staircases, temples, terraces, palaces, towers, fountains, and a famous sundial; Museo de Sitio museum; near the Urubamba is the Temple of the Moon; approached from Cuzco by rail.

Macintosh A model of personal computer known particularly for its use of windows and icons to communicate with the user. It is very popular among users involved in aspects of graphic design work. Macintosh is a trade mark of Apple Computer Inc of California.

Macintosh, Charles (1766–1843) Manufacturing chemist, born in Glasgow, W Scotland, UK. While trying to find uses for the waste products from gasworks, he developed in 1823 a method of waterproofing cloth, which resulted in the manufacture of the raincoat, or *macintosh*.

Mackay (of Clashfern), James Peter Hymers Mackay, Baron (1927–) Jurist, born in the village of Scourie, Highland, N Scotland, UK. He studied mathematics and natural philosophy at Edinburgh, and later taught mathematics at St Andrews University, before switching to law. He was called to the bar in 1955, and in 1965 became a QC, specializing in tax law. In 1979 he was made Lord Advocate for Scotland, and became a life peer. As Lord Chancellor (1987–97), he created consternation among the English bar by proposing radical reforms of the legal profession. Since 1998, he has been editor-in-chief of *Halsbury's Laws of England*.

McKay, Heather [muhkiy], *née* **Blundell** (1941–) Squash player, born in Queanbeyan, New South Wales, SE Australia. During her career she completely dominated the game, from 1962 to 1979 winning every competition she entered. She won the British squash championship for 16 consecutive years (1962–77), and also regularly won the Australian championship (1960–73). She moved to Canada in 1975, and later became a successful racketball competitor.

Macke, August [mahkuh] (1887–1914) Painter, born in Meschede, WC Germany. He studied at Düsseldorf, and designed stage scenery. Profoundly influenced by Matisse, whose work he saw in Munich in 1910, he founded the *Blaue Reiter* group together with Franz Marc. He was a sensitive colourist, working in watercolour as well as oil, and painted the kind of subject-matter favoured by the Impressionists – figures in a park, street scenes, children, and animals (eg 'The Zoo', 1912). He was killed in action in Champagne, France.

McKellen, Sir Ian (Murray) [muhkelen] (1939–) Actor, born in Burnley, Lancashire, NW England, UK. He played in several repertory theatres before making his London debut in 1964. He joined the National Theatre in 1965, the touring Prospect Theatre Company in 1968, and with Edward Petherbridge founded the Actors' Company in 1972. He played many memorable parts for the Royal Shakespeare Company (1974–8), including the title role of the 1976 Trevor Nunn production of *Macbeth* with Judi Dench. In 1998–9 he led the first resident ensemble company at the West Yorkshire Playhouse, directed by Jude Kelly. His films include *Scandal* (1988), *Richard III* (1995), *Cold Comfort Farm* (1996), *Gods and Monsters* (1998), *X-Men* (2000), and the *Lord of the Rings* trilogy (2001–3). He is also known for his solo recitals on a wide range of themes. He was knighted in 1991.

Mackenzie, Sir (Edward Montague) Compton (1883–1972) Writer, born in West Hartlepool, Co Durham, NE England, UK, the brother of Fay Compton. He studied at Oxford, and began on the stage, but turned to literature, publishing his first novel in 1911. He served at Gallipoli in World War 1, and in 1917 became director of the Aegean Intelligence Service in Syria. He wrote a large number of novels, notably *Sinister Street* (1913–14) and *Whisky Galore* (1947). He lived in Scotland after 1928, and became a strong nationalist. He was knighted in 1952.

McKenzie, Kevin (1954–) Ballet dancer and choreographer, born in Burlington, Vermont, USA. He trained at the Washington School of Ballet and became a leading dancer there. After a spell with the Joffrey Ballet, he joined the American Ballet Theatre as soloist (1979) and principal dancer (1980), and was appointed artistic director of the company in 1992.

Mackenzie, William Lyon (1795–1861) Politician, born in Dundee, E Scotland, UK. He emigrated to Canada in 1820, established the *Colonial Advocate* in 1824, and entered politics in 1828. In 1837 he published in his paper a declaration of Canadian independence, headed a band of reform-minded insurgents, and after a skirmish with a superior force, fled to the USA, where he was imprisoned. He returned to Canada in 1849, becoming a journalist and MP (1850–8).

Mackenzie Range Mountain range in Northwest Territories, NW Canada; extends c.800 km/497 mi SE–NW; rises to 2972 m/9750 ft at Keele Peak; watershed for tributaries of Mackenzie and Yukon Rivers; Nahanni nature park in the S; mountains and river both named after Scottish explorer Sir Alexander Mackenzie (?1755–1820).

Mackenzie River River in Northwest Territories, NW Canada; issues from W end of Great Slave Lake; flows NW to enter the Beaufort Sea through a wide delta near the boundary with Yukon Territory; length 4241 km/2635 mi; navigable in summer (Jun–Oct); hydroelectricity, oil and mineral transportation.

mackerel Surface-living fish (*Scomber scombrus*) widespread and locally abundant in the N Atlantic; undertakes long seasonal migrations; length up to 60 cm/2 ft; body slender, rounded in section, tail deeply forked, small finlets between dorsal and anal fins; bright blue or green with dark blue or black bars, underside silvery white; extensively fished commercially using nets or lines; changes in distribution and migration patterns led to a failure of the major fisheries off Cornwall and the Minch, Scotland, during the 1970s. The name is also used for other species in the families Scombridae and Scomberesocidae. (Family: Scombridae.)

mackerel shark Large, powerful shark (*Lamna nasus*) found in open ocean waters of the N Atlantic and Mediterranean; feeds mostly on fish and squid; not normally offensive; good sport fish, and taken commercially on long lines; also called **porbeagle**. (Family: Lamnidae.)

mackerel sky A patterning of cirrocumulus and altocumulus clouds resembling fish markings. These are found at altitudes above 5000 m/16 000 ft.

Mackerras, Sir (Alan) Charles (MacLaurin) [muhkeras] (1925–) Conductor, born in Schenectady, New York, USA. He played oboe with the Sydney Symphony Orchestra (1943–6), was a staff conductor at Sadler's Wells Opera (1949–53), and returned there in 1970 as musical director, having established an international reputation. Subsequent conducting posts have included the BBC Symphony Orchestra, Sydney Symphony Orchestra, Royal Liverpool Philharmonic Orchestra, and Welsh National Opera (musical director, 1987–92). He was principal guest conductor, Scottish Chamber Orchestra (1992–5), and with the Czech Philharmonic from 1996. A noted scholar of the music of Janáček, he was knighted in 1979, and made a Companion of Honour in 2003.

Mckillop, Mary Helen [muhkilop], known as **Mother Mary of the Cross** (1842–1909) Religious, born in Fitzroy, Melbourne, Victoria, SE Australia. With Father Tenison-Woods she founded in 1866 the Society of the Sisters of St Joseph of the Sacred Heart in Penola, South Australia. Excommunicated in 1871, she was reinstated two years later by Pope Pius IX, who approved the Sisterhood. In 1875 she was confirmed as superior-general of the order. The case for her beatification was made in 1925, and in 1975 her cause was formally introduced by the Vatican, when it was announced that she would become Australia's first saint. She was declared venerable by Pope John Paul II in 1992, and her beatification was approved in 1993.

McKinley, William (1843–1901) US statesman and 25th president (1897–1901), born in Niles, Ohio, USA. He served in the Civil War, then became a lawyer. He was elected to Congress in 1877, and in 1891 was made Governor of Ohio, his name being identified with the high protective tariff carried in the *McKinley Bill* of 1890. He secured a large majority in the presidential elections of 1896 and 1900 as the representative of a gold standard and high tariffs. In his first term the war with Spain (1898) took place, with the conquest of Cuba and the Philippines. At the beginning of his second term, he was shot by an anarchist at Buffalo, and died a few days later.

McKinley, Mount 63°04N 151°00W. Mountain in SC Alaska, USA; in Denali National Park and Preserve; highest peak in the USA and in North America; covered almost completely by glaciers; consists of two peaks (6194 m/20 321 ft, 5934 m/19 468 ft); Indian name Denali; first climbed (1913) by Hudson Stuck (US).

MacKinnon, Roderick (1956–) Biochemist, born in Burlington, Massachusetts, USA. He studied chemistry at Brandeis University (1978) and attended Tufts University School of Medicine (1982), later joining the faculty at Harvard Medical School. In 1996 he moved to the Howard Hughes Medical Institute, Rockefeller University, NY, where he became head of the Laboratory of Molecular Neurobiology and Biophysics. He shared the 2003 Nobel Prize for Chemistry for discoveries concerning channels in cell membranes, his contribution involving the structural and mechanistic studies of ion channels.

Mackintosh, Sir Cameron (Anthony) (1946–) British impresario. Following a childhood ambition to stage musical shows, he became a stage hand at the Theatre Royal, Drury Lane, London, in the early 1960s. He produced his first musical in 1969, and in association with the Arts Council supplied road-show musicals to regional theatres in the 1970s. He agreed to finance Lloyd Webber's *Cats*, and has subsequently produced, in London and New York City, such musicals as *Little Shop of Horrors* (1983), *Les Misérables* (1985), *Phantom of the Opera* (1986), and *Miss Saigon* (1989). Later London productions include *Moby Dick* (1992), *Martin Guerre* (1996), *Oklahoma!* (1998), and *The Witches of Eastwick* (2000). He was knighted in 1996, and received the Variety Club of Great Britain Special Award in 1997.

Mackintosh, Charles Rennie (1868–1928) Architect, designer, and painter, born in Glasgow, W Scotland, UK. He attended evening classes at Glasgow School of Art, joined the established firm of Honeyman and Kepple in 1889, and in 1900 married **Margaret Mackintosh** (1865–1933), with whom he worked in close collaboration. He became a leader of the 'Glasgow Style', a movement related to Art Nouveau. His work exercised considerable influence on European design, and included the Glasgow School of Art (1896–1909), and Hill House in Helensburgh (1902–6). His designs included detailed interiors, textiles, furniture, and metalwork. His work was exhibited at the Vienna Secession Exhibition in 1900, and in his later years he turned to painting, producing a series of watercolours (1923–7). He left Glasgow in 1914, and eventually settled in London.

MacLaine, Shirley, stage name of **Shirley Maclean Beaty** (1934–) Film actress and writer, born in Richmond, Virginia, USA, the sister of **Warren Beatty**. Having begun studying ballet at age two, she left for New York after graduating from high school, and entered show business as a teenager when she joined the chorus of *Oklahoma* in New York City (1950). Her first Broadway experience was in the chorus line of *Me and Juliet* (1953). Understudy to Carol Haney in *The Pajama Game* (1954), she replaced the injured Haney after the third performance and was almost immediately signed up by Hollywood, making her screen debut in *The Trouble with Harry* (1955). She proved to be a versatile actress in films ranging from musicals such as *Irma La Douce* (1963) to sentimental dramas such as *Terms of Endearment* (1983), for which she won an Oscar as best actress. Later films include a sequel, *Evening Star* (1997), *Steel Magnolias* (1989), and *Postcards from the Edge* (1990). .She led an equally varied career offscreen as an activist for liberal causes, leader of the first American women's delegation to China (which resulted in her documentary, *The Other Half of the Sky: A China Memoir* , 1975), a tireless tourer in her one-woman variety shows, and author of several best-sellers. She was also the butt of much teasing for her professed belief in reincarnation.

McLaughlin, Audrey [muhgloklin] (1936–) Canadian politician, born in Dutton, Ontario, SE Canada. She was MP for the Yukon Territory (1987–97), and leader of the federal New Democratic Party (1989–95).

McLaughlin, Isabel [muhgloklin] (1903–) Painter, born in Oshawa, Ontario, SE Canada. She studied at the Ontario College of Art, then in Toronto and Paris, and became one of Canada's leading women artists, a past president of the Canadian Group of Painters. She is known for her highly imaginary paintings depicting botanical studies, noted for their bright colours, vibrant brush strokes, and strong sense of design. She is benefactor and patron of the Robert McLaughlin Art Gallery in Oshawa.

Maclean, Alistair [muhklayn] (1922–87) Writer, born in Glasgow, W Scotland, UK. He studied at Glasgow University, served in the Royal Navy (1941–46) and, while a schoolteacher, won a short-story competition held by the *Glasgow Herald*. At the suggestion of William Collins, the publishers, he produced a full-length novel, *HMS Ulysses* (1955), and this epic story of wartime bravery became an immediate best seller. He followed it with *The Guns of Navarone* in 1957, and turned to full-time writing. One of the most successful and prolific writers of adventure stories, many of his books were made into films, including *Ice Station Zebra* (1963), *Where Eagles Dare* (1967), and *Puppet on a Chain* (1969).

Maclean, Donald (Duart) [muhklayn] (1913–83) British diplomat and Soviet intelligence officer, born in London, UK. He studied at Cambridge at the same time as Anthony Blunt, Guy Burgess, and Kim Philby, and was similarly influenced by Communism. He joined the diplomatic service in 1934, and was recruited by Soviet intelligence as an agent. During his diplomatic career he held the post of Head of Chancery at the British Embassy in Washington, where he made information available to the Soviet Union on the establishment of the North Atlantic Treaty Organization. He also served as secretary of the Combined Policy on Atomic Development, and finally (1950) as head of the American Department at the Foreign Office, where he had access to highly classified information, especially about the progress of the war in Korea. He was warned by Philby (1951) that he was under suspicion, and disappeared with Burgess, reappearing in Russia in 1956; later (1979) it transpired that he had escaped with the help of Blunt.

Maclean, Sorley [muhklayn], Gaelic **Somhairle MacGill-Eain** (1911–96) Gaelic poet, born at Osgaig, I of Raasay, off Skye, Highland, N Scotland, UK. He read English at Edinburgh University (1929–33), and by the end of the 1930s was an established figure on the Scottish literary scene. In 1940 he published *Seventeen Poems for Sixpence*, which he produced with Robert Garioch, and in 1943, *Dàin do Eimhir* (Poems to Eimhir), addressed to the legendary Eimhir of the early Irish sagas. A teacher and headmaster until his retirement in 1972, his major collection of poems, *Reothairt is Contraigh* (Spring Tide and Neap Tide), appeared in 1977. Translations of his work from Gaelic (often made by himself) have been issued in bilingual editions all over the world.

MacLeish, Archibald [muhkleesh] (1892–1982) Poet, born in Glencoe, Illinois, USA. He studied at Yale and Harvard, was librarian of Congress (1939–44), and became professor of rhetoric at Harvard (1949–62). His first volumes of poetry appeared in 1917, and he won Pulitzer Prizes for *Conquistador* (1932), *Collected Poems 1917–52* (1953), and his social drama in modern verse, *J B* (1959). A strong supporter of Franklin D Roosevelt, he was assistant secretary of state (1944–5).

MacLennan, (John) Hugh (1907–90) Novelist and essayist, born in Nova Scotia, SE Canada. He studied at Dalhousie, Oxford, and Princeton universities, then taught at McGill (1967–79). A highly esteemed writer, he was the first major English-speaking novelist to attempt to portray Canada's national character and regional relationships. He won the Governor-General's Award three times for fiction – *Two Solitudes* (1945), *The Precipice* (1948), and *The Watch that Ends the Night* (1959) – and twice for non-fiction, with *Cross Country* and *Thirty and Three*.

Macleod, Iain (Norman) [muhklowd] (1913–70) British statesman, born in Skipton, North Yorkshire, N England, UK. He studied at Cambridge, became a Conservative MP (1950), minister of health (1952–5), minister of labour (1955–9), secretary of state for the Colonies (1959–61), and chairman of the Conservative Party (1961–3). Refusing to serve under Home, he spent two years editing the *Spectator* (1963–5). Highly popular, and a gifted speaker, he was appointed shadow Chancellor (1965–70) under Heath, and after the Conservative victory (1970) became Chancellor of the Exchequer. However, a month later he died suddenly at the age of 57.

Macleod, J(ohn) J(ames) R(ickard) [muhklowd] (1876–1935) Physiologist, born in Clunie, Perth and Kinross, E Scotland, UK. He studied at Aberdeen, Leipzig, and Cambridge, and became professor of physiology at Cleveland, OH (1903), Toronto (1918), and Aberdeen (1928). In 1922 he discovered insulin with Sir Frederick Banting and Charles Best, and shared the 1923 Nobel Prize for Physiology or Medicine.

McLuhan, (Herbert) Marshall [muhklooan] (1911–80) Writer, born in Edmonton, Alberta, W Canada. He studied English literature at the universities of Manitoba and Cambridge. In 1946 he became professor at St Michael's College, Toronto, and in 1963 was appointed director of the University of Toronto's Centre for Culture and Technology. He held controversial views on the effect of the communication media, claiming that it is the media, not the information and ideas which they disseminate, that influence society. His books include *The Gutenberg Galaxy* (1962), *Understanding Media* (1964), *The Medium is the Message* (with Q Fiore, 1967), and *Counter-Blast* (1970).

Macmahon, Marie Edme Patrice Maurice de, duc de (Duke of) **Magenta** [makmahon] (1808–93) Marshal and second president of the Third Republic (1873–9), born in Sully, C France. He was a commander in the Crimean War (1854–6), and for his services in the Italian campaign (1859) was made marshal and a duke. In the Franco-Prussian War (1870–1) he was defeated at Wörth, and surrendered at Sedan. After the war he suppressed the Commune (1871), and succeeded Thiers as president. Failing to assume dictatorial powers, he resigned in 1879, thus ensuring the supremacy of parliament.

McMahon, Sir William [muhkmahn] (1908–88) Australian statesman and prime minister (1971–2), born in Sydney, New South Wales, SE Australia. He studied at the university there, and qualified and practised as a solicitor. After service in World War 2 he became active in the Liberal Party and was elected to the House of Representatives in 1949. He held a variety of posts in the administrations of Sir Robert Menzies, Harold Holt, and John Gorton, until he took over the premiership when Gorton lost a vote of confidence in 1971. The following year the Liberals lost the general election, but he continued to lead his party until 1977, when he was knighted.

McManaman, Steve [muhkmanaman] (1972–) Footballer, born in Liverpool, Merseyside, NW England, UK. A midfielder, he served an apprenticeship at Liverpool, then joined the club, moving to Real Madrid in 1999. He signed for Manchester City FC for the start of the 2003–4 season. By 2004 he had won 37 caps playing for England.

Macmillan, Daniel (1813–57) and **Alexander Macmillan** (1818–96) Booksellers and publishers, brothers, born in Upper Corrie, I of Arran, and Irvine, North Ayrshire, Scotland, UK respectively. Daniel was apprenticed to booksellers in Scotland and Cambridge from the age of 11 when his father died, and in 1843 he and his brother Alexander opened a bookshop in London. In Cambridge they started publishing textbooks (1844), then novels, including *Westward Ho!* and *Tom Brown's Schooldays*. In the year after Daniel's death the firm opened a branch in London, and by 1893 had become a limited company, with Daniel's son, **Frederick** (1851–1936), as chairman.

Macmillan, (Maurice) Harold, 1st Earl of Stockton (1894–1986) British statesman and prime minister (1957–63), born in London, UK, the grandson of Daniel Macmillan. He studied at Oxford, and became a Conservative MP in 1924. He was minister of housing (1951–4), minister of defence (1954–5), foreign secretary (1955), and Chancellor of the Exchequer (1955–7), and succeded Eden as premier. He gained unexpected popularity with his infectious enthusiasm, effective domestic policy ('most of our people have never had it so good'), and resolute foreign policy, and he was re-elected in 1959. After several political setbacks, he resigned through ill health in 1963, and left the House of Commons in 1964. He became Chancellor of Oxford University in 1960, and was made an earl on his 90th birthday in 1984.

MacMillan, Sir Kenneth (1929–92) Ballet dancer, choreographer, and ballet company director, born in Dunfermline, Fife, E Scotland, UK. He joined the Sadler's Wells Theatre Ballet in 1946, and began to choreograph in 1953. He directed the Berlin Opera (1966–9), and was artistic director of the Royal Ballet (1970–7), becoming its principal choreographer in 1977. His works include *Romeo and Juliet* (1965), *Manon* (1974), and *Mayerling* (1978). He was knighted in 1983.

Macmillan, Kirkpatrick (1813–78) Blacksmith, born near Thornhill, Dumfries and Galloway, SW Scotland, UK. In 1837 he built a 'dandy' horse – a kind of bicycle on which the rider pushed himself along with his feet. Three years later he had applied the crank to his machine to make the world's first pedal cycle, with wooden frame and iron-tyred wheels. His invention was never patented, and for many years it was credited to one of his imitators, Gavin Dalzell.

McMillan, Terry (1951–) Novelist, born in Port Huron, Michigan, USA. She studied at Berkeley and Columbia universities and later taught at the universities of Wyoming (1987–90) and Arizona (1990–2). She began writing in her mid-thirties, publishing *Mama* (1987) followed by a string of best-selling novels including *Disappearing Acts* (1989), *Waiting to Exhale* (1992; filmed 1995), *How Stella Got Her Groove Back* (1996), and *A Day Late and a Dollar Short* (2001). She is also editor of *Breaking Ice: An Anthology of Contemporary African-American Fiction* (1990).

McMurtry, Larry (Jeff) [muhkmertree] (1936–) Writer, bookseller, and academic, born in Wichita Falls, Texas, USA. He studied at North Texas State College. His first novel *Horseman, Pass By* (1961, Jess H Jones Award) was filmed as the Academy Award-winning *Hud* (1963). This and subsequent early novels were semi-autobiographical and centred on the frustrations of ranch life. He wrote the screenplay for his novel *The Last Picture Show* (1966; Oscar Best Picture, 1972). He went on to write a trilogy of novels with urban settings comprising *Moving On* (1970), *All My Friends Are Going to Be Strangers* (1972), and *Terms of Endearment* (1977). His best-selling frontier epic *Lonesome Dove* (1985) won a Pulitzer Prize in 1986.

McNaghten rules [muhknawtn] A legal set of principles which state when a defendant who is believed to be insane should not be convicted of a crime or offence. The rules provide that accused persons must show that they suffer from a defect of reason arising from serious mental disease; also that, because of this, they did not know what they were doing or did not know that what they were doing was wrong. The rules were developed subsequent to the 19th-c murder trial of Daniel McNaghten, a case in which insanity was proved. They serve as the legal standard for insanity in England, Wales, Canada, New Zealand, India, Sri Lanka, and many US and Australian jurisdictions. Although not applicable in Scotland, similar tests are used by the courts there.

Macnamara, Dame (Annie) Jean (1899–1968) Physician, born in Beechworth, Victoria, SE Australia. She studied at Melbourne University, worked in local hospitals, and during the poliomyelitis epidemic of 1925 tested the use of immune serum. Later, with Sir Macfarlane Burnet, she found that there was more than one strain of the polio virus, a discovery which led to the development of the Salk vaccine. She was also involved in the controversial introduction of myxomatosis as a means of controlling the rabbit population of Australia in 1951.

McNamara, Robert S(trange) (1916–) US Democratic politician and businessman, born in San Francisco, California, USA. After service in the air force (1943–6), he worked his way up in the Ford Motor Co to president by 1960, and in 1961 joined the Kennedy administration as secretary of defense, being particularly involved in the Vietnam War. In 1968 he resigned to become president of the World Bank (a post he held until 1981). In the 1980s he emerged as a critic of the nuclear arms race, and among his publications are *Blundering into Disaster* (1987) and *In Retrospect: The Tragedy and Lessons of Vietnam* (1995).

MacNeice, (Frederick) Louis [muhknees] (1907–63) Poet, born in Belfast, NE Northern Ireland, UK. He studied at Oxford, and became a lecturer in Classics at Birmingham (1930–6), and in Greek at the University of London (1936–40). He was closely associated with the new British left-wing poets of the 1930s, especially Auden, with whom he wrote *Letters from Iceland* (1937). Other volumes include *Blind Fireworks* (1929), *Collected Poems* (1949), and *Solstices* (1961). In 1941 he joined the staff of the BBC. He was the author of several verse plays for radio, notably *The Dark Tower* (1947), as well as translations of Aeschylus and of Goethe's *Faust*.

Mâcon [makõ], ancient **Matisco** 46°19N 4°50E, pop (2000e) 40 300. Manufacturing city and capital of Saône-et-Loire department, C France, on the W bank of the R Saône; episcopal see from the 6th-c until the Revolution; road and rail junction; commercial centre of major wine area; textiles, agricultural machinery, casks; remains of 12th-c cathedral; birthplace of Lamartine; prehistoric site at Solutre, 8 km/5 mi W.

Maconchy, Dame Elizabeth [muhkongkee] (1907–94) Composer, born in Broxbourne, Hertfordshire, SE England, UK. She studied under Vaughan Williams at the Royal College of Music, then went to Prague, where her first major work, a piano concerto, was performed in 1930. Her most characteristic work was in the field of chamber music, and among her best-known compositions are her *Symphony* (1953) and the overture *Proud Thames* (1953). She also wrote choral, operatic, and ballet music, as well as orchestral works and songs. She was made a dame in 1987. She married writer **William Richard LeFanu** in 1930; their daughter, **Nicola (Frances) LeFanu** (1947–), is also a composer.

McPhee, John (Angus) (1931–) Writer, born in Princeton, New Jersey, USA. He graduated from Princeton (1953), studied in the UK at Cambridge (1953–4), then became a television playwright for *Robert Montgomery Presents* (1955–7), co-editor of *Time* magazine (1957–64), and a staff writer for the *New Yorker* (from 1964). His non-fiction books cover wide-ranging subjects, including a series on geology beginning with *Basin and Range* (1981).

McPherson, Aimée Semple, *née* **Kennedy** (1890–1944) Pentecostal evangelist and healer, born near Ingersoll, Ontario, SE Canada. Widowed shortly after her first marriage, she became hugely successful as an evangelist. In 1918 she founded the Foursquare Gospel Movement in Los Angeles, and for nearly two decades conducted a flamboyant preaching and healing ministry in the Angelus Temple, which cost her followers $1·5 million to construct. She had her own radio station, Bible school, and magazine. She married three more times, had many legal actions against her over the alleged misuse of church funds, and mysteriously disappeared for five weeks in 1926, claiming to have been kidnapped.

Macquarie, Lachlan [muhkworee] (1761–1824) Soldier and colonial administrator, born on the I of Ulva, Argyll and Bute, W Scotland, UK. He joined the Black Watch in 1777, and after service in North America, India, and Egypt, was appointed Governor of New South Wales in 1810 following the deposition of Bligh. The colony, populated largely by convicts, and exploited by monopolists, was raised by his administration to a state of prosperity. In 1821, political chicanery by the monopolists and his own ill health compelled him to return to Britain. Known as 'the father of Australia' he has given his name to the Lachlan and Macquarie rivers, and to Macquarie I.

Macquarie Island 54°30N 158°56W, area 123 sq km/47 sq mi. Island lying 1345 km/835 mi SW of Tasmania, Australia; average height 240 m/800 ft, rises to 425 m/1400 ft; meteorological and geological research stations; nature reserve (1933); breeding ground of royal penguin; colony of fur seals re-established there, 1956; made world heritage site, 1997.

McQueen, (Terence) Steve(n) (1930–80) Film actor, born in Slater, Missouri, USA. After periods in a reform school and in the marines, he trained at the Neighbourhood Playhouse and Uta Hagen School, New York City. He made his film debut as an extra in *Somebody Up There Likes Me* (1956). The television Western series *Wanted Dead or Alive* (1958) revealed his film potential, and led to a co-starring role in *The Magnificent Seven* (1960). He became the archetypal 1960s cinema hero/rebel with his performances in *The Great Escape* (1963), *The Cincinnati Kid* (1965), and *Bullitt* (1968). He was married (1973–8) to actress **Ali McGraw** (1938–), and died after a long struggle with cancer.

macramé [makrahmee] A type of coarse lace produced by knotting and plaiting, which enjoyed a widespread revival in the mid-19th-c. It was used to make decorative fringed borders for costumes as well as furnishings such as window blinds, antimacassars, and cushions.

Macready, William Charles [muhkreedee] (1793–1873) Actor, born in London, UK. He made his debut at Birmingham in 1810, and in 1816 appeared at Covent Garden, developing his restrained acting techniques which later became a major influence on modern stagecraft. He re-established some of the text of Shakespeare in its original form, purging it of the adaptations introduced by Colley Cibber and others. In 1837 he was appointed manager of Covent Garden, and extended his techniques to production. After two seasons he moved to Drury Lane (1841–3), then played in the provinces, Paris and America. His last visit to the USA was marked by terrible riots (1849), in which 22 people died, as a result of a feud started by the US actor Edwin Forrest.

macrobiotics A 'perfect diet', influenced by Zen Buddhist philosophy at the beginning of the 20th-c, thought to improve health and prolong life. All foods are seen as either *yin* (eg fruit) or *yang* (eg bread), and a strict balance of intake is prescribed. Seven levels of a macrobiotic diet are established, with the role of cereals increasing from 40% to up to 100% of the foods eaten. Such a diet is low in quality protein and has been associated with several cases of malnutrition in the USA, especially in children subjected to such diets by over-enthusiastic parents.

macroeconomics The study of economic aggregrates and averages. These include levels of national income, employment and

Madagascar

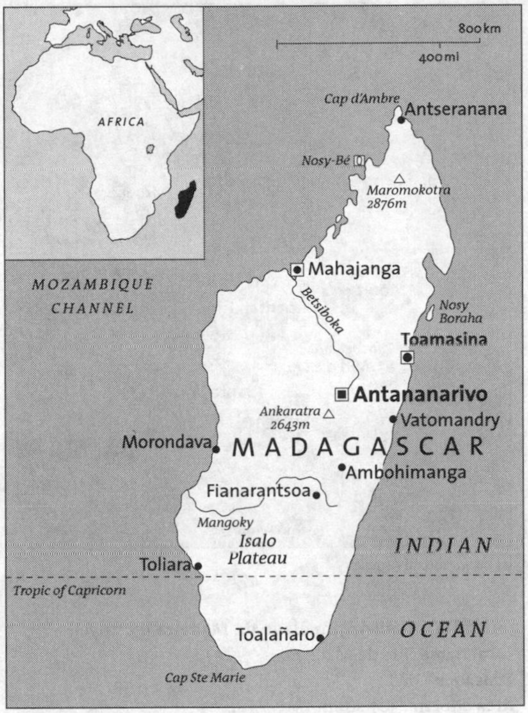

☐ International Airport

[madagasker], official name **Republic of Madagascar**, Malagasy **Repoblikan'i Madagasikara**

Local name Madagasikara

Timezone GMT +3

Area 587 041 km²/226 658 sq mi

Population total (2002e) 16 473 000

Status Republic

Date of independence 1960

Capital Antananarivo

Languages Malagasy (official), with French widely spoken

Ethnic groups Malagasy (99%) (including Merina 26%, Betsimisaraka 15%, Betsileo 12%)

Religions Traditional animist beliefs (47%), Christian (48%) (Roman Catholic 26%, Protestant 23%), Muslim (5%)

Physical features World's fourth largest island, length (N–S) 1580 km/982 mi; dissected N–S by a ridge of mountains (Tsaratananan Range), rising to 2876 m/9436 ft at Maromokotra; cliffs (E) drop down to a coastal plain through tropical forest; terraced descent (W) through savannah to coast, heavily indented in N.

Climate Tropical, variable rainfall; average annual rainfall 1000–1500 mm/40–60 in, higher in tropical coastal region; average annual temperatures 21°C (Jan), 15°C (Jul).

Currency 1 Malagasy Franc (FMG, MgFr) = 100 centimes

Economy Chiefly agricultural economy; rice, manioc, coffee, sugar, vanilla, cotton, peanuts, tobacco, livestock; food processing, tanning, cement, soap, paper, textiles, oil products; graphite, chrome, coal, ilmenite.

GDP (2002e) $12·59 bn, per capita $800

Human Development Index (2002) 0·469

History Settled by Indonesians in 1st-c AD and by African traders in 8th-c; visited by Portuguese, 16th-c; French established trading posts in late 18th-c; claimed as a protectorate by the French, 1895; autonomous overseas French territory (Malagasy Republic), 1958; independence, 1960; became Madagascar, 1977; new multi-party constitution, 1992; new constitution in 1998; governed by a President, who appoints a Council of Ministers and is guided by a Supreme Revolutionary Council; National People's Assembly is elected every five years; crisis followed 2001 elections, when President Ratsiraka refused to yield power; opposition leader Marc Ravalomanana appointed president, May 2002; legislative elections (Dec) followed by new cabinet, 2003.

Head of State
1993–6 Albert Zafy
1996 Norbert Ratsirahonana *Interim*
1997–2002 Didier Ratsiraka
2002– Marc Ravalomanana

Head of Government
1993–5 Francisque Ravony
1995–6 Emmanuel Rakotovahiny
1996–7 Norbert Ratsirahonana
1997–8 Pascal Rakotomavo
1998–2002 Tantely Andrianarivo
2002– Jacques Sylla

unemployment, price levels and inflation, short-term fluctuations, and long-term growth rates in the economy. This involves analyzing the behaviour of various sectors of the economy: the determinants of consumption, investment, and foreign trade and payments, and the policies followed by the government and monetary authorities. The techniques of macroeconomics include logical models or theories, the study of institutions such as banks and insurance companies, and the application of statistical techniques through econometrics. Macroeconomics is contrasted with *microeconomics*, which studies the decisions of individuals and firms, treating macroeconomic facts as a background.

macronutrients *nutrients*

macro-photography or **photomacrography** The photography of small objects or details using normal or special purpose camera lenses, in contrast to *photomicrography*, which uses two-stage magnification by objective and eyepiece lenses. In practice, photomacrography refers to images on film reproduced at life size or larger. Smaller images are given by *close-up photography*, but both require the lens to focus very close to the subject.

McTaggart, John (McTaggart Ellis) (1866–1925) Philosopher, born in London, UK. He taught at Cambridge (1897–1923). His systematic metaphysics is set out in *The Nature of Existence* (2 vols, 1921, and posthumously 1927). He is regarded as the most important of the Anglo-Hegelian or Idealistic philosophers who dominated British and American thought in the late 19th-c and early 20th-c.

McVeigh, Timothy (James) [muhkvay] (1968–2001) Convicted perpetrator of the 1995 Oklahoma City bombing, born in Pendleton, New York, USA. He joined the army in 1988, took part in Operation Desert Storm, and was discharged in 1991. He became internationally known when he was charged with the bombing of the Alfred P Murrah US government building in Oklahoma City in 1995, in which 168 people died. At his trial in 1997, a Denver jury found him guilty of conspiracy and murder, and he was sentenced to death by lethal injection, although a series of appeals was expected to follow. Failing all appeals he was executed by lethal injection in 2001. Two other conspirators, Terry Nichols (1955–) and Michael Fortier (1969–), were also later convicted.

Macy, William H (1950–) Theatre and film actor, born in Miami, Florida, USA. He studied drama in Reading, UK, and later under David Mamet at Goddard College, Vermont. He co-formed the *St Nicholas Company* with Mamet and Steven Schachter, and during the 1970s–80s appeared in numerous stage and television productions. He became a household name in 1994 when he appeared in the television series *ER*, and in 2003 he won an Emmy for his role in the TV mini-series *Door to Door*. His films include *Fargo* (1996, Oscar nomination), *Magnolia* (1999), *State and Main* (2000), and *Seabiscuit* (2003).

Madagascar *p.941*

Madagascar jasmine *stephanotis*

Madara Rider An 8th-c bas-relief, carved out of the sheer cliff face in the village of Madara, E Bulgaria; a world heritage monument. The near life-size sculpture depicts a man on horseback trampling a lion beneath his horse's hooves.

Madariaga (y Rojo), Salvador de [ma<u>th</u>ariahga] (1886–1978) Writer, scholar, and diplomat, born in La Coruña, NW Spain. He studied at Madrid and Paris, and became a journalist in London (1916–21), a member of the League of Nations secretariat (1922–7), professor of Spanish studies at Oxford (1928–31), and Spanish ambassador to the USA (1931) and France (1932–4). During 1933 he was briefly minister of education in the Spanish Republican government. An opponent of the Franco regime, he was in exile 1936–76. He wrote many historical works, especially on Spain and Spanish-America, including *Latin America between the Eagle and the Bear* (1962, trans title).

mad cow disease *bovine spongiform encephalopathy*

madder An evergreen perennial (*Rubia tinctoria*), native to the Mediterranean; stems 4-angled, trailing or scrambling by means of small downwardly directed hooks; leaves narrow, stiff, in whorls of 4–6; flowers small, yellow, 5-petalled; berries reddish-brown. The roots produce the dye alizarin. (Family: Rubiaceae.)

Madeira (Islands) *see panel*

Madeira, River [madayra] River in NW Brazil, the longest tributary of the Amazon, and third longest river in South America; flows N along the Bolivia–Brazil border, then NE to join the Amazon 152 km/94 mi E of Manaus; length with its headstream, the Mamoré, is over 3200 km/2000 mi; navigable from Pôrto Velho.

Maderna, Bruno [madairna] (1920–73) Composer and conductor, born in Venice, NE Italy. A child prodigy violinist and conductor, he went on to study composition and conducting. Early in his musical career he composed for films and radio, and taught at the Venice Conservatory, then in 1955 he began to do research into the possibilities of electronic music, founding with Luciano Berio the Studio di Fonologia Musicale of Italian Radio. He became music director of Milan Radio, and wrote pieces for combinations of live and taped music, such as *Compositions in Three Tempi*, and a number of pieces for electronic music, such as *Dimensions II* (1960).

Madhya Pradesh [madya pradaysh] pop (2001e) 60 385 100; area 442 841 sq km/170 937 sq mi. State in C India, between the Deccan and the Ganges plains; largest state in India; crossed by numerous rivers; ruled by the Gonds, 16th–17th-c, and Marathas, 18th-c; occupied by the British, 1820; called Central Provinces and Berar, 1903–50; formed under the States Reorganization Act, 1956; capital, Bhopal; governed by a 90-member Upper House and an elected 320-member Lower House; major irrigation schemes; sugar cane, oilseed, cotton, forestry; steel, electrical engineering, aluminium, paper, textiles, machine tools, food processing, handicrafts; coal, iron ore, manganese, bauxite.

Madison 43°04N 89°24W, pop (2000e) 208 100. Capital of state in Dane County, S Wisconsin, USA; on L Mendota and L Monona; state capital, 1836; city status, 1856; birthplace of Karole Armitage; airfield; railway; university (1836); trading and manufacturing centre in agricultural region; farm machinery, meat-packing, medical equipment; World Dairy Exposition (Oct).

Madison, James (1751–1836) US statesman and fourth president (1809–17), born in Port Conway, Virginia, USA. He studied at the College of New Jersey (Princeton University), and entered politics in 1776. He played a major role in the Constitutional Convention of 1787, becoming known as 'the

Madeira (Islands)

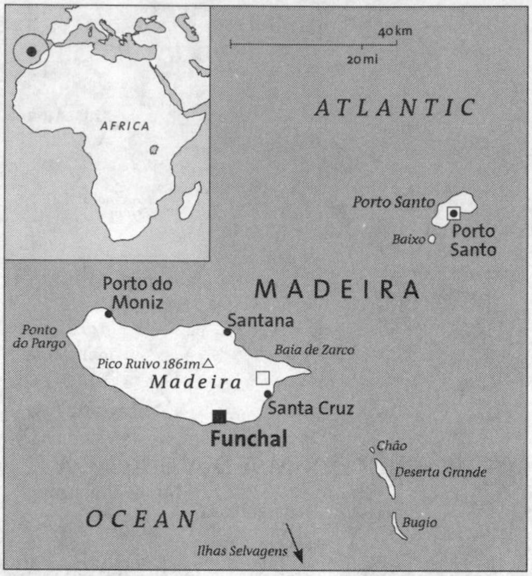

□ International Airport

[madeera], Port **Arquipélago da Madeira** (Portugal)

Local name Ilha de Madeira

Timezone GMT

Area 796km^2/307 sq mi

Population total (2000e) 259 000

Status Semi-autonomous region of Portugal

Capital Funchal (on Madeira Island)

Physical features Main island in an archipelago off the coast of N Africa, 980 km/610 mi SW of Lisbon; consists of Madeira, Porto Santo and three uninhabited islands; highest point, Pico Ruivo de Santana, 1862 m/6111 ft on Madeira.

Economy Agriculture; sugar cane, fruit, fishing, Madeira (a fortified wine); embroidery, crafts; tourism.

History Occupied by the Portuguese, 15th-c; occupied by Britain, 1801, and 1807–14; gained partial autonomy, 1980, but remains a Portuguese overseas territory; locally-elected government, and Assembly.

father of the Constitution', and he collaborated in the writing of *The Federalist Papers*. Elected to the first national Congress, he became a leader of the Jeffersonian Republican Party. He was secretary of state under Jefferson, and president for two terms from 1809. His period in office saw the Napoleonic Wars and the conflict with Britain (the War of 1812).

Madison Avenue A street in Manhattan, New York City, USA, extending N to the Harlem R from Madison Square. With its glittering skyscrapers and expensive boutiques, it is seen as the centre of the advertising industry.

Madonna, in full **Madonna Louise Ciccone** (1958–) Pop singer, born in Rochester, Michigan, USA. She trained as a dancer at Michigan University before moving to New York City, where she began her professional career as a backing singer to a number of New York groups. She hired Michael Jackson's manager prior to releasing *Madonna* (1983), an album which included five US hit singles. Subsequent albums have included *Like a Virgin* (1984), *True Blue* (1986), *Music* (2000), and *American Life* (2003). She has also acted in films, including *Desperately Seeking Susan* (1985) and *Shanghai Surprise* (1986). Her defiant and raunchy stage appearances became an important role model for teenagers in the 1980s and 1990s, and her international success has been secured by clever promotion and image-making. This was reinforced in several media in the early 1990s, with the publication of a controversial collection of erotic photographs of herself in *Sex* (1992), alongside an album, *Erotica*. Later films include *Body of Evidence* (1993), and *Evita* (1996). She made her London West End stage debut in 2002 in *Up for Grabs*. Her first children's book, *The English Roses*, was published in 2003.

Madras [madras], official name **Chennai** (Nov 1996) 13°08N 80°19E, pop (2000e) 6 296 000. Capital of Tamil Nadu, SE India; on R Coom, 1360 km/845 mi SW of Kolkata (Calcutta); fourth largest city in India, and chief port of Tamil Nadu; founded by the British, 17th-c; airport; railway; university (1857); textiles, chemicals, tanning, glass, engineering, jewellery, clothing, cars, bicycles; trade in leather, wool, cotton, tobacco, mica, magnesite; Fort St George (1639), Kapaleeswara temple, Pathasarathy temple (8th-c), San Thome Cathedral; St Mary's Church (1680), thought to be the oldest Anglican church in Asia; Mount St Thomas nearby, traditional site of martyrdom of the apostle.

Madrid [madrid] 40°25N 3°45W, pop (2000e) 2 948 000. Industrial capital and largest city of Spain; capital of Madrid province; in C Spain, on R Manzanares; altitude, 655 m/2149 ft, the highest capital city in Europe; archbishopric; airport; railway; metro; two universities (1508, 1968); textiles, engineering, chemicals, leather goods, agricultural trade; site of a Moorish fortress until 11th-c, under siege for nearly three years in the Civil War; capital (replacing Valladolid), 1561; El Escorial, a world heritage site; Royal Palace (18th-c), Prado Museum, Villahermosa Palace, Lazaro Galdiano Museum, El Retiro Park, archaeological museum, national library; Fiesta of Almudena (Nov), pilgrimage of St Isidore (May); 200 killed by terrorist bombings at railway stations (Mar 2004).

madrigal A polyphonic song, usually secular and without instrumental accompaniment. It was cultivated especially in Italy during the 16th-c by Palestrina, Lassus, Gabrieli, Marenzio (1553–99), and others, and is characterized by a judicious mixture of contrapuntal and chordal style and by serious, Petrarchan, and usually amorous verses. In the early 17th-c, Italian madrigals, notably those of Monteverdi, absorbed some Baroque features, including solo vocal writing, continuo accompaniment, and instrumental obbligatos, and were superseded by the new cantata.

Madura foot *mycetoma*

Madurai [maduriy] 9°55N 78°10E, pop (2000e) 1 117 000. City in Tamil Nadu, S India; on the R Voigai, 425 km/264 mi SW of Chennai (Madras); capital of the Pandyan kingdom and the Nayak dynasty; occupied by the British, 1801; airfield; railway; university (1966); silk and muslin weaving, woodcarving, brassware, trade in coffee, tea, cardamom; large Dravidian temple complex (14th–17th-c).

Madurese An Austronesian-speaking people of the island of Madura, Kangean Is, and nearby coastal areas of NE Java, Indonesia. They cultivate rice and raise export cattle on Madura, and are well-known in Java as migrant labourers, traders, fishermen, and sailors. Population c.5 million.

Maecenas, Gaius (Cilnius) [miyseenas] (?–8 BC) Roman politician of ancient Etruscan lineage, who together with Agrippa played a key role in the rise to power of Octavian/Augustus, and his establishment of the empire after 31 BC. Besides being a trusted counsellor and diplomatic agent, he also helped the new regime by his judicious patronage of the arts, encouraging such poets as Horace, Virgil, and Propertius.

maenads [meenads] In Greek mythology, 'mad women', who followed Dionysus (Bacchus) on his journeys; they were dressed in animal-skins, and so strong that they could uproot trees and kill wild animals, eating the flesh raw. They are also known as **Bacchae** or **Bacchantes**.

Maes, Nicholas [mays] (1634–93) Painter, born in Dordrecht, The Netherlands. He studied in Rembrandt's studio in Amsterdam (c.1648–50), returning to Dordrecht by 1654. He specialized in small genre subjects, especially kitchen scenes (eg 'Woman Scraping Parsnips' 1655, National Gallery, London) and old women praying. After a visit to Antwerp (c.1665), he turned to portraiture in a style derived from van Dyck.

Maes Howe [mayz how] A chambered tomb of the early 3rd millennium BC on Orkney, N Scotland, UK, outstanding for its construction and preservation. Beneath a mound 35 m/115 ft in diameter, a 7·3 m/24 ft long drystone-walled entrance passage gives onto a cross-shaped burial chamber with a corbelled vault 3·8 m/12 ft high. Above the door slab is a slot allowing the setting Sun to penetrate the burial chamber at the midwinter solstice. Inside are 24 runic inscriptions scratched by Viking raiders in the mid-12th-c AD.

maestà [miysta] (Ital 'majesty') In art, the Virgin represented as Queen of Heaven, flanked by angels and saints. The most splendid examples were painted in Italy in the 13th–14th-c by Cimabué, Duccio, and Martini.

Maeterlinck, Maurice (Polydore Marie Bernard) [mahterlingk], also known as **comte** (Count) **Maeterlinck** (1862–1949) Playwright, born in Ghent, NW Belgium. He studied law at Ghent University, became a disciple of the Symbolist movement, and in 1889 produced his first volume of poetry, *Les Serres chaudes* (Hot House Blooms). His masterpiece was the prose-play *Pelléas et Mélisande* (1892), on which Debussy based his opera. He wrote many other plays, which have been widely translated, and was awarded the Nobel Prize for Literature in 1911.

Mafeking, Siege of (1899–1900) The most celebrated siege of the second Boer War. Colonel Robert Baden-Powell and a detachment of British troops were besieged by the Boers from October 1899 until May 1900. The news of their relief aroused public hysteria in Britain, the celebrations being known as 'mafficking'. The truth about the siege may have been rather different from the heroic action depicted by the British press. It has been alleged that the white garrison survived in reasonable comfort as the result of appropriating the rations of the blacks, who were faced either with starvation or with running the gauntlet of Boers by escaping from the town.

Mafia (Ital 'swank') A powerful and well-defended criminal organization, originating as a secret society in 13th-c Italy. It developed (along with its modern name) in the 19th-c, and from Italy moved to the USA, where it became known as *Cosa Nostra* ('Our Affair'). There have been many attempts to suppress the Mafia, but its system of family loyalty and code of silence makes progress difficult. A widespread protest against the Mafia spread in Italy during 1993, following the murder of several senior people involved in anti-Mafia law enforcement, and a number of public figures were accused of corruption and forced to resign.

Magallanes y Antártica Chilena [magalyanays ee antarteeka cheelayna] Region of S Chile extending S from 48°40'S; area 132 034 sq km/50 979 sq mi; comprises the provinces of Ultima Esperanza, Magallanes, Tierra del Fuego and Antártica Chilena; Chile lays claim to the slice of Antarctica between 53°W and 90°W; capital, Punta Arenas; sheep, cattle, forestry, oil, natural gas, food canning; several national parks; Cueva de Miladón, where remains of the sloth *Mylodon listai* found in 1895, c.8000 years old.

Magdalena, River [magdalayna] (Span **Río**) Major river of Colombia, rising in the Cordillera Central; flows N 1600 km/1000 mi to enter the Caribbean 14 km/9 mi NW of Barranquilla in a wide delta; navigable for most of its course; fertile valley in upper and mid course, producing coffee, sugar cane, tobacco, cacao, cotton.

Magdalenian [magdaleenian] The last Upper Palaeolithic archaeological culture of W Europe, named after the cave of La Madeleine, Dordogne, SW France, excavated in 1863. Many sites dated c.17 000–12 000 BC are known from Spain, France, Belgium, Britain, Germany, Switzerland, and the Czech Republic. Most notable are the painted caves of Lascaux and Altamira.

Magdeburg [mahkdeboorg] 52°08N 11°36E, pop (2000e) 289 000. River-port capital of Magdeburg county, C Germany; on R Elbe SW of Berlin; former capital of Saxony, and important mediaeval trading town at centre of N German plain; access to the Ruhr and Rhine Rivers via the Mittelland Canal; badly bombed in World War 2; railway; college of medicine; college of technology (1953); iron and steel, engineering, chemicals, sugar refining, textiles; 13th–16th-c cathedral.

Magellan, Ferdinand [majelan] (c.1480–1521) Navigator, born in Sabrosa or Porto, Portugal. After serving in the East Indies and Morocco, he offered his services to Spain. He sailed from Seville (1519) around the foot of South America (Cape of the Virgins) to reach the ocean which he named the Pacific (1520). He was killed in the Philippines, but his ships continued back to Spain (1522), thus completing the first circumnavigation of the world. The *Strait of Magellan* is named after him.

Magellanic Clouds Two dwarf galaxies, satellites of the Milky Way, visible as cloudy patches in the S night sky, first recorded by Magellan in 1519, 52 and 58 kiloparsec away, and each containing a few thousand million stars. They are of immense astrophysical importance, because the individual stars within them can be studied and are essentially all at the same distance from us. This removes a great source of uncertainty compared to the situation within our own Galaxy, where actual distances to individual stars are hard to determine.

Magellan project A US space mission that between late 1990 and 1992 successfully mapped Venus in its entirety, using an orbiter with side-looking radar to provide sub-kilometre resolution images. Radar is used because of the global cloud cover, the created images being interpreted much as are television images. The technique of Venus radar mapping was first used by the Pioneer Venus Orbiter in 1978 and by Soviet Venera 15 and 16 spacecraft in 1983. The single Magellan spacecraft was managed by NASA's Jet Propulsion Laboratory and was launched using the space shuttle in 1989. Following the completion of its mapping mission, it was used to demonstrate the technique of aerobraking in the upper Venusian atmosphere; after many orbits the spacecraft entered the atmosphere and burned up.

Magen David *Star of David*

Magendie, François [mazhãdee] (1783–1855) Physiologist and physician, born in Bordeaux, SW France. As professor of anatomy in the Collège de France (1831), he studied nerve physiology and the veins, and was the first to experiment on hypersensitivity to foreign substances (anaphylaxis). His research demonstrated the functional differences in the spinal nerves, and the effects of drugs on the body.

Maggiore, Lake (Ital **Lago**) [majawray], ancient **Verbanus Lacus** area 212 sq km/82 sq mi. Second largest of the N Italian lakes; N end in the Swiss canton of Ticino; length 65 km/40 mi; width 3–5 km/1¾–3 mi; maximum depth 372 m/1220 ft; major tourist area; lake resorts include Ispra, Stresa, Arona, and (Swiss) Locarno; Borromean Is on W arm of the lake.

maggot The grub-like larval stage of many true flies. (Order: Diptera.)

Maghreb [magreb], Eng **Maghrib** area c.9 million sq km/3·5 million sq mi. Area of NW Africa including the countries of Morocco, Algeria, and Tunisia; largely occupied by the Kabyle, Shluh, and Tuareg. In Arabic, it refers to Morocco only.

Magi [mayjiy] **1** A Greek term used in antiquity with a variety of connotations: magi were members of the priestly clan of the Persians, but classical Greek and Roman writers used the term in a derogatory sense and with no necessary connection with Persia to refer to sorcerers and even 'quacks'.

2 A group of unspecified number guided by a mysterious star (*Matt* 2.1–12), who came from 'the East' and presented gifts to the infant Jesus in Bethlehem, after inquiring of his whereabouts from Herod. Origen (3rd-c AD) suggested they were three because of the three gifts of gold, frankincense, and myrrh. Tertullian (AD c.160–220) deduced that they were kings. Later Christian tradition named them as Caspar, Melchior, and Balthazar.

magic Beliefs and practices which promise a power to intervene in natural processes, but which have no scientific basis. Two common principles of magical belief are said to be 'like affects like' (eg that a cloud of smoke rising to the sky will bring rain) and 'part affects whole' (eg burning a person's hair-cuttings will cause that person to be damaged). In modern industrial societies, belief in magic remains strong, since it offers some hope that malign chance can be combated. Everywhere, magical beliefs are strongest in situations of uncertainty – as Hume remarked, when he commented on the notorious superstitiousness of sailors.

Magic Circle An organization of amateur and professional magicians, formed in London in 1905, and now with c.1500 members throughout the world. There are categories of associate membership, for those with an interest in magic, and various degrees of full membership (achieved through examination), restricted to those who have a knowledge of, and practical ability in magic, as well as a commitment to secrecy (the circle's motto is *indocilis privata loqui*, 'not apt to disclose secrets').

magic mushroom A mushroom, chiefly the British liberty-cap *Psilocybe semilanceata*, which contains the hallucinogen *psilocybin*. Its use is cultish among young people, who take it as an infusion, adding it to boiling water, in which the active ingredients dissolve.

magic numbers *nuclear structure*

magic realism or **magical realism** A type of post-modernist fiction that mixes elements of fantasy, fable, and folklore with realistic narrative, imbuing it with a fabulous or dreamlike quality. It mixes the depiction of everyday events with fantastic elements to create an apparent discordance which undermines the text and eventually the authority of the novel form itself. The term was first applied in the 1940s by the Cuban novelist Alejo Carpentier and introduced into the critical vocabulary by Alistair Reid. It is particularly associated with Latin-American writers such as Carlos Fuentes, Mario Vargas Llosa, Miguel Angel Asturias, Julio Cortázar, and Gabriel Garcia Márquez. European writers most influenced by magic realism include Italo Calvino and Milan Kundera; writers in English include Salman Rushdie, Graham Swift, Julian Barnes, and Angela Carter. The term is also applied to the work of a group of German painters in the 1920s known as the *Neue Sachlichkeit* (New Objectivity) movement, distinguished by their realistic, often cynical style of painting (in contrast to the prevailing style of Expressionism and Abstraction).

Maginot Line [mazhinoh] French defensive fortifications stretching from Longwy in Belgium to the Swiss border, named after André Maginot (1877–1932), French minister of defence (1924–31) who directed its construction. The line was constructed (1929–34) to act as protection against German invasion, but Belgium refused to extend it along her frontier with Germany. The chief effect it had was to create a false sense of security; the German attack of 1940 through the Low Countries largely bypassed the Maginot Line, whose name became synonymous with passive defence and defeatism.

magistrate *justice of the peace; stipendiary magistrate*

Maglemosian [maglemohzian] A N European Mesolithic culture extending from Britain to S Scandinavia and NW Russia c.8000–5600 BC; its name derives from the Danish *Magle Mose* ('Great Bog') on Zeeland, where notable early finds were made. Fishing, fowling, and the hunting of elk and wild cattle constituted its subsistence base – activities archaeologically attested by finds of bows and arrows, barbed spear and harpoon heads, fish hooks, nets, traps, and boats.

magma Molten rock, formed by the partial melting of the Earth's mantle. Under certain geological conditions it may migrate upwards and solidify within the crust to form an igneous intrusion, or may reach the surface, where it loses its volatile constituents and is erupted as lava.

Magna Carta The 'Great Charter', imposed by rebellious barons on King John of England in June 1215 at Runnymede, designed to prohibit arbitrary royal acts by declaring a body of defined law and custom which the king must respect in dealing with all his free subjects. Of its 63 clauses, many of which concerned John's misuse of his financial and judicial powers, the most famous are clause 39 – 'No freeman shall be taken or imprisoned except by the lawful judgment of his equals or by the law of the land' – and clause 40 – 'To no one will we sell, to no one will we deny or delay right or justice'. The principle that kings should rule justly was of long standing, but in Magna Carta the first systematic attempt was made to distinguish between kingship and tyranny. While failing to resolve all the problems raised by the nature of the English crown's relations with the community, it endured as a symbol of the sovereignty of the rule of law, and was of fundamental importance to the constitutional development of England and other countries whose legal and governmental systems were modelled on English conventions.

Magna Graecia [**griy**sha] Literally (Lat), 'Great Greece'; the collective name in antiquity for the Greek cities of S Italy. Most (eg Cumae, Sybaris) were founded by settlers from mainland Greece and the Aegean area, but some were offshoots of the Greek colonies in Italy themselves (eg Naples was founded by Cumae, and Paestum by Sybaris).

Magnani, Anna [manyahnee] (1908–73) Actress, born in Alexandria, N Egypt. Raised in poverty, she first made her living as a nightclub singer, but married the director Goffredo Alessandrini (annulled 1950) and worked in films from 1934, achieving recognition in Rossellini's *Roma città aperta* (1945, Rome, Open City). She received an Oscar for her first Hollywood film *The Rose Tattoo* (1955), but much of her later work was for the Italian stage and television, although she appeared in Fellini's *Roma* (1972). She died unexpectedly following a minor operation.

magnesia Magnesium oxide (MgO), also called **periclase**; a white solid, melting point 2850°C, obtained from heating magnesium carbonate, used as a heat-resisting material. **Milk of magnesia** is a suspension of hydrated magnesia used as a laxative.

magnesite A magnesium carbonate ($MgCO_3$) mineral formed by the alteration of magnesium-rich rock by fluids. It forms pale, massive ore deposits which are an important source of magnesium.

magnesium Mg, element 12, melting point 649°C. A silvery metal, always found combined in nature, but mainly as the carbonate in magnesite ($MgCO_3$) and dolomite ($CaMg(CO_3)_2$). In practice, magnesium is obtained by electrolysis of $MgCl_2$ from brines. It is used in alloys for its lightness (density 1·7 g/cm^3), and for flares and flash bulbs because of the bright white light produced by its very exothermic reaction with oxygen. In its compounds, it almost always shows oxidation state +2; salts of Mg^{2+} are, after those of Ca^{2+}, the main cause of hard water. Hydrated magnesium sulphate is known as *Epsom salts*.

magnet A source of magnetic field; always with two poles, named N (north) and S (south), since no isolated single pole exists; like poles repel; opposite poles attract. A permanent magnet is usually made from a ferromagnetic material which at some time has been exposed to a magnetic field. An **electromagnet** is some suitable core material around which is wrapped a current-carrying coil.

magnetic cooling A technique used to cool a sample to temperatures as low as 10^{-3}K (approximately −273°C). If a paramagnetic sample is cooled by conventional means while subjected to a magnetic field, and is then thermally insulated and the field removed, the individual magnetic moments in the material are free to become disordered, but in doing so they take up heat from the sample, causing it to cool. This is an adiabatic process, as no heat flows into or out of the sample.

magnetic declination The direction of the Earth's magnetic field in terms of the angle, measured in the horizontal plane, which the field makes with the meridian, ie the deviation of the field from true N; also termed the magnetic *variation*.

magnetic dip The direction of the Earth's magnetic field in terms of the angle at which the field is inclined to the horizontal; also termed the magnetic *inclination*.

magnetic dipole moment *magnetic moment*

magnetic disk A disk coated with magnetizable material on one or both sides. Magnetic disks are an important type of computer storage medium. Data is written to or read from a set of concentric tracks on the disk by magnetic read/write heads. Two general classes exist: the so-called *hard* disks made of rigid material, which store large quantities of data, and *floppy* disks, formerly made of flexible plastic, which store much smaller amounts. Disks may be removable from the disk drive (eg floppy disks) or non-removable (eg Winchester disks). In comparison with magnetic tapes, data can be very rapidly retrieved from magnetic disk media.

magnetic domain In a ferromagnetic material, a region in which individual atomic magnetic moments are all aligned parallel, even in the absence of an external field. In unmagnetized material, the direction of magnetic orientation of different domains is unrelated; in magnetized material, they are parallel.

magnetic field A region of magnetic influence around a magnet, moving charge, or current-carrying wire; denoted by B, the magnetic flux density, units T (tesla), and by H, the magnetic field strength, units A/m (amps per metre). There are many technological applications, including generators and motors.

magnetic flux The flow of magnetic influence from the N to S poles of a magnet, or around a current-carrying wire; symbol Φ, units Wb (weber). It is the product of magnetic flux density B (sometimes called 'magnetic field') and area. B is related to magnetic field intensity H via permeability μ: $B = \mu H$.

magnetic hysteresis In ferromagnetic materials such as iron, the dependence of the magnetic field in the material on the magnetizing field and prior magnetization. It is an important source of energy loss in transformers and motors.

magnetic ink character recognition *character recognition*

magnetic moment A property of magnets, currents circulating in loops, and spinning charged particles that dictates the strength of the turning force exerted on the system by a magnetic field, B; symbol μ, units A.m^2 (amp.metre-squared) or J/T (joules per tesla); a vector quantity; also called the **magnetic dipole moment**. Turning force (torque), Γ, is $\Gamma = \mu B \sin\theta$, where θ is the angle between μ and B directions.

Spinning charged particles such as electrons and protons behave like minute current-carrying coils, and so have magnetic moments. Neutrons, despite having zero net charge, also have a magnetic moment, since they spin and are composed of charged particles; their magnetic moment is exploited in neutron diffraction experiments. Atomic nuclei have magnetic moments which are exploited in nuclear magnetic resonance. For certain atoms, the magnetic moment contributions from various electrons, either from their spins or motion about the atomic nucleus, do not cancel. Such atoms have large net atomic magnetic moments, which form the basis of magnetic properties of bulk materials such as paramagnetism and ferromagnetism.

For a magnet in a magnetic field, a force acts that tries to align its poles in the direction of the field (which is how a compass works). Spinning particles precess in a magnetic field, ie the direction of their spins (hence magnetic moments) rotates about the field direction. The magnetic moment of the electron ($9{\cdot}285 \times 10^{-24}$ J/T) is due solely to the fact that the electron is a spinning charge. For comparison, this is equivalent to a current loop the size of an atomic nucleus carrying a current of 300 000 A. The magnetic moment of a single loop of radius 1 cm carrying a current of 1 A is 3×10^{-4} J/T.

magnetic monopole A lone magnetic pole – non-existent, according to classical electromagnetism. Paul Dirac proposed that monopoles could be present in quantum theories (1931), and they have been predicted in modern gauge theory (1974). Unified theories of fundamental forces predict monopoles of mass 10^{16} greater than proton mass. No monopoles have ever been detected.

magnetic permeability *permeability*

magnetic poles The two points on the Earth's surface to which a compass needle points. The N and S magnetic poles have geographical co-ordinates 78·5°N 69°W and 78·5°S 111°E, and move very slowly with time.

magnetic resonance A resonance effect in which atoms or nuclei precessing in a magnetic field absorb energy from incident radio waves; also called **spin resonance**. The magnetic moments of atoms and nuclei precess about the direction of an applied magnetic field. When such a system is subjected to radio waves of certain frequencies related to the precession frequency, a resonance condition is satisfied, and energy is absorbed from the radio beam. The effect provides the basis for important analytical techniques in chemistry.

magnetic resonance imaging (MRI) *nuclear magnetic resonance*

magnetic storm A disturbance in the Earth's magnetic field causing global disruption of radio signals and the occurrence of auroras. There is a tendency for such events to be periodic. They are caused by the interaction of charged solar particles with the Earth's magnetic field.

magnetic susceptibility The ratio of magnetization M to magnetic field strength H; symbol K, expressed as a pure number. It expresses the dependence of a magnetic field in a material on an external field which results only from current in the magnetizing coils. It is related to permeability, and constant except for ferromagnetic materials.

magnetic tape 1 A clear plastic film coated with crystalline magnetic particles embedded in varnish, first demonstrated as an effective sound recording and reproducing medium in the 1930s. It came increasingly into use after World War 2, and has more recently been extended to video recording, and data storage for computers. Professional recording practice of the 1980s employed multiple-track open-reel tape, storing the sounds in digital form, while domestic use came to be dominated by the compact cassette introduced first by Philips in 1964. To the convenience of the latter has been added increasing quality with new coatings (chrome dioxide, metal) and noise reduction systems.

2 A storage medium used on larger computers, the most common being 2400 ft (c.750 m) reels of 0·5 in (12·7 mm)-wide tape. In recent years, smaller format magnetic cartridge tape systems have been used as archiving ('back-up') systems for microcomputers, especially those employing Winchester disks. Another variation has been the use of standard audio tapes for digital data storage in low-cost microcomputer systems; but the decreasing cost of floppy disk systems is gradually ousting the rather unreliable audio-tape system. All magnetic-tape systems are relatively slow, compared to magnetic disks, since the access time required to obtain a particular piece of information depends on its position on the tape.

magnetic vector potential A vector quantity whose rate of change with distance is related to magnetic field in a complex way; symbol A, units Wb/m (webers per metre). Electric current is the source for magnetic vector potential, as electric charge is for electrostatic potential. Magnetic vector potential supports a special transformation (a *gauge transformation*) which leaves the related magnetic field equations unchanged.

magnetism Phenomena associated with magnetic fields and magnetic materials, and the study of such phenomena. All magnetic effects ultimately stem from moving electric charges, and all materials have magnetic properties. Electric coils, currents in wires, and permanent magnets are all sources of magnetic field.

magnetite or **lodestone** An iron oxide mineral (Fe_3O_4) with a very strong natural magnetism. It is a valuable ore of iron.

magnetization Magnetic moment per unit volume, resulting from the individual magnetic moments contributed by atoms or molecules of the material; symbol M, units A/m (amps per metre); expresses how much a material is magnetized. For diamagnetic materials, magnetization opposes the external field; for paramagnetic materials, it reinforces it. In these cases, the magnetization is proportional to the external field. For ferromagnets this proportionality fails, and M can be large, even with no external field.

magneto A simple machine which generates alternating current, using the principle that a current is generated when a conductor moves through a magnetic field. One type comprises a coil of thin wire spinning between the poles of a powerful horseshoe magnet. It is used with combustion engines to provide the power for the sparking plugs.

magneto-fluid-mechanics *magnetohydrodynamics*

magnetohydrodynamics The mechanics of electrically conducting fluids, such as liquid metals and plasmas, when subject to electric and magnetic fields; also called **magneto-fluid-mechanics**. The study is relevant to plasma nuclear fusion, liquid metal cooling systems, and electrical power generation from hot plasmas. Magnetohydrodynamic propulsion systems for ships and submarines pass an electric current through sea water in the presence of a powerful magnetic field to produce a jet of water which provides thrust.

magnetometer A device for measuring the strength and direction of magnetic fields. Gauss built an early magnetometer in 1832, comprising a freely rotating magnet suspended from a torsion wire in which the period of oscillation of the magnet measured the field strength. Modern magnetometers include the *fluxgate* magnetometer, in which paired electromagnets driven by an external alternating voltage generate an electrical signal in a coil surrounding the pair in response to the field under test, and *cryogenic* or *SQUID* magnetometers. Magnetometers are used in many systems where magnetic fields are present, and also in geophysics.

magneto optical effects *Faraday effect; Zeeman effect*

magnetosphere The region surrounding Solar System bodies having magnetic fields, in which the field is confined under the influence of the streaming solar wind. It is a teardrop-shaped region whose size and shape are constantly readjusting to the variations of the solar wind. Charged particles from both solar wind and Earth's atmosphere are stored in the terrestrial magnetosphere, which has been extensively explored since Van Allen radiation belts were discovered by Explorer 1 in 1958. Stored particles are periodically ejected into N and S regions of the atmosphere along the magnetic field and accelerated to high speeds by mechanisms which are poorly understood. Collisions with atmospheric atoms cause emissions of light seen as aurora. Other planets known to have magnetospheres include Jupiter, Saturn, Uranus, Neptune, and Mercury.

magnetostriction The change in length of ferromagnetic materials when subject to a magnetic field. For example, nickel will contract along the field direction, and expand in the transverse direction. The effect results from the alignment of magnetic domains under the influence of the external field. It is exploited in ultrasonic transducers.

magnetron A device for generating microwaves. It comprises an evacuated chamber with a central cathode surrounded by a circular anode. Electrons expelled from the cathode circle it under the influence of electric and magnetic fields. Microwave production results from resonances between the moving electrons and cavities in the anode. Developed during the 1940s for radar, it is today widely used in microwave ovens.

magnification A measure of an optical system's power to reduce or enlarge an image. For a simple lens, magnification equals the ratio of the angle subtended at the eye with the lens to the angle subtended at the eye without the lens. It is approximately equal to the ratio of size of image to size of object.

Magnitogorsk [magnyitogaw(r)sk], formerly **Magnitnaya** 53°28N 59°06E, pop (2000e) 442 000. Industrial town in Chelyabinskaya oblast, SW Siberian Russia, on the R Ural; built, 1929–31; airfield; railway; iron and magnetite deposits; one of the largest centres of the Russian metallurgical industry; clothing, footwear; Palace of Metallurgists (1936).

magnitude A measure of the brightness of a celestial object, first used (120 BC) by Hipparchus, who referred to the brightest stars visible to the eye as 'first magnitude' and the dimmest as 'sixth magnitude'. The system was given a scientific basis in 1856: equal magnitude steps are in logarithmic progression, such that a magnitude difference of one unit corresponds to a brightness ratio of 2·512, and five magnitudes correspond to a ratio of 100 in actual brightnesses. The zero of the magnitude scale is essentially arbitrary. The **apparent magnitude** of a star is its brightness measured at the Earth, which depends on distance and luminosity. More useful physically is **absolute magnitude**; this is the observed apparent magnitude converted to what the object would have at an (arbitrary) distance of 10 parsec. Properties of stars and galaxies can be properly compared only via absolute magnitudes.

magnolia A deciduous or evergreen shrub or tree native to E North America and E Asia; leaves often glossy; flowers generally large, cup-shaped, with several whorls of white or pink perianth segments; fruit an almost cone-like strobilus of many carpels. Many species are popular ornamentals. Various characteristics, including the construction of its flower and fruit, make them often regarded as the most primitive flowering plants. (Genus: *Magnolia*, 80 species. Family: Magnoliaceae.)

magnon In magnetic materials, oscillations in the relative orientations of atomic spins, which correspond to magnetization waves. Magnons are quantum spin waves, appearing as particles capable of scattering with neutrons. Experimentally observable, they are important in understanding the thermodynamic and magnetic properties of magnetic materials.

Magnusson, Magnus (1929–) Writer and broadcaster, born in Edinburgh, EC Scotland, UK of Icelandic parents. He studied at Oxford, and became a journalist, then a broadcaster. He is chiefly known for presenting a wide range of radio and television programmes, such as *Chronicle*, *Tonight* and, most famously, the annual series of *Mastermind* (1972–97). His books include *Introducing Archaeology* (1972), *Vikings!* (1980), and *Treasures of Scotland* (1981), and he has translated many books from Icelandic (with Hermann Pálsson). He was the editor of the 5th edition of the *Chambers Biographical Dictionary* (1990). He was Rector of Edinburgh University (1975–8), and has been much involved with heritage and conservation organizations.

Magog *Gog and Magog*

magot [magoh] *Barbary ape*

magpie A bird of the crow family (13 species); especially the **black-billed magpie** (*Pica pica*). The name is also used for black-and-white birds in the families Cracticidae (the **bell/black-backed/white-backed magpie**), Anatidae (the **magpie goose**), Estrildidae (the **magpie mannikin**), Grallinidae (the **magpie lark**), Sturnidae (the **magpie starling**), Thraupidae (the **magpie tanager**), and Turdidae (the **magpie robin**).

Magritte, René (François Ghislain) [magreet] (1898–1967) Surrealist painter, born in Lessines, SC Belgium. He studied at the Académie Royale des Beaux-Arts (1916–18) in Brussels, and became a wallpaper designer and commercial artist. He was a leading member of the newly formed Belgian Surrealist group (1924), and produced works of dreamlike incongruity, such as 'Rape', in which he substitutes a torso for a face. His major paintings include 'The Wind and the Song' (1928–9) and 'The Human Condition' (1934, 1935). He was acclaimed in the US as an early innovator of the Pop Art of the 1960s.

Magyar A Uralic language spoken as a national language by c.11 million people in Hungary, and by a further 3 million in the surrounding areas.

Mahabalipuram monuments [mahahbalipuram] A collection of Hindu monolithic temples and cave temples at Mahabalipuram in Tamil Nadu, S India; a world heritage site. The temples date from the 7th–8th-c, and are noted for their rich carvings, particularly the rock sculpture known as 'The Descent of the Ganges' or 'Arjuna's Penance'.

Mahabharata [mahabhahrata] A major epic of Hindu culture and history, and a holy book. Dating from the first millennium BC, its 110 000 couplets make it the longest epic in the world. It was orally transmitted and later became literature printed in Sanskrit and other languages. Various editions were brought together and published in the 19th-c as the Mahabharata. The central plot concerns the conflict between two related families, the Kurus (spirits of evil) and Pandus (spirits of good). Woven around this story are myths, legends, folk tales, and philosophical pieces, including the *Bhagavadgita*.

Mahamuni Pagoda or **Arakan Pagoda** A temple built near Mandalay, Myanmar, by King Bodawpaya in 1784 to house the famous 'Mahamuni', a 4 m/13 ft high image of Buddha probably cast in Arakan in the 2nd-c. The statue has been covered with gold leaf to a depth of several centimetres by Buddhist pilgrims.

Maharashtra [mahahrashtra] pop (2001e) 96 752 000; area 307 762 sq km/118 796 sq mi. Large state in W India, bounded W by the Arabian Sea; crossed by several mountain ranges and rivers; ruled by the Mughals, 14th–17th-c; heart of the Maratha Empire under Shivaji (17th-c); British control, early 19th-c; became a state in 1960; capital, Mumbai (Bombay); governed by a 78-member Legislative Council and an elected 287-member Legislative Assembly; rice, sugar cane, groundnuts, cotton; textiles, electrical equipment, machinery, chemicals, oil products; industry largely in Mumbai, Pune (Poona), and Thana; coal, chromite, iron ore, bauxite.

Maharishi [maharishee] (Sanskrit, 'great sage') The Hindu title for a guru or spiritual leader. In the West, the teaching of Transcendental Meditation by the Maharishi Mahesh Yogi is well known.

Mahayana [mahayahna] (Sanskrit, 'greater vehicle') The form of Buddhism commonly practised in China, Tibet, Mongolia, Nepal, Korea, and Japan. It dates from about the 1st-c, when it arose as a development within Buddhism in N India. It emphasizes various forms of popular devotion based on its theory of the bodhisattvas.

Mahdi (divine leader) [mahdee] (Arabic, 'divinely guided one') The name given by Sunni Muslims to those who periodically revitalize the Muslim community. Sunnis look forward to a time before the Last Day when a Mahdi will appear and establish a reign of justice on Earth. Shiites identify the Mahdi with the expected reappearance of the hidden Imam. Many Muslim leaders have claimed the title, such as Mohammed Ahmed, who established a theocratic state in the Sudan in 1882. His great-grandson, Sadiq al-Mahdi, became prime minister of the Sudan in 1986.

Mahé [mah-hay] 4°41S 55°30E; pop (2000e) 72 000; area 153 sq km/59 sq mi. Main island of the Seychelles, Indian Ocean; c.1600 km/1000 mi E of Mombasa (Kenya); Victoria, capital of the Seychelles, on the NW coast; airport; tourism; Morne Seychelles National Park.

mah-jong or **mah-jongg** A Chinese game, originally played with cards, introduced to the West under its present name after World War 1. It is usually played by four people using 144 small tiles divided into three suits (circles, bamboos, characters) and four sets of honour tiles (winds, dragons, seasons, flowers). (Sets containing 136 tiles are also used.) The aim is to collect sequences of tiles, in the manner of rummy card games. In 1937 the National Mah-Jong League was founded in the USA. The name means 'sparrow', a bird of mythical great intelligence, which appears on one of the tiles.

Mahler, Gustav (1860–1911) Composer, born in Kaliště, C Czech Republic (formerly Bohemia, Austrian Empire). He studied at the Vienna Conservatory, and worked as a conductor, becoming artistic director of the Vienna Court Opera in 1897. He resigned after 12 years to devote himself to composition and the concert platform. His mature works consist entirely of songs and nine large-scale symphonies, with a 10th left unfinished. He is best known for the song-symphony *Das Lied von der Erde* (1908–9, The Song of the Earth).

mahlstick A stick, with a pad at one end, on which a painter steadies the hand while executing delicate passages in a picture. Mahlsticks can occasionally be seen in artists' self-portraits.

mahogany An evergreen tree (*Swietenia mahogani*) native to Central America and the Caribbean Is; leaves pinnate; flowers 5-petalled, yellowish, in loose clusters. It is one of several timbers commercially called mahogany, a reddish wood of high quality, heavy, hard, and easily worked. (Family: Meliaceae.)

Mahomet *Mohammed*

Mahon, Derek [mahn] (1941–) Poet, born in Belfast, NE Northern Ireland, UK. He was educated at Belfast Institute and Trinity College, Dublin, and was a teacher before turning to journalism and other writing. Drawn to squalid landscapes and desperate situations, his acknowledged influences are Louis MacNeice and W H Auden. *Twelve Poems* was published in 1965, since when there have been a number of others, including *The Hunt by Night* (1982), *A Kensington Notebook* (1984) *The Yellow Book* (1997), and *Collected Poems* (1999).

mahonia *Oregon grape*

Mahratta *Maratha*

Mahy, Margaret [mayhee] (1936–) Children's author, born in Whangarei, New Zealand. A librarian with a taste for writing, she published her first story in 1961, and by 1993 had published 110 books. Since 1986, with *The Trickster*, the settings of her stories have increasingly had a more distinctively New Zealand flavour. She has twice won the Carnegie Award for children's literature.

Maiden Castle A spectacular Iron Age hillfort near Dorchester, Dorset, S England, UK, its multiple earthwork ramparts and ditches enclosing 18 ha/44 acres, and having an internal perimeter of 2·5 km/1·6 mi. Constructed after 350 BC on the site of an earlier Neolithic camp, the existing defences date to c.150 BC, their complex entrances remodelled c.70 BC. Capital of the native tribe of the Durotriges, it is thought to have been captured by Vespasian's Second Legion following the Roman invasion of Britain in AD 43, and abandoned.

maidenhair fern A graceful and delicate perennial fern, found almost everywhere, but especially in the tropics; fronds with slender, black, wiry stalks; leaflets stalked, irregularly fan-shaped, the margins turned under and bearing sori. (Genus: *Adiantum*, 200 species. Family: Polypodiaceae.)

maidenhair tree *ginkgo*

Maidstone 51°17N 0°32E, pop (2001e) 139 000. County town in Kent, SE England, UK; on the R Medway, S of Chatham; birthplace of William Hazlitt; railway; paper, fruit canning, brewing, cement, confectionery; 14th-c All Saints Church, 14th-c Archbishop's palace, Chillington Manor, Tyrwhitt Drake museum of carriages.

Maier, Ulrike [miyer] (1965–94) Skier, born in Austria. She won the world Supergiant slalom skiing championship twice before her fatal accident during a practice run at Garmisch-Partenkirchen. She was the first woman skier to be killed in a World Cup race.

Maier, Hermann [miyer] (1972–) Skier, born in Flachau, Salzburg, Austria. His parents ran a skiing school, and he took part in his first skiing races at the age of five. His achievements include the European Cup (1996) and World Cup (1998, 2000, 2001, 2004), and in March 2001 he equalled the World Cup season record of 13 wins.

Mailer, Norman (Kingsley) [mayler], originally **Nachum Malech Mailer** (1923–) Novelist and journalist, born in Long Branch, New Jersey, USA. He studied at Harvard, and served in the Pacific in World War 2. His first novel, *The Naked and the Dead* (1948), became a best seller, and established him as a leading novelist of his generation. His miscellany of pieces, *Advertisements for Myself* (1959), also attracted considerable interest. As a protester he was prominent throughout the 1960s, publishing *Armies of the Night* (1968, Pulitzer), whose subject is the 1967 protest march on the Pentagon. Later books include *Ancient Evenings* (1983), *Tough Guys Don't Dance* (1984), *Harlot's Ghost* (1991), *Oswald's Tale* (1995), *The Gospel According to the Son* (1997), *Barbary Shore* (1998), and *The Time of Our Time* (1999).

Maillol, Aristide (Joseph Bonaventure) [mayol] (1861–1944) Sculptor, born in Banyuls-sur-Mer, C France. He studied at the Ecole des Beaux-Arts, and spent some years designing tapestries. The latter half of his life was devoted to the representation of the nude female figure in a style of monumental simplicity and classical serenity, such as 'Mediterranean' (c.1901, Museum of Modern Art, New York City) and 'Night' (1902, Dina Vierny Collection, Paris).

mailmerge A word-processing facility which allows inserts to be placed in a standard document. It is widely used for the bulk mailing of circulars in letter form, as it gives these the semblance of having been individually produced.

Maiman, Theodore H(arold) [miyman] (1927–) Physicist, born in Los Angeles, California, USA. He studied physics at Colorado and Stanford universities, and joined Hughes Research Laboratories, Miami, in 1955. He was much interested in the maser, devised in 1953 to produce coherent microwave radiation. He improved its design, and by 1960 devised the first working laser, which gave coherent visible light. From the 1960s he founded companies to develop laser devices, and in 1977 joined TRW Electronics of California.

Maimonides, Moses [miymonideez], originally **Moses ben Maimon** (1138–1204) Philosopher, born in Córdoba, S Spain. He studied Aristotelian philosophy and Greek medicine from Arab teachers, and migrated to Egypt, where he became physician to Saladin. A major influence on Jewish thought, he wrote an important commentary on the Mishna, and a great philosophical work, the *Dalalat al-ha'irin* (1190, Guide of the Perplexed), arguing for the reconciliation of Greek philosophy and religion. He was an influence on a range of philosophers and traditions – Jewish, Muslim, and Christian – and was also the author of one of the most important codes of Jewish law.

Mainbocher [maynboshay], originally **Main Rousseau Bocher** (c.1890–1976) Fashion designer, born in Chicago, Illinois, USA. He studied and worked in Chicago, and after service in World War 1 stayed on in Paris, eventually becoming a fashion artist with *Harper's Bazaar* and editor of French *Vogue*. He started his couture house in Paris in 1930. One of his creations was the wedding dress designed for Mrs Wallis Simpson, the Duchess of Windsor (1937). He opened a salon for ready-to-wear clothes in New York City in 1940, but returned to Europe in 1971.

Maine pop (2000e) 1 274 900; area 86 153 sq km/33 265 sq mi. New England state in the NE corner of the USA, divided into 16 counties; bounded N by Canada, W by New Hampshire, E by the Atlantic; the 'Pine Tree State' or 'Lumber State'; explored by the Cabots in the 1490s; settled first by the French in 1604, and by the English in 1607; separated from Massachusetts in 1820, when admitted to the Union as 23rd state; capital, Augusta; largest town, Portland; the Kennebec and Penobscot Rivers run S to the Atlantic Ocean; crossed by the Appalachian Mts which rise to 1605 m/5266 ft at Mt Katahdin in Baxter State Park; dotted with over 1600 lakes, largest L Moosehead; N 80% forested; S coastal strip mainly arable; main industries include agriculture (especially potatoes), forestry, fishing, paper manufacturing, tourism.

mainframe computer A somewhat dated term still used to refer to very large capacity computers, and to distinguish them from the smaller computers now widely available. However, the distinction between mainframe and other computers is not always clear. The term **minicomputer**, for example, is sometimes used to refer to computers which do not fall into the category of either microcomputer or mainframe computer. Minicomputers are normally used for specific operations, such as the control of a chemical process, or to serve a small department in a manufacturing company.

main sequence In astronomy, a broad band in the Hertzsprung–Russell diagram, in which most stars lie. A star spends most of its life on this main sequence, while it burns hydrogen to helium. Once the hydrogen in the core is consumed, the star evolves away from the main sequence, becoming first a red giant. The Sun is a main sequence star.

mainstreaming The introduction of children with special educational needs, many of whom were formerly known as 'handicapped', into ordinary schools. In both the USA and UK, it was decided in the late 1970s and early 1980s to reduce the number of such children who attended special schools. The argument in favour was that many children in special schools were set targets which were too low, and also that they would gain from being educated alongside so-called 'normal' children. Reservations were expressed about most schools' ability, without substantial training for staff and extra resources, to offer skilled specialist help to children with different needs.

maintained school In the UK, a school which receives its money from a local education authority. It is often known popularly as a 'state school', though this term is inappropriate in a country where the state does not run schools.

maintenance A term used in England and Wales for money payments paid by one marriage partner to help support the other and/or their children, whether or not they are legitimate, during or following legal separation or divorce. This is more correctly known now as *financial provision* or *financial relief*. The payments are often referred to as *alimony*, but terminology varies (eg it is called *aliment* or *periodical allowance* in Scotland).

Maintenon, Françoise d'Aubigné, Marquise de (Marchioness of) [mĩtenõ], (1635–1719) Second wife of Louis XIV of France, born in Niort, W France. Orphaned, she married her guardian, the crippled poet Paul Scarron in 1652, and on his death was reduced to poverty. In 1669 she discreetly took charge of the king's two sons by her friend Madame de Montespan, and became the king's mistress. By 1674 the king had enabled her to purchase the estate of Maintenon, near Paris, which was converted to a marquisate. After the queen's death (1683), Louis married her secretly. She was accused of having great influence over him, especially over the persecution of Protestants. On his death in 1715 she retired to the educational institution for poor noblewomen which she had founded at St Cyr (1686).

Mainz [miynts], Fr **Mayence** 50°00N 8°16E, pop (2000e) 186 000. Old Roman city and capital of Rheinland-Pfalz province, WC Germany; on left bank of R Rhine opposite mouth of R Main; important traffic junction and commercial centre; railway; university (1477); headquarters of radio and television corporations; centre of the Rhine wine trade; glass materials, electronics, publishing; Gutenberg set up his printing press here; cathedral (mostly 11th–13th-c); Mainzer Fastnacht (Shrovetide); tourist river cruises along the Rhine to Cologne.

maiolica [mayolika], also (19th-c) spelled **majolica** Tin-glazed earthenware produced in Italy since before 1250. In the Renaissance period the decoration was often similar to the work of the most important contemporary Italian painters of complex religious and secular scenes.

Maitland, F(rederic) W(illiam) (1850–1906) Jurist and historian of English law, born in London, UK. He studied at Trinity College, Cambridge (1873–6) and Lincoln's Inn, and was called to the bar in 1876. After practising law he became reader in English law (1884) and professor (1888) at Cambridge. His contribution was to apply historical and comparative methods to the study of English institutions, and with Frederick Pollock he wrote the classic *The History of English Law before the Time of Edward I* (1895). In 1887 he co-founded the Selden Society for the study of English law.

maize The only cereal (*Zea mays*) native to the New World, originally tropical and developed as a major food crop from wild types by the Indians of Central America; also called **sweet corn** and **Indian corn**, and always called **corn** in the USA. Modern strains are suitable for temperate regions. It is a robust annual; male flowers in a terminal tassel; females forming a woody cob, bearing rows of plump, white, yellow, red, or purple grains. Its heads are eaten ripe or unripe as a vegetable. The grains and foliage are used for animal fodder, and it also yields flour, starch, syrup, alcohol, and paper. (Family: Gramineae.)

majlis [majles] (Arabic 'council') Any of a number of political institutions in the Middle East, ranging from parliaments to advisory councils for rulers.

Major, John (1943–) British statesman and prime minister (1990–7), born in London, UK. He had a career in banking before becoming Conservative MP for Huntingdonshire in 1979. He entered Margaret Thatcher's government as a junior minister in 1981, and rose to become Treasury chief secretary under Chancellor Nigel Lawson in 1987. Thereafter, having caught the eye of the prime minister, his progress was spectacular. In 1989 he replaced Sir Geoffrey Howe as foreign secretary, then the same year returned to the Treasury as Chancellor, when Lawson dramatically resigned. He remained loyal to Thatcher in the first round of the 1990 Conservative Party leadership election; then, when she stood down, and indicated that he was her preferred candidate, he ran successfully against Michael Heseltine and Douglas Hurd to become prime minister. He resigned as leader of the Conservative party after they lost the 1997 general election but remained active as an MP until he stepped down at the general election in 2001. He was made a Companion of Honour in 1998. His autobiography appeared in 1999.

Majorca [mayaw(r)ka], Span **Mallorca**, ancient **Balearis Major** pop (2000e) 600 000; area 3640 sq km/1400 sq mi. Largest island in the Balearics, W Mediterranean, 240 km/150 mi N of Algiers; chief town, Palma; tree-covered Sierra del Alfabia rises to 1445 m/4741 ft at Torrellas; taken in 1229 by James I of Aragón; in the Middle Ages, famous for its porcelain (maiolica); popular tourist resort; pottery, brandy, jewellery, mining, sheep, timber, fishing; many Roman, Phoenician, and Carthaginian remains.

majuscule [majuhskyool] A form of writing in which the letters are of uniform height, as if contained within a pair of horizontal lines. Usually called CAPITAL letters, the Greek and Roman alphabets were originally written in this way. It is contrasted with the later system known as **minuscule** [**min**uhskyool], in which parts of some letters extend above and below the horizontal lines ('small letters'), such as *h*, *g*. Minuscule writing was a gradual development, in regular use for Greek by the 7th–8th-c AD. The 'dual alphabet', using both capital and small letters, dates from the 8th-c.

Makale *Mekele*

Makarios III [makaryos], originally **Mihail Khristodoulou Mouskos** (1913–77) Archbishop and primate of the Orthodox Church of Cyprus, and president of Cyprus (1960–74, 1974–7), born in Ano Panayia, W Cyprus. He was ordained priest in 1946, elected Bishop of Kition in 1948, and became archbishop in 1950. He reorganized the *enosis* (union) movement, was arrested and detained in 1956, but returned to a tumultuous welcome in 1959 to become chief Greek-Cypriot Minister in the new Greek–Turkish provisional government. Later that year he was elected president. A short-lived coup removed him briefly from power in 1974. On his death, the posts of archbishop and head of state were separated.

Makassar *Ujung Pandang*

Makassar or **Macassar Strait** [makasah(r)], Indonesian **Selat** Stretch of water between the islands of Borneo in the W and Sulawesi (Celebes) in the E, linking the Java Sea (S) to the Celebes Sea (N); length 720 km/447 mi.

Makhmalbaf, Mohsen (1951–) Film director, born in Tehran, Iran. He founded the Centre for Propagation of Islamic Thought and Arts (1981) where he wrote short stories and scripts before his directorial film debut in 1982 with *Nassouh Repentant*. Later films include *Nun Va Goldoon* (1996, Moment of Innocence) and *Silence* (1998). His daughter **Samira Makhmalbaf** (1980–), also born in Tehran, is also an internationally acclaimed director, her films include the award-winning semi-documentary feature film *Sib* (1998, The Apple), and *Takhte Siah* (2000, The

Blackboard), scripted by Mohsen, which won the Jury Prize at the Cannes Film Festival.

Makonde [makohnday] A Bantu-speaking agricultural group of N Mozambique and SE Tanzania. Many work as migrant labourers on the E African coast, and are famous as woodcarvers, often drawing on Makonde folklore for themes.

Maksutov telescope [maksootof] An optical telescope in which the principal image-forming lens and mirror surfaces are spherical, and therefore easy to make. The design was published by the Russian optician D D Maksutov (1896–1964) in 1944.

Makua [makwah] A Bantu-speaking agricultural people of N Mozambique and S Tanzania. Strongly influenced by E African coast Arabs, many converted to Islam. Population c.3·8 million.

Malabo [malaboh], formerly **Clarencetown** or **Port Clarence**, and **Santa Isabel** 3°45N 8°50E, pop (2000e) 14 000. Seaport capital of Equatorial Guinea, W Africa; on island of Bioko, Gulf of Guinea; founded by British in 1827; airfield; coffee, cocoa, timber trade.

malabsorption The failure of intestinal absorption of nutrients taken as food. In general, this results in diarrhoea, abdominal pain and distension, loss of weight, anaemia, and features of specific vitamin deficiencies. Underlying causes include the tropical disease sprue, which may have an infective cause; abnormal bacterial proliferation in the small intestine, due to congenital or acquired blind loops of intestine; Crohn's disease, a non-specific chronic inflammation of the alimentary tract that affects young people; and pancreatic disease. The most important cause in the UK is coeliac disease.

Malacca or **Melaka** [malaka] pop (2000e) 726 000; area 1657 sq km/640 sq mi. State in SW Peninsular Malaysia; bounded W by the Strait of Malacca; one of the former Straits Settlements; capital, Malacca, pop (2000e) 136 000; centre of a great trading empire since the 15th-c; Islam spread from here throughout the Malayan Peninsula; held at various times by the Portuguese, Dutch, and British; large Chinese population; rubber, tin, rice; state museum, St John's Fort, St Peter's Church (1710), Cheng Hoon Teng Temple (oldest Chinese temple in Malaysia), Kampung Kling Mosque, Vinayagar Moorthi Temple.

Malacca, Strait of [muhlakuh] Channel between the Malaysia Peninsula and the Indonesian island of Sumatra; 800 km/500 mi long by 50–320 km/30–200 mi wide; links the Andaman Sea to the S China Sea; an important shipping lane; largest port, Singapore.

Malachi or **Malachias, Book of** [malakhiy] The last of the 12 so-called 'minor' prophetic writings of the Hebrew Bible/Old Testament; probably anonymous, since *malachi* in Hebrew means 'my messenger'; possibly the work of a 'cult prophet' in view of the strong criticism of priestly neglect of cultic requirements. Usually dated c.510–460 BC, in the period before the reforms of Ezra and Nehemiah, it stresses the need for faithfulness to the covenant with Yahweh, the need for fidelity in marriage, and the threat of a coming day of judgment.

malachite [malakiyt] A hydrated copper carbonate mineral ($Cu_2CO_3(OH)_2$) found in weathered copper ore deposits. It is bright green in colour.

malachite green [malakiyt] A green dye, named for its similarity in colour to the mineral malachite; there is no structural relationship. It is an example of a large class of dyes called *triphenylmethanes* on account of their structure.

Malachy, St [malakhee], originally **Máel Máedoc úa Morgair** (c.1094–1148) Monk and reformer, born in Armagh, Co Armagh, SE Northern Ireland, UK. He became Abbot of Bangor (1121), Bishop of Connor (1125) and Archbishop of Armagh (1134). He substituted Roman for Celtic liturgy, and renewed the use of the sacraments. In 1139 he journeyed to Rome, visiting St Bernard at Clairvaux, and introduced the Cistercian Order into Ireland on his return in 1142. In 1190 he became the first Irishman to be canonized. Feast day 3 November.

Málaga [malaga], ancient **Malaca** 36°43N 4°23W, pop (2000e) 519 000. Port and capital of Málaga province, Andalusia, S Spain; at the mouth of R Guadalmedina, 544 km/338 mi S of Madrid; founded by the Phoenicians, 12th-c BC; part of Spain, 1487; bishopric; airport; railway; car ferries to Casablanca, Tangier, Genoa; university (1972); tourism, textiles, beer, wine, chemicals, food processing, fruit trade; birthplace of Picasso; Moorish Alcazaba, cathedral (16th–18th-c), Roman theatre, fine arts museum; Museu Picasso (2003); Fiesta of La Virgen del Monte Carmel (Jul), fair (Aug), Festival of Spain (Aug–Sep), Costa del Sol Rally (Dec).

Malagasy [malagasee] The peoples of the island of Madagascar, comprising about 50 ethnic groups of diverse origins, but the strongest element from Indonesia; Malagasy languages are Austronesian. There are also Swahili and Bantu groups from the African mainland living in the NW, where there is a strong Muslim minority. The traditional economy is based on agriculture, with rice grown as a staple, and cattle farming important in many areas. Before colonial rule, groups were autonomous and politically uncentralized, except for the Merina of the C highlands, who established a powerful kingdom in the 16th-c. Most Malagasy are Protestant Christians.

Malamud, Bernard [malamuhd] (1914–86) Novelist and writer of short stories, born in New York City, USA. He studied at Columbia University, and taught at Oregon State University (1949–61) and Bennington College, VT (1961–86). His novels reflect his keen interest in Jewish-American life, notably in *The Assistant* (1957) and *God's Grace* (1982), and in his short stories, including *The Stories of Bernard Malamud* (1983). *The Fixer* (1966) won the Pulitzer Prize and the National Book Award.

malamute [malamyoot] *Alaskan malamute*

Malan, Daniel (François) [malan] (1874–1959) South African statesman and prime minister (1948–54), born in Riebeek West, SW South Africa. He studied at Victoria College, Stellenbosch, and Utrecht University, and in 1905 joined the ministry of the Dutch Reformed Church, but left to become editor of *Die Burger* (1915), the Nationalist newspaper. He became an MP in 1918, and in 1924 held the portfolios of the interior, education, and public health. He broke with Hertzog in 1934, and formed the Purified (Afrikaans *Gesuiwerde*) National Party. In 1939 Hertzog resigned from the government, and joined Malan in the Reunited (Afrikaans *Herenigde*) National Party. He was Leader of the Opposition, and in 1948 became premier and minister for external affairs, introducing the controversial apartheid policy. He was a strong believer in a strict white supremacy and a rigidly hierarchical society.

malaria A disease, endemic in tropical countries, caused by infection with one of four species of *Plasmodium*, a parasite transmitted by *Anopheles* mosquitoes. The parasites multiply in the liver and in red blood cells, which are destroyed with each life cycle, producing characteristic symptoms of high fever, shaking, and aches. *Plasmodium vivax* and *ovale* produce symptoms on alternate days; *Plasmodium malariae* produces symptoms every three days, associated with an enlarged spleen. *Plasmodium falciparum* infection is the most serious, giving rise to more continuous symptoms and a range of complications. Parasites and cell debris block capillaries, resulting in organ damage; involvement of the brain can lead to convulsions, coma, and death. Diagnosis is made by observation of the parasite under a microscope. Several drugs are available for treatment, but increasing resistance to these is now being seen, particularly by *Plasmodium falciparum*. Travellers should consult an expert centre for provision of anti-malarial medication.

Mälar, Lake [melah(r)], Swed **Mälaren** area 1140 sq km/440 sq mi. Lake in SE Sweden, extending 113 km/70 mi inland from the Baltic Sea; city of Stockholm on both sides of the strait connecting the lake with the Baltic Sea.

Malatesta Lords of the state of Rimini in NE Italy from the 13th-c to the 16th-c; among the most durable of several families of *signori* who dominated political life in the Italian Renaissance. Originally the political 'vicars' of the papacy, the Mala-

Malawi

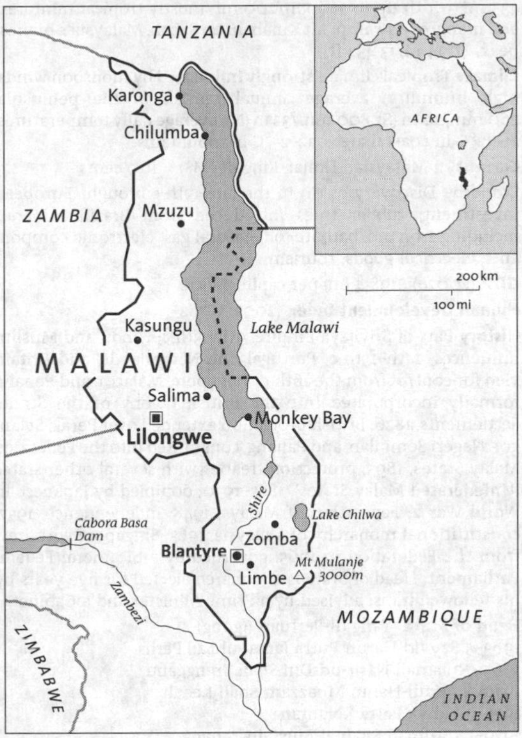

□ International Airport

[malahwee], official name **Republic of Malawi**

Local name Malawi (Malaêi)

Timezone GMT +2

Area 118 484 km^2/45 735 sq mi

Population total (2002e) 10 520 000

Status Republic

Date of independence 1964

Capital Lilongwe

Languages English and Chichewa (official)

Ethnic groups Maravi (including Nyanja, Chewa, Tonga, Tumbuka) (60%), Lomwe (18%), Yao (13%), Ngoni (7%), also Asian and European minorities

Religions Protestant (55%), Roman Catholic (20%), Muslim (20%), traditional animist beliefs (3%)

Physical features Crossed N–S by the Great Rift Valley; contains Africa's third largest lake, L Malawi; main river, Shire; Shire highlands (S) rise to nearly 3000 m/10 000 ft at Mt Mulanje.

Climate Tropical climate in S; high year-round temperatures, 28–37°C; average annual temperatures 23°C (Jan), 16°C (Jul) in Lilongwe; average annual rainfall, 740 mm/30 in; more moderate temperatures in central areas.

Currency 1 Kwacha (MK) = 100 tambala

Economy Based on agriculture (employs 90% of population); tobacco, sugar, tea, cotton, groundnuts, maize; textiles, matches, cigarettes, beer, spirits, shoes, cement.

GDP (2002e) $6·811 bn, per capita $600

Human Development Index (2002) 0·400

History Visited by the Portuguese, 17th-c; European contact established by David Livingstone, 1859; Scottish church missions in the area; claimed as the British Protectorate of Nyasaland, 1891; British colony, 1907; in the 1950s joined with N and S Rhodesia to form the Federation of Rhodesia and Nyasaland; independence, 1964; republic, 1966; governed by a President, Cabinet and National Assembly.

Head of State/Government
1966–94 Hastings Kamuzu Banda
1994– Bakili Muluzi

Vice President
2003– Justin Malewezi

testa state was overthrown in 1500 by a coalition of the papacy and the French.

Malawi *see panel*

Malawi, Lake *Nyasa, Lake*

Malay (language) The language of the Malay Peninsula, which has provided the modern standard language, **Bahasa Indonesia**, known as **Bahasa Malaysia** in Malaysia. A pidginized form, **Bazaar Malay**, has been a lingua franca in the region for many centuries, before the advent of Western trade and colonialism. A further variety, **Baba Malay**, is used by Chinese communities in Malaysia. Inscriptions in Malay date from the 7th-c.

Malay (people) A cluster of Malay-speaking (Austronesian) peoples of the Malay Peninsula (where they are 54% of the population), and neighbouring islands and territory, including parts of Borneo and Sumatra. Most became Hindu before being converted to Islam in the 15th-c, and Hindu Indian influence on their culture is still strong. Most Malay villages are along the rivers and coasts in tropical forest. They grow wet rice and rubber, a major cash crop.

Malayalam [malayahlam] The Dravidian language associated with the S Indian state of Kerala. It has c.34 million speakers.

Malay bear *sun bear*

Malayo-Polynesian languages *Austronesian languages*

Malaysia *p.952*

Malcolm III, nickname **Malcolm Canmore** ('Big Head') (c.1031–93) King of Scots (1058–93), the son of Duncan I, who was slain by Macbeth in 1040. He returned from exile in 1054, and conquered S Scotland; but he did not become king until he had defeated and killed Macbeth (1057) and disposed of Macbeth's stepson, Lulach (1058). He married as his second wife the English Princess Margaret (later St Margaret), sister of Edgar the Ætheling, and launched five invasions of England between 1061 and his death in a skirmish near Alnwick, Northumberland.

Malcolm, George (John) (1917–97) Harpsichordist and conductor, born in London, UK. He studied at the Royal College of Music and at Oxford, and was Master of the Music at Westminster Cathedral (1947–59), after which he earned a wide reputation as a freelance harpsichord soloist and a conductor. He was made a papal Knight of the Order of St Gregory in 1970.

Malcolm X, originally **Malcolm Little** (1925–65) African-American nationalist leader, born in Omaha, Nebraska, USA. Imprisoned for burglary in 1946, he was converted to the Black Muslim sect led by Elijah Muhammad. On his release in 1953, he assumed his new name, and won a large following on speaking tours on behalf of the sect, pressing for black separatism and the use of violence in self-defence. In 1964, following a trip to Mecca, his views changed, and he founded the Organization of Afro-American Unity. A factional feud ensued, culminating in his assassination by Black Muslim enemies during a rally in Harlem.

Maldives *p.953*

Malé [malee], Dhivehi **Daviyani** 4°00N 73°28E, pop (2000e) 76 000; area 2 sq km/0·77 sq mi. Chief atoll and capital of the Maldives; over 700 km/435 mi WSW of Sri Lanka; airport; commercial centre; trade in breadfruit, copra, palm mats.

Malebranche, Nicolas [malbrãsh] (1638–1715) Philosopher, born in Paris, France. He joined the Catholic Oratorians in 1660, and studied theology until Descartes' works drew him to philosophy. His major work is *De la recherche de la vérité* (1674, Search after Truth), which defends many of Descartes'

Malaysia

☐ International Airport

[malayzha]

Local name Malaysia

Timezone GMT +8

Area 329 749 km²/127 283 sq mi

Population total (2002e) 24 370 000

Status Republic

Date of independence 1957

Capital Kuala Lumpur

Languages Bahasa Malaysia (Malay) (official), also Chinese, English, and Tamil widely spoken

Ethnic groups Malay (59%), Chinese (32%), Indian (9%)

Religions Muslim (53%), Buddhist (17%), Chinese folk-religionist (12%), Hindu (7%), Christian (6%)

Physical features Independent federation of states located in SE Asia, comprising 11 states and a federal territory in Peninsular Malaysia, and the E States of Sabah and Sarawak on the island of Borneo; mountain chain of granite and limestone running N–S, rising to Mt Tahan, 2189 m/7182 ft; peninsula length 700 km/435 mi, width up to 320 km/200 mi; mostly tropical rainforest and mangrove swamp; Mt Kinabalu on Sabah, Malaysia's highest peak, 4094 m/13 432 ft.

Climate Tropical climate strongly influenced by monsoon winds; high humidity; average annual rainfall in the peninsula, 260 mm/10 in (S), 800 mm/32 in (N); average daily temperatures, 21–32°C in coastal areas, 12–25°C in mountains.

Currency 1 Malaysian Dollar/Ringgit (M$) = 100 cents

Economy Discovery of tin in the late 19th-c brought European investment; rubber trees introduced from Brazil; minerals including iron ore, bauxite; oil, natural gas; electronic components, electrical goods; tourism.

GDP (2002e) $198·4 bn, per capita $8800

Human Development Index (2002) 0·782

History Part of Srivijaya Empire, 9th–13th-c; Hindu and Muslim influences, 14th–15th-c; Portugal, the Netherlands, and Britain vied for control from the 16th-c; Singapore, Malacca, and Penang formally incorporated into the British Colony of the Straits Settlements, 1826; British protection extended over Perak, Selangor, Negeri Sembilan, and Pahang, constituted into the Federated Malay States, 1895; protection treaties with several other states (Unfederated Malay States), 1885–1930; occupied by Japanese in World War 2; Federation of Malaya, 1948; independence, 1957; constitutional monarchy of Malaysia, 1963; Singapore withdrew from the Federation in 1965; governed by a bicameral Federal Parliament; Head of State is a Monarch elected for five years by his fellow sultans; advised by a Prime Minister and a Cabinet.

Head of State (Yang di-Pertuan Agong)
1963–5 Sayyid Harun Putra Jamal-ul-Lail Perlis
1965–70 Ismail Nasir-ud-Din Shah Trengganu
1970–5 Abdul-Halim Muazzam Shah Kedah
1975–9 Yahya Petra Kelantan
1979–84 Ahmad Shah al-Mustain Pahang
1984–9 Mahmud Iskandar Shah Johore
1989–4 Azlan Muhibbuddin Shah Perak
1994–9 Ja'afar ibn Abdul Rahman
1999–2001 Salehuddin Abdul Aziz Shah
2001 Mizan Zainal Abidin *Acting*
2001– Syed Sirajuddin

Head of Government
1970–6 Abdul Razak bin Hussein
1976–9 Haji Hussein bin Onn
1979–97 Mahathir bin Mohamad
1997 Anwar Ibrahim *Acting*
1997–2003 Mahathir bin Mohamad
2003– Abdullah Ahmad Badawi

views, but explains all causal interaction between mind and body by a theory of divine intervention known as *occasionalism*.

maleic acid [malayik] $C_4H_4O_4$, IUPAC ***cis*-butenedioic acid**, melting point 139°C. A geometrical isomer of fumaric acid, but as the carboxyl groups are on the same side of the double bond, it forms an internal hydrogen bond, indicated in the formula, and thus has a much lower melting point than fumaric acid. It easily forms an anhydride by the loss of a water molecule with the formation of a ring.

Malenkov, Georgiy Maksimilianovich [malyenkof] (1902–88) Soviet statesman and prime minister (1953–5), born in Orenburg, W Russia. He joined the Communist Party in 1920 and was involved in the collectivization of agriculture and the purges of the 1930s under Stalin. He became a member of the Politburo and deputy prime minister in 1946, succeeding Stalin as Party first secretary and prime minister in 1953. He resigned in 1955, admitting responsibility for the failure of Soviet agricultural policy, and in 1957 was sent to Kazakhstan as manager of a hydroelectric plant.

Malesherbes, Chrétien (Guillaume de Lamoignon) de [malzairb] (1721–94) French statesman, born in Paris, France. He became a counsellor of the *Parlement* of Paris (1744), and was made chief censor of the press (1750). At Louis XVI's accession (1774) he became secretary of state for the royal household, instituting prison and legal reforms in tandem with Turgot's economic improvements. He resigned in 1776 on the eve of Turgot's dismissal. Despite his reforming zeal, he was mistrusted as an aristocrat during the Revolution. Arrested as a Royalist (1794), he was guillotined in Paris.

Malevich, Kazimir (Severinovich) [malayevich] (1878–1935) Painter and designer, born in Kiev, Ukraine. He studied in Moscow in 1902 and, together with Mondrian, was one of the earliest pioneers of pure abstraction, founding the Suprematist movement. He claimed to have painted the first totally abstract picture, a black square on a white background, as early as 1913. Certainly he was exhibiting similar work by 1915, and went on to paint a series entitled 'White on White'.

Mali *p.954*

malic acid HOOC–CH_2–CH(OH)–COOH, IUPAC **2-hydroxybutanedioic acid**, melting point 100°C. An acid found in unripe fruit, especially apples. Loss of water produces maleic and fumaric acids.

Maldives

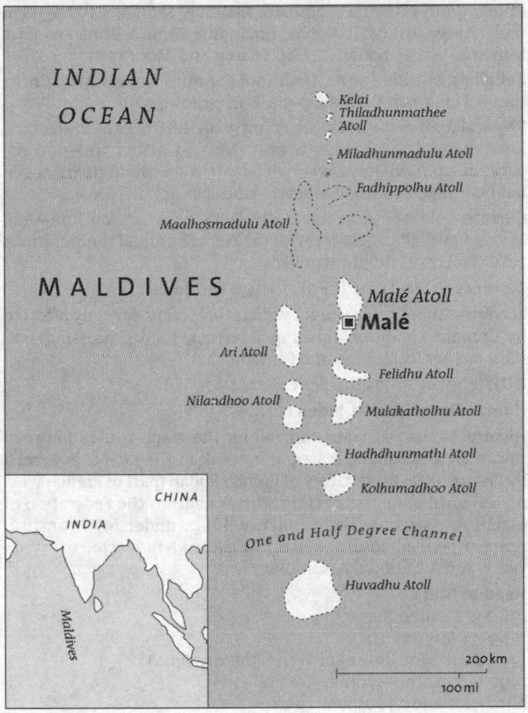

□ International Airport

[moldiyvz], formerly **Maldive Islands**, official name **Republic of Maldives**, Dhivehi **Dhivehi Jumhuriya**

Local name Dhivehi Jumhuriya

Timezone GMT +5

Area 300 km²/116 sq mi

Population total (2002e) 281 000

Status Independent republic within the Commonwealth

Date of independence 1968

Capital Malé

Languages Dhivehi (official), Arabic, Hindi, and English widely spoken

Ethnic groups Sinhalese (Dravidian extraction mainly), also Arab, Negrito, African influences

Religion Almost 100% Sunni Muslim

Physical features Island archipelago in the Indian Ocean; comprises c.1190 islands (202 inhabited) in a chain of 20 coral atolls; many small and low-lying with sandy beaches fringed with coconut palms; none of the islands rising above 1·8 m/5 ft; 10% of land arable, 3% forested.

Climate Generally warm and humid; wet season created by SW monsoons (Apr–Oct), dry season by NE monsoon (Dec–Mar); average annual rainfall, 2100 mm/83 in; average daily temperature 22°C.

Currency 1 Rufiyaa (MRf, Rf) = 100 laaris

Economy Agriculture; breadfruit, banana, mango, cassava, sweet potato, millet; fishing, shipping, tourism.

GDP (2002e) $1·25 bn, per capita $3900

Human Development Index (2002) 0·743

History Former dependency of Ceylon (Sri Lanka); British protectorate, 1887–1965; became a Republic within the Commonwealth, 1953; Sultan restored, 1954; independence outside the Commonwealth, 1965; rejoined Commonwealth, 1982; governed by a president, a ministers' Majlis (cabinet), and a citizens' Majlis of 48 members elected for five years.

Monarch (Sultan)
1954–68 Muhammad Farid Didi

Head of State/Government
1968–78 Ibrahim Nasir
1978– Maumoon Abdul Gayoom

Malinke [malingkay] or **Mandingo** A cluster of autonomous Mande-speaking agricultural peoples of Mali, Guinea, Senegal, and neighbouring areas. All groups are under the authority of a hereditary noble class. Malinke groups founded the Mandingo Empire of Mali (13th–16th-c).

Malinowski, Bronislaw (Kasper) [malinofskee] (1884–1942) Anthropologist, born in Kraków, S Poland. He studied at the Jagiellonian University, Kraków, and at Leipzig, went to London in 1910, and taught at the London School of Economics, where he became a professor (1927). In 1938 he went to the USA, where he accepted a post at Yale. His most famous work is *Argonauts of the Western Pacific* (1922) in which he pioneered 'participant observation' as a method of fieldwork (notably in the Trobriand Is). He was a major proponent of functionalism in anthropology.

Malipiero, (Gian) Francesco [malipyayroh] (1882–1973) Composer, born in Venice, NE Italy. He studied in Vienna, Venice, and Bologna, visited Paris, and became professor of composition at the Parma Conservatory (1921), and director of institutes at Padua and Venice (1939–52). He wrote symphonic, operatic, vocal, and chamber music, and edited Monteverdi and Vivaldi.

mallard A dabbling duck (*Anas platyrhynchos*) found near water throughout the N hemisphere; blue patch on wing; male with green head and thin white neck ring; the ancestor of nearly all domestic ducks. Originally the name was used only for the male. (Family: Anatidae.)

Mallarmé, Stéphane [malah(r)may] (1842–98) Symbolist poet, born in Paris, France. He taught English in Paris and elsewhere, visiting England on several occasions. He translated the poems of Poe, and in his own writing became a leader of the Symbolist school. His works included *Hérodiade* (1864), *L'Après-midi d'un faune* (1865), which inspired Debussy's prelude, and the remarkable experimental poem, *Un Coup de dés* (1914, A Dice Throw).

Malle, Louis [mal] (1932–95) Film director, born in Thumeries, N France. He studied political science at the Jesuit College, Fontainebleau, and the Sorbonne, after which he entered the Institut des Hautes Etudes Cinématographiques (1950). His first feature film was *Ascenseur pour l'échafaud* (1957, trans Frantic) for which he won the Prix Delluc. The success of his second film *Les Amants* (1958, The Lovers) brought recognition, and he went on to establish an international reputation, receiving critical acclaim for such works as *Calcutta* (1969), *Le Souffle au coeur* (1971, trans Dearest Love), and *Atlantic City* (1980, BAFTA). Later films included *Au Revoir les enfants* (1987, Goodbye, Children) and *Damage* (1993). He married actress **Candice Bergen** (1946–) in 1980.

mallee [malee] A scrubland vegetation zone in the semi-arid parts of SE and SW Australia. Dwarf eucalyptus shrubs dominate, growing to 2 m/6 ft in height.

mallee fowl A megapode bird (*Leipoa ocellata*) native to Australia; brown with white spots on wings; inhabits dry scrubland, especially **mallee scrub** (dwarf eucalyptus); eats seeds, flowers, insects, and lizards; need not drink; also known as **lowan**. (Family: Megapodiidae.)

Mallon, Seamus (1936–) Northern Ireland politician, born in Markethill, Armagh, Northern Ireland. Educated at Newry and Belfast, he was a primary school headteacher before being elected to Armagh District Council (1973–86) and the Northern

Mali

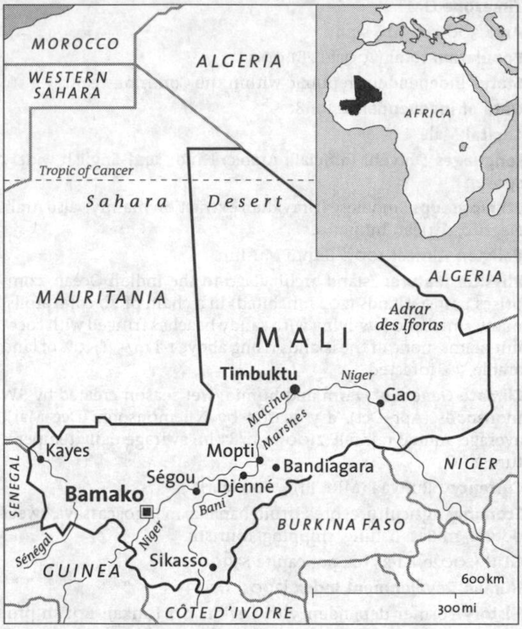

□ International Airport

[mahlee], official name **Republic of Mali**, Fr **République de Mali**

Local name Mali

Timezone GMT

Area 1 240 192 km²/478 714 sq mi

Population total (2002e) 11 340 000

Status Republic

Date of independence 1960

Capital Bamako

Languages French (official), local languages (including Bambara) widely spoken

Ethnic groups Mande (Bambara, Malinke, Sarakole) (50%), Peul (Fulani nomads) (17%), Voltaic (including Senufo, Bura, Senouto, Minianka) (12%), Songhai (6%), Tuareg and Moor (5%)

Religions Muslim (90%), traditional animist beliefs (9%), Christian (1%) (Roman Catholic 0·5%, Protestant 0·5%)

Physical features Landlocked country on the fringe of the Sahara; lower part of the Hoggar massif (N); arid plains 300–500 m/1000–1600 ft; mainly savannah land in the S; main rivers, Niger, Bani, Sénégal; featureless desert land (N).

Climate Subtropical in S and SW, with rainy season (Jun–Oct); average rainfall c.1000 mm/40 in; average annual temperatures 24°C (Jan), 27°C (Jul) in Bamako.

Currency 1 CFA Franc (CFAFr) = 100 centimes

Economy Mainly subsistence agriculture; crops severely affected by drought conditions; fishing, livestock, food processing, textiles, leather, cement; some tourism.

GDP (2002e) $9·775 bn, per capital $900

Human Development Index (2002) 0·386

History Mediaeval state controlling the trade routes between savannah and Sahara, reaching its peak in the 14th-c; governed by France, 1881–95; territory of French Sudan (part of French West Africa) until 1959; partnership with Senegal as the Federation of Mali, 1959; separate independence, 1960; under 1979 constitution (suspended, 1991) governed by a President elected every six years, and a National Assembly.

Head of State
1960–8 Modibo Keita
1969–91 Moussa Traoré
1991–2 Amadou Toumani Touré *Military Junta*
1992–2002 Alpha Oumar Konaré
2002– Amadou Toumani Touré

Head of Government
1986–8 Mamadou Dembelé
1988–91 *No Prime Minister*
1991–2 Soumana Sacko
1992–3 Younoussi Touré
1993–4 Abdoulaye Sekou Sow
1994–2000 Ibrahim Boubakar Keita
2000–2 Mande Sidibe
2002 Modibo Keita
2002– Mohammed Ag Amani

Ireland Assembly (1973–4). A member of the Social Democratic and Labour Party, he was appointed to the Republic of Ireland Senate (1981–2), and was elected a UK MP (1986–). An active campaigner for the peace process and supporter of the Good Friday Agreement, he was elected to the new Northern Ireland Assembly in 1998, becoming deputy first minister (1999–2001).

mallow N temperate annual and perennial herb; palmately lobed or divided leaves; flowers with an epicalyx, calyx and five heart-shaped to deeply notched petals, rose, purple, or white, often with dark veins; stamens numerous, united into a central column; fruit a flat whorl of 1-seeded segments, resembling small cheeses. It is related to both cotton and hibiscus, with very similar flowers. (Genus: *Malva*, 40 species. Family: Malvaceae.)

Mallowan, Max *Christie, Agatha*

Malmö [malmoe] 55°35N 13°00E, pop (2000e) 245 000. Fortified seaport and capital of Malmöhus county, SW Sweden; on The Sound opposite Copenhagen, Denmark; end-point of Øresund bridge from Copenhagen (17 km/10·5 mi), opened 2000; third largest city in Sweden; under Danish rule until 1658; railway; engineering, shipbuilding, foodstuffs, textiles, cement; town hall (16th-c); Church of St Peter (14th-c).

malnutrition A deficiency of one or more of the essential ingredients of a diet. Undernutrition occurs when insufficient food energy is taken, and when prolonged may lead to profound weight loss. The insufficiency may be more specific and involve one or several vitamin deficiencies. Examples include water-soluble vitamins (B-vitamins, C, folates) and fat-soluble vitamins (A, D, E). Electrolyte deficiencies and inadequate amounts of essential fatty and amino acids may also occur. These may give rise to a wide range of clinical abnormalities and metabolic defects.

Malory, Sir Thomas (?–1471) Writer, known for his work *Le Morte Darthur* (The Death of Arthur). From Caxton's preface (1485), we are told that Malory was a knight, that he finished his work in the ninth year of the reign of Edward IV (1461–70), and that he 'reduced' it from some French book. Probably he was the Sir Thomas Malory of Newbold Revel, Warwickshire, whose quarrels with a neighbouring priory and (probably) Lancastrian politics brought him imprisonment.

Malouf, David [maloof] (1934–) Novelist, born in Brisbane, Queensland, NE Australia. He studied at Queensland University, teaching there and at Sydney. Previously concentrating on poetry, his first novel was *Johnno* (1975). He became a full-time writer in 1978, and in 1979 was awarded the New South Wales Premier's Literary Award for *An Imaginary Life* (1978). Other novels include *Fly Away Peter* (1982), *Harland's Half Acre* (1984), *The Great World* (1991, Miles Franklin Award), *Remembering*

Malta

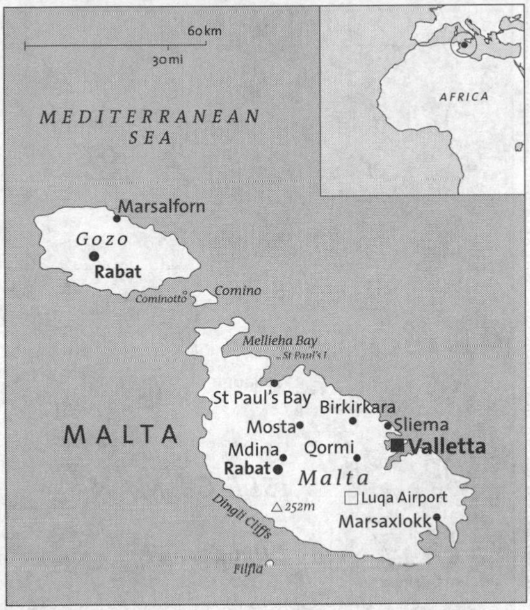

□ International Airport

official name **Republic of Malta**, Maltese **Repubblika ta' Malta**, ancient **Melita**

Local name Malta

Timezone GMT +1

Area 316 km²/122 sq mi

Population total (2002e) 386 000

Status Independent republic within the Commonwealth

Date of independence 1964

Capital Valletta

Languages English and Maltese (official)

Ethnic groups Maltese (mixed Arabic, Sicilian, Norman, Spanish, English, Italian racial origin) (95%), English (2%)

Religions Roman Catholic Apostolic (97%), Anglican Communion (2%)

Physical features Archipelago, comprising the islands of Malta (246 km²/95 sq mi), Gozo (67 km²/26 sq mi), and Comino (2·7 km²/1 sq mi), with the uninhabited islets of Cominotto, Filfla, and St Paul; highest point, 252 m/830 ft, on island of Malta; well-indented coastline with natural harbours, rocky coves; no rivers.

Climate Mediterranean, hot, dry summers, cool, rainy winters; rainy season (Oct–Mar); average annual rainfall 400 mm/16 in; average annual temperatures 13°C (Jan), 26°C (Jul) in Valletta.

Currency 1 Maltese pound (LM) = 100 cents

Economy Tourism; ship repair (naval dockyards now converted to commercial use); developing as a trans-shipment centre for the Mediterranean; tobacco, plastic and steel goods, paints, detergents; potatoes, tomatoes, oranges, grapes.

GDP (2002e) $6·818 bn, per capita $17 200

Human Development Index (2002) 0·875

History Controlled at various times by Phoenicia, Greece, Carthage, and Rome; conquered by Arabs, 9th-c; given to the Knights Hospitallers, 1530; British Crown Colony, 1815; important strategic base in both World Wars; for its resistance to heavy air attacks, the island was awarded the George Cross, 1942; achieved independence, 1964; republic, 1974; British military base closed, 1979; governed by a President, Prime Minister, Cabinet and House of Representatives.

Head of State
1994–9 Ugo Mifsud Bonnici
1999– Guido de Marco

Head of Government
1996–8 Alfred Sant
1998– Eddie Fenech Adami

Babylon (1993), which was shortlisted for the Booker Prize, and won the 1996 IMPAC Dublin Literary Award. *Conversation at Curlow Creek* (1997), and *Dream Stuff* (2000).

Malraux, André (Georges) [malroh] (1901–76) Statesman and novelist, born in Paris, France. He studied oriental languages and spent much time in China, where he worked for the Guomindang and was active in the 1927 revolution. He also fought in the Spanish Civil War, and in World War 2 escaped from a prison camp to join the French resistance. He was minister of information in de Gaulle's government (1945–6), and minister of cultural affairs (1960–9). He is known for his novels, notably *La Condition humaine* (1933, trans Man's Fate; Prix Goncourt) and *L'Espoir* (1937, trans Man's Hope).

Malta *see panel*

Maltese (language) A language spoken by 300 000 people on the island of Malta, related to the W dialects of Arabic. It has changed substantially from the linguistic structure of its source, through the influence of the Romance languages. It is the only variety of Arabic written in the Roman alphabet.

Maltese (zoology) A small toy spaniel developed in Italy (name probably derived from the Sicilian town of Melita); colour uniform; hair straight, coat very long and thick, reaching ground; legs short, hidden by coat.

Malthus, Thomas Robert (1766–1834) Economist, born near Dorking, Surrey, SE England, UK. He studied at Cambridge, and was ordained in 1797. In 1798 he published anonymously his *Essay on the Principle of Population*, which argued that the population has a natural tendency to increase faster than the means of subsistence, and that efforts should be made to cut the birth rate, either by self-restraint or birth control – a view which later was widely misrepresented under the name of *Malthusianism*. In 1805 he became professor of political economy in the East India College at Haileybury, where he wrote *Principles of Political Economy* (1820) and other works.

maltose [mawltohs] $C_{12}H_{22}O_{11}$. A condensation dimer of two molecules of glucose which are recovered when it is hydrolyzed; also known as **malt sugar**. It is derived from the limited hydrolysis of starch, of which it is the repeating unit.

malt sugar *maltose*

Malvern [mawlvern] or **Great Malvern** 52°07N 2°19W, pop (2000e) 31 700. Town in Hereford and Worcester, WC England, UK; popular health resort in the Malvern Hills, 12 km/7 mi SW of Worcester; railway; engineering, plastics, tourism; Malvern College (public school); Elgar lived and is buried here; Malvern Festival (May).

Malvinas [malveenas] *Falkland Islands*

Mamaev Kurgan [mamyef koorgan] or **Mamai Hill** An area in the heart of Volgograd, Russia, and the scene of the most severe conflict during the Battle of Stalingrad (1942–3). The Soviet victory is commemorated by the Motherland monument, a 52 m/171 ft statue designed by E V Vuchetich, which dominates the hill, and the dead are mourned in the Square of Heroes and the Square of Grief below. The Mamaev Kurgan memorial was erected in 1963–7.

Mamai Hill *Mamaev Kurgan*

mamba A venomous African snake of the family Elapidae; may climb trees; eats lizards and birds; strong venom; not usually aggressive (although the fastest snake ever recorded was a black mamba which reached 11 kph/7 mph while chasing a man who had been teasing it); two species: the **black mamba** (*Dendroaspis polylepis*), correctly the **black-mouthed mamba**, with body dark brown or grey, never black; and the **green mamba** (*Dendroaspis angusticeps*).

Mamet, David (Alan) [mamet], sometimes credited as **Richard Weisz** (1947–) Playwright, screenplay writer, and film director, born in Chicago, Illinois, USA. He studied at Goddard College, VT, then became an actor in New York City. His plays, such as *American Buffalo* (1976) and *Speed the Plow* (1987), address the psychological and ethical issues that confront modern urban society. Other works include the plays *The Woods* (1977) and *The Cryptogram* (1994), the screenplays *The Postman Always Rings Twice* (1981) and *The Untouchables* (1986), and the films (as director) *House of Games* (1986) *The Spanish Prisoner* (1998), *The Winslow Boy* (1999), and *State and Main* (2000). A novel, *The Village*, appeared in 1994. In 1984 he was awarded the Pulitzer Prize in Drama for *Glengarry Glen Ross*. He also wrote the screenplay for *Hannibal* (2001), a sequel to *The Silence of the Lambs*.

Mamluks or **Mamelukes** Slave soldiers who constituted the army of the Ayyubid sultanate established in Egypt by Saladin in the 1170s. Their commanders (*amirs*) created a professional army of high quality. In 1250 they overthrew the Ayyubids, and established Mamluk dynasties until conquered by the Ottomans in 1516–17. They continued to rule in Egypt with Ottoman sanction until the French invasion in 1798; their remnants were massacred by Mohammed Ali in 1811.

mammal An animal characterized by having mammary glands in the female, along with several other features: a covering of hair (very sparse in some mammals); each side of the lower jaw formed from one bone (the *dentary*); three small bones in the middle ear (the *hammer, anvil*, and *stirrup*); seven vertebrae in the neck (only six in the manatee); and no nucleus in the red blood cells. Whales, dugongs, and manatees have lost their hind legs. Mammals are divided into **placental mammals**, in which the young develop in a womb (the *uterus*) where they are nourished from the blood of the mother and are born at an advanced stage of development; **marsupials**, in which the young are not nourished in a womb but are born at a very early developmental stage and develop outside the mother's body, usually in a pouch, nourished with milk from the mammary gland; and **monotremes** (or **egg-laying mammals**), in which the young hatch from an egg outside the body of the mother and are then nourished with milk. (Class: Mammalia, c.4000 species.)

mammary gland In female mammals, a gland responsible for the production and release of milk to feed their young. The number varies between 2 and 20. They are located on the surface of the chest or abdomen, and may be concentrated into an udder. They are probably derived from highly modified sweat glands.

mammoth A specialized elephant originating in Africa, which spread in the early Pleistocene epoch through Eurasia and North America. The **woolly mammoth** was abundant in tundra regions, had long hair and a thick fat layer for insulation, fed on grasses and legumes in summer, and on shrubs and bark in winter. It died out c.12 000 years ago. (Order: Proboscidea.)

Mammoth Cave A system of subterranean passages and caverns created by limestone erosion and extending over 480 km/300 mi in W Kentucky. The area was designated a national park in 1936, and is a world heritage site.

mammoth tree A massive evergreen conifer (*Sequoiadendron giganteum*) confined to the W slopes of the Sierra Nevada Mts, CA; also called **California** or **giant redwood**, **California big tree**, or **wellingtonia**. It is sometimes claimed as the oldest living organism; age estimates range from 400–4000 years. Several of the finest specimens are named after famous Americans. (Family: Taxodiaceae.)

Man, Isle of *see panel*

management information system (MIS) *executive information system*

Managua [managwa] 12°06N 86°18W, pop (2000e) 1 414 000. Commercial centre and capital city of Nicaragua, on the S shore of Lago de Managua, 45 km/28 mi inland from the Pacific Ocean; badly damaged by earthquake in 1931 and 1972; airport; railway; university (1961); textiles, matches, cigarettes, cement; archaeological site of Huellas de Acahualinca nearby; Fiesta of Santo Domingo (Aug).

Man, Isle of

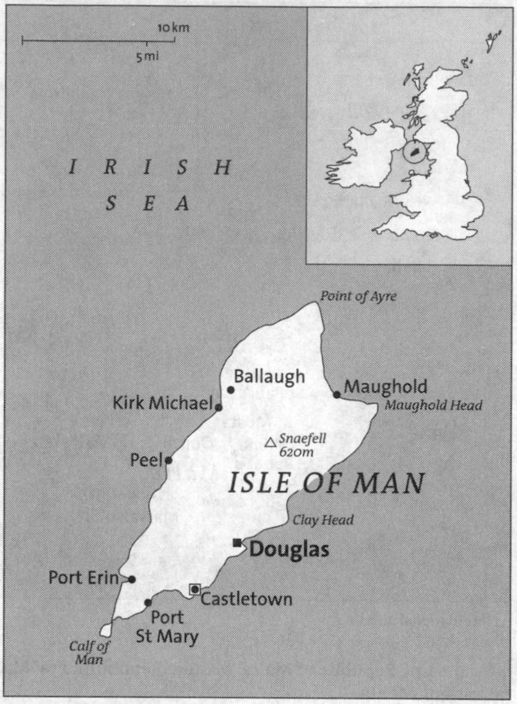

□ International Airport

(UK British Islands)

Timezone GMT

Area 572 km²/221 sq mi

Population total (2000e) 76 200

Status Crown dependency of the United Kingdom

Capital Douglas

Languages English (Manx survived as an everyday language until 19th-c)

Physical features Island in the Irish Sea; rises to 620 m/2036 ft at Snaefell.

Economy Tourism, agriculture, fishing, light engineering; used as a tax haven; not part of European Community. Annual Tourist Trophy motorcycle races held here.

History Ruled by the Welsh, 6th–9th-c; then by the Scandinavians, Scots, and English; purchased by the British Government between 1765 and 1828; the island has its own Parliament, the bicameral Court of Tynwald, which consists of the elected House of Keys and the Legislative Council; Acts of the British Parliament do not generally apply to Man.

manakin A small bird native to C and tropical South America; short bill, wings, and (usually) tail; toes partially joined; inhabits forests; eats insects and small fruits picked in flight; noted for its complex display. (It should not be confused with the mannikin.) (Family: Pipridae, c.53 species.)

Manama [manama], Arabic **al-Manamah** 26°12N 50°38E, pop (2000e) 176 000. Seaport capital of Bahrain, on N coast of Bahrain I in the Persian Gulf; connected by a causeway with

Muharraq I to the NE; a free trade port with facilities at Mina Sulman near Sitra Wharf; oil refining, commerce, banking.

Mana Pools area 2196 sq km/848 sq mi. National park in N Zimbabwe; a world heritage site; established in 1963; partly bordered NW by the R Zambezi, the frontier with Zambia; extensive wildlife; in the dry season animals migrate towards the river in huge numbers.

Manas A wildlife sanctuary in Assam, on the Indian border with Bhutan; a world heritage site. Occupying jungle-clad hills in the watershed of the Mana, Beki, and Hakua Rivers, it is noted as a refuge for a wide variety of bird and animal life, particularly the rare pygmy hog and golden langur.

Manasseh, Prayer of [manase] Short, eloquent writing of the Old Testament Pseudepigrapha (but often considered part of the Apocrypha even though not clearly in the Septuagint), ostensibly the work of Manasseh, a notoriously wicked king of Judah (c.687–642 BC), expressing his personal confession of sin and petition for pardon. Most scholars date the work from the 2nd-c BC to the 1st-c AD, considering it a late elaboration based on parts of 2 *Chron* 33.

Manasseh, tribe of [manase] One of the 12 tribes of ancient Israel, but said to be descended from Joseph's elder son, who with Ephraim was adopted by Jacob to share in his blessing (*Gen* 48–9). Perhaps originally it was a half tribe. Its territory in C Palestine extended on both sides of the Jordan R, located between the tribes of Ephraim and Issachar in the W.

manatee [manatee] An aquatic mammal, found from Brazil to SE USA, and in W Africa; inhabits shallow coastal seas and rivers; large rounded body; short head with square muzzle; front legs are flippers; no hind legs; tail ends in a flat horizontal disc; eats underwater plants. (Order: Sirenia. Family: Trichechidae, 3 species.)

Manaus or **Manáos** [manãos] 3°06S 60°00W, pop (2000e) 1 285 000. River-port capital of Amazonas state, N Brazil, on the N bank of the R Negro just above its influx into the Amazon; the collecting point for produce of a vast area; founded, 1660; free zone established, 1967; airfield; university (1965); timber, rubber, natural fibres, nuts; cathedral; Teatro Amazonas opera house (1896, rebuilt 1929, restored 1974, 1987); folklore festival (Jun).

Manchester (New Hampshire) 43°00N 71°28 W, pop (2000e) 107 000. City in Hillsborough Co, New Hampshire, USA; on the R Merrimack, 24 km/15 mi S of Concord; largest city in New Hampshire; railway; airfield; New Hampshire College (1932); textiles, leather products, vehicle parts, paper; museum, library, art gallery.

Manchester (UK), Lat **Mancunium** 53°30N 2°15W, pop (2001e) 392 800. Metropolitan district in Greater Manchester urban area, NW England, UK, on the R Irwell, 256 km/159 mi NW of London; Roman town, located at a major crossroads; became centre of local textile industry in 17th-c, and focal point of English cotton industry during the Industrial Revolution; became a city in 1853; University of Manchester (1880), University of Manchester Institute of Science and Technology (1824); Manchester Metropolitan University (1992, formerly Manchester Polytechnic); railway; airport; connected to the Irish Sea by the 57 km/35¼ mi Manchester Ship Canal (1894); UK's second largest commercial centre; textiles, chemicals, engineering, paper, foodstuffs, rubber, electrical equipment, printing; cultural centre for NW; art gallery, Royal Exchange (theatre), Cotton Exchange (leisure centre); Hallé Orchestra; 15th-c cathedral; Chetham's Hospital and Library, the oldest public library in England; Free Trade Hall (1843); Liverpool Road Station, the world's oldest surviving passenger station; football league teams, Manchester City (Blues), Manchester United (Reds).

Manchester, Greater pop (2001e) 2 482 400; area 1287 sq km/497 sq mi. Metropolitan county of NW England, UK, consisting of 10 boroughs (Bolton, Bury, Manchester, Oldham, Rochdale, Salford, Stockport, Tameside, Trafford, Wigan); metropolitan council abolished in 1986; county town, Manchester; Ship Canal, Old Trafford cricket ground.

Manchester School A group of economists, working from Manchester, England, in the early 19th-c, who advocated free trade and laissez-faire. The focus of their attention was the repeal of the Corn Laws: the *Anti-Corn Law League* was headed by Bright and Cobden.

Manchester Ship Canal An artificial waterway in the UK linking Manchester with the Mersey estuary. The canal, which is 57 km/35 mi long, was opened in 1894 and allowed the city to develop as a sea port.

Manchester United Football Club English Association football club, based in Manchester, UK. Founded in 1878, it turned professional in 1885. The team have been winners of the Premier League seven times (1993–4, 1996–7, 1999–2000, 2001) and FA Cup winners 10 times (1909, 1948, 1963, 1977, 1983, 1985, 1990, 1994, 1999). They were European Champions in 1968 and winners of the European Cup Winners' Cup in 1991. In the 1998–9 season, they became the first British club to win the Premier League Championship, the FA Cup, and the European Cup.

Manching A massive hillfort of the Middle La Tène period (2nd–1st-c BC) near Ingolstadt, Bavaria, S Germany. The native capital of the Vindelici and one of Europe's earliest towns, it was a major trading centre, manufacturing iron, glass, pottery, leather, and textiles, and minting coins.

Manchukuo or **Manzhouguo** [manchookwoh] A Japanese puppet-state established in 1932 in Manchuria, which Japanese forces had invaded in 1931. Puyi, the last Qing emperor, was its nominal head. The regime ended with the defeat of Japan in 1945.

Manchuria A region of NE China, including the provinces of Heilongjiang, Jilin, and Liaoning; mountainous area, sparsely populated by nomadic tribes; Chinese protectorate, 7th-c; Manchus replaced Ming dynasty to become the last Chinese emperors (Qing dynasty, 1644–1912); vast natural resources of timber and minerals (coal, iron, magnesite, oil, uranium, gold); Russian military control, 1900; captured by Japan, 1931, and became part of puppet state of Manchukuo; Russian control re-asserted, 1945; Chinese sovereignty recognized, 1950, but border area with Russia a continuing focus of political tension.

Manchus A nomadic people of Jürchen stock in Manchuria (an area that included present-day Liaoning, Jilin, and Heilongjiang) who ruled all China from 1644 to 1912 under the Qing dynasty. The ruler Hong Taiji adopted the term *Manchu* (Chin *Manzhou*), probably a Buddhist term, for his people in 1635. There are now about 2·5 million Manchu people in China.

Mancini, Henry [manseenee], popular name of **Enrico Mancini** (1924–94) Composer, born in Cleveland, Ohio, USA. His studies at the Juilliard School of Music, New York City, were interrupted by World War 2, but while in service he met Glenn Miller, later joining his band as an arranger and pianist. His Oscar-winning compositions include the songs 'Moon River' (1961) and 'Days of Wine and Roses' (1962), and the film scores for *Breakfast at Tiffany's* (1961) and *Victor/Victoria* (1982). Other hits include theme tunes for the *Pink Panther* film and the *Peter Gunn* television series. During his career he composed more than 80 film scores and won 20 Grammy Awards.

Mandaeans [mandeeanz] A small Gnostic sect in Iran and Iraq who believe that the spiritual soul will be freed from its imprisonment in the evil material world by the redeemer, Manda d'Hayye ('the knowledge of life').

mandala [mandala] Circular, complex geometric designs in Hindu and Buddhist religious art, representing the universe or other aspects of their beliefs. They are used as a focus and aid to concentration in worship and meditation.

Mandalay [mandalay] 21°57N 96°04E, pop (2000e) 731 200. River-port capital of Mandalay division, C Myanmar; on R Ayeyarwady (Irrawaddy), N of Rangoon; airfield; railway; university (1964); commercial centre, tourism; Kuthodaw Pagoda contains 729 marble slabs on which are inscribed the entire Buddhist Canon; Shwenandaw Kyaung monastery; old city of

Pagan to the W, founded AD 109, contains largest concentration of pagodas and temples in Myanmar (mainly 11th–13th-c).

Mandarin *Chinese*

mandarin A citrus fruit (*Citrus reticulata*) with yellow to deep orange-red fruits, very like small oranges but with thin, loose rind. Its species include satsumas and tangerines. (Family: Rutaceae.)

mandarin duck A perching duck native to E Asia (*Aix galericulata*), and introduced in N Europe; male multicoloured with shaggy head and sail-like feathers on wings; inhabits fresh water among trees; eats seeds, small fish, and insects; nests in hole in tree; also known as **mandarin**.

mandates A system under which former territories of the German and Ottoman Empires were to be administered by the victorious powers of World War 1 under international supervision. The mandates were granted by the League of Nations, and annual reports had to be submitted to its Permanent Mandates Commission. Britain and France acquired mandates in the Middle East (Palestine, Iraq, Transjordan, Syria, Lebanon) and Africa (Tanganyika, Togo, Cameroon) while Belgium acquired Rwanda-Urundi, South Africa acquired South-West Africa, and Australia and New Zealand acquired New Guinea and Western Samoa. The functions of the Commission were later taken over by the Trusteeship Council of the United Nations.

Mande [manday] A cluster of Mande-speaking agricultural peoples of W Sudan, Sierra Leone, Liberia, and Côte d'Ivoire. They founded the mediaeval empires of Ghana and Mali, and were also important traders. They include the Bambara (well-known for their art), Dyula (Islamic converts who dominated the African end of the Sahara trade), Malinke, Mende, and Soninke.

Mandela, Nelson (Rolihlahla) [mandela] (1918–) South African statesman and president (1994–99), born in Transkei, SE South Africa. He was a lawyer in Johannesburg, then joined the African National Congress in 1944. For the next 20 years he directed a campaign of defiance against the South African government and its racist policies, orchestrating in 1961 a three-day national strike. In 1964 he was sentenced to life imprisonment for political offences. He continued to be such a potent symbol of black resistance that the 1980s saw a co-ordinated international campaign for his release. His first wife, Winnie, was also frequently subjected to restrictions on her personal freedom. He was released from prison in 1990, after President F W de Klerk had unbanned the ANC, removed restrictions on political groups, and suspended executions. Mandela immediately urged foreign powers not to reduce their pressure on the South African government for constitutional reform. He was elected president of the African National Congress in 1991, stepping down in 1997. He and Winnie separated in 1992 and he married Graça Machel in 1998. In 1993 he shared the Nobel Prize for Peace with de Klerk for their work towards dismantling apartheid, and in 1995 was awarded the Order of Merit. He retired from active politics at the 1999 general election.

Mandela, Winnie [mandela], also **Madikizela-Mandela**, popular name of **Nomzano Zaniewe Winifred Mandela** (1934–) Former wife of Nelson Mandela, born in Bizana, E South Africa. After qualifying as a social worker, she married Mandela in 1958. Her first arrest took place three months later, and in 1962 she was banned for the first time. For the next 20 years she was banned, restricted, detained, and jailed a number of times. In 1990, when her husband was released from prison, she took an increasingly prominent role in the African National Congress (ANC), until her conviction on charges of kidnapping and assault. In 1992, the Mandelas divorced. She continued to operate as a militant and maverick figure under ANC colours, making a political comeback in late 1993, and given a role in the 1994 government as deputy minister for arts, culture, science, and technology (dismissed in 1995). A controversial and charismatic figure, she figured prominently in the proceedings of the Truth and Reconciliation Commission in 1997. In 2003 she was convicted for fraudulently obtaining bank loans from the ANC Women's League, of which she was president, and sentenced to four years in jail.

Mandelbrot, Benoit (1924–) Mathematician, born in Warsaw, Poland. He studied at the Ecole Polytechnique, Paris, and at the California Institute of Technology, then became professor of mathematics at Geneva (1955–7) and the Ecole Polytechnique (1957–8). He joined IBM in 1958, and became professor of mathematics at Yale in 1987. A central figure in the development of fractals, his book *The Fractal Geometry of Nature* (1982) was important in demonstrating the potential application of fractals to natural phenomena. His name is applied to a particular set of complex numbers which generate one type of fractal (the **Mandelbrot set**), whose visually attractive properties have captured public interest since the 1980s.

Mandelson, Peter [mandelson] (1954–) Politician, born in London, UK, the grandson of Herbert Morrison. He studied at Oxford, became a television producer for *Weekend World* (1982–5), and was then appointed Labour Party Director for Campaigns and Communications (1985–90). Elected as MP for Hartlepool in 1992, he became a Labour whip, and in 1996 worked exclusively on the Labour Party election campaign. After Labour's landslide victory in 1997 he became a minister without portfolio – an influential member of the cabinet, responsible for assisting the prime minister in policy matters. He was appointed president of the Board of Trade and secretary of state for trade and industry in 1998. He resigned from the government in 1998 following his failure to declare, in the Member's Register of Interests, a private mortgage loan from his cabinet colleague, Geoffrey Robinson (paymaster general). After 10 months without office, he was appointed Northern Ireland Secretary, playing a significant part in negotiations that led to the establishment of the Northern Ireland Assembly. He resigned from the cabinet in 2001.

Mandelstam, Osip Emilevich [manduhlstam] (1891–1938) Poet, born in Warsaw, Poland. He was a leader of the Acmeist movement. His early success with *Kamen* (1913, Stone), *Tristia* (1922, Sad Things), and *Stikhotvorenia 1921–25* (1928, Poems) was followed by suspicion and exile (1934) by the Soviet authorities. He continued to write poetry, committed to memory by his wife **Nadezhda** (1899–1980) and published abroad more than 20 years after his death as *Sobranie sochineny* (Collected Works) in three volumes (1964–71). His wife wrote their story in *Hope Against Hope* (1970) and *Hope Abandoned* (1974).

Mandeville, Jehan de or **Sir John** [mandevil] (14th-c) The name assigned to the compiler of a famous and fanciful book of travels (*The Voyage and Travels of Sir John Mandeville, Knight*), published apparently in 1366, and soon translated from the French into all European tongues. It may have been written by a physician, **Jehan de Bourgogne**, otherwise **Jehan à la Barbe**, who died in Liège in 1372, and who is said to have revealed on his death-bed his real name of Mandeville (or Maundevylle), explaining that he had had to flee from his native England for a homicide. Some scholars, however, attribute it to **Jean d'Outremeuse**, a Frenchman.

Mandingo *Malinke*

mandolin A plucked string instrument, about 60 cm/2 ft long, developed in the 18th-c from the earlier mandora and mandola. It has a pear-shaped body somewhat like a lute's, a fretted fingerboard, and a pegbox set back at an angle. There are four pairs of steel strings, tuned like a violin's and played with a plectrum.

mandrake A thick-rooted perennial (*Mandragora officinalis*) native to Europe; leaves in a rosette; flowers blue; berries yellow to orange. Once widely regarded for its medicinal and narcotic properties, it has been the subject of many superstitions, such as the claim that it screams when uprooted. (Family: Solanaceae.)

mandrill A baboon (*Mandrillus sphinx*) native to W African forests; stocky with short limbs and thick coat; tail minute; buttocks red-blue; naked face with scarlet muzzle and bright blue, ridged cheeks (especially in male); lives on ground in small family groups.

maned jackal *aardwolf*

maned sheep *aoudad*

Manes [mayneez, mahneez] In Roman religion, 'the dead'. The concept developed from (1) the spirits of the dead in general, to (2) the gods of the Underworld, **Di Manes**, (3) the ancestors of the family, and (4) the spirits of individuals in grave-stone inscriptions.

Manet, Edouard [manay] (1832–83) Painter, born in Paris, France. Intended for a legal career, he became an artist, and exhibited at the Salon in 1861. His 'Dejeuner sur l'herbe' (1863, Luncheon on the Grass), which scandalized the traditional Classicists, was rejected, and although the equally provocative 'Olympia' was accepted in 1865, the Salon remained hostile, and Manet's genius was not recognized until after his death. He exhibited in the *Salon des Refusés*, and helped to form the group out of which the Impressionist movement arose.

mangabey [manggabee] An Old World monkey, native to tropical Africa; slender with long tail, long coat; pronounced whiskers on sides of face; inhabits forests; some species spend time on the ground. (Genus: *Cercocebus*, 4 species.)

manganese Mn, element 25, melting point 1244°C. A transition metal, density about 7·4 g/cm^3, always found combined in nature, but mainly as the dioxide, MnO_2. The metal is produced by heating this to give Mn_3O_4, and then reducing with aluminium. The metal, which has three irregular structures not found for any other metal, is mainly used in alloy steels. It forms a wide range of compounds, commonly showing oxidation states +2, +3, +4, +6, and +7. The last is found in *permanganates*, which contain the ion MnO_4. Potassium permanganate is a convenient and strong oxidizing agent in aqueous solution.

manganese nodules Nodule-shaped masses of metal oxides a few centimetres across, which form at the sea floor. They were first discovered by the HMS *Challenger* expedition in 1873, and have now been found to occur widely in all the major ocean basins except the Arctic. They are also known as *ferromanganese* or *polymetallic* nodules because of their mixture of metal oxides. Though primarily iron- and manganese-rich, some nodules contain copper, nickel, cobalt, titanium and other economically valuable metals. Interest in the commercial exploitation of nodules helped both spark and stall the Law of the Sea treaty.

Mangbetu [mangbetoo] A cluster of C Sudanic-speaking peoples in NE Democratic Republic of Congo. In the 19th-c they were a powerful kingdom ruled by an aristocracy to which alone the name Mangbetu was given. They are renowned for their craftwork, especially in wood and iron. Population c.1 million.

mange [maynzh] A contagious skin disease of domestic animals. It results from infestation with several types of mites which burrow into the skin, causing itching and irritation.

mangel-wurzel *beet*

mangetout [mãzh **too**] *pea*

mango An evergreen tree (*Mangifera indica*) growing to 18 m/60 ft, native to SE Asia; leaves roughly oblong; flowers tiny, white, with 4–5 petals; fleshy fruit 7–10 cm/2¾–4 in, oval to kidney-shaped, yellow flushed with red. It is grown for the sweet-tasting, edible fruit. (Family: Anacardiaceae.)

mangosteen A small evergreen tree native to Malaysia (*Garcinia mangostana*); leaves up to 20 cm/8 in, oval to elliptical; flowers red, 4-petalled; fruit round, with thick purplish rind and sweet, white, edible flesh. (Family: Guttifereae.)

mangrove Any of several unrelated tropical or subtropical trees, all sharing similar structure and biology, growing on coastal and estuarine mud-flats. All possess either aerial roots or *pneumatophores*, special breathing roots which help aerate the root system in swampy ground. The seeds germinate while still on the parent tree, allowing them to become quickly established when shed in the shifting tidal environment. Mangroves often cover extensive tracts, forming a distinctive vegetation type. (Main genera: *Rhizophora*, 7 species, and *Brugeria*, 6 species. Family: Rhizophoraceae; and *Avicennia*, 14 species. Family: Avicenniaceae.)

mangrove snake Any snake usually found in the trees of mangrove swamps. The name is used especially for several SE Asian snakes of the family Colubridae: the **mangrove tree snake** (*Boiga dendrophila*), the **white-bellied mangrove snake** (*Fordonia leucobalia*), and **Gray's mangrove snake** (*Myron richardsonii*).

Manhattan pop (2000e) 1 537 200; area 72 sq km/28 sq mi. An island forming one of the five boroughs of the City of New York, New York State, E USA; at the N end of New York Bay, bounded W by the Hudson R; co-extensive with New York Co; settled by the Dutch as part of New Netherlands in 1626, bought from local Indians for trinkets and cloth worth c.$24; taken by the British in 1664; major financial and commercial centre based around Wall Street and the World Trade Center, the scene of a terrorist attack on 11 Sep 2001; headquarters of the United Nations; Broadway, Empire State Building, Greenwich Village; six universities – Columbia (1754), New York (1831), City University of New York (1847), Yeshiva (1886), Rockefeller (1901), Pace (1906), and a satellite campus of Fordham at the Lincoln Center; named after a local tribe of Indians.

Manhattan project The codename for the most secret scientific operation of World War 2, the development of the atomic bomb, undertaken successfully in the USA from 1942 onwards. The project culminated in the detonation of the first atomic weapon at Alamogordo, New Mexico (16 Jul 1945).

manic depressive psychosis A severe illness with repeated episodes of depressed and/or elevated mood; also called **bipolar disorder**. There is often the loss of normal social inhibitions, irritability, hyperactivity, elation, accelerated thought and speech, delusions, and occasionally hallucinations in the manic episodes. In the depressive phase there is loss of energy, feelings of worthlessness, and altered physiological functioning, such as disturbed sleep.

Manichaeism [manikeeizm] or **Manichaeanism** A religious sect founded by the prophet Manes (or Mani) (c.216–76), who began teaching in Persia in 240. His teaching was based on a primaeval conflict between the realms of light and darkness, in which the material world represents an invasion of the realm of light by the powers of darkness. The purpose of religion is to release the particles of light imprisoned in matter, and Buddha, the Prophets, Jesus, and finally Manes have been sent to help in this task. Release involved adherence to a strict ascetic regimen. The Zoroastrians condemned the sect and executed Manes, but it spread rapidly in the West, surviving until the 10th-c. It also spread rapidly in Tang China after its introduction by Persians in 694, especially after its adoption as the official religion of the Uighur Turks in Mongolia and N China in 763. It was banned in China from 843, though some influence remained in astronomy and the calendar, in both China and Japan.

Manila [manila] 14°36N 120°59E, pop (2000e) 1 961 000. Capital of the Philippines, on R Pasig, Manila Bay, SW Luzon I; founded, 1571; important trade centre under the Spanish; occupied by the British 1762–3; taken by the USA during the Spanish-American War, 1898; badly damaged in World War 2; airport; railway; several universities (earliest, 1611); shipbuilding, chemicals, textiles, timber, food processing.

Manila hemp *abaca*

manioc *cassava*

Manipur [manipoor] pop (2001e) 2 388 600; area 22 356 sq km/8629 sq mi. State in NE India; British rule in 1891; administered from the state of Assam until 1947, when it became a union territory; became a state in 1972; capital, Imphal; governed by a 60-member Legislative Assembly; weaving, sugar, cement; wheat, maize, pulses, fruit, bamboo, teak; problems of soil erosion being reduced by terracing of valley slopes.

Manipuri A form of Indian classical dance from the hill region of NE India. It has two strands: a ritualistic form, dedicated to the god Shiva and incorporating stories of immortal lovers, and social forms performed at major festivals, such as the New Year (in mid-April). Unusually, in Indian dance, the face is not used for expressive purposes.

Manitoba [manitohba] pop (2000e) 1 223 000; area 649 950 sq km/250 945 sq mi. Province in W Canada; boundaries include Hudson Bay (NE) and USA (S); known as the 'land of 100 000 lakes', the result of glaciation, notably Lakes Winnipeg, Winnipegosis, Manitoba; drained by several rivers flowing into L Winnipeg or Hudson Bay; land gradually rises in W and S to 832 m/2730 ft at Mt Baldy; capital, Winnipeg; major town, Brandon; cereals (especially wheat), livestock, vegetables, fishing, timber, hydroelectric power, food processing, mining (oil, gold, nickel, silver, copper, zinc), machinery, tourism; aboriginal population includes Cree, Ojibwa, Assiniboine, and Chippewyan; trading rights given to Hudson's Bay Co, 1670; several forts established because of English–French conflict, including Fort Rouge, 1738 (site of Winnipeg); French claims in the N ceded to the British under the Treaty of Utrecht (1713) and, in the S, the Treaty of Paris (1763); settlement on the Red R from 1812, with many Scottish and Irish settlers; purchased from Hudson's Bay Company by Canada in 1869, provoking insurrection under Riel; joined confederation in 1870; boundaries extended, 1881 and 1912; major development of area after railway reached Winnipeg in the 1880s; governed by a lieutenant-governor and an elected 57-member Legislative Assembly.

manitou [manitoo] A term used by the Algonkin Indians of the E Woodlands of North America to designate the supernatural world and to identify any manifestation of it, such as spirits encountered in visions, or certain powers of nature. Human beings and animals may also exhibit the 'spirit' of manitou.

Manizales [manisalays] 5°03N 75°32W, pop (2000e) 325 200. Capital of Caldas department, C Colombia; in Cordillera Central at 2153 m/7064 ft; founded, 1848; airfield; university (1950); centre of coffee area; textiles, leather, chemicals; experimental coffee plantation and freeze-dried coffee plant at Chinchiná; Teatro de los Fundadores; cathedral (unfinished); skiing and mountain climbing at Nevado del Ruiz; coffee festival (Jan).

Mankowitz, (Cyril) Wolf [mangkohvits] (1924–98) Writer, playwright, and antique dealer, born in London, UK. He studied at Cambridge. His publications in the art domain include a study of Josiah Wedgwood, and *The Concise Encyclopedia of English Pottery and Porcelain* (1957). His fiction includes the novel *A Kid for Two Farthings* (1953), the play *The Bespoke Overcoat* (1954), the films *The Millionairess* (1960), *The Long, the Short, and the Tall* (1961), and *Casino Royale* (1967), and the musicals *Expresso Bongo* (1958–9), *Pickwick* (1963), and *Stand and Deliver!* (1972). Later works include the novels *Gioconda* (1987) and *A Night with Casanova* (1991).

Mann, Thomas (1875–1955) Novelist, born in Lübeck, N Germany. He left school at 19, and spent some time at Munich University before becoming a writer, like his brother Heinrich. His early masterpiece, *Buddenbrooks* (1901), traced the decline of a family over four generations. He produced several short stories and novellas, such as *Der Tod in Venedig* (1913, Death in Venice; filmed, 1971; opera by Britten, 1971–3), and then wrote *Der Zauberberg* (1924, The Magic Mountain). He was awarded the Nobel Prize for Literature in 1929. He left Germany for Switzerland in 1933, was deprived of his German citizenship, and settled in the USA in 1936. He returned to Switzerland in 1947, and produced his greatest work, a modern version of the mediaeval legend, *Doktor Faustus* (1947).

manna The name of several edible plant products, some of which have been proposed as the biblical food dropped from heaven during the Israelites' flight from Egypt. Lichen (*Lecanora esculenta*) from Asia Minor, the source of lichen bread and manna jelly, curls into balls when dry and blows in the wind. Stems of tamarisk (*Tamarisk mannifera*) produce a honey-like substance in response to scale insect attack.

manna ash A species of ash (*Fraxinus ornus*), native to the Mediterranean, and often planted in streets and parks, displaying large clusters of fragrant flowers with creamy-white petals. The dried sap is rich in the sugar-alcohol mannitol, and forms the manna of commerce. (Family: Oleaceae.)

Mannerheim, Carl Gustav (Emil), Vapaaherra (Baron) **[manerhiym]** (1867–1951) Finnish soldier, statesman, and president (1944–6), born in Villnäs, SW Finland. Trained as an officer in the Tsarist army, he rose to the rank of general and, defeating the Finnish Bolsheviks (1918), he expelled the Russian forces from Finland. When Finland declared independence (1918), he became supreme commander and regent. Defeated in the presidential election of 1919, he was appointed chief of the National Defence Council (1930–9) and planned the *Mannerheim Line*, a fortified line of defence across the Karelian Isthmus to block any potential aggression by the Soviet Union. When Soviet forces attacked (1939), he was appointed commander-in-chief in the Winter War of 1939–40. He continued to command the Finnish forces in alliance with Germany until 1944, when he became president of the Finnish Republic. In March 1939 he brought Finland into the war against Germany.

Mannerism A form of art and architecture prevalent in France, Spain, and especially Italy during the 16th-c, characterized by overcrowded detail, and an irrational manipulation of classical elements, for playful or startling effect. Vasari (1550) used the word *maniera* for a type of refined and artificial beauty, as seen in such works as Raphael's 'St Cecilia' and Michelangelo's 'Victory'. In art, leading Mannerists included Giulio Romano, Pontormo, and Parmigiano, whose pictures are painted with jewel-like colours, and sculptors such as Cellini. In architecture, the style is typified by the Laurentian Library vestibule, Florence (1526), architect Michelangelo.

Mannheim [manhiym] 49°30N 8°28E, pop (2000e) 320 000. Commercial and manufacturing river port in Karlsruhe district, SWC Germany; on right bank of R Rhine, at the outflow of the canalized R Neckar, 70 km/43 mi SW of Frankfurt; one of the largest inland harbours in Europe; seat of the Electors Palatine (18th-c), when it became a cultural centre; badly bombed in World War 2; railway; university (1907); machinery, vehicles (Daimler-Benz), electrical engineering, oil refining, chemicals, pharmaceuticals, plastics, sugar refining, cables, tourism; castle, town hall, National Theatre, Reiss Museum; folk festival (May).

mannikin A small seed-eating bird, native to Africa S of the Sahara, India, and SE Asia; inhabits forest, open country, and cultivation. (Genus: *Lonchura*, 23 species. Family: Estrildidae.)

Manning, Henry Edward, Cardinal (1808–92) Roman Catholic clergyman, born in Totteridge, Hertfordshire, SE England, UK. He studied at Oxford, became a priest in the Church of England (1833), converted to Catholicism in 1851, and in 1865 was appointed Archbishop of Westminster. At the Council of 1870, he was a zealous supporter of the infallibility dogma. Appointed cardinal in 1875, he continued as a leader of the Ultramontanes.

manometer A device for measuring pressure exerted by or within a fluid (gas or liquid). It usually refers to various U-tube methods, pressure being shown by the difference in the height of the fluid (such as mercury) in the two arms of a U-tube, one arm being connected to the fluid whose pressure is being measured. The term is also sometimes used for other types of pressure gauge, in which pressure is exerted on a surface linked mechanically or electrically with an indicator or recorder.

manorial system or **seignorial system** A basic feature of European society from the 11th-c to the 15th-c, which poses many problems of definition. The 'typical' manor used to be regarded as an agricultural estate coincident with the village, and comprising the lord's estate (demesne) or home farm, attached villein tenements providing labour services on the demesne, and free tenements owing rents. In reality, there was a pronounced lack of uniformity. Manors, which might be concentrated or dispersed, frequently cut across villages; some consisted solely or largely of demesne; others contained only peasant tenements; and labour dues, often commuted for money by the 13th-c, varied widely in their onerousness. Typically, the demesne was divided into arable, meadow (the commons), woodland, and waste. The arable was held by the peasants, usually with holdings in strips; the meadow was generally held in common. Small local industry was also a function of the manorial system, and dues owed to the estate included such items as cloth, building materials, and ironware. The lord or his agent presided over the manorial courts, which were the centre of the administration of justice. The manor was also the unit for the raising of taxes and for public improvements. The manorial system declined with the spread of trade, the wide development of towns and capitalistic commerce, and, in England, the enclosure of estates.

Mansard or **Mansart, François** [mãsah(r)] (1598–1666) Architect, born in Paris, France. He brought a simplified adaptation of the Baroque style into use in France. His first major work, the N wing of the Château de Blois, featured the double-angled high-pitched roof which now bears his name. His churches include Sainte-Marie de Chaillot, Sainte-Marie de la Visitation, and Val-de-Grâce, and he built or remodelled several notable buildings in Paris and elsewhere.

Mansell, Nigel [mansl] (1954–) Motor-racing driver, born in Birmingham, West Midlands, C England, UK. He entered Formula 1 racing in 1980. From 176 Grand Prix starts, he won 29 races from 26 pole positions. In 1992 he retired from Formula 1 racing after winning the driver's championship with eight wins. He joined the Haas-Newman Indy car racing team in the USA, becoming Indy car champion in 1993, his first year, briefly returned to Formula 1 in 1995, driving for McLaren, then retired.

Mansfield, Katherine, pseudonym of **Kathleen Mansfield Murry**, *née* **Beauchamp** (1888–1923) Short-story writer, born in Wellington, New Zealand. She studied at Queen's College, London, then took up music for two years in New Zealand before returning to London to pursue a literary career. In 1918, after some traumatic early experiences that marked her work, she married the writer John Middleton Murry. Her first major work was *Prelude* (1917), a long, delicate evocation of the New Zealand of her childhood. *Bliss, and Other Stories* (1920), containing the classic stories 'Je ne parle pas français' and 'Prelude', confirmed her standing as an original and innovative writer, influenced by Chekhov. The only other collection published before her premature death from tuberculosis was *The Garden Party, and Other Stories* (1922). Posthumous works include *Poems* (1923), *Something Childish, and Other Stories* (1924), and her revealing *Journal* (1927) and *Letters* (1928).

Mansfield, Sir Peter (1933–) Physicist, born in London, England, UK. He left school at 15 to work in a printing shop and later joined the army. He studied for his A levels at night-school and entered Queen Mary College, University of London, gaining his PhD in 1962. After various academic posts he became professor of physics at Nottingham University (1979). In 2003 he shared the Nobel Prize for Physiology or Medicine for discoveries concerning magnetic resonance imaging (MRI). He was knighted in 1993.

manslaughter An English legal term for a form of unlawful homicide which does not amount to murder, covering a wide spectrum of culpability, including behaving recklessly or negligently but without an intention to kill; known as *culpable homicide* in Scottish law. Mitigating factors, such as provocation, diminished responsibility, or a suicide pact may reduce an offence from murder to manslaughter (often called **voluntary manslaughter** in the USA). Grossly negligent behaviour or omission, in certain circumstances, which results in unintended death may also constitute the offence (often called **involuntary manslaughter** in the USA). There is a separate statutory offence of causing death by reckless driving; this is often called *vehicular homicide* in the USA, and requires a lesser degree of negligence than involuntary manslaughter. In England and Wales, the Crime (Sentences) Act (1997) provides for compulsory life sentence for those convicted of manslaughter for a second time.

Manson, Charles (1934–) Cult leader, born in Cincinnati, Ohio, USA. Released from prison in 1967, he set up a commune based on free love and devotion to himself. Members of his cult conducted a series of grisly murders in California in 1969, including that of actress **Sharon Tate** (1943–69). He and his accomplices were sentenced to death, but were spared the death penalty due to a Supreme Court ruling against capital punishment.

manta ray Largest of the devil rays, exceeding 6 m/20 ft in width and 1300 kg/2800 lb in weight; mouth broad, situated across front of head; feeds on plankton and small fish filtered from water passing over gill arches. (Genus: *Manta*. Family: Mobulidae.)

Mantegna, Andrea [mantenya] (c.1431–1506) Painter, born in Vicenza, NE Italy. He was apprenticed to the tailor-painter Francesco Squarcione in Padua, and seems to have been adopted by him. In 1459 he was persuaded by Ludovico Gonzaga, Duke of Mantua, to work for him. His most important works were nine tempera pictures of 'The Triumph of Caesar' (1482–92), which were acquired by Charles I and are now at Hampton Court, and his decoration of the ceiling of the Camera degli Sposi in Mantua.

Mantel, Hilary (Mary) (1952–) Novelist, born in Hadfield, Derbyshire, N Engand, UK. Early novels – *Every Day is Mother's Day* (1985) and *Vacant Possession* (1986) – reflected her experience in social work. Later she lived in Saudi Arabia, which became the setting for a thriller, *Eight Months on Ghazzah Street* (1988). In 1987 she won the first Shiva Naipaul Prize. Her novel *Fludd* (1989) was followed by *A Place of Greater Safety* (1992), *A Change of Climate* (1994), and *An Experiment in Love* (1995). *The Giant, O'Brien* (1999), a thought-provoking narrative set in the 18th-c, won her much critical acclaim.

mantis A medium to large insect that has a well-camouflaged body and a mobile head with large eyes; waits motionless for insect prey to approach before striking out with its grasping, spiny forelegs; c.1800 species, in some of which the female eats the male head-first during copulation. (Order: Mantodea.)

mantis shrimp A shrimp-like crustacean, found in abundance in shallow tropical seas; c.350 species, all fierce, grasping predators, typically inhabiting burrows or crevices from where they emerge to spear or smash prey with their powerful claws (Class: Malacostraca. Order: Stomatopoda.)

Mantle, Mickey (Charles) (1931–95) Baseball player, born in Spavinaw, Oklahoma, USA. A great centrefielder, baserunner, and hitter, he was a member of the renowned New York Yankees team of the 1950s and 1960s. He once hit a home run measured at a record 177 m/565 ft. The American League's Most Valuable Player in 1956, he won a rare Triple Crown in batting, home runs, and runs batted in. He was elected to the Baseball Hall of Fame in 1974.

Mantoux test [mantoo] Intradermal injection of an extract prepared from tuberculosis bacilli. The skin reaction measures the immune response to tuberculosis. When positive, the patient is known to suffer from or to have suffered from tuberculosis, or to have been vaccinated. It is named after French physician Charles Mantoux (1877–1947).

mantra [mantruh] The prescribed words or word of power used in Hindu ritual, which depend on correct recitation for its efficacy; also, the belief that the repetition of a special phrase or word in meditation and devotion helps to concentrate the mind and aids in the development of spiritual power. A disciple of a spiritual leader may be given an individual mantra as an initiation.

Mantua [mantyua], Ital **Mantova** 45°10N 10°47E, pop (2000e) 61 000. Capital town of Mantua province, Lombardy, N Italy, on R Mincio; founded in Etruscan times; railway; sugar refining, brewing, tanning, printing, tourism; birthplace of Virgil nearby; ringed by ancient walls and bastions; Church of Sant'Andrea (1472–94), cathedral (10th–18th-c), Palazzo Ducale (16th-c), Castello San Giorgio (1395–1406); Fiera Di Sant' Anselmo (Mar).

Manu [manoo] In Hindu mythology, the forefather of the human race, to whom the Manu Smirti ('Lawbook of Manu') is attributed.

Manú [manoo] area 15 328 sq km/5917 sq mi. Largest national park in SE Peru; a world heritage site; established in 1973.

Manuel I *Emanuel I*

manure Organic material which is used to fertilize land. It usually consists of livestock excrement, generally mixed with straw or other litter used in the animals' housing. The generic term for dung mixed with straw is **farmyard manure** (FYM); animals housed in systems requiring little or no straw (commonly intensive systems) produce *slurry*, which is excrement plus water. Another type of manure derives from seaweed/kelp harvested from the sea or seashore. *Composts* can be made from any organic material, processed under controlled conditions to form new organic compounds. Other manures include sewage sludge and domestic sewage sludge, the latter often containing high levels of potentially toxic elements, notably zinc.

Manuzio, Aldo *Aldus Manutius*

Manx cat A breed of domestic cat, native to the Isle of Man; a British short-haired type; thick double-layered coat; no tail (but this does not always breed true, as some kittens may have tails or stumps of tails); also known as a **rumpy**.

many body theory In physics, a general term describing attempts to explain the properties of systems of a number of interacting particles or objects, irrespective of the type of particles and the form of interaction between them. Nucleons moving in the nucleus, electrons around the atom, and planets around the Sun are examples where many-body approximation techniques can be used. In 1994 mathematician Zhihong Xia showed that the classic three-body problem, in which three objects interact via Newtonian gravitational forces, has no simple mathematical solution: it is 'non-integrable'.

Manyoshu [manyohshoo] Anthology of 4516 Japanese poems, compiled some time after AD 760. The poems, mainly in the 31-syllable, 5-line *tanka* genre, were written in Chinese characters.

many worlds interpretation In physics, a proposal that, when a measurement is performed on a quantum system, all possible outcomes of the measurement actually occur; made by US physicist Hugh Everett in 1957. This contrasts with the conventional view, that only one state of many possible states is observed. The many-worlds view leads to the conclusion that the universe is constantly dividing to give vast numbers of alternative universes which co-exist but do not interact with one another, and that we live in a single one of these many universes. The theory does resolve difficulties in the quantum theory of measurement, but in a philosophically dubious manner.

Manzoni, Alessandro [mantsohnee] (1785–1873) Novelist and poet, born in Milan, N Italy. He published his first poems in 1806, and spent the next few years writing sacred lyrics and a treatise on the religious basis of morality. The work which gave him European fame is his historical novel, *I promessi sposi* (1825–7, The Betrothed), one of the most notable works of fiction in Italian literature. He was a strong advocate of a united Italy, and became a senator of the kingdom in 1860. When he died he was given a state funeral. Verdi composed his *Requiem* in Manzoni's honour.

Maoism Specifically, the thought of Mao Zedong (Tse-tung), and more broadly a revolutionary ideology based on Marxism–Leninism adapted to Chinese conditions. Maoism shifted the focus of revolutionary struggle from the urban workers or proletariat to the countryside and the peasantry. There were three main elements: strict Leninist principles of organization, Chinese tradition, and armed struggle as a form of revolutionary activity. Mao gained political power in 1949 through a peasant army, his slogan being 'Political power grows through the barrel of a gun'. While there were attempts to take account of the views of the masses, the Chinese Communist Party was organized along strict centralist, hierarchical lines, and increasingly became a vehicle for a personal dictatorship. In domestic terms Mao pursued a radical and far-reaching attempt to transform traditional Chinese society and its economy, using thought reform, indoctrination, and the psychological transformation of the masses. Maoism was regarded in the 1960s at the height of the Cultural Revolution as a highly radical form of Marxism–Leninism that was distinct from the bureaucratic repression of the Soviet Union, and had a strong appeal among the New Left. Since his death, Mao's use of the masses for political purposes, his economic reforms, and his conception of political power have been increasingly criticized inside and outside China as seriously misguided and too rigid.

Maori [mowree] Polynesian people who were the original inhabitants of New Zealand. The first of them arrived, probably from the Marquesas Is, about AD 800, bringing with them dogs and rats, and some cultivated plants, including the kumara (sweet potato). They also ate fern roots, fish, and birds, including the large flightless moa, which they hunted to extinction. By 1200 they had explored the whole country, and by 1800 numbered over 100 000. They were skilful carvers of wood and greenstone (jade). Politically they were divided into loose tribes linked by trade and sporadic warfare, and ruled by hereditary chiefs. In the 19th-c they came to be outnumbered and dominated by European (*pakeha*) settlers. Their culture declined; they lost most of their land; and by 1896 their population had shrunk to 42 200. There was some improvement in the 20th-c. Numbers rose (523 000 in the 1996 census), and after the 1970s they became politically more assertive, with a number of seats in parliament. The Maori language has been officially encouraged, and they have obtained the return of some of their land.

Mao Zedong [mow dzuhdoong], also spelled **Mao Tse-tung** (1893–1976) Leader and leading theorist of the Chinese communist revolution, born in the village of Shaoshan, Hunan Province, SEC China, the son of a farmer. He graduated from Changsha teachers' training college, then worked at Beijing University, where he was influenced by Chen Duxiu and Li Dazhao. He took a leading part in the May Fourth Movement (1919), becoming a Marxist and a founding member of the Chinese Communist Party (1921). During the first united front with the Guomindang (Nationalist Party), he concentrated on political work among the peasants of his native province, and advocated a rural revolution, creating a soviet in Jiangxi province in 1928. After the break with the Guomindang in 1927, the Communists were driven from the cities, and with the assistance first of Zhu De, later of Lin Biao, he evolved the guerrilla tactics of 'people's war'. In 1934 the Guomindang was at last able to destroy the Jiangxi Soviet, and in the subsequent Long March the Communist forces retreated to Shanxi to set up a new base. This established Mao's supremacy in the Party.

When in 1936, under the increasing threat of Japanese invasion, the Guomindang renewed their alliance with the Communists, Mao restored and vastly increased the political and military power of his Party. His claim to share in the government led to civil war; the regime of Jiang Jieshi was ousted from the Chinese mainland; and the new People's Republic of China was proclaimed (1949) with Mao as both Chairman of the Chinese Communist Party and President of the Republic. He followed the Soviet model of economic development and social change until 1958, then broke with the USSR and launched his Great Leap Forward, which encouraged the establishment of rural industry and the use of surplus rural labour to create a new infrastructure for agriculture. The failure of the Great Leap lost him most of his influence, but by 1966, with China's armed forces securely in the hands of his ally Lin Biao, he launched the Great Proletarian Cultural Revolution, and the Great Leap strategy was revived (with caution) when the left wing was victorious in the ensuing political struggles (1966–71). He died after a prolonged illness, which may have weakened his judgment. A strong reaction then set in against 'cult of personality' and the excessive collectivism and egalitarianism which had emerged during his time in power. A political, military, social, and economic essayist, he was also a significant minor poet.

map The graphic representation of spatial information about a place on a plane surface through the use of symbols and signs. Maps are generally produced for specific purposes (eg *cadastral* maps show land ownership; *topographical* maps show relief and terrain features; and *thematic* maps illustrate particular features, such as maps of population density). The earliest surviving maps are of estates of wealthy Babylonians (c.2500 BC) on clay tablets. The European traditions of map making date back to the Ancient Greeks.

maple A member of a large genus of deciduous trees, native to N temperate regions; leaves variable in shape but typically palmately lobed with 3–13 toothed lobes, sometimes pinnate; flowers in clusters, small, greenish, purple, or red; characteristic fruit of two winged seeds fused at base, eventually splitting apart, the wings acting as propellers. Many species produce striking autumn colours, especially reds and purples, and are planted for ornament. Maple syrup is obtained from the sap of the **sugar maple** (*Acer saccharum*). (Genus: *Acer*, 200 species. Family: Aceraceae.)

Mappa Mundi [mapa mundee] (Lat 'map of the world') A celebrated 13th-c map of the world, owned by Hereford Cathedral, Hereford, UK. The map is on vellum, measuring 163 × 137 cm/ 64 × 54 in, and shows the world as a round plate, with Jerusalem centrally located and Britain on its fringes. It comprises c.500 illustrations, and gives information on routes of pilgrimage, trade and travel, architecture, place names, history, mythology, flora, and fauna. In 1988 there was a public outcry over proposed plans to sell the map, to help raise funds for the Cathedral. The proposal was subsequently withdrawn, following assistance given by the National Heritage Memorial Fund.

Mapplethorpe, Robert (1946–89) Photographer, born in New York City, USA. He studied painting and sculpture at the Pratt Institute in New York, after which he concentrated on photography, mounting his first exhibition in 1976. A major retrospective of his often controversial work was presented by the Whitney Museum of American Art in 1988. He died of AIDS the following year.

map projection *see panel*

map projection

Mercator's projection

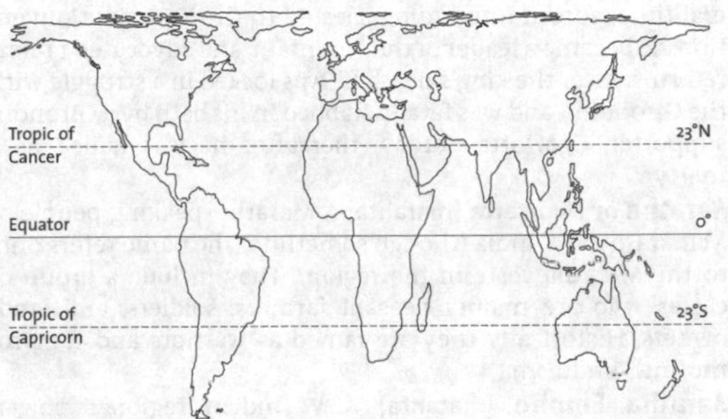

Peters' projection

The method of portraying the spherical surface of the Earth on a flat surface. Because a sphere is three-dimensional in form, and a map two-dimensional, there is inevitably some distortion: the representation of distance (true scale), direction (true bearing), area, and shape cannot be shown correctly together on the same map. Consequently different map projections have been developed, according to purpose, which show for example true distance, or true area. The greatest distortions occur when a large area, such as the whole of the Earth's surface, is being mapped. For the mapping of smaller areas, such as topographical maps, a compromise is made to minimize the distortion of all four properties.

Maputo [mapootoh], formerly **Lourenço Marques** (to 1976) 25°58S 32°32E, pop (2000e) 1 329 000. Seaport capital of Mozambique, on Maputo Bay, 485 km/300 mi E of Johannesburg; visited by the Portuguese, 1502; explored by the trader Lourenço Marques; capital of Portuguese East Africa, 1907; airport; railway; university (1962); steel, textiles, ship repair, footwear, cement, furniture; an outlet for several SE African countries.

maquette [maket] A small model made by a sculptor as a preliminary study or sketch for a full-size work. A maquette is usually in clay, wax, or plaster.

maquis *macchia*

Maquis [makee] The local name given to the dense scrub in Corsica; name adopted in German-occupied France by groups of young men who from 1942 hid in the hills and forests to escape forced labour in Germany. Supported by the French Communist Party, they were organized into resistance groups, but were not centrally controlled. They were active in the national rising against the Germans on and after D-Day.

marabou A large stork (*Leptoptilos crumeniferus*) native to Africa S of the Sahara (*Leptoptilos crumeniferus*); also known as the **marabou stork**; head and neck naked; inhabits dry regions; eats carrion and small animals; nests in trees. (Family: Ciconiidae.)

Maracaibo [marakiyboh] 10°44N 71°37W, pop (2000e) 1 460 400. Capital of Zulia state, NW Venezuela, on NW shore of L Maracaibo; second largest city in Venezuela; airport; two universities (1891, 1973); oil production and processing, petrochemicals.

Maracaibo, Lake [marakiyboh] (Span **Lago de**) area 13 000 sq km/5000 sq mi. Lake in NW Venezuela; length, c.210 km/ 130 mi; linked to the Gulf of Venezuela through narrows and the Tablazo Bay; contains one of the world's greatest oilfields, discovered in 1914; major pollution problem from oil spills; Maracaibo Lowlands noted for the highest annual average temperatures in Latin America.

maracas [muhrakuhs] A pair of rattles, originally gourds filled with dried seeds, used as a rhythm instrument in Latin-American and occasionally Western orchestral music.

Maradona, Diego [maradona] (1960–) Footballer, born in Lanus, Argentina. He became Argentina's youngest ever international in 1977, transferred to Boca Juniors for £1 million as a teenager, and in 1982 became the world's most expensive footballer when he joined Barcelona for £5 million. He broke the record again in 1984 when the Italian club Napoli paid £6·9 million for him. He captained Argentina to their second World Cup in 1986, only for his career to founder amid accusations of drug-taking. Following a 15-month ban, he returned by popular demand, though without a club, to the World Cup side as captain in 1994, but was again suspended from the team following a positive drug test. He signed for Santos in 1995 and announced his retirement in 1997.

maral *red deer*

Maralinga 30°13S 131°24E. Ghost town, South Australia, on the E Nullarbor Plain, N of the transcontinental railway; area used by the British as a nuclear testing site in the 1950s; British government agreed to pay compensation to Aboriginal inhabitants in 1993.

Marañón, River [maranyohn] River in Peru, one of the Amazon's major headstreams; rises in the Andes, 137 km/85 mi E of the Pacific; joins the R Ucayali to form the Amazon 88 km/55 mi SW of Iquitos; estimated length is 1600 km/1000 mi; navigable as far as the Pongo de Manseriche gorge.

marasmus [marazmus] The childhood equivalent of adult starvation, usually occurring after six months of life, and caused by insufficient intake of protein and of energy. Affected children are extremely thin and wizened.

Marat, Jean Paul [mara] (1743–93) French revolutionary politician, born in Boudry, W Switzerland. He studied medicine at Bordeaux, and lived in Paris, Holland, Newcastle, and London. At the Revolution he became a member of the Cordelier Club, and established the radical paper *L'Ami du peuple* (The Friend of the People). His virulence provoked hatred, and he was several times forced into hiding. Elected to the National Convention, he became a leader of the Mountain, and advocated radical reforms. After the king's death he was locked in a struggle with the Girondins, and was fatally stabbed in his bath by a Girondin supporter, Charlotte Corday; thereafter he was hailed as a martyr.

Maratha or **Mahratta** [marahta] A Marathi-speaking people of Maharashtra, W India (though sometimes the name refers only to the Maratha caste in the region). They include a group of castes who are mainly peasant farmers, soldiers, and landowners. Historically they are famed as warriors and for promoting Hinduism.

Maratha Empire [marahta] A W Indian regional power, founded by Maratha warrior-leader Shivaji (1627–80), that waged campaigns against the Mughals and began their decline. It later became a confederacy of leading families (Bhonsle, Gaekwad, Holkar, Sindhia) under hereditary chief ministers (Peshwas). The kingdom was defeated by Afghans at Panipat (1761). It sought British protection but was destroyed by British intervention in 1818.

Marathi [marahtee] *Indo-Aryan languages*

marathon A long-distance running race, normally on open roads, over the distance 42 km 195 m/26 mi 385 yd. The race was introduced at the first modern Olympic Games in 1896 to commemorate the run of the Greek courier (according to legend, Pheidippides) who ran the c.39 km/24 mi from Marathon to Athens in 490 BC with the news of a Greek victory over the Persian army. After proclaiming the victory, he collapsed and died. The current marathon distance was first used at the 1908 London Olympics, its exact distance being fixed so that competitors could finish in front of the royal box. The distance was standardized in 1924. It is now a popular event for the non-competitive enthusiast, with many thousands taking part in the annual marathons in London, Boston, and New York City. In the 1980s, the **half-marathon** also became popular, over the distance 21 km/13 mi 192½ yd.

Marathon, Battle of (490 BC) The decisive Athenian victory over the Persians on the E coast of Attica, which brought the First Persian War to an end.

Marbella [mah(r)baya] 36°30N 4°57W, pop (2000e) 78 000. Port and resort on the Costa del Sol, Málaga province, Andalusia, S Spain; watersports; large bathing beaches; tourism, iron and steel, furniture; Fiesta del Sol (Jan), Fiestas of San Bernabe (Jun), Semana del Sol (Aug), Costa del Sol Rally (Dec).

marble A metamorphic rock formed by the recrystallization of limestone and dolomite. It is white when pure, but its impurities give it a distinctive coloration. It is easily sculpted and polished, and is also used as a building stone.

Marburg [mah(r)boorg] 50°49N 8°36E, pop (2000e) 75 400. City in Giessen district, WC Germany; on the R Lahn, 74 km/46 mi N of Frankfurt; railway; university (1527); pharmaceuticals, optical equipment; St Elizabeth's Church (1235–83), Gothic castle (15th–16th-c).

Marburg disease *green monkey disease*

Marc, Franz (1880–1916) Artist, born in Munich, SE Germany. He studied in Munich, Italy, and France, and with Kandinsky founded *Der Blaue Reiter* (The Blue Rider) Expressionist group in Munich in 1911. Most of his paintings were of animals, such as the famous 'Tower of the Blue Horses' (1911, Walker Art Center, Minneapolis), portrayed in forceful colours.

Marc Antony *Antonius, Marcus*

marcasite [mah(r)kaseet] An iron sulphide mineral (FeS_2) with the same chemical composition as pyrite, but formed at lower temperatures. It is found in sedimentary rocks, and is also associated with major ore deposits of the Mississippi Valley.

Marceau, Marcel [mah(r)soh] (1923–) Mime artist, born in Strasbourg, NE France. He studied at the Ecole des Beaux-Arts in Paris, and with Etienne Decroux. In 1948 he founded the Compagnie de Mime Marcel Marceau, developing the art of mime, becoming himself the leading exponent. His white-faced character, Bip, based on the 19th-c French Pierrot, a melancholy vagabond, is famous from his appearances on stage and television throughout the world. Among the many original performances he has devised are the mime-drama *Don Juan* (1964), and the ballet *Candide* (1971). He has also created about 100 pantomimes, such as *The Creation of the World*. In 1978 he became head of the Ecole de Mimodrame Marcel Marceau.

Marcellus, Marcus Claudius [mah(r)selus] **1** (c.268–208 BC) Roman general of the time of the Second Punic War. Nicknamed the 'Sword of Rome', his main exploits were the defeat of the Insubrian Gauls (222 BC) and the capture of Syracuse (212 BC).

2 (42–23 BC) Nephew of the Emperor Augustus by his sister Octavia, and his first intended successor. His early death was widely regarded as a national calamity.

march Music designed to accompany soldiers marching in step, and therefore virtually always in duple or quadruple metre and (except for funeral marches) in a moderate or quick tempo. Concert pieces in march style include the 'Marche au supplice' in Berlioz's *Symphonie fantastique* (1830) and Elgar's five *Pomp and Circumstance* marches (1901–7).

Marches, the, Ital **Marche** pop (2000e) 1 446 000; area 9693 sq km/3741 sq mi. The area of EC Italy between the Apennines and the Adriatic Sea, centred on Ancona. Except for the narrow coastal plain, it is mostly mountainous, but with very fertile uplands; production of majolica; tourism.

marchioness *marquess*

March on Rome The largely symbolic culmination of the pseudo-revolutionary process surrounding Italian fascism's entry into government and Mussolini's appointment (1922) as premier. Planned as part of an insurrection which only half occurred, the actual march was a celebration of a victory achieved by nominally constitutional means.

March to the Sea *Sherman, William Tecumseh*

Marciano, Rocky [mah(r)siahnoh], originally **Rocco Francis Marchegiano**, nickname **the Rock from Brockton** (1923–69) Heavyweight boxing champion, born in Brockton, Massachusetts, USA. He first took up boxing as a serviceman in Britain during World War 2, turned professional in 1947, and made his name when he defeated the former world champion, Joe Louis, in 1951. He won the world title from Jersey Joe Walcott the following year, and when he retired in 1956 was the only undefeated world heavyweight champion, with a professional record of 49 bouts and 49 victories, including 43 by knockout. He died in an air-crash in Newton, IA.

Marconi, Guglielmo [mah(r)kohnee] (1874–1937) Physicist and inventor, born in Bologna, N Italy. He studied at the Technical Institute of Livorno, and started experimenting with a device to convert electromagnetic waves into electricity. His first successful experiments in wireless telegraphy were made at Bologna in 1895, and in 1899 he erected a wireless station at La Spezia, and formed the Marconi Telegraph Co in London. In 1899 he transmitted signals across the English Channel, and in 1901 across the Atlantic. He later developed short-wave radio equipment, and established a worldwide radio telegraph network for the British government. He shared the 1909 Nobel Prize for Physics.

Marco Polo *Polo, Marco*

Marco Polo's sheep *argali*

Marcos, Ferdinand (Edralin) [mah(r)kos] (1917–89) Philippines statesman and president (1965–86), born in Ilocos Norte, Philippines. He trained as a lawyer, and as a politician obtained considerable US support as an anti-Communist. His regime as president was marked by increasing repression, misuse of foreign financial aid, and political murders (notably the assassination of Benigno Aquino in 1983). He declared martial law in 1972, but was overthrown in 1986 by a popular front led by Corazon Aquino. He went into exile in Hawaii, where he, and his wife **Imelda** (1930–), fought against demands from US courts investigating charges of financial mismanagement and corruption. His body was returned to the Philippines for burial in 1993, and soon afterwards Imelda was convicted of corruption and sentenced to 18 years imprisonment. She was released on bail, appealed against her sentence, and was acquitted in 1998. Still commanding a great deal of popular support, she was re-elected to congress for Leyte province in 1996.

Marcus Aurelius Antoninus (121–180) *Aurelius*

Marcuse, Herbert [mah(r)koozuh] (1898–1979) Marxist philosopher, born in Berlin, Germany. He studied at Berlin and Freiburg, and became an influential figure in the Frankfurt School. He fled to Geneva in 1933, and after World War 2 moved to the USA, working in intelligence. He later held posts at Columbia (1951), Harvard (1952), Brandeis (1954), and California, San Diego (1965–76). His books include *Reason and Revolution* (1941), *Eros and Civilization* (1955) and, more famously, *One Dimensional Man* (1964), condemning the 'repressive tolerance' of modern industrial society which both stimulated and satisfied the superficial material desires of the masses at the cost of more fundamental needs and freedoms.

Mar del Plata [mah(r) thel plata] 38°00S 57°30W, pop (2000e) 466 500. Port on the Atlantic coast in SE Buenos Aires province, E Argentina; founded in 1874; one of the prime holiday resorts of South America, with 8 km/5 mi of beaches; two universities (1958, 1962); railway; airfield; meat packing, fish canning, tourism; museums, casino.

Mardi Gras [mah(r)dee grah] The French name (literally 'fat Tuesday') for Shrove Tuesday, the day before the beginning of Lent; Mardi Gras carnivals, beginning some time before Shrove Tuesday, are held in various places; among the most famous are those of Rio de Janeiro and New Orleans.

Marduk [mah(r)duk] Originally the patron deity of the city of Babylon. He later became the supreme god of Babylonia, taking over the functions of Enlil.

mare's tail An aquatic perennial native to Europe, Asia, and N Africa (*Hippuris vulgaris*); stems growing to 150 cm/5 ft, usually less, emerging above water; narrow leaves in whorls of 6–12; flowers tiny, green, on emergent portion of stem. (Family: Hippuridaceae.)

Marfan's syndrome [mah(r)fan] An inherited disease of connective tissue. The arms and legs grow to abnormal lengths with excessively mobile joints, and the fingers and toes are long and spidery; also known as **arachnodactyly**. There may also be heart disease and dislocation of the lenses of the eyes. There is a lack of subcutaneous tissue, so affected individuals are underweight in spite of being extremely tall. It is named after French paediatrician Bernard Jean Antoinin Marfan (1858–1942). President Abraham Lincoln probably suffered from it.

Margaret (of Scotland), St (c.1046–93) Scottish queen, born in Hungary. She moved to England, but after the Norman Conquest fled to Scotland with her younger brother, Edgar the Ætheling. She married the Scottish king, Malcolm Canmore, and did much to civilize the realm, and to assimilate the old Celtic Church to the rest of Christendom. She was canonized in 1250. Feast day 16 November or 19 June.

Margaret (Rose), Princess (1930–2002) British princess, born at Glamis Castle, Angus, E Scotland, UK, the second daughter of George VI and sister of Elizabeth II. In 1955, when she was third in succession to the throne, she denied rumours of her possible marriage to **Group-Captain Peter Townsend** (a divorcé), amid a great deal of publicity and concern that a constitutional crisis could be precipitated by such a marriage. In 1960 she married Antony Armstrong-Jones (divorced, 1978), who was created Viscount Linley and Earl of Snowdon in 1961. The former title devolved upon their son, **David Albert Charles** (1961–), who married Serena Alleyne Stanhope in 1993; children are **Charles Armstrong-Jones** (1999–) and **Margarita Armstrong-Jones** (2002–). Their daughter is **Sarah Frances Elizabeth** (1964–), who married Daniel Chatto in 1994; children are **Samuel Chatto** (1996–) and **Arthur Chatto** (1999–).

Margaret of Anjou [ãzhoo] (1430–82) Queen of England, probably born in Pont-à-Mousson, NE France. The daughter of René of Anjou, she was married to Henry VI of England in 1445. Owing to his mental weakness she was in effect sovereign, and the war of 1449, in which Normandy was lost, was laid by the English to her charge. In the Wars of the Roses, after a brave struggle of nearly 20 years, she was finally defeated at Tewkesbury (1471), and imprisoned for four years in the Tower, until ransomed by Louis XI. She then retired to France, where she died in poverty.

Margaret Tudor (1489–1541) Queen of Scotland, born in London, UK, the eldest daughter of Henry VII. She became the wife of James IV of Scotland (1503), and the mother of James V, for whom she acted as regent. After James IV's death in 1513 she married twice again, to the Earl of Angus (1514), and Lord Methven (1527). She was much involved in the political intrigues between the pro-French and pro-English factions in Scotland. Her great-grandson was James VI of Scotland and I of England.

Margareta or **Margaret** (1353–1412) Queen of Denmark, Norway, and Sweden, born in Søborg, E Denmark. She became Queen of Denmark in 1375, on the death of her father, Waldemar IV, without male heirs; by the death of her husband Haakon VI in 1380, she became ruler of Norway; and in 1388 she aided a rising of Swedish nobles against their king, Albert of Mecklenburg, and became Queen of Sweden. She had her infant cousin, Eric of Pomerania, crowned king of the three kingdoms at Kalmar in 1397, but remained the real ruler of Scandinavia until her death.

margarine A butter-substitute that does not contain dairy fat, usually made from vegetable oils and skimmed milk, and supplemented with vitamins A and D. In the 1860s a French chemist, Hippolyte Mège-Mouriès (1817–80), extracted a fraction of beef fat at 30–40°C which he termed *oleo-margarine*. This was used as the basis of a butter substitute until 1903, when a process of hardening vegetable oils by hydrogenation was patented. Since then, butter substitutes have developed in sophistication, although most of these are still based on hydrogenated vegetable or marine oils. The degree of hydrogenation of the original oil determines how much remains of the original polyunsaturates.

margay [mah(r)gay] A rare member of the cat family (*Felis wiedii*), found from N Mexico to N Argentina; pale with ring-like dark spots; inhabits forest; hunts in trees; rear feet adapted for climbing (capable of rotating through 180°); sometimes reared as pets.

marginal cost In economics, the cost of producing one extra unit, or the total cost saved if one less unit is produced. In accountancy, it is the variable cost of producing a unit. **Marginal costing** is a system where only variable costs (ie costs which vary directly with the volume made or sold, such as materials) are related to the unit. *Fixed costs* (ie those remaining unchanged whatever the volume, such as rent) are not allocated to the unit.

marginal productivity An economic concept defining the additional output (*marginal output*) generated by the last, additional input of labour (or other input). The concept is used as a theory of wage determination, in that firms employ workers only as long as the revenue from the marginal worker is greater than his or her cost.

Margrethe II [mah(r)**gre**tuh] (1940–) Queen of Denmark (1972–), born in Copenhagen, Denmark, the daughter of Frederick IX. She studied at Copenhagen, Cambridge, Århus, the Sorbonne, and London, and qualified as an archaeologist. Also an accomplished artist, she illustrated a 1977 edition of J R R Tolkien's *Lord of the Rings* using the pseudonym **Ingahild Grathmer**. In 1967 she married a French diplomat, **comte Henri de Laborde de Monpezat**, now **Prince Henrik** of Denmark. Their children are the heir apparent, **Prince Frederik André Henrik Christian** (1968–), and **Prince Joachim Holger Waldemar Christian** (1969–). She is one of Denmark's most popular monarchs. Her people can arrange to meet her to discuss an issue in the same way that a British MP holds a 'surgery' for constituents.

marguerite [mah(r)ge**reet**] *ox-eye daisy*

Mari [**mah**ree] The most important city on the middle Euphrates in the third and second millennia BC until its destruction c.1759 BC by the Babylonians. It was the centre of a vast trading network in NW Mesopotamia. Since 1933, c.20 000 cuneiform tablets dating from c.18th-c BC have been discovered, providing a great deal of information about the period. Although none mentions any actual Biblical character or place, several offer interesting parallels to practices in the patriarchal period of Israel's history.

maria [**ma**riya] (singular **mare** [**mah**ray]) Dark regions mainly on the nearside of the Moon. They are flat plains of basalt formed 3–3·9 thousand million years ago. Dense concentrations of material beneath the maria are known as *mascons*.

Mariana Islands *see panel*

Mariana Islands

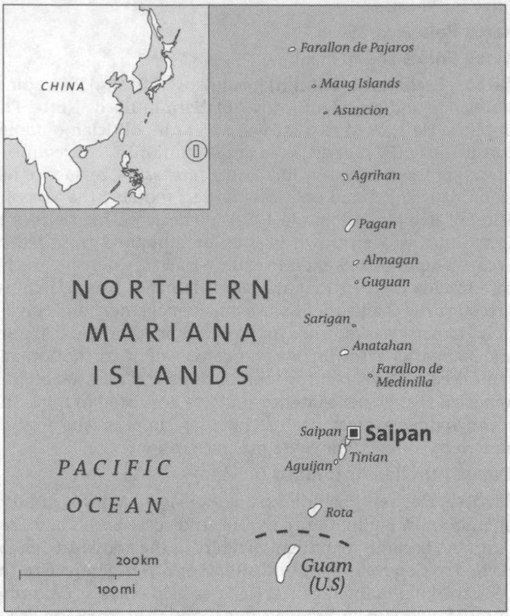

☐ International Airport

in full **Commonwealth of the Northern Mariana Islands** pop (2000e) 72 000; area 471 sq km/182 sq mi. Group of 14 islands in the NW Pacific, c.2400 km/1500 mi E of the Philippines; capital, Saipan; mainly volcanic (three still active); includes Saipan, Tinian, Rota, Pagan, Guguan; held by the USA under UN mandate after World War 2 as part of the US Trust Territory of the Pacific Is, 1947–78; self-governing commonwealth of the USA, 1978–90; trusteeship ended 1990; tourism, sugar cane, coconuts, coffee.

Marianas Trench An oceanic trench running SW to N off the I of Guam and the N Marianas Is, Pacific Ocean. Its deepest point, Challenger Deep, 11 040 m/36 220 ft, is the Earth's maximum ocean depth.

Maria Theresa (1717–80) Archduchess of Austria, and Queen of Hungary and Bohemia (1740–80), born in Vienna, Austria, the daughter of Emperor Charles VI (ruled 1711–40). In 1736 she married **Francis, Duke of Lorraine**, and in 1740 succeeded her father in the hereditary Habsburg lands. Her claim, however, led to the War of the Austrian Succession, during which she lost Silesia to Prussia. She received the Hungarian crown (1741), and in 1745 her husband was elected Holy Roman Emperor. Although her foreign minister, Kaunitz, tried to isolate Prussia by diplomatic means, military conflict was renewed in the Seven Years' War, and by 1763 she was finally forced to recognize the status quo of 1756. In her later years she strove to maintain international peace, and reluctantly accepted the partition of Poland (1772). Of her 10 surviving children, the eldest son succeeded her as Joseph II.

mariculture The cultivation of marine fish, shellfish, and algae; distinguished from **aquaculture**, which includes both freshwater and saltwater organisms. Mariculture operations range from small subsistence 'farms' to large commercial enterprises. Practices vary from raising fish, shellfish, and algae in protected enclosures to releasing salmon from hatcheries in the hope of catching them years later when they return to the same waters to spawn. Shellfish farming is successfully practised in France (oysters) and Spain (mussels) by growing the animals on suspended frames in productive coastal waters. The development of artificial reefs is sometimes considered to be a form of mariculture, in that it can stimulate nearshore fish production in otherwise barren coastal areas.

Marie Antoinette (Josèphe Jeanne) (1755–93) Queen of France, born in Vienna, Austria, the daughter of Maria Theresa and Francis I. She was married to the Dauphin, afterwards Louis XVI (1770), to strengthen the Franco-Austrian alliance, and exerted a growing influence over him. Capricious and frivolous, she aroused criticism by her extravagance, disregard for conventions, devotion to the interests of Austria, and opposition to reform. From the outbreak of the French Revolution, she resisted the advice of constitutional monarchists (eg Mirabeau), and helped to alienate the monarchy from the people. However, the famous solution to the bread famine, 'let them eat cake', is unjustly attributed to her. In 1791 she and Louis tried to escape from the Tuileries to her native Austria, but were seized at Varennes and imprisoned in Paris. After the king's execution, she was arraigned before the Tribunal and guillotined.

Marie Celeste An American 103-ft brigantine, found abandoned in the mid-Atlantic in 1872. She had left New York on 7 November, sailing for Genoa, and was encountered by an English ship, the *Dei Gratia*, on 4 December, c.400 miles off the Portuguese coast. There were plenty of supplies on board, as well as the crew's personal possessions, and no sign of disturbance, but the steering wheel was left running free, suggesting that everyone had left in a hurry; there was no sign of what had happened to Captain Briggs, his wife and daughter, and the seven-man crew. The ship's lifeboat was missing, as were several navigational papers and instruments, suggesting that everyone had left anticipating some danger, and had been unable to return. Several speculative and fictitious accounts of the mystery were propounded at the time, including one by Arthur Conan Doyle, and the event continues to intrigue over a century later. The ship continued in service, despite its unlucky reputation, eventually sinking off Haiti in 1885.

Marie de France (12th-c) Poet, born in Normandy, NW France. She spent much of her life in England, where she wrote several verse narratives based on Celtic stories. Her *Lais*, dedicated to 'a noble king' (probably Henry II), were a landmark in French literature.

Marie de Médicis [maydeesees], Ital **Maria de' Medici** [maydichee] (1573–1642) Queen consort of Henry IV of France, born in Florence, NC Italy, the daughter of Francesco de' Medici, Grand Duke of Tuscany. She married Henry in 1600, following his divorce from his first wife Margaret, and gave birth to a son (later Louis XIII) in 1601. After her husband's death (1610) she acted as regent, but her capricious behaviour and dependence on favourites led to her confinement in Blois when Louis assumed royal power in 1617. She continued to intrigue against Louis and her former protégé, Richelieu, who had become the king's adviser. She was banished to Compiègne, but escaped to Brussels (1631). Her last years were spent in poverty.

Marie Louise (1791–1847) Empress of France, born in Vienna, Austria, the daughter of the Holy Roman Emperor, Francis II. She married Napoleon in 1810 (after his divorce from Joséphine), and in 1811 bore him a son, who was created King of Rome and who became Napoleon II. On Napoleon's abdication she returned to Austria. By the Treaty of Fontainebleau (1814) she was awarded the Duchies of Para, Piacenza, and Guastalla in Italy.

marigold A name applied to several different species of the daisy family, Compositae.

Mariinsky Theatre of Opera and Ballet *Kirov Ballet*

marijuana or **marihuana** *cannabis*

marimba In modern orchestras and pop groups, a percussion instrument resembling a xylophone, with slender wooden bars and metal resonators, but with a lower compass and played with soft beaters.

Mariner programme A series of increasingly complex 3-axis stabilized spacecraft launched by NASA to begin the exploration of the inner and outer Solar System. The programme included the first planetary flyby (Mariner 2, Venus, Dec 1962), the first planetary orbiter (Mariner 9, Mars, Nov 1971), the first mission to Mercury (Mariner 10, Mar 1974, Sep 1974, and Mar 1975), and the first detailed observations of Jovian, Saturnian, and Uranian systems (Mariner *Jupiter-Saturn* – renamed *Voyager* – 1979–86). The spacecraft were built and operated by NASA's Jet Propulsion Laboratory and derived from the early lunar impact spacecraft *Ranger*. The Viking Mars orbiter was also a member of the Mariner family.

Marines Soldiers, under naval command, who nevertheless are equipped and organized to make war on land. Originally posted in small units aboard warships, in the two world wars, Marines have been used as combat forces in their own right, specializing in such operations as commando raiding and amphibious assault.

Marinetti, Filippo (Tommaso) Emilio [marinetee] (1876–1944) Italian writer, born in Alexandria, N Egypt. He studied in Paris and Genoa, then worked as a journalist in Milan. He published the original Futurist manifesto in *Figaro* in 1909. In his writings he glorified war, the machine age, speed and 'dynamism', and condemned all traditional forms of literature and art. In 1919 he became a Fascist. His publications include *Le futurisme* (1911) and *Teatro sintetico futuristo* (1916, Synthetic Futurist Theatre).

Marini, Marino [mareenee] (1901–80) Sculptor and painter, born in Pistoia, NC Italy. He studied in Florence, and taught at the Scuola d'Arte di Villa Reale, Monza (1929–40), before moving to Milan, where he was professor at Brera Academy (1940–70). His work, mainly in bronze, was figurative, his best-known theme being the horse and rider. He liked to combine different techniques, including colour, as in 'Dancer' (1949–54). He also executed portraits of Stravinsky, Chagall, Henry Miller, and others.

Marino, Dan [mareenoh] (1961–) Player of American football, born in Pittsburgh, Pennsylvania, USA. An outstanding quarterback with the Miami Dolphins, in the 1984 season he gained 5084 yards passing, and passed for 48 touchdowns, both NFL records. His career totals of 58 913 yards and 408 touchdown passes are both NFL records, but he went into the 1999 season, his 17th, still looking for a Super Bowl ring. He announced his retirement in 2000.

marionettes *puppetry*

Maritain, Jacques [mareetĩ] (1882–1973) Philosopher and diplomat, born in Paris, France. He studied in Paris and Heidelberg, and converted to Catholicism in 1906. He was professor at the Institut Catholique in Paris (1914–40), and taught mainly in North America, at Toronto, Columbia, Chicago, and Princeton universities (1948–60). As French ambassador to the Vatican (1945–8), he later became a strong opponent of the Vatican Council and the neo-Modernist movement. His main works include *Les Degrés du savoir* (1932, The Degree of Knowledge), *Art et scolastique* (1920, Art and Scholasticism), and *La Philosophie morale* (1960, Moral Philosophy).

Maritime Provinces The provinces in mainland Canada which border the Atlantic coast and the Gulf of St Lawrence: New Brunswick, Nova Scotia, and Prince Edward Island. Taken together with Newfoundland, they are described as the **Atlantic Provinces**.

Maritime Trust A national organization in the UK to restore, maintain, and display ships of historic or technical importance. It has preserved many ships including HMS *Warrior*, the *Cutty Sark*, and *Gypsy Moth IV*. It was set up in 1969, on the initiative of Prince Philip.

Mariupol [mariupol], formerly **Zhdanov** 47°05N 37°34E, pop (2000e) 512 000. Seaport in Donetskaya oblast, Ukraine; at the mouth of the R Kalmius, on the Sea of Azov; founded, 1779; airfield; railway; noted mud-bath resort; coal trade, iron and steel, chemicals, fertilizers, metallurgical equipment, fishing.

Marius, Gaius (c.157–86 BC) Roman general and politician, born in Arpinum. Of comparatively humble extraction, his military talents and ruthless ambition enabled him to rise to the very top in Rome, where he held an unprecedented number of consulships (seven), and married into the heart of the aristocracy – the Julian gens. Famous in his lifetime for his victories over Jugurtha (105 BC), the Teutones (102 BC), and the Cimbri (101 BC), it was by his army reforms that he made his greatest impact on the state. His final years were dominated by his rivalry with Sulla. The violence with which he recaptured Rome for Cinna from the forces backing Sulla (87 BC) permanently damaged his reputation.

Marivaux, Pierre (Carlet de Chamblain de) [mareevoh] (1688–1763) Playwright and novelist, born in Paris, France. Trained as a lawyer, he published his first play at the age of 20. He wrote several comedies, of which his best is *Le Jeu de l'amour et du hasard* (1730, The Game of Love and Chance). His best-known novel, *La Vie de Marianne* (1731–41, The Life of Marianne) was never finished, and is marked by an affected style which has been dubbed *Marivaudage*. Although he became director of the Académie Française in 1759, his work was not fully appreciated until after his death.

marjoram [mah(r)joram] A somewhat bushy perennial (*Origanum vulgare*), native to limestone and chalky soils in Europe, the Mediterranean, and Asia; stems square; leaves oval, in opposite pairs; flowers small, 2-lipped, white or purplish-pink, in dense spikes. It is cultivated as a culinary herb, often under the name **oregano**. The plants grown in warm countries are the most strongly aromatic. (Family: Labiatae.)

Mark, St, also called **John Mark** (fl.1st-c) Christian disciple. He is described in the New Testament as 'John whose surname was Mark' (*Acts* 12.12, 25), and a helper of the apostles Barnabas and Paul during their first missionary journey. He is often considered the Mark who is accredited in 2nd-c traditions with the writing of the second Gospel, described by Papias (early 2nd-c bishop in Asia Minor) as the 'interpreter of Peter'. Feast day 25 April.

Mark, Gospel according to The second book of the New Testament canon, the shortest of the four gospels, and argued by many scholars also to be the earliest; anonymous, but traditionally attributed to John Mark. Because it contains less teaching material than the other Gospels, it places relatively greater emphasis on Jesus's miracle-working, opposers, and death. It also draws attention to the mystery of Jesus's role and activities. The Gospel begins abruptly (compared with the other Gospels), and may have ended equally abruptly, since the disputed stories of the resurrection appearances in *Mark* 16.9–20 are likely to be a late addition.

Mark Antony *Antonius, Marcus*

Markarian galaxy *galaxy*

market economy An economic system where prices, wages, and what is made and sold are determined by market forces of supply and demand, with no state interference. The contrast is with a *command economy*, where the state takes all economic decisions. Most Western economies these days are mixed, with varying degrees of state control.

market forces or **market mechanism** The network of interactions between buyers and sellers which determines the price and quantity of products and goods, prices being set by the forces of supply and demand. The process assumes that there is no interference by, for example, government.

market gardening The intensive production of horticultural crops on smallholdings, especially fruit and vegetables for local markets; also known as **truck gardening** in the USA. It may incorporate pick-your-own enterprises, where labour is scarce.

marketing The management of a business with the customer in mind. It aims to identify a market where a potential exists for profitable business, and to take the necessary steps to satisfy that market by careful planning of the 'marketing mix' or the 'Four Ps': product, price, place, and promotion (including advertising).

marketing board A statutory body which has the power to control some aspect(s) of production, processing, or marketing for a specific commodity. It is usually created through a majority vote of producers, and financed through compulsory levy. Most frequently used to manage the marketing and promotion of agricultural commodities, it may also fund research and the collection and dissemination of information. Marketing boards are used widely throughout the non-communist world, and are particularly common in North America.

market research A technique to find out more about the market in which a business is operating, or may operate in the future. Survey techniques are often used, seeking the opinions of individuals who might be buyers, and providing information about the potential size and characteristics of a particular market segment. Market research also enables advertising agencies to target their campaigns more accurately.

market socialism A variant of socialism which seeks to marry the benefits of the market system with those of socialism and thus avoid the negative aspects of both; associated with the Polish economist Oskar Lange (1904–65). It combines the efficiency of the market-place, as a way of providing the goods and services demanded by the consumers, with the social justice associated with the allocation of profits on the basis of need through some socially controlled mechanism.

markhor [**mah(r)**kaw(r)] A wild goat (*Capra falconeri*) native to the mountains of S Asia; the largest goat; male with long beard covering throat; long horns extremely thick, close (or joined) at base, with sharp spiral ridge around outside; inhabits woodlands.

Markievicz, Constance (Georgine), Countess [mah(r)**kyay**vich], *née* **Gore-Booth** (1868–1927) Irish nationalist, born in London, UK. She married the Polish Count Casimir Markievicz, fought in the Easter Rising (1916), and was sentenced to death, but reprieved. Elected the first British woman MP in 1918, she did not take her seat, but was a member of the Dáil from 1923.

Markova, Dame Alicia [mah(r)**koh**va], originally **Lilian Alicia Marks** (1910–) Prima ballerina, born in London, UK. She danced with Ballets Russes in 1924, and on her return to Britain appeared for the Camargo Society and the Vic-Wells Ballet. There followed a period of partnership with Anton Dolin (1904–83) which led to the establishment of the Markova–Dolin Company in 1935. They made guest appearances together around the world, and were famed for their interpretation of *Giselle*. She retired in 1962, was created a dame in 1963, became a director of the Metropolitan Opera Ballet (1963–9), and took up an appointment as professor of ballet and the performing arts at the University of Cincinnati in 1970. In 1986 she became president of the London Festival Ballet (now the English National Ballet).

Markov chain In mathematics, a chain of events in which the probability of moving from one state to another depends on the existing state. These are often displayed in matrices, and a two-state Markov chain, one in which there are two possible states at each stage, is illustrated by the matrix

$$\begin{bmatrix} a & 1-a \\ 1-b & b \end{bmatrix}.$$

For example, a man travels home from work either by car or by train. If he travels by car any one day, the probability that he travels by car the next might be 0·4; if he travels by train one day, the probability that he travels by train the next might be 0·3. These would be shown in the transition matrix

$$\begin{bmatrix} 0{\cdot}4 & 0{\cdot}6 \\ 0{\cdot}7 & 0{\cdot}3 \end{bmatrix}.$$

The notion is named after the Soviet mathematician Andrey Andreyevich Markov (1856–1922).

Markowitz, Harry M [**mah(r)**kovits] (1927–) Economist, born in Chicago, Illinois, USA. He taught at Los Angeles, Pennsylvania, and Rutgers universities, and at Baruch College, New York City (from 1982). He was also chairman of the board at Consolidated Analysis Centers (1963–8) and president of Arbitrage Management Co (1969–72). He shared the 1990 Nobel Prize for Economics for developing the theory of the rational behaviour involved in portfolio selection under uncertainty.

Marks (of Broughton), Simon Marks, Baron (1888–1964) Businessman, born in Leeds, West Yorkshire, N England, UK. In 1907 he inherited the 60 Marks and Spencer penny bazaars which his father **Michael Marks**, with Thomas Spencer, had built up from 1884. In collaboration with Israel (later Lord) Sieff (1899–1972), his brother-in-law, he developed Marks and Spencer, with its pioneering policy of 'Don't ask the price – it's a penny', into a major retail chain. 'Marks and Sparks' used their considerable purchasing power to encourage British clothing manufacturers to achieve demanding standards, and their 'St Michael' brand label became a guarantee of high quality at a reasonable price. He was knighted in 1944 and created a baron in 1961.

marl Carbonate-rich clay deposits formed by the weathering of impure limestones.

Marlborough, John Churchill, 1st Duke of [**mah(r)l**bruh] (1650–1722) English general, born in Ashe, Devon, SW England, UK. He was commissioned in the Guards (1667), and further promoted when in 1678 he married **Sarah Jennings**, an attendant of Princess Anne. On James II's accession (1685), he was elevated to an English barony and given the rank of general. He took a leading part in quelling Monmouth's rebellion at Sedgemoor, but deserted to the Prince of Orange in 1688, serving the Protestant cause in campaigns in Ireland and Flanders. Under Queen Anne he was appointed supreme commander of the British forces in the War of the Spanish Succession (1701–13), and he became captain-general of the Allied armies. His military flair and organizational skills resulted in several great victories – Donauwörth and Blenheim (1704), Ramillies (1706), Oudenaarde and the capture of Lille (1708) – for which he was richly rewarded with Blenheim Palace and a dukedom. Forced by political interests to align himself with the Whig war party (1708), his influence waned, and when his wife fell from royal favour the Tories pressed for his downfall. He was dismissed on charges of embezzling, and left England for continental Europe (1712), returning after George's accession (1714). Though restored to his former offices, his health was impaired, and he died not long afterwards.

Marley, Bob, popular name of **Robert Nesta Marley** (1945–81) Singer, guitarist, and composer of reggae music, born near Kingston, Jamaica. He made his first record at the age of 19, and in 1965 formed the vocal trio, The Wailers, with Peter Tosh and Bunny Livingstone. Their music developed political themes with an artless lyricism and infectious rhythm, and in the 1970s Marley brought it around the world. He was a disciple of Rastafarianism, and a charismatic spokesman not only for his religion but also his culture and generation. His albums include *Catch a Fire* (1972), and *Uprising* (1980), and his most famous songs include 'No Woman, No Cry' and 'I Shot the Sheriff'.

marlin Any of several large, fast-swimming, highly agile billfishes widespread in warm seas; length up to 4·5 m/14¾ ft; very important commercially, and highly prized as sport fish, especially the **blue marlin** (*Makaira nigricans*) and the **striped marlin** (*Tetrapturus audax*). (Genera: *Makaira, Tetrapturus*. Family: Istiophoridae.)

Marlowe, Christopher (1564–93) Playwright and poet, born in Canterbury, Kent, SE England, UK. He studied there and at Cambridge, and was the most significant of Shakespeare's predecessors in English drama. His *Tamburlaine the Great* (c.1587) shows his discovery of the strength and variety of blank verse, and this was followed by *The Jew of Malta* (c.1590), *The Tragical History of Dr Faustus* (c.1592), partly written by others, and *Edward II* (c.1592). He wrote several translations and poems, such as the unfinished *Hero and Leander*, and much of his other work has been handed down in fragments. He led an irregular life, and was on the point of being arrested for disseminating atheistic opinions when he was fatally stabbed, under mysterious circumstances, apparently in a tavern brawl in Deptford; research suggests he was murdered by an agent of Walsingham, for reasons unknown.

Marmara [mah(r)mara] or **Marmora, Sea of**, Turkish **Marmara Denizi**, ancient **Propontis** area 11 474 sq km/4429 sq mi. Sea in NW Turkey, between Europe (N) and Asia (S); connected (E) with the Black Sea through the Bosporus and (W) with the Aegean Sea through the Dardanelles; length, c.200 km/125 mi; Istanbul is on its NE shore; Marmara I (from which the sea gets its modern name) is in the W, a source of marble, slate, and granite.

Marmes Man Prehistoric human remains found in 1965 on R J Marmes's ranch in Washington state, USA. About 11 000 years old, they rank as early evidence for the peopling of North America from E Asia.

marmoset [mah(r)moset] A monkey-like primate, native to South America; thick fur, long tail; head may have ornamental tufts; thumb not opposable; nails long, curved, pointed; inhabits tropical forest. (Family: Callitrichidae, 17 species.)

marmot [mah(r)mot] A large, ground-dwelling squirrel native to Europe, Asia, and North America; length, c.75 cm/30 in; inhabits open country; lives in burrows; hibernates for up to 9 months; eats vegetation and insects. (Genus: *Marmota*, 11 species.)

Marne, Battle of the (1914) A battle early in World War 1, in which General Joffre's French armies and the British Expeditionary Force halted German forces which had crossed the Marne and were approaching Paris, thus ending German hopes of a swift victory. The German line withdrew across the R Aisne, dug in, and occupied much the same positions until 1918.

Marne, River, ancient **Matrona** River in C France rising in the Langres Plateau; flows NW and W across Champagne to meet the R Seine near Paris; length 525 km/326 mi; navigable to St Dizier; scene of two major battles in World War 1 (1914, 1918).

Maronite Church A Christian community originating in Syria in the 7th-c, claiming origin from St Maro (d.407). Condemned for its Monothelite beliefs in 680, the Church survived in Syria and elsewhere, and since 1182 has been in communion with the Roman Catholic Church.

Marprelate Tracts Seven pamphlets covertly published in London, 1587–9. The pseudonymous author, 'Martin Marprelate', satirized the Elizabethan Church and bishops, and favoured a Presbyterian system. One alleged author, John Penry (1559–93), was executed; another, John Udall (1560–92), died in prison; a third, Job Throckmorton (1545–1601), successfully refuted the accusations. The Tracts led to statutes against dissenting sects and sedition (1593).

Marquesas Islands [mah(r)kaysaz], Fr **Iles Marquises** pop (2000e) 9300; area 1189 sq km/459 sq mi. Mountainous, wooded volcanic island group of French Polynesia, 1184 km/736 mi NE of Tahiti; comprises Nuku Hiva (where Herman Melville lived), Ua Pu, Ua Huka, Hiva Oa (where Gauguin painted), Tahuata, Fatu Hiva, and five smaller uninhabited islands; acquired by France, 1842; chief settlement, Taiohae (Hiva Oa); copra, cotton, vanilla.

marquess or **marquis** In the UK, a nobleman holding a title in the second rank of the peerage. The word (from Latin *marchio*) originally denoted a commander of a *march*, or frontier area. The wife of a marquess is a **marchioness**.

marquetry Veneers (thin sheets of highly polished woods of different colours) applied to furniture in ornamental patterns, frequently of fruit, flowers, and foliage. A popular technique throughout W Europe in the later 17th–18th-c, it became particularly widely used in England after the accession of William and Mary in 1688. The finest examples were by French cabinet-makers of the reigns of Louis XIV, XV, and XVI. **Parquetry** is marquetry arranged in geometrical patterns, sometimes to give an effect of perspective. It was popular in England in the second half of the 17th-c.

Márquez, Gabriel (Gabo) García [mah(r)kes] (1928–) Novelist, born in Aracataca, Colombia. He studied law and journalism at Bogotá and Cartagena, and began writing while working as a journalist in Europe (1950–65), publishing his first novel, *La hojarasca* (trans Leaf Storm) in 1955. His masterpiece is *Cien años de soledad* (1967, One Hundred Years of Solitude). Later works include *El amor en los tiempos del cólera* (1985, Love in a Time of Cholera), *Of Love and Other Demons* (1995), and *Los Funerales De La Mama Grande* (1999, Funerals of the Great Matriarch). The first of three volumes of autobiography, *Living to Tell the Tale*, appeared in 2003. He received the Nobel Prize for Literature in 1982.

marquis *marquess*

Marrakesh or **Marrakech** [marakesh] 31°49N 8°00W, pop (2000e) 640 000. City in Tensift province, C Morocco; in N foothills of the Haut Atlas, 240 km/150 mi S of Casablanca; one of Morocco's four imperial cities, founded in 1062; second largest city in Morocco; airport; railway; university; leather, carpets, tourism; Koutoubia mosque (12th-c); Medina, a world heritage site.

marram grass A tough perennial (*Ammophila arenaria*) with creeping rhizomes, native to coasts of W Europe; leaf-blades inrolled, panicles spike-like. It is a pioneer colonizer, adapted to dry conditions, and able to withstand burial by drifting sand. It is often planted on dunes as a sand-binder. (Family: Gramineae.)

marriage In anthropology, the legitimate long-term mating arrangement institutionalized in a community. If a union is called marriage, this implies that husband and wife have recognized claims over their partners, often including material claims; and it renders the children born of such a union legitimate heirs to both parents. Marriage also creates relationships of affinity between a person and his or her spouse's relatives, and perhaps even directly between the relatives of the husband and wife. In many parts of the world a man may legitimately marry more than one wife (*polygyny*), but it is very unusual for a woman to be permitted more than one husband (*polyandry*). Polygyny is often associated with the payment of a bride-price by the groom or his family to the relatives of the bride. In other societies the wife may bring a dowry to her husband, particularly where a woman is expected to marry into a higher social class.

Generally, certain marriages are prohibited or discouraged: some are ruled out by incest restrictions; others by virtue of religion, social class, ethnicity, and (above all) by age, since almost universally the bride is expected to be younger than her husband. The actual pool of marriage partners is in practice often very restricted. Anthropologists have made a special study of societies where there is also a positive requirement, or a preference, for marriage with a woman who stands in a particular kinship relationship to her prospective husband. Many Muslim communities, for example, favour marriage between a man and his father's brother's daughter. In a number of other societies there is a strong preference for marriage with a mother's brother's daughter. The contemporary Western belief that young men and women should be free to choose their own marriage partner is historically very unusual. In most societies – including many Western communities – these decisions have been taken by the older generation.

marrow (anatomy) *bone marrow*

marrow (botany) A trailing or climbing vine (*Cucurbita pepo*) native to America, long cultivated as a vegetable; leaves palmately-lobed; male and female flowers yellow, 12·5 cm/5 in diameter, funnel-shaped; fruit up to 90 cm/3 ft or more long, cylindrical, oval, or round; rind green or yellow, leathery, smooth or rough, with thick flesh surrounding numerous seeds. (Family: Cucurbitaceae.)

Marryat, Frederick (1792–1848) Naval officer and novelist, born in London, UK. After a life at sea, including commanding the *Ariadne* (1828), he retired and wrote novels based on his experiences, of which some of the best known are *Frank Mildmay* (1829), *Peter Simple* (1833), and *Mr Midshipman Easy* (1836). He toured the USA and wrote other books before settling in Langham, Norfolk, where he spent his days farming and writing stories for children. His best-known work is *The Children of the New Forest* (1847).

Mars (astronomy) The fourth planet from the Sun; the outermost of the terrestrial-type planets, with an eccentric orbit at a mean distance of 1·52 AU, and a diameter about half that of Earth. Its basic planetary characteristics are: mass $6{\cdot}42 \times 10^{23}$ kg; equatorial radius 3397 km/2111 mi; mean density 3·93 g/cm^3; equatorial gravity 372 cm/s^2; day (sidereal) 24 h 37 min 22 s; year 687 days; obliquity 25°11'; orbital eccentricity 0·093. A characteristically red planet, known to the ancients, it has been the subject of popular interest as a possible abode of life. There are two small natural satellites, Phobos and Deimos. Modern understanding dates back to the first spacecraft flyby of the planet in 1965 (NASA's Mariner 4) with later knowledge derived from Mariners 6 and 7, from the first planetary orbiter Mariner 9, from Viking landers and orbiters, and a series of orbiters and landers beginning with Mars Global Surveyor and the Pathfinder lander (with the Sojourner rover) which arrived in 1997, and continuing (after several failed missions) with the Mars Exploration Rover (Spirit) in Jan 2004. It is a dry, cold planet with a thin, 95% carbon dioxide atmosphere. The atmospheric circulation has similarities to Earth's, but is marked by annual episodes of violent dust-storm activity that often escalate to planet-wide storms.

There is a complex surface of cratered uplands, lowland plains, and massive volcanic regions. The tilt of the rotational axis is similar to Earth's, and leads to marked seasonal variations. Seasonal polar caps of carbon dioxide grow to middle latitudes by the end of winter. There is an apparently permanent cap of water ice at the N pole. Polar regions show extensive sedimentary deposits with periodic layering – apparent evidence of periodic climate change. A variety of channel-like features (in popular tradition called 'canals') are observed – 'runoff' channels a few tens of kilometres long and having tributaries; 'outflow' channels of great size (tens of kilometres wide and hundreds long); and 'fretted' channels that are wide and steep-walled. The 'runoff' channels suggest that water once flowed on Mars, and this was confirmed in 2004, when Mars Exploration Rover Opportunity revealed that rocks were once in contact with water.

Volcanism is widespread, especially in the regions of Tharsis and Elysium. Tharsis volcanos are the largest and youngest, and lie on a pronounced crustal bulge – Olympus Mons reaches 27 km/16 mi in height, is c.700 km/435 mi across, and is capped by a caldera 80 km/50 mi across. The Valles Marineris is an equally spectacular canyon system, stretching a quarter of the way around the planet (over 4000 km/2500 mi), measuring 150–700 km/100–450 mi in width, and reaching depths of 2–7 km/1–4 mi. Soil coloration is due to the oxidation of iron minerals. Viking lander soil analysis revealed no organic material, even from meteorite falls, and indicates that the soil/atmospheric chemistry destroys organics. It is thought highly unlikely that Mars is, today, an abode for life. The possibility of biotic or prebiotic molecular evolution in earlier eras remains an intriguing question.

Mars (mythology) The Roman god of war, second only to Jupiter. The month of March is named after him. His mythology is borrowed from Ares, though various annual ceremonies at Rome indicate that he was originally an agricultural deity who guarded the fields.

Marsalis, Wynton [mah(r)**sah**lis] (1961–) Trumpeter and composer, born in New Orleans, Louisiana, USA. At 14 he performed Haydn's trumpet concerto with the New Orleans Philharmonic Orchestra – the first of many engagements as a classical virtuoso – and went on to study at the Berkshire Music Center, MA, and the Juilliard School, New York City. Recruited in 1980 to Art Blakey's Jazz Messengers (along with his brother, **Branford** (1960–), on tenor and soprano saxophones), he left in 1982 to lead the first of a succession of small groups. He played acoustic jazz in the 1960s tradition of Mingus and Davis, and his recordings include *Standard Time* (1987) and an ambitious suite for orchestra, *Citi Movement* (1993). He won Grammy awards in 1984 for both a jazz and a classical recording, and in 1997 was awarded the Pulitzer Prize for Music.

Marseille [mah(r)**say**], also Eng **Marseilles**, ancient **Massilia** 43°18N 5°23E, pop (2000e) 837 000. Principal commercial port and capital of Bouches-du-Rhône department, S France; on NE shore of the Gulf of Lyon, 130 km/81 mi WSW of Nice; second largest city in France and leading port of the Mediterranean; founded c.600 BC by Greeks; Old Port (Vieux Port) on a rocky peninsula; airport; railway; metro; archbishopric; university; shipbuilding, chemicals, trade in minerals, oil refining, engineering, soap, glass, cigarettes, beverages, dairy produce, trade in fruit, wine, olive oil, vegetables, spices, hides; known for its bouillabaisse (fish soup); Church of St-Victor (11th–14th-c), 19th-c neo-Byzantine basilica of Notre-Dame-de-la-Garde, town hall (1663–83), Cathédrale de la Major (1852–93), Cathédrale St Lazare (11th–12th-c), Musée des Beaux Arts, New Harbour (Port Moderne); Basin de la Joliette used by passenger ships; international trade fair (Apr–Sep).

Mars Express mission A spacecraft mission to Mars undertaken by the European Space Agency launched by a Soyuz rocket from Baikonur in June 2003. The mission includes a remote sensing orbiter and a small lander named Beagle 2. It has the goal of recovering some of the orbital science objectives of the Russian-European Mars '96 mission that was lost at launch. Beagle 2, instrumented to address questions of exobiological interest, has been supplied by a consortium of mainly British university and industry institutions, and is scheduled to reach Mars on 25 December 2003. Although apparently on course, by February 2004 no signal had been received from the lander, and the mission was classed as lost.

Marsh, Dame Ngaio (Edith) [**niy**oh] (1899–1982) Detective-story writer, born in Christchurch, New Zealand. She moved to England, UK in 1928, and published her first novel, *A Man Lay Dead* (1934). It was followed by a series of novels and short stories featuring Superintendent Roderick Alleyn of Scotland Yard. These include *Vintage Murder* (1937), *Opening Night* (1951), and *Black as He's Painted* (1974). She was made a dame in 1948.

Marshall, George C(atlett) (1880–1959) US soldier and statesman, born in Uniontown, Pennsylvania, USA. He studied at the Virginia Military Institute, and was commissioned in 1901. As chief-of-staff (1939–45) he directed the US army throughout World War 2. After two years in China as special representative of the president, he became secretary of state (1947–9), and originated the **Marshall Aid** plan for the post-war reconstruction of Europe. He was awarded the Nobel Peace Prize in 1953.

Marshall, John (1755–1835) Jurist, born in Germantown, Virginia, USA. He studied law, but served in the Continental army in the American Revolution (1775–9). In 1788 he was elected to the Constitutional Convention, and in 1799 to Congress, serving as secretary of state (1800–1). He became Chief Justice of the USA (1801–35), during which time he dominated the Supreme Court, and established the US doctrine of judicial review of federal and state legislation.

Marshall, Thurgood (1908–93) Judge, born in Baltimore, Maryland, USA. He studied at Lincoln University and Howard University Law School, then began work for the National Association for the Advancement of Colored People (1936), becoming head of its legal staff (1940). As an attorney he won a historic victory in the case of *Brown* v. *Board of Education of Topeka* (1954) which declared that racial segregation in public schools was unconstitutional. Further notable successes followed in cases concerning prejudice against African-Americans. He was nominated to the US Court of Appeals (1961), named solicitor general (1965), and became the first African-American member of the Supreme Court (1967–91).

Marshall Islands *see panel*

Marshall Plan The popular name for the *European Recovery Program*, a scheme for large-scale, medium-term US aid to war-ravaged Europe, announced in 1947 by US secretary of state, George Marshall. 'Marshall Aid' was rejected by the USSR and the Eastern bloc, but during 1948–50 it materially assisted W Europe's economic revival, particularly in West Germany. Reasons for US aid included the importance of the European market for US goods; US fears that communism would spread in Europe; and the integration of West Germany (a vital industrial nation and twice in one century a major aggressor) into Europe.

marsh gas *methane*

marsh harrier A hawk found throughout the Old World (*Circus aeruginosus*); brown body, paler head, and grey tail; inhabits marshland (sometimes grassland in Australasia); eats frogs and other small animals; nests among reeds; also known as **swamp hawk**. (Family: Accipitridae.)

marsh marigold *kingcup*

marsh samphire *glasswort*

marsh tern *tern*

Marsh test A test for arsenic and antimony involving the reduction of their compounds to volatile AsH_3 and SbH_3, which deposit the metals as a mirror on a glass surface. It is named after British chemist James Marsh (1794–1846), assistant to Michael Faraday at the Royal Military Academy, London.

Marsilius of Padua [mah(r)silius] (c.1275–c.1342) Political theorist and philosopher, born in Padua, NE Italy. He was rector of the University of Paris from 1313, where he lectured on natural philosophy, engaged in medical research, and involved himself in Italian politics. In 1324 he completed *Defensor pacis*, a political treatise which argued against the temporal power of clergy and pope. When the authorship of the work became known, he was forced to flee Paris (1326). Excommunicated by Pope John XXII, he took refuge at the court of Louis of Bavaria in Munich.

Mars Observer project A NASA-led programme of Mars exploration missions of relatively low cost and mass. The first orbiter spacecraft was launched in 1992, designed to acquire global maps of the surface chemistry, mineralogy, and elevations, as well as to provide very high resolution (3 m/7 ft) surface images and measurements of magnetic field and atmosphere dynamics. Contact with the spacecraft was lost in 1993, three days before the scheduled Mars orbit insertion. It was followed by the Surveyor programme.

Mars programme A Soviet series of robotic Mars exploration projects (1962–74), including flybys, orbiters, and hard-landers. It was less successful than other Soviet planetary missions. Mars 5 (1974) returned images from Mars orbit. The Soviets

Marshall Islands

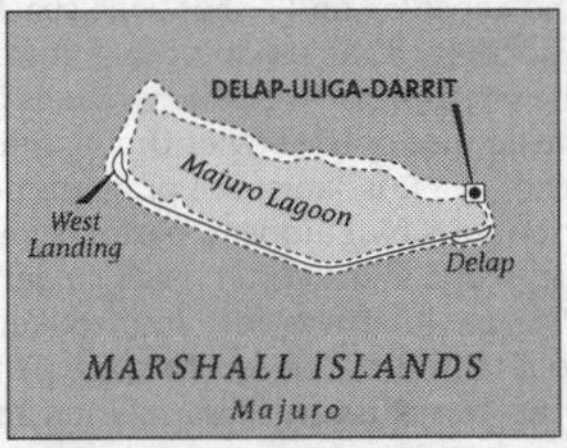

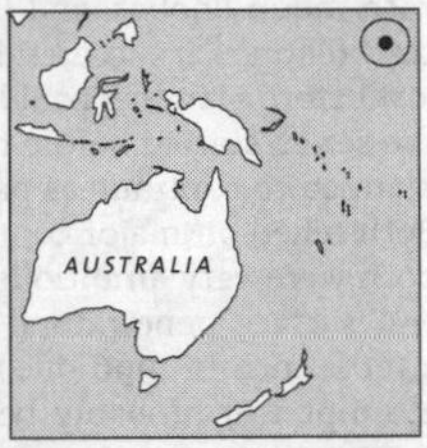

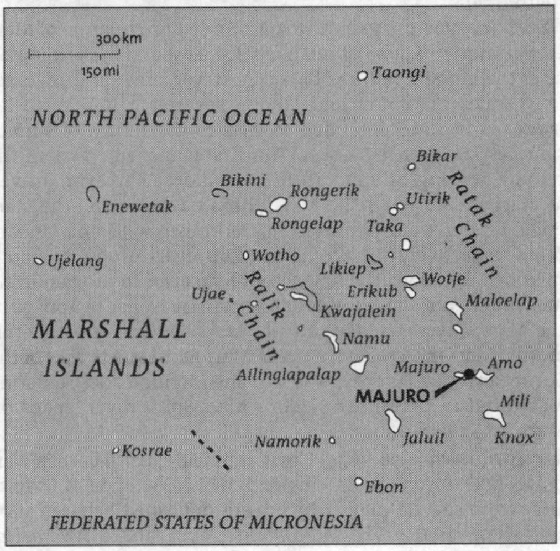

☐ International Airport

Timezone GMT +12

Area c.180 km²/70 sq mi

Population total (2002e) 56 600

Status Republic

Date of independence 1986

Capital Delap-Uliga-Darrit (municipality on Majuro Atoll)

Languages Marshallese (Kajin-Majol) (official), English and Japanese also spoken

Ethnic group Micronesian (99%)

Religions Christian (Protestant 90%, Roman Catholic 8%)

Physical features Archipelago in C Pacific Ocean; comprising 34 islands, including Kwajalein and Jaluit, and 870 reefs; two parallel chains of coral atolls, Ratik (E) and Ralik (W), extending c.925 km/800 mi in length; volcanic islands, rise no more than a few metres above sea level.

Climate Hot and humid; wet season (May–Nov); typhoon season (Dec–Mar); average annual temperature 27°C.

Currency 1 US Dollar (US$) = 100 cents

Economy Farming; fishing; tropical agriculture; coconuts, tomatoes, melons, breadfruit.

GDP (2001e) $115 mn, per capita $1600

History Explored by the Spanish, 1529; part of UN Trust Territory of the Pacific, 1949–78, administered by the USA; US nuclear weapon tests held on Bikini and Eniwetak atolls, 1946–62; self-governing republic, 1979; compact of free association with the USA in 1986 with US recognizing independence; trusteeship ended, 1990; governed by a President elected by a Parliament.

Head of State/Government
1979–96 Amata Kabua
1996–7 Kunio Lemari *Acting*
1997–2000 Imata Kabua
2000– Kessia Note

resumed Mars exploration in 1988, with dual launches of new generation interplanetary spacecraft to orbit Mars, rendezvous with moon Phobos, and land capsules on Phobos. One spacecraft (Phobos 2) successfully achieved the rendezvous, but was lost before a landing could be attempted. Two more missions in the series, started before the demise of the Soviet Union, were planned to continue as part of the Russian space programme. Both relied on major contributions by European partners and both were very ambitious in scope – an orbiter, hard landers, and surface penetrators. The payload was lost immediately after launch in 1996 due to a failure of the fourth stage. This attempt will probably be the last Russian Mars mission for many years.

Mars Surveyor programme A NASA-led programme of Mars exploration missions of relatively low cost and mass, initiated after the in-flight failure of Mars Observer, providing a decade-long series of orbital and landed spacecraft. It began with launches in 1996, intended to lead to the return of surface samples to Earth by 2008. The first-launched mission, the remote sensing orbiter called Mars Global Surveyor, arrived at Mars in late 1997. The Mars Climate Orbiter and the Mars Polar Lander were launched in December 1998 and January 1999 respectively for arrival at Mars in late 1999, but both missions were lost (the first through an error in programming measurements, the second for unknown reasons). In April 2001 the Mars Odyssey spacecraft was launched and entered orbit around Mars in October that year. Mars Express, a project of the European Space Agency, was launched in June 2003, entering Mars orbit in December. NASA's Mars Spirit rover landed on Mars in January 2004.

Marston, John (1576–1634) Playwright and satirist, born in Wardington, Oxfordshire, SC England, UK. He studied at Oxford, and wrote several plays which were published between 1602 and 1607, notably *The Malcontent* (1604), and *Eastward Ho!* (1605), a satirical comedy written in conjunction with Chapman and Jonson. In 1607 he gave up playwriting, took orders (1609), and held the living of Christ Church, Hampshire (1616–31).

Marston Moor, Battle of (1644) A major conflict in the English Civil War, in which a force of 27 000 parliamentary and Scottish troops defeated 18 000 royalists. The royalist cavalry was led by Prince Rupert; the parliamentary horse by Oliver Cromwell. The defeat led to the fall of the royalist stronghold of York, and the virtual collapse of Charles I's cause in the N.

marsupial A mammal, native to Australasia and the New World; young often develop in a pouch which opens forwards (climbing species) or backwards (burrowing species); vagina is branched; penis usually forked; second and third toes of foot often small and joined, forming a comb for grooming. (Order: Marsupialia, 266 species.)

marsupial mole An Australian marsupial (*Notoryctes typhlops*); mole-like with pale yellow coat; eyes and ears hidden by fur; nose pad enlarged to cover front of head; large claws for digging; tail very short; female with pouch opening backwards; inhabits dry sandy areas; burrows collapse behind them as they dig. (Family: Notoryctidae.)

Martello towers [mah(r)**tel**oh] Small circular forts with thick walls. Many were erected on the S and SE coast of England in the early 19th-c to provide observation posts and defence against a projected French invasion. The name comes from Cape Mortella, Corsica, where such a tower was captured by a British Fleet in 1794.

marten A mammal of genus *Martes* (7 species), native to Europe, Asia, and North America; solid body with sharp nose and long bushy tail; usually inhabits upland forests; eats small mammals, birds, and carrion. (Family: Mustelidae.)

martensite [**mah(r)**tinziyt] The principal component of hard steel, formed by quenching from high temperatures. It consists of intergrown plate-like crystals with a distorted cubic structure arising from the presence of carbon atoms in the iron structure.

Martha's Vineyard Island in the Atlantic off the SE coast of Massachusetts, USA; part of Duke's County; area 280 sq km/108 sq mi; chief town, Edgartown; former whaling and fishing centre; summer resort; so called because the first English settlers found an abundance of wild grapes growing here.

Martial, in full **Marcus Valerius Martialis** (c.40–c.104) Latin poet and epigrammatist, born at Bilbilis, Spain. He went to Rome in 64, and became a client of the influential Spanish house of the Senecas, through which he found a patron in Calpurnius Piso. He is remembered for his 12 books of epigrams, mainly satirical comments on contemporary events and society.

martial arts Styles of armed or unarmed combat developed in the East. In modern times most of these arts have developed into popular sports in the West.

martial law The imposition of military rule on the civilian population, either by the leader of an occupying army, or by a territory's own government. In the latter case, it most commonly occurs after there has been a military coup or during a period of colonial rule. Many countries' constitutions have provision for the introduction of martial law in times of foreign threats and emergencies, although in many liberal democracies there are severe restrictions on its implementation which render it largely impractical. The military in such countries can, however, be more readily mobilized in support of the civil authorities.

Martin, St (c.316–c.400) Patron saint of France, born in Sabaria, Pannonia. He studied at Pavia, travelled to Gaul, and founded the first monastery near Poitiers in c.360. He became famous for his sanctity and as a worker of miracles. He was drawn by force from his retreat in 371–2, and made Bishop of Tours, but chose to live in a new monastery which he founded at Marmoutier, near Tours. Feast day 11 (W) or 12 November (E).

Martin, Pierre Emile [mah(r)**tĩ**] (1824–1915) Metallurgist, born in Bourges, C France. In his father's iron and steel works, he devised an improved method of producing high-quality steel in an open-hearth furnace using the heat-regeneration process introduced by Siemens. The products of the Siemens–Martin process won a gold medal at the Paris Exhibition of 1867, and the open-hearth furnace became the major source of the world's steel. Martin spent his later years in poverty while others profited from his process, until in 1907 an international benefit fund restored his finances to a level of modest comfort.

Martin, Steve (1945–) Film actor, born in Waco, Texas, USA. As a comedy writer for television he won an Emmy Award for *The Smothers Brothers Comedy Hour* (1968) and a nomination for *Van Dyke and Company* (1975). He made his film debut in *The Absent Minded Waiter* (1977), which received an Oscar nomination for best short film. An inspired performance of lunacy in *All Of Me* (1984) brought him a New York Film Critics' Best Actor Award. Later films include *Parenthood* (1989), *Housesitter* (1992), *Father of the Bride* and its sequel (1991, 1995), *Bowfinger* (1999), and *Bringing Down the House* (2003).

martin A bird of the swallow family. Those with short tails are usually called 'martins', those with long tails 'swallows'. The names are not applied consistently. (Family: Hirundinidae, 23 species.)

Martín de Porres, St [**poh**res] (1579–1639) South American saint, who spent his entire life in the Dominican Order in Lima, Peru, ministering to the sick and poor. He was also noted for his way with animals. Beatified in 1837, he was canonized in 1962. He is the patron saint of social justice. Feast day 3 November.

Martin du Gard, Roger [mah(r)**tĩ** dü **gah(r)**] (1881–1958) Novelist, born in Neuilly, NC France. He is best known for his eight-novel series, *Les Thibault* (1922–40), dealing with family life during the first decades of the 20th-c. Author also of several plays, he was awarded the Nobel Prize for Literature in 1937.

Martini, Simone [mah(r)**tee**nee] (c.1284–1344) Painter, born in Siena, C Italy. A pupil of Duccio, he was the most important artist of the 14th-c Sienese school, notable for his grace of line and exquisite colour. He worked in Assisi (1333–9), and at the papal court at Avignon (1339–44). His 'Annunciation' is in the Uffizi Gallery.

Martinique [mah(r)tineek] pop (2000e) 416 000; area 1079 sq km/416 sq mi. Island in the Windward group of the Lesser Antilles, E Caribbean, between Dominica and St Lucia; capital, Fort-de-France; timezone GMT -4; population mainly of African or mixed descent; chief religion, Roman Catholicism; official language, French, with creole widely spoken; unit of currency, the euro; length, 61 km/38 mi; width, 24 km/15 mi; rises steeply from the sea, particularly on N coast; highest point, Mt Pelée (1397 m/4583 ft); tropical climate with high humidity; average temperature at Fort-de-France, 21–29°C (Jan–Mar), 23–31°C (Jun–Oct); wet season (Jul–Nov); visited by Columbus, 1502; French colony, 1635; overseas department of France, 1946; administered by a commissioner-general and an elected 41-member Regional Council; two senators and four deputies sent to National Assembly in Paris; economy based largely on agriculture; sugar cane, bananas, pineapples; construction, rum distilling, cement, oil refining, light industry, tourism.

Martin Luther King Day In the USA, the third Monday in January; a federal public holiday in honour of the civil rights leader, commemorated in about half of the US states. There are several variations on the name of the day, and the date of the celebration also varies, from state to state.

Martinmas In the UK, the feast of St Martin (11 Nov), a day on which traditionally rents were paid, servants hired, and livestock slaughtered for winter salting; a quarter-day in Scotland.

Martinson, Harry (Edmund) (1904–78) Poet and novelist, born in Jämshög, S Sweden. After a harsh childhood as parish orphan, he went to sea as a stoker in 1919 and travelled worldwide, before making his name as a poet. His autobiographical novels include *Nässlorna blomma* (1935, Flowering Nettle), and *Vägen ut* (1936, The Way Out). His poetic space epic, *Aniara* (1956), was set to music as an opera by Karl-Birger Blomdahl. He was elected to the Swedish Academy in 1949, and he shared the 1974 Nobel Prize for Literature with Eyvind Johnson.

Martinů, Bohuslav [mah(r)tinoo] (1890–1959) Composer, born in Polička, C Czech Republic. Expelled from the Prague Conservatory, he was readmitted in 1920, studying under Joseph Suk (1875–1935), before working in Paris. He fled to America in 1941, and produced a number of important works, including his first symphony, commissioned by Koussevitzky for the Boston Symphony Orchestra (1942). A prolific composer, he ranges from 18th-c orchestral works to modern programme pieces evoked by unusual stimuli such as football (*Half Time*) or aeroplanes (*Thunderbolt P 47*). His operas include the miniature *Comedy on a Bridge*.

Marvell, Andrew [mah(r)vl] (1621–78) Poet, politician, and satirist, born in Winestead, Hull, NE England, UK. He studied at Cambridge, travelled widely in Europe (1642–6), worked as a tutor, and became Milton's assistant (1657). He is remembered for his pastoral and love poems, notably 'To His Coy Mistress' and 'Upon Appleton House' (c.1652–3). Ranked among the metaphysical poets, his works were largely ignored until they were revived in the 20th-c, notably by T S Eliot, who recognized in them an integration of thought and feeling. After becoming an MP (1659), his writing was devoted to pamphlets and satires attacking intolerance and arbitrary government.

Marx, Karl (Heinrich) (1818–83) Social philosopher and founder of international communism, born in Trier, W Germany. The son of a Jewish lawyer, he studied law at Bonn and Berlin, but took up philosophy, particularly Hegelian philosophy, and Feuerbach's materialism. In 1841 he received a doctorate from the University of Jena. He edited a radical newspaper, and after it was suppressed in Germany he moved to Paris (1843) and Brussels (1845). There, with Engels as his closest collaborator, disciple, and sponsor, he reorganized the Socialist League of the Just, later renamed the Communist League, which met in London in 1847. In 1848, in conjunction with Engels, he finalized the *Communist Manifesto*, which interprets history as the history of class struggle and attacks the state as the instrument of oppression. It predicts a social revolution led by the proletariat, and attacks capitalism, private property, the family, religion, and morality as ideologies of the bourgeoisie. Expelled from most European countries, he settled in 1849 in London, where he studied economics, and wrote the first volume of his major work, *Das Kapital* (1867, two further volumes, compiled by Engels from Marx's drafts were added posthumously in 1884 and 1894). In these, he expanded his theory of global and political revolution as a result of the conflict between the working classes and the bourgeoisie. His goal was to unite all workers in the world in order to achieve political power and transcend national boundaries. He was a leading figure in the First International from 1864 until its demise in 1872. The last decade of his life was marked by increasing ill health. He is buried in Highgate Cemetery, London.

Marx Brothers Family of film comedians, born in New York City, USA, comprising Julius (1895–1977), or **Groucho**; Leonard (1891–1961), or **Chico**; Arthur (1893–1961), or **Harpo**; and Herbert (1901–79), or **Zeppo**. They began their stage career in vaudeville in a team called the Six Musical Mascots that included their mother, **Minnie** (d.1929), and an aunt; another brother, Milton (?1897–1977), known as **Gummo**, left the act early on. They later appeared as the Four Nightingales, and finally as the Marx Brothers. Their main reputation was made in a series of films, such as *Animal Crackers* and *Monkey Business* (both 1932). Herbert retired from films in 1935, and the others had further successes, such as *A Night at the Opera* (1935), and *A Day at the Races* (1937). Each had a well-defined stencil: Groucho with his wisecracks, cigar, and moustache; Chico, the pianist with his own technique and Italian accent; and Harpo, the dumb clown and harp maestro. The team broke up in 1949, and the brothers then pursued individual careers. Groucho wrote the autobiographical *Groucho and Me* (1959), and *Memoirs of a Mangy Lover* (1964), and Harpo published his autobiography, *Harpo Speaks* (1961).

Marxism The body of social and political thought informed by the writings of Karl Marx. According to Marx, the whole history of humankind is to be equated with the history of the class struggle. In Marx's view, the driving force of social change would be the contradiction between the structure of 'productive forces' and social order. These contradictions gradually increase, and eventually can only be abolished by a social revolution removing the ruling class and replacing it by another one. Only the working class, which will eventually defeat capitalism, can in the end establish a classless communist society. In communist interpretation, dialectical materialism is a higher stage of materialism, based on the English utopian socialism of, for example, Sir Thomas More, as well as on materialist philosophy (mainly as defined by Ludwig Feuerbach), and on Hegelian dialectics.

Marxism is thus essentially a critical analysis of capitalist society, contending that such societies are subject to crises which create the conditions for proletarian revolutions and the transformation to socialism. Much of Marx's writing, especially *Das Kapital*, was concerned with the economic dynamics of capitalist societies, seeing the state as an instrument of class rule supporting private capital and suppressing the masses. Because of private capital's need to earn profits or extract surplus value, wages have to be kept to a subsistence minimum. This produces economic contradictions, because it restricts the purchasing power of workers to consume the goods produced. Capitalism is, therefore, inherently unstable, being subject to crises of booms and slumps. Marx's view was that these crises would become increasingly worse, and eventually lead to revolution, whereby the working class would seize the state and establish a dictatorship of the proletariat, productive power would be in public hands, and class differences would disappear (socialism). This classless society would eventually lead to the withering away of the state, producing a communist society. Marxism sought to extend this method of analysis to contemporary conditions. In particular, Western Marxism examined the ability of state intervention to smooth out the crises of capitalism and establish a legitimacy for the existing capitalist order through its control over education and the media. In non-industrialized societies Marxism was adapted to account for revolution in countries where there was no extensive development of capitalism, in contrast to Marx's view of history. It is generally recognized that Marx's writings regarding the transformation to socialism and the nature of socialism lacked detail. In consequence, Marxism has attracted a wide range of interpretations by political theorists.

Marxism–Leninism A distinct variant of Marxism, considered as a combination of dialectical and historical materialism; the pragmatic ideology of most communist parties until 1989. It was formulated by Lenin, who prior to the Bolshevik revolution argued for direct rule by workers and peasants, and advocated direct democracy through the soviets (councils). In practice, the Bolshevik revolution did not produce a democratic republic, but gave a 'leading and directing' role to the party, seen as the vanguard of a working class which had insufficient political consciousness to forge a revolution; such a well-organized and disciplined party, operating according to the principles of democratic centralism, would be able to exploit the revolutionary situation. Leninist principles of a revolutionary vanguard became the central tenet of all communist parties. All were organized according to the idea of democratic centralism which affords the leadership, on the grounds of its revolutionary insight, the right to dictate party policy, to select party officials from above, and to discipline dissenting party members. Lenin modified Marx's theory of historical materialism, contending that revolutionary opportunities should be seized when they arose, and not when the social and economic conditions of capitalist crisis leading to proletarian revolution existed. He also developed a theory of imperialism which held that it was the last stage of a decaying capitalism. This was used to justify revolution in feudal Russia, because it was an imperial power, and later to justify communist intervention in underdeveloped countries as part of the struggle between socialism and imperialism. Marxism–Leninism was subsequently equated with the dictatorship of the proletariat under the leadership of the communist party (the 'people's democracy' or transitional phase between capitalism and communism) in the Soviet satellite states. This was redefined as 'realistic' socialism in the Brezhnev era.

Mary I, Tudor (1516–58) Queen of England and Ireland (1553–8), born in Greenwich, EC Greater London, UK, the daughter of Henry VIII by his first wife, Catherine of Aragon. She was a devout Catholic, and during the reign of Edward, her half brother, she lived in retirement, refusing to conform to the new religion. Despite Northumberland's conspiracy to prevent her succession on Edward's death (1553), she relied on the support of the country, entered London, and ousted Lady Jane Grey. Thereafter she proceeded cautiously, repealing anti-Catholic legislation and reviving Catholic practices, but her intention was to restore papal supremacy with the assistance of Cardinal Pole, and to cement a Catholic union with Philip II of Spain. These aspirations provoked Wyatt's rebellion, followed by the execution of Jane Grey and the imprisonment of Mary's half-sister, Elizabeth, on suspicion of complicity. Mary's unpopular marriage to Philip (1554) was followed by the repeal of the antipapal laws of Henry VIII, the restoration of ecclesiastical courts and the laws against heresy (1555), and the burning at the stake of some 300 Protestants. This earned her the name of 'Bloody Mary' in Protestant hagiography, though her direct responsibility is unlikely. The persecutions of her reign were no more severe than many on the European continent, but were unprecedented in England. She died allegedly of cancer.

Mary II (1662–94) Queen of Britain and Ireland from 1689, born in St James's Palace, London, UK, the daughter of the Duke of York (later James II) and his first wife, **Anne Hyde** (1638–71). She was married in 1677 to her first cousin, William, Stadtholder of the United Netherlands, who in November 1688 landed in Torbay with an Anglo-Dutch army in response to an invitation from seven Whig peers hostile to the arbitrary rule of James II. When James fled to France, she came to London from Holland and was proclaimed queen, sharing the throne with her husband, who became William III. Both sovereigns accepted the constitutional revolution implicit in the Declaration of Rights. She was content to leave executive authority with William (except when he was abroad or campaigning in Ireland), but she was largely responsible for raising the moral standard of court life, and enjoyed a popularity which her husband never attained. She died of smallpox, and left no children.

Mary, Queen of Scots (1542–87) Queen of Scotland (1542–87) and queen consort of France (1559–60), born in Linlithgow Palace, West Lothian, EC Scotland, UK, the daughter of James V of Scotland by his second wife, Mary of Guise. Queen of Scotland at a week old, her betrothal to Prince Edward of England was annulled by the Scottish parliament, precipitating war with England. After the Scots' defeat at Pinkie (1547), she was sent to the French court and married the Dauphin (1558), later Francis II, but was widowed at 18 (1560) and returned to Scotland (1561). In 1565, ambitious for the English throne, she married her cousin, Henry Stewart, Lord Darnley, a grandson of Margaret Tudor, but became disgusted by his debauchery, and was soon alienated from him. The vicious murder of Rizzio, her Italian secretary, by Darnley and a group of Protestant nobles in her presence (1566) confirmed her insecurity. The birth of a son, the future James VI, failed to bring a reconciliation. While ill with smallpox, Darnley was mysteriously killed in an explosion at Kirk o' Field (1567); the chief suspect was the Earl of Bothwell, who underwent a mock trial and was acquitted. Mary's involvement is unclear, but she consented to marry Bothwell, a divorcé with whom she had become infatuated. The Protestant nobles under Morton rose against her; she surrendered at Carberry Hill, was imprisoned at Loch Leven, and compelled to abdicate. After escaping, she raised an army, but was defeated again by the confederate lords at Langside (1568). Placing herself under the protection of Queen Elizabeth, she found herself instead a prisoner for life. Her presence in England gave rise to countless plots to depose Elizabeth and restore Catholicism. Finally, after the Babington conspiracy (1586) she was brought to trial for treason, and executed in Fotheringay Castle, Northamptonshire.

Mary (mother of Jesus), also known as **Our Lady** or **the Blessed Virgin Mary** (?–c.63) Mother of Jesus Christ. In the New Testament she is most prominent in the stories of Jesus's birth (in the Gospels of Matthew and Luke), where the conception of Jesus is said to be 'of the Holy Spirit' (*Matt* 1.18), and she is described as betrothed to Joseph. She only occasionally appears in Jesus's ministry, but (*John* 19.25) she was present at Jesus's crucifixion, and was committed by him to the care of the disciple, John. According to the Acts of the Apostles, she remained in Jerusalem during the early years of the Church, and tradition places her tomb in Jerusalem. She has become a subject of devotion in her own right, especially in Roman Catholic doctrine and worship, and apocryphal traditions were attached to her in works such as the *Gospel of Mary* and *Gospel of the Birth of Mary*. The belief that her body was taken up into heaven is celebrated in the festival of the Assumption, defined as Roman Catholic dogma in 1950. Her Immaculate Conception has been a dogma since 1854. Belief in the apparitions of the Virgin at Lourdes, Fatima, Medugorje and in several other places attracts many thousands of pilgrims each year. In Roman Catholic and Orthodox Christianity, she holds a special place as an intermediary between believers and God.

Mary of Teck, in full **Victoria Mary Augusta Louise Olga Pauline Claudine Agnes** (1867–1953) Queen-consort of Great Britain, the wife of George V, born in Kensington Palace, London, UK, the only daughter of Francis, Duke of Teck, and Princess

Mary Adelaide of Cambridge, a grand-daughter of George III. In 1891 she accepted a marriage proposal from the Duke of Clarence, who within six weeks died from pneumonia. She then married his brother, the Duke of York, in 1893. After his accession (as George V) in 1910, she accompanied him to Delhi as Empress of India for the historically unique Coronation Durbar of December 1911. Although by nature stiff and reserved, she was more sympathetic to changing habits than her husband, whom she helped to mould into a 'people's king'. After the abdication of her eldest son, Edward VIII, she once again strengthened the popular appeal of the monarchy throughout the reign of her second son, George VI, whom she survived by 13 months.

Maryland pop (2000e) 5 296 500; area 27 090 sq km/10 460 sq mi. State in E USA, divided into 23 counties and one city; the 'Old Line' or 'Free State'; the first settlement (1634) located at St Mary's (state capital until 1694); seventh of the original 13 states to ratify the Constitution, 1788; gave up territory for the establishment of the District of Columbia; abolished slavery, 1864; capital, Annapolis; other chief city, Baltimore (85% of the population live in this area); bounded E by Delaware and the Atlantic Ocean; Chesapeake Bay stretches N through the state, almost splitting it in two; the Potomac R forms most of the S border; the Susquehanna and Patuxent Rivers cross the state, emptying into Chesapeake Bay; highest point Mt Backbone (1024 m/3360 ft); to the N and W is the rolling Piedmont, rising up to the Blue Ridge and Pennsylvania Hills; to the S and E is Chesapeake Bay with indented shores forming a popular resort area; the Eastern Shore with over 12 000 sq km/4500 sq mi of forest is noted for its scenic beauty; iron and steel, shipbuilding, electrical equipment, machinery, processed foods; poultry, dairy products, corn, soybeans, tobacco.

Mary Magdalene, St [magdalen] (1st-c) Disciple of Jesus. Very little is known about her; *Magdalene* possibly means 'of Magdala', in Galilee. Luke (8.2) reports that Jesus exorcised seven evil spirits from her; thereafter she appears only in the narratives of Jesus's passion and resurrection where, seemingly with other women, she appears at the Cross and later at the empty tomb. John (20) relates a private encounter with the resurrected Jesus. Her identification with Mary, the sister of Martha (*John* 11–12), is very tenuous. Feast day 22 July.

Mary Rose A warship built in 1511 for Henry VIII and rebuilt in 1536. In 1545, while in action against the French off Portsmouth, she capsized and sank with the loss of most of her crew. Her remains were salvaged in 1982 in a complex and much-publicized operation, and are now exhibited at Portsmouth.

Masaccio [masachio], originally **Tommaso de Giovanni di Simone Guidi** (1401–28) Painter and pioneer of the Renaissance, born in Castel San Giovanni di Altura, Duchy of Milan. In his short life he brought about a revolution in the dramatic and realistic representation of biblical events. This was recognized by his contemporaries, and had a great influence on Michelangelo and through him on the entire 16th-c. His greatest work is the fresco cycle in the Brancacci Chapel of the Church of S Maria del Carmine in Florence (1424–7).

Masada [masahda] or **Mezada** A Roman hilltop fortress established 37–31 BC by the Palestinian ruler Herod in barren mountains W of the Dead Sea; within Israel since 1947. Seized by zealots during the First Jewish Revolt in AD 66–70, it was taken by the Roman army in 73 after a lengthy siege which culminated in the mass suicide of all 400 defenders. As a political symbol of Jewish solidarity and resistance down the ages, it remains unparalleled.

Masai or **Maasai** [masiy] A people of the Rift Valley area of Kenya and Tanzania, speaking a Nilotic language. They are nomadic and semi-nomadic cattle herders, organized in a complex age-set system which provided warriors under control of ritual leaders. In some regions they are being encouraged to turn to sedentary farming. Masai possess the typical bodily adaptation to the hot climate of the E African savannah, with long, narrow torso and limbs, giving them average body height of 1 m 80 cm/6 ft or more.

Masaryk, Tomáš (Garrigue) [masarik] (1850–1937) Founder-president of the Czechoslovakian Republic (1918–35), born in Hodonin, SE Czech Republic. He was a professor of philosophy in Prague (1882–1914), supported Czech national causes in parliament in Vienna (1891–3, 1907–14), and exposed as forgeries documents intended by the Habsburg authorities to discredit the political leaders of the Slav minorities. During World War 1 he worked with Beneš in London, where he became chairman of the Czech National Council, organizing the Czech independence movement. He was re-elected president on three occasions, before resigning in 1935 in favour of Beneš.

Mascagni, Pietro [maskanyee] (1863–1945) Composer, born in Livorno, W Italy. After leaving the Milan Conservatory prematurely (disliking the discipline there), he joined a travelling opera company. In 1890 he produced the brilliantly successful one-act opera, *Cavalleria rusticana*. His many later operas failed to repeat this success, though arias and intermezzi from them are still performed.

Mascarene Islands [maskareen], Fr **Archipel des Mascareignes** Island group in the Indian Ocean, 700–800 km/450–500 mi E of Madagascar; includes Réunion, Mauritius, and Rodrigues; named after the 16th-c Portuguese navigator, Mascarenhas.

mascon *maria*

Masefield, John (Edward) (1878–1967) Poet and novelist, born in Ledbury, Hereford and Worcester, WC England, UK. Trained for the merchant service, he served his apprenticeship on a sailing ship. Ill health drove him ashore, and after three years in New York he returned to England to become a writer in 1897, first making his mark as a journalist. His earliest and best-known poetical work, *Salt Water Ballads* (containing 'Sea Fever'), appeared in 1902. His finest narrative poem is probably 'Reynard the Fox' (1919), and other works include the novels *Sard Harker* (1924) and *The Hawbucks* (1929), and the plays *The Trial of Jesus* (1925) and *The Coming of Christ* (1928). He became poet laureate in 1930.

maser A device which produces microwaves from excited atoms or molecules, devised in 1954 by Charles Townes and others; the name is an acronym of *microwave amplification by the stimulated emission of radiation*. The first device relied on thermally excited ammonia molecules, other gases such as hydrogen are now also used. Masers employ the same physical principles as lasers, but produce lower frequency radiation. They are used as sensitive low-noise amplifiers for radar and satellite communications.

Maseru [maseeroo] 29°19S 27°29E, pop (2000e) 148 000. Capital of Lesotho; on the R Caledon, 130 km/81 mi E of Bloemfontein (South Africa); altitude 1506 m/4941 ft; founded, 1869; airport; railway terminus; university (1964); experimental crop station; administration, commerce, diamond processing, tourism.

Mashhad [mashhad] or **Meshed** 36°16N 59°34E, pop (2000e) 2 021 000. Capital city of Mashhad district, Khorasan, NE Iran; near the Turkmenia border, just S of the R Kashaf; second largest city in Iran; industrial and trade centre; airport; railway; university (1956); carpets, gemstones; 9th-c shrine of Imam Ali Reza.

masochism *sadomasochism*

Masolino (da Panicale) [masohleenoh], originally **Tommaso di Cristoforo Fini** (1383–c.1447) Painter, born in Panicale, Romagna. He matriculated in the Florentine Guild in 1423. His early style, close to the Gothic manner of Lorenzo Monaco, yielded briefly to the influence of the more realistic art of Masaccio, with whom he worked on the frescoes of the Life of St Peter in the Brancacci Chapel of the Church of S Maria del Carmine in Florence. His greatest work is the fresco cycle in the Baptistery and Collegiata of Castiglione d'Olona near Como (1430s), which were discovered only in 1843.

Mason, James (1909–84) Actor, born in Huddersfield, West Yorkshire, N England, UK. He studied architecture, then made his stage debut in 1931. He appeared at the Old Vic and with the Gate Company in Dublin before making his film debut in 1935. He became one of the most prolific, distinguished, and reliable of cinema actors. He was nominated for an Oscar for *A Star Is Born* (1954), *Georgy Girl* (1966), and *The Verdict* (1982). Other respected performances from more than 100 films include *Lolita* (1962) and *The Shooting Party* (1984).

mason bee A solitary bee that collects soft malleable materials such as mud, resin, or chewed leaves, and shapes them into a nest either inside an existing hole in timber or under stones, or on branches or exposed rock surfaces. (Order: Hymenoptera. Family: Megachilidae.)

Mason–Dixon Line The border between Maryland and Pennsylvania, USA, drawn in 1763–7 by British astronomers Charles Mason (1730–87) and Jeremiah Dixon (1733–79). It is regarded as the boundary between 'the North' and 'the South'.

Masoretes or **Massoretes** [masohreets] (Heb 'transmitters of tradition') Jewish scholars considered responsible for preserving traditions regarding the text of the Hebrew Bible, and especially for creating a system of vowel signs to reflect the pronunciation of the Hebrew consonantal text in their day. The resulting vocalized text (c.9th–10th-c) was known as the **Masoretic Text**, the basis for the text of the Hebrew Bible normally used today.

masque A courtly celebration composed of poetry, song, dance, and (usually) elaborate mechanical scenery, unified by a theme or emblematic story. It was often performed at banquets when the masked performers would engage spectators in the fictional game, and encourage participation in the dancing. Shakespeare introduced a short masque in *The Tempest* (1611), and music for Milton's masque *Comus* (1634) was written by Henry Lawes. The Royal masques of Tudor and Stuart England are best known for the collaboration of Ben Jonson and Inigo Jones (1605–31).

mass An intrinsic property of all matter and energy, the source of gravitational field; symbol *m*, units kg (kilogram). It is perceived as an object's weight (the downward-acting force due to gravity) or its inertia (its reluctance to change its motion). The mass of an object increases with its velocity, according to special relativity, tending towards infinity as the object's velocity approaches the speed of light.

Mass (Lat *missa*, from *missio* 'dismissal') The sacrament of the Eucharist (Holy Communion) in the Roman Catholic Church and some other churches. Bread and wine are consecrated by a priest, and the elements (usually bread alone) distributed among the faithful. According to the doctrine of the Council of Trent (counteracting the teaching of the 16th-c Reformers) the bread and wine become the body and blood of Christ (*transubstantiation*), and the sacrament is to be understood as a divine, propitiatory sacrifice. Masses perform different functions in the life of the Church, eg a Requiem Mass for the dead, a Nuptial Mass for a marriage.

Massachusetts pop (2000e) 6 349 000; area 21 455 sq km/8284 sq mi. New England state in NE USA, divided into 14 counties; the 'Bay State' or 'Old Colony'; third most densely populated state; one of the original states of the Union, sixth to ratify the Constitution, 1788; capital, Boston; other chief cities, Cambridge, Springfield, Worcester; rises from an indented coastline to a stony, upland interior and gentle, rolling hills to the W; Connecticut R flows N–S across the W part of the state, Housatonic R flows S near the W border, Merrimack R enters the Atlantic Ocean in the NE; Berkshire Hills rise between the Housatonic and Connecticut Rivers; highest point Mt Greylock (1049 m/3442 ft); electronics, printing and publishing, timber, nursery and greenhouse produce, vegetables, cranberries; many coastal resorts; Pilgrim Fathers settled at Plymouth in 1620; colony of Massachusetts founded 1629; first shots of the War of Independence fired at Lexington in 1775.

mass action, law of A law in chemistry: the rate of reaction of a substance is proportional to its 'active mass', or essentially its concentration. Hence, the speed of a simple chemical reaction is proportional to the product of the concentrations of the reactants. Most chemical reactions must, however, be analysed in terms of a sequence of such simple reactions.

massage *aromatherapy; cardiac resuscitation*

Massawa [masahwa] or **Mitsiwa** 15°37N 39°28E, pop (2000e) 58 900. Seaport in Eritrea, on the Red Sea coast, 65 km/40 mi NE of Asmara; occupied by Italy, 1885; capital of Italian Eritrea until 1897; largely rebuilt after earthquake in 1921; railway; commercial centre; fish and meat processing, cement, salt, tourism; naval base.

Masséna, André [masayna] (1758–1817) French general of the Revolutionary and Napoleonic Wars, born in Nice, SE France. He distinguished himself in Napoleon's Italian campaign (1796–7), defeating the Russians at Zürich (1799), and successfully defending Genoa (1800). He was created a marshal of the empire in 1804, took command of the army in Italy, and after further successes was made Duke of Rivoli (1807). After the Austrian campaign (1809) he was made Prince of Essling. However, forced to retreat in the Iberian Peninsula by Wellington's forces, he was relieved of his command (1810).

mass–energy relation A relationship in physics, stated by Einstein, expressed as $E = mc^2$, where E is energy, c is the velocity of light, and m is mass, as measured for a moving object. It corresponds to the statement that all energy has mass (rather than 'mass and energy are interconvertible'). In typical nuclear decay, the sum of the masses of decay fragments as measured at rest is less than the initial rest mass by the amount E/c^2, where E is the energy evolved in the process. In general, energy and mass are conserved, rest mass is not.

Massenet, Jules (Emile Frédéric) [masenay] (1842–1912) Composer, born in Montaud, SW France. He studied at the Paris Conservatoire, where he was professor (1878–96). He made his name with the comic opera *Don César de Bazan* (1872). Other operas followed, including *Manon* (1884), considered by many to be his masterpiece, *Le Cid* (1885), and *Werther* (1892). Among his other works are oratorios, orchestral suites, music for piano, and songs.

Massey, Raymond (Hart) (1896–1983) Actor, born in Toronto, Ontario, SE Canada. He made his stage debut in 1922, and played Lincoln in *Abe Lincoln* (1938–9). On film he played leading parts in more than 60 films, including *Arsenic and Old Lace* (1942) and *East of Eden* (1955). He is remembered for his long-running television role as 'Dr Gillespie' in the *Dr Kildare* series during the 1960s.

Massey, William Ferguson (1856–1925) New Zealand statesman and prime minister (1912–25), born in Limavady, Co Londonderry, NW Northern Ireland, UK. He emigrated to New Zealand in 1870 and became a farmer, taking the leadership of farming associations. Elected to the House of Representatives (1894) as a Conservative, he became Leader of the Opposition (1894–1912), and then prime minister. He held this office until his death, leading the coalition during World War 1.

Massif Central [maseef sõtral] Area of ancient rocks in SEC France, occupying about a sixth of the country; generally over 300 m/1000 ft; highest peak, Puy de Sancy in the Monts Dore (1885 m/6184 ft); massive limestone beds with gorges, crags, and caves, as well as volcanic rocks such as the Monts Dômes; source of Loire, Allier, Cher, and Creuse Rivers; farming, several industrial centres, tourism; winter sports at Le Mont-Dore, Super-Besse, Super-Lioran.

Massine, Léonide [maseen], originally **Leonid Fyodorovich Miassin** (1896–1979) Ballet dancer, choreographer, and mime, born in Moscow, Russia. He trained with the Imperial Ballet School at St Petersburg, then became principal dancer, replacing Nijinsky in Diaghilev's Ballets Russes, and going on to choreograph such acclaimed works as *La Boutique fantasque* (1919) and *The Rite of Spring* (1920). He settled in Europe, working independently for various companies, including Sadler's Wells and Ballets des Champs Elysées. He created his own parts in the ballet films *The Red Shoes* (1948), and *The Tales of Hoffmann* (1950). He became an American citizen in 1944.

Massinger, Philip (1583–1640) Playwright, born near Salisbury, Wiltshire, S England, UK. After leaving Oxford without a degree, he became a playwright apprenticed to Henslowe. Much of his work after 1613 is in collaboration with others, especially Fletcher. *The City Madam* (1632) and *A New Way to Pay Old Debts* (1633) are among his best-known satirical comedies. He is credited with having contributed, with Shakespeare, to portions of *Henry VIII* and of *The Two Noble Kinsmen*, both printed in 1634.

mass media *media*

mass number *nucleon number*

mass observation A set of social research techniques developed in the late 1930s for gathering a substantial amount of data on the lives of 'ordinary' people, including ethnographic community studies using informal interviews, participant observation, and similar methods. Both professional and lay volunteer observers and informants were used to produce a broad, richly detailed profile of a number of urban communities. Today the technique is less fashionable, though the revolution in communications technology makes the approach more feasible.

mass spectrometer A machine for measuring the proportions and masses of the atomic species in some sample; invented in 1919 by British scientist Francis Aston (1877–1945). Ions formed from a gaseous sample are passed through a magnetic field, where they are deflected by an amount depending on their mass. Different isotopes can be distinguished. It is an important analytical device for determining atomic and isotopic compositions.

Massys or **Matsys, Quentin** [masees] (c.1466–c.1530) Painter, born in Louvain, C Belgium. In 1491 he joined the painters' Guild of St Luke in Antwerp. His paintings are mostly religious and genre pictures, treated with a reverent spirit, but with decided touches of Realism (as in 'The Banker and His Wife'). He also ranks high as a portrait painter, his best works including a portrait of Erasmus.

mastaba [mastaba] An ancient Egyptian funerary tomb built of brick or stone; rectangular, flat-topped with sloping sides. An outer chamber for offerings links to an inner chamber, and from there a shaft leads downwards to the actual grave below ground level.

mast cells Cells with granules containing histamine, heparin, and other chemicals. They are absent from blood, but present in the loose connective tissue surrounding the blood vessels and lymphatics, especially in the respiratory and digestive tracts. Tissue injury and infection causes the release of the granular contents, resulting in inflammatory and allergic responses.

mastectomy A surgical procedure involving the removal of all or part of the breast, sometimes including the excision of the associated lymph nodes under the arm. The operation is performed in the treatment of malignant breast tumours.

master An artistic status achieved within the mediaeval guild system. Artists and craftsmen followed several years' apprenticeship before becoming 'masters', through production of a 'masterpiece'. Only then could they open workshops of their own and take apprentices. The term **Old Master** is used loosely to refer to any major painter from Giotto to Cézanne, regarded as a model of traditional excellence.

Masters, Edgar Lee (1869–1950) Poet and novelist, born in Garnett, Kansas, USA. He studied at Knox College, Galesburg, IL, was admitted to the bar in 1891, and became a successful lawyer in Chicago. His most memorable work is the *Spoon River Anthology* (1915), a book of epitaphs in free verse in the form of monologues about a small town community.

Master, John (1914–83) Writer and soldier, born in Calcutta, India. He grew up in India and was educated at Wellington and the Royal Military College, Sandhurst. During his army career he served in India, Myanmar (Burma), and the Middle East. After Indian independence he moved to the USA and wrote a series of novels about the Savage family in India. *Nightrunners of Bengal* (1951) and *Bhowani Junction* (1953) became immediate best-sellers. He also wrote a trilogy about World War 1, *Loss of Eden: Now God Be Thanked* (1979), and a biography of Casanova (1969).

Masters The popular name for the **US Masters** golf tournament, played every April over four rounds at Augusta National Golf Club in Augusta, GA. An invitational event, only the world's top players take part. The Masters was the idea of the former leading US amateur golfer Robert Tyre ('Bobby') Jones (1902–71), who lived in Georgia. The first Masters was in 1934, and won by Horton Smith (USA). The winner receives (for a year) a coveted green jacket as part of the prize.

Masters and Johnson Human sexuality researchers and authors: **William H(owell) Masters** (1915–2001) and **Virginia E(shelman) Johnson** (1925–), born in Cleveland, Ohio, and Springfield, Missouri, USA, respectively. He studied medicine at Rochester University, joined Washington University School of Medicine (St Louis) in 1947, and began his research work into sexuality in 1954. She studied at University of Missouri, and began work with Masters as a research associate in 1957. In 1964 they established the Reproductive Biology Research Foundation, where the study of the psychology and physiology of sexual intercourse was carried out using volunteer subjects under laboratory conditions. They published *Human Sexual Response* in 1966, which became an international best seller. They continued to publish sexual studies, including *Human Sexual Inadequacy* (1970) and *On Sex and Human Loving* (1986). They married in 1971 and divorced in 1992.

Mastersingers *Meistersinger*

mastic An evergreen shrub, sometimes a small tree (*Pistacia lentiscus*) growing to 8 m/26 ft, native to the Mediterranean region; leaves pinnate with 6–12 leaflets on a winged stalk; flowers tiny, in dense axillary heads; fruits round, red becoming black, very aromatic. The mastic resin is used both in medicine and as a varnish sealant. (Family: Anacardiaceae.)

mastiff A large domestic dog; originally any large dog, but now restricted to three breeds: the **Old English mastiff** (short pale coat, long legs and tail, heavy head with short pendulous ears, deep muzzle and jowls), the rare **Tibetan mastiff**, and the **Japanese tosa**. The name is also used in **bull-mastiff**.

mastodon A browsing, elephant-like mammal found in woodland savannahs during the Miocene epoch, almost worldwide in distribution; became extinct in the Pleistocene epoch; characterized by dentition; often with upper and lower pairs of tusks, lower tusks sometimes shovel-like. (Order: Proboscidea.)

mastoiditis [mastoydiytis] Acute bacterial inflammation in the honeycomb of air-containing spaces within the mastoid bone of the skull. Symptoms include earache, fever, and pain behind the ear. Formerly a common complication of infection in the nose or throat, the use of antibiotics has greatly reduced its frequency. Complications of mastoiditis include meningitis, brain abscess, and deafness.

mastoid process The large bony prominence behind the ear. It is part of the temporal bone, and contains air cells (**mastoid air cells**) which communicate with the middle ear cavity. It gives attachment to the *sternomastoid* muscle (which in thin individuals stands out as it passes downwards and medially towards the sternum).

Mastroianni, Marcello [mastroyahnee] (1924–96) Actor, born in Fontana Liri, C Italy. A survivor of a wartime Nazi labour camp, he studied at the University of Rome, was involved in amateur dramatics and, sponsored by the university, joined a leading theatrical troupe. He made his film debut in 1947, and by 1960 was established as an international star with his role in Fellini's *La dolce vita*. Co-starring in many films with Sophia Loren, he received Oscar nominations for *Divorzio all'Italiano* (1962, Divorce, Italian Style), *Una giornata particolare* (1977, A Special Day), and *Oci ciornie* (1987, Dark Eyes). His last film was *Three Lives and Only One Death* (1996).

masturbation A normal process in which there is manual or mechanical stimulation of the sex organs for the purpose of sexual gratification. It is usually accompanied by sexual fantasies.

Matabeleland [matabeeleeland] Region of W and S Zimbabwe, between the Zambezi and Limpopo Rivers; named after the Matabele Bantu, a Zulu tribe originally located in Natal and the Transvaal; acquired by the British South Africa Company, 1889; part of Southern Rhodesia, 1923; chief town, Bulawayo.

Mata Hari [mahta hahree], (Malay 'sun'), pseudonym of **Margaretha Geertruide MacLeod**, *née* **Zelle** (1876–1917) Dancer and spy, born in Leeuwarden, N Netherlands. In 1895 she married Campbell MacLeod, a British-born captain in the Dutch army, but the marriage broke up. Billing herself as a Javanese dancer, she began to perform erotic dances for private gatherings (1905), adopting the stage name of Mata Hari. In 1907 she joined the German secret service, and became the courtesan of men in high military and governmental positions (on both sides during the war). Found guilty of espionage for the Germans, she was shot by the French in Paris. Her name has become synonymous with the alluring female spy.

matamata [matamata] A side-necked turtle from South America (*Chelus fimbriatus*); large head shaped like an arrowhead; shell with a jagged irregular surface, often with a growth of water weed; lies camouflaged on river beds and ambushes passing fish. (Family: Chelidae.)

materialism The philosophical view that everything is composed exclusively of physical constituents located in space and time. Materialists thus deny the independent existence of minds, mental states, spirit, or abstract entities such as universals and numbers. Forms of materialism go back as far as Democritus and Epicurus; the main 20th-c variants were physicalism and dialectical materialism.

materials science The study of the engineering properties of materials, as dictated by their microscopic structure. It draws on standard mechanical testing techniques from engineering, and methods of structural study derived from physics and chemistry (eg electron microscopy), to understand how bonds are formed between different components of material. It has been responsible for the development of several new materials, such as conducting rubber, metallic glasses, ceramics for use in car engines, special metals for aircraft, and the fibreglass and carbon fibre composites used in sports equipment.

mathematical linguistics The study of language using mathematical concepts, of particular importance in the formalization of linguistic theory within generative grammar. Statistical techniques are also widely employed, eg in the study of the frequency and distribution of specific forms in texts, to decide cases of uncertain authorship (**statistical linguistics**).

mathematical logic The application of mathematical rigour and symbolic techniques to the study of logic, such as the development of formal languages and axiom systems for constructing logical proofs; also known as **symbolic logic**. Modern work in the field was inspired by Boole, and carried forward by Frege, Whitehead and Russell, Gödel, and Tarski.

mathematics A systematic body of knowledge built on certain axioms and assumptions, principally relating to numbers and spatial relationships. Thus, **arithmetic** was developed from the natural (or counting) numbers (1, 2, 3, 4...) to negative integers (−3,−2,−1...), rationals ($-\frac{3}{4}$, $-\frac{1}{2}$, $\frac{1}{2}$...), irrationals ($\sqrt{2}$...), and transcendentals (π, e...). **Geometry** was developed from Euclid's axioms, and later from variants of them. **Algebra** was generalized from arithmetic algebra, where an unknown x represented a number, to abstract algebras, in which not only were the operations defined differently (eg multiplication is not necessarily commutative, $a \times b$ is not equal to $b \times a$), but the operations themselves are not defined on numbers, eg Boolean algebra is defined on sets.

Virtually all civilizations had some idea of counting, albeit as a one-to-one correspondence between the number of animals to be counted and the number of marks on a stick. The idea of a number came next, then that of a numeral to represent that number; but by c.1000 BC peoples such as the Chinese, Hindus, Babylonians, and Egyptians had made significant advances in arithmetic. The study of geometry was developed by the Greeks from c.600 BC, with Thales of Miletus, Pythagoras, and their disciples developing it from stated axioms; much of their work was summarized in Euclid's *Elements* (c.300 BC). The greatest mathematician of pre-Christian times was Archimedes. The invention of algebra is credited to the Arabs (notably al-Khawarizmi, AD c.800), who had also introduced to Europe the system of numerals on which our present system is based.

Euclidean geometry had been virtually exhausted by the 17th-c, but Descartes' invention of co-ordinate geometry opened exciting new prospects, and later Gauss, Lobachevsky, and others varied the postulates on which Euclidean geometry was based. The invention of the calculus by Newton and Leibniz enabled scientists to solve a vast range of physical problems, including the motion of the celestial bodies. In 17th-c France, Fermat and Pascal pioneered the study of probability, furthered by Abraham Demoivre (1667–1754, a close friend of Isaac Newton), and others. The 19th-c saw Gauss, the greatest mathematician of that century, contribute to almost every field of mathematics then known, his own favourite being number theory. At the same time, abstract ideas were being developed, such as set theory by Cantor, group theory by Evariste Galois (1811–32), and matrix algebra. Developments in the past 40 years have been stimulated by the electronic computer, advances being made in fields as diverse as numerical analysis and the theory of fractals.

Abstract ideas in mathematics may be classified as **pure mathematics**, and their applications as **applied mathematics**; but it is remarkable how many abstract ideas (eg set theory, matrix algebra) have had practical applications (the pattern of a snow flake, electrical networks) and how practical problems (eg the fair distribution of lottery prizes) have stimulated abstract ideas (the concept of a random number). Since the 1960s, many new topics (set theory, matrices, and vectors) have been taught in schools. These are sometimes, usually abusively, called 'new maths'.

Mather, Cotton [ma<u>th</u>er] (1663–1728) Colonial minister and writer, born in Boston, Massachusetts, USA. He studied at Harvard, and became a colleague to his father, Increase Mather (1639–1723), at the Second Church, Boston, succeeding him in 1683. His reputation suffered because of his involvement in the Salem witchcraft trials of 1692, but he nevertheless supported smallpox inoculation and other progressive ideas. A polymath, he reported on American botany, and was one of the earliest New England historians.

Matilda of Flanders (c.1031–83) Queen consort of William I of England, born in Flanders, France. She married William in 1050 in Normandy, and during his absences in England the duchy of Normandy was under her regency, with the aid of their son, Robert Curthose. The embroidery of the Bayeux Tapestry was once wrongly attributed to her.

Matisse, Henri (Emile Benoît) [matees] (1869–1954) Painter, born in Le Cateau, N France. He studied law in Paris, then worked as a lawyer's clerk. An interest in art came unexpectedly in his 20s, and in 1892 he took classes in Paris, first at the Académie Julian, then at the Ecole des Beaux-Arts. From 1904 he was the leader of the Fauves (Fr 'wild beasts', the name given by a hostile critic), and although he painted several pictures influenced by Cubism and Impressionism, his most characteristic paintings display a bold use of brilliant areas of primary colour, organized within a rhythmic two-dimensional design. During the early 1930s he travelled in Europe and the USA, and in 1949–51 he decorated a Dominican chapel at Vence, near Nice.

Matlock 53°08N 1°32W; pop (2000e) 14 500. County town in Derbyshire, C England, UK; 14 km/9 mi SW of Chesterfield; railway; transport equipment, engineering; formerly a spa town.

Mato Grosso [matoh grosoh], formerly **Matto Grosso** pop (2000e) 2 330 000; area 881 000 sq km/340 000 sq mi. State in Centro-Oeste region, CW Brazil, bordered SW by Bolivia; capital, Cuiabá; food processing; cattle, coffee, cotton, timber, rubber, metallurgy; drained by tributaries of the Amazon (N), Paraguai (S), and Araguaia (E); half the area under forest; 611 sq km/ 236 sq mi Cará-Cará biological reserve in the SW (1971); Pantanal conservation area in the SW is a world heritage site; Xingu National Park in the NE; states of Mato Grosso (N) and Mato Grosso do Sul (S), pop (2000e) 1 905 000, capital Campo Grande, separated in 1977; the name also given to the whole plateau area in the S (the Planalto de Mato Grosso), which extends beyond the state.

Matra Mountains Mountain range in N Hungary; a S spur of the Carpathian Mts; rises to 1014 m/3327 ft at Mt Kékes, highest peak in Hungary.

matrilineal descent A descent system in which family or clan membership, inheritance, and succession is traced through the mother's daughters. It does not mean that women control all property, or hold all positions of authority. One of the most famous examples was found on the Trobriand Is, New Guinea.

matrix In mathematics, an ordered array of numbers subject to certain laws of composition. These laws can be demonstrated by the matrices.

$$A = \begin{bmatrix} a & b \\ c & d \end{bmatrix} \text{and } B = \begin{bmatrix} p & q \\ r & s \end{bmatrix}.$$

We define addition by

$$A + B = \begin{bmatrix} a+p & b+q \\ c+r & d+s \end{bmatrix}$$

and multiplication by

$$A \cdot B = \begin{bmatrix} ap+br & aq+bs \\ cp+dr & cq+ds \end{bmatrix}$$

Matrices can have any number of rows and columns, a matrix with *m* rows and *n* columns being called an *m by n* (written $m \times n$) matrix. **Matrix algebra** was developed by Camille Jordan, German Leopold Kronecker (1823–91), and others on the basis of early work by Cayley in the 19th-c, partly in an attempt to develop a non-commutative algebra, as $\mathbf{A} . \mathbf{B} \neq \mathbf{B} . \mathbf{A}$ in general. Matrices have in the past 40 years been found to have many applications, such as in probability theory (Markov chains), electricity, and the theory of games.

Matrix Churchill *Scott Report*

Matsys, Quentin *Massys, Quentin*

Matteotti, Giacomo [matiotee] (1885–1924) Italian politician, born in Fratta Polesine, NE Italy. A member of the Italian Chamber of Deputies, he began to organize the United Socialist Party (1921), and was an outspoken opponent of Mussolini's Fascists (1922–4). His protests against Fascist election outrages led to his murder in 1924, provoking a crisis which nearly brought the Fascist regime to an end.

matter The substances of which everything in the universe is composed. At one level, this is taken to mean atoms bound together into bulk matter. At the ultimate level, matter means the spin ½ particles such as electrons and quarks, bound together by spin 1 force particles such as photons and gluons.

Matterhorn, Fr **Mont Cervin**, Ital **Monte Cervino** 45°59N 7°39E. Mountain peak in Switzerland, SW of Zermatt; in the Pennine Alps, on the Swiss–Italian border; height, 4478 m/14 691 ft; first climbed by British mountaineer Edward Whymper in 1865.

matte shot A motion picture scene in which a mask, or matte, restricts the image area exposed so that a second image can be added subsequently. The matte may be a card or metal cut-out mounted in front of the lens during photography, or a strip of film with opaque and transparent areas used during printing.

Matthau, Walter [matow], originally **Walter Matuschanskavasky** (1920–2000) Film actor, born in New York City, USA. The son of Russian-Jewish immigrants, he studied at the New School for Social Research Dramatic Workshop, began working in Yiddish theatre, and made his Broadway debut in 1948. His film debut was in *The Kentuckian* (1955), and for many years he was cast as a villain. It was the 1967 Neil Simon comedy film *The Odd Couple* which pushed him into major film parts. Later films include *Hello Dolly* (1969), *Cactus Flower* (1969), *Pirates* (1986), *I.Q.* (1995), *Out to Sea* (1997), and *The Odd Couple II* (1998). His final film was *Hanging Up* (2000).

Matthew, St (1st-c) One of the 12 apostles in the New Testament. He was a tax gatherer before becoming a disciple of Jesus, and is identified with Levi (in *Mark* 2.14 and *Luke* 5.27). According to tradition he was the author of the first Gospel, a missionary to the Hebrews in Judaea, Ethiopia, and Persia, and suffered martyrdom, but nothing is known with certainty about his life. Feast day 22 July.

Matthew, Gospel according to The first work of the New Testament canon; one of the four canonical Gospels, until the 20th-c widely thought to have been the earliest Gospel written; anonymous, but 2nd-c traditions assign it to the apostle and former tax-collector, Matthew. It is noteworthy for its story of the Magi at Jesus's birth, its wealth of moral instruction (as in the Sermon on the Mount), and its emphasis on Jesus as the fulfilment of the Old Testament expectations.

Matthew Paris (c.1200–59) Chronicler and Benedictine monk. He entered the monastery at St Albans, Hertfordshire, SE England, UK in 1217, and became abbey chronicler there in 1236. His main work is the *Chronica majora*, the fullest available account of events in England between 1236 and 1259, and which also included interesting details of many other European countries. He is especially famous for his maps and drawings.

Matthews, Sir Stanley (1915–2000) Footballer, born in Hanley, Staffordshire, C England, UK. He started his sporting career with Stoke City in 1931, before a controversial transfer to Blackpool in 1947. Medals eluded him until 1953, when he played a significant role in the Football Association Cup Final. He returned to Stoke in 1961, and continued to play First Division football until after he was 50. He played for England 54 times, was twice Footballer of the Year (1948, 1963), and was the inaugural winner of the European Footballer of the Year Award in 1956. He later managed Port Vale, and was knighted in 1965.

Matthias I, known as **Matthew Corvinus**, Hung **Mátyás Corvin** (c.1443–90) King of Hungary (1458–90), born in Koloszvár, Hungary (now Cluj-Napoca, Romania), the second son of János Hunyady. He drove back the Turks, and made himself master of Bosnia (1462), Moldavia and Wallachia (1467), Moravia, Silesia, and Lusatia (1478), Vienna, and a large part of Austria proper (1485). His rule was arbitrary and his taxes heavy, but he greatly encouraged arts and letters, founded the Corvina library, promoted industry, and reformed finances and the system of justice.

Matthias, William (James) (1934–92) Composer, born in Whitland, Pembrokeshire, SW Wales, UK. He studied in London, and became lecturer (1959–68) and professor (1970–88, then research professor) at University College, Bangor. His works include an opera, *The Servants* (1980), three symphonies, several concertos, and much chamber, choral, and church music. Among his choral works is an anthem written for the wedding ceremony of the Prince and Princess of Wales (1981). He was artistic director of the North Wales Music Festival from 1972 until his death.

MATV (Master Antenna Television) The use of a single antenna to serve a number of TV receivers. The system can be introduced directly, as in an apartment block, or from a central station by way of a cable distribution service.

Mau [mow] A nationalist movement (1926–35) challenging New Zealand colonial rule in W Samoa. On 'Black Sunday' (28 Dec 1929) police fired on a peaceful crowd and killed eight Mau supporters. W Samoa was ruled by New Zealand from 1914 to 1961.

Maudling, Reginald (1917–79) British Conservative statesman, born in London, UK. He studied at Oxford, was called to the bar (1940), and served in the air force during World War 2. He entered parliament in 1950, became minister of supply (1953–7), paymaster-general (1957–9), President of the Board of Trade (1959–61), colonial secretary (1961), Chancellor of the Exchequer (1962–4), and deputy leader of the Opposition in

1964. In 1970 he became home secretary in the Heath government, but resigned in 1972 when he became implicated in the bankruptcy proceedings of architect John Poulson.

Mauger, Ivan (Gerald) [mawger] (1939–) Speedway rider, born in Christchurch, New Zealand. He rode for Wimbledon, Rye House, Eastbourne, Newcastle, Belle Vue, Exeter, and Hull between 1957 and 1982, and won the world individual title a record six times (1968–70, 1972, 1977, 1979). He also won two pairs world titles, four team titles, and the world long-track title three times.

Maugham, W(illiam) Somerset [mawm] (1874–1965) Novelist, playwright, and short-story writer, born in Paris, France. Orphaned at 10, he studied at Canterbury and Heidelberg, qualifying as a surgeon at St Thomas's Hospital, London. His first novel, *Liza of Lambeth* (1897), was a minor success, and he turned to writing full-time. Four of his plays ran simultaneously in London in 1908, and he wrote many others, notably *The Moon and Sixpence* (1919), *The Circle* (1921), *East of Suez* (1922), and *Cakes and Ale* (1930). His novels include the semi-autobiographical *Of Human Bondage* (1915). He is best known for his short stories, particularly 'Rain', originally published in the collection, *The Trembling of a Leaf* (1921). *The Complete Short Stories* (3 vols) was published in 1951.

Maui [mowee] pop (2000e) 128 100; area 1885 sq km/728 sq mi. Second largest island of the US state of Hawaii; forms Maui County with the islands of Lanai and Molokai; chief town, Wailuku; resort at Kanapali; former capital of Hawaii at Lahaina; rises to 3055 m/10 023 ft at Haleakala; has the only railway in the Pacific; sugar, tourism.

Mau Mau A secret society which led a revolt of the Kikuyu people of Kenya in the 1950s. It began in 1952, with the murder of white settlers and Kikuyu 'loyalists'. British troops were deployed in its suppression, but the cost in men and money convinced Britain that decolonization was imperative.

Mauna Kea [mowna kaya] 19°50N 155°28W. Dormant volcano in NC Hawaii, USA; rises to 4201 m/13 783 ft; highest island mountain in the world; numerous cinder cones; snow-capped in winter; several large telescopes at the summit.

Mauna Kea Observatory [mowna kaya] The best accessible site for ground-based astronomy between 320 nm and 1 mm wavelengths, located on Mauna Kea, Hawaii. Founded in 1964, the observatory comprises many major telescopes on the summit (4200 m/13 800 ft) and shield of the dormant volcano, among the most powerful of their kind.

Mauna Loa [mowna loha] 19°28N 155°35W. Active volcano in C Hawaii, USA; in Hawaii Volcanoes National Park; rises to 4169 m/13 678 ft; numerous craters, notably Kilauea, the second largest active crater in the world (containing Halemaumau fiery pit); on its summit is Mokuaweoweo Crater, also large and active; eruptions in 1855–6, 1926, 1950, 1984.

Maundy Thursday [mawndee] The Thursday before Easter, so called from Lat *mandatum*, 'commandment', the first word of the anthem traditionally sung on that day. In memory of Christ's washing his disciples' feet (*John* 13.4–10) it was once the custom for monarchs to wash the feet of poor people on Maundy Thursday; in Britain, special money (**Maundy money**) is given by the sovereign to the same number of elderly poor people as there are years in the sovereign's age.

Maupassant, (Henri René Albert) Guy de [mohpasã] (1850–93) Novelist, born probably at the Château de Miromesnil, Dieppe, NW France. He studied at Rouen, and spent his life in Normandy. After serving as a soldier and a government clerk, he took to writing, encouraged by Flaubert, a friend of his mother's, and joined the Naturalist group led by Zola. His stories range from the short tale to the full-length novel. His first success, *Boule de suif* (1880, Ball of Fat), a short story about a prostitute's life during the Franco-Prussian War, led to his being in great demand by newspapers. There followed about 300 stories and several novels, including *Une Vie* (1883, trans A Woman's Life), and the supposedly autobiographical *Bel-Ami* (1885). His stories 'Le Horla' (Hallucination) and 'La Peur' (Fear) describe madness and fear with a horrifying accuracy which foreshadows the insanity which beset Maupassant in 1892, when he was committed to an asylum in Paris.

Maupertuis, Pierre Louis Moreau de [mohpertwee] (1698–1759) Mathematician, born in St Malo, W France. A member of the Académie de Sciences from 1731, he led the French Academicians sent to Lapland in 1736 to measure the length of a degree of the meridian, in order to verify Newton's theories of the shape of the Earth. Frederick II made him president of the Berlin Academy in 1746. Maupertuis is best known for his 'principle of least action' in mechanics, and formed a theory of heredity which was a century ahead of its time.

Mauriac, François [mohriak] (1885–1970) Novelist, born in Bordeaux, SW France. He studied at Bordeaux, was of strict Roman Catholic parentage, and became regarded as the leading novelist of that faith. He started as a poet, publishing his first volume of verse in 1909. His novels explore temptation, sin, and redemption, and include *Le Baiser au lépreux* (1922, The Kiss to the Leper) and *Le Noeud de vipères* (1932, Viper's Tangle). He was awarded the 1952 Nobel Prize for Literature.

Maurice, Prinz van Oranje, Graaf van Nassau (Prince of Orange, Count of Nassau) (1567–1625) Stadtholder of the United Provinces of the Netherlands, born in Dillenburg, the son of William the Silent. He was elected stadtholder of Holland and Zeeland (1587) and later (1589) of Utrecht, Overyssel, and Gelderland, also becoming captain-general of the armies of the United Provinces during their War of Independence from Spain. He checked the Spanish advance, and by his steady offensive (1590–1606) liberated the N provinces. He became Prince of Orange in 1618, on the death of his elder brother. In the renewed conflict with the Habsburgs, he commanded the new republic, seeking help from England and France (1624).

Maurists [mawrists] A French Benedictine congregation of St Maur, founded in the early 17th-c. The monks were chiefly noted for their literary and historical work. Suspected of being influenced by Jansenism, they were eventually dissolved in 1818.

Mauritania *p.981*

Mauritius *p.982*

Maurois, André [mohrwah], pseudonym of **Emile Herzog** (1885–1967) Writer and biographer, born in Elbeuf, NW France. During World War 1 he was a liaison officer with the British army, and began his literary career with a book of shrewd and affectionate observation of British character, *Les Silences du Colonel Bramble* (1918, The Silences of Colonel Bramble). His many biographies include studies of Shelley (1923), Disraeli (1927), Voltaire (1935), and Proust (1949).

Mauroy, Pierre [mohrwah] (1928–) French politician and prime minister (1981–4). He was a teacher before becoming involved with trade unionism and Socialist politics, and was prominent in the creation of a new French Socialist Party in 1971. He became Mayor of Lille in 1973, and was elected to the National Assembly in the same year and then to the Senate (in 1992). A close ally of Mitterrand, Mauroy acted as his spokesman during the Socialists' successful election campaign.

mausoleum *Gur Amir; Lenin Mausoleum; Mausolus, Tomb of; Mount Li; Taj Mahal*

Mausolus, Tomb of [mowzolus] A huge, ornate tomb built at Halicarnassus in SW Asia Minor around 350 BC by Mausolus's widow, Queen Artemisia II of Caria (reigned c.353–350 BC). It is the source of the word 'mausoleum'.

Maw, (John) Nicholas (1935–) Composer, born in Grantham, Lincolnshire, EC England, UK. He studied in London (1955–8) and Paris (1958–9), taught at Cambridge and Yale universities, and became professor of music at Milton Avery Graduate School of Arts, Bard College, NY, in 1990. His music, traditional in idiom but original in expression, includes two comic operas, *One Man Show* (1964) and *The Rising of the Moon* (1970), two string quartets, and many orchestral works, including *Spring Music* (1983), *Odyssey* (1987), and *Violin Concerto* (1993).

Mauritania

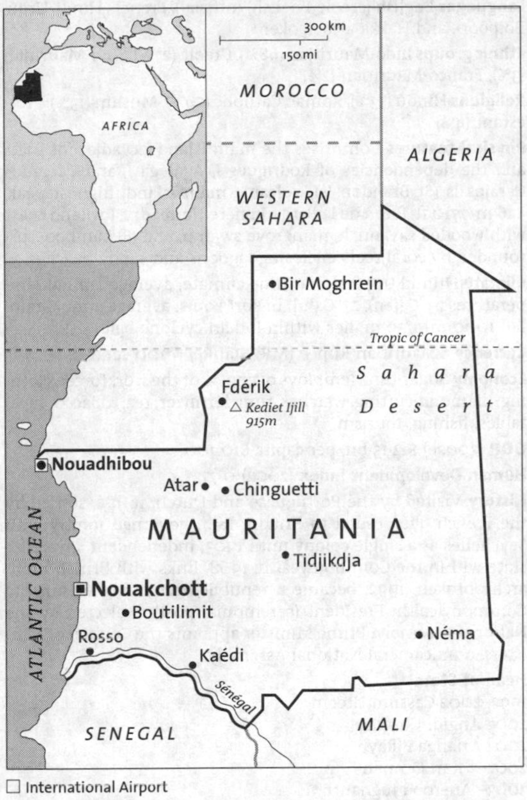

[moritaynia], Fr **Mauritanie**, Arabic **Muritaniyah**, official name **Islamic Republic of Mauritania**, Fr **République Islamique de Mauritanie**

Local names Mūritāniyā (Arabic), Mauritanie (French)

Timezone GMT

Area 1 029 920 km^2/397 549 sq mi

Population total (2002e) 2 656 000

Status Islamic republic

Date of independence 1960

Capital Nouakchott

Languages Arabic (official), French and local languages also spoken

Ethnic groups Moor (30%), black (30%), mixed (40%)

Religions Sunni Muslim (99%), Roman Catholic (1%)

Physical features Saharan zone in N comprises two-thirds of the country; coastal zone has minimal rainfall; Sahelian zone, with savannah grasslands; Sénégal R zone, the chief agricultural region; highest point, Kediet Ijill, 915 m/3002 ft in the NW.

Climate Dry, tropical climate, with sparse rainfall; average annual temperatures 22°C (Jan), 28°C (Jul) in Nouakchott; rainy season (May–Sep) in S, with occasional tornadoes; average annual rainfall 158 mm/6·2 in.

Currency 1 Ouguija (U, UM) = 5 khoums

Economy Subsistence agriculture (employs 80% of population); crop success constantly under threat from drought; livestock, cereals, vegetables, dates; mining of iron ore, copper, gypsum.

GDP (2002e) $4·891 bn, per capita $1700

Human Development Index (2002) 0·438

History Visited by Portuguese, 15th-c; French protectorate within French West Africa, 1903; French colony, 1920; independence, 1960; military coup, 1979; new constitution, 1991; became a republic, 1992; governed by an executive President (6-year term), Prime Minister, National Assembly, and Senate.

Head of State

1979–80 Mohammed Mahmoud Ould Ahmed Louly
1980–4 Mohammed Khouna Ould Haydalla
1984– Moaouiya Ould Sid Ahmed Taya

Head of Government

1992–6 Sidi Mohammed Ould Boubaker
1996–7 Cheikh el Avia Ould Mohamed Khouna
1997–8 Mohamed Lemine Ould Guig
1998–2003 Cheikh el Avia Ould Mohamed Khouna
2003– Sghair Ould M'barek

Maxim, Sir Hiram (Stevens) (1840–1916) Inventor and engineer, born in Sangerville, Maine, USA. He became a coachbuilder in an engineering works in Fitchburg, MA (1865), and from 1867 took out patents for a wide range of inventions, including electric lamps and gas equipment. An interest in automatic weapons took him to England in 1881, where he perfected the *Maxim machine-gun* in 1883. He also invented a pneumatic gun, a smokeless powder, a mousetrap, and carbon filaments for light bulbs. He became a British subject in 1900, and was knighted in 1901.

maximal aerobic power The highest oxygen uptake an individual can achieve during physical work while breathing air at sea-level, commonly used as a test of cardiovascular fitness; also known as **maximal oxygen uptake**. Genetic constitution is the most important determining factor, but the level can still be raised by appropriate training.

Maximilian I (1459–1519) Holy Roman Emperor (1493–1519), born as Archduke of Austria in Wiener Neustadt, NE Austria, the eldest son of Emperor Frederick III and Eleanor of Portugal. Elected King of the Romans (1486), he inherited the Habsburg territories and assumed the imperial title in 1493. He pursued an ambitious foreign policy, based on dynastic alliances, with far-reaching results for Habsburg power. His marriage to Mary of Burgundy brought his family the Burgundian inheritance, including Holland, followed by union with the Spanish kingdoms of Castile and Aragon when the Spanish crown passed to his grandson, Charles (1516). A double marriage treaty between the Habsburgs and the Jagiellons (1506) eventually brought the union of Austria–Bohemia–Hungary (1526). He was involved in conflict with the Flemish, the Swiss, the German princes, and especially with the Valois kings of France. Financial difficulties weakened his campaigns, and he was later forced to cede Milan (1504) to Louis XII. He incurred the hostility of the Venetians and, despite the League of Cambrai (1508), suffered defeat. He was succeeded by his grandson, as Charles V.

Maximilian, Ferdinand Joseph (1832–67) Emperor of Mexico (1864–7), born in Vienna, Austria, the younger brother of Emperor Francis Joseph, and an archduke of Austria. In 1863, he accepted the offer of the crown of Mexico, supported by France; When Napoleon III withdrew his troops, he refused to abdicate, and made a brave defence at Querétaro, but was betrayed and executed.

Maxwell, James C(lerk) (1831–79) Physicist, born in Edinburgh, EC Scotland, UK. He studied at Edinburgh and Cambridge, became professor at Aberdeen (1856) and London (1860), and was the first professor of experimental physics at Cambridge (1871), where he organized the Cavendish Laboratory. In 1873 he published his great *Treatise on Electricity and Magnetism*, which gives a mathematical treatment to Faraday's theory of electrical and magnetic forces. He also contributed to the study of colour vision, and to the kinetic theory of gases, but his greatest work was his theory of electromagnetic radiation, which established him as the leading theoretical physicist of the century.

Mauritius

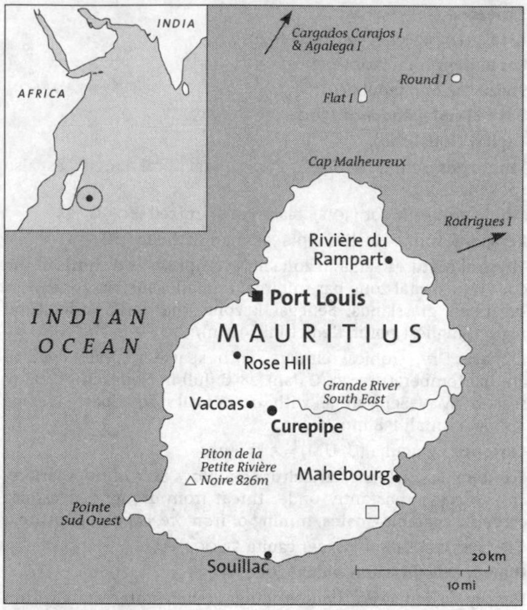

☐ International Airport

[morishuhs]

Local name Mauritius

Timezone GMT +4

Area 1 865 km²/720 sq mi

Population total (2002e) 1 211 000

Status Republic within the Commonwealth

Date of independence 1968

Capital Port Louis

Languages English (creole-English) (official), French, Hindi, Urdu, Bojpoori, and Hakka also spoken

Ethnic groups Indo-Mauritian (68%), Creole (27%), Sino-Mauritian (3%), Franco-Mauritian (2%)

Religions Hindu (53%), Roman Catholic (26%), Muslim (13%), Protestant (4%)

Physical features Comprises the main island, 20 adjacent islets and the dependencies of Rodrigues I, Agalega I, and Cargados Carajos Is (St Brandon Is); volcanic main island; highest peak, 826 m/2710 ft, Piton de la Petite Rivière Noire; dry, lowland coast with wooded savannah, mangrove swamp, and (E) bamboo; surrounded by coral reefs enclosing lagoons and sandy beaches.

Climate Humid tropical-maritime climate; average annual temperatures 23°C (Jan), 27°C (Jul) in Port Louis; average annual rainfall 1000 mm/39 in; lies within Indian cyclone belt.

Currency 1 Mauritian Rupee (MR, MauRe) = 100 cents

Economy Sugar-cane (employs over 25% of the workforce); clothing; diamond-cutting, watches, rum, fertilizer; tea, tobacco, vegetables; fishing; tourism.

GDP (2002e) $12·15 bn, per capita $10 100

Human Development Index (2002) 0·772

History Visited by the Portuguese and Dutch, 16th-c; settled by the French, 1715; ceded to Britain, 1814; governed jointly with Seychelles as a single colony until 1903; independent sovereign state within the Commonwealth, 1968; links with British monarchy broken, 1992, became a republic, remaining within the Commonwealth; President (ceremonial post) is elected by the National Assembly; Prime Minister appoints the Council of Ministers; a unicameral National Assembly.

Head of State
1992–2002 Cassum Uteem
2002 Angidi Chettiar
2002 Arianga Pillay
2002–3 Karl Offman
2003– Anerood Jugnauth

Head of Government
1995–2000 Navin Ramgoolam
2000–3 Anerood Jugnauth
2003– Paul Berenger

Maxwell, (Ian) Robert, originally **Ludvik Hoch** (1923–91) Publisher and politician, born in Slatinske Dòly, Czech Republic. Self-educated, he served in World War 2 before founding the Pergamon Press. A former Labour MP (1964–70), he had many business interests, including film production and television. He became chairman of the Mirror group of newspapers in 1984, but was forced to float the company on the London stock market in 1991. Following his death in mysterious circumstances (his body was found in the sea near the Canary Is, after he disappeared from his luxury yacht), it transpired that he had secretly siphoned large sums of money from two of his companies, and from employee pension funds, to preserve his financial empire.

Maxwell–Boltzmann distribution A description of the distribution of energy amongst the atoms or molecules of a (perfect) gas; made by James Clerk Maxwell and Ludwig Boltzmann in 1868. It is essential to understanding how the bulk thermodynamic properties of a gas are related to the behaviour of large numbers of individual gas atoms.

Maxwell Davies, Sir Peter *Davies, Sir Peter Maxwell*

may *hawthorn*

Mayakovsky, Vladimir (Vladimirovich) [miyakofskee] (1893–1930) Poet and playwright, born in Bagdadi, WC Georgia. He began writing at an early age, and was regarded as the leader of the Futurist school. During the Russian Revolution (1917) he emerged as the propaganda mouthpiece of the Bolsheviks. His plays include *Misteriya-Buff* (1918, Mystery-Bouffe), and the satirical *Klop* (1929, The Bedbug) and *Banya* (1930, The Bath-House). Towards the end of his life he was severely castigated by more orthodox Soviet writers and critics for his outspoken criticism of bureaucracy and his unconventional opinions on art, and this appears to have contributed towards his suicide.

Mayas [miyaz] The best-known civilization of the classic period of Middle America (AD 250–900). The Maya rose to prominence c.300 in present-day S Mexico, Guatemala, N Belize, and W Honduras. Inheriting the inventions and ideas of earlier civilizations, such as the Olmec and Teotihuacán, they developed astronomy, calendrical systems, hieroglyphic writing, and ceremonial architecture, including pyramid temples. The tropical rainforest area was cleared for agriculture, and rain water was stored in numerous reservoirs. They also traded with other, distant people, clearing routes through jungles and swamps. Most people farmed, while centres such as Tikal and Bonampak were largely ceremonial and political, with an elite of priests and nobles ruling over the countryside. Maya civilization started to decline, for reasons unknown, c.900, although some peripheral centres still thrived, under the influence of Mexico.

maybug *cockchafer*

Mayer, Louis B(urt) [mayer], originally **Eliezer Mayer** (1885–1957) Film mogul, born in Minsk, Belarus. In 1907 he purchased a house in Haverhill, MA, refurbished it as a nickelodeon, and opened one of the earliest custom-designed cinemas. He later acquired a chain of theatres in New England, moving into film production with the formation of Metro Films (1915) and Louis

B Mayer Productions (1917), which later joined with Sam Goldwyn to form Metro–Goldwyn–Mayer in 1924. The first vice-president in charge of production, he was instrumental in the creation of Hollywood as a dream factory and the establishment of the star system, with such successes as *Ben Hur* (1926), *Grand Hotel* (1932), the Andy Hardy series, *Ninotchka* (1939), and countless others. He received an honorary Academy Award in 1950.

Mayfair A district in London, UK where throughout the 17th-c a fair was held in May. It became a fashionable residential area in the late 19th-c and early 20th-c, but is now largely given over to offices. It lies between Piccadilly and Oxford St to the N and S, and between Hyde Park and Regent St to the E and W.

Mayflower A three-masted carrack in which the Pilgrims sailed from Plymouth to North America in 1620. The ship was only 27·5 m/90 ft in length, and the voyage took 66 days. Her 100 passengers, Puritan refugees from religious intolerance, became 101 by the end of the journey (there were two births and one death during the passage).

mayfly A winged insect with a short adult life. Mayflies live as aquatic larvae for up to four years, then emerge as non-feeding, flying adults that survive only 2–72 hours, during which time mating takes place. (Order: Ephemeroptera, c.2000 species.)

May Fourth Movement A 5000-student demonstration in Beijing on 4 May 1919 against the Western powers' Versailles decision granting Japan rights over Shandong (Shantung). The protest crystallized nationwide aspirations for a new China, and inspired both revolutionary and gradualist strands in the New Culture Movement.

mayhem A common-law crime and civil injury involving the intentional disfigurement of another person; also referred to as **maiming**. The disfigurement has to be of a permanent, though not necessarily disabling character, such as cutting off an ear or a finger. England and most US jurisdictions now incorporate the offence of mayhem into assault statutes.

Maynooth 53°23N 6°35W, pop (2001e) 10 000. Historic town in Co Kildare, E Ireland; located 25 km/15 mi W of Dublin; birthplace of George Barrington; railway; university; Maynooth College (1795) training seminary for priests; castle (1175) was home of the Fitzgeralds (earls of Kildare) and the political capital of the country during 15th–16th-c; St Mary's Church (originally 13th-c); rapidly growing commuter town for Dublin; service and retail centre.

Mayo [mayoh], Ir **Mhuigheo** pop (2000e) 112 000; area 5398 sq km/2084 sq mi. County in Connacht province, W Ireland; bounded N and W by the Atlantic Ocean; drained by R Moy (noted for salmon fishing); Achill I lies off W coast; Nephin Beg Range to the NW; capital, Castlebar; sheep and cattle farming, potatoes, oats; Knock, scene of apparition of Virgin Mary in 1879, major place of pilgrimage, served by new airport; Croagh Patrick, Ireland's holy mountain, scene of annual pilgrimage (Jul).

Mayo, Charles Horace [mayoh] (1865–1939) Surgeon, born in Rochester, Minnesota, USA. He studied at Chicago Medical College, went into private practice with his father, **William Worrall Mayo** (1819–1911), and made a special study of goitre. In 1905, he helped his brother **William James Mayo** (1861–1939) to organize at Rochester the Mayo Clinic, which their father had founded. Charles' son, **Charles William Mayo** (1898–1968), also became a surgeon. The family were pioneers in the practice of group medicine.

mayor The political head of a town or city government. The name is used in a vast range of political systems, but the role and to some extent the status of mayors vary considerably. In some cases the mayor can have significant executive powers of decision-making and appointment, while in others the position is one of chairing local councils while enjoying few special powers; in a few instances the role is largely a ceremonial one.

Mayotte [mayot], Eng **Mahore** pop (2000e) 156 900; area 374 sq km/144 sq mi. Small island group of volcanic origin, E of the Comoros Is at the N end of the Mozambique Channel, W Indian Ocean; administered by France; two main islands; Grande Terre (area 360 sq km/140 sq mi), rising to 660 m/2165 ft at Mt Benara; La Petite Terre or Ilot de Pamandzi (area 14 sq km/5 sq mi); capital, Dzaoudzi; chief languages, French, Mahorian; French colony, 1843–1914; attached with the Comoros Is to Madagascar; overseas territory of France; when the rest of the group became independent in 1974, Mayotte voted to remain a French dependency; airport; fishing, vanilla, coffee, copra, ylang-ylang.

maypole Traditionally in Britain and continental Europe, a tall pole decorated with vegetation and ribbons on the first of May, and the focus of festivities on that day to welcome Spring and ensure fertility. Since the later 19th-c a shorter pole is sometimes substituted, around which adults or children perform a plaited-ribbon dance at many open-air festivities.

Mays, Willie (Howard), nickname **the Say Hey Kid** (1931–) Baseball player, born in Westfield, Alabama, USA. He played for the New York (1951–7) and San Francisco (1958–72) Giants, and the New York Mets (1972–3). A magnificent fielder, batter, and baserunner, only he and Hank Aaron have performed the double of more than 3000 hits and 600 home runs; he alone has stolen more than 300 bases while compiling more than 400 home runs. He was twice voted the Most Valuable Player (1954, 1965), and became the Baseball Player of the Decade (1960–9). He was elected to the Baseball Hall of Fame in 1979.

Mazar-e-Sharif [mazah(r) ay shareef] 36°43N 67°05E, pop (2001e) 232 800. Capital of Balkh province, N Afghanistan; 56 km/35 mi S of Uzbekistan border; connected by road and air with Kabul, 320 km/200 mi SE; Blue Mosque and shrine mark the reputed site of the tomb of the caliph Ali, son-in-law of Mohammed; a Taliban stronghold with many guerilla training camps, some believed run by Osama bin Laden; camps targeted by US-led attack (Oct 2001) in response to Taliban government's refusal to give up bin Laden; chemical fertilizers from natural gas; textiles, bricks, flour milling.

Mazarin, Jules [mazarĩ], known as **Cardinal Mazarin**, originally **Giulio Raimondo Mazzarino** (1602–61) Neopolitan clergyman, diplomat, and statesman, born in Pescine, C Italy. He studied at Rome and in Spain, became papal nuncio to the French court (1634–6) and entered the service of Louis XIII in 1639. Through the influence of Richelieu he was elevated to cardinal, succeeding his mentor as first minister in 1642. After Louis' death (1643), he retained his authority under the queen-regent, Anne of Austria. Blamed by many for the civil disturbances of the Frondes, he twice fled the kingdom, and returned to Paris in 1653 after the nobles' revolt had been suppressed. His foreign policy was more fruitful: he concluded the Peace of Westphalia (1648), whose terms increased French prestige, and negotiated the Treaty of the Pyrenees (1659), ending the prolonged Franco–Spanish conflict. He was a patron of the arts and learning, founding the Royal Academy of Painting and Sculpture (1648) and building up an important library in Paris.

Mazatlán [masatlan] 23°11N 106°25W, pop (2000e) 376 000. Seaport in Sinaloa state, W Mexico; on the Pacific coast S of the Gulf of California; airfield; railway; largest Mexican port on the Pacific Ocean; main industrial and commercial centre in the W; fishing, textiles, sugar refining, distilling, trade in tobacco and bananas, tourism.

mazurka A quick Polish dance in triple metre, with a strong accent on the second or third beat. Chopin wrote numerous examples for piano.

Mazzini, Giuseppe [matseenee] (1805–72) Patriot and republican, born in Genoa, NW Italy. He was trained as a lawyer, and became an ardent liberal, founding the Young Italy Association (1833). Expelled from France, he travelled Europe advocating republicanism and insurrection. In 1848 he became involved in the Lombard revolt, and collaborated with Garibaldi in attempting to keep the patriotic struggle alive in the Alps. In 1849 he became one of the triumvirate governing the Roman Republic, overthrown after two months by French intervention. During the events of 1859–60 he and his supporters worked strenuously but vainly to make the new Italy a republic.

Mbabane [mbabanay] 26°18S 31°06E, pop (2000e) 53 000. Capital of Swaziland, 320 km/200 mi E of Johannesburg (South Africa) and 160 km/100 mi WSW of Maputo (Mozambique); capital, 1902; administrative and commercial centre; iron ore.

MBE *British Empire, Order of the*

Mbeki, Thabo (Mvuyelwa) [mbekee] (1942–) Leader of the African National Congress (ANC) from 1997, and president of South Africa (1999–), born in Idutywa, SE South Africa. He joined the ANC Youth League as a teenager, and in 1959 was expelled from school for political activities. By the time his father, Govan Mbeki (1910–2001), was sentenced to life at the Rivonia Trial of 1964, Thabo was in exile. He then studied in England and the USSR. Elected to the National Executive Committee of the ANC in 1975, he became one of its most influential leaders. After the organization was unbanned in 1990, he returned to South Africa, and played a major role in the negotiations for a new political dispensation. In 1994 he was appointed first deputy president in Nelson Mandela's administration, and in 1997 succeeded him as president of the ANC.

Mc surnames *as if spelled* Mac

McAleese, Mary [makalees] (1951–) President of Ireland (1997–), born in Belfast, NE Northern Ireland, UK. She studied at Queen's University, Belfast, moving in 1975 to Trinity College Dublin as professor of criminal law. She also worked as a television journalist (1979–81), and in the 1980s became known as an outspoken campaigner for a wide range of social causes. In 1987 she moved into university administration at Queen's, becoming the first woman and Catholic pro-vice-chancellor in 1994. Despite her northern background, she became the presidential successor to Mary Robinson in the 1997 election.

MCC Abbreviation of **Marylebone Cricket Club**, whose headquarters are at Lord's Cricket Ground, N London. It was founded in 1787 by a group of noblemen headed by the Earl of Winchilsea, Lord Charles Lennox, the Duke of York, and the Duke of Dorset. It retained responsibility for the running of the game until 1968, and is still custodian of the laws.

Meacher, Michael (Hugh) [meecher] (1939–) British statesman, born in Hemel Hempstead, Hertfordshire, SE England, UK. Educated at Oxford and the London School of Economics, he was a university lecturer before being elected Labour MP for Oldham West (1970–). He held junior posts in the 1970s, became a member of Labour's national executive committee (1983–8), and served as minister for the environment (1997–2003).

Mead, George Herbert (1863–1931) Social psychologist, born in South Hadley, Massachusetts, USA. He studied at Harvard, Leipzig, and Berlin, taught at Michigan University (1891–4), then moved to the philosophy department at Chicago (1894–1931). His main interest lay in the theory of the mind, the notion of the self, and how this is developed through communication with others. His work gave rise to Symbolic Interactionism, a social science approach concerned with the meanings that people give to the world, and how these are worked out through interpersonal interaction. His main works, published shortly after his death, are *Mind, Self and Society* (1934) and *The Philosophy of the Act* (1938).

Mead, Margaret (1901–78) Anthropologist, born in Philadelphia, Pennsylvania, USA. She studied at Columbia University under Franz Boas, then carried out a number of field studies in the Pacific, writing both academic and popular books, such as *Coming of Age in Samoa* (1928) and *New Lives for Old* (1956). She held a position for many years at the American Museum of Natural History, but increasingly became a freelance media heavyweight, one of the most famous women of her generation, particularly well known for her views on educational and social issues.

mead An alcoholic beverage derived from fermented honey. It was widely drunk in Anglo-Saxon England, and was known as *hydromel* by the Romans.

Meade, James Edward (1907–95) Economist, born in Swanage, Dorset, S England, UK. He worked for the League of Nations in the 1930s, and was a member, then director, of the economic section of the Cabinet Office (1940–6). He then became professor of economics at London School of Economics (1947–57) and of political economy at Cambridge (1957–68). A prolific writer, his principal contributions have been in the area of international trade, including *The Theory of International Economic Policy* (2 vols, 1951–5). He shared the 1977 Nobel Prize for Economics.

Meade, Richard (John Hannay) (1938–) Equestrian rider, born in Chepstow, Monmouthshire, SE Wales, UK. One of Britain's most successful Olympians, he won three gold medals – the Three-day Event team golds in 1968 and 1972, and the individual title in 1972 (on *Laurieston*). He also won world championship team gold medals (1970, 1982), European championship team gold medals (1967, 1971, 1981), Burghley in 1964 (on *Barberry*), and Badminton in 1970 (on *The Poacher*) and 1982 (on *Speculator III*).

meadow grass A perennial grass (*Poa pratensis*) with creeping, rooting stems forming rather stiff tufts; variable and widespread throughout the temperate N hemisphere. It is important as a pasture grass. (Family: Gramineae.)

meadowlark A bird native to the New World; plumage streaked and mottled on back; inhabits grassland and cultivation; eats insects and seeds; nests on ground. (Genus: *Sturnella*, 5 species. Family: Icteridae.)

meadow saffron A plant with corms, native to Europe (*Colchicum autumnale*); leaves 12–30 cm/5–12 in, lance-shaped, glossy, absent when flowers appear in autumn; flowers lilac, goblet-shaped, the six perianth-segments fused below to form a tube 5–20 cm/2–8 in long; fruit ripening in spring as leaves appear; also called **autumn crocus**. It is the source of the alkaloid colchicine, used in genetic research to inhibit chromosome separation. (Family: Liliaceae.)

meadow-sweet An erect perennial (*Filipendula ulmaria*) growing to 120 cm/4 ft, native to Europe, W Asia, and N Africa; leaves pinnate with pairs of small leaflets alternating with five pairs of large ones; flowers 5-petalled with reflexed sepals, creamy, fragrant, forming an irregular terminal mass, carpels spirally twisted. (Family: Rosaceae.)

Meads, Colin (Earl), nickname **Pine Tree** (1936–) Rugby union player, born in Cambridge, New Zealand. A lock forward, New Zealand rugby's 'unsmiling giant', he wore the All Black jersey in 133 matches, including a then-record 55 internationals, between 1957 and 1971. He was only the second player ever sent off in an international, against Scotland in 1967. A sheep farmer, he served as national coach and selector and union president after retiring.

Meale, Richard Graham (1932–) Composer, conductor, and teacher, born in Sydney, New South Wales, SE Australia. He studied at the New South Wales Conservatory and the University of California, where he researched the music of Japan, Java, and Bali. Returning to Australia he made an immediate impact with his compositions *Los Alboradas* (1963) and *Homage to Garcia Lorca* (1964). From 1969 he was reader in music at Adelaide University. His first opera *Voss* (1982), with a libretto by David Malouf based on the novel by Patrick White, demonstrates the strength of his orchestral and vocal writing, and is part of the Australian Opera's repertoire. His second opera, *Mer de Glace*, again with a libretto by Malouf, was premiered in 1991.

mealworm The larva of a darkling ground beetle, *Tenebrio molitor*, which feeds on stored flour; a cylindrical larva up to 25 mm/1 in long, well-adapted to life in very arid conditions. (Order: Coleoptera. Family: Tenebrionidae.)

mealybug A scale insect that infests all parts of its host plants; adult female flattened, males enclosed in cocoon-like sac; can lay eggs or bear live young; worldwide, including many pests of cultivated plants. (Order: Homoptera. Family: Pseudococcidae, c.1100 species.)

mean In mathematics, the sum of *n* scores, divided by *n*; colloquially called the 'average'. The **arithmetic mean** is obtained by adding a set of scores and dividing the total by the number of scores; for example, the arithmetic mean of the scores 6, 2, 8, 4 is 5 (6 + 2 + 8 + 4 = 20; 20 ÷ 4 = 5). If the scores are $x_1, x_2, x_3 ... x_n$, the mean *m* is

$$\frac{1}{n}(x_1 + x_2 + x_3 ... x_n),$$

written

$$\frac{1}{n}\sum x_i.$$

The **geometric mean** of *n* scores is the *n*th root of the product of those scores; for example, the geometric mean of 2, 9, 12 is 6, since 2 × 9 × 12 = 216, and

$$\sqrt[3]{216} = 6.$$

The *n* numbers $a_1, a_2, a_3 ... a_n$, have the geometric mean

$$\sqrt[n]{a_1 a_2 a_3 ... a_n}.$$

mean free path The average distance travelled by some atom or molecule before colliding with another, typically about 60 nm in gases; symbol *l*, units m (metre). It is important in understanding the properties of gases, such as diffusion, and the movement of such particles as electrons and neutrons through solids.

mean life In atomic, nuclear, and particle physics, the average time taken for an excited atom to lose energy or for a particle to decay; symbol τ, units s (second). It is related to half-life $T_{1/2}$ by $T_{1/2} = \tau \log 2 = 0{\cdot}693\tau$; $1/\tau$ is the decay rate.

means test A method of assessing an individual or family's eligibility for some kind of financial assistance, used by government agencies and local authorities. The 'means' refers to a person's income and other sources of money. Aid is given on a sliding scale, and above a certain level no help is given. The expression is used infrequently nowadays, because of its emotive overtones, and has largely been replaced by 'assessment'.

measles A viral childhood disease spread by airborne infected droplets. It begins with a cough and runny nose, followed by a generalized blotchy red rash and fever. Complications include pneumonia and secondary bacterial middle-ear infection. Diffuse viral infection of the brain (*encephalitis*) also occurs rarely and can result in permanent brain damage. The incidence of the illness in developed countries has been substantially reduced by the widespread use of vaccination. However in developing countries it remains common and carries a significant mortality.

meat The edible muscle of animals, the most common forms including beef, pork, bacon, lamb, and poultry. The flesh of many other species is also eaten as meat, including the horse, buffalo, camel, dog, deer, rabbit, and monkey, though cultural practices vary. Meat is rich in protein, iron, and zinc. The amount of fat in meat is determined by age, the method of husbandry, and butchering method.

Meath [meeth], Ir **na Midhe** pop (2000e) 107 000; area 2339 sq km/903 sq mi. County in Leinster province, E Ireland; bounded E by Irish Sea; drained by Boyne and Blackwater Rivers; crossed by the Royal Canal; former kingdom; capital, Trim; sheep, cattle, potatoes, oats.

Mecca [meka], Arabic **Makkah**, ancient **Macoraba** 21°30N 39°54E, pop (2000e) 1 005 000. Islamic holy city in Mecca province, WC Saudi Arabia; 64 km/40 mi E of its Red Sea port, Jedda; birthplace of Mohammed and site of the Kaba, the chief shrine of Muslim pilgrimage; between 1·5 and 2 million pilgrims visit Mecca annually; city closed to non-Muslims; large bazaars, al-Harram Mosque with the Kaba and sacred Black Stone.

mechanical advantage The ratio of the resistance or load to the applied force or effort of a machine; for example, the weight lifted by a lever divided by the effort required. It is an essential property of a machine, which can be less than, equal to, or greater than 1. The actual mechanical advantage of a working machine is always less than that predicted because some extra effort is always needed to overcome frictional resistance.

mechanical engineering The branch of engineering concerned with the design, construction, and operation of machines of all types. It is also concerned with the production and application of mechanical power. Hence mechanical engineers design, operate, and test engines that produce power from steam, petrol, nuclear energy, and other sources, and a wide range of associated equipment. The field became a separate branch of engineering when steam power was introduced into manufacturing in the 1800s.

mechanical hysteresis *elastic hysteresis*

mechanical properties of matter Properties such as tensile strength and stiffness, dictated by the nature of the bonds between atoms of the material. These bonds also control whether the material is metallic, crystalline, glass-like, or of some other character.

mechanics The study of the motion of objects as a result of the forces acting on them. Motion in a straight line is called *linear* or *rectilinear* motion, and is described using mass *m*, velocity *v*, acceleration *a*, momentum *p*, and force *F*; *rotational* motion is described using moment of inertia *I*, angular velocity ω, angular acceleration α, angular momentum *L*, and torque Γ. **Quantum mechanics** governs objects the size of atoms (10^{-10} m) or less. **Classical mechanics** corresponds to all other aspects of mechanics, and includes **Newtonian mechanics**, **celestial mechanics** (the motion of stars and planets), general relativity, **fluid mechanics**, and **relativistic mechanics** (for objects moving at high velocity).

mechanism The view that everything in nature can be explained by means of deterministic causal processes, most clearly exemplified in Newtonian mechanics. Mechanism is opposed both to teleology and vitalism, and is incompatible with orthodox interpretations of quantum mechanics.

mechanization The use of machines wholly or partly to replace the human operator. Unlike automation, in which there is no reference to the operator at all, mechanization requires some input from people, in terms of feeding in data and giving instructions. Early mechanization replaced the craftsman by the machine operator, and involved the use of machines such as levers and pulleys. Computers are the major example of modern mechanization and automation.

Mechnikov or **Metchnikoff, Ilya** [mechnikof] (1845–1916) Biologist, born in Ivanovka, Ukraine. He became professor of zoology and comparative anatomy at Odessa (1870), and in 1888 joined Pasteur in Paris. He shared the 1908 Nobel Prize for Physiology or Medicine for his work on immunology, in which he discovered the cells (*phagocytes*) which devour infective organisms.

Mecklenburg Declaration of Independence (1775) Resolutions adopted in Mecklenburg County, North Carolina, during the American Revolution, denying all British authority. The resolutions were ignored by the Continental Congress, which at that point was much more interested in reconciliation with Britain than in independence from it.

Mecoptera [mekoptera] *scorpion fly*

medal A piece of metal, often in the form of a coin or cross, bearing a device or inscription, struck or cast in commemoration of an event or as a reward for merit. Medals may be awarded for personal bravery (eg Victoria Cross, Medal of Honor), for participation in an event or battle (eg Victoria Medal, awarded to soldiers of all Allied nations in World War 1), or for sports (eg Olympic gold, silver, and bronze medals).

Medal of Honor (MH, MOH) In the USA, the highest decoration awarded for heroism, instituted in 1861; it is worn on a blue ribbon decorated with white stars.

Medawar, Sir Peter (Brian) [medawah(r)] (1915–87) Zoologist and one of the world's leading immunologists, born in Rio de Janeiro, Brazil. He studied zoology at Oxford, was appointed professor of zoology at Birmingham University (1947–51) and professor of comparative anatomy at University College London (1951–62), where he pioneered experiments in the prevention of rejection in transplant operations. He was director of the National Institute for Medical Research from 1962. In 1960 he shared the Nobel Prize for Physiology or Medicine for researches on immunological tolerance in relation to skin and organ grafting. He was also well known for his writing on scientific method, as in *The Art of the Soluble* (1967). He was knighted in 1965.

Medea [medeea] In Greek mythology, a witch, the daughter of Aeetes, the King of Colchis, who assisted Jason in obtaining the Golden Fleece. On their return to Iolcos, she renewed the youth of an aged ram by boiling it in a cauldron, and tricked the daughters of Pelias into performing a similar ritual, so that they destroyed their own father. When deserted by Jason at Corinth, she fled in her aerial chariot after killing her children.

Médecins Sans Frontières [maydsĩ sã frõtyair] ('Doctors Without Borders') An independent medical agency, founded in France in 1971. It is devoted to providing rapid professional help to victims of natural and human disasters wherever it is needed, regardless of race, religion, politics, or sex, and to raising public awareness of their plight. It received the Nobel Peace Prize in 1999 for its pioneering humanitarian work.

Medellín [medeyeen] 6°15N 75°36W, pop (2000e) 1 665 000. Industrial and commercial capital of Antioquia department, NWC Colombia; founded by Jewish refugees from Spain, 1616; leading industrial centre; airport; railway; five universities; coffee trade, steel, textiles, chemicals, pharmaceuticals, food processing; rubber, wood, and metal products; focal point for illegal drugs activities; cathedral of Villanueva (1868–1931) in Parque Bolívar; Museo El Castillo, 18th-c churches (San Ignacio, San Juan de Dios, San Antonio); zoo.

Medes [meedz] An ancient people living to the SW of the Caspian Sea, often wrongly identified with the Persians. At their peak in the 7th-c and 6th-c BC, they conquered Urartu and Assyria, and extended their power as far west as C Turkey. In the E they ruled most of Iran. Their empire passed to the Persians c.550 BC.

media The means of producing and disseminating news, information, and entertainment to a universal audience, typically through the press (both tabloid and broadsheet), magazines, cinema, radio and television, and even paperback publishing and pornography. Developing historically with industrialization and urbanization, the mass media have come to play an influential role in every nation's economic, political, and cultural life. The mass media have been hailed at times as bulwarks of democracy and key contributors to social cohesion and well-being, and at other times reviled as agents of repression, or as promoting anti-social behaviour and perverting cultural standards. In countries with authoritarian or totalitarian governments, government ownership or control directly affect the mass media. Most media organizations are operated commercially, though some are state-owned or, like the British Broadcasting Corporation (BBC), public corporations. Mergers and acquisitions, as well as the integration of production, distribution, and equipment supply, have produced media empires operating on a multinational or indeed worldwide basis. Advances in satellite broadcasting have further strengthened the position of exporters of information and entertainment and have given rise to accusations of 'cultural imperialism' by the West at the expense of local values. The Internet poses a contemporary challenge by virtue of its freedom of access and interactive character.

mediaeval art The arts of Europe and the Middle East during the thousand years between the fall of Rome and the establishment of modern nation states around the time of the Renaissance. Reflecting the spiritual and intellectual dominance of the Catholic Church, the greatest achievements of mediaeval art include Byzantine ivories and mosaics, illuminated manuscripts such as prayer books, and the cathedrals of the 'High Middle Ages', with their lavish sculpture and stained glass. In Protestant countries such as Britain, much mediaeval art (especially wall-painting and sculpture) was destroyed at the Reformation.

median In mathematics, the middle score, when the scores are arranged in order of size; for example, the scores 1, 5, 3, 7, 2 are re-arranged 1, 2, 3, 5, 7, and the middle score is 3. If we have an even number of scores, the median is the mean of the two middle scores; thus for 1, 4, 5, 2, the median is $\frac{1}{2}(2 + 4)$, ie 3. For a continuous distribution, the median M is such that half the scores are less than M, and half greater.

Medicaid and **Medicare** Two US schemes to provide health care, introduced by the federal government in 1965. **Medicaid** is operated by state governments, and provides financial assistance to low-income persons covering physician, hospital, and other medical needs. **Medicare** is for persons over the age of 65, providing basic hospital insurance and supplementing insurance for doctors and other health care services. Similar schemes operate in several other countries, such as Australia.

medical ethics The branch of medicine that deals with the incorporation of an individual's interests, societal values, legal issues, and moral arguments into medical practice. Examples of the areas covered include consent to treatment, confidentiality, research on human subjects, contraception and abortion, rationing of health care, and the prolonging of life in the event of serious irreversible brain damage.

medical insurance *health insurance*

Medici [maydeechee], Fr **Médicis** A banking family which virtually ruled Florence from 1434 to 1494, though without holding formal office. They were overthrown by the republic in 1494, but restored to power in 1512, and from 1537 became hereditary dukes of Florence, and from 1569 Grand Dukes of Tuscany. They produced three popes (Leo X, Clement VII, and Leo XI), two queens of France (Catherine de' Medici and Marie de' Medici), and several cardinals of the Roman Catholic Church. The magnificence and liberality of many members of the house, who were generous patrons of the arts, literature, and learning, allowed Florence to become the richest repository of European culture of the period. They were patrons of artists, including Botticelli and Michelangelo (who later designed their 16th-c funerary chapel).

medicine The science and practice of preventing, alleviating, and curing human illness. From the earliest times, trial-and-error revealed plants and parts of animals to be poisonous, edible, or useful in disease; this led to medical folklore and herbal remedies. Prior to the scientific revolution of the 19th-c, attempts to cope with serious disease were frustrated by the lack of a satisfactory theory of disease or knowledge of causes. Although the study of anatomy grew rapidly from the time of Aristotle and the Alexandrian medical school in 300 BC, physiology and ideas of organ function remained rudimentary. Speculations untested by experiments were by present-day standards grotesque, and gave rise to such practices as trephining, bleeding, cupping, and purging, often accompanied by magic rituals and incantations. Nevertheless, in a few societies doctors accurately recorded relevant events, such as Indian physicians who in 1000 BC were listing features of several common disabling diseases. Chinese medicine is documented from 600 BC, and the first Chinese medical text was written in 1st-c BC. The major contribution of Greek medicine was in the field of medical ethics, and the Hippocratic code of conduct is still invoked today. Roman medicine was pre-eminent in public health, with its emphasis on clean water, sewage disposal, and public baths. The emphasis by early Christians on miracles was balanced by the impulse to comfort and nurse the sick. Arabian medicine made significant contributions to chemistry and drugs, and set up the first organized medical school in Salerno (c.900). From there the torch was passed to Padua, where Vesalius corrected the anatomical misconceptions of Galen, and thereafter to Montpelier, Leyden, Edinburgh, and London.

The major medical discovery of the 17th-c was the circulation of the blood; 100 years later, oxygen and its relationship to blood. In the 18th-c, clinical bedside teaching became the favoured method of doctor training, as it is today. The value of post-mortem studies was demonstrated by Morgagni in Padua. New methods of examination were introduced, notably the stethoscope (by Laënnec) and percussion of the chest. Jenner showed the benefit of vaccination to prevent smallpox (though such procedures were known in 16th-c China). The germ theory of disease dominated the 19th-c, and Pasteur virtually created the science of bacteriology, from which Lister was inspired to develop the concept of antisepsis. By the end of the century, mosquitoes were known to carry malaria and yellow fever. Röntgen discovered X-rays, and the Curies discovered radium. Freud developed psychiatry.

Progress in the 20th-c was unparalleled, being distinguished by the growth in modern technology and the development of rigorous experimental testing. Thus the claim for the efficacy of a new drug, for example, does not rest on anecdote, but on carefully planned double-blind animal and human trials in statistically controlled populations. Progress was stimulated rather than hindered by World Wars 1 and 2, in such areas as rehabilitation after injury, blood transfusion, anaesthesia, and chemotherapy, including the development of antibiotics and vitamins and the discovery of insulin and cortisone. New concepts have included genetic disease, the adverse effects of some lifestyles and environmental pollution, vaccination for a number of infectious diseases, artificial organ and life-support systems, organ transplantation, and the science of immunology.

Medicine Hat 50°03N 110°41W, pop (2000e) 48 800. City in SE Alberta, Canada, on S Saskatchewan R; railway arrived, 1873; city status, 1906; airfield; natural gas, glass blowing, chemical fertilizers, petrochemicals, clay products; Dinosaur Provincial Park, 104 km/65 mi W; oldest rodeo in Alberta (Jul).

medick An annual and perennial, native to Europe, W Asia, and N Africa; leaves with three toothed leaflets; pea-flowers small, mostly yellow; fruit usually a spirally coiled pod, often spiny, less commonly sickle-shaped. (Genus: *Medicago*, 100 species. Family: Leguminosae.)

Medina [medeena], Arabic **Madinah, Al** 24°35N 39°52E, pop (2000e) 813 000. Islamic holy city in Medina province, Saudi Arabia; 336 km/209 mi N of Mecca; second most important holy city of Islam (after Mecca), containing the tomb of Mohammed; after his flight from Mecca, Mohammed sought refuge here; important pilgrimage trade, served by the Red Sea port of Yanbu al-Bahr; city closed to non-Muslims; airfield; Islamic university (1961); centre of a large date-growing oasis, producing also fruit, grain, clover; numerous mosques, Islamic monuments.

meditation Devout and continuous reflection on a particular religious theme, practised in many religions and serving a variety of aims, such as deepening spiritual insight, or achieving union with the divine will. Some religions hold that disciplined breathing, posture, and ordering of thoughts deepen meditation.

Mediterranean Sea, ancient **Mediterraneum** or **Mare Internum** area 2 516 000 sq km/971 000 sq mi. World's largest inland sea, lying between Africa, Asia, and Europe; connected with the Atlantic by the 14·5 km/9 mi-wide Straits of Gibraltar, with the Black Sea by the Dardanelles, Sea of Marmara, and Bosporus, and with the Indian Ocean by the Suez Canal and Red Sea; subdivided into the Ligurian, Adriatic, Aegean, Ionian, and Tyrrhenian Seas; length, 3860 km/2400 mi; maximum width, 1610 km/1000 mi; maximum depth, 4405 m/14 452 ft; higher salinity than the Atlantic; 'Mediterranean climate' of hot, dry summers (intensified by the Sirocco wind) and mild winters with rainstorms; seaboard highly favoured as holiday and health resort; maritime highway since ancient times for the Phoenicians, Greeks, Venetians, and Crusaders, connecting Europe with the E; eclipsed in the 14th–16th-c because of Turkish dominance and opening of ocean highway around Africa; Suez Canal (1869) restored much of its importance; pollution a major problem; strategic importance demonstrated during and after World War 2.

medium (art) The liquid into which pigment is mixed to make paint. Its purpose is to enable the pigment to be spread on the surface of the picture, and to stick. Various substances have been used for this, including oil, glue, size, egg, vegetable gum, and wax.

medium (parapsychology) Especially in spiritualism, a person through whom spirits of the dead are claimed to demonstrate their presence by means of spoken or written messages, or apparently paranormal physical effects.

Medjugorje [medyoogorye] 43°20N 17°49E. Village in Bosnia and Herzegovina, S of Mostar; since 1981, claimed to be the scene of regular appearances by the Virgin Mary to a group of local children; now a major site of pilgrimage, having attracted over 10 million visitors in the 1980s; in the 1990s, number of pilgrims much reduced by civil war.

medlar A small deciduous tree or shrub (*Mespilus germanica*), growing to 6 m/20 ft, native to SE Europe, and cultivated and naturalized elsewhere; leaves oblong, yellowish; flowers solitary, 3–6 cm/1¼–2½ in diameter, white; sepals leafy, longer than petals; fruit 2–3 cm/¾–1¼ in, brown, becoming soft and edible when over-ripe. (Family: Rosaceae.)

Médoc [maydok] District in Gironde department, SW France; flat alluvial plain on W bank of Gironde estuary, N of Bordeaux; bounded W by the Atlantic Ocean; famous for its clarets, notably at Haut-Médoc; chief towns, Lesparre and Pauillac.

medulla oblongata [meduhla oblonggahta] The lower part of the brain stem, continuous with the pons above and the spinal cord below. It contains the 'vital centres' (so-called because damage to them is often fatal) concerned with the reflex control of the cardiovascular and respiratory systems. It also helps to govern swallowing, sneezing, coughing, and vomiting.

medusa [medyooza] The free-swimming phase in the life-cycle of a coelenterate. The body is typically discoid or bell-shaped, usually radially symmetrical, with marginal tentacles and a centrally located mouth on the underside. The medusa contains the reproductive organs, and is the sexual phase in the coelenterate life cycle.

Medusa [medyooza] In Greek mythology, the name of one of the Gorgons, whose head is portrayed with staring eyes and snakes for hair.

Medway Towns Urban area in Kent, SE England, UK; includes Gillingham and Rochester (merging as Medway unitary authority, 1998), Chatham, and Strood on the R Medway, E of London; railway.

Mee, Arthur (Henry) (1875–1943) Journalist, editor, and writer, born in Stapleford, Nottinghamshire, C England, UK. He was most widely known for his *Children's Encyclopaedia* (1908) and *Children's Newspaper*. He also wrote a wide range of popular works on history, science, and geography.

Meech Lake Accord A Canadian constitutional package, put together by the government of Brian Mulroney in 1987 at a conference at Meech L, N of Ottawa. It proposed a fresh federal structure for Canada, giving the provinces more authority, and recognized Quebec as a 'distinct society'. The Accord died after it failed to receive the support of all 10 Provinces and First Nations leaders in 1990.

Meegeren, Han van *van Meegeren, Han*

meerkat A mongoose native to S Africa; three species: the **suricate** or **slender-tailed meerkat** (*Suricata suricata*); the **yellow** or **thick-tailed meerkat**, or **yellow mongoose** (*Cynictis penicillata*); and the **gray meerkat** or **Selous mongoose** (*Paracynictis selousi*).

meerschaum [meershuhm] or **epiolite** A hydrated magnesium silicate mineral, which forms fine, fibrous masses like white clay and is easily carved. It is porous when dry, and is used for pipe bowls. Asia Minor is the main source.

megabyte *byte*

megalith (Gr *mega*, 'large' + *lithos*, 'stone') In European prehistory, a monument built of large, roughly-dressed stone slabs;

sometimes anachronistically called a **cromlech**. Most are of Neolithic date. Outside Europe, comparable (though unrelated) megalithic monuments are found in S India, Tibet, SE Asia, Japan, and Oceania.

Megaloceros [megaloseros] *Irish elk*

megalomania An extremely inflated view of one's own significance and abilities. This may take on a delusional quality in which, for example, the individual may believe himself to be Jesus Christ. In this situation the description of the thoughts is referred to as *delusions of grandeur*.

Megaloptera [megaloptera] *alderfly; dobsonfly*

megaparsec *parsec*

megapode An Australasian ground-living bird; usually inhabits rainforest; eats mainly fruit and insects; sturdy body with large legs and feet; eggs usually incubated by natural heat in mound of decaying vegetation; young fly within hours of hatching; also known as **mound bird**, **mound builder**, or **incubator bird**. It includes **scrub-fowl** of the genus *Megapodius*. (Family: Megapodiidae, 12 species.)

Megatherium [megatheerium] The largest ground sloth, found in Central and South America during the Pleistocene epoch; a two-legged browser and grazer in grassy woodlands and pasture; forelimbs large, hindlimbs short but massive; toes clawed; walked on outer edge of foot. (Order: Xenarthra.)

megaton *kiloton* (TNT)

megavitamin therapy A form of nutritional therapy based on the work of Linus Pauling, who believed that very large doses of vitamin C could cure or prevent the common cold by having a direct anti-viral effect and also by enhancing the effect of the immune system. Large doses of various vitamins have been used in psychiatry to treat patients with a wide variety of disorders, such as schizophrenia, depression, and hyperactivity, on the assumption that these problems may be the result of vitamin deficiency. It has been shown that some people cannot absorb adequate amounts of vitamins and minerals from their diet, and that cancer patients require vitamins in much larger quantities than usual to avoid significant deficiency. However, some vitamins taken in excessive amounts may cause toxic effects, and such treatments should only be given under medical supervision.

megawatt *watt*

Megiddo [megidoh] In antiquity, an important town in N Palestine controlling the main route from Egypt to Syria. Under Israelite control from around 1000 BC, it was rebuilt by Solomon (c.970–933 BC) as a military and administrative centre. Among its most impressive remains are the 9th-c stables of the Israelite kings.

megohm *ohm*

Mehta, Ved (Parkash) [mayta] (1934–) Writer, born in Lahore, NE Pakistan (formerly India). Blind from the age of four, he went to the USA for his education when he was 15, and attended the Arkansas School for the Blind at Little Rock, and Pomona College, before going to Oxford and Harvard universities. While at Pomona he published his first book, the autobiography *Face to Face* (1957). He has had a distinguished career as a journalist, contributing chiefly to *The New Yorker*. Employing amanuenses, he has written biographies, stories, essays, and portraits of India, including *The New India* (1978) and *Rajiv Gandhi and Rama's Kingdom* (1995), and in 1999 appeared *Remembering Mr Shawn's New Yorker*. His enduring achievement, however, is *Continents of Exile*, an acclaimed series of autobiographical books (1972–89). He became a US citizen in 1975.

Mehta, Zubin [mayta] (1936–) Conductor, born in Mumbai (Bombay), W India. Born into a musical family, he later studied music in Vienna. He became associate conductor of the Royal Liverpool Philharmonic (1958), and went on to be conductor and musical director of many prestigious orchestras, notably the Los Angeles Philharmonic (1962–78) and the New York Philharmonic (1978–91). He is now the musical director (for life) of the Israel Philharmonic Orchestra.

Meidan Emam [maydan emam] A public square built in Isfahan, C Iran, by Abbas I (1571–1629) in the late 16th-c; a world heritage site. The square is flanked by four notable buildings: the former Royal Mosque, the Sheikh Lotfollah Mosque, the Ali Qapu Palace, and the gateway to the Qeyssariyeh.

Meiji Restoration (1868) [mayjee] An important point in Japanese history, when the last shogun was overthrown in a short civil war, and the position of the emperor (Mutsuhito, who ruled until 1912) was restored to political importance. Powerful new leaders set about making Japan into an industrial state. The four hereditary classes of Tokugawa Japan were abolished. New technology and technical experts were brought from the West.

Meiji Shrine [mayjee] An important pilgrimage centre in Tokyo. The shrine was completed in 1920 and dedicated to Emperor Meiji. The present building is a reconstruction of the original which was destroyed in World War 2.

Meiji Tenno *Mutsuhito*

Meiningen Players [miyningen] The private theatre company of the Duke of Saxe-Meiningen (1826–1914) which, through its European tours of the 1880s, influenced the development of Western theatre. The advantages of the unifying hand of a director could be seen in the organization of the crowd scenes and the integration of scenic design with the movements of the actors.

meiosis [miyohsis] One of the principal mechanisms of nuclear division in living organisms, resulting in the formation of gametes (in animals) or sexual spores (in plants). During meiosis a diploid nucleus (ie one possessing a double set of chromosomes) undergoes two successive divisions. This results in the production of four cells, each receiving only one member of each chromosome pair. The halving of chromosome numbers compensates for the doubling that occurs when two haploid gametes (ie each possessing a single set of chromosomes) unite to form a zygote during sexual reproduction. The phases of meiosis are *leptotene* (the appearance of chromosomes as threads in the nucleus), *zygotene* (the pairing of chromosomes to form bivalents), *pachytene* (the separation of bivalents), and *diplotene* (the moving apart of chromosomes). Meiosis is an important process in sexual reproduction, providing the opportunity for recombination to occur, as genetic material can be exchanged by crossing over between homologous chromosomes during the pachytene phase.

Meir, Golda [mayeer], originally **Goldie Myerson**, *née* **Mabovitch** (1898–1978) Israeli stateswoman and prime minister (1969–74), born in Kiev, Ukraine. Brought up in Milwaukee, WI, from 1906, she became a teacher and an active Zionist. After her marriage to **Morris Myerson** (1917), she emigrated to a kibbutz in Palestine in 1921, and became a leading figure in the Labour movement. She was Israeli ambassador to the Soviet Union (1948–9), minister of labour (1949–56), then Hebraized her name when appointed foreign minister (1956–66). As prime minister of a coalition government, her plans to maintain a 'security frontier' along the Jordan river were halted by the fourth Arab–Israeli War (1973), and she was forced to resign as a result of the Israeli losses incurred.

Meissen porcelain [miysn] Porcelain made at Meissen, near Dresden; the first factory in Europe to make true hard-paste porcelain. The secret was discovered in 1708 by Johann Friedrich Böttger (1682–1719). The factory, founded in 1710, was the most influential in Europe, and is still in production.

Meissner effect [miysner] In superconductivity, the exclusion of magnetic fields from the body of the superconducting material; discovered by German physicist Walther Meissner in 1933. If a block of metal is placed in a magnetic field, the field will exist throughout the material. When the temperature is lowered to below a certain substance-dependent critical temperature, the field vanishes from inside the material, being forced to flow round it.

Meissonier, (Jean Louis) Ernest [maysonyay] (1815–91) Painter, born in Lyon, SC France. His works were largely of military and historical scenes, painted with careful attention to detail, including several of the Napoleonic era.

Meistersinger [**mysterzinger**] Members of German guilds of the 14th–16th-c devoted to the encouragement of poetry and music in strict traditional forms. Their activities form the basis for Wagner's opera *Die Meistersinger von Nürnberg* (1868).

Meitner, Lise [**miytner**] (1878–1968) Physicist, born in Vienna, Austria. She studied at Vienna, and became a professor in Berlin (1926–38), where she was also a member of the Kaiser Wilhelm Institute for Chemistry (1907–38). In 1917 she shared with Otto Hahn the discovery of the radioactive element protactinium, and became known for her work on nuclear physics. In 1938 she fled from Nazi Germany to the Nobel Physical Institute, Sweden, moving from there to the Royal Swedish Academy of Engineering Sciences, Stockholm, in 1947. With her nephew Frisch she devised the idea of nuclear fission in late 1938. She retired to England in 1960.

Mekele or **Makale** [**makalay**] 13°32N 39°33E, pop (2000e) 94 200. Capital of Tigray region, NE Ethiopia; airport; salt trade, resin; major refugee centre during the severe drought of 1983.

Meknès [**meknes**] 33°53N 5°37W, pop (2000e) 465 000. City in Centre-Sud province, N Morocco; in the Moyen Atlas, 50 km/31 mi SW of Fez; one of Morocco's four imperial cities, founded in the 12th-c; several palaces built under Moulay Ismail (1672–1727) to rival the Versailles of Louis XIV; capital until 1728; railway; leather, wine, carpets, pottery; Musée des Arts Marocains, Bou Inania Médersa (14th-c, religious college), Grand Mosque, Moulay Ismail's tomb, gardens of El Haboul.

Mekong River [**meekong**], Chin **Lancang Jiang** River in IndoChina, SE Asia; rises in Tibet (Xizang) as the Ziqu and Zhaqu, which join as the Langcang Jiang; flows S and SW, forming the boundary between Laos and Myanmar, SE to form the Laos–Thailand boundary, then generally E and S into Cambodia and Vietnam, splitting into four major tributaries at its delta on the South China Sea; linked to the Tonlé Sap lake in C Cambodia, which acts as its flood reservoir during the wet season; length c.4000 km/2500 mi; navigable for c.550 km/340 mi.

Melaka *Malacca*

Melanchthon, Philipp [**melangkthon**], originally **Philipp Schwartzerd** (1497–1560) Protestant reformer, born in Bretten, SW Germany. His name is a Greek translation of his German surname, 'black earth'. He studied at Heidelberg and Tübingen, and in 1516 became professor of Greek at Wittenberg and Luther's fellow worker. His *Loci communes* (1512) is the first great Protestant work on dogmatic theology. He also composed the Augsburg Confession (1530).

Melanesia One of the three broad geographical–cultural areas of the Pacific. It includes the islands of New Guinea, the Solomons, Vanuatu, and New Caledonia. (Fiji is more usefully included in Polynesia, on account of the authority it accords hereditary chiefs.) The peoples of Melanesia typically have dark skin, kinky hair, large jaws, and a high incidence of blood group B. Numerous languages are spoken among them. The name comes from Greek *melas*, 'black' and *nesos*, 'island'.

melanins [**melaninz**] Dark brown pigments which in different concentrations give coloration (shades of yellow and brown) to the eyes, skin, hair, feathers, and scales of many vertebrates. They are present in the pigment-bearing cells (*melanophores*) of amphibians, reptiles, and fish, as well as in the outer skin cells (*melanocytes*) of mammals. In humans they help protect the skin against the damaging effects of sunlight (ultraviolet radiations). The amount present in the skin is determined by both genetic and environmental factors.

melanocyte-stimulating hormone (MSH) [**melanohsiyt**] A hormone (a polypeptide) present in the intermediate lobe of the pituitary gland of vertebrates; also known as **intermedin**. It stimulates the synthesis and dispersion of melanins.

melanoma [**melanohma**] A pigmented tumour due to overgrowth of melanin-producing cells in the basal cell layer of the skin. Increasingly in recent years a proportion are becoming malignant, enlarge rapidly, and spread to other parts of the body (*malignant melanoma*). Prevention is by protecting the skin from bright sunlight.

melatonin [**melatohnin**] A hormone produced from serotonin, mainly within the pineal gland. Little is known about its precise function. Its secretion from the pineal gland and its concentration within blood both fluctuate, being highest during darkness. In humans it may be associated with the synchronization of circadian rhythms.

Melba, Dame Nellie, professional name of **Helen Armstrong**, *née* **Mitchell** (1861–1931) Prima donna, born in Melbourne, Victoria, SE Australia, from which she took her name. A talented pianist, she studied singing after her marriage in 1882. She appeared at Covent Garden in 1888, and the purity of her coloratura soprano voice won her worldwide fame. She was created a dame in 1918. 'Peach Melba' and 'Melba toast' were named after her.

Melbourne 37°45S 144°58E, pop (2000e) 3 339 000. Port and state capital in Victoria, Australia; on the Yarra R, at the head of Port Phillip Bay; founded in 1835, named after the British prime minister, Lord Melbourne; state capital, 1851; capital of Australia when federal parliament sat here, 1901–27; Melbourne statistical division contains 56 local government areas; many large parks and fine 19th-c buildings; two airports; railway; underground; five universities (1855, 1958, 1964, 1991, 1992); Australia's biggest cargo port; major financial and communications centre; heavy engineering, textiles, paper, electronics, chemicals, foodstuffs, metal processing, cars, shipbuilding; two cathedrals; Melbourne Cricket Ground; Flemington racecourse (holds the Melbourne Cup horse race); Moomba 10-day festival of street parades, sporting events and cultural activities (Mar); Melbourne Royal Agricultural Show (Sep); Melbourne Cup Day (Nov); site of 1956 Olympic Games.

Melbourne, William Lamb, 2nd Viscount (1779–1848) British statesman and prime minister (1834, 1835–41), born in London, UK. He studied at Cambridge and Glasgow, became a Whig MP in 1805, and was made chief secretary for Ireland (1827–8). Succeeding as second viscount (1828), he became home secretary (1830–4) under Grey. He formed a close, almost avuncular relationship with the young Queen Victoria. Defeated in the election of 1841, he resigned and thereafter took little part in public affairs. His wife wrote novels as **Lady Caroline Lamb** (1785–1828), and was notorious for her 9-months' devotion (1812–13) to Lord Byron.

Melbourne Cup Australia's principal horse race, first run in 1861, for 3-year-olds and upwards. It is now run over 3200 m (2 mi) of the Flemington Park racecourse in Victoria. Held on the first Tuesday in November, Melbourne Cup day is a social occasion like Royal Ascot.

Melchett, Baron *Mond, Alfred*

Melchites [**melkhiyts**] Christians who follow the Byzantine rite, and who belong to the Patriarchates of Alexandria, Antioch, and Jerusalem. During the 5th-c, they supported the Byzantine emperor in his opposition to the Monophysites (hence their name, which is from the Syriac word for 'royalist').

Meleager [**meleeayger**] A Greek hero, at whose birth the Moerae appeared and prophesied that he would die when the brand then on the fire had burnt away. His mother, Althaea, removed it and kept it. When the quarrel over the Calydonian boar took place and her brothers were killed by Meleager, she threw the brand onto the fire, so that he died.

Méliès, Georges [**maylyes**] (1861–1938) Illusionist and film maker, born in Paris, France. He made his name in Paris as a stage magician. Immediately after the invention of the cinema, he began making short films, and from 1895 was a pioneer in trick cinematography to present magical effects. His films include *Voyage to the Moon* (1902) and *20,000 Leagues Under the Sea* (1907). He fell into obscurity after 1913, and died in poverty.

Melilla [**mayleelya**], ancient **Russadir** 35°21N 2°57W, pop (2000e) 67 000. Free port and modern commercial city on N African coast of Morocco; with Ceuta, forms a region of Spain;

founded as a port by the Phoenicians; free port since 1863; re-occupied by Spain in 1926; airport; car ferries to Málaga; trade in iron ore; naval shipyard; old town, Church of the Purisima Concepción (16th-c).

melilot [**mel**ilot] Typically an annual or biennial, native to Europe, Asia, and N Africa, often smelling strongly of new-mown hay on drying; leaves with three toothed leaflets; pea-flowers small, yellow or white, in long, narrow, spike-like inflorescences. Several species are grown for fodder, and it is also used for flavouring cheeses. (Genus: *Melilotus*, 20 species. Family: Leguminosae.)

Mellon, Andrew W(illiam) (1855–1937) Financier, philanthropist, and statesman, born in Pittsburgh, Pennsylvania, USA. Trained as a lawyer, he entered his father's banking house in 1874, became its president, and made a reputation for himself as an industrial magnate, becoming one of the richest men in the USA by the early 1920s. Entering politics, he was secretary of the Treasury (1921–32) under presidents Harding, Coolidge, and Hoover, and made controversial fiscal reforms, drastically reducing taxation of the wealthy. He endowed the National Gallery of Art at Washington, DC.

Mellor, David (John) (1949–) British statesman. He studied at Cambridge, and was called to the bar in 1972. He was elected Conservative MP for Putney in 1979, and after holding various junior posts became minister of state at the Home Office (1986–7, 1989–90), Foreign and Commonwealth Office (1987–8), and the Department of Health (1988–9). He was minister for the arts in 1990, then chief secretary to the Treasury (1990–2) and secretary of state for national heritage (1992). His political career ended when he was forced to resign from the government in 1992 following revelations about an extra-marital affair. He went on to present a football programme on BBC's Radio 5, and was voted BBC Radio Personality of the Year in 1995. He failed to retain his seat in the 1997 election, but later that year was appointed head of a football Task Force by the Labour minister for sport.

melodrama A theatrical genre in vogue after the French Revolution and popularized by Pixerécourt (1773–1884), which became a mass entertainment in Europe and the USA throughout the 19th-c. Originating in London in operatic theatre, melodrama is a style which emphasizes the depiction of story, the creation of suspense, and the use of sensational episodes. Well-known examples are Douglas Jerrold's *Black-Eyed Susan* (1829), the anonymous *Maria Marten* (c.1830), and *Sweeny Todd, the Demon Barber of Fleet Street* (1842). Spectacular melodramas were staged at the Drury Lane Theatre, with shipwrecks, earthquakes, and horse racing.

melody A basic constituent of music, being a succession of pitches arranged in some intelligible order. In Western music, melody is found independently of music's other basic elements (harmony and rhythm) only in plainchant and some folksong. Between c.1675 and 1925, melodic inspiration (a gift for composing 'good tunes') became more and more highly prized as the token of a composer's originality. Since then, many composers have sought to express their musical personalities in other ways, through the use of texture, rhythm, etc.

melon A trailing or climbing vine (*Cucumis melo*) with tendrils, probably native to Africa, but cultivated from early times; leaves heart-shaped, palmately-lobed; male and female flowers yellow, c.3 cm/1¼ in diameter, funnel-shaped; fruit up to 25 cm/10 in long, round or ovoid; rind green or yellow, leathery, sometimes with a net pattern; edible flesh thick, sweet, surrounding numerous seeds. The types include cantaloupe, casaba, honeydew, and musk. (Family: Cucurbitaceae.)

Melos [**mee**los], Gr **Mílos** area 151 sq km/58 sq mi. Southwesternmost island of the Cyclades, Greece, in the S Aegean Sea; main town, Plaka; minerals, fruit, olives, cotton, tourism; 'Venus de Milo' sculpture (Louvre, Paris) discovered here in 1820.

Melpomene [mel**pom**inee] The Greek Muse of tragedy.

meltdown A catastrophic event in a nuclear reactor. If control of the release of thermal energy is lost, the temperature of the reacting core rises to a point at which the fuel rods melt, and radioactive material may be released into the environment.

melting point The temperature at which a solid becomes liquid. If heat is applied to a solid, its temperature rises until the melting point is reached, when heat energy is then absorbed to form liquid from the solid. Temperature continues to rise once the melting is complete.

Mélusine or **Mélisande** In French folklore, a half-human fairy who locked her father into a mountain and was condemned to change into a fish from the waist down every Saturday. Her husband, Raymond de Poitiers of Lusignan, broke his promise never to see her on Saturdays, and she disappeared, to be heard lamenting whenever one of her descendants was about to die.

Melville, Herman (1819–91) Novelist, born in New York City, USA. He became a bank clerk, but left in search of adventure, and joined a whaling ship bound for the South Seas (1841). His journeys were the subject matter for his first novels, *Typee* (1846) and *Omoo* (1847). In 1847 he married, and after three years in New York City took a farm near Pittsfield, MA. During this period he wrote his masterpiece, *Moby-Dick* (1851), a classic among sea stories. After 1857, he wrote only some poetry, leaving his long story *Billy Budd, Foretopman* in manuscript. Now regarded as one of America's greatest novelists, he was not so acclaimed during his life; even *Moby-Dick* was unappreciated.

membrane potential The voltage differential maintained across the plasma membranes of most living cells, with the inside of the cell being negatively charged with respect to the outside; also known as *transmembrane potential*. Its magnitude is determined by differences in the concentrations of ions on the two sides of the membrane, varying from about −9 to −100 mv according to the nature of the cell.

membranophone Any musical instrument in which the sound is generated by the vibrations of a stretched membrane. The most important are the various kinds of drum. Membranophones form one of the main categories in the standard classification of Hornbostel and Sachs (1914).

Memlinc or **Memling, Hans** [**mem**ling] (c.1435–1494) Religious painter, born in Seligenstadt, SWC Germany. He lived mostly in Bruges, and was probably a pupil of Rogier van der Weyden. His works include the triptych of the 'Madonna Enthroned' at Chatsworth (1468), and the 'Marriage of St Catherine' (1479) and the 'Shrine of St Ursula' (1489), both at Bruges. He was also an original and creative portrait painter.

Memnon [**mem**non] In Greek mythology, a prince from Ethiopia, the son of Eos and Tithonus, who was killed at Troy by Achilles. The Greeks thought that one of the gigantic statues at Thebes represented him; it gave out a musical sound at sunrise.

Memorial Day A national holiday in the USA, held on the last Monday in May in honour of American war dead; originally instituted as **Decoration Day** in 1868 in honour of soldiers killed in the American Civil War.

memory The ability to access information in the mind relating to past events or experiences. Theories of memory deal with the causes of forgetting (pure decay or interference from other material), and the possibility that there may be two or more distinct stores from which information is forgotten at different rates (**short-term** and **long-term** memory). They also analyze the distinction between **episodic** memory (memory for specific events experienced by the individual) and **semantic** memory (knowledge), and the way incoming information and previous knowledge interact in language comprehension and problem solving ('working memory'). Practical issues include the reliability of eye-witnesses' memories (eye-witnesses are easily biased by information they receive after the witnessed event).

Memphis (Egypt) An important town in ancient Egypt on the W bank of the Nile, S of the Delta. The capital of Lower Egypt under the pharaohs, it declined in importance under the Ptolemies, who made Alexandria their capital instead. The necropolis of Memphis is at Saqqarah.

Memphis (USA) [memfis] 35°08N 90°03W, pop (2000e) 650 000. Seat of Shelby Co, SW Tennessee, USA; a port on the Mississippi R; largest city in the state; site of military fort, 1797; city established, 1819; captured by Union forces during the Civil War (battle of Memphis, 1862); severe yellow-fever epidemics in the 1870s; airfield; railway; two universities (1848, 1912); important market for cotton, hardwood lumber, livestock, poultry; food and paper products, chemicals, textiles, fabricated metals; music recording industry; Martin Luther King Jr assassinated here (1968); Graceland, home of Elvis Presley; Beale Street, made famous by W C Handy and regarded as the birthplace of the blues; Mud Island Park.

Menai Straits [meniy] Channel separating Anglesey from the mainland of NW Wales, UK; length 24 km/15 mi; width varies from 175 m/575 ft to 3·2 km/2 mi; crossed by the Menai Suspension Bridge, built by Telford (1819–26), length 176 m/580 ft, and the Britannia railway/road bridge (1980), rebuilt after fire in 1970 seriously damaged the original tubular railway bridge of Robert Stephenson (1846–9).

Menander [menander] (c.343–291 BC) Greek comic playwright, born in Athens, Greece. He wrote more than 100 comedies, but only a few fragments of his work were known until 1906, when a papyrus containing 1328 lines from four different plays was discovered in Egypt. In 1957, however, the complete text of the comedy *Dyskolos* ('The Bad-Tempered Man') was brought to light in Geneva.

menarche [menah(r)kee] The first menstrual bleeding of the human female, which occurs during puberty (10 to 15 years of age depending on genetic, nutritional, and emotional status). It signifies the approach of reproductive maturity, but does not indicate the attainment of full fertility, which is delayed until the adult pattern of pituitary and gonadal hormone secretion is established, and menstrual cycles become both regular and accompanied by ovulation.

Menchik-Stevenson, Vera (Francevna), *née* **Menchik** (1906–44) Chess player, born in Moscow, Russia. She became a British citizen on her marriage in 1937. Recognized as the finest of all female chess players, she held the world title from 1927 (the first champion) to 1944, when she was killed during a London air-raid.

Mencius [menshius], Latin name **Meng-tzu** (Master Meng) (c.371–c.289 BC) Philosopher and sage, born in Shantung, E China. He founded a school modelled on that of Confucius, and travelled China for some 20 years searching for a ruler to implement Confucian moral and political ideals. The search was unsuccessful, but his conversations with rulers, disciples, and others are recorded in a book of sayings compiled after his death (*Book of Meng-tzu*). His ethical system was based on the belief that human beings are innately and instinctively good, but require the proper conditions and support for moral growth. He also made many practical recommendations about taxes, road maintenance, and poor law.

Mencken, H(enry) L(ouis) (1880–1956) Philologist, editor, and satirist, born in Baltimore, Maryland, USA. He studied at Baltimore Polytechnic, became a journalist and literary critic, and greatly influenced the US literary scene in the 1920s. His major work, *The American Language*, was first published in 1918, and in 1924 he founded the *American Mercury*, editing it until 1933.

Mendel, Gregor (Johann) (1822–84) Biologist and botanist, born in Heinzendorf, Austria. Entering an Augustinian cloister in 1843, he was ordained a priest in 1847. After studying science at Vienna (1851–3), he became abbot at Brno (1868). He researched the inheritance characters in plants, especially edible peas, and his experiments in hybridity in plants led to the formulation of his laws of segregation and independent assortment (1866). His principle of factorial inheritance and the quantitative investigation of single characters have provided the basis for modern genetics. Recognition came many years after his death, when his key article, 'Experiments with plant hybrids' (1866), was discovered.

Mendeleyev, Dmitri Ivanovich [mendelayef] (1834–1907) Chemist, born in Tobolsk, WC Russia. He became a teacher, then studied at Odessa, St Petersburg, and Heidelberg, becoming professor of chemistry at St Petersburg from 1866. He devised the periodic classification (or table) of chemical elements (1869), by which he predicted the existence of several elements which were subsequently discovered. Element No 101 (*mendelevium*) is named after him.

Mendel's laws The fundamental principles of inheritance, proposed by Gregor Mendel in 1866. In a series of experiments on garden peas, he crossed varieties differing in particular features (eg tall by short), and observed the effects on the individuals in each generation. His *principle of gametic purity* states that inherited pairs of factors segregate at germ cell formation and recombine at fertilization, ie that a sex cell (sperm, ovum, pollen) can carry only one from each pair of factors available to it. This showed that characteristics are not transmitted directly from generation to generation as previously thought, but that there are discrete factors responsible for their appearance. The *law of independent segregation* states that when more than one pair of factors are involved in a cross, each pair segregates independently of the others. The mechanisms which Mendel described in his laws remain the basis for much of modern genetics.

Mendelssohn(-Bartholdy), (Jakob Ludwig) Felix [mendlsuhn] (1809–47) Composer, born in Hamburg, N Germany, the grandson of Moses Mendelssohn, and the son of a Hamburg banker who added the name Bartholdy. He studied piano and composition in Berlin, making his first public appearance at the age of nine. A prolific composer even as a boy, among his early successes was the *Midsummer Night's Dream* overture (1826). In London in 1829 he conducted his C minor symphony. A tour of Scotland inspired him with the *Hebrides* overture (1830) and the *Scottish Symphony*. He founded an Academy of Arts at Berlin in 1841, and a music school at Leipzig in 1843. Other major works include his oratorios *St Paul* (1836) and *Elijah* (1846).

Mendelssohn, Moses [mendelsuhn] (1729–86) Philosopher, literary critic, and biblical scholar, born in Dessau, EC Germany. He studied at Berlin and became the partner to a silk manufacturer. A zealous defender of enlightened monotheism, he was an apostle of deism. His major works include *Phädon* (1767), on the immortality of the soul; *Jerusalem* (1783), which advocates Judaism as the religion of reason; and *Morgenstunden* (1785) which argues for the rationality of belief in the existence of God.

Menderes, Adnan [menderes] (1899–1961) Turkish statesman and prime minister (1950–60), born near Aydin, W Turkey. Though educated for the law, he became a farmer, and entered politics in 1932. In 1945 he became one of the leaders of the new Democratic Party, and was made prime minister when it came to power in 1950. Re-elected in 1954 and 1957, in May 1960 he was deposed and superseded after an army coup. He appeared as defendant with over 500 officials of his former Democratic Party administration at the Yassiada trials (1960–1), was sentenced to death, and hanged.

Mendes, Sam(uel Alexander) [mendez] (1965–) Theatre and film director, born in Reading, SE England, UK. After graduating from Cambridge he launched himself onto the theatrical scene with innovative stage productions in London and at the Chichester Festival Theatre. He joined the Royal Shakespeare Company in 1992, then became artistic director of London's Donmar Warehouse (1992–2002), in 1998 producing the world premiere of *The Blue Room*. He made his film debut to great acclaim in 1999 with *American Beauty* (Oscars for Best Director and Best Picture). Later films include *Road to Perdition* (2002). He married actress Kate Winslet in 2003.

Mendès-France, Pierre [mendez frãs] (1907–82) French statesman and prime minister (1954–5), born in Paris, France. A lawyer, he entered parliament in 1932, was imprisoned by the

Vichy government, and in 1941 escaped to join the Free French forces in England. He was minister for national economy under Charles de Gaulle in 1945, and became a prominent member of the Radical Party. As prime minister, he ended the war in Indo-China, but his government was defeated on its N African policy. A firm critic of de Gaulle, he lost his seat in the 1958 election. He became increasingly opposed to the autocratic use of presidential power by de Gaulle, and retired from political life in 1973.

Mendicant Orders (Lat *mendicare*, 'to beg') Religious Orders in which friars were not permitted to hold property, either personally or in common. Such Orders were able to survive only through the charity of others.

Mendip Hills Hill range in SW England, UK; extending 37 km/ 23 mi NW–SE from Weston-super-Mare to near Shepton Mallet; rises to 326 m/1069 ft at Blackdown; includes limestone caves of Cheddar Gorge; traces of former Roman lead mines.

Mendoza [menthohsa] 32°48S 68°52W, pop (2000e) 135 300. Capital of Mendoza province, W Argentina; at foot of Sierra de los Paramillos range, on the R Tulumaya; altitude 756 m/ 2480 ft; colonized by Chile in 1561; belonged to Chile until 1776; destroyed by fire and earthquake in 1861; four universities (1939, 1959, 1960, 1968); airport; railway; trading and processing centre for a large, irrigated agricultural area, dealing mainly in wine; annual wine festival (Feb–Mar).

Menelaus [menilayus] In Greek legend, the younger brother of Agamemnon. He was King of Sparta, and married to Helen. After several years of marriage, she was abducted by Paris, and this was the cause of the Trojan War, in which Menelaus was second-in-command of the Greek army. He was delayed in Egypt on his return. Finally he settled down again at Sparta with Helen.

Mengistu, Haile Mariam [menggistoo] (1937–) Ethiopian soldier, politician, and president (1987–91), born in the Harar region, E Ethiopia. He studied at Holetu military academy, and joined the Ethiopian army, rising to the rank of colonel. He took part in the 1974 coup which removed Emperor Haile Selassie, then in 1977 led another coup which ousted the military regime. Despite Ethiopia's perilous economy, guerrilla fighting, and frequent droughts throughout the 1970s and 1980s, he managed to retain power with help from Russia and the West. In 1987 he sanctioned the return of one-party civilian rule under the Marxist–Leninist Workers Party, with himself as president. In 1991 when rebel groups closed in on Addis Ababa, he fled the country, and his government fell. He now lives in Zimbabwe.

Mengs, Anton Raphael (1728–79) Painter, born in Aussig, E Germany. He studied under his father at Dresden, eventually settled at Rome, and directed a school of painting. A close friend of Winckelmann, he became the most famous of the early Neoclassical painters. In Madrid (1761–70, 1773–6) he decorated the dome of the grand salon in the royal palace with the 'Apotheosis of the Emperor Trajan'.

menhir [meneer] (Welsh *maen*, 'stone' + *hir*, 'long') In European prehistory, a single standing stone or megalith. A striking example is the tapering granite pillar at Locmariaquer near Carnac, Brittany, known as 'Le Grand Menhir Brisé'; now lying in four pieces, this formerly stood 20 m/67 ft high and weighed an estimated 256 tonnes.

Ménière's disease [menyair, muhnyair] Repeated attacks of vertigo (a subjective sense of rotation), usually abrupt in onset, accompanied by tinnitus and progressive deafness, and sometimes associated with sweating, nausea, pallor, and vomiting. It is a disorder of the inner ear of unknown cause, affecting mainly middle-aged and elderly persons. It is named after French physician Prosper Ménière (1799–1862).

meningitis [meninjiytis] An infection of the membranes (pia and arachnoid) covering the brain. It may be caused by bacteria (eg *Neisseria meningitidis*, pneumococci, haemophilus, tuberculosis, or other species), viruses, or more rarely by fungi (eg *Cryptococcus*). The infectious agent enters through the nose or bloodstream. **Viral meningitis** is usually short-lived and harmless; **bacterial meningitis** is more serious and may cause death. The onset is usually sudden, with headache, fever, stiffness of the neck on flexion, and dislike of the light (*photophobia*), followed by drowsiness, fits, and coma. Symptoms may be less obvious in infants, who may just appear drowsy or irritable. Diagnosis is made by lumbar puncture, which allows the organism to be identified and appropriate antibiotics given.

meniscus [muhniskuhs] *surface tension*

Mennonites [menoniyts] Dutch and Swiss Anabaptists who later called themselves Mennonites after one of their Dutch leaders, Menno Simons (1496–1559). They adhere to the Confession of Dordrecht (1632), baptize on confession of faith, are pacifists, refuse to hold civic office, and follow the teachings of the New Testament. Most of their 1 million adherents live in the USA.

Menon, Krishna *Krishna Menon*

menopause Strictly defined as the cessation of menstruation, but more commonly used to refer to the period of time (up to eight years prior to the cessation of menstruation) when the menstrual cycle becomes less regular, due to the loss of responsiveness of the ovaries to gonadotrophins; also known as **climacteric**. Even though menstruation may be irregular, reproductive capacity is not lost. The complete cessation of menstruation usually occurs between 45 and 50 years. It is often accompanied by physical (sweating, hot flushes, vaginitis) and psychogenic (depression, insomnia, fatigue) disturbances, which generally respond to oestrogen therapy. Menopause is unique to the human female, but its significance is unclear.

menorah [menohra] A candelabrum of seven branches, with three curving upwards on each side of a central shaft, an ancient symbol of Judaism, and the official symbol of the modern State of Israel. In the Bible, it was originally part of the furnishings of the Tabernacle in the wilderness, and eventually of the Jerusalem Temple. The Hanukkah candleholder has eight arms, and in many synagogues the arms number other than seven, so as to avoid direct imitation of that in the Temple (forbidden in the Talmud).

menorrhagia [menorayjia] Excessive menstrual bleeding due to menstruation that is too heavy, too long, or too frequent. It commonly results from local abnormalities of the uterus, but also arises from disorders of the hormones controlling normal menstruation.

Menotti, Gian Carlo [menotee] (1911–) Composer, born in Cadegliano, N Italy. He studied in Milan, then emigrated to the USA. A student in Philadelphia, he achieved international fame with a series of operas that began with *Amelia Goes to the Ball* (1937). *The Consul* (1950) and *The Saint of Bleecker Street* (1954) both won Pulitzer Prizes. *Amahl and the Night Visitors* (1951) was a successful television opera. In 1958 he founded the Festival of Two Worlds in Spoleto. Later works include a symphony (1976), a Mass, *O Pulchritudo* (1979), and several other operas.

Mensa (Lat 'table') An inconspicuous constellation in the S sky. It was named by Lacaille after Table Mountain, Cape Province, South Africa, where he had an observatory.

Mensa International An organization of people whose members are admitted only after they 'have established by some standard intelligence test, that their intelligence is higher than 98% of the population'. Founded in England in 1945, branches now exist in around 100 countries.

men's health A recent branch of medicine that deals with preventing and treating illnesses that particularly affect men. It involves health promotion to increase awareness of diseases such as testicular and prostatic cancer, and to encourage healthy lifestyles including exercise, good diet, and sensible alcohol consumption. It also includes measures to prevent accidents and suicides, a major cause of death among young males, and treatment of male disorders such as impotence and hair loss.

Mensheviks [mensheviks] (Russ 'minority-ites') Members of the moderate faction of the Marxist Russian Social Democratic

Labour Party, led by J Martov (pseudonym of Yulii Osipovich Tsederbaum, 1878–1923), which split with Lenin's Bolsheviks at the party's second Congress in 1903. The Mensheviks opposed Lenin's policies on party organization and his revolutionary tactics. In 1917 some Mensheviks joined the provisional government. The Menshevik Party was abolished by the communist authorities in the 1920s and many of its members were liquidated.

menstruation In humans and some of the higher primates, a periodic discharge from the vagina of blood, mucus, and debris from the disintegrating mucous membrane of the uterus, in response to hormone changes when the ovum is not fertilized. In humans, it lasts 3–7 days as a rule. In women of child-bearing age (13–50 years), it occurs at approximately 4-week intervals, reflecting the changing hormone production in the ovaries. The first menstrual period in life is known as *menarche*, the last as *menopause*. Menstruation does not occur during pregnancy, and for some time after (up to three months), because of the change in balance of reproductive hormones. Breast feeding delays the resumption of menstrual cycles. Menstrual regularity may be disrupted by a number of factors, of which nutritional status and emotion are perhaps the most common.

mental disorders A group of conditions with psychological or behavioural manifestations which may be accompanied by impaired functioning. This may be a result of current distress or an increased risk of morbidity or mortality. The range of causes includes biological, psychological, genetic, social, and physical disturbances. The features of a mental disorder exclude normal reactions to distressing events and deviant behaviours. The disorders do not have discrete boundaries, nor do people suffering from the same disorder necessarily display many features in common. Examples include anxiety, dementia, drug addictions, eating disorders, schizophrenia, and sleep disorders. Mental retardation and disorders of development are usually considered separately.

mental handicap A condition in which people have an intelligence quotient of less than 70, with deficits in their ability to live independently, evidenced before age 18. Four types are generally recognized: **mild** (IQ 50–70), **moderate** (IQ 35–49), **severe** (IQ 20–34), and **profound** (IQ $<$ 20). The cause is unknown in c.75% of cases. Theories include currently undetectable brain damage and environmental deprivation. Known causes include genetic conditions (eg Down's syndrome), infectious diseases (eg rubella), and noxious chemicals (eg thalidomide). Accidents are one of the major causes in early childhood.

mental underdevelopment The delay or premature arrest of a child's intellectual, behavioural, and social development. It may be due to a large number of different disorders: genetic defects (eg Down's syndrome); hormonal disorders (eg hypothyroidism); brain damage during birth due to lack of oxygen; and maternal infections during pregnancy (eg rubella and toxoplasmosis). Intelligence quotient (IQ) is sometimes used to describe the degree of mental handicap, with scores below 50 indicating severe handicap.

menthol $C_{10}H_{20}O$, a terpene alcohol, melting point 43°C. A waxy solid, the main constituent of oil of peppermint, it is used as a flavouring, a mild antiseptic, a decongestant, and a local anaesthetic. Its structure is closely related to that of camphor.

menu (computing) A set of options presented to the user by a computer program. A program which communicates with the user solely by providing choices from interlinked menus is said to be **menu-driven**. The menu facility is used extensively, in addition to icons, in graphic user interfaces.

Menuhin, Yehudi Menuhin, Baron [menyooin] (1916–99) Violinist, born in New York City, USA. He achieved fame at the age of seven when he appeared as soloist with the San Francisco Symphony Orchestra. This was followed by appearances all over the world as a prodigy, and after 18 months' retirement for study, he continued his career as a virtuoso, winning international renown especially for his interpretation of Bartók and Elgar. Largely based in Switzerland and England after World War 2, he conducted as often as he played. In 1962 he founded a school for musically gifted children near London. He was awarded an honorary knighthood in 1965, took British nationality in 1985, and was made a member of the Order of Merit in 1987 and a life peer in 1993. His sister **Hephzibah** (1920–81) was a gifted pianist.

Menzies, Sir Robert Gordon [menzees] (1894–1978) Australian statesman and prime minister (1939–41, 1949–66), born in Jeparit, Victoria, SE Australia. He studied in Melbourne, practised as a barrister before entering politics, became a member of the Victoria parliament (1928), a KC (1929), and moved to the Federal House of Representatives (1934). He was Commonwealth attorney general (1935–9), then became prime minister. He again took office as premier of the coalition government in 1949, which he led for the next 25 years, maintaining strong political links with Britain and cultivating a close economic and military alliance with the USA. In 1956 he headed the Five Nations Committee, which sought to come to a settlement with Nasser on the question of Suez. He was knighted in 1963.

Mercalli intensity scale [merkalee] A scale of 12 points, devised by Italian seismologist Giuseppe Mercalli (1850–1914), for measuring the intensity of an earthquake. The scale is based on the damage done, rather than on the total energy released, and so varies from place to place. It has been superseded by the Richter scale.

mercantilism The view that exports add to a country's wealth, and imports detract from it. This is allied to the view of international trade as a zero-sum game, in which one country's gain is another country's loss. This school of thought has led to protectionist policies in the past, and is by no means extinct. It contrasts with the free-traders' view that exports are a cost to an economy and imports a benefit, and that international trade is a source of potential gains to all parties. It can be argued that there is some merit in both views: the mercantilist view of the world has some application in the short run in times of economic depression; the free-traders' view is more appropriate in the long run and in times of economic prosperity.

Mercator, Gerardus [merkayter], originally **Gerhard Kremer** or **Cremer** (1512–94) Mathematician, geographer, and mapmaker, born in Rupelmonde, N Belgium. He graduated at Louvain, and by the time he was 24 was proficient as an engraver, calligrapher, and scientific-instrument maker. He is best known for introducing the map projection to aid navigators (1569) which bears his name, and which has been used for nautical charts ever since. In 1585 he was the first to use the word *atlas* to describe a book of maps (completed by his son in 1595), with a cover drawing of Atlas holding a globe on his shoulders.

Mercator's map projection [merkayter] A map projection devised in 1569 by Gerardus Mercator, which was the first of real use for navigation purposes. It is based on parallels equal in length to that of the Equator. The distance between the meridians is stretched away from the Equator. As a result, a line of constant bearing appears as a straight line on Mercator's projection, rather than the curved line on a globe. The major distortion is that area is exaggerated at high latitudes; for example Greenland appears as large as South America even though it is only c.10% of the latter's area.

Mercedario, Cerro [mersaydarioh] 31°58S 70°10W. Andean peak rising to 6770 m/22 211 ft in San Juan province, W Argentina, near the Chilean border.

Mercer, David (1928–80) Playwright, born in Wakefield, West Yorkshire, N England, UK. He left school at 14, coming back to study painting, then took a degree in fine arts at Durham (1953). After a period as a teacher, he became a full-time writer in the early 1960s. Winner of the 1965 *Evening Standard* Award for most promising playwright, his stage work includes *Ride a Cock Horse* (1965) and *Cousin Vladimir* (1978). His screenplays include *Morgan* (1965), and *Providence* (1977). He continued to address issues of personal alienation and the class system in later television plays such as *Huggy Bear* (1976) and *Rod of Iron* (1980).

mercerizing The chemical treatment of cotton with strong alkalis, to make it stronger, lustrous, and more silk-like. The process was devised in 1844 by English chemist John Mercer (1791–1866).

Merchant, Ismail, originally **Ismail Noormohamed Abdul Rehman** (1936–) Film producer, born in Mumbai (Bombay), W India. In 1961 he collaborated with James Ivory (1928–) in setting up a film production company, Merchant-Ivory Productions. They made their first film, *The Householder*, in 1963, and achieved international success with *Shakespeare Wallah* (1965). Later works include *The Bostonians* (1984), the Oscar-nominated *A Room With A View* (1985), *Howards End* (1992), *The Remains of the Day* (1993), *Surviving Picasso* (1996), and *Goldfish Bowl* (2000). He has also worked as a director, his films including *The Proprietor* (1996) and *Cotton Mary* (1999). In 2002 he was awarded, with James Ivory, a BAFTA Fellowship for outstanding contributions to world cinema.

Merchant Adventurers Local guilds exporting woollen cloth from 14th-c London. Formed in 1407, they increasingly dominated trade at the expense of smaller ports; from 1496, their headquarters were in Antwerp. Although numbering only a few dozen, they were important in economy and finance until the mid-17th-c, because woollen cloth was the country's leading export.

merchant bank A UK bank specializing in trading and company financial matters; similar to a US *investment bank*. The term is traditionally used to describe members of the Accepting Houses Committee, dealing primarily with bills of exchange. Its functions include financing overseas trade; raising new finance for companies; helping exporters hedge against currency fluctuations; advising companies on mergers and takeovers; and issuing and marketing Eurodollars and other Eurocurrency.

Merchant Navy The commercial ships of a nation, a term first used by King George V in a speech in 1922. The mercantile marine was classed as an armed service throughout World War 2, and developed a highly efficient manning and recruiting service which was reconstituted for peace time. The US Merchant Marine Academy, for example, is a training institution for the US merchant fleet. In recent years the amount of merchant shipping in the world has been steadily decreasing. In 1939 there were over 9000 ships in Britain's Merchant Navy, but by the 1990s the number had dwindled to under 2000.

Mercia A kingdom of the Anglo-Saxon heptarchy, with its main centres at Tamworth, Lichfield, and Repton. Settled by Angles in c.500, Mercian supremacy over the other Anglo-Saxon kingdoms reached its height under Offa, whom Charlemagne treated as an equal. He had the great Offa's Dyke built to protect W Mercia from the Welsh. In 874 Mercia succumbed to the invading Danish army, and ultimately the E part became (886) a portion of the Danelaw, while the W part was controlled by Alfred of Wessex.

Merckx, Eddy [merks], nickname **the Cannibal** (1945–) Racing cyclist, born in Woluwe St Pierre, C Belgium. He won the Tour de France a record-equalling five times (1969–72, 1974), the Tour of Italy five times, and all the major classics, including the Milan–San Remo race, seven times. World Amateur Road Race champion in 1964, he won the professional title three times. He won more races (445) and more classics than any other rider. He retired in 1978 and established his own bicycle manufacturing company.

Mercosur (Span), **Mercosul** (Portuguese) ('Southern Common Market') A common market agreement, signed in 1991 between Argentina, Brazil, Paraguay, and Uruguay, which aimed to introduce free movement of goods and services; inaugurated on 1 January 1995. Its secretariat is in Montevideo, Uruguay. Chile and Bolivia joined as associate members in 1996. It is the world's fourth largest free trade grouping, with over 200 million people. In 1999 Mercosur proposed a free trade agreement with the European Union, dependent on future policies of the World Trade Organization.

Mercouri, Melina [merkooree], originally **Anna Amalia Mercouri** (1923–94) Film actress and politician, born in Athens, Greece. She studied drama at the National Theatre in Athens, made her stage debut in 1944, and established her reputation as Blanche in Tennessee Williams' *A Streetcar Named Desire* (1949). She began in films in 1955, and found international fame in 1960 in *Never on Sunday*. Always politically involved, she was exiled from Greece (1967–74), during which time she played in several British and US productions, such as *Topkapi* (1964) and *Gaily, Gaily* (1969). She returned to be elected to parliament as a socialist in 1977, and became minister of culture (1981–9, 1993–4). She devoted the last years of her life to a world-wide campaign for the return of the Elgin Marbles.

Mercredi, Ovide [mairkredee] (1946–) Canadian aboriginal affairs activist, born in Grand Rapids, Manitoba, C Canada. A Cree Indian, he studied law at the University of Manitoba, and practised as a criminal lawyer. A leading advocate of native people's rights, he supported a policy of nonviolent civil activism, and became National Chief of the Assembly of First Nations in 1991. His book, *In the Rapids: Navigating the Future of First Nations* appeared in 1993.

Mercury (astronomy) The innermost planet of the Solar System; an airless, lunar-like body with the following characteristics: mass $3{\cdot}30 \times 10^{23}$ kg; radius 2439 km/1516 mi; mean density 5·4 g/cm^3; rotational period 58·65 days; orbital period 88 days; obliquity $\sim 0°$; orbital eccentricity 0·206; mean distance from the Sun $57{\cdot}9 \times 10^6$ km/$36{\cdot}0 \times 10^6$ mi. It has a relatively high orbital ellipticity and slow rotation rate, making three rotations for every two revolutions about the Sun. The equatorial surface temperatures reach 430°C, while on the night side temperatures may drop to −180°C. It has a weak magnetic field (c.1% of Earth's), and a very tenuous atmosphere. It is a high temperature 'end member' of the family of planets, with a greater proportion of iron (65–70% by mass) than others, and the correspondingly highest density. One hemisphere of the surface was mapped by Mariner 10 (1974–5), the other is still unknown. It has an apparently lunar-like crust, shaped by asteroidal bombardment and episodes of volcanic flooding. Its most notable surface feature is the 1300 km/800 mi diameter *Caloris* basin impact feature. Planet-wide evidence of crustal faulting in the form of elongated scarps suggests tidal despinning early in its history because of the Sun's gravitational interaction.

mercury (chemistry) Hg (from Lat *hydrargyrum*), element 80, melting point −39°C, boiling point 357°C. Silver in colour, unique among metals by being a liquid at normal temperatures; also known as **quicksilver**. A relatively unreactive metal, it is found free in nature, but is much more common as the sulphide (HgS), called *vermilion* when used as a pigment. This is roasted in air to give the metal directly: $HgS + O_2 \rightarrow Hg + SO_2$. The metal is used in both temperature- and pressure-measuring equipment. In its compounds, it shows oxidation states +1 and +2, the +1 state being the unusual dimeric ion Hg_2^{2+}. Hg_2Cl_2 was formerly much used as a purgative; the fulminate, $Hg(CNO)_2$, is a detonator. The vapour and soluble salts are toxic and cumulative; a particularly virulent form in the environment is the ion CH_3Hg^+.

Mercury (mythology) or **Mercurius** A Roman god, principally of trading, who was identifed with Hermes, and inherited his mythology.

Mercury programme The first US crewed spaceflight programme, the precursor to the Gemini and Apollo programmes, using a one-man crew. The first suborbital flight (5 May 1961) was piloted by Alan Shepard; the first orbital flight (20 Feb 1962) by John Glenn. The spacecraft demonstrated a life support system and the basic elements of recovery – retro-rocket de-orbit, drag braking re-entry, and water landing and recovery. There were two suborbital flights, and four orbital flights.

Meredith, George (1828–1909) Writer, born in Portsmouth, Hampshire, S England, UK. He was educated privately and in

Germany, and on his return to London rejected a career in law. Although his best-known work, *The Ordeal of Richard Feverel*, was written in 1859, he achieved no real literary success to begin with, and lived in poverty, forced to eke out a living by becoming a manuscript reader. Later works, such as *The Egoist* (1879) and *Diana of the Crossways* (1885), brought him financial reward. His main poetic work is *Modern Love* (1862), based partly on his first, unhappy marriage. Other books include *Evan Harrington* (1860), *Harry Richmond* (1871), and *Beauchamp's Career* (1875). His prose works include *Poems and Lyrics of the Joy of Earth* (1883). He was awarded the Order of Merit in 1905, and enjoyed much recognition towards the end of his life. His unfinished short story, 'Celt and Saxon', published posthumously in 1910, was influential in creating popular awareness of these two cultures.

merganser [merganser] A sea duck native to the N hemisphere and SE Brazil; slender serrated bill; inhabits marine and inland waters; dives for food; eats fish and crustaceans; also known as **saw-bill**. (Genus: *Mergus*, 5 species. Subfamily: Anatinae. Tribe: Mergini.)

merger A business arrangement in which two companies bring together their operations and form a single company. The share capital of the two companies is replaced by an issue of shares in the new company, shareholders of the old companies receiving new shares on a formula basis. The extent to which operations are merged depends on the nature of the companies, ranging from total merging (as when two building firms merge) to the merging of head office activities only (where the two firms are in different business sectors).

meridian (acupuncture) *acupuncture*

meridian (astronomy) At any location, the great circle on the Earth at right angles to the Equator passing from N to S Poles. All celestial objects reach their highest point in the sky when they cross the celestial meridian, and the Sun is on the meridian at local noon.

meridian circle A telescope specially designed to observe celestial objects only when they cross the meridian; also called a **transit circle**. On a fixed E–W axis which can swing only N–S, it is used for timing the passage of stars across the local meridian. In the past of crucial importance for determining star positions, it is now used for tracking the irregular rotation of the Earth. The excellent instrument at Greenwich, near London, secured the selection of Greenwich as the prime meridian in 1884.

Mérimée, Prosper [mayreemay] (1803–70) Writer, born in Paris, France. He studied law, visited Spain in 1830, and held posts under the ministries of the navy, commerce, and the interior. He was appointed inspector-general of historical remains in France in 1833, and became a senator in 1853. He wrote novels and short stories, archaeological and historical dissertations, and travel stories, all of which display exact learning, keen observation, and humour. Among his novels are *Colomba* (1840), *Carmen* (1845, popularized by Bizet's opera), and *La Chambre bleue* (1872, The Blue Room). He also wrote plays, and the famous *Lettres á une inconnue* (1873, Letters to an Unknown Girl).

merino A breed of sheep which produce a heavy thick white fleece of very high quality. Originating in Spain, and developed primarily in Australia over the past 200 years, merinos are now found in many parts of the world, being well adapted to hot climates. Australia is by far the largest producer of merino wool.

Merionethshire *Gwynedd*

meristem A region of growth or potential growth in a plant, such as the tips of shoots and roots, or buds. It consists of actively dividing cells (the *initials*) and their undifferentiated daughter cells which will form the new tissues.

Merleau-Ponty, Maurice [mairloh põtee] (1908–61) Philosopher, born in Rochefort-sur-mer, W France. He studied in Paris, taught in various lycées, and served as an army officer in World War 2, before holding professorships at Lyon (1948) and Paris (from 1949). He helped Sartre and de Beauvoir found the journal *Les Temps Modernes* in 1945, and was a fellow-traveller with Sartre in the Communist Party in the early post-war years. His two main philosophical works are *La Structure du comportement* (1942, The Structure of Behaviour) and *Phénoménologie de la perception* (1945, Phenomenology of Perception) which investigate the nature of consciousness, and reject the extremes of both behaviouristic psychology and subjectivist accounts.

merlin A small falcon native to the N hemisphere (*Falco columbarius*); lacks white cheeks of other falcons; inhabits open country, hills, and desert; eats mainly birds (some small mammals and insects); nests on ground or in abandoned nests of other species in trees; also known as **pigeon hawk**. (Family: Falconidae.)

Merlin In the Arthurian legends, a good wizard or sage whose magic was used to help King Arthur. He was the son of an incubus and a mortal woman, and therefore indestructible; but he was finally entrapped by Vivien, the Lady of the Lake, and bound under a rock for ever. He was famous for his prophecies.

Merneptah [mernepta] (13th-c BC) King of Egypt (1236–1223 BC), the son of Rameses II. He is famous principally for his great victory near Memphis over the Libyans and Sea Peoples (1232 BC).

Meroe *Kush*

meroplankton *plankton*

Merovingians [merohvinjianz] The original Frankish royal family, formerly chiefs of the Salians, named after the half-legendary Merovech or Meroveus (the 'sea-fighter'). Clovis was the first Merovingian king to control large parts of Gaul; the last to hold significant power was Dagobert I (d.638), though the royal dynasty survived until Childeric III's deposition in 751.

Mersey, River [merzee] River in NW England, UK; formed at junction of Goyt and Tame Rivers; flows 112 km/70 mi W past Warrington, Runcorn, Birkenhead, and Liverpool to form a wide estuary into the Irish Sea at Liverpool Bay; tributaries include the Weaver and Irwell Rivers and the Manchester Ship Canal.

Merseyside pop (2001e) 1 362 000; area 652 sq km/252 sq mi. County of NW England, UK created in 1974 from parts of Lancashire and Cheshire; metropolitan council abolished in 1986; on both sides of the R Mersey estuary; chemicals, vehicles, electrical equipment; chief town, Liverpool; Prescot Museum, Croxteth Hall and Country Park, Speke Hall.

Merthyr Tydfil [merther **tid**vil], Welsh **Merthyr Tudful** pop (2001e) 56 000; area 111 sq km/43 sq mi. County (unitary authority from 1996) in S Wales, UK; administrative centre, Merthyr Tydfil.

Merton, Robert C (1944–) Economist, born in New York City, USA. He graduated from MIT in 1970, joined the MIT faculty (1970–88), then went on to Harvard Business School. He shared the 1997 Nobel Prize for Economics for his contribution to a new method of determining the value of derivatives.

Merton, Robert K(ing), originally **Meyer Robert Schkolnick** (1910–2003) Sociologist, born in Philadelphia, Pennsylvania, USA. He studied at Temple and Harvard, going on to teach at Harvard (1934–9), Tulane (1939–41), and Columbia universities (1941–79). He was also associate director of the Bureau of Applied Social Research. He is regarded as the founder of the sociology of science, in which he developed an analysis of the norms guiding scientists' behaviour, the competition and reward system in science, and how both of these operate in historical and contemporary contexts. His main works include *Social Theory and Social Structure* (1949) and *The Sociology of Science* (1973). He shared the Nobel Prize for Economics in 1997.

Merton, Thomas (1915–68) Catholic monk and writer, born in Prades, S France. He studied and taught English at Columbia University, became a convert to Roman Catholicism, and in 1941 joined the Trappist order at Our Lady of Gethsemane Abbey, Kentucky. His best-selling autobiography, *The Seven Storey Mountain* (1946), prompted many to become monks, and brought him international fame. His other works ranged from personal journals and poetry to social criticism. His growing interest in Eastern spirituality led him to attend a conference in Bangkok, where he was accidentally electrocuted by a faulty fan.

Meru, Mount In Hindu cosmology, a mythical golden mountain (popularly identified with one of the Himalayan peaks), considered the central axis of the universe and the paradisial abode of the gods. It is the subject of many myths, also in Buddhism. Brahma's square city of gold is said to be found at its summit; beneath the mountain are said to be seven underworlds.

mesa [maysa] An area of high, flat land (tableland) with steep escarpments formed by the remnants of horizontal resistant rocks, and underlain by softer rock. Further erosion forms buttes.

Mesa Verde [maysa verday] (Span 'green table') An area of precipitous canyons and wooded volcanic mesa in SW Colorado, USA, 55 km/34 mi W of Durango; a world heritage site. The most visited archaeological site in the USA, and a National Park since 1906, it is renowned for its Anasazi Indian cliff-dwellings – notably the 4-storey Cliff Palace of the 13th-c AD, which has 220 rooms and 23 kivas (underground meeting chambers), and held an ancient population of c.250–350.

mescal *century plant*

mescal button *peyote*

mescaline [meskalin, -leen] A hallucinogenic drug from the Mexican cactus *Lophophora williamsi*, also known as *Anhalonium lewinii*. Having been used for centuries for its ability to cause hallucinations, it was made famous in the 1950s by Aldous Huxley in *The Doors of Perception*, and was widely used during the 'psychedelic era' of the 1960s.

mesembryanthemum *Livingstone daisy*

mesh A topology for a computer network in which each computer is linked directly to every other computer in the network. Although it could be used as a topology for a local area network, this rarely happens; a mesh topology is normally appropriate only for a metropolitan area or wide area network.

Meshed *Mashhad*

Mesmer, Franz Anton [mezmer] (1734–1815) Physician, born near L Constance, W Austria. He studied and practised medicine at Vienna, and c.1772 took up the idea that there exists a power which he called 'animal magnetism'. This led to the founding of *mesmerism*, precurser of hypnotism in modern psychotherapy. In 1778 he went to Paris, where he created a sensation by curing diseases at seances. In 1785, when a learned commission denounced him as an imposter, he retired to Switzerland.

Mesoamerica or **Middle America** The area covered by Central America and Mexico together. Because Mexico is geographically a part of North America, this term is often used to identify features of cultural or historical importance which both regions share.

Mesoamerican ballgame A ritual athletic contest of notable brutality, widespread in Mexico from c.1000 BC to the Spanish Conquest in 1519. Played with a large, solid rubber ball by two opposing teams on a purpose-built court – at Chichén Itzá 83 m/272 ft by 61 m/200 ft with walls 8 m/27 ft high – the ball represented the Sun, the court the cosmos. Post-game ceremonies included the sacrifice of the losers.

Mesolithic The Middle Stone Age, the epoch of hunter-gatherers (c.12 000–8000 years ago) that followed the Palaeolithic at the end of the last ice age, and in Europe and W Asia preceded the Neolithic. Archaeologically it is characterized by small stone tools called microliths.

meson [meezon] In particle physics, a collective term for strongly interacting subatomic particles having integer spin, each comprising a quark–antiquark pair. Mesons, especially pi-mesons (pions), are responsible for holding together protons and neutrons in atomic nuclei.

mesopelagic zone The depth zone in the open sea extending from just beneath the epipelagic zone down to a depth of approximately 1000 m/3000 ft. In this depth range, not enough light penetrates for photosynthesis, but there may be enough light for vision. The zone also includes the main ocean thermocline and the zone of minimum dissolved oxygen for most parts of the world's oceans.

Mesopotamia [mesopotaymia] Literally, 'the land between the rivers'; the name in antiquity for the area between the Tigris and Euphrates. It was conventionally divided into two: **Lower Mesopotamia**, the home of the Sumerian and Babylonian civilizations, stretched from the alluvial plain at the head of the Persian Gulf to Baghdad (C Iraq); **Upper Mesopotamia**, the home of the Assyrians, extended from Baghdad to the foothills of E Turkey. Historically, the former is more important: here the world's first urban civilization emerged during the fourth millennium BC; the Mesopotamian Empire was established c.2300 BC.

Mesosaurus A lightly built, aquatic reptile known from the late Carboniferous to the early Permian periods in South America and S Africa; up to 1 m/3¼ ft long; lived in fresh water. (Class: Anapsida. Order: Mesosauria.)

mesosphere A region of the atmosphere from c.50–80 km/30–50 mi, separated from the stratosphere below by the stratopause, and from the thermosphere above by the mesopause. It is characterized by rapidly falling temperature with height, from around 0°C to −100°C. Pressure is very low, from c.1 mb at 50 km/30 mi to 0·01 mb at 80 km/50 mi.

Mesozoa [mezozoha] A small phylum of multicellular animals found as internal parasites of marine invertebrates such as cephalopod molluscs; covered by hair-like cilia; body organized into two layers, not differentiated into tissues.

Mesozoic era [mezozohik] A major division of geological time extending from c.250 to 65 million years ago; subdivided into the Triassic, Jurassic, and Cretaceous periods. It was the age of the giant reptiles and the beginning of mammalian life.

Messager, André (Charles Prosper) [mesazhay] (1853–1929) Composer and conductor, born in Montluçon, C France. He was artistic director of Covent Garden Theatre, London (1901–7), and director of Opéra Comique, Paris (1898–1903, 1919–20). His operettas were popular in England as well as France, and include *La Bearnaise* (1885), *Madame Chrysanthème* (1893), and *Monsieur Beaucaire* (1919). He also wrote piano pieces and several ballets, notably *Les Deux pigeons* (1886, The Two Pigeons).

Messenia [meseenia] In ancient Greece, the SW part of the Peloponnese. Conquered by the Spartans in the 8th-c and 7th-c BC, its inhabitants were reduced to a state of serfdom called *helotry*. They regained their independence in 369 BC with Theban help.

Messerschmitt, Willy [mesershmit], popular name of **Wilhelm Messerschmitt** (1898–1978) Aircraft engineer and designer, born in Frankfurt, WC Germany. He studied at the Munich Institute of Technology, and in 1926 joined the Bayerische Flugzeugwerke as its chief designer and engineer. In 1938 the company became the Messerschmitt-Aitken-Gesellschaft, producing military aircraft. His Me109 set a world speed record in 1939, and during World War 2 he supplied the *Luftwaffe* with its foremost types of combat aircraft. In 1944 he produced the Me262 fighter, the first jet-plane flown in combat.

Messiaen, Olivier (Eugène Prosper Charles) [mesiã] (1908–92) Composer and organist, born in Avignon, SE France. He studied at the Paris Conservatoire, where his teachers included Paul Dukas. He became professor at the Schola Cantorum (1936–9) and (after a period of war-time imprisonment) professor of harmony at the Paris Conservatoire in 1941. He composed extensively for organ, orchestra, voice, and piano, and made frequent use of new instruments. His music was motivated by religious mysticism, and he is best known for *Vingt regards sur l'enfant Jésus* (1944, Twenty Looks at the Infant Jesus), and the mammoth *Turangalila* symphony. His great interest in birdsong proved the stimulus for several works, including the *Catalogue d'oiseaux* for piano (1956–8).

Messiah [mesiya] (Heb 'anointed one') In Jewish writings from c.2nd-c BC onwards, one who would help deliver Israel from its enemies, aid in its restoration, and establish a worldwide kingdom. Many different representations of this figure can be discovered in early Judaism and Christianity. In Christian thought, the role is interpreted as fulfilled in Jesus of Nazareth: 'Christ' is derived from the Greek rendering of the Hebrew word for 'messiah'.

messianism Jewish movements expressing the hope for a new and perfected age. Jewish Orthodoxy reflects this through traditional beliefs in the coming of a personal Messiah who would re-establish the Temple in Jerusalem and from there rule over a redeemed world. Reformed Judaism anticipates the world's perfection by the example of Judaism in human achievements such as social reforms and justice, though still concerned with preserving the identity of the Jewish race within existing states. In contrast, Zionism places emphasis on the physical restoration of the Jewish state in Palestine and the return of exiled Jews there.

Messier, Charles [mesyay] (1730–1817) Astronomer, born in Badonviller, NE France. He had a keen interest in comets, discovering 15, and is mainly remembered for the *Messier Catalog* which, by 1781, contained 103 star clusters, nebulae, and galaxies. Objects were given alphanumeric names (M1, M2, etc) – a convention which continues to be used in astronomy.

Messina, Strait of, ancient **Fretum Siculum** Channel between Sicily and the Italian mainland, separating the Ionian and Tyrrhenian Seas; minimum width (N) 5 km/3 mi; length 35 km/22 mi; chief ports, Messina (Sicily) and Reggio di Calabria (mainland).

ME syndrome An abbreviation for **myalgic encephalomyelitis syndrome**; also known as **chronic fatigue syndrome**. It is characterized by weakness, mild fever, diffuse muscle and joint pains, depression, visual disturbance, and headaches, which persist for several months and ultimately resolve. The cause is unknown; some believe it follows certain viral infections; others believe that it has a psychological origin.

metabolism The complete range of biochemical processes taking place within living organisms. It comprises those processes which produce complex substances from simpler components, with a consequent use of energy (**anabolism**), and those which break down complex food molecules, thus liberating energy (**catabolism**). In the context of nutrition, it refers to the process by which cells catabolize food substances to give the body the energy it needs for its various functions. These include all forms of physical exertion, as well as the maintenance of the body's vital functions, such as the heart beat. **Basal metabolism** is the minimum energy expenditure needed to maintain all the vital functions of the body, such as heart beat, urine formation, respiration, and brain function. It is usually measured when the subject is lying down at complete physical and mental rest and at least 12 hours after the last meal. In such a case, the energy expended is approximately 1 kilocalorie (4 kilojoules) per minute – slightly more for men and less for women.

Metabolism A Japanese architectural concept and group originally founded in 1960 by Kiyonori Kikutake, Kisho Kurokawa, and Noboru Kawazoe. It is characterized by the use of forms strongly reminiscent of science fiction, and by the synthesis of the public realm with private spaces. The latter often consist of minimal, high-technology capsules.

metabolism, inborn error of Inherited disorders caused by defects in complex biochemical processes. They may affect the way the body makes or breaks down cells (eg in the blood) or the way it handles substances such as carbohydrates, amino acids, lipids, steroids, purines, and heavy metals.

metahistory A branch of historical study concerned with the philosophy of history and with the formulation of laws governing the process of change. It also includes a critique of the nature of history, and the means by which historical reasoning is conducted.

metal An element whose solid phase is characterized by high thermal and electrical conductivities. Pure metals are all lustrous, opaque, cold to the touch, and more or less malleable. The large majority of the elements are metals, and metallic properties increase from lighter to heavier elements in each group of the periodic table and from right to left in each row.

metal fatigue A weakness which develops in a metal structure that has been subjected to many repeated stresses, even though they may be intermittent. As a result, the structure may fail under a load which it could initially have sustained without fracture. The condition was known and studied in the late 19th-c, but it became a subject of particularly serious study after the Comet aircraft disaster of 1954. The causes of metal fatigue remain obscure, but experiment and design now aim at obviating it.

metallic glass Metal in an amorphous condition (ie the atoms of the metal have no regular or crystalline arrangement); first produced in 1960 by US materials scientist William Klement (1937–). Metals, normally crystalline in internal structure, can be converted to this condition (analogous to that of glass) by the rapid cooling of a melt, or by very fine subdivision. Metallic glasses are useful for transformer cores, and for forming (by powder metallurgy methods) very strong components such as gears.

metallocene *ferrocene*

metallography The study of the structure of metals, usually implying the use of microscopy or X-ray diffraction. A metal has several kinds of structure, arising from grain, crystalline structure, and the inclusion of impurities. Many types of examination may be made. In microscopic methods, pioneered in Sheffield in the 1860s by English chemist Henry Clifton Sorby (1826–1908), a polished etched surface is examined at several degrees of magnification. For electron microscopy, a plastic impression is made for use as the specimen. X-ray diffraction may be used to study internal atomic arrangements.

metalloids Elements midway between being metals and non-metals. They make a diagonal band across the periodic table, and are generally considered to include boron, silicon, germanium, arsenic, antimony, tellurium, and polonium.

metallurgy The technique and science of extracting metals from their ores, converting them (often as alloys with other metals) into useful forms, and establishing the conditions for their fabrication. Metallurgy is one of the most ancient arts. Traditional methods were transformed in the latter half of the 19th-c by the application of chemistry, physics, and microscopy. The changes undergone by metals during fabrication and treatment are now important aspects of metallurgy, as are the physics and chemistry of corrosion prevention. The development of metallurgical theory has promoted the growth of a wide practice of testing and inspection.

metamorphic rock Rock formed by the alteration of pre-existing rock by intense heat and/or pressure, and often accompanied by the action of hot fluids in the Earth's crust. The changes characteristically involve the growth of new minerals that are stable under these conditions, and a change of texture. *Contact metamorphism* is localized, and produced by the heat of an igneous intrusion. *Regional metamorphism* is associated with large-scale mountain-building processes in the crust. Slates, schists, and gneisses are characteristic rocks formed at progressively higher grades of metamorphism.

metamorphosis In biology, an abrupt structural change, as seen in the marked changes during the development of an organism, especially the transformation from larva to adult, or from one larval stage to the next. Metamorphosis may be progressive, such as the transformation of tadpole into frog, or may involve an intermediate quiescent phase within a cocoon or chrysalis, during which tissue reorganization takes place.

metaphor (Gr 'carrying from one place to another') A figurative device in language where something is referred to, implicitly, in terms of something else: the Moon is a goddess, life a dark wood, the world a stage. An explicit comparison ('Life, like a dome of many-coloured glass') is a **simile**. Language is inherently metaphorical, making different aspects of experience intelligible in terms of each other. It is for this reason that metaphor is considered essential to poetic expression: enabling us 'To see a world in a grain of sand/And Heaven in a wild flower;/Hold infinity in the palm of your hand,/And eternity in an hour' (Blake).

metaphysical painting A modern art movement which flourished c.1915–18 in Italy. It was founded by Chirico, who painted mysterious empty landscapes inhabited by tailors' dummies, and classical busts casting threatening shadows.

metaphysical poetry A term applied to some English poetry of the late 16th-c and early 17th-c, on account of its use of unusual and sometimes difficult ideas in relation to emotional states. Dryden remarked that the chief proponent of the genre, John Donne, 'affects the metaphysics', and Dr Johnson referred to the way in which in this poetry 'heterogeneous ideas [are] yoked by violence together'. The metaphysicals had a profound influence on 20th-c English poetry, thanks, in part, to the critical appreciation of T S Eliot and others.

metaphysics A traditional branch of philosophy which deals at the most general level with the nature of existence – what it is, what sorts of things exist, of what categories, and in what structure. The term is popularly used to refer to the suprasensible, beyond the realm of experience. The origin of the term is a reference to the text Aristotle wrote 'after the Physics'.

Metastasio, Pietro [metastahzioh], originally **Pietro Armando Dominico Trapassi** (1698–1782) Poet, born in Rome, Italy. A gift for versifying attracted the attention of Fian Vincenzo Gravin, a man of letters who educated him, and left him his fortune (1718). He gained his reputation by his masque *The Garden of Hesperides* (1722), wrote the libretti for 27 operas, including Mozart's *Clemenza di Tito*, and became court poet at Vienna in 1729.

metastasis [metastasis] The occurrence of tumour tissue in organs distant from the site of the primary tumour. It is characteristic of malignant tumours, where cancer cells are transported by way of the blood stream or lymphatics.

Metaxas, Ioannis [metaksas] (1871–1941) General and dictator of Greece (1936–41), born in Ithaka. He fought against the Turks in 1897, studied military science in Germany, and in 1913 became chief of the general staff. On the fall of Constantine I in 1917 he fled to Italy, but returned with him in 1921. In 1935 he became deputy prime minister, and as premier in 1936 established a Fascist dictatorship. He led the resistance to the Italian invasion of Greece in 1940, and remained in office until his death.

metazoan [metazohan] A multicellular animal with its body organized into specialized tissues and organs; a member of the subkingdom Eumetazoa.

Metchnikoff, Ilya *Mechnikov*

meteor A piece of dust or rock which gives off a streak of light seen when it burns up in the Earth's atmosphere; popularly known as a *shooting star*. A **meteor shower** can be seen when the Earth passes through a trail of dust left by a comet in interplanetary space. An unusual number of meteors (dozens per hour) can then be seen emanating from one part of the sky (the *radiant*). (*see panel*)

Meteora [metayora] 39°44N 21°38E. Rock formations in Trikala department, N Greece, rising to 300 m/1000 ft from the Pinios plain; site of monasteries, first settled 9th-c AD.

Meteor Crater or **Barringer Crater** An impact crater 1·3 km/0·8 mi across near Flagstaff, Arizona, USA; estimated age 20 000 years. Its origin was determined by geologist Eugene Shoemaker in the 1950s, thereby illuminating the significance of meteoritic impacts on the history of Earth and the planets. It is believed to be the result of the impact of a meteorite c.10 m/11 yd across.

meteoric water *groundwater*

meteorite A lump of interplanetary debris that survives a high-speed passage through the atmosphere and hits the ground. Meteorites mostly derive from asteroids, with a few from the Moon and some even from Mars. The types are stony, iron, and stony-iron; some stony meteorites have intriguing inclusions of organic material. They often show clear signs of heat abrasion. The biggest known (60 tonnes) is an iron meteorite that lies where it fell in prehistoric times in Namibia. Meteor Crater, Arizona, was formed by a meteorite. The oldest are dated at 4·7 thousand million years. A meteorite is known as a **meteoroid** while travelling in space.

meteoroid *meteorite*

meteorology The scientific study of global atmospheric processes: the receipt of solar radiation, evaporation, evapotranspiration, and precipitation, and the determination of, and changes in, atmospheric pressure (and, therefore, wind). Meteorology is generally concerned with the short-term processes (ie hours and days rather than months and seasons) operating in the troposphere and mesosphere, which are the atmospheric layers of the Earth's weather systems. Satellites are now the main source of meteorological data, the first purpose-built device being the American *Tiros I*, launched in 1960. The data are used for weather forecasting, and in meteorological and climatological research.

meter (literature; physics) *metre* (literature) ; *metre* (physics)

methanal *formaldehyde*

methane [meethayn, methayn] CH_4. The simplest of the alkane or paraffin hydrocarbons; the tetrahedral shape of methane is fundamental to all organic compounds. Formed by the anaerobic decomposition of organic matter, it is the main constituent of natural gas, and was originally called **marsh gas**.

methanogen *Archaebacteria*

methanoic acid *formic acid*

methanol [methanol] CH_3OH, also called **methyl** or **wood alcohol**, boiling point 65°C. A colourless liquid, originally produced by the dry distillation of wood, but now synthesized from hydrogen and carbon monoxide. It is an important starting chemical in synthesis, a solvent, and a denaturing agent for ethyl alcohol. It is poisonous, causing blindness and eventually death when drunk.

Method, the Both a style of acting and a system of training for the working actor, developed in the USA by Lee Strasberg. He was inspired by what he knew of Stanislavsky's system, particularly that part which is concerned with the actor's work on himself. The method stresses inner motivation and psychological truth. It was adapted by the Group Theater in the USA in the 1930s, and came into prominence when it was taken on by the Actors' Studio. A well-known exponent of this style is Marlon Brando.

Methodism A Christian denomination founded in 1739 by John Wesley as an evangelical movement within the Church of England, becoming a separate body in 1795. The movement spread rapidly as he travelled the country on horseback and sent other evangelical leaders to the American colonies, where the movement flourished. In the 19th-c, doctrinal disputes caused divisions both in Britain and the USA. These were healed in Britain in 1932, and partially so in the USA, with the uniting of the

Annual major meteor showers

Name	*Dates of maximum*	*Hourly rate*
Quadrantids	3–4 January	100
Lyrids	21–22 April	10
Eta Aquarids	5–6 May	35
Delta Aquarids	28–29 July	20
Perseids	12–13 August	75
Orionids	22 October	25
Taurids	4 November	10
Leonids	17–18 November	10
Geminids	13–14 December	75

three main bodies of Methodists. The principal doctrines of the Church are laid down in Wesley's sermons, his notes on the New Testament, and his Articles of Religion. In 2004 there were c.34 million Methodists worldwide.

Methodius, St *Cyril, St*

Methuen, Sir Algernon (Methuen Marshall) [methyooen], originally **Stedman** (1856–1924) Publisher, born in London, UK. He was a teacher of classics and French (1880–95), and began publishing as a sideline with Methuen & Co in 1889 to market his own textbooks. His first publishing success was Kipling's *Barrack-Room Ballads* (1892), and he also published works of Belloc, R L Stevenson, and Oscar Wilde. He was created a baronet in 1916.

Methuselah [mithoozela] The eighth and longest-lived of the Hebrew patriarchs, who lived before the Flood. His supposed 969 years makes him the paragon of longevity.

methyl alcohol *methanol*

methylated spirits Ethyl alcohol with additives to make it poisonous and unpalatable, and hence unsuitable for beverage use; also called **denatured alcohol**. The major additives are methanol, pyridine, and benzene.

methylbenzene *toluene*

methylbutane *pentane*

methyl orange A dye of the diazo type, containing the group –N=N–. It is a pH indicator, being red in its acid form and yellow-orange in base, the change occurring about pH 4.

Metis [meetis] A tiny natural satellite of Jupiter, discovered in 1979; distance from the planet 128 000 km/79 000 mi; diameter 40 km/25 mi.

Métis [maytee] The mixed blood offspring of primarily French-Canadian and native Indian marriages; in the west, the descendants of the *coureurs de bois*.

metonymy [metonimee] (Gr 'name change') The substitution of an attribute of something for the thing itself, such as *the stage* for the theatrical profession, *the crown* for the monarchy. It can be compared with **synechdoche** (Gr 'taking up together'), where the part stands for the whole: *hand* for man, *head* for cattle.

metre (UK) **/ meter** (US) (literature) (Gr *metron* 'measure') The recurrence of a rhythmic pattern in poetry, within the line and over larger units (*stanzas*). The subject is problematical, because different languages measure different things to establish metre. In the classical languages, it is length (or 'quantity'); in Chinese, it is pitch; in Japanese, the syllable; in Germanic languages, stress. French metre respects classical quantity. Some English metre works by stress count, overriding the syllable (as in Old English and Old Welsh poetry, Gerard Manley Hopkins), some by counting both stressed and unstressed syllables (as in the traditional iamb, dactyl, etc). But there is no definitive system of English prosody.

metre (UK) **/ meter** (US) (physics) Base SI unit of length; symbol *m*; defined (since 1984) as the length of the path travelled by light in a vacuum during an interval of 1/299 792 458 of a second; commonly used as **kilometre** (*km*, 1000 m), **centimetre** (*cm*, 1/100 m) and **millimetre** (*mm*, 1/1000 m).

metric In mathematics, a rule for measuring distance along curves and angles between curves in some space, and containing information on the curvature of the space. It is central to general relativity, which establishes equations relating the metric (and hence curvature) to matter distribution.

metronome A device for indicating and determining the tempo of a musical work. The type in common use, patented in 1815 by Johann Nepomuk Maelzel (1770–1838), works like a pendulum clock; its rate of swing, and therefore of 'tick' also, is controlled by an adjustable weight on the upper extension of the pendulum arm, visible outside the wooden box which encloses the rest. There are now electronic models.

metropolitan area network (MAN) A computer network which serves an area roughly equal to a city or large town, and thus falls between a local area network and a wide area network. An example of a MAN is a cable TV network, which could be used also for two-way data transmission.

Metropolitan Museum of Art A museum opened in New York City, USA in 1872. It houses a vast and comprehensive collection displaying the artistic achievements of many cultures, ancient and modern.

Metropolitan Opera Company The chief operatic organization in New York City, USA. The company began in 1883, and soon acquired an international reputation. In 1966 it moved from its Broadway location to the Lincoln Center.

Metternich, Klemens (Wenzel Nepomuk Lothar), Fürst von (Prince of) [meternikh] (1773–1859) Austrian statesman, born in Koblenz, W Germany. He studied at Strasburg and Mainz, was attached to the Austrian embassy at The Hague, and became Austrian minister at Dresden, Berlin, and Paris. In 1809 he was appointed Austrian chancellor and foreign minister, and negotiated the marriage between Napoleon and Princess Marie Louise. He took a prominent part in the Congress of Vienna (1814), obstructing Russia's intended annexation of Poland and Prussia's acquisition of the state of Saxony. Between 1815 and 1848 he was the most powerful influence for conservatism in Europe. In setting up a German confederation under Austrian leadership, he managed to maintain the status quo in Germany ('papering over the cracks'), but failed in his attempt to use the Quadruple Alliance as a means of preventing revolution. However, he remained Europe's leading statesman until he was ousted by the 1848 Revolutions, having contributed much to the tension that produced those upheavals. After the fall of the imperial government in that year, he fled to England, and in 1851 retired to his castle of Johannesberg on the Rhine.

Metz [mets], ancient **Divodurum Mediomatricum** 49°08N 6°10E, pop (2000e) 125 000. Fortified town and capital of Moselle department, NE France; on R Moselle near German border, 285 km/177 mi NE of Paris; strategic focus of crossroads; residence of Merovingian kings, 6th-c; later, part of Holy Roman Empire; taken by France, 1552; part of Germany from 1871 until after World War 1; scene of major German defence in 1944 invasion; World War 1 military cemetery nearby; airport; road and rail junction; bishopric; university (1971); trade in coal, metals, wine; brewing, tanning, foodstuffs, cement, footwear; Gothic Cathedral (1250–1380), St-Pierre-aux-Nonnains (7th-c), Eglise Ste-Thérèse, town hall (18th-c), Porte des Allemands (13th-c); Mirabelle Plum Festival (Sep).

Meung, Jean de *Jean de Meung*

Meuse, River [moez], Dutch **Maas**, ancient **Mosa** River in NE France, Belgium, and The Netherlands, rising on the Langres Plateau, NE France; flows N through the Ardennes into Belgium, then W into The Netherlands as the Maas; enters the North Sea through Hollandsch Diep in the Rhine delta; length 950 km/590 mi; navigable for 578 km/359 mi; scene of severe fighting during the German invasions in both World Wars.

Mexican architecture The architecture of Mexico, since the Spanish conquest of Central America involving the introduction of W European architectural forms, first Gothic, then Spanish Renaissance and the Baroque, typified by Mexico Cathedral, Mexico City (1563–1667). In the 20th-c, the influence of the French Beaux Arts was quickly replaced by International Style tenets. Since the 1950s, the work of Felix Candela and Pedro Ramirez Vásquez has met with increasing recognition, as have the simple vernacular building forms developed by Luis Barragán and others during the 1920s.

Mexican art The art associated with Mexico. Before the Spanish conquest (1520–42), the Aztecs produced powerful religious sculpture in stone, richly ornamental frescoes, and polychrome pottery. Since the Revolution (1910), artists such as José Clementi Orozco, David Alfaro (1898–1974), and Diego Rivera have dedicated their talents to overtly political ends, painting huge murals for the edification of the masses. Modern Mexican art is strongly figurative, tending to caricature, and draws on popular rather than 'high art' traditions.

Mexico

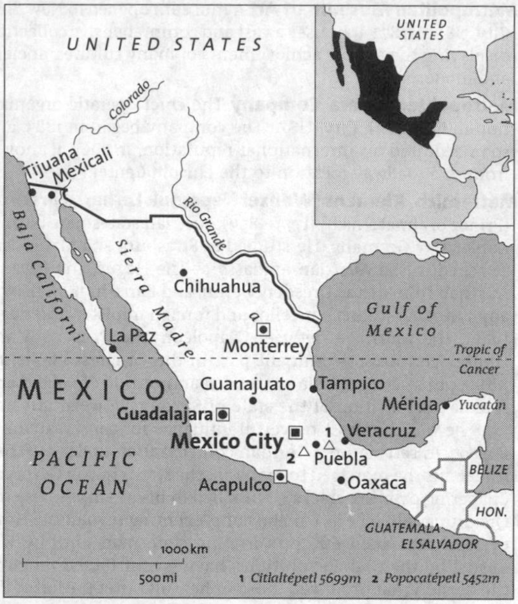

□ International Airport

Span **México** or **Méjico**, official name **United Mexican States**, Span **Estados Unidos Mexicanos**

Local name México

Timezone GMT −8 to −6

Area 1 978 800 km²/763 817 sq mi

Population total (2002e) 100 977 000

Status Republic

Date of independence 1821

Capital Mexico City

Languages Spanish (official), indigenous languages

Ethnic groups Indian-Spanish (mestizo) (60%), Amerindian (30%), White (9%)

Religions Roman Catholic (80%), Protestant (3%)

Physical features Narrow coastal plains; land rises steeply to C plateau, c.2400 m/7800 ft; volcanic peaks to S, notably Citlaltépetl, 5699 m/18 697 ft; limestone lowlands of the Yucatán peninsula stretch into the Gulf of Mexico (SE); region subject to earthquakes.

Climate Tropical climate in S; severe, arid conditions N and W; average annual temperatures 13°C (Jan), 16°C (Jul) in Mexico City; average annual rainfall 747 mm/29·4 in.

Currency 1 Mexican Peso (Mex$) = 100 centavos

Economy Wide range of mineral exports; major discoveries of oil and natural gas in the 1970s (now world's fourth largest producer); fluorite and graphite (world's leading producer); large petrochemical industry; important trading relationship with USA, especially after free-trade-area agreement in 1993.

GDP (2002e) $924·4 bn, per capita $8900

Human Development Index (2002) 0·796

History Centre of Indian civilizations for over 2500 years; Gulf Coast Olmecs based at La Venta, Zapotecs at Monte Albán near Oaxaca, Mixtecs at Mitla, Toltecs at Tula, Maya in the Yucatán, Aztecs at Tenochtitlán; Spanish arrival in 1516; Vice-royalty of New Spain established; struggle for independence from 1810; federal republic, 1824; lost territory to the USA, 1836, and after the Mexican War, 1846–8; civil war, 1858–61; occupation of Mexico City by French forces, 1863–7; revolution, 1910–17; major earthquake in Mexicio City, 1985; revolt in S state of Chiapas by Zapatista National Liberation Army, 1994; negotiations over Indian rights in late 1990s, ongoing; major economic crises, 1994, followed by package of loan guarantees from the USA, 1995; governed by a President, Cabinet, and bicameral Congress with a Senate and a Chamber of Deputies.

Head of State/Government

1940–6 Manuel Avila Camacho
1946–52 Miguel Alemán
1952–8 Adolfo Ruiz Cortines
1958–64 Adolfo López Mateos
1964–70 Gustavo Díaz Ordaz
1970–6 Luis Echeverría
1976–82 José López Portillo
1982–8 Miguel de la Madrid Hurtado
1988–94 Carlos Salinas de Gortari
1994–2000 Ernesto Zedillo
2000– Vincente Fox

Mexican War (1846–8) A war between Mexico and the USA, declared by the US Congress after it received a message from President Polk calling for war. The war began in territory disputed between Texas (annexed by the USA but claimed by Mexico) and Mexico. US troops invaded the heart of Mexico and forced a capitulation in which Mexico ceded most of the present-day SW United States.

Mexico, Gulf of area 1 543 000 sq km/596 000 sq mi. Gulf on the SE coast of North America, forming a basin enclosed by the USA (N) and Mexico (W) as far as the Yucatán Peninsula; deepest point, Sigsbee Deep (3878 m/12 723 ft); receives the Mississippi and Rio Grande del Norte Rivers; low, sandy shoreline with many marshes, lagoons, deltas; oil and natural gas resources on continental shelves.

Mexico *see panel*

Mexico City, Span **Ciudad de México** 19°25N 99°10W, pop (2000e) 11 431 000; 'Metromex' urban region, pop (2000e) 26 000 000. Federal district and capital of Mexico; in C Mexico, altitude 2200 m/7200 ft, in intermontane basin, area 50 sq km/20 sq mi; largest city in the world; oldest capital in continental America; built on the site of the Aztec capital, Tenochtitlán; city centre a world heritage site; capital of the Viceroyalty of New Spain for 300 years until independence; airport; railway; seven universities; vehicles, iron and steel, chemicals, tobacco, glass, food processing, textiles; cathedral (16th–19th-c), National Palace (1692), Castle of Chapultepec (now the national museum of history), national museum of anthropology; ruins of Teotihuacán, 40 km/25 mi NE; location of 1968 summer Olympic Games; scene of a major industrial accident (Nov 1984), when a liquefied gas tank exploded at the San Juan Ixhuatepec storage facility; major earthquake (Sep 1985) killed c.20 000.

Meyerbeer, Giacomo [miyerbayer], originally **Jakob Liebmann Meyer Beer** (1791–1864) Operatic composer, born in Berlin, Germany. At seven he played Mozart's D-minor piano concerto in public, and at 15 was received into the house of Abt Vogler at Darmstadt. He attracted attention as a pianist in Vienna, and after studying in Italy produced operas in the new style (Rossini's), which were well received. He lived mostly in Berlin (1824–31), then studied French opera, writing the highly successful *Robert le Diable* (1831) and *Huguenots* (1836). He was appointed *Kapellmeister* at Berlin (1842), and continued to write successfully.

Meyerhold, Vsevolod Emilievich [miyerhohld] (1874–c.1940) Actor and director, who played a major role in the emergence of Soviet theatre, born in Penza, Russia. He joined the Moscow Art Theatre as an actor, and was appointed by Stanislavsky as director of the new Studio on Povarskaya Street in 1905. He later became director of the Theatre of the Revolution (1922–4) and of the Meyerhold Theatre (1923–38). His system of Bio-Mechanics, in which actors were required to suppress their individuality, and the stage setting was minimal, was eventually condemned by the Stalinist regime. He was arrested in 1939 after delivering a defiant speech at a theatre conference, and either died in a labour camp or was executed.

Mezada *Masada*

mezereon [mezeerion] A small deciduous shrub growing to c.1 m/3¼ ft (*Daphne mezereon*), native to chalky areas in Europe and Asia; leaves oval, entire; flowers pink-purple, sometimes white, tubular with four spreading lobes, fragrant, appearing before the leaves. It is often cultivated for ornament. (Family: Thymeleaceae.)

mezzanine [mezaneen] An intermediate floor in a building, placed between two main (usually lower) storeys; also known as an **entresol**.

Mezzogiorno [metzohjaw(r)noh] pop (2000e) 20 383 000. Geographical region of S Italy comprising Abruzzo, Molise, Campania, Basilicata, Apulia, Calabria, and the islands of Sicily and Sardinia; contains 35% of population of Italy, with much emigration; name ('midday') refers to the heat of the region; oil refining and petrochemicals; a largely agricultural area; devastated by earthquake (1980).

mezzotint [metzohtint] A technique of engraving which gives tonal rather than linear effects, and which was therefore very suitable for reproducing oil paintings. Invented c.1640, it was rendered obsolete by photography in the 19th-c.

Miami [miyamee] 25°47N 80°11W, pop (2000e) 362 500. Seat of Dade Co, SE Florida, USA; a port on Biscayne Bay, at the mouth of the Miami R; settled around a military post in the 1830s; since 1945, one of the country's most famous and popular resorts; airport; railway; major tourist industry with extensive recreational facilities (c.13 million visitors each year); the processing and shipping hub of a large agricultural region; printing and publishing, fishing, clothing, aluminium products, furniture, transportation equipment; air gateway to Latin America; large numbers of immigrants (over half the metropolitan population is Hispanic); professional teams, Dolphins (football), Heat (basketball), Marlins (baseball); Dade Co Art Museum, Seaquarium, Villa Vizcaya, the Everglades, Biscayne Boulevard; Orange Bowl Festival (Dec).

Miami Beach 25°47N 80°08W, pop (2000e) 87 900. Town in Dade Co, SE Florida, USA, on an island across Biscayne Bay from Miami; area developed in 1920s; railway; connected to Miami by four causeways; popular year-round resort, famous for its 'gold coast' hotel strip.

Miao [myow] A Sino-Tibetan-speaking mountain people of SE Asia and S China, constituting many different groups, each with its own language or dialect, customs, and dress. They are agricultural, growing opium as a cash crop. Population more than 4 million, mostly in China.

miasm [miyazm] A derangement of the body's energy fields which can result in persistent disease or increased susceptibility to disease. The concept was developed by Samuel Hahnemann, who believed that miasms may be inherited as a result of illness suffered by an ancestor which influenced genetic function, or they may be acquired, but when the acute phase of an illness or infection passes, the miasm remains as a persisting influence which causes chronic problems. Miasms are detected by 'supersensitive' methods, and there is no direct equivalent pathogenic factor described by orthodox medicine.

Micah, Book of [miyka] or **Micheas, Book of** One of the 12 so-called 'minor' prophetic books of the Hebrew Bible/Old Testament, attributed to the prophet Micah of Moresheth-gath (in the hill country of Judah), a contemporary of Isaiah in Judah and active in the late 8th-c BC. The work is noted for its attack on social injustices against the poorer classes, as well as for predicting the punishment of Samaria and Jerusalem because of the sins of their people. Some parts of the work may be of later date (6th–5th-c BC).

micas [miykaz] An important group of common rock-forming minerals characterized by a layer structure which gives the crystals a platy form and a perfect basal cleavage. Micas are chemically complex hydrous sheet silicates, commonly containing aluminium, potassium, sodium, magnesium, and iron. Important members are *muscovite* (white mica), a light, silvery-coloured potassium aluminium silicate, and *biotite*, which is dark brown, and contains additional iron and magnesium.

Michael VIII Palaeologus [payleeologus] (c.1224–1282) Byzantine emperor (1261–82), born in Nicaea into the Greek nobility. He rose to be a successful general in the empire of Nicaea. In 1258 he became a regent for, and soon co-ruler with, the eight-year-old emperor, John IV Lascaris, whom he later had blinded and imprisoned. In 1261 he became emperor of Constantinople, incurring the enmity of the papacy and Charles of Anjou (1227–85) who aimed to re-establish the Latin empire. The forced reunion of the Orthodox Church with Rome aroused great discontent among his subjects but warded off attacks until 1281. The hostile Pope Martin IV (pontiff 1281–5) proclaimed a crusade against him, but Michael incited discontent in Sicily, which was invaded by his allies the Aragonese, thereby ending the Angevin threat.

Michael (of Romania) (1921–) King of Romania (1927–30, 1940–7), born in Sinaia, C Romania, the son of Carol II. He first succeeded to the throne on the death of his grandfather Ferdinand I, his father having renounced his own claims in 1925. In 1930 he was supplanted by his father (reigned 1930–40), but was again made king in 1940 when the Germans gained control of Romania. In 1944 he played a considerable part in the overthrow of the dictatorship of Antonescu. He announced the acceptance of the Allied peace terms, and declared war on Germany. Forced in 1945 to accept a Communist-dominated government, he was later compelled to abdicate (1947), and has since lived in exile near Geneva.

Michael (angel) An angel described as the guardian of Israel (*Dan* 10, 12). He appears as a great patron, intercessor, and warrior in later Jewish non-canonical works (eg 1 *Enoch*, the Ascension of Isaiah, the War Scroll at Qumran). In *Jude* 9, he is depicted as an 'archangel' disputing with the Devil over Moses' body, and in *Rev* 12.7 as warring against 'the dragon'. In the later Christian Church, the benefits of his patronage were claimed by Christians, and his feast day is known as 'Michaelmas'.

Michael, George, originally **Yorgos Kyriatou Panayiotou** (1963–) Singer and songwriter, born in Finchley, NW Greater London, UK. A partner with **Andrew Ridgeley** (1963–) of the band Wham!, he released his debut solo single 'Careless Whisper' in 1985, which reached number 1 in the UK charts, while Wham!'s popularity continued to rise. In 1985 he became the youngest ever recipient of the Ivor Novello Songwriter of the Year award (he won it again in 1989). His second solo single 'A Different Corner' (1986) topped the UK charts before the final Wham! concert. His debut solo album, *Faith*, topped the UK and US charts, staying in the US charts for over a year. A tangle with the law at a public convenience in the USA did not affect the success of *Ladies and Gentlemen* (1998). Later albums include *Songs From the Last Century* (1999) and *Patience* (2004).

Michael Faraday Award Award established in 1986 and given annually to the individual working scientist who, in the opinion of the Council of the Royal Society, has done most to further an understanding of the role of science, engineering, or technology in society in the UK. A silver gilt medal and a prize of £2500 are presented by the president of the Royal Society at the annual anniversary meeting, and the winner is invited to give a lecture as part of the Society's annual public programme of events.

Michaelmas [miklmas] In the Christian Church, the feast of St Michael and All Angels (29 Sep); a quarter-day in England and Wales.

Michaelmas daisy [miklmas] A member of a large group of perennial cultivars of aster, mostly derived from the North American *Aster novi-belgii*; stems tall, erect; leaves alternate; flower-heads daisy-like, often in large clustered inflorescences;

spreading outer florets blue, pink, red, or white; inner disc florets yellow. (Genus: *Aster*. Family: Compositae.)

Micheas (OT book) [mikayas] *Micah, Book of*

Michelangelo [miyklanjeloh], in full **Michelangelo di Lodovico Buonarroti Simoni** (1475–1564) Sculptor, painter, and poet, born in Caprese, NC Italy. As a boy he was placed in the care of a stonemason at Settignano, and in 1488 spent three years in Florence with Ghirlandaio. He received the patronage of Lorenzo de' Medici, and after his death (1492) spent three years in Bologna. His 'Cupid' was bought by Cardinal San Giorgio, who summoned him to Rome (1496), where he stayed for four years. He then returned to Florence, where he sculpted the marble 'David'. Though he did not wholly neglect painting, his genius was essentially plastic, and he was far more interested in form than in colour. In 1503 Julius II summoned him back to Rome, where he was commissioned to design the pope's tomb; but interruptions and quarrels left him able to complete only a fragment. Instead, he was ordered to decorate the ceiling of the Sistine Chapel with paintings, which he did with reluctance (1508–12). In 1528 danger to Florence forced him to the science of fortification, and when the city was besieged (1529) he was foremost in its defence. His last pictorial achievement was 'The Last Judgement' (1537), and the next year he was appointed architect of St Peter's, to which he devoted himself until his death.

Michelin, André [michelin], Fr [meeshlĩ] (1853–1931) Tyre manufacturer, born in Paris, France. He and his younger brother **Edouard** (1859–1940) established the Michelin tyre company in 1888, and were the first to use demountable pneumatic tyres on motor cars. They also initiated the production of high-quality road maps and guide books.

Michelson, A(lbert) A(braham) [mikelsn] (1852–1931) Physicist, born in Strzelno, C Poland. His family emigrated to the USA in 1854. He trained at the Naval Academy, Annapolis, MD, studied physics at various centres in Europe, and became professor of physics at Chicago from 1892. He established the speed of light as a fundamental constant, and in 1907 became the first US scientist to be awarded the Nobel Prize for Physics. He invented an interferometer and an echelon grating, and did important work on the spectrum, but is chiefly remembered for the **Michelson–Morley** experiment (1887) to determine ether drift, the negative result of which set Albert Einstein on the road to the theory of relativity.

Michigan [mishigan] pop (2000e) 9 938 400; area 151 579 sq km/ 58 527 sq mi. State in NC USA, divided into 83 counties; split into two peninsulas by L Michigan and L Huron; the 'Great Lake State' or the 'Wolverine State'; 26th state admitted to the Union, 1837; settled by the French, 1668; ceded to the British, 1763; handed over to the USA in 1783 and became part of Indiana Territory; Territory of Michigan established, 1805; boundaries greatly extended in 1818 and 1834; capital, Lansing; other chief cities, Detroit, Grand Rapids, Warren, Flint; the Montreal, Brule, and Menominee Rivers mark the Wisconsin border; the border with Canada is formed by the St Clair R (between L Huron and L St Clair) and the Detroit R (between L St Clair and L Erie); 99 909 sq km/38 565 sq mi of the Great Lakes lie within the state boundary; highest point Mt Curwood (604 m/ 1982 ft); the upper peninsula and N part of the lower peninsula are mainly forested, containing several state parks; a major tourist area; the S part of the state is highly industrialized; motor vehicles and parts, machinery, cement, iron and steel (second in the country for iron ore production); corn and dairy products.

Michigan, Lake Third largest of the Great Lakes (area 58 020 sq km/22 400 sq mi) and the only one lying entirely within the USA; 494 km/307 mi long; maximum width 190 km/ 118 mi; maximum depth 281 m/922 ft; Green Bay indents the Wisconsin shore; linked in the NE with L Huron via the Strait of Mackinac; linked to the Mississippi by canals and rivers; ports include Michigan City, Gary, Chicago, Evanston, Waukegan, Kenosha, Racine, Milwaukee, Manitowoc, Escanaba, Muskegon, Grand Haven.

Michiko *Akihito*

Mickiewicz, Adam (Bernard) [mitskyayvich] (1798–1855) The national poet of Poland, born near Navahrudak, WC Belarus (formerly Novogrodek). He studied at Wilno, and published his first poems in 1822. After travelling in Germany, France, and Italy, he wrote his masterpiece, the epic *Pan Tadeusz* (1834, Thaddeus). He taught at Lausanne and Paris, and in 1853 went to Italy to organize the Polish legion.

MICR (Magnetic Ink Character Recognition) *character recognition*

microbe *micro-organism*

microchip A tiny wafer of semiconductor material, such as silicon, processed to form an integrated circuit. With progress in circuit fabrication technology, the integration size of an IC (integrated circuit) chip was improved through **large-scale integration (LSI)**, which made it possible to pack thousands of transistors and related electronic components on to a single chip. Further advances led to the integration size being increased to **very large-scale integration (VLSI)**, in which hundreds of thousands of transistors and related electronic components are packed on to each IC chip. When memory and logic circuits are built in, the microchip becomes known as a microprocessor. The costs of microchip technology are relatively small. As a result, microprocessors are now commonly used in calculators, washing machines, video games, and even on credit cards. Microchips can be made to hold an indefinitely large number of integrated circuits by using nanotechnology to manipulate individual atoms.

microclimatology The study of climatic conditions in small areas on or near to surfaces where plants and animals live. The microclimate of an area is determined by the processes operating at the surface: the absorption of solar radiation by plants and soil; the use of heat in evaporation and evapotranspiration; and the effect of air flowing across the surface.

microcomputer A computer based on a single chip microprocessor plus necessary memory and input and output devices. The term (often abbreviated to **micro**) was first applied to the small desktop computers which first appeared in the 1970s, based originally on 8-bit microprocessors. Since then 16-bit and 32-bit single chip microprocessors have become widely available, and the power and speed of microcomputers based on these have increased dramatically. The distinction in terms of performance between microcomputers and minicomputers is no longer clear.

microeconomics The study of decision-making by individuals and firms. This includes personal decisions about training, earning and spending income, and retirement. It includes decisions about setting up or closing down firms, what funds should be lent or borrowed, what investments to make in productive equipment, how many people to employ, what to produce, at what price and by what methods it can be sold, and what attitude is taken to risk. The techniques of microeconomics include logical models or theories, institutional and historical studies of family and firm behaviour and the way in which markets are organized, and statistical surveys of consumption, investment, and employment. Much of microeconomics uses the assumption that individuals try to maximize utility, and firms try to maximize profits. While this leads to many insights, critics point out that information on what actions are possible is limited and expensive, so that both individuals and firms have to *satisfice*, ie seek some reasonably satisfactory course of action, rather than looking for an optimum. Microeconomics is contrasted with *macroeconomics*, which is concerned with the behaviour of economic aggregates, taking individuals' and firms' decision-making as a background.

microelectronics A branch of electronics concerned with producing and using microcircuits – miniaturized electronic circuits consisting of tiny transistors, integrated circuits, and other electronic components often contained in one microchip. Microelectronic circuiting is used in computers, inertial guidance systems, and spacecraft.

microfarad *farad*

microfiche [**miy**krohfeesh] A sheet of film with an array of microfilmed images. The film size is from 76 × 127 mm/3 × 5 in to 152 × 229 mm/6 × 9 in with 30 to 100 images. The original documents are typically copied at 24 times reduction onto unperforated 16 mm film, cut into six strips of 10 images, and loaded into a plastic film jacket of A6 size. This set of negatives is then contact-printed onto diazo-type materials to provide a sheet of images for reading in a suitable viewer.

microfilm Black-and-white photographic material of extremely fine grain and high resolution for document copying on a greatly reduced scale. Microfilms are usually read by enlarged projection.

microfloppy disk *minidisk*

microgravity A state of free-fall weightlessness experienced in spacecraft. In Earth orbit, the force of gravity is counterbalanced by centrifugal acceleration due to rotation; equivalently, an object in orbit around the Earth may be considered to be always falling towards Earth, while Earth's curvature causes its surface to retreat at the same rate. In practice, due to gravitational effects of the spacecraft itself, and accelerations produced by spacecraft attitude control, it is difficult to obtain less than one-millionth Earth gravity for experimentation. There are limited opportunities for microgravity experiments in the small space stations presently available.

microlight *hang glider*

micromachine A fully functional device, such as a tiny motor, or robot, which may be no bigger than a speck of sand. The tiny size of micromachines allows them to be used in locations where people are unable to operate, such as inside other working machines, in the heart of nuclear reactors, or in pipes full of poisonous substances. Fitted with cameras, they can be used inside the human body to give surgeons a unique insight into problems. Some micromachines are designed as pressure sensors, consisting of tiny resistors buried in a diaphragm of silicon; changes in pressure cause the diaphragm to bend, and alter the resistance values. Others are designed as accelerometers, consisting of two sets of microscopic interlocking teeth which shift in alignment with changes in acceleration; for example, sudden deceleration can be used to trigger an air bag in a car. The microscopic components of micromachines are made using laser technology, photolithography, and x-ray lithography.

micrometer [miy**krom**iter] A gauge for making precise measurements of size, consisting of a spindle moved by a finely-threaded screw. An object is held between the screw's spindle and anvil. The leg of the micrometer is calibrated so that the size of the object can be read from the scale on the barrel. Digital readout versions are now available.

micrometre *micron*

microminiaturization The construction of very small electronic circuits and systems to save weight, size, and cost. This process began with the replacement of valves by transistors in the early 1950s, and continued with the development of integrated circuits. It is used extensively in satellite technology and computers.

micron Unit of length; symbol μ; defined as 10^{-6} m, a length more properly known as the **micrometre**. The micron is used in biological sciences.

Micronesia A collection of island groups in the N Pacific. Included are the Marianas, Carolines, Marshalls, Kiribati (Gilbert Is), and Nauru. Most are of atoll formation, and very small. Their small size and limited resources, and the distances between them, ensured that the power of traditional chiefs was both limited and localized. The people are outwardly distinguishable from Melanesians and Polynesians, having straight hair, and analysis of their blood typing suggests that they are a distinctive racial grouping. The name comes from Greek *micros*, 'small' and *nesos*, 'island'.

Micronesia, Federated States of *p.1004*

micronutrients *nutrients*

micro-organism An organism of microscopic size, typically not visible to the unaided eye; commonly includes bacteria, blue-green bacteria, yeasts, and some other fungi, viroids, and viruses; also referred to as a **microbe**.

microphone A device that converts acoustic waves in air to electrical signals for transmission, recording, and reproduction. First developed by Bell and Edison in 1876–7 for telephony, microphones are widely employed in telecommunications, sound recording, and hearing aids. In all types, impinging sound waves cause corresponding oscillations of a diaphragm. These movements in their turn vary a resistance (**carbon microphones**, as in telephone receivers), capacitance (**condenser microphones**), electromagnetic field (**dynamic** and **coil microphones**), or the shape of a piezo-electric crystal (**crystal microphones**), each producing a variation in electrical output. There are various patterns of reception: *omni-directional*, more or less equally sensitive in all directions; *bi-directional* with marked front and rear sensitivity in a figure-of-eight pattern; and *uni-directional*, in which the sensitivity falls off to each side in a cardioid pattern. This last characteristic is further emphasized by a slotted tube in front of the diaphragm in the highly-directional gun- or rifle-microphone. A *lavallier* [lav**al**yay] is a small personal microphone worn by the speaker on a neck-cord or coat lapel, allowing freedom of movement.

microprocessor *microchip; microcomputer*

micro-satellite DNA *satellite DNA*

microscope An optical instrument for producing enlarged images of minute objects. The compound microscope, in which a second lens further magnifies the image produced by a primary lens, was invented in the Netherlands in the late 16th-c; after 1830 it was widely used, following Joseph Lister's refinements which minimized chromatic and spherical distortions. The effectiveness of compound light microscopes is limited by the resolving power of the lens; magnifications can be achieved up to a maximum of 2000. Electron microscopes use a beam of electrons instead of light, thus allowing viruses and other molecular phenomena to be studied at magnifications of over 50 000.

Microscopium (Lat 'microscope') A small, faint S constellation, introduced by Lacaille in the 18th-c.

Microsoft A computer company which came into prominence with the design and supply of the operating system (MS-DOS) for the IBM personal computer. The system is supported by spreadsheet and word-processing packages and more recently by the Windows application software. During the 1990s, Microsoft became the world's leading computer company, and found itself having to defend its practices when the US government brought an initially successful anti-trust (monopoly) action against it in 1999, arguing that Microsoft unfairly used the dominance of its Windows computer operating system to squeeze out smaller rivals. In 2000 a judge ordered that Microsoft be split into two companies. This ruling was overturned in June 2001 by the US Court of Appeals, and later that year Microsoft and the Justice Dept. agreed on a settlement, though a group of states continued to press for tougher penalties. In November 2003 Microsoft faced a European challenge in Brussels along similar lines.

microsurgery The performance of surgical procedures on very small structures under microscopic control; examples include the joining of tiny blood vessels severed by injury, or operations on the inner ear. Miniaturized precision surgical instruments are employed.

microteaching A technique used in the training of teachers which involves the trainee practising a specific teaching skill (such as questioning or explaining) for a short time with a small group of children, receiving feedback such as a tutor's com-

Micronesia, Federated States of

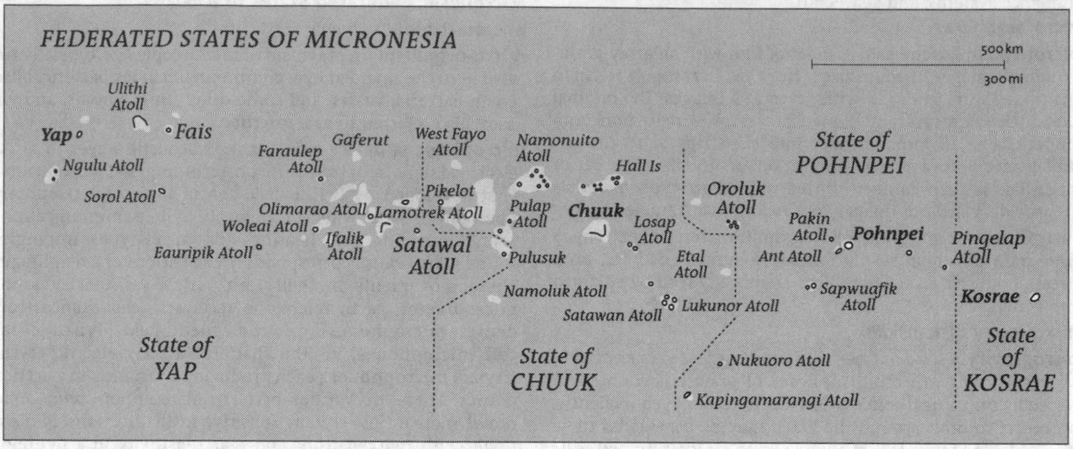

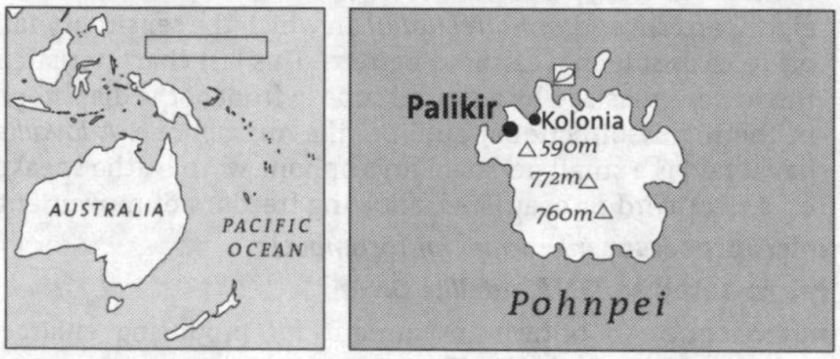

☐ International Airport

(USA Formal Dependencies)

Timezone GMT +11

Area 700 km²/270 sq mi

Population total (2002e) 109 000

Status Republic

Date of independence 1991

Capital Palikir (on Pohnpei Island)

Languages English (official), with several indigenous languages also spoken

Ethnic groups Trukese (41%), Pohnpeian (26%)

Religions Roman Catholic (50%), Protestant (47%)

Physical features Group of four states in the W Pacific Ocean (Yap, Truk, Pohnpei, Kosrae); comprises all the Caroline I except Belau; islands vary from high mountainous terrain to low coral atolls.

Climate Tropical climate, with occasional typhoons; heavy rainfall all year.

Currency 1 US Dollar (US$) = 100 cents

Economy Agriculture; farming and fishing; tropical fruits, coconuts, vegetables; few mineral resources.

GDP (2002e) $277 mn, per capita $2000

History Settled by Spanish seafarers, 1565; formally annexed by Spain, 1874; sold to Germany, 1899; control mandated to Japan by League of Nations, 1920; American Navy took control following Japan's defeat in World War 2, 1945; part of UN Trust Territory of the Pacific, 1947; compact of free association with the US, 1982; trusteeship ended, 1990; independent state, 1991, under Compact of Free Association, the US continues to control its defence and foreign relations; governed by a President and a National Congress.

Head of State/Government
1991–6 Bailey Olter
1996–9 Jacob Nena
1999–2003 Leo Falcam
2003– Joseph Urusemal

ments, a written appraisal, or seeing a videotape of the minilesson. A second attempt follows with another small class.

microtone A musical interval smaller than a semitone. Microtones are indigenous to some musical cultures, especially in the East, and they occur naturally in the harmonic series. In Western art music, where the smallest interval is normally the semitone, some 20th-c composers (eg Hába, Bloch, Bartók, Boulez) used microtones (especially quarter-tones) for their exotic effect or to extend their means of expression.

microwave background radiation *cosmic background radiation*

microwave link Communication using radio transmission at frequencies above 1 gHz, usually by highly directional beams between dish antennae. The method is important in telephone transmission, and also in television distribution, both for temporary outside broadcast links to the main studio and as permanent stages in a broadcast network.

microwave oven An oven, first constructed in 1947, which uses microwave radiation (electromagnetic waves) to heat food. The radiation used (wavelength 0·12 m) penetrates inside food, where it is absorbed primarily by water molecules, causing heat to spread through the food. This penetration effect makes heating much faster than in conventional ovens. Microwave ovens are sometimes combined with conventional ovens to provide quick heating plus surface browning. Many materials, such as glass and ceramics, are unaffected by microwave radiation.

microwaves Electromagnetic radiation of wavelength between 1 mm and 10 cm, less than radio waves and more than infrared. They are produced by klystrons and magnetrons, and used in radar, communications, and microwave ovens.

micturition *urine*

Midas [miydas] A legendary King of Phrygia, of whom many stories are told. In one story, as a reward for helping the satyr, Silenus, Dionysus gave Midas a wish, and he asked that anything he touched should turn to gold. However, this caused so many difficulties (eg in eating and drinking) that he asked to be released; he was told to bathe in the River Pactolus, which thereafter had golden sands.

Middle Ages The period of European history between the collapse of the Roman Empire in the West and the Renaissance (c.500–c.1500); sometimes, however, the term is restricted in its use to the four or five centuries after the year 1000. By the early 16th-c, humanists regarded the civilization that followed the fall of Rome as distinctly different from the classical culture that preceded it and the classical revival of their own day. The notion of a separate but inferior mediaeval civilization has since been transformed into a more positive appreciation of the age and its achievements, notably the emergence of national states, separate kingdoms, and the development of forms of government. Trade and urban life began to flourish, while the establishment of monastic houses encouraged learning and husbandry. A growth in the power of the papacy led to clashes between the pope and secular rulers. Society was organized on a military, hierarchical basis, with the feudal system providing land and tenure in exchange for military service. The Middle Ages saw the foundation of universities and the flowering of scholarship, art, architecture, and music. In the 15th-c and 16th-c the Renaissance in Italy and humanism in N Europe marked a new spirit of sceptical inquiry which heralded the end of mediaevalism in much of Europe.

Middle America A geographical region encompassing Mexico, Central America, and the West Indies; includes the Gulf of Mexico and the Caribbean.

Middle East A loosely defined geographical region encompassing the largely Arab States to the E of the Mediterranean, together with Cyprus, Turkey, and the countries of North Africa. The region conventionally includes the countries of Syria, Lebanon, Israel, Jordan, Egypt, Iraq, Iran, Kuwait, Saudi Arabia, Bahrain, Qatar, Oman, United Arab Emirates, Yemen, Sudan, Libya, Tunisia, Algeria, and Morocco.

Middlesbrough [midlzbruh] 54°35N 1°14W, pop (2001e) 134 800. Port town and (from 1996) unitary authority, NE England, UK; on the R Tees; rapid expansion as a town around the iron industry in the 19th-c; part of the Teesside conurbation; railway; University of Teesside (1992, formerly Polytechnic); iron and steel, engineering, chemicals, fertilizer; former Town Hall (1846), Town Hall (1889), Custom House (1840), Captain Cook birthplace museum; Transporter Bridge (1911, largest in world).

middle school A type of school in the UK for children aged 8–12 or 9–13. The former are regarded as primary, the latter as secondary schools.

Middlesex Former county of England, UK, which lost its official identity after local government reorganization in 1965. Most of its area was subsumed under Greater London, with some districts transferred to Surrey and Hertfordshire. The name continues to be used by many local organizations.

Middle Temple *Inns of Court*

Middleton, Thomas (c.1570–1627) Playwright, probably born in London, UK. After spending two years at Oxford and writing verse, he wrote satirical and romantic comedies for producer Philip Henslowe, collaborating with Dekker on plays such as *The Honest Whore* (1604). In 1620 he was appointed city chronologer, commissioned to write and produce the Lord Mayors' pageants. His stage masterpieces include *Women Beware Women* (c.1621) and *The Changeling* (1622, with William Rowley (c.1585–c.1642)). He also wrote popular pageants and masques for city ceremonials.

Middle West or **Midwest** The NC region of the USA, comprising the states between the Great Lakes and the upper Mississippi R valley: Illinois, Indiana, Iowa, Kansas, Minnesota, Missouri, Nebraska, Michigan, Ohio, and Wisconsin. Much of this area is within the corn-belt agricultural region.

Midgard [midgah(r)d] Middle Earth, the land in which human beings live, according to Norse mythology.

midge A small, delicate fly that gathers in vast swarms at dusk near standing water; adults gnat-like but non-biting, as mouthparts are poorly developed; larvae typically aquatic, feeding on algae or detritus, occasionally predatory. (Order: Diptera. Family: Chironomidae, c.5000 species.)

midget *dwarfism*

Mid Glamorgan pop (2000e) 551 500; area 1018 sq km/393 sq mi. Former county in S Wales, UK; created in 1974, and replaced in 1996 by Merthyr Tydfil, Caerphilly, Bridgend, and Rhondda Cynon Taff counties.

MIDI [midee] *digital media*

Midianites [midianiyts] An ancient semi-nomadic people dwelling in the desert area of the Transjordan; in *Gen* 25, reputedly descended from the offspring (Midian) of one of Abraham's concubines (Keturah). Later they are portrayed as enticing the Israelites into idolatry, but are overcome by Gideon (*Jud* 6–8). They were noted for their use of camels in raids.

Midland Canal *Mittelland Canal*

Midler, Bette [bet] (1945–) Comedienne and actress, born in Honolulu, Hawaii, USA. After studying drama at the University of Hawaii she was hired as a film extra, and made her stage debut in New York City in 1966. She then developed a popular nightclub act as a chanteuse and purveyor of outrageously bawdy comic routines. Her album *The Divine Miss M* (1974) won her a Grammy award as Best New Artist, and the same year she received a Tony award for her record-breaking Broadway show. Her dramatic performance in the film *The Rose* (1979) earned her an Oscar nomination, and she has since enjoyed considerable commercial success in a string of films including *Outrageous Fortune* (1987), *Big Business* (1988), *Scenes from a Mall* (1991), *The First Wives Club* (1996), and *Get Bruce* (1999).

midnight sun A phenomenon during the summer period within the Arctic and Antarctic circles, when the Sun remains continuously above the horizon. Correspondingly, there is an equal period in winter when the Sun does not rise at all.

midrash [midrash] In general terms, teaching linked to a running exposition of scriptural texts, especially found in rabbinic literature. The scriptural interpretation is often a relatively free explanation of the text's meaning, based on attaching significance to single words, grammatical forms, or similarities with passages elsewhere so as to make the text relevant to a wide range of questions of rabbinic interest. The term can also apply to the genre of rabbinic writings which consist of such interpretations.

midshipman Bottom-dwelling fish found on or in muddy bottoms along Atlantic and Pacific coasts of North America; length up to 35 cm/14 in; head rather flattened, body tapering to tiny tail fin; dorsal and anal fins long; underside bearing numerous small light organs; may produce audible grunts or whistles. (Genus: *Porichthys*. Family: Batrachoididae.)

midsummer The summer solstice or 'longest day', which falls in the northern hemisphere on 21 or 22 June, depending on the locality. Ceremonies in honour of the Sun have been held on this day from the earliest times. **Midsummer Day**, a quarter-day in England and Wales, is 24 June, the feast day of John the Baptist. It is preceded by **Midsummer Night**, when supernatural beings are said to roam abroad.

Midway Islands 28°15N 177°25W; pop (2000e) 450; area 3 sq km/1 sq mi. Circular atoll enclosing two small islands (Sand, Eastern) in the C Pacific Ocean 1850 km/1150 mi NW of Oahu, Hawaii; annexed by USA, 1867; submarine cable station since 1905; commercial aircraft stopover since 1935; military airbase since 1941; Allied air victory in the Battle of Midway (1942) was a turning point in World War 2.

midwifery The practice of attending women before, during, and after childbirth. The profession is known from the earliest times (eg in the Hebrew Bible), but the formal training of midwives dates only from the late 19th-c. In some places (such as the UK), midwives are licensed, though the status and practice of the profession varies greatly, and in some places (such as a number of US states) they are not formally recognized. Midwifery is not restricted to women, though not everyone has been enthusiastic about the arrival of the 'male midwife'.

midwife toad A European frog of the family Discoglossidae; lives away from water; may dig burrows; mates on dry land; male wraps eggs around his legs and carries them until they hatch, then puts tadpoles in water; two species: the **common midwife toad** (*Alytes obstetricans*) and the **Iberian midwife toad** (*Alytes cisternasii*).

Mies van der Rohe, Ludwig [mees van duh rohuh], also spelled **Miës**, originally **Ludwig Mies** (1886–1969) Architect and designer, born in Aachen, W Germany. A pioneer of glass skyscrapers, he designed high-rise flats for the Weissenhof Exhibition in 1927, and the German Pavilion for the Barcelona International Exposition (1929). He also designed tubular-steel furniture, particularly the 'Barcelona chair'. He was director of the Bauhaus in Dessau (1930–3), before becoming professor of architecture at the Illinois Institute of Technology in Chicago (1937–58). Among his major works are the two glass apartment towers on Lake Shore Drive in Chicago, the Seagram Building in New York City (1956–8), and the Public Library in Washington, DC (1967).

mifepristone *contraception*

mignonette [minyonet] An annual native to N Africa (*Reseda odorata;*) leaves lance-shaped; spikes of creamy, fragrant flowers; petals 4–7, lobed, those at the back larger with deeper, more numerous lobes. (Family: Resedaceae.)

migraine A recurrent, severe, usually one-sided headache, often accompanied by vomiting and visual disturbances which take the form of bright streaks of light. It tends to occur in young people, lasts a few hours, and lessens in severity and frequency with age. In the majority of cases the condition, though troublesome, is benign. It is believed to arise from the constriction of small arteries within the brain followed by their dilation. Some foods such as chocolate and cheese containing substances affecting the degree of constriction or dilation of blood vessels appear to be responsible in some cases. Other aggravating factors are stress, anxiety, alcohol, and menstruation.

migration **1** In anthropology and sociology, a movement of population within or between countries. Migration within countries has been preponderantly towards urban centres, seen possibly by migrants as attractive alternatives to rural overpopulation and its associated deprivation. International migration (*emigration*) may be a response to other factors, such as political threats against minority groups or warfare. Migrants may not always be given the right to settle in those regions to which they travel, and may be treated as temporary refugees or stateless migrant labourers. In advanced, prosperous societies there has been a considerable out-migration of people from the cities to the surrounding countryside, a phenomenon known as 'population turnaround'.
2 In biology, the movement of organisms or their dispersal stages (seeds, spores, or larvae) from one area to another. It includes one-way movement into and out of an area, but is commonly restricted to the periodic two-way movements that take place over relatively long distances and along well-defined routes. Such seasonal migration between summer and winter feeding areas, for example, is usually triggered by day length.

Mihailović, Dragoljub [mihiylohvich], nickname **Drazha** (1893–1946) Serbian soldier, born in Ivanjica, WC Serbia. After World War 1, he rose to the rank of colonel in the Yugoslav army. In 1941 when Germany occupied Yugoslavia, he remained in the mountains and organized resistance, forming groups (Chetniks) to wage guerrilla warfare. He became minister of war for the Yugoslavian goverment in exile (1943), then allied himself with the Germans, and then with the Italians in order to fight the Communists. After the war he was captured and executed by the Tito government for collaboration.

Mikonos or **Mykonos** [meekonos] pop (2000e) 5800; area 85 sq km/33 sq mi. Island of the Cyclades, Greece, in the Aegean Sea; airfield; ferry service to Delos and other islands; several noted resorts; Agios Panteleimon monastery, many churches built by sailors.

Mikoyan, Anastas Ivanovich [mikoyan] (1895–1978) Politician, born in Sanain, N Armenia. He studied theology, then joined the Bolsheviks in 1915. A member of the Central Committee in 1922, he supported Stalin against Trotsky, and in 1926 became minister of trade, doing much to improve Soviet standards of living, and introducing several ideas from the West. He was vice-chairman of the Council of Ministers (1955–64), and President of the Presidium of the Supreme Soviet (1964–5).

Milan, Ital **Milano** 45°28N 9°12E, pop (2000e) 1 431 000. Commercial city and capital of Milan province, Lombardy, N Italy, on R Olna; second largest city in Italy; Gallic town, taken by the Romans in 222 BC; chief city of the Western Roman Empire (AD 292); from 12th-c, ruled by the dukes of Milan; Duchy of Milan held by Spain, 16th-c; ceded to Austria, 1714; capital of Napoleon's puppet kingdom of Italy, 1797–1814; held by Austria, 1815–59; Mussolini founded Fascist Party here, 1919; linked by shipping canals with the Ticino and Po Rivers, and with Lakes Maggiore and Como; two airports (Malpensa, Linate); railway junction; underground; two universities (1920, 1923); birthplace of Visconti; a leading financial and commercial centre; textiles, iron and steel, metalworking, paper making, cars, aircraft, chemicals, pharmaceuticals, electrical apparatus, computers, foodstuffs, porcelain, engineering, publishing, fashion; Churches of San Lorenzo (early Christian), Sant'Ambrogio (founded 386); Santa Maria delle Grazie (15th-c, with Leonardo da Vinci's 'Last Supper' on the wall of the adjoining monastery), a world heritage site; Gothic cathedral began (14th-c), Palazzo dell'Ambrosiana (1603–9), Castello Sforzesco (1368), La Scala opera house (1775–8); Milan trade fair (Apr).

mildew Any fungal disease of a plant in which the thread-like fungal strands (together forming the mycelium) are visible on the leaves of the host plant as pale or white patches.

Mildura [mildyoora] 34°14S 142°13E, pop (2000e) 22 600. Town in NW Victoria, Australia, on the Murray R; railway; airfield; citrus growing, wine; Aboriginal Arts Centre; the bar in the Mildura Working Men's Club is said to be the longest in the world at 90·8 m/298 ft with 27 beer taps.

Miles, Bernard (James) Miles, Baron (1907–91) Actor, stage director, and founder of the Mermaid Theatre, born in Uxbridge, W Greater London, UK. His career as an actor flourished from the 1930s onward, but it was as the founder of the Mermaid Theatre that he made his greatest contribution to the British theatre. In 1951 he founded a small private theatre in the grounds of his home at St John's Wood, London; it was re-erected in the City of London, and in 1959 a permanent, professional Mermaid Theatre, financed by public subscription, was built at Puddle Dock, Blackfriars. It opened with his own musical play, *Lock Up Your Daughters*, adapted from Fielding. He was knighted in 1969.

Milesians [miyleezhnz] A group of Presocratic philosopher-scientists who came from Miletus in Ionia and who were active in the 6th-c BC. Thales, Anaximander, and Anaximenes are usually regarded as the first Greek (and therefore the first Western) philosophers, in the sense that they offered rational rather than supernatural accounts of cosmology and the basis of matter.

Miletus [miyleetus] A prosperous, commercially-oriented, Greek city-state in Ionia on the W coast of Asia Minor. It was the birthplace of the early Greek philosophers called the **Milesians**.

milfoil *yarrow*

Milhaud, Darius [meeoh] (1892–1974) Composer, born in Aix-en-Provence, SE France. He studied under Widor and d'Indy at the Paris Conservatoire. While attached to the French Embassy at Rio de Janeiro (1917–18), he met the playwright Paul Claudel, with whom he frequently collaborated, as on the opera *Christopher Columbus*. Returning to France, he was for a while a member of *Les Six*. He was professor of music at Mills College, California (1940–7), and taught at the Paris Conservatoire from 1947. His ballets include the jazz ballet *La Création du monde* (1923, The Creation of the World), and he composed several operas, much incidental music for plays, symphonies, and orchestral, choral, and chamber works.

Militant Tendency A British political group which came to prominence in the 1980s. (*Militant* is a newspaper published originally by Labour Party members espousing Marxist positions.) Its supporters infiltrated a number of local Labour Parties and the Young Socialists (its youth wing), and a number were elected as Labour MPs. Fearing the adverse electoral publicity resulting from Militant activities, the Labour Party moved to expel members of Militant on the grounds that they were members of a separate political party, which is against the Party's constitution. Many of those expelled took the Party to court, but their cases were not upheld. After this, Militant's influence in the Party declined, though the Tendency began to field its own candidates and achieved some success in local elections. In 1993 Militant ceased activity within the Labour Party and renamed itself *Militant Labour*. In 1996 it became the *Socialist Party*.

Military Cross (MC) A military award in the UK, instituted in 1914, awarded to captains, lieutenants, and warrant officers in the Army for acts of gallantry or devotion to duty, these ranks not being eligible for the DSO. The ribbon has equal stripes: white, purple, white.

military intelligence The collection and evaluation of information relevant to military decision making. Intelligence can be gathered by many means, such as listening to enemy electronic emissions (electronic intelligence, or *elint*), monitoring signals traffic (*Sigint*), the use of surveillance satellites, and traditional espionage techniques. Most armed forces have specifically trained intelligence units attached to them (whose role would include such activities as interrogating prisoners after a battle, or listening in to enemy radar traffic), but more well-known are the national agencies which collate information at a strategic level, such as the US Defense Intelligence Agency (DIA) and the British Secret Intelligence Service (SIS). The practice of resisting and frustrating hostile attempts to gain military, political, or scientific intelligence is known as **counter-intelligence**.

military monkey *patas monkey*

military science The theoretical study of warfare and of the strategic, tactical, and logistic principles behind it. Studied from ancient times to the computerized war-game 'scenarios' of today, military science concerns itself with such unchanging principles as the primacy of the objective, concentration of force, economy of force, surprise, and manoeuvre. Notable theoreticians and writers on military science include the Chinese general Sun Tzu (c.500 BC), the German general Karl von Clausewitz (1780–1831), and the British writer Basil Liddell Hart (1895–1972), who did much to inspire the German concept of Blitzkrieg.

military starling *starling*

military textiles High-performance textiles used for military purposes. Some were first used in this field, for example Orlon (for parachutes) and Kevlar (for bullet-proof vests and flash suits).

militia A military force raised (usually in times of emergency) for national defence, separate from the regular army. These national forces are raised by government decree, and can thus be distinguished from guerrilla forces.

milk A white or whitish liquid secreted by the mammary glands of female mammals to nourish their young. The milk of many species has been consumed by humans from earliest times, especially cow's milk, with goat's, ewe's, and buffalo milk also making a significant contribution in various parts of the world. Milk is about 88% water, 4·8% lactose, 3·2% protein, and 3·9% fat. *Cream*, an oil-in-water emulsion, is the yellowish surface layer of fat which forms when milk is allowed to stand. This may be removed, leaving **skimmed milk**. Low-fat milk, which is increasing in popularity, is produced by partially removing the fat (by 50% – **semi-skimmed milk**). Butter is made by churning the cream, while both yogurt and cheese are made by fermenting milk using different bacteria. Most milks are *pasteurized* before being sold for human consumption: this heat treatment greatly removes the risk of the consumer being exposed to bacteria which cause brucellosis and tuberculosis. The shelf life of milk can be greatly increased by ultra-high-temperature (UHT) treatment, although the palatability declines somewhat.

milk of magnesia A suspension of magnesium hydroxide ($Mg(OH)_2$) used as an antacid to sooth an acid stomach. It can also be used as a mild laxative.

milkweed A latex-producing perennial, sometimes shrubby, native to America; leaves in pairs or whorls of three; flowers in small umbels, each flower with a short, tubular corolla and five stamens united with the style into a tube with five valve-like appendages. (Genus: *Asclepias*, 120 species. Family: Asclepiadaceae.)

milkweed butterfly A large, colourful butterfly; wings brownish, bearing black and white markings; caterpillars brightly banded or striped as warning coloration; feed on milkweed plants containing chemicals that make them distasteful to predators. (Order: Lepidoptera. Family: Nymphalidae.)

milkwort A perennial herb or small shrub, found almost everywhere; leaves usually alternate; flowers in spikes, five sepals, two inner large, often petaloid and brightly coloured, enclosing three petals fused with eight stamens to form a tube. In **common milkwort** (*Polygala vulgaris*), the flowers are white, pink, or blue, sometimes all on the same plant. (Genus: *Polygala*, 500–600 species. Family: Polygalaceae.)

Milky Way A diffuse band of light across the sky, first resolved by Galileo into a 'congeries of stars' resulting from the combined light of thousands of millions of faint stars in our Galaxy. Strictly it means the belt of light seen in the night sky, but the term is used freely, even by professional astronomers, as the name of the Galaxy to which our Sun belongs. The name, from ancient Greek, was adopted also by the Romans.

Mill, James (1773–1836) Philosopher, historian, and economist, the father of John Stuart Mill, born in Northwater Bridge, Angus, E Scotland, UK. He studied for the ministry at Edinburgh, and became a teacher, then a journalist. A disciple and friend of Jeremy Bentham, he was an enthusiastic proponent of utilitarianism, and took a leading part in the founding of University College London (1825). His first major publication was the *History of British India* (1817–18), which secured him a permanent position with the East India Co, where he rose to become head of the Examiner's Office in 1830. He continued writing utilitarian essays for such publications as the *Westminster Review* and the *Encyclopaedia Britannica*, and wrote *Analysis of the Phenomenon of the Human Mind* (1829), his main philosophical work, which provides a psychological basis for utilitarianism. A member of the circle of 'Philosophical Radicals', his *Elements of Political Economy* was an important influence on Marx.

Mill, John Stuart (1806–73) Empiricist philosopher and social reformer, born in London, UK. His father, the Scottish philosopher James Mill, imposed on him a precocious education: he was taught Greek at the age of 3, Latin and arithmetic at 8, logic at 12, and political economy at 13. In 1823 he began a career under his father at the India Office, where he advanced to become head of his department. One of the major intellectual figures of the 19th-c, he was leader of the Benthamite utilitarian movement, helped form the Utilitarian Society, was a major contributor to the *Westminster Review*, and became a regular participant in the London Debating Society. He published his major work, *A System of Logic*, in 1843. In 1851 he married **Harriet Taylor**, who helped him draft the brilliant essay *On Liberty* (1859), the most popular of all his works. His other main works include *Utilitarianism* (1863) and *Three Essays on Religion* (1874). He was elected to parliament in 1865, campaigning for women's suffrage and liberalism. A major figure in the British empiricist tradition, he greatly influenced such figures as Bertrand Russell (to whom he was godfather 'in a secular sense') and J M Keynes.

Millais, Sir John Everett [milay] (1829–96) Painter, born in Southampton, Hampshire, S England, UK. He studied at the Royal Academy from the age of 11, and became a founder member of the Pre-Raphaelite Brotherhood, his works in this style including the controversial 'Christ in the House of His Parents' (1850, Tate, London). His later works were largely portraits, and some landscapes, and he also became well known for his woodcut illustrations for magazines. He became a baronet in 1885. A late painting, 'Bubbles' (1886), achieved huge popularity.

Millay, Edna St Vincent [milay] (1892–1950) Poet, born in Rockland, Maine, USA. Her first poem was published when she was a student at Vassar College, NY. Moving to Greenwich Village, then at its height as a meeting place for artists and writers, she published *A Few Figs from Thistles* (1920), from which the line 'My candle burns at both ends' came to represent youthful escapades. In 1923 came *The Harp Weaver and Other Poems*, for which she was awarded a Pulitzer Prize. She published many other works, including three verse plays, and wrote the libretto for the successful American opera, *The King's Henchman* (1927).

millenarianism [milinaireeuhnizm] The belief held by some Christians that there will be a thousand-year (millennium) reign of the saints, either before or immediately after the return of Christ. The belief is usually based on an interpretation of *Rev* 20. 1–7. The main body of Christians has not endorsed millenarianism, but it had its advocates from the earliest years of Christianity, and in the 19th-c there was a renewal of apocalyptical and millennial ideas, such as the Plymouth Brethren and the Adventists. In recent decades, the term has been used more broadly by social scientists, referring to any religious group looking forward to a sudden and early transformation of the world. Such movements tend to arise in periods of great social change or during social crises, and usually aim to advance a suppressed social group, as in the Melanesian cargo cults.

Millennium Dome The centrepiece of the UK's millennial celebrations, opened on 31 December 1999, designed by the Richard Rogers Partnership, and built in Greenwich, at a cost of £758 million: diameter 320 m/1050 ft, height 50 m/164 ft, circumference 1 km/0·62 mi, floor space 8 hectares/20 acres. Its contents included 14 thematic areas: Home Planet (space travel), Living Island (seaside environment), Shared Ground (the importance of community), Play (interactive digital games), Body (including the world's largest representation of the human form, 27 m/88 ft high and weighing 600 tonnes), Learning (in school and workplace), Mind (in art and science), Faith (diversity of belief), Self Portrait (sculptures and images of Britain), Journey (travel in the future), Money (exploring finance), Our Town Story Theatre (community theatre), Rest (contemplative environment), and Talk (world of communication), with a large central area for performances, and a cinema complex (Skyscape) outside. Its early months were accompanied by controversy, with opening-night difficulties followed by lower-than-expected attendances, senior management changes, and further financial aid. It closed at the end of 2000.

Millennium Stadium *Cardiff Arms Park*

Millennium Wheel *London Eye*

Miller, Arthur (1915–) Playwright, born in New York City, USA. After his father's ruin in the Depression, he worked to pay for his education at the University of Michigan, where he began writing plays. He achieved recognition with *All My Sons* (1947), but *Death of a Salesman* (1949) won the Pulitzer Prize and brought him international fame. This and *The Crucible* (1957) have been performed all over the world, making him America's best-known playwright. In 1957 he was tried and found guilty of contempt of Congress for refusing to reveal to the House Un-American Activities Committee the names of a literary circle suspected of Communist affiliations. He was briefly married to Marilyn Monroe, from whom he was divorced in 1961. He wrote many other plays, a screenplay, adaptations for television, short stories, and a collection of theatre essays. His autobiography *Timebends* was published in 1987. In 1995 *Homely Girl, a Life, and Other Stories* was published to commemorate his eightieth birthday. In 1999 he was awarded the Prix Molière.

Miller, (Alton) Glenn (1904–44) Trombonist and bandleader, born in Clarinda, Iowa, USA. He studied at Colorado, joined the Ben Pollack Band before completing his studies, then moved to New York City in 1928, where he worked as a freelance musician and arranger. From 1937 he led a succession of popular dance orchestras, and joined the US Army Air Force in 1942, forming the US Air Force band to entertain the troops. He achieved a distinctive sound with a saxophone–clarinet combination, his many successes including 'Moonlight Serenade' (his theme song), 'Little Brown Jug', and 'In the Mood' (1939). While the band was stationed in Europe, he was a passenger in a small aircraft lost without trace over the English Channel. Several theories have been proposed for the disappearance, such as bad weather, but records have suggested that his aircraft may have been hit by bombs jettisoned over the Channel by Allied bombers returning from a mission aborted through bad weather. The big band sound he created has continued to be performed with great popularity since his death, and the film *The Glenn Miller Story* (1953) has kept his memory alive.

Miller, Henry (Valentine) (1891–1980) Writer, born in New York City, USA, of Bavarian descent. With money from his father, which was intended to finance him through Cornell, he travelled throughout SW USA and Alaska. In 1930 he moved to France for nine years, during which time he published *Tropic of Cancer* (1934) and *Tropic of Capricorn* (1938), much of which is autobiographical and repetitiously sexual. American editions of the *Tropics* were not published until the early 1960s, and he briefly became one of the most widely read US authors. Other books include *Black Spring* (1936), *The Air-Conditioned Nightmare* (1945), and *The Rosy Crucifixion* trilogy (1965).

Miller, Sir Jonathan (Wolfe) (1934–) Actor and director, born in London, UK, He qualified as a doctor at Cambridge, and his career has combined medical research with contributions to stage and television. He came to public attention as part of the *Beyond the Fringe* team (1961–4), and in 1962 he directed John Osborne's *Under Plain Cover* at the Royal Court, which led to work in New York City, and an associate directorship of the National Theatre (1973–5), as well as much freelance work. From 1964 to 1965 he was editor and presenter of the BBC Television arts programme, *Monitor*. From 1974 he specialized in productions for the English National Opera and other major companies, and was artistic director at the Old Vic, London (1988–90). He wrote and presented the BBC television series *The Body in Question* (1977) and *States of Mind* (1982), and in 1985 became a research fellow in neuropsychology at Sussex University. He has written several books, including *Subsequent Performances* (1986). He was knighted in 2002.

Miller, Keith (Ross) (1919–) Cricketer, born in Melbourne, Victoria, SE Australia. In the great Don Bradman Test side that won the Ashes series 4–0 in 1948, he established himself as the world's leading all-rounder of the time, a flamboyant figure renowned for aggressive strokes and fast bowling. During his career he scored 2598 runs in 55 Test matches, including seven centuries, and took 170 wickets. After retirement in 1956 he became a sports journalist.

Miller, Merton (1923–2000) Economist, born in Boston, Massachusetts, USA. He taught at the Carnegie Institute of Technology, and in 1961 moved to Chicago University. In 1990 he shared the Nobel Prize for Economics for his contributions in applying economic theory to the field of corporate finance.

miller's thumb *bullhead*

Millet, Jean François [meeay] (1814–75) Painter, born in Gruchy, France. He farmed with his peasant father before being placed with a painter at Cherbourg. In 1837 he worked under Delaroche in Paris, achieving recognition at the Salon in 1844. Later he settled in Barbizon, painting the rustic life of France with sympathetic power. His famous 'Sower' was completed in 1850. His 'Peasants Grafting' (1855) was followed by 'The Gleaners' (1857), and other masterpieces. He also produced charcoal drawings of high quality, and etched a few plates. He received little public notice, but after the Great Exhibition in Paris (1867) he was awarded the *Légion d'honneur*.

millet A small-grained, rather inferior cereal from the tropics and warm temperate regions, grown in poor areas or as emergency crops mainly for animal feed and bird seed. It was cultivated in China from 5000 BC (the Sanskrit word for millet means 'Chinese'), and later in India and Egypt. **Common millet** (*Panicum miliaceum*) has branching heads; **foxtail** or **Italian millet** (*Setaria italica*) and **bulrush millet** (*Pennisetum glaucum*) have dense heads. (Family: Gramineae.)

millibar *bar* (physics)

Milligan, Spike, popular name of **Terence Alan Patrick Sean Milligan** (1918–2002) Humorist, born in Ahmadnagar, W India. A singer and trumpeter, he made his radio debut in *Opportunity Knocks* (1949), and co-wrote and performed in *The Goon Show* (1951–9). His unique perspective on the world, allied to an irrepressible sense of the ridiculous, has been expressed in all the artistic media and has left an indelible influence on British humour. As well as numerous stage and television appearances, and small roles in feature films, he published a variety of children's books, poetry, and comic novels including *Puckoon* (1963), *Adolf Hitler, My Part in His Downfall* (1971), and *Black Beauty: According to Spike Milligan* (1996). He wrote two volumes of autobiography, *Where Have All the Bullets Gone?* (1985) and *Peacework* (1991). He was awarded an honorary knighthood in 2001.

Millikan, Robert (Andrews) (1868–1953) Physicist, born in Morrison, Illinois, USA. He studied at Columbia University, Oberlin College, Berlin, and Göttingen, taught physics at Chicago University (1896–1921), then became head of California Institute of Technology. He determined the charge on the electron, for which he was awarded the Nobel Prize for Physics in 1923, and did important work on cosmic rays, showing them to come from space.

millilitre *litre*

millimetre *metre* (physics)

millipede A long-bodied, terrestrial arthropod; typically with double body segments, each bearing two pairs of walking legs; mostly small, found in soil or litter; many are able to roll into a ball or coil for protection. (Class: Diplopoda, c.10 000 species.)

Mills, C(harles) Wright (1916–62) Political scientist, born in Waco, Texas, USA. Educated at Texas and Wisconsin, he taught at the universities of Maryland and Columbia. A radical US political sociologist, his works were concerned to lay open the power structure of modern capitalist America. His *White Collar* (1951) examined the changes that had occurred in the nature of the American middle class since the early 19th-c. In *The Power Elite* (1956), he identified a largely self-perpetuating group that dominates the rest of the society. His work provided the major but non-Marxist critique of the USA in the post-World War 2 years.

Mills, Enos (Abijah) (1870–1922) Naturalist and writer, born near Kansas City, Kansas, USA. A frail child, he went to Colorado for his health, settling in a cabin at the foot of Long's Peak mountain. He began studying nature, became a writer, lecturer, and mountain guide, and in 1901 opened the Long Peak Inn, a haven for nature lovers. His lobbying efforts led to the establishment of the Rocky Mountain National Park in 1915.

Mills, Sir John (Lewis Ernest Watts) (1908–) Actor and director, born in Felixstowe, Suffolk, E England, UK. He first appeared on stage in 1929, becoming a popular actor in light comedies and musicals in the 1930s. He was best known as a film star, appearing in many patriotic war films as well as such epics as *Scott of the Antarctic* (1948), *The Colditz Story* (1954), and *Oh! What a Lovely War* (1969). For two generations of film audiences he represented the figure of a fundamentally decent and reliable Englishman, and took few unsympathetic roles. He was awarded an Oscar for his role as the village idiot in *Ryan's Daughter* (1970), and appeared in *Gandhi* (1982) and *Deadly Advice* (1994). His stage career indicates a wider acting range, including *The Petition* at the National Theatre in 1986. He was knighted in 1976, and is the father of actresses **Juliet** and **Hayley** (1946–). In 2002 he received a BAFTA Fellowship for outstanding contributions to world cinema.

Mills, Juliet (Maryon) (1941–) Film actress, born in London, UK, the daughter of Sir John Mills. She appeared in several films as a baby and young child, beginning with *In Which We Serve* (1942), and made her debut as an adult in *No My Darling Daughter* (1961). Later films include *Carry on Jack* (1964), *Oh! What a Lovely War* (1969), and *Jonathan Livingston Seagull* (1973), as well as several television movies, such as *Waxwork II* (1992) and *A Stranger in the Mirror* (1993).

Milne, A(lan) A(lexander) (1882–1956) Writer, born in London, UK. He studied at Cambridge, where he edited the undergraduate magazine *Granta*. He joined the staff of *Punch* as assistant editor, and became well known for his light essays and comedies, notably *Wurzel-Flummery* (1917), *Mr Pim Passes By* (1919), and *The Dover Road* (1922). In 1924 he achieved world fame with his book of children's verse, *When We Were Very Young*, written for his son, Christopher Robin, who was immortalized with his toy bear Winnie-the-Pooh in further children's classics such as *Winnie-the-Pooh* (1926), *Now We Are Six* (1927), and *The House at Pooh Corner* (1928), later made into a series of successful cartoon films.

Milo of Croton [miyloh, meeloh] (6th-c BC) Legendary Greek wrestler from the Greek colony of Croton in S Italy. He won the wrestling contest at five successive Olympic Games, and swept the board at all other festivals. A man of huge stature, he boasted that no one had ever brought him to his knees. It is said that he carried a live ox upon his shoulders through the stadium at Olympia, then ate it all in a single day. He played a leading part in the military defeat of Sybaris in 511 BC. Tradition has it that in his old age he tried to split a tree, which closed upon his hands and held him there until he was devoured by wolves.

Milosevic, Slobodan [milosuhvich] (1941–) President of Serbia (1990–2000) and Yugoslavia (1997–2000), born in Pozarevac, Serbia. He studied law at Belgrade University, then began a career in management and banking before entering politics. He is the founder and president of the socialist party of Serbia. He became the focus of world attention during the Kosovo crisis and NATO confrontation in early 1999, but following a wave of popular unrest he lost power in October 2000, and was replaced as president by Vojislav Kostunica. Following considerable international political and economic pressure, the new government arrested Milosevic (April 2001), and in June 2001 he was handed over to UN investigators to face a war crimes tribunal in The Hague. His trial began in February 2002 and was ongoing in 2004. In a separate investigation, in 2003 he was indicted with ordering the murder of former Serbian president, Ivan Stambolic, and with the attempted murder of oposition leader, Vuk Draskovic.

Miłosz, Czeslaw [meewosh, chezhwof] (1911–) Poet and man of letters, born in Szetejnie, N Lithuania. A founder of the catastrophist school of Polish poetry, co-founder of the literary periodical *Zagary*, and author of a book of essays called *The Captive Mind* (trans title), he was a leader of the avant garde before World War 2. During the War he worked for the Warsaw underground, then became a member of the Polish diplomatic service (1946–50). Rejecting the Communist government, he exiled himself to Paris to write (1951–60), then emigrated to America, becoming professor of Slavic languages and literature at the University of California, Berkeley. His poetry includes *Hymn of the Pearl* (1981), *Hymn of the Earth* (1986), and *Road-Side Dog* (1998) (trans titles). A selection of his wartime essays, *Legends of Modernity* (trans title), appeared in 1996, and his *Collected Poems* in 1997. He was awarded the Nobel Prize for Literature in 1980.

mi lou *Père David's deer*

Milstein, César [milstiyn] (1927–2002) Molecular biologist and immunologist, born in Bahía Blanca, Argentina. He studied at Buenos Aires University and at Cambridge, then joined the Medical Research Council Laboratory of Molecular Biology in Cambridge in 1963. He worked on antibody research, and in 1975 developed monoclonal antibodies with **Georges Köhler** (1946–95), which revolutionized biological research, and for which they shared the 1984 Nobel Prize for Physiology or Medicine.

Miltiades, the Younger [miltiyadeez] (c.550–489 BC) Athenian general and statesman. From an immensely wealthy family, he was reduced to becoming a vassal of Darius I of Persia, and accompanied him on his Scythian expedition (c.514). He returned to Athens in 493, and masterminded the Greek victory against the Persians at Marathon (490). He was the father of Cimon by the Thracian princess, Hegesipyle.

Milton, John (1608–74) Poet, born in London, UK. He studied at Cambridge, and spent six years of studious leisure at Horton, which he regarded as preparation for his life's work as a poet. There he wrote *L'Allegro* and *Il Penseroso* (1632), the masque, *Comus* (1633), and *Lycidas* (1637). He concluded his formal education with a visit to Italy (1638–9). The fame of his Latin poems had preceded him, and he was received in the academies with distinction. His revolutionary ardour during the Civil War silenced his poetic outpourings for 20 years, except for occasional sonnets, most of which were published in a volume of *Poems* in 1645. On his return to London in 1639 he emerged as the polemical champion of the revolution in a series of pamphlets against episcopacy (1642), on divorce (1643), in defence of the liberty of the press, *Areopagitica* (1644), and in support of the regicides (1649), and became official apologist for the Commonwealth. Blind from 1652, he dictated his poems to his daughters, nephews, and disciples, among them Andrew Marvell. After the Restoration he went into hiding for a short period, then devoted himself wholly to poetry, becoming widely esteemed as a poet second only to Shakespeare. The theme of his epic sacred masterpiece, *Paradise Lost*, on the biblical story of a man's fall from grace, had been in his mind since 1641. The first three books reflect the triumph of the godly; the last of the 12, written in 1663, are tinged with despair – as if to acknowledge that God's kingdom is not of this world. It was followed by *Paradise Regained* and *Samson Agonistes* (both 1671). Milton's influence on 18th-c poets was immense.

Milton Keynes [keenz] 52°03N 0°42W, pop (2001e) 207 100. Industrial new town (since 1967) and unitary authority (from 1997) in Buckinghamshire, SC England, UK; 80 km/50 mi NW of London; designed on a grid pattern; Open University (1969); railway; wide range of light industries; real-snow slopes recreational centre; festival (Feb).

Milwaukee [milwawkee] 43°02N 87°55W, pop (2000e) 597 000. Seat of Milwaukee Co, SE Wisconsin, USA, on the W shore of L Michigan; major lake port; largest city in the state; settled by German immigrants in the mid-19th-c; airfield; railway; two universities (1857, 1908); heavy machinery, electrical equipment; leading manufacturer of diesel and petrol engines; home of several breweries, and famed for its beer-producing tradition; professional teams, Brewers (baseball), Bucks (basketball); Pabst Museum, brewery tours, Mitchell Park Horticultural Conservatory, Milwaukee Public Museum, art museum.

Mimas [miymas] A natural satellite of Saturn, discovered in 1789 by W Herschel; distance to the planet 186 000 km/116 000 mi; diameter 390 km/240 mi; orbital period 0·942 days.

Mimbres [mimbresh] A native Mogollon Indian culture of the Mimbres R, SW New Mexico, USA, AD c.1000–1250. It is celebrated artistically for its painted pottery, particularly bowls bearing stylized humans and animals in black, brown, and orange on white.

mime In terms of ancient theatre, both a short dramatic sketch and a professional entertainer. In ancient Rome it became a spoken form of popular, farcical drama with music which was played without masks. In the 5th-c the Church excommunicated all performers of mime for burlesquing the sacraments and for indecency. The Middle Ages had mime players, while the actors of the *commedia dell'arte* relied heavily on mime. It became an essential part of ballet. The work of Jean-Baptiste Gaspard Deburau popularized mime in France in the 19th-c. In 20th-c theatre, it signified the art of silent corporeal expression as espoused by Etienne Decroux and popularized by Marcel Marceau. In recent years a new form of mime has developed, in which dialogue is not prohibited, but arises out of improvization.

MIME [mimee] *digital media*

mimicry The close resemblance of one organism (the mimic) to another (the model) in order to deceive a third. There are two main types of mimicry: **Batesian mimicry**, in which harmless or palatable species mimic a venomous or unpalatable model in order to deceive a predator; and **Mullerian mimicry**, in which several different mimic species, all of which are unpalatable, display a similar warning coloration pattern.

mimosa *wattle*

mimulus An annual or perennial, found almost everywhere, many from North America; leaves oval, in opposite pairs; flowers usually yellow with red blotches, 2-lipped, the upper lip 2-lobed, lower 3-lobed with two projecting flaps in the throat. (Genus: *Mimulus*, 100 species. Family: Scrophulariaceae.)

minaret *Islamic architecture*

Minas Gerais [meenas zheriys] pop (2000e) 18 159 000; area 587 172 sq km/226 648 sq mi. State in Sudeste region, SE Brazil; a wedge of land between Goiás (N) and São Paulo (S), known as the Triângulo Mineiro (Mineral Triangle) because it accounts for half of Brazil's mineral production; capital Belo Horizonte; coffee, iron ore, gold, diamonds, metal-working, timber, textiles, food processing, cattle, mineral waters; national monument of Ouro Prêto (1933); caves and grottoes.

mind An entity usually contrasted with the body or matter, as the mental is with the physical, but variously understood in the history of thought. In its broadest sense (included in or conflated with the meaning of *soul*) it is taken to be the distinction between the animate and the inanimate; in a narrower sense it is taken to be the distinguishing feature of *persons*, and related to self-consciousness and identity. It has posed problems of definition and explanation for philosophers, psychologists, and cognitive scientists, who from their different standpoints have tried to relate it to the brain and to behaviour and have considered analogies with computer software.

Mindanao [mindanahoh] pop (2000e) 16 321 000; area 99 040 sq km/38 229 sq mi. Island in the S Philippines; bounded by the Celebes Sea (SW), Sulu Sea (W), and Bohol Sea (N); many bays and offshore islets; mountainous, rising to 2954 m/9691 ft at Mt Apo; major rivers include the Agusan and Mindanao; largest lake, Laguna Lanao; chief towns, Davao, Zamboanga; hemp, pineapples, maize, timber, gold; Islamic secessionist movement since mid-1970s; Autonomous Region of Muslim Mindanao created, 1989; peace agreement, 1996.

Mindelo [meendayloo] 16°54N 25°00W, pop (2000e) 41 900. City and chief port (Porto Grande) of Cape Verde; on NW shore of São Vicente I; important refuelling point for transatlantic ships; submarine cable station.

Mindoro [mindohroh] pop (2000e) 1 003 000; area 9732 sq km/3756 sq mi. Island of the Philippines, SW of Luzon I; bounded by the Sulu Sea (S) and South China Sea (W); rises to 2585 m/8481 ft at Mt Halcon; wide coastal plains to the E; chief town, Calapan; timber, coal.

Mindszenty, József, Cardinal [mindsentee], (1892–1975) Roman Catholic clergyman, born in Mindszent, SE Hungary. Primate of Hungary (1945), and created cardinal (1946), he became internationally known in 1948 when, having refused to let the Catholic schools be secularized, he was arrested and charged with treason by the Communist government in Budapest, and sentenced to life imprisonment. Temporarily released in the wake of the 1956 uprising, he was granted asylum in the US legation at Budapest, where he remained as a voluntary prisoner until 1971, when he went to Rome. He criticized the Vatican's policy towards Hungary, and was asked by Pope Paul VI to resign his primacy. He settled in Vienna, and spent his last years in a Hungarian religious community.

mine An explosive device hidden underground or in water in order to destroy vehicles, ships, or people as they pass over or near it. Land and underwater mines were deployed in Ming

China (1569) and were used extensively in 20th-c conflicts on land and at sea. Over 500 types of mines have been developed, encased in metal, plastic, glass, or wood, and containing an explosive device such as trinitrotoluene (TNT). There are four types of submarine mines: contact mines explode when they are hit by a vessel; acoustic mines are triggered by the sound of a passing ship; pressure mines are detonated by changes in pressure when a ship passes nearby; and magnetic mines react to the magnetic field around the mine when a ship passes by. Anti-personal landmines may be designed to kill or maim by spraying high-speed fragments or steel balls. Buried landmines may be set off by trip-wire or surface pressure, while submarine mines may be exploded by contact with a vessel or through a magnetic mechanism. **Mine detectors** are used to locate metal mines, and probe rods and flail tanks are used to detect and disable landmines made of plastic or wood. An estimated 100 million uncharted landmines in more than 60 countries are left over from post-World War 2 conflicts; they are now estimated to kill 10 times as many civilians as soldiers. In 1997 a treaty banning the production, use, transfer, and stockpiling of landmines was signed by 125 countries, but not the USA, Russia, and China.

mineralocorticoids [mineralohk**aw(r)**tikoydz] Steroid hormones synthesized and released from the adrenal cortex of many vertebrates. They are important in the body's sodium and potassium balance, and in the maintenance of extracellular fluid volume. In humans the main mineralocorticoid is aldosterone.

mineralogy The study of the chemical composition, physical properties, and occurrence of minerals. Major aspects of the subject include identification, classification and systematics, crystallography, and mineral associations in rocks and ore deposits.

mineral oil A term used to distinguish lubricating oils of mineral origin. Early lubrication used oils of vegetable or animal origin, but the extensive development of machinery in the mid-19th-c demanded other supplies, which were found in the newly exploited subterranean sources of oil.

minerals Naturally occurring substances, generally inorganic and crystalline, with a homogeneous structure and a chemical composition defined within specified limits; classified by chemical composition and crystal structure. They are the constituents of rocks in the Earth. *Mineral ores* are the source of most elements, and also have wide use as fluxes and catalysts in industry. Well-crystallized examples of durable minerals are often prized as gemstones.

mineral waters Naturally occurring groundwaters rich in dissolved minerals derived from the rocks through which they flow. They are associated with medicinal properties, and may be used for bathing or as drinking water, depending on the composition.

miners' right A document granting the holder the legal right to prospect and mine for minerals in Australia. Replacing a licence system after the Eureka Stockade clash (1854), the new system was introduced in Victoria in 1855, and spread throughout Australia.

Minerva [m**er**va] The Roman goddess of handicrafts and intellectual activity, later identified with Athena as the goddess of wisdom.

minesweeper A small vessel designed or adapted to cut the moorings of mines, thus allowing them to float to the surface where they are destroyed by gunfire.

Ming dynasty (1368–1644) Major Chinese dynasty, established by Hongwu (r.1368–98) and consolidated by Yongle (r.1403–24). Its orderly government, social stability, cultural homogeneity, and grandeur surpassed even the Tang and Song periods. In 1421, its capital was shifted from Nanjing to Beijing, which was rebuilt, as was the Grand Canal, and a 600-mi extension was made to the Great Wall. The army increased to at least 3 million, there was much annexation of neighbouring territories, regular Western trade began, and a new legal code was issued (1373). The period is known for its philosophical, historical, and literary writing, its porcelain, lacquer, and cloisonné, its opulent lifestyle, and its developments in manufacturing (eg steel production) and medicine (eg smallpox immunization). Economic chaos and political confusion under later emperors led to dynastic collapse. The last Ming hanged himself as rebels entered Beijing; the Manchu took over, and Qing rule began.

Minghella, Anthony [mingg**e**la] (1954–) Director and screenwriter, born in Ryde, Isle of Wight, S England, UK. The son of Italian parents, he studied at the University of Hull and began a career as playwright and theatre director. His credits as film director/writer include *Truly, Madly, Deeply* (1991), *The English Patient* (1996, Oscars for Best Film and Best Director), *The Talented Mr Ripley* (1999), and *Cold Mountain* (2003).

Mingus, Charles [m**i**ngguhs] (1922–79) Jazz bassist, composer, and bandleader, born in Nogales, Arizona, USA. He played the cello with the Los Angeles Junior Philharmonic Orchestra before becoming a bassist with traditional-style bands. During the 1940s, he worked with big bands, and from 1953 led groups called the 'Jazz Workshop', which experimented with atonality and other devices of European symphonic music. His most powerful and individualistic music came later, such as *Wednesday Night Prayer Meeting* (1959) and *Fables of Faubus* (1960).

miniature camera Originally, a small still camera using short lengths of perforated 35 mm film, first produced in the mid-1920s. The term **compact camera** has been preferred, since the 1970s, using formats of 24 × 36 mm or smaller. Perforated and unperforated film is used, or even circular discs, supplied in cassettes or cartridges.

miniature painting A term sometimes used for the small pictures in illuminated manuscripts, and (more often, and properly) for the 'portraits in little' that were so popular in Elizabethan England. There is a comprehensive collection in the Victoria and Albert Museum, London.

minicomputer *mainframe computer*

minidisk A very compact magnetic disk storage medium for microcomputers, sometimes known as a **microfloppy disk**. There are presently at least four different sizes varying from about 1·5 in to 4 in (c.3·8 cm–10 cm) in diameter; the most common size is 3·5 in. Minidisks are enclosed in a rigid jacket, and are better protected from accidental damage.

minilab Automated machinery for the rapid production of colour prints. Exposed colour film is usually sent to a laboratory for processing and printing, but a minilab may be set up almost anywhere there is a power supply. No drain is needed, as waste is collected for disposal. Miniaturized equipment is used. Colour-print film is developed in an automated machine and the negatives placed in an automatic printer/processor using a long roll of colour paper. The exposure paper is processed immediately, and dry finished prints emerge. The exposure and processing are under microprocessor control. Results are available in an hour or less.

Minimal Art A modern art movement that has flourished since the 1950s, mainly in the USA. Typical products are the blank or monochrome canvases of US painter Ad Reinhardt (1913–67), and the prefabricated firebricks of US sculptor Carl André (1935–). In all cases the art content may be described as minimal.

minimalism In music, a style of composition, increasingly prominent since the 1960s, which abjures the complexities of many earlier 20th-c techniques in favour of simple harmonic and melodic units repeated many times, usually with phased modifications and superimpositions, in an unchanging, 'mechanical' metre. Among those who have espoused the style have been Cornelius Cardew, Philip Glass, Steve Reich, and Terry Riley. The term is shared with several other art forms (eg painting, theatre) which make use of their medium in a reduced or simplified way.

minimum lending rate (MLR) Formerly the minimum rate of interest at which the Bank of England would lend to discount houses. Used as an instrument of government policy, it superseded the bank rate in 1973, and was itself superseded in 1981 by the *bank base rate*, on which all other interest rates are set.

minimum wage A minimum rate of pay imposed by a government in certain sectors of the economy, or in general, with the aim of raising standards of living among the poorer sections of the community. Economists argue that the interference with free market forces may lead to higher unemployment among the less skilled and to wage inflation, as workers with wages little above the minimum rate demand pay increases to maintain their traditional differentials.

mining The extraction of useful mineral substances from the Earth, either near the surface or at some depth. It was practised in prehistoric times, widely used in classical times, and became highly developed after the introduction of mechanical power. In surface, strip, and open-cast mining, the soil is stripped away, and the ore, coal, clay, or mineral is dug directly. At greater depths the deposits are approached by horizontal tunnels dug from vertical shafts (*drifts*). Variants of these digging methods are adopted for different geological situations. Other methods of mining may be devised for particular substances. Tin ore (from Malaysia) is dredged from lake bottoms. Sulphur is raised from depth by concentric bore-holes down one of which is passed a stream of very hot water that melts the sulphur (the *Frasch process*). Salt is sometimes raised by leaching with water, and recovered by evaporation of the brine.

Minitab A computer package designed to enable users of personal computers to carry out statistical analyses of data.

Minitel A videotex service provided in France and similar to the Prestel service in the United Kingdom. It has achieved greater penetration because the service was introduced as a substitute for the printed telephone directory. Hence the Minitel terminal was available to every telephone subscriber.

minivet A small brightly-coloured bird, native to India and SE Asia; inhabits forest, scrub, and cultivation; eats insects, spiders, and buds. (Genus: *Pericrocotus*, 11 species. Family: Campephagidae.)

mink A mammal of genus *Mustela*; weasel-like, with a thick dark brown coat important to the fur trade (other colours produced by captive breeding); inhabits woods near water; swims well; two living species: most important commercially is the **American mink** from North America (introduced elsewhere); also, the **European mink**. The extinct **sea mink** lived along the E shore of the USA until the 1880s. (Family: Mustelidae.)

Minkowski space [minkofskee] The space–time of special relativity, comprising one time and three space dimensions; formulated by Russo-German mathematician Hermann Minkowski (1864–1909). His notion of flat space (ie no gravity, so zero curvature), with a geometry expressed in a special metric, is consistent with the requirements of special relativity. It is distinct from the flat space of Newtonian mechanics.

Minneapolis [mineeapolis] 44°59N 93°16W, pop (2000e) 382 600. Seat of Hennepin Co, SE Minnesota, USA; largest city in the state; a port on the Mississippi R to the W of its twin city, St Paul; part of Fort Snelling military reservation, 1819; later developed as a centre of the timber and flour milling industries; city status, 1867; airport; railway; university (1851); important processing, distributing, and trade centre for enormous grain and cattle area; machinery, electronic equipment and computers, food processing and flour milling; the financial capital of the upper Midwest, with a Federal Reserve Bank; wide streets, parks, and lakes; professional teams, Minnesota Twins (baseball), Minnesota Vikings (football), Minnesota North Stars (ice hockey), Minnesota Timberwolves (basketball); Institute of Arts, Guthrie Theatre, American Swedish Institute, Grain Exchange; Aquatennial (Jul).

Minnelli, Liza (May) [minelee] (1946–) Singer and actress, born in Los Angeles, California, USA, the daughter of Vincente Minnelli and Judy Garland. She first appeared on screen in her mother's film *In the Good Old Summertime* (1949), and became the youngest-ever actress to win a Tony award, for *Flora, the Red Menace* (1965). On television and in cabaret, her vocal talents and emotional rendition of plaintive songs earned comparisons with her mother. Dramatic roles in such films as *Charlie Bubbles* (1967), *The Sterile Cuckoo* (1969), and *Tell Me that You Love Me, Junie Moon* (1970) revealed her as a skilled portrayer of social outcasts. She won an Oscar for *Cabaret* (1972), and a television special, *Liza with a Z* (1972), confirmed her many talents. Subsequent dramatic appearances include *New York, New York* (1977), *Stepping Out* (1991), and the *Arthur* films with Dudley Moore. Her work for television includes *West Side Waltz* (1995) and the comedy sitcom *Arrested Development* (2003). In 2002 she married her fourth husband, producer David Gest, but the marriage ended acrimoniously in 2003.

Minnesinger [minuhzinger] Aristocratic German minstrels who performed songs of courtly love in the 12th–14th-c.

Minnesota [minisohta] (Siouan 'watery cloud') pop (2000e) 4 919 500; area 218 593 sq km/84 402 sq mi. State in N USA, divided into 87 counties; bounded N by Canada; the 'North Star State' or the 'Gopher State'; 32nd state admitted to the Union, 1858; the land E of the Mississippi R included in the North-west Territory, 1787; the land to the W became part of the USA with the Louisiana Purchase, 1803; permanently settled after the establishment of Fort Snelling, 1820; area became Minnesota Territory in 1849 and the 32nd state in 1858; Sioux Indian rebellion in S Minnesota, 1862; settled by many Scandinavians in the 1880s; capital, St Paul; other chief cities, Minneapolis and Duluth; Mississippi R source in the NC region; Minnesota and St Croix Rivers empty into the Mississippi; over 11 000 lakes scattered throughout the state; 5729 sq km/22 114 sq mi of L Superior within the state boundary; Sawtooth Mts in the extreme NE; highest point Mt Eagle (701 m/2300 ft); glaciated terrain in the N, with boulder-strewn hills, marshland, and large areas of forest; major tourist area; iron ore mined in the E mountains; prairies in the S and W; agriculture the leading industry; nation's second biggest producer of dairy products, hay, oats, rye, turkeys; processed foods, machinery, electrical equipment, paper products.

minnow Small, freshwater fish (*Phoxinus phoxinus*) widely distributed and locally abundant in lakes and streams of N Europe and Asia; length up to 13 cm/5 in; body slender, cylindrical, mouth small; variable greenish-brown above, underside yellowish; breeding males have bright orange underside. (Family: Cyprinidae.)

Minoan and Mycenaean / Mycenean architecture [miyseneean] A form of architecture prevalent in the Aegean c.3000–1100 BC. It mainly uses post-and-lintel masonry construction without mortar; characterized by thick walls covered with stucco, and asymmetrically planned. The most famous example is the Palace of Knossos on Crete, with a labyrinthine series of rooms, courtyards, and passages, which was destroyed by an earthquake in 1450 BC.

Minoan art [minohan] The art associated with the Minoan civilization of the Aegean, notably in Crete c.2300–1100 BC. The well-known amphora painted with an octopus and seaweed patterns attests to a powerful feeling for decoration. The frescoes in the Palace of Minos at Knossos, representing figures vaulting over the backs of charging bulls, show Egyptian influence.

Minoan civilization [minohan] The brilliant Bronze Age culture which flourished in the Aegean area in the third and second millennia BC, reaching its zenith around the middle of the second millennium (1700–1450 BC). Its most impressive remains come from Crete: the large palace-like structures at Knossos, Phaestus, Mallia, and Zakron reveal a sophisticated society, a complex centrally-controlled economy, a highly developed bureaucracy, and evidence of trading contacts far beyond the Aegean itself (eg the Levant and Egypt). Minoan civilization came abruptly to an end c.1450 BC. The cause is unknown: earthquakes, tidal waves, and invading Mycenaeans are all possible.

Minogue, Kylie [minohg] (1968–) Singer and actress, born in Melbourne, Victoria, NE Australia. She began acting in TV at age

12 in the soap opera *Skyways*, but later achieved worldwide fame for her role in the soap opera *Neighbours*. In 1987 she began a successful recording career, and her 1988 single 'I Should Be So Lucky', had huge sales. Numerous hit singles in Europe, Australia, and Japan followed. All 15 of the singles she first released in Britain reached the Top 10. In 2001 she topped the UK singles and album charts with 'Can't Get You Out Of My Head' (from *Fever*), and made number one again with 'Slow' from the album *Body Language* (2003). Her sister **Danni** is also a pop singer.

Minor, William Chester (1835–1920) Murderer and lexicographer, born in Ceylon (now Sri Lanka). He graduated from Yale Medical School, enlisted as assistant army surgeon, and fought in the American Civil War. In 1871 he moved to London, where in a fit of paranoid insanity he shot dead George Merritt, a brewery stoker. He spent the next 38 years as a certified criminal lunatic in Broadmoor. Answering an appeal by James Murray in the early 1880s for volunteer readers to help create the *New English Dictionary*, Minor became one of the most prolific, scholarly, and respected contributors, presenting thousands of lexicographical items for inclusion. His story is told in *The Surgeon of Crowthorne* (1998) by Simon Winchester.

minor In the UK, a person who has not yet reached the age of 18, often referred to technically as an *infant* (in England and Wales); in Scots law, a distinction is drawn between *pupils* (up to age 12 for girls, 14 for boys) and *minors* (from those ages to age 18); in the USA, the age of majority varies across jurisdictions and for different purposes. Minors cannot validly enter certain contracts, such as a contract for a loan. A British citizen who has reached the age of 18 (the *age of majority*) is entitled to vote in parliamentary and local elections and, until the age of 65, may be called on to serve as a juror, if ordinarily resident in the UK for at least five years. Other rights (such as the right to marry with consent and the right to have sexual intercourse) are governed by different age limits, often 16. The Twentysixth Amendment to the US constitution (1971) gave 18-year-olds the right to vote.

Minorca [minaw(r)ka], Span **Menorca**, ancient **Balearis Minor** pop (2000e) 63 000; area 700 sq km/270 sq mi. Second largest island in the Balearics, W Mediterranean, NE of Majorca; length, 47 km/29 mi; breadth, 10–19 km/6–12 mi; low-lying, rising to 357 m/1171 ft at Monte Toro; occupied by the British, 18th-c; airport at Mahón, the island capital; tourism, lead, iron, copper.

minor planet *asteroids*

Minos [miynos] A legendary King of Crete (or several kings), preserving the memory in the Greek mind of what we now call Minoan civilization. In Greek mythology, he was the son of Zeus and Europa, and expected a tribute from Athens of fourteen youths and maidens every year. In the Underworld he became a judge of the dead.

Minot, George (Richards) [miynuht] (1885–1950) Physician, born in Boston, Massachusetts, USA. Professor of medicine at Harvard (1928–48), he first introduced, with William P Murphy, a diet of raw liver for the treatment of pernicious anaemia, which led to the preparation of vitamin B_12. They shared the 1934 Nobel Prize for Physiology or Medicine.

Minotaur [miynotaw(r)] The son of Pasiphae and a bull from the sea, half bull and half human; the name means Minos's bull. It was kept in a labyrinth made by Daedalus, and killed by Theseus with the help of Ariadne.

Minsk 53°51N 27°30E, pop (2000e) 1 653 000. Capital city of Belarus, on the R Svisloch; one of the oldest towns in the state, c.11th-c; under Lithuanian and Polish rule; part of Russia, 1793; badly damaged in World War 2; large Jewish population killed during German occupation; airport; railway junction; university (1921), machine tools, vehicles, instruments, electronics, electrical engineering; Bernardine convent (17th-c), Cathedral of the Holy Spirit (17th-c).

Mint *Royal Mint*

mint A perennial native to temperate regions, especially in the N hemisphere; creeping rhizomes; square stems; oval leaves in opposite pairs; whorls of small pale pink to purplish flowers, sometimes forming heads; sometimes called **balm**. Its characteristic pungent scent is due to the presence of essential oils containing menthol. Mints hybridize easily, both in cultivation and in the wild, and are grown for their culinary value as herbs and flavourings. Many have distinctive odours, including ginger mint (*Mentha* × *gentilis*), peppermint, eau de Cologne mint (both *Mentha* × *piperita*), spearmint (*Mentha spicata*), and pineapple mint (*Mentha suaveolens*). (Genus: *Mentha*, 25 species. Family: Labiatae.)

Mintoff, Dom(inic) (1916–) Maltese statesman and prime minister (1955–8, 1971–84), born in Cospicua, SE Malta. He studied at Malta and Oxford universities, afterwards becoming a civil engineer. In 1947 he joined the Malta Labour Party, and in the first Labour government was minister of works and deputy prime minister. As premier from 1955, his demands for independence and the accompanying political agitation over the transfer of the naval dockyard to a commercial concern led directly to the suspension of Malta's constitution in 1959. He resigned in 1958 to lead the Malta Liberation Movement, and became Leader of the Opposition in 1962. In a second term as prime minister (1971–84), he followed a policy of moving away from British influence.

Minton ceramics One of the principal British potteries of the 19th–20th-c, founded in 1796 by Thomas Minton (1765–1826). They produced pottery and porcelain, making large quantities of willow pattern. Mid-19th-c wares included finely-painted pieces in the Sèvres style, and *majolica*, a new type of earthenware (not to be identified with *maiolica*).

minuet A French dance in triple metre and moderate tempo, popular among the European aristocracy in the 17th–18th-c. It became a standard movement in the symphony and related genres of the classical period, in the form minuet–trio–minuet.

minuscule [minuhskyool] *majuscule*

Minutemen Militiamen, particularly in New England, who were prepared to take up arms at very short notice. They were important in the first months of the US War of Independence, before the creation of a regular Continental Army under Washington.

Miocene epoch [miyoseen] A geological epoch of the Tertiary period, from c.24 to 5 million years ago. It was characterized by great mountain-building episodes, which formed the Alps and Himalayas, and the development of most modern mammalian groups.

MIPS [mips] Acronym for **millions of instructions per second**. It is a measure of the speed at which computers can operate.

Mira [miyra] (Lat 'the Wonderful') A star (*omicron Ceti*) in the constellation Cetus, first recorded in 1596 and recognized as a variable in 1638. It is a red giant, varying on a cycle of 331 days from 10th magnitude (minimum) to 2nd magnitude (maximum). It reached 1·2 magnitude, among the top 20 brightest stars in the sky, in 1779. It is the prototype for **Mira variables** – variable stars with long periods of months or more.

Mirabeau, Honoré Gabriel Riqueti, comte de (Count of) [meeraboh] (1749–91) Revolutionary politician and orator, born in Bignon, C France. At 17 he entered a cavalry regiment, but was imprisoned on several occasions for his disorderly behaviour. While hiding in Amsterdam, having eloped with a young married woman, he wrote the sensational *Essai sur le despotisme* (Essay on Despotism). Sentenced to death, he was imprisoned at Vincennes in 1777 for over three years, where he wrote his famous *Essai sur les lettres de cachet* (2 vols, 1782). Elected to the Estates General by the Third Estate of Marseille (1780), his political acumen made him a force in the National Assembly, while his audacity and eloquence endeared him to the people. He advocated a constitutional monarchy on the English model, but failed to convince Louis XVI. As the popular movement progressed, his views were also rejected by the revolutionaries. He was nonetheless elected president of the Assembly in 1791, but died soon afterwards.

miracle play *mystery play*

mirage An optical illusion caused by the refraction of light through thin surface layers of air with different temperature and hence density, causing objects near the horizon to become distorted. It appears as a floating and shimmering image on the horizon, particularly in deserts, on very hot days.

Miranda A natural satellite of Uranus, discovered in 1948; distance from the planet 130 000 km/81 000 mi; diameter 480 km/300 mi. Its very complex surface, observed by Voyager 1 in 1986, suggests a history of almost total destruction and subsequent re-accretion.

Miranda warning *right to silence*

Miró, Joán [meeroh, hwan] (1893–1983) Artist, born in Barcelona, NE Spain. After an unhappy period as a clerk, he studied in Paris and Barcelona, and exhibited with the Surrealists in 1925. In his early years he had great admiration for primitive Catalan art and the Art Nouveau forms of Gaudi's architecture. In 1920 he settled in Paris and invented a manner of painting using curvilinear, fantastical forms which suggest all kinds of dream-like situations. His paintings are predominantly abstract, and his humorous fantasy makes play with a restricted range of pure colours and dancing shapes, as in 'Catalan Landscape' (1923–4, New York City). His other work includes ballet sets, sculptures, murals, and tapestries.

Mirren, Dame Helen (1945–) Actress, born in London, UK. A member of the Royal Shakespeare Company, she appeared in a wide range of classical theatre roles, and won the Best Actress award at the Cannes Film Festival for *Cal* (1984). Later films include *The Cook, The Thief, His Wife and Her Lover* (1989), *The Madness of King George* (1994), *Some Mother's Son* (1997), *Gosford Park* (2001), and *Calendar Girls* (2003). Her role as Jane Tennison in the television series *Prime Suspect* (from 1991) made her a household name in the UK. She was made a dame in 2003.

Mirrlees, James (Alexander) (1936–) Economist, born in Minnigaff, Dumfries and Galloway, SW Scotland, UK. He studied mathematics at Edinburgh and Cambridge, then taught at Oxford (1969–95) and Cambridge. He shared the Nobel Prize for Economics in 1996 for his work in analyzing the consequences of incomplete financial information

mirror A smooth surface which reflects large amounts of light, usually made of glass with a highly reflective metal deposit on the front or back, or of highly polished metal. *Plane mirrors* form a virtual image the same size as the object, but with left and right reversed. *Convex mirrors* distort the image, but *concave mirrors* with a parabolic surface are used in astronomical telescopes to collect and focus light. Large astronomical mirrors can be over 5 m/16 ft across, but mirrors of all sizes are used in optical instruments. Half-silvered mirrors are used as one-way mirrors between a well-lit and a dim room.

Mir (Russ 'peace') **space station** A Russian (formerly Soviet space station) (launched Feb 1986) which evolved from Salyut, having more power (solar panels) and more docking ports (five) than previous spacecraft, allowing for the build-up of a modular station. It is used for long-duration spaceflight experience, and for biomedical, science, and applications experiments. Yuri Romanenko occupied Mir for 326 days in 1987. The current space endurance record for men is held by Russian cosmonaut Valeri Poliakov, who lived in space for 438 days (Jan 1994–Mar 1995), and for women by US astronaut Shannon Lucid (188 days, Mar–Sep 1996). The space station was employed as an important element in the planning of the construction phase of the International Space Station (ISS): the Shuttle–Mir programme was begun in 1995 and led to nine docking missions and more than two years of continous stays by astronauts. The station underwent difficult repairs during the second half of 1997, after an unmanned cargo ship collided with one of its modules. Mir was abandoned in 1999, and the Russian Space Agency and NASA planned a controlled destructive re-entry of the station. It re-entered the Earth's atmosphere and its remains plunged into the Pacific Ocean 1800 miles east of New Zealand in March 2001.

MIRV [merv] Acronym for **Multiple, Independently-targeted Re-entry Vehicle**, a nuclear-armed warhead, numbers of which may be incorporated in the front end of a large ballistic missile to be dispensed over a target area. A 'MIRVed' missile may therefore make attacks on several targets at once.

miscarriage *abortion*

miscarriage of justice A criminal case where an injustice has or may have been committed, either in the preparation of the case or at trial, resulting in an innocent person being convicted or an 'unsafe and unsatisfactory' verdict of guilt being returned. There can be several reasons for such a miscarriage, including non-disclosure of evidence, inappropriate questioning, or the giving of partisan evidence by prosecution scientists. In many cases where there has been an alleged miscarriage of justice, the convictions have been quashed, following an appeal.

misdemeanour / misdemeanor At common law, any offence other than treason or a felony; in most US jurisdictions, a criminal offence other than a felony, with a punishment of a fine or less than one year in a local prison. The felony/misdemeanour distinction in the UK was abolished by the Criminal Law Act of 1967, which created summary, indictable, and either-way offences (offences which can be proceeded on summarily or through indictment). A *wobbler* in the USA is a crime which can be charged as either a misdemeanour or a felony, and is roughly equivalent to an either-way offence in the UK.

Mishima, Yukio, pseudonym of **Hiraoka Kimitake** (1925–70) Writer and right-wing activist, born in Tokyo, Japan. He studied at Tokyo University, became a civil servant, then embarked on a prolific writing career which, as well as 40 novels, produced poetry, essays, and modern *Kabuki* and *Noh* drama. His first major work was *Confessions of a Mask* (1949) which dealt with his discovery of his own homosexuality, and the ways in which he attempted to conceal it. His great tetralogy, *Sea of Fertility* (1965–70) with a central theme of reincarnation, spanned Japanese life and events in the 20th-c. Passionately interested in the chivalrous traditions of imperial Japan, he believed implicitly in the ideal of a heroic destiny. He became an expert in the martial arts of *karate* and *kendo*, and in 1968 founded the Shield Society, a group of a 100 youths dedicated to a revival of *bushido*, the Samurai knightly code of honour. In 1970 he publicly committed suicide by ritually disembowelling himself (*seppuku*) with his sword after a carefully staged attempt to rouse the nation to a return to pre-war nationalist ideals.

Mishnah [mish**nuh**], (Heb 'repetition', referring to the practice of learning by repetition) An important written collection of rabbinic laws, supplementary to the legislation in Jewish Scriptures. The laws are classified under six main headings (*sedarim*): Seeds (agricultural tithes), Set Feasts, Women, Damages, Holiness (offerings), and Purities. Although the Mishnah's general arrangement can be traced to Rabbi Akiba (AD c.120), its final editing was due to Rabbi Judah the Prince (AD c.200).

Miskolc [meeshkolts] 48°07N 20°50E, pop (2000e) 192 000. Capital of Borsod-Abaúj-Zemplén county, NE Hungary, on R Sajo; second largest city in Hungary; airfield; railway; technical university of heavy industry (1870); iron and steel, chemicals, engineering, food processing, textiles, wine; National Theatre; castle of Diósgyör, 15th-c church on Avas Hill, Fazola furnace.

Missal The liturgical book of the Roman Catholic Church, containing liturgies for the celebration of Mass throughout the year. It includes all the prayers, Biblical readings, ceremonial, and singing directions.

missile *guided missile*

missing mass *dark matter*

missions, Christian The promotion of Christian faith among non-Christian people. Missionary activity has been a permanent feature of Christianity, particularly in the Roman Catholic and Protestant Churches. In the past, it was often associated with the expansion of European or American power, but modern missions recognize the importance of early establishing indigenous churches, with worship expressed in terms of local culture.

Mississippi pop (2000e) 2 844 700; area 123 510 sq km/ 47 689 sq mi. State in S USA, divided into 82 counties; the 'Magnolia State'; held by France, Britain, and Spain in turn, becoming part of the USA in 1795; the 20th state to join the Union, 1817; seceded, 1861; re-admitted in 1870, but white supremacy was maintained, particularly by the constitution of 1890; highest black population of any state (35%); capital, Jackson; other chief cities, Biloxi, Meridian, Hattiesburg, Greenville, Gulfport; bounded S by the Gulf of Mexico and Louisiana; main rivers the Mississippi (forms the W border), Pearl (part of S border), and Tennessee (NE border); highest point Mt Woodall (246 m/807 ft); much of the S state covered in pine woods; fertile coastal plain; land rises in the NE; major cotton-producing area between Mississippi and Yazoo Rivers; soybeans, cattle, dairy products, poultry; petroleum, natural gas (over a third of the land given over to oil and gas development); clothing, wood products, foods, chemicals; fisheries prominent along the Gulf coast; the lowest per capita income in the USA; a centre of the civil rights movement in the 1960s; Old Spanish Fort, Vicksburg National Military Park, historic Natchez.

Mississippian period *Carboniferous period*

Mississippi River River in C USA; rises in N Minnesota; source, L Itasca; flows S to form the border between the states of Minnesota, Iowa, Missouri, Arkansas, and Louisiana on the W and Wisconsin, Illinois, Tennessee, and Mississippi on the E; enters the Gulf of Mexico in SE Louisiana, near New Orleans; length estimates vary, because of the extensive delta; from L Itasca, MN to the delta, 3766 km/2340 mi; the **Upper Mississippi** runs from L Itasca to the confluence with the Missouri R, 1884 km/ 1171 mi; when the Missouri is considered part of the main stream, length from the Missouri's Upper Red Rock source to the delta is 6020 km/3740 mi; major tributaries the Minnesota, Des Moines, Missouri, Arkansas, and Red (on the W), and the Illinois and Ohio (on the E); drains an area of about 3·25 million sq km/2 million sq mi between the Appalachian and the Rocky Mts, including part of Alberta and Saskatchewan; several artificial levees on the banks of the lower river help to cope with flooding; delta consists of salt marsh, wooded swampland and low-lying alluvial tracts, dissected by numerous distributaries (*bayous*); practically no tides; navigable as far as Minneapolis; steamboat era in the 19th-c; now a busy commercial waterway; major ports New Orleans, St Louis, Memphis, St Paul, Minneapolis, Baton Rouge.

Missoni, (Tai) Otavio [misohnee] (1921–) Knitwear designer, born in Yugoslavia. He founded the Missoni company in Milan with his wife, Rosita, in 1953. At first manufacturing knitwear to be sold under other labels, they later created, under their own label, innovative knitwear notable for its sophistication and distinctive colours and patterns.

Missouri [mizooree] pop (2000e) 5 595 200; area 180 508 sq km/ 69 697 sq mi. State in C USA, divided into 114 counties; the 'Show Me State'; became part of USA with the Louisiana Purchase, 1803; a territory in 1812, but its application for admission as a state (1817) was controversial, as it had introduced slavery; eventually admitted as the 24th state in 1821 under the Missouri Compromise; capital, Jefferson City; other chief cities, St Louis, Kansas City, Springfield, Independence; E and W borders largely defined by the Mississippi, Missouri, and Des Moines Rivers; Ozark Plateau in the SW; highest point Mt Taum Sauk (540 m/1772 ft); split into two parts by the Missouri R; to the N, open prairie-land with corn and livestock, particularly hogs and cattle; to the S, foothills and the Ozarks, much of which is forested; more farms than any other state except Texas; automobiles, aircraft and aerospace components, processed foods and chemicals, machinery, fabricated metals and electrical equipment; mines yield over 90% of the nation's lead; position at the junction of the nation's two greatest rivers led to its development as a transport hub, and as the starting point for the pioneering advance W across the continent.

Missouri Compromise (1820) An agreement to admit Missouri, with slavery, and Maine (separated from Massachusetts), without it, to statehood simultaneously, in order to preserve a sectional balance in the US Senate. The compromise also forbade slavery in the rest of the Louisiana Purchase, N of 36°30.

Missouri River Major river in the USA, and chief tributary of the Mississippi; formed in SW Montana by the confluence of the Jefferson, Madison, and Gallatin Rivers; flows through North and South Dakota, then forms the borders between Nebraska and Kansas (W) and Iowa and Missouri (E); joins the Mississippi just N of St Louis; length 3725 km/2315 mi (with longest headstream, 4125 km/2563 mi); major tributaries the Musselshell, Milk, Yellowstone, Little Missouri, Grand (of South Dakota), Moreau, Cheyenne, Bad, White, Niobrara, James, Platte, Kansas, Grand (of Iowa and Missouri), Gasconade, Osage; used for irrigation, flood-control, and hydroelectricity; major dams the Canyon Ferry, Hauser L, Holter L, Fort Peck L, Garrison, Oahe, and Fort Randall; navigation (as far as Fort Benton) is dangerous.

Mistinguett [meestīget], originally **Jeanne-Marie Bourgeois** (1875–1956) Dancer, singer, and actress, born in Enghien-les-Bains, NC France. Making her debut in 1895, she became the most popular French music-hall artiste of the first three decades of the century, reaching the height of success with Maurice Chevalier at the Moulin Rouge, the Casino de Paris, and the Folies Bergère.

Misti, Volcán El or **El Misti** [meestee] Dormant volcano in S Peru, in the Andean Cordillera Occidental; height, 5843 m/ 19 170 ft; last eruption, 1600; of religious significance to the Incas; observatory established by Harvard University near its summit.

mistle thrush A thrush (*Turdus viscivorus*) native to Europe (N Africa during winter), and E to Siberia and N India; cream breast with bold spots; wing feathers with pale edges; inhabits open woodlands; nests high in forks of trees; also known as **stormcock**.

mistletoe A hemiparasitic evergreen shrub (*Viscum album*) native to Europe, N Africa, and Asia; stem growing to 1 m/ 3¼ ft, branches regularly forked; leaves leathery, yellowish, in opposite pairs; flowers small, in tight clusters of 3–5, greenish-yellow, males and females on separate plants; berries white. Mistletoe usually grows on deciduous trees (often apples, but also others), rarely on evergreens. The germinating seed sends haustorial roots into the vascular system of the host, from which it draws nutrients. All members of the mistletoe family (*Loranthaceae*) are hemiparasites. The plant was venerated by the druids, who cut it ceremonially from their sacred oaks with a golden knife. It was widely held to cure sterility and counteract poisons. Nowadays it is used as a Christmas decoration. (Family: Loranthaceae.)

Mistral A strong, cool wind common in S France. It originates in the Massif Central, and blows down the Rhône Valley between the Massif Central and French Alps. When it occurs in spring it may damage early crops. A similar wind is the Bora on the Adriatic Coast of Croatia. Both are examples of katabatic winds.

Mistral, Frédéric [meestral] (1830–1914) Poet, born in Maillane, SE France. He became a founder of the Provençal renaissance movement (the *Félibrige* school), and is best known for his long narrative poems, such as *Miréio* (1859) and *Calendau* (1861), and for his Provençal French dictionary (1878–86). He was awarded the Nobel Prize for Literature in 1904.

Mistral, Gabriela [meestral], pseudonym of **Lucila Godoy de Alcayaga** (1889–1957) Poet, diplomat, and teacher, born in Vicuña, Chile. A teacher from the age of 15, she taught at Columbia University, Vassar College, and in Puerto Rico, and combined her writing with a career as a diplomat and cultural minister. She established herself as a poet with 'Sonetos de la muerte' (1914, Sonnets of Death), taking her name from Gabriele d'Annunzio and Frédéric Mistral. Her poem 'Dolor' from the collection *Desolación* (1922, Desolation) is based on the suicide of her lover. She never married, and her work is inspired by a Romantic preoccupation with sorrow and death. She was awarded the Nobel Prize for Literature in 1945.

Mitchell, George (John) (1933–) US lawyer and politician, born in Waterville, Maine, USA. He became a lawyer, and a US attorney and district judge in Maine. Appointed senator for Maine in 1980, he achieved national prominence for his interrogation of Oliver North during the Iran-Contra investigation, and was elected Senate majority leader in 1989. He retired from the Senate in 1995, but was asked by Clinton to organize a conference on the IRA ceasefire in Northern Ireland, and to chair the talks on paramilitary decommissioning of arms. He became internationally known as the mediator in charge of the talks leading to the Good Friday agreement in April 1998.

Mitchell, Joni, *née* **Roberta Joan Anderson** (1943–) Singer and songwriter, born in McLeod, Alberta, W Canada. Her compositions, highly original and personal in their lyrical imagery, first attracted attention among folk-music audiences in Toronto while she was still in her teens. She moved to the USA in the mid-1960s, and in 1968 recorded her first album, *Joni Mitchell* (1968). Other highly successful albums followed, including *Clouds, Ladies of the Canyon* (1969), and *Blue* (1970). Many of her songs, notably 'Both Sides Now' (1971), have been recorded by other singers.

Mitchell, Margaret (1900–49) Novelist, born in Atlanta, Georgia, USA. She studied for a medical career, but turned to journalism, writing for *The Atlanta Journal* (1922–6). After her marriage to **John R Marsh** in 1925, and an injury to her ankle which forced her retirement, she began the 10-year task of writing her only novel, *Gone with the Wind* (1936), which won the Pulitzer Prize, sold over 25 million copies, was translated into 30 languages, and was the subject of an Oscar-winning-film (1939).

Mitchell, R(eginald) J(oseph) (1895–1937) Aircraft designer, born in Talke, Staffordshire, C England, UK. Trained as an engineer, he joined the Vickers Armstrong Supermarine Co in 1916, where he soon became chief designer. He designed sea-planes that won many of the Schneider trophy races (1922–31) and from them evolved the famous Spitfire, whose triumph in World War 2 he did not live to see.

Mitchison, Naomi (Mary Margaret), *née* **Haldane** (1897–1999) Writer, born in Edinburgh, EC Scotland, UK, the sister of E S, J S, and R B Haldane. Educated at the Dragon School, Oxford, she won instant attention with her brilliant and personal evocations of Greece and Sparta in such novels as *The Conquered* (1923), *When the Bough Breaks* (1924), *Cloud Cuckoo Land* (1925), and *Black Sparta* (1928). In 1931 came the erudite *Corn King and Spring Queen*, which brought to life the civilizations of ancient Egypt, Scythia, and the Middle East. She travelled widely, and in 1963 was made Tribal Adviser and Mother to the Bakgatla of Botswana.

Mitchum, Robert (1917–97) Film actor, born in Bridgeport, Connecticut, USA. After a youth spent as a labourer, vagrant, and professional boxer, he went to Hollywood, where he found employment in the film industry as an extra (1943). A prolific leading man particularly associated with the post-war film noir thriller, his laconic, heavy-lidded manner was deceptively casual, disguising a potent screen presence. His films included *Out of the Past* (1947), *Night of the Hunter* (1955), *The Sundowners* (1960), and *Farewell My Lovely* (1975, as Philip Marlowe). Among later films were *Mr North* (1988), *Cape Fear* (1991), and *Dead Man* (1996). He also appeared in several television films and series.

mite A small, short-bodied arthropod with head and abdomen fused into a compact body; typically with four pairs of walking legs; mouthparts include a pair of fangs; c.30 000 described species, including both free-living and parasitic forms, many of which are pests of economically important crops. (Class: Arachnida. Order: Acari.)

Mitford, Nancy (Freeman) (1904–73) Writer, born in London, UK, the sister of Diana, Jessica, and Unity Mitford. Educated at home, she established a reputation with her witty novels such as *The Pursuit of Love* (1945) and *Love in a Cold Climate* (1949). After the war she settled in France and wrote major biographies, including *Madame de Pompadour* (1953), *Voltaire in Love* (1957), and *Frederick the Great* (1970). As one of the essayists in *Noblesse Oblige*, edited by herself (1956), she popularized the famous 'U' (upper-class) and 'non-U' classification of linguistic usage and behaviour.

mithan *gaur*

Mithr or **Mithras** A god worshipped in the early Roman Empire, of Persian origin, and identified with the Sun. The cult was predominantly military, and restricted to males; it was practised in caves, and involved baptism. Other resemblances to Christianity include Mithras's miraculous birth and his adoration by shepherds. The main story was of his fight with the bull, which he conquers and sacrifices.

Mithridates VI (Eupator) [mithri**day**teez], also spelled **Mithradates**, known as **the Great** (?–63 BC) King of Pontus (c.115–63 BC), a Hellenized ruler of Iranian extraction in the Black Sea area, whose attempts to expand his empire over Cappadocia and Bithynia led to a series of wars (the Mithridatic Wars) with Rome (88–66 BC). Though worsted by Sulla (c.86 BC) and Lucullus (72–71 BC), he was not finally defeated until Pompey took over the E command (66 BC). He avoided capture, but later took his own life.

Mitla [**meet**la] 16°54N 96°16W. Ancient city in C Oaxaca, S Mexico, in the Sierra Madre del Sur, 40 km/25 mi SE of Oaxaca; former centre of the Zapotec civilization; well-preserved ruins include temples, subterranean tombs, and a building known as the 'hall of monoliths'.

mitochondrion [miytoh**kon**drion] A typically oval-shaped structure, often about 2 μm long, found in large numbers in eucaryotic cells. It comprises a double membrane, the inner forming folds and ridges (*cristae*) which penetrate the central matrix. It functions as a major site for metabolic activities that release energy by breaking down food molecules.

mitosis [miy**toh**sis] The normal process of nuclear division and separation that takes place in a dividing cell, producing two daughter cells, each containing a nucleus with the same complement of chromosomes as the mother cell. During mitosis, each chromosome divides lengthwise into two chromatids, which separate and form the chromosomes of the resulting daughter nuclei. The phases of mitosis are: *prophase* (the shortening and thickening of chromosomes), *metaphase* (the arrangement of chromosomes around the equator of a spindle), *anaphase* (the separation of chromatids), and *telophase* (the chromosomes return to an extended state, and the nuclear membrane is reformed).

mitre / miter (Gr *mitra*, 'turban') The liturgical headwear of a bishop of the Western Christian Church. It takes the form of a shield-shaped, high, stiff hat, representing the 'helmet of salvation'.

MIT school In linguistics, a label applied to the group of US linguists associated with the Massachusetts Institute of Technology (MIT), who have developed the concept of generative grammar under the influence of Noam Chomsky.

Mitsiwa *Massawa*

Mittelland Canal [**mit**eland] (Ger 'Midland Canal') A system of German canals and rivers linking the Dortmund–Ems Canal with Magdeburg. The waterway, which together with side canals provides an important transportation network, was completed in the late 1930s. It is 325 km/202 mi in length.

Mitterrand, François (Maurice Marie) [meetuhrã] (1916–96) French statesman and president (1981–95), born in Jarnac, W France. He studied law and politics at the University of Paris. During World War 2 he served with the French forces, was wounded and captured, but escaped and joined the French resistance. He was a deputy in the French National Assembly almost continuously from 1946, representing the constituency of Nievre (near Dijon), and held ministerial posts in 11 centrist governments (1947–58). He opposed de Gaulle's creation of the Fifth Republic, and lost his assembly seat in the 1958 election. For many years he remained a stubborn opponent of de Gaulle. He worked for unification of the French Left, and became secretary of the Socialist Party in 1971. Following his victory in 1981, he embarked on a programme of nationalization and job creation in an attempt to combat stagnation and unemployment. With Kohl, he forged the Treaty of Maastricht on European union in 1991. Following Rocard's resignation in 1991 he appointed the controversial Edith Cresson as prime minister. Bérégovoy, who replaced her, committed suicide following allegations which implicated Mitterrand in deliberately misleading the French public over the economic situation. During his retirement, revelations emerged of his friendship with wartime Vichy collaborators, political corruption, and extramarital affairs.

mix; mixing *dissolve; dubbing*

mixed-ability groups *streaming*

mixed economy *market economy*

mixed tide A tidal cycle intermediate between a diurnal tide and a semi-diurnal tide. It normally exhibits two low and two high tides per lunar day, but the highs and lows are of unequal magnitude. This type of tide is common around the Pacific Ocean basin.

mixture In chemistry, distinguished from a compound in the following respects. A *mixture of A and B* is of indefinite composition, contains properties of A and B, and is easily separated into A and B. A *compound AB* has a definite ratio of A to B, contains properties unrelated to A and B, and needs a reaction to regain A and B.

Mjøsa, Lake [myoesa] or **Mjøsen** area 368 sq km/142 sq mi. Elongated lake in SE Norway, from Eidsvoll (S) to Lillehammer (N); length 100 km/62 mi maximum depth 443 m/1453 ft; Norway's largest lake; heavily stocked with trout; chief towns, Lillehammer, Hamar, Gjøvik.

Mnemosyne [neemozinee] In Greek mythology, a Titan, daughter of Earth and Heaven, and mother of all the Muses. The name means 'Memory'.

Mo, Timothy (Peter) [moh] (1950–) Novelist, born in Kowloon, Hong Kong. He studied at Oxford University, attracting attention with his first novel, *The Monkey King* (1978), set in Hong Kong, followed by *Sour Sweet* (1982, Hawthornden Prize), a densely realistic portrait of London's Chinese community. Later novels include *The Redundancy of Courage* (1991), *Brownout on Breadfruit Boulevard* (1995), *Renegade or Halo Squared* (1999).

moa An extinct bird native to New Zealand; a large ratite (up to 3 m/10 ft high) with long neck and legs, no wings; slow-moving; inhabited forests; ate berries, seeds, and shoots. Some may have survived into the 19th-c. (Family: Dinornithidae, c.12 species.)

Moabites [mohabytes] An ancient Semitic people who in Old Testament times inhabited the area to the SE of the Dead Sea. Like the Ammonites, they were believed to be descended from Lot.

Moabite Stone [mohabiyt] An inscribed basalt slab, discovered in 1868 and subsequently broken up, which describes the successful revolt of Mesha, king of Moab, against the Israelites during the reign of Ahab (9th-c BC) or possibly of his son Jehoram (2 *Ki* 1.1). It is important for the linguistic and historical light cast on the Hebrew Biblical narratives.

Mobile [mohbeel] 30°41N 88°03W, pop (2000e) 198 900. Seat of Mobile Co, SW Alabama, USA; a major US port on Mobile Bay; settled by the French, 1711; ceded to the British, 1763; city status, 1819; scene of a Federal victory at the naval battle of Mobile Bay, 1864; railway; university (1963); Alabama's only seaport; shipbuilding, oil refining, paper, textiles, aluminium, chemicals; Mardi Gras, Azalea Trail Festival (Mar–May).

mobile A name first applied by Marcel Duchamp to the hanging wire-and-metal sculptures of Alexander Calder. From c.1931 Calder perfected these popular and widely-imitated abstract constructions, sometimes adding a motor, sometimes relying on air currents to set them turning.

mobile communications A system which provides a simple, convenient means of communication for people who wish to keep in touch when travelling. The first mobile communication system was ship-borne radio, and there have since been widespread developments in the field of military communications. In modern times the term also refers to personal communication systems such as CB radio, radio paging, and car and pocket phones which use cellular radio. Cellular radio employs local radio transmitters, covering small areas (*cells*), which receive and transmit calls in association with the telecommunications network. Direct-dial calls using special handsets were a major development of the 1990s.

mobile phone (UK) or **cellphone** (US) A portable telephone handset, used with a cellular radio or other mobile communication system, small enough to fit into the pocket. It enables users to make direct-dial telephone calls wherever they are.

Möbius, August Ferdinand [moebius] (1790–1868) Mathematician, born in Schulpforta, EC Germany. As professor at Leipzig he worked on analytical geometry, topology, and theoretical astronomy, but is chiefly known for the discovery of the *Möbius strip* (a one-sided surface formed by giving a rectangular strip a half-twist, then joining the ends together) and the *Möbius net*, important in projective geometry. He also introduced barycentric co-ordinates into geometry.

Möbius strip *see panel*

Mobutu, Sese Seko [mobootoo], originally **Joseph Désiré Mobutu** (1930–97) Zairean politician and president (1965–97), born in Lisala, N Democratic Republic of Congo (formerly Zaire, and earlier, Belgian Congo). He worked as a journalist in the Belgian colonial army, becoming a sergeant-major, and in 1958 joined Lumumba's Congolese National Movement Party. In 1960, immediately after independence, the government in Leopoldville was so indecisive in its dealings with dissidents in Katanga province that Mobutu stepped in and took over, five months later handing back power to the civilian government. After the civil war of 1963–5 he again took over, but this time retained power. As president, with a new constitution and a new name

Möbius strip

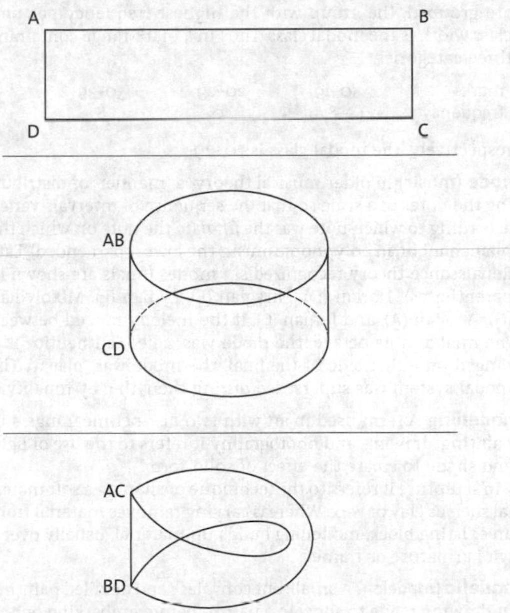

[moebius] In topology, a one-sided surface bounded by a single continuous line. Take a long, thin rectangle *ABCD*, and join *A* to *B*, and *C* to *D*. This forms a cylinder, with two surfaces, an inside and an outside. Now take a similar rectangle *ABCD*, and join *A* to *C*, *B* to *D*. Starting at any point *P* on the surface now formed, we can draw a continuous line over the surface to reach the point at the 'other' side of *P*.

for his country, he adopted a new name for himself and the rank of marshal. His regime was harsh and highly personalized. He was re-elected president in 1984, and elections scheduled for 1991 were postponed. He was forced to stand down in May 1997 following an uprising led by Laurent Kabila (1939–2001).

Mobutu Sese Seko, Lake *Albert, Lake*

moccasin flower *lady's slipper*

Moche [mochay] An ancient Andean city near Trujillo, Peru, the capital AD c.200–550 of the Moche (or Mochica) state. Particularly celebrated are its twin pyramids of the Sun and Moon, the former 160 m/525 ft by 34 m/112 ft square and 40 m/130 ft high, with 130 million adobe bricks. Moche metalwork, textiles, and especially ceramics are notable.

mockingbird A bird native to the New World; thrush-like with sharp, slightly curved bill and long tail; sings well; excellent mimic; inhabits forest and bushy areas; eats invertebrates and fruit; also known as **mocking-thrush**. (Family: Mimidae, 16 species.)

mock orange A deciduous, temperate shrub, mainly from E Asia; leaves oval, opposite, with prominent veins; flowers fragrant, usually white, bowl-shaped, with four petals and numerous stamens; fruit a capsule. It is named for the resemblance of its flowers to those of the orange, but in horticulture it is sometimes called **syringa**, the botanical name for lilac. (Genus: *Philadelphus*, 75 species. Family: Hydrangaceae.)

Mod The annual autumn musical and literary festival of Gaelic-speaking Scotland organized by An Comunn Gaidhealach (the Gaelic language society) on the model of the Welsh eisteddfod; first held in Oban in 1892.

modal logic A branch of logic dealing with inferences involving statements of necessity or possibility. Its investigation has led to important debates in metaphysics and the philosophy of language.

mode (mathematics) In mathematics, the commonest of a set of scores; for example, the mode of 1, 2, 3, 4, 4, 5 is 4. If the scores are grouped, the group with the highest frequency per unit class width is the modal class. Thus in a mark-range containing three categories,

marks	0–19	20–29	30–39
frequency	8	10	8

respectively, the modal class is 20–29.

mode (music) In older musical theory, a 'manner' of distributing the notes of a scale so that the sequence of intervals varied according to which note was the *final* (ie the note on which the plainchant or, in polyphonic music, the lowest part ended). Late Renaissance theory recognized six modes (finals are shown in parentheses): Dorian (D), Phrygian (E), Lydian (F), Mixolydian (G), Aeolian (A), and Ionian (C). If the melody ranged between the final and its octave, the mode was called 'authentic'; if it ranged on either side of the final, the mode was 'plagal'. The modal system was superseded during the 17th-c by tonality.

modelling A term used in art with two distinct meanings. **1** In painting, drawing, and photography it refers to the use of light and shade to create the effect of solid form.

2 In sculpture it refers to the technique of shaping a soft material such as clay or wax. Whereas carving removes material from an existing block, modelling builds up material, usually over a wire armature or frame.

modello [modeloh] A small, but complete and detailed painting or drawing made to show to a patron before embarking on the full-size work. At this stage the patron might suggest changes. Superb oil *modelli* exist by Rubens and Tiepolo.

modem [mohdem] Acronym for **MOdulator/DEModulator**, a device which converts digital information from computers into electrical signals that can be transmitted over telephone lines and vice versa.

moderator A person who presides over Presbyterian Church courts, such as the kirk session, presbytery, synod, or General Assembly. In Reformed Churches generally, the term is applied to the chairman of official Church gatherings.

modern art A term used widely but imprecisely to refer to all the 'progressive' movements in 19th–20th-c art. Accounts vary: some consider Goya the first modern artist; others prefer Manet. What is agreed is that towards the end of the 19th-c a number of artists, including Cézanne, Gauguin, van Gogh, Ensor, and Munch, challenged in various ways the traditional approach to painting based on such notions as naturalistic figure-drawing and Renaissance perspective. Their innovations inspired the younger generation around 1904–5 (in Paris, Rouault, Matisse, Picasso; in Dresden, Kirchner, Heckel, Schmitt-Rottluff). Picasso and Braque developed Cubism (1906–8), the most widely influential of all modern movements. The *Blaue Reiter* group in Munich pushed further away from imitation (1912–14), and a purely abstract art soon emerged in the hands of Kandinsky and Klee. In Moscow in 1917 Malevich developed a totally abstract art which he called 'Suprematism'. By 1916 a nihilist reaction known as 'Dadaism' was already emerging in Zürich; it attacked all artistic values, but itself contributed to the ideas of the early Surrealists, who launched their first manifesto in Paris in 1924.

modern dance A theatre form of dance which began c.1910 and continues to evolve. It shares the revolutionary assumptions of all modern movements in the arts, rejecting the established form of dance and ballet. Greek myths, psychological states, political comment, reflections on the mechanization of life, and alienation of modern society have been common themes, demonstrating a serious modern consciousness. Isadora Duncan and Ruth Saint Denis are often credited with originating the modern movement in the first two decades of the 20th-c, the former in returning to natural movements, the latter in using exotic Oriental influences. Later, Martha Graham and Doris Humphrey emerged as major figures, each developing a particular way of moving and a distinctive repertoire. Merce Cunningham was one of the major innovators of modern dance, redefining its concept as an emphasis on form rather than content. The emphasis in modern dance lies in the expressiveness of the human body in showing emotional states, and this required a new vocabulary of movement using 'natural' actions such as walking, running, and breathing. The choreographer Rudolf Laban developed theories of movement which remain important, and a comprehensive notation system. In Germany in the 1970s–80s, Pina Bausch's dramatic theatrical works continued the modern, expressionist movement. Audio and visual technology have offered a new dimension. Since the 1960s there has been a massive expansion of small modern dance companies in Europe and North America.

Modernism A generic term referring to experimental methods in different art forms in the earlier part of the 20th-c. These experiments were stimulated by a sharpened sense of the arbitrariness of existing artistic conventions, and doubts about the human place and purpose in the world. Dada, Surrealism, and various anti-genres are all manifestations of Modernism. Notable works include Joyce's *Ulysses* (1922) and T S Eliot's *Waste Land* (1922); the plays of Pirandello, Brecht, and Ionesco; the Cubist paintings of Picasso and Braque; and the twelve-tone music of Webern and Schoenberg.

Modern Movement *Bauhaus; International Style* 2

modern pentathlon *pentathlon*

Modigliani, Amedeo [mohdeelyahnee] (1884–1920) Painter and sculptor of the modern school of Paris, born in Livorno, W Italy. His early work was influenced by the painters of the Italian Renaissance, and in Paris by Toulouse-Lautrec and the Fauves. In 1909, encouraged by the Rumanian sculptor Brancusi, he produced a number of elongated stone heads in African style. He continued to use this style when he resumed painting, with a series of richly coloured, elongated portraits. In 1918 in Paris he opened his first one-man show, which included some very frank nudes, and the exhibition was closed for indecency on the first day. His health was delicate, and his life was marred by poverty, drink, and drug addiction. It was only after his death that he obtained recognition, and the prices of his paintings soared.

Modigliani, Franco [mohdeelyahnee] (1918–2003) US economist, born in Rome, Italy. Having taken a law degree in Rome in 1939, he held professorships at a number of small institutions in the USA (1942–8), then at Illinois (1949–52), Carnegie-Mellon (1952–60), and Northwestern (1960–2) universities, and at Massachusetts Institute of Technology (from 1962). He was awarded the 1985 Nobel Prize for Economics for his work on two fundamental theories – personal saving and corporate finance.

Modigliani–Miller theory An economic theory developed by US economists Franco Modigliani and Merton H Miller in 1958, which broke new ground in business finance. Their thesis is that if two companies differ only in the way they are financed and in their total market value (ie the value of their shares on the stock market), then investors will sell shares in the over-valued company, and buy shares in the undervalued company until the market value for both is the same.

modulation (physics) The imposition of regular changes on some background, usually a beam of particles or radiation, and often as a means of conveying information via the beam. A broadcast signal is used to modulate the electron beam inside a television set to reproduce the picture. Certain crystals and liquids when subjected to electric fields may be used to modulate beams of light.

module A unit measure of proportion in architecture used to regulate all the parts of a building. In classical architecture, this meant the diameter of the column at the base of the shaft. The name derives from Latin *modulus*, 'measure'. Since World War 2, it is particularly used as the common unit of measure that co-ordinates the sizes of all the components in a standardized or 'modular' building, so that they may be fitted together with maximum ease and flexibility.

modulus of compression *bulk modulus*

modulus of elasticity *Young's modulus*

modulus of rigidity *shear modulus*

Moerae or **Moirai** [moyree, moyriy] In Greek mythology, the fates; a trio of goddesses, mentioned in Homer, who control human destiny and sometimes overrule the gods. In later writers, they are assigned names and functions: **Lachesis** [**lak**esis] ('the distributor'), who allots the destinies of human beings; **Clotho** [**kloh**thoh] ('the spinner'), who spins the thread of life; and **Atropos** [**a**tropos] ('the inflexible'), who cuts it. They may originally have been birth-goddesses.

Mogadishu [mogadishoo], Somali **Muqdisho**, Ital **Mogadiscio** 2°02N 45°21E, pop (2000e) 633 000. Seaport capital of Somalia, on the Indian Ocean coast; founded, 10th-c; taken by the Sultan of Zanzibar, 1871; sold to Italy, becoming capital of Italian Somaliland, 1905; occupied by British forces in World War 2; airport; university (1954); commerce, oil refining, uranium, food processing; fort, mosques (13th-c), cathedral (1928).

Mogadon *benzodiazepines*

Mogao or **Mo-kao Caves** [mogow] A complex of 496 Buddhist cave temples on the edge of the Takla Makan desert, Gansu, China; a world heritage site. The caves were sculptured in the 4th–14th-c, and are noted for their wall paintings, particularly those executed during the 6th–9th-c.

Mogollon [moguhyohn] A prehistoric culture of the American SW AD c.300–1350, artistically notable for its vigorous ceramics. Extending from S Arizona and New Mexico to the Chihuahuan and Sonoran deserts of Mexico, its villages of c.15–20 pithouses were typically sited for defence on mountain-tops until c.600, when there was a movement towards river valleys to facilitate more intensive maize agriculture. The Zuni of Arizona are their modern descendants.

Mogul *Mughal*

mohair *Angora goat*

Mohammed or **Mahomet** (Western forms of Arabic **Muhammad**) (c.570–c.632) Prophet of Islam, born in Mecca, the son of Abdallah, a poor merchant. Orphaned at six, he was cared for first by his grandfather, then by his uncle, and earned his living by tending sheep. At 25 he led the caravans of a rich widow, whom he later married. He continued as a merchant, but spent much of his time in solitary contemplation. When he was 40, the angel Gabriel appeared to him on Mt Hira, near Mecca, and commanded him in the name of God to preach the true religion. Four years later he was told to come forward publicly as a preacher. The basis of his teaching was the Qur'an, which had been revealed to him by God, and which he began dictating in 625. He attacked superstition, and exhorted people to a pious, moral life, and belief in an all-powerful, all-just, and merciful God, who had chosen him as his prophet. God's mercy was principally to be obtained by prayer, fasting, and almsgiving. At first dismissing him as a poet, the Meccans finally rose against him and his followers. He sought refuge at Medina in 622 (the date of the Mohammedan Era, the *Hijra* or *Hegira*), and assumed the position of highest judge and ruler of the city. He then engaged in war against the enemies of Islam. In 630 he took Mecca, where he was recognized as leader and prophet, and thus secured the new religion in Arabia. In 632 he undertook his last pilgrimage to Mecca, and there on Mt Arafat fixed the ceremonies of the pilgrimage (*Hajj*). He fell ill after his return, and died at the house of his favourite wife, Aïshah, the daughter of Abu-Bakr.

Mohammed II or **Mehmet II**, known as **the Conqueror** (1432–81) Sultan of Turkey (1451–81), and founder of the Ottoman empire, born in Adrianople. He took Constantinople in 1453, renaming it Istanbul, thus extinguishing the Byzantine empire and giving the Turks their commanding position on the Bosphorus. Checked by Janos Hunyady at Belgrade in 1456, he nevertheless annexed most of Serbia, all of Greece, and most of the Aegean Is. He threatened Venetian territory, was repelled from Rhodes by the Knights of St John (1480), and took Otranto (1480). He died in a campaign against Persia.

Mohammed Ahmed, known as **the Mahdi** (1844–85) African political and religious leader, born in Dongola, N Sudan. A student of religion from his youth, in 1881 he proclaimed his divine mission to purify Islam and the governments that defiled it. He became a relentless and successful rebel against Egyptian rule in E Sudan, becoming known as the Mahdi, or Muslim messiah (1882). He made El Obeid his capital in 1883, and annihilated an Egyptian army under **William Hicks** ('Hicks Pasha', 1830–83). In 1885 Khartoum was taken, and General Gordon killed.

Mohammed Ali or **Mehemet Ali** (c.1769–1849) Governor and later viceroy of Egypt (1805–49), born in Macedonia, the founder of the Egyptian royal family which reigned until the 1952 revolution. He was sent to Egypt in 1801 to join an Albanian force which was trying to expel the French. After the latters' departure he skilfully manoeuvred himself into supreme power. As viceroy he massacred the Mamluks (1811), and formed a regular army. In 1816 he reduced part of Arabia through the generalship of his eldest son **Ibrahim Pasha** (1789–1848), in 1820 he annexed Nubia, and his troops occupied Morea and Crete against the Greeks (1821–8). In 1831 Ibrahim began the conquest of Syria, and the victory at Nezib (1839) might have elevated his father to the throne of Constantinople. However, the intervention of four European powers (1840) in Constantinople demanding withdrawal, and a British naval landing in Acre, forced Ibrahim to return to Cairo and compelled Mohammad Ali to limit his ambitions to Egypt.

Mohawk [**moh**hawk] An Iroquoian-speaking, semi sedentary, North American Indian group, living around L Champlain. A member of the Iroquois League, they were defeated by US troops in 1777, and crossed into Canada, settling permanently in Ontario. They now work as farmers and migrant structural steel workers.

Mohenjo-daro [mohenjoh **da**roh] A prehistoric walled city on the R Indus, in Sind, Pakistan, c.320 km/200 mi NE of Karachi; a world heritage site. Occupied c.2300–1750 BC and excavated since 1922, it covered 100 ha/250 acres and held an ancient population of c.30–40 000. Its two mounds have buildings entirely of mudbrick. To the W, there is a citadel encircled by a 13 m/42 ft-high embankment containing civic, religious, and administrative buildings (notably the 3 m/10 ft-deep Great Bath for ritual bathing). To the E, there is a regularly planned lower city of two-storied houses for the bulk of the population.

Mohiniyattam A classical dance from Kerala, India that combines elements of Bharata Natyam and Kathakali with local folk dances. It is a secular, flowing, graceful dance performed by women dressed in white and gold costume.

Mohole [moh**hohl**] An attempt by US geologists and engineers to drill a borehole into the upper mantle beyond the Mohorovičić discontinuity. It was begun in the 1950s but abandoned in 1966 due to rising costs.

Moholy-Nagy, László [moh**hoy nodj**] (1895–1946) Artist and photographer, born in Bácsborsód, S Hungary. He studied law in Budapest, painted with Dada and Constructionist groups in Vienna and Berlin (1919–23), and produced his first 'photograms' (non-representational photographic images made directly without a camera) in 1923. He joined the Bauhaus under Walter Gropius in 1925. He was quickly recognized as a leading avant-garde artist in the New Photographers movement in Europe (1925–35), his work including film-making and typography integrated with photographic illustration. He was invited to the USA in 1937 to head the New Bauhaus school in Chicago, later the Institute of Design. Here he taught photography, becoming a US citizen shortly before his death.

Mohorovičić discontinuity [moh**hor**oh**vichich**] (or **Moho**) The zone separating the Earth's crust from the mantle, characterized by an abrupt change in density and the speeds of seismic waves travelling through them. It lies at c.6 km/3·5 mi below the ocean floor but up to 70 km/45 mi below the surface of the continents. It is named after its discoverer, Croatian geophysicist Andrija Mohorovičić (1857–1936) who identified it from earthquake shock-wave data in 1909.

Mohs scale *hardness*

Moi, Daniel Arap [moy] (1924–) Kenyan politician and president (1978–), born in the Rift Valley Province, Kenya. He was educated at mission schools, then worked as a teacher (1949–57). In 1957 he was elected to the Legislative Council as a member of the Kenya African Democratic Union. He served as a minister from 1961, and became vice-president under Kenyatta in 1967. When Kenyatta died in 1978, few people expected him to be capable of surviving under that enormous shadow, but, adopting the motto *nyayo* (footsteps to freedom), he gradually asserted his authority. He purged the army, launched a development plan, and in 1982 made the Kenyan African National Union the only legally permitted party. Despite his increasingly firm style of government, he was re-elected in 1983 and 1988. In late 1992 he held multi-party elections, which he won, though they were followed by some accusations of ballot-rigging.

Mojave or **Mohave Desert** [moh**hah**vee] Desert in S California, USA, part of the Great Basin; a series of flat basins with interior drainage separated by low, bare ranges; area c.65 000 sq km/25 000 sq mi; annual rainfall c.120 mm/4·7 in; agriculture only where artesian water occurs; the Mojave R flows mainly underground into the Mojave sink.

molasses A brownish syrup, obtained as a by-product of the sugar-beet or sugar-cane industry; it is what remains once the sugar has been refined. It is widely used as an animal feed supplement, especially for dairy cows, and in the production of rum and treacle.

Mold, Welsh **Yr Wyddgrug** 53°10N 3°08W, pop (2000e) 9500. Administrative centre of Flintshire, NE Wales, UK; on the R Alyn, 18 km/11 mi WSW of Chester; railway; agricultural trade, light industry; Theatre Clwyd.

Moldavia and Wallachia [mol**day**via, wo**lay**kia] Two independent Balkan principalities formed in the 14th-c: Moldavia lies in NE Romania, SW of the R Prut; Wallachia lies in S Romania, S of the Transylvanian Alps. In the 16th-c they were incorporated into the Ottoman Empire, but the Russo–Turkish wars during the 18th–19th-c weakened Turkish control of the Balkans, and the two states gained autonomy under a Russian protectorate by the Treaty of Adrianople (1829). In 1862 Moldavia and Wallachia merged to form the unitary Principality of Romania; Moldavia became a Soviet Socialist Republic in 1940, but gained independence after the collapse of the USSR in 1991.

Moldova *p.1021*

mole (medicine) Usually a small flat congenital lesion in the skin resulting from the proliferation of small blood vessels and containing scattered pigment cells (*birthmarks*). Occasionally these are more extensive, and form raised patches (*plaques*) which may necessitate surgical removal or other treatment.

mole (physics) Base SI unit of amount of substance; symbol *mol*; defined as the amount of substance of a system which contains as many elementary entities as there are atoms in 0·012 kg of carbon-12.

mole (zoology) A mammal native to lowlands in Europe, Asia, and North America; an insectivore; dark with minute eyes, short tail; enlarged forelimbs used for digging; most moles feed in their burrows; **star-nosed mole** catches food in water; **shrew moles** feed above ground. (Family: Talpidae, 27 species.)

mole cricket A burrowing, grasshopper-like insect; body large, to 48 mm/2 in, and heavily armoured; forelegs powerful, spade-like, used for digging; digs galleries underground; feeds on insects, seedlings and tubers; c.50 species, all of which produce sound by vibration (*stridulation*). (Order: Orthoptera. Family: Gryllotalpidae.)

molecular beam epitaxy A method of producing thin crystal films, in which the film composition can be carefully controlled. It relies on a number of heated sources, each of a different element, from which beams of atoms pass through an evacuated chamber and strike a crystalline target. The precise composition of the atomic layers built up on the crystal is controlled by source temperatures and systems of shutters. The method is used to produce novel semiconductor devices, such as in integrated optics and quantum Hall effect research.

molecular biology The study of the structure and function of the large organic molecules associated with living organisms, especially the nucleic acids (DNA and RNA) and proteins.

molecular cloud An interstellar nebula, unusually rich in molecules (as opposed to atoms), detected from microwave radiation. The Galactic centre and Orion Nebula have very rich clouds of this sort.

molecular weight The mass of a mole of a substance, based on a mole of ^{12}C having a mass of 12 units; more accurately called the **relative molecular mass**. It is calculated in practice by summing the relative atomic masses of the atoms making up the formula of the substance.

molecule A finite group of two or more atoms, which is the smallest unit of a substance having the properties of that substance. Molecular compounds include water, most organic compounds, globular proteins, and viruses. Non-molecular compounds include metals, ionic compounds, and diamond.

mole rat A mouse-like rodent of family Muridae (16 species); three subfamilies: the **blind mole rat** from the Middle East and surrounding area (Spalacinae); the **E Asian** or **C Asiatic mole rat**, or **zokor** (Myospalacinae); and the **African mole rat** (Tachyoryctinae). The name is also used for the cavy-like rodent of family Bathyergidae (8 species), the **African mole rat** or **blesmol**.

mole viper *asp*

Molière [mol**yair**], pseudonym of **Jean Baptiste Poquelin** (1622–73) Playwright, born in Paris, France. He studied with the Jesuits at the Collège de Clermont. In 1643 he embarked on a theatrical venture under the title of L'Illustre Théâtre, which lasted for over three years in Paris. The company then proceeded to the provinces, and had sufficient success to keep going from 1646 to 1658, obtaining the patronage of Philippe d'Orléans. In 1658 he played before the king, and organized a regular theatre. From the publication of *Les Précieuses ridicules* (1659, trans

Moldova

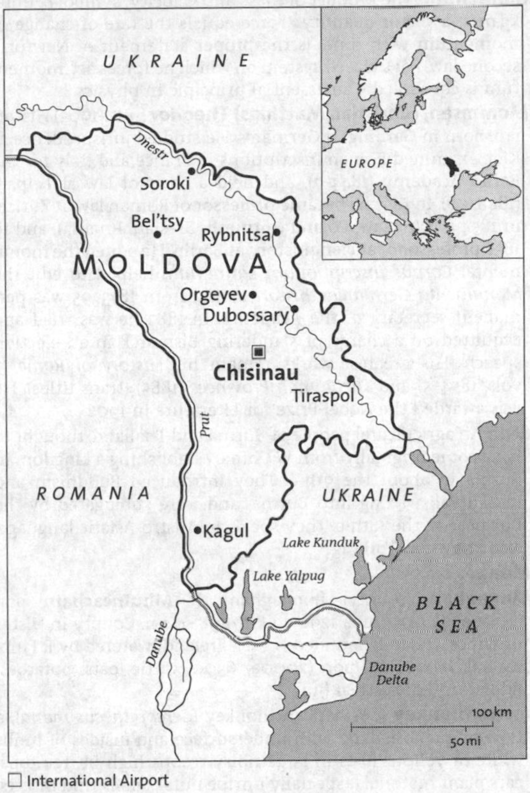

[moldohva], official name **Republic of Moldova**, formerly (to 1990) **Moldavian SSR**, Russ **Moldavskaya**

Local name Moldova

Timezone GMT +2

Area 33 700 km²/13 008 sq mi

Population total (2002e) 4 231 000

Status Republic

Date of independence 1991

Capital Chisinau (Kishinev)

Languages Moldovan (official), Ukrainian also spoken

Ethnic groups Moldovan (64%), Ukrainian (14%), Russian (13%), Gagauzi (4%), Jewish (2%)

Religions Christian (mainly Russian Orthodox, also Baptist and Roman Catholic)

Physical features Landlocked area consisting of hilly plains, average elevation of 147 m/482 ft, cut by river valleys, ravines, and gullies; uplands in C, Kodry Hills, reach highest point, Mt Balaneshty, 429 m/1409 ft; chief rivers, the Dnestr and Prut; level plain of Bel'tsy Steppe and uplands (N); eroded Medobory-Toltry limestone ridges border R Prut (N).

Climate Warm, moderately continental; long dry periods in S; average annual temperatures -5°C (N), -3°C (S) (Jan), 20°C (N), 23°C (S) (Jul); average annual rainfall 450–550 mm/18–22 in.

Currency 1 Moldovan leu = 100 bani

Economy Main exports include wine, tobacco, food-canning, machinery, electrical engineering, knitwear, textiles, fruit.

GDP (2002e) $11·51 bn, per capita $2600

Human Development Index (2002) 0·701

History Formerly part of Romania (the region known as Bessarabia); W part remained in Romania, Bessarabia in E became the Moldavian Soviet Socialist Republic in 1940; occupied by Romania, who allied with Germany in World War 2; recaptured by USSR, 1944; Moldavian language granted official status, 1989, leading to tension between ethnic Russians and Moldovans; declaration of independence, 1991, joined Commonwealth of Independent States; tension due to separatist pressure from Gagauz and Dnestr Russian minorities, 1990–1; new constitution, 1994; governed by a President, Prime Minister and Supreme Soviet.

Head of State
1991–6 Mircea Snegur
1996–2001 Petru Lucinschi
2001– Vladimir Voronin

Head of Government
1991–2 Valeriu Muravschi
1992–7 Andrei Sangeli
1997–9 Ion Cebuc
1999 Ion Sturza
1999–2001 Dumitru Barghis
2001– Vasile Tarlev

The Affected Young Ladies), no year passed without at least one major dramatic achievement, such as *L'Ecole des femmes* (1622, The School for Wives), *Tartuffe* (1664), *Le Misanthrope* (1666, The Misanthropist), and *Le Bourgeois Gentilhomme* (1670). He died after acting in a performance of his last play, *Le Malade imaginaire* (1673, The Imaginary Invalid). Widely recognized as one of the greatest French dramatists, many of his plays have also been translated for performances in English theatres, giving him a considerable reputation abroad.

Molina, Luis de [mohleena] (1535–1600) Jesuit theologian, born in Cuenca, EC Spain. He studied at Coimbra, and was professor of theology at Evora (1568–83). His principal writings include the celebrated treatise on grace and free will *Concordia liberi arbitrii cum gratiae donis* (1588, The Harmony of Free Will with Gifts of Grace). He asserts that predestination to eternal happiness or punishment is consequent on God's foreknowledge of the free determination of human will. This view (*Molinism*) was attacked as a revival of Pelagianism, causing the dispute between Molinists and Thomists. A papal decree in 1607 permitted both opinions.

mollusc [moluhsk] An unsegmented invertebrate animal, typically with an underside muscular foot and a mantle above, covered by calcareous scales or a solid calcareous shell. A posterior cavity contains gills (*ctenidia*) for respiration. Most have a well-developed head, with eyes and a rasping jaw apparatus (*radula*). Visceral organs are typically protected by a shell secreted by the mantle. Most are free-living in aquatic or damp terrestrial habitats; some are parasitic. There are c.80 000 species. (Phylum: Mollusca.)

molly Small, colourful, freshwater fish (*Poecilia sphenops*) found in rivers and lakes of Central America; length up to 12 cm/4¾ in; greenish-brown above, rows of orange spots along sides, dorsal fin with orange and black markings; popular amongst aquarists; many varieties produced through captive breeding. (Family: Poeciliidae.)

Molly Maguires A secret organization of (primarily Irish) miners, involved in industrial disputes in Pennsylvania during the 1870s. The prosecution of their leaders led to hangings and imprisonments, which crushed the group.

Molnár, Ferenc [mohlnah(r), ferents] (1878–1952) Novelist and playwright, born in Budapest, Hungary. He trained as a lawyer, but became a journalist and war correspondent. He had considerable success with his short stories, but is best known for his novel *The Paul Street Boys* (1907), and his plays *The Devil* (1907), *Liliom* (1909), and *The Good Fairy* (1930), all of which have achieved success in English translation.

Moloch [mohlok] In the Bible, a god of the Canaanites and other peoples, in whose cult children were sacrificed by fire. He is a rebel angel in Milton's *Paradise Lost*. The name is used for any excessive and cruel religion.

moloch [mohlok] An agamid lizard (*Moloch horridus*) native to W Australia; entire body covered with large thorn-like spines; spiky tail shorter than head and body; inhabits deserts; eats ants; also known as **thorny devil** or **horny devil**.

Molokai [molokiy] area 670 sq km/260 sq mi. Island of the US state of Hawaii, in Maui Co; Kalaupapa leper settlement (pop 130) on the N coast; cattle.

Molotov, Vyacheslav Mikhailovich [molotof] (from Rus *molot*, 'hammer'), originally **Vyacheslav Mikhailovich Skriabin** (1890–1986) Russian statesman and prime minister (1930–41), born in Kukaida, Russia. An international figure from 1939, when he became foreign minister (1939–49, 1953–6), he was Stalin's chief adviser at Teheran and Yalta, and was present at the founding of the UN (1945). After World War 2, he emerged as the uncompromising champion of world Sovietism; his *nyet* ('no') at meetings of the UN became a byword, and fostered the Cold War. He resigned in 1956, and was demoted by Krushchev. He was expelled from the Communist party's Presidium and sent into virtual exile as ambassador to Outer Mongolia. In the 1960s he retired to his home near Moscow. His name is preserved in **Molotov cocktail** – a bottle of inflammable liquid used as a weapon – which he put into production during World War 2.

Moltke, Helmuth (Karl Bernhard), Graf von (Count of) [moltkuh] (1800–91) Field marshal, born in Parchim, N Germany (formerly Prussia). He entered Prussian service in 1822, and became chief of the general staff in Berlin (1858–88). His reorganization of the Prussian army led to success in the wars with Denmark (1863–4), Austria (1866), and France (1870–1).

Moluccas [moluhkas], Indonesian **Maluku**, or **Spice Islands** pop (2000e) 2 182 000; area 74 505 sq km/28 759 sq mi. Island group and province of Indonesia, lying between Sulawesi (W) and New Guinea (E); includes c.1000 islands, notably Halmahera, Seram, Buru; mostly volcanic and mountainous; visited by the Portuguese, 1512; under Dutch rule, early 17th-c; secession movement in the S Moluccas followed Indonesian independence (1949), still continuing in The Netherlands; capital, Ambon; copra, spices, sago, coconut oil, tuna.

molybdenum [molibdenum] Mo, element 42, density 10·2 g/cm^3, melting point 2610°C. A grey metal, occurring most commonly as the disulphide, MoS_2; it is roasted in air to give MoO_3, which is then reduced with hydrogen. It is an ingredient of several steel alloys, and MoS_2 is important as a high temperature lubricant.

Molyneux, Edward (Henry) [molinyoo] (1891–1974) Fashion designer, born in London, UK. After studying art, he worked for Lucile in London and abroad. After service as a captain in the British army in World War 1, in which he lost an eye, he opened his own couture house in Paris in 1919, with branches in London, Monte Carlo, Cannes, and Biarritz. He became famous for the elegant simplicity of his tailored suits with pleated skirts, and for his evening wear.

Mombasa [mombasa] 4°04S 39°40E, pop (2000e) 697 000. Seaport in Coast province, SE Kenya; Kenya's main port; on Mombasa I, connected to mainland by Mukapa causeway; Kilindini harbour; capital of British East Africa Protectorate, 1888–1907; used as a British naval base in World War 2; airport; railway terminus; car assembly, oil refining, tourism; Fort Jesus (1593), now a museum.

moment In physics, a general term referring to a system's ability to rotate under the application of an external force. The moment of force in mechanics is called *torque*.

moment of force *torque*

moment of inertia In mechanics, the notion that, for a rotating object, the turning force required to make the object turn faster depends on how the object's mass is distributed about the axis of rotation; symbol *I*, units kg.m^2. For example, the force needed to spin a disc more quickly about its centre will be greater if the disc's mass is concentrated towards its rim. For a uniform disc of radius *r* and mass *m* spinning horizontally about its centre, $I = mr^2/2$.

momentum The product of mass and velocity; symbol *p*, units kg.m/s; a vector quantity. 'Force equals the rate of change of momentum with time' is the proper statement of Newton's second law. For a closed system on which no forces act, momentum is conserved – an essential principle in physics.

Mommsen, (Christian Matthias) Theodor (1817–1903) Historian, born in Garding, N Germany. He studied jurisprudence at Kiel, examined Roman inscriptions in France and Italy for the Berlin Academy (1844–7), and held a chair of law at Leipzig (1848–50). In 1852 he became professor of Roman law at Zürich, in 1854 at Wrocław, Poland (formerly Breslau, Prussia), and in 1858 professor of ancient history at Berlin. He edited the monumental *Corpus inscriptionum Latinarum*, helped to edit the *Monumenta Germaniae historica*, and from 1873–95 was permanent secretary of the Academy. In 1882 he was tried and acquitted on a charge of slandering Bismarck in an election speech. His greatest works remain his *History of Rome* (3 vols, 1854–5) and *The Roman Provinces* (1885) (trans titles). He was awarded the Nobel Prize for Literature in 1902.

Mon An agricultural people of Burma and Thailand, thought to have come originally from W China, establishing a kingdom in Burma in about the 9th-c. They introduced Buddhism and Indian Pali writing into Burma, and were subjugated by the Burmese in the 18th-c. They speak an Austro-Asiatic language, also known as **Tailang**.

Monaco *p.1023*

Monaghan (county) [monaghan], Ir **Mhuineachain** pop (2000e) 52 000; area 1290 sq km/498 sq mi. County in Ulster province, Ireland; bounded N by N Ireland; watered by R Finn; capital, Monaghan pop (2000e) 6300; cattle, oats, potatoes; fiddler of Orie festival (Jul).

mona monkey A W African monkey (*Cercopithecus mona*), a type of guenon; dark, with undersurface and insides of limbs white or yellow; lives in large noisy troops high in tree tops; eats plant material (especially unripe nuts), snails, and insects.

monarch butterfly A large, colourful butterfly; wings brownish orange, marked with black patterns; slow fliers, migrating over great distances, from Mexico to Canada. (Order: Lepidoptera. Family: Nymphalidae.)

monarchy A political system in which a single person is a political ruler, whose position normally rests on the basis of divine authority, backed by tradition. The position is usually hereditary, passing through the male line. In Europe, the democratic revolutions of the 18th–20th-c saw an end to what was until then the most widely known form of government. A number of countries, however, maintained the position of monarch, establishing **constitutional monarchies**, where the sovereign acts on the advice of government ministers who govern on his or her behalf. The monarchy's political power is thus largely formal and its role largely ceremonial, but its influence may increase in times of political crisis or when there is a vacuum in parliamentary politics.

monasticism A form of religious life found in both Christianity (mostly in Roman Catholic and Orthodox circles) and Buddhism, emphasizing the perfection of the individual either through a solitary ascetic existence or more often through life in a consecrated community. Members of such communities are known as **monks**. In Christianity the movement is often traced back to Antony and Pachomius of Egypt (late 3rd-c). Although initially a lay movement, it soon became dominated by clergy, often marked by voluntary poverty and a life of devotion and worship. The most significant early monastic legislation was the rule of Benedict (480–543), which became a standard in Western Christianity. In the Middle Ages, monks were increasingly involved in scholarly research and copying manuscripts. In the 13th-c several new orders emerged, known as *friars* or *mendicant orders*, which combined monastic life with missionary preaching to those outside. Periods of decline and reform followed from the 14th-c to the 16th-c.

Monaco

[monakoh], official name **Principality of Monaco**
Local name Monaco (*see map, p.584*)
Timezone GMT +1
Area 1·95 km^2/0·75 sq mi
Population total (2002e) 32 000
Status Principality
Capital Monaco-Ville
Languages French (official), English, Italian, and Monegasque also spoken
Ethnic groups French (58%), Italian (16%), Monegasque (16%)
Religion Roman Catholic (95%)
Physical features Located on Mediterranean Riviera, close to the Italian frontier with France; surrounded landward by the French department of Alpes-Maritimes; steep and rugged landscape; area available for commercial development has been extended by land reclaimed from sea.
Climate Mediterranean; warm, dry summers, mild, wet winters; average annual temperatures 10°C (Jan), 23°C (Jul); average annual rainfall 758 mm/30 in.
Currency 1 euro = 100 cents (previous to February 2002, 1 French Franc (Fr) = 100 centimes).
Economy Tourism; chemicals, printing, textiles, plastics.
GDP (1999e) $870 mn, per capita $2700
History Under the protection of France since the 17th-c, apart from a period under Sardinia, 1815–61; 1911 constitution ended power of the Prince as an absolute ruler; constitution of 1911 suspended in 1959; new constitution adopted, 1962; governed by a Prince as Head of State, a Minister of State, heading a Council of Government, and a National Council.
Head of State (Prince)
1949– Rainier III
Head of Government (Minister of State)
1991–4 Jacques Dupont
1994–7 Paul Dijoud
1997–2000 Michel Lévêque
2000– Patrick Leclerq

monazite [monaziyt] A phosphate mineral containing rare-earth metals (*lanthanides*) such as lanthanum, cerium, yttrium, and thorium, and important as the major source of these metals. It occurs in granitic rocks and placer deposits.

Monck, George *Monk, George*

Mond, Ludwig (1839–1909) Chemist and industrialist, born in Kassel, C Germany. Settling in England in 1864, he perfected at Widnes a sulphur recovery process. He founded in 1873, with John Tomlinson Brunner, a great alkali-works at Winnington, Cheshire, and made discoveries in nickel manufacture. In 1896 he gave to the Royal Institution for the nation a physico-chemical laboratory costing £100 000.

Mondale, Walter F(rederick) (1928–) US politician and vice-president (1977–81), born in Ceylon, Minnesota, USA. He studied at the University of Minnesota Law School, and made his reputation as a local Democrat in his home state, before serving in the US Senate (1964–76). He was selected as Jimmy Carter's running-mate in the 1976 presidential election, and served as an active vice-president, but was defeated with Carter in their bid for re-election in 1980. In 1984 he was the Democratic presidential nominee, but was crushingly defeated by the Republican, Ronald Reagan. Following this reverse, Mondale retired from national politics to resume his law practice, then was appointed US ambassador to Japan (1993–97) by President Clinton. He was narrowly defeated for a seat in the Senate in the mid-term elections in 2002.

Mondrian, Piet [mondrian], originally **Pieter Cornelis Mondriaan** (1872–1944) Artist, born in Amersfoort, The Netherlands. One of the founders of the *De Stijl* movement, he began by painting landscapes in a traditional sombre Dutch manner, but after moving to Paris in 1909 he came under the influence of Matisse and Cubism. He then began painting still-lifes, becoming increasingly abstract. During World War 1 he concentrated on rectilinear compositions which depend for their beauty on the simple relationships between the coloured areas. His work has been a major influence on all purely abstract painters, and he is considered the leader of Neoplasticism.

Monet, Claude [monay] (1840–1926) Painter, born in Paris, France. He spent his youth in Le Havre, where he met Boudin, who encouraged him to work in the open air. Moving to Paris, he associated with Renoir, Pissarro, and Sisley, and exhibited with them at the first Impressionist Exhibition in 1874; one of his works at this exhibition, 'Impression: soleil levant' (Impression: Sunrise, 1872, Paris), gave the name to the movement. Later he worked much in Argenteuil. With Pissarro, Monet is recognized as being one of the creators of Impressionism, and he was one of its most consistent exponents. He visited England, The Netherlands, and Venice, and spent his life expressing his instinctive way of seeing the most subtle nuances of colour, atmosphere, and light in landscape. Apart from many sea and river scenes, he also executed several series of paintings of subjects under different aspects of light, such as 'Haystacks' (1890–1, Chicago) and the almost abstract 'Water Lilies' (the Orangerie, Paris).

monetarism An economic policy based on the control of a country's money supply. It assumes that the quantity of money in an economy determines its economic activity, and particularly its rate of inflation. If the money supply is allowed to rise too quickly, prices will rise, resulting in inflation. To curb inflationary pressures, governments therefore need to reduce the supply of money and raise interest rates. This view was a major influence on British and US economic policy in the 1980s.

Monetary Compensation Amount *green pound*

money A generally acceptable and convenient medium of exchange, in order to avoid the problems of barter; also a representation of value and a means of storing value. It is usually in the form of coins or notes, but it can be any generally accepted object. Originally coins of gold or silver had an intrinsic value of their own; today, the intrinsic value of coins is virtually nothing. Until the 1920s, money was backed by gold (the *gold standard*): a pound note or dollar bill could be exchanged for a given amount of gold (hence such words on banknotes as 'promise to pay') and the amount of money issued by banks was related to the amount of gold held. The first bank notes issued in Europe were by the Bank of Stockholm in 1661. Money is now increasingly not in tangible form, but consists of balances in accounts at banks, exchange being by means of cheques, credit-cards or charge-cards, and by *credit-transfer*, where one account is reduced (debited) and another increased (credited) by the same amount electronically. Modern systems are reducing the dependence on cash, hence the emergence of the phrase, the 'cashless society'. Many definitions of money are in use. In the UK, for example, the narrow definition, M0, refers to the stock of notes and coins in circulation, banks' till money, and bankers' balances at the Bank of England. Also in use are M1, M2, M3, and other measures, each containing additional items.

money market In economic terms, the supply of and demand for money. In a free market, the increasing demand for money leads to pressure to raise interest rates. If the monetary authorities then raise these rates (in the UK through the Bank of England; in the USA, through the Federal Reserve Bank), the demand falls. The term also refers to the place where money is traded – banks, discount houses, and foreign exchange dealers (*money brokers*).

money-market funding An economic system created in the 1970s in the USA when interest rates were rising. Interest-rate ceilings were placed on Savings and Loan Associations (US building societies), who were thus unable to offer depositors competitive interest rates. Money-market institutions would

Mongolia

☐ International Airport

Mongolian **Mongol Uls**, formerly **Mongolian People's Republic** (1924–92)

Local name Mongol Uls

Timezone GMT +7 (W), +8 (C), +9 (E)

Area 1 566 500 km²/604 800 sq mi

Population total (2002e) 2 457 000

Status State

Date of independence 1911

Capital Ulaanbaatar

Languages Khalka (official), Russian and Chinese spoken by respective minorities

Ethnic groups Mongol (Khalka, Dorbed, Buryat, Dariganga) (90%), Kazakh (4%), Russian (2%), other (4%)

Religions Formerly Tibetan Buddhist (now only a single monastery remains in UlaanBaator); unreliable data on current situation as a result of religious suppression in 20th-c.

Physical features Landlocked mountainous country; highest point, Tavan-Bogdo-Uli, 4373 m/14 347 ft; high ground mainly in W, with mountains lying NW–SE to form Mongolian Altai chain; lower SE area runs into the Gobi Desert; lowland plains; mainly arid grasslands.

Climate Extreme continental climate, with hard and long-lasting frosts in winter; arid desert conditions prevail in the S; average annual temperatures -26°C (Jan), 16°C (Jul); average annual rainfall 208 mm/18·2 in.

Currency 1 Tugrik (Tug) = 100 möngö

Economy Traditionally a pastoral nomadic economy; series of 5-year plans aiming for an agricultural-industrial economy; 70% of agricultural production derived from cattle raising; foodstuffs, animal products; coal, gold, uranium, lead.

GDP (2002e) $5·06 bn, per capita $1900

Human Development Index (2002) 0·655

History Originally the homeland of nomadic tribes, which united under Genghis Khan in the 13th-c to become part of the great Mongol Empire; assimilated into China, and divided into Inner and Outer Mongolia; Outer Mongolia declared itself an independent monarchy, 1911; changed name to Mongolian People's Republic, 1924, not recognized by China until 1946; governed by a Great People's Khural (parliament), a Council of Ministers, and a Presidium; chairman of Presidium is Head of State; changed name to State of Mongolia, 1992, and new constitution established.

Head of State
1990–7 Punsalmaagiyn Ochirbat
1997– Natsagiyn Bagabandi

Head of Government
1992–6 Puntsagiyn Jasray
1996–8 Mendsayhany Enhsayhan
1998 Tsakhiagiin Elbegdorj
1998–9 Janlaviyn Narantsatsralt
1999 Nyam-Osoriyn Tuyaa (*acting*)
1999–2000 Rinchinnyamiyn Amarjargal
2000– Nambariin Enkhbayar

take the deposits and invest them in short-term bonds, such as treasury bills. The system also offered limited banking facilities to investors as well as high interest rates.

money spider A small, dark-coloured spider that constructs a sheet-like web on vegetation; adults hang on underside of web and run out to catch prey; very abundant in N hemisphere; can travel long distances attached to silk threads blown by the wind. The name is derived from the folk belief that a spider on one's clothes was a sign of good luck or money coming. (Order: Araneae. Family: Liniphiidae.)

money supply The amount of money in circulation in an economy. The notion plays an important role in economic theory. Money is used in all transactions, and forms a major part of the wealth of individuals and firms. Monetarists believe that changes in the money supply are important signals of use in economic forecasting, and that the control of the money supply is vital to economic policy. This theory is difficult to apply in practical macroeconomics, as there are several definitions of the money supply in any one country, and modern firms may also hold large balances in foreign currencies.

Monge, Gaspard, comte de (Count of) **Péluse** [mõzh] (1746–1818) Mathematician, physicist, and founder of descriptive geometry, born in Beaune, E France. He was professor of mathematics at Mézières (1768), and professor of hydraulics at the Lycée in Paris (1780). He helped to found the Ecole Polytechnique (1794), and became professor of mathematics there. The following year there appeared his *Leçons de géométrie descriptive*, in which he stated his principles regarding the general application of geometry to the arts of construction (descriptive geometry). During the Revolution he was minister for the navy, and in charge of the national manufacture of arms and gunpowder. He was made a senator (1805), but lost his honours at the Restoration, and died in poverty.

Mongo A cluster of Bantu-speaking peoples of forested regions of C Democratic Republic of Congo, organized into many small chiefdoms. They live by farming, hunting, and gathering, and have a rich oral and music tradition.

Mongol *Altaic*

Mongolia *see panel*

Mongolian wild horse *Przewalski's horse*

mongolism *Down's syndrome*

Mongoloid *race*

Mongols Mongolian and S Siberian tribes who created the largest empire in ancient history (including C Asia, China, Korea, Russia, and Persia), of key importance in the process of cultural diffusion. It probably facilitated movement to Europe of Chinese printing, porcelain, explosives, and other technology, and the importation of new plants to China. Expansion began c.1200 under Genghis Khan, and culminated under Kublai Khan, by the end of the century. The core of Mongol power was the 130 000-strong army, known for its rapid movement, tactical skill, and horsemanship. The empire was linked by roads and couriers, and there was a written language based on Uighur, and a written legal code. There survives a 13th-c eye-witness account of the court's splendours. Lacking political organization, dominated by an alien militarism, and without formalized dynastic succession, the empire disintegrated in the 14th-c. About 3 million Mongols now live in Chinese Inner Mongolia, and about 2 million in Mongolia proper.

Mongo-Ma-Loba *Cameroon, Mount*

mongoose A carnivorous mammal, native to S and SE Asia and Africa (introduced elsewhere); adept at killing snakes and rats, and often introduced to areas for this purpose (usually disastrously, as they also eat other mammals, birds, and birds' eggs). (Family: Viverridae, 36 species.)

monism In philosophy, the metaphysical doctrine either that only one substantial thing really exists in the universe, as in the systems of Parmenides, Spinoza, and Hegel, and thus opposed to pluralism; or that there is only one *kind* of thing, as in materialism (matter) and idealism (mind).

monitor (navy) A floating gun platform, lying low above the waterline, moving at slow speed. It achieved relatively high firepower while offering a small target silhouette. Used mainly for coastal bombardment, modern weapons have made it obsolete. The name derives from the USS *Monitor*, built by the Unionists in the American Civil War (1861–5), which fought a famous but inconclusive action against CSS *Virginia* (previouly *Merrimac*); both were ironclads. *Monitor*, capable of only 4 knots, and unseaworthy, eventually foundered off Cape Hatteras 9 months after the initial action.

monitorial system A concept of early 19th-c British education, developed by British educationists Andrew Bell (1753–1832) and Joseph Lancaster (1778–1838), to train young school leavers to act as teachers' assistants or 'monitors'. It involved only a few hours' training.

monitor lizard A lizard native to Africa, S and SE Asia, and Australia; long pointed head and long neck; long tail which cannot voluntarily be shed; long claws; long forked tongue; teeth narrow with sharp cutting edges. (Genus: *Varanus*, 31 species. Family: Varanidae.)

Moniz, António Egas *Egas Moniz, António*

Monk or **Monck, George, 1st Duke of Albemarle** (1608–70) General, born in Great Potheridge, Devon, SW England, UK. He fought in the Low Countries, and with the Royalists in Scotland, then joined the Commonwealth cause and served successfully in Ireland, Scotland, and in the first Dutch War (1652–4). He feared a return to Civil War during and after Richard Cromwell's regime (1658–9), and was instrumental (as commander of the army in Scotland) in bringing about the restoration of Charles II, for which he was created Duke of Albemarle.

Monk, Thelonious (Sphere) (1917–82) Jazz pianist and composer, born in Rocky Mount, North Carolina, USA. He worked as a freelance musician, and studied briefly at the Juilliard School, New York City. He worked under a succession of leaders in New York City (1939–45), and first recorded while playing with the Coleman Hawkins Sextet in 1944. He formed his own small group in 1947, and from that time performed chiefly with small groups. Although once called the 'High Priest of Bebop', and credited with helping to create the jazz style of the 1940s, his angular, idiosyncratic melodies stood apart from the main currents of the day, and some of his audiences never quite caught up with him. His most memorable compositions include 'Round Midnight' (1947) and 'Criss Cross' (1951).

monk *monasticism*

monkey A primate of the group Anthropoidea; two subgroups: the **Platyrrhine** or **flat-nosed monkeys** from the New World (includes New World monkeys and marmosets), and the **Catarrhine** or **downward-nosed monkeys** from the Old World.

monkey bread *baobab*

monkey nut *peanut*

monkey-puzzle An evergreen conifer (*Araucaria araucana*) native to Chile and Argentina; branches in open whorls, covered with hard, sharp-pointed, triangular, overlapping leaves; also known as **Chile pine**. It is often planted in parks and gardens as a curiosity. (Family: Araucariaceae.)

Monkey Trial *Scopes Trial*

monkfish Largest of the angelsharks (*Squatina squatina*) common in the E North Atlantic and Mediterranean; length up to 1·8 m/6 ft; body shape intermediate between sharks and rays; head flattened, mouth anterior, gill openings lateral, pectoral fins very broad, tail slender; also called **angelfish**. (Family: Squatinidae.)

monkshood A perennial (*Aconitum napellus*) with blackish, tuberous roots, native to Europe and NW Asia; leaves deeply-divided; flowers mauve, with a cowl-shaped helmet or hood; also called **aconite**. It is used as a narcotic and painkiller, but is highly poisonous because of the presence of alkaloids, including aconitin. (Family: Ranunculaceae.)

Monmouth, James Scott, Duke of (1649–85) Illegitimate son of Charles II of England by Lucy, daughter of Richard Walters of Haverfordwest, born in Rotterdam, The Netherlands. He was created Duke of Monmouth in 1663, and became captain-general in 1670. He had substantial popular support, and as a Protestant became a focus of opposition to James II. After the discovery of the Rye House Plot (1683), he fled to the Low Countries. In 1685 he landed at Lyme Regis, and asserted his right to the crown. He was defeated at the Battle of Sedgemoor, captured, and beheaded in the Tower of London.

Monmouth, Battle of (1778) An engagement in New Jersey between British and American troops during the US War of Independence. It was notable for Washington's suspension of General Charles Lee (1731–82) from command, and for the discipline of American troops under fire.

Monmouthshire [monmuhthsheer], Welsh **Sir Fynwy** pop (2001e) 84 900; area 851 sq km/328 sq mi. County (unitary authority from 1996) in SE Wales, UK; drained by R Wye and R Usk; Brecon Beacons in NW; administrative centre, Cwmbran; other chief towns, Abergavenny, Monmouth, Chepstow; agriculture; tourism, especially in Wye Valley; castles at Abergavenny, Caldicott, Chepstow, Monmouth, Raglan, Usk; Tintern Abbey (12th-c).

Monnet, Jean [monay] (1888–1979) French statesman, born in Cognac, W France. He was educated locally, and in 1914 entered the Ministry of Commerce. A distinguished economist and expert in financial affairs, he became in 1947 commissioner-general of the 'Plan de modernisation et d'équipement de la France' (the **Monnet plan**) that advocated the restoration of a strong French economy by means of centralized planning. Monnet was an internationalist and campaigned for European integration, working out the details of the Schuman Plan. He became president of the European Coal and Steel High Authority (1952–5), and in 1956 was president of the Action Committee for the United States of Europe. His influence on European unification was immense.

Monoceros [monoseros] (Gr 'unicorn') A N constellation in the Milky Way, next to Orion, containing several clusters and nebulae.

monoclonal antibody [monohklohnal antibodee] A pure antibody produced in bulk by artificial means, used in medicine for treating diseases (eg some cancers) and in scientific research. It is produced by immunizing an animal with a particular antigen. The animal's lymphocytes which raise antibodies against the antigen are subsequently fused with myeloma cells (B-lymphocyte tumours) to form hybrid cells. These cells multiply rapidly, and produce the antibody in large amounts.

monocotyledons [monohkotileedndz] One of two major divisions of the flowering plants, often referred to simply as **monocots**; contrasting with *dicotyledons* (*dicots*). The seed embryo has only one cotyledon, and the primary root of the seedling soon withers, leaving only a fibrous root system. Monocots usually have narrow leaves with parallel unbranched veins, and flowers with parts arranged in threes or multiples of three. The vascular bundles are scattered through the stem; there is usually no cambium, and thus no secondary vascular tissue; and while there are tree-like monocots such as palms, both their manner of growth and their timber are very different from those of dicots. Monocots form a much smaller group than dicots, with about 60 families currently recognized, although some of them (eg grasses, palms, orchids, lilies) are among the largest families of flowering plants. (Subclass: Monocotyledonae.)

monoculture The growing of one type of crop on the same land over a period of years with hardly any crop rotation. Such systems are widespread in the developed world. However, it has been shown that monocultural cultivation is more susceptible to pests and diseases, and therefore requires relatively high inputs of fungicide and insecticide to protect it. Its widespread adoption, while increasing yield, has reduced the range of species and crops used for food production; its dependence on the use of mechanized processes and large field size has led to a decrease in the biodiversity of plants and animals. The term may also refer to single-species tree plantations.

Monod, Jacques (Lucien) [monoh] (1910–76) Biochemist, born in Paris, France. He studied at Paris University, served in the French Resistance during World War 2, then joined the Pasteur Institute in Paris. He became head of the cellular biochemistry department in 1954, and director in 1971, as well as professor of molecular biology at the Collège de France from 1967. With François Jacob (1920–) he discovered genes that regulate other genes (*operons*), for which they shared the 1965 Nobel Prize for Physiology or Medicine with Andrè Lwoff (1902–94).

monody In music, a single vocal or instrumental line, in contrast to polyphony. Gregorian chant and unaccompanied folksong are both examples of monody, but the term is often applied more specifically (though perhaps less accurately) to the continuo-accompanied solo vocal music of the early 17th-c.

monomer [monomer] A simple molecule which can add to or condense with itself to form a *polymer*. An amino acid is a monomer of a protein; ethylene ($CH_2{=}CH_2$) is the monomer of polyethylene ($(-CH_2-CH_2-)_n$).

mononucleosis, infectious *glandular fever*

monopack *integral tripack*

Monophysites [monofisiyts] (Gr 'one nature') Adherents to the doctrine that Christ did not have two natures after his Incarnation – one human and one divine – but rather had only one nature, which was effectively divine since the divine apparently dominated the human. This view grew out of controversies over the nature and person of Christ from the 4th–6th-c, associated especially with Eutyches (c.378–454, head of a monastery in Constantinople), and condemned by Pope Leo (449) and the Council of Chalcedon (451); yet variant forms continued to arise in subsequent centuries, especially influencing Coptic, Syrian, and Armenian churches.

Monopolies Commission or **Monopolies and Mergers Commission** A UK government body set up in 1948 as the *Monopolies and Restrictive Practices Commission*, whose powers were extended by the Restrictive Trade Practices Act (1980); comparable to the US Federal Trade Commission. It has wide powers to investigate activities which may be against the public interest, particularly with respect to mergers, takeovers, and monopoly situations. It can require companies to sell off parts of their operations.

monopoly A business situation where there is only one supplier of a good or service. This is unusual except where there is only one possible source of supply (**natural monopoly**) or the state excludes competition (eg in postal services). In economics, the term refers to a lack of competition. Monopoly is often opposed, as it is believed to result in excessive prices, either to boost profits or because of a lack of incentive to keep down costs through efficient or innovative operations. Monopoly is defended where there are large economies of scale, or it is thought that profits will help consumers in the long run by financing research. A **bilateral monopoly** exists when there is both only one buyer and only one seller of a good. This is even rarer than monopoly.

monopsony A business situation where there is only one buyer – a 'buyer's monopoly'. It is very rare on any significant scale.

monorail A railway using a single rail for the support of the train. The rail may be above or below the train, and the train may be stabilized if necessary by guide wheels and gyroscopes. The rail may be made of steel or concrete. Considerable research has gone into investigating non-wheeled methods of support, such as using air cushions and magnetic levitation. Monorails are used almost exclusively for public transport, with the two best-known systems running in Tokyo and Seattle.

monosaccharide [monosakariyd] A simple sugar, the monomer of a polysaccharide, formed from it by condensation polymerization.

monosodium glutamate (MSG) A flavouring agent used to enhance the meat flavour of many processed foods containing meat or meat extracts. It is commonly associated with the 'Chinese Restaurant Syndrome', an array of symptoms associated with eating a Chinese meal in which excess MSG has been used. All objective studies suggest that sensitivity to MSG is extremely rare. MSG is absorbed as glutamic acid, and since this is the most abundant natural amino acid in blood, it is difficult to elevate blood glutamate through ingesting MSG. Some of the reported side-effects of MSG may be due to impurities. Most are psychosomatic. MSG is not permitted in foods manufactured for babies and infants.

monotheism The belief that only one God exists. It developed within the Jewish faith, and remains a feature of Judaism, Christianity, and Islam. It is opposed to both polytheism and pantheism. Christian belief in the Trinity is thought by Muslims and Jews to deny monotheism.

Monothelites [monotheliyts] A Christian group who believed that in the person of Jesus Christ there was only one will, not two (one human, one divine). They were condemned at the Council of Constantinople in 680.

monotreme [monohtreem] An egg-laying mammal; lays soft-shelled eggs which hatch after 10 days; suckles young for 3–6 months; no teeth as adults. (Order: Monotremata, 3 species.)

Monotype (art) In art, a one-off print made by painting on a sheet of glass or a metal plate, and pressing a sheet of paper against the wet surface. Castiglione used this method in the 17th-c, Blake used a form of monotype in the 18th-c, and Degas in the 19th-c, frequently in combination with other media such as pastel.

Monotype (printing) *typesetting*

Monroe, James (1758–1831) US statesman and fifth president (1817–25), born in Westmoreland Co, Virginia, USA. After serving in the Revolution he entered politics, becoming a member of the US Senate (1790–4). He was governor of Virginia (1799–1802), and in 1803 helped to negotiate the Louisiana Purchase. In 1811 he was again Governor of Virginia, then secretary of state (1811–17), and also secretary of war (1814–15). In 1816 he was elected president, and in 1820 re-elected almost unanimously. His most popular acts were the recognition of the Spanish American republics, and the promulgation in a message to Congress (1823) of the *Monroe Doctrine*, embodying the principle 'that the American continents ... are henceforth not to be considered as subjects for future colonization by any European power'.

Monroe, Marilyn, stage name of **Norma Jean Mortenson** or **Baker** (1926–62) Film star, born in Los Angeles, California, USA. After a childhood spent largely in foster homes, she became a photographer's model in 1946. Following small film parts, she starred as a beautiful, sexy 'dumb blonde' in such films as *How to Marry a Millionaire* and *Gentlemen Prefer Blondes* (both 1953). Wanting more serious roles, she studied at Lee Strasberg's Actors' Studio, and went on to win acclaim in *Bus Stop* (1956) and *The Misfits* (1961), written for her by her third husband, Arthur Miller. She went to London to make *The Prince and* *the Showgirl* (1957) with Sir Laurence Olivier. Divorced from Miller in 1961, her death in 1962, apparently from an overdose of sleeping pills, shocked the world, and has become a symbol of Hollywood's ruthless exploitation of beauty and youth. Media investigations into the circumstances surrounding her death have continued into the 2000s.

Monroe Doctrine A major statement of American foreign policy, proclaimed in 1823, attributed to President James Monroe, but written by secretary of state John Quincy Adams. The doctrine was issued after renewed interest in the Americas by European powers, especially Britain and Russia, following the Spanish-American revolutions for independence. It announced (1) the existence of a separate political system in the Western hemisphere, (2) US hostility to further European colonization or attempts to extend European influence, and (3) non-interference with existing European colonies and dependencies or in European affairs.

Monrovia [monrohvia] 6°20N 10°46W, pop (2000e) 741 000. Seaport capital of Liberia, W Africa; 362 km/225 mi SSE of Freetown (Sierra Leone); on an area divided by lagoons into islands and peninsulas; main port and industrial sector on Bushrod Island; founded by the American Colonization Society, 1822; original name Christopolis, changed to Monrovia after the US president; airport; railway terminus; university (1862); Firestone rubber plantation and processing centre nearby; oil, cement.

Mons [mõs], Eng [monz], Flemish **Bergen** 50°28N 3°58E, pop (2000e) 93 800. Commercial and cultural city, capital of Hainaut province, S Belgium; inland harbour, handling mostly coal from the Borinage, major mining region; built on site of one of Caesar's camps; often a battlefield, notably in World War 1 (Aug 1914); railway; university (1965); textiles, leather, pharmaceuticals, metal processing, aluminium products; Gothic cathedral, town hall (15th-c); annual Battle of the Lumecon.

Monsarrat, Nicholas (John Turney) [monsarat] (1910–79) Novelist, born in Liverpool, Merseyside, NW England, UK. He studied at Cambridge, abandoned law for literature, and wrote three novels, and a play, *The Visitors*, which reached the London stage. During World War 2 he served in the navy, and out of his experiences emerged his best-selling novel, *The Cruel Sea* (1951, filmed 1953). *The Story of Esther Costello* (1953) repeated that success, followed by *The Tribe That Lost Its Head* (1956) and *The Pillow Fight* (1965). He settled in Ottawa, Canada, as director of the UK Information Office (1953–6), after holding a similar post in South Africa. He wrote a two-volume autobiography *Life is a Four-Letter Word* (1966, 1970).

monsoon climates Climates characterized by distinct wet and dry seasons, resulting from the seasonal migration of the intertropical convergence zone and changes in wind direction; they are found in tropical areas, especially Asia. For the Asiatic monsoon, heating over the Asian landmass in summer results in low pressure over the continent. Warm, moist air is drawn in from the oceans (the SW monsoon) and rain falls. In the autumn the thermal contrast between land and sea declines, and areas of low and high pressure reverse. Cooler, drier winds blow down from the Himalayas (the NE monsoon) and persist until the spring. Much of the agriculture of Asia is dependent on the monsoon, but the timing of its arrival is variable, and if it is late there is generally less rainfall.

monstera [monstera] A tall climber or liane (*Monstera deliciosa*) native to tropical America; stems with tough aerial roots; leaves large, heart-shaped, entire when young, developing deep notches and sometimes holes as tissue between veins ceases to grow; spadix surrounded by a large, coloured spathe; also called **Swiss cheese plant**. A popular house plant, the flowers and edible fruits rarely appear when grown indoors. (Family: Araceae.)

monstrance A liturgical vessel, usually of gold or silver frame with a glass window, used to display the Eucharistic host or consecrated bread. It enables the host to be venerated by worshippers.

montage [montahzh] **1** In art, a technique whereby illustrations or photographs are cut from papers or magazines, arranged in new ways, and mounted. A development of collage, it was used by the Dadaists and Surrealists, and persists in modern advertising.
2 In film editing, a sequence containing a series of rapidly changing images, often dissolving together or superimposed to convey a visually dramatic effect. Pioneered by D W Griffith in his film *The Avenging Conscience* (1914), early examples of montage can be seen in Franz Borzage's *Seventh Heaven* (1927), Sergey Eisenstein's *The Battleship Potemkin* (1925), *October* (1928), and *The General Line* (1929), and in Abel Gance's powerful and melodramatic *La Roue* (1922, The Wheel).

Montagu, Lady Mary Wortley [montagyoo], *née* **Pierrepont** (1689–1762) Writer, born in London, UK. The daughter of the Duke of Kingston, she married Edward Wortley Montague in 1712, and lived in London. A poet and essayist as well as a feminist and a beauty, she gained a brilliant reputation among literary figures. While in Constantinople with her husband, she wrote her entertaining *Letters*, published in 1763 after her death, describing Eastern life. She also brought the smallpox inoculation from Turkey, introducing it to England, her own beauty having been marked by an attack while she was a young woman.

Montaigne, Michel (Eyquem) de [mõten] (1533–92) Essayist and courtier, born at Château de Montaigne, Périgord, SW France. He spoke no language but Latin until he was six, received his early education at Bordeaux, then studied law. He obtained a post in connection with the *Parlement* of Bordeaux, and for 13 years was a city counsellor, later becoming mayor. A translation (1569) of the *Natural History* of a 15th-c professor at Toulouse was his first attempt at literature, and supplied the text for his *Apologie de Raymon Sebond*. In 1571 he succeeded to the family estate at Montaigne, and lived the life of a country gentleman, varied by visits to Paris and a tour in Germany, Switzerland, and Italy. He is remembered for his *Essais* (1572–80, 1588) on the new ideas and personalities of the time, which introduced a new literary genre to accommodate what Matthew Arnold was later to call 'the dialogue of the mind with itself'. Quoted by Shakespeare, imitated by Bacon, and incorporated into the discourse of the novel, Montaigne's essays have provided a major contribution to literary history.

Montale, Eugenio [montahlay] (1896–1981) Poet, born in Genoa, NW Italy. He was the leading poet of the modern Italian 'Hermetic' school, and his primary concern was with language and meaning. His works include *Ossi di seppia* (1925, Cuttlefish Bones), *Le occasioni* (1939, The Occasions), *La bufera e altro* (1956, The Storm, and Other Poems), *Satura* (1962), and *Xenia* (1966). He was awarded the Nobel Prize for Literature in 1975.

Montana [montana] pop (2000e) 902 200; area 380 834 sq km/147 046 sq mi. State in NW USA, divided into 56 counties; the 'Treasure State'; most of the state acquired by the Louisiana Purchase, 1803; border with Canada settled by the Oregon Treaty, 1846; became the Territory of Montana, 1864; gold rush after 1858 discoveries; ranchers moved into the area in 1866, taking over Indian land; conflict with the Sioux resulted in the defeat of General Custer at the Battle of the Little Bighorn, 1876; six Indian reservations now in the state; 41st state to join the Union, 1889; new state constitution, 1973; capital, Helena; other chief cities, Billings and Great Falls; bounded N by the Canadian provinces of British Columbia, Alberta, and Saskatchewan; fourth largest US state; crossed by the Missouri and Yellowstone Rivers; Bitterroot Range, part of the Rocky Mts, lies along much of the W border; highest point Granite Peak (3901 m/12 798 ft); the Great Plains (E) are largely occupied by vast wheat fields and livestock farms; W dominated by the Rocky Mts, covered in dense pine forests; part of Yellowstone National Park in the S; Glacier National Park in the W; tourism a major state industry; hunting, fishing, skiing, hiking, boating (glacier lakes); copper, silver, gold, zinc, lead, manganese in the mountainous W; petroleum, natural gas, large coal-mines in the E; timber, wood products, refined petroleum, processed foods; cattle, wheat, hay, barley, dairy products.

Montana, Joe [montana], popular name of **Joseph C Montana, Jr** (1956–) Player of American football, born in New Eagle, Pennsylvania, USA. A former Notre Dame quarterback, he led the San Francisco 49ers to victories in four Super Bowls during the 1980s. An inspirational leader and talented passer, he was named the National Football League's most valuable player in 1989. He joined the Kansas City Chiefs 1993–5, before retiring.

Montand, Yves [mõtã, eev], originally **Ivo Livi** (1921–91) Actor-singer, born in Monsummano Alto, NWC Italy. He worked at a variety of jobs before performing as a singer and impressionist in Marseille and Paris. A protégé of Edith Piaf, he made his film debut with her in *Etoile sans lumière* (1946, Star Without Light). He appeared in *Le Salaire de la peur* (1953, The Wages of Fear), and ventured abroad for such films as *Let's Make Love* (1960). His acting reputation was enhanced by an association with the director Constantin Costa-Gavras in such films as *Z* (1968) and *L'Aveu* (1970, The Confession). He was married to actress **Simone Signoret** from 1951 until her death in 1985. In the 1980s he became a distinguished elder statesman of the French film industry, his films including *Jean de Florette* and *Manon des sources* (both 1986).

Montanism [montanizm] A popular Christian movement derived from Montanus of Phrygia (AD c.170) and two women, Prisca and Maximilla, whose ecstatic prophecies and literal expectation of the imminent end of the age won a wide following of churches in Asia Minor. These features and its austere ethical and spiritual ideals were opposed by the Catholic Church, which defended the importance of the institutional ministry and apostolic tradition.

Mont Blanc [mõ blã] Highest alpine massif of SE France, SW Switzerland, and NW Italy; 25 peaks over 4000 m/13 000 ft; highest peak, Mont Blanc (4807 m/15 771 ft); frontiers of France, Switzerland, and Italy meet at Mt Dolent (3823 m/12 542 ft); road tunnel (12 km/7½ mi long) connects France and Italy; closed by fire which killed over 40 people, March 1999, reopened in 2002; first climbed in 1786 by J Balmat and M G Paccard; chief resort, Chamonix.

montbretia [monbreesha] A perennial (*Crocosmia* × *crocosmiiflora*) growing to 90 cm/3 ft, producing corms and spreading by stolons; leaves sword-shaped, in narrow fans; flowers 2·5–5 cm/1–2 in diameter, orange, slightly zygomorphic, funnel-shaped, in one-sided sprays. It is a hybrid of garden origin, first raised in France in 1880. (Family: Iridaceae.)

Montcalm (de Saint Véran), Louis Joseph de Montcalm-Grozon, marquis de [mõkalm] (1712–59) French general, born in Condiac, S France. During the Seven Years' War he took command of the French troops in Canada (1756), and captured the British post of Oswego and Fort William Henry. In 1758 he defended Ticonderoga, and proceeded to the defence of Quebec, where he died in the battle against General Wolfe on the Plains of Abraham.

Monte Albán [montay alban] The ancient capital of the Zapotecs of S Mexico, strategically placed at an elevation of 400 m/1300 ft above the Valley of Oaxaca; a world heritage site. In use c.400 BC–AD 800, it occupied an area of 40 sq km/15 sq mi at its peak (c.200–700) with a population of c.20 000. Its artificially-levelled hilltop plaza (300 m/1000 ft by 200 m/650 ft) contains platform pyramids and a ballcourt, while the slopes below are terraced to form c.2000 house and farm plots.

Monte Carlo [montay kah(r)loh] 43°46N 7°23E. Resort town on a rocky promontory of the Mediterranean Riviera, in Monaco, on the N side of the harbour opposite the town of Monaco; famous Casino, providing c.4% of national revenue, built in 1878; Palais des Congrès (Les Spélugues); annual car rally, world championship Grand Prix motor race.

Montefiore, Sir Moses (Haim) [montefyohray] (1784–1885) Philanthropist, born in Livorno, W Italy. He retired with a fortune from stockbroking in 1824, and from 1829 was prominent in the struggle for Jewish equality. After long exclusion and repeated re-election, he was admitted sheriff of London in 1837. Between 1827 and 1875 he made seven journeys to Palestine in the interests of his oppressed co-religionists in Poland, Russia, Rumania, and Damascus. He was knighted in 1837, and became a baronet in 1846.

Montego Bay [monteegoh], locally **Mobay** 18°27N 77°56W, pop (2000e) 89 000. Port and capital city of St James parish, Cornwall county, NW coast of Jamaica; free port and principal tourist centre of the island; airport; railway; trade in bananas, sugar; Rose Hall Great House (1770), old British fort, 18th-c church.

Montenegro [monteneegroh], Serbo-Croatian **Crna Gora** pop (2000e) 681 000; area 13 812 sq km/5331 sq mi. Republic in the Union of Serbia and Montenegro (former federation of Yugoslavia); timezone GMT +2; capital, Podgorica; mountainous region; Mediterranean climate on coast, winter snow in mountains; independent monarchy until 1918; became constituent republic of Yugoslavia, 1946; in favour of maintenance of Yugoslavia as a federation, 1991; focus of NATO air-strikes, along with Serbia, in Kosovo crisis, 1999; growing movement for independence from Serbia; livestock, grain, tobacco; German mark replaced the dinar as official currency, 1999; the euro became the official currency in 2002.

Montespan, Françoise Athenaïs de Rochechouart, marquise de (Marchioness of) [mõtespã] (1641–1707) Mistress of Louis XIV, born in Tonnay-Charente, W France, the daughter of the Duc de Mortemart. In 1663 she married the Marquis de Montespan, and joined the household of Queen Maria Theresa as lady-in-waiting. She became the king's mistress in c.1667, and after her marriage was annulled (1674), was given official recognition of her position. She bore the king seven children, who were legitimized (1673). Supplanted first by Mademoiselle de Fontanges and later by Madame de Maintenon, she left court in 1687 and retired to the convent of Saint-Joseph in Paris, eventually becoming the superior.

Montesquieu, Charles Louis de Secondat, Baron de la Brède et de [mõteskyoe] (1689–1755) Philosopher and jurist, born at Château La Brède near Bordeaux, SW France. Educated at Bordeaux, he became an advocate, but turned to scientific research and literary work. He settled in Paris (1726), then spent some years travelling and studying political and social institutions. His best-known work is the comparative study of legal and political issues, *De l'esprit des lois* (1748, The Spirit of Laws), which was a major influence on 18th-c Europe and inspired the American Constitution and the Declaration of the Rights of Man. He is best remembered for his theory of the separation of powers. Dividing authority into legislative, executive, and judicial powers, his argument was that each of these three powers should be independent of the other.

Montessori, Maria [montesawree] (1870–1952) Physician and educationist, born in Rome, Italy. She studied at Rome, where she was the first woman in Italy to graduate in medicine. Later, she joined the psychiatric clinic, and became interested in the problems of mentally handicapped children. She opened her first 'children's house' in 1907, developing a system of education for children of three to six, based on freedom of movement, the provision of considerable choice for pupils, and the use of specially designed activities and equipment. **Montessori schools** were also later developed for older children throughout the world.

Monteux, Pierre [mõtoe] (1875–1964) Conductor, born in Paris, France. He trained at the Paris Conservatoire, where he began his career as a viola player. He conducted Diaghilev's Ballets Russes in Paris (1911–14, 1917), and in 1914 organized the 'Concerts Monteux', whose programmes gave prominence to new French and Russian music. Founding and directing the Orchestre Symphonique de Paris, in 1936 he took over the newly organized San Francisco Symphony Orchestra, and in 1941 established a summer school for student conductors at Hanover, NH. From 1960 until his death he was principal conductor of the London Symphony Orchestra, and became one of the

20th-c's leading conductors, his interpretations equally admired in ballet, opera, and symphonic music.

Monteverdi, Claudio [montayvairdee] (1567–1643) Composer, born in Cremona, N Italy. A proficient violist, he learned the art of composition in Cremona, publishing a set of three-part choral pieces at the age of 15. About 1590 he was appointed court musician to the Duke of Mantua, whose *maestro di capella* he became in 1602, moving on to a similar post at St Mark's, Venice, in 1613, where he remained until his death. His eight books of madrigals, which appeared at regular intervals between 1587 and 1638, show his originality and pioneering spirit. The two surviving operas of his later period, *Il Ritorno d'Ulisse* (1641, The Return of Ulysses) and *L'Incoronazione di Poppea* (1642, The Coronation of Poppaea), both written when he was well past 70, show development towards the Baroque style and foreshadow the use of the *leitmotif*. His greatest contribution to church music is the *Mass* and *Vespers of the Blessed Virgin* (1610), which contained tone colours and harmonies well in advance of his time.

Montevideo [montevidayoh] 34°55S 56°10W, pop (2000e) 1 374 500. Federal and provincial capital of Uruguay, on the R Plate; founded, 1726; capital, 1830; airport; railway; university (1849); meat packing, food processing, tanning, footwear, soap, matches, trade in meat, skins, wool; cathedral (1790–1804), Cabildo (1808), several museums and parks, sports stadium (Estadio Centenario), fort on Cerro hill; the German battleship *Graf Spee* was scuttled offshore during the Battle of the River Plate (1939).

Montez, Lola [montez], originally **Marie Dolores Eliza Rosanna Gilbert** (1818–61) Dancer, born in Limerick, SW Ireland. An outstanding beauty, she trained to be a Spanish dancer, and appeared at Her Majesty's Theatre in London. While touring Europe, she went to Munich (1846), where she gained influence over the eccentric artist-king, Ludwig I of Bavaria (reigned 1825–48), who created her Countess of Landsfeld. The 1848 revolution forced her to flee, and she then travelled in Australia and the USA. She settled in California, where she lectured on fashion and beauty, but never regained her former standing, and died in poverty.

Montezuma II [montezooma] (1466–1520) The last Aztec emperor (1502–20). A distinguished warrior and legislator, he died during the Spanish conquest of Hernán Cortés. One of his descendants was viceroy of Mexico (1697–1701).

Montfort, Simon de, Earl of Leicester (c.1208–1265) English statesman and soldier, born in Montfort, C France. Well received by Henry III of England in 1230, he was confirmed in his title and estates in 1232, and in 1238 married the king's youngest sister, **Eleanor**. As the king's deputy in Gascony (1248), he put down disaffection with a heavy hand. He returned to England in 1253, became the leader of the barons in their opposition to the king, and defeated him at Lewes (1264). He then became virtual ruler of England, calling a parliament in 1265; but the barons soon grew dissatisfied with his rule, and the king's army defeated him at Evesham, where he was killed.

Montgolfier brothers [mõgolfyay] Aeronautical inventors: **Joseph Michel Montgolfier** (1740–1810) and **Jacques Etienne Montgolfier** (1745–99), born in Annonay, SC France. In 1782 they constructed a balloon whose bag was lifted by lighting a cauldron of paper beneath it, thus heating and rarifying the air it contained. A flight of 9 km/5½ mi, at 3000 ft, carrying Pilatre de Rozier and the Marquis d'Arlandes, was achieved in 1783 – the world's first manned flight. Further experiments were frustrated by the outbreak of the French Revolution.

Montgomery (Alabama) 32°23N 86°19W, pop (2000e) 201 600. Capital of state in Montgomery Co, C Alabama, USA, on the Alabama R; state capital, 1847; the Confederate States of America formed here, 1861; occupied by Federal troops, 1865; railway; university (1874), important market centre for farming produce; cotton, livestock, dairy products; diverse industries, including machinery, glass, textiles, furniture, foods, paper; scene of the 1955 bus boycott by blacks protesting against segregation, which contributed to the growth of the civil rights movement.

Montgomery (of Alamein), Bernard Law Montgomery, 1st Viscount (1887–1976) British field marshal, born in London, UK. He trained at Sandhurst Military Academy, and was commissioned into the Royal Warwickshire Regiment in 1908. In World War 2, he gained renown as arguably the best British field commander since Wellington. A controversial and outspoken figure, he was nevertheless a 'soldier's general', able to establish a remarkable rapport with his troops. He commanded the 8th Army in N Africa, and defeated Rommel at El Alamein (1942). He played a key role in the invasion of Sicily and Italy (1943), and was appointed commander-in-chief, ground forces, for the Allied invasion of Normandy (1944). On his insistence, the invasion frontage was widened, and more troops were committed to the initial assault. Criticized for slow progress after D-Day, he uncharacteristically agreed to the badly planned airborne landings at Arnhem (Sep 1944), which resulted in the only defeat of his military career. In 1945, German forces in NW Germany, The Netherlands, and Denmark surrendered to him on Lünenberg Heath. Appointed field marshal (1944) and viscount (1946), he served successively as Chief of the Imperial General Staff (1946–8) and deputy supreme commander of NATO forces in Europe (1951–8). His books include *History of Warfare* (1968).

month The time for the Moon to orbit the Earth, relative to a reference point. Lunar motion is very complex. The Moon orbits the Earth in 27·32 days (relative to the stars), passing through the familiar cycle of lunar phases. The lunar month of 29·53 days is the interval between successive new Moons. Twelve lunar months is less than one solar year, so the calendar months are arbitrarily longer than lunar months.

Montherlant, Henri (Marie Joseph Millon) de [mõtairlã] (1896–1972) Novelist and playwright, born in Paris, France. He was severely wounded in World War 1, after which he travelled in Spain, Africa, and Italy. His major work is an elegantly written four-novel cycle, beginning with *Les jeunes filles* and *Pitié pour les femmes* (1936, published together as Pity for Women), in which he portrays women as willing and shallow tools of men. After 1942 he wrote several plays, including *Malatesta* (1946) and *Don Juan* (1958). He committed suicide in 1972.

Monti, Eugenio [montee] (1928–) Bobsleigh driver, born in Dobbiaco, NE Italy. The winner of a record six Olympic bobsleighing medals, he won golds in the two- and four-man events at the 1968 Games, after winning the silver in both events in 1956, and the bronze in 1964. He was also a member of 11 Italian world championship winning teams between 1957 and 1968. After retiring in 1968, he was appointed manager to the Italian national team.

Montoneros [montonairos] Argentine urban guerrillas claiming allegiance to Peronism and (from 1970) staging terrorist actions against the military regime then in power. Repudiated by Juan Domingo Perón himself (1974), the Montoneros renewed their attacks on the regime installed in 1976, meeting with severe repression.

Montpelier [montpeelyer] 44°16N 72°35W, pop (2000e) 8000. Capital of Vermont, USA; in Washington Co, N Vermont, on the Winooski R; settled, 1780; state capital, 1805; railway; Vermont College (1834); notable skiing areas nearby at Pinnacle Mt, Judgement Ridge, Glen Ellen, Bolton Valley, Sugarbush Valley, Mad River Glen; birthplace of Admiral George Dewey; textiles, machinery, wood products, granite quarrying, printing.

Montpellier [mõpelyay] 43°37N 3°52E, pop (2000e) 217 000. Industrial and commercial city, and capital of Hérault department, S France; 123 km/76 mi NW of Marseille; founded around a Benedictine abbey, 8th-c; airport; railway; bishopric; university (1289); wine trade, textiles, printing, concrete, machinery, wood products; birthplace of Comte; Gothic Cathedral of St Pierre (1364), many 17th–18th-c patricians' and merchants' houses, Doric triumphal arch (1691), Château d'Eau (aqueduct terminal); Jardin des Plantes, France's first botanical garden (1593); Musée Fabre, Atger Museum.

Montreal [montreeawl], Fr **Montréal** [mõrayal] 45°30N 73°36W, pop (2000e) 1 139 000. River-port city in S Quebec province, Canada; on Montreal I, on the St Lawrence R (ice-free May–Nov); second largest city in Canada, and second largest French-speaking city in the world; first visited by Cartier, 1535; fort, 1611; developed as a fur-trading centre; surrendered to British, 1760; capital of Canada, 1844–9; British garrison withdrawn, 1870; two airports; railway; metro; four universities (1821, 1876, 1969, 1974), two English-speaking and two French-speaking; major commercial centre; aircraft, railway equipment, oil refining, meat packing, clothing, plastics, footwear, cement, brewing, publishing; trade in grain, timber, paper; Montreal Symphony Orchestra, Les Grands Ballets Canadiens; professional teams, Montreal Expos (baseball), Montreal Canadiens (ice hockey); neo-Gothic Notre Dame Church (1829), Christ Church Cathedral, St James Cathedral, Séminaire de Saint-Sulpice (1658), Maisonneuve Monument (1895), Château de Ramezay (now a museum); location of 1967 World's Fair (Expo) and 1976 Olympic Games.

Montreux [mõtroe] 46°27N 6°55E, pop (2000e) 20 200. Winter sports centre and resort town in Vaud canton, SW Switzerland; at E end of L Geneva, SE of Lausanne; railway; figs, vines, walnuts, tourism; casino; 13th-c Château de Chillon nearby; Golden Rose Television Festival (spring), International Jazz Festival (Jun–Jul), Music Festival (Sep).

Montrose, James Graham, 1st Marquess of (1612–50) Scottish soldier and royalist. He studied at St Andrews and travelled in Europe, returning in 1637, and was one of the four noblemen who drew up the National Covenant in support of Presbyterianism (1638). He served in the Covenanter army in 1640, but transferred his allegiance to Charles I, and led the Royalist army to victory at Tippermuir (1644). After the Royalist defeat at Naseby (1645), his army became disaffected, and his remaining force was defeated at Philiphaugh. He fled to Europe, returning to Scotland after Charles's execution to avenge his death; but his army was largely lost by shipwreck, and the remnant defeated at Invercharron (1650). He was taken prisoner, and hanged in Edinburgh.

Mont-Saint-Michel [mõ sĩ mishel] A rocky isle off the coast of Normandy, NW France, famous for its Gothic abbey; a world heritage site. A Benedictine settlement was first established here in the 8th-c, but the most impressive elements of the abbey date from the early 13th-c.

Montserrat *see panel*

Monty Python, in full **Monty Python's Flying Circus** An anarchic satirical series, shown on BBC television between 1969 and 1974, starring Graham Chapman (1941–89), John Cleese, Eric Idle, Terry Jones, and Michael Palin. The series changed the face of British television humour, with its inspired lunacy, surreal comedy, and animated graphics (by Terry Gilliam), and generated a cult following which was eventually international. The troupe later collaborated on such films as *The Life of Brian* (1979) and *The Meaning of Life* (1983), before developing their individual careers. They occasionally come together for charity revues and suchlike events.

Monument, the A Doric column in C London, UK, surmounted by a representation of a flame-encircled globe, designed by Wren and erected (1671–7) to commemorate the Fire of London. The structure is 61·5 m/202 ft high and stands in Fish Street Hill, London.

Moody, Dwight L(yman) (1837–99) Evangelist, born in Northfield, Massachusetts, USA. A shoe salesman in Boston, in 1856 he went to Chicago to engage in missionary work, and founded the Moody Church. In 1870 he was joined by **Ira David Sankey** (1840–1908). In 1873 and 1883 they visited Great Britain as evangelists, Moody preaching and Sankey singing; afterwards they worked together in America. In 1899 he founded the Moody Bible Institute in Chicago.

Moody, Helen (Newington) Wills (1905–98) Tennis player, born in Centerville, California, USA. She studied at the University of California (1927) and from then until her retirement (1939) she dominated women's tennis. She won her first US women's singles title in 1923, then went on to win it six more times by 1931. She also won the Wimbledon singles championship eight times, the French singles four times, various doubles championships, and two gold medals in the 1924 Olympics. Married to **Frederick Moody**, she competed between 1929–39 as Helen Wills Moody. Divorced and remarried, she competed in senior tournaments as **Mrs Roark**.

Montserrat

[montsuhrat], also **Emerald Isle** (UK British Overseas Territory) *(see map, p.1099)*

Timezone GMT - 4

Area 106 km²/41 sq mi

Population (1997e) 11 000 (pre-disaster), (2001e) 4500

Capital Plymouth (abandoned in 1997), new buildings at Brades Estate, NW Montserrat

Physical features Volcanic island in the Leeward Is, E Caribbean; mountainous, heavily forested; highest point, Chance's Peak, 914 m/3000 ft; seven active volcanoes.

Climate Tropical climate, with low humidity; average annual rainfall 1500 mm/60 in; hurricanes occur (Jun-Nov).

Currency 1 East Caribbean Dollar (EC$) = 100 cents

Economy Tourism (accounts for 25% of national income); cotton, peppers, livestock, electronic assembly, crafts, rum distilling, postage stamps.

GDP (2002e) $29 mn, per capita $3400

History Visited by Colombus, 1493; colonized by English and Irish settlers, 1632; plantation economy based on slave labour; British Crown Colony, 1871; joined Federation of the West Indies, 1958–62; island severely damaged by hurricane Hugo, 1989; half the island, including the capital, destroyed by eruption of Soufriere Hills volcano, June 1997; 8000 people left the island, with returnees (from 1998) limited by lack of housing; British sovereign represented by a Governor, with an Executive Council and a Legislative Council.

Moog synthesizer *synthesizer*

Moon *pp.1032–3*

moon bear *black bear*

moon daisy *ox-eye daisy*

moonfish Large, midwater fish (*Lampris guttatus*) widespread in tropical and temperate seas at depths of 100–500 m/300–1600 ft; length up to 1·5 m/5 ft; body deep, compressed, fins well-developed, protruding mouth, lacking teeth; colour very characteristic, deep blue on back spotted with white, underside silver, fins deep red; also called **opah**. (Family: Lampridae.)

Moonies A derisive name applied to members of the religious movement founded in 1954 by Korean evangelist Sun Myung Moon (1920–). Known as the **Unification Church** (in full, the Holy Spirit Association for the Unification of World Christianity), and more recently the **Association of Families for Unification and World Peace**, the organization was founded in 1954 in South Korea, and moved to Tarrytown, NY, in the 1970s. Its doctrines are presented in Moon's book, *The Divine Principle* (1952), and stress the leading role of the family, through which God's purpose will manifest itself on Earth; mass marriages, which may involve a thousand or more couples, are one of the movement's more public activities. Rev Moon and his wife, Hak Ja Han, are seen as the Lord and Lady of the Second Advent, and called Father and Mother by their disciples. The missionary activities of the Church have attracted a great deal of criticism, especially from parents who believe that their children have been brainwashed. The organization's financial affairs have also been the subject of investigation, and in 1982 Moon was fined and sentenced to 18 months imprisonment for US tax evasion. He has continued to live chiefly in the USA, where he owns several companies, but has encountered increasing opposition to his movement there, and also in several countries where he has tried to expand, especially in C and S America. In the late

1990s he began to develop a centre at Jardim, W Brazil, as a new 'garden of Eden'.

moonrat A SE Asian insectivorous mammal; resembles closely related hedgehogs, but lacks spines and has a longer tail; several species reputed to be the most evil-smelling animals (scent from anal glands resembles rotting garlic); they live alone; also known as **hairy hedgehog** or **gymnure**. (Family: Erinaceidae, 5 species.)

moonstone A semi-precious gemstone variety of the mineral potassium feldspar. It has a pale opalescent lustre because of its fine-scale oriented microstructure, which diffracts light.

Moore, Archie, originally **Archibald Lee Wright**, nickname **the Mongoose** (1913/16–98) Boxer, born in Benoit, Michigan, USA. His actual date of birth is uncertain (by his own account), but he was still the oldest man to hold a world title; he also reigned longer than any light-heavyweight champion – nine years, one month. He was 39 (or 36) when he beat Joey Maxim for the light-heavyweight title in 1952. He had 228 professional bouts and won 194, knocking out a record 141 opponents. He lost to Cassius Clay in 1962, and retired in 1965.

Moore, Bobby, popular name of **Robert Frederick Chelsea Moore** (1941–93) Footballer, born in London, UK. In a long career with West Ham United (1958–74) and later Fulham (1974–7), he played 1000 matches at senior level, receiving an FA Cup-winner's Medal in 1964 and a European Cup-winner's Cup Medal in 1965. He was capped 108 times (107 in succession), 90 of them as captain, a total only surpassed by Peter Shilton. He played in the World Cup finals in Chile in 1962, and captained the victorious England side in the 1966 World Cup.

Moore, Brian (1921–99) Writer, born in Belfast, NE Northern Ireland, UK. After World War 2 he became a journalist and adopted Canadian citizenship. He spent time in New York before moving to California. He was particularly admired for his portrayal of women, as seen in *The Lonely Passion of Judith Hearne* (1955, filmed 1987). *The Great Victorian Collection* (1975) was awarded the James Tait Black Memorial Prize, and both *The Doctor's Wife* (1976) and *Black Robe* (1985) were short-listed for the Booker Prize. Later books include *The Colour of Blood* (1987), *No Other Life* (1993), *The Statement* (1995), and *The Magician's Wife* (1998). The play *Lies of Silence* (1990, filmed 1991) is an exile's view of the troubles in Northern Ireland.

Moore, Demi, originally **Demetria Guynes** (1962–) Film actress, producer, and director, born in Roswell, New Mexico, USA. She worked in television before making her film debut in *Choices* (1981), but her major breakthrough came with *St Elmo's Fire* (1984). Later films include *Ghost* (1990), *Indecent Proposal* (1992), *The Scarlet Letter* (1995), *Striptease* (1996), *G.I.Jane* (1997), and *Charlie's Angels: Full Throttle* (2003). She co-founded a production company, Moving Pictures, with Suzanne Todd; their work includes *Austin Powers: The Spy Who Shagged Me* (1999). She was married to actor Bruce Willis (1987–98).

Moore, Dudley (Stuart John) (1935–2002) Actor, comedian, and musician, born in London, UK. He studied at Oxford. Small in stature but big in personality he was one of the successful *Beyond the Fringe* team (1960–64). He joined Peter Cook for the TV series *Not Only ... but also* (1964–70), and starred in several films including *10* (1979), *Arthur* (1981), *Santa Claus – The Movie* (1985), *Arthur 2 – On the Rocks* (1988), *Crazy People* (1990), and *Blame it on the Bellboy* (1992). An accomplished musician, he performed for radio and TV with his own jazz piano trio, and composed for several films and plays. In 1991 he co-presented the television series *Orchestra!* with Sir Georg Solti. In 1999 he was diagnosed with a degenerative brain disease, progressive supranuclear palsy.

Moore, G(eorge) E(dward) (1873–1958) Philosopher, born in London, UK. He studied at Dulwich College and Cambridge, and left classics for philosophy, where he first embraced then rejected the claims of Hegelian idealism. His major ethical work was *Principia Ethica* (1903), in which he argued against the naturalistic fallacy. At Cambridge he became a lecturer in moral science (1911), and professor of mental philosophy and logic (1925–39). He was a leading influence on the Bloomsbury group. He also edited the journal *Mind* (1921–47), and made it the major English-language journal in the field.

Moore, Gerald (1899–1987) Pianoforte accompanist, born in Watford, Hertfordshire, SE England. He studied music at Toronto, and established himself as an outstanding accompanist of the world's leading singers and instrumentalists. He was a regular performer at international music festivals, and a notable lecturer and television broadcaster on music.

Moore, Henry (Spencer) (1898–1986) Sculptor, born in Castleford, West Yorkshire, N England, UK. He studied at the Royal College of Art, London, where he taught sculpture (1924–31), moving to the Chelsea School of Art (1931–9). Recognized as one of the most original and powerful modern sculptors, his style is based on the organic forms and undulations found in landscape and natural rocks, and influenced by primitive African and Mexican art. He achieved the spatial, three-dimensional quality of sculpture by the piercing of his figures. Principal commissions included the 'Madonna and Child' in St Matthew's Church, Northampton (1943–4), the decorative frieze (1952) on the Time Life building, London, and the monumental female reclining figures for the UNESCO building in Paris (1958) and the Lincoln Center in New York City (1965). Major collections can be seen at the Henry Moore Sculpture Center, Toronto, The Tate Gallery, London, and at his former home in Much Hadham, Hertfordshire.

Moore, Sir John (1761–1809) British soldier, born in Glasgow, W Scotland, UK. From 1794 he served in many countries in Europe and in the West Indies, but is remembered for his command of the English army in Spain (1808–9), where he was forced to retreat to Coruña. There he defeated a French attack, but was mortally wounded (as recounted in the poem by Wolfe).

Moore, Julianne, originally **Julie Anne Smith** (1961–) Actress, born in Fayetteville, North Carolina, USA. She studied drama at Boston University's School of Performing Arts, and after a number of stage parts became known for her role in the US television soap *As The World Turns* (1985–8). Feature film credits include *The Hand That Rocks the Cradle* (1991), *The Fugitive* (1993), *Nine Months* (1995), and *The Hours* (2002). She has twice been nominated for a best actress Oscar, for *Boogie Nights* (1997) and *Far From Heaven* (2002).

Moore, Marianne (Craig) (1887–1972) Poet, born in St Louis, Missouri, USA. She studied at Bryn Mawr College, PA, and taught at Carlisle Commercial College before becoming a branch librarian in New York City (1921–5). She contributed to *The Egoist* from 1915, and edited *The Dial* from 1926 until its demise in 1929. She was acquainted with such seminal Modernists as Pound and T S Eliot, and associated with the Greenwich Village group, Idiosyncratic. A consummate stylist, and unmistakably modern, her first publication was *Poems* (1921). *Selected Poems* appeared in 1935, and *Complete Poems* in 1967.

Moore, Michael (1954–) Film director, producer, writer, and political activist, born in Davison, Flint, Michigan, USA. He studied at the University of Michigan, Flint, and began working as a newspaper journalist. Moving into film production, he began with the groundbreaking documentary *Roger and Me* (1989), chronicling events as the General Motors corporation abandoned its hometown of Flint, MI. Topical issues in American society are explored in the films *Canadian Bacon* (1995) and *Bowling for Columbine* (2002, Oscar for best documentary). Among his books are *The Awful Truth* (1999), the best-selling *Stupid White Men* (2001), a critique of corporate America, and *Dude, Where's My Country?* (2003), a commentary on the Bush administration.

Moore, Sir Patrick (Alfred Caldwell) (1923–) British amateur astronomer, writer, broadcaster, and musician. He was educated at home due to childhood illness. He is best known as the enthusiastic and knowledgeable presenter of the long-running BBC television programme *The Sky at Night* (1957–). He is an accomplished xylophone player, and has composed several works, including *Perseus and Andromeda* (1975). The recipient

Moon

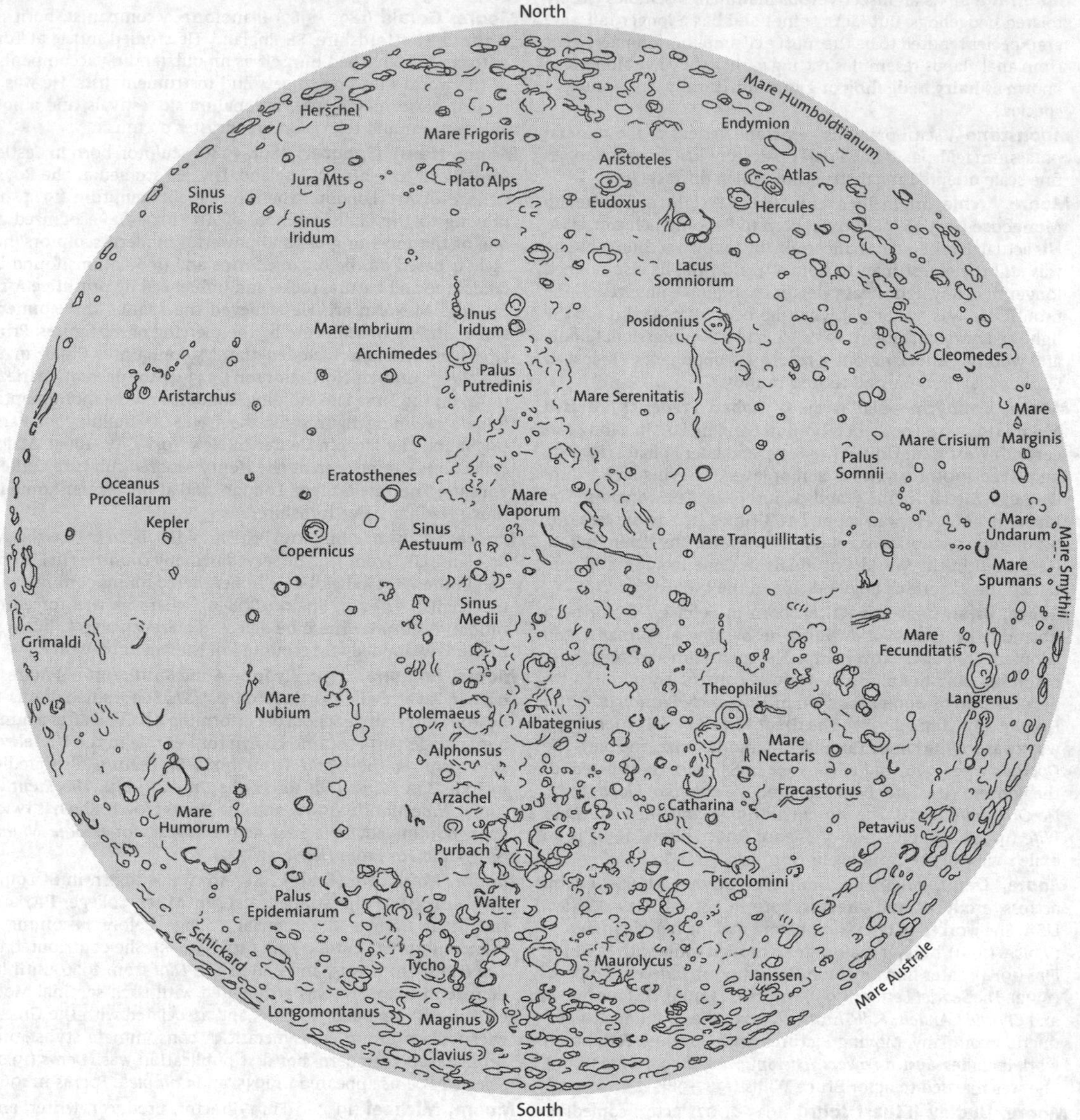

The Earth's only natural satellite, lacking any atmosphere; about a quarter the size of the Earth, and treated as one of the family of terrestrial planets. It has the following characteristics: mass 0·073 × 10^{27} g; radius 1738 km/1080 mi; mean density 3·34 g/cm^3; equatorial gravity 162 cm/s; rotational period 27·3 days; orbital period 27·3 days; average distance from Earth 384 400 km/238 850 mi. Overall density is low, because of a major iron deficiency. Apollo seismic measurements indicate that the interior is solid to a depth of c.1000 km/600 mi; the nature of the core is still uncertain. There is no global magnetic field, but evidence of past magnetization is contained in individual rock samples. The equality of rotational and orbital rates is due to tidal despinning of the Moon into a stable synchronous period, so that the same hemisphere of the Moon always faces the Earth.

The brighter surface regions (*highlands*) represent the original lunar crustal material shaped by saturation bombardment of meteoritic material. The dark surface regions (*mare*

of many awards for his services to astronomy, he has published over 60 books, including *The Amateur Astronomer* (1970), *The A–Z of Astronomy* (1986), *Mission to the Planets* (1990), and *Teach Yourself Astronomy* (1995). He received a knighthood in 2001.

Moore, Sir Roger (George) (1927–) Film star, born in London, UK. An art school student of painting, he made his film debut as an extra in 1945, and appeared in small roles on stage and in films prior to army service. He appeared on Broadway in *A Pin to See the Peepshow* (1953) and in the Hollywood film *The Last Time I Saw Paris* (1954). On television he won stardom as the action-man hero of such series as *Ivanhoe* (1958), *The Alaskans* (1960–1), and *The Persuaders* (1972–3), but most especially, *The Saint* (1962–9). His own wittiest critic, he brought a lightweight

Moon (far side)

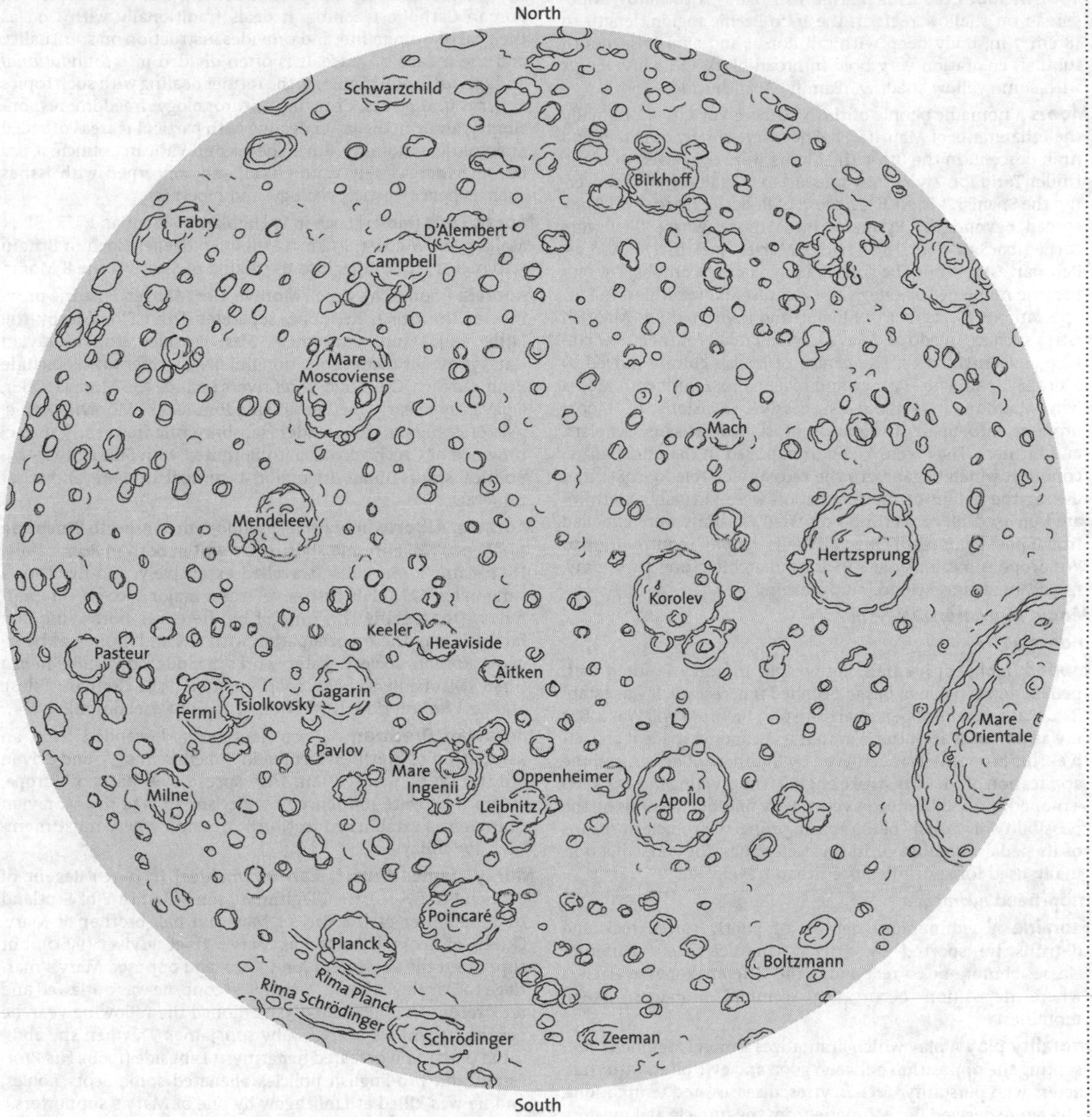

regions), located mainly on the side observable from Earth, represent basaltic (volcanic) flooding of basins created by major asteroidal impacts. Apollo and Luna sample isotopic dating places mare basalts in the range of 3–4 thousand million years, in contrast to 4·2–4·5 thousand million for highland samples. Lunar evolution models based on Lunar Orbiter mapping of the Moon and on Apollo and Luna sample analyses suggest five principal episodes: accretion and large-scale melting; crustal separation and concurrent massive meteoritic bombardment; partial melting at depth; diminished bombardment with further melting at depth and emplacement of mare basalts; and cessation of volcanism and gradual internal cooling. The popular current theory for the creation of the Moon involves the impact of a Mars-sized object with the Earth, occasioning a catastrophic disruption of the Earth, and the accretion of the Moon in Earth orbit from debris torn from the Earth's mantle.

insouciance to the role of James Bond in seven films between *Live and Let Die* (1973) and *A View to a Kill* (1985). Recent films include *Spice World* (1997). He was knighted in 2003.

Moores, Sir John (1896–1993) Businessman, born in Eccles, Greater Manchester, NW England, UK. He founded Littlewoods football pools in 1923, distributing 4000 coupons by hand in Liverpool. Following a visit to America, he established a mail-order business in Britain (1932), and opened the first store in the Littlewoods chain in 1937. When Liverpool Polytechnic was awarded university status in 1992, it took the name of Liverpool John Moores University.

moorhen Either of two species of rail of the genus *Gallinula*, especially the **moorhen**, **common gallinule**, or **Florida gallinule** (*Gallinula chloropus*), found worldwide; also the **lesser** or

little moorhen (*Gallinula angulata*), found in sub-Saharan Africa; long legs and toes; inhabit water margins; related to coots.

moorish idol Colourful marine fish (*Zanclus cornutus*) widespread on shallow reefs in the Indo-Pacific region; length to 18 cm/7 in; body deep with tall dorsal and anal fins; mouth tubular; coloration very bold in broad black and white bands with some yellow shading. (Family: Acanthuridae.)

Moors A nomadic people of the N seaboard of Africa, originally the inhabitants of Mauritania. They were chiefly of Berber and Arab descent. In the 8th-c the Moors were converted to Islam. Under Tariq ibn Ziyad they crossed to Gibraltar (711) and overran the Spanish Visigoth kingdom of Roderick (r.710–?711). They spread beyond the Pyrenees into France, where they were turned back at Tours by Charles Martel (732). In 776, Abd ar-Rahman established the Umayyad dynasty at Cordoba. The city became renowned as one of the greatest and wealthiest in Europe, famous as a centre of Muslim and Jewish culture. Moorish cities such as Toledo and Seville were famed for their new culture and universities. The centre of Jewish culture moved to Moorish Spain (7th–15th-c), and reached its zenith with Moses ben Maimon (1135–1204). Successive invasions of Moors brought into Spain thousands of skilled artisans, scholars, and farmers. They were killed or expelled in the Christian reconquest which began with the recovery of Toledo (1085), and during the height of the Inquisition were virtually exterminated. In 1502 all remaining professed Muslims were expelled from Spain by order of Queen Isabella. Moorish contribution to W Europe is incalculable – in art and architecture, astronomy, music, medicine, science, and learning.

Moors Murderers *Brady, Ian*

moose *elk*

moped [**moh**ped] A small, lightweight motorcycle fitted with pedals, and capable of being pedalled if necessary. It was established as a means of personal transport before World War 2, but it was not until after the War that its economy made it attractive. This economy was achieved by lightness of design and the application of the two-stroke engine. The dividing line between a moped and a light motorcycle is very fine, but depends on the possibility of actually being able to propel the vehicle by means of its pedals. Because of its characteristics, the moped is normally used for short distance urban travel.

mop-head *hydrangea*

moraine A sedimentary deposit of poorly sorted rock and detritus transported by glaciers and ice-sheets. Different classes of moraine correspond to the different zones of glaciers where deposition occurs (eg terminal moraines, lateral moraines).

morality play A play which dramatizes a moral argument, presenting the opposition between good and evil, often with characters who personify virtues, vices, diseases, and temptations. The genre derived its technique from the miracle and mystery play, and its subject matter from sermons. It was popular in England, Scotland, France, and The Netherlands in the 15th-c and early 16th-c. Unlike the mystery play, it was not tied to religious festivals, and was performed by professional actors. The earliest surviving example in English is the *Castle of Perseverance* (1420), and the best-known is *Everyman* (c.1510).

Moral Majority A US political action committee founded in 1979 which has played a leading part in the revival of the New Right. It campaigns for the election of morally conservative politicians and for changes to public policy in such areas as abortion, homosexuality, and school prayers. It is associated with Christian fundamentalists, who in the 1980s came to play a prominent role in US politics.

Moral Rearmament A movement founded by Frank Buchman in 1938 to deepen the spirituality and morality of Christians. It succeeded the 'Oxford Group' movement (founded 1921; not to be confused with the earlier Oxford Movement), and the original individualistic and pietistic emphasis was expanded to include political and social concerns.

moral theology A theological discipline concerned with ethical questions considered from a specifically Christian perspective. Its sources include scripture, tradition, and philosophy. In Roman Catholic teaching, it deals traditionally with God as the goal of human life, and provides instruction on spirituality and the means of grace. It is often divided into *foundational* and *special* moral theology, the former dealing with such topics as scriptural ethics, Christian anthropology, freedom, responsibility, and sin; the latter dealing with particular areas of social and political morality. Since the Second Vatican Council, it has become increasingly ecumenical, and concerned with issues such as peace, justice, ecology, and bioethics.

Morar, Loch [**mo**rer] Loch in W Highland, W Scotland, UK; SE of Mallaig, on W coast; 19 km/12 mi long; deepest loch in Britain (310 m/1017 ft); drains into the Sound of Sleat via the R Morar.

Moravia [mo**ray**via], Czech **Morava**, Ger **Mähren** Historic province of the Czech Republic; separated from Slovakia by the Little and White Carpathian Mts; corridor (the Moravian Gate) provides communication link (N–S); chief towns include Brno, Ostrava, Olomouc; chief rivers include the Morava, Oder, Opava, Dyje; early mediaeval kingdom (Great Moravia), 9th-c; part of Bohemia, 1029; under Habsburg rule from early 16th-c; province of Czechoslovakia, 1918; united with Silesia, 1927–49; political status under discussion, 1991; coal, iron ore, and other minerals.

Moravia, Alberto [mo**ray**via], pseudonym of **Alberto Pincherle** (1907–90) Novelist and short-story writer, born in Rome, Italy. He became a journalist, travelled extensively, and lived for a time in the USA. His first novel was a major success, *Gli indifferenti* (1929, trans The Time of Indifference), portraying in a fatalistic way the preoccupation with sex and money of bourgeois Roman society. Later works include *La disubbidienza* (1948, Disobedience), *Racconti romani* (1954, Roman Tales), and *La Vita Interiore* (1978, trans Time of Desecration).

Moravian Brethren A Protestant body descended from an association of Brethren formed in Bohemia in 1457, and driven out in 1722 by persecution. They spread over parts of Europe, where they were influenced by Pietism. In 1734 the Moravian Church was established in North America, where most members live today.

Moray, James Stuart, Earl of [**muh**ree] (1531–70) Regent of Scotland (1567–70), the illegitimate son of James V of Scotland by a daughter of the Earl of Mar, and half-brother of Mary, Queen of Scots. He acted as Mary's chief adviser (1560), but supported the Protestant John Knox and opposed Mary's marriage to Darnley. After an attempted coup, he was outlawed and took refuge in England (1565). Pardoned the following year, he became regent for Mary's baby son, James VI, when she abdicated (1567), and defeated her army at Langside (1568). His Protestant and pro-English policies alienated some Scots nobles, and he was killed at Linlithgow by one of Mary's supporters.

moray eel Any of the family Muraenidae of marine eels, widespread in tropical and warm temperate seas; dorsal and anal fins continuous, pelvics and pectorals absent; teeth well-developed; largest species may exceed 3 m/10 ft in length; includes *Muraena helena*, found in the Mediterranean and E Atlantic; length up to 1·3 m/4·3 ft; mottled brown and yellow; may be extremely aggressive.

morbidity *disease frequency*

Morceli, Noureddine [maw(r)**se**lee] (1970–) Athlete, born in Tenes, N Algeria. World champion over 1500 m in 1991 – the youngest ever – he repeated his success in 1993 and 1995. During the latter year he held the world record for 1500 m, the mile, 2000 m and 3000 m, and in 1996 was Olympic 1500 m champion.

Mordecai [**maw(r)**dekiy] (c.5th-c BC) Biblical hero. He is described in the Book of Esther as a Jew in exile in Persia, who cared for his orphaned cousin Esther and gained the favour of King Xerxes after uncovering a plot against him. He used his subsequent influence to protect Jews from an edict issued against them. The event is commemorated by the annual Jewish feast of Purim.

More, Henry [moor] (1614–87) Philosopher and theologian, born in Grantham, Lincolnshire, EC England, UK. He studied at Cambridge, where he remained all his life, and became a leading figure in the circle of 'Cambridge Platonists' which included Whichcote and Cudworth. He devoted himself entirely to study, despite the turbulent political times in which he lived, and developed a particular affinity for Plato, Plotinus, and Descartes. He wrote in prose and verse, his main works being *Philosophical Poems* (1647), *The Immortality of the Soul* (1659), and *Divine Dialogues* (1668).

More, Sir Thomas [moor], also **St Thomas More** (1478–1535) English statesman and scholar, born in London, UK. He studied at Oxford, became a lawyer, then spent four years in a Carthusian monastery to test his vocation for the priesthood. He did not take holy orders, and under Henry VIII became Master of Requests (1514), Treasurer of the Exchequer (1521), and Chancellor of the Duchy of Lancaster (1525). On the fall of Wolsey (1529), he was appointed Lord Chancellor, but resigned in 1532 following his opposition to Henry's break with the Roman Catholic Church. On refusing to recognize Henry as head of the English Church, he was imprisoned and beheaded. A leading humanist scholar, as revealed in his Latin *Utopia* (1516) and many other works, he was canonized in 1935, and declared the patron saint of politicians in 2000; feast day 22 June.

Moreau, Gustave [moroh] (1826–98) Painter, born in Paris, France. He studied at the Ecole des Beaux-Arts, where he was appointed professor of painting in 1892. He was an eccentric Symbolist who painted colourful but usually rather sinister scenes from ancient mythology and the Bible, as in 'Salome' (1876).

Morecambe, Eric, originally **Eric Bartholomew** (1926–84) Comedian, born in Morecambe, Lancashire, NW England, UK. Having appeared in working men's clubs since the age of 11, he teamed up in 1943 with fellow entertainer, **Ernie Wise** (originally **Ernest Wiseman**) (1925–99). They made their West End debut in the revue *Strike a New Note* in 1943. In 1947 they teamed up again and, as **Morecambe and Wise**, subsequently became the finest British comedy double-act for many years, working in music-hall, summer-shows, pantomimes, radio, films, and television. In 1968, Morecambe had a heart attack; they reduced their work-load, concentrating on their television shows – programmes of sketches interspersed with the double-act routine. Their films, such as *The Magnificent Two* (1967), were not successful; the small screen and the stage were their media, and quick-fire repartee their true forte.

morel [morel] An edible fungus (*Morchella esculenta*); fruiting body consists of a pale stalk (*stipe*) and brownish, egg-shaped head with a pitted or ridged surface; found singly, sometimes in rings, in rich alkaline soils in woods, pastures, and bonfire sites. (Subdivision: Ascomycetes. Order: Pezizales.)

morello cherry *cherry*

Morgagni, Giovanni Battista [maw(r)ganyee] (1682–1771) Physician, born in Forli, NEC Italy. He studied at Bologna, worked as an anatomical demonstrator, and became professor of medicine at Padua in 1711. In his writings, he correlated pathological lesions with symptoms in over 700 cases, and is traditionally considered to be the founder of the science of pathological anatomy, 'the father of morbid anatomy'.

Morgan, Edwin (George) (1920–) Poet, born in Glasgow, W Scotland, UK. He studied at Glasgow University, where he later taught literature. He is a versatile writer, having produced both powerful 'social' poems (the Glasgow Sonnets in *From Glasgow to Saturn*, 1973) as well as much experimental writing, including concrete and computer poems. His work is well represented in *Poems of Thirty Years* (1982). Later works include *You: Anti-War Poetry* (1991) and *Collected Poems* (1996).

Morgan, Sir Henry (c.1635–88) Buccaneer, born in Llanrumney, S Wales, UK. Kidnapped as a child in Bristol and shipped to Barbados, he joined the buccaneers, leading many raids against the Spanish and Dutch in the West Indies and Central America. His most famous exploit was the sacking of Porto Bello and Panama (1671). Transported to London under arrest (1672) to placate the Spanish, he was subsequently knighted (1674) on the renewal of hostilities. He moved to Jamaica, where he became a wealthy planter and deputy-governor.

Morgan, J(ohn) P(ierpont) (1837–1913) Banker, financier, and art collector, born in Hartford, Connecticut, USA. The son of the financier **Junius Spencer Morgan** (1813–90), he built his father's firm into the most powerful private banking house in the USA. His house, along with the Rothschilds, provided a loan to help the US government during the depression of 1893. It later developed the railroad system, and formed the US Steel Corporation (1901). He compiled one of the greatest private art collections of his day, which he bequeathed to the Metropolitan Museum of Art in New York City. He was also noted for his extensive philanthropic benefactions. His son, **John Pierpont Jr** (1867–1943), succeeded him, and raised loans for Britain during World War 1.

Morgan, Thomas Hunt (1866–1945) Geneticist and biologist, born in Lexington, Kentucky, USA. He studied zoology at Kentucky State College and Johns Hopkins University, and became professor of experimental zoology at Columbia (1904–28) and the California Institute of Technology (1928–45). He carried out experiments with the *Drosophila* fruit fly, and established a chromosome theory of heredity involving genes for specific tasks aligned on chromosomes, which earned him the 1933 Nobel Prize for Physiology or Medicine.

Morgan A breed of strong horse, developed in the 19th-c in the USA; descended from one stallion called *Justin Morgan* (originally called *Figure*); height, 14–15½ hands/1·4–1·6 m/4½–5¼ ft; brown or black; good riding or carriage horse.

Morgan le Fay In Arthurian legend, an enchantress, 'Morgan the Fairy', King Arthur's sister, and generally hostile towards him. She was one of the three queens who received him at his death.

Morisot, Berthe (Marie Pauline) [morisoh] (1841–95) Painter and printmaker, born in Bourges, C France, the grand-daughter of painter Jean Fragonard (1732–1806). The leading female exponent of Impressionism, she painted chiefly women and children. Her early work shows the influence of Corot, who was her friend and mentor, but her later style owes more to Renoir. She herself exercised an influence on Manet, whose brother Eugène she married.

Morley, Edward Williams (1838–1923) Chemist and physicist, born in Newark, New Jersey, USA. He was taught at home, and studied at Williams College. He became a Congregational minister, like his father, but taught science at the college which became Western Reserve University, OH (1869–1906). His early research was on the oxygen content of air, and he also studied the relative atomic mass of oxygen (measured to within 1 in 10 000). He worked with Albert Abraham Michelson in their famous experiments to detect the 'ether-drift' (1887).

Morley, Robert (1908–92) Actor and writer, born in Semley, Wiltshire, S England, UK. He trained in London, and appeared on the London and Broadway stages. In his film career, from 1938, he played many individual character parts, including the title role in *Oscar Wilde* (1960). His appearances continued into the 1980s, with *Loophole* (1980) and *Sky High* (1986). He was well known for his edited collections, such as *Robert Morley's Book of Bricks* (1979), and humorous anecdotal writing, such as *Morley Matters* (1980).

Mormons [mawmuhnz] A religious movement based on the visionary experiences of Joseph Smith, who organized it as the 'Church of Jesus Christ of Latter-Day Saints' in 1830 at Fayette, NY. Smith claimed to have been led to the Book of Mormon, inscribed on golden plates and buried 1000 years before in a hill near Palmyra, NY. An account of an ancient American people to whom Christ appeared after his ascension, it teaches Christ's future establishment of the New Jerusalem in America. It is regarded as equal with the Bible. Subjected to persecution, the Mormons moved W, and Brigham Young finally led most of them to the valley of the Great Salt Lake, Utah (1847). Their practice of plural marriage (until 1890) was one of several issues which brought persecution of the Church, culminating in the assassination of Joseph Smith in 1844. Mormons now actively engage in missionary work and give two years' voluntary service to the Church. There were over 11 million worldwide in 2004.

Mornay, Philippe de, seigneur du (Lord of) **Plessay-Marly** (1549–1623) French Huguenot leader and polemicist, born in Buhy, NW France. Converted to Protestantism in 1560, he was nicknamed the 'Pope of the Huguenots' for his role in the Wars of Religion (1562–98). A trusted counsellor of Henry of Navarre, he undertook many embassies for the Protestant cause; however, he lost the king's favour after Henry's conversion to Catholicism (1593) and played no further part in national affairs.

morning-after pill *contraception; DES*

morning glory An annual (*Ipomoea tricolor*) growing to 3 m/10 ft, native to tropical America; climbing by means of twining stems; leaves oval to heart-shaped; flowers up to 12·5 cm/5 in diameter, funnel-shaped, blue with yellow throat, sometimes purple or red. It is a relative of the sweet potato and bindweeds, and a popular ornamental. (Family: Convolvulaceae.)

morning sickness Nausea and vomiting during the first three months of pregnancy, which affects c.50% of women. It tends to subside thereafter, and is believed to result from associated hormonal changes.

Moro, Aldo [moroh] (1916–78) Italian statesman and prime minister (1963–4, 1964–6, 1966–8, 1974–6, 1976), born in Maglie, SE Italy. He was professor of law at the University of Bari, and published several books on legal subjects. After World War 2 he was elected deputy to the Constituent Assembly and to the Legislature and held various cabinet posts. He took office as secretary of the Christian Democrats (1959) and, although leader of the centrist group within the Party, was sympathetic to the Socialists. He was Italian premier on five occasions, then became Leader of the Christian Democrats (1976), which afforded him powerful influence in Italian politics. Red Brigade left-wing terrorists kidnapped him in Rome in 1978 and subsequently murdered him.

Morocco *p.1037*

Moroni [morohnee] 11°40S 43°16E, pop (2000e) 26 300. Capital of Comoros, and chief town of Njazidja (formerly Grande Comore I); airport; vanilla, coffee, cacao, soft drinks, metal and wood products; several mosques; pilgrimage centre at Chiouanda.

Morpeth 55°10N 1°41W, pop (2000e) 15 200. County town of Northumberland, NE England, UK, on the R Wansbeck, 23 km/14 mi N of Newcastle upon Tyne; railway; light engineering, market gardening, mineral water; remains of Morpeth Castle (14th-c).

Morpheus [maw(r)fyoos] In Roman mythology, one of the sons of Somnus ('sleep') who sends or impersonates images of people in the dreamer's mind. Later, as in Spenser, he is the god of sleep.

morphine A drug derived from opium, used to ease severe pain. Because of its addictive potential, its use is controlled. In overdoses it causes death by suppressing respiration. It is also used in anti-diarrhoeal preparations.

morpho A large to very large butterfly with bright, metallic wings; colours produced by scales on wings rather than by pigments; caterpillars with divided last abdominal segment; feeding on leguminous plants. (Order: Lepidoptera. Family: Nymphalidae.)

morphology (biology) The form and structure of an individual organism, with special emphasis on its external features.

morphology (linguistics) In linguistics, the study of **morphemes**, the smallest indivisible units of meaning in the structure of a word (eg *anti-lock-ing, un-worthi-ness, horse-s*). It recognizes such notions as roots, inflections, prefixes, suffixes, and compound words, and tries to establish the rules governing the way words are formed and inter-related within specific languages and language in general.

Morris, Desmond (John) (1928–) British zoologist and writer. He studied at Birmingham and Oxford, then did research into animal behaviour under Nikolaas Tinbergen. His later career as head of Granada TV's Film Unit at London Zoo (1956–9), and curator of mammals for the Zoological Society (1959–67), developed his interest in the explanation and demonstration of animal behaviour to the public. Already the author of scientific papers, his study of human behaviour in *The Naked Ape* (1967) became a best seller, popularizing sociology and zoology, and was followed by many television programmes on animal and social behaviour. His other books include *The Human Zoo* (1969), *Manwatching* (1977), *The Soccer Tribe* (1981), *Catwatching* and *Dogwatching* (both 1986), *Animal-Watching* (1990), *Illustrated Babywatching* (1995), *Body Guards* (1999), and *Peoplewatching* (2002).

Morris, Estelle (1952–) British stateswoman, born in Manchester, Greater Manchester, NW England, UK. She studied at Coventry College of Education and Warwick University, and took up a teaching post at a comprehensive school in Coventry (1974–92). Elected Labour MP for Birmingham Yardley in 1992, she became minister of state for the Department for Education and Employment (1997–8), minister for school standards (1997–2001), secretary of state for education and skills (2001–2), and arts minister (2003–).

Morris, Robert L(yle) (1942–) Psychologist, born in Canonsburg, Pennsylvania, USA. He studied at the University of Pittsburgh and Duke University. In 1985 he was appointed the first Koestler professor of parapsychology at the University of Edinburgh.

Morris, Robert (1931–) Sculptor and mixed media artist, born in Kansas City, Missouri, USA. He studied engineering and art, and after moving to San Francisco in 1950 became active as a painter and in improvisatory theatre. He settled in New York City in 1961, specializing in minimalist works, earthwork projects, and scatter pieces.

Morris, William (1834–96) Craftsman, poet, and political activist, born in Walthamstow, NC Greater London, UK. Educated at Marlborough College, he studied for holy orders at Oxford, but renounced the Church, studied architecture, then became a professional painter (1857–62). In 1861, after designing and furnishing his marital home, he founded the firm of Morris, Marshall, Faulkner & Co, which revolutionized the art of house decoration and furniture in England. His literary career began with a volume of poetry. He visited Iceland twice (1871, 1873), and was inspired to write *The Story of Sigurd the Volsung and the Fall of the Nibelungs* (4 vols, 1876), regarded as the greatest of his many works. His belief that the excellence of mediaeval arts and crafts was destroyed by Victorian mass-production and capitalism led him to join the Social Democratic Federation in 1883, and he subsequently organized the Socialist League. In 1890 he founded the Kelmscott Press at Hammersmith, issuing his own works and reprints of classics.

morris dance A form of traditional dance dating back to the 15th-c, found in England but with continental European equivalents. Its distinctive features are stamping and hopping performed by rows or circles of performers usually dressed in white and always carrying some prop – a stick, handkerchief, or garland, and traditionally a hobby-horse or inflated pig's bladder. They are accompanied by accordion or concertina with bass drum. What was once an exclusively male dance is now increasingly performed by women's or mixed groups.

Morrison (of Lambeth), Herbert Stanley Morrison, Baron (1888–1965) British statesman, born in London, UK. Largely self-educated, he helped to found the London Labour Party, and became its secretary in 1915. As leader of the London County Council from 1934, he grouped together London's passenger transport system, and much of the credit for the 'Green Belt' was due to him. First elected an MP in 1923, in Churchill's war

Morocco

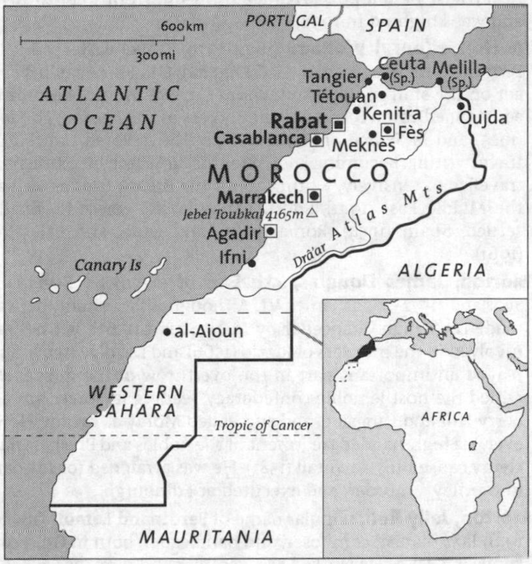

☐ International Airport

[muhrokoh], official name **The Kingdom of Morocco**, Arabic **al-Mamlakah al-Maghribiyah**

Local name al-Magrib

Timezone GMT

Area 409 200 km²/157 951 sq mi

Population total (2002e) 29 632 000

Status Kingdom

Date of independence 1956

Capital Rabat

Languages Arabic (official), Berber, Spanish, and French also widely spoken

Ethnic groups Arab-Berber (99%), non-Moroccan (0·7%), Jewish (0·2%)

Religions Sunni Muslim (98%), Christian (1%), Jewish (0·2%)

Physical features Dominated by a series of mountain ranges, rising in the Atlas Mts (S) to 4165 m/13 664 ft at Jebel Toubkal; broad coastal plain; main rivers, Drâ'ar (S and SW) and Moulouya (N) draining into the Mediterranean.

Climate Mediterranean climate on N coast; semi-arid in S; Sahara virtually rainless; average annual temperatures 13°C (Jan), 22°C (Jul) in Rabat; average annual rainfall 564 mm/22·2 in.

Currency 1 Moroccan Dirham (DH) = 100 Moroccan francs

Economy Agriculture (employs over 50% of population); largest known reserves of phosphate in world; fishing, textiles, cement, soap, tobacco, chemicals, paper, timber products; tourism centred on the four imperial cities and the warm Atlantic resorts.

GDP (2002e) $121·8 bn, per capita $3900

Human Development Index (2002) 0·602

History N coast occupied by Phoenicians, Carthaginians, and Romans since 12th-c BC; invasion by Arabs, 7th-c AD; conflicting French and Spanish interest in the region in 19th-c; Treaty of Fez in 1912, established Spanish Morocco (capital, Tétouan) and French Morocco (capital, Rabat); Tangier became an international zone, 1923–56; protectorates gained independence, 1956; became Kingdom of Morocco, 1957; Spanish withdrew from former Spanish Sahara (Western Sahara) in 1975; Morocco laid claim to this area using the 'Green March' as a gesture of peaceful occupation; Mauritania withdrew from southern third of territory in 1979, leaving Morocco fighting with the Polisario for the whole of Western Sahara; ceasefire agreement signed, 1990; 'constitutional' monarchy, but the King presides over his appointed Cabinet, which is led by a Prime Minister; a unicameral Chamber of Representatives.

Head of State (Monarch)

1957–61 Mohammed V
1961–99 Hassan II
1999– Mohammad VI

Head of Government

1955–8 Si Mohammed Bekkai
1958 Ahmad Balfrej
1958–60 Abdullah Ibrahim
1960–3 *As monarch*
1963–5 Ahmad Bahnini
1965–7 *As monarch*
1967–9 Moulay Ahmed Laraki
1969–71 Mohammed Ben Hima
1971–2 Mohammed Karim Lamrani
1972–9 Ahmed Othman
1979–83 Maati Bouabid
1983–5 Mohammed Karim Lamrani
1985–92 Azzedine Laraka
1992–4 Mohammed Karim Lamrani
1994–8 Abdellatif Filali
1998–2002 Abderrahmane el-Yousifi
2002– Driss Jettou

cabinet he was home secretary and minister of home security. A powerful figure in the post-war social revolution, he was deputy prime minister (1945–51), Lord President of the Council, and Leader of the House of Commons. In 1951 he became deputy Leader of the Opposition, but was defeated by Hugh Gaitskell in the contest for the leadership of the Labour Party in 1955. He was created a life peer in 1959.

Morrison, Toni, *née* **Chloe Anthony Wofford** (1931–) Novelist, born in Lorain, Ohio, USA. She studied at Howard and Cornell universities, then taught at Howard before moving to New York City in 1965. She worked in publishing as a senior editor at Random House before becoming a novelist. She explores in rich vocabulary and cold-blooded detail the story of rural African-Americans. Her early titles include *The Bluest Eye* (1970) and *Song of Solomon* (1977). Two later novels, *Tar Baby* (1981) and *Beloved* (1988, Pulitzer), confirmed her as one of the most important novelists of her generation, and she received the Nobel Prize for Literature in 1993. Later books include *Jazz* (1993), *Paradise* (1998), and *Love* (2003).

Morrison, Van, popular name of **George Ivan Morrison** (1945–) Singer, musician, and songwriter, born in Belfast, NE Northern Ireland, UK. After leaving school at the age of 15, he played guitar and later saxophone in several teenage groups, making his first recordings as a member of Them during the 1960s. His first solo hit was 'Brown-Eyed Girl' (1967) and a year later he released the highly acclaimed, surreal album *Astral Weeks*. Other successes of that period included 'Caravan' (1970) and the albums *Moondance* (1970) and *Tupelo Honey* (1971). In the 1980s his work developed a more mystical dimension. He continued to record into the 2000s, with such albums as *The Healing Game* (1996) and *Down the Road* (2002). A celebrated live performer, he insisted that every note be recorded live for the acclaimed album 'It's Too Late To Stop Now' (1974).

Morrison, Mount *Yu Shan*

Morse, Samuel F(inley) B(reese) (1791–1872) Artist, and inventor of the telegraph and Morse code, born in Charlestown, Massachusetts, USA. He graduated from Yale in 1810, and studied painting in England. Founder and first president of the National Academy of Design in New York City (1826), he taught art at New York University from 1832. Interested in chemistry and electricity, from 1832–5 he worked on the development of a magnetic telegraph, which he exhibited to Congress in 1837, and attempted in vain to patent in Europe. He struggled on with scanty means until 1843, when Congress voted him $30 000 for an experimental telegraph line between Washington and Baltimore, built by Ezra Cornell (1807–74), over which he sent the historic message, 'What hath God wrought?' on 24 May 1844. His system, widely adopted, together with that of Morse code (1838), brought him honours and rewards.

Morse code A binary code for the transmission of verbal messages, devised during the 1830s by Samuel Morse. Each letter of the alphabet, numeral, and punctuation mark was assigned a distinctive combination of (short) dots and (long) dashes. Thus the distress call SOS was rendered ···---···. An improved version, known as the International Morse Code, was devised at a European conference in 1851. Morse has continued to be used in ship-to-shore communication and various other contexts, but modern telegraphy has made greater use of the more economical **Baudot code**, devised in 1874 by French engineer Jean Maurice Emile Baudot. Although Morse code was officially replaced by the Global Maritime Distress and Safety System (GMDSS) in 1999, it will continue to be used by amateur radio enthusiasts and others.

mortality *disease frequency*

mortar (building) Any one of many mixtures of lime and sand or (modern) cement and sand with water, which provide a bond between bricks, masonry, or tiles.

mortar (military) A weapon, used typically by infantry forces, which projects a small bomb at a high trajectory to fall on enemy forces at short range.

mortar and pestle A device known in various forms since ancient times for grinding granular material into powder. The **mortar** is a bowl of hard material. The **pestle** is a conical piece of similar material with a rounded end, with which the material to be ground is forced against the bowl. Simple forms are used in the kitchen or in simple pharmacy. Modern sophisticated mechanized versions are used in industry.

mortgage [mawgij] An arrangement whereby a lender (the **mortgagee**) lends money to a borrower (the **mortgagor**), the loan being secured on the mortgagor's assets (commonly land or buildings). Mortgages have played a significant role in permitting the spread of home ownership. However, mortgages are not confined to loans used to buy homes or land. Mortgages of chattels are possible, but the complexity of the relevant law has meant that such mortgages are uncommon. A mortgage is unlike a hire-purchase agreement in that the mortgaged property belongs to the borrower. Mortgages of various kinds (eg endowment, capped, interest-only, and repayment) are typically extended by building societies, banks, and insurance companies to businesses and individual house-buyers. The mortgage lapses when the loan is fully repaid along with all the interest due.

Mortier, Edouard Adolphe Casimir Joseph, duc de Trevise (Duke of Treviso) [maw(r)tyay] (1768–1835) French soldier who fought in the Revolutionary and Napoleonic Wars, born in Cateau-Cambrésis, N France. Promoted to general (1799) and Marshal of the Empire (1804), he campaigned in Germany, Russia, and Spain. He was prime minister and minister of war (1834–5) under Louis Philippe, at whose side he was killed during an assassination attempt on the king's life in Paris.

Mortimer, Sir John (Clifford) (1923–) Playwright, novelist, and barrister, born in London, UK. He studied at Oxford, was called to the bar in 1948, and became a QC in 1966. He became known as a dramatist with his one-act play *The Dock Brief* (1957). An autobiographical play, *A Voyage Round My Father* (1970), was filmed for television in 1982. He has written several TV screenplays, including *I, Claudius* (1976) and *Brideshead Revisited* (1981). His series of novels featuring the disreputable barrister, Horace Rumpole, were adapted for television as *Rumpole of the Bailey*, and won him the British television writer of the year award in 1980. His other novels include *Paradise Postponed* (1985), *Under the Hammer* (1994), and *Summer of a Dormouse* (1999). Among other works are a volume of autobiography, *Clinging to the Wreckage* (1982), and *Where There's a Will* (2003), a collection of his observations on life. He was married to novelist **Penelope Mortimer** (1918–99) from 1949 to 1972, and was knighted in 1998.

Morton, H(enry) V(ollam) (1892–1979) Travel writer, born in Birmingham, West Midlands, C England, UK. He began his career on the staff of the *Birmingham Gazette* in 1910, becoming assistant editor in 1912. After the success of *The Heart of London* (1925) and *In Search of England* (1927), he devoted himself to travel writing, becoming known for his 'In Search of ...' titles. He travelled extensively, writing about the British Isles as well as the Middle East (1941), South Africa (1948), where he finally settled, Spain (1954), Rome (1957), and Israel and Palestine (1961).

Morton, James Douglas, 4th Earl of (c.1516–81) Regent of Scotland (1572–8) for James VI. Although a Protestant, he was made Lord High Chancellor by Mary Stuart (1563); yet he was involved in the murders of Rizzio (1566) and Darnley (1567), and played an important part in the overthrow of the queen. He joined the hostile noble confederacy, leading its forces at Carberry Hill and Langside, and succeeded Moray as regent. However, his high-handed treatment of the nobles and Presbyterian clergy caused his downfall (1581). He was arraigned for his part in Darnley's murder, and executed at Edinburgh.

Morton, Jelly Roll, popular name of **Ferdinand Lemott** (1890–1941) Jazz pianist, composer, and bandleader, born in Gulfport, Louisiana, USA. He worked as a gambler and pimp as well as a piano entertainer. His genius as a jazz pioneer is revealed in the recordings he made (1923–7) while living in Chicago. His unaccompanied piano solos made best sellers of such tunes as 'King Porter Stomp', 'Wolverine Blues', and 'Jelly Roll Blues'. His orchestral arrangements for his band, the Red Hot Peppers, blended lyricism with stomping rhythms, and ensemble subtlety with improvisation. He died, all but forgotten, in Los Angeles, but his recordings were rediscovered with considerable fanfare a few years later.

Morton, John (c.1420–1500) Statesman and cardinal, probably born in Milborne St Andrew, Dorset, S England, UK. He practised as a lawyer, and strongly supported Henry VI, but after the Battle of Tewkesbury made his peace with Edward IV, and became Master of the Rolls (1473) and Bishop of Ely (1479). Richard III imprisoned him in 1483, but he escaped, and after the accession of Henry VII was made Archbishop of Canterbury (1486), Chancellor (1487), and a cardinal (1493).

Morton, John Cameron (Andrieu Bingham Michael), pseudonym **Beachcomber** (1893–1979) British writer and journalist. After serving in World War 1, he took up writing and published many books of humour, fantasy, and satire, as well as a number of historical works, including several on the French Revolution. From 1924 to 1975 he contributed a regular humorous column, 'By the Way', to the *Daily Express* under his pseudonym.

mosaic The technique of making decorative designs or pictures by arranging small pieces (*tesserae*) of coloured glass, marble, or ceramic in a bed of cement. It was much used by the Romans for pavements, by the early Christians and Byzantines for murals in churches, and also by Islamic artists. Interest in mosaic revived in Italy in the later 19th-c.

Mosaic Law *Torah*

mosasaurus [mohsasawrus] A very large, marine lizard abundant in Cretaceous seas around N Europe and America; swimming mainly by movements of tail; paddle-like limbs used for steering; head long, teeth long and sharp; typically fed on fishes and other vertebrates. (Order: Squamata.)

moschatel [moskatel] A perennial (*Adoxa moschatellina*) native to the N hemisphere, 5–10 cm/2–4 in high; rhizomatous; leaves divided into three toothed leaflets; flowers greenish-yellow, forming an almost square head, each face formed by a 5-petalled flower (hence the alternative name, **town hall clock**) plus a 4-petalled flower at the top. (Family: Adoxaceae.)

Mosconi, Willie [moskohnee], popular name of **William Joseph Mosconi** (1913–93) Pocket billiards player, born in Philadelphia, Pennsylvania, USA. After pocketing $75 in a Depression tournament, he took the first of many world titles in 1941. A tireless promoter of the game, he was technical adviser for the movie *The Hustler* (1961), and wrote *Willie Mosconi on Pocket Billiards* (1959).

Moscow, Russ **Moskva** 55°45N 37°42E, pop (2000e) 9 400 000. Capital and largest city of Russia, on the R Moskva; linked by canal to the R Volga; known from the 12th-c; capital of the principality of Muscovy, 13th-c; invaded by Napoleon, 1812; capital of the Russian SFSR, 1918; capital of the USSR, 1922; airport; railway; underground; universities (1755, 1960); Academy of Sciences; solar research, clothing, footwear, textiles, oil refining, chemicals, publishing, tourism; Moscow Art Theatre, Bolshoi Theatre of Opera and Ballet, Moscow State Circus; Kremlin (1300); Spassky Tower (symbol of Moscow), Uspenski (Assumption) Cathedral (1475–9), Cathedral of the Archangel (1333, rebuilt 1505–9), Blagoveshchenski (Annunciation) Cathedral, Great Palace (1838–49), Granovitaya Palace (1487–91), Oruzheinaya Plata or Armoury (1849–51), Palace of the Patriarchs (17th-c), Red Square, St Basil's Cathedral (16th-c), Lenin Mausoleum; numerous theatres, art galleries, museums notably the Lenin Museum and the Museum of the Revolution; scene of the 1980 Olympic Games.

Moscow Art Theatre Now one of the most prestigious of Russian theatrical institutions, which began in 1898 as a company of student and amateur actors. Its fame rests on its founders – Stanislavsky and Nemirovich-Danchenko – and their determined advocacy of theatre as a serious and important art; on its meticulous and innovative productions of Chekhov and Gorki; and on its studios, established from 1913 onwards for training and experimental work. It is now a state theatre dedicated to Maxim Gorky.

Moselle, River [mohzel], Ger **Mosel**, ancient **Mosella** River in Germany, Luxembourg, and NE France; rises in the French Vosges; flows N and NE to enter the R Rhine at Koblenz; length 514 km/319 mi; navigable length 240 km/150 mi; canalized since 1964, with a series of 10 dams to regulate its flow; a major wine area.

Moser-Pröll, Annemarie [mohzer proel], *née* **Pröll** (1953–) Alpine skier, born in Kleinarl, Austria. She won a women's record 62 World Cup races (1970–9), and was overall champion (1979), downhill champion (1978, 1979), Olympic downhill champion (1980), world combined champion (1972, 1978), and world downhill champion (1974, 1978, 1980). She temporarily retired in 1975–6, after her marriage, and finally retired after the 1980 Olympics.

Moses [mohziz] (c.13th-c BC) Major character of Israelite history, portrayed in the Book of Exodus as the leader of the deliverance of Hebrew slaves from Egypt and the recipient of the Ten Commandments at Mt Sinai. In Exodus, stories about his early life depict his escape from death as an infant by being hidden in the bulrushes, his upbringing in the Egyptian court, his flight to Midian, and his divine call to lead the Hebrews out of Egypt. Stories of this deliverance describe Moses predicting a series of miraculous plagues designed to persuade the Pharaoh to release the Hebrews, the Passover narrative, and the miraculous escape led by Moses through the 'sea of reeds'. Traditions then describe Moses' leadership of the Israelites during their 40 years of wilderness wandering, and his death E of the Jordan R before the Hebrews entered Canaan, the Promised Land. He was traditionally considered the author of the five books of the Law, the Pentateuch of the Hebrew Bible, but this is doubted by modern scholars.

Moses, Ed(win Corley) (1955–) Hurdler, born in Dayton, Ohio, USA. Between August 1977 and June 1987 he ran a record 122 races without defeat. He was the World Cup gold medal winner at the 400 m hurdles in 1977, 1979, and 1981, the world champion in 1983, and Olympic champion in 1976 and 1984, only the US boycott of the 1980 Olympic games preventing a possible hat trick. He won the bronze medal at the 1988 Olympics. Between 1976 and 1983 he broke the world record four times.

Moses, Grandma, popular name of **Anna Mary Robertson Moses** (1860–1961) Artist, born in Greenwich, New York, USA. She began to paint childhood country scenes at about the age of 75, when arthritis made it difficult for her to sew, such as 'Catching the Thanksgiving Turkey' and 'Over the River to Grandma's House'. She had her first show in New York City in 1940, and achieved great popular success throughout the USA.

Moshoeshoe II [moshweshwe], originally **Constantine Bereng Seeiso** (1938–96) King of Lesotho (1966–90, 1994–6). He studied at Oxford, was installed as Paramount Chief of the Basotho people (1960), and proclaimed king when Lesotho became independent six years later. His desire for political involvement led to his being twice placed under house arrest, and in 1970 an eight-month exile in The Netherlands ended when Moshoeshoe agreed to take no further part in the country's politics. A military coup in 1986 replaced the government with a military council with the king as nominal executive head. When Moshoeshoe refused to sanction certain changes in 1990, he was forced to abdicate in favour of his son, **Letsie III**, but returned as king in 1994.

Moslem *Islam*

Mosley, Nicholas [mohzlee], **Baron Ravensdale** (1923–) Writer, born in London, UK. He studied at Oxford, joined the army (1942–6), and published his first novel, *Spaces of the Dark* in 1951. Later novels include *The Rainbearers* (1955), *Accident* (1964, filmed by Joseph Losey in 1967), *Hopeful Monsters* (1990, Whitbread Prize), and *Children of Darkness and Light* (1996). Other works include a 2-volume biography of his parents, Sir Oswald and Lady Cynthia Mosley (1982–3), and a volume of autobiography, *Efforts at Truth* (1995).

Mosley, Sir Oswald (Ernald) [mohzlee] (1896–1980) Politician, born in London, UK. He was successively a Conservative, Independent, and Labour MP, and a member of the 1929 Labour government. He resigned from Labour and founded the New Party (1931). Following a visit to Italy, he joined the British Union of Fascists, of which he became leader, and which is remembered for its anti-Semitic violence in the East End of London and its support for Hitler. Detained under the Defence Regulations during World War 2, he founded another racialist party, the Union Movement, in 1948. His second wife (in 1936) was a member of the Mitford family, **Diana Mitford** (1910–2003).

mosquito, also known as **gnat** A small, slender fly with a piercing proboscis; females feed on blood, males on plant juices; eggs laid in water; larvae aquatic, feeding by filtering plankton from water; pupa comma-shaped, active, lives beneath surface film, suspended by its breathing tube; blood-feeding females act as intermediate hosts of malaria, yellow fever, filariasis, dengue, and other disease organisms; worldwide. (Order: Diptera. Family: Culicidae, c.3000 species.)

Mosquito Coast Undeveloped lowland area in E Honduras and E Nicaragua, Central America, following the Caribbean coast in a 65 km/40 mi-wide strip of tropical forest, lagoons, and swamp; inhabited by Black Creoles and the Miskito, Sumo, and Rama Indians; controlled by the British, 1665–1860; timber, bananas.

Moss, Sir Stirling (1929–) Motor-racing driver, born in London, UK. He won many major races in the 1950s, including the British Grand Prix (twice), the Mille Miglia, and the Targa Florio. He never won a world title, though he was runner-up to Fangio (1955–7) and to Mike Hawthorn (1958). He won 16 races from 66 starts (1951–61). A bad crash at Goodwood in 1962 ended his career. He then became a journalist and broadcaster, returning to saloon car racing in 1980. He was knighted in 1999.

moss A small, spore-bearing, non-vascular plant of the Class Musci, related to liverworts and hornworts. Mat- or cushion-forming, the visible plant is the gametophyte which begins as an undifferentiated body (*thallus*) or, more usually, a thread-like structure (*protonema*) reminiscent of a green alga. This develops into the more familiar plant with stems, simple, delicate leaves, and multicellular rhizoids. The sporophyte consists of a stalked capsule containing a central pillar and numerous spores. The capsule matures after the stalk has elongated, and the spores are released via pores, slits or, in some species, explosively. Mosses are found almost everywhere, most often in damp, shady places. However, some species are better able to withstand drying out, and a few even inhabit very dry places such as walls.

moss animal *Bryozoa*

Mössbauer effect [moesbower] The recoil-free absorption and subsequent re-emission of gamma rays by matter; discovered in 1958 by German physicist Rudolf Mössbauer (1929–). Usually after an atom has absorbed a gamma ray photon, it will re-emit the photon and recoil, thereby increasing the wavelength of the emitted radiation. Mössbauer discovered that at low temperatures atomic nuclei can absorb then re-emit gamma ray photons without recoiling individually. The recoil is passed instead to the bulk of the material, and thus has negligible effect on the emitted radiation. This finding provides the basis for a spectroscopic technique, which has been used to observe gravitational redshift.

Mossi A Gur-speaking people of Burkina Faso. They are sedentary farmers, comprising several chiefdoms united under a powerful paramount chief, the Morho Naba of Ouagadougou, who rules a feudally organized kingdom.

Mosul [mohsool] 36°21N 43°08E, pop (2000e) 884 000. Capital town of Neineva governorate, NW Iraq, on W bank of R Tigris, 352 km/218 mi NW of Baghdad; chief town of N Mesopotamia, 8th–13th-c; airfield; railway; university (1967); agricultural market centre; power generation, oil refining, cement, textiles; ruins of ancient Nineveh nearby.

motet A sacred musical work, originating in the 13th-c and cultivated (especially at Vespers) during the Renaissance as an unaccompanied polyphonic piece, reaching its highest point of development in the works of such composers as Desprez, Lassus, Palestrina, and Byrd. After 1600, motets often included instrumental accompaniment, notably the *grands motets* of Marc-Antoine Charpentier (1634–1704), Lalande, and others performed at the French court, but the term continued to distinguish sacred works in Latin from others (cantatas and anthems) in the vernacular. Some German composers (notably Bach and Brahms), however, used the term *Motette* for pieces in the vernacular without independent instrumental support.

moth An insect belonging to the order Lepidoptera, which comprises the butterflies and moths. Moths are distinguished from butterflies by being active mostly at night, by folding their wings flat over the body when at rest, and by having complex comb-like tips to their antennae; but there are exceptions.

motherese The speech used by adults to young children while they are learning to speak; also known as **caretaker speech**. It typically has shorter expressions than the ones adults normally use, is grammatically simple, and has clear pronunciation, often with exaggerated intonation patterns.

mother-in-law's-tongue A perennial (*Sansevieria trifasciata*) native to W Africa; rhizomatous; leaves to 1 m/3¾ ft, stiff, erect, sword-shaped, fleshy, dark green with pale bands; flowers greenish white; berries orange. It is a widely grown house plant, also called **sanseveria** and **snake plant**, from the patterning on its leaves. (Family: Agavaceae.)

Mother Lode The gold-mining region in the W foothills of the Sierra Nevada, California, USA. It was the centre of the Californian gold rush, with peak production in 1852.

Mother's Day A day set apart in honour of mothers: in the UK, **Mothering Sunday**, the fourth Sunday of Lent; in Australia, Canada, and the USA, the second Sunday in May.

Motherwell 55°48N 4°00W, pop (2000e) 29 600. Administrative centre of North Lanarkshire, C Scotland, UK; 20 km/12 mi SE of Glasgow; united with Wishaw burgh in 1920; railway; engineering; pilgrimages to Grotto of Our Lady of Lourdes at Carfin, 3 km/1¾ mi N.

Motherwell, Robert (Burns) (1915–91) Artist, born in Aberdeen, Washington, USA. He briefly attended the California School of Fine Arts in San Francisco, and studied philosophy at Stanford, Harvard, Grenoble, and Columbia universities. He wrote a good deal on the theory of modern art, and helped found the abstract expressionist group in New York City in the 1940s. His interest in Freud and psychoanalysis led him to spontaneous painting, his huge images often resembling semi-automatic doodles of a kind that the Surrealists had explored. He married the artist Helen Frankenthaler (1928–) in 1955.

moth owl *owl; owlet frogmouth*

Motion, Andrew (1952–) Poet, biographer, and novelist, born in London, UK. He studied at Oxford, and became an English lecturer at Hull University (1976–80), and later professor of creative writing at the University of East Anglia (1995–). His works include *The Lamberts* (1986, Somerset Maugham Award), a biography of Philip Larkin *A Writer's Life* (1993, Whitbread), a biography of Keats (1997), and *Wainewright the Poisoner* (2000). His collections of poetry include *Love in a Life* (1991), *Selected Poems 1976-1997* (1998), and *Public Property* (2002). He has also published novels including *The Invention of Dr Cake* (2003). He succeeded Ted Hughes as poet laureate in 1999.

motion pictures *cinema; cinematography*

motmot A bird native to the New World tropics; related to kingfishers; tail feathers long, usually with barbless zone near tip; inhabits deep forest; eats insects, lizards, and fruit. (Family: Motmotidae, 8 species.)

moto-cross A specialist form of motorcycle racing over a circuit of rough terrain, and taking advantage of natural hazards such as streams and hills. The motorcycles are sturdier than those for road use, and for competition are usually categorized by engine size. The first moto-cross was held in Camberley, Surrey, UK, in 1924. The sport is also often known as **scrambling**.

motorcycle A two-wheeled vehicle designed to carry a rider and frequently a passenger for transport and pleasure, using a two- or four-stroke internal combustion engine to drive the rear wheel, with steering being accomplished by the rider turning the front wheel. The first such vehicle, a motor tricyle, was built in England in 1884, and in Germany in 1885 Gottlieb Daimler and Wilhelm Maybach (1846–1929) used their petrol engines to drive a bicycle. A sidecar was often fitted to provide extra passenger accommodation, but this has become increasingly rare since the 1960s. The range, style, and design of motorcycles has varied enormously since they became a practical proposition in the mid-1890s. Since the 1960s, motorcycle production has been dominated by a number of Japanese firms, though the US Harley-Davidson has considerable prestige.

motorcycle racing The racing of motorcycles, first organized by the *Automobile Club de France* in 1906, from Paris to Nantes and back. The most famous races are held on the roads of the Isle of Man each June, and are known as the *TT* (*Tourist Trophy*) races; first held in 1907. A season-long grand prix world championship takes place each year, and a series of races is held for each of the following engine-size categories: 80 cc, 125 cc, 250 cc, 500 cc, and sidecar. Other forms of motorcycle racing include speedway moto-cross (scrambling), and motorcycle trials riding.

motorcycle trials One of the oldest forms of motorcycle competition. Trials riding is a severe test of the machine's durability, held over tough predetermined courses normally 50–60 km/30–40 mi in length. The Scottish Six Days Trial is the toughest trial in the world. The test calls for all the riders' skills of balance, as well as speed, because they must remain on their machines over rugged undulating surfaces.

motor insurance A system by which motorists pay premiums, often annual, to an insurance company, which will then pay costs arising from accident, damage, or theft. In many countries there is a legal requirement to have *third party* insurance before using public roads; this covers damage and injury except to the insured and to the insured's own vehicle and passengers. *Comprehensive* insurance is needed in order to cover damage and injury in these other cases. Premiums are related to age, occupation, and driving experience of drivers, the age, power, and value of the vehicle, and the area where it is expected to be used. An *excess* means that the insured bears the first part of any claim; a *no-claims bonus* means that, if no claim has been made, the premium on renewal is reduced. Insurance policies may or may not cover legal costs.

motor neurone disease A rare disorder of the central nervous system in which the nerve cells responsible for muscular movement slowly degenerate. Affected persons have progressive difficulty in speaking, swallowing, moving the limbs, and eventually breathing. Occasionally there are associated psychological symptoms or dementia. The cause is unknown, and there is no effective remedy.

motor racing The racing of finely tuned motor cars, which can either be purpose-built or modified production vehicles. The most popular form of motor racing is Formula One grand prix racing for high-powered purpose-built cars which can average well over 240 kph/150 mph. A season-long world championship (Mar–Nov), involves usually 16 races at different venues worldwide. Other popular forms include Formula 3000, Formula Three, rallying, sports car, Indy car racing in the USA, Formula Ford, hill climbing, and production car races. Safety precautions are very strict in all countries where racing takes place. The first race was in 1894, from Paris to Rouen; the first grand prix was the French, in 1906. Past famous races include the Mille Miglia in Italy and Targa Florio in Sicily. Current famous races include the Le Mans 24-hour endurance race, the Monte Carlo Rally, the Paris to Dakar Rally, and the Indianapolis 500.

Motown A black-owned record company, founded in 1959 by Berry Gordy (1929–) in Detroit, MI ('Motortown'). Early Motown hits by Smokey Robinson and the Miracles, Mary Wells, and the Marvelettes were followed by dozens more rhythm-and-blues and soul classics in the 1960s, many written by Robinson or by the songwriting team of Holland, Dozier, and Holland, and recorded by the Supremes, the Jackson Five, the Temptations, the Four Tops, Marvin Gaye, Junior Walker, the Isley Brothers, and many others. In 1971 the company moved to Los Angeles.

Mott, Lucretia, *née* **Coffin** (1793–1880) Feminist and reformer, born in Nantucket, Massachusetts, USA. Educated at a Friends' boarding school, she became a teacher, earning half the salary of her male colleagues, which prompted her interest in women's rights. She married fellow-teacher **James Mott** in 1811, and together they campaigned against slavery, offering refuge to runaway slaves after the Fugitive Slave Law of 1850. With Elizabeth Stanton she organized the first Woman's Rights Convention in 1848, from which time she remained prominent and active in the feminist movement.

Mott, Sir Nevill F(rancis) (1905–96) Physicist, born in Leeds, West Yorkshire, N England, UK. He studied at Cambridge, and became a lecturer and fellow there, working with Ernest Rutherford. He later became professor at Bristol, and in 1954 at Cambridge. He shared the 1977 Nobel Prize for Physics for his independent work on the electronic properties of disordered materials. He was influential in showing how to model the complexity of physical problems such as fracture of metals and electronic processes in disordered semiconductors. He was knighted in 1962.

motte and bailey A quickly constructed earth and timber fortification of Norman date. It consisted of an artificial mound or *motte* – characteristically shaped like an upturned basin – surrounded by a ditch, a separately defended outer court or *bailey* adjoining to one side. Common particularly in England in the late 11th-c and 12th-c, four examples are depicted on the Bayeux Tapestry.

mouflon [mooflon] A wild sheep with a short tail and thick curling horns; short dark fleece with white legs and underparts; two species: **Asiatic mouflon** or **red sheep** (*Ovis orientalis*), the ancestor of domestic sheep, from the mountains of SW Asia; and the **mouflon** or **European mouflon** (*Ovis musimon*) from Corsica and Sardinia (introduced elsewhere).

mould Any fungus, particularly one with an abundant, woolly mycelium of thread-like strands, often with visible spore-bearing structures.

moulting The shedding of an external covering, such as the periodic loss of hair by mammals and feathers by birds. Feather shedding and replacement in birds is usually gradual and does not affect flight, but in some birds (eg ducks) all flight feathers are shed simultaneously, and the bird is temporarily flightless. The shedding of the hard outer covering (*exoskeleton*) of arthropods is known as *ecdysis*.

mound bird / builder *megapode*

Mountain, the A group of Jacobin extremist deputies in the French Convention, led by Robespierre, so-called because they sat high up at the back of the Assembly where they overlooked their political opponents, the Girondins, and the uncommitted majority who were known collectively as 'the Plain'.

mountain A very high, steep natural prominence, often of bare rock, commonly forming part of a chain. Mountains have various origins. All the major mountain chains involve folding of the Earth's crust, but many mountains result from other geological processes. Some are cones built up from volcanoes; some are the result of plateau erosion; some are individual mounds of intrusive igneous rock; some are produced by fault movements. The highest mountain in the world is Mount Everest at height (1999 calculation) 8850 m/29 035 ft;. Principal mountain ranges include the Alps (Europe), Andes (South America), Himalayas (C Asia), Pyrenees (Europe), Rockies (North America), and Urals (Russia). (*see p.1042*)

mountain ash *rowan*

mountain avens [avinz] A dwarf, creeping, evergreen shrub to 8 cm/3 in (*Dryas octopetala*) native to arctic regions and high mountains; leaves oval with rounded teeth; flowers 7–10-petalled, white, heliotropic; fruits with feathery plume. The flowers act as parabolic mirrors, raising the temperature at the centre several degrees above ambient, thus attracting pollinating insects and enabling them to be more active in the warmth. (Family: Rosaceae.)

mountain beaver A squirrel-like rodent (*Aplodontia rufa*) native to the Pacific coast of North America; not a true beaver; the most primitive living rodent; stocky with a minute hairy tail; white spot under each ear; inhabits burrows in cool moist regions (not necessarily mountains); also known as **sewellel**, **boomer**, or **whistler**. (Family: Aplodontidae.)

mountaineering The skill of climbing a mountain aided by ropes and other accessories, such as crampons. It is a very dangerous pastime if undertaken with the wrong pre-approach and equipment. Its forms include **rock climbing**, practised especially in countries with relatively low peaks, and **snow and ice climbing**, practised on the higher peaks of the world. For tall peaks, the climb can take weeks, and often assistance is needed from guides, such as the Sherpas who assist with climbs in the Himalayas. All the world's highest peaks have now been conquered, and present-day mountaineering expeditions aim to climb previously untried routes. Major climbs include: Mont Blanc (1786, Michel Paccard, Jacques Balmat), The Matterhorn (1865, Edward Whymper), Annapurna I (1950, Maurice Herzog, Louis Lachenal), Everest (1953, Edmund Hillary, Tenzing Norgay), and K2 (1954, Achille Compagnoni, Lino Lacedelli).

mountain goat *Rocky Mountain goat*

mountain laurel An evergreen shrub or small tree (*Kalmia latifolia*) native to North America; leaves elliptical, leathery; flowers saucer-shaped, 5-lobed, white, pink, or red; also called **calico bush**. (Family: Ericaceae.)

mountain lion *cougar*

mountain sheep *bighorn*

Mount Athos, Gr **Ayíon Oros** pop (2000e) 1620; area 336 sq km/130 sq mi. Autonomous administration in Macedonia region, Greece; Mt Athos, rising to 1956 m/6417 ft, is the 'Holy Moun-

Highest mountains

Name	Height* m	ft	Location
Mt Everest	8 850	29 035	China/Nepal
K2 (Mt Godwin-Austen)	8 610	28 250	Kashmir–Jammu
Kangchenjunga	8 590	28 170	India/Nepal
Lhotse	8 500	27 890	China/Nepal
Kangchenjunga, S Peak	8 470	27 800	India/Nepal
Makalu I	8 470	27 800	China/Nepal
Kangchenjunga, W Peak	8 420	27 620	India/Nepal
Llotse E Peak	8 380	27 500	China/Nepal
Dhaulagiri	8 170	26 810	Nepal
Cho Oyu	8 150	26 750	China/Nepal
Manaslu	8 130	26 660	Nepal
Nanga Parbat	8 130	26 660	Kashmir–Jammu
Annapurna I	8 080	26 500	Nepal
Gasherbrum I	8 070	26 470	Kashmir–Jammu
Broad-highest	8 050	26 400	Kashmir–Jammu
Gasherbrum II	8 030	26 360	Kashmir–Jammu
Gosainthan	8 010	26 290	China
Broad-middle	8 000	26 250	Kashmir–Jammu
Gasherbrum III	7 950	26 090	Kashmir–Jammu
Annapurna II	7 940	26 040	Nepal
Nanda Devi	7 820	25 660	India
Rakaposhi	7 790	25 560	Kashmir
Kamet	7 760	25 450	India
Ulugh Muztagh	7 720	25 340	Tibet
Tirich Mir	7 690	25 230	Pakistan
Muz Tag Ata	7 550	24 760	China
Communism Peak	7 490	24 590	Tajikistan
Pobedy Peak	7 440	24 410	Kyrgyzstan
Aconcagua	6 960	22 830	Argentina
Ojos del Salado	6 910	22 660	Argentina/Chile

*Heights are given to the nearest 10 m/ft.

tain' of the Greek Church, associated with the monastic order of St Basil since the 9th-c; declared a theocratic republic in 1927.

Mountbatten (of Burma), Louis (Francis Albert Victor Nicholas) Mountbatten, 1st Earl (1900–79) British Admiral of the Fleet and statesman, born in Windsor, S England, UK, the younger son of Prince Louis of Battenberg and Princess Victoria of Hesse, the granddaughter of Queen Victoria. He trained at Dartmouth, and joined the Royal Navy in 1916. In World War 2 he became chief of Combined Operations Command (1942), and played a key role in preparations for D-Day. In 1943 he was appointed supreme commander in SE Asia, where he defeated the Japanese offensive into India (1944), and worked closely with Slim to reconquer Burma (1945). He received the Japanese surrender at Singapore, and in 1947 was sworn in as last Viceroy of India prior to independence. Created an earl in 1947, he returned to the Admiralty, and became First Sea Lord (1954) and chief of the defence staff (1959). Retiring in 1965, he remained in the public eye, and was assassinated by Irish terrorists while fishing off Mullaghmore near his summer home, Classiebawn Castle, Co Sligo, Ireland.

Mountbatten, Prince Philip *Edinburgh, Duke of*

Mounties The popular name of the **Royal Canadian Mounted Police**, the federal police force of Canada. Its headquarters is in Ottawa. The organization was founded in 1873, and until 1920 was known as the North West Mounted Police. The red jacket and broad-brimmed hat worn by its officers are features of their distinctive uniform.

Mount Li The burial place of Qin Shihuangdi, the first Emperor of China (259–210 BC); a world heritage site. On the Wei R 32 km/20 mi E of Xi'an, Shaanxi, it is renowned for the discovery in 1974 of a life-size army of c.7500 painted terracotta figures deployed in military formation in chambers underground. Pit 1 (210 m/690 ft by 60 m/200 ft) holds an armed infantry unit of c.6000, in 11 parallel corridors, with crossbowmen and six chariots containing officers at the head. Pit 2 has c.1400 cavalry and 90 chariots drawn by four-horse teams arranged in 14 corridors.

Mount of Olives *Olives, Mount of*

Mount Palomar Observatory *Palomar Observatory*

Mount Sinai *Sinai, Mount*

Mount Vernon The family home of George Washington, on the Potomac R in Virginia. The 18th-c building and its gardens were purchased by the Mount Vernon Ladies' Association in 1858, and furnished and decorated as in Washington's time. Washington and his wife, Martha, are buried there.

Mount Wilson Observatory Observatory on Mt Wilson, near Pasadena, California, USA, established in 1904 by the Carnegie Institution, Washington, DC. The main telescope of 2·5 m/100 in (1917) contributed to our knowledge of the distant galaxies in the early 20th-c; its observations in the 1920s established that the universe is expanding. Observing conditions have been severely affected by the night sky brightness of the West Coast urban areas.

Mourne Mountains [mawn] Mountain range in SE County Down, SE Northern Ireland, UK; extends 24 km/15 mi from Carlingford Lough NE to Dundrum Bay; a granitic hill range which supplies most of Belfast's water; rises to 852 m/2795 ft at Slieve Donard.

mourning dove A dove (*Zenaida macroura*) native to North America and the Caribbean; short legs, thin bill, and long tail; inhabits woodland, semi-desert, and town outskirts; eats seeds and invertebrates; nests in trees, buildings, or on ground. (Family: Columbidae.)

mouse (computing) A computer input device which can be moved around on a flat surface causing a cursor to move around the computer screen in response. It usually has at least one selection button, and can be used to choose options pointed to on the screen.

mouse (zoology) A name used for many small unrelated species in the rodent family, found worldwide, especially for members of genus *Mus* (36 species throughout Old World); **house mouse** (*Mus musculus*), from Asia, has dispersed globally in association with humans; spreads some diseases, but is not as guilty as rats; the white **laboratory mouse** is a form of *Mus musculus*. (Family: Muridae.)

mousebird *coly*

mouse deer *chevrotain*

mouse hare *pika*

Mouskouri, Nana [muskooree] (1936–) Singer, born in Athens, Greece. She made her first record in Greece in 1959, and went on to record 'The White Rose of Athens' (1962), which became a major European hit. In the early 1970s she had a series of hit albums in the UK. She was a member of the European Parliament (1994–9)

Moussorgsky, Modest (Petrovich) [musaw(r)gskee], also spelled **Mussorgsky** or **Musorgsky** (1839–81) Composer, born in Karevo, W Russia. He was educated for the army, but resigned his commission in 1858 and began the serious study of music under Balakirev. A member of the Glinka-inspired nationalist group in St Petersburg, he first made a name with his songs; but his masterpiece is the opera *Boris Godunov*, first performed in St Petersburg in 1874. His piano suite *Pictures from an Exhibition* (1874) has also kept a firm place in the concert repertoire. Other operas and large-scale works remained uncompleted as the composer sank into the chronic alcoholism which hastened his early death. His friend Rimsky-Korsakov undertook the task of musical executor, arranged or completed many of his unfinished works, and rearranged some of the finished ones.

Mousterian [moosteerian] A European archaeological culture of the Middle Palaeolithic Age (c.70 000–40 000 BC), named after the cave at Le Moustier, Dordogne, SW France, excavated from c.1863. Its stone tools are probably the work of Neanderthals.

Comparable material is also found in the Middle East and N Africa.

mouth The first part of the gastro-intestinal tract; the space bounded by the lips, cheeks, and palate, lined with mucous membrane, and containing the teeth, the tongue, salivary glands, nerves, and blood vessels. In mammals one of its characteristic features is the movable muscular lips and cheeks, which are intimately related to chewing, and in humans to speech and the expression of emotion. It is continuous behind with the upper part of the pharynx.

mouthbrooder Freshwater fish (*Sarotherodon niloticus*) widespread in C Africa and along the Nile; length up to 50 cm/20 in; body deep, compressed; feeds on a variety of aquatic invertebrates; female broods eggs in mouth; an important food fish in some areas. (Family: Cichlidae.)

mouth organ *harmonica*

mouth-to-mouth respiration *artificial respiration*

movement In music, a self contained section of a longer work, such as a concerto or symphony. It may be linked to the movement that precedes or follows it, with which it is usually contrasted in tempo or key (often both).

movies *cinema; cinematography*

Movietone The trade name for one of the first sound-on-film recording and reproducing systems, launched by Fox in 1927. It was used initially for newsreels, and subsequently for all their feature film production.

Mowlem, Mo [mohlem], popular name of **Marjorie Mowlem** (1949–) British stateswoman, born in Watford, Hertfordshire, SE England, UK. She studied at Durham, UK and Iowa, USA, then worked as a university lecturer in Florida and Newcastle and as an administrator at Northern College, Barnsley, before becoming Labour MP for Redcar (1987–2001). She held various posts in opposition, before being appointed as secretary-of-state for Northern Ireland (1997–9), and minister for the cabinet office and chancellor of the Duchy of Lancaster (1999–2001) in the Labour government. She played a key part in achieving the Good Friday Agreement and in the establishment of the Northern Ireland Assembly. Her political memoir, *Momentum*, appeared in 2002.

moxibustion Local heat applied directly or indirectly to an acupuncture point. Direct application of heat is usually accomplished by the burning of *moxa*, made from the dried leaves of the plant *Artemisia vulgaris* (of the chrysanthemum family). It is available in the form of sticks, cones, and as 'punk', a wool-like product which can be rolled and fastened to acupuncture needles. The technique is thought to have originated in the cold mountainous regions of N China, the penetration of the heat augmenting and encouraging the flow of energy in the body. It is used mostly in traditional Chinese medicine for the treatment of cold and for chronic conditions such as osteoarthritis.

Moynihan, Daniel P(atrick) (1927–2003) Academic and politician, born in Tulsa, Oklahoma, USA. He studied at the City College of New York and Tufts University, then taught at Syracuse, Harvard, and the Massachusetts Institute of Technology. He served in the administrations of Presidents Johnson and Nixon, acquiring notoriety as the author of *The Negro Family: the Case for National Action* (1965), which held that many of the educational problems of African Americans could be traced to the instability of black urban families, and urged a programme of reform. He was ambassador to India (1973–4), and won a seat in the US Senate as a Democrat in 1976. Widely regarded as an important senator and influential policy thinker, he is the only person in American history to have served in four successive administrations. He retired from the Senate in 2001.

Mozambique *p.1044*

Mozart, Wolfgang Amadeus [mohtsah(r)t] (1756–91) Composer, born in Salzburg, C Austria, the son of the violinist and composer Leopold Mozart (1719–87). A child prodigy, he made his first professional tour (as a pianist) through Europe when he was six. He was a prolific composer, and travelled widely, but failed to find a permanent position. After some years in Salzburg as *Konzertmeister* to the archbishop, he resigned (1781) and settled in Vienna. His operas *The Marriage of Figaro* (1786) and *Don Giovanni* (1787) made it impossible for the court still to overlook the composer, and he was appointed court composer to Joseph II in 1787. His compositions, numbering over 600 in Köchel's catalogue, include several other operas – notably *Die Entführung aus dem Serail* (1782, The Abduction from the Harem), *Così fan tutte* (1790) and *The Magic Flute* (1791) – 41 symphonies, and many concertos, chamber works, and sonatas. In writing the Requiem Mass commissioned for Count Walsegg, he felt he was writing his own requiem; he died before it was finished.

MPEG [empeg] *digital media*

Mphahlele, Es'kia [mpahlaylay], popular name of **Ezekiel Mphahlele** (1919–) Novelist, autobiographer, and critic, born in Pretoria, South Africa. His ghetto childhood bulks large in his autobiography, *Down Second Avenue* (1959). He spent the years 1957 to 1978 in Nigeria, France, Kenya, Zambia, and the USA. By the time he published a second volume of autobiography, *Afrika My Music* (1984), he had also written four volumes of short stories and three novels. His influential criticism includes *The African Image* (1962), a pioneering analysis of African literature in its political context. He returned to South Africa in 1978.

Mpumalanga [mpumalangga] (Swati 'land of the rising sun') One of the nine new provinces established by the South African constitution of 1994, in NE South Africa, situated largely on high plateau grasslands; formerly constituted part of Transvaal; borders Mozambique and Swaziland in the E; capital, Nelspruit, pop (2000e) 2 784 000; area 81 816 sq km/31 581 sq mi; chief languages, Siswati (40%), Zulu (28%), Afrikaans; tourism (game reserves, including Kruger National park), manufacturing, mining, electricity, agriculture, forestry.

MS Access A computer package for data management, developed by Microsoft to run on the IBM personal computer. It is intended to interface to, and provide the data storage for, applications developed in Visual Basic.

MS-DOS An operating system developed by Microsoft for the IBM personal computer; it is a registered trade mark. This system has contributed largely to the success of the IBM product.

MS Excel A computer package for operations on a spreadsheet developed by Microsoft to run on the IBM personal computer. It is a registered trade mark.

MS Word A computer package for word processing produced by Microsoft to run on the IBM personal computer. A version is also now available for Macintosh computers.

M-II [em too] The trade name for a videotape recording system of broadcast standard introduced in 1986 by Matsushita. It uses ½ in metal particle tape at a speed of 6·63 cm/s in a cassette 189 × 104 × 25 mm, with component recording of luminance and compressed chrominance on adjacent parallel tracks.

Mubarak, (Mohammed) Hosni (Said) [mubarak] (1928–) Egyptian statesman and president (1981–), born in al-Minufiyah, NE Egypt. A former pilot and flying instructor who rose to become commander of the Egyptian Air Force, he was vice-president under Anwar Sadat from 1975 until the latter's assassination in 1981. As president he has struggled to further Egypt's economic development, to meet the threat posed by Muslim extremists, and to follow a balanced foreign policy, including adhering to the peace treaty with Israel (1979) and supporting the military coalition against Iraq during the Gulf War (1991).

mucous membrane [myookuhs] A sheet of fibrous tissue that lines every cavity or canal of the body which opens to the exterior (eg the alimentary and urogenital tracts). It consists of a surface layer of epithelium, and an underlying connective tissue layer (the *lamina propria*). The surface may contain simple glands. It provides a barrier between the cells that form the body and the external environment.

Mudéjar [moothehah(r)] The name given to those Moors who remained after the Christian conquest of Spain. It refers particularly to a style of architecture built by Muslim craftsmen in

Mozambique

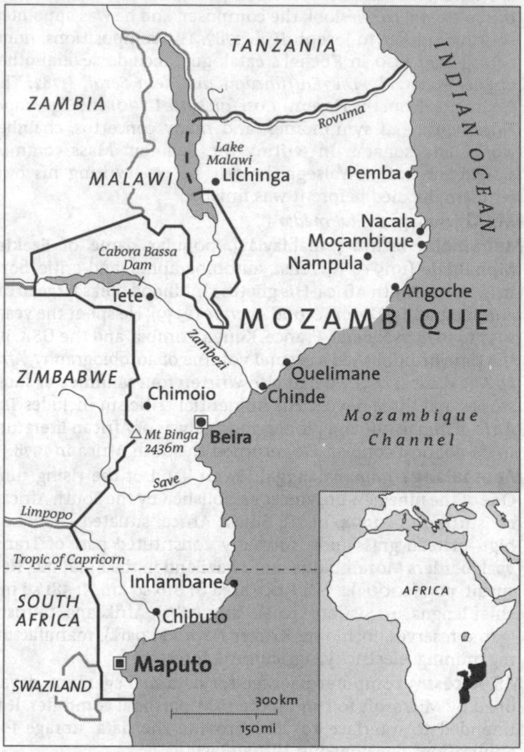

☐ International Airport

[mohzambeek], official name (from 1991) **Republic of Mozambique**, Port **República de Moçambique**

Local name Moçambique

Timezone GMT +2

Area 799 380 km²/308 641 sq mi

Population total (2002e) 18 083 000

Status Republic

Date of independence 1975

Capital Maputo

Languages Portuguese (official)

Ethnic groups Makua/Lomwe (52%), Thonga (24%), Malawi (12%), Shona (6%), Yao (3%)

Religions Local animist beliefs (60%), Christian (majority Roman Catholic) (30%), Muslim (10%)

Physical features Located in SE Africa; main rivers, the Zambezi and Limpopo provide irrigation and hydroelectricity; savannah plateau inland, mean elevation 800–1000 m/2600–4000 ft; highest peak, Mt Binga, 2436 m/7992 ft; S of Zambezi is low-lying coast with sandy beaches and mangroves; low hills of volcanic origin inland, Zimbabwe plateau further N.

Climate Tropical with high humidity; rainy season (Dec–Mar); drought conditions in S; average annual temperatures 26°C (Jan), 18°C (Jul) in Maputo; average annual rainfall 560 mm/30 in.

Currency 1 Metical (Mt, MZM) = 100 centavos

Economy Badly affected by drought (1981–4), internal strife, and lack of foreign exchange; agriculture (employs 85% of population); cashew nuts, tea, cotton, sugar cane, copra, sisal, groundnuts, fruit, rice, cereals, tobacco; forestry; livestock; reserves of gemstones and minerals; Great Limpopo Transfrontier Park game reserve established, 2002.

GDP (2002e) $19·52 bn, per capita $1100

Human Development Index (2002) 0·322

History Originally inhabited by Bantu peoples from the N, 1st–4th-c AD; coast settled by Arab traders; visited by Portuguese explorers by late 15th-c; part of Portuguese Africa since 1751; Mozambique Portuguese East Africa in late 19th-c; overseas province of Portugal, 1951; independence movement formed in 1962, the Frente de Libertaçao de Moçambique (FRELIMO), with armed resistance to colonial rule; independence as the People's Republic of Mozambique, 1975; continuing civil war, with first peace talks in 1990; socialist one-party state, 1975–90; new constitution and change of name to Republic of Mozambique, 1990; peace accord signed between Chissanó (President of Mozambique) and Dhlakama (leader of the Renamo-Mozambique National Resistance), 1992; President (term of 5 years) rules with an Assembly of the Republic.

Head of State

1975–86 Samora Moïses Machel

1986– Joaquim Alberto Chissanó

Head of Government

1986–94 Mario de Graça Machungo

1994– Pascoal Mocumbi

their native style for Christian monuments, such as the Alcazar at Seville. The style later became absorbed into Spanish Gothic.

mudfish *bowfin*

mudhopper Very distinctive fish (*Periophthalmus koelreuteri* and *Periophthalmodon schlosseri*) widespread in the Indo-Pacific; locally common on mud flats of estuaries and mangrove swamps, living much of the time out of water; length 15–25 cm/6–10 in; eyes raised on top of head; paired fins used as props and for locomotion across the mud; also called **mudskipper**. (Family: Gobiidae.)

mudlark Either of two species of bird of the genus *Grallina*, also known as **mudnester** or **mudnest builder**: the black-and-white **magpie lark** (*Grallina cyanoleuca*) from open woodland in Australia; and the **torrent lark** (*Grallina bruijni*) from mountain streams in New Guinea. They build nests from mud, hence the name. (Family: Grallinidae.)

mudnest builder / mudnester *mudlark*

mudpuppy A salamander from North America (*Fecturus maculosus*); spends entire life in water; brown-grey with feathery gills; limbs with four toes; deep narrow tail; inhabits diverse waterbodies; eats invertebrates and fish. (Family: Proteidae.)

mudskipper *mudhopper*

muesli [myoozlee] A popular breakfast cereal now available in a wide variety of mixtures, which include cereals, nuts, and fruits. These mixtures have been developed from the raw food diet of Dr Max Birchner-Brenner (1867–1939), which included oatmeal, grated apples, berries, and milk, and which was high in fibre and low in fat.

muezzin [mooezin] In Islam, an official of the mosque who issues the call to prayer to the faithful. The name means 'announcer'.

mufti In Islamic religion, a man trained in the *Sharia*, or Muslim divine law, and who can give a legal opinion (*fatwa*) on questions concerning Islamic practice.

Mufulira [mufuleera] 12°30S 28°12E, pop (2000e) 270 700. Mining city in Copperbelt province, Zambia; world's second largest underground copper mine nearby; railway; clothing, explosives.

Mugabe, Robert (Gabriel) [mugahbay] (1924–) First prime minister (1980–) and president (1987–) of Zimbabwe, born in Kutama, Zimbabwe (formerly Southern Rhodesia). Largely self-educated, he became a teacher in 1942. After short periods in the National Democratic Party and Zimbabwe African People's Union (ZAPU), he was briefly detained, but escaped to co-found, with Ndabaningi Sithole, the Zimbabwe African

National Union (ZANU). After a 10-year detention in Rhodesia (1964–74) he spent five years in Mozambique gathering support in preparation for Zimbabwe's independence in 1980. His ZANU and the ZAPU forces of Joshua Nkomo united in 1976 to form the Patriotic Front, and later, a coalition government. Though Mugabe formerly espoused a pragmatic Marxism and declared his intention of turning Zimbabwe into a one-party state, multi-party elections were held in 1990 (which he won), and his party dropped all references to 'Marxism–Leninism', and 'scientific socialism' from its constitution in 1991. He came to world attention in 2000 for initiating a land redistribution policy aimed at local white farmers, which resulted in intimidation, civil disturbance, some deaths, and much international condemnation. He won a fifth term in office in 2002, but controversy surrounding the election process led to Zimbabwe being suspended from the Commonwealth for a year, and following the decision to reaffirm the suspension in 2003 he announced that he would withdraw from the organization.

mugger A rare crocodile (*Crocodilus palustris*) native to India and Sri Lanka; formerly common in the R Ganges; broad snout; young may be 1 m/3¾ ft long after only one year.

Muggeridge, (Thomas) Malcolm (1903–90) Journalist, born in Croydon, London, UK. A lecturer at the Egyptian University in Cairo (1927–30), he then became a journalist. Serving with the Intelligence Corps during World War 2, he received the Legion of Honour and the Croix de Guerre. Resuming his journalistic career, he worked with the *Daily Telegraph* (1946–52), and was editor of *Punch* (1953–7). He contributed regularly to the television programme *Panorama* (1953–60), and had his own series *Appointment With ...* (1960–1) and *Let Me Speak* (1964–5). He wrote *Chronicle of Wasted Time* (1982), and other books. A controversial rector of Edinburgh University (1967–8), he resigned over student liberalism and promiscuity. He characterized his life as a spiritual journey towards a greater understanding of faith, and in 1982 became a Roman Catholic.

Mughal or **Mogul Empire** An important Indian Muslim state (1526–1857), founded by Babur (1526–30). It temporarily declined under Humayun (1530–40), who lost control to the Afghan chieftain Sher Shah (1540–5). His son, Akbar (1556–1605), defeated the Afghan challenge at Panipat (1556) and extended the empire to include territory between Afghanistan and the Deccan. This was a period of religious freedom, in which a policy of conciliation was pursued with the Rajput states. Akbar was succeeded by Jehangir (1605–27) and Shah Jehan (1627–58). Its last great emperor was Aurangzeb (1658–1707), who extended the limits of the empire further S; however, religious bigotry alienated non-Muslim supporters and undermined the empire's unity. The empire disintegrated under Maratha and British pressure. By the mid-18th-c it ruled only a small area around Delhi. Its last emperor, Bahadur Shah II (1837–57) was exiled by the British to Yangon (Rangoon) after the 1857 uprising.

mugwort An aromatic perennial growing to 120 cm/4 ft, native to many temperate areas; leaves deeply divided, dark green above, silvery with woolly hairs below; flower-heads reddish-brown, numerous but rather insignificant, crowded on long leafy stems. The young leaves are used as a condiment for goose, duck, and pork. (Genus: *Artemisia*. Family: Compositae.)

mugwump (Alonkin Indian 'great chief') A name for Independent Republicans in the US election of 1884 who preferred reform to party discipline, particularly on the question of ending the spoils system. They included journalist E L Godkin (1831–1902), author and leader of civil service reform George William Curtis (1824–92), journalist Carl Schurz (1829–1906), and lawyer and businessman Charles Francis Adams (1807–86).

Muhammad *Mohammed*

Muharram [muharam] The first month of the Muslim year; also used as the name of the religious celebration culminating in Ashura.

Muir, Edwin [myoor] (1887–1959) Poet and critic, born in Deerness, Orkney Is, NE Scotland, UK. Educated in Kirkwall, he moved to Glasgow at 14, and in 1919 married the novelist **Willa Anderson** (1890–1970), with whom he settled in London. They travelled in mainland Europe (1921–4), where they collaborated in notable translations of Kafka and other authors. He also worked in Rome, Scotland, and Harvard (1955–6, as professor of poetry). His poems appeared in eight slim volumes, dating from 1925, notably in *The Voyage* (1946) and *The Labyrinth* (1949). His other writing includes a controversial study of John Knox, studies on D H Lawrence, and a volume of autobiography (1954).

Muir, Frank [myoor] (1920–98) Writer and broadcaster, born in London, UK. He served in the RAF (1940–6), and joined Denis Norden to become one of the best-known teams of comedy script-writers (1947–64), contributing to many shows on radio and television. After a short period in television management he returned to facing the camera in *Call My Bluff* (1970), and began the radio series *Frank Muir Goes into...* (1971). With Norden he published a number of books on the theme *My Word*, such as *The Complete and Utter 'My Word!' Collection* (1983), and by himself a series of children's books based on the dog 'What-a-Mess'.

Muir, Jean (Elizabeth) [myoor] (1933–95) Fashion designer, born in London, UK. Educated at Dame Harper School, Bedford, she started as a salesgirl with Liberty's in London in 1950, then moved to Jaeger in 1956. In 1961 she worked on her own as Jane & Jane, establishing in 1966 her own company, Jean Muir. Her clothes are noted for classic shapes, softness, and fluidity.

Mujahideen [moojahadeen] ('holy warriors') Muslim guerrillas who resisted the Soviet occupation of Afghanistan after the invasion (Dec 1979). Based in Iran and Pakistan, they formed various armed bands united by their common aim of defeating the invaders, and the conflict was proclaimed a *jihad* ('holy war'). The Soviets withdrew from Afghanistan in 1989, and the Mujahideen subsequently experienced much internal dissent over their role in the country's future. By 1998, a new movement dedicated to establishing a strict Islamic state, the *Taliban*, had taken control of 90 per cent of the country. In 1999, the warring factions agreed to work towards a permanent ceasefire and to share power. The term is also used more generally than in relation to the Afghan conflict, referring to any Muslim whose armed struggle can be said to be in the interest of the faith.

mujtahid [moojtahhid] A religious scholar who exercises personal interpretation of the *Sharia* or Muslim divine law. Shiism allows such interpretations, while Sunnism has usually refused them.

Mukden *Shenyang*

mulberry A deciduous tree, of oriental origin, but long cultivated; heart-shaped, toothed leaves; male and female flowers in separate catkin-like spikes; individual fruits juicy, coalescing so that the whole spike forms the 'berry'. The **black mulberry** (*Morus nigra*) has purplish fruits. The leaves of the **white mulberry** (*Morus alba*) are food for silkworms. (Genus: *Morus*, 10 species. Family: Moraceae.)

Muldoon, Sir Robert (David) [muhldoon] (1921–92) New Zealand statesman and prime minister (1975–84), born in Auckland, New Zealand. He served as an infantryman in World War 2 before becoming an accountant and president of the New Zealand Institute of Cost Accountants. He was first elected to parliament (as a National Party MP) in 1960, and after five years as minister of finance became deputy prime minister. From 1974 he was Party leader and Leader of the Opposition, and led the National Party to victory in the 1975 elections. After serving as prime minister, he gave up leadership of the National Party, but remained an MP until 1991, and served as shadow foreign affairs spokesman. He was knighted in 1984.

mule (textiles) A spinning frame invented by Samuel Crompton in 1779, which fully mechanized the hand spinning process. It was regarded as a hybrid of two previous inventions, hence its name. Initially used for cotton, it was adapted for merino and other fibres. Because it is an intermittent (rather than continuous process) it is now superseded.

mule (zoology) An animal produced from the mating of a male donkey with a female horse. If a male horse mates with a female donkey the result is a **hinny**. Both are usually sterile, and have the front end resembling the father and the rear end resembling the mother.

Mulhouse [muhlooz], Ger **Mulhausen** 47°45N 7°21E, pop (2000e) 114 000. Industrial and commercial river port in Haut-Rhin department, NE France; on R Ill and Rhine–Rhône Canal, 35 km/22 mi S of Colmar; second largest town in Alsace; imperial free city from 1308; allied with the Swiss, 1515–1648; independent republic until 1798, then voted to become French; under German rule in 1871, reverting to France in 1918; railway; university; linen-weaving and spinning, printed fabrics, dyes, machinery, chemicals, fertilizers, cars; Renaissance town hall (1552), Church of St-Etienne, Musée National de l'Automobile, French Railway Museum, 31-storey Tour de l'Europe.

mullah [mula] (Arabic, 'master') In Islam, a scholar, teacher, or man of religious piety and learning. It is also a title of respect given to those performing duties related to Islamic Law.

mullein [muluhn] Typically a biennial or perennial, often very hairy, with a tall, erect stem, native to Europe and Asia; rosette leaves oval to oblong up to 50 cm/20 in or more; flowers in long dense spikes, 5-petalled, yellow, pink, purple, or white; the stamen filaments often with conspicuous white, yellow, or purple hairs. (Genus: *Verbascum*, 360 species. Family: Scrophulariaceae.)

mullet *grey mullet; red mullet*

Mulligan, Gerry, popular name of **Gerald Joseph Mulligan** (1927–96) Jazz musician, born in New York City, USA. He was one of many white jazz musicians to emerge in the USA after World War 2. Alto playing with Miles Davis, he moved to California in 1952, and formed his own quartet. A technically accomplished musician, he experimented to produce a distinctive sound which proved popular and commercially successful. His motion pictures include *Jazz on a Summer's Day*, *I Want to Live* (both 1958), and *The Subterraneans* (1960).

Mulliken, Robert (Sanderson) (1896–1986) Chemist and physicist, born in Newburyport, Massachusetts, USA. He studied at the Massachusetts Institute of Technology and the University of Chicago, then taught briefly at New York (1926–8), before settling as a professor at Chicago. He was awarded the Nobel Prize for Chemistry in 1966 for his work on chemical bonds and the electronic structure of molecules.

Mullingar [muhlingah(r)], Ir **Muileann Cearr** 53°32N 7°20W, pop (2000e) 12 000. Market town and capital of Westmeath county, Leinster, E Ireland; on the Royal Canal, WNW of Dublin; railway; cattle trade; cathedral.

Mulready, William [muhlreedee] (1786–1863) Painter, born in Ennis, Co Clare, W Ireland. He studied at the Royal Academy, London, and specialized in genre paintings, becoming best known for his rural scenes such as 'Interior of an English Cottage' (1828). He also worked at portraiture and book illustration, and designed the first penny-postage envelope.

Mulroney, (Martin) Brian (1939–) Canadian politician and prime minister (1984–93), born in Baie Comeau, Quebec, SE Canada. He attended St Francis Xavier University in Nova Scotia, and studied law at Laval University, taking up a career first in law, then in business. He became leader of the Progressive Conservative Party in 1983, and won a landslide election victory in 1984. He negotiated a free trade agreement with the USA in 1988 and a North American Free Trade Agreement which extends to Mexico (1992). His period in office was marked by controversial proposals regarding the position of French-speaking Quebec. He resigned in 1993 when the party's popularity was at an all-time low.

Multan [multan] 30°10N 71°36E, pop (2000e) 1 193 000. City in Punjab province, Pakistan, 314 km/195 mi SW of Lahore; ruled by the emperors of Delhi 1526–1779, and by the Afghans until 1818, when the city was seized by the Sikhs; under British rule, 1849; airfield; railway; trade in grain, cotton, wool, fruits; 14th-c tombs of Muslim saints.

multicultural education The education together of more than one cultural or ethnic group. The term is also used to describe education which stresses pluralism, and the contribution to learning which can come from many social and cultural sources, not solely the single predominant national one.

multilateralism In economics, a system where a group of countries negotiate trade and payments arrangements, rather than dealing bilaterally. In trade, multilateralism is summed up by the 'most favoured nation' clause, whereby imports from any member country are to be treated no less favourably than those from any other member. The extreme form of this is a free trade area. In payments, multilateral settlement means that a country need only be concerned to balance its payments with other countries in total, and need not keep its payments in bilateral balance. The alternative, bilateral, system has the merit that two parties may find it easier to reach agreement than several parties would. Multilateralism can also be applied to countries with foreign aid, where intermediaries such as the International Development Association are multilateral channels for aid.

multilingualism *bilingualism*

multimedia (computing) The tools and techniques used in computing to allow computer programs to handle sound, picture, and video components. In a multimedia system one could use the computer to select extracts from a piece of music which could then be broadcast with a full video picture of the orchestra and hi-fi sound, or could be broadcast in sound only with the video displaying the score. The computer would control the movements of the score to keep it in line with the sound.

multimedia (projection) The audio-visual presentation from groups of slide projectors programmed to show a complex sequence of images on a very wide screen with accompanying sound from tape recording. The pictures can be separate or blended together to fill the whole screen, with fast or slow dissolves between successive images and superimposed effects.

multinational corporations *transnational corporations*

multiple sclerosis A disease in which the normal coating of neurones (*myelin*) in the brain and spinal cord is lost. This affects the transmission of impulses along the nerves, impairing the function of the body systems that they control. It is found in 1 in 2000 people and is more common in women than men. The cause is uncertain, but it may be related to an auto-immune process. Clinical features are diverse, and include weakness of the limbs, double vision, speech difficulties, vertigo, a sensation of pins and needles, and inability to co-ordinate movements (*ataxia*), all of which can be transient but recurrent, and slowly become more severe. There is no specific treatment.

multiple star Three or more stars gravitationally bound in complex orbits. The star complex Alpha Centauri is an example of such a system.

multiplexer A device in data communications which enables the inputs from a number of communication lines to be concentrated and fed down a single line.

multipolarity A theory of international politics which contends that power is likely to become concentrated in the hands of a few major powers: the USA, W Europe, Russia, Japan, and China. It superseded the idea of **bipolarity**, which had currency in the 1950s, where power was said to be concentrated in the hands of the two superpowers. Multipolarity gives greater emphasis to economic power relative to military (especially nuclear) power, hence the inclusion of Japan and W Europe. It is suggested that a multipolar system leads to more flexible and stable relationships in international politics.

Mumbai, official name (1995) of **Bombay** 18°55N 72°50E, pop (2000e) 12 500 000. Port capital of Maharashtra, W India; India's largest city, and the only natural deep-water harbour on the W coast; built on a group of islands linked by causeways;

ceded to Portugal, 1534; ceded to Britain, 1661; headquarters of the East India Company, 1685–1708; airport; railway; two universities (1916, 1957); textiles, carpets, machinery, chemicals, oil refining; nuclear reactor at Trombay; Afghan church (1847), Gateway of India (archway commemorating visit to India of King George V and Queen Mary, 1911), Mani Bhavan (Gandhi memorial), Raudat Tahera mosque and mausoleum, Prince of Wales Museum; Elephanta Caves on Elephanta I in Mumbai harbour; city damaged by series of terrorist bomb attacks during 2003; film industry (Bollywood) and a major centre for the making of Hindi and Marathi language films.

Mumford, Lewis (1895–1990) Sociologist and writer, born in Flushing, New York, USA. He studied at the City College of New York, became a literary critic and journal editor, and began to write on architecture and urbanization in such works as *The Story of Utopias* (1922) and *The City in History* (1961), stressing the unhappy effects of technology on society. A prolific author, he held academic posts at several universities, including the chair of city and regional planning at the University of Pennsylvania (1951–9).

mummers English traditional actors providing entertainment at seasonal festivals. In the 18th-c the mummers' Christmas play evolved, based on a legend of St George, with a duel between champions ending in the death of one of them and his revival by a doctor.

mumps A viral infection spread by droplets, especially common among children and young adults. A characteristic feature is pain and swelling of one or both parotid glands near the angle of the jaw; the testes, pancreas, meninges, and ovaries may also be affected. The parotid gland swelling usually subsides in a few days, but complications may occur including deafness, meningitis, and infertility. A vaccination is available to prevent the disease.

Munch, Edvard [mungk] (1863–1944) Painter, born in Löten, E Norway. He studied in Oslo, travelled in Europe, and finally settled in Norway in 1908. In Paris he came under the influence of Gauguin. He was obsessed by subjects such as death and love, which he illustrated in an Expressionist Symbolic style, using bright colours and a tortuously curved design, as in 'The Scream' (1893). His engravings influenced *die Brücke* in Germany.

Münchhausen, (Karl Friedrich Hieronymus), Freiherr von (Baron) [munchhowzen] (1720–97) Soldier, born in Bodenwerder, C Germany. Proverbial as the narrator of ridiculously exaggerated exploits, he served in Russian campaigns against the Turks. A collection of stories attributed to him, and describing his surreal adventures, was first published in English as *Baron Munchhausen's Narrative of his Marvellous Travels and Campaigns in Russia* (1785) by **Rudolf Erich Raspe** (1737–94). In medicine, *Münchhausen's syndrome* has come to be attributed to individuals who wander round the country presenting themselves at different hospitals with different but spurious physical complaints.

Münchhausen's syndrome [münshhowzn] The falsification of illness in order to attract attention and sympathy, but not for immediate financial or personal gain. Typically, individuals feign or even self-induce symptoms, and present themselves to health-care providers for investigation and treatment. In **Münchhausen's syndrome by proxy**, an individual falsifies illness in another person, usually a child. It is named after an 18th-c baron, notorious for his tales and romances.

Muncie [muhnsee] 40°12N 85°23W, pop (2000e) 67 400. Seat of Delaware Co, E Indiana, USA, on W fork of the White R; settled, 1824; city status, 1865; railway; university (1918); electrical equipment, glassware, furniture, vehicle parts; represented as the 'average American town' in the 1929 sociological study *Middletown* by R & H Lynd.

Munda An Austroasiatic-speaking people settled in hilly and forested regions of E and C India. Physically indistinguishable from Indians, and culturally similar to other Indians, they have retained a separate identity and religion.

Mundell, Robert A(lexander) (1932–) Economist, born in Ontario, SE Canada. He studied at the Massachusetts Institute of Technology, then held posts at Chicago, Stanford, and Johns Hopkins universities, before joining the International Monetary Fund (1961). Later posts include professorships at the universities of Chicago (1966–71) and Columbia, New York (from 1974). He was awarded the 1999 Nobel Prize for Economics for his analysis of monetary and fiscal policy under different exchange rate regimes and his analysis of optimal currency areas.

mung bean A bushy annual (*Vigna radiata*) growing to 90 cm/3 ft or more, native to tropical Asia; leaves with three hairy leaflets; pea-flowers yellow, in small stalked clusters; pods slender, up to 15-seeded. It is widely cultivated, especially in the Orient for the edible pods and nutritious seeds eaten boiled, or germinated to produce 'bean sprouts'. (Family: Leguminosae.)

Munich [myoonikh], Ger **München** 48°08N 11°35E, pop (2000e) 1 270 000. Capital of Bavaria province, S Germany, on the R Isar; third largest city in Germany; founded, 1158; capital of Bavaria, from 1506; home of the Nazi movement, 1920s; badly bombed in World War 2; railway; university (1471); technical university (1868); chemicals, pharmaceuticals, cosmetics, rubber, precision engineering, machinery, vehicles, aircraft, defence systems, printing and publishing, clothing, foodstuffs, brewing, wine, agricultural produce; Church of St Peter (1181), town hall (1470), cathedral (15th-c), Nymphenburg Palace (17th-c), opera house, art gallery; Pinakothek der Moderne (opened 2002); Oktoberfest (beer festival); site of summer Olympic Games (1972).

Munich Agreement An agreement endorsed (29 Sep 1938) at a conference in Munich by the British prime minister Chamberlain, the French prime minister Daladier, Mussolini, and Hitler. In return for the secession of the Sudeten area of Czechoslovakia to Germany, the rest of Czechoslovakia was to be guaranteed against unprovoked aggression. Poland and Hungary also seized long-desired areas of Czech territory in Moravia, Slovakia, and Ruthenia. Germany took over the rest (rump) of Czechoslovakia in March 1939, thereby rendering the Munich Pact null and void. Britain responded by guaranteeing Poland. Hitler signed a non-aggression pact with the Soviet Union on 23 August 1939. On September 1, he invaded Poland, instigating World War 2. Neither Czechoslovakia nor the Soviet Union were invited to the conference, nor were they consulted about the agreement.

Munich Putsch The abortive attempt by Hitler to overthrow the state government of Bavaria in 1923, as a prelude to the March on Berlin and the establishment of the Nazi regime in Germany. It was supported by General Ludendorff, but badly planned, and it disintegrated in the face of firm Bavarian police action. Hitler was tried for treason, and sentenced to five years' imprisonment. He served eight months of his sentence, during which he wrote *Mein Kampf* (1925, My Struggle).

municipal court *County Court*

Munnings, Sir Alfred (1878–1959) Painter, born in Suffolk, E England, UK. A specialist in the painting of horses and sporting pictures, he became president of the Royal Academy (1944–9). His work is in many public galleries. He was well known for his forthright criticism of modern art.

Munro, H(ector) H(ugh) [muhnroh], pseudonym **Saki** (1870–1916) Novelist and short-story writer, born in Akyab, W Myanmar (formerly Burma). Educated in England at Bedford Grammar School, he returned to Burma and joined the police force in 1893. He went to London in 1896, took up writing for the *Westminster Gazette*, and from 1902 was the Balkans correspondent for the *Morning Post*. He is best known for his short stories, humorous, satiric, supernatural, and macabre, which are highly individual, full of eccentric wit and unconventional situations. Collections include *Reginald* (1904) and *Beasts and Superbeasts* (1914). His novels *The Unbearable Bassington* (1912) and *When William Came* (1913) show his gifts as a social satirist of his contemporary upper-class Edwardian world. He was killed on the Western Front during World War 1, having volunteered for active service despite being over 40.

Munsell Color System A system for measuring and naming colours, devised by US painter Albert H Munsell (?–1918). The *Munsell Book of Color* contains 1200 samples grouped according to minimum discriminable intervals of hue, saturation, and brilliance.

Munster [muhnster] pop (2000e) 1 022 000; area 24 127 sq km/ 9313 sq mi. Province in S Ireland; bounded S and W by the Atlantic Ocean; comprises the counties of Clare, Cork, Kerry, Limerick, Tipperary (N and S Ridings), and Waterford; a former kingdom.

Münster [munster] 51°58N 7°37E, pop (2000e) 268 000. Capital city of Münster district, W Germany; on the R Aa and the Dortmund–Ems Canal, 125 km/78 mi NE of Cologne; member of the Hanseatic League; capital of former province of Westphalia; Treaty of Westphalia (1648) signed here; bishopric; railway; university (1780); service industries, civil engineering, gases; cathedral (1225–65).

muntjac or **muntjak** A true deer, native to India and SE Asia; face with 'V'-shaped ridge; arms of 'V' continued as freely projecting bony columns; ends of columns in male bearing short antlers; both sexes with projecting canine teeth; call resembles a dog barking; also known as **barking deer** or **rib-faced deer**. (Genus: *Muntiacus*, 5 species.)

Müntzer, Thomas [müntser], also spelled **Münzer** or **Monczer** (c.1489–1525) Religious reformer and Anabaptist, born in Stolberg, E Germany. He studied theology, and in 1520 began to preach at Zwickau. His socialism and mystical doctrines soon brought him into collision with the authorities. After preaching widely, in 1525 he was elected pastor of the Anabaptists at Mülhausen, where his communistic ideas soon aroused the whole country. He joined the Peasants' Revolt (1524–5), but was defeated at Frankenhausen, and executed a few days later.

muon A fundamental particle, produced in weak radioactive decays of pions; symbol μ; mass 106 MeV; charge −1; spin ½. It behaves like a heavy electron, but decays to an electron, a neutrino, and an antineutrino. It was discovered in 1937 by Carl Anderson in cosmic ray experiments.

Muppets *Henson*

Murad, Ferid (1936–) Pharmacologist, born in Whiting, Indiana, USA. He studied at Western Reserve University, later working at the University of Virginia (1975–81), Stanford University (1981–8), and the University of Texas at Houston (1997–). He shared the 1998 Nobel Prize for Physiology or Medicine for his contribution to the discovery of nitric oxide as a signalling molecule in the cardiovascular system.

mural A painting or carving on a wall. Murals, representing human and animal motifs as well as pure pattern, have existed since prehistoric times, and various techniques have been used. A great deal of impressive wall decoration survives from the Ancient Near East: the Egyptians, for instance, used distemper or gouache for decorating their tombs, while the Babylonians and Assyrians made extensive use of stone low-relief sculpture. Although Greek wall-painting has almost all perished, we know a good deal about the various styles of Roman wall decoration from the excavations at Pompeii, Herculaneum, and Stabiae (2nd-c BC–AD 79). Both fresco and mosaic were employed: mosaic was much favoured during the Byzantine period in Italy, fresco during the later Middle Ages and Renaissance. The genre continued to be practised in the 20th-c, and may be seen in many popular manifestations, such as identifying sectarian attitudes and areas in Belfast, Northern Ireland.

muramidase *lysozyme*

Murasaki, Shikibu [murasahkee] (978–c.1031) Lady of the court, and writer, born in Kyoto, C Japan. She wrote the world's earliest surviving long novel, also considered the greatest Japanese literary work, *Genji Monogatari* or *The Tale of Genji* (first translated into English by Arthur Waley, 6 vols, 1925–33).

Murat, Joachim [mürah] (1767–1815) French marshal and king of Naples (1808–15), born in La Bastide-Fortunière, SC France. He enlisted in the cavalry on the eve of the French Revolution (1787), and was promoted to general of division in the Egyptian campaign (1799). He married Napoleon's sister, Caroline, after helping him become First Consul. He failed to gain the Spanish crown (1808), and was proclaimed King of the Two Sicilies. After taking part in the Russian campaign, he won Dresden and fought at Leipzig, but concluded a treaty with the Austrians, hoping to save his kingdom. On Napoleon's return from Elba, he recommenced war against Austria, but was twice defeated, and failed to recover Naples. He was captured and executed at Pizzo, Calabria.

Murcia, Eng [mersha], Span [moorthya] pop (2000e) 1 046 000; area 11 313 sq km/4367 sq mi. Region and province of SE Spain; thinly populated, except in the river valleys; oranges, lemons, dates, coastal tourism, lead, zinc, iron; capital, Murcia, pop (2000e) 323 000, on R Segura; former capital of Moorish kingdom; bishopric; airport; railway; university (1915); agricultural market, silk, textiles, flour, pharmaceuticals, tinned food, leather goods; cathedral (14th-c), Salzillo museum; Spring Festival, Our Lady of La Fuensanta (Sep).

murder Unlawful homicide other than manslaughter, infanticide (where separately recognized, as in England and Wales), or causing death by reckless driving. In England and Wales, a person can be convicted of murder only where the crime was committed with malice aforethought (*mens rea*, Lat 'guilty mind'); also the victim must have died within a year and a day of the commission of the crime. Murder is subject to the special defences of provocation, suicide pact, and diminished responsibility. In many US jurisdictions (and also in Scotland), the notion of 'malice aforethought' is not relevant: in these jurisdictions, murder is the intentional killing of another without justification, excuse, or mitigating circumstances, or in the perpetration of a felony (US). In the UK, the sentence on conviction is life imprisonment, which is compulsory, but several countries and jurisdictions provide for capital punishment. In some countries, such as the USA, **first-degree murder** is defined as premeditated, deliberate killing that occurs with specified felonies such as robbery, rape, or kidnapping. **Second-degree murder** may be defined as the act of unintentionally causing another's death at the scene of crime.

Murdoch, Dame (Jean) Iris (1919–99) Novelist and philosopher, born in Dublin, Ireland. She studied at Oxford, then worked at the Treasury (1938–42) and for a UN relief organization (1944–6). She was fellow and tutor in philosophy at Oxford (1948–63), and took up novel writing as a hobby. A prolific writer, she produced a series of successful books exploring complex human relationships with subtlety and humour, such as *Under the Net* (1954), *The Bell* (1958), *The Black Prince* (1973), *The Sea, The Sea* (1978, Booker), *The Philospher's Pupil* (1983), *The Message to the Planet* (1989), and *Jackson's Dilemma* (1995). She also wrote plays and several philosophical and critical studies, including *Sartre* (1953). Many themes are recapitulated in *Metaphysics as a Guide to Morals* (1992). She was made a dame in 1987. A memoir by her husband, John Bayley, *Iris*, including an account of her decline through Alzheimer's disease, was published to great acclaim in 1998 (filmed, 2001).

Murdoch, Lachlan (Keith) (1971–) Media executive, born in London, UK, the son of Rupert Murdoch. He graduated in philosophy from Princeton University, and became general manager of Queensland Newspapers, part of News Limited, the Australian company which itself is the original arm of the News Corporation empire. In 1995 he became publisher of *The Australian* newspaper, and his meteoric rise continued, so that by 1997 he was the executive chairman of News Limited. One of a trio of possible heirs to Rupert, Lachlan is the only sibling with a seat on News Corporation's board.

Murdoch, (Keith) Rupert (1931–) Media proprietor, born in Melbourne, Victoria, SE Australia. He studied at Oxford, then worked for two years on the *Daily Express*, returning to Australia in 1952, where he inherited *The News* in Adelaide on the death of his father. He built a substantial newspaper and magazine publishing empire in Australia, the USA, Hong Kong, and the UK, including the *News of the World* and the *Sun* which, boosted by his 'page three' feature, maintained its lead in the circulation war. In 1981 his company, News International, acquired *The Times* and *The Sunday Times* after a bitter struggle. He moved into the American market in 1976 with the purchase of the New York *Post*, then acquired The New York Magazine Company, whose titles include *The New York Magazine*, *New West*, and *Village Voice*. He became a US citizen in 1985. He also has major business interests in other media industries, especially television, films and publishing, on three continents. He is owner of the Twentieth Century Fox film studio and the Fox television network in the US, and satellite broadcaster BSkyB in the UK. In 2003 his son, **James Murdoch**, was appointed chief executive of BSkyB amid much controversy.

Murdock, William (1754–1839) Engineer, and pioneer of coal gas for lighting, born in Old Cumnock, East Ayrshire, SW Scotland, UK. He worked with Boulton and James Watt of Birmingham, and was sent to Cornwall to erect mining engines. At his home in Redruth he constructed the model of a high-pressure engine to run on wheels (1784), introduced labour-saving machinery, a new method of wheel rotation, an oscillating engine (1785), and a steam-gun. He also improved Watt's engine. His distillation of coal gas began at Redruth in 1792, when he illuminated his own home with it, but it was not until 1803 that Boulton's engineering works at Soho had gas lighting.

murex [myooreks] A carnivorous marine snail, characterized by its elaborate shell bearing spiny outgrowths; many species feed on bivalve molluscs, forcing the valves apart and eating the contents; species of Mediterranean murex are the principal source of Royal Purple dye. (Class: Gastropoda. Order: Neogastropoda.)

Murillo, Bartolomé Esteban [mooreelyoh] (1618–82) Painter, born in Seville, SW Spain. In 1645 he painted 11 remarkable pictures for the convent of San Francisco, which made his name. He founded the Academy of Seville (1660), of which he became first president. He frequently chose the Immaculate Conception or the Assumption of the Virgin as a subject, and treated them much alike. His pictures naturally fall into two groups – scenes from low life, such as gipsies and beggar children (mostly early works), and religious paintings. In 1681 he fell from a scaffold when painting an altarpiece at Cadiz, and died soon after.

Müritz, Lake, Ger **Müritz-See** Lake in Neubrandenburg county, Germany; largest natural lake in former East Germany; area 117 sq km/45 sq mi.

Murmansk [moormansk], formerly **Romanov-na-Murmane** (to 1917) 68°59N 33°08E, pop (2000e) 470 000. Seaport capital of Murmanskaya oblast, Russia; on the E coast of Kola Bay, 50 km/31 mi from the open sea; founded, 1916; most important Russian fishing port (ice-free); airfield; railway; fishing, fish processing, shipbuilding and repairing, tourism.

Murngin *Yolngu*

Murphy, Eddie, popular name of **Edward Reagan Murphy** (1961–) Comic performer and film director, born in New York City, USA. A popular prankster and mimic at school, he hosted a talent show at the Roosevelt Youth Center in 1976 and subsequently decided to pursue a career in show-business. He first came to national prominence on the television show *Saturday Night Live* (1980–4). A charismatic, self-confident humorist, his debut in the film *48 Hrs* (1982) was followed by an unbroken string of box-office hits including *Trading Places* (1983) and *Beverly Hills Cop* (1984, and its sequel, 1987). Later films include *The Nutty Professor* (1996), *Dr Dolittle* (1998), *Bowfinger* (1999), and *Daddy Day Care* (2003). His best-selling albums include *Eddie Murphy Comedian* (1982) and *How Could it Be?* (1984). He made his directorial debut with *Harlem Nights* (1989).

Murphy, Lionel (Keith) (1922–86) Lawyer and politician, born in Sydney, New South Wales, SE Australia. He studied chemistry at the University of Sydney, but turned to law. Unusually, he was admitted to the New South Wales bar in 1947 before graduating as a lawyer from the University of Sydney in 1949. He was elected as Labor senator for New South Wales in the 1962 Federal Parliament, became Opposition leader in 1967, and was appointed attorney-general in 1972. He oversaw several items of landmark legislation, including the Family Law Act, the Law Reform Commission, the Trade Practices Act, and the Human Rights Commission. In 1975 he was appointed to the High Court of Australia, where he made many progressive decisions. Accused in 1984 of having attempted to pervert the course of justice, he was exonerated in 1986, but died soon after. A controversial figure who challenged political and legal boundaries, the impact of his reforms on Australian society is widely acknowledged.

Murphy, Thomas Bernard (1935–) Playwright, born in Tuam, Co Galway, W Ireland. His first play, *A Whistle in the Dark*, was produced in England in 1961, and from then until 1970 he lived and wrote in London. His major works date from his return to Ireland, and include *The Sanctuary Lamp* (1975), *The Blue Macushla* (1980), *The Gigli Concert* (1983), and *Bailegangáire* (1985).

Murphy, William P(arry) (1892–1987) Haematologist, born in Stoughton, Wisconsin, USA. He was a staff member of several New England hospitals before starting private practice in Brookline, MA (1923–87), concurrently working at Peter Bent Brigham Hospital, Boston (1923–73), and Harvard Medical School (1923–58). Inspired by the work of Whipple, and in conjunction with Minot, he shared the 1934 Nobel Prize for Physiology or Medicine for devising dietary liver extract therapy for patients with pernicious anaemia.

Murphy-O'Connor, Cormac, Cardinal (1932–) Roman Catholic cardinal, born in Reading, Berkshire, SE England, UK. He trained at the English College in Rome, was ordained (1956), and worked in Portsmouth and Southampton before his appointment to the English College as rector (1971–7). In 1977 he became Bishop of Arundel and Brighton and later succeeded Cardinal Basil Hume as Archbishop of Westminster (2000). He was made a cardinal in 2001.

Murray, (George) Gilbert (Aimé) (1866–1957) Classical scholar and writer, born in Sydney, New South Wales, SE Australia. He studied at Oxford, and was appointed professor of Greek at Glasgow (1889) and at Oxford (1908). His work as a Classical historian and translator of Greek playwrights brought him world acclaim. His celebrated verse translations of Greek plays, including *The Trojan Women*, *Medea*, and *Electra*, were performed at London's Court Theatre from 1902. His many works on Classics include *History of Ancient Greek Literature* (1897) and *Four Stages of Greek Religion* (1912). As a lifelong Liberal, he stood for parliament, unsuccessfully, six times. President of the League of Nations Union (1923–38), he was the first president of the UN Association General Council.

Murray, Sir James (Augustus Henry) (1837–1915) Philologist and lexicographer, born in Denholm, Scottish Borders, SE Scotland, UK. A grammar school teacher (1855–85), his *Dialects of the Southern Counties of Scotland* (1873) established his reputation. The great work of his life, the editing of the Philological Society's *New English Dictionary* (later called the *Oxford English Dictionary*), was begun at Mill Hill in 1879, and completed in 1928 at Oxford. He edited about half the work, but he created the organization and the inspiration for its completion. He was knighted in 1908.

Murray, Les(lie Allan) (1938–) Poet, born in Nabiac, New South Wales, SE Australia. His childhood and adolescence were spent on a dairy farm, and he studied at Sydney University. He has worked mostly as a freelance writer, contributing literary journalism to newspapers and magazines. His poetry, which has made him one of Australia's leading literary figures, is revered for its evocation of rural life, though its personal style and often polemical tone are also noted. Significant collections include *The Ilex Tree* (with G Lehmann, 1965), *The People's Otherworld* (1983), *Dog Fox Field* (1990), and *Subhuman Redneck Poems* (1996, T S Eliot Prize). Later works include *Fredy Neptune: A Novel in Verse* (1999) and *Collected Poems 1961-2002* (2002).

Murray, Len, popular name of **Baron Lionel Murray of Telford** (1922–) Trade union leader, born in Hadley, Shropshire, WC England, UK. He studied at London and Oxford, and joined the staff of the Trades Union Congress (TUC) in 1947. He progressed from the economic department to become assistant general secretary (1969–73), then general secretary (1973–84). He played a major role in the 'social contract' partnership between the TUC and the Labour governments of Harold Wilson and James Callaghan (1974–8) but, from 1979, had an unhappy relationship with the Conservative administration of Margaret Thatcher. He was made a life peer in 1985.

Murray cod Large, freshwater fish (*Maccullochella macquariensis*) found in rivers and lakes of Australia; length up to 1·8 m/6–10 ft; body robust with large head and powerful jaws; dark green mottled with blue; good sport fish. (Family: Serranidae.)

Murray River Longest river in Australia; rises in the Australian Alps near Mt Kosciusko; length 2570 km/1600 mi; enters the Southern Ocean at Encounter Bay SE of Adelaide; forms the border between New South Wales and Victoria for 1930 km/1200 mi; receives the Darling R 640 km/400 mi from its mouth (the Murray–Darling is 3750 km/2330 mi long); the river system extends into four states, covering a seventh of the continent; used extensively for irrigation and hydroelectric power; navigation now generally confined to tourist steamers; major tributaries the Darling, Murrumbidgee, Mitta Mitta, Goulburn, Campaspe, Loddon.

Murrow, Ed(ward Roscoe), originally **Egbert Roscoe Murrow** (1908–65) Journalist and broadcaster, born in Greensboro, North Carolina, USA. He first visited Europe as assistant director of the Institute of International Education (1932–5). Joining CBS in 1935, he returned to Europe in 1937, and became a compassionate conveyor of the wartime spirit in Britain. In post-war America he became a producer and presenter of such hard-hitting, current affairs programmes as *See It Now* (1951–8) and *Person to Person* (1953–60). Committed to the pursuit of truth and excellence, his questioning of Senator McCarthy in 1954 contributed to the latter's fall from grace. He received five Emmy Awards (1953–8), then retired from television journalism to head the United States Information Agency (1961–4).

Murrumbidgee River [muhruhmb**i**jee] River in New South Wales, Australia; rises in the Snowy Mts; flows 1759 km/1093 mi N through Australian Capital Territory, then W to join the Murray R on the Victoria border; major tributary the Lachlan R; floodplain irrigates a large agricultural basin.

Murry, John Middleton (1889–1957) Writer and critic, born in London, UK. He studied at Oxford, and became editor of *Rhythm*. He then edited the *Athenaeum* (1919–21), and wrote poetry and many volumes of essays and criticism which had a strong influence on the young intellectuals of the 1920s. In 1918 he married Katherine Mansfield, and introduced her work in the *Adelphi*, another literary magazine, of which he was founder and editor (1923–48). He produced posthumous selections from Katherine Mansfield's letters and diaries, and a biography in 1932. He became a pacifist, and edited *Peace News* (1940–6). Towards the end of his life he became interested in agriculture, starting a community farm in Norfolk. His major works include critical studies on *Keats and Shakespeare* (1925), his friend *D H Lawrence* (1931), *William Blake* (1933), and *Swift* (1954).

Mururoa [mururoha] 139°00W 22°00S, pop (2000e) 3500. Remote atoll in French Polynesia, used by France as a nuclear testing site. Between 1966 and 1974 tests were carried out in the atmosphere; since then they have been held underground within an extinct volcano.

Musaceae [myuzasee-ee] A small family of Zingiberales comprising c.35 species of coarse, tree-like perennial herbs dying back to the ground after flowering; confined to tropical and subtropical regions of the Old World; includes bananas and plantains; leaves with an expanded simple blade; flowers strongly nectar-producing and adapted for pollination by birds and bats, producing a fleshy fruit; flowers finger-shaped, arranged in racemes with brightly coloured bracts, each with 6 petals and stamens.

Musca (Lat 'fly') A small S constellation near Crux.

muscarine [muhskarin, -reen] A substance isolated from the poisonous mushroom *Amanita muscaria*. Peoples of E Siberia used dried mushrooms for their intoxicating effects. In W Europe, extracts were used as fly-killing agents (the common name for the mushroom is *fly agaric*). Purified muscarine has been formative in constructing the theory of information transmission in nerves.

Muscat [muhskat], Arabic **Masqat** 27°37N 58°36E, pop (2000e) 423 000. Seaport capital of Oman, on a peninsula in the Gulf of Oman; occupied by the Portuguese, 1508–1650; a former commercial centre, with much trade now lost to Matrah; airport; residence of the Sultan; natural gas, chemicals; two forts (16th-c).

muscle A contractile tissue consisting of fibres bound together by connective tissue and specialized to convert chemical energy into mechanical energy for movement. It is traditionally classified as skeletal, smooth, and cardiac, depending on certain characteristics, but recently myoepithelial cells (of sweat glands) have become recognized as a type of muscle. **Skeletal muscle** is generally attached to bone, and being under central nervous control is principally concerned with voluntary movement. There are two types of skeletal muscle fibre: *red fibres* contain large amounts of myoglobin, which provides the fibre with a store of oxygen, and are generally more numerous in postural muscles, while *white fibres* are found in muscles performing rapid movements. **Smooth muscle** is present mainly in the walls of hollow organs (eg the gut, uterus, blood vessels, ducts). Contraction and relaxation of the fibres is slower than in skeletal muscle, and may be spontaneous or controlled by the autonomic nervous system. **Cardiac muscle** is present only in the heart: its inherent continuous rhythmical contractility is modified by the specialized conducting system, which in turn is under the influence of the autonomic nervous system as well as by circulating adrenaline. Medical problems affecting muscle include convulsions, cramp, fibrositis, muscular dystrophy, myasthenia gravis and rheumatism.

muscovite *micas*

muscovy duck A large duck (*Cairina moschata*) native to Central and tropical South America; wild male black/green with white patches on wing; dark bare skin on face; inhabits water in woodland; eats plants, seeds, small fish, and insects, especially termites. Domestic breeds are grey, white, or speckled, with a scarlet skin patch. It is the only duck other than the mallard to be domesticated. (Family: Anatidae.)

muscular dystrophy A group of genetically determined disorders in which muscle fibres undergo progressive degeneration and are replaced by fibrous tissue (*fibrosis*). The nervous system is not involved. The condition appears early in life, and causes symmetrical weakness and wasting of groups of muscles, such as those of the lower limbs, shoulder, girdle, and face. The most common form of the disease (*Duchenne* type), is due to a defect on the X chromosome, and only affects boys. The muscle cell membrane lacks a specific protein (*dystrophin*), which normally prevents the muscle structure from being destroyed by its own contractions.

Musée d'Orsay [müzay daw(r)say] A museum in Paris, developed on the site of the former railway station and hotel, the Gare d'Orsay, and incorporating several of its architectural features. It contains a wide range of artistic works produced chiefly between 1848 and 1914, and includes painting, sculpture, photography, architecture, and decoration and industrial art. Originally designed by French architect Victor Laloux (1850–1937), the building was converted into a museum in 1984–5.

Muses In Homer, the nine daughters of Zeus and Mnemosyne, who inspire the bard. In later writers they are located on Helicon and Parnassus, and are associated with fountains, such as the Pierian Spring. They were then given names and functions, though there are variations: **Calliope**, epic poetry; **Clio**, history;

Erato, lyric poetry, hymns; **Euterpe**, flute; **Melpomene**, tragedy; **Polyhymnia**, acting, music, dance; **Terpsichore**, lyric poetry, dance; **Thalia**, comedy; **Urania**, astronomy.

museum *American Museum of Natural History; art gallery; Ashmolean / British / Imperial War / London / Natural History / Peace Memorial / Science / Victoria and Albert Museum; Hagia Sophia; Louvre; Musée d'Orsay; Pergamum* (Berlin) ; *Pinakothek, Alte; Pitti Palace; Prado; Terme; Uffizi*

Museum of Modern Art (New York City) Museum founded (1929) in New York City, USA by three private citizens, Lillie P Bliss, Mary Quinn Sullivan, and Abby Aldrich Rockefeller, as the first US museum to devote its collections entirely to the modern art movement. It houses more than 100 000 works divided into six areas: architecture and design, drawings, film and video, painting and sculpture, photography, and prints and illustrated books.

Museveni, Yoweri Kaguta [moosevaynee] (1945–) Soldier, politician, and president of Uganda (1986–). He studied at Dar es Salaam University, then worked for President Milton Obote until his overthrow by Idi Amin (1971). From exile in Tanzania he formed the Front for National Salvation, and took part in the defeat of Amin in 1979. He became minister of defence (1979–80), but was in disagreement with Obote, who returned to the presidency in 1980 with the help of Tanzanian troops. When they withdrew in 1982, a virtual civil war ensued, and reasonable normality did not return until 1986 when Museveni became president, pledging to follow a policy of national reconciliation.

Musgrave Ranges [muhzgrayv] Mountain ranges in South Australia, close to the Northern Territory border; extend 80 km/ 50 mi; rise to 1440 m/4724 ft at Mt Woodroffe, highest point in the state.

Musharraf, Pervez [musharaf] (1943–) Pakistani military leader and president (1999–), born in New Delhi, NC India. He emigrated with his family to Karachi, Pakistan in 1947, joined the army, and was a career soldier for 35 years. He fought in the 1965 and 1971 wars against India and was awarded a medal for bravery in 1965. He rose through the ranks and in 1998 was appointed army chief by Nawaz Sharrif, supporting the Pakistani invasion of the Indian-held territory of Jammu–Kashmir (1999). Angered by the decision to withdraw from the territory, he seized power after learning that he had been sacked as army chief. He became head of the military government, suspended the constitution, dissolved parliament, and established a National Security Council. In 2001, he played a major role in relation to the international movement against terrorism, focused on adjoining Afghanistan. In 2002 he received overwhelming support in a controversial nationwide referendum to extend his term of office for another five years. The same year he was again at the centre of international attention, during the confrontation between Pakistan and India over Jammu–Kashmir. He survived an assassination attempt by Islamic extremists in 2002 and again in December 2003.

mushroom The cultivated mushroom (*Agaricus bisporus*); fruiting body comprises a short white stalk (*stipe*) and rounded cap with brownish gills on the underside; also used as a general name for any similar-shaped fungus. (Subdivision: Basidiomycetes. Order: Agaricales.)

Musial, Stan(ley Frank) [myoozial], nickname **Stan the Man** (1920–) Baseball player, born in Donora, Pennsylvania, USA. He spent his entire career with the St Louis Cardinals, making his debut in 1941. He topped the National League's batting list seven times and was three times voted the league's Most Valuable Player. He retired in 1963 with a ·331 batting average, 475 home runs, and a then National League record of 3630 hits to his credit.

music An orderly succession of sounds of definite pitch, whose constituents are melody, harmony, and rhythm. Almost as fundamental to a perception of the nature of music, however, is *articulation*, which embraces not only the phrasing, dynamics, etc that breathe life into a musical performance, but also the composer's creative use of silence. Music, even when it is imagined silently without an interpreter, exists in time, which means that, except for certain types of composition in which words are paramount (such as operatic recitative and some plainchant), virtually all musical structures entail a degree of audible repetition, even if this cannot always be fully grasped at a first hearing. Music is therefore a kind of aural patterning rather than aural painting – abstract rather than representational. This is not to deny its capacity to elicit a strong emotional response, mainly by creating and eventually resolving harmonic and rhythmic tensions which somehow mirror those of the human body and mind, but the essential nature of music is possibly closer to mathematics than to any of its sister arts.

musical A distinctive genre of musical theatre, evolving in the USA during the 1920s, a strong story is fused with a musical score and professional choreography, found in both theatre and cinema. The first musical of real importance was Jerome Kern's *Showboat* (1927). Feature films with spectacular show-business song-and-dance themes followed rapidly on the introduction of sound-film in 1927, with the direct transcription of theatrical productions or built around a backstage story. For the cinema audiences of the depressed 1930s and the war-restricted 1940s, lavish musicals provided outstanding popular escapism. Memorable musicals of the 1950s include *Guys and Dolls* (1950), *An American in Paris* (1951), *Singin' in the Rain* (1952), and Bernstein's *West Side Story* (1957). Their appeal then decreased, except for transfers of established stage successes or as vehicles for current pop stars, but revived in the 1980s, due largely to the string of successes associated with Andrew Lloyd Webber.

musical comedy A show derived from burlesque and light opera in the 1890s. The formative productions at the Gaiety Theatre in London had their counterpart across the Atlantic, and this kind of entertainment proved popular in England and the USA for some 40 years.

musical glasses An instrument, also known as the **glass harmonica**, consisting of glass vessels of various sizes and pitches which were struck or stroked to produce musical, bell-like sounds. Various types, including Franklin's 'armonica' (1761) were popular in the 18th-c, and several composers, including Mozart, wrote music for them.

musical instruments Devices for producing musical sounds, among the oldest cultural artefacts known. They have changed and developed over the ages in response to technical advances, the discovery of new materials, the invention of new designs, and the expressive demands of composers. Many old instruments have become obsolete, or have been revived in modern times for performing early music. The instruments of the modern symphony orchestra are commonly divided into four types: *woodwind*, *brass*, *percussion*, and *strings*; it is in that order (reading from top to bottom) that they are grouped in orchestral scores. Another way of classifying all instruments (not merely those of the orchestra) would be according to the method of playing them: whether they are bowed, blown, struck, plucked, strummed, or (as with keyboard instruments) touched. However, a different classification, now generally regarded as standard, was devised by musicologists Erich von Hornbostel (1877–1935) and Kurt Sachs (1881–1959), and published in the *Zeitschrift für Ethnologie* in 1914. Building on the work of Charles Victor Mahillon (1841–1924), they divided instruments into four main classes according to the physical characteristics of the sound source (ie the vibrating agent): *aerophones* (in which the sound is generated by air), *chordophones* (by one or more strings), *idiophones* (by the body of the instrument itself), and *membranophones* (by a stretched membrane). To these a fifth class has since been added: *electrophones*, in which the sound is produced by electromagnets, oscillators, or other non-acoustic devices. Each class is then subdivided according to other characteristics.

musical notation The modern method of notating music on five-line staves (*staff notation*) is a development of a mediaeval system for the preservation and uniform dissemination of plainchant. Until the 13th-c only the pitch, and not the length, of notes was indicated, but the development of polyphony in the later Middle Ages necessitated the invention of some form of notation showing note length. Other ways of notating music have included several systems of tablature.

music hall Mass entertainment of the Victorian era which developed in the music rooms of London taverns. After Charles Morton organized a building specifically for this purpose alongside his tavern in 1849, such special 'halls' were opened throughout the country, 'worked' by itinerant performers who perfected short turns with stage business and comic songs to suit their individual style. With the advent of the cinema, the popularity of the music-hall faded.

musicology The scientific and scholarly study of music, embracing the recovery and evaluation of source material, the study of music's historical context, the analysis of particular works and repertories, and several other disciplines. Modern musicology may be said to have originated in the Enlightenment, with the compilation of dictionaries (such as J G Walther's *Musikalisches Lexikon*, 1732; J-J Rousseau's *Dictionnaire*, 1768), the writing of music histories (such as those by Burney and Hawkins), and the publication of specialized journals. Such activities proliferated in the 19th-c, when German scholars took the lead with carefully prepared collected editions (of Handel, Bach, Palestrina, etc). Modern musicologists need to command many specialized skills, including a knowledge of palaeography, paper-types, watermarks, and rastrology (the study of how music staves are drawn). It is an advantage if they are good practical musicians as well.

music theatre A staged performance of a dramatic kind, with music and (usually) singing. The term is applied mainly to small-scale avant-garde works written since World War 2 which reject the aims and values of traditional opera, but it might be extended to include such earlier works as Stravinsky's *The Soldier's Tale* and the musical plays of Brecht and Weill.

Musil, Robert (Elder von) [**moo**sil] (1880–1942) Novelist, born in Klagenfurt, S Austria. He was trained as a scientist (he invented a chromatometer) and as a philosopher. During World War 1 he was an officer, and drew on his experience for *Die Verwirrungen des Zöglings Törless* (1906, trans Young Törless), a story of life inside a military academy. *Der Mann ohne Eigenschaften* (1930–42, The Man Without Qualities, 1969), his unfinished masterpiece, depicting a society on the brink of an abyss, is widely acknowledged as one of the great novels of the 20th-c, despite the confusion of final drafts which the author did not have time to tidy up before his death.

musique concrète [müzeek kõkret] Music composed of 'natural' (ie non-electronic but not necessarily musical) sounds, which are then mixed and manipulated on tape and heard through loudspeakers. Both the term and the technique originated with French composer Pierre Schaeffer (1910–95) in the 1940s.

musk A species of mimulus (*Mimulus moschatus*) with yellow flowers, native to North America from British Columbia to the California region. It was formerly cultivated for the musky scent given off by sticky hairs on all parts of the plant, but this characteristic has been lost, and the plants are nowadays scentless. (Family: Scrophulariaceae.)

musk deer A deer native to wet mountain forests in E Asia; rear legs longer than front legs; kangaroo-like head has no antlers; male with long canine teeth and gland on abdomen, producing a pungent oily jelly (*musk*); musk collected and used in perfumes to make the scent longer-lasting. (Genus: *Moschus*, 3 species. Family: Moschidae.)

muskeg The poorly drained sphagnum moss peat bog and marshland found in the tundra and taiga areas of N Canada. It is underlain by permafrost, the upper surfaces of which partially thaw in summer, providing good breeding conditions for mosquitoes.

muskellunge [**muh**skeluhnj] Largest of the pike fishes (*Esox masquinongy*) confined to well-weeded habitats in the Great Lakes of North America and associated rivers; length up to 2·4 m/8 ft; an agile predator, much prized by anglers as a sport fish. (Family: Esocidae.)

musket A heavy firearm, the most important infantry weapon from the late 17th-c to the mid-19th-c, dominant particularly in the Napoleonic era. Smooth-bored and muzzle-loading, the musket required a high degree of training to operate. It was inaccurate, requiring massed ranks of infantrymen firing their muskets in volleys at short range to prove effective.

Muskie, Edmund S(ixtus) (1914–96) US lawyer and statesman, born in Rumford, Maine, USA. He studied at Bates College and Cornell University, and after war service and private law practice entered the Maine legislature in 1947. He became Governor of Maine (1955–9), then state senator (1959–80), resigning to accept appointment as secretary of state under President Carter. He was Democratic candidate for the vice-presidency in 1968.

musk ox A large goat-antelope (*Ovibos moschatus*) native to the Arctic tundra of North America; very thick long shaggy dark-brown coat; short pale brown legs with splayed hooves; head large, held low, with flat horns meeting in mid-line as a helmet, horn tips curving forwards; lives in herds.

muskrat A large nocturnal water rat (*Ondatra zibethicus*) native to North America; tail flattened from side to side; thick fur exploited commercially; has a musky smell; inhabits wetlands; builds 'houses' (large domes of vegetation and mud); also known as **musquash**. The name **round-tailed muskrat** is used for the Florida water rat. (*Neofiber alleni*).

Muslim *Islam*

Muslim art *Islamic art*

Muslim Brotherhood An Islamic movement, founded in Egypt in 1928 by an Egyptian schoolteacher, Hasan al-Banna, its original goal being the reform of Islamic society by eliminating Western influences and other decadent accretions. In the early 1980s the Muslim Brotherhood was revived in Egypt, its members attacking government buildings and personnel. In Syria in 1980–2 it led an armed revolt against the secular Baathist regime. In 1988 an offshoot of the Brotherhood, HAMAS, was one of the three leading factions in the intifada against Israeli occupation of the West Bank and Gaza.

musquash *muskrat*

mussel A sedentary bivalve mollusc found in estuaries and shallow seas, attached to a substrate by means of tough filaments (*byssus* threads); feeds by filtering particles of matter from water passing over gills; commonly used for human consumption. (Class: Pelecypoda. Order: Mytiloida.)

Musset, (Louis Charles) Alfred de [müsay] (1810–57) Poet and playwright, born in Paris, France. After studying first the law, then medicine, he published his first collection of poems, *Contes d'Espagne et d'Italie* (1829, Tales of Spain and Italy). This won the approval of Victor Hugo, who accepted him into his *Cénacle*, the inner shrine of militant Romanticism, even though Musset had already begun to poke gentle fun at the movement. His first excursion into drama failed, and from then on he conceived an 'armchair theatre' with plays intended for reading only. In 1833 Musset met George Sand, and there began the stormy love affair which, according to his autobiographical poem *La Confession d'un enfant du siècle* (1835, The Confession of a Child of the Age), coloured much of his work after that date. His *Nuits* (1835–7, Nights), trace the emotional upheaval of his love for George Sand from despair to final resignation.

Mussolini, Benito (Amilcare Andrea), known as **il Duce** ('the Leader') (1883–1945) Dictator and prime minister of Italy (1922–43), born in Predappio, Romagna. From a poor family, he was expelled from two schools for knife-assaults on other students, and soon became one of Italy's most intelligent and menacing young Socialists. He broke with the Italian Socialist Party after advocating Italian intervention in World War 1. In 1919 he helped found the *Fasci di Combattimento* as a would-be revolutionary force, and in 1922 became prime minister, his success symbolized by the March on Rome (Oct 1922). By 1925 he had established himself as dictator. His rule saw the replacement of parliamentarism by a 'Corporate State' and an officially totalitarian system; the establishment of the Vatican state (1929); the annexation of Abyssinia (1935–6) and Albania (1939); and the formation of the Axis with Germany. His declaration of war on Britain and France exposed Italy's military unpreparedness, and was followed by a series of defeats in N and E Africa and in the Balkans. Following the Allied invasion of Sicily (Jun 1943), and with his supporters deserting him, he was overthrown and arrested (Jul 1943). Rescued from imprisonment by German paratroopers, he was placed in charge of the puppet Italian Social Republic, but in 1945 he was captured by the Italian Resistance, shot and then hanged, his body being exposed to insult in Como and in Milan, the old headquarters of Fascism.

Mussorgsky, Modest *Moussorgsky, Modest*

mustang A breed of horse, developed naturally in North America as a wild horse; descended from Spanish horses introduced by the Conquistadors; first horses used by American Indians; height, 14–15 hands/1·4–1·5 m/4 ft 8 in; used for riding.

Mustapha Kemel Atatürk *Atatürk, Mustapha Kemal*

mustard An erect annual growing to 1 m/3¾ ft; deeply lobed leaves; yellow, cross-shaped flowers. Commercial mustard is produced from ground seeds of two species cultivated on a large scale: **white mustard** (*Brassica alba*) is native to Europe; seeds milled to produce fine powder, or wet-milled to form paste; commercial production mainly in Canada, E Europe, E England; **black mustard** (*Brassica nigra*), origin unknown but widely naturalized, also yields mustard oil. (Family: Cruciferae.)

mustard gas A light-yellow, oily liquid which becomes a gas above 14°C, acting as a powerful vesicant (producer of blisters) that attacks the human skin, eyes, and lungs. It may have been used in China before the 3rd-c BC, and blown against enemies by bellows. In modern times, it is known for its use as a poison gas on the battlefield of Ypres by the Germans in July 1917. Chemically, it is 2,2'-dichlorodiethylsulphide, $(Cl–CH_2–CH_2)_2S$, boiling point 216°C.

Muste, A(braham) J(ohn), originally **Abraham Johannes Muste**, known as **A J** (1885–1967) Labour leader and pacifist, born in Zierikzee, The Netherlands. His family moved to the USA in 1891, where he became a minister of the Dutch Reformed Church of America (1909–14), then of the Congregational Church (1914–18) and of the Society of Friends (1918–26). During World War 1 he joined the Quaker-sponsored pacifist group, the Fellowship of Reconciliation (FOR), and became executive secretary of the Amalgamated Textile Workers (1919–21) and director of Brookwood Labor College (1921–33), where he helped to train labour activists ('Musteites'). As executive secretary of the American Workers Party (1933–5) and the Workers Party of the United States (1935–6), he supported strike actions, and developed a Marxist revolutionary stance. A mystical experience brought him back to Christian pacifism, advocating non-violence, and he became director of the Labor Temple (1937–40), and executive secretary of the FOR (1940–53). During the 1950s he was active in several civil rights and world peace movements, and in the 1960s was one of the leaders of opposition to the Vietnam War. Sometimes called 'America's Gandhi', he was a leading influence on 20th-c social movements in the USA.

Mustelidae [muhstelidee] A family of carnivorous mammals (67 species), found worldwide except in Australasia and Madagascar; usually with long thin body, short legs, long tail; species include the badger, otter, and weasel.

mutation An abrupt change in the genetic characteristics of an organism. In **chromosomal mutations**, there is a deletion, breakage, or re-arrangement of chromosome material. In **molecular mutation**, there is a physico-chemical change in the DNA sequence, either within a codon, or involving the loss, duplication, or re-arrangement of longer sections of DNA. An example of the first would be a baby born with the 'cat-cry' syndrome (in which the mutation is a deletion of the short arm of chromosome 5). An example of the second would be a baby born with or developing Duchenne muscular dystrophy in a family with no previous history.

mute swan The largest swan (*Cygnus olor*) up to 15 kg/33 lb, native to Europe and Asia, and introduced in the USA; inhabits lakes, often near habitation; eats water plants; orange bill with black swelling at base; does not 'honk' when flying; feet black. One form with pink feet is called the **Polish swan**. (Family: Anatidae.)

Mutsuhito [mutsuheetoh], **Meiji Tenno** (1852–1912) Emperor of Japan (1867–1912) who became the symbol of Japan's modernization, born in Kyoto, C Japan, son of the titular Emperor, Komei, whom he succeeded. Within a year he had overthrown the last of the shoguns, who had exercised dictatorial authority in Japan for 700 years. His long reign saw the rapid political and military westernization of Japan. The feudal system was abolished in 1871; most restrictions on foreign trade were removed; a constitution providing for an advisory cabinet and an imperial Diet was promulgated in 1889; and a navy was created on the British model and an army on the German. Military success against China in 1894 and 1895 was followed by Japan's victories in the Russo–Japanese War (1904–5), and by the economic penetration of Korea and Manchuria.

muttonbird The alternative name of the **short tailed shearwater** (*Puffinus tenuirostris*) from S Australia and the Pacific, or the **sooty shearwater** (*Puffinus griseus*) from New Zealand. The young of both are harvested commercially as food and for their down.

mutual fund *open-ended investment company*

mutualism An association between two different species of organisms in which both species benefit from the relationship. Usage is sometimes restricted to those obligatory relationships where neither species can survive in the absence of the other. The relationship between termites and the protozoans living in their gut is mutualistic: the protozoans digest the cellulose in wood and make its nutrients available to the termites, receiving in return a suitable protected environment and a supply of food.

Muzorewa, Abel (Tendekayi) [muzoraywa] (1925–) Clergyman and politician, born in Umtali (now Mutare), E Zimbabwe. Ordained in 1953, he studied in the USA and in 1968 became the first black bishop of the United Methodist Church. In 1971 he became president of the African National Council (ANC), a non-violent organization intended to pave the way for an internal settlement of the political situation in Rhodesia. In 1975 the ANC split into two factions – the gradualists, led by Muzorewa, working for a transition to majority rule, and the more extreme elements, led by Joshua Nkomo. Muzorewa was prime minister of 'Zimbabwe Rhodesia' for six months in 1979, but after independence his movement was defeated by the parties of Robert Mugabe and Joshua Nkomo.

MX missile An abbreviation used for **Missile Experimental**, the codename of a US third-generation land-based intercontinental ballistic missile. Under development from the late 1960s, it was eventually deployed as the 'Peacekeeper' missile from 1987 onwards in land-based silos in the US Mid-west. This followed much political and strategic debate about the best way of basing these very large and very powerfully armed long-range missiles, to keep them out of reach of a potential Soviet 'first strike'. Eventually it was decided to base 100 in fixed underground silos.

Myall Creek massacre In Australian history, the massacre of 28 Aborigines in NE New South Wales (1838) by a party of assigned convicts for an alleged attack on cattle. Seven of the men charged with the massacre were found guilty and hanged. The accused attracted considerable support from other colonists, who regarded Aborigines as less than human; thereafter the murder of Aborigines was carefully concealed.

Myanmar

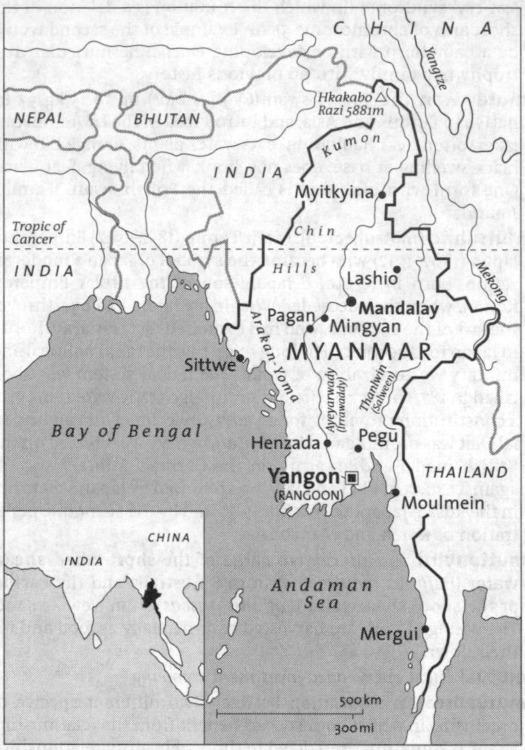

☐ International Airport

[myanmah(r)], formerly (to 1989) **Burma**, official name **Union of Myanmar**, Burmese **Pyidaungzu Myanma Naingngandaw**

Local name Pyidaungzu Myanma Naingngandaw

Timezone GMT +6·5

Area 678 576 km²/261 930 sq mi

Population total (2002e) 42 238 000

Status Union

Date of independence 1948

Capital Yangon (Rangoon)

Languages Burmese (official), also tribal languages spoken

Ethnic groups Burman (Tibeto-Chinese) (72%), Shan (9%), Karen (7%), Chinese (3%), Indian (2%)

Religions Theravada Buddhist (85%), animist, Muslim, Hindu, Christian minorities (15%)

Physical features Bordered in the N, E, and W by mountains rising (N) to Hkakabo Razi, 5881 m/19 294 ft; located on Chinese frontier, forming part of Kumon Range; Chin Hills (W) descend into upland forests of the Arakan-Yoma range (S); principal rivers, Ayeyarwady (Irrawaddy), Thanlwin (Salween), and Sittang.

Climate Tropical monsoon climate; equatorial on coast; humid temperate in extreme N; SW monsoon season (Jun–Sep); cool, dry season (Nov–Apr); hot, dry season (May–Sep); average annual temperatures 23°C (Jan), 27°C (Jul) in Yangon; average annual rainfall 2616 mm/103 in.

Currency 1 Kyat (K) = 100 pyas

Economy Largely dependent on agriculture; rice, pulses, sugar cane; forestry (hardwoods); textiles, pharmaceuticals, petroleum refining, and mining of minerals.

GDP (2002e) $73·69 bn, per capita $1700

Human Development Index (2002) 0·552

History First unified in the 11th-c by King Anawrahta; invasion by Kubla Khan, 1287; second dynasty established under King Tabinshweti in 1486, but plagued by internal disunity and wars with Siam from 16th-c; new dynasty under King Alaungpaya, 1752; annexed to British India following Anglo-Burmese wars (1824–86); separated from India, 1937; occupied by Japanese in World War 2; independence as Union of Burma under Prime Minister U Nu, 1948; military coup under U Ne Win, 1962; single-party socialist republic, 1974; army coup in 1988, leading to formation of a State Law and Order Restoration Council, headed by a Chairman; name changed to Union of Myanmar in 1989 and renamed capital Yangon; Aung San Sun Kyi (Nobel Peace Prize, 1991), main opposition leader, placed under house arrest in 1989–95, 2000–2, 2003–; constitutional conference ongoing since 1992.

Union of Burma

President

1948–52 Sao Shwe Thaik
1952–7 Agga Maha Thiri Thudhamma Ba U
1957–62 U Wing Maung
1962 Sama Duwa Sinwa Nawng

Revolutionary Council – Chairman

1962–74 Ne Win (Maung Shu Maung)

State Council – Chairman

1974–81 Ne Win (Maung Shu Maung)
1981–8 U San Yu
1988 U Sein Lwin
1988 Maung Maung
1988–9 Saw Maung

Union of Myanmar

1989–92 Saw Maung
1992– Than Shwe

Prime Minister

1947–56 Nu U (Thakin Nu)
1956–7 U Ba Swe
1957–8 U Nu
1958–60 Ne Win (Maung Shu Maung)
1960–2 U Nu
1962–74 Ne Win (Maung Shu Maung)
1974–7 U Sein Win
1977–8 U Maung Maung Ka
1988 U Tun Tin
1988–92 Saw Maung
1992–2003 Than Shwe
2003– Khin Nyunt

Myanmar *see panel*

myasthenia gravis [miyastheenia grahvis] A condition characterized by the inability to sustain a contraction of voluntary (*somatic*) muscles. It results from the presence of an auto-antibody which blocks the action of motor nerve impulses that initiate muscle contraction. The muscles become rapidly fatigued, but recover temporarily after a period of rest.

Mycenae [miyseenee] A fortified town in the Argolid, associated in Greek tradition with Agamemnon, the conqueror of Troy. While its extensive Bronze Age remains do indicate that Mycenae was the seat of a powerful warrior chieftain in the 16th-c BC, this is no longer thought to be that of Agamemnon himself.

Mycenaean architecture *Minoan and Mycenaean architecture*

Mycenaean / Mycenean art [miyseneean] The art of Homeric (ie late Bronze Age) Greece. Minoan influence was strong, as in the famous gold cup from Vaphio (c.16th–12th-c BC) with its vigorous representation of bulls captured in nets (National Museum, Athens).

Mycenaean / Mycenean civilization [miyseneean] A brilliant Bronze Age culture which flourished in Greece and the Aegean in the second millennium, reaching its high point in Greece in the 13th-c BC. Important sites are Mycenae, Pylos, and Tiryns. These show the existence in Greece of the palace system of government with its complex redistributive economy, found earlier in Minoan Crete. An important difference, however, is the existence in Mycenaean society of a distinct warrior class. The chief Mycenaean palace sites were destroyed or abandoned towards the end of the 13th-c. Internal warfare may have been the cause; invading Dorians are no longer considered responsible.

mycetoma [miysetohma] A painless mass arising from a fungal infection produced when the fungus grows within the body and becomes matted together with the body's tissues. Fungi such as *Actinomyces* can enter the skin through wounds. The lesion commonly affects the lower limbs, and is also known as **Madura foot**. There may be deeply penetrating chronic abscesses, and the discharge of pus. Another fungus, *Aspergillus*, can grow in the lungs in cavities left by tuberculosis.

mycology [miykolojee] The study of fungi, including the identification, description, and classification of the great diversity of fungi. Fungi are usually identifiable only when they are fruiting, as their vegetative bodies consist of a mass of filamentous threads (*hyphae*), and are similar in appearance in the majority of species.

Mycoplasma The smallest, self-replicating micro-organisms, usually 150–300 nm in diameter. A distinct nucleus is lacking, as are cell walls. They vary in shape from spherical to filamentary. There are c.60 species, all except one being parasitic on vertebrates, plants, and insects. (Kingdom: Monera. Class: Mollicutes.)

mycorrhiza [miykoriyza] A common symbiotic association formed between a fungus and the roots of a plant. In **ectotrophic** mycorrhiza, found in many trees, the fungus grows mainly outside the root, forming a sheath and replacing the root hairs; in **endotrophic** mycorrhiza, found in orchids and heaths, the fungus grows within and between the cells of the root. Mycorrhizal systems have enhanced absorption abilities, and infected plants compete better than non-infected ones, while the fungus benefits from nutrients supplied by the plant. In many cases the plants which form these associations will not grow properly – if at all – in the absence of the fungal partner.

myelin [miyelin] A soft, white substance (a complex of protein lipids) forming a multilayered insulating sheath around the large-diameter axons of vertebrate and crustacean neurones. This increases the speed of conduction of the action potential along the axon. The progressive breakdown of the sheath is associated with the disruption of normal neurone conduction (as in human multiple sclerosis).

myeloma [miyelohma] A malignant proliferation of antibody-producing cells derived from type B lymphocytes (plasma cells) in the bone marrow. Normal bone marrow cells are destroyed and replaced, leading to a reduction in the number of circulating red and white blood cells, and platelets. Patients thus become anaemic and vulnerable to infection, and blood clotting is impaired. The bones are weakened and prone to fractures. Production of large quantities of abnormal antibody can damage the kidneys. The prognosis is poor.

Myers, F(rederic) W(illiam) H(enry) (1843–1901) Poet and essayist, born in Keswick, Cumbria, NW England, UK. A classical scholar, he studied at Cambridge, and became a school inspector (1872–1900). He wrote poems (collected 1921), essays, a book on *Wordsworth* (1881), and *Human Personality and its Survival of Bodily Death* (1903). He was one of the founders of the Society for Psychical Research in 1882, and for the rest of his life he was one of its most productive researchers.

Myers, Mike (1963–) Actor, comedian, writer, and director, born in Scarborough, Ontario, Canada. In 1988 he became a comedian on the television programme *Saturday Night Live*, where he introduced the character 'Wayne Campbell'. He took the character to the big screen in the film *Wayne's World* (1992) which proved an unlikely smash hit. Later films include three *Austin Powers* movies (1997, 1999, 2002) and the voice of Shrek (*Shrek*, 2001, 2004).

Mykonos *Mikonos*

My Lai incident [mee liy] The massacre of several hundred unarmed inhabitants of the S Vietnamese village of My Lai by US troops (Mar 1968), an incident exposed by *Life* magazine photos in 1969. The officer responsible, Lieutenant Calley, was court-martialled in 1970–1.

mynah / myna A bird of the starling family (13 species), native to India and SE Asia, and introduced widely elsewhere; inhabits forest and cultivation, often near habitation; eats mainly fruit, grain, and insects; kept as pets, and known for their vocal mimicry.

myocardial infarction [miyohkah(r)dial] The death of muscle cells of the heart, occurring when they are deprived of oxygen. It may be preceded by attacks of angina pectoris. The cardinal symptom is severe pain over the chest, which unlike that of angina does not subside with rest but persists for several hours. It is often accompanied by shortness of breath, sweating, and vomiting. Diagnostic changes are seen on an electrocardiogram. Effects vary with the site and extent of the muscle involved. It may cause little bodily disturbance beyond a few days of tiredness, but it may lead to heart failure, cardiac arrhythmias, and cardiac arrest with sudden death. Uncomplicated cases can recover fully. Emergency treatment involves prompt administration of drugs to dissolve blood clots in the coronary arteries.

Myolodon [miyolodon] The last of the ground sloths, surviving in Patagonia until recent times, now extinct; samples of its red-haired skin with embedded bony structures have been found in caves. (Order: Xenarthra.)

myopia *eye*

Myrdal, (Karl) Gunnar [mürdahl] (1898–1987) Economist, politician, and international civil servant, born in Gustafs Dalecarlia, Sweden. He studied at Stockholm, where he became professor of political economy (1933). He wrote a classic study of race relations in the USA (*An American Dilemma*, 1944), then was minister of trade and commerce in Sweden (1945–7), and executive secretary of the UN Economic Commission for Europe (1947–57). His later works include *The Challenge of Affluence* (1963). He was awarded the 1974 Nobel Prize for Economics, principally for his work on the critical application of economic theory to Third World countries.

Myriapoda [miriapoda] A diverse group of terrestrial arthropods containing the millipedes (class: Diplopoda), centipedes (class: Chilopoda), and two small classes, Symphyla and Pauropoda. All have a segmented trunk that is not differentiated into thorax and abdomen.

Myrmidons [mermidnz] In Greek legend, a band of warriors from Thessaly who went to the Trojan War with Achilles.

myrobalan *cherry plum*

Myron [miyron] (fl.c.480–440 BC) Sculptor, born in Eleutherae, Greece. A contemporary of Phidias, he lived mostly in Athens. He worked in bronze, and is best known for his studies of athletes in action, particularly the celebrated 'Discobolos' and 'Marsyas'.

myrrh 1 A spiny, deciduous shrub, native to Africa and W Asia; leaves oval or widest above the middle; flowers tiny, males and females on separate plants. Several species from E Africa and Arabia exude the aromatic resin myrrh used in incense and perfume. (Genus: *Commiphora*, 185 species. Family: Burseraceae.) 2 *sweet cicely*

myrtle An evergreen shrub of the family Myrtaceae, found mainly in South America, but also in Australia, New Zealand, the Mediterranean, and warm parts of N Europe and North America; common myrtle grows to over 5 m/16 ft; leaves thick, oil-bearing; solitary white flowers, c.1·8 cm/0·7 in long; purple-black berries; oil formerly used as an antiseptic. (Genus: *Myrtus*, c.16 species.)

Mysore [miysaw(r)] 12°17N 76°41E, pop (2000e) 564 000. City in Karnataka state, SW India; 850 km/528 mi SE of Mumbai; formerly the dynastic capital of Mysore state; founded, 16th-c; railway; university (1916); textiles, food processing, chemicals; known as 'the garden city of India' because of its wide streets and numerous parks; maharaja's palace, within an ancient fort (rebuilt, 18th-c); statue of Nandi (sacred bull of Shiva) on Chamundi Hill (SE), a place of pilgrimage.

mystery play A mediaeval play based upon a Biblical episode. Cycles of plays (notably, those of York, Chester, and Wakefield) tell a continuous story, often portraying the Christian vision from the Creation to the Day of Judgment. They were performed in towns across Europe, and various episodes were presented by trade guilds (then known as 'mysteries'). These plays, and the later **miracle plays** on the Virgin and saints' lives, represent an important phase in the evolution of secular drama from religious ritual.

mystery religions Religious cults of the Graeco-Roman world, full admission to which was restricted to those who had gone through certain secret initiation rites or mysteries. The most famous were those of Demeter at Eleusis in Greece, but the cults of Dionysus, Isis, and Mithras also involved initiation into mysteries.

mysticism The spiritual quest in any religion for the most direct experience of God. Characteristically, mysticism, widely practised in Eastern religions, concentrates on prayer, meditation, contemplation, and fasting, so as to produce the attitude necessary for what is believed to be a direct encounter with God. Christian mysticism tends to focus on the person and sufferings of Christ, attempting to move beyond image and word to the immediate presence of God. In contrast with other forms of mysticism, Christian mystics reject the idea, common in some other religions, of the absorption of the individual into the divine, and retain the distinction between the individual believer and God. Notable Christian mystics include such diverse figures as St Augustine, St Francis of Assisi, and St Teresa of Ávila.

mythology The traditional stories of a people, often orally transmitted. They usually tell of unbelievable things in a deliberate manner, so that a 'myth' can mean both 'an untrue story', and 'a story containing religious truth'. The subject-matter of myths is either the gods and their relations with human or other beings, or complex explanations of physical phenomena. Until recently *mythology* meant Greek mythology, which is distinct in its concentration on stories of heroes and heroines, and its avoidance of the bizarre episodes in contemporary Near Eastern myths. Greek mythology was largely derived from Homer; it referred to a specific historical period (before the Trojan War); and it was, to a certain extent, rationalized and beautified by later writers. The use of this mythology in Elizabethan and Romantic poets indicates a wish to break out of narrowly Christian patterns of behaviour. Some writers (such as Blake, Tolkien, and Yeats) have created mythical systems of their own by synthesizing disparate materials. Recent scholarship has been either folklorist or structuralist, finding unexpected parallels in myths from widely different sources, and showing their function in determining social behaviour.

myxoedema / myxedema [miksuhdeema] The deposition of a substance (*mucopolysaccharide*) under the skin, producing thickening, swelling, and pallor, and a characteristic puffy facial appearance. It is almost invariably associated with severe primary hypothyroidism.

myxomatosis [miksomatohsis] A contagious viral disease of rabbits, characterized by the presence of jelly-like tumours (*myxomata*); harmless to cottontails (occurs naturally in the South American forest rabbit, or tapiti (*Sylvilagus brasiliensis*), but is fatal to European rabbits); introduced to Australia in 1951 to control the vast population of introduced rabbits; devastated wild rabbit populations in Europe in the 1950s.

M'Zab Valley An oasis in a fertile gorge along the Oued M'zab watercourse in the Saharan region of C Algeria; a world heritage site. The area was settled in the 11th-c by the M'zabites, a nonconformist Islamic sect who came here to escape persecution. It is renowned for its five ancient towns, its 4000 wells, and its palm groves.

n

Naas [nays], Ir **Nás na Riogh** 53°13N 6°39W, pop (2000e) 11 300. Market town and capital of Kildare county, Leinster, EC Ireland; on branch of the Grand Canal, SW of Dublin; former capital of the kings of Leinster; noted horse-racing area.

Nabis, Les [nabee] A small group of artists working in Paris c.1890–c.1900 under the influence of Gauguin. Its leading members were Denis, Bonnard and Vuillard.

Nablus [nabloos] 32°13N 35°16E, pop (2000e) 120 000. Capital town of Nablus governorate, Israeli-occupied West Bank, NW Jordan; 48 km/30 mi N of Jerusalem; market centre for the surrounding agricultural region; wheat, olives, sheep, goats; Great Mosque (rebuilt, 1167, as Crusader church); Jacob's Well nearby.

Nabokov, Vladimir [nabohkof] (1899–1977) Writer, born in St Petersburg, NW Russia. He went to school in St Petersburg, and when his family emigrated to Berlin in 1919 he studied at Cambridge. He then rejoined his family, living in Berlin for the next 15 years. There he had his first literary success, a translation of some of Heine's songs, and he published his first novels, all written in Russian under the pseudonym **Vladimir Sirin**, beginning with *Mashenka* (1926). After a time in Paris (1937–40), he emigrated to the USA, where he took out US citizenship in 1945 and taught at Wellesley College and Cornell University. Writing now in English, he published many short stories and novels, including the controversial *Lolita* (1955, filmed 1962 and 1998), dealing with the desire of a middle-aged intellectual for a 12-year-old girl, which brought him fame and wealth, and allowed him to abandon teaching and devote himself full time to writing. Other works include *The Real Life of Sebastian Knight* (1941), *Bend Sinister* (1947), *Pale Fire* (1962), and *Ada* (1969), as well as his lyrical autobiography *Speak, Memory* (1967). Among 20th-c novelists he is highly regarded for his linguistic versatility and intellectual range. His critical approach is illustrated by the collection *Lectures on Literature* (1980). From 1958 he lived in Switzerland.

Nader, Ralph [nayder] (1934–) Lawyer and consumer activist, born in Winsted, Connecticut, USA. He studied at Princeton and Harvard, and was admitted to the Connecticut bar in 1959. Since then he has campaigned for improved consumer rights and protection, encouraging the establishment of powerful civic interest lobbies of which the US Congress, state legislatures, and corporate executives have had to take note. His best-seller about the automobile industry, *Unsafe at Any Speed* (1965), led to the passing of improved car safety regulations in 1966. His other books include *The Menace of Atomic Energy* (1977), *Good Works* (1993), and *No Contest* (1996). He became head of the Public Citizen Foundation in 1980. In 2000 he ran for the US presidency as a Green Party candidate but received only three per cent of the vote.

nadir [naydeer] A point on the celestial sphere immediately below an observer, therefore unobservable. Its opposite, the point vertically above the observer, is the **zenith**.

Naevius, Gnaeus [neevius] (c.264–c.194 BC) Poet and playwright, probably born in Campania. He served in the first Punic War (264–241 BC), and started producing his own plays in 235. A plebeian, for 30 years he satirized the Roman nobles in his plays, and was compelled to leave Rome, ultimately retiring to Utica in Africa. Fragments of an epic, *De bello Punico*, are extant.

naevus *birthmark*

Nafud [nafood] Desert area in N part of the Arabian Peninsula; c.290 km/180 mi long and 225 km/140 mi wide; occasional violent windstorms have formed crescent-shaped dunes, rising to heights of c.200 m/600 ft; dates, vegetables, barley, and fruit are grown in oases, especially near the Hejaz Mts.

Nagaland [nahgaland] pop (2001e) 1 988 600; area 16 527 sq km/6379 sq mi. State in NE India; administrative centre, Kohima; governed by a 60-member State Assembly; rice, sugar cane, pulses, forestry, weaving; former territory of Assam; became a state in 1961; strong movement for independence amongst Naga tribesmen; talks with the Naga tribes underground movement resulted in the Shillong Peace Agreement, 1975.

Nagarjuna [nagah(r)juna] (c.150–c.250) Indian Buddhist monk-philosopher. He was the founder of the Madhyamika or Middle Path school of Buddhism.

Nagasaki [nagasakee] 32°45N 129°52E, pop (2000e) 455 000. Capital of Nagasaki prefecture, W Kyushu, Japan; visited by the Portuguese, 1545; centre for Jesuit missionaries from 16th-c; one of the power centres of the Tokugawa Shogunate; target for the second atomic bomb of World War 2 (9 Aug 1945), killing or wounding c.75 000, and destroying over a third of the city; airport; railway; university (1949); fishing, shipbuilding, engineering, metal products; stone bridges across the R Nakajima, including Spectacles Bridge (1634); Sofukuji pavilions; peace statue in Peace Park; Statue of the Martyrs (1962); Suwa Shrine festival (Oct).

Nag Hammadi texts [nahg hamahdee] A library of religious texts recorded in Coptic and discovered in 1945 in Egypt near the town of Nag Hammadi. It consists of some 12 books containing 52 tractates, the scriptures of the Christian Gnostic movement in Egypt, although some works are neither openly 'Gnostic' or 'Christian' but are rather of a philosophical or Jewish character. It is valuable evidence for this early form of 'heretical' Christianity, and contains many previously-unknown works.

Nagorno-Karabakh [nagaw(r)noh karabakh], Russ **Nagorno-Karabakhskaya** area 11 400 sq km/4400 sq mi. Autonomous region in Azerbaijan, established in 1923 after the reversal (on Stalin's instigation) of a decision taken in 1921 by the Bureau of Caucasian Affairs to unite the region with Armenia; administrative centre, Stepanakert; in Karabakhsky and Murovdag ranges of the Caucasus; climate ranges from −10°C in winter to 25°C in summer; majority of population Armenian, leading to claims by Armenia for its incorporation into that republic; opposed by Azerbaijan and former Soviet Union, leading to military conflict from 1988 onwards; ceasefire agreement signed, 1994; mineral springs, agriculture, horticulture, livestock, marble, minerals, sericulture, vineyards.

Nagoya [nagoya] 35°08N 136°53E, pop (2000e) 2 154 000. Port capital of Aichi prefecture, C Honshu, Japan, on NE shore of Ise-wan Bay; founded as a castle, 17th-c; fourth largest city of Japan; munitions centre, heavily bombed in World War 2; airport; railway; two universities (1939, 1950); engineering, metal prod-

Namibia

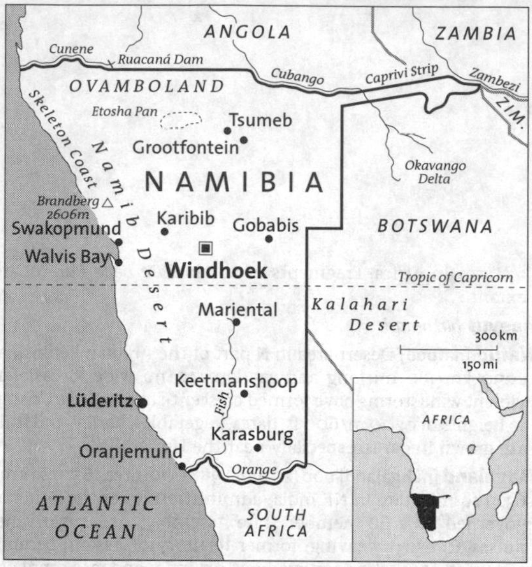

☐ International Airport

[namibia], formerly **Southwest Africa** (to 1968), earlier **German South-West Africa**

Local name Namibia

Timezone GMT +2

Area 824 292 km²/318 261 sq mi

Population total (2002e) 1 837 000

Status Republic

Date of independence 1990

Capital Windhoek

Languages English (official), Afrikaans, German, local languages

Ethnic groups African (chiefly Ovambo) (85%), white (7%), mixed (8%)

Religions Christian (Lutheran, Roman Catholic, Dutch Reformed, and Anglican) (90%), traditional animist beliefs (10%)

Physical features Located in SW Africa; Namib Desert runs parallel along the Atlantic Ocean coast; inland plateau, mean elevation 1500 m/5000 ft; highest point, Brandberg, 2606 m/8550 ft; Kalahari Desert to the E and S; Orange R forms S frontier with South Africa.

Climate Arid, continental tropical climate; average maximum daily temperature, 20–30°C; 49°C (Nov–Apr) in coastal desert (Namib); average annual rainfall 360 mm/14 in at Windhoek.

Currency 1 Namibian Dollar (R) = 100 cents

Economy Agriculture (employs c.60% of population); indigenous subsistence farming in N; major world producer of diamonds and uranium; fishing; brewing; textiles; plastics.

GDP (2002e) $13·15 bn, per capita $6900

Human Development Index (2002) 0·610

History Visited by British and Dutch missionaries from late 18th-c; German protectorate, 1884; mandated to South Africa by the League of Nations, 1920; UN assumed direct responsibility in 1966, changing name to Namibia, 1968, and recognizing the Southwest Africa People's Organization (SWAPO) as representative of the Namibian people, 1973; South Africa continued to administer the area as Southwest Africa; SWAPO commenced guerrilla activities, 1966; bases established in S Angola, involving Cuban troops in 1970s; interim administration installed by South Africa, 1985; full independence, 1990; governed by a President, Prime Minister and Cabinet, and an elected National Assembly.

Head of State

1990– Sam Daniel Nujoma

Head of Government

1990–2002 Hage Geingob

2002– Theo-Ben Gurirab

ucts, cars, machinery, textiles; Nagoya Castle (rebuilt, 1959), Atsuta Shrine (c.1st-c), Tokugawa art museum.

Nagpur [nahgpoor] 21°08N 79°10E, pop (2000e) 1 905 000. City in Maharashtra, WC India; on R Pench, 675 km/419 mi NE of Mumbai; founded, 18th-c; scene of the final British overthrow of the Marathas, 1817–18; former capital of Berar and Madhya Pradesh states; airfield; railway; university (1923); cotton textiles, paper, metallurgy, trade in oranges.

Nagy, Imre [noj, imray] (1895–1958) Hungarian statesman and prime minister (1953–5), born in Kaposvar, SW Hungary. He had a minor post in the Béla Kun revolutionary government in Hungary. He then went to Moscow (1929), and became a member of the Institute for Agrarian Sciences. Returning with the Red Army (1944), he was minister of agriculture, and as premier introduced milder political control. When Soviet forces began to put down the 1956 revolution, he appealed to the world for help, but was displaced by the Soviet puppet, János Kádár, and executed in Budapest.

Nahanni National park in NW Canada; area 4770 sq km/1842 sq mi; habitat of the peregrine falcon, golden eagle, grey wolf, and grizzly bear, as well as many other rare species; a world heritage site.

Nahum, Book of [nayhum] One of the 12 so-called 'minor' prophetic writings of the Hebrew Bible/Old Testament, attributed to a prophet named Nahum, about whom little else is known. The oracle vigorously announces the imminent downfall of Assyria and the destruction of Nineveh (612 BC), which is interpreted as the Lord's judgment upon its wickedness and as good news for Judah. It was perhaps intended to encourage Judean stirrings for independence from the occupying power.

naiad [niyad] In Greek mythology, a nymph who inhabits springs, rivers, and lakes.

Naidoo, Jay (Jayaseelan) [niydoo] (1954–) South African labour leader and opponent of apartheid, born in Durban, E South Africa. In 1979 he became a trade union organizer, and rose to prominence in the labour movement. When the Congress of South African Trade Unions (COSATU) was founded in 1985, he was elected general secretary. In this capacity he played a leading role during the mass-based protest politics of the 1980s, and led COSATU into formal alliance with the African National Congress and the South African Communist Party. From December 1990, he was active in the negotiations for a new political dispensation in South Africa.

nails Rectangular plates of horny tissue found on the back of the end bones (*terminal phalanges*) of each digit. They are specialized modifications of the outer two layers of the epidermis. Each nail is partly surrounded by a fold of skin (the *nail wall*) and is firmly anchored to the underlying *nail bed*. They grow at c.1 mm/0·04 in per week, faster in summer than in winter.

Naipaul, Sir V(idiadhar) S(urajprasad) [niypawl] (1932–) Novelist, born in Chaguanas, W Trinidad. He studied at Port of Spain, and Oxford, became editor of *Caribbean Voices* for the BBC, and was a journalist, before publishing his first novel, *The Mystic Masseur* in 1957. The book which made his name was *A House for Mr Biswas* (1961), a satire spanning three Trinidadian generations. Thereafter the Caribbean figured less prominently in his work, which grew steadily darker and more complex, as seen in *In a Free State* (1971, Booker) and *A Bend in the River* (1979), a re-creation of what it is like to live under an African dictatorship. *The Enigma of Arrival* (1987) returns the scene to England. He has also written several travel books, including *An*

Area of Darkness: an Experience of India (1964) and *Among the Believers: an Islamic Journey* (1981). His *Reading and Writing: a Personal Account* appeared in 2000, and a further novel, *Half a Life*, in 2001. He was knighted in 1990, and was awarded the Nobel Prize for Literature in 2001.

Nairobi [niyrohbee] 1°17S 36°50E, pop (2000e) 1 833 000. Province and capital of Kenya; on the central Kenya plateau, 450 km/280 mi NW of Mombasa; largest city in E Africa; former seat of the British governor of Kenya; airport; railway; university (1956); centre of communications and commerce; textiles, chemicals, glass, agricultural trade; headquarters of the United Nations Environment Programme Secretariat; cathedral (1963), Sikh temple, national museum (including largest collection of African butterflies in the world), Snake Park.

naive art *primitivism*

Nakasone, Yasuhiro [nakasohnay] (1918–) Japanese statesman and prime minister (1982–7), born in Takasaki, C Japan. He studied at Tokyo University, was a junior naval officer in World War 2, and entered the ministry of home affairs in 1945. Elected to the Diet at age 29 for the Liberal–Democratic (Conservative) Party, he held a range of ministerial posts (1959–82). As premier, he supported the renewal of the US–Japan Security Treaty, and maintained close relations with President Ronald Reagan.

Namaqualand [namakaland], Afrikaans [namakwalant] Region in S Namibia and W South Africa; comprises **Little Namaqualand**, extending S from the Orange R, chief town Springbok, and **Great Namaqualand**, extending N from the Orange R, chief town Keetmanshoop; European presence since 1665; indigenous peoples known as Namaquas or Nama; diamond mines.

Namath, Joe, popular name of **Joseph William Namath**, nickname **Broadway Joe** (1943–) Player of American football, born in Beaver Falls, Pennsylvania, USA. He joined the New York Jets from the unbeaten University of Alabama team in 1965, and became one of the leading quarterbacks in the 1960s. He led the Jets to a Super Bowl victory in 1969, beating Baltimore for the first win by an American Football League team over the established National Football League. His lifestyle outside football attracted a great deal of publicity, hence his nickname. After his retirement (1978), he remained in the public eye, with appearances in films and on television.

Namatjira, Albert [namatjeera] (1902–59) Artist, born in Hermannsburg Lutheran mission, near Alice Springs, Northern Territory, Australia, a member of the Aranda Aboriginal people. He achieved wide fame almost overnight for his European-influenced watercolour landscapes. In 1957 he was in the unique position of being made an Australian citizen, 10 years before other Aboriginal people. Divided by two cultures, his last years became a nightmare. A retrospective exhibition of his work was held in Alice Springs in 1984.

Namen [namen] *Namur*

Namib Desert [namib] Desert in W Namibia, along most of the Atlantic seaboard of Namibia; length, c.1300 km/800 mi; width, 50–160 km/30–100 mi; contains the highest sand dunes in the world.

Namibia *p.1058*

Namier, Sir Lewis (Bernstein) [naymyer], originally **Ludwik Bernstein Niemirowski** (1888–1960) Historian, born near Warsaw, Poland. He moved to England in 1906, studied at Oxford, and took British nationality. He became professor of modern history at Manchester (1931–52), creating a school of history in which the emphasis was on the detailed analysis of events and institutions, particularly parliamentary elections, so as to reveal the motivation of the individuals involved in them. One of his most important works is *The Structure of Politics at the Accession of George II* (1929).

Namur [namür], Eng [namoor], Flemish **Namen** 50°28N 4°52E, pop (2000e) 105 500. Capital city of Namur province, SC Belgium, at confluence of Sambre and Meuse Rivers; key strategic point of the Belgian defence line on the R Meuse; conquered by the Germans in 1914 and 1940; railway; private university (1831); glass, porcelain, enamel, paper, steel; cathedral (1751–67), citadel (17th-c).

Nanak [nanak], known as **Guru Nanak** (1469–1539) Religious leader, the founder of Sikhism, born at Talwandi, near Lahore, NE Pakistan (formerly India). A Hindu by birth, he left his home at around the age of 30, and spent 20 years travelling widely in search of spiritual truth. He eventually settled in Kartarpur, in the Punjab, where he attracted many followers. He was a revolutionary in his thought, denouncing many contemporary religious practices as idolatrous, speaking out against caste and discriminatory rituals, and preaching equality for all. His doctrine was set out later in the *Adi-Granth*.

Nana Sahib [nana saheeb], originally **Brahmin Dundhu Panth** (c.1820–c.1859) Prominent rebel of the Indian Mutiny, the adopted son of the ex-peshwa of the Marathas **Baji Rao II** (1796–1818). At the outbreak of the Indian Mutiny (1857) he became the leader of the Sepoys in Cawnpore, and organized the massacre of the British residents. After the collapse of the rebellion he escaped into Nepal, and died in the hills some time later.

NANC An abbreviation of **non-adrenergic, non-cholinergic**: a description of autonomic nerve fibres in which the neurotransmitter is neither noradrenaline nor acetylcholine. Important areas supplied by such nerves include the airways, bladder, intestine, and genitals. Possible NANC transmitters include some purines (eg adenosinetriphosphate) and various peptides (eg vasoactive intestinal polypeptide).

Nanchang or **Nan-ch'ang** [nanchang] 28°38N 115°56E, pop (2000e) 1 527 000, administrative region 3 935 000. Industrial capital of Jiangxi province, SE China; founded 201 BC during the E Han dynasty; centre of abortive uprising (1927) led by pro-communist Guomindang officers under Russian direction; airfield; railway; university; distribution centre for kaolin clay; cotton, machinery, paper, food processing, chemicals; Jiangxi Provincial Museum; Bada Shanren Exhibition Hall.

Nancy [nãsee] 48°42N 6°12E, pop (2000e) 104 000. Manufacturing city and capital of Meurthe-et-Moselle department, NE France; on R Meurthe and Marne–Rhine Canal, 285 km/177 mi E of Paris; former capital of Lorraine; part of France, 1766; road and rail junction; episcopal see; university (1572); iron and steel, boilers, catering equipment, glass, footwear, tobacco, yeast, brewing; 17th-c town hall, 13th-c ducal palace, 15th-c Eglise des Cordeliers, 14th-c Porte de la Craffe, cathedral (1703–42); noted for its 18th-c Baroque architecture: Place Stanislas, Place de la Carrière, and Place d'Alliance comprise a world heritage site.

nandu *rhea* (ornithology)

Nanjing [nahnjing] or **Nanking** 32°03N 118°47E, pop (2000e) 2 987 000, administrative region 5 762 000. Capital of Jiangsu province, SE China, on the Yangtze R; founded, 900 BC; capital of China 220–589, 907–79, 1356–68 (renamed Nanjing, or 'southern capital'), 1928–49; centre of Taiping Rebellion (1850–64); river port and trade centre; open port after the Opium War (1842), which concluded with the Treaty of Nanjing; airfield; railway; university (1902); coal, metallurgy, petroleum refining, engineering, shipbuilding; major Yangtze bridge; many historical sites and relics; Nanjing museum, Sun Yatsen Mausoleum, Ming Xiaoling (Ming Emperors' Tombs), Zijin Mountain astronomical observatory and museum, Yuhuatai Park.

Nanking *Nanjing*

Nanning or **Nan-ning** 22°50N 108°06E, pop (2000e) 1 298 000, administrative region 2 908 000. Capital of Guangxi Zhuang autonomous region, S China; founded during the Yuan dynasty; military supply town during Vietnam War; closed to foreigners until 1977; airfield; railway; agricultural trade; food processing, coal, bauxite, leather, paper, machinery; Dragon Boat Regatta (May–Jun).

nanotechnology The science of construction in which dimensions of the components are less than 100 nanometres (nm; 10^{-9} of a metre), this is c.100 000 times thinner than a human hair. The term was introduced by Nomo Taniguchi in 1974 to refer to mechanical machining methods. *Top-down* nanotechnology concentrates on manufacturing on this very small scale. Techniques such as photolithography are used to make transistors for integrated circuits; the smaller the transistor, and the closer together they are packed, the higher the processing power of the chip. An Intel Pentium chip has about 1·5 million transistors. A specialized **Dynamic Random Access (DRAM)** chip carries 64 million transistors. *Bottom-up* nanotechnology builds with individual atoms. A **Scanning Tunnelling Microscope (STM)** is used to manipulate and arrange individual atoms exactly as required. Another development has been the **Nanomanipulator**, which senses the electric fields of the atoms; this uses 3-D computer graphics and virtual reality technology to allow the scientists to 'see' and 'feel' the atoms as they move them. In 1985, naturally occurring crystals called *fullerenes* were discovered. One type is the Buckminsterfullerene (nicknamed a *Buckyball*), a hollow carbon ball which is so strong that it can be used as tiny ball bearings. Rolling up a sheet of carbon atoms produces a tube which is only a nanometre wide. If metals are 'sucked' up the tiny tube and the 'straw' then dissolved, the result is a **nanowire** which can be used in microelectric circuits. The application of nanotechnology may result in revolutionary methods of atom-by-atom manufacturing and surgery on a cellular scale, as well as the creation of computers of great compactness and power.

Nansen, Fridtjof [**fri**tyof] (1861–1930) Explorer, born near Oslo, Norway. He studied at Oslo University and later at Naples. In 1882 he made a voyage into the Arctic regions in the sealer *Viking*, and on his return was made keeper of the natural history department of the museum at Bergen. In 1888 he journeyed across Greenland E–W, but his great achievement was his scheme for reaching the North Pole by letting his ship, *The Fram*, get frozen into the ice N of Siberia (1883) and drift with a current setting towards Greenland; the boat reached 84°4', and after a further voyage on foot, he achieved 86°14', the highest latitude then attained. The first Norwegian ambassador in London (1906–8), he was awarded the Nobel Prize for Peace for Russian relief work (1922), and he did much for the League of Nations.

Nantes [nãt], Breton **Naoned**, ancient **Condivincum**, later **Namnetes** 47°12N 1°33W, pop (2000e) 256 000. Manufacturing and commercial seaport, and capital of Loire-Atlantique department, W France; at head of Loire estuary, 171 km/106 mi W of Tours; seventh largest city in France; 16th–18th-c centre of sugar and ebony trade; France's leading port in 18th-c; 19th-c decline, halted by construction of harbour at St-Nazaire and river dredging; major bomb damage in World War 2; railway; university (1962); oil refining, sugar refining, boatbuilding, tobacco, soap, textiles, food products, building materials; birthplace of Jules Verne; Gothic Cathedral, museum of fine arts, Château des Ducs (10th-c, rebuilt 1466), where Edict of Nantes was signed.

Nantes, Edict of [nãt] (1598) A law promulgated by Henry IV of France at Nantes granting religious and civil liberties to his Protestant Huguenot subjects at the end of the Wars of Religion. Richelieu annulled its political clauses (1629) as a threat to his centralizing policies; and the same motive led Louis XIV to order the infamous revocation of the edict (1685). Thousands of Protestants fled abroad to escape the system of Dragonnades, whereby soldiers were billeted in houses where they were encouraged to commit outrages against the persons and property of the Huguenots.

Nantucket (Algonquian 'narrow-tidal-river-at') pop (2002e) 9000. Island in the Atlantic off the SE coast of Massachusetts, USA; with Muskeget and Tuckernuck Is, forms Nantucket Co; area 122 sq km/47 sq mi; formerly an important whaling centre; now a summer resort.

Naomi [nay**oh**mee] (Heb 'my delight') Biblical character described in the stories of the Book of Ruth as the mother-in-law of Ruth and Orpah. After Naomi was widowed, she returned from Moab to Bethlehem with her daughter, and attempted to arrange the marriage of Ruth with Boaz, one of the secondary kinsmen of Naomi's deceased husband. The offspring of this union was said to be the grandfather of David

napalm [**nay**pahm] A munition (usually air-launched in canisters by aircraft) containing petroleum gel which uses flame for its destructive effects. It is designed for use against hard targets such as bunkers and armoured vehicles. Chemically, it is an aluminium soap of naphthenic and palmitic acids (which give the substance its name).

Napata [na**pah**ta] An ancient city, situated on the W bank of the Nile in what is now the Sudan. It was the capital of the kingdom of Cush c.750–590 BC. Although political dominance passed to Meroe in that year, Napata remained the religious capital.

Naphtali, tribe of [**naf**talee] One of the 12 tribes of ancient Israel, said to be descended from Naphtali, Jacob's second son by Bilhah (Rachel's maid). Its tribal territory was in N Palestine, immediately W of the Sea of Galilee and upper Jordan R. The tribe is described in the Book of Judges as consisting of courageous warriors.

naphtha [**naf**tha] A mixture of hydrocarbons obtained either from coal tar or from petroleum. It has a boiling range of about 100–180°C. Naphtha from coal tar is mainly aromatic, containing much toluene, while that from petroleum is mainly aliphatic.

naphthalene [**naf**thaleen] $C_{10}H_8$, melting point 80°C. A white, waxy solid, containing two fused benzene rings; obtained from the distillation of coal tar. It forms many derivatives, and is important as a starting material in the synthesis of dyestuffs and plastics. It is familiar as the main ingredient of mothballs.

naphthol [**naf**thol] $C_{10}H_7OH$. Two isomeric phenols, obtained by substituting –OH for one hydrogen atom of naphthalene. Both are present in coal tar, and are starting materials for dyes.

Napier [**nay**pyer] 39°29S 176°58E, pop (2000e) 57 000. Seaport in Hawke's Bay on the E coast of North Island, New Zealand; largely destroyed by earthquake in 1931; much of the business area rebuilt in Art Deco style; a modern seaside city built largely on reclaimed land; airfield; railway; centre of a rich farming area; electronics, food processing, trade in wool, meat, fruit, pulp, tobacco.

Napier, John [**nay**pyer] (1550–1617) Mathematician, the inventor of logarithms, born at Merchiston Castle, Edinburgh, EC Scotland, UK. He studied at St Andrews, travelled in Europe, then settled down to a life of literary and scientific study. He described his famous invention in *Mirifici logarithmorum canonis descriptio* (1614, Description of the Marvellous Canon of Logarithms), and also devised a calculating machine, using a set of rods called **Napier's bones**.

Naples, Ital **Napoli**, Lat **Neapolis** 40°50N 14°15E, pop (2000e) 1 205 000. Seaport and capital city of Naples province, Campania, SW Italy; on the Tyrrhenian Sea, 189 km/117 mi SE of Rome; founded c.600 BC by refugees from Greek colony of Cumae; capital of Napoleon's Parthenopean Republic (1799) and of the Sicilian kingdom (1806); joined Kingdom of Italy, 1860; severely damaged in World War 2, and by earthquakes, 1980; archbishopric; airport; railway; car ferries to Sardinia and Sicily; university (1224); commerce, textiles, cars, aerospace, telecommunications, glass, food processing, tourism; several areas economically deprived; Cathedral of San Gennaro (13th–15th-c), Church of San Lorenzo Maggiore (1266–1324), Porta Capuana (15th–16th-c), Church of San Giovanni a Carbonara (14th–15th-c), national museum; folk song festival (Sep).

Napoleon I, Fr **Napoléon Bonaparte**, Ital **Napoleone Buonaparte** (1769–1821) French general, consul, and emperor (1804–15), a titanic figure in European history, born in Ajaccio, Corsica. He entered the military schools at Brienne (1779) and Paris (1784), commanded the artillery at the siege of Toulon (1793), and was promoted brigadier-general. In 1796 he married Joséphine, widow of the Vicomte de Beauharnais, and soon after left for Italy, where he skilfully defeated the Piedmontese and Austrians (at Lodi), and made several gains through the Treaty of Campo Formio (1797). Intending to break British trade by conquering Egypt, he captured Malta (1798), and entered Cairo, defeating the Turks; but after the French fleet was destroyed by Nelson at the Battle of the Nile in 1798 (also known as The Battle of Aboukir Bay), he returned to France (1799), having learned of French reverses in Europe. The *coup d'état* of 18th Brumaire followed (9 Nov 1799) in which Napoleon assumed power as First Consul, instituting a military dictatorship. He then routed the Austrians at Marengo (1800), made further gains at the Treaty of Luneville (1801), and consolidated French domination by the Concordat with Rome and the Peace of Amiens with England (1802).

Elected consul for life, he assumed the hereditary title of emperor in 1804. His administrative, military, educational, and legal reforms (notably the *Code Napoléon*) made a lasting impact on French society. War with England was renewed, and extended to Russia and Austria. Forced by England's naval supremacy at Trafalgar (1805) to abandon the notion of invasion, he attacked the Austrians and Russians, gaining victories at Ulm and Austerlitz (1805). Prussia was defeated at Jena and Auerstadt (1806), and Russia at Friedland (1807). After the Peace of Tilsit, he became the arbiter of Europe. He then tried to cripple England with the Continental System, ordering the European states under his control to boycott British goods. He sent armies into Portugal and Spain, which resulted in the bitter and ultimately unsuccessful Peninsular War (1808–14).

In 1809, wanting an heir, he divorced Joséphine, who was childless by him, and married the Archduchess Marie Louise of Austria, a son being born in 1811. Believing that Russia was planning an alliance with England, he invaded (1812), defeating the Russians at Borodino, before entering Moscow, but he was forced to retreat, his army broken by hunger and the Russian winter. In 1813 his victories over the allied armies continued at Lützen, Bautzen, and Dresden, but he was routed at Leipzig, and France was invaded. Forced to abdicate, he was given the sovereignty of Elba (1814). The unpopularity which followed the return of the Bourbons motivated him to return to France in 1815. He regained power for a period known as the Hundred Days, but was defeated by the combination of Wellington's and Blücher's forces at Waterloo. He fled to Paris, abdicated, surrendered to the British, and was banished to St Helena, where he died. In all the areas of Europe under Napoleonic rule, the Code Napoléon became law. A great number of political and social reforms resulted, including the abolition of feudalism and serfdom, freedom of religion in most occupied states, the granting of constitutions, universal male suffrage, and parliaments. Administrations, judiciary systems, and a free education system based on the French model were set up. Higher education was made available to all qualified applicants regardless of religion or social class.

Napoleon II, in full **François Charles Joseph Bonaparte** (1811–32) Son of Napoleon I by the Archduchess Marie Louise, born in Paris, France. He was styled King of Rome at his birth. After his father's abdication he was brought up in Austria, and in 1818 given the title of the Duke of Reichstadt, though allowed no active political role.

Napoleon III, until 1852 **Louis Napoleon**, originally **Charles Louis Napoleon Bonaparte** (1808–73) Third son of Louis Bonaparte, king of Holland (the brother of Napoleon I) and Hortense Beauharnais; the president of the Second French Republic (1848–52) and emperor of the French (1852–70), born in Paris, France. After the death of Napoleon II he became the head of the Napoleonic dynasty. He made two abortive attempts on the French throne (1836, 1840), for which he was imprisoned. He escaped to England (1846), but when the Bonapartist tide swept France after the 1848 revolution he was elected first to the Assembly and then to the presidency (1848). Engineering the dissolution of the constitution, he assumed the title of emperor, and in 1853 married **Eugénie de Montijo de Guzman** (1826–1920), a Spanish countess, who bore him a son, the Prince Imperial, **Eugène Louis Jean Joseph Napoleon** (1856). He actively encouraged economic expansion and the modernization of Paris, while externally the Second Empire coincided with the Crimean War (1854–6), the expeditions to China (1857–60), the annexation (1860) of Savoy and Nice, and the ill-starred intervention in Mexico (1861–7). Encouraged by the empress, he unwisely declared war on Prussia in 1870, and suffered humiliating defeat, culminating in the Battle of Sedan. Confined at Wilhelmshohe until 1871, he went into exile in England.

Napoleonic Wars (1800–15) The continuation of the Revolutionary Wars, fought to preserve French hegemony in Europe. They were initially a guarantee for the political, social, and economic changes of the 1789 Revolution, but increasingly became a manifestation of Napoleon's personal ambitions. The wars began with Napoleon's destruction of the Second Coalition (1800). After a peaceful interlude (1802–3) Britain resumed hostilities, prompting Napoleon to prepare for invasion, and encouraging the formation of a Third Coalition (1805–7). While Britain retained naval superiority (1805), Napoleon established territorial domination, sustained by economic warfare, resulting in the invasions of Spain (1808) and Russia (1812). Gradually the French were overwhelmed by the Fourth Coalition (1813–14); the Hundred Days' epilogue ended with Waterloo (1815).

nappe [nap] A large-scale geological fold structure in which rocks have been overturned and transported several kilometres or more by compressional stresses during mountain-building processes. The Alps consist of several such nappes.

Nara [nahra] 34°41N 135°49E, pop (2000e) 359 000. Capital of Nara prefecture, S Honshu, Japan, 29 km/18 mi E of Osaka; first urban capital of Japan, 710; cultural and religious centre; centre of Japanese Buddhism; railway; women's university (1908); textiles, dolls, fans; Todaiji (East Great Temple, founded 743), housing massive bronze statue of Buddha (22 m/72 ft tall) in world's largest wooden building, and Nara national museum (the Shosoin); Toshodaishi Temple (8th-c); Horyuji (6th-c) nearby, oldest temple complex in Japan, and world's oldest wooden buildings.

Nara period An episode in Japanese history when the first permanent capital was established at Nara (Heijo) between modern Kyoto and Osaka in AD 710. The oldest surviving Japanese poetry anthologies and histories date from this period, besides major Buddhist temples. Nara was abandoned as the capital in 784, and replaced in 794 by Heian (modern Kyoto).

Narayan, R(asipuram) K(rishnaswami) [nariyan] (1906–2001) Novelist and short-story writer, born in Chennai (Madras), SE India. He studied there and at Maharaja's College in Mysore. His first novel, *Swami and Friends* (1935), and its successors, including *Mr Sampath* (1949), *The Vendor of Sweets* (1967), and *A Tiger for Malgudi* (1983) are set in the enchanting fictional territory of 'Malgudi'. His novel *The Guide* (1958) won him the National Prize of the Indian Literary Academy. He also published stories, travel books, books for children, and essays. One of the most highly acclaimed Indian novelists of his generation, his publication in Britain was brought about by Graham Greene. Later works include the novels *Talkative Man* (1986), *The World of Nagaraj* (1990), and *The Grandmother's Tale* (1993). His autobiography, *My Days*, was published in 1975.

Narayanganj [narayangganj] 23°36N 90°28E, pop (2000e) 557 300. City in Narayanganj district, SE Bangladesh; on R Meghna, E of Dhaka; river port for Dhaka, and one of the busiest trade centres; collection centre for jute, hides, and skins; major industrial region, including jute mills, cotton textiles, leather, glass, shoes.

narcissism A condition of self-infatuation stemming from difficulties at an early stage of psychological development. It may manifest as exhibitionism, indifference to criticism, a presumption of special entitlement, and fantasies of unlimited sexual prowess, intelligence, or attractiveness.

narcissus [nah(r)**sis**uhs] A bulb native to Europe, the Mediterranean region, and W Asia; leaves strap-shaped; flowers solitary or several on a long stalk, central trumpet or cup (the *corona*), surrounded by six spreading perianth-segments, white, yellow, or pink; the corona often contrasting, sometimes red. Horticulturally a division is made into *daffodils*, with the corona equalling or longer than the perianth, and *narcissi*, with the corona shorter than the perianth. Many species and numerous cultivars are grown in gardens and for the cut-flower trade. (Genus: *Narcissus*, 60 species. Family: Amaryllidaceae.)

Narcissus [nah(r)**sis**us] In Greek mythology, a beautiful youth who fell in love with his reflection in a pool; he pined away and was changed into a flower. Ovid says this was because of his cruelty to Echo.

narcolepsy An extreme tendency towards excessive sleepiness often associated with cataplexy, in which sleep onset is accompanied by dreaming. Sleep paralysis and hypnagogic (during the process of falling asleep) hallucinations are accompanying features. Genetic factors have recently been shown to be involved.

narcotics Drugs related to morphine which, in the literal sense, induce **narcosis**, or stupor. In common parlance the term has been adopted to include all addictive drugs. Narcotics such as morphine, heroin, and cocaine are used illegally for the euphoric sensations they induce, and are highly addictive.

Narmada [nah(r)mada] or **Narbada, River** River of India, rising in the Maikala range of Madhya Pradesh; flows generally SW across Gujarat to meet the Gulf of Cambay; length 1245 km/ 774 mi; a sacred river to Hindus; many pilgrimage centres and bathing ghats along its course.

Narnia [nah(r)nia] A mythical country, the scene of a sequence of novels by C S Lewis, beginning with *The Lion, The Witch, and The Wardrobe* (1950).

narrowcasting *broadcasting*

Narses [nah(r)seez] (c.478–573) Persian statesman and general, born in Armenia. He rose in the imperial household in Constantinople to be keeper of the privy purse to Justinian I. In 538 he was sent to Italy, but recalled the next year. In 552 Belisarius was recalled from Italy, and Narses succeeded him, defeated the Ostrogoths, took possession of Rome, and completely extinguished the Gothic power in Italy. Justinian appointed him prefect of Italy in 554, but he was charged with avarice, and on Justinian's death he was deprived of his office.

narthex A transverse vestibule in a basilica church, either inside and before the nave, or outside the main facade. Alternatively, it may refer to any enclosed, covered space before the main entrance.

Narvik [nah(r)vik] 68°26N 17°25E, pop (2000e) 19 400. Seaport in Nordland county, N Norway; at W end of a peninsula in the Ofoten Fjord, opposite the Lofoten Is; airfield; terminus of the Lappland railway from the Kiruna iron-ore mines in Sweden; ice-free harbour; occupied by Germany, 1940; scene of World War 2 naval battles in which two British and nine German destroyers were lost.

narwhal [nah(r)wuhl] A small, toothed whale (*Monodon monoceros*) native to the Arctic seas; mottled brown; no dorsal fin; two teeth (at front of upper jaw); in male, left tooth grows forwards forming a straight tusk half as long as body; eats fish, squid, and crustaceans. (Family: Monodontidae.)

NASA (National Aeronautics and Space Administration) An independent agency of the US Government responsible for the civil space programme. It was established in 1958 by President Eisenhower based on the old National Advisory Committee for Aeronautics (NACA). Its headquarters is in Washington, DC, where programme plans originate. Individual projects are implemented at different field centres: *Ames Research Center* (Mountain View, CA) for astrobiology and information systems; *Dryden Flight Research Center* (Edwards, CA) for aeronautic flight research; *Goddard Space Flight Center* (Greenbelt, MD) for astronomy and Earth sciences; *Jet Propulsion Laboratory* (Pasadena, CA) for Solar System exploration; *Johnson Space Center* (Houston, TX) for manned missions; *Kennedy Space Center* (Cape Canaveral, FL) for launch operations; *Langley Research Center* (Norfolk, VA) for aeronautics; *Glenn* (formerly *Lewis*) *Research Center* (Cleveland, OH) for space technologies; and *Marshall Space Flight Center* (Huntsville, AL) for launch vehicles and space science.

Naseby, Battle of [nayzbee] (14 Jun 1645) A major conflict of the English Civil War in the E Midlands, C England, UK. The Royalist forces of Charles I, outnumbered by two to one, were defeated by Parliament's New Model Army led by Fairfax, with Cromwell commanding the cavalry. Royalist cavalry, led by Prince Rupert, left the main battle, fatally weakening Charles's forces.

Nash, John (1752–1835) Architect, born in London, UK. He trained as an architect, practised in London, and gained a reputation by his country-house designs. He came to the notice of the Prince of Wales (the future George IV), and was engaged to plan the layout of the new Regent's Park and its environs of curved terraces (1811–25). He laid out Regent Street to link the Park with Westminster, built Carlton House Terrace, and laid out Trafalgar Square and St James's Park. He recreated Buckingham Palace from old Buckingham House, designed the Marble Arch which originally stood in front of it (moved to its present site in 1851), and rebuilt Brighton Pavilion in Oriental style. On the strength of a patent for improvements to the arches and piers of bridges (1797), he claimed much of the credit for introducing steel girders.

Nash, John F (1928–) Economist, born in Bluefield, West Virginia, USA. He studied at the Carnegie Institute of Technology and Princeton University, moved to MIT, then returned to Princeton. He shared the Nobel Prize for Economics in 1994 for his contribution to the analysis of equilibria in the theory of non-co-operative games.

Nash, (Frederic) Ogden (1902–71) Humorous writer, born in Rye, New York, USA. He studied at Harvard, then tried teaching, editing, selling bonds, and copy writing, before his poetry became successful enough for him to make a living from it. Taking outrageous liberties with the English language ('I would live all my life in nonchalance and insouciance / Were it not for making a living, which is rather a nouciance'), he soon became the most popular modern versifier, frequently published in the *New Yorker*, whose sophisticated tone he helped establish. His subject-matter was the everyday life of middle-class America, which he described in a witty and acute manner, in an idiosyncratic style involving long digressions and striking rhyme schemes. He published many collections, including *Hard Lines* (1931) and *Parents Keep Out: Elderly Poems for Youngerly Readers* (1951).

Nash, Paul (1889–1946) Painter, born in London, UK. He studied at St Paul's and the Slade School of Art, London, and became an official war artist in 1917 (remembered particularly for his poignant 'Menin Road', 1919). Developing a style which reduced form to bare essentials, he won renown as a landscape painter, and also practised scene painting, commercial design, and book illustration. For a while he taught at the Royal College of Art. In 1939 he again filled the role of war artist, this time for the Air Ministry and the Ministry of Information, producing such pictures as 'Battle of Britain' and 'Totes Meer' (1940–1, Tate, London). Shortly before his death he turned to a very individual style of flower painting.

Nash, Richard, nickname **Beau Nash** (1674–1762) Dandy, born in Swansea, SC Wales, UK. He studied at Oxford, held a commission in the army, and in 1693 entered the Middle Temple. He then made a shifty living by gambling, but in 1704 became master of ceremonies at Bath, where he conducted the public balls with a splendour never before witnessed. His reforms in manners, his influence in improving the streets and buildings, and his leadership in fashion helped to transform Bath into a fashionable holiday centre. Although he died a pauper, he was buried with pomp in Bath Abbey.

Nashe or **Nash, Thomas,** pseudonym **Pasquil** (1567–1601) Playwright and satirist, born in Lowestoft, Suffolk, E England, UK.

He studied at Cambridge, travelled in Europe, then went to London as a writer, where he plunged into the Martin Marprelate controversy, displaying a talent for vituperation, and attacking the Puritans in *Pierce Penilesse, his Supplication to the Divell* (1592). Other works include the satirical masque, *Summer's Last Will and Testament* (1592), and the picaresque tale, *The Unfortunate Traveller or the Life of Jacke Wilton* (1594). His play *The Isle of Dogs* (1597), now lost, drew such attention to abuses in the state that it was suppressed, the theatre closed, and he was thrown into the Fleet prison for some months.

Nashville–Davidson, commonly **Nashville**, nickname **Music City, USA** 36°10N 86°47W, pop (2000e) 556 000. Capital of state in Davidson Co, N Tennessee, USA; port on the Cumberland R; settled as Nashborough, 1779–80; renamed Nashville, 1784; state capital, 1843; merged with Davidson, 1963; airfield; railway; three universities (1867, 1872, 1909); chemicals, glass, clothing, publishing, railway engineering; famed for its music industry (country and western); centre for religious education; the Capitol (tomb of James K Polk), Country Music Hall of Fame, Opryland USA (family entertainment complex); Country Music Fan Fair (Jun).

Nasik [nahsik] 20°02N 75°30E, pop (2000e) 848 000. City in Maharashtra state, WC India, on a tributary of the Darna R, 145 km/90 mi NE of Mumbai; a holy place of Hindu pilgrimage; cattle, poultry, brassware, printing; many Vishnuite temples and shrines; Buddhist caves, 2nd-c AD.

Nassau (Bahamas) [nasaw] 25°05N 77°20W, pop (2000e) 14 400. Capital of the Bahamas on NE coast of New Providence I; frequented by pirates during the 18th-c and captured briefly by Americans in 1776; Fort Nassau (1697), Fort Charlotte (1787–94), and Fort Fincastle (1793) built to protect the city from Spanish invasion; airport; a popular winter tourist resort.

Nassau (European history) [nasow] A Burgundian noble family, who rose as servants of the Habsburgs, then rebelled against their authority in the Low Countries. They were made *stadtholders* of Holland, Zeeland, and Friesland, Counts of Nassau, and Princes of Orange by Charles V. The heirs to the titles, William of Orange (1533–84), and his brother Louis (1538–74), Count of Nassau, supported and led the Dutch Revolt (1566–1648) against their former masters.

Nasser, Gamal Abdel (1918–70) Egyptian statesman, prime minister (1954–6), and president (1956–70), born in Alexandria, N Egypt. An army officer, he became dissatisfied with the corruption of the Farouk regime, and was the prime mover in the Free Officers' coup of 1952. He assumed the premiership in 1954, and then presidential powers, deposing his fellow officer, General Mohammed Neguib. Officially elected president in 1956, he nationalized the Suez Canal, which prompted Britain and France to seek his forcible overthrow, gaining Israeli co-operation in the invasion of Sinai. In 1958 he created a federation with Syria (the United Arab Republic), but Syria withdrew in 1961. After the six-day Arab–Israeli War (1967), heavy losses on the Arab side led to his resignation, but he was persuaded to stay on, and died still in office.

Nasser, Lake, Arabic **Buheiret en-Naser** Lake in S Egypt; length 500 km/310 mi; area c.5000 sq km/1930 sq mi; created after building the Aswan High Dam (1971); named after former President of Egypt.

nastic movement A non-directional plant response to an external stimulus, such as the opening and closing of flowers and the collapse of leaflets of the sensitive plant. It is attained by differential growth, or by controlled water movement within specialized cells.

nasturtium [nastershuhm] An annual or perennial, trailing or climbing by twining leaf-stalks, native to Mexico and temperate South America; leaves rounded or lobed, stalk attached to centre of blade; flowers large, slightly zygomorphic, roughly trumpet-shaped with five petals and a backward-projecting spur, in shades of yellow, orange, and scarlet. Various species and numerous cultivars are grown for ornament. (Genus: *Tropaeolum*, 90 species. Family: Balsaminaceae.)

Natal (Africa) *KwaZulu Natal*

Natal (Brazil) [natahl] 5°46S 35°15W, pop (2000e) 692 200. Port capital of Rio Grande do Norte state, NE Brazil; on the Atlantic coast at mouth of R Potengi, N of Recife; airfield; railway; university (1958); trade in sugar, cotton; cashew plantations; textiles; Marine Research Institute at Praia da Areia Preta; rocket base of Barreira do Inferno, 20 km/12 mi S; cathedral, 16th-c fort, Museu Câmara Cascudo.

Nataraja [natarahja] One of the names of the Hindu deity, Shiva. As the Lord of the Dance he dances the creation of the universe.

Natchez Trace A road built by the US army in the early 19th-c to link Nashville, TN, with the then pioneer outpost of Natchez in Mississippi, 725 km/450 mi distant. The road, which follows an earlier American Indian track, was designated a national parkway in 1939.

Nathanael [nathanial], (Heb 'God has given') (fl.1st-c) New Testament character, who appears only in *John* (1.45–51 and 21.2). He is said to have been brought to Jesus by Philip, and is one of the first to confess Jesus as 'Son of God, King of Israel'. He does not appear by this name in any list of disciples in the synoptic Gospels, however; possibly he was not one of the 12 or even a historical individual at all, despite some attempts to identify him with Bartholomew or Matthew in the synoptic lists of the 12 disciples.

Nation, Carry (Amelia), *née* **Moore** (1846–1911) Temperance agitator, born in Garrard Co, Kentucky, USA. Trained as a teacher, she entered the temperance movement in 1890. A large, powerful woman of volcanic emotions, she went on hymn-singing, saloon-smashing expeditions with a hatchet in many US cities, attacking what she considered to be illegal drinking places. Frequently imprisoned and fined for breach of the peace, she would sell her hatchets as souvenirs to raise money.

National Academy of Design The main official academy of art in the USA. Founded in 1826, it still exists as an exhibiting society for the more traditionally-minded artists.

national accounts A set of accounts showing how much a nation has produced and consumed during some period, normally a year. This will cover the composition of goods and services produced, by sector; the division of expenditures between consumption, investment, government, imports, and exports; and the division of incomes between wages, profits, rents, interest, taxes, and transfer payments. It will also include a balance sheet of the nation's internal and external assets at some date. All these are usually given both at current prices, before and after taxes, and at some base year prices to facilitate comparisons over time.

National Aeronautics and Space Administration *NASA*

national anthem The official song of a nation. Examples include: Canada's *O Canada*, composed by Calixa Lavallée and adopted in 1980; France's *La Marseillaise*, composed by Claude-Joseph Rouget de Lisle and adopted in 1795; Japan's *Kimigayo* ('His Majesty's Reign'), composed by Hayashi Hirimori, but not officially adopted; Germany's *Deutschlandlied* ('Song of Germany'), composed by Haydn and adopted in 1950; the UK's *God Save the Queen/King*, of unknown composition, adopted in the 18th-c; the USA's *The Star-Spangled Banner*, composed by John Stafford Smith and adopted in 1931; and the Russian Federation's *State Hymn*, composed by Mikhail Glinka and adopted in 1991. Australia's *Advance Australia Fair*, composed by Peter Dodds McCormick and adopted in 1977, is the national tune; the official anthem is *God Save the Queen/King*, played when a regal or vice-regal personage is present.

national archives *archives*

National Assembly for Wales *Welsh Assembly*

National Association for the Advancement of Colored People (NAACP) A group, open to all Americans, which aims to extend awareness among the country's African-American population of their political rights; founded in the USA in

1909. It has successfully used the courts, in the face of opposition from politicians, to remove certain legal barriers to the equal rights of blacks. It was also active in encouraging blacks to register for the vote during the voter registration drives in the Southern states during the 1960s. Its aim is an integrated society.

National Audubon Society [awduhbon] A US private conservation organization named after the US artist and naturalist, John James Audubon. It manages more than 60 wildlife sanctuaries in the USA.

National Basketball Association (NBA) A professional sports league that gained worldwide acclaim for managing its players and marketing their skills. Founded just after World War 2, the league grew slowly during the 1950s. In 1980 Larry Bird (1956–) and Earvin 'Magic' Johnson started a decade where the league gained international acceptance. Player salaries skyrocketed and television exposure became pervasive. The emergence of Michael Jordan in the mid-1980s brought the league's greatest superstar to national consciousness. Participation in the 1992 and 1996 Olympic Games made the NBA the world-class standard for basketball. An owner-inspired lockout in 1998 left a residue of bitterness with fans and players, but the NBA continued to be a major sports and marketing phenomenon into the 21st-c.

National Bureau of Standards *National Institute of Standards and Technology*

National Council of the Churches of Christ in the USA An association of Protestant, Eastern Orthodox, and National Catholic Churches formed in 1950 in the USA. Affiliated to the World Council of Churches, it is committed to the principle of manifesting the oneness of the Church of Christ.

national curriculum A curriculum for all the schools in a country, usually devised by the central authority in the capital city. Some countries (eg France) have had one for many years; some (eg the USA) do not have one at all. England and Wales introduced one in 1988, consisting of three 'core' subjects (English, maths, science), and seven 'foundation' subjects (art, geography, history, music, physical education, technology, and, in secondary schools only, a modern language). Variation in practices may need to be introduced, to take account of different situations. In Wales, for example, Welsh is a core subject in Welsh-speaking areas and a foundation subject in non-Welsh speaking areas.

national debt The amount owed by the government of a country, including both central government and local authorities, as the result of borrowing and repayments over the years. Debt may be held domestically or by foreigners. The annual payments due in interest and repayment of loans is known as **debt service**. The public sector borrowing requirement (approximately equal to the budget deficit) represents the yearly addition to the national debt.

National Economic Development Council (NEDC), nickname **Neddy** A UK forum set up in 1962 where government, industry, and union representatives could meet to discuss economic affairs. The Council was supported by a secretariat, the National Economic Development Office (NEDO). Many 'little Neddies' were created, relating to specific industries. NEDC was closed in 1992.

National Front (NF) A strongly nationalist political party in Britain which centres its political programme on opposition to immigration, and calls for the repatriation of ethnic minorities even if they were born in the UK. The party was created in 1960 by the merger of the White Defence League and the National Labour Party, and in its early years was a small neo-Nazi grouping. In the mid- and late 1970s it had some minor impact in elections and its membership grew. It tried to develop a more respectable face and recruited some members from the right of the Conservative Party to widen its base beyond hard-line neofascists. Its political appeal declined with the election of a Conservative government in 1979, and it has largely withdrawn from any move to enter the mainstream of politics. Many of the Front's leaders are avowedly racist and anti-semitic, and many of those associated with the party are widely believed to be involved in racial and latterly football violence. In common with many extreme parties, it has suffered a number of schisms, but makes occasional gains in local elections.

National Gallery An art gallery in London housing the largest collection of paintings in Britain, and one of the finest collections in the world. It was opened in 1824 in Pall Mall, but moved to its present premises in Trafalgar Square in 1838. A spacious extension, the Sainsbury Wing, designed by Robert Venturi, opened in 1991 to house the early Renaissance pictures.

National Gallery of Art A gallery endowed by Andrew W Mellon and opened in Washington, District of Columbia, USA in 1941. Although the museum is a branch of the Smithsonian Institution, it is administered independently.

National Gallery of Australia An art gallery on the shores of L Burley Griffin in Canberra, opened in 1982. It houses a permanent collection showing the history of Australian art, including Aboriginal art, and includes collections of Asian and Pacific art, as well as international graphic arts and photography, African and Pre-Columbian art, a sculpture garden, and European art of all periods.

National Geographic Society In the USA, a scientific and educational organization, founded in 1888. The knowledge gained from the exploration and research it funds is published in its monthly journal *National Geographic*. It had over 10 million members in 2004.

National Grid Reference System A unique grid reference for mapping purposes for any part of the UK, using letters and numbers. The country has been divided by the Ordnance Survey into a number of grid squares, 100 × 100 km (62·14 mi), each with its own identifying letters. Each square is further subdivided into numbered 1 km (0·62 mi) squares.

national guard A militia or reserve military force. The US National Guard is organized on a state-by-state basis, its members voluntarily enlisting for military training and for service in aiding the civil power when called upon by the state governor.

National Health Service (NHS) A system of health care established in the UK in 1948. World War 2 revealed the need for reform of the health and hospital services which had served up to that time. The new service was to be, and largely remains, a free service available to the whole population, without income limit, and funded out of general taxation. Existing municipal and voluntary hospitals were nationalized and came under the control of regional Health Boards (subsequently called Area Health Committees). Hospital consultants and specialists were salaried (full-time and part-time). General practitioners (GPs) remained self-employed, and received capitation fees based on the number of individuals who registered with them as patients. GPs are now organized into *Primary Care Groups* that serve defined geographical populations of around 100 000 people. They provide primary and community care for their patients, and purchase specialist care from hospital services. The NHS is supported by nurses, technical and scientific staff, and ancillary workers, and is the largest single employer of labour in the UK.

National Heritage Memorial Fund A fund set up in 1980 by the National Heritage Memorial Act as a memorial to those who have died in service for the UK. It is the successor of the National Land Fund, and is administered by the Department of the Environment. The fund is used for the purpose of helping in the acquisition, maintenance, and preservation of land, buildings, and objects of outstanding scenic, historic, architectural, artistic, and scientific interest.

National Hockey League The pre-eminent association of professional ice hockey teams in Canada and the USA. Established in 1917 at Montreal, it was originally composed of four teams from Ontario and Quebec, and later expanded to include larger numbers of teams from American cities. A championship series is played annually for the Stanley Cup.

national hunt racing *horse racing*

national income A measure of the aggregate level of economic activity in a country. This is calculated in a number of ways. Gross domestic product (GDP) is the total value of production in a country, before allowing for depreciation of its capital stock. Gross national product (GNP) is GDP plus net property income from abroad. To get from GDP to GNP the profits of foreign firms operating domestically and interest paid abroad are deducted, and the profits of domestic firms operating abroad and interest received from abroad are added. National income as a technical term is GNP minus depreciation of the capital stock. As depreciation is not a set of market transactions that can be observed, but only an estimate, the figure for national income is not widely used, and most economists prefer GDP or GNP. In considering how a national economy has progressed over time, national income figures on any definition are revalued at constant prices, to get a real measure. In considering national welfare, the aggregate national income needs to be divided by the population, to get national income per capita.

National Institute of Standards and Technology (NIST) A US government facility, established by Congress in 1901, researching and developing measurement methods, standards, and technology in support of industry, commerce, scientific institutions, and government; formerly known as the **National Bureau of Standards**. Its laboratories are located mainly at Boulder, CO, or at the NIST headquarters in Gaithersburg, MD.

national insurance A system whereby the state insures all its residents against illness, disability, unemployment, and old age. In the UK, for example, the National Insurance Scheme is funded by compulsory contributions on all workers above a low exemption limit and their employers. The National Insurance Fund then makes payments to individuals who are ill, unemployed, or retired. The contributions cover only a small part of the total cost of the scheme, the remainder coming from central government revenues.

nationalism A political doctrine which views the nation as the principal unit of political organization. Underlying this is the assumption that human beings hold the characteristic of nationality, with which they identify culturally, economically, and politically. A primary aim of nationalists, therefore, is to secure the right to belong to an independent state based on a particular national grouping. Nationalism is thus associated with attempts by national groupings to secure independence from dominance by other nation-states and to maintain that position against threats to it. It is often associated with the struggle against colonialism. More broadly, nationalism can be seen as a general political stance which holds that the principal aim of political activity should be to serve the national interest as opposed to that of a particular class or grouping. In practice, the national interest is, except in extreme cases such as war, open to different interpretations, and nationalism is often no more than an attempt to give legitimacy to a particular political standpoint. Nationalism, with the exception of anti-colonial movements, is based around a conservative, and sometimes romantic political philosophy that emphasizes the nation's past.

Nationalist Party (China) *Guomindang*

nationalization Taking into public ownership an entire industry, normally a public utility. Nationalization takes place with social as well as commercial objectives. The main reasons are that an industry (a) is crucial to the economy and in need of government direction, (b) is a natural monopoly, (c) has suffered a period of decline which needs to be reversed, (d) produces a good or service which would not be available to all areas if commercial profit were the only criterion for supply, or (e) is important to national defence. There is also the view, based on a socialist ideology, that public ownership is desirable to prevent the earning of private profit extracted from labour and the concentration of economic power in private hands. Nationalized industries in the UK are normally constituted as *public corporations* accountable to a government minister, although their numbers and importance have declined dramatically as a result of the policy of privatization pursued by the Conservative governments of 1979–97 and continued by the New Labour goverment of 1997.

National League A baseball league that grew out of the first professional league, the National Association (NA). It was founded in 1876 by William Hulbert, then owner of the NA Chicago White Stockings. The NA was a weak league beset by failing franchises and undisciplined players. As president of the new National League (1877–82), Hulbert introduced regular schedules, banned alcohol from baseball grounds, and worked to eliminate game-fixing. At his death (1882) the league was firmly established and the reputation of professional baseball enhanced.

National Library of Australia One of Australia's principal libraries, established in 1901 as the parliamentary library of the new federal government. In 1912, it became entitled to a copy of all Australian material. Re-housed in Canberra in 1968, it now holds over four million items.

National Library of Wales A library established by Royal Charter in 1907 and opened on its present site in Aberystwyth, W Wales, UK in 1916; the main building was not completed until 1955. It is one of the six largest libraries in Britain, and as a Copyright (Legal Deposit) Library, it has the right to claim any work (books, periodicals, newspapers, music, maps) published in the British Isles.

National Lottery *lottery*

National Museum of Photography, Film, and Television A museum which explores the world of the media through a combination of permanent galleries, temporary exhibitions, and film shows; part of the National Museum of Science and Industry, it was founded in 1983, and is located in Bradford, W Yorkshire, UK. Its collection includes over 3 million items of social, historical, and cultural value in photography and film making. These include the world's first negative, the earliest television footage, and what is regarded as the world's first example of moving pictures – Louis Le Prince's 1888 film of Leeds Bridge. The museum explores key areas of technological change, including the World Wide Web, computer vision, virtual reality, and the world of special effects, animations, and video games.

National Park According to the United Nations, an area of educational and scientific importance for habitat and wildlife, of great beauty, and of recreational value, but which has suffered little human impact, so remaining a relative wilderness. It should also be protected from resource development and be relatively unpopulated. Examples include Yosemite National Park, USA, and Wood Buffalo National Park, Canada. According to these criteria, the national parks of England and Wales do not qualify for inclusion in the United Nations list, because they are situated near populated areas where forestry, agriculture, and limited industrial activities are permitted. National parks date back to 19th-c USA, where the first was established around the Yellowstone R, WY, in 1872. The first parks in England and Wales were designated in 1951, and there were eleven in 2004. The first Scottish park was established in 2002.

National Party (Australia) The third largest party in Australia since 1920, originally named the **Country Party**. It grew out of rural dissatisfaction with the way governments had favoured urban areas, and concern over loss of population to the towns. The party is conservative in social matters, generally favours policies of free trade and low tariffs, and supports government public expenditure. Since 1923 it has been in coalition with the Conservative Party. The National Party achieved its greatest success when it governed with the Liberal Party nationally (1949–72). It has been most dynamic in Queensland under Premier Johannes Bjelke-Peterson (1968–87), where it has governed in its own right since 1983 (in a coalition with Liberals from 1992), the only state where this has happened. In 1988, the party claimed the largest membership of any Australian political party (140 000), but attracted the lowest vote of the three largest parties (11·5%) in the 1987 national election. A National/Liberal coalition continued, 1987–96.

National Physical Laboratory A UK state laboratory established in 1900 at Teddington, near London, to research and develop industrial and scientific standards of measurement. As Britain's national standards laboratory, it supports basic units of measurement such as the amp and the metre. It has custody of the UK primary standard mass (copy number 18 of the International Prototype Kilogram, the original of which is at Sèvres, Paris). NPL developed the first accurate caesium atomic clock (1955).

National Portrait Gallery A gallery of portraits of distinguished people in British history. Opened in London in 1859, it was moved to its present position adjoining the National Gallery in 1895.

national product *gross domestic product*

National Radio Astronomy Observatory (NRAO) The principal radio astronomy observatory of the USA, with powerful telescopes at Green Bank, WV; Kitt Peak, AZ; and Socorro, NM (Very Large Array), and headquarters at Charlottesville, VA. The NRAO was established in the mid-1950s and acquired its first operational radio telescope in 1959. Instruments at Green Bank include a 100 × 110 m dish, the world's largest fully steerable radio telescope, completed in 1999.

National Road A road built in the early 19th-c from Cumberland, MD, to Vandalia, IL, and eventually to St Louis, MO. Its construction and repair were financed initially by government sales of land, but in the 1830s this became the responsibility of the states through which it passed. The National Road played an important role in the expansion of the West.

National Savings A range of financial instruments provided by the UK government for use by small savers. There is a variety of securities in the system. All have full state guarantees for both capital and interest, are available at post offices without fees in small quantities, and are repayable on sight or relatively short notice. Some are tax-free; some are available only to pensioners; and some are indexed to the Retail Price Index (RPI). The amounts which can be held by any individual are limited, and they cannot be held by institutions. National Savings tend to have yields lower than the best obtainable by larger and more sophisticated investors, but their safety, at least in money terms, makes them attractive to small savers whose funds and information are both limited.

National Security Adviser A member of staff who is responsible for advising the US president on security matters. He is regarded as a senior figure in the White House; his views sometimes serve to balance or compete with those of the secretary of state.

National Security Council A body created by Congress in 1947 to advise the US president on the integration of domestic, foreign, and military policies relating to national security. It was designed to achieve effective co-ordination between the military services and other government agencies and departments, and is composed of the president, vice-president, secretary of state, secretary of defense, and the director of the Office of Emergency Planning.

national service *conscription*

National Socialism *Nazi Party*

National Socialist German Worker's Party *Nazi Party*

National Society for the Prevention of Cruelty to Children (NSPCC) A child welfare society, founded in 1884 as the London Society for the Prevention of Cruelty to Children. The NSPCC has over 200 inspectors in England, Wales, and Northern Ireland who investigate reports of cruelty to or neglect of children. In Scotland, the **Royal Scottish Society for the Prevention of Cruelty to Children** (also founded in 1884) performs a similar function.

national theatre A theatre which is endowed by the state and is usually situated in the national capital. Today found throughout the world, such endowed companies have a long history in many European countries. The oldest national theatre is the Comédie Française in Paris, founded in 1680 by Louis XIV; this was followed by five other French national theatres. Other long-established national theatres are to be found in Denmark (1772), Sweden (1773), and Norway (1899). In Britain, though advocated from the time of Garrick, a National Theatre was not inaugurated until 1962, under the direction of Laurence Olivier. Peter Hall replaced Olivier (1973–88), he was followed by Richard Eyre (1988–1997), Trevor Nunn (1997–2002), and Nicholas Hytner (2002–). Since 1976 the company has occupied its own building on the South Bank. The year 1999 saw the creation of the first National Theatre Ensemble Company, which received critical acclaim.

National Trust In the UK, a charity founded in 1895 with the full name 'The National Trust for Places of Historic Interest and Natural Beauty'. Its membership stands at over 1 million, making it the largest and most influential conservation body in Britain. The Trust owns historic houses, gardens, and sites of natural beauty, which it opens to the public; those who are not members pay a fee to enter. It has a branch for US members, the Royal Oak. The National Trust for Scotland is a separate organization run on similar lines.

National Youth Ballet A trust which organizes an annual school for youth dance companies from across Britain to work with top professional choreographers and teachers. The National Youth Ballet has been in existence since 1985. It auditions countrywide, selecting 25 dancers aged 16–20 to tour with a programme of commissioned works.

Nation of Islam *Black Muslims*

nations *countries of the world*

Nations, Battle of the *Leipzig, Battle of*

Native American Church An indigenous 19th-c religious movement among North American Indians, combining native religion with certain elements of Christianity; formally founded in 1918. Its main ritual centres on the sacramental and curative use of the non-narcotic hallucinogen mescaline, derived from the peyote plant.

Nativity, the The story of the miraculous birth of Jesus of Nazareth to Mary, the accompanying events of which are variously described in the opening chapters of the Gospels of Matthew and Luke. Matthew's Gospel emphasizes the subsequent coming of the Magi, Herods' slaughter of the infants, and the flight to Egypt. Luke's Gospel describes a census and the coming of the shepherds. Although the year of Jesus's birth is unknown, it is usually fixed at c.6 BC, two years before the death of Herod the Great (*Matt* 2.1, 16–20). The observance of the birth, the festival of Christmas, has been celebrated throughout most of Christendom since the 4th–5th-c on 25 December.

NATO [naytoh] Acronym for **North Atlantic Treaty Organization**. An organization established by a treaty signed in 1949 by Belgium, Canada, Denmark, France, Iceland, Italy, Luxembourg, The Netherlands, Norway, Portugal, the UK, and the USA; Greece and Turkey acceded in 1952, West Germany in 1955, and Spain in 1982. Poland, the Czech Republic, and Hungary formally joined in 1999. Its headquarters is in Brussels. NATO was established as a military alliance to defend W Europe against Soviet aggression. The treaty commits the members to treat an armed attack on one of them as an attack on all of them, and for all to assist the country attacked by such actions as are deemed necessary. The alliance forces are based on contributions from the member countries' armed services and operate under a multi-national command. The remit includes the deployment of nuclear, as well as conventional, weapons. Its institutions include a Council, an International Secretariat, the Supreme Headquarters Allied Powers, Europe (SHAPE), and various committees to formulate common policies. In the 1970s and 1980s, NATO policy of a first-strike nuclear attack to fend off a Soviet conventional attack became controversial in W Europe, where many thought it increased the possibility of nuclear war. In 1966 France under de Gaulle withdrew all its forces from NATO command, but it remains a member. After the 1989 changes in E Europe, a NATO summit in London (1990) began the process of redefining NATO's military and political goals, and in 1997 NATO and Russia signed a Founding Act on Mutual Relations, allowing for NATO's eastward expansion. NATO's Partnership for Peace is a political structure which has involved over 20 C and E European states. In 1999, NATO authorized air-strikes in Yugoslavia, in response to Serbian measures against the ethnic Albanian population in Kosovo. In May 2002 Russia became a strategic partner when the NATO–Russian Council (NRC) was formed to frame policy on terrorism and other shared concerns. Estonia, Latvia, Lithuania, Bulgaria, Romania, Slovenia, and the Slovak Republic formally joined in 2003. NATO's first peacekeeping role outside Europe took place in 2003, when it assumed control of the International Security Assistance Force in Afghanistan.

natterjack A European true toad (*Bufo calamita*); rough green skin with thin yellow line along spine; short legs; inhabits sandy areas; the loudest European toad (croak may be heard 2 km/1¼ mi away).

Natufian [natoofian] A Mesolithic culture of SW Syria, Lebanon, and Palestine (c.12 800–10 500 BC), named after the Palestinian site of Wadi en-Natuf. Though largely restricted to 65 km/40 mi of the Mediterranean coast, animal herding, the harvesting of wild cereals, and increasingly permanent settlement point to incipient agriculture. Open sites like Jericho were occupied, as well as caves and rock shelters.

natural childbirth Successful labour entirely without or with minimal use of drugs or outside assistance. It is helped by exercises to strengthen the abdominal muscles and encourage relaxation of the pelvic muscles, which are undertaken throughout pregnancy. It is facilitated by a full awareness of the nature of childbirth, developing psychological attitudes which reduce anxiety and fear, and increase pain tolerance. It is safest in the absence of physical disorders of the mother or fetus.

natural gas Gas which occurs in subterranean accumulations, often in association with petroleum deposits. It mainly consists of simple hydrocarbons, mostly methane, with some propane; there may also be nitrogen, helium, and hydrogen sulphide. 'Wet gas' has recoverable amounts of higher hydrocarbons (eg butane, pentane) which have commercial value as Liquefied Petroleum Gas. Natural gas is one of the most widely used and versatile of fuels, and a source of other chemicals. When used as a gas supply, it is adulterated with other gases to give it an odour. Natural gas was used by the Chinese as early as the 2nd-c AD.

Natural History Museum The popular name for the British Museum (Natural History), housed since 1881 in S Kensington, London. The exhibition was originally built up in the 17th–18th-c around the collections of Sir Hans Sloane and Sir Joseph Banks.

Naturalism A term used in art criticism for the faithful copying of nature, with no attempt to 'improve' or idealize the subject; used in this sense in 1672 by Giovanni Pietro Bellori (1615–96) to characterize the work of Caravaggio and his followers. It later became used to describe the incorporation of scientific method into art, especially literature. This was advocated by the French novelist Emile Zola in the late 19th-c, at a time when confidence in science ran high. Zola claimed the writer should be a dispassionate observer of phenomena, his imagination a laboratory. The Naturalist movement provided a philosophical framework for the earlier Realist initiative, but was soon undermined by Symbolist ideas. Naturalism had an after-life in England (with Bennett), in the USA (with Dreiser), and in Germany (with Hauptmann).

naturalistic fallacy A term in ethics, coined by G E Moore: the mistake of thinking that goodness is some natural or empirical property of things, such as their capacity to produce pleasure; more generally, the alleged mistake identified by Hume of inferring normative conclusions from factual premises – an 'ought' from an 'is'.

natural justice A legal concept, originally developed by the courts of equity, incorporating broad rules or principles aimed at ensuring that judicial and quasi-judicial proceedings are governed by fairness. It includes two main principles: everyone should have a right to be heard in his or her own case; and judges should be unbiased in hearing a case and without personal interest. These rules apply not only to those accused before courts, but also to those persons subject to the decisions of bodies acting judicially or exercising an administrative power affecting a person's status, rights, or obligations. Any such decision which contravenes natural justice is void. An interested party alleging lack of natural justice may seek a judicial review.

natural law 1 In the natural sciences, a descriptive law which purports to explain the nature or behaviour of the physical world. An example is Newton's laws of mechanics.
2 In ethics and jurisprudence, a prescriptive law which defines how people *ought* to behave, and which is said to be rooted in human nature and rationality, not in convention or civil legislation. Notable natural law theorists include the Stoics, Aquinas (for whom natural law derived ultimately from divine law), Grotius, and Kant.

natural selection The complex process by which the totality of environmental factors determines the non-random and differential reproduction of genetically different organisms. It is viewed as the force which directs the course of evolution by preserving those variants or traits best adapted to survive.

natural units A system of units used in particle physics in which equations are simplified by setting $c = (h/2\pi) = 1$, where c is the velocity of light and h is Planck's constant; requires that both length and time have units of one divided by mass.

Nature Conservancy Council *English Nature*

Nature Reserve A protected area for the conservation and management of wildlife and habitat. In the UK these range from National Nature Reserves, in the care of English Nature, to reserves managed by the National Trust, local authorities, and county naturalist trusts. In 2004 there were 214 National Nature Reserves, which represent the best-known examples of coastal, freshwater, marshland, bog, moorland, heathland, grassland, woodland, and alpine habitats.

naturopathy [natyuropathee] A holistic approach to health care which aims to create favourable conditions in which the body's own natural powers of healing will eliminate any illness and then continue to maintain health. The symptoms of an illness are seen as part of the healing process, so these are not suppressed; instead, the body is encouraged to correct its own disturbed equilibrium. Treatment usually begins with fasting to eliminate any toxins, including the substances which may be causing the disease, then proceeds to a natural diet which usually consists of whole and unrefined foods, with fruit and juices to consolidate the benefits of fasting. Patients are encouraged to take responsibility for their own health, and are taught the basic principles of nutrition, hygiene, and systematic exercise so that they can maintain a healthy lifestyle.

Naughtie, (Alexander) James [**nokh**tee] (1951–) Journalist and broadcaster, born in Scotland, UK. He studied at Aberdeen University and Syracuse University, NY, then worked on various British newspapers, including *The Scotsman* (1977–84) and *The Guardian* (1984–8). He then became presenter of the BBC's *The World At One* (1988–94), and joined the team of *Today* in 1994. He has also presented several documentary series, such as *A Nearby Country* (1991) and *The Thin Blue Line* (1993), and was Sony Radio Awards Personality of the Year in 1991.

Naukratis [nawkratis] A Greek town in the Delta of Egypt, established by the Milesians c.675 BC. It was the commercial and industrial centre of the Greeks in Egypt until the foundation of Alexandria by Alexander the Great (c.331 BC).

Nauru *p.1068*

Nausicaa [nawsikaya] In Homer's *Odyssey*, the daughter of King Alcinous. When Odysseus landed in Phaeacia, alone and naked,

Nauru

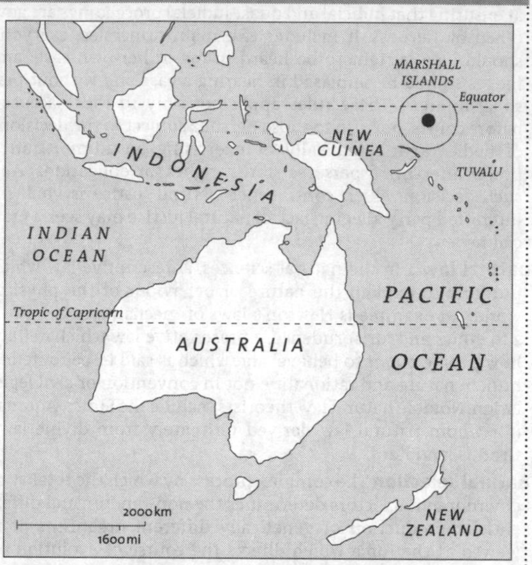

[naooroo], official name **Republic of Nauru**

Local name Naeoro (Nauruan)

Timezone GMT +12

Area 21·3 km^2/8·2 sq mi

Population total (2002e) 12 300

Status Republic

Date of independence 1968

Capital Yaren District (No official capital)

Languages Nauruan (official), English

Ethnic groups Nauruans (62%), Pacific islanders (26%), Asian (9%), Caucasian (3%)

Religions Christian (Nauruan Protestant, Roman Catholic)

Physical features Small isolated island in WC Pacific Ocean, 4000 km/2500 mi NE of Sydney, Australia; ground rises from sandy beaches to give fertile coastal belt, c.100–300 m/300–1000 ft wide, the only cultivable soil; central plateau inland, highest point 65 m/213 ft; mainly phosphate-bearing rocks.

Climate Tropical, hot, and humid; average annual temperatures 27°C (Jan), 28°C (Jul); average annual rainfall 1520 mm/60 in; monsoon season (Nov–Feb).

Currency 1 Australian Dollar ($A) = 100 cents

Economy Based on phosphate mining, now limited reserves; coconuts, some vegetables; tourism; tax haven.

GDP (2001e) $60 mn, per capita $5000

History Under German administration from 1880s to 1914; after 1919, League of Nations mandate, administered by Australia; occupied by Japan, 1942–5; independence movement, 1960s; self-government, 1966; full independence, 1968; unicameral Parliament, elects a President, who appoints a Cabinet.

Head of State/Government
1999–2000 René Harris
2000–1 Bernard Dowiyogo
2001–3 René Harris
2003 Bernard Dowiyogo
2003 Derog Gioura
2003 Ludwig Scotty
2003– René Harris

she was doing the laundry by the sea-shore; she took him home to her father's palace.

nautilus [nawtilus] A primitive cephalopod mollusc with an external spiral shell containing gas in its chambers; numerous tentacles present around mouth; four gills; eyes like a pinhole camera in design, without lenses; only a single living genus known, but the group has an extensive fossil record. (Class: Cephalopoda. Subclass: Nautiloidea.)

Navajo or **Navaho** [navahoh] Athapascan-speaking North American Southwest Indians, who migrated to the SW some time after AD 1000, and who are today the second largest Indian group in the USA, numbering c.269 000 (2000 census). They carried out raids on Spanish settlers in the area, but were themselves eventually defeated by US troops (1863–4), and settled in 1888 on a reservation in Arizona (presently 15 million acres). They adopted the long-established weaving traditions of SW US peoples, such as the Hopi; and many are now commercially-successful weavers. Many work as migrant labourers throughout the SW, and some have settled in the cities and on irrigated farming lands. They are known for their skills in weaving and making jewellery.

Navaratri [navarahtree] A Hindu festival held in the autumn (Asvina S 1–10) in honour of various goddesses (especially Durga), and also commemorating the victory of Rama over Ravana, the Demon King; also known as **Durga Puja** [**dur**ga **poo**ja].

Navarre [navah(r)], Span **Navarra** pop (2000e) 523 000; area 10 421 sq km/4022 sq mi. Region and former kingdom of N Spain, co-extensive with the modern province of Navarre; early centre of resistance to the Moors; united with Castile, 1515; capital, Pamplona; cereals, vegetables, vines, food canning, cement, footwear, textiles, clothes, electrical equipment, iron and steel, furniture, metal products.

nave The W part of a church open to the laity, as opposed to the chancel or choir. More specifically, it refers to the middle section of the W limb between the side aisles.

navel *umbilical cord*

Navier–Stokes equation An important but complex equation describing the mechanics of a viscous fluid, relating changes in the velocity of the fluid to the pressure and viscous forces acting on it; formulated by French engineer Claude Navier (1785–1836) and British mathematician George Stokes (1819–1903). It can be solved only for certain special cases.

navigation The means of finding the way from one place to another in safety. *Celestial navigation* is the oldest and most traditional type of navigation. Navigators could calculate their craft's latitude from the angle of the sun or other stars above the horizon, measured using a sextant. Longitude was calculated by knowing the local time exactly compared to that at 0° longitude, at Greenwich, London. Time is based on the time of rotation of the Earth, and is measured aboard ship using a very accurate chronometer. The simplest form of navigation is called *dead reckoning* (from the term *deduced reckoning*): the position of a ship or aircraft is simply calculated by knowing its speed (measured in knots), the direction it is heading from a compass reading (the bearing), and the time it has been travelling. Navigators can improve on the dead reckoning position if they take account of effects of wind and tide pushing their craft off course. The result is a plot of their estimated position. Another type of navigation, known as *piloting*, uses features along the route as landmarks (eg tall buildings, hills). The disadvantage of these systems is that they do not work in poor visibility conditions. *Electronic navigation* can be used in all weather conditions. *Satellites* are also increasingly being used for navigation, sending out signals which can be received and used as position finders. The Global Positioning System (GPS) gives an almost instant fix of position in latitude and longitude. *Radar navigation* works by sending out signals and representing the reflection from obstacles on a display. *Inertial navigation* is a completely self-contained system, unaffected by weather, magnetic fields, electric storms, etc. It uses the outputs from three gyroscopes and three accelerometers to measure changes in rotation and position accurately in three dimensions (roll, pitch, and yaw).

Navigation Acts Protective legislation in Britain passed between 1650 and 1696, designed to increase England's share of overseas carrying trade. The laws stated that all imports to England had to be in English ships or in those of the country of origin. The laws were frequently contentious in the 18th-c, adding to the 13 American colonies' sense of grievance against the mother country. They were not repealed until 1849.

navigation satellite An artificial object placed in orbit around the Earth, which acts as an aid to navigation. By giving position references and acting as signal relays, navigators of aeroplanes and ships can obtain an accurate fix on their position.

Navratilova, Martina [navratil**oh**va] (1956–) Tennis player, born in Prague, Czech Republic. For three years she played for Czechoslovakia in the Federation Cup, but in 1975 defected to the USA and turned professional, becoming a US citizen in 1981. Her rivalry with Chris Evert was one of the great features of the game from 1975. The winner of a record nine singles titles at Wimbledon (1978–9, 1982–7, 1990), she won 167 singles titles (including 18 Grand Slam events) and 165 doubles titles with her partner Pam Shriver (including 37 Grand Slam events), becoming the most prolific winner in women's tennis. In 1994 she retired from competitive singles tennis. She won the Australian Open mixed doubles title with Leander Paes in 2003, and in doing so broke the record for the oldest ever winner of a Grand Slam crown. Later that year she secured a record-equalling 20th Wimbledon title when she won (with Paes) the mixed doubles final. She has become known as a spokeswoman on several social issues, notably gay rights, animal rights, and ecology, as well as on issues to do with the status of women and young players in tennis.

navy The branch of the armed forces whose main function is the projection of military power at and by sea. The role of naval forces is manifold, primarily the protection of lines of communication for the safe transport of troops and supplies (and its converse, denying the enemy the freedom of the seas). Navies have been important since early times. The Greek naval victory over the Persians in 480 BC was crucial to world history. The Chinese navy had armed warships by the 10th-c, and totalled 50 000 men. In the two World Wars, naval power was critical, with the added dimensions of submarine, amphibious, and carrier warfare. Since the 1960s, with the advent of the ballistic missile-firing submarine, navies have had the additional responsibility of nuclear deterrence.

Naxos [**nak**sos] pop (2000e) 15 300; area 428 sq km/165 sq mi. Largest island of the Cyclades, Greece, in the S Aegean Sea; length 35 km/22 mi; width 26 km/16 mi; rises to 1002 m/3287 ft; chief town, Naxos; airfield; potatoes, fruit, marble, tourism.

Nazarene, Church of the A union of independent Christian Churches, formed in Texas in 1908, and now with headquarters in Kansas City, MO. Conciliar in polity, it is evangelical and missionary in emphasis, with an extensive overseas outreach.

Nazarenes **1** A name used occasionally in the New Testament apparently to depict 'someone from Nazareth', and most frequently describing Jesus Christ. In *Acts* 24.5, it seems to designate 'Christians', and later traditions indicate that this was the name by which Christians were known among the Jews. Yet by the 4th-c, Epiphanius refers to it as representing a heretical Christian sect with Judaizing tendencies, and implies the existence of a *Gospel of the Nazoraeans*.
2 A derisive nickname given to a group of German artists in Rome 1810–c.1820. Leading members, including Johann Friedrich Overbeck (1789–1869), Franz Pforr (1788–1812), and Peter von Cornelius (1783–1867), were inspired by 15th-c styles, and dedicated to the revival of mediaeval and Renaissance religious art.

Nazareth, Hebrew **Nazerat** 32°41N 35°16E, pop (2000e) 70 000. Capital town of Northern district, N Israel; above the Jezreel plain; mainly Christian population; home of Jesus for most of his life; tourism, market centre; Church of the Annunciation, Church of St Joseph.

Nazca [**nas**ka] A pre-Columbian culture located along the S Peruvian coast, and flourishing between c.200 BC and AD 500. It was noted for its distinctive style of pottery and large-scale 'lines' (best seen from the air) on the desert surface.

Naze, the, Norwegian **Lindesnes** 57°59N 7°03E. Cape on the S extremity of Norway, projecting into the North Sea at the entrance to the Skagerrak; first beacon light in Norway established here.

Nazi Party A German political party which dominated Germany from 1933 to 1945. It originated as the *Deutsche Arbeiterpartei* (German Worker's Party), founded in Munich in 1919 to protest against the German surrender of 1918 and the Treaty of Versailles, and renamed the *Nationalsozialistische Deutsche Arbeiterpartei* (National Socialist German Worker's Party, or Nazi Party) in 1920. Adolf Hitler became the party's leader the following year. Its ideology was extremely nationalist, imperialist, and racist, maintaining that the world was divided into a hierarchy of races: Aryans, of whom Germans were the purest example, were the supreme culture-bearing race, while the Jews were the lowest. It was also contended that the Jews were intent on world conquest through infesting the Aryan race. These ideas were set out by Hitler in *Mein Kampf* (1925). It was not until the 1930s that the Nazi Party gained a position of significant support: in 1932 with 37·3% of the vote they became the largest party in the Reichstag. Support came from people of all backgrounds, but was most prominent among Protestants, the middle class, and the young. In 1933 Hitler was appointed chancellor in a coalition government, a position from which he, aided by the party, was able to build up a personal dictatorship, through legal measures, terror, and propaganda. Once in power, the Nazis ruthlessly crushed opposition, indoctrinated the public with their ideas, engaged in extensive rearmament, and in the late 1930s invaded Austria, the Sudetenland, and the rest of Czechoslovakia, which according to the ideology was necessary for obtaining land for the 'master race'. During World War 2, their actions included slave labour, plunder, and mass extermination. Nazism as a political ideology is now viewed very much as the expression of extreme inhumanity, fanatical nationalism, and the logic of nihilism. Resentment against immigrants to Germany precipitated a renewal of neo-Nazi demonstrations in the 1990s.

Ndebele [nduh**bee**lee] or **Matabele** A Bantu-speaking people of SW Zimbabwe and N South Africa, originating in the 19th-c as an offshoot of Nguni groups who moved N, conquering some of the indigenous Shona peoples, and establishing a highly stratified state. In the 1890s they resisted white pioneers' encroachment on their land, but were ruthlessly suppressed.

N'djamena [nja**mee**na], formerly **Fort Lamy** 12°10N 14°59E, pop (2000e) 791 000. Capital of Chad, NC Africa, and capital of Chari-Baguirmi prefecture, WC Chad; at confluence of Logone and Chari Rivers; junction of caravan routes; founded by French, 1900; bombed by Italians, 1942; airport; university (1971); trade in cotton, cattle; several research institutes; National Museum.

Ndola [n**doh**la] 13°00S 28°39E, pop (2000e) 514 900. Capital of Copperbelt province, C Zambia, 275 km/171 mi N of Lusaka; airport; railway; technical college; commercial centre of a major mining area; cement, oil refining, paint, adhesives, tyres, furniture, clothing, mining equipment, food processing.

Neagh, Lough [lokh **nay**] area 396 sq km/153 sq mi. Large lake in C Northern Ireland, UK; length, 29 km/18 mi; width, 18 km/11 mi; largest lake in the British Isles; well-known for its eels; outlet is the R Bann, which flows N to the coast; lignite mining around the lake.

Neanderthal Man [nee**an**dertahl] *Homo sapiens neanderthalensis*. A distinctive form of archaic *Homo sapiens*, with a long, flat, braincase (capacity 1200–1800 cm), a retreating frontal, heavy brow ridge, and a projecting face with a large nose. Contrary to early reconstructions, Neanderthals were fully upright, but had stocky, muscular body build (height 1·55–1·8 m/5 ft 1 in–5 ft 10 in; average 1·66 m/5 ft 4 in). Fossil evidence indicates Neanderthal characters evolved slowly from about 0·5 million years ago, but the full set of features only occur after c.0·1 million years ago in Europe, S Russia, and the Middle East (SW Asia). There is a particular concentration of finds in W Europe, where Neanderthals disappear c.33 000 years ago with the arrival of anatomically modern humans (*H. sapiens sapiens*); in SW Asia the two subspecies coexisted for c.60 000 years (100 000–40 000 years ago).

neap tide An especially small tidal range occurring twice monthly. It is produced by the tidal forces of the Sun and Moon acting in opposition. These minimum monthly tides occur when the Moon is in its first and third quarters.

near-death experience (NDE) A striking experience sometimes reported by those who have recovered from being close to death. It generally includes an out-of-the-body experience in which one travels through a dark void or tunnel towards a bright light, and then may encounter religious figures or deceased loved ones. It is often accompanied by strong feelings of peacefulness.

Near Earth Object (NEO) An asteroid or comet in the Solar System with an orbit that brings it close to the Earth, presenting a potential collision hazard. There are estimated to be approximately 2000 NEOs larger than 1 km/0·6 mi in diameter, and more than a million larger than 50 m/165 ft in diameter, the size above which they would penetrate the Earth's atmosphere. From this size up to about 1 km in diameter, an NEO impact on Earth would cause immense local damage. The impact of an NEO larger than about 2 km/1·2 mi (energy greater than a million megatons) would produce severe environmental damage around the globe, probably an 'impact winter' with loss of crops worldwide, and subsequent starvation and disease. Still larger impacts can cause mass extinctions, such as the one (15 km/9 mi diameter and c.100 million megatons) that ended the age of the dinosaurs 65 million years ago.

nearsightedness *eye*

Neath and Port Talbot, Welsh **Castell-Nedd a Phort Talbot** pop (2001e) 134 500; area 442 sq km/171 sq mi. County (unitary authority from 1996) in SC Wales, UK; drained by R Neath and R Avan; administrative centre, Port Talbot; other chief towns, Neath, Pontardawe; steel, engineering, light industry; castle, abbey and Roman fort at Neath.

Neblina, Pico da [peekoh da nebleena] 1°45N 66°01W. Mountain in Amazonas state, N Brazil; rises to 3014 m/9888 ft in the Serra Imeri range on the frontier with Venezuela; now known to be the highest mountain in Brazil; situated in a 22 000 sq km/8500 sq mi national park established in 1979.

Nebraska [nebraska] pop (2000e) 1 711 300; area 200 342 sq km/77 352 sq mi. State in C USA, divided into 93 counties; the 'Cornhusker State'; part of the Louisiana Purchase, 1803; Bellevue first permanent settlement; became a territory stretching to the Canadian border in 1854, but its area was reduced in 1863; the 37th state admitted to the Union, 1867; the Union Pacific Railroad completed its transcontinental line, 1869, resulting in a land boom; capital, Lincoln; other chief cities, Omaha and Grand Island; Missouri R forms the E border; Platte R crosses the state to empty into the Missouri; highest point Johnson Township (1654 m/5426 ft); E region undulating fertile farmland, growing corn; further W, on the Great Plains, grass cover helping to stabilize eroded land; in the far W, foothills of the Rocky Mts; agriculture dominates the economy; cattle (second largest producer in the country), corn, hogs, wheat, sorghum; food processing, electrical machinery, chemicals.

Nebuchadnezzar II [nebookadnezer], also spelled **Nebuchadrezzar** (c.630–562 BC) King of Babylon (605–562 BC). He succeeded his father Nabopolassar, and during his 43-year reign recovered the long-lost provinces of the kingdom, once more making Babylon a supreme nation. He not only restored the empire and rebuilt Babylon, but almost every temple throughout the land underwent restoration at his hands. Every mound opened by explorers has contained bricks, cylinders, or tablets inscribed with his name. In 597 he captured Jerusalem, and in 586 destroyed the city, removing most of the inhabitants to Chaldea.

nebula A cloud of gas and dust in space, appearing either light or dark. Some nebulae are areas where stars form; others are produced by the death of stars. **Star-forming nebulae** include the large and bright Orion Nebula, the gas of which is excited to luminescence by the ultraviolet light from the stars within it. **Dark nebulae** have no illuminating stars; examples are the Coalsack and the Horsehead Nebula. Shells of gas thrown off by old stars are known as **planetary nebulae**, such as the Helix Nebula. Other nebulae are produced by supernova explosions, such as the Crab Nebula.

neck That part of the body which connects the head and the thorax as well as the upper limbs to the trunk. The various structures within the neck are contained within coverings of connective tissue (*fascia*), organized in well-defined sheets and membranes. The most superficial cylindrical layer of fascia encloses and covers all structures within the neck (except the platysma muscle, which lies in the subcutaneous tissue). Deeper layers of fascia surround specific structures. The cylindrical organization of these various fasciae emphasizes that they form longitudinal compartments transmitting structures from one region to another. The neck contains the continuations of many structures: the vertebral column, alimentary and respiratory tracts, blood vessels and their branches, lymph nodes and lymphatic vessels, groups of muscles, and several cranial and cervical nerves.

Necker, Jacques (1732–1804) Statesman and financier, born in Geneva, SW Switzerland. Initially a banker's clerk, he moved to Paris (1762), founded a bank, and became a wealthy speculator. In 1776–7 he was director of the French Treasury and director-general of finances. He attempted some administrative reforms, but tried to finance French involvement in the War of American Independence by heavy borrowing, while concealing the large state deficit. He was dismissed in 1781, but recalled in 1788 to deal with the impending financial crisis. He summoned the States General, but his proposals for social and constitutional change aroused royal opposition, and he was dismissed. His dismissal helped to provoke the public disorder that ended in the storming of the Bastille, and he was hastily recalled in 1789, but resigned the following year.

necropsy *post mortem*

nectar A sugary fluid secreted by specialized glands (*nectaries*) usually found in flowers, sometimes also in other organs. It is used to attract insect pollinators.

nectarine A smooth-skinned variety of peach (*Prunus persica*, variety *nectarina*). (Family: Rosaceae.)

Neddy *National Economic Development Council*

Nederlands *Dutch*

Needham, Joseph [needam] (1900–95) Historian of science, born in London, UK. He studied at Cambridge, where he taught (1924–66), becoming Master of Gonville and Caius College (1966–76) and director of the Needham Research Institute (1976–90). He trained as a biochemist, and published a pioneering *History of Embryology* (1934) before developing a consuming interest in the Chinese tradition of science, technology, and medicine. His major work is the multi-volume series *Science and Civilisation in China* (from 1956).

needlefish Slender-bodied fish with very long jaws forming a narrow bill; widespread in tropical and warm temperate seas; dorsal and anal fins placed close to tail; includes W Atlantic, *Strongylura marina*, a voracious surface-living predator; length up to 1·2 m/4 ft; also called **garfish**. (Family: Belonidae.)

Ne'eman, Yuval (1925–) Physicist and politician, born in Tel Aviv, Israel. Active against the British in Palestine (1946–7), he became a captain in the Israeli Defence Force (1947), deputy director of defence intelligence (1955–7), and defence attaché in London (1958–60). He was professor of physics at Tel Aviv (1965–73), then at the University of Texas, Austin, and (1979–

97) director of the Sackler Institute of Advanced Studies. He founded the Tehiya political party and became a member of the Knesset in 1981, and has held ministerial posts in the areas of science and development. In 1983 he founded the Israeli Space Agency. In physics he has worked on the role of symmetry in particle physics, and co-authored the influential book *The Eight-Fold Way* with Murray Gell-Mann.

Neer, Aernout or **Aert van der** (1603/4–77) Painter, born in Amsterdam, The Netherlands. He specialized in moonlit canal and river scenes. Although his paintings are now regarded as major works of the Dutch school, he received little recognition in his own time. In 1658 he gave up painting in order to open a wineshop. He was no more successful in this venture, and returned to painting in 1662 after being declared bankrupt. Two of his sons became artists: **Eglon** (1634–1703) and **Jan** (1638–65).

Neeson, Liam (1952–) Film actor, born in Ballymena, NE Northern Ireland, UK. He performed with the Abbey Theatre, Dublin, and the Lyric Players Theatre, Belfast, making his film debut in *Excalibur* (1981). He received an Oscar nomination for his role as Schindler in *Schindler's List* (1993), and went on to play the title roles in *Rob Roy* (1995) and *Michael Collins* (1996). Later films include *Star Wars Episode 1: The Phantom Menace* (1999) and *Kinsey* (2003). He is married to actress Natasha Richardson.

Nefertiti [neferteetee] (14th-c BC) Egyptian queen, the consort of Akhenaton, by whom she had six children, and whose new religious cult of the Sun god Aton she supported. She is immortalized in the beautiful sculptured head found at Amarna in 1912, now in the Berlin Museum. Little is known of her background, but she is believed to have been an Asian princess from Mitanni.

negative An image in which the tonal scale of the original scene is inverted, light areas being reproduced as dark and vice versa. In a **colour negative** the hues of the original are also represented in their complementary colours. Film exposed in a camera is usually processed to yield a negative, from which a positive print must be made to reproduce the original scene.

negative income tax A scheme where the poorest sections of the community receive a state-funded 'income support payment' instead of various grants and supplementary benefits. The notion applies to low earning workers, and is intended to raise their income to a suitable level.

Negeri Sembilan [negree sembilahn] pop (2000e) 900 000; area 6643 sq km/2564 sq mi. State in SW Peninsular Malaysia; bounded W by the Strait of Malacca, SE by Malacca, NW by Selangor, NE by Pahang; capital, Seremban; rubber, rice, tin.

Negev [negev] Hilly desert region of S Israel, extending in a wedge from Beersheba in the N to Eilat on the Gulf of Aqaba; hilly in the S, reaching 1935 m/6348 ft at Har Ramon; N irrigated by a conduit leading from L Tiberias; increasing kibbutz settlement.

negligence A tort (or delict, in Scotland) applicable to a very wide range of situations. To succeed in negligence, the plaintiff must prove that the defendant owed him or her a duty of care, that is, the legal obligation to take reasonable care to avoid causing damage. There is a duty to take care in most situations in which a person's actions may cause physical damage to others or to their property. The plaintiff must also prove that the duty was breached in this instance, and that the breach caused damage to the plaintiff (known as *actual* or *proximate cause* in the USA). Road accidents are a common source of negligence claims. It is not sufficient to show that there has been an incident; negligence must be proved, although only to the standard of 'the balance of probabilities'. In the case of pure economic loss, where no physical damage is involved (eg poor investment advice), it may also be necessary to establish a relationship of special trust, often called a *fiduciary relationship* based on reliance by the plaintiff on the defendant's actions or statements.

Negoiul, Mount [negoyul] 45°35N 24°31E. Mountain in the Transylvanian Alps of SC Romania, rising to 2548 m/8359 ft; highest mountain in Romania.

Negro, River (Argentina) [naygroh] (Span **Río**) Patagonian river in SC Argentina; formed by junction of Neuquén and Limay Rivers; flows S and SE to the Atlantic 32 km/20 mi SE of Viedma; navigable for 400 km/250 mi upstream; used for hydroelectric power; vineyards in irrigated valleys; length of the Neuquén–Negro, 1130 km/702 mi.

Negro, River (Brazil) [negroh] (Port **Rio**) Important N tributary of the Amazon, N Brazil; rises in SE Colombia, flows generally SE through the Amazon tropical rainforest, joining the Amazon 18 km/11 mi below Manaus; length c.2250 km/1400 mi; a major transport channel, connected to the Orinoco R via the Casiquiare Canal; contains numerous islands; up to 32 km/20 mi wide above Manaus, narrows to 2·5 km/1½ mi at its mouth.

Nehemiah, Book of [neehemiya] A book of the Hebrew Bible/Old Testament, originally joined to the Book of Ezra, and probably also to 1 and 2 Chronicles. This historical writing was named after a Jewish official of the King of Persia, Nehemiah, who apparently led a return to Judea by Jewish exiles in Persia. He had two periods of governorship in Judea during the reign of Artaxerxes I (465–424 BC) or possibly Artaxerxes II (404–359 BC). There is some chronological confusion in the work, because of the presence of some sections which appear to belong to the Book of Ezra.

Nehru, Jawaharlal [nairoo], known as **Pandit** ('Teacher') **Nehru** (1889–1964) Indian statesman and prime minister (1947–64), born in Allahabad, NE India, the son of Motilal Nehru. He studied at Cambridge, became a lawyer, and served in the Allahabad High Court. He joined the Indian Congress Committee (1918), was influenced by Gandhi, and was imprisoned several times by the British. In 1929 he was elected president of the Indian National Congress. He became India's first prime minister and minister of external affairs (1947), and followed a policy of neutrality during the Cold War. He introduced a policy of industrialization, reorganized the states on a linguistic basis, and brought the dispute with Pakistan over Kashmir to a peaceful solution.

Nei Mongol *Inner Mongolia*

nekton Swimming marine organisms, capable of locomotion for extended periods of time at speeds greater than those of ocean currents; distinct from plankton, which are drifters. Nekton range in size from tiny fish to giant sperm whales.

Nelson, (John) Byron, Jr (1912–) Golfer, born in Fort Worth, Texas, USA. He won a record 18 tournaments on the US Professional Golfers Association (PGA) tour in 1945, 11 of them successive, and also won the US Open (1939), the US PGA Championship (1940, 1945), and the US Masters (1937, 1942) – a total of 52 US Tour events. He captained the 1965 US Ryder Cup team at Birkdale, and became a notable golf teacher and broadcaster after he retired from tournament play.

Nelson, Horatio (1758–1805) British admiral, born in Burnham Thorpe, Norfolk, E England, UK. He joined the navy in 1770, and was sent to the West Indies (1784) to enforce the Navigation Act against the newly independent United States. There he married Frances Nisbet (1761–1831), and in 1787 retired with her to Burnham Thorpe. In 1794 he commanded the naval brigade at the reduction of Bastia and Calvi where he lost the sight of his right eye, and in an action at Santa Cruz had his right arm amputated. In 1798 he followed the French fleet to Egypt, destroying it at Aboukir Bay. On his return to Naples, he fell in love with Emma, Lady Hamilton, and began a liaison with her which lasted until his death. In 1801 he was made rear-admiral, and led the attack on Copenhagen. Previously created a baron, he then became a viscount, and commander-in-chief. In 1805 he gained his greatest victory, against the combined French and Spanish fleet at Trafalgar. During the battle he was mortally wounded on his flagship, HMS *Victory*. His body was brought home and buried in St Paul's.

Nelson, Willie (1933–) Country singer, songwriter, and guitarist, born in Abbott, Texas, USA. After writing and recording many country-music hits in the 1960s, he gained a wider audience in the 1970s with such albums as *Shotgun Willie* (1972) and *Stardust* (1978). Success continued in the 1980s through further collaborations with Waylon Jennings, Merle Haggard, and other country stars, and albums like *Always on my Mind* prospering in the pop music market.

Nelson Lakes area 961 sq km/371 sq mi. National park, N South Island, New Zealand; contains Rotoiti and Rotoroa lakes; surrounded by rugged, forest-clad mountains rising to over 1800 m/6000 ft; established in 1956.

nematode An unsegmented worm, typically circular in section; body covered with cuticle; head end with terminal mouth, surrounded by lips and three rings of sense organs; abundant in aquatic sediments, in soil, and as parasites of plants and animals; c.12 000 species described; also known as **eelworms**, **roundworms**, or **pinworms**. (Phylum: Nematoda.)

Nematomorpha [nematomaw(r)fa] *horsehair worm*

Nemertea [nemertia] *ribbon worm*

nemesia [nemeezha] An annual (*Nemesia strumosa*) growing to 60 cm/2 ft, native to S Africa; leaves oblong, toothed; flowers with 2-lobed upper lip and large, spreading 3-lobed lower lip, in a range of colours. It is a popular garden plant, especially in dwarf forms. (Family: Scrophulariaceae.)

Nemesis [nemesis] In Greek mythology, the goddess of retribution. She primarily represents the penalty the gods exact for human folly, excessive pride, or too much good fortune.

Nemirovich-Danchenko, Vladimir (Ivanovich) [nemirohvich danchengkoh] (1858–1943) Theatre director, writer, and teacher, born in Ozurgety, Russia. Co-founder with Stanislavsky of the Moscow Art Theatre, he became sole director following the latter's death in 1938. Among his most notable productions were *The Brothers Karamazov* (1910) and *Nikolai Stavrogin* (1913). After 1919, his interest in opera led to some of his most original work as a director.

Nemrut Dag The mountain site of the tomb-sanctuary of King Antiochus of Commagene (64–32 BC), S Anatolia, Turkey; a world heritage monument. The peak is 220 m/722 ft above sea-level, while the tomb is a conical tumulus 50 m/160 ft high and 150 m/500 ft in diameter at its base.

nene [naynay] *Hawaiian goose*

Nenets A Uralic-speaking ethnic group living in N Russia, originally known as **Samoyed** or **Yurak**. They are reindeer keepers, and also fishermen and hunters (of wild reindeer). Formerly nomadic, they are now settled in villages.

Nennius (fl.796) Writer, from Wales, reputedly the author of the early Latin compilation known as the *Historia Britonum*, an account of British history from the time of Julius Caesar to towards the end of the 7th-c. The book gives a mythical version of the origins of the Britons, and recounts the Roman occupation, the settlement of the Saxons, and the historical Arthur's 12 victories over the Saxons. There are several versions of the *Historia*: the North-Welsh, the South-Welsh, the Irish, and the English. Although it contains material of doubtful historical significance, its real value lies in its preservation of material needed for the study of early Celtic literature in general, and the Arthurian legend in particular.

NEO *Near Earth Object*

Neoclassicism (art and architecture) A classical revival affecting all the visual arts, including architecture and the decorative arts, which flourished from c.1750 onwards, lasting well into the 19th-c. A reaction against the decorous excesses of Baroque and the 'frivolity' of Rococo, it began in Rome, but spread throughout W Europe and North America. Partly inspired by the excavations at Pompeii, Herculaneum, and Paestum, it received its theoretical underpinning from Winckelmann, whose essay on the 'noble simplicity and calm grandeur' of Greek art (1755) was followed by a pioneering history of antique art (1764). In painting, the style reached its peak in the powerful and dramatic works of David (eg 'Oath of the Horatii', 1784, Louvre), while the rather frigid side of Neoclassicism is well exemplified by the sculpture of Canova. In architecture, theorists proposed a reasoned approach based on the 'primitive hut' and clear structural principles. The buildings are usually characterized by pure geometric form, restrained decoration, unbroken contours, an overall severe appearance, and sometimes monumental proportions. The chief exponents were Etienne Louis Boullée and Claude Nicolas Ledoux in France, and John Soane in England.

Neoclassicism (music) A 20th-c music movement which sought to restore the ideals, and to some extent the style and vocabulary, of the 18th-c classical period. Since Bach often provided the model for Neoclassical works, the movement might be as accurately described as 'neo-Baroque', but its main motivation was in any case anti-Romantic. It is associated particularly with Stravinsky's middle-period works (c.1920–30), but touched many other composers, including Prokofiev and Hindemith.

neo-corporatism *corporatism*

Neoexpressionism A vague term sometimes used for all forms of abstract art which are regarded as conveying strong emotions, or which seem to have been produced by the artist in a heightened emotional state. Examples include Kandinsky's work after c.1920, or US Action Painting.

neofascism Fascist ideas and movements that have continued after the demise of the inter-war fascist dictatorships. Apart from considerably less political influence, it is hard to detect significant differences between contemporary fascism and its earlier counterparts. Neofascism in W Europe has, however, been opposed to immigration from former colonial and Balkan countries, and has used this as a major campaigning platform. The economic problems brought on by the reunification of East and West Germany, and the collapse of communism in Eastern Europe, gave rise to an upsurge in neofascist ideas and violence in these countries against immigrants, Jews, Roms, and the mentally handicapped.

Neo-Freudian Applied to psychoanalysts who base their theories and practice on those elaborated by Freud, but who have made specific modifications to Freud's theories. They include the German psychoanalyst Karen Horney (1885–1952) and the American psychiatrist Harry Stack Sullivan (1892–1949), but not Freud's contemporaries.

Neoimpressionism *Divisionism*

Neo-Kantianism A philosophical movement in Germany between c.1870 and 1920, concerned to revive a Kantian approach to epistemology, and opposed to the speculative metaphysics of Hegel on the grounds that this was inadequate to account for mathematical and scientific knowledge. Leading figures in this rather diverse trend were Helmholtz (1821–94), Lange (1828–75), Rickert (1863–1936), Windleband (1848–1915), Natorp (1854–1924), and Cassirer.

Neo-Keynesianism or **new Keynesianism** [kaynzianizm] A term introduced in 1982 by James Meade, related to the economic theories of J M Keynes, but modified to apply to the economic situation of the time. The approach recognizes three government economic targets: growth, balance of payments equilibrium, and adequate investment. These aims can be met by tax policy, exchange rates, and interest rates.

Neolithic The New Stone Age, the latest period of the Stone Age, traditionally associated with the beginnings of settled agriculture and towns. In the Near East, farming began as early as 10 000 years ago, but it took several thousand years to reach N Europe.

neologism [neeolojizm] A term referring to any newly coined word, usually identifying a new concept. In the 1980s, English neologisms included *yuppie*, *glitz*, *pocket phone*, and *user-friendly*. The term is also used in the field of language pathology, where it refers to the coining of a word of obscure or no meaning; the phenomenon is found in aphasia, schizophrenia, and several other disorders.

Neo-Malthusianism A modern version of the theory of Malthus, that excessive poverty and mortality in populations results from imbalance between population size and available resources. It is used by some conservative theorists with reference to the Third World today.

Neo-Marxism The doctrines of Marxists who draw upon Marx's early writings, which had a more romantic and utopian emphasis than his later works concerned with economics and historical materialism. Strongly influenced by Hegelian philosophy, a key feature of Neo-Marxism is its self-critical approach, which accepts the need for a review of theory, rather than a rigid acceptance of dogma, as prevalent under Soviet communism. This critical approach, at its peak in the 1960s and 1970s, has seen a number of competing schools.

neon Ne, element 10. The second noble gas, forming c.0·002% of the atmosphere, and obtained by the fractional distillation of liquid air. It forms no known compounds, and is used mainly in gas discharge tubes and gas lasers, where it emits a characteristic red glow.

neopentane *pentane*

neoplasm *tumour*

Neoplasticism A term invented c.1917 by Mondrian to describe his own particularly severe form of abstract art. He permitted only primary colours, black, white, and grey, and restricted his shapes to squares or rectangles defined by vertical and horizontal lines.

Neoplatonism A school of philosophy founded by Plotinus, which synthesized with Platonism the thought of Aristotle, the Stoics, and the Pythagoreans, and also assimilated much popular religion and myth. Neoplatonist philosophy remained dominant for a millennium, and was revived in the Renaissance by Ficino, Pico, and others.

Neoptolemus [neeoptolemus] In Greek legend, the son of Achilles and Deidameia, his original name being Pyrrhus. He went with Odysseus to persuade Philoctetes to come to Troy. At the end of the war he killed Priam and enslaved Andromache; for this, Apollo prevented him from reaching his home, and he was killed in a dispute at Delphi. The name means the 'young warrior'.

neorealism In cinema, a style of film-making which arose in Italy soon after World War 2, emphasizing themes of social reality even in fictional stories, rather than the escapism of artificial middle-class drama. It used actual settings and non-professional artists, at least in minor roles. An example of the techniques of neorealism is Roberto Rossellini's *Roma, Citta Aperta* (1945, Rome, Open City), in which he used non-professional actors, a low-quality 'grainy' standard of film, and minimal technical standards. Italian neorealism has influenced directors as diverse as Satyajit Ray, John Ford, Jean Renoir, and the Japanese film director Mizoguchi Kenji (1898–1956) in his World War 2 film, *Ugetsu Monogatari* (1955, Tales of Moonlight and Rain).

neoteny [neeotenee] A relative slowing down of bodily (*somatic*) development, so that sexual maturity is attained in an organism while retaining some juvenile characters. In an evolutionary perspective, this gives rise to descendants that retain as adults juvenile features of their ancestors. An example is the Mexican axolotl, a newt which becomes sexually mature before metamorphosing into the adult, so that it retains juvenile characters, such as external gills, even as an adult.

Neo-Thomism [neeohtohmizm] A philosophical movement in the late 19th-c and 20th-c which sought to revive interest in the thought of St Thomas Aquinas. 'Thomism' was declared the official theology of the Roman Catholic Church in 1879, and Neo-Thomism (and the natural theology associated with it) remains an important feature of Roman Catholic and some Anglican thought.

Nepal *p.1074*

nephanalysis (Gr *nephos* 'cloud') A meteorological term for the study of clouds, in particular the amount and frequency of different cloud forms. Satellite imagery of cloud cover is often used in weather forecasting.

nephrite *jade*

nephritis *glomerulonephritis*

nephrons *kidneys*

nephrotic syndrome [nefrotik] A clinical syndrome which results from the chronic loss of large amounts of plasma proteins in the urine, leading to a fall in their concentration in the blood and to generalized oedema. It arises as a complication of persistent glomerulonephritis.

Neptune (astronomy) The eighth planet from the Sun, the outermost of the four 'gas giant' planets; discovered in 1846 as a result of a prediction by Leverrier to explain anomalies in the observed orbit of Uranus; encountered by Voyager 2 (24 Aug 1989). There are eight known moons, including Triton, which has a thin atmosphere, and Nereid. Neptune's main characteristics are: mass $1{\cdot}02 \times 10^{26}$ kg; equatorial radius 24 766 km/15 389 mi; mean density 1·7 g/cm^3; rotational period 16·11 hours; orbital period 164·8 years; inclination of equator 28·3°; eccentricity of orbit 0·010; mean distance from Sun 30·07 AU. It is an apparent twin of Uranus internally, composed of hydrogen and helium, but with much more carbon, nitrogen, and oxygen than Jupiter and Saturn. It is thought to lack sharp internal boundaries between a rock-rich core, an ice-rich mantle, and a deep atmosphere. Its bluish-green coloration is produced by methane in the upper atmosphere. It has cirrus clouds of methane above high-level clouds of methane and ammonia, with lower water clouds. There are storm systems resembling Jupiter's, including a Great Dark Spot in the S hemisphere seen by Voyager. It has a magnetic field of 0·1 gauss, tilted 47° from the rotation axis. There are five rings between 42 000 km/26 000 mi and 63 000 km/39 000 mi from Neptune's centre. The outer ring has clumpy sections, termed *arcs*, probably associated with small moonlets.

Neptune (mythology) The Roman water-god (the Romans originally had no sea-gods). He was later identified with Poseidon, whose characteristics and mythology he acquired.

Nereid [neereeid] The outermost natural satellite of Neptune, discovered in 1949; distance from the planet 5 510 000 km/3 424 000 mi; diameter 340 km/210 mi. It has a highly inclined (28°), eccentric orbit about Neptune, and is probably a captured object.

nereid [neereeid] In Greek mythology, a sea-nymph, one of the 50 or (in some accounts) 100 daughters of Nereus and Doris. They lived with their father in the depths of the sea. Thetis and Galatea were nereids.

Nereus [neeryoos] In Greek mythology, a sea-god, the wise old man of the sea who always tells the truth. Heracles had to wrestle with him to find the location of the Golden Apples.

Nergal [nergahl] The Mesopotamian god of the Underworld; at first, a solar deity capable of killing enormous numbers of people in the heat of noon-day. He forced Ereshkigal, the original goddess of the Underworld, to share her power with him.

Neri, St Philip [nairee] (1515–95) Mystic, born in Florence, NC Italy, the founder of the Oratory. He went to Rome at the age of 18, and for many years spent most of his time in works of charity and instruction, and in solitary prayer. In 1551 he became a priest, and gathered around him a following of disciples which became the Congregation of the Oratory (1564), and later received the approbation of the pope. The community was finally established at Vallicella, where he built a new church (Chiesa Nuova) on the site of Santa Maria. He was canonized in 1622; feast day 26 May.

neritic zone The marine life zone in the water over the continental shelves. It is strongly influenced by its proximity to land, hence neritic organisms must be able to tolerate greater change in temperature and salinity than oceanic organisms.

Nernst, Walther Hermann (1864–1941) Physical chemist, born in Briesen, E Germany. He was professor of chemistry in Göttingen (1891), Berlin (1905), and director of the Berlin Physical Institute in 1925. He proposed the heat theorem (the third law

Nepal

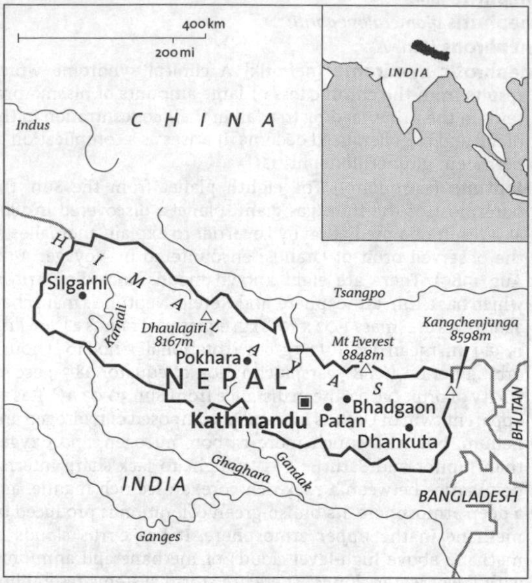

☐ International Airport

[nepawl, naypal], official name **Kingdom of Nepal**, Nepali **Nepal Adhirajya**

Local name Nepāl

Timezone GMT +5¾

Area 145 391 km^2/56 121 sq mi

Population total (2002e) 23 692 000

Status Kingdom

Capital Kathmandu

Languages Nepali (official), Maithir, Bhojpuri

Ethnic groups Nepalese (58%), Bihari (19%), Tamang (4%), Tharu (3%), Newar (3%)

Religions Only official Hindu state in the world: Hindu (90%), Buddhist (5%), Muslim (3%), Christian (0·2%)

Physical features Landlocked, rises steeply from the Ganges basin in India; high fertile valleys in the 'hill country' at 1300 m/4300 ft, notably the Vale of Kathmandu (a world heritage site); dominated by the Himalayas (glaciated), highest peak, Mt Everest, 8848 m/29 028 ft.

Climate Varies from subtropical lowland with hot, humid summers and mild winters, to an alpine climate over 3300 m/10 800 ft, with permanently snow-covered peaks; average annual temperatures 0°C (Jan), 24°C (Jul) in Kathmandu; monsoon season (Jun–Sep); average annual rainfall 1428 mm/56 in.

Currency 1 Nepalese Rupee (NRp, NRs) = 100 paise/pice

Economy Agriculture (employs 90% of population); rice, jute, cereals, sugar cane; agricultural and forest-based goods; carpets; garments, handicrafts; hydroelectric power developing; tourism increasingly important.

GDP (2002e) $37·32 bn, per capita $1400

Human Development Index (2002) 0·490

History Originally a group of independent hill states, united in 18th-c; parliamentary system introduced, 1959; replaced by village councils (panchayats), 1960; a constitutional monarchy ruled by hereditary King; period of unrest in 1990, followed by reduction of King's powers, a new constitution and fresh elections, 1991; King now rules with a Council of Ministers, a bicameral Parliament consisting of an elected House of Representatives and a National Council; Crown Prince Dipendra allegedly murdered 10 members of his immediate family, including his father King Birendra and his mother Queen Aishwarya, before killing himself, 2001; state of emergency following new conflict with Communist Party rebels, Nov 2001; ceasefire and peace-talks begun (Jan 2003), but broke down (Aug).

Head of State (Monarch)
1972–2001 Birendra Bir Bikram Shah Deva
2001 Dipendra Bir Bikram Shah
2001– Gyanendra Bir Bikram Shah

Head of Government
1970–1 *As king*
1971–3 Kirti Nidhi Bista
1973–5 Nagendra Prasad Rijal
1975–7 Tulsi Giri
1977–9 Kirti Nidhi Bista
1979–83 Surya Bahadur Thapa
1983–6 Lokendra Bahadur Chand
1986–90 Marich Man Singh Shrestha
1990 Lokendra Bahadur Chand
1990–1 Krishna Prasad Bhattarai
1991–4 Girija Prasad Koirala
1994–5 Man Mohan Adhikari
1995–7 Sher Bahadur Deupa
1997 Lokendra Bahadur Chand
1997–8 Surya Bahadur Thapa
1998–9 Girija Prasad Koirala
1999–2000 Krishna Prasad Bhattarai
2000–1 Girija Prasad Koirala
2001–2 Sher Bahadur Deuba
2002–3 Lokendra Bahadur Chand *Interim*
2003– Surya Bahadur Thapa

of thermodynamics) in 1906, investigated the specific heat of solids at low temperature in connection with quantum theory, and also proposed the atom chain-reaction theory in photochemistry. He was awarded the Nobel Prize for Chemistry in 1920.

Nero [neeroh], in full **Nero Claudius Caesar**, originally **Lucius Domitius Ahenobarbus** (37–68) Emperor of Rome (54–68), the son of Gnaeus Domitius Ahenobarbus and the younger Agrippina, daughter of Germanicus. He owed his name and position to the driving ambition of his mother, who engineered his adoption by the Emperor Claudius, her fourth husband. Initially his reign was good, thanks to his three main advisers: his mother, the philosopher Seneca, and the Praetorian Prefect Burrus. But after her murder (59), and their fall from favour, Nero, more interested in sex, singing, acting, and chariot-racing than government, neglected affairs of state, and corruption set in. He was blamed for the Great Fire of Rome (64), despite assiduous attempts to make scapegoats of the Christians. A major plot to overthrow him (the Conspiracy of Piso) was formed (65) but detected, and Rome had to endure three more years of tyranny before he was toppled from power by the army, and forced to commit suicide.

Neruda, Pablo [nerootha], pseudonym of **Neftali Ricardo Reyes y Basualto** (1904–73) Poet, born in Parral, Chile. He studied at Santiago, and made his name with *Veinte poemas de amor y una canción desesperada* (1924, Twenty Love Poems and a Song of Despair). From 1927 he held diplomatic posts in various East Asian and European countries. Returning to Chile (1943), he joined the Communist Party, and was elected to the Senate (1945). He travelled in Russia and China (1948–52), and was later the Chilean ambassador in Paris (1970–2). His other works include *Residencia en la tierra* (1925–31, Residence on Earth) and *Canto general* (1950, General Song). He was awarded the Nobel Prize for Literature in 1971.

nerve (cell) *neurone*

nerve gas An agent of chemical warfare, whose deadly effects are achieved by attacking the human body's central nervous system. Paralysis and death come within seconds of absorption (which may be via the skin).

nerve growth factor (NGF) A biologically active peptide found widely (eg in the eye, heart, salivary glands, vas deferens) in many animals, including humans. It controls the growth and development of sympathetic nervous tissue and some sensory neurones. It is classified as a hormone by some authorities.

Nervi, Pier Luigi [nairvee] (1891–1979) Architect and engineer, born in Sondrio, N Italy. After graduating as an engineer, he set up as a building contractor. His many works include the Berta Stadium in Florence (1930–2), a complex of exhibition halls in Turin (1948–50), and the Pirelli building (the first skyscraper in Italy, 1955). He achieved an international reputation with his designs for the two Olympic stadia in Rome (1960), in which bold and imaginative use is made of concrete for roofing in the large areas. He also designed San Francisco cathedral (1970). He was professor at Rome from 1947 to 1961.

nervous system That part of the body concerned with controlling and integrating the activity of its various parts, providing a mechanism whereby the animal can respond to a changing external environment while still maintaining a constant internal environment. It is composed of nerves (*neurones*) and supporting cells. The transfer of information between nerve cells (at *synapses*) is usually by the release of small quantities of *transmitter substances*. Communication with other body tissues may be by the direct release of transmitter substances on to the tissue (usually in the presence of some other substance, such as an enzyme) or by the release of hormones into the blood stream (either directly from the nervous system or from endocrine glands under its control).

In all activities involving the nervous system, regardless of their complexity, there are three components involved: a *receptive* or *sensory* component, an *integrative* component, and an *effector* or *motor* component. In higher animals the integrative component has undergone the greatest development, and forms the major part of the nervous system. In its simplest form, as in coelenterates, the nervous system merely consists of a diffuse network of interconnecting cells. With increasing complexity of the animal, the network becomes organized into a longitudinal cord. This is followed by the grouping and centralization of the motor and sensory cells, and the eventual development of a large integrating centre (the brain). In mammals the nervous system is divided into **central** and **peripheral** parts, both parts working together as a functioning unit: the central part comprises the brain and spinal cord, while the peripheral part comprises the remainder. Disorders, diseases, and infections of the nervous system include neuralgia, paralysis, prion disease, and tetanus.

Nesbit, E(dith), maiden name and pseudonym of **Mrs Hubert Bland** (1858–1924) Writer, born in London, UK. She was educated at a French convent, and began her literary career by writing poetry, having met the Rossettis and their friends. She is best remembered for her children's stories, which reacted against the moralizing then prevalent. They include *The Story of the Treasure Seekers* (1899), *The Would-be-Goods* (1901), and *The Railway Children* (1906, filmed 1970). She also wrote novels and ghost stories.

Nesebar A town, formerly Menebria, situated on the E coast of Bulgaria; a world heritage site. It has a wealth of ancient buildings and archaeological sites which testify to its 3000-year history as a Thracian settlement, a Greek colony, and a Byzantine city.

Nesselrode, Karl (Robert) Vasilyevich, Graf (Count) [neselrohduh] (1780–1862) Russian statesman, born in Lisbon, Portugal, the son of the Russian ambassador. He represented Russia at the Congress of Vienna (1814–15), and was one of the most active diplomats of the Holy Alliance. He became foreign minister (1822), and dominated Russian foreign policy for 30 years. His Balkan policy of trying to curb France's influence over the Ottoman empire contributed to the outbreak of the Crimean War (1854).

Ness, Loch Loch in Highland, N Scotland, UK; extending NE from Fort Augustus along the Great Glen to 9 km/6 mi SW of Inverness; 38 km/24 mi long; average width 2 km/1¼ mi; maximum depth 230 m/755 ft (near Castle Urquhart); part of the Caledonian Canal; drained by R Ness (N) to the Moray Firth; said to be inhabited by a 12–15 m/40–50 ft-long 'monster'; several unconfirmed sightings, but no clear results from scientific investigations; Loch Ness Monster Exhibition Centre at Drumnadrochit (W shore).

nest A domicile or home constructed, typically by birds, for the purpose of containing and protecting eggs and young; young birds before they leave the nest are known as *nestlings*. They may continue to be fed by their parents even after leaving the nest. Young birds that remain in the nest for a prolonged period after hatching are known as *nidicolous*; those that leave soon after hatching are known as *nidifugous*.

Nestor [nestaw(r)] A senior Greek leader in the Trojan War, the son of Neleus. In the *Iliad*, Homer portrays him as a long-winded sage, whose advice is often not taken. In the *Odyssey*, he is still living at Pylos, where a Mycenaean palace was discovered in the 1930s.

Nestorians Followers of Nestorius, Bishop of Constantinople (died c.451), who is alleged to have taught the doctrine, later declared heretical, of two persons (one human, one divine) as well as two natures in the incarnate Christ. They formed a separate Church which survived in parts of Persia.

Netanyahu, Benjamin [netanyahoo], nicknamed in Israel **Bibi** (1949–) Israeli politician and prime minister (1996–9), born in Tel Aviv, Israel. His family moved to the USA when he was a child, and he was educated at Harvard and MIT. He joined the Israeli embassy in Washington, became Israel's ambassador to the UN, and was elected to the Israeli parliament in 1988, becoming leader of the Likud Party in 1993. A hard-liner on security issues, he campaigned on a platform of peace with security, and defeated Shimon Peres by a narrow margin in the 1996 elections. He was succeeded in 1999 by Ehud Barak.

netball A women's seven-a-side court game, invented in the USA in 1891 and developed from basketball. The court is 100 ft (30·5 m) long and 50 ft (15·25 m) wide. The object is to score goals by throwing the ball through the opponent's net, which is attached to a circular hoop suspended on a post 10 ft (3·05 m) high. Players must not run with the ball.

Netherlands, Austrian and Spanish Ten provinces in the S of the Low Countries, predominantly Catholic, and united to Spain through Emperor Charles V, who inherited them from his grandfather Maximilian. They remained Spanish after the Dutch secession (1648), were ceded to the Austrian Habsburgs by the Treaty of Utrecht (1713), and achieved independence from Austria (1794) in the French Revolutionary Wars.

Netherlands Antilles *p.1076*

Netherlands East Indies The name applied to Indonesia until 1945, when Dr Sukarno declared independence: the area included the islands of Java, Sumatra, the Celebes, most of Borneo, the Molveens, and Bali. The Dutch recognized Indonesia's independence in 1948.

Netherlands, The *p.1077*

nettle *dead-nettle; stinging nettle*

nettle rash *urticaria*

network *local area network*

network topology A method of arranging the linking of computers which are to form a wide area or local area network. Standard topologies include bus, mesh, ring and star.

Neuchâtel [noeshatel], Ger **Neuenburg** 44°60N 6°56E, pop (2000e) 34 500. Capital town of Neuchâtel canton, W Switzerland, on W shore of L Neuchâtel, 40 km/25 mi W of Bern; railway; university (1909); research centre for the Swiss watch industry; scientific instruments, electronics, tobacco, wine trade; university church (13th-c), castle (mainly 16th-c).

Netherlands Antilles

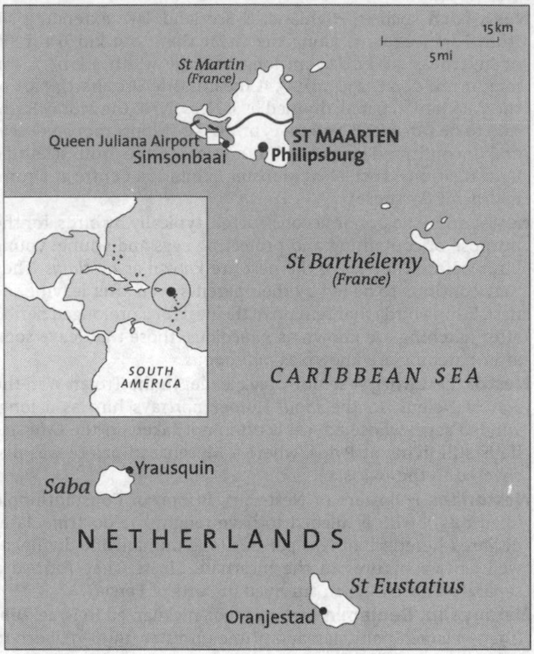

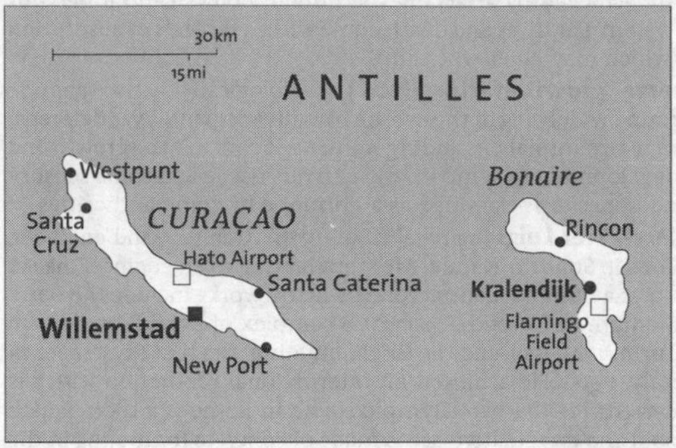

[antileez], Dutch **Nederlandse Antillen**

Local name Nederlandse Antillen

Timezone GMT −4

Area 993 km²/383 sq mi

Population total (2000e) 210 000

Status Self-governing region of The Netherlands

Capital Willemstad (on Curaçao Island)

Languages Dutch (official), Papiamento, English, and Spanish widely spoken

Ethnic groups Large majority of mixed European/Caribbean Indian descent

Religions Christian (mainly Roman Catholic)

Physical features Islands in the Caribbean Sea, comprising the Southern group (Leeward Is) of Curaçao and Bonaire, 60–110 km/37–68 mi N of the Venezuelan coast, and the Northern group (Windward Is) of St Maarten, St Eustatius, and Saba; terrain generally hilly, with volcanic interiors.

Climate Tropical maritime climate; average annual temperature 27·5°C; average annual rainfall varies from 500 mm/20 in (S) to 1000 mm/40 in (N); Northern group subject to hurricanes (Jul–Oct).

Currency 1 Netherland Antilles Guilder/Florin = 100 cents

Economy Based on refining of crude oil imported from Venezuela; aim of industrial diversification; ship repairing; tourism.

GDP (2002e) $2·4 bn, per capita $11 400

History Visited by Columbus, initially claimed for Spain; small-scale Spanish colonization in Curaçao, 1511; occupied by Dutch settlers, 17th-c; acquired full internal self-government within Kingdom of the Netherlands, 1954; Aruba separated from the other islands, 1986; Sovereign of The Netherlands is Head of State, represented by a Governor, a Council of Ministers and a unicameral legislature.

Head of State
(Dutch monarch represented by Governor-General)
1983–90 Rene Romer
1990–2002 Jaime Saleh
2002– Fritz Goedgedrag

Head of Government
1988–94 Maria Liberia Peters
1994–8 Suzie Rommer
1998–2002 Miguel Pourier
2002–3 Etienne Ys
2003 Ben Komproe *Acting*
2003– Mirna Louise-Godett

Neuchâtel, Lake [noeshatel] (Fr **Lac de**) area 218 sq km/84 sq mi. Largest lake to lie wholly within Switzerland, running SW–NE at the foot of the Jura Mts, W Switzerland; major wine-growing area; boat services link lakeside towns; chief towns on the shore include Neuchâtel (NW) and Yverdon (S).

Neue Künstlervereinigung [noyer kunstlerfriynigung] (Ger 'new association of artists') A group of modern 'fauvist' artists founded in Munich in 1909. Leading members included Vasily Kandinsky, Alexey von Jawlensky, and Gabriele Münter (1877–1962).

Neue Sachlichkeit [noyer sakhlikhkiyt] (Ger 'new objectivity') A movement in German art c.1920, a reaction against the abstract and expressionist tendencies of modern art and a return to 'true objectivity', ie a kind of literal and deliberately seamy realism. The chief exponents of this short-lived style were Georg Grosz (1852–1944), and Otto Dix (1898–1969).

Neumann, (Johann) Balthasar [noyman] (1687–1753) Architect, born in Cheb, W Czech Republic (formerly Eger, Bohemia). He was at first a military engineer in the service of the Archbishop of Würzburg, but after visiting Paris and absorbing new ideas, he became professor of architecture at Würzburg. Many outstanding examples of the Baroque style were designed by him, notably the Würzburg Palace, Schloss Bruchsal, and the pilgrimage church of Vierzehnheiligen.

Neumann, John Von [noyman] *Von Neumann, John*

neuralgia [nyooraljia] Pain arising from a sensory nerve, and felt over the surface of the body supplied by the affected nerve. In the most common type, **trigeminal neuralgia**, pain, usually severe and paroxysmal, is felt over the forehead, face, or jaw supplied by one or more of the branches of the trigeminal (Vth cranial) nerve. The cause is unknown but it may be triggered by speech, eating, or other facial movements. Other forms include **post-herpetic neuralgia**, which may follow herpes zoster infection (shingles), and **brachial neuralgia**, affecting the nerves of the upper arm (the brachial plexus), and resulting in aching and pain over the shoulders and down the arms. It often arises from abnormal pressure on the spinal nerves in the neck.

neural network An arrangement of computers linked together in a way which attempts to mimic the activity of the brain. The individual computers undertake specific tasks and relate the outcome of those tasks to other computers in the network.

neurasthenia [nyoorastheenia] A neurosis which takes the form of complaints of excessive fatigue and tiredness. No physical cause of the condition has been found.

Netherlands, The

or **Holland**, Dutch **Nederland**, official name **Kingdom of the Netherlands**, Dutch **Koninkrijk der Nederlanden**

Local name Nederland

Timezone GMT +1

Area 33 929 km^2/13 097 sq mi

Population total (2002e) 16 142 000

Status Kingdom

Date of independence 1830

Capital Amsterdam

Language Dutch (official)

Ethnic groups Dutch (Germanic/Gallo-Celtic descent) (99%), Indonesian/Surinamese (1%)

Religions Roman Catholic (38%), Protestant (Dutch Reformed Church and other Protestant churches) (30%)

Physical features Generally low and flat, except SE where hills rise to 321 m/1053 ft; much of coastal area below sea-level, reaching lowest point -6·7 m/-19·7 ft N of Rotterdam; protected by coastal dunes and artificial dykes; highest point, Vaalserberg, in SE; 27% of land area is below sea level, an area inhabited by c.60% of population.

Climate Cool, temperate maritime climate, with continental influences. Average annual temperatures 1·7°C (Jan), 17°C (Jul); average annual rainfall exceeds 700 mm/27 in, evenly distributed throughout the year.

Currency 1 euro = 100 cents (previous to February 2002, 1 Guilder (Gld)/ Florin (f) = 100 cents).

Economy Rotterdam and newly-constructed Europort are the major European ports of transshipment, handling goods for EC member countries; Amsterdam is a world diamond centre; world's largest exporter of dairy produce; highly intensive agriculture; horticulture; engineering, chemicals, oil products, natural gas, high technology and electrical goods; fishing; tourism.

GDP (2002e) $437·8 bn, per capita $27 200

Human Development Index (2002) 0·935

History Part of Roman Empire to 4th-c AD; part of Frankish Empire by 8th-c; incorporated into the Holy Roman Empire; lands passed to Philip II, who succeeded to Spain and the Netherlands, 1555; attempts to stamp out Protestantism led to rebellion, 1572; seven N provinces united against Spain, 1579; United Provinces independence, 1581; overrun by the French, 1795–1813, who established the Batavian Republic; united with Belgium as the Kingdom of the United Netherlands until 1830, when Belgium withdrew; neutral in World War 1; occupied by Germany, World War 2, with strong Dutch resistance; joined with Belgium and Luxembourg to form the Benelux economic union, 1948; conflict over independence of Dutch colonies in SE Asia in late 1940s, joined NATO, 1949; independence granted to former colonies, Indonesia, 1949, with the addition of W New Guinea, 1963, and Suriname, 1975; a parliamentary democracy under a constitutional monarchy; government led by a Prime Minister; States General (Staten-Generaal) consists of a 75-member First Chamber, and a 150-member Second Chamber; resignation of entire cabinet, 2002, following critical report on Dutch peace-keeping role in Bosnia in 1995.

Head of State (Monarch)
1890–1948 Wilhelmina
1948–80 Juliana
1980– Beatrix

Head of Government
1939–40 Dirk J de Geer
1940–5 Pieter S Gerbrandy (in exile)
1945–6 Willem Schemerhorn/ Willem Drees
1946–8 Louis J M Beel
1948–51 Willem Drees/Josephus R H van Schaik
1951–8 Willem Drees
1958–9 Louis J M Beel
1959–63 Jan E de Quay
1963–5 Victor G M Marijnen
1965–6 Joseph M L T Cals
1966–7 Jelle Zijlstra
1967–71 Petrus J S de Jong
1971–3 Barend W Biesheuvel
1973–7 Joop M den Uyl
1977–82 Andreas A M van Agt
1982–94 Rudd Lubbers
1994–2002 Wim Kok
2002– Jan-Peter Balkenende

Neurath, Otto [noyraht] (1882–1945) Philosopher and social theorist, born in Vienna, Austria. A member of the influential 'Vienna Circle', he was particularly associated with 'physicalism', which aimed to establish an entirely materialist foundation of knowledge. His best philosophical work was published in the group's journal *Erkenntnis*, but he also wrote books on sociology, education, and social policy, including *International Picture Language* (1936) and *Modern Man in the Making* (1939). Active in public affairs as an independent Marxist, he was an energetic organizer, and was involved with such diverse bodies as the Carnegie Endowment for International Peace (1911–13), and the International Unity of Science movement (1934–40).

neuritis *neuropathy*

neuroanatomy *anatomy*

neurohormone A chemical messenger secreted by nerve cells and carried by the blood to the target cells, where its effects are mediated. For example, two neurohormones secreted by the neurohypophysis (a collection of nerve terminals) of the pituitary gland are *antidiuretic hormone* and *oxytocin*, which promote water re-absorption by kidneys and milk ejection from breasts, respectively.

neurolinguistic programming (NLP) A system of training which aims to develop the ability to communicate, to achieve rapid learning, to improve behaviour patterns, and to change destructive habits in oneself and others. The system is based on the work of three psychotherapists (Milton Erickson, Fritz Perls, Virginia Satir), who studied how outstanding individuals managed to achieve their excellence, and developed a theory about the way the brain organizes and stores information. The technique can be intergrated with other forms of treatment.

neurolinguistics The study of the neurological basis of language use: in particular, how the brain controls the processes of speech and comprehension. Important data comes from the study of clinical linguistic conditions (eg aphasia, stuttering) and everyday 'errors', such as hesitations and slips of the tongue, which throw light on the way in which the basic speech system can break down.

neurology The branch of medicine which deals with the study of the central nervous system (the brain and spinal cord) and its peripheral nerves, in health (*neurophysiology*) and disease (*neuropathology*).

neurone / neuron [nyoorohn, -ron] The functional unit of the nervous systems of animals; also known as a **nerve cell**. Neurones process and transmit information to target tissues (other neurones, muscles, glands), usually through the mediation of chemicals (*neurotransmitters*). Vertebrate neurones typically consist of a cell body (with a well-developed nucleus surrounded by a mass of cytoplasm), an *axon* (with terminal branches specialized to carry information from the cell body across connections to target tissues), and *dendrites* (projecting from the cell body and receiving information from axon terminals of other neurones for integration by the neurone). Most invertebrate neurones lack dendrites.

neuropathology The study of the disease processes which affect the nervous system. These include haemorrhage in various parts of the brain; infections and tumours of the brain and its enveloping membranes; degenerative disorders such as prion disease, Parkinsonism and dementia; metabolic disorders; neuropathies; and demyelinating disorders such as multiple sclerosis.

neuropathy [nyooropathee] A term which covers all pathological processes that affect peripheral somatic and autonomic nerves. Many disorders affect peripheral somatic nerves and induce similar clinical features. These consist of the sensation of pins and needles (*paraesthesiae*), loss of sensation, and muscle weakness. Very often the most distal part of the nerve in the extremities (hands and feet) is affected first or most severely. Causes include ischaemia (eg diabetes and polyarteritis), vitamin deficiencies (B and B_{12}), alcoholism and other poisons, inflammation of the nerves (*neuritis*), infections such as leprosy, and some viruses. When there is widespread involvement of many nerve fibres, the condition is known as **polyneuropathy**.

neurophysiology The study of the functions of the nervous systems of animals. Neurophysiologists use a variety of methods to elucidate aspects of nervous function. Common techniques are ablation (the removal or destruction of nervous tissue); the electrical stimulation of, or recording from, single nerve cells (eg squid axons, retinal photoreceptors) and groups of nerve cells (eg the basal ganglia and motor cortex areas of mammalian brains), using electrodes; and techniques borrowed from other disciplines (eg computer-assisted tomography, histofluorescence techniques, autoradiography).

neuropsychology The study of psychological phenomena in the light of what is known about brain organization and function. Neuropsychologists are often concerned with patients suffering from brain damage. The aim of their work is to identify these patients' disabilities, discover methods of rehabilitation, and use this information to make inferences about the functioning of the normal mind and brain.

Neuroptera [nyooroptera] An order of primitive winged insects, including the snakeflies, lacewings, and antlions; typically two pairs of similar wings with lace-like veins; mouthparts of a simple, biting type; adults and larvae typically feed on sap-sucking insects.

neurosis A mental illness often associated with high levels of anxiety, and fears which the sufferer understands are irrational, and representing exaggerated and/or unconscious ways of dealing with conflicts. The symptoms are distressing to the individual and considered to be unacceptable. The condition is enduring, and throughout reality remains intact. Examples include hypochondriasis, obsessive-compulsive disorders, and phobic disorders.

neurotoxins Naturally occurring or synthetic substances which specifically or predominantly affect the nervous system. Examples are aconitum (from aconite), an early poison used by ancient warriors on darts and spears, chickpeas (resulting in lathyrism), synthetic organophosphorous compounds (eg nerve gas), and toxins of bacterial origin such as tetanus toxin and the toxin of *Clostridium botulinum*, one of the most powerful poisons known.

neurotransmitter A chemical substance (eg acetylcholine, noradrenaline) released as a messenger from nerves. It enables the transmission of a nervous impulse across the narrow gap (*synapse*) between a nerve ending and a muscle, gland, or another nerve. Its rapid breakdown by enzymes or its re-uptake by the nerve terminates its effect.

neutrality In foreign policy, a situation where a state will not provide military and sometimes diplomatic support to another state. When the term refers simply to a state's policy, it is synonymous with *neutralism*, but it also has a more precise legal meaning. Under international laws of neutrality, a non-belligerent enjoys certain rights and obligations in times of war. It may not permit the use of its territory as a base for military operations nor furnish military assistance to the belligerents. A neutralized state enjoys the right of passage on the open seas for its non-military goods. It may, however, show sympathy with one belligerent as long as this is not reflected in its actions. A member of an alliance may remain neutral in a conflict between another member of the alliance and a third state, if the alliance is not established for the purposes of conflict with that third state (eg members of NATO during the UK's conflict with Argentina over the Falkland Is).

neutralization In acid–base reactions, the mixing of chemically equivalent amounts of acid and base to give a solution near pH 7. Weak, non-toxic acids and bases are often used to neutralize spills, since excess will not cause the inverse problem to that being treated.

neutrino A fundamental particle; symbol ν; mass not known exactly, but small, possibly zero; charge 0; spin $\frac{1}{2}$, with spin direction always opposing the direction of motion; senses only gravitational and weak nuclear forces; produced in weak radioactive decays; very unreactive and difficult to detect. Three species of neutrino are known, corresponding to the electron, muon, and tau. Neutrinos were predicted by Wolfgang Pauli in 1930, and first observed in 1956 in nuclear reactor experiments. Results from the giant underground Super Kamiokaude detector, Japan, reported in 1998, indicate the existence of neutrino oscillations, in which the different species of neutrino evolve one into another. Neutrino oscillations imply that neutrinos have mass. Neutrinos having mass are a candidate for dark matter.

neutrino astronomy A term applied to attempts to detect neutrinos from the Sun, to discover the conditions existing in the solar core, and also from supernovae. Experiments conducted since the 1960s have shown a detected rate of solar neutrinos rather less than predicted by theories of nucleosynthesis.

neutron A component particle of the atomic nucleus; symbol *n*; mass $1{\cdot}675 \times 10^{-27}$ kg (939·6 MeV), charge 0, spin $\frac{1}{2}$; held in the nucleus by strong nuclear force; discovered by James Chadwick in 1932. Free neutrons decay to protons, electrons, and antineutrinos, with a half-life of 10·1 minutes.

neutron bomb More precisely an **enhanced radiation (ER) weapon**, a nuclear munition small enough to be used on the battlefield, fired as an artillery shell or short-range missile warhead, which on detonation produces radiation effects rather than blast and heat. The destructive effect is therefore aimed against living things (such as the crews of tanks inside their machines, which the gamma radiation released on detonation can penetrate) rather than vehicles and buildings.

neutron diffraction An interference effect using neutrons scattered, for example from different layers of atoms in a solid, to give distinctive intensity patterns which can be used to determine the solid's structure. Because neutrons have no electric charge they are very penetrating, and their magnetic moment makes them useful for determining the magnetic aspects of materials, such as high-temperature superconducting compounds. They also interact via the strong interaction with atomic nuclei in the sample, so are sensitive to isotopes in the sample. Some experimental neutron sources rely on nuclear reactors to provide continuous neutron beams; others use particle beams to create a pulsed neutron source. Neutron scattering is used to study many systems including plastics, ceramics, liquid crystal, proteins, and biological materials.

neutron star A star that has collapsed so far under gravity that it consists almost entirely of neutrons. Once the nuclear fuel in a star is exhausted, it cools and contracts. Stars of more than 1·5 solar masses shrink until pressure between the neutrons balances the inward pull of gravity. They are only 10 km/6 mi across, and have a density of 10^{17} kg/m^3 at this stage. Formed in supernova explosions, they are observed as pulsars.

Nevada [**nev**ah**da**] pop (2000e) 1 998 300; area 286 341 sq km/110 561 sq mi. State in W USA, divided into 16 counties; the 'Sage Brush State', 'Battle Born State', or 'Silver State'; part ceded by Mexico to the USA in the Treaty of Guadalupe Hidalgo, 1848; included in Mormon-ruled Utah Territory, 1850; settlement expanded after the Comstock Lode silver strike, 1859; a separate territory, 1861; joined the Union as the 36th state, 1864; capital, Carson City; other chief cities, Las Vegas and Reno; rivers include the Colorado (part of the Arizona border) and Humboldt; L Pyramid and L Winnemucca in the W; L Tahoe on the Californian border; highest point, Boundary Peak (4006 m/13 143 ft); mainly within the Great Basin, a large arid desert interspersed with barren mountain ranges; an area of internal drainage, with most of the rivers petering out in the desert or ending in alkali sinks; in the rain shadow of the Sierra Nevada Mts of California; the driest of all the states; mostly unpopulated and uncultivated, with a few oases of irrigation; Hoover Dam creates L Mead; federal government owns 85% of Nevada's land; mining (mercury, barite, silver, and several other minerals); a major gold supplier; oil discovered 1954; agriculture not highly developed; cattle, sheep, dairy products, hay, alfalfa; food processing, clay and glass products, chemicals, copper smelting, electrical machinery, high technology industries, lumber; tourism, notably the shores of L Tahoe, Death Valley National Monument (partly in Nevada), and the gambling resorts of Las Vegas and Reno (which attract around 20 million visitors each year; gaming taxes a primary source of state revenue); liberal divorce laws an attraction to many from outside the state; very rapid population growth (50% increase between 1980 and 1990).

Nevado (mountain) *Ampato / Illampu / Ruiz / Salcantay, Nevado (de/del)*

Never Never Land Area of Northern Territory, Australia, SE of Darwin; chief town, Katherine; first explored by Leichardt in 1844; featured in Mrs Aeneas Gunn's book, *We of the Never Never*.

nevus *birthmark*

New Age A period of time recognized as our Solar System passes through one sign of the Zodiac to the next. It takes c.2000 years to travel through each star sign, each of which constitutes an 'age'. The Piscean age (represented by water) started with the beginning of the Roman Empire, and we entered the new age of Aquarius (an air sign) in 1997. It is said that the dawning of a new age will bring teachers who will guide humanity in the right direction, and the coming of a new age is predicted in many religious texts. The increasing interest in Eastern cultures, techniques of meditation, and methods for increasing consciousness and spirituality, as well as disenchantment with the materialistic way in which Western culture has developed, are cited as signs of the imminent arrival of a new age in which the human race will accept responsibility for the world that it has created, and will make conscious efforts to undo the damage being done to our own planet and to live in harmony with each other and with the rest of the universe. In the early 1990s, various groups of people united chiefly by their unattached lifestyle came to be called 'new age travellers' by the UK media.

New Amsterdam *New York City*

Newark (UK) [**nyoo**ah(r)k], properly **Newark-on-Trent** 53°05N 0°49W, pop (2000e) 33 400. Town in Nottinghamshire, C England, UK; at junction of a branch of the Trent and Devon Rivers, 25 km/15 mi SW of Lincoln; railway; foodstuffs, brewing, engineering, agricultural machinery, gypsum, limestone; Newark Castle place of King John's death; repeatedly under siege in Civil War.

Newark (USA) [**nyoo**erk], locally [**noo**erk] 40°44N 74°10W, pop (2000e) 273 500. Seat of Essex Co, NE New Jersey, USA; port on the Passaic R and Newark Bay; largest city in the state (but a 16% decline in population between 1980 and 1990); an important road, rail, and air centre; settled by Puritans from Connecticut, 1666; city status, 1836; scene of race riots, 1967; airport; railway; university (1934); chemicals, electrical equipment; insurance and financial centre; linked to New York City by underground rail; Trinity Cathedral, Newark Museum.

Newbery, John (1713–67) Publisher and bookseller, born in Berkshire, S England, UK. He settled in London in c.1744 as a seller of books and patent medicines. He was the first to publish books specifically for children, and was part-author of some of the best of them, notably *Goody Two-Shoes*. In 1758 he started the *Universal Chronicle*, or *Weekly Gazette*, in which the 'Idler' appeared. In the *Public Ledger* (1760) appeared Goldsmith's 'Citizen of the World'. Since 1922 the Newbery Medal has been awarded annually for the best American children's book.

New Britain, formerly **Neu-Pommern** pop (2000e) 318 000; area 37 800 sq km/14 600 sq mi. Largest island of the Bismarck Archipelago, Papua New Guinea; separated from New Ireland by St George's Channel; Solomon Sea (S) and Bismarck Sea (N); length, 480 km/298 mi; width, 80 km/50 mi; capital, Rabaul; oil palm, copra, cocoa, coconuts, timber, copper, gold, iron, coal.

New Brunswick pop (2000e) 810 200; area 73 440 sq km/28 355 sq mi. Province in E Canada, boundaries include the USA (W), Gulf of St Lawrence (E), and Bay of Fundy (S); forested, rocky land, generally low-lying, rising in the NW; several rivers and lakes, especially Grand Lake (area 174 sq km/67 sq mi); capital, Fredericton; major towns include Saint John and Moncton; paper and wood products, potatoes, seafood, mining (zinc, lead, silver, potash, bismuth), tourism, food processing, dairy products, livestock, poultry; aboriginal population includes Micmac, Abenaki, Malecite; first settled by French fur traders and farmers; 'Acadia' ceded to Britain by the Treaty of Utrecht (1713); many United Empire Loyalist immigrants, and separation from Nova Scotia, 1783; joined confederation, 1867, governed by a lieutenant-governor and an elected 58-member Legislative Assembly.

Newbury 51°25N 1°20W, pop (2001e) 34 800. Town in W Berkshire, S England, UK; on R Kennet, 27 km/17 mi SW of Reading; birthplace of Francis Baily and Sir Alastair Pilkington; two English Civil War battles fought here (1643, 1644); racecourse; Greenham Common nearby; controversial by-pass opened, 1998; Vodaphone headquarters, engineering, furniture, paper, cardboard, electronics, pharmaceuticals.

New Caledonia, Fr **Nouvelle Calédonie** pop (2000e) 200 500; area 18 575 sq km/7170 sq mi. Territory in the SW Pacific Ocean, 1100 km/680 mi E of Australia, comprising New Caledonia, Loyalty Is, Isle des Pins, Isle Bélep, and the uninhabited Chesterfield and Huon Is; capital, Nouméa; timezone GMT +11; chief ethnic groups, Melanesians (43%), Europeans (37%); official language, French, with English widely spoken; chief religion, Roman Catholicism; unit of currency, the French Pacific franc; long, narrow main island, 400 km/250 mi in length; rises to 1639 m/5377 ft at Mt Panie; C mountain chain; dry W coast covered mostly by gum-tree savannah; tropical E coast; mild Mediterranean-type climate; average temperatures 19·9°C (Jul), 25·8°C (Jan); warm and humid; visited by Captain Cook, 1774; annexed by France as a penal settlement, 1853; French Overseas Territory, 1946; governed by a high commissioner and four Regional Councils, members of which serve on the national 46-member Territorial Council; serious disturbances in the mid-1980s when indigenous Melanesians began their struggle for independence; decision to stay part of France, after referendum of voters, 1987; agreement (Noumea Accord, 1998) provides for referendum on independence within 15–20 years, and gradual transfer of powers; beef, pork, poultry, coffee, maize, fruit, vegetables; copra, nickel (world's third largest producer), chrome, iron; chlorine and oxygen plants, cement, soft drinks, clothing, foodstuffs, tourism.

Newcastle (Australia) **[nyookahsl]** 32°55S 151°46E, pop (2000e) 472 300. City and major port in New South Wales, Australia; on the E coast, situated at the mouth of the Hunter R, 160 km/100 mi N of Sydney; founded as a penal settlement, 1804; scene of Australia's biggest earthquake (1989); the lower Hunter region contains the wine growing and resort area of Pokolbin; airfield; railway; university (1965); City Art Gallery has collections by Sir William Dobell; coal mining, iron and steel, shipbuilding, railway engineering, chemicals, fertilizers, textiles; trade in coal, grain, wool, dairy produce.

Newcastle (UK) **[nyookahsl]**, locally **[nyookasl]**, in full **Newcastle upon Tyne**, Lat **Pons Aelii** 54°59N 1°35W, pop (2001e) 259 600. Administrative centre of Tyne and Wear, NE England, UK; part of Tyneside urban area; 440 km/273 mi N of London, on R Tyne, crossed by eight bridges; cultural, commercial, and administrative centre for the NE of England; site of a Roman bridge and fort; by legend an Anglo-Saxon monastic centre and town ('Monkchester'); Norman castle founded 11th-c, rebuilt 12th-c, for defence against the Scots; city status, 1882; university (1963); University of Northumbria (1992, formerly Newcastle-upon-Tyne Polytechnic); railway; underground; ferries to N Europe; heavy engineering, aircraft, chemicals, pharmaceuticals, coal trade; Stephenson's iron works established here (1820s); Roman remains, mediaeval walls, 12th-c castle keep, 15th-c Cathedral of St Nicholas, Roman Catholic Cathedral (1844), art gallery, museums, Guildhall (1658); football league team, Newcastle United (Magpies).

Newcastle, Duke of *Cavendish, William; Pelham, Thomas*

Newcastle disease *fowl pest*

Newcastle-under-Lyme 53°00N 2°14W, pop (2001e) 122 000. Town in Staffordshire, C England, UK; 3 km/1¾ mi W of Stoke-on-Trent; railway; high-technology industries, brick and tile manufacturing.

New Comedy Athenian comic theatre of the late 4th-c and early 3rd-c BC, exemplified in the work of Menander and the Roman imitations by Plautus and Terence. There is a regular division into five acts, and the dramatic chorus, once the representative of forces larger than life, had either completely disappeared or become a band of musicians and dancers who provide light entertainment.

Newcomen, Thomas [nyookuhmen] (1663–1729) Inventor, born in Dartmouth, Devon, SW England, UK. A blacksmith by trade, he developed a piston engine using steam at atmospheric pressure and the vacuum created when the steam was condensed to pump water from mines. In 1698 he began working with Thomas Savery, who had just patented a high pressure steam engine. Together they constructed practical working engines that were widely used in collieries.

New Criticism A critical theory and method which concentrates on the text itself, the 'words on the page', to the exclusion of extrinsic information. It was developed by such critics as Cleanth Brooks (1906–94) and John Crowe Ransom (1888–1974) in the USA in the 1930s and 1940s, under the influence of Symbolist and Russian Formalist ideas; and in its turn provided a theoretical basis for the technique of *practical criticism*.

New Deal The administration and policies of US President Roosevelt, who pledged a 'new deal' for the country during the campaign of 1932. He embarked on active state economic involvement to combat the Great Depression, setting the tone in a hectic 'first hundred days'. Although some early legislation was invalidated by the Supreme Court, the New Deal left a lasting impact on US government, economy, and society, not least by the effective creation of the modern institution of the presidency. Major specific initiatives included the National Industrial Recovery Act (1933), the Tennessee Valley Authority (1933), the Agricultural Adjustment Act (1933), the National Youth Administration (1935), the National Labor Relations Act (1935), and the Social Security Act (1935). Historians often distinguish the **first New Deal** (1933–4), concerned primarily with restarting and stabilizing the economy, from the **second New Deal** (1935–9), aimed at social reform. From 1940 onwards Roosevelt was primarily concerned with foreign affairs.

New Delhi *Delhi*

New Democratic Party (NDP) A Canadian political party which succeeded the Co-operative Commonwealth Federation as Canada's social democratic political party in 1961. Formally supported by the Canadian Labour Congress, the NDP has formed provincial governments in Saskatchewan, Manitoba, British Columbia, and Ontario, though it has never risen above third party status nationally.

New England A region of NE USA, comprising the states of Maine, New Hampshire, Massachusetts, Vermont, Rhode Island, and Connecticut. The main area of English settlement in the 17th-c, several of the colonies initially formed themselves into a New England Confederation. A century later, the region was the centre of the independence movement in the years before the American Revolution, and at other times has been a leader in educational and intellectual movements.

New England Confederation (1643–84) An agreement of the American colonies of Massachusetts, Plymouth, Connecticut, and New Haven to establish a common government for the purposes of war and Indian relations. The Confederation declined in importance after 1664.

New English Art Club A British society founded in 1886 by a group of artists whose 'progressive work', largely inspired by recent French painting, was being rejected by the Royal Academy. Leading members have included George Clauser (1852–1944), Wilson Steer (1860–1942), John Singer Sargent (1856–1925), John Lavery (1856–1941), and Walter Richard Sickert (1860–1942).

New English Bible An English translation of the Bible from the original languages undertaken by an interdenominational committee of scholars under the auspices of the University Presses of Cambridge and Oxford since 1948. The first edition of the New Testament was completed in 1961, and the first complete Bible was produced in 1970. The goal was to present the text in good English literary idiom rather than in 'Biblical English', and to reflect the results of recent Biblical scholarship. It was substantially revised in 1989 under the title of the **Revised English Bible**.

New Forest An area of heath, woodland, and marsh covering c.37 300 ha/92 200 acres of S Hampshire, England; a popular tourist area. William the Conqueror appropriated the area for his new 'forest' (royal hunting land) in 1079. Known for its ponies, it is now administered by 10 Verderers, the head Verderer being appointed by the Crown.

New Forest pony A breed of horse, developed naturally in the New Forest, Hampshire, England, from many breeds roaming the area; classed as two types: **Type A** (height, 12–13·2 hands/1·2–1·4 m/4 ft–4 ft 6 in) and the more solid **Type B** (height, 13·2–14·2 hands/1·4–1·5 m/4 ft 6 in–4 ft 10 in).

Newfoundland (Canada) **[nyoofnland]** pop (2000e) 636 200; area 405 720 sq km/156 648 sq mi. Island in E Canada, part of the province of Newfoundland and Labrador, separated from Labrador by the Strait of Belle Isle; a roughly triangular island, rising to 814 m/2671 ft (W); mainly a rolling plateau with low hills; a deeply indented coastline; several peninsulas, lakes, and rivers; Gros Morne National Park on W coast (area 1942 sq km/750 sq mi, established 1970); capital, St John's; food processing, pulp and paper, mining (iron ore), fishing, oil, hydroelectric power, dairy products, poultry; aboriginal population included Micmac (S) and Beothuk (extinct c.1829); Vikings visited Labrador AD c.1000; coastline explored by Cabot, 1497; British sovereignty declared, 1583 (Britain's first colony); self-governing colony, 1855; placed under a Commission of Government appointed by Britain, 1934; voted to unite with Canada, 1949; Newfoundland the name of the whole province, changed to Newfoundland and Labrador, 1965; governed by a lieutenant-governor and an elected 52-member House of Assembly.

Newfoundland (zoology) **[nyoofnland]** A breed of dog, developed in Newfoundland; large, very thick-set, with an enormous heavy head; broad deep muzzle and small ears and eyes; very thick, black, double-layered, water-resistant coat; webbed feet.

Newfoundland and Labrador (Canada) *Labrador; Newfoundland*

New France North American colonies claimed by France from the 16th-c, including Canada, Acadia, and Louisiana. Their economy was based largely on the fur trade, subsistence agriculture, and fisheries. The population totalled 70 000 at its peak. Canada and Acadia were lost to the British incrementally up to 1763; Louisiana was sold to the USA in 1803.

New Frontier The administration and policies of US President Kennedy (1961–3). It was characterized by a high international profile and a liberal domestic stance.

Newgate From the 13th-c to 1902, the main prison of the City of London, whence many convicted criminals were taken to Tyburn for hanging. It became a generic description for a prison. In the 16th-c several Roman Catholic martyrs, as well as the Protestant martyr, Anne Askew (1521–46), were imprisoned there before being burnt at the stake at Smithfield. It was finally demolished in 1902 to make way for the Central Criminal Court.

New General Catalogue (NGC) An astronomical catalogue published in 1888 by J L E Dreyer, Armagh Observatory, Northern Ireland, listing 7840 nebulae, galaxies, and clusters. The numbering system is still regularly used by professional astronomers.

New Granada, Span **Nueva Granada** The official name in the Spanish-American Empire for the area now covered by the Republic of Colombia. It was also the name (1739–1810) of a Spanish viceroyalty embracing Venezuela and Quito in addition to New Granada.

New Grange A megalithic passage grave of c.3200 BC in the Boyne R valley, Ireland, 40 km/25 mi N of Dublin. The 19 m/60 ft slab-roofed passage gives onto a cross-shaped burial chamber with a 6 m/20 ft-high corbelled vault, the earthen mound above being c.80–85 m/260–280 ft in diameter and c.11 m/36 ft high, retained by a kerb and sheathed with white quartz pebbles. At the winter solstice, the Sun could shine through a slot above the entrance to illuminate the burial chamber. The pecked abstract ornament of the kerb, passage, and chamber is among Europe's finest prehistoric art.

New Guard In Australian history, an extreme right-wing organization formed in New South Wales in 1932 by Eric Campbell, which claimed 100 000 members by 1933. Its principal achievement was the disruption of the official opening of Sydney Harbour Bridge (1932). In some respects a fascist organization, the Guard was defunct by 1935.

New Hampshire pop (2000e) 1 235 800, area 24 032 sq km/9279 sq mi. State in NE USA, divided into 10 counties; bounded N by Canada; the 'Granite State'; explored by Champlain and Pring, 1603–5; first settlement at Little Harbor, 1623; ninth of the original 13 states to ratify the Federal Constitution, 1788; capital, Concord; other chief cities, Manchester, Nashua, Portsmouth; Connecticut R forms the W border; Merrimack R flows S through the C into Massachusetts; forested mountains in the N (White Mts), highest point Mt Washington (1917 m/6289 ft); the S largely devoted to arable farming and grazing; chief agricultural products dairy and greenhouse products, maple syrup, hay, apples, eggs; diverse manufacturing industries, tourism, forestry.

New Haven, formerly **Quinnipiac** (to 1640) 41°18N 72°55W, pop (2000e) 123 600. Port town in New Haven County, S Connecticut, USA; on Long Island Sound; founded by Puritans, 1638; joint capital of state with Hartford, 1701–1875; railway; Yale University (1701); diverse industrial development; inventions developed here include vulcanized rubber (Charles Goodyear) and the repeating revolver (Samuel Colt); firearms, aircraft parts, hardware.

New Hebrides *Vanuatu*

New Ireland, formerly **Neu-Mecklenburg** pop (2000e) 107 000; area 8647 sq km/3338 sq mi. Second largest island in the Bismarck Archipelago, Papua New Guinea, separated from New Britain (SW) by St George's Channel; length, 480 km/298 mi; average width, 24 km/15 mi; capital, Kavieng; tuna fishing, copra.

New Jersey pop (2000e) 8 414 300, area 20 168 sq km/7787 sq mi. State in E USA, divided into 21 counties; the 'Garden State'; one of the original states of the Union, third to ratify the Federal Constitution, 1787; colonized after the explorations of Verrazano (1524) and Hudson (1609); capital, Trenton; other chief cities, Newark, Jersey City, Paterson, Elizabeth; many of the state's communities are satellites of New York City; Hudson R follows the NE border, and the Delaware R the W border; Appalachian Highlands fall down through Piedmont Plateau to low coastal plains, broken by ridges of the Palisades; highest peak Mt High Point (550 m/1804 ft); 40% of the land forested, mostly in the SE; NE highly industrialized and densely populated; the rest mainly arable and grazing, producing dairy products, hay, soybeans; a major industrial and commercial area; chemicals, pharmaceuticals, electronics, metals, machinery, textiles, processed foods; many tourist centres; casino gambling at Atlantic City.

New Jerusalem, Church of the A religious sect based on the teachings of the Swedish scientist and seer, Emanuel Swedenborg, who believed he had direct contact with the spiritual world through visionary experiences. There he saw that a first dispensation of the Christian Church had ended and a new one was beginning, the 'New Jerusalem'. His first church was organized in London in 1783.

New Labour A movement in the UK Labour Party which accepts a policy of combining traditional socialist values with a concern to respond to the new ideals and aspirations of the individual. The term had previously been used in New Zealand in 1989, when the left wing of the Labour Party there split off from the main body. In Britain, it is associated with the approach of Tony Blair, especially in his concern to develop a 'stakeholder economy', where each member of society has an interest in the state's economic progress. It involved a rethinking of several traditional principles, such as the rewriting of Clause Four of the Labour Party constitution, which had affirmed the commitment to common ownership of industry and services. Those who do not share these views are sometimes referred to as 'Old Labour'.

New Left A Neo-Marxist movement which espoused a more libertarian form of socialism compared to orthodox Marxism. In part, it was inspired by the earlier writings of Marx, which were essentially humanistic, and the ideas of Italian politician Antonio Gramsci regarding the importance of ideological hegemony. It also drew on dialectical sociology, Trotskyism, anarchism, and radical forms of existentialism. It is, however, difficult to pinpoint any central ideas specific to the New Left. The movement had some influence in the 1960s, particularly in student politics and in opposition to the Vietnam War, but it never became an effectively organized political force. Its importance declined, and it gave way in part to the New Right.

newly industrialized countries The formerly less developed countries which have built up considerable industrial production and exports over recent decades. This group includes the four 'Asian Tigers', Hong Kong, Singapore, South Korea, and Taiwan, and also countries such as China, India, Malaysia, and Thailand in Asia, and Brazil and Mexico in Latin America. Newly industrialized countries account for an increasing proportion of world trade, including intra-industry trade and trade in high-tech products, and provide formidable competition for the longer established OECD industrial countries.

Newman, John Henry, Cardinal (1801–90) Theologian, born in London, UK, into a Calvinist family. He studied at Oxford, became a fellow of Oriel College, and was ordained in 1824. He was a vigorous member of the Oxford Movement, composing a number of its tracts, notably Tract 90, which argued that the intention of the Thirty-nine Articles was Catholic in spirit. This led to the end of the Movement, and his own conversion to Catholicism (1845). He went to Rome, and joined the Oratorians, returning to set up his own community in Birmingham. He published several essays, lectures, and sermons, as well as a spiritual autobiography, *Apologia pro vita sua* (1864, Apology for His Life). A moderate in the controversies of the Vatican Council, he was made a cardinal in 1879.

Newman, Nanette (1939–) British actress and writer. She trained at the Italia Conti Stage School and the Royal Academy of Dramatic Art, London, and appeared as a child in several films for the Children's Film Foundation. In 1959 she married Bryan Forbes, and has appeared in a number of his films, including *The L-Shaped Room* (1962), *The Raging Moon* (1971), and *The Stepford Wives* (1974). She was a frequent member of the panel on the television quiz shows *Call My Bluff* and *What's My Line*, and had her own series *The Fun Food Factory*. She has written many popular books, such as *God Bless Love* (1972, reprinted 16 times), *Fun Food Feasts* (1978), *Charlie the Noisy Caterpillar* (1989), and *There's a Bear in the Classroom* (1996).

Newman, Paul (Leonard) (1925–) Film actor and director, born in Cleveland, Ohio, USA. He turned to acting after a knee injury ended a promising sports career. Studying at the Yale School of Drama and the Actor's Studio in New York City, he made his film debut in 1954, and became one of the key stars of his generation, portraying idealistic rebels in such popular films as *Cool Hand Luke* (1967) and *Butch Cassidy and the Sundance Kid* (1969). He later pursued interests in motor-racing, politics, and food production, but returned as a powerful character actor and director of such sensitive works as *The Glass Menagerie* (1987). He has been nominated seven times for an Academy Award, receiving a special Oscar for his services to film in 1986, and winning a Best Actor Award for *The Color of Money* the same year. Later films include *Nobody's Fool* (1995) and *Road to Perdition* (2002). He married the actress Joanne Woodward in 1958.

Newman, Randy (1943–) Singer and songwriter, born in Los Angeles, California, USA. He began studying the piano at age seven and was writing songs professionally when he was 17. After letting others such as Judy Collins, Peggy Lee, Ella Fitzgerald, and Joni Mitchell sing his songs, he took to performing at colleges and nightclubs in the late 1960s and earned a reputation for his inimitable piano and vocal style. He composed film scores such as *Cold Turkey* (1970), *Ragtime* (1981), and *The Paper* (1994), and released several popular albums including *Randy Newman* (1968), *Sail Away* (1972) and *Little Criminals* (1978).

new mathematics A term used to denote mathematical topics which are introduced into the school curriculum later than other more traditional activities, and which are thus usually less familiar to parents and the general public. The actual mathematics is not in itself 'new', and would include such topics as 'tessellations' (the fitting together of regularly chequered pattern shapes), and learning to draw a Venn diagram showing the separateness or overlapping of sets.

New Mexico pop (2000e) 1 819 000; area 314 914 sq km/ 121 593 sq mi. State in SW USA, divided into 33 counties; the 'Land of Enchantment'; first explored by the Spanish in the early 1500s; first white settlement at Santa Fe, 1609; governed by Mexico from 1821; ceded to the USA in the Treaty of Guadalupe Hidalgo, 1848; organized as a territory (1850), including Arizona and part of Colorado; admitted to the Union as the 47th state, 1912; capital, Santa Fe; other chief cities, Albuquerque, Las Cruces, Roswell; over a third of the population Hispanic (higher percentage than any other state); bounded S by Texas and Mexico; rivers include the Pecos and the Rio Grande (forms part of S border); highest point Wheeler Peak (4011 m/ 13 160 ft); mainly broad deserts, forested mountain wildernesses, and towering barren peaks; isolated mountain ranges, part of the Rocky Mts, flank the Rio Grande; forests mainly in the SW and N; mostly semi-arid plain with little rainfall; farming in the well-irrigated valley of the Rio Grande; cattle, dairy products, sheep, hay, wheat, cotton; processed foods, chemicals, electrical equipment, lumbering; nation's chief producer of uranium, potash, perlite; oil, coal, natural gas; tourism important (warm, dry climate and striking scenery); the Carlsbad Caverns National Park, Aztec ruins, White Sands, Chaco Canyon, Gila Cliff Dwellings, Gran Quivira; several military establishments and atomic energy centres; Los Alamos atomic research centre built 1943; first atomic bomb explosion at White Sands proving grounds, July 1945; several mountain Indian reservations.

New Model Army An English army established by Parliament (15 Feb 1645) to strengthen the Roundheads' forces in the Civil War against the Royalists. The county and regional armies of Essex, Manchester, and Waller were merged into a successful national force of 22 000 men. The cavalry and artillery were augmented; the battle tactics and military training of Gustavus Adolphus adopted; discipline and pay improved; and religious toleration introduced. The army became known as **the Ironsides**, with Oliver Cromwell as the lieutenant-general. It was inextricably involved in national developments until the Restoration, and formed the basis of government during the Commonwealth.

New Netherland A Dutch colony in the valley of the Hudson R. The first settlement was Fort Orange (Albany), founded in 1617; Nieuw Amsterdam (New York City) followed in 1624. Conquered by the English and named New York in 1664, it was reconquered in 1674 after a second brief period of Dutch rule. Initially established on feudal social lines, the colony prospered on the basis of the fur trade.

new novel *nouveau roman*

New Orleans [aw(r)leenz] 29°58N 90°04W, pop (2000e) 407 000. Parish seat of Orleans parish, SE Louisiana, USA, between the Mississippi R and L Pontchartrain; 'Crescent City', located on a bend in the river; founded by the French, 1718; capital of French Louisiana, 1722; ceded to Spain, 1763; passed to the US in the Louisiana Purchase 1803; French influence still evident in the city today; prospered in the 19th-c as a market for slaves and cotton; gained a lasting reputation for glamour and wild living; fell to Union troops during the Civil War; industrial growth in the 20th-c after the discovery of vast deposits of oil and natural gas in the region; New Orleans musicians contributed to early development of jazz, late 19th-c (birthplace of Louis Armstrong); airport; railway; five universities; one of the nation's busiest ports, at the head of the Mississippi; oil and petrochemical industries; shipbuilding yards; professional team, Saints (football); important creole culture; the French Quarter, the Cabildo, St Louis Cathedral, Jazz Museum, Isaac Delgado Museum of Art; Mardi Gras (Feb–Mar), Jazz and Heritage Festival (Apr).

Newport (Isle of Wight) 50°42N 1°18W, pop (2000e) 21 800. River port, market town, and administrative centre of Isle of Wight, S England, UK; on the R Medina, 8 km/5 mi from its mouth; Parkhurst prison nearby; construction equipment, valves, printing; 12th-c Carisbrooke Castle.

Newport (Rhode Island) 41°29N 71°19W, pop (2000e) 26 500. Seat of Newport Co, SE Rhode Island, USA; port at the mouth of Narragansett Bay; settled, 1639; city status, 1853; haven for religious groups, including Quakers and Jews; railway; several US Navy establishments; shipbuilding, electrical goods, jewellery, precision instruments; many palatial mansions (eg the Breakers), the sloop *Providence*, Tennis Hall of Fame; Newport Jazz Festival held here 1954–71; music festival (Jul); yachting (including America's Cup races).

Newport (Wales), Welsh **Casnewydd** pop (2001e) 137 000; area 191 sq km/74 sq mi. County (unitary authority from 1996) in SE Wales, UK; administrative centre, Newport, on R Usk; steel, aluminium, electronics, chemicals, market gardening; Roman fort at Caerleon.

New Providence pop (2000e) 199 000; area 207 sq km/80 sq mi. Island in the NC Bahamas, on the Great Bahama Bank; length 32 km/20 mi; capital Nassau; contains more than half the total population of the group; airport; popular tourist resort.

New Right A wide-ranging ideological movement associated with the revival of conservatism in the 1970s and 1980s, particularly in the UK and USA. Its ideas are most prominently connected with classical liberal economic theory from the 19th-c. It is strongly in favour of state withdrawal from ownership, and intervention in the economy in favour of a free-enterprise system. There is also a strong moral conservatism – an emphasis on respect for authority, combined with a strong expression of patriotism and support for the idea of the family. Politically, the New Right adopts an aggressive style which places weight on pursuing convictions rather than on generating a consensus. In the USA in the 1980s it was associated with the emergence of Christian fundamentalism (eg the Moral Majority).

New River Gorge Bridge Longest single arch steel span bridge in the world, and second highest bridge in the USA, located on the New River N of Fayetteville, West Virginia; length 923 m/3030 ft; arch span 518 m/1700 ft; height 267 m/876 ft; completed in 1977; annual Bridge Day on the third Saturday in October.

New Ross, Ir **Baila Nua** 52°24N 6°56W, pop (2000e) 6100. Mediaeval town and river port in Wexford county, Leinster, SE Ireland; on R Barrow, NE of Waterford; home of the Kennedy family in Dunganstown, 8 km/5 mi S; J F Kennedy Memorial Park nearby.

news agency An organization providing a general or specialized news service. Agencies range from large, publicly-quoted companies (eg Reuters) and state-owned concerns (eg Xinhua) to small private operations. Clients, especially the media, subscribe to the continuous (*wire*) service provided by the major agencies, or buy individual items locally.

newsgroup *USENET*

New Siberian Islands, Russ **Novosibirskiye Ostrova** area 28 250 sq km/10 900 sq mi. Uninhabited Russian archipelago in the Arctic Ocean, between the Laptev Sea (W) and the E Siberian Sea (E), NE Russia; rises to 374 m/1227 ft; chief islands are Kotelnyy, Faddeyevskiy, and New Siberia; separated from the Lyakhov Is (S) by the Proliv Sannikova strait; mammoth fossils.

New South Wales pop (2000e) 6 333 000; area 801 428 sq km/309 400 sq mi. State in SE Australia, bordered E by the South Pacific Ocean and Tasman Sea; the first British colony, named by Captain Cook, who landed at Botany Bay, 1770; first settlement at Sydney, 1788; comprises 12 statistical divisions; coastal lowlands give way to tablelands, formed by the Great Dividing Range (highest point Mt Kosciusko, 2228 m/7310 ft); fertile irrigated plains further W comprise two-thirds of the state; main coastal rivers the Hawkesbury, Hunter, Macleay, Clarence; main inland rivers the Darling, Murray, Murrumbidgee, Lachlan, Macquarie-Bogan; capital, Sydney; principal cities, Newcastle, Wollongong; beef cattle, dairy farming, wool, cereals, fishing, forestry, textiles, electrical machinery, chemicals, food processing; lead, zinc, and coal mining; the most populous and most heavily industrialized state in Australia; state holidays Bank Holiday (Aug); Labour Day (Oct).

New Spain, Span **Nueva España** The formal title of the Spanish viceroyalty covering the area of modern Mexico.

newspaper A regularly published account of recent events. Modern newspapers are printed, usually by offset lithography, on large sheets, folded once and inserted one within another, and published at daily, weekly, or (occasionally) monthly frequencies. Predecessors of the modern newspaper included official information sheets, as in the Roman *Acta Diurna*, hung in public places, and mediaeval manuscript news pamphlets, printed in Germany and the Netherlands. The modern newspaper can be traced back to the British publications, the *Corante* (1621) and *Weekly Newes* (1622). Many publications were suppressed during the 17th-c, but censorship was relaxed after the 1688 revolution. The first daily paper was the *Daily Courant* (1702), and the first true evening paper the *Courier* (1792). The reign of George III was marked by bitter conflict over the freedom of the press, not least the reporting of speeches in the House of Commons. In the USA the first newspapers (in Boston, 1689) avoided controversy, but the *Boston Gazette* (and the *Massachusetts Spy*, 1770) engaged in political debate. The *New York Times* was founded in 1851, its editors setting a pattern for the future by appealing to a cultured, intellectual readership instead of a mass audience.

In the 19th-c, fast rotary presses, the change to cheap paper, and the abolition of the Stamp Duty (1855) encouraged a great growth in publication. Technical improvements since then have successively brought in mechanized metal typesetting, photoengraved illustrations, phototypesetting, offset lithography, and facsimile transmission of text and pictures. The revolution in newsgathering and editorial preparation has equalled the technical advances. Recent developments include the use of electronic databases, facilities for journalists to type stories straight into the phototypesetter computer, make-up screens on which whole pages can be laid out and reviewed, and the inclusion of four-colour half-tone illustrations. Newspaper design and marketing saw rapid development in the 20th-c, with the tabloid circulation wars, price competition, and a reduction in the number of newspapers published. In the early 2000s, c.18 000 newspapers were being published around the world, with particularly important countries being Russia (over 4800), India (over 2000), Ukraine (over 1700), and the USA (over 1600); Canada had 110, the UK 99, Australia 71, and South Africa 20. Over 200 million newspapers are printed in the world daily.

New Style date The dating system which followed the adoption of the Gregorian calendar by Great Britain and its American colonies (14 Sep 1752); previous dates are referred to as **Old Style** dates. The new system eliminated 11 days to get in step with Europe, and moved the day on which the count of years changes from the Feast of the Annunciation (25 Mar) back to 1 January.

New Sweden A Swedish colony, founded at Fort Christina (Wilmington) on the Delaware R in 1633, with Dutch investment and involvement. It was absorbed by New Netherland in 1655.

newt An amphibian of order Urodela; resembles the salamander, but adults spend summer or entire year in water; breeds in water; young (called the *eft* stage) live on land for 1–7 years. (Genera: *Triturus*, *Taricha*, *Notophthalmus*, *Pleurodeles*, *Echinotriton*. Family: Salamandridae.)

New Territories area 950 sq km/367 sq mi. Region of Hong Kong; N of the Kowloon Peninsula, includes part of the mainland and over 200 islands; leased to Britain until 1997, when Hong Kong was restored to China under the Sino–British Agreement of 1984.

New Testament Along with the Old Testament, the sacred literature of Christianity. It is called 'New Testament' because its writings are believed to represent a new covenant of God with his people, centred on the person and work of Jesus Christ, as distinct from the old covenant with Israel which is described in the 'Old Testament'. The 27 New Testament writings were originally composed in Greek, mainly in the 1st-c AD, unlike the Old Testament writings which are primarily in Hebrew and from earlier centuries. The New Testament writings focus upon the ministry of Jesus, the origins of the Christian Church, and the ministries of Paul and other early apostles. They are usually grouped as follows: 4 Gospels (Matthew, Mark, Luke, John), the Acts of the Apostles, 13 letters attributed to Paul (Romans, 1 and 2 Corinthians, Galatians, Ephesians, Philippians, Colossians, 1 and 2 Thessalonians, 1 and 2 Timothy, Titus, Philemon), the Letter to the Hebrews, 7 General or 'Catholic' letters (James; 1 and 2 Peter; 1, 2 and 3 John; Jude) and the Book of Revelation. This corpus largely achieved recognition in the Christian Church by the end of the 2nd-c, but a few works continued to be contested in later centuries.

Newton, Sir Isaac (1642–1727) Physicist and mathematician, born in Woolsthorpe, Lincolnshire, EC England, UK. He studied at Cambridge. In 1665–6 the fall of an apple is said to have suggested the train of thought that led to the law of gravitation. He studied the nature of light, concluding that white light is a mixture of colours which can be separated by refraction, and devised the first reflecting telescope. He became professor of mathematics at Cambridge in 1669, where he resumed his work on gravitation, expounded finally in his famous *Philosophiae naturalis principia mathematica* (1687, Mathematical Principles of Natural Philosophy). In 1696 he was appointed warden of the Mint, and was master of the Mint from 1699 until his death. He also sat in parliament on two occasions, was elected president of the Royal Society in 1703, and was knighted in 1705. During his life he was involved in many controversies, notably with Leibniz over the question of priority in the discovery of calculus.

newton SI unit of force; symbol *N*; named after Isaac Newton; defined as the force which causes an acceleration of 1 m/s^2 for an object of mass 1 kg.

Newtonian mechanics A theory of mechanics which considers the relationships between force and motion for 'everyday' objects, ie objects much larger than atoms and moving slowly relative to the speed of light; formulated by Isaac Newton. The theory is expressed as Newton's three laws of motion. Time is regarded as fixed and absolute, the same for all observers, and distinct from space; mass and energy are separate.

Newtonian telescope The first usable astronomical telescope with a parabolic mirror rather than a lens to focus light, and an internal flat mirror to deflect the image to an eyepiece, thus eliminating colour distortions. This optical arrangement is still popular for low-cost amateur telescopes.

Newton's laws The basic expression of Newtonian mechanics; formulated in 1687 by Isaac Newton. **First law**: the velocity of an object does not change unless a force acts on it. **Second law**: a force F applied to an object of mass m causes an acceleration a according to $F = ma$. **Third law**: every action has an equal and opposite reaction.

new town A British solution to problems of city growth: a planned, self-contained settlement designed to relieve urban congestion. Some (eg Peterborough) incorporated existing settlements; others (eg Peterlee) were built on new sites. Dating from the 1946 New Towns Act, 14 were designated between 1947 and 1950, and seven more since then. They incorporate features designed to ensure independence from the parent community, minimum commuting, and a balance of social groups. Examples include Cumbernauld, Cwmbran, Harlow, and Milton Keynes.

new universities Orginally, universities built to accommodate the expanding numbers entering higher education in Britain during the post-war period: Keele (1949); Sussex (1961); Essex (1961); York (1963); Lancaster (1964); East Anglia (1964); Kent (1965); Warwick (1965); Stirling (1967); Open (1969). The term does not generally include those 19th-c colleges which were converted into universities in the 20th-c, such as Newcastle. Since 1992, the term has come to be applied to polytechnics in Britain which acquired university status that year. For example, Leicester Polytechnic became De Montfort University.

New Wave *Nouvelle Vague*

New World monkey A monkey inhabiting Central and South America; nostrils wide apart and opening to the side (unlike Old World monkeys); thumb not opposable; some species with prehensile (grasping) tails. (Family: Cebidae, 32 species.)

New Year's Day The first day of the year (1 Jan in countries using the Gregorian calendar). Communities using other calendars celebrate New Year on other dates: the Jewish New Year, for example, is Rosh Hashanah (1 Tishri), which falls in September or October, and the Chinese New Year falls between 21 January and 19 February.

New York (state) pop (2000e) 18 976 500; area 127 185 sq km/ 49 108 sq mi. State in NE USA, divided into 62 counties; the 'Empire State'; second most populous state; one of the original states of the Union, 11th to ratify the Federal Constitution, 1788; explored by Hudson and Champlain, 1609; Dutch established posts near Albany, 1614, settled Manhattan, 1626; New Netherlands taken by the British, 1664; scene of several battles in the American Revolution (eg Saratoga); capital, Albany; other chief cities, New York City, Syracuse, Yonkers, Rochester, Buffalo; Hudson R flows S through the E state, St Lawrence R part of the N border, Delaware R part of the S border; Niagara Falls in W; Adirondack Mts rise in the N, Catskill Mts in the S; highest point in the Adirondacks at Mt Marcy (1629 m/5344 ft); state contains 11 334 sq km/4375 sq mi of the Great Lakes, as well as L Oneida and the Finger Lakes in the C; extensive woodland and forest in the NE, elsewhere a mixture of cropland, pasture, and woodland; clothing, pharmaceuticals, publishing, electronics, automotive and aircraft components; dairy products, corn, beef; New York City the chief ethnically mixed centre of population in the USA.

New York City or **New York** 40°43N 74°00W, pop (2000e) 8 008 300. County seat of New York Co, SE New York, USA; at the mouth of the Hudson R; largest city in the USA and largest port, with 1200 km/750 mi of waterfront, including that in neighbouring New Jersey; originally the site of a trading post established in 1624; colonized by the Dutch and named New Amsterdam 1625; captured by the British in 1664 and named New York after the king's brother, the Duke of York; scene of the reading of the Declaration of Independence (4 Jul 1776); held by the British throughout the War of Independence; George Washington inaugurated here as first US president; rapid commercial and industrial growth after the opening of the Erie Canal, 1825; Ellis Island the main centre of American immigration, late 19th–early 20th-c; movement away from the city to the suburbs by many middle-class residents since World War 2; emergency loans saved city from bankruptcy in mid-1970s; divided into five boroughs, each co-extensive with a county – Bronx (Bronx Co), Brooklyn (Kings Co), Manhattan (New York Co), Queens (Queens Co – in 1990 census, the most racially diverse community in the USA), Staten Island (Richmond Co); eight universities; railway; two airports (La Guardia, Kennedy); major world financial centre, with Stock Exchange in Wall Street; advertising, the media, printing and publishing, textiles, food processing, metal products, scientific equipment, vehicles, shipbuilding, machinery, pharmaceuticals; professional teams, Mets, Yankees (baseball), Knickerbockers (basketball), Giants, Jets (football), Islanders, Rangers

New Zealand

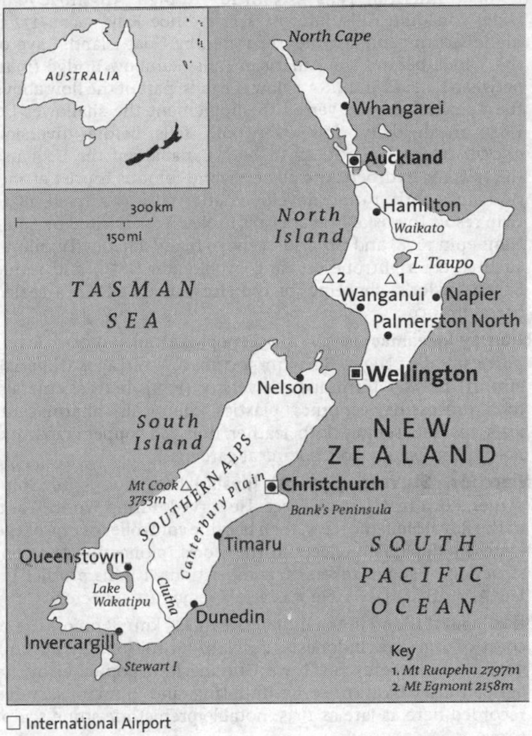

Maori **Aotearoa**

Local name Aotearoa (Maori)

Timezone GMT +12

Area 268 812 km^2/103 761 sq mi

Population total (2002e) 3 893 000

Status Independent member of the Commonwealth

Date of independence 1947

Capital Wellington

Languages English and Maori (official)

Ethnic groups European (mainly British, Australian and Dutch) (87%), Maori (9%)

Religions Christian (59%) (Anglican 25%, Presbyterian 18%, Roman Catholic 16%)

Physical features Consists of two principal islands (North and South) separated by the Cook Strait, and several minor islands; North Island mountainous in the centre with many hot springs; peaks rise to 2797 m/9176 ft at Mt Ruapehu; South Island mountainous for its whole length, rising in the Southern Alps to 3753 m/12 313 ft at Mt Cook, New Zealand's highest point; many glaciers and mountain lakes; largest area of level lowland is the Canterbury Plain, E side of South Island; L Taupo, largest natural lake, occupies an ancient volcanic crater; major lakes include Te Anau and Wakatipu.

Climate Cool, temperate climate, almost subtropical in extreme N; Mean temperature range, 18°C in N, 9°C in S; lower temperatures in South Island; highly changeable weather, all months moderately wet; average daily temperature 16–23°C (Jan), 8–13°C (Jul) in Auckland; average annual rainfall 1053 mm/41 in; subject to periodic sub-tropical cyclones.

Currency 1 New Zealand Dollar ($NZ) = 100 cents

Economy Farming, especially sheep and cattle; one of the world's major exporters of dairy produce; third largest exporter of wool; Kiwi fruit, venison; textiles; timber, food processing; substantial coal and natural gas reserves; hydroelectric power; tourism.

GDP (2002e) $78·4 bn, per capita $20 100

Human Development Index (2002) 0·917

History Settled by Maoris from E Polynesia by c.1000 AD; first European sighting by Abel Tasman in 1642, named Staten Landt; later known as Nieuw Zeeland, after the Dutch Province; visited by Captain Cook, 1769; first European settlement, 1792; dependency of New South Wales until 1840; annexed by Britain 1840; outbreaks of war between immigrants and Maoris, 1860–70; Dominion of New Zealand, 1907; independent within the Commonwealth, 1947; governed by a Prime Minister, a Cabinet and a unicameral, 97-member House of Representatives; elections every 3 years.

Head of State
(British monarch represented by Governor-General)
1996–2001 Michael Hardie Boys
2001– Dame Silvia Cartwright

Head of Government
1906 William Hall-Jones *Lib*
1906–12 Joseph George Ward *Lib/Nat*
1912 Thomas Mackenzie *Nat*
1912–25 William Ferguson Massey *Ref*
1925 Francis Henry Dillon Bell *Ref*
1925–8 Joseph Gordon Coates *Ref*
1928–30 Joseph George Ward *Lib/Nat*
1930–5 George William Forbes *Un*
1935–40 Michael Joseph Savage *Lab*
1940–9 Peter Fraser *Lab*
1949–57 Sidney George Holland *Nat*
1957 Keith Jacka Holyoake *Nat*
1957–60 Walter Nash *Lab*
1960–72 Keith Jacka Holyoake *Nat*
1972 John Ross Marshall *Nat*
1972–4 Norman Eric Kirk *Lab*
1974–5 Wallace Edward Rowling *Lab*
1975–84 Robert David Muldoon *Nat*
1984–9 David Russell Lange *Lab*
1989–90 Geoffrey Palmer *Lab*
1990 Michael Kenneth Moore *Lab*
1990–7 James Brendan Bolger *Nat*
1997–9 Jenny Shipley *Nat*
1999– Helen Clark *Lab*
Lab Labour *Ref* Reform *Lib* Liberal *Un* United *Nat* National

Overseas territories
Name / Area (km^2/sq mi) / Capital / Population
Cook Islands / 238/92 / Avarua / (2000e) 20 400
Niue / 263/101 / Alofi / (2000e) 2100
Ross Dependency / 413 550 /159 600 / uninhabited
Tokelau / 10/4 / Nukunonu / (2000e) 1000

(ice hockey); the country's centre for fashion, arts, and entertainment, with many museums and galleries; Central Park. A New York landmark, the World Trade Center, collapsed after two aircraft were deliberately flown at the 1360-ft twin towers in a terrorist attack on 11 September 2001.

New York City Ballet Resident ballet company of the New York State Theater at the Lincoln Center for the Performing Arts and the Saratoga Performing Arts Center, both in New York, USA. First named the **Ballet Company**, it was founded in 1946 by George Balanchine and Lincoln Kirstein (1907–96) as a private subscription organization. In 1948 it was renamed the New York City Ballet, and in 1964 it moved to its present home. Its aim was to explore a new, contemporary repertory with works by choreographers such as Balanchine, Jerome Robbins (ballet master 1969–90), and Ashton. Peter Martins, one of the company's former principle dancers, became ballet master in 1983.

New York Public Library One of the most famous architectural structures in New York City, of Beaux-Arts design with marble colonnade and a pair of grand marble lions flanking the Fifth Avenue entrance. When originally built (1911) the library housed the collections of the Lenox Library and the Astor Library. Today, it holds over 6 million books, 12 million periodicals, and almost 3 million pictures. Notable among the permanent exhibits are Gilbert Stuart's portrait of George Washington and Charles Dickens' desk.

New York School A term sometimes applied rather loosely (for it was never a school in the formal sense) to the group of US painters who, after 1945, centred around Jackson Pollock (1912–56), Arshile Gorky (1904–48), Willem de Kooning (1904–97), and Mark Rothko (1903–70).

New York Yankees Baseball team, founded as the New York Highlanders in 1903 and renamed the Yankees in 1913. They are winners of a record 26 World Series and 38 American League championships, including five consecutive World Series wins (1949–53). Less successful in the 1980s and early 1990s, the Yankees won the World Series again in 1996, 1998, 1999, and 2000. The club moved to Yankee Stadium in 1923; rebuilt in 1973–5, it has a current capacity of 57 746.

New Zealand *p.1085*

Ney, Michel, duc d' (Duke of) **Elchingen** [nay] (1769–1815) French marshal, born in Saarlouis, Germany (formerly NE France). He fought in the Revolutionary Wars, became a general of division (1799), and a marshal of the empire. Created Duke of Elchingen (1805), he distinguished himself at Jena (1806), Eylau, and Friedland (1807). He commanded the third corps of the Grand Army in the Russian campaign (1813), for which he received the title of Prince of Moskowa. After Napoleon's abdication (1814), he accepted the Bourbon restoration, but instead of obeying orders to retake Bonaparte (1815), Ney deserted to his side and led the centre at Waterloo. On Louis XVIII's second restoration, he was condemned for high treason, and shot in Paris.

Ngorongoro Crater [nggohronggohroh] Crater in N Tanzania, in the Rift Valley; its rim is at an altitude of c.2100 m/6900 ft, and its floor lies c.600 m/2000 ft below this level; area, c.260 sq km/100 sq mi; centre of a conservation region, a world heritage site, covering 7800 sq km/3000 sq mi; provides a cattle-farming area for the Masai, and a wildlife range for wildebeeste, gazelle, zebra.

Ngugi wa Thiong'o [ngoogee wa tyonggoh], formerly **James Ngugi** (1938–) Writer, born in Limuru, WC Kenya. He studied at Makerere and Leeds universities, and taught English at Nairobi University, where he became chairman of the department of literature (1972–7). His award-winning novel *Weep Not, Child* (1964) was the first novel in English by an East African. The theme of Kenya's struggle for independence is further explored in later novels, *The River Between* (1965), *A Grain of Wheat* (1967), and *Petals of Blood* (1977). He then gave up using English as the medium for his fiction (though continuing to use it for translation and other purposes), arguing that the continuing use of local languages (Kikuyu, in his case) was a prerequisite for political reform. He wrote several plays, notably *The Trial of Dedan Kimathi* (1977), and co-wrote *Ngaahika Ndeenda* (I Will Marry When I Want), which led to his year-long detention without trial (1978). His ordeal is described in *Detained* (1981). He has lived in exile since 1982. In 1996 he received the Fonlon-Nichols Award, given annually for excellence in African creative writing and contributions to the struggle for human rights and freedom of expression.

Nguni [ngoonee] A cluster of Bantu-speaking peoples of S Africa. Originally occupying present-day Natal and Transkei, they expanded rapidly in the early 19th-c in a series of migrations. The main groups today include the Zulu, Swazi, and Xhosa of South Africa and Swaziland; the Ndebele of Zimbabwe; and the Ngoni of Zambia, Malawi, and Tanzania. All groups are organized under the control of powerful chiefs aided by councils. In South Africa they lost much of their land and power to Europeans from the 18th-c onwards.

nhandu *rhea* (ornithology)

niacin *nicotinic acid*

Niagara Falls Two waterfalls in W New York, USA and S Ontario, Canada; between L Erie and L Ontario, on the international border; American Falls 55·5 m/182 ft high, 328 m/1076 ft wide; Canadian Falls, known as Horseshoe Falls, 54 m/177 ft high, 640 m/2100 ft wide; separated by Goat Island; Cave of the Winds behind the American Falls; Rainbow Bridge (1941) between Canada and USA below the falls; part of the flow above the Canadian Falls diverted to supplement the shallower US Falls; mean daily flow over both falls before diversion c.5000 cu m/200 000 cu ft; both Canada and the USA use the falls for hydroelectric power; world-famous tourist attraction since early 19th-c, developed after railway arrived, 1836; twin resort towns of Niagara Falls in New York (visited by Louis Hennepin 1678) and Ontario; scene of many daredevil exploits, such as the tightrope crossing by Blondin (1859) and Annie Edson Taylor's 'shooting' of the Horseshoe Falls in a sealed barrel in 1901.

Niamey [neeamay] 13°32N 2°05E, pop (2000e) 569 000. River-port capital of Niger; 800 km/500 mi NW of Lagos (Nigeria); airport; railway terminus; university (1971); textiles, metals, food processing, ceramics, plastics, chemicals, pharmaceuticals; markets selling cloth, leather, iron and copper craftwork; national museum, zoo, botanical gardens.

Niarchos, Stavros (Spyros) [nyah(r)khos] (1909–96) Shipowner, born in Athens, Greece. He served during World War 2 in the Royal Hellenic navy, then became controller of one of the largest independent fleets in the world, pioneering the construction of supertankers, in competition with his brother-in-law Aristotle Onassis. He was also a major art collector.

Nias [neeas] Island in the Indian Ocean, 125 km/78 mi off the W coast of Sumatra, Indonesia; 240 km/159 mi long by 80 km/50 mi wide; airfield; chief town, Gunungsitoli; populated by the agricultural Niah tribe; headhunting and human sacrifice recorded here as late as 1935; notable prehistoric stone sculptures.

Nibelungen [neebelungen] In mediaeval German legends, a race of dwarfs who live in Norway and possess a famous treasure. The *Nibelungenlied* recounts how Siegfried obtained the treasure and his later misfortunes. Wagner conflated this with other legends for his opera cycle.

Nicaea, Council of [niyseea] **1** (325) The first ecumenical Council of the Church, called by Emperor Constantine to settle the doctrinal dispute between the Arians and the Orthodox on the person of Christ.

2 (787) A Council of the Church called to deal with the question of the veneration of images.

NICAM An acronym for **near instantaneously companded** [ie compressed and expanded] **audio multiplex**, a digital system used in television transmissions which provides high-quality stereophonic sound. First used by the BBC in 1986, it is now found in several other countries. A decoder attached to a television set enables the viewer to receive stereo sound along with any television programme which has recorded it.

Nicaragua *p.1087*

Nicaragua, Lago de [nikaragwa] or **Gran Lago** area 8026 sq km/3098 sq mi. Largest lake of Nicaragua and Central America, separated from the Atlantic Ocean (W) by a 15 km/9 mi-wide isthmus; length 148 km/92 mi; width 55 km/34 mi; contains over 300 small islands, notably Isla de Ometepe, with two volcanoes; Granada is on the NW shore.

Nice [nees], Ital **Nizza**, ancient **Nicaea** 43°42N 7°14E, pop (2000e) 358 000. Fashionable coastal resort on the Mediterranean Sea, and capital of Alpes-Maritimes department, SE France; encircled by hills on the Baie des Anges, 157 km/98 mi NE of Marseille; fifth largest city in France; airport; railway; university (1965); leading tourist centre; textiles, perfume, soap, olive oil, fruit, furniture; flower market in old town; cathedral (1650), several 17th–18th-c Baroque churches, 17th-c Palais Lascaris, Palais de la Mediterranée, Palais des Expositions, 19th-c opera house, casinos, palm-lined Promenade des Anglais; Carnival

Nicaragua

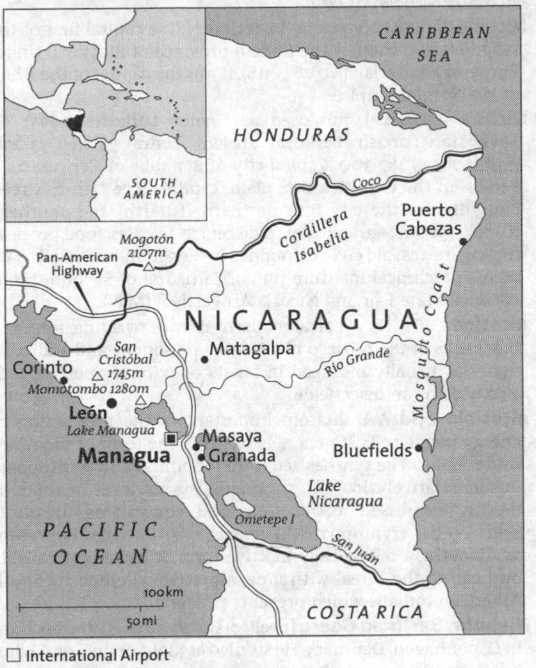

[nikaragwa], official name **Republic of Nicaragua**, Span **República de Nicaragua**

Local name Nicaragua

Timezone GMT −6

Area 148 000 km²/57 128 sq mi

Population total (2002e) 5 024 000

Status Republic

Date of independence 1821

Capital Managua

Languages Spanish (official), indigenous Indian languages and English (creole-English)

Ethnic groups Mestizo (69%), white (17%), black (9%), Indian (Sumu, Mikito, Ramaguie peoples) (5%)

Religions Roman Catholic (95%), Protestant (5%)

Physical features Mountainous W half, with volcanic ranges rising to over 2000 m/6500 ft (NW); two large lakes, L Nicaragua and L Managua, behind the coastal mountain range; rolling uplands and forested plains to the E; many short rivers flow into the Pacific Ocean and the lakes.

Climate Tropical climate; average annual temperatures, 26°C (Jan), 30°C (Jul) at Managua; rainy season (May–Nov), high humidity; average annual rainfall 1140 mm/45 in; country devastated by hurricane Mitch in 1998.

Currency 1 New Córdoba (C$) = 100 centavos

Economy Agriculture (accounts for over two-thirds of total exports); cotton, coffee, sugar cane, rice, corn, tobacco; oil, natural gas. Gold, silver, chemicals, textiles.

GDP (2002e) $11·16 bn, per capita $2200

Human Development Index (2002) 0·635

History Colonized by Spaniards, early 16th-c; independence from Spain, 1821; left the Federation of Central America in 1838; dictatorship under Anastasio Somoza, 1938; Sandinista National Liberation Front seized power in 1979, and established a socialist junta of national reconstruction; under the 1987 constitution (revised in 1994), a President and a Constituent Assembly are elected for 6-year terms; former supporters of the Somoza government (the Contras), based in Honduras and supported by the USA, carried out guerrilla activities against the junta from 1979; ceasefire and disarmament agreed in 1990.

Head of State/Government

1950–6 Anastasio Somoza García
1956–63 Luis Somoza Debayle
1963–6 René Schick Gutiérrez
1966–7 Lorenzo Guerrero Gutiérrez
1967–72 Anastasio Somoza Debayle
1972–4 *Triumvirate*
1974–9 Anastasio Somoza Debayle
1979–84 *Government junta of National Reconstruction*
1984–90 Daniel Ortega Saavedra
1990–6 Violeta Barrios de Chamorro
1996–2001 Arnoldo Aleman Lacayo
2001– Enrique Bolaños Geyer

(before Lent), book festival (May), international dog festival (Jun); ballet festival (Jul–Aug).

Nicene Creed [niyseen] An expanded formal statement of Christian belief, based on the creed of the first Council of Nicaea (325). This is still publicly recited as part of the Eucharistic liturgies of the Orthodox and Roman Catholic Churches, as well as many Protestant Churches.

Nichiren Buddhism [nichiren] A sect founded by the Japanese Buddhist reformer Nichiren (1222–82); sometimes called the **Lotus** sect, because of his claim that the Lotus Sutra contained the ultimate truth. He attacked other forms of Buddhism, and called the nation to convert to true Buddhism. There are almost 40 subsects today.

Nicholas I (1796–1855) Tsar of Russia (1825–55), born near St Petersburg, NW Russia, the third son of Paul I. An absolute despot, he engaged in wars with Persia and Turkey, suppressed a rising in Poland, and attempted to Russianize all the inhabitants of the empire. He helped to quell the 1848 Hungarian insurrection, and drew closer the alliance with Prussia. The re-establishment of the French empire confirmed these alliances, and led him to think of absorbing Turkey, but the opposition of Britain and France brought on the Crimean War, during which he died.

Nicholas II (1868–1918) The last tsar of Russia (1895–1917), born near St Petersburg, NW Russia, the son of Alexander III. His reign was marked by the alliance with France (1894), an entente with Britain, a disastrous war with Japan (1904–5), and the establishment of the national assembly, or Duma (1906). When forced by the 1905 Revolution to accept a constitutional monarchy, he continued to believe that he was responsible only to God. He took command of the Russian armies against the Central Powers in 1915, leaving the government of the country to the empress Alexandra and Rasputin. His mismanagement of the war and government chaos led to his abdication in 1917, and subsequent imprisonment. In July 1918 the Bolsheviks moved him and his family to Siberia, where they were executed at Ekaterinburg. The Russian Orthodox Church bestowed sainthood on Nicholas, his wife and five children in 2000.

Nicholas, St (4th-c) Bishop of Myra, Lucia, and patron saint of Russia, widely associated with the feast of Christmas. He was imprisoned under Diocletian and released under Constantine, and his supposed relics were conveyed to Bari in 1087. He is the patron of youth, merchants, sailors, travellers, and thieves. His identification with Father Christmas began in Europe, and spread to America, where the name was altered to *Santa Claus*. The tradition of exchanging gifts on Christmas Day derives from a legend of his benevolence. Feast day 6 December.

Nicholas or **Nicolaus of Cusa** [kyooza] (1401–64) Cardinal and philospher, born in Cusa, W Germany. He studied at Heidelberg and Padua, and took a prominent part in the Council of Basel. Ordained in 1440, he became a cardinal in 1448, and as papal legate visited Constantinople to promote the union of the Eastern and Western Churches. A Renaissance scientist in advance of his time, he wrote on astronomy, mathematics, philosophy, and biology.

Nicholson, Ben (1894–1982) Artist, born in Denham, Buckinghamshire, SC England, UK, the son of Sir William Nicholson. He exhibited with the Paris Abstraction-Création group (1933–4) and at the Venice Biennale (1954). He designed a mural panel for the Festival of Britain (1951), and executed another for the Time Life building in London (1952). As one of the leading abstract artists, he gained an international reputation, and won the first Guggenheim Award in 1957. Although he produced a number of purely geometrical paintings and reliefs, in general he used conventional still-life objects as a starting point for his finely drawn and subtly balanced and coloured variations. Three times married, his second wife was Barbara Hepworth.

Nicholson, Jack (1937–) Film actor, script-writer, and director, born in Neptune, New Jersey, USA. An office boy at MGM, he worked with the Players Ring Theater before making his film debut in 1958. A supporting role in *Easy Rider* (1969) brought him belated critical recognition. His intense charisma and acute sense of humour have illuminated a wide range of characters in such diverse films as *Chinatown* (1974), *The Shining* (1980), and *Prizzi's Honor* (1985). He has also written scripts, and occasionally directs. Nominated many times for an Academy Award, he won Oscars for *One Flew Over the Cuckoo's Nest* (1975), *Terms of Endearment* (1983), and *As Good As It Gets* (1997). Other film credits include *The Witches of Eastwick* (1987), *Batman* (1989), *About Schmidt* (2002, Golden Globe; Oscar nomination), and *Something's Gotta Give* (2003).

Nicias [nikias, nisias] (?–413 BC) Wealthy politician and general, from Athens, prominent during the Peloponnesian War. A political moderate, he was opposed to the strident warmongering of Cleon and Alcibiades, and arranged the short-lived peace named after him (421 BC). Appointed commander in Sicily (416 BC), his lack of sympathy with his mission, along with bad luck, ill health, and sheer incompetence, led to the total destruction of the Athenian forces, and his own death at the hands of the Syracusans.

nickel Ni, element 28, density 8 g/cm^3, melting point 1450°C. A silvery metal, most commonly obtained from pentlandite, a complex sulphide of nickel and iron; it occurs uncombined only in some meteorites. The metal, which is weakly ferromagnetic, forms a protective oxide coating, and is used in coinage and cutlery, both as the free metal and as an alloy with copper (*German silver*). It is also an important catalyst for hydrogenation (*Raney nickel*), and is an ingredient of many stainless steels. Its compounds mainly show oxidation state +2.

nickel-silver *Britannia metal*

Nicklaus, Jack (William) [niklows] (1940–) Golfer, born in Columbus, Ohio, USA. He won the US Amateur title in 1959 and 1961, then turned professional. Runner-up to Arnold Palmer in the 1960 US Open, as amateur, he has since won all the world's major tournaments: the (British) Open (1966, 1970, 1978), the US Open (1962, 1967, 1972, 1980), the US Professional Golfers Association tournament a record-equalling five times (1963, 1971, 1973, 1975, 1980), and the US Masters a record six times (1963, 1965–6, 1972, 1975, 1986). His win in 1986 was at the age of 46 years 82 days, the oldest winner of the event. His 18 professional majors is a world record. He continues to play, but is also involved in golf course and golf club design.

Nicobar Islands *Andaman and Nicobar Islands*

Nicolai, (Carl) Otto (Ehrenfried) [nikoliy] (1810–49) Composer, born in Königsberg, Prussia (now Kaliningrad, Russia). He studied in Berlin and Rome, becoming court conductor in Vienna (1841) and conductor of the Berlin Opera (1847). His opera *The Merry Wives of Windsor* was produced just before he died.

Nicolaus *Nicholas of Cusa*

Nicomedia [niykohmeedia] In antiquity, the capital first of the kingdom and then of the Roman province of Bithynia. Under Emperor Diocletian (AD 284–316), it was the capital of the E half of the Roman Empire.

Nicosia [nikoseea], proposed new name **Lefkosia** (1995), Gr **Levkosia**, Turkish **Lefkosa**, ancient **Ledra** 35°11N 33°23E, pop (2000e) 187 300. Capital city of Republic of Cyprus; on R Pedias, in the C of Mesaoria plain; capital since 12th-c; 'Green Line' divides the city into northern (Turkish) and southern (Greek) sectors; agricultural trade centre; textiles, food processing, cigarettes; old city surrounded by Venetian-built walls (late 16th-c); technical institute (1968); Cathedral of St John; International State Fair and Nicosia Art Festival (May).

nicotine $C_{10}H_{14}N_2$. An alkaloid derived from pyridine, found in the leaves of the tobacco plant. It is a poisonous and addictive material, usually indulged in for its relaxing properties. It is also used as an insecticide.

nicotinic acid A B vitamin important in the production of energy inside cells. It generally exists in the form of **nicotinamide**, and can be synthesized from the amino acid tryptophan, but at relatively low rates; nonetheless its level in foods is usually expressed as nicotinic acid equivalents (nicotinic acid + 0·017 tryptophan). In cereals, nicotinic acid is present as **niacytin**, a biologically inactive form. It becomes available on heating the cereal with lime, a practice adopted by South American Indians which prevents pellagra.

Niebuhr, Barthold Georg [neeboor] (1776–1831) Historian, born in Copenhagen, Denmark. He studied at Kiel, London, and Edinburgh, in 1816 became Prussian ambassador at the Vatican, and on his return in 1823 lectured at Bonn. His main work, the *Römische Geschichte* (1811–32, History of Rome), based on the constructive analysis of historical source material, marked him out as a founder of the 19th-c school of German historical scholarship.

Nielsen, Carl (August) [neelsen] (1865–1931) Composer, born in Nørre-Lyndelse, C Denmark. He studied at the Copenhagen Conservatory (1884–6), and became conductor at the Royal Theatre (1908–14) and with the Copenhagen Musical Society (1915–27). He is particularly known for his six symphonies, and he also wrote concertos, choral and chamber music, the tragic opera *Saul and David* (1902), the comic opera *Masquerade* (1906), and a huge organ work, *Commotio* (1931).

Niemöller, (Friedrich Gustav Emil) Martin [neemoeler] (1892–1984) Lutheran pastor and outspoken opponent of Hitler, born in Lippstadt, WC Germany. He was a leading submarine commander in World War 1, then studied theology, and was ordained in 1924, becoming pastor at Berlin-Dahlem in 1931. Summoned with other Protestant Church leaders before Hitler, he publicly opposed the Nazi regime, and was arrested and placed in various concentration camps (1937–45). Released by Allied forces in 1945, he was responsible for the 'Declaration of Guilt' by the German Churches for not opposing Hitler more strenuously, but he also condemned the abuses of the de-Nazification courts. A controversial pacifist, he later became president of the Evangelical Church in Hesse and Nassau (1947), and president of the World Council of Churches (1961).

Niepce, (Joseph) Nicéphore [nyeps] (1765–1833) Chemist, born in Chalon-sur-Saône, EC France. One of the inventors of photography, he served in the army, and in 1795 became administrator of Nice. At Chalon in 1801 he devoted himself to chemistry, and in 1822 succeeded in obtaining a photographic copy of an engraving superimposed on glass. At length he succeeded in producing a permanent photographic image on metal (1826), said to be the world's first. From 1829 he co-operated with Louis Daguerre in further research.

Nietzsche, Friedrich (Wilhelm) [neechuh] (1844–1900) Philosopher and critic, born in Röcken, EC Germany. He was a strongly religious child and a brilliant undergraduate, accepting the chair of classical philology at Basel (1869–79) before graduating. Influenced by Schopenhauer, he dedicated his first book, *Die Geburt der Tragödie* (1872, The Birth of Tragedy) to his friend Wagner, whose operas he regarded as the true successors to Greek tragedy, but broke with him in 1876, and resigned his university position in 1878 in fast-deteriorating mental and physical health. The characteristic themes of his major work, *Also sprach Zarathustra* (1883–5, Thus Spake Zarathustra), are the vehement repudiation of Christian and liberal ethics, the detestation of democratic ideals, the idea of the *Übermensch* 'overman' who can create and impose his own law, the death of God, and Schopenhauer's 'will to power'. Other works include *Jenseits von Gut und Böse* (1886, Beyond Good and Evil), *Zur genealogie der Moral* (1887, On the Genealogy of Morals), and his autobiography *Ecce Homo* (1908). Much of his esoteric doctrine appealed to the Nazis, and he was a major influence on existentialism. In 1889 he had a mental breakdown, from which he never recovered.

Niger *see panel*

Niger, River [niyjer] River in W Africa; length c.4100 km/ 2550 mi; third longest river in Africa; rises 280 km/175 mi from the Atlantic coast; flows NE through Guinea and Mali; dammed at Markala and Sansanding in Mali; splits into several courses and a cluster of lakes in the Macina depression; part of Niger's SW border with Benin; dammed to form the Mainji reservoir, Nigeria; flows SE and S, spreading into a delta c.320 km/200 mi across, entering the Gulf of Guinea; known as **Upper Niger** or Djoliba as far as Timbuktu, **Middle Niger** from there to Jebba in W Nigeria, and **Lower Niger** or Kovarra (Kawarra, Kwara) from Jebba to its delta; navigable in sections and seasonally; frequently interrupted by rapids; first explored by Mungo Park, 1795–6.

Niger–Congo languages The largest language family in Africa, with 1000 languages spread over almost the entire continent S of the Sahara. It is usually divided into six sub-groups of languages: Adamawa-Eastern, Benue–Congo, Kwa, Mande, Voltaic, and West Atlantic. Among the important Niger–Congo languages are Igbo, Swahili, Wolof, Yoruba, and Zulu. The largest group is the Benue–Congo, which comprises c.700 languages; of these, c.500 belong to the *Bantu* group.

Nigeria *p.1040*

night ape / monkey *douroucouli*

night blindness Reduced ability to adapt to the dark and to see in dim light, resulting from deficiency of vitamin A (retinol). This vitamin is an essential component of rhodopsin, a retinal pigment responsible for colour vision.

nighthawk *goatsucker*

night heron A short, stocky heron, found worldwide; inhabits water margins; eats small aquatic animals; usually feeds at night. (Tribe: Nycticoracini, 8 species.)

Niger

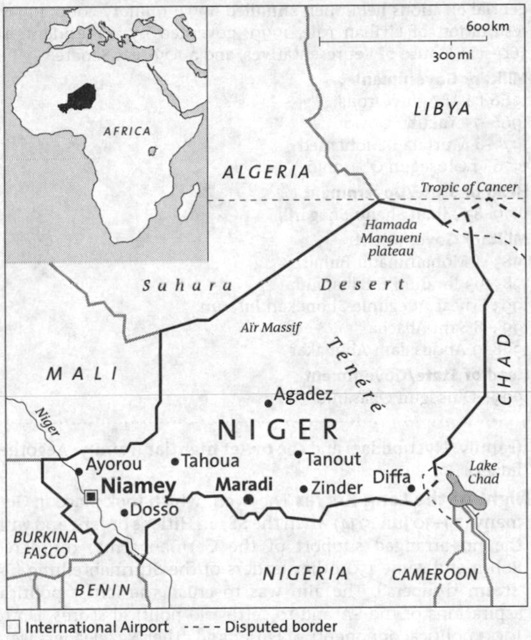

□ International Airport - - - - Disputed border

[niyjer], official name **Republic of Niger**, Fr **République du Niger**

Local name Niger

Timezone GMT +1

Area 1 267 000 km²/489 191 sq mi

Population total (2002e) 10 640 000

Status Republic

Date of Independence 1960

Capital Niamey

Languages French (official) with Hausa, Songhai, Fulfulde, Tamashek, and Arabic widely spoken

Ethnic groups Hausa (54%), Djerma and Songhai (22%), Fulani (9%), Tuareg (8%), Beriberi (4%), Arab (2%)

Religions Muslim (80%), traditional beliefs and small Christian minority (primarily Roman Catholic) (20%)

Physical features Occupies S fringe of Sahara Desert, on a high plateau; Hamada Mangueni plateau (far N); Aïr Massif (C); Ténéré du Tafassasset desert (E); W Talk desert (C and N); water in quantity found only in the SW (R Niger) and SE (L Chad).

Climate One of the hottest countries in the world; average annual temperature 16°C (Jun-Oct), 41°C (Feb-May); rainy season in S (Jun-Oct); rainfall decreases N to almost negligible levels in desert areas; average annual rainfall at Niamey, 554 mm/22 in.

Currency 1 CFA Franc (CFAFr) = 100 centimes

Economy Dominated by agriculture and mining; production badly affected by severe drought conditions in 1970s; uranium, tin, phosphates, coal, salt, natron; building materials, textiles, food processing.

GDP (2002e) $8·713 bn, per capita $800

Human Development Index (2002) 0·277

History Occupied by the French, 1883–99; territory within French West Africa, 1904; independence, 1960; military coup, 1974; governed by a Higher Council for National Orientation led by a President who appoints a Council of Ministers; elected National Assembly, 1989; constitution suspended, 1991; multi-party constitution adopted, 1992.

Head of State
1993–6 Mahamane Ousmane
1996–9 Ibrahim Barre Mainassara
1999 Daouda Malam Wanke
1999– Mamadou Tandjo

Head of Government
1990–1 Aliou Mahamidou
1991–3 Amadou Cheiffou *Interim*
1993–4 Mahamoudou Issoufou
1994–5 Abdoulaye Souley
1995–6 Hama Amadou
1996 Boukary Adji
1996–7 Amadou Boubacar Cisse
1997–2000 Ibrahim Assane Mayaki
2000– Hama Amadou

Nigeria

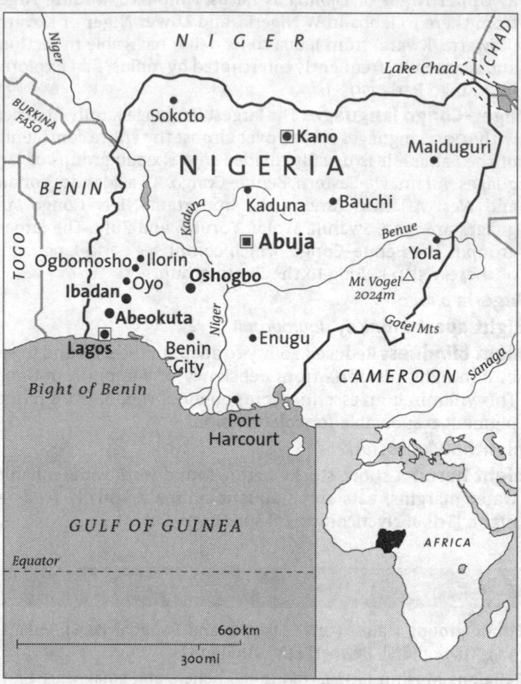

☐ International Airport ---- Disputed border

official name **Federal Republic of Nigeria**
Local name Nigeria
Timezone GMT +1
Area 923 768 km^2/356 669 sq mi
Population total (2002e) 129 935 000
Status Republic
Date of independence 1960
Capital Abuja
Languages English (official), Hausa, Yoruba, Ibo, and other Niger-Congo dialects widely used
Ethnic groups Over 250 tribal groups, notably Hausa and Fulani, Yoruba and Ibo (65%); Kanuri, Tiv, Edo, Nupe, and Ibidio (25%)
Religions Muslim (50%), Christian (34%), indigenous animist beliefs (10%)
Physical features Long, sandy shoreline with mangrove swamp, dominated by R Niger delta; undulating area of tropical rainforest and oil palm bush behind a coastal strip; open woodland and savannah further N; numerous rivers, notably the Niger and the Benue; Gotel Mts on SE frontier, highest point, Mt Vogel, 2024 m/ 6640 ft.
Climate Tropical; uniformly high temperatures; average annual temperatures 21–7°C (Jan), 25–6°C (Jul); dry season in the N (Oct–Apr); average annual rainfall 1836–2497 mm/54–98 in; subject to influence of the Saharan Harmattan in N.
Currency 1 Naira (N) = 100 kobos
Economy Oil (provides c.90% of exports); agriculture (employs 50% of population); palm oil, groundnuts, cotton, cassava, rice, sugar cane, tobacco; fishing, livestock, forestry; natural gas, tin, iron ore, columbite (world's largest supplier), tantalite, limestone; pulp, paper, textiles, rubber.
GDP (2002e) $112·5 bn, per capita $900
Human Development Index (2002) 0·462
History Centre of the Nok culture, 500 BC-AD 200; Muslim immigrants, 15th–16th-c; British colony at Lagos, 1861; protectorates of N and S Nigeria, 1900; amalgamated as the Colony and Protectorate of Nigeria, 1914; federation, 1954; independence, 1960; federal republic, 1963; military coup, 1966; E area formed Republic of Biafra, 1967; civil war, and surrender of Biafra, 1970; military coups 1983 and 1985; major civil and religious unrest, 1992; presidential elections held, then annulled, 1993; military coup, 1993; restoration of civilian rule, 1999; governed by a President, a 360-seat House of Representatives, and a 109-seat Senate.

Military Government
1966 J T U Aguiyi-Ironsi
1966–75 Yakubu Gowon
1975–6 Murtala R Mohamed
1976–9 Olusegun Obasanjo
Head of State/Government
1979–83 Alhaji Shehu Shagari
Military Government
1983–4 Mohammadu Buhari
1985–93 Ibrahim B Babangida
1993 Ernest Adegunle Shonekan *Interim*
1993–8 Sani Abacha
1998–9 Abdusalam Abubakar
Head of State/Government
1999– Olusegun Obasanjo

Nightingale, Florence, known as **the Lady of the Lamp** (1820–1910) Hospital reformer, born in Florence, NC Italy. Raised in England, she trained as a nurse at Kaiserswerth and Paris. During the Crimean War, after the Battle of Alma (1854), she led a party of 38 nurses to organize a nursing department at Scutari. There she found grossly inadequate sanitation, but soon established better conditions and had 10 000 wounded under her care. She returned to England in 1856, where she formed an institution for the training of nurses at St Thomas' Hospital, and spent several years on army sanitary reform, the improvement of nursing, and public health in India.

nightingale Either of two species of thrush of the genus *Luscinia*, native to Europe, Asia, and N Africa; mid-brown with paler breast; male renowned for its song; often sings at night. The **nightingale** (*Luscinia megarhynchos*) is found in dry woods and hedgerows; the **thrush nightingale**, or **nightingale thrush** (*Luscinia luscinia*), in damp woodland near water. (Family: Turdidae.)

nightjar A nocturnal bird of the widespread family Caprimulgidae (c.70 species); mottled brown with short bill; spends day camouflaged on ground or along branch; inhabits woodland or desert; eats insects. The name is also used for the **tree nightjar** (Family: Nyctibiidae) and the **owlet nightjar** (Family: Aegothelidae).

Night of the Long Knives The event which took place in Germany (29–30 Jun 1934) when the SS, on Hitler's orders, and with the pre-arranged support of the German army, murdered Röhm and some 150 other leaders of the Sturmabteilung (SA 'storm troopers'). The aim was to crush the leftist political aspirations of the SA and to settle old political scores. Up to 1000 political opponents of Hitler and other Nazi leaders were eliminated. The incident completed Hitler's seizure of total power, and led to the nazification of the army.

nightshade *deadly nightshade; woody nightshade*

nihilism (Lat, literally 'nothing-ism') A term invented by Turgenev in connection with his character, the revolutionary Bazarov, in *Fathers and Sons* and later applied to other members of the Russian radical intelligentsia. It popularly denotes the disillusioned rejection of conventional moral values and institutions.

Niigata [neegata] 37°58N 139°02E, pop (2000e) 490 000. Port capital of Niigata prefecture, N Honshu, Japan; on the East Sea (Sea of Japan) at the mouth of R Shinano; mountainous region with many plateaus, Niigata was previously one of the most remote and inaccessible areas of Japan; airport; railway; three universities; oil refining, machinery, chemicals, textiles; rice, tulips, pears, watermelons, radishes; leading producer of *sake* (rice wine); Niigata Stadium Big Swan (2001).

Nijinska, Bronislava [nizhinska] (1891–1972) Ballet dancer and choreographer, born in Minsk, Belarus, the sister of Vaslav Nijinsky. She studied at St Petersburg, and became a soloist with the Maryinski company. She danced with the Ballets Russes company in Paris and London (1909–14) before returning to Russia during World War 1, where she danced and started a school in Kiev. She joined Diaghilev in 1921 as principal choreographer, the only woman to achieve this status. After working in Buenos Aires and Paris, she briefly formed her own company (1932), and after 1938 lived and worked mainly in the USA. Noted for the modern, stark realism of her ballets, two works remain in popular repertory: *Le Noces* (1923) and *Les Biches* (1924).

Nijinsky, Vaslav [nizhinskee] (1890–1950) Ballet dancer, born in Kiev, Ukraine, the brother of Bronislava Nijinska. Considered one of the greatest and most innovative male dancers of the 20th-c, he was, like his sister, trained at the Imperial Ballet School in St Petersburg, and first appeared in ballet at the Mariinski Theatre. As the leading dancer in Diaghilev's Ballets Russes, taken to Paris in 1909, he became phenomenally successful, and in 1911 he appeared as Petrouchka in the first performance of Stravinsky's burlesque ballet. His choreographic portfolio is slim but has two high points, *L'Après-midi d'un faune* (1912, Afternoon of a Fawn), and *Sacre du printemps* (1913, The Rite of Spring), which at the time was regarded as outrageous in its subversion of conventional ballet and its use of Stravinsky's rhythmically complex score. He married in 1913, and was interned in Hungary during the early part of World War 1. He rejoined Diaghilev for a world tour, but retired in 1917 when he was diagnosed a paranoid schizophrenic.

Nijinsky [nijinskee] Racehorse. In 1970, he was the first horse to win over £100 000 (in fact, £159 681) in a single British flat racing season. His wins included three Classics – the Derby, 2000 Guineas, and St Leger.

Nijmegen or **Nimeguen** [niymuhkhn, niymaygn], Ger **Nimwegen**, ancient **Noviomagus** 51°50N 5°52E, pop (2000e) 153 000. City in S Gelderland province, E Netherlands; on the R Waal, 19 km/12 mi S of Arnhem; founded as a hilltop Roman fort, AD 69; former residence of the Carlovingian kings; member of the Hanseatic League; railway; university (1923); metalworking, electrical engineering, textiles, printing, foodstuffs, chemicals; town hall (16th-c), Groote Kerk (13th-c); remains of Charlemagne's Valkhof Palace (8th-c).

Nijo-jo Castle [nijohjoh] A stronghold built in 1603 in Kyoto, Japan, by Tokugawa Ieyasu, founder of the Tokugawa shogunate. The complex is set in fine landscaped gardens and surrounded by a moat; it includes the Ninomaru Palace and the famous Karamon gate (originally from Fushimi Castle).

Nike [niykee, neekay] The Greek goddess of Victory, either in war or in an athletic contest. She is the frequent subject of sculpture, often shown as a winged figure, as in Nike of Samothrace. The Roman equivalent was Victoria.

Nile, River *see panel*

Nile, Battle of the *Aboukir Bay, Battle of* 1

nilgai [nilgiy] An Indian spiral-horned antelope (*Boselaphus tragocamelus*), the largest Indian antelope; male bluish with short slightly curved horns, tuft of dark hairs on throat; female brown without horns; also known as **blue bull** or **bluebuck**. The name *bluebuck* is also used for an extinct African antelope (*Hippotragus leucophaeus*).

Nilgiri Hills [neelgiree] Hills linking the Eastern Ghats with the Western Ghats, Tamil Nadu state, S India; connected to the S Deccan Plateau; highest point, Doda Betta (2636 m/8648 ft); many coffee and tea plantations.

Nilotes [niylohteez] Peoples of NE Africa who originated in the Nile regions and moved S probably before the 16th-c. Pastoralists, they mingled with agriculturalists creating new ethnic groupings. The Acholi and Alur of N Uganda, and the Luo who inhabit the E shores of L Victoria, all belong to this group. It is also thought that some Nilotic migrants, known as the Bito, became the aristocracies of some of the states of Uganda, notably Buganda, Bunyoro, and Toro.

Nile, River

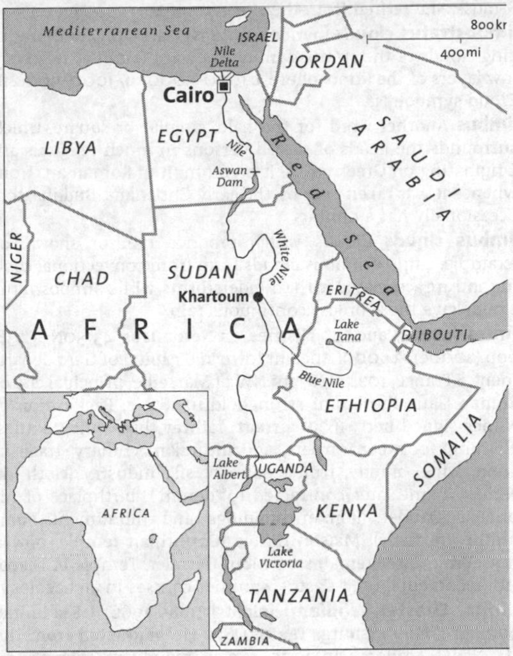

□ International Airport

[niyl], Arabic **Nahr en-Nil** River in E and NE Africa; longest river in the world; length from its most remote headstream (Luvironza R), 6695 km/4160 mi; Luvironza rises in SC Burundi, and flows generally NE and N under various names, entering L Victoria in W; Victoria Nile flows N through L Kyoga into NE end of L Albert; Albert Nile flows N through NW Uganda, becoming known as the White Nile at the Sudanese frontier; joined by the Blue Nile at Khartoum, to become the Nile proper, c.3000 km/1900 mi from its delta on the Mediterranean Sea; joined (E) by R Atbara, the only significant tributary; on entering Egypt, flows into L Nasser, created by the Aswan High Dam; opens out into a broad delta N of Cairo, from Alexandria (W) to Port Said (E), 250 km/155 mi E–W and 160 km/100 mi N–S; flows through two mouths (Rosetta and Damietta), both c.240 km/150 mi long; Egypt's population and cultivated land almost entirely along the floodplain; European discovery of Blue Nile's source made by James Bruce, 1768–73; L Victoria established as Nile's main reservoir by J H Speke, 1858.

Nilsen, Dennis (1948–) British convicted murderer. He admitted the murder and mutilation of between 12 and 16 young men in England between 1978 and 1983. He was sentenced to life imprisonment, with a recommendation that he serve a minimum of 25 years on six counts of murder and two of attempted murder.

Nilsson, (Märta) Birgit (1922–) Operatic soprano, born in Karup, SW Sweden. She studied at the Stockholm Royal Academy of Music. Following her debut in 1946, she sang with the Stockholm Royal Opera (1947–51), and at Bayreuth Festivals (1953–70). She was the leading Wagnerian soprano of that period, having a voice of exceptional power, stamina, and intense personality. She sang at most of the great houses and festivals of the world, and her repertoire included Verdi, Puccini, and Strauss. She retired from the stage in 1982.

nimbostratus clouds [nimbohstratuhs] Dark-grey, rain-producing clouds of the stratus family. They are found at relatively low layers of the atmosphere, c.1000–3000 m/3000–9000 ft. Cloud symbol: Ns.

nimbus Another word for the halo, circular or square, which surrounds the heads of sacred persons in much religious art. Originating on Greek vases, it is common in Roman art, from whence it was taken over by the early Christians. Buddha, too, occasionally has a nimbus.

nimbus clouds Clouds which produce rain or snow. For example, cumulonimbus clouds form from convectional cooling and are associated with thunderstorms, while nimbostratus clouds give more or less continuous rain.

Nîmes [neem], ancient **Nismes** or **Nemausus** 43°50N 4°23E, pop (2000e) 134 000. Ancient town and capital of Gard department, S France; 102 km/63 mi NW of Marseille; principal city of Roman Gaul; Protestant stronghold in 16th-c; Pacification of Nîmes signed here, 1629; airport; railway; bishopric; textiles, clothing, footwear, carpets, agricultural machinery, trade in grain, wine, brandy, fruit; centre of silk industry (cloth 'de Nîmes', name later contracted to 'denim'); birthplace of Alphonse Daudet; Roman buildings and monuments, amphitheatre (1st-c), Maison Carrée (Corinthian temple, now a museum), tower remains on Mont Cavalier, Temple of Diana, 11th-c Cathedral of St-Castor; summer courses in archaeology.

Nimitz, Chester W(illiam) [nimits] (1885–1966) US admiral, born in Fredericksburg, Texas, USA. He graduated from the US Naval Academy in 1905, served mainly in submarines, and by 1938 had risen to the rank of rear-admiral. Chief of the Bureau of Navigation at the outset of World War 2 (1939–41), he commanded the US Pacific fleet and Pacific Ocean areas (1941–5), contributing to the defeat of Japan. He was made a fleet admiral in 1944, and signed the Japanese surrender documents for the USA on board the USS *Missouri* in Tokyo Bay (1945). Later posts include chief of naval operations (1945–7), and special assistant to the secretary of the navy (1947–9).

Nimoy, Leonard [nimoy] (1931–) Actor, director, producer, and writer, born in Boston, Massachusetts, USA. He studied at Boston College, moved to Los Angeles and joined a theatre group. His film work began in 1951, with *Queen for a Day*, but he eventually came to be identified in the public mind with the half-Vulcan/half-human character of Spock in the *Star Trek* series (1966–9). When the series was reprised as feature films (1979–91), he produced the third and fourth instalments, and scripted the fourth. In addition to many other acting roles in theatre, film, and television, he has worked as a director, his films including *Three Men and a Baby* (1987) and *Holy Matrimony* (1994). He has also written several books, including combinations of poetry and photography, as well as the book-pair *I Am Not Spock* (1975), in which he tried to break away from his screen image, and *I Am Spock* (1995), in which he accepted it.

Nimrod In the Table of Nations (*Gen* 10), purportedly the son of Cush and great-grandson of Noah. He was a legendary warrior and hunter, and allegedly one of the first to rule over a great empire after the Flood, becoming King of Babylon and S Mesopotamia as well as of Assyria, where he is said to have founded Nineveh. In some rabbinic traditions, he was also considered the builder of the Tower of Babel (*Gen* 11), but it is uncertain whether he was a historical individual at all.

Nimrud The Upper Mesopotamian city which became the royal seat and military capital of the Assyrian Empire in the 9th-c BC.

Nin, Anaïs [neen, anaees] (1903–77) Novelist and short-story writer, born in Neuilly, NC France. She studied in New York City, then returned to Paris, where she became acquainted with many well-known writers and artists, and began to write herself. Her early work includes a study of D H Lawrence (1932) and several novels, as well as a collection of erotically-driven short stories, *Under a Glass Bell* (1944). However, her somewhat controversial reputation as an artist and seminal figure in the new feminism of the 1970s rests on her *Journals* (1966–83). Spanning the years 1931 to 1974 they are a record of an era, as well as a passionate, explicit, and candid account of one woman's voyage of self-discovery.

Nineteen Counties An unsuccessful attempt by the government of New South Wales to limit the spread of settlement. The counties were proclaimed by Governor Darling in 1829, covering 9 million ha/22 million acres, and bounded (N) by the Manning R, (W) by the Wellington Valley, (S) by the Goulburn Plains, and (E) by the Pacific Ocean. The boundaries of the counties were ignored, and Pastoralists 'squatted' on the land outside them. In 1836 Governor Bourke permitted squatters to graze their sheep outside the counties for an annual licence fee. In 1847, the Nineteen Counties were absorbed into a new administrative division of the Colony.

ninety-five theses A series of points of academic debate with the pope, posted by Martin Luther on the church door at Wittenberg in 1517. They attacked many practices of the Church, including indulgences and papal powers. This act is generally regarded as initiating the Protestant Reformation.

Nineveh [ninevuh] One of the most important cities of ancient Assyria, located E of the Tigris, and the site of royal residences from c.11th-c BC. It was founded in pre-historic times, although some Biblical legends associate its origin with Nimrod, and the temple of Ishtar is noted there in the Code of Hammurabi. It was at its height of importance in the 8th–7th-c BC under Sennacherib, but fell in 612 BC to the Medes and Persians. Its royal libraries, containing thousands of clay tablets, are one of the best surviving sources for ancient Mesopotamian history.

Ningbo or **Ning-po** [ningboh] 29°54N 121°33E, pop (2000e) 1 274 000, administrative region 5 295 000. Port city in Zhejiang province, E China, at confluence of Fenghua, Tong, and Yuyao Rivers; traditional outlet for silk and porcelain; important during Song dynasty, 10th–13th-c; centre of trade under early Ming, 14th–16th-c; burned by Japanese pirates, 1523; opened to Western trade, 1842; designated a special economic zone; railway; fishing, food processing, shipbuilding, textiles, high technology; Tianyi Ge Library (1561, oldest in China); Tianfeng Ta pagoda (1330).

ninjutsu An armed Japanese martial art, whose origins are obscure because of the secrecy surrounding the *Ninja*, who were assassins. In the 1980s it became popular as a cult in the cinema and video world.

Niño, El *El Niño*

Niobe [niyohbee] In Greek mythology, the daughter of Tantalus and the wife of Amphion. She had twelve children (or more) and said she was better than any mother, including Leto. This provoked Leto's children, Apollo and Artemis, who killed all (or most of) the children, and turned the weeping Niobe into a weeping rock on Mt Sipylos.

Niokolo-Koba [nyokohloh **koh**ba] area 9130 sq km/3524 sq mi. National park and game reserve in E Senegal, W Africa; established in 1953; principally watered by the R Gambia; Mt Asirik rises to 311 m/1020 ft; a world heritage site.

Nippur [nipoor] The religious centre of the Sumerians, where their kings were crowned and perhaps also buried. It was never a political capital, but the seat of the god, Enlil, the head of the Sumerian pantheon.

Nirvana [neervahna] In Buddhism, the attainment of supreme bliss, tranquillity, and purity, when the fires of desire are extinguished. The goal of Buddhists, it is neither personal immortality nor the annihilation of the self, but more like absorption into the infinite.

Niš or **Nish** [neesh], ancient **Naisus** 43°20N 21°54E, pop (2000e) 178 000. Industrial town in SEC Serbia, on R Nišava; formerly a stronghold on the road to Byzantium; occupied by Bulgaria until 1918; airfield; railway; university (1965); locomotives, wine, grain, cattle trade, electronics; open-air theatre, Tower of Skulls, Turkish citadel; Constantine's villa at Mediana; film festival.

nisnas monkey *patas monkey*

nit An egg laid by a louse of the order Phthiraptera, especially used of eggs of the human head and body lice.

Niterói [neeteroy] 22°54S 43°06W, pop (2000e) 553 300. Port in Rio de Janeiro state, SE Brazil, on SE shore of Guanabara Bay opposite Rio de Janeiro; founded 1573; former state capital; connected to Rio by a bridge, length 14 km/9 mi; railway; ferries to Rio; university (1960); commerce, shipbuilding, canning, fishing, tourism; colonial forts of Santa Cruz (16th-c), Barão do Rio Branco (1633), Gragoatá, Nossa Senhora da Boa Viagem; Church of Boa Viagem (1633); archaeological site and museum.

nitinol An elastic type of metal wire containing nickel and titanium.

nitrate A salt of nitric acid, containing the NO_3^- ion, or a compound containing the covalently bonded $-O-NO_2$ group. Potassium and sodium nitrates occur in nature (*saltpetre* or *Chile saltpetre*), and are used in food preservation, fertilizers, and explosives. Organic nitrates are highly explosive.

nitre [niyter] *potassium*

nitric acid HNO_3, melting point −42°C. A strong, oxidizing acid, made commercially by the oxidation of ammonia (the Ostwald process), the overall reaction being: $NH_3 + 2O_2 \rightarrow HNO_3 + H_2O$. It is important in the manufacture of agricultural chemicals and explosives.

nitric oxide NO, boiling point −152°C. A colourless gas, an intermediate in the oxidation of ammonia to nitric acid. It reacts spontaneously with oxygen to give nitrogen dioxide (NO_2).

nitrite A salt of nitrous acid (HNO_2), containing the ion NO_2^-, or a compound containing covalently bonded $-O-N=O$. Nitrites are the most effective means of reducing the growth of the bacteria causing botulism. Sodium nitrite plays a particular role in food preservation.

nitro- The name for the group $-NO_2$, isomeric with the nitrite group, but bonded through nitrogen. Most organic nitro- compounds are explosive, such as trinitrotoluene (TNT). *Nitroglycerine* is better called *glyceryl trinitrate*, as it is the nitrate ester of glycerol. It is mixed with sawdust or other filler to make dynamite.

nitrocellulose A chemical compound formed by the action of nitric acid on cellulose; first made in 1845 by German chemist Christian Friedrich Schonbein (1799–1868). Its explosive properties proved unmanageable until about 20 years later, when it was turned into the form known as *gun cotton*. Mixed with nitroglycerine, it forms the main constituent of some blasting explosives and propellants. Some forms of cellulose nitrate, less explosive but still highly inflammable, were for many years used in plastics and as a film base.

nitrogen N, element 7, boiling point −196°C. In the form of diatomic molecules (N_2), it is the most abundant gas in the atmosphere, of which it makes up 78%. It is obtained by the fractional distillation of air. The strength of the triple bond in NÙN makes the gas almost inert, and it is commonly used when an inert atmosphere is required. Conversion of nitrogen to water-soluble forms, such as ammonia and nitrates, is called **nitrogen fixation**. This can be carried out by soil bacteria, and industrially by the Haber process. Most other compounds of nitrogen, especially nitrites and nitrates, are derived from ammonia. The main uses of its compounds are in agricultural fertilizers and in explosives, which make use of the large amount of energy released when N_2 is reformed.

nitrogen cycle The dynamic system of changes in the nature of nitrogen-containing compounds circulating between the atmosphere, the soil, and living organisms. It includes the fixation of gaseous molecular nitrogen into nitrogenous compounds by micro-organisms, lightning, or other processes; the oxidation of ammonia to nitrite and of nitrite to nitrate by aerobic organisms (*nitrification*); the decomposition of organic matter by putrefaction; and the eventual release of gaseous nitrogen by the reduction of nitrates and nitrites, typically by anaerobic micro-organisms (*denitrification*).

nitrogen fixation A means of converting atmospheric nitrogen to compounds usable as fertilizers. The need for such means, in the face of potential food shortage for a growing population, was seen to be an acute world problem in the late 19th-c. Attention was called to it in a famous speech to the British Association by Sir William Crookes in 1898. Nitrogen, which is essential for the nutrition of plants, is not directly absorbed by them from the atmosphere. In nature, soil bacteria carry out the necessary conversion of gaseous nitrogen to assimilable compounds. The best solution to the problem was that of Haber and Bosch (via ammonia); most nitrogenous fertilizers are now derived from atmospheric nitrogen through this type of fixation process.

nitrogen mustard *cyclophosphamide*

nitroglycerine An explosive liquid made by the action of nitric acid (mixed with sulphuric acid) on glycerol. When first made in 1846 by Italian chemist Ascanio Sobrero (1812–88), it was considered impossibly dangerous, but was put to some use with careful handling. Then from 1867 Nobel made its use more general by mixing it with moderators. It is a constituent of several mixed explosives (eg gelignite). In medicine, the inhaled vapour rapidly relieves the pain of angina.

nitrous oxide Boiling point −88°C. Dinitrogen oxide, N_2O, isoelectronic with carbon dioxide; also called **laughing gas**. It has a slightly sweet odour, and is used as a general anaesthetic for short periods, especially in dentistry. It is produced by the decomposition of ammonium nitrate: $NH_4NO_3 \rightarrow N_2O + 2H_2O$.

Niue [nyooay] 19°02S 169°55W; pop (2000e) 2100; area 259 sq km/100 sq mi. Coral island in the S Pacific Ocean, 2140 km/1330 mi NE of New Zealand; main settlement, Alofi; timezone GMT +12; chief religion, Christianity; official language, English; New Zealand currency used; mainly coral, with a flat, rolling interior and porous soils; highest point, 70 m/230 ft; subtropical and damp climate; hurricanes in the hot season (Dec–Mar); rainfall throughout the year; visited by Captain Cook, 1774; European missionaries in mid-19th-c; British protectorate, 1900; annexed to New Zealand, 1901; since 1974, internal self-government in free association with New Zealand, which still maintains responsibility for defence and foreign affairs, governed by an elected 24-member Legislative Assembly, headed by a premier; mainly agricultural economy; passionfruit, copra, bananas, crafts; severely damaged by cyclone Heta, Jan 2004.

Niven, David, popular name of **James David Graham Nevins** (1909–83) Actor, born in Kirriemuir, Angus, E Scotland, UK. He trained at Sandhurst Military Academy, served in the army, and had a variety of jobs before he arrived in Hollywood, where he joined the social set led by Errol Flynn and Clark Gable, and worked as an extra in *Mutiny on the Bounty* (1935). Signed by Samuel Goldwyn, he developed into a polished light comedian and gallant hero in such films as *The Charge of the Light Brigade* (1936) and *The Dawn Patrol* (1938). After service as an army officer in World War 2, he spent 30 years as an urbane leading man, perfectly cast as the gentlemanly voyager Phineas Fogg in *Around the World in 80 Days* (1956), and winning an Oscar for *Separate Tables* (1958). An inimitable raconteur, he published two volumes of lighthearted autobiography: *The Moon's a Balloon* (1972) and *Bring on the Empty Horses* (1975).

nix or **nixie** In European folk-tales, a water-sprite, who occasionally entraps people into her pool; not to be confused with the deity Nyx in Greek mythology.

Nixon, Richard (Milhous) (1913–94) US statesman and 37th president (1969–74), born in Yorba Linda, California, USA. He studied at Whittier College and Duke University, became a lawyer, served in the US navy, and was elected to the US House of Representatives in 1946. He became senator in 1950, and vice-president under Eisenhower (1953–61). In 1959 on a visit to Moscow he achieved notoriety by his outspoken exchanges with Nikita Khrushchev. As the Republican candidate, he lost the presidential election (1960) to John F Kennedy by a tiny margin. Standing for the governorship of California in 1962, he was again defeated. He won the presidential election in 1968 by a small margin, and was re-elected in 1972 by a large majority. His presidency saw the end of the Vietnam War, imposed wage and price controls, and presidential visits to China. During an official investigation into a break-in attempt in June 1972 at the Democratic National Committee's headquarters in the Watergate Hotel, Washington, he lost credibility by at first claiming executive privilege for senior White House officials to prevent them being questioned, and by refusing to hand over tapes of relevant conversations. He resigned in August 1974 under the threat of impeachment, after several leading members of his government had been found guilty of being involved in the Watergate scandal. The following month he was given a full pardon by President Gerald Ford.

Nizhni Novgorod [nizhnee novgorod], formerly **Gorky** (1929–91) 56°20N 44°00E, pop (2000e) 1 430 000. River-port and industrial capital of Gorkovskaya oblast, E European Russia; at the confluence of the Volga and Oka Rivers; founded as a frontier post, 1221; famous for its annual trade fairs (1817–1930); renamed in honour of Maxim Gorky; airport; railway; university (1918); machines, chemicals, woodworking, foodstuffs.

Njazidja [njazeeja], formerly **Grande Comore** 11°45S 43°15E; pop (2000e) 250 800; area 1148 sq km/443 sq mi. Largest island of the Comoros group in the Mozambique Channel; chief town, Moroni; steep mountains rise to the peak of Kartala, an active volcano (2361 m/7746 ft); timber.

Nkomo, Joshua (Mqabuko Nyongolo) [nkohmoh] (1917–99) Zimbabwean statesman, born in Semokwe, Zimbabwe. Educated mainly in South Africa, he became a member of the African National Congress in 1952, and president of the Zimbabwe African People's Union (ZAPU) in 1961. There followed a long period during which he was placed under government restrictions, but in 1976 he formed the Popular Front with Robert Mugabe to press for black majority rule in an independent Zimbabwe, and was given a cabinet post in the Mugabe government in 1980. However, tension between his party and Mugabe's led to his dismissal in 1982. Although Nkomo's native Matabeleland continued to harbour dissidents from Mugabe's rule, some reconciliation was achieved as Zimbabwe moved towards a one-party state.

Nkrumah, Kwame [nkrooma] (1909–72) Ghanaian statesman, prime minister (1957–60), and president (1960–6), born in Nkroful, SW Ghana (formerly Gold Coast). He studied in both the USA (Lincoln University) and the UK (London School of Economics), returning to the Gold Coast in 1947, and in 1949 formed the nationalist Convention People's Party. In 1950 he was imprisoned, but elected to parliament while still in jail. Released in 1951, he became leader of business in the Assembly, and then premier. Called 'the Gandhi of Africa', he was a significant leader both of the movement against white domination and of pan-African feeling. He was the moving spirit behind the Charter of African States (1961). Economic reforms led to political opposition and several attempts on his life, interference with the judiciary, and the formation of a one-party state in 1964. His regime was overthrown by a military coup during his absence in China, and he sought asylum in Guinea, where he was given the status of co-head of state.

Noah [nohuh] Biblical character, depicted as the son of Lamech. He is described as a 'righteous man' who was given divine instruction to build an ark in which he, his immediate family, and a selection of animals were saved from a widespread flood over the Earth (*Gen* 6–9). In the Table of Nations (*Gen* 10), Noah's sons (Japheth, Ham, and Shem) are depicted as the ancestors of all the nations on Earth. A similar flood legend was told of a Babylonian character, Utanapishtim, in the Gilgamesh epic.

Nobel, Alfred Bernhard [nohbel] (1833–96) Chemist and industrialist, the inventor of dynamite and the founder of the Nobel Prizes, born in Stockholm, Sweden. He moved to Russia as a child, studied chemistry in Paris, worked in the USA (1852–6) under John Ericsson, and settled in Sweden in 1859. An explosives expert like his father, in 1866 he invented a safe and manageable form of nitroglycerine he called *dynamite*, and later, smokeless gunpowder and (1875) gelignite. He helped to create an industrial empire manufacturing many of his other inventions, and amassed a huge fortune, much of which he left to endow annual prizes (first awarded in 1901) for physics, chemistry, physiology or medicine, literature, and peace. (A sixth prize, for economics, was instituted in his honour in 1969.)

Nobel Prizes [nohbel] Prizes awarded each year from the income of a trust fund established by the will of Swedish scientist and industrialist Alfred Nobel to those who, in the opinion of the judges, have contributed most in the fields of physics, chemistry, physiology or medicine, literature, and peace. The first prizes were awarded in 1901. A sixth prize, for economics, was established by the Swedish National Bank in 1968, and awarded for the first time in 1969. Each prizewinner receives a gold medal and a sum of money.

Nobile, Umberto [nohbilay] (1885–1978) Aviator, born in Lauro, S Italy. He became an aeronautical engineer and built the airships *Norge* and *Italia*. He flew across the North Pole in the *Norge* with Amundsen and Lincoln Ellsworth (1880–1951) in 1926. A general in the Italian air force and professor of aeronautical engineering at Naples, in 1928 he was wrecked in the airship *Italia* when returning from the North Pole, and was judged to be responsible for the disaster. He resigned his commission, but was later reinstated.

noble gases The final or zeroth group of the periodic table; also called the **rare** or **inert gases**. They are all gases at normal temperatures, and were called 'noble' because they were long thought to form no chemical compounds.

noble metals Metals which are intrinsically unreactive and not readily subject to corrosion. Gold, silver, and the 'platinum metals' are the best examples. Metals such as aluminium and chromium, whose corrosion resistance is due to an adhering coat of oxide, are called *passive*.

Nobunaga, Oda [nobunahga] (1534–82) The first of the three great historical unifiers of Japan, followed by Hideyoshi and Tokugawa, born into a noble family near Nagoya, EC Japan. He became a general, and was invited by the emperor to establish order in the old capital, Kyoto (1568), destroying the power of the Buddhist Church, and favouring Christianity as a counterbalance. He built Azuchi Castle, near Kyoto, as his headquarters. He was assassinated by one of his own generals, in Kyoto.

Noctiluca [noktilooka] An unusually large, single-celled marine organism; a dinoflagellate, moving by means of whip-like flagella; bioluminescent, producing flashes of light when disturbed; feeds mainly by ingestion of small particles. (Class: Dinophyceae.)

noctilucent cloud Very high altitude (80 km/50 mi) dusty clouds visible as a rippled or veiled structure after sunset during summer in each hemisphere. They consist of water ice frozen onto a dust core.

noctuid moth [noktyooid] Any of a large family, the Noctuidae, of typically drab, nocturnal moths; larvae feed on leaves, flowers, and buds, or bore into plant stems; c.21 000 species, many of which cause serious damage to crops, including cutworms and armyworms; also known as the **owlet moth**. (Order: Lepidoptera.)

noctule A type of bat, native to Asia, Europe, Madeira, and the Azores; dark or yellow brown; inhabits woodland but may feed in open areas; often eats beetles (once observed to eat mice). (Genus: *Nyctalus*, 5 species. Family: Vespertilionidae.)

nocturnal In astronomy, an instrument analogous to a sundial, consisting of an arm and a disc, used to determine local time at night. It works by aligning the arm parallel to the Pointers in Ursa Major, and reading the time from engraved scales.

nocturne A piece of music, usually in a meditative, languid style. The title has been used for piano pieces by John Field (its inventor), Chopin, and Fauré, and for orchestral pieces by Mendelssohn and Debussy.

noddy *tern*

Noel-Baker (of the City of Derby), Philip (John) Noel-Baker, Baron (1889–1982) British statesman, born in London, UK. He studied at Cambridge, and captained the British Olympic team in 1912, where he won a silver medal in the 1500 m. He served on the secretariat of the League of Nations (1919–22), became professor of international relations at London (1924–9), and was elected a Labour MP (1929–31, 1936–70). He was secretary of state for air (1946–7) and of commonwealth relations (1947–50), and minister of fuel and power (1950–1). A lifelong campaigner for peace through multilateral disarmament, he was awarded the Nobel Peace Prize in 1959, and created a life peer in 1977.

Noether, (Amalie) Emmy [**noe**ter] (1882–1935) Mathematician, born in Erlangen, SC Germany. She studied at Erlangen and Göttingen. Though invited to Göttingen in 1915 by David Hilbert, as a woman she could not hold a full academic post at that time, but worked there in a semi-honorary capacity until she emigrated to the USA in 1933 to Bryn Mawr and Princeton. One of the leading figures in the development of abstract algebra, the theory of **Noetherian rings** has been an important subject of later research.

no-fault principle In law, the principle that it should be possible to claim compensation for injury without proving fault against a defendant. In an action for negligence, it is necessary to prove that the damage was caused through a breach of a duty of care owed to the plaintiff by the defendant; if the defendant is not shown to be at fault, the case fails. The no-fault principle seeks to fill this gap by means of an insurance scheme. The compensation scheme for personal injuries in New Zealand is a notable example of the principle in operation, but the scope of the original scheme has been reduced in the UK. Industrial disablement benefit is a form of no-fault compensation. Many US states have adopted no-fault schemes for motor insurance policies in an attempt to reduce policy premiums.

Nogier, Paul *auricular therapy*

Noh Classical theatre of Japan in which imitation, gesture, dance, mask-work, costume, song, and music are fused in a concise stage art. The philosophy, style and much of the repertoire was established by Kan'ami (1333–84) and his son Zeami (1363–1443). Five schools of Noh exist, and most of the plays they perform were written before 1600.

Nolan, Sir Sidney (Robert) (1917–92) Painter, born in Melbourne, Victoria, SE Australia. Largely self-taught, he took up full-time painting in 1938 and made his name with a series of 'Ned Kelly' paintings begun in 1946, following this with an 'explorer' series. He first went to Europe in 1950, and although he has worked in Italy, Greece, and Africa, he remains best known for his Australian paintings. He also designed the Covent Garden productions *The Rite of Spring* (1962), *Samson and Delilah* (1981), and the Australian Opera's *Il Trovatore* (1983), has illustrated books by Robert Lowell and Benjamin Britten, and published a volume of poems, drawings and paintings, *Paradise Garden* (1972). He was knighted in 1981.

Nolan Committee (Committee on Standards in Public Life) A committee chaired by Lord Nolan (1928–) and established by UK prime minister John Major in 1994, in the wake of accusations of sleaze involving members of the government and others in public life. It published its first report in 1995 and laid down seven principles by which those involved in public life should conduct themselves: selflessness, integrity, objectivity, accountability, openness, honesty, leadership.

Nolde, Emil [**nol**duh], pseudonym of **Emil Hansen** (1867–1956) Artist and printmaker, born in Nolde, W Germany. One of the most important Expressionist painters, he was briefly a member of the Expressionist *die Brücke* (1906–7), but produced his own powerful 'blood and soil' style of distorted forms in violent religious pictures such as 'The Life of Christ' (1911–12). He also produced a large number of etchings, lithographs, and woodcuts.

Nollekens, Joseph [**nol**ekenz] (1737–1823) Neoclassical sculptor, born in London, UK. He worked in Rome for 10 years from 1760, and became a member of the Royal Academy in 1772. He executed likenesses of most of his famous contemporaries, including Garrick, Sterne, Goldsmith, Johnson, Fox, Pitt, and George III.

nomadism A way of life characterized by moving from one place to another, with no fixed residence, though often temporary centres. Mobility may be cyclical or periodic, determined by the availability of food supplies, rainfall, weather, employment, etc. Most nomadic people (eg the Bedouin, the Kirghiz) are either hunter-gatherers or pastoralists. Some are described as **semi-nomadic** (eg the Fulani), as they remain settled in one area for a span of time and cultivate crops. As various governments have restricted movements of people, nomadism has declined in recent decades.

nominalism In metaphysics, the view that only individual things exist in the full sense. Universals and properties (eg 'redness') have no independent reality, but are just names.

non-aligned movement A movement of states which positively espoused the position of not taking sides in the major division within world politics between the USA and USSR. Non-alignment differs from neutralism in that it is associated with moves to mediate between the superpowers, and aims to make a direct contribution to the achievement of peace. The neutrality of non-aligned states is supposed to afford them increased diplomatic influence. Attempts in the early 1960s to give impetus to the movement by Mediterranean, African, and Asian countries were badly shaken by superpower hostility. However, a number of recently de-colonized countries have favoured non-alignment as a mark of their independence. A formal Non-aligned Movement began in 1961, and holds conferences every three years; there were 114 members in 2004 (Yugoslavia being suspended).

Nonconformists Originally, those Protestants in England and Wales in the 17th-c who dissented from the principles of the Church of England. It has subsequently been applied to such denominations as Baptists, Congregationalists, and Methodists, and generally refers to Christians who refuse to conform to the doctrine and practice of an established or national Church.

Non-Co-operation Movement An unsuccessful nationalist campaign (1919–22) led by Gandhi and Congress to force the British to grant Indian independence. It was strengthened by joining forces with Indian Muslims campaigning against British policy towards the Ottoman Empire. The movement involved the boycott of Government institutions and foreign goods, and was abandoned when the protest became violent.

non-Euclidian geometries *geometries, non-Euclidian*

nonfigurative art *abstract art*

non-flam *safety film*

nonjurors Those who refused to swear an oath of loyalty to William III and Mary II in 1689, since to do so would infringe the divine right of monarchical succession. Most were clerics, including Archbishop William Sancroft of Canterbury (1617–93), five other bishops, and about 400 clergy. They were deprived of their offices.

nonlinear physics The study of systems in which the response to a stimulus is not directly proportional to the size of the stimulus. For example, when small weights are suspended from a spring, doubling the weight doubles the extension (Hooke's law) and the system is termed linear. If too much weight is added, the extension is not governed by such a simple law: the system is nonlinear. A pendulum undergoing large swings is a nonlinear system. High intensity light, such as laser light, induces nonlinear responses when interacting with atoms.

Nono, Luigi [**noh**noh] (1924–90) Composer, born in Venice, NE Italy. He studied at the Venice Conservatoire under Malipiero and Maderna, with whom he and Luciano Berio helped to establish Italy in the forefront of contemporary music. He worked for a time at the electronic studio in Darmstadt, and became a leading composer of electronic, aleatory, and serial music. A strongly politically committed artist, *Il canto sospeso* (1956, The Suspended Song), based on the letters of victims of wartime oppression, brought him to international notice. His other works include *Intolleranza* (1961, Intolerance) and *Canto per il Vietnam* (1973, A Song for Vietnam).

non-objective art *abstract art*

Nonpartisan League An organization of farmers, founded in 1915 in North Dakota and spreading across the N wheat belt. Quasi-socialist, the League advocated public ownership of public utilities. It declined after 1920, in part because of opposition to involvement in World War 1.

Non-Proliferation Treaty (NPT) A treaty signed in 1968 by the USA, Soviet Union, UK, and an open-ended list of over 100 other countries. It sought to limit the spread of nuclear weapons by restricting their transfer by the signatories, and for non-nuclear weapon states to pursue only peaceful uses of nuclear energy.

non-renewable resources Resources (ie objects of material or economic use to society, such as minerals, timber, and fish) which have evolved or formed over such long time periods that their exploitation is not sustainable. They cannot be used without danger of exhaustion because of the timescale needed for new stocks to form. Examples include fossil fuel deposits (coal, oil, gas) and mineral deposits (iron, gold). Some non-renewable resources can be recycled (eg metallic ores).

nonsense verse Verse which is written in defiance of sense and logic to satisfy the ear and the spirit rather than the intelligence. Edward Lear wrote famous examples, as did Lewis Carroll in the two *Alice* books; Spike Milligan (of the Goons) has made a modern contribution to the genre. Occasionally, previously non-existent words, such as *chortle* in Carroll's celebrated *Jabberwocky* poem, have passed into the language.

non-sporting dog A category of domestic dog; name used for breeds bred as pets/companions (except very small such breeds, which are called **toy dogs**); includes dogs formerly bred for sport (eg bulldog, some poodles); sometimes includes **working dogs** (eg collies).

non-tariff barriers Barriers to international trade other than tariffs. Tariffs, or taxes on imports, have been greatly reduced during successive rounds of international negotiation under the General Agreement on Tariffs and Trade (GATT). On some trade flows, especially industrial exports from less developed countries (LDCs), tariffs have been replaced by the growth of non-tariff barriers (NTBs). These include import quotas, especially on textiles under the Multi-Fibre Arrangement (MFA), and voluntary export restraint agreements (VERs), under which exporters 'volunteer' to restrict the volume or value of their exports to given markets. The growth of new export markets is also hindered by the rise of *contingent protection*, for example under anti-dumping procedures. Investment in facilities to produce and market new exports is not encouraged by the knowledge that contingent restrictions may be imposed if one is too successful. The limitation or elimination of NTBs should provide work for many future rounds of international trade negotiation under the World Trade Organization (WTO).

non-verbal communication (NVC) Those forms of interpersonal communication beyond the spoken or written word; often referred to as body language. The messages communicated may be deliberate (eg winking or bowing), or unintentional (eg blushing or shivering). Cultural codes largely determine what meaning, if any, there is in a facial expression, gesture, or posture.

non-woven fabrics Fabrics constructed from sheets of fibres, with or without fibre orientation, by stitching, glueing, or otherwise bonding the fibres together. Such non-woven fabrics are widely used as low-cost or disposable products, such as curtaining, medical textiles, and cleaning cloths.

Noonuccal, Oodgeroo [nunuhkl, ujuhroo], originally **Kath(leen Jean Mary) Walker** (1920–93) Poet and Aboriginal rights activist, born in Brisbane, Queensland, NE Australia. She was brought up with the Noonuccal tribe on Stradbroke I, Queensland, where many of the old Aboriginal customs survived. She became the first Aboriginal writer to be published in English, with her collection of poems *We Are Going* (1964), followed by *The Dawn is at Hand* (1966). She published a book of stories in traditional Aboriginal form, *Stradbroke Dreamtime* (1972). She visited the USA on a Fulbright Scholarship (1978–9), lecturing on Aboriginal rights, and was active on many Aboriginal interest committees including the Aboriginal Arts Board. She ran a Centre for Aboriginal Culture on Stradbroke I, for children of all races, and adopted her tribal name.

Nootka An American Indian group of the Northwest Pacific Coast, on the W side of Vancouver I, speaking an Algonkian–Wakashan language. They were famous as whalers, using dugout canoes and harpoons, and became wealthy during the late 18th-c through the fur trade.

noradrenaline (UK) [naw(r)**a**drenalin] / **norepinephrine** (US) [naw(r)epi**nef**rin] A chemical substance (a catecholamine) which functions in many animals as a neurotransmitter in the sympathetic nerves and brain, released (in association with adrenaline) from the adrenal medulla. Its widespread actions include cardiac stimulation, blood vessel constriction, and the relaxation of the bronchioles and gastro-intestinal tract. Within the brain, it is involved in the regulation of body temperature, food and water intake, and cardiovascular and respiratory control.

Norbertines *Premonstratensians*

Norden, Denis (1922–) British script-writer and broadcaster. He was educated in London, and with Frank Muir formed a comedy script-writing duo (1947–64). They contributed to many shows, including *Take It From Here* (1947–58) and *Bedtime with Braden* (1950–4), and have been resident on many panel shows, such as *My Word* (from 1956) and *My Music* (from 1967), and co-operated in writing a number of books. From 1964 he worked as a solo writer for films and television, especially *It'll Be Alright on the Night* (1977–), which he also presents.

Nordenskjöld, Nils (Adolf Erik), Baron [naw(r)denshoel] (1832–1901) Arctic navigator, born in Helsinki, Finland. A naturalized Swede, he made several expeditions to Spitsbergen, mapping the S of the island. After two preliminary trips proving the navigability of the Kara Sea, he accomplished the navigation of the Northeast Passage (on the *Vega*) from the Atlantic to the Pacific along the N coast of Asia (1878–9). He later made two expeditions to Greenland.

Nördliche Kalkalpen [nerdlikhuh kal**kal**pen] Mountain range of the E Alps in C Austria, rising to 2995 m/9826 ft at Hoher Dachstein.

norepinephrine *noradrenaline*

Norfolk (UK) [naw(r)fuhk] pop (2001e) 796 700; area 5368 sq km/2073 sq mi. County in E England, UK; low-lying, with fens in W; Norfolk Broads in E; drained by Yare, Ouse, Waveney, and Bure Rivers; county town, Norwich; other chief towns King's Lynn and Great Yarmouth, a major resort and fishing port; offshore natural gas; agriculture, turkeys, fishing, tourism; Grime's Graves (Neolithic flint mines), Sandringham royal residence, Shrine of Our Lady of Walsingham, Halvergate Marshes wildlife preserve.

Norfolk (USA) [nawfuhk] 36°51N 76°17W, pop (2000e) 234 400. Seaport and independent city, SE Virginia, USA, on the Elizabeth R; settled, 1682; city status, 1845; centre of fighting in the American Revolution and the Civil War; largest city in the state; airfield; railway; Norfolk State College (1935); headquarters of the US Atlantic Fleet, largest naval base in the world; shipbuilding, automobiles, chemicals machinery, trade in coal, grain, tobacco, timber, vegetables; Chrysler Museum, Douglas Mac-

Arthur Memorial, Hampton Roads Naval Museum, Botanical Gardens; Azalea Festival (Apr).

Norfolk, Duke of *Howard, Thomas*

Norfolk Island [naw(r)fuhk] 29°04S 167°57E, pop (2000e) 2200; area 35 sq km/13 sq mi; length 8 km/5 mi. Fertile, hilly island in the W Pacific Ocean, 1488 km/925 mi NE of Sydney, Australia; a British penal settlement in 1788–1806 and 1826–55; many people from the Pitcairn Is transferred here, 1856; an Australian external territory since 1913, governed by the Norfolk Island Legislative Assembly, and represented in Australia by an administrator appointed by the governor-general; English and Tahitian spoken; postage stamps, tourism.

Noriega, Manuel (Antonio) [noriayga] (1939–) Soldier and politician, born in Panama City, Panama. He studied at the university there and at a military school in Peru. The ruling force behind the Panamanian presidents (1983–9), he had been recruited by the CIA in the late 1960s, and supported by the US government until 1987. Alleging his involvement in drug trafficking, the US authorities ordered his arrest in 1989: 13 000 US troops invaded Panama to support the 12 000 already there. He surrendered in January 1990 after taking refuge for 10 days in the Vatican nunciature. He was taken to the USA for trial, found guilty in 1992, and sentenced to 40 years imprisonment.

Norma (Lat 'level') A small, faint S hemisphere constellation.

normal school *college of education*

Norman, Barry (Leslie) (1933–) British writer and television film critic. In 1973 he joined BBC television as host of *Film '73*, then wrote and presented the show (1973–81, 1983–97) until joining Sky television in 1998. He also wrote and presented the series *The Hollywood Greats* (1977–9, 1984–5) and *Talking Pictures* (1988). His books include *100 Best Films of the Century* (1992) and *The Mickey Mouse Affair* (1995). In 1990 he was voted Radio Times Columnist of the Year, and in 1995 was given a special award by the London Film Critics Circle and was honoured with a Special Achievement Award by the Guild of Provincial Film Writers.

Norman, Greg(ory John), nickname **the Great White Shark** (1955–) Golfer, born in Mount Isa, Queensland, NE Australia. A professional since 1976, and ranked the world's top player more often than anybody, he won the (British) Open (1986, 1993) and the World Matchplay Championship (1980, 1983, 1986) while topping the annual money-winners on the US PGA Tour three times (1986, 1990, 1995). With more than 50 victories worldwide, golf has made him a multimillionaire.

Norman, Jessye (1945–) Soprano, born in Augusta, Georgia, USA. Winning a scholarship to study voice, she graduated from Howard University, and studied further at Michigan. She made her operatic debut in *Tannhaüser* at Berlin (1969), and in *Aïda* at both La Scala and Covent Garden in 1972. She has since toured widely at music festivals and concerts, and is widely admired in opera and concert music for her beauty of tone, breadth of register, and mastery of dynamic range.

Norman architecture The form of architecture prevalent in 11th-c and 12th-c England, corresponding to the European Romanesque. Notable examples include Durham, Ely, Winchester, and Worcester cathedrals.

Norman Conquest A fundamental watershed in English political and social history, though some of its consequences are much debated. It not only began the rule of a dynasty of Norman kings (1066–1154), but entailed the virtual replacement of the Anglo-Saxon nobility by Normans, Bretons, and Flemings, many of whom retained lands in N France. The language of government, law, and of the court was Norman French. Moreover, between 1066 and 1144 England and Normandy were normally united under one king-duke, and the result was the formation of a single cross-Channel state. The Angevin conquest of Normandy (1144–5) and takeover of England (1154) ensured that England's fortunes would continue to be linked with France, even after the French annexation of Normandy in 1204.

Normandy, Fr **Normandie** Former duchy and province in NW France, along the littoral of the English Channel between Brittany and French Flanders; now occupying the regions of Haute-Normandie and Basse-Normandie; leading state in Middle Ages; William Duke of Normandy conquered England in 1066; focus of English–French dispute in 12th–14th-c, until became part of France in 1449; scene of Allied invasion, 1944; fertile agricultural area; sheep, dairy farming, flax, fruit.

Normandy Campaign (1944) A World War 2 campaign ('Operation Overlord') the biggest amphibious landing in history, which began on D-Day (6 Jun 1944). Allied forces under the overall command of General Eisenhower began the liberation of W Europe from Germany by landing on the Normandy coast between the Orne R and St Marcouf. Artificial harbours were constructed along a strip of beach so that armoured vehicles and heavy guns could be unloaded. US forces, under the command of General Omar Bradley, encountered the strongest German resistance at Omaha Beach. Allied air supremacy was vital in securing territory against German resistance. British misinformation deceived the Germans as to where the landings would take place – to the extent that Hitler persisted with the notion that the main attack would come N of the Seine and, fatally for the German forces, kept valuable troops there. Heavy fighting ensued for three weeks, before Allied troops captured Cherbourg (27 Jun). Tanks broke through the German defences, and Paris was liberated (25 Aug), followed by the liberation of Brussels (2 Sep), and the crossing of the German frontier (12 Sep). During the campaign more than 2 million troops, 4 million tonnes of supplies, and 450 000 vehicles had been landed, at the cost of some 224 000 Allied casualties.

Normans By the early 11th-c, a name (derived from 'Northmen', ie Vikings) applied to all the people inhabiting Normandy, a duchy (and later province) in N France, though probably only a small element was actually of Scandinavian descent. During the second half of the 11th-c and the first decades of the 12th-c, their achievements, especially as conquerors, were remarkable. They completed the conquest and aristocratic feudalization and colonization of England and a large part of Wales following a series of rebellions. They established a kingdom in S Italy and Sicily, founded the Norman principality of Antioch, fought against the Muslims in Spain, and settled peacefully in Scotland. They built motte and bailey castles and rebuilt churches throughout England, N France, and S Italy. The impact of Norman administration in Britain is reflected in the Domesday Book. Norman French became the language of law in England until the 17th-c.

norm-referenced test A test which compares candidates with each other, usually spreading marks over a normal distribution, with most in the middle and few at each extreme. Most conventional tests which give percentages of A to E grades are of this kind.

Norns In Norse mythology, the equivalent of the Fates, three sisters who sit under the tree Yggdrasil and spin the web of Destiny, including that of individual human beings. Even Odin cannot unpick the web of the Norns. Their names are Urd (who knows the past), Verlandi (the present), and Skuld (the future). They also water the principal root of the world-tree.

North, Frederick, 8th Baron North (1732–92) British statesman and prime minister (1770–82), born in London, UK. He became a Lord of the Treasury (1759) and Chancellor of the Exchequer (1767), and as prime minister brought George III a period of political stability. He was widely criticized both for failing to avert the Declaration of Independence by the North American colonies (1776) and for failing to defeat them in the subsequent war (1776–83). He annoyed the king by resigning in 1782, then formed a coalition with his former Whig opponent, Fox (1783), but it did not survive royal hostility. After this coalition was dismissed (1783), he remained an Opposition politician until his death.

North, Oliver (1943–) US soldier, born in San Antonio, Texas, USA. He trained at the US Naval College, Annapolis, and during the Vietnam War led a counter-insurgency marines platoon, winning a Silver Star and Purple Heart. Appointed a deputy-

North America

ARCTIC OCEAN
ASIA
Bering Strait
Brooks Range
Beaufort Sea
Ellesmere Island
Greenland
(to Denmark)
Bering Sea
UNITED STATES OF AMERICA
Victoria Island
Baffin Bay
Davis Strait
Baffin Island
Aleutian Islands
Aleutian Range
Mackenzie
Great Bear Lake
Foxe Basin
Gulf of Alaska
Mackenzie Mountains
Labrador Sea
Hudson Strait
Great Slave Lake
Hudson Bay
Lake Athabasca
ROCKY MOUNTAINS
CANADA
Queen Charlotte Islands
Reindeer Lake
St Pierre & Miquelon
(to France)
Lake Winnipeg
Vancouver Island
PACIFIC OCEAN
Lake Superior
St Lawrence
Lake Huron
Lake Michigan
Lake Ontario
Lake Erie
Missouri
ATLANTIC OCEAN
Great Salt Lake
Colorado
UNITED STATES OF AMERICA
Ohio
Appalachian Mountains
Arkansas
Mississippi
Lower California
Gulf of California
Rio Grande
Mississippi Delta
Gulf of Mexico
BAHAMAS
Turks & Caicos Islands
CUBA
MEXICO
HAITI
Greater Antilles
Cayman Islands
(to UK)
Navassa Island
Yucatan Peninsula
JAMAICA
BELIZE
Caribbean Sea
GUATEMALA
HONDURAS
EL SALVADOR
NICARAGUA
Lake Nicaragua
COSTA RICA
PANAMA

director of the National Security Council by President Reagan in 1981, he played a key role in a series of controversial military and security actions. Implicated in the Irangate scandal, involving the supply of arms to Iran in exchange for US hostages, and the operation of a secret slush fund to aid the Contra guerrillas in Nicaragua, he was forced to resign in 1986. Found guilty on three of 12 charges arising from the affair, he was given a three-year suspended jail sentence, and fined $150 000. In 1990, the three convictions were set aside, and he was cleared of all charges in 1991. He heads a political action group, V-PAC, and gives radio broadcasts. In 1991 he published *Under Fire: An American Story*.

North, Sir Thomas (1523–?1601) Translator, born in London, UK. He is known for his translation of Plutarch's *Lives of the Noble Grecians and Romans* in 1579, from which Shakespeare drew his knowledge of ancient history for many of his plays. He was knighted in 1591.

North African Campaign (1940–3) A campaign fought during World War 2 between Allied and Axis troops. After an initial Italian invasion of Egypt, Italian forces were driven back deep into Libya, and Rommel was sent to N Africa with the specially trained Afrika Corps to stem a further Italian retreat. The British were driven back to the Egyptian border, though they defended Tobruk. They counter-attacked late in 1941, and fighting continued the following year, with Rommel once more gaining the initiative. In October, British troops under Montgomery defeated Rommel at the Battle of El Alamein, and drove the German troops W once more. In February 1943, the Germans attacked US troops in Tunisia, were driven back, and finally 250 000 Axis troops, half of them German, were caught in a pincer movement by Allied forces advancing from E and W.

North America Third largest continent, extending 9600 km/6000 mi from 70°30N to 15°N; area c.24 million sq km/9¼ million sq mi; separated from Asia by the Bering Strait; bounded by the Beaufort Sea (NW), Arctic Ocean (N), Baffin Bay and Davis Strait (NE), Atlantic Ocean (E), and Pacific Ocean (W); includes Canada, USA, and Mexico; numerous islands, including Baffin I, Newfoundland, and the West Indies; ranges include the Rocky Mts, Alaska Range (including Mt McKinley, highest point), and Appalachian Mts; major lake system, the Great Lakes; major rivers include the Mississippi, Missouri, Rio Grande, and St Lawrence.

North American Free Trade Agreement (NAFTA) An association of the USA, Canada, and Mexico, established in 1992 to create a free-trade area covering all of North America, eliminating over a period of time customs duties and other restrictions; Chile likely to join in due course. In addition, it would open Mexico's closed financial industries to American and Canadian competition, erect barriers to prevent overseas companies from bypassing American tariffs by shipping goods via Mexico, and create trilateral commissions to resolve disputes involving health, environmental, and labour regulations. Finally ratified in late 1993, the bloc is the second largest free-trade area in the world (after the European Economic Area), with c.360 million customers.

Northampton 52°14N 0°54W, pop (2001e) 194 500. County town in Northamptonshire, C England, UK; on R Nene, SE of Coventry and 97 km/60 mi NW of London; originally a Saxon town; Thomas Becket tried here in 1164; destroyed by fire in 1675; designated a 'new town' in 1968; railway; footwear, leather goods, cosmetics, vehicle parts; 12th-c Church of the Holy Sepulchre, one of four round churches in England; All Saints' Church and the Church of St Peter; football league team, Northampton Town (Cobblers).

Northamptonshire pop (2001e) 629 700; area 2367 sq km/914 sq mi. Agricultural county in C England, UK; drained by the Welland and Nene Rivers; county town, Northampton; cereals, livestock, sugar beet, potatoes, iron mining, shoemaking, printing, engineering.

North Atlantic Treaty Organization *NATO*

North Cape, Norwegian **Nordkapp** 71°10N 25°48E. Cape on N Magerøy I, N Norway; considered to be the most northerly point of Europe.

North Carolina pop (2000e) 8 049 300; area 136 407 sq km/ 52 669 sq mi. State in SE USA, divided into 100 counties; the 'Tar Heel State' or 'Old North State'; unsuccessful settlement on Roanoke I in the 1580s; part of the Carolina grant given by Charles II, 1663; named North Carolina, 1691; a royal province, 1729; location of Mecklenburg Declaration of Independence (1775); twelfth of the original 13 states to ratify the Constitution, 1789; withdrew from the Union, 1861; slavery abolished, 1865; re-admitted to the Union, 1868; capital, Raleigh; other major cities, Charlotte, Greensboro, Winston-Salem, Durham; bounded E by the Atlantic Ocean; crossed by the Roanoke and Yadkin (becomes the Pee Dee) Rivers; highest point Mt Mitchell (2037 m/6683 ft); a chain of coastal islands with constantly shifting sand dunes, enclosing several lagoons; a major tourist area; flat, swampy, mainland coastal strip; low land gives way to the rolling hills of the Piedmont; fast-flowing rivers provide hydroelectric power for manufacturing industries; in the W the Blue Ridge and Great Smoky Mts; four national forests; 40% of all US tobacco; cotton, silk goods, synthetic fibres, furniture, electrical machinery, chemicals; poultry, corn, soybeans, peanuts, hogs; feldspar, mica, lithium; industrial growth greatest of any Southern state since World War 2.

Northcliffe, Lord *Harmsworth, Alfred*

North Dakota [dakohta] pop (2000e) 642 400; area 183 111 sq km/70 702 sq mi. State in NC USA, divided into 53 counties; 'Sioux State', 'Flickertail State'; became part of USA in the Louisiana Purchase, 1803; included in Dakota Territory, 1861; separated from South Dakota to become the 39th state admitted to the Union, 1889; capital, Bismarck; other chief cities, Fargo, Grand Forks, Minot; sparsely populated; crossed by the Missouri R; the Red R follows the E state border; highest point White Butte (1069 m/3507 ft); semi-arid conditions in the W; cultivation possible only in river valleys, rest of the land covered in short prairie grasses, where cattle are grazed; E region a flat fertile plain, covered almost entirely by crops, chiefly spring wheat, barley, sunflowers, and flaxseed (nation's leading producer of all these crops); major cattle state; oil (NW) and lignite coal (W); processed foods and machinery; several Indian reservations.

North Downs Way Long-distance footpath in S England; length 227 km/141 mi; follows the crest of the North Downs from Farnham to Dover.

Northeast Passage A shipping route through the S Arctic Ocean along the N coast of Europe and Asia, connecting the Atlantic and Pacific Oceans. Its crossing was first attempted in 1550, but it was not successfully travelled until 1878–9. A regular shipping lane is maintained by Russia.

Northern Cape One of the nine new provinces established by the South African constitution of 1994, in W South Africa; formerly part of Cape Provinces; largely semi-arid; NW frontier with Namibia formed by the Orange R; largest province, smallest population; pop (2000e) 785 000; area 363 389 sq km/ 140 268 sq mi; capital, Kimberley; chief languages, Afrikaans (65%), Setswana (22%), Xhosa; diamonds, tourism (Kalahari-Gemsbok National Park).

Northern Ireland *p.1101*

Northern Ireland Assembly A 108-member governing body for Northern Ireland, established (following a referendum) as part of the Good Friday Agreement. It has responsibility for the policy areas of agriculture, economic development, education, environment, and health and social services. Elections (by proportional representation) to the body were held in 1998 with 10 parties represented, the largest being the Ulster Unionist Party (28 members), the Social and Democratic Labour Party (24), the Democratic Unionist Party (20), and Sinn Féin (18). The assembly, meeting in Stormont Castle, Belfast, is overseen by a presiding officer appointed by the secretary-of-state for Ireland, and elects its own officers and executive committee. David Trimble (UUP) was elected the inaugural first minister and Seamus Mallon (SDLP) the inaugural deputy minister. The full establishment of the Assembly was held up by continued disagreement over the participation of Sinn Féin in the executive committee before the decommissioning of weapons held by republican paramilitaries, a demand which was dropped in November 1999. The Assembly came into effect in December; however, a perceived lack of progress on the decommissioning issue led to the reimposition of UK rule in February–May 2000, and there was a further suspension of devolution in October 2002.

northern lights *aurora* (astronomy)

Northern Province, renamed **Limpopo** (Feb 2002) One of the nine new provinces established by the South African constitution of 1994, in N South Africa; borders Botswana (NW), Zimbabwe (N), and Mozambique (NE); Limpopo R to the N; formerly part of Transvaal, and includes former homelands of Lebowa and Gazankulu; capital, Polokwane (formerly, Pietersburg); pop (2000e) 4 343 000; area 119 606 sq km/46 168 sq mi; chief language, Pedi (56%), Shangaan (22%), Venda; largely bushveld, with some mountains and forests; lowest per capita income in the country; mining, agriculture, forestry, tourism (game parks).

Northern Territory pop (2000e) 194 400; area 1 346 200 sq km/ 520 000 sq mi. One of the two mainland territories of Australia, covering about a sixth of the continent; part of New South Wales, 1824; annexed by South Australia, 1863; transferred to Federal Government control, 1911; achieved self-government, 1978; bordered N by the Arafura Sea and the Gulf of Carpentaria; mainly within the tropics; from Arnhem Land in the N the land rises S to the Macdonnell Ranges, reaching 1525 m/5000 ft at Mt Liebig; good pasture land in the N (Barkly Tableland), largely flat and arid in the S (Simpson Desert); many islands off the N coast (notably Groote Eylandt, Melville and Bathurst Is); Ayers Rock in Uluru national park; major rivers in the N the Victoria, Daly, South Alligator, East Alligator, McArthur, Roper; rivers in the interior flow only after heavy rain; capital and chief port, Darwin; chief towns Alice Springs, Katherine, Nhulunbuy; beef cattle, fishing, minerals (bauxite, bismuth, uranium, gold, manganese, copper), oil, gas; many Aboriginal settlements; Aboriginal art found throughout the area; state holidays: May Day, Picnic Day (Aug).

Northern War *Great Northern War*

North German Confederation The state system and constitutional arrangement created in 1866 by Bismarck, chancellor of Prussia, following the Prussian defeat of Austria and the dissolution of the German Confederation. Utterly dominated by Prussia, the new Confederation was itself dissolved with the creation of the German Empire in 1871.

North India, Church of A Church established in Nagpur in 1970 by the union of six different, originally missionary churches in India, including the Anglicans, United Church of North India, Methodists, Baptists, Brethren, and Disciples of Christ. Its constitution combines episcopal and conciliar government.

northing A grid line which runs W to E on a map, but which is numbered northwards. It is related to the **easting**, a grid line which runs N to S, and which is numbered eastwards. The northing number associated with a place is always given after the number of the easting when citing a grid reference.

North Island pop (2000e) 2 790 000; area 114 834 sq km/ 44 326 sq mi. The smaller but more densely populated of the two major islands of New Zealand; separated from South Island by the Cook Strait; irregularly shaped with a long peninsula projecting NW; several mountain ranges; highest volcanic mountain, Ruapehu (2797 m/9176 ft); contains the largest of New Zealand's lakes, L Taupo (606 sq km/234 sq mi); many hot springs, NC; fertile plains in the coastal areas; chief towns include Wellington, Auckland, Napier, Hastings, New Plymouth, Palmerston North; wine, farming, horse breeding, fruit,

Northern Ireland

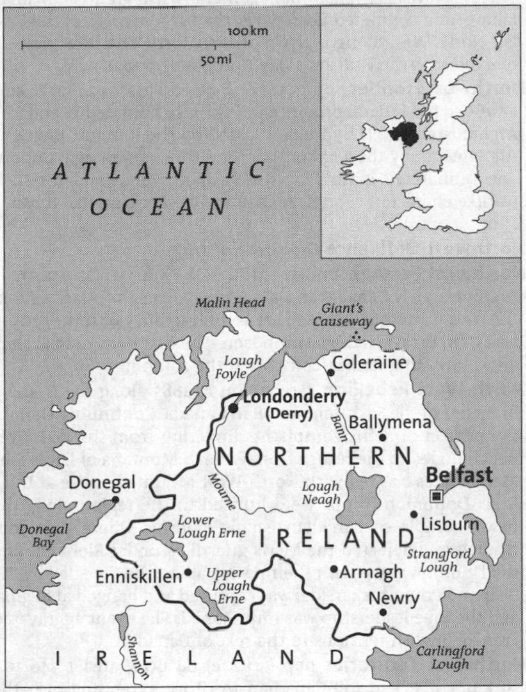

□ International Airport ∴ World heritage site

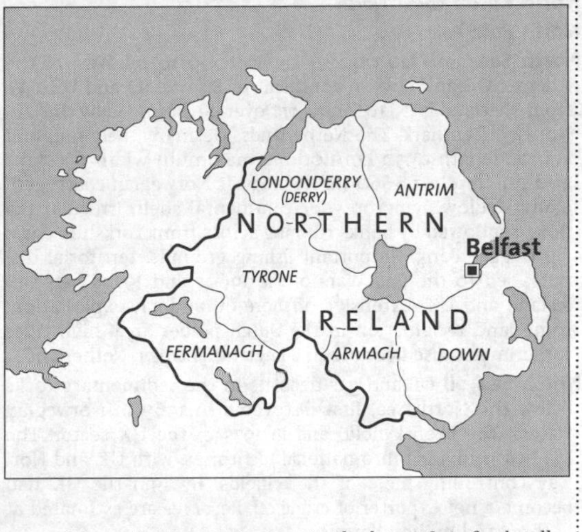

also **Ulster** (UK)

Area 14 120 km²/5450 sq mi

Population total (2001e) 1 685 300

Status Constituent division of the United Kingdom

Capital Belfast

Languages English, Irish Gaelic

Religions Christian (Roman Catholic 28%, Presbyterian 23%, Church of Ireland 19%)

Physical features Occupies the NE part of Ireland, centred on Lough Neagh; Mourne Mts in SE; highest point, Slieve Donard, 847 m/2786 ft, in the former Co. Down; R Mourne, 82 km/51 mi in length.

Economy Agriculture; service industries, shipbuilding, engineering, chemicals; linen, textiles; economy badly affected by the sectarian troubles since 1969.

History Separate Parliament established in 1920, with a 52-member House of Commons and a 26-member Senate; Protestant majority in the population, generally supporting political union with Great Britain; many of the Roman Catholic minority look for union with the Republic of Ireland; violent conflict between the communities broke out in 1969, leading to the establishment of a British army peace-keeping force; sectarian murders and bombings continued both within and outside the province; as a result of the disturbances, Parliament was abolished in 1972; powers are now vested in the UK Secretary of State for Northern Ireland; formation of a 78-member Assembly, 1973; replaced by a Constitutional Convention, 1975; Assembly re-formed in 1982, but Nationalist members did not take their seats; under the 1985 Anglo-Irish agreement, the Republic of Ireland was given a consultative role in the government of Northern Ireland; all Northern Ireland MPs in the British Parliament resigned in protest, 1986; continuing controversy in the late 1980s; fresh talks between all main parties and the Irish government, 1992; breakthrough in December 1993 with the Downing Street Declaration; IRA and loyalist ceasefires, 1994; joint Irish/British Framework Document, February 1995; new IRA campaign, 1996; start of all-party talks (initially with Sinn Féin excluded), 1996; Good Friday agreement, 1998, introduces Northern Ireland Assembly; problems over arms decommissioning by the IRA hinder implementation of the agreement, 1999 and ongoing; review of the peace process by US senator George Mitchell announced (Jul 1999), leading to a compromise formula and the inauguration of the Assembly in December; reimposition of UK rule (Feb–May 2000); further suspension of devolution (Oct 2002); multiparty peace talks to restore devolution resumed (Mar 2003) but suffer setback as scheduled elections (May) to the Assembly are postponed; elections reset (Nov) with success for the anti-Agreement Democratic Unionist Party; post-election talks begin.

Districts of Northern Ireland

Name / Area (km² / sq mi) / Population total (2000e) / Admin
Antrim / 563 / 217 / 44 700 / Antrim
Ards / 369 / 142 / 67 900 / Newtownards
Armagh / 672 / 259 / 52 100 / Armagh
Ballymena / 638 / 246 / 57 800 / Ballymena
Ballymoney / 419 / 162 / 25 500 / Ballymoney
Banbridge / 444 / 171 / 34 600 / Banbridge
Belfast / 140 / 54 / 285 800 / Belfast
Carrickfergus / 87 / 34 / 35 000 / Carrickfergus
Castlereagh / 85 / 33 / 53 600 / Belfast
Coleraine / 485 / 187 / 52 100 / Coleraine
Cookstown / 623 / 240 / 31 800 / Cookstown
Craigavon / 383 / 147 / 77 800 / Craigavon
Down / 646 / 249 / 63 000 / Downpatrick
Dungannon / 779 / 301 / 49 900 / Dungannon
Fermanagh / 1876 / 715 / 54 100 / Enniskillen
Larne / 338 / 131 / 30 400 / Larne
Limavady / 587 / 227 / 23 700 / Limavady
Lisburn / 444 / 171 / 103 000 / Lisburn
Londonderry (Derry) / 382 / 147 / 102 000 / Londonderry (Derry)
Magherafelt / 573 / 221 / 37 500 / Magherafelt
Moyle / 495 / 191 / 15 000 / Ballycastle
Newry and Mourne / 895 / 346 / 75 600 / Newry
Newtownabbey / 152 / 59 / 77 900 / Newtownabbey
North Down / 73 / 28 / 74 500 / Bangor
Omagh / 1129 / 436 / 47 900 / Omagh
Strabane / 870 / 336 / 37 400 / Strabane

coal, natural gas; spas and health resorts; Maori mostly live on North Island.

North Korea *Korea, North*

North Pole *Poles*

North Sea area 520 000 sq km/201 000 sq mi. Arm of the Atlantic Ocean between continent of Europe (E) and UK (W), from Shetland Is (N) to Straits of Dover (S); bounded by the UK, Norway, Denmark, The Netherlands, Germany, Belgium, and France; length c.950 km/600 mi; maximum width 650 km/400 mi; depths of 660 m/2165 ft near Norwegian coast; generally shallow, lying on wide continental shelf; irregular sea floor, shallowed by banks running across from Yorkshire coast (eg Dogger Bank); important fishing grounds; territorial disputes led to the Cod Wars of the 1960s and 1970s between Iceland and UK; extensive offshore oil and gas exploitation; some land reclamation in the Dutch polder area; high tides sometimes cause flooding in E England and The Netherlands.

North Sea oil Oil and gas deposits in the sedimentary rocks below the North Sea, first discovered in 1969 in Norwegian waters (the Ekofisk field) and in 1975 in the UK sector. The sea-bed is divided into national territories, with UK and Norway controlling most of the oilfields. By 1981 the UK had become a net exporter of crude oil. Reserves are estimated at 12 thousand million barrels.

Northumberland pop (2001e) 307 200; area 5032 sq km/1943 sq mi. County in NE England; bounded N by Scotland, E by the North Sea; Pennines in the W; rises in the N to 755 m/2477 ft at The Cheviot; drained by the Tyne, Blyth, Wansbeck, Coquet, Aln, and Till Rivers; Holy I and the Farne Is lie off the coast; Kielder Water (artificial lake, 1982); county town, Morpeth; chief towns include Berwick-upon-Tweed, Ashington, Blyth, Alnwick; sheep, barley, oats, fishing, forestry, coal; many Roman remains, especially Hadrian's Wall; castles at Alnwick and Bamburgh.

Northumberland, Dukes of *Percy*

Northumberland National Park National park in NE England; area 1031 sq km/398 sq mi; established in 1956; bounded S by Hadrian's Wall and N by the Cheviot Hills.

Northumbria The largest kingdom of the Anglo-Saxon heptarchy. It was originally composed of two independent kingdoms, Bernicia and Deira, divided by the river Tees, both settled by invading Angles c.500. Aethelfrith of Bernicia (593–616) united the kingdoms to form Northumbria, and added Scottish and Welsh territory. Edwin of Deira (612–32) accepted Roman Christianity in 627. After a period of anarchy Edwin was killed by Oswald of Bernicia (633–41), who introduced Celtic Christianity under St Aidan. Oswald's successor, Osin (641–70), established the Roman Church over the Celtic Church at the Synod of Whitby (663). In the 7th-c it established a broad dominance in Britain both N and S of the Humber, while in the 8th-c the Northumbrian monasteries gained a European-wide reputation for sanctity and learning. The kingdom came to an end in 876 after the sacking of York by the Danes, and by the 12th-c Northumbria was equivalent to the earldom or county of Northumberland.

North West One of the nine new provinces established by the South African constitution of 1994, in NW South Africa; completely land-locked; borders Botswana in the N; capital Mmabatho; pop (2000e) 3 201 000; area 118 710 sq km/45 822 sq mi; diamonds, gold, platinum; maize, sunflower seeds, groundnuts; cattle, food production; tourism (resort complex at Sun City).

Northwest Coast Indians North American Indians living along the Pacific coastline from Alaska to NW California, consisting of a number of different groups who were wealthy, hierarchical, and had highly developed artistic traditions. They included the Haidas, Tsimshians, Kwakiutls, Nootkas, Tlingits, and Yuroks. One of their famous ceremonial institutions was the potlatch. Many died in the conflict with white settlers and traders, and their way of life was transformed.

North West Company A trading partnership based in Montreal and Fort William, Canada, from the 1780s to 1821. It combined Scottish/Loyalist management with French-Canadian labour, and competed fiercely for the fur resources of the British North West along a chain of land forts. The 'Nor'Westers' merged into the Hudson's Bay Company in 1821.

Northwest Frontier pop (2000e) 18 085 000; area 74 521 sq km/28 765 sq mi. Federal province in Pakistan; bounded W and S by Afghanistan and N by India; crossed by the R Indus; linked to Afghanistan by the Khyber Pass, and thus of strategic importance; inhabited mainly by the Pathans, renowned for their warlike character; capital, Peshawar; livestock, grains, tobacco, fruit.

Northwest Ordinance *Ordinance of 1787*

Northwest Passage A route through the S Arctic Ocean, Arctic Archipelago, N Canada, and along the N coast of Alaska. From the 16th-c attempts were made to find it, but not until 1903–6 was it first traversed by Amundsen. The first commercial ship, an ice-breaking tanker, completed the route in 1969.

North-West Rebellion A rebellion in 1885 along the N and S branches of the Saskatchewan R in Canada. Continuing Dominion neglect of Métis complaints lingering from the Red River Rebellion led to the return from exile in Montana of Louis Riel. Métis forces clashed with North-West Mounted Police at Duck Lake. Dominion troops were hurried to the region along the newly-completed Canadian Pacific Railway, where they confronted and defeated the Métis guerrillas under Riel and Gabriel Dumont, along with their native allies, the Cree, led by Big Bear and Poundmaker. Riel was captured and hanged at Regina, and the Cree leadership was imprisoned. The event aggravated French–English tensions in the rest of Canada.

Northwest Territories pop (2000e) 64 600; area 1 346 106 sq km/519 597 sq mi. Canadian territory extending over the N of Canada, consisting of the Arctic islands, the islands in Hudson and Ungava Bays, and the land N of 60°N, between Hudson Bay and the Yukon territory; sparsely populated, two-thirds Athapaskan-speaking peoples and Inuit; capital, Yellowknife (since 1967); mining (lead, zinc, gold), handicrafts, fur products, fishing, tourism, oil; land held by the Hudson's Bay Company (Rupert's Land and North West Territory) changed to the present name on entering Canadian federation, 1870; present form of administration adopted, 1905; governed by a commissioner and an elected 24-member Legislative Assembly; the new Canadian territory of Nunavut was created in 1999 from a region formerly in E Northwest Territories.

North York Moors National park chiefly in North Yorkshire, England; area 1432 sq km/553 sq mi; established in 1952; follows the coast N of Scarborough to Hambleton Hills (W); headlands and sandy beaches, open moorland and wooded valleys; Mount Grace Priory, Rievaulx Abbey, Byland Abbey.

North Yorkshire *Yorkshire, North*

Norway *p.1103*

Norway spruce The most common species of spruce (*Picea abies*) native to Europe and planted on a vast commercial scale. It is a source of timber, pitch, spruce beer, and, in Britain, Christmas trees. (Family: Pinaceae.)

Norwegian *Germanic languages; Scandinavian languages*

Norwegian literature The ballads, folk songs, and legends of the later Middle Ages, taken by Norwegian colonists to Iceland, provided the materials for the great sagas in Old Norse. Copenhagen provided the literary focus until the 18th-c; modern Norwegian literature followed independence from Denmark in 1814. Poet Henryk Wergeland (1808–45) and his novelist sister Camilla Collett (1813–95) expressed the new nationalist spirit, where Johan Welhaven (1807–73) looked to former links. Henrik Ibsen (1828–1906) began with themes from Norwegian legend, but moved to contemporary subjects for his best-known plays (eg *Hedda Gabler*, 1890), as did Björnstjerne Björnson (1832–1910); these transformed European drama. The Norwegian novel of this time was also important, in the hands of Alexander Kielland (1849–1906) and Jonas Lie (1833–1908). The greatest

Norway

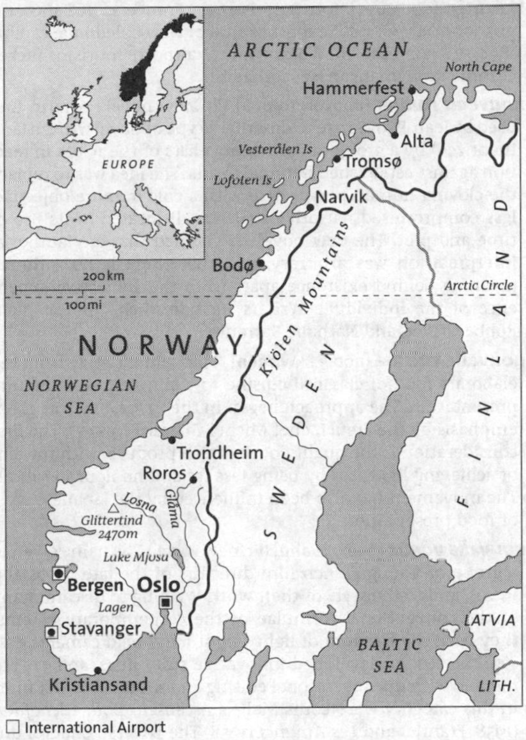

Norwegian **Norge**, official name **Kingdom of Norway**, Norwegian **Kongeriket Norge**

Local name Norge

Timezone GMT +1

Area 323 895 km^2/125 023 sq mi

Population total (2002e) 4 537 000

Status Kingdom

Date of independence 1905

Capital Oslo

Languages Norwegian (official) (in the varieties of Bokmål and Nynorsk), Lappish- and Finnish-speaking minorities

Ethnic groups Germanic (Nordic, Alpine, Baltic descent) (97%), Sami/Lapp minority in far N

Religions Evangelical Lutheran (95%), Baptist, Pentecostalist, Methodist, and Roman Catholic (5%)

Physical features Mountainous country; Kjölen Mts form the N part of the boundary with Sweden; Jotunheimen range in SC Norway; much of the interior over 1500 m/5000 ft; numerous lakes, the largest being L MjÝsa, 368 km^2/142 sq mi; irregular coastline with many small islands and long deep fjords.

Climate Arctic winter climate in interior highlands, snow, strong winds and severe frosts; comparatively mild conditions on coast; average annual temperatures -4°C (Jan), 17°C (Jul) in Oslo; average annual rainfall 683 mm/27 in; rainfall heavy on W coast.

Currency 1 Norwegian Krone (NKr) = 100 øre

Economy Based on extraction and processing of raw materials, using plentiful hydroelectric power; oil and natural gas from North Sea fields; land under cultivation, less than 3%; productive forests covered 21% of land area in 1985.

GDP (2002e) $149·1 bn, per capita $33 000

Human Development Index (2002) 0·942

History A united kingdom achieved by St Olaf in the 11th-c, whose successor, Cnut, brought Norway under Danish rule; united with Sweden and Denmark, 1389; annexed by Sweden as a reward for assistance against Napolcon, 1814, growing nationalism resulted in independence, 1905; declared neutrality in both World Wars, but occupied by Germany, 1940–5, after heavy resistance; Free Norwegian government based in London; joined NATO, 1949; joined European Free Trade Association, 1960; a limited, hereditary monarchy; government led by a Prime Minister; Parliament (Storting) comprises upper (Lagting) and lower (Odelsting) chambers.

Head of State (Monarch)
1872–1905 Oscar II *Union with Sweden*
1905–57 Haakon VII
1957–91 Olav V
1991– Harald V

Head of Government
1973–6 Trygve Bratteli
1976–81 Odvar Nordli
1981 Gro Harlem Brundtland
1981–6 Kåre Willoch
1986–9 Gro Harlem Brundtland
1989–90 Jan P Syse
1990–6 Gro Harlem Brundtland
1996–7 Thorbjoern Jagland
1997–2000 Kjell Magne Bondevik
2000–1 Jens Stoltenberg
2001– Kjell Magne Bondevik

name in Norwegian literature since then is Knut Hamsun (1859–1952), whose vitalist fiction anticipated 20th-c themes. But novelists such as Sigrid Undset (1882–1949), Olav Duun (1876–1939), Johan Borgen (1902–79) and latterly Dag Solstad (1941–), and poets such as Olaf Bull (1883–1933) and the libertarian socialist Arnulf Overland (1889–1968) continue a distinguished tradition.

Norwegian Sea area 1 383 000 sq km/534 000 sq mi. N Atlantic sea bounded by NW coast of Norway and E coast of Iceland; depths in the Norwegian Basin reach 1240 m/4068 ft, and in the Jan Mayen Fracture Zone, close to the continental shelf, 2740 m/8989 ft; generally ice-free because of influence of warm N Atlantic Drift.

Nor-wester *Föhn / Foehn wind*

Norwich (UK) [**nor**ich] 52°38N 1°18E, pop (2001e) 121 600. County town in Norfolk, E England; near the confluence of the Yare and Wensum Rivers, 160 km/100 mi NE of London; provincial centre for the largely agricultural East Anglia; major textile centre in 16th–17th-c; University of East Anglia (1964); North Sea reached via R Yare and Great Yarmouth (32 km/20 mi E); railway; commerce, engineering, printing, chemicals, electrical goods, silk, foodstuffs, trade in grain and livestock; Norman cathedral (1096), Church of St Peter Mancroft (1430–55); football league team, Norwich City (Canaries).

Norwich School A group of provincial English landscape painters, in oil and watercolour, working in Norwich 1803–34. Leading masters were Cotman and Crome.

nose The protrusion from the front of the face above the mouth and below the eyes. Part of the respiratory tract, it consists of an external part (with a skeleton of bone and cartilage) and an inner cavity. The nasal cavity has a large surface area, because of the presence of scrolls of bone (the *conchae*) projecting into it from the side walls. It is covered mainly with respiratory epithelium, except in its most superior part where the epithelium is specialized to subserve the sense of smell. The functions of the nasal cavity are olfaction (smell) and changing the nature of the inspired air. Various glands moisten the air, and produce a sticky substance which traps inspired particles (afterwards conveyed by cilia towards the nasopharynx for swallowing).

The rich vascular network also warms the air. Because of this network, the nose has a tendency to bleed profusely if it is hit.

noseeum [nohseeum] *biting midge*

Nostradamus [nostradahmus], Latin name of **Michel de Notre-dame** (1503–66) Physician and astrologer, born in St Rémy, SE France. He became doctor of medicine in 1529, and practised in Agen, Lyon, and other places. He set himself up as a prophet in c.1547. His *Centuries* of predictions in rhymed quatrains (two collections, 1555–8), expressed generally in obscure and enigmatical terms, brought their author a great reputation. Charles IX on his accession appointed him physician-in-ordinary. Books continue to be published applying his predictions to present-day situations.

notebook A very compact form of personal computer which can be accommodated inside a briefcase. Even so, most notebooks offer the same facilities as a desk-top personal computer.

note-cluster In music, a group of adjacent notes, especially on a keyboard instrument, sounded together for their percussive or sonorous effect. Clusters are associated with some 20th-c composers, such as Cowell and Bartók, but they appear also in the sonatas of Scarlatti.

nothosaur [nothosaw(r)] A long-necked, marine reptile; flourished during the Triassic period, but extinct by the early Jurassic period; limbs well adapted for swimming. (Order: Sauropterygia. Suborder: Nothosauria.)

notochord [nohtohkaw(r)d] A rod-like structure which extends almost the entire length of the body in larvae and some adult chordates. It lies behind the gut but below the nerve cord, providing flexible support for the body. It is replaced by the vertebral column in most vertebrates, but retained throughout life in certain marine animals (eg cephalochordates, lampreys).

Notre Dame (de Paris) [notruh dam duh paree] An early Gothic cathedral on the Ile de la Cité in Paris. It was commissioned by Maurice de Sully, Bishop of Paris, in 1159 and constructed over a period of two centuries (1163–1345). The tremendous weight of its masonry has caused it to subside several feet.

not-self *self / not-self*

Nottingham, Anglo-Saxon **Snotingaham** or **Notingeham** 52°58N 1°10W, pop (2001e) 267 000. City and (from 1998) unitary authority in Nottinghamshire, C England, UK; on the R Trent, 200 km/125 mi NW of London; university (1948); Nottingham Trent University (1992, formerly Nottingham Polytechnic); founded by the Danes; became a city in 1897; Civil War started here in 1642; connected to both the Irish and North Seas by canal; railway; cigarettes, lace (former major centre), textiles, tanning, engineering, bicycles, furniture, typewriters, printing, pharmaceuticals; 17th-c Nottingham Castle, 15th-c St Mary's Church; Theatre Royal; Playhouse; nearby, Newstead Abbey (home of Byron) and Eastwood (home of D H Lawrence); Goose Fair during the first week in Oct; football league teams, Nottingham Forest (Reds), Nottingham County (Magpies).

Nottinghamshire pop (2001e) 748 500; area 2164 sq km/836 sq mi. County in the R Trent basin of C England, UK; Pennines in W, remains of Sherwood Forest in SW; county town, Nottingham (unitary authority from 1998); chief towns include Worksop, Newark, Mansfield; arable and dairy farming, coal, gypsum, limestone, textiles, chemicals.

Notungulata [notuhngyoolahta] A large order of extinct, South American, plant-eating mammals, known from the late Palaeocene to the Pleistocene epochs; typically with short skulls; ear structure unique in having two large chambers; third digit of feet forming main axis.

Nouadhibou [nooadeeboo], Fr **Port Etienne** 20°54N 17°00W, pop (2000e) 83 000. Seaport capital of Dakhlet-Nouadhibou region, Mauritania, at N end of the Bay of Levrier; Mauritania's main seaport; linked by rail to the iron ore mines near Zouîrât; airport; iron ore trade, fish processing and refrigeration, industrial gas.

Nouakchott [nwakshot] 18°09N 15°58W, pop (2000e) 553 000. Capital of Mauritania, near the Atlantic coast; harbour 7 km/4 mi SSW; founded on an important caravan route, 1960; airport; salt, cement, insecticides, matches, trade in gums and grains; camel markets.

Nouméa [noomaya], formerly **Port de France** 22°16S 166°26E, pop (2000e) 79 000. Seaport capital of New Caledonia; capital, 1854; US air base in World War 2; airport; tourism, nickel, chrome, iron, manganese; cathedral.

nouveau roman [noovoh rohmã] (Fr 'new novel') A term first used by Jean-Paul Sartre to describe a type of novel written (and theorized) by a group of French novelists of the 1950s in reaction against established fictional forms. The idea was to replace the cloying human perspective with a colder, more objective, less compromised narrative that was dislocated in its use of time and plot. The new novelists claimed that any authorial interpretation was arbitrary, and that there is no ultimate meaning behind existence apart from the subjective experience of the individual. Writers include Michel Butor, Alain Robbe-Grillet, and Nathalie Sarraute.

nouvelle cuisine [noovel kwizeen] A movement away from the elaborate food of classical cuisine to a simpler, more natural presentation. The approach began in the 1970s, and was given emphasis by the French chef Michel Guérard (1933–). The first consideration is the quality of the fresh produce, with the aim of achieving lightness by using less fat and no flour in sauces. The movement has also been influenced by the Japanese style of food presentation.

nouvelle vague [noovel vahg] (Fr 'new wave') The name given to a group of young French film directors of the late 1950s and 1960s, and to the style of their work. Wishing to discard many of the conventional formulae of the contemporary cinema, they used the freedom of lightweight hand-held cameras outside the studio, developed innovative story-lines, and experimented with unconventional editing and sound. The first films in this category were Louis Malle's *Ascenseur pour l'échafaud* (1958, Frantic) and *Les Amants* (1958, The Lovers). Chabrol directed *Le Beau Serge* (1958) and *Les Cousins* (1959); Truffaut made *Les Quatre Cents Coups* (1959, The 400 Blows); and Alain Resnais broke new ground with *Hiroshima mon amour* (1959), which moves constantly between past and present, and *L'Année dernière à Marienbad* (1961, Last Year at Marienbad), a virtually plotless story set in a surreal, sculptured world. Godard was another innovator, who in *A bout de souffle* (1960, Breathless) uses hand-held cameras, jump-cuts, and real locations.

nova In a binary star system near the end of its life, the phenomenon where one star becomes a giant, and its atmosphere spills over to its companion, a white dwarf. A nuclear explosion is triggered on the white dwarf, whose luminosity increases by 10 000 times (10 magnitudes) or more for a few months. The phenomenon can recur.

Novak, Kim, originally **Marilyn Pauline Novak** (1933–) Film actress, born in Chicago, Illinois, USA. She made her screen debut in *The French Line* (1954), then starred in *The Pushover* (1954), and soon became a leading box-office attraction of the 1950s – perhaps the last of the 'sex goddesses' produced by the Hollywood star system. Her films include *The Man With The Golden Arm* (1955), *Pal Joey* (1957), *Vertigo* (1958), *The Amorous Adventures of Moll Flanders* (1965), and *The Mirror Crack'd* (1980). She was largely absent from the screen in the 1980s, following her marriage, but still takes occasional roles, as in *Liebestraum* (1991).

Novak, Michael [nohvak] (1933–) Lay Roman Catholic theologian, economist, and political philosopher, born in Johnstown, Pennsylvania, USA. He studied at the Holy Cross Seminary at the University of Notre Dame, MA, and the Gregorian University in Rome, but left the Congregation of Holy Cross in 1960 soon after his ordination to the priesthood, and was accepted into Harvard on a graduate fellowship later that year. His books include *The Open Church* (1964) and *The Spirit of Democratic Capitalism* (1982). In 1981 he was appointed US ambassador for the UN Human Rights Commission, and in 1994 received the Templeton Prize for Progress in Religion.

Novalis [nohvalis], pseudonym of **Friedrich Leopold von Hardenberg** (1772–1801) Romantic poet and novelist, born in Oberwiederstedt, EC Germany. At Weissenfels (1795) he fell in love with a girl whose early death left a lasting impression upon him, and in whose memory he wrote the prose lyrics of *Hymnen an die Nacht* (1800, Hymns to the Night). He also published *Geistliche Lieder* (1799, Sacred Songs). He left two philosophical Romances, both incomplete, *Heinrich von Ofterdingen* and *Die Lehrlinge zu Sais* (The Novices of Sais). He is sometimes called 'the prophet of Romanticism'.

Nova Scotia [nohva skohsha] pop (2000e) 1 050 000; area 55 490 sq km/21 424 sq mi. Province in SE Canada; boundaries include the Atlantic Ocean (E, S, W), Bay of Fundy (W), Northumberland Strait (N), and Gulf of St Lawrence (NE); includes Cape Breton I to the NE, separated by the Strait of Canso, 3 km/1¾ mi wide, connected by causeway; province linked to the Canadian mainland by the isthmus of Chignecto; deeply indented coastline, low hill ranges, many lakes and small rivers; capital, Halifax; other chief towns, Dartmouth, Sydney, Glace Bay, Truro, New Glasgow; dairy farming, fruit, fishing (especially lobster), timber, coal, gypsum, tin, tourism; home to the Micmac nation; probably visited by Vikings and European fishermen; settled by the French as Acadia, 1604–5; mainland assigned to Britain in the Treaty of Utrecht (1713), Cape Breton I remaining French until seized in 1758; many United Empire Loyalists settled here after the American Revolution; Cape Breton I a separate province from 1784, re-incorporated into Nova Scotia, 1820; joined the Canadian federation, 1867; governed by a lieutenant-governor and an elected 52-member House of Assembly.

Novaya Zemlya [novaya zimlya] area 81 279 sq km/31 374 sq mi. Archipelago in the Arctic Ocean, between the Barents Sea (W) and Kara Sea (E), NW Russia; two large islands separated by a narrow strait; numerous offshore islands; length, 960 km/596 mi; glaciated land (N) gives way to tundra lowland (S); an extension of the Ural Mts, rising to heights above 1000 m/3000 ft; some settlement on heavily indented W coast; copper, lead, zinc, asphaltite; formerly used for thermonuclear testing.

novel A work of fiction, most often in prose. The term (literally meaning 'new' or 'news') came into general use in the 18th-c to describe that form of fiction, deriving from classical epic and romance but incorporating features from other modes such as autobiography and travel writing, which centred on the life of an individual, as in *Robinson Crusoe* (1719) and *Tom Jones* (1749). Major Japanese novels (eg the tale of *Genji* (c.1000)) were published from the 11th-c, and Chinese novels from the 14th-c. Satisfying the taste of the new reading public for a personal perspective on familiar and unfamiliar experiences, the novel quickly became the dominant literary form in the West, as it was already in the East. Spanish writers such as Cervantes with his novel *Don Quixote de la Mancha* (1605, 1615) led the way. In the 19th-c writers such as Scott, Jane Austen, the Brontë sisters, Dickens, George Eliot, Balzac, Zola, Dostoevsky, Tolstoy, Melville, and Harriet Beecher Stowe helped create the moral and imaginative climate of their age. While retaining its traditional function, in the 20th-c the novel was developed (some would say destroyed) by persistent experimentation, by (among others) Joyce, Proust, Virginia Woolf, Nabokov, Cortazar, and Calvino. An important contribution to the evolution of the novel was made in the second half of the 20th-c by Latin-American writers such as Carlos Fuentes (*The Death of Artemio Cruz*, 1962), Mario Vargas Llosa (*The Time of the Hero*, 1966), and Gabriel Garcia Marquez (*One Hundred Years of Solitude*, 1970). Their new genre of 'magic realism' set out to transcend the local world through a magical and timeless unity which mixes realistic narrative with fantastic and fabulous elements.

novella (Ital 'tale', 'news') Originally a short story, as in Boccaccio's *Decameron*. The term is now used to define (if somewhat precariously) a prose fiction which is longer than a short story but shorter than a novel. Chinese novellas date from the 3rd-c BC. The genre was popular under the Tang (7th–10th-c) and constantly refined until the 18th-c.

Novello, Ivor [noveloh], originally **David Ivor Davies** (1893–1951) Actor, composer, songwriter, and playwright, born in Cardiff, S Wales, UK. He studied at Oxford, where he was a chorister. His song 'Keep the Home Fires Burning' was one of the most popular of World War 1. He first appeared on the regular stage in London in 1921 and enjoyed great popularity, his most successful and characteristic works being his 'Ruritanian' musical plays such as *Glamorous Night* (1935), *The Dancing Years* (1939), and *King's Rhapsody* (1949).

novel proteins Proteins derived from processed or textured vegetable proteins or from bacterial or fungal proteins; also known as **single-cell proteins**. The micro-organisms can be grown on a wide variety of industrial waste products, such as hydrocarbon waste from petroleum, or grain waste from milling; they are then harvested, and their protein isolated for animal or human nutrition.

Novgorod [nofgorod] 58°30N 31°20E, pop (2000e) 232 000. Capital city of Novgorodskaya oblast, NW European Russia; on R Volkhov, 6 km/4 mi from L Ilmen; one of the oldest cities in Russia, known in the 9th-c; badly damaged in World War 2; railway; centre of an important agricultural area; electrical engineering, woodworking, ship repairing, foodstuffs, tourism; St Sophia's Cathedral (1045–50), Dukhov monastery (12th-c); since 1945, major excavations of deep waterlogged deposits, revealing two-storied log cabin houses of the mediaeval town, arranged along timber roadways.

Novi Sad [novee sahd], Ger **Neusatz** 45°15N 19°51E, pop (2000e) 181 000. Commercial and industrial capital of the autonomous province of Vojvodina, N Serbia; on R Danube; formerly an important stronghold against the Turks; railway; university (1960); wine, fruit and vegetable trade, leather, textiles, tobacco; Niška Banja health resort nearby; bishop's palace, Petrovaradin castle, cathedral; international agricultural show (May), Danube international rowing regatta (Aug), autumn fair (Oct).

Novocaine A proprietary name for *procaine*, a local anaesthetic. Procaine was first manufactured in 1905 to displace cocaine, whose stimulant and addictive properties were disadvantageous. *Lignocaine* is now more frequently used.

Novosibirsk [novosyibyeersk], formerly **Novonikolaevsk** (1903–25) 55°00N 83°05E, pop (2000e) 1 440 000. River-port capital of Novosibirskaya oblast, S Siberian Russia, on the R Ob; founded, 1893; on the Trans-Siberian Railway; university (1959); leading economic centre of Siberia; Kuznetsk Basin coal and iron deposits nearby; machines, metallurgy, chemicals, foodstuffs.

Noyori, Ryoji (1938–) Chemist, born in Kobe, C Japan. He studied at Kyoto University, later joining the Research Center for Materials Science at Nagoya University. He shared the 2001 Nobel Prize for Chemistry for work on chirally catalysed hydrogenation reactions.

NTSC Abbreviation of **National Television Systems Commission**, responsible for the coding system for colour television introduced in the USA in 1954, and since then generally adopted throughout the Americas and Japan for all 525-line 60 Hz transmission. The two colour difference signals are 90° out of phase and combined to form the chrominance signal. The colour of the final picture is critically dependent on the correct phase relation being maintained throughout broadcast transmission, and the receiver requires a hue control.

Nu, U [noo] ('uncle'), originally **Thakin Nu** (1907–95) Burmese statesman and prime minister (1948–56, 1957–8, 1960–2), born in Wakema, S Myanmar (formerly Burma). He studied at Rangoon University, and came to prominence through student political movements (1934). Imprisoned by the British for sedition (1940), he was released by the Japanese and served in Ba Maw's puppet administration. In 1946 he became president of the Burmese Constituent Assembly, and then the first prime minister of the independent Burmese Republic. He was finally overthrown by a military coup in 1962, and imprisoned, but released in 1966. He then lived abroad organizing resistance to the military regime, but returned to Burma in 1980 to become a Buddhist monk. Following the uprising in 1988, he formed an Alliance for Peace and Democracy, which led to his house arrest until 1992.

Nubian Desert [nyoobian] area c.400 000 sq km/155 000 sq mi. Desert in NE Sudan; a sandstone plateau between the Red Sea and the R Nile; the ancient state of Nubia occupied the area from the First Cataract of the Nile to Khartoum.

Nubian monuments [nyoobian] A group of world heritage monuments around L Nasser in Ethiopia, many of which were rescued from flooding during the construction of Aswan High Dam. They include the 13th-c BC temples of Ramses II at Abu Simbel; Philae, the island of sanctuaries, sacred to Isis from the 4th-c BC; Amada, with its temples from the 15th-c and 13th-c BC; Kalabsha, built during the reign of Augustus; the 11th-c monastery of St Simeon; and 11th–12th-c Islamic cemeteries.

nuclear disarmament A political movement which emerged soon after the advent of nuclear weapons, demanding their control, the limitation of their spread to non-nuclear weapon states, and their eventual abolition. Although the US and Soviet governments had some success in reaching arms limitation treaties, such as the Partial Test-Ban Treaty (1963), the Anti-Ballistic Missile Treaty (1972, the US withdrew in 2002), and the Intermediate range Nuclear Forces (INF) agreement (1987), mass political movements such as the British Campaign for Nuclear Disarmament (CND) continued to attract support during the 1980s, but their significance has declined with the emergence of post-Warsaw Pact E Europe.

nuclear family *family*

nuclear fission The splitting of a heavy atomic nucleus into two approximately equal portions, with the emission of free neutrons and energy; discovered by Otto Hahn in 1938. Induced fission is initiated by collisions with neutrons. Spontaneous fission is comparatively rare. Fission in uranium and plutonium forms the basic mechanism of nuclear power and atomic bombs.

nuclear fusion The fusing together of two lightweight atomic nuclei, typically isotopes of hydrogen or lithium, having a total rest mass which exceeds that of the products. The mass difference is made up by energy released in the process. To initiate fusion, the reacting species must be brought close enough together so that short-range nuclear forces come into play, as is possible in the high-temperature environments of the Sun and nuclear explosions. Fusion reactors attempt to reproduce such conditions. Some achieve this using *magnetic confinement*, confining a hot, reacting plasma of interacting ions into a doughnut-shaped region using strong magnetic fields, as for example in conventional tokamaks such as the JET facility. Alternative plasma configurations are possible, for instance spherical torus facilities such as the Mega-Amp Spherical Tokamak at Culham, UK. *Inertial confinement* fusion works by using massive lasers to implode tiny fuel pellets, the pressure of implosion causing the plasma compression and confinement, for example at the National Ignition Facility at the Lawrence Livermore National Laboratory, CA. An alternative route to fusion is *muon catalysed* fusion, in which an elementary particle called a muon replaces the electron of a tritium atom. Because the muon is 207 times more massive than the electron, it is closely bound to the tritium nucleus. When the deuterium and muonic tritium are combined, the result is a much smaller molecule than normal, in which the two atomic nuclei have a good chance of coming close enough to fuse. Muon catalysed fusion is observed experimentally.

nuclear magnetic resonance (NMR) An analytic technique, important in chemistry, which relies on magnetic resonance involving protons. A sample is subjected to a strong magnetic field, causing the proton magnetic moments to precess. An additional variable radio-frequency magnetic field is applied, and the spectrum of absorbed frequencies measured. This spectrum reflects the proton's environment, so indicating the sample's structure. NMR is an important imaging technique in medicine, complementary to X-ray imaging, known as **magnetic resonance imaging** (MRI).

nuclear magnetron *Bohr magnetron*

nuclear physics The study of the properties and composition of the atomic nucleus. Early nuclear physics experiments include the study of natural radioactivity, and the demonstration of the existence of the nucleus in 1911. Modern experiments include the study of rapidly rotating 'superdeformed' nuclei, and of dense nuclear matter (quark-gluon plasma) formed by collisions of heavy nuclei. The nucleus is probed using X-rays, neutrons, mesons, and electrons. The applications of nuclear physics include nuclear power, nuclear weapons, and radio-isotopes in medicine.

nuclear power *nuclear fission / fusion / reactor*

nuclear proliferation The spread of nuclear weapons. Attempts at prevention include export controls, international inspection and verification agencies, and bans on both testing and production of weapons-grade material. The 1968 Nuclear Non-Proliferation Treaty (NPT) requires non-nuclear signatories to reject nuclear weapons research and development. Non-signatories include Israel, India, and Pakistan, all of which have tested nuclear weapons and are nations in conflict. Iraq, a signatory, has begun developing nuclear and biological weapons and already has chemical weapons. Many countries claim the Non-Proliferation Treaty discriminates, and refuse to sign it until the nuclear nations disarm. Fear of nuclear war between superpowers has been superseded with fear of possible nuclear strikes in regional conflicts, and of terrorists acquiring nuclear materials from former Soviet sources.

nuclear reactor A device for producing a continuous supply of heat energy from nuclear fission. Certain radioactive atomic nuclei, on being struck by neutrons, generate additional neutrons. This is self-sustaining if the speed of the neutrons is not too great. A nuclear reactor therefore has (i) a 'fuel', which may be uranium 235 or 238, or plutonium 239; (ii) a moderator, to control the speed and number of neutrons; and (iii) a heat exchange system, to utilize the heat generated (generally by operating the steam-driven turbines of a conventional electric power station). A **boiling water reactor** uses the cooling water itself as the source of steam for the turbines. In a **pressurized water reactor**, the coolant is water under such pressure that it reaches a high temperature without evaporation, and is used to heat boiler water via a heat exchanger. A **gas-cooled reactor** uses carbon dioxide or some other gas as a coolant, heating turbine water via a heat exchanger. A **fast reactor** has no moderator, and generally uses liquid sodium as a coolant. A **breeder reactor** uses uranium 238 enriched with plutonium 239; it produces more Pu 239, and is the type of reactor used to generate material for atomic weapons. Some nuclear reactors are built and used solely for research purposes. Nuclear power sources are an important source of energy in several countries (2001 figures) such as Lithuania (78%) and France (77%); compare UK (23%) and USA (20%).

nuclear structure The structure of the atomic nucleus, composed of protons and neutrons, collectively termed *nucleons*. For virtually all nuclei the number of neutrons, N, is larger than the number of protons, Z, especially for the nuclei of heavier elements – the imbalance linked to the electrostatic repulsion acting between protons but not neutrons. About 2000 nuclear species, or different neutron and proton combinations, are known, though only 283 are either long-lived or stable. On a chart of the nuclei with neutron number along the horizontal axis and proton number along the vertical axis (a Segrè chart), the nuclei form a broad, almost diagonal band running below the line where neutron number equals proton number. The stable nuclei lie along the centre of the band. Those nuclei lying away from the centre of the band have an imbalance of protons or neutrons and are unstable. Neutron-rich nuclei appear below the centre of the band, proton-rich nuclei appear above. Some neutron-rich nuclei have a *neutron halo*, some a skin surrounding a central nuclear core.

There is evidence that nucleons can form clusters within the nucleus, eg Beryllium-12 (4 protons and 8 neutrons) may behave like two alpha particles bonded together by four neutrons. Nuclei can be excited, such as during collisions in accelerators, and lose energy to become de-excited by emitting gamma rays. The spectrum of gamma ray energies shows that protons and neutrons can be excited into discrete energy levels within the nucleus, on analogy with the energy level pattern of excited electrons in atoms. Protons and neutrons move in well-defined orbits within the nucleus. Long-lived states in which protons or neutrons are excited into higher-energy states within the nucleus are called *nucleur isomers*. Most nuclei are deformed, ie not exactly spherical, and the departure from spherical is manifested as a measurable electric quadrupole moment. Superdeformed nuclei are those having an ellipsoidal shape (like a rugby ball) in which the major axis is twice as long as the minor axis. A few nuclei are known in which the excited state has a high angular momentum but cannot decay, yielding a long-lived excited state called a *spin trap*, eg the naturally occurring isotope tantalum-180.

Various models of nuclear structure have been developed to try to explain particular features of the nucleus. The *liquid drop model*, which views the nucleus as a homogenous drop of 'nuclear liquid', is useful in understanding the bulk properties of nuclei. These include the overall size of the nucleus, and its binding energy, the difference between the mass of all the nucleons in the nucleus, and the actual mass of the nucleus itself. The *shell model*, in which a nucleon moves in a 'potential well' due to the combined effect of all its companions, accounts for the existence of energy levels in the nucleus, the shells equating to groups of energy levels having very similar energies. The *collective model* considers the motion of the nucleus as a whole, such as pulsations of the entire nucleus, or other motions of collections of nucleons, such as the relative oscillation of protons to neutrons giving rise to giant resonances.

Nuclear Test-Ban Treaty A 1963 treaty prohibiting the testing of nuclear weapons on or above the surface of the Earth, originally put forward by the USA, USSR, and UK as an indirect means of slowing down the proliferation of countries with nuclear weapons. The impact of the treaty was somewhat diminished by its boycott by two nuclear nations, France and China. All five nations signed a Comprehensive Test Ban Treaty (CTBT) in 1996, and this had received 171 member signatures and 109 ratifications by early 2004.

nuclear weapons Weapons of mass destruction employing the energy-liberating nuclear phenomena of fission or fusion for their effects. According to their size and the means of delivery, they may be classified as **tactical short-range weapons** for use against enemy battlefield forces; **theatre medium-range weapons** for use against deep military targets; and **strategic long-range weapons** for use against enemy cities and command centres.

nucleic acids Large molecules which store genetic information, produced by living cells, and composed of a chain of nucleotides. Two forms are found: deoxyribonucleic acid (DNA) and ribonucleic acid (RNA), which may be either single- or double-stranded. DNA is found primarily in the nucleus, but also in small quantities in mitochondria and other structures. RNA is found in the nucleus and cytoplasm.

nucleolus [nyookleeohlus] A clearly defined and typically spherical structure within the nucleus of a eucaryotic cell, functioning as the site of the origin of ribosomes. It is composed of densely packed fibres and granules, rich in RNA and protein.

nucleon A collective term for both proton and neutron. It was suggested by Werner Heisenberg in 1932 that protons and neutrons appear to the strong nuclear force as two possible states of a single underlying particle. This particle, the nucleon, was described in terms of a new quantum number called isospin.

nucleonics The technology associated with nuclear reactors and their functioning. It entails the study of the techniques of assembling the radioactive material safely and in a form allowing it to produce its energy, the transfer of heat energy to boilers and turbines for the production of electricity, and the installation of all these units in structures which will be safe in normal use and in the event of malfunction. It is also concerned with the design and use of instruments which monitor and control radioactivity, as well as with the disposal of radioactive waste material.

nucleon number The total number of protons plus neutrons in an atomic nucleus; symbol *A*; also called the **mass number**. This total differs for different isotopes, and so is useful for labelling them. The number of neutrons equals $A-Z$, where Z is the proton number.

nucleophile An entity with an excess of electrons which tends to react at a positively charged centre. Anions and molecules with lone pairs of electrons (eg H_2O and NH_3) are nucleophiles.

nucleosome The basic unit into which the DNA is packed in the chromatin of eucaryotes. A nucleosome contains an octomer of proteins consisting of two copies each of histones H2A, H2B, H3, and H4, around which is wrapped two-and-a-half turns (146 base pairs) of DNA. Other proteins will be involved in the packing; these will vary according to whether the DNA is active or silent.

nucleosynthesis The creation of chemical elements by nuclear reactions in stars and other cosmic explosions. Current theory suggests that the very early universe consisted only of hydrogen and helium. Hydrogen burning in stars, and nuclear explosions at the end of a star's life, have formed all other elements by transmutation. Carbon atoms in the ink on this page were made thousands of millions of years ago in an exploding star by fusing together three helium nuclei at a temperature of 10^{7-8} degrees.

nucleotide A portion of a nucleic acid consisting of a purine or pyrimidine base, a sugar molecule, and a phosphate group bonded together. There are four principal nucleotides in DNA: deoxyadenylic, deoxycytidylic, deoxyguanylic, and deoxythmidylic acids. In RNA, they are adenylic, cytidylic, guanylic, and uridylic acids. When the phosphate is missing, the residue is called a *nucleoside*.

nucleus (astronomy) The central core of a comet, about 1–10 km/½–6 mi across, consisting of icy substances and dust, or the central part of a galaxy or quasar, possibly the seat of unusually energetic activity within the galaxy.

nucleus (biology) The chromosome-containing structure found in the great majority of non-dividing eucaryotic cells; delimited from the surrounding cytoplasm by a double membrane; typically ovoid or spherical, sometimes irregularly shaped. The nucleus is essential for the long-term survival of the cell. However, it disappears temporarily during cell division, and may be lost in certain mature cells, such as mammalian red blood cells.

nucleus (physics) The core of an atom, comprising various numbers of protons and neutrons, making up c.99·975% of an atom's mass. The number of protons equals the total positive charge of the nucleus, and equals the number of electrons in a complete atom. The nuclear components are bound together by strong nuclear force, sufficient to overcome electrical repulsions between the protons. The nucleus diameter is approximately 10^{-14} m. The nucleus of common hydrogen is a single proton; the nucleus of uranium-238 contains 92 protons and 146 neutrons.

nuclide In nuclear physics, a nucleus having a particular number of protons and neutrons. The proton number (lower) and nucleon number (upper) must both be given. For example, the two nuclides corresponding to two of the isotopes of carbon are $_6C^{12}$ and $_6C^{14}$ which both contain 6 protons, but 6 and 8 neutrons respectively.

Nudibranchia [nyoodibrangkia] *sea slug*

nuée ardente [nüay ah(r)dãnt] ('burning cloud') An incandescent cloud of hot gas and volcanic ash erupted from a volcano and travelling at great speed down its flanks.

Nuesslein-Volhard, Christiane [nüsliyn **fol**haht] (1942–) Developmental biologist, born in Magdeburg, EC Germany. She studied at the University of Tübingen, where she joined the Max-Planck Institute for Developmental Biology. She shared the Nobel Prize for Physiology or Medicine in 1995 for her research into how genes control early development of the human embryo. Using the fruit fly, her contribution, in collaboration with Wieschaus, was to identify a number of genes which determine the body plan and formation of body segments. She was the first German woman to receive a science Nobel Prize.

Nueva Esparta [nwayva espah(r)ta] pop (2000e) 339 600; area 1150 sq km/440 sq mi. State consisting of Caribbean islands, off the coast of Venezuela; consists of Margarita I, Coche, Cubagua and several smaller islands; capital, La Asunción; fishing, tourism.

Nuffield, William Richard Morris, 1st Viscount (1877–1963) Motor magnate and philanthropist, born in Worcester, Hereford and Worcester, WC England, UK. He started in the bicycle repair business, and was the first British manufacturer to develop the mass production of cheap cars (Morris). He was made a baronet in 1929 and a viscount in 1934. He used part of his vast fortune to benefit hospitals, charities, and Oxford University. In 1937 he endowed Nuffield College, Oxford, and in 1943 established the Nuffield Foundation for medical, scientific, and social research.

Nuffield Radio Astronomy Laboratories An institution at Jodrell Bank, Cheshire, NWC England, UK, founded in 1945, operated by the University of Manchester. It contains the first fully steerable radio telescope (76 m/250 ft), completed in 1957, now called the Lovell telescope. It is responsible for the MERLIN array telescope, with antennae throughout England, as well as an educational centre and a public planetarium.

nuisance A tort (or delict, in Scotland) which involves unreasonable interference by act or omission with the use or comfortable enjoyment of neighbouring property, such as by noise, smell, or smoke. The interference must be continuing and substantial to be actionable, and may depend on the locality and other circumstances. Nuisance may also be committed in relation to certain rights over land, such as a right of support of buildings. A nuisance affecting a number or class of people may in some jurisdictions (eg England) amount to a crime of public nuisance (eg in the obstruction of a road). The Attorney-General may in such a case bring a civil action on behalf of the public. The usual remedy is an injunction to have the nuisance stopped. The Protection from Harassment Act (1997) enables individuals in England and Wales to be prevented from harassing their neighbours.

Nujoma, Sam Daniel [nu**joh**ma] (1929–) Namibian nationalist leader, and first president of independent Namibia (1990–), born in Ongandjera, N Namibia. Educated at a Finnish missionary school in Windhoek, he entered active politics in 1958, founding the South West Africa People's Organisation of Namibia. Exiled in 1960 and again in 1966, he established a military wing, the People's Liberation Army of Namibia, in the mid-1960s, and his long struggle for Namibia's independence eventually bore fruit in 1989.

Nuku'alofa [nookualohfah] 21°09S 175°14W, pop (2000e) 23 500. Port and capital town of Tonga, S Pacific; on Tongatapu I, 690 km/430 mi SE of Suva, Fiji; university; coconut processing; royal palace (1867).

Nullarbor Plain [nuhl**la**baw] Vast plateau in SW South Australia and S Western Australia, between the Great Victoria Desert and the Great Australian Bight; extends 480 km/300 mi W from Ooldea, South Australia to Kalgoorlie, Western Australia; maximum height 305 m/1000 ft; consists of sand dunes and sparse vegetation (*Nullarbor*, 'treeless'); crossed by the Trans-Australian Railway, the world's longest straight stretch of railway (478 km/297 mi); Nullarbor national park on the coast (area 2319 sq km/895 sq mi).

nullification A US legal doctrine that a state has the power to render laws of the federal government void within its borders. It was first tested by South Carolina during the 'Nullification Crisis' in 1832, over the issue of enforcing a federal tariff. That immediate issue was resolved by the Jackson administration's Force Bill. But in larger terms the problem was not resolved until the Civil War, and in some ways until the civil rights movement.

numbat An Australian marsupial (*Myrmecobius fasciatus*); narrow pointed head with horizontal black line through eye; shoulders reddish-brown; hindquarters with grey and white hoops; long bushy grey tail; female without a pouch; inhabits woodlands; eats termites; also known as **banded anteater** or **marsupial anteater**. (Family: Myrmecobiidae.)

number line In mathematics, a straight line marked at equal intervals to show the positive and negative numbers.

numbers A concept used initially in counting, to compare the sizes of groups of objects. **Natural numbers** (or *cardinal numbers*) are the numbers used in counting, 1,2,3,4,5.... These are always *whole numbers*. The set of *integers* comprises all the natural numbers (the *positive integers*), *zero*, and the *negative numbers*...−3,−2,−1. The **rational numbers** are all the numbers that can be expressed in the form m/n, where m and n are two integers, positive or negative. Rational numbers include *proper fractions* (those whose numerator is less than their denominator, eg $\frac{3}{8}$) and *improper fractions* (those whose numerator is greater than their denominator, eg $\frac{8}{3}$). **Mixed numbers** are the sum of an integer and a proper fraction, eg $2\frac{1}{2}$. *Decimal fractions* are those with denominator a power of 10, written as 0·3, 0·345, etc. *Recurring decimals* are decimal fractions where a sequence of digits is repeated, eg 0·037037037..., which can be written $0{\cdot}\dot{0}3\dot{7}$, and is equal to $\frac{37}{999}$, or $\frac{1}{27}$. All recurring decimals can be expressed as rational numbers.

Irrational numbers are all real numbers that are not rational. Some can be expressed as the roots of algebraic equations with rational coefficients, eg $\sqrt{3}$ is a root of $x^2 = 3$. Those that cannot be so expressed are called **transcendental numbers**, eg π, e, e^2. **Real numbers** are all numbers that do not contain an **imaginary number** (a square root of a negative number). The positive square root of −1 is denoted by i (occasionally j). **Complex numbers** have a real and an imaginary part, eg $3 + 4i$. Either part of a complex number can be zero, so that all real numbers can be considered to be complex. The majority of real numbers are transcendental – a surprising proposition, but true, for π, π^2, π^3..., etc are all transcendental numbers. To any non-transcendental number, say k, there correspond an infinite number of transcendentals, such as $k + \pi$, $k + \pi^2$, $k + \pi^3$,....

Numbers, Book of A book of the Hebrew Bible/Old Testament, the fourth book of the Pentateuch; entitled in the Hebrew text 'In the Wilderness' or 'And He Spoke', but called 'Numbers' in Greek tradition because of the census of the tribes recorded in the first chapters. It describes the wilderness wanderings of Israel after the Exodus, starting with the preparations for leaving Sinai, and including the journeys to Kadesh-barnea and to the Transjordan prior to the entry into Canaan. Moses is the dominant character in the narrative, but there is also much ritual and legal material (often assigned to a priestly source).

number theory The abstract study of the relationship between numbers, by which is meant positive rational numbers. An early problem was one of several solved by Diophantus: 'Find three numbers such that their sum is a perfect square, and the sum of any two is a perfect square' (41, 80, 320). In the 17th-c Fermat proved many results in number theory, leaving us his famous 'last theorem'. The following theorem is said to have been his own favourite. 'All the primes greater than 3 can be divided into two classes, those such as 5, 13, 17, 29, 37... of the form $4n + 1$, where n is an integer), and those such as 7, 11, 19, 23, 31... of the form $4n + 3$. All the primes of the first class, and none of the second, can be expressed as the sum of two squares, eg $5 = 1^2 + 2^2, 13 = 2^2 + 3^2, 17 = 1^2 + 4^2$.' German mathematician Gauss asserted: 'Mathematics is the queen of the sciences, and the theory of numbers is the queen of mathematics.'

numeral In mathematics, the symbol used to represent a number. The commonest system of numerals today is the Hindu-Arabic, possibly invented by the Hindus and brought to Europe by the Arabs. This uses the symbols 0, 1, 2, 3,...9 and the idea of place-value to represent each whole number. Other systems of numerals include the Roman and the Greek. The latter used the letters of the alphabet to represent the numbers, α (alpha) for 1, β (beta) for 2,... with ι (iota) for 10, κ (kappa) twenty,... and ρ (rho) for 100. As there were only 24 letters in the Greek alphabet, even for some numbers below 1000 it was necessary to use obsolete characters.

numerical analysis Methods of calculation involving successive approximations, such as iterative methods. For example, to find $\sqrt{10}$ to any required degree of accuracy, if x_n is a good approximation to $\sqrt{10}$, use the algorithm

$$x_{n+1} = \frac{1}{2}[x_n + \frac{10}{x_n}]$$

to find $x_n + 1$, a better approximation. Great developments have been made recently in this field, encouraged by the suitability of computers for numerical methods.

numerical control The branch of computer science related to the computer control of machine tools in the manufacturing industry. Analog, digital, and hybrid computers have all been used in this area, although digital computers now predominate.

numerology The mystical study of numbers, derived mainly from Hindu and Arabic teaching, but also from Jewish and Chinese traditions. In the Chinese tradition, odd numbers are yang in quality and symbolize the celestial world, whereas even numbers are yin in quality and represent the terrestrial world. Pythagoras believed that the character of each of the nine numbers is linked to cosmic influences, and that numbers can be used to interpret the energies available at a particular hour, day, week, month, or year. Each number has a size, quality, vibration, and mystical value, and the study of their symbolism can be used as a method of divination.

Numidia [nyumidia] The Roman name for the region in N Africa to the W and S of Carthage. It roughly corresponds to modern Algeria.

numismatics The study and collecting of coins, notes, and other similar objects, such as medals. The first known coins were issued by the Lydians of Anatolia in the 7th-c BC. The first containing an accurate likeness of a reigning English monarch were minted in 1504, with the head of Henry VII. The first coins with milled edges were minted in France in 1639. The history of coin collecting dates from the Italian Renaissance, one of the first collectors being the 14th-c poet, Petrarch. Collectors in the 17th-c were the first to catalogue their collections. Coin collectors worldwide were brought together in 1936, when the International Numismatics Foundation was set up. Most museums now have extensive collections.

nummulites An important group of fossil protozoans known from the middle Palaeocene to the middle Oligocene epochs; shells disc-shaped, many-chambered, and containing calcium. They are used as zone fossils in stratigraphic analysis.

nun A member of a religious order of women living under vows of poverty, chastity, and obedience. The term includes women living in enclosed convents, as well as sisters devoted to service of the sick or poor.

Nunavut [noo nah voot] (Inuktitut, 'Our land') A Canadian territory (area 2 093 190 sq km/807 971 sq mi) created from a region formerly in E Northwest Territories, Canada, stretching from Manitoba to the North Pole; capital, Iqaluit. Its establishment was agreed in 1991 following negotiations between the federal government of Canada and Inuit leaders, and it was officially created on 1 April 1999. The population of c.29 000 is mainly Inuit (Eskimo).

Nunn, Sir Trevor (Robert) (1940–) Stage director, born in Ipswich, Suffolk, E England, UK. He studied at Cambridge, then joined the Belgrade Theatre, Coventry, as a trainee director, and moved to the Royal Shakespeare Company in 1965. In 1968 he succeeded Peter Hall as the company's artistic director, being joined as co-artistic director by Terry Hands 10 years later. He directed many outstanding productions for the Royal Shakespeare Company (RSC), and during his directorship (1968–87) the RSC took many strides forward, including the opening of two new theatres in Stratford: The Other Place (1974) and The Swan (1986). He has also directed the Andrew Lloyd Webber musicals *Cats* (1981), *Starlight Express* (1984), and *Aspects of Love* (1989). Appointed director of the Royal National Theatre (1997–2003), he created Ensemble Companies (in 1999 and 2000) with a core group of actors forming different casts in a series of plays. He was knighted in 2002. In 2003 he was honoured with a Lifetime Achievement Award by the Directors Guild of Great Britain.

Nuremberg [nyooremberg], Ger **Nürnberg** 49°27N 11°05E, pop (2000e) 511 000. Commercial and manufacturing city in Mittelfranken district, SC Germany; on the R Pegnitz and the Rhine-Main-Danube Canal, 147 km/91 mi NW of Munich; second largest city in Bavaria; scene of Mastersingers' contests during the Renaissance; annual meeting place of Nazi Party after 1933; badly bombed in World War 2; scene of German war criminal trials (1945–6); railway; electronics, electrical equipment, pharmaceuticals, metal products, cars, office machinery, toys, foodstuffs, brewing; birthplace of Dürer, Pachelbel, and Hans Sachs; S Lawrence's Church (13th–15th-c), S Sebald's Church (13th-c), Our Lady's Church (14th-c), Imperial Castle (12th–16th-c), Town Hall (founded, 1340), Holy Ghost Hospital (1331); city walls; Hitler Stadium, Nazi Congress Hall; Annual International Toy Fair.

Nuremberg Laws [nyooremberg] Two racial laws promulgated in Nuremberg in 1935 at a Reichstag meeting held during a Nazi Party rally. They formed the hallmark of Nazi ideology – anti-Semitism – following 1933 legislation to ban Jews from the professions, civil service, and the judiciary. The first law deprived of German citizenship those not of 'German or related blood'; the second made marriage or extra-marital relations illegal between Germans and Jews. Additional laws defined a Jew as one with a Jewish grandparent, banned non-Jewish domestic staff in Jewish households, introduced 'J' stamps in Jewish passports, and forced Jews to take surnames identifiable as Jewish. The laws were the first steps in the process of separating off Jews and other 'non-Aryans' in Nazi Germany, a process which culminated in the Holocaust in World War 2.

Nuremberg Trials [nyooremberg] Proceedings held by the Allies at Nuremberg after World War 2 to try Nazi war criminals, following a decision made in 1943. An International Military Tribunal was set up in August 1945, and sat from November until October 1946. The charges were conspiracy against peace, crimes against peace, violations of the laws and customs of war, and crimes against humanity. Twenty-one Nazis were tried in person, including Goering and Ribbentrop (who were sentenced to death), and Hess (who was given life imprisonment). In all, ten prisoners were executed, two committed suicide, and most of the remainder were condemned to life imprisonment.

Nureyev, Rudolf (Hametovich) [noorayef] (1938–93) Ballet dancer, born in Irkutsk, in southern Siberian Russia. He studied at the Leningrad Choregraphic School, and became a soloist with the Kirov Ballet. While touring with the Ballet in 1961, he obtained political asylum in Paris, and became an Austrian citizen in 1982. He made his debut at Covent Garden with the Royal Ballet in 1962, and became Fonteyn's regular partner. His virtuosity and expressiveness made him one of the greatest male dancers of the 1960s, in both classical and modern ballets. He began to choreograph and dance for many European companies, and became ballet director of the Paris Opéra Ballet (1983–9) and principal choreographer (1989–92). In his later years he also began to conduct, leading orchestras in the

USA, Europe, and the former Soviet Union. His autobiography, *Nureyev*, appeared in 1962.

Nurmi, Paavo (Johannes) [noormee] (1897–1973) Athlete, born in Turku, SW Finland. He won nine gold medals at three Olympic Games (1920–8), and set 22 world records at distances ranging from 1500 m to 10 000 m. His first world record was in 1921, when he clocked 30 min 40·2 sec for the 10 000 m. He retired from racing in 1933. His statue stands outside the Helsinki Olympic Stadium.

Nürnberg *Nuremberg*

Nurse, Sir Paul (M) (1949–) Biochemist and cell biologist, born in London, UK. He studied at the universities of Birmingham and East Anglia, and later at Bern, Edinburgh, and Sussex (1973–84). He headed the Cell Cycle Laboratory of the Imperial Cancer Research Fund in London (1984–7) and returned to it in 1993 after a period holding a chair at Oxford. He shared the 2001 Nobel Prize for Physiology or Medicine for his contributions to understanding the key regulators of the cell cycle. He was knighted in 1999.

nursery rhymes Traditional rhymes, essentially adult-inspired, passed on from parent to child as nursery entertainment. Most date in print from no earlier than the 18th-c, but are probably older. Some celebrate contemporary personalities; some are 'counting-out' rhymes, chanted while selecting a 'victim' from a group. Included in the earliest printed collections (1744 and 1780) are: 'Little Tommy Tucker', 'Baa, Baa, Black Sheep', 'There was a Little Man', 'Sing a Song of Sixpence', 'Who Killed Cock Robin?', 'Jack and Jill', 'Ding Dong Bell' and 'Hush-a-bye Baby'. A major collection of nursery rhymes and children's books, made by Iona Opie (1923–) and Peter Opie (1918–82), is housed in the Bodleian Library, Oxford.

nursery school A school for children under the age at which schooling becomes compulsory. The teachers are usually trained, by comparison with *playgroups*, which make greater use of volunteer helpers. Provision varies, when it is non-statutory, according to where one lives.

nurse shark Very large inoffensive shark (*Ginglymostoma cirratum*) found in shallow waters of the tropical and subtropical Atlantic; length up to 4 m/13 ft; head broad with conspicuous barbels close to nostrils, fins broad; yellowish brown. (Family: Orectolobidae.)

nursing The branch of medicine which provides care for the sick and injured, and assumes responsibility for the patient's physical, social, and spiritual needs that encourage recovery. Nurses comprise the largest single group of health workers. In developed countries the profession undergoes formal training prior to registration. Nurses are responsible for monitoring therapies, and increasingly have the authority to prescribe specific medical or surgical remedies or drugs, as well as assisting doctors and surgeons in carrying out treatment. With advances in medical practice, many nurses have become specialized in one of several subdisciplines, including hospital, paediatric, psychiatric, home-visiting, and intensive care nurses. They also have responsibility for training junior nurses and nursing aides in practical procedures, and in encouraging self-help and self-care by patients themselves where this is feasible. They also have a role in promoting health.

Nusayri *Alawi* (Islam)

nut A dry, non-splitting fruit with a woody shell, often seated in a cup-like structure and containing several seeds, only one of which develops fully. In non-specialist use, the term is often applied to any woody fruit or seed.

nutation In astronomy, the irregular 'nodding' of a rotation axis, particularly for Earth, discovered in 1748 by British astronomer James Bradley. It has an amplitude of 9 arc seconds and a period of 18·6 years, and results from the gravitational attractions of the Sun and Moon on the Earth's equatorial bulge.

nutcracker Either of two species of crow of the genus *Nucifraga*: the **nutcracker** (*Nucifraga caryocatactes*) of Europe and Asia; and **Clark's nutcracker** (*Nucifraga columbiana*) of W North America. They inhabit coniferous forest, and eat insects, seeds, and young birds. (Family: Corvidae.)

nuthatch A small bird of the family Sittidae (c.23 species), inhabiting rocks or woodland in the N hemisphere; short tail, sharp straight bill; eats insects (sometimes nuts); hunts by walking 'head first' down treetrunks or rock faces. The name is also used for the **coral-billed nuthatch** (Family: Hyposittidae) and the **pink-faced nuthatch** (Family: Daphoenosittidae).

nutmeg An evergreen tree (*Myristica fragrans*) growing to 9 m/30 ft, native to the Moluccas, Indonesia; leaves oblong, fragrant; flowers waxy, yellow, 3-lobed bells; fruit 5–9 cm/2–3½ in, fleshy, pear-shaped, containing a single, large seed (the nutmeg) surrounded by a red aril from which mace is made. Both spices contain a narcotic, and are poisonous in large quantities. (Family: Myristicaceae.)

nutria *coypu*

nutrients All components of foods and all diet supplements which fall into one or other of the following categories. **Macronutrients** are energy-yielding substances, proteins, carbohydrates, and fats; **micronutrients** are minerals, vitamins, and various chemical substances present in tiny quantities (the *trace elements*). Dietary fibre is not a nutrient.

nutrition The scientific study of all aspects of what organisms (in particular, human beings) eat. It involves the analysis of what people eat, the psychology of why they eat, what happens to food in the body, and how the balance of food affects health. Nutrition is deeply rooted in biochemistry and physiology, but also involves chemistry, psychology, sociology, statistics, economics, agriculture, and medicine. An expert in nutrition is known as a **nutritionist** (often wrongly referred to as a 'nutritionalist').

nutritional medicine The study of the interaction of nutritional factors within the human body to find ways of treating disease and maintaining health. It includes the study of the properties of the nutrients themselves, and the physiology of digestion, absorption, and biochemical utilization. Practitioners of nutritional medicine are usually medically qualified, and base their diagnosis upon orthodox medical assessment, with laboratory tests such as vitamin and mineral assays or assessment of bowel function. Treatment may be given by correcting any micronutrient deficiencies using appropriate supplements, and by dietary manipulation to avoid any food items that have been shown to be contributing to illness.

nutritional minerals Elements found in all cells and fluids of the body that are essential in the diet, though only in very small quantities. Examples include: potassium, vital to the maintenance of intracellular fluid levels; calcium, required to build bones and teeth and for the process of transmitting nervous impulses to muscles; iron, used by the body to make haemoglobin, an oxygen-carrying pigment in the blood; and iodine, necessary for the synthesis of thyroid hormone.

Nuzi [noozee] An ancient town in Upper Mesopotamia, E of the Tigris. It was a flourishing Hurrian community in the second millennium BC, with strong commercial interests.

nyala An African spiral-horned antelope; greyish-brown with thin vertical white lines; male with shaggy coat; two species: **nyala** (*Tragelaphus angasi*), found in dense undergrowth near water in SE Africa; and **mountain nyala** (*Tragelaphus buxtoni*), from high forest in Ethiopia.

Nyasa [niasa] or **Malawi, Lake**, Mozambique **Niassa** area 28 500 sq km/11 000 sq mi. Lake in SEC Africa; third largest lake in Africa, in the S section of the Great Rift Valley; within Malawi and Mozambique, and bordering Tanzania; 580 km/365 mi long; 24–80 km/15–50 mi wide; altitude, 437 m/1434 ft; navigation possible over the whole of the lake; sometimes known as the 'Calendar Lake' because it is 365 miles long and 52 miles across, at its widest point; a world heritage site.

Nyerere, Julius (Kambarage) [nyerairay] (1922–99) Tanzanian statesman and president (1962–85), born in Butiama, N Tanzania (formerly Tanganyika). He became a teacher at Makerere, then studied at Edinburgh. He reorganized the nationalists into the Tanganyika African National Union (1954), of which he became president, and in 1960 became chief minister. He was premier when Tanganyika was granted internal self-government (1961), and was made president on independence (1962). In 1964 he negotiated the union of Tanganyika and Zanzibar as Tanzania. He led his country on a path of Socialism and self-reliance, but his policies failed, and he retired in 1985.

nylon A generic term for the most widely-produced type of synthetic fibre, used commercially since 1938. It is a polyamide whose lightness and elasticity make it available for use both in fibre and solid form. It is also an extremely strong and hard-wearing material. Its uses are therefore varied, including ropes, tyre cords, engineering components, furnishings, and apparel.

Nyman, Michael [niyman] (1944–) Pianist and composer, born in London, UK. He formed the Michael Nyman Band in 1977, for which he composed several works characterized by highly charged, stylized, rhythmical chord progressions, much influenced by Purcell, in which his own piano playing is a driving force. His compositions include scores for the films of Peter Greenaway, and for the films *Carrington* (1995) and *The Piano* (1993), as well as a chamber opera *The Man Who Mistook His Wife for a Hat* (1986). Later works include string quartets, concertos for piano (1994) and trombone (1995), and the opera *Facing Goya* (2000). A selection of film music, *The Very Best of Michael Nyman 1980–2001*, appeared in 2001.

nymph (entomology) A feeding and growth stage in the development of insects, between hatching and the reorganization involved in attaining adulthood. The term is used only in relation to those insects in which the wings develop gradually and externally.

nymph (mythology) In Greek mythology, one of the 'young women', nature-spirits, who live in streams (*naiads*), trees (*hamadryads*), the sea (*nereids*), as well as rocks and mountains; also those of a particular locality, who sometimes have a special name. They are long-lived but not immortal, and are fond of music and dancing. Unfortunately, people who see them become *nympholept*, filled with madness.

nymphalid butterfly A butterfly of the family Nymphalidae; typically colourful, with long hair-like scales; forelegs reduced, non-functional; eggs ribbed; caterpillars with spines; c.8200 species, including admirals, emperors, fritillaries, and tortoiseshell butterflies. (Order: Lepidoptera).

Nymphenburg porcelain Porcelain made at the Nymphenburg factory near Munich, Germany, which from 1753 produced fine table wares and figures. Their most celebrated modeller was Franz Anton Bustelli (1723–63), who made elegant Rococo miniature sculptures of stylized humans in contemporary dress.

nymphomania *satyriasis*

Nyoro [nyoroh] A Bantu-speaking agricultural people of W Uganda. The original feudal kingdom of Bunyoro-Kitara was founded in the 14th–15th-c with a pastoralist ruling class (Hima) and farming peasants (Iru). It was the most powerful kingdom in the area during the 19th-c, but was destroyed by the British in the 1890s. The kingship was abolished by the Ugandan government in 1966.

Nyx *nix*

O

Oahu [ohahhoo] pop (2000e) 920 000; area 1526 sq km/ 589 sq mi. Third largest island of the US state of Hawaii; part of Honolulu County; chief town, Honolulu; rises to 1233 m/ 4045 ft at Kaala; sugar, fruit, tourism; naval base at Pearl Harbor.

oak A member of a large genus of often massive and long-lived trees and also small shrubs, native to the N hemisphere; leaves deciduous or evergreen, usually shallowly lobed or with wavy margins; flowers tiny, perianth 4–7-lobed, males in catkins, females solitary or in clusters; fruit an acorn seated in a scaly cup. It is a traditional source of excellent timber, and also of cork and bark for tanning. Some North American species are planted for their fine autumn colours. **Oak-apples** are woody galls produced by wasp larvae. (Genus: *Quercus*, 450 species. Family: Fagaceae.)

Oakeshott, Michael Joseph (1901–90) Philosopher and political theorist, born in Harpenden, Hertfordshire, SE England, UK. He studied at Cambridge, taught there (1929–49), and was professor of political science at the London School of Economics (1950–69). His first and main philosophical work was *Experience and its Modes* (1933), written broadly from within the English idealist tradition. This view of human experience and conduct is developed in his political theory, which tends to be conservative, pragmatic, and sceptical of systematization and ideology, as represented in the later works *Rationalism in Politics* (1962) and *On Human Conduct* (1975).

Oakland 37°49N 122°16W, pop (2000e) 399 500. Port capital of Alameda Co, W California, USA, on the E shore of San Francisco Bay; founded, 1850; linked by the San Francisco–Oakland Bay Bridge (1936); major earthquake, 1989; airports (Oakland, Hayward); railway; vehicles, chemicals, paint, food processing, metal products, office equipment; observatory; art gallery; museums; professional teams, A's (baseball), Golden State Warriors (basketball).

Oakley, Annie, popular name of **Phoebe Anne Oakley Moses** (1860–1926) Rodeo star and sharp-shooter, born in Woodland (now Willowdell), Darke Co, Ohio, USA. She learned to shoot at an early age, and married **Frank E Butler** in 1876 after beating him in a shooting match. They formed a trick-shooting act, and from 1885 toured widely with the Buffalo Bill Wild West Show. A tiny woman just under five feet tall, from 30 paces she shot cigarettes from her husband's lips and the lips of Kaiser Wilhelm II, and through the pips of a playing card tossed in the air. 'Annie Oakley' became a synonym for a complimentary ticket, because of the hole traditionally punched in it. Her story was fictionalized in the Irving Berlin musical comedy *Annie Get Your Gun* (1946), starring Ethel Merman.

Oak Ridge 36°01N 84°16W, pop (2000e) 27 400. Town in Anderson Co, E Tennessee, USA, on the Clinch R; founded by the US Government in 1942 to house workers developing the uranium-235 and plutonium-239 isotopes for the atomic bomb; the community was kept secret until after the first bombs were dropped in 1945; centre of atomic energy and nuclear physics research; nuclear fuel, nuclear instruments, electronic instrumentation; American Museum of Atomic Energy.

Oaks *Classics*

oarfish Very long, ribbon-shaped fish (*Regalecus glesne*) widespread in tropical and warm temperate seas; length up to 7 m/ 23 ft; body extremely slender, compressed, tapering posteriorly; dorsal fin extending full length of body, tail fin absent, pelvis reduced to long filaments. (Family: Regalecidae.)

OAS 1 Abbreviation of **Organisation de l'Armée Secrète** ('Secret Army Organization'), the clandestine organization of French Algerians, led by rebel army generals Jouhaud and Salan, active (1960–2) in resisting Algerian independence. It caused considerable violence in Algeria and metropolitan France until thrown into rapid decline by the Franco-Algerian ceasefire (Mar 1962), Salan's capture (Apr 1962), and Algerian independence (Jul 1962).
2 *Organization of American States*

Oasis British pop group, formed in 1992 with five members, all but one from Manchester, NW England, UK: **Liam Gallagher** (1972– , vocals), **Noel Gallagher** (1967– , lead guitar, backing vocals, songwriter), **Paul 'Bonehead' Arthurs** (1965– , rhythm guitar), replaced in 1999 by **Gem Archer**, **Paul 'Guigsy' McGuigan** (1971– , bass guitar), replaced in 1999 by **Andy Bell**, and **Tony McCarroll** (drums), replaced in 1995 by **Alan White** (1972– , born in London). Their first single, 'Supersonic' (1994), became an immediate number 1 hit, and was followed by a series of hits, such as 'Shakermaker' (1994), 'Wonderwall' (1995), 'Don't Look Back in Anger' (1996), and 'D'You Know What I Mean' (1997). Their first album, *Definitely Maybe* (1994), was the fastest selling debut album in British pop history, later albums including *What's The Story (Morning Glory)* (1995), *Be Here Now* (1997), *Standing On the Shoulders of Giants* (2000), and *Heathen Chemistry* (2002). The group rose to become the leading UK band of the 1990s, touring widely, the flamboyant personal lives of the Gallagher brothers attracting the kind of media attention that had not been seen since the Beatles (with whom – along with God – they readily compared themselves).

Oates, Joyce Carol (1938–) Novelist and essayist, born in Lockport, New York, USA. She studied at Syracuse University and at the University of Wisconsin, taught English at Detroit (1961–7), then became professor of English at Windsor, Ontario. Her first novel was *With Shuddering Fall* (1964), and *Them* (1969), her fourth novel, won a National Book award. Later books include *Marya: A Life* (1986), *We Were the Mulvaneys* (1996), *Broke Heart Blues* (1999), and *Middle Age: A Romance* (2001). She has published poetry, essays, and criticism, and her short-story collections include *The Wheel of Love* (1970) and *Raven's Wing* (1987).

Oates, Lawrence (Edward Grace) (1880–1912) Explorer, born in London, UK. He was educated at Eton, joined the army, and served in South Africa. In 1910 he joined Scott's Antarctic Expedition in charge of the ponies, and was one of the party of five to reach the South Pole in 1912. On the return journey the explorers became weatherbound. Lamed by severe frostbite, and convinced that his condition would fatally handicap his companions' prospect of survival, he walked out into the blizzard, sacrificing his life. His last words have become famous: 'I am just going outside, I may be some time'.

Oates, Titus (1649–1705) Conspirator and perjurer, born in Oakham, Leicestershire, C England, UK. He studied at Cambridge, and took Anglican orders, but was dismissed from his curacy for misconduct. Having feigned conversion to Catholicism and attended Jesuit seminaries on the continent, in 1678 he made public details of a fictitious Jesuit plot to murder Charles II and restore Catholicism. This 'Popish Plot' caused widespread panic, and at least 35 innocent people were tried and executed for complicity in it; but suspicion of Oates gradually grew and two years later he was found guilty of perjury, flogged, and imprisoned for life. The Revolution of 1688 set him at liberty, and he was granted a pension.

oath A solemn expression from a person giving evidence in court or making a sworn written statement. The traditional wording is 'I swear by Almighty God that the evidence which I shall give shall be the truth, the whole truth, and nothing but the truth'. Alternatively, it is possible to *affirm*, that is to solemnly promise to tell the truth. Other traditional or religious practices are often recognized; for example a Chinese witness may break a plate to emphasize solemnity. The deliberate giving of false testimony under oath is called *perjury*.

oats A cereal (*Avena sativa*), probably native to the Mediterranean basin, and cultivated in temperate regions, especially in the N hemisphere, tolerating a wide climatic range, and growing where other cereals fail. Its inflorescence is a graceful, spreading panicle. It is an important human and animal food, though less so in recent times. It is rich in protein, but unlike wheat cannot be used for bread. (Family: Gramineae.)

Ob, River [op] Chief river of the W Siberian Lowlands, C Russia; formed by the union of the Biya and Katun Rivers, in the N foothills of the Altay Mts; flows generally NW and W to the mouth of the R Irtysh at Khanty-Mansiysk; turns N and divides into numerous channels, to enter Ob Bay, an inlet of the Kara Sea; length, 3650 km/2268 mi; with the R Irtysh, its chief tributary, length 5570 km/3461 mi, the world's fourth longest river; frozen for 5–6 months of the year; important transport route; vast oil reserves within its basin.

Obadiah, Book of [ohbadiya] One of the 12 so-called 'minor' prophetic writings of the Hebrew Bible/Old Testament, and the shortest book of the Hebrew Bible; named after the otherwise unknown prophet, whose name means 'Servant of God'; sometimes called **Book of Abdias**. The work may have originated soon after the fall of Jerusalem in 587/6 BC, but it is not always seen as a unified composition deriving from one time. It prophesies the fall of Edom in retribution for taking sides against Jerusalem, predicting judgment on the nations and the restoration of Israel at the final day of the Lord.

Obelia [ohbeelia] A genus of marine invertebrate animals; hydroids, living in colonies, commonly found growing on seaweeds in the intertidal zone on shores; polyps on erect stems connect by root-like horizontal branches; a horny sheath (theca) forms a protective cup around each polyp; free-swimming medusa stage. (Phylum: Cnidaria. Class: Hydrozoa.)

obelisk A tall pillar, usually made of granite, square in section, tapering upwards, and ending in a small pyramid. Obelisks were common in ancient Egypt, being used for commemorative or religious purposes. Well-known examples are Cleopatra's Needles (c.1475 BC), one of which is now located on the Victoria Embankment, London, the other in Central Park, New York City.

Oberammergau Passion Play [ohberamergow] A dramatization every 10 years of the Passion of Christ, performed by villagers of Oberammergau in Bavaria, S Germany. It is performed in fulfilment of a vow made in 1663, when the village was saved from plague.

Oberon (astronomy) [ohberon] The second-largest satellite of Uranus, discovered in 1787 by William Herschel; distance from the planet 583 500 km/362 600 mi; diameter 1524 km/947 mi.

Oberon (mythology) [ohberon] In European literature, the name of the king of the fairies, as in Shakespeare's *A Midsummer Night's Dream* and Wieland's *Oberon*.

Oberpfälzer Wald [ohberfeltser vahlt] Low NW section of the Bohemian Forest, between the Fichtelgebirge and Bavarian Forest; highest peak in former West Germany, the Entenbuhl (901 m/2956 ft).

obesity [ohbeesitee] Extreme overweight, with an excessive amount of body fat; the most common nutritional disease in affluent societies. It is associated with a high mortality, and predisposes to serious diseases, including diabetes mellitis, hypertension, and coronary heart disease. It may be related to genetic factors, or to hormonal disorders such as hypothyroidism or Cushing's syndrome. However the majority of cases are a consequence of excessive food intake and inadequate physical exercise.

objective test A test which is scored according to strict rules, rather than on the subjective judgment of the tester. The scorer usually operates to a marking system based on predetermined acceptable answers. Often the test will be scored by someone other than the person who gave it, for even greater objectivity.

object-oriented paradigm An approach to building software where programs are created as chunks of code known as *objects*, each object relating to a conceptual unit involved in the system (eg an interface object might be a screen or a window, a business object might be a customer or a purchase order). The same coded objects can be used in many different systems, providing re-use of the same code. This enables new applications to be *component engineered* by assembling and tailoring already existing objects from a library provided by software manufacturers. Object-oriented programming languages began to be used extensively throughout the 1980s and 1990s. Object-oriented databases developed during the 1990s, and a number of important object-oriented database management systems are now in the market place. Object-oriented analysis and design methodologies came into prominence only during the late 1990s, but they have taken over from structured systems development methodologies as the dominant approach to the design and creation of business application systems.

obliquity of the ecliptic The angle at which the celestial equator intersects the ecliptic, now decreasing by 0·47 arc seconds per year, due to precession and nutation. It varies between 21°55' and 24°18'. Its value in AD 2000 was 23°26'21".

obo [ohboh] A term derived from 'oil/bulk ore', a vessel designed to carry oil and bulk ore either together or separately. This is a relatively new class of vessel, first built in the mid-1960s. By 2000, total obo tonnage was 20 million gross tonnes, over 37 million deadweight tonnes.

oboe A musical instrument made of wood in three jointed sections, opening to a small bell; it is fitted with a double reed. It first appeared in recognizable form in the mid-17th-c and was widely used in the 18th-c. Since then its mechanism has been developed, particularly by the addition of keys. In the orchestra it is normally the oboe that sets the pitch for the other instruments. A lower-pitched instrument, the **oboe d'amore**, was also used in the 18th-c, but fell into disuse later.

Obote, (Apollo) Milton [ohbohtay] (1924–) Ugandan statesman, prime minister (1962–71), and president (1967–71, 1981–5), born in Lango, Uganda. He studied at Makerere College, Kampala, was elected to the Legislative Council (1957), founded the Uganda People's Congress (1960), and became leader of the opposition (1961–2). At independence in 1962 he became the new nation's first prime minister. In 1966 he mounted a coup, deposed King Mutesa II, declared a republic, and made himself executive president. In 1971 he was, in turn, deposed by Idi Amin, and took refuge in Tanzania. After Amin's removal in 1979, he was re-elected president in 1981. Ousted by Brigadier Basilio Okello in 1985, he was granted political asylum in Zambia.

O'Brien, (Donal) Conor (Dermod David Donat) Cruise (1917–) Historian, critic, and Irish statesman, born in Dublin, Ireland. He studied at Dublin, and became an outstanding historian and critic. His best-known work is *To Katanga and Back* (1962), an autobiographical narrative of the Congo crisis of 1961. An MP from 1969, he became minister for posts and telegraphs (1973–7). He was subsequently editor-in-chief of *The Observer*, as well as the author of studies on Albert Camus and Edmund Burke, and remains a contributor to a wide variety of print media.

O'Brien, (Josephine) Edna (1930–) Novelist and short-story writer, born in Tuamgraney, Co Clare, W Ireland. She studied at the Pharmaceutical College of Dublin, and practised pharmacy briefly before becoming a writer. Much of her writing is concerned with the position of women in society – their lack of fulfilment and the repressive nature of their upbringing. Her celebrated books include *The Country Girls* (1960), *Girls in Their Married Bliss* (1963), and *August Is a Wicked Month* (1965). *The Collected Edna O'Brien*, containing nine novels, was published in 1978. Later works include *Time and Tide* (1992), *House of Splendid Isolation* (1994), *Down by the River* (1996), and *Wild Decembers* (1999). Her short stories are also highly regarded, the best from several collections appearing in *The Fanatic Heart* (1985), and in 1990 she published *Lantern Slides*.

O'Brien, Flann, pseudonym of **Brian O'Nolan**, also known as **Myles na Gopaleen** (1911–66) Writer and journalist, born in Strabane, Co Tyrone, W Northern Ireland, UK. He studied at Dublin, and his first and major novel was *At Swim-Two-Birds* (1939, translated into Gaelic, 1956). A civil servant, he contributed a column to the *Irish Times* for some 20 years under his Irish pseudonym. Best known as an idiosyncratic newspaper columnist, various anthologies appeared after his death – *The Best of Myles* (1968), *The Various Lives of Keats and Chapman and the Brother* (1976), and *Myles From Dublin* (1985).

O'Brien, William (1852–1928) Journalist and nationalist, born in Mallow, Co Cork, S Ireland. He studied at Queen's College, Cork, became editor of the weekly *United Ireland*, and sat in parliament as a Nationalist (1883–95). Several times prosecuted, and imprisoned for two years, he later returned to parliament (1900–18), founded the United Irish League (1898), and the All-for-Ireland League (1910).

observatory The instruments and associated buildings for conducting astronomical research. This broad definition includes the structures of native proto-astronomers, such as the builders of Stonehenge and Meso-American pyramids, the great mountain observatories of professionals in Hawaii, Australia, and Chile, the backyard shed of the keen amateur, and satellites carrying telescopes far above the atmosphere. Modern optical observatories are situated on mountain tops to get above cloud and atmospheric pollution, with oceanic islands being particularly satisfactory. The astronomers at most large observatories welcome enquiries from the general public, and many are open for self-guided tours. Local astronomical societies often have observatories where it is possible to view the planets, stars, and galaxies on clear nights.

obstetrics [obste**t**riks] The medical and surgical care of pregnancy and childbirth. It involves the prenatal care and assessment of the woman's ability to undergo labour, the assessment of the size and health of the fetus in the womb, the detection of diseases related to pregnancy (eg eclampsia), the diagnosis of the position of the fetus in the uterus, and the conduct of the delivery via the vagina. In special circumstances, delivery may need to be assisted by the use of obstetrical forceps to ease the passage of the head through the pelvic outlet, by vacuum extraction, or by caesarian section. Also important are the control of pain, the use of drugs to influence uterine contraction, and the diagnosis and treatment of complications during pregnancy and in the following period.

ocarina [okare**e**na] A simple, egg-shaped musical instrument belonging to the flute family, with a protruding mouthpiece, six fingerholes, and two thumbholes. It is made from terracotta, and is played by children, and also as a folk instrument.

O'Casey, Sean, originally **John Casey** (1880–1964) Playwright, born in Dublin, Ireland. From an impoverished Protestant family, he suffered from poor health during his boyhood. Trachoma permanently damaged his eyesight and interrupted his education. During years of physical hardship in labouring work, he became involved with the Irish Citizen Army, but resigned in 1914 in protest against its anti-Union attitudes. His first publication was a broadside, *The Story of Thomas Ashe* (1917), about a friend in the Citizen Army who died on hunger strike, but he was already interested in the work of the Abbey Theatre. After rejecting at least three of his plays, the Abbey staged *The Shadow of a Gunman* (1923) and *Juno and the Paycock* (1924). Later he became more experimental and impressionistic. His anti-war drama *The Plough and the Stars* (1926) provoked a full-scale riot, and caused him to leave Ireland for good. Other works include *The Silver Tassie* (1929), *Cockadoodle Dandy* (1949), and *The Bishop's Bonfire* (1955). He also wrote essays, such as *The Flying Wasp* (1936), and was awarded the Hawthornden Prize in 1926.

occasionalism A philosophical theory, associated particularly with Malebranche and Geulincx, which espouses Descartes' dualism of mind and body but tries to explain all causal interaction between them by God's direct intervention. God 'occasions' all processes and events, and mind and body operate in a separate but perfectly synchronized way, like two clocks.

occluded front A meteorological term, also called an **occlusion**, used to describe the situation in a depression when the cold front catches up with the warm front, and lifts the warm air off the ground. The depression then fills in, and atmospheric pressure rises.

occultation An astronomical phenomenon observed when a planet or moon passes across the line of sight to another body. It is useful for getting information on the position, size, and atmosphere of the body causing the occultation. The rings around Uranus were detected when the planet occulted light from a star.

occultism Activities purporting to achieve communication with the supernatural. The term includes magic, divination, certain types of spiritualism, and witchcraft. Occult knowledge is often held to be secret, for initiates only.

occupational diseases Diseases which arise in the course of employment; also known as **industrial disease**, in the context of industrial work. They have been recognized from antiquity and throughout history: Ecclesiastes recognized that blacksmiths suffered from deafness because of the noise of their work; Venetian gilders suffered from mercury poisoning; and the Industrial Revolution caused atmospheric pollution with many toxic substances. Such conditions affect almost every bodily system. Many chemicals and dyes induce dermatitis. Inhalation of industrial products affects the lungs, and may lead to pneumoconiosis or asbestosis. Agricultural workers may suffer damage from the inhalation of vegetable dust and fungal spores. Ionizing radiation may cause leukaemia. Compressed-air workers suffer damage to their ears and fingers; and welders may damage their eyes. Health workers can acquire infections. Liver disease may follow exposure to organic solvents. Such events have led to the development of *industrial medicine*, by which environmentally-produced disease is identified, indices of well-being of vulnerable groups are established and monitored, and the limiting factors in the environment or work place which cause disorder are defined. In most countries there are arrangements for the compensation of those who suffer from occupational diseases. Several countries have also developed agencies to monitor the situation; for example, in the USA the Occupational Safety and Health Administration enforces federal regulations.

occupational psychology The application of psychological methods to the study and resolution of problems in industry in the widest sense. It includes the study of work skills and the working environment, vocational guidance, personnel selection, all forms of training, principles of management, organization structure and function, principles of advertising and salesmanship, and consumer motivation, preference, and satisfaction.

occupational therapy A range of treatments designed to minimise the impact of physical and psychiatric conditions on life in order to help people reach their maximum level of function

Oceans

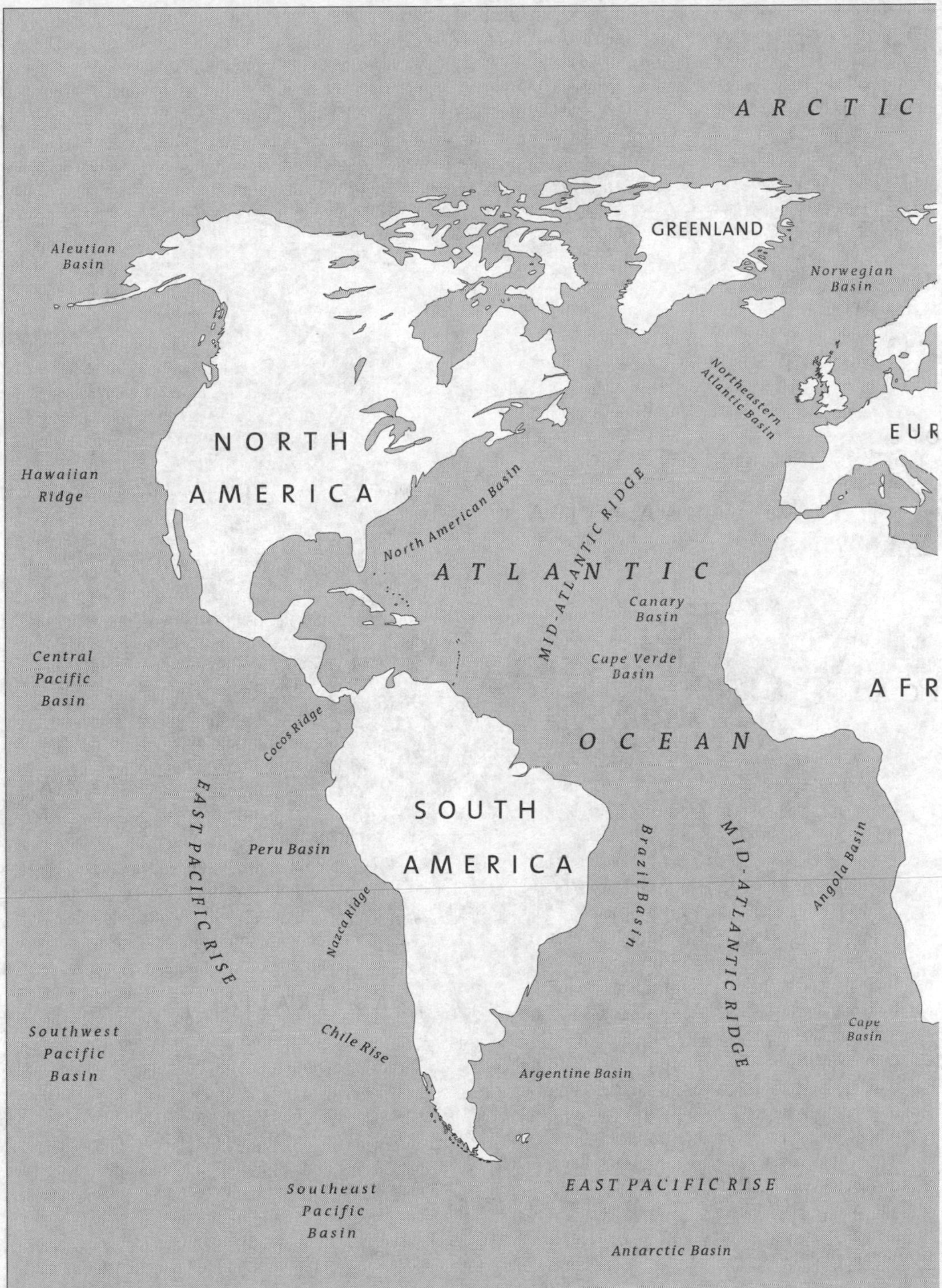
ARCTIC
GREENLAND
Aleutian Basin
Norwegian Basin
Northeastern Atlantic Basin
EUR
NORTH AMERICA
Hawaiian Ridge
North American Basin
MID-ATLANTIC RIDGE
ATLANTIC
Canary Basin
Cape Verde Basin
Central Pacific Basin
AFR
Cocos Ridge
OCEAN
EAST PACIFIC RISE
SOUTH AMERICA
Peru Basin
Brazil Basin
MID-ATLANTIC RIDGE
Angola Basin
Nazca Ridge
Southwest Pacific Basin
Chile Rise
Cape Basin
Argentine Basin
Southeast Pacific Basin
EAST PACIFIC RISE
Antarctic Basin

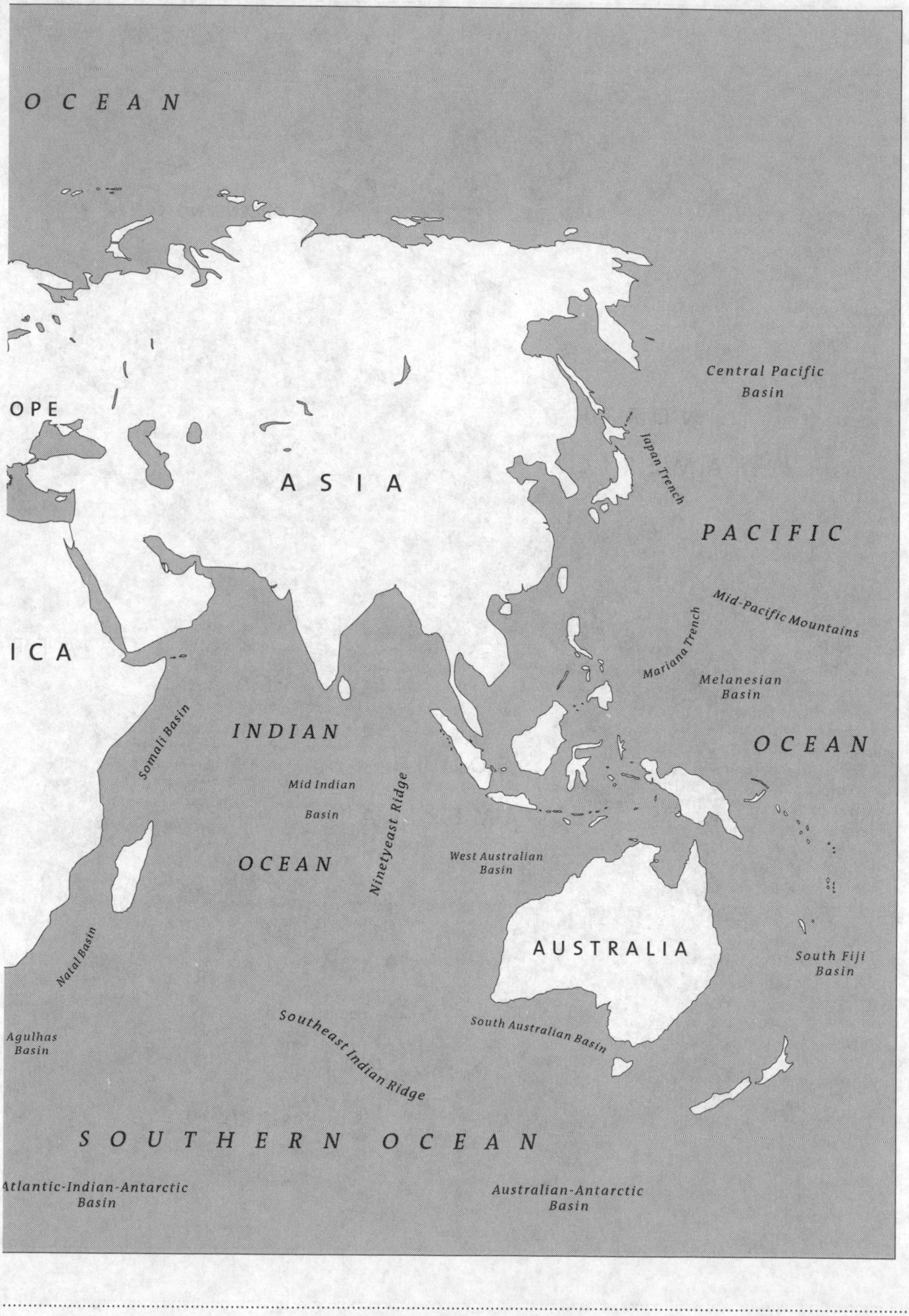
OCEAN
OPE
ASIA
ICA
Central Pacific
Basin
Japan Trench
PACIFIC
Mid-Pacific Mountains
Mariana Trench
Melanesian
Basin
OCEAN
Somali Basin
INDIAN
Mid Indian
Basin
Ninetyeast Ridge
OCEAN
West Australian
Basin
AUSTRALIA
South Fiji
Basin
Natal Basin
Agulhas
Basin
Southeast Indian Ridge
South Australian Basin
SOUTHERN OCEAN
Atlantic-Indian-Antarctic
Basin
Australian-Antarctic
Basin

and independence in all aspects of daily living. It includes provision of physical aids, such as stair rails, and activities such as vocationally orientated workshops and arts and crafts classes.

oceanarium *aquarium*

Oceania [ohshiahnia], also **Oceanica** A general name applied to the isles of the Pacific Ocean, including Polynesia, Melanesia, Micronesia, Australasia, and sometimes the Malaysian islands.

oceanic bank *seamount*

oceanic ridges Giant undersea mountain ranges, rising above the surrounding sea floor 1–4 km/½–2½ mi, which wind their way around the globe for over 80 000 km/50 000 mi and cover 35% of the sea floor. Average depth of a ridge crest is c.2·5 km/1·5 mi; ridge width is 2000–4000 km/1250–2500 mi, with the relief becoming more subdued away from the crest as the surface slopes down to the ocean basin. The axes of all oceanic ridges are offset by numerous fractures called *transform faults*, which are seismically active, being the sites of numerous shallow earthquakes. The Mid-Atlantic Ridge is the best-known ridge system, divided into *crest* and *flank* provinces. The crest province consists of a *high fractured plateau*, *rift mountains*, and a *rift valley* which lies along the axis of the ridge, 25–50 km/15–30 mi wide, and 1–2 km/½–1 mi deeper than the adjacent mountains. A series of steps going from the high fractured plateau to the ocean basin forms the flank province. The overall gradient of this ridge is 1:100. The East Pacific Rise, on the other hand, is a wide, low bulge with a gradient of 1:500. It further differs from the Mid-Atlantic Ridge in having no prominent valley along its crest.

Large areas of the sea floor which rise more than several hundred metres above the level of the ocean basin floor are **oceanic rises**. Unlike ridge systems, these features are generally aseismic, lacking significant earthquake activity. Examples are the Ninety East Ridge in the Indian Ocean, Jan Mayen Ridge in the N Atlantic, and the Shatsky Rise in the N Pacific. (*see pp.1115–16*)

oceanic rise *oceanic ridges*

oceanic trenches A long, narrow depression in the seafloor. Typically 50–100 km/30–60 mi wide, up to several thousand km long, descending three to four km deeper than the surrounding ocean floor. Though trenches are found in the Atlantic (Puerto Rico and South Sandwich) and Indian Oceans (Java Trench), most occur in the Pacific Ocean, which is virtually surrounded by trenches (eg the Peru-Chile, Aleutian, Japan, and Tonga-Kermedac). The greatest depth on Earth is found in the Challenger Deep section of the Mariana Trench, which reaches 11 034 m/36 412 ft.

oceanic zone The marine life zone of the open ocean past the edge of the continental shelf. Oceanic organisms live in an environment showing little change in temperature or salinity, hence they cannot tolerate fluctuations.

Oceanides [ohseeanideez] In Greek mythology, the innumerable nymphs who inhabit the ocean and other watery places. They are the daughters of Oceanus and Tethys.

oceanography The study of the oceans, also referred to as **oceanology**. It is usually divided into four sub-disciplines. **Geological oceanography** deals with the structure and origin of the ocean floor, the processes which operate along the shoreline, the sediments which cover the ocean floor, and the origin and distribution of marine mineral resources. **Chemical oceanography** deals with the chemical properties of seawater, the components dissolved in seawater, and the chemical reactions which take place in the ocean, at the sea floor, and at the sea surface. **Physical oceanography** covers the physical processes in the ocean, including ocean currents, waves, tides, and the interaction between the atmosphere and the ocean. **Biological oceanography** deals with marine organisms and their relationship with their environment, including the effects of the physical, chemical, and geological conditions in the sea on the distribution and abundance of organisms, and the effects of the organisms on the marine environment. (*see pp.1115–16*)

ocean thermal energy conversion (OTEC) A technique for converting difference in ocean temperature between warm surface waters and cold deeper waters into a usable energy resource. A typical OTEC plant might use tropical ocean surface water to evaporate ammonia, which would cause a turbine to generate electricity. Cold deep water would be used to condense the ammonia to start the cycle again. Part of the electrical power is used to operate pumps to bring the cold water to the ocean surface.

Oceanus [ohseeanus] In Greek mythology, a Titan, the son of Uranus and Gaia. He is a benign god who personifies the stream of Ocean which was assumed to surround the world, as known to the Greeks.

ocelot [oselot] A rare member of the cat family (*Felis pardalis*), found from S USA to N Argentina; pale with dark spots and lines; inhabits diverse habitats; eats small mammals, birds, snakes, and fish; sometimes reared as pets; also known as **painted leopard** or **tigrillo**.

Ochoa, Severo [ohchoha] (1905–93) Biochemist, born in Luarca, NW Spain. He studied medicine at Madrid University, then carried out research at Heidelberg and Oxford. He emigrated to the USA in 1941, joining the staff of the New York University Medicine School. His work on the biological synthesis of nucleic activities brought him a share of the 1959 Nobel Prize for Physiology or Medicine.

ochre Earth consisting of a mixture of hydrated iron oxides and clay, light yellow to brown in colour. It is ground to a powder and used as a pigment.

Ockham, William of *William of Ockham*

O'Connell, Daniel, known as **the Liberator** (1775–1847) Irish Catholic political leader, born near Cahirciveen, Co Kerry, SW Ireland. He became a lawyer, and in 1823 formed the Catholic Association, which successfully fought elections against the landlords. His election as MP for Co Clare precipitated a crisis in Wellington's government, which eventually granted Catholic Emancipation (1829), enabling him to take his seat in the Commons. In 1840 he founded the Repeal Association, and agitation to end the union with Britain increased. In 1844 he was imprisoned for 14 weeks on a charge of sedition. In conflict with the Young Ireland movement (1846), and failing in health, he left Ireland in 1847.

O'Connor, Feargus Edward (1794–1855) Chartist leader, born in Connorville, Co Cork, S Ireland. He studied at Dublin, became a lawyer, and entered parliament in 1832. Estranged from O'Connell, he devoted himself to the cause of the working classes in England. His Leeds *Northern Star* (1837) became the most influential Chartist newspaper. He attempted, without great success, to unify the Chartist movement via the National Charter Association (1842), and presented himself as leader of the Chartist cause. Elected MP for Nottingham in 1847, in 1852 insanity caused his withdrawal from public life.

O'Connor, (Mary) Flannery (1925–64) Writer, born in Savannah, Georgia, USA. She studied at the University of Iowa, and was brought up a Roman Catholic in the Bible-belt of the Deep South. *Wise Blood* (1952), the first of her two novels, is a bizarre tragi-comedy, and its theme of vocation is taken up again in her second, *The Violent Bear It Away* (1960). Regarded as one of the finest short-story writers of her generation, her collections include *A Good Man Is Hard To Find, and Other Stories* (1955) and *Everything That Rises Must Converge* (1965). She was crippled for more than 10 years by lupus erythematosus, from which she died.

O'Connor, Sandra Day, *née* **Day** (1930–) Jurist, the first female justice of the US Supreme Court, born in El Paso, Texas, USA. She studied law and was admitted to the bar in California, but then took up practice in Arizona, where she became assistant attorney-general (1965–9) and then a state senator. She was a Superior Court judge of Maricopa Co (1974–9) and a judge of the Arizona Court of Appeals (1979–81) before President Reagan named her as the first woman justice of the US Supreme Court in 1981.

octadecanoic acid *stearic acid*

octane number The measure of ability of a fuel to resist knocking (premature ignition) in the cylinder of an internal combustion engine. The properties of a mixture of iso-octane (which resists knocking) and heptane (which knocks easily) are matched to the behaviour of the fuel under test.

Octans (Lat 'octant') An inconspicuous S constellation, containing the S celestial pole. The nearest naked-eye star to the S celestial pole is Sigma Octantis.

octet A group of eight; used in chemistry in connection with the elements between boron and calcium (atomic numbers 5 to 20) and many heavier ones, whose most stable compounds have an octet of valence electrons associated with each atom, either by ion formation or by sharing electrons in covalent bonding. An octet of valence electrons is also called a *noble gas configuration*.

October Revolution (1917) The overthrow of the Russian provisional government by Bolshevik-led armed workers (Red Guards), soldiers, and sailors (25–26 Oct 1917). The revolution was organized by the Military Revolutionary Committee of the Petrograd Soviet. The members of the provisional government were arrested and replaced by the Soviet of People's Commissars (*Sovnarkom*), chaired by Lenin – the first Soviet government.

October War *Arab–Israeli Wars*

octopus A carnivorous marine mollusc with a short, sac-like body and eight arms largely connected by webbing; reaches 5·4 m/18 ft in length, and with a maximum outstretched arm-span of nearly 9 m/30 ft; shell usually absent; contains a funnel, used for swimming by jet propulsion; prey caught using suckers on arms; when alarmed, may eject a cloud of ink. (Class: Cephalopoda. Order: Octopoda.)

octopush A form of hockey played underwater, first introduced in South Africa in the 1960s. Teams consist of six players who use miniature hockey sticks and a puck replacing the ball. To score a goal, the puck must hit the opposing end of the swimming pool.

odd function *even functions*

ode (Gr 'song') A lyric poem, usually of some length and formal complexity. The form of the ode is not prescribed, but determined in each case by the theme, subject, and situation. Pindar in Greek, Horace in Latin, Milton and Keats in English, and Ronsard, Leopaldi, Schiller, and Claudel were notable practitioners.

Odense [ohdensuh] 55°24N 10°25E, pop (2000e) 182 600. Port and chief town on Fyn I, Denmark; third largest city of Denmark; railway; university (1964); engineering, foodstuffs, textiles, timber; St Knud's Church (reconstructed 13th-c), 18th-c palace; birthplace of Hans Christian Andersen.

Oder, River [ohder], Czech, Polish **Odra**, ancient **Viadua** River in C Europe rising in E Sudetes Mts of the Czech Republic; flows N through Poland, eventually meeting the Baltic Sea near Szczecin; length 854 km/531 mi; navigable for 711 km/442 mi; canal links to W and E Europe.

Oder–Neisse Line [ohder niysuh] The Polish–German border, following the Oder and W Neisse rivers from the Baltic Sea to the Czechoslovak border, drawn by the Allies (1944–5), and involving the transfer to Poland of large areas of pre-war Germany. A source of contention between the German Federal Republic and the German Democratic Republic, it was finally recognized by the former in 1970.

Odessa [ohdesa] 46°30N 30°46E, pop (2000e) 1 095 000. Seaport capital of Odesskaya oblast, Ukraine, on NW shore of the Black Sea; centre of the battleship *Potemkin* mutiny in the 1905 Revolution; railway; university (1865); naval base and home port for a fishing and Antarctic whaling fleet; leading Black Sea port, trading in grain, sugar, machinery, coal, oil products, cement, metals, jute, timber; icebreakers ensure that the port is ice-free throughout the year; large health resorts nearby; fishing, solar research, machines, oil refining, metalworking, chemicals; Uspensky Cathedral (1855–69).

Odets, Clifford [ohdets] (1906–63) Playwright and actor, born in Philadelphia, Pennsylvania, USA. In 1931 he joined the Group Theater, New York City, becoming a leading US playwright in the 1930s. His works are marked by a strong social conscience, and grow largely from the conditions of the Great Depression. They include *Waiting for Lefty*, *Till the Day I Die* (both 1935), and *Golden Boy* (1937). His film scripts include *The General Died at Dawn* (1936), *None but the Lonely Heart* (1944, which he directed), and *The Big Knife* (1955).

Odette, popular name of **Odette Hallowes**, formerly **Churchill** (to 1955) and **Sansom** (to 1946), née **Brailly** (1912–95) French wartime resistance heroine, born in Amiens, N France. Brought up in France, she married an Englishman in 1931 and moved to London. Through responding to a BBC appeal in 1942 for information about the coast of N Europe, she came to the attention of the French section of the Special Operations Executive, who trained her, and sent her to France as an agent. Arrested by the Germans in 1943, she was tortured by the Gestapo in Paris, and sent to Ravensbruck concentration camp. Awarded the George Cross in 1946, her wartime exploits were retold in a successful film, *Odette* (1950), starring Anna Neagle, which made her and her then husband, Peter Churchill, national figures.

Odin [ohdin] In Norse mythology, the All-Father, the god of poetry and the dead; also known as **Woden** (English) or **Wotan** (German). He gave one eye to the Giant Mimir in exchange for wisdom. He rides the eight-legged horse Sleipnir, and keeps two ravens to bring him news. Often he wanders the world as a hooded one-eyed old man.

Odissi A soft, lyrical and erotic style of classical dance for women, found in E India. It is characterized by the sensuous movement of the dancers, abruptly frozen into sculptured poses.

Odo [ohdoh] (c.1036–97) Anglo-Norman clergyman, Bishop of Bayeux, and half-brother of William I. He fought at the Battle of Hastings (1066) and was created Earl of Kent. He played a conspicuous part under William in English history, and was regent during his absences in Normandy, but left England after rebelling against William II. He rebuilt Bayeux Cathedral, and may have commissioned the Bayeux tapestry.

Odoacer [ohdohayser], also found as **Odovacar** (?–493) Germanic warrior who destroyed the W Roman empire, and became the first barbarian king of Italy (476–93). An able ruler, he was challenged and overthrown by the Ostrogothic King Theodoric (489–93) at the instigation of the E Roman Emperor, Zeno.

Odonata [ohdonata] *damselfly; dragonfly*

Odysseus [odisyoos] A Greek hero, known in Latin as **Ulixes**, from which Ulysses is derived. The son of Laertes, King of Ithaca, he took part in the Trojan War, where he was respected for his intelligence. In later writers he is made cunning and devious. He took ten years to return from Troy, encountering many romantic adventures, described in Homer's *Odyssey*. Eventually he returned to Ithaca, slaughtered the suitors who were besieging his wife Penelope, and, to appease Poseidon, the main cause of his troubles, set out to find a country where the oar on his shoulder would be taken for a winnowing-fan. Dante and Tennyson credit him with one final journey of exploration into the Atlantic Ocean.

Oe, Kenzaburo [ohay] (1935–) Novelist and short-story writer, born in Shikoku, S Japan. He studied French at the University of Tokyo, and became known for his short stories capturing the mood of post-war Japan, such as *The Catch* (trans 1959, Akutagawa Prize). His major books include *Hiroshima Notes* (1965; trans 1981), *A Personal Matter* (1964; trans 1968), *The Silent Cry* (1967; trans 1974, Tanizaki Prize), and *A Healing Family* (trans 1996). He received the Nobel Prize for Literature in 1994. Later work includes *Grand Street 55* (1999).

oedema / edema [eedeema] The accumulation of excess amounts of body fluids (water and salts) within the tissues of the body. It occurs when the hydrostatic pressure forcing fluid out of the blood vessels exceeds the osmotic pressure pulling it back in. The influence of gravity ensures that fluid accumulates in the feet and legs. The most common causes are heart, kidney, and liver failure. In heart and kidney failure, the body retains water and salts, expanding the blood volume and forcing fluid out into the tissues. Liver failure leads to a fall in the levels of proteins in the blood, reducing its osmotic pressure and allowing fluid to escape into the tissues.

Oedipus [eedipus] In Greek legend, a Theban hero of whom it was foretold that he would kill his father and marry his mother. He was exposed at birth, and lamed with a spike through his feet (his name means 'swell-foot'). Brought up in Corinth, he fled from his adoptive parents when an oracle revealed his destiny. On the way to Thebes he killed his father Laius by chance, and, having guessed the riddle of the sphinx, was made the new ruler of the city and married its queen, Jocasta. When all was revealed, he blinded himself. He died either at Thebes (Homer) or at Colonus in Attica (Sophocles).

Oedipus complex [eedipus] A psychoanalytic term describing the erotic feelings of a son for his mother, and an associated sense of competitiveness towards the father. The female equivalent is the **Electra complex**, describing a daughter's jealousy of her mother, love for her father, and blame for the mother's depriving her of a penis. Both terms were coined by Freud to understand phases of normal child development.

Oersted *Ørsted, Hans Christian*

Oesling *Ösling*

oesophagus / esophagus [eesofaguhs] A long, muscular tube passing from the lower part of the pharynx through the thorax to the stomach; also known as the **gullet**. In adult humans it is c.24 cm/9·5 in long. Lined by stratified squamous (wear and tear) epithelium, it is the most muscular part of the digestive tract. It squeezes solids and liquids (taken in by the mouth) by waves of contraction of its muscle layers towards the stomach. During its course it has several constrictions, which are of clinical importance because ingested material will be momentarily held up on its way to the stomach; consequently there will be a greater degree of damage to the lining membrane at these points, should corrosive materials (eg turpentine) be swallowed.

oestrogens / estrogens [eestrojenz] Steroid sex hormones (eg *oestradiol, oestriol, oestrone*) produced in the ovary, placenta, testis, and adrenal cortex. They are responsible for the devel opment of female secondary sexual characteristics in humans, as well as promoting sexual readiness (*oestrus*, eg in rats and mice), and preparing the uterus for implantation. They are used in oral contraceptives and in the treatment of certain cancers (eg of the prostate). They are also found in plants.

oestrus / estrus [eestruhs] The period of maximum sexual receptivity, or heat, in female mammals. It is usually also the time of release of the egg from the ovary.

'Of'- (organizations) *regulator*

Offa (?–796) King of Mercia (757–96). He was the greatest Anglo-Saxon ruler in the 8th-c, treated as an equal by Charlemagne. He asserted his authority over all the kingdoms S of the Humber, and regarded their rulers as subordinate provincial governors. He was responsible for constructing Offa's Dyke, stretching for 70 mi along the Welsh border, and established a new currency based on the silver penny which, with numerous changes of design, remained the standard coin of England for many centuries. His reign represents an important but flawed attempt to unify England, with the Mercian supremacy collapsing soon after his death.

offal All the organs of slaughtered animals other than muscles and bones. Several of these organs (such as the liver and kidneys) are eaten; others (such as the gut) are usually discarded.

Offaly [ofalee], Ir **Ua bhFailghe** pop (2000e) 59 000; area 1997 sq km/771 sq mi. County in Leinster province, C Ireland; bounded W by R Shannon; Slieve Bloom Mts rise in the SW; capital, Tullamore; cattle, grain; large tracts of peat used as fuel for power stations.

Offa's Dyke An interrupted linear earthwork 130 km/80 mi long – the gaps originally thick forest – linking the R Dee near Prestatyn, N Wales, UK, with the Severn Estuary at Chepstow. Erected in the late 8th-c AD by Offa, King of Mercia, to define the W boundary of his kingdom, it marks the traditional boundary between England and Wales. Offa's Dyke Path, opened in 1971, follows most of its course.

Off-Broadway *Broadway*

Offenbach, Jacques [ofenbahkh], originally **Jacob Eberst** (1819–80) Composer, born in Cologne, W Germany. He moved to Paris in 1833, directing the Théâtre-Français orchestra in 1848, and becoming manager of the *Bouffes-Parisiens* in 1855. He composed many light, lively operettas, such as *Orphée aux enfers* (1858, trans Orpheus in the Underworld). He also produced one grand opera, *Les contes d'Hoffmann* (The Tales of Hoffmann), which was not produced until 1881, after his death.

Office, Divine or **Holy** In the pre-Reformation Western Church and in the Roman Catholic Church, prayers which must be said by priests and religious every day, originally at fixed hours. The practice dates from early monasticism, and derives from Jewish tradition.

office automation The use of computers for the performance of conventional office tasks, such as document preparation, diary management, and simple file management. Frequently computers in individual offices are connected through a local area network, which enables documents to be shared between offices, and meetings within departments to be organized.

Office of Fair Trading A non-ministerial government department in England and Wales, headed by the Director-General of Fair Trading. It keeps under review commercial activities which supply goods or services to the consumer, and collects information about these activities. The Fair Trading Act (1993) set up the office, and laid down a framework of law to eliminate or control unfair consumer practices. The director-general also monitors commercial activities which relate to monopoly situations.

Office of Management and Budget (OMB) The office which the US president uses to control the financial operations of government, created in 1970 out of the Bureau of the Budget. In recent times, particularly under President Reagan, it has been used more overtly as an instrument of policy, by controlling domestic spending. It is an important political arm of the presidency and not just a technical budget advisory office.

offset lithography *lithography*

O'Flaherty, Liam (1897–1984) Writer, born on Inishmore in the Aran Is, Co Galway, W Ireland. He studied at Rockwell College, Tipperary, and University College, Dublin, and fought in the British army during World War 1, and with the Republicans in the Irish Civil War. He went to London in 1922 to become a writer, and published his first novels, *Thy Neighbour's Wife* (1923) and *The Black Soul* (1924). *The Informer* (1925) won the James Tait Black Memorial Prize and was a popular success. A leading figure of the Irish Renaissance, he has also published collections of short stories.

Ogaden [ogaden] Geographical area in SE Ethiopia; dry plateau intermittently watered by Fafen Shet and Jerer Rivers; part of Abyssinia, 1890; part of Italian East Africa, 1936–41; largely inhabited by Somali-speaking nomads; area claimed by Somalia in 1960s; Somali invasion in 1977 repulsed by Ethiopian forces; fighting continued throughout the 1980s.

Ogam or **Ogham** [ogam] A writing system used from around the 4th-c for writing Irish and Pictish. Memorial inscriptions occur on stone monuments, particularly in Ireland and S Wales. The alphabet has 20 letters composed of sets of parallel straight lines (numbering from one to five), cut to and across the vertical corners of stone monuments, some lying horizontally and others falling diagonally from left to right.

Ogbomosho [ogbomoshoh] 8°05N 4°11E, pop (2000e) 804 000. Market town in Oyo state, W Nigeria, 88 km/55 mi NNE of Ibadan; third largest city in Nigeria; agricultural trade, crafts, cloth, shoes, tobacco; festivals of Ebo Oba Ijeru (Feb), Egungun (Jul), and Ashun (Aug).

Ogden, C(harles) K(ay) (1889–1957) Linguistic reformer, born in Fleetwood, Lancashire, NW England, UK. He studied classics at Cambridge, was founder-editor of the *Cambridge Magazine* (1912–22), and founder in 1917 of the Orthological Institute. In the 1920s he conceived the idea of 'Basic English', a simplified system of English as an international language with a restricted vocabulary of 850 words, which he developed with the help of I A Richards.

Ogdensburg Agreement A pact signed in August 1940 between US President Roosevelt and Canadian Prime Minister Mackenzie King. It established the means for developing continental economic and military planning through the Permanent Joint Board on Defence, and marked a loosening of ties between Canada and Britain.

Ogdon, John (Andrew Howard) (1937–89) Pianist, born in Mansfield Woodhouse, Nottinghamshire, C England, UK. He studied in Manchester, and in 1962 was joint prizewinner in the Tchaikovsky Competition in Moscow. He had a powerful technique, a remarkable memory, and a huge repertory. He also composed, his works including a piano concerto. Illness forced him to give up playing for several years.

Ogham *Ogam*

Ogilvie Thompson, Julian (1934–) Businessman, born in Cape Town, SW South Africa. He studied at Diocesan College, Rondebosch, and became a personal assistant to Harry Oppenheimer at Anglo American Corporation of SA, South Africa's largest corporation. Formerly chairman of De Beer's Consolidated Mines, and Minorco SA, he became chairman of Anglo American in 1990. He is also a governor of the Urban Foundation.

Ogilvy, Mrs Angus *Alexandra, Princess*

O'Hara, John (Henry) (1905–70) Novelist and short-story writer, born in Pottsville, Pennsylvania, USA. When his father died, instead of going to Yale as planned, he travelled and became a reporter in New York City. His first novel was *Appointment in Samarra* (1934); its naturalistic account of three days that culminate in the suicide of Julian English, a victim of his own reckless sexual appetite, made it a quick success. His best-known works – *Butterfield 8* (1935) and *Pal Joey* (1940) – became film and stage successes. His short-story collections include *The Doctor's Son* (1935) and *Waiting for Winter* (1967).

O. Henry *Henry, O*

O'Higgins, Bernardo, known as **the Liberator of Chile** (1778–1842) Revolutionary, and first president of the Republic of Chile (1817–23), born in Chillán, Chile. He was the illegitimate son of **Ambrosio O'Higgins** (c.1720–1801), the Irish-born viceroy of Chile (1789) and of Peru (1795). He played a great part in the Chilean revolt of 1810–17, and became president, but was deposed after a revolution and retired to Peru.

Ohio [ohhiyoh] pop (2000e) 11 353 000; area 107 040 sq km/ 41 330 sq mi. State in E USA, divided into 88 counties; the 'Buckeye State'; visited by La Salle in 1669 and settled by fur traders from 1685; 17th state to join the Union, 1803; capital, Columbus; other chief cities, Cleveland, Cincinnati, Toledo, Akron, Dayton; part of the Allegheny plateau; drained by the Muskingum, Scioto, and Great Miami Rivers which flow to meet the Ohio R and L Erie; grain, soybeans, vegetables, dairy cattle, livestock; coal (E and SE Appalachian coalfield), natural gas, stone, sand, gravel; major industrial centre, including steel, metal products, vehicles, paper, chemicals, rubber, clothing, electrical goods, foodstuffs.

Ohio Company **1** Virginia-based speculators who acquired a Crown grant of 200 000 acres (80 000 ha) in 1749 in the area between the Ohio R, Great Kanawha R, and Allegheny Mts. **2** An organization of speculators in 1786 who used depreciated currency and securities to acquire large amounts of Ohio land. They were indirectly responsible for the passage of the Ordinance of 1787, establishing a political basis for Westward expansion.

Ohio River River in EC USA; formed at Pittsburgh by the union of the Monongahela and Allegheny Rivers; flows generally SW for 1578 km/980 mi to join the Mississippi at Cairo, Illinois; forms the state boundary between Ohio, Indiana, and Illinois (N) and West Virginia and Kentucky (S); chief tributaries the Kanawha, Licking, Kentucky, Tennessee (left); the Scioto, Miami, Wabash (right); navigable all the way, with the help of a canal at Louisville; length 2101 km/1306 mi (including the Allegheny).

Ohlin, Bertil (Gotthard) (1899–1979) Economist and politician, born in Klippan, S Sweden. He studied in Sweden and at Harvard, and became professor at Copenhagen (1925–30) and Stockholm (1930–65). He was a member of the Swedish parliament (1938–70), and leader of the Liberal Party (1944–67). As an economist he is best known for the **Heckscher–Ohlin theorem**, which states that countries will export goods that are produced with their relatively abundant factors of production, and import those goods produced with their scarce factors. He shared the 1977 Nobel Prize for Economics for his work on the dynamics of trade.

Ohm, Georg Simon (1787–1854) Physicist, born in Erlangen, Bavaria, SC Germany. He became professor at Nuremburg (1833–49) and Munich (1849–54), after a long struggle to get due recognition for the importance of his work. **Ohm's law** had been published in 1827 as a result of his research in electricity, and the measure of resistance is now called the **ohm**.

ohm SI unit of electrical resistance; symbol Ω; a resistance of 1 ohm exists between two points of a conductor if a potential difference of 1 volt causes a current of 1 amp to flow between them; named after Georg Ohm; commonly used as **kilohms** ($k\Omega$, 10^3 ohms) and **megohms** ($M\Omega$, 10^6 ohms). In 1990 the von Klitzing constant, $R_{K\text{-}90}$, became the international standard of resistance measurement.

ohmmeter A small portable instrument for measuring resistances in an electrical circuit. It consists of an ammeter together with one variable and one fixed resistance. The unknown resistance is found by measuring the difference in current flow between closed circuit conditions and when the unknown resistance is introduced between the connectors of the ohmmeter.

Ohm's law In electrical circuits, the result that potential difference U and current I satisfy $U = IR$ for resistance R; for alternating current circuits, $U = IZ$, where Z is impedance; stated by Georg Ohm in 1827.

Ohrid [okhrid], Ital **Ohrida** 41°06N 20°49E, pop (2000e) 69 000. Town in the SW of the Former Yugoslav Republic of Macedonia; on the shores of L Ohrid; airfield; tourism, fishing, agriculture; old town, a world heritage site; Cathedral of St Sophia, St Clement's Church (13th-c), castle; old town festival (May, Aug), Balkan folk festival (Jul), summer festival (Jul–Aug).

Ohrid, Lake [okhrid], Serbo-Croatian **Ohridsko Jezero** Lake situated on the frontier between Albania and the Former Yugoslav Republic of Macedonia, to the E of Elbasan; area 350 sq km/ 135 sq mi; two-thirds in Macedonia; boat service joining the picturesque town of Ohrid, now a national monument, to Sveti Naum at the S end; tourist resort at Struga.

oil (botany) A fluid secreted by special glands in many plants, often forming food reserves in fruits and seeds such as olives, palms, rape, and flax. Volatile *essential oils* are produced by aromatic plants, especially in dry regions, and may help reduce transpiration or provide protection against animals. *Edible oils* are obtained from many plants, including soy beans, maize, olives, sunflowers, coconut, and rapeseed.

oil (earth sciences) A fossil fuel that is chemically a complex mixture of hydrocarbons, formed from organic remains by the action of heat and pressure over millions of years; known as *natural* or *crude* oil. It occupies the pore spaces between grains in sedimentary rock, and accumulates when its upward migration is trapped by a suitable impervious 'cap' rock. It occurs together with natural gas and solid hydrocarbons (collectively termed *petroleum*) as well as water. When refined it is used as a primary fuel for industry, and hence has great economic importance.

oil beetle A brightly-coloured beetle; adults produce a chemical (*cantharidin*) that causes skin blisters; larvae louse-like, feeding on insect eggs or on food stores in bees' nests. (Order: Coleoptera. Family: Meloidae, c.3000 species.)

oilbird A nightjar-like bird (*Steatornis caripensis*) native to N South America and Trinidad; roosts in caves; uses echolocation; eats fruit picked in flight; also known as the **guacharo**, or **diablotin**. It is the only nocturnal fruit-eating bird. Its fledglings are very fat, and were formerly boiled to extract oil, used for cooking. (Family: Steatornithidae.)

oil painting A method of painting which employs drying oils (such as linseed oil) in the medium. In use since Roman times for decorating shields, etc, the technique was perfected and adapted to painting pictures in the 15th-c.

oil palm A tree (*Elaeis guineensis*) reaching 15 m/50 ft, native to tropical Africa; leaves 4·5 m/15 ft, feathery. The numerous oval, orange fruits are rendered down for oil. (Family: Palmae.)

oil pollution Damage to the seas and coasts as a result of major oil spillages from oil tankers. In 1967, the *Torrey Canyon* spilt more than 100 000 tonnes of oil off the Cornish coast. In 1978, the *Amoco Cadiz* ran aground off Brittany, losing 220 000 tonnes of oil. In March 1989 the supertanker *Exxon Valdez* ran aground on an Alaskan reef, spilling 45 000 tonnes of oil into the fishing waters of Prince William Sound, putting the fishing industry at risk and devastating wildlife over an area of 2500 sq km/1000 sq mi. In January 1992 a major oil slick in the Persian Gulf was caused when Iraqis opened valves at a Kuwaiti export terminal, and this was followed by further massive pollution when retreating Iraqi forces sabotaged two-thirds of Kuwait's wells. In January 1993 the tanker MV *Braer* was washed onto rocks in the Shetland Is, losing all of its 85 000-tonne cargo of light oil. The consequences of such pollution are long-lasting, because of the contaminated food chain.

oil rig An artificial platform set up above deposits of oil and gas at sea to support drilling equipment. The tall towers are known as *jackets*, which are made on land and towed out to sea on their sides before being erected. *Shallow-water rigs* are built on barges which are towed into position and then sunk to provide a steady base for the derrick and drilling gear. In deep water, *fixed-leg rigs* stand on the seabed and are held by steel pins; these are so heavy and strong that they can withstand almost all rough weather conditions. *Compliant rigs* are designed to sway slightly in storms, and are less likely to fall over; they stand on narrow columns on the seabed, and are held upright by guy ropes. The drill bit which cuts through the rock to the oil deposit is made of hard material such as diamond or tungsten. It is at the end of a long pipe called the *drill string*, which is made up of sections 9 m (30 ft) long. The rock chippings are carried up and out of the hole by pumping a specific mud constituted of chemicals and water down through the drill string. The mud also helps to keep the drill bit cool. By steering the drill bit, an oil rig platform can drill up to 40 wells under the seabed at different angles, allowing more access to the oil deposit.

Oireachtas [erakhtas] An annual Irish gathering organized, on the lines of the Welsh eisteddfod, by the Gaelic League; first held in 1898.

Oistrakh, David (Fyodorovitch) [oystrak] (1908–74) Violinist, born in Odessa, S Ukraine. He studied at Odessa Conservatory, graduating in 1926. In 1928 he went to Moscow, and began to teach at the Conservatory there in 1934, being appointed professor in 1939. He made concert tours in Europe and America, and was awarded the Stalin Prize in 1945 and the Lenin Prize in 1960. His son **Igor Davidovitch Oistrakh** (1931–), born in Odessa, is also a noted violinist.

Ojibwa [ohjibwa] An Algonkin North American Indian group originally concentrated around L Superior and L Huron; called **Chippewa** by the Europeans; c.150 000 (2000 census). Hunters and nomads, they were impoverished following the decline of the fur trade.

Ojos del Salado, Cerro [ohkhohs thel salathoh] 27°05S 68°35W. Andean peak rising to 6908 m/22 664 ft on the Argentina–Chile border; second highest peak in the W hemisphere, after Aconcagua; world's highest active volcano.

Oka pop (2000e) 1860. A town W of Montreal, Quebec, Canada. It was the scene of violence and an armed stand-off between Canadian troops and Mohawk people, July–September 1990. It stimulated renewed public concern to resolve outstanding aboriginal issues.

okapi [ohkahpee] A mammal of the giraffe family (*Okapia johnstoni*) native to Democratic Republic of Congo; reddish-brown with long neck, large ears, and extremely long tongue (can lick its own eyes); face and lower legs pale; upper legs and hindquarters with thin horizontal stripes; male with two blunt 'horns'; inhabits dense wet forest; eats leaves and fruit.

Okavango, River [ohkavanggoh] Third largest river in S Africa, flowing through Angola, Namibia, and Botswana; rises in C Angola, and flows S (600 km/375 mi) then E (400 km/250 mi), forming part of the border between Angola and Namibia; then flows S into Botswana, where it drains into the Okavango delta (Makgadikgadi Pans, c.15 000 sq km/6000 sq mi), containing forest, swamp, marsh, and lagoon, a major wildlife area, where all the water evaporates; flooding here fills nearby rivers and sometimes L Ngami; length 1600 km/1000 mi.

Okayama [ohkayama] 34°40N 133°54E, pop (2000e) 610 000. Port capital of Okayama prefecture, SW Honshu, Japan, 112 km/70 mi W of Osaka; railway; university (1949); commerce, cotton, electronics, porcelain; dominated by the 'Castle of the Crow' (16th-c), Koraku-en Gardens (17th-c).

Okeechobee, Lake [ohkeechohbee] Lake in SC Florida, USA; linked to the Atlantic by the St Lucie and Miami Canals; largest lake in S USA (area 815 sq km/315 sq mi, maximum depth 4·6 m/15 ft); rivers drain S through the Everglades.

O'Keeffe, Georgia (1887–1986) Painter, born on a farm in Sun Prairie, Wisconsin, USA. She studied at the Art Institute of Chicago (1905–6) and at the Art Students' League in New York City (1907–8), where she met photographer Alfred Stieglitz, whom she married in 1924. As early as 1915 she pioneered abstract art in the USA (such as 'Blue and Green Music', 1919), but later moved towards a more figurative style, painting flowers and architectural subjects, frequently with a Surrealist flavour. In her later years, she painted a great deal in New Mexico, and many paintings came from her worldwide travels.

Okefenokee Swamp [ohkefenohkee] (Muskogean 'water-shaking') Area of swamp land in SE Georgia and NE Florida, USA; drained SW by the Suwannee R; important wildlife refuge; tourist centre.

Okhotsk, Sea of, Russ **Okhotskoye More** area 1 528 000 sq km/590 000 sq mi. NW arm of the Pacific Ocean, bounded E by the Kamchatka Peninsula, SE by the Kuril Is, SW by the Japanese island of Hokkaido, W by the island of Sakhalin and the far E coast of Russia; maximum depth 3365 m/11 039 ft; rich in marine life; ice-bound (Nov–Jun) and subject to heavy fogs.

Okinawa [ohkinawa] pop (2000e) 1 278 000; area 2263 sq km/874 sq mi. Region of Japan comprising the S part of the Ryukyu group; bounded W by the East China Sea, E by the Pacific Ocean; island of Okinawa is the largest in the group (area 1176 sq km/454 sq mi), 528 km/328 mi SSW of Kyushu; important sugar trade in the early modern period; Japanese sovereignty accepted by China, 1874; taken by the USA in World War 2; returned to Japan, 1972; capital, Naha; tobacco, pineapples, textiles, sugar cane, fish.

Okinoshima [okeenosheema] area 348 sq km/134 sq mi. Island group in Chugoku region, Japan; in the East Sea (Sea of Japan), 56 km/35 mi N of SW Honshu; includes Dogo (largest island) and Dozen (group of three islands); generally mountainous and forested; Dogo rises to 608 m/1995 ft; timber, fishing; chief town and port, Saigo on Dogo.

Oklahoma [ohkla**hoh**ma] (Muskogean 'red people') pop (2000e) 3 450 700; area 181 083 sq km/69 919 sq mi. State in SW USA, divided into 77 counties; the 'Sooner State'; mostly acquired by the USA in the Louisiana Purchase, 1803; Indians forced to move here in the 1830s (Indian Territory); Allem Wright, a Choctaw chief, coined the name to describe the land held by his people; Indians then lost the W region to whites (Oklahoma Territory, 1890); merged Indian and Oklahoma territories admitted into the Union as the 46th state, 1907; capital, Oklahoma City; other chief cities, Tulsa and Lawton; rivers include the Red (forms the S border), Arkansas, Canadian, Cimarron; Ouachita Mts in the SE; Wichita Mts in the SW; highest point Black Mesa (1516 m/4974 ft); in the W, high prairies part of the Great Plains; major agricultural products livestock and wheat; cotton, dairy products, peanuts; large oil reserves and associated petroleum industry; machinery, fabricated metals, aircraft.

Oklahoma City 35°30N 97°30W, pop (2000e) 506 000. State capital in Oklahoma Co, C Oklahoma, USA, on the N Canadian R; settled around a railway station, 1889; state capital, 1910; developed rapidly after oil discovered, 1928; largest city in the state; airport; railway; university (1911); terrorist bomb destroyed federal office block, April 1995; oil production; distribution and processing centre for livestock, grain, cotton; aircraft, machinery, electrical equipment; Tinker Air Force Base; National Cowboy Hall of Fame, Western Heritage Centre, state historical museum; festival of arts (Apr), Quarter Horse Show (Nov).

okra [**oh**kra, **o**kra] A vegetable crop (*Hibiscus esculentis*), originating in tropical Africa, and producing cylindrical edible fruits up to 20 cm/8 in long which are eaten immature, either cooked or fresh; also known as **ladies' fingers** or **gumbo**. The crop is widely cultivated in the tropics and sub-tropics. (Family: Malvaceae.)

Okri, Ben [**o**kree] (1959–) Novelist and short-story writer, born in Minna, C Nigeria. He studied in Nigeria, then at the University of Essex, UK. His first books were the autobiographical novels *Flowers and Shadows* (1980) and *The Landscapes Within* (1981). Later works include two books of short stories (1986, 1988) and the novels *The Famished Road* (1991, Booker Prize), *Dangerous Love* (1996), *Infinite Riches* (1998), and *In Arcadia* (2002). A book of poems, *An African Elegy*, appeared in 1992.

Olah, George A [**o**la] (1927–) Chemist, born in Budapest, Hungary. He studied at the Technical University of Budapest, and worked at the Hungarian Academy of Sciences, but left Hungary in 1956 for Canada, then the USA. He taught at Case Western Reserve University (1965–77), then moved to the University of Southern California, Los Angeles, becoming director of the Loker Hydrocarbon Research Institute in 1991. He received the 1994 Nobel Prize for Chemistry for the study of hydrocarbons, and of new ways to use them, identifying an intermediate stage of short-lived compounds ('carbocations') in organic chemical reactions.

Öland [**oe**land] pop (2000e) 26 500; area 1344 sq km/519 sq mi. Elongated Swedish island in the Baltic Sea, off the SE coast of Sweden; separated from the mainland by Kalmar Sound; length, 136 km/84 mi; largest island in Sweden; chief town, Borgholm; potatoes, sugar beet, cattle, sugar refining, quarrying; Borgholm castle (12th–13th-c). The southern part of the island is a world heritage site.

Olav V [**oh**laf] (1903–91) King of Norway (1957–91), born near Sandringham, Norfolk, E England, UK, the son and successor of Haakon VII and Maud, daughter of Edward VII of Britain. He studied in Norway and at Oxford, and was an outstanding sportsman and Olympic yachtsman in his youth. He stayed in Norway when it was invaded by Germany in 1940, and was appointed head of the Norwegian armed forces. Later he escaped with his father to England, returning in 1945. In 1929 he married **Princess Martha of Sweden** (1901–54), and had two daughters and a son, **Harald** (1937–), who succeeded to the Norwegian throne as Harald V in 1991.

Olbers' paradox A paradox expressed in 1826 by German astronomer Heinrich Wilhelm Olbers (1758–1840): why is the sky dark at night? In an infinitely large, unchanging, universe populated uniformly with stars and galaxies, the sky would be dazzling bright, which is not the case. This simple observation implies that the universe is not an infinite static arrangement of stars. In fact, modern cosmology postulates a finite expanding universe.

Old Bailey A street in the City of London, and, by association, the Central Criminal Court located there. The first courthouse was erected in 1539. The present building dates from 1907; the bronze statue of Justice surmounting its dome is a notable London landmark.

Old Believers Russian Orthodox traditionalists who rejected the reforms instituted in 1666. Although persecuted, they survived, established their own hierarchy in 1848, and were recognized by the state in 1881.

Oldcastle, Sir John, nickname **Good Lord Cobham** (c.1378–1417) Lollard leader and knight of England, born in Hereford and Worcester, WC England, UK. After serving in the Scottish and Welsh wars, and becoming an intimate of Henry V when Prince of Wales, he was tried and convicted on charges of heresy in 1413. He escaped from the Tower, and conspired with other Lollards to capture Henry V at Eltham Palace, Kent, and take control of London. The rising was abortive. He remained free until caught near Welshpool in 1417, and was hanged and burned. Shakespeare's Falstaff is based partly on him.

Old Catholics A group of Churches separated at various times from the Roman Catholic Church, including the Church of Utrecht (separated 1724), and German, Austrian, and Swiss Catholics who refused to accept papal infallibility (1870); also some former Poles and Croats in North America. They enjoy intercommunion with Anglicans.

Old Church Slavonic *Slavic languages*

Old Comedy Athenian comic theatre of the 5th-c BC. It has a unique structure that includes an *agon* (a contest) and a *parabasis* (a choral address to the audience on a contemporary social issue). Its grotesque costume, with the phallus worn for male roles, symbolizes the irreverence that governs the plays. The only complete plays extant are by Aristophanes.

Oldenburg, Claes (Thure) (1929–) Sculptor, born in Stockholm, Sweden. He studied at Yale and the Art Institute of Chicago before moving to New York City in 1956, where he became part of the milieu from which Pop Art developed. In 1963 he introduced soft sculptures of normally hard objects such as light switches, for which he became best known. His projects for huge monuments in public places have occasionally been realized, as in the 'Colossal Ashtray with Fagends' at the Pompidou Centre, Paris.

Old English The language of the Anglo-Saxons in England, as distinct from the original continental Saxons, in the period before the Norman Conquest; also known as **Anglo-Saxon**. It was a highly inflected language. Glosses to Latin texts survive from the 8th-c; the epic poem *Beowulf* (composed in the 8th-c) is preserved in an 11th-c manuscript; and there are several poems, historical narratives, prose sagas, and legal documents. It was written in an Irish form of the Latin alphabet, introduced by monks.

Old English sheepdog A breed of dog, developed in Britain in the 18th-c to protect cattle; large with hindquarters higher than shoulder; covered in long, untidy coat, often hiding ears and eyes; usually white with large dark patches; short tail.

Oldfield, Bruce (1950–) Fashion designer, born in London, UK. He taught art, then studied fashion in Kent (1968–71) and in London (1972–3), after which he became a freelance designer. He designed for Bendel's store in New York City, and sold sketches to Yves Saint Laurent. He showed his first collection in London in 1975. He designs evening dresses for members of the royal family and film-stars, as well as making ready-to-wear clothes.

Old High German *Germanic languages*

Oldman, Gary (1959–) Film actor, producer, and director, born in London, UK. He was a member of the Glasgow Citizen's Theatre, and became known following his portrayal of punk rocker Sid Vicious in the film *Sid and Nancy* (1986) and of playwright Joe Orton in *Prick Up Your Ears* (1987). Later films include *Bram Stoker's Dracula* (1992), the role of Beethoven in *Immortal Beloved* (1994), *Basquiat* (1996), *Lost in Space* (1998), and *Harry Potter and the Prisoner of Azkaban* (2004). He produced and directed *Nil by Mouth* (1997).

Old Masters *master*

Old Persian *Iranian languages*

Old Style date *New Style date*

Old Testament The sacred literature of Judaism, in which the corpus of writings is known simply as the Jewish Scriptures or Hebrew Bible, or even sometimes the Torah; it was also adopted by Christians as part of their sacred writings, and they began to call it the 'Old Testament' as distinct from the Christian writings that constitute the 'New Testament'. The Old Testament writings span stories from Creation and the origin of the Jewish people to the centuries of Israelite history describing the rise of Davidic monarchy, the division of the kingdom, exile, and return from exile. The canon of the Jewish religious community, which was fixed AD c.100, was arranged into three parts – the **Law**, the **Prophets**, and the **Writings** – although the precise arrangement and divisions of the books have varied through the centuries. The Law consists of the five books of the Pentateuch (Genesis, Exodus, Leviticus, Numbers, Deuteronomy). The Prophets have been divided since about the 8th-c AD into the *former* and *latter* prophets: the former prophets consist of the narratives (presumed written by prophets) found in Joshua, Judges, Samuel, and Kings, and the latter prophets consist of Isaiah, Jeremiah, Ezekiel, and the Book of the Twelve Prophets (Hosea, Joel, Amos, Obadiah, Jonah, Micah, Nahum, Habakkuk, Zephaniah, Haggai, Zechariah, Malachi). The Writings contain all remaining works: Psalms, Proverbs, Job, Song of Songs, Ruth, Lamentations, Ecclesiastes, Esther, Daniel, Ezra-Nehemiah, and Chronicles.

All the books of the Hebrew Bible appear in the versions of the Old Testament used by Protestant Churches today, but divided so as to number 39 in total. Roman Catholic versions of the Old Testament, however, accept 46 works, the additions not appearing in the Hebrew Bible but being found in Greek versions and the Latin Vulgate. These extra works are considered part of the Old Testament Apocrypha by Protestants.

Olduvai Gorge [olduviy] 2°58S 35°22E. A gorge within the Ngorongoro conservation area of the Rift Valley, N Tanzania. It is an important hominid site, with deposits extending from just under 2 million years ago down to recent. It was excavated by Louis and Mary Leakey, who recovered much archaeological and faunal material as well as important fossils of *Australopithecus boisei*, *Homo habilis*, and *Homo erectus*. Besides these finds, the Gorge has provided valuable evidence of the ecology and behaviour of early hominids.

Old Vic Theatre Theatre in London, UK, first opened in 1818 as the Royal Coburg Theatre and renamed the Royal Victoria Theatre in 1833. After 1880 it became the Royal Victorian Music Hall, popularly known as the Old Vic. Under the management of Lilian Mary Baylis from 1912, the theatre was devoted to the production of opera and the plays of Shakespeare. In 1946 the Bristol Old Vic was established as a permanent repertory company, and the London-based Young Vic was created in 1973.

Old World monkey A monkey of family Cercopithecidae (76 species); nostrils close together and opening downwards or forwards (unlike New World monkeys); tails never grasping, sometimes short; buttocks may have naked patches of skin; some species ground-dwelling.

oleander [oliander] An evergreen shrub (*Nerium oleander*) growing to 5 m/16 ft, native to the Mediterranean region; leaves lance-shaped, leathery; flowers 4 cm/1½ in diameter, in terminal clusters, tubular with five spreading lobes, pink or white. It is widely cultivated in warm regions as an ornamental; all parts are poisonous. Cultivars have larger (often double) flowers, ranging from white to crimson or purple. (Family: Apocynaceae.)

oleaster [oliaster] A deciduous, sometimes thorny, shrub or tree (*Elaeagnus angustifolia*) growing to 13 m/42 ft, native to W Asia; leaves narrow, dull green above, covered with minute silvery scales beneath; flowers 1 cm/0·4 in long, tubular with four spreading lobes, silver outside, yellow inside, fragrant; berries silvery-yellow. (Family: Eleagnaceae.)

olefin(e)s [ohluhfinz] *alkenes*

Oléron, Ile d' [eel dolayrõ], ancient **Uliarus** Wooded fertile island in E Bay of Biscay, W France; France's second largest off-shore island (after Corsica); 3 km/1¾ mi from mainland; linked by modern toll-bridge; area 175 sq km/68 sq mi; length 30 km/19 mi; main towns, Le Château d'Oléron, St-Pierre d'Oléron; oysters, farming, tourism.

oligarchy In ancient Greece, the term applied to city-states such as Corinth and Thebes, where political power was in the hands of a minority of its male citizens. They contrasted with democracies such as Argos, where power was held by the majority.

Oligocene epoch [oligoseen] A geological epoch of the Tertiary period from c.37 to 25 million years ago, and characterized by colder climate, the general retreat of the seas, and the evolution of many modern mammals.

oligomer [oligomer] A small polymer, generally consisting of three to ten monomer units; examples include oligopeptides and oligosaccharides.

oligopoly [oligopolee] An economic situation where an industry is dominated by a few suppliers. In economic theory, it constitutes one type of imperfect competition. Oligopolists may have monopoly power and the ability to affect prices and to make above-normal profits. Many of the former communist states such as Russia have adopted a crude form of capitalism, which is open to abuse by oligopolists.

olingo [olinggoh] A nocturnal mammal, native to C and N South America; superficially resembles the lemur; pale brown with small rounded ears, large eyes and very long, darkly banded tail; inhabits trees; eats mainly fruit. (Genus: *Bassaricyon*, 5 species. Family: Procyonidae.)

Oliphant, Sir Mark, in full **Marcus Laurence Elwin Oliphant** (1901–2000) Nuclear physicist, born in Adelaide, South Australia. He studied there and at Cambridge, where he did valuable work on the nuclear disintegration of lithium. Professor at Birmingham (1937), he designed and built a 60-in cyclotron. He worked on the atomic bomb project at Los Alamos (1943–5), but later strongly argued against the US monopoly of atomic secrets. He became Australian representative of the UN Atomic Energy Commission in 1946, designed a proton-synchrotron for the Australian government, and was appointed research professor at Canberra (1950–63). He was knighted in 1959, and became Governor of South Australia in 1971–6.

Olivares, Gaspar de Guzman y Pimental, conde-duque de (Count-Duke of) [olivahrez] (1587–1645) Spanish statesman, favourite and chief minister (1623–43) of Philip IV (reigned 1621–65), born in Rome, Italy. He cultivated the arts, and tried to moderate Spain's anachronistic administration and to build up military resources, but his introduction of the Union of Arms brought revolts in Portugal and Catalonia (1640–3). He took Spain into renewed conflict with the United Provinces and challenged France over the Mantuan Succession (1628–31) and in the Thirty Years' War (1635–48). After the Spanish fleet was destroyed at the Battle of the Downs (1639) and Roussillon was overrun by the French, he was dismissed (1643), and went into exile in Toro.

olive A long-lived evergreen tree (*Olea europaea*) native to the Mediterranean region, growing to 15 m/50 ft; trunk silvery, gnarled with numerous cavities; leaves opposite, narrow, pointed, leathery, dark green above, pale beneath; flowers small, white, four petals; fruit succulent, oily, green, ripening over one year to black. The wild form (variety *sylvestris*) is bushy with spiny branches and small fruits; the cultivated olive (variety *europaea*) has been grown since early times as an important source of olive oil obtained from pressed fruit. The fruits are also pickled, both green and ripe. The trees yield timber. (Family: Oleaceae.)

Oliver, King, popular name of **Joseph Oliver** (1885–1938) Cornettist, composer, and bandleader, born in Abend, Louisiana, USA. Raised in New Orleans, his first instrument was the trombone, and as a youth he played in various parade bands as well as in early jazz groups. He then moved to Chicago, where in 1922 he formed his Creole Jazz Band, and is remembered for his discovery of Louis Armstrong. Although Oliver worked as a musician until 1937, he made no recordings after 1931, when he developed severe dental problems, and he faded into obscurity. His compositions, such as 'Dippermouth Blues' and 'Dr Jazz', have become part of the standard traditional repertoire.

Oliver, Jamie (Trevor) (1975–) Chef, born in Clavering, Essex, SE England, UK. His parents ran a successful pub/restaurant in Cambridge, where he grew up, and from an early age he helped in the kitchens for pocket money. He trained at Westminster Catering College, then joined Antonio Carluccio's London restaurant before moving to the River Café Restaurant as a sous-chef. In 1999 he made the successful cooking series *The Naked Chef* for BBC television, with an accompanying cookbook. Later books include *The Return of the Naked Chef* (2000) and *Happy Days with the Naked Chef* (2001), and he writes a regular column for the Saturday *Times* magazine.

Olives, Mount of or **Mount Olivet** [olivet] A rocky outcrop overlooking the Old City of Jerusalem across the Kidron Valley, a site of sanctuaries during the reigns of David and Solomon, and a traditional Jewish burial ground. In Jesus' ministry this marks the location of his discourse about the coming of the end of the age (*Mark* 13). It is also near the site of the Garden of Gethsemane where Jesus was arrested, and the supposed location of the ascension of the risen Jesus (*Acts* 1.6–12).

olive shell A carnivorous or scavenging marine snail found in warm seas; usually active at night, moving around at a depth of 1–2 cm/0·4–0·8 in below the surface of the sediment; prey caught using a large muscular foot. (Class: Gastropoda. Order: Neogastropoda.)

Olivier (of Brighton), Laurence (Kerr) Olivier, Baron (1907–89) Actor, producer, and director, born in Dorking, Surrey, SE England, UK. He trained in London, and began his career at Birmingham in 1926, joining the Old Vic, London, in 1937. He played all the great Shakespearean roles, while his versatility was underlined by his virtuoso display in *The Entertainer* (1957) as a broken-down low comedian. After war service he became co-director of the Old Vic (1944). His films include *Henry V*, *Hamlet*, and *Richard III*. Divorced from his first wife, **Jill Esmond** in 1940, in the same year he married English actress **Vivien Leigh**. They were divorced in 1961, and he then married English actress **Joan Plowright**. He became first director of the Chichester Theatre Festival (1962) and of the National Theatre (1963–73). After 1974 he appeared chiefly in films and on television, notably in *Brideshead Revisited* (1982) and *King Lear* (1983). He was knighted in 1947, and made a life peer in 1970.

olivine [oliviyn] A silicate mineral ranging in composition from Fe_2SiO_4 (*fayalite*) to Mg_2SiO_4 (*forsterite*); glassy, hard, and typically olive-green in colour. It is important in rocks poor in silica, and is a primary constituent of the upper mantle of the Earth. Its gem quality crystals are termed *peridot*.

olm A salamander (*Proteus anguinus*) native to underground limestone caves in the Balkan peninsula and NE Italy; spends entire life in water; thin pale body (length, up to 30 cm/12 in), red feathery gills, extremely thin limbs, no eyes. (Family: Proteidae.)

Olmecs Members of a highly elaborate Middle American Indian culture on the Mexican Gulf Coast, at its height 1200–600 BC. The Olmecs influenced the rise and development of the other great civilizations of Middle America. They probably had the first large planned religious and ceremonial centres, at San Lorenzo, La Venta, and Tres Zapotecs, where the resident elite and their families lived, served by much larger populations dispersed throughout the lowland area. The centres had temple mounds, monumental sculptures, massive altars, and sophisticated systems of drains and lagoons. They were probably also the first people in the area to devise glyph writing and the 260-day Mesoamerican calendar.

Olmsted, Frederick (Law) (1822–1903) Landscape architect, born in Hartford, Connecticut, USA. After a limited education because of an eye problem, he attended Yale University to study science and engineering, then became a journalist. An interest in landscape led to his appointment as architect-in-chief of the improvement scheme for Central Park, New York City. He was thereafter commissioned to design other important public park schemes, including those at Brooklyn, Philadelphia, and Belle Isle Park, Detroit, as well as the grounds surrounding Washington, DC, and the campus at Berkeley, University of California. He worked to have Yosemite created a state reservation, and was among those proposing a system of protected wilderness areas for the USA.

Olympia (Greece), Gr **Olímbia** 37°38N 21°39E. Village and national sanctuary in Ilia department, S Greece, on N bank of R Alfios; chief sanctuary of Zeus, from c.1000 BC; site of the Panhellenic religious festival held every 4 years from 776 BC, the ancestor of the modern Olympic Games; railway; major excavations in 19th-c; Temple of Zeus (5th-c BC), Hera's Temple, Stadium.

Olympia (USA) 47°03N 122°53W, pop (2000e) 42 500. Seaport capital of Washington State and seat of Thurston Co, W Washington, USA; at the S end of Puget Sound, at the mouth of Deschutes R; founded at the end of the Oregon Trail, 1850; capital of Washington Territory, 1853; railway; lumbering, fishing, mining.

Olympians In Greek mythology, a collective name for the major gods and goddesses, who were thought to live on Mt Olympus, the highest mountain in Ancient Greece, situated in a range between Macedonia and Thessaly.

Olympic Games A sports gathering held every 4 years by athletes from all over the world, each celebration taking place at a different venue. They evolved from the ancient Greek games, held at Olympia, which go back at least to the 8th-c BC. They were banned in AD 393 by the Christian Emperor Theodosius I, probably because of their pagan practices, and were revived in 1896 by French educator Pierre de Fredi, Baron de Coubertin (1863–1937), with Athens as the first venue. In the 2000 games more than 10 000 competitors from 198 nations competed, in 28 different sports. Since 1924 a separate Winter Olympic Games has been staged, and was held in the same year as the Summer Games, until 1992, when it was decided to stage it midway between the Summer Games. The Games are governed by the International Olympic Committee.

Olympic National Park National park in the Olympic Mountains, Washington, USA; area 3678 sq km/1420 sq mi; a world heritage area; noted for the variety of its scenery, which includes glaciers and a stretch of the Pacific coastline, and as a refuge for the rare Roosevelt elk; also many rare varieties of flowers.

Olympus, Mount (Cyprus) [olimpuhs] 34°56N 32°52E. Mountain in the Troödos range of C Cyprus, rising to 1951 m/6401 ft; highest peak on the island.

Olympus, Mount (Greece) [olimpus], Gr **Olimbos** Range of mountains between Macedonia and Thessalia regions, N Greece, highest point, Mitikas (2917 m/9570 ft); traditionally the abode of the dynasty of gods headed by Zeus.

Olympus Mons [olimpuhs monz] A huge volcanic mountain on Mars, lying on the edge of a region of intense Martian volcanism ('Tharsis'), a broad upwarp in the crust. It is enormous by terrestrial standards, with a summit 27 km/17 mi high, and a diameter of 700 km/435 mi. It was discovered by Mariner 9 orbiter in 1972, and extensively studied by Viking orbiters, but was previously known to astronomers as a region of persistent

Oman

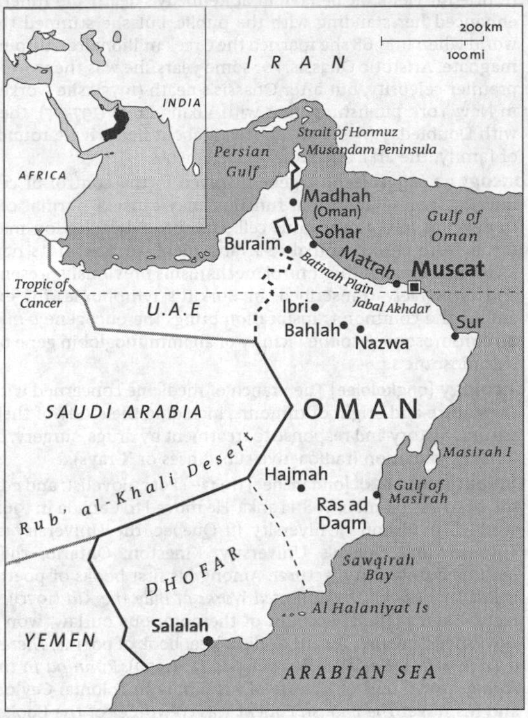

☐ International Airport - - - Border awaiting demarcation

[ohman], formerly **Muscat and Oman**, official name **Sultanate of Oman**

Local name 'Umān

Timezone GMT +4

Area 300 000 km^2/115 800 sq mi

Population total (2002e) 2 522 000

Status Sultanate

Date of independence 1951

Capital Muscat

Languages Arabic (official), English, Baluchi (and other Mahri languages), Urdu and Indian dialects also spoken

Ethnic groups Arab, with small Baluchi, Iranian, Indian, Pakistani, and W European minorities

Religions Ibadhi Muslim (75%), Sunni Muslim, Shi'a Muslim and Hindu (25%)

Physical features Located on the SE corner of the Arabian peninsula; the tip of the Musandam peninsula in the Strait of Hormuz is separated from the rest of the country by an 80 km/50 mi strip belonging to the United Arab Emirates; several peaks in the Hajjar Mt range, Jabal Akhdar ridge rises to 3000 m/10 000 ft; vast sand desert in NE; Dhofar uplands in SW.

Climate Desert climate, hot and arid; hot, humid on coast (Apr–Oct); average annual temperature 22°C (Jan), 33°C (Jul); light monsoon rains in S (Jun–Sep); average annual rainfall 99 mm/3·9 in.

Currency 1 Omani Rial (RO) = 1000 baizas

Economy Oil discovered, 1964, now provides over 90% of government revenue; natural gas an important source of industrial power; c.70% of the population relies on agriculture; alfalfa, wheat, tobacco, fruit, vegetables, fishing.

GDP (2002e) $22·4 bn, per capita $8300

Human Development Index (2002) 0·751

History Dominant maritime power of the W Indian Ocean in 16th-c; independent from UK, 1951; separatist tribal revolt in Dhofar, 1964, led to a palace coup that installed the present Sultan in 1970; opened airbases to Western forces, following Iraqi invasion of Kuwait, 1990; independent state ruled by a Sultan who is both Head of State and Premier, and who appoints a Cabinet and a 59-member Consultative Council.

Head of State/Government (Sultan)

1888–1913 Faisal Bin Turki
1913–32 Taimur Bin Faisal
1932–70 Said III bin Taimur
1970– Qaboos bin Said

brightenings ('Nix Olympica'), now realized to be diurnal cloud formations.

Olynthus [olinthus] In antiquity, the chief city-state on the Chalcidic peninsula in the N Aegean. It was destroyed in 348 BC by its former ally, Philip II of Macedon, for deserting his cause and throwing in its lot with Athens.

Om [om, ohm] A mystical and sacred monosyllable in Hindu tradition, the sound of which was believed to have a divine power. It was used at the beginning and end of prayers, as a mantra for meditation, and as an invocation itself. In the Upanishads it is mentioned as the primary sound syllable.

Omagh [ohmah], Ir **An Omaigh** 54°36N 7°18W, pop (2000e) 18 100. Town in Omagh district, Tyrone, WC Northern Ireland, UK, on R Strule; administrative centre of the district of Omagh, pop (2000e) 46 600; footwear, engineering, salmon fishing, dairy produce, tourism; inside the 19th-c Catholic parish church is the Black Bell of Drumragh (9th-c); town centre badly damaged by bomb-attack (Aug 1998), which killed 29, the worst incident of the Northern Ireland troubles since the 1960s.

Omaha (Indians) [ohmaha] A Siouan-speaking North American Plains Indian group, originally from the Atlantic seaboard, who migrated to Minnesota in response to European colonial settlement. In the late 17th-c the Dakotas, who had obtained guns through trade, pushed them into Nebraska, where they farmed and hunted buffalo. In 1854 they sold most of their land to white settlers, but were granted some land by the government in 1882. They now live on reservations in Nebraska.

Omaha (Nebraska) [ohmaha] 41°17N 96°01W, pop (2000e) 390 000. Seat of Douglas Co, E Nebraska, USA; a port on the Missouri R; fur-trading post established here, 1812; city status, 1867; largest city in the state; airport; railway; two universities (1878, 1908); major livestock market and meat-processing centre; farm machinery, electrical equipment, fertilizers; centre for medical treatment and research; air force base; site of strategic Air Command since 1948; Joslyn Art Museum, aerospace museum, Boys Town; College World Series (Jun).

Oman *see panel*

Oman, Gulf of NW arm of the Indian Ocean, lying between Oman and Iran; linked to the Persian Gulf by the Strait of Hormuz, and (SE) to the Arabian Sea; vital waterway for ocean traffic to and from the Gulf states; 480 km/300 mi long.

Omar or **Umar I** [ohmah(r)] (c.581–644) The second caliph. He was father of Hafsa, one of Mohammed's wives, and succeeded Abu-Bakr in 634. With his generals he built up an empire comprising Persia, Syria, and Egypt. He was assassinated in Medina by a Persian slave.

Omar Khayyám [kayam], also spelled **Umar Khayyám** (c.1050–c.1122) Poet, mathematician, and astronomer, born in Nishapur, Persia. Summoned to Merv by the sultan, he reformed the Muslim calendar, and was known to the Western world as a mathematician, until in 1859 Edward FitzGerald published a translation of his *Rubáiyát* ('Quatrains'). The work is now regarded as an anthology of which little or nothing may be by Omar.

OMB *Office of Management and Budget*

ombudsman [ombudzman] (Swed 'agent' or 'representative') An official who investigates complaints regarding administrative action by governments – so-called 'mal-administration'. The complaint may not necessarily be confined to illegal action, but can cover broader injustices in administrative decisions. Most ombudsmen's powers are of necessity widely defined, but they normally do not investigate issues that can be considered by the courts or tribunals. Their findings do not have the force of law, and are put in the form of reports from which it is hoped remedial action will result. The first such institution was created in Sweden at the beginning of the 19th-c, and today most countries have followed the lead, with the exception of those in Central and South America and communist states. A number of industries (eg insurance, banking) have set up their own, non-statutory, voluntary ombudsmen to oversee their business activities.

Omdurman [omdoorman] 15°37N 32°29E, pop (2000e) 816 000. Major suburb of Khartoum, C Sudan; connected to the main city by a tramline bridge over the White Nile; military headquarters of Mohammed Ahmed, 1884; captured by the British, 1898; university (1961); agricultural trade, textiles, crafts; ruins of the Mahdi's tomb.

Omdurman, Battle of [omdoorman] (1898) An engagement outside Khartoum, across the Nile, which confirmed the British reconquest of the Sudan. The British campaign under Kitchener had been authorized in 1895, and instituted with powerful Anglo-Egyptian forces in 1896. The overwhelming defeat of the massed forces of the Khalifa (the successor of Mohammed Ahmed, the Mahdi), with many casualties, illustrated the power of modern weapons.

OMNIMAX *IMAX*

omnivore Any animal, or human, whose diet includes both the flesh of animals and vegetable material; there may be specialized teeth to deal with the varied foodstuffs. The term contrasts with *carnivore* (a flesh-eater, such as the lion) and *herbivore* (a plant-eater, such as the cow).

Omo National park in S Ethiopia; area 4015 sq km/1550 sq mi; lower valley, a world heritage site.

Omri (9th-c BC) King of Israel (c.886 BC–c.875 BC). An army commander, he was made king after Zimri assassinated Elah and seized the throne. He is the first Israelite monarch found to be mentioned in historical records other than the Bible itself. The Moabite Stone states that 'Omri, king of Israel, oppressed Moab many days and his sons after him'. Omri founded the city of Samaria on a hill and was buried there. He was succeeded by his son Ahab.

Omsk 55°00N 73°22E, pop (2000e) 1 161 000. River-port capital of Omskaya oblast, W Siberian Russia; at the confluence of the Irtysh and Om Rivers; founded as a fortress, 1716; the greenest city in Siberia with 25 sq km/10 sq mi of boulevards and gardens; airport; on the Trans-Siberian Railway; university (1974); oil refining, chemicals, engineering, clothing, footwear.

onager [onajer] *ass*

Onassis, Aristotle (Socrates) [ohnasis] (1906–75) Millionaire shipowner, born in Smyrna, W Turkey. At 16 he left Smyrna for Greece as a refugee, and from there went to Buenos Aires, where he made a fortune in tobacco and was for a time Greek consul. Buying his first ships (1932–3), he built up one of the world's largest independent fleets, and was a pioneer in the construction of super-tankers. His first marriage, to **Athina**, daughter of Stavros Livanos, a Greek ship-owner, ended in divorce (1960). He then had a long relationship with Maria Callas, and in 1968 married Jacqueline Kennedy.

Onassis, Jacqueline Kennedy, *née* **Jacqueline Lee Bouvier**, popularly known as **Jackie Kennedy** (1929–94) US first lady (1961–3), born in Southampton, New York, USA. She studied at Vassar College, the Sorbonne, and Washington University, and worked as a reporter before marrying John F Kennedy in 1953. She was not always comfortable with the demands of being the wife of a Kennedy and a politician, but as first lady she promoted her personal agenda of the arts, history, and high style. Her first child was stillborn, and she lost an infant in 1963, but they had two other children, **Caroline** (1957–) and **John** (1960–99). Her stoic behaviour at Kennedy's death and funeral enhanced her standing with the public, but she stunned the world when in 1968 she married the Greek millionaire shipping magnate, Aristotle Onassis. For some years she was the world's premier celebrity, but after Onassis's death (1975), she worked in New York publishing, first with Viking Press (1975–7), then with Doubleday (1978–94), and went about her private rounds of family, the arts, and social engagements.

oncogene [ongkojeen] A gene involved in the control of cell division, whose abnormal function may cause a normal cell to develop into a cancerous cell. Oncogene dysfunction may result from chromosomal re-arrangement, so that in its new location it escapes the control mechanisms previously present, and is actively transcribed. In Burkitt's lymphoma, for example, the common translocation brings the oncogene *c-myc* on chromosome 8 to the vicinity of an immunoglobin gene on chromosome 14.

oncology [ongkolojee] The branch of medicine concerned with the nature and origin of tumours, including the study of their natural history and response to treatment by drugs, surgery, or ionizing radiation (radioactive substances or X-rays).

Ondaatje, Michael [ondahchee] (1943–) Poet, novelist, and editor, born in Colombo, W Sri Lanka. He moved to Canada in 1962, studied at Bishop's University in Quebec, the University of Toronto, and Queen's University, Kingston, Ontario, then became a university lecturer. Among his first books of poetry is *Rat Jelly* (1973). *The Collected Works of Billy the Kid* (1970), a factual and fictional account of the notorious outlaw, won a Governor-General's Award, as did a later book of poems, *There's a Trick with a Knife I'm Learning to Do* (1979). *Running in the Family* (1982) tells of the life of his family in colonial Ceylon, and his novel *The English Patient* was co-winner of the Booker Prize in 1992 (filmed 1996, Oscar). *Handwriting: Poems* appeared in 1999, and the novel *Anil's Ghost* in 2000. His work characteristically blends the factual and imaginary, has a cinematic quality, and depends on an imagery of exoticism.

ondes Martenot [õd mah(r)tenoh] An electronic musical instrument invented in 1928 by Maurice Martenot; the name derives from Fr *ondes* '[musical] waves'. A keyboard, capable of producing a vibrato, is played by the right hand; the left operates the controls for timbre and dynamics. The sound is heard through loudspeakers, often of unusual design. The instrument has been used especially by French composers, including Messiaen and Boulez.

O'Neal, (Patrick) Ryan (1941–) Film actor, born in Los Angeles, California, USA. He became well known as Rodney Harrison in the television series *Peyton Place*, a character he played for nearly five years. His films include *Love Story* (1970), *Paper Moon* (1973), *Irreconcilable Differences* (1984), *Chances Are* (1989), *Faithful* (1996), *Hacks* (1997), and *People I Know* (2002).

Onega, Lake [onyega], Russ **Ozero Onezhskoye** area 9720 sq km/3752 sq mi. Second largest lake in Europe, NW European Russia, close to the Finnish border; between L Ladoga (S) and the White Sea (NE); length 250 km/155 mi; maximum depth 120 m/394 ft; narrow bays (N) extend up to 112 km/70 mi inland; numerous islands (N); connected by canal to the R Volga and the White Sea; chief ports include Petrozavodsk, Voznesenye, Povenets; freezes over (Nov–May).

Oneida [ohniyda] An Iroquoian-speaking North American Indian agricultural group, the smallest tribe of the Iroquois League, originally based in C New York State. They supported the colonists during the American Revolution and were attacked by pro-British Iroquois. They later divided into factions settling in Ontario, Wisconsin, and New York.

O'Neill, Susie, properly **Susan O'Neill** (1973–) Swimmer born in Brisbane, Queensland, Australia. One of Australia's most successful swimmers, she holds a record 35 Australian titles. At the 1996 Olympic Games she won gold, silver, and bronze medals. At the Commonwealth Games in 1998 at Kuala Lumpur she won a record eight medals, including six gold. She won a gold medal in the 200 m butterfly at the 1998 World Championships. In the Pan Pacific Championships in 1999 she won six medals, including gold in the 200 m butterfly and the 200 m freestyle. At the Sydney Olympics in 2000 she broke Mary T Meagher's 19-year-old 200 m butterfly record with a time of 2:05·81.

O'Neill, Eugene (Gladstone) (1888–1953) Playwright, born in New York City, USA. Born into a volatile theatrical family, his education was fragmented, and for six years he went to sea, living the life of a tramp at docksides, and making an attempt at suicide. After a spell in a sanatorium recovering from tuberculosis, he began writing plays as a means of making sense of his disturbed emotions. He was sent to study play-writing at Harvard (1914), and joined the Provincetown Players in 1915, for whom *Beyond the Horizon* (1920, Pulitzer) was written. The most widely produced and translated US playwright of his time, he gained three more Pulitzer Prizes – for *Anna Christie* (1922), *Strange Interlude* (1928), and his masterpiece *Long Day's Journey Into Night* (published posthumously, 1956). Other classics include *Desire Under The Elms* (1924), *Mourning Becomes Electra* (1931), and *The Iceman Cometh* (1946). He was awarded the Nobel Prize for Literature in 1936, the first US dramatist to be thus honoured.

O'Neill (of the Maine), Terence (Marne) O'Neill, Baron (1914–90) Northern Ireland politician and prime minister (1963–9), born in Co Antrim, NE Northern Ireland, UK. He was educated at Eton, and served in the Irish Guards during World War 2. A member of the Northern Ireland parliament (1946–70), he held junior posts before becoming minister for home affairs (1956), minister of finance (1956–63), then prime minister. A supporter of closer cross-border links with the Republic, he angered many Unionists. Following a general election in 1969, dissension in the Unionist Party increased, and he resigned the premiership soon after. Made a life peer in 1970, he continued to speak out on Northern Ireland issues.

One Nation Australian political party, formed in 1997 by Pauline Hanson, an Australian businesswoman elected as an independent MP in 1996 (after being expelled from the Liberal Party for attacking Aborigines and immigrant Asians in her election campaign). It advocates curbs on Asian immigration, the removal of Aboriginal welfare programmes, and a protectionist economic policy. It received strong support in the 1998 Queensland state elections, winning 11 seats in the legislature. However, increasing nationwide condemnation of its policies brought a major setback in the 1998 federal elections, winning no seat in the House, and only one in the Senate, with Hanson losing her Queensland seat.

One Thousand Guineas *Classics*

onion Any of several species of the genus *Allium*, probably originating in Asia, and all grown as vegetables. The ordinary onion (*Allium cepa*) has solitary, globular, or flask-shaped bulbs, often of great size; flattened, tubular leaves semi-circular in cross-section; and inflated stalks bearing white flowers. **Spanish onion** is a variety with white-skinned bulbs; the **shallot** a variety with clusters of small, oval bulbs. **Egyptian** and **everlasting onions** are varieties with narrow bulbs growing in clumps, and bulbils mixed with the flowers. **Welsh onion** (*Allium fistulosum*) has narrow bulbs, leaves circular in cross-section, and yellowish flowers. (Family: Liliaceae).

on-line processing The use of computers to undertake tasks where transactions are initiated and data entered from terminals located in the users' offices. Common examples are the booking of airline tickets, holidays, hotels, and car hire, and transactions in building societies and some banks.

Onnes, Heike Kamerlingh [ohnes] *Kamerlingh-Onnes, Heike*

Ono, Yoko *Lennon, John*

onomastics [onohmastiks] The study of the history, development, and geographical distribution of proper names. All categories of names are included, such as people's first names and surnames, place names, home names, and the names of boats, trains, and pets.

onomatopoeia [onomatopeea] (Gr 'name-making') The imitation of a natural (or mechanical) sound in language. This may be found in single words (*screech*, *babble*, *tick-tock*) or in longer units. It is especially heard in poetry, where Pope said that 'The sound must give an echo to the sense'; for example, 'the slithering and grumble/as the mason mixed his mortar' (Seamus Heaney). Different languages have different potential in this respect. Japanese has over three times as many sound symbolic expressions as English, expressing a much wider range of meanings, eg *fura-fura* ('roam') and *dabu-dabu* ('baggy').

onsen [onsen] A Japanese hot spring. The country's volcanic geography means there are many hot spring resorts, or spas, a favourite destination of private or company excursions. *Onsen* hotels can have public baths as large as swimming pools.

Ontario pop (2000e) 11 293 000; area 1 068 580 sq km/ 412 578 sq mi. Province in SE Canada; boundaries include Hudson Bay (N), James Bay (NE), and USA (S), largely across the Great Lakes; rocky Canadian Shield in N, with clay belt suitable for farming; several rivers flow into Hudson and James Bays, the St Lawrence, and the Great Lakes; many lakes; N area sparsely populated, densely wooded; capital, Toronto, largest city in Canada; major cities include Ottawa, Thunder Bay, Hamilton; most populated and second largest province; tobacco, corn, livestock, poultry, dairy products, fur, vehicles and parts, food processing, iron and steel, machinery, mining (nickel, copper, uranium, zinc, gold, iron), hydroelectricity; indigenous societies included Ojibwa, Cree, Nipissing, Huron (Wyandot), Petun, Neutral, and other Iroquoian speakers; widely explored by French fur traders and missionaries, 17th-c; British territory, 1763; many United Empire Loyalist immigrants after the American War of Independence; constituted as Upper Canada, 1791; rebellion against executive government, 1837–8; joined to Lower Canada, 1840; modern province established at time of confederation, 1867; governed by a lieutenant-governor and a 130-member legislature.

Ontario, Lake Smallest of the Great Lakes, North America, on US–Canadian border; length 311 km/193 mi; breadth 85 km/ 53 mi; maximum depth 244 m/800 ft; area 19 011 sq km/ 7338 sq mi, just over half in Canada; connected (SW) with L Erie via the Niagara R and the Welland Ship Canal; outlet, the St Lawrence R (NE); canals link with Hudson R, L Huron, and Ottawa; ports include (in Ontario) Kingston, Hamilton, and Toronto, and (in New York State) Rochester and Oswego; never ice-bound.

ontological argument One of the traditional arguments for the existence of God, first developed by Anselm. God is defined as the being than which nothing greater can be conceived; something which exists must be greater than something which does not; therefore God must exist.

ontology A central part of metaphysics: the theory of what sorts of things really exist. A materialist, for example, will argue that matter is the only fundamental existent, in terms of which everything else must be explained.

Onychophora [onikofora] A sub-phylum of primitive arthropods, comprising the velvet worms; sometimes classified as a separate phylum.

onyx *agate*

oolite [ohuhliyt] A limestone composed of *ooliths*, ie rounded grains made of concentric layers of radiating fibres of carbonate, usually aragonite or calcite. It is formed by the precipitation and growth of consecutive layers of carbonate on a nucleus of a sand or shell fragment, as it is moved about on a warm, shallow sea floor. Coarser oolites (> 3 mm/⅛ in diameter) are termed *pisolites*.

Oort cloud [aw(r)t] A hypothesized source of the long-period comets; a spherical 'halo' about the Sun at a distance of c.50 000 AU; named after Dutch astronomer Jan Hendrik Oort (1900–92), who first noted the clustering of aphelia of new comets in this region. It is at the boundary of the Sun's gravitational sphere of influence, about a third of the distance to the nearest star. Comets are believed to have originated in the outer Solar System 4·6 thousand million years ago when the system was being formed, and to have been scattered outward by the gravitational effects of the giant planets.

Oostende [ohstenduh] *Ostend*

opah [ohpa] *moonfish*

opal A natural form of amorphous (non-crystalline) silica (SiO_2), containing varying amounts of water, and formed at relatively low temperatures from solutions associated with igneous activity and supersaturated in silica. It is usually white, but gems have a characteristic play of rainbow colours. The best occurrences are in Australia.

Op Art An abbreviation for **Optical Art**, a modern art movement of the 1960s which exploited the illusionistic effects of abstract spiral or wavy patterns, stripes, spots, etc. Hungarian-born French painter Victor Vasarely (1908–97) and British painter Bridget Riley (1931–) were leading exponents.

OPEC (Organization of Petroleum Exporting Countries) [ohpek] An international economic organization set up in 1960 with its headquarters in Vienna; the longest-surviving major cartel, originally consisting of 13 oil-producing countries (now 11). The founder members were Iran, Iraq, Kuwait, Saudi Arabia, and Venezuela; and they were later joined by Algeria, Ecuador (withdrew, 1992), Gabon (withdrew, 1996), Indonesia, Libya, Nigeria, Qatar, and the United Arab Emirates (formerly Abu Dhabi). Its purpose is to co-ordinate the petroleum policy of members to protect their interests, especially in relation to the fixing of prices for crude oil and the quantities to be produced.

open-cast mining *mining*

open cluster A family of a few dozen to a few hundred relatively young stars (typically no more than a few hundred million years old) formed simultaneously and still physically close together; also called a **galactic cluster**. There are c.1000 in our Galaxy. Pleiades and Hyades are examples visible to the naked eye.

Open Door US foreign policy towards China and other countries, formulated in response to the weakness of the Chinese Manchu empire. Begun in September 1899 and modified in July 1900, the Open Door policy was secured by the American secretary of state, John Hay, to preserve Chinese integrity by opposing the development of spheres of influence dominated by particular countries. The principle became a major assumption of American policy in Asia until the establishment of the Communist regime in China in 1949.

open-ended investment company An investment company which pools the funds of its shareholders, and invests in a diversified portfolio of stocks and shares, also called a **mutual fund**. It grows by continually offering new shares for sale. Such a company contrasts with a **closed-end investment company**, which has a fixed amount of share capital.

open enrolment In the UK, a policy which permits parents to enrol their child at any school which has a place available; this is in contrast with a policy based on strictly defined geographical catchment areas. In the USA, the term applies to colleges that allow the enrolment of any high-school graduate.

Open Golf Championship Annual British golfing championship, first contested at Prestwick, South Ayrshire (17 Oct 1860), and won by Willie Park. Regarded as the world's leading golf tournament, it is played over 72 holes at a different venue each year. All courses are seaside links. The winner receives a silver claret jug, as well as a sizeable cheque.

open government A demand made by several groups in the 1970s and 1980s, particularly in the UK, for less secrecy in policy making. Such groups pressed for reform of the 'catch-all' Section 2 of the Official Secrets Act, and the introduction of a Freedom of Information Act. The UK government introduced reform proposals in the late 1980s, but critics argued that these were likely to prove even more restrictive. The 1997 Labour government produced a white paper on Freedom of Information, but there has been little further movement on the issue.

open-hearth process A steel-making process devised in 1860 by William Siemens (1823–83) and first successfully operated in 1864 by Pierre Emile Martin (1824–1915). The molten pig iron from which the steel is to be made is not in direct contact with the fuel providing the heat, but only with the hot flames from combustion which play on a shallow hearth containing pig-iron, scrap, and a flux. The steel can be withdrawn continuously. It will operate with iron derived from ores, with which the Bessemer process is ineffective.

open-market operations An economic situation where a central bank actively engages in selling or buying government bonds to influence liquid reserves in the banks. If the central bank buys securities, the money paid out increases the commercial banks' reserves, and therefore the amount of money that can be lent. The opposite consequences obtain when the central bank engages in selling.

open plan An arrangement of rooms in a building in which the internal doors and walls have been reduced to a minimum, or even omitted altogether. It is particularly associated with the International Style architecture of the 1920s and 1930s, and subsequently with offices and private housing of the period after World War 2.

open-plan school A school with few interior walls or box-shaped classrooms. Instead, open-plan areas permit freedom of movement and team teaching. Usually there are special areas for noisier activities or for painting and drama, as well as a resources centre.

open shop *closed shop*

open stage Any stage in a theatre building which is in the same space as the auditorium, and which has no part of the acting or scenic area separated from the audience by a wall or an abrupt variation in ceiling height. A descendant of the Elizabethan platform stage, it is designed to draw the audience closer to the drama.

open systems interconnection (OSI) An international standard for the definition of connections between computers, which allows computers of different makes and architectures to communicate with each other for the transfer of data. The organization committed to the establishment of software and standards to enable computers to fulfil these requirements is the **Open Software Foundation (OSF)**.

Open Theater A US experimental theatre company which performed from 1963 until 1973. Under the leadership of Joseph Chaikin, it concentrated on extending the actor's resources for image-making and encouraged collaboration, through a creative rehearsal period, between actors and writers.

Open University An institution of higher education, such as has been established in a number of countries, which enables students to study for a degree without attendance. Courses are usually based on a credit system, and the student graduates when sufficient credits have been amassed. The teaching is frequently carried out through correspondence units and broadcast or taped supporting programmes, though often with some face-to-face tutoring at local study centres. Entry qualifications are often more permissively framed than in conventional universities, and in many cases no formal qualifications are required, because beginners can take foundation or access courses.

opera A stage work in which music plays a continuous or substantial role. The genre originated in Chinese musical plays from the 10th-c, and in Europe at Florence c.1600, and was well established throughout Italy by the end of the 17th-c; by the middle of the 18th-c it had conquered most of W Europe. In Italy, opera, whether serious or comic, has usually been sung throughout; elsewhere other types have developed which alternate songs with spoken dialogue (*semi-opera* in England, *opéra comique* in France, *Singspiel* in Germany). The history of opera has largely been one of reforms introduced to correct an imbalance between the demands of music and those of the drama.

Wagner's music dramas aimed at a *Gesamtkunstwerk* which united the arts of music, poetry, gesture, and painting. The hope was that this would provide the 'music of the future'; but the course of opera since then has been dictated as much by financial as by artistic considerations.

opera buffa Italian comic opera, especially of the 18th-c, with dialogue in recitative. Mozart's *Le nozze di Figaro* (1786, The Marriage of Figaro) is an outstanding example of the genre.

opéra comique French opera, with spoken dialogue, originally comic but later including such dramatic operas as Bizet's *Carmen* (1875).

operant A term of instrumental learning, introduced by US psychologist B F Skinner. An *operant* is an action which has an effect on the environment, and which can be modified according to its consequences.

opera seria Italian serious opera of the 18th-c and early 19th-c, exhibiting a rigid separation of aria (and the occasional ensemble) and recitative. It reached its highest point of development as a poetic form in the librettos of Metastasio, and as a musical genre in Mozart's *Idomeneo* (1781) and *La clemenza di Tito* (1791).

operating system A computer program which supervises the running of all other programs on a computer. Common microprocessor operating systems are CP/M, MS-DOS, and Microsoft Windows.

operationalism A radically empiricist programme, enunciated by P W Bridgman in 1927, which defines scientific concepts in terms of the actual physical operations used to measure them. Length, for example, is nothing more than what is specified by the activities of measurement.

operetta Light opera, with spoken dialogue and usually dancing, exemplified in the stage works of Offenbach, Strauss, and Sullivan.

operon A group of closely linked genes which affect different steps in a single metabolic sequence and which function as an integrated unit. The term was introduced by the French geneticist, François Jacob, in 1960.

Ophir [ohfer] A land of unknown location, mentioned in the Bible as famous for its resources of gold; 1 *Kings* 9–10, 22 suggest that it was reached from Palestine by ship, so it is variously placed in Arabia, India, or E Africa. Solomon is said to have sent a fleet there from Ezion-Geber, but the fame of the 'gold of Ophir' is known also from archaeological inscriptions.

Ophiuchus [ofyookus] (Gr 'serpent bearer') A large constellation on the celestial equator, including several globular clusters and the nearby object, Barnard's star.

ophthalmia [op-, ofthalmia] Inflammation of the conjunctival membrane covering the eye in the newborn. It may be caused by gonorrhoea infection (*ophthalmia neonatorum*) or arise as a consequence of injury to the other eye (*sympathetic ophthalmia*).

ophthalmology [op-, ofthalmolojee] The branch of medical practice concerned with disorders and diseases of the eyes. It includes general or systemic diseases that may affect the eye, and their medical or surgical treatment.

Ophuls or **Opüls, Max** [opüls], originally **Max Oppenheimer** (1902–57) Film director, born in Saarbrücken, SW Germany, who chose French nationality in the plebiscite of 1934. He worked in films from 1930, first in Germany and later in France. In 1941 he emigrated to the USA, and in 1947–9 made *The Exile*, *Caught*, and *The Reckless Moment*. He then returned to France, where he made his greatest successes, *La Ronde* (1950) and *Lola Montez* (1955).

Opie, John [ohpee] (1716–1807) Portraitist and historical painter, born in St Agnes, Cornwall, SW England, UK. His portraits interested his teacher **John Wolcot** (1738–1819, pseudonym **Peter Pindar**), by whom he was taken to London in 1789 to become the 'Cornish Wonder'. He became renowned as a portraitist of contemporary figures, and also painted historical pictures like the well-known 'Murder of Rizzio' (1787). He became professor of painting at the Royal Academy in 1805.

opinion poll The taking of opinions from a sample of the electorate regarding their voting intentions, their views of political leaders, and wider political attitudes. They are also used to assess consumer preferences. Polls originated in the USA in the 1930s, and today are commonplace both at and between elections. Although based on small samples, if the sample is systematically drawn and representative of the population, the poll is accurate to within a few per cent. There is concern that the publishing of polls forecasting the results of elections could themselves influence voting intentions, and some countries restrict poll publication before an election.

opioid peptides [ohpioyd peptiydz] A family of chemical substances (peptides), including *enkephalins*, *endorphins*, and *dynorphins*, which are found in the brain, spinal cord, pituitary gland, gastro-intestinal tract, and adrenal medulla; also known as **endogenous opioids**. In the brain and spinal cord they appear to be neurotransmitters or neuromodulators involved in pain perception. Central nervous system effects in humans include potent analgesia, euphoria, and respiratory depression. They are probably also involved in gut motility and pituitary hormone release.

Opitz (von Boberfeld), Martin (1597–1639) Poet, born in Bolesławeic, SW Poland (formerly Bunzlau, Germany). He studied at Frankfurt, Heidelberg, and Leyden, served several German princes, and became historiographer to Władysław IV of Poland. He wrote in a scholarly and stilted style which influenced German poetry for 200 years, and introduced Renaissance poetic thinking into Germany.

opium The dried extract of the unripe seed capsules of the opium poppy, *Papaver somniferum*, which contains several narcotic alkaloids, including morphine. It was used by many ancient cultures including the Babylonians, Egyptians, Greeks, and Romans for its properties of relieving pain, inducing sleep, and promoting psychological effects of peace and well-being. Opium is still occasionally used as an anti-diarrhoeal preparation.

opium poppy A bluish or greyish-green annual (*Papaver somniferum*) growing to 1 m/3¾ ft, native to Europe and Asia; leaves oblong, shallowly lobed, clasping stem; flowers 4-petalled; capsule pepper-pot shaped, with a ring of pores around the rim. In the garden form (subspecies *hortense*), the flowers are mauve with a dark centre; in the drug-producing form (subspecies *somniferum*), the flowers are white. Opium is obtained by making incisions in the young fruit capsules, which weep latex containing the drug. The refinement of raw opium yields other drugs, such as morphine. (Family: Papaveraceae.)

Opium Wars Two wars (1839–42, 1856–60) between China and the Western powers, especially Britain, fought over the question of commercial rights in China, specifically relating to the opium trade. Imports of opium from Bengal were dominated by the British East India Company, and Chinese payments in silver helped to finance British India. When the Chinese attempted to stop the imports (1839), a British force besieged Guangzhou (Canton), occupied Shanghai, and imposed the Treaty of Nanjing (Nanking) in 1842. This opened Guangzhou, Nanjing, Shanghai, Fuzhou (Foochow), and Xiamen (Amoy) to Western trade. The Second Opium War, or **Arrow War**, began when Chinese boarded a Hong Kong ship (*The Arrow*), flying a British flag but suspected of piracy (1856). British troops occupied Guangzhou, and an Anglo-French army marched on Beijing. The Treaties of Tianjin (Tientsin) in 1858 between China and Britain, France, Russia, and the USA opened 10 more ports and legalized the opium traffic. Beijing was subsequently sacked by allied troops (1860). These 'unequal treaties', not abrogated until 1949, established a strong, threatening Western influence in China, and helped stir up nationalist sentiments which led to the 1911 revolution and the rise of political radicalism.

Oporto [opaw(r)toh], Port **Porto** 41°08N 8°40W, pop (2000e) 307 000. Capital of Oporto district, N Portugal; 272 km/169 mi N of Lisbon, on N bank of R Douro near its mouth; second largest city in Portugal; bishopric; railway; university

(1911); port wine, fruit, olive oil, cork; cathedral (12th-c), stock exchange palace, Clérigos Tower; festival of São João (Jun).

opossum [oposm] A marsupial of family Didelphidae (75 species), native to the New World; hind foot with opposable 'thumb', and lacking the 'comb' of many Australian marsupials; most climb trees; often have grasping tail; not all females have pouches; New World marsupials called opossums; Australian marsupials of similar appearance called **possums**. The name is also used for 7 species of New World **shrew** or **rat opossums** (family: Caenolestidae).

Oppenheimer, Sir Ernest [openhiymer] (1880–1957) Mining magnate, politician, and philanthropist, born in Friedberg, WC Germany. From the age of 17 he worked for a London firm of diamond merchants and, sent out to Kimberley as their representative in 1902, soon became one of the leaders of the diamond industry. In 1917, with John Pierpont Morgan Jr, he formed the Anglo-American Corporation of South Africa, and at the time of his death his interests extended over 95% of the world's supply of diamonds. He became Mayor of Kimberley (1912–15) and an MP (1924–38). A philanthropist and public figure, he was knighted in 1921.

Oppenheimer, J(ulius) Robert [openhiymer] (1904–67) Nuclear physicist, born in New York City, USA. He studied at Harvard, Cambridge, Göttingen, Leyden, and Zürich universities, then taught physics at the California Institute of Technology (1929). In 1942 he joined the atom bomb project, and became director of the Los Alamos laboratory (1943–5). He was chairman of the advisory committee to the US Atomic Energy Commission (1946–52), and in 1947 became director and professor of physics at the Institute for Advanced Study, Princeton. In 1953 he was suspended from secret nuclear research by a security review board for his past Communist associations, although many people disagreed with the charges brought against him. He delivered the BBC Reith Lectures (1953), and received the Enrico Fermi Award in 1963.

opposition (astronomy) The moment when a planet is opposite the Sun, as observed in our sky. The planet crosses the meridian at local midnight, which is therefore the best time for observing.

opposition (politics) The right of parties and political movements not holding government office to criticize the government and seek to replace it by offering alternative policies. In democratic systems the **Opposition** normally consists of those parties which oppose the government through parliamentary channels, their activities being regarded as a necessary activity, and recognized in parliamentary and electoral procedures. Opposition can also occur from parties or movements outside parliament, either because they are too weak or not inclined to gain parliamentary representation. Interest groups may oppose governments on specific issues. In non-democratic systems, oppositions are often outlawed and sometimes repressed, although covert opposition continues.

Ops The Roman goddess of plenty, the consort of Saturn, identified with Rhea.

optical activity The ability of certain materials to rotate the plane of polarization of light passing through them. The degree of rotation depends on the thickness of material traversed. Substances which rotate light clockwise (when looking along the beam towards the light source) are termed *dextrorotatory*; those which rotate to the left, *levorotatory*. Sugar, quartz, and turpentine are optically active.

optical character reader (OCR) A machine which can read standard texts into a computer using a combination of optical and computer techniques.

optical fibres Fibres of transparent optical material, usually glass, for transmitting images or data. Each fibre consists of a core and an outer cladding of lower refractive index: light travels through the core and is contained within it by refraction (total internal reflection) at the core/cladding boundary. In telecommunications, optical fibres, made from very pure materials, transmit data very long distances (up to 50 km/30 mi at one stretch). Optical fibre cables contain bundles of very thin fibres allowing high transmission capacity combined with flexibility. Because of the flexibility and small diameter of the optical fibre bundle, the technique is also used in medicine for viewing inaccessible parts of the body (*endoscopy*).

optical sensing Sensors which detect light and convert it into electrical signals. Human eyes are very adaptable optical sensors, able to respond to a wide range of light levels but of a restricted range of wavelengths: the light stimulation results in electrical impulses to the brain, which are then interpreted. Artificial optical sensors include photo-electric cells, which may be sensitive to infra-red or ultra-violet wavelengths, and photographic light meters.

optical stress analysis *photoelasticity*

optics The study of light and of instruments using light. The subject has a long history. Mirrors were used by the ancient Egyptians c.2000 BC, and Greek philosophers developed simple theories of light (the law of reflection being stated by Euclid in 300 BC). The Greeks also knew of lenses (burning glasses) and studied refraction. Optics was studied at the Chinese Imperial Medical College from AD 620. The idea of using lenses to correct vision is probably due to Roger Bacon (13th-c). Galileo devised one of the earliest telescopes (1609), and Newton built the first reflecting telescope (1668). The compound microscope (consisting of two or more elements) is thought to have been invented c.1590 by Dutch spectacle-maker Zacharias Janssen (1588–1632). The modern formulation of geometrical optics, including reflection and refraction, began in the early 17th-c. Geometrical optics treats light as rays which travel in straight lines, changing direction only at the interface between materials. Diffraction was noted later that century, leading to early ideas that light may be wave-like. The *wave* theory of light was supported by the work of Dutch physicist Christian Huygens, but opposed by Isaac Newton, who maintained that light was composed of particles called corpuscles (the *corpuscular* theory). The demonstration by British physicist Thomas Young of interference effects in light (1804) supported the wave theory. Light as a (transverse) wave provided an explanation of the polarization effects observed by Newton and Huygens in calcite crystals. The modern understanding of light embraces both wave and particle viewpoints. The 'rays' of geometrical optics correspond to the direction of wave propagation. Physical optics includes wave effects. Modern optical developments include optical fibres and their use in communications; optical logic elements and potentially optical computers; the application of Fourier analysis techniques, in particular spatial filtering (eg allowing the removal of unwanted horizontal lines from photographs); the mass production of plastic lenses with complicated curved surfaces; lasers; and holography.

opting out (education) *grant-maintained school*

options market A market in which traders can buy the right to buy ('call') or sell ('put') shares or commodities at a pre-agreed 'exercise price' at some future date or within some future period. If the market price rises above the exercise price, the holders of 'put' options will not want to use them, since they could get more in the market; they will have lost the money paid for their option. If the market price falls below the exercise price, holders of 'call' options will not want to use them, since they could get the share cheaper in the market; again the cost of the option will have been lost. Options may be used to speculate on an expected rise or fall in the market price without the risk of actually holding the underlying share or commodity. Equally, however, they may be used to 'hedge', ie to buy safety. If one must hold commodities in the course of trade, a 'put' option avoids the risk of large losses if the market price collapses. If one is going to need a commodity at a future date, a 'call' option puts an upper limit on what it can cost. Options markets exist only for widely traded shares and commodities. Traded options markets opened in Chicago in 1973 and in London in 1978.

optoelectronics The study of the production and control of light by electronic devices, such as semiconductor lasers, liquid crystals, and light-emitting diodes. It provides the technology for electronic displays in watches and calculators, and the interconversion of optical and electronic signals in optical fibre communications.

optometry [optometree] The assessment of the function of the eye, with special reference to errors of refraction, and the provision of appropriate corrective lenses and spectacles. It also now includes the specialized examination of the eye to diagnose a wide range of defects, such as disorders of fields of vision; disorders affecting the lens, aqueous humour, and retina, as revealed by ophthalmoscopic examination; and the estimation of intra-ocular pressure to detect glaucoma. These assessments are carried out by qualified and registered *optometrists*.

opuntia [opuhnsha] A large genus of cacti with stems made up of flattened, spiny, pear-shaped segments; native to the Americas, but widely introduced elsewhere. They spread easily, forming impenetrable thickets and often becoming troublesome weeds. They are sometimes cultivated for their juicy fruits, or grown as hedging plants and ornamentals. *Opuntia cochenillifera* is a food plant for cochineal insects. (Genus: *Opuntia*, 250 species. Family: Cactaceae.)

Opus Dei [ohpus dayee] (Lat 'work of God') The title of a Roman Catholic society, founded in 1928, to promote the exercise of Christian virtues by individuals in secular society. In some countries and at certain periods (eg Spain in the mid-20th-c) it acquired a measure of political power. The term was formerly used by the Benedictines, referring to the divine office, to express the duty of prayer.

ora *Komodo dragon*

orache [orich] A member of a genus of annuals or perennials, found almost everywhere, some forming small shrubs; the whole plant often mealy white; flowers tiny, green, males with five perianth-segments, females enclosed in two small bracts. The garden form of the annual **common orache** (*Atriplex patula*) is rich in vitamin C, and was once used as a vegetable. (Genus: *Atriplex*, 200 species. Family: Chenopodiaceae.)

oracle Divine prophetic declarations about unknown or future events, or the places (such as Delphi) or inspired individuals (such as the Sibyls) through which such communications occur. In ancient Greek stories, these revelations were usually given in response to questions put to the gods. In Biblical traditions, however, oracles are sometimes distinguished from 'prophecies', in that the latter are unsolicited, although the Old Testament also testifies to interrogations of the divine being. Sometimes oracles were not expressed as verbal messages, but were associated with casting lots or other methods of the divination of signs.

Oracle (computing) A computer package for implementing relational databases, offering query-languages and CASE tools; also, the name of the company which markets the Oracle database and associated software.

Oracle (telecommunications) The teletext system operated by the UK Independent Broadcasting Association (later, the Independent Television Commission) as a commercial service since 1981. The name is an acronym for *Optional Reception of Announcements by Coded Line Electronics*. In 1993 it was renamed *Teletext on 3*, and later became known as *ITV-text* or just *Teletext*.

oracle bones Inscribed shoulder blades of pig, ox, and sheep (later tortoise shells) used for divination by the Shang monarchs of N China, 16th–11th-c BC. The patterns of cracks made by hot brands applied to the bones were read as guidance from royal ancestors, this information being recorded alongside, using an ideographic script of 2000 characters – the earliest-known Chinese writing. Since 1928 c.200 000 bones have been recovered. Their decipherment is comparable in importance to that of Egyptian hieroglyphs. They detail births, illnesses, rituals, wars, hunting, agriculture, and the weather, plus a chronology of Shang kings and officials.

oracy The ability to express oneself coherently and to listen with good comprehension. The fostering of these skills has come to be seen as an important goal of childhood education, alongside the traditional focus on reading and writing. The term itself was coined on analogy with *literacy* and *numeracy*.

oral contraceptives *contraception*

oral history The means of discovering information about the past by interviewing subjects, a technique increasingly used since the 1970s by social historians and anthropologists to augment the written record, especially in areas where 'orthodox' sources are deficient or unobtainable. Some argue that oral history is now a discipline in its own right, rather than simply a means of acquiring information.

oral surgery *dentistry*

Oran [orahn] or **Wahran** 35°45N 0°38W, pop (2000e) 850 900. Seaport in Oran department, N Algeria, N Africa; 355 km/221 mi W of Algiers; founded 8th-c; first ruled by Arabs, then Spaniards (1509–1708), Turks (1708–32), and French (1831–1962); landing point for Allied forces in World War 2; former French naval base nearby at Mers el Kabir; university (1965); airport; railway; iron, textiles, food processing, footwear, cigarettes; trade in grain, wool, vegetables, esparto grass; 16th-c Santa Cruz fortress, municipal museum.

O'Rane, Patricia *Dark, Eleanor*

Orange (France) [orãzh] 44°08N 4°48E, pop (2000e) 29 400. Town in Vaucluse department, SE France, on the R Rhône, N of Avignon; market centre, glass, food processing; developed around a group of Roman monuments, now a world heritage site; vast well-preserved theatre, with 4 m/12 ft statue of Augustus (probably late 1st-c BC); 18 m/60 ft-high triumphal arch, commemorating Julius Caesar's victories over local Gauls.

Orange, Princes of *William I* (of the Netherlands); *William III* (of Great Britain)

orange A citrus fruit 7–10 cm/2¾–4 in diameter, globular with thick, often rough rind. The familiar edible fruit is the **sweet orange** (*Citrus sinensis*). The **Seville orange** (*Citrus aurantium*) has sour fruits, and is cooked for marmalade. **Bergamot orange** (*Citrus bergamia*) is grown as a source of bergamot oil, obtained from the rind of the yellow fruit, and oil of Neroli from the flowers. (Genus: *Citrus*. Family: Rutaceae.)

Orange Free State *Free State*

Orange Order An association that developed from the Orange Society, which had been formed in 1795 to counteract growing Catholic influence in Ireland and 'to maintain the laws and peace of the country and the Protestant constitution'. The name was taken from the Protestant Dutch dynasty represented by William III, who defeated the exiled Catholic king James II at the Battle of the Boyne in 1690. Organized in 'Lodges', it provided the backbone of resistance to Home Rule proposals from the mid-1880s, and has operated as a force for conservative Protestantism in Northern Ireland since partition. The Orangemen's celebration of the anniversary of the Battle of the Boyne (July 12) in a display of street parades is regarded by Nationalists and others as supremacism. As a result, violence has often accompanied Orange marches routed through Catholic areas, leading to the setting up of a Parades Commission to regulate the routes.

Orange Prize A literary prize established in 1996, given annually to fiction written by women and published in the UK. Worth £30 000, it is the UK's largest annual literary award for a single novel.

Orange River, Afrikaans **Oranjerivier** River in Lesotho, South Africa, and Namibia; rises in the Drakensberg Mts in NE Lesotho, and flows S into South Africa, then generally W and NW, following the border between South Africa and Namibia, to enter the Atlantic Ocean at Alexander Bay; length 2100 km/1300 mi; dammed in several places as part of the **Orange River Project** (begun 1963) to provide irrigation and power.

orang-utan An ape (*Pongo pygmaeus*) native to forests of Sumatra and Borneo; height, 1·5 m/5 ft; sparse covering of long shaggy red-brown hair; armspan up to 2·25 m/7½ ft; adults with large naked 'double chin'; adult male with large naked fatty folds around face; sleeps in trees.

Oratorians 1 A community of priests, followers of St Philip of Neri (16th-c), living together without vows, and devoted to prayer, preaching, and attractive services of worship. They still flourish in many countries, including Italy, France, and England where they were introduced by Cardinal Newman. Their home in London is Brompton Oratory.

2 Priests of the French Oratory, or **Oratory of Jesus Christ**, founded in 1611 and following a modified form of the rule established by St Philip Neri, dissolved in 1791 and re-established in 1852. This community is noted for educating priests and furthering popular devotion.

oratorio A non-liturgical, quasi-dramatic sacred work, usually for solo voices, chorus, and orchestra. It takes its name from the Italian 'prayer-hall' in which the earliest oratorios were performed in the mid-17th-c, but until c.1750 it existed also in secular settings as an alternative to the serenata and opera, especially during Lent. Handel's oratorios, originally performed in the London theatres, represent this type at its finest, but by the time they influenced Haydn's *The Creation* (1798) the oratorio had come to be regarded as a religious rather than a dramatic work, and since then cathedral festivals have frequently provided the occasion for an oratorio performance. Among composers of oratorio after Haydn, Mendelssohn and Elgar were particularly important.

oratory The art and practice of public speaking. Effective oratory requires that the choice of language, its style, and mode of delivery should be appropriate for a given audience, location, and occasion. Its major forms (legal, political, ceremonial) can be traced back to earliest times, notably to the Greek orators of the 4th-c BC (eg Demosthenes), and the Roman orators of the 1st-c BC (eg Cicero). Other categories developed later, such as religious oratory, following the rise of Christianity and other religions, and commercial oratory. In modern times, oratory has been effectively practised, as can be seen in the speeches of Hitler, Churchill, John F Kennedy, and Martin Luther King Jr, and the radio or television debates and 'fireside chats' used by leading politicians.

orbit In astronomy, the path followed by any celestial object or satellite moving through a gravitational field. For the case of two bodies only, the orbit can be calculated analytically with arbitrary precision, and is one of the conic sections: parabola, ellipse, or circle. For three or more, the problem is immensely complex, and has to be solved numerically by computer. A **geostationary orbit** is one followed by a satellite above the Equator at 35 900 km/22 300 mi, where it keeps in exact step with the Earth's rotation and is thus always in the same part of the sky. This is essential for satellite communications and television.

orb weaver A spider that spins orb-shaped webs; legs armed with many long spines; fangs with many teeth; prey caught in web are cut out and wrapped in silk. (Order: Araneae. Family: Araneidae.)

Orcagna [aw(r)kanya], originally **Andrea de Cione** (c.1308–c.1368) Painter, sculptor, and architect, born in Florence, NC Italy. A member of a family of painters, his greatest paintings are frescoes, an altarpiece in Santa Maria Nobella, and the 'Coronation of the Virgin' (National Gallery, London). Many consider him second in the 14th-c only to Giotto, who influenced him.

orchestra Originally the name for the semi-circular space in front of a stage, later extended to the body of instrumentalists that performed there. Large instrumental ensembles were often used in the Renaissance period, but these were not orchestras in the modern sense of a regular constituted body of string players, with additional woodwind, brass, and percussion as required. Opera 'orchestras' in the mid-17th-c were mostly small, with only one player to a part, and the development of the orchestra took place mainly in the courts, those of London, Paris, and Vienna being particularly important. The advent of the concerto in the late 17th-c stimulated the formation of four-part string orchestras in all the major musical centres, and by the end of the 18th-c the standard orchestra for the symphonies of Haydn and Mozart included also pairs of flutes, oboes, bassoons, horns, trumpets, timpani, and (sometimes) clarinets. Each section expanded further during the 19th-c, and the modern symphony orchestra of about 100 players will normally include 60 or more string instruments, triple or quadruple woodwind and brass, and (in addition to the instruments mentioned above) at least three trombones, tuba, harp, and a vast array of percussion.

orchestration The scoring of a piece of music for the instruments of the orchestra. The study of orchestration as a discipline separate from composition originated in the 19th-c, when one of the most influential treatises was written on the subject by Berlioz (1843).

orchid A monocotyledonous plant belonging to the family Orchidaceae, one of the largest and most advanced flowering-plant families, containing some 17 000 species. Orchids are found in virtually all parts of the world except Antarctica, but are especially abundant in the tropics. Nearly half the species are epiphytic; the remainder are terrestrial, a few Australian species even having a completely subterranean life-cycle. All are perennial herbs with sometimes tuberous rhizomes. The epiphytic species have clinging and aerial roots as well as normal feeding roots. A common feature is the development of *pseudobulbs* – cylindrical or bulb-like swellings of the stems just above soil level, which store nutrients and water, and from which leaves and flowers arise. The fleshy, frequently spotted or blotched leaves sheath the stem at their bases. Orchids are best known for their complex, often spectacular and exotic flowers, and for their highly developed pollination mechanisms. The flower typically consists of a slender ovary surmounted by three petaloid sepals and two similar petals, with the third petal forming a lower lip or *labellum* which differs from the others in form and colour. It is variously expanded, enlarged, lobed, frilled, or divided, sometimes spurred, and usually strikingly marked or ornamented. Within the flower the three stigmas and one or two stamens are fused into a column, the exact form of which depends greatly on the pollinator species to which these organs must be presented. Insects, bats, and even frogs may act as pollinators, and many are species specific. The pollen is usually held in sticky, stalked masses called *pollinia*, which become attached with special quick-setting glue to the pollinator. Despite pollinator specificity, orchids interbreed with great facility, and very many hybrids are known in the wild as well as in cultivation. Orchid seeds take up to 18 months to ripen, and up to four years to reach the flowering stage. They are minute, with a poorly developed embryo, and germination is successful only if mycorrhizal fungi are present. Because of these problems, commercial orchid breeding relies heavily on tissue culture and similar propagation techniques. Orchids exert a strong fascination for many people, and numerous species are now commonly cultivated, with whole societies devoted to their study and care. (Family: Orchidaceae.)

Orczy, Emma (Magdalena Rosalia Marie Josepha Barbara), Baroness [awtsee, awksee] (1865–1947) Novelist and playwright, born in Tarna-Eörs, NEC Hungary. The family settled in London in 1880. *The Scarlet Pimpernel* (1905) was the first success in her long writing career. It was followed by many popular adventure romances, including *The Elusive Pimpernel* (1908). The first of the Scarlet Pimpernel films appeared in 1934, directed by Alexander Korda, with Leslie Howard in the leading role.

ordered pairs In mathematics, pairs of numbers, say (a,b) and (c,d) which are equal only if $a = c$, $b = d$. Rational numbers are examples of equivalence classes of ordered pairs, as 2/3 is not the same as 3/2, but is the same as 4/6. Further examples are the Cartesian co-ordinates of points in a plane, for the point (3,4) is not the same as the point (4,3). Ordered triples, etc are defined similarly.

Order in Council In British government, legislation made by the Monarch in Council allowed by act of parliament, but which does not need to be ratified by parliament. It is the main means through which the powers of the royal prerogative are exercised. In practice the decisions are taken by government ministers, not by the monarch.

Order of Merit (OM) In the UK, a decoration for those who have provided pre-eminent service to the country; the letters OM may be used after their name. Instituted by Edward VII in 1902 and limited to 24 members, it comprises a military and a civil class. The ribbon is blue and scarlet.

order of reaction The dependence of a rate of reaction on the concentration of a reactant. If a rate of reaction varies directly with the concentration of one reactant, the reaction is said to be *first order*; if with the square of the concentration, *second order*; and so on. The overall order of reaction is the sum of the orders with respect to each reactant.

Orders *(Orders of) Australia / Bath / British Empire / Canada / Companions of Honour / Garter / Royal Victorian / St Michael and St George / Thistle*

Orders, Holy Grades of ministry in Orthodox, Roman Catholic, and Anglican Churches. **Major Orders** consist of ordained ministers, bishops, priests, and deacons (and, in the Western Church, subdeacons). **Minor Orders** include, in the Western Church, lectors, porters, exorcists, acolytes; in the Eastern Church, subdeacons. Major Orders constitute the hierarchy of the Church, to be distinguished from the laity. A distinction is also drawn between **First Orders** (fully professed men), **Second Orders** (fully professed women), and **Third Orders** (those affiliated usually to one of the Mendicant Orders). A member of a Third Order (a 'Tertiary') may live in a religious community, or in the world.

orders of architecture *p.1134–5*

Ordinance of 1787 An Act of the American Continental Congress establishing procedures by which newly-settled Western territories could enter the American union on the basis of full political equality with the original states. It was one of several **Northwest Ordinances** passed in 1784–7.

ordinary language philosophy *linguistic philosophy*

Ordnance Datum (OD) The mean sea level in the UK, used as a fixed reference from which the elevations of all points in the country are surveyed. It was determined by hourly measurements of sea level made between 1915 and 1921 at Newlyn, Cornwall. The equivalent in the USA is the **Sea Level Datum**, calculated from the mean sea level for the whole US coastal area.

Ordnance Survey of Great Britain The survey and mapping agency established by the 1841 Ordnance Survey Act, although founded initially in 1791 as the Trigonometrical Survey. Maps were originally produced at a scale of 1 in to the mile and are now available at a number of scales. Scales are expressed as a representative fraction, such as 1: 63 360 (1 in to 63 360 in, or 1 mi). The basic scales are 1: 1250 (1 cm to 1250 cm or 1 in to 1250 in, ie 50 in to the mile), 1: 2500 (or c.50 in to the mile), and 1: 10 000, which supersedes the 1: 10 350 (c.6 in to the mile). These are produced by ground fieldwork, topographical survey, and aerial photography, kept up-to-date by a system of continuous revision. All other map series (1: 25 000, 1: 50 000, and 1: 250 000) are derived from the detail of the basic maps. The survey also produces archaeological and historical maps. The Ordnance Survey of Northern Ireland is separate.

Ordovician period [aw(r)dovishian] The second of the geological periods of the Palaeozoic era, extending from c.505 to 438 million years ago. All animal life was restricted to the sea; numerous invertebrates flourished, including graptolites, trilobites, brachiopods, and corals; and the first vertebrates appeared (jawless fish). The proto-Atlantic ocean opened.

ore A mineral deposit from which metallic and non-metallic constituents can be extracted. Ores may be formed directly from crystallizing magma, or precipitated from hydrothermal fluids associated with igneous activity or concentrated in alluvial deposits after weathering.

Örebro [erebroh] 59°17N 15°13E, pop (2000e) 127 000. Capital city of Örebro county, SC Sweden; at W end of L Hjälmaren, 160 km/100 mi W of Stockholm, at mouth of R Svartån; former meeting place of the parliament (*Riksdag*); railway; university (1967); machinery, chemicals; St Nicholas's Church (18th-c), castle (16th-c, restored 19th-c), town hall (1856–62).

oregano [origahnoh, oreganoh] *marjoram*

Oregon [origuhn] pop (2000e) 3 421 400; area 251 409 sq km/ 97 073 sq mi. State in NW USA, divided into 36 counties; the 'Beaver State'; established as a fur-trading post on the site of the present town of Astoria, 1811; occupied by both Britain and the USA, 1818–46, when the international boundary was settled on the 49th parallel; became a territory, 1848; joined the Union as the 33rd state, 1859; population grew after 1842 with settlers following the Oregon Trail, and again in the late 19th-c after the completion of the transcontinental railway; capital, Salem; other chief cities, Albany, Eugene, Portland, Springfield; bounded W by the Pacific Ocean; rivers include the Columbia, Snake, Willamette; split by the Cascade Range; fertile Willamette R valley in the W, with the Coast Ranges beyond; High Desert in the E, a semi-arid plateau used for ranching and wheat-growing; Blue Mts and Wallowa Mts in the NE; Fremont Mts and Steens Mts in the S; highest point Mt Hood (3424 m/ 11 234 ft); several small lakes in the S, including Upper Klamath L and L Albert; about half the area forested; produces over a quarter of the USA's softwood and plywood; electronics, food processing, paper, fishing; livestock, wheat, dairy produce, fruit, vegetables; major tourist region; Crater Lake National Park in the SW.

Oregon boundary dispute A disagreement between the British and US governments over the frontier between respective possessions on the W coast of North America. Britain claimed the NW drainage of the Columbia R to its mouth at Fort Vancouver, while the US sought a much more northerly boundary. The Oregon Treaty (1846) settled on the 49th parallel, dipping S at Juan de Fuca Strait to maintain British claims to Vancouver Island. Residual disputes over the disposition of the Gulf/San Juan Is in the strait were settled by arbitration in 1872.

Oregon grape An evergreen shrub (*Mahonia aquifolium*), native to W North America; leaves glossy, with ovoid, spiny leaflets; flowers yellow, in short spikes; edible berries c.8 mm/ 0·3 in, blue-black with a whitish bloom. (Family: Berberidaceae.)

Oregon Trail The main route for emigration to the far W of the USA in the 1840s. The trail began at Independence, Missouri, crossed the Rockies at South Pass in Wyoming, and terminated at the mouth of the Columbia R.

Orestes [oresteez] In Greek legend, the son of Agamemnon and Clytemnestra. After his father's murder he went into exile, but returned to kill Aegisthus and his mother, for which he was pursued by the Erinyes. His character was made psychologically interesting by the Greek tragic poets.

orfe [aw(r)f] Freshwater fish (*Leuciscus idus*) widespread in lowland rivers and lakes of E Europe and C Russia; length up to 40 cm/16 in; greenish-brown on back, sides silver, underside white; also known as **ide**; **golden orfe** is an ornamental variety with orange coloration. (Family: Cyprinidae.)

Orff, Carl (1895–1982) Composer, born in Munich, SE Germany. He studied at Munich, where he helped found the Günther music school (1925). The influence of Stravinsky is apparent in his compositions. He is best known for his secular oratorio based on a 13th-c poem, *Carmina Burana* (1937). Later works include *Oedipus* (1959) and *Prometheus* (1966).

organ The name of various types of musical instruments, but without further qualification referring to an instrument in which air from a windchest, fed by bellows, is released under pressure into metal or wooden pipes of various lengths and

orders of architecture

The arrangement of the parts of a column and an entablature in classical architecture according to one of five accepted principles, or orders: Tuscan, Doric, Ionic, Corinthian, Composite. Originally developed by the ancient Greeks, the earliest surviving codification is by the 1st-c Roman Vitruvius, subsequently analysed in much greater detail by European architectural theorists from the Renaissance onwards.

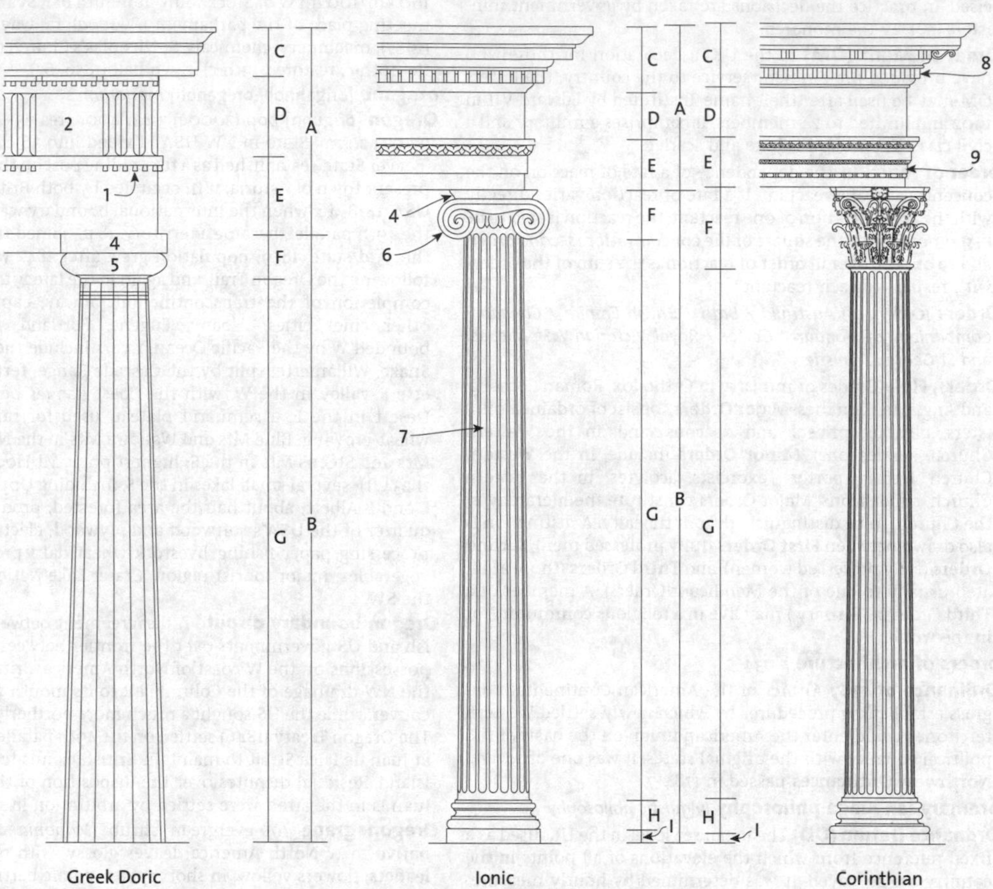

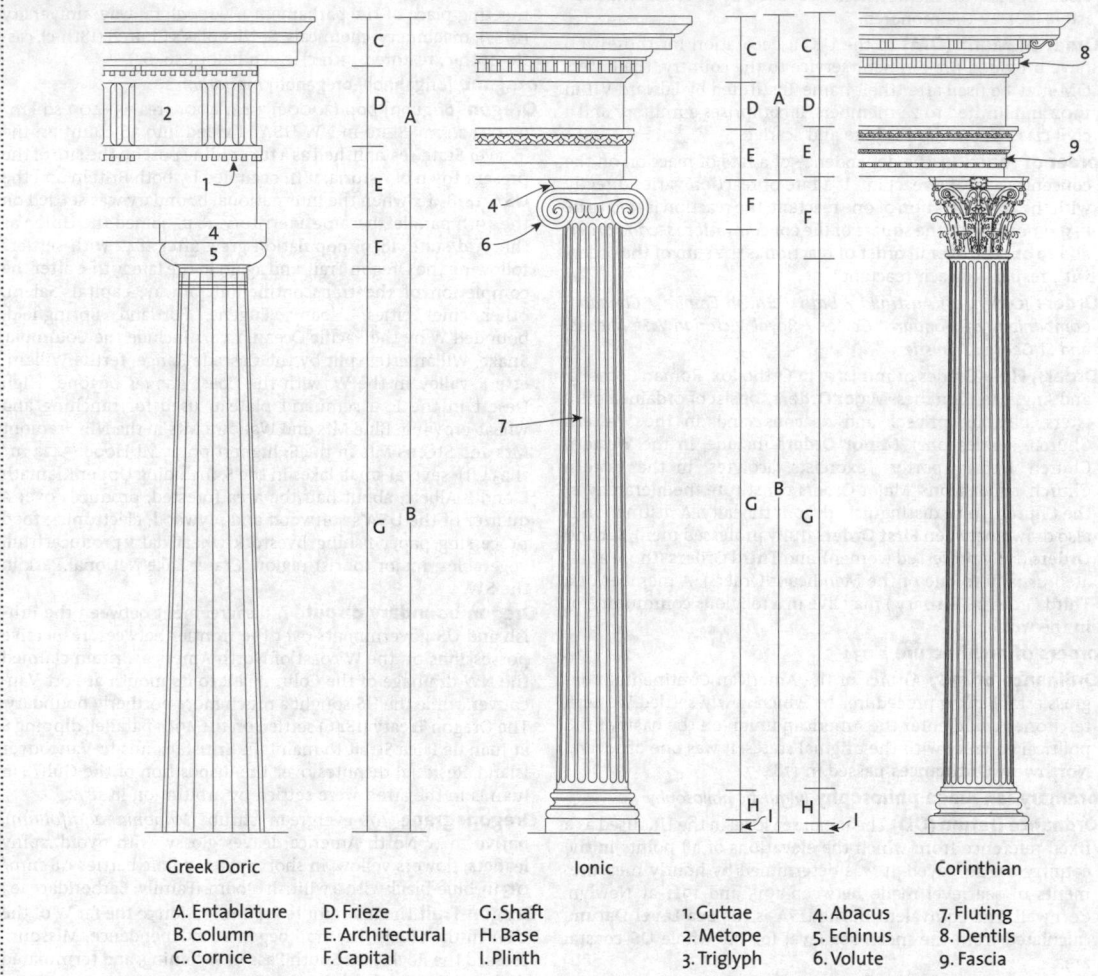

Greek Doric | Ionic | Corinthian

A. Entablature	D. Frieze	G. Shaft	1. Guttae	4. Abacus	7. Fluting
B. Column	E. Architectural	H. Base	2. Metope	5. Echinus	8. Dentils
C. Cornice	F. Capital	I. Plinth	3. Triglyph	6. Volute	9. Fascia

bores by the action of keys operated by the player's fingers or feet. The ranks of pipes, which vary in pitch, volume, and timbre according to their length, material, width of bore, and the method by which the air is made to vibrate in them, are brought into action by means of drawknobs (or *stops*); players can select a *registration* (or combination of stops) appropriate to the music they wish to play.

The earliest organs had only one manual keyboard. Most modern church organs have at least two: a 'Great' and, above that, a 'Swell', so called because the pipes it operates are enclosed within a shuttered swell-box, enabling gradations of volume to be made without changing the stops. Large organs have also a 'Choir' manual below the Great, and very large instruments often have a fourth or even a fifth manual situated above the Swell. In addition, a pedalboard, operated by the feet, is provided, and couplers enable pipes belonging to one keyboard to be sounded on another.

The **cinema organ**, with its distinctive 'voicing' and its special effects (train hooter, telephone bell, etc) was developed in the early 20th-c, especially by the Wurlitzer Company in the USA, to accompany silent films and to play popular medleys during intervals. In **electronic organs**, an invention of the 1920s, the pipes are replaced by other means of tone production, such as electromagnets and oscillators. Since they occupy only a small space and are inexpensive compared to a pipe organ, they have been installed in many churches, and are popular as domestic instruments, as well as in pop and rock groups.

organ-grinder's monkey *capuchin*

organic architecture A conception of architecture in which elements are placed in harmony rather than in juxtaposition with each other. It usually involves the rejection of classical notions of a given set of rules or solutions, and instead treats form as something latently present in the problem at hand. In particular, it is concerned with the relation of human beings and the building to the rest of nature. Stylistically, it ranges from the ornate naturalistic decoration of Antonio Gaudí to the geometric compositions of Alvar Aalto.

organic chemistry That part of chemistry which deals specifically with the structures and reactions of the compounds of carbon. Since carbon has a tendency to form chains and rings to a far greater extent than other elements, its compounds are much more numerous than those of the other elements.

organic farming Farming without synthetic chemical fertilizers, sprays, or pharmaceuticals. Fertility is maintained through the addition of animal manures and composts, and through rotations which include nitrogen-fixing plants such as clover. Weeds and diseases are controlled through rotations and cultivations, including hand weeding. In some countries there is a premium market for certified organic produce, including livestock which are guaranteed to have been fed exclusively on organically grown feedstuffs, and to have been reared as far as possible in their natural environment. There have been sharp increases in organic farming in recent years, especially in Europe, where there was a tenfold increase from 12 000 ha in 1985 to 1·2 m ha in 1996. Even with this rapid growth, organic farming still represents a very small fraction of the total land in agricultural production.

Organisation de l'Armée Secrète *OAS* 1

Organization for Economic Co-operation and Development (OECD) An international organization set up in 1961 to assist member states to develop economic and social policies aimed at high sustained economic growth with financial stability. Essentially, membership is limited only by a country's commitment to a market economy and a pluralistic democracy. Exchanges between OECD governments flow from information and analysis of trends, economic developments, patterns of trade, environment, agriculture, technology, and taxation. The USA is the biggest financial contributor, followed by Japan. The organization's 30 members are Australia, Austria, Belgium, Canada, Czech Republic, Denmark, Finland, France, Germany, Greece, Hungary, Iceland, Ireland, Italy, Japan, Luxembourg, Mexico, The Netherlands, New Zealand, Norway, Poland, Portugal, Slovakia, Spain, Sweden, Switzerland, Turkey, Korea, the UK, and the USA. The OECD is located in Paris.

Organization for European Economic Co-operation (OEEC) An organization established in 1948 by 16 W European countries and by the occupying forces on behalf of West Germany. Its formal aims were to promote trade, stability, and expansion, and it provided a framework for handling aid from the USA. It was replaced in 1961.

Organization for International Economic Co-operation *COMECON*

Organization for Security and Co-operation in Europe (OSCE), formerly known as **Conference on Security and Co-operation in Europe (CSCE)** A political grouping first established in 1975 and which came to prominence after the European political revolution of 1989–90. Its purpose is conflict prevention, crisis management, and post-conflict rehabilitation. It embraces Europe, USA, and Canada (with Albania the only European non-participant). Its secretariat opened in Prague in 1991. There were 55 members in 2004.

Organization of African Unity *African Union*

Organization of American States (OAS) A regional agency established in 1948 for the purpose of co-ordinating the work of a variety of inter-American agencies, recognized within the terms of the United Nations Charter. The organization operates through the Inter-American Conference, which meets every 5 years to decide issues of policy; consultative meetings of foreign ministers, which decide on more pressing matters; a council of representatives of all member states; its central organ, the Pan-American Union; and a series of special conferences and inter-governmental organizations. All 35 independent countries of the Americas have ratified the OAS Charter, but Cuba remains excluded (since 1962).

Organization of Arab Petroleum Exporting Countries (OAPEC) An organization formed under the umbrella of the Organization of Petroleum Exporting Countries (OPEC) in 1968 by Saudi Arabia, Kuwait, and Libya, with its headquarters in Kuwait. By 1972 all the Arab oil producers had joined.

Organization of Central American States An agency established in 1951 by Costa Rica, El Salvador, Guatemala, Honduras, and Nicaragua (Panama refused to join) to promote economic, social, and cultural co-operation. In 1965 this was extended to include political and educational co-operation. The organization has also been involved in legal reform.

Organization of Petroleum Exporting Countries *OPEC*

Organization of the Islamic Conference An organization of sovereign Muslim states, formed in 1971, with the aims of promoting Islamic solidarity, safeguarding Muslim holy places, and promoting the rights of all Muslim peoples. It had 57 members in 2004.

organum [**aw(r)**ganum] An early type of mediaeval polyphony in which one or more parts were added to a plainchant, moving mainly in parallel intervals with it.

orgone therapy [**aw(r)**gohn] A form of therapy devised by a pupil of Sigmund Freud, Wilhelm Reich (1897–1957), who claimed to have discovered a unique form of energy that he called 'primordial or cosmic orgone energy', named after his research centre at Orgonon, USA. He designed **orgone accumulators** – boxes made of alternating layers of metal and wood said to concentrate and store this energy, which was then supposedly available for healing purposes. He claimed that patients placed in these accumulators were cured of serious diseases, including cancer; but following investigation by the Federal Food and Drugs Administration in 1954 he was prosecuted as a charlatan, and died in prison.

Orhon Gol, River [**aw(r)**kon **gol**] River in Mongolia; flows for 1117 km/694 mi from the NE edge of the Gobi Desert to the W of Altanbulag, where it joins the Selenge R.

oribi [**o**ribee] A dwarf antelope (*Ourebia ourebi*) native to Africa S of the Sahara; pale brown with tufts of long hairs on the knees; naked glandular area beneath each ear; males with short spike-like horns; inhabits grasslands.

Oriental dance *East Asian dance*

orienteering A form of cross-country running with the aid of a map and compass. The sport was devised by Swedish youth leader Ernst Killander in 1918, and based on military training techniques. Popular in the Nordic countries, it developed as an international sport in the 1960s. Competitors have to reach specifically designated control points on the course by using their map and compass, and skill in using these is as important as athletic stamina.

origami [**o**rigahmee] The art of making models of animals or other objects by folding sheets of paper into shapes with the minimum use of scissors or other implements. It originated in the 10th-c AD in Japan, where it is widely practised. In many countries, it is used primarily as an educational aid for young children.

Origen [**o**rijen] (c.185–c.254) Christian biblical scholar and theologian of Alexandria, N Egypt, who became head of the catechetical school in Alexandria. He was a layman until c.230, when he was ordained in Palestine. Exiled from Alexandria by Bishop Demetrius, he established a new school in Caesarea. He was imprisoned and tortured during the persecution under Decius in 250. His writings were prolific, but his views on the unity of God and speculations about the salvation of the devil were condemned by Church Councils in the 5th–6th-c.

Original Dixieland Jazz Band The first band to make a jazz record. It consisted of Nick LaRocca (1889–1961), cornet; Eddie Edwards (1891–1963), trombone and violin; Larry Shields (1893–1953), clarinet; Henry Ragas (1890–1919), piano; and Tony Sbarbaro (1897–1969), drums. All were born in New Orleans, LA, apart from Ragas's replacement, J Russell Robinson (1892–1963), born in Palmdale, CA. The band created a sensation in New York playing at a club called the Paradise, but their recordings on 26 February 1917 of 'Livery Stable Blues' and 'Dixieland Jazz Band One-Step' rocked the nation and launched jazz as an international phenomenon.

original sin The traditional Christian doctrine that, by virtue of the Fall, every human being inherits a 'flawed' or 'tainted' nature in need of regeneration and with a disposition to sinful conduct. There have been various interpretations of the Fall and humanity's sinful condition, ranging from the literal to various symbolic accounts.

oriole A bird of the Old World family Oriolidae (**Old World orioles**, 28 species) or the New World family Icteridae (**American orioles**, c.90 species). The name is also used for the **oriole finch** (Family: Fringillidae).

Orion (astronomy) [**o**riyon] Perhaps the most conspicuous of all constellations, although only 26th in size. Equatorial, and thus visible in both hemispheres, it is a dominant sight in the midwinter sky of the N hemisphere. Its brightest stars are Rigel, the seventh-brightest star in our sky, one of the most luminous of all stars (distance 237 parsec), and Betelgeuse, a red supergiant, somewhat variable in luminosity, over 500 times the diameter of the Sun (distance 131 parsec). The **Orion nebula** is found in the 'sword' of Orion. A line of three stars marks Orion's belt. It is the nearest and brightest emission nebula, 500 parsec away, visible to the naked eye, and a veritable cosmic factory, making new stars and interstellar molecules. It is a strong radio and infrared source. Even binoculars will show its structure. In Greek mythology, Orion was a hunter who was stung to death by a scorpion for his boastfulness; in the sky, Orion sets as his slayer, in the form of the constellation Scorpius, rises.

Orion (mythology) [**o**riyon] In Greek mythology, a gigantic hunter, beloved by Eos and killed by Artemis. He was changed into a constellation, and this generated further astronomical stories – for example, that he pursues the Pleiades.

Orissa [**o**risa] pop (2000e) 37 009 000; area 155 782 sq km/60 132 sq mi. State in E India, bounded E by the Bay of Bengal; ceded to the Marathas, 1751; taken by the British, 1803; subdivision of Bengal until 1912, when province of Bihar and Orissa created; separate province, 1936; became a state, 1950; capital, Bhubaneswar; governed by a 147-member Legislative Assembly; R Mahanadi dammed to form the Hirakaud Reservoir

(1957), largest earth dam in the world; 65% of population depend on agriculture; rice, wheat, oilseed, sugar cane, jute, forestry, fishing; chromite, dolomite, graphite, iron ore, limestone; cement, fertilizer, sugar, glass, machinery, textiles, crafts; tourism in the Golden Triangle (Konark, Puri, Bhubaneswar); major flooding caused by cyclone (Oct 1999).

Orkney [aw(r)knee] pop (2000e) 20 400; area 976 sq km/ 377 sq mi. Group of islands off NE Scotland, UK; separated from Scottish mainland (S) by the Pentland Firth; 15 main islands (especially Mainland, South Ronaldsay, Sanday, Westray, Hoy), and many smaller islands; c.20 islands inhabited; generally low-lying, with steep cliffs on W side; capital, Kirkwall, on Mainland; Norse dependency from 9th-c; annexed by Scotland from Norway and Denmark, 1472; fishing, farming, weaving; North Sea oil terminal on Flotta; oil service bases on Mainland and Hoy; several prehistoric remains, notably Standing Stones at Stenness (W Mainland), c.3000 BC, and Neolithic village at Skara Brae (W Mainland); isolated stack (height 137 m/449 ft), Old Man of Hoy (NW of Hoy); Scapa Flow, sea area within the islands, used in World Wars 1 and 2 as a major naval anchorage; German Fleet surrendered there in 1918, but in 1919 was scuppered by its skeleton crews.

Orlando 28°33N 81°23W, pop (2000e) 186 000. Seat of Orange Co, C Florida, USA; settled c.1844; airfield; railway; tourism, aerospace, and electronic industries, trade in citrus fruit and vegetables; Walt Disney World.

Orleans [aw(r)leeanz], Fr **Orléans**, ancient **Aurelianum** 47°54N 1°52E, pop (2000e) 110 000. Ancient town and capital of Loiret department, C France; on right bank of R Loire, 92 km/57 mi SSW of Paris; associated with Joan of Arc, 'The Maid of Orleans', who raised the English siege here in 1429; road and rail junction; bishopric; university (1309); centre of fruit and vegetable region; textiles, clothing, blankets, food processing, sparkling wines, agricultural equipment; cathedral (13th–16th-c), town hall (16th-c), episcopal palace, museum of fine art; Feast of Joan of Arc (May).

Orléans, Charles, duc d' (Duke of) [aw(r)layã] (1391–1465) French soldier, nobleman, and poet, born in Paris, France. In 1406 he married his cousin Isabella, the widow of Richard II of England. He commanded at Agincourt (1415), and was taken prisoner and carried to England, where he lived for 25 years, composing courtly poetry in French and English. Ransomed in 1440, he then maintained a kind of literary court at Blois. His son became Louis XII.

Orléans, Louis Philippe Joseph, duc d' (Duke of) [aw(r)layã], known as **Philippe Egalité** ('equality') (1747–93) Bourbon prince, born in Saint-Cloud, NC France, the cousin of Louis XVI and father of Louis Philippe. He became the Duc de Chartres in 1752, and inherited his father's title in 1785. At the Revolution he proved a strong supporter of the Third Estate against the privileged orders, and in 1792 renounced his title of nobility for his popular name. At the Convention he voted for the king's death, but was himself arrested, after the defection of his eldest son to the Austrians (1793), and guillotined.

Orléans, House of The junior branch of the Valois and Bourbon dynasties in France, the title of which fell to four individual lines: Philippe de Valois (1336–75), created duke in 1344 but died without issue; Louis I de Valois (1372–1407), whose descendants held the title until 1544; Gaston (1608–60), the Bourbon third son of Henry IV, made duke in 1626; and Louis XIV's younger brother Philippe (1640–1701), from whom descended the Regent Orléans (1674–1723), Philippe 'Egalité' (1747–93), who died in the French Revolution, and Louis Philippe (1773–1850), 'King of the French'. The latter's son, Ferdinand Philippe (1810–42), was the last to hold the ducal title.

Ormandy, Eugene [aw(r)mandee], originally **Jenö Ormandy** (1899–1985) Conductor, born in Budapest, Hungary. A child prodigy, he studied the violin in Budapest, became an orchestral player in Berlin, then emigrated to the USA (1921), and became a US citizen (1927). He took up conducting, and headed the Minneapolis Symphony (1931–6) before taking the podium of the Philadelphia Orchestra in 1936 (for two years co-conductor with Stokowski). He remained at that post until his retirement in 1980, maintaining the voluptuousness of sound for which the orchestra was both praised and criticized.

ormer *abalone*

ormolu or **ormulu** A gilded metal alloy of copper, zinc, and tin used in France since the 17th-c for candelabra, clocks, and other decorative luxury objects, and for mounting elaborate furniture. It was adopted more sparingly in England from the mid-18th-c.

Ornithischia [aw(r)nithiskia] The bird-hipped dinosaurs, characterized by the backwards pointing pubis bone in the pelvic girdle, similar to that of birds. They comprise four exclusively plant-eating groups: the ankylosaurs, the ceratopsians, the stegosaurs, and the ornithopods such as the hadrosaurs and *Iguanodon*.

Ornitholestes [aw(r)nitholesteez] *Coelurus*

ornithology The study of birds. It includes observations on the evolutionary relationships of the different groups, the distribution of species and populations, ecology, conservation, migration, behaviour of individuals, birdsong, anatomy, physiology, biochemistry, and genetics. More than most other scientific disciplines, ornithology has benefited from the enthusiastic involvement of amateurs and the co-ordination of their observations.

orogeny [orojenee] A period of mountain-building involving intense deformation and subsequent uplift of rocks when crustal plates collide. The plate boundaries define an **orogenic belt** which forms a fold-mountain chain. Metamorphism and igneous intrusion take place at depth in the orogenic belt. Examples include the Pacific belt, where the continental crust collides with the oceanic crust, and the Himalayas, which resulted from the collision of the Indian and Asian continental plates.

orographic rain [orografik] A type of precipitation which occurs when an airstream crosses a mountain barrier. It is forced to rise, cool, and (if moist) condense. Rain falls on the windward side of the barrier, and dry air descends on the leeward or sheltered side.

Oromo A cluster of Cushitic-speaking peoples of Ethiopia and N Kenya; the largest group in Ethiopia, their former name **Galla** (Amharic: 'slave') is no longer in official use. Traditionally pastoralists, the groups in N Ethiopia are farmers, while the S Oromo are still cattle herders. The S Oromo have preserved much of their traditional social organization and religion; the N Oromo have mostly become Christian or Muslim.

Orozco, José Clemente [oroskoh] (1883–1949) Painter, born in Ciudad Guzmán (formerly Zapotlán el Grande), W Mexico. He studied engineering and architectural drawing in Mexico City, and art at the Academia San Carlos (1906–10). One of the greatest mural painters of the 20th-c, he decorated many public buildings in Mexico and the USA. His work frequently embraced the themes of the Mexican Revolution, and the mechanization and dehumanization of life in the metropolis. His best-known works include 'Soldadero' (c.1917), 'Christ Destroys His Cross' (1922), 'Omniscience' (1925), and 'Juárez Reborn' (1948).

Orpheus [aw(r)fyoos] A legendary Greek poet from Thrace, able to charm beasts and even stones with the music of his lyre. In this way he obtained the release of his wife Eurydice from Hades. He was killed by the maenads, and his head, still singing, floated to Lesbos.

Orphism A modern art movement which flourished c.1912, experimenting with pure colour in ways that heralded abstract painting. The leading exponent was Delaunay.

orris A white-flowered species of iris (*Iris germanica*, variety *florentina*), with fleshy rhizomes which provide **orris root**, used in perfumery. (Family: Iridaceae.)

Ørsted, Hans Christian [oe(r)sted], also spelled **Oersted** (1777–1851) Physicist, born in Rudkøbing, S Denmark. He became a professor at Copenhagen (1806), where in 1820 he discovered the magnetic effect of an electric current. The unit of magnetic field strength used to be named after him.

Ortega y Gasset, José [aw(r)tayga ee gaset] (1883–1955) Philosopher and existentialist humanist, born in Madrid, Spain. He studied at Madrid and in Germany, and became professor of metaphysics at Madrid (1910). His critical writings on modern authors made him an influential figure, and his *La rebelión de las masas* (1930, The Revolt of the Masses) foreshadowed the Civil War. His 'perspectivism' asserted the uniqueness and equal validity of the infinity of different possible interpretations of the world, and he grounded ultimate reality in the life of the individual ('I am I and my circumstances'). He lived in voluntary exile in South America and Portugal (1936–48).

Ortelius [aw(r)teelius], Lat name of **Abraham Ortels** (1527–98) Cartographer and engraver, born in Antwerp, N Belgium. He was trained as an engraver, and became interested in map-making in c.1560. His *Theatrum orbis terrarum* (1570, trans Epitome of the Theatre of the World) was the first great atlas.

orthicon An electron tube used extensively in early television cameras, but now superseded by photoconductive vidicon tubes or charge-coupled devices. The orthicon tube made broadcast television practical, converting the optical image into an electrical signal.

orthoclase [aw(r)thoklayz] A form of the mineral potassium feldspar; usually pink and a primary constituent of granite.

orthodontics *dentistry*

Orthodox Church or **Eastern Orthodox Church** A communion of self-governing Churches (with adherents estimated at over 220 million in 2004) recognizing the honorary primacy of the Patriarch of Constantinople and confessing the doctrine of the seven Ecumenical Councils (from Nicaea I, 327, to Nicaea II, 787). It includes the patriarchates of Alexandria, Antioch, Constantinople, and Jerusalem, and the Churches of Russia, Bulgaria, Cyprus, Serbia, Georgia, Romania, Greece, Poland, Albania, and the Czech and Slovak Republics. It developed historically from the Eastern Roman or Byzantine Empire. In doctrine it is strongly trinitarian, and in practice stresses the mystery and importance of the sacraments, of which it recognizes seven. Episcopal in government, the highest authority is the Ecumenical Council.

orthographic projection A system of related two-dimensional views of an object with all lines drawn to scale. The object is considered to be enclosed within a glass box, and the drawing consists of the three views observed through (or projected onto) the top, front, and side of the box, which is then unfolded to give a flat sheet containing the three views. The view through (or on) the top of the box is known as the *plan*; the other two views are the *front elevation* and *end elevation*. Internal detail is shown by sectional views.

orthopaedics / orthopedics [aw(r)thopeediks] The branch of surgery concerned with injuries and disorders affecting the skeleton, ie the bones and joints and associated connective tissues and muscle tendons. It includes the diagnosis and treatment of fractures and dislocations, the correction of congenital and acquired deformities and abnormalities of posture, and the surgical re-alignment or replacement of diseased or damaged joints by artificial prostheses. It also provides surgical and medical treatment for tumours and bone infections, for complaints such as backache and sciatica, and for prolapsed intervertebral and degenerative disorders of the spine.

Orthoptera [aw(r)thoptera] An order of medium to large insects found in all terrestrial habitats, from soil burrows to tree canopies; hindlegs usually modified for jumping; forewings leathery or parchment-like; many produce sound by rubbing their limbs or wings (*stridulation*).

ortolan [aw(r)tohlan] A bunting found from Europe to Mongolia (*Emberiza hortulana*) (winters in N Africa), inhabiting bushy open country, rocky hillsides, and cultivation; eats seeds and insects. also known as the **ortolan bunting** or **garden bunting**.

Orton, Joe, popular name of **John Kingsley Orton** (1933–67) Playwright and actor, born in Leicester, Leicestershire, C England, UK, and trained at the Royal Academy of Dramatic Art, London. His exuberant tastelessness established him as a pioneer of a style of black farce. His play *What the Butler Saw* (1969) carried the farce tradition of threatened adultery into the forbidden realms of incest and sexual violence. Two years before its performance he was bloodily murdered by his male lover, who subsequently took his own life. Other works include *Entertaining Mr Sloane* (1963) and *Loot* (1964–5). *The Orton Diaries* (1986) contain startling revelations.

Orust [ooruhst] area 346 sq km/134 sq mi. Swedish island in the Kattegat, off SW coast of Sweden; separated from the mainland by a narrow channel 1·6–5 km/1–3 mi wide; length, 22 km/14 mi; width, 16 km/10 mi; second largest island in Sweden.

Orwell, George, pseudonym of **Eric Arthur Blair** (1903–50) Novelist and essayist, born in Motihari, Bengal, E India. He was educated at Eton, and served in Burma in the Indian Imperial Police (1922–7), but rejected the political injustice of imperial life (recounted in the novel *Burmese Days*, 1934) to live a life of poverty in the East End of London and in Paris, which became the subject for his book *Down and Out in Paris and London* (1933). Similarly researched experiences led to the writing of *A Clergyman's Daughter* (1935), *Keep the Aspidistra Flying* (1936), *The Road to Wigan Pier* (1937), *Homage to Catalonia* (1938) and *The Lion and the Unicorn* (1941). His experience of fighting for the Republicans in the Spanish Civil War intensified his political commitment to the Left. During World War 2, he was war correspondent for the BBC and the *Observer*, and wrote for the *Tribune*. His intellectual honesty motivated his biting satire of Communist ideology in *Animal Farm* (1945) – a masterpiece which was equalled by his novel *1984* (1949), a pessimistic satire about the threat of totalitarianism and the mechanistic society of the future. He died of tuberculosis a few months after its publication.

Orycteropodidae [orikteropodidee] A family of insectivorous mammals (Tubulidentata) found in open grassland and brushland of the Ethiopian region; only member, the aardvark.

oryx [oriks] A grazing antelope with very long slender horns; pale with striking white and dark markings on face and underparts; three species: the **oryx** (also known as the **Cape oryx**, **beisa oryx**, **fringe-eared oryx**, or **gemsbok**) (*Oryx gazella*) and the **scimitar** or **white oryx** (*Oryx dammah*), both from Africa; and the **Arabian** or **white oryx** (*Oryx leucoryx*) from the Middle East.

Osaka [ohsaka], formerly **Naniwa** 34°40N 135°30E, pop (2000e) 2 672 000. Port capital of Osaka prefecture, S Honshu, Japan, on NE shore of Osaka-wan Bay; one of the power centres of Hideyoshi, and then during the Tokugawa shogunate, 17th–19th-c; major shipping and trade developments from 18th-c; leading centre for traditional puppet theatre (*bunraku*); focus of abortive peasant revolt, 1837; city almost completely destroyed in World War 2; now third largest city in Japan; airport; railway; subway; several universities; part of the Osaka–Kobe industrial area; commerce, steel, textiles, chemicals, brewing, printing; famous puppet theatre; Osaka Castle, municipal museum, electric science museum, Fujita museum, Shintennoji temple (6th-c), Sumiyoshi Shrine (present buildings, 1808); Nagai Stadium (1996); Tenjin Matsuri river races (Jul); Great Exhibition (1970).

Osama bin Laden, also **Usama bin Ladin** [usama bin laden] (1958–) Wealthy Saudi guerrilla leader, born in Riyadh of a Yemeni family. After succeeding in business he moved to Afghanistan, where he supported and supplied the Mujahideen fighting against the Soviet occupation. He then founded al-Qaeda (see separate entry), and called for a jihad against the 'Judao-Christian alliance occupying Islamic sacred land in Palestine and the Arabian Peninsula'. In 1991 he moved to the Sudan, from where he was expelled in 1996 for organizing bombing and assassination campaigns. He was accused by the USA of being behind the 1998 bomb attacks on their embassies in Kenya and Tanzania, and the bombing of the USS *Cole* warship in the port of Aden, Yemen in 2000. Subsequently he conducted his terrorist campaigns under the protection of the Taliban in Afghanistan. He was named as the chief suspect in the assaults on the World Trade Center, New York, and the Pentagon, Washington, in September 2001, with subsequent events clarifying his role in the event, but his whereabouts became unknown as the US-led attack on the Taliban progressed later that year. Since 2002 occasional tape-recordings purporting to come from him have been made public.

Osborne, John (James) (1929–94) Playwright, film producer, and actor, born in London, UK. Educated at public school in Devon, he was briefly a copywriter, and he wrote his first plays while working as an actor in repertory theatres. *Look Back in Anger* (1956, filmed 1958), his first play as sole author, established him as the first of the 'Angry Young Men'. *The Entertainer* (1957, filmed 1959), confirmed his position as the leading young exponent of British social drama. Among other works are *Luther* (1960, filmed 1971), *Inadmissible Evidence* (1964, filmed 1965), and *West of Suez* (1971), while *Déjàvu* (1991) rediscovers Jimmy Porter a generation later. He also wrote the screenplay of *Tom Jones* (1964, Oscar), and two volumes of outspoken and acerbic autobiography, *A Better Class of Person* (1981, televised 1985) and *Almost a Gentleman* (1991).

Osbourne, Ozzie, popular name of **John Michael Osbourne** (1948–) Rock musician and television entertainer, born in Aston, Birmingham, UK. After a troubled childhood, he made a career in music, forming Rare Breed, which eventually developed into Black Sabbath. He achieved international recognition following the success of a weekly MTV show, *The Osbournes* (2002–), a mixture of reality television and family sitcom chronicling events in the life of himself and his family.

Oscar The familiar name for the statuette awarded annually by the American Academy of Motion Picture Arts and Sciences for outstanding performances and creative and technical achievement in films shown during the preceding year. There are many accounts of the origin of the name, all speculative: in one account, it arose when a secretary at the Academy said that the figure reminded her of her Uncle Oscar. The statuette is 34·3 cm (13·5 in) high and weighs about 4 kg (8·5 lb); the gold plated bronze human figure was executed by the American sculptor George Stanley, based on sketches by the art director Cedric Gibbons.

oscillation A repetitive periodic change. Electrical currents in radio receivers oscillate, for example. Mechanical oscillations, such as those in a building caused by passing traffic or in a plucked guitar string, are usually called *vibrations*.

oscillator A circuit for converting direct current (DC) into alternating current (AC), of a required frequency. Part of the output is returned via a feedback circuit to the input. By varying the components of the feedback circuit, the oscillator can be 'tuned' to a certain frequency.

Osee *Hosea, Book of*

O'Shane, Pat(ricia) June (1941–) Magistrate, born in Mossman, Queensland, NE Australia. She studied at the University of New South Wales, and in 1978 became the first person of Aboriginal descent to be called to the bar. In 1981 she became head of the New South Wales State Ministry of Aboriginal Affairs. She was appointed a magistrate in the local courts of New South Wales in 1986, and has made a number of progressive, well-publicized decisions concerning women and Aboriginal people.

Osheroff, Douglas D [osherof] (1945–) Physicist, born in Aberdeen, Washington, USA. He studied at Cornell University, working under Lee and Richardson as part of the team which in 1972 discovered the superfluidity of helium-3. He shared the Nobel Prize for Physics in 1996.

osier A species of willow forming a shrub or small tree (*Salix viminalis*), growing to 3–5 m/10–16 ft; native to Europe and Asia, and often grown as a source of *withies*, long pliant stems produced in numbers when the plants are coppiced and used, for example, in basketwork. (Family: Salicaceae.)

Osiris [ohsiyris] Ancient Egyptian god, the husband of Isis. Originally he was the king of Egypt; his brother Seth murdered him and scattered the pieces of his body. These were collected by Isis; and Osiris, given renewed life, was made the king of the Underworld. After the cult of the dead was developed during the Middle Kingdom, Osiris was seen as the judge of the soul after death.

Ösling or **Oesling** [oesling] Geographical region in the Ardennes, N Luxembourg; wooded and less fertile than the Gutland ('good land') to the S, but largely agricultural; occupies 828 sq km/320 sq mi (32%) of Luxembourg.

Oslo [ozloh], formerly **Christiania** or **Kristiania** 59°55N 10°45E, pop (2000e) 483 000. Capital city of Norway, at the head of Oslo Fjord, SE Norway; founded, 11th-c; under the influence of the Hanseatic League, 14th-c; destroyed by fire, 1624; rebuilt by Christian IV of Denmark and Norway and renamed Christiania; cultural revival, 19th-c; capital, 1905; renamed Oslo, 1925; bishopric; airports; railway; university (1811); metalworking, foodstuffs, clothing, shipbuilding, trade in timber, paper; largest port in Norway, the base of a large merchant shipping fleet; cathedral (17th-c), royal palace (1825–48), Akershus Castle (13th-c), Norwegian folk museum, national gallery, national theatre.

osmiridium [ozmiridium] A naturally occurring alloy of osmium and iridium in which the iridium content is less than 35%; *iridosmine* has osmium greater than 35%. It occurs with platinum ores.

osmosis *osmotic pressure*

osmotic pressure [ozmotik] The pressure that must be exerted on a solution containing a given concentration of solute separated from a sample of the pure solvent by a membrane permeable only to the solvent, in order to prevent the solvent's passage through the membrane from solvent to solution. It is usually directly proportional to the concentration, and thus may be used to determine the molecular weights of unknown solutes. Exerting a pressure greater than the osmotic pressure causes solvent to pass through the membrane from solution to solvent; this 'reverse osmosis' is a method of purifying water. Osmosis is an important process in living organisms, especially aquatic organisms. Many are **osmoregulators**, maintaining the osmotic concentration of their body fluids at a level independent of that of the surrounding medium.

Osnabrück [ohznabrük] 52°17N 8°03E, pop (2000e) 168 000. Manufacturing city in SW Lower Saxony province, Germany, 48 km/30 mi NE of Münster; badly bombed in World War 2; railway; linked to the Mittelland Canal; bishopric; university (1973); iron and steel, machine tools, cars, textiles, paper; cathedral (13th-c), episcopal palace (17th-c).

osprey A large bird of prey (*Pandion haliaetus*), inhabiting sea coasts or inland waters worldwide, also known as **fish hawk** or **fish eagle**; dives on fish, grasping them in its talons; soles of feet have spines to aid grip. (Family: Pandionidae.)

Ossa, Mount Highest mountain in Tasmania (1617 m/5305 ft); situated within the Cradle Mt–L St Clair national park (area 1319 sq km/509 sq mi).

Ossian or **Oisín** Legendary Irish poet and warrior, the son of the 3rd-c hero Fingal or Fionn MacCumhail. The Scottish poet **James Macpherson** (1736–96) professed to have collected and translated his works, though it was later shown that the poems, such as the epic *Fingal*, were largely of his own devising. Nonetheless they were well received in Europe, and influenced the Romantic movement.

Ossory An ancient Irish kingdom, co-extensive with the diocese of Ossory (seat, Kilkenny), conquered by Anglo-Norman invaders in the late 12th-c. Thereafter the most powerful families in the area were the Marshals, Earls of Pembroke, Wales, and Lords of Leinster (1199–1245), and the Butlers, created Earls of Ormond (1328) and Ossory (1528).

Ostade, Adriaen van [ostahduh] (1610–85) Painter and engraver, born in Haarlem, The Netherlands. He was a pupil of Frans Hals, and his use of chiaroscuro shows the influence of

Rembrandt. His subjects are taken mostly from everyday life, for example tavern scenes, farmyards, markets, and village greens. His 'Alchemist' is in the National Gallery. His brother **Isaak** (1621–49) treated similar subjects, but excelled at winter scenes and landscapes.

Ostend, Flemish **Oostende**, Fr **Ostende** 51°13N 2°55E, pop (2000e) 69 700. Seaport in West Flanders province, W Belgium, on the North Sea coast; principal ferry port for UK (Dover and Folkestone); most important seaport and largest seaside resort in Belgium; headquarters of the Belgian fishing fleet; railway; shipbuilding, fish processing, soap; spa resort, promenade, casino, racecourse, Chalet Royal; Blessing of the Sea (Jul).

osteoarthritis A common disease of joints of humans and other animals; also known as **osteoarthrosis**. Over 80% of those over middle age are affected. The condition is a primary degeneration and disintegration of the articular cartilage, which tends to affect the weight-bearing joints such as the hips; but no joint is immune. The cause is unknown, though wear and tear is often invoked. Osteoarthritis may occur at an earlier age in joints affected by bone fracture or by other diseases, such as rheumatoid arthritis, in which the alignment of joint surfaces has been affected. The main symptom is pain and stiffness of the joint. When this is severe and affects the hip or knee joints, replacement by an artificial joint of steel and polyethelene may be successful.

osteogenesis imperfecta *brittle bone syndrome*

osteology The scientific study of bone and bones, involving both their microscopic and macroscopic structure. It is used in anthropology for species identification and carbon dating, in clinical medicine for the assessment of development and nutritional status of the individual, and in forensic medicine for the reconstruction and sexing of victims.

osteomalacia [ostiohmal**ay**sha] A metabolic disorder of bone caused by a lack of vitamin D. In children and adolescents, normal growth is retarded, and the condition is called *rickets*. In adults, the bones become demineralized and often show small fractures at points of stress, such as in the pelvis. Generalized bone and muscle pain are common symptoms.

osteomyelitis [ostiohmiyel**iy**tis] Infection within bone. It arises either as a result of blood-borne infection or, less commonly, following direct injury. It causes local pain and fever, and if untreated leads to bone destruction. A variety of micro-organisms may be responsible, most commonly *Staphylococci*.

osteopathy [ostiopathee] A system of treatment originally based on the belief that abnormalities in the skeletal system are responsible for a wide range of diseases by interfering with the blood and nerve supply to the region affected. Today less ambitious claims are made, and osteopaths concentrate on the treatment of backache, and pains in the legs, neck, and head. Like chiropractors they use massage and manipulation, stretch various joints, and apply high-velocity thrusts. Most of the evidence for their success is anecdotal, and today there is no clear distinction between chiropractic and osteopathy.

osteoporosis [ostiohporohsis] Thinning and weakening of bones because of a loss of tissue substance. It is obvious on X-rays as a reduction in bone density. It is common in elderly women, and is related to a reduction in the level of sex hormones. Affected women develop a characteristic stooping posture due to collapse of the vertebrae, and are prone to fractures, especially of the hip. Sex hormone replacement therapy can prevent osteoporosis in menopausal women. Regular exercise also helps, since the stress on the bones stimulates them to maintain their density.

Ostia [**os**tia] The ancient town situated at the mouth of the Tiber in W Italy. It was Rome's main naval base during the Punic Wars. Under the Roman empire, it was the main port; here the precious grain cargoes were unloaded and warehoused before being taken up the Tiber to the capital.

Ostpolitik [ostpoliteek] The policy initiated in West Germany in the 1960s to normalize relations with communist countries which recognized the German Democratic Republic (GDR), and to reduce hostility between West Germany and its Eastern neighbours. It led to peace treaties with Poland and the USSR, the recognition of the Polish border (the Oder–Neisse Line) and, most significantly, the recognition of the GDR. Largely masterminded by Willy Brandt, the policy had the broader aim of generally improving relations between West and East, and can be viewed as a forerunner of detente.

ostracism In ancient Athens, the means whereby unpopular citizens could be banished for up to 10 years without loss of property or citizenship. Votes were cast by writing on *ostraka* (potsherds) the names of the citizens to be banished.

ostracod A small, short-bodied crustacean with a hinged bivalved shell that completely encloses the body; legs typically adapted for walking over substrate; over 10 000 fossil species and 5700 living species known from marine, freshwater, and occasionally terrestrial habitats. (Class: Ostracoda.)

Ostrava [ostrava] 49°50N 18°13E, pop (2000e) 333 000. Industrial capital of Severomoravský region, Czech Republic; near junction of Oder and Ostravice Rivers; important strategic position in mediaeval times; airport; railway; metal industries, coal mining, chemicals, machinery, rolling stock.

ostrich The largest living bird (*Struthio camelus*) (height up to 2·75 m/9 ft); unable to fly; fastest animal on two legs (c.70 kph/45 mph); largest egg of any living bird (the same volume as 40 hen's eggs); inhabits dry areas of Africa; eats plants and some lizards. The **American ostrich** is an obsolete name for the rhea. (Family: Struthionidae.)

Ostrogoths A Germanic people, forming one of the two great Gothic tribes, who entered Italy in 489 and established a kingdom under Theodoric, traditionally a descendant of the Ostrogothic chieftain Hermanaric, defeated by the Huns in 375. The kingdom collapsed in the mid-6th-c, but was revived by the Lombards.

O'Sullivan, Ronnie, popular name of **Ronald Antonio O'Sullivan** (1975–) Snooker player, born in Wordsley, Wolverhampton, West Midlands, C England, UK. Brought up in Essex, he proved a talented young player and turned professional in 1992. His achievements to date include the British Open (1994), three UK Championship titles (1993, 1997, 2001), World Championship title (2001), and the European Open (2003). Nicknamed 'the Rocket', he also compiled the fastest-ever 147 maximum break (5 min 20 sec), completed during the 1997 World Championships.

Oswald, St (c.605–642) Anglo-Saxon king of Northumbria (633–41), the son of Ethelfrith of Benicia. Having been converted at Iona, he established Christianity in Northumbria with St Aidan's help. He fell in battle with the pagan King Penda. Feast day 5 August.

Oswald, Lee Harvey (1939–63) Alleged killer of President John F Kennedy, born in New Orleans, Louisiana, USA. A Marxist and former US marine, he lived for a while in the USSR (1959–62). He was arrested some hours after Kennedy's assassination (22 November 1963) on a charge of murdering a police officer in another incident. The following day he was also charged with the murder of President Kennedy. Before he could come to trial, he was shot at close range by nightclub owner Jack Ruby. The Warren Commission (1964) held him to be responsible for the assassination, although the belief that he was part of a conspiracy still persists.

Oswega / Oswega tea [osweeguh] *bergamot* 1

Otaka, Tadaaki [ohtaka] (1947–) Japanese conductor. He studied at the Toho Gakuen School of Music and the Vienna Hochschule, and was a student with the NHK (Japanese Broadcasting Corporation) Symphony Orchestra (1968–70), making his professional debut with the NHK (1971), and his US debut in 1985. He became conductor of the Tokyo Philharmonic Orchestra (1971–91, laureate 1991–), principal conductor of the BBC National Orchestra of Wales (1987–95, laureate 1996–), and music adviser and principal conductor of the Kioi Sinfonietta, Japan (1995–).

Otis, Elisha (Graves) [ohtis] (1811–61) Inventor, born in Halifax, Vermont, USA. A master mechanic in a bedstead factory, he was put in charge of the construction of a new factory at Yonkers, NY. There he designed a spring-operated safety device which would hold lifting platforms securely if there was any failure of tension in the rope (1852). He opened a shop, patented his 'elevator', and exhibited it dramatically in a rope-cutting incident at an Exposition in New York City in 1854, after which orders came in rapidly for passenger as well as goods lifts. He also patented a new type of steam-powered lift in 1861.

O'Toole, Peter (Seamus) (1932–) Actor, born in Connemara, Co Galway, W Ireland. A journalist and member of the submarine service, he attended the Royal Academy of Dramatic Art, London, before joining the Bristol Old Vic, where he made his professional debut in 1955. West End success and a season with the Royal Shakespeare Company established his stage reputation, while his performance in *Lawrence of Arabia* (1962) made him an international film star. Adept at drama, comedy, or musicals, he has tackled many of the great classical roles, frequently being cast as mercurial or eccentric characters. Nominated seven times for an Oscar, his films include *The Lion in Winter* (1968), *Goodbye Mr Chips* (1969), *The Stunt Man* (1980), *My Favorite Year* (1982), *The Last Emperor* (1987), and *Molokai* (1999). He received critical acclaim for his portrayal of Jeffrey Bernard in the play *Jeffrey Bernard is Unwell*, which was televised in 1999. In 2003 he was awarded an honorary Oscar.

Ottawa 45°25N 75°43W, pop (2000e) 351 300. Capital of Canada, in E Ontario, Canada, on the Ottawa R at its junction with the Rideau Canal and R; founded as Bytown, 1826; present name, 1854; capital of United Provinces, 1858; national capital, 1867; two-thirds English-speaking, one-third French; airport; railway; two universities (1848, 1942); pulp and paper, aluminium, steel, bronze, clothing, food processing, watches and clocks, glass; Peace Tower in parliament buildings, 88 m/289 ft high; Eternal Flame on Parliament Hill, lit 1967; National War Memorial, War Museum, National Library, National Art Gallery of Canada, National Museum of Natural Sciences, Museum of Science and Technology, National Archives; professional teams, Ottawa Senators (ice hockey), Ottawa Rough Riders (football); Changing of the Guard on Parliament Hill, Tulip Festival (May).

Ottawa Agreements A series of agreements concluded in Canada in 1932 at an economic conference held between Britain and its Dominions at the height of the world depression. The conference decided in favour of a limited amount of imperial preference following the adoption of a new protective tariff by the British government earlier that year.

Ottawa River, Fr **Rivière des Outaouais** Canadian river, the largest tributary of the St Lawrence; rises in the Canadian Shield, flows W, then S and SE to the St Lawrence SW of Montreal; length 1270 km/780 mi; forms the Ontario–Quebec border for most of its course; hydroelectric power; connected to L Ontario via the Rideau Canal; its river valley was an important early travel route.

otter A mammal of family Mustelidae; streamlined, with a flattened muzzle; brown with paler underparts; tail thick at base; feet usually webbed; inhabits streams and lakes; eats fish and invertebrates; 12 species in genera *Lutra* (**river otters**), *Aonyx* (**clawless otters**), and *Pteronura* (the **giant otter**).

otter hound A breed of dog, used in Britain since the 14th-c to hunt otters; excellent sense of smell; large, with short erect tail, large head, and long, pendulous ears; coat coarse, wiry, water-resistant; feet webbed.

otter shrew A mammal of the tenrec family (3 species); an insectivore, native to WC Africa; resembles the otter, with brown back and white underparts, small eyes, long flat muzzle, and tail flattened from side to side.

Ottey, Merlene (Joyce) (1960–) Athlete, born in Jamaica. She has been ranked in the world's top ten women sprinters each year since 1980. She won 73 successive sprint finals and 15 heats during 1989–91, and three Commonwealth Games titles – 200 m in 1982 and 100 m and 200 m in 1990. She has set seven Commonwealth records at 200 m and five at 100 m. She won her eighth Olympic medal in Sydney in 2000, where she was anchor runner for Jamaica, a record women's total in athletics. In 2001 she set the world veteran indoor record over 100 m with a time of 11·21 s, the third fastest time ever.

Otto I, known as **the Great** (912–73) King of the Germans (from 936) and Holy Roman Emperor (from 962). He subdued many turbulent tribes, maintained almost supreme power in Italy, and encouraged Christian missions to Scandinavian and Slavonic lands.

Otto, Nikolaus (August) (1832–91) Engineer, born near Schlangenbad, WC Germany. In 1876 he built the first internal combustion engine that operated on a four-stroke cycle, now generally known as the **Otto cycle**, even though the principle of four-stroke operation had been patented in 1862 by the French engineer **Alphonse Eugène Beau de Rochas** (1815–93).

otto *attar*

Ottoman Empire A Muslim empire founded c.1300 by Sultan Osman I (1259–1326), and originating in Asia Minor. Ottoman forces entered Europe in 1345, conquered Constantinople in 1453, and by 1520 controlled most of SE Europe (including part of Hungary), the Middle East, and N Africa. Following the 'golden age' of Sulaiman the Magnificent, the empire began a protracted decline. During the 19th-c and early 20th-c, Ottoman power was eroded by the SE European ambitions of Russia and Austria, the N African ambitions of France, Britain, and Italy, the emergence of the Balkan nations, and internal loss of authority. It joined the Central Powers in 1914, and collapsed following their defeat in 1918.

Ottonian art Art of the 10th–11th-c in Germany, named after the Holy Roman Emperors Otto I–III. Carolingian elements are combined with early Christian and Byzantine motifs. The bronze doors of Hildesheim Cathedral (1015), with their expressive biblical scenes, attest to the high standards achieved.

Otway, Thomas (1652–85) Playwright, born in Trotton, West Sussex, S England, UK. He studied at Oxford, but left without a degree, then failed as an actor and became a writer. He translated Racine and Molière, and wrote Restoration comedies, but his best-known works are the tragedies *The Orphan* (1680) and his masterpiece *Venice Preserved, or a Plot Discovered* (1682).

Ötztal Alps [oetstal], Ger **Ötztaler Alpen** Mountain range in Tirol state, W Austria, rising to 3774 m/12 382 ft at Wildspitze, Austria's second highest peak.

Ouagadougou [wagadoogoo] 12°20N 1°40W, pop (2000e) 725 300. Capital of Burkina Faso, W Africa; part of the Ivory Coast until 1947; capital of Mossi empire from 15th-c; captured by French, 1896; airfield; terminus of railway line from Abidjan (Nigeria); university (1969); textiles, soap, vegetable oil; trade in groundnuts, millet, livestock; neo-romanesque cathedral; palace of Moro Naba (Mossi Emperor).

Oudenaarde [oodenah(r)d], Fr **Audenarde** 50°50N 3°37E, pop (2000e) 27 400. Town in East Flanders province, W Belgium; site of defeat of French by Marlborough and Prince Eugene (1708); railway; traditional centre for carpet-weaving and tapestries; town hall (1526–37), Church of Onze Lieve Vrouw Pamele (begun 1235).

Ouija board [weeja, weejee] A board bearing letters, words, and numbers, upon which an indicator such as an upturned glass is placed. Several people rest their fingers on the indicator, which then moves without their conscious volition across the board. It can then purportedly spell out messages which provide information about events or situations unknown to the people present. It is alleged that information may also be received from deceased persons. The word originates from the French and German words for *yes* (*oui* and *ja*).

Oulu [ohloo], Swed **Uleåborg** 65°00N 25°26E, pop (2000e) 104 000. Seaport and capital of Oulu province, W Finland, on the Gulf of Bothnia, at mouth of R Oulu; established, 1605; destroyed by fire, 1822; airfield; railway; university (1958); shipbuilding, timber; Tar Ski Race, cross-country ski race founded in 1889; Oulu Music Summer (Jul–Aug).

ounce (zoology) *snow leopard*

Ouranus *Uranus* (astronomy)

Our Lady *Mary* (mother of Jesus)

Ouro Prêto [**ohroh praytoh**], formerly **Vila Rica** Town founded in 1711 in Minas Gerais, the mining area of NE Brazil; declared national monument, 1933; a world heritage site; centre of gold and diamond trading during the colonial era, with wealth reflected in its architecture; showcase of the work of the sculptor Antônio Francisco (Aleijadinho) Lisboa (1738–1814); on 24 June Ouro Preto becomes capital of Minas Gerais for that day only.

Ouse, River (S England) [ooz] **1** River in East Sussex, S England; rises 10 km/6 mi SW of Crawley and flows E and S for 48 km/30 mi to meet the English Channel at Newhaven.
2 River in Yorkshire, NE England; formed at the junction of the Ure and Swale Rivers near Boroughbridge; flows 96 km/60 mi SE to meet the R Trent where it becomes the Humber estuary.
3 River rising NW of Brackley in Northamptonshire, C England; flows 256 km/159 mi past Buckingham and Bedford and through the S fenland, to meet the Wash NW of King's Lynn; also known as the **Great Ouse**.
4 Tributary of the Great Ouse river, E England; flows 38 km/24 mi W along part of the Norfolk–Suffolk border to meet the Great Ouse at Brandon Creek; also known as the **Little Ouse**.

ousel *ouzel*

out-of-the-body experience (OOBE or **OBE)** An experience in which people have the sensation that their conscious self exists in a separate location from their body, such that they perceive their surroundings as if their conscious self had actually left their body. The experience often feels as real to them as normal everyday life reality.

ouzel or **ousel** A thrush (*Turdus torquatus*) native to Europe, N Africa, and SW Asia; dark with pale wings and white crescent on breast; inhabits high moorland and hillsides; also known as the **ring ouzel**. The name was formerly used for the blackbird *Turdus merula*. **Water-ouzel** is used for the unrelated dipper (*Cinclus cinclus*).

ouzo [oozoh] A traditional Greek spirit flavoured with aniseed, and usually drunk with water.

Oval, the One of the largest cricket grounds in England, located at Kennington, S London. It is owned by the Duchy of Cornwall, and is the headquarters of Surrey County Cricket Club.

Ovamboland [ohv**am**bohland] Region in N Namibia, extending W along the Namibia–Angola frontier from the Okavango R; Etosha national park in the S; chief indigenous peoples, the Ovambo; area of conflict during 1970s and 1980s between SWAPO guerrilla forces based in S Angola and South African forces.

ovarian follicle A structure within the mammalian ovary, part of which may develop into a mature ovum to be released at ovulation; also known as a **Graafian follicle** [**grah**fian], after the Dutch physiologist, Reinier de Graaf (1641–73). Each follicle consists of a primordial germ cell (*ovum*), surrounded by epithelial cells. At birth the human female may have as many as 400 000 follicles contained within the ovaries (of which only 300–400 come to maturity); at this stage they are known as primary follicles. During the early years of life, the primary follicles remain quiescent but many degenerate during this period. With the onset of puberty and menstruation several follicles each month begin to develop further, resulting in usually just one follicle discharging its ovum from the ovary into the abdominal cavity (*ovulation*). The stimulus to further development of the follicles is due to the ovaries coming into full function in response to the secretion of follicle-stimulating hormone (FSH) and luteinizing hormone (LH).

During the first half of the menstrual cycle, stimulation of the ovary by FSH causes the development and maturation of the follicle and increased oestrogen secretion. In many mammals, secretion of oestrogen at this time causes the female to be 'on heat' (in *oestrus*), this being the only time she is receptive to the male. In humans, ovulation is about halfway through the menstrual cycle. When oestrogen secretion reaches its peak in the human female, secretion of LH causes the follicle to enlarge quickly and rupture into the abdominal cavity, where the maturing ovum is collected by the uterine (Fallopian) tube. If fertilization occurs, it does so inside the uterine tube, usually within 24 hours of release of the ovum. LH secretion also causes the remains of the follicle to develop into the *corpus luteum*, which secretes progesterone and some oestrogen. Unless pregnancy occurs, the *corpus luteum* does not last for more than 12 days (progesterone is therefore not continuously secreted in the non-pregnant female). The secretion of progesterone prepares the lining of the uterus (*endometrium*) for implantation. If implantation does not result, the cessation of progesterone secretion (which occurs with regression of the corpus luteum) causes the endometrium to disintegrate and bleed (menstruation).

ovary The reproductive organ in a female animal in which the eggs are produced, and which may also produce hormones. Ovaries are typically paired, and release their eggs down *oviducts* or uterine tubes. In plants the hollow base of the carpel, containing the ovules, is termed the ovary. Its wall contributes to the fruit containing the seeds.

Overland Telegraph A telegraph line crossing Australia and linking it with the outside world; opened in 1872. The line covered 3175 km/1972 mi between Port Augusta (South Australia) to Darwin (Northern Territory), where it joined an undersea cable to Java.

overpopulation A density of population such that the available resources of an area are unable to support the resident people; contrasted with **underpopulation**, where the area is able to support a greater density. It is impossible to derive a precise figure for overpopulation, as the concept is subjective and rarely related to any agreed minimum standard of living. It is important to take account of the area under consideration. For example, the crude population density of Chad is only 7 people per sq km/19 per sq mi (2003), yet the country could be regarded as overpopulated because the harsh physical conditions mean that the land is unable to support that density. The daily (1978–80) per capita calorific intake was 1808, which is 76% of the United Nations Food and Agricultural Organization recommended minimum requirement.

over-the-counter drugs (OTCs) Those drugs which may be purchased directly from a pharmacy without a prescription, such as aspirin. Some problems arise with OTCs, such as their inappropriate use (eg an overdose) and their dangerous interactions with some prescription drugs.

over-the-counter (OTC) trading Trading in stocks and shares other than via the stock exchange. Over-the-counter shares are issued by companies too small for Stock Exchange listing; they are often considered to be a very risky investment. Dealing in these shares takes place through companies specializing in this type of stock, and not through a stockbroker. In the USA, the National Association of Securities Dealers' Automated Quotations (NASDAQ) has been described as an 'electronic over-the-counter stock market': the system does not work through the New York Stock Exchange, but directly by computer to brokers and market makers.

overture An orchestral prelude to an opera or other work, or (since the early 19th-c) an independent, usually descriptive, concert piece of similar length. The 'French overture' of the 17th–18th-c consisted of a slow section followed by a quick one, often ending with a partial return of the opening material; the contemporary 'Italian overture' was on the pattern fast–slow–fast.

Ovett, Steve [ohvet], popular name of **Steven Michael James Ovett** (1955–) Athlete, born in Brighton, East Sussex, SE England, UK. Gold medallist in the 800 m at the 1980 Olympics, he also won a bronze in the 1500 m. He broke the world record at 1500 m (three times), at one mile (twice) and at two miles. An outspoken and sometimes controversial figure, he occasionally upset the press, but remained generally popular with his fellow athletes and the spectators. As his competitive career faded he began a new role as a television commentator.

Ovid [ovid], in full **Publius Ovidius Naso** (43 BC–AD 17) Latin poet, born in Sulmo, Italy. He trained as a lawyer, but devoted himself to poetry, and visited Athens. His first success was the tragedy *Medea*, followed by *Heroides*, love letters from legendary heroines to their lords. His major poems are the three-book *Ars amatoria* (Art of Love) and the 15-book *Metamorphoses* (Transformations), written in hexameters and imitated by Goethe and Pushkin. With its startling insights into psychological states and symbolism, this is one of the most influential works from antiquity. In AD 8 he was banished, for some reason unknown, to Tomi on the Black Sea.

Oviedo [ovyaythoh] 43°25N 5°50W, pop (2000e) 197 000. Capital of Oviedo province, Asturias, NW Spain, 451 km/280 mi NW of Madrid; bishopric; airport; railway; university (1608); former capital of Asturias; commerce, cement, pharmaceuticals, domestic appliances, metal products; cathedral (14th-c); Fiesta of La Ascension (May), Fiesta of San Mateo (Sep).

Ovimbundu [ovimbundoo] A Bantu-speaking agricultural people of the Benguela Highlands of Angola, comprising some 20 indigenous chiefdoms. They formerly traded over much of C Africa, and supplied slaves to the Portuguese.

ovo-lacto vegetarians *vegetarianism*

ovulation *ovarian follicle*

ovule The female sex-cell of seed plants which, after fertilization, forms the seed. In gymnosperms the ovules lie exposed on the scales of the female cone; in flowering plants they are enclosed within an ovary.

ovum *egg*

Owen, Alun (Davies) (1926–94) Playwright, born in Liverpool, Merseyside, NW England, UK. He began as an actor in Birmingham, then became a prolific writer for television and radio. His works include *The Rough and Ready Lot* (1958), *Progress to the Park* (1959), and a musical collaboration with Lionel Bart, *Maggie May* (1964).

Owen (of the City of Plymouth), David (Anthony Llewellyn), Baron (1938–) British statesman, born in Plymouth, Devon, SW England, UK. He studied at Cambridge and London, trained in medicine, then became Labour MP for Plymouth (1966). He was under-secretary to the navy (1968), secretary for health (1974–6), and foreign secretary (1977–9). One of the so-called 'Gang of Four' who formed the Social Democratic Party (SDP) in 1981, he succeeded Roy Jenkins as its leader in 1983. Following the Alliance's disappointing result in the 1987 general election, he opposed Liberal leader David Steel over the question of the merger of the two parties. In 1988, after the SDP voted to accept merger, he led the smaller section of the Party to a short independent existence. He retired from parliament and was created a peer in 1992. With Cyrus Vance he was appointed by the UN to try to establish peace between the warring factions in former Yugoslavia (1992–3). He was made a Companion of Honour in 1994. In 1998 he launched a campaign against the proposed entry of Britain into European monetary union. He is Chancellor of Liverpool University.

Owen, Michael (James) (1979–) Footballer, born in Chester, Cheshire, NWC England, UK. A centreforward, he joined Liverpool FC in 1996, and rapidly established a reputation, becoming FA Young Player of the Year in 1997–8. In February 1998 he became the youngest player in the 20th-c to receive an England cap. By mid-1998 he had won five caps for his country, and was a member of the 1998 World Cup team, scoring one of the tournament's most memorable goals. He played in the Euro 2000 competition and the 2002 World Cup, and in April 2002 stood in for an injured David Beckham as captain, becoming the youngest England captain for 40 years. By 2004 he had won 53 caps. He was voted Sports Personality of the Year in 1998, and European Footballer of the Year in 2001. In April 2003 he notched up his 100th goal for Liverpool.

Owen, Robert (1771–1858) Social and educational reformer, born in Newtown, Powys, E Wales, UK. Apprenticed to a draper, in 1800 he became manager and part owner of the New Lanark cotton mills, Lanarkshire (now a world heritage site), where he set up a social welfare programme, and established a 'model community'. His socialistic theories were put to the test in other experimental communities, such as at Orbiston, near Glasgow, and New Harmony in Indiana, but all were unsuccessful. He was later active in the trade-union movement, and in 1852 became a spiritualist.

Owen, Wilfred (Edward Salter) (1893–1918) Poet, born at Plas Wilmot, near Oswestry, Shropshire, WC England, UK. He studied at the Birkenhead Institute and at Shrewsbury Technical School, left England to teach English in Bordeaux (1913), and began to write. Wounded in World War 1, he was sent to recuperate near Edinburgh, where he met Siegfried Sassoon, who encouraged his poetry writing. One of the most important poets of World War 1, his poems, expressing a horror of the cruelty and waste of war, were first collected in 1920 by Sassoon and reappeared in 1931 with a memoir by Edmund Blunden. Several were set to music by Britten in his *War Requiem* (1962). *The Collected Poems*, edited by C Day Lewis, were published in 1963. He was killed in action on the Western Front on his return to France, a week before the armistice.

Owens, Jesse, popular name of **James** or **John Cleveland** (1913–80) Athlete, born in Danville, Alabama, USA. Within 45 min on 25 May 1935 at Ann Arbor, MI, he set five world records (100 yd, long jump, 220 yd, 220 yd hurdles, and 200 m hurdles). His long-jump record of 26 ft 8¼ in stood for 25 years. In 1936 he showed his dominance at the Berlin Olympics, much to Hitler's annoyance, when he won four gold medals, a feat equalled only in 1984 by Carl Lewis.

owl A predatory nocturnal bird, found worldwide; large head and broad flat face; forwardly directed eyes; acute sight and hearing; kills prey with talons and swallows whole, regurgitating bones, fur, etc as pellets. There are two families: **typical owls** (Strigidae, c.120 species) and **barn owls**, **grass owls**, and **bay owls** (Tytonidae, 11 species). Tytonidae differ in having smaller eyes, long slender legs, a serrated middle claw, and a heart-shaped face. Some typical owls have ear-like tufts on their head. The name *owl* is also used for unrelated **moth owls** of the family Aegothelidae. (Order: Strigiformes.)

owlet frogmouth A nightjar-like bird found from Tasmania to New Guinea; small with long tail; inhabits forests; eats insects; also known as **owlet nightjar** or **moth owl**. (Genus: *Aegotheles*, 8 species. Family: Aegothelidae.)

owlet moth *noctuid moth*

owlet nightjar *nightjar; owlet frogmouth*

owl monkey *douroucouli*

owl parrot *kakapo*

ox A ruminant mammal of genus *Bos* (5 species); an artiodactyl. The name is used especially for the domestic bullock used as a draught animal.

oxalic acid [oksalik] IUPAC **ethanedioic acid**, HOOC–COOH, commonly occurs as the colourless crystalline dihydrate, melting point 101°C. It occurs in many plants, especially rhubarb, and is poisonous. It is a moderately strong acid, partially neutralized solutions having a pH of about 2·5. Its salts, *oxalates*, form chelates with transition metals, and are thus useful in removing rust and blood stains from clothing.

oxalis A perennial, sometimes an annual, found almost everywhere, but many native to South America and S Africa; leaves clover-like with three (sometimes more) leaflets, often folding up at night; flowers 5-petalled, funnel-shaped; fruits with catapult mechanism for dispersing seeds. Some species are grown as ornamentals. Several are serious weeds. (Genus: *Oxalis*, 800 species. Family: Oxalidaceae.)

Oxenstierna or **Oxenstern, Axel Gustafsson, Greve** (Count) [oksensherna, oksenstern] (1583–1654) Swedish statesman, born near Uppsala, E Sweden. From 1612 he served as chancellor, and negotiated peace with Denmark, Russia, and Poland; and though he sought to prevent Gustavus Adolphus from plunging into the Thirty Years' War, he supported the war effort, even after the king's death (1632). During most of the minority of Queen Christina he was effective ruler of the country (1636–44), vindicating his policies by the terms of the Peace of Westphalia (1648).

ox-eye daisy A variable clump-forming perennial (*Leucanthemum vulgare*), growing to 1 m/3¼ ft, native to Europe; lower leaves spoon-shaped with toothed margins; flower-heads up to 5 cm/2 in or more across, long-stalked, solitary; spreading outer florets white, inner disc florets yellow; also called **marguerite** and **dog** or **moon daisy**. It is widely grown as a garden ornamental and for cut flowers, and was formerly used as a medicinal herb. (Family: Compositae.)

OXFAM A British charity based in Oxford, dedicated to alleviating poverty and distress throughout the world; an abbreviated form of **Oxford Committee for Famine Relief**. Founded in 1942, most of its funds are now used to provide long-term development aid to Third World countries. Oxfam International now works in over 80 countries.

Oxford (UK), Lat **Oxonia** 51°46N 1°15W, pop (2001e) 134 200. County town of Oxfordshire, SC England, UK; on Thames and Cherwell Rivers, 80 km/50 mi NW of London; 12th-c university, granted its first official privileges in 1214; Oxford Brookes University (1992, formerly Oxford Polytechnic); Royalist headquarters in Civil War; airfield; railway; industry located in the suburb of Cowley (notably vehicles); steel products, electrical goods, paper; 12th-c cathedral; Sunrise Service (May Day); Eights Week (Jun–Jul); St Giles Market (Sep); football league team, Oxford United ('U's').

Oxford, Provisions of (1258) A baronial programme imposing constitutional limitations on the English crown. Henry III had to share power with a permanent council of barons, parliaments meeting three times a year, and independent executive officers (chancellor, justiciar, treasurer). In 1261 the pope absolved Henry from his oath to observe the Provisions.

Oxford Movement A movement within the Church of England, beginning in 1833 at Oxford, which sought the revival of high doctrine and ceremonial; also known as **Tractarianism**. Initiated by 'tracts' written by Keble, Newman, and Pusey, it opposed liberal tendencies in the Church and certain Reformation emphases. It led to Anglo-Catholicism and ritualism, and has remained influential in certain quarters of Anglicanism.

Oxfordshire pop (2001e) 605 500; area 2608 sq km/1007 sq mi. County in the S Midlands of England; Cotswold Hills to the NW, Chiltern Hills to the SW; county town, Oxford; agriculture, vehicles, paper, textiles; River Thames, Vale of the White Horse; Atomic Energy Authority laboratories at Culham.

Oxford University The oldest university in Britain, having its origins in informal groups of masters and students gathered in Oxford in the 12th-c. The closure of the University of Paris to Englishmen in 1167 accelerated Oxford's development into a *universitas*. Prestigious university institutions include the Bodleian Library, the Ashmolean Museum, the Sheldonian Theatre (1644–8), and the Oxford University Press (founded in 1585). (*see panel*)

oxidation The loss of electrons, always accompanied by reduction (the gain of the same electrons). Chemical reactions in which electrons are transferred from one atom to another are called **oxidation–reduction** or **redox** reactions. Elements in compounds are conveniently given an **oxidation state** or **oxidation number** which relates to their redox properties. These states may usually be assigned by the following rules: (1) oxygen is −2 except in the element (O) and in peroxides (−1); (2) hydrogen is +1 except in the element (O) and saline hydrides (−1); (3) halogens bonded to elements other than oxygen are −1; (4) other elements are calculated to make the sum of all the oxidation states of the atoms in an ion or molecule equal to the net charge. Thus, the oxidation state of Mn in MnO_4^- is +7, and the average for sulphur in $S_2O_3^{2-}$ is +2. The oxidation state is expressed using Roman numerals, as in manganese(VII) or Mn^{VII}.

Oxford University

College	Founded
University College	1249
Balliol	1263
Merton	1264
St Edmund Hall	1278
Exeter	1314
Oriel	1326
Queen's	1340
New College	1379
Lincoln	1427
All Souls	1438
Magdalen	1458
Brasenose	1509
Corpus Christi	1517
Christ Church	1546
Trinity	1554
St John's	1555
Jesus	1571
Wadham	1612
Pembroke	1624
Worcester	1714
St Catherine's	1868
Keble	1870
Hertford	1874
Lady Margaret Hall	1878
Somerville	1879
St Hugh's	1886
St Hilda's[1]	1893
St Peter's	1929
Nutfield[2]	1937
St Antony's[2]	1950
St Anne's	1952
Linacre[1]	1962
Wolfson[2]	1965
St Cross[2]	1965
Green[2]	1979
Rewley House[3]	1990

[1]Women's colleges
[2]Graduate colleges
[3]Continuing and part-time education college

oxides Compounds of oxygen, especially those containing the ion O^{2-}. Oxides of non-metals are called **acidic oxides**, as they react with water to give acids; for example, sulphur trioxide (SO_3) gives sulphuric acid (H_2SO_4); carbon dioxide (CO_2) gives carbonic acid (H_2CO_3). Oxides of metals are **basic oxides**, and react with water to give hydroxides, eg sodium oxide (Na_2O) gives sodium hydroxide (NaOH). **Amphoteric oxides** are those such as aluminium oxide (Al_2O_3), which reacts with strong acid as a base and with strong base as an acid.

oxidizing agent A substance which oxidizes another in a chemical reaction, being itself reduced in the process. The most important is oxygen gas (O_2), which is reduced to O^{2-}, OH^-, or H_2O when it oxidizes a metal.

oxlip A perennial with a rosette of crinkled leaves, drooping flowers at the tip of a common stalk, and a tubular calyx. The true oxlip (*Primula elatior*), from C and N Europe, has pale yellow flowers all hanging on one side of the stalk. A plant referred to as the **common oxlip** is a hybrid between the cowslip and the primrose (*Primula veris × vulgaris*), similar to the cowslip but with larger, paler flowers. (Family: Primulaceae.)

oxopropanoic acid *pyruvic acid*

oxpecker An African bird of the starling family; narrow but deep bill, short legs, and stiff tail; inhabits grassland; clings to large mammals, especially ungulates; eats flies and ticks from host's skin; also known as **tickbird**. (Genus: *Buphagus*, 2 species.)

Oxus, River *Amudarya, River*

oxyacetylene welding A technique much used in cutting metal and in joining two pieces of metal by melting them together at the point of contact (*welding*). The temperature obtained by burning acetylene with oxygen is the highest obtainable by any gas–oxygen flame (over 3200°C).

oxygen O, element 8, boiling point −183°C. By far the commonest element in the Earth's crust, of which it makes up nearly 50% in various combined forms. It also constitutes 21% of the atmosphere as diatomic molecules (O_2). Although this is very reactive, it is constantly replenished by photosynthesis. All higher forms of life depend on oxygen. The element boils at 13°C higher than nitrogen, and is isolated by the fractional distillation of air. Liquid oxygen is pale blue in colour, and is used as an oxidant. Oxygen occurs widely in organic and inorganic compounds, mainly showing oxidation state −2.

oxygen cycle The dynamic system of changes in the nature of oxygen-containing compounds circulating between the atmosphere, the soil, and living organisms. The oxygen cycle is interwoven with other cycles, such as the nitrogen cycle and the global water cycle. The main biological phase involves the use of gaseous oxygen during respiration in animals and plants, with the consequent production of water and carbon dioxide, and the use of these products by green plants during photosynthesis, resulting in the liberation of gaseous oxygen.

oxytocin [oksitohsin] A hormone (a peptide) present in the rear part of the pituitary gland (the *neurohypophysis*) of many vertebrates. In humans, it is produced in the hypothalamus, but stored in and released from the pituitary gland. In lactating females it is released when the newborn suckle, thereby promoting milk-ejection. It also induces contractions of the uterus during labour. Its role in males is unknown.

oyan *linsang*

oyster Bivalve mollusc with unequal valves, the left valve typically being cemented to a hard substrate; shell valves closed by a single muscle; often cultured for human consumption, regarded as a delicacy. Some species used for the production of pearls. (Class: Pelecypoda. Order: Ostreoida.)

oystercatcher A large plover-like bird, inhabiting coasts worldwide (except mid-ocean and polar regions) and cultivated areas; black or black-and-white; long reddish bill and legs; eats invertebrates, especially bivalve shellfish; also known as the **sea pie**. (Genus: *Haematopus*, 4 species. Family: Haematopodidae.)

Oz, Amos, originally **Amos Klausner** (1939–) Novelist, born in Jerusalem, Israel. He studied at the Hebrew University there and at Oxford, served in the Israeli army, and worked part-time as a schoolteacher as well as a writer. His novels describe the tensions of life in modern Israel, and include (trans titles) *Elsewhere, Perhaps* (1966), *My Michael* (1968), *In the Land of Israel* (1982), and *Don't Call it Night* (1995). Later books include *Panther in the Basement* (1997) and *The Same Sea* (2001).

ozalid process *photocopying*

Ozark Mountains [ohzahk] (Fr *aux arks*, 'at the arks') Highlands in SC USA, between the Arkansas and Missouri Rivers; area c.129 500 sq km/50 000 sq mi, altitude generally 300–360 m/1000–1200 ft; Boston Mts rise to 747 m/2450 ft; hydroelectricity from Bagnell Dam (Lake of the Ozarks); mining, forestry, tourism.

Ozawa, Seiji [ozahwa] (1935–) Conductor, born in Hoten, NE China. Trained in Japan, Paris, and the USA, he then conducted the Toronto and San Francisco Symphonies, before beginning in 1973 his long tenure as conductor of the Boston Symphony. He joined the Vienna State Opera in 2002.

ozone A form of oxygen having molecules O_3. It is formed by the action of ultraviolet radiation on ordinary oxygen, and is a gas, boiling point −112°C. It is unstable and a strong oxidizing agent, with bacteriocidal properties, but is corrosive to humans in any but very low concentration. Its presence in the upper atmosphere is important in protecting the Earth from excessive ultraviolet radiation.

ozone layer The part of the stratosphere at a height of c.22 km/14 mi in which the gas ozone (O_3) is most concentrated. It is produced by the action of ultraviolet light from the Sun on oxygen (O_2) in the air. The ozone layer shields the Earth from the harmful effects of solar ultraviolet radiation, but can be decomposed by complex chemical reactions, notably involving chlorofluorocarbons (CFCs), used as the pressurized propellant in some aerosol sprays, in refrigerating systems, and in the production of foam packaging. An area of 50–75% depletion of total ozone has been called an **ozone hole**, defined geographically as the area in which the total ozone amount is less than 220 Dobson Units. (1 Dobson Unit is defined as 0.01 mm thickness at standard temperature and pressure of 0°C and 1 atmosphere pressure.) During the 1980s, reports of holes above the Arctic and Antarctic led to renewed efforts in Europe to reach agreement on an accelerated reduction in CFC consumption. The main focus of attention was in the Antarctic, where the hole, steadily increasing since the 1980s, was estimated to be c.28 million sq km in September 2003. In 1987 the Montreal Protocol was signed by around 40 countries to limit the use of ozone-depleting substances (in force from 1990, since ratified by 180 countries), with the intention that consumption of CFCs would be frozen by 1999, reduced by 50% by 2005, and eliminated by 2010. Between 1986 and 1999, world global consumption of CFCs was reduced from 1·1 million to 150 000 tons, raising hopes that ozone levels would now begin to recover.

P

Pabst, G(eorg) W(ilhelm) (1885–1967) Film director, born in Raudnitz, NWC Czech Republic (formerly Raudnice, Bohemia). He began directing in 1923, and his darkly realistic, almost documentary style was acclaimed in *Die Liebe der Jeanne Ney* (1927, The Love of Jeanne Ney). Other works include his pacifist *Westfront 1918* (1930) and his great co-production with France, *Kameradschaft* (1931, Comradeship), all examples of the New Realism. The left-wing stance he took in *Die Dreigroschenoper* (1931, The Threepenny Opera), from the stage production by Bertolt Brecht and Kurt Weill, contributed to his work being banned by the Nazis after they came to power in 1933. Between 1933 and 1941 Pabst worked in France and the USA. In 1941 he moved to Vienna, where his last two films were released: *Der Letzte Akt* (The Last Ten Days of Adolf Hitler) and *Es Geschah am 20 Juli* (Jackboot Mutiny), which depicts the attempts made by Claus von Stauffenberg to assassinate Hitler.

paca [paka] A cavy-like rodent native to Central and South America; inhabits forests near water; resembles the agouti, but with a larger snout, and body marked with pale spots and horizontal lines. (Genus: *Cuniculus*, 2 species. Family: Dasyproctidae.)

pacarana [pakarana] A rare cavy-like rodent (*Dinomys branickii*); resembles the paca, but has a short bushy tail; also known as **false paca** or **Branick's paca**. (Family: Dinomyidae.)

pacemaker A cell or object that determines the rhythm at which certain events occur. In vertebrates, pacemaker cells are present in the heart and in the longitudinal muscle of the stomach and ureter. Such cells depolarize and repolarize spontaneously at basic rhythms (which can be modified by the autonomic nervous system), thereby establishing the rate of contraction. In patients with heart block (a malfunction of the sinu-atrial node or conducting system) artificial pacemakers (usually battery-operated and implanted under the skin) stimulate the heart electrically to restore and maintain higher rates of cardiac contraction.

Pachelbel, Johann [pakhelbel] (c.1653–1706) Composer and organist, born in Nuremberg, SC Germany. He held a variety of organist's posts before he returned to Nuremberg as organist of St Sebald's Church (1695). His works, which include six suites for two violins, and organ fugues, profoundly influenced J S Bach. His best-known composition is the Canon in D Major.

pachinko [pachingkoh] The Japanese game of pinball, the word coming from the sound of a steel ball running round a pinball machine. Many pachinko halls are found in all Japanese towns, with bright lighting, neon signs, and loud music. They have row upon row of vertically installed machines, with facing seats for customers.

Pachomius, St [pakohmius] (4th-c) Founder of communal monasticism, from Egypt. He superseded the system of solitary reclusive life by founding (AD c.318), the first monastery on the island of Tabenna on the Nile, with its properly regulated communal life and rule. He founded 10 other monasteries, including two convents for women. Feast day 9 May.

pachyderm [pakiderm] A mammal of the (now obsolete) group Pachydermata ('with thick skin'). The name was used for those ungulates which do not 'chew the cud', especially the elephants, but also rhinoceroses, hippopotamuses, horses, pigs, and other perissodactyls.

Pacific Community, formerly **South Pacific Commission** (to 1997) An organization set up in 1947 by Western states then exercising colonial rule in the S Pacific. The purpose was to advance the economic and social interests of the peoples under their control within a framework of regional co-operation. The S Pacific nations also joined, from the 1960s, as they became independent.

Pacific Islands *United States Trust Territory of the Pacific*

Pacific Islands Forum *South Pacific Forum*

Pacific Ocean area c.181 300 000 sq km/70 000 000 sq mi. Ocean extending from the Arctic to the Antarctic, between North and South America (E) and Asia and Oceania (W); covers a third of the Earth and almost half the total water surface area; S part sometimes known as the South Sea; chief arms, the Bering, Ross, Okhotsk, Japan, Yellow, E China, S China, Philippine, Coral, Tasman, Arafura, and Celebes Seas; narrow continental shelves on E shores, wider on W; rim of volcanoes ('Pacific Ring of Fire'), deep open trenches, and active continental margins; sea-floor contraction, Pacific and North American Plates converging at 5·2–5·6 cm/2·05–2·2 in per year (NW), also at the Nazca Plate (SE), 17·2 cm/6·8 in per year; greatest known depth, Challenger Deep in the Marianas Trench, 11 040 m/36 220 ft; major ridge system, the E Pacific Ridge (Albatross Cordillera); ocean floor largely a deep sea-plain, average depth 4300 m/14 100 ft; many islands, either volcanic (eg Hawaii) or coral, mainly in the W section; Spain, Portugal, the UK, and The Netherlands held colonies from the 17th-c, France and Russia in the 18th-c, and the USA, Germany, and Japan in the 19th-c; commercial importance has increased since opening of Panama Canal (1920).

Pacific Scandal Funds of c.$350 000 supplied by railroad promoters to the Conservative Party of Canada during the general election of 1872. The discovery of widespread attempts to use the money for bribing the electorate led to the resignation of the Macdonald government in 1873.

pacifism The doctrine of opposition to all wars, including civil wars. Its most obvious feature is the personal commitment to non-participation in wars, except possibly in a non-combatant role. Pacifists also advocate efforts to maintain peace and support disarmament, especially through the strengthening of international organizations and law. They have long been associated with Christian sects, but in the 20th-c they included many who opposed war from secular moral bases. Pacifism is often associated with support for non-violent political action. A more limited form is **nuclear pacifism**, which is opposed to nuclear, but not conventional, war.

Pacino, Al(fredo) [pacheenoh] (1940–) Film actor, born in New York City, USA. He studied at the Herbert Berghov Studio under Charles Laughton, and at the Actors Studio, and is renowned for his detailed and thoroughly researched acting style. His first main role came as Michael in *The Godfather* (1972), which he followed with acclaimed performances in *Serpico* (1973) and *The Godfather, Part II* and *III* (1974, 1990). Among many later films are *Scarface* (1983), *Sea of Love* (1989), *Scent of a Woman* (1992, Oscar), *Donnie Brasco* (1997), *Insomnia* (2002), and *The Recruit*

(2003). He made his directorial debut with *Looking for Richard* (1996). In 2001 he received the Cecile B DeMille Award for his outstanding contribution to entertainment.

packet switching A service provided by Posts, Telegraph and Telephones Authorities which allows one computer to send a message to a second computer in the form of a set of packets which are transmitted over specially dedicated telephone lines. Packets from different subscribers are all sent down the same line in sequence. This removes the need for the telephone line to be dedicated to the two computers for the whole of the time that they are communicating and is, therefore, much cheaper for the users than a continuous link would be. The mode of operation is akin to sending a letter rather than having a continuous telephone conversation. A **package assembler disassembler (PAD)** is a device in data communications which enables a conventional computer to interface to a packet switching service.

pack rat A rat native to Central and North America; grey-brown with pale undersides; tail may be bushy or naked; builds nests with whatever is available, including man-made items; also known as **trade rat** or **wood rat**. (Genus: *Neotoma*, 20 species.)

Pact of Paris *Kellogg–Briand Pact*

Padang [padang] 1°00S 100°21E, pop (2000e) 865 000. Capital of Sumatra Barat province, Indonesia; main seaport on the W coast of Sumatra; third largest city in Sumatra; airfield; railway; university (1956); outlet for exports of rubber, copra, tea, coffee at Telukbajur, 6 km/4 mi S.

Padania [padania] Area in N Italy declared to be an independent republic by the secessionist Northern League (led by Umberto Bossi) in 1996. It comprises over a third of the country, including all the land around the R Po, and extending to the S of Florence, from coast to coast. The declaration received widespread publicity, but limited support, and was condemned by the Italian government.

paddlefish Archaic, sturgeon-like, freshwater fish of family Polyodontidae, with only two living representatives; *Polyodon spathula* (length up to 2 m/6½ ft), found in the Mississippi basin, USA; *Psephurus gladius* (length up to 7 m/23 ft), from the Yangtze R, China; head produced into a long snout; known as fossils from the Eocene and Upper Cretaceous periods.

paddle tennis A bat-and-ball game played as singles or doubles, invented in the USA in 1898. It is played on a court which is roughly a third of the size of lawn tennis with a wooden paddle and a deadened tennis ball. In most respects the rules are the same as lawn tennis.

Paderewski, Ignacy (Jan) [paduhrefskee] (1860–1941) Pianist, composer, and patriot, born in Kurylowka, SE Poland. He studied at Warsaw, becoming professor at the Conservatory in 1878. In 1884 he taught at the Strasbourg Conservatory, and became a virtuoso pianist, appearing throughout Europe and America. He became director of Warsaw Conservatory in 1909. In 1919 he served briefly as the first premier of Poland, but soon retired from politics, went to live in Switzerland, and resumed concert work. He was elected president of Poland's provisional parliament in 1940.

Padua [padyooa] Ital **Padova**, ancient **Patavium** 45°24N 11°53E, pop (2000e) 217 000. City in NE Italy; on the R Bacchiglione; railway junction; 16th-c university; tomb of St Antony of Padua, a pilgrimage site; cathedral (16th-c); botanical garden (Orto Botanico) a world heritage site.

paediatrics / pediatrics [peediatriks] The medical care of infants and children, and the study of the diseases which affect them. It encompasses the care of the newborn child, including problems such as failure to breathe, jaundice, failure to thrive, congenital malformations, and special care units. In older children many common diseases behave differently from the same condition in adult life, and require specialized attention. *Community paediatrics* is a developing branch of the discipline, covering such aspects as behavioural disorders and child abuse.

paedophilia / pedophilia A sexual interest in children (of either sex). Active interference is illegal, and there is often long-term psychological trauma experienced by the child. It has been suggested that paedophiles act in the way they do because they have difficulties in establishing normal adult relationships, and find children less threatening.

Paestum [peestum] An ancient Greek town in SW Italy in the region of Naples, founded c.600 BC by Sybaris. It was renowned in antiquity for its magnificent Doric temples, impressive remains of which still survive.

Páez, José Antonio [paez] (1790–1873) Venezuelan general and president (1831–5, 1839–43, 1861–3), born in Aragua, Venezuela. He commanded forces of *llaneros* ('cowboys') in the war of independence as principal lieutenant of Simón Bolívar. On the break-up of Gran Colombia, he became president.

Paganini, Niccolo [paganeenee] (1782–1840) Violin virtuoso, born in Genoa, NW Italy. He gave his first concert in 1793, began touring professionally in Italy in 1805, and created a sensation in Austria, Germany, Paris, and London (1828–31). Much admired for his dexterity and technical brilliance, he revolutionized violin technique, his innovations including the use of stopped harmonics. He published several concertos and, in 1820, the celebrated *24 Capricci*.

Page, Sir Frederick Handley (1885–1962) Pioneer aircraft designer and engineer, born in Cheltenham, Gloucestershire, SWC England, UK. In 1909 he founded the firm of aeronautical engineers which bears his name. His twin-engined 0/400 (1918) was one of the earliest heavy bombers, and his Hampden and Halifax bombers were used in World War 2. His civil aircraft include the Hannibal, Hermes, and Herald transports. He was knighted in 1942.

PageMaker® A desk-top publishing package in which page composition, including full graphics, is the principal objective.

pager A small radio receiver used in one-way communication to alert an individual or deliver a short message; not normally used with voice transmission. A radio-paging system has three parts: a pager, a radio transmitter, and an encoder. It works within a small area using one low-power transmitter, or over larger areas using multiple transmitters.

Paget's disease [pajet] A chronic disorder of the adult skeleton, of unknown origin, in which normal bone growth and replacement is disturbed; named after English surgeon James Paget (1814–99), and also known as **osteitis deformans**. Some bones or parts of bones become overcalcified and dense, and others become demineralized. This produces pain in the bones and they are prone to fractures. Occasionally there are cancerous changes in the bones.

pagoda [pagohda] Originally, a Buddhist reliquary cairn or mound (*stupa*), now a shrine or memorial building. Modified by Chinese architectural principles, it developed over time into the stone, brick, and wooden pagodas found throughout E Asia. It is a multi-storied tower, with each storey having a roof of glazed tiles.

Pahang [pahang] pop (2000e) 1 313 000; area 35 965 sq km/ 13 882 sq mi. State in E Peninsular Malaysia, bounded E by the South China Sea; watered by R Pahang; formerly part of the kingdom of Malacca; capital, Kuantan; timber, rubber, tin, rice, tourism.

Pahang, River Longest river in Peninsular Malaysia; flows 456 km/283 mi E into the South China Sea, S of Kuantan.

Pahari [pahahree] An Indo-Aryan-speaking agricultural people of Nepal and the adjoining Himalayan region of India. They are predominantly Hindu, but with a less elaborate caste system than most other Hindus. Population c.10 million.

Paharpur Vihara [paha(r)poor vihahra] The ruins of a Buddhist monastery (*vihara*) at Paharpur, NW Bangladesh; a world heritage site. Said to have been founded by King Dharma Aal in AD 700, this is the largest Buddhist building S of the Himalayas, and a major archaeological site.

Pahlavi, Mohammad Reza [pahlavee] (1919–80) Shah of Persia, born in Tehran, Iran, who succeeded on the abdication of his father, Reza Shah (1878–1944), in 1941. His reign was for many years marked by social reforms and a movement away from the old-fashioned despotic concept of the monarchy, but during the later 1970s the economic situation deteriorated, social inequalities worsened, and protest at western-style 'decadence' grew among the religious fundamentalists. He introduced harsh measures of control, which failed to restore stability. He was forced to leave the country, and a revolutionary government was formed under Ayatollah Khomeini (1979). He was in the USA for medical treatment when the Iranian government seized the US embassy in Teheran (1979) and held many of its staff hostage for over a year, demanding his return to Iran. He made his final residence in Egypt at the invitation of President Sadat.

Paige, Elaine (1951–) Actress and singer, born in London, UK. She joined the West End cast of *Hair* in 1969, but it was her performances in *Jesus Christ Superstar* (1972) and *Billy* (1974) that established her as a musical actress. She appeared at Chichester Festival Theatre, and at Stratford East, before she became a star as *Evita* in 1978. Later shows include *Cats* (1981), *Chess* (1986), *Anything Goes* (1989), *Piaf* (1993), *Sunset Boulevard* at the Adelphi, London (1994–5) and New York (1996), *The Misanthrope* (1998), and *The King and I* (2000).

Päijänne, Lake [piyane] Lake in SC Finland; largest single lake in Finland; area 1090 sq km/420 sq mi; drained S to the Gulf of Finland by R Kymi; boat and hydrofoil service links Jyväskylä and Lahti.

pain An unpleasant sensation – in the simplest case, the stimulation of nerve endings by a strong stimulus, such as heat, cold, pressure, or tissue damage. Pain receptors are located over most of the body surface and at many internal sites. When stimulated, they initiate reflex responses within the spinal cord, and convey information to the brain, where pain is perceived. The degree of pain is determined not only by the intensity of the stimulus, but also by psychological factors which can increase or decrease the release of pain-killing peptides (endorphins and enkephalins) within the brain and spinal cord. Pain which disappears with healing is called *acute*. *Chronic* pain persists after healing (eg pain from a phantom limb), suggesting a pain memory stored in the brain. Many factors modify pain experience. Soldiers in combat may not find wounds painful initially. Stimulation of one body region can reduce pain in another. The converse also happens: recurrent pain in one area can sensitize other areas to become trigger zones, where even a light touch can trigger pain. In *referred pain*, pain from an internal organ is felt as if located in a skin area supplied by the same nerve which supplies the organ (eg angina pain from heart muscle is felt in the left arm). Acute pain is protective: people born with insensitivity to pain, or who develop it due to disease of the nervous system, can inflict serious injuries on themselves.

Paine, Thomas (1737–1809) Revolutionary philosopher and writer, born in Thetford, Norfolk, E England, UK. A corset-maker from the age of 13, he became a sailor, a schoolmaster, and an exciseman. In 1774 he sailed for Philadelphia, where his pamphlet *Common Sense* (1776) argued for complete independence. He served with the US army, and was made secretary to the Committee of Foreign Affairs. In 1787 he returned to England, where he wrote *The Rights of Man* (1791–2) in support of the French Revolution. Arraigned for treason, he fled to Paris, where he was elected a Deputy to the National Convention, but imprisoned for his proposal to offer the king asylum in the USA. At this time he wrote *The Age of Reason*, in favour of deism. Released in 1796, he returned to the USA in 1802.

paint A colouring substance consisting of two basic elements, pigment and medium, used as a decorative and protective coating for architectural and constructed surfaces, and also as an artistic medium. Pigments have been derived from earths (eg yellow ochre), minerals (eg malachite), and dyes (organic and, since the mid-19th-c, synthetic). These are reduced to powder, and dispersed in whatever medium (eg oil) the artist is using. In the 20th-c there were many developments in the technology of paint production, including such qualities as rapid drying, fire resistance, external vs internal use, and corrosion resistance, as well as improved textures for different surfaces and a much wider range of colours (available through paint-mixing equipment).

painted lady A medium-sized butterfly; wings brick-red with black patches, and white patches on point of forewings; caterpillar blackish green, with branching spikes, up to 50 mm/2 in long. (Order: Lepidoptera. Family: Nymphalidae.)

painted leopard *ocelot*

painter *cougar*

painting An art which originated in prehistoric times; but the modern sense of the word, the skilful arrangement of colours on a surface to create an independent work, has been current only since the Renaissance. In many societies, including that of mediaeval Europe, painting has been devoted largely to religious ends; but the Romans decorated their houses with secular murals, and from the 15th-c onwards various types of painting have developed: history, portrait, landscape, genre, and still life.

pair production The production of an electron-positron pair from a high energy X-ray or gamma ray photon, in which the photon loses energy equivalent to at least double the mass of an electron. It occurs in the passage of gamma rays through matter, and is the principal mechanism of high-energy gamma ray absorption.

Paisley [payzlee] 55°50N 4°26W, pop (2000e) 84 500. Administrative centre of Renfrewshire, W Scotland, UK; 11 km/7 mi W of Glasgow; railway; University of Paisley (1992, formerly Paisley College of Technology); sugar refining, distilling, engineering, jam, chemicals, textiles (especially Paisley shawls); observatory, museum, art gallery; Paisley abbey (1163, restored 20th-c).

Paisley, Bob [payzlee], popular name of **Robert Paisley** (1919–96) Football manager, born in Hetton-le-Hole, Durham, NE England, UK. A player with the amateur side Bishop Auckland, he joined Liverpool in 1939, and spent nearly 50 years at the club. It was during his spell as manager (1974–83) that Liverpool enjoyed their greatest years, and became the most successful club side in England. Manager of the Year on six occasions, he continued to be involved with the club as director and adviser.

Paisley, Rev Ian (Richard Kyle) [payzlee] (1926–) Militant Protestant clergyman and politician, born in Armagh, Co Armagh, SE Northern Ireland, UK. Ordained in 1946, he formed his own Church (the Free Presbyterian Church of Ulster) in 1951, and from the 1960s became deeply involved in Ulster politics. He founded the Protestant Unionist Party and stood as its MP for four years until 1974, and has since been the Democratic Unionist Party (DUP) MP for North Antrim. He has been a member of the European Parliament since 1970. A rousing orator, he is strongly pro-British, fiercely opposed to the IRA, Roman Catholicism, and the unification of Ireland. In 1998 he was elected to the newly formed Northern Ireland Assembly, but refused to sit in the Assembly when it met in December 1999 and (after it was reconvened) in May 2000. He led the DUP to success in the Assembly elections in November 2003.

Paiute [piyoot] Two separate Numic-speaking American Indian groups, traditionally hunter-gatherers, divided into the S Paiute (Utah, Arizona, Nevada, California) and the N Paiute (California, Nevada, Oregon). The S Paiute, who had relatively peaceful relations with whites, were put into reservations in the 19th-c. The N group fought intermittently with white prospectors and farmers until 1874, when the US government appropriated their land.

Pakistan *p.1149*

PAL [pal] Acronym for **Phase Alternating Line**, the coding system for colour television developed in Germany and the UK from 1965, and widely adopted for 625-line 50 Hz transmission in Europe and many other parts of the world. To overcome the critical phase relation of the colour difference signals in the NTSC system, their phase is reversed line by line so that small differences are cancelled out; no hue control is necessary in the receiver.

Pakistan

□ International Airport ∴ World heritage site
-- India/Pakistan line of control

official name **Islamic Republic of Pakistan**

Local name Pākistān

Timezone GMT +5

Area 803 943 km²/310 322 sq mi

Population total (2002e) 145 960 000

Status Republic

Date of independence 1947

Capital Islamabad

Languages Urdu and English (official), Punjabi, Sindhi, Pashto, Urdu, Baluchi, and Brahvi mainly spoken

Ethnic groups Punjabi (66%), Sindhi (13%), Baluchi (3%), Pathan and Muhajir minorities, also Afghan refugees in W Pakistan

Religions Muslim (97%) (Sunni 77%, Shi'a 20%), Christian, Hindu, Parsee, Buddhist minorities

Physical features R Indus flows from Himalayas to Karachi, forming a vast, fertile, densely populated alluvial floodplain in E; bounded N and W by mountains rising to 8611 m/28 250 ft at K2, and 8126 m/26 660 ft at Nanga Parbat; mostly flat plateau, low-lying plains and arid desert to the S; major rivers include Jhelum, Chenab, Indus, Sutlej.

Climate Continental, with many temperature and rainfall variations; dominated by the Asiatic monsoon; severe winters in mountainous regions; average annual temperatures 10°C (Jan), 32°C (Jul) in Islamabad; average annual rainfall in Punjab, 250 mm/10 in in SW, 635 mm/25 in in NE; rainy season (Jun–Oct).

Currency 1 Pakistan Rupee (PRs, Rp) = 100 paisa

Economy Agriculture (employs 55% of labour force); cotton production important, supporting major spinning, weaving, and processing industries; sugar cane; textiles; natural gas; tobacco; salt; uranium.

GDP (2002e) $295·3 bn, per capita $2000

Human Development Index (2002) 0·499

History Remains of Indus Valley civilization over 4000 years ago; Muslim rule under the Mughal Empire, 1526–1761; British rule over most areas, 1840s; separated from India to form a state for the Muslim minority, 1947; consisted of West Pakistan (Baluchistan, North-West Frontier, West Punjab, Sind) and East Pakistan (East Bengal), physically separated by 1610 km/1000 mi; occupied Jammu and Kashmir, 1949 (disputed territory with India, and the cause of wars in 1965 and 1971); proclaimed an Islamic republic, 1956; differences between E and W Pakistan developed into civil war, 1971; E Pakistan became an independent state (Bangladesh); military coup by General Zia ul-Haq, 1977, with execution of former prime minister Bhutto in 1979; new constitution (1985) strengthened Zia's powers; Benazir Bhutto elected prime minister, 1988, deposed 1990, re-elected 1993; deposed 1996; ethnic (Muslim/Sindh) violence, especially in Karachi, 1994, and ongoing; military coup, 1999; coup leader, General Musharraf, declared president in 2001; sensitive border area with Afghanistan, following the US-led anti-Taliban campaign, 2001, focusing on Afgan refugees, Pakistani pro-Taliban fighters, and Taliban escapees; ongoing tension with India over Kashmir, with some fighting, 2001, escalating into a major crisis, mid-2002; ceasefire announced (Nov 2003) and diplomatic ties and transport links resumed; governed by an elected President and a bicameral Federal Parliament.

Head of State
1988–93 Ghulam Ishaq Khan
1993–7 Farooq Ahmed Leghari
1997–2001 Mohammad Rafiq Tarar
2001– Pervez Musharraf

Head of Government
1973–7 Zulfikar Ali Bhutto
1977–85 *No Prime Minister*
1985–8 Mohammad Khan Junejo
1988 Mohammad Aslam Khan Khattak
1988–90 Benazir Bhutto
1990 Ghulam Mustafa Jatoi
1990–3 Mian Mohammad Nawaz Sharif
1993–6 Benazir Bhutto
1996–7 Malik Meraj Khalid
1997–9 Mian Mohammad Nawaz Sharif
1999–2001 General Pervez Musharraf (Chief Executive Officer)
2002– Zafarullah Khan Jamali

pala [pahla] An altarpiece consisting of a single large picture, instead of several small ones; also known as a **pala d'altare**. The type first appeared in Florence c.1430.

Palach, Jan [palakh] (1948–69) Czech philosophy student. As a protest against the invasion of Czechoslovakia by Warsaw Pact forces (Aug 1968), he burnt himself to death in Wenceslas Square, Prague in January 1969. He became a hero and symbol of hope, and was mourned by thousands. Huge popular demonstrations marking the 20th anniversary of his death were held in Prague in 1989, and a stone effigy to him now stands in the Charles University.

Palaeocene / Paleocene epoch [paliohseen] The first of the geological epochs of the Tertiary period, from c.66 to 55 million years ago. The vast majority of dinosaurs had disappeared, and mammals suddenly diversified.

palaeoclimatology / paleoclimatology An interdisciplinary subject which studies past climatic conditions, and attempts to model the responsible atmospheric processes. It involves components of a wide range of academic disciplines.

palaeoecology / paleoecology [palioheekolojee] The application of ecological concepts to the study of the interactions between members of fossil communities and their environment. The basic assumption is that the animals and plants of the geological past lived under essentially the same conditions as their living relatives. A palaeoecological study of a fossil community would involve the construction of a faunal and floral list, an assessment of the relative abundances of these organisms, and some interpretation of their feeding (*trophic*) relationships, as in any ecological study.

palaeogeography / paleogeography The study of the geography of former geological periods. This is achieved through the reconstruction of prevailing geographical conditions from the presence of fossils, and an interpretation of the environment under which rocks were formed.

palaeography / paleography The study of the styles of handwriting used by scribes in ancient and mediaeval times. The aim is to establish the provenance or authenticity of specific texts, by relating the hand of a particular scribe, in a particular document, to the styles prevailing in the relevant historical period. There are many pitfalls for the palaeographer: the earliest manuscripts had no spaces between words; documents were made available only by laborious copying; scribes frequently miscopied (often, they were not conversant with the language of the text they were copying), and abbreviations were often used, which could lead to ambiguity, eg Latin *imperator* ('emperor') might appear as *imp*.

palaeolimnology / paleolimnology *limnology*

Palaeolithic / Paleolithic The Old Stone Age, the first and longest part of the Stone Age, which began some 2·6 million years ago in Africa and ended 12 000–10 000 years ago with the Mesolithic. In Europe it is usually divided into **Lower Palaeolithic** (to c.200 000 years ago), **Middle Palaeolithic** (c.200 000–40 000 years ago), and **Upper Palaeolithic** (c.40 000–12 000 years ago).

Palaeolithic / Paleolithic art The art of the Old Stone Age, created c.30 000 years ago, the oldest known. Preserved in limestone caves in France and Spain are impressive murals representing hunting scenes, with realistic drawings of horses, bulls, and many animals now extinct or no longer found in Europe. Small sculptures were also made, the best known being the 'Venus of Willendorf', a stylized 11·5 cm/4½ in stone carving of a pregnant woman. Such works were not made as 'art' in the modern sense; the paintings are often found only in virtually inaccessible chambers deep within the ground, and were presumably done for magical purposes.

palaeomagnetism / paleomagnetism The magnetism preserved in rocks which contain iron-bearing minerals such as magnetite and hematite. It results from the alignment of the internal magnetic fields of the mineral grains to the prevailing Earth's field during the formation of the rock, either by sedimentation, crystallization from a magma, or chemical reaction. By measuring the direction of this 'fossil magnetism' in rocks, it is possible to measure the palaeolatitude at which the rock formed, and the position of the Earth's Poles at the time.

palaeontology / paleontology The study of fossils; especially, the reconstruction of the organism from its fossil remains and the study of the processes of fossilization.

palaeopathology / paleopathology The study of ancient human diseases using skeletal material and, where it survives through mummification or bog preservation, soft tissue. Arthritis, tuberculosis, leprosy, syphilis, tumours, dental disease, fractures, and congenital deformities can be diagnosed, as well as dietary deficiency diseases, such as rickets and yaws. Relative frequencies of occurrence and life-expectancy statistics throw light on ancient demography.

Palaeozoic / Paleozoic era [paleeoh**zoh**ik] A major division of geological time extending from c.590 to 250 million years ago; subdivided into the Cambrian, Ordovician, and Silurian periods (the **Early Palaeozoic** era), and the Devonian, Carboniferous, and Permian periods (the **Late Palaeozoic** era).

palaeozoology / paleozoology The study of animal fossils, including their tracks and other trace fossils, such as burrows and faeces.

palantype [**pal**antiyp] The UK trade name of a shorthand typewriter; known by the trade name **stenotype** in the USA. Using a silent keyboard, the operator produces on bands of paper a phonetic version of ongoing utterances (eg court proceedings). Both hands are used, and several keys are pressed simultaneously. The output is later transcribed to produce a normal typescript.

palate A structure forming the roof of the mouth and the floor of the nasal cavity. A complete palate is a characteristic of mammals, being associated with the ability to suck. It is divided into the **hard palate**, towards the front (formed by bone) and the mobile fibro-muscular **soft palate**, towards the back (which is continuous with the hard palate). The soft palate hangs downwards into the pharynx (separating its nasal and oral parts), and consists mainly of muscle attached to a fibrous base. It may be tensed and raised to close off the nasopharynx, as in swallowing or when producing certain sounds. The muscles of the soft palate pass to both the pharynx and the tongue. Failure of the two halves of the palate to meet and fuse in the midline gives rise to the condition of *cleft palate*.

Palatinate, the A German Rhenish principality, capital Heidelberg. Acquired by the Wittelsbach family (1214), it was elevated to an imperial Electorate by the Golden Bull of 1356, and became increasingly wealthy and important in the 13th–15th-c. After the introduction of Calvinism by Frederick III (r.1559–76), it was the leading Protestant German state and head of the Protestant Union (1608), before its division and systematic devastation in the Thirty Years' War (1618–48) and later by France (1685). In the 18th-c it lost significance, being successively re-unified as a single state (1706), linked dynastically with Bavaria (1777), and occupied by the French (1793–4). Shared between Baden and Bavaria (1815), it was finally absorbed into the German Reich (1871).

Palau *Belau*

Palawan [pa**lah**wan], formerly **Paragua** (1902–5) pop (2000e) 467 000; area 11 780 sq km/4547 sq mi; Island of the W Philippines; long, narrow, with a mountain chain running almost the whole length; Mindoro I to the NE, separated by Mindoro Strait; bounded by the Sulu Sea (E) and South China Sea (W); rises in the S to 2054 m/6739 ft at Mt Mantalingajan; chief town, Puerto Princesa; timber, chromite, fishing.

Pale The 'land of peace' where English rule prevailed in late mediaeval times on the edges of English territory around Calais (until its loss in 1558), Scotland, and a large part of E Ireland. The phrase 'beyond the pale' has been used to imply something is outside the boundaries of normal behaviour – that is, being beyond the extent of English law. In Ireland, the Pale shrank under Elizabeth I because of aggrandizement by Anglo-Irish nobles (the earls of Desmond, Kildare, and Ormond), and continued to diminish until its reconquest under Henry VIII. It was defined as the four counties of Dublin, Kildare, Louth, and Meath in 1464, but the Act of 1495 under Poynings' rule showed a smaller area. Another Pale is known in W Russia, created by Catherine the Great. It consisted of enclaves for Jews living in those areas of Poland that had been annexed by Russia after 1792 and ultimately were extended to include all of Lithuania, Belorussia, and much of Ukraine.

Palembang [pa**lem**bang] 2°59S 104°45E, pop (2000e) 1 152 000. River-port capital of Sumatra Selatan province, Indonesia; on R Musi, S Sumatra I; former capital of the Srivijaya Empire (7th–17th-c); airfield; university (1960); oil refining, trade in oil, rubber, fertilizers, textiles.

Palenque [pa**leng**ke] A Mayan city of AD 600–800 on the slopes of the Chiapas Mts, S Mexico, celebrated for its beauty and distinctive architecture: a world heritage site. Its monuments include a labyrinthine palace complex; temple pyramids of the Sun, Cross, and Foliate Cross; and the Temple of Inscriptions, built to house the tomb of Pacal, ruler of Palenque 615–84.

Paleo-, paleo- *see under Palaeo-, palaeo-*

Palermo [pa**ler**moh] 38°08N 13°23E, pop (2000e) 733 000. Seaport and capital of Palermo province, on N coast of Sicily, S Italy; founded by Phoenicians, 7th–8th-c BC; archbishopric; airport; railway; ferries; university (1777); construction, shipbuilding, steel, glass, chemicals, furniture, service industries, food processing, tourism; trade in fruit, wine, olive oil; cathedral (12th-c), Church of San Cataldo (12th-c), ruined Church of San

Giovanni degli Eremiti (1132), Church of La Martorana (1143), Teatro Massimo (1875–97); trade fair (May–Jun).

Palestine (Middle East) A country in the Middle East whose boundaries were transformed by political considerations across the 20th-c. Following the break-up of the Ottoman Empire in the settlement after World War 1, Palestine was created as a British mandate in 1922. Britain had pledged its support for Zionist national aspirations in the 1917 Balfour Declaration, prior to the formation of Palestine and in disregard of the interests of the 88% Arab majority. These competing national aspirations made Britain's position in Palestine untenable, and in 1947 it relinquished control to the UN, which voted in November to partition the territory and impose a two-state solution, one Jewish and one Arab, with Jerusalem under international control. Rejected by the Arabs and accepted by the Zionists, partition ultimately was superseded by the outcome of the 1948 Arab–Israeli War, which left the new state of Israel in possession of 77% of the mandated territory. As Jordan annexed the West Bank, including East Jerusalem (1948), and Egypt administered the small Gaza Strip, Palestine effectively disappeared from the map. Israel occupied East Jerusalem, the West Bank, and the Gaza Strip in the June 1967 War, since which time these regions have been collectively referred to as the **Occupied Territories**. In July 1988, King Hussein of Jordan severed administrative and legal ties to the West Bank in deference to the PLO's claim to be the legitimate representative of the Palestinian people. At the 19th meeting of the Palestine National Council in Algiers (Nov 1988), the PLO proclaimed the State of Palestine. The boundaries of that state were never specified, the declaration amounting to PLO recognition of the principle of partition rejected in 1947, although the PLO Charter still denied Israel's right to exist. Over 100 states have since recognized the State of Palestine, and PLO offices in those countries are recognized as embassies. In 1993, a historic peace agreement was signed in Washington between the PLO and Israel, which provided for an Israeli withdrawal from the Gaza Strip and the West Bank town of Jericho. These two areas would be under full Palestinian authority, and a degree of self-rule would be allowed in parts of the rest of the West Bank. The agreement was internationally acclaimed (though greeted with hostility by many Israelis and Palestinians), but was only haltingly implemented by Israel. Yasser Araft, the chairman of the Palestine National Authority (see separate entry), became president in 1996. A period of stalemate was broken by the US-brokered Wye agreement (1998), by which Israel would redeploy its forces from further West Bank areas, and the Palestinians would strengthen anti-terrorist measures and cancel anti-Israel provisions in their national charter. However, disagreement over troop withdrawals, Israeli settlements, the return of Palestinian refugees, and the status of Jerusalem continued to hinder peace negotiations, and threatened the projected deadline for the declaration of an independent state in 2000. Violent clashes between Israeli troops and Palestinian police and civilians intensified in 2001. Israeli Prime Minister Ariel Sharon maintained a hard-line approach to the crisis and the conflict escalated when he ordered Israeli troops into the territory controlled by the Palestinian National Authority. Following a wave of attacks on Israel by suicide-bombers, further incursions took place, 2002–4. US President Bush published (Apr 2003) a peace initiative, known as the 'road map', for a phase-by-phase route to ending conflict in the Middle East and to full Palestinian statehood. Palestinian and Israeli moderates launched an alternative peace plan, the Geneva Accord, in December 2003.

Palestine Liberation Organization *PLO*

Palestine National Authority (PNA) pop (2002e) West Bank 2 164 000; Gaza Strip 1 226 000 Autonomous authority created by charter in 1968 and established in May 1994 to give self-government to the Palestinians of Gaza and certain areas on the West Bank (by 1997, Jericho, Jenin, Tulkarem, Nablus, Qalqiliya, Bethlehem, Ramallah, and 80% of Hebron); chief ethnic groups: Palestinian Arab and other 99·4% (West Bank), 83% (Gaza), Jewish 0.6% (West Bank), 17% (Gaza); religions: Muslim 98.7 (Gaza), 75% (West Bank), Jewish 0.6% (West Bank), 17% (Gaza), Christian and other 0.7% (West Bank), 8% (Gaza); GDP (2002) $2.1 bn (West Bank), $750 mn (Gaza); headquarters, Ramallah; governed by a cabinet and Legislative Council, with security maintained by an army and police force; first cabinet resigned in 1997 facing charges of corruption; foreign financial aid allowed PNA to develop industry, trade, and communications; opening of Gaza airport, 1998; avowed aim of PNA to declare a Palestinian state (see separate entry). Head of state (president): Yasser Arafat (1994–. Head of government (prime minister): Mahmoud Ridha Abbas ('Abu Mazen') (2003); Ahmed Qureia (2003–).

Palestrina, Giovanni Pierluigi da [palestreena] (c.1525–94) Composer, born in Palestrina, WC Italy. At Rome he learned composition and organ playing, and became organist and *maestro di canto* at the cathedral of St Agapit, Palestrina (1544). In 1551 he became master of the Julian choir at St Peter's, the first of several appointments in Rome. The most distinguished composer of the Renaissance, he composed over 100 Masses, motets, hymns, and other church pieces, and in 1577 began a revision of the Gradual (which he later abandoned).

palette In art, a term with two main senses: **1** A flat wooden plate, oval or rectangular, on which painters arrange their colours.

2 The range of colours used by an artist. Thus, Rembrandt's palette was occasionally restricted to just four or five basic colours, while an Impressionist might use a dozen. By extension, this sense has come to be used in computing, referring to the range of colours available on a computer using computer graphics.

Palgrave, Francis Turner [palgrayv] (1824–97) Poet and critic, born in Great Yarmouth, Norfolk, E England, UK. He studied at Oxford, and after a variety of posts in education and administration became professor of poetry there (1886–95). He is best kown as the editor of the *Golden Treasury of Songs and Lyrical Poems* (1861; second series, 1896), known to generations of schoolchildren as 'Palgrave's Golden Treasury'.

Palin, Michael (Edward) [paylin] (1943–) Script-writer and actor, born in Sheffield, Yorkshire, N England, UK. He studied at Oxford, then joined the BBC team writing and acting in *Monty Python's Flying Circus* (1969–74) and the Monty Python films. He won a BAFTA award for *A Fish Called Wanda* (1988) and appeared in the sequel *Fierce Creatures* (1997). A versatile writer, his works include a play, *The Weekend* (1994), and a novel, *Hemingway's Chair* (1995). He has also presented a popular series of travel documentaries for BBC TV, beginning with *Around the World in Eighty Days* (1989), following this with a journey from North to South Pole along the 30° meridian (*Pole to Pole*, 1992), and another around the Pacific rim (*Full Circle*, 1997). In 1999 *Michael Palin's Hemingway Adventure* took him to Spain, Africa, Cuba and the USA.

palindrome A word or phrase which reads the same backwards as forwards, such as 'madam', 'radar', and 'Draw, o coward!'. Longer sequences are usually nonsensical, but there are exceptions, as in: 'Doc, note, I dissent. A fast never prevents a fatness. I diet on cod'.

palio An Italian festival held annually in several cities. Palios were first held in mediaeval times, the highlight being the bareback horse races in which jockeys race for the *palio* (a silk standard bearing a painted image of the Virgin Mary). The most famous is the Palio of Siena, first held in 1482.

Palissy, Bernard [paleesee] (c.1510–90) Potter, born in Agen, SW France. He began as a glass-painter, then settled in Saintes (1539), where he devised new techniques for glazing earthenware. His products, bearing in high-relief plants and animals coloured to represent nature, soon made him famous, and although imprisoned as a Huguenot in 1562, he was speedily released and taken into royal favour. In c.1565 he established his workshop at the Tuileries, and was specially exempted from the St Bartholomew's Day massacre (1572). In 1588 he was again arrested as a Huguenot, and died in prison.

Palladianism [palaydianizm] An architectural style of the 17th-c and 18th-c derived from the Renaissance buildings and writing of Andrea Palladio, and characterized by the use of symmetrical planning and the pedantic application of Roman architectural forms. Especially popular in England, it was first used by Inigo Jones for the Banqueting House, London (1619–22), and followed and promoted by the publications of Lord Burlington. The style was also used in Italy, Germany, Holland, Russia, and the USA.

Palladio, Andrea [paladioh], originally **Andrea di Pietro della Gondola** (1508–80) Architect, born in Vicenza, NE Italy. He founded modern Italian architecture, as distinguished from the earlier Italian Renaissance. The *Palladian* style, modelled on the ancient Roman, can be seen in many places and villas in the Vicenza region, notably the Villa Rotonda (1550–1). *I quattro libri dell' architettura* (1570, The Four Books of Architecture) greatly influenced his successors.

Palladium In Greek legend, an image of Pallas Athene which fell from heaven, and became 'the luck of Troy'. Odysseus and Diomedes stole it, and it was supposed to have reached Argos, Athens, or Sparta. The Romans believed Aeneas had brought it to Rome.

Pallas The second asteroid to be found (1802), discovered by the German astronomer and physician, Wilhelm Olbers (1758–1840), 540 km/335 mi across. It was named after Pallas Athene, the goddess of wisdom.

Pallas's cat A member of the cat family (*Felis manul*), found from SE Siberia to Iran; same size as the domestic cat; heavy body; short legs; thickest coat of any wild cat; silvery grey or dirty brown; inhabits open and rocky country; lives in a den; eats small mammals and birds.

pallium or **pall** A circular white woollen band with six purple crosses, signifying episcopal power and union with the Holy See (of the Roman Catholic Church). It is worn by the pope, and by archbishops to whom he grants the right.

palm A woody plant found throughout the tropics, typical of and prominent on oceanic islands, with a few species reaching warm temperate regions. Palms are monocotyledons, and display the typical characters of parallel-veined leaves and floral parts arranged in whorls of three, or multiples of three. Some species are climbers, but most are trees and, as is typical in monocots, lack secondary growth from a vascular cambium. Unlike dicot trees, which increase in size and girth each year, palms achieve their full diameter as seedlings, subsequent growth increasing only their height.

The trunk is covered with old leaf-sheaths, or their scars, and has a crown of leaves. At the tip is a single, large, apical bud; if the bud is removed or damaged, the plant dies. Leaves are mostly fan- or feather-shaped, with numerous, pleated segments, and can reach 20 m/65 ft in length. The huge inflorescences can contain an estimated 250 000 flowers; in some species they are produced only once, after which the plant dies. Such a massive burst of flowering requires great energy, and in these species the trunk often contains large quantities of starch or sugar. The fruits are 1-seeded berries, dry, fleshy or fibrous, oily rather than starchy, often brightly coloured, sometimes very hard. They show a great size range, and include the world's largest seed, that of the *coco de mer* (20 kg/44 lb, c.50 cm/20 in long).

Palms are of immense economic importance, especially in the tropics, where they provide a range of basic products, including vegetables, starch, fruits and nuts, timber, fibre, sugar, alcohol, and wax. They are a very old plant group; fossils of a salt water palm, *Nypa*, date from 100–110 million years ago, making it the seventh oldest-known flowering plant. (Family: Palmae.)

Palma (de Mallorca) [palma] 39°35N 2°39E, pop (2000e) 300 000. Seaport and chief city of Majorca I, Balearic Is; bishopric; airport; university (1967); shipyard, footwear, metalwork, beer, clothes, pottery, tourism; Bellver Castle (14th-c), Church of St Francis, cathedral (13th–16th-c), Spanish Pueblo open-air museum.

palmate In botany, the shape of a leaf in which four or more leaflets arise from the same point, and spread like the fingers of a hand.

Palmer, Arnold (Daniel) (1929–) Golfer, born in Latrobe, Pennsylvania, USA. US Amateur champion in 1954, he won the Canadian Open (1955), the (British) Open (1961–2), the US Open (1960), and the US Masters (1958, 1960, 1962, 1964). The first golfer (1968) to win $1 million in his career, he has been credited with turning golf from an exclusive sport into a popular pastime.

Palmer, Nettie, popular name of **Janet Gertrude Palmer Higgins** (1885–1964) Writer and critic, born in Bendigo, Victoria, SE Australia. She studied in Melbourne and London, where she married Vance Palmer. Her prolific literary journalism in the 1920s and 1930s was extremely important in the development of Australian literary culture. She was a familiar broadcaster on ABC radio in the 1940s and 1950s, and was well known in international literary circles. She published two volumes of poetry, books of criticism including *Modern Australian Literature 1900–23*, a study of Henry Handel Richardson, and various histories and memoirs. A vigorous promoter of Australian writing, she also edited a number of anthologies.

Palmer, Vance (1885–1959) Writer and critic, born in Bundaberg, Queensland, SE Australia. He rejected the notion of a university education and chose to travel widely instead. A leading member of the Pioneer Players theatre group, he published poetry but was better known as a novelist, publishing a number of outback novels including *The Passage* (1930). By the 1940s he had a reputation as a pre-eminent cultural figure, and wrote a number of essays and literary and historical studies. Vance and Nettie Palmer were a remarkable literary partnership of great importance to Australia's cultural life.

Palmerston (Australia) *Darwin* (Australia)

Palmerston (of Palmerston), Henry John Temple, 3rd Viscount (1784–1865) British statesman and Liberal prime minister (1855–8, 1859–65), born in Broadlands, Hampshire, S England, UK. He studied at Edinburgh and Cambridge, became a Tory MP in 1807, served as secretary of war (1809–28), joined the Whigs (1830), and was three times foreign secretary (1830–4, 1835–41, 1846–51). His brusque speed, assertive manner, and robust defences of what he considered to be British interests abroad secured him the name of 'Firebrand Palmerston'. A more comfortable nickname was **Pam**, and his frequently xenophobic foreign policy won him substantial popular support in Britain. He is associated with 'Gunboat Diplomacy', whereby Britain employed, or threatened to employ, its unchallengeable naval supremacy to resolve overseas differences in its favour. Home secretary in Aberdeen's coalition (1852), he became premier in 1855, when he vigorously prosecuted the Crimean War with Russia. His authority after resuming the premiership in 1859 was unchallenged, and he became Britain's oldest prime minister. A sturdy opponent of further parliamentary reform in the early 1860s, he died in office.

Palmerston North 40°20S 175°39E, pop (2000e) 77 000. City in North Island, New Zealand, NE of Wellington; airfield; railway; university (1926); agricultural research centre; dairy products, pharmaceuticals, textiles, electrical goods; Manawatu rugby museum.

palmitic acid [palmitik] $C_{15}H_{31}COOH$, IUPAC **hexadecanoic acid**, a saturated fatty acid, melting point 63°C. It is obtained from many animal and plant sources, especially milk and palm oil (from which the name is derived).

palm oil A major edible oil, obtained from the flesh of the fruit of several types of palm tree. It is produced in large quantities, and widely used for the manufacture of margarine, as well as in soap, candles, and lubricating grease.

Palm Springs 33°50N 116°33W, pop (2000e) 42 800. Resort city in Riverside Co, S California, USA, in the N Coachella Valley; founded, 1876; developed as a luxurious desert resort in the early 1930s; airfield; nearby Palm Canyon (an ancient grove of native palms), Tahquitz Bowl (a natural amphitheatre); hot springs; golf courses.

Palm Sunday In the Christian Church, the Sunday before Easter, commemorating the entry of Jesus into Jerusalem, when the crowd spread palm branches in front of him (*Mark* 11, *John* 13).

Palmyra (Pacific Ocean) [**palmiyra**] 5°52N 162°05W. Uninhabited atoll enclosing 50 small islets in the Pacific Ocean 1600 km/1000 mi S of Honolulu; annexed by USA, 1912; important air transport base in World War 2; since 1962 under jurisdiction of US Department of the Interior; site for nuclear waste disposal since 1986.

Palmyra (Roman history) [**palmiyra**] In Roman times, a flourishing oasis town on the E fringe of the Empire, whose wealth came from controlling the desert trade routes between N Syria and Babylonia. At the height of its power in the 3rd-c AD, it briefly gained independence before being brought to heel and destroyed by the Romans in 273.

Palo Alto 37°27N 122°10W, pop (2000e) 58 600. City in Santa Clara Co, W California, USA; near the SW end of San Francisco Bay, 48 km/30 mi SSE of San Francisco; at the centre of 'Silicon Valley' high technology area; birthplace of Clarence Roderic Allen and Douglas Dunn; railway.

Palomar Observatory An observatory on Mount Palomar near San Diego, California, USA, owned by the California Institute of Technology (Caltech). It is the site of the 5 m/200 in Hale reflector telescope (1948), which has made numerous contributions to observational astronomy and cosmology. The 1·2 m/48 in Schmidt telescope at this observatory is used to survey the sky photographically. The first Palomar Observatory Sky Survey in the 1950s is a primary database used by all observatories. A second epoch survey using new photographic emulsions was carried out in the 1980s. Measurement of plates from both epochs will enable the proper motions of thousands of stars to be calculated.

palomino [**palomeenoh**] A horse with a distinctive type of colouring, found in various breeds, and actively selected by some breeders, especially in the USA; pale golden brown with white mane and tail (occasionally white on face or legs); also known as **California sorrel**.

Palouse *Appaloosa*

Paltrow, Gwyneth [**paltroh**] (1972–) Film actress, born in Los Angeles, California, USA. Brought up in a show business family, she abandoned her art history studies at the University of California, Santa Barbara, to pursue an acting career. Her films include *Hook* (1991), *Malice* (1993), and *Seven* (1995). It was her 1996 performance in the title role of Emma Woodhouse, adapted from the novel by Jane Austen, that led to her being offered the role of Viola in *Shakespeare in Love* (1998, Oscar). In 1997 she broke off her much publicized engagement to the actor Brad Pitt and went on to film *A Perfect Murder* (1998), *The Talented Mr Ripley* (1999), and *Sylvia* (2003). She made her London West End stage debut in *Proof* in 2002. She married Chris Martin, singer with the UK pop band Coldplay, in 2003.

palynology [**paylinolojee**] The analysis of pollen grains preserved in ancient sediments and soils to reconstruct variations in vegetation over time; blanket bog, acid moorland podzols, and lake deposits provide particularly good data. The impact of prehistoric peoples and early agriculture on the natural environment is a subject of much contemporary interest.

pampa(s) The extensive grassland (prairie) region of Argentina and Uruguay around the R Plate estuary. It is a major centre for cattle ranching.

pampas cat A member of the cat family (*Felis colocolo*) native to South America; same size as the domestic cat; thick greyish brown or pale coat, marked with spots and lines; inhabits forest and grassland; eats small mammals (eg guinea pigs) and birds.

pampas grass A large perennial grass (*Cortaderia selloana*) forming dense tufts of arching bluish leaves and tall, erect stems 3 m/10 ft high, bearing silvery-white, sometimes pink, plume-like panicles. Native to Brazil, Argentina, and Chile, it is widely grown as an ornamental. (Family: Gramineae.)

Pamplona [**pamplohna**], Lat **Pampeluna** or **Pompaelo** 42°48N 1°38W, pop (2000e) 182 000. Capital of Navarre province, N Spain; on R Arga, 407 km/253 mi N of Madrid; archbishopric; capital of the Kingdom of Navarre, 10th-c; airport; railway; university (1952); agricultural centre, paper, rope, pottery, chemicals, kitchenware; cathedral (14th–15th-c), museum; Fiesta of San Fermin (Jul), with bull-running in the streets; Chiquita (Sep).

Pamporovo [**pamporohvoh**] 41°43N 24°39E. International ski resort in Smolyan province, S Bulgaria; 15 km/9 mi N of Smolyan in the Rhodopi Mts; altitude 1650 m/5413 ft; on Snezhanka ('Snow White') Peak there are several ski runs up to 3800 m/12 500 ft in length.

Pan (astronomy) The 18th natural satellite of Saturn, discovered in 1990 from photographs taken nine years earlier by the Voyager 2 space probe; distance from the centre of Saturn 133 600 km/83 000 mi; diameter 20 km/12 mi; orbital period 0·58 days.

Pan (mythology) A Greek god, the 'nourisher' of flocks and herds, originally a rural goat-god from Arcadia, depicted with goat-like ears, horns, and legs. His pan-pipe is made of reeds, and he can cause groups of people to be seized with uncontrollable fear ('panic').

Pan-Africanism A movement founded by US and W Indian blacks to promote the interests of black people everywhere. It held meetings in 1900, 1919 (in association with the Peace Conference at Versailles), and 1945, and influenced the intellectual development of nationalism in Africa. Nasser made Cairo a centre of Pan-African influence, a role subsequently taken over by Addis Ababa.

Pan-Africanist Congress (PAC) A black political party in South Africa which broke away from the African National Congress in 1958 under the leadership of Robert Sobukwe (1924–78). Sobukwe objected to the relative moderation of the ANC leadership of Lutuli and Mandela, particularly its relationship with the white-dominated Congress of Democrats, and used the PAC to pursue a distinctly black and radical policy. In 1960, it upstaged the ANC by instituting resistance to pass laws, and its campaign led to the Sharpeville Massacre. Its militant wing, Poqo, began a campaign of violence. Sobukwe was imprisoned on Robben I, and was 'banned' on being released in 1969. After his death the PAC remained active in the guerrilla campaigns. It was one of the political parties unbanned by President de Klerk.

Panama *p.1154*

Panama Canal A canal bisecting the Isthmus of Panama and linking the Atlantic and Pacific Oceans. It is 82 km/51 mi long, and 150 m/490 ft wide in most places; built by the US Corps of Engineers (1904–14). In 1979, US control of the Panama Canal Zone (8 km/5 mi of land flanking the canal, formerly the site of a US military installation) was passed to the Republic of Panama, which guaranteed the neutrality of the waterway itself when it took over operational control of the canal in 2000.

Panama City, Span **Panamá** 8°57N 79°30W, pop (2000e) 713 000. Capital city of Panama, on the N shore of the Gulf of Panama, near the Pacific end of the Panama Canal; founded, 1673; airport; railway; two universities (1935, 1965); industrial and transportation centre of Panama; on the Pan-American Highway; Church of San José; historic district and Salón Bolivar, a world heritage site.

Pan-American Games A multi-sport competition for athletes from North, South, and Central American nations. First held at Buenos Aires, Argentina, in 1951, they now take place every four years.

Pan-American Highway A network of designated roads extending 27 000 km/17 000 mi across the Americas from Alaska to Chile. The proposal, which was put to the 5th International Conference of American States in 1923, was originally for a single route, but several alternative routes have since been designated.

Panama

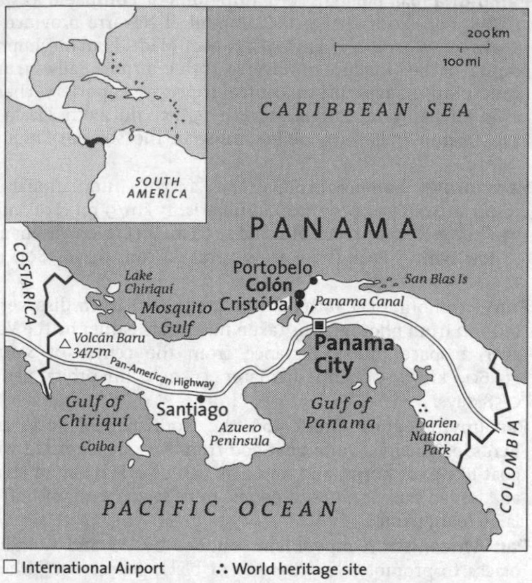

Span **Panamá**, official name **Republic of Panama**, Span **República de Panamá**

Local name Panamá

Timezone GMT −5

Area 77 082 km^2/29 753 sq mi

Population total (2002e) 2 915 000

Status Republic

Date of independence 1903

Capital Panama City

Languages Spanish (official), English and indigenous languages (including Cuna, Chibchan, Choco)

Ethnic groups Mestizo (mixed Spanish-Indian) (70%), West Indian (14%), white (10%), Indian (6%)

Religions Christian (Roman Catholic 93%, Protestant 6%), Jewish, Muslim, and Baha'i minorities

Physical features Mostly mountainous; Serranía de Tabasará (W) rises to 3475 m/11 401 ft at Volcán Baru; Azuero peninsula (Peninsula de Azuero) in the S; lake-studded lowland cuts across the isthmus; dense tropical forests on the Caribbean coast; Panama Canal, 82 km/51 mi long, connects Pacific and Atlantic oceans.

Climate Tropical, with uniformly high temperatures; average annual temperature 26°C (Jan), 27°C (Jul) in Panama City; dry season (Jan–Apr) only; average annual rainfall 1770 mm/69·7 in.

Currency 1 US dollar, local Balboa (B, Ba) = 100 cents

Economy Canal revenue (accounts for 80% of country's wealth); great increase in banking sector since 1970; attempts to diversify include oil refining, cigarettes, paper products; tourism; copper, gold, silver; bananas, coffee, cacao, sugar cane.

GDP (2002e) $18·06 bn, per capita $6200

Human Development Index (2002) 0·787

History Visited by Columbus, 1502; under Spanish colonial rule until 1821; joined the Republic of Greater Colombia; separation from Colombia after a US-inspired revolution, 1903; assumed sovereignty of the 8 km/5 mi-wide Canal zone, previously administered by the USA, 1979; military rule under Manuel Noriega, 1983–9; US invasion in 1989, deposed Noriega; governed by a President, Cabinet, and unicameral Legislative Assembly.

Head of State/Government

1960–4 Roberto Francisco Chiari
1964–8 Marco A Robles
1968 Arnulfo Arias Madrid
1968 *Military junta*
1968–9 Omar Torrijos Herrera
1969–78 Demetrio Basilio Lakas
1978–82 Aristides Royo
1982–4 Ricardo de la Espriella
1984 Jorge Enrique Illueca Sibauste
1984–5 Nicolás Ardito Barletta
1985–8 Eric Arturo Delvalle
1988–9 Manuel Solís Palma
1989–94 Guillermo Endara
1994–9 Ernesto Pérez Balladares
1999– Mireya Moscoso de Gruber

Pan-American Union An organization founded in 1890 to foster political and economic co-operation among American states, and to draw North and South America closer together; first called the **International Bureau for American Republics**. Until World War 2 the Union concluded many agreements covering trade, migration, and neutrality zones around their coasts, despite fears among many members of domination by the USA. In 1948 it became part of the wider Organization of American States, and now forms its permanent administrative and advisory machinery. It has four departments: economic and social affairs; international law; cultural affairs; and administrative services.

pan-and-scan A method of adapting a wide-screen motion picture to the narrower video format by selecting a limited area of the frame covering the most important action, which is continuously followed as though by 'panning' a camera. The selection is in fact made electronically in the telecine process.

Panathenaea [panatheniya] A festival held annually at Athens in honour of Athene, the patron goddess of the city. It consisted of a procession from the town to the Acropolis, the sacrifice at the great altar there of a hekatomb (100 cattle), and then athletic contests.

Pancake Day *Shrove Tuesday*

Panchen Lama [panchen lahma] A spiritual leader and teacher in Tibetan Buddhism, second in importance to the Dalai Lama, and said to be the reincarnation of the Buddha Amitabha. The late Panchen Lama (1938–89), the 10th reincarnation, became the ward of the Chinese in his childhood, and some Tibetans disputed his status.

pancreas [pangkrias] A soft gland made up of small lobes (*lobules*) associated with the alimentary canal of vertebrates with jaws, and producing both exocrine and endocrine secretions. It consists of the *secretory alveoli* (the exocrine part) and the *islets of Langerhans* (the endocrine part). In humans it is c.12–15 cm/4·5–6 in long, and lies on the rear abdominal wall in front of the upper two lumbar vertebrae, extending to the left. The secretory alveoli produce an alkaline mixture of digestive enzymes (the **pancreatic juices**), which are discharged into the duodenum. The islets of Langerhans (consisting of A, B, and D cells in humans) synthesize and secrete hormones involved in carbohydrate metabolism.

panda A mammal of family Ailuropodidae, related to raccoons and bears; inhabits bamboo forests in mountains; two species: **giant panda** (*Ailuropoda melanoleuca*) from China; bear-like with large round head; white with black legs, shoulders, chest, ears, and area around eyes; front paw with elongated wrist bone which acts like a sixth digit; grasps bamboo shoots between this extra 'thumb' and the first and second true digits; also the **red panda**, **lesser panda**, or **cat bear** (*Ailurus fulgens*) found from S China to N Burma; raccoon-like; red-brown with black underparts and tail tip; dark rings around tail; white markings on face.

Pandarus [pandarus] In Homer's *Iliad*, a Trojan prince, killed by Diomedes. In later developments of the story of Troilus and

Cressida, he became her uncle and their 'go-between' (hence 'pander').

Pandit, Vijaya Lakshmi, *née* **Swarup Kumari Nehru** (1900–90) Indian diplomat, born in Allahabad, NE India, the sister of Nehru. She was active in the nationalist movement, and was three times imprisoned. In the Legislative Assembly of the United Provinces (later, Uttar Pradesh) she was minister for local self-government and public health (1937–9), the first Indian woman to hold a cabinet post. Leader of the Indian UN delegation (1946–8, 1952–3), she also held several ambassadorial posts (1947–51). In 1953, she became the first woman president of the UN General Assembly, and was Indian High Commissioner in London (1954–61).

Pandora [pandawra] In Greek mythology, the first woman, made by Hephaestus, and adorned by the gods with special qualities; she was sent to be the wife of Epimetheus. Zeus gave her a box (or she found a storage-jar) from which all the evils which plague mankind came out; only Hope was left in the bottom of the box. The name means 'all gifts'.

panegyric [panejirik] A speech, poem, or song of praise addressed to an individual, group, or institution. Examples include Pliny's eulogy of Trajan, and Mark Antony's oration on Caesar in Shakespeare's *Julius Caesar*. Less creditable instances are addresses by authors to patrons, and periodic tributes to royalty by the English poets laureate.

Pangaea [panjeea] The name given to the hypothesized 'supercontinent' comprising Gondwanaland and Laurasia which made up the Earth's continental crust before the Jurassic period. It then began to split, as a result of continental drift, eventually forming the present-day distribution of the continents.

pangamic acid A component of many seeds, whose chemical name is n-di-isopropyl-glucuronate. Although it is promoted as a vitamin (B_{15}), pangamic acid serves no known nutritional function.

pangolin [panggohlin] A mammal native to Africa and S and SE Asia; pointed head with small eyes; long broad tail; long tongue and no teeth; eats ants and termites; covered in large overlapping horny plates (resembles a tiled roof); curls into an armoured ball; the only member of order Pholidota; also known as **scaly anteater**. (Genus: *Manis*, 7 species.)

pangram A meaningful sentence which contains all the letters of the alphabet, ideally only once each. A familiar example, though with duplications, is the typists' test sentence *The quick brown fox jumped over the lazy dog.* A 26-letter English pangram (albeit with rather obscure words) is *Veldt jynx grimps waqf zho buck.*

Pangu or **P'an-ku** The first being of the Chinese creation myth, documented from the 3rd-c BC. He breaks open the primal egg from within, holds up the sky, and prevents it from bearing down upon the Earth. Then the world is made from parts of him, so that his body becomes the mountains, his hair the stars, and his eyes the Sun and Moon. His body lice provided the world's animals and people.

Panhandle Any territory comprising a narrow strip of land running out from a large area in the shape of a pan handle; in the USA, applied to areas in (1) NW Texas (the Texas Panhandle), (2) NW Oklahoma, (3) N Idaho, (4) NE West Virginia (Eastern Panhandle), (5) N West Virginia, (6) SE Alaska, (7) Nebraska, and (8) an extension of the Golden Gate Park in San Francisco.

panicle A branched, racemose type of inflorescence. The term is often used for any complexly-branched inflorescence.

Paninari [paninahree] An Italian youth cult of the 1980s named from the sandwich bars where its members gathered. They wore expensive 'designer' clothes (from the US and Italy), presenting a tough militaristic image – leather jackets, belts with large buckles, dark glasses – which accorded with their right-wing views.

Panjabi *Indo-Aryan languages*

Pankhurst, Emmeline, *née* **Goulden** (1857–1928) Suffragette, born in Manchester, Greater Manchester, NW England, UK. In 1879 she married **Richard Marsden Pankhurst** (d.1898), a radical Manchester barrister who had been the author of the first women's suffrage bill in Britain and of the Married Women's Property Acts of 1870 and 1882. She founded the Women's Franchise League (1889), and in 1903, with her daughter **Christabel Harriette** (1880–1958), the Women's Social and Political Union. From 1905 she fought for women's suffrage by violent means, on several occasions being arrested and going on hunger strike. After the outbreak of World War 1, she worked instead for the industrial mobilization of women. Of her daughters and fellow workers, **Dame Christabel** turned later to preaching Christ's Second Coming; and **Sylvia** (1882–1960) diverged to pacificism, internationalism, and Labour politics.

panorama In art, a painting of a landscape which is too large to be viewed all at once but which is either unrolled before the spectator, bit by bit, or displayed all around a room, which may be circular in plan. The huge panorama of Scheveningen by Hendrik Willem Mesdag (1831–1915) is one of the tourist attractions of The Hague.

panoramic camera A camera that gives a picture which is long and narrow, ie of high aspect ratio as the proportion of length to width, rather like wide-screen cinema. A conventional camera may use a film gate of the same proportions as the picture, either selectable as an alternative by a removable mask, or using a different film back. A true panoramic camera uses an integral rotating lens and slit shutter arrangement to cover a horizontal angle of up to 120° while exposing the film in a curved gate. Alternative designs use a rotating camera with the film moved progressively past a slit in the focal plane, or a rotating prism assembly in front of the lens.

panpipes A musical instrument made of various lengths of hollowed cane or wood joined together in a row. The player blows across the top to sound a different pitch from each pipe. Of great antiquity, panpipes are still widely used in certain folk cultures, such as those of South America.

pansy Any of several species or varieties of violet, in which the flat, 5-petalled flowers are held in a vertical plane and often resemble a face, the effect being heightened by honey-guide markings on the petals. The cultivated pansy, developed as a cottage garden flower c.1830, has large flowers with overlapping petals in a wider range of colours. (Genus: *Viola*. Family: Violaceae.)

pantheism The belief that God and the universe are ultimately identical. It may equate the world with God or deny the reality of the world, maintaining that only the divine is real and that sense experience is illusory. It is a characteristic feature of Hinduism and certain schools of Buddhism.

pantheon A temple in Rome dedicated to all the gods, begun by Agrippa in 27 BC and rebuilt by Hadrian (AD 100–125), and now S Maria Rotonda. The name is also used for many derivatives of the original, and more generally for any burial place of heroes or Temple of Fame.

panther A member of the cat family, but not a distinct species. The name is used for the black form of the leopard (especially in the combination **black panther**) or as an alternative name for the cougar.

pantomime In most European languages the term denotes what in English is usually referred to as a mime. In England the term signifies a specific form of entertainment developed from the harlequinade in the 19th-c. It is performed during the Christmas season as a mixture of songs, dances, slapstick, topical jokes, male and female impersonations, magic, and spectacle, with a storyline that is loosely connected to a fairy-tale or nursery-rhyme. The word was also used for the mimed Pierrot plays of Jean-Baptiste Gaspard Deburau, based on the *commedia dell'arte* masque. *Pantomimus* was the name given to a performer in Imperial Rome, who by movement and gesture alone represented the different characters in a short scene based on classical history or mythology. The *pantomimus* wore a mask with no mouthpiece, changing it with each character portrayed.

pantonality An attribute of music which fluctuates rapidly from one key centre to another, so that it cannot be said to be in any particular key. Some late Wagner and early Schoenberg works might be described as pantonal.

pantothenic acid A B vitamin which acts as a co-factor in several enzyme reactions. Because it is found so widely in nature, a deficiency in humans has not yet been recorded.

Panzer (Ger 'armour') A term used in the German armed forces, applied to warships (*Panzerschiffe*, 'armoured ship') but more particularly to armoured fighting vehicles. The Panzer divisions (essentially tank forces) were the most important component of the German army's fighting strength during World War 2.

papacy *pope*

Papa Doc *Duvalier, François*

Papago [papagoh] A Uto-Aztecan-speaking North American Indian group who lived on the Arizona–Mexico border. Seminomadic food gatherers, they later raised cattle and cultivated some crops. They are concentrated on three reservations in Arizona.

Papal States The 'States of the Church', straddling rural, mountainous areas of C Italy, comprising territories received by treaties and donations in the Middle Ages. The papal government was often ineffective, and relied upon local lords (Malatesta of Rimini, Montefeltro of Urbino) who were appointed as 'vicars in temporal matters'. They were annexed by Italy in 1870, but the papacy refused to recognize their loss until the Lateran Treaty (1929), which established the Vatican papal state.

papaw [papaw] A small, unbranched tree (*Carica papaya*) growing to 6 m/20 ft, with very soft wood and copious latex; a crown of long-stalked, palmate leaves up to 75 cm/30 in wide; flowers yellow, males and females on separate plants; fruit up to 30 cm/12 in long, oval, yellow; also called **papaya** and **pawpaw**. Its origin is unknown, but it is possibly a hybrid. It is widely cultivated throughout the tropics for its juicy but bland fruits. Latex from the leaves and young fruits contains the enzyme **papain**, which is used in the medical, meat, and leather industries. (Family: Caricaceae.)

papaya *papaw*

Papeete [papayaytay] 17°32S 149°34W, pop (2000e) 99 300. Capital and chief port of French Polynesia, on NW coast of Tahiti; airport; copra, vanilla, mother-of-pearl.

Papen, Franz von [papen] (1879–1969) German politician, born in Werl, WC Germany. He was military attaché in Mexico and Washington, chief-of-staff with a Turkish army, and took to Centre Party politics. As Hindenburg's chancellor (1932) he suppressed the Prussian Socialist government, and as Hitler's vice-chancellor (1933–4) signed a concordat with Rome. He later became ambassador to Austria (1936–8) and Turkey (1939–44). Taken prisoner in 1945, he was acquitted at the Nuremberg Trials.

paper Material in sheet form used for a wide range of functions, notably writing, drawing, printing, and packaging. Invented in China in AD 105, it was originally produced from pulped rags or plant fibres. It came quickly into common use in China; in 143 a scholar apologized for no longer writing on silk; toilet-paper was produced in 590 – its use noted with disgust by Arab merchants; and paper money was being circulated by the 8th-c. It was introduced to mediaeval Europe by the Moors, eventually superseding parchment as the standard material for written and printed documents. From the 19th-c, wood pulp and cellulose have largely been used in its manufacture, but plant fibres (eg esparto grass) and rags continue to be used, especially for paper of strength or high quality, and the recycling of waste paper nowadays is increasingly practised on ecological grounds. Early paper was hand made, and consisted of single sheets. Machines for making continuous rolls (or *webs*) of paper were introduced in France at the end of the 18th-c. The world uses some 200 million tons of paper each year.

paper-bark birch A species of birch with peeling white bark (*Betula papyrifolia*), which is used to make canoes. It is native to North America. (Family: Betulaceae.)

paper nautilus [nawtilus] An octopus-like marine mollusc (*Argonauta*); two tentacles modified in the female to secrete a fragile external egg case, the so-called shell; female c.30 cm/12 in long, male only 1 cm/0·4 in long; widely distributed in tropical and subtropical seas. (Class: Cephalopoda.)

Paphos [pafos] 34°45N 32°23E, pop (2000e) 31 700. Holiday resort and capital town of Paphos district, SW Cyprus, on the Mediterranean Sea; capital of Cyprus during Roman times; old city founded probably in Mycenaean period, a world heritage site; remains of Roman villa (House of Dionysos), 7th-c Byzantine castle, 3rd-c BC 'Tombs of the Kings', Saranda Kolones (remains of Byzantine castle), Chrysopolitissa Basilica (early Christian basilica).

papilionid butterfly [papilyonid] A butterfly of the family Papilionidae; medium to very large, and often brightly coloured; hindwings commonly extended into tails; adults and caterpillars usually distasteful to predators; c.550 species, including swallowtails, Apollo butterflies, and the birdwings. (Order: Lepidoptera.)

papilloma [papilohma] Localized overgrowths of cells on epithelial surfaces such as the skin, intestinal lining, or bladder lining. Many papillomas are benign, but some tend to recur and become malignant.

papillon [papilon] A toy breed of dog developed in France several centuries ago; small with long fine coat thickest on chest, neck, and upper legs; ears with fringes of hair, resembling a butterfly's wings.

Papineau, Louis Joseph [papeenoh] (1786–1871) French-Canadian leader, born in Montreal, Quebec, SE Canada. He was Speaker of the House of Assembly for Lower Canada (1815–37), opposed the union with Upper Canada, and agitated against the imperial government. His leadership of the *Patriotes* during the rebellion of 1837 led to a warrant being issued against him for high treason. He escaped to Paris, but returned to Canada after the general amnesty of 1844.

Papp, Joe, originally **Joseph Papirofsky** (1921–91) Stage director and producer, born in New York City, USA. Following acting and backstage experience, he formed a Shakespeare Workshop which in 1954 started performing free shows in Central Park; in 1960 this Workshop officially became the New York Shakespeare Festival. A permanent open-air theatre, the Delacorte, was built in the Park for the company in 1962. In 1967 he founded the off-Broadway Public Theater, dedicated to new work by US writers, opening with the original production of the rock musical, *Hair*. Later musicals include *A Chorus Line* (1975, Pulitzer Prize) as well as over 350 plays. He was later director of the theatres at the Lincoln Center (1973–8).

Pappus of Alexandria (4th-c) Greek mathematician, whose eight-book *Synagoge* (Collection) is extant in an incomplete form. Some of our knowledge of ancient Greek mathematics derives exclusively from his work.

paprika *pepper 1*

Papua New Guinea *p.1157*

papyrus [papiyruhs] An aquatic perennial (*Cyperus papyrus*) native to N Africa; stems growing to 4 m/13 ft, triangular in cross-section; leaves grass-like; flowers tiny, yellowish, lacking perianth, in spikelets forming large spherical heads. The ancients made paper by pressing wet strips of the pithy stems side by side. (Family: Cyperaceae.)

parable A metaphor in narrative form (although sometimes considered a simile) with the purpose not so much of imparting propositional truths or general moral lessons as challenging the perspective of the hearer. In the Bible, parables are frequently used by Jesus in his preaching about the kingdom of God, and include well-known stories about the Good Samaritan, the Prodigal Son, the Sower, and many others. These parables were often subjected to allegorical interpretation by the Church fathers.

Papua New Guinea

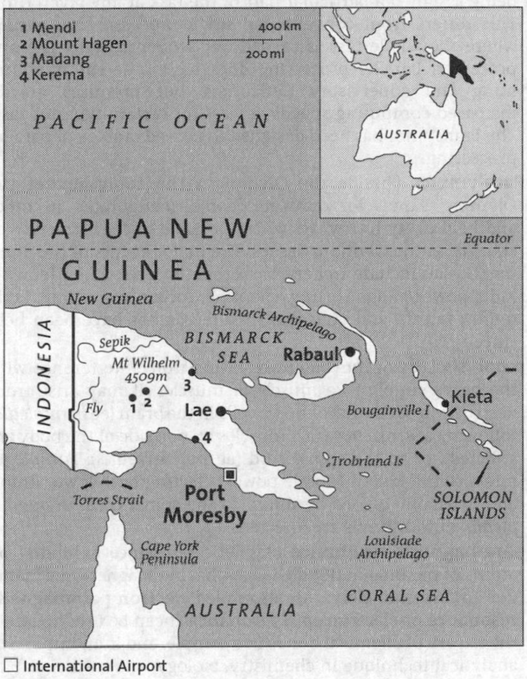

official name **Independent State of Papua New Guinea**

Local name Papua New Guinea

Timezone GMT +10

Area 462 840 km²/178 656 sq mi

Population total (2002e) 5 426 000

Status Independent state within the Commonwealth

Date of independence 1975

Capital Port Moresby

Languages Pidgin English and Hiri Motu (official parliamentary languages), Tok Pisin, and c.750 indigenous languages spoken

Ethnic groups Papuan (80%), Melanesian (15%), Polynesian, Chinese, and European minorities

Religions Christian (Protestant 64%, Roman Catholic 33%), local beliefs

Physical features Island group in SW Pacific Ocean, comprising E half of the island of New Guinea, the Bismarck and Louisiade archipelagos, the Trobriand and D'Entrecasteaux Is, and other off-lying groups; complex system of mountains, highest point, Mt Wilhelm, 4509 m/14 793 ft; mainly covered with tropical rainforest; vast mangrove swamps along coast; archipelago islands are mountainous, mostly volcanic and fringed with coral reefs.

Climate Typical monsoon, with temperatures and humidity constantly high; average annual temperature 28°C (Jan), 26°C (Jul); average annual rainfall 2000–2500 mm/80–100 in.

Currency 1 Kina (K) = 100 toea

Economy Farming, fishing, and forestry (engages c.75% of workforce); vegetables, sugar, peanuts; natural gas; brewing; tourism.

GDP (2002e) $10·86 bn, per capita $2100

Human Development Index (2002) 0·535

History British protectorate in SE New Guinea, 1884; some of the islands under German protectorate, 1884; German New Guinea in NE in 1899; German colony annexed by Australia in World War 1; Australia mandated to govern both British and German areas, 1920; combined as the United Nations Trust Territory of Papua and New Guinea, 1949; independence within the Commonwealth, 1975; a Governor-General represents the British Crown; governed by a Prime Minister and a Cabinet, with a unicameral National Parliament.

Head of State
(British monarch represented by Governor-General)
1991–7 Wiwa Korowi
1997–2003 Sir Silas Atopare
2003– Bill Skate *Acting*

Head of Government
1980–2 Julius Chan
1982–5 Michael Thomas Somare
1985–8 Paias Wingti
1988–92 Rabbie Namiliu
1992–4 Paias Wingti
1994–7 Julius Chan
1997 John Giheno (caretaker)
1997–9 Bill Skate
1999–2002 Mekere Morauta
2002– Michael Thomas Somare

parabola *p.1158*

Paracas A barren peninsula on the S coast of Peru, renowned for its ornate prehistoric pottery and colourful embroidered textiles. Most of the artefacts have been recovered from mummified burials and dated c.600–100 BC.

Paracelsus [paraselsus], originally **Philippus Aureolus Theophrastus Bombastus von Hohenheim** (1493–1541) Alchemist and physician, born in Einsiedeln, NC Switzerland. He travelled widely in Europe and the Middle East, learning about alchemy, and acquiring great fame as a medical practitioner (1526) introducing laudanum, sulphur, lead, and mercury into Western therapeutics. He became town physician and lecturer at Basel (1527), but his controversial views caused his exile in 1538. He travelled through Europe until settling at Salzburg in 1541. He established the use of chemistry in medicine, gave the most up-to-date description of syphilis, and was the first to argue that small doses of what makes people ill can also cure them.

paracetamol [parasetamol] A mild painkiller commonly used for headache, menstrual pain, etc. It will also reduce body temperature during fever. Although very safe, overdose leads to irreversible liver damage, and can be fatal.

parachuting The act of jumping out of an aircraft and eventually landing with the aid of a parachute. As a sport, the competitor free-falls for a few thousand feet before opening the chute, normally at approximately 750 m/2500 ft. In competition, the object is to land within a predetermined target area. Parachuting first became popular as a variety act. French aeronaut André-Jacques Garnerin (1769–1823) made the first recorded descent over Paris in October 1797, when he was released from a balloon.

paracrine [parakriyn] A chemical messenger (eg prostaglandins, pancreatic somatostatin, kinins) synthesized by specific cells and released into the extracellular fluid for transport to adjacent cells, where it has a regulatory effect. It is rapidly inactivated by local enzymes. It may function as a hormone, a neurohormone, or a neurotransmitter elsewhere in the body. By convention, neurotransmitters themselves are not classified as paracrines.

Paradise A term, probably of Persian origin, referring to a walled garden or park; in the Bible, applied variously to the Garden of Eden (*Gen* 2–3, in the Septuagint only) and to forests, but only later to a blessed, future heavenly state and place of bliss (2 *Cor* 12.4; *Rev* 2.7). In ancient and modern thought, Para-

parabola

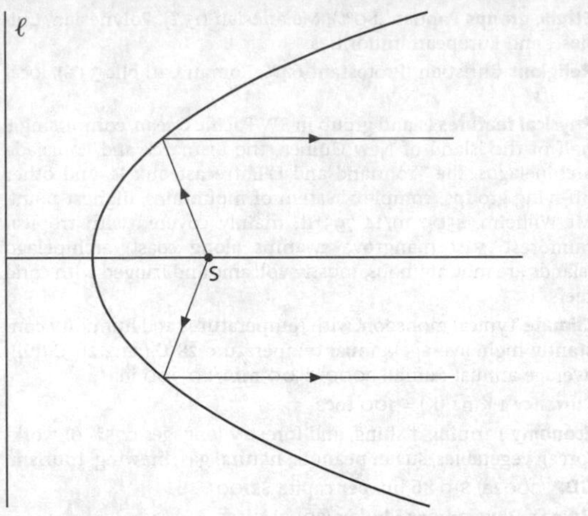

In mathematics, the locus of a point whose distance from a fixed point *S* (the *focus*) is equal to its distance from a fixed line *l* (the *directrix*). It is one of the classical conic sections. The parabola has the property that the tangent at any point *P* is equally inclined to the line *PS*, and the line through *P* parallel to the *x*-axis of the parabola. Thus rays emitted from *S* and reflected by the curve will be parallel. This notion underlies the technique for obtaining parallel rays of light, and for transmitting parallel radio waves.

dise has been visualized not only as gardens, but also as mountains and islands.

paradox In logic, a contradictory or implausible conclusion which seems to follow by valid argument from true premisses. 'This sentence is false' appears to be true if false, and false if true. Such self-referential paradoxes played an important role in the work of Russell and Frege on the foundations of mathematical logic.

paraffin *kerosene*

paraffin wax Solid hydrocarbon wax, originally produced from shale c.1850, but now made from petroleum. It is used for candles (for which it was socially very useful in the later 19th-c), waterproofing, textile conditioning, polishes, and ointments. It owes some of its properties to its micro-crystalline structure.

Paraguay *p.1159*

Paraguay, River [paragwiy] (Span **Río**), Port **Rio Paraguai** River in C South America; a chief tributary of the R Paraná; rises in Brazil (Mato Grosso), flows S, forming part of Brazil–Bolivia, Brazil–Paraguay, and Paraguay–Argentina borders, flowing into the Paraná above Corrientes, Argentina; length 2300 km/1450 mi; used widely by local river traffic.

Paraguayan War *Triple Alliance, War of the*

parakeet The name used for some small parrots with long pointed tails (c.37 species).

paraldehyde [paraldehiyd] $(C_2H_4O)_3$. An oligomer containing three molecules of acetaldehdyde; a liquid boiling at 128°C. Acetaldehyde is conveniently stored in this form, from which it is regenerated by heating with acid.

Paralipomenon [paralipomenon] *Chronicles, Books of*

parallax In astronomy, an apparent displacement in the position of any celestial object caused by a change in the position of the observer; specifically, a change because of the motion of the Earth around the Sun. It is often loosely used by astronomers to be synonymous with distance, because it is inversely proportional to distance.

parallel computing *parallel processing*

parallel distributed processing *connectionism*

parallel processing The use of two or more processors simultaneously to carry out a single computing task, each processor being assigned a particular part of the task at any given time. This differs from conventional single-processor computing, where the whole task is carried out sequentially by the one processor. Parallel processing does have inherent programming and supervisory difficulties, but promises greatly increased computing speeds at least for certain types of task. The Transputer has been designed to take advantage of parallel processing.

Paralympics ('beside the Olympics') The equivalent of the Olympic Games for disabled people, inaugurated in 1960, and held every four years where possible in the same city or country as the Olympic Games. The major events of the Summer Games include archery, basketball, boccia, cycling, fencing, judo, power/weight lifting, shooting, soccer, swimming, table tennis, tennis, and volleyball; Winter Games have been held since 1976.

paralysis Loss of movement resulting from interference with the nerve supply to a muscle or muscles. It may arise from destruction of the motor nerve cells in the brain (eg *hemiplegia*, following a stroke in which muscles on one side of the body are affected), or in the spinal cord (eg poliomyelitis). *Paraplegia* refers to the loss of muscle power affecting both lower limbs, and is usually caused by injury to the spinal cord. In *quadriplegia* all four limbs are affected.

paramagnetic resonance Magnetic resonance exhibited by atoms of paramagnetic substances, having magnetic moments due to unpaired electrons; also called **electron paramagnetic resonance** or **electron spin resonance**. It can be used to study the nature of chemical bonds in a sample, and is an important analytical technique in chemistry, biology, and medicine.

paramagnetism A magnetic effect present in many materials (eg aluminium and oxygen at room temperature) in which individual atoms' magnetic moments align in support of an applied magnetic field, the material being attracted towards the source of the applied field. It is characterized by positive magnetic susceptibility, and exploited in magnetic cooling.

Paramaribo [paramareeboh] 5°54N 55°14W, pop (2000e) 261 000. Federal capital of Suriname; chief port and only large town of Suriname, on the R Suriname; capital of British Suriname, 1651; under Dutch rule, 1814–1975; airport; university (1968); trade in bauxite, coffee, timber, fruit; People's Palace (former Governor's Mansion), Fort Zeelandia; cathedral (1885) built entirely of wood, said to be largest wooden building in the Americas.

Paramecium [parameesium] A genus of single-celled micro-organisms, ovoid in shape, length up to 0·33 mm/0·013 in; cells contain two types of nucleus (macronucleus and micronucleus); feeds by ingestion of bacteria; hair-like processes (*cilia*) arranged uniformly over cell surface; common in aquatic habitats. (Phylum: Ciliophora.)

paramedic A medical specialist responsible for collecting injured or unwell people (eg from the site of an accident), administering life-saving procedures where necessary, and initiating emergency treatment while transporting the casualty to a hospital, usually in an ambulance or helicopter.

Paraná, River [parana] (Span **Río**), in Brazil **Alto Parana** Major river of South America; forms with its tributaries (notably the Paraguay) and the R Uruguay South America's second largest drainage system; rises in SEC Brazil and flows generally S along Paraguay's E and S border into Argentina, where it joins the Uruguay after 3300 km/2000 mi to form the R Plate estuary on the Atlantic; dammed at various points for hydroelectricity, with a major scheme at Itaipú in Brazil.

parana pine *araucaria*

paranoia An excessive tendency to suspiciousness and sensitivity to being rebuffed. Paranoid individuals may presume by merely seeing a police car that there is an elaborate plot to put them in jail, and that the plot has been directed by an unknown authority. This definition is of a symptom, but in addition the

Paraguay

[paragwiy], official name **Republic of Paraguay**, Span **República del Paraguay**

Local name Paraguay

Timezone GMT – 4

Area 406 750 km²/157 000 sq mi

Population total (2002e) 5 774 000

Status Republic

Date of independence 1811

Capital Asunción

Languages Spanish (official), but Guaraní also spoken

Ethnic groups Mestizo (mixed Spanish-Guaraní Indian) (91%), Amerindian, black, European, and Asian minorities

Religions Roman Catholic (96%), Mennonite, Baptist/Anglican minorities

Physical features Landlocked, in C South America; divided into two regions by the R Paraguay; Gran Chaco in the W, mostly cattle country or scrub forest; more fertile land in the E; Paraná plateau at 300–600 m/1000–2000 ft, mainly wet, treeless savannah.

Climate Tropical NW, with hot summers, warm winters; temperate in SE; average annual temperatures 27°C (Jan), 18°C (Jul) in Asunción; average annual rainfall 1316 mm/52 in.

Currency 1 Guaraní (G) = 100 céntimos

Economy Agriculture (employs 43% of the labour force); oilseed, cotton, wheat, tobacco, corn, rice, sugar cane; pulp, timber, textiles, cement, glass.

GDP (2002e) $25·19 bn, per capita $4300

Human Development Index (2002) 0·740

History Originally inhabited by Guaraní Indians; arrival of the Spanish, 1537; arrival of Jesuit missionaries, 1609; independence from Spain, 1811; War of the Triple Alliance against Brazil, Argentina, and Uruguay, 1865–70; Chaco War with Bolivia, 1932–5; civil war, 1947; General Alfredo Stroessner seized power, 1954, forced to stand down following a coup in 1989; new constitution, creating post of Vice-President, 1992; governed by a President, an appointed Council of Ministers, and a bicameral National Congress.

Head of State/Government

1940–8 Higinio Moríñigo
1948 Juan Manuel Frutos
1948–9 Juan Natalicio González
1949 Raimundo Rolón
1949 Felipe Molas López
1949–54 Federico Chaves
1954 Tomás Romero Pareira
1954–89 Alfredo Stroessner
1989–93 Andres Rodriguez
1993–8 Juan Carlos Wasmosy
1998–9 Raúl Cubas Grau
1999–2003 Luis Gonzalez Macchi
2003– Nicanor Duarte Frutos

term has been used to describe a syndrome, and in this sense it was brought into common usage by the German physician Karl Ludwig Kahlbaum (1828–99) in 1863.

paranormal Beyond the bounds of what can be explained in terms of currently held scientific knowledge. Thus, to describe an event as paranormal requires that all other possible explanations for the event, based on known principles, be ruled out. However, the use of the term does not imply that the eventual explanation, as science discovers more about allegedly paranormal events, will be non-physical; it allows for the possibility that new discoveries in physics may account for events which are now classified as paranormal. This is in contrast with the term *supernatural*, which implies a non-physical explanation for events that lie forever beyond natural laws.

paraplegia *paralysis*

parapsychology The scientific study of certain aspects of the paranormal, primarily those in which an organism appears (i) to receive information from its environment through some means not presently understood (also known as **extrasensory perception**, or ESP), or (ii) to exert an influence on its environment through some means not presently understood (also known as **psychokinesis**, or **PK**), in the laboratory or in everyday life. Although the terms *parapsychology* and *psychical research* are roughly equivalent, some topics considered to be the subject matter of psychical research in its early days, such as hypnosis, had become part of 'orthodox' psychology and medicine by the time the term *parapsychology* came into use, and so the latter incorporates only those topics which seem to have a paranormal component according to today's knowledge.

In addition, the term has tended to be applied to studies of the paranormal which have used scientific methodology, no doubt because it was popularized in the English-speaking world by J B Rhine, who in the 1930s gained prominence with his application of laboratory methods. Publication of the positive results of Rhine's research had considerable impact on scientists, although interest declined when others found it difficult to repeat his results themselves. In the present day, the reality of paranormal phenomena remains controversial, but increasingly sophisticated approaches to experimentation offer hopes of increasing the level of repeatability between different laboratories. Meanwhile, the scientific approach of parapsychology appears to be gaining respectability, with the acceptance of the Parapsychological Association as an affiliate by the American Association for the Advancement of Science in 1969, and the establishment of the Koestler Chair of Parapsychology at the University of Edinburgh in 1985.

parasitic plant A plant which obtains some or all of its food and/or shelter from another plant. The arrangement may be temporary or permanent. **Obligate parasites** can survive only by this means; **facultative parasites** are more flexible, and under certain conditions are able to survive without the host, for example by changing to a saprophytic lifestyle. Many fungi and some plants have adopted this lifestyle.

Among flowering plants total parasites include broomrapes, rafflesias, and dodders. They are brown or reddish, completely lacking chlorophyll, have very reduced leaves and roots, and hence are unable to manufacture any food of their own. Rafflesias are unusual within flowering plants in being **endoparasites**, living entirely within the host's tissues, except for the flowers, which break out through the body of the host in order to be pollinated and to shed their seeds. Broomrapes and dodders are examples of **ectoparasites**, living outside the host, but attached to it by modified feeding organs (*haustoria*) which penetrate the host vascular system to draw off nutrients.

A much larger group are the semi-parasitic plants, which possess green leaves and are able to manufacture at least some nutrients, but have root systems capable of forming haustorial attachments, usually to other root systems, and thus supplement their food supply from a host. They are termed **hemiparasites**, and include mistletoe and eyebrights. Not all plants that augment their food supply from outside sources are parasites. Some, such as orchids and members of the pea family, live together in a relationship of symbiosis; others are saprophytes; and a few are predatory.

parasitology [parasitolojee] The study of organisms which live on and at the expense of another living creature (the *host*) and of their interactions. Strictly these organisms include both harmless and disease-producing viruses and bacteria, but common usage restricts the study to (1) *Protozoa* such as *Amoeba*, *Giardia*, *Trichomonas*, *Trypanosoma*, *Leishmania*, and *Toxoplasma*, (2) worms such as round and flat worms, tapeworms, *Trichinella*, *Schistosoma*, *Echinococcus*, and others, and (3) *arthropods* which cause harm to humans by producing venom, sucking blood, and carrying disease (eg mosquitoes, sandflies, and lice), or merely by inhabiting the skin and causing itching (eg scabies).

parasympathetic nervous system *autonomic nervous system*

parathormone *parathyroid hormone*

parathyroid glands In humans a set of glands, usually four in number, closely associated with the back of the thyroid gland within its capsule. Each gland consists of *chief* cells, which produce parathyroid hormone, and *oxyphil* cells, whose function is unknown. The removal of all parathyroid glands in mammals causes death within a few days.

parathyroid hormone A hormone (a polypeptide) synthesized and secreted by the chief cells of the parathyroid glands, released in response to lowered blood calcium levels; also known as **parathormone**. It has the opposite effect to calcitonin: it raises extracellular calcium levels by stimulating the removal of calcium from bone and from the renal tubule into the blood, and it promotes the conversion of vitamin D to an active form, which stimulates intestinal calcium absorption.

paratyphoid fever A disease caused by a species of *Salmonella*, similar to but less serious than typhoid fever. It is acquired through contaminated food or drink.

Parcae [pah(r)see, pah(r)kiy] The fates. The name originally referred to a Roman birth-goddess. She was later trebled, and identified with the Moerae, the goddesses who allot the destiny of human beings.

parchment A prepared but untanned animal skin, usually of a sheep, goat, or calf, developed by the Greeks c.2nd-c BC as a medium of writing. In mediaeval Europe, before the introduction of paper, parchment was used for manuscripts and later for printed books. Nowadays, its use is reserved for commemorative and other important documents. A high quality, fine-grained parchment is known as *vellum*.

parchment-bark *pittosporum*

parchment worm A filter-feeding bristleworm that inhabits a leathery or parchment-like tube embedded in soft sediment; fragile body divided into three distinct regions; c.45 species, all marine. (Class: Polychaeta. Order: Chaetopterida.)

pardalote *diamondbird*

parenteral nutrition *intravenous feeding*

Pareto, Vilfredo [paraytoh] (1848–1923) Economist and sociologist, born in Paris, France. Brought up in Italy, he studied at Turin University, became an engineer, and directed a railway company in Italy. He then studied philosophy and politics, and became professor of political economy at Lausanne from 1893. He wrote several influential textbooks on the subject, in which he demonstrated a mathematical approach. In sociology, his *Trattato di sociologica generale* (1916, trans The Mind and Society) enquired into the nature of individual and social action; it presented a theory of the superiority of an elite class which anticipated some of the principles of Fascism.

Paretsky, Sara [paretskee] (1947–) Writer of detective fiction, born in Ames, Iowa, USA. She studied at the universities of Kansas and Chicago, and worked for an insurance company before writing full time from 1985. All her novels are set in and around Chicago, and most feature V I Warshawski, a female private detective. Her first Warshawski novel, *Indemnity Only*, appeared in 1982. Many of her books, such as *Bitter Medicine* (1987) and *Burn Marks* (1990), explore social issues. *Ghost Country* (1998) does not feature her heroine, though she returns to Warshawski in *Hard Time* (1999). *Blood Shot* (1988) is often said to to be her best work. She is a founder of Sisters in Crime, which promotes the work of other women writers of detective fiction. She received the Diamond Dagger Award of the Crime Writers Association of Great Britain in 2002.

Paricutín [pareekooteen] 19°29N 102°17W. Active volcano in W Michoacán, WC Mexico; height 2774 m/9101 ft; 1943 eruption buried the Indian town of San Juan; church spires are all that can be seen of the former village.

Paris (France), ancient **Lutetia** 48°50N 2°20E, pop (2000e) 2 251 000. Capital of France and of Ville de Paris department, on R Seine; originally a Roman settlement; capital of Frankish kingdom, 6th-c; established as capital, 987; R Seine spanned here by 30 bridges, oldest the Pont Neuf (1578–1604); tourist river boats ('bateaux mouches'); bounded by Bois de Boulogne (W), Bois de Vincennes (E); divided into 20 arrondissements; 'Left Bank' (formerly associated with the aristocracy, later with writers and artists) and 'Right Bank' (formerly associated with the middle class); headquarters of many international organizations (notably UNESCO); airports at Orly (S), Charles de Gaulle (Roissy) and Le Bourget (NE); main railway stations, Gare du Nord, Gare de l'Est, Gare d'Austerlitz, Gare de Lyon, Gare St-Lazare, Gare Montparnasse; métro; Sorbonne University (13th-c); one of the world's main tourist centres, with famous hotels, nightclubs, theatres, restaurants, and shops; world centre of high fashion and production of luxury goods; wide range of heavy and light industry in suburbs; *Right Bank*: Arc de Triomphe, Champs Elysées, Place de la Concorde, Centre Pompidou (1977), Louvre, Church of La Madeleine, Montmartre, Basilica of Sacré Coeur, L'Opéra (1861–75), Tuileries gardens; *Left Bank*: Eiffel Tower (1889), Hôtel des Invalides, Musée d'Orsay, Jardin des Plantes (1626), Palais du Luxembourg, Notre Dame Cathedral (1163), Montparnasse and Latin Quarter, associated with artists and writers; horse racing at Longchamp, Vincennes, Auteuil; Euro Disney theme park to E of city; international air show at Le Bourget (every second June), Festival du Quartier du Marais (Jun–Jul), international film festival (Oct).

Paris (mythology) In Greek mythology, a prince of Troy, the son of Priam and Hecuba; also called **Alexander**. Because of a prophecy, he was exposed at birth on Mt Ida, where he was loved by Oenone, a nymph. There he also chose Aphrodite as the fairest of three goddesses ('the judgment of Paris'). She offered him Helen, the most beautiful woman in the world; he abducted Helen, and so caused the Trojan War. He was wounded by Philoctetes, and in his death-agony asked Oenone for help, which she refused.

Paris, Matthew *Matthew Paris*

Paris, School of In art history, a term with two applications: in the 13th-c, when Paris was the European centre for illuminated manuscripts; and in the 20th-c, when Paris was the focus of most of the modern art movements (c.1900–50).

Paris, Treaties of 1 (1761–3) The peace settlement ending the Seven Years' War (1756–63), signed by Britain, France, and Spain. Spain surrendered Florida to the British, but received the Louisiana Territory and New Orleans from France, and Havana and Manila from Britain. In exchange for minor concessions, France ceded Canada, America E of the Mississippi, Cape Breton and the St Lawrence islands, Dominica, Tobago, the Grenadines, and Senegal to Britain. In the short term, Britain was isolated by the French determination for revenge, but the final consequence was British colonial supremacy.
2 (1814–15) Successive peace settlements involving France and the victorious coalition of Britain, Austria, Prussia, Russia, Sweden, and Portugal, restoring the Bourbon monarchy to France in place of the Napoleonic Empire, before and after the Hundred Days (1815). In 1815 a large indemnity and army of occupation replaced the generous terms of 1814.

Paris, Treaty of (1951) *European Coal and Steel Community; European Community*

Paris, University of The three schools of Notre-Dame, Ste Geneviève, and St Victor, which flourished during the 12th-c in Paris, may be regarded as the foundation of the university. Founded in large part c.1208, as shown in a Bull of Innocent III, it is situated on the left bank of the R Seine. Thomas Aquinas, Bonaventure, and Alexander of Hales were among those who taught there during the 13th-c, and in 1253 the prestigious college of Sorbonne was founded as part of the university by Robert de Sorbon (1201–74). In the 14th-c it was pre-eminent among European universities. As a result of student demands for educational reform in May 1968, the university was reorganized into 13 independent faculties, known as *Universités de Paris I à XIII*.

parish council The smallest unit of local elective government in the UK, dating from the 16th-c and originally based on an area covered by one church. It is not normally elected along party political lines, but has close links with the local community. Councils of this kind have various names in different countries, such as community councils, townships, rural communes, and (in India) panchayats.

Paris Opéra Ballet The oldest national ballet company in the world. It was established in France in 1661 by Louis XIV as the Académie Royale de Danse, and amalgamated with the Académie Royale de Musique in 1672. Its first great director was Lully, who pioneered the opera-ballet form in which dancers became as important a part of the performance as the virtuoso singers. As part of the Théâtre National de l'Opéra, the company exercised great influence over European theatrical dance of the 18th and early 19th-c. In 1875 the Paris Opéra Ballet moved to the purpose-built Palais Garnier. Brigitte Lefèvre was appointed director of dance in 1995.

Paris Pacts (1954) A series of amendments and protocols to the Treaty of Brussels and the Brussels Treaty Organization. Italy and the Federal Republic of Germany became members of what became known as the Western European Union. Germany agreed not to manufacture atomic, bacteriological, or chemical weapons, thus clearing the way for its rearmament and membership of NATO.

Paris Peace Conference 1 (1919–20) A meeting of 32 'allied and associated powers' who met in Paris to draw up a peace settlement after World War 1. Five treaties were concluded – with Germany (Treaty of Versailles, 1919), Austria (Treaty of St Germain, 1919), Hungary (Treaty of Trianon, 1920), Bulgaria (Treaty of Neuilly, 1919), and Turkey (Treaties of Sèvres, 1920, and Lausanne, 1923).
2 (1946) A meeting of the five members of the Council of Foreign Ministers (UK, France, USA, Russia, China) and 16 other nations involved in the war against the Axis Powers. It drew up peace treaties with Bulgaria, Finland, Hungary, Romania, and Italy. Despite repeated divisions, agreement was finally reached and the treaties signed in the spring of 1947.

parity (economics) A term used when central banks undertake to limit fluctuations in exchange rate; abbreviated as **par**; the **par rate** is that around which the margin of fluctuation is measured. A security stands at par if its market price is equal to its face value. Parity has also been used in US agricultural policy as the name for a notional fair price for certain crops.

parity (physics) In quantum mechanics, a quantity which monitors the behaviour of a system under change from left- to right-handed co-ordinates; symbol *P*. A multiplicative parity quantum number can be ascribed to quantum systems and particles, and is conserved by electromagnetic and strong nuclear forces but not by weak nuclear force. Weak radioactive decays have an overall handedness; neutrinos are described as left-handed.

parity check A simple means of detecting errors in transmitted binary data. Each byte contains a **parity bit** which is set to indicate whether the byte contains an odd or even number of 1s. This bit is then checked on reception to ensure that it is consistent. This simple system will not detect all errors, eg it will detect if one bit is in error but not if two are in error. Much more complicated and reliable systems such as Hamming Codes are now in general use.

Park, Mungo (1771–1806) Explorer of Africa, born in Foulshiels, Scottish Borders, SE Scotland, UK. He became a surgeon at Edinburgh, and in 1792 served on an expedition to Sumatra. In 1795–6 he made a journey along the Niger R, as recounted in *Travels in the Interior of Africa* (1799). He settled as a surgeon in Peebles, then in 1805 undertook another journey to the Niger. The expedition reached Bussa, where he was drowned following an attack by natives.

Parker, Sir Alan (1944–) Film director and actor, born in London, UK. He began his career in advertising, then progressed via script writing to directing short films. He made his feature-length cinema debut with *Bugsy Malone* (1976). Later films include *Midnight Express* (1978), *Birdy* (1985), *The Commitments* (1991, BAFTA best film and director), *Evita* (1996), *Angela's Ashes* (1998), and *The Life of David Gale* (2002). He received a knighthood in 2001.

Parker, Charlie, popular name of **Charles (Christopher) Parker**, nickname **Bird** or **Yardbird** (1920–55) Jazz saxophonist, born in Kansas City, Kansas, USA. He worked with Jay McShann's orchestra, and his first recordings in 1941 already reveal technical grace on the alto saxophone and melodic inventiveness. In New York City, he joined Dizzy Gillespie, Thelonious Monk, and other musicians in expanding the harmonic basis for jazz. The new music, called 'bebop', developed an adventuresome young audience at the end of World War 2. He began using heroin as a teenager, and died at 34. In 1988 the film, *Bird*, directed by Clint Eastwood, presented an entertaining but sanitized version of his life.

Parker, Dorothy, *née* **Rothschild** (1893–1967) Journalist and short-story writer, born in West End, New Jersey, USA. Educated at a convent, in 1916 she sold some of her poetry to the editor of *Vogue*, and was given an editorial position on the magazine. She became drama critic of *Vanity Fair* (1917–20), and was at her most trenchant in book reviews and stories in the early issues (1927–33) of the *The New Yorker*, a magazine whose character she did much to form. Her work continued to appear in the magazine at irregular intervals until 1955. Her reviews were collected in *A Month of Saturdays* (1971). She also wrote for *Esquire*, and published poems and sketches. Her poems appeared in *Not So Deep as a Well* (1936) and *Enough Rope* (1926), which became a best seller. Her short stories were collected in *Here Lies* (1939).

Parker, Matthew (1504–75) The second Protestant Archbishop of Canterbury, born in Norwich, Norfolk, E England, UK. He was chaplain to Anne Boleyn (1535), and held several church posts, becoming Dean of Lincoln. Deprived of his preferments by Queen Mary, he was made Archbishop of Canterbury by Elizabeth I (1559). He strove to bring about more general conformity, adopting a middle road between Catholic and Puritan extremes, and was in charge of the formulation of the Thirty-nine Articles.

Parkes, Sir Henry (1815–96) Australian statesman, born in Stoneleigh, Warwickshire, C England, UK. He emigrated to New South Wales in 1839, and became a well-known journalist in Sydney. A member of the colonial parliament in 1854, from 1872 he was five times premier of New South Wales. Knighted in 1877, he helped draft a constitution for a federated Australia (1891).

Parkinson, C(yril) Northcote (1909–93) Political scientist, born in Barnard Castle, Durham, NE England, UK. He studied at Cambridge, and at Kings College, London, then became professor of history at the University of Malaya (1950–8), and a visiting professor at Harvard and Illinois. He wrote many works on historical, political, and economic subjects, but achieved wider renown by his serio-comic tilt at bureaucratic malpractices in *Parkinson's Law: the Pursuit of Progress* (1957). 'Parkinson's law' – that work expands to fill the time available for its completion, and subordinates multiply at a fixed rate, regardless of the amount of work produced – has passed into the language.

Parkinson's disease A disorder of the central nervous system, named after British physician James Parkinson (1755–1824); also known as **paralysis agitans**. It affects the basal ganglia, the part of the brain that controls the co-ordination of movements. Neurones in this area become depleted of dopamine, the chemical that they use to transmit nerve impulses. Muscles become rigid, and it is difficult to initiate movements. Facial expression is lost, and there is a characteristic 'pill-rolling' tremor of the hands. Relief is obtained by providing dopamine as a drug, or by transplanting dopamine-secreting brain tissue.

Parlement [pah(r)luhmã] The French court of law in *ancien régime* France, originally a single institution, the *Parlement* of Paris, which developed from the mediaeval King's Court or *curia regis*, and subsequently assumed both political and judicial functions, its moves dictated by the interests of its almost exclusively noble members. From the late 16th-c onwards, the *parlements* systematically opposed royal reform measures. Their members joined the Frondes (1648–53), the abortive aristocratic revolution against Cardinal Mazarin. A century later, the *parlements* blocked the tax on all income from property. Between the 14th-c and 17th-c a network of provincial *parlements* emerged but, as bastions of conservatism and privilege, the *parlements* were among the first institutions be to abolished in the early days of the French Revolution (1790).

parliament The general term in most English-speaking countries for the national legislative body, normally elected by popular vote. Its role is to pass legislation and keep a check on the activities of the government or executive. In a parliamentary governmental system it is also responsible for choosing and sustaining a government, though the individual members of the government will be chosen by the prime minister. In some presidential systems (eg France) parliament can also be integral to supporting the government, but not the president, who is elected separately and who can be a member of a party which does not hold a parliamentary majority. In other systems, the executive may exist independently of the parliament, as is the case with the US president. In the UK, the national parliament is constituted by the House of Lords and the elected House of Commons. Proposed laws must go through a defined procedure in both Houses and receive the royal assent, before becoming statutes. Since 1999, Scotland (the Scottish Parliament), Northern Ireland (the Northern Ireland Assembly) and Wales (the Welsh Assembly) have been given their own directly elected legislative bodies, though the Northern Ireland body was suspended (Feb–May 2000, Oct 2002–) following lack of progress in relation to IRA arms decommissioning.

Parliamentary Commissioner for Administration The British ombudsman for central administration, established in 1967, who examines complaints of maladministration. The commissioner is a servant of parliament and works closely with a House of Commons select committee. Peers have no access to him; all complaints have to be channelled through MPs.

Parma [pah(r)ma] 44°48N 10°19E, pop (2000e) 181 000. Capital city of Parma province, Emilia-Romagna, N Italy; on R Parma, 126 km/78 mi SE of Milan; major cultural centre in Middle Ages; railway; university (13th-c); agricultural trade, oil refining, ham, salami, pasta, cheese (Parmesan), food processing, glass, fertilizers, textiles, perfume; birthplace of Toscanini; baptistery (12th–13th-c), cathedral (12th-c), Palazzo della Pilotta (begun 1583), Church of the Madonna della Steccata (1521–39), modelled on St Peter's in Rome; international food fairs (May, Oct); Palio (Sept).

Parmenides [pah(r)menideez] (c.515–c.445 BC) The most influential of the Presocratic philosophers, a native of the Greek settlement of Elea in S Italy, and founder of the Eleatic school. He is the first philosopher to insist on a distinction between the world of appearances and reality, and his remarkable poem, 'On Nature', foreshadows the dualism of Plato's metaphysics.

Parmigianino [pah(r)mijianeenoh], also called **Parmigiano**, originally **Girolamo Francesco Maria Mazzola** (1503–40) Painter of the Lombard school, born in Parma, N Italy. He began to paint in Parma, moving to Rome in 1523, but was forced to flee to Bologna when the city was sacked in 1527. At Bologna he painted his famous Madonna altarpiece for the nuns of St Margaret before returning to Parma in 1531.

Parnassians A group of poets in 19th-c France, associated with the journal *Le Parnasse Contemporain* (1866–76); among them Charles Leconte de Lisle, José Hérédia (1842–1905), and Sully-Prudhomme. In reaction against Romanticism, and in the scientific spirit of the age, they favoured a more austere and objective poetry.

Parnell, Charles Stewart [pah(r)nel, pah(r)nel] (1846–91) Irish politician, born in Avondale, Co Wicklow, E Ireland. He studied at Cambridge, and in 1875 became an MP, supporting Home Rule, and gained great popularity in Ireland by his audacity in the use of obstructive parliamentary tactics. In 1879 he was elected president of the Irish National Land League, and in 1886 allied with the Liberals in support of Gladstone's Home Rule Bill. He remained an influential figure until 1890, when following his affair with Katharine O'Shea, he was cited as co-respondent in a divorce case, and forced to retire as leader of the Irish nationalists.

parody (Gr 'burlesque poem/song') An imitation of a work of art, or convention, often for comic and satirical purposes. Examples include Cervantes' *Don Quixote* (1606–16) and Pope's *Rape of the Lock* (1714). Parody also serves the evolution of art through the exposure of outworn styles, as in Shakespeare's parody of Petrarchanism ('My mistress' eyes are nothing like the sun') or Jane Austen's parody of the Gothic novel in *Northanger Abbey* (1818). In the 20th-c, parody often served a pluralist function, revealing cultural gaps and fault-lines, as in Joyce's allusion to the Odyssey in *Ulysses* (1922), and Derek Walcott's in *Omeros* (1991). It has been pervasive in the other arts also – painting (Magritte), music (Satie), and the often self-regarding cinema – and may be thought of as an inevitable and healthy reflex in an evolving culture.

parole A conditional release given to a prisoner who still has part of a sentence left to serve. In England and Wales, parole has now been abolished for prisoners serving four years or less. They are automatically released on licence after serving one half of their sentence. Prisoners with longer sentences, except life sentences, must be paroled after serving two thirds of their sentences, and may be given parole after serving half their sentences. Under the Crime (Sentences) Act (1997), the Parole Board, rather than the home secretary, is responsible for the release of juveniles who are convicted of murder. A local review committee reports to the Parole Board which then advises the home secretary (in England and Wales) or (in the case of Scotland) the secretary of state for Scotland. In certain cases, the minister may act on the advice of the local committee alone. Release is conditional, and those paroled are supervised by a probation officer. In the USA, a parole board considers release, based on extensive guidelines, usually after a fixed portion of the sentence has been served. In 2002, the European Court of Human Rights ruled that judges, not politicians, should decide on the length of a life sentence, once the minimum tariff has been served.

Paros [pahros] area 195 sq km/75 sq mi; pop (2000e) 8470. Third largest island of the Cyclades, Greece, in the S Aegean Sea, W of Naxos; chief town, Parikia; beaches at Drios, Alikes, Pisso Livadi; famous for its marble and churches.

parousia [parooseea] (Gr 'coming', 'arrival', 'presence') In Christian thought, normally the future return or 'second coming' of Christ, which will be marked by a heavenly appearance, God's judgment of all humanity, and the resurrection of the dead. Belief in the imminence of Christ's return is particularly prominent in Paul's letters. Protracted delay of the event led to some reformulation of the belief, although some Christian movements continue to await the literal fulfilment of this predicted event and the signs associated with it.

Parque Nacional de Los Glaciares [glasyarays] Andean national park in SW Santa Cruz province, Patagonia, Argentina; area 4459 sq km/1721 sq mi; established in 1937; includes the E parts of L Viedma and L Argentino; borders Chile in the W; a world heritage site.

parquetry *marquetry*

Parr, Catherine (1512–48) Sixth wife of Henry VIII, the daughter of Sir Thomas Parr of Kendal. She first married Edward Borough, then Lord Latimer, and in 1543 became Queen of England by marrying Henry VIII. A learned, tolerant, and tactful woman, she persuaded Henry to restore the succession to his daughters, Mary I and Elizabeth, and showed her stepchildren much kindness. Very soon after Henry's death (1547) she married a former suitor, Lord Thomas Seymour of Sudeley, but died in childbirth the following year.

Parra, Violeta [para] (1917–67) Internationally celebrated Chilean folklorist, songwriter, and singer, born in San Carlos, Chile. She had a varied career, including a period in Paris (1961–5), and her work inspired the New Chilean Song movement of the later 1960s.

parrot A colourful bird, native to warm regions worldwide; bill large, hooked; nostrils on fleshy band (*cere*); inhabits forests or open country; eats mainly fruit and seeds (some insects); manipulates food with foot; good at mimicking human voice. (Family: Psittacidae, c.330 species.)

parrot disease *psittacosis*

parrotfish Colourful fish belonging to the family Scaridae (4 genera), in which jaw teeth are fused into a parrot-like beak used for scraping algal and coral growth from reefs; flat grinding teeth; body compressed, length 20–100 cm/8–40 in. The name is also used for the Indo-Pacific family Oplegnathidae.

parrot's bill An evergreen shrub (*Clianthus puniceus*), growing to 3·5 m/11 ft or more, native to New Zealand; also called **glory pea** and **lobster claw**, referring to the curiously-shaped, long curving lower petals of the flowers; leaves pinnate; flowers to 6·5 cm/2½ in, long, scarlet, in large pendulous clusters. (Family: Leguminosae.)

Parry, Sir (Charles) Hubert (Hastings) (1848–1918) Composer, born in Bournemouth, Dorset, S England, UK. He studied at Oxford, was professor at the Royal College of Music (1883), and in 1895 became its director. He composed three oratorios, an opera, five symphonies, and many other works, but is best known for his unison chorus 'Jerusalem' (1916), words by William Blake, sung as an unofficial anthem at the end of each season of Promenade Concerts in London.

Parry, Joseph (1841–1903) Musician, born in Merthyr Tydfil, S Wales, UK. He studied at the Royal Academy of Music, London, and became professor at University College, Cardiff. He composed oratorios, operas, and songs, and became one of the leading hymn-writers in the Welsh tradition, his best known hymn tune being 'Aberystwyth'.

parsec (pc) A unit of length, used for distances beyond the Solar System. The term is a contraction of **parallax second**, and is the distance at which the astronomical unit (AU) subtends one second of arc; it equals 206 265 AU, $3{\cdot}086 \times 10^{13}$ km/$1{\cdot}918 \times 10^{13}$ mi, 3·26 light years. (The light year is never used in professional astronomy.) The larger units **kiloparsec** (kpc) and **megaparsec** (Mpc) for 1000 and 1 000 000 pc respectively are also widely used in galactic and extragalactic contexts.

Parseeism [pah(r)seeizm] The religion of the descendants of the ancient Zoroastrians, who fled Persia after its conquest and settled in India in the 8th-c. They live mainly in the region round Mumbai, and preach a rule of life conforming to the purity of Ahura Mazda.

Parsifal *Perceval, Sir*

parsing The analyzing and labelling of the grammatical components of a sentence, according to their function within some grammatical framework, such as 'subject', 'verb', and 'object'. Thus, in one widely used system, a sentence such as *The cat sat on the dog* would be parsed as Subject + Predicate, with the Predicate parsed into Verb + Adverb Phrase, viz. *The cat + sat + on the dog*. Further divisions would identify the definite articles and preposition. Exercises of this kind were universally practised in schools during the 19th-c and in the first half of the 20th-c, but fell into disfavour during the 1950s because of their mechanical, uninspiring techniques. During the 1980s a move to re-introduce some form of parsing, as an antidote to the perceived widespread ignorance of grammar, received increasing support.

parsley A biennial or perennial (*Petroselinum crispum*), growing to 75 cm/30 in, but usually smaller; leaves triangular, shining, divided into wedge-shaped segments, lobed and also often curly in cultivated varieties; flowers yellowish, in long-stemmed, flat-topped umbels up to 5 cm/2 in across, petals notched; fruit ovoid. Its origin is uncertain, but it is widely cultivated as a flavouring. (Family: Umbelliferae.)

parsnip A biennial growing to 1·5 m/5 ft, but usually smaller, native to Europe and W Asia, and introduced in North and South America and Australasia; leaves divided into oblong-oval toothed segments up to 10 cm/4 in long; flowers yellow, without sepals, in umbels 3–10 cm/1¼–4 in across; fruit ellipsoid, broadly winged. It is grown commercially for the sweet, fleshy tap-roots, which are eaten as a vegetable and used as fodder for livestock. (Family: Umbelliferae.)

parson bird *tui*

Parsons, Sir Charles (Algernon) (1854–1931) Engineer, born in London, UK. He studied at Dublin and Cambridge, became an engineering apprentice, and in 1884 developed the high-speed steam turbine. He also built the first turbine-driven steamship, the *Turbinia*, in 1897.

Parsons, Talcott [tawlcot] (1902–79) Sociologist, born in Colorado Springs, Colorado, USA. He studied at Amherst College, the London School of Economics, and Heidelberg University, and became one of the most prominent US sociologists, based throughout his career at Harvard. He developed a functionalist analysis of social systems through his principal publications, *The Structure of Social Action* (1939) and *The Social System* (1951).

Parsons, Tony (1953–) Journalist and novelist, born in Romford, Essex, SE England, UK. He first worked in a gin distillery before joining the New Musical Express as a journalist. After leaving the paper he became a roving reporter for magazines *GQ* and *Elle*, and also wrote three 'potboiler' novels. During the 1990s he became a newspaper columnist and a regular panellist on BBC Two's *Late Review* programme. His novel, *Man and Boy* (1998), won Book of the Year at the British Book Awards, and later novels include *One for My Baby* (2001) and *Man and Wife* (2003).

parthenocarpy *fruit*

parthenogenesis [pah(r)thenohjenesis] The development of an individual from an egg without fertilization by a male gamete (*sperm*). Eggs that develop parthenogenetically are usually diploid (possessing two chromosome sets) and genetically identical with the mother. Many organisms (eg water fleas) pass through several parthenogenetic generations consisting only of females, but will produce males and reproduce sexually at the onset of adverse environmental conditions.

Parthenon The principal building of the Athenian Acropolis, a Doric temple of Pentelic marble dedicated to Athena *Parthenos* ('the Maiden'); a world heritage site. It was built 447–433 BC to the plans of Ictinus and Callicrates under the supervision of Phidias, the sculptor responsible for its 9 m/30 ft-high gold and ivory cult statue. Converted subsequently into a church, then a mosque, it was reduced to a shell by explosion in 1687 while housing a powder magazine during the Turkish–Venetian war.

Parthians The inheritors of the E territories of the Seleucids, from the 3rd-c BC ruling an empire that stretched from the Euphrates to the Indus. Rome's main rivals for power in the E, they resisted conquest by her in the 50s BC, but failed in their turn to take over her E provinces. In the end, both had to settle for uneasy co-existence.

participant observation A research technique in social science in which the researcher observes social action directly by becoming a member of the group under observation. Such membership may be overt (ie the observer tells the group that he/she is a researcher) or covert (ie the observer adopts a role in the group to disguise this fact).

particle accelerators Machines for accelerating charged subatomic particles, usually electrons or protons or their respective antiparticles, to high velocity. The basic configurations are straight (linear accelerators) or circular (synchrotrons). In the latter, magnetic fields control the beam path. Both use radiofrequency electric fields to provide acceleration. The beams of particles collide either with stationary targets (eg liquid hydrogen) or another oncoming particle beam (colliding beam machines).

particle beam weapons The use of high-energy subatomic particles, generated in nuclear accelerators and turned into a directable beam, as a practical weapon. One of the goals of late 20th-c military research was to prove the technology of this approach, which would be used, for example, to shoot down missiles in space.

particle detectors Devices for detecting and identifying subatomic particles in particle physics experiments. They are designed to measure total energy, charge to mass ratio, velocity, position, and time. Since no single instrument can perform all these tasks, detectors often comprise several distinct units, each performing a different task.

particle physics The study of the fundamental components of matter and the forces between them; also called **high energy physics** or **elementary particle physics**. Most particle physics experiments involve the use of large particle accelerators, necessary to force particles close enough together to produce interactions. All theories in particle physics are quantum theories, in which symmetry is of central importance.

The material world is composed of atoms. Each atom in turn comprises a central nucleus surrounded by electrons, and the nucleus is composed of protons and neutrons. These protons, neutrons, the particles from which they are made, and other related objects are the entities studied in particle physics. Subatomic particles thought to be indivisible into smaller particles are known as *fundamental particles*: these are the matter particles (quarks, neutrinos, electrons, muons, and taus) and the force particles (gluons, photons, and W and Z bosons). The important forces acting between these particles are the electromagnetic, strong nuclear, and weak nuclear forces. Gravity is ignored.

By the late 1930s, protons, neutrons, and electrons were all known; nuclear fission had been observed; and the subject of nuclear physics was established. Particle physics explores the structure of matter at one level beneath nuclear physics. The earliest particle physics experiments involved measuring tracks left by cosmic rays in photographic emulsions. In this way muons (1937) and pions (1947) were discovered. Originally the pion was thought to be the fundamental carrier of nuclear force, in line with an early theory of nuclear force proposed by Hideki Yukawa in 1935. This view has now been superseded, although in low energy nuclear physics the force between protons and neutrons can be discussed in terms of mediation by pions.

During the 1950s, further cosmic ray studies and early accelerator experiments revealed other particles of various masses. Some exhibited unusual or 'strange' behaviour. Such particles were produced easily, suggesting they formed via strong interactions, but decayed slowly via weak interactions. A new quantum number called *strangeness*, conserved in strong but not in weak interactions, was invented to explain these results. Other similar quantum numbers having equally unlikely names have subsequently been introduced to account for observed particle interactions. During the 1950s and 1960s, many particles and resonances were discovered, including the antiproton (confirming that antiparticles exist) and the neutrino.

A scheme of particle classification based on symmetry, in which particles were labelled by quantum numbers such as isospin and strangeness, was introduced in 1961 by Murray Gell-Mann and Yuval Ne'eman. In 1964 Gell-Mann and US physicist George Zweig (1937–) proposed quarks as abstract entities underlying symmetry patterns. However, experiments (1968) at the Stanford Linear Accelerator Center in the USA, which involved firing electrons at protons, suggested that objects within protons have the properties of quarks. Although no quarks have ever been observed directly, it is widely assumed they are the ultimate components of protons, neutrons, and most other subatomic particles.

The full theory of strong interaction, in which the strong force between quarks is carried by gluons, dates from 1973, and is called **quantum chromodynamics**. Weak interactions, governing radioactive beta decay, are understood in terms of the decay of individual quarks. For a neutron decaying to a proton (plus electron and antineutrino), a single u quark in the proton decays to a d quark plus electron and antineutrino. The weak force is carried by W and Z particles, and is well described by Glashow–Weinberg–Salam theory (1968). Purely electromagnetic interactions are described by quantum electrodynamics. Current research focuses on resolving difficulties in existing theories, constructing unified theories of strong, weak, and electromagnetic forces, and incorporating gravity to give a complete theory of the physical universe.

***Parti Québecois* (PQ)** [kaybekwah] A separatist political party in Canada, established in 1968. Led by René Lévesque until 1985, the *péquistes* formed the government in Quebec in 1976, and were elected for a second term in 1981. The PQ's goal of sovereignty-association failed to win sufficient support in Quebec in a 1980 referendum.

partita [pah(r)teeta] In music of the Baroque period, one of a set of instrumental variations (*partite*), such as Bach's *Partite diverse* on the chorale melody 'O Gott, du frommer Gott'; or a set of instrumental dances, such as Bach's three partitas for violin and six for keyboard.

partition coefficient *distribution coefficient*

Partition of Ireland (1949) The division of Ireland between an independent Irish Republic and Northern Ireland (Ulster), where the Protestant majority wanted to remain British. The Ulster Plantation in the 17th-c had established a Protestant ascendancy over the native Catholic population. A partition movement arose during the 1880s series of Home Rule Bills. Increased support for Sinn Féin followed the Easter Rising (1916), and the IRA's guerrilla campaign spread to Ulster. Protestant attacks in Catholic areas of Ulster caused deaths as well as retaliations by the IRA. The Anglo-Irish Treaty (1921) established an Irish Free Sate that excluded the six counties of Ulster. The formation of an independent Republic of Ireland in 1949 led to Britain guaranteeing Northern Ireland the status of a self-governing province of the UK, as long as this was supported by a majority vote in the Northern Ireland parliament (Stormont).

partnership A form of business organization where the owners share all the profits – or take all the losses – according to some predetermined formula. Liability is normally unlimited, but sometimes a 'limited partnership' is set up. There are usually not more than 20 partners, though larger partnerships do exist, as in the case of solicitors and firms of chartered accountants.

Parton, Dolly (Rebecca) (1946–) Country singer, songwriter, and actress, born in Locust Ridge, Tennessee, USA. Her early success was with Porter Wagoner (1927–), on television and record; she later took country-based music into the pop mainstream, well-known hits including 'Jolene' (1974) and 'Islands In The Stream' (1984). From 1982 she had success as a film actress, and also began to operate her own theme park, 'Dollywood'.

Partridge, Eric (Honeywood) (1894–1979) Lexicographer, born in Waimata Valley, Gisborne, New Zealand. He studied at Queensland and Oxford universities, was elected Queensland travelling fellow at Oxford after World War 1, and briefly lectured at Manchester and London universities (1925–7). For most of his life he worked as a freelance writer, carrying out a vast amount of painstaking personal research into the history and meaning of words. He is best known for his specialized studies of slang and other aspects of colloquial language. His works in this field include the pioneering *Dictionary of Slang and Unconventional English* (1937), *Usage and Abusage* (1947), and *A Dictionary of the Underworld, British and American* (1950), as well as many individual essays on the history and usage of English words.

partridge A drab, plump, short-tailed bird of the pheasant family; found from Europe to SE Asia, and in Africa; inhabits open country (sometimes tropical rainforest); eats insects when young, plant material as adult. (Family: Phasianidae, 84 species.)

par value *parity* (economics)

parvovirus A group of small, single-stranded DNA viruses that can infect animals or humans. Animal parvoviruses are responsible for commonly occurring blood disorders in cats and dogs, and a type of parvovirus designated B19 causes disease in humans. Infection of young children leads to an illness known as *erythema infectiosum* or *fifth disease*; fever, cough, and headache are accompanied by a rash affecting the cheeks, which gives a characteristic 'slapped cheek' appearance. Infection during pregnancy may lead to severe damage or death of the fetus.

Pasargadae [pasah(r)gadiy] The site in S Iran chosen by Cyrus the Great in 546 BC to be the capital of the new Achaemenid empire. It was also the site of Cyrus's tomb.

Pascal, Blaise [paskal] (1623–62) Mathematician, physicist, theologian, and man-of-letters, born in Clermont-Ferrand, C France. He invented a calculating machine (1647), and later the barometer, the hydraulic press, and the syringe. Until 1654 he spent his time between mathematics and the social round in Paris, but a mystical experience that year led him to join his sister, who was a member of the Jansenist convent at Port-Royal, where he defended Jansenism against the Jesuits in *Lettres provinciales* (1656–7). Fragments jotted down for a case book of Christian truth were discovered after his death and published as the *Pensées* (1669, Thoughts).

PASCAL A high-level computer programming language, named after the French mathematician, Blaise Pascal, which was developed from ALGOL in the late 1960s. It has become a popular language in the educational field, and is widely used with microcomputers. Versions of the language have been generated to incorporate the object-oriented paradigm.

pascal SI unit of pressure; symbol *Pa*; named after Blaise Pascal; defined as the pressure due to a force of 1 newton acting on an area of 1 square metre.

Pascua, Isla de *Easter Island*

Pashtun or **Pathan** [patahn] A cluster of Pashto-speaking agricultural and herding people of NW Pakistan and SE Afghanistan; possibly originally from Afghanistan, with several groups migrating to Pakistan in the 13th–16th-c. Traditionally warriors, many are employed in the national armies. They are the most numerous and dominant group in Afghanistan, numbering 6·2 million; 6·7 million live in Pakistan.

Pašić, Nikola [pasheetch] (c.1846–1926) Serbian statesman, born in Zaječar, E Yugoslavia. Condemned to death in 1883 for his part in the plot against King Milan, he survived on the accession of King Peter to be prime minister of Serbia (five times, from 1891) and later of Yugoslavia (1921–4, 1924–6), which he helped to found.

Pasiphae (astronomy) [pasifayee] The eighth natural satellite of Jupiter, discovered in 1908; distance from the planet 23 500 000 km/14 603 000 mi; orbital period 735 days; diameter 50 km/30 mi.

Pasiphae (mythology) [pasifayee] In Greek mythology, the daughter of Helios, and wife of Minos, King of Crete. She loved a bull sent by Poseidon, and became the mother of the Minotaur.

Pasmore, (Edwin John) Victor (1908–98) Artist, born in Chelsham, Surrey, SE England, UK. Largely self-taught, he was one of the founders of the London 'Euston Road School' (1937). He became an art teacher, and after World War 2 began to paint in a highly abstract style, in which colour is often primarily used to suggest relief. His works include *Rectangular Motif* (1949) and *Inland Sea* (1950, Tate, London). He became a Companion of Honour in 1981.

Pasolini, Pier Paolo [pasohleenee] (1922–75) Film director and writer, born in Bologna, N Italy. He became a Marxist following World War 2, moved to Rome, and began to write sordid novels of slum life in the city. In the 1950s he also worked as a scriptwriter and actor. He made his debut as a director in 1961, and became known for controversial, bawdy literary adaptations such as *Il Vangelo secondo Matteo* (1964, The Gospel According to St Matthew), *Il Decamerone* (1971, The Decameron), and *The Canterbury Tales* (1973). He was murdered, probably as the result of a homosexual encounter.

passacaglia [pasakahlya] A musical structure in which a continuously repeated bass line or harmonic progression provides the basis for a set of uninterrupted variations. Bach's *Passacaglia in C Minor* for organ is a well-known example.

passage rites *initiation rites*

Passchendaele, Battle of [pashendayl] (1917) The third battle of Ypres during World War 1; a British offensive which was continued despite no hope of a break-through to the Belgian ports, the original objective. It was notable for appallingly muddy conditions, minimal gains, and British casualties of at least 300 000. In the final action, Canadians captured the village of Passchendaele, 10 km/6 mi NE of Ypres.

passenger pigeon An extinct long-tailed pigeon (*Ectopistes migratorius*) from E North America; formed flocks of millions of birds; inhabited forests; nested in trees; migrated; hunted to extinction in the wild by 1894. The last specimen died in Cincinnati Zoo (1 Sep 1914, at 1 pm).

passerine Any bird of the worldwide order Passeriformes ('perching birds'); includes the **songbirds** (suborder: Oscines); comprises more than half the living species of birds; four toes, one pointing backwards and opposing the others; wing has 9–10 primary feathers; tail usually with 12 main feathers. They are land birds, crossing seas only when migrating.

passion flower A member of a large genus of climbers with twining tendrils, native to America, a few to Asia and Australia; leaves oval, crescent-shaped or deeply palmately-lobed; flowers large, showy, with five coloured sepals alternating with five petals, said to symbolize the crucifixion, with the inner corona of filaments representing the crown of thorns, and the styles the cross and nails; yellow or purple edible berry (known as **passion fruit** or **granadilla**), up to 10 cm/4 in long. (Genus: *Passiflora*, 500 species. Family: Passifloraceae.)

passion fruit *passion flower*

Passionists A religious order, founded in Italy in 1720 by St Paul of the Cross; properly known as the **Congregation of the Barefooted Clerics of the Most Holy Cross and Passion of our Lord Jesus Christ**. With houses in Europe and the USA, their declared objective is to maintain the memory of Christ's sufferings and death.

passive smoking Inhalation by non-smokers of tobacco smoke introduced into the atmosphere by smokers. It increases the risk of lung cancer and coronary heart disease.

Passover An annual Jewish festival, occurring in March or April (15–22 Nisan), commemorating the exodus of the Israelites from Egypt; named from God's passing over the houses of the Israelites when he killed the first-born children of the Egyptians (*Ex* 13); also known as **Pesach** [**pay**sakh]. It is marked by a special meal including unleavened bread and bitter herbs.

pasta A mixture of water, durum wheat flour (hard), and occasionally egg, originating in Italy. The dough is extruded through dies of various shapes, and dried to provide a wide variety of types (eg cannelloni, farfalle, fettucine, fusilli, lasagne, macaroni, noodles, ravioli, spaghetti, tagliatelle, tortellini, and vermicelli). Pastas are rich in starch, and are often served with a meat-based sauce.

pastel Powdered pigment mixed with a little gum or resin and shaped into sticks like crayons. The artist works directly onto the paper, which may be slightly tinted, without using a medium of any sort. Pastel painting enjoyed a considerable vogue in the 18th-c, especially in France.

Pasternak, Boris (Leonidovich) [**pas**ternak] (1890–1960) Lyric poet, novelist, and translator, born in Moscow, Russia. He studied law and musical composition, then switched to philosophy. He wrote autobiographical and political poetry, and some outstanding short stories, some of which were collected in *The Childhood of Lyuvers* (1924). Unable to publish his own poetry during the years under Stalin, he became the official translator into Russian of Shakespeare, Verlaine, and Goethe. He caused a political earthquake with his first novel, *Dr Zhivago*, which was banned in the Soviet Union, but became an international success after its publication in Italy in 1957. A fragmentary, poet's novel, it describes with intense feeling the Russian Revolution as it impinged upon one individual. Expelled by the Soviet Writers' Union, he had to take the unprecedented step of refusing the 1958 Nobel Prize for Literature.

Pasteur, Louis [**pas**ter] (1822–95) Chemist and microbiologist, born in Dôle, E France. He studied at Besançon and Paris universities, and held academic posts at Strasbourg, Lille, and Paris, where in 1867 he became professor of chemistry at the Sorbonne. He established that putrefaction and fermentation were caused by micro-organisms, thus providing an impetus to microbiology and leading to his 'pasteurization' process for milk. In a famous experiment in 1881, he showed that sheep and cows 'vaccinated' with the attenuated bacilli of anthrax received protection against the disease. In 1888 the Institut Pasteur was founded at Paris for the treatment of rabies, and he worked there until his death.

pasteurization A mild heat treatment used to kill micro-organisms in milk. The process heats the milk at 63–66°C for 30 minutes or 72°C for 15 seconds. This destroys pathogenic bacteria, and somewhat aids the shelf-life of the milk. It was discovered by the French chemist, Louis Pasteur, after whom it was named.

Paston Letters An invaluable collection of over 500 letters of a 15th-c gentry family from Norfolk, England, providing pictures of family life, estate management, local feuds, and national politics during the Wars of the Roses (1455–87). They are particularly valuable because the Pastons were of middling rank and, therefore, were more typical of landed society than the great lords dominant on the national scene.

pastoral (Lat 'pertaining to shepherds') A poem or other work expressing love of and longing for an idealized rural existence. Deriving from Theocritus, whose faithful lovers Daphnis and Chloe have become proverbial, the pastoral mode has been much imitated and adapted. Other forms include the pastoral romance and drama.

pastoralism A way of life characterized by keeping herds of animals, such as cattle, sheep, camels, reindeer, goats, or llamas. It is common in dry, mountainous, or severely cold climates not suitable for agriculture, although some groups combine pastoralism with agriculture. Many pastoralists are nomadic, having to move around in search of good grazing ground, but the amount of nomadism varies considerably, some living in settled areas for most of their lives. Because they travel around and can use their animals to transport goods, many pastoralists have become important long-distance traders. During the colonial period, pastoral migration and movements were severely curtailed in many parts. As agriculture expanded into areas which had previously served pastoralists (eg in Masailand, Kenya), pastoral communities found themselves confined to a diminishing area, which was inadequate, particularly in the dry season. As a result, many pastoralists have been victims of devastating famines.

Pastoral Letters or **Pastoral Epistles** Three New Testament writings – the First and Second Letters to Timothy and the Letter to Titus – so named since about the 18th-c because they purport to give Paul's advice to his colleagues Timothy and Titus about Church leadership. Their direct authorship by Paul, however, is now widely questioned on grounds of vocabulary, theology, and setting.

pastoral staff A crook-shaped stick carried by bishops; otherwise called a **crozier**. The symbol of episcopal office, it represents the rod of correction and the crook of care.

Patagonia [patago**h**nia] area 489 541 sq km/188 963 sq mi. Region of S Argentina, comprising the provinces of Chubut, Rio Negro, Santa Cruz, and the territory of Tierra del Fuego; name sometimes applied to the whole of the S part of South America, including Chilean territory; in 1520 Magellan sailed along the Patagonian coast, passing through the strait now bearing his name; a semi-arid tableland rising in terraces from the Atlantic coast to the base of the Andes; several rivers; chief towns include Trelew, Rio Grande, Ushuaia, Comodoro Rivadavia, Viedma, Puerto Madryn, Rio Gallegos, and the resort town of Bariloche; sheep, oil, iron ore, coal, copper, uranium, bauxite, manganese; irrigated crops; many immigrants in 19th-c, especially from Wales.

Patan [**pa**tan], also **Lalitpur** 27°40N 85°20E, pop (2000e) 245 000. City in C Nepal, 5 km/3 mi SE of Kathmandu, in the Kathmandu Valley; founded, 7th-c; built in a circular plan with Buddhist stupas on the four points of the compass; capital of the Nepali kingdom, 17th-c; captured by the Gurkhas, 1768; wool, leather; centre of the Banra sect of goldsmiths and silversmiths; known as the 'city of artists'; 16th-c Palace of the Malla Kings, Temple of Lord Krishna, Royal Bath (*Tushahity*).

patas monkey [pa**tah**] An Old World monkey (*Erythrocebus patas*) native to grasslands of W and C Africa; coat red-brown; male with mane of long hairs and white moustache; can run at up to 50 kph/30 mph; also known as **red guenon**, **military monkey**, **hussar monkey**, or **nisnas monkey**.

patch clamp analysis An electrophysiological technique which isolates a small area of the plasma membrane of a living, excitable cell (eg a muscle, nerve, or gland cell), and studies single receptors within it, with respect to their interaction with chemical transmitters, hormones, drugs, or other substances applied directly to them.

Patchett, Ann (1963–) Writer and novelist, born in Los Angeles, California, USA. She grew up in Nashville, TN and studied at the Sarah Lawrence College in New York (1984) and the University of Iowa (1987). In 1997 she was appointed Tennessee Williams fellow in creative writing at the University of the South, Nashville. Her novels include *The Patron Saint of Liars* (1992), *Taft* (1994), and *Bel Canto* (2001, PEN/Faulkner Award, Orange Prize). She has also written short stories and works of non-fiction.

patchouli A shrubby aromatic perennial (*Pogostemon cablin*) growing to 1 m/3¼ ft or more, native to the tropics and subtropics of SE Asia; stems square; leaves oval, toothed, in opposite pairs; flowers white, tubular, 2-lipped, in whorls. It yields an aromatic essential oil used in perfumery. (Family: Labiatae.)

paten [**pa**tn] A circular metal plate, often of silver or gold, on which bread is placed at the celebration of the Eucharist.

Patenier, Joachim (de) [patenyay], also spelled **Patinir** or **Patinier** (c.1485–1524) Painter, probably born in Bouvignes, S Belgium. Little is known of his early life, although it has been suggested that he studied under Hieronymus Bosch. In 1515 he is recorded as a member of the Antwerp painters' guild. He was arguably the first Western artist to paint scenes in which the natural world, while not the whole subject of the painting, clearly dominates the religious narrative.

patent A formal document which gives inventors the exclusive right for a period of years to exploit the product or process they have created, either by operating it themselves or by licensing others to use it. Patents thus form part of general intellectual property legislation, like copyright, or the registration of trademarks. The exclusive monopoly is not conferred automatically, as in the case of copyright. Patentees must define and disclose the invention to their national Patent Office, which investigates whether the invention is new and non-obvious. Patents can also be applied for through the Patent Co-operation Treaty, an international system for the multiple filing of patent applications, or the European Patent Convention, which grants protection to an invention in all countries that are parties to the convention. Patents have the disadvantage of restricting the diffusion of new techniques, but the merit of increasing the incentive to spend on research and development.

patent medicine A medicine for which a patent was granted, or one to which the preparer affixed his or her name to indicate sole rights of sale. Patent medicines stemmed from the 1624 Statute of Monopolies in England which granted 14 years of protected monopoly for the sale of a branded medicine. Preparers of these medicines had the right to use 'secret ingredients', until the Pharmacy and Medicines Act of 1941 required their disclosure for safety reasons. The sale of patent medicines expanded rapidly in the 18th-c, and English patent medicines were popular in the USA by mid-century. In the 19th-c, US-produced patent medicines took over the market. In 1796, Samuel Lee, Jnr became the first American to patent a medicine: 'Bilious Pills'. By 1804 there were already more than 80 patent medicines, promoted aggressively by newspaper advertising, signboards, pamphlets, and tours. Today in the USA, the term refers to proprietary drugs, available without prescription; they are regulated by the US Food and Drug Administration.

patent theatre A theatre with letters patent from the Crown granting it the privilege of presenting plays publicly in London. Two such companies, ultimately resident at Covent Garden and Drury Lane, held these exclusive rights from 1660 until 1843, though Samuel Foote was granted a Patent at the Haymarket for the summer months from 1766.

Pater, Walter (Horatio) [payter] (1839–94) Critic and essayist, born in London, UK. He studied at Canterbury and Oxford, where he worked as a scholar, and became known with his *Studies in the History of the Renaissance* (1873). His philosophical romance, *Marius the Epicurean* (1885), appealed to a wider audience, dealing with the spread of Christianity in the days of catacombs. He developed a highly polished prose style, and exercised considerable influence on the aesthetic movements of his time.

Pater Noster [pahter noster] *Lord's Prayer*

Paterson, A(ndrew) B(arton), nickname **Banjo Paterson** (1864–1941) Journalist and poet, born at Narambla, New South Wales, SE Australia. He lived at Illalong station until he was 10, when he went to school in Sydney, and later contributed some early verse to the Sydney *Bulletin*. A World War 2 correspondent, he wrote several books of light verse, including *The Man From Snowy River and Other Verses* (1895), and *The Animals Noah Forgot* (1933). He is probably best known for 'Waltzing Matilda' (1895), adapted from a traditional ditty, which became very popular in Australia.

Paterson, William (1658–1719) Financier and chief projector of the plan to establish the Bank of England, born in Tinwald, Dumfries and Galloway, SW Scotland, UK. He spent some years trading in the West Indies, and then promoted a scheme for a colony in Darien, Central America. After making a fortune by commerce in London, he was instrumental in founding the Bank of England, and was one of its first directors (1694). A firm supporter of free trade, he sailed with the expedition to Darien (1698), and after its failure returned in ill health to England (1699). In 1715 the government awarded him an indemnity for his Darien losses.

Paterson's curse A herb (*Echium lycopsis*) introduced into Australia c.1869, named after a landowner in Victoria thought to have been responsible for its spread. A noxious weed in agricultural areas, it is also known as 'Salvation Jane' and 'Lady Campbell Weed'.

Pathan *Pashtun*

Pathé, Charles [pathay], Fr [patay] (1863–1957) Film pioneer, born in Paris, France. In 1896 he founded Société Pathé Frères with his brothers **Emile**, **Théophile**, and **Jacques**, first for cinema presentation, but expanding into manufacture. By 1912 it had become one of the largest film production organizations in the world, including a hand-coloured stencil process, *Pathécolor*. They introduced the newsreel in France in 1909, and shortly after in the USA and Britain, as well as the screen magazine *Pathé Pictorial*. Charles retired in 1929, but the company continued, and in England became Associated British Pathé Ltd (1949).

pathology The scientific study of disease in humans and other living organisms. It involves the application of a wide range of analytical techniques to body cells, tissues, and fluids. Originally limited to gross post-mortem dissection of the body, ready access to blood and to tissue biopsies today allows the investigation of the living person. It encompasses the study of the causes of diseases, the detection of micro-organisms and of chromosome and enzyme defects, the microscopic (including ultramicroscopic) study of cells and tissues, cell culture and immunological reactions, and microchemical analyses.

Patmore, Coventry (Kersey Dighton) (1823–96) Poet, born in Woodford, Essex, SE England, UK. He was assistant librarian at the British Museum, and associated with the Pre-Raphaelite Brotherhood. His major work, *The Angel in the House* (1854–62), describing married love, was followed by the death of his wife **Emily** in 1862, and his conversion to Catholicism under the influence of **Marianne**, who became his second wife. Thereafter he wrote mainly on mystical or religious themes, as in *The Unknown Eros* (1877).

Patmos area 34 sq km/13 sq mi; pop (2000e) 2700. Island of the Dodecanese, Greece, in the Aegean Sea, off W coast of Turkey; chief town, Hora; St John the apostle lived here for 2 years; Monastery of St John (19th-c); resort beaches.

Patna [patna] 25°37N 85°12E, pop (2000e) 1 077 000. Winter capital of Bihar, E India; on S bank of R Ganges, 467 km/290 mi NW of Kolkata (Calcutta); on site of ancient city of Pataliputra, capital of 6th-c Magadha kingdom; French trading post, 1732; university (1917); major rice-growing region; noted for its handicrafts (brassware, furniture, carpets); Sikh temple, mosque of Sher Shah.

Paton, Alan (Stewart) [paytn] (1903–88) Writer and educator, born in Pietermaritzburg, E South Africa. He studied at the University of Natal, began work as a teacher, and became principal of the Diepkloof Reformatory for young offenders (1935), where he was known for the success of his enlightened methods. From his deep concern with the racial problem in South Africa sprang several novels, notably *Cry, the Beloved Country* (1948), *Too Late the Phalarope* (1953), and *Ah, but Your Land is Beautiful* (1981). Also an acclaimed biographer, he was president of the Liberal Association of South Africa (1953–68).

Patou, Jean [patoo] (1880–1936) Fashion designer, born in Normandy, NW France. The son of a prosperous tanner, in 1907 he joined an uncle who dealt in furs. He opened Maison Parry in Paris (1912), and in 1913 sold his collection outright to a US buyer. After war service, he successfully opened again as couturier in 1919. He was noted for his designs for sports stars, actresses, and society ladies, and for his perfume, 'Joy'.

patriarch 1 The head of a family or tribe. In Biblical literature, usually applied either to the 10 purported ancestors of the human race prior to the Flood (*Gen* 5), or more commonly to Abraham, Isaac, Jacob, and Jacob's 12 sons (*Gen* 12–50). The 12 tribes of Israel are traced to the 12 sons of Jacob.
2 An ecclesiastical title used since about the 6th-c for the bishops of the five important ecclesiastical centres of the early Christian Church: Alexandria, Antioch, Constantinople, Jerusalem, and Rome. These bishops exercised influence and jurisdiction over the churches in the areas surrounding their cities.

patricians In ancient Rome, the members of a select number of aristocratic clans or *gentes*, such as the Julii. The precise origins of this elite are obscure and still much debated.

Patrick, St (c.385–461) Apostle of Ireland, born (perhaps) in South Wales. At 16 he was carried to Ireland by pirates, and sold to an Antrim chief. Six years later he escaped and became a monk in France. Ordained a bishop at 45, he then became a missionary to Ireland (432), travelling widely among the chiefs, and in 454 fixed his see at Armagh. He died at Saul (Saulpatrick), and was probably buried at Armagh. The only authentic literary remains of the saint are his *Confession*, and a letter addressed to a British chieftain, Coroticus. Feast day 17 March.

Patriotic Front (Zimbabwe) A union of nationalist movements formed to respond to efforts by US secretary of state Henry Kissinger to find a solution to the problem of white minority rule in Rhodesia (Zimbabwe), entrenched since the Unilateral Declaration of Independence (Nov 1965). The guerrilla forces of the Zimbabwe National Liberation Army and the Zimbabwe People's Revolutionary Army stepped up their action, and by 1979 the white Rhodesian leader, Ian Smith, was forced into an internal settlement. An election brought Bishop Abel Muzorewa to power as the country's first African prime minister, but the guerrilla campaign continued. In 1980 the Lancaster House Agreement created fresh elections, in which the Patriotic Front won 87% of the votes. The Front broke up, but Nkomo and Mugabe were later reconciled in moves towards the creation of a one-party state.

patristics *Fathers of the Church*

Patroclus [patro**klus**] In Greek legend, the son of Menoetius; the faithful follower of Achilles at Troy. He went into battle wearing Achilles' armour, but was cut down by Hector. His death made Achilles return to the battle.

patron saint A saint who, by tradition or otherwise, has been chosen as the special intercessor and advocate in heaven of a particular place, person, occupation, or organization. The custom of having patron saints for churches arose from the practice of building churches over the tombs of martyrs.

Patrons of Husbandry *Granger movement*

Pattadakal An old town in Karnataka, SW India, which reached the height of its glory in the 7th–8th-c, when most of its temples (now designated world heritage monuments) were built. The most notable is the Lokeshwari or Virupaksha temple, a huge structure with sculptures that narrate episodes from Hindu epics.

Pattaya [pat**iya**] 12°57N 100°53E. Beach resort in E Thailand; on the NE shore of the Gulf of Thailand S of Bang Phra; the 'Riviera' of Thailand, with resort facilities.

Patten, Chris(topher Francis) (1944–) British politician, born in London, UK. He studied at Oxford, joined the Conservative Party's research department, worked in the cabinet office, and became personal assistant to the party chairman (1972–4). When the Conservatives returned to power in 1979, he held a number of non-cabinet posts, then became minister for overseas development (1986), secretary of state for the environment (1989), and party chairman (1991). Credited with master-minding the Tory victory in the 1992 election, he lost his own seat and was appointed the last Governor of Hong Kong (1992–7), where his proposals (1993) for greater democracy brought him into conflict with the Chinese government. He was made a Companion of Honour in 1998. Following the 1998 Good Friday Agreement on the Northern Ireland peace process, he was appointed chair of the Independent Commission on Policing for Northern Ireland. He became a European Commissioner (with responsibility for external relations and European Union enlargement) in 1999. In 2003 he was elected Chancellor of Oxford University.

pattern recognition *character recognition*

Patterson, James (1949–) Novelist, born in New York City, USA. He studied English at Manhattan College, and published his first novel *The Thomas Berryman Number* in 1976. His later best-selling novels include *Along Came A Spider* (1993), *Kiss The Girls* (1995; filmed 1997), *See How They Run* (1997), *Cradle and All* (2000), and *The Big Bad Wolf* (2003).

Patton, George (Smith), Jr (1885–1945) US general, born in San Gabriel, California, USA. Trained at West Point, he became one of the most daring and flamboyant US combat commanders of World War 2. He played a key role in the Allied invasion of French N Africa (1942), led the US 7th Army in its assault on Sicily (1943), commanded the 3rd Army in the invasion of France, and contained the German counter-offensive in the Ardennes (1944). He was fatally injured in a motor accident.

Pau [poh] 43°19N 0°25W, pop (2000e) 88 000. Economic centre and capital of Pyrénées-Atlantiques department, SW France; on right bank of R Gave de Pau, 174 km/108 mi S of Bordeaux; former capital of Béarn province, 1464; health resort, winter sports centre; road and rail junction; engineering, textiles, brewing, tanning, tourism; natural gas nearby; birthplace of Henry IV of France, Charles XIV of Sweden; 12th–15th-c castle, Musée des Beaux-Arts, Musée Bernadotte, Boulevard des Pyrénées.

Paul I (of Greece) (1901–64) King of the Hellenes (1947–64), born in Athens, Greece. In 1922 he served with the Greek navy against the Turks; but in 1924, when a Republic was proclaimed, went into exile, returning to Greece as crown prince in 1935. In World War 2 he served with the Greek general staff in the Albanian campaign, and was in exile in London (1941–6). His reign covered the latter half of the Greek Civil War (1946–9) and its difficult aftermath. During the early 1960s his personal role, and that of his wife Queen Frederika, became sources of bitter political controversy.

Paul, St, originally **Saul of Tarsus** (?10–65/67 AD) Apostle to the Gentiles and important theologian of the early Christian Church, born of Jewish parents at Tarsus, Cilicia. He reputedly trained as a rabbi in Jerusalem, becoming a fervent Pharisee and persecutor of Christians. On his way to Damascus (AD c.34), he was converted to Christianity by a vision of Christ, and after several months in Nabatea began to preach the Christian message and undertake missionary journeys, first in Cyprus, Antioch of Pisidia, Iconium, Lystra, and Derbe. Around 49–51, he had to address an apostolic conference in Jerusalem on the disputed issue of how Gentiles and Jews were to be admitted to the Church (*Gal* 2.1–10; *Acts* 15.1–21), and a form of resolution was apparently reached which allowed him to continue his mission to the Gentiles, although a later dispute with Peter did arise in Antioch.

The precise chronology of his missionary activities is confused (beginning c.46), but other journeys took Paul, with Silvanus (Silas), to Asia Minor and through Galatia and Phrygia to Macedonia and Achaia, where in Corinth he was especially successful. An extensive mission was also undertaken in Ephesus, amid many difficulties, leading eventually to a final visit to Macedonia and Corinth. On his return to Jerusalem, he was apparently imprisoned for two years, following disturbances against him by the Jews. He was transferred to Caesarea and to Rome after appealing to Caesar; and according to later tradition, he was executed by Nero c.64 (although some traditions suggest that he was released and went to Spain). Thirteen New Testament letters are traditionally attributed to him, as well as some extracanonical works. Feast day 29 June.

Patron Saints Of Occupations

Accountants	Matthew
Actors	Genesius, Vitus
Advertisers	Bernadino of Siena
Architects	Thomas (Apostle)
Artists	Luke, Angelico
Astronauts	Joseph (Cupertino)
Astronomers	Dominic
Athletes	Sebastian
Authors	Francis de Sales
Aviators	Our Lady of Loreto
Bakers	Honoratus
Bankers	Bernardino (Feltre)
Barbers	Cosmas and Damian
Blacksmiths	Eligius
Bookkeepers	Matthew
Book trade	John of God
Brewers	Amand, Wenceslaus
Builders	Barbara, Thomas (Apostle)
Butchers	Luke
Carpenters	Joseph
Chemists	Cosmas and Damian
Comedians	Vitus
Cooks	Lawrence, Martha
Dancers	Vitus
Dentists	Apollonia
Doctors	Cosmas and Damian, Luke
Editors	Francis de Sales
Farmers	Isidore
Firemen	Florian
Fishermen	Andrew, Peter
Florists	Dorothy, Thérèse of Lisieux
Gardeners	Adam, Fiacre
Glassworkers	Luke, Lucy
Gravediggers	Joseph (Arimathea)
Grocers	Michael
Hotelkeepers	Amand, Julian the Hospitaler
Housewives	Martha
Jewellers	Eligius
Journalists	Francis de Sales
Labourers	James, John Bosco
Lawyers	Ivo, Thomas More
Librarians	Jerome, Catherine of Alexandria
Merchants	Francis of Assisi
Messengers	Gabriel
Metalworkers	Eligius
Midwives	Raymond Nonnatus
Miners	Anne, Barbara
Motorists	Christopher
Musicians	Cecilia, Gregory the Great
Nurses	Camillus de Lellis, John of God
Philosophers	Thomas Aquinas, Catherine of Alexandria
Poets	Cecilia, David
Policemen	Michael
Postal workers	Gabriel
Priests	Jean-Baptiste Vianney
Printers	John of God
Prisoners	Leonard
Radio workers	Gabriel
Sailors	Christopher, Erasmus, Francis of Paola
Scholars	Thomas Aquinas
Scientists	Albert the Great
Sculptors	Luke, Louis
Secretaries	Genesius
Servants	Martha, Zita
Shoemakers	Crispin, Crispinian
Singers	Cecilia, Gregory
Soldiers	George, Joan of Arc, Martin of Tours, Sebastian
Students	Thomas Aquinas
Surgeons	Luke, Cosmas and Damian
Tailors	Homobonus
Tax collectors	Matthew
Taxi drivers	Fiacre
Teachers	Gregory the Great, John Baptist de la Salle
Theologians	Augustine, Alphonsus Liguori Thomas Aquinas
Television workers	Gabriel
Undertakers	Dismas, Joseph of Arimathea
Waiters	Martha
Writers	Lucy

Paul III, originally **Alessandro Farnese** (1468–1549) Pope (1534–49), born in Canino, WC Italy. The first of the popes of the Counter-Reformation, in 1538 he issued the bull of excommunication and deposition against Henry VIII of England, and also the bull instituting the Order of the Jesuits in 1540. He summoned the Council of Trent in 1545.

Paul VI, originally **Giovanni Battista Montini** (1897–1978) Pope (1963–78), born in Concesio, Italy. He graduated at the Gregorian University of Rome, was ordained in 1920, and entered the Vatican diplomatic service, where he remained until 1944. He was then appointed Archbishop of Milan, in which important diocese he became known for his liberal views and support of social reform. Made a cardinal in 1958, he succeeded John XXIII, many of whose opinions he shared. He travelled more widely than any previous pope, and initiated important advances in the move towards Christian unity.

Pauli, Wolfgang [powlee] (1900–58) Theoretical physicist, born in Vienna, Austria. He studied under Arnold Sommerfeld (1868–1951) in Munich and Niels Bohr in Copenhagen, then taught at Hamburg and Zürich (1928–55, apart from a wartime period at the Institute for Advanced Study, Princeton, 1940–6). He formulated the 'exclusion principle' (1924) in quantum physics, and in 1931 postulated the existence of an electrically neutral particle called the neutrino, first detected by Frederick Reines (1953). He was awarded the 1945 Nobel Prize for Physics, and became a US citizen in 1946, later returning to Zürich.

Pauli exclusion principle [powlee] The principle that no two electrons (or other fermions) may occupy exactly the same quantum state; formulated by Wolfgang Pauli in 1925. The principle is necessary to explain why electrons in atoms do not all collapse into a single state. It is a fundamental principle of quantum theory.

Paulin, Tom [pawlin] (1949–) Poet, born in Leeds, West Yorkshire, N England, UK. He grew up in Belfast, and studied at the universities of Hull and Oxford. His central themes are the Irish predicament, and in particular Protestant identity, beginning with *A State of Justice* (1977). Later books include *The Riot Act* (1985), *Seize the Fire* (1990), and *The Invasion Handbook* (2002). He edited the Faber books of political verse (1986) and vernacular verse (1990), and his critical works include *The Day-Star of Liberty: William Hazlitt's Radical Style* (1999). He is also known in the UK as a contributor to television discussion programmes on the arts.

Pauline Letters or **Pauline Epistles** A set of New Testament writings ascribed to the apostle Paul, usually numbering 13, excluding the letter to the Hebrews, which rightly does not claim Pauline authorship. Modern scholars are confident of Paul's authorship in only seven cases (Romans, 1 and 2 Corinthians, Galatians, Philippians, 1 Thessalonians, and Philemon), and debate the authenticity of 2 Thessalonians, Colossians, Ephesians, and the Pastoral Letters. The widely accepted writings were actual letters to specific churches and situations in areas where Paul had a pastoral or missionary interest, and were not general systematic treatises.

Pauling, Linus (Carl) [pawling] (1901–94) Chemist, born in Portland, Oregon, USA. He studied at Oregon State University and the California Institute of Technology, and at several centres in Europe, and became professor of chemistry at the California Institute of Technology in 1927. He applied quantum theory to chemistry, and was awarded the Nobel Prize for Chemistry in 1954 for his contributions to the theory of valency. His work on molecular structure (mainly using X-ray diffraction) revolutionized both inorganic chemistry and biochemistry. He became a controversial figure from 1955 as the leading scientific critic of US nuclear deterrent policy, forcibly setting out his views in *No More War* (1958). Awarded the Nobel Prize for Peace in 1962, he was the first person to have received two full Nobel Prizes.

pavane [pavan] A stately dance of the 16th–17th-c, probably of Italian origin; the name may derive from the town of Padua. It was often linked to a livelier dance, generally in triple time, known as a *galliard* (from Fr 'merry').

Pavarotti, Luciano [pavarotee] (1935–) Tenor, born in Modena, N Italy. He abandoned a career in school-teaching to become a singer, and won the international competition at the Teatro Reggio Emilia in 1961, making his operatic debut there in *La Bohème* the same year. He took part in the La Scala tour of Europe in 1963–4, toured Australia with Joan Sutherland in *Lucia di Lammermoor* in 1965, and made his US debut in 1968. His voice and performance are very much in the powerful style of the traditional Italian tenor. He is now internationally known as a concert performer, and has achieved a large popular following through his recordings and television appearances. He appeared in the film *Yes, Giorgio* in 1981, and published a volume of autobiography the same year.

Pavese, Cesare [pavayzay] (1908–50) Writer, born in Cuneo, NW Italy. He worked as a translator and publisher before turning to writing. His short stories, such as *La bella estate* (1949, The Beautiful Summer), were well-received, but he is best known for his novel *La luna e i falò* (1950, The Moon and the Bonfires). His unsentimental celebration of Italian rural life exerted a strong influence on later Italian fiction and film making.

Pavia [paveea], ancient **Ticinum** 45°12N 9°09E, pop (2000e) 86 000. Capital town of Pavia province, Lombardy, N Italy, on R Ticino; linked with Milan by canal; railway; university (1361); iron and steel castings, textiles, sewing machines; cathedral (begun 1487), Church of San Michele (1155), Church of San Pietro in Ciel d'Oro (1132, restored 19th-c); Pavia–Venice motorboat race (Jun).

Pavlov, Ivan Petrovich [pavlov] (1849–1936) Physiologist, born in Ryazan, W Russia. He studied medicine at St Petersburg, conducted research in Wrocław, Poland (formerly Breslau, Prussia), and Leipzig, and returned to St Petersburg, where he became professor (1890) and director of the Institute of Experimental Medicine (1913). He worked on the physiology of circulation and digestion, and from 1902 studied what later became known as *Pavlovian conditioning* (or classical conditioning) in animals, summarizing this work in *Lectures on Conditioned Reflexes* (1926). A major influence on the development of behaviourism in psychology, he was awarded the Nobel Prize for Physiology or Medicine in 1904.

Pavlova, Anna [pavlova] (1881–1931) Ballerina, born in St Petersburg, NW Russia. She trained at the Imperial Ballet School there, and became world famous, creating roles in work by Fokine, in particular *The Dying Swan* (1905). After a period with Diaghilev's Ballets Russes, she began touring Europe with her own company (1909). She choreographed over a dozen works, of which the best known are *Snowflakes* (1915) and *Autumn Leaves* (1918). Conservative and romantic in her aesthetic, she did much to create the stereotyped image of the ballerina.

Pavo [pahvoh] (Lat 'peacock') A constellation in the S hemisphere.

pawnbroking A system of money-lending in which an article, usually personal property, is deposited with an agent (the **pawnbroker**) as security for the loan. The article can be redeemed within a given time on repayment of the loan plus interest. Articles which are unredeemed at the end of the period become the property of the pawnbroker and may be sold in order to repay the loan. The system has a very long history, and was popular with the poorer classes in earlier times. It has declined in recent years with the growth of hire-purchase and easier credit facilities.

pawpaw *papaw*

Paxman, Jeremy (Dickson) (1950–) British television presenter and journalist, born in Leeds, West Yorkshire, N England, UK. He studied at Cambridge, then joined BBC 1 as presenter on *Tonight* (1977–9), *Panorama* (1979–84), the *Six O'Clock News* (1985–6), and *Breakfast Time* (1986–9). Programmes on BBC 2 include *Newsnight* (1989–), on which he developed a reputation as a tough but fair interviewer, *Did You See?* (1991–3), and *University Challenge* (1994–). He received the BAFTA Richard Dimbleby Award in 1996. A regular contributor to newspapers and magazines, his books include *Fish, Fishing and the Meaning of Life* (1994), *The English: A Portrait of A People* (1999), and *The Political Animal* (2002).

Paxton, Sir Joseph (1801–65) Gardener and architect, born near Woburn, Bedfordshire, SC England, UK. He was a working gardener to the Duke of Devonshire, at Chiswick and Chatsworth, where he remodelled the gardens, and built the conservatory and lily house. He designed a revolutionary building of prefabricated sections of cast-iron and glass for the Great Exhibition of 1851 (nicknamed 'the Crystal Palace'), which he re-erected in Sydenham in 1854. It was destroyed by fire in 1936.

Payachata, Nevados de [payachata] 18°10S 69°10W. Andean massif on Chile–Bolivia border; 129 km/80 mi NW of Arica; includes two snow-capped peaks, Cerro de Pomarepe (6240 m/20 472 ft) and Cerro de Parinacota (6342 m/20 807 ft).

PAYE An abbreviation of **pay as you earn**, a UK taxation system whereby income tax is deducted from a worker's pay by an employer before handing over the wage. The employer is therefore responsible for collecting the tax on behalf of the government. The amount to be collected is determined from tables issued by the tax authorities, and by reference to each person's *tax code*, calculated at the start of each fiscal year. Several other countries have a payroll deduction plan of this kind.

Payton, Walter (1954–99) Player of American football, born in Columbia, Mississippi, USA. In his career with the Chicago Bears (1975–88), he rushed for 16 726 yards, a National Football League record. In one game (1977) he rushed for a record 275 yards. His 110 rushing touchdowns were a record at the time of his retirement in 1988. He was elected to the Hall of Fame in 1993.

pay TV The non-broadcast distribution of video entertainment to a restricted audience of subscribers who pay for the programmes viewed. The programmes are received either by individual cable connection or by scrambled microwave or satellite transmission requiring a rented decoder.

Paz, Octavio (1914–98) Poet, born in Mexico City, Mexico. He studied at the National University of Mexico, and fought on the Republican side in the Spanish Civil War. A career diplomat, he served as the Mexican ambassador to India (1962–8), and taught at Texas, Harvard, and Cambridge universities. He was a writer of great energy and versatility, with 30 volumes from 1933; his *Collected Poems* (1957–87), in Spanish and English, were published in 1988. He also wrote important prose works, notably *Tiempo Nublado* (1984, trans One Earth, Four or Five Worlds), and later works include *The Double Flame: Essays on Love and Eroticism* (1996). He received the Nobel Prize for Literature in 1990.

Paz, La *La Paz*

Paz Estenssoro, Victor [pahs estensawroh] (1907–2001) Bolivian politician, revolutionary, and president (1952–6, 1960–4, 1985–9), born in Tarija, Bolivia. He studied at the University Mayor de San Andres, and held a number of financial posts before entering politics in the 1930s, and in 1942 founding the National Revolutionary Movement. He went into exile in 1946, returning to win the presidency in 1952. He was re-elected in 1960 and again in 1985, returning from near-retirement at the age of 77. During a long career he was Bolivian ambassador in London (1956–9) and a professor at London University (1966).

Pazyryk [pazuhrik] In the Altai Mts, C Siberia, a group of frozen tombs of prehistoric nomad chieftains perfectly preserved by permafrost since their deposition in timber-lined burial chambers in the 4th-c BC. Embalmed, tattooed bodies survived, as well as furniture, wooden plates, horse trappings, clothing, felt rugs, and Chinese silk. Cannabis-smoking equipment was also recovered.

PC *personal computer*

PCBs Abbreviation of **polychlorobiphenyls**, usually a mixture of compounds in which chlorine is substituted for many of the hydrogen atoms in biphenyl, $C_{12}H_{10}$, a molecule in which two phenyl groups are joined to one another. Their stability makes them excellent flame retardants and electrical insulators, but their eventual degradation products are toxic. In 1999 it was revealed in Belgium that a batch of animal food which had been contaminated with dioxin also contained PCBs many times the safety limit for food. Like dioxin, PCBs accumulate in body fat and act like a slow poison.

PCP *angel dust*

pea A botanical term used as a suffix, referring to several plants of the family Leguminosae, but especially to members of the genus *Pisum*. The distinctive flower is typical of most of the family, having an upright petal (the standard), two spreading petals (the wings), and two lower petals which are partly joined along their length, and surround the ovary and stamens (the keel); the whole is sometimes rather butterfly-like in appearance. The best-known species are **sweet pea** (*Lathyrus odoratus*) and **garden pea** (*Pisum sativum*), a climbing annual growing to 2 m/6½ ft, native to S Europe and N Africa; leaves with 1–3 pairs of oval leaflets and a terminal branched tendril; flowers up to 3·5 cm/1½ in long, white, pink or purplish, in small clusters of 1–3; pods up to 12 cm/4¾ in long, oblong, containing up to 10 seeds. It has been cultivated since prehistoric times for the edible seeds (*peas*) eaten as a vegetable, fresh, dried, frozen, or canned. Many cultivars are also widely grown, including the smaller-seeded *petit pois*, and also *mangetout*, where the whole pod is consumed. (*Pisum sativum*. Family: Leguminosae.)

Peace Corps An agency of volunteers funded by the US government, established in 1961. Volunteers, who usually offer vocational training, numbered more than 10 000 in 52 countries in 1966, but in the 1980s the corps was asked to leave some countries hostile to US policies. Development has paralleled that of similar agencies in France, Germany, and the UK, with more emphasis now on the recruitment of skilled, mature volunteers. There were 7500 voluntees in 71 countries in early 2004

Peace Memorial Museum A museum in the Heiwa Koen ('Peace Park'), Hiroshima, Japan, housing information and exhibits chronicling the effects of the atomic bomb which destroyed the city in 1945.

Peace River River in W Canada, rising in the Omineca Mts, British Columbia, as the Finlay R; flows SE, then E and N to enter the Slave R near its outflow from L Athabasca; length 1923 km/1195 mi to the head of Finlay R; used for hydroelectricity.

peace studies Educational courses designed to explore the role of the military in society, international strategic relationships, and those conditions that most promote peace and human welfare in society. They have a strong association with the liberal left tradition in academia, and are therefore viewed with some suspicion by conservative educationists.

peach A small deciduous tree (*Prunus persica*), growing to 6 m/20 ft; leaves elliptical to oblong, pointed, toothed; flowers pink, rarely white, appearing before leaves; fruit globular, velvety 4–8 cm/1½–3 in, yellow flushed red with thick sweet flesh, stone grooved. Its origin is obscure: possibly native to China, it has long been cultivated, often as an espalier. (Family: Rosaceae.)

Peacock, Thomas Love (1785–1866) Novelist and poet, born in Weymouth, Dorset, S England, UK. He entered the service of the East India Company in 1819 after producing three satirical romances, *Headlong Hall* (1816), *Melincourt* (1817), and *Nightmare Abbey* (1818), and later produced four other works along similar lines. In each case a company of humorists meet in a country house, and the satire arises from their conversation rather than from character or plot.

peacock Either of two species of pheasant (Genus: *Pavo*) from the forests of India and SE Asia: especially the **Indian peafowl** (*Pavo cristatus*); also *Afropavo congensis* from the Congo basin; alternatively known as **peafowl**; the female sometimes called **peahen**. The two species can interbreed. The peacock is known for its resplendent train (extending to some 1·5 m/5 ft), in which each feather ends with a brightly coloured, ring-shaped feature (the 'eye'). The peacock displays his tail by raising it above and behind his head. Males are mainly blue-green or green-bronze; females are green or brown, and lack a train. The birds are known for their ill temper. The name is also used for **peacock pheasants** of the genus *Polyplectron* (6 species).

peacock butterfly A medium-sized butterfly with a prominent eyespot on each reddish-brown wing; caterpillars feed on stinging nettles; early caterpillars spin silk webs on nettle leaves. (Order: Lepidoptera. Family: Nymphalidae.)

peacocking The methods used by illegal land occupiers ('squatters') to protect their holdings from the Free Selection Acts in New South Wales and Victoria from the 1860s. A common method was to retain areas with water or good pastures, making the rest of the land useless for closer settlement. Another method was to use agents or 'dummies' to buy up land on the squatters' behalf. Because of the dryness of much of Australia, 'peacocking' often succeeded. The allusion is to the eye-like markings on the tail of a peacock: the squatters 'picked the eyes' (ie the most desirable parts) out of the land.

pea crab A small crab that lives inside marine bivalve molluscs, such as mussels and oysters, usually in shallow waters; pale in colour; last pair of legs armed with hooks for holding onto the host. (Class: Malacostraca. Order: Decapoda.)

peafowl *peacock*

Peak District National park in NC England, UK; area 1404 sq km/542 sq mi; established in 1951; mainly in Derbyshire, with parts in adjacent counties; limestone uplands and woodlands (S, E); limestone caves, major tourist attraction, notably at Peak Cavern, near Castleton; moorlands and crags (N), walking and climbing area; highest point, Kinder Scout, 727 m/2088 ft.

Peake, Mervyn (Laurence) (1911–68) Writer and artist, born in Kuling, EC China, where his father was a missionary. Educated in China and Kent, he became a painter, and taught at the Westminster School of Art. He is best known for his Gothic fantasy trilogy of novels, *Titus Groan* (1946), *Gormenghast* (1950, televised 2000), and *Titus Alone* (1959), and for the novel *Mr Pye* (1953). He also published books of verse, and illustrated several classics, including *The Ancient Mariner*, and children's books.

peanut An annual (*Arachis hypogaea*), growing to 50 cm/20 in, native to South America; leaves divided into four elliptical or oval leaflets; pea-flowers yellow, growing downwards after fertilization and drawing the young pods into the soil, where they ripen underground; also called **groundnut** or **monkey nut**. It is widely grown for the edible seeds (*peanuts*), used in confectionery and as a source of peanut oil; they are often roasted and salted, and eaten as a savoury. (Family: Leguminosae.)

peanut worm An unsegmented marine worm that lives in burrows in sediment, in calcareous rock, or in coral; body usually divided into stout trunk and slender retractable proboscis, encircled by tentacles; gut U-shaped; larvae found in plankton; c.320 species. (Phylum: Sipuncula.)

pear A deciduous, usually thorny tree or shrub, native to Europe and Asia; leaves narrowly lance-shaped to broadly oval; flowers white or pinkish, in flat-topped clusters, appearing before or with the leaves; fruit round or top-shaped as well as pear-shaped. Its characteristic gritty texture is caused by the presence of stone-cells in the flesh of the fruit. It is widely grown as an orchard tree and ornamental. (Genus: *Pyrus*, 30 species. Family: Rosaceae.)

Pearce, Stuart (1962–) Footballer, born in Shepherds Bush, SW London, UK. A left back, he played for Wealdstone and Coventry City before moving to Nottingham Forest (1985–97), where he also acted for a time as player/manager, Newcastle United (1997–9), West Ham (1999), and Manchester City (2001). A member of the World Cup team in 1990, and of the European Cup teams in 1992 and 1996, he won 78 caps for England (captain in 1992).

pearlfish Elongate and very slender fish widespread in tropical and warm temperate seas, living inside sea cucumbers, sea urchins, and other marine invertebrates; length up to 30 cm/12 in; tail pointed, dorsal and anal fins long, pelvics absent; includes European *Echiodon drummondi*. (Family: Carapidae, 2 genera.)

Pearl Harbor US deep-water naval base on the island of Oahu in the US Pacific Ocean state of Hawaii, adjacent to Honolulu. A treaty of 1887 granted the USA rights as a coaling and repair base, and a naval base was established in 1908, with completion of a major military dry dock in 1919. The surprise bombing of the base by the Japanese (7 Dec 1941), sinking or disabling 11 battleships and cruisers, plus smaller vessels, and destroying 177 aircraft, with 4491 casualties, brought the USA into World War 2. Simultaneous attacks were made on Hong Kong, Malaya, the Philippines, and Singapore. US carriers which escaped Pearl Harbor led to the Japanese defeat at Midway (1942), which turned the course of the War.

Pearl Islands, Span **Archipiélago de las Perlas** pop (2000e) 3900. Panamanian island group in the Gulf of Panama, Central America; over 180 islands, the largest being Isla del Rey, chief town San Miguel; pearl fishing in colonial times; now a wide range of fishing.

pearlite A type of steel formed by an intimate intergrowth of iron with iron carbide. It has a lustrous sheen.

Pearl River *Zhu Jiang*

Pears, Sir Peter (Neville Luard) [peerz] (1910–86) Tenor, born in Farnham, Surrey, SE England, UK. He was organ scholar at Oxford, then studied singing at the Royal College of Music (1933–4). He toured the USA and Europe with Benjamin Britten, and in 1943 joined Sadler's Wells. After the success of *Peter Grimes* (1945), he joined Britten in the English Opera Group, and was co-founder with him of the Aldeburgh Festival (1948). Knighted in 1978, he was noted for his understanding of modern works.

Pearse, Patrick (or **Pádraic**) **Henry** [peers] (1879–1916) Writer, educationist, and nationalist, born in Dublin, Ireland. He wrote poems, short stories, and plays in English and Irish. A leader of the Gaelic revival, he joined the Gaelic League in 1895, became editor of its journal, and lectured in Irish at University College. In 1915 he joined the Irish Republican Brotherhood, and in the 1916 Easter Rising was commander-in-chief of the insurgents, and proclaimed president of the provisional government. After the revolt had been quelled he was arrested, court-martialled, and shot, along with his brother **William**.

Pearson, Lester B(owles) (1897–1972) Canadian statesman and prime minister (1963–8), born in Newtonbrook, Ontario, SE Canada. He studied at Toronto and Oxford universities, and was leader of the Canadian delegation to the UN, becoming president of the General Assembly (1952–3). Minister of external affairs (1948–57), his efforts to resolve the Suez Crisis were rewarded with the Nobel Peace Prize in 1957. As Liberal prime minister, he introduced a comprehensive pension plan, socialized medicine, and the maple-leaf flag.

Peary, Robert (Edwin) [peeree] (1856–1920) Naval commander and explorer, born in Cresson Springs, Pennsylvania, USA. He made eight Arctic voyages to Greenland, all starting from the W coast of Greenland. He crossed the Greenland ice-sheet to the E coast in 1892 and 1895. In 1900 he reached and named Cape Morris Jessup, the N tip of Greenland. In 1906 he reached 87° 6' N lat, and on 6 April 1909 attained the North Pole. His claim to be first to reach the North Pole was disputed by his fellow explorer Frederick Cook, who claimed to have reached the Pole in 1908, though doubt still exists about whether Cook actually reached 90°N.

Peary Land Region of N Greenland on the Arctic Ocean, forming a mountainous peninsula; its N cape, Kap Morris Jesup, is the most northerly point of land in the Arctic; not covered by ice; explored by Peary in 1892 and 1900.

peasants Cultivators whose primary aim is to cater for their own subsistence. In a peasant economy, the market production is subordinate, and takes place only when the household's subsistence needs have been satisfied. Peasants are typically incorporated into a centralized political system, and obliged to pay tribute or provide compulsory labour service to their superiors.

Peasants' Revolt An English popular rising of June 1381, among townsmen as well as peasants, based in Essex, Kent, and London, UK, with associated insurrections elsewhere. It was precipitated by the three oppressive poll taxes of 1377–81, the underlying causes being misgovernment, the desire for personal freedom, and an assortment of local grievances. It was quickly suppressed.

Peasants' War (1524–5) Probably the largest peasant uprising in European history, raging through Germany, from the Rhineland to Pomerania. It sought to defend traditional agrarian rights and establish social equality and justice against lords and princes. Appealing to notions of divine law fostered by the Lutheran Reformation, it was denounced by Luther, and suppressed by the princes. Over 100 000 rebels were eventually slaughtered.

peat The partially decomposed remains of plants which accumulate and are preserved in waterlogged conditions in areas of cool, humid climate. Because it is an anaerobic environment, it is a good medium for the preservation of archaeological remains and also bodies, such as Grauballe Man (whose death is radiocarbon-dated to between 1540 and 1740 years ago) in Denmark. It is the first stage in the formation of coal, and is widely used as a form of fuel (eg in Ireland and Russia).

pecan A deciduous tree (*Carya pecan*) growing to 45 m/150 ft, native to E North America; leaves pinnately divided into toothed leaflets; flowers small, green, lacking petals; males in catkins, females in clusters; nut 4–5 cm/1½–2 in, roughly oblong, reddish-brown, edible. (Family: Juglandaceae.)

peccary [pekaree] A mammal native to forest and dry scrubland in Central and South America; an artiodactyl, a New World equivalent of the Old World pig, but smaller, with three (not four) toes on each hind foot; tusks grow downwards (not upwards). (Family: Tayassuidae, 3 species.)

Peck, (Eldred) Gregory (1916–2003) Film star, born in La Jolla, California, USA. After two years with the Neighbourhood Playhouse in New York City, his Broadway debut in 1942 led to a flood of film offers. One of the first major independent postwar film stars, his good looks and soft-spoken manner were used to portray many men of action and everyday citizens distinguished by their sense of decency. Nominated five times for an Oscar, he received the Award for his portrayal of a liberal Southern lawyer in *To Kill a Mockingbird* (1962). Among his best-known films were *Spellbound* (1945), *Twelve O'Clock High* (1949), *The Gunfighter* (1950), and *The Omen* (1976), and later appearances included *Old Gringo* (1989) and *Cape Fear* (1991). He also produced films, including *The Trial of the Catonsville Nine* (1972), an anti-Vietnam war drama reflecting his own off-screen involvement with liberal causes and support of the Democratic Party. In 1999 he received the American film industry's Lifetime Achievement Award.

Peckinpah, Sam [pekinpah] (1925–84) Film director, born in Fresno, California, USA. He started work on television Westerns, and directed his first feature, *The Deadly Companions*, in 1961. He portrayed a harshly realistic view of the lawless US West, accentuating the inherent violence, as in *Major Dundee* (1965) and *The Wild Bunch* (1969). His personal life was equally turbulent, his heavy drinking and quarrels with the studios restricting his creative output in his later years, and although he retired to a mountain retreat in 1978, he died in Los Angeles not long after.

Pecos River [paykohs] River in S USA; chief branch of the Rio Grande; rises in New Mexico in the Sangre de Cristo Mts; flows S through Texas to join the Rio Grande NW of Del Rio; length 1490 km/925 mi; used for irrigation.

Pécs [paych], Ger **Fünfkirchen**, Lat **Sopianae** 46°05N 18°15E, pop (2000e) 166 000. Industrial capital of Baranya county, S Hungary; capital of E Pannonia under Roman rule; bishopric; university (1367, refounded 1922), university of medicine (1923); centre of a noted wine-producing area; leather, coal.

pectin A complex molecule (a homopolysaccharide) especially rich in galacturonic acid. It functions as a cement-like material in plant cell walls, particularly young primary cell walls, and is abundant in fruits such as apples.

pediatrics *paediatrics*

pediment (architecture) In classical architecture, a triangular section of wall above the entablature and enclosed by the sloping cornices, ie a low-pitched gable. A **broken pediment** is one where the sloping sides do not meet at the apex.

pediment (earth science) A gently sloping surface cut into bedrock where there is a change in gradient, such as at the foot of a steep mountain slope, and extending towards an alluvial or river plain. There is some controversy as to their origin: competing explanations include erosion by rivers flowing from the mountainous area, and the transport of soil downslope by running water not confined to channels.

pedology The study of soil as a natural phenomenon, including its formation, development, and physical characteristics. It embraces soil mapping, the study of soil formation and development, and the subdisciplines of soil chemistry, soil physics, and soil microbiology. The term derives from Greek *pedon* 'ground'.

pedometer A device for counting the number of paces taken by the wearer. It usually consists of a free pendulum, operating a ratchet, which moves a toothed wheel one tooth per pace; this is then connected to a dial counter. The device will be calibrated to correspond to the length of the user's pace.

pedophilia *paedophilia*

Pedra Furada [pedra furahda] Rock shelter in Piaui region, Brazil, the earliest human settlement yet known in the Americas. Dated by radiocarbon, and still controversial, it suggests that early modern humans reached the New World more than 30 000 years ago, around the time they arrived in Europe and Australia, and much earlier than previously thought. Pedra Furada and the nearby shelter of Perna also boast red-painted human figures 10–12 000 years old, the earliest dated rock art in the New World.

Pedro I (1798–1834) Emperor of Brazil (1822–31), born in Lisbon, Portugal, the second son of John VI of Portugal (reigned 1816–26). He fled to Brazil with his parents on Napoleon's invasion, and became prince-regent of Brazil on his father's return to Portugal (1821). A liberal in outlook, he declared for Brazilian independence in 1822, and was crowned as Emperor Pedro I in 1826. The new empire did not start smoothly, and in 1831 he abdicated and withdrew to Portugal, where he had succeeded his father as Pedro IV (1826), but abdicated that throne in favour of his daughter, Maria.

Peebles 55°39N 3°12W, pop (2000e) 7500. Town in Scottish Borders, SEC Scotland, UK; on R Tweed, 33 km/20 mi S of Edinburgh; textiles, tourism; Tweeddale museum; mediaeval Neidpath Castle nearby; 13 km/8 mi SE, Traquair House (oldest inhabited house in Scotland); birthplace of William and Robert Chambers.

Peel, John, popular name of **John Robert Parker Ravenscroft** (1939–) Radio disc jockey and presenter, born in Heswall, Merseyside, NW England, UK. He was educated at Shrewsbury School, and after completing his national service (1957–9) he went to the USA and became a disc jockey for Radio WRR in Dallas. He returned to England in 1967 and began a long career with Radio 1. Since 1998 he has presented Radio 4's *Home Truths*, which won four Sony Radio awards in 1999. He also won the honorary gold Sony Radio Award in 2002.

Peel, Sir Robert (1788–1850) British statesman and prime minister (1834–5, 1841–6), born near Bury, Greater Manchester, NW England, UK. He studied at Oxford, and became a Tory MP in 1809. He was made secretary for Ireland (1812–18), where he displayed a strong anti-Catholic spirit, and was fiercely attacked by O'Connell, earning the nickname 'Orange Peel'. As home secretary (1822–7, 1828–30), he carried through the Catholic Emancipation Act and reorganized the London police force (who became known as *Peelers* or *Bobbies*). As prime minister, his second ministry concentrated upon economic reforms, including the introduction of income tax, but his decision to phase out agricultural protection by repealing the Corn Laws (1846) split his party and precipitated his resignation. He remained in parliament as leader of the *Peelites* (1846–50), until a riding accident caused his death.

Peele, George (c.1558–96) Elizabethan playwright and poet, born in London, UK. He studied at Oxford, then moved to London, where for 17 years he lived a Bohemian life as actor, poet, and playwright. His best-known works are *The Arraignment of Paris* (1584), a dramatic pastoral containing ingenious flatteries of Elizabeth, the historical play *Edward I* (1593), and the popular play *The Old Wives' Tale* (1595). The latter is a satire on the romantic dramas of the time, one of the first English works of its kind.

peepul A species of strangler fig (*Ficus religiosa*) native to SE Asia, and regarded as sacred in India; also called **pipal** or **bo-tree**. (Family: Moraceae.)

peerage In the UK, holders of the title of duke, marquess, earl, viscount, or baron (whether hereditary or for life), who make up, in that order of precedence, the titled nobility. Their privileges have been much reduced in recent years, especially after the 1999 reform of the House of Lords, but they remain exempt from jury service. The Peerage Act 1963 permits a person inheriting a peerage to disclaim it for life, as did Viscount Stansgate (Tony Benn) and the Earl of Home (Lord Home of the Hirsel) without the subsequent descent of the peerage being affected.

peewit An alternative name for the lapwing (*Vanellus vanellus*); also known as **pewit**. It was formerly an alternative name for the **black-headed gull** (*Larus ridibundus*).

Pegasus (astronomy) (Lat 'winged horse') The seventh-largest constellation, conspicuous in the N hemisphere, and best known for its large square of four stars, one of which actually belongs to the neighbouring constellation of Andromeda.

Pegasus (mythology) In Greek mythology, a winged horse, which sprang from the body of the Medusa after her death. Bellerophon caught it with Athene's assistance. Various fountains sprang from the touch of its foot, such as Hippocrene on Mt Helicon. Finally it was placed in the sky as a constellation.

pegmatite [pegmatiyt] Very coarse-grained igneous rocks with varied and sometimes exotic mineralogy due to concentrations of the rarer elements. They are commonly associated with the later stages of granite crystallization in dykes and sills, and are the source of many gem-quality and uncommon minerals.

Pei, I(eoh) M(ing) [pay] (1917–) Architect, born in Canton, SE China. He emigrated to the USA in 1935, where he studied at the Massachusetts Institute of Technology. He became a US citizen in 1954, and the following year founded his own firm. His principal projects include Mile High Center, Denver, the 60-storey John Hancock Tower, Boston, the glass pyramids at the Louvre, Paris, and the Miho Museum, Kyoto, Japan (1998). A controversial, adventurous designer, he was awarded the 1983 Pritzker Prize for architecture.

Peierls, Sir Rudolph (Ernest) [pairlz] (1907–95) Physicist, born in Berlin, Germany. He studied at Berlin, Munich, and Leipzig, becoming Pauli's assistant at Zürich. He travelled widely before becoming a professor at Birmingham (1937–63), Oxford (1963–

74), and the University of Washington, Seattle (1974–7). He applied quantum theory to solids and to magnetic effects, and then turned to nuclear physics. In 1940 with Frisch he reported to the British government that an atomic bomb based on uranium fission was feasible, and worked on this (the Manhattan project) throughout World War 2.

Peiping; Pei-p'ing *Beijing*

Peirce, Charles Sanders [peers] (1839–1914) Philosopher, logician, and mathematician, born in Cambridge, Massachusetts, USA. He studied at Harvard, and worked for the US Coast and Geodetic Survey from 1861. In 1879 he became a lecturer in logic at Johns Hopkins University, but left in 1894 to devote the rest of his life to private study. His enormous output of papers was collected and published posthumously in eight volumes (1931–58). A pioneer in the development of modern, formal logic and the logic of relations, he is best known as the founder of pragmatism, which he later named 'pragmaticism' to distinguish it from the work of William James. His theory of meaning helped establish the field of semiotics.

pekan *fisher*

Pekinese or **Pekingese** A toy breed of dog, developed in China 2000 years ago; long body with short legs; tail curved over back; long, pendulous ears; flat face, muzzle virtually non-existent; coat very long, fine, thickest on neck and chest; also known as **peke**.

Peking *Beijing*

Peking Man *Zhoukoudian*

Pelagianism *Pelagius*

pelagic environments The marine life zone in the water, as opposed to the environments at the sea floor (*benthic*). Pelagic environments have been subdivided into *neritic* and *oceanic*, based on proximity to land, and into *epipelagic*, *mesopelagic*, and *bathypelagic*, based on depth.

Pelagius [pelayjius] (c.360–c.420) British or Irish monk. He settled in Rome c.400, where he disputed with St Augustine on the nature of grace and original sin. His view that salvation can be achieved by the exercise of human powers (*Pelagianism*) was condemned as heretical by Church Councils in 416 and 418, and he was excommunicated and banished from Rome. Nothing more is known of him after that date.

pelargonium An annual or perennial, native mainly to S Africa; often slightly succulent, leaves rounded or ivy-shaped, variously lobed; flowers in a range of colours in clusters. They include the so-called 'geraniums' of horticulture, which fall into three main types: **regals** have spectacular flowers; **zonals** have leaves with bands of colour; and **ivy-leaved** have lobed leaves and trailing stems. (Genus: *Pelargonium*, 250 species. Family: Geraniaceae.)

Pelasgians [pelazgianz] The name given by the Greeks to the indigenous, pre-Greek peoples of the Aegean region.

Pelau *Belau*

Pelé [pelay], popular name of **Edson Arantes do Nascimento** (1940–) Footballer, widely held to be the best player in the game's history, born in Três Corações, Brazil. He made his international debut at 16, and at 17 appeared for Brazil in the 1958 World Cup Final, scoring two goals in the 4–2 win over Sweden. He won a second winner's medal in 1962, and a third in 1970. His first-class career was spent at Santos (1955–74), then with the New York Cosmos (1975–7). He appeared in 1363 first-class games (1955–77) and scored 1281 goals, winning 91 caps. In Brazil, he is a national hero. He was appointed a sports minister in the Brazilian cabinet in 1994, and received an honorary British knighthood in 1997.

Pelecypoda [pelesipoda] *ark shell; bivalve*

Pelée, Mount [pelay], Fr **Montagne Pelée** 14°18N 61°10W. Active volcano on Martinique I, E Caribbean; height, 1397 m/4583 ft; erupted in 1902 killing over 26 000 people in the town of St Pierre.

Peleus [peelyoos] In Greek mythology, the King of Phythia in Thessaly, who had to capture Thetis, a nereid, before he could marry her. The gods attended the wedding feast. He was the father of Achilles.

Pelevin, Victor (1962–) Writer, born in Moscow, Russia. He is considered the leading Russian novelist of his generation and a satirist of both the human and the Russian condition. His first novel, *Omon Ra* (1992), was acclaimed for its high satire and youthful enthusiasm. This was followed by a collection of stories, *The Blue Lantern and Other Stories* (1993), and a novel, *The Yellow Arrow* (1994), both of which were awarded literary prizes in Russia. Another satirical novel, *The Life of Insects* (1998), reflects the collapsing Soviet empire. *Babylon* (2000) is a humorous dig at the westernization of Russia following the influx of American goods and ideas, while *Clay Machine Gun* (2000) is a satire on Russian crime and corruption.

Pelham, Henry [pelam] (1696–1754) British statesman and prime minister (1743–54), born in London, UK, the younger brother of Thomas Pelham. He took an active part in suppressing the Jacobite Rising of 1715, became secretary for war in 1724, and was a zealous supporter of Walpole. Events during his ministry (reconstructed in 1744 as the 'broad-bottom administration') were the Austrian Succession War, the Jacobite Rising of 1745, the Financial Bill of 1750, the reform of the calendar, and the Earl of Hardwicke's Marriage Act.

Pelham (-Holles), Thomas, 1st Duke of Newcastle [pelam] (1693–1768) British statesman and prime minister (1754–6, 1757–62), the brother of Henry Pelham. He became Earl of Clare (1714) and Duke of Newcastle (1715). A Whig and a supporter of Walpole, he was appointed secretary of state in 1724, and held the office for 30 years. Extremely influential during the reigns of George I and II, in 1757 he was in coalition with Pitt during the Seven Years' War, but resigned after hostility from the new king, George III.

pelican A large aquatic bird from warm regions worldwide; bill long, with lower part sack-like; face naked; eats fish and crustaceans. (Genus: *Pelecanus*, 8 species. Family: Pelecanidae.)

pellagra [pelaygra] A nutritional disease which results from a deficiency of niacin (a vitamin of the B group). It is common in Africa due to a combination of a low niacin diet and malabsorption of food. In severe form it is characterized by dermatitis, diarrhoea, and dementia.

Pelopidas [pelopidas] (c.410–364 BC) Theban general and statesman. Together with his friend Epaminondas, he established the short-lived Theban hegemony over Greece in the 360s BC. After playing a prominent part in the Theban victory over Sparta at Leuctra (371 BC), he subsequently operated mainly to the N of Greece in Thessaly and Macedonia. He was killed in battle against Alexander of Pherae.

Peloponnese [peloponeez], Gr **Pelopónnisos** pop (2000e) 1 125 000; area 21 379 sq km/8252 sq mi. Peninsular region of Greece, the most southerly part of the Greek mainland, to which it is linked by the Isthmus of Corinth; bordered N by a range of hills, highest peak Killini (2376 m/7795 ft); chief towns, Argos, Corinth, Patras, Pirgos, Sparta, Calamata; a popular holiday region.

Peloponnesian War [peloponeeshan] (431–404 BC) The war waged throughout the Greek world on land and sea by the Spartans and their allies against Athens and her allies. The underlying cause was Athenian imperialism and the fear this produced in the chief mainland city-states, notably Corinth and Sparta itself. Despite its length, there were few decisive engagements; in fact, so evenly balanced were the two sides that the war ended only when the Persians intervened and threw their weight behind the Spartans. The result was defeat for the Athenians, the dismantling of their empire, and the installation in Athens of a Spartan-backed puppet regime, the so-called Thirty Tyrants.

Pelops [pelops] In Greek mythology, the son of Tantalus. As a child, his father served him up to the gods; Demeter ate part of his shoulder, but it was replaced with ivory and Pelops was brought back to life. In order to marry Hippodameia, he bribed Myrtilus, the charioteer of her father Oenomaus, to put a wax linch-pin in his chariot-wheel; after Oenomaus' death he also killed Myrtilus, and this brought a curse upon Atreus and Thyestes, his sons.

pelota [pelohta] The generic name for various hand, glove, racket, or bat-and-ball court games which all developed from the French *jeu de paume* ('palm [of hand] game'). The most popular form is *Pelote Basque*, which was first played in the Basque region on the French/Spanish border; also known as **jai alai** (Basque 'merry festival'), the name given to it when it was introduced into Cuba in 1900. It uses a walled court, known as a *trinquete*. Players wear a shaped wicker basket attached to their forearm in which they catch and propel the ball. Pelota is one of the world's fastest games. In some US states there is legalized public betting on the outcome of games.

Peltier effect *thermoelectric effects*

pelvic inflammatory disease An infection of the uterus, uterine tubes, ovaries, and surrounding tissues. It is usually caused by bacteria spreading from the lower genital tract (vagina and cervix). Infection may occur during delivery of a baby or insertion of contraceptive intrauterine devices, but is most commonly due to sexually transmitted organisms, especially *chlamydia trachomatis* and *neisseria gonorrhoea*. Infection may lead to pain in the lower abdomen, vaginal discharge, irregular or heavy menstrual periods, and general features of illness such as fever and fatigue; however, it may be completely symptomless. The infection can be treated with antibiotics, but if left untreated can seriously and permanently damage the organs of the upper genital tract, reducing fertility, and greatly increasing the risk of ectopic pregnancy if pregnancy does occur. Prevention is by avoiding unsafe sexual intercourse.

pelvis **1** The lowest region of the abdominal cavity. It contains part of the gastro-intestinal tract (coils of the small intestine, appendix (sometimes), sigmoid colon, and rectum), part of the urinary system (the bladder), and some of the internal reproductive organs (the ovaries and uterus in females; the vas deferens, seminal vesicles, and prostate gland in males).
2 A ring of bone which forms the limb girdle of the lower limb, and serves to transmit forces from the lower limbs to the trunk. It consists of the two hip bones, the sacrum, and the coccyx. It gives attachment to muscles of the trunk and lower limbs.

pelycosaur [pelikosaw(r)] A carnivorous fossil reptile known from the Carboniferous to the late Permian periods, mostly in North America; skull mammal-like with a single opening behind orbit for insertion of jaw muscles; typically with expanded sail along back, used for temperature regulation and possibly for signalling. (Subclass: Synapsida. Order: Pelycosauria.)

Pemba pop (2000e) 354 000; area 981 sq km/379 sq mi. Island region of Tanzania, in the Indian Ocean, N of Zanzibar and E of Tanga; capital, Chake Chake; cloves (world's largest producer), copra.

Pembrokeshire, Welsh **Sir Penfro** pop (2001e) 112 900; area 1590 sq km/614 sq mi. County (unitary authority from 1996) in SW Wales, UK; drained by the R Cleddau; administrative centre, Haverfordwest; other chief towns, Fishguard, Pembroke, Tenby; ferries to Ireland (Rosslare) from Fishguard; agriculture, oil refining (Milford Haven), dairy products, fishing, tourism; Caldy I priory and monastery; castles at Pembroke, Cilgerran, Carew; St David's Cathedral.

Pembrokeshire Coast National park in SW Wales, UK; area 579 sq km/223 sq mi; established in 1952; long stretches of coastline alternating between cliffs and sandy beaches; includes Milford Haven harbour, St David's Cathedral, several Norman castles.

PEN Initials standing for 'poets, playwrights, editors, essayists, novelists', an international association, founded by C A Dawson Scott in 1921, to promote friendship and understanding between writers, and to defend freedom of expression within and between all nations. Publications include *PEN International* (reviews), and *PEN New Fiction* and *PEN New Poetry*, in alternate years.

pen A writing or drawing implement used with ink. The modern pen developed from brushes (as used in Chinese calligraphy), reeds, and quills. By the mid 19th-c, metal pen nibs fixed to wooden stems had largely replaced quill pens, though they also needed to be dipped continually in ink. This problem was finally solved in 1884 by L E Waterman's invention of the **fountain pen**, with its reservoir and capillary action. The ball-point pen has remained in common use since the late 1930s, though rivalled by the **felt-tip pen** from the 1960s and the **rollerball** from the 1970s.

Penal Laws Collectively, statutes passed chiefly against the practice of Roman Catholicism in Britain and Ireland, when Catholic nations were perceived as a threat in the 16th–17th-c, but also against Protestant Nonconformists. They prevented Catholics from voting and holding public office. Fines and imprisonment were prescribed for participation in Catholic services, while officiating priests could be executed. In England, Catholics were subjected to laws limiting their property and means of education. In Ireland the Penal Laws were extended and made extremely oppressive during the 18th-c. As a result, Catholics could neither teach their children nor send them abroad; persons of property could not enter into mixed marriages; a Catholic could not inherit property if there was any Protestant heir; a Catholic could not hold a seat in the Irish Parliament (1692), nor hold public office, vote (1727), or practise law. The laws were repealed in stages, from the late 18th-c, the last not until 1926.

penal settlements Places of secondary punishment in Australia where convicts found guilty of serious offences were sent; also used for colonial criminals sentenced to transportation, and (after 1842) for British convicts transported for life. About 10% of the 162 000 convicts transported to Australia spent some time in these settlements, which were mainly at Newcastle (1801–24), Port Macquarie (1821–30), Morton Bay (1825–38), Macquarie Harbour (1822–33), Port Arthur (after 1830), and Norfolk I (after 1825). Life in these settlements varied from hard to savage, with hard labour and frequent and severe floggings; the last three named had deservedly fearsome reputations.

penance (Lat *poena*, 'punishment') Both the inner turning to God in sorrow for sin, and the outward discipline of the Church in order to reinforce repentance by prayer, confession, fasting, and good works. In the Orthodox and Roman Catholic Churches, penance is a sacrament.

Penang [penang], also **Pulau Pinang** pop (2000e) 1 421 000; area 1044 sq km/403 sq mi. State in NW Malaysia; a coastal strip on the NW coast of the Malay Peninsula and the island (*pulau*) of Penang in the Strait of Malacca; first British settlement in Malaya; capital, Pinang (formerly George Town); rice, rubber, tin.

Penates [penayteez, penahteez] In Roman religion, the guardians of the storeroom; 'Lares and Penates' were the household gods. The *penates publici* were the 'luck' of the Roman state, originally brought by Aeneas from Troy and kept at Lavinium.

pencil In art, originally a brush, a meaning still found in the 18th-c. Drawing sticks of graphite encased in wood were in use by the 17th-c, but modern hard and soft pencils, in which the graphite is mixed with clay and fired in a kiln, were first devised in France c.1790 by French inventor Nicholas-Jacques Conté (1755–1805). Readily erasable, the pencil lends itself to sketches and temporary notes, and is widely used by artists and draftsmen, as well as for everyday purposes. The term 'lead pencil' is a misnomer, arising from the early belief that graphite was a type of lead. The hardness of a pencil depends on the amount of clay used along with the graphite, and is indicated by a hardness rating, such as 8B (very soft) to 10H (very hard). The blackness of a pencil depends on the size and number of particles it deposits when making a mark. A wide range of coloured pencils is also manufactured, especially for children.

Penda (c.575–655) King of Mercia (c.632–55). He established mastery over the English Midlands, and was frequently at war with the kings of Northumbria. His forces defeated and killed Edwin at Hatfield in Yorkshire (633), and also Edwin's successor, Oswald, when he invaded Penda's territories (642); but Penda was himself slain in battle near Leeds while campaigning against Oswald's successor, Oswiu.

Penderecki, Krzysztof [pendreskee] (1933–) Composer, born in Debica, SE Poland. He studied at Kraków Conservatory, and became a leading composer of the Polish avant garde, exercising considerable influence as a teacher. He first attracted international attention with his *Threnody for the Victims of Hiroshima* (1960). Later works include the opera *The Devils of Loudun* (1969), two further operas, a St Luke Passion, and several other orchestral and vocal compositions.

Pendleton, Don(ald Eugene) (1927–95) Author, born in Little Rock, Arkansas, USA. An aerospace engineer, who turned to full-time writing at the age of 40, he contributed to many popular genres, including science fiction and mystery, but is best known for his series of 38 'Executioner' novels, starring Mack Bolan. Launched in 1969 with *War Against the Mafia*, the series led to the emergence of a new genre of 'action/adventure' writing in the 1970s, especially popular in North America. He also published under the names of Dan Britain and Stephan Gregory.

pendulum In its simplest form, a weight, suspended by a wire or rod from a firm support, allowed to swing freely to and fro under the influence of gravity. For a support of length l, the time taken for a there-and-back complete swing, the period T, is

$$T = 2\pi\sqrt{\frac{l}{g}},$$

where g is acceleration due to gravity. The period does not depend on the weight of the bob nor on the size of the swing (for small swings), which is why pendulums are used in clocks.

Penelope In Greek legend, the wife of Odysseus, who faithfully waited 20 years for his return from Troy. She tricked her insistent suitors by weaving her web (a shroud for Odysseus' father, Laertes, which had to be finished before she could marry), and undoing her work every night.

penetrance The extent to which the effects of a gene can be seen in the phenotype. A gene is *fully* penetrant if all individuals carrying it show its effects, as in achondroplastic dwarfism. A gene is of *reduced* penetrance if it has no detectable effect in some individuals proved by pedigree studies to be carrying it, as in brachydactyly (abnormal shortness of fingers and toes).

penetration aid Devices built into the 'front-end' of a nuclear-armed missile which, when the real warheads separate from their carrier (known as the *post boost-vehicle*), fly out and on to confuse enemy radars into believing that they are real rather than dummy warheads. This makes interception by anti-ballistic missile defences much more difficult.

Penghu Qundao [punghoo] or **P'eng-hu Ch'ün-tao**, Span, Port **Pescadores** pop (2000e) 103 000; area 127 sq km/49 sq mi. Island archipelago and county of Taiwan, in the Taiwan Strait, astride the Tropic of Cancer; consists of 64 islands, one-third uninhabitable; 85% of the population lives on the largest island, Penghu; Penghu Bay Bridge is the largest inter-island bridge in the Far East (5541 m/18 179 ft long); fishing, vegetables, coral; many temples (oldest, 1593 in honour of Matsu, Goddess of the Sea).

penguin A flightless seabird, native to S hemisphere; wings modified as flippers; feathers small, waterproof; mouth lined with fleshy, backward-pointing spines; eats fish, squid, krill, etc. (Family: Spheniscidae, 18 species.)

penicillin An antibiotic produced by the mould *Penicillium*. In 1928 at St Mary's Hospital, London, Fleming first noted its activity against the bacterium *Staphylococcus* when his culture plate accidentally became contaminated with the mould. The work was taken up and developed 10 years later by Florey, Chain, and others at Oxford. Its remarkable clinical activity in infectious diseases was first demonstrated in 1941. Today penicillin is still one of the most important antibiotics. Several types are used, such as ampicillin and benzylpenicillin (penicillin G).

Penicillium A genus of fungi with a white network of filaments (*mycelium*) bearing greenish powdery masses (*conidia*) on its surface; grows on decaying organic matter; many species produce important antibiotics, such as penicillin. (Subdivision: Ascomycetes. Order: Eurotiales.)

Peninsular Campaign (1862) In the American Civil War, an extended attempt by the Union army under General McClellan to take Richmond, VA (the Southern capital), by moving up the peninsula between the James and York Rivers. The effort failed, but Confederate troops were unable to drive the Northerners off the peninsula.

Peninsular War (1808–14) The prolonged struggle for the Iberian peninsula between the occupying French and a British army under Wellington (formerly Wellesley), supported by Portuguese forces. Known in Spain as the *War of Independence* and to Napoleonic France as 'the Spanish ulcer', it started as a Spanish revolt against the imposition of Napoleon's brother Joseph as King of Spain, but developed into a bitter conflict, as British troops repulsed Masséna's Lisbon offensive (1810–11) and advanced from their base behind the Torres Vedras to liberate Spain. Following Napoleon's Moscow campaign (1812), French resources were over-extended, enabling Wellington's army to invade SW France (1813–14).

penis A part of the male urogenital system composed mainly of erectile tissue and traversed by the *urethra*. It has a fixed root and a mobile body. The erectile tissue consists of three longitudinal columns (two *corpora cavernosa* and the *corpus spongiosum*). The urethra traverses the corpus spongiosum, which is considerably smaller than the corpora cavernosa. The free end of the corpus spongiosum expands to form the *glans penis* (which has the slit-like external urethral orifice near its summit). The erectile masses at the root of the penis are covered on their outer surfaces by muscle. The skin over the body of the penis is thin, delicate, freely mobile, and largely free from hairs. Towards the base of the glans penis it forms a free fold (the *prepuce* or *foreskin*) which overlaps the glans to a variable extent (the foreskin is surgically removed in circumcision so that the glans is always visible). The size of the penis varies with the amount of blood present within the erectile tissue. Erection builds up as a consequence of various sexual stimuli (pleasurable sights, sound, smell, and other psychic stimuli) reinforced by direct sensory touch (of the body and genital skin). This results in an increase in length and diameter of the penis until it assumes the erect position. Once sexual excitement abates, it returns to its flaccid state. In some mammals (eg dog, bear, baboon) a bone (the *os penis*) develops in the septum between the two corpora cavernosa.

penitential psalms A set of seven Old Testament psalms – *Psalms* 6, 32, 38, 51 (*Miserere*), 102, 130 (*De Profundis*) and 143, although differently numbered in the Vulgate and many Catholic versions – which have been used in Christian liturgy since at least the early Middle Ages, when they were regularly recited on Fridays during Lent. They are mainly laments, although not all are directly concerned with repentance of sin.

Penn, Sean (Justin) (1960–) Actor, writer, producer, and director, born in Santa Monica, California, USA. Born into a show-business family, he appeared on television in a number of small parts before gaining his first feature-film role in *Taps* (1981). Later films include *Colors* (1988), *Dead Man Walking* (1995, Oscar nomination for best actor), *The Thin Red Line* (1998), and *Mystic River* (2003, Best Actor Oscar). Among his films as writer/director are *The Indian Runner* (1991) and *The Crossing Guard* (1995). His first wife was Madonna (1985–9).

Penn, William (1644–1718) Quaker reformer and colonialist, the founder of Pennsylvania, born in London, UK. Sent down from Oxford for refusing to conform to the restored Anglican Church, he joined the Quakers in 1666, was imprisoned for his writings (1668), and while in the Tower wrote the most popular of his books, *No Cross, No Crown*. In 1681 he obtained a grant of land in North America, which he called Pennsylvania in honour of his father, Admiral Sir William Penn (1621–70). He sailed in 1682, and governed the colony for two years. After his return, he supported James II, and worked for religious tolerance. In 1699 he made a second visit to Pennsylvania, where his constitution had proved unworkable, and much had to be altered. After a permanent Charter was agreed (1701), he returned to England, where he remained until his death.

Penney, William (George) Penney, Baron (1909–91) Physicist, born in Gibraltar. He studied at London, Wisconsin, and Cambridge universities, was appointed professor of mathematics at the Imperial College of Science, London, worked at Los Alamos, CA, on the atom bomb project (1944–5), and was an observer when the atomic bomb was dropped on Nagasaki. He became director of the Atomic Weapons Research Establishment at Aldermaston (1953–9), and was chairman (1964–7) of the UK Atomic Energy Authority. He was the key figure in the UK's success in producing its own atomic (1952) and hydrogen bombs (1957). Knighted in 1952, he was created a life peer in 1967, and became Rector of Imperial College London (1967–73).

Pennines or **Pennine Chain**, nickname **the backbone of England** Mountain range in N England, UK; extends S from Northumberland to Derbyshire; fold of carboniferous limestone and overlying millstone grit, worn into high moorland and fell; separated from the Cheviot Hills (N) by the Tyne Gap; dissected by the Yorkshire Dales (S); rises to 893 m/2930 ft at Cross Fell; main watershed for rivers of N England; **Pennine Way** footpath extends 402 km/250 mi from Derbyshire to the Scottish Borders.

Pennsylvania [pensilvaynia] pop (2000e) 12 281 000; area 117 343 sq km/45 308 sq mi. State in E USA, divided into 67 counties; the 'Keystone State'; one of the original states of the Union, second to ratify the Federal Constitution, 1787; first settled by the Swedish, 1643; taken by the Dutch, and then by the British in 1664; region given by King Charles II to William Penn, 1681; scene of many battles in the American Revolution and Civil War; capital, Harrisburg; other chief cities, Philadelphia, Pittsburgh, Erie; Delaware R forms the E border; other rivers the Susquehanna, Allegheny, Monongahela, the latter two forming the Ohio R at Pittsburgh; major industrial state; coal mining, oil drilling (first oil-well in USA, 1859); steel and other metals, machinery, electrical equipment; dairy products, grain, vegetables, apples, hay, tobacco, grapes.

Pennsylvania, University of *Ivy League*

Pennsylvanian period *Carboniferous period*

pennyroyal A species of mint (*Mentha pulegium*) native to Europe and the Mediterranean, and also found in N America, with creeping, mat-forming stems, pale green leaves, mauve flowers, and strong, slightly peppermint, scent. It is used for soups and stuffings, and is sometimes grown as a lawn plant. As a mildly spicy tea, it is sometimes recommended for its physiological effects or as a herbal remedy. However, its oils contain pulegone, which is extremely toxic, and in some circumstances (eg when used in an attempt to induce abortion) it has proved lethal. (Family: Labiatae.)

Penrose, Sir Roger (1931–) Mathematical physicist, born in Colchester, Essex, SE England, UK. He studied at University College London and Cambridge. From 1956 he held posts at several British and American universities before taking an appointment at Birkbeck College, London (1964) and Oxford (1973). His research interests span topology and gravitation. In 1965 he showed that Einstein's general relativity predicts that stars can collapse under their own weight to form black holes. Subsequently, he and Hawking showed that general relativity predicts a 'big bang' creation of the universe (1970). He invented *twistors*, geometrical entities that can be used to describe space-time. The *Penrose triangle* is an impossible figure that inspired M(aurits) C(ornelius) Escher's 'Ascending and descending'. He was knighted in 1994.

pension A payment made to an individual who has retired from work, on a weekly or monthly basis, related to the wage or salary being earned before retirement. **Company pension schemes** operate by receiving contributions from employees and employers; the funds are invested, and the pensions are paid from the proceeds of the investment. In the UK, a **state-pension scheme** (SERPS, or State Earnings Related Pension Scheme) is available for individuals without a company pension. The state also pays a basic old-age pension (introduced 1909). Private pensions are schemes where the individual secures a pension privately, using the investment process. Several countries have made special arrangements to ensure that their workers are covered, usually with tax benefits, using a state social security programme, and often supplementing this with additional facilities, such as the Individual Retirement Account (IRA) system in the USA. In developing countries and in many of the former communist countries, old-age pensions rarely cover more than a small minority of people, or are severely curtailed by inflation.

Pentagon The central offices of the US military forces and the Defense Department, in Arlington, Virginia, USA. The complex, which was designed by G E Bergstrom and built 1941–3, covers 14 ha/34 acres. It is composed of five 5-storey, pentagonal buildings. A section of the complex was destroyed on 11 September 2001 when an aircraft was deliberately flown into it in a terrorist attack.

pentameter (Gr 'five measures') A line of verse of five feet: 'The lyf so short, the craft so long to lerne'. Since Chaucer (quoted here), and in this form (the iambic pentameter), it has been the most common verse form in English.

pentane C_5H_{12}, an alkane hydrocarbon with five carbon atoms. There are three structural isomers: **n-pentane**, $CH_3CH_2CH_2CH_2CH_3$ (boiling point 36°C); **isopentane** (IUPAC **methylbutane**), $CH_3CH_2CH(CH_3)CH_3$ (boiling point 28°C); and **neopentane** (IUPAC **dimethylpropane**), $CH_3C(CH_3)_2CH_3$ (boiling point 10°C).

Pentateuch [pentatyook] The five Books of Moses in the Hebrew Bible/Old Testament, comprising Genesis, Exodus, Leviticus, Numbers, and Deuteronomy; also called the *Torah*. Although attributed to Moses since ancient times, the works as a whole are believed by modern scholars to be composed of several discrete strands of traditions from various periods (such as an early Judean source 'J'; a N Israelite source 'E'; a priestly source 'P', perhaps from exilic times; and a source 'D' responsible for most of Deuteronomy). Together they trace Israel's origins from the earliest times, through the patriarchs, to the Exodus and Sinai periods prior to the entry to Canaan; they also contain much cultic and legal instruction.

pentathlon A five-event track-and-field discipline for women, seldom contested, having been replaced in 1981 by the seven-event heptathlon: the events of the pentathlon were the 100 m hurdles, shot put, high jump, long jump, and 800 m. Another form is the **modern pentathlon**, a five-sport competition based on miltary training. The events are cross-country riding on horseback, epée fencing, pistol shooting, swimming, and cross-country running. It is a modern Olympic event.

pentatonic scale A musical scale with five notes in the octave, most commonly equivalent to the first, second, third, fifth, and sixth degrees of the major scale.

Pentecost [pentekost] **1** A festival day in the Christian calendar, some 50 days after the death and resurrection of Jesus (seven weeks after Easter Sunday), commemorating the event in *Acts* 2 when the Holy Spirit was said to have come upon Jesus's apostles in Jerusalem, enabling them to 'speak in other tongues' to those present. In *Acts* 2.1, this occurred on the Jewish feast of Pentecost. In the English Church, this day is sometimes called 'Whitsunday'. The term *Pentecost* may also be used for the entire period between Easter Sunday and Pentecost Sunday. **2** *Shabuoth*

Pentecostal Churches *Pentecostalism*

Pentecostalism [pentikostalizm] A modern Christian renewal movement inspired by the descent of the Holy Spirit experienced by the Apostles at the first Christian Pentecost (*Acts* 2). It is marked by the reappearance of speaking in tongues, prophecy, and healing. The movement began in 1901 at Topeka, KS, and became organized in 1905 at Los Angeles. Rejected by their own churches, new churches were established, commonly called 'Pentecostal', and since then their missionary zeal has reached every part of the world. Pentecostal churches are characterized by a literal interpretation of the Bible, informal worship during which there is enthusiastic singing and spontaneous exclamations of praise and thanksgiving, and the exercise of the gifts of the Holy Spirit. There are over 22 million Pentecostals worldwide. Since the 1960s, Pentecostalism (usually referred to as 'charismatic renewal') has appeared within the established Protestant, Roman Catholic, and Greek Orthodox Churches.

Pentheus [penthyoos] In Greek mythology, a king of Thebes who did not welcome Dionysus. Disguising himself as a woman, he tried to spy on the orgiastic rites of the maenads, who tore him to pieces, his mother leading them on.

pentyl *amyl*

penumbra An area of partial shadow. A partial eclipse of the Sun is visible from within the penumbra of the Moon's shadow when it falls on the Earth. The term is also used for the lighter periphery of a sunspot, around the dark central umbra.

Penzance [penzans] 50°07N 5°33W, pop (2000e) 21 100. Town in Cornwall, SW England, UK; chief resort town of 'the Cornish Riviera', 40 km/25 mi SW of Truro; railway; ferry and helicopter services to Scilly Is; tourism, horticulture, clothing; Chysauster Iron Age village (N).

Penzias, Arno (Allan) [penzias] (1933–) Astrophysicist, born in Munich, SE Germany. A refugee with his family from Nazi Germany, he studied at Colombia University, joining the Bell Telephone Laboratories in 1961. In 1965 he and his colleague Robert Wilson, exploring the Milky Way with a radio telescope, discovered cosmic microwave background radiation – a discovery which has provided some of the strongest evidence for the 'big bang' theory for the origin of the universe. They shared the Nobel Prize for Physics in 1978.

peony A perennial herb or shrub, native to Europe (especially Greece), Asia, and W North America; leaves divided into lobed leaflets; flowers large, showy, ranging in colour from white or yellow to pink or red, up to 15 cm/6 in across, with 5–10 petals and numerous stamens. Many species, hybrids, and cultivars are grown as ornamentals. (Genus: *Paeonia*, 33 species. Family: Paeoniaceae.)

people's democracy A term applied by Soviet Communists and their allies in the Soviet satellite states to the stage of society during or soon after the takeover of power by themselves. They regarded the 'people's democracy' as a transitional stage of a society's development from capitalism to socialism, under close control by the Communist Party. In a people's democracy there was some form of machinery for mass participation in public affairs, but not for democratic elections. Given the very restricted opportunity afforded to the people to make any choices under such regimes, the term was something of a misnomer when used by non-Communists. It was used by the Communists as a more palatable term than the *dictatorship of the proletariat* when they sought to obtain broader political support and acknowledgement by the citizens of their own country or from outside. Following the collapse of Communism in 1990, the name was dropped from the official title of most countries that had previously used it.

People's Liberation Army *Red Army* (China)

People's Party *Populist Party*

Pepin III, known as **Pepin the Short** (c.714–68) King of the Franks (751–68), founder of the Frankish dynasty of the Carolingians, the father of Charlemagne. The son of Charles Martel, he was chosen king after the deposition of Childeric, the last of the Merovingians. He led an army into Italy (754), and defeated the Lombards. The rest of his life was spent in wars against the Saxons and Saracens.

pepper **1** An annual native to the New World tropics. Related to the potato and tomato, it has similar white flowers but entire, glossy leaves and large, fleshy, edible berries in a variety of shapes and colours. Its hot, spicy flavour is due to the chemical *capsaicin*, contained in the placenta. Used whole or ground into powder, peppers include paprika, chillies, cayenne pepper, and red pepper, plus numerous purely local types; the familiar green peppers are simply unripe red peppers. (Genus: *Capsicum*, 50 species. Family: Solanaceae.)
2 A tropical shrub or climber (*Piper nigrum*) with long, slender spikes of minute flowers and small hard fruits. The dried, unripe fruits are called *black peppercorns*. Removal of the outer layer yields *white peppercorns*. Both are used whole or ground as spice or condiment. (Family: Piperaceae.)

peppered moth A moth found in two colour forms: white wings with dark speckling, and dark wings with white speckling. It is regarded as a classic example of industrial melanism, ie birds selectively prey upon a light form when settled on a dark (polluted) background, and upon a dark form settled on a light (unpolluted) background, so that the dark form predominates in polluted industrial areas. (Order: Lepidoptera. Family: Geometridae.)

pepperidge *tupelo*

peppermint *mint*

pepsin A digestive enzyme, present in the gastric juice of vertebrates, which breaks down dietary protein into polypeptides of various sizes. It is secreted into the cavity of the stomach by the chief cells of the stomach, as an inactive pro-enzyme precursor (*pepsinogen*), and converted into pepsin by gastric HCl. It is active only in the acid environment of the stomach. Seven related pepsins have been identified in humans.

peptic ulcer The ulceration of a small part of the lining of either the stomach or the duodenum, caused by erosion by gastric acid. Symptoms range from mild indigestion to episodes of severe upper abdominal pain, nausea, and vomiting. Complications include haemorrhage, which may be severe, and perforation, which can lead to peritonitis. Predisposing factors include smoking, alcohol, stress, and irritant drugs such as aspirin. Many cases are associated with colonization of the upper intestinal tract with the bacterium *helicobacter pylori*.

peptide A molecule obtained by the partial hydrolysis of proteins, a short chain (oligomer) of amino acids. Longer polymers (generally 50 or more amino acids) are called **polypeptides** or proteins. The amide linkage in proteins is known as a **peptide linkage**.

Pepys, Samuel [peeps] (1633–1703) Diarist and naval administrator, born in London, UK. He studied at Cambridge, rose rapidly in the naval service, and became secretary to the Admiralty in 1672. He lost his office and was imprisoned in the Tower of London because of his alleged complicity in the Popish Plot (1678–9), but was reappointed in 1684 and in that same year became president of the Royal Society. At the Revolution (1688) he was again removed from office. The celebrated diary, which ran from 1 January 1660 to 31 May 1669, the year his wife died and his eyesight failed him, is of interest both as the personal record (and confessions) of a man of abounding love of life, and for the vivid picture it gives of contemporary life, including naval administration and Court intrigue. The highlights are probably the restoration and coronation of Charles II (1660), the Great Plague (1665–6), the Great Fire of London (1666), and the arrival of the Dutch fleet (1665–7). It was written in Thomas Shelton's Shorthand, and not decoded until 1825.

Perak [perak] pop (2000e) 2 765 000; area 21 005 sq km/ 8108 sq mi. State in W Peninsular Malaysia; bounded W by the Strait of Malacca; watered by the R Perak; capital, Ipoh; one of the wealthiest states in Malaysia since the discovery of tin in the 1840s; Kinta Valley, the leading tin-mining area; rubber, coconuts, rice, timber.

Perceval, Sir, or **Parsifal** In the Arthurian legends, a knight who went in quest of the Holy Grail. In the German version (*Parzival*) his bashfulness prevented him from asking the right questions of the warden of the Grail castle, so that the Fisher King was not healed.

Perceval, Spencer (1762–1812) British statesman and prime minister (1809–12), born in London, UK. He studied at Cambridge, was called to the bar (1786), and became an MP in 1796. He was solicitor general (1801), attorney general (1802), and Chancellor of the Exchequer (1807), before becoming premier. An efficient administrator, his Tory government was firmly established when he was shot while entering the lobby of the House of Commons by a bankrupt Liverpool broker, John Bellingham, who was later hanged for the murder.

perch Name used for many of the freshwater fish in the families Percidae and Centropomidae, as well as several similar species in other groups; includes European *Perca fluviatilis*, widespread in lakes and quiet rivers; deep-bodied, length up to 50 cm/20 in; green and brown with dark vertical bands; popular with anglers, and fished commercially in some areas.

Percheron [pershuhron] A heavy breed of horse, developed in France, with much Arab blood; height, 15·2–17 hands/1·6–1·7 m/5 ft 2 in–5 ft 5 in; black or grey; deep, solid body with strong neck and short, very muscular legs; the most popular heavy draught horse worldwide.

perching duck A duck of the tribe Cairinini (8 species), including the genera *Aix*, *Nettapus*, *Callonetta*, *Cairina*, *Chenonetta*, and *Sarkidiornis*. They nest in holes or (**muscovy duck**) in hollows. The tribe also includes four species of geese, called **perching geese**.

percussion A category of musical instruments, essentially idiophones and membranophones, which are played by being struck or shaken. Some produce notes of definite pitch (eg timpani, xylophone); others do not (eg cymbals, side drum). The percussion instruments commonly used in the modern orchestra are the timpani, side drum, bass drum, cymbals, tam-tam, tubular bells, and xylophone; except for the side drum, bass drum, and timpani, they are all idiophones.

percussion cap A small container holding an explosive charge – a development of firearm technology in the early 19th-c which led to the modern centre-fire cartridge used in small arms. The fall of a hammer ignites the percussion cap, which in turn detonates the main propellant charge in the cartridge.

Percy A noble N England family, whose founder, **William de Percy** (c.1030–96), travelled to England with the Conqueror. The most famous member of the family was **Henry** (1364–1403), the famous 'Hotspur', who fell fighting against Henry IV at Shrewsbury. His father, who had helped Henry of Lancaster to the throne, was dissatisfied with the king's rewards, and with his son plotted the insurrection.

Père David's deer A true deer (*Elaphurus davidianus*) native to China, extinct in the wild for nearly 2000 years; a herd survived in the Chinese Imperial Hunting Park until 1900; descendants of these now in parks and zoos; large with long tail; antlers may grow twice in one year, tines pointing backwards; original habitat unknown, but broad feet and willingness to swim suggest wetlands; also known as **mi lou**.

peregrine falcon A fast, agile falcon (*Falco peregrinus*), found virtually worldwide, often near sea cliffs or in mountains; eats birds; dives vertically on prey, or chases in flight; also known as **duck hawk**. A popular choice for falconry, its numbers are declining because of insecticide poisoning, as they feed on seed-eating birds which have eaten treated grain.

perennial A plant which lives for several years. **Herbaceous perennials** die back to ground level each year, surviving as underground organs such as bulbs or rhizomes. **Woody perennials** retain their aerial stems, which put out further growth each year.

Peres, Shimon [perez], originally **Shimon Perski** (1923–) Israeli statesman and prime minister (1984–6, 1995–6), born in Valozhyn, W Belarus (formerly Wołożyn, Poland). He was raised on a kibbutz, then studied at New York and Harvard universities. In 1948 he became head of naval services in the new state of Israel, and later director-general of the defence ministry (1953–9). In 1959 he was elected to the Knesset, and became minister of defence (1974–7), chairman of the Labour Party, and Leader of the Opposition (1977). He then entered into a unique power-sharing agreement with the leader of the Consolidation Party (Likud), Yitzhak Shamir, becoming prime minister from 1984 to 1986, when Shamir took over. After the inconclusive 1988 general election, Peres eventually rejoined Shamir in a new coalition, which collapsed in 1990. He then opposed Shamir's government until replaced as Labour Party leader by Itzhak Rabin (1992), and shared the Nobel Peace Prize with him in 1994. In 1995–6 Peres served a second term as prime minister. He joined Ariel Sharon's government as minister of foreign affairs (2001–2), and was elected interim Labour leader in opposition in 2003.

perestroika [perestroyka] The process of 'reconstructing' Soviet society through a programme of reforms initiated from 1985 by General Secretary Gorbachev. Such reforms, meant to be consistent with the ideals of the 1917 revolution, were directed at relaxing state controls over the economy, eliminating corruption from the state bureaucracy, and democratizing the Soviet communist party and the workplace to strengthen workers' control.

Pérez de Cuellar, Javier [peres duh kwayah(r)] (1920–) Peruvian diplomat, and secretary-general of the UN (1982–91), born in Lima, Peru. He studied at Lima University, and embarked on a career in the Peruvian diplomatic service, representing his country at the first UN assembly in 1946. As secretary-general, he played a prominent role in trying to secure a peaceful solution to the Falklands crisis, a ceasefire in the Iran–Iraq War, the release of the Iranian hostages in 1991, and the achievement of independence for Namibia. He became prime minister and foreign minister in the Peruvian transitional cabinet in the aftermath of President Fujimori's resignation in 2000.

Pérez Galdós, Benito [peres galdos] (1843–1920) Novelist and playwright, born in Las Palmas, Canary Is, Spain. He switched from law to journalism, and then to writing historical novels. Regarded as Spain's greatest novelist after Cervantes, his 46 short *Episodios nacionales* (National Episodes) give a vivid picture of 19th-c Spain from the viewpoint of the people. Some of his longer novels have been translated, including *Doña Perfecta* (1876, trans 1886). His plays, many of them based on his novels, have also been successful.

perfect competition A market situation described in economic theory where there are many buyers, many sellers, products are indistinguishable from each other, and there is perfect knowledge. The actions of any one individual cannot affect the market.

perfect numbers In mathematics, a number where the sum of its divisors is equal to the number itself. Thus the divisors of 6 are 1, 2, 3, and $1 + 2 + 3 = 6$; the divisors of 28 are 1, 2, 4, 7, 14, and their sum is 28; the next perfect number is 496. In Euclid's *Elements* a formula is given for finding perfect numbers: if $2^n - 1$ is prime, then $2^{n-1}(2^n - 1)$ is a perfect number.

performance *competence*

Pergamum (Asia Minor) [pergamum] or **Pergamon** An ancient city in NW Asia Minor, which in Hellenistic times was the capital of the Attalids. Under their patronage it became a major centre of art and learning; its school of sculpture was internationally renowned, and its library came second only to that of Alexandria.

Pergamum (Berlin) A branch of the Staatliche (state) museum in Berlin, Germany, housing one of the world's finest collections of Greek, Roman, Middle Eastern, and Eastern art and antiquities. The Pergamum altar, erected in the 2nd-c BC at the Greek settlement of Pergamum in Turkey, is on display there.

Pergolesi, Giovanni Battista [pergolayzee] (1710–36) Composer, born in Jesi, EC Italy. He attended the Conservatorio dei Poveri di Gesù Cristo at Naples, became a violinist, and in 1732 was appointed *maestro di cappella* to the Prince of Naples. His comic intermezzo *La serva padrona* (1732) was highly popular, and influenced the development of *opera buffa*. He wrote much church music, and in 1736 left Naples for a Capuchin monastery at Pozzuoli, where he composed his great *Stabat Mater*.

peri [peeree] In Persian mythology, the generic name given to a good fairy or genie. Peri-Banou, for example, was the name of a beautiful fairy in *The Arabian Nights*.

perianth The two outer whorls of floral parts (sepals and petals) taken together. When the whorls are not clearly distinguishable from each other, the individual parts are referred to as **perianth segments**. When the entire perianth is petaloid, as in many monocot flowers, the individual segments are sometimes termed *tepals*.

periapsis The closest point of approach of an orbiting body (planet, comet, spacecraft, etc) to the primary body; contrasted with **apoapsis**, the furthest point. For orbits about the Sun, **perihelion** is the point of closest approach; **aphelion** the furthest distance. For orbits about the Earth, the closest point is **perigee**; the furthest distance **apogee**.

pericarditis Inflammation of the pericardium, the sac of fibrous tissue that surrounds the heart. It may arise due to infections, especially viruses, connective tissue diseases such as systemic lupus erythematosus, as a complication of heart attack, or with no obvious cause. The predominant clinical feature is a sharp chest pain, aggravated by inspiration, and accompanied by fever. Auscultation of the heart usually reveals a characteristic rubbing sound. The major complication is a build-up of fluid between the pericardium and the heart (*pericardial tamponade*), which exerts pressure on the heart and prevents it from pumping effectively, leading to shock. Urgent drainage of the fluid with a needle may be required.

periclase *magnesia*

Pericles [perikleez] (c.495–429 BC) General and statesman, of the aristocratic Alcmaeonid family, who presided over the 'Golden Age' of Athens, and was virtually its uncrowned king (443–429 BC). Politically a radical, he helped push through the constitutional reforms that brought about full Athenian democracy (462–461 BC). A staunch opponent of Sparta, it was his unremitting hostility to her and her allies that brought about the Peloponnesian War (431–404 BC). Renowned for his oratory, his 'Funeral Speech' (431/430 BC), as recorded by Thucydides, is an impassioned apologia for Athens' democratic principles and system of government.

peridot *olivine*

peridotite [peridohtiyt] A coarse-grained igneous rock rich in the mineral olivine together with pyroxene and other ferromagnesian minerals. It is thought to be a major constituent of the Earth's mantle.

perigee *periapsis*

Périgord [payreegaw(r)] Part of the former province of Guyenne, SW France, now mostly in the department of Dordogne; chief town, Périgueux; extensively forested, chalky area, known for truffles; Palaeolithic (Perigordian) caves near Montignac, Rouffignac, and Le Bugue.

perihelion *periapsis*

perinatal mortality rate *infant mortality rate*

perinatology The study of disorders of the newborn that occur in the perinatal period, between 24 weeks of gestation and one week of life. It includes the care of such disorders as distressed breathing, bleeding, jaundice of the newborn, and birth injuries.

period (geology) *geological time scale*

period (physiology) *menstruation*

periodical A magazine or journal published at advertised intervals. No rigid distinction can be drawn: magazines are generally published speculatively by commercial publishers and sold retail in newsagents, bookshops, and bookstalls; journals are edited and published by or for institutions, clubs, and societies for sale predominantly to their members. However, many magazines may be bought on subscription. The weekly *Tatler* (1709–11) and *Spectator* (1711–14) were the earliest periodicals, quickly achieving considerable circulations. In the 18th-c, c.800 magazine titles were published, the longest-running being the *Gentleman's Magazine* (1731–1907). In the 20th-c, there was a great increase in the number of weekly and monthly magazines published, and in the range of their subject matter. Similarly, journal publishing increased, sponsored by learned societies, commercial and university-press publishers, and government and other official bodies. A recent development is the electronic journal, which may be received on-line direct to the subscriber's computer, and which may or may not be accompanied by the publication of a printed form of the same text. There were over 15 000 periodicals being published around the world in the 1990s.

periodic function In mathematics, a function such that $f(x + a) = f(x)$ for all x. If a is the smallest positive constant for which this is true, a is called the period. The commonest periodic functions are sine and cosine; the period of sin kx is $2\pi/k$.

periodic motion Any motion which repeats itself in a regular way, such as the swing of a pendulum, a weight bouncing on a spring, or wave motion. It is characterized by time T, the time taken for a complete cycle, and a restoring force that is always directed towards some rest position, resulting in motion about that rest position.

periodic table *p.1181*

periodontics *dentistry*

Peripatus [peripatus] A genus of velvet worm typically found in humid forest litter; body segmented, length up to 150 mm/6 in; head with a pair of antennae and jaws; legs lobe-like; mostly nocturnal, feeding on invertebrates. (Phylum: Arthropoda. Subphylum: Onychophora.)

peripheral nervous system (PNS) That part of the nervous system arranged into a large number of nerves, which connects the central nervous system with other tissues of the body. It is divided into an **autonomic** part, involved in involuntary (automatic) responses, and a **somatic** part, comprising in humans the 12 pairs of *cranial nerves* and some 31 pairs of *spinal nerves*, which are involved in voluntary acts and in monitoring the external and (in part) the internal environments of the body.

periscope An optical instrument for viewing an object concealed from view by a barrier (usually higher than the observer's eye-level). The basic principle is the use of two mirrors, parallel but separated by some distance: light from the object being observed reaches the first mirror, is reflected downwards, then reflected again at the second mirror, its whole path being somewhat in the form of a Z. The efficiency of the instrument may be assisted by additional optical devices such as an internal telescope or range finder system, as in the periscope used in a submerged submarine for viewing an object above sea-level, or in tanks for steering.

perissodactyl [perisohdaktil] ('odd-toed ungulate') A hoofed mammal of order Perissodactyla (16 species); foot with one or three functional toes (the first absent on all feet, the fifth absent on hindfeet); weight carried on toe 3 or toes 2–4.

peristyle [peristiyl] A series of columns surrounding an open court, temple, or other building. It is particularly used in classical architecture, such as the Lincoln Memorial, Washington, DC (dedicated, 1922).

peritoneum [peritoneeum] The fluid-secreting lining of the abdominal cavity and part of the pelvic cavity. During embryonic development it becomes twisted and folded, because of the relative growth of different parts of the gastro-intestinal tract. The majority of the tract is suspended from the rear abdominal wall by folds of peritoneum. Peritoneal ligaments attach less mobile structures to the abdominal walls.

peritonitis [peritoniytis] Inflammation of the peritoneum, the membrane lining the abdominal cavity, by infection or by irritant substances. The peritoneum may be regarded as the 'policeman' of the abdomen, in the sense that leakage from the stomach or intestine (as occurs in a perforation) causes layers of the peritoneum to stick to each other and confine the infection to a limited area; for example, a perforated appen-

periodic table

1	2	3	4	5	6	7	8	9	10	11	12	13	14	15	16	17	18
1 H Hydrogen 1.00794																	2 He Helium 4.00260
3 Li Lithium 6.941	4 Be Berylium 9.01218											5 B Boron 10.81	6 C Carbon 12.011	7 N Nitrogen 14.0067	8 O Oxygen 15.9994	9 F Flourine 18.998403	10 Ne Neon 20.179
11 Na Sodium 22.98977	12 Mg Magnesium 24.305	Transition series										13 Al Aluminium 26.98154	14 Si Silicon 28.0355	15 P Phosphorus 30.97376	16 S Sulphur 32.066	17 Cl Chlorine 35.453	18 Ar Argon 39.948
19 K Potassium 39.0983	20 Ca Calcium 40.08	21 Sc Scardium 44.9559	22 Ti Titanium 47.88	23 V Vanadium 50.9415	24 Cr Chromium 51.996	25 Mn Manganese 54.9380	26 Fe Iron 55.847	27 Co Cobalt 58.9332	28 Ni Nickel 58.69	29 Cu Copper 63.546	30 Zn Zinc 65.38	31 Ga Gallium 69.72	32 Ge Germanium 72.59	33 As Arsenic 74.9216	34 Se Selenium 78.96	35 Br Bromine 79.904	36 Kr Krypton 83.80
37 Rb Rubidium 85.4678	38 Sr Strontium 87.62	39 Y Yttrium 88.9059	40 Zr Zirconium 91.22	41 Nb Niobium 92.9064	42 Mo Molybdenum 95.94	43 Tc Technetium (98)	44 Ru Ruthenium 101.07	45 Rh Rhodium 102.9055	46 Pd Palladium 106.42	47 Ag Silver 107.8682	48 Cd Cadmium 112.41	49 In Indium 114.82	50 Sn Tin 118.69	51 Sb Antimony 121.75	52 Te Tellurium 127.60	53 I Iodine 126.9045	54 Xe Xenon 131.29
55 Cs Caesium 132.9054	56 Ba Barium 137.33	57–71 Lanthenide series (rare earth elements) ★	72 Hf Hafnium 178.49	73 Ta Tantalum 180.9479	74 W Tungsten 183.85	75 Re Rhenium 186.207	76 Os Osmium 190.2	77 Ir Iridium 192.2	78 Pt Platinum 195.08	79 Au Gold 196.9665	80 Hg Mercury 200.59	81 Tl Thallium 204.383	82 Pb Lead 207.2	83 Bi Bismuth 208.9804	84 Po Polonium (209)	85 At Astatine (210)	86 Rn Radon (222)
87 Fr Francium (223)	88 Ra Radium 226.0254	89–103 Actinide series (radioactive rare earth elements) ☆	104 Rf Rutherfordium (261)	105 Db Dubnium (262)	106 Sg Seaborgium (263)	107 Bh Bohrium (262)	108 Hs Hassium (265)	109 Mt Meitnerium (266)	110 Uun Ununnilium (269)	111 Uuu Unununium (272)	112 Uub Ununbium (277)	← under investigation →					

atomic number — symbol

86 Rn Radon (222)

element name

atomic weight (most stable isotope of radioactive elements in parenthesis)

★	57 La Lanthanum 138.9055	58 Ce Cerium 140.12	59 Pr Praseodymium 140.9077	60 Nd Neodymium 144.24	61 Pm Promethium (145)	62 Sm Samarium 150.36	63 Eu Europium 151.96	64 Gd Gadolinium 157.25	65 Tb Terbium 158.9254	66 Dy Dysprosium 162.50	67 Ho Holmium 164.9304	68 Er Erbium 167.26	69 Tm Thulium 168.9342	70 Yt Ytterbium 173.04	71 Lu Lutetium 174.967
☆	89 Ac Actinium 227.0278	90 Th Thorium 232.0381	91 Pa Protactinium 231.0359	92 U Uranium 238.0289	93 Np Neptunium 237.0482	94 Pu Plutonium (244)	95 Am Americium (243)	96 Cm Curium (247)	97 Bk Berkelium (247)	98 Cf Californium (252)	99 Es Einsteinium (254)	100 Fm Fermium (257)	101 Md Mendelevium (258)	102 No Nobelium (259)	103 Lr Lawrencium (260)

The method of listing the chemical elements in terms of increasing atomic number, so that the rows represent increasing occupancy of an electron subshell, and the columns represent equivalent numbers of valence electrons. The original table of Mendeleyev (1869) was based on atomic weight, but had several successes in predicting the existence and chemical properties of undiscovered elements.

dix may lead to a localized appendiceal abscess. Sometimes however the infection spreads throughout the peritoneal cavity, resulting in a generalized peritonitis, which is an acute surgical emergency with a high mortality. The surface of the peritoneum is very large, and generalized infection leads to the exudation of large volumes of fluid from the circulation, and so to shock. Chemical irritants to the peritoneum include gastric hydrochloric acid, bile juice leaking from a perforated duodenal ulcer, or pancreatic enzymes released into the peritoneum following acute pancreatitis.

periwinkle (botany) An evergreen, creeping herb of the dogbane family (Apocynaceae), originally native to the island of Madagascar, now found in Europe, W Asia, and N Africa; slender, arching, or trailing stems; leaves oval, in opposite pairs; flowers white, mauve, or blue-purple, tubular with five flat, asymmetric lobes. Main species: **common periwinkle** (Genus: *Catharanthus roseus*) and **lesser periwinkle** (Genus: *Vinca minor*); both also known as **myrtle**; historically attributed with medicinal properties.

periwinkle (zoology) A marine snail commonly found in the intertidal zone on shores; shells lack a mother-of-pearl layer; aperture closed off by a horny plate (*operculum*) on the foot; feeds by grazing on seaweeds and lichens. (Class: Gastropoda. Order: Mesogastropoda.)

perjury A crime committed by a person who, when giving evidence in a court under oath (or having affirmed or declared), deliberately makes a false statement or a statement which he or she does not believe to be true even if it is in fact true. The crime is essentially one of disregarding the oath: someone who makes several such false statements during a single case may be convicted of only a single perjury (though the number of instances could affect the severity of the sentence). Some offences in England and Wales which are related to perjury, such as making a false statement in any document required by statute, are punishable by two years imprisonment.

Perkins, Anthony (1932–92) Actor, born in New York City, USA. He studied at Columbia University, and made his film debut in 1953 while still a student. After several early films, such as *Friendly Persuasion* (1956), he achieved international fame as the maniacal Norman Bates in Hitchcock's *Psycho* (1960), with its three sequels (1983, 1986, 1990). Although he played many other parts on stage and screen, this role was the peak of his career.

Perkins, Charles (Nelson) (1936–2000) Bureaucrat and activist, born in Alice Springs, Northern Territory, C Australia of Arunta and European descent. He studied at the University of Sydney, becoming the first Aborigine to graduate from a university. He was a leader of the Aboriginal movement in the 1960s, his 'freedom rides' bringing injustice to Aboriginal people to public attention. He was chairman of the Aboriginal Development Commission (1981–4) and permanent head of the department of Aboriginal Affairs in Canberra (1984–9). He had been a member of the Australia Council Aboriginal Arts Committee since 1990.

Perkins, Kieren (John) (1973–) Swimmer, born in Brisbane, Queensland, SE Australia. He won the silver medal in the 1500 m freestyle at the 1990 Commonwealth Games, and set four world records (at 800 m and 1500 m) in the year leading up to the 1992 Barcelona Olympics, where he won the 1500 m final, breaking the Games record in the process, and regaining the title at the Atlanta Olympic Games in 1996. In 1994, he broke his own world 1500 m record with a time of 14 min 41·66 sec.

Perl, Martin (Lewis) (1927–) Physicist, born in Brooklyn, New York, USA. He studied at Columbia University (1955), taught at the University of Michigan (1955–63), then joined Stanford University (1963). His study of elementary particles led to his detection of the tau lepton – a short-lived, heavy-weight cousin of the electron, and one of the fundamental building blocks of matter. He shared the 1995 Nobel Prize for Physics with Frederick Reines.

Perlis [perlis] pop (2000e) 233 000; area 818 sq km/316 sq mi. State in NW Peninsular Malaysia, bounded N by Thailand, SW by the Strait of Malacca; smallest state in Malaysia; Langkawi Is lie offshore; capital, Kangar; rice, rubber, coconuts, tin.

Perm, formerly **Molotov** (1940–57) 58°01N 56°10E, pop (2000e) 1 092 000. Industrial capital city of Permskaya oblast, NE European Russia, on R Kama; founded, 1723; airfield; railway; university (1916); heavy engineering, chemicals, oil refining, clothing, footwear.

permafrost Perennially frozen ground in low temperature regions of the Earth. It is underlain at depth by unfrozen ground, and also overlain by an active surface layer which thaws in summer and refreezes in the autumn. The pressure produced by the downfreezing from the surface on the unfrozen and moisture-laden lower part of this active zone may be released by cracking of the frozen surface layer, causing severe problems for the construction of roads, buildings, and pipelines. Also the removal of insulating vegetation in permafrost regions deepens the active zone by melting the permafrost, often resulting in subsidence at the surface.

permalloy An alloy of iron and nickel or iron and cobalt, which is easily magnetized and demagnetized, developed by Swedish engineer Gustav Waldemar Elmen (1876–1957). The high magnetic permeability of permalloys is very useful for parts of electrical machinery subject to rapidly alternating magnetic fields. Their importance was realized in 1920 by the communication and telephone industry to make deep-sea communication telegraph cables capable of handling large numbers of messages.

permanent magnet *magnet*

permanent set *plastic deformation*

permeability The ratio of magnetic flux density B in some material to the applied magnetic field strength H; symbol μ, units H/m (henrys per metre); $B = \mu H$. The permeability of the vacuum $\mu_0 = 4\pi \times 10^{-7}$ H/m is a fundamental constant appearing throughout magnetism. Equivalently, permeability μ is the ratio of magnetic field (the magnetic flux density B) produced in a material enclosed by some solenoid to the magnetic field that would be produced in empty space within the same solenoid, all multiplied by μ_0. For paramagnetic materials, μ is larger than μ_0, and the field in the material is larger than the corresponding field in empty space. For diamagnetic materials, μ is less than μ_0, and the field is reduced. For ferromagnetic materials, μ is usually much larger than μ_0, and the field much larger. The property is related to magnetic susceptibility.

Permian period A geological period of the Upper Palaeozoic era, extending from c.286 to 250 million years ago. It was marked by the extinction of many groups of marine invertebrate animals and the diversification of reptiles. There were hot deserts in many parts of the Earth, with periods of glaciation in the S continents.

permittivity A measure of the degree to which molecules of some material polarize (align) under the influence of an electric field; symbol ε, units F/m (farads per metre). The permittivity of the vacuum is exactly $1/(\mu_0 c^2)$, where μ_0 is the permeability of the vacuum and c is the velocity of light, giving the permittivity as $\varepsilon_0 = 8{\cdot}854 \times 10^{-12}$ F/m, a universal constant appearing throughout electricity. For dielectric materials, ε is a material-dependent constant (the dielectric constant for that material under specified conditions) multiplied by ε_0.

permutational art A form of modern art in which certain features of the work are subject to change. Such changes (size, arrangement, number of parts, etc) may be predetermined by the artist (as in computer graphics) or left to chance.

Perón, (Maria) Eva (Duarte de) [peron], known as **Evita** (1919–52) The second wife of Argentinian President Juan Perón, born in Los Toldos, Argentina. A radio and screen actress before her marriage in 1945, she became a powerful political influence and the mainstay of the Perón government. She was idolized by the poor, and after her death in Buenos Aires, support for her husband waned. Her body was stolen, taken to Europe, and kept in secret until 1976. The successful musical *Evita* (1979) was based on her life.

Perón, Isabelita [peron], popular name of **Maria Estela Perón** *née* **Martínez Cartas** (1931–) President of Argentina (1974–6), born in La Rioja Province, Argentina. She was a dancer, who became the third wife of Juan Perón in 1961, living with him in Spain until his return to Argentina as president in 1973, when she was made vice-president. She took over the presidency at his death in 1974, but her inadequacy in office led to a military take-over in 1976. She was imprisoned for five years on a charge of abuse of public property, and on her release in 1981 settled in Madrid.

Perón, Juan (Domingo) [peron] (1895–1974) Argentinian soldier and president (1946–55, 1973–4), born in Lobos, Buenos Aires. He took a leading part in the army coup of 1943, gained widespread support through his social reforms, and became president in 1946. He was deposed and exiled in 1955, having antagonized the Church, the armed forces, and many of his former Labour supporters. He returned in triumph in 1973, and won an overwhelming electoral victory, but died the following year.

Peronism [peronizm] A heterogeneous Argentine political movement formed in 1945–6 to support the successful presidential candidacy of Juan Domingo Perón and his government thereafter. The movement later underwent division, some left-wing Peronists forming the Montoneros guerrilla group, but it survived Perón's death (1974). Despite continued internal disputes, the party won the presidency again in 1989. The ideology of Peronism (formally labelled *Justicialism* in 1949) has proved difficult to describe, and can perhaps best be viewed as a unique amalgam of nationalism and social democracy, strongly coloured by loyalty to the memory of Perón.

Perot, (Henry) Ross [peroh] (1930–) Businessman and politician, born in Texarkana, Texas, USA. After working as a salesman with IBM, he founded the Electronic Data Systems Corporation Inc, Dallas, in 1962, which grew to have over 50 000 employees. He was its chairman and chief executive (1982–6) until a buy-out by General Motors. He became internationally known when he stood as an independent candidate in the 1992 US presidential election. He withdrew in July, but then re-entered the campaign three weeks before the election, on the grounds that neither of the main candidates had addressed the need to reduce the federal deficit. Though attracting a great deal of popular support, he received no electoral votes. He stood again in the 1996 elections, with similar results.

peroxide A compound containing the ion O_2^{2-} or the group –O–O–. **Hydrogen peroxide** (H_2O_2) is an important oxidizing agent and bleach. Organic peroxides are explosive.

Perpendicular Style The form of English Gothic architecture prevalent from the late 14th-c to the 16th-c, derived from the Decorated style. It is characterized by a stress on horizontals and slender verticals, large expanses of windows, panel tracery and, in particular, fan vaults. The most dramatic example is King's College Chapel, Cambridge (1446–1515).

perpetual motion Literally, motion which is never ending. The term usually refers to 'perpetual motion machines' that invariably violate energy conservation and represent their inventors' optimism. An example would be a car powered by a windmill whose blades are driven by the flow of air due to the car's motion. Superfluidity and the flow of electrical current in superconductors are examples of literal perpetual motion.

Perpignan [perpeenyã] 42°42N 2°53E, pop (2000e) 111 000. Market town and resort capital of Pyrénées-Orientales department, S France; near the Spanish border, 154 km/96 mi S of Toulouse; settled in Roman times; capital of former province of Roussillon; chartered, 1197; scene of Church Council, 1408; united to France, 1659; road and rail junction; university (14th c), trade in olives, fruit, wine; tourism; citadel (17th–18th-c), chateau (14th-c, now a museum), town hall (13th–17th-c), Cathedral of St-Jean (14th–17th-c), Church of St-Jacques (14th–18th-c), Church of Notre-Dame-la-Réal (14th-c); Midsummer Festival (Jun).

Perrault, Charles [peroh] (1628–1703) Writer, born in Paris, France. He became a lawyer, and in 1663 was a secretary to Colbert. He wrote several poems, and engaged in debate over the relative merits of the ancients and the moderns, but is best known for the fairy tales published by him under the title *Histoires ou contes du temps passé* (1697), with the further title on the frontispiece, *Contes de Ma Mère l'Oye* (Mother Goose's Tales). They were translated into English by Robert Samber (1729). Collected from fables current in different times and among different peoples, the tales are among the most archetypal of their kind, such as 'Sleeping Beauty', 'Red Riding Hood', 'Blue Beard', 'Puss in Boots', 'Cinderella', and 'Tom Thumb'.

Perry, Fred(erick John) (1909–95) Lawn tennis and table tennis player, born in Stockport, Greater Manchester, NW England, UK. He won the world table tennis title (1929) and the men's lawn tennis singles title at Wimbledon (1934–6), the last British male champion. He also won the singles title at the French, Australian, and US championships, and was the first man to win all four major titles. He later became a US citizen, and served with the US armed forces. A notable writer, after retiring he was also proprietor of a sports goods firm.

Perry, Matthew (1969–) Actor, born in Williamstown, Massachusetts, USA. He moved with his mother to Ottawa as a child, and became an accomplished teenage tennis-player, but after moving to Los Angeles, he opted for acting. He had a variety of parts in television sitcoms, eventually achieving success with his role as Chandler Bing in the acclaimed television series *Friends* (1994–2004). Roles in feature films include *Fools Rush In* (1997), *Three to Tango* (1999), and *The Whole Nine Yards* (2000).

perry An alcoholic beverage made from fermenting pears. Sour pears contain a high level of tannin, which make them unsuitable for eating. Perry is produced commercially in the UK, Germany, and France, and is especially popular in the UK.

Perseids [perseeidz] A major meteor shower visible for a week or so before and after peaking on 12 August each year, the date on which the Earth crosses the orbit. The maximum hourly rate is c.70 meteors. They appear to radiate from the constellation Perseus, from which they take their name. This shower is associated with Comet Swift-Tuttle (discovered in 1862, reappeared in 1992), and consists of stony debris left by the comet along its orbit.

Persephone [persefonee] In Greek mythology, the daughter of Demeter and Zeus, originally called Kore ('maiden'); known as **Proserpine** in Latin. She was gathering flowers at Enna in Sicily when Hades abducted her and made her queen of the Underworld. There she ate the seeds of the pomegranate, which meant (in fairy lore) that she was bound to stay; but a compromise was arranged so that she returns for half of every year (an allegory of the return of Spring).

Persepolis [persepolis] The site in the mountains of Iran of the palaces and graves of the Achaemenid rulers of Persia; a world heritage site. Selected originally by Darius I, the site was extensively developed by his successors Xerxes and Artaxerxes. It was sacked by Alexander the Great in 331 BC.

Perseus (astronomy) [persyoos] A N hemisphere constellation, in the Milky Way. Fairly easy to see, it includes a double cluster of stars visible to the naked eye, as well as the famous variable star Algol. The Perseid meteors radiate from it every August.

Perseus (mythology) [persyoos] In Greek mythology, the son of Zeus and Danae. Danae's father put her and the young Perseus in a chest which floated to Seriphos, and he grew up on the island. The king ordered Perseus to fetch the head of Medusa, otherwise he would take Danae by force. With Athene's help Perseus asked the way of the Graiae, killed the Gorgon, and used its head to rescue Andromeda and save his mother.

Pershing, John J(oseph), nickname **Black Jack** (1860–1948) US general, born in Laclede, Missouri, USA. At first a schoolteacher, he went to West Point, becoming military instructor there and at Nebraska University. He served on frontier duty against the Sioux and Apache Indians (1886–98), in the Cuban War in 1898, during the Moro insurgencies in the Philippines (1903), in the Japanese army during the Russo–Japanese War (1904–5), and in Mexico in 1916. In 1917 he was appointed commander-in-chief of the US Expeditionary Force in Europe, and later became chief-of-staff of the US army (1921–4).

Pershing missile A medium-range, land-based missile with a nuclear warhead, deployed by the US Army in West Germany from 1983 onwards as part of NATO's theatre nuclear force modernization programme. The Pershing II supplanted the earlier Pershing I.

Persia *Iran*

Persian *Iranian languages*

Persian architecture The architecture associated with Iran (Persia), the earliest examples being fortified buildings in W Iran (8th-c–7th-c BC). Later buildings of the Achaemenid dynasty disclose an architecture heavily dependent on columns and thick walls, made of stone and mud-bricks and brilliantly decorated with reliefs, glazed bricks, and carved stucco. Most impressive is the Palace of Persepolis (c.518–460 BC), including the 'Hall of the Hundred Columns' throne room. Persia also contributed the cruciform mosque to Islamic architecture, such as the Masjid-i-Shah, Isfahan (1612–38).

Persian art The art associated with Iran (Persia), which has flourished since remote antiquity. Pottery dating from 4000–3000 BC is decorated with abstract and stylized animal designs, which were soon adapted by craftsmen in bronze and gold. Alexander the Great's conquest (333 BC) introduced new ideas, including Greek conventions for drapery and gestures. The Sassanian period (AD 224–642), one of the most creative periods of all, reacted by reviving traditional forms. The Arab conquest (7th-c) introduced Islamic ideas: splendid mosques were built, and calligraphy and manuscript illumination flourished.

Persian cat A type of long-haired domestic cat; round head and short face; many breeds. The name was formerly used for any long-haired cat, and is still used in the USA for breeds which in Britain are called *long-hairs* (eg *blue Persian* = *blue long-hair*).

Persian Empire An empire created by the Achaemenids in the second half of the 6th-c BC through their conquests of the Medes, Babylonians, Lydians, and Egyptians, extending from NW India to the E Mediterranean. Although it was overthrown by Alexander the Great in the 330s BC, its administrative structure, the satrapal system, survived.

Persian Gulf, also **The Gulf**, **Arabian Gulf** Lat **Sinus Persicus** area 238 800 sq km/92 200 sq mi. Arm of the Arabian Sea, connected to it via the Gulf of Oman and the Strait of Hormuz; bounded N by Iran, NW by Iraq and Kuwait, W by Saudi Arabia and Qatar, and S by the United Arab Emirates; largest islands, Bahrain and Qeshm (Iran); length 885 km/550 mi; maximum width 322 km/200 mi; average depth 100 m/325 ft; important source of oil; pipeline (N) links offshore oilfields with Iran and Saudi Arabia via terminal on Khârg I; scene of great tension during Iran–Iraq War in the 1980s, and during the Gulf War against Iraq in 1991.

Persian literature A literature which begins with 10th-c court poetry, represented by Rudagi (died 954). Firdausi (935–1020) composed the *Shahnama* or Book of Kings, the vast national epic on legends of Iran, establishing a Golden Age that lasted until the 15th-c. Earlier in this period we have the quatrains or *rubaiyyat* of the mathematician Omar Khayyam (1034–1130), the odes or *qasida* of Anvari (12th- c) and Khaqani (1106–85), and the *mathnavi*, narrative poems on a complex rhyme scheme, of Nizami (1141–1202). The influence of Islamic mysticism is evident later, in the *mathnavi* of Jalal-ud-din Rumi (c.1326–c.1390), whose collection *Divan* has been frequently translated; and the lyrical poems of Jami (1414–92). Important prose works were written on science by Avicenna (980–1037), on religion by Ghazzali (1058–1111), and on ethics – the celebrated *Gulistan* – by Saadi (1184–1291). Prose was also used for biographical and historical writings. Drama and prose fiction were introduced from the West in the late 19th-c, and there are now some interesting short-story writers. Modern Iran has produced the great novelist and short-story writer Sadiq Hidayat (1903–51), who is widely known through translations into European languages.

Persian Wars The name given to the two punitive expeditions launched by the Persian kings, Darius I and Xerxes, against Greece in 490 and 480–479 BC. The first was in retaliation for Greek intervention in the Ionian revolt of 499 BC, and was directed only at Athens and Eretria; it ended in catastrophe for the Persians at Marathon. The second was to wipe out the disgrace of Marathon; it ended in the twin defeats for the Persians at Plataea and Mycale.

persimmon [persimon] Any of several species of ebony, widely cultivated for their fleshy berries, which are edible but very astringent until fully ripe; also called **date plums**. The best known are the Chinese or Japanese persimmon, or **kakee** (*Diospyros kaki*), fruit 7·5 cm/3 in, globose, yellow to orange, native to E Asia; the **American persimmon** (*Diospyros virginiana*), fruit c.3·5 cm/1½ in diameter, orange, native to North America; and the **common date plum** (*Diospyros lotus*), fruit 1·5 cm/0·6 in, yellow or blue-black, native to Asia. (Family: Ebonaceae.)

personal computer (PC) A term used to describe microcomputers in general, and also used by the firm of IBM in its range of microcomputers. However, with microcomputers becoming increasingly powerful and widely used in industry and commerce, the initial significance of the term has begun to wane.

personal electronic organizer A hand-held electronic device which typically functions as a filing and indexing system for personal information, such as would be found in an address book, diary, or task list. It usually has a small screen for displaying the information, and keys for entering alphanumeric characters, although some devices use a pointer or pen-like device, and may include handwriting recognition. Unlike the personal computer, it cannot be programmed by the user.

personality A set of individually evolved characteristic patterns of behaviour which determine daily functioning on both conscious and unconscious levels. It is said to represent the balance between innate drives and a combination of conscience and external controls. A **personality disorder** is said to exist when features of personality limit the formation and maintenance of satisfying interpersonal relationships. As a result of inflexible and/or maladaptive personality traits, the individual's ability to function is impaired, or there is extreme objective distress. The description of personality disorders varies greatly in different psychiatric classifications. Examples include dependent and schizoid personalities.

person-centred therapy *client-centred therapy*

perspective In art, any method whereby the illusion of depth is achieved on a flat surface. Various methods have existed in addition to the 'scientific' one-point system invented by Brunelleschi c.1420. Most are based on the fact that objects appear smaller in proportion to their distance from the beholder, and that receding parallel lines appear to meet on the horizon at what is called the *vanishing point*. The Greeks developed scientific perspective as a by-product of their interest in optics and geometry, but it was unknown to the Egyptians. Alberti, Uccello, Dürer, and Leonardo were pioneers of the theory of perspective, and many textbooks were written on the subject in the 17th–18th-c.

Perspex The proprietary name for a flat sheet form of polymethylmethacrylate resin, of notably high transparency. It first gained importance through its use for aircraft windows in World War 2.

perspiration *sweat*

Perth (Australia) 31°58S 115°49E, pop (2000e) 1 263 000. State capital of Western Australia, near the mouth of the Swan R; the commercial, cultural, and transportation centre on the W coast; founded, 1829; city status, 1856; rapid development after the discovery of gold and the opening of Fremantle harbour (1897); fourth largest city in Australia; airport; railway; four universities (1911, 1975, 1987, 1990); two cathedrals; textiles, clothes, cement, furniture, motor vehicles, gold and diamond mining,

Peru

☐ International Airport ∴ World heritage site

official name **Republic of Peru**, Span **República del Peru**

Local name Perú

Timezone GMT −5

Area 1 284 640 km²/495 871 sq mi

Population total (2002e) 26 749 000

Status Republic

Date of independence 1821

Capital Lima

Languages Spanish and Quechua (official), Aymará also spoken

Ethnic groups South American Indian (47%), Mestizo (mixed Indian and European) (33%), white (12%), black, Japanese, and Chinese (3%)

Religions Roman Catholic (90%), Anglican, Methodist, Peruvian Baha'i minorities

Physical features Arid plains and foothills on the coast, with areas of desert and fertile river valleys; Central Sierra, average altitude 3000 m/10 000 ft, contains 50% of the population; highest peak, Mt Huascarán, 6768 m/22 204 ft, in W; forested Andes and Amazon basin (E), with major rivers flowing to the Amazon.

Climate Mild temperatures all year on coast; dry, arid desert in the S; typically wet, tropical climate in Amazon basin; average annual temperatures 23°C (Jan), 17°C (Jul) in Lima; average annual rainfall 48 mm/1·9 in.

Currency 1 New Sol = 100 céntimos

Economy One of the world's leading producers of silver, zinc, lead, copper, gold, iron ore; 80% of Peru's oil extracted from the Amazon forest; cotton, potatoes, sugar, olives; tourism, especially to ancient sites.

GDP (2002e) $138·8 bn, per capita $5000

Human Development Index (2002) 0·747

History Highly developed Inca civilization; arrival of Spanish, 1531; Vice-royalty of Peru established; independence declared, 1821; frequent border disputes in 19th-c (eg War of the Pacific, 1879–83); several military coups; terrorist activities by Maoist guerrillas; bicameral Congress consists of a Senate and a National Chamber of Deputies; an elected President appoints a Council of Ministers.

Head of State
1985–90 Alan García Pérez
1990–2000 Alberto Keinya Fujimori
2000–1 Valentin Paniagua Corazao *Interim*
2001– Alejandro Toledo

Head of Government
1999–2000 Alberto Bustamante Belaúnde
2000 Frederico Salas Guevara
2000–1 Javier Pérez de Cuellar *Transitional*
2001–2 Roberto Danino
2002–3 Luis Maria Solari de la Fuente
2003 Beatriz Merino
2003– Carlos Ferrero Costa

agricultural trade; tourism; Western Australian Museum; Old Court House; the most isolated of Australia's state capitals (Adelaide is 2250 km/1400 mi away); scene of the Commonwealth and Empire Games 1962.

Perth (Scotland) 56°24N 3°28W, pop (2000e) 42 900. Administrative centre of Perth and Kinross, E Scotland, UK; on R Tay, 50 km/30 mi N of Edinburgh; scene of assassination of James I (1437); railway; whisky, insurance, glass making, printing, agricultural supplies, tourism; Dalhousie castle, art gallery and museum, St John's Kirk (15th-c); festival of arts (May); agricultural show (Jun).

perturbation In astronomy, any small deviation in the equilibrium motion of a celestial object caused by a change in the gravitational field acting on it. Two bodies in mutual orbit trace a perfect ellipse. Any deviations from such a path indicate the presence of additional objects. Perturbations in the orbit of Uranus led directly to the discovery of Neptune in 1846.

perturbation theory A mathematical technique frequently used to obtain approximate solutions to equations describing physical systems that are too complicated to solve exactly. The problem is rewritten in two portions: one which can be solved exactly, and a smaller part (the **perturbation**) which allows the calculation of corrections to the first answer in terms of a sequence of ever-decreasing terms. The technique is essential in many branches of physics, particularly quantum theory.

pertussis *whooping cough*

Peru *see panel*

Perugia [payroojia] 43°07N 12°23E, pop (2000e) 145 000. Capital town of Perugia province, Umbria, C Italy, on a hill 493 m/1790 ft above the Tiber valley, 141 km/88 mi N of Rome; founded by Etruscans; taken by Romans, 295 BC; archbishopric; railway; university (1276); agricultural products, textiles, cement, printing, tanning, furniture, pasta, chocolate, cultural activities, tourism; Cathedral of San Lorenzo (15th-c), town hall (13th-c), Arco d'Augusto (Etruscan town gate), Church of San Pietro dei Cassiensi; jazz festival (Jul); music festival (Sep).

Perugino [perujeenoh] (Ital 'the Perugian'), originally **Pietro di Cristoforo Vannucci** (c.1450–1523) Painter, born in Città della Pieve, Umbria, C Italy. He established himself in Perugia, and had Raphael as a pupil in Florence (1486–99). He painted several frescoes in the Sistine Chapel, Rome, notably 'Christ Giving the Keys to Peter' (1481–2).

Perutz, Max (Ferdinand) [peruhts] (1914–2002) Biochemist, born in Vienna, Austria. He studied at Vienna and Cambridge, and worked at the Cavendish Laboratory on the molecular stucture of haemoglobin, using the technique of X-ray diffraction. He became director of the Medical Research Council's unit for molecular biology, shared the Nobel Prize for Chemistry in 1962, and was awarded the Order of Merit in 1988.

Pesach *Passover*

Peshawar [peshahwa(r)] 34°01N 71°40E, pop (2000e) 907 000. Capital of North-West Frontier province, Pakistan; 172 km/ 107 mi W of Islamabad and 16 km/10 mi E of the Khyber Pass; city of the Pathan people; under Sikh rule, early 19th-c; occupied by the British, 1849; airfield; railway; university (1950); major trade centre on the Afghan frontier; textiles, leather, food processing, copperware; Balahisar fort, Mosque of Mahabat, Qissa Khawani bazaar.

Pestalozzi, Johann Heinrich [pestalotsee] (1746–1827) Educationist, and pioneer of mass education for poor children, born in Zürich, N Switzerland. He worked as a farmer (1769), then tried to educate waifs and strays in his home (1774). After several failed attempts, he managed to open a school at Berthoud (Burgdorf), where he wrote *Wie Gertrud ihre Kinder lehrt* (1801, How Gertrude Educates her Children), the recognized exposition of the Pestalozzian method, in which the process of education is seen as a gradual unfolding, prompted by observation, of the children's innate facilities. *Pestalozzi International Children's Villages* have been established at Trogen, Switzerland (1946) and Sedlescombe, Surrey, UK (1958).

pesticide A natural or synthetic agrochemical used to kill insects, rodents, weeds, fungi, or other living things which are harmful to plants, animals, or foodstuffs. Pesticides are designed to target a specific pest in a specific environment, without harming other organisms. However, exposure to long-term or large doses of some pesticides may be toxic to humans and animals, and biological controls are increasingly used to reduce or replace pesticides.

Pétain, (Henri) Philippe (Omer) [paytĩ] (1856–1951) French soldier and statesman, born in Cauchy-à-la-Tour, N France. During World War 1 he became a national hero for his defence of Verdun (1916), and was made commander-in-chief (1917) and marshal of France (1918). When France collapsed in 1940, he negotiated the armistice with Germany and Italy, and became chief-of-state, establishing his government at Vichy. His aim to unite France under the slogan 'Work, Family and Country', and keep it out of the war, involved active collaboration with Germany. After the liberation, he was tried in the French courts, his death sentence for treason being commuted to life imprisonment on the Ile d'Yeu, where he died. His role remains controversial, and some still regard him as a patriot rather than a traitor.

petal One of the second whorl of flower parts, collectively termed the *corolla*. It is usually large and brightly coloured to attract pollinators, but is sometimes pale, reduced, or absent.

Peter I (of Russia), known as **the Great** (1672–1725) Tsar of Russia (1682–1721) and emperor (1721–5), born in Moscow, Russia, the son of Tsar Alexey and his second wife Natalia Naryshkin. He became accomplished in mechanics, with an abiding interest in military and naval technology. He was joint tsar with his mentally retarded half-brother, Ivan, under the regency of their sister, Sophia (1682–9). In 1697–8 he travelled to Germany, Holland, England, and Hapsburg Vienna; his chief aims being to recruit foreign technicians and craftsmen. On Ivan's death (1696) he became sole tsar, and embarked on a series of sweeping military, fiscal, administrative, educational, cultural, and ecclesiastical reforms, many of them based on W European models. He brought the boyars under the authority of Church and throne; encouraged industry, trade, and education; modernized the state administration; and introduced Arabic numerals into the Russian alphabet. During his reign the first Russian-language newspaper was published and the Academy of Sciences was established. All classes of society suffered from the impact of the reforms and the brutality of their implementation; his own son, Alexis, died under torture (1718), suspected of leading a conspiracy against his father. Nevertheless, his efforts to modernize Russia turned it from a backward country into an empire to be feared. Peter fought major wars with the Ottoman empire, Persia, and in particular Sweden, which Russia defeated in the Great Northern War (1700-21). This victory established Russia as a major European power, and gained a maritime exit on the Baltic coast, where Peter founded his new capital, St Petersburg (1703). He failed to nominate a successor, and was succeeded by his wife, Catherine I.

Peter, St, originally **Simon** or **Simeon bar Jona** ('son of Jona') (1st-c) One of the 12 apostles of Jesus Christ, at first a fisherman living in Capernaum. He was renamed by Jesus as **Cephas** (Peter, meaning 'rock') in view of his leadership amongst the disciples. In the Gospels he is often the spokesman for the other disciples, and leader of the inner group which accompanied Jesus at the Transfiguration and Gethsemane. Immediately after Jesus's resurrection and ascension, Peter appears also as the leader of the Christian community in Jerusalem. Later he may have engaged in missionary work outside Palestine, certainly visiting Antioch, but little is directly known of these activities. Tradition says that he was executed with his head downward in Rome (c.64). His presence in Rome is uncertain, but he is regarded by the Roman Catholic Church as the first Bishop of Rome. Two New Testament letters bear his name, but the authenticity of both is often disputed. Other apocryphal writings also exist in his name, such as the Acts of Peter and the Apocalypse of Peter. Feast day 29 June.

Peter the Hermit (c.1050–c.1115) Monk, a preacher of the first Crusade, born in Amiens, N France. He served as a soldier, became a monk, and in 1095 preached throughout Europe, generating enthusiastic support for the Crusade. He led the second army, which reached Asia Minor, but was defeated by the Turks at Nicaea. He then accompanied the fifth army in 1096, which reached Jerusalem.

Peter, Letters of New Testament writings attributed to the apostle Peter, although both are widely considered by modern scholars to be pseudonymous. The first letter claims to be written from 'Babylon' (possibly a cipher for Rome) to Christians in Asia Minor, encouraging them to stand fast amidst persecution, and reminding them of their Christian vows and obligations. It has been variously dated between the Neronian persecution of AD 64 and the Domitian persecution c.95. The second, shorter letter yields no direct references to its situation, but appears to oppose teachers who deny the second coming of Christ and espouse gnostic-tending doctrines. It is sometimes dated in the first half of the 2nd-c, and its canonical status was at times disputed in the early Church.

Peter and Paul Fortress A stronghold founded in 1703 by Peter the Great on a small island in the Neva R delta, then called Ingermanland, an area seized from Sweden during the Northern War (1700–21), and around which the city of St Petersburg sprang up. The fortress, which was notorious throughout the 19th-c for its political prison, has been a museum since 1922.

Peter Lombard *Lombard, Peter*

Peterloo Massacre (1819) The name given to the forcible breakup of a mass meeting about parliamentary reform held at St Peter's Fields, Manchester, NW England, UK. The Manchester Yeomanry charged into the crowd of some 60 000, killing eleven people. The incident strengthened the campaign for reform. 'Peterloo' was a sardonic pun on the Waterloo victory of 1815. The immediate effect was the passing of Six Acts (1819) by Parliament restricting the organization of public meetings and the dissemination of seditious literature.

Peters' map projection An equal area map projection, produced in 1973 by German cartographer and mathematician, Arno Peters (1916–2002). It shows continents and oceans in proportion to their relative sizes, allowing comparisons to be made. More traditional projections exaggerate the importance of the N hemisphere (eg in maps based on Mercator's Projection, the N hemisphere covers two thirds of the map area and the S hemisphere the remaining third). The Peters' projection avoids the Eurocentric view of the world, and shows the densely populated equatorial regions in correct proportion to each other.

Peterson, Oscar (Emmanuel) (1925–) Jazz pianist and composer, born in Montreal, Quebec, SE Canada. He could already play the piano when he began formal studies at six, his extraordinary keyboard facility winning him numerous awards and making him a local celebrity. In 1949 he became an international star when he joined a concert tour called 'Jazz at the Philharmonic' in New York. He travels globally, and has probably recorded more than any other jazz musician.

Petipa, Marius [peteepa] (1818–1910) Ballet-master, dancer, and choreographer, credited with the development of Russian classical ballet, born in Marseille, S France. After touring France, Spain, and the USA, he went to St Petersburg in 1847 as the principal dancer at the Imperial Theatre. There he staged his first ballet, *Pharaoh's Daughter* (1858), setting the style of *ballet à grand spectacle* which was to dominate Russian ballet for the rest of the century. In 1867 he became ballet-master at the Mariinsky Theatre in St Petersburg, creating 50 original ballets and restagings, the most famous being Tchaikovsky's *The Sleeping Beauty* (1890).

Petit, Roland [puhtee] (1924–) Choreographer and dancer, born in Paris, France. He trained at the Paris Opéra Ballet, and became its leading dancer (1943). In 1948 he founded Les Ballets de Paris de Roland Petit, which toured widely in Europe and the USA. He created a repertory of new ballet, and was also responsible for the ballet sequences in the film *Hans Christian Andersen* (1952), danced by his wife, **Zizi (Renée) Jeanmaire** (1924–). In 1972 he founded the Ballet de Marseille, and became its director.

petition of right *Crown Proceedings Act*

petit mal [petee mal] *epilepsy*

petit pois [petee pwah] *pea*

Petöfi, Sandor [petoefee] (1823–49) Poet, born in Kiskörös, SC Hungary. He was successively actor, soldier, and literary hack, but by 1844 had secured his fame as a poet, his most popular work being *János vitéz* (1845, Janos the Hero). In 1848 he threw himself into the revolutionary cause, writing numerous war songs, and fell in battle at Segesvár.

Petra [petra], Arabic **Wadi Musa** 30°20N 35°26E. Ancient rock-cut city in Maan governorate, East Bank, SW Jordan; capital of the Nabataean Arabs until their conquest by Rome in the early 2nd-c AD; wealthy commercial city for several centuries, controlling the international spice trade; approached only via a series of narrow ravines; numerous temples, tombs, houses, shrines, altars, and a great theatre carved out of red sandstone cliffs; a world heritage site.

Petrarch [petrah(r)k], in full **Francesco Petrarca** (1304–74) Poet and scholar, born in Arezzo, NC Italy. He studied at Bologna and Avignon, where he became a clergyman. In 1327 at Avignon he first saw Laura (possibly Laure de Noves, married in 1325 to Hugo de Sade), who inspired him with a passion which has become proverbial for its constancy and purity. As the fame of his learnings grew, royal courts competed for his presence, and in 1341 he was crowned poet laureate at Rome. The earliest of the great Renaissance humanists, he wrote widely on the classics, but he is best known for the series of love poems addressed to Laura, the *Canzoniere*, written in vernacular Italian. The work mirrors the poet's internal struggle between reality and dream, spirituality and the pleasures of the flesh. He left Avignon in 1353 after Laura's death, and lived the rest of his life in N Italy. His writing proved to be a major influence on many authors, notably Chaucer. His chief inspiration lay, however, in his sonnet form, which was adopted, among others, by Surrey, Wyatt, and Shakespeare.

petrel A seabird of the order Procellariiformes (**tubenoses**): small species called *petrels*; larger species called *albatrosses*. They include fulmars, prions, shearwaters, gadfly petrels (all from the family Procellariidae), storm petrels (Family: Hydrobatidae), and diving petrels (Family: Pelecanoididae). Their body contains much fat; sailors used to push a wick through the bird and use it as a candle.

Petrie, Sir (William Matthew) Flinders [peetree] (1853–1942) Archaeologist and Egyptologist, born in Charlton, Kent, SE England, UK. He surveyed Stonehenge (1874–7), but turned entirely to Egyptology from 1881, beginning by surveying the pyramids and temples of Giza and excavating the mounds of Tanis and Naucratis. The author of more than 100 books, renowned for his energy and spartan tastes, he became the first Edwards professor of archaeology at London (1892–1933), continuing excavations in Egypt and Palestine until well into his 80s.

petrified forest The results of a fossilizing process in which wood is gradually replaced by silica, commonly chalcedony or opal, by the infiltration of mineral-rich water. The fine structural detail may be perfectly preserved during the process, as in the Petrified Forest National Park in Arizona, USA (area 377 sq km/145 sq mi, established 1962).

petrochemicals Organic chemicals made from products of the petroleum industry or from natural gas. It is possible to make them all from other source materials, but the petroleum source is cheap and plentiful, and simple chemical reactions on distillates provide materials for conversion to plastics, fibres, detergents, etc. Many important solvents are the direct products of distillation.

petrocurrency or **petro-dollar** A currency surplus available in oil-producing countries on their balance of payments, which is surplus to their own requirements; sometimes termed 'footloose' money. The term came to prominence after the 1973 oil crisis. The currency is available for investment elsewhere, mainly in the USA and W Europe. Funds are usually held in US dollars, pounds sterling, or German deutschmarks.

petrogenesis; petrography *petrology*

petrol (UK) or **gasoline** (US) A liquid fuel for use in those internal combustion engines in which the fuel–air mixture is ignited by a spark. It consists of a mixture of many volatile hydrocarbons derived from the distillation and cracking of petroleum. It normally contains additives such as lead compounds to improve performance (the prevention of premature ignition) or rust inhibitors. In the 1980s, environmental concern led to a rapid increase in the use of *unleaded* petrol, but criticisms of reduced performance led to the development of a *superunleaded* petrol, with the addition of benzene and other compounds. Debate continues over the environmental impact of these additives.

petroleum Crude oil, probably of biological origin, occurring as accumulations under impervious rock. Normally liquid, it ranges from being light and mobile to very viscous, and is often associated with gas or water. Its main constituents are a variety of hydrocarbons, but there may also be sulphur, nitrogen, or oxygen compounds. It is found chiefly in the USA, several republics of the former USSR, Middle East, Venezuela, North Africa, and the North Sea.

petrology The study of rocks: their composition, mineralogy, mode of occurrence, and origin. The subdisciplines include *sedimentary*, *igneous*, and *metamorphic* petrology. **Petrography** is concerned with the textural and mineralogical description of rocks, often studied by optical microscopy of thin slices, while **petrogenesis** is concerned with their origin.

Petronas Twin Towers At the beginning of 2003, the tallest building in the world (each tower is 451·9 m/1483 ft), completed in Kuala Lumpur in 1996. It has 88 storeys, and was designed by Cesar Pelli and Associates.

Petronius Arbiter [petrohnius ah(r)bitair] (1st-c) Latin writer, supposed to be the Gaius Petronius whom Tacitus called *arbiter elegantiae* (arbiter of taste) at the court of Nero. He is generally believed to be the author of *Satyricon*, a satirical romance in prose and verse about the licentious life of the upper class in S Italy, fragments of which have been preserved. Accused of conspiring against Nero, he committed suicide.

Petrov affair The defection by Soviet embassy third secretary, Vladimir M Petrov, in Canberra in April 1954; he was granted political asylum by the Australian government. The Soviet government tried to fly Petrov's wife back to Moscow, but the aircraft was intercepted at Darwin, and she too was granted asylum. Later the Petrovs revealed they had been spying in Australia, and in one of their documents they implicated two members of the staff of Dr H V Evatt, the Federal leader of the Labor opposition. Evatt defended his staff before a Royal Commission (1954–5), but it refused to clear them. The affair helped to split the Labor Party, contributing to its failure to win national government for nearly 20 years.

petunia A bushy, free-flowering annual (*Petunia* × *hybrida*) native to South America, with large, funnel-shaped flowers. It is a relative of the potato, and a popular garden plant grown for its brightly coloured, often striped flowers. (Family: Solanaceae.)

Peul *Fulani*

Pevsner, Antoine (1886–1962) Constructivist sculptor and painter, born in Oryol, W Russia. In Moscow he helped to form the Suprematist group, but in 1920 he broke away from the Suprematists, and issued the *Realist Manifesto* with his brother. This ultimately caused their exile from Russia, and he migrated to Paris. Several of his completely nonfigurative constructions (mainly in copper and bronze) are in the Museum of Modern Art, New York City.

Pevsner, Sir Nikolaus (Bernhard Leon) (1902–83) Art historian, born in Leipzig, EC Germany. He was lecturer in art at Göttingen University until the Nazis came to power (1933), when he fled to Britain and became an authority on English architecture. He wrote the enormously popular book, *An Outline of European Architecture* (1942), and became art editor of Penguin Books (1949). He produced the monumental series for Penguin Books, *The Buildings of England* (50 vols, 1951–74), and was professor of fine art at Cambridge (1949–55). He was knighted in 1969.

pewit *peewit*

pewter A grey alloy consisting mainly of tin with other constituents. Lead was formerly used, to increase hardness, but because of its toxicity this has now been replaced by antimony. Pewter is traditionally used in candlesticks, drinking vessels, and other utensils.

peyote or **peyot** [payohtee] A small cactus (*Lophophora williamsii*) native to Mexico and Texas; stem globular, bluish, with tufts of hairs but no spines; also called **mescal button**. It was used by American Indians to produce a drug containing the hallucinogen *mescalin*, used in religious rites. (Family: Cactaceae.)

Pfeiffer, Michelle [fiyfer] (1958–) Film actress, born in Santa Ana, California, USA. A winner of the Miss Orange County beauty pageant, she had a variety of film and television roles before impressing audiences with her performance in *Scarface* (1983). She won acclaim for her role in *The Witches of Eastwick* (1987) and *Married to the Mob* (1988), and gained a Best Supporting Actress Oscar nomination for *Dangerous Liaisons* (1988), and a Best Actress Oscar nomination for *The Fabulous Baker Boys* (1989). Other films include *Frankie and Johnny* (1991), *Batman Returns* (1992), *Up Close and Personal* (1996), *A Midsummer Night's Dream* (1999), *The Story of Us* (1999), and *What Lies Beneath* (2000).

pH A measure of the acidity of a solution; it is approximately the negative of the common logarithm of the concentration of hydrogen ions in a solution, measured in moles per litre. In water, the product of the concentrations of hydrogen and hydroxide ions is about 10^{-14} at normal temperatures. The pH of an aqueous solution normally lies between 0 (strongly acidic) and 14 (strongly basic). A neutral solution has pH = 7.

Phaedra [feedra] In Greek legend, the daughter of Minos and the second wife of Theseus. While he was away she fell in love with her step-son Hippolytus. He rejected her, so she accused him of trying to rape her. Theseus called on Poseidon to punish him with death, after which Phaedra hanged herself in remorse.

Phaedrus or **Phaeder** [feedrus, feeder] (1st-c) The translator of Aesop's fables into Latin verse, born a slave in Macedonia. He went to Italy, where he was the freedman of Emperor Augustus. He published five books of fables, many his own invention, which were still widely read in mediaeval Europe.

Phaeophyceae [feeohfiysee-ee] The class of seaweeds comprising the brown algae; also known as the **Phaeophyta**.

Phaethon [fayithohn] or **Phaeton** [fayiton, fayton] In Greek mythology, the son of Helios the Sun-god and Clymene. He found his way to his father's palace and asked to drive the chariot of the Sun. He swung it too near the Earth, and so Zeus destroyed him with a thunderbolt. He fell into the R Eridanos.

phagocyte [fagosiyt] Any cell which engulfs and usually digests particles, micro-organisms (bacteria), or harmful cells. Many unicellular animals are phagocytic. In most multicellular animals, phagocytes fulfil a protective and cleansing role. In humans and other mammals, they occur in the blood (neutrophils, basophils, and monocytes), connective tissue, and the reticulo-endothelial system (tissue macrophages).

phalanger [falanjer] An Australasian nocturnal marsupial; thick fur, small ears, large forward-facing eyes, long grasping tail (often naked at tip); inhabits trees; eats mainly plant material; also known as **cuscus**. (Genus: *Phalanger*, 10 species. Family: Phalangeridae.)

Phalaris [falaris] (?–554 BC) Tyrant of Acragas (modern Agrigento) in Sicily, notorious for his cruelty. On his overthrow, he suffered the same fate as his former victims: he was roasted alive in a bronze bull.

phalarope [falerohp] A sandpiper of the genus *Phalaropus* (3 species); widespread; breeds in N hemisphere, winters in S tropics; adapted for swimming; inhabits shallow water. The larger female is more colourful than the male, and takes several mates.

Phanerozoic time [fanerozohik] A geological term used to describe the period of c.590 million years from the end of the Precambrian era to the present. Phanerozoic rocks were once thought to be the only ones which contain fossils.

pharaoh The title applied to the god-kings of ancient Egypt from the New Kingdom (c.1500 BC) onwards. Pharaohs were the chief mediators between their mortal subjects and the gods, and after death were believed to become gods themselves, as their mummified forms show; all have the attributes of the god Osiris – plaited beard, crook, and flail. Best known of the New Kingdom pharaohs are Tutankhamun (c.1352 BC), Rameses II (the pharaoh of the Exodus), and Rameses III (the conqueror of the Sea Peoples).

Pharaoh hound A medium-sized breed of dog, developed in Egypt; similar in stature to the greyhound, but with ears large, broad, pointed, and held erect; coat short, reddish-brown or white with grey or reddish patches.

Pharaoh's rat *ichneumon* (mammal)

Pharisees [fariseez] An influential minority group within Palestinian Judaism before AD 70, mainly consisting of laymen; possibly originating out of the Hasidim who opposed the political aspirations of John Hyrcanus I (c.2nd-c BC). They were noted for their separation from the common people, and for their punctilious observance of written and oral laws regarding ritual purity, cleansings, and food laws, assuming even the obligations placed upon priests. In the New Testament Gospels, they are often portrayed as the opponents of Jesus. After the fall of Jerusalem in 70, it was from Pharisaic circles that the rabbinic movement arose.

Phar Lap New Zealand chestnut gelding which became Australia's most famous racing horse in the late 1920s and early 1930s. He won 37 of his 51 races in this period, but his greatest win was the 1930 Melbourne Cup. Taken to North America, he won a major race in Mexico but died several weeks later in San Francisco, probably from eating highly fermentable green pasture and not, as widely believed, from poisoning by US gangsters. The autopsy showed his heart was twice normal size.

pharmacology A branch of medical science which studies the actions, uses, and undesirable side-effects of drugs. The first descriptions of remedies from plant sources were made by the ancient Greeks and Chinese: over 30 drugs were known in 4th-c BC China, and a great 1st-c BC pharmacopoeia listed 365. Dioscorides' *De materia medica* (AD c.60) was the first basic Western pharmacopoeia. The Chinese knew 1748 drugs and 16 000 prescriptions by 992. The subject became a scientific discipline in the West in the 19th-c, when pioneers began to study more precisely the physiological actions of purified drugs. Magendie performed one of the first experimental analyses of the actions of a pure drug (strychnine), and described the actions and uses of various others in his *Formulaire* (1821). Building on this approach, German scientists developed the subject in both the commercial and academic worlds from the late 19th-c. Oswald Schmeideberg (1838–1921) researched the actions of digitalis and muscarine; Hans Horst Meyer (1853–1939) the mechanism of action of anaesthetics. Paul Ehrlich (1854–1915) contributed to the modern theory of drug action by defining the interactions between drugs and their target tissues as being the same as those involved in conventional chemical bonds. John J Abel (1857–1938) returned to the USA after studying in Germany, and was a major influence on the development of the subject there. Pharmacological research is carried out in drug companies, universities, and research institutes, and has led to the development of over 200 essential drugs, as defined by the World Health Organization. In recent years, specialized branches have developed, such as molecular pharmacology, immunopharmacology, and neuropharmacology, which cross the boundaries of other biological disciplines.

pharmacopoeia [fah(r)makopeea] A book of standards for drugs, advising on identity, purity, and identification. In most countries there is an official pharmacopoeia, and any dispensed drug must comply with its standards.

pharmacy Originally the science of preparing, compounding, and dispensing medicines. Since more potent drugs have become available (mid-1940s), the scope of pharmacy has become increasingly concerned with more clinical functions, such as the checking of doses and drug interactions.

Pharos of Alexandria [fairos] A marble watch tower and lighthouse on the island of Pharos in the harbour of Alexandria, built by Ptolemy II (285–246 BC). It was the first of its kind.

pharyngeal tonsils *adenoids*

pharyngitis [farinjiytis] A sore throat; one of the commonest medical complaints, usually the result of bacterial or viral infection of the lining tissues of the pharynx.

pharynx A space formed by mucous membrane-covered muscle situated behind and communicating with the nose, mouth, and larynx. It extends from the base of the skull, and is continuous with the oesophagus below. The nasal part of the pharynx receives the opening of the auditory tube. In the oral part, the digestive and respiratory tracts cross, and during swallowing respiration is temporarily suspended. In the lower part, the narrow slits on either side of the larynx (the *piriform fossae*) are the regions where sharp objects (eg large fish bones) may become lodged if swallowed. The upper areas contain accumulations of lymphoid tissue (the tonsils) which, it is thought, help to guard against airborne infection.

phase 1 In wave motion, the fraction of a wave cycle completed by a time variable, where one complete cycle corresponds to 2π radians; alternatively, an argument of a function describing a wave. The phase difference, ϕ radians, represents the degree to which one wave leads or lags behind another; for $\phi = 0$ or 2π, the waves are in phase; for $\phi = \pi$, the waves are antiphase. **Phase shift** refers to a change in phase, eg by π radians for light waves reflected by a mirror. Two waves having a constant phase difference are called *coherent*.
2 In circuit theory, current and potential difference may be out-of-phase. If these are changing in time in a periodic way, then the maximums in current flowing through components such as inductors and capacitors will occur at different times from maximums in potential difference across these components. There will be a phase difference between the two.
3 In relation to matter, the different states: solid, liquid, and gas.

phases of matter The three possible states of matter: solid, liquid, and gas. The phase of a particular substance depends on temperature and pressure. A change from one phase to another, as in boiling or melting, is called a **phase transition**. A **phase diagram** shows the phases of a substance for various temperatures and pressures.

phase transition *phases of matter*

Phasmida [fazmida] An order of large insects with either elongate bodies and limbs (stick insects) or flattened, leaf-like bodies and limbs (leaf insects); length up to 30 cm/1 ft; c.2500 species, all of which are foliage feeders, mostly tropical or subtropical in distribution.

phatic communion A use of language which is not intended for giving or getting information, but for setting up social relationships, or being polite. It includes many formulae for greeting and leave-taking, as well as dance-hall routines (*Do you come here often?*) and conversations about the weather.

pheasant A large, plump, ground-feeding bird, native to Africa (1 species) and Asia, and introduced elsewhere; short wings and fast, low flight; male brightly coloured with long tail; inhabits woodland or scrub; eats plant material and insects; many species bred and hunted for sport. (Family: Phasianidae, 48 species.)

Pheloung, Barrington (1954–) Composer and conductor, born in Sydney, New South Wales, SE Australia. A guitarist in a blues band, he came to England and studied at the Royal College of Music in London and Surrey University (1977). He became principal conductor to the London Contemporary Dance Theatre (1979–90) and has also composed for ballet, dance, and theatre. His work for television includes *Boon* (1985), *Inspector Morse* (1986), and *Dalziel and Pascoe* (1995), and among his film scores are *Truly, Madly, Deeply* (1990), *Hilary and Jackie* (1998), and *Touching Wild Horses* (2002). He now lives in England.

Phelps, Michael (1985–) Swimmer, born in Baltimore, Maryland, USA. At age 15 he competed in the Olympic Games at Sydney (2000) and came 5th in the 200 m butterfly. The next year, at the World Championships, he won the same event in record time. He established himself further at the 2003 World Championships in Barcelona, where he won three gold medals and set new record times in the 200 m butterfly (1:53.93), 200 m individual medley (1:56.04), and the 400 m individual medley (4:09.09); he also won silver in the 100 m butterfly.

phenanthrene [fenanthreen] $C_{14}H_{10}$, melting point 101°C. A crystalline solid, an aromatic hydrocarbon containing three fused benzene rings. It occurs in coal tar, and it and its derivatives are carcinogenic. One of its bonds is easily broken, yielding derivatives of diphenyl (C_6H_5–C_6H_5).

phencyclidine *angel dust*

phenobarbitone *barbiturates*

phenol [feenol, fenohl] C_6H_5OH, IUPAC **hydroxybenzene**, also called **carbolic acid**, used as an antiseptic in situations where its corrosive properties are not a problem. A major constituent of coal tar, it is also synthesized in large quantities, as it has applications in the manufacture of fibres, resins, dyes, drugs, and explosives.

phenology [fenolojee] The branch of biology which studies the timing of natural phenomena. Examples include seasonal variations in vegetation, and their relationship with weather and climate.

phenomenalism In philosophy, the theory that statements about physical objects are in the end equivalent to statements about actual or possible perceptual experiences. The theory is associated with radically empiricist theories, such as those of Hume, Mill, and Ayer.

phenomenology A loosely defined philosophical movement begun by Husserl and developed by Scheler, Heidegger, Sartre, and Merleau-Ponty. In its broadest sense it is a descriptive philosophy of experience. Its central method is to describe carefully one's conscious processes, concentrating on subjective experiences and suspending all beliefs and assumptions about their 'external' existence and causation. The result is supposed to be a non-empirical, intuitive enquiry into the real essences or meanings that are common to different minds. The movement was influential in continental Europe in the 20th-c, but is contrasted in style and method to the analytical philosophy dominant in the English-speaking world.

phenothiazines [feenoh**thiy**azeenz] A class of drugs introduced in the 1950s and used in the treatment of psychiatric disorders such as schizophrenia and mania. Chlorpromazine (Largactil) was the first example.

phenotype The outward appearance of a specific single gene. For example, the dominant mutation A^y in mice (the genotype) will give the phenotype of a yellow coat and obesity.

phenyl [**fee**niyl, **fe**nil] C_6H_5–. A group derived by the removal of one hydrogen atom from a benzene ring.

phenylamine *aniline*

phenylketonuria [fenilkeetonyo**o**ria] A rare inherited disorder due to a defect in the metabolism of phenylalanine (an amino acid contained in protein). Phenylalanine accumulates in the body, and may cause mental deficiency. It can be detected in infancy by a screening test applied to urine, and if a strict phenylalanine-free diet is maintained, childhood development is normal.

phenylmethanal *benzaldehyde*

phenylmethyl *benzyl*

pheromone [**fe**romohn] A chemical substance secreted to the outside by an animal, which has a specific effect on another member of the same species. **Releasing** pheromones elicit a particular behavioural response, such as mating or aggression. **Priming** pheromones cause a change in the physiology of the recipient, such as an effect on reproductive hormones. Pheromones are common in insects; they are also found in rodents and monkeys, and more may be discovered. They are exploited in agriculture to control the time and frequency of mating in farm animals, and the movement of insects.

Phidias [**fiy**dias] (5th-c BC) The greatest sculptor of Greece, born in Athens. He received from Pericles a commission to execute the chief statues for the city, and became superintendent of all public works. He constructed the Propylaea and the Parthenon, carving the gold and ivory 'Athena' there and the 'Zeus' at Olympia. Charged by his enemies with appropriating gold from the statue, he disappeared from Athens, presumably into exile.

Philadelphia 39°57N 75°10W, pop (2000e) 1 517 500. Major deep-water port in Philadelphia Co, SE Pennsylvania, USA, at the confluence of the Schuylkill and Delaware Rivers; noted centre for culture, education, and medical research; fifth largest city in the USA; first settled by Swedes in the 1640s; British settlement organized by William Penn in 1681, and the town laid out in 1682; many Scottish and Irish immigrants settled in the 18th-c; birthplace of the nation, where the Declaration of Independence was signed, 1776; Constitutional Convention met here and adopted the Constitution of the United States, 1787; US capital, 1790–1800; heavily involved in the anti-slavery movement and the Civil War; site of Centennial Exposition, 1876; airport; railway; four universities (1740, 1851, 1884, 1891); financial centre; textiles, machinery and electronic equipment, chemicals, printing and publishing; service economy supplanting the dwindling manufacturing industry; naval dockyard; professional teams, Phillies (baseball), 76ers (basketball), Eagles (football), Flyers (ice hockey); Liberty Bell (Independence Hall), Pennsylvania Academy of the Fine Arts (oldest art museum in USA), Museum of Art, Franklin Institute Science Museum and Planetarium, Independence National Historical Park.

philadelphus [fila**del**fuhs] *mock orange*

philately fi**lat**elee] The collecting and study of stamps and related matter, popularly known as **stamp collecting**. Rarity is the main cause of the high prices paid by some enthusiasts. Commemorative sets available for limited periods and stamps issued and franked on the first day of issue ('first-day covers') have a special appeal. Sales of these play an important role in the economies of some developing countries. Philately also comprises stamped envelopes, postmarks, and more recently phonecards. The British Museum owns the world's largest philatelic collection. The first stamp-collector is thought to have been John Tomlynson, who started collecting stamps on 7 May 1840, the day after the issue of the world's first postage stamp, the 'penny black'.

Philby, Kim, popular name of **Harold Adrian Russell Philby** (1912–88) Double agent, born in Ambala, N India. He studied at Cambridge, where, like Burgess, Maclean, Blunt, and others, he became a Communist. Already recruited as a Soviet agent, he was employed by the British Secret Intelligence Service (1944–6) as head of anti-Communist counter-espionage. He later became first secretary of the British embassy in Washington, working in liaison with the CIA (1949–51), and from 1956 worked in Beirut as a journalist. In 1963 he disappeared to Russia, where he was granted citizenship.

Philemon and Baucis [fiy**lee**mon, **baw**sis] An old couple, man and wife, who were the only ones to entertain the Greek gods Zeus and Hermes when they visited the Earth to test people's hospitality. In return they were saved from a flood, made priest and priestess, and allowed to die at the same time, when they were changed into trees.

Philemon, Letter to [fiy**lee**mon] The shortest of Paul's letters, usually accepted as genuinely from the apostle to an individual Christian named Philemon, whose runaway slave Onesimus had been converted by Paul in prison. Paul asks Philemon to forgive and receive Onesimus as a fellow Christian, and not to seek punishment under Roman law. It probably dates from the late 50s or the early 60s AD.

Philip II (of France), known as **Philip Augustus** (1165–1223) King of France (1179–1223), born in Paris, France, the son of Louis VII (reigned 1137–79). His reign formed a key period in the development of the mediaeval kingdom of France. He embarked on the Third Crusade in 1190, but returned the following year to concentrate on attacking the continental lands of the Angevin kings of England. By the time he died, Capetian power was firmly established over most of France.

Philip II (of Macedon) (382–336 BC) King of Macedon (359–336 BC), the father of Alexander the Great. He used his military and diplomatic skills first to create a powerful unified state at home (359–353 BC), then to make himself the master of the whole of independent Greece. His decisive victory at Chaeronea (338 BC) established Macedonian hegemony there for good. The planned Macedonian conquest of Persia, aborted by his assassination in 336 BC, was eventually carried out by his son.

Philip II (of Spain) (1527–98) King of Spain (1556–98) and Portugal (as Philip I, 1580–98), born in Valladolid, NWC Spain, the only son of Emperor Charles V and Isabella of Portugal. Following the death of his first wife, **Maria of Portugal**, at the birth of their son, Don Carlos (1545), he married **Mary I** of England (1554), becoming joint sovereign of England. Before Mary's death (1558) he had inherited the Habsburg possessions in Italy, the Netherlands, Spain, and the New World. To seal the end of the Valois–Habsburg conflict he married **Elizabeth of France**, who bore him two daughters. His brief fourth marriage to his cousin **Anna of Austria** (1570) produced another son, the future Philip III. As the champion of the Counter-Reformation, he tried to destroy infidels and heretics alike. He sought to crush Protestantism, first in the Low Countries (from 1568), then in England and France. The destruction of the Armada (1588) and the continuing revolt of the Netherlands, along with domestic economic problems and internal unrest, suggest a reign marked by failure. However, among his political achievements were the curbing of Ottoman seapower after the Battle of Lepanto (1571) and the conquest of Portugal (1580).

Philip III (of Burgundy), known as **Philip the Good** (1396–1467) Duke of Burgundy (1419–67), born in Dijon, E France, the grandson of Philip the Bold. He at first recognized Henry V of England as heir to the French crown, but concluded a separate peace with the French in 1435. Philip created one of the most powerful

Philippines

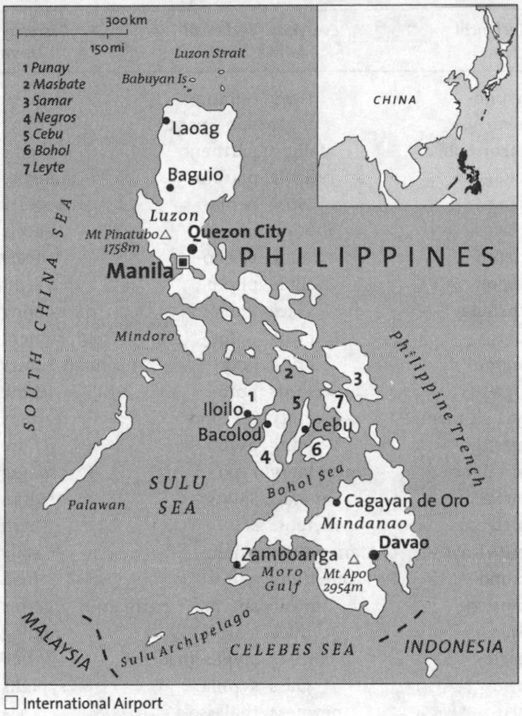

[filipeenz], official name **Republic of the Philippines**, Pilipino **Republika ng Pilipinas**

Local name Filipinas

Timezone GMT +8

Area 299 679 km²/115 676 sq mi

Population total (2000e) 80 961 000

Status Republic

Date of independence 1946

Capital Manila

Languages Tagalog (Pilipino), and English (official), over 87 local languages, including Cebuano, Ilocano, Bicol, and Samar-Leyte

Ethnic groups Filipino, with Chinese, Spanish, and American minorities

Religions Roman Catholic (83%), Protestant (9%), Muslim (5%), Buddhist (3%)

Physical features An archipelago of more than 7100 islands and islets, NE of Borneo; largest island, Luzon 108 172 km²/41 754 sq mi; Mindanao, 94 227 km²/36 372 sq mi, has active volcano Apo, 2954 m/9690 ft, and mountainous rainforest; Mount Pinatubo volcano, 1758 m/5770 ft, situated 90 km/56 mi NW of Manila; largely mountainous islands.

Climate Tropical, maritime; warm and humid throughout year; average annual temperature 25°C (Jan), 28°C (Jul) in Manila; average annual rainfall 2083 mm/82 in; frequent typhoons and occasional earth tremors and tsunamis (tidal waves).

Currency 1 Philippine Peso (PP, P-) = 100 centavos

Economy Farming (employs c.50% of workforce); rice, pineapples, mangos, vegetables, livestock, sugar, tobacco, rubber, coffee; oil, copper, gold; textiles; vehicles; tourism.

GDP (2002e) $379·7 bn, per capita $4600

Human Development Index (2002) 0·754

History Claimed for Spain by Magellan, 1521; ceded to the USA after the Spanish-American War, 1898; became a self-governing Commonwealth, 1935; occupied by the Japanese in World War 2; independence, 1946; Communist guerrilla activity in N; Muslim separatist movement in S; martial law following political unrest, 1972–81; exiled political leader Benigno Aquino assassinated on returning to Manila, 1983; coup in 1986 ended the 20-year rule of President Ferdinand Marcos; new constitution, 1987; attempted coup, 1989, with continuing political unrest; eruption of Mount Pinatubo, 1991; governed by a President and a bicameral legislature, comprising a Senate and a House of Representatives.

Head of State/Government

First Republic

1946–8 Manuel A Roxas
1948–53 Elpidio Quirino
1953–7 Ramon Magsaysay
1957–61 Carlos P Garcia
1961–5 Diosdado Macapagal
1965–72 Ferdinand Edralin Marcos

Martial Law

1972–81 Ferdinand Edralin Marcos

Second Republic

1981–6 Ferdinand Edralin Marcos
1986–92 (Maria) Corazon Aquino
1992–8 Fidel Ramos
1998–2001 Joseph Arap Estrada
2001– Gloria Macapagal Arroyo

states in later mediaeval Europe. A committed crusader, he maintained a fleet for operations against the Ottoman Turks.

Philip V (1683–1746) First Bourbon king of Spain (1700–46), born in Versailles, NC France, the grandson of Louis XIV and Maria Theresa, and great-grandson of Philip IV of Spain. After a long struggle with the rival Habsburg candidate for the Spanish succession, Philip gained the throne at the Peace of Utrecht (1713), but lost the Spanish Netherlands and Italian lands. Twice married, he fell under the influence of his second wife, **Elizabeth Farnese of Parma**, whose desire to secure Italian possessions for her sons brought Spain into conflict with Austria, Great Britain, France, and the United Provinces.

Philip VI (1293–1350) First Valois king of France (1328–50), the nephew of Philip IV, who became king on the death of Charles IV. His right was denied by Edward III of England, son of the daughter of Philip IV, who declared that females, though excluded from the succession by the Salic law, could transmit their right to their children. The Hundred Years' War with England thus began (1337), and in 1346 Edward III landed in Normandy, defeating Philip at Crécy, just as the Black Death was about to spread through France.

Philip, St (1st-c) One of the disciples of Jesus, listed among the 12 (in *Mark* 3.14 and *Acts* 1). He is especially prominent in John's Gospel, where he is said to come from Bethsaida in Galilee, leads Nathanael to Jesus (1.43), is present at the feeding of the 5000 (6.1), and brings 'the Greeks' to Jesus (12.21). His later career is unknown, but traditions suggest he was martyred on a cross. He is probably not the same person as Philip 'the Evangelist' (*Acts* 6.5). Feast day 3 May (W) or 14 November (E).

Philip, Prince *Edinburgh, Duke of*

Philippi, Battle of [filipiy] (42 BC) The decisive battle in N Greece in which Antony and Octavian (later the Emperor Augustus) defeated Brutus and Cassius, and thus avenged the murder of Julius Caesar.

Philippians, Letter to the [filipianz] New Testament writing, widely accepted as genuinely from the apostle Paul to a Christian community that he had founded earlier at Philippi in Macedonia, although the unity of the work has been debated. Writing while imprisoned (AD mid-50s?), Paul thanks them for a gift sent to him, appraises them of his situation and difficul-

An A To Z Of Phobias

Technical term	Everyday term	Technical term	Everyday term	Technical term	Everyday term	Technical term	Everyday term
acero-	sourness	claustro-	closed spaces	hypno-	sleep	ourano-	heaven
achulo-	darkness	cnido-	stings	ideo-	ideas	pan- (panto-)	everything
acro-	heights	cometo-	comets	kakorraphia-	failure	partheno-	girls
aero-	air	crystallo-	crystals	katagelo-	ridicule	patroio-	heredity
agora-	open spaces	cyno-	dogs	keno-	void	penia-	poverty
aichuro-	points	demo-	crowds	kineso-	motion	phasmo-	ghosts
ailouro-	cats	demono-	demons	klepto-	stealing	phobo-	fears
akoustico-	sound	dermato-	skin	kopo-	fatigue	photo-	light
algo-	pain	dike-	justice	kristallo-	ice	pnigero-	smothering
amaka-	carriages	dora-	fur	lalo-	stuttering	poine-	punishment
amatho-	dust	elsoptro-	mirror	linono-	string	poly-	many things
andro-	men	elektro-	electricity	logo-	words	poto-	drink
anemo-	wind	enete-	pins	lysso- (-mania)-	insanity	pterono-	feathers
angino-	narrowness	entomo-	insects	mastigo-	flogging	pyro-	fire
anthropo-	man	eoso-	dawn	mechano-	machinery	rypo-	soiling
antlo-	flood	eremo-	solitude	metallo-	metals	Satano-	Satan
apeiro-	infinity	ergo-	work	meteoro-	meteors	sela-	flash
arachno-	spiders	erythro-	blushing	miso (myso-)-	contamination	sidero-	stars
astheno-	weakness	geno-	sex	mono-	one thing	sito-	food
astra-	astral	geuma- (geumato-)	taste	musico-	music	sperma- (spermato-)	germs
ate-	ruin	grapho-	writing	muso-	mice	stasi-	standing
aulo-	flute	gymno- (gymnoto-)	nudity	necro-	corpses	stygio- (hadeo-)	hell
Auroro-	Northern Lights	gyno-	women	nelo-	glass	syphilo-	syphilis
bacillo-	Microbes	hamartio-	sin	neo-	newness	thalasso-	sea
baro-	gravity	hapto-	touch	nepho- (nephelo-)	clouds	thanato-	death
baso-	walking	harpaxo-	robbers	noso- (patho-)	disease	thasso-	sitting
batracho-	amphibians	hedono-	pleasure	ocho-	vehicles	theo-	God
belone-	needles	hemato-	blood	odonto-	teeth	thermo-	heat
bronto- (tonitro-)	thunder	helmintho-	worms	oiko-	home	toxi-	poison
cheima- (cheimato-)	cold	hodo-	travel	olfacto-	smell	tremo-	trembling
chiono-	snow	homichlo-	fog	ommato-	eyes	triskaideka-	thirteen
chrometo- (chremato-)	money	horme-	shock	oneiro-	dreams	xeno-	strangers
chromo-	colour	hydro-	water	ophidio-	snakes	zelo-	jealousy
chrono-	duration	hypegia-	responsibility	ornitho-	birds	zoo-	animals

ties, warns them of sectarian teaching, but generally displays a warm regard for their commitment.

philippic A denunciation in speech or writing, direct and often abusive. The term derives from Demosthenes' orations (c.350 BC) attacking Philip of Macedon. Cicero's *In Verrem* (70 BC), Swift's *Drapier's Letters* (1724), and the *Letters* of Junius (1769–72) are notable examples.

Philippines *p.1191*

Philistines The ancient warlike inhabitants of the coastal area of the SE Mediterranean between present-day Jaffa and Egypt. They were constantly at odds with the Israelites of the hinterland – a struggle epitomized by the stories of Samson and of David and Goliath.

Phillip, Arthur (1738–1814) Admiral, founder and first governor of New South Wales, born in London, UK. He trained at Greenwich, joined the merchant navy at 16 and the Royal Navy at 23, saw service in the Mediterranean, and was at the taking of Havana. He retired from the navy after the Seven Years' War (1763), married, and settled as a gentleman farmer in Hampshire. After the failure of the marriage, he returned to the sea, serving with the Portuguese navy, and in 1778 rejoining the Royal Navy. In 1787 he was appointed commander of the 'First Fleet' carrying convicts to Australia, and founded a penal colony settlement at Sydney the following year. He returned to England in poor health in 1792, and was made vice-admiral in 1810. He married again, and retired to Bath. The site and foundations of his 1788 Government House still exist in Bridge Street, Sydney, the oldest piece of colonial heritage in the country.

Phillips, Mark, Captain (1948–) Former husband of Princess Anne, and a noted horseman. He trained at Sandhurst Military Academy, and joined the Queen's Dragoon Guards in 1969. In 1973 he married Princess Anne (now the Princess Royal), but they divorced in 1992. He was a regular member of the British equestrian team (1970–6), and won many team events, including the gold medal at the Olympic Games in Munich in 1972.

Phillips, William D (1948–) Physicist, born in Wilkes-Barre, Pennsylvania, USA. He graduated in 1976 from MIT, joining the National Institute of Standards and Technology in Gaithersburg, MD. In 1997 he shared the Nobel Prize for Physics for his contribution to the development of methods to cool and trap atoms with laser light.

Phillips curve In economics, the shape of a curve in a diagram which shows the relationship between inflation and levels of unemployment. It derives from the work of the New Zealand economist A W Phillips (1914–75) in the early 1960s. It is normally assumed to show inflation as a decreasing function of unemployment, but curved so that high levels of unemploy-

Everyday term	Technical term	Everyday term	Technical term	Everyday term	Technical term	Everyday term	Technical term
air	aero-	feathers	pterono-	meteors	meteoro-	smothering	pnigero-
amphibians	batracho-	fire	pyro-	mice	muso-	snakes	ophidio-
animals	zoo-	flash	sela-	microbes	bacillo-	snow	chiono-
astral	astra-	flogging	mastigo-	mirrors	eisoptro-	soiling	rypo-
birds	ornitho-	flood	antlo-	money	chrometo-	solitude	eremo-
blood	hemato-	flute	aulo-	motion	kineso-	sound	akoustico-
blushing	erythro-	fog	homichlo-	music	musico-	sourness	acero-
carriages	amaka-	food	sito-	narrowness	angino-	spiders	arachno-
cats	ailouro-	fur	dora-	needles	belone-	standing	stasi-
closed spaces	claustro-	germs	sperma- (spermato-)	newness	neo-	stars	sidero-
clouds	ncpho- (nephelo-)	ghosts	phasmo-	Northern Lights	Auroro-	stealing	klepto-
cold	cheima- (cheimato-)	girls	partheno-	nudity	gymno- (gymnoto)-	stings	cnido-
colour	chromo-	glass	nelo-	one thing	mono-	strangers	xeno-
comets	cometo-	God	theo-	open spaces	agora-	string	linono-
contamination	miso-, myso-	gravity	baro-	pain	algo-	stuttering	lalo-
corpses	necro-	heat	thermo-	pins	enete-	syphilis	syphilo-
crowds	demo-	heaven	ourano-	pleasure	hedono-	taste	geuma- (geumato-)
crystals	crystallo-	heights	acro-	points	aichuro-	teeth	odonto-
darkness	achulo-	hell	stygio- (hadeo-)	poison	toxi-	thirteen	triskaideka-
dawn	eoso-	heredity	patroio-	poverty	penia-	thunder	bronto- (tonitro-)
death	thanato-	home	oiko-	punishment	poine-	touch	hapto-
demons	demono-	ice	kristallo-	responsibility	hypegia-	travel	hodo-
disease	noso-, patho-	ideas	ideo-	ridicule	katagelo-	trembling	tremo-
dogs	cyno-	infinity	apeiro-	robberies	harpaxo-	vehicles	ocho-
dreams	oneiro-	insanity	lysso- (-mania)	ruin	ate-	void	keno-
drinks	poto-	insects	entomo-	Satan	Satano-	walking	baso-
duration	chrono-	jealousy	zelo-	sea	thalasso-	water	hydro-
dust	amatho-	justice	dike-	sex	geno-	weakness	astheno-
electricity	elektro-	light	photo-	shock	horme-	wind	anemo-
everything	pan- (panto-)	machinery	mechano-	sin	hamartio-	women	gyno-
eyes	ommato-	man	anthropo-	sitting	thasso-	words	logo-
failure	kakorraphia-	many things	poly-	skin	dermato-	work	ergo-
fatigue	kopo-	men	andro-	sleep	hypno-	worms	helmintho-
fears	phobo-	metals	metallo-	smell	olfacto-	writing	grapho-

ment are less effective in cutting inflation than low levels of unemployment are at increasing it. In the 'expectations-augmented' Phillips curve, the level of the curve varies according to current expectations about future price increases.

Philoctetes [filokteeteez] A Greek hero, the son of Poeas, who inherited the bow of Heracles and its poisoned arrows. On the way to Troy he was bitten by a snake, and the wound stank, so that he was left behind on the island of Lemnos. It was prophesied that only with the arrows of Heracles could Troy be taken, so Diomedes and Odysseus came to find Philoctetes. His wound was healed and he entered the battle, killing Paris.

philodendron [filodendron] An evergreen shrub, climber, or epiphyte with both clinging and aerial roots, native to warm regions of the New World; leaves varying with species, age, and position on plant, lance- to spear- or heart-shaped, sometimes deeply lobed; flowers tiny, grouped in a spadix surrounded by a large, showy spathe. Many are popular house plants. (Genus: *Philodendron*, 275 species. Family: Araceae.)

Philo Judaeus [fyloh judayus] (c.20 BC–c.AD 40) Hellenistic Jewish philosopher, born in Alexandria. His work brought together Greek philosophy and the Hebrew Scriptures and greatly influenced subsequent Greek Christian theologians such as Clement and Origen. His commentaries on the Pentateuch interpret it according to the philosophical ideas of Plato and Aristotle; their doctrines in turn were modified by him in the light of Scripture. In c.40 he headed a deputation to Emperor Caligula in support of Jewish rights.

Philomela and Procne [filuhmeela, proknee], or **Philomel, Progne** In Greek mythology, the daughters of Pandion, King of Athens. Procne married Tereus, King of Thrace, who raped Philomela and removed her tongue; but she was able to tell Procne by a message in her embroidery. So Procne served up her son Itys, or Itylos, in a meal to his father. While pursuing the sisters, the gods changed Tereus into the hoopoe, Philomela into the swallow, and Procne into the nightingale. In Latin authors, the birds of the sisters are reversed.

Philosophes [filozof] The leaders of the French Enlightenment – political commentators, writers, and propagandists – who were critical of the *ancien régime* and advocates of rational criteria and social reform. The group included such philosophers as the Marquis de Condorcet, Diderot, Helvétius, d'Alembert, Rousseau, and Voltaire. They were forerunners of, and in some cases participants in, the French Revolution. Their great collective work was the *Encyclopédie* (1751–80).

philosophy Literally 'love of wisdom', a subject which deals with the most general questions about the universe and our place in it. Is the world entirely physical in its composition and processes? Is there any purpose to it? Can we know anything for certain? Are we free? Are there any absolute values? Philosophy differs from science, in that its questions cannot be answered empirically, by observation or experiment; and from religion, in that its purpose is entirely intellectual, and allows no role for faith or revelation. Philosophy tends to proceed by an informal but rigorous process of conceptual analysis and reasoning. Its major branches are *metaphysics*, *epistemology* (or theory of knowledge), *ethics*, and *logic* (especially the theory of meaning, formal logic now being regarded more as part of mathematics). Philosophy is thus concerned with the common core of human knowledge and experience but also with the concepts, modes of argument, and foundations of other special subjects, so that there are, for example, philosophies of science, history, art (aesthetics), politics, and religion.

Western philosophy is conventionally divided into several overlapping periods or traditions: **Greek and Roman**, from the 6th-c BC to the 6th-c AD, with Plato and Aristotle setting the agenda for almost all that follows; **Mediaeval**, from Augustine in the 4th-c to the 15th-c, a period when Muslims, Jews, and Christians all tried to relate the classical inheritance, particularly from Aristotle, to their different religious traditions; **Renaissance**, the humanism of the 14th-c to the 16th-c; **Early Modern**, 16th-c and 17th-c, when such figures as Descartes, Locke, and Leibniz began to work out the philosophical implications of the scientific revolution; **Enlightenment**, the consequent liberalism and empiricism of the 18th-c; and **Modern**, the 19th-c and 20th-c, marked by the separation from philosophy of separate sciences, such as logic and psychology, and the professionalism of the subject around the core questions of epistemology, metaphysics, and the theory of meaning. There are of course other non-Western philosophical traditions, some of which intersected at various points with Western philosophy (Islam, Judaism) and some of which take quite separate paths (Indian, Chinese).

philosophy of science A branch of philosophy, often approached through the history of science, which studies the nature of scientific theories, explanations, and descriptions, and relates them to general philosophical issues in epistemology, logic, or metaphysics. Organized empirical knowledge of the kind represented by successful science has often been taken as a model of human knowledge, against which other claimants can be measured; but its privileged status has been undermined by some recent theorists.

Phipps, Sir William (1651–95) Colonial governor, born in Pemmaquid, Maine, USA. He was successively shepherd, carpenter, and trader, and in 1687 recovered £300 000 from a wrecked Spanish ship off the Bahamas. This gained him a knighthood and the appointment as provost-marshal of New England. In 1690 he captured Port Royal (now Annapolis) in Nova Scotia, but failed in 1691 in a naval attack upon Quebec. In 1692 he became governor of Massachusetts, and the force behind the Salem witchcraft trials of 1692 burned itself out when his wife was accused of witchcraft.

Phiz *Browne, Hablot Knight*

phlebitis [flebiytis] Inflammation of a vein, commonly associated with varicose veins. It often arises in association with thrombosis of the blood within veins, when it is referred to as **thrombophlebitis**. The veins of the leg are commonly affected, and the disorder may follow childbirth, a surgical operation, or stagnation of the blood from a prolonged dependency on the legs, such as during a long journey. Severe degrees of phlebitis may lead to ulceration of the overlying skin and oedema of the affected leg. The most important complication is embolism, especially to the lung.

phloem [flohem] Tissue, composed of conducting cells and often supporting fibres, which transports sap from the leaves to other parts of a plant. It is either located in the vascular bundles or forms the inner bark of woody plants. It is complementary to xylem, but composed of living cells.

phlogiston theory [flojistn] A theory, popular in the 18th-c, whereby a material undergoing combustion was held to lose a substance (*phlogiston*, from Gr 'flame') to the atmosphere. The theory was strongly defended, but became increasingly untenable as it became clear that the products of combustion always weigh more than the material burnt.

phlogopite [flogopiyt] A member of the mica group of minerals, common in igneous rocks. Its composition is similar to biotite.

phlox A mat-forming or erect annual or perennial, almost exclusively native to North America and Mexico; leaves in opposite pairs; flowers tubular with five notched lobes, often white, pink, or blue, sometimes fragrant, in dense terminal heads. (Genus: *Phlox*, 67 species. Family: Polemoniaceae.)

Phnom Penh [(p)nom pen] 11°35N 104°55E, pop (2000e) 1 122 000. River port capital of Cambodia, at the confluence of Mekong R and Tonlé Sap (lake); founded by the Khmers, 1371; capital, 1434; abandoned as capital several times, but became permanent capital in 1867; under Japanese occupation in World War 2; after the communist victory of 1975, the population was removed to work in the fields; railway; several universities; commerce, food processing, textiles; royal palace, several museums and pagodas; current population uncertain, because of continuing refugee problem.

phobia A reaction of extreme fear to an object or situation not ordinarily considered dangerous (eg open spaces, spiders, birds). Avoidance behaviour may occur. The major forms of phobia are **simple phobia** (in which people are afraid of a specific object or situation) and **social phobia** (in which they are concerned about their behaviour in front of others). (*see pp.1192–3*)

Phobos [fohbos] The larger of the two natural satellites of Mars, discovered in 1877 by American astronomer Asaph Hall (1829–1907); distance from the planet 937 800 km/582 700 mi; diameter 27 km/17 mi; orbital period 7 h 39 min. Close approaches by several spacecraft have revealed an irregular, cratered, dark surface with low density, suggesting a similarity to carbonaceous meteorites and primitive asteroids. It is presumed to be a captured asteroid.

Phocis [fohkis] The region in C Greece to the W of Boeotia, in which Delphi and the Delphic oracle were situated.

Phoebe (astronomy) [feebee] The ninth natural satellite of Saturn, discovered in 1898; distance from the planet 12 950 000 km/8 047 000 mi; diameter 220 km/137 mi; orbital period 550·5 days.

Phoebe (mythology) [feebee] In Greek mythology, a Titaness, identified with the Moon. Later she was confused with Artemis.

Phoenicia [fuhneesha] The narrow strip in the E Mediterranean between the mountains of Lebanon and the sea, where the cities of Arad, Byblos, Sidon, and Tyre were located. It derived its name from the Phoenicians; descendants of the Canaanites, they were the dominant people of the area from the end of the second millennium BC, and this was their base first for trading all over the Mediterranean and then, from the 8th-c BC, for establishing trading posts and colonies in the W Mediterranean, such as Leptis Magna and Carthage in N Africa. From here came their most important contribution to Western culture – the alphabet.

Phoenician [fuhneeshn] An extinct language of the Semitic family. Its consonantal alphabet was adapted by the Greeks, through the addition of vowel symbols, and ultimately it became the model for all Western alphabets.

Phoenix, River (1970–93) Film actor, born in Madras, Oregon, USA. He made his film debut in *Explorers* (1985), and received a Best Actor Oscar nomination for his role in *Running on Empty* (1988). Later films include *Indiana Jones and the Last Crusade* (1989) and *Love You To Death* (1990). He was finishing the filming of *Dark Blood*, when he collapsed and died from a massive drug overdose.

Phoenix (USA) [feeniks] 33°27N 112°04W, pop (2000e) 1 321 000. State capital in Maricopa Co, SC Arizona, USA, on the Salt R;

largest city in the state, and seventh largest in the USA; settled, 1870; state capital, 1889; airport; railway; hub of the rich Salt River Valley; important centre for data-processing and electronics research; computer components, aircraft, machinery, food products, textiles; popular winter and health resort, with its dry, sunny climate; professional teams, Suns (basketball), Cardinals (football); Heard Museum of Anthropology and Primitive Arts, Pueblo Grande Museum, Desert Botanical Garden, Pioneer Arizona Museum; Cowboy Artists Exhibition (Nov).

Phoenix (astronomy) [**fee**niks] A S hemisphere constellation.

phoenix / phenix (mythology) [**fee**niks] A legendary bird, which lives a long time. It kills itself on a funeral pyre, but is then reborn from the ashes. The idea of resurrection appealed to Christian allegorists.

Phoenix Islands pop (2000e) 50 (all on Kanton I). Coral island group of Kiribati, S Pacific Ocean, c.1300 km/800 mi SE of the Gilbert Is; formerly an important source of guano; most inhabitants were resettled in the Solomon Is in 1978.

Phoenix Park murders The murder in Dublin on 6 May 1882 of the recently appointed chief secretary for Ireland, Lord Frederick Cavendish (1836–82), and his under-secretary, Thomas Henry Burke (1829–82), by a terrorist nationalist group called 'The Invincibles'. More murders followed during the summer. The British government responded with a Coercion Act. Five of the Phoenix Park murderers were arrested and hanged.

phoneme The smallest unit in the sound system of a language, capable of signalling a difference of meaning between words. For example, the English words *pail* and *tail* are distinguished by the initial consonant phonemes /p/ and /t/. The same phoneme will vary in its phonetic character, depending on the context in which it occurs; /t/, for instance, is pronounced with lips spread, in the word *tan*, but with lips rounded in *too*. These phonetic variants of a phoneme are known as **allophones**. The number of phonemes in a language varies greatly, from less than a dozen to over 80. English has about 44 (depending on the accent and the method of analysis used). No two languages or dialects have the same phonemic system.

phonetics The study of the range of sounds which can be produced by the human vocal organs. **Articulatory phonetics** studies the movements of the vocal organs (such as the tongue, lips, and larynx); **acoustic phonetics**, the physical properties of the sound waves produced in speech; and **auditory phonetics**, the way in which the listener uses ear and brain to decode sound waves. Any study of speech which employs instruments to measure such features as airflow or the frequencies of sound waves is known as **instrumental phonetics**, and these studies typically take place within **experimental phonetics**. The study of the properties of speech as a human capacity is known as **general phonetics**, while other studies describe the particular range of phonetic characteristics in specific languages (**descriptive phonetics**).

phonics A general method of teaching children to read by recognizing the relationship between individual letters and sounds. It builds up the pronunciation of new words by saying them sound by sound, as with the one-to-one correspondences between *cat* and [k-a-t]. More complex correspondences are gradually introduced, such as between the split sequence *a...e* and the pronunciation [ay] in *dame*. Many phonic approaches have now been devised.

phonograph The first practical device for recording and reproducing sounds stored as grooves cut in cylinders, mainly of wax, rotated beneath a stylus by hand or clockwork. Demonstrated by Edison in 1877, it was initially intended as an office dictating machine, but came to be widely applied in home musical entertainment during the next half-century.

phonology The study of the sound system of a language, and of the general properties of sound systems. The human vocal apparatus is capable of a wide variety of speech sounds, but only a small number is used distinctively in any one language. Phonologists study the way the sound segments (or **phonemes**) are organized in languages (**segmental phonology**), and also the patterns of pitch, loudness, and other voice qualities which can extend over syllables, phrases, and sentences (**non-segmental** or **suprasegmental phonology**).

phonon A wave which passes like a ripple through a solid, causing momentary displacement of atoms. Phonons are the quantum of lattice vibration, and exhibit particle-like properties, including the ability to scatter other particles, as observed in neutron diffraction. A grain of salt at room temperature contains about 10^{18} phonons.

phosphates Salts of phosphoric acid, usually containing one of the tetrahedral ions PO_4^{3-}, HPO_4^{2-}, or $H_2PO_4^-$. Phosphates occur in various minerals, especially apatite, and are mined for use as fertilizers. Phosphates are an essential constituent of RNA and DNA. Solutions containing mixtures of the ions HPO_4^{2-} and $H_2PO_4^-$ are buffered at $pH \approx 7$.

phospholipid A special category of fats where a part of the molecule (the head) is highly polar and thus, unlike most fats, soluble in water (*hydrophilic*), while the remainder (the tail) is highly insoluble (*hydrophobic*). The head varies from one phospholipid class to another. Phospholipids are the main components of all biological membranes. In addition, they store arachidonic acid, a precursor of the prostaglandins.

phosphor *luminescence*

phosphorescence Light produced by an object excited by a means other than heat, where the light emission continues after the energy source has been removed; a type of delayed luminescence. The emission may continue for a fraction of a second or for hours, depending on the substance. The long after-glow on a television screen, after the television has been switched off, is an example of phosphorescence.

phosphoric acid H_3PO_4. A tribasic acid, with three series of salts. It is generally a syrupy liquid, very hygroscopic; dehydration gives phosphorus pentoxide (P_2O_5), which is an excellent drying agent.

phosphorus P, element 15, the second element of the nitrogen group. It is not found free in nature, but may be prepared both as a very reactive, molecular, white form (P_4), melting point 44°C, and as a variety of less reactive, high-melting polymeric solids with colours ranging from red to black. It is found in many minerals, particularly apatite, mainly as calcium phosphate. The white form of the element is prepared by the reduction of calcium phosphate with carbon. It reacts spontaneously with air to give phosphorus pentoxide (P_2O_5), the anhydride of phosphoric acid. Phosphorus in compounds shows oxidation state +3 or (more commonly) +5. It is essential to life, being required for DNA and RNA. Industrial uses for phosphorus compounds include matches and agricultural fertilizers.

photic zone *epipelagic environments*

photino *supersymmetry*

Photius, St [**foh**tius] (c.820–91) Patriarch of Constantinople (858–67, 877–86), born in Constantinople (Istanbul). On the deposition of Ignatius from the patriarchate, he was hurried through all the stages of holy orders, and installed in his stead. In 862, Pope Nicholas I called a Council at Rome, which declared Photius's election invalid, and reinstated Ignatius. Supported by the emperor, Photius assembled a Council at Constantinople (867), which withdrew from communion with Rome. He was then deposed and reinstated on several occasions, and excluded the *Filioque* clause from the Creed (879) before being finally exiled to Armenia (886). Feast day 6 February (E).

photocell *photoelectric cell*

photochemistry The study of chemical reactions brought about by the absorption of visible and ultraviolet light, and of those reactions that produce light. Reactions of the first type include those which convert light energy into electrical energy in solar cells. The decomposition or dissociation of molecules by exposure to light is known as **photolysis**.

photoconductivity The increase in conductivity of a material (usually a semiconductor, such as silicon or germanium arsenide) resulting from the exposure to light. Incoming light photons above a certain energy level cause the production of electron-hole pairs that aid conduction. The effect is exploited in light-sensitive detectors and switches, and in television cameras.

photocopying The photographic reproduction of written, printed, or graphic work. Two processes can be used. In **xerography** an image of the original is focused on to a photosensitive surface (a selenium plate or cylinder), which converts light into electric charge. This electrostatic image attracts charged ink powder (toner), and the image is then transferred to a paper or other support, and permanently fixed by heating. The **ozalid process** (also called the **diazo process**) uses paper coated with diazonium compounds. This is exposed to ultraviolet light through a transparent original. Only the diazo in the shadows of the original is developed by ammonia vapour to give a positive print. The latest photocopiers use a laser to scan the image and store it in computer memory where it can then be enlarged, reduced, or enhanced as necessary. A colour photocopier takes four pictures of the original: one in black and white and one each in cyan (blue), magenta (red), and yellow. Each picture goes to a separate printing drum with that coloured ink. Paper is fed through each drum in turn, picking up another layer of colour until the copy is complete.

photoelasticity The change in the light-transmitting properties of a solid (eg glass or plastic) caused by stress; also called **mechanically induced birefringence**. It alters the polarization of transmitted light, and is observable by placing a suitable material between crossed Polaroids (ie having the transmission directions at right angles) and stressing the material. The coloured patterns formed are useful in engineering stress analysis.

photoelectric cell, also known as **photocell** A device sensitive to light which responds to radiation with an electrical effect. It is generally based on a semi-conductor (eg selenium, germanium or silicon, suitably prepared or modified). The radiation releases bound electrons, and, according to the constitution of the cell, the result may be a change in conductivity (*photoconductive cells*), the production of an electromotive force (*photovoltaic cells*), or some other effect. They are used in light meters (eg in photography), light detectors (eg in burglar alarms), and spacecraft power supplies.

photoelectric effect The emission of electrons from the surface of a metal as a result of irradiation with light. No electrons are emitted unless the wavelength of the light is less than some critical value, which depends on the material; and the energy of the emitted electrons depends not on the intensity of the light but on its wavelength. The correct interpretation, that light must comprise well-defined units having energy related to wavelength (photons, quanta of light), is due to Einstein (1905). The effect was discovered by Heinrich Hertz in 1887, and was crucial to the development of quantum theory.

photoemission spectroscopy A technique for studying the structure of atoms and molecules. Electromagnetic radiation directed on to a sample causes the emission of electrons, which are then detected. The use of X-rays allows the study of inner electrons; ultraviolet rays allow the study of bonding electrons.

photoengraving Techniques for the creation of metal printing plates on cylinders carrying the image of continuous-tone ('line') and half-tone text and, particularly, illustrations for letterpress and gravure printing. Film produced by photographing the image to be communicated is exposed on the metal plate, which is already coated with a light-sensitive solution. After exposure and subsequent etching, the printing image will remain in relief on a letterpress plate, or etched into a gravure cylinder.

Photometry

Photometric Quantities	*Symbols*	*Units*	*Corresponding Radiometric Quantities*
luminous flux	ϕ	lumen (lm)	radiant power
luminous intensity	I	candela (cd)	radiant intensity
luminance	L	cd/m^2	radiance
illuminance	E	lux (lx)	irradiance

photogrammetry The use of photographic records to determine precise measurements. It is principally applied in mapmaking by aerial survey, but is also used for medical, forensic, and architectural purposes, where dimensional grids may be included or superimposed.

photography The recording and reproduction of images on light-sensitive materials by chemical processes. In 1816 Nicéphore Niepce in France tried to record the optical image formed in a camera obscura, and in 1822 succeeded in obtaining a photographic copy of an engraving superimposed on glass. By 1839 Daguerre had established a reliable process. About the same time in England, Fox Talbot discovered the process of developing and fixing the exposed image as a negative and making a positive print. Scott Archer (1813–57) in 1851 invented the collodion 'wet plate', and dry plates coated with sensitized emulsion were produced commercially in the mid-1870s, followed by celluloid-based film from 1889.

In a camera, light reaching the photo-sensitive emulsion containing silver halide crystals forms a latent (invisible) image, which can be made visible by chemical development, reducing the exposed crystals to black metallic silver. The remaining unaffected halide is then removed by fixing to leave a permanent negative record of the exposure. By exposing another photo-sensitive material to light passing through this negative, a print can be made which, after developing and fixing, yields a positive image representing the original scene. In a reversal system, the film exposed in the camera is processed to produce a positive rather than a negative image by removing the initially exposed halide.

photo-ionization The production of ions by light or other electromagnetic radiation of sufficient energy to remove an electron from an atom. For example, the Earth's ionosphere is caused by ultraviolet light forming ions from atoms in the atmosphere. Light falling on semiconductors causes the production of charge-carrying electrons and holes that are essential to solar cells.

photoluminescence *luminescence*

photolysis *photochemistry*

photomacrography *macro-photography*

photomechanical reproduction The multiple printing of photographs in ink on paper, usually from metal or plastic plates in which the image is made up of solid dots. Gradation in the picture is produced by variations in the dot size, not the density of the ink. Plates are prepared by re-photographing flat copy through a screen with a line-ruling appropriate to the printing process and product: from 26–34 lines per cm for newsprint; up to 53–120 per cm for high quality book illustration. For colour reproduction, separate plates are made for each of the inks to be used, normally yellow, magenta, cyan, and black.

photometry The measurement of light and its rate of flow. In contrast to radiometry, photometry considers visible frequencies only, and takes account of the uneven sensitivity of the eye to light of different frequencies; it is important in photography and lighting design. Photometric quantities are measured using **photometers**. (*see panel*)

photomicrograph A photograph of an object as observed through a microscope. Optical means can provide magnifications up to about × 2000, and image enhancement techniques such as dark-ground illumination, phase contrast, and polarization in colour can be used. For an electron microscope, the scanned image must be photographed from a high-resolution display tube, using long exposure time to eliminate scanning line-structure; magnifications of $\times 10^6$ or more can be achieved.

photo-montage An assembly of selected images achieved either by physically mounting cut-out portions of prints on a backing, or by combination printing from several separate negatives in succession. It is widely used in the preparation of advertising display material, and sometimes for artistic creations.

photomultiplier A device for the electronic detection of light. Incoming light causes the emission of electrons from a surface via the photoelectric effect. A sequence of electrodes accelerates away the electrons, and gives a measurable current which signals the detection of a photon.

photon The quantum or particle of light. Light and all other electromagnetic radiation comprises a stream of photons, each of which has energy $E = h\nu$, where h is Planck's constant and ν is frequency. Photons of yellow light have energy $3{\cdot}4 \times 10^{-19}$J. A household light emits c.10^{20} photons every second. Photons have no (rest) mass and are spin 1. In quantum theory they transmit electromagnetic force.

photonic crystal An artificial crystal composed of regularly spaced light-reflecting elements, eg a square lattice of reflecting columns spaced about a micron apart. Light waves entering the side of the lattice are reflected from different columns and interfere, blocking the transmission of light of certain frequencies. Missing columns or missing rows of columns serve to trap light, so photonic crystals can be used to manipulate very fine light beams. Three-dimensional photonic crystals operating in the visible part of the spectrum have been produced, and may provide the means of 'wiring' for optical microcircuits for use in telecommunications applications. A much larger scale photonic crystal blocks the transmission of sound, and has been proposed as a soundproofing technique.

photoperiodism The response of an organism to periodic changes, either in light intensity or, more usually, in the duration of the light period (daylength) in a natural or artificial light-dark cycle. Photoperiodism controls the timing of many events in the annual life cycle of plants, and in the seasonal reproductive cycles of some animals.

Photorealism A style of modern painting, also called *Hyperrealism* or *Superrealism*. Pictures, often quite large, are meticulously painted in a style of extreme naturalism like a sharply-focused coloured photograph. Photorealism has flourished since the 1960s, especially in the USA.

photosphere The visible surface of the Sun or a star. About 500 km/300 mi thick, it is the zone where the Sun's layers progress from being completely opaque to radiation to being transparent, hence the zone from which the light we see actually comes. The temperature is c.6000 K. When viewed at very high resolution, the photosphere has a mottled appearance (*granulation*).

photosynthesis The complex process in which light energy is used to convert water and carbon dioxide into simple carbohydrates. Light-absorbing pigments, notably chlorophyll, found in chloroplasts, are essential to the process, which can be carried out only by green plants and photosynthetic bacteria. Plants are the main source of atmospheric oxygen, released as a by-product of photosynthesis.

phototherapy Body exposure to cool blue light (420–480 nm), free of ultraviolet light. It is used in the treatment of jaundice occurring in the newborn. The pigment bilirubin is degraded into water-soluble products that are more readily eliminated in the urine.

phototypesetter A machine for composing type and creating an image of the composed type on film or paper, ready for exposure to a plate for printing. The individual characters may be stored in the machine either as images on film, or digitally within the machine's computer memory; they may be exposed one after another, or line by line using a raster scan; the light source may be a flash, cathode-ray tube, or laser-beam.

photovoltaic effect The production of electrical current by light falling on some material, usually a semiconductor. The charge carriers are produced by photo-ionization. To produce a useful current, this must occur at a p–n semiconductor junction, so that the potential difference across the junction separates the charge carriers. The effect is the basic mechanism of solar cells.

phreaker A term applied to a hacker who uses hacking expertise to gain entry to telephone company computer systems. The aim is usually to make free telephone calls.

phrenology [frenolojee] The analysis of mind and character by the study of the shape and contours of the skull. It is based on the erroneous belief that this reflects the degree of development of the underlying regions of the brain, particularly those areas concerned with higher mental functions. It was popular in Europe during the early 19th-c.

Phrygia [frijia] The name of the kingdom in antiquity with which the legendary Midas is associated. At its widest extent around the beginning of the first millennium, it consisted of the C plateau of Asia Minor and its W flank. After its conquest by Lydia in the 6th-c BC, it never regained its political independence.

Phryne [friynee] (4th-c BC) Greek courtesan of antiquity, who reputedly was Praxiteles' model for his statue of Aphrodite. Accused of profaning the Eleusinian Mysteries, she was defended by the orator Hyperides, who threw off her robe, showing her loveliness, and so gained the verdict.

Phuket [pooket], formerly **Salang** or **Junkseylon** Largest island of Thailand, in the Andaman Sea, 900 km/560 mi S of Bangkok; a resort area; notable limestone caves and columns at Phang Nga Bay; marine biological centre; major outlet to the Indian Ocean; vegetarian festival (Oct).

phylloxera [filokseera] A dwarf, aphid-like insect that can kill grape vines; some larvae are short-beaked, and cause galls on vine leaves; others are long-beaked and suck at roots. (Order: Homoptera. Family: Phylloxeridae.)

phylogeny [fiylojenee] The relationships between groups of animals as determined by their evolutionary history, so that groups are linked together on the basis of the recency of common ancestry. This is assessed primarily by the recognition of shared derived characters. The pattern of evolutionary relationships within and between groups can be depicted in the form of a branching diagram (an evolutionary tree) showing the lines of descent.

phylum [fiyluhm] In animal classification, one of the major groupings, forming the principal category below *kingdom*, and comprising classes and lower categories. Phyla represent the major types of animals, each having its own basic structural plan that is clearly different from that of other phyla.

physalis [fisalis] A soft-leaved annual or perennial; found almost everywhere, but many species native to America; salver-shaped, 5-petalled flowers, in which the calyx becomes enlarged and bladder-like, enclosing the berry in fruit. Several are important local crops. (Genus: *Physalis*, 100 species. Family: Solanaceae.)

physical chemistry The study of the dependence of physical properties on chemical composition, and of the physical changes accompanying chemical reactions.

physical fitness The conditioning of the body so that it is able to endure longer and more strenuous periods of aerobic exercise. The capacity of the lungs, heart, and muscles to absorb oxygen, pump it round the body, and use it to generate energy are increased. Physical fitness is important to health because it is protective against illness, especially cardiovascular disease.

physicalism In philosophy, the view that any empirical proposition can be expressed as a statement about publicly observable physical objects and events. The doctrine was developed by logical positivists such as Neurath and Carnap.

physical medicine *physiotherapy*

physician Someone who is authorized to practice medicine, having passed an approved medical training course; commonly known as a **doctor**. A distinction is drawn with a **surgeon**, who is trained to practice surgery. The Royal College of Physicians of London was founded in 1518 by Thomas Linacre, with a charter from Henry VIII, and membership of the College is the standard qualification for medical specialists in the UK. In Scotland, the Royal College of Physicians of Edinburgh was founded in 1681, and Glasgow has its own Royal College of Physicians and Surgeons, founded in 1599. The Royal College of Surgeons of London received its charter in 1800, having evolved from the 15th-c guilds which protected the interests of surgeons and barbers, and there is also a Royal College of Surgeons in Edinburgh. In the British tradition, physicians are given the title of *Dr*, whereas surgeons (and dentists) retain the title of *Mr, Mrs, Miss, or Ms*; in the USA, *Dr* is used for physicians, dentists, and surgeons.

physics The study of matter and forces, at the most basic level. Physics as a discernible discipline began during the Renaissance, with Copernicus' model of planetary motion and Galileo's mechanics. Astronomy and mechanics continued to dominate the field, with the work of Newton, Kepler, and others; Newton and Leibniz developed calculus, which Newton used to express his theorems of mechanics. Galileo, Newton, and Kepler all studied optics. Huygens was the first to envisage light as a wave, an idea strongly disputed by Newton. Galileo built one of the earliest telescopes, and the compound microscope was (probably) invented c.1590 by Zacharias Janssen. Thermodynamics dates from the work of Carnot, Joule, and others in the 19th-c. About this time, steam power was becoming important: Watt introduced his improved steam engine in 1769, and Stephenson's 'Rocket', a steam-powered railway engine, dates from 1829. Franklin was the first to clarify the idea of electric charge; the electric battery was invented by Volta. The foundation of modern electromagnetism was laid by Ampère and Faraday, and electric motors and dynamos were invented at this time.

Newton's mechanics dominated physics for two centuries, and was in part responsible for a mechanistic philosophy that attempted to explain all phenomena in terms of mechanics. The physicists' view of the world has changed dramatically due to two major developments in the early part of the 20th-c. The first was Einstein's theory of special relativity, which grew in part from Maxwell's work in electromagnetism in the second half of the 19th-c. From the special theory, Einstein went on to his general theory of relativity, a theory of gravity, which was possible only because of mathematical developments by Riemann in the study of geometry. The second was the development of quantum theory and atomic theory by Schrödinger, Bohr, and many others. This was made possible by work in thermodynamics, electromagnetism, and the new radiations. It has led to modern solid state physics, as well as atomic, nuclear and particle physics. From these have developed electronics and hence computers, lasers, nuclear power, and much more.

Physiocrats A group of French economic and political thinkers of the later 18th-c, led by Quesnay, and committed to *a priori* principles of reason and natural law. Their theories made them critics of internal trade barriers, and controls and advocates of systematic economic reform.

physiological psychology The study of the physiological processes in brain and body which underlie behaviour and psychological experience. This includes the physiology of the senses, the study of the electrical and chemical activity of the brain, the effects of drugs and hormones, the physiological correlates of mental disorders, and the consequences of brain damage.

physiology An experimental science concerned with the study of the functions of living things. Its scope is wide: some studies are concerned with processes that go on in cells (eg phagocytosis, photosynthesis); others with how tissues or organs work, and how they are controlled and integrated within the whole organism; yet others deal with how living things respond to their environment. Physiology makes use of many investigative procedures including those employed in the related disciplines of anatomy, biochemistry, biophysics, cell biology, histology, and pharmacology.

physiotherapy A process of physical rehabilitation to help restore normal bodily function after injury, surgery, or disease. Treatment varies widely, but includes active and passive exercises, massage, and the application of heat by diathermy. Wasting and weakness of muscle from enforced disuse (eg following a fracture) occurs very rapidly, and associated joints become stiff. Graded exercises over long periods are essential if proper function is to be restored. Post-operative or bed-ridden individuals are prone to chest infection, and deep-breathing exercises with pummelling of the back of the chest encourages the expectoration of retained secretions. Exercises are also applied to paralysed limbs following nerve injury or strokes.

phytic acid A store of phosphorus present in most cereals and legumes; also called *inositol hexaphosphate*. This acid can bind such minerals as calcium, iron, and zinc, and reduce their bioavailability. Thus, iron may be less available from some vegetable sources than from some animal sources. However, its availability can be increased by consuming vitamin C at the same time.

phytochrome [fiytokrohm] A pigment found in most groups of plants, which is involved in photoperiodic responses. A protein compound, it exists in two forms which absorb different kinds of light, and acts as a switch mechanism linked to environmental light conditions, such as daylength. It controls many activities, such as flowering and growth.

phytogeography The study of the factors responsible for the past and present distribution of plants on the Earth's surface. It is part of the larger discipline of biogeography.

phytoplankton *plankton*

phytosaur [fiytosaw(r)] An extinct reptile with a crocodile-like body; teeth inserted in sockets (*thecodontic*); known from the late Triassic period of North America, Europe, and Asia. (Subclass: Archosauria.)

phytotherapy *herbalism*

pi (π) [piy] In mathematics, the ratio of a circle's circumference to its diameter, (3·14159...). This was often taken to be 3 (for example, in the Old Testament, 1 *Kings* 7.23; 2 *Chron* 4.2). The Babylonians used several values, such as $3\frac{1}{8}$. The Egyptians (in the Rhind papyrus) used $\pi \approx (4/3)^4 \approx 3{\cdot}1604$. By successive approximations of inscribed and circumscribed polygons, Archimedes proved that $223/71 < \pi < 22/7$, ie $3{\cdot}1408 < \pi < 3{\cdot}14285$. The Chinese, c.500 knew that $\pi \approx 355/113 \approx 3{\cdot}1415929...$ – an approximation whose digits (1, 1, 3, 3, 5, 5) make it easy to recall. Thanks to a simple mathematical formula for π, it is now known to over ten million decimal places, a triumph in computing sciences' ability to handle large numbers efficiently.

Piacenza [pyachentsa], ancient **Placentia** 45°03N 9°41E, pop (2000e) 111 000. Capital town of Piacenza province, Emilia-Romagna, N Italy; on R Po, 50 km/31 mi SE of Milan; railway; agricultural trade and machinery, cannaries, machine tools, pasta, leather goods, chemicals, pharmaceuticals; Palazzo Gotico (begun 1281), cathedral (12th–13th-c), Church of Sant'Antonino (11th–12th-c), Church of Santa Maria di Campagna (1522–8); well-preserved circuit of 16th-c walls; Festa di San Prospero (Nov); agricultural and livestock exhibition.

Piaf, Edith [peeaf], popular name of **Edith Giovanna Gassion** (1915–63) Singer, born in Paris, France. Abandoned by her mother at birth and raised by her grandmother, she was blind for four years, and it was her father, an acrobat, who encouraged her to sing. She started her career by singing in the streets, graduating to cabaret, and becoming known as *Piaf*, from the Parisian slang for 'sparrow'. She appeared in plays and films, but it was for her songs, with their undercurrent of sadness and nostalgia, that she became legendary, travelling widely in Europe and America. Despite her phenomenal success, her life was marred by unhappiness and illness. Among her best-remembered songs are 'Milord', 'La vie en rose', and 'Non, je ne regrette rien'.

Piaget, Jean [pyahzhay] (1896–1980) Psychologist and pioneer in the study of child intelligence, born in Neuchâtel, W Switzerland. After studying zoology he turned to psychology, became professor of psychology at Geneva University (1929–54), director of the Centre d'Epistémologie Génétique, and a director of the Institut des Sciences de l'Education. He is best known for his research on the development of cognitive functions in children, in such pioneering studies as *La Naissance de l'intelligence chez l'enfant* (1948, The Origins of Intelligence in Children).

Piagetian psychology [pyazhetian] A psychological approach which aims to understand the persistent philosophical problem of how, as biological organisms, people acquire knowledge; derived from the work of Jean Piaget. For Piagetians, development involves the gradual acquisition of logical abilities, which we gain simply through interacting with the environment. Babies, for example, have to learn that objects and people still exist when they cannot be seen. School-aged children have to discover the principles of perspective-taking and conservation, which reflect an ability to reconcile two conflicting pieces of information. Largely as a result of Piaget's ideas, primary education now relies much upon self-discovery, since the theory holds that children progress through a set sequence of intellectual stages which cannot be rushed.

piano The most important domestic and recital instrument for over 200 years, first made by Cristofori in Florence in the last years of the 17th-c. The main difference between its mechanism and that of the earlier clavichord is that the hammers (tipped with felt) rebound after they have struck the string, and this made possible the dynamic contrasts from which the instrument derived its full name (**pianoforte** = quiet/loud). During the 19th-c a succession of famous makers, including John Broadwood (1732–1814), Sébastien Erard (1752–1831), Karl Bechstein (1826–1900), Julius Ferdinand Blüthner (1824–1910), and Heinrich Engelhard Steinway (1797–1871), developed the piano to increase its volume and sustaining power, extend its compass, and refine its action (especially in the direction of rapid articulation).

The earliest pianos were built with the strings extending away from the keyboard, as in the harpsichord and the modern grand, or (in the case of the 'square' piano) at right-angles to the keys, as in the clavichord. In the 19th-c the upright model, with the strings set perpendicularly, was developed in response to the need for a sonorous, full-compass instrument that could stand in a small room. The modern piano is fitted with a mechanism operated by two pedals: the left ('soft') pedal makes the tone quieter; the other sustains it after the keys have been released. Some modern grand pianos have a third, central pedal which allows the player to sustain some notes while dampening others. In modern pianos all but the very lowest (single) strings are tuned in pairs, or threes, an important consideration in the case of some types of popular music, for which pianos are often tuned with the unisons slightly but perceptibly out of tune, giving a distinctive 'honky-tonk' timbre.

pianola A trade name for a type of player piano manufactured by the Aeolian Corporation in the USA.

piapiac [peeapeeak] A crow native to C Africa (*Ptilostomus afer*); black with thick black bill and very long tail; inhabits open country and palm trees; eats insects (sometimes taken from the backs of large mammals) and palm fruit. (Family: Corvidae.)

Piatra or **Piatra-Neamţ** [pyatra nyamts] 46°53N 26°23E, pop (2000e) 116 000. Industrial town and capital of Neamţ county, NE Romania, on R Bistriţa; railway; chemicals, food processing, textiles, pharmaceuticals; Bistriţa monastery (1402).

pica [piyka] The consumption of non-food items, including in particular the consumption of soil, known as *geophagia* or *geophagy*. Animals deprived of some minerals may chew at non-foods to overcome their deficiency. Among humans, geophagy is especially common in W Africa, where village industries exist to supply the demand for rock-based pellets.

Picabia, Francis [pikahbia] (1879–1953) Painter, born in Paris, France. He was one of the most anarchistic of modern artists, involved in Cubism, Dadaism, and Surrealism. He helped to intoduce Dadaism to New York in 1915. His anti-art productions, often portraying senseless machinery, include 'Parade Amoureuse' (1917) and many of the cover designs for the American anti-art magazine *291*, which he edited.

Picardy [pika(r)dee], Fr **Picardie** pop (2000e) 1 893 000; area 19 399 sq km/7488 sq mi. Region and former province of N France, comprising departments of Aisne, Oise, and Somme; bounded NW by the English Channel; flat landscape, crossed by several rivers (eg Somme, Oise) and canals; chief towns, Abbeville, Amiens, St-Quentin, Laon, Beauvais, Compiègne; chemicals, metalworking; scene of heavy fighting during World War 1.

picaresque novel (Span *picaro* 'rogue') A novel which dealt originally with the comic misfortunes of a low-life character, as in the anonymous Spanish *Lazarillo de Tormes* (1553). It is now applied more loosely to the miscellaneous adventures of any character living on his or her wits, and often on the road.

Picasso, Pablo [pikasoh] (1881–1973) Artist, the dominating figure of early 20th-c art, born in Málaga, S Spain. He studied at Barcelona and Madrid, and in 1901 set up a studio in Montmartre, Paris. His 'blue period' (1902–4), a series of striking studies of the poor in haunting attitudes of despair and gloom, gave way to the gay, life-affirming 'pink period' (1904–6), full of harlequins, acrobats, and the incidents of circus life. He then turned to brown, and began to work in sculpture. His break with tradition came with 'Les Demoiselles d'Avignon' (1906–7, New York), the first exemplar of analytical Cubism, a movement which he developed with Braque (1909–14). From 1917 he became associated with Diaghilev's Ballets Russes, designing costumes and sets. His major creation is 'Guernica' (1937, Madrid), expressing in synthetic Cubism his horror of the bombing of this Basque town during the Civil War. During World War 2 he was mostly in Paris, and after the liberation joined the Communists. A great innovator, he also illustrated classical texts, and experimented in sculpture, ceramics, and lithography. The Museu Picasso was opened in Málaga in 2003. Housed in a former palace, the museum was founded in collaboration with the artist's family, who have donated many works on display.

Piccard, Auguste (Antoine) [peekah(r)] (1884–1962) Physicist, born in Basel, N Switzerland, the twin brother of Jean Piccard (1884–1963). He studied at Zürich, and became professor of applied physics at Brussels (1922), and held posts at Lausanne, Chicago, and Minnesota universities. In 1932 he ascended in a balloon 16 940 m/55 563 ft into the stratosphere, and in 1948 explored the ocean depths off West Africa in a bathyscaphe of his own design. His son **Jacques (Ernest Jean) Piccard** (1922–) was a member of the team which established a world record by diving 10 900 m/35 800 ft in the US bathyscaphe *Trieste* into the Marianas Trench of the Pacific Ocean (1960).

piccolo A small transverse flute pitched one octave higher than the standard instrument.

Pichincha [peecheencha] 0°10S 78°35W. Andean volcano in Pichincha province, NC Ecuador; 10 km/6 mi NW of Quito; rises to 4794 m/15 728 ft; last eruption, 1981, and still emits gases; site of decisive battle (1822) in fight for independence.

pickerel Small, freshwater pike (*Esox americanus*) found in slow weedy streams and lakes in E North America; length up to c.30 cm/12 in; feeds on small fish and invertebrates. (Family: Esocidae.)

Pickering, William H(ayward) (1910–2004) Rocket scientist, born in Wellington, New Zealand. He studied in the USA, and in 1944 joined the Jet Propulsion Laboratory, which he went on to direct (1954–76). He oversaw the first orbit of the Earth by a US satellite (1958), the first US soft landings on the Moon, the first mission to orbit Mars (Mariner IX) and the first missions to Venus and Mercury (Mariner X). He received an honorary knighthood in 1976.

picketing The action by a trade union in an industrial dispute to try to persuade fellow-workers and others not to go to work, or do business with the company involved in the dispute. Pickets stand outside the gates of the factory or offices, and lobby all who would go in. Trade union legislation in the UK now limits picketing to the place where the picket actually works (**primary picketing**), and requires that it be carried out peacefully. Employers may be able to take legal action to stop other forms of action, such as the picketing of locations where the company in dispute is not directly involved (**secondary picketing**), or the use of **flying pickets**, workers not employed by the company in dispute, who are nonetheless ready to travel to the scene of the industrial action to help in the picketing. Picketing was formerly illegal in the USA, but is now allowed under a variety of state regulations, some of which correspond to the UK's *primary* category.

Pickford, Mary, originally **Gladys Mary Smith** (1893–1979) Actress, born in Toronto, Ontario, SE Canada. She first appeared on the stage at the age of five, and made her film debut in 1909. Her beauty and ingenuous charm won her the title of 'The World's Sweetheart', her many successful films including *Rebecca of Sunnybrook Farm* (1917), *Poor Little Rich Girl* (1917), and *The Taming of the Shrew* (1929). She made her first talkie, *Coquette*, in 1929, and retired from the screen in 1933. She founded United Artists Film Corporation in 1919. Her second husband was Douglas Fairbanks, Snr.

pick-up A term from the electrical period of recorded sound reproduction, describing the stylus, cantilever, and cartridge of a record player (or turntable). The undulations in the record groove are first converted into stylus lever vibrations. The light, stiff cantilever conveys these movements to the cartridge, and the resulting electrical oscillations are then sent via the amplifier to the loudspeakers. The advent of the long-playing record and stereophonic recordings required the development of diamond styli with progressively smaller tips.

Pico della Mirandola, Giovanni, comte (Count) [peekoh, mirandola] (1463–94) Renaissance philosopher, born in Mirandola, NE Italy. He studied in Italy and France, and in 1486 wrote his *Conclusions*, offering to dispute his 900 theses on logic, ethics, theology, mathematics, and the *Kabbala* against all-comers in Rome, but the debate was forbidden by Pope Innocent VIII on the grounds that some of the theses were heretical (a charge from which he was absolved in 1493). His philosophy was an attempt to reconcile Platonic and Aristotelian ontological doctrines. He also wrote Latin epistles and elegies, a series of Italian sonnets, and a major study of free will, *De hominis dignitate oratio* (1486, Oration on the Dignity of Man).

Pico de Orizaba *Citlaltépetl*

picofarad *farad*

picric acid $C_6H_2(NO_2)_3OH$, 2,4,6-trinitrophenol, melting point 122°C. A yellow solid, made by nitrating phenol. A weak acid, but stronger than phenol, it is a yellow dye and an explosive.

pictography The study of writing systems, which make use of symbols called **pictographs** or **pictograms** – direct, stylized representations of objects in the real world, drawn in outline. Pictographic writing is the oldest form of writing known, and occurs very widely throughout the world; the earliest discovered in Egypt is dated to c.3000 BC. Pictographs must be sufficiently suggestive of their referents to be recognized unambiguously. They have one potential advantage over other writing systems, in that they represent objects, and not linguistic elements; in this way, they are independent of any specific language system, and might be thought to cross over language boundaries. However, they are difficult to interpret outside the artistic and other representational conventions specific to the culture in which they were devised; consequently very many remain undeciphered, because we cannot be certain what a particular arrangement of lines and curves stands for. They are inherently ambiguous linguistically, too; for example, they cannot convey when an event occurred, or whether it is completed, on-going, or to happen in the future.

Pictor (Lat 'easel') A small, inconspicuous S constellation, near the Large Magellanic Cloud.

Picts (Lat *picti* 'painted people') A general term coined by the Romans in the 3rd-c for their barbarian enemies in Britain N of the Antonine Wall, and then used to describe the subjects of kings ruling N and S of the E Grampians. The name derives from the local custom of body tattooing. They disappear from history soon after being united with the Scots under Kenneth I. Traces of their language and art – notably the enigmatic Pictish symbol stones – survive.

Picturesque A word used vaguely nowadays to mean 'as pretty as a picture', but in the 18th-c much discussed as an aesthetic category in its own right, somewhere between 'beautiful' and 'sublime'. It was applied mainly to rugged landscapes with rocks, waterfalls, and winding paths.

piculet *woodpecker*

piddock A marine bivalve mollusc that bores into hard substrates such as chalk or wood on the lower shore in shallow waters; lives in a hollowed-out chamber in the substrate; takes in water by means of long siphons. (Class: Pelecypoda.)

pidgin A language with a highly simplified grammar and vocabulary, the native language of no one, which develops when people who lack a common language attempt to communicate. Pidgins flourish in areas of trade contact, and were particularly common in the East and West Indies, Africa, and the Americas, based on English, French, Spanish, and Portuguese, during the days of colonial exploration. Some pidgins have developed into important systems of communication, such as Tok Pisin in Papua New Guinea, which is used on the radio and in the press. Pidgins become *creoles* when they are used by people as a mother-tongue.

Piedmont [peedmont], Ital **Piemonte** pop (2000e) 4 334 000; area 25 400 sq km/9800 sq mi. Region of N Italy; centre of Italian unification in 19th-c; capital, Turin; other chief towns, Cuneo, Saluzzo, Asti, Alessandria; bounded (S) by the Appenines and (N, W) Alps; industries (metalworking, machinery, cars, textiles, leather, foodstuffs) around Turin, Ivrea, Biella; fruit-growing, vineyards, arable farming, cattle in Po valley; tourism in hill regions.

Pied Piper of Hamelin In German legend a 13th-c piper who charmed Hamelin's rats out of the city with his music. He was refused his fee, and in revenge lured all the children away from the city. Both Goethe and Robert Browning retell the tale.

Pierce, Lorne (Albert) (1890–1961) Canadian editor and writer. As editor of Ryerson Press for forty years, he contributed greatly to the development and appreciation of Canadian literature. In 1926 he established a medal to be awarded for achievement in imaginative or critical literature written in either English or French. Known as the Lorne Pierce Medal, the award is decided by the Canadian Académie des lettres et des sciences humaines, and usually given every two years.

Pierce, Franklin (1804–69) US statesman and 14th president (1853–7), born in Hillsborough, New Hampshire, USA. Admitted to the bar in 1827, he was elected to Congress as a Jacksonian Democrat, and in 1837 to the US Senate. He advocated the annexation of Texas with or without slavery, and was made brigadier-general in the Mexican War. Elected president in 1853, he defended slavery and the fugitive slave law. Among the events of his administration was the repeal of the Missouri Compromise and the passing of the Kansas–Nebraska Act, which kindled a flame that ultimately led to the Civil War. The unpopularity of this Act led to his enforced retirement from politics in 1857.

Pierce, Mary [peers] (1975–) French tennis player, born in Montreal, Canada. Her tournament victories include the Australian Open in 1995, the first Frenchwoman to win this title since 1967, and the French Open in 2000. She reached the Masters semifinal in 1993 and the Roland-Garros final in 1994.

Piero della Francesca [pyayroh, franchayska] (c.1420–92) Painter, born in Borgo San Sepolcro, NC Italy. His major work is a series of frescoes illustrating 'The Legend of the True Cross'

(1452–66) in the choir of S Francesco at Arezzo. An unfinished 'Nativity' in the London National Gallery shows some Flemish influence. He also wrote a treatise on geometry and a manual on perspective.

Piero di Cosimo [pyairoh di kohzimoh], originally **Piero di Lorenzo** (c.1462–c.1521) Painter, born in Florence, NC Italy. He was a pupil of Cosimo Rosselli, whose name he adopted. His later style was influenced by Signorelli and Leonardo da Vinci, and among his best-known works are 'The Death of Procris' (c.1500, National Gallery, London) and 'The Rescue of Andromeda' (c.1515, Uffizi).

Pierre [pyayr] 44°22N 100°21W, pop (2000e) 13 900. Capital of state in Hughes Co, C South Dakota, USA, on the Missouri R; founded as a railway terminus, 1880; state capital, 1889; centre of a grain and dairy farming region; L Oahe and the Oahe Dam nearby.

Pierrot An evocative fictional character with a rich theatrical, literary, and artistic history. Originally **Pedrolino**, a servant role in the *commedia dell'arte*, Pierrot gained his white face and white floppy costume on the French stage. Pierrot developed as the clown counterpart of Harlequin, the earliest French version being created in 1682 in Paris. His childlike manner and his pathos, dumb and solitary, was the creation of the great 19th-c pantomimist Deburau at the Fenambules theatre in Paris. It survives in many clowns today.

pierrot show A British form of concert party created, due to the popularity of Pierrot, in the 1890s. Dressed in white or black, with pompoms, ruffs, and – for the men – a dunce's cap, the pierrot-troupes performed their form of variety on the beaches and piers of seaside towns.

pietà [peeuhta] (Ital 'pity') In art, the representation of the dead Christ mourned by angels, apostles, or holy women. Michelangelo's famous marble 'Pietà' (c.1500) in St Peter's, Rome, shows Christ lying peacefully in the lap of his mother, represented as young and beautiful; but most representations of the subject are dramatic and emotional.

Pietermaritzburg [peetermaritzberg] or **Maritzburg** 30°33S 30°24E, pop (2000e) 266 000. City in KwaZulu Natal province, E South Africa, 73 km/45 mi WNW of Durban; founded by Boers from Cape Colony, 1838; capital of former province of Natal; railway; university (1910); centre of rich farming area; footwear, aluminium, rubber, furniture, rice; Voortrekker Museum, Macrorie House Museum.

Pietism [piyetizm] Originally, a movement within Lutheranism in the 17th-c and 18th-c stressing good works, Bible study, and holiness in Christian life. It was a reaction against rigid Protestant dogmatism, and influenced other groups, such as Moravians, Methodists, and Evangelicals.

piezo-electric effect [piyeetzoh] The appearance of an electric field in some material as a result of the application of stress, as in quartz and bone. Stress distorts the crystals, causing unbalanced electrical forces in the material. The effect is exploited in gas cooker lighters, load sensors, and transducers.

pig A mammal native to woodland in Europe, S Asia, and Africa; an artiodactyl; stout body with short legs and coarse hair; short thin tail; very long face in front of ears; small eyes; snout muscular, flattened, disc-like (often used for digging); lower and/or upper canine teeth may form upward-pointing tusks; eats plant and animal food; male called *boar*, female called *sow*, young called *piglets*; also known as **hog** or **swine**. The name *pig* is usually used for the domestic pig (*Sus scrofa*). (Family: Suidae, 9 species.)

pigeon A bird of the widespread family Columbidae (c.255 species); plump with round bill; nostrils on fleshy band (*cere*); strong flier; inhabits diverse areas; eats fruit, seeds, and some invertebrates; many domestic breeds. The name is also used for the **pigeon guillemot** (Family: Alcidae) and the **Cape pigeon** (Family: Procellariidae).

pigeon hawk *merlin*

pigeon pea A short-lived, shrubby, perennial, leguminous crop (*cajanus cajan*), grown in tropical countries, especially India and the West Indies; also known as **red gram**. The seeds of the crop are usually harvested when mature, and provide an important source of protein, especially in drier areas, where its deep root system enables it to survive periods of drought. (Family: Leguminosae.)

Piggott, Lester (Keith) (1935–) Flat racing jockey, born in Wantage, Oxfordshire, SC England, UK. He rode his first winner at the age of 12, and his first Epsom Derby winner, *Never Say Die*, in 1954. He subsequently rode a record nine winners of the race, and a record 29 Classic winners between 1954 and 1985. During his career he rode 4493 winners in Britain (1948–85), a figure bettered only by Gordon Richards, and was champion jockey 11 times. After retiring, he took up training at Newmarket, but was imprisoned (1987–8) for tax offences, then returned to the saddle in 1990 and won his 30th Classic, the 2000 Guineas, in 1992. He retired in 1995.

pig-iron The product of the blast furnace. The molten iron is run into channels which have moulds led off them, fancifully likened to pigs in a litter. This cast-iron has a high proportion of carbon (c.4%) which has to be reduced to under 1% to form steel.

pigments Colouring materials. (1) **Biological** pigments are substances, usually similar to dyestuffs, which give colour to tissues. (2) **Industrial** pigments give colour and opacity to paints, plastics, and other materials by being dispersed through them. A good pigment must be suitably stable to light and chemical attack.

pignut *earthnut*

pigweed *amaranth*

pika [peeka, piyka] A mammal of order Lagomorpha, native to C and NE Asia and W North America; resembles a small rabbit, with short legs, short rounded ears, and minute tail; inhabits rocky areas or open country; also known as **cony**, **coney**, **rock rabbit**, **slide rat**, **little chief hare**, **mouse hare**, **haymaker**, **squeak rabbit**, **whistling hare**, or **calling hare**. (Family: Ochotonidae, 14 species.)

pike Any of the large predatory freshwater fish of the family Esocidae; distinguished by an elongate body with dorsal and anal fins set close to the tail; snout pointed, jaws large; includes familiar *Esox lucius*, found in well-weeded rivers and lakes throughout N Europe, Russia, and North America; length up to 1·5 m/5 ft; mottled greenish-brown; feeds on fish and other aquatic vertebrates, including birds; highly prized by anglers.

pikeperch *zander*

piket *skunk*

pilaster [pilaster] A rectangular pillar that projects only slightly from the wall of a building. In classical architecture it is usually designed according to one of the five orders.

Pilate, Pontius [ponshus], Lat **Pontius Pilatus** (1st-c) Roman prefect of Judea. He was appointed by Tiberius in c.26, having charge of the state and the occupying military forces, but subordinate to the legate of Syria. Although based in Caesarea, he also resided in Jerusalem. He caused unrest by his use of Temple funds to build an aqueduct, by his temporary location of Roman standards in Jerusalem, and by his slaughter of Samaritans in 36 (for which he was recalled). His fame rests entirely on his role in the story of Jesus of Nazareth, permitting his execution by crucifixion at the prompting of the Jewish authorities.

Pilates [pilahteez] An exercise-based system that aims to develop the body's 'centre' in order to create a stable core for all types of movement; named after its deviser, German gymnast Joseph Pilates (1880–1967). Originally referred to as *contrology*, the method tones, stretches, and mobilizes the body through regular sessions, so that the body's structure realigns and a balance is achieved within the muscular-skeletal system.

pilchard Small, herring-like, surface-living fish (*Sardina pilchardus*) widespread and locally abundant in the E North Atlantic and Mediterranean; length up to 25 cm/10 in; greenish-blue above, underside silver; important commercial fish, usually canned for marketing; also called **sardine**. The name is also used for several similar clupeid species in the genera *Sardinella* and *Sardinops*. (Family: Clupeidae.)

piles *haemorrhoids*

Pilger, John (Richard) [**pil**jer] (1939–) Journalist and documentary film-maker, born in Sydney, New South Wales, SE Australia. A provocative and controversial journalist who has worked mainly in Britain, he has twice won the British Journalist of the Year award and is a winner of the UNESCO Peace Prize. His film *Year Zero* (1979) exposed the atrocities of Pol Pot to the world. Later films include *Vietnam: The Last Battle* (1995) and *Inside Burma: Land of Fear* (1996). His published works include the collected writings *Heroes* (1986), *Hidden Agendas* (1998), and *The New Rulers of the World* (2002). His book, *The Secret Country* (1989), is a critical appraisal of the position of Aboriginal people in Australia.

Pilgrimage of Grace (Oct 1536–Jan 1537) A major Tudor rebellion in England, a series of armed demonstrations by Roman Catholics in six N counties. It was directed against the policies and ministers of Henry VIII, and combined upper-class and popular discontent over religious and secular issues. It was led by Lord Thomas Darcy (1467–1537), Robert Aske (?–1537), and 'pilgrims' carrying banners of the Five Wounds of Christ. The leaders and over 200 others were executed.

Pilgrims or **Pilgrim Fathers** The English religious dissenters who left to establish Plymouth Colony in America in 1620, after crossing the Atlantic aboard the *Mayflower*. Many originally came from Lincolnshire and N Nottinghamshire. They had spent an extended period in the Netherlands, to avoid persecution, before migrating to America.

Pilgrims' Way A long-distance footpath in Surrey and Kent, S England, UK, opened in 1972. The path is pre-Roman; its name derives from the popular belief that it was used by mediaeval pilgrims travelling from Winchester to Canterbury.

pill *contraception*

Pillars of Hercules The ancient mythological name for the promontories flanking the Strait of Gibraltar: the Rock of Gibraltar and Cueta, N Africa. They guard the entrance to the Mediterranean Sea.

pillars of Islam *Islam*

pilotfish Marine fish (*Naucrates ductor*) which derives its name from the behaviour of juveniles that swim alongside ships or larger fish such as sharks; adults tend to be solitary; length up to 60 cm/2 ft; greyish-blue on back with banding on sides; widely distributed in tropical and warm temperate seas. (Family: Carangidae.)

pilotis [**pil**otee, **pil**oteez] Posts or columns used on the ground floor of a building to raise most of the main body to first-floor level, thus leaving unenclosed space below. Usually slender and circular in section, they are particularly associated with the work of the 20th-c architect Le Corbusier.

pilot whale A toothed whale of family Delphinidae; black with bulbous overhanging snout; eats squid (and some fish); two species: **long-finned pilot whale**, **blackfish**, or **ca(a)'ing whale** (*Globicephala melaena*) from N Atlantic and cool temperate S oceans; **Pacific pilot whale** (*Globicephala sieboldii*) from tropical and warm temperate oceans.

Pilsen *Plzeň*

Piłsudski, Józef (Klemens) [pil**suds**kee] (1867–1935) Polish marshal, statesman, and first president (1918–22), born in Zulow, N Poland. Often imprisoned in the cause of Polish independence, he became leader of the Polish Socialist Party (1892), and formed a band of troops which fought on the side of Austria during World War 1. He declared Poland's independence in 1918, and became the country's first president. Following a military coup in 1926, he refused the post of president, but served as a powerful minister of defence in the new government.

Piltdown Man A supposed early fossil man found in 1912 near Piltdown, East Sussex, SE England, UK; named *Eoanthropus* ('Dawn Man'). Later study proved the find a forgery, with a modern human cranium and the jawbone of an orang-utan.

pimento *allspice*

pi-meson *pion*

pimpernel A sprawling annual weed (*Anagallis arvensis*); cosmopolitan; leaves paired, shiny, oval; flowers on long slender stalks, five petals. Scarlet and blue pimpernels are different coloured forms of the same plant. (Family: Primulaceae.)

PIN [pin] Acronym for **Personal Identification Number**; a unique number allocated to the users of computer-based equipment which allows the identity of each user to be established. It is often used in modern banking systems, where users can draw cash from machines on presentation of their card plus their PIN.

Pinakothek, Alte [**al**tuh peena**koh**tek] A museum founded in 1836 in Munich, EC Germany. It houses one of the finest collections of German, Dutch, Flemish, and Spanish paintings from the 14th-c to the 18th-c. The adjacent Neue [**noy**uh] Pinakothek was established in 1853, and houses 19th-c and 20th-c paintings and sculptures.

Pinang (city) [**pin**ang], or **Penang**, formerly **George Town** 5°26N 100°16E, pop (2000e) 379 000. Capital of Pinang state, W Peninsular Malaysia, on NE coast; named after King George III of Great Britain; Malaysia's chief port; railway; ferry to Butterworth on the mainland; large Chinese population; electronics, textiles, silk, toys; trade in tin, rubber; Fort Cornwallis, St George's Church (oldest Anglican Church in SE Asia).

Pinang (state) [**pin**ang], or **Pulau Pinang**, formerly **Penang** pop (2000e) 1 421 000; area 1044 sq km/403 sq mi. State in NW Malaysia; a coastal strip on the NW coast of the Malay Peninsula and the island (*pulau*) of Pinang in the Strait of Malacca; first British settlement in Malaya; capital, Pinang (formerly George Town); rice, rubber, tin.

pinchbeck An alloy of copper and zinc, but with less zinc than in brass. It is named after London watchmaker Christopher Pinchbeck (1670–1732) who used it to simulate gold.

Pinckney, Charles (Cotesworth) (1746–1825) US statesman, born in Charleston, South Carolina, USA. He studied at Oxford and at Caen Military Academy, then settled as a barrister in Charleston. He was Washington's aide-de-camp at Brandywine and Germantown, but was taken prisoner at the surrender of Charleston (1780). A member of the Constitutional Convention (1787), he introduced the clause forbidding religious tests. In 1796 he was appointed minister to France, but the French Directory refused to receive him. He was twice Federalist candidate for the presidency (1804, 1808).

Pincus, Gregory (Goodwin) (1903–67) Physiologist, born in Woodbine, New Jersey, USA. He studied at Cornell, Harvard, Cambridge, and Berlin universities, then founded his own consultancy in experimental biology at Shrewsbury, MA. In 1951, impressed by the work of the birth-control campaigner, Margaret Sanger, he began research into the nature of reproduction, and found that some of the new synthetic hormones controlled fertility effectively. Field trials in 1954 were successful, leading to the development of the contraceptive pill.

Pindar (518–438 BC) The chief lyric poet of Greece, born near Thebes. He studied in Athens, and became famous as a composer of odes, hymns, and paeans for people in all parts of the Greek world. Although he wrote for all kinds of circumstances, only his *Epinikia* (Triumphal Odes) have survived entire, four books celebrating the victories won in the Olympian, Pythian, Nemean, and Isthmian games. The **Pindaric Ode** is characterized by the irregularity in the number of feet in the lines, and by the arbitrary arrangement of the rhymes.

Pindus Mountains, Gr **Píndhos Oros** Mountain range in WC and NW Greece; length c.500 km/310 mi, from the Albanian frontier to near the Gulf of Corinth; highest peak, Smolikas (2633 m/8638 ft); watershed between rivers flowing to the Aegean Sea and to the Ionian Sea.

pine A member of a large genus of evergreen conifers widespread throughout the N hemisphere. The branches and twigs are in whorls, each whorl representing one year's growth. The leaves are of three kinds: (1) seedling leaves, narrow, toothed; (2) adult scale leaves, borne on long shoots but soon falling; (3)

adult needle leaves in bundles of 2, 3, or 5, according to species, borne on short shoots in the axils of the scale leaves. The cones are woody, at least two years old when ripe. Pines are of great commercial importance, and are planted on a vast scale. The timber is resistant to decay because of a high content of resin, rich in oil of turpentine. This yields turpentine, tar, and pitch on distillation, and is also the source of the distinctive foliage scent. (Genus: *Pinus*, 70–100 species. Family: Pinaceae.)

pineal gland [pinial] A small gland of vertebrates situated above the third ventricle of the brain, and lying outside the blood-brain barrier. It synthesizes the hormone *melatonin*, whose release is under the control of sympathetic fibres, and whose activity is synchronized with the light-dark cycle. It has an important role in determining seasonal breeding patterns in some mammals.

pineapple An evergreen perennial native to South America (*Ananas comosus*); leaves stiff, arching, sword-shaped, spiny, grey-green; flowers 3-petalled, blue, in a dense cone-like inflorescence topped by a leafy spire; individual fruits fusing to form a fleshy, yellow, multiple fruit up to 30 cm/12 in long. It is an important crop in much of the tropics. The cultivars include seedless forms, and variegated ornamentals. The juice from the fruit is rich in vitamins A and B. (Family: Bromeliaceae.)

pineapple mint *mint*

pine marten A marten often found in trees; brown with pale markings on undersurface; nests in holes; two species: **European pine marten** (*Martes martes*) from coniferous and deciduous forests in Europe and Asia, and **American pine marten** (*Martes americana*) from coniferous forests of North America.

Pinero, Sir Arthur (Wing) [pinairoh] (1855–1934) Playwright, born in London, UK. He studied law, but in 1874 made his debut on the stage in Edinburgh, and in 1875 joined the Lyceum Company. He wrote several farces, but is best known for his social dramas, notably *The Second Mrs Tanqueray* (1893) and *Trelawny of the Wells* (1898), which made him the most successful playwright of his day. He was knighted in 1909.

pingo An Inuit word used to describe an ice-cored hill found in areas of permafrost. As an ice lens forms in the ground, it pushes the overlying earth up into a mound. Pingos in the Northwest Territories, Canada, can reach 70 m/230 ft in height.

pinhole glasses Spectacles with opaque lenses which have many perforations allowing light to pass through to the eye, and which are said to make focusing easier. The glasses were originally developed in Germany during the late 19th-c. Claims have been made of improvement in vision in a wide variety of visual defects, including shortsightedness, longsightedness, and astigmatism.

pink An annual, biennial, or perennial herb with grass-like, paired, often bluish leaves, native to the temperate N hemisphere; flowers with short, tubular epicalyx and tubular calyx; five petals, spreading, toothed or slightly frilly, pink, also red or white, often scented. Many species are cultivated in gardens. The genus includes the well-known carnations and sweet williams of horticulture. (Genus: *Dianthus*, 300 species. Family: Caryophyllaceae.)

Pinkerton, Allan (1819–84) Detective, born in Glasgow, W Scotland, UK. He was a Chartist who in 1842 settled in Dundee, IL, became a detective and deputy-sheriff, and in 1850 founded the Pinkerton National Detective Agency. He headed a Federal intelligence network during the Civil War, and his agency later took a leading part in breaking up the Molly Maguires and in policing other labour disputes.

pink salmon Comparatively small salmon species (*Oncorhynchus gorbuscha*), native to the N Pacific, but now introduced to the Atlantic; length up to 75 cm/30 in; dorsal surface with small black spots; spawning males have a distinctive humped back and red coloration; commercially important as a food fish. (Family: Salmonidae.)

pinnate The shape of a leaf divided into several lobes or leaflets arranged in two opposite rows along the stalk. In **bi-pinnate** leaves, the leaflets are themselves pinnate.

Pinochet (Ugarte), Augusto [peenohshay] (1915–) Chilean dictator (1973–90), born in Valparaíso, Chile. A career army officer, he led the military coup overthrowing the Allende government in 1973, establishing himself at the head of the ensuing military regime. In 1980 he enacted a constitution giving himself an eight-year presidential term (1981–9). A plebiscite held in 1988 rejected his candidacy as president beyond 1990, but he retained his post as commander-in-chief of the army until 1998. In October 1998 he became the centre of international attention when he was arrested in London, following a request from Spain for his extradition to stand trial for 'crimes of genocide and terrorism', in which some of the victims had been Spanish nationals. The arrest caused tension between UK and Chile, and civil unrest in Chile between Pinochet supporters and opponents. At the beginning of 2000, Pinochet remained under house arrest in the UK, pending the outcome of legal procedures, but in April the UK government returned him to Chile on the grounds of ill health. Chile's Court of Appeal decided to strip Pinochet of immunity from prosecution (August) and he was later ordered to stand trial. In 2001 a Santiago appeals court voted in favour of suspending proceedings against him on the grounds that he was mentally unfit to stand trial, a decision confirmed by the Supreme Court in July 2002.

pinochle [peenuhkl] A card game derived from bézique. Two packs of 24 cards are used, all cards from 2–8 having been discarded. The object is to win tricks, as in whist, and to score points according to the cards won. Cards have the following values: ace–11, ten–10, king–4, queen–3, jack–2, nine–0.

Pinsent, Matthew (Clive) (1970–) Rower, born in Dorset, S England, UK. He studied at Eton and Oxford, where he was a member of the University Boat Race team. He made his rowing debut at senior international level in 1989, and in 1990 teamed up with Steve Redgrave for the coxless pairs. His many honours include eight gold medals in the World Championship Coxless Pairs (1991, 1993–5, 1997–9, 2002) and Olympic gold Coxless Pairs (1992, 1996) and Coxless Fours (2000). He became a member of the International Olympic Committee in 2002.

pint *litre*

pinta [pinta] An infection with *Treponema carateum*, a bacterium endemic in Central and South America. It causes a number of skin lesions depending on the stage of the illness.

pintail A dabbling duck of the genus *Anas* (3 species): two species are native to South America and the Caribbean; one to the N hemisphere (*Anas acuta*). The male has long central tail feathers. *Anas acuta* may be the most abundant duck in the world.

Pinter, Harold (1930–) Playwright and director, born in London, UK. He became a repertory actor, first writing poetry, then turning to drama with *The Room* (1957). His first major play, *The Birthday Party* (1958), was badly received, but was revived after the success of *The Caretaker* (1960, film 1963), and has been televised twice (1960, 1987) and filmed (1968). Other plays include *The Homecoming* (1965), *Old Times* (1971), and *No Man's Land* (1975). His television play *The Lover* (1963) won the Italia Prize. Early screenplays include *The Servant* (1962), *The Pumpkin Eaters* (1963), *Accident* (1967), and *The Go-Between* (1969). His work is highly regarded for the way it uses the unspoken meaning behind inconsequential everyday talk to induce an atmosphere of menace. Closely associated with the director Peter Hall, he became an associate director of the National Theatre after Hall became director in 1973. He wrote a number of filmscripts during the 1980s, including *The French Lieutenant's Woman* (1981) and *Reunion* (1989), as well as several short plays, such as *A Kind of Alaska* (1982) and *Mountain Language* (1988), in which there is an explicit commitment to radical political causes. Later plays include *Moonlight* (1993) and *Ashes to Ashes* (1996), and in 1998 appeared *Various Voices*. He was made a Companion of Honour in 2002.

Pintupi A people of Australia's Western Desert. Their traditional country spans the border between Western Australia and the Northern Territory. Some Pintupi continued to live entirely by hunting and gathering until severe drought during the 1950s and 1960s forced them onto government settlements. Most now live in or around the communities of YaiYai, Docker River, and Haast's Bluff. Pintupi artists were influential early members of the art school which developed at Papunya in the 1970s, whose work is characterized by the traditional art style of C Australia, in which circles, arcs, and footprints predominate, painted in a dot technique, using a brush or the end of a twig to apply the paint.

pinworm *nematode*

pin-yin *Chinese*

pion [piyon] A strongly interacting subatomic particle of the meson family; symbol π; three possible charges: +1, −1 (π^+, π^-, mass 140 MeV each), and 0 (π^0, mass 135 MeV); spin zero; also called a **pi-meson**. Charged pions decay to muons and neutrinos; neutral pions decay to gamma rays. Discovered in cosmic ray experiments in 1947, in nuclear physics pions are carriers of strong nuclear force.

Pioneer programme A series of relatively simple spin-stabilized spacecraft launched by the USA 1958–78. Pioneers 1 to 3 were Air Force 'lunar' flights that were only partially successful. Pioneers 4 to 9 explored the interplanetary medium from orbits around the Sun at about the same distance as Earth. Pioneers 10 and 11 (launched in 1972 and 1973) achieved the first flybys of Jupiter (Dec 1973, Apr 1974) and of Saturn (Pioneer 11 in 1979), and the first exploration of the boundary of the Sun's influence (heliopause). Pioneer 12 was the first US Venus orbiter, and Pioneer 13's four probes successfully explored Venus' atmosphere (1978). The programme was managed and operated by NASA's Ames Research Center.

pipa A Chinese lute with a pear-shaped body, short neck, fretted soundboard, and four silk strings plucked with the fingernails.

pipal *peepul*

pipefish Distinctive fish with a very slender segmented body, small mouth on a tubular snout, and delicate fins; with seahorses and seadragons it comprises the family Syngnathidae (11 genera); feeds on plankton and fish larvae; length up to 60 cm/2 ft, typically much smaller; eggs carried by males, in some species within a special brood pouch.

Piper, John (1903–92) Artist, born in Epsom, Surrey, SE England, UK. An abstract artist in the 1930s, he developed a representational style, as seen in his pictures of war damage and his topographical pictures, notably the watercolours of Windsor Castle commissioned by the Queen (1941–2). He is also known for his theatre sets, as well as the stained glass designs in Coventry Cathedral.

Piper, Leonora E (1857–1950) US medium, discovered in 1885 by William James. Mrs Piper's trance speech and writing were studied extensively (1885–1911) by James and other members of the American and British Societies for Psychical Research. She became for William James his 'white crow', when he became convinced of the paranormal origin of some of her trance utterances.

Piper Alpha An oil-drilling platform in the North Sea, off the coast of Scotland, which was destroyed by an explosion in July 1988. The disaster killed 167, and resulted in insurance claims approaching 1·5 thousand million dollars.

Pipe Rolls Records of the English Exchequer containing county by county the annual accounts of sheriffs and other royal officials. They were so called because they consisted of sheets of parchment rolled into the shape of pipes. The earliest Pipe Roll to survive is that of 1130, and they form a virtually complete series from 1156 until discontinued in 1832.

pipes of Pan *panpipes*

pipistrelle [pipistrel] A bat of family Vespertilionidae; genus *Pipistrellus* (46 species), found worldwide except South America; includes the smallest bats; among the first bats to fly in the evening; erratic in flight; also genus *Glischropus* (2 species), called **thick-thumbed pipistrelles**.

pipit A wagtail of the worldwide genus *Anthus* (34 dull-coloured species), or the more colourful African genera *Tmetothylacus* (1 species) and *Macronyx* (8 species, the 'longclaws'). They sing during fluttering, descending flights.

Piquet, Nelson [peekay], originally **Nelson Souto Maior** (1952–) Motor-racing driver, born in Rio de Janeiro, Brazil. He changed his name so that his parents would not find out about his racing exploits. He was British Formula Three champion in 1978, and world champion in 1981, 1983 (both Brabham), and 1987 (Williams). He won 23 grand prix between 1978 and a serious accident in 1991.

Piraeus [piyreeus], Gr **Piraiéus** 37°57N 23°42E, pop (2000e) 212 000. Major port in Attica department, Greece; on a hilly peninsula, 8 km/5 mi SW of Athens; the port of Athens since the 5th-c BC; main harbour, Kantharos, with two ancient harbours still used on the E coast; rail terminus; ferries to the Greek islands; Navy Week (Jun–Jul).

Pirandello, Luigi [pirandeloh] (1867–1936) Playwright, novelist, and short-story writer, born in Girgenti, Sicily, S Italy. He studied philology at Rome and Bonn, becoming a lecturer in literature at Rome (1897–1922). After writing powerful and realistic novels and short stories, such as *Il fu Mattia Pascal* (1903, The Late Mattia Pascal), he turned to the theatre and became a leading exponent of contemporary drama. Among his plays are *Sei personaggi in cerca d'autore* (1921, Six Characters in Search of an Author), *Enrico IV* (1922, Henry IV) and *Come tu mi vuoi* (1930, As You Desire Me). In 1925 he established a theatre of his own in Rome, the Teatro d'Arte, and his company took his plays all over Europe. Many of his later plays have been filmed. In 1934 he was awarded the Nobel Prize for Literature.

Piranesi, Giambattista [piranayzee], or **Giovanni Battista** (1720–78) Architect and copper-engraver of Roman antiquities, born in Mestre, near Venice, NE Italy. He went to Rome in 1740 as a draftsman for the Venetian ambassador, and settled there permanently in 1745. He studied with the leading printmakers and developed his own techniques, producing innumerable etchings of the city both in ancient times and in his own day.

piranha [pirahna, pirahnya] Any of several voracious, predatory freshwater fishes widespread in rivers of South America; body deep and robust; length up to 60 cm/2 ft; strong jaws and sharp interlocking teeth; extremely aggressive flesh-eating fish, often feeding in large shoals.

Pirani gauge [pirahnee] An instrument for measuring the degree of vacuum. Electrically heated thin wire, initially in equilibrium, loses heat faster or slower as pressure changes; consequent change in the resistance of the wire is thus a measure of the change of pressure of the surrounding gas.

Pire, Dominique (Georges) [peer] (1910–69) Dominican priest, born in Dinant, S Belgium. He lectured in moral philosophy at Louvain (1937–47) and was awarded the Croix de Guerre for resistance work as priest and intelligence officer in World War 2. After the war he devoted himself to helping refugees and displaced persons, and was awarded the 1958 Nobel Prize for Peace for his scheme of 'European villages', including the 'Anne Frank village' in Germany for elderly refugees and destitute children.

Pisa [peeza] 43°43N 10°24E, pop (2000e) 107 000. Capital town of Pisa province, Tuscany, W Italy, on both banks of the R Arno, 10 km/6 mi from the Ligurian Sea; formerly a major port, now distanced from the sea through river silting; archbishopric; airport; railway; university (1338); glass, pottery, furniture, pharmaceuticals, motorcycles, yachts, tourism; birthplace of Galileo; cathedral (11th–12th-c), baptistery (12th–14th-c), Campo Santo cemetery (1278–1463); campanile (the 'Leaning Tower', 1173–1372), Piazza del Duomo is a world heritage site; carnival (Feb); Regata Storica di San Renieri, historic boat races (Jun).

Pisanello, Antonio [peesaneloh], originally **Antonio Pisano** (c.1395–1455) Court painter, born in Pisa, W Italy. The foremost draughtsman of his day, his drawings are marked by an accurate observation of reality, and a naturalism which contrasts with the stylized manner of his great contemporary, Gentile da Fabriano. These drawings became models for later Renaissance artists. His most famous picture is 'The Vision of Saint

Pitcairn Islands

(UK British Dependent Territory)
Timezone GMT −9
Area 27 km²/10 sq mi
Population total (2003e) 48
Capital Adamstown
Physical features Volcanic island group in the SE Pacific Ocean, E of French Polynesia; comprises Pitcairn Island, 4.5 km²/1.7 sq mi, and the uninhabited islands of Ducie, Henderson, and Oeno; Pitcairn Island rises to 335 m/1099 ft.
Climate Equable climate; average annual temperatures 24°C (Jan), 19°C (Jul); average annual rainfall 2000 mm/80 in.
Currency 1 New Zealand Dollar ($NZ) = 100 cents
Economy Postage stamps; tropical and subtropical crops; crafts, forestry.
History Visited by the British, 1767; occupied by nine mutineers from HMS Bounty, 1790; overpopulation led to emigration to Norfolk I, 1856; some returning in 1864; transferred to Fiji, 1952; now a UK Dependent Territory, governed by the High Commissioner in New Zealand.

Eustace', but his frescoes have all been lost except for two in Verona. He was also considered the greatest medallist of his time.

Pisano, Andrea [peesahnoh], also known as **Andrea da Pontedera** (c.1270–1349) Sculptor, born in Pontedera, W Italy. He became famous as a worker in bronze and a sculptor in marble, settling in Florence. In 1337 he succeeded Giotto as chief artist in the cathedral at Florence, and later became chief artist in the cathedral at Orvieto (1347), working on reliefs and statues.

Pisano, Nicola [peesahnoh] (c.1225–78/84) Sculptor, architect, and engineer, probably born in Apulia, SE Italy. His first great work was the sculpted panels for the pulpit in the Baptistery in Pisa, finished in 1260, whose powerful dramatic composition was carved in high relief. He collaborated with his son Giovanni on a pulpit for the cathedral at Siena (1268), and on the Fontana Maggiore in Perugia. Although working in a traditional Gothic style, he studied classical sculpture, and incorporated this into his own work.

Pisces [piyseez] (Lat 'fishes') A large N constellation of the zodiac which lacks bright stars, and so is hard to identify. It lies between Aquarius and Aries, and contains the vernal equinox.

Piscis Austrinus [piysis ostriynus] (Lat 'southern fish') A small S hemisphere constellation, which includes the first magnitude star Fomalhaut, 7·7 parsec away.

Pisistratus [piysistratus], also spelled **Peisistratos** (c.600–527 BC) Tyrant of Athens (561–c.556 BC, 546–527 BC). A moderate and far-sighted ruler, he did much to improve the lot of the small farmer in Attica, and to boost Athenian trade abroad, especially in the Black Sea area. A patron of the arts, he invited the leading Greek poets of the day to settle in Athens, where he set about fostering a sense of national unity by instituting or expanding great religious and cultural festivals. He was succeeded by his sons Hippias and Hipparchus, the so-called *Pisistratidae*, but the dynasty was overthrown in 510 BC.

Pissarro, Camille [peesaroh] (1830–1903) Impressionist artist, born in St Thomas, West Indies. He went to Paris (1855), where he was much influenced by Corot's landscapes. Most of his works were painted in the countryside round Paris, such as 'Boulevard Montmartre' (1897, National Gallery, London). The leader of the original Impressionists, he was the only one to exhibit at all eight of the Group exhibitions in Paris from 1874 to 1886. He also experimented with Divisionism.

Pissis, Monte [peesees] 27°45S 68°40W. Andean peak rising to 6882 m/22 578 ft on the border between Catamarca and La Rioja provinces, Argentina.

pistachio [pistahshioh] A small deciduous tree (*Pistacia vera*) growing to 6 m/20 ft, native to W Asia; leaves pinnate with 3–5 leaflets and slightly winged stalk; flowers greenish, in long, loose heads; fruit 2–2·5 cm/¾–1 in, red-brown, nut-like. It is widely cultivated for its edible seeds, used in confectionery. (Family: Anacardiaceae.)

pistil *carpel*

pistol A hand-held firearm first developed from 'hand-cannons' in the 14th-c. The application of the revolver principle in the 1830s by Samuel Colt made the pistol a multi-shot weapon, while the development of 'automatic' weapons c.1900 (such as the Luger and Browning) was a further refinement.

pit bull terrier *bull terrier*

Pitcairn Islands *see panel*

pitch (acoustics) An aspect of auditory sensation which makes listeners judge a sound as relatively 'high' or 'low'. The pitch at which a musical note sounds, and to which instruments are tuned, has varied considerably from one period to another, and often within a particular period. The present standard, *a*' = 440 Hz, was adopted by the International Organization for Standardization in 1955. Anyone who can name accurately the pitch of an isolated note is said to possess 'absolute' or 'perfect' pitch.

pitch (chemistry) The black, semi-solid residue left after the distillation of tar, used in bitumen and road-surfacing. It contains a complex mixture of hydrocarbons and resins, and is soluble in some organic solvents.

pitchblende or **uraninite** Uranium oxide (UO_2), the chief ore of uranium; hard, very dense, and radioactive. It is found in high temperature veins related to igneous rocks.

pitcher plant Any of the members of three separate families of carnivorous plants, in which the leaves are modified to form lidded pitcher traps containing water and enzymes. The pitchers are often flushed or blotched with red, and have honey glands and sometimes translucent 'windows' on the inner surface, or emit odours to attract insect prey; below the honey glands is a smooth 'slide zone' down which the insects fall. A second zone of downward-pointing hairs prevents the prey from climbing out, and it drowns in the fluid-filled base, where it is digested by the plant. The family Sarraceniaceae, native to E North America, California, and tropical South America, are perennial herbs with basal rosettes of long, curved pitchers, flowers nodding, solitary or several on a leafless stem. The family Nepenthaceae, native to the tropics of SE Asia, Australia, and Madagascar, are herbs, shrubs, often epiphytes and climbing by means of tendrils formed from an extension of the leaf midrib. In most species the end of the tendril expands to form a jug-shaped pitcher; flowers small, in spikes, males and females on separate plants; petals absent, but 4–5 sepals often brightly coloured. The family Cephalotaceae contains a single species, the **flycatcher plant** (*Cephalotus follicularis*), native to W Australia; a perennial herb with a basal rosette in which some leaves form jug-shaped pitchers; flowers with six coloured sepals, borne on a leafless stem.

Pitești [peetesht] 44°51N 24°51E, pop (2000e) 160 000. Capital of Argeș county, Romania, on R Argeș; railway junction; petrochemicals, vehicles, electric motors, textiles, wine, fruit.

Pithecanthropus [pithekanthropus] A name formerly used for the fossil ape-man, *Homo erectus*, which includes Java Man and Peking Man.

Pitjantjatjara The principal Aboriginal language of Australia's Western Desert, spoken by several thousand people in South Australia, Western Australia, and the Northern Territory. Many Pitjantjatjara worked in the cattle industry from the late 19th-c to the 1970s. Since then, mechanization has reduced the role of Aboriginal stockmen and women. An active Pitjantjatjara literacy programme has resulted in it becoming one of the most widely-used written Aboriginal languages.

Pitman, Sir Isaac (1813–97) Educationist, and inventor of a shorthand system, born in Trowbridge, Wiltshire, S England, UK. First a clerk, he became a schoolmaster at Barton-on-Humber, and at Wotton-under-Edge, where he issued his *Stenographic Sound Hand* (1837). Dismissed from Wotton because he had joined the New Jerusalem (Swedenborgian) Church, he established a Phonetic Institute for teaching shorthand in Bath (1839). In 1842 he brought out the *Phonetic Journal*, and in 1845 opened premises in London. He was knighted in 1894.

Pitney, Gene (1941–) Singer and songwriter, born in Hartford, Connecticut, USA. His first hit as a writer came with 'Rubber Ball' (1961), recorded by Bobby Vee. He also wrote 'Hello Mary Lou', a hit for Ricky Nelson in 1961, and one of his most revived songs. Among his hits as a singer were 'I Wanna Love My Life Away' (1961), '24 Hours From Tulsa' (1963), and 'Something's Gotten Hold Of My Heart' (1967). He was inducted into the Rock and Roll Hall of Fame in 2002.

Pitot tube [peetoh] An instrument for measuring the velocity of a flowing fluid; named after French engineer Henri Pitot (1695–1771). An open-ended tube faces the direction of the flow: the pressure observed by an attached manometer is a function of velocity.

Pitt, Brad (1963–) Film actor, born in Shawnee, Oklahoma, USA. He studied graphic design at the University of Missouri but left early and headed for Hollywood to try his luck at acting. He became known after his appearance in *Thelma & Louise* (1991), and later films include *A River Runs through It* (1992), *Seven* (1995), *Twelve Monkeys* (1995), *Fight Club* (1999), *Spy Game* (2001), and *Troy* (2004).

Pitt, William, 1st Earl of Chatham, also known as **Pitt the Elder** (1708–78) Statesman and orator, born in London, UK. He studied at Oxford, joined the army (1731), then entered Parliament for the family borough of Old Sarum (1735). He led the young 'Patriot' Whigs, and in 1756 became nominally secretary of state, but virtually premier. The king's enmity led him to resign in 1757, but public demand caused his recall. Again compelled to resign when his cabinet refused to declare war with Spain (1761), he vigorously attacked the peace terms of the Treaty of Paris (1763) as too generous to France. He formed a new ministry in 1766, but ill health contributed to his resignation in 1768.

Pitt, William, also known as **Pitt the Younger** (1759–1806) British statesman and prime minister (1783–1801, 1804–6), the second son of William Pitt, Earl of Chatham, born in Hayes, Greater London, UK. He studied law at Cambridge, but then became an MP (1781), his first post being Chancellor of the Exchequer under Shelburne (1782). He became First Lord of the Treasury 1783, and accepted the premiership after the collapse of the short-lived Portland government, at the age of 24, to become Britain's youngest prime minister. His first ministry lasted for 18 years, during which he carried through important reforms, his policy being influenced by the political economy of Adam Smith. He negotiated coalitions against France (1793, 1798), but these had little success. After the Irish rebellion of 1798, he proposed a legislative union which would be followed by Catholic emancipation. The union was effected in 1800, but Pitt resigned office in 1801 rather than contest George III's hostility to emancipation. He was persuaded to return to office in 1804, in the face of the mounting Napoleonic threat, formed a coalition with Russia, Austria, and Sweden, and with the defeat of the French at Trafalgar (1805) was hailed as the saviour of Europe. He drank very heavily, and this contributed to his early death while still prime minister.

Pitti Palace [pitee] A palace in Florence, NC Italy, designed by Brunelleschi in the 15th-c. It was originally the residence of the Grand Dukes of Tuscany and (1866–70) of Victor Emanuel II. The palace now houses museums of silverware and of modern art, and the Palatine Gallery, a magnificent art collection principally of Italian masters.

pittosporum [pitosporum] An evergreen shrub or small tree, mostly native to Australasia but also to parts of Africa and Asia; leaves leathery; flowers 5-petalled, purple, white, or greenish-yellow, and often fragrant; also called **parchment-bark**. (Genus: *Pittosporum*, 150 species. Family: Pittosporaceae.)

Pittsburgh 40°26N 80°01W, pop (2000e) 334 600. Seat of Allegheny Co, W Pennsylvania, USA; at the confluence of the Allegheny and Monongahela Rivers where they form the Ohio R; Fort Duquesne built here by the French; taken by the British and renamed Fort Pitt, 1758; city status, 1816; airport; railway; three universities (1787, 1878, 1900); city's traditional steel industry largely replaced by service industries; machinery, chemicals; third largest US corporate headquarters; noted for recent urban redevelopment and a dramatic reduction in air and water pollution; professional teams, Pirates (baseball), Steelers (football), Penguins (ice hockey); Carnegie Institute, Frick Art Museum, Point State Park, Heinz Hall, Phipps Conservatory; arts festival (Jun).

Pittsburg Landing, Battle of *Shiloh, Battle of*

pituitary gland [pityooitree] A vertebrate endocrine gland situated within the skull in a small concavity on the sphenoid bone, and connected to the hypothalamus by the infundibulum; also known as the **hypophysis**. Anatomical differences exist between species, but it generally consists of two parts – an *adenohypophysis* at the front, and a *neurohypophysis* at the back. It acts mainly by controlling the activities of many of the other endocrine glands; hence its colloquial description as 'leader of the endocrine orchestra'.

pit viper A viper of the subfamily Crotalinae (142 species), sometimes treated as a separate family (Crotalidae, with the remaining vipers called *true vipers*); absent from Africa; front of face with small heat-sensitive pit on each side; can hunt and attack in total darkness by sensing prey's body heat.

Pius V, St, originally **Michele Ghislieri** (1504–72) Pope (1566–72), born near Alessandria, N Italy. He became a bishop in 1556, and a cardinal in 1557. As pope he implemented the decrees of the Council of Trent (1545–63), excommunicated Elizabeth I (1570), and organized the expedition against the Turks, that resulted in the naval engagement of Lepanto (1571). He was canonized in 1712. Feast day 30 April.

Pius VII, originally **Gregorio Barnaba Chiaramonti** (1742–1823) Pope (1800–23), born in Cesena, E Italy. He became a cardinal in 1785. He arranged a concordat with Napoleon, and in 1804 was compelled to consecrate him as emperor. In 1809 the French annexed the Papal States. Pius was removed to Grenoble, then to Fontainebleau, and forced to sign a new concordat sanctioning the annexation. The fall of Napoleon (1814) allowed his return to Rome, and papal territory was restored by the Congress of Vienna.

Pius IX, known as **Pio Nono**, originally **Giovanni Maria Mastai-Ferretti** (1792–1878) Pope (1846–78), born in Senigallia, E Italy. He became Archbishop of Spoleto in 1827, and a cardinal in 1840. He introduced several reforms, but after the 1848 revolutions (during which he was forced to flee from Rome) he became progressively more conservative, and condemned modernism in theology. He decreed the dogma of the Immaculate Conception in 1854, and called the Vatican Council (1869–79), which proclaimed papal infallibility. He refused to recognize the new state of Italy, into which Rome was incorporated in 1870, after which he lived a voluntary 'prisoner' within the Vatican until his death. His pontificate is the longest in papal history. His beatification was announced in 2000.

Pius XI, originally **Ambrogio Damiano Achille Ratti** (1857–1939) Pope (1922–39), born in Desio, N Italy. A great linguist and scholar, he was librarian of the Ambrosian (Milan) and Vatican libraries. He became Cardinal Archbishop of Milan in 1921. As pope, he signed the Lateran Treaty (1929), which brought into existence the Vatican State, and made concordats with many countries.

Pius XII, originally **Eugenio Maria Giuseppe Giovanni Pacelli** (1876–1958) Pope (1939–58), born in Rome, Italy. Ordained in 1899, he became a papal diplomat, cardinal (1929), and secretary of state to the Holy See. Under his leadership during World War 2 the Vatican did much humanitarian work, notably for prisoners of war and refugees. There has been continuing controversy, however, over his attitude to the treatment of Jews in Nazi Germany, critics arguing that he could have used his influence with Catholic Germany to prevent the massacres, others

Planetary Data

Planet	Distance from sun maximum million km	maximum million mi	minimum million km	minimum million mi	Sidereal period	Axial rotation (equatorial)	Diameter (equatorial) km	Diameter (equatorial) mi
Mercury	69.4	43.0	46.8	29.0	88 d	58 d 16 h	4 878	3 032
Venus	109.0	67.6	107.6	66.7	224.7 d	243 d	12 104	7 520
Earth	152.6	94.6	147.4	91.4	365.26 d[1]	23 h 56 m 4s	12 756	7 926
Mars	249.2	154.5	207.3	128.5	687 d	24 h 37 m 22 s	6 794	4 222
Jupiter	817.4	506.8	741.6	459.8	11.86 y	9 h 55 m 41 s	142 984	88 846
Saturn	1 512	937.6	1 346	834.6	29.46 y	10 h 14 m	120 536	74 898
Uranus	3 011	1 867	2 740	1 699	84.01 y	17.2 h[2]	51 118	31 764
Neptune	4 543	2 817	4 466	2 769	164.79 y	16.11 h[2]	49 532	30 778
Pluto	7 364	4 566	4 461	2 766	248.5 y	6.387 d	2 274	1 412

[1] 365 d 5 h 48 m 46 s.

[2] Different latitudes rotate at different speeds.

y:years d:days h:hours m:minutes s:seconds km:kilometres mi:miles

that any attempt to do so would have proved futile and might have worsened the situation. In the post-war years he was particularly concerned with the plight of persecuted churchmen in Communist countries.

pixel From *pic*ture *el*ement, the smallest resolved unit of a video or computer-generated image which has specific luminance and colour; also an individual light-sensitive unit in an array forming a solid-state sensor in a camera. Pixel dimensions may be fixed during manufacture or determined in a raster display by the number of scanning lines and the resolution along each line.

Pizarro, Francisco [peethah**roh**] (c.1478–1541) Conquistador, born in Trujillo, WC Spain. He served in Italy, and with the expedition which discovered the Pacific (1513). In 1526 he and Almagro sailed for Peru, and in 1531 began the conquest of the Incas. He killed the Inca king, Atahualpa, then worked to consolidate the new empire, founding Lima (1535) and other cities. In 1537, dissension with Almagro over the control of Cuzco led to conflict. Too old to take the field himself, Pizarro entrusted the command of his forces to his brothers, who defeated and executed Almagro soon afterwards. In revenge Almagro's followers assassinated Pizarro.

PK *psychokinesis*

Plaatje, Sol(omon Tshekisho) [**plah**chee, **pliy**kee] (1879–1932) Writer and South African political figure, born in Boshof, C South Africa. He was a versatile intellectual and politician, an author, journalist, linguist, and polemicist. Proficient in at least eight languages, he established the first Tswana-language newspaper, published collections of Tswana proverbs, translated four Shakespeare plays into Tswana, and wrote a novel, *Mhudi* (1930). He is perhaps best remembered for his graphic *Native Life in South Africa* (1916), a moving appeal against the 1913 Land Act. He was a founder member of the African National Congress, and that body's first secretary-general.

placebo [pla**see**boh] An inactive substance given as a drug to a patient, who may benefit from the belief that the drug is active. Because patients can improve under this illusion, new drugs are usually tested for clinical efficacy in trials where a placebo is given to one group. The active drug must prove itself to be more efficacious than the placebo.

placenta (anatomy) [pla**sen**ta] An organ which develops in the uterus of all pregnant mammals, except the monetremes. It is attached to the uterus of the mother, and connected to the fetus by the umbilical cord. It is derived from both the fetal and maternal tissues, and subserves the needs of the developing fetus by allowing maternal and fetal blood to come into close association for the exchange of respiratory gases, nutrients, and waste products. It secretes a number of hormones (such as oestrogen, progesterone, and chorionic gonadotrophin) essential for pregnancy.

placenta (botany) [pla**sen**ta] Tissue to which the ovules or spores of plants are attached. The arrangement of ovules is termed **placentation**, and is an important diagnostic character in many plants.

Placid, Lake *Lake Placid*

Placodermi [plako**der**mee] An extinct class of primitive, jawed fishes known primarily from the Devonian period, mostly dwelling on sea bottom; large head covered by shield composed of bony plates; body depressed, heavily armoured.

plagioclase [**play**jioklayz] *feldspar*

plague The most notorious epidemic disease of all time, caused by infection with *Yersinia* (formerly *Pasteurella*) *pestis*, carried by fleas that infest rats and squirrels, which then bite humans. There are two forms of the disease. **Bubonic plague** is a severe illness with the development of 'buboes', swollen pus-filled lymph nodes. Untreated, it is fatal in over 50% of cases. **Pneumonic plague** is rare but almost always fatal. It can also be spread by inhalation of infected respiratory secretions. Outbreaks of plague (*black death*) have afflicted communities over many centuries. There have been two major epidemics, in the 17th and 14th centuries, and the latter killed half the population of Europe. Today it occurs only in isolated cases or as small local outbreaks. It can now be treated with antibiotics.

plaice Common European flatfish (*Pleuronectes platessa*) widespread in continental shelf waters from N Norway to the Mediterranean; length up to 90 cm/3 ft; both eyes on right side; upper surface brown with orange spots, underside white; supports very important commercial fisheries, especially around the British Is. (Family: Pleuronectidae.)

Plaid Cymru [pliyd **kuhm**ree] The Welsh National Party, founded in 1925, with the aim of achieving independence for Wales. It stands for election throughout Wales, but finds support mainly in the N of the country. It had three MPs following the 1987 general election, and four in 1992 and 1997. In 1986 the party agreed with the Scottish Nationalist Party to form a single parliamentary grouping in the Westminster Parliament. In 1999 it formed the second largest political party in the Welsh Assembly.

Plaidy, Jean *Hibbert, Eleanor*

Plain, the, known as the ***Marais*** The majority of deputies in the French Revolutionary Convention, politically uncommitted to a particular faction, although broadly aligned with the Girondins. They were ultimately outmaneouvred by extremists, the Jacobins of the Mountain.

plainchant The unaccompanied, single-strand music to which the Mass and other parts of the Roman liturgy were sung (and to some extent still are). It is notated, without precise indications of rhythm, on a four-line staff.

Plains Indians North American Indian groups who lived on the Great Plains between the Mississippi R and the Rocky Mts in the USA and Canada. Most were nomadic or semi-nomadic buffalo hunters living together in small bands, and engaged in various conflicts with one another; some were sedentary farmers. Their lives were dramatically changed by the introduction of horses by the Spanish, which led to intensified warring between groups, and hunting over much greater expanses. Eventually, overhunting brought the buffalo near extinction, and white settlers finally destroyed the Indians' power, confining them to reservations.

plainsong *plainchant*

plains wanderer A small, plump, ground-dwelling bird from open country in SE Australia (*Pedionomus torquatus*); mottled plumage; four toes on each foot; eats insects, seeds, and plants; also known as the **collared hemipode**. (Family: Pedionomidae.)

plaintiff *defendant*

planarian [planairian] A free-living predatory flatworm commonly found in aquatic and damp terrestrial habitats; intestine divided into an anterior and two posterior branches; feeds using a posteriorly-directed pharynx. (Phylum: Platyhelminthes. Order: Tricladida.)

Planchon, Roger [plãshõ] (1931–) Theatre director, playwright, and actor, born in the Ardèche, E France. He founded a theatre company in a disused printing works in Lyon in 1952, moving to the Théâtre de la Cité in Villeurbanne in 1957. His company was the recipient of the title, subsidy, and touring obligations of the Théâtre National Populaire in 1972.

Planck, Max (Karl Ernst Ludwig) (1858–1947) Theoretical physicist, born in Kiel, N Germany. He studied at Munich and Berlin, where he became professor of theoretical physics (1889–1926). His work on thermodynamics and black body radiation led him to abandon classical principles and introduce the quantum theory (1900), for which he was awarded the Nobel Prize for Physics in 1918. Several research institutes now carry his name.

Planck length A length scale thought to be of importance in quantum gravity, which may represent the shortest possible distance between points; equals $\sqrt{Gh/2\pi c^3}$, where *G* is the gravitational constant, *h* is Planck's constant, and *c* is the velocity of light; value $1{\cdot}62 \times 10^{-35}$ m; stated by Max Planck. The corresponding Planck mass is $2{\cdot}18 \times 10^{-8}$ kg.

Planck mass *Planck length*

Planck's constant A fundamental constant appearing in all equations of quantum theory; symbol *h*, value $6{\cdot}626 \times 10^{-34}$ J.s (joule.second); introduced by Max Planck in 1900, via the study of blackbody radiation. It relates the energy *E* of a quantum of light to its frequency ν by $E = h\nu$. It is sometimes used in the form $\hbar$, which is equal to $h/2\pi$.

plane (mathematics) In mathematics, a surface such that if any two points in that surface are joined by a straight line, all the points on the straight line lie on the surface. This can be seen as a generalization in three-dimensional space of a straight line. Two planes are either parallel or meet in a straight line. A plane is uniquely determined by three points not in a straight line, or by two straight lines meeting in a point, or by a point in the plane and a direction perpendicular to the plane. The equation of a general plane in rectangular Cartesian co-ordinates is $ax + by + cz + d = 0$.

planet A nonluminous body gravitationally bound to the Sun or a star. The basic distinction between a star and a planet is that a star generates its own heat and light, through nuclear reactions, whereas a planet shines only through reflected light. The theory of planetary formation suggests that they condense from material left over during primary star formation. They should therefore be common, but they are extremely hard to detect, being so much fainter than their parent stars. The first extrasolar planet, 51 Pegasi B, was detected in 1995, and 115 such planets had been detected by 2004, including the oldest and most distant (in the M4 star cluster in the constellation Scorpius, c.12·7 thousand million years old). In the Solar System there are nine major planets and innumerable minor planets, or *asteroids*. In the Solar System there are nine major planets and innumerable minor planets, or *asteroids*. Large numbers of comets are stored in a spherical shell (the *Oort Cloud*) at great distances from the Sun, some of which occasionally enter the inner Solar System and a few of which are trapped there. The major planets comprise two types; the *inner*, terrestrial planets (Mercury, Venus, Earth, Mars), and the giant gaseous *outer* planets (Jupiter, Saturn, Uranus, Neptune), together with unique, distant Pluto. All except Mercury and Venus have associated moons or, for the giant planets, systems of moons. All are believed to have been formed about 4·6 thousand million years ago, soon after the formation of the Sun from a collapsing cloud of gas and dust.

The inner planets are dense, and made primarily of metals and of metal silicates. They are internally differentiated into zones: an iron-rich *core*, an iron-magnesium silicate *mantle*, and a *crust* of lighter metal silicates. Venus, Earth, and Mars have atmospheres believed to be outgassed from the interiors over geological time. The outer planets are much less dense, and made primarily of gases and ices together with a core equivalent to a large terrestrial planet. They are also internally differentiated into zones: an outer core of hydrogen in a solid phase, a mantle of liquid hydrogen/helium, and a deep gaseous atmosphere. Jupiter is by far the most massive planet, containing over two-thirds of the material in the Solar System apart from the Sun. Many searches have been made for a tenth planet in our Solar System; since the discovery of the Kuiper Belt it now seems certain that no such body exists, though new proposals are regularly made (e.g. Sedna, 2004). (*see panel p.1207*)

planetarium A special building with a dome in which a projector produces an impression of the stars in the night sky. Planetary motions and many sorts of astronomical phenomena can be demonstrated for teaching and entertainment purposes. Famous examples are the Hayden Planetarium in New York City (part of the American Museum of Natural History) and the London Planetarium.

planetary nebula A shell of glowing gas surrounding an evolved star, from which it was ejected. There is no connection with planets: the name derived from the visual similarity at the telescope between the disc of such a nebula and the disc of a planet. They are late stages in the evolution of stars 1–4 times as massive as the Sun. Some thousands are known in our Galaxy.

plane tree A tall, long-lived deciduous tree, native to S Europe, Asia, and especially North America; distinctive flaking bark, revealing large creamy or pink patches; leaves palmately lobed; fruiting heads pendulous globes, persisting on the tree through the winter. The **London plane** (*Platanus* × *hispanica*) is a garden hybrid resistant to air pollution, widely planted in city streets. (Genus: *Platanus*, 10 species. Family: Platinaceae.)

planimeter A mathematical instrument for measuring the area enclosed by an irregular curve. A pointer moved around the perimeter is connected by lever arms to an integrating mechanism.

plankton Organisms without effective means of locomotion; drifters. They have been subdivided into plant (**phytoplankton**) and animal (**zooplankton**) types. Some plankton are capable of limited swimming ability, but cannot move faster than the ocean currents in which they may be carried, hence they cannot effectively swim. Most plankton are microscopic in size. Some are the larval stages of organisms with larger, adult phases (**meroplankton**); examples include sea urchins, starfish, bivalves, and larval fish. Others remain planktonic for their entire life-cycle (**holoplankton**); examples include copepods, arrow worms, and krill.

planned economy An economy in which the government decides what should be produced and who should get it. This is contrasted with a *market economy*, in which individuals and firms decide for themselves what to produce and consume. The advantages claimed for a planned economy are that wasteful duplication of effort and unemployment can be avoided, and goods can be distributed fairly. The process of deciding what commands to issue in a command economy, and checking that orders are carried out, requires an enormous amount of information and civil servants to manipulate it. Critics of planned economies claim that they are bad at discovering what people really want and at motivating anybody to supply it, and are inflexible in the face of a rapidly changing environment. The former Soviet Union was the world's largest example of a centrally planned economy; its successors have started to move towards a market economy. Most real world economies fall somewhere between full central planning and a pure market economy. In the UK, for example, the government decides what should be provided in several large sectors, including defence, roads, education, and health.

planographic printing *printing*

plant An organism which typically uses sunlight as an energy source via photosynthetic pathways involving the green pigment chlorophyll (kingdom: *Plantae*). Plants are mostly nonmotile and lack obvious excretory and nervous systems, and sensory organs. They are eucaryotic, and typically possess cell walls composed largely of cellulose. Traditionally the chlorophyll-containing single-celled algae have been regarded as plants, even though they may be motile and can feed by ingesting organic matter. The fungi have also been grouped with plants, although they lack chlorophyll and feed by absorbing organic substances.

Plantagenets The name given by historians to the royal dynasty in England from Henry II to Richard II (1154–1399), then continued by two rival houses of younger lines, Lancaster and York, until 1485. The dynasty was so called because, allegedly, Henry II's father Geoffrey, Count of Anjou, sported a sprig of broom (Old Fr, *plante genêt*) in his cap. Of Angevin descent, Geoffrey married Matilda of France, daughter of King Henry I of England. Their son became (1154) the first Angevin (or Plantagenet) king of England as Henry II.

plantain 1 Typically an annual or perennial, sometimes a shrub, often a weed; very widespread; a rosette of narrow, lance-shaped to broadly oval, strongly veined leaves; flowers tiny, with four brownish or green, membranous petals, packed into a dense, erect spike. (Genus: *Plantago*, 265 species. Family: Plantaginaceae.)
2 *banana*

plantain-eater *turaco*

plantain lily *hosta*

plantation A system of agriculture generally found in the tropics and subtropics. Plantations were a product of colonialism – large, company-owned, and labour intensive. With the independence of former colonies many plantations were nationalized, and some divided into smaller units. Plantation farming is associated with the production of cash crops such as coffee, tea, rubber, and cotton, but the term is also applied to planted and managed forests in temperate regions.

Plantation of Ulster *Ulster Plantation*

plant breeding The improvement of agriculturally or horticulturally important plants, either by selecting improved varieties from mixtures or by hybridization followed by the selection of desirable genotypes. Once a simple *ad hoc* process largely based on the laws of inheritance established by Gregor Mendel and involving hybrids within or between related species or genes, plant breeding developed in the second half of the 20th-c into an increasingly sophisticated science which may involve the introduction of characters from widely differing plants or even animals. The moral and ecological aspects of the genetic modifications involved have given rise to great controversy, particularly when the new products are used in human or animal food.

plant genetic resources The range of genetic variability to be found in the wild and cultivated forms of any species. The plants comprising this variability are an essential source of raw material for plant breeders. For many important species, they are maintained under controlled conditions in gene banks supervised by the International Board for Plant Genetic Resources or at nationally-supervised centres.

plant hopper A small, hopping insect that feeds by sucking sap or cell contents of plants; species include pests of economically important crops, such as rice and sugar cane. (Order: Homoptera. Family: Delphacidae, c.1300 species.)

plasma (physics) A fourth state of matter comprising a fluid of ions and free electrons, formed for example by the extreme heating of a gas, and characterized by powerful electrical forces between the particles. Fluorescent lights and the interiors of stars contain plasmas. Plasma properties are studied in **plasma physics**. The main interest is the creation of controlled nuclear fusion, with the ultimate aim of power generation. The principal features are the containment of the plasma using magnetic fields (*plasma confinement*) and the heating of the plasma by passing electrical currents through it, by injecting particles into it, or by the application of radio-frequency waves.

plasma (physiology) [**plaz**ma] The fluid portion of whole blood, in which the blood cells are suspended. It transports nutrients, metabolic waste products, and chemicals involved in the clotting process, as well as hormones and drugs, to their target cells. It clots readily, and can be obtained by centrifuging or sedimentation. The term is also used for the fluid portion of semen, in which spermatozoa are suspended.

plasmapheresis [plazmaferesis] or **plasma exchange** The circulation of whole blood outside the body, during which centrifugal force separates the cellular component and plasma, which is discarded and replaced by fresh plasma or plasma albumin. The purpose is to remove a damaging plasma component such as an abnormal antibody.

plasma screen A form of display screen used with computers in which the screen can be made very flat. It is therefore suitable for notebook and laptop computers.

Plasmodium [plazmohdium] A genus of parasitic protozoans containing the micro-organisms that cause malaria in humans; life cycle complex, involving stages in an intermediate host, the mosquito, and stages in the blood or other organs of a final vertebrate host. (Phylum: Apicomplexa. Class: Sporozoa.)

Plassey, Battle of [plasee] (1757) A decisive British victory under Clive over Nawab Siraj ud Daula, Nawab of Bengal, India. Clive's success was aided by the treachery of Nawab's general, Mir Jafar, whom the British subsequently placed on the throne. The victory was an important step in the British acquisition of Bengal.

plaster *gypsum*

plastic deformation The irreversible deformation of a material stressed to beyond its elastic limit (*yield point*). Further increases in stress cause disproportionately large deformations until a fracture point is reached. *Ductile* materials are those which undergo large plastic deformations (eg most metals); *brittle* materials undergo small plastic deformations.

plastics Originally any soft, formable material; now commonly used for synthetic organic resins which can be softened by heating, and then shaped or cast. Some (called *thermoset*, eg phenol-formaldehyde resin) are then resistant to softening on further heating; others (called *thermoplastic*, eg polyethylene and polystyrene) may be repeatedly softened. Plastics may be designed with almost any desired property, ranging from great heat stability to rapid natural decomposition in soil, and from good electrical insulators to conductors.

plastic surgery The grafting of skin and subcutaneous tissue from a healthy site on the body to one that has suffered damage from disease, trauma, or burns. The manoeuvre is sometimes carried out in several stages, and its purpose is to cover areas denuded of skin and to fill in areas deficient in tissue. It also includes surgical operations undertaken for cosmetic purposes, such as face-lifting, reshaping noses, breast augmentation, and removing unsightly fat.

Plataea [plateea] A Greek city-state in Boeotia, which shared with Athens the honour of defeating the Persians at Marathon, and was the site in 479 BC of a decisive Greek victory over the Persians.

Plate, River, Span **Río de la Plata** A wide, shallow estuary of the Paraná and Uruguay Rivers on the E coast of South America, between Argentina (S and W shore) and Uruguay (N shore); area 35 000 sq km/13 510 sq mi; length 320 km/200 mi; width 220 km/140 mi at its mouth and 45 km/28 mi at Buenos Aires; European discovery, 1516; Buenos Aires on S shore, Montevideo on N shore; scene of a naval engagement (Dec 1939) between three out-gunned British cruisers and the formidable German pocket-battleship *Graf Spee* (**Battle of the River Plate**); the *Graf Spee* inexplicably disengaged, and was trapped in the neutral port of Montevideo, to be scuttled a few days later.

plate 1 A photographic material with a sensitive emulsion coated on a sheet of glass.
2 In special effects cinematography, a positive picture print on slide or film, used in back projection and similar processes as the background scene against which the foreground action is to appear.

Plateau Indians North American Indian groups who lived on the plateau between the Rocky Mts and the Cascade Range. Most groups lived in camps during the summer, hunting and fishing; during the severe winters, they sheltered in earth lodges in permanent villages located along the rivers. This way of life was radically affected by fur traders and trappers arriving from the E, bringing in European diseases, to which many succumbed, and weapons. In the 18th-c, Plains Indians introduced horses, and during the 19th-c European settlers and prospectors fought with the Indians over land. In the ensuing wars, most groups were decimated, and the survivors forced into reservations.

platelets Small disc-like structures (2–4 μ in diameter) found in the blood of all mammals, produced in bone marrow. They contain factors important in the arrest of bleeding (eg serotonin), and in wound healing (eg platelet-derived growth factor). The number of circulating platelets is regulated by a hormone (*thrombopoietin*) of unknown origin. Any deficiency (*thrombocytopenia*) results in severe bleeding, either spontaneously or when wounded.

Plater, Alan (Frederick) [**play**ter] (1935–) Playwright, born in Jarrow-on-Tyne, Tyne and Wear, NE England, UK. Trained as an architect, his writing was first published in *Punch* (1958). He became a regular writer for *Z Cars* (1963–5), *Softly Softly* (1966–76), and other television series. His television plays include *Close the Coalhouse Door* (1968), *The Land of Green Ginger* (1974), and *The Last of the Blonde Bombshells* (2000). His screenplays include the film *The Virgin and the Gypsy* (1969) and *It Shouldn't Happen to a Vet* (1974), and the television adaptations *The Barchester Chronicles* (1981) and *Fortunes of War* (1987). Among plays written for the theatre are a jazz musical *Rent Party* (1989) and *I Thought I Heard a Rustling* (1991). He has also written novels, notably *The Beiderbecke Affair* (1985), *The Beiderbecke Tapes* (1986), and *The Beiderbecke Connection* (1992), based on his television series.

plate tectonics A model of the structure and dynamics of the Earth's crust, developed in the 1960s to explain and relate observations such as continental drift, mid-ocean ridges and ocean trenches, the distribution of earthquakes, and volcanic activity. The theory proposes that the Earth's lithosphere is made up of a number of relatively thin, rigid plates which may include both continental and ocean crust and which move relative to one another. Plate boundaries are defined by major earthquake zones and belts of volcanic activity. New plate material is generated by basaltic lava erupted along mid-ocean ridges and eventually consumed at subduction zones at the site of deep ocean trenches. Plate collisions result in the formation of mountain belts such as the Alps and Himalayas. Plate motion is most probably driven by convection currents within the mantle on which the plates float.

platform tennis A variation of paddle tennis, a cross between lawn tennis and squash, and played with a sponge ball. Side and rear screens can be used to bring the ball into court. Invented in c.1920, it is a popular outdoor winter sport in the USA, where the US Platform Tennis Association was formed in 1934.

Plath, Sylvia (1932–63) Poet and novelist, born in Boston, Massachusetts, USA. Driven by a desire to write, she won a Fulbright Fellowship to Newnham College, Cambridge, in 1956, where she studied English, and met and married the poet Ted Hughes. After some time spent teaching in the USA, they settled in England, first in London, then in Devon, but separated in 1962. Her severe depressions drove her to suicide. Often termed a 'confessional poet', her earlier, highly controlled work gave way to a poetry of visionary expression and personal intensity, which has since come to be highly regarded. Her collections include *A Winter Ship* (1960), which was published anonymously, *The Colossus* (1960) and, posthumously, *Ariel* (1965), and *Winter Trees* (1972). Her collected poems were edited by Ted Hughes in 1981. Her only novel, *The Bell Jar* (1963), which describes a student's mental breakdown, was published under the pseudonym **Victoria Lucas** just before her own suicide.

platinum Pt, element 78, density 21·5 g/cm^3, melting point 1772°C. A precious metal, which occurs occasionally uncombined but more importantly as a sulphide. It is a valuable impurity in nickel deposits, and is generally found along with the other *platinum metals*. Similar to gold in its unreactivity, it is used for jewellery and for laboratory vessels. It is also an important catalyst for hydrogenations; finely divided platinum can absorb large volumes of hydrogen gas.

platinum metals A series of elements which occur together in nature, and have similar properties: ruthenium (Ru), rhodium (Rh), palladium (Pd), osmium (Os), iridium (Ir), and platinum (Pt).

Plato (c.428–347 BC) Greek philosopher, probably born in Athens, Greece of an aristocratic family. Little is known of his early life, but he was a devoted disciple of Socrates. He travelled widely, then in about 367 BC founded his Academy at Athens, where Aristotle was his most famous pupil. He remained there for the rest of his life, apart from visits to Syracuse, where he was involved in political experiments. His 30 or more dialogues are conventionally divided into three periods. The early dialogues have Socrates as the principal character engaged in ironic and inconclusive interrogations about the definition of different moral virtues (piety in the *Euthyphro*, courage in the *Laches*, and so on). In the middle, highly literary dialogues, such as the *Symposium*, *Gorgias*, *Phaedo*, and *Republic*, he increasingly develops his own positive doctrines, such as the theory of knowledge as recollection, the immortality of the soul, the tripartite division of the soul, and above all the theory of forms (or 'ideas') which contrasts the transient, material world of 'particulars' (objects merely of perception, opinion, and belief) with the timeless, unchanging world of universals or forms (the true objects of knowledge). The *Republic* also describes Plato's celebrated political utopia, ruled by philosopher-kings who have mastered the discipline of 'dialectic'. The third group of later dialogues (including the *Parmenides*, *Theaetetus*, and *Sophist*) represents a series of highly sophisticated criticisms of the metaphysical and logical assumptions of his middle period, and contain some of his most demanding and original work. Taken as a whole, his philosophy has been so enormously influential that the whole subsequent Western tradition was described by Whitehead as a series of 'footnotes to Plato'.

Platonic solids In mathematics, solids whose faces are congruent regular polygons meeting in the same numbers at each vertex. There are five such solids: the *tetrahedron* (four faces, each an equilateral triangle); the *cube* (six faces, each a square); the *octahedron* (eight faces, each a pentagon); the *dodecahedron* (12 faces, each a hexagon); and the *icosahedron* (20 faces, each an equilateral triangle). All five were described by Plato, who showed how to construct models of the solids using triangles, squares, and pentagons for their faces.

Platt, David (Andrew) (1966–) Footballer, born in Chadderton, Greater Manchester, NW England, UK. A midfielder, he played for Crewe Alexandra, Aston Villa, Bari, Juventus, and Sampdoria, before moving to Arsenal (1995–8). A former England captain (1994–6), he won 62 caps for England. He was the Professional Footballers' Association Player of the Year in 1990. Retiring as a player in 1998, he became coach of Sampdoria, but resigned in 1999 after a series of disastrous results, and joined Nottingham Forest as manager. He became coach of the England Under-21 side in 2001.

Platyhelminthes [plateehelminths] A phylum of flattened, worm-like animals comprising parasitic groups, such as the tapeworms (class: Cestoda) and flukes (class: Trematoda), and free-living groups, such as the planarians (class: Tricladida).

platypus *duck-billed platypus*

Plautus, Titus Maccius [plawtus] (c.250–184 BC) Comic playwright, born in Sarsina, Italy. He worked in the theatre, then in foreign trade, before beginning to write plays (c.224 BC). About 130 plays have been attributed to him, but many are thought to be the work of earlier playwrights which he revised. Varro limited the genuine comedies to 21, and these 'Varronian comedies' are the ones which have survived. Extremely popular, and still being performed five centuries later, the plays are full of robust life and vigorous dialogue, and influenced many other playwrights, such as Shakespeare and Molière.

Player, Gary (Jim) (1935–) Golfer, born in Johannesburg, NE South Africa. He is one of only four golfers to win each of the four Grand Slam events. His first major success was the 1959 (British) Open, a title he also won in 1968 and 1974. He was the first non-American for 45 years to win the US Open (1965), and the first to win the US Professional Golfers Association title (1962, 1972) and the US Masters (1961, 1974, 1978). He won the South African Open 12 times, and the World Matchplay title a record five times, since matched by Ballesteros. He now breeds horses in South Africa, and is a leading member of the US Seniors Tour.

player piano A mechanism attached to a piano (or a piano fitted with such a mechanism) in which a perforated roll passes over a brass 'tracker bar' and causes those keys to be depressed to which the perforations correspond. The mechanism is driven by suction generated by pedals operated by the player's feet. In the earliest models, made from c.1890 onwards, tempo, dynamics, and 'expression' were at the command of the player, but later they were incorporated into the rolls themselves, some of which were cut by such artists as Gershwin and Rachmaninov. The popularity of the player piano declined in the 1920s and 1930s as other means of mechanical reproduction were developed.

Playfair, John (1748–1819) Mathematician and geologist, born in Benvie, Dundee, E Scotland, UK. He studied at St Andrews University, became joint professor of mathematics at Edinburgh (1785), and professor of natural philosophy (1805). He wrote an important textbook on geometry, and also investigated glaciation and the formation of river valleys.

playgroup An informal gathering of children under normal school age, and many of their parents, where the emphasis is on play and enjoyment of each other's company. There are usually rules governing the running of such groups, mainly about the suitability of premises, health aspects, and the ratio of adults to children, but though playgroup leaders may be trained people, many of the volunteer helpers are parents themselves.

playing cards Small rectangular cards used for playing card games. A standard pack contains 52 cards divided into four *suits*; hearts, clubs, diamonds, and spades. Each suit is subdivided into 13 cards numbered as follows: ace, 2–10, and the court (or picture) cards, jack, queen, and king. Most packs also contain two cards known as jokers, which can be given any value, but they are used in very few games. The earliest playing cards were used in China in the 10th-c. When they first appeared in Europe (in Italy) in the 14th-c, the pack consisted of 78 cards. It was standardized at 52 in the 15th-c.

plea bargaining A controversial administrative device of resolving criminal cases, in which the defendant pleads guilty to a lesser offence or one carrying a lighter punishment, with the consent of the court and the prosecution, in order to conserve resources by moving cases through the system more quickly. The US Supreme Court has acknowledged the constitutionality of plea bargaining, noting that the defendant merely trades the right to trial in order to avoid its attendant uncertainties and obtain a more lenient sentence, as long as the bargain is entered into knowingly and voluntarily and is accepted by the prosecution. In England and Wales, any negotiations taking place between the judge and defence counsel must be in the presence of prosecuting counsel. The accused is not a party to the negotiations, is not bound to agree, and must be allowed to decide freely about the negotiations. Plea bargaining is controversial, because there is concern that the innocent might plead guilty to secure lesser sentences, to avoid long trials, or under pressure from their lawyers; conversely, when cases are disposed of without a complete disclosure of all the facts, defendants may escape with lighter sentences.

Pleasence, Sir Donald [plezuhns] (1919–95) Actor, born in Worksop, Nottinghamshire, C England, UK. He made his first appearance in Jersey in 1939, served in the RAF during World War 2, and returned to the stage in 1946. He worked at various repertory theatres, including Birmingham and the Bristol Old Vic, but scored a huge success as the malevolent tramp, Davies, in Harold Pinter's *The Caretaker* (1960). After the 1960s, his London stage appearances were rare, but he made many TV appearances, including *The Barchester Chronicles* (1982), and was in constant demand for film work, often as a villain, as in *Dr Crippen* (1962), *Cul-de-Sac* (1966), and many others, known for his piercing stare, menacing voice, and bald head. He was knighted in 1994.

plebeians [plebeeanz] or **plebs** In early Rome, citizens other than the patricians, who were the ruling elite. By the late Republic, some plebeian clans (such as the Claudians) had come to be part of the ruling aristocracy, and the distinction between them and the patricians became blurred.

plebiscite *referendum*

Plecoptera [plekoptera] *stonefly*

plectrum A short length of metal, tortoise-shell, ivory, plastic, or other material worn on the fingers or held between them, to pluck a string instrument such as the guitar and mandolin.

Pléiade, La [playad] (Fr 'the Pleiades') A group of French poets of the 16th-c who sought to emancipate the French language (and literature) from mediaevalism by introducing Greek and Latin models. The best known were Ronsard and du Bellay, whose *Défense et illustration de la langue française* (1549) served as a manifesto.

Pleiades (astronomy) [pleeadeez, pliyadeez] An open cluster of stars in Taurus, familiarly known as the **Seven Sisters**, although only six stars are readily visible to the naked eye, while people with sharp vision claim to see twice as many. The most prominent of the open clusters, it was noted as early as 2357 BC in literature and mythology. The cluster is c.50 million years old, and contains several hundred stars. Distance: 116 parsec.

Pleiades (mythology) [pliyadeez] In Greek mythology, the seven daughters of Atlas and Pleione: Maia, Taygete, Elektra, Alkyone, Asterope, Kelaino, and Merope. After their deaths they were changed into the star-cluster of the same name.

pleiotropy [pliyotropee] The multiple effects of a single gene. The 'vestigial' gene in *Drosophila* reduces the size of the wings, but among other changes, also modifies the balancers (*halteres*), changes the direction of particular bristles, and alters the number of egg strings in the ovaries. Many genes for human syndromes are pleiotropic; for example, the gene for arachnodactyly (Marfan's syndrome) produces not only the slender spidery physique, with elongation especially of the end portions of the limbs, but also joint hypermobility, often dislocation of the lens of the eye, and diseases of the heart.

Pleistocene epoch [pliystoseen] The earlier of the two geological epochs of the Quaternary period, from 2 million years ago to 10 000 years ago; termed the *Ice Age* in the N hemisphere, where it was characterized by several periods of glacial advance and retreat. It was marked by the extinction of mammals such as the mammoth and the mastodon, and the evolution of man and familiar mammalian life.

Plekhanov, Georgiy Valentinovich [plekahnof] (1856–1918) Marxist philosopher, historian, and journalist, 'the father of Russian Marxism', born in Gundalovka, W Russia. He left Russia in 1880, and in 1883 founded the first Russian Marxist group (the Liberation Labour Group) in Geneva, where he remained until 1917. He was a major intellectual influence on the young Lenin, but sided with the Mensheviks against Lenin's Bolsheviks, and denounced the October Revolution.

plesiosaur [plesiosaw(r)] A marine reptile known from the Mesozoic era; body broad and compact, with large limbs developed as paddles; neck typically long, head small with a long snout bearing sharp teeth for feeding on fish; short-necked forms known as *pliosaurs*. (Order: Sauropterygia.)

pleurisy [ploorizee] Inflammation of membranes in the chest cavity (*pleura*) by micro-organisms, especially bacteria or viruses. It induces sharp pain on one or other side of the chest, aggravated by breathing. The pain often lessens with the passage of time, as fluid is exuded and separates the layers of pleura.

Plimsoll, Samuel (1824–98) Social reformer, known as 'the sailors' friend', born in Bristol, SW England, UK. He became an MP in 1868, and having accumulated a large file on the unseaworthiness of ships, caused the Merchant Shipping Act (1876) to be passed. Every owner was ordered to mark upon the side of a ship a circular disc, with a horizontal line drawn through its centre (the *Plimsoll line*), down to which the vessel might be loaded. This convention was legally enforced in 1894.

Pliny (the Elder), in full **Gaius Plinius Secundus** (23–79) Roman scholar, born in Novum Comum (now Como), Gaul. He studied at Rome, served in the army in Germany, and later settled in Como, where he devoted himself to study and writing. Nero appointed him procurator in Spain, and through his brother-in-law's death (71) he became guardian of his nephew Pliny (the Younger), whom he adopted. He continued his studies, and wrote a 37-volume encyclopedia, the *Historia naturalis* (77, Natural History), his only work to survive. In 79 he was in command of the Roman fleet when the great eruption of Vesuvius was at its height. He landed at Stabiae (Castellamare), to observe more closely, and was killed by volcanic fumes.

Pliny (the Younger), in full **Gaius Plinius Caecilius Secundus** (c.62–c.114) Roman writer and administrator, born in Novum Comum (now Como), Gaul, the nephew and adopted son of Pliny the Elder. He became a lawyer and a highly proficient orator, much in demand. He served as a military tribune in Syria, and progressed to be quaestor, praetor, and (100) consul, holding several posts throughout the empire. He was the master of epistolary style, his many letters providing an insight into the life of the upper class in the 1st-c. His letters written as governor of Bithynia in present-day Turkey contain some of the earliest pagan accounts of Christians.

Pliocene epoch [pliyoseen] The last of the geological epochs of the Tertiary period, from 5 to 2 million years ago and immediately preceding the Pleistocene epoch.

pliosaur [pliyosaw(r)] A powerfully built plesiosaur known from Mesozoic seas; a short neck and an enormous head; predatory on large aquatic animals. (Order: Sauropterygia.)

PLO (Palestine Liberation Organization) An umbrella organization for the diverse factions which sought the creation of a Palestinian state in part or the whole of British Mandated Palestine. **Fatah**, the Movement for the Liberation of Palestine, founded by Yasser Arafat, is the largest of the groups. The other major factions are the **Democratic Front for the Liberation of Palestine (DFLP)** founded by Nayef Hawatmeh, the **Popular Front for the Liberation of Palestine (PFLP)** founded by George Habash, the **PFLP-General Command** headed by Ahmed Jibril, the Syrian-sponsored **Saiqa**, and the Iraqi-sponsored **Arab Liberation Front**. After its withdrawal from Beirut during the Israeli siege of 1982, the PLO was based in Tunis. In 1988 the PLO accepted Israel's right to exist and renounced terrorism, and in 1993 the PLO and Israel agreed to recognize each other. Since the establishment of the Palestine National Authority, the PLO has largely been superseded and remains mainly as a negotiator. Its unofficial headquarters are in Jerusalem.

Ploieşti [ployesht] 44°57N 26°01E, pop (2000e) 246 000. Capital of Prahova county, SC Romania; railway; major centre for the petroleum industry, with pipelines to Giurgiu, Bucharest, and Constanţa; oil refining, oilfield equipment, petrochemicals, textiles, paper, furniture.

Plotinus [plotiynus] (c.205–70) The first systematic philosopher of the Neoplatonic school, probably born in Lycopolis, C Egypt. He studied in Alexandria and Persia, and settled in Rome (244), where he became a popular lecturer, advocating asceticism and the contemplative life. When 60, he attempted to found a platonic 'Republic' in Campania, but died in Minturnae. His 54 works were edited by his pupil, Porphyry, who arranged them in six groups of nine books, or *Enneads*. They established the foundations of Neoplatonism as a philosophical system, which combined Platonic with Pythagorean, Aristotelian, and Stoic doctrines and greatly influenced early Christian theology.

plotter *X–Y plotter*

Plough, the A familiar pattern of seven bright stars within Ursa Major; also called the **Big Dipper** (chiefly US) and **Charles's Wain**. The two stars furthest from the handle, Merak and Dubhe (the Pointers), point almost directly to Polaris, the North Star.

plough An implement used for cutting furrows and turning over the soil into ridges and furrows, so that surface vegetation is buried and seed-bed preparation can begin. The earliest ploughs were scratch-ploughs, consisting of a wooden wedge and fastened to a handle or beam which was pulled by men or oxen and capable only of breaking, not turning the soil. The first recorded furrow-plough was in 3rd-c AD China. From the 10th-c AD wheeled ploughs were used in Europe, using a vertically attached metal knife or coulter and a mould-board, which turned the soil. Modern ploughs are made of steel and are tractor-drawn. They commonly turn multiple furrows in one pass. Recent years have seen the widespread adoption of the reversible plough. In this machine a second set of bodies which turn the soil to the left is mounted on the beam in opposition to the right-hand set. By using alternate sets of bodies, the reversible plough can work across a field from one side to the other with no marking-out, no ridges or furrows, and a minimum of idle time on the headlands.

Plough Monday In the UK, the Monday after Twelfth Night. Traditionally this was the time when ploughmen and others resumed work after the Christmas festivities.

Plovdiv [plovdif], formerly **Philippopoli**, Lat **Evmolpia**, Thracian **Pulpudeva** 42°08N 24°25E, pop (2000e) 352 000. Capital of Plovdiv province, C Bulgaria; on the R Maritsa, 156 km/97 mi SE of Sofia; second largest city in Bulgaria; airport; railway; higher educational institutions; metal products, food processing, textiles, chemicals; trading centre for livestock and tobacco; International Trade Fair since 1892; Roman amphitheatre; Old Plovdiv has many buildings from the Middle Ages and the National Revival Period.

plover A small to medium-sized bird (Family: Charadriidae, 63 species), found worldwide; short tail, long legs; bill straight, same length as head; inhabits shores, grasslands, or deserts; eats invertebrates; moves by repeated short runs and pauses; includes lapwings and dotterels. The name is also used for the **crab-plover** (Family: Dromadidae), the **Egyptian plover** (Family: Glareolidae), the **upland plover** (Family: Scolopacidae), the

Norfolk plover and **stone-plover** (Family: Burhinidae), and the **quail-plover** (Family: Turnicidae).

Plowright, Dame Joan (1929–) Actress, born in Brigg, Lincolnshire, EC England, UK. Trained at the Laban Art of Movement Studio, Manchester, and the Old Vic Theatre School, she became a member of the English Stage Company at the Royal Court Theatre, London, in 1956. There she played opposite Laurence Olivier, whom she married in 1961. She played Jean Rice in Osborne's *The Entertainer* (1957) and Beattie in Arnold Wesker's *Roots* (1959), and in 1963 joined the National Theatre in its first season. A formidably talented classical actress, she has also appeared on television and in films, including *The Entertainer* (1960), *The Dressmaker* (1988), *Avalon* (1991), *Enchanted April* (1993, Golden Globe), and *Tea with Mussolini* (1998). She has also worked as a stage producer and director. She was made a dame in 2004.

plum Any of various species of the genus *Prunus*. The widely grown plum of orchards (*Prunus domestica*) is a small deciduous tree or shrub; white blossom appearing simultaneously with leaves; ovoid yellow, red, purplish, or black fruit; sweet flesh enclosing a large stone. It is thought to be a hybrid between the sloe and the cherry plum. (Family: Rosaceae.)

plume moth A delicate, long-legged moth which holds its rolled wings sideways, at an angle to its body, when at rest; wings often divided; caterpillars small and spiny. (Order: Lepidoptera. Family: Pterophoridae, c.500 species.)

pluralism (philosophy) Any metaphysical theory which is committed to the ultimate existence of two or more kinds of things. For example, mind–body dualists, such as Descartes, are pluralists.

pluralism (politics) Both a description of and prescription for circumstances where political power is widely dispersed, so that no one interest group or class predominates. The principal conditions for pluralism are free elections, many and overlapping interests, low barriers to ways of organizing pressure on government, and a state that is responsive to popular demands. The term is commonly applied to liberal democracies, where it is argued that the large number of pressure groups complement electoral politics in allowing citizens to get their preferences reflected in government decisions. However, the argument that pluralism is democratic is criticized by some on the grounds that social and economic inequalities make political competition unequal.

Plutarch [**ploo**tah(r)k], Gr **Ploutarchos** (c.46–c.120) Historian, biographer, and philosopher, born in Chaeronea, Boeotia, Greece. He studied in Athens and made several visits to Rome, where he gave public lectures in philosophy. His extant writings comprise *Opera moralia*, a series of essays on ethical, political, religious, and other topics, and several historical works, notably *Bioi paralleloi* (Parallel Lives), a gallery of 46 portraits of the great characters of preceding ages, each book consisting of a Greek and a Roman figure, sharing some resemblance. North's translation of his work into English (1579) was the source of Shakespeare's Roman plays.

Pluto (astronomy) The ninth and most distant planet from the Sun, smaller than our Moon, discovered in 1930 by Clyde Tombaugh after an extensive search. It is an anomalous planet in the outer Solar System, bearing no resemblance to the 'gas giants'. It is accompanied by a relatively large moon, Charon, discovered in 1978. Pluto's known characteristics are: mass $0{\cdot}125 \times 10^{23}$ kg; radius 1137 km/706 mi; mean density 2·0 g/cm^3; inclination of equator 122°; rotational period 6·387 days; orbital period 248·0 years; eccentricity of orbit 0·249; mean distance from the Sun 39·48 AU. It is an extremely difficult object to study telescopically. It is probably similar to Neptune's largest moon, Triton, and has a notably low density, suggesting the admixture of significant quantities of methane ice in its make-up. There is a thin atmosphere of methane gas, and evidence for distinct reflectivity differences on the surface. Surface temperatures are c.55K.

Pluto (mythology) In Greek mythology, originally the god of wealth, **Plutos**; but Hades was also called Pluton, 'the Rich One', perhaps to avoid naming him. The name later became a synonym for Hades.

plutocracy A political system ruled by the wealthy. It is difficult to identify any example of a country that has strictly been a plutocracy (though the Venetian republic probably comes closest), and no set of rulers would ever claim to be plutocrats. The label is commonly used in a looser sense to mean a government heavily influenced by wealth, or as a term of abuse.

plutonic rock An igneous rock which has a coarse grain size because of the slow crystallization of magma at depth in the Earth's crust. Granites and gabbros are typical plutonic rocks.

plutonium Pu, element 94, essentially a synthetic element, density 19·8 g/cm^3, melting point 641°C. It was first prepared in a nuclear reactor in 1940 by a deuteron bombardment of uranium. Its most important isotope (^{239}Pu) has a half-life of nearly 25 000 years. It forms an extensive series of compounds with oxidation states +3, +4, and +6, but is mainly important as a fissile nuclear fuel.

Plymouth (Montserrat) [**plim**uhth] 16°44N 62°14W, pop (1997e) 3500 (pre-disaster). Former port and capital town of Montserrat, Lesser Antilles, E Caribbean; on the SW tip of the island; tourism, crafts, agricultural trade; abandoned after 1997 volcano eruption, with new buildings at Brades Estate, NW Montserrat.

Plymouth (UK) [**plim**uhth] 50°23N 4°10W, pop (2001e) 240 700. Seaport and (from 1998) unitary authority in Devon, SW England, UK; on Plymouth Sound, at the confluence of the Tamar and Plym Rivers, 340 km/211 mi SW of London; home port of Sir Francis Drake; Pilgrim Fathers set out from here in the *Mayflower* (1620); much rebuilding after severe bombing in World War 2; a major base for the Royal Navy; ferry links to Santander (Spain), Roscoff, and St Malo; railway; airfield; University of Plymouth (1992, formerly Polytechnic of the South West); light industries; Plymouth Hoe, where Drake is said to have finished his game of bowls before leaving to fight the Spanish Armada; Eddystone Lighthouse 22 km/14 mi offshore; navy week (Aug); football league team, Plymouth Argyle (Pilgrims).

Plymouth (USA) [**plim**uhth] 41°57N 70°40W, pop (2000e) 51 700. Seat of Plymouth Co, SE Massachusetts, USA; on Plymouth Bay; first permanent European settlement in New England, founded by Pilgrims in 1620; railway; fishing, textiles, rope, tourism; Plymouth Rock, replica *Mayflower II*, 'living history' community at Plimouth Plantation.

Plymouth Brethren A religious sect founded by a group of Christian evangelicals in 1829 in Dublin, Ireland. It spread to England, where in 1832 a meeting was established at Plymouth, Devon. Millenarian in outlook, the sect is characterized by a simplicity of belief, practice, and style of life based on the New Testament. By 1848 they had split into the 'Open' and the 'Exclusive' Brethren.

Plynlimon Fawr [plin**lim**on **vowr**] 52°28N 3°47W. Mountain rising to 752 m/2467 ft on the Cardiganshire–Powys border, C Wales, UK; 23 km/14 mi NE of Aberystwyth.

Plzeň [**puhl**zen], Ger **Pilsen** 49°40N 13°10E, pop (2000e) 176 000. Modern industrial capital of Západočeský region, Czech Republic; at junction of Uhlava, Uslava, Radbuza and Mže Rivers, SW of Prague; railway; beer (Pilsen lager), metallurgy, aircraft, armaments, motor vehicles, chemicals, clothing.

PMS; PMT *premenstrual syndrome / tension*

pneumatophore [nyoo**mat**ofaw(r)] A root with numerous lenticels which projects into the air some distance from the plant. It aids aeration of the root system in plants such as mangroves, which grow in swampy or water-logged ground.

pneumococcus [nyoomoh**kok**us] A common name for the bacterium *Streptococcus pneumoniae*, one of the causative agents of pneumonia. (Kingdom: Monera. Family: Streptococcaceae.)

pneumoconiosis [nyoomohkony**oh**sis] A lung disease caused by the inhalation of air containing fine particles, which are dispersed throughout the lungs and cause progressive scarring (*fibrosis*). A common industrial disorder, it occurs among coal and other miners and those working with silica and asbestos. It leads to a cough and progressive shortness of breath.

pneumonia [nyoo**moh**nia] Inflammation of the lungs from infection by micro-organisms, usually bacteria or viruses. In contrast to bronchitis, which affects the airways, the infection involves the alveoli deep in the lungs, where oxygen exchange normally takes place. The alveoli become inflamed, and fill with fluid and inflammatory cells. This impairs gaseous exchange, and a fall in the oxygen content of the blood occurs. It is usually an acute illness of sudden onset, with shortness of breath, fever, a productive cough, haemoptysis, and pleurisy. When the inflammatory reaction involves one or more lobes or parts of a lobe, the pneumonia is referred to as **lobar pneumonia**. A further type is **bronchopneumonia**, where patches of infection are scattered throughout both lungs.

pneumothorax [nyoomoh**thaw**raks] The presence of air in the space between the two layers of membrane covering each lung (the *pleural space*). The resulting increase in pressure around the lung prevents it from expanding properly, and may cause it to collapse completely. The air may enter the pleural space from the lung through an area of weakness (*spontaneous pneumothorax*) or be introduced from the outside through a wound in the chest wall.

Po, River [poh], ancient **Padus**, Gr **Eridanos** River in N Italy, rising in the Cottian Alps at Monviso near the French frontier; flows generally E to enter the Adriatic Sea, 56 km/35 mi S of Venice; length 652 km/405 mi; longest river in Italy; its valley is the most fertile agricultural region in the country; irregular flow, tending to silt up and alter its course; artificial embankments below Piacenza since ancient times.

Pobedy, Peak [pobedee] 42°25N 80°15E. Highest peak in the Tian Shan range, on the China–Kyrgyzstan frontier; height, 7439 m/24 406 ft.

Pocahontas [pohka**hon**tas], personal name **Matoaka** (1595–1617) American-Indian princess, born near Jamestown, Virginia, USA, the daughter of Powhatan. An American folk heroine, she helped maintain peace between the colonists and Indians, and saved the life of English adventurer John Smith when he was at the mercy of her tribe. In 1612 she embraced Christianity and was baptized **Rebecca**. The following year she married **John Rolfe** (1585–1622), and in 1616 came with him to England, where she was received by royalty. She died of smallpox, and left one son; several Virginia families claim descent from her.

pochard [**poh**cherd] A duck of the worldwide tribe Aythyini (15 species), comprising the diving-duck genera *Aythya* and *Netta*. It nests on the ground.

Pockels cell *electro-optic effects*

pocket borough British parliamentary boroughs, especially before the First Reform Act (1832), where the electorate was so small that the local landed proprietor had the borough 'in his pocket' – that is, he was able to return his own nominee. The number of voters in such boroughs was usually very small, making control easier. The number of seats controlled by leading landowners was an indication of their political power in the 18th-c.

pocket gopher A squirrel-like rodent, native to North and Central America; rat-like with large head and strong jaws; cheeks infolded as fur-lined 'pockets'; digs burrows with incisor teeth; inhabits open country; also known as **pouched rat** or **gopher**. (Family: Geomyidae, 34 species.)

Podgorica [podgoritsa], formerly **Titograd** (1946–92) 42°28N 19°17E, pop (2000e) 120 000. Capital of Montenegro on R Morava, N of L Scutari; badly damaged in World War 2; originally named after Marshal Tito; airfield; railway; university (1973); aluminium, metalwork, furniture, tobacco; birthplace of Diocletian.

Podgorniy, Nikolay Victorovich [pod**gaw(r)**nee] (1903–83) Soviet statesman, party official, and chairman of the Presidium of the Supreme Soviet (1965–77), born in Karlovka, EC Ukraine. In 1930 he joined the Communist Party, and after World War 2 took a leading role in the economic reconstruction of the liberated Ukraine. He held various senior posts (1950–65), and after the dismissal of Khrushchev (1964) became chairman of the Presidium. He was relieved of his office in 1977 and replaced by Brezhnev.

podiatry [po**di**yatree] *chiropody*

Poe, Edgar Allan (1809–49) Poet and story writer, born in Boston, Massachusetts, USA. Orphaned by the age of three, he was adopted by John Allan (1815–20) and brought up partly in England, UK. He began to write poetry, publishing *Tamerlane and other Poems* in 1827. He became a journalist in Richmond, VA, then settled in Philadelphia, PA, where he worked for literary magazines. He published *Tales of the Grotesque and Arabesque* in 1840, and several short stories, notably 'The Murders in the Rue Morgue' (1841), the first detective story. His weird and fantastic stories, dwelling by choice on the horrible, were both original and influential. In 1844 he moved to New York City, where his poem 'The Raven' (1845) won him immediate fame. His wife died in 1847, after which he wrote little. He became mentally disturbed, and attempted suicide in 1848.

poetic licence The poet's practice of taking liberty with known facts in the interests of telling a more interesting or more effective story. The historical Hotspur was 20 years older than Prince Henry; in *Henry IV*, for dramatic purposes, Shakespeare makes them the same age. The term can also refer to licence taken, for poetic effect, with the rules of grammar.

Poet Laureate A poet appointed by the British sovereign with the duty (no longer obligatory) of writing verse upon significant royal and national occasions. The first was John Dryden, who held office in 1668–88. From then until the 19th-c the post was held by inferior poets, but it gained great prestige with the tenure (1850–96) of Alfred, Lord Tennyson. The post is now also recognized in the USA.

poetry (Gr *poiein* 'to make') Originally, any creative literary work; the term is still so defined in Shelley's *Defence of Poetry* (1821). With the development and diversification of literary forms, 'poetry' came to be used for metrical composition in any mode, as distinct from writing in prose. But the weakening of such distinctions (with the prose poem and the poetic novel) has meant that a strict separation is not maintainable, the only evident distinction being between prose and verse. The term therefore has resumed an evaluative rather than descriptive significance, and is often used for any literary work of a distinctly imaginative or elaborate kind, or indeed (by extension), the lyrical mode in any other art form. The theory and practice of poetry, concerning itself with such fundamental questions as what poetry is, what it does, and how it should be written, is known as **poetics**.

Pogonophora [pogo**no**fera] *beardworm*

Pohnpei *Ponape*

poikilotherm [poy**ki**lohtherm] An animal that has no internal mechanism for regulating body temperature, so that it fluctuates with changes in ambient temperatures. It is often termed *cold-blooded*, but body temperatures may be maintained at a high level as a result of activity, or by behaviour patterns such as basking.

Poincaré, (Jules) Henri [pwĩkaray] (1854–1912) Mathematician, born in Nancy, NE France, the cousin of Raymond Poincaré. He studied at Paris, where he became professor in 1881. He was eminent in physics, mechanics, and astronomy, and contributed to many fields of mathematics. He created the theory of automorphic functions, using new ideas from group theory, non-Euclidean geometry, and complex function theory. The origins of the theory of chaos are in a famous paper of 1889 on real differential equations and celestial mechanics. Many of the basic ideas in modern topology, triangulation, and homology are due to him. He gave influential lecture courses on such topics as thermodynamics, and almost anticipated Einsteins's theory of special relativity, showing that the Lorentz transformations form a group. In his last years he published several

Poland

Polish **Polska**, official name **The Republic of Poland**

Local name Polska

Timezone GMT +1

Area 312 683 km²/120 695 sq mi

Population total (2002e) 38 644 000

Status Republic

Date of independence 1918

Capital Warsaw

Language Polish (official)

Ethnic groups Polish (99%), Ukrainian, Belorussian, and Jewish minorities

Religions Roman Catholic (94%), small Jewish and Muslim minorities

Physical features Part of the great European plain, with the Carpathian and Sudetes Mts (S) rising in the High Tatra to 2499 m/ 8199 ft at Mt Rysy; Polish plateau in N, cut by the Bug, San, and Wisła (Vistula) rivers; richest coal basin in Europe in the W (Silesia); flat Baltic coastal area; forests cover 20% of land.

Climate Continental climate, with severe winters, hot summers; average annual temperatures -4°C (Jan), 19°C (Jul) in Warsaw; average annual rainfall 550 mm/22 in.

Currency 1 Złoty (Zl) = 100 groszy

Economy Nearly 50% of the land under cultivation; major producer of coal; zinc, lead, sulphur; shipbuilding, machinery, vehicles, electrical equipment, textiles.

GDP (2002e) $373·2 bn, per capita $9700

Human Development Index (2002) 0·833

History Emergence as a powerful Slavic group in 11th-c; united with Lithuania, 1569; divided between Prussia, Russia, and Austria, 1772, 1793, 1795; semi-independent state after Congress of Vienna, 1815; incorporated into the Russian Empire; after World War 1, declared an independent Polish state, 1918; partition between Germany and the USSR, 1939; invasion by Germany, 1939; major resistance movement, and a government in exile during World War 2; People's Democracy established under Soviet influence, 1944; rise of independent trade union, Solidarity, 1980; state of martial law imposed, 1981–3; loss of support for communist government and major success for Solidarity in 1989 elections; proclaimed Polish Republic, 1989, and constitution amended to provide for a bicameral National Assembly.

Head of State
1989–90 Wojciech Jaruzelski
1990–5 Lech Wałęsa
1995– Alexander Kwasniewski

Head of Government
1989–91 Tadeusz Mazowiecki
1991 Jan Krzysztof Bielecki
1991–2 Jan Olszewski
1992 Waldemar Pawlak
1992–3 Hanna Suchocka
1993–5 Waldemar Pawlak
1995–6 Jozef Oleksy
1996–7 Wlodzimierz Cimoszewicz
1997–2001 Jerzy Buzek
2001– Leszek Miller

books on the philosophy of science and scientific method, and was also well known for his popular expositions of science.

Poincaré, Raymond (Nicolas Landry) [pwĩkaray] (1860–1934) French statesman, prime minister (1912–13, 1922–4, 1926–9), and president (1913–20), born in Bar-le-Duc, NE France. He studied law, then became a deputy (1887) and senator (1903), held ministerial posts in public instruction, foreign affairs, and finance, was three times premier, and president of the Third Republic during World War 1. He occupied the Ruhr in 1923, and his national union ministry averted ruin in 1926.

poinsettia [poynsetia] A deciduous shrub native to Mexico (*Euphorbia pulcherrima*). The flower is in fact a specialized inflorescence (*cyathium*) with large vermilion bracts resembling petals. Pot plants are commonly treated with growth retardant to retain shape and stature. (Family: Euphorbiaceae.)

Pointe-à-Pitre [pwĩt a **pee**truh] 16°14N 61°32W, pop (2000e) 105 000. Seaport and capital town of Guadeloupe, on SW coast of island of Grande-Terre; largest town in Guadeloupe; airport; commercial centre, agricultural trade, tourism.

Pointe-Noire [pwĩt nwah(r)] 4°48S 11°53E, pop (2000e) 552 800. Seaport in Kouilou province, SW Congo, W Africa; on the Atlantic coast 385 km/239 mi. WSW of Brazzaville; W terminus of railway from Brazzaville; harbour facilities begun in 1934, completed after 1945; airfield; centre of Congo's oil industry; oil refining, banking, timber, shoes.

pointer A sporting dog belonging to one of several breeds developed to detect game; stands rigidly, like a statue, with the muzzle pointing towards the prey animal.

Pointers *Plough, the*

Pointillism *Divisionism*

point-of-sale (POS) terminal The name given to a special kind of computer-controlled till containing a barcode reader and links to a central computer. The barcode of a product is read by the terminal, the type and the price of good is identified by the central computer, and this data is communicated to the terminal. The shopper receives a printout of goods bought with prices, and the central computer records the details of all the items which have been sold and – if an account card is used – of the customers who have bought them.

point-to-point An event featuring horse races for amateur riders over a cross-country course, normally on farmland. They are organized by hunts, and the horses used are regular hunting horses. Original courses went from one point to another, hence the name, but are now often over circular or oval courses with a mixture of artificial and natural fences.

Poiret, Paul [pwaray] (1879–1944) Fashion designer, born in Paris, France. The son of a cloth merchant, he started to make sketches and sell them, eventually joining Jacques Doucet in 1896, and later Worth. In 1904 he set up on his own. He loosened and softened women's clothes, producing a more natural outline; his 'hobble' skirt became famous. In 1914 he was the first president of Le Syndicat de Défence de la Grande Couture Française, formed to protect the copyright of couturiers.

poise [pwahz] *viscosity*

poison A chemical substance that is harmful to the body if ingested, inhaled, or inoculated. Damage may occur by a variety of different processes and may happen acutely or gradually over time with repeated exposure. The poison may be an artificial chemical, a naturally occurring element, or an organic substance derived from a bacterium, animal, or plant. Many drugs that are therapeutic at the correct dose are poisonous at high doses. Examples include carbon monoxide, which prevents the blood from transporting oxygen if inhaled; cyanide, strychnine, and arsenic, which are sometimes used with malicious intent; paracetamol, which in high doses damages the liver; and lead, which causes a variety of adverse effects in children with prolonged exposure.

poison-arrow frog *arrow-poison frog*

poison gas Chemical munitions fired in artillery shells or released from containers which spread toxic or disabling gases onto the battlefield. Such gases (used in World War 1) included mustard, phosgene, and chlorine.

poison ivy A shrub or woody vine, native to North America (*Rhus toxicodendron*); a very variable plant, the leaves with three leaflets, smooth and glossy or hairy, toothed or lobed; flowers white. Plants which form erect shrubs and have leaves blunt-tipped and lobed to resemble oak leaves are often called **poison oak**, regarded as a separate species by some authorities. All parts produce a resin containing the chemical urushinol, which is poisonous to the touch, causing severe dermatitis. The resin is non-volatile, and can be carried on clothing, soil, and even smoke, and take effect far from the plant itself. (Family: Anacardiaceae.)

poison oak *poison ivy*

Poisson, Siméon Denis [pwasõ] (1781–1840) Mathematician, born in Pithiviers, C France. He studied medicine, then turned to mathematics, studying under Laplace and Lagrange, and became professor at the Ecole Polytechnique in 1806. He is known for his research into celestial mechanics, electromagnetism, and also probability, where he established the law governing the distribution of rare and randomly occurring events (the *Poisson distribution*).

Poisson's ratio The (negative) ratio of strain in a direction perpendicular to an applied stress to the strain in the direction of the stress; symbol μ, expressed as a number; stated by Siméon Poisson. It expresses the decrease in diameter of a rod stretched lengthways. Typical values are between 0·1 and 0·4.

Poitier, Sidney [pwatyay] (1924–) Actor and director, born in Miami, Florida, USA. A student at the American Negro Theater in New York City, he appeared on stage and in films before making his Hollywood debut in 1950. Cast mainly in supporting roles, he won an Oscar for *Lilies of the Field* (1963), and became the cinema's first African-American superstar. Handsome and unassuming, he brought dignity to the portrayal of noble and intelligent characters in such films as *In the Heat of the Night* (1967) and *Guess Who's Coming to Dinner* (1967). During the 1970s he also began to direct, producing a number of lowbrow comedies such as *Stir Crazy* (1980) and *Ghost Dad* (1990). He returned to acting after a 10-year absence, appearing in *Shoot to Kill* (1988), *Little Nikita* (1988), *Sneakers* (1992), and *One Man, One Vote* (1997). In 2002 he received an honorary Oscar.

Poitiers [pwatyay] 46°35N 0°20E, pop (2000e) 86 300. Market town and capital of Vienne department, W France; 160 km/100 mi ESE of Nantes; Roman settlement; former capital of ancient province of Poitou; site of French defeat by English (1356); road and railway junction; bishopric; university (1431); chemicals, hosiery, trade in honey, wine, wool; 4th-c Baptistry (France's oldest Christian building), cathedral (12th–13th-c), Church of Notre-Dame-de-la-Grande (11th–12th-c), town hall (1869–76) containing the Musée des Beaux-Arts, Romanesque Church of St-Hilaire-le-Grand (11th–12th-c).

Poitou [pwatoo] Former province in W France, now occupying the departments of Vendée, Deux-Sèvres, and Vienne; chief town, Poitiers; held by England until 1369.

poker A gambling card game for two to eight players which started in the USA in the 19th-c. The object is to get (or convince your opponents that you have) a better hand than theirs. Hands are ranked, the best being a Royal Flush, ie 10–jack–queen–king–ace all of the same suit. There are several varieties of poker, the most popular being 5-card draw, 5-card stud, and 7-card stud.

pokeweed A herbacious perennial, native to North America (*Phytolacca americana*); stems c.2 m/6½ ft; leaves oval; flowers small, white, 4-lobed, in dense spikes; berries dark purple with poisonous seeds. The leaves are used in salads. The berries yield a red dye, hence the alternative name, **red ink plant**. (Family: Phytolaccaceae.)

Pokhara Valley [pohkara] Valley in Nepal, C Asia, 203 km/126 mi NW of Kathmandu; town of Pokhara at an altitude of 913 m/2995 ft; centre of one of Nepal's Development Regions; dominated by the Himalayas, notably Machhapuchhre, height 7993 m/26 223 ft; road and air flights from Kathmandu; several lakes; fishing, boating, trekking.

Poland *p.1215*

Poland, Partitions of Agreements between Russia, Austria, and Prussia to partition and take over Poland in the late 18th-c. There were three partitions (1772, 1793, 1795), under the provisions of which Poland lost its independent statehood, and its territories were divided between the three empires. Throughout the 19th-c, the Poles constantly struggled for national liberation and political autonomy. In the first Partition, a constitution was imposed which safeguarded against Polish resurgence. Education was completely modernized. In the second Partition, Russian armies occupied all of E Poland, with the Prussians occupying the W. In 1794 Polish forces won temporary victory over the Russians; however, the Poles were outnumbered. The third Partition carved up the remaining Polish territory, Russia gaining one-half and Prussia and Austria one-quarter each.

Polanski, Roman [polanskee] (1933–) Polish film-maker, born in Paris, France. An actor on radio and in the theatre, he attended the State Film School in Łódź (1954–9), making a number of short films. His feature-length debut, *Nóz w Wodzie* (1962, Knife in the Water), brought him international recognition, and he later worked in London, Paris and Los Angeles on such films as *Repulsion* (1965), *Rosemary's Baby* (1968), *Tess* (1979), *Frantic* (1988), *Bitter Moon* (1992), *Death and the Maiden* (1995), *The Ninth Gate* (1999), and *The Pianist* (2002, Cannes Palme d'Or; BAFTA; Oscar). A traumatic life that includes his internment in a German concentration camp, where his mother died, and the horrifying murder of his second wife, actress **Sharon Tate** (1943–69), has been reflected in his artistic concern with alienation, and the understanding of evil. On stage, he has directed *Lulu* (1974) and *Rigoletto* (1976) and acted in *Amadeus* (1981) and *Metamorphosis* (1988).

Polanyi, Michael [polanyee] (1891–1976) Physical chemist and social philosopher, born in Budapest, Hungary. He studied there and at Karlsruhe, lectured at Berlin, emigrated to Britain after Hitler's rise to power, and was professor of physical chemistry (1933–48) and of social studies (1948–58) at Manchester. He did notable work on reaction kinetics and crystal structure, and wrote much on the freedom of scientific thought, philosophy of science, and social science.

polarization

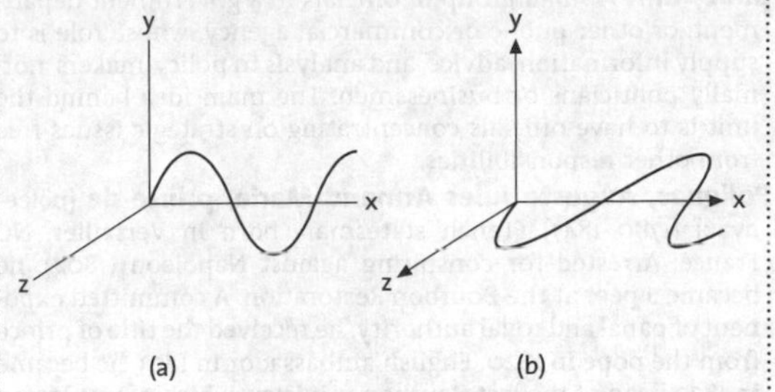

A property of (transverse) waves in which wave oscillations occur in a direction which is either constant or varies in a well-defined way. Illustration (a) shows a wave moving in x direction along a rope, polarized in the y direction, and illustration (b) in the z direction. These are both linear polarizations, since each portion of rope moves up and down in straight lines. General linear polarization can be represented as a sum of x and z polarizations, not necessarily in equal amounts. The x and z polarized waves may be combined such that they are not in step, ie their phases differ. The y polarized wave may lead the x wave by a phase difference of $\pi/2$, corresponding to elliptical polarization, ie when looking back along the direction of motion, the rope traces out an ellipse. The precise shape of the ellipse depends on the phase difference and amplitudes of the two waves. A special case is equal amplitude linear waves, differing in phase by $\pi/2$, which gives circular polarization. If, when looking back along the direction of motion, the rope appears to move clockwise, the polarization is described as right circular; if anticlockwise, it is left circular. A plate with a slit cut in it placed in the path of a wave will allow that portion of the wave in the direction of the slit to pass; the slit acts as a polarizer. Corresponding polarization effects to those oberved in the rope can be seen elsewhere. Polarization in electromagnetic radiation (including light) is dictated by the electric part of the wave. Skylight, reflected light, and scattered light are all (partially) polarized.

polar bear A bear native to the Arctic ice pack and surrounding seas (*Thalarctos maritimus*); white with long neck and small head; swims well; eats mainly seals, also small mammals, birds, reindeer (can outrun reindeer over short distances), fish, vegetation.

Polar Circle *Arctic Circle*

polar co-ordinates In mathematics, a method of determining the position of a point P by its distance r from a pole O and the angle θ between OP and a base line. This system is particularly convenient for points related to one fixed point, eg the polar equation of a circle centre O is merely $r = a$; the polar equation of a circle passing through O, base line the diameter through O, is $r = 2a \cos \theta$. Loops and similar curves have easy polar equations, eg $r = a \sin n\theta$.

polar front The main area of frontal weather systems in the N Pacific and N Atlantic. It forms the boundary between polar (cold) and subtropical (warmer) air masses, along which depressions or cyclones develop. The position of the front is associated with the polar jet stream, and shifts according to season. In winter it is further S (40°–50°N), and frontal activity is responsible for the cold, wet weather of N Europe. In summer it migrates N, and its location is more variable.

polarimetry An analytic technique in which linearly polarized light is passed through an optically active sample, and the degree of rotation of the plane of polarization is measured. It is used especially in chemistry and biology to identify and measure concentrations of transparent solutions, such as sugar solutions.

Polaris [polahris] The brightest star in the constellation Ursa Minor, currently lying (by chance) within 1° of the N celestial pole; also called the **Pole Star**. Its altitude is approximately equal to the latitude of the observer. This star was much used for simple navigation.

Polaris missile [pohlahris] A first-generation US submarine-launched ballistic missile under development from the mid-1950s. The US Navy's first Polaris deterrent patrol was made in 1960, and the system was operational with the Royal Navy in 1968. It is no longer operational with the US Navy, but a modified version with three separate warheads and advanced penetration aids continued with the Royal Navy's four Polaris-equipped submarines, until the Trident system began to replace them during the 1990s.

polarity In chemistry, a permanent property of a substance, implying an inherent separation of electric charge. The notion contrasts with **polarizability**, which is an induced property of a substance.

polarity therapy A form of therapy devised by Randolph Stone (1890–1983), a student of osteopathy, naturopathy, and chiropractic, who taught that the body has five energy centres corresponding to the five elements (earth, water, fire, air, and ether), and that most illnesses are caused by a blockage in the flow of energy between these centres. He used exercise, massage, and manipulation to stimulate the imbalance of life energy in the body and to remove any blockages caused by bad living or an adverse environment. As well as physical therapy, present-day practitioners employ counselling to develop self-awareness and positive attitudes to the body, and also give dietary advice to eliminate toxins and maintain a healthy lifestyle.

polarization *see panel*

polarizing filter A filter which transmits only light polarized in a specific dimension. It is used in general photography to suppress specular reflections from non-metallic surfaces and to darken blue skies. Other applications include stereoscopy, stress analysis, and mineral structures in photomicrography.

polar molecule *electric dipole moment*

polarography The study of the relationship between current and voltage in an electrochemical cell. Generally, the voltage of a working electrode relative to a standard reference is changed systematically in an electrolysis cell while the current passing is measured. Sharp rises in current at particular voltages are characteristic of specific ions in solution, and may be used in both qualitative and quantitative analysis.

Polaroid **1** A trade name for doubly refracting material; developed by US physicist Edwin Land in 1938. A dyed plastic sheet is strained so as to align its molecules, thus making it transmit light preferentially, ie linearly polarized in one direction, otherwise it is absorbed. It is familiar in sun-glasses to reduce the glare from light polarized on reflection, and is also used in some optical equipment.
2 The trade name of an instant photography system developed by Land for black-and-white (1947) and colour (1963). The film is processed with viscous chemical reacting substances in integral pods applied inside the camera immediately after exposure or by a separate machine.

polder [polder] A Dutch term for a flat area of land reclaimed from the sea or a river flood-plain, and protected from flooding by dykes (eg the partial reclamation of the Zuider Zee in The Netherlands). They are often below sea level, so pumping is needed to keep them clear of water.

Pole, Reginald, Cardinal (1500–58) Roman Catholic archbishop, born at Stourton Castle, Staffordshire, C England, UK. He studied at Oxford and Padua, received several Church posts, and was at first high in Henry VIII's favour; but after opposing the king on divorce, he left for Italy, and lost all his preferments. In 1536 the pope made him a cardinal, and he served on a commission that looked at abuses within the Church, recommending reforms in *Consilium de emendanda ecclesia* (1537, Plan for Church Reform). In 1554, in the reign of Mary I, he returned to England as papal legate. He became one of her most powerful advisers, returned the country to Rome, and became Archbishop of Canterbury.

pole *magnetic poles; Poles*

polecat A mammal of family Mustelidae; resembles a large weasel (length, 60 cm/24 in); dark with pale marks on face and ear tips; two species: **European polecat**, **foul marten**, **foumart**, or **fitchet** (*Mustela putorius*); **steppe polecat** (*Mustela eversmanni*) from Asia. The name is also used for the **marbled polecat** of genus *Vormela*; for the zorilla; and (in the USA) for skunks of genus *Mephitis*.

Poles The two diametrically opposite points at which the Earth's axis cuts the Earth's surface; known as the **geographical poles**. The North Pole is covered by the Arctic Ocean, and the South Pole by the land mass of Antarctica. The **magnetic poles** are the positions towards which the needle of a magnetic compass will point. They differ from the geographical poles by an angle known as the *declination* or *magnetic variation*, which itself varies at different points of the Earth's surface and at different times. The South Pole was first reached by Amundsen on 14 December 1911, a month before the British team, led by Scott, which arrived on 17 January 1912; the North Pole was first reached by Robert E Peary on 6 April 1909.

Pole Star *Polaris*

pole vault An athletics field event in which competitors attempt to vault, with the aid of a flexible pole, over a bar set at a predetermined height without knocking the bar off. The person clearing the greatest height or (if two or more tie) the person with the fewest misses at lower heights is the winner. The height of the bar is gradually increased, and competitors are allowed three attempts to clear each new height; they are eliminated if they fail. The current world record for men is 6·14 m/20 ft 1·68 in, achieved by Sergey Bubka (1963–) of Ukraine in 1994 at Sestriere, Italy; for women, it is 4·81 m/15 ft 9·37 in, achieved by Stacy Dragila (1971–) of the USA in 2001 at California, USA.

Poliakoff, Stephen [polyakof] (1952–) Playwright and film director, born in London, UK. He studied at Cambridge, and started to write plays as a teenager. A run of his plays produced by the Bush Theatre, including *Hitting Town* and *City Sugar* (both 1975) established him as a prolific, original playwright with an instinct for powerful contemporary metaphors. He was writer-in-residence at the National Theatre (1976–7), and had several plays produced by the Royal Shakespeare Company, including *Shout Across the River* (1978), *Breaking the Silence* (1984), and *Playing with Trains* (1989). Later plays include *Sienna Red* (1992), *Blinded by the Sun* (1996), and *Sweet Panic* (2003). He wrote and directed the film *Close My Eyes* (1991), and the television plays *Caught on a Train* (1980), *Shooting the Past* (1999), *Perfect Strangers* (2001), and *The Lost Prince* (2003).

police The body of civilian officers responsible for and concerned with the enforcement of law and maintenance of civil order. The police receive their authority from the legislature and act in the public interest. Some police forces have a role in both the prosecution and the investigation of crimes, but in most countries, particularly Western countries, these tend to be separated, with the police concentrating on the prevention and investigation of crime, and a body such as the Crown Prosecution Service in England and Wales, the Procurator Fiscal Service in Scotland, or the District Attorney in the USA taking the decision independently whether to prosecute. In addition to national forces, there are a number of specialized police forces concerned with riot control or the security and protection of particular areas, such as military establishments or railway stations. Most police services make a distinction between uniformed and plain-clothed operations. The former patrols the streets, while the latter are detectives who investigate crime in co-operation with intelligence bodies. In 1984 in the UK, the Police Complaints Authority was established by the Police and Criminal Evidence Act, to supervise complaints against the police.

policy unit A small group of officials in a government department, or other public or commercial agency, whose role is to supply information, advice, and analysis to policy-makers, normally politicians or businessmen. The main idea behind the unit is to have officials concentrating on strategic issues free from other responsibilities.

Polignac, Auguste Jules Armand Marie, prince de [poleenyak] (1780–1847) French statesman, born in Versailles, NC France. Arrested for conspiring against Napoleon (1804), he became a peer at the Bourbon Restoration. A committed exponent of papal and royal authority, he received the title of prince from the pope in 1820. English ambassador in 1823, he became in 1829 head of the last Bourbon ministry, which promulgated the Saint-Cloud Ordinances that cost Charles X his throne (1830). He was imprisoned until 1836, then lived in exile in England, returning in 1845 to Paris.

poliomyelitis [pohliohmiyeliytis] A disease due to a virus transmitted in contaminated food and water, particularly affecting children. It initially infects cells lining the intestine, causing a diarrhoeal illness. In 1% of cases, it then migrates to motor neurone cells in the spinal cord, the nerves that supply muscles. Destruction of these cells leads to paralysis that may affect a limb or the respiratory muscles, resulting in death. The disease was responsible for killing and disabling large numbers of people in the early 20th-c, when it was known as **infantile paralysis**. It has now been virtually eliminated by improved sanitation and the use of vaccines.

polis [polis, polays] (plural **poleis**) Conventionally translated 'city-state', the principal political and economic unit of classical Greece. There might be differences of political colouring between one polis and another. Some (eg Athens) were full-blown democracies, while others (eg Corinth, Thebes, Sparta) were more oligarchical in character. But all possessed the same basic organs of government – an assembly of male citizens, an advisory council, and elected executive officers. Always self-governing, they were usually economically self-sufficient as well.

Polish *Polish literature; Slavic languages*

Polish Corridor An area of formerly German territory granted to Poland by the Treaty of Versailles (1919). It linked the Polish heartland with the free city of Danzig, and gave Poland access to the Baltic Sea, but divided E Prussia from the rest of Germany. Its recovery was one of Hitler's aspirations during the late 1930s, and its invasion by Germany in 1939 led to the outbreak of World War 2.

Polish literature The *Bogurodzica*, an early 15th-c hymn to the Virgin, initiates a literature which reflects Polish history, at the crossroads (often the battleground) of East and West. The 'father of Polish literature', Rej (1509–69), bridged the mediaeval and early modern world, while Copernicus still wrote in Latin; the poet Jan Kochanowski (1530–84) was the first Renaissance figure. The 17th-c Baroque was reflected in the poetry of Jan Morsztyn (1621–93), the epic chronicles (1660–1) of Samuel Twardowski, and the memoirs of Jan Pasek (1636–1701). The later 18th-c was a period of intense activity, with the first theatre opening (in Warsaw) in 1765, and such writers as Ignacy Krasicki (1735–1801) and Julian Niemcewicz (1757–1841). The early 19th-c finds three great Romantic poets writing in exile: the national poet Adam Mickiewicz, Juliusz Slowaci (1808–49), and Zygmunt Krasiński (1812–59), while the Modernist precursor Cyprian Norwid (1821–83) endured both exile and neglect. Political realities ushered in the novel, in the hands of Eliza Orzeszkowa (1841–1910), Boleslaw Prus (1845–1912), and the epic narrator Henryk Sienkiewicż (Nobel Prize, 1905). The writers of Young Poland, before 1918, reflected the experimentalism of the time – among them the poet Jan Kasprowicz (1860–1926), the novelist Stefan Żeromski (1864–1925), and the innovatory dramatist Stanislaw Wyspiański (1868–1907). Between the wars, independent Poland produced many important novelists, including Maria Dąbrowska (1889–1965), Michal Choromański (1904–72), Witold Gombrowicz (1904–69), and Jerzy Andrzejewski (1909–83); also the poetry of Julian Tuwim (1894–1953) and the Surrealist theatre of Stanislaw Witkiewicz (1885–1939). Between 1945 and the end of communist rule, writers such as the novelist Tadeusz Konwicki (1926–), poets Zbigniew Herbert and Czeslaw Miłosz, the playwright Slawomir Mrożek (1930–), and Stanislaw Lem (1921–), with his prophetic science fiction, expressed an embattled but undefeated consciousness.

Polish swan *mute swan*

Politburo [**pol**itbyooroh] The Political Bureau of the Central Committee of the Communist Party of the Soviet Union; at various times, known as the **Presidium**. It was the highest organ of the party, and, therefore, of the entire Soviet political system. Elected by the Central Committee, there were twelve members plus seven candidate members who had no votes, but in practice membership was decided by the politburo itself under the General Secretary, who presided over it. Its functions may be compared to those of a cabinet, though its authority varied over the years, becoming more firmly established during the Brezhnev era.

political action committee A non-party organization in the USA, which contributes money to candidates for public office. Since 1971 each committee has been able to give only $5000 per election to each candidate. The committees are created by various organized interests, such as unions, trade associations, and groups with strong political beliefs. There is increasing concern about their 'buying' influence.

political correctness A pejorative term for the view which demands that all instances of real or perceived linguistic discrimination against social groups should be eradicated. The movement emerged strongly in the 1980s, espoused especially by US political liberals, and has focused on those aspects of language which seem to preserve demeaning attitudes towards disadvantaged or oppressed groups, such as the use of *man* to mean 'humanity' (thereby perpetuating the subordinate role of women) or the use of *black* with negative overtones (as in the idiom *be in my black books*). The most sensitive domains are to do with race (racism), gender (sexism), sexual affinity, ecology, and (physical or mental) personal development. The view was at first supported by many moderate members of progressive or activist groups, concerned with the rights of minorities, but by attracting hard-line extremists it has attracted increasing antagonism and ridicule (eg people who are less than beautiful might be described as 'aesthetically challenged'). The inflexible condemnation of 'incorrect' vocabulary has itself been condemned for its intolerance, reminding some of the 'thought police' of futuristic novels.

political economy The name given to economics in the late 18th-c and early 19th-c. The term has not been much used in modern times, apart from in professorial titles, reflecting the fact that the scope of economics is today much wider, dealing with many more issues than national economic affairs and the role of government. The name does however indicate that economics is not an exact science, but a social science which often has to take into account 'political' considerations.

political philosophy The philosophical study both of the concepts, values, and arguments used in political science and of the substantive issues involved in the exercise and distribution of political power. Among the leading theorists historically have been Plato, Aristotle, Augustine, Aquinas, Machiavelli, Hobbes, Locke, Marx, Rousseau, and Mill, addressing such issues as the nature of the state, the relations between Church and state, individual rights, democracy, and law and freedom. There has been a revival since the 1970s, associated with work on rights by American theorists such as Rawls, and with such themes as feminism, civil disobedience, and green issues.

political science The academic discipline which describes and analyses the operations of government, the state, and other political organizations, and any other factors which influence their behaviour, such as economics. A major concern is to establish how power is exercised, and by whom, in resolving conflict within society. There is a range of approaches, some of which draw upon other academic studies, such as sociology, economics, and psychology, and which can be regarded as subdisciplines of the subject. **Empirical analysis** draws conclusions by observing and generating data about state organizations and wider societal groupings and their interrelationships. **Political theory** (of which **political philosophy** is a subbranch) has two principal concerns: the clarification of values in order to demonstrate logically the purpose of political activity, and thereby the way in which society 'ought' to proceed (eg in allocating resources); and the rigorous derivation and testing of theories drawn from empirical research. In everyday life, **politics** focuses on the policies and actions of individuals and groups (**political parties**) as they compete for power at national or local levels. **Politicians** are those who are actively involved in conducting the business of government at some level: the notion is a wide-ranging one, and includes members of parliament, local councillors, senators, ministers of state, prime ministers, members of the House of Lords, members of a military junta, dictators, and others. When politicians act on behalf of a government, especially in relation to international affairs, they are often referred to as **statesmen** or **stateswomen**. This is how the latter term is used in the present encyclopedia, ie for those politicians who have achieved ministerial standing.

political sociology The academic study of the relationship between social structures and political behaviour. It seeks to explain political phenomena in terms of social factors, in particular social conflict and consensus. Its range of coverage is extensive and growing, having established itself in the latter half of the 20th-c as a separate field of study. Much of the work is based upon the comparative analysis of different countries.

politics *political science*

Polk, James K(nox) (1795–1849) US statesman and 11th president (1845–9), born in Mecklenburg Co, North Carolina, USA. Admitted to the bar in 1820, he entered Congress as a Democrat (1825), and became Governor of Tennessee (1839). During his presidency, Texas was admitted to the Union (1845), and after the Mexican War (1846–7) the USA acquired California and New Mexico. The Oregon boundary was settled by a compromise with England. He also condemned the anti-slavery agitation, and was committed to states' rights, a revenue tariff, and an independent treasury.

polka A quick dance of Bohemian origin, in duple metre, with an accent on the second beat. Performed by couples, it was a favourite 19th-c ballroom dance, and numerous examples were composed by the Strauss family.

poll *opinion poll*

Pollack, Sydney (1934–) Film director and producer, born in South Bend, Indiana, USA. He began as an actor, moved to television directing, and made his debut as a feature film director with *Slender Thread* (1965). Later films include *They Shoot Horses Don't They?* (1969), *Sabrina* (1995), and *Random Hearts* (1999). He received an Oscar nomination for Best Director in 1982 for *Tootsie*, and won two Oscars (as Best Director and Best Producer) in 1985 for *Out of Africa*. In 1998 he directed *Sliding Doors*, and in 1999 he played the part of Victor Ziegler in *Eyes Wide Shut*. He directed *Up at the Villa* in 2000.

pollack Cod-like fish (*Pollachius pollachius*) found in inshore waters of the N Atlantic from Norway to the Mediterranean; length up to 1·3 m/4¼ ft; lower jaw protrudes beyond upper; chin barbel absent; greenish-brown on back, sides pale yellow, underside white; feeds mainly on other fishes; taken commercially by net and on lines; also popular with sea anglers. (Family: Gadidae.)

Pollaiuolo, Antonio [poliy**woloh**] (c.1432–98) Goldsmith, medallist, metal-caster, and painter, born in Florence, NC Italy. He cast sepulchral monuments in St Peter's in Rome for Popes Sixtus IV and Innocent VIII. One of the first painters to study anatomy and apply it to his art, he was skilled in suggesting movement. His brother **Piero** (1443–96) was associated with him in his work.

pollen The male sex-cells of seed plants, produced in large numbers in the anthers of flowering plants and the pollen-sacs of gymnosperms. On reaching the stigma of a flower or the scale of a female cone, the pollen grain grows a tube through which its contents are transferred to fertilize the ovule. Pollen grains vary greatly in size, shape, and surface sculpturing, which may all play a part in dispersal. Wind-born pollen is smooth and light; that carried by insects is often heavier and sticky. The outer coat of the grain (*exine*) is very resistant to decay, and fossilized pollen can be used to investigate the vegetation of prehistoric times.

pollen analysis *palynology*

pollination The transfer of pollen from anther to ovary within a flower, necessary for fertilization and seed production. It is usually a complex and sophisticated process, demanding structural and physiological specialization within the flower, and often involving outside agents, principally insects, birds, wind, or water. The entire package of adaptations and modifications found in any particular flower may be referred to as the *pollination syndrome*. The control of outside agents such as animals may be achieved by the use of very specific signals from the flower (eg colour, scent) to stimulate responses only in specific pollinators, thus increasing the chances of successful transfer, and requiring relatively low pollen production. Inanimate agents such as wind and water are much more haphazard, and plants using them must produce larger amounts of pollen to ensure success. Pollination may occur between the stamens and ovary of the same flower, but in the interests of outbreeding, many species have one or more mechanisms to prevent this, including the spatial arrangement and differential ripening of the floral parts, and chemical compatability systems which prevent pollen of the wrong sort from fertilizing the ovules.

Pollock, (Paul) Jackson (1912–56) Artist, born in Cody, Wyoming, USA. He studied at the Art Students' League in New York City, and became the first exponent of Action Painting in America. His art developed from Surrealism to abstract art and the first drip paintings of 1947. This technique he continued with increasing violence and often on huge canvases, as in *One* (1950), which is 17 ft long. Other striking works include *No. 32* (1950), and the black and white *Echo and Blue Poles*. He was killed in a motor accident.

pollock *saithe*

poll tax *community charge*

pollution The direct or indirect introduction of a harmful substance into the environment. The degree of pollution depends on the nature and amount of the pollutant, and the location into which it is introduced; fertilizers become pollutants when used to excess, and when they become concentrated in run-off water entering streams. Different categories of pollution include air pollution (eg acid rain), freshwater pollution (eg discharge of chemical effluent from industry into rivers), marine pollution (eg oil spills from tankers), noise pollution (eg from aircraft), land pollution (eg the burial of toxic waste), and visual pollution (eg the intrusion of industry into an area of scenic beauty).

Pollux *Gemini*

pollywog *tadpole*

Polo, Marco (1254–1324) Merchant and traveller, born in Venice, NE Italy. After a previous visit to Kublai Khan in China (1260–9), his father and uncle made a second journey (1271–5), taking Marco with them. He became an envoy in Kublai Khan's service, and served as Governor of Yangzhou. He left China in 1292, returned to Venice (1295), and fought against the Genoese, but was captured. During his imprisonment, he compiled an account of his travels, *Il milione* (trans The Travels of Marco Polo), which became widely read. The book gives a vivid description of Kublai Khan and his palace, Chinese daily life, the Grand Canal and Yangtze, and many cities, including the unfinished Beijing. The historicity of his account has been questioned – he failed to mention several important features (such as the Great Wall), and there is in fact no record in Chinese archives of his presence or governorship there. His details could have come from Arab merchants.

polo A stick-and-ball game played on horseback by teams of four. When the side lines of the ground are boarded, the playing area measures 300 yd/274 m by 160 yd/146 m, making it the largest of all ball games. The object is to strike the ball with a hand-held mallet into the opposing goal, which measures 8 yd/7·3 m wide by 10 ft/3 m high. Each game is divided into 7-minute periods known as *chukkers*. The number of chukkers varies according to each competition. Polo was first played in C Asia c.500 BC, its name deriving from the Tibetan *pulu*. There are Chinese references from AD 710; emperors played from the 8th-c onwards; and a 10th-c emperor executed a critic.

polonaise A Polish dance in a moderate triple metre. It was used by many composers, but is chiefly associated with Chopin, whose 13 examples for piano express his intense patriotism. The dance itself dates from the 16th-c or earlier, when it was performed at peasant and court processions by couples arranged in line by rank.

Polonnaruwa [pohlonahruva] 7°56N 81°02E, pop (2000e) 14 600. Capital of Polonnaruwa district, Sri Lanka, on the N shore of L Parakrama Samudra; many buildings of the 11th–14th-c, when it was the island's capital; a world heritage site; King Parakrama Bahu's Palace, Kumara Pokuna; formerly fortified by three concentric walls.

Pol Pot [pol **pot**], also called **Saloth Sar** (1926–98) Cambodian politician and prime minister (1976–9), born in Kompong Thom Province, C Cambodia. He was active in the anti-French resistance under Ho Chi-Minh, and in 1964 joined the pro-Chinese Communist Party. He then studied in Paris (1949–53), worked as a teacher (1954–63), and became leader of the Khmer Rouge guerrillas, defeating Lon Nol's military goverment in 1976. As prime minister, he set up a totalitarian regime which caused the death, imprisonment, or exile of around 2 million. Overthrown in 1979, when the Vietnamese invaded Cambodia, he withdrew to the mountains to lead the Khmer Rouge forces. He announced his retirement in 1985, but continued to be an influential figure within the movement. He defected from the Khmer Rouge in 1996. Later he was blamed as sole perpetrator of genocide, and in 1997 he was captured by his former comrades. After a show trial deep in the Cambodian jungle he died while still in captivity, having been condemned to life imprisonment.

Poltava [poltahva] 49°35N 34°35E, pop (2000e) 314 000. Industrial capital city of Poltavskaya oblast, Ukraine, on R Vorskla; one of the oldest settlements in the Ukraine, known since the 7th-c; site of Swedish defeat by Peter the Great, 1709; railway; agricultural trade, machinery, metalworking, foodstuffs, clothing, glass; cathedral of the Krestovozdvizhenskii monastery (1689–1709).

poltergeist A disembodied spirit thought to be capable of causing unusual physical disturbances, such as movement and/or breakage of objects, malfunctioning of electrical devices, and loud raps. In some accounts, these events are portrayed as depending upon the presence of a particular living person (the 'agent' or 'focus').

Polunin, Slava [poloonin] (1950–) Mime artist and clown, born in Orel, W Russia. At age 17 he studied mime at St Petersburg and in the early 1980s he founded the Theatre of the Art of Modern Clowning. He has travelled around the world performing *Snowshow* (1993), a popular family entertainment which has received several awards.

polyamides Large molecules formed by the condensation polymerization of diamines with dicarboxylic acids, such as 1,6-diaminohexane, $H_2NCH_2CH_2CH_2CH_2CH_2CH_2NH_2$ with 1,6-hexanedioic acid (adipic acid) $HOOCCH_2CH_2CH_2CH_2COOH$ to give nylon. These complementary molecules give the same type of amide linkage as that found in natural protein fibres, such as silk and wool, where the monomers are amino acids.

polyanthus [polianthuhs] A garden hybrid (*Primula × polyanthus*) derived mainly from the primrose and the cowslip, with the large flowers of the former, borne in heads like the latter. (Family: Primulaceae.)

polyarchy A political term characterizing the processes and institutions of modern, Western, liberal democracies. The main features of polyarchies are opposition and the absence of strictly hierarchical organizations. They tend to be segmented, with people participating in political processes of direct interest to them; but universal elections remain of importance.

Polybius [polibius] (c.200–c.120 BC) Greek politician, diplomat, and historian, from Megalopolis in the Peloponnese, who wrote of the rise of Rome to world power status (264–146 BC). Only five of the original books survive. The 18 years he spent in Rome as a political hostage (168–150 BC) gave him a unique insight into Roman affairs, and led to lasting friendships with some of the great figures of the day, notably Scipio Aemilianus.

polycarbamates *polyurethanes*

Polycarp, St (c.69–c.155) Greek bishop of Smyrna who bridges the little-known period between the age of his master, the apostle John, and that of his own disciple, Irenaeus. His only extant writing is the *Epistle to the Philippians*, incomplete in the original Greek, but complete in a Latin translation. He visited Rome to discuss the question of the timing of Easter, and was martyred on his return to Smyrna – an event graphically described in an early document, *The Martyrdom of Polycarp*. Feast day 23 February.

polycentrism A political term, first used by the Italian Communist Party leader, Palmiro Togliatti (1893–1964) after the 20th Congress of the Soviet Communist Party (1956), to indicate the growing independence of communist parties from the Soviet Party after the Stalin era. The trend began in Yugoslavia under Tito, and was adopted to varying degrees by other national parties as a means of taking account of local conditions.

polychlorobiphenyls *PCBs*

polychromy In art, the practice of colouring sculpture; also in architecture, the employment of coloured marbles, bricks, flint, stone, etc on buildings for decorative effect.

Polyclitus or **Polycleitos** [polikliytus] (5th-c BC) Greek sculptor from Samos, Greece, a contemporary of Phidias, known for his statues of athletes, which were often copied. One of his greatest works is the bronze *Doryphorus* ('Spear Bearer').

Polycrates [polikrateez] (6th-c BC) Tyrant of Samos (540–522 BC). One of the earliest of Greek tyrants, he turned Samos into a major naval power, the ally of Egypt, Cyrene, and later Persia, and made her the cultural centre of the E Aegean. Among the poets who enjoyed his patronage was Anacreon.

polycythaemia / polycythemia [poleesiytheemia] An excessive number of circulating red blood cells. It arises as a result of oxygen deficiency, as occurs for example by living at high altitudes, and rarely as a spontaneous disease related to leukaemia.

polyembryony [poliembrionee] The formation of numerous embryos from a single fertilized egg (*zygote*), ovule, or other cell.

polyesters Large molecules formed by the condensation polymerization of dialcohols with dicarboxylic acids (eg ethylene glycol $HOCH_2CH_2OH$ with terephthalic acid $HOOC–C_6H_4–COOH$). Synthetic fibres include Terylene (ICI) and Dacron (Du Pont): they impart crease-resistant and easy-care properties to domestic textiles. Their high strength, abrasion resistance, and chemical inertness are also exploited industrially – for example, combined with other plastics and glass fibre, as reinforced plastic for construction.

polyethylene A family of thermoplastics of a waxy nature, made by subjecting ethene (ethylene) to high pressures at moderate temperatures. Commonly known as **polythene**, it was first produced commercially in 1939. Valuable as an insulator, it is easy to work into vessels with high chemical resistance, and was important in the development of radar.

polygamy A form of marriage where a person has more than one spouse at the same time. The concept includes *polygyny*, the most common, where a man has more than one wife, and *polyandry*, where a woman has more than one husband.

polygene [polijeen] A gene of small effect, acting in combination with many others. Variation in observable characteristics is of two types: *discrete* (eg blood groups A or O), where assignment is to one category or another; and *quantitative* (eg stature) where measurement is against a continuous scale without distinct categories. Inheritance of the latter type of character is largely under the control of polygenes.

polygon In mathematics, a plane figure whose boundaries are segments of straight lines. If there are n sides of the polygon, the sum of the interior angles is $(2n-4)$ right angles. A **regular polygon** has sides equal in length, and all the interior angles at the vertices are equal. A regular polygon with three sides is an equilateral triangle; one with four sides is a square. There is an infinite number of regular figures.

polyhedron In mathematics, a solid completely bounded by plane surfaces. It can be proved that there are only five regular polyhedra, those bounded by congruent regular polygons. If there are v vertices, e edges, f faces, and a angles in a polyhedron, $v + f - e = 2 - g$ (Euler's formula), and $a = 2e$, $a \geqslant 3f$, $v \leqslant e$, $f \leqslant \frac{2}{3}e$, $f \leqslant 2v-4$, where g is the genus of the surface. Polyhedra are of great importance in crystallography and mineralogy.

Polyhymnia [poleehimnia, polimnia] In Greek mythology, one of the Muses, associated with dancing or mime.

polymerase chain reaction (PCR) The exponential production of a double-stranded DNA fragment from a specific DNA template. The template is mixed with 5 and 3 oligonucleotide DNA primers of 20–40 base pairs in length which define the ends of the fragment, individual nucleotides, and a heat-stable enzyme called *DNA polymerase* (derived from bacteria that survive and grow in hot springs). Using temperatures which melt apart the two strands of the DNA helix, and then permit annealing of the primers to the DNA template, allowing the polymerase to work, the number of copies of the DNA increases as a chain reaction. RNA can also be used as a template, but a DNA copy must first be produced using the enzyme reverse transcriptase; this is called *RT-PCR*.

polymerization The forming of a large molecule, a **polymer**, by the combination of smaller ones (*monomers*). Combinations of two molecules are called **dimers**; of three, **trimers**. Small polymers (usually of three to ten monomers) are known as **oligomers**. The monomers may be all of the same type, as in polyethylene, or they may be two complementary molecules, as in polyester or polyamide formation. There are two main types of reaction: *condensation*, in which a side product is formed, and *addition*, in which it is not. Polymers may contain anything from 100 to over 10 000 monomer residues.

polymethylmethacrylate *Perspex*

polymorphism (biology) The coexistence of two or more genetically distinct forms of an organism within the same interbreeding population, where the frequency of the rarest type is not maintained by mutation alone. The polymorphism may be balanced and persist over many generations, or may be transient. Human eye colour is an example of a readily observable polymorphism, but there are many invisible polymorphisms detectable only by special techniques, such as DNA analysis.

polymorphism (chemistry) The existence of two or more substances with the same chemical composition but different crystal structures. Examples include graphite and diamond or calcite and aragonite.

polymyositis [polimiyohsiytis] A rare diffuse inflammatory disorder of muscle, connective tissue, and skin. An auto-immune process may be involved.

Polynesia A large triangular area in the EC Pacific extending from Hawaii in the N to New Zealand in the S and to Easter I in the E. Among other island groups, it includes Tuvalu (Ellice Is),

Tokelau, Samoa, Tonga, Cook Is, Marquesas Is, and Society Is (Tahiti). The striking cultural, linguistic, and physical similarities between the people of these islands are due to their common descent from the Lapita people who first settled in Tonga. Polynesians are typically of medium height, stocky build, with light-to-medium skin colour, wavy hair, and little body hair; there is a high rate of blood group N, a low rate of B, and an absence of Rh-negative.

polyneuropathy *neuropathy*

Polynices or **Polyneices** [poliniyseez] A Greek hero, the second son of Oedipus, who led the Seven against Thebes. Creon's refusal to bury him led eventually to the death of Antigone.

polynomial An algebraic expression containing several terms added to or subtracted from each other, eg $a + 2b - 3c$. If these terms are multiples of powers of a single variable, say x (eg $a_0x^n + a_1x^{n-1} + a_2x^{n-2} + ...a^n$, where $a_0 \neq 0$), the polynomial is said to be of degree n in x. A polynomial of degree 2 is a *quadratic*; of degree 3 is a *cubic*.

polyp (medicine) A small tumour growing from the lining surface of an organ, such as the large intestine, nose, or larynx. It may bleed and need surgical removal. Often benign, it may become malignant or recurrent.

polyp (zoology) The individual, soft-bodied, sedentary form of a coelenterate; body consists of a cylindrical trunk with an apical mouth surrounded by tentacles; attached basally in solitary forms, or to a branching tubular system in colonies. (Phylum: Cnidaria.)

polypeptide *peptide*

Polyphemus [polifeemus] In Greek mythology, one of the Cyclopes, who imprisoned Odysseus and some of his companions in his cave. They blinded his one eye, and told Polyphemus that 'No one' had hurt him. As a result, when he called on the other Cyclopes for help, and they asked who had attacked him, they did not understand his answer. Odysseus' band escaped by hiding under the sheep when they were let out of the cave to graze.

polyphony [polifonee] Music in more than one part. In general usage the term implies counterpoint, rather than simple chordal texture (**homophony**). One might thus talk of 'Renaissance polyphony' with reference to the Masses, motets, and madrigals of the 16th-c, but not of 'Romantic polyphony' with reference to 19th-c music as a whole, even though virtually all Romantic music is in the strictest sense polyphonic.

polyploidy [poliploydee] The condition in which an individual has more than the normal two sets of homologous chromosomes found in diploid organisms; particularly common in plants. It is caused by replication of the entire chromosome set within the nucleus, but without any subsequent nuclear division. It includes triploid (three sets), tetraploid (four sets), and octoploid (eight sets).

polypody [polipodee] A perennial fern with creeping rhizomes, found almost everywhere; often epiphytic; fronds solitary, deeply lobed, or divided; sori without indusia, forming 1–3 rows on the underside of the frond. (Genus: *Polypodium*, 75 species. Family: Polypodiaceae.)

polypropylene A thermoplastic made by passing propene (propylene) over a phosphoric acid catalyst at a moderately high temperature, or by passing propene into heptane with a catalyst. It is useful as a moulding material, or as an extruded film.

polysaccharides [poleesakariydz] Large carbohydrate molecules resulting from the condensation polymerization of sugars to form ether linkages between the monosaccharide units. Hydrolysis of a polysaccharide leads to the formation of simpler sugars. Common polysaccharides include starch and cellulose, both polymers of glucose.

polystyrene *styrene*

polytechnic An institution of higher education devoted to the teaching of many subjects, as opposed to a *monotechnic*, such as a college of education, which teaches only one kind of course. What distinguishes it from a university is that more of its courses have a strong vocational bias, often involving actual work experience during the course. However, it is not exclusively devoted to vocational work, and may offer liberal studies as well. Research is also undertaken, especially in conjunction with industry. In Britain, polytechnics were given university status in 1992.

polytetrafluorethylene (PTFE) A thermosetting plastic polymer with important surface-modifying properties. PTFE has a low coefficient of friction which makes it valuable in non-lubricated bearings, ski-surfaces, etc. Its anti-stick properties make it useful in cooking utensils. It has a high chemical resistance, a high softening point, and is a good insulator.

polytheism The belief in or worship of many gods, characteristic not only of primitive religions but also of the religions of classical Greece and Rome. It is an attempt, contrasting with monotheism, to acknowledge a divine presence in the world.

polythene *polyethylene*

polytonality The property of music in which two or more keys are used simultaneously. In Holst's *Terzetto* (1924), the parts for flute, oboe, and viola are each written in a different key.

polytope In mathematics, the four-dimensional analogue of a polyhedron. With each point in 2-dimensional space, we can associate a number-pair (x,y); with each point in 3-dimensional space, we associate the ordered triple (x,y,z), so we are encouraged to go on and think of n-dimensional space as ordered sets of numbers $(x_1, x_2, x_3,...x_n)$. This leads at once to 4-dimensional space. Regular polytopes have 3-dimensional regular polyhedrons as their 'faces'; it has been proved that whereas there are only five regular polyhedrons in 3-dimensional space, there are six regular polytopes in 4-dimensional space, and three in 5-dimensional space.

polyunsaturated fatty acids Dietary fats largely comprised of glycerol combined with three fatty acids, the whole molecule being a *triglyceride*. Fatty acids can be **saturated**, **mono-unsaturated**, or **polyunsaturated** depending on the number of carbon-to-carbon bonds which are not fully saturated with hydrogen atoms. The greater the number of such unsaturated bonds, the more polyunsaturated the fat. Polyunsaturated fats are liquid at room temperature, and are industrially hydrogenated to produce a harder, more saturated fat used in many margarines. An adequate intake of these fats can contribute to the maintenance of acceptable levels of blood cholesterol. All marine oils and most vegetable oils (but not palm and coconut oils) are rich in polyunsaturated fatty acids. The main such fatty acid in nature is linoleic acid, an essential component of the human diet (one of the **essential fatty acids**); it is needed for the synthesis of arachidonic acid and prostaglandins, but is obtainable only from vegetable oils. We require c.3% of our daily energy in the form of linoleic acid.

polyurethanes [poliyoorethaynz] or **polycarbamates** Large molecules formed from the addition polymerization of butane-1,4-diol and hexane-1,6-di-isocyanate, which give lightweight, flexible or rigid foams. They are widely used in coatings and adhesives, and the flexible form is found in swimsuits and corsets. Their combustion releases very poisonous isocyanate fumes, which leads to restrictions on their use (eg in furnishings).

polyuria *diabetes mellitus*

polyvinylacetate [poliviynilasetayt] A polymer of vinyl acetate monomer ($CH_2COO.CH{=}CH_2$) used in adhesives, plasticizers, and concrete additives.

polyvinylchloride (PVC) [poliviynilklawriyd] A family of polymers of vinyl chloride ($CH_2 = CHCl$). It is generally mixed with additives or fillers to give materials useful for their limited flexibility, such as floor coverings, luggage, furnishing, and electric wire coating.

polywater A temporary excitement of the 1960s, when a silicate gel was mistaken for a new polymorph of water, with apparent formula about H_8O_4. Had this existed and been stable with respect to ordinary water, a catalyst might have been discovered which would have ended life on Earth by converting all water to this form!

Pombal, Sebastião (José) de Carvalho (e Mello), marquês de (Marquess of) [põbal] (1699–1782) Portuguese statesman and chief minister (1756–77), born near Coimbra, C Portugal. He became ambassador to London (1739) and Vienna (1745), and secretary of foreign affairs (1750). He showed great resourcefulness in replanning the city of Lisbon following the disastrous earthquake of 1755, and became chief minister. He opposed Church influence, reorganized the army, and improved agriculture, commerce, and finance. He was made count (1758) and marquess (1770), but fell from office on the accession of Maria I (reigned 1777–1816).

pomegranate A deciduous, sometimes spiny, shrub or tree (*Punica granatum*) growing to 9 m/30 ft, native to SW Asia, and cultivated in Europe since ancient times; leaves up to 8 cm/3 in, shiny, oblong, opposite; flowers 2–4 cm/¾–1½ in, calyx and petals scarlet; fruit 5–8 cm/2–3 in, globose with yellow or reddish, leathery skin; seeds numerous, each embedded in translucent, purplish, juicy and sweet flesh. (Family: Punicaceae.)

Pomerania [pomeraynia], Ger **Pommern**, Polish **Pomorze** Region of NC Europe along the Baltic Sea from Stralsund (Germany) to the R Vistula in Poland; a disputed territory, 17th–18th-c; divided among Germany, Poland, and the free city of Danzig, 1919–39; divided between East Germany and Poland, 1945; many lakes; chief towns, Gdańsk, Szczecin, Koszalin.

Pomeranian A toy breed of dog developed from spitz breeds in Britain during the 19th-c; thick double-layered coat, longest on neck, legs and rear end; tail curled only at tip, carried across the back.

Pomona [pomohna] Roman goddess of fruit-trees and their fruit, especially apples and pears.

Pompadour, Jeanne Antoinette Poisson, marquise de (Marchioness of) [pompadoor], known as **Madame de Pompadour** (1721–64) Mistress of Louis XV, born in Paris, France. A woman of remarkable grace, beauty, and wit, she became a queen of fashion, and attracted the eye of the king at a ball. Installed at Versailles (1745), and ennobled as marquise de Pompadour, she assumed the entire control of public affairs, and for 20 years swayed state policy, appointing her own favourites. She founded the royal porcelain factory at Sèvres, and was a lavish patroness of architecture, the arts, and literature. She was largely blamed for the French defeats in the Seven Years' War.

pompano [pompanoh] Any of several large deep-bodied marine fish which with jacks and scads comprise the family Carangidae (11 genera); body typically compressed, head with steep profile, tail deeply forked; widespread in open oceanic waters, especially warm seas; many are excellent sport and food fishes.

Pompeii [pompayee], Ital **Pompei** [pompay] 40°45N 14°27E, pop (2000e) 24 000. Ruined ancient city in Naples province, Campania, SW Italy, at the S foot of Vesuvius, 20 km/12 mi SE of Naples; world heritage site; an important port and agricultural, wine, and perfume centre in Roman times; damaged by a violent earthquake in AD 63; great eruption of Vesuvius in AD 79 covered the whole city with a layer of ashes and pumice-stone 6–7 m/20–23 ft deep; systematic excavation since 18th-c has revealed a city roughly elliptical in shape, 3 km/1¾ mi in circumference, with eight gates, and many buildings well-preserved by the volcanic ash; two-fifths of the city still remains buried; modern town lies to the E, with the pilgrimage church of Santuario della Madonna del Rosario.

Pompey [pompee], in full **Gnaeus Pompeius Magnus**, known as **Pompey the Great** (106–48 BC) Roman politician and general of the late Republic, whose outstanding military talents, as shown by his victories over the Marians (83–82 BC), Sertorius (77 BC), Spartacus (71 BC), the pirates (67 BC), and Mithridates VI (66 BC), put him at the forefront of Roman politics from an early age. He was also an organizer of genius, and his settlement of the East after the Mithridatic Wars (63 BC) established the pattern of Roman administration there for well over a century. Consistently outmanoeuvred in the 50s BC by Julius Caesar, he was finally defeated by him in the Battle of Pharsalus (48 BC), and was assassinated in Egypt shortly after.

Pompidou, Georges (Jean Raymond) [põpeedoo] (1911–74) French statesman, prime minister (1962, 1962–6, 1966–7, 1967–8), and president (1969–74), born in Montboudif, C France. He trained as an administrator, joined de Gaulle's staff in 1944, and held various government posts from 1946. He helped to draft the constitution for the Fifth Republic (1958), negotiated a settlement in Algeria (1961), and played a key role in resolving the political crisis of 1968. Dismissed by his increasingly jealous patron, Charles de Gaulle, he was elected president following the latter's resignation. The Pompidou Centre in Paris is named after him; designed by Richard Rogers (1933–) and Renzo Piano (1937–), it was opened in 1977.

Pompidou Centre *Centre Beaubourg*

Ponape or **Pohnpei** [ponpay] pop (2000e) 41 100; area 345 sq km/133 sq mi. One of the Federated States of Micronesia, W Pacific; comprises the island of Ponape (303 sq km/117 sq mi) and eight outlying atolls; capital, Kolonia; copra, tropical fruit, tourism.

Ponce [ponsay] 18°01N 66°36W, pop (2000e) 155 000. Second largest city in Puerto Rico, E Caribbean; port at Playa de Ponce on the S coast, 70 km/43 mi SW of San Juan; airfield; iron, sugar, canning; colonial mansions, Ponce fort (1760).

Ponce de León, Juan [ponthay thay layon] (1460–1521) Explorer, born in San Servas, Spain. A page at the Aragonese court, he was a member of Columbus's second expedition (1493) and served as deputy to Ovando (1508–9), exploring and settling Puerto Rico (1510). In 1513 he discovered Florida and, while acting governor, occupied Trinidad, but failed to conquer his new subjects, the Carib Indians. On a second expedition to Florida (1521) he returned to Cuba, where he died from a poisoned-arrow wound.

Pondicherry [pondicheree] pop (2001e) 973 800; area 492 sq km/190 sq mi. Union territory in S India; founded, 1674, the chief French settlement in India; transferred to India, 1954; union territory, 1962; capital, Pondicherry; governed by a Council of Ministers responsible to a Legislative Assembly; railway; rice, millet, groundnuts, sugar cane, cotton; textiles, paper, brewing.

pond skater An aquatic bug which lives and moves over the surface of rivers, lakes, and even the ocean, supported by surface tension; its body and legs have a water repellant and unwettable surface; feeds mainly on drowning insects. (Order: Heteroptera. Family: Gerridae, c.400 species.)

pond turtle *terrapin*

pondweed An aquatic perennial, native to freshwater habitats everywhere; submerged leaves translucent; floating leaves, if present, opaque, green; flowers inconspicuous, in oval heads, wind- or water-pollinated; seeds buoyant. (Genus: *Potamogeton*, 100 species. Family: Potamogetonaceae.)

Ponta Delgada [põta delgahda] 37°29N 25°40W, pop (2000e) 21 000. Largest town in the Azores, on S coast of São Miguel I; commercial centre, tourism; Churches of São Sebastião and São Pedro, Convent of Santo Andre; Cavalhadas de São Pedro mediaeval equestrian games (Jun), Divino Espírito Santo folk festival (Jun–Aug).

Pontedera, Andrea da *Pisano, Andrea*

Ponte Vecchio [pontay vekyoh] A bridge across the R Arno at Florence, completed in 1345 by Taddeo Galli. The lower walkway is lined with jewellers' shops above which an upper corridor, built by Vasari, links the Pitti Palace with the Uffizi.

Pontiac's Conspiracy or **Rebellion** (1763) An attempt by American Indians of the Ohio and Great Lakes country to drive whites out of the area W of Niagara. It was led by Pontiac (c.1720–69), chief of the Ottawa tribe, and inspired by the religious leader known as the Delaware Prophet. The movement reached its peak with an unsuccessful siege of Detroit, and a final peace was signed in 1766.

pontoon A popular card game which is a variation of blackjack. It can be played by any small number of players, ideally six. The

Popes

Antipope refers to a pontiff set up in opposition to one asserted to be canonically chosen.

until *c.* 64	Peter
c. 64–*c.* 76	Linus
c. 76–*c.* 90	Anacletus
c. 90–*c.* 99	Clement I
c. 99–*c.* 105	Evaristus
c. 105–*c.* 117	Alexander I
c. 117–*c.* 127	Sixtus I
c. 127–*c.* 137	Telesphorus
c. 137–*c.* 140	Hyginus
c. 140–*c.* 154	Pius I
c. 154–*c.* 166	Anicetus
c. 166–*c.* 175	Soter
175–89	Eleutherius
189–98	Victor IV
198–217	Zephyrinus
217–22	Calixtus I
217–*c.* 235	Hippolytus *Antipope*
222–30	Urban I
230–5	Pontian
235–6	Anterus
236–50	Fabian
251–3	Cornelius
251–*c.* 258	Novatian *Antipope*
253–4	Lucius I
254–7	Stephen I
257–8	Sixtus II
259–68	Dionysius
269–74	Felix I
275–83	Eutychianus
283–96	Caius
296–304	Marcellinus
308–9	Marcellus I
310	Eusebius
311–14	Miltiades
314–35	Sylvester I
336	Mark
337–52	Julius I
352–66	Liberius
355–65	Felix II *Antipope*
366–84	Damasus I
366–7	Utsinus *Antipope*
384–99	Siricius
399–401	Anastasius I
402–17	St Innocent I
417–18	St Zosimus
418–22	Boniface I
418–19	Eulalius *Antipope*
422–32	Celestine I
432–40	Sixtus III
440–61	Leo I 'the Great'
461–8	Hilarus
468–83	Simplicius
483–92	Felix III (II)
492–6	St Gelasius I
496–8	Anastasius II
498–514	(Coelius) Symmachus
498, 501–5	Laurentius *Antipope*
514–23	Hormisdas
523–6	John I
526–30	Felix IV (III)
530–2	Boniface II
530	Dioscorus *Antipope*
533–5	John II
535–6	Agapetus I
536–7	Silverius
537–55	Vigilius
556–61	Pelagius I
561–74	John III
575–9	Benedict I
579–90	Pelagius II
590–604	St Gregory I 'the Great'
604–6	Sabinianus
607	Boniface III
608–15	Boniface IV
615–18	Deusdedit *or* Adeodatus I
619–25	Boniface V
625–38	Honorius I
640	Severinus
640–2	John IV
642–9	Theodore I
649–55	St Martin I
654–7	St Eugenius I[1]
657–72	Vitalian
672–6	Adeodatus II
676–8	Donus
678–81	Agatho
682–3	Leo II
684–5	Benedict II
685–6	John V
686–7	Cono
687	Theodore *Antipope*
687	Paschal *Antipope*
687–701	Sergius I
701–5	John VI
705–7	John VII
708	Sisinnius
708–15	Constantine
715–31	St Gregory II
731–41	St Gregory III
741–52	St Zacharias
752	Stephen II (*not consecrated*)
752–7	Stephen II (III)
757–67	Paul I
767–9	Constantine II *Antipope*
768	Philip *Antipope*
768–72	Stephen III (IV)
772–95	Adrian I
795–816	Leo III
816–17	Stephen IV (V)
817–24	Paschal I
824–7	Eugenius II
827	Valentine
827–44	Gregory IV
844	John *Antipope*
844–7	Sergius II
847–55	Leo IV
855–8	Benedict III
855	Anastasius Bibliothecarius *Antipope*
858–67	St Nicholas I 'the Great'
867–72	Adrian II
872–82	John VIII
882–4	Martin II (Marinus I)
884–5	Adrian III
885–91	Stephen V (VI)
891–6	Formosus
896	Boniface VI
896–7	Stephen VI (VII)
897	Romanus
897	Theodore II
898–900	John IX
900–3	Benedict IV
903	Leo V
903–4	Christopher *Antipope*
904–11	Sergius III
911–13	Anastasius III
913–14	Lando
914–28	John X
928	Leo VI
928–31	Stephen VII (VIII)
931–5	John XI
936–9	Leo VII
939–42	Stephen IX
942–6	Martin III (Marinus II)
946–55	Agapetus II
955–64	John XII (Octavian)
963–5	Leo VIII
964–6	Benedict V
965–72	John XIII
973–4	Benedict VI
974, 984–5	Boniface VII *Antipope*
974–83	Benedict VII
983–4	John XIV
985–96	John XV
996–9	Gregory V
997–8	John XVI *Antipope*
999–1003	Sylvester II
1003	John XVII
1004–9	John XVIII
1009–12	Sergius IV
1012–24	Benedict VIII
1012	Gregory *Antipope*
1024–32	John XIX
1032–44	Benedict IX
1045	Sylvester III
1045	Benedict IX (*second reign*)
1045–6	Gregory VI
1046–7	Clement II
1047–8	Benedict IX (*third reign*)
1048	Damasus II (Poppo)
1048–54	Leo IX (Bruno of Toul)
1055–7	Victor II (Gebhard of Hirschberg)
1057–8	Stephen IX (X) (Frederick of Lorraine)
1058–9	Benedict X (John of Tusculum) *Antipope*
1059–61	Nicholas II (Gerard of Burgundy)
1061–73	Alexander II (Anseim of Lucca)
1061–72	Honorius II (Peter Cadalus) *Antipope*
1073–85	Gregory VII (St Hildebrand)
1080, 1084–1100	Clement III (Guibert of Ravenna) *Antipope*
1086–7	Victor III (Desiderius)
1088–99	Urban II (Odo of Chatillon)
1099–1118	Paschal II (Raneiro da Bieda)
1100–2	Theodoric *Antipope*
1102	Albert *Antipope*
1105–11	Sylvester IV *Antipope*
1118–19	Gelasius II (John of Gaeta)
1118–21	Gregory VIII (Maurice of Braga) *Antipope*
1119–24	Callistus II (Guy of Burgundy)

[1] Elected during the banishment of Martin I [2] different individuals [3] There was no John XX

1124–30	Honorius II (Lamberro dei Fagnani)
1124	Celestine II *Antipope*
1130–43	Innocent II (Gregory Parareschi)
1130–8	Anacletus II *Antipope*
1138	Victor IV[2] *Antipope*
1143–4	Celestine II (Guido di Castello)
1144–5	Lucius II (Gherardo Caccianemici)
1145–53	Eugenius III (Bernardo Paganelli)
1153–4	Anastasius IV (Corrado della Subarra)
1154–9	Adrian IV (Nicholas Breakspear)
1159–81	Alexander III (Orlando Bandinelli)
1159–64	Victor IV[2] (Ottaviano di Monticelli) *Antipope*
1164–8	Paschal III (Guido of Crema) *Antipope*
1168–78	Calixtus III (John of Struma) *Antipope*
1179–80	Innocent III (Lando da Sessa)
1181–5	Lucius III (Ubaldo Allucingoli)
1185–7	Urban III (Uberto Crivelli)
1187	Gregory VIII (Alberto di Morra)
1187–91	Clement III (Paolo Scolari)
1191–8	Celestine III (Giacinto Boboni-Orsini)
1198–1216	Innocent III (Lotario de' Conti)
1216–27	Honorius III (Cancio Savelli)
1227–41	Gregory IX (Ugolino di Segni)
1241	Celestine IV (Goffredo Castiglione)
1243–54	Innocent IV (Sinibaldo de' Fieschi)
1254–61	Alexander IV (Rinaldo di Segni)
1261–4	Urban IV (Jacques Pantaléon)
1265–8	Clement IV (Guy le Gros Foulques)
1271–6	Gregory X (Tebaldo Visconti)
1276	Innocent V (Pierre de Champagni)
1276	Adrian V (Ottoboni Fieschi)
1276–7	John XXI[3] (Pietro Rebuli-Giuliani)
1277–80	Nicholas III (Giovanni Gaetano Orsini)
1281–5	Martin IV (Simon de Brie)
1285–7	Honorius IV (Giacomo Savelli)
1288–92	Nicholas IV (Girolamo Masci)
1294	Celestine V (Pietro di Morrone)
1294–1303	Boniface VIII (Benedetto Caetani)
1303–4	Benedict XI (Niccolo Boccasini)
1305–14	Clement V (Raymond Bertrand de Got)
1316–34	John XXII (Jacques Duèse)
1328–30	Nicholas V (Pietro Rainalducci) *Antipope*
1334–42	Benedict XII (Jacques Fournier)
1342–52	Clement VI (Pierre Roger de Beaufort)
1352–62	Innocent VI (Étienne Aubert)
1362–70	Urban V (Guillaume de Grimoard)
1370–8	Gregory XI (Pierre Roger de Beaufort)
1378–89	Urban VI (Bartolomeo Prignano)
1378–94	Clement VII (Robert of Geneva) *Antipope*
1389–1404	Boniface IX (Pietro Tomacelli)
1394–1423	Benedict XIII (Pedro de Luna) *Antipope*
1404–6	Innocent VII (Cosmato de' Migliorati)
1406–15	Gregory XII (Angelo Correr)
1409–10	Alexander V (Petros Philargi) *Antipope*
1410–15	John XXIII (Baldassare Cossa) *Antipope*
1417–31	Martin V (Oddone Colonna)
1423–9	Clement VIII (Gil Sanchez Muños) *Antipope*
1425–30	Benedict XIV (Bernard Garnier) *Antipope*
1431–47	Eugenius IV (Gabriele Condulmer)
1670–6	Clement X (Emilio Altieri)
1439–49	Felix V (Amadeus VIII of Savoy) *Antipope*
1447–55	Nicholas V (Tommaso Parentucelli);
1455–8	Calixtus III (Alfonso de Borja)
1458–64	Pius II (Enea Silvio de Piccolomini)
1464–71	Paul II (Pietro Barbo)
1471–84	Sixtus IV (Francesco della Rovere)
1484–92	Innocent VIII (Giovanni Battista Cibo)
1492–1503	Alexander VI (Rodrigo Borgia)
1503	Pius III (Francesco Todoeschini-Picolomini)
1503–13	Julius II (Giuliano della Rovere)
1513–21	Leo X (Giovanni de'Medici)
1522–3	Adrian VI (Adrian Dedel)
1523–34	Clement VII (Giulio de'Medici)
1534–49	Paul III (Allessandro Farnese)
1550–5	Julius III (Gianmaria del Monte)
1555	Marcellus II (Marcello Cervini)
1555–9	Paul IV (Giovanni Pietro Caraffa)
1559–65	Pius IV (Giovanni Angelo Medici)
1566–72	Pius V (Michele Ghislieri)
1572–85	Gregory XIII (Ugo Buoncompagni)
1585–90	Sixtus V (Felice Peretti)
1590	Urban VII (Giambattista Castagna)
1590–1	Gregory XIV (Niccolo Sfondrati)
1591	Innocent IX (Gian Antonio Facchinetti)
1592–1605	Clement VIII (Ippolito Aldobrandini)
1605	Leo XI (Alessandro de' Medici Ottaiano)
1605–21	Paul V (Camillo Borghese)
1621–3	Gregory XV (Alessandro Ludovisi)
1623–44	Urban VIII (Maffeo Barberini)
1644–55	Innocent X (Giambattista Pamfili)
1655–67	Alexander VII (Fabio Chigi)
1667–9	Clement IX (Julio Rospigliosi)
1670–6	Clement X (Emilio Altieri)
1676–89	Innocent XI (Benedetto Odescalchi)
1689–91	Alexander VIII (Pietro Vito Ottoboni)
1691–1700	Innocent XII (Antonio Pignatelli)
1700–21	Clement XI (Gian Francesco Albani)
1721–4	Innocent XIII (Michelangelo dei Conti)
1724–30	Benedict XIII (Pietro Orsini)
1730–40	Clement XII (Lorenzo Corsini)
1740–58	Benedict XIV (Prospero Lambertini)
1758–69	Clement XIII (Carlo Rezzonico)
1769–74	Clement XIV (Lorenzo Ganganelli)
1775–99	Pius VI (Giovanni Braschi)
1800–23	Pius VII (Luigi Barnaba Chiaramonti)
1823–9	Leo XII (Annibale della Genga)
1829–30	Pius VIII (Francesco Saven Castiglioni)
1831–46	Gregory XVI (Bartolomeo Alberto Capellari)
1846–78	Pius IX (Giovanni Maria Mastai Ferretti)
1878–1903	Leo XIII (Vincenzo Gioacchino Pecci)
1903–14	Pius X (Giuseppe Sarto)
1914–22	Benedict XV (Giacomo della Chiesa)
1922–39	Pius XI (Achille Ratti)
1939–58	Pius XII (Eugenio Pacelli)
1958–63	John XXIII (Angelo Giuseppe Roncalli)
1963–78	Paul VI (Giovanni Battista Montini)
1978	John Paul I (Albino Luciani)
1978–	John Paul II (Karol Jozef Wojtyła)

object is to try to obtain a total of 21 with your cards, and is thus also known as *vingt-et-un* (Fr '21').

pontoon bridge A floating bridge supported by pontoons. The structure may be temporary, as for military usage, or permanent, where deep water and adverse ground conditions make piers expensive. Typically the pontoons consist of flat bottomed boats, hollow metal cylinders, or concrete rafts. Three permanent concrete pontoon bridges cross L Washington in Seattle, USA.

Pontormo, Jacopo da [pontaw(r)moh], originally **Jacopo Carrucci** (1494–1557) Painter, born in Pontormo, NC Italy. A pupil of Andrea del Sarto and other masters, his works include several frescoes, notably of the Passion (1522–5) in the Certosa near Florence. His masterpiece is 'The Deposition' (c.1525), a chapel altarpiece in Santa Felicità, Florence.

Pontus In antiquity, the territory in NE Asia Minor lying E of Bithynia and S of the Black Sea. In the early 1st-c BC, it was the centre of the empire of Mithridates VI; with his defeat the area became a Roman province.

Pontypridd [pontiprith] 51°37N 3°22W, pop (2000e) 32 300. Valley town in Rhondda Cynon Taff, S Wales, UK; on the R Taff, 18 km/11 mi NW of Cardiff; railway; Glamorgan University (1992, formerly Polytechnic of Wales); chemicals, electronics, chains and cables.

pony *Dales / Dartmoor / Exmoor / Highland / New Forest / Shetland / Welsh pony; horse*

Pony Club A worldwide organization with the aim of establishing good horsemanship among children through championships and rallies. It was established in 1929.

pony express A rapid mail service from St Joseph, MO, to San Francisco, CA, using relays of riders and horses. Established in 1860, the service was withdrawn after the completion of the first transcontinental telegraph line a year later.

poodle A French breed of dog, developed originally for hunting; three sizes: *standard* (taller than 38 cm/15 in), *miniature*, and *toy* (less than 28 cm/11 in); narrow head with pendulous ears; tail docked; thick coat often clipped for ornamental effect.

pool An American table game played in many forms. It uses 16 balls, and a cue similar to that used in billiards and snooker. The most popular form is the variation known as **8-ball pool**. The object is to sink all balls of a certain design (usually striped or solid), and then finally the black ball (the No. 8 ball, hence the name). It is played on a table approximately half the size of a standard billiard table, with six round pockets.

Poole 50°43N 1°59W, pop (2001e) 138 300. Port town in Dorset, S England, UK; located 6 km/4 mi W of Bournemouth; unitary authority from 1997; birthplace of John Le Carré; Poole harbour is Europe's largest natural harbour with cross-channel sailings to France and the Channel Is; ferries to the Isle of Wight and to nearby Brownsea Is, owned by the National Trust and home to the red squirrel; railway; Poole pottery and Purbeck pottery produced locally; Waterfront Museum, Compton Acres gardens, deer sanctuary; tourism.

Poona or **Pune** 18°34N 73°58E, pop (2000e) 1 831 000. Industrial city in Maharashtra state, W India, 120 km/75 mi SE of Mumbai; former capital of the Marathas; under British rule, 1818; important colonial military and administrative centre; airfield; railway; university (1949); many medical, agricultural, and engineering colleges; cotton, engineering, munitions, chemicals, metalwork, vehicles, soap, paper; 17th–18th-c palaces and temples.

Poopó, Lake [pohohpoh] (Span **Lago**) Lake in Oruro department, W Bolivia; 56 km/35 mi S of Oruro; second largest lake in Bolivia; area 2512 sq km/970 sq mi; length 97 km/60 mi; width 32–48 km/20–30 mi; c.2·5 m/8·2 ft deep.

Poor Clares *Franciscans*

Poor Laws Legislation in Britain originally formulated in 1598 and 1601, whereby relief of poverty suffered by members of a parish was the responsibility of individual parishes under the supervision of Justices of the Peace and the administration of Overseers. Funds were provided by local property rates sufficient to meet the cost of maintaining the poor and to find employment for the able-bodied. Vagrants and vagabonds were sent to houses of correction, which became mandatory in all shires after 1601. Poorhouses were set up to accommodate the sick, the infirm, and the insane. Apprenticeships were provided for able-bodied needy children, who were separated from their parents. As the population grew and rates rose at the end of the 18th-c, the poor laws were increasingly criticized. The Poor Law Amendment Act of 1834 radically changed the system.

Pop Art A modern art form based on the commonplace and ephemeral aspects of 20th-c urban life, such as soup cans, comics, movies, and advertising. Pioneer British Pop artists included Eduardo Paolozzi (1924–) and Richard Hamilton (1922–) in the mid-1950s, and leading US contributors in the 1960s include Jasper Johns, Andy Warhol, and Roy Lichtenstein. American Pop is tougher and more deliberately shocking than British, with strong reminiscences of Dada. Humour is an important element, though art critics have been inclined to take it all very solemnly.

Popayán [popayan] 2°27N 76°22W, pop (2000e) 171 900. Historic city and capital of Cauca department, SW Colombia; founded, 1536; serious earthquake, 1983; cathedral; university (1827); coffee, food processing, tanning.

Pope, Alexander (1688–1744) Poet, born in London, UK, to a Roman Catholic family in the year of the Protestant Revolution. In 1700 the family settled at Binfield, Bracknell Forest. Debarred from university because of his religion, and largely self-taught, he suffered from poor health caused by tuberculosis, and asthma, and had a curvature of the spine, his resulting diminutive stature (4 ft 6 in) providing a target for critics, since he was frequently engaged in literary vendettas. He became well known as a satirical poet, and a master of the heroic couplet, notably in *The Rape of the Lock* (1712–14). He turned to translation with the *Iliad* (1715–20), whose success enabled him to set up a home in Twickenham, but he was forced to remove himself from London following further anti-Catholic measures after the Jacobite rebellion of 1715. However, he formed a friendship with his neighbour, Lady Mary Wortley Montagu, which was very important to him but soured after 1723. There he wrote his major poem, *The Dunciad* (1728, continued 1742), the *Epistle to Doctor Arbuthnot* (1735), the philosophical *Essay on Man* (1733–4), and a series of satires imitating the epistles of Horace (1733–8).

pope (Lat *papa*, Gk *papas*, 'father') The title of the Bishop of Rome as head or Supreme Pontiff of the Roman Catholic Church; also, the title given to the head of the Coptic Church. The Bishop of Rome is elected by a conclave of the College of Cardinals, his authority deriving from the belief that he represents Christ in direct descendancy from the Apostle Peter, said to be the first Bishop of Rome. After the decline of the ancient churches of the Eastern Roman Empire, resulting from the spread of Islam, the pope in Rome became the undisputed centre of the Christian Church, and enjoyed considerable political power as the temporal sovereign of extensive papal states in Europe (now restricted to the Vatican City in Rome). The claim to infallibility was formalized at the First Vatican Council in 1870. (*see pp.1124–5*)

pop group An ensemble which performs pop music, often pursuing one particular musical style, and adopting a corresponding image. It typically includes two or three electric guitars, drums (with other percussion), keyboards, and vocalist(s), nearly always with amplification. Several highly successful pop groups – including the Monkees in the late 1960s and Take That! and the Spice Girls in the 1990s – have assumed an image which was created by a record company, manager, or producer, and designed to appeal to a very specific adolescent market.

Popish Plot An apocryphal Jesuit conspiracy in 1678 to assassinate Charles II of England, burn London, slaughter Protestants, and place his Roman Catholic brother James, Duke of York, on the throne. It was invented by opportunist rogues, Titus

Oates (1649–1705) and Israel Tonge (1621–80). A nation-wide panic ensued, resulting in 35 executions, bills in three Parliaments for the exclusion of James from the succession, and the fall of the Danby government.

poplar A deciduous, N temperate tree; triangular-ovoid to almost heart-shaped leaves; flowers tiny, in pendulous catkins appearing before leaves; seeds with cottony white hairs, which aid wind-dispersal and give rise to the American name **cottonwood**. Very fast-growing, it is used for cheap timber, matchwood, paper pulp, and as ornamentals. Some species (**balsam poplars**) have aromatic timber. (Genus: *Populus*, 35 species. Family: Salicaceae.)

Pople, Sir John A (1925–2004) Chemist, born in Burnham-on-Sea, Somerset. He graduated from Cambridge in mathematics in 1951, and taught at Northwestern University, IL. He shared the 1998 Nobel Prize for Chemistry for his contribution to methods that can be used for theoretical studies of the properties of molecules and the chemical processes in which they are involved – specifically, for his development of computational methods in quantum chemistry. He was knighted in 2003.

pop music Popular commercial music, with its audience mainly among the young, current since the late 1950s. In c.1900 the name 'pops' was given to a series of concerts of light music promoted annually by the Boston Symphony Orchestra. But the singular, *pop*, refers to the kind of music inaugurated by rock and roll, and which has since diversified to such an extent that it is now most easily defined in terms of its market. The Beatles in the 1960s were one of the first groups to experiment radically with the basic rock format. Since then, pop music has taken in and adapted elements from a diverse range of musical sources, including blues, soul, reggae, country and western, and various ethnic styles. Pop musicians have also been very quick to exploit the possibilities of electronic music, particularly for such dance styles as hip-hop and rap music. Pop music is generally played, presented, and marketed for a teenage audience, with success measured in terms of the various pop charts (particularly in the UK the Music Week/Gallup/BBC chart, and in the USA the Billboard chart), which list records in order of sales attained.

Popocatépetl [popohkataypetl] 19°01N 98°38W. Dormant volcano in C Mexico, 72 km/45 mi SE of Mexico City; height 5452 m/17 887 ft; second highest peak in Mexico, with a snow-capped symmetrical cone; crater c.1 km/¾ mi in circumference and 402 m/1319 ft deep; erupts intermittently, last eruption, 2003; in Ixtaccihuatl–Popocatépetl National Park, area c.250 sq km/100 sq mi; established in 1935.

Poppaea Sabina [popaya sabeena] (?–65) Roman society beauty and voluptuary who before her marriage to the Emperor Nero (62) had been the wife of his playboy friend, the future Emperor Otho. She shared the then fashionable interest in Judaism, and has been thought by many to have encouraged Nero in his vicious attack on the Christians in the aftermath of the Fire of Rome (64).

Popper, Sir Karl (Raimund) (1902–94) Philosopher, born in Vienna, Austria. He studied at Vienna University, where he associated with the 'Vienna Circle' of philosophers, though he was strongly critical of their logical positivism. In 1935 he published his first book on scientific methodology, *Die Logik der Forschung* (1934, The Logic of Scientific Discovery), which stressed the importance of 'falsifiability' as a defining factor of true scientific theories, which he contrasted with such 'pseudosciences' as Marxism and psychoanalysis. He left Vienna during Hitler's rise to power, lectured in New Zealand (1937–45), finally becoming professor of logic and scientific method at London (1949–69). Later books include *The Open Society and its Enemies* (1945), a polemic directed against all systems with totalitarian implications, particularly Marxism, and *The Poverty of Historicism* (1957). He was knighted in 1965.

pop poetry A term derived from 'pop [ie popular] music' in the 1970s to describe poetry written for public performance rather than for private reading. It is often topical, satirical, 'protest poetry', and accompanied by music; as with John Cooper Clarke and Lynton Kwesi Johnson (1952–).

poppy The name given to many members of the family Papaveraceae. All produce latex, are often brightly coloured, and have flowers with two sepals and four overlapping petals, often crumpled when they first open. Red poppies, which grew wild in the fields of Flanders, are used in November as a symbol of remembrance of those who died in the two World Wars.

Popski's Private Army A British fighting unit in World War 2. It was raised in October 1942 by Lt-Col Vladimir Peniakoff (1897–1951), known as 'Popski', a Belgian of Russian parentage. It had a maximum strength of 195 men, and engaged in intelligence-gathering and hit-and-run attacks behind enemy lines in N Africa and Italy.

popular culture A term which, used in a narrow sense, describes mass cultural phenomena, such as soap operas, spectator sports, and pop music; more broadly, it describes the mentality and way of life of most people as opposed to elites. Popular culture is now the subject of serious study, with museums and university courses devoted to it.

popular front A strategy of the communist movement begun in the 1930s as a means of fostering collaboration among left and centre parties to oppose the rise of right-wing movements and regimes, most obviously fascist ones. There were popular front governments in France, Spain, and Chile. The strategy virtually died with the signing of the Nazi Soviet Pact (1939), but re-emerged after Hitler invaded the Soviet Union.

population The inhabitants of a region or country who together comprise its native and immigrant people. While it is often used to define the boundary of the citizenry of a sovereign state, it is also used more specifically to refer to a group or category of people sharing specific characteristics, eg 'the working class population', 'the coloured population', and so on.

population biology The branch of biology dealing with the study of the distributions of populations of living organisms in time and space. It includes the study of the dynamic changes that occur within populations, and the factors that cause those changes.

population density A measure of the number of people living within a standard unit of area, useful for comparative purposes. For example, the population density of The Netherlands (2001) was 384·5 per sq km/996 per sq mi, and for Australia (2001) 2·5 per sq km/6·5 per sq mi. However, these are crude measurements, and take no account of the area of habitable land. Accordingly, population density may be calculated to relate population to cultivable land or some other economic indicator.

population genetics The study of the genetic constitutions of populations acting in consort with the environment, the processes that affect gene and genotype frequencies, and the mathematical theorems that describe them. The basic theorems were established in the period 1908–30, with the work of British geneticists R A Fisher (1890–1962), J B S Haldane (1892–1964), and US geneticist Sewall Wright (1889–1988). In human population genetics, a great deal is now known about the distribution of gene frequencies for blood groups in different peoples, and rather less for serum proteins and enzymes. DNA technology suggests that there is much variation in DNA sequences, but the frequencies of these variant sequences (*restriction fragment length polymorphisms*) in different populations are as yet little known.

populism Essentially a political outlook or mentality rather than an ideology, identified by a popular reaction to dramatic change, such as rapid industrialization. People feel that events are beyond their control, which is blamed on some conspiracy of foreigners, ethnic groups, economic interests, or intellectuals. The populist reaction is to 'regain' control from the suggested centres of power, usually through some form of participation, and to seek revenge and redemption. Beyond that, populism is an obscure and variable outlook, and has failed to establish political parties successfully. It is often found in underdeveloped countries as a reaction against more developed countries. In the USA, it developed as a political stance that minimized the importance of elite leadership. The Populist Party sought the presidency twice (1888, 1892) on a platform supporting the interests of farmers. It briefly won control of several states, as well as a number of seats in Congress. After 1892 it was absorbed into the Democratic Party.

Populist Party (1892–6) A US political party that grew from agrarian and labour discontent, especially in the S and mid-W; also known as the **People's Party**. In 1892 the Populists' presidential candidate gained over a million votes. In 1896 the party endorsed the Democratic candidate William Jennings Bryan (1860–1925).

porbeagle *mackerel shark*

porcelain A hard, vitreous, translucent, resonant material, contrasting with opaque, more porous pottery. It contains china clay (kaolin) and chinastone (petuntse), and is fired at a temperature of c.1200–1350°C, whereas pottery does not contain chinastone, and is fired at a lower temperature. Porcelain was first manufactured by the Chinese in the Tang dynasty (7th–10th-c), when production of the famous jade-green celadon ware began. At least nine major variants were produced under the Song (10th–13th-c). It found its way to W Europe from c.1300, and was prized as a semi-precious material, often mounted in gold or silver. The first European attempts to make it were at the Medici factory in Florence in the 1570s, but real success was only achieved at Meissen in the early 18th-c.

porcupine A cavy-like rodent; some hairs modified as long sharp spines; lives in diverse habitats; 22 species in two families: ground-dwelling family Hystricidae (**Old World porcupines**) from Africa and S Asia, and tree-climbing family Erethizontidae (**New World porcupines**), widespread in the New World.

porcupine-fish Large, bottom-living fish (*Diodon hystrix*) widespread in shallow waters of tropical seas; length up to 90 cm/3 ft; body covered with long sharp spines; inflates body as a defence to become almost spherical with spines erect; mouth has a parrot-like beak, bearing strong crushing teeth; feeds on molluscs, echinoderms, and crustaceans. (Family: Diodontidae.)

porgy *sea bream*

Porifera [porifera] *sponge*

porky *filefish*

pornography The presentation of erotic behaviour intended to cause sexual arousal, typically using film, graphic, or written media. It is widely considered to be a demeaning representation of sexuality and the body. Most authorities distinguish between 'soft' and illegal 'hard core' pornography, but many, especially feminists, argue that the 'softer' version should be banned as well. In the US, pornography is a major industry – bigger, for example, than the film and record industries combined. There is evidence to suggest that pornographic material which shows women 'enjoying' rape, degradation, or other forms of sexual violence may encourage men to become sexually violent. However, difficulties of definition and changing social attitudes have led to problems of control and law enforcement.

porosity A mechanical property of solids, a measure of their ability to allow the passage of a fluid. The narrow channels that make a material porous allow it to absorb fluid via capillarity, as a sponge absorbs water. Oil exists underground in porous rock; water drains through sand.

porphyria [paw(r)firia] A group of inherited disorders involving the excess production of chemical substances known as *porphyrins*. They cause a wide range of abnormalities, including sensitivity of the skin to sunlight, pigmentation of the skin, abdominal pain, and mental confusion. It entered the British royal family through Mary, Queen of Scots, and symptoms were displayed by the Stuarts. It then passed to the Hanoverians, and was most acutely displayed in the supposed 'madness' of George III. It is sometimes called 'the royal malady', not because of its royal connections, but due to the production of purple urine.

Porphyry [paw(r)fuhree] (c.233–304) Neoplatonist philosopher, born in Tyre or Batanea. After studying at Athens he went to Rome (c.263), where he studied under Plotinus, becoming his disciple and biographer. He wrote a celebrated treatise against the Christians, of which only fragments remain. His most influential work was the *Isagoge*, a commentary on Aristotle's *Categories*, widely used in the Middle Ages.

porpoise *dolphin*

Porres, St Martín de *Martín de Porres, St*

Porsche, Ferdinand [paw(r)shuh] (1875–1951) Automobile designer, born in Hafersdorf, Germany. He designed cars for Daimler and Auto Union, then set up his own studio, and in 1934 produced the plans for a revolutionary type of cheap car with the engine in the rear, to which the Nazis gave the name *Volkswagen* ('people's car'). The Porsche sports car was introduced in 1950.

port A sweet, fortified wine, first produced in the upper Douro valley, N Portugal. Grapes have been grown on the steeply-terraced hillsides since the 17th-c. The wine used to be transported down the fast-flowing river to Oporto (hence the name), but is today taken by road. 'Vintage' port is unblended. All port is aged in *pipes* (115-gallon wooden barrels).

Port Augusta 32°30S 137°27E, pop (2000e) 16 100. Town in South Australia, at the head of the Spencer Gulf; airfield; railway; wool and grain trade, engineering; starting point for the 'Ghan' train to Darwin and the Indian Pacific train to Perth; base for the flying doctor service.

Port-au-Prince [paw(r)t oh prĩs] 18°33N 72°20W, pop (2000e) 859 000. Seaport capital of Haiti; on the Gulf of Gonâve, W coast of Hispaniola I; commercial and processing centre at W end of the fertile Plaine du Cul-de-Sac; airport; archbishopric; university (1944); coffee, sugar; 18th-c cathedral.

Port Elizabeth 33°58S 25°36E, pop (2000e) 846 000 (metropolitan area). Seaport in Eastern Cape province, South Africa, on Algoa Bay, Indian Ocean, 725 km/450 mi E of Cape Town; Fort Frederick built here by British forces, 1799; founded, 1820; airfield; railway; university (1964); locomotives, motor vehicles, food processing, steel, wool, mohair, skins, tyres, citrus fruits; Addo Elephant national park nearby.

Porter, Cole (1891–1964) Composer, born in Peru, Indiana, USA. He studied law at Harvard before entering the Schola Cantorum in Paris. Attracted to musical comedy, he composed lyrics and music for many stage successes. In 1937 he was severely hurt in a riding accident, leaving him in permanent pain, but he continued to compose, reaching the height of his success with the shows *Kiss Me Kate* (1948) and *Can-Can* (1953). His highly personal style and dramatic sense is illustrated by such popular songs as 'Night and Day' (1932), 'Begin the Beguine' (1935), and 'Ev'ry Time We Say Goodbye' (1944).

Porter, (of Luddenham), Sir George Porter, Baron (1920–2002) Physical chemist, born in Stainforth, North Yorkshire, N England, UK. He studied at Leeds, and worked with radar as a naval officer in World War 2. In 1945 he moved to Cambridge, where he studied very fast reactions in gases, using a combination of electronic and spectroscopic techniques. He shared the Nobel Prize for Chemistry in 1967. He became director of the Royal Institution (1966–85), president of the Royal Society (1985–90), and chairman of the Centre For Photomolecular Sciences (1990–2002). He was knighted in 1972 and created a life peer in 1990.

Porter, Katherine Anne (Maria Veronica Callista Russell) (1890–1980) Short-story writer and novelist, born in Indian Creek, Texas, USA. Educated in a convent, she worked as a journalist and teacher in Mexico. Her first book of stories, *Flowering Judas* (1930), was followed by *Pale Horse, Pale Rider* (1939). She is also known for a long allegorical novel, *The Ship of Fools* (1962), about a journey from Mexico to Germany on the eve of Hitler's rise to power. *The Collected Stories of Katherine Anne Porter* (1965) received both the Pulitzer Prize and the National Book Award.

Porter, Peter (Neville Frederick) (1929–) Poet, born in Brisbane, Queensland, NE Australia. He studied at Brisbane University, then worked as a journalist before coming to England in 1951. His collections *Once Bitten, Twice Bitten* (1961) and *Poems Ancient and Modern* (1964) are descriptive and satirical of Britain in the 1960s, while later volumes such as *The Cost of Seriousness* (1978) and *The Automatic Oracle* (1987, Whitbread) are more reflective and elegiac. His *Collected Poems* appeared in 1983, and consolidated his international reputation. A later collection, *Dragons in their Pleasant Palaces*, appeared in 1997, and he edited the *Oxford Book of Australian Verse* (1998). In 2002 he won the Queen's Gold Medal for Poetry and the Forward Poetry Prize. He is well known in Britain as a reviewer and broadcaster.

Porter, Rodney Robert (1917–85) Biochemist, born in Liverpool, Merseyside, NW England, UK. He studied there and at Cambridge, worked at the National Institute for Medical Research (1949–60), St Mary's Hospital Medical School, London (1960–7), and became professor at Oxford (1967). His work on antibodies from 1949, together with studies by Gerald Edelman and others, enabled him to propose an overall molecular structure for antibodies. His ideas helped to link the biochemistry of antibodies with immunology, and he shared the Nobel Prize for Physiology or Medicine with Gerald Edelman in 1972.

porter *beer*

portfolio theory The analysis of how investors allocate their wealth between the various types of asset available. It assumes that all would prefer the best available return for any given degree of risk, and the lowest degree of risk for any expected rate of return. Various efficient portfolios are available which have these properties; different investors choose between expected profits and safety differently, to suit their own wealth and temperament. The *capital asset pricing model* studies how differences in risk and expected return affect the prices of different assets. The work in this area of US economist James Tobin secured him the Nobel Prize for Economics in 1981.

Port Harcourt [hah(r)kert] 4°43N 7°05E, pop (2000e) 452 000. Seaport capital of Rivers state, S Nigeria; on R Bonny, 65 km/40 mi from the sea; Nigeria's second largest port; established in 1912; airport; railway link to the Enugu coalfields; university (1975); metals, glass, liquid propane gas, oil refining, petrochemicals, fishing.

portico [paw(r)tikoh] A colonnaded and roofed space attached to a building and forming an entrance way. It is usually classical in style, with detached or attached columns and a pediment above.

Portillo, Michael (Denzil Xavier) [paw(r)tiloh] (1953–) British Conservative statesman. He studied at Cambridge, and became an MP in 1984. After several appointments as a special adviser to government departments, he became minister of state for transport (1988–90) and the environment (1990–2), chief secretary for the Treasury (1992–4), secretary of state for employment (1994–5), and defence secretary (1995–7). He lost his seat in the 1997 general election, but won a by-election in Kensington and Chelsea in 1999. He became shadow chancellor in 2000. Following his defeat in the Conservative leadership contest in 2001 he announced that he would leave front-line politics. He declined a post in Michael Howard's shadow cabinet (Nov 2003) and made known his intention to leave politics after the next general election.

Portland (Maine) 43°39N 70°16W, pop (2000e) 64 200. Business capital and chief port of Maine, USA; seat of Cumberland Co; on the coast of Casco Bay, SE of Sebago Lake; established, 1632; city status, 1832; state capital, 1820–32; railway; Westbrook Junior College (1831); fisheries, ship repair, paper, chemicals, oil trade; birthplace of Longfellow.

Portland (Oregon) 45°32N 122°37W, pop (2000e) 529 100. Freshwater port and capital of Multnomah Co, NW Oregon, USA, on the Willamette R; largest city in the state; laid out, 1845; served as a supply point in the 1850s during the California gold rush and later (1897–1900) during the Alaska gold rush; airport; railway; university (1901); machinery, electrical equipment, food processing, wood products, metal goods; trade in timber, grain, aluminium; tourism; professional team, Trail Blazers (basketball).

Portland, Isle of Rocky peninsula on Dorset coast, S England, UK; extends into the English Channel; connected to the mainland by a shingle ridge (Chesil Beach); area 12 sq km/4·6 sq mi; naval base at Portland Harbour; Portland Stone (limestone) used in many London buildings; Portland Castle built by Henry VIII (1520).

Portland, Duke of *Bentinck, William Henry Cavendish*

Portland Cement *cement*

Portlaoighise [paw(r)tlayish] or **Port Laoise**, formerly **Maryborough** 53°02N 7°17W, pop (2000e) 8500. Capital of Laoighis county, Leinster, Ireland; SW of Dublin; railway; jail; small industrial estate.

Port Louis [loois] 20°18S 57°31E, pop (2000e) 159 000. Seaport capital of Mauritius; established, 1735; trade developed until the building of the Suez Canal; handles almost all of the trade of Mauritius; sugar, textiles, clothes, diamond cutting, watches, electrical and electronic equipment, sunglasses; university (1965); two cathedrals.

Port Moresby [maw(r)zbee] 9°30S 147°07E, pop (2000e) 240 000. Seaport capital of Papua New Guinea, on the S coast of New Guinea; Allied base in World War 2; airport; university (1965); base for overseas telecommunications and national broadcasting; light industry; Hiri Moale Festival (Aug–Sep), arts festival (Sep).

Port Natal *Durban*

Port of Spain 10°38N 61°31W, pop (2000e) 50 000. Seaport capital of Trinidad and Tobago, NW coast of Trinidad; capital of Trinidad, 1783; airport; principal commercial centre in the E Caribbean; oil products, rum, sugar; botanical gardens, two cathedrals, San Andres Fort (1785).

Porton Down A research centre established by the Ministry of Defence in Wiltshire, S England, UK, for the investigation of biological and chemical warfare.

Porto Novo 6°30N 2°47E, pop (2000e) 341 300. Seaport capital of Benin, W Africa, on a lagoon in Ouémé province; settled by the Portuguese, centre for slave and tobacco trading; though the official capital, there is little political and economic activity, this taking place in Cotonou; railway; palm oil, cotton; Palace of King Toffa and museum.

Portree 57°24N 6°12W, pop (2000e) 1970. Port in Highland, NW Scotland, UK; on Loch Portree, E coast; largest town on Skye.

Port Royal [royal] A French religious and intellectual community occupying the former convent of Port-Royal-des-Champs, near Paris. It was associated with the Jansenist movement, and founded by the Abbé de Saint-Cyran (1637), a friend and admirer of the theologian, Cornelius Jansen, himself a devotee of Augustinian philosophy. The community was dispersed in 1665, and the convent destroyed (1710–11).

Portrush, Ir **Port Rois** 55°12N 6°40W, pop (2000e) 5800. Town in Coleraine district, Antrim, NE Northern Ireland, UK, on the N coast; railway; engineering; tourist centre for the Giant's Causeway, 11 km/7 mi NE.

Port Said [saeed], Arabic **Bur Said** 31°17N 32°18E, pop (2000e) 551 500. Seaport capital of Port Said governorate, NE Egypt; on Mediterranean coast at N end of Suez Canal, 169 km/105 mi NE of Cairo; founded in 1859 at beginning of Canal construction; shipping services, trade in rice, cotton, salt.

Port San Carlos 51°30S 58°59W. Settlement on the W coast of East Falkland, Falkland Is; British Task Force landed near here in May 1982, during the Falklands War.

Portsmouth (UK) 50°48N 1°05W, pop (2001e) 186 700. Seaport city and (from 1997) unitary authority in Hampshire, S England, UK; on Portsea I, 133 km/83 mi SW of London; major naval base; railway; Portsmouth University (1992, formerly Polytechnic); ship repairing, electronics, engineering; ferries to the Channel

Portugal

□ International Airport

official name **Republic of Portugal**, Port **República Portuguesa**, ancient **Lusitania**
Local name Portugal
Timezone GMT +1
Area 91 630 km^2/35 370 sq mi
Population total (2002e) 10 384 000
Status Republic
Capital Lisbon
Languages Portuguese (official), with many dialectal variations
Ethnic groups Homogeneous (Mediterranean stock), with small African minority
Religions Roman Catholic (97%), Protestant (1%), Muslim minority
Physical features Located on W side of Iberian peninsula; includes semi-autonomous Azores and Madeira Is; chief mountain range, the Serra da Estrêla (N), rising to 1991 m/6532 ft; main rivers, Douro, Tagus, Guadiana, are the lower courses of rivers beginning in Spain.
Climate Cool, maritime climate in N; warmer Mediterranean type in S; most rainfall in winter; average annual temperature 11°C (Jan), 22°C (Jul) in Lisbon; average annual rainfall 686 mm/27 in; record temperatures caused widespread forest fires in C and S regions, August 2003.
Currency 1 euro = 100 cents (previous to 2002, 1 Escudo (Esc) = 100 centavos)
Economy Several labour-intensive areas, including textiles, leather, wood products, cork, ceramics; timber; wine, fish; chemicals, electrical machinery, steel, shipbuilding; minerals, cereals, pulses, fruit, olive oil; c.20% of land is forested.
GDP (2002e) $195·2 bn, per capita $19 400
Human Development Index (2002) 0·880
History Became a kingdom under Alfonso Henriques in 1140; major period of world exploration and beginning of Portuguese Empire in 15th-c; under Spanish domination, 1580–1640; invaded by the French, 1807; island of Azores granted semi-autonomy, 1895; monarchy overthrown and republic established, 1910; dictatorship of Dr Salazar, 1928–68; military coup in 1974, followed by 10 years of political unrest under 15 governments; island of Madeira gained partial autonomy, 1980; Macao still administered by Portugal; joined EC, 1986; governed by a President, elected for five years, a Prime Minister and Council of Ministers, and a unicameral Assembly of the Republic.
Head of State
1976–86 António dos Santos Ramalho Eanes
1986–96 Mário Alberto Nobre Lopez Soares
1996– Jorge Sampaio
Head of Government
1978–9 Carlos Alberto de Mota Pinto
1979 Maria de Lurdes Pintassilgo
1980–1 Francisco de Sá Carneiro
1981–3 Francisco Pinto Balsemão
1983–5 Mário Alberto Nobre Lopez Soares
1985–95 Aníbal Cavaco Silva
1995–2001 António Guterres
2002– Jose Manuel Durao Barroso

Is, France, and the I of Wight; birthplace of Charles Dickens; Nelson's flagship *HMS Victory*; Tudor warship, *Mary Rose*; Royal Navy Museum; Royal Marines, Museum; Southsea Castle including Round Tower and Point Battery; Fort Widley (Portsdown Hill); Navy Week (Aug); football league team, Portsmouth (Pompey).

Portsmouth (Virginia) 36°50N 76°18W, pop (2000e) 100 600. Port and independent city, SE Virginia, USA, on the Elizabeth R; founded, 1752; a base for British and then Revolutionary troops during the War of Independence; evacuated and burned by Union troops during the Civil War (1861), then retaken (1862); part of a US naval complex; railway; shipbuilding (the *Chesapeake* and the ironclad *Merrimack* were built here), railway engineering, fishing; trade in tobacco and cotton.

Port Sudan [soodan] 19°38N 37°07E, pop (2000e) 319 000. Seaport capital of Eastern region, Sudan, on the Red Sea coast; Sudan's main port; founded, 1906; airfield; railway; NE terminus of an oil pipeline from Khartoum; handles most of the country's trade.

Port Talbot *Neath and Port Talbot*

Portugal *see panel*

Portuguese *Portuguese literature; Romance languages*

Portuguese literature Troubadour songs from the 13th-c represent the earliest Portuguese literature. This genre flourished, to be joined by court poetry collected in the *Cancioneiro Geral* (1516, General Song-Book). Saints' lives and legends were popular material. Drama developed after Gil Vicente (1470–1537), the tragedies of Antonio Ferreira (1528–69) being particularly notable. Classical influences from Italy and Spain affected court circles in the 16th-c, but Camões' *Os Lusíadas* (1572, The Lusiads), the Portuguese epic, confirmed nationalist feeling. This was depressed during Spanish rule, when even the language was threatened; but in the 18th-c Francisco do Nascimento (1734–1819) and Manuel du Bocage (1756–1805) revived earlier traditions. The Romantic movement, stimulated by the revolutionary João Almeida-Garrett (1799–1854), was represented by Alexandre Herculano (1810–77), Antero de Quental (1842–91), and Cesário Verde (1855–86). Júlio Dinis (1839–71) and Eça de Queirós (1845–1900), the 'Portuguese Zola', introduced the Realist novel, to be followed by Alves Redol (1911–69). But as often happens, it is the poets who best survived the political turmoil of the 20th-c. The most remarkable is Fernando Pessoa (1888–1935), who wrote from four different 'personalities'; but the Symbolist Eugénio de Castro (1869–1944), the speculative Teixeira de Pascões (1879–1952), José Régio (1901–69) with his explorations of loss, and Miguel Torga (1907–95), with his countervailing optimism, all made important contributions. Meanwhile, over two centuries of Brazilian literature have also been written in Portuguese.

Portuguese man-of-war A jellyfish-like coelenterate which floats at the ocean surface, held up by a gas-filled float; lives as a colony; individuals within the colony are specialized for particular tasks, such as feeding or reproduction; catches prey using long stinging tentacles that hang down from the float; can inflict painful stings on swimmers. (Phylum: Cnidaria. Order: Siphonophora.)

Porvoo [paw(r)voh], Swed **Borgå** 60°24N 25°40E, pop (2000e) 20 900. Picturesque town in Uudenmaa province, SE Finland; near mouth of Porvoonjoki (river); second oldest town in Finland, established, 1346; bishopric; boat service to Helsinki; publishing, brewing, tourism; home of national poet, Johan Runeberg; cathedral (15th-c); cycle race and Porvoo day (Jun); Postmaki Festival (Jul).

porwiggle *tadpole*

Poseidon [posiydn] In Greek mythology, the brother of Zeus, god of water and the sea, depicted with a trident in his hand. He is a violent god, responsible for earthquakes and similar destructive forces. He is also connected with horse-taming.

Poseidon weed [posiydn] A grass-like, totally submerged, marine plant (*Posidonia marina*) common in shallow parts of the Mediterranean sea. Leaves and rhizomes are often washed ashore in great quantities, as are **Poseidon balls**, brown globes formed of the fibrous debris by wave action. (Family: Posidoniaceae.)

positivism In philosophy, the position that all genuine knowledge is derived from and validated by science. Developed from the British empiricist tradition, it was first explicitly formulated in the 19th-c by Comte, and was taken up by the utilitarians (Bentham and Mill), Herbert Spencer, Mach, and others, who were optimistic about the benefits of scientific progress for humanity and who were hostile to theology and metaphysics.

positron The antiparticle partner to the electron; symbol e^+; mass and spin same as electron, but charge +1; discovered in 1932 by US physicist Carl Anderson and British physicist Patrick Blackett (1897–1974), by observing tracks left in cloud chambers by cosmic rays. It annihilates with electrons to give gamma rays, and is emitted by some radioactive sources, such as sodium-22. It is used in positron emission tomography in medicine, and in studies of the electron properties of solids.

possession The alleged control of a living person by an entity lacking a physical body. In the Middle Ages, the Christian Church generally saw possession in terms of demonic control, while in other cultures, shamans who appear to be taken over by a different personality may be thought of as being controlled by (often benign) spirits. These days, cases of apparent possession are frequently interpreted as being instances of multiple personality, or indicative of some other disorder.

possible worlds A philosophical concept first used by Leibniz, who claimed that God chose to create this world because it is the best of all the infinitely many worlds he might have created. Contemporary philosophers have exploited the notion in modal logic; for example, the distinction between necessary and contingent truths can be expressed as a distinction between propositions that are true in all possible worlds and propositions that are true only in some.

possum An Australian marsupial of family Burramyidae (**pygmy possum**, 7 species), family Pseudocheiridae (**ringtail possum**, 16 species), family Phalangeridae (**scaly-tailed possum** plus 3 species of **brushtail possum**), or family Petauridae (**Leadbetter's possum** plus 2 species of **striped possum**). The name is commonly used for **opossum** in the USA.

postage stamp An adhesive printed or embossed stamp or label indicating the prepayment of a fee for the conveyance of letters, postcards, parcels etc. The first postage stamps were issued in England in the 1840s, but soon became a global phenomenon. Definitive stamps are those which are normally available for purchase, while commemorative stamps are issued periodically to mark special occasions. The latter in particular have become a design specialism.

postal service The collection, sorting, and delivery of mail. National postal services have existed since the early 19th-c, using a network of post offices and post boxes for the collection of letters, cards, parcels, and other missives. Deliveries are usually to-the-door, but may also be made to a private PO Box or Poste Restante at a post office. The sorting of mail has become quicker in recent years with the introduction of postal or zip codes and new electronic technology. In some countries, private operators now provide competition for the former monopoly state suppliers. Post offices may also offer a range of additional counter services, such as savings accounts and currency exchange.

post and lintel / lintol A form of architectural construction consisting of vertical, loadbearing posts supporting horizontal lintels to create openings. It is typified by Greek architecture, in contrast to arched or arcuated construction. The technique is also known as **trabeated** construction.

poster art The development of posters as an art form, dating from the late 19th-c, when there were improvements in printing techniques, especially colour lithography. Toulouse-Lautrec was an early master who achieved some of his most striking effects through this medium; and the work of Czech artist Alphonse Mucha (1860–1939) has enjoyed a wide revival.

Postimpressionism An imprecise term coined by the art critic Roger Fry c.1910 to cover the more progressive forms of French painting since c.1880. The painters included van Gogh, Gauguin, Cézanne, and Matisse.

post-industrial society An economically and technologically advanced society no longer dependent for its productivity on large-scale, labour-intensive industrial manufacture. The term was coined by the US sociologist Daniel Bell (1919–) in 1973.

postmodern dance Originally, a chronological label to describe dance forms that rejected the theories and practices of modern dance. The term was first coined to describe the reaction against the formalized systems of codified movement in dance. It was based on a rejection of stylized techniques, introducing in their stead 'natural' movements such as walking, running, and breathing. Postmodern dance could be intensely theatrical or abstract and sparse in style (minimalist), as seen in the works of Merce Cunningham, whose compositional work provided the starting point for the postmodern movement in the 1960s. Together with Douglas Dunn, he formed the Judson Dance Theater in Greenwich Village, New York. In Germany, Pina Bausch's *Ausdruckstanz* (expressionist dance) exposed the alienation of the individual from the group, and used male and female relationships to configure the social predicament. As the century advanced, the term 'postmodern' became so diffuse as to lose its definition.

Postmodernism A term used in architecture to describe a style or concept that supersedes 20th-c modernism and the International Style in particular. Often used in a polemical and self-consciously intellectual way, it is generally applied to buildings which draw upon an eclectic range of stylistic precedents, especially classical, such as the A T & T building, New York (1978–83), architects Johnson & Burgee. In recent years the term has been increasingly used to identify a basic rejection of previously widely-held architectural beliefs, and has also emerged in relation to such fields as literature and cinema.

post mortem The dissection of a body after death in order to determine the cause of death; also known as **necropsy**. A post mortem is carried out whenever the cause of death is uncertain, particularly when death has occurred in suspicious circumstances. As well as gross dissection of the body and examination of the internal organs, it may also involve microscopic examination of the tissues and tests for micro-organisms and chemical substances in the body fluids.

post-natal depression A disturbance in a mother's mood during the period following delivery of a baby. It is related to sudden drops in hormone levels, fatigue, and a reaction to the momentous events of childbirth. Mild emotional upset is common, usually limited tearfulness and irritability lasting a few days. More serious depression may occur, particularly in cases where social support is poor, with feelings of anxiety and groundless fears about the baby; a few mothers even react with revulsion, forming the notion that their baby is not their own. Rarely, a severe mental illness develops (*puerperal psychosis*), with a manic depressive or schizophrenic-type episode that requires treatment on a psychiatric ward.

post office *postal service*

postpartum haemorrhage / hemorrhage Bleeding in the mother in excess of 500 ml (c.1 pt) occurring in the first 24 hours after the birth of the baby. It may be a result of retention of a placental fragment, inadequate uterine contraction after the birth, lacerations, or maternal bleeding disorders. Urgent blood transfusion is required while dealing with the cause, which in severe cases may necessitate hysterectomy.

post-production The completion stages of a film after shooting up to the first public showing. The picture is finally edited to the director's satisfaction, and the original negative cut to conform; music and sound effects are recorded and mixed with the actors' dialogue in dubbing the final track. This magnetic record is transferred to a photographic sound negative for printing along with the cut picture negative to produce the *answer print*. After the director's approval, a *show print* is made for the premiere presentation. Corresponding stages are followed for a video production: the editing and sound track preparation results in the 'on-line' transfer of the original videotape to produce the final master for transmission or duplication.

PostScript A computer language which has been developed to provide a uniform means of describing pages of text and/or graphics. It is widely used in desk-top publishing. PostScript-compatible printers contain a microcomputer system called a *raster image processor* (RIP) which can interpret a PostScript program and produce the relevant printed page(s).

Posts, Telegraph and Telephones Authority (PTT) A government appointed agency which, in most countries, provides a telecommunications service and at the same time controls electromagnetic transmission. Before any private organization can install its own telecommunications, it must obtain permission from the PTT.

post-traumatic stress disorder A severe anxiety reaction that occurs in some people exposed to a traumatic event involving witness to, threat of, or experience of death or serious harm; it often affects war veterans. The traumatic event is re-experienced in the form of images or thoughts ('flashbacks'), accompanied by sweating, a rapid heart beat, and a feeling of fear. Flashbacks are often precipitated by cues that resemble the original event, and stimuli that are associated with the trauma are avoided, which may substantially disrupt normal life. The condition also predisposes to depression and addiction. It may be prevented by offering counselling or other psychiatric interventions to people who have experienced extremely stressful situations.

Potala Palace An imposing 13-storey stronghold constructed on a rocky outcrop near Lhasa, Tibet, in the 17th-c. Once the religious and political centre of Tibet, the complex includes the Red Palace (former seat of the Dalai Lamas) as well as many halls, chapels, and prisons. A world heritage site.

potash Potassium oxide, K_2O. The term is generally used for any potassium compounds used as fertilizers whose potassium content is reported in terms of the equivalent amount of K_2O, or about 1·2 times the percentage by weight of potassium.

potassium K (Lat *kalium*), element 19, melting point 63°C. One of the most reactive metals, and the third of the alkali metal group. It is not found free in nature, but obtained chiefly from mineral deposits of the chloride (KCl) and the nitrate (KNO_3, also known as *nitre* or *saltpetre*). The metal is prepared by the electrolysis of molten KCl or KOH. It is an important strong reducing agent, and must be kept away from water, with which it reacts explosively. In virtually all of its compounds, it has oxidation state +1. These are important mainly as agricultural chemicals and explosives.

potassium–argon dating A radiometric method for dating rocks more than 100 000 years old. It uses the fact that radioactive isotope potassium-40 decays with a known half-life to yield argon-40, and hence the amount of each isotope in a rock can be used to determine its age. It has proved crucial for dating the early human remains found in the E African Rift Valley at such sites as Olduvai, Laetoli, Hadar, and Koobi Fora.

potato A well-known tuber-producing plant and staple crop throughout temperate regions of the world; an erect to somewhat sprawling perennial; pinnate leaves; clusters of drooping, white or purple flowers, with a 5-lobed corolla and five yellow stamens forming a prominent cone. The fruit is a berry similar in appearance to that of the tomato (a relative), but usually greenish, and unlike the tomato it is poisonous. The value of the potato as a vegetable lies in the stem tubers which are produced in abundance at the ends of stolons and which are rich in starch, vitamin C, and proteins. The tubers vary greatly in size, shape, colour, keeping and cooking qualities, and taste. The skins can be white, yellow to brown, pink, red, or purplish-black, and the flesh white to yellow, pink, or purple. The 'eyes' on a potato are dormant buds, which in favourable conditions give rise to new stems. Plants grown from tubers are clones of the parent; this is commercially useful, as any desired characters are conserved. There are thousands of varieties, all regarded as belonging to a single species, *Solanum tuberosum*. There are also some 160 wild species, not all closely related.

The potato is native to South America, where it has a long history as a cultivated plant, primitive varieties being a staple crop from at least AD 200. Prior to the Spanish conquest, it was confined to the high Andes from Colombia to N Argentina and to Chile. Exactly when and how it was introduced to Europe is still a matter for conjecture, but despite various legends it probably first arrived in Spain from Colombia or Peru c.1565, and separately in England towards the end of the 16th-c (though not, as legend would have it, brought by Sir Walter Raleigh). Whatever its exact origin, 90% of the world's production now comes from the Old World, mainly E Europe, and as a crop it is rivalled only by wheat and rice. Potatoes are susceptible to a number of diseases, including viruses and potato blight (*Phytophthora infestans*). Production of better quality, higher-yielding, and especially of disease-resistant strains is a priority for crop breeders. Wild species and primitive strains, many of which are disease-resistant and have other desirable traits, are nowadays recognized as being very important as a gene pool for improving modern strains. (Family: Solanaceae.)

potato blight A widespread disease of potato and related plants caused by the fungus *Phytophthora infestans*, especially in wet weather; symptoms include brown patches on leaves and in tubers; white mould often visible beneath leaves. A severe outbreak in Ireland in the 1840s caused the great Irish potato famine. (Class: Oomycetes. Order: Peronosporales.)

Potemkin, Grigoriy Alexandrovich [potyomkin] (1739–91) Russian field marshal, born near Smolensk, W Russia. He entered the Russian army, attracted the notice of Catherine II, and became her intimate favourite, heavily influencing Russian foreign policy. There is some reason to believe they were secretly married. He distinguished himself in the Russo–Turkish Wars (1768–74, 1787–92), during which Russia gained the Crimea and the N coast of the Black Sea.

potential A scalar quantity associated with a force whose rate of change with distance is proportional to the strength of that force; symbol *V*. In a gravitational field, it is the potential energy of an object of mass 1 kg; in an electric field it is the potential energy of a charge of 1 C.

potential difference A quantity in physics, often called **voltage**; symbol *U*, units V (volt). A potential difference is said to exist between two points if work must be done against an electric field to carry a charge from one point to the other. A potential difference divided by the distance between the two points gives the strength of the electric field between the points. The potential difference between the terminals of a battery indicates the battery's ability to drive current around a circuit.

potential energy The energy stored by an object by virtue of its position in the region of influence of some force; symbol *V*, units J (joule). For example, an object acquires potential energy equal to the work done against the force of gravity in raising it above the Earth's surface; when released, the object falls to the ground, and its potential energy is converted into kinetic energy, the energy of motion. Work done in compressing a spring is stored as elastic potential energy in the spring. The potential energy of a positive electric charge may be increased by bringing it closer to another positive charge.

potentilla A member of a large genus of annuals or perennials, sometimes creeping, rarely small shrubs, native to N temperate regions; leaves with three leaflets, or pinnately or palmately divided into leaflets; flowers with epicalyx, 4–5 sepals, 4–5 petals;. They can be roughly divided into two groups: **cinquefoils** with 5-petalled flowers, and **tormentils** with 4-petalled flowers. Several, especially the shrubby species, are widely grown ornamentals. (Genus: *Potentilla*, 500 species. Family: Rosaceae.)

potentiometer An instrument for the accurate measurement or control of electrical potential. A known potential drop is created in a long (usually coiled) wire by a battery, and a sliding contact is used to tap off any proportion of this drop. Potentiometers are used in electronic circuits, especially as volume controls in transistor radios.

potholing *speleology*

potlatch A feast celebrating an important event, or following personal humiliation, at which the host gives away his wealth (slaves, blankets, canoes, etc). People receiving wealth in this way would later give their own potlatches, ensuring circulation of some of the property. It was a common practice among North American Indians of the Northwest Pacific coast, becoming increasingly competitive under pressure from colonial trade goods and disease, and culminating in dramatic destruction of property. The potlatch was outlawed in the late 19th-c, but made legal again in the 1950s.

pot marigold An annual to perennial (*Calendula officinalis*), growing to 70 cm/27 in; slightly sticky to the touch; leaves paddle-shaped; flower-heads solitary, up to 7 cm/2¾ in across; outer ray florets orange or yellow, often in several rows; fruit boat-shaped. Of unknown origin, it is a popular garden plant. The dried petals were once used for colouring butter. (Family: Compositae.)

Potomac River [potohmak] River in West Virginia, Virginia, and Maryland, USA; formed at the junction of two branches rising in the Allegheny Mts; flows through Washington, DC, into Chesapeake Bay; length 460 km/286 mi; navigable for large craft as far as Washington; main tributary the Shenandoah; the Great Falls lie 24 km/15 mi above Washington.

potoroo *rat kangaroo*

Potosí [potohsee] 19°34S 65°45W, pop (2000e) 136 400. Capital of Potosí department, SW Bolivia; altitude 4070 m/13 353 ft; highest city of its size in the world; founded by Spanish in 1545; major silver-mining town in 17th–18th-c, becoming the most important city in South America at the time; airfield; railway; university (1892); tin, silver, copper, lead; chief industrial centre of Bolivia; Convent of Santa Teresa (art collection); Las Cajas Reales (Cabildo and Royal Treasury); cathedral; mint (Casa Real de Moneda), founded 1572, rebuilt 1759, now a museum; thermal baths at the Laguna de Tarapaya; city is a world heritage site.

Potsdam 52°23N 13°04E, pop (2000e) 145 000. Capital of Potsdam county, E Germany; on R Havel, W of Berlin; former residence of German emperors and Prussian kings; badly bombed in World War 2; scene of the 1945 Potsdam Conference; railway; Academy of Political Science and Law; colleges of cinematographic and television art; Central Meteorological Centre; food processing, pharmaceuticals, electrical equipment, textiles, film industry; Sans Souci palace and park (1745–7), 18th-c garrison church.

Potsdam Conference A conference which met during the final stages of World War 2 (17 Jul–2 Aug 1945). Churchill (and later Attlee), Stalin, and Truman met to discuss the post-war settlement in Europe. Soviet power in E Europe was recognized, and it was agreed that Poland's W frontier should run along the Oder–Neisse line. The decision was made to divide Germany into four occupation zones and to transfer the German population of certain E European territories (over 10 million people) to Germany. It established a Council of Foreign Ministers to handle peace treaties, made plans to introduce representative and elective principles of government in Germany, discussed reparations (on which the Soviet Union was subsequently to default), outlawed the Nazi Party, and decentralized the German economy. Political differences between the USA and USSR, and the breaching of the agreement by Stalin, marked the start of the Cold War. The **Potsdam Declaration** (26 July 1945) demanded from Japan the choice between unconditional surrender or total destruction.

Potter, (Helen) Beatrix (1866–1943) Writer and illustrator of books for children, born in London, UK. A repressed and lonely child, she grew up longing for the country and animals. She taught herself to draw and paint, and her famous characters started as sketches of pet animals dressed as human beings, along with letters to amuse the sick son of her former governess, which she privately published as *The Tale of Peter Rabbit* (1900) and *The Tailor of Gloucester* (1902). A publisher reprinted them, and she became the outstanding writer and artist of picture-story books of her time, widely translated and reprinted. *Peter Rabbit*, *Jemima Puddle-Duck*, *Mrs Tiggy-Winkle*, *Benjamin Bunny*, and her other creations have become classics of children's literature. In 1913 she married **William Heelis**, stopped writing, and spent the rest of her life raising Herdwick sheep. *The Journal of Beatrix Potter*, written in code, was transcribed by Leslie Linder (1966).

Potter, Dennis (Christopher George) (1935–94) Playwright, born in the Forest of Dean, Gloucestershire, SWC England, UK. He studied at Oxford, and was a journalist and TV critic before he began writing plays. Although he wrote for the stage (*Sufficient Carbohydrate*, 1984), he was primarily a television dramatist. His first success was *Vote, Vote, Vote for Nigel Barton* (1965). Other plays include *Brimstone and Treacle* (1976), *Blue Remembered Hills* (1979, BAFTA), *Cream in my Coffee* (1982, Prix Italia), *The Singing Detective* (1986), and *Lipstick on Your Collar* (1993). Several dealt with controversial topics, such as the treatment of the self-doubting Christ in *Son of Man* (1969). His work was often technically innovative, as in *Pennies from Heaven* (1978), which required the actors to mime to popular songs of the 1920s and 1930s that intercut the action. His work includes a novel, *Hide and Seek* (1973). He completed *Karaoke* and *Cold Lazarus* just before his death.

Potter, Paul (1625–54) Painter and etcher, born in Enkhuizen, The Netherlands. He worked in Delft and The Hague, moving in 1652 to Amsterdam. His best pictures are small pastoral scenes with animal figures, but he also painted large pictures, notably the life-size 'Young Bull' (1647, The Hague).

Potter, Stephen (Meredith) (1900–69) British writer and radio producer. He joined the BBC in 1938, and was co-author with Joyce Grenfell of the *How* series. He wrote a novel, *The Young Man* (1929), and an educational study, *The Muse in Chains* (1937), but made his name with a series of humorous books on the art of demoralizing the opposition – *The Theory and Practice of Gamesmanship; or the Art of Winning Games Without Actually Cheating* (1947), *One-Upmanship* (1952), and *Supermanship* (1958).

Potteries, The NW Midlands urban area in the upper Trent valley of Staffordshire, C England, UK; extends c.14 km/9 mi (NW–SE) by 5 km/3 mi (W–E); includes several towns within Stoke-on-Trent; railway; since the 18th-c, the heart of the English china and earthenware industry, based on local clay and coal.

potter wasp A solitary, hunting wasp; adults make flask-shaped nests of clay and saliva; females provision nests with paralysed caterpillars or other insect larvae before egg laid; adults feed on nectar. (Order: Hymenoptera. Family: Eumenidae.)

pottery Vessels made out of fired clay, produced by mankind since the earliest civilizations. They can be hand-built, moulded, or in more sophisticated societies thrown on a wheel. Pottery tends to be soft and rather porous, and is therefore normally protected by a **glaze**, which also gives a shiny decorative appearance. Glaze is applied after the first firing, when the pot is placed in the kiln for the second time at a lower temperature.

potto A primitive primate (*Perodicticus potto*) native to Africa; resembles the slow loris, but has a dark face and short tail; four spines (elongated vertebrae) on back of neck. (Family: Lorisidae.) The name **golden potto** is used for the related **angwantibo**.)

pouched rat A type of rat native to Africa; three species resemble rats, two resemble hamsters; all have internal cheek pouches; rat-like species often have blind wingless earwigs (of genus *Hemimerus*) in their fur. (Subfamily: Cricetomyinae, 5 species.)

Poulenc, Francis [poolãk] (1899–1963) Composer, born in Paris, France. He became a member of *Les Six*, and was prominent in the reaction against Impressionism. His works include much chamber music and the ballet *Les Biches*, produced by Diaghilev in 1924; but he is best known for his considerable output of songs, such as *Fêtes galantes* (1943).

Pound, Ezra (Weston Loomis) (1885–1972) Poet and critic, born in Hailey, Idaho, USA. He studied chiefly at the University of Pennsylvania, then travelled widely in Europe, working as a journalist and editor. He became part of literary movements in London, where his publications included *Personae* (1909) and *Homage to Sextus Propertius* (1919). From 1924 he made his home in Italy, where he caused resentment by making pro-Fascist broadcasts in the early stages of World War 2. In 1945 he was escorted back to the USA and indicted for treason, but judged insane, and placed in an asylum. Released in 1958, he returned to Italy. He was an experimental poet, whom T S Eliot regarded as the motivating force behind modern poetry. His main work is *The Cantos*, a loosely knit series of poems, which he began during World War 1, and which were published in many instalments (1930–59).

pound (economics) The unit of currency of the UK (the **pound sterling**), and certain other countries. The £ symbol is derived from letter *L* for *libra*, a measure of weight. It was formerly divided into 20 shillings and 240 pence; but since decimalization in 1971 it is divided into 100 pence (*new pence*). One-pound gold coins called sovereigns were made for circulation in Britain from 1489 to 1931, after which paper pound notes were in general circulation. In 1983 the British government introduced a one-pound coin to replace the one-pound note, which it stopped issuing on 31 Dec 1984.

pound (physics) *kilogram*

Poussin, Nicolas [poosĩ] (1594–1665) Painter, born near Les Andelys, NW France. He went to Rome in 1624, and spent the rest of his life there, apart from a short visit (1640–2) to Paris. The greatest master of French Classicism, deeply influenced by Raphael and the Antique, his masterpieces include two sets of the 'Seven Sacraments' (1636–40, 1644–8).

Poussinisme *Rubénisme*

poverty trap An anomaly in a social welfare and taxation system which occurs when individuals, previously unemployed and claiming various social benefits, obtain work, and find that they are taxed, so ending up with less net income than before. The same situation may also apply to low-paid workers who obtain a small rise and find they have lost the right to certain benefits. It is also used more generally to describe situations where, because of the loss of means-tested benefits, the return to working is too small to be worth the effort, or the return to accepting promotion is too small for the extra responsibility.

POW Abbreviation of **prisoner-of-war**, whose treatment was first codified by International Treaty at the Hague Conference of 1899. This stated that POWs must be humanely treated, and not obliged to divulge military information other than name, rank, and number.

powder metallurgy Making metal shapes by compressing powdered metal into a finished or near-finished shape. First used for tungsten lamp filaments, it is now used for such products as tungsten carbide cutting tools and self-lubricating bearings. It can be used on iron, tin, nickel, copper, aluminium, and titanium. The powders are made a specific and regular size by atomization (cooling a spray of molten metal) or controlled chemical precipitation. The material is pressed into shape and then heat-treated (*sintered*). In an alternative method, the powder is fed from a hopper into a gap between rollers to produce a strip. The advantages of powder metallurgy are economy of manufacture and porosity where needed.

Powell, Anthony (Dymoke) (1905–2000) Novelist, born in London, UK. He studied at Oxford, worked in publishing and journalism before World War 2, and by 1936 had published four satirical novels, beginning with *Afternoon Men* (1931). After the war he began the series of novels he called *A Dance to the Music of Time* (1951–75; televised, 1997) – 12 volumes, covering 50 years of British upper middle-class life and attitudes. *At Lady Molly's* (1957) won the James Tait Black Memorial Prize, and *Temporary Kings* (1973) won the W H Smith Literary Award. He also published four volumes of memoirs under the general title *To Keep the Ball Rolling* (1976–82). Later books include the novel *The Fisher King* (1986) and a volume of criticism, *Under Review* (1992). He was made a Companion of Honour in 1988.

Powell, Bud, popular name of **Earl Powell** (1924–66) Jazz pianist, born in New York City, USA. Playing from the age of six, he became involved with the modern jazz movement in the 1940s, with encouragement from Thelonious Monk. A head injury sustained in an attack heralded a series of visits to mental hospitals; nevertheless, he was the most influential jazz pianist of his time. He was the first choice to work and record with top New York players until he moved to Paris (1959–64), where he led a trio featuring US expatriate drummer, Kenny Clarke. The film *Round Midnight* (1986) was partly based on his life.

Powell, Colin (Luther) [**koh**lin] (1937–) US army general, born in New York City, USA. He studied at the City College of New York, and took an army commission, later serving in Vietnam (1962–3, 1968–9). After holding a series of senior commands, he was appointed head of the National Security Council by President Reagan (1987–9), took over the Army Forces Command, and was made chairman of the joint chiefs-of-staff by President Bush (1989–93), the first African-American officer to receive this distinction. He had overall responsibility for the US military operation against Iraq in 1990–1. Britain awarded him an honorary knighthood in 1993. He retired from the army in 1993, and wrote a best-selling autobiography, *My American Journey* (1995), emerging as a popular and high-profile national figure. He was chairman of America's Promise (1997–2000). A Republican, he announced he was not interested in running for president in 1996. George W Bush appointed him secretary of state (2001–).

Powell, (John) Enoch (1912–98) British statesman, born in Birmingham, West Midlands, C England, UK. He studied at Cambridge, was professor of Greek at the University of Sydney (1937–9), and became a Conservative MP in 1950. He held several junior posts before becoming minister of health (1960–3). His outspoken attitude on the issues of non-white immigration and racial integration came to national attention in 1968, and as a consequence of this he was dismissed from the shadow cabinet. He was elected an Ulster Unionist MP in 1974, losing his seat in 1987. His many publications include works on Herodotos, books of poetry (collected works, 1990), and general socio-political texts, such as *A Nation Not Afraid* (1965), *Medicine and Politics* (1966), and *No Easy Answers* (1973). In 1994 appeared *The Evolution of the Gospel*.

Powell, Michael (1905–90) Film director, scriptwriter, and producer, born in Bekesbourne, Kent, SE England, UK. He worked as a director on minor productions in the 1930s, and co-directed on *The Thief of Baghdad* (1940) for Korda, who introduced him to the Hungarian scriptwriter, **Emeric Pressburger** (1902–88). Powell and Pressburger formed The Archers Company in 1942, and for more than 10 years made a series of unusual and original features, many with an exceptional use of colour, such as *Black Narcissus* (1947) and *The Tales of Hoffman* (1951). After the break-up of the partnership, Powell's productions were infrequent, including the controversial *Peeping Tom* (1960) and *The Boy Who Turned Yellow* (1972), from a script by Pressburger.

Powell, Robert (1944–) Actor, born in Salford, Lancashire, NW England, UK. He worked in repertory, appeared with the Royal Shakespeare Company, and toured with the Bristol Old Vic. He became widely known through his role in the television series *Jude the Obscure* (1971), and for his title role in the Franco Zeffirelli film for television, *Jesus of Nazareth* (1977). His feature film roles include *Secrets* (1971), *The Thirty-Nine Steps* (1978), *Frankenstein* (1984), and *The Mystery of Edwin Drood* (1993). Later television work includes *The Detectives* (1989) – reprised in a 1992 comedy series with Jasper Carrott – and *The First Circle* (1991).

power (mathematics) *exponent*

power (physics) The rate of change of work with time; symbol *P*, units W (watt). To lift an object some distance into the air requires a fixed amount of work, but to do the job more quickly requires more power.

powerboat racing The racing of boats fitted with high-powered and finely-tuned engines. The first boat to be fitted with a petrol engine was by Frenchman Jean Joseph Lenoir (1822–1900) in 1865, when he introduced his boat on the R Seine in Paris. The first race was c.1900, and the first race of note was from Calais to Dover in 1903. Races take place both inshore and offshore.

Powhatan Confederacy [powuhtan] A group of Algonkin North American Indian tribes inhabiting the Tidewater region of Virginia at the time of the first white contact; named after chief Powhatan. Initially receptive, the Indians grew suspicious of the newcomers, and in 1622 and 1644 launched massive attacks on them, but were defeated both times. Over 1000 scattered descendants of these tribes were still to be found in Virginia in the mid-20th-c.

Powys [powis] pop (2001e) 126 300; area 5077 sq km/1960 sq mi. Mountainous county in E Wales, UK; created in 1974, and status reaffirmed in 1996; bounded E by England; drained by the Usk, Wye, Taff and Tawe Rivers; Lake Vyrnwy (reservoir) source of water for Liverpool and Birmingham; administrative centre, Llandrindod Wells; other chief towns, Brecon, Newtown, Welshpool; agriculture, forestry, tourism; Brecon Beacons National Park.

Powys, John Cowper [powis] (1872–1963) Writer and critic, born in Shirley, Derbyshire, C England, UK, the brother of Llewelyn (1884–1939) and Theodore Francis Powys (1875–1953). He studied at Cambridge, then worked as a teacher and lecturer, much of the time in the USA. He wrote poetry and essays, but is best known for his long novels on West Country and historical themes, such as *A Glastonbury Romance* (1932) and *Owen Glendower* (1940). His *Autobiography* was published in 1934.

Poyang Hu or **P'o-yang Hu** [pohyahng hoo] Lake in N Jiangxi province, SE China; China's largest freshwater lake; area 3583 sq km/1383 sq mi; much reduced from earlier size by silt deposits and land reclamation; merges with the Yangtze R in N.

Poynings' Law, also known as the **Statues of Drogheda** Statutes enacted by the Irish Parliament at the direction of Sir Edward Poynings (1459–1521), English lord deputy of Ireland, in 1494, removing its right to meet without the English government's agreement and to pass laws without prior approval by the English king. The immediate object was to crush Yorkist support, but over the long term it bolstered English claims to sovereignty and conquest of Ireland. It was effectively repealed in 1782.

Poznań [poznan], Ger **Posen** 52°25N 16°93E, pop (2000e) 595 000. Capital of Poznań voivodship, W Poland, on R Warta; capital of Poland until 13th-c; bishopric; airfield; railway; two universities (1918, 1919); metallurgy, machinery, chemicals, clothing, food processing, transport; noted for its choirs and the Polish Theatre of Dance; Franciscan church (17th–18th-c), 13th-c castle with museum of crafts, national museum, Great Poland army museum, cathedral (18th-c, largely rebuilt); festival of Polish contemporary music (spring), international violin competitions (every five years), fair of commerce (Jun).

PR *public relations*

Prado [prahdoh] The Spanish national museum in Madrid, housing the world's finest collection of Spanish art, as well as many exhibits from other major European schools. The gallery, which evolved from the private collections of the Spanish royal house, was opened to the public in 1819 by Ferdinand VII.

Praesepe [priyseepee] *Cancer*

Praetorian Guard [pritawrian] An elite corps in imperial Rome – effectively, the emperor's bodyguard. Their real influence dates from the 20s AD, when they were concentrated in a single barracks in Rome itself, and put under the control of a single commander.

Praetorius, Michael [pritawrius] (1571–1621) Composer, born in Creuzburg, C Germany. He studied in Torgau, Frankfurt an der Oder, and Zerbst, and became court organist and (from 1604) *Kapellmeister* at the court of Wolfenbüttel. As well as being one of the most prolific composers of his time (especially of church music), he wrote an important treatise, *Syntagma musicum* (1614–20).

praetors [preeterz] In ancient Rome, the chief law officers of the state, elected annually, second only to the consuls in importance. The office could not be held before the age of 33.

pragmatics In linguistics, the study of the way context influences the use and understanding of language, particularly in interactive situations such as addressing, replying, being polite, joking, or being persuasive. This includes the study of speech acts – the way language is used to *do* things; for example, *I promise*, used in appropriate circumstances, *is* to promise.

Pragmatic Sanction A Habsburg family law devised in 1713 by Charles VI to alter an earlier pact in favour of the undivided succession of his heirs, male or female, to the Habsburg lands (1713). Later, much effort was deployed in achieving internal and international guarantees for his daughter Maria Theresa's claims, though these were repudiated by Frederick II of Prussia (1740).

pragmatism A philosophical theory of truth and meaning developed by the American philosophers Peirce, William James, and Dewey. Essentially, it is the view that theoretical disputes can be resolved by examining their practical consequences: beliefs are true if and because they work not vice versa.

Prague, Czech **Praha** 50°05N 14°25E, pop (2000e) 1 219 000. Industrial and commercial capital of Czech Republic, on R Vltava; important trading centre since 10th-c; capital of newly-created Czechoslovakia, 1918; occupied by Warsaw Pact troops, 1968; historical centre declared a conservation area, 1971; archbishopric; airport (Ruzyně); railway; metro; Charles University

(1348); technical university (1707); chemicals, machine tools, locomotives, aircraft, glass, motorcycles, furniture, soap, perfumes; Hradčany Castle, Cathedral of St Vitus, Royal Palace (Královský Palác), St Nicholas Cathedral, Wallenstein Palace, St George (10th-c Romanesque church), National Gallery.

Praia [prahya] 14°53N 23°30W, pop (2000e) 43 000. Port and capital of the Republic of Cape Verde, on S shore of São Tiago I; airport connecting with Dakar and neighbouring islands; naval shipyard, light industry, fishing, commerce.

prairie The extensive grassland and treeless region of N USA and Canada. Originally the vegetation was coarse grass and habitat for the bison. Its fertile soils encouraged ploughing and cultivation, and the prairies are now a major arable area. Cattle ranching is also important. Little natural prairie survives. Prairies are known as *steppe* in Europe and Asia, and as *pampa(s)* in South America.

prairie chicken A grouse native to C USA (*Tympanuchus cupido*); upright tail; long upright feathers on head; inflatable orange neck sacs; inhabits prairie; eats fruit, seeds, and insects.

prairie dog A North American squirrel; length, up to 45 cm/18 in, with short tail; inhabits open country; digs extensive burrow systems called 'towns' (composed of 'wards' which contain social units called 'coteries'). (Genus: *Cynomys*, 5 species.)

prairie schooner A type of wagon used by emigrants making the journey W across the USA in the 19th-c, with cloth covers stretched over hoops. They were commonly known as **covered wagons**, and also as **Conestoga wagons**, from the place in Pennsylvania where they were originally manufactured.

prairie wolf *coyote*

Pramoedya, Ananta Toe [pramudya], also spelled **Pramudya Ananta Tur** (1925–) Novelist, born in Blora, Java, Indonesia. He is Indonesia's most celebrated writer, best known for his 'Buru Quartet', named after the prison island where he was incarcerated in 1965 as a political prisoner. Banned by the Suharto regime, the theme of the novels, such as *This Earth of Mankind* (1982) and *A Child of All Nations* (1984), is Indonesia's effort to create a national identity. In the early 1960s, as a communist sympathizer, he had become a key member of the Institute for People's Culture in which he denounced other writers. This tarnished his reputation, and there were protests when, in 1995, he was awarded the Magsaysay prize.

Prasad, Rajendra [prasad] (1884–1963) Indian statesman and first president (1950–62), born in Zeradei, E India. He studied law, but left legal practice to become a follower of Mahatma Gandhi. A member of the Working Committee of the All-India Congress in 1922, he was president of the Congress several times between 1934 and 1948. In 1946 he was appointed minister for food and agriculture, and president of the Indian Constituent Assembly, becoming president of the Republic in 1950. He wrote several books, including *India Divided at the Feet of Mahatma Gandhi*.

Pratchett, Terry (1948–) Writer, born in Beaconsfield, Buckinghamshire, SC England, UK. He is best known for his series of fantasy novels, Discworld, which began in 1983 with *The Colour of Magic* and which had reached a 31st novel, *The Monstrous Regiment*, in 2003. *The Science of Discworld* appeared in 1999, with a second volume in 2002. Other works include the 'Truckers' trilogy (called the 'Bromeliad' trilogy in the USA), and a series of Johnny Maxwell novels. Several books have been adapted for stage and television.

pratincole [pratingkohl] A bird of the Old World family Glareolidae, subfamily Glareolinae (8 species); long wings, short tail; short black bill with reddish base; short legs (Genus: *Glareolus*, 7 species) or long legs (Genus: *Stiltia*); lives near water; eats insects.

prawn A general name for many shrimp-like crustaceans. *Prawn* and *shrimp* are interchangeable common names, with usage varying according to local tradition; in the USA, for example, *shrimp* is the more commonly used term. (Class: Malacostraca. Order: Decapoda.)

Praxiteles [praksiteleez] (4th-c BC) Sculptor from Athens, considered one of the greatest of Greek sculptors. His works have almost all perished, though his 'Hermes Carrying the Boy Dionysus' was found at Olympia in 1877. Several of his statues are known from Roman copies.

prayer Turning to God in speech or silent concentration. A major characteristic of most religions, it includes petition, adoration, confession, invocation, thanksgiving, and intercession. It can be silent (mental) or vocal, public or private, individual or corporate, liturgical or free. It is generally considered an essential feature of worship.

praying mantis A large, green mantis which lies motionless in wait for its prey, holding its grasping forelegs in an attitude suggestive of prayer; found in Europe. (Order: Mantodea. Family: Mantidae.)

Precambrian era A geological time before the Phanerozoic, from the formation of the Earth (c.4600 million years ago) to c.590 million years ago; subdivided into the Archean and the Proterozoic eons. Precambrian rocks outcrop over vast areas of continental interiors.

precedent A doctrine of law, present in most legal systems, whereby an earlier court's decision or judgment on the same point of law involving similar facts is followed by another court at a later date. Some precedents, where they are 'in point' and have been decided by a higher court, are binding and must be followed. Prior decisions by courts of equal or lesser authority or courts of another jurisdiction may be persuasive to varying degrees, and can be followed if it is felt appropriate. Precedent is sometimes referred to as 'judge-made law', as opposed to statute law; but precedent can be overruled by statute, and where any conflict exists the statute takes precedence. The term is also applied to the copy of a legal document, such as a will or a deed, which is used or adapted as a model or style for drafting other documents.

precession In rotational mechanics, the progressive change in orientation of the axis of rotation. For example, a child's spinning top spins about its own axis, but also wobbles or precesses about the vertical. The Earth precesses in a complicated way.

precession of the equinoxes A phenomenon which results from slow changes in the direction in space of the Earth's rotation axis. The gravitational attractions of the Sun and Moon tug at the Earth's equatorial bulge, leading to a turning force or 'couple' that swings the rotation axis through a cone in space, at an angle of 23·5° to the equatorial plane, on a period of 25 800 years. An important consequence of precession is that the positions of all celestial objects change continuously: the origin of the co-ordinate system is where the Equator and ecliptic cross (the first point of Aries) and this moves W along the ecliptic at 50 arc seconds a year. Star catalogues always list the year to which the positions apply, so that the exact position at any moment has to be computed. Another consequence is that the celestial pole describes a circle 47° in diameter, and in 14 000 years Vega, rather than Polaris, will be the North Star.

precious stones *gemstones*

precipitate Insoluble material formed during a chemical reaction in solution. Examples include the deposition of scale in a kettle and the formation of soap scum by hard water.

precipitation A climatic term covering rainfall, drizzle, snow, sleet, hail, and dew. As rising air cools, it condenses around dust particles to form water droplets and clouds. If the droplet grows to a critical size, it will fall as precipitation; the type reaching the ground depends on the air temperature between the cloud and the ground. In many parts of the world, rain and snow are the main contributors, and often the words 'rainfall' and 'precipitation' are used interchangeably.

Precise Positioning Service *Global Positioning System*

Pre-Columbian art and architecture The arts of the North, Central, and South American Indians, before the European conquests of the 16th-c. The more advanced 'high cultures' developed in the Peruvian (C Andean) area of South America and in Central America and Mexico. In Peru, the Incas (15th-c)

Length Of Pregnancy In Some Mammals

Animal	Gestation period*	Animal	Gestation period*
camel	406	kangaroo	40
cat	62	lion	108
chimpanzee	280	mink	50
cow	237	monkey, rhesus	164
dog	62	mouse	21
dolphin	276	opossum	13
elephant, African	640	orangutan	245–275
ferret	42	pig	113
fox	52	rabbit	32
giraffe	395–425	rat	21
goat	151	reindeer	215–245
guinea pig	68	seal, northern fur	350
hamster	16	sheep	148
hedgehog	35–40	skunk	62
horse	337	squirrel, grey	44
human	266	tiger	105–109
hyena	110	whale	365

*average number of days

built with huge stone blocks, worked smooth and fitted tightly together. In Central America, truncated pyramids served as bases for temples; the Maya (Guatemala, Honduras, Mexico) were great builders and inventive sculptors in stone, pottery, and jade, as were the Aztecs of Mexico. Most pre-Columbian cultures produced textiles and metalwork.

predella [pridela] A row of small pictures attached to the lower edge of an altarpiece. Predella panels normally illustrate scenes from the life of the saint who appears on the main *pala* above.

predestination In Christian theology, the doctrine that the ultimate salvation or damnation of each human individual has been ordained beforehand. A source of endless dispute, the doctrine has been interpreted in many ways. It was first fully articulated by Augustine during his controversy with the Pelagians, who upheld the doctrine of free will. The Protestant Reformers Luther and Calvin defended the doctrine, though in varying degrees. Jakob Arminius (1560–1609) rejected the Calvinist view of predestination, and argued that the divine sovereignty was compatible with human free will. According to the teaching of Islam, human beings cannot ultimately oppose God's will, but they have the freedom to accept or reject God, along with the fateful consequences incurred by the latter choice.

pre-eclampsia [pree-eklampsia] A potentially serious, abnormal condition of late pregnancy, with high blood pressure, protein in the urine, and swelling (*oedema*) of the limbs; also known as **pregnancy induced hypertension**. It is an uncommon condition, and the cause is unknown, but it is more common in multiple pregnancies and in women under 16 and over 40 years of age. Blood pressure is monitored regularly during pregnancy to check for the condition. Once detected, admission to hospital and bed rest usually result in the resolution of the disorder and the birth of a normal baby; otherwise, liver damage and eclampsia may develop.

pre-emptive strike *strategic capability*

prefabrication In architecture, the manufacture of parts or the whole of a building in a factory or other place away from the construction site. It was famously used for the rapid construction of the Crystal Palace, London (1851), architect Joseph Paxton. First considered in earnest during the 1920s, it was subsequently put into practice on a wide scale during the post-war years. Although successfully used for many building types, particularly industrial ones, the prefabricated houses of the 1950s and 1960s ('prefabs') have met with structural and social problems. Since the 1960s, the practice has been increasingly referred to as **systems building**.

prefect In local government, a senior official who is a direct agent of central government. The prefectorial system contrasts with systems of local government that allow for local participation and autonomy, and is found most notably in France since Napoleon, and in Italy since the *Risorgimento*. It has been criticized for its high degree of centralization, and the power of prefects has declined over the years.

preference shares Shares issued by a company, without voting rights, which carry a fixed rate of dividend (or interest). The holders have a prior claim on the profits of the company over ordinary shareholders.

prefix *affix*

pregnancy A physiological process in which female, live-bearing mammals nurture their developing young within the uterus; also known as **gestation**. It begins when the fertilized ovum embeds itself in the uterine wall (*implantation*), and ends with the birth of the offspring (*parturition*). During pregnancy in humans, which lasts on average 40 weeks from the first day of the last menstrual period, menstruation is absent (in response to circulating hormones), the uterus enlarges, the breasts increase in size in preparation for lactation, and there are other major physiological changes. The duration of pregnancy is species-specific: smaller animals with large litters generally have short gestation periods (eg hamsters, 16 days), whereas humans and African elephants have gestation periods of 266 days and 640 days respectively. (*see panel*)

prehistoric art *Palaeolithic art*

prejudice Making judgments about individuals based on inadequate or biased information. In the 20th-c, racism – together with the Holocaust and the influx of refugee psychologists and sociologists into the USA in the 1930s – made the study of prejudice a key area of contemporary social psychological research. The search for the roots of prejudice in terms of the individual pathology of the prejudiced led to both social cognitive (the phenomenon of stereotyping) and developmental (the 'authoritarian personality') explanations. A different social climate has seen more recent attention being paid to prejudice towards women and homosexuals. Marxist and other critical theorists object to the individualism of this approach, and its failure to recognize societal and structural bases of prejudice.

prelude A piece of instrumental music which precedes a longer work, such as a suite of dances or an operatic act, or is coupled with another of comparable length, especially a fugue. Until the 17th-c, independent preludes were often written, or improvised, to test an instrument's tuning, and several 19th-c composers (including Chopin) extended this tradition to sets of independent preludes in all the major and minor keys.

premenstrual syndrome / tension (PMS, PMT) A condition in which a variety of symptoms occur in relation to menstruation which interfere with normal life. It is of variable duration, has components that are both physical (eg constipation, abdominal pain, asthma, sleep disturbance) and mental (eg irritability, lethargy, and depression), and does not usually commence at the very beginning of puberty. In some societies it has been considered a cause of 'temporary insanity'. The causes are unknown, but psychological, social, and biological factors have been invoked. Treatment has included psychotherapy, progesterone hormones, and drugs to promote the passage of urine to eliminate the bloated feeling that many sufferers have.

premier *prime minister*

Premier Division The name of the English football league first division, comprising the top 20 English sides, established as a separate organization in the 1992–3 season. The three lower divisions (2, 3, and 4) were renamed 1, 2, and 3, respectively.

Preminger, Otto [preminjer] (1906–86) Film director and producer, born in Vienna, Austria. He studied law at Vienna University, then became a theatre director there, and directed his first film in 1931. He emigrated to the USA in 1935, and became a

US citizen in 1943. After some years of directing on the Broadway stage, he made *Laura* (1944), a *film noir*, often considered his best film. In the 1950s he made good use of the new wide-screen technology in such productions as *Carmen Jones* (1954) and *Bonjour Tristesse* (1959). Later films included *Porgy and Bess* (1959), *Anatomy of a Murder* (1959), *Exodus* (1960), and *The Human Factor* (1979).

premiss A sentence which is explicitly assumed in an argument. In *Paris is larger than London; therefore London is smaller than Paris*, 'Paris is larger than London' is the only premiss. A sentence need not be true, or be believed to be true, to function as a premiss.

premium bond A UK government security, introduced in 1956, and issued in numbered units of one pound. The accumulated interest on bonds sold is distributed through a lottery in the form of weekly and monthly tax-free cash prizes. Winning numbers are selected by a computer known as ERNIE (Electronic Random Number Indicator Equipment).

Premonstratensians [preemonstra**ten**sianz] A religious order founded by St Norbert at Prémontré, France, in 1120; also known as the **Norbertines** or **White Canons**. They are noted for parish education and mission work, and continue chiefly in Belgium.

prenatal diagnosis The assessment of the well-being of the fetus and the detection of abnormalities. Traditional clinical methods have been greatly reinforced by three recent techniques. *Ultrasound* is simple and safe, and is performed routinely in some countries to establish gestational age, confirm multiple pregnancies, and detect congenital abnormalities, such as spina bifida. *Amniocentesis* and *chorionic villus sampling*, as well as the sampling of fetal blood, are carried out at an earlier stage of pregnancy, when the information obtained may be of great value to counselling the mother with a view to obtaining an early abortion. As these methods entail some additional risks to the fetus, they tend to be used in selective cases where genetic disease is suspected.

preparatory school In the UK, an independent fee-paying school for children up to the age when they might move to a public school, or to a maintained secondary school if parents no longer wish to pay fees. It usually caters for pupils up to the age of 13. In the USA, a preparatory school is one which prepares students for college, equivalent to the British public school.

prepared piano A piano into which extraneous objects have been inserted, usually between the strings, to alter the timbre of all or selected notes. US composer John Cage and other avant-garde composers have used it since the 1940s.

Pre-Raphaelite Brotherhood (PRB) A group of artists formed in London in 1848 with the aim of revolutionizing early Victorian art; their preference for the styles of the 15th-c (ie pre-Raphael) led to someone (it is unclear who) suggesting the name c.1847. Leading members were Millais, Hunt, and D G Rossetti. They rejected the sentimental mediaevalism and academic formulae of the time, seeking instead a new truth to nature and fresh subjects, often taken from Romantic poetry (eg Keats, Tennyson, Patmore). The public was deeply suspicious until Ruskin came to their defence. PRB pictures (the initials appear on some early pictures) are recognizable by their bright colours, hard-edged forms, shallow picture-space, and meticulous attention to detail.

presbyopia *eye*

presbyter *elder* (religion)

Presbyterianism The conciliar form of Church government of the Reformed Churches, deriving from the 16th-c Reformation led by John Calvin in Geneva and John Knox in Scotland. Government is by courts at local congregational (eg kirk session), regional (presbytery), and national (General Assembly) levels. *Elders* (ordained laymen) as well as ministers play a leading part in all courts. Through emigration and missionary activity from Scotland, Ireland, and England, Presbyterianism has spread worldwide. The World Presbyterian Alliance was formed in 1878, to be succeeded in 1970 by the World Alliance of Reformed Churches.

presbytery **1** The E part of the chancel of a church, behind the choir.

2 The traditional name for the dwelling-house of priests in the Roman Catholic Church.

3 In Presbyterianism, a church court composed of equal numbers of elders and ministers, presided over by a moderator, and overseeing a geographical grouping of congregations.

preschool education The provision of education for children under the statutory school age. This can either be in nursery or kindergarten, where there will usually be trained personnel, or in playgroups, where parent volunteers work with playgroup leaders. In some countries the provision of preschool education is widespread, but in others it is almost nonexistent.

Prescott, John (Leslie) (1938–) British politician, born in Prestatyn, Denbighshire, NC Wales, UK. He served in the merchant navy (1955–63), and studied at Oxford and Hull universities. In 1968 he became an officer of the National Union of Seamen, and a Labour MP in 1970. Although opposed to Britain's membership of the European Community, he was elected to the European Parliament in 1975, and became leader of the Labour group (1976–9). In the shadow cabinet he was spokesman for employment, energy, and transport, and he was deputy leader of the party (1994–7). In the 1997 Labour government, he was appointed deputy prime minister and secretary of state for the Environment, Transport and the Regions. After the general election he retained his position as deputy prime minister and became first secretary of state at the Cabinet office and chancellor of the Duchy of Lancaster (2001–2), and after a Cabinet reshuffle in 2002 was given responsibility for local government and the regions.

prescription An order for drugs written by a physician to a pharmacist, who will supply the correct medicine to the patient. Originally the sign ℞ was used to instruct the pharmacist to assemble the ingredients according to written instructions. This sign now simply indicates requests for prepared drugs. Until the 1940s prescriptions were written entirely in Latin.

prescriptivism An approach to language use which lays down 'rules of correctness', without taking account of real norms of usage, but by appealing to historical or imagined 'standards'. Examples of prescriptive rules in English state that one should say *I shall* not *I will* to express future time, and that one should never end a sentence with a preposition. Such rules date from the end of the 18th-c, and were widely taught in British public schools during the 19th-c, thereby gaining prestige, as they came to be associated with educated speech and writing. They usually bear little correspondence to the way the majority of people speak, and the question of whether one should or should not adhere to them is thus hotly debated.

president The name used by a head of state who is not appointed on a hereditary basis. The powers and means of selection can take a variety of forms: some are elected and others appointed. In parliamentary systems, the president performs a largely formal and ceremonial role, ensuring that a government is formed (eg Ireland). In constitutional hybrid systems the president shares the government of the state with the prime minister, cabinet, and legislature (eg France). Under a presidential system, the president is usually elected separately from the legislature for a fixed term of office. He or she is chief executive and commander-in-chief of the armed forces, as well as head of the government (eg the USA and Russia).

Presidential Medal of Freedom The highest American award for civilians in peacetime, given for contributions to the interests of the USA, or to world peace, or for cultural achievements.

presiding officer The name given to the officer who oversees the conduct and business of a legislative chamber. It is used in the Scottish Parliament, and in the Northern Ireland and Welsh Assemblies.

Presidium *Politburo*

Presley, Elvis (Aaron) (1935–77) Rock singer, born in Tupelo, Mississippi, USA. He began singing in his church choir and taught himself to play the guitar, his early models being black Gospel and blues singers. In 1953 he recorded some sides for Sun Records in Memphis, TN, which came to the attention of the entrepreneur, 'Colonel' Tom Parker, and led to aggressive promotion of Presley's career. In 1956 'Heartbreak Hotel' sold millions of copies, and his performances, featuring much hip-swaying, incited hysteria in teenagers and outrage in their parents. He served two years in the US army in Germany, and became increasingly reclusive on his return to civilian life. He made many records that sold in the millions, including 'Hound Dog', 'Love Me Tender', and 'Jailhouse Rock'. His Hollywood films such as *Loving You* (1957), *King Creole* (1958), and *GI Blues* (1960) became enormous moneymakers. Suffering from obesity and narcotics-dependence, he died at Graceland, his Memphis mansion, which is now a souvenir shrine for his many fans. A remix of an earlier song 'A Little Less Conversation' topped the UK charts in 2002, giving Elvis his 18th number one hit in Britain.

Presocratics The first Greek (and therefore Western) philosophers, who came 'before Socrates' in the 6th-c and 5th-c BC. They sought natural and rational rather than mythological explanations for phenomena, and their interests were scientific as well as philosophical (in the narrower, modern sense).

Pressburg *Bratislava*

press freedom The right claimed by newspapers, journals, etc to disseminate such information, news, and opinions as they judge to be in the public interest. Specific press freedoms include the right to found a newspaper free from licensing restraints; editorial freedom; the right of access to public institutions; and the confidentiality of the journalist's sources. The concept is regarded as an essential feature of modern democracies. In democratic countries, press freedom may conflict with other rights, such as the individual's right to privacy or the right to reply to adverse comments made by the press. In repressive societies and totalitarian states, press freedom is non-existent; its denial is characterized by censorship and the punitive treatment of independently minded editors and journalists. However, even in democratic countries press freedom is usually limited by legal constraints, proprietors' interests, economic factors, and professional codes.

press-moulded glass An industrial glass-making technique introduced in the USA in the 1820s and in England from 1831. Tableware and ornaments were made by pressing molten glass between metal moulds which formed their contours and decoration in one operation. Initially the upper mould or plunger was pressed down by a hand-operated lever or screw, but from 1894 steam presses came into use. Birmingham, Stourbridge, Manchester, and Tyneside were important centres in the 19th-c, and production continued in the 20th-c with improved technology.

pressure Force per unit area; symbol p, units Pa (pascal). A given weight acting on a smaller area corresponds to larger pressure. For an object immersed in a fluid, such as water or air, pressure acts on all sides of the object. It is measured using barometers or pressure gauges. Other common units of pressure are bar and torr.

pressure gauge A gauge which measures pressure, consisting of a hook-shaped tube called the *Bourdon tube*. When the pressure inside exceeds that outside, the tube straightens. This movement is transferred through levers and gears to move a pointer around a calibrated dial. A microscopic pressure sensor is made from a diaphragm of silicon, less than 10 micrometers thick, with tiny resistors buried in it. Changes in pressure cause the diaphragm to bend and the resistors to change their value. The change in pressure can then be measured.

pressure group A voluntary organization formed to articulate particular political or commercial interests or causes; also called an **interest group**; sometimes known as **lobbyists**. It can directly represent its members (a *sectional* group) or act on behalf of others (a *promotional* group). In the main, it tries to influence government and legislature, but may also attempt to influence public opinion. It differs from a political party in that it does not seek political office.

pressurized water reactor *nuclear reactor*

Prestel An interactive computer-based information system provided over the telephone network in the UK by British Telecom. It provides access to a wide variety of information sources.

Prester John A mythical Christian priest-king of a vast empire in C Asia. Reports of his existence, wealth and military might, substantiated by a letter purporting to have come from him in 1165, raised the morale of Christian Europe as it faced the Muslim threat. The story probably arose both from reports of Nestorian Christians in Asia and more obviously of the African Christian kingdom of Ethiopia, which had been cut off by the Islamic conquest of Egypt. 'Prester' comes from Old French *prestre*, 'priest'.

Preston 53°46N 2°42W, pop (2001e) 129 600. City and county town of Lancashire, NW England, UK; 45 km/28 mi NW of Manchester, on the R Ribble; site of Royalist defeat in the Civil War (1648); 19th-c centre of the cotton industry; birthplace of Richard Arkwright; city status granted 2002; railway; University of Central Lancashire (1992, formerly Lancashire Polytechnic); electrical goods, engineering, textiles, plastics, chemicals; Harris museum; Preston Guild Fair every 20 years; football league team, Preston North End (Lillywhites).

Prestonpans [prestnpanz] 55°57N 3°00W, pop (2000e) 8080. Town in East Lothian, E Scotland, UK; on S shore of Firth of Forth, 5 km/3 mi NE of Musselburgh; railway; coal processing; site of Scottish victory over the English (1745).

Prestwick 55°30N 3°12W, pop (2000e) 13 700. Town in South Ayrshire, SW Scotland, UK; on the W coast, 4·8 km/3 mi N of Ayr; airport (the official international gateway for Scotland); railway; aerospace engineering.

Pretoria [pritawria] 25°45S 28°12E, pop (2000e) 613 000 (metropolitan area). Administrative capital of South Africa, and alternative capital of Gauteng province; 48 km/30 mi NE of Johannesburg; altitude 1369 m/4491 ft; founded, 1855; capital of South African Republic, 1881; railway; two universities (1873, 1908); railway engineering, vehicles, iron and steel, chemicals, cement, leather; Voortrekker Memorial, Paul Kruger Memorial, Transvaal Museum.

Pretorius, Andries (Wilhelmus Jacobus) [pretawrius] (1799–1853) Afrikaner leader, born in Graaff-Reinet, S South Africa (then Cape Colony). A prosperous farmer, he joined the Great Trek of 1836 into Natal, where he was chosen commandant-general. He later accepted British rule, but after differences with the governor he trekked again, this time across the Vaal. Eventually the British recognized the Transvaal Republic, later the South African Republic, whose new capital was named Pretoria after him.

Pretorius, Marthinus (Wessel) [pretawrius] (1819–1901) Afrikaner soldier and statesman, president of the South African Republic (1857–71), born in Graaff-Reinet, S South Africa, the son of Andries Pretorius. He succeeded his father as commandant-general in 1853, and was elected president of the South African Republic, and of the Orange Free State (1859–63). He fought against the British again in 1877, until the independence of the Republic was recognized (1881), then retired.

prevalence (of disease) *disease frequency*

preventive medicine A branch of medical practice that is concerned with the prevention of disease. This is achieved by measures that (1) control the environment, such as clean air legislation, (2) ensure a hygienic and suitable food and water supply, (3) promote mass medication (eg schemes of immunization), (4) organize programmes for the eradication of disease (eg smallpox, diphtheria), and (5) promote safer life styles largely by education (eg the reduction in smoking to prevent cancer of the lung, and the promotion of condoms to reduce the possibility of AIDS).

Prévert, Jacques [prayvair] (1900–77) Poet, born in Neuilly-sur-Seine, NC France. He was involved with the Surrealists, and wrote songs, pieces for cabaret, and scenarios for Renoir, as well as the screenplay for the celebrated film, *Les Enfants du Paradis* (1946, The Children of Paradise). The piquant mixture of wit and sentiment in his poetry proved very popular; collections include *Paroles* (1946, Words), *La Pluie et le beau temps* (1955, Rain and Fine Weather), and *Choses et autres* (1972, Things and Others).

Previn, André (George) [previn] (1929–) Conductor and composer, born in Berlin, Germany. His family fled from Nazi Germany to the USA in 1938. He studied music mainly in California and Paris, spent some years as a jazz pianist, and became musical director of symphony orchestras at Houston (1967–9), London (1968–79), Pittsburgh (1976–86), and Los Angeles (1986–9). He became composer laureate of the London Symphony Orchestra in 1991, and conductor laureate the following year. He has composed musicals, film scores, and orchestral works, and achieved popular success both on television and in the concert hall by bringing classical music to the attention of a wide public. His books include *Music Face to Face* (1971) and *André Previn's Guide to Music* (1983). He was given an honorary knighthood in 1996.

Prévost, (Antoine François), l'Abbé [prayvoh] (1697–1763) Novelist, born in Hesdin, N France. He spent some years in the army, became a Benedictine monk, then lived in exile in England and Holland. He wrote many novels and translations, but is best known for *Manon Lescaut* (1731), originally published as the final part of a seven-volume novel. Having returned to France by 1735, he was appointed honorary chaplain to the Prince de Conti.

Priam [priyam] In Greek legend, the King of Troy. He was son of Laomedon, and husband of Hecuba, and is presented in the *Iliad* as an old man. When Hector was killed, he went secretly to Achilles to beg his son's body for burial. At the sack of Troy, he was killed by Neoptolemus.

Pribilof Islands [pribilof] Group of four islands in the Bering Sea, Alaska, USA; two inhabited (St Paul, St George); area 168 sq km/65 sq mi; centre of seal fur trade.

Price, (Mary Violet) Leontyne (1927–) Soprano, born in Laurel, Mississippi, USA. She studied at the Juilliard School, New York City. A notable Bess (1952–4) in Gershwin's *Porgy and Bess*, she was the first black opera singer on television, in *Tosca* for NBC (1955). An outstanding Verdi singer, she was also much associated with Barber's music.

Price, Nick, popular name of **Nicholas Raymond Leige Price** (1957–) Golfer, born in Durban, E South Africa. His family moved to Zimbabwe, where he began playing golf as a child. At age 17 he won the Junior World Tournament in San Diego, and turned professional in 1977. Notable wins include the PGA World Series (1983), the United States PGA Championship (1992, 1994), and the British Open (1994). He finished the 1994 PGA tour as top money winner, having earned nearly $1·5 million.

Price, Vincent (Leonard) (1911–93) Actor and writer, born in St Louis, Missouri, USA. He travelled in Europe, studied at Yale, and became an actor. He made his screen debut in 1938, and after many minor roles he began to perform in low-budget horror movies such as *House of Wax* (1953), achieving his first major success with *The Fall of the House of Usher* (1960). Known for his distinctive, low-pitched, creaky, atmospheric voice, and his quizzical, mock-serious facial expressions, he went on to star in a series of acclaimed Gothic horror movies, such as *The Pit and the Pendulum* (1961) and *The Abominable Dr Phibes* (1971). He abandoned films in the mid-1970s, going on to present cookery programmes for television – he wrote *A Treasury of Great Recipes* (1965) with his second wife, Mary Grant – but he had two last roles in *The Whales of August* (1987) and *Edward Scissorhands* (1991).

price index *retail price index*

prices and incomes policy An attempt by government to control inflation by acting directly on prices and wages, either by persuasion or by law. This contrasts with the view that inflation should be controlled by monetary or fiscal policies to influence demand, or supply-side measures to improve productivity. The correct structure of prices and wages is controversial, and the government's power to control prices and wages is uneven. Economists tend to agree that prices and wages policy is not a permanent substitute for monetary, fiscal, and supply-side policies, but disagree over how useful incomes policies can be as an occasional supplement to other policies to improve or speed up their working. It is impossible for governments to avoid prices and incomes policy entirely, as they are themselves major purchasers of goods and employers of labour. Efforts at prices and incomes policy have been sporadic, in the UK in the 1960s and 1970s, and in France in the early 1980s.

prickly heat A common generalized skin disorder in tropical countries that may also affect local areas of skin in temperate climates. Obstruction to the ducts of sweat glands results in a crop of small red pimples (*papules*) associated with itching.

prickly pear A species of opuntia (*Opuntia vulgaris*) often cultivated for its reddish, juicy, edible fruits. (Family: Cactaceae.)

Pride, Sir Thomas (?–1658) English parliamentarian during the Civil War, born (possibly) near Glastonbury, Somerset, SW England, UK. Little is known of his early life. He commanded a regiment at Naseby (1645), and served in Scotland. When the House of Commons indicated it might effect a settlement with Charles I, he was appointed by the army (1648) to expel its Presbyterian Royalist members (**Pride's Purge**). He sat among the king's judges, and signed the death warrant. He was knighted by Cromwell in 1656.

pride of India A deciduous tree (*Koelreuteria paniculata*) growing to 15 m/50 ft, native to E Asia; leaves pinnate, leaflets toothed; inflorescence pyramidal; flowers 1 cm/0·4 in diameter, yellow, 4-petalled; fruit a papery capsule; also called **golden-rain tree**. It is widely planted for ornament. (Family: Sapindaceae.)

priest The person authorized to sacrifice. In Christianity, the term derives from the Old Testament sacrificial system, and developed in the New Testament with Jesus Christ as great High Priest. Now, mainly in Roman Catholic, Orthodox, and Anglican usage, it refers to an ordained officer authorized to administer the sacraments, in particular the Eucharist (the sacrifice of the Mass).

Priestley, J(ohn) B(oynton) (1894–1984) Writer, born in Bradford, West Yorkshire, N England, UK. He studied at Bradford and Cambridge, made a reputation with his critical writings, and gained wide popularity from his novel, *The Good Companions* (1929). It was followed by other humorous novels, such as *Angel Pavement* (1930), and he established his reputation as a playwright with *Dangerous Corner* (1932), *Time and the Conways* (1937), and other plays on space-time themes, as well as popular comedies, such as *Laburnum Grove* (1933). He married the archaeologist Jacquetta Hawkes in 1953. He refused both a knighthood and a peerage, but accepted the Order of Merit in 1977.

Priestley, Joseph (1733–1804) Chemist and clergyman, born in Fieldhead, West Yorkshire, N England, UK. In 1755 he became a Presbyterian minister, and after moving to Leeds in 1767 took up the study of chemistry. He is best known for his research into the chemistry of gases, and for his discovery of oxygen (1774). He also wrote an English grammar and books on education and politics. His controversial views on religion and political theory (he was a supporter of the French Revolution) led him in 1794 to leave in fear of his life for America, where he was well received.

primary In politics, an election to choose the candidates for an election to public office. It differs from other forms of candidate selection in that the primary election is not organized by political parties, but by the government authority for which the election is to be held. The procedure is most commonly associated with the USA, but there are various forms of primary, and several ways in which political parties can be directly or indirectly involved.

primary colours There are three primary colours recognized in physiology and physics: red, green, and blue. The primary pigments of painting and colour printing are cyan, magenta, and yellow. In theory all other colours can be made by mixing these pigments, but a good deal depends on the chemical constitution of the actual pigments employed.

primary education The first phase of statutory education, usually covering the years from 5 or 6 up to 11 or 12. In most countries, the emphasis is on the coverage of a wide range of subjects and themes usually taught by the class teacher. In some countries there is more specialist teaching, especially in fields such as music, mathematics, and science, and children may have specialist rather than generalist teachers for these subjects. There is also emphasis on social and personal development in the primary phase, and on 'learning by doing'. Primary schools tend to be much smaller in size than secondary schools.

primate (religion) The most senior bishop of a given area; for example, in the Church of England the Archbishop of Canterbury is primate of All England. Originally, the name applied to the metropolitan of a province, and then to the patriarch.

primate (zoology) A mammal of the order Primates (c.180 species); most inhabit tropical forests; both eyes face forwards; hands and (usually) feet with grasping 'opposable thumb', used for climbing; cerebral hemispheres of brain well developed. Their classification is unsettled, but living species are usually placed in two suborders: the Strepsirhini (**prosimians**) and the Haplorhini (**tarsiers** and **Anthropoidea**).

prime minister The leader of and usually head of a government; also known as a **premier**. In general, prime ministers have to work through collective decision-making in a *cabinet*, although they can enjoy certain separate powers. In electoral systems, they are usually the leader of the largest party or coalition in parliament; unlike presidents, their power base is more that of the party than that of personality.

prime number In mathematics, a positive integer greater than 1 that has no divisors other than 1 and itself. Primes have always had an important place in the theory of numbers. Number theorists have tried to devise functions $f(n)$ which produce only prime numbers for positive integer values of n, but so far, all have failed. The function $f(n) = n^2 - n + 41$ yields primes for all $n < 41$; $f(n) = n^2 - 79n + 1601$ produces primes for $n < 80$. Fermat conjectured that $2^{2^n} + 1$ is prime for all non-negative integer n, but this has been proved incorrect.

prime rate The US bank base lending rate, at which the bank will lend to its best ('prime') customers. This rate applies to only 50 or so large US corporations, all others paying higher rates. An increase in the prime rate is a signal for all other interest rates to follow, making borrowing generally more expensive.

primitivism In modern art, the deliberate rejection of Western techniques and skills in the pursuit of 'stronger' effects found in such domains as African tribal or Oceanic art. The word may therefore be applied to Gauguin, and to Picasso's work from c.1906. It is sometimes referred to as 'naive art'.

Primo de Rivera (y Orbaneja), Miguel [preemoh thay rivera] (1870–1930) Spanish general, born in Jerez de la Frontera, SW Spain. He served in Cuba, the Philippines, and Morocco, and in 1923 led a military coup, inaugurating a dictatorship which lasted until 1930. During 1928–9 he lost the support of the army, the ruling class, and King Alfonso XIII, and in 1930 gave up power. His son, **José Antonio Primo de Rivera** (1903–36), founded the Spanish Fascist Party (*Falange Española*) in 1933, and was executed by the Republicans in 1936.

primrose A stemless perennial (*Primula vulgaris*) native to Europe, W Asia, and N Africa; a rosette of crinkled, tongue-shaped leaves; flowers long-stalked with a tubular calyx and spreading, pale yellow, rarely pink petals. It is a plant of woods and hedges, decreasing in some places because of excessive picking. The garden polyanthus is derived from a hybrid with the cowslip. (Family: Primulaceae.)

Prince, stage name by which **Prince Roger Nelson** is most widely known (1958–) Pop-singer and composer, born in Minneapolis, Minnesota, USA. Named after the Prince Roger Trio, a jazz band in which his father was a pianist, he was signed to Warner Brother Records as a teenager, and released *For You* in 1978. Subsequent albums included *Prince* (1979), *Dirty Mind* (1980), and *Controversy* (1981), which attracted increasing controversy with their tendency to mix religious and overtly sexual themes. International success followed the release of *1999* (1982), the film and album *Purple Rain* (1984), and *Batman* (1989), which confirmed him as one of America's most commercially successful pop artists. He changed his name to the unpronounceable glyph O(+> in 1993, and has since adopted the designation of **The Artist (formerly known as Prince)**.

Prince, Hal, popular name of **Harold Smith Prince** (1928–) Stage director and producer, born in New York City, USA. A stage manager on Broadway, he became a successful producer and director of stage musicals. His first production was *The Pajama Game* (1954), and other memorable shows include *West Side Story* (1957), *Fiddler on the Roof* (1964), and *Cabaret* (1968). He has maintained a long association with Stephen Sondheim, producing and directing many of the composer's shows, including *Sweeney Todd* (1979). He also directed *Evita* (1978) and *The Phantom of the Opera* (1986) for Andrew Lloyd Webber. Later productions include *Whistle Down the Wind* (1997) and *Candide* (1997).

Prince Edward Island pop (2000e) 145 600; area 5660 sq km/2185 sq mi. Province in E Canada; island in the Gulf of St Lawrence, separated from the mainland (SW) by Northumberland Strait; irregular coastline; rises to 142 m/466 ft; capital, Charlottetown; other towns include Summerside, Tignish, Souris; occupied first by Micmac nation; visited by Cartier, 1534; French claim as Île St Jean; settled by Acadians; captured by British, 1758; annexed to Nova Scotia, 1763; separate province, 1769; modern name, after Queen Victoria's father, 1798; joined Canada, 1873; governed by a lieutenant-governor and a 32-member elected Legislative Assembly; potatoes, tobacco, vegetables, grains, dairy products, fishing, food processing, tourism.

Prince of Wales In the UK, the title conferred (by custom, not law) on the sovereign's eldest son. Wales was ruled by a succession of independent princes from the 5th-c; the first to be acknowledged by an English king was Llewelyn ap Gruffudd (r.1246–82) in 1267. Tradition holds that after the death of Llewelyn in battle (against the English) and the execution of his brother, Edward I presented his own infant son to the Welsh people at Caernarfon Castle as their prince. The title has been used since that time.

Princess Royal A title sometimes bestowed on the eldest, or only, daughter of a sovereign. George V's daughter Mary was Princess Royal until her death in 1965; the title was conferred by the Queen on Princess Anne in 1987.

Princeton 40°21N 74°40W, pop (2000e) 14 200. Borough in Mercer Co, WC New Jersey, USA, on the Millstone R; founded by Quakers, 1696; scene of a British defeat by George Washington, 1777; a noted centre for education and research; university (1746); birthplace of Paul Robeson; home of Einstein after his emigration to the USA.

principle of equivalence *equivalence principle*

principle of least action *least-action principle*

printed circuit A technique which replaces individual wiring between components in electronic circuits. It is made by depositing a network of thin, metallic connections on to a board, the electronic components usually being soldered to pins on the other side of the board or, since c.1990, surface-mounted. The technique is commonly used to mount integrated circuits or chips together on boards for use as plug-in units in computers, televisions, or other electronic components. Printed circuit boards can be mass-produced, and their use enables circuit assembly to be easily automated. The most complicated boards have several layers and many components.

printer *computer printer*

printing A set of techniques for placing an image on a foundation in a controlled sequence of identical copies. The image may be verbal, illustrative or abstract, in one or many colours; the foundation is generally paper; and the colouring agent is generally ink. The techniques include *relief*, *planographic* (surface), and *intaglio* (recess) printing. The principal forms of relief printing are *letterpress* and *flexography*; those of planographic printing, *lithography* and the obsolescent *collotype*. Intaglio printing is typified by *gravure*, but most of the techniques used by artists in printmaking (engraving, drypoint, mezzotint, and etching) also fall into this category. Screen-process printing and stencilling are sometimes categorized as planographic processes, but are better viewed as unique processes. The oldest form of printing, letterpress, depends upon pressure for the satisfactory transfer of ink to paper, so the early history of printing is the history of wooden printing presses as well as of movable type and blocks.

Printing probably originated in 6th-c China (a text survives from 594), demand being stimulated by the need for examination textbooks and Buddhist texts, and newspaper was first printed c.860. The world's oldest known printed book is Wang Jie's *Diamond Sutra* (868), and the Confucian classics (130 vols) were printed in 932–53. Printing with metal plates developed in the 11th-c; moveable metal type c.1050. Europe may have learned of printing from the Arabs, or from Egyptian block printing (first recorded in 1300). The first European block printing dates from 1375. Gutenberg began printing in 1436, and Caxton in 1475. Later design improvements included the 'Dutch' press developed in Amsterdam and introduced into N America in 1639. The wooden handpress was superseded in 1795 by the first all-metal press, the Stanhope. The 19th and 20th-c saw the development of increasingly elaborate mechanical presses capable of printing on one side, then on both sides of the sheet, in one and then two colours, and faster machines in which the relief image is carried on a curved plate attached to one of the cylinders (*flexography*). Offset lithography developed at the beginning of the 20th-c, and came into widespread use. Techniques of typesetting can now create the typographic image direct, either on film or on paper, thus cutting out the need for typesetters to set and store metal type. Modern printing presses are either sheet-fed (printing one or more pages or other images at a time, in one or more colours, on ready-cut sheets of paper or other substrate) or web-fed (printing sets of one or more pages on a continuous reel, which is cut up into sheets after printing). The printed sheets each comprise two or more pages of the final book, and are folded and trimmed before binding.

prion A petrel, native to S oceans; uses very stout bill with sieve-like edge to strain minute crustaceans from water. (Genus: *Pachyptila*, perhaps 6 species; experts disagree. Family: Procellariidae.)

prion disease [**pri**yon] An unusual category of disease, thought to be transmitted by infectious agents composed of protein; the name is derived from **proteinaceous infectious particles**. It is found in humans (eg Creutzfeldt-Jacob disease, kuru) and animals (eg bovine spongiform encephalopathy in cows, scrapie in sheep). There is progressive degeneration of the central nervous system, with characteristic pathological changes including small holes (vacuoles) in the cells, which has led to the term *spongiform ecephalopathy*, and deposits of an abnormal, highly folded protein. All the functions of the brain are affected, most obviously resulting in movement disorders and dementia. The disease can be inherited or occur sporadically, and may be transmitted within and possibly between species. Hereditary cases have a genetic mutation that causes them to produce the prion. Infectious transmission is thought to occur as a result of inoculation or ingestion of tissue from an infected source. The possibility of transmission from cattle to humans has raised major anxieties, particularly in the UK.

Prior, Matthew (1664–1721) Diplomat and poet, born in Wimborne, Dorset, S England, UK. He studied at Cambridge, became an MP (1700), and carried out diplomatic work in Holland, being instrumental in concluding the Treaty of Utrecht (1713). He wrote several political and philosophical poems, but is best known for his light occasional verse collected as *Poems on Several Occasions* (1709).

Priscian [**pri**shian], Lat **Priscianus** (6th-c) Latin grammarian, born in Caesarea. At the beginning of the 6th-c he taught Latin at Constantinople. As well as his 18-volume *Institutiones grammaticae*, which was influential in the Middle Ages, he wrote six smaller grammatical treatises and two hexameter poems.

prism In mathematics, a solid geometrical figure: its section is a rectilineal figure, with parallel edges. In optics, it is a transparent object used to produce or study the refraction and dispersion of light. It may be made of glass, plastic, or liquid in a hollow prism.

prison That part of the penal system where criminals are held in custody for varying lengths of time determined by the courts as punishment for offences. Prisons developed rapidly from the early 19th-c; before then, banishment and corporal or capital punishment were the main ways of dealing with offenders. Subsequently, imprisonment itself came to be seen as both an adequate penalty and acceptable means of social control or 'deterrence'. Conditions in the earliest municipal prisons were usually atrocious, and were improved only through the work of penal reformers such as Elizabeth Fry. Problems of overcrowding still dog many prisons today, making efforts of rehabilitation of prisoners much more difficult.

Priština [**preesh**tina] 42°39N 21°10E, pop (2001e) 190 500. Capital town of Kosovo autonomous province, S Serbia; former capital of Serbia; airfield; railway; university (1976); population decimated by forced removal of ethnic Albanian population (Mar–Apr 1999); severely damaged in the ensuing Yugoslavia/NATO conflict; vehicle parts, crafts; many Turkish buildings, including the Sultan Murad mosque; nearby marble cave of Donje and monastery of Gračanica.

Pritchett, Sir V(ictor) S(awdon) (1900–97) Writer and critic, born in Ipswich, Suffolk, E England, UK. He studied in London, became a foreign newspaper correspondent in France, Morocco, and Spain, and published his first novel, *Claire Drummer*, in 1929. He became known for his critical works, such as *The Living Novel* (1946), short stories, and travel books. He was knighted in 1975, and also published two volumes of autobiography, *A Cab at the Door* (1968) and *Midnight Oil* (1973). He was made a Companion of Honour in 1993.

Pritzker Architecture Prize Architecture prize established by Jay A Pritzker in 1979. Worth $100 000, the prestigious prize is awarded annually by the Chicago-based Hyatt Foundation to honour the achievements of a living architect. Thomas J Pritzker, eldest son of the founder, is president of the Foundation.

private enterprise An economic system where individuals, singly or collectively, may engage in a business venture using their own resources and without needing state approval or control, as long as the venture does not contravene existing laws and rules. It contrasts with **public enterprise**, where the activity is carried out by a state-owned or -controlled organization.

privateering *buccaneers*

private sector Those aspects of an economy which are not controlled by the state, but which are in the hands of individuals or companies, and thereby answerable to the owners. The notion contrasts with the **public sector**.

privatization The return to private ownership of organizations formerly owned by the state. The government issues shares in the company to be privatized, and offers them for sale to the public. The company therefore becomes answerable to the shareholders and not to the government. Several cases of privatization took place in Britain in the 1980s, including British

Telecom and British Gas. The government was able to raise considerable sums of money by this means, thus helping to reduce its borrowing requirements and cut tax rates. The privatization of certain public-sector utilities such as the railway system has led to criticism of the companies' safety procedures in favour of cost-cutting.

privet A mostly temperate, evergreen or deciduous shrub or small tree; leaves opposite, leathery; flowers tubular with four spreading lobes, creamy, fragrant, in loose conical inflorescences; berries black or purple, poisonous. Several species are commonly used for garden hedges. (Genus: *Ligustrum*, c.40 species. Family: Oleaceae.)

Privy Council A body which advises the British monarch, appointed by the crown. In previous times, particularly the Tudor period, it was a highly influential group, and might be regarded as the precursor of the cabinet. Today its role is largely formal, enacting subordinate legislation (proclamations and Orders in Council). Its membership is over 300, but the quorum is three.

Prix de l'Arc de Triomphe [pree duh **lahk** duh treeõf] The richest horse race in Europe, held at the end of the season over 2400 m/2625 yd at Longchamp, near Paris, on the first Sunday in October. First run in 1920, it is the leading race in Europe for horses at least three years old.

Prix Goncourt France's most prestigious literary prize for fiction, given annually since 1903 by the Académie Goncourt (founded by Edmond de Goncourt). The award carries a symbolic prize of 50 francs but guarantees huge sales for the author.

Prizren [preezren] 42°12N 20°43E, pop (2001e) 114 900. Town in Kosovo autonomous province, SW Serbia; on R Prizrenska Bistrica, near the Albanian frontier; built on the site of a Roman town (Theranda); important mediaeval trade centre; part of Albania, 1941–4; railway; tourism, gold and silver work; old town, mosques.

probability theory The mathematical study of relative probabilities in processes involving uncertainty, for example tossing a coin or rolling dice. The foundations of the subject were laid by Pascal and Fermat in the 17th-c, and it was further systematized in the 20th-c by the Russian mathematician Andrei Nicolaevich Kolmogorov (1903–87).

probate The official proving of a will. The executor of the will applies to the court (eg in England and Wales, the High Court, Family Division, and in the USA, generally Probate Courts or Registrars) for a certificate confirming the validity of the will and the authority of the executor to administer the estate of the deceased. The term is not used in all jurisdictions (eg in Scotland, where the equivalent term is *confirmation*).

probation A method of dealing with offenders over the age of 16 where, instead of a sentence of imprisonment, a court may order the offender to be supervised for a fixed period of no longer than three years by a **probation officer**. Offenders must agree to be placed on probation after the obligations under the order are explained to them. A court may in addition require the offender to perform unpaid work for a specified number of hours, or to attend a specified day training centre. They are most usually imposed on first offenders, young offenders, elderly offenders who need support, and offenders whose crimes are not serious.

proboscis monkey [probosis] An Old World monkey (*Nasalis larvatus*) native to Borneo; pale with darker 'cap' on head, and dark back; long tail; protruding nose, which in adult males becomes bulbous and pendulous; excellent swimmer; inhabits forest near fresh water; eats leaves.

procaryote or **prokaryote** [prohkarioht] An organism that lacks an organized nucleus separated from the surrounding cytoplasm by a nuclear membrane. They are predominantly single-celled micro-organisms, such as the bacteria and blue-green algae, or infectious agents of cells, such as the viruses.

procedural programming A form of computer programming in which statements which instruct the computer to carry out operations and data are organized in sequence. Most procedural programming languages can be compiled into a set of instructions for the computer to obey. Examples of procedural languages are FORTRAN and PASCAL.

processing (photography) Treating exposed photographic material to produce a permanent visible image. This is normally carried out through a series of chemical reactions such as developing and fixing, interspersed with washes to remove residues, and completed by drying, so that the result may be safely handled.

processionary caterpillar A caterpillar that lives in colonies with its siblings inside a silk tent constructed on its food plant. Periodically, the caterpillars leave the tents and migrate in long, nose-to-tail lines over the ground. (Order: Lepidoptera.)

Proclus [**proh**klus] (c.412–85) Greek Neoplatonist philosopher, born in Constantinople. He studied at Alexandria and Athens, and became the last head of Plato's Academy. His approach, based on Plotinus, combined the Roman, Syrian and Alexandrian schools of thought in Greek philosophy into one theological metaphysic. His works were translated into Arabic and Latin, and were influential in the Middle Ages.

Proconsul *Dryopithecus*

Procop(ius) *Prokop*

Procopius [pro**koh**pius] (c.499–565) Byzantine historian, born in Caesarea (now in Israel). He studied law, and accompanied Belisarius against the Persians (526), the Vandals in Africa (533), and the Ostrogoths in Italy (536). He was highly honoured by Justinian, and seems to have been appointed prefect of Constantinople in 562. His principal works are histories of the Persian, Vandal, and Gothic wars, and an attack on the court of Justinian.

Procrustes [proh**kruh**steez] In the legend of Theseus, a robber, living in Attica, who made travellers lie on his bed, and either cut or lengthened them to fit it; his name means 'the stretcher'. Theseus gave him the same treatment, and killed him.

procurator fiscal A public offical in Scotland who, acting on behalf of the Lord Advocate, is responsible for initiating and pursuing the prosecution of crimes and offences, reported to them by the police, in the sheriff court and the district court. The 'fiscal' is also responsible for reporting serious crimes to the Crown Office, which may merit prosecution in the High Court, as well as for investigating all cases of sudden, accidental, or suspicious deaths and for initiating fatal accident inquiries.

Prodi, Romano [prodee] (1939–) Italian statesman, prime minister (1996–8), and president of the European Commission (1999–), born in Scandiano, Emilia-Romagna, N Italy. He studied in Milan and at the London School of Economics, and worked in universities in Italy and the USA before becoming an MP. He was industry minister (1978–9) and twice president of IRI (Istituto per la Ricostruzione Industriale) (1982–9, 1993–4). In 1995 he headed a centre-left alliance called *L'Ulivo*, which was successful in the 1996 elections and he became prime minister. He was appointed president of the European Commission following the mass resignation of all the commissioners over a highly critical report detailing severe maladministration, and introduced a new code of conduct.

producer In the motion picture industry, the person who brings the initial concept to practical reality – organizing finance and budgetary control, choosing the director, and holding the balance between the director and other important members of the production team, including the principal artists. Producers exercise day-to-day administration to ensure that the shooting schedule is maintained and unforeseen crises dealt with. They are also concerned with publicity and distribution for the international market, and exploitation on television and video. In major television organizations, producers tend to specialize in particular categories (eg drama, comedy, current affairs), and one producer is often in charge of a series of programmes, working with several different directors or presenters. In radio broadcasting, the producer has a dual role, being also the person who actually controls the making of the programmes (the province of the *director*, in other media).

producer gas A gas formed by passing air through hot coke, the chemical reaction being $C+\frac{1}{2}O_2 \rightarrow CO$. This reaction is exothermic, but produces gas of low calorific value – it contains about 60% nitrogen. It is often produced alternately with water gas.

productivity The ratio of output to input in an industrial context. It usually refers to the quantity of goods or commodities produced in relation to the number of employees engaged in the operation (**labour productivity**). **Total productivity** includes the input of capital also. Low productivity is the major cause of a company's decline, since it results in high costs per unit, and therefore high prices that are not competitive. The notion is important in wage negotiations: **productivity bargaining** balances a proposed increase in wages with an anticipated rise in productivity.

Professional Chess Association *chess*

profit The difference for a company between its sales revenue and the costs attributable to those sales. Profit may be calculated before or after deducting interest payments, and before or after deducting taxation charges. The surplus may be paid out to shareholders as a dividend, or retained by the business (as *reserves*) to finance capital expenditure. **Profit sharing** is a scheme whereby a percentage of the profits of a company is given to staff in the form of an additional bonus payment; it may be in the form of cash or of shares in the company. **Profit maximization** is the economic concept that firms will aim to do everything possible to achieve the maximum possible profits – a view which is not considered realistic or possible by some authorities in economics. **Profitability** is the measurement of how effectively a company has used the resources available to it. The ratio of profit to capital employed (ie equity capital, or assets) is commonly used. There are also many **non-profit-making** companies, where a surplus is ploughed back into the company, or (as in the case of charities) used for charitable purposes.

Profumo, John (Dennis) [prof**yoo**moh] (1915–) British statesman. He studied at Oxford, and became a Conservative MP (1940). He held several government posts before becoming minister of state for foreign affairs (1959–60) and secretary of state for war (1960–3). He resigned in 1963 as a result of a scandal following his admission that he had earlier been guilty of a grave misdemeanour in deceiving the House of Commons about the nature of his relationship with Christine Keeler, who was at the time also involved with a Russian diplomat. He later engaged in a great deal of social and charitable work, and was chairman (1982–5) then president of Toynbee Hall, London.

progesterone [proh**jes**terohn] A steroid hormone present in both sexes of all vertebrates. In mammals it is critical for the establishment and maintenance of pregnancy. In humans it is primarily secreted by the ovaries and placenta. It acts to prepare the uterus for implantation of the embryo, inhibits ovulation during pregnancy, and prepares the breasts for lactation. It also acts to raise body temperature.

prognosis In medicine, an assessment of the likely outcome of a disease and its treatment. A good prognosis implies that the patient is likely to recover completely; a poor prognosis implies that the disease is likely to prove terminal within a short period.

program; programmer *computer program*

programmed learning A form of learning developed in the 1960s, based on the behaviourist learning theories of US psychologist B F Skinner. He stressed the need for short frames of information to be given, followed by an active response and the immediate reinforcement of correct answers. The element of self-pacing was also important. Specially designed teaching machines were developed, some on a linear basis with the learner following a fixed sequence of frames, others on a branching principle which permitted a variety of paths through the programme. Though no longer as popular as it was in the 1960s, programmed-learning principles have been influential in the development of microcomputer software and the interactive video disk.

programme music Music which paints a scene or tells a story. Among early examples are the violin concertos by Vivaldi called *The Four Seasons*, but it was in the 19th-c, with the increased resources of the symphony orchestra, that composers most widely and effectively gave musical expression to literary and other extra-musical ideas. The concert overture and the symphonic poem proved to be ideal vehicles for this, and in many cases (such as in Smetana's cycle of symphonic poems, *Má Vlast* (1874–9, My Country), they embodied nationalistic ideals and aspirations. The capability of music to convey a 'programme' without the aid of a written commentary is severely limited, but its illustrative powers have been proved many times.

programming language An artificial language which allows people to instruct computers to carry out specific tasks; also known as a **computer language**. Many programming languages have been developed; among the relatively common high-level languages are ADA, APL, ALGOL, BASIC, C, C++, COBOL, CORAL, FORTH, FORTRAN, LISP, PASCAL, PROLOG, and JAVA (*see separate entries*). In addition there are numerous low-level languages which, unlike high-level languages, are specific to particular processors.

Progressive Conservative (PC) Party A Canadian political party, mainly active at the federal level, but with branches in most provinces and territories. It originated in C Canada in the 1850s, though with roots going back to 18th-c Toryism. In 1942 the Party lurched briefly to the left, adding on prominent members of the Progressive Party. The PCs have formed the government nationally five times since, but were resoundingly defeated in the general election in 1993.

progressive education A term used to denote teaching which places greater emphasis on the wishes of the child. It usually involves greater freedom of choice, activity, and movement than traditional forms of teaching. Progressive education has been pioneered in certain schools such as Summerhill and Dartington Hall, UK, but its influences have spread to other schools, particularly in the primary sector.

Progressive Party (1912–16, 1924) The name used by three separate third-party political initiatives in the USA. The first, essentially a breakaway from the Republicans, centred on former president Theodore Roosevelt (in office 1901–9), who was its presidential candidate in 1912. The second developed in 1924 from midwestern farmer and labour discontent. Its presidential candidate, Senator Robert La Follette (1855–1925) of Wisconsin, won four million votes. The third Progressive candidacy was by former vice-president Henry A Wallace in 1948, on a programme of opposition to the developing Cold War.

progressive taxation Taxation system designed to make the proportion of income paid in tax increase with incomes. For income tax this is often achieved by making incomes below some minimum level exempt, then levying higher rates on successive parts of income. For indirect taxes it can be achieved by having exemption or low tax rates for goods consumed largely by the relatively poor, and high rates on luxuries.

Progress spacecraft An uncrewed version of the Soviet Soyuz crewed spacecraft, modified as a resupply vehicle for the Salyut and Mir space stations. After unloading, the spacecraft is separated and removed from orbit to burn up in the atmosphere.

Prohibition (1920–33) An attempt to stop the sale of alcoholic drinks in the USA, authorized by the Eighteenth Amendment to the Constitution (1919) and the Volstead Act (1920). Prohibition met great resistance, especially in urban immigrant communities, and generated a large bootlegging industry. It was ended by the repeal of the 18th amendment in 1933.

projection television A television system in which images are projected through special wide-aperture lenses on a large external screen, usually using three high-brightness cathode ray tubes in the component colours red, green, and blue. Electronic adjustment allows accurate registration of the three colour images, but the limited brightness output limits the width of an external high-reflection screen to c.4 m/13 ft. Single-lens versions use dichroic mirrors for beam combination, or 'light valves' of liquid crystal diode construction. For larger areas a xenon lamp with video image modulation must be used, as in the eidophor system.

projective geometry The study of what geometric figures have in common with their shadows – for example, the properties of being a line, or a curve defined by a polynomial of a given degree. The subject was invented by Girard Desargues (1591–1661) and used to simplify the study of conics: all ellipses, parabolas, and hyperbolas are projectively equivalent. Newton similarly reduced all cubic curves to five types. The subject then lapsed, to be rediscovered by Frenchman Jean Victor Poncelet (1788–1867) and August Ferdinand Möbius in the early 1820s, when it became the most fundamental branch of geometry. Properties involving distance are not preserved by projective transformations, and projective properties of figures are few but basic. Projective geometry is the best setting for enumerative questions about the number of curves of a given kind, and so for the geometrical study of the solution of equations.

projective tests In psychology, a number of somewhat contentious procedures for assessing personality. Their use involves the presentation of ambiguous, vague, or unstructured material onto which the testee is assumed to project his/her personality. They are believed capable of revealing unconscious wishes, complexes, and conflicts, but test results may be influenced by current mood and recent experiences. The most famous is the Rorschach Psychodiagnostic Technique, which requires subjects to describe what they see in 10 bilaterally symmetrical inkblots. Other tests include pictures from which subjects make up stories, and the completion of incomplete sentences.

projector An apparatus for presenting an enlarged image on a screen from a transparency such as a photographic slide or film. In a motion picture projector, each frame is held stationary at an illuminated aperture for a brief period, and then advanced by an intermittent sprocket or reciprocating claw, the light being cut off by a rotating shutter during the movement. The sound track on the film is reproduced at a separate sound head where the film is moved continuously at constant speed. Cinema presentation on large screens requires powerful light sources, originally carbon lamps, now xenon lamps of 2 kW to 5 kW, whose light is concentrated on the aperture by a large parabolic mirror. 35 mm film is fed and taken up on large spools, up to 4000 ft (1800 m) capacity, mounted above and below the projector body. Continuous loop systems are also widely employed, which can run a complete programme of 4½ hours duration with as much as 24 500 ft (7500 m) of film fed from horizontal turntables, termed *platters*. 16 mm projectors for smaller screens generally have tungsten-halogen lamps of 250 to 500 W, and use 1600 ft (500 m) film spools.

prokaryote *procaryote*

Prokofiev, Sergey Sergeyevitch [prohkofief] (1891–1953) Composer, born in Sontsovka, SE Ukraine. He began to compose at the age of five, studied at the St Petersburg Conservatory, and won a reputation as a virtuoso pianist. During World War 1 he lived in London, then moved to the USA, returning to the USSR in 1934. He wrote many occasional works for official celebrations, in addition to popular pieces such as *Peter and the Wolf* (1936) and film music. His works have a vast range, including seven symphonies, nine concertos, ballets, operas, suites, cantatas, sonatas, and songs.

Prokop or **Procop(ius)** [prohkop, prokohpius], known as **the Bald** or **the Great** (c.1380–1434) Bohemian Hussite leader, a follower of Žižka, and on his death, the leader of the Taborites. He carried out raids into Silesia, Saxony, and Franconia, and repeatedly defeated German armies. With his colleague, **Prokop (the Younger)**, he fell in battle in Lipany, Hungary.

prolactin [prohlaktin] A hormone secreted by the front part of the pituitary gland (*adenohypophysis*) which initiates lactation in mammals and stimulates the production of another hormone, progesterone, by the corpus luteum.

prolapsed intervertebral disc A condition which arises when the nucleus of the disc situated between the bodies of the vertebrae is forced outwards through the surrounding joint capsule; commonly known as a **slipped disc**. It is caused by an excessive load being placed on the joints between the bodies of the spinal vertebrae, such as in heavy or awkward lifting, and is followed by sudden or rapidly developing back pain or sciatica. Common levels for disc prolapse are in the lower back (between lumbar vertebrae 4–5 and lumbar 5 and sacral vertebrae 1) and in the neck.

proletariat In radical and socialist philosophy, a term coined to denote the **working class**, ie those who live by their labour and do not own property. It is particularly important in Marxist and communist ideology. *Lumpenproletariat* was coined by Marx to refer to the underclass in big cities from whom class identification could not be expected.

pro-life movement Organized opposition to the legality of induced abortion, and to laboratory experiments on human embryos. There are a number of national organizations and pressure groups, such as Operation Rescue in the USA, the Society for the Protection of the Unborn Child (SPUC), and LIFE. Active support comes from members of several religions, notably Roman Catholics, but also Muslims and Jews.

PROLOG A high-level programming language based on mathematical logic, widely used in artificial intelligence applications. It was developed at the University of Aix-Marseille in France and in the UK at Imperial College and Edinburgh University. PROLOG has to some extent replaced LISP, mainly in Europe.

PROM [peerom] Acronym for **programmable read-only memory**, a special type of integrated circuit read-only memory (ROM) into which the user can write data after manufacture. Once written, the data cannot be altered.

promenade concert A musical performance, especially by an orchestra, during which some at least of the audience are offered floor space, without seats, at reduced prices. The London 'proms' were started at the Queen's Hall by Sir Henry Wood in 1895; they transferred to the Royal Albert Hall in 1941.

Prometheus [prohmeethyoos] In Greek mythology, a Titan, son of Iapetus and brother of Epimetheus; originally a trickster who outwits Zeus; his name means 'the foreseeing'. He made human beings out of clay, and taught them the arts of civilization. He stole fire from heaven to help mankind, whom Zeus wished to destroy, and was punished by being chained to a rock in the Caucasus; every day an eagle fed on his liver, which grew again in the night. He knew a secret which concerned Zeus' future, and bargained for his release. Heracles, passing through the Caucasus, shot the eagle and set Prometheus free.

promissory note A signed document containing a written promise to pay a sum of money on or by a specific date. The document is legally binding and is signed, for example, when a bank customer takes out a loan. A particular form is a *commercial paper*, issued by large companies, which can be bought and sold.

promoter (genetics) The non-coding region immediately next to the start of a gene which acts as a 'switch' to allow transcription. Various proteins (known as *transcription factors*) bind to the promoter DNA sequences which ultimately have the effect of recruiting the enzyme RNA polymerase. This begins the process of transcription of the gene.

pronation [pronayshn] A movement of the forearm so that the palm of the hand is brought to face backwards, with the thumb towards the body. In this position the radius lies across the ulna.

prongbuck *pronghorn*

pronghorn A North American antelope (*Antilocapra americana*); male called **prongbuck**; pale brown with prominent eyes; female horns short; male horns with frontal 'prong' and backward-curving tips; outer layer of horns shed each year; will approach moving objects (including predators); inhabits grasslands.

proof spirit *alcohol strength*

propane C_3H_8, boiling point −42°C. The third in the alkane series of hydrocarbons; a gas obtained from petroleum and natural gas, used as a fuel and a refrigerant.

propanone *acetone*

propellant **1** An explosive which produces a violent but steady pressure, such as is needed to expel a projectile from a gun. Gunpowder, suitably graded, was the first. After the high explosive properties of nitroglycerine and nitrocellulose had been discovered, attempts were made to moderate their disruptive effect to make them useful as propellants. Success was achieved with various gelatinized mixtures, notably Cordite. **2** A rocket fuel which functions not by exerting pressure but by the recoil effect of the expulsion of gases at high speed (which is why a rocket can be propelled in empty space). Many forms exist, some solid, some liquid (eg hydrazine with dinitrogen tetroxide).

propeller A device used principally by ships and aeroplanes to transform the rotational energy of an engine into directed thrust. To accomplish this, the propeller is fitted with blades radiating from a central hub, each blade being of aerofoil cross section. As the propeller rotates, the water or air is accelerated backwards, producing an opposite reactive force in the propeller and its shaft. This reactive force acts in the forward direction, which is transmitted to the craft as the propulsive force.

Propertius, Sextus [propershius] (c.48–c.15 BC) Latin elegiac poet, probably born in Asisium (Assisi), Italy. He travelled to Rome (c.34 BC), where he became a poet, winning the favour of Maecenas and Emperor Augustus. The central figure of his inspiration was his mistress, to whom he devoted the first of his four surviving books, *Cynthia*. Much of his work was published after his death, in Rome.

property Something owned or possessed – a notion whose precise definition varies greatly between different jurisdictions. In Anglo–US law, **real property** includes lands and buildings; also, intangible interests in land, such as easements. Other kinds of property are known as **personal property**. Leases are classified as personal property, and are also referred to as 'chattels real'. **Chattels** are movable goods, classed as personal property. A gift of personal property made by will is a **legacy**; in England and Wales, a gift of real property made by will is a **devise**. A devise may specify the property involved; it may be worded to cover all property; or it may deal only with the residue of property, following a specific devise. **Intellectual property** is a general term covering intangible rights in the product of intellectual effort. It includes copyright in published work, and patents granted to protect new inventions. In Scotland, the terms **heritable** and **movable property** are used instead of *real* and *personal property*, and the term *devise* is not used, all gifts being legacies. Some things are not deemed ownable, such as outer space.

propfan An aircraft propeller designed for a turbo-engine, enabling large amounts of power to be delivered by increasing the number and area of the blades in comparison with a conventional aircraft propeller. A particular feature of such propellers is the swept back or 'skew' nature of the blades, which allows quieter operation for the rotational speeds involved.

prophet One who is inspired to reveal a message from a divine being; an important figure in many religious traditions, sometimes with cultic functions, but sometimes a lone figure opposing the established cult or social order (eg Jeremiah, Amos, and Hosea in the Hebrew Bible). Although their messages may acquire an enduring relevance, they usually address a specific situation or problem. In the New Testament, 'prophets' are listed after 'apostles' in Paul's lists of Christian ministries (1 *Cor* 12.28; *Eph* 4.11), but the problem of false prophets is also of concern in some works (*Matt* 7.15; 1 *John* 4.1).

proportional counter A device for monitoring the path of charged particles produced in particle physics experiments. Arrays of wire electrodes give an electric field which accelerates ions produced by a passage of charged particles. The ions cause pulses in electrodes that are recorded electronically to give a map of the particle track. Drift chambers and multi-wire proportional chambers are common forms of proportional counter. French physicist Georges Charpak (1924–) was awarded the 1992 Nobel Prize for Physics for his invention of the multi-wire proportional chamber.

proportional representation Any system of voting designed to ensure that representatives are elected in numbers proportionate to their support among those voting in an election. There are many voting methods, none of which achieves perfect proportionality. In the *list system* the number of candidates on a party's list who are elected depends on the proportion of votes they receive in national elections. In the *single transferable vote*, votes are cast in multi-member constituencies and an ordered preference for all the candidates can be expressed on the ballot paper, votes being transferred from one candidate to another to enable them to gain the necessary quota to be elected. Proportional representation comes close to meeting the democratic principle of majority government; examples can be found in most European countries. The case against it is that it does not in fact produce majority party government, but unstable coalitions, and breaks the bond between MPs and their constituencies.

proprioception *kinaesthesis*

propyl [prohpiyl, -pil] $CH_3CH_2CH_2$-. A group derived from propane. **Isopropyl** is the isomeric $(CH_3)_2CH$–. Propyl and isopropyl alcohols (propan-1-ol and propan-2-ol) are both used as solvents and as substitutes for ethanol in non-beverage applications.

propylaeum or **propylaea** [prohpileeum, prohpileea] An important entrance gateway or vestibule. It is usually in front of a sacred building, as on the Acropolis, Athens (437–432 BC).

proscenium An arch and opening of a stage wall separating the auditorium of a theatre from the acting and scenic area. From its origins in the stagecraft of Peruzzi (1481–1537), Serlio (1475–1554) and others, its development, linked to a concept of theatrical illusion, dominated Western drama until the early 20th-c. In its early form, it was a frame for perspective scenery, and a permanent structure, with doors for actors' exits and entrances, embracing a deep acting area (which was also known as the proscenium). In time it became the narrowest of picture frames enclosing a common world of scenery and action. The process culminated – through the coincidence of naturalism and the ability to darken the auditorium – in the notion of the proscenium as a 'fourth wall' through which the audience, sitting in darkness, could see and eavesdrop.

prose (Lat *prosa oratio* 'straightforward discourse') Non-metrical writing, or indeed speech (Molière's M Jourdain was impressed to realize that he spoke prose). There is a natural tendency to regard prose as direct and unadorned, the clear pane of expression beside the stained glass of poetry. Such limpid prose was recommended to the members of the Royal Society in 1667 – an attitude which continues to be found in such works as Ernest Gowers' *Plain Words* (1948). But prose may be as elaborate, complex, and figurative as any poetry, as may be seen in the works of Cicero, Rabelais, Swift, Dickens, Proust, Woolf, and Joyce.

prosecution The initiation and pursuance of criminal proceedings against an individual in a criminal court. Prosecutions are typically the province of the state, though several jurisdictions (including Scotland and England) do, in theory, permit private prosecutions (although they are extremely rare and are mostly for assault). Common law systems are *accusatorial*, with the burden of proof normally resting with the prosecution to prove the offence beyond reasonable doubt. In Britain, while the police have the responsibility to investigate crimes and offences, the responsibility for prosecution generally lies with the Crown Prosecution Service in England and Wales (which exercises the functions previously undertaken by the Director of Public Prosecutions), and with the Lord Advocate and the Procurator Fiscal Service in Scotland. In the USA it is the District Attorney who is responsible for the majority of criminal prosecutions. Civil law systems, such as France and Germany, are termed *inquisitorial* systems, whereby the prosecutor presents the case to court, but it is the responsibility of the judge to investigate the facts of the case and if necessary to call and question witnesses.

prose poem A composition printed continuously, as prose, but sharing many features (rhythm, imagery) with poetry. Aloysius Bertrand's *Gaspard de la nuit* (1842), followed by Baudelaire's *Petits poèmes en prose* (1869), established the genre, which overlaps with the very short story, as practised by Kafka and others.

Proserpine *Persephone*

prosimian A primate of the suborder Strepsirhini (40 species); wet nose with slit-like nostrils; tip of nose, between nostrils, with an obvious vertical groove; also known as **primitive primate**.

prosody The pitch, loudness, tempo, and rhythm of speech. A particular application of prosodic study is in relation to poetry, where it provides a means of analyzing the rhythmical properties of lines (*metrics*), as part of the study of versification. Prosodic features play an important role in forming the stress patterns within words and phrases, and the intonation patterns within sentences.

prosopography The study of human behaviour through collective biography, aiming to explain people's actions through knowledge of their personal backgrounds – sex, education, age, wealth, class, and family relations. It was applied to 18th-c British history by Sir Lewis Namier, but found to be of limited value in periods of ideological division, such as the 16th-c and 17th-c.

Prost, Alain [prost], nickname **the Professor** (1955–) Motor-racing driver and team owner, born in St Chamond, SW France. He was the first Frenchman to win the world title. He won in 1985–6 (both for McLaren–Porsche), was runner-up in 1983–4 and 1988, and won again in 1989 (for Maclaren–Honda) and 1993, when he announced his retirement. During his Formula 1 career he won 51 races from 199 starts, and his 798·5 championship points is a world record. He returned to Formula 1 as a team owner with Team Prost (1997 to 2001) but was less successful.

prostaglandins [prostaglandins] A family of unsaturated fatty acids produced by virtually every tissue of the body in response to particular stimuli. They are largely derived from arachidonic acid present in the plasma membrane, and probably act locally at sites of production. Their physiological role is unclear, but they are implicated in the breakdown of the corpus luteum, platelet function, the natural prevention of ulcers, and the causes of inflammation.

prostate gland A partly muscular, partly glandular, accessory male sex organ in mammals, lying within the pelvis below the bladder, encircling part of the urethra. The ejaculatory ducts pass through the gland to enter the urethra. It is small at birth and grows rapidly during puberty to attain adult size within a year. During sexual arousal it contributes (via numerous ducts opening into the urethra) an alkaline fluid to semen, accounting for approximately one-third of its volume and giving it its characteristic odour. The gland can be divided into a number of lobes: a mainly muscular lobe towards the front, lateral lobes at the sides, a middle lobe, and a lobe towards the back (often the site of cancer of the prostate). After age 50 the gland may atrophy; however, an excessive increase in the size of the middle lobe may also occur, compressing the urethra and bulging into the bladder, and adversely affecting the functioning of the kidneys. Treatment involves the removal of part or all of the gland.

prosthesis [prostheesis] An artificial substitute for a part of the body. Examples include a mechanical arm or leg, artificial heart valves, dentures, and tooth implants.

Protagoras [prohtagoras] (c.490–421 BC) The earliest self-proclaimed Greek Sophist, born in Abdera, Greece. He taught mainly in Athens, presenting a system of practical wisdom fitted to train people for citizen's duties, and based on the doctrine that 'man is the measure of all things'. His doctrine that all beliefs are true was examined in great detail and rejected by Plato. All his works are lost except a fragment of his treatise *On the Gods*.

protea [prohtia] A shrub or small tree, native to tropical and especially S Africa, where they are very diverse; leaves entire or divided, leathery. The large and often spectacular 'flowers' are actually inflorescences containing numerous small true flowers in the centre, surrounded by stiff, often brightly-coloured, petal-like bracts. (Genus: *Protea*, 130 species. Family: Proteaceae.)

protectionism A government policy of protecting domestic industries against foreign competition. Devices used include tariffs, quotas on imports, subsidies for domestic firms, and preference in state purchasing. The industries may be chosen for protection as 'infants', which the government would like to grow, as declining sectors where the government wants to avoid unemployment, or because they are thought vital for national defence. If protection succeeds it may damage exporters, either through foreign retaliation or because the protected country's currency appreciates. Protection is supposed to be checked by international treaties, including the General Agreement on Tariffs and Trade.

protective coloration / colouration The coloration pattern of an animal, serving a protective function. **Cryptic coloration** camouflages the animal against its background. **Disruptive coloration** delays recognition of the whole animal by attracting the predator's attention to elements of the colour pattern. **Warning coloration** is conspicuous, and advertises the unpalatable, poisonous, or otherwise harmful properties of an animal to a potential predator.

Protectorate A regime established by the Instrument of Government, the work of army conservatives, England's only written constitution. The Lord Protectors, Oliver Cromwell (ruled 1653–8) and his son Richard (ruled 1658–9), issued ordinances and controlled the armed forces, subject to the advice of a Council of State and with Parliament as legislative partner. It failed to win support, and its collapse led to the Restoration.

protectorate A territory over which the protecting state enjoys power and jurisdiction short of full sovereignty; not formally annexed, it can come about by treaty, grant, or usage. A *protected state* is a form of protectorate where the territory is more like a unified state and has its own identifiable rulers. The commonest types were the 19th–20th-c colonial protectorates, Botswana being a British example, all of which have now achieved independence.

protein One of the three essential types of energy foods. It is a natural condensation polymer of amino acids occurring mainly as structural tissue in animals (fibrous proteins, mainly water insoluble, eg silk) but also as enzymes in both animals and plants (globular proteins, largely water soluble, eg haemoglobin). Nearly all proteins are derived from 20 amino acids.

Proterozoic eon The later of the two geological eons into which the Precambrian era is divided; the period of time from 2500 million years ago until the beginning of the Cambrian period 590 million years ago.

Protestant Ethic The term coined by the German sociologist Max Weber to describe the conduct and attitudes of the non-conformist religious groups of the Reformation period, such as the Lutheran and Calvinist forms of Protestantism; also called the **Protestant Work Ethic**. Weber drew most attention to the idea common to all such groups that believers must be diligent, disciplined, and fully committed to their worldly duties and tasks in order to 'glorify God'. He argued that the sort of conduct this inspired at work and at home helped to promote the growth of industry and capitalist enterprise. The careful use of one's resources, being thrifty, investing wisely, and acting with moderation not only made good religious sense but led to sound business practice as well.

Protestantism The generic term for expressions of Christian faith originating from the 16th-c Reformation as a protest against Roman Catholicism. Common characteristics include the authority of scripture, justification by faith alone, and the priesthood of all believers. The original groupings were those who followed Luther, Calvin, and Zwingli, and the term now embraces most non-Roman Catholic or non-Orthodox denominations. There were over 350 million Protestants in 2004.

Proteus [proh**t**yoos] A genus of typically rod-shaped bacteria that move by means of flagella. Many strains exhibit swarming behaviour. They are found primarily in the intestines and faeces of humans and other animals. Some species cause disease. (Kingdom: Monera. Family: Enterobacteriaceae.)

Proteus [proh**t**yoos] In Greek mythology, a sea god, associated with seals, and a shape-changer; he will give answers to questions after a wrestling match. He is sometimes to be found on the island of Pharos, in Egypt, where Menelaus wrestled with him.

protista *Protoctista*

Protoceratops [prohtoh**ser**atops] A primitive ceratopsian dinosaur, known from the Upper Cretaceous period of E Asia; rear frill on skull well developed; teeth for shearing, and powerful enough to cope with extremely tough plants; probably lived in herds and shared common nursery sites for egg-laying. (Order: Ornithischia.)

protochordate [prohtoh**kaw(r)**dayt] An informal name for any of the chordates (phylum: Chordata) that lack a vertebral column. These invertebrate chordates include the amphioxus (subphylum: Cephalochordata) and the tunicates (subphylum: Tunicata).

Protocols of the Elders of Zion A fraudulent document, originally printed in Russia (1903) and much translated, ostensibly reporting discussions among Jewish elders of plans to subvert Christian civilization and erect a world Zionist state. Exposed as forgeries in *The Times* (1921), the 'Protocols' have nevertheless been, and remain, a staple of anti-Semitic propaganda, most specifically by Hitler during his campaign against the Jews (1933–45).

Protoctista [prohtok**tis**ta] A kingdom of relatively simple, eucaryotic organisms, comprising the single-celled protozoans and those algae and fungi that possess flagellated spores. They typically possess, at some stage in their life-cycle, a true flagellum (a whip-like organelle containing a ring of nine microtubules surrounding two central tubules). They vary greatly in size, from the smallest micro-organisms (eg *Chlorella*) to the giant kelps. The smallest members of this kingdom, generally composed of a single cell, or only a few cells, are known as **protists**, in some classifications.

Proto-Indo-European *Indo-European languages*

proton A component particle of the atomic nucleus; symbol *p*; mass $1{\cdot}673 \times 10^{-27}$ kg (938·3 MeV), charge +1, spin $\frac{1}{2}$. It is held in the nucleus by strong nuclear force, sufficient to overcome the repulsion due to other protons. Free protons are not known to decay.

proton number The number of protons in an atomic nucleus, equal to the number of electrons in an atom; symbol *Z*; also called **atomic number**. Each element has a unique proton number. Isotopes of an element have the same proton number, but a different nucleon number.

protoplasm The complex, translucent substance that makes up every living cell. It includes the plasma membrane, but excludes such elements as ingested material and masses of secretion. In eucaryotes, protoplasm is divisible into *nucleoplasm* (the protoplasm in the nucleus) and *cytoplasm* (the protoplasm in the rest of the cell).

protostar A collapsing sphere of gas, of sufficient mass to make a star, but in which nuclear reactions have not yet started. Such objects can be detected with infrared telescopes because of the heat released by the collapse. The phase lasts 10^5–10^7 years.

Protozoa A diverse group of unicellular micro-organisms found free-living, as consumers of organic matter, in all kinds of habitats, and as parasites or associates of other organisms; typically possess a single nucleus, sometimes two or more; usually reproduce by splitting in two (*binary fission*), but sexual reproductive processes are known to occur; includes many disease-causing organisms.

protozoology The study of the *Protozoa*, a diverse group of single-celled eucaryotic micro-organisms which feed by ingesting or absorbing organic matter.

Protura [prot**yoo**ra] An order of small, primitively wingless insects that lack eyes and antennae; use forelegs as feelers; possess three pairs of rudimentary limbs (*styli*) on abdominal segments; found under stones and bark, or in rotting vegetation; c.120 species.

Proudhon, Pierre Joseph [proodõ] (1809–65) Socialist and political theorist, born in Besançon, NE France. In Paris he wrote his first important book, *Qu'est-ce que la propriété?* (1840, What is Property?), affirming the bold paradox 'property is theft', because it involves the exploitation of the labour of others. He then published his greatest work, the *Système des contradictions économiques* (1846, System of Economic Contradictions). During the 1848 Revolution, the violence of his utterances brought him three years' imprisonment, and after further arrest (1858) he retired to Belgium. He was amnestied in 1860.

Proulx, E(dna) Annie [proo] (1935–) Novelist, born in Norwich, Connecticut, USA. She studied at the University of Vermont (1969) and Sir George Williams University, Montreal (1973). Married and divorced three times, she regularly wrote for magazines to support her family, and in 1988 her collected stories were published as *Heart Songs and Other Stories*. She turned to novel writing with *Postcards* (1992), and won the Pulitzer Prize for her second book, *The Shipping News* (1994). Later works include *Accordion Crimes* (1996), *Close Range: Wyoming Stories* (1999), and *That Old Ace in the Hole* (2002).

Proust, Marcel [proost] (1871–1922) Novelist, born in Auteuil, NC France, of Jewish descent. A semi-invalid from asthma, he was looked after by his mother, and her death in 1905 caused him to withdraw from society, living in a sound-proofed flat, and giving himself over almost entirely to introspection. He then devoted himself to writing, and in 1912 produced the first part of what was to be the greatest novel of the 20th-c, his 13-volume masterpiece, *A la recherche du temps perdu* (trans Remembrance of Things Past), published the next year at his own expense. The second volume of this work, delayed by World War 1, won the Prix Goncourt in 1919. The next volumes brought him an international reputation, and he was able to complete the last six volumes (but not revise them) before his death. His massive novel, exploring the power of the memory and the unconscious, as well as the nature of writing itself, has been profoundly influential.

Provence [provãs], Lat **Provincia** Former province in SE France on the Mediterranean coast, now occupying departments of Bouches-du-Rhône, Var, Basses-Alpes, and parts of Alpes-Maritimes and Vaucluse; formerly part of the kingdom of Arles; part of France, 1481; distinctive Romance dialect; coal, bauxite, lead, zinc, salt; market-gardening, grapes, olives, perfumes, tourism (especially on Riviera).

Proverbs, Book of A book of the Hebrew Bible/Old Testament, attributed in the opening title to Solomon, but probably consisting of collected wisdom traditions from several centuries. It contains several sub-collections: Chapters 1–9 include poems about personified Wisdom, and moral admonitions of a father to his son; Chapters 10–29 present sets of individual sayings on virtues and vices with little thematic arrangement, similar to ancient Egyptian wisdom instructions such as *The Instruction of Amenemope*; Chapters 30–31 are two appendices, ending with a poem about the virtuous wife.

providence The belief that all things are ultimately ordered and governed by God towards a purpose. Some form of this belief features in Judaism, Islam, and Christianity, and is implied in the belief in the trustworthiness, goodness, and power of God.

Human free will is not generally denied, it being claimed that God either overrules it or works through it.

Providence 41°49N 71°24W, pop (2000e) 173 600. Capital of Rhode Island, USA; the smallest state capital in land area; port at the head of Providence R, in Providence County; established, 1636; city status, 1832; an early haven for religious dissenters; airport; railway; Brown University (1764); jewellery and silverware, fabricated metals, equipment; first Baptist and Unitarian churches, State Capitol, museum of art; oldest existing synagogue in USA (1763); its excellent harbour makes it a popular sailing resort, as well as a major port for oil tankers.

Providencia *San Andrés–Providencia*

Provincetown Players A US theatre group (1915–29) remembered for the work of its leading playwright Eugene O'Neill and designer Robert Edmond Jones.

Provisional IRA *IRA*

Provisional Sinn Féin *Sinn Féin*

Provisions of Oxford *Oxford, Provisions of*

proxemics [prokseemiks] The study of how people use physical space as an aspect of non-verbal communication. It is concerned with the intimate, personal, social, and public distances that individuals, classes, and cultures maintain in their interactions with each other. Several research studies have now been made of such behaviours as how closely people sit together, how much they touch each other while talking, and how they vary their practices of hand-shaking, and significant cultural and personal differences have been demonstrated.

Proxima Centauri [proksima sentawree] *Centaurus*

Prozac *antidepressants*

Prudhoe Bay [proodoh] Bay on N coast of Alaska, USA, on the Beaufort Sea; pipeline links Arctic oil fields with Valdez on the Gulf of Alaska.

Prud'hon, Pierre Paul [prüdõ] (1758–1823) Painter, born in Cluny, EC France. He studied in Dijon, trained with engravers in Paris, and went to Rome. He returned to work in a refined style not in accord with revolutionary Paris. Patronized, however, by the empresses of Napoleon, he was made court painter, and among his best work is a portrait of Joséphine.

prunus A tree or shrub of a large temperate genus containing many well-known ornamentals and orchard fruits, such as cherry, plum, peach, and almond; flowers with five petals and usually 20 stamens; fruit a single stony seed surrounded by a fleshy outer layer. (Genus: *Prunus*, 400 species. Family: Rosaceae.)

Prusiner, Stanley B (1942–) Neurologist, born in Des Moines, Iowa, USA. He graduated from the University of Pennsylvania in 1968, then worked at the University of California, Berkeley and San Francisco. He shared the 1998 Nobel Prize for Physiology or Medicine for his discovery of prions.

Prussia A N European state, originally centred in the E Baltic region as a duchy owing suzerainty to Poland. Prussia was inherited by the German house of Brandenburg in the early 17th-c. Brandenburg-Prussia was consolidated and expanded, and Polish sovereignty thrown off, by Frederick William the 'Great Elector' (1620–88). The kingdom of Prussia was founded in 1701; under Frederick William I (1713–40) and Frederick II ('the Great') (1740–86) it acquired W Prussia and Silesia, and gained considerable territory in W Germany at the Congress of Vienna (1815). Frederick expanded the Prussian army, and the state's organization was reconstructed around the military elite. The army became Europe's most effective force, and enhanced Prussia's status in Europe. During the 19th-c it emerged as the most powerful German state, and ultimately the focus of German unification. Within the German Empire (1871–1918) and the Weimar Republic (1919–33), it retained considerable autonomy and influence. As a legal entity, Prussia ceased to exist with the post-1945 division of Germany and the establishment of a revised E German–Polish frontier.

prussic acid *cyanide; hydrocyanic acid*

Prynne, William [prin] (1600–69) Puritan pamphleteer, born in Swanswick, Somerset, SW England, UK. He studied at Oxford, and was called to the bar, but was early drawn into controversy. In 1633 appeared his *Histrio-Mastix: the Players Scourge*, which contained an apparent attack on the queen (Henrietta Maria); for this he was tortured, fined, and imprisoned. Released in 1640 by the Long Parliament, he prosecuted Laud (1644), and became an MP (1648). Purged from the House in 1650, he was again imprisoned (1650–2). After Cromwell's death he returned to parliament as a Royalist, for which he was made Keeper of the Tower Records.

Przewalski's horse [pruhzhuhvalskee] A rare wild horse, native to the steppes fringing the Gobi Desert; thought to be a 'steppe type' ancestor of modern domestic breeds; reddish-brown with stiff, erect black mane and white muzzle; named after 19th-c Russian soldier and explorer Nikolai Przewalski; also known as **Mongolian wild horse**, or **Asiatic wild horse**.

Psalms, Book of A book of the Hebrew Bible/Old Testament, designated *tehillim* (Heb 'songs'), but the name 'Psalms' deriving from the Greek translation; also known as the **Psalter**. It consists of 150 hymns or poems of various types, including songs of thanksgiving, individual and community laments, wisdom poetry, and royal and enthronement songs. Many of the poems have individual titles and attributions, and the collection represents material from several centuries, brought together in its present form probably in the post-exilic period. The Psalter is regularly used in Jewish and Christian worship, its hymns admired for the religious insights of their composers. It was the most important type of mediaeval illustrated book.

Psalter *Psalms, Book of*

psaltery A mediaeval zither, constructed in various shapes, with a wooden soundbox and strings played by the fingers or with a plectrum. It is considered the ancestor of the dulcimer, which replaced it in the 15th-c. The word *psaltery* was earlier used for any plucked string instrument.

Psamtik I [samtik] King of Egypt (664–610 BC) who liberated Egypt from Assyrian control, and founded the XXVIth dynasty.

psephology [sefolojee] The study of elections and voting. It is popularly associated with the analysis of voting figures and the forecasting of outcomes, but covers all aspects of elections including legal frameworks, candidate selection, sociological and geographical analysis of voting patterns, and electoral systems.

Pseudepigrapha [syoodepigrafa] An ancient Jewish (and sometimes Christian) body of literature which is not part of the Jewish Scriptures or of major Christian versions of the Old Testament or of the Apocrypha, but which is similar to the Old Testament in character, in that its works claim to present a divine message, derived from Old Testament characters or ideas. Strictly the term means works 'written under a false name', but this does not adequately distinguish this literature from the Old Testament or Apocrypha. This large collection of writings spans roughly the period 200 BC–AD 200, although it was first collected by Johannes Fabricius (1668–1736). It includes apocalypses (eg 1 Enoch, 4 Ezra), testaments (eg Testaments of the 12 Patriarchs), wisdom literature, prayers and psalms (eg Prayer of Manasseh, Psalms of Solomon), and additions to Old Testament stories (eg Life of Adam and Eve).

Pseudo-Isidorian Forgeries A collection of genuine and spurious materials made by Frankish churchmen c.850, primarily to stress the authority and independence of bishops. It incorporates forged decretals (papal decrees) which 'Isidorus Mercator' claimed to have gathered together. Regarded as authoritative by 11th-c popes, these helped justify papal claims during the Investiture Controversy.

pseudopodium [syoodoh**poh**dium] A lobe-like protrusion, usually temporary, of the cell body of amoeboid cells, brought about by cytoplasmic streaming. Pseudopodia function as a means of locomotion, and also as a way of feeding (by engulfing food particles).

psi [psiy, siy] A parapsychological term for certain paranormal processes, embracing both extrasensory perception and psychokinesis. The term was introduced by British psychologist

R H Thouless, being the letter of the Greek alphabet most appropriate to stand for things considered as psychic.

psi-missing A parapsychological term applied to formal tests of extrasensory perception or psychokinesis in which the person being tested produces results that are actually below the level expected by chance. It is analogous to consistent 'bad luck'.

psittacosis [(p)sitakohsis] A disease caused by infection with *Chlamydia psittaci*. The micro-organism normally infects birds, but can be transmitted to humans in infected droppings. Alternative names for the disease are *parrot fever* and *pigeon fancier's lung*. There is a flu-like illness with pneumonia, often severe. Treatment is with the antibiotic tetracycline.

Pskov School [pskof] Russian icon and mural painters active c.1200–c.1500 in the city of Pskov. Byzantine influence is very evident.

psoriasis [(p)soriyasis] A common persisting or recurring skin disorder, in which small red scaly itching patches form in the superficial layers of the skin. The lesions particularly affect the elbows, knees, scalp, and nails. The cause is unknown, but the turnover of the basal cells of the skin is increased. The condition causes a great deal of personal distress. It rarely threatens life, but may do so when it becomes widespread and severe (*exfoliative psoriasis*).

Psyche [siykee] In Greek mythology, 'the soul', usually represented by a butterfly. In the story told by Apuleius, she was beloved by Cupid, who hid her in an enchanted palace, and visited her at night, forbidding her to look at him. Her sisters persuaded her to light a lamp; she saw Cupid, but was separated from him, and given impossible tasks by Venus, who impeded her search for him. The story is an allegory of love and the soul.

psychedelic art An art style that flourished in the late 1960s, influenced by the craze for hallucinatory drugs, especially LSD. Typical designs feature abstract swirls of high-key colour, sometimes accompanied by calligraphy in a curvilinear style derived from Art Nouveau.

psychedelic drugs *hallucinogens*

psychiatry A branch of medicine concerned with the study, diagnosis, prevention, and treatment of mental and emotional disorders. Its pattern of practice derives from many other disciplines (such as philosophy, psychology, biology, and ethology) and incorporates a wide range of treatment modalities. Within psychiatry, there is a range of sub-specialties including **child psychiatry**, **liaison psychiatry** (the study of patients with other physical illnesses concurrent with psychological and mental difficulties), **forensic psychiatry** (the study and treatment of patients who have broken the law), and **psychotherapy**. The range of conditions treated by psychiatrists is wide, and includes patients suffering from psychoses (in which there is a loss of contact with reality), neuroses (in which anxiety is a major component), eating disorders, disorders of dependence, mental retardation, and sleep disorders. The term *psychiatry* was coined in 1847. Society's attitude to the mentally ill has undergone a series of changes, and has often been influenced by those working outside of the psychiatric domain. Important contributors to modern attitudes concerning the mentally ill were the French physician Philippe Pinel (1745–1826) and the British philanthropist William Tuke (1732–1822). There has been a range of contributors to various aspects of psychiatry. Freud, Adler, Jung and many others have contributed to the psychological and psychoanalytic schools. Pavlov, Skinner, Solpe, and Beck have contributed to behavioural aspects. The German psychiatrist Emil Kraepelin (1856–1926) contributed the definition of clinical syndromes.

psychical research *parapsychology*

psychic healing A form of therapy in which the healer uses a patient's aura to diagnose the problem or illness that has brought about the consultation, and then transmits to the patient the energy that is needed for healing. In **psychic surgery**, healers work upon a patient by moving their hands over the diseased parts, which may result in the appearance of blood and pieces of tissue, though no evidence of an incision can be seen after the procedure. Anecdotal accounts of such 'operations' have come from several locations, such as the Espiritista Church in the Philippines.

psychoanalysis The theory and clinical practice of a form of psychology which emphasizes unconscious aspects of the mental life of an individual. The treatment, pioneered by Freud, is a form of therapy which attempts to eliminate conflict by altering the personality in a positive way. Freud introduced ideas concerning the use of the study of dreams as a way of understanding people's deeper emotions; he emphasized the introspective study of the self and, with colleagues such as Adler, Karl Abraham (1877–1925), and Jung, advanced ideas about normal and abnormal psychological processes. The first Psychoanalytic Society was in Austria, but both a combination of differences of views and wider political events led to psychoanalysis having a greater impact on North American as opposed to European psychiatry.

psychodrama A technique involving a combination of behavioural and psychoanalytic psychotherapy which makes use of the dramatic presentation of personal life situations. Through these, the patient learns new ways of dealing with both emotional and interpersonal problems.

psychohistory A method of historical study using psychoanalytic methods, especially those of Sigmund Freud, who attempted analyses of Leonardo da Vinci and Woodrow Wilson. Its leading practitioner was Erik H Erikson (1902–94), whose *Young Man Luther* (1958) shocked traditional historians by connecting the reformer's theological breakthrough with an 'identity crisis', the result of an allegedly unhappy childhood, uneasy relations with parents as an adolescent, and chronic constipation. Psychohistory has also studied Charles I, Archbishop Laud, Gandhi, and President Nixon. While sometimes successful in showing the relationship between personalities and history, psychohistory suffers from a concentration upon individuals and from a failure to explain larger movements.

psychokinesis (PK) One of the two major categories of allegedly paranormal phenomena studied by parapsychologists (the other being extrasensory perception). It is defined as the influencing by a living agent of a physical system or object by means other than those currently understood by the physical sciences. The phenomenon was earlier referred to as **telekinesis**.

psycholinguistics The study of the psychology of language. Psycholinguists are variously concerned with first and second language acquisition, language production and comprehension, and linguistic deficits such as aphasia and dyslexia. The central goal of the subject is to marry the methods and theories of the linguist with those of the psychologist. For example, a linguist might propose a grammar that accurately describes the structure of English, but the psycholinguist must try to explain how such a grammar could be learned by an infant with limited perceptual and mnemonic capacities.

psychologism The theory that philosophical problems are really questions of fact about the workings of the human mind, to be investigated by psychology. The theory was developed in the 19th-c by German philosophers. It was applied by Mill to the case of logic, but was strongly resisted by Frege and Husserl.

psychology The science of mental life – a succinct definition used by William James in 1890. Modern psychology began with the great advances in science and medicine of the 19th-c, including the work of Darwin on comparative studies of behaviour, Galton on inheritance and variation in human abilities, Helmholtz and others on the functions of the nervous system, Fechner on the basis of psychophysics, and Freud on the explanation of 'irrational' behaviour. In 1879, Wundt established in Leipzig the first laboratory entirely devoted to experimental psychology. The turn of the century saw the publication of Binet and Simon's work on testing the intelligence of French school children. Pavlov's work on the conditioned reflex had a profound influence on theories of learning and their practical applications. At the same time, Thorndike's studies of animal learning in the USA laid the basis for behaviourism, developed by Watson, and later by Skinner, in an attempt to give a complete account of human behaviour without any reference to mental states.

Contemporary psychology has seen a revival of interest in cognitive processes, with new interpretations using concepts from communication theory, information processing systems, control systems, and goal-seeking devices, and computer systems for the organization and representation of knowledge. The application of psychological methods pervades many aspects of everyday life. These methods are used, for example, in learning methods, the assessment of food preferences, the investigation of attitudes, opinions, and prejudices, the design of work and leisure environment, personnel selection and management, counselling, and therapy.

psychometrics A branch of psychology concerned with the measurement of psychological characteristics, especially intelligence, abilities, personality, and mood states. Psychometric tests are carefully constructed and standardized to provide measures of the highest possible reliability and validity.

psychometry In parapsychology, the apparent ability of a person to gain information paranormally from an inanimate object about events associated with it or its owner.

psychopathology A term used in psychiatry and clinical psychology, referring to any form of mental illness or aberration.

psychopharmacology The science of the mechanisms, uses, and side-effects of drugs that modify psychological function and behaviour.

psychophysics Methods originated by Gustav Fechner in 1860 in an attempt to quantify, as psychophysical laws, the relationships between physical stimulation and sensations. Measures of *sensitivity* have been developed into rigorous techniques (eg using signal detection theory), nowadays used principally to establish and describe the constraints on perception provided by the sensory apparatus. *Scaling* methods, which have been controversial, assess the magnitude of the effect of different amounts of stimulation. Both types of method are also used to study more complex perceptual abilities, such as face, speech, or music perception.

psychophysiological disorder *psychosomatic disorder*

psychosis A psychiatric term with a variety of uses. It is most clearly used when referring to psychiatric illnesses in which there is a loss of contact with reality, in the form of delusions or hallucinations. Less optimally, it is an indication that a psychiatric illness is severe rather than mild or moderate in its impact on the individual. It is also used with reference to two main groups of psychiatric illnesses: **organic psychoses** are caused by diseases affecting the brain; **functional psychoses** do not have a known physical cause. The term may in addition be used for illnesses in which there is a qualitative change in the emotions; those in which there is regression to immature forms of behaviour; and situations of marked withdrawal and a lack of relating to others.

psychosomatic disorder A set of real physical symptoms (eg headaches, high blood pressure) which have been caused, maintained, or exacerbated by psychological factors; also called a **psychophysiological disorder**. The cause is thought to involve intense and prolonged activity of the sympathetic branch of the autonomic nervous system in response to stress.

psychosurgery A procedure in which there is surgery on a brain regarded as histologically normal, with the intention of influencing the course of a behaviour disorder. The term was first employed by the US neurologist Walter Freeman (1895–1972) and US neurosurgeon James Winston Watts (1904–94) in 1942, but the procedure was first used in 1935. The intention in psychosurgery is to create a lesion in the brain to remove pathological thoughts and feelings with the preservation of normal functions. These procedures were initially referred to as **lobotomy** in the USA and **leucotomy** in Europe.

psychotherapy The treatment of emotional problems by a trained therapist, with the object of removing or modifying maladaptive feelings or behaviours and the promotion of what is referred to as 'personal growth and development'. There are various styles of treatment, including individual psychotherapy, marital counselling, family psychotherapy, and group psychotherapy. The question of the effectiveness of psychotherapy has often been raised, and there is now convincing research that in particular conditions, such as psychosomatic illnesses, psychotherapy (often using a combination of techniques) is effective in approximately two-thirds of patients.

psychotomimetic drugs *hallucinogens*

psyllid [silid] A jumping plant louse; feeds by sucking sap; some induce formation of galls on plant; immature stages almost immobile and unable to jump; worldwide. (Order: Homoptera. Family: Psyllidae, c.1300 species.)

Ptah [tah, ptah] An early Egyptian god associated with Memphis, and represented in human shape. Originally the creator of the world, he is later the god of craftsmanship. The name 'Egypt' is a Greek misunderstanding of 'Hut-ka-Ptah', which means 'the mansion of Ptah'. Herodotos equated him with Hephaestus.

ptarmigan [tah(r)migan] A grouse of the N hemisphere, inhabiting the high-altitude Alpine zone and tundra; moults three times a year; plumage mottled grey in summer, white in winter, with thickly feathered feet and toes acting as snowshoes. (Genus: *Lagopus*, 3 species.)

Pteranodon [teranodon] A huge pterosaur from the late Cretaceous period of North America; wingspan up to 7 m/23 ft; long toothless beak counterbalanced by a bony crest arising at neck joint; tail reduced to short stump; probably ate fish. (Order: Pterosauria.)

Pteraspis [teraspis] A fossil jawless vertebrate; known from the late Ordovician to the Devonian periods; body eel-like, without paired fins; skeleton not composed of true bone; related to the hagfish. (Class: Pteraspidimorphi.)

pteridophyte [teridohfiyt] Any spore-bearing vascular plant, in some classifications forming the Division Pteridophyta. They include ferns, whisk ferns, clubmosses, and horsetails.

pterodactyl [terodaktil] *pterosaur*

pteropod [teropod] *sea butterfly*

pterosaur [terosaw(r)] An extinct, flying reptile known from the late Triassic to the end of the Cretaceous period; ranged in size from sparrow-like to a wingspan of 15 m/50 ft; narrow, leathery wings supported by elongated fourth finger, probably flapped in active flight; bodies hairy; mostly predators; formerly known as **pterodactyls**. (Subclass: Archosauria. Order: Pterosauria.)

Ptolemaic system [tolemayik] The planetary system described in the 2nd-c AD by Claudius Ptolemaeus of Alexandria. It is Earth-centred, with the planets moving in circular orbits. To represent the observed positions of the planets as closely as possible, each planet is allowed to move on a small circle (the *epicycle*) which in turn travels along a larger circle (the *deferent*). It can predict positions to within 1° or so, and was widely used as the definitive description of the Solar System until overthrown by Copernicus in 1543.

Ptolemy I Soter [tolemee] ('Saviour') (c.366–c.283 BC) Macedonian general in the army of Alexander the Great, who became ruler of Egypt after Alexander's death (323 BC). In 304 BC he adopted the royal title, and thus founded the Ptolemaic dynasty. An able ruler, he secured control over Palestine, Cyprus, and parts of Asia Minor, and placed his regime everywhere on a sound military and financial basis. In 305 BC he defended the Rhodians against Demetrius, and received from them the title of *Soter*. Abroad, the empire was maintained, and in Egypt, Alexandria (with its royally founded museum and library) became the chief centre for learning in the Mediterranean world. On his abdication in 285 BC, he was succeeded by his son as Ptolemy II Philadelphus.

Ptolemy [tolemee], in full **Claudius Ptolemaeus** [tolemayus] (fl.127–145) Greek astronomer and geographer, who worked in the great library in Alexandria. Considered the greatest astronomer of late antiquity, his book known as *Almagest* ('the greatest') is the most important compendium of astronomy produced until the 16th-c. His system, an Earth-centred universe (the *Ptolemaic system*), held sway until dislodged by Copernicus. He also compiled a *Geographia*, containing a catalogue of places with latitude and longitude, wrote on the musical scale and chronology, and constructed several maps, including a map of the world.

puberty The period of change from childhood to adulthood, characterized by the attainment of sexual maturity and full reproductive capacity. It begins earlier in girls (about age 11) than in boys (about age 13), and lasts between 3 and 5 years. Its onset depends on both genetic and environmental influences (such as nutritional status). In both sexes there is an accelerated growth of the body (the adolescent/pubertal growth spurt), the final maturation of the gonads, and the development of secondary sexual characteristics: the development of breasts, appearance of pubic hair, and onset of menstruation in girls; the appearance of pubic and facial hair, enlargement of the penis and scrotum, and deepening of the voice in boys.

public corporations *nationalization*

public debt The total amount of government borrowings, both short-term, such as treasury bills, and long-term bonds; also known as the **government debt** or the **national debt**. The total UK public debt in the 1990s was over £190 thousand million, while that of the USA was over $3500 thousand million. Today, the finances involved in contracting and redeeming the public debt of a country are a sizeable proportion of its government budget. As the money for redemption of the public debt is raised principally through taxation, the size of the national debt is a factor in determining taxation rates.

public health *community medicine*

public house In the UK, an establishment licensed to sell alcoholic drinks; the 'pub' is, like the café in Europe, a place to meet and relax. Many pubs have names of great antiquity, often of historical interest; the common image of the pub is of a quaint building in the country, dating from Tudor times (or earlier), but many different forms exist, and true 'traditional' pubs are becoming rarer.

Public Interest Immunity *Scott Report*

public prosecutor *district attorney*

Public Record Office (PRO) The British national depository of government papers, selected archives, and legal documents to be permanently preserved, spanning 1000 years. Its holdings include Magna Carta, Domesday Book, and Shakespeare's will. It was established by Act of Parliament in 1838. Formerly based in Chancery Lane, C London, its headquarters is now at Kew, Surrey, with a Family Records Centre also in C London.

public relations (PR) The practice of managing reputation and of building goodwill on behalf of organizations, both externally and internally. It developed as a management and, later, academic discipline in the USA and in the UK in the early 20th-c, but is now practised worldwide in the commercial and public sectors. PR is commonly associated with ploys to ensure positive media coverage. In reality, public relations today is a multifaceted activity, which includes crisis management, political lobbying, dealings with the financial world, community involvement, and internal communications. Each of these recognizes a specific 'public' with which an organization has a key relationship.

Public Safety, Committee of A French Revolutionary political body, set up in the war crisis (Apr 1793) to organize defence against internal and external enemies. Its members, elected by the National Convention, came to exercise dictatorial powers during the Reign of Terror, particularly under Robespierre's leadership. After his downfall (Jul 1794), its powers were strictly limited.

public school In England, a fee-paying school for pupils of secondary age, often over 11 for girls and over 13 for boys; famous examples include Charterhouse, Eton, Harrow, Merchant Taylors', Radley, Roedean, Rugby, and Westminster. In the USA, it is the exact opposite: a school run by public authorities where fees are not paid.

public sector The parts of an economy owned by government. This includes both central and local government, and intermediate levels such as states of the USA, or Länder in Germany. It also includes public corporations operating state-owned industries, such as coal-mines or railways.

public sector borrowing requirement (PSBR) The amount of money a government needs to raise in a fiscal year by borrowing. The need arises from tax revenues and other income being less than total spending of the various government departments. The budget deficit has to be borrowed. This is normal in the UK, though general economic growth and the sale of government-owned enterprises led to budget surpluses in the late 1980s. In the USA the Federal government had massive deficits throughout the 1980s. Reducing the PSBR has been seen in the UK as important in restricting the growth of the money supply, and thus for the control of inflation.

public switched telephone network (PSTN) The conventional telephone network provided by the Posts, Telegraph and Telephones Authorities for normal voice communication, often referred to today as POTS (Plain Old Telephone Service). It is of particular interest to computer specialists since, by using modems, data communication between computers can be effected over a public telephone line. The line is in use, and has to be paid for, for the whole of the time of transmission. A preferred system for linking computers where the amount of data to be transferred is small is packet switching.

publishing The complex commercial activity in which a publisher selects, edits, and designs verbal and illustrative material, arranges its manufacture, and offers it for sale. The commodity in which publishers trade is information, interpreted widely to include entertainment, verbal and visual art, and propaganda. The media employed for publication embrace books, periodicals, newspapers, television and radio, audio and video tapes and discs, optical discs such as CD-ROM, and computer-driven on-line services. The great bulk of material published at any one time is in copyright, and broadly speaking copyrights are a publisher's stock-in-trade.

The complexity and size of the publishing trade are phenomena of modern times, and have grown in parallel with the rise of the professional author, the spread of literacy, the modernization of retailing, the use of computers to assist writing and typesetting, and other such factors. All publishing is characterized by investment in plant followed by speculative mass-production. For centuries, early printers had to be publishers too, until this role was assumed by booksellers, who often collaborated to share the initial costs of printing. Most publishing houses over 100 years old have their origins in printing or bookselling or both. The trade has changed greatly since the 1950s: the largest publishers have grown, partly by natural expansion but also particularly by acquisition; medium-sized and smaller firms have merged or been taken over; but new houses continue to spring up.

Pucci, Emilio, marchese (Marquess) **di Barsento** [poochee] (1914–92) Fashion designer, born in Naples, SW Italy. He studied in Italy and the USA, gaining a doctorate in political science in 1941. A member of the Italian ski team (1934), in 1947 he was photographed wearing ski clothes he had designed. He then began to create and sell clothes for women, opening his couture house in 1950, and becoming famous for his use of bold patterns and brilliant colour. He became a member of the Italian parliament in 1965.

Puccini, Giacomo (Antonio Domenico Michele Secondo Maria) [pucheenee] (1858–1924) Operatic composer, born in Lucca, NW Italy. An organist and choirmaster, his first compositions were for the Church. In 1880 he attended the Milan Con-

Puerto Rico

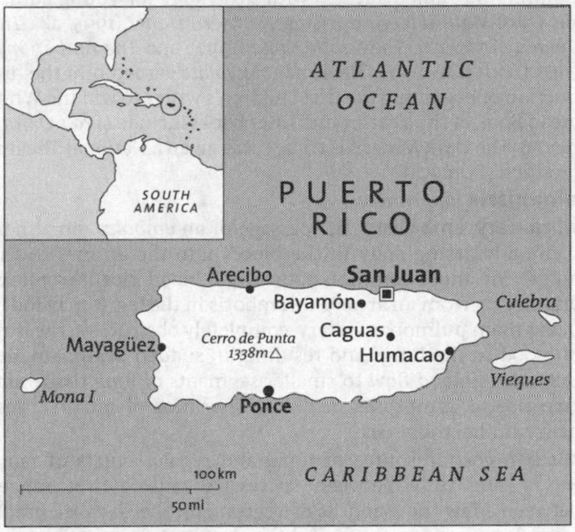

□ International Airport

[pwairtoh reekoh], formerly **Porto Rico** (to 1932), official name **Commonwealth of Puerto Rico** (USA Formal Dependencies)

Local name Puerto Rico

Timezone GMT −4

Area 8897 km^2/3434 sq mi

Population total (2000e) 3 808 600

Status Commonwealth

Capital San Juan

Languages Spanish (official), with English widely spoken

Religion Roman Catholic

Physical features Easternmost island of the Greater Antilles; almost rectangular in shape; crossed W–E by mountains, rising to 1338 m/4389 ft at Cerro de Punta; coastal plain belt in N; islands of Vieques and Culebra also belong to Puerto Rico.

Climate Tropical maritime climate; average annual temperature 25°C; high humidity.

Currency 1 US Dollar (US$) = 100 cents

Economy Manufacturing the most important sector of the economy; food processing, petrochemicals, electrical equipment, pharmaceuticals; textiles, clothing; livestock, tobacco, sugar, pineapples, coconuts; tourism.

GDP (2002e) $43·01 bn, per capita $11 100

History Originally occupied by Carib and Arawak Indians; visited by Columbus, 1493; remained a Spanish colony until ceded to the US, 1898; high levels of emigration to the US from 1940s–50s; became a semi-autonomous Commonwealth in association with US, 1952; executive power exercised by a Governor; a bicameral Legislative Assembly consists of a Senate and House of Representatives.

servatory. His first great success was *Manon Lescaut* (1893), but this was eclipsed by *La Bohème* (1896), *Tosca* (1900), and *Madame Butterfly* (1904). His last opera, *Turandot*, was left unfinished at his death.

Pucelle, Jean [püsel] or **Pucello, Johan** (c.1300–c.1355) French painter who ran an important workshop in Paris from the 1320s onwards, specializing in illuminated manuscripts. The 'Belleville Breviary' (Bibliothèque Nationale, Paris) and the 'Hours of Jeanne d'Evreux' (Metropolitan Museum, New York City) are among the greatest masterpieces of early French painting, fusing Italian Renaissance with traditional French elements.

Pucello, Johan *Pucelle, Jean*

puddling process 1 A process for converting pig-iron (high carbon) into wrought iron (very low carbon) by melting it in a small furnace in which it is worked to remove carbon (by exposure to oxidation by air) and the slag (by extrusion). This was formerly carried out by hand, but is now done mechanically. 2 The agitation of a concrete mix to promote settling and uniformity of texture.

Pudney, John (Sleigh) (1909–77) Writer, born in Langley, Buckinghamshire, SC England, UK. Educated at Gresham's School, Holt, he joined the BBC as a radio producer and scriptwriter, then worked on the *News Chronicle* and later *The Daily Express* and *News Review*. His poem 'For Johnny', written during an air raid in London in 1941, became immediately popular, later appearing in the collection *Dispersal Point and Other Air Poems* (1942). In addition to volumes of verse he also published many novels, such as *The Net* (1952) and *Thin Air* (1961), children's books, and numerous works of non-fiction, including a history of lavatories, *The Smallest Room* (1954).

Pudovkin, Vsevoled (Illarianovich) [pudofkin] (1893–1953) Film director and writer, born in Penza, W Russia. He joined the State Institute for Cinematography in Moscow, and in his first feature, *Mat* (1926, Mother), applied his concepts of montage and cross-cutting in editing. There followed the silent classics, *Konets Sankt-Peterburga* (1927, The End of St Petersburg) and *Potomok Chingis-Khan* (1928, trans Storm Over Asia), and sound films such as *Dezertir* (1933, Deserter). Much of his work portrays heroic characters in the context of historical turmoil. His books and lectures also had great international influence.

Puebla [pwaybla] or **Heróica Puebla de Zaragoza** 19°03N 98°10W, pop (2000e) 1 269 000. Capital of Puebla state, SC Mexico; SE of Mexico City; altitude 2150 m/7054 ft; damaged by earthquake, 1973; railway; two universities (1937, 1940); agricultural trade, textiles, pottery, cement, onyx; famous for its glazed tiles which cover the domes of many of its 60 churches; cathedral (17th-c), Church of Santo Domingo (1659), archbishop's palace (16th-c), Teatro Principal (1790); historic centre now a world heritage site.

Pueblo (Indians) [pwebloh] North American Indians of SW USA, living in settlements called *pueblos* in multi-storied, permanent houses made of clay. Culturally and linguistically diverse, they are divided into E and W Pueblo, the latter including the Hopi and Zuni. They are famed for their weaving, basketry, sand paintings, and pottery, and have preserved much of their traditional culture intact.

puerperal fever [pyooerperal] A fever greater than 38°C arising in a mother in the first 14 days after childbirth. It may be a consequence of genital, breast, or urinary tract infection. It was formerly a serious complication of childbearing, when infection was introduced to the genital tract by the hands of doctors or midwives. Today it is a rare cause of maternal death.

Puerto Cortes [pwairtoh kortays] 15°50N 87°55W, pop (2000e) 42 800. Port town in Cortés department, NW Honduras; at mouth of R Ulúa, on the Caribbean Sea; principal port of Honduras; free zone opened in 1978; railway; oil refining.

Puerto Rico *see panel*

puff adder A viper which inhabits grassland; two species: the **puff adder** (*Bitis arietans*) from Africa and the Middle East; length up to 2 m/6$\frac{1}{2}$ ft; very thick mottled brown body; very loud hiss; puffs up the body with air when alarmed; the **dwarf puff adder** (*Bitis peringueyi*) from SW Africa; length, 30 cm/ 12 in.

puffball A globular, often spherical fruiting body of certain fungi (the Gasteromycetes); found above ground; spores released when the wall of the puffball ruptures. (Subdivision: Basidiomycetes. Order: Lycoperdales.)

puffer Any of several stout-bodied marine and freshwater fish which can inflate the body with air or water to become almost spherical; widespread in shallow warm seas, especially over reefs and sea grass beds; body often spiny, jaws bearing four teeth forming a parrot-like beak; some organs and tissue extremely poisonous. Fishes of this family are considered a delicacy in Japan, where they are prepared by specialist chefs. (Family: Tetraodontidae, 7 genera.)

puffin Any of four species of auk of the genus *Fratercula* (2 species), *Cerorhinca* (1 species), or *Lunda* (1 species); bill large, deep, multicoloured; eats young fish and sand eels; nests in burrows or rock crevices. *Cerorhinca* is nocturnal.

pug A toy breed of dog developed in China; similar origins to the Pekinese, but with a short coat; now taller and heavier than the Pekinese, but face still flat, and tail carried over back.

Pugachev, Yemelyan Ivanovich [pugachef], also spelled **Pugachov** (1726–75) Russian Cossack, pretender to the Russian throne, and leader of a mass rebellion against Catherine II (1773–5), born in Zimoveyskaya-na-Donu, Russia. He proclaimed himself to be Peter III, Catherine's murdered husband, and promised to restore ancient freedoms. The rebellion was marked by great ferocity, and Pugachev's name later became a byword for the spirit of peasant revolution in Russia. He was captured in 1774 and taken to Moscow, where he was tortured and executed.

Pugin, Augustus (Welby Northmore) [pyoojin] (1812–52) Architect, born in London, UK. Trained by his father, he worked with Charles Barry, designing a large part of the decoration and sculpture for the new Houses of Parliament (begun 1840). He became a Catholic (c.1833), and most of his plans were made for churches within that faith, such as the Catholic cathedrals at Birmingham and Newcastle. His designs and publications, especially *Contrasts* (1836), did much to revive Gothic architecture in England.

Pugwash Conference A series of conferences first held in Pugwash, Nova Scotia, in 1957, which brought together scientists concerned about the impact on humanity of nuclear weapons. It owed much to the initiative of Bertrand Russell. The 1963 conference saw the USA give the USSR information regarding a safety system for nuclear weapons as part of an effort in arms control. Its president, Joseph Rotblat, and the Pugwash Conferences, were awarded the Nobel Peace Prize in 1995.

Pula [poola], Ital **Pola**, Lat **Pietas Iulia** 44°52N 13°52E, pop (2000e) 60 100. Seaport and resort town in W Croatia, on the Adriatic coast; built on the site of a former Roman colony; airport; railway; car ferries to Italy; naval and commercial port, shipyards, tourism; Roman amphitheatre, Temple of Augustus, cathedral, castle (17th-c); folk displays and concerts (Jun–Aug), film festival (Jul–Aug).

puli [poolee] A medium-sized breed of dog developed in Hungary for hunting and as a sheepdog; ears pendulous; tail curls over back; coat thick and long, covering eyes and ears, often reaching the ground and tangled into rope-like cords.

Pulitzer, Joseph [poolitser] (1847–1911) Newspaper proprietor, born in Makó, SE Hungary. In 1864 he emigrated and joined the US army. Discharged the following year, he moved penniless to St Louis. There he became a reporter, was elected to the State legislature, and began to acquire and revitalize old newspapers. The acquisition of the *New York World* (1883) sealed his success, and he became wealthy. He endowed the Columbia University School of Journalism, and in his will established annual Pulitzer Prizes in the fields of literature, drama, history, music, and journalism.

pulley A simple machine: a wheel with a grooved rim in which a rope can run. This changes the direction of force applied to the rope, and so can be used to raise heavy weights by pulling downwards.

Pullman, George (Mortimer) (1831–97) Inventor and businessman, born in Brocton, New York, USA. A cabinet-maker, he became a contractor in Chicago and a storekeeper in Colorado, before designing a Pullman railroad sleeping-car (1865). The Pullman Palace Car Co was formed in 1867, and in 1868 he introduced dining-cars. In 1880 he founded Pullman City for his workers, since absorbed by Chicago.

Pullman, Philip (1946–) Novelist, born in Norwich, Norfolk, E England, UK. He studied English at Oxford and had various jobs before training as a teacher. From 1988 he worked as a part-time lecturer at Westminster College in Oxford, but left in 1996 to devote himself entirely to writing. Publishing works mostly for children, he gained success with his trilogy for young adults, *His Dark Materials*, comprising *Northern Lights* (1995, aka *The Golden Compass*), *The Subtle Knife* (1997), and *The Amber Spyglass* (2000). In 2002, *The Amber Spyglass* earned him the distinction of becoming the first children's writer to win the Whitbread Book of the Year Award. Later books include *Lyra's Oxford* (2003). The Dark Materials trilogy was given a National Theatre production in 2004.

pulmonaria *lungwort*

pulmonary embolism The passage of an *embolus* (an abnormally circulating body in the blood) into the arteries to the lungs. The most common source is a blood clot (*thrombus*) originating from an area of thrombosis in the leg. It may lodge in the main pulmonary artery, completely obstructing the flow of blood to the lungs and resulting in sudden death. Smaller clots block blood flow to smaller segments of lung tissue and give rise to symptoms including shortness of breath, chest pain, and haemoptysis.

pulsar A cosmic source of rapid and regular bursts of radio waves. The time between successive radio pulses ranges between a few thousandths of a second for the so-called 'millisecond pulsars' to over 4 s for the slowest pulsars. Pulsars are collapsed neutron stars, having a mass similar to the Sun, but a diameter of only 10 km/6 mi or so. Over 1000 are known.

pulsating star A variable star whose outer layers regularly expand and contract. Cepheid variables are of particular importance, because their period of pulsation gives a measure of absolute luminosity, and therefore enables stellar distances to be found for these stars by comparing apparent and absolute brightness.

pulse (botany) A general name applied to peas, beans, and lentils, the edible ripe seeds of several plants of the pea family. Pulses are often rich in protein and nutritious. (Family: Leguminosae.)

pulse (physiology) A pressure wave generated by the ejection of blood from the left ventricle into the vascular system. The number of pulsations per minute reflects heart rate, which in humans is between 70 and 90 at rest (exercise, anger, and fever increase pulse rate, whereas depression lowers it). The alternate expansion and recoil of arteries lying near to the body surface can readily be felt (and sometimes seen) as a throbbing. The pulse rate is commonly taken by placing the finger tips on the inside of the forearm just above the wrist (the *radial pulse*).

puma *cougar*

pumice A very light and porous igneous rock, usually granitic in chemical composition, formed by solidifying the froth caused by vigorous degassing of volatile substances from a lava during eruption. It is used as an abrasive.

pump A machine for moving a fluid or gas from one place to another; commonly used to move fluids, often water, through pipes. The earliest recorded mechanical pumps (square-pallet chain pumps) were in 1st-c BC China. The simplest pump, which uses the pressure of the air, can lift water through a height of only c.10 m/33 ft. More complex pumps provide mains water for the home, and circulate water to cool car engines. *Pressure pumps* are used to blow up bicycle tyres and footballs. *Evacuation pumps* suck air from sealed containers to make a partial vacuum. The heart is also a type of pump, moving blood through the veins in the body.

pumpkin A trailing or climbing vine (*Cucurbita maxima*) native to America; leaves palmately-lobed; male and female flowers 12·5 cm/5 in diameter, funnel-shaped; fruit usually globular, often reaching great size and weight; rind and flesh orange, rather fibrous, surrounding numerous seeds; cultivated as a vegetable. It is also often used to make Hallowe'en lanterns by placing a candle in the hollowed-out centre, and carving a face in the rind, through which the light shines. (Family: Cucurbitaceae.)

Punch and Judy A glove-puppet show – named after the man and wife who are its central characters – which developed in Britain from the marionette plays based on Pulcinella, the impudent hunchback of the *commedia dell'arte*. The Victorian era was the heyday of the itinerant puppeteer with his portable open-air booth, but the tradition has survived and its major features have remained constant. Being a one-man show, only two hand-puppets can appear at a given time. Punch, operated by the right hand, is a constant figure, while the challenges of the left hand introduce character after character to be defeated by Punch's anarchic vigour. The French equivalent of the British Punch, German **Hanswurst** or **Kasperl**, Russian **Petroushka**, is the **Guignol**. In Paris the name attached itself in the 1890s to cabarets which specialized in short puppet plays of violence, murder, and ghostly apparitions. Its home now remains in the portable booths and small theatres of Montmartre.

punctuation The part of a language's writing system which provides clues to the way a text is organized. Early writing systems made little or no use of punctuation. Punctuation marks were first introduced by Ancient Greek and Roman authors, from around the 2nd-c BC, as an aid to reading a text aloud, and they retain some of that function in modern languages. They are primarily a visual prompt to the lexical and grammatical structure of a text, with two main functions. Some conventions organize the text into grammatical or semantic units, such as paragraphs and words (spaces), sentences and clauses (full-stop, comma, colon, semi-colon); parentheses and the dash can both substitute for commas, while quotation marks identify extracts of speech. Other conventions carry meaning of their own: the question mark identifies a sentence type, the apostrophe marks possession (*John's*) and contractions (*I'm, must've*), while the exclamation mark conveys such features of meaning as surprise.

Pune *Poona*

Punic Wars [pyoo**nik**] The three wars fought and won in the 3rd-c and 2nd-c BC by Rome against her only remaining rival for supreme power in the W Mediterranean, the Phoenician (Punic) city, Carthage. The first (264–241 BC) resulted in Rome's acquisition of her first overseas province, Sicily, hitherto a Carthaginian territory. The second war (218–201 BC) saw Carthage surrender to Rome all her remaining overseas possessions, and become a dependent, tribute-paying ally. The third (149–146 BC) ended in the capture and total destruction of Carthage itself.

Punjab (India) [**pun**jahb] pop (2001e) 24 289 300; area 50 362 sq km/19 440 sq mi. State in NW India, bounded W and NW by Pakistan; capital (jointly with Haryana), Chandigarh; major cities include Amritsar, Jalandhar, Faridkot, Ludhiana; population c.60% Sikh in Indian Punjab, mainly Muslim in Pakistani Punjab; part of the Mughal Empire until end of 18th-c; annexed by the British after the Sikh Wars (1846, 1849); autonomous province, 1937; partitioned between India and Pakistan into East and West Punjab on the basis of religion, 1947; Indian state renamed Punjab, reformed as a Punjabi-speaking state, 1956 and 1966; governed by a 117-member Legislative Assembly; Alkai Dai Party campaigns for Sikh autonomy; wheat, maize, rice, sugar cane, cotton; textiles, sewing machines, sugar, fertilizers, bicycles, electrical goods, machine tools, scientific instruments.

Punjab (Pakistan) [**pun**jahb] pop (2000e) 77 280 000; area 205 334 sq km/79 259 sq mi. Province in Pakistan, bounded E and S by India and the Thar Desert and N by Baltistan; crossed by the Sutlej, Chenab, Jhelum, Ravi, and Indus Rivers; chiefly Muslim population; capital, Lahore; grains, cotton, sugar cane, fruit, vegetables; textiles, foodstuffs, metal goods, bicycles, machinery.

Punjabi *Indo-Aryan languages*

punkie *biting midge*

punk rock A type of anarchistic rock music, originating in the late 1970s with such UK groups as Generation X, The Buzzocks, and The Sex Pistols. Their very loudly amplified performances were characterized by the public use of swear words, outrageous behaviour, and clothes and hairstyles which sought to challenge establishment values.

Punt, land of In antiquity, the area to the S of Egypt near the mouth of the Red Sea. From the third millennium BC, it was the source for the Egyptians of incense, myrrh, gold, and ivory.

Punta Arenas [punta ar**ay**nas] 53°09S 70°52W, pop (2000e) 141 000. Port and capital of Magallanes y Antártica Chilena region, Chile; most southerly city in Chile, on Brunswick Peninsula facing the Straits of Magellan; founded as penal colony in 19th-c; airfield; sheep-farming trade, exporting wool, skins, and frozen meat; most southerly brewery in world; crude oil and gas; museum at Colegio Salesiano, Museum of Regional History, Patagonian Institute; Festival Folclórica de la Patagonia (July); skiing on Cerro Mirador (9 km/5 mi W), the most southerly resort in the world, with a sea view.

pupa The life-cycle stage of an insect during which the larval form is reorganized to produce the definitive adult form. It is commonly an inactive stage, enclosed in a hard shell (*chrysalis*) or silken covering (*cocoon*).

pupil *eye*

puppetry The art and craft of manipulating inanimate figures for performance. There are three major means of manipulation: from above, by strings, as with **marionettes**; from below, behind or beside, by inserting a hand into the costume, head or limbs of the puppet, as with **glove puppets**; and from below or behind, by a central support (sometimes with additional strings) activating the head and body, and by separate supports controlling the limbs, as with **rod-puppets**. The last method is sometimes used to manipulate two-dimensional figures so as to form silhouettes on a screen; these are known as **shadow puppets**. Movable puppets are known to have existed in ancient Egypt, ancient Greece, and throughout the Roman empire. Until the 20th-c puppetry was an important part of popular entertainment and folk culture throughout Europe, Asia Minor, and Asia, the best known being the Javanese shadow puppets and the Turkish *Karagöz*. In India, shadow puppets survive mainly in Kerala. Rod puppets, still used in India and Java, are full-length figures. Controlled from below, they are slow and measured in their movements. The **bunraku** figures of Japanese drama are about two-thirds life-size, their on-stage operators working in teams, no puppet being workable by one operator alone. In the second half of the 20th-c some theatre companies, notably the Magic Lantern theatre in Prague, successfully pioneered the merging of performances by live actors and puppets. Puppet shows have also achieved a presence on television, both to provide children's entertainment and for political satire.

Puppis [**pup**is] (Lat 'ship's stern') A S constellation, partly in the Milky Way, which includes many notable star clusters.

Puranas [pur**ah**nas] In Indian tradition, a set of sacred compositions dating from the Gupta period (AD c.4th-c onwards), dealing with the mythology of Hinduism. They are very important in popular Hinduism.

Purcell, E(dward) M(ills) [**per**sel] (1912–97) Physicist, born in Taylorville, Illinois, USA. He studied at Purdue, Karlsruhe, and Harvard universities, worked on microwave radar at Massachusetts Institute of Technology during World War 2, and was appointed professor of physics at Harvard (1949). He developed nuclear magnetic resonance methods of analysis which have become a major tool in chemistry, and was the first to detect the interstellar microwave radiation predicted by van de Hulst. He shared the Nobel Prize for Physics in 1952 for his work on the magnetic moments of atomic nuclei.

Purcell, Henry [**per**sel], earlier [per**sel**] (1659–95) Composer, born in London, UK. He was a Chapel Royal chorister, and held posts as organist there and at Westminster Abbey, as well as becoming keeper of the king's instruments (1683). Though his harpsichord pieces and his trio-sonatas for violins and continuo have retained their popularity, he is best known for his vocal and choral works. In his official capacity he produced a number of pieces in celebration of royal birthdays, St Cecilia's Day, and other occasions. He also wrote a great deal of incidental stage music, including *The Fairy Queen* (1692) and *The Tempest* (1695), and an opera, *Dido and Aeneas* (1689). Of his many songs, 'Nymphs and Shepherds' is probably the best known.

Purcell, William Gray *Elmslie, George Grant*

purchase tax An excise tax levied on consumer goods, and added to the price paid by the customer; the rate varied with the type of goods. In the UK it was replaced by value-added tax in 1973.

purchasing power parity (PPP) An economic theory that the true rate of exchange between two currencies can be determined by what can be bought with a unit of each currency. Parity is achieved when what can be purchased is the same.

Pure Land Buddhism A school of Buddhism founded, it is said, by the Chinese monk, Hui Yuan (334–417). It is characterized by devotion to the Bodhisattva Amitabha, who rules over a 'pure land'. The goal of those devoted to Amitabha and the pure land is to be reborn there, and attain enlightenment. The school also spread to Japan.

purgative *laxative*

purgatory In Roman Catholic and some Orthodox teaching, the place and state in which the souls of the dead suffer for their sins before being admitted to heaven. Those in purgatory may be assisted by the prayers of the faithful on Earth.

Purim [pyurim, pureem] The Jewish Feast of Lots, celebrated on 14 or 15 Adar (about 1 Mar), commemorating the deliverance of the Jews from a plot to have them massacred, as related in the Book of Esther.

purines [pyooreenz] A group of organic bases, the most important of which are adenine and guanine, part of the nucleotide chains of DNA and RNA.

Purism A modern art movement founded in 1918 by French artist Amédée Ozenfant (1886–1966) and the architect Le Corbusier. They rejected Cubism, and sought an art of pure and impersonal forms based, however, on the observation of real things. Although no great pictures resulted, Purism influenced modern architecture and design.

Puritanism The belief that further reformation was required in the Church of England under Elizabeth I and the Stuarts. It arose in the 1560s out of dissatisfaction with the 'popish elements', such as surplices, which had been retained by the Elizabethan religious settlement. It was not always a coherent, organized movement; rather, a diverse body of opinions and personalities, which occasionally came together. It included the anti-episcopal Presbyterian movement of John Field (1545–88) and Thomas Cartwright (1535–1603) in the 1570s and 1580s; the separatist churches that left England for Holland and America from 1590 to 1640; the 'presbyterian', 'independent', and more radical groups which emerged during the Civil War and interregnum; and the nonconformist sects persecuted by the Cavalier Parliament's 'Clarendon Code' under Charles II. Whether there existed, as some sociologists have maintained, a distinctive 'puritan ethic' with economic ethics and behaviour that fostered capitalism, is very doubtful.

Purkinje, Johannes (Evangelista) [poorkinyay] (1787–1869) Histologist and physiologist, born in Libochovice, NW Czech Republic. He graduated in 1818 with a thesis on vision, which gained him the friendship and support of Goethe. Helped by this, he became professor in Wrocław, Poland (formerly Breslau, Prussia) and later at Prague. An early user of the improved compound microscope, he discovered a number of new and important microscopic anatomical structures, some of which are named after him. He was also a very early user of the microtome for cutting sections.

Purple Heart In the USA, a decoration instituted in 1782 as an award for gallantry; it was revived in 1932, since when it has been awarded for wounds received in action. The ribbon is purple with white edges.

purpura [perpyoora] A condition in which there is spontaneous bleeding into the skin or mucous membranes, giving rise to small scattered areas of bruising. It has many causes, including damage to small blood vessels, disorders of blood platelets, and defects in blood clotting.

purslane A name applied to several different plants. **Common purslane** (*Portulacca oleracea*), a weed very widespread in warm regions and cultivated as a pot herb, is a fleshy-leaved annual with yellow, 4–6-petalled flowers. The related **pink purslane** (*Claytonia sibirica*), native to W North America, is an annual or perennial with long-stalked leaves and white or pink 5-petalled flowers. (Family: Portulaccaceae.)

pus Yellow liquid formed after localized inflammation, such as an abscess, or on the surface of a wound, produced by infection with certain bacteria (known as *pyogenic* bacteria). It consists of dead tissue, white blood cells, and micro-organisms.

Pusan or **Busan** [poosahn] 5°05N 129°02E, pop (2000e) 4 170 000. Seaport and special city in SE Korea with provincial status, on SE coast on Korea Strait; Korea's second largest city; airport; railway; international ferry; hydrofoil; two universities (1946–7); engineering, shipbuilding, tourism, fishing, trade in salt, fish, rice, soybeans; municipal museum; UN Memorial Cemetery from the Korean War, Yongdu san park, Pusan Tower, T'aejongdae park, Tongnae Hot Springs nearby, Pomosa Buddhist temple nearby (founded 678); Pusan Stadium (2001).

Pusey, E(dward) B(ouverie) [pyoozee] (1800–82) Theologian, born in Pusey, Oxfordshire, SC England, UK. He studied at Oxford, where he became professor of Hebrew in 1828, retaining the position until his death. His main aim was to prevent the spread of Rationalism in England, and he joined Newman in the Oxford Movement (1833), contributing several tracts, notably those on baptism and the Eucharist. After Newman's conversion, he became the leader of the Movement, defending his own position in several publications.

Pushkin, Alexander Sergeyevich [pushkin] (1799–1837) Poet, born in Moscow, Russia. In 1817 he entered government service, but his liberalism caused his exile to S Russia (1820) until after the accession of Nicholas I (1826). Hailed in Russia as its greatest poet, his first success was the romantic poem 'Ruslan and Lyudmila' (1820), followed by the verse novel *Eugene Onegin* (1828), the historical tragedy *Boris Godunov* (1831), and several other large-scale works. He also wrote many lyrical poems, tales, and essays, and was appointed Russian historiographer. His marriage (1831) to **Nikolayevna Goncharova** proved unhappy and led to his early death, defending his wife's honour in a duel with her brother-in-law, brought about by his enemies at court.

puss moth A prominent moth with white forewings bearing black zigzag markings; hindwings white in male, grey in female; caterpillar green with reddish head, found on willow and poplar. (Order: Lepidoptera. Family: Notodontidae.)

Putin, Vladimir (Vladimirovich) (1952–) Russian politician and president (1999–), born in Leningrad (now St Petersburg), NW Russia. He graduated from Leningrad State University in 1975 and began his career in the KGB as an intelligence officer stationed mainly in East Germany (1975–89). Following the collapse of the Soviet Union in 1991, he retired from the KGB, and became first deputy mayor of Leningrad (1994), moving to Moscow in 1996. In 1998 he was appointed deputy head of management in Boris Yeltsin's presidential administration, then head of the Federal Security and of Yeltsin's Security Council, and was promoted prime minister in August 1999. In December 1999 Yeltsin resigned as president, appointing Putin acting president until official elections were held (in early 2000). He was re-elected in 2004.

Putnam, Hilary (1926–) Philosopher, born in Chicago, Illinois, USA. He held teaching positions at Northwestern University and Princeton, and became professor of the philosophy of science at the Massachusetts Institute of Technology (1961–5) and professor of philosophy at Harvard in 1965. He argues strongly for a conception of philosophy that makes it essential to a responsible view of the real world and our place in it. His books include *Meaning and the Moral Sciences* (1978) and *Reason, Truth and History* (1982).

putrefaction The anaerobic decomposition of protein-rich organic matter by bacteria. It results in the formation of methane and other foul-smelling gaseous products.

Puttnam (of Queensgate), David (Terence) Puttnam, Lord (1941–) Film-maker and educationist, born in London, UK. He left school at 16, then had a very successful background in advertising and photography, which led him to produce his first feature film *S.W.A.L.K.* (1969). Subsequently he helped encourage new directorial talents with stylish, low-budget features such as *Bugsy Malone* (1976) and *The Duellists* (1977). *Chariots of Fire* (1981), which won four Oscars, epitomized the type of intelligent, humanist drama he wanted to make, and its international commercial appeal allowed him to progress to larger scale explorations of human and moral dilemmas in such films as *Local Hero* (1983), *The Killing Fields* (1984), and *The Mission* (1986). In 1986 he became chairman and chief executive of Columbia Pictures, but returned to Britain after a year. Later films include *Memphis Belle* (1990), *Meeting Venus* (1991), *Being Human* (1994), and *My Life So Far* (1997). He was knighted in 1995, and received a life peerage in 1997. He now works principally in the field of education, serving as an adviser to a number of UK government departments. He is Chancellor of the University of Sunderland, and a governor and lecturer at the London School of Economics. In 2000 he took up his appointment as chairman of the General Teaching Council, and in 2002 he became president of UNICEF (UK).

putty A cement made of fine, powdered chalk or white lead, mixed with linseed oil. It is used for filling wood, and for fixing glass in frames. It hardens slowly on exposure to air. **Putty powder** is a fine, tin oxide powder used for polishing glass and granite.

Puvis de Chavannes, Pierre (Cécile) [püvee duh shavan] (1824–98) Painter, born in Lyon, SC France. He is best known for his murals on public buildings, notably of the life of St Geneviève in the Panthéon, Paris, and the large allegorical works such as 'Work' and 'Peace' on the staircase of the Musée de Picardie, Amiens.

Puyi, Pu Yi, or **P'u-i** [pooyee], personal name of the **Xuantong** Emperor (1906–67) Last emperor of China (1908–12) and the first of Manchukuo (1934–5), born in Beijing, China. Emperor at the age of two, after the 1912 revolution he was given a pension and a summer palace. Known in the West as **Henry Puyi**, in 1932 he was called from private life by the Japanese to be provincial dictator of Manchukuo, under the name of **Kangde**. Taken prisoner by the Russians in 1945, he was tried in China as a war criminal (1950), pardoned (1959), and became a private citizen. The story of his life was made into a successful film (*The Last Emperor*) in 1988.

PVC *polyvinylchloride*

Pycnogonida [piknuhgonida] *sea spider*

pyelitis *pyelonephritis*

pyelonephritis [piyelohnefriytis] A bacterial inflammation of the kidney, usually associated with infection in the lower urinary tract, such as the bladder. The infection usually reaches the kidney by ascending the ureters, and is encouraged to do so by a lesion causing obstruction to the free flow of urine, such as urinary stones, or enlargement of the prostate. Infection is accompanied by high fever and back pain and needs treatment with appropriate antibiotics, since persisting or recurrent infection may lead to renal failure.

Pygmalion [pigmaylion] In Greek mythology, a king of Cyprus, who made a statue of a beautiful woman. He prayed to Aphrodite, and the sculptured figure came to life.

Pygmies A small-statured people living in C Africa (averaging 1·50 m/4·9 ft in height), the best known of which are the forest-dwelling Mbuti of the Democratic Republic of Congo and the Twa of the Great Lakes savannahs. Traditionally hunter-gatherers, most Pygmy bands live in a close relationship with non-Pygmy groups, and many have become farmers and herders in surrounding savannah areas. All speak the Bantu languages of their non-Pygmy neighbours.

pygmy hippopotamus *hippopotamus*

pygmy owl A small owl, native to the Americas, Europe, and Asia; inhabits woodland; nests in holes. (Genus: *Glaucidium*, 6 species. Family: Strigidae.)

pylon **1** The flanking towers to the gateway of an ancient Egyptian temple; usually rectangular in plan with tapering, truncated sides.
2 In modern times, a tall, usually metal structure that carries power cables or acts as a guiding post at an airfield.

Pylos [piylos] A town on the W coast of the Peloponnese, associated in Greek tradition with Nestor, a Greek chief at the time of the Trojan War. Excavations have revealed a large, unfortified Mycenaean palace there.

Pym, Barbara (Mary Crampton) (1913–80) Novelist, born in Oswestry, Shropshire, WC England, UK. She studied at Liverpool and Oxford universities, and for most of her adult life worked at the International African Institute in London. She is best known for her series of satirical novels on English middle-class society, including *Excellent Woman* (1952) and *Quartet in Autumn* (1977).

Pym, John [pim] (1584–1643) English politician, born in Brymore, Somerset, SW England, UK. He left Oxford without taking a degree, studied law, and entered parliament (1614). In 1641 he took a leading part in the impeachment of Strafford, helped to draw up the Grand Remonstrance, and in 1642 was one of the five members whom Charles I singled out by name. He stayed in London during the Civil War, and died soon after being appointed lieutenant of the Ordnance.

Pynchon, Thomas (Ruggles) [pinchon] (1937–) Novelist, born in Glen Cove, New York, USA. He studied at Cornell, then worked as a technical writer for Boeing before leaving to write fiction. His novels, such as *V* (1963), *The Crying of Lot 49* (1966), *Gravity's Rainbow* (1973, National Book Award), and *Vineland* (1992) all display a preoccupation with codes, quests, and coincidences that determines the form of the narrative. Later works include *Mason and Dixon* (1997). An experimentalist, esoteric and elusive, his books largely abandon the normal conventions of the novel. He has also written several short stories, published in *Slow Learner* (1984), which also contains a revealing essay on his acknowledged influences.

Pyongyang [pyuhngyang], Jap **Heijo** 39°00N 125°47E, pop (2000e) 2 906 000. Capital of North Korea, overlooking the R Taedong; Korea's oldest city, founded allegedly in 1122 BC; capital of Choson kingdom, 300–200 BC; colony of China, 108 BC; centre of Han Chinese colonial administration; taken by Japanese, 1592–3; retaken by China, 1593; capital of North Korea since 1948; rebuilt after the Korean War; airport; railway; university (1946); iron and steel, machinery, textiles, aircraft, sugar; 1st-c tombs.

pyorrhoea / pyorrhea [piyoreea] *dentistry*

pyracantha *firethorn*

pyralid moth [piralid] A moth of the family Pyralidae; adults often slender with long hindlimbs; caterpillars typically plant feeders, sometimes scavengers or parasites; c.20 000 species, many pests of crops and dried vegetable products. (Order: Lepidoptera.)

pyramid An architectural structure on a triangular, square, or polygonal base, with triangular sides meeting in a single point. In Egyptian architecture, it is a sepulchral stone monument with a square base. In Pre-Columbian architecture, it is an artificial hill with a flat top. The phrase **the Pyramids** usually refers to the Fourth Dynasty pyramids of the Giza plateau on the SW outskirts of modern Cairo. The Great Pyramid of Cheops (c.2589–2566 BC) is 146 m/480 ft high, 230 m/755 ft square, and 2 352 000 cu m/27 688 000 cu ft in volume, made up of 2·5 million limestone blocks each of 2·5 tonnes.

pyramid healing A form of healing which uses the electromagnetic energy thought to be mystically concentrated within the dimensions of a pyramid. (The height of the Great Pyramids is

Pythagoras's theorem

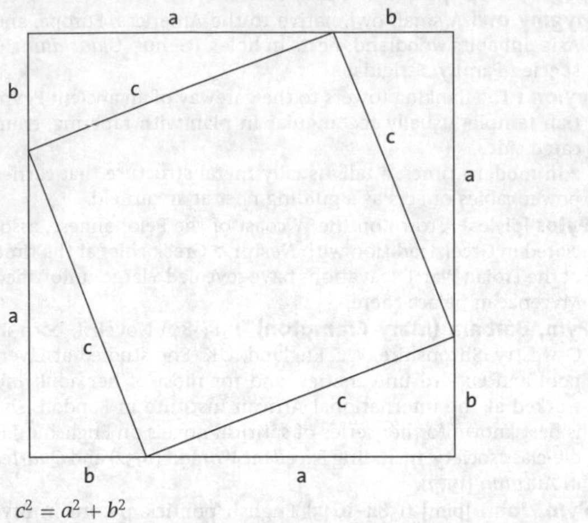

$c^2 = a^2 + b^2$

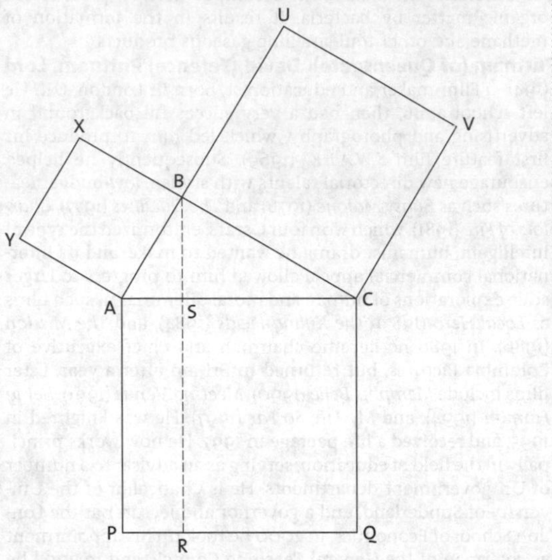

$AC^2 = AB^2 + BC^2$

[piythagoras] A mathematical proposition advanced by Pythagoras, that in any right-angled triangle, the square on the hypotenuse is equal to the sum of the squares on the other two sides. The converse of the theorem is also true: in any triangle in which the square on the longest side is equal to the sum of the squares on the other two sides, the angle opposite the longest side is a right angle. Although known to the Babylonians, tradition ascribes to Pythagoras himself the first proof, probably based on the first diagram. The commoner proof (the second diagram), proving first that the area of square *ABXY* is equal to that of the rectangle *APRS*, was given by Euclid. Pythagorean triples - three integers (eg 3,4,5) that can be the sides of right-angled triangles - have long fascinated people. The formula 2k*mn*, k($m^2 + n^2$), k($m^2 - n^2$) generates all Pythagorean triples. The theorem was probably independently conceived and proved in 2nd-c AD China.

the radius of a circle whose circumference is the same as the circumference of the square base.) Pyramids have been reported to enhance plant growth. Sleeping with the head inside a pyramid is claimed to improve the quality of sleep, and possibly to induce changes in hormone levels which have been reported to cause alterations in the menstrual cycle. Pyramidal storage containers are claimed to keep razor blades sharp, and to prolong the life of fruit and vegetables.

pyramids A ball game played on a standard billiard table in which 15 coloured balls, usually red, are placed in a triangle with the apex ball on the pyramid spot (the pink-ball spot). The object is to sink more balls than your opponent. Pyramids was the forerunner of snooker in the 19th-c.

Pyramus and Thisbe [piramus, thizbee] In a story told by Ovid, two lovers who were kept apart by their parents. They conversed through a crack in the wall between their houses, and agreed to meet at Ninus's tomb outside the city of Babylon. Finding Thisbe's blood-stained cloak, Pyramus thought she had been killed by a lion, and committed suicide. When she found him, Thisbe killed herself on his sword. The story is incorporated into Shakespeare's *A Midsummer Night's Dream*.

Pyrenean mountain dog A breed of dog developed in the Pyrenees several centuries ago to protect sheep; large powerful body with heavy head; thick, usually pale-coloured, coat.

Pyrenees [pireneez], Fr **Pyrénées**, Span **Pirineos** Mountain range extending W–E from the Bay of Biscay to the Mediterranean Sea, separating the Iberian Peninsula from the rest of Europe; stretches 450 km/280 mi along the French–Spanish frontier; includes Andorra; highest point, Pic de Aneto (3404 m/11 168 ft); Gouffre de la Pierre St Martin, one of the deepest caves in the world; Grotte Casteret, highest ice cave in Europe; observatory at Pic du Midi de Bigorre.

Pyrenees, Treaty of the (1659) A treaty between France and Spain ending the hostilities of the Thirty Years' War. It followed a series of Spanish Habsburg defeats since 1643 (the Austrian Habsburgs made a separate peace in the Treaty of Westphalia, 1648). The French gained border regions, but withdrew from most of Italy. It marked the end of Spanish military and political dominance in W Europe.

pyrethrum [piyreethruhm] A perennial, growing to 45 cm/18 in (*Tanacetum cinerariifolium*), native to parts of the Balkan peninsula, but extensively cultivated, especially in E Africa and South America; leaves divided, silvery-grey; flower-heads solitary, daisy-like, spreading outer florets white. An insecticide, known in China by the 2nd-c AD, is prepared from the extracts of the powdered and dried flower-heads. (Family: Compositae.)

Pyrex® A trade name for a borosilicate glass with a high silica content, some boron, and some aluminium. It is useful chemically because of its high mechanical strength, and its resistance to strong alkalis and acids. It is useful physically because of its low coefficient of thermal expansion (giving resistance to thermal shock). These properties favour its extensive domestic and scientific use.

pyrexia *fever*

pyridine [pirideen] C_5H_5N, boiling point 115°C. An organic base with a vile odour. It occurs in a fraction of coal tar, and is carcinogenic. Many alkaloids are pyridine derivatives.

pyridoxine A B vitamin (B_6) which exists in the form of *pyridoxine* in vegetable foods and *pyridoxal* and *pyridoxamine* in animal foods. In the body, all food forms of this vitamin are converted to pyridoxal phosphate. It acts as a co-enzyme for the enzymes involved in the interconversion and metabolism of amino acids. Deficiency is rare, but large doses of B_6 are frequently used as a treatment for several disorders, including premenstrual syndrome and mild depression, though its efficacy is disputed. Prolonged excessive intakes have been associated with nervous disorders.

pyrimidines [pirimideenz] A group of organic bases, the most important of which are cytosine, thymine, and uracil, part of the nucleotide chains of DNA and RNA.

pyrite A metallic yellow iron sulphide (FeS_2) mineral, common and widespread, often occurring as well-formed cubic crystals; also termed 'fool's gold' because of its colour. It is used as a source of sulphur and in the manufacture of sulphuric acid.

pyroclastic rock A general name given to rocks formed from fragments of lava ejected from a volcano into the atmosphere. Examples are ignimbrites, consolidated volcanic ash (*tuff*), and volcanic agglomerate.

pyroelectrics Crystalline materials having an overall electric dipole moment that changes with temperature but is insensitive to an applied electric field, eg lithium niobate, $LiNbO_3$. They are related to ferroelectrics.

pyrolysis The decomposition of a substance by heating in the absence of oxygen, usually resulting in simpler compounds being formed. The most important example is the pyrolysis or 'cracking' of petroleum, by which alkanes are converted into alkenes and shorter alkanes, eg propane may be converted to ethene and methane: $CH_3CH_2CH_3 \rightarrow CH_2{=}CH_2 + CH_4$.

pyrometer A type of thermometer for measuring high temperatures. In the optical pyrometer, the heat colour of the hot object is compared to that of a heated filament through which a controlled current is passed. When the colours match, the sample temperature is known via the previous calibration of the filament.

pyrope [piyrohp] *garnet*

pyroxenes [piyrokseenz] A large group of silicate minerals including many important rock-forming minerals; similar to amphiboles, but with a single-chain structure of silicate tetrahedra and without hydroxyl ions. Important members of the group are enstatite, diopside, augite, pigeonite, and jadeite. They are widely distributed in igneous and metamorphic rocks.

Pyrrho [piroh] (c.360–c.270 BC) Philosopher, born in Elis, Greece. He travelled in Persia and India with Alexander the Great, then returned to Elis. His opinions are known from the writings of his pupil, Timon. He taught that we can know nothing of the nature of things, but that the best attitude of mind is suspense of judgment, which brings with it 'an imperturbable peace of mind'. *Pyrrhonism* is often regarded as the foundation of scepticism.

Pyrrhus [pirus] (c.318–272 BC) King of Epirus (modern Albania) (307–303 BC, 297–272 BC), an ambitious ruler whose aim was to revive the empire of his second cousin, Alexander the Great. Unsuccessful in this goal (283 BC), he turned to the West, where he became embroiled in Italian affairs and hence conflict with Rome. Though he won two battles (280–279 BC), his losses, particularly at Asculum (279 BC), were so great that they gave rise to the phrase *Pyrrhic victory*.

pyruvic acid [piyroovik] CH_3–CO–COOH, IUPAC **2-oxopropanoic acid**. The non-chiral oxidation product of lactic acid. It occurs in several metabolic reaction pathways.

Pythagoras [piythagoras] (6th-c BC) Philosopher and mathematician, born in Samos, Greece. He settled at Crotona, S Italy (c.530 BC) where he founded a moral and religious school. He eventually fled from there because of persecution, settling at Megapontum in Lucania. *Pythagoreanism* was first a way of life, of moral abstinence and purification, not solely a philosophy; its teaching included the doctrine of the transmigration of souls between successive bodies. He is associated with discoveries involving the chief musical intervals, the relations of numbers, and with more fundamental beliefs about the representation of the world of nature through numbers. The famous geometrical theorem attributed to him was probably developed later by members of the Pythagorean school. Pythagorean thought exerted considerable influence on Plato's doctrines.

Pythagoras's theorem *see panel p.1258*

Pytheas [pithias] (4th-c BC) Mariner, born in Massilia (Marseille), Gaul. He sailed past Spain, Gaul, and the E coast of Britain (c.330 BC), and reached the island of 'Thule', six days' sail from N Britain (possibly Iceland). His account of the voyage is lost, but referred to by several later writers.

Pythian Games [pithian] In ancient Greece, one of the main Pan-Hellenic festivals, held every four years in the sanctuary of Apollo Pythios at Delphi. 'Pythios' or 'python slayer' was the name under which Apollo was worshipped there.

Pythias (of Syracuse) *Damon and Pythias*

python A snake of family Pythonidae (27 species), sometimes included in the boa family; native to Africa, S and SE Asia, Australasia, and (a single species) Central America; a constrictor; minute remnants of hind limbs; eye with vertical slit-like pupil; females lay eggs and often incubate these until they hatch.

pyx A small metal box used in the Roman Catholic Church for carrying the Blessed Sacrament to the sick; also a larger receptacle for exposing the host or consecrated bread.

Pyxis [piksis] (Lat 'compass') A S constellation, small and faint, lying between Puppis and Hydra.

Qaboos bin Said [kaboos] (1940–) Sultan of Oman (1970–), born in Muscat, Oman, the son of Said bin Taimar, and the 14th descendant of the ruling dynasty of the Albusaid family. He studied in England and trained at Sandhurst Military Academy, from where his father recalled him and kept him prisoner for six years. In 1970 he overthrew his father in a bloodless coup and assumed the sultanship. He then headed the rapid and stable modernization of his country.

Qaddafi, Muammar *Gaddafi, Muammar*

Qaeda, al- *Osama bin Laden*

QALY Abbreviation of **Quality Adjusted Life Year**; a standardized method of assessing health care on the basis of cost and benefit, which takes both life expectancy and quality of life into account.

Qatar *see panel*

Q fever An infection caused by *Coxiella burnettii*, a micro-organism that is widespread in nature, infesting cattle and sheep. It is contracted by humans in rural areas from direct contact with infected animals or inhalation of dust from contaminated premises. There is a flu-like illness, which may be complicated by pneumonia or endocarditis (infection of the lining of the heart and heart valves). It can be treated with the antibiotic tetracycline.

Qatar

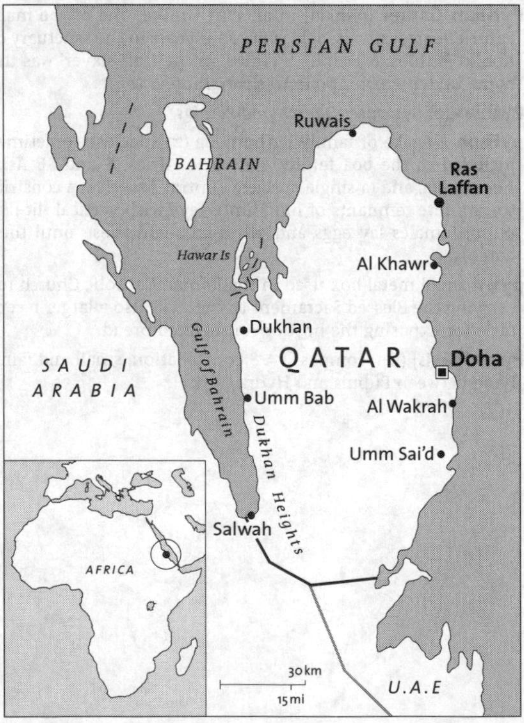

[katah(r)], official name **State of Qatar**, Arabic **Dawlat al-Qatar**

Local name Qatar

Timezone GMT +3

Area 11 437 km²/4415 sq mi

Population total (2002e) 606 000

Status Independent state

Date of independence 1971

Capital Doha

Languages Arabic (official), English

Ethnic groups Arab (40%), Pakistani (18%), Indian (18%), Iranian (10%)

Religion Sunni Muslim (95%)

Physical features Low-lying state on the E coast of the Arabian Peninsula, comprising the Qatar Peninsula and numerous small offshore islands; peninsula, 160 km/100 mi long and 55–80 km/34–50 mi wide, slopes gently from the Dukhan Heights 98 m/321 ft, to the E shore; barren terrain, mainly sand and gravel; coral reefs offshore.

Climate Desert climate; average temperatures 23°C (Jan), 35°C (Jul); high humidity; sparse rainfall; average annual rainfall 62 mm/2·4 in.

Currency 1 Qatar Riyal (QR) = 100 dirhams

Economy Based on oil; offshore gas reserves thought to be an eighth of known world reserves; oil refineries, petrochemicals, liquefied natural gas, fertilizers, steel, cement, ship repairing, engineering; fishing.

GDP (2002e) $15·91 bn, per capita $20 100

Human Development Index (2002) 0·803

History British protectorate after Turkish withdrawal, 1916; independence, 1971; palace coup brought Khalifah bin Hamad to power, 1972; long-standing territorial dispute with Bahrain over Hawar Is, awarded to Bahrain, 2001; a hereditary monarchy, with an Emir who is both Head of State and Prime Minister; Council of Ministers is assisted by a Consultative Council; country's first constitution approved in a national referendum (Apr 2003), provides for establishment of 45-member Advisory Council, of whom 30 members to be elected by Quatari citizens and 15 appointed by the Amir.

Head of State/Government (Emir)

Family name: al-Thani
1960–72 Ahmad bin Ali
1972–95 Khalifa bin Hamad
1995– Hamad bin Khalifa

Head of Government
1996– Abdulla bin Khalifa

Qianlong [chyan lung], also spelled **Ch'ien-Lung** (1711–99) Seventh emperor of the Manchurian Qing (Ch'ing) dynasty, and the fourth to rule China. He succeeded at the age of 24. Wanting to be thought the greatest ruler in China's history, he ordered (1773) a great literary catalogue by 15 000 scribes (36 000 vols), studied painting and calligraphy, wrote 42 000 poems, published notes on his studies (1736) and a prose/verse collection (1737), patronized the arts and scholarship, and built a sumptuous summer palace. After three major campaigns (1755–9) he annexed E Turkestan (re-named Xinjiang, 'New Dominion'), conquered Burma (1769) and Nepal (1790–1), and suppressed revolt in Taiwan. This expensive foreign policy, allied to governmental corruption, provoked a rebellion which he was unable to suppress, and he abdicated in 1795.

Qin dynasty or **Ch'in dynasty** [chin] (221–206 BC) A dynasty which began the first great imperial phase of Chinese history, and established many of the ingredients of traditional China. Originally one of the later Zhou warring states, the Qin, from their capital on a Yellow River tributary near modern Xian, extended imperial authority over substantial areas of C and S China beyond the Yangtze. The dynasty collapsed shortly after the death of Shihuangdi ('First Emperor'). Its achievements included the standardization of the Chinese script, weights, and measures, and the construction of roads, canals, and the Great Wall.

Qingdao, Tsingtao, or **Ch'ing-tao** [chingdow] 36°04N 120°22E, pop (2000e) 2 343 000, administrative region 6 931 000. Resort seaport city in Shandong province, E China, on the Yellow Sea; a small fishing village until after 1898, when developed by Germans into a modern city; occupied by Japan in World War 1; railway; airfield; cars, trains, consumer goods, brewing.

Qing dynasty [ching] (1644–1912) The last imperial Chinese dynasty. Originating from the Tungusic tribes to the NE, and the Jin dynasty which ruled the N in the Song period (12th–13th-c), they took the appellation Manchu in 1635, and the dynastic title Qing in 1636. Building a power base in Manchuria, Mongolia, and Korea, then invited (1644) to suppress rebellion in China, they subsequently extended supremacy over all China, especially under the Kangxi Emperor (r.1662–1722). Rule was by an unequal Manchu–Chinese partnership – for example, cities had Manchu garrisons – but gentry support was ensured through non-intervention in land ownership, producing an administration seen by Europeans as a model of stability (especially since Christianity was tolerated). The 17th–19th-c saw a rapid increase in prosperity and cultural richness. It was a major period for art, porcelain, philosophy, literature, and science. Taiwan, Outer Mongolia, Turkestan, Tibet, Burma, and Nepal were conquered. However, serious reversals took place in the 19th-c: China was defeated by Britain and France in the Opium Wars (1840–2, 1857–60), forcing ports to be opened and leading to the sack of Beijing; defeat by France in 1884 lost China control of Indo-China; defeat by Japan in 1894 lost Korea and Taiwan; and the Boxer Rising (1900) provoked a second sack of Beijing and huge indemnities. There were revolts in China proper, such as the Taiping Rebellion (1850–64), and efforts at reform were negated by Ci-Xi. The dynasty was overthrown by revolutionaries in 1911, a revolutionary government was established, and the last emperor abdicated in 1912.

Qinghai Hu [chinghiy hoo] Salt lake in NE Qinghai province, WC China; area 4583 sq km/1769 sq mi; altitude 3196 m/10 485 ft; largest salt lake in China; island in centre of lake a nature protection zone, well known for its water birds.

Qinghai–Tibet Plateau *Tibet Plateau*

Qinhuangdao or **Ch'in-huang-tao** [chinhwahngdow] 39°55N 119°37E, pop (2000e) 581 400, administrative region 2 568 000. Port in Hebei province, N China, on NW coast of Bohai Gulf; designated a special economic zone in 1985; linked by pipeline to the Daqing oil field; railway; metallurgy, fibreglass, glass, textiles, fertilizer, chemicals; trade in fruit, chestnuts, fish, grain, coal, oil; Shanhaiguan (N), the E end of the Great Wall.

Qin Shihuangdi [chin shihwangdee], also spelled **Ch'in Shih Huang-ti** (259–210 BC) First true emperor of China, who forcibly unified much of modern China following the decline of the Zhou dynasty. His achievements in unifying, centralizing, and bureaucratizing China may have been influenced by those of Darius I of Persia, and followed precepts laid out by the legalist philosopher Xunzi. Aided by his chief minister Li Si he consolidated N defences into a Great Wall, and drove the Xiongnu (Huns) from S of the Yellow R. He conquered the S, built canals and roads, divided China into 36 military prefectures, destroyed feudalism, and disarmed nobles. He also standardized Chinese script, and harmonized axle lengths, weights, measures, and laws. His principal palace, accommodating 10 000, was connected to 270 others by a covered road network. He was buried in a starry mausoleum with 6000 life-size terracotta guards. The tomb has been excavated since 1974.

Qoheleth [kohheleth] *Ecclesiastes, Book of*

Qom [koom] 34°39N 50°57E, pop (2000e) 761 000. Industrial town in Qom district, Markazi, Iran; on R Anarbar, 120 km/75 mi SW of Tehran; road and rail junction; gas pipeline; pilgrimage centre for Shiite Muslims; shrine of Fatima.

Quadragesima [kwodrajesima] In the Western Christian Church, another name for the festival of Lent, or specifically for the first Sunday in Lent, so called from its being approximately 40 days before Easter (Lat *quadragesimus*, 'fortieth') and by analogy with *Quinquaqesima*.

quadratic equations *equations*

quadrature The position of a planet or the Moon when the angular distance from the Sun, as measured from the Earth, is 90°. The Moon is at half phase when at quadrature.

quadrature of the circle One of the classical problems of geometry, to draw a square equal in area to a circle, using only straight edge and compasses. Although it has been proved impossible with these instruments, many 'solutions' have been found. One of the earliest was given by the Egyptians, who used a square side equal to $(8/9)d$, where d is the diameter of the circle. This gives a square area $(64/81)d^2$, instead of $(\pi/4)d^2$, whence $\pi \approx 3{\cdot}160$... The metaphor of squaring the circle for accomplishing the impossible was used to comic effect as early as Aristophanes.

quadrille A popular 19th-c dance, performed to music (often arranged from contemporary tunes) in a lively duple time.

quadriplegia *paralysis*

quadrivium (Lat 'the place where four roads meet') The four scientific disciplines of astronomy, geometry, arithmetic, and music, which together with the *trivium* of grammar, rhetoric, and logic constituted the university curriculum of the seven liberal arts in the Middle Ages.

quadrophonic sound A system attempting greater authenticity in reproducing concert-hall musical performances by the use of four signal channels and four loudspeakers placed in a square around the listener. Unconvincing results, additional equipment costs, and no single industry standard restricted this to being an episode of the 1970s.

Quadruple Alliance **1** (1718) A treaty signed by Britain, France, and the Habsburg emperor, to which the Dutch were expected to accede, to ensure the principle of collective security in W Europe. It provided for mutual guarantees of titles, possessions, and rights of succession, despite Spain's hostility to Italian territorial provisions, and secured peace for a generation (1718–33). **2** (1815) A treaty signed initially by Austria, Prussia, Russia, and Britain, and acceded to by France in 1818, confirming the 1815 Paris and Vienna provisions for 20 years. It was part of Castlereagh's scheme to guarantee peace through a permanent Concert of Europe.

quaestors [kweesterz] Junior, annually elected, financial officers at Rome. The quaestorship was the lowest rank in the hierarchy of offices, the *cursus honorum*, and could not be held before the age of 25. Tenure conferred automatic membership of the Senate.

quagga [kwaga] An extinct zebra native to S Africa (*Equus quagga*); stripes only on head and shoulders; brown body, white legs and tail; last individual died in Amsterdam zoo in 1883.

Quaid, Dennis [kwayd] (1954–) Film actor, born in Houston, Texas, USA. He appeared in a number of small films before *The Right Stuff* (1983) established him as a leading man. He proved his versatility in such films as *Innerspace* (1987), *The Big Easy* (1987), and *Postcards from The Edge* (1990). Later films include *Wyatt Earp* (1994), *The Parent Trap* (1998), *Any Given Sunday* (1999), and *Far From Heaven* (2002). His television work includes the highly rated *Bill* (1981) and its sequel *Bill: On His Own* (1983).

Quai d'Orsay [kay daw(r)say] The embankment on the left bank of the R Seine in Paris, and by association the French Foreign Ministry located there.

quail A small, short-tailed bird of the pheasant family Phasianidae; native to the New World (29 species) and the Old World (10 species). Indian **bush quails** are actually small partridges. The name is also used for the unrelated **bustard/button-quail** and **lark quail/quail plover** (Family: Turnicidae), the **quail dove** (Family: Columbidae), **quail finch** (Family: Estrildidae), and **quail thrush** (Family: Timaliidae).

Quakers *Friends, Society of*

quaking grass A slender grass, native to temperate regions, with pyramidal panicles of oval, flattened spikelets hanging on thread-like stalks which tremble in the slightest breeze, hence the name. (Genus: *Briza*, 20 species. Family: Gramineae.)

quality circles Groups of 10–20 workers who were given responsibility for the quality of products in Japan after World War 2, using techniques introduced from the USA. These Circles helped make Japanese products famous for quality and reliability. The approach has been adopted by many Western companies since the 1980s.

quango A shortened form of the term **quasi-non-governmental organization**, a type of organization which became common in the USA, being established by the private sector but largely or entirely financed by the federal government. In the UK the term has been applied to non-departmental bodies (the exact definition varies) that are neither part of a central government department nor part of local government, such as the Monopolies Commission. Many are merely advisory bodies, but a number do have important regulatory functions (eg the Scottish Environmental Protection Agency). In the late 1970s there was increasing concern about these bodies because of their lack of accountability, their cost, and their use as a source of patronage. The concern declined, but quangos did not, and the number grew again in the 1980s and 1990s.

Quant, Mary [kwont] (1934–) Fashion designer, inventor of the mini-skirt and hot pants, born in London, UK. She studied at Goldsmith's College of Art and designed hats for the fashionable Danish milliner, Erik. She began fashion design when she opened a small boutique in Chelsea in 1955, and married one of her partners, **Alexander Plunket Greene**. Her designs were an immediate success, and within seven years she had expanded to the USA and Europe, heading a multi-million dollar business. The geometric simplicity of her designs, especially the mini-skirt, and the originality of her colours, became an essential feature of the new young Chelsea look. In the 1970s she extended into cosmetics and textile design. She received the British Fashion Council's Hall of Fame Award in 1990.

quantity theory of money A theory in economics which states that the money supply (M) × the 'velocity of circulation' (V) (ie the number of times a year it changes hands) must equal the price level (P) × the real volume of transactions (T): in algebraic terms, $MV = PT$. Monetarists have argued that inflation is therefore mainly due to changes in the quantity of money, since the velocity of circulation depends on business practices, and the real level of activity depends on supply-side factors, neither of which changes quickly. Large increases in M must therefore lead to large rises in P, ie inflation. While this is true for large changes in M, business practices do change, and a large proportion of actual transactions are in capital markets; the real level of activity is also subject to short-run variations in the trade cycle. For small changes in M, the connection with the price level is therefore very weak, and even large changes in M produce results subject to long and variable time lags.

Quantrill, William (Clarke) [kwontril] (1837–65) Guerrilla chief and soldier, born in Canal Dover, Ohio, USA. He lived on the frontier as a gambler and thief, then settled in the area. When the Civil War broke out, he formed a group of irregulars, known as **Quantrill's Raiders**, which included Jesse James, that robbed mail coaches, fought skirmishes, and attacked Union communities – the most notorious raid being the massacre of some 150 free-soilers in Lawrence, KS (1863). As the war was ending, he set out for Washington, DC, evidently to assassinate President Lincoln, but Federal troops mortally wounded him in Kentucky.

quantum chromodynamics A widely accepted theory of strong nuclear force in which quarks are bound together by gluons; proposed in 1973; also known as **QCD**. Quarks interact because of a 'colour' quantity on each in a way analogous to the interaction between charged particles because of the charge on each particle.

quantum computer A computer which makes explicit use of the rules of quantum mechanics. Pioneered by David Deutsch in 1985, it relies on quantum entanglement to achieve a highly parallel operation in which many manipulations are effectively processed simultaneously, offering greatly improved speed over conventional computers, including parallel computers, for certain types of calculation. Elementary calculations and simple logic circuits have been demonstrated, but a complete quantum computer has not yet been built.

quantum electrodynamics A modern theory of electromagnetic interactions, developed by US physicists Richard Feynman and Julian Schwinger (1918–94), Japanese physicist Sinichiro Tomonaga (1906–79), and others during the 1940s; also called **QED**. Charged subatomic particles interact via photons, the quantum of electromagnetic radiation. The theory predicts the electron *g*-factor and atomic energy levels to high precision. It is a prototype gauge theory on which theories of nuclear forces are modelled.

quantum entanglement A fundamental property of quantum systems, first described by Erwin Schrödinger, in which two quantum systems can become correlated in a way which is impossible in classical physics. The two systems retain this correlation such that, under certain circumstances, subsequent action on one system can then have implications for the outcome of a measurement on the other. Explicitly verified by experiment, its applications include quantum computing and secure telecommunications via quantum cryptography. Entanglement also explains the destruction of the interference pattern in the double-slit experiment when either of the paths is monitored, an effect often explained using the Heisenberg uncertainty principle. Two quantum systems are said to be entangled if the wave function describing the combination of those two systems cannot be simply factored into a product of two wave functions corresponding to two separate systems.

quantum field theory The most sophisticated form of quantum theory, in which all matter and force particles are expressed as sums over simple waves. It is essential for understanding the processes in which particles are created or destroyed, as when electrons and positrons annihilate at the same time, and is applied to solid state and particle physics. Quantum electrodynamics, quantum chromodynamics, and the Glashow–Weinberg–Salam theory are all quantum field theories.

quantum gravity Gravitation acting at submicroscopic length scales where quantum effects are important. Theories of quantum gravity seek to combine features of quantum mechanics and general relativity. In quantum gravity, gravitational interaction would occur via the exchange of gravitons, the proposed quantum of gravitation. However, the view has no experimental support, and as yet no consistent theory has been developed.

quantum Hall effect Regular steps in the Hall conductivity effect at low temperatures in high magnetic fields for electrons constrained to move in a plane, such as in the junction region of silicon-metal oxide semiconductor devices; first observed in 1980 by Klaus von Klitzing and others; sometimes termed the **integer quantum Hall effect**. It results from the quantized orbiting motion of electrons in a magnetic field. The conductivity has values that are integer multiples of e^2/h, where e is the electron charge and h is Planck's constant. In 1982 Horst Störmer and Daniel Tsui discovered the **fractional Hall effect**, in which the conductivity has certain fractional multiples of e^2/h. This result was explained by Robert Laughlin as due to a new type of quasi-particle formed from electrons and microscopic magnetic whirlpools. These quasi-particles form a 'quantum fluid' with parallels in liquid helium and superconductors. Störmer, Tsui, and Laughlin were awarded the 1998 Nobel Prize for Physics.

quantum mechanics A system of mechanics applicable at distances of atomic dimensions, 10^{-10} m or less, and providing for the description of atoms, molecules, and all phenomena that depend on properties of matter at the atomic level. Among the many technologically important applications of quantum mechanics are superconductors, lasers, and electronics. In 1900, the study of blackbody radiation (electromagnetic radiation emitted by objects on account of their temperature) led Max Planck to the idea that light is composed of photons – minute packets of light each of energy $E = h\nu$, where h is Planck's constant and ν is the frequency of light. Further evidence that light exists in packets (*quanta*) came from the photoelectric effect (1905) and the Compton effect (1923). Light, thought to be wave-like, thus appeared to behave like particles.

In 1923 Louis de Broglie suggested that matter particles may in turn behave like waves. He proposed that particles such as electrons have associated with them a wavelength λ given by $\lambda = h/p$, where p is the particle momentum. The wave-like character of electrons was confirmed in 1927 by US physicists Clinton Davisson (1881–1958) and Lester Germer (1896–1971), by diffracting electrons with crystals. In 1926, Erwin Schrödinger devised an expression for the behaviour of matter waves. When applied to the hydrogen atom, Schrödinger's equation predicted spectral lines in good agreement with observation. Werner Heisenberg also devised a form of quantum mechanics equivalent to that of Schrödinger (1925), but more difficult to understand. Other essential elements of quantum mechanics are Heisenberg's uncertainty principle (1927) and Pauli's exclusion principle (1925). The development of quantum mechanics applicable to particles moving at high speed was due to Paul Dirac (1928), and is known as **relativistic quantum mechanics**. A further development of quantum theory, incorporating the creation and destruction of particles, took place during the 1940s and is called **quantum field theory**.

The wave-like nature of electrons and other particles is expressed by wavefunctions, the most fundamental way of describing either simple particles or other more complicated quantum systems. The behaviour of wavefunctions is governed by the Schrödinger equation. Particles such as electrons are no longer considered as point-like objects, but are spread out in a way governed by wavefunctions. The square of the wavefunction measures the probability of finding a particle at a given point. Quantum mechanics necessarily means dealing with a probabilistic description of nature, and thus contrasts with classical mechanics, in which the precise properties of every object are in principle calculable. The attributes of quantum systems have measurable values which are discrete. For example, the energy of an electron in an atom does not have a continuous spectrum of values, but only allows certain values; the energy is said to be *quantized*. When an electron in an excited atom jumps from one possible energy state to another of lower energy, a quantum of light is emitted. Measurements on quantum states will give one of the possible discrete values, with a probability controlled by the wavefunction.

quantum numbers Simple numbers or vectors that specify the state of a quantum system and the results of observations performed on that system. The values are usually discrete. Charge is a simple quantum number; spin is a vector quantum number. Conservation laws are expressed in terms of quantum numbers; subatomic particles and atomic states are classified by quantum numbers.

quantum statistical mechanics An extension of statistical mechanics in which quantum conditions on individual particles are taken into account, especially restrictions imposed by the uncertainty principle.

quantum teleportation A way of transferring quantum information from one place to another. It was proposed by US physicist Charles Bennett and collaborators in 1993, and first demonstrated by Anton Zeilinger and others in 1996. Teleportation involving photons can impose the state of a 'message' photon, for example its spin orientation, on to a distant 'recipient' photon. The state of the original message photon is destroyed. Quantum teleportation exploits the phenomenon of quantum entanglement; it offers reliable movement of quantum information from point to point, as in a quantum computer, avoiding problems caused by fragility of quantum states, but it does not imply the ability to move large objects from place to place.

quantum tunnelling A feature specific to quantum systems, in which particles have a certain probability of existing beyond barriers, ie they are able to penetrate barriers that classically would be expected to constrain them. The feature arises from the wave description of quantum systems. Alpha decay, the tunnelling electron microscope, and the Josephson junction all display quantum tunnelling.

Quantz, Johann Joachim (1697–1773) Flautist and composer, born near Göttingen, C Germany. He spent many years in the service of the King of Saxony, toured extensively in Italy, France, and England, and became teacher of Frederick II, and later his court composer. Author of a treatise on flute-playing, he composed some 300 concertos for one or two flutes as well as a vast quantity of other music for this instrument.

quarantine A period during which people or animals suspected of carrying a contagious disease are kept in isolation. Originally quarantine was an attempt to prevent the spread of plague in the 14th-c: ships arriving at port were kept isolated and offshore for 40 days (Ital *quarantina*) – perhaps because this was the period spent in isolation in the desert by Moses and Jesus. Later the principle was applied to many infectious diseases, and the time shortened to relate to the incubation period of the particular infection. The practice is now rarely used in human illness: possible infected suspects are merely kept under medical supervision at home or in hospital. It is still applied to dogs and other animals imported from overseas into some countries, as a defence against the spread of rabies; a 6-month period is normal. In March 2000, *pet passports* were introduced in the UK, allowing pet owners to take their dogs and cats to EU countries without the animals having to spend time in quarantine upon return. Plants also are subject to international quarantine laws.

quark A fundamental component of matter; symbol *q*. Though there is experimental support for quarks, none has been observed directly. Six quark types are known, identified by their 'flavours': *up*, *down*, *strange*, *charm*, *top*, and *bottom*. The most recently discovered quark is the top quark, seen in proton–antiproton collisions at Fermilab in 1994; it has a mass of about 177 GeV, about as much as an entire gold atom, and vastly more than any other quark species, especially the light u, d, and s quarks. Each flavour quark carries one of three possible 'colours'. Quarks have spin $\frac{1}{2}$, and charges of $\pm\frac{1}{3}$ or $\pm\frac{2}{3}$. For example, the up quark (u) has charge $+\frac{2}{3}$ and the down quark (d) charge $-\frac{1}{3}$. Protons comprise uud, neutrons udd. According to current theory, subatomic particles composed of quarks are bound together by gluons. Baryons are made of three quarks; mesons of quark/antiquark pairs.

quark–gluon plasma A state of matter comprising a gas (plasma) of free quarks and gluons. Normally quarks, which make up subatomic particles such as protons and neutrons, are bound together and prohibited from becoming free via the mechanism of confinement. Gluons, the carriers of the strong force through which quarks interact, are likewise confined. The theory of quark and gluon interactions (quantum chromodynamics) suggests that at sufficient temperatures and pressures, quarks and gluons are no longer bound within conventional particle states, but form a plasma of freely moving quarks and gluons. Evidence exists for the creation of a quark–gluon plasma from collisions between heavy nuclei observed at CERN, Geneva (1997, 2000). Quark–gluon plasma is thought to have existed in the moments following the 'big bang'.

Quark XPress® A desk-top publishing package which offers facilities for both text and graphic manipulation.

Quarles, Francis [kwaw(r)lz] (1592–1644) Religious poet, born near Romford, Essex, SE England, UK. He studied at Cambridge and London, and was successively cup-bearer to the Princess Elizabeth (1613), secretary to Archbishop Ussher (c.1629), and chronologer to the City of London (1639). A royalist and churchman, many of his books and manuscripts were destroyed during the Civil War. His best-known work is the emblem book (a series of symbolic pictures with verse commentary) called *Emblems* (1635), and a prose book of aphorisms, *Enchyridion* (1640).

quarrying Making an open excavation for the extraction of stone for direct use, as distinct from *open-cast mining*, in which minerals are extracted for subsequent conversion. The stone may be used as it is in blocks, or crushed for such uses as gravel in concrete.

quarter-day Any of the four days in the year (ie one every quarter-year) on which rents and similar charges are traditionally paid, leases begin and expire, and servants and farm-labourers were formerly engaged and dismissed; in England and Wales, the quarter-days are Lady Day (25 Mar), Midsummer Day (24 Jun), Michaelmas (29 Sep) and Christmas Day (25 Dec); Scottish quarter-days are Candlemas (2 Feb), Whitsunday (15 May), Lammas (1 Aug) and Martinmas (11 Nov). They are different in the USA (1 Jan, 1 Apr, 1 Jul, 1 Oct). There is much folklore and tradition behind these days, which were probably determined largely because they were important days in the Christian calendar approximately 3 months apart at convenient points in the agricultural year.

quarter horse The oldest American breed of horse, developed for sprinting a quarter of a mile; height, 15·2–16·5 hands/1·5–1·7 m/5 ft 2 in–5 ft 5 in; muscular body and hindquarters; slender legs; popular with cowboys; also known as **American quarter horse**, or **short horse**.

Quarton, Enguerrand [kah(r)tõ], also found as **Charonton** or **Charrenton** (15th-c) Gothic religious painter, born in Laon, N France. Documents relating to six of his important paintings survive, one of which, for a Coronation of the Virgin, is one of the most complete and interesting documents of early French art. His style united French and Italian influences, and some have attributed to him, on stylistic grounds, the most famous of 15th-c French paintings, the 'Pietà' of Villeneuve-lès-Avignon.

quartz The crystalline form of silicon dioxide (SiO_2), one of the most common minerals in the Earth's crust. The clear crystals are known as *rock crystal*, but it is commonly white and translucent. Semi-precious varieties (eg amethyst) may be coloured. It may occur as microcrystalline varieties, such as chalcedony, agate, and flint. It is very important industrially because of its piezo-electric properties.

quartzite A rock produced by the recrystallization of sandstone by metamorphism, and consisting of interlocking crystals of quartz (**metaquartzite**). It is also a sandstone with purely siliceous cement (**orthoquartzite**).

quasar [kwayzah(r)] A distant, compact object far beyond our Galaxy, which looks starlike on a photograph, but has a redshift characteristic of an extremely remote object. The word is a contraction of **quasi-stellar object**. The distinctive features of quasars are an extremely compact structure and high redshift corresponding to velocities approaching the speed of light. Implied distances run into thousand millions of parsecs, making them the most distant and luminous objects in the universe, millions of times brighter than normal galaxies. They are thought to be young galaxies with massive black holes at their centres into which gas and stars are falling.

quasi contract *restitution*

quasi-crystals Solid substances which on a small scale exhibit symmetries similar to those of crystals, but which lack the perfect overall ordering of true crystals. They were first observed in 1984 as an unexpected five-fold symmetry in Al_6Mn alloy.

Quasimodo, Salvatore [kwazeemohdoh] (1901–68) Poet, born in Syracuse, Sicily, S Italy. He studied at Palermo and Rome, became an engineer, then turned to writing, becoming professor of literature in Milan. His early work was Symbolist in character, as in *Ed è subito sera* (1942, And Suddenly It's Evening), and he became a leader of the 'hermetic' poets. After World War 2 his poetry dealt largely with social issues and a deep concern with the fate of Italy, as in *La vita non è sogno* (1949, Life is not a Dream).

quasi-particles Excitations that behave in a particle-like way, or real particles whose behaviour is modified by their environment. An example of the first type is the phonon, a crystal lattice vibration; an example of the second is the motion of electrons in solids, where the electrons can appear to have an effective mass far greater than a free electron mass. Other important quasi-particles are excitons and magnons.

quassia [kwoshia] A shrub or small tree (*Quassia amara*) native to tropical America; leaves pinnate; flowers tubular, red. It is cultivated for ornament, and for the bitter wood containing the chemical *quassiin*, used medicinally to counter dysentery. (Family: Simaroubaceae.)

Quaternary period [kwaternaree] A geological period of the Cenozoic era extending from 2 million years ago to the present day; subdivided into the Pleistocene and Holocene epochs. It is characterized by extensive glaciations in the N Hemisphere and the emergence of mankind.

quaternions In algebra, a set of four ordered real numbers subject to certain laws of composition. The laws of composition are illustrated by $(a, b, c, d) + (p, q, r, s) = (a + p, b + q, c + r, d + s)$ and $(a, b, c, d) . (p, q, r, s) = (ap - bq - cr - ds, aq + bp + cs - dr, ar + cp + dq - bs, as + br + dp - cq)$. Quaternions were developed by Irish mathematician Sir William Hamilton (1803–65), and provide an example of a non-commutative algebra, as multiplication is not commutative. The name *quaternion* was suggested because there are four ordered numbers in each. The so-called 'complex part' (b, c, d) was separated off by physicists, who preferred to work with vectors.

Quayle, Sir Anthony [kwayl] (1913–89) Actor and director, born in Ainsdale, Lancashire, NW England, UK. He trained at the Royal Academy of Dramatic Art, London, and started in vaudeville, graduating to the Old Vic Company in 1932. After World War 2 he joined the Shakespeare Memorial Theatre Company at Stratford-upon-Avon as actor and theatre director (1948–56), where he elevated the company to international standing, and provided much of the foundation work for the creation of the Royal Shakespeare Company (1960). In Europe and America he appeared in several contemporary plays now established as classics, and also had a successful screen career, with roles in many major films, such as *Lawrence of Arabia* (1962). He founded the Compass Theatre Company in 1982.

Quayle, (James) Dan(forth) [kwayl] (1947–) US politician and vice-president (1989–93), born in Indianapolis, Indiana, USA. He studied at DePauw and Indiana universities, then worked as a lawyer, journalist, and public official, becoming a Republican member of the Congress (1977–81) and US Senate (1981–8). He was elected vice-president under George Bush in 1988, and announced in 1999 that he would run for president in 2000, but later withdrew (Sep 1999). Because of some verbal slips, he became a figure of fun for many in the media.

qubit [**kyoo**bit] The basic element of information in quantum computing; an abbreviation of **quantum bit**. In conventional computing, the basic element of information is the bit, having values of either '0' or '1'. In quantum computing, information is also encoded using two states, but the quantum system is not restricted to existing merely in one or other, and can exist as a combination of both simultaneously. The qubit is in a superposition of two quantum states, a '0' state and a '1' state. Reading a qubit gives a certain probability of finding a '0' state, and a certain probability of finding a '1' state, and in the process destroys the special character of the qubit.

Quebec (city) [**kwebek**], Fr **Québec** [kaybek] 46°50N 71°15W, pop (2000e) 187 800. Capital of Quebec province, Canada, on the St Lawrence R where it meets the St Charles R; built on Cape Diamond, cliff rising 100 m/328 ft; only walled city in North America; 92% French-speaking; site of Iroquoian village Stadacona, 16th-c; visited by Cartier, 1535; French colony founded, 1608; taken by the English, 1629; returned to France, 1632; capital of New France, 1663; captured by the British under Wolfe, 1759; ceded to Britain, 1763; capital of Lower Canada (1791) and Quebec (1867); airport; railway; two universities (1852, 1968); shipbuilding, paper, clothing, food processing, footwear, electrical goods, tobacco, tourism; professional team, Quebec Nordiques (ice hockey); Château Frontenac (setting for World War 2 meetings with USA and UK), N America's oldest lift (links Upper and Lower Town), Musée du Fort, Citadel fortress (a world heritage site), Battlefield Park (including Provincial Museum and Plains of Abraham), Quebec Museum; Quebec Winter Carnival Canoe Race (Feb).

Quebec (province) [**kwebek**], Fr **Québec** [kaybek] pop (2000e) 7 722 000; area 1 540 680 sq km/594 856 sq mi. Largest province in Canada; boundaries include James and Hudson Bays (NW), Hudson Strait and Ungava Bay (NE), Gulf of St Lawrence (E), and USA (S); Canadian Shield in N four-fifths, a rolling plateau dotted with lakes; tundra in extreme N; rises to 1588 m/5210 ft at Mont d'Iberville; Notre Dame Mts in the S; several rivers flow into the St Lawrence and James and Hudson Bays; several islands in the St Lawrence; S part intensely cultivated; most population in St Lawrence valley; capital, Quebec; major cities include Montreal, Laval, Sherbrooke, Verdun, Hull, Trois Rivières; agriculture, timber, paper, hydroelectric power, aluminium, bauxite, iron ore, copper, gold, zinc, asbestos, textiles, high-technology industries, tourism; first nations include Inuit, Innu, Cree, Montagnais, Algonquin, Naskapi, and Mohawk; claimed for France by Cartier, 1534; province of New France, 1608; captured by British, 1629; restored to France, 1632; invaded by British, 1759; transferred to Britain by Treaty of Paris, 1763; constituted as Lower Canada, 1791; united to Upper Canada as Canada E, 1841; province of Quebec, 1867, with English and French as official languages; founding partner in Confederation, 1867; strong separatist movement emerged in 1960s, but 1980 referendum decided against sovereignty-association, and a further referendum was narrowly defeated in 1995; governed by a lieutenant-governor and a 125-member elected National Assembly.

Quechua [**kech**wa] A South American Indian language of the Andean–Equatorial group. The official language of the Incas, it is now spoken by 8 million from Colombia to Chile, and is widely used as a lingua franca. It has a literary history which dates from the 17th-c.

Queen, Ellery *Dannay, Frederic*

Queen Anne's lace *cow parsley*

Queen Anne Style The architecture, furniture, and silver designed during the reign of Queen Anne (1702–14), notable for carefully calculated proportions and a lack of applied ornament. Generous Baroque shapes and robust carved legs characterized chairs, cabinets, and several other objects. The style was revived in English architecture in the last third of the 19th-c, characterized by compositions of mullioned windows, handsome brickwork, and imposingly grouped chimneys.

Queen Anne's War (1702–1713) The second of the four intercolonial wars waged by Britain and France for control of colonial North America, known in Europe as the **War of the Spanish Succession**. Both sides made considerable use of Indian allies. Settled by the Treaty of Utrecht (1713), the war resulted in British control of Newfoundland, Acadia, and Hudson Bay. Britain also gained the *asiento*, an agreement to send slaves to Spanish America, and to engage in general trade.

Queen Charlotte Islands, Haida **G'waii** pop (2000e) 5900; area 9790 sq km/3779 sq mi. Archipelago of c.150 islands off the W coast of British Columbia, W Canada; extend over c.100 km/60 mi; timber, fishing.

Queen Elizabeth Islands area over 390 000 sq km/150 000 sq mi. Northernmost islands of the Canadian Arctic Archipelago, situated N of latitude 74°N; include Ellesmere, Devon, Prince Patrick, and Cornwallis Is, and the Sverdrup and Parry groups; named in 1953.

Queen Maud Land, Norwegian **Dronning Maud Land** Main part of Norwegian Antarctic Territory (between 20°W and 45°W and S of 60°S), extending to the S Pole; claimed by Norway in 1939; scientific bases at Sanae (S Africa) and Novo Lazarevskaya (Russia).

Queens pop (2000e) 2 229 400; area 283 sq km/109 sq mi. Borough of New York City, USA; co-extensive with Queens Co; at the W end of Long Island; connected to the mainland by the Hell Gate Bridge, and with Manhattan by the Queensboro Bridge; a borough since 1898; contains the two New York airports; area of greatest ethnic diversity in the USA.

Queen's Award In the UK, an award given annually on the Queen's birthday (21 Apr). Established in 1965, there are now two separate awards, one for export achievement, the other for technological achievement.

Queensberry, Sir John Sholto Douglas, 8th Marquess of (1844–1900) British aristocrat, a keen patron of boxing, who supervised the formulation in 1867 of new rules to govern that sport, since known as the **Queensberry Rules**. In 1895 he was tried and acquitted for publishing a defamatory libel on Oscar Wilde – an event which led to Wilde's trial and imprisonment.

Queen's Counsel (QC) A senior member of the English or Scottish bar, when the monarch is a queen; the equivalent term under a king is **King's Counsel** (**KC**). A practising barrister or advocate of 10 years' standing may apply to become a Queen's Counsel (or 'take silk' – a reference to the gowns which they wear). New appointments (made on the recommendation of the Lord Chancellor) are announced annually on Maundy Thursday.

Queensland pop (2000e) 3 290 000; area 1 727 200 sq km/666 900 sq mi. Second largest state in Australia; established as a penal colony, 1824; open to free settlers, 1842; part of New South Wales until 1859; contains 11 statistical divisions; bordered N by the Gulf of Carpentaria, the Torres Strait, and the Coral Sea, and E by the South Pacific Ocean; Cape York Peninsula in the N; the Great Dividing Range runs N–S, separating a fertile coastal strip to the E from dry plains to the W; tropical climate in the N; Scenic Rim Mountains on the border with New South Wales; most population in the SE; capital, Brisbane; principal cities Gold Coast, Townsville, Cairns, Ipswich, Toowoomba, Rockhampton; provides 22% of Australia's agricultural production, with sugar the main export crop; wheat, sorghum, tomatoes, citrus and tropical fruit; bauxite, coal, copper, zinc, lead, phosphate, nickel, oil, gas; machinery, chemicals, textiles, food processing, furniture, plastics, rubber products, forest products, paper, motor vehicles; total coastline 5200 km/3200 mi; Great Barrier Reef runs parallel to the Pacific coast; Noosa to Bribie I is known as the 'sunshine coast', while E of Brisbane to the New South Wales border is the 'gold coast', major resort areas with fine surfing beaches.

Queensland arrowroot *arrowroot; canna*

Queen Victoria water lily A giant water lily (*Victoria amazonica*), native to the Amazon, growing in water 1–2 m/3–6 ft deep; prickly, floating leaves up to 2 m/6½ ft diameter, with upturned rim several cm deep, resembling a shallow dish; flowers up to 30 cm/12 in diameter, white, fading to purple. It was named in honour of Queen Victoria. (Family: Nymphaeaceae.)

quelea [kweelia] An African weaverbird, inhabiting grassland, woodland, and marsh; eats seeds. The **red-billed quelea** (*Quelea quelea*) is a serious agricultural pest, plaguing grain crops. (Genus: *Quelea*, 3 species.)

Queluz [kiluzh] 38°45N 9°15W, pop (2000e) 60 700. Market town in Lisbon district, C Portugal, 15 km/9 mi NW of Lisbon; Queluz Palace, former summer residence of the Braganza kings; Queluz fair (Sep).

Queneau, Raymond [kenoh] (1903–76) Novelist and poet, born in Le Havre, NW France. He studied at the Sorbonne. The best of his poetry is contained in *Les Ziaux* (1943) and *Si tu t'imagines* (1952, If You Suppose). His novels include *Le Chiendent* (1933, The Bark Tree) and *Zazie dans le métro* (1959, Zazie in the Metro, filmed 1960), and are often self-reflective, anticipating some of the devices of the *nouveau roman*.

Quennell, Sir Peter (Courtney) [kwenel] (1905–93) Biographer, born in Bickley, SE Greater London, UK. He studied at Oxford, became professor of English at Tokyo for a year, then returned to London as a writer. Author of several books of verse and a novel, and editor of the *Cornhill Magazine* (1944–51), he is best known for his many biographical studies, including those of Byron (1935, 1941), Ruskin (1949), Shakespeare (1963), and Pope (1968). He also edited many volumes of literary studies. He was knighted in 1992.

Quercia, Jacopo della *Jacopo della Quercia*

Querétaro [keraytaroh] 20°38N 100°23W, pop (2000e) 547 000. Capital of Querétaro state, C Mexico, 200 km/124 mi NW of Mexico City; altitude, 1865 m/6119 ft; important in the 1810 independence rising; scene of the surrender and execution of Emperor Maximilian, 1867; railway; university (1618); textiles, opals, mercury, pottery; Church of Santa Cruz, Convent of San Francisco, federal palace; agricultural fair (Dec).

query language A computer language provided by many database management systems to enable users to frame a general enquiry about the data held on the database. The most common query language is SQL.

Quesada, Elwood (Richard) [kesahda] (1904–93) Aviator, born in Washington, District of Columbia, USA. During World War 2, he commanded the 9th Fighter Command in England (1943) and, as head of the 9th Tactical Air Command, directed thousands of sorties in preparation for the Allied landings in Normandy in 1944. He retired from the service in 1951, and in 1959 became the first head of the newly formed Federal Aviation Administration.

Quesada, Gonzalo Jiménez de [kaysahtha] (c.1497–1579) Conquistador, born in Córdoba or Granada, S Spain. Appointed magistrate at Santa Marta, in 1536 he headed an expedition, and after many hardships and loss of men conquered the Chibchas in the E. This he called New Granada, and its chief town Santa Fé de Bogotá. In 1569, during a later expedition in search of El Dorado, he reached the R Guaviare not far from the point where it meets the Orinoco.

Quesnay, François [kenay] (1694–1774) Physician and economist, born in Mérey, NC France. He studied medicine at Paris, and by his death had risen to be first physician to the king. His fame depends chiefly on his essays in political economy. He became a leader of the *Economistes*, also called the Physiocratic School, and contributed to Diderot's *Encyclopédie*.

Quesnel, Pasquier [kenel] (1634–1719) Jansenist theologian, born in Paris, France. He studied at the Sorbonne, and in 1662 became director of the Paris Oratory, where he wrote *Nouveau Testament en français avec des réflexions morales* (1687–94, New Testament in French with Thoughts on Morality). Having refused to condemn Jansenism in 1684, he fled to Brussels. Hostility to his work led to his imprisonment (1703), but he escaped to Amsterdam.

Quetta [kweta] 30°15N 67°01E, pop (2000e) 465 000. Capital of Baluchistan province, W Pakistan; in the C Brahui Range, 590 km/367 mi N of Karachi; altitude 1650 m/5500 ft; strategic location on the trade route between Afghanistan and the Lower Indus valley; controls the Bolan Pass and the Khojak Pass; acquired by the British, 1876; badly damaged by earthquake, 1935; airfield; railway; centre of a fruit-growing area; linked to Shikarpur by natural gas pipeline in 1982.

quetzal A Central American bird (*Pharomachrus mocinno*), inhabiting mountain forests; eats fruit, insects, frogs, lizards, and snails; male with red underparts, green head and back, and very long trailing tail; also known as the **resplendent quetzal** or **resplendent trogon**. Revered by the Mayans and Aztecs, it was associated with the god Quetzalcoatl, and is the national bird of Guatemala. Its numbers are now seriously diminishing. The name is also used for four South American species of *Pharomachrus*.

Quetzalcoatl [ketzlkohatl] The feathered serpent god of the pre-Columbian Aztec and Mayan cultures of Central America. A powerful figure, in some contexts he is represented as a culture hero, in others as a deity and creator, and in others as the Aztec high priest. He is associated with the invention of the calendar and the re-creation of human life. He provoked the anger of another god, and fled in a boat made of serpent skin promising to return – a promise used to advantage by the invader Cortés.

Quevedo y Villegas, Francisco Gómez de [kevaythoh ee veelyaygas] (1580–1645) Spanish writer, born in Madrid, Spain. He studied at Alcalá and Valladolid universities, and was a distinguished poet, but chose a political career, becoming counsellor to the Duke of Osuna (1613–20). One of the most prolific Spanish poets, his greatest work remains the brilliant picaresque novel, *La vida del buscón* (1626, The Life of a Scoundrel).

Quezaltenango [kesaltenanggoh], or **Xela** [shayla] 14°50N 91°30W, pop (2000e) 118 000. Capital town of Quezaltenango department, SW Guatemala; surrounded by volcanic peaks; Guatemala's second industrial and trading centre; largely rebuilt since earthquakes of 1818 and 1902; branch of San Carlos University.

Quezon, Manuel (Luis) [kayson] (1878–1944) First Philippine president (1935–44), born in Baler, Philippines. He studied at Manila, and went to Washington as one of the resident Philippine commissioners (1909). President of the Philippine Senate (1916–35), he was elected the first president of the Philippine Commonwealth, establishing a highly centralized government. He displayed great courage during the Japanese onslaught on General MacArthur's defences in 1941, refusing to evacuate to the USA until appealed to by President Roosevelt. Quezon City, the former capital (1948–76) of the Philippines on the island of Luzon, is named after him.

Quezon City [kayson] 14°39N 121°01E, pop (2000e) 2 044 000. Residential city in Capital province, Philippines; on Luzon I, NE of Manila; laid out in 1940; former capital, 1948–76; university (1908); textiles, tourism; night procession of La Naval de Manila (Oct).

quicklime *calcium*

quicksilver *mercury* (chemistry)

quickthorn *hawthorn*

Quiet Revolution A term used to describe the process of accelerated social and economic modernization in Quebec during the 1960s. Under the liberal regime of Jean Lesage, The *Révolution Tranquille* was characterized by expanded opportunities for French Canadians in higher education, government, and major development projects. The period saw a decline in the influence of the Catholic Church and a rise in Québecois nationalism.

quill A pen made from the tapered stem of a bird's feather, especially the outer wing feathers of geese. Quills were the chief writing implement from the 6th-c AD until the advent of steel pens in the mid-19th-c.

Quiller-Couch, Sir Arthur (Thomas) [kwiler kooch], pseudonym **Q** (1863–1944) Man of letters, born in Bodmin, Cornwall, SW England, UK. He studied at Oxford, where he became a lecturer in classics (1886–7), then moved to Cambridge (1912) as professor of English literature. He edited *The Oxford Book of English Verse* (1900), and published several volumes of essays and criticism. He also wrote poems, short stories, and several humorous novels. He was knighted in 1910.

quillwort A spore-bearing vascular plant related to clubmosses, mostly aquatic pteridophytes distributed throughout the world; tufted leaves grass-like but cylindrical, enclosing sporangia in their swollen bases. (Genus: *Isoetes*, 75 species. Family: Isoetaceae.)

Quilter, Roger (1877–1953) Composer, born in Brighton, East Sussex, SE England, UK. He studied in Germany and lived entirely by composing, holding no official posts and making few public appearances. His works include an opera (*Julia*), a radio opera (*The Blue Boar*), and the *Children's Overture*, based on nursery tunes, but he is best known for his songs.

Quimper [kīpair] or **Quimper Corentin** 48°00N 4°09W, pop (2000e) 65 400. Manufacturing and commercial capital of Finistère department, NW France; on estuary of R Odet, 179 km/111 mi W of Rennes; capital of old countship of Carnouailles; railway; pottery (Quimper or Brittany ware) since 16th-c; textiles, tourism; 13th-c Gothic Cathedral of St-Corentin; former bishop's palace (early 16th-c), now a museum; folk festival (Jul).

quince A deciduous shrub or small tree (*Cydonia oblonqa*) reaching 1·5–7·5 m/5–25 ft, native to Asia; leaves oval; flowers pale pink, bowl-shaped, resembling apple blossom; fruit apple- or pear-shaped, 5–12 cm/2–4¾ in diameter in cultivated plants, fragrant but hard when ripe, mainly used in preserves. It is cultivated and naturalized in much of Europe. (Family: Rosaceae.)

Quincy, Josiah (1772–1864) US statesman, born in Braintree (now Quincy), Massachusetts, USA. He studied at Harvard, was called to the bar in 1793, and became a leading member of the Federalist Party. Elected in 1804 to Congress, he denounced slavery, and distinguished himself as an orator. He declined re-election to Congress (1812), but became a member of the Massachusetts legislature, served as Mayor of Boston (1823–8), and was President of Harvard (1829–45).

Quine, Willard Van Orman [kwiyn] (1908–2000) Philosopher and logician, born in Akron, Ohio, USA. He studied at Prague, Oxford, and Harvard, and became professor of philosophy at Harvard (1948–78, now emeritus). Much influenced by Carnap, the Vienna Circle, and the empiricist tradition, he went on to make his own distinctive and original contributions to philosophy. His philosophy of language challenges the standard distinctions between analysis and synthetic truths and between science and metaphysics. His books include *Mathematical Logic* (1940), *Word and Object* (1960), *The Roots of Reference* (1974), *The Logic of Sequences* (1990), and *From Stimulus to Science* (1995).

Quinet, Edgar [keenay] (1803–75) Poet, historian, and politician, born in Bourg-en-Bresse, E France. He studied at Strasbourg, Geneva, Paris, and Heidelberg. His first major work was a translation of Herder's *Philosophy of History* (1825), and his reputation was established with the epic poem *Ahasvérus* (1833). Appointed professor of foreign literature at Lyon (1839), his lectures caused so much excitement that the government suppressed them in 1846, and after the coup of February 1848 he was exiled. His historical works include *La Révolution religieuse au XIXe siècle* (1857, The Religious Revolution in the 19th-c), *Histoire de la campagne de 1815* (1862, History of the 1815 Campaign), and *La Révolution* (1865).

quinine A drug used in the prevention of malaria, and sometimes in its treatment. It is present in the bark of various *Cinchona* trees native to the Andes, but it is also cultivated in Sri Lanka, India, and Java. Pure quinine was first isolated from the bark in 1820, and this form of the drug was the only real antimalarial drug in use until the 1920s. Since the development of resistance to new synthetic antimalarial drugs, it has regained a certain popularity.

Quinn, Anthony (1915–2001) Film actor, born in Chihuahua, Mexico. Of Irish-Mexican parentage, he grew up in the USA, and after a few stage roles made his film debut in *Parole!* (1936). For many years he was confined to small parts as an ethnic or exotic, usually as a menacing foreigner or Indian. He won Oscars for *Viva Zapata* (1952) and *Lust for Life* (1956) and he gained critical acclaim in Fellini's *La Strada* (1954), but his looks and manner kept him playing exotics, the most notable being *Zorba the Greek* (1964). He later appeared in a musical version of this, and starred in the television series, *The Man and the City* (1971–2). He was also a serious painter for many years.

Quinnipiac *New Haven*

quinoline [kwinolin] C_9H_7N, boiling point 238°C. An organic base, related to pyridine. Both it and the isomeric **isoquinoline** are oily liquids, constituents of coal-tar. Quinine and other alkaloids are derivatives of quinoline.

quinone $C_6H_4O_2$. One of two isomers derived from benzene (*benzoquinones*) or derivatives of these. They are highly coloured, and a quinone group is often a chromophore of a dyestuff.

Quinquagesima [kwinkwajesima] In the Western Christian Church, the Sunday before Lent, so called from its being 50 days before Easter, counting inclusively (Lat *quinquagesimus*, 'fiftieth').

quinsy [kwinzee] The formation of an abscess in and around the tonsils. It is a complication of severe tonsillitis caused by a bacterial infection, usually a haemolytic streptococcus. Treatment is with appropriate antibiotics and drainage of the pus. Later surgery to remove the tonsils (*tonsillectomy*) may be considered.

Quintana, Manuel José [keentahna] (1772–1857) Poet and advocate, born in Madrid, Spain, where his house became a resort of advanced liberals. Besides his classic *Vidas de los Españoles célebres* (1807–34, Lives of Famous Spaniards), he published tragedies and poetry written in a classical style, the best of which are his odes, ardently patriotic yet restrained. On the restoration of Ferdinand VII he was imprisoned (1814–20), but recanted, and by 1833 had become tutor to the future Queen Isabella II (r.1833–68). He was crowned national poet by Isabella in 1855. Longfellow translated some of his poetry into English.

Quintero, Serafin Alvarez *Alvarez Quintero, Serafin*

Quintilian [kwintilian], in full **Marcus Fabius Quintilianus** (c.35–c.100) Roman rhetorician, born in Calagurris, Spain. He studied oratory at Rome, returned there in 68, and became eminent as a pleader and state teacher of the oratorical art. His reputation rests securely on his great work, *Institutio Oratoria* (Education of an Orator), a complete system of rhetoric in 12 books.

quipu [keepoo] An accounting system of knotted cords developed by the Peruvian Incas and others. The system was a complex one, with strings and knots of various lengths, shapes, and colours, and was used for keeping detailed records, such as census information, and for sending messages.

Quirigua [keereegwa] The ruins of a Maya city, dating from 600–900, in a 30 ha/75 acre forest preserve in E Guatemala; a world heritage site. The ruins are notable for their massive sandstone stelae (one is 11 m/35 ft tall), altars, and animal carvings.

Quirinal One of the seven hills of Rome, NE of Capitoline Hill, the site of several ancient shrines. A papal palace was built in Quirinal Square (begun c.1585) in accordance with Pope Gregory XIII's will. Later known as the Quirinal palace, it became the residence of the kings of Italy during 1870–1946, and from 1947 it has been the home of the presidents of Italy.

Quirk, (Charles) Randolph, Baron (1920–) Grammarian and writer on the English language, born in the Isle of Man, UK. He was educated at University College London, where he lectured in English (1947–54), then taught at Durham (1954–60). He returned to a chair at University College (1960–81), where he also directed the Survey of English Usage. Major grammars in which he was involved are *A Grammar of Contemporary English* (1972) and *A Comprehensive Grammar of the English Language* (1985). He was also Vice-Chancellor of London University (1981–5). He was made a life peer in 1994.

Quisling, Vidkun (Abraham Lauritz Jonsson) [kwizling] (1887–1945) Diplomat and fascist leader, born in Fyresdal, S Norway. He was an army major, a League of Nations official, had the care of British interests in Russia (1927–9), and was defence minister in Norway (1931–3). In 1933 he founded the *Nasjonal Samling* (National Party) in imitation of the German National Socialist Party, and became puppet prime minister in occupied Norway. He gave himself up in May 1945, was tried and executed. His name has since been used for anyone who aids an enemy.

Quit India Movement A campaign launched (Aug 1942) by the Indian National Congress calling for immediate independence from Britain, and threatening mass non-violent struggle if its demands were not met. Gandhi and other Congress leaders were arrested, and the movement quickly suppressed. As a result there were two years of relative quiet in Indian politics.

Quito [keetoh] 0°14S 78°30W, pop (2000e) 1 358 000. Capital of Ecuador in the Andean Sierra of NC Ecuador; second largest city; at E foot of Pichincha volcano; altitude 2850 m/9350 ft, giving it a temperate climate; former Inca capital (old city designated a world heritage site); captured by Spanish, 1534; airport; railway; three universities (1769, 1869, 1946); commerce, mining (clay, sand), food processing, textiles, pharmaceuticals, iron and steel, motor vehicles; cathedral, archbishop's palace, government palace, Parque Alameda (with oldest astronomical observatory in South America), Casa de la Cultura Ecuatoriana, church and monastery of San Francisco (1535), La Compañía Jesuit church, church and monastery of La Merced (with twin clock to London's Big Ben, 1817); Cerro Panecillo, 183 m above city with statue on top to Virgen de las Americas; Carnival (pre-Lent).

Qumran, community of [kumran] (c. 2nd-c BC–1st-c AD) An exclusive Jewish sect, located near the NW corner of the Dead Sea, apparently closely related to the Essene sect mentioned by Josephus. They opposed the Hasmonean highpriesthood of the 2nd-c BC, and considered themselves alone to be the true Israel awaiting God's new kingdom, being kept pure by their strict practices of legal observance and community discipline. They were destroyed during the Jewish revolt of AD 66–70, but many of their writings were discovered in 1947 as part of the Dead Sea Scrolls.

quoits An outdoor game demanding great accuracy, which involves the throwing of a metal ring at a peg. It has been a popular sport in England since the middle of the 14th-c. From quoits has developed horseshoe pitching.

quota (IMF) The share of a member country in the International Monetary Fund (IMF). Its quota determines the amount of its own and other currencies a member has to subscribe on joining. The voting power of a member on decisions by the IMF, and the amount it can borrow if necessary, are both proportional to its quota. A large quota for a rich country such as the USA implies a large subscription and a large say in decisions. A larger quota for a poor country means larger access to various forms of loan if it encounters balance of payments problems. IMF quotas are revised periodically, by negotiation between members.

quota (OPEC) The maximum quantity of oil that a member of the Organization of Petroleum Exporting Countries (OPEC) is supposed to sell in a given period. OPEC sets quotas by periodical negotiation in order to maintain world crude oil prices. As any individual member of a cartel can gain by selling more than its quota while others stick to theirs, there is some suspicion that OPEC quotas are not fully effective.

quotas, import A means of restricting imports of a commodity or product by limiting the quantity that can be imported in a particular period. The aim is to protect domestic industry and preserve foreign currency reserves. They were extensively imposed in the UK in the late 1940s and 1950s, but have now been eliminated for most goods.

Qur'an or **Koran** [korahn] The sacred book of Islam. It is held to be the direct word of God, inscribed in heaven, and revealed piecemeal to the Prophet Mohammed over a period of 20 years (begining in 625) by the angel Gabriel as a message for all humanity. The text itself is regarded as sacred; a Muslim should be ritually pure before touching it, and it is a sacrilege to imitate its literary style. It is a book of poetry rather than prose, and is chanted for liturgical and devotional purposes. It is generally written as in the voice of God, and is primarily instructive; its pronouncements are generally regarded as infallible; and it is the highest authority on all religious and legal matters. It is roughly the same extent as the New Testament, divided into 114 chapters (*surahs*) of unequal length. The early surahs deal with God as creator, his oneness, greatness, and authority, the role of Mohammed as his messenger, and of Islam in history. Later surahs deal with legal, social, and ethical issues.

Qutb Minar or **Kutab Minar** [kutb minah(r)] A famous city landmark in Delhi, India. Built in 1199 as a Muslim tower of victory, the Qutb Minar is 72·5 m/263 ft high.

Qu Yuan or **Chü Yüan** [choo yooan] (3rd-c BC) The earliest named Chinese poet, of royal ancestry. His work is characterized by rich lyricism and philosophical depth. His major work, the 374-line *Li Sao* ('Encountering Sadness') may be an allegory on his own life: a minister to royalty, he had been banished. His suicide by drowning is commemorated in the Chinese Dragon Boat Festival.

QwaQwa [kwakwa] Former national state or non-independent black homeland in South Africa; self-governing status, 1974; incorporated into KwaZulu Natal following the new South African constitution of 1994.

r

Rab [rap], ancient **Arba** 44°46N 14°44E, pop (2000e) 9300. Island in the Adriatic Sea off the coast of W Croatia; a leading resort island since the 1950s; noted for fruit and wine.

Rabat (Malta) [rabat] 35°53N 14°25E, pop (2000e) 14 000. Town in SWC Malta, 10 km/6 mi SW of Valletta; St Paul lived in a cave here during his 3-month stay on the island after shipwreck, AD 60; Roman villa and museum of Roman antiquities, St Paul's Grotto, Verdala Castle, St Agatha and St Paul's Catacombs.

Rabat (Morocco) [rabat] 34°02N 6°51W, pop (2000e) 756 000. Capital of Morocco, 90 km/56 mi NE of Casablanca at the mouth of the Bou Regreg; one of Morocco's four imperial cities; originally a fortified monastery; city founded, 12th-c; French colonialists established a Residency-General, 1912; airport; railway; university (1957); textiles, carpets, cement bricks, flour milling; mausoleum of Mohammed V, Hassan Tower, 14th-c Chella fortress, arts museum, archaeological museum.

rabban *rabbi*

rabbi (Heb 'my lord', or 'my master/teacher') In Judaism after AD 70, a title for accredited Jewish teachers or sages, who often exercised judicial functions too; prior to 70, used less technically as a form of respectful address, as presumably in the New Testament Gospels. The teachings of these early sages are preserved in the Mishnah, the Talmud, and many other forms of rabbinic literature. **Rabban** is a superior form of the title, used in the Mishnah for four early scholars: Gamaliel the Elder, Johanan ben Zakkai, Gamaliel II, and Simeon ben Gamaliel II. Today rabbis also have pastoral functions and a role in worship, much like ministers or clergy of other faiths.

rabbit A mammal of the order Lagomorpha, family Leporidae (23 species); differs from the closely related **hare** in several respects (different skull features, smaller, gives birth to naked young, lives in groups, burrows to produce complex warrens, lacks black ear tips); also called **con(e)y** – a name often used for rabbit skin. The **domestic rabbit**, also known as the **European rabbit** or **Old World rabbit** (*Oryctolagus cuniculus*), is common as a pet, with many breeds. The **white laboratory rabbit** used in medical research is a form of the domestic rabbit. The name *hare* is used in describing some species.

rabbitfish *chimaera* (zoology)

Rabelais, François [rabelay], pseudonym (an anagram of his name) **Alcofribas Nasier** (?1494–1553) Satirist, physician, and humanist, born in or near Chinon, WC France. After a period with a Franciscan order, he studied medicine at Montpellier, and became a physician at Lyon. Here he began the sequence of books for which he is remembered, beginning with the comic and satirical *Pantagruel* (1533) and *Gargantua* (1535), published under his pseudonym, and both highly successful, though condemned by the Church for their unorthodox ideas and mockery of religious practices. In 1546 he published his *Tiers Livre* (1546, Third Book) under his own name. It was again condemned, and he fled to Metz, where for a while he practised medicine. He later published a *Quart Livre* (1552, Fourth Book), and there is a *Cinquiesme Livre* (1564, Fifth Book), published after his death, whose authorship is uncertain. His influence on literature, notably in Britain, has been widespread.

rabies [raybeez] A virus infection that affects a wide range of animals, such as dogs, cats, foxes, skunks, and vampire bats; also known as **hydrophobia**. It is transmitted to humans by bites, or by licks on skin abrasions or intact mucous membranes. The central nervous system is affected, leading to restlessness, convulsions, paralysis and loss of sensation, delusions, and hallucinations. The alternative name stems from the violent contractions of the larynx and inspiratory muscles induced by drinking. Death from the established condition is almost invariable, but immediate immunization is usually successful.

Rabin, Itzhak [rabeen] (1922–95) Israeli soldier, statesman, and prime minister (1974–7, 1992–5), born in Jerusalem, Israel. After studies at agricultural school he embarked on an army career, completing his training in Britain. He fought in the War of Independence (1948–9), and represented the Israeli Defence Forces at the armistice in Rhodes. He rose to become chief-of-staff in 1964, heading the armed forces during the Six-Day War (1967). After serving as ambassador to the USA (1968–73) he became Labour Party leader and prime minister, resigning in 1977 when involved in a scandal over accounts he kept in the USA. He later served as defence minister (1984–90), was re-elected as Labour Party leader in 1992, and became prime minister again later that year. He shared the Nobel Peace Prize in 1994. He was assassinated by Yigal Amir, a 27-year old right-wing Israeli law student.

raccoon A mammal of genus *Procyon* (7 species), native to North and Central America; grey with dark bands around tail; face pale with black band across eyes; inhabits woodland and scrubland near water; eats fruit, nuts, and small animals. (Family: Procyonidae.)

raccoon dog An E Asian member of the dog family (*Nyctereutes procyonoides*) (introduced in Russia); fox-like, with short legs and heavy body; thick yellow-brown coat; face resembles raccoon; inhabits woodland near water; eats small animals (mainly frogs) and fruit; also known in the fur trade as the **Japanese fox** or **Ussuri(an) raccoon**.

RACE [rays] Acronym for **Research in Advanced Communications in Europe**, a European special programme of research in telecommunications particularly related to data communications.

race A biologically distinctive major division of a species, in which the differences between recognized races exceed the variation within them. While useful in describing variation in many plants and animals, where race is often equated with subspecies, the concept has little or no value for describing human biological diversity. This is because the pattern of human variation is predominantly one of within-group variation, so that it is impossible to delineate clear boundaries between groups. Although the concept of human races is long-established and persistent, it is not consistent with actual classificatory categories. Biological differences between groups result from the isolation of breeding populations, but evidence indicates contact between human groups since at least the Middle Pleistocene (0·6 million years ago). In the past 500 years, with the expansion of trade, colonization, etc, long-range contacts have greatly increased; gene pools are in constant flux, and the biological contrasts between populations are slight, relative to their internal variability. Traditional 'racial' classifications typically emphasize external features such as skin colour or hair type, but other genetically-determined traits such as blood groups or enzyme variants tend to cross-cut the classical categories based on superficial features.

Racial schemes typically assume (*i*) that races are real, whereas race is a concept that may or may not be useful in summarizing patterns of variations, and (*ii*) that the characters used to identify races are selectively neutral, so that degrees of similarity and difference reflect evolutionary relatedness. In fact, genetic traits and environments interact, and similar environments may select for the independent evolution of similar features in otherwise unrelated groups (eg there are clear correlations between aspects of body proportions, skin colour, facial features and hair form, and climatic variation). Earlier workers assumed that biological races could be clearly demarcated, and that racial groups varied not only in external features, but also in intelligence and personality. Despite many attempts to establish correlations, there is no evidence for biologically-determined differences between populations in such ability or character traits, nor of any consistent relationship with cultural systems or institutions.

racehorse *thoroughbred*

raceme *inflorescence*

racer *black snake*

Rachel Biblical character, the daughter of Laban and wife of Jacob, and the mother of Joseph and Benjamin. According to *Genesis* 29, Jacob worked 14 years to earn Rachel as his wife, after having once been tricked into taking her elder sister Leah. At first, Rachel was said to be barren, but she died when giving birth to her second son, Benjamin.

Rachmaninov, Sergey Vasilyevich [rakh**man**inof], also spelled **Rachmaninoff** and **Rakhmaninov** (1873–1943) Composer and pianist, born in Nizhni Novgorod, W Russia. He studied at St Petersburg and at Moscow, where he won the gold medal for composition. Having fled from the Russian Revolution, he settled in the USA (1918). He wrote operas, orchestral works, and songs, but is best known for his piano music, which includes four concertos, the popular *Prelude in C Sharp Minor*, and his last major work, the *Rhapsody on a Theme of Paganini* (1934) for piano and orchestra.

racial discrimination Treating someone in a particular way because of their race or ethnicity; also known as **racialism** or **racism**. The term is usually understood to mean negative discrimination, that is, treating people in a way which will disadvantage them relative to other social groups. Negative racial discrimination often occurs in housing and employment and is illegal in most modern societies, though often difficult to prove in a court of law.

Racine, Jean (Baptiste) [ra**seen**] (1639–99) Dramatic poet, born in La Ferté-Milon, N France. He studied at Beauvais and Port Royal, then went to Paris, where his verses quickly made him known. He began to write plays in 1664, his major verse tragedies including *Andromaque* (1667), *Britannicus* (1669), *Bajazet* (1672), *Phèdre* (1677), and *Bérénice* (1679). Widely regarded as the master of tragic pathos, he then left the theatre, married, and lived in domestic retirement. He later wrote two religious plays on Old Testament subjects, *Esther* (1689) and *Athalie* (1691), intended for performance by the girls at the school of Saint-Cyr.

racism An ideology that claims to explain an alleged inferiority of certain racial or ethnic groups in terms of their biological or physical characteristics. Racist beliefs have been used to justify genocide, chronic poverty, and the maintenance of systems of inequality (such as South African apartheid and the so-called 'ethnic cleansing' of Bosnia). **Institutional racism** consists of the collective failure of an organization to provide an appropriate and professional service to people because of their colour, culture, or ethnic origins.

rackets (UK) / **racquets** (US) A racket-and-ball game played on a walled court by two or four players; also called **racquetball** (US). It is thought to have originated in the Middle Ages, and to have developed at the Fleet debtor's prison, London, in the 18th-c. It is regarded as the forerunner of many racket/bat and ball games.

Rackham, Arthur [**rak**am] (1867–1939) Artist, born in London, UK. A water-colourist and book illustrator, he was well known for his typically Romantic and grotesque pictures in books of fairy tales, such as *Peter Pan* (1906), and his own work, *The Arthur Rackham Fairy Book* (1933).

racoon *raccoon*

racquetball *rackets / racquets*

rad In radioactivity, an old unit for absorbed dose; symbol rad; 1 rad is equivalent to 0·01 J/kg, or 0·01 Gy (gray, SI unit); an abbreviation of **radiation**; classed as a unit in temporary use with SI units.

radar Acronym for **radio detection and ranging**, a system developed in the 1930s whereby the position and distance of objects can be determined by measuring the time taken for radio waves to be reflected and returned. **Continuous wave radar** detects returned signals by their different frequencies. **Pulsed radar** transmits short pulses at regular intervals from a directional antenna. Some types of radars, called 'track-while-scan' are able to compute a target's position and speed without interrupting the continuous scanning. A receiver converts the echo pulses to a video signal displayed on a cathode ray tube. The most usual display is the plan position indicator, used by air traffic control. **Secondary radar**, with a separate antenna and receiver, is also used in air traffic control. An aircraft detects this secondary radar and automatically responds with an identifying coded signal. Radar is also used in navigation, fire control, the detection and location of underground objects, storm detection, and for speed control by police.

radar astronomy The use of pulses of radio waves to detect the distances and map the surfaces of objects in the Solar System. It has been applied with great success to Venus and several asteroids, and in measuring the diameters of the nuclei of comets.

Radcliffe, Ann, *née* **Ward** (1764–1823) Novelist, born in London, UK. She lived a retired life, and became well known for her Gothic novels, notably *The Romance of the Forest* (1791), *The Mysteries of Udolpho* (1794), and *The Italian* (1797). Her contemporary reputation was considerable, and she influenced Byron, Shelley, and others, many of whom imitated her 'gothick romances'.

Radcliffe, Paula (1973–) Athlete, born in Northwich, Cheshire, NWC England, UK. She won the world junior cross-country title in 1992 and steadily developed as a distance runner, twice winning the world cross-country long-course gold medal (2001, 2002). Other achievements include the 5000 m gold at the 2002 Commonwealth Games, the 10 000 m gold at the 2002 European Championships, twice women's winner of the London Marathon (2002, 2003), and winner of the Chicago Marathon (2002), where she set a new women's world record time of 2 hr 17 min 18 sec. She was named female athlete of the year by the International Association of Athletics Federations in 2002.

Radek, Karl Bernhardovich [**rah**dek], originally **Karl Sobelsohn** (1885–?1939) Russian revolutionary and politician, born in Lvov (Lwow), W Ukraine (formerly Austria). He studied at Kraków and Bern, and became a journalist. He organized the German Communists during their revolution (1918), and was imprisoned (1919). Returning to the Soviet Union, he became a leading member of the Communist International, but lost standing with his growing distrust of extremist tactics. He was charged as a Trotsky supporter, and expelled from the Party (1927–30). In 1937 he was a victim of one of Stalin's show trials.

Radhakrishnan, Sir Sarvepalli [rahda**krish**nan] (1888–1975) Indian philosopher, statesman, and president (1962–7), born in Tiruttani, Chennai (Madras), SE India. He studied at Madras, taught at Mysore and Calcutta universities, and became professor of Eastern religions and ethics at Oxford (1936–52). In 1946 he was chief Indian delegate to UNESCO, becoming its chairman in 1949. A member of the Indian Assembly in 1947, he was Indian ambassador to the Soviet Union (1949), vice-president of India (1952–62), then president. He was knighted in 1931.

radian SI unit for measuring angles in a plane: symbol *rad*; 1 radian is the angle subtended at the centre of a circle by an arc along the circumference equal in length to the circle's radius; thus π radians = 180°.

radiance; radiant intensity / power *radiometry*

radiation A general term for the processes by which energy is lost from a source without physical contact. It refers to various radioactive and electromagnetic emissions. Heat radiation, for example, is electromagnetic radiation emitted from an object on account of its temperature.

radiation sickness An acute affect on the body of high doses of ionizing radiation, which may be a complication of radiotherapy for the treatment of cancer. It results in weakness, nausea, vomiting, and diarrhoea, and damage to epithelial surfaces with hair loss, red patches on the skin (*erythema*), and mouth ulcers.

radical An unstable molecule containing unpaired electrons (eg CH_3, methyl). The term is also used as a synonym for 'group' in the sense of 'part of a molecule'.

radicalism Any set of ideas, of either left or right, which argues for more substantial social and political change than is supported in the political mainstream. What is radical is a matter of judgment, and so the term is very widely applied. In a number of countries there are Radical Parties which are left of centre.

radiesthesia [raydiestheezha] The use of dowsing as a method of diagnosing disease and selecting a suitable treatment, usually in the form of a herbal or homeopathic remedy. One method, using a pendulum, developed in France at the beginning of the 20th-c, was introduced to the UK in 1939 by Dr George Laurence, who founded the Medical Society for the Study of Radiesthesia. The technique does not require the actual presence of the patient, since it can be applied to a 'witness', such as a sample of hair, nail clippings, blood, or saliva. Diagnosis is made by comparing the response of the pendulum to that observed with reference samples taken in various disease states.

radio The transmission of sound signals through space by means of radio-frequency electromagnetic waves. In 1888 the German physicist Heinrich Hertz produced and detected radio waves, developing the equations made by James Clerk Maxwell. Guglielmo Marconi constructed a device to translate radio waves into electrical signals, and in 1901 transmitted signals across the Atlantic Ocean. Prior to World War 1, radio messages were sent between land stations and ships, and between land and aircraft. In 1918, a radiotelegraph message was transmitted from Wales to Australia. Radio broadcasting became routinely available during the 1920s, when such institutions as the BBC (1922) came into being. Since the 1920s, radio transmission has improved enormously. The introduction of transistors (1948) and integrated circuits revolutionized receivers, and higher radio frequencies have been introduced (for example, *FM* or *frequency modulation*). The development of stereo has proved particularly suitable for the broadcasting of music. Both FM and AM (*amplitude modulation*) radio depend on analog technology. Most radio broadcasters are now developing digital audio broadcasting, which offers a higher quality of sound and allows a massive increase in the number of radio channels that can be fitted to the world's electromagnetic spectrum. Wavebands for international communication now rely on satellites for transmission. The clockwork or wind-up radio, commercially marketed since 1996, has further revolutionized the scope of radio broadcasting. Needing neither batteries nor electricity, its power-source is an internal spring-driven generator powered by hand, enabling people in remote parts of the world where affordable energy is scarce to keep abreast of current developments.

radioactive dating *radiocarbon dating*

radioactive fallout The radioactive substances produced by a nuclear explosion (eg above-ground weapons testing; the accident at Chernobyl nuclear power station in 1986). These substances are carried away from the explosion site by winds, and are deposited (either from dry air as particles, or dissolved in rain) causing contamination, possibly up to thousands of kilometres away. Fallout from the Chernobyl accident included caesium-134, caesium-137, iodine-131, plutonium-239, and strontium-90.

radioactive tracer A radioactive isotope of an element substituted specifically in a compound in order to 'tag' it. Much has been learned about the mechanisms of reactions in this way, as the reactant supplying a specific atom to a product can be identified.

radioactive waste A byproduct of the many processes involved in the generation of nuclear power. Despite nearly 30 years of commercial nuclear power generation, there is no acceptable solution to the problem of radioactive waste disposal. Three levels of waste are produced: low, intermediate, and high. *Low-level* and *intermediate-level* waste is generally buried in pits: at Drigg, adjacent to the Sellafield nuclear complex in the UK, and in abandoned salt mines in Germany. *High-level* waste is generally stored in stainless steel tanks, and continually cooled. One possibility for storage is vitrification (solidification in glass), to reduce the volume of waste. Proposals exist for the burial of high-level waste either under the seabed or deep underground on land. The production and storage of radioactive waste is a major international environmental issue, with strong opposition from such pressure groups as Greenpeace.

radioactivity The spontaneous decay of atomic nuclei, resulting in the emission of particles and energy; discovered by Antoine Henri Becquerel in 1896. The possible emissions are alpha particles, beta particles, and gamma rays. The exact moment of decay for any one nucleus cannot be predicted, though for a large sample the fraction of nuclei that will decay in a suitable time interval can be determined. Radioactivity is detected and measured using Geiger counters.

radioactivity units The activity of a radioactive source, expressed in **becquerels** (*Bq*), where 1 Bq is one decay per second. Particles from different substances may be produced in similar numbers but with very different energies. This is taken into account using a second unit, the **gray**, (*Gy*), which measures the energy deposited in some object by the radiation: the *absorbed dose*. Different types of radiation cause different degrees of biological damage, even if the total energy deposited is the same; for example, 1 Gy of alpha radiation causes 20 times as much damage as 1 Gy of beta radiation. This potential for causing harm is expressed as *dose equivalent*, units **sievert**, (*Sv*), which is the product of absorbed dose in Gy and a *relative biological effectiveness* (RBE) factor. Radiation limits for working places and the environment are expressed in Sv.

Radioactivity Units

Name	*Definition*	*Unit*	*Old Unit*
activity	rate of disintegrations	Bq	Ci (curie)
absorbed dose	energy deposited in object divided by mass of object	Gy	rad
dose equivalent	absorbed dose × RBE	Sv	rem

RBE	*Radiation*
20	alpha
10	neutron
1	beta, gamma, X-ray

radio astronomy The exploration of the universe by detecting radio emission from celestial objects. The frequency range is very great, from 10 mHz to 300 gHz. A variety of antennas are used, from single dishes to elaborate networks of telescopes forming intercontinental radio interferometers. The principal sources of cosmic radio emission are the Sun, Jupiter, interstellar gas, pulsars, supernova remnants, radio galaxies, quasars, and the cosmic background radiation of the universe itself.

radio beacon A fixed radio transmitting station, sending out a coded signal characteristic of that station. This helps aircraft pilots and ships' captains to navigate safely, especially in bad weather conditions. Using two or more radio beacons, a direction finder aboard a vessel can accurately pinpoint the vessel's position.

radiobiology The branch of biology concerned with the effects of radioactive materials on living organisms, and with the use of radioactive tracers to study metabolic processes.

radio broadcasting 1 *broadcasting*

2 In computing, a form of data transmission in which the data is broadcast over radio waves and received by large numbers of computer users. This is an important means of communicating data when the number of receivers is large and there is no requirement for them to respond to the message which has been sent. It is particularly relevant where the receivers are mobile.

radiocarbon dating A radiometric method for measuring the decay of the radioactive isotope carbon-14 in organic material up to 80 000 years old, developed in 1948–9 by Willard Libby. Living animals and plants take in carbon, which contains some radioactive carbon-14. When the organism dies, it stops taking in carbon, and as the carbon-14 decays, its proportion to the total amount of carbon decreases in a way which is directly related to the time elapsed since death. Using samples principally from wood and charcoal, the technique revolutionized archaeological dating across the world. Recent refinements allow reliable determinations of date from no more than a few fibres of cloth or a grain of wheat. Radiocarbon dating was the technique by which in 1988 a fragment of the Turin Shroud was shown to date from the 14th-c.

radiochemistry The production and use of radioisotopes to study chemical compounds and their reactions. An example is the synthesis of compounds incorporating radioactive atoms in specific sites, to see whether those atoms are present in a product of a subsequent chemical reaction.

radio galaxy A galaxy which is an intense source of cosmic radio waves – about one galaxy in a million. In such objects, an active galactic nucleus (almost certainly a black hole) is producing immense quantities of electrons travelling at almost the speed of light. When these encounter a magnetic field, they spiral around the field lines, emitting synchrotron radiation as radio waves. Some radio galaxies are extremely large, with radio emission coming from regions up to 300 kiloparsec from the associated galaxy. Investigations of these objects led directly to the discovery of quasars.

radiogram A single device capable of both receiving radio broadcasts and playing gramophone records. It was developed during the 1930s, with the wider domestic use of radio sets and electricity, and incorporated a record player which made use of the radio's amplifier and speaker. Popular for its convenience and for aesthetic reasons, it was the forerunner of the music centre.

radiography Producing a photographic image (actually a shadow-image) of a structure which is penetrated by X-rays, gamma-rays, or electrons. These radiations are, in general, differentially absorbed by the different parts of any structure, and produce corresponding densities of exposure on a photographic film. The first radiograph was made by Röntgen in 1895, and the technique is now highly developed for medical diagnosis and for non-destructive industrial testing. In **miniature radiography**, the X-ray image on a large fluorescent screen in contact with the subject is photographed with a 35 mm camera.

radio-immunoassay A method using radioactively-labelled material corresponding to a substance to be measured, together with a specific antibody to the substance. After mixing, the degree of binding of the antibody to the labelled substance can be estimated, and used to calculate the amount of substance present in a biological fluid, such as blood.

radioisotope An isotope which spontaneously undergoes radioactive decay. It may be naturally occurring or artificially produced. All isotopes of all elements with an atomic number above 83 are radioisotopes. Carbon-14 is an isotope continuously produced in the upper atmosphere by cosmic ray bombardment, and used in the technique of carbon dating.

radioisotope thermo-electric generator (RTG) A source of electrical power for spacecraft operating at great distances from the Sun (replacing insufficiently powerful solar arrays) or on planetary surfaces (where solar array operation is impractical). Radioactive material is used to generate heat, and electricity is generated by temperature differential across dissimilar metals. The fuel is usually plutonium-238, which has a half-life of 77 years and can therefore generate copious heat in small quantities to power spacecraft having mission lifetimes of a decade or so. RTGs have been used for many US and Soviet space missions, including Apollo seismometer packages, Viking landers, Pioneers 10 and 11, Voyagers 1 and 2, Galileo, Ulysses, and Cassini–Huygens. Because nuclear fuel is used, the devices are built to survive launch and spacecraft accidents, and even to withstand atmospheric re-entry. The use of such power sources has provoked legal actions in the USA because of concerns about launch safety.

Radiolaria [raydiohlairia] An informal grouping of marine single-celled organisms (protozoans). They have a typically spherical cell body, with an elaborate skeleton consisting of radiating spikes of silica. (Class: Actinopoda.)

radiometric dating A method for determining the absolute age of a rock by measuring the amount of radioactive element present and comparing it to the amount of stable element into which it decays. This ratio, in conjunction with the known half-life of the radiometric element, is used to calculate the age of the rock or mineral being measured.

radiometry The measurement of radiated electromagnetic energy, especially infrared. *Radiant power* is the total power from a source; *radiant intensity* is radiant power per unit solid angle, and is used to describe sources that do not radiate uniformly in all directions; *radiance* is radiant intensity per unit area; *irradiance* is total power per unit area. Radiometric quantities are measured using radiometers. (*see panel*)

radionics An application of radiesthesia using an instrument devised by Dr Albert Abrams (d.1924). Although his 'black box' contained no power source or electronic circuitry, Abrams claimed that it could be tuned into the energy waves emanating from a biological sample ('the witness') by rotating a small bar magnet. A series of dials on the instrument are set to correspond with various disease conditions. Disease can be diagnosed in humans, animals, or even plants, and then healing waves transmitted from the instrument so that the actual presence of the patient is not necessary for treatment to take place.

Radiometry

Radiometric quantity	*Symbol*	*Units*
radiant power	Φ	W
radiant intensity	I	W/sr
radiance	L	W/sr.m²
irradiance	E	W/m²

radiosonde (radiosounding) balloon [raydiohsond] A package of instruments sent up with a weather balloon to measure pressure, temperature, and humidity as the balloon rises to high altitudes (20 000 m/65 000 ft). Pressure measurements are used to calculate altitude. Information is transmitted back to ground-receiving stations by radio signals, and the instruments are recovered after descent by parachute. A **rawindsonde** (radar wind sounding) [**ray**winsond] balloon is a version of radiosonde which also measures wind speed and direction. The balloon carries a radar target so that its course can be plotted.

radio telescope *telescope*

radiotherapy The use of radiation (especially X-rays) to treat disease, especially malignant tumours, which are more sensitive to certain kinds of radiation than are normal tissues. When X-rays are used to control a tumour, they are directed into the patient in a beam from several different angles, carefully positioned so that the tumour receives the maximum concentration, leaving adjacent healthy tissues little affected. Radioactive materials can also be used (eg a tiny pellet), implanted directly into the tumour to give a carefully calculated total dose. The technique has proved particularly successful in the treatment of various kinds of cancer.

radio waves Electromagnetic radiation of wavelength greater than about 10 cm. It is produced by oscillating electric currents in antennas, and travels at the velocity of light. Modulated radio waves are used in communications.

radish An annual or biennial (*Raphanus sativus*) with a tuberous root, irregularly lobed leaves, and cross-shaped, white to purplish flowers. Its origin is unknown, but it has been used as a vegetable since Ancient Egyptian times. Summer radishes are small and fast-growing; winter radishes are large, up to 250 g/9 oz, and slower-growing. The related **wild radish** (*Raphanus raphanistrum*) has slender roots and often yellow flowers. (Family: Cruciferae.)

radium Ra, element 88, melting point 700°C. A metal, with all its isotopes radioactive. The most stable isotope, ^{226}Ra, has a half-life of only 1620 years, but it occurs in uranium ores as a product of radioactive decay, and its main source is extraction from these ores. Its chemical properties are similar to those of barium, but all its uses relate to its radioactivity, and it is usually used as a salt, such as $RaCl_2$. It is a source of α-particles, and combined with beryllium, a neutron source. Radium salts exhibit fluorescence, and were formerly used in luminous watch dials.

radius (anatomy) *arm*

radon Rn, element 86, boiling point −62°C. The heaviest of the noble gases. It has several isotopes: that with the longest half-life (4 days) is ^{222}Rn, formed with radium. It is continuously liberated to the atmosphere by natural radioactive decay; on average, a litre of air contains about 1000 atoms of Rn (1 part in 10^{20}). Its few compounds, mainly fluorides, are similar to those of xenon; its primary use is in radiotherapy. High levels of radon exposure are associated with areas of granite rock (eg Dartmoor in the UK). It can penetrate buildings through floors and walls and accumulate in the lungs, causing respiratory damage including lung cancer. Regulations now ensure proper sealing of floors and walls and adequate ventilation of buildings in high-risk areas.

Raeburn, Sir Henry [**ray**bern] (1756–1823) Portrait painter, born near Edinburgh, EC Scotland, UK. He first produced watercolour miniatures, then worked in oils. After his marriage to a wealthy widow, he studied in Rome (1785–7), then settled in Edinburgh, where he painted the leading members of Edinburgh society in a typically bold, strongly shadowed style. He was knighted in 1822.

Raeder, Erich [**ray**der] (1876–1960) German grand admiral, born in Wandsbek, N Germany. He joined the navy in 1894, and became a chief-of-staff during World War 1. In 1928 he was made commander-in-chief of the navy, and encouraged the building of submarines and capital warships despite the ban imposed by the Treaty of Versailles. He became grand admiral in 1939, but disagreed with Hitler on the deployment of the navy and was removed from command in 1943 At the Nuremberg Trials (1946), he was sentenced to life imprisonment, but released in 1955.

RAF *Royal Air Force*

raffia palm A tree growing to 7·5 m/25 ft, native to Africa; leaves 18 m/60 ft, feathery. The surface of the young leaflets is stripped to provide raffia fibre. (Genus: *Raffia*, 30 species. Family: Palmae.)

Raffles, Sir (Thomas) Stamford (1781–1826) Colonial administrator, born at sea, off Port Morant, Jamaica. He had limited formal schooling, became a clerk in the East India Company, and after studying by himself gained a position as assistant secretary in Penang. He quickly rose to become Lieutenant-Governor of Java (1811–16), where he completely reformed the administration. In 1815 he visited the Borobudur Temple and ordered the excavation, surveying, and restoration of the site. He also undertook a study of the natural history of Indonesia; the genus of flowering plants *Rafflesia* is named after him. In 1816 ill health brought him home to England, where he was knighted. As Lieutenant-Governor of Bengkulu (1818–23), he established a settlement at Singapore (1819), and was thus largely responsible for the development of the British empire in the Far East.

rafflesia The best-known member of an entirely parasitic family of flowering plants from the tropics and subtropics. All are obligate parasites, in which the plant is reduced to a web of cells, most closely resembling the hyphae of fungi, which spread through the body of the host plant. Only the flowers are recognizable as belonging to a flowering-plant, developing as buds within the host tissue and bursting through before opening. Some members of the family have small flowers and parasitize herbs; rafflesia, native to Malaysia, parasitizes woody vines and has enormous flowers. The flowers of *Rafflesia arnoldii* are the largest in the world, reaching 1 m/3¼ ft in diameter. They are bowl-shaped, with 4–5 spreading lobes, and are typical carrion flowers, the whole structure being fleshy, mottled, and coloured to resemble rotting meat. They produce a strong putrid smell to complete the illusion, and attract flies to pollinate them. (Genus: *Rafflesia*, 12 species. Family: Rafflesiaceae.)

Rafsanjani, Ali Akbar Hashemi [rafsanjah**nee**] (1934–) Iranian politician and president (1989–97), born in Rafsanjan, C Iran. He supported Ayatollah Khomeini after the latter's exile in 1963, and became a wealthy property speculator in the 1970s. He spent three years in prison (1975–7) for his political activities on behalf of the exiled Khomeini. After the 1979 revolution, he helped to found the ruling Islamic Republican Party, and in 1980 was chosen as Speaker of the Majlis (Lower House), representing the moderates who favour improved relations with the West. In the 1980s he was the most influential figure in Iran after Khomeini, and his successor. In office, his policies, particularly in the economic sphere, were more pragmatic. He condemned both the USA and Iraq during the Gulf War in 1991, and after the war strove to renew close ties with the West.

raga In Indian music, the equivalent of the Western 'mode', but with broader connotations of melodic contour, performance style, ornamentation, etc.

ragged robin A perennial herb (*Lychnis flos-cuculi*), native to Europe and Asia, usually in marshy or damp places; opposite leaves; flowers pink, rarely white, five petals, each divided into four narrow segments and with two cleft scales at the base, giving the 'ragged' effect. (Family: Caryophyllaceae.)

ragged school In the UK, a school where education was offered free to the children of the poor, who often came to school without shoes and in ragged clothing. It was a development of the early 19th-c by John Pounds of Portsmouth (1766–1839).

Raglan (of Raglan), Lord Fitzroy James Henry Somerset, Baron (1788–1855) British general, born at Badminton, Gloucestershire, SWC England, UK, the son of the Duke of Beaufort. He joined the army in 1804, fought at Waterloo (1815), became an MP, and was made a baron in 1852. In 1854 he led an ill-prepared force against the Russians in the Crimea, but though victorious at Alma did not follow up his advantage. His ambiguous order led to the Charge of the Light Brigade (1854) at Balaclava. His name was given to the *raglan sleeve*, which came into use in the 1850s.

Ragnarök [ragnaroek] In Norse mythology, the final battle between the gods and the monstrous forces hostile to them. Though gods and monsters die, a new world will arise.

ragtime A type of syncopated US music popular from c.1890 to c.1920, when it yielded to (and influenced) the new jazz style. Despite the popularity of Irving Berlin's song, *Alexander's Ragtime Band* (1911), 'rags' were composed mainly for piano, and ragtime was popularized by Scott Joplin and other pianist–composers. Its revival in the 1970s was mainly due to the advocacy of US scholar, pianist and conductor, Joshua Rifkin (1944–).

ragworm A free-swimming, carnivorous worm found close to the sea bed; catches prey using an outward-turning muscular tube (*proboscis*) armed with strong jaws; swims using lateral lobes (*parapodia*) on its body segments, armed with bristles. (Phylum: Annelida. Class: Polychaeta.)

ragwort A robust biennial or perennial (*Senecio jacobaea*), growing to 1·5 m/5 ft, native to Europe and W Asia, but widely introduced elsewhere; leaves with irregularly toothed lobes; flower-heads numerous, up to 2·5 cm/1 in across, bright golden yellow and daisy-like, in dense flat-topped clusters. It is poisonous to livestock if eaten in quantity, and is usually avoided by grazing cattle. (Family: Compositae.)

Rahman, Shaikh Mujibur [rahman] (1920–75) First prime minister (1972–5) and president (1975) of Bangladesh, born in Tongipara, S Bangladesh (formerly East Bengal). After studying law at Dacca, he helped found the Awami League (1949). In 1954 he was elected to the East Pakistan Provincial Assembly, and took an opposition role during the 1960s. In 1966 he was arrested and imprisoned for two years for provoking separatism. After winning an overall majority in the Pakistani elections of 1970, but being denied office, he launched a non-co-operation campaign which escalated into civil war and the creation of Bangladesh. After becoming president in 1975, he and his wife were assassinated in a military coup.

Rahner, Karl (1904–84) Roman Catholic theologian, born in Freiburg, SW Germany. He studied at Freiburg and Innsbruck, and taught at Innsbruck, Munich, and Münster. In his voluminous writings (such as his multivolume *Theological Investigations*), he uses insights of the philosophy of existentialism while remaining true to the tradition of Aquinas. He played a major role as a consultant at the Second Vatican Council (1962–5).

Raikes, Robert [rayks] (1735–1811) Philanthropist and pioneer of the Sunday-School movement, born in Gloucester, Gloucestershire, SWC England, UK. In 1757 he succeeded his father as proprietor of the *Gloucester Journal*. His pity for the misery and ignorance of many children in his native city led him to start a Sunday school (1780) where they might learn to read and repeat the Catechism. He lived to see such schools spread throughout England.

rail A bird of the worldwide family Rallidae (c.130 species), possibly the most widespread group of terrestrial birds; large legs, short rounded wings, and short tails; many (not all) found near water; many extinct species. The name is also used for **rail-babblers** (Family: Timaliidae) and **Bensch's rail** (Family: Mesitornithidae).

rail gun 1 A heavy artillery piece mounted on a railway carriage. **2** A proposed component of the Strategic Defense Initiative, a land-based, short-range system for the last-ditch defence of individual land targets. It uses electrical energy to accelerate kinetic energy munitions to very high velocities.

railway The general name given in the UK to a transport system that has as its central feature the operation of a locomotive hauling passenger carriages or freight trucks on specially mounted tracks or rails, called the *permanent way*. The geographical area covered by the rails forms a **rail network**, and the operation of all trains on the network together with their scheduling, control, and engineering support services form a **railway system**. North American usage retains the historical name of **railroad** to describe the above definition of railway, and uses the term **railway** to describe the permanent way, ie the rails, their fixings, and associated engineering.

The first important development, the Stockton and Darlington railway, was opened in Yorkshire in 1825, and was used mainly for the carriage of coal and other goods, and some passengers, employing both steam locomotives and horses for traction. It was not until 1830, and the opening of the Liverpool and Manchester Railway, that a full passenger-carrying railway with all its associated handling features, and solely dependent on steam locomotives, became operational. From this early start, railways quickly spread across Europe and the USA, where in 1830 the 'Best Friend of Charleston' pulled the first train on US soil. By 1869 it was possible to cross the USA by rail. Railways spread across the rest of the world by colonial and trade expansion, as happened in India in 1851. However, such introductions quickly developed into different types to suit local conditions, even though most of the equipment was still manufactured in Europe or the USA and exported.

Because of the strategic nature of railways, governments have always taken a strong interest in their building and operation, and indeed most railways in the world are at present state-owned, running at a loss. These losses arise from the high cost of investment needed to replace old machinery and buildings, and the strong increase in competition from road transport. After 1947, the entire British railway system was state-owned, and various attempts at rationalization were undertaken in an endeavour to reduce non-economic operation. The most famous of these rationalizations, which gave rise to a large number of line closures, was the implementation of the Beeching Report of 1963. Rather similar problems in the USA led to the formation of AMTRAK in 1971. AMTRAK is wholly owned by the US government, but unlike most nationalized railways is responsible only for intercity passenger rail services; freight is handled by private companies. British Rail privatization took place in the mid-1990s, with Railtrack being set up with responsibility for railway infrastructure from 1994. In an effort to counter the competition of both road transport and aircraft, new fast trains have been developed, most notably in Japan (the 'Bullet' train) and France (the TGV, short for 'Train à Grande Vitesse'). The success of the TGV has led to a new network of such trains being introduced throughout France.

railway signalling A system for controlling the movement of trains, formerly using flags and hand-operated mechanical signals, and in recent years radio and electronic systems. In the UK in the 1980s, British Rail installed computer-controlled 4-aspect signalling, designed to interlock with the points system. Trackside colour light signals give the driver instructions: green (go), red (stop), double yellow (caution), single yellow (greater caution). These are supplemented by audio and visual signals in the driver's cab. Drivers must acknowledge yellow signals by braking or pressing a reset button, otherwise the train is automatically stopped. Despite these precautions, accidents still occur. A collision in Clapham, London, UK, in 1988 was caused by defective wiring; a crash at Purley, Greater London, UK, in 1989 was caused by a driver going through a red light, as was the one at Ladbroke Grove Junction, near Paddington, London, UK, in 1999. Some European countries use a system whereby a microcomputer in the cab can override the driver.

rainbow An arc of light comprising the spectral colours, formed when the Sun's rays are refracted and internally reflected by raindrops acting as prisms or lenses. It is visible when the Sun is behind the observer and the rain is in front. A **double rainbow** may occur when some of the light is refracted twice.

rainbow guide *scouting*

Rainbow Snake In Australian aboriginal religion, the great fertility spirit, both male and female, creator and destroyer; known as **Julunggul**. It is associated with streams and waterholes, from which it emerges in the creation-story and leaves special markings on the ground.

Raine, Craig (Anthony) (1944–) Poet, born in Shildon, Co Durham, NE England, UK. He studied at Oxford University and lectured there before becoming poetry editor at Faber and Faber (1981–91). He published his first book, *The Onion, Memory*, in 1978. Later books include *Rich* (1984), *Selected Poetry* (1992), and *Collected Poems* (1999). He also wrote the libretto for *The Electrification of the Soviet Union* (1986), an opera by Nigel Osborne, commissioned by Glyndebourne.

rainfall A type of precipitation in which water droplets reach the ground in liquid state. When water droplets are small, rain may be called *drizzle*. In temperate and humid regions, rainfall may form the major contribution to annual precipitation totals, while at high latitudes snow may be the main contributor. The amount of rainfall is measured with a rain gauge.

rainforest The vegetation type found in wet equatorial regions and other areas of high precipitation, such as the Coast Mountains of NW USA, and New Zealand. Tropical rainforests are characterized by a great diversity of plant and animal species, a closed canopy layer which allows little light to reach the forest floor, and rapid nutrient cycling within the forest. Despite the luxuriant growth of these forests, when cut down the soils are relatively infertile, because most of the nutrients are in the vegetation, and soils are rapidly washed away. Many of the trees have considerable commercial value (eg mahogany, teak), and large areas are being cleared. Deforestation is also occurring to create new agricultural areas (cattle ranching) and industry (mining). The United Nations Food and Agricultural Organization estimates that c.100 000 sq km/c.40 000 sq mi are cleared each year. This rate of disappearance is alarming many conservationists, because of the extinction of unique plant and animal species. Tropical rainforests also play an important role in the global climate system, which could also be disrupted by clearance.

rain gauge A meteorological instrument used to measure the amount of rainfall for a given period. It is commonly in the form of a bucket, with an opening of known size, which funnels rain into a measuring cylinder below. To maintain standards, measurements are made at set times using standardized instruments. Automatic rain gauges recording time and amount of rain are used to calculate rainfall intensity.

Rainier, Mount [raynyer] 46°51N 121°46W. Dormant volcano in WC Washington, USA; height 4395 m/14 419 ft; highest point in the Cascade Range; the largest single-peak glacier system in the USA; Mt Rainier National Park; 26 glaciers, notably Emmons (c.8 km/5 mi long) and Nisqually (c.6 km/3¾ mi long).

Rainier III [raynyay], in full **Rainier Louis Henri Maxence Bertrand de Grimaldi** (1923–) Prince of Monaco (1949–), born in Monaco. In 1956 he married US film actress Grace Kelly. They had two daughters, **Princess Caroline Louise Marguerite** (1957–) and **Princess Stephanie Marie Elisabeth** (1965–), and a son, **Prince Albert Alexandre Louis Pierre** (1958–).

Rais or **Raiz, Baron** *Retz, Baron*

raisins Black or white grapes, dried naturally or artificially. They have a high sugar content, and are used widely in cake- and bun-making to impart sweetness.

rajah or **raja** A title formerly used in India by a local prince or chief; the equivalent female title was **rani** or **ranee**, though this was also used for the wife of a rajah. **Maharaja(h)** and **maharani/maharanee** were higher-ranking titles used in some areas. Other Indian princely titles include **nawab, nizam, rao** (**maharao**), and **rawal** (**maharawal**). Areas which used these titles include (*raja*) Cannanore, Cochin; (*maharaja*) Baroda, Bharatpur, Gwalior, Indore, Kolhapur, Lahore, Mysore; (*rana*) Mewar, Udaipur; (*nawab*) Bhopal, Tonk; (*rao*) Bundi, Cutch, Kotah; (*nizam*) Hyderabad; and (*rawal*) Jaisalmer. The princely system became less significant following the independence of India and Pakistan, and it ceased to be recognized after the Princely Derecognition Act of 1971. The title of *raja(h)* was also used in a few other areas, such as Perlis (Malaysia), and by the Brookes in Sarawak (1841–1946).

Raja Ram Mohan Rai *Rammohun Roy*

Rajasthan [rahjastahn] pop (2001e) 56 473 100; area 342 214 sq km/132 095 sq mi. State in NW India, bounded W by Pakistan; formed in 1948; capital, Jaipur; governed by a 200-member Legislative Assembly; crossed by numerous rivers; Thar desert in the W; Anavalli range to the S; pulses, sugar cane, oilseed, cotton; textiles, cement, glass, sugar; phosphate, silver, asbestos, copper, feldspar, limestone, salt.

Rakhmaninov, Sergei *Rachmaninov*

Rakoczi [rakohtsee] A princely family of Hungary and Transylvania which became extinct in 1780. The most important member was the popular **Francis II** (1676–1735), who in 1703 led a Hungarian revolt against Austria. He had little success but was hailed by his countrymen as a patriot and a hero. His later years were spent as a Carmelite monk in France and in Turkey.

Raleigh [rahlee] 35°46N 78°38W, pop (2000e) 276 100. Capital of state in Wake Co, EC North Carolina, USA; established, 1788; named after Sir Walter Raleigh; airfield; railway; two universities (1865, 1887); foods, textiles, electrical equipment; birthplace of President Andrew Johnson.

Raleigh, Sir Walter [rawlee, ralee], also spelled **Ralegh** (1552–1618) Courtier, explorer, soldier, and writer, born in Hayes Barton, Devon, SW England, UK. He studied at Oxford before serving in the Huguenot army in France (1569). A rival of the Earl of Essex for the queen's favours, he served (1580) in Elizabeth's army in Ireland, distinguishing himself by his ruthlessness at the siege of Smerwick and by the plantation of English and Scots Protestants in Munster. Elizabeth rewarded him with a large estate in Ireland, knighted him (1585), and gave him trade privileges and the right to colonize America. In 1587 he explored from N Carolina to present-day Florida, naming the region *Virginia* in honour of Elizabeth, the 'Virgin Queen'. In 1587 Raleigh sent an ill-fated second expedition of colonists to Roanoake. In 1588 he took part in the victory over the Spanish Armada. He led other raids against Spanish possessions and returned with much booty. Raleigh forfeited Elizabeth's favour by his courtship of and subsequent marriage to one of her maids-of-honour, Bessy Throckmorton, and he was committed to the Tower (1592). Hoping, on his release, to recover his position, he led an abortive expedition to Guiana to search for El Dorado, a legendary land of gold. Instead, he helped to introduce the potato plant and tobacco use in England and Ireland. Elizabeth's successor, James I, distrusted and feared Raleigh, charged him with treason and condemned him to death, but commuted the sentence to imprisonment in the Tower (1603). There Raleigh lived with his wife and servants, and wrote his *History of the World* (1614). He was released in 1616 to search for gold in South America. Against the king's undertaking to the Spanish, he invaded and pillaged Spanish territory, was forced to return to England without booty, and was arrested on the orders of the king. His original death sentence for treason was invoked, and he was executed at Westminster. A gifted poet, writer, and scholar, many of his poems and writings were destroyed. A pioneer of the Italian sonnet-form in English, he was a patron of the arts, notably of Edmund Spenser in his composition of *The Faerie Queene* (1589–96).

rally A form of motor racing which demands skill and endurance from driver and navigator. Rallies are raced over several days (sometimes weeks) both on open roads and in forests, national parks, etc, where special stages are organized. Drivers use modified production cars. Famous rallies include the Monte Carlo Rally, the RAC Lombard Rally, and the Safari Rally.

RAM [ram] Acronym for **random access memory** (sometimes **read-and-write memory**), a type of computer memory, usually integrated circuits, which can be read from and written to. RAM is used in all computers; data contained in RAM is lost when the electrical power is removed.

ram *sheep*

Ramadan [rama**dahn**] The ninth month of the Muslim year, observed as a month of fasting during which Muslims abstain from eating, drinking, and sexual intercourse between sunrise and sunset; the Ramadan fast, which ends in the festival of Id-al-Fitr, is one of the five 'pillars', or basic duties, of Islam.

Ramadan War *Arab–Israeli Wars*

Ramakrishna [rama**krish**na], originally **Gadadhar Chatterjee** (1836–86) Hindu religious teacher, born in the Hooghly district of Bengal, E India, the son of a poor Brahmin family with little formal education. He became a priest at Dakshineswar Kali temple, near Kolkata (Calcutta), eventually forming his own religious order. He believed in self-realization and God-realization – expressing God by the way one lives and worships – and taught that all religions were different paths to the same goal. His most noteworthy disciple was Vivekananda. Several books of his sayings were later published by his followers.

Raman, Sir Chandrasekhara (Venkata) [**rah**man] (1888–1970) Physicist, born in Trichinopoly, now Tiruchchirappalli, S India. He studied at Chennai (Madras), and became professor of physics at Calcutta (1917–33) and director of the Indian Institute of Science at Bangalore. In 1929 he was knighted, and in 1930 awarded the Nobel Prize for Physics for his discoveries relating to the scattering of light (the **Raman effect**).

Ramana Maharishi [ra**mah**na maha**ri**shee], also known as **Sri Ramana** and **Sri Bhagavan** (1879–1950) Philosopher, born in Tiruchuli, S India. At the age of 17 a religious experience led him to become a hermit at the holy mountain of Arunachala, where he remained until his death. Much of the time he lived in caves and avoided publicity, but he later allowed devotees to establish an *ashram*. His philosophy of seeking self-knowledge through integration of the personality in the 'cave of the heart' became known to Westerners through the books of Paul Brunton as well as his own *Collected Works* (1969) and other anthologies.

Raman scattering [**rah**man] Light scattering from a material in which the scattered light comprises substance-dependent spectral lines centred on and symmetric about the frequency of the incident light; described by Chandrasekhara Raman in 1928. The frequency shift is due to an energy exchange between the incident light photons and the scattering atoms. Raman spectroscopy using lasers is an important means of studying the structure of molecules.

Ramanuja [ra**mah**nuja] (traditionally c.1017–1137) Hindu theologian and philosopher, born in Sriperumbudur, Tamil Nadu, S India. He organized temple worship, founded centres to disseminate his doctrine of devotion to Visnu and Siva, and provided the intellectual basis for the practice of *bhakti*, or devotional worship.

Ramanujan, Srinivasa [ra**mah**nujan] (1887–1920) Mathematician, born in Erode, S India. The child of poor parents, he taught himself from an elementary English textbook. Although he attended college, he did not graduate. While working as a clerk, he was persuaded to send over 100 theorems that he had discovered to Godfrey Hardy at Cambridge, including results on elliptic integrals, partitions, and analytic number theory. Hardy was so impressed that he arranged for him to come to Cambridge in 1914. He was the first Indian to be elected a fellow of the Royal Society.

Ramaphosa, Cyril (Matamela) [rama**poh**za] (1952–) South African politician and trade unionist, born in Johannesburg, NE South Africa. He entered politics as a student at the University of the North, and was detained for the first time in 1974. He qualified as a lawyer, and worked initially in the legal department of a trade union grouping. In 1982 he was elected as the first general secretary of the National Union of Mineworkers, which rapidly grew to become the largest trade union in South Africa. He played a prominent part in the protest politics of the 1980s, and in 1991 became the secretary-general of the African National Congress, resigning in 1996. He was perhaps the Congress's most effective representative during the formal negotiations that began in December 1991.

Ramapithecus [rama**pith**ekus] A fossil ape, known from the Miocene epoch of E Europe, Asia, and E Africa; ground-dwelling, walked on all fours; jaws robust; cheek teeth large, with thick enamel; canine teeth low as in early hominids; probably fed on coarse foodstuffs gathered in mixed woodland and savannah. (Family: Pongidae.)

Ramayana [rama**yah**na] One of the two great Sanskrit epics of ancient India, which tells the story of Rama, his wife Sita, and the evil forces ranged against them. Though ascribed to the sage Valmiki, it derives from oral tradition. Its 24 000 couplets make it one-quarter the length of the *Mahabharata*. A critical edition was published in 1997.

Rambert, Dame Marie [**rom**bair], originally **Cyvia Rambam** (1888–1982) Ballet dancer and teacher, born in Warsaw, Poland. She was sent to Paris to study medicine, but became involved in artistic circles and instead took up dancing. In 1913 she worked on Stravinsky's *Rite of Spring* with Diaghilev's Ballets Russes. She moved to London, where she became a British citizen (1918). From 1926 she formed small companies to present classical and new ballets, promoting collaboration between painters, musicians, and choreographers. In 1935 she formed the Ballet Rambert, and remained closely associated with it through its change to a modern dance company in the 1960s. A strong supporter of young British choreographers, dancers, and designers, she was created a dame in 1962.

Rambert Dance Company [**rom**bair] Britain's oldest established dance company, dating its existence to 1926 when the ballet teacher Marie Rambert persuaded one of her pupils, Frederick Ashton, to choreograph his first ballet, *A Tragedy of Fashion*, for a review at the Lyric Theatre, Hammersmith, London. The company developed at the Mercury Theatre as the Ballet Club, first performing under the name of Ballet Rambert in 1935. A leading force in contemporary dance, in 1966 it was re-established as a smaller, more innovative ensemble with an emphasis on the creation of new works. In 1987 the company changed to its present name, and in 1994 the dancer and choreographer Christopher Bruce was appointed artistic director, followed by Mark Baldwin in 2002.

Ramblers' Association A British federation of local rambling clubs, established in 1935. It campaigns for access to open countryside, defends outstanding landscape and rights-of-way, and is one of the main advocates of long-distance footpaths, such as the Pennine Way.

Rameau, Jean Philippe [ra**moh**] (1683–1764) Composer, born in Dijon, E France. He became an organist, and in 1722 settled in Paris, where he published his *Traité de l'harmonie* (1722, Treatise on Harmony), a work of fundamental importance in the history of musical style. He wrote many operas, notably *Hippolyte et Aricie* (1733) and *Castor et Pollux* (1737), as well as ballets, harpsichord pieces, and vocal music.

Rameses or **Ramses II** [**ram**(e)seez], known as **the Great** (13th-c BC) King of Egypt (1304–1237 BC), whose long and prosperous reign marks the last great peak of Egyptian power. Despite his doubtful victory over the Hittites at Kadesh in N Syria (1299 BC), he managed to stabilize his frontier against them, making peace with them (1283 BC) and later marrying a Hittite princess (1270 BC). An enthusiastic builder, he has left innumerable monuments, among them the great sandstone temples at Abu Simbel.

Rameses or **Ramses III** [**ram**(e)seez] (12th-c BC) King of Egypt (1198–1166 BC), famous primarily for his great victory over the Sea Peoples, invaders from Asia Minor and the Aegean Is. Tradition identifies him with the pharaoh who oppressed the Hebrews of the Exodus.

ramjet A type of jet engine in which fast-moving air is slowed down by a diffuser, which produces a corresponding increase in the air's pressure. This high-pressure air then has fuel injected into it, and the mixture is continuously burned. The resulting hot gases are ejected rearwards in the form of a jet of gas. This method of jet propulsion is practical up to speeds of eight times the speed of sound.

Rammohun Roy or **Raja Ram Mohan Rai** (1774–1833) Religious reformer, born in Bengal of high Brahman ancestry. He came early to question his ancestral faith, and studied Buddhism in Tibet. He published various works in Persian, Arabic, and Sanskrit, with the aim of uprooting idolatry, and helped in the abolition of sati. He issued an English abridgment of the *Vedanta*, and published *The Precepts of Jesus* (1820) and pamphlets hostile both to Hinduism and to Christian Trinitarianism. In 1828 he began the Brahmo Samaj Association, and in 1830 the Emperor of Delhi bestowed on him the title of raja.

Ramos-Horta, José [ramos haw(r)ta] (1950–) East Timorese activist. He was exiled by the Portuguese in 1970 for his support of the independence movement in East Timor, then returned to take part in the civil war (1972–5), becoming a guerrilla member of Fretilin. He withdrew to Australia following the invasion by Indonesia in 1975, becoming East Timor's international spokesman, and has since sought international support for a peaceful solution. He shared the Nobel Prize for Peace in 1996.

Ramsay, Allan (c.1685–1758) Poet, born in Leadhills, South Lanarkshire, WC Scotland, UK. He was known as a poet by 1718, having issued several short humorous satires. His works include the pastoral comedy, *The Gentle Shepherd* (1725), and an edited collection of Scots poetry, *The Evergreen* (1724). He was the father of the artist Allan Ramsay.

Ramsay, Sir William (1852–1916) Chemist, born in Glasgow, W Scotland, UK. He studied at Heidelberg, and became professor of chemistry at Bristol (1880–7) and University College London (1887–1912). In conjunction with Lord Rayleigh he discovered argon in 1894. Later he identified helium, neon, krypton, and xenon, and was awarded the Nobel Prize for Chemistry in 1904.

Ramses *Rameses*

Ramsey, Frank (Plumpton) (1903–30) Philosopher and mathematician, born in Cambridge, Cambridgeshire, EC England, UK. He read mathematics at Cambridge, and went on to be elected fellow of King's College when he was only 21. In his tragically short life (he died after an operation) he made outstanding contributions to philosophy, logic, mathematics, and economics, to an extent which was only properly recognized years after his death. The best of his work is collected in *Philosophical Papers* (edited by D H Mellor, 1990).

Ramsey (of Canterbury), (Arthur) Michael Ramsey, Baron (1904–88) Archbishop of Canterbury (1961–74), born in Cambridge, Cambridgeshire, EC England, UK. He studied theology at Cambridge, was ordained in 1928, and became professor at Durham (1940–50) and Cambridge (1950–2). He was Bishop of Durham (1952–6) and Archbishop of York (1956–61). As Archbishop of Canterbury he worked for Church unity, making a historic visit to Pope Paul VI in the Vatican in 1966, but was disappointed in his attempts to forge a reconciliation with the Methodist Church. His books include *The Resurrection of Christ* (1945) and *Be Still and Know* (1982). He retired in 1974, and was given a life peerage.

Ramsgate 51°20N 1°25E, pop (2000e) 38 700. Port town in Kent, SE England, UK; S of Margate on the English Channel; resort made popular by George IV; railway; hovercraft service to France; yachting, fishing, tourism; St Augustine's Abbey and Church; model village; Celtic cross marks the spot where St Augustine is supposed to have landed in 597.

Ram Singh [rahm sing] (1816–85) Sikh philosopher and reformer, born in Bhaini, E Pakistan (formerly India). As a boy, he was a member of the Namdhari movement, of which he later became leader. Having entered the army of Ranjit Singh, he formed a sect to rejuvenate Sikhism. He built up a *khalsa*, or private army, and prophesied that British rule would be broken. Following attacks on Muslims in 1872, he was exiled to Rangoon as a state prisoner.

Ramus, Petrus [ramü], Lat name of **Pierre de la Ramée** (1515–72) Humanist and philosopher, born in Cuts, N France. He studied in Paris, became a lecturer on Classical authors, and undertook to reform the science of logic. His attempts excited much hostility among the Aristotelians, and his *Dialectic* (1543) which presented a controversial new system of logic was at first suppressed, but in 1551 he became professor of philosophy at the Collège de France. He later became a Protestant (c.1561) which made him politically vulnerable, and he fled from Paris to travel in Germany and Switzerland (1568–70). Returning to France in 1571, he was killed in the massacre of St Bartholomew.

Rancagua [rankagwa] 34°10S 70°45W, pop (2000e) 225 800. Capital of Liberatador General Bernardo O'Higgins region, C Chile; S of Santiago; scene of a royalist victory (1814) in the Spanish–American Wars of Independence; railway; agricultural trade; El Teniente, world's largest underground copper mine, nearby; thermal springs of Cauquenes to the S; Merced Church (national monument); historical museum; Festival del Poroto (Bean Festival) (Feb); national rodeo championships (Mar).

rancidity The reaction of atmospheric oxygen with fats, which produces unpleasant odours and flavours, and reduces vitamin A and E levels in foods. Antioxidants are commonly added to foods to prevent the development of rancidity. Vitamin E is nature's own antioxidant.

Rand *Witwatersrand*

Randolph, A(sa) Philip (1889–1979) Labour leader and civil rights activist, born in Crescent City, FL. He studied at City College, New York, co-founded an employment agency and the African-American labour monthly, the *Messenger* (1917), and built the first successful African-American trade union, the Brotherhood of Sleeping Car Porters (1925). He influenced President Truman to desegregate the armed forces in 1948, formed the Negro American Labor Council in 1960, and directed the civil rights march on Washington (1963).

randomized controlled trial A scientific method used in medicine to determine whether a new drug or other medical intervention is effective. It is designed to ensure that therapies are thoroughly evaluated before being widely used. A group of people is allocated at random to receive either the active treatment or a dummy treatment (*placebo*). The proportion of people in each group who benefit is then compared to see whether the active treatment has a statistically greater beneficial effect than the dummy treatment. To avoid the *placebo effect*, which occurs when individuals attribute a beneficial effect to a drug regardless of whether it is genuine, neither the people receiving the intervention nor the medical practitioners administering it are aware of whether each group has received the active or the dummy treatment (*double blinding*).

random number In mathematics, a number chosen from a given set of numbers so that each has the same probability of being chosen. If the given set of numbers is the set of integers from 0 to 9 inclusive, each number has a probability of 0·1 of being chosen. A **random number table** is a table of digits chosen at random, each digit having a probability of 0·1 of being chosen, and each choice being independent of the other choices. In order to choose fairly the prize-winning numbers in a national lottery, random numbers may be generated electronically. In the UK premium bonds lottery, ERNIE stands for 'Electronic Random Number Indicator'.

random processes In physics, processes comprising a sequence of events in which the outcome of one event has no bearing on the outcome of any other; also termed **stochastic processes**. Such processes cannot be predicted exactly; for example, an atom diffusing through gas moves from one collision with a gas atom to another, giving rise to a random path. Random processes involving large numbers of particles are amenable to statistical techniques.

Randstad Urban conurbation of settlements in NW Netherlands, forming a horse-shoe shape around a central agricultural zone; contains most of the Dutch population; chief cities, Amsterdam, Rotterdam, Utrecht, The Hague.

range-finder An optical device for measuring subject distance by determining the angular convergence of the lines of sight from two points a known distance apart. It is sometimes provided as a focusing aid in photography, directly coupled to the camera lens movement.

Ranger programme The first US series of lunar spacecraft missions, built and managed by NASA's Jet Propulsion Laboratory, designed to study the surface characteristics of the Moon prior to the Apollo manned landings. Launched on Atlas vehicles, the spacecraft were targeted to impact the Moon after telemetering images of increasingly high resolution. The first successful mission was Ranger 7 (Aug 1964), which impacted the Moon in the Mare Nubium (Sea of Clouds) region. The following two Rangers were also successful. They were the technological forerunner to the Mariner series of planetary spacecraft.

Rangoon *Yangon*

Ranji [rahnjee] A sky-father in the creation stories of New Zealand Maori religion. He and the Earth-mother Papa are the creators of gods and human beings.

Ranjit Singh [ranjit sing], known as **the Lion of the Punjab** (1780–1839) Sikh ruler, born in Budrukhan, NE Pakistan (formerly India). Succeeding his father as ruler of Lahore, he fought to unite all the Sikh provinces, and, with the help of a modernized army trained by Western soldiers, became the most powerful ruler in India. In 1813 he procured the Koh-i-noor diamond from an Afghan prince, as the price of assistance in war.

Rank (of Sutton Scotney), J(oseph) Arthur Rank, Baron (1888–1972) Film magnate, born in Hull, NE England, UK. He became chairman of many film companies, including Gaumont-British and Cinema-Television, and did much to promote the British film industry at a time when Hollywood seemed to have the monopoly, owning a chain of 600 cinemas, and being active in film production, exhibition, and distribution. An active supporter of the Methodist Church, he was keenly interested in social problems. He was made a life peer in 1957.

Rankine temperature *temperature*

Ransome, Arthur (Michell) (1884–1967) Writer, born in Leeds, West Yorkshire, N England, UK. He studied at Rugby, worked for a publisher, and became a war correspondent in World War 1, covering the Russian Revolution. After a stormy relationship with his first wife, they divorced in 1924, and he married Trotsky's secretary, **Evgenia Shelepin**, with whom he fled from Russia. He wrote critical works and travel books before making his name with books for young readers, notably *Swallows and Amazons* (1930).

ransoms A perennial growing to 45 cm/18 in (*Allium ursinum*), native to Europe and Asia; narrow bulb consisting of a single leaf base, 2–3 broadly elliptical leaves, and a flat-topped umbel of white, star-shaped flowers. It is often found carpeting woodland floors. The whole plant smells strongly of garlic. (Family: Liliaceae).

Rantzen, Esther (Louise) (1940–) Television presenter and producer, born in Berkhamsted, Hertfordshire, SE England, UK. She studied at Oxford, and joined the BBC in 1963, making sound effects for radio drama. She went on to be a researcher, then reporter, and during 1973–94 produced and presented *That's Life*, a populist consumer programme. She has campaigned against issues of child abuse and drug problems in a variety of documentaries, such as *Childwatch* (1987), and founded the charity 'Childline' (1986). In 1988 she received the Richard Dimbleby Award for her contributions to factual television. She married broadcaster **Desmond Wilcox** (1931–2000) in 1977, their joint publications including *Kill the Chocolate Biscuit* (1981) and *Baby Love* (1987). She began presenting the talk-show *Esther* for BBC2 in 1995, and a new series of issue-based journalism for ITV in 1998.

rape (botany) A biennial herb (*Brassica rapus*, variety *arvensis*) growing to 1 m/3¼ ft, related to the swede, but with a non-tuberous root; bluish-green leaves; yellow, cross-shaped flowers. It is grown for fodder and, increasingly, as a source of rape-oil, obtained from crushed seeds, and rape-seed cake, made from the residue. (Family: Cruciferae.)

rape (law) The crime committed when a person forces a male or female to have sexual intercourse without consent. An honest and reasonable belief that the woman or man has consented is a valid defence, though there have been some highly controversial judgments on this point in recent years. The law now recognizes rape by a husband against his wife. The maximum sentence is life imprisonment. **Statutory rape** occurs when sexual advantage is taken of someone deemed unable to understand the nature of sexual intercourse, such as a severely mentally-handicapped person, someone too young to understand the nature of the act or below the age of consent, or (in some jurisdictions) someone in a subordinate role, such as an employee. Sometimes a man reasonably believes a woman to be over the age of consent, or perhaps she lied about her age; nevertheless, the man is generally held guilty of statutory rape.

Raphael [rafael], in full **Raffaello Sanzio** (1483–1520) Painter, born in Urbino, EC Italy. He studied at Perugia under Perugino, whose style is reflected in his earliest paintings, such as 'The Crucifixion' (c.1503, National Gallery, London). In c.1504 he went to Florence, where he was strongly influenced by Leonardo and Michelangelo. He completed several Madonnas, as well as such works as 'The Holy Family' (Madrid) and 'The Deposition' (1507, Borghese). In 1508 he went to Rome, where he produced his greatest works, including the frescoes in the papal apartments of the Vatican, and the cartoons for the tapestries of the Sistine Chapel (1515–16). In 1514 he succeeded Bramante as architect of St Peter's. His last work, 'The Transfiguration' (Vatican), was nearly finished when he died.

Raphael, Frederic (Michael) (1931–) Novelist, playwright, screenwriter, and biographer, born in Chicago, Illinois, USA. He studied at Charterhouse and St John's College, Cambridge. He has adapted several of his novels for the screen, including *Richard's Things* (1973) and *The Glittering Prizes* (1976), which became a popular television series. In 1966 he won an Oscar for the screenplay of his novel *Darling* (1965). His biographies include *W Somerset Maugham and his World* (1977, revised 1989), *Byron* (1982), and *Eyes Wide Open* (1999), about the writing of the screenplay for Kubrick's *Eyes Wide Shut* (1999).

rap music A musical style which started in the streets of New York with inner-city high-school students chanting crude incantations over rock records customized by reversing the turntable and distorting the amplification. In 1983, 'It's Like That' by Run DMC., a trio of schoolmates from the borough of Queens, sold 500 000 copies, heralding the music conquest of the suburbs. Along with the standard electronic arsenal of rock music, rap music often mixes in wailing saxophones, but the main effect comes from a tortuous backbeat. The parlando lyrics went unnoticed until increasingly flagrant advocacy of drug use, promiscuity, authority-bashing, and rioting led to bans and legal threats. The rappers seemed genuinely surprised that anyone would take their doggerel so seriously. On Run DMC.'s 'Ooh, Watcha Gonna Do' (1993), the lyrics say, in part 'I'm a feasible fellow / teasable mellow / easily diesel / 'cause it's ego from the ghetto'. Really.

rare earths *lanthanides*

rare gases *noble gases*

Ras al-Khaimah [ras al khiyma] pop (2000e) 119 900; area 1690 sq km/652 sq mi. Northernmost of the United Arab Emirates, bounded W by the Persian Gulf; capital, Ras al-Khaimah; offshore oil production began in 1984; industrial development largely at Khor Khuwair; cement, pharmaceuticals, limestone.

Rasmussen, Knud (Johan Victor) [razmusen] (1879–1933) Explorer and ethnologist, born in Jacobshavn, Greenland. From 1902 onwards he directed several expeditions to Greenland in support of the theory that the Inuit and the North American Indians were both descended from migratory tribes from Asia. In 1910 he established Thule base on Cape York, and crossed by dog-sledge from Greenland to the Bering Strait (1921–4).

raspberry A deciduous shrub (*Rubus idaeus*) growing to c.2 m/6½ ft, native to Europe and Asia; straight, slender prickles;

woody, biennial stems from buds on the roots; leaves pinnately divided into 3–5 toothed leaflets; flowers 5-petalled, white. The red 'berry' is an aggregate of 1-seeded carpels separating cleanly from a conical receptacle when ripe. It is cultivated for fruit. (Family: Rosaceae.)

Raspe, Rudolf Erich *Münchhausen, Baron von*

Rasputin, Grigoriy Yefimovich [raspyootin] (?1871–1916) Peasant and self-styled religious 'elder' (*starets*), born in Pokrovskoye, WC Russia. A member of the schismatic sect of *Khlysty* ('flagellants'), he was introduced into the royal household, where he quickly gained the confidence of the emperor (Nicholas II) and empress (Alexandra of Hesse) by his ability to control through hypnosis the bleeding of the haemophiliac heir to the throne, Tsarevich Alexey. He created a public scandal through the combination of his sexual and alcoholic excesses, and his political influence in securing the appointment of government ministers. He was murdered by a group of right-wing patriots, led by Prince Felix Yusupov, a distant relative of the Tsar, and his body dumped in the frozen R Neva.

Ras Shamra texts [rahs shahmra] Some 350 texts, inscribed on tablets, found 1928–60 on the site of ancient Ugarit in NW Syria, many written in a previously unknown cuneiform script now described as 'Ugaritic', and others in Babylonian. The texts include several epics, with stories about the Canaanite gods El, Baal, Astarte, and Asherah. Dated c.1400 BC, they are important not only for descriptions of pre-Israelite Canaanite religious practices and ideas, but also for light shed on practices recorded in the Hebrew Bible.

Rastafarianism A religious movement from the West Indies, followed by about a million people. It largely derives from the thought of Jamaican political activist Marcus Garvey (1887–1940), who advocated a return to Africa as a means of solving the problems of black oppression. When Haile Selassie was crowned Emperor of Ethiopia in 1930, he came to be viewed as the Messiah, with Ethiopia seen as the promised land. Rastafarians follow strict taboos governing what they may eat (eg no pork, milk, coffee); ganja (marijuana) is held to be a sacrament; they usually wear their hair in long dreadlocks; and they cultivate a distinctive form of speech.

raster The rectangular pattern of horizontal scanning lines by which the picture image is analysed in a video camera, and reproduced on the display screen of a cathode-ray tube.

raster graphics A form of picture generation by computer in which the computer drives a television monitor in order to produce the picture as 625 or more lines. The image is refreshed at regular intervals – in the UK, every 1/25 of a second. A similar technique is used to generate images on a pixel-based printer such as a laser printer or an ink-jet printer.

rat A mouse-like rodent of family Muridae; name used generally for many unrelated species in this family, especially for members of genus *Rattus* (c.80 species throughout the Old World); also used for some species in other families. The Malaysian **black rat**, **house rat**, or **roof rat** (*Rattus rattus*) and Chinese **brown rat**, **sewer rat**, or **Norway rat** (*Rattus norvegicus*) have dispersed globally in association with humans. Both species spread human diseases (bubonic plague was spread by fleas of the black rat). The **laboratory rat** is a white form of *Rattus norvegicus*.

Ratana Church A Christian sect founded in 1918 by Wiremu Ratana with the purpose of uniting the Maori people of New Zealand. Although not successful, it came to exert great political influence among the Maori.

ratel A badger-like mammal (*Mellivora capensis*) native to Africa and S Asia, dark brown with top of head and centre of back pale yellowish-grey; fearless, with very tough skin; eats small animals, carrion, and vegetation; follows honeyguides to beehives and takes the honey; also known as **honey badger**. (Family: Mustelidae.)

rates The system of local taxation in use in the UK up to 1990 (for England and Wales; up to 1989 for Scotland). The **rateable value** of properties was decided by public valuers, and the rate per pound was set by the local authority. Rates were the main source of local authority funds after grants from central government. Because rates were paid only by occupiers of property, this system was regarded as unfair, since other residents had votes for the bodies determining the level of rates, but did not pay for the cost of the policies. Rates were therefore replaced by the community charge, though rating valuations stayed as the basis for charges by water companies. However, after much opposition, in 1993 there was a return to the system of basing local taxation on property values. Business rates, levied on commercial and industrial properties, continued after 1990.

ratfish *chimaera* (zoology)

Rathenau, Walther [rahtenow] (1867–1922) Industrialist and statesman, born in Berlin, Germany. He organized German war industries during World War 1, and in 1921, as minister of reconstruction, and after February 1922 as foreign minister, dealt with reparations. His attempts to negotiate a reparations agreement with the victorious Allies, and the fact that he was Jewish, made him extremely unpopular in nationalist circles, and he was murdered by extremists.

Rather, Dan (Irvin) [rather] (1931–) Television news presenter and writer, born in Wharton Texas, USA. Educated at Sam Houston State Teachers College, he became a television journalist for CBS in Dallas, then White House correspondent and London bureau chief (1963–74), becoming nationally known for his reports on such major events as the Kennedy assassination, Vietnam, and the Watergate affair. His national profile grew when he became co-editor of *60 Minutes* (1975–81), and he went on to become anchor of *CBS Evening News* (from 1981). He has been involved in many other TV specials, and has written several books on television journalism.

Rathlin Island area 14 sq km/5½ sq mi. Island in N Antrim, N Northern Ireland, UK, 5 km/3 mi NW of Fair Head; length, 8 km/5 mi; up to 5 km/3 mi wide; rises to 137 m/449 ft; St Columba founded a church here, 6th-c; ruins of a castle where Robert the Bruce is thought to have taken refuge in 1306.

rational-emotive therapy An approach developed by US clinical psychologist Albert Ellis (1913–), based on the premise that emotional problems arise as a result of the unrealistic beliefs people hold about themselves (eg 'I must be loved by everyone', 'I must be perfect in everything I do'). Negative evaluations of the self – and consequent adverse emotions such as anxiety and depression – are thought to arise when these beliefs are not supported. By cajoling, teasing, and arguing, the therapist challenges the client's beliefs in an attempt to make them more realistic and rational.

rationalism (architecture) A 20th-c conception of architecture which pursued the most logical possible solution to every aspect of building. Although to some extent inherent in a great part of 20th-c architecture, it is particularly associated with the work of most of the Bauhaus and International Style architects of the 1920s and 1930s, especially in Italy.

rationalism (philosophy) The tradition represented by the great 17th-c figures Descartes, Leibniz, and Spinoza, who believed that the general nature of the world could be established by reason alone, through *a priori* knowledge independent of sense-experience. It is usually contrasted with *empiricism*. In a popular sense, a commitment to reason as opposed to faith, convention, or emotion. It is therefore contrasted with *irrationalism*.

rational number *numbers*

ratio of specific heats For gases, the ratio of specific heat at constant pressure to specific heat at constant volume; symbol γ, expressed as a pure number. The former is larger, since at constant pressure gas does work expanding against its surroundings. Typical values are between 1·2 and 1·6. The ratio is related to the ideal gas constant, R, and is important in the study of the thermodynamic properties of gases.

Ratitae [ratiytee] (Lat *ratis* 'raft') An obsolete term for flightless running birds, such as the ostrich and emu (which are still referred to as **ratites**). With loss of flight, the breastbone in these birds has lost its keel and become flat (or 'raft-like').

rat kangaroo An Australian marsupial, resembling a small kangaroo (head and body length up to 50 cm/20 in) but differing in the structure of the teeth and in having a more general diet; eats plant material and invertebrates; smallest species have rat-like heads. The three species of the genus *Potorous* are called *potoroos*. (Family: Potoroidae, 10 species.)

rat-tail Deep-water fish with large head and narrow tapering body; dorsal and anal fins continuous; may have light organs on underside; some species make sounds by resonating the swim bladder; also called **grenadier**. (Family: Macrouridae.)

rattan palm [ratan] A member of a large genus of tropical climbing palms with slender, extremely long stems up to 180 m/600 ft. The plants climb by means of hooked spines at the tips, or along midribs of the feathery leaves which cling to surrounding vegetation and support stems as they grow upward. The stems are stripped to make rattan canes, widely used for furniture, baskets, and other items; also the very strong malacca cane used for walking sticks. (Genus: *Calamus*, 375 species. Family: Palmae.)

Rattigan, Sir Terence (Mervyn) (1911–77) Playwright, born in London, UK. He studied at Oxford, and scored a great success with his comedy *French Without Tears* (1936). Several later works were acclaimed, notably *The Winslow Boy* (1946), *The Browning Version* (1948), *Separate Tables* (1954), and *Ross* (1960). He was knighted in 1971.

Rattle, Sir Simon (Denis) (1955–) Conductor, born in Liverpool, Merseyside, NW England, UK. He studied at the Royal Academy of Music, London, won the Bournemouth International Conducting Competition at the age of 17, and made his London debut at both the Royal Albert and Festival Halls in 1976. He was assistant conductor of the BBC Scottish Symphony Orchestra (1977–80), then joined the City of Birmingham Symphony Orchestra as principal conductor (1980), becoming music director there (1990–8), and has been principal guest conductor of the Los Angeles Philharmonic since 1981. He joined the Berlin Philharmonic orchestra as chief conductor and artistic director in 2002. He was knighted in 1994.

rattlesnake A New World pit viper of genus *Crotalus* (28 species); tail with a segmented rattle (except in the **Santa Catalina rattlesnake**, *Crotalus catalinensis*); rattle made from modified scales (one segment added at each moult, but old segments are lost); venom attacks blood cells. The name is also used for the **pygmy** or **ground rattlesnakes** of genus *Sistrurus* (3 species).

Rau, Johannes [row] (1931–) German politician and president (1999–), born in Wuppertal-Barmen, W Germany. He was first a bookseller's apprentice and then a manager in a publishing company before becoming a full-time politician. First elected to the North Rhine–Westphalia state parliament in 1957, he became a member of the Social Democratic Party Executive (1968–99). He was minister for science and research in the state government (1970–8), and then minister president (1978–98), before being elected federal president.

Rauschenberg, Robert [rowshenberg] (1925–) Avant-garde artist, born in Port Arthur, Texas, USA. He studied art at the Kansas City Art Institute, in Paris, and at Black Mountain College, NC. His collages and 'combines' incorporate a variety of rubbish (rusty metal, old tyres, stuffed birds, fragments of clothing, etc) splashed with paint. Sometimes categorized as a Pop artist, his work has strong affinities with Dadaism, and with the 'ready-mades' of Duchamp.

Ravel, Maurice [ravel] (1875–1937) Composer, born in Ciboure, SW France. He studied under Fauré at the Paris Conservatoire, and won recognition with the *Pavane pour une infante défunte* (1899, Pavane for a Dead Princess). He wrote several successful piano pieces, *Rapsodie espagnole* (1908, Spanish Rhapsody), and the music for the Diaghilev ballet *Daphnis et Chloé* (first performed, 1912). After World War 1, in which he saw active service, his works included the 'choreographic poem' *La Valse* (1920), the opera *L'Enfant et les sortilèges* (1925, The Child and the Enchantments), and *Boléro* (1928), intended as a miniature ballet.

raven A large crow, especially the **great raven** (*Corvus corax*) of the N hemisphere; other species found in the N hemisphere and Australia; omnivorous; territorial; does not nest in colonies. (Genus: *Corvus*, 9 species.)

Ravenna [ravena] 44°25N 12°12E, pop (2000e) 142 000. Capital town of Ravenna province, Emilia-Romagna, NE Italy; 10 km/6 mi from the Adriatic Sea, connected by canal; capital of W Roman Empire in AD 409, and of later Ostrogothic and Byzantine rulers; archbishopric; railway; oil refining, natural gas, textiles, wine; Church of San Vitale (begun 526), with famous mosaics; cathedral (18th-c), octagonal baptistery (5th-c) in Church of Sant' Apollinare Nuovo, tomb of Empress Galla Placidia (5th-c), tomb of Theodoric (c.520); Dante celebrations (mid-Sep).

Ravi [rahvee] **River,** ancient **Hydraotes** River in NW India and Pakistan; one of the five rivers of the Punjab; rises in the SE Pir Panjal range; flows generally SW across the Pakistan Punjab, past Lahore, to join the R Chenab 53 km/33 mi NE of Multan; length 765 km/475 mi; part of the border between Pakistan and India.

Rawalpindi [rahwalpindee] 33°40N 73°08E, pop (2000e) 1 300 000. City in Punjab province, Pakistan, 258 km/160 mi NW of Lahore; strategically important location controlling routes to Kashmir; occupied by the British, 1849; interim capital, 1959–69; airfield; railway; military and commercial centre; oil refining, railway engineering, iron, chemicals, furniture, trade in grain, timber, wool.

rawindsonde [raywinsond] *radiosonde balloon*

Rawlings, Jerry J(ohn) (1947–) Ghanaian leader (1979, 1981–2001) and president (1992–2001), born in Accra, Ghana. He was at the centre of a coup in 1979, returning power to a civilian government a few months later. Despite being forcibly retired from the armed forces and discredited by the government he helped install, his popularity remained high, and he returned with his Armed Forces Revolutionary Council to seize power again at the end of 1981. Under pressure from aid donors to institute democratic reforms, in 1992 he announced a return to multi-party elections and was elected as president.

Rawls, John (Bordley) (1921–2002) Philosopher, born in Baltimore, Maryland, USA. He studied at Princeton, and taught at Princeton and Cornell before going to Harvard as professor in 1962. His best-known work, *A Theory of Justice* (1971), has probably been the most discussed text in social and political philosophy since World War 2, reviving an interest in social contract theory, rights, and liberalism.

Rawsthorne, Alan (1905–71) Composer, born in Haslingden, Lancashire, NW England, UK. He trained as a dentist, then turned to music, studying in Manchester and Berlin. He settled in London in 1935, and wrote a wide range of works, including three symphonies, eight concertos, choral and chamber music, and several film scores.

Ray, John (1627–1705) Naturalist, born in Black Notley, Essex, SE England, UK. He studied at Cambridge, where he became a fellow of Trinity College (1649), but lost his post at the Restoration for religious reasons. With a pupil, **Francis Willoughby** (1635–72), he travelled widely in Europe studying botany and zoology. His classification of plants, with its emphasis on the species as the basic unit, was the foundation of modern taxonomy, his major work being the three-volume *Historia Plantarum* (1686–1704).

Ray, Man, originally **Emanuel Rudnitsky** (1890–1976) Painter, photographer, and film-maker, born in Philadelphia, Pennsylvania, USA. He studied art in New York City, became a major figure in the development of Modernism, and co-founder of the New York Dadaist movement. He experimented with new techniques in painting and photography, became interested in filming, and in France made Surrealist films such as *Anemic Cinema* (1924) with Marcel Duchamp. During the 1930s he published and exhibited photographs and *rayographs* (photographic montages made without a camera).

Ray, Satyajit [riy] (1921–92) Film director, born in Kolkata (Calcutta), E India. He studied at Santiniketan University, then worked as a commercial artist while writing screenplays. His first film, *Pather Panchali* (1954, On the Road), was undertaken in his spare time with very limited finance. Its international success at the Cannes Film Festival allowed him to complete the trilogy with *Aparajito* (1956, The Unvanquished) and *Apu Sansar* (1959, The World of Apu), and he continued as India's leading film-maker. Later features include *The Kingdom of Diamonds* (1980), *Pickoo* (1982), *The Home and The World* (1984), and *An Enemy of the People* (1989). He received an Academy Lifetime Achievement Award in 1991.

ray Any of the numerous small to large bottom-dwelling cartilaginous fishes in families Anacanthobatidae, Pseudorajidae, Rajidae (skates and rays), Gymnuridae (butterfly ray), Rhinopteridae, Mobulidae (devil rays), Torpedinidae (electric rays), and Myliobatidae (eagle rays); front part of the body strongly flattened with broad pectoral fins; mouth and gill openings on the underside; tail typically slender and cylindrical; dorsal and tail fins very small.

Rayleigh scattering The scattering of light by objects which are small compared to the wavelength of light; varies as $(\text{frequency})^4$; described by British physicist Lord Rayleigh (1842–1919). The Rayleigh scattering of sunlight by air molecules makes the sky appear blue, since blue light is scattered more than other frequencies.

rayon A textile fibre formed from cellulose (a constituent of wood pulp), first produced late in the 19th-c. Improvements in manufacturing methods have made modern rayon fibres important as domestic and industrial materials.

Razi *Rhazes*

Razin, Stepan Timofeyevich [razeen], known as **Stenka Razin** (c.1630–71) Russian Cossack, and leader of a Cossack and peasant revolt (1670–1) directed against the boyars and landowning nobility. In April 1671 he was captured, taken to Moscow and publicly executed. He became a folk-hero celebrated in later legend and song as the embodiment of popular rebellion against authority.

razorbill An auk native to the N Atlantic (*Alca torda*); black bill, with vertical white stripe near tip; nests in colonies, often with guillemots.

razor shell A burrowing marine bivalve with two similar elongate shell valves; shell closed by two muscles; burrows actively in sand using a muscular foot. (Class: Pelecypoda. Order: Veneroida.)

Re [ray] or **Ra** [rah] In Egyptian religion, the ancient Sun-god of Heliopolis. As the creator, he emerged from the primaeval waters at the beginning of time. He is depicted as a falcon with the Sun's disc on his head: at night he appears as a ram-headed god who sails through the Underworld.

reactance In alternating current circuits containing inductors and capacitors, the factor which determines the phase relationship between current and voltage; symbol X, units Ω (ohms). It is the imaginary part of impedance, controlling the power input to the circuit.

reaction time (RT) The interval between the onset of a signal and the initiation of a voluntary response to it. The time (rarely less than a fifth of a second) varies according to the complexity of the situation, the number of possible alternative signals, and the choice of available responses. Measures of RT are used by psychologists to make inferences about processes in the central nervous system, and in applications such as the improvement of high-speed skills (eg in car-driving, piloting aircraft, ball-games).

reactive armour A form of protection for military vehicles such as tanks against the kind of 'hollow-charge' warhead typically used in infantry-fired antitank missiles; developed in Chobham, Surrey, it is also known as **Chobham armour**. This warhead is designed to burn its way through the armoured metal skin of the vehicle in a hot jet of gas and molten metal, rather than to smash its way in using simple kinetic energy. On impact from such a hollow-charge weapon, reactive armour itself detonates locally, neutralizing the attacking weapon's effects.

Read, Sir Herbert (Edward) (1893–1968) Poet and art critic, born near Kirkby Moorside, North Yorkshire, N England, UK. He was an assistant keeper at the Victoria and Albert Museum, London, then professor of fine art at Edinburgh (1931–3). He held several other academic posts, and became known as a poet and a writer on aesthetics in such works as *The Meaning of Art* (1931) and *The Philosophy of Modern Art* (1946). His *Collected Poems* were published in 1946. He was also director of the first major British design consultancy, the Design Research Unit. He was knighted in 1953.

Reading (UK) [reding] 51°28N 0°59W, pop (2001e) 143 100. Unitary authority (from 1998) and former county town of Berkshire, S England, UK; at the junction of the Kennet and Thames Rivers, 63 km/39 mi W of London; a centre of the textile industry in mediaeval times; railway; university (1926); rapidly developing commercial centre; brewing, boatbuilding, food processing, metal products, engineering, electronics, printing; 12th-c Benedictine abbey, burial place of Henry I; Hexagon (theatre), museum of English rural life (1951), museum of Greek archaeology; football league team, Reading (Royals).

readymade In modern art, any object not made by the artist but chosen by him or her and exhibited as a 'work of art'. Thus Duchamp exhibited a bottle-rack in 1914 and (most notoriously) a urinal, which he 'signed' R. Mutt and entitled 'Fountain' in 1917.

Reagan, Ronald (Wilson) [raygn] (1911–) US statesman and 40th president (1981–9), and former film and television actor, born in Tampico, Illinois, USA. He studied at Eureka College, IL, became a radio sports announcer, went to Hollywood (1937), and made over 50 films, beginning with *Love Is On the Air* (1937). Although originally a Democrat and supporter of liberal causes, he became increasingly anti-Communist, and in 1962 joined the Republican Party as an extreme right-winger. He became Governor of California in 1966, and stood unsuccessfully for the Republican presidential nomination in 1968 and 1976. In 1980 he defeated Jimmy Carter, and won a second term in 1984, defeating Walter Mondale. He introduced a major programme of economic change aimed at reducing government spending and inflation, took a strong anti-Communist stand, especially in the Middle East and Central America, and introduced the Strategic Defense Initiative. In 1981 he was wounded in an assassination attempt. During his second term, he backed off from his previous attitude of confrontation with the USSR, reaching a major arms-reduction accord with Soviet leader Gorbachev. His domestic popularity remained high throughout his presidency, despite charges of corruption against his aides, and his inability to get much of his programme through Congress.

Realism (art and literature) In art criticism, a term (especially with a capital R) referring to the deliberate choice of ugly or unidealized subject-matter, sometimes to make a social or political point. Thus Courbet's 'Stonebreakers' (1849) represented the hardship of the poorest class in France. Realism with a small 'r' is often used rather vaguely as the opposite of 'abstract'. More generally, in literature and art, the term refers to the advocacy of verisimilitude, as encountered in the Realist movement of mid-19th-c France, which flourished (as Naturalism) in the revolutionary scientific confidence of that era. The dislocation of reality in the 20th-c undermined conventional or 'naive' Realism, and a further qualification is now needed to make the term meaningful (eg 'surrealism', 'magic realism').

realism (philosophy) **1** The theory supporting the commonsense view that the world and its contents do not depend for their existence on the fact that some mind (whether human or divine) is aware of them. It is opposed to *idealism* and *phenomenalism*.

2 The theory held by Plato and others that universals (eg 'redness') or abstract entities (eg numbers) have a real existence outside the mind and apart from their instances. It is opposed to *nominalism*.

3 In the philosophy of science, the theory that scientific theories do describe the way the world really is, and succeed each other as progressive approximations to a fuller truth. It is opposed to *instrumentalism*.

Real Madrid [rayal madrid] Spanish football club, based in Madrid. Founded in 1902, it was a founder member of the Spanish League in 1928. Real have never been relegated and have been champion a record 27 times and cup winners 17 times. Their rivalry with Barcelona reflects regional and political tensions within Spain. The club was made world famous by winning the first five European Cup finals between 1956 and 1960, and its total of nine victories – subsequent wins in 1966, 1998, 2000, and 2002 – is still a record. Real were also UEFA Cup winners in 1985 and 1986. They were named 'Team of the Century' by FIFA in 1998, and later that year won the International Cup, to become World Club Champions. Its stadium, Estadio Santiago Bernabeu, was opened in 1947, and was the venue for the 1982 World Cup Final. Current capacity: 109 000.

real numbers *numbers*

real presence The belief that the body and blood of Christ are actually present in the bread and wine at communion (Eucharist/Mass). The nature of Christ's presence became the subject of great controversy at the Reformation.

real tennis An indoor racket-and-ball game played on a walled court, similar to rackets, but containing specifically designed hazards. A derivation of the French *jeu de paume* ('palm [of hand] game'), which was first played in the 11th-c. The racket developed in the 16th-c, and the game became very popular in the following century. Today, however, it is a minority sport, having been eclipsed by lawn tennis and other derivatives. It is also known as 'royal' or 'court' tennis.

real-time computing A notion which applies to those computing systems where near-simultaneous response to input data is a necessary requirement; examples include air-traffic control, point-of-sale terminals, military applications, and vehicle control. Interactive computing on larger computers is generally time-shared, and does not place the user in a real-time computing environment.

Reardon, Ray(mond) [reerdn] (1932–) Snooker player, born in Tredegar, Blaenau Gwent. SE Wales, UK. The first of the great snooker players of the modern era, he was dominant in the 1970s. Welsh amateur champion six times (1950–5), he turned professional in 1968, after careers as a miner and policeman. He was world professional champion six times (1970, 1973–6, 1978), and until 1982 was top of the snooker ratings.

reasoning Mental activity in which the reasoner moves from given information to a novel conclusion, in a series of steps that the reasoner can justify. Reasoning may be **deductive**, arriving at a conclusion from a set of premises (eg proving a theorem in mathematics), or **inductive**, when we try to create a new generalization based on available evidence. Psychologists have debated whether reasoning is based on some sort of internal mental logic, or whether more informal procedures (images, scenarios, or 'mental models') are used. Experimental investigations suggest that, when we attempt to reason, we are poor at handling negative information, and reluctant to seek evidence that will disconfirm currently-held beliefs.

Réaumur, René Antoine Ferchault de [rayohmür] (1683–1757) Polymath, born in La Rochelle, W France. He carried out research in metallurgy and glassmaking, and produced a major work on entomology. His thermometer (with spirit instead of mercury) has 80 degrees between the freezing-point and boiling-point.

Rebecca Riots A popular protest movement by Welsh peasants and agricultural labourers in W Wales in the late 1830s and early 1840s. An important target of the hostility was the heavy tolls imposed at toll-gates, but the riots were an expression of more general discontent with low wages and poor conditions. The rioters took their text from *Genesis* 24:60: 'And they blessed Rebecca and said unto her, let thy seed possess the gates of those which hate thee'. Each band of rioters had a Rebecca for a leader – often a man disguised as a woman. In 1844 an Act to 'consolidate and amend the Laws relating to Turnpike Trusts in Wales' ended the protest.

Rebellions of 1837 **1** A rebellion in Lower Canada (Quebec) generated by stalemate between the elected Legislative Assembly and the appointed Executive Council over control of provincial revenues. Led by Papineau and his Parti Patriote, it sought to locate authority in the largely Canadian Assembly. It was crushed by government troops after several brief confrontations.

2 Later in 1837, a rebellion in Upper Canada (Ontario), which opposed the oligarchical control exercised by the Family Compact, and the position of preferment enjoyed by the Church of England. Armed Radicals led by Mackenzie marched on Toronto to seize the government, but were repulsed by pro-government troops and volunteers. Mackenzie and Papineau both fled to the USA.

Reber, Grote [rayber] (1911–2002) Radio astronomer, born in Wheaton, Illinois, USA. An amateur ham radio operator, he was so intrigued by reports of Karl Jansky's 'cosmic static' that he built a parabolic dish, the first radio telescope, in his yard in Wheaton (1937). As the world's first radio astronomer, he published a radio map of the sky in 1944. He moved to Tasmania (1954), where he presided over a field of dipoles (antennas) 3500 ft in diameter while continuing his private research.

rebirthing A form of psychotherapy based on the idea that traumatic experiences at birth may result in negative thoughts and attitudes in later life. Regression back to birth and reliving the experience may allow these attitudes to be corrected. Various methods of regression are practised. **Water rebirthing** involves being submerged in a bath of water. In **group rebirthing**, the person to be reborn is enclosed tightly in a 'womb' formed by the bodies of the other members of the group, who press tightly against the candidate using cushions as buffers.

Rebuck, Gail (Ruth) [reebuhk], married name **Gould** (1952–) Publisher, born in London, UK. She studied at the University of Sussex, and entered publishing in 1975, first joining Grisewood & Dempsey, then moving to Robert Nicholson Publications (1976) and the Hamlyn Group (1978). Appointed publishing director at Century Publishing in 1982, she stayed with the company when it became Century Hutchinson (1985) and also when this was taken over by Random House (1989), and in 1991 became chair and chief executive of Random House UK.

rebus [reebuhs] The enigmatic representation in visual form of the sounds of a name or word. As a form of visual pun, rebuses are often used to puzzle or amuse, such as a drawing of a raygun (= 'Reagan'), or the letters CU (= 'see you'); some have become part of everyday writing, such as IOU (= 'I owe you'). They are an ancient means of communication, being found in early forms of picture-writing.

Récamier, (Jeanne Françoise) Julie (Adélaide) [ruhkamyay], *née* **Bernard** (1777–1849) Hostess, born in Lyon, SC France. Her salon became a fashionable meeting place, especially for former Royalists and those opposed to Napoleon. When her husband was financially ruined, she was forced to leave Paris (1805), returning in 1815. The most distinguished friend of her later years was Chateaubriand.

receptacle In flowering plants, the area at the tip of the flower-stalk to which the floral parts are attached. Usually convex, it may become swollen or expanded to enclose the carpels, and plays an important role in fruit formation.

receptors In physiology, specialized sites, usually within the cell membrane, which have evolved to bind and mediate the effects of neurotransmitters and hormones, but which also mediate the effects of many substances foreign to the body (such as drugs); also known as **binding sites**. As a consequence of the binding, intermediate factors are activated which trigger a cellular response.

recession An economic situation where demand is sluggish, output is not rising, and unemployment is on the increase. Not as severe a downturn as a depression, a recession is usually identified when gross domestic product falls for two successive quarters. Recession in the UK occurred in 1974–5 and 1980–2, and was internationally widespread in 1990–3.

recessive In genetics, a characteristic which becomes apparent only when an individual has inherited two copies of similar or identical alleles. The adjective is often misused, and should strictly be applied only to characteristics, and not to genes or alleles. In human genetic diseases inherited as autosomal recessives (eg cystic fibrosis), symptomless parents may each pass one mutant allele to their child, and the double dose leads to development of the disorder. In X-linked recessive diseases, the symptomless mother may pass a mutant allele to her son, who with a single X chromosome will then develop the disorder.

Recife [reseefay] 8°06S 34°53W, pop (2000e) 1 586 000. Port capital of Pernambuco state, NE Brazil, at the mouth of the R Capibaribe; consists of Recife proper (on a peninsula), Boa Vista (on the mainland), and Santo António (on an island between the two), all connected by bridges; most important commercial and industrial city in the NE; airport (Guararapes); two universities (1951, 1954); sugar, sugar refining, cotton, distilling, tourism; location of first Brazilian printing house, 1706; São Francisco de Assis Church (1612), Church of Conceição dos Militares (1708), Church of Nossa Senhora das Prazeres (1656), Forte do Brum (1629), Cinco Pontas (fort, built by Dutch 1630, altered by Portuguese 1677), Casa da Cultura (old prison), Museu do Açúcar (Sugar Museum).

Reciprocity A movement begun in British North America during the 1840s for the bilateral reduction of tariffs between the British colonies and the USA; it resulted in the Reciprocity Treaty of 1854. The treaty negotiations represented an important step in the growth of Canadian political autonomy. Arrangements became a source of discord in Washington, however, and the Treaty was dissolved by the USA in 1866. Attempts to renew Reciprocity failed up to 1911, when the idea was finally shelved until the 1980s.

recitative A type of musical declamation which allows the words to be delivered naturally and quickly, and is therefore indispensable in those types of all-sung opera, oratorio, and cantata in which dialogue and narrative are interrupted by long or numerous arias. 'Simple recitative' (*recitativó semplice* or *secco*) is accompanied only by continuo; 'accompanied recitative' (*recitativó accompagnato* or *stromentato*) by the orchestra.

recombinant DNA Hybrid (recombinant) nucleic acid molecules generated by genetic engineering technology through the use of *restriction enzymes* (present in many micro-organisms) that can cut double-stranded DNA molecules at a specific sequence, usually 4–8 base pairs. Each enzyme recognizes a different base sequence. DNA fragments produced by the cleavage with a particular restriction enzyme can be joined and the joint resealed through the use of an enzyme called DNA ligase, so that the molecules composed of the DNA segments from unrelated organisms may be artificially recombined to produce genes which do not occur in nature. The resulting recombinant genes are initially propagated in bacteria (or sometimes yeast) as part of independent circular DNA molecules known as plasmids. This technology is at the basis of numerous applications, including research into gene structure and function, screening for the presence of a particular disease gene (eg Huntington's chorea, cystic fibrosis, haemophilia), somatic gene therapy, and the generation of genetically modified organisms.

recommended daily allowance (RDA) A standard against which a population's intake of nutrients may be measured. The RDA for a nutrient is calculated to allow for individuals whose metabolic requirements are naturally high. For most nutrients this is achieved by increasing the RDA from the mean requirement to the mean plus two standard deviations. Some nutritionists feel that many RDAs are set excessively high by some expert committees.

RECONSAT An abbreviation of ***recon**naissance **sat**ellite*, a military space system placed into Earth orbit. It is equipped with cameras and other sensors capable of recording objects (such as military units) and activities on the ground, and relaying that information to Earth stations for analysis by intelligence experts.

reconstruction (linguistics) The process by which the sound system of an undocumented parent language can be 'constructed', by comparing the words in languages known (or suspected) to be related; also called **internal reconstruction**. Thus, the Indo-European form *pəter* ('father') is reconstructed by comparing such variants as Latin *pater* and Gothic *fadar*. An analysis of the systematic correspondences between *p*- and *f*- in these and other related languages leads to the postulation of *p* as the earlier first consonant in these words.

Reconstruction The period after the American Civil War when the South was occupied by Northern troops, while major changes went forward in its way of life. These included the destruction of slavery and the attempted integration of the freed black people. Reconstruction brought three amendments to the US Constitution, as well as bitter dispute over the extent of the needed changes. Resistance to it among white Southerners resulted in the founding of the Ku Klux Klan in 1866. Once scorned by historians as a 'tragic era' of corruption, Reconstruction is now seen as a period of necessary but incomplete social change. The era ended in 1877, when a bargain among politicians gave a disputed presidential election to the Republicans in return for 'home' (ie white) rule in the South. Once white rule was fully restored, a policy of racial segregation was imposed to keep black people firmly subordinate.

recorder (law) In the legal system of England and Wales, a part-time judge. Those appointed are barristers or solicitors. Recorders sit mainly in the Crown Court. There are also Recorder's Courts in the USA, chiefly handling criminal cases at the municipal level.

recorder (music) A type of end-blown duct flute in two or three jointed sections, with seven fingerholes and a thumbhole. It is made of wood or (in recent times) plastic in various sizes, the most common being the **descant** and the **treble**. By the end of the 18th-c it was superseded by the transverse flute, but it was revived in the 20th-c as a school instrument and for playing early music, and several modern composers have written for it.

recording *sound recording*

record player The successor to the gramophone, following the advent in the 1920s of the use of electricity in the recording and reproducing processes. It was essentially a turntable, pick-up, and arm which reproduced the music or other sounds recorded on discs (gramophone records), usually through its own amplifier and speaker.

rectifier A device that changes alternating current (AC), which continuously reverses direction, into direct current (DC), by allowing it to flow in one direction only. Electric lights and motors use alternating current, but in general most electronic equipment needs direct current. Semiconductor diodes can be used as rectifiers.

rectilinear motion *mechanics*

rector In the Church of England, the parish priest receiving full tithe rents; in other Anglican churches, generally a parish priest. In Roman Catholicism, the term denotes the priest in charge of a religious house, college, or school. In some countries (eg Scotland), it refers to the senior officer of a university, elected by students.

rectum That part of the gastro-intestinal tract between the sigmoid colon and the anal canal. When gastro-intestinal contents enter the rectum, the individual has the urge to defaecate. Partial (mucous membrane and submucosa layer) or complete (whole thickness of the rectal wall) prolapse of the rectum is relatively common, and has many causative factors (eg muscle damage during childbirth, poor muscle tone in the elderly).

recycling Putting waste substances back into productive use, a procedure advocated by many conservationists. It is a means of reducing the demand on non-renewable resources, and of preventing problems of pollution and waste disposal. Examples include the pulping of waste paper to make recycled paper, the existence of bottle banks to collect used glass, and the smelting of metals from scrap. Incentives for recycling can be provided by government subsidies or by a deposit tax on containers.

red admiral A large butterfly found widely in the N hemisphere; upperside of wings black with scarlet bands and patches of white and blue; caterpillars commonly found on nettles; overwinter as adults. (Order: Lepidoptera. Family: Nymphalidae.)

red algae A large and diverse group of alga-like plants, ranging in form from single cells to large differentiated bodies; reddish colour stems from the mixture of photosynthetic pigments, chlorophyll *a*, phycobiliproteins, and carotenoids inside the cells; reproduction involves the production of an egg cell inside a specialized organ (*oogonium*) receptive to the male gamete. (Class: Rhodophyceae.)

Red Army (China) Communist army built up by Zhu De at Mao Zedong's Jiangxi soviet after 1927. It was distinguished by more egalitarian command, disciplined treatment of civilians, the dissemination of political ideas, and the use of guerrilla tactics. It retreated N on the Long March (1934–5) to escape Nationalist pressure. Between 1936 and 1945 it grew from 22 000 to 900 000. In the civil war after 1945, it defeated the Nationalist forces, having been reorganized as the **People's Liberation Army (PLA)** in 1946. Since the establishment of the People's Republic (1949), the army has occupied Tibet (1950) and suppressed rebellion there (1959), intervened in Korea (1950–3), defeated India in the Himalayas (1962), and restored order (1967) during the Cultural Revolution. PLA forces also carried out the Beijing massacre (1989). Reversals on the Russian border (1969) and the unsuccessful invasion of Vietnam (1979) led to the army's reconstruction in the 1980s, and its reduction from four to three million.

Red Army (USSR) The Red Army of Workers and Peasants (*RKKA*, *Rabochekrest'yanshi Krasny*), the official name of the army of the Soviet Union (1918–45). It was the most important land force engaged in the defeat of Nazi Germany (1941–5), and later became the most powerful land force in the world.

red-brick universities Those English universities founded in the late 19th-c or first half of the 20th-c in the provincial cities: Manchester (1880; new charter 1903), Liverpool (1903; affiliated to Manchester, 1884–1903), Leeds (1904; affiliated to Manchester, 1887–1904), Birmingham (1900), Sheffield (1905), Bristol (1909), Reading (1926), Southampton (1952, University College 1902), Exeter (1955, University College, 1922), and Leicester (1957, University College 1918).

Red Brigade, Ital **Brigate Rosse** A left-wing Italian terrorist group which began operating in 1974 as a response to the failure of the New Left, involved in bombings and killings. Its activities were largely directed at the kidnapping and killing of Italian judges, politicians, and businessmen, such as the former Italian premier Aldo Moro in 1978. In 1984 it split into two factions Several leading members were imprisoned, and the gang became less prominent during the following decade.

red cedar A species of *arbor vitae* (*Thuja plicata*), native to North America, which yields red timber. (Family: Cupressaceae.) It is also the commercial name for timber from the American species of juniper, *Juniperus virginiana*, often used for pencils.

Red Crescent *Red Cross*

Red Cross An international agency founded by the Geneva Convention (1864) to assist those wounded or captured in war. There are national branches; the British Red Cross performs relief duties throughout the world; the American Red Cross also runs a blood supply service. All branches use the symbol of the red cross on a white ground, except Muslim branches, which use the red crescent, Israel, which uses a red Star of David, and Iran, which uses a red lion and sun.

red currant A species of currant (*Ribes rubrum*) native to W Europe. It produces edible red berries on old wood. The **white currant** is merely a white-berried form. (Family: Grossulariaceae.)

red deer A true deer (*Cervus elephas*) widespread in the temperate N hemisphere (introduced in Australia and New Zealand); also known as the **Bactrian deer**, **Yarkand deer**, **maral**, **shou**, **hangul**, or (in North America) **wapiti** or **elk**; sometimes farmed; pale brown in summer, darker in winter. Each antler usually has five tines (the *Swedish* form); if each has six, the stag is a *Royal*; if each has seven, it is a *Wilson*.

red dwarf A small, cool star, 0·5–0·1 the mass and diameter of the Sun, and 100–100 000 times fainter than the Sun. Red dwarfs are probably the most abundant type of star, but are difficult to see because they are so dim. Two of the nearest stars to the Sun, Proxima Centauri and Barnard's Star, are red dwarfs.

redemption The belief that through the work of Jesus Christ humanity is enabled to be released from a state of sin to a state of grace with God. The term was originally applied to the purchase of the liberty of a slave.

Redford, (Charles) Robert (1937–) Actor and director, born in Santa Barbara, California, USA. He dropped out of college to study art and acting, and good performances on Broadway and on television led to engagements in Hollywood, but without great success until the film version of his stage role in *Barefoot in the Park* (1967). Major star parts soon followed, as in *Butch Cassidy and the Sundance Kid* (1969), *The Sting* (1973), *All the President's Men* (1976), and *Out of Africa* (1985). Later films include *Indecent Proposal* (1993) and *Up Close and Personal* (1996). As a director he made the Olympics-based skiing film *Downhill Racer* in 1969, was awarded an Oscar for *Ordinary People* (1980), and directed *A River Runs Through It* (1993), acclaimed for its cinematography. In 1998 he directed and starred in *The Horse Whisperer*, and later appearances include *Spy Game* (2001) and *The Clearing* (2003). He established the Sundance Institute in 1981 to encourage new talent and the creation of independent feature films. He received an Academy Lifetime Achievement Award in 2002.

red fox A fox native to Europe (*Vulpes vulpes*), temperate Asia, N Africa, and North America (introduced in Australia); usually red-brown with white underparts (**red fox**); sometimes black (**black fox**), silvery grey (**silver fox**), or with a black cross on the back (**cross fox**).

red giant A cool red star, 10–100 times the radius of the Sun, and hundreds of thousands of times as luminous, but of similar mass. It develops in a late stage of stellar evolution, after the main sequence, when hydrogen in the core is exhausted and the outer layers expand.

red gram *pigeon pea*

Redgrave, Sir Michael (Scudamore) (1908–85) Actor, born in Bristol, SW England, UK. He studied at Cambridge, became a teacher, and began his acting career at the Liverpool Playhouse in 1934. His many notable stage performances included Richard II (1951), Prospero (1952), Antony (1953), and Uncle Vanya (1962), and he also had a distinguished film career, starting with his appearance in Hitchcock's *The Lady Vanishes* (1938). He was knighted in 1959, and his autobiography *In My Mind's Eye* appeared in 1983. He married the actress **Rachel Kempson** (1910–2003) in 1935, and their three children are all actors; **Vanessa**, **Corin** (1939–), and **Lynn** (1944–).

Redgrave, Steve, properly **Sir Steven Geoffrey Redgrave** (1962–) Rower, born in Marlow, Buckinghamshire, SE England, UK. His main event is the heavyweight coxless pairs. He was the winner of five consecutive gold Olympic medals from 1984 to 2000, a feat accomplished by no other Olympic athlete. He was also the winner of six World Championship gold medals and three Commonwealth Games gold medals, more than any other rower. In 2003 he received the Golden Personality award at the 50th anniversary BBC Sports Personality of the Year awards. He received a knighthood in 2001.

Redgrave, Vanessa (1937–) Actress, born in London, UK, the daughter of actor Michael Redgrave. She trained at the Central School of Speech and Drama, London, joined the Royal Shakespeare Company in the 1960s, and took the lead in several feature films, including *Morgan, a Suitable Case for Treatment* (1966), *The Devils* (1971), and *Julia* (1977, Oscar). Later films include *The Bostonians* (1983), *The Ballad of the Sad Cafe* (1991), *Howard's End* (1992), *Mission Impossible* (1996), *Wilde* (1997), *Mrs Dalloway* (1998), and *The Cradle Will Rock* (1999). Other work includes *The Gathering Storm* (2002) for television, and in 2003 she won a Tony Award for her performance in a revival of *Long Day's Journey into Night*. She is also well known for her active support of left-wing causes. In 1999 she turned down the opportunity to become a dame, refusing to accept the honour from a government run by Tony Blair.

red grouse A reddish-brown grouse, native to the British Is; originally considered a separate species, *Lagopus scoticus*; now treated as a subspecies of the widespread N hemisphere **willow grouse** (*Lagopus lagopus*).

Redgrove, Peter (William) (1932–2003) Poet and writer, born in Kingston-upon-Thames, Surrey. He was educated at Taunton School and at Cambridge, where he became a friend of Ted Hughes and a founder member of an association of poets, the Group. His books include *The Moon Disposes: Poems 1954–87* (1987), and he also wrote numerous novels, plays, and non-fiction works, including a pioneering work with his second wife, **Penelope Shuttle** (1947–): *The Wise Wound: Menstruation and Every Woman* (1978). In 1996 he was awarded the Queen's Medal for Poetry.

Red Guards Young radical Maoist activists (mostly students) who spread the 1966 Cultural Revolution across China, destroying whatever was 'old', and rebelling against all 'reactionary' authority. The first Red Guards were a group formed in Qinghua University in Beijing on whom Mao bestowed his blessing at a mass rally in the capital in 1966.

red-hot poker A perennial native to S Africa (*Kniphofia uvaria*); leaves greyish, narrow, tapering; flowers tubular, downward-angled, red, turning orange then yellow with age, in dense, poker-shaped spikes on stems up to 2 m/6½ ft high. Numerous hybrids of various stature and flower colour are cultivated for ornament. (Family: Liliaceae.)

red ink plant *pokeweed*

red mullet Colourful marine fish widespread in tropical and warm temperate seas; body elongate, underside rather straight, upper surface of head strongly curved; mouth with pair of large chin barbels; includes commercially important European species, *Mullus surmuletus*; also called **goatfish**. (Family: Mullidae, 3 genera.)

Redon, Odilon [ruhdõ] (1840–1916) Artist, born in Bordeaux, SW France. He is usually regarded as a pioneer Surrealist, because of his use of dream images in his work. He made many charcoal drawings and lithographs, but after 1900 painted, especially in pastel, pictures of flowers and portraits in intense colour.

redpoll Either of two species of finch of genus *Carduelis*, especially the **common redpoll**, with subspecies **mealy redpoll**, **lesser redpoll**, and **Greenland redpoll** (*Carduelis flammea*); also the **Arctic redpoll** or **Hornemann's redpoll** (*Carduelis hornemanni*); native to the N hemisphere, and introduced in New Zealand. (Family: Fringillidae.)

Red River (China), Chin **Yuan Jiang**, Vietnamese **Song Hong** River rising in C Yunnan province, China, SW of Kunming; flows SE into Vietnam to meet the Gulf of Tongking in a large delta, 32 km/20 mi E of Haiphong; length, c.800 km/500 mi.

Red River (USA) River in S USA; rises in N Texas in the Llano Estacado; forms the Texas–Oklahoma and Texas–Arkansas borders; above Baton Rouge, enters two distributaries; the Atchafalaya R flows S to the Gulf of Mexico; the Old R joins the Mississippi; length 1966 km/1222 mi; major tributaries the Pease, Wichita, Washita, Little, Black; used for flood-control, irrigation, hydroelectricity; navigable to Shreveport.

Red River Colony A British colony founded by the Earl of Selkirk in Rupert's Land (Manitoba) on the Assiniboine and Red Rivers in 1812. It was an English- and Gaelic-speaking colony in an area dominated by Indian and Métis fur traders and farmers. It was the focus of ethnic, racial, and commercial rivalries, culminating in the Battle of Seven Oaks (1816). From the 1820s, anglophone Protestant 'country-born' settlers and francophone Catholic Métis developed side by side in relative harmony until 1869–70.

Red River Rebellion A movement for self-determination in 1869–70 by the resident Métis population of Red River Colony, Canada (now Manitoba), which broke out when control over trading rights passed from the Hudson Bay Company to the Dominion of Canada. Led by Louis Riel, the Métis and anglophone 'mixed-bloods' established a provisional government (1870). Armed conflict followed, and a leader of a failed Anglo-Protestant counter-rising, Thomas Scott, was executed by the Métis. Although Canada agreed to the terms of the rebels (in the Manitoba Act, 1870), Orange opinion in Ontario was so outraged by the execution of Scott that Riel was obliged to flee the country.

Red Rum Racehorse. He is the only horse to have won the Grand National steeplechase three times – in 1973 and 1974, ridden by Brian Fletcher, and in 1977, ridden by Tommy Stack.

red salmon *sockeye*

Red Sea, ancient **Sinus Arabicus** area c.453 000 sq km/175 000 sq mi. NW arm of the Indian Ocean, between the Arabian Peninsula and Egypt, Sudan, and Ethiopia; occupies the rift valley which stretches S into the African continent; connected to the Mediterranean Sea by the Suez Canal; divided into the Gulfs of Suez and Aqaba by the Sinai Peninsula (NW); a narrow sea, up to 360 km/225 mi wide, 2335 km/1450 mi long; maximum depth, 2200 m/7200 ft near the centre; many islands; coral reefs parallel to shores; high salinity; name probably derives from reddish seaweed found here; major trade route, especially since Suez Canal (1869).

red setter *Irish setter*

redshank Either of two species of sandpiper of genus *Tringa*, especially the **common redshank** (*Tringa totanus*), from Europe and Asia; also the **spotted redshank** (*Tringa erythropus*), from Scandinavia, Europe, and Asia; long red legs; long dark bill with red base.

red sheep *mouflon*

redshift The displacement of features in the spectra of astronomical objects, particularly galaxies and quasars, towards the longer wavelengths. This is generally interpreted as a result of the Doppler effect resulting from the expansion of the universe.

Red Spot, Great *Jupiter* (astronomy)

Red Square The central square of Moscow. Its Russian name (*Krasnaya Ploshchad*) derives from the Old Slavonic *krasny* ('beautiful' or 'red'). The translation of 'red' became established only in the 20th-c. Historically the site of executions, demonstrations, and processions, the square became the scene of parades every May and November.

red squirrel A small tree-dwelling squirrel; coat reddish-brown (dark brown or white forms exist); inhabits woodland, especially coniferous forest; four species: the **European red squirrel** (*Sciurus vulgaris*) from Europe and Asia, and the **North American red squirrels** or **chickarees** of genus *Tamiasciurus*.

redstart An Old World thrush of genus *Phoenicurus* (11 species), *Sheppardia* (2 species), or *Rhyacornis* (2 species); also, a New World warbler of genus *Myioborus* (11 species) or *Setophaga* (1 species).

Red Terror (1918–21) The Bolshevik campaign of terror and anarchy that followed the Russian Revolution of 1917. It was carried out systematically by the Cheka (Secret Police) and loosely-organized Red Army forces during and after the Russian Civil War (1918–20) against potential political opponents and 'class enemies' – especially the bourgeoisie, former aristocracy, and peasants who resisted the seizing of grain for the war. Atrocities were committed on both sides. The tsar and his family were executed along with 200 000 other Russians, as territory changed hands between the Red Army and the White Russian forces in the Crimea, Poland, Siberia, Moscow, N Russia and Vladivostok. Lenin justified terror as a means of obtaining and maintaining power; class, not deeds, was enough to confirm guilt.

reduced instruction set computer (RISC) A computer using a very small and relatively simple instruction set, which allows faster processing and greater compatibility in design between computers.

reducing agent A substance which reduces another in a chemical reaction, being itself oxidized in the process. An important example is hydrogen gas (H_2), which is oxidized to water when it reduces a metal oxide.

reduction A chemical process involving the gain of electrons, always accompanied by oxidation, the loss of electrons. It often involves the gain of hydrogen or the loss of oxygen by a compound.

reductionism In philosophy, an attempt to explain or define one set of concepts or theories in terms of another which is more basic or less complex. For example, the view that human behaviour can be 'reduced to' animal behaviour, or animal behaviour to the physical laws of matter (so that psychology and biology reduce to physics).

redundancy Dismissal of employees whose work is no longer needed. This may occur through a fall in the demand for their products, through new labour practices of outsourcing the work to a self-employed worker, or through technical progress leading to mechanization or automation of production. If the need for labour falls slowly, adjustment may be possible through natural wastage, ie not replacing those who leave. If demand falls quickly, redundancies occur. In some countries, workers may have a legal right to minimum compensation for redundancy by statutory instrument; in the UK, for example, this usually applies to full-time workers with over 2 years service. Payments may be greater, and may include some workers without a legal entitlement, as the price of industrial peace. Employers often prefer to offer sufficiently favourable terms to induce voluntary redundancy, to preserve the morale of their remaining workforce; where this fails, compulsory redundancies may occur.

red valerian *valerian*

redwing A thrush native to Europe, Asia, and N Africa (*Turdus iliacus*); speckled breast, red sides, and cream 'eyebrow'; migrates S in autumn, often with fieldfares. The name is also used for the **red-winged blackbird** (Family: Icteridae) and the **redwing francolin** (Family: Phasianidae).

redwood *coast redwood; dawn redwood*

Redwood National park in N California, USA, on the Pacific coast; protects the Coast redwood trees (*Sequoia sempervirens*), among the tallest in the world; area 228 sq km/88 sq mi.

Redwood, John (1951–) British politician, born in Dover, Kent, SE England, UK. Educated at Oxford, he worked with a merchant bank before being appointed head of Margaret Thatcher's Policy Unit in 1983. Elected Conservative MP for Wokingham in 1987, he became a junior minister in the Department of Trade and Industry before being made secretary of state for Wales (1993–5). He came to national attention when he resigned from the cabinet in 1995 to challenge John Major as leader of the Conservative Party, expressing the views of the party's right wing. His vigorous campaign attracted unexpected levels of support, and he was a strong but unsuccessful contender for leadership of his party, following Major's resignation in 1997. He became shadow secretary-of-state for trade and industry (1997-2000) under William Hague.

Reed, Sir Carol (1906–76) Film director, born in London, UK. He studied at Canterbury, and became an actor and director, joining the cinema in 1930. He produced or directed several major films, such as *Kipps* (1941), *The Fallen Idol* (1948), and *Oliver!* (1968, Oscar), but is best known for *The Third Man* (1949), depicting the sinister underworld of post-war, partitioned Vienna, based on the book by Graham Greene. He was knighted in 1952.

Reed, Walter (1851–1902) Army surgeon, born in Belroi, Virginia, USA. He entered the medical corps in 1875, and was appointed professor of bacteriology in the Army Medical College, Washington, DC, in 1893. Investigations carried out by him in 1900 proved that the transmission of yellow fever was by mosquitoes, and his research led to the eventual eradication of this disease from Cuba. The Walter Reed Hospital in Washington is named after him.

reed A tall grass (*Phragmites australis*) with far-creeping rhizomes, found almost everywhere; stout, erect stems 2–3 m/6–10 ft high; panicle nodding, soft, dull purple. It forms vast beds in swamps or shallow water, and is used for good-quality thatch. (Family: Gramineae.)

reedbuck An African grazing antelope of genus *Redunca*; pale brown with white underparts; male with horns curving forward at tip; female without horns; inhabits long grass and reeds near water; three species: **southern**, **mountain** and **bohor reedbucks**.

reed instrument Any woodwind instrument whose sound is produced by a stream of air causing a 'reed' (which may be of cane, metal, or plastic) to vibrate. The reed may be single (as in the clarinet) or double (as in the oboe); it may vibrate freely (as in the harmonica and the crumhorn) or be controlled by the player's lips (as in all orchestral reed instruments). Each type has a distinctive timbre, which is further affected by the size and shape of the instrument. The main orchestral reed instruments are the oboe, cor anglais, clarinet, bass clarinet, bassoon, and double bassoon.

reedling A small, long-tailed babbler (*Panurus biarmicus*), native to S Asia and Europe; male pale brown with grey head and black vertical bar on face; inhabits reedbeds and swamps; eats insects, berries, and seeds; also known as the **bearded reedling**, or **bearded tit**.

reedmace An aquatic perennial (*Typha latifolia*), more or less cosmopolitan; stems robust, growing to 2·5 m/8 ft; leaves grass-like; flowers tiny, grouped into a distinctive inflorescence, the hairy female florets forming a furry, brown cylinder surmounted by a plume composed of male flowers all reduced to clusters of stamens; also called **cat's-tail**, **false bulrush** and, erroneously, **bulrush**. It often forms extensive reed-swamps. (Family: Typhaceae.)

reed organ A musical instrument in which reeds, brought into play by means of one or more keyboards, are made to vibrate freely by air under pressure from bellows. Smaller models, such as the harmonium, have only one manual, and the bellows are powered by a foot treadle; larger ones may have two manuals and a pedalboard, the bellows being operated by a separate lever or by an electric motor. Reed organs were at one time popular as domestic instruments and also in small churches, being less expensive and requiring less space than pipe organs. In the 20th-c the demand gradually switched to electronic organs.

reed warbler An Old World warbler, especially the **reed warbler** (*Acrocephalus scirpaceus*) from Europe, SW Asia, and Africa; inhabits reed beds and parks; eats insects, berries, and molluscs. (Genus: *Acrocephalus*, 14 species.)

reef *atoll*

reefer A vessel designed to carry refrigerated cargoes in specially cooled and insulated compartments. Modern cargoes include carcases of beef, dairy produce, and most kinds of fruit.

reel In photography, (1) a flanged spool on which long lengths of film or tape may be wound, or (2) the roll of motion picture film that forms a convenient length for handling a section of a programme during editing and printing. A typical feature film comprises 5 or 6 reels, each 500–600 m/1600–2000 ft in length.

Reeve, Christopher (1952–) Film actor, born in New York City, USA. He had various stage and television roles before becoming universally known as the star of *Superman* and its sequels (1978, 1980, 1983, 1987). Later films include *Noises Off* (1992) and *Morning Glory* (1994). In 1994 he became paralysed from the neck downwards and wheel-chair bound following a horse-riding accident, but acted again in *Village of the Damned* (1995) and various television productions, including *Rear Window* (1998). He is also much involved in campaigns supporting handicapped children and paraplegics.

reeve *ruff*

Reeves, Keanu [keeahnoo] (1964–) Film actor, born in Beirut, Lebanon. He acted in several Canadian television plays, and had a small part in *Youngblood* (1986) before gaining attention for his performance in *The River's Edge* (1986). *Bill and Ted's Excellent Adventure* (1989), and its sequel, *Bill and Ted's Bogus Journey* (1991), brought him international recognition. Later films include *Much Ado About Nothing* (1993), *Speed* (1994), and *The Matrix* (1999) and its sequels, *The Matrix Reloaded* and *Matrix Revolutions* (both 2003).

referendum A device of direct democracy whereby the electorate can pronounce, usually for or against, on some measure put before it by government; also known as a **plebiscite**. In some countries a petition of sufficient voters can put an issue to a referendum. Most commonly referenda are held on constitutional changes (eg women's suffrage, as in Switzerland), rather than on government policy.

reflation In economics, government action designed to stimulate an economy which is in a period of recession. Strategies include increasing government expenditure, lowering taxes, and reducing interest rates.

reflectance *reflection*

reflecting telescope *telescope*

reflection In physics, the bouncing off from a suitable surface of a beam of light, sound, or other wave at an angle equal to that of the incident beam. Light is reflected by shiny (eg metal) surfaces, and at a change in refractive index (eg in passing from air to glass). Sound is reflected by hard, smooth surfaces and in passing through a change in air density. **Reflectance** is the measured ratio of incident intensity to reflected intensity.

reflex A rapid, involuntary, and stereotyped action made by an animal in response to a particular stimulus involving the central nervous system. An example is the rapid withdrawal of the hand after touching a very hot surface.

reflex camera A camera in which an image of the scene being photographed is shown on the viewfinder screen by way of a mirror. In **single-lens reflex** (**SLR**) types, the mirror is at 45° behind the camera lens and is automatically swung out of the way immediately before exposure. The **twin-lens reflex** has two matched lenses coupled for focusing, one for the viewfinder alone and the other with shutter and diaphragm for the camera proper.

reflexology An ancient system of diagnosis and treatment, dating from c.3000 BC, based on the belief that an image of the entire body, including the internal organs, is represented on the surface of the foot. Although reflexology zones do not correspond exactly to acupuncture meridians, diagnosis is based on the same principles as found in traditional Chinese medicine, where illness is seen as due to blockage of energy flow. Palpation of the feet locates sites of tenderness or crystalline deposits beneath the skin which relate to the sites of blockage, and treatment is given by pressure and massage to disperse the blockages and stimulate the internal organs. Although reflexology is not effective for treatment of surgical problems or structural abnormalities, there are many reports of success in treating functional disorders such as headaches, constipation, and stress-induced disorders.

reflex projection In special effects cinematography, a system of front projection onto a highly reflective directional beaded screen by way of a semi-silvered mirror. Foreground action and projected background can then be photographed together through the mirror by a camera whose lens axis coincides with that of the projector – hence also known as **front axial projection**.

Reform Acts Legislation in Britain which altered parliamentary constituencies, increased the size of the electorate, and enfranchised the majority of the adult population of the country. The main Acts were: **1832** (known as the **Great Reform Act**), which gave the vote to almost all male members of the middle classes, introduced a uniform £10 franchise in the boroughs and enfranchised the new industrial towns, which had hitherto been unrepresented. However, the bulk of the population (all women and five-sixths of the men) were still without a vote. The Reform Act of **1867** gave the vote to all settled tenants in the boroughs thus creating a substantial working-class male franchise for the first time. The Act of **1884** extended a similar franchise to rural and mining areas and to domestic servants. The Act of **1885** aimed to create parliamentary constituencies of broadly equal size. The Representation of the People Act of **1918** created a universal male suffrage and gave the vote to propertied, educated women of 30 years and over. Universal suffrage for everyone over 21 was finally achieved in **1928**. In **1969** the minimum voting age was lowered from 21 years to 18. The 1832 Reform Act was the subject of furious controversy, and was preceded by widespread radical agitation, as was the Representation of the People Act of 1918, which led to riots, hunger strikes, and imprisonment.

Reformation The Protestant reform movements in the Christian Church, inspired by and derived from Martin Luther, John Calvin, and others in 16th-c Europe. A complex phenomenon, various factors are common to all reforms: a Biblical revival and translation of the Word of God into the vernacular; an improvement in the intellectual and moral standards of the clergy; emphasis on the sovereignty of God; and insistence that faith and scriptures are at the centre of the Christian message. Non-religious factors aiding the spread of the Reformation included the invention of the printing press; the political, social and economic uncertainties of the age; and a general feeling of revival caused by the Renaissance.

In Germany, Luther's 'ninety-five theses' (1517) questioned the authority of the Church and led to his excommunication. The Lutheran Church then spread rapidly, in Switzerland under Zwingli and later under Calvin, neither of whom allowed any form of worship or devotion not explicitly warranted by scripture. The authority of scripture, the cornerstone of the Reformation, required a degree of ecclesiastical authority (and power) to justify and maintain it. The doctrine of the priesthood of all believers and the importance placed on preaching the Word of God led to an educated clergy, and decentralized church communities were better able to prevent abuse of ecclesiastical privilege. In England, Henry VIII declared that the king was the supreme head of the English Church, and appropriated Church property; in 1549 the Book of Common Prayer, embodying Reformation doctrine, was published, and under Elizabeth I a strong anti-papal stance was taken. In Scotland, under the influence of Calvin and the leadership of John Knox, the Presbyterian Church of Scotland was established in 1560, and remains the national Church. The Reformation also took root as Lutheran and Reformed Churches in France, Scandinavia, Czechoslovakia, Hungary, Romania, and Poland.

Reformation, Catholic *Counter-Reformation*

Reformed Churches Churches deriving from Calvin's Reformation in 16th-c Geneva, adopting a conciliar or presbyterian form of Church government. They are now worldwide in extent, with most being members of the World Alliance of Reformed Churches.

Reformed Church in America A Christian denomination established in 1628 with the organization of the Collegiate Church for the early Dutch Reformed settlers. It gained its independence in 1770, was incorporated as the Reformed Protestant Church in 1819, and adopted its current name in 1867. In 1784 it established the New Brunswick Theological Seminary, the oldest Protestant seminary in the USA.

reformism Any doctrine or movement that advocates gradual social and political change rather than revolutionary change; most commonly applied to socialism. The underlying premise is that democratic procedures provide the most suitable means through which to build social change.

Reform Judaism A movement beginning in early 19th-c Germany for the reform of Jewish worship, ritual, and beliefs in the light of modern scholarship and knowledge. Greater emphasis is placed on the ethical teachings of the prophets than on ritual law, and reason and experience are primary in the assessment of belief.

Reform Party A Canadian political party, established to articulate discontent in the W of the country. It captured the third largest number of seats in the 1993 general election, almost all from Alberta and British Columbia.

refracting telescope *telescope*

refraction *see panel*

refractive index A measurement of the ratio of velocity of light (or other electromagnetic wave) in a vacuum to that in matter; symbol n; always greater than 1; n(air) = 1·0003, n(water) = 1·33, so the velocity of light in water is about 75% of that in air.

refractories Materials which are neither deformed nor chemically changed by exposure to high temperatures. This makes them suitable for containers, structural materials, and components, particularly in metallurgical operations, such as furnace linings. Naturally occurring refractories include silica, fireclay, and alumina. Synthetic refractories include the high-melting carbides and nitrides used in nuclear power plant.

refrigerator An insulated enclosed space, with a cooling mechanism to reduce its temperature, which preserves foodstuffs for short periods. The earlier *ice-house* used ice as a coolant, but from c.1875 mechanical means were introduced (originally for ship's refrigerators), compressing a coolant outside to allow it to expand inside and thus absorb heat. From c.1910 domestic models were available, and became largely universal by the late 1960s; they run at 4°C. A colder-running version (at c.–20°C) is the *deep freeze*, which can store food for some months.

refraction

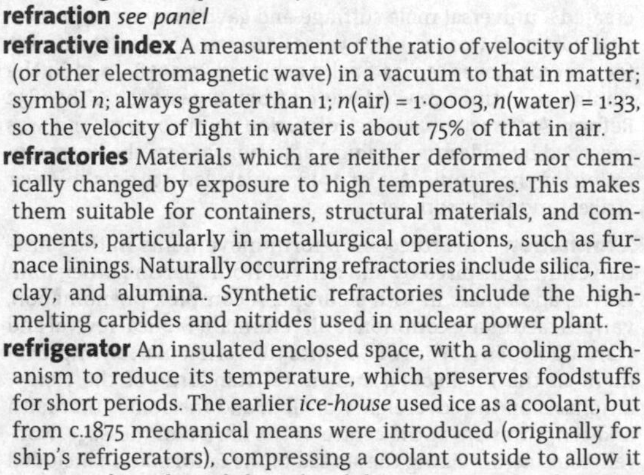

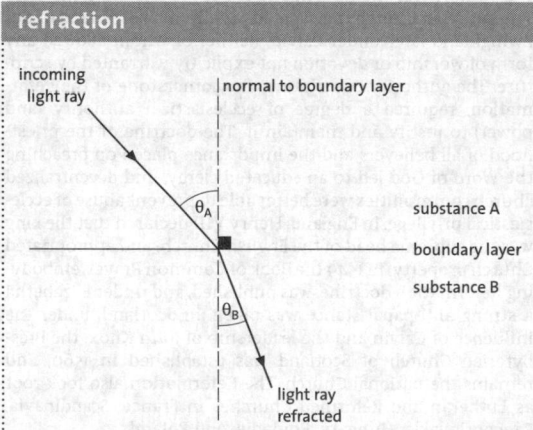

A change in the direction of a wave as it passes from one medium to another in which the wave velocity is different, for example a sound wave passing from hot to cold air. It is expressed by Snell's law, $\sin \theta_A / \sin \theta_B$ = constant. The illustration shows a wave having a velocity in substance B which is less than its velocity in substance A. If the wave was light and substance A was a vacuum, $\sin \theta_{vac} / \sin \theta_B = n_B$, the refractive index of substance B. Light passing into a substance of higher refractive index is bent towards normal. The distortion of partially submerged objects, rainbows, and mirages are all caused by the refraction of light.

refuse-derived fuel 1 Garbage from which metallic and mineral inclusions have been removed, so that it can be fed into a suitably designed furnace. It is often used for generating electricity or district heating.
2 The product of small-scale fermentation of domestic and animal waste to produce gas (*methane*) for domestic use. The process has been promoted particularly in some rural areas in Third World countries.

regal A small portable reed organ, in use during the 16th–17th-c. The wind pressure was maintained by two small bellows directly behind the keyboard.

Regency Style An elegant Neoclassical style current in England at the beginning of the 19th-c, with late 18th-c antecedents. Like the Empire Style in France, it made bold use of Greek motifs, such as the key-pattern, and Egyptian devices inspired by the campaigns against Napoleon on the Nile (1798–1800). The work of John Nash was particularly important.

Regensburg [**ray**gnzboorg], Fr **Ratisbon**, ancient **Castra Regina** 49°01N 12°07E, pop (2000e) 126 000. Commercial city in Oberpfalz district, Germany; at confluence of R Regen and R Danube, 104 km/65 mi NE of Munich; well-preserved mediaeval city; Imperial Diets held here (1663–1806); bishopric; railway; river harbour; university (1962); electrical engineering, chemicals, clothing, sugar refining, carpets, river craft, brewing; Gothic cathedral (13th–16th-c), old town hall, Benedictine monastery of St Emmeram (7th-c).

regent The person appointed to act for the monarch if he/she is incapacitated, unavailable, or under 18. In the UK, it is customary for the next heir to the throne to be regent: from 1811 to 1820 the Prince of Wales (later George IV) acted as regent because of the supposed insanity of his father, George III.

reggae [**reg**ay] A type of popular music, of Rastafarian Jamaican origin but drawing on Afro-American traditions and later influenced by rock. Many reggae songs spring from a social malaise; they are usually accompanied by electric guitars, piano, organ, and drum set. Among prominent reggae artists were Bob Marley and the Wailers.

Reggio di Calabria [**re**jioh dee ka**lab**ria] 38°06N 15°39E, pop (2000e) 182 000. Seaport and capital of Reggio di Calabria province, Calabria, S Italy; on E side of the Strait of Messina; founded by Greek colonists, 8th-c BC; archbishopric; airport; railway; ferry to Sicily; fruit, oil of bergamot, railway carriages, paper making, tourism; agricultural fair (Mar–Apr).

Reggio nell'Emilia [**re**jioh nelay**mee**lia] 44°42N 10°37E, pop (2000e) 135 000. Capital town of Reggio nell'Emilia province, Emilia-Romagna, N Italy; founded by the Romans; birthplace of Ariosto; railway; agricultural trade, wine, cheese, food packaging, canning, cement, engineering; cathedral (13th–15th-c), Church of the Madonna della Chiaira (1597–1619).

Regina [re**jiy**na] 50°30N 104°38W, pop (2000e) 188 800. Capital of Saskatchewan province, on Moosejaw Creek, SC Canada; founded, 1882 as capital of Northwest Territories; named in honour of Queen Victoria; provincial capital, 1905; centre of grain, potash, and oil industries; airport; railway; university (1917); grain trade, oil refining, steel, engineering, meat processing, canning; Royal Canadian Mounted Police Museum, Wascana Park, Diefenbaker Homestead, Saskatchewan Centre of Arts, Museum of Natural History; professional team, Saskatchewan Rough Riders (football); Buffalo Days (pioneer celebration, Jul), Canadian Western Agribition (autumn).

Regiomontanus [rejiohmon**tay**nus], Lat name of **Johannes Müller** (1436–76) Mathematician and astronomer, born in Königsberg (Lat *Mons Regius*, hence his pseudonym), Prussia (now Kaliningrad, Russia). He studied at Vienna, and in 1471 settled in Nuremberg where a rich patrician, Bernard Walther, offered him an observatory. He established the study of algebra and trigonometry in Germany, and wrote on a variety of applied topics. In 1474 he was summoned to Rome by Sixtus IV to help reform the calendar.

regionalism 1 In planning, the division of a country into regions for political, developmental, and administrative purposes. The

division is based on the underlying assumption of unifying characteristics (eg social, economic) within a region.
2 A movement whereby the inhabitants of a region stress their individual or separate identity from other regions. This can be based on factors such as linguistic differences (eg in Belgium), religious differences (eg Northern Ireland), and ethnic differences (eg the Kurdish population in Iraq). It may result in war, as seen in the 1990s conflict between the regions of former Yugoslavia.

register A variety of language defined by the social context in which it is deemed appropriate for use, such as religion, law, science, advertising, journalism, or conversation. Each register can be identified by a range of linguistic features which together distinguish it from other registers in the language. Traditional religious language is usually one of the most distinctive in English, making use of such forms as *goeth*, *knowest*, *vouchsafe*, and *O*.

regolith The layer of fine powdery material on the Moon produced by the repeated impact of meteorites. It is up to 25 m/ 80 ft thick. Similar dust probably covers many other objects in the Solar System.

regression One of many defence mechanisms in which the individual returns to behaviour more apposite to an earlier age. This can be a component of a psychotherapy process and can also occur in physical illness; for example, a man with a severe injury to the spine but who was able to feed himself insisted on his wife feeding him with a spoon during the acute phase of his illness.

regulator The non-ministerial head of a government department which controls privatized industries in England and Wales. In the 1980s and 1990s, a large number of state-owned enterprises were sold off as monopolies, in some cases without any real competition. Many of these corporations provided essential services to the public, so control and accountability were not transferred to the purchasers. These functions are vested in independent regulators who head **regulatory agencies** such as the Office of Telecommunications (OFTEL), the Office of Gas Supply (OFGAS), and the Office of the Rail Regulator (OFRAIL). They are responsible for protecting the consumer interest and obtaining redress for grievances, as well as setting standards and monitoring prices.

Regulator Movements Rural insurgencies in South Carolina and North Carolina, just prior to independence. The South Carolina events took place in the mid-1760s, and the North Carolina movement followed a few years later, meeting military defeat in 1771. Both disputes pitched the slave-holding seacoast against small farmers of the interior, but otherwise the causes and outcomes were different. The ensuing bitterness spilled over into the American Revolution. The term *regulator* was also used elsewhere in early America to describe other popular insurrectionary movements.

Regulus, Marcus Atilius [regyulus] (3rd-c BC) Roman general and statesman of the First Punic War, whose heroic death at the hands of the Carthaginians earned him legendary status. After capture by the Carthaginians, he was sent to Rome on parole to sue for peace. Having dissuaded the Senate from agreeing to their terms, he voluntarily returned to Carthage, where he was tortured to death.

rehabilitation In medicine, the process of helping a patient return to normal life or attain the best possible lifestyle following a serious illness or injury. It may involve physiotherapy and occupational therapy to help the body regain its optimal level of functioning.

Rehnquist, William H(ubbs) [renkwist] (1924–) Jurist, born in Milwaukee, Wisconsin, USA. He studied at Harvard and the Stanford Law School, then practised law, and became active in the Republican Party. In his post as head of the Office of Legal Council in the justice department (1969), he supported such controversial measures as pre-trial detention and wire-tapping, impressing President Nixon, who appointed him Associate Justice of the Supreme Court in 1972. In 1986 he was appointed Chief Justice, and after 1989, when a 'new right' majority had been established by President Reagan, he framed a series of conservative rulings on abortion, affirmative action, and capital punishment.

Reich [riykh] The term used to describe the German Empire. The Holy Roman Empire (962–1806) was regarded as the **First Reich**, and unified Germany after 1870 was referred to as the **Second Reich** (*Kaiserreich*). After 1933, the enlarged Germany envisaged in Hitler's plans was known as the **Third Reich**.

Reich, Wilhelm [riykh] (1897–1957) Psychoanalyst, born in Dobrzcynica, Austria-Hungary (part of modern Poland). He became a practising psychoanalyst while still a medical student in Vienna, but broke from the Freudian school, developing a theory in which neuroses resulted from repressed, undissipated feelings or sexual energy. In *The Function of Orgasm* (1927), and other works, he expounded on the necessity of regular orgasms for the mental health of both men and women. He was expelled from the German Communist Party in 1933 and the International Psychoanalytical Association in 1934, and emigrated to the USA in 1939. He established the pseudo-scientific 'Orgone' Institute, but died in gaol after being prosecuted for promoting a fraudulent treatment. During the sexual revolution of the 1960s, he became something of a cult figure in the USA. His other works include *Character Analysis* (1933) and *The Sexual Revolution* (1936–45).

Reichenbach, Hans [riykhenbakh] (1891–1953) Philosopher of science, born in Hamburg, N Germany. He studied in Berlin, Munich, Göttingen, and Erlangen, then became professor of philosophy at Berlin (1926–33), Istanbul (1933–8) and Los Angeles (from 1938). He was an early associate of the Vienna School of logical positivists, and with Rudolph Carnap founded the journal *Erkenntnis* in 1930 (which reappeared in 1975 in the USA). He made an important technical contribution to probability theory, in which two truth tables are replaced by the multivalued concept of 'weight', and wrote widely on logic and the philosophical bases of science in such works as *Theory of Probability* (1935), *Elements of Symbolic Logic* (1947), and *The Rise of Scientific Philosophy* (1951) (trans titles).

Reichian therapy A system of psychotherapy developed by Wilhelm Reich, based on the idea that memories of unpleasant experiences and feelings in the unconscious mind create both psychological problems and physical tension ('body armouring'). Treatment by physical manipulation can relax the body armouring, thereby releasing tension and freeing repressed emotions.

Reichstag fire [riykhstag] The deliberate burning down of Germany's parliament building (27 Feb 1933), shortly after the Nazi accession to power. A deranged Dutch ex-communist, van der Lubbe, was accused of arson and executed. The new Nazi government, insisting that the act was evidence of a wider communist conspiracy, used the situation to ban and suppress the German Communist Party. Communist conspiracy was certainly not behind the fire; nor, probably, were the Nazis themselves, though it was long believed to be so. It is now increasingly agreed that, however convenient the fire may have been to the regime, van der Lubbe acted alone.

Reid, Thomas (1710–96) Philosopher, born in Strachan, Aberdeenshire, NE Scotland, UK. He studied at Aberdeen, becoming professor there in 1751, and later succeeded Adam Smith in the chair of moral philosophy at Glasgow (1764–80). He was leader of the 'Scottish' school, which rejected the scepticism of David Hume. His main publications include *Essays on the Intellectual Powers of Man* (1785) and *Essays on the Active Powers of Man* (1788).

Reign of Terror (1793–4) The extreme phase of the French Revolution, characterized by the systematic execution of political opponents of the Jacobins and supposed sympathizers of the Counter-Revolution, who were brought before the Revolutionary Tribunal and guillotined. 40 000 people are thought to have been killed in Paris and the provinces.

Reims *Rheims*

reincarnation The belief that, following death, some aspect of the self or soul can be reborn in a new body (human or animal), a process which may be repeated many times. This belief is fundamental to many Eastern religions, such as Hinduism and Buddhism, and is also found in more modern, Western belief systems such as theosophy. Alleged past-life regressions, where a hypnotized person appears to 'remember' past lives, have recently fuelled Western interest in reincarnation, although such cases may only represent the person trying to meet the implied demands of the hypnotist.

reindeer A true deer (*Rangifer tarandus*) native to high latitudes of the N hemisphere (introduced on South Georgia I); first domesticated 3000 years ago; the most northerly deer, inhabiting open tundra; the only deer in which females have antlers, and the only one in which the lowest, forward-pointing tine is branched; long coat of hollow hairs; nose covered with hairs; feet make clicking sound when walking; hooves broad; in winter, digs in snow with antlers to eat lichens; also known as **caribou** ('shoveller').

Reiner, Rob [riyner] (1945–) Film actor, director, and producer, born in New York City, USA. He appeared in a number of small films before becoming known for his role in *All in the Family* (1971–8, 2 Emmies), later roles including *Postcards from the Edge* (1990), *Sleepless in Seattle* (1993), *The First Wives Club* (1996), and *EDtv* (1999). He made his directorial debut in 1984 with *This Is Spinal Tap*, and acted as producer as well as director for several other films, notably *When Harry Met Sally* (1989) and *Ghosts of Mississippi* (1996), and directed *The Story of Us* (1999).

Reines, Frederick (1918–98) Physicist, born in Paterson, New Jersey, USA. He studied at New York University (1944), worked on the atomic bomb at Los Alamos (1944–9), taught at Case Western Institute of Technology (1959–66), then joined the University of California, Irvine (1966–88). For his discovery of the neutrino, one of the fundamental particles of the universe, he shared the 1995 Nobel Prize for Physics with Martin Perl.

Reinhardt, Django [riynhah(r)t], popular name of **Jean Baptiste Reinhardt** (1910–53) Jazz guitarist, born in Liverchies, Belgium. He was born in the family caravan in a Rom (Gypsy) community, and taught himself the guitar. At 18, injury in a fire caused the fusing of the fourth and fifth fingers of his left hand, but he simply devised a new chording method for his guitar, and continued to play. He played in the Quintet of the Hot Club of France with Stephane Grappelli (1934–9), producing many renowned recordings, and became the first European jazz musician to influence the music.

Reinhardt, Max [riynhah(r)t], originally **Max Goldmann** (1873–1943) Theatre director, born in Baden, NC Germany. An introverted child, he was sent to drama school, and was a shy actor before turning to directing at the Kleines Theatre in Berlin (1902). He became famous overnight with his 1905 production of *A Midsummer Night's Dream*. An innovator in theatre art and technique, his work often involved spectacular, large-scale productions, as in *The Miracle* (London, 1911), which used over 2000 actors. As co-founder of the Salzburg Festival (1920), he left Germany in 1933, and moved to Hollywood, where he opened a theatre workshop.

Reinitzer, Friedrich [riynitser] (1857–1927) Botanist, born in Austria. In 1888, while observing the chemical reactions of cholesterol benzoate, he noted that this compound had two different melting points: at 149°C the solid became an opaque liquid, and at 179°C it became clear. He communicated his findings to German physicist Otto Lehmann (1855–1922) who discovered that, during its opaque phase, the salt in question showed areas of crystalline molecular structures which he termed 'liquid crystals'.

Reisz, Karel [riys] (1926–2002) Film and theatre actor, director, and producer, born in Ostrava, Czechoslovakia (now Czech Republic). As a child he was sent to England in 1938, and later studied at Cambridge. His film credits include *Saturday Night and Sunday Morning* (1959), *Night Must Fall* (1963), *Morgan: A Suitable Case for Treatment* (1966), *The Gambler* (1974), and *The French Lieutenant's Woman* (1981). In later years he worked mainly as a theatre director. In 1999 he appeared in the film documentary *Cinéma Vérité: Defining Moments*, directed by Peter Wintonick.

Reith (of Stonehaven), John (Charles Walsham) Reith, Baron [reeth] (1889–1971) British statesman and engineer, born in Stonehaven, Aberdeenshire, NE Scotland, UK. He studied at Glasgow, entered the field of radio communication, and became the first general manager of the BBC (1922), then its director-general (1927–38). He was the architect of public service broadcasting in the UK. He became an MP in 1940, and was minister of works and buildings (1940–2). The BBC inaugurated the Reith Lectures in 1948 in honour of his influence on broadcasting, and he was created a baron in 1940.

relapsing fever A group of diseases resulting from infection with spirochaete bacteria of the genus *Borrelia*, transmitted to humans by body lice or ticks. One of these is *Lyme disease*. There is a 'bulls eye' rash at the site of the bite accompanied by fever, headache, fatigue, and muscle aches. Complications include widespread skin rashes and inflammation of the joints, heart, and brain. It tends to occur in epidemics and to afflict refugees.

relational database A form of organizing data in a computer in which each entity type is stored separately as a table, and the relationships between entities are stored as another table. In the database for the present encyclopedia, for example, the individual entries are stored in one file, and the relationships between entries (such as the indexing of the words in the entries, which controls the alphabetical order) are stored separately.

relative atomic mass The mass of atoms, expressed in atomic mass units u, eg carbon-12 is 12·0000 u by definition, nitrogen-14 is 14·0031 u; symbol A_r; formerly called **atomic weight**. The periodic table lists masses for naturally occurring isotopic mixtures, eg naturally occurring nitrogen is 14·0067 u.

relative biological effectiveness *radioactivity units*

relative density Density measured relative to some standard, typically water at 20°C; symbol *d*, expressed as a pure number; measured using hydrometers; formerly called **specific gravity**. For example, for alcohol, density ρ = 789 kg/m^3, d = 0·791.

relativism The view that there are no objective or universally valid truths and values; they are all dependent on and 'relative to' the culture, society, or circumstances of the individual. This doctrine often arises from observations of human diversity of an anthropological kind; in philosophy it goes back at least as far as Protagoras and the Sophists.

relativistic quantum mechanics Quantum mechanics consistent with special relativity, and thus applicable to fast-moving systems; originally developed by Paul Dirac in 1928. It predicts the observed fine detail of atomic spectra, and is essential in particle physics.

relativity *general relativity; special relativity*

relaxation meter *biofeedback*

relay An electrical or solid-state device, operated by changes in input, which is used to control or operate other devices connected to the output. Most relays are used in electrical circuits, though they may have mechanical input or output. They have a range of applications in telephone exchanges, switches, and automation systems.

releasing factor *releasing hormone*

releasing hormone One of a group of hormones produced in different parts of the hypothalamus, and stored and released by the neurones of the median eminence of the hypothalamus in response to stimuli from the brain. It is transported to the front lobe of the pituitary gland, where it stimulates or inhibits the release of a specific pituitary hormone (eg growth-hormone-releasing hormone). Previously known as a **releasing factor**, this term is now confined to hypothalamic hormones whose chemical structures are unknown (eg prolactin-releasing factor).

relics Material remains (eg bones, skin) of, or objects which have been in contact with, a saint or person worthy of special religious attention. In many religions, and in the Christianity of Roman Catholic and Orthodox Churches, these are objects of veneration, and the churches in which they are housed places of pilgrimage.

relief printing A print, made from a block (usually wood or lino) which has been cut away in those parts intended to be left white; the method contrasts with intaglio or surface prints. The ink adheres to the raised (relief) parts only, and when the block is pressed against a sheet of paper only those parts print.

relief sculpture A type of sculpture in which the forms are raised above the background, but not shaped fully 'in the round'. In **low relief** (or **bas-relief**) the design is hardly raised above the surface, as on a coin, while in **high relief** the forms may be almost free-standing, as on a Roman sarcophagus, or the pediments of many classical buildings.

religion A concept which has been used to denote: (1) the class of all religions; (2) the common essence or pattern of all supposedly genuine religious phenomena; (3) the transcendant or 'this-worldly' ideal of which any actual religion is as an imperfect manifestation; and (4) human religiousness as a form of life which may or may not be expressed in systems of belief and practice. These usages suffer from a tendency to be evaluative, presuppose a commitment of some sort, or are so general as to provide little specific guidance. What is clear is that no single definition will suffice to encompass the varied sets of traditions, practices, and ideas which constitute different religions. Some religions involve the belief in and worship of a god or gods, but this is not true of all. Christianity, Islam, and Judaism are theistic religions, while Buddhism does not require a belief in gods, and where it does occur, the gods are not considered important. There are theories of religion which construe it as wholly a human phenomenon, without any supernatural or transcendent origin and point of reference, while others argue that some such reference is the essence of the matter. Several other viewpoints exist, and there are often boundary disputes regarding the application of the concept. For example, debate continues as to whether Confucianism is properly to be considered a religion; and some writers argue that Marxism is in important respects a religion.

Religion, Wars of (1562–98) A series of religious and political conflicts in France, caused by the growth of Calvinism, noble factionalism, and weak royal government. After 1559 there were a number of weak and/or young Valois kings whose mother, Catherine de' Medici, attempted abortive compromises. Calvinist or 'Huguenot' numbers increased from the 1550s, fostered by the missionary activities of Geneva. The noble factions of Bourbon, Guise, and Montmorency were split by religion as well as by family interests. Civil wars were encouraged by Philip II of Spain's support of the Catholic Guise faction and by Elizabeth I's aid to the Huguenots. They ended when Henry of Navarre returned to Catholicism and crushed the Guise Catholic League (1589–98).

rem In radioactivity, an old measure of dose equivalent; symbol *rem*; equal to absorbed dose in rad multiplied by relative biological effectiveness, 1 rem = 0·01 Sv (sievert, SI unit); an abbreviation of **röntgen equivalent in man**; classed as a unit in temporary use with SI units.

Remarque, Erich Maria [ruhmah(r)k], originally **Erich Paul Remark** (1898–1970) Novelist, born in Osnabrück, NWC Germany. He served in World War 1, and worked as a sports journalist while writing his famous war novel, *All Quiet on the Western Front* (1929). An immediate international success, it was filmed in 1930. The Nazis ordered it to be burned, and he was deprived of his German citizenship. Other titles, none of which were as critically acclaimed, include its sequel, *The Road Back* (1931). His novels were banned by the Nazis (1933), and in 1939 he emigrated to the USA, where he wrote more novels, married the film star **Paulette Goddard** (1911–90), and became a naturalized citizen. Later novels include *The Black Obelisk* (1957) and *The Night in Lisbon* (1962).

Rembrandt (Harmenszoon van Rijn) [rembrant] (1606–69) Painter, born in Leyden, The Netherlands. He studied under various masters, and was introduced to Italian art. His early works include religious and historical scenes, unusual in Protestant Holland. He settled in Amsterdam (1631), where he ran a large studio and took numerous pupils. 'The Anatomy Lesson of Dr Nicolaes Tulp' (1632, The Hague) assured his reputation as a portrait painter. In 1634 he married Saskia van Ulenburgh (1613–42), and in the year of her death produced his masterpiece, 'The Night Watch' (Amsterdam), which was well received, and which was followed by other important commissions. His extravagance, especially as a collector, led to bankruptcy in 1656, but he continued to work with undiminished energy and power. His preserved works number over 650 oil paintings, 2000 drawings and studies, and 300 etchings. He died in relative obscurity.

Remembrance Sunday In the UK, the Sunday nearest 11 November (formerly Armistice Day), on which are commemorated those who died in the two world wars. A two-minute silence is observed at 11 am. There are special church services, and wreath-laying ceremonies at war memorials.

Remington, Eliphalet (1793–1861) Firearms manufacturer and inventor, born in Suffield, Connecticut, USA. While still a young man he made for himself a flintlock rifle which, although not original, was very accurate. In 1828 he built a factory beside the Erie Canal, and pioneered several improvements in small arms manufacture, including a method of straightening gun barrels and the first successful cast steel rifle barrel in the USA.

Remington, Frederic (Sackrider) (1861–1909) Painter, sculptor, and illustrator, born in Canton, New York, USA. He studied at the Yale Art School (1878–9) and the Art Students League, New York City (c.1885), then moved West and became a cowboy and rancher. Offered a commission to illustrate Geronimo's Apache campaign for *Harper's Weekly* (1882), he began his career as a painter of the American West. He recorded the Indian Wars of 1890–91, created his first bronze sculpture, 'Bronco Buster' (1895), and wrote and illustrated several books that recounted his adventures.

Remonstrants Christians adhering to the Calvinistic doctrine of Jacobus Arminius (17th-c Holland), whose followers were also known as **Arminians**. They were named after the 'Remonstrance', a statement of Arminian teaching dating from 1610. Small in number, they were influential among Baptists, and in Methodism and Calvinism.

remora [remuhra] Slender-bodied fish (*Remora remora*) widespread in warm seas; large sucking disc on upper surface of head, with which it attaches firmly to other fish, especially sharks; length up to 45 cm/18 in; also called **shark-sucker**. (Family: Echeneidae, 3 genera, 8 species.)

remote sensing A method of measuring the characteristics of an object without touching it. The term is usually applied to images of the Earth taken by satellites, and to cameras in aircraft which can be used to map different phenomena; examples include cloud cover from METEOSAT, and land-use patterns from LANDSAT.

Renaissance From the French for 're-birth', referring to the revival of classical literature and artistic styles at various times in European history. Such renaissances occurred in the 8th–9th-c, in the 12th-c, and in the 14th–16th-c. The first, or **Carolingian Renaissance**, centred upon the recovery of classical Latin texts in cathedral schools. The second, or **Twelfth-century Renaissance**, was marked by the foundation of universities and the rediscovery of Aristotle's ethical and philosophical works. The third (which is usually called **the Renaissance** and is the best-known), was distinguished for the development of naturalistic works of art, the study of ancient Greek authors, above all Plato, and the critical study of Christian texts. It began in Italy and spread to the rest of Europe which, in the Middle Ages, was feudal, fragmented, and dominated by the Church.

Although varied in content and institutional focus, all three renaissances therefore included elements of revived classicism. Yet it was the third such revival between c.1300 and c.1600 that historians since Michelet and Burckhardt in the mid-19th-c have thought marked the beginnings of modern times. Since they wrote, however, a number of criticisms have been levelled against their interpretations. One is that the two earlier renaissances diminish the supposed unique importance of the third. A second is that few major scientific and technological discoveries, which are crucial to modern societies, were made during the third renaissance. A third is that mass movements – another hallmark of 'modernity' – were almost totally absent from the third renaissance, which was a distinctly elite affair. A final objection is that the Renaissance according to Burckhardt was almost entirely limited to N Italy.

Recent scholarship has indeed confirmed certain elements of the Burckhardtian theory. Chief among them is the rise of secular and urban states and values. These changes included new institutions such as permanent embassies and spies, standing armies, and regular taxation. New attitudes were also involved. In the 14th-c, Marsiglio of Padua rejected all clerical authority; in the 15th-c, 'civic humanists' made service to the city-state a moral imperative; and in the early 16th-c, Machiavelli stated that power should be pursued without reference to Christian commandments. In philosophy, Ficino and Pico della Mirandola suggested that human perfection was possible through the intellectual study of pagan sources, as well as Christian ones, and through Platonic love. Artistic production, although its subjects often remained religious, also acknowledged secular values, as in the geometric naturalism of Piero della Francesca's paintings.

The changes brought about by the Italian Renaissance of the 14th–16th-c should not be compared with modern political and social revolutions. But it did contain fundamental changes in values and institutions, the effects of which were not confined to Europe's elites. The wealthy cities financed the great artistic achievements of this Renaissance. Humanism, perfect artistic endeavour, and bodily perfection were ideas made more readily accessible by the invention of printing.

Renaissance architecture The rediscovery and application of classical and especially Roman architectural forms and principles in 15th-c and 16th-c W Europe. It is particularly associated with Italy, and the work of such architects as Alberti, Bramante, Brunelleschi, Michelangelo, Palladio, Raphael, Giulio Romano, Giuliano da Sangallo, and Vignola. Renaissance architecture is also to be found in England, such as the Queen's House, Greenwich (1616), architect Inigo Jones, and in Belgium, France, Germany, The Netherlands, and Spain.

Renaissance art A movement which began in Florence in the early 15th-c, when Masaccio, Donatello, and Brunelleschi turned to ancient Roman art and architecture for inspiration. Parallel to the new humanism in literature, a new self-consciousness arose about style. Piero della Francesca, Mantegna, and others sought classical proportions for their figures, while the new system of perspective helped to rationalize the picture-space. Ghiberti, Verrocchio, and Michelangelo were the greatest sculptors after Donatello; Leonardo and Raphael painted portraits, and religious and historical works. The period c.1500–20 is known as the **High Renaissance**. In the 16th-c, Renaissance style spread throughout Italy, especially to Venice, and to much of W Europe.

Renault, Mary [renoh], pseudonym of **Eileen Mary Challans** (1905–83) Novelist, born in Forest Gate, London, UK. She was educated in Bristol and at St Hugh's College, Oxford. Her first novel, *Purposes of Love* (1939), was a frank account of heterosexuality and lesbianism. In 1948 she emigrated to South Africa where she wrote *The Charioteer* (1953), a serious study of homosexual love. The theme was continued in the *Last of the Wine* (1956), the first of eight accounts of life in Ancient Greece. She also wrote a novel about Alexander the Great, *The Nature of Alexander* (1975).

Rendell (of Babergh), Ruth Rendell, Baroness [rendl], originally **Ruth Barbara Grasemann**, occasional pseudonym **Barbara Vine** (1930–) Detective-story writer, born in London, UK. She went to school in Loughton, Essex, and spent some time as a journalist and managing director of a local newspaper before publishing her first novel *From Doon with Death* in 1964. Several of her detective stories feature Chief Inspector Wexford, such as *Shake Hands Forever* (1975), *Simisola* (1994), and *Harm Done* (1999), and she has also written mystery thrillers including *A Judgement in Stone* (1977), and books of short stories. Later novels include *The Rottweiler* (2003). Books written under her pseudonym include *The House of Stairs* (1988), *Gallowglass* (1990), *The Brimstone Wedding* (1995), and *Grasshopper* (2000). Many of her stories have been filmed or televised, notably in the series *The Ruth Rendell Mysteries*. Among her awards is the 1981 Arts Council National Book Award for Genre Fiction. She received a life peerage in 1997.

renewable resources Resources with a yield which is sustainable and which may be used without danger of exhaustion, such as solar power, wind energy, and hydroelectric power, all of which are directly or indirectly due to solar energy. Some renewable resources (eg crops, timber, fish) are sustainable in the long term only through careful management, so that they are not overexploited (eg overcropping, overgrazing) or misused in the short term.

Renfrew (of Kaimsthorn), (Andrew) Colin Renfrew, Baron (1937–) Archaeologist, born in Stockton-on-Tees, Durham, NE England, UK. He studied at Cambridge. His work has ranged widely, but exhibits a central preoccupation with the nature of cultural change in prehistory. He has excavated in Greece (1964–76) and Orkney (1972–4), notably at the chambered tomb of Quanterness. He became professor of archaeology at Cambridge in 1981, and Master of Jesus College, Cambridge, in 1986. His books include *The Emergence of Civilization* (1972), *The Archaeology of Cult* (1985), and *The Cycladic Spirit* (1991). He has also contributed to several pioneering archaeological programmes on BBC television, notably in the *Chronicle* series. He was made a life peer in 1991.

Reni, Guido [raynee] (1575–1642) Baroque painter, born near Bologna, N Italy. He studied in Bologna, and worked both there and in Rome. The fresco painted for the Borghese garden house, 'Aurora and the Hours' (1613–14) is usually regarded as his masterpiece, but some critics rank higher the unfinished 'Nativity' in San Martino, Naples. He later settled again in Bologna.

renin A hormone, produced by the kidneys, which promotes the conversion of *angiotensinogen* (a plasma protein) into *angiotensin I*, the inactive precursor of the physiologically active *angiotensin II*. The function of the latter is to constrict the arterioles (thereby raising blood pressure), and to stimulate aldosterone secretion and thirst. It is the most important blood vessel constrictor known.

Renner, Karl (1870–1950) Austrian statesman, chancellor (1918–20, 1945), and president (1945–50), born in Unter-Tannowitz, Austria. He trained as a lawyer, joined the Austrian Social Democratic Party, and became the first chancellor of the Austrian Republic. Imprisoned as a Socialist leader, following the brief civil war (Feb 1934), he was chancellor again after World War 2, and first president of the new republic.

Rennes [ren], Breton **Roazon**, ancient **Condate** 48°07N 1°41W, pop (2000e) 207 000. Industrial and commercial city, and capital of Ille-et-Vilaine department, NW France; at confluence of canalized Ille and Vilaine Rivers, 309 km/192 mi SW of Paris; capital of Brittany, 10th-c, and now its economic and cultural centre; largely rebuilt after major fire, 1720; badly bombed in World War 2; airport; road and rail junction; archbishopric; university (1461); oil refining, textiles, chemicals, electronics, cars; Baroque town hall (1734), Palais de Justice, former abbey church of Notre-Dame (11th–13th-c), cathedral (largely rebuilt, 19th-c), La Porte Mordelaise, Thabor Gardens.

rennet An extract from the stomach of most young animals, but particularly the calf and the lamb, which contains the enzyme *rennin*. It causes the main milk protein *casein* to precipitate, thus allowing the milk to clot, forming a hard curd with the release of a watery whey rich in sugar (*lactose*) and whey protein. Rennet is commercially available, sometimes being used in recipes and the manufacture of cheese. A vegetable-derived rennet is also available.

Rennie, John (1761–1821) Civil engineer, born in Phantassie, East Lothian, E Scotland, UK. He studied at Edinburgh University, entered the employment of Boulton & Watt (1784), set up in London as an engineer (1791), and soon became famous as a bridge-builder – building Kelso, Leeds, Musselburgh, Newton Stewart, Boston, New Galloway, and the old Southwark and Waterloo Bridges, and designing London Bridge. He made many important canals, drained fens, designed the docks in London and several other ports, and improved others. He also constructed the celebrated breakwater at Plymouth (1811–41).

Reno [reenoh] 39°31N 119°48W, pop (2000e) 180 500. Seat of Washoe Co, W Nevada, USA, on the Truckee R; settled, 1859; developed with arrival of railway, 1868; airport; university (1874); noted for its casinos; formerly (before laws generally became less restrictive), couples wanting a quick divorce would drive to Reno; Reno Rodeo (Jun), National Air Races (Sep).

Reno, Janet [reenoh] (1938–) US attorney general (1993–2001), born in Miami, Florida, USA, the first woman to become US attorney general and the longest serving occupant of that cabinet post. She studied at Harvard Law School, became the county prosecutor in Dade County, FL (1978–93), and was then appointed attorney general. She became one of the most respected members of the Clinton administration in its first term, known for launching innovative programmes designed to steer non-violent drug offenders away from jail and espousing the rights of criminal defendants. Her readiness to nominate special prosecutors to investigate the president drew fire from the White House, but her political position was unassailable. The anti-trust suit against Microsoft, Inc (1998–9) was the most publicized policy action of her tenure.

Renoir, Jean [renwah(r)] (1894–1979) Film director, born in Paris, France, the son of Pierre Auguste Renoir. After serving in World War 1 (where he won the Croix de Guerre), he studied ceramics, then began writing screenplays, and turned to silent film-making. His version of Zola's *Nana* (1926), *La Grande Illusion* (1937, The Great Illusion), *La Règle du Jeu* (1939, The Rules of the Game), *The Diary of a Chambermaid* (1946), and *Le Déjeuner sur l'herbe* (1959, Lunch on the Grass) are among the masterpieces of the cinema. He left France in 1941 during the German invasion, and became a US citizen. His last films were *Le Caporal épinglé* (1962, The Vanishing Corporal) and *Le Petit théâtre de Jean Renoir* (1969, The Little Theatre of Jean Renoir). He received an honorary Academy Award in 1975.

Renoir, Pierre Auguste [ruhnwah] (1841–1919) Impressionist artist, born in Limoges, C France. He first painted porcelain and fans, began to paint in the open air c.1864, and from 1870 obtained several commissions for portraits. He exhibited with the Impressionists (1874–9, 1882). His picture of sunlight filtering through leaves – *Le Moulin de la Galette* (1876, Louvre) – epitomizes his colourful, happy art. His visit to Italy in 1880 was followed by a series of 'Bathers' in a more cold and Classical style. He then returned to reds, orange, and gold to portray nudes in sunlight, a style which he continued to develop until his death.

renormalization A mathematical procedure in quantum field theories for avoiding infinite results in calculations by a careful redefinition of basic quantities such as mass and charge. The requirement of renormalization, as displayed for example by quantum electrodynamics, is regarded as prerequisite for a useful theory.

Renshaw, Willie, popular name of **William (Charles) Renshaw** (1861–1904) Tennis player, the first great tennis champion, born in Cheltenham, Gloucestershire, SWC England, UK. He started playing at Cheltenham School with his twin brother **Ernest Renshaw** (1861–99), who also became a champion. Willie was Wimbledon singles champion in 1881–6 and 1899, and won the All-England doubles title with Ernest in 1884–6 and 1888–9.

reparations Payments imposed on the powers defeated in war to cover the costs incurred by the victors. For example, they were levied as part of the Versailles peace settlement by the Allies on Germany at the end of World War 1, though the final sum of £6000 million plus interest was not fixed until April 1921. The Dawes (1924) and Young (1929) Plans reduced the scale of the payments, which were finally abandoned in the Lausanne Pact of 1932, because of the Depression. They aroused great bitterness in Germany, and fuelled nationalism and the rise of the Nazis. After World War 2 reparations took the form of Allied occupation of Germany and Japan. Britain, France, and the USA ended reparation collections in 1952. Stalin systematically plundered the East German zone by the stripping of assets and industrial equipment. In Japan, the USA administered the removal of capital goods, and the Soviet Union seized Japanese assets in Manchuria and the Kuril (*Chishima*). Since 1948 West Germany has paid in excess of $37 billion (£20·7 billion) to Israel as reparations for the Holocaust.

repertory grid A technique developed by the US psychologist George Kelly (1905–66) for eliciting a respondent's view of some aspect of the world. Respondents produce their own list of characteristics (*constructs*) on which they rate items (eg colleagues). The structure of this grid of constructs and items can be used to describe how the respondent sees the world. The technique has been much used in management training and speech therapy.

repetitive strain injury (RSI) A term used to describe a variety of types of soft tissue injury caused by repetitive motion, poor posture, or excessive stress of a body part. It includes tendinitis, carpal tunnel syndrome (affecting the thumb and hand), and some sports injuries such as tennis elbow. Injuries may be work-related, due to typing or using tools, and may be prevented by a suitable working environment, eg correct seating and avoiding long periods spent at repetitive tasks.

replete *honey ant*

representative action In English law, an action taken by one person representing and on behalf of a number of others who have an identical claim against the defendant; the term is not used in Scots law; in the USA, it is usually referred to as a **class action**. For example, it might be used by one or more individual shareholders against alleged wrongdoers in control of a company (usually called a *shareholders derivative action* in the USA). An analogous procedure is a *test action* (or *test case*), where several people agree to be bound by the result of an action brought by one or more of those persons. A representative action cannot generally be brought if each member of the group has a separate claim for damages.

Representatives, House of *House of Representatives*

repression A psychoanalytic term representing one of many defence mechanisms. There is the unconscious exclusion of painful memories and unacceptable feelings. In psychotherapy there is often the exploration of this defence mechanism with the release of information into conscious awareness. However, in certain forms of treatment (eg repressive–inspirational group psychotherapy) there is an attempt to bolster rather than to penetrate the patient's defences.

reproduction The act or process of producing offspring; one of the essential properties of a living organism. Reproduction in its simplest form is an asexual process involving the division of an organism into two or more parts by fission, budding, spore formation, or vegetative propagation. Sexual reproduction involves the formation of specialized gametes (such as sperm and egg) by meiosis, and the fusion of a pair of gametes to form a zygote. In demographic research, the **reproduction rate** is the rate at which a population produces new members by birth.

reptile An animal of the class Reptilia (6547 species), which evolved from primitive amphibians; most live on land; breathe with lungs, not gills; dry waterproof skin with horny scales (not separated, like those of a fish, but folds of skin); may moult outer skin regularly; one small bone (the *columella* or *stapes*) in the ear, and several bones forming either side of the lower jaw (unlike mammals); use Sun's rays to maintain body temperature; young do not develop in water (born live, or hatch from shelled eggs laid on land); classified in four orders: Squamata (lizards and snakes), Chelonia (Testudinata or Testudines – tortoises and turtles), Crocodilia (or Loricata – crocodiles, alligators, etc), and Rhyncocephalia (the tuatara); many extinct species, including dinosaurs, plesiosaurs, pterosaurs, and ichthyosaurs.

Repton, Humphry (1752–1818) Landscape designer, born in Bury St Edmunds, Suffolk, E England, UK. The successor to Lancelot 'Capability' Brown, he completed the change from formal gardens of the early 18th-c to the 'picturesque'. He designed gardens at Uppark in Sussex and Sheringham Hall in Norfolk, and wrote *Observations on the Theory and Practice of Landscape Gardening* (1803).

republic A form of state and government where, unlike a monarchy (which is hereditary), the head of state and leader of the government are periodically appointed under the constitution. It thus covers most modern states, and in this respect the term has lost something of its earlier meaning and appeal as an alternative to systems where political power was hereditary. Republics now vary considerably in form, ranging from liberal democratic states to personal dictatorships.

Republican Party One of the two main parties in US politics, created in 1854 out of the anti-slavery movement that preceded the Civil War. It found almost immediate success when Abraham Lincoln was elected president in 1860, and held the presidency except for four terms until Franklin D Roosevelt in 1933, when the Depression led to a major turnaround in Republican fortunes, and the Democrats became the clear majority party for 20 years. Since then there has been a period of split party control, with the Republicans often winning the presidency, and the Democrats holding the majority in Congress. Traditionally supported by voters with high income, education, and social status, its largest support is in NE industrial and W farming areas, and more recently in the southern 'Sunbelt'. It is identified with big business rather than unions, and with white Anglo-Saxons rather than ethnic minorities. It advocates limited central government, the protection of states' rights, and an active and interventionist foreign policy stance. In the 1980s, it became much more conservative in outlook. During the 1990s the party regained control of the House of Representatives (1994), ending a half century out of power. At the same time it lost the 1992 and 1996 presidential elections. It went on to win the presidential election in 2000 amid controversy over voting procedure.

requiem [rekwee-em] (Lat 'rest') In the Roman Catholic Church, a Mass for the dead. In addition to its liturgical use, it has become a musical form, of which there are many outstanding examples, eg requiems by Mozart, Fauré, and Britten.

requirements analysis *systems analysis*

requirements engineering A branch of computer science which studies business requirements as part of an overall computer system development process. It addresses the investigation and analysis stages of the systems development life cycle rather than the design and construction stages, and incorporates examination of the social and cultural aspects of the system as well as the functional and data aspects.

reredos [reeredos] *altarpiece*

resale price maintenance (RPM) The action of manufacturers in fixing the prices at which their products may be resold by retailers. While RPM does not necessarily imply a price-fixing cartel by manufacturers, it makes such a cartel much easier to enforce. RPM was stopped in the UK by the Restrictive Trade Practices Act (1956) and the Retail Prices Act (1964), except for a few special cases, such as the (now abandoned) Net Book Agreement. Manufacturers can now set only a 'recommended' resale price.

research and development (R&D) The process of using labour, materials, and capital to enable a firm to produce a particular product in the future. New products and techniques require expensive testing for effectiveness, durability, and safety. R&D is carried on in a wide variety of sectors, but is concentrated in what are termed 'high-tech' industries, including electronics, aviation, atomic energy, and pharmaceuticals. All the world's major industrial countries spend heavily on R&D, funded both by business and, largely because of its defence applications, by governments.

reserpine [reserpin] A drug present in the shrub *Rauwolfia serpentina* which has been widely used for centuries in Hindu medicine for the treatment of a variety of diseases, including hypertension, insomnia, and mental disorders. More recently it has been used in the West as a sedative, and in psychosis. It has now been superseded by more potent, safer drugs. It is still sometimes used in hypertension.

reserve currency A currency which countries choose to hold as foreign exchange reserves. In theory this could be issued by an international institution such as the International Monetary Fund, but historically national currencies have been used. A country needs two things to make its currency appear attractive to others to hold as reserves. Its currency must be expected to maintain its value relative to others, which implies having stable prices, or relatively low inflation. The country must also be sufficiently large and wealthy that there is enough of its currency available to hold. In the 19th-c and part of the 20th-c, the UK pound sterling was used by many countries. For most of the 20th-c, the US dollar was widely used. If the European currency is a success, the Euro may well become the 21st-c's main reserve currency.

reserves Gold and convertible currency held by countries as a result of receiving payment for exports. Falling reserves occur as a result of imports being greater than exports. In banking, the term refers to the notes and coins banks must hold in case of a sudden demand (a 'run on the bank'). In accountancy, it refers to the profits which have been ploughed back into a company.

reservoir A tank or artificial lake where water is stored. Reservoirs are filled either by damming streams and rivers at times of excess flow, or by pumping water to them. The water can then be released in a controlled manner for domestic or industrial consumption, irrigation, or to generate electric power.

resin A natural or synthetic polymer which softens on heating. The term is loosely used to include any polymer, as in 'ion-exchange resins'.

resistance A measure of the potential difference U needed to produce direct current I in an electrical circuit component; symbol R, units Ω (ohm); $R = U/I$ by definition. It measures a component's ability to restrict current flow. Resistance causes energy loss from a circuit by heating. I/R is called conductance.

Resistencia [reseestensia] 27°28S 58°59W, pop (2000e) 243 900. Agricultural, commercial, and industrial capital of Chaco province, N Argentina; on the R Barranqueras; founded as a Jesuit mission, mid-18th-c; airport; railway; cotton, sugar cane, cattle, timber.

resistivity The electrical resistance of a metre cube of material, constant for a given material at a specific temperature; symbol ρ, units Ω.m (ohm.metre). At 0°C, for copper (a good conductor), $\rho = 1{\cdot}55 \times 10^{-8}$ Ω.m; for germanium (a semiconductor), $\rho = 0{\cdot}5$ Ω.m approximately; for glass (an insulator), $\rho = 10^{11}$Ω.m approximately. $1/\rho$ is conductivity.

resistor A component in an electrical circuit designed to introduce a known resistance to the flow of current. Resistance changes with temperature rise, increasing in metals, and falling in semiconductors. It also varies with the size of the conductor, rising as it becomes longer or thinner.

Reşiţa [resheetsa] 45°16N 21°55E, pop (2000e) 110 000. Capital of Caraş-Severin county, W Romania, in the W foothills of the Transylvanian Alps; railway; iron foundries opened in 1770s;

metallurgy, steel, coal, iron ore, marine diesel engines, food processing.

Resnais, Alain [ruhnay] (1922–) Film director, born in Vannes, NW France. He studied in Paris, and made a series of prize-winning short documentaries, such as *Van Gogh* (1948, Oscar) and *Guernica* (1950). His first feature film was *Hiroshima mon amour* (1959, Hiroshima, My Love), and this was followed by the controversial *L'Année dernière à Marienbad* (1961, Last Year at Marienbad), hailed as a Surrealistic and dreamlike masterpiece by some, as a confused and tedious failure by others. His later films include *Mon Oncle d'Amérique* (1980, My American Uncle), *La vie est un roman* (1983, Life is a Novel), *Mélo* (1986), *Smoking/No Smoking* (1993), and *On Connaît la Chanson* (1997, Same Old Song).

resonance A condition obtained when the frequency of the force driving an oscillating system matches a natural frequency of the system. It is characterized by especially large amplitudes of oscillation at these specific frequencies.

resonances In particle physics, strongly interacting particle-like entities that decay after about 10^{-23} s into more stable particles. This is too short a time to correspond to a particle having a well-defined mass-energy in the usual sense. Large numbers of resonances have been detected and documented.

resonant ionization spectroscopy A sensitive analytical technique for determining trace amounts of materials to better than 1 part in 10^{14}. It uses a pair of tuned dye lasers to ionize atoms or molecules in a vapour sample. The resulting ions are counted or passed to a mass spectrometer for identification.

Respighi, Ottorino [respeegee] (1879–1936) Composer, born in Bologna, N Italy. He studied at Bologna and St Petersburg, and in 1913 became professor of composition at the St Cecilia Academy in Rome. His works include nine operas, the symphonic poems *Fontane di Roma* (1916, Fountains of Rome) and *Pini di Roma* (1924, Pines of Rome), and the ballet *La Boutique fantasque*, produced by Diaghilev in 1919.

respiration A physiological term with a range of related meanings: (1) the act of breathing, whereby terrestrial animals move air in and out of their lungs, and aquatic animals pump water through their gills; (2) the uptake of oxygen from and the release of carbon dioxide to the environment; and (3) the metabolic processes by which organisms derive energy from foodstuffs by utilizing oxygen (**aerobic respiration**) or without the involvement of oxygen (**anaerobic respiration**); often referred to as **tissue** or **cell respiration**. In humans, breathing is achieved by periodic changes in the volume of the thoracic cage (produced principally by the contraction of the diaphragm and the movement of the ribs) which draws air into the lungs (*inhalation*) or expels air from them (*exhalation*). Oxygen diffuses from the alveoli into the pulmonary capillaries, and is carried to the tissues for use in aerobic respiration. Carbon dioxide (the main end product of aerobic respiration) is carried by blood to the lungs for release into the environment.

respirator A mechanical method of delivering oxygen to and removing carbon dioxide from patients who are unable to breathe for themselves. It expands the lungs intermittently through a tube introduced into the trachea. Simple portable apparatus is available that can be operated by hand when short-term ventilation is required. For more prolonged use, a number of automated machines are available. The original respirator was referred to as an 'iron lung'; this was a large box enclosing the patient's body, excluding the head and neck. Entry of air into the lungs was achieved by intermittently lowering the air pressure within the chamber, thus expanding the patient's lungs and chest. This type of respirator was classically used with patients suffering from respiratory paralysis due to poliomyelitis, but it is no longer used.

restitution An equitable remedy to restore property to its owner; also, a substantive legal doctrine to prevent the unjust enrichment of a defendant who has caused goods or money to be transferred by mistake, compulsion, illegality, or lack of authority. It is designed to prevent a defendant from the benefit of his or her own wrongful act. It is known as **quasi contract** in civil law.

Restoration The return of Charles II to England (Jun 1660) at the request of the Convention Parliament, following the collapse of the Protectorate regime; but many royal prerogative powers and institutions were not restored. The bishops and the Church of England returned, but Parliament took the lead in passing the Clarendon Code (1661–5) outlawing dissent from the Book of Common Prayer (1662). The severe religious controls stood in sharp contrast to a new ribaldry in public life and at Court, where 'gallantry' was a euphemism for sexual intrigue. However, theatres, which had been banned by the Puritans, staged a revival with a new form of social comedy of manners characterized by glittering, cynical, licentious, and extravagant language and plot. Women's roles, until then played by boys, were taken by actresses, the most notable among them being Nell Gwynne of the King's Company of Players. A more opulent style of dress, interior decoration, furniture, and textiles became fashionable, caricatured by contemporary engravers such as William Hogarth.

restriction fragment length polymorphism Cloned sequences of DNA which can be used for gene mapping by traditional methods of genetic analysis. In agriculture, the use of RFLP has greatly assisted the mapping and analysis of quantitative characters such as disease resistance, processing quality, or yielding capacity, thus simplifying and accelerating the breeding of genotypes carrying desired combinations of characters.

restrictive covenant An obligation created by deed whereby one person (the **covenantor**) undertakes a negative obligation for the benefit of another (the **covenantee**). In the context of land, a restrictive covenant may be transmitted to burden subsequent owners of a property – for example, a promise not to build. In many jurisdictions, such as in England and Wales and the USA, discriminatory restrictive covenants (eg, a promise not to sell to a black person) are unenforceable.

restrictive practices Agreements between firms which restrict competition. Such agreements may refer to prices, division of markets, or collusion over matters such as selling practices or the granting of credit. Some forms of restrictive practice are forbidden by law in the UK; for example, resale price maintenance (RPM), by which producers could dictate the prices at which distributors sold their products to the public, was forbidden in the 1960s, subject to a few exceptions such as the now-lapsed Net Book Agreement. Other restrictive practices are controlled on a case-by-case basis, with a Registrar who compiles information on restrictive agreements, and a Restrictive Practices Court (RPC) to which cases can be referred. Parliament has provided general guidance to the RPC on the criteria which should be applied in ruling whether or not particular agreements are in the public interest. Many other countries, including the USA and the member states of the European Union, have laws forbidding restrictive practices and procedures for regulating them.

resurrection A form of re-animation of a person after death, the belief in which can be traced to late Biblical Judaism and early Christianity. The nature of the new corporeality, the timing of the transformation, and the matter of whether all people would be raised from the dead or only the 'just' have been variously expressed in Jewish and Christian literature, but the emphasis on some form of revival of the body after death is distinct from many views about the immortality of the soul. Christian faith affirms the resurrection of Jesus Christ in particular, signifying God's vindication of Jesus.

retable *altarpiece*

Retail Price Index (RPI) A means of calculating the general trend of prices of goods and services; also called the **consumer price index (CPI)**, popularly known as the **cost of living index**. It is used as the main indicator of inflation, and is calculated each month by identifying the prices that an average household will have paid for a basket of goods and services. Any increase or decrease is expressed in terms of an index number, where the base at a certain date was 100. If prices on average rose by 4% in the month, then the index would have moved from 100 to 104, or an equivalent amount. The 'basket' is reformed periodically to keep in line with changing consumer spending habits.

Reticulum [retikyulum] (Lat 'net') A small S constellation near the Large Magellanic Cloud.

retina The innermost lining of the vertebrate eyeball, which transmits information about the visual world to the brain. It consists of an outer pigmented layer and an inner (cerebral) layer of photosensitive cells (*rods* and *cones*) and neurones. The cerebral layer radiates out from the *optic disc* (the region where the nerve fibres leave the eyeball to form the optic nerve) to the periphery, gradually reducing in thickness. The optic disc is nonpigmented and insensitive to light, because of the absence of both retinal layers, and is known as the *blind spot*. Within the cerebral layer is the *macula* (a small oval area in the visual axis) having a central depression (the *fovea centralis*). The fovea has the highest resolving power of any part of the retina, because it contains only tightly packed cones, which almost reach the internal surface; consequently an image on this region is least distorted. Light focused by the lens forms an inverted image on the retina. This stimulates the rods and cones to generate impulses which are transmitted via the optic nerve to reach the visual areas of the cortex for interpretation. The pigmented and cerebral layers occasionally separate (*detachment of the retina*), leading to partial blindness. Reattachment is often possible using cryoscopy or photocoagulation by laser beam.

retinol The active form of vitamin A. In the diet, retinol is found in margarine, oily fish, and dairy fats. It acts to maintain the integrity of skin and lung (epithelial tissue) and is also involved in the synthesis of visual purple, which determines our ability to adapt vision to darkness. Vitamin A deficiency leads to a reduced ability to adapt to darkness, and a severe deficiency leads to permanent blindness. Retinol can be synthesized from dietary carotene found in carrots and green leafy vegetables – hence the belief that carrots help eyesight.

retriever A sporting dog belonging to one of several breeds developed to assist hunters. When game has been shot, the retriever is sent to the point where it fell to collect it and bring it to the hunter.

retrograde motion E→W motion of a body in orbit, or rotation on its axis, in contrast to the normal W→E motion in the Solar system. The term is particularly used for the temporary E→W movement of a planet through our sky. Planetary paths are normally from W to E. However, because the Earth is also on an orbit, the two motions sometimes combine to make the planet temporarily backtrack, and seem to move for a time in the reverse direction. The effect is most marked for Mars.

retrovirus A virus c.100 nm in diameter, with an outer envelope enclosing the core. The genetic information is stored in a molecule of single-stranded ribonucleic acid. It is characterized by the occurrence of a special enzyme (*reverse transcriptase*) within the virus particle. (Family: Retroviridae.)

Returned Services League In Australia, an organization recruited from men and women with military service overseas (motto 'The price of liberty is eternal vigilance'). Its functions are social (welfare care and clubs) and political: it forms a major pressure group, with direct access to the cabinet.

Retz (Jean François Paul de Gondi), Cardinal de (1614–79) Clergyman, born in Montmirail, NC France. He plotted against Mazarin, and exploited the Parlementary Fronde (1648) to further his own interests and the power of the Church. After transferring his allegiance between the rebel factions and the crown, he received a cardinal's hat, though in 1652 he was imprisoned on Louis XIV's personal orders. After making peace with Louis (1662), he received the abbacy of St Denis. In his last years he wrote his *Mémoires*, a classic in 17th-c French literature.

Retz, Gilles de Laval, Baron de, also spelled **Rais** or **Raiz** (1404–40) Breton nobleman, born in Champtocé, E France. He fought by the side of Joan of Arc at Orléans, and became Marshal of France at 25, but soon retired to his estates, where for over 10 years he is alleged to have indulged in satanism and the most infamous orgies. He was hanged and burned at Nantes, after being tried and condemned for heresy.

Reuben, tribe of [roobn] One of the 12 tribes of ancient Israel, portrayed as descended from Jacob's first son by Leah. Reuben is also said to have encouraged his brothers to cast Joseph into a pit, rather than to kill him. The tribe's territory included the region E of the Dead Sea and S of Gad.

Réunion [rayoonyon], formally **Bourbon** pop (2000e) 730 000; area 2512 sq km/970 sq mi. Island in the Mascarenes archipelago, Indian Ocean, 800 km/500 mi E of Madagascar; capital, St-Denis; timezone GMT +4; established as a French penal colony, 1638; overseas department, 1946; part of an administrative region, 1973; administers several uninhabited small islands nearby; several volcanoes, one active, rising to Le Piton des Neiges at 3071 m/10 075 ft; governed by a commissioner, a 47-member General Council, and a 45-member Regional Council, both elected for 6-year terms; tourism, sugar, rum, maize, potatoes, tobacco, vanilla.

Reuter, Paul Julius, Freiherr (Baron) **von** [royter], originally **Israel Beer Josaphat** (1816–99) Founder of the first news agency, born in Kassel, C Germany. Of Jewish parentage, he became a Christian and adopted his new name in 1844. He published political pamphlets, moved to Paris during the revolution (1848), and sent news items back to German newspapers via a pigeon carrier service (1850). He developed the idea of a telegraphic news service, and in 1851 moved his headquarters to London, becoming a naturalized British subject. His news service extended worldwide with the development of undersea cables. He was created a baron in 1871.

revelation Generally, the disclosure of what was previously unknown or not clearly apprehended, usually by divine or preternatural means. In religion, it is used to refer to disclosures by God or the divine as distinguished from that attained by the human processes of observation, experiment, and reason.

Revelation, Book of or **the Apocalypse of St John** The last book in the New Testament, whose author is named as 'John', an exile on the island of Patmos (1.9), although scholars differ about his precise identity, and parts of the Eastern Church were slow to accept the work as canonical. Chapters 1–3 are letters of exhortation to seven churches in Asia Minor, but Chapters 4–22 consist of symbolic visions about future tribulations and judgments marking the End times and the return of Christ. It may have been an attempt to offer hope to a church facing persecution in the early 90s.

reverberatory furnace A furnace in which the contents are not heated directly by the burning fuel, but by hot flames diverted by the roof of the furnace so as to play down on the material to be heated. Although mainly known in steel making, it is also used in other processes such as glass making or ceramics.

Revere, Paul [reveer] (1735–1818) US patriot, born in Boston, Massachusetts, USA. A silversmith and copperplate printer, he was one of the party that destroyed the tea in Boston harbour (1773), and was at the head of a secret society formed to watch the British. On 18 April 1775, the night before Lexington and Concord, he started out for Concord, where arms were secreted. He was turned back by a British patrol, and his mission was completed by Dr Samuel Prescott (1751–?77). It was Revere, however, whom the poet Longfellow immortalized for the 'midnight ride'.

reversal process A photographic method by which film exposed in a camera yields a positive picture rather than a negative. After the original negative image has been developed, it is bleached and removed, leaving the previously unexposed silver halides in the emulsion to be given a second development and form the complementary positive. With colour materials, the first development is to silver only, and after its removal the second developer forms the colour-coupled images.

Revised English Bible *New English Bible*

revisionism Most commonly, a doctrinal deviation from the ideological stance of a communist party or state; also, the critical re-assessment of Marxist theories. In general, the term has polemical overtones, and is applied to opponents thought to have broken with Marxist–Leninist orthodoxy. In the era of polycentrism in the communist movement, it has been used by communist parties to attack each other's claims to represent the orthodox position. The term is sometimes used in much the same manner by other political parties claiming to have some deep rooted ideological position, such as the British Labour Party. Given its negative associations, few would ever adopt the revisionist label.

Revolt of the Netherlands (1568–1648) Uprisings and wars against Spanish Habsburg rule by 17 provinces in the Low Countries, also called the **War of Independence**, the **Eighty Years' War**, and the **Dutch Revolt**. The provinces, previously separate fiefs, were united by Charles V (r.1519–58). Resistance to centralization and religious persecution began in the 1550s. The wars devastated the 10 southern provinces retained by the Spanish. The rebels, led by William of Orange and his Protestant naval force of 'sea beggars' (*Watergeuzen*), took refuge in seven northern provinces, chiefly Holland, which was declared a republic in 1609, with the Orange family as *Stadtholder*. Independence was recognized by Spain in 1648.

revolution A change of regime in a country followed by a major reconstitution of the political, social, and economic order. The emphasis is on complete change, though continuities have been a feature of almost all major revolutions. This is notable in Marxism, which not only advocates social and political change by revolution, but also how revolution comes about. Revolutions are normally viewed as involving violent overthrow and the use of force, but this is not a necessary condition. It can be distinguished from the sudden overthrow of a ruler by force in a *coup d'état*, through its emphasis on socio-economic change.

Revolution of 1905 A series of nationwide strikes, demonstrations, and mutinies in Russia, sparked off by the massacre of peacefully demonstrating workers by imperial soldiers in St Petersburg on *Bloody Sunday* (9 Jan 1905). Mutiny broke out on the battleship *Potemkin* and a 'soviet' or council of workers' delegates was formed in St Petersburg. Faced with continuing popular unrest from industrial workers, peasants, and armed forces protesting against mounting taxation, Nicholas II was forced to make concessions, including the legalization of political parties, and elections to a national assembly – the State Duma. However, the Social Democrats continued to fight for a total overthrow of the system, and were met with harsh reprisals.

Revolutions of 1848 A succession of popular, violent uprisings in various W and C European countries during 1848–9, some fuelled by political and economic grievances against established governments, often inspired by liberal and socialist ideas, others by demands for national independence from foreign rule, as in the Italian states, Bohemia, and Hungary. Nobles and the middle class wanted more representation in government; workers and peasants revolted against poverty resulting from the changes wrought by the Industrial Revolution. In France the abdication of Louis Philippe was followed by the Second Republic and the socialist experiment of National Workshops; liberal constitutions were granted in Austria and in many German states; Britain experienced Chartism. The revolutions collapsed from internal weakness or military suppression, and aroused reaction; but they presaged the ultimate triumph of nationalism, if not liberalism, as a precursor of Italian and German reunification.

revolver A single-barrelled pistol with a revolving breech containing chambers for cartridges (usually six), which automatically brings a new cartridge into alignment for firing after each shot. The first practical example was produced by Samuel Colt in 1835, using the action of cocking the firing hammer to revolve the cylinder barrel.

rex A domestic cat with an unusually thin curly coat; a *foreign short-haired* variety; three forms: **Cornish**, **Devon**, and **German**. A rex with a dark face, legs, and tail (like a Siamese) is called a **si-rex**. The name *rex* is also used for a rabbit with a short outer coat.

Reye's syndrome [ray] A rare but frequently fatal illness that tends to follow a viral infection, although aspirin has also been implicated. There are fatty deposits in the liver, and swelling of the brain leading to confusion and coma. It is named after an Australian pathologist, R D K Reye (1912–78), who wrote about the condition in 1963.

Reykjavík [raykyaveek] 64°09N 21°58W, pop (2000e) 106 000. Capital and chief port of Iceland, on Faxa Bay, SW Iceland; founded, 874; chartered, 1786; seat of Danish administration, 1801; capital, 1918; seat of Icelandic parliament; Lutheran bishopric; airport; university (1911); heating system uses nearby hot springs; commerce, fishing, fish processing; national museum, open air museum; meeting place of US and USSR leaders in October 1986 to discuss arms control.

Reymont, Władysław (Stanisław) (1868–1925) Novelist, born in Kobiele Wielkie, SC Poland. His works include *Chlopi* (4 vols, 1904–9, The Peasants) and *Ziemia obiecana* (1899, The Promised Land), best known as a film in different language versions. He was awarded the Nobel Prize for Literature in 1924.

Reynaud, Paul [raynoh] (1878–1966) French statesman and prime minister (1940), born in Barcelonnette, SE France. Originally a barrister, he held many French government posts, and was premier (Apr to Jun) during the fall of France in 1940. He resigned rather than agree to an armistice with Germany, and was imprisoned by the Germans for the duration of World War 2. Afterwards he re-entered politics until losing his seat in 1962, and was a delegate to the Council of Europe (1949).

Reynolds, Sir Joshua [renuhldz] (1723–92) Portrait painter, born in Plympton, Devon, SW England, UK. He studied art in London, and also in Rome (1749–52), then established himself in London, and by 1760 was at the height of his fame as a portrait painter. His works include 'Dr Samuel Johnson' (c.1756, National Portrait Gallery, London) and 'Sarah Siddons as the Tragic Muse' (1784, San Marino, CA). He became the first president of the Royal Academy (1768), and was knighted in 1769. He left well over 2000 works, from which 700 engravings have been made.

Reynolds' number In fluid mechanics, an empirical relationship between viscosity η and flow pattern; symbol *Re*, expressed as a pure number; named after British engineer Osborne Reynolds (1842–1912). For a fluid of density ρ flowing at velocity v along a pipe of diameter d, $Re = vd\rho/\eta$. An increase in the value of *Re* corresponds to a change in flow pattern from smooth to turbulent, such as when the *Re* for water changes from 2000 to 3000 as water velocity is increased.

Reza Pahlavi, Mohammed *Pahlavi, Mohammed Reza*

Rhadamanthus or **Rhadamanthys** [radamanthus] In Greek mythology, a Cretan, son of Zeus and Europa. He did not die but was taken to Elysium, where he became the just judge of the dead.

Rhaetian [reeshn] *Romance languages*

rhapsody A piece of music in which the composer allows his imagination to range more or less freely over some theme, story, or idea, without regard for any prescribed structure. Lizst's *Hungarian Rhapsodies* and Rachmaninov's *Rhapsody on a Theme of Paganini* (a set of free variations) are examples of what is essentially a Romantic genre.

Rhätikon [raytikon] Mountain range of the E or Rhaetian Alps on the frontier between Austria, Switzerland, and Liechtenstein, rising to 2965 m/9728 ft at Schesaplana; major skiing area.

Rhazes or Razi [rayzeez, rayzee], in full **Abu Bakr Muhammad ibn Zakariya ar-Razi** (10th-c) Physician and alchemist, who lived in Baghdad. Considered the greatest physician of the Arab world, he gave full accounts of smallpox and measles, and wrote an immense Graeco-Arabic encyclopedia. This was translated into Latin, and had considerable influence on medical science in the Middle Ages.

Rhea (astronomy) **[reea]** The fifth natural satellite of Saturn, discovered in 1672; distance from the planet 527 000 km/ 327 000 mi. It is the second largest moon of Saturn, diameter 1530 km/950 mi; orbital period 4·518 days.

Rhea or **Rheia** (mythology) **[reea]** In Greek mythology, a Titan, sister and wife of Cronus, and mother of Zeus and other Olympian gods. When Cronus consumed his children, Rhea gave him a stone instead of Zeus, who was saved and later rebelled against his father.

rhea (ornithology) **[reea]** A South American ratite, resembling the ostrich, but smaller (up to 1·5 m/5 ft), duller plumage, and larger wings; inhabits open country with long-stemmed vegetation; eats plants, insects, and small vertebrates; can swim; also known as the **ema**, **nandu** (**nhandu**), or **American ostrich**. (Family: Rheidae, 2 species.)

Rhee, Syngman (1875–1965) Korean statesman and president of South Korea (1948–60), born near Kaesong, S North Korea. Imprisoned (1897–1904) for his part in an independence campaign, he later went to the USA, returning to Japanese-annexed Korea in 1910. After the unsuccessful rising of 1919, he became president of the exiled Korean Provisional Government. On Japan's surrender (1945) he returned to become the first elected president of South Korea. Re-elected for a fourth term (1960), he was obliged to resign after a month following major riots and the resignation of his cabinet. He went into exile in Honolulu.

Rheims [reemz], Fr **Reims** [rĩs], ancient **Durocortorum**, later **Remi** 49°15N 4°02E, pop (2000e) 189 000. Historic town in Marne department, NE France; on right bank of R Vesle, 133 ENE of Paris; port on Aisne–Marne Canal; bishopric since 4th-c, now an archbishopric; former coronation site of French kings; extensive damage in World War 1; scene of German surrender, 1945; road and rail junction; university (1967); textiles, chemicals, metallurgy, building, wholesale grocery, stained-glass workshops; major wine-producing centre (especially champagne), with an extensive network of storage caves; Gothic cathedral (13th-c, badly damaged in World War 1, now restored), 11th-c Church of St-Rémi, Musée St-Denis; Roman remains, including the Porte de Mars (2nd-c AD).

Rhenish Slate Mountains, Ger **Rheinisches Schiefergebirge** Extensive plateau of Germany, dissected by the Rhine and its tributaries, between the Belgian border (W), the Lahn R (E), Bingen (S), and Bonn (N); highest peak, the Grosser Feldberg (879 m/2884 ft) of the Taunus range.

rheology [reeolojee] The study of the deformation and flow of materials subjected to force. It includes the viscosity of liquids and gases, strain and shear due to stresses in solids, and plastic deformation in metals.

rhesus factor A series of closely related but distinct antigens (*agglutinogens*) usually present in the plasma membranes of human red blood cells. They give rise to the Rh (Rhesus) blood group system. Individuals with the factor are **Rh+**; those without are **Rh−**. An Rh− woman carrying her first Rh+ child may produce anti-Rh antibodies during the period immediately following the birth. During a subsequent pregnancy, these antibodies may cross the placenta, and if the fetus is Rh+ they may cause haemolysis and haemolytic disease of the newborn (*erythroblastosis foetalis*). The risk is minimized by reducing the formation of maternal antibodies, achieved by the administration of anti-Rh+ antibodies to the mother immediately after the birth of the first child. In Britain 85% of the population is Rh+. The ratio of Rh+ to Rh− differs between ethnic populations.

rhesus monkey A macaque (*Macaca mulatta*) native to S Asia from Afghanistan to Indochina; stocky; sandy-brown; inhabits a wide range of habitats, including towns; used widely for medical research; also known as **rhesus macaque**. The *rhesus factor* of blood is named after this species.

rhetoric The spoken and written language of persuasion. Rhetoric has had a chequered history. In the classical and mediaeval world, it was a formal branch of learning concerned with the techniques and devices required to persuade or convince an audience. Leading early analysts included Aristotle, Cicero, and Quintilian, who developed theories of successful speech-making. Subsequently it came to signify elaborate and pompous language, which is nonetheless empty and insincere. In recent years, however, there has been a renewed interest in its role in interpersonal and mass communication, as attention has focused on the rules and conventions that enable language and other sign systems to convey meaning, and to present a message in the most effective way.

rheumatic fever A common disease of children and adolescents in Asia and Africa, arising from an immunological reaction to preceding infection with certain strains of *Streptococcus* (eg scarlet fever). It is characterized by fever, a flitting arthritis (in which pain and swelling moves from joint to joint), and inflammation of the heart (*carditis*). While joint involvement rarely leads to persisting deformity, serious rheumatic heart disease can produce permanent distortion, narrowing, and incompetence of the valves of the heart.

rheumatism A non-specific name given to aches and pains in muscles, particularly in the shoulders and back, and common in older people. The absence of fever and serological abnormalities distinguishes the condition from inflammatory rheumatic diseases.

Rhine, J(oseph) B(anks) (1895–1980) Psychologist, the pioneer of parapsychology, born in Juniáta, Pennsylvania, USA. He studied botany at Chicago, switched to psychology under William McDougall at Duke University, and in 1937 became professor of psychology there, co-founding the Parapsychology Laboratory (1930). He later founded the Institute of Parapsychology in Durham, NC (1964). His laboratory-devised experiments involving packs of specially designed cards attempted to establish the phenomena of extrasensory perception and telepathy on a statistical basis.

Rhine, River *p.1299*

Rhine canals A canal system linking the Rhine to other rivers. The chief systems are the Rhine–Rhone, length 349 km/217 mi, built 1784–1833; the Rhine–Marne, length 314 km/195 mi, built 1838–53; the Dortmund–Ems, length 266 km/165 mi, built 1892–9; the Rhine–Herne, length 39 km/24 mi, built 1907–14; and the Rhine–Main–Danube, length 171 km/106 mi, built 1921–92. The Dortmund–Ems and Rhine–Herne canals link the Rhine and Ruhr valleys to the German port of Emden.

rhinitis Inflammation of the lining of the nose, leading to a discharge, and producing a stuffy, running nose. It may be caused by allergic conditions such as hay fever, or by infections such as the common cold.

rhinoceros The second largest land animal (after the elephant), native to S and SE Asia and Africa; a perissodactyl mammal of the family Rhinocerotidae; skin tough, usually with few hairs; long head with small eyes placed well forward; nose with 'horn(s)' made from fibrous outgrowths of the skin; five species: **Indian** (or **greater one-horned**) **rhinoceros**, with stud-like lumps on skin; **Javan** (or **lesser one-horned**) **rhinoceros**, with smoother skin; **Sumatran** (or **Asian two-horned**) **rhinoceros**, with a covering of red-brown hair; African **black** (or **hook-lipped**) **rhinoceros** and African **white** (or **square-lipped**) **rhinoceros**, both with two horns; many extinct species; also known as **rhino**.

rhizoid A uni- or multicellular thread-like structure found in algae, mosses, liverworts, and the gametophytes of ferns. Rhizoids anchor the plant to the substrate and absorb water, but unlike true roots are not differentiated into separate tissues.

rhizome A horizontally growing underground stem. It is either slender and fast-growing, allowing the plant to spread vegetatively, or fleshy and acting as a food store.

Rhine, River

Ger **Rhein**, Dutch **Run**, Fr **Rhin**, ancient **Rhenus** River in C and W Europe, rising in SE Switzerland, in the Rheinwaldhorn glacier; flows N to L Constance, W to Basel, then generally N, forming part of the Germany–France border; divides into two major branches in The Netherlands, the Lek and Waal, before entering the North Sea; length, 1320 km/820 mi; main waterway of W Europe, flowing through major industrial areas; widely connected by canals to other rivers; tourism in the Rhine Valley and on the Rhine itself.

Rhizopoda [riyzopoda] A large group of protozoans distinguished on the basis of their types of pseudopodia; includes the amoebae and foraminiferans.

Rhode Island pop (2000e) 1 048 300; area 3139 sq km/1212 sq mi. New England state in NE USA, divided into five counties; 'Little Rhody' or the 'Ocean State'; smallest US state, but the second most densely populated; one of the original states, 13th to ratify the Federal Constitution, 1790; gave protection to Quakers in 1657 and to Jews from the Netherlands in 1658; capital, Providence; major cities, Warwick, Cranston, Pawtucket; rises from the Narragansett Basin in the E to flat and rolling uplands in the W; highest point Jerimoth Hill (247 m/810 ft); textiles, electronics, silverware, jewellery, potatoes, apples, corn.

Rhodes, Gr **Ródhos**, Ital **Rodi** pop (2000e) 95 400; area 1398 sq km/540 sq mi. Largest island of the Dodecanese, Greece, in the SE Aegean Sea, off SW coast of Turkey; length 72 km/45 mi; maximum width 35 km/22 mi; fourth largest Greek island; crossed by a long ridge of hills, rising to 1215 m/3986 ft; originally settled by Mycenean Greeks, 1400 BC; statue of the Sun-god Chares was one of the Seven Wonders of the World; Knights of the Order of St John settled here, 1309–1522; held by Italy, 1912–47; airfield; ferries to Cyprus, Italy, Turkey; capital, Rhodes, pop (2000e) 45 600; wine, cereals, fruit, tobacco, tourism; acropolis, Temple of Aphrodite (3rd-c BC); Hospital of the Knights (1440–89), now an archaeological museum; Navy Week (Jun–Jul).

Rhodes, Cecil (John) (1853–1902) British colonial statesman, and prime minister of Cape Colony, South Africa (1890–6), born in Bishop's Stortford, Hertfordshire, SE England, UK. Suffering from a lung weakness, he was sent for his health to a brother's cotton farm in South Africa; he subsquently made a fortune at the Kimberley diamond diggings, and amalgamated the several diamond companies to form the De Beers Consolidated Mines Co (1888). Dividing his time between Kimberley and England, he studied at Oxford, and entered the Cape House of Assembly, securing Bechuanaland as a protectorate (1884) and the charter for the British South Africa Company (1889), whose territory was later to be named Rhodesia after him. He became prime minister of Cape Colony, but was forced to resign in 1896 because of complications arising from the Jameson raid. He was a conspicuous figure during the Boer War (1899–1902), when he organized the defences of Kimberley. His will founded scholarships at Oxford for Americans, Germans, and colonials (*Rhodes scholars*).

Rhodes, Wilfred (1877–1973) Cricketer, born in Kirkheaton, West Yorkshire, N England, UK. He played for Yorkshire and England, and during his career (1898–1930) took a world record 4187 wickets and scored 39 722 runs. He took 100 wickets in a season 23 times, and performed the 'double' of 1000 runs and 100 wickets 16 times – first-class cricket records. The oldest man to play Test cricket, he was 52 years 165 days when he played for England against the West Indies at Kingston in April 1930.

Rhodes, Zandra (1940–) Fashion designer, born in Chatham, Kent, SE England, UK. She studied textile printing and lithography at Medway College of Art, then won a scholarship to the Royal College of Art. She designed and printed textiles and, with others, opened the Fulham Road Clothes Shop in 1967, afterwards setting up on her own. She showed her first collection in 1969, and is noted for her distinctive, exotic designs in floating chiffons and silks. In London in 1975 she co-founded Zandra Rhodes (UK) Ltd and Zandra Rhodes (Shops) Ltd, and began licensing her name in the USA, Australia, and Japan. In addition to innovative clothes design, she expanded into cosmetics, jewellery, and home furnishings. In 2003 she opened the Zandra Rhodes Fashion and Textile Museum in Bermondsey, London.

Rhodesia *Zambia; Zimbabwe*

Rhodesian ridgeback A national breed of dog of South Africa; large muscular body with thick neck and long muzzle; ears pendulous; short golden coat; hairs along spine grow forwards, forming a ridge; originally used to hunt lions.

rhododendron An evergreen shrub or small tree, sometimes an epiphyte, native to N temperate regions but concentrated in the area where the great Asian rivers break through the E Himalayas and in New Guinea, and found only on acid soils; leaves alternate, usually oval, leathery; flowers in clusters at tips of main branches, funnel or bell-shaped; sepals sometimes reduced to a rim; 5–10 petals and stamens. Several hundred cultivars are known, with flowers varying greatly in size and colour. Azaleas belong to the same genus and have the same features, except they are deciduous. (Genus: *Rhododendron*, c.1200 species. Family: Ericaceae.)

Rhodope Mountains [rodopee], Bulgarian **Rhodopi** Range of mountains stretching NW–SE in SW Bulgaria and NE Greece, rising to 2925 m/9596 ft at Musala; length 290 km/180 mi; a major climatic divide between C Bulgaria and the Aegean; Bulgarian forestry area.

Rhondda, Cynon, Taff [rontha, kuhnon, taf] pop (2001e) 232 000; area 126 sq km / 49 sq mi. County (unitary authority from 1996) in S Wales, UK; extends along the Rhondda Fawr and Rhondda Fach valleys; administrative centre, Cardiff; other chief towns, Aberdare, Mountain Ash, Pontypridd; former major coal mining area; light engineering, electrical goods, clothing; Royal Mint at Llantrisant.

Rhône, River River in C and SW Europe, rising in the Rhône glacier in S Switzerland, and flowing through L Geneva then W and S between the Jura and the Alps to its delta on the Mediterranean; length, 812 km/504 mi; joined at Lyon by its largest tributary, the Saône; extensive source of hydroelectricity and irrigation; strong current allows little navigation until well below Lyon; canal system between Lyon and the coast; Rhône valley an important routeway, renowned for its scenery.

rhubarb A long-lived perennial herb (*Rheum rhaponticum*), related to dock, and native to Siberia; basal leaves large, heart-shaped, wavy, with green or red stalks; leaves can be poisonous; flowers small, white, 6-petalled, in large spreading inflorescence. A number of hybrids and cultivars are grown for the edible leaf-stalks. During the first Opium War, the Chinese believed the interruption of Chinese rhubarb exports would incapacitate British soldiers because of constipation; the ploy failed. (Family: Polygonaceae.)

Rhyl [ril] 53°19N 3°29W, pop (2000e) 24 400. Seaside resort town in Denbighshire, NE Wales, UK; in Abergele-Rhyl-Prestatyn urban area; at mouth of Clwyd R; railway; furniture, tourism; funfair, promenade, Floral Hall, Sun Centre, Pavilion Theatre.

rhyme The repetition of the same or a similar syllable, for rhetorical effect, typically at the end of a poetic line. Rhyme was rarely found in the classical literatures, developing only with late Latin – it is suggested, to aid memorizing and recitation. There is a limitless variety of rhyme schemes, from the simple rhyming couplet to 'open' rhyme schemes such as that employed in Milton's *Lycidas*. Several 20th-c poets explored half-rhyme, as in Wilfred Owen's 'Strange Meeting', where *friend/frowned* and *killed/cold* are rhymes.

rhyming slang A form of expression, used by Cockney speakers (from London, UK), which hides the identity of a word in a rhyming phrase that has little or no meaningful relationship to it. The expression typically consists of two or three words, the last of which rhymes with the target. Examples include *Cain and Abel* for 'table' and *Hampstead Heath* for 'teeth'. Often the expression is abbreviated, keeping the first word only, as in *china* from *china plate*, 'mate'. The practice is found from the early 19th-c, and may have developed from a form of criminal secret language.

rhyolite [riyoliyt] A silica-rich volcanic igneous rock with a composition approximately equivalent to granite. It is fine-grained or glassy, because of rapid cooling, and occurs in several forms.

Rhys, Jean [rees], pseudonym of **Ella Gwendolen Rees Williams** (1894–1979) Novelist, born in Roseau, Dominica. She moved to England in 1910 to train at the Royal Academy of Dramatic Art, London, but her father's death after only one term obliged her to join a touring theatre company. After World War 1, she lived in Paris, where she wrote short stories and several novels on the theme of female vulnerability, including *The Left Bank* (1927), *After Leaving Mr Mackenzie* (1931), and *Good Morning Midnight* (1939). Returning to Cornwall, she lived in retirement for nearly 30 years, then published in 1966 her best-known novel, *Wide Sargasso Sea*, a 'prequel' to Charlotte Bronte's *Jane Eyre*. Further short stories followed in 1968 and 1976, and an autobiography, *Smile Please*, was published posthumously in 1979.

Rhys-Jones, Sophie *Edward, Prince*

rhythm A pattern marked by the regular recurrence of elements, found in speech, music, dance, and other forms of behaviour, and more generally in the cyclical changes of nature (such as the seasons). In speech, rhythm is most noticeable in the metrical patterns of poetry. In music, it is the constituent that has to do with metre, note-lengths, and accent rather than with pitch. Music is said to be 'strongly rhythmic' when the basic pulse is firmly emphasized (as in much pop music) or when a rhythmic pattern is insistently repeated (such as 'Mars' from Holst's *The Planets*); but rhythmic subtlety in music depends more on the play between an established pulse and the melodic or harmonic accents that disturb it, or between one rhythmic pattern and another (**cross-rhythm**).

rhythm and blues A type of popular music dating from the 1940s and 1950s which combined melodic and textual features of the blues with the rhythm section of a pop group (electric guitars, keyboards, and drum set). It was an important forerunner both of rock and roll and of soul music.

rhythm method *contraception*

Rialto Bridge [realtoh] A bridge spanning the Grand Canal in Venice. It was built in 1588–92 by Antonio da Ponte.

rib A curved, twisted strip of bone passing around the thorax from the vertebral column to articulate indirectly with the sternum by its costal cartilage. There are twelve pairs in humans, of which the eleventh and twelfth are not attached at the front (**floating ribs**). As they pass around the thorax the ribs curve downwards as well as forwards. They provide protection for the lungs, heart, and great vessels. During breathing they move to bring about changes in the volume of the thorax.

Ribbentrop, Joachim von [ribentrop] (1893–1946) German statesman, born in Wesel, W Germany. He became a member of the National Socialist Party in 1932 and, as Hitler's adviser in foreign affairs, was responsible for the Anglo-German naval pact (1935). He became ambassador to Britain (1936) and foreign minister (1938–45). Captured by the British in 1945, he was condemned and executed at Nuremberg.

Ribble, River River rising in the Pennine Hills of North Yorkshire, N England, UK; flows 120 km/75 mi S and SW past Preston to meet the Irish Sea in a broad estuary.

ribbonfish Elongate, slender-bodied fish (*Lepidopus caudatus*) widespread in the tropical and warm temperate N Atlantic, and in parts of the Indian and Pacific Oceans; length up to 2 m/6½ ft; head pointed, jaws bearing powerful teeth; body compressed and tapering, tail fin reduced or absent; dorsal fins extend entire length of body, pelvics absent; also called **scabbardfish**. (Family: Trichiuridae.)

ribbon worm An unsegmented, bilaterally symmetrical worm found mainly on or in shallow marine sediments, occasionally in fresh water; typically predators or scavengers that feed using an outward-turning muscular tube (*proboscis*); may reach lengths of over 20 m/65 ft. (Phylum: Nemertea.)

Ribera, José or **Jusepe de** [reevera], known as **Lo Spagnoletto** ('the Little Spaniard') (1588–1656) Painter and etcher, born in Játiva, E Spain. He settled in Naples, and became court painter there. He is noted for the often gruesome realism with which he treated religious and mythological subjects, such as the martyrdom of the saints, as well as portraits, such as 'Portrait of a Bearded Woman' (1631, Spain). Later works were calmer and more subtle, and include his paintings of the Passion.

rib-faced deer *muntjac*

riboflavin A B vitamin (B_2), an essential active component (*coenzyme*) involved in energy transfers in cells, found especially in green vegetables, milk, eggs, liver, and yeast. A simple deficiency of riboflavin is rare; where one occurs, it is usually associated with multiple deficiencies of several vitamins.

ribonucleic acid *RNA*

ribose [riybohs] $C_5H_{10}O_5$. A pentose or 5-carbon sugar, occurring in the structure of ribonucleic acids (RNA). Two of its atoms (OH, HO) are connected to the phosphate groups in RNA.

ribosome A complex of RNA (**ribosomal RNA** or **rRNA**) and several proteins which exist in bacteria and the cytoplasm of nucleated (eucaryotic) cells. Ribosomes occur both as free particles within the cell and as particles attached to the membranes of the endoplasmic reticulum in eucaryotic cells. Ribosomes account for a large proportion of the total RNA in a cell. In combination with other molecules (in particular, transfer RNA or tRNA), ribosomes function as the machinery that decodes the genetic information present in mRNA, converting this into the amino acid sequence of protein molecules through the process known as *translation*. Proteins then migrate to other parts of the cell for use.

Ricardo, David [rikah(r)doh] (1772–1823) Political economist, born in London, UK. He set up in business as a young man, and by 1814 had made a fortune. In 1817 appeared the work on which his reputation chiefly rests, *Principles of Political Economy and Taxation*. The founder, together with Adam Smith, of British classical economics, he made important contributions to the labour theory of value, the theory of rents, and the theory of comparative advantage, notably in international trade. In 1819 he became an MP, and was influential in the free-trade movement.

Ricci, Matteo [reechee] (1552–1610) Founder of the Jesuit missions in China, born in Macerata, E Italy. He studied at Rome, then travelled to India, where he was ordained (1580). He went on to China in 1583, and from 1602 was employed at the court in Beijing. He mastered Chinese, wrote works to a standard which received much commendation from the Chinese literati, and met with great success as a missionary. His journal (over 600 pages in English translation) gives close detail on Ming China.

Ricci, Nina, originally **Maria Nielli** (1883–1970) Fashion designer, born in Turin, NW Italy. She became an apprentice in a Paris couture house in 1900, joined Raffin in 1908, and stayed with him for 20 years, eventually becoming his partner. She showed her first collection in 1932, and her fragrances in 1941, and developed a wide range of further products in cosmetics, furs, and fashion accessories. After her retirement in 1959, the firm continued to grow, and by the mid-1990s it had boutiques in over 130 countries.

Ricci, Sebastiano [reechee] (1659–1734) Painter, born in Belluno, NE Italy. He trained in Venice, and after extensive travel in Italy worked for two years in Vienna (1701–3). In 1712 he travelled to England, via Holland, with his nephew Marco Ricci. The only complete work to survive from this time is a 'Resurrection' in the apse of Chelsea Hospital chapel. His colourful style influenced the young Tiepolo.

Riccio, David *Rizzio, David*

Rice, Condoleezza [kondoleetsa] (1955–) US academic and Republican politician, born in Birmingham, Alabama, USA. She studied political science at the University of Denver, graduating at the age of 19, then continued in political science at Notre Dame and at Denver. She started political life as a Democrat, but changed parties in 1982 as a result of Jimmy Carter's Afghanistan policy. She joined Stanford University in 1981, becoming a professor in the political science department and a Hoover Institution fellow (1985–6, 1991–3), and was the first woman and first African-American to become a Stanford provost (1993–9). After a period in Washington in the mid-1980s as a fellow attached to the Joint Chiefs-of-Staff, she became director of Soviet and East European affairs with the National Security Council (1989), and special assistant to George Bush. She is co-author (with Philip Zelikow) of *Germany Unified and Europe Transformed* (1995). She was appointed national security adviser by George W Bush in 2001.

Rice, Tim, popular name of **Sir Timothy Miles Bindon Rice** (1944–) Lyricist, writer, and broadcaster, born in Buckinghamshire, SC England, UK. He studied at Lancing College, then took up law, but left a lawyer's firm to join the EMI recording company. He has co-written lyrics on many award-winning records, has appeared on numerous radio and TV quiz shows, and written several books. He is best known for writing the lyrics to music by Andrew Lloyd Webber for *Joseph and the Amazing Technicolour Dreamcoat* (1968), followed by *Jesus Christ Superstar* (1971) and *Evita* (1978). Later works include the lyrics for *Chess* (recorded 1984), *Cricket* (1986), *Starmania* (1991), and *Beauty and the Beast* (1997). He was knighted in 1994.

rice An important cereal grass (*Oryza sativa*), with open panicles, drooping with numerous grains. It is the premier food plant of Asia, and was grown in China from before 4000 BC. It is cultivated in flooded paddy fields, with many varieties adapted to different water-levels. Recent breeding programmes have produced successful, high-yielding, semi-dwarf varieties. Upland rice is low-yielding, but does not require flooding, and can be grown in cooler, drier regions. (Family: Gramineae.)

rice blast A fungal disease (*Pyricularia oryzae = Magnoportha grisea*) which produces lesions on the leaves, stems, and panicles of rice, causing serious loss of yield or even crop failure in paddy rice; also known as **tungro**. It was the main cause of the Bengal famine, which caused great loss of life in E India and Bangladesh in the late 1940s, but losses are now infrequent following the introduction of resistant varieties. (Order: Ascomycetes.)

Rich, Adrienne (Cecile) (1929–) Poet, born in Baltimore, Maryland, USA. She studied at Radcliffe College, lived briefly in The Netherlands, then taught at several institutions, notably at Cornell from 1981. Based in New York City, she won many awards, and became known for her highly personal poetry, as in *Diving into the Wreck: Poems 1971–2* (1973). Later works include *An Atlas of the Difficult World: Poems 1988–1991* (1991) and *Midnight Salvage: Poems 1995–1998* (1999).

Richard I, known as **Richard Coeur de Lion** or **Richard the Lionheart** (1157–99) King of England (1189–99), born in Oxford, Oxfordshire, SC England, UK, the third son of Henry II and Eleanor of Aquitaine. Of his 10-year reign, he spent only five months in England, devoting himself to crusading and defending the Angevin lands in France. Already recognized as an outstanding soldier, he took Messina (1190), Cyprus, and Acre (1191) during the Third Crusade, and advanced to within sight of Jerusalem. On the return journey, he was arrested in Vienna (1192), and remained a prisoner of the German Emperor Henry VI until he agreed to be ransomed (1194). The rest of his reign was occupied in warfare against Philip II of France, while the government of England was conducted by the justiciar, Hubert Walter. Richard was mortally wounded while besieging the castle of Châlus, Aquitaine.

Richard II (1367–1400) King of England (1377–99), born in Bordeaux, SW France, the younger son of Edward the Black Prince, who succeeded his grandfather, Edward III, at the age of 10. He displayed great bravery in confronting the rebels in London during the Peasants' Revolt (1381); but already parliament was concerned about his favourites, and the reign was dominated by the struggle between Richard's desire to act independently, and the magnates' concern to curb his power. He quarrelled with his uncle, John of Gaunt, and his main supporters were found guilty of treason in the 'Merciless Parliament' of 1388. After Richard had declared an end to his minority (1389), he built up a stronger following, and during 1397–8 took his revenge by having the Earl of Arundel executed, the Duke of Gloucester murdered, and several lords banished, the exiles including Gaunt's son, Henry Bolingbroke (later Henry IV). His final act of oppression was to confiscate the Lancastrian estates after Gaunt's death (1399). Having failed to restrain the king by constitutional means, the magnates resolved to unseat him from the throne. Bolingbroke invaded England unopposed, and Richard was deposed in his favour (Sep 1399). He died in Pontefract Castle, Yorkshire, possibly of starvation.

Richard III (1452–85) King of England (1483–5), born in Fotheringay Castle, Northamptonshire, C England, UK, the youngest son of Richard, Duke of York. He was created Duke of Gloucester by his brother, Edward IV, in 1461, accompanied him into exile (1470), and played a key role in his restoration (1471). Rewarded with part of the Neville inheritance, he exercised viceregal powers in N England, and in 1482 recaptured Berwick-upon-Tweed from the Scots. When Edward died (1483) and was succeeded by his under-age son, Edward V, Richard acted first as protector, but within three months, he had overthrown the Woodvilles (relations of Edward IV's queen), seen to the execution of Lord Hastings (c.1430–83), and had himself proclaimed and crowned as the rightful king. Young Edward and his brother were probably murdered in the Tower on Richard's orders (though not all historians agree). He tried to stabilize his position, but failed to win broad-based support. His rival Henry Tudor (later Henry VII), confronted him in battle at Bosworth Field, and Richard died fighting bravely against heavy odds. Though ruthless, he was not the absolute monster Tudor historians portrayed him to be, nor is there proof he was a hunchback.

Richard, Cliff, popular name of **Sir Harry Roger Webb** (1940–) Pop-singer, born in Lucknow, NC India. He moved to England at the age of eight, began his professional career playing with the Dick Teague Group, and formed his own band in 1958. Originally called The Drifters, the group changed its name to The Shadows to avoid confusion with a US vocal group of the same name. Following the success of 'Living Doll' (1959), The Shadows were hailed as Britain's answer to American rock. He made a series of family musical films during the 1960s, including *The Young Ones* (1961) and *Summer Holiday* (1962), and played the leading role in the musicals *Time* (1986) and *Heathcliff* (1996). Following his conversion to Christianity, his clean-cut image damaged his reputation with rock fans, but he has nevertheless become a British entertainment institution. His many recorded albums have included *21 Today* (1961), *Rock and Roll Juvenile* (1979), *Love Songs* (1981), *Silver*, released in 1983 to celebrate 25 years as a recording artist, *Mistletoe and Wine* which topped the charts for four weeks at Christmas in 1988, and *Cliff at Christmas* (2003). He was number one again with his single *Millennium Prayer* in December 1999. He was knighted in 1995.

Richard Alston Dance Company Britain's largest independent dance company. Founded by its artistic director Richard Alston in 1994, it focuses on new choreography but combines this with the re-creation of seminal past works from Alston's career. It is resident at The Place, London, Britain's largest National Dance Agency, one of the busiest venues in Europe and home to the London Contemporary Dance School.

Richards, Emma (1975–) Yachtswoman, born in Helensburgh, Argylle and Bute, W Scotland, UK. She studied at Glasgow University and later settled in Hampshire, S England. In her 18 m/ 60 ft yacht *Pindar*, she became the first woman and youngest person to complete the 29 000-mile Around Alone solo race. She departed from New York (Sep 2002) and after 135 days at sea crossed the finishing line at Newport, RI (May 2003) in fourth place.

Richards, Frank, pseudonym of **Charles (Harold St John) Hamilton** (1875–1961) Children's writer, born in London, UK. Educated privately, he wrote stories for magazines and comics while still a schoolboy. As a professional writer, he produced 70 000 words a week under various pseudonyms for *Gem*, *Magnet*, and other papers. He created 'Billy Bunter' and 'Greyfriars School' for *The Magnet*, and after World War 2, wrote numerous books about 'Billy Bunter' and 'Tom Merry', becoming the most prolific author in the history of juvenile fiction.

Richards, Sir Gordon (1904–86) Jockey and trainer, born in Oakengates, Shropshire, WC England, UK. Between 1921 and 1954 he rode a record 4870 winners in Britain, and was champion jockey a record 26 times (1925–53). On 12 occasions he rode 200 winners in a season, and his 269 winners in 1947 remained a record until broken by Tony McCoy in 2002. He won 14 English Classics (1930–53), and rode 12 consecutive winners (1933), including all six at Chepstow. He won his only Epsom Derby in 1953 on *Pinza*, six days after receiving a knighthood. He took up training after retirement in 1954.

Richards, I(vor) A(rmstrong) (1893–1979) Literary critic and scholar, who pioneered the detailed critical study of literary texts in the 20th-c, born in Sandbach, Cheshire, NWC England, UK. With C K Ogden he wrote *The Meaning of Meaning* in 1923. His later books include the influential *Principles of Literary Criticism* (1924) and *Practical Criticism* (1929). During the 1930s he helped to develop Basic English, worked in China (1929–30, 1936–8), and became professor of English at Harvard (1944), where his publications included poetry as well as critical essays.

Richards, Viv, popular name of **Sir Isaac Vivian Alexander Richards** (1952–) Cricket player, born in Antigua. In 1976 he scored a record 1710 Test runs in one calendar year. He captained the West Indies (1985–91), and scored 8540 runs in 121 Test matches, including 24 centuries. In England he played county cricket for Somerset (1974–86) and Glamorgan (1990–3). He received a knighthood in 1999.

Richardson, Henry Handel, pseudonym of **Ethel Florence Lindesay Robertson**, *née* **Richardson** (1870–1946) Novelist, born in Melbourne, Victoria, SE Australia. She travelled and studied in Europe, and after her marriage to **John George Robertson** (1895) lived in Strasbourg and then England (1904). She attained distinction with the third part of her trilogy, published as *The Fortunes of Richard Mahony* (1929), which traces the career of a gold-rush migrant .

Richardson, H(enry) H(obson) (1838–86) Architect, born in Priestley Plantation, Louisiana, USA. Educated at Harvard, he studied architecture in Paris, and initiated the Romanesque revival in the USA, leading to a distinctively American style of architecture. He designed a number of churches, especially Trinity Church, Boston (1872–7), the Allegheny Co Buildings in Pittsburgh, and halls of residence at Harvard (1879–84).

Richardson, Miranda (1958–) Actress, born in Southport, Lancashire, NW England, UK. She made her West End debut in *Moving* (1980–1), and her film debut in *Dance With a Stranger* (1985). Later films include *Empire of The Sun* (1987), *Damage* (1992, BAFTA for Best Supporting Actress), *Tom and Viv* (1994), *The Apostle* (1997), *Sleepy Hollow* (1999), *Get Carter* (2000), and *Spider* (2002). Television roles include Queen Elizabeth in the BBC comedy series *Blackadder* (1990), and *A Dance to the Music of Time* (1997).

Richardson, Sir Ralph (David) (1902–83) Actor, born in Cheltenham, Gloucestershire, SWC England, UK. He made his debut at the Little Theatre, Brighton (1921), and gained an early reputation with the Birmingham Repertory Theatre, which he joined in 1926. His association with the Old Vic Company commenced in 1930, and he was asked to lead its post-war revival. His many stage appearances include *West of Suez* (1971), *The Cherry Orchard* (1978), and *The Understanding* (1982), and he had major roles in such films as *Anna Karenina* (1948), *The Heiress, Oh! What a Lovely War* (1969), *A Doll's House* (1973), and *Invitation to the Wedding* (1983). He was knighted in 1947.

Richardson, Robert C (1937–) Physicist, born in Washington, District of Columbia, USA. He studied at Duke University, then moved to Cornell, where with Lee and Osheroff he contributed to the discovery of the superfluidity of helium-3. He shared the Nobel Prize for Physics in 1996.

Richardson, Samuel (1689–1761) Novelist, born in Mackworth, Derbyshire, C England, UK. He was apprenticed to a printer, married his master's daughter, and set up in business for himself in London, where he became the centre of a wide circle of friends. *Pamela* (1740), his first novel, is 'a series of familiar letters now first published in order to cultivate the Principles of Virtue and Religion', and this was the aim of all his works. He also wrote *Clarissa* (1748), published in seven volumes, and *Sir Charles Grandison* (1754). In using the epistolary method (which suggested authenticity at a time when mere fiction was frowned upon), he helped to develop the dramatic scope of the novel, then little regarded as a literary form.

Richelieu, Armand Jean du Plessis, Cardinal, duc de (Duke of) [**reeshlyoe**] (1585–1642) French statesman and first minister of France (1624–42), born in Richelieu, WC France. A protégé of the queen mother, Marie de Medicis, he became minister of state (1624), and as chief minister was the effective ruler of France. His twin aims, to secure universal obedience to the Bourbon monarchy and to enhance France's international prestige, were achieved at the expense of recalcitrant groups in French society. His principal achievement was to check Habsburg power, ultimately by sending armies into the Spanish Netherlands, Alsace, Lorraine, and Roussillon. He founded the French Academy in 1634.

Richler, Mordecai (1931–2001) Writer, born in Montreal, Quebec, SE Canada. He was brought up in Montreal's Jewish ghetto, attended university in Montreal, then lived in Paris (1951–2). His best-known novel is *The Apprenticeship of Duddy Kravitz* (1959), which was later filmed, although *St Urbain's Horseman* (1971) is a more ambitious work. Later books include *Solomon Gursky was Here* (1990) and *Barney's Version* (1997). He wrote essays, scripts for cinema, radio, and television, and a memoir, *This Year in Jerusalem* (1994).

Richmond (UK), properly **Richmond-upon-Thames [temz]** 51°28N 0°19W, pop (2001e) 172 300. Borough of SW Greater London, UK; on the R Thames; includes the suburbs of Twickenham, Richmond, and Barnes; railway; engineering, plastics; Hampton Court Palace, Royal Botanic Gardens (Kew Gardens), Ham House.

Richmond (Virginia) 37°33N 77°27W, pop (2000e) 197 800. Port and capital of state in E Virginia, USA, on the James R; settled as a trading post (Fort Charles), 1645; state capital, 1779; scene of Virginia Convention (1788) for the ratification of the Federal Constitution; Confederate capital during the Civil War; captured by Union forces, 1865; airfield; railway; three universities (1804, 1832, 1865); corporate headquarters centre; tobacco, aluminium products, industrial fibres; Virginia Museum of Fine Arts, Museum of the Confederacy, National Battlefield Park.

Richter, Hans (1843–1916) Conductor, born in Raab, NW Hungary. He studied at Vienna, became conductor at Munich, Budapest, and Vienna, gave a series of annual concerts in London (1879–97), and was conductor of the Hallé Orchestra (1897–1911). He was an authority on the music of Wagner, with whom he was closely associated in the Bayreuth festivals.

Richter, Johann Paul (Friedrich), pseudonym **Jean Paul** (1763–1825) Novelist and humorist, born in Wunsiedel, E Germany. He studied theology in Leipzig, then turned to literature, and after several years struggling to publish, began to teach (1787). He produced a wide range of works, achieving success with such romances as *Die unsichtbare Loge* (1793, The Invisible Lodge), *Hesperus* (1795), and the four-volume *Titan* (1800–3).

Richter, Sviatoslav (Teofilovich) (1915–97) Pianist, born in Zhitomir, WC Ukraine. He studied at the Moscow Conservatory (1937–42), and won the Stalin Prize in 1949. He made extensive concert tours, with a wide repertoire, and was associated with the music festivals at Aldeburgh and Spoleto.

Richter scale A logarithmic scale, devised in 1935 by US geophysicist Charles Francis Richter (1900–85), for representing the energy released by earthquakes. A figure of two or less is barely perceptible, while an earthquake measuring over five may be destructive, and eight or more is a major earthquake.

Richthofen, Ferdinand (Paul Wilhelm), Baron von [rikhthohfn] (1833–1905) Geographer, geologist, and traveller, born in Karlsruhe, SW Germany. He studied at Wrocław, Poland (formerly Breslau, Prussia) and Berlin, in 1860 accompanied a Prussian expedition to E Asia, then travelled in Java, Siam, Burma, California (1863–8), China, and Japan (1868–72). After his return he became professor of geology at Bonn (1875), and of geography at Leipzig (1883) and at Berlin (1886), his research helping to develop the field of geomorphology.

ricin [riysin, risin] An extremely toxic protein present in the castor bean (*Ricinus communis*) of the family Euphorbiaceae, which has been used as a deadly poison in political assassinations. It has been proposed as a chemical warfare agent.

rickets A disorder of infants and growing children resulting from a deficiency of vitamin D. There is a failure to calcify the growing ends of long bones (eg the femur and radius), and the soft bones are prone to deformities; bowing of the legs and curvature of the spine are typical. Swelling and enlargement of the ends of the ribs in front of the chest is known as the 'rickety rosary'.

Rickettsia [riketsia] A genus of typically rod-shaped micro-organisms with bacteria-like cell walls. Rickettsias multiply inside or in close association with cells of animal hosts. The primary hosts are usually arthropods, which often serve as carriers to vertebrate hosts. They include the causative agents of scrub typhus, trench fever, and other human diseases. (Kingdom: Monera. Family: Rickettsiaceae.)

Rickman, Alan (1946–) Actor, born in London, UK. He studied at Chelsea School of Art, the Royal College of Art, and the Royal Academy of Dramatic Art, London, and played a wide range of theatre roles during the 1980s, including seasons at the RSC in 1978–9 and 1985–6. He became well known for his film work, beginning with *Die Hard* (1988), and including *Truly, Madly, Deeply* (1991), *Robin Hood, Prince of Thieves* (1991, BAFTA Best Supporting Actor), *Michael Collins* (1996), *Rasputin* (1996, Emmy), *Galaxy Quest* (1999), *Harry Potter and the Philosopher's Stone* (2001), and *Love Actually* (2003). He made his directorial debut with *The Winter Guest* (1998).

Ricoeur, Paul [reekoe(r)] (1913–) Philosopher, born in Valence, SE France. He studied at the University of Paris, and became professor at Strasbourg (1948–56), Paris-Nanterre (1956–70), and Chicago (1970). He has been an influential figure in French and Anglo-American philosophy, engaging critically with various contemporary methodologies – structuralism, phenomenology, psychoanalysis, and hermeneutics – across a whole range of problems. His publications include *Philosophie de la volonté* (3 vols, 1950–60, Philosophy of the Will) and *La Métaphore vive* (1975, The Living Metaphor).

riddle An utterance, often cast in a traditional form, whose intention is to mystify or mislead; a linguistic guessing game. In Europe, riddles tend to be short questions, usually posed for humorous purposes, and generally restricted to children's games and conversation. In Africa, however, they are widely used by adults, often comprising cryptic statements of a philosophical character. In ancient Greece, they had a serious purpose, being used by judges, oracles, and others to test a person's wisdom.

Ridgeley, Andrew *Michael, George*

Ridgeway A long-distance footpath in England running 137 km/85 mi from Beacon Hill, Buckinghamshire, SC England, to Overton Hill, Wiltshire, S England, UK. The modern path follows the **Great Ridgeway**, a prehistoric trading route (used by drovers in the 18th c); it also follows the old Icknield Way for a stretch.

Ridgway, Matthew (Bunker) (1895–1993) US soldier, born in Fort Monroe, Virginia, USA. He trained at West Point, and commanded the 82nd Airborne Division in Sicily (1943) and Normandy (1944), the 18th Airborne Corps in the North West Europe campaign (1944–5), and the US 8th Army in UN operations in Korea (1950). He succeeded Douglas MacArthur in command of US and UN forces (1951), and was supreme Allied commander in Europe in succession to Eisenhower (1952–3), and chief of US army staff (1953).

Riding for the Disabled The organized riding of horses and ponies to enrich the lives of seriously disabled people, especially children. People with Down's syndrome, cerebral palsy, spina bifida, and other such disabilities are taught to ride suitable mounts under careful supervision. Subjects usually confined to a wheelchair are able to benefit from a superior viewpoint, and to have a measure of control of their activities, sometimes for the first time in their lives.

riding the marches A Scottish ritual, also called **common riding**, the equivalent of English *beating the bounds*. It is performed on horseback, chiefly in the towns of S Scotland.

Ridley, Nicholas (c.1500–1555) Protestant martyr, born near Haltwhistle, Northumberland, NE England, UK. Educated at Cambridge, he was ordained c.1524, and studied in Paris and Louvain (1527–30). He then held a variety of posts, including chaplain to Cranmer and Henry VIII, and Bishop of Rochester (1547). An ardent reformer, he became Bishop of London (1550), and helped Cranmer prepare the Thirty-nine Articles. On the death of Edward VI he espoused the cause of Lady Jane Grey, was imprisoned, and executed.

Rie, Dame Lucie [ree] (1902–95) Studio potter, born in Vienna, Austria. Trained at the *Kunstgewerbeschule*, in 1938 she moved as a refugee to England, where she shared a workshop with Hans Coper, producing ceramic jewellery and buttons while continuing her individual work. She later produced stoneware, tin-glazed earthenware, and porcelain pots, with a precision and technical control that has influenced many of today's leading potters. A retrospective exhibition of her work was held at Norwich in 1981. She was created a dame in 1991.

Riefenstahl, Leni [reefenshtahl], popular name of **Berta Helene Amalie Riefenstahl** (1902–2003) Film-maker, born in Berlin, Germany. After acting in several films she formed her own company, and made *Triumph des Willens* (1935, Triumph of the Will), a compelling record of a Nazi rally at Nuremberg. It vividly illustrated Hitler's charismatic appeal, but tainted her career, prompting criticism that she had glorified the event. *Olympiad* (1938), her epic two-part documentary of the 1936 Berlin Olympic Games, was given a gala premiere on Hitler's 49th birthday. During World War 2 she made *Tiefland*, a non-musical and non-political version of d'Albert's opera of that name. This was premiered in 1954, after she had been released from imprisonment for her collaboration with the Nazis. In the 1970s she published several controversial photographic studies of Africa. Her autobiography, *Leni Riefenstahl, a Memoir*, was published in 1993.

Riel, Louis [ree-el] (1844–85) Canadian political leader, born in Red River Settlement, Rupert's Land, Canada. He succeeded his father as a leader of the Métis, and headed the Red River Rebellion in 1869–70. As president of the provisional government, he was able to secure better terms for the new province of Manitoba in the Confederation. Following a period of exile in the USA, he returned to lead a second uprising of Métis (1885), in what is now Saskatchewan. His subsequent arrest and trial led to his execution.

Riemann, (Georg Friedrich) Bernhard [reeman] (1826–66) Mathematician, born in Breselenz, NC Germany. He studied at Göttingen and Berlin universities, and became professor of mathematics at Göttingen (1859). His early work was on the theory of functions, but he is best remembered for his development of non-Euclidian geometry, important in modern physics and relativity theory. His profound conjecture (the **Riemann hypothesis**) about the behaviour of the zeta (or Riemann) function, which he showed determines the distribution of the prime numbers, has resisted proof since its publication in 1857.

Rienzi, Cola di [rienzee], also spelled **Rienzo** (1313–54) Italian patriot, born in Rome, Italy. In 1347 he incited the citizens to rise against the rule of the nobles. The senators were driven out, and he was made tribune. Papal authority then turned against him, and he fled from Rome. He returned in 1354, and tried to re-establish his position, but was killed in a rising against him. Wagner's opera on his story was completed in 1840.

Riesman, David [reezman] (1909–) Sociologist, born in Philadelphia, Pennsylvania, USA. He studied at Harvard, then worked as a clerk, teacher, and assistant district attorney before becoming professor at the University of Chicago (1946–58) and then at Harvard. His most notable work is the co-authored study of the urban middle class, *The Lonely Crowd* (1950). He has also written extensively on policy for higher education.

Rievaulx Abbey [reevoh] A ruined 12th-c Cistercian abbey, located in a deep valley in the North Yorkshire Moors National Park, Ryedale district, North Yorkshire, England, UK. The monastery was founded during the Christianizing mission of St Bernard of Clairvaux in N England.

Rif or **Riff** A cluster of Berber agricultural and herding groups of NE Morocco. Famed as warriors, in the 1920s they defeated the Spanish, but were eventually conquered by combined French and Spanish forces in 1926. They later served in the French and Spanish regiments in Morocco.

Rifkind, Sir Malcolm (Leslie) (1946–) British Conservative statesman, born in Edinburgh, EC Scotland, UK. He studied at Edinburgh, was called to the bar in 1970, and was elected an MP in 1974. After a ministerial post in the Foreign and Commonwealth office (1983–6), he became secretary of state for Scotland (1986–90), transport (1990–2), defence (1992–5), and foreign secretary (1995–7). He lost his seat in the 1997 general election, the year he received a knighthood.

rifle A type of firearm developed into a practical weapon in the mid-19th-c in which the barrel of the gun is internally grooved in a spiral form. The bullet is spun as it passes down the bore, the spin stabilizing it in flight and thus increasing its accuracy. Bolt-action magazine rifles firing smokeless powder cartridges transformed infantry firepower by the end of the 19th-c, but their technology remained more or less static until the middle of World War 2, when the gas-operated automatic rifle made its appearance. Today's military **assault rifles** are lightweight, fully automatic weapons with great range and accuracy. The rifling concept has also been developed in producing barrels for large artillery pieces, to assist accuracy.

riflebird A bird of paradise, native to NE Australia and New Guinea; males with metallic plumage on throat; short rounded wings; displays high in trees; inhabits forests; eats invertebrates and fruit. (Genus: *Ptiloris*, 3 species.)

rifleman A small, wren-like bird (*Acanthisitta chloris*), native to New Zealand and nearby islands; male with green back and pale underparts; inhabits woodland; feeds in trees on insects and spiders; nests in hole in tree; formerly also called **riflebird**. (Family: Xenicidae.)

rift valley An elongated trough in the Earth's crust bounded by normal faults; also termed a **graben**. It is a region of tension in the Earth's crust arising from crustal plates moving apart, and is associated with volcanoes, such as Kilimanjaro in the East African Rift valley. Rift valleys also form along mid-ocean ridges.

Rift Valley or **Great Rift Valley** Major geological feature running from the Middle East S to SE Africa; from Syria (35°N) to Mozambique (20°S), covering a sixth of the Earth's circumference; a depression interrupted by plateaux and mountains; parts filled by seas and lakes; contains the Sea of Galilee, Dead Sea, Gulf of Aqaba, and Red Sea; runs between the Ethiopian highlands and the Somali plains; branches in Kenya, S of L Turkana; E branch lakes include Baringo Nakuru, Naivasha, and Magadi; W branch (also known as the Albertine Rift), along the edge of the Congo basin, includes lakes Albert, Edward, Kivu, and Tanganyika; once rejoined, the rift holds L Nyasa, follows the R Zambezi valley, and ends on the Mozambique coastal lowlands.

rig(ging) *sailing rig*

Riga [reega] 56°53N 24°08E, pop (2000e) 836 000. Seaport capital of Latvia; on the R Daugava, near its mouth on the Gulf of Riga; founded as a trading station, 1201; member of the Hanseatic League, 1282; capital of independent Latvia, 1918–40, and from 1991; occupied by Germany in World War 2; airport; railway; university (1919); military base; shipbuilding, machinery, metalworking, woodworking, chemicals, electronics, fishing; cultural centre and seaside resort; Riga Castle (1330), Lutheran cathedral (13th-c, rebuilt 16th-c); historic centre, a world heritage site.

Rigel [riyjuhl] *Orion* (astronomy)

Rigg, Dame Diana (1938–) Actress, born in Doncaster, S Yorkshire, N England, UK. She studied at the Royal Academy of Dramatic Art and joined the Royal Shakespeare Company at Stratford (1959–64). After playing Emma Peel in the popular *The Avengers* television series, she joined the National Theatre (1972), making regular appearances during the 1970s. In New York her role in *Medea* (1993–4) earned her a Tony Award. Among her films are *Evil Under the Sun* (1982) and *A Good Man in Africa* (1994). Her television work includes *Mother Love* (1990, BAFTA), *The Mrs Bradley Mysteries* (2000), and *King Charles II: The Power and the Passion* (2003). She was made a dame in 1994.

right ascension One of the two co-ordinates, used with declination for specifying position on the celestial sphere; the celestial equivalent of longitude. It is the angular distance measured E along the celestial equator from the vernal equinox to the intersection of the hour circle passing through the body. Units are hours, minutes, and seconds, and one hour of right ascension is 15°.

rightsizing A strategy for organizing the use of mainframe, mini, and personal computers in an organization, in such a way that data is held on the type of computer and at the location for which it is most suited.

right to silence In most legal jurisdictions, a right which protects criminal suspects from answering questions put to them by the relevant authority or from giving any evidence. In the UK, police are required to *caution* suspects about their right to silence and right to legal advice. The drawing of any adverse inference from this silence is in the court's discretion. However, if suspects fail to account for objects in their possession or their presence at a particular place, inferences of guilt may be drawn. The right to a fair trial enshrined in the European Convention on Human Rights includes a right to remain silent, and for suspects not to incriminate themselves. In the USA, police are required to give all suspects a *Miranda warning*, based on the United States Supreme Court case *Miranda v. Arizona* (1966), in which the court held that prosecutors may not use incriminating statements of suspects unless strict procedural safeguards are followed to guarantee the suspect's awareness of the constitutional right to remain silent and to have an attorney. Any waiver of these rights must be free and voluntary, and the questioning must cease if the suspect wishes to remain silent or requests an attorney.

right whale A baleen whale; large head (up to 40% of total length); three species: **right whale** (*Balaena glacialis*) from temperate seas; **bowhead** or **Greenland right whale** (*Balaena mysticetus*) from the Arctic, with the longest baleen plates (4·5 m/14¾ ft) of any whale; **pygmy right whale** (*Caperea marginata*) from sub-Antarctic seas. The name is also used for **right whale dolphins** (genus: *Lissodelphis*, 2 species). (Family: Balaenidae.)

right wing One end of the political continuum, originally identifying those who supported the institutions of the monarchy during the French Revolution. In the 19th-c the term was applied to those who were conservative in their view, supporting authority, the state, tradition, property, patriotism, and institutions such as the Church and family. Those on the right were strongly opposed to socialism. In the 20th-c, while the right was still associated with such a position, it also developed a radical, non-conservative side. On the one hand, this was associated with extreme nationalism (fascism), and, on the other, with attempts to reverse what are viewed as socialist developments.

rigidity *shear modulus*

rigor mortis [riger maw(r)tis] A temporary stiffening of the body after death because of the depletion of adenosine triphosphate and phosphoryl creatinine within skeletal muscle fibres. The time of onset depends to some extent on the cause of death and environmental temperature, but usually begins 3 hours after death, and is completed by 12 hours. The effects persist for 3–4 days, after which flaccidity returns.

Rijeka [riyeka], Ital **Fiume** 45°20N 14°27E, pop (2000e) 172 900. Seaport town in W Croatia, on R Rečina, where it meets Rijeka Bay on the Adriatic coast; Croatia's largest port; former Roman base (Tarsatica); occupied by the Slavs, 7th-c; naval base of the Austro-Hungarian Empire until 1918; ceded to Italy, 1924; ceded to Yugoslavia, 1947; airfield; railway; ferries; university (1973); shipyards, oil refineries; Trsat castle, Jadran palace, cathedral, national museum.

Rijksmuseum [riyksmoozayum] ('state museum') A Dutch word generally used to indicate the national art gallery in Amsterdam, The Netherlands. The collection, which is amongst the finest in Europe and is unrivalled in its holdings of Dutch masters, derives from that of the Nationale Kunst-Galerij, opened in 1800. The present building was designed by Petrus Cuypers and erected in 1877–85.

Rila Monastery [reela] A monastery in the Rila Mountain range, Bulgaria, founded by Ivan Rilski (876–946), which became a great spiritual centre. In the 14th-c, when it was at the height of its wealth and power, a vast monastery was erected – most of which was destroyed by fire in 1833. The present complex was built in 1834–60, and is a world heritage site.

Rila Mountain [reela], Bulgarian **Rila Planina** Mountain in W Bulgaria, forming the NW part of the Rila–Rhodopes Mountain Massif; the highest range in the Balkan peninsula, rising to 2925 m/9596 ft at Musala; forestry and livestock grazing.

Riley, Bridget (1931–) Artist, born in London, UK. She studied at Goldsmith's College of Art (1949–52) and the Royal College of Art (1952–5). Her first one-woman exhibition was in London at Gallery One in 1962, followed by others worldwide. She is a leading practitioner of Op Art, manipulating overall flat patterns, originally in black and white but later in colour, using repeated shapes or undulating lines, often creating an illusion of movement, as seen in 'Fall' (1963, Tate, London). She was the first English painter to win the major painting prize at the Venice Biennale (1968). She was made a Companion of Honour in 1998.

Rilke, Rainer Maria [rilkuh] (1875–1926) Lyric poet, born in Prague, Czech Republic. He studied at Prague, Munich, and Berlin. His three-part poem cycle, *Das Stundenbuch* (1905, The Book of Hours), written after visiting Russia, shows the deep influence of Russian Pietism. Mysticism was abandoned for the aesthetic ideal in *Gedichte* (1907–8, Poems), seen also in his two major works, *Die Sonnette an Orpheus* (Sonnets to Orpheus) and *Duineser Elegien* (Duino Elegies), both written in 1923.

rille [ril] A straight or winding valley on the Moon. **Linear rilles** are caused by faults in the Moon's crust. **Sinous rilles**, with a U-shaped cross-section, are related to the lava tubes in volcanic regions such as Hawaii, and mark places where molten lava has flowed in the past.

Rimbaud, (Jean Nicolas) Arthur [rĩboh] (1854–91) Poet, born in Charleville, NE France. One of the most revolutionary figures in 19th-c literature, he published his first book of poems in 1870, following this with his most famous work, *Le Bateau ivre* (1871, The Drunken Boat). In 1871, Verlaine invited him to Paris, where they led a life of ill repute together. Before the relationship ended (1873), Rimbaud wrote *Les Illuminations*, a series of prose and verse poems, which show him to be a precursor of Symbolism, and which were published by Verlaine in 1876, when he believed Rimbaud to be dead. Disappointed at the cold reception given to his *Une Saison en enfer* (1873, A Season in Hell), he stopped writing, and spent the rest of his life wandering in Europe and the NE regions of Africa.

rime A form of precipitation in which surfaces are coated in opaque ice. It forms when ice accretes on objects through the freezing, on impact, of supercooled water droplets, because the surfaces are at temperatures well below the freezing point of water.

Rimet, Jules [reemay] (1873–1956) French football administrator. He founded the Red Star Club of Paris, became president of the French football league (1910), and was president of the French Football Federation (1919–49). He promoted the Fédération Internationale de Football Association (FIFA), of which he was president (1921–56), and founded the World Cup competition (1930), his name being added to the title in 1946.

Rimington, Stella *intelligence service*

Rimini, Lat **Arminium** 44°04N 12°34E, pop (2001e) 131 400. City in Emilia-Romagna region of N Italy, on the Riviera del Sole of the Adriatic; at the junction of the Roman Aemilian Way and Flaminian Way; occupied by Romans (268 BC); under Papal States control (1509); annexed to the Kingdom of Italy (1860); railway; Roman Arch of Augustus (c.27 BC); amphitheatre; Malatesta Temple; Palazzo dell'Arengo (1204); castle (1446); developed as a popular beach resort during the 20th-c.

Rimsky-Korsakov, Nikolai (Andreyevich) [rimskee kaw(r)sakof] (1844–1908) Composer, born in Tikhvin, NW Russia. Educated at the naval academy in St Petersburg, his early musical education was perfunctory, but his interest was kindled after meeting Balakirev in 1861. He sailed as a midshipman on a sailing ship (1862–5), after which he wrote his first symphony (1865). In 1871 he was made a professor at the St Petersburg Conservatory, where he was able to develop his technique. He produced three great orchestral masterpieces, *Capriccio Espagnol*, *Easter Festival*, and *Scheherazade* (1887–8), but his main works after that were operas, such as *The Golden Cockerel* (1907). Ever conscious of his earlier technical shortcomings, he rewrote almost all his early work. He also edited and completed works by Borodin and Mussorgsky.

rinderpest [rinderpest] An infectious disease of ruminant mammals; also known as **cattle plague**. It is characterized by blood in the faeces, fever, and swelling of the mucous membranes.

ring (chemistry) In chemistry, a closed group of atoms. For carbon compounds, rings of five or six atoms are the most stable.

ring (computing) A computer network topology in which the computers are connected to the linking cable in the form of a ring. Messages are sent around the ring from one computer to the next, and picked up by the one to which the message is addressed.

ringdove *wood pigeon*

ringed lizard *amphisbaena*

Ring nebula *Lyra*

ring of fire A belt of major earthquake and volcanic activity around the Pacific Ocean, defining the boundary between crustal plates.

ring ouzel *ouzel*

ringtail *cacomistle*

ring-tailed monkey *capuchin*

ringworm A common skin disease resulting from a fungal infection of the outer layers of the skin. The infection spreads outwards from a single site, forming a reddened ring, while the centre tends to heal. It usually affects the scalp, groin, and the clefts of the toes.

Rinzai Zen *Zen Buddhism*

Rio de Janeiro [reeoh duh zhaneeroh], known as **Rio** 22°53S 43°17W, pop (2000e) 6 968 000. Port capital of Rio de Janeiro state, SE Brazil, on the Bahia de Guanabara; covers an area of 20 km/12 mi along a narrow strip of land between mountains and sea; Pão de Açucar (Sugar Loaf Mountain) rises to 396 m/1299 ft; two airports (Galeão, Santos Dumont); railway; metro; three universities (1920, 1940, 1950); discovered, 1502; first settled by the French, 1555; taken by the Portuguese, 1567; seat of the Viceroy, 1763; capital of Brazil, 1834–1960; trade in coffee, sugar, iron ore; shipbuilding, sugar refining, pharmaceuticals, textiles, food processing, engineering, printing; major international tourist centre, with famous beaches at Copacabana, Ipanema, Leblon; suburb of Santa Teresa contains many colonial and 19th-c buildings; figure of Christ on the highest peak, Corcovado (710 m/2329 ft); monastery of São Bento (1641), 17th-c convent (Ordem do Terceiro do Monte do Carmo), Church of Nossa Senhora da Glória do Outeiro (1791); municipal theatre, replica of the Paris Opera House; national museum; world-famous Carnival, on the days preceding Lent, with parades, competitions, and fancy-dress balls; festival of Iemanjá (31 Dec).

Rio Grande (Mexico) [**reeoh grand, granday**] **Río Bravo**, **Río Bravo del Norte**. River in SW USA and N Mexico; rises in the Rocky Mts, SW Colorado; flows SE through New Mexico, then along the Texas–Mexico border; enters the Gulf of Mexico E of Brownsville; length 3033 km/1885 mi; major tributaries the Pecos and Conchos; used for irrigation and flood-control; navigation forbidden by international agreement beyond Brownsville.

Rioja [reeohkha] pop (2000e) 265 000; area 5034 sq km/1943 sq mi. Region of N Spain co-extensive with the modern province of Logroño; watered by the R Ebro and its tributaries; the best-known wine-producing area in Spain; capital, Logroño.

Río Muni [reeoh moonee] area 26 016 sq km/10 042 sq mi. Mainland territory of Equatorial Guinea, WC Africa; bounded W by the Gulf of Guinea, E and S by Gabon, and N by Cameroon; chief town, Bata; R Mbini (Benito) flows from the mountains to the coast.

Riot Act Legislation in Britain concerned to preserve public order, first passed at the beginning of the Hanoverian era in 1714. When 12 or more people were unlawfully assembled and refused to disperse, they were, after the reading of a section of this Act by a person in authority, immediately considered felons having committed a serious crime. Frequent use was made of the Act in the 18th-c. Its use declined in the 19th-c and it was repealed in 1911.

ripieno [ripyaynoh] *concerto grosso*

Ripken, Cal, popular name of **Calvin James Ripken Jr** (1960–) Baseball player, born in Havre de Grace, Maryland, USA. The Baltimore Orioles 'Iron Man' shortstop, he is famed for his all-time record of 2632 consecutive major league games from 1982 to 1999, beating the previous record of 2130 games held by Lou Gehrig in 1995. Ripken made his major league debut in 1981 and was the American League's Most Valuable Player in 1983 and 1991, winning the Golden Gloves in 1991 and 1992. He converted to third base in 1998, and by early 2000 he had career totals of 415 home runs and 3040 hits. He retired from major league baseball in 2001. His father, **Cal Ripken Sr**, played and coached at major league level.

Ripon [ripn] 54°08N 1°31W, pop (2000e) 13 700. Town in North Yorkshire, N England, UK; reckoned to be England's second oldest town; light engineering; racecourse; Cathedral of St Peter and St Wilfrid (7th–15th-c); 13th-c Wakeman's House; Fountains Abbey ruins nearby.

risk analysis A technique used in insurance and in business which attempts to calculate the effect of the 'worst possible' outcome of a venture. In business, the profits from a project costing many millions of pounds are unknown, but may be very high or unacceptably low. Risk analysis looks at all possible outcomes, assigning probabilities to each so that all the options are quantified. In insurance, actuaries calculate probabilities for the purpose of determining premiums.

Risorgimento [rizaw(r)zhimentoh] (It 'resurgence', 'rebirth') The 19th-c movement by which Italy achieved unity and nationhood. Although its origins lay in the 18th-c Enlightenment and the Napoleonic period, the Risorgimento proper began with the 1830 revolutions and, after failure in 1848–9, reached fruition under the leadership of Piedmont/Sardinia during 1859–70. In 1859–61 the Austrians were expelled from Lombardy, and the C Italian duchies, the Papal States, and Naples/Sicily united with Sardinia to form the Kingdom of Italy. Venetia (1866) and Rome (1870) were added later.

rites of passage *initiation rites*

Rivaldo, popular name of **Rivaldo Vitor Borba Ferreira** (1972–) Footballer, born in Recife, Brazil. He signed for FC Santa Cruz in 1991, then played for Mogi-Mirim, SC Corinthians, and SE Palmeiras. Joining Deportivo de La Coruña in 1996, he notched up 21 goals in his first season.The next year he transferred to FC Barcelona as a replacement for Ronaldo, and in 2002 joined Serie A side AC Milan, who released him in 2003. His many awards include the Ballon d'Or and the FIFA World Footballer of the Year in 1999. He was named in the FIFA All-Star Team of the 1998 and 2002 World Cup tournaments.

river A body of flowing water restricted to a relatively narrow channel by banks. It typically originates as a stream in high ground from springwater or run-off from rainwater or a glacier, and moves downhill, eroding a channel which grows as tributaries join the flow, and often carving out major valleys. In its middle stages the river flows more slowly, and meanders begin to form; while in its mature stages deposition of sediment and the formation of broad flood-plains and deltas is characteristic. Rivers are the most significant modifiers of the landscape, and their course has also determined the pattern of settlement, agriculture, and trade. (*see p.1307*)

Rivera, Diego [rivayra] (1886–1957) Painter, born in Guanajuato, SC Mexico. In 1921 he began a series of murals in public buildings depicting the life and history of the Mexican people. He also executed frescoes in the USA (1930–4), mainly of industrial life. His art is a blend of folk art and revolutionary propaganda, with overtones of Byzantine and Aztec symbolism.

river blindness An infection endemic in Africa caused by the filaria *Onchocerca volvulus*; also known as **onchocerciasis**. The micro-organism is conveyed by blackflies that live near rivers and which inflict a painful bite. Eye involvement causes itch-

Longest Rivers

Name	Outflow	Length* km	mi
Nile-Kagera-Ruvuvu-Ruvusu-Luvironza	Mediterranean Sea (Egypt)	6 690	4 160
Amazon-Ucayali-Tambo-Ene-Apurimac	Atlantic Ocean (Brazil)	6 570	4 080
Mississippi-Missouri-Jefferson-Beaverhead-Red Rock	Gulf of Mexico (USA)	6 020	3 740
Chang Jiang (Yangtze)	E China Sea (China)	5 980	3 720
Yenisey-Angara-Selenga-Ider	Kara Sea (Russia)	5 870	3 650
Amur-Argun-Kerulen	Tartar Strait (Russia)	5 780	3 590
Ob-Irtysh	Gulf of Ob, Kara Sea (Russia)	5 410	3 360
Plata-Parana-Grande	Atlantic Ocean (Argentina/Uruguay)	4 880	3 030
Huang Ho (Yellow)	Yellow Sea (China)	4 840	3 010
Congo (Zaire)-Lualaba	Atlantic Ocean (Angola-D.R. Congo)	4 630	2 880
Lena	Laptev Sea (Russia)	4 400	2 730
Mackenzie-Slave-Peace-Finlay	Beaufort Sea (Canada)	4 240	2 630
Mekong	S China Sea (Vietnam)	4 180	2 600
Niger	Gulf of Guinea (Nigeria)	4 100	2 550

*Lengths are given to the nearest 10 km/mi, and include the river plus tributaries comprising the longest watercourse.

ing, excessive secretion of tears (*lachrymation*), inflammation of the iris, glaucoma, and blindness.

River Brethren *Brethren (in Christ)*

Rivers, Joan, professional name of **Joan Alexandra Molinsky** (1933–) Comedienne and writer, born in Larchmont, New York, USA. She appeared as a film extra in 1951, and after graduating from college, became a fashion co-ordinator. She had parts in minor plays before working with the Chicago improvisational troupe Second City (1961–2), where she developed her acid-comedy routines. Success came with an appearance on *The Tonight Show* in 1965. She made her Las Vegas debut in 1969, wrote a regular column in the *Chicago Tribune* (1973–6), and became the regular guest host of *The Tonight Show* (1983–6). She hosted *The Late Show* (1986–7), *Hollywood Squares* (from 1987), and her own daytime talk show in 1989, and has also directed films, recorded albums, and written books, including *Having a Baby Can Be a Scream* (1974) and *Bouncing Back* (1997).

Riviera The Mediterranean coast between Toulon, France, and La Spezia, Italy. It is a narrow coastal strip bordered by the Alps to the N, and includes many holiday resorts.

Rix, Brian, popular name of **Brian Norman Roger Rix, Lord Rix of Whitehall and of Hornsea** (1924–) Actor and manager, born in Cottingham, East Riding of Yorkshire, NE England, UK. He studied in York, joined the Donald Wolfit players in 1943, served with the RAF, and formed his own company in Ilkley, Yorkshire (1948) and in Margate (1949). He established a reputation for farce at the Whitehall Theatre with such productions as *Reluctant Heroes* (1950) and *Dry Rot* (1954). He also appeared in a number of films, such as *Don't Just Lie There, Say Something* (1974). He left the stage for charity work with the mentally handicapped, and became chairman of Mencap (1988–98). He has published two volumes of autobiography, *My Farce from My Elbow* (1975) and *Farce About Face* (1989). He was knighted in 1986 and became a life peer in 1992.

Riyadh [riyad], Arabic **Ar Riyad** 24°41N 46°42E, pop (2000e) 3 044 000. Capital city of Saudi Arabia; formerly a walled city; airport; railway; three universities (1950, 1957, 1984); communications centre; commerce, oil refining, dates, fruit, grain; over 1000 mosques, royal palace; 'Solar Village' to the N, a prototype project for use of solar power; target of terrorist suicide bomb attacks, May 2003.

Rizzio, David [ritsioh], also spelled **Riccio** (?1533–1566) Courtier and musician, born in Pancalieri, NW Italy. After travelling to Scotland with the Duke of Savoy's embassy, he entered the service of Mary, Queen of Scots (1561), became her favourite, and was made her French secretary in 1564. He negotiated her marriage with Darnley (1565), who became jealous of his influence, and plotted his death with a group of nobles, including Morton and Ruthven. Rizzio was dragged from the queen's presence and murdered.

RNA or **ribonucleic acid** A nucleic acid found throughout the cell, distinguished from DNA by the substitution of the pyrimidine base (uracil) for thymidine, and the sugar component (ribose) for deoxyribose. RNA is involved in many crucial cellular processes, in particular the synthesis of proteins. It is synthesized as a complementary strand to a section of DNA base sequences by a class of enzymes known as **RNA polymerases**. RNA copies of protein coding genes are processed (introns being spliced out) to give **mature messenger RNA (mRNA)**, which is then transported through the nuclear membrane to the ribosomes in the cytoplasm. **Transfer RNA (tRNA)** is copied from tRNA genes and collects the free amino acids in the cytoplasm, transporting them to the ribosomes (which contain ribosomal RNA or rRNA copied from rRNA genes). The amino acids transported by the tRNA molecules are joined in a sequence dictated by the mRNA. Therefore, once the mRNA is attached to the ribosomes, it serves as a template for the production of protein polypeptide chains. Another class of RNAs, known as **small nuclear RNA (snRNA)**, forms part of complexes with proteins called snRNPs, which are involved in the removal of introns (splicing) to produce mRNA.

Roach, Hal, popular name of **Harald Eugene Roach** (1892–1992) Film-maker, born in Elmira, New York, USA. After an adventurous life as a mule-skinner and gold prospector in Alaska, he entered the film industry as a stuntman and extra in 1911. He began producing short comedy films, becoming an expert in the mechanics of slapstick, and helped to foster the careers of Laurel and Hardy. He also devised the series of Our Gang films, and won Oscars for *The Music Box* (1932) and *Bored of Education* (1936). His range of full-length productions includes *Way Out West* (1937), *Of Mice and Men* (1939), and *One Million BC* (1940), which he co-directed. After World War 2 he diversified into television production. His final film was the compilation feature *The Crazy World of Laurel and Hardy* (1967), and in 1984 he received a special Academy Award.

Roach, Max(well) (1924–) Jazz drummer, bandleader, and composer, born in New Land, North Carolina, USA. He has played with many of the pioneers of 'bop' and modern jazz, including Dizzy Gillespie, Coleman Hawkins, Charlie Parker, Lester Young, and Miles Davis. He was also a teacher of music, and professor of music at the University of Massachusetts.

roach Freshwater fish (*Rutilus rutilus*) found in rivers and lakes of Europe; body moderately deep, length up to 45 cm/18 in; greenish-brown on back, sides silver, pelvic and anal fins red;

feeds on invertebrates and some plant material; popular with anglers, and fished commercially in some parts of E Europe. (Family: Cyprinidae.)

road rage Aggressive behaviour while driving a motor vehicle on a public highway. There is no specific road rage offence in many jurisdictions, but such behaviour may involve a breach of other laws. If the aggressor causes injury, he or she may face conviction for murder, causing death by reckless driving, battery, or some other offence.

roadrunner A ground-dwelling cuckoo, native to SW USA and Central America; long tail and legs; head with short crest; inhabits dry open country; eats invertebrates, small vertebrates and eggs; territorial; nests in tree or cactus. (Genus: *Geococcyx*, 2 species.)

Road Town 18°26N 64°32W, pop (2000e) 3600. Seaport and capital town of the British Virgin Is, Greater Antilles, E Caribbean; on E coast of Tortola I; agricultural trade, tourism.

roan antelope A grazing antelope (*Hippotragus equinus*) native to Africa W of the Rift Valley; also known as **horse antelope**; pale horse-like body with short mane of stiff hairs, short horns, and tips of ears with long tufts of hairs; inhabits savannah.

Roanoke [rohanohk] 37°16N 79°56W, pop (2000e) 94 900. Independent city, SW Virginia, USA, on the Roanoke R; settled, 1740; gateway to the Shenandoah valley; airfield; railway; railway engineering, electrical equipment, furniture, textiles, metal products.

Roaring Forties *westerlies*

Robards, Jason, Jr [rohbah(r)dz] (1922–2000) Actor, born in Chicago, Illinois, USA. The son of a once-famous stage and film actor, **Jason Robards Sr** (1892–1963), he served seven years in the US Navy, survived the attack on Pearl Harbor, and was awarded the Navy Cross. He went to New York City and supported himself by taxi-driving and teaching while gaining acting experience. He gained public and critical acclaim as a stage actor in Eugene O'Neill's *The Iceman Cometh* (1956) and *Long Day's Journey Into Night* (1957). He made his film debut in *The Journey* (1959), and won Best Supporting Actor Oscars in *All the President's Men* (1976) and *Julia* (1977). Later film appearances include *Philadelphia* (1993), *Enemy of the State* (1998), and *Beloved* (1998). He was awarded the National Medal of Arts in 1997.

Robbe-Grillet, Alain [rob greeyay] (1922–) Novelist, born in Brest, NW France. He studied in Paris, and worked as an agronomist, then in a publishing house. After his first novel, *Les Gommes* (1953, The Erasers), he emerged as the leader of the *nouveau roman* group, contributing to the genre such novels as *Le Voyeur* (1955, The Voyeur) and *La Jalousie* (1959, Jealousy), and the theoretical work *Pour un nouveau roman* (1963, Towards the New Novel). Later novels include *Un Régicide* (1978) and *La Belle Captive* (1995). He also wrote essays and film scenarios, notably *L'Année dernière à Marienbad* (1961, Last Year at Marienbad).

robber crab A large terrestrial crustacean related to the hermit crab; cuticle of abdomen hard and resistant to drying out; found in tropical and subtropical areas scavenging near the sea shore; able to climb trees and to crack open coconuts, hence its alternative name of **coconut crab**. (Class: Malacostraca. Order: Decapoda.)

robber fly An active, predatory fly commonly found in open sunny habitats; forelegs robust, armed with strong bristles for gripping insect prey caught in flight; many species mimic bees and wasps. (Order: Diptera. Family: Asilidae, c.5000 species.)

robbery The taking of personal property from the person or immediate presence of another against his or her will through the use of violence or intimidation. A threat of violence is sufficient. Robbery and assaults with intent to rob are punishable with a maximum sentence of life imprisonment.

Robbia, Luca della (c.1400–82) Sculptor, born in Florence, NC Italy. Between 1431 and 1440 he executed 10 unequalled panels of angels and dancing boys for the cathedral there, for whose sacristy he also made a bronze door with 10 panels of figures in relief (1448–67). He is also known for his figures in terracotta, including medallions and reliefs, white or coloured. He established a business producing glazed terracottas which was carried on by his nephew **Andrea della Robbia** (1435–1525) and Andrea's son **Giovanni della Robbia** (1469–c.1529).

Robbins, Frederick C(hapman) (1916–2003) Physiologist and paediatrician, born in Auburn, Alabama, USA. He studied at Harvard and served in the US Army's medical laboratory virus section during World War 2. He then joined Enders and Weller at the Children's Hospital, Boston, where he helped devise techniques for cultivating the poliomyelitis virus. He was professor of paediatrics at Case Western Reserve University, Cleveland (1952–80), and shared the 1954 Nobel Prize for Physiology or Medicine.

Robbins, Jerome (1918–98) Dancer and choreographer, born in New York City, USA. He studied ballet and modern dance, worked initially as an actor, then joined the American Ballet Theatre (1940). He became associate director then director of New York City Ballet (1949–59), and joint ballet master (1983–9). His collaboration with Leonard Bernstein resulted in his most famous musical, *West Side Story* (1957), for which he won two Oscars in the 1961 Hollywood version. Other Broadway successes included *Gypsy* (1959) and *Fiddler on the Roof* (1964), and later works include *Watermill* (1972), *Glass Pieces* (1983), and (with Mikhail Baryshnikov) *A Suite of Dances* (1994).

Robbins (of Clare Market), Lionel Charles Robbins, Baron (1898–1984) Economist and educationist, born in Sipson, S Greater London, UK. Professor at the London School of Economics (1929–61), he directed the economic section of the war cabinet, then became chairman of the *Financial Times* (until 1970). He also chaired the *Robbins Committee*, which led to the major expansion of higher education in the UK (1961–4). His best-known work is *An Essay on the Nature and Significance of Economic Science* (1932), which has become a classic of methodology. He became a life peer in 1959, and a Companion of Honour in 1968.

Robbins, Tim (1958–) Film actor, director, and writer, born in West Govina, California, USA. He grew up in New York City, moved to Los Angeles in 1981, and helped found the Actors Gang, an alternative theatre group. To fund this venture he took roles in such films as *Fraternity Vacation* (1985) and *Howard the Duck* (1986). He wrote, directed, and composed the songs for the critically acclaimed *Bob Roberts* (1992). Later films include (as actor) *The Shawshank Redemption* (1994) and *Arlington Road* (1999) and (as producer, director, and writer) *Dead Man Walking* (1995). He directed *The Cradle Will Rock* (1999) and received a Best Supporting Actor Oscar for his role in *Mystic River* (2003).

Robert I *Bruce, Robert*

Robert II (1316–90) King of Scots (1371–90), the son of Walter, hereditary steward of Scotland. He acted as sole regent during the exile and captivity of David II. On David's death, he became king in right of his descent from his maternal grandfather, Robert I, and founded the Stuart royal dynasty.

Robert, Duke of Normandy *Henry I* (of England)

Roberts (of Kandahar, Pretoria, and Waterford), Frederick Sleigh Roberts, 1st Earl (1832–1914) British field marshal, born in Cawnpore, N India. He trained at Sandhurst Military Academy, and took an active part in the Indian Mutiny, winning the VC in 1858. He became commander-in-chief in India (1885–93), and served as supreme commander in South Africa during the Boer War, relieving Kimberley (1900). He was created earl in 1901, and died while visiting troops in the field in France.

Roberts, Julia originally **Julie Fiona Roberts** (1967–) US film actress, born in Smyrna, Georgia, USA. She made her screen debut in *Baja Oklahoma* (1988), and became well known following *Mystic Pizza* (1988) and *Steel Magnolias* (1989, Oscar nomination for Best Supporting Actress). Later films include *Pretty Woman* (1990), *Michael Collins* (1996), *Notting Hill* (1999), *Erin Brockovich* (2000, BAFTA, Best Actress; Golden Globe), *America's Sweethearts* (2001), and *Mona Lisa Smile* (2003).

Roberts, Tom (1856–1931) Painter, born in Dorchester, Dorset, S England, UK. He emigrated as a child, and studied at the Carlton School of Design and at the National Gallery School, both in Melbourne, before returning to London to attend the Royal Academy Schools. His best work, which deals with pioneering life in the bush, was produced in Australia in the late 1880s and 1890s. He was commissioned to paint the official opening of the first Australian federal parliament, a subject which required over 250 individual portraits.

Robertson (of Port Ellen), George (Islay MacNeill) Robertson, Baron (1946–) British statesman, born on the island of Islay, W Scotland, UK. He studied at Dundee University, became Scottish organizer of the General and Municipal Workers' Union (1969–78), and was elected an MP in 1978. He was the opposition spokesman on Scotland (1979–80), defence (1980–1), and foreign and commonwealth affairs (1981–93), then joined the shadow cabinet, and was spokesman on Scotland (1993–7). He served as defence secretary (1997–9) in the Labour government, and was appointed secretary-general of NATO in 1999, stepping down at the end of 2003. He was awarded a peerage in the same year.

Robertson, Pat, popular name of **Marion Gordon Robertson** (1930–) Religious broadcaster and politician, born in Lexington, Virginia, USA. He studied at Washington and Lee University, Lexington, VA, Yale Law School, and the New York Theological Seminary. He founded the Christian Broadcast Network in 1960 and began his popular religious talk show, the '700 Club', in 1968. He realized early the possibilities of cable television for reaching a targeted audience, and became one of the most watchable and influential 'televangelists' of the 1980s. His failed run for the Republican presidential nomination in 1988 showed the limits of his political appeal.

Robeson, Paul (Bustill) [**rohb**sn] (1898–1976) Singer and actor, born in Princeton, New Jersey, USA. He was admitted to the US bar before embarking on a stage career in New York City in 1921, appearing in Britain in 1922. Success as an African-American actor was matched by popularity as a singer, and he appeared in works ranging from *Show Boat* to plays by O'Neill and Shakespeare. He was known particularly for his Othello, a part which he first played in London in 1930. He toured widely giving song recitals, notably of black spirituals, and appeared in numerous films. In the 1950s his outspoken opposition to racial discrimination, and his Communist sympathies, led to professional ostracism at home, and he retired from public life in the 1960s.

Robespierre, Maximilien François Marie Isidore de [**rohbs**-pyair] (1758–94) French revolutionary leader, born in Arras, N France. He became a lawyer, was elected to the States General (1789), became a prominent member of the Jacobin Club, and emerged in the National Assembly as a popular radical, known as 'the Incorruptible'. In 1791 he was public accuser, and in 1792 presented a petition to the Legislative Assembly for a Revolutionary Tribunal. Elected first deputy for Paris in the National Convention, he emerged as leader of the Mountain, strenuously opposed to the Girondins, whom he helped to destroy. In 1793 he became a member of the Committee of Public Safety, and for three months dominated the country, introducing the Reign of Terror and the cult of the Supreme Being. But as his ruthless exercise of power increased, his popularity waned. He was attacked in the Convention, arrested, and guillotined on the orders of the Revolutionary Tribunal.

Robey, Sir George [**roh**bee], originally **George Edward Wade** (1869–1954) Comedian, born in Herne Hill, Kent, SE England, UK. He first appeared on the stage in 1891, made a name for himself in musical shows such as *The Bing Boys* (1916), and later emerged as a Shakespearean actor in the part of Falstaff. He was famous for his bowler hat, black coat, hooked stick, and thickly painted eyebrows. He was knighted in 1954.

robin A bird of the thrush family Turdidae (44 species), usually with a red breast; especially the Eurasian/N African robin (*Erithacus rubecula*). The name is also used for some Australasian flycatchers (28 species) and for the **Jamaican tody** (Family: Todidae).

Robin Goodfellow In English 16th-c and 17th-c popular belief, a mischievous fairy who would do housework if duly rewarded. He was also called **Puck** or **Hobgoblin**. His characteristic activities are listed in *A Midsummer Night's Dream* (2.i).

Robin Hood Legendary 13th-c outlaw who lived in Sherwood Forest in the N Midlands, England, celebrated in ballads dating from the 14th-c. He protected the poor, and outwitted, robbed, or killed the wealthy and unscrupulous officials of Church and state. The legend may have had its origins in the popular discontent that led to the Peasants' Revolt of 1381.

Robinson, Anne (1944–) Journalist and television presenter, born in Liverpool, Merseyside, UK. She was educated at Farnborough Hill Convent, Hampshire, and in Paris. She joined the *Daily Mail* (1966–7) and *Sunday Times* (1968–77), becoming a columnist for the *Daily Mirror* (1980–93), *Today* (1993–5), *The Times* (1994–5), and *The Sun* (1995). For BBC television she presented *Points of View* (1988) and the consumer programme *Watchdog* (1993–2001). In 2000 she became known as the formidable presenter of the quiz game *The Weakest Link*, and successfully took the show to NBC television in the USA the following year.

Robinson, Edward G, originally **Emanuel Goldenberg** (1893–1973) Film actor, born in Bucharest, Romania. His family emigrated to the USA in 1903, and he studied at the American Academy of Dramatic Arts in New York City. He started in silent films, but became famous with his vivid portrayal of a vicious gangster in *Little Caesar* (1930). He brought magnetism and a refreshing humanity to a rogues' gallery of larcenous hoodlums in such films as *The Whole Town's Talking* (1935) and *Key Largo* (1948). His support of democratic causes brought disfavour at the time of the McCarthy witch-hunts. Subsequently he continued in strong character parts, such as in *Double Indemnity* (1944) and *All My Sons* (1948), many of his later appearances being in international co-productions, such as *The Cincinnati Kid* (1965). His autobiography, *All My Yesterdays*, was published in 1973, and he was posthumously awarded a special Academy Award the same year.

Robinson, Edwin Arlington (1869–1935) Poet, born in Head Tide, Maine, USA. He was brought up in the town of Gardiner, Maine, which provided the background for 'Tilbury Town', the fictional New England village setting of his best poetry. He studied at Harvard, and went to New York City to find work. He made his name with an early collection of poetry *The Children of the Night* (1897), and was three times a Pulitzer prizewinner, for his *Collected Poems* (1922), *The Man Who Died Twice* (1924), and *Tristram* (1927), one of his several modern renditions of Arthurian legends.

Robinson, (William) Heath (1872–1944) Artist, cartoonist, and book-illustrator, born in London, UK. He trained at the Islington School of Art, and in 1897 illustrated an edition of *Don Quixote*, the first of many works, including editions of *The Arabian Nights* (1899), *Twelfth Night* (1908) and *Water Babies* (1915). His fame rests mainly on his humorous drawings – in his ability to poke fun at the machine age with intricate drawings of countless 'Heath Robinson contraptions' of absurd and fantastic design to perform simple and practical operations, such as the raising of one's hat, the shuffling and dealing of cards, or the recovering of a collar-stud which has slipped down the wearer's back.

Robinson, Jackie, popular name of **Jack Roosevelt Robinson** (1919–72) Baseball player, the first African-American player to play major league baseball, born in Cairo, Georgia, USA. Excelling in sports at the University of California, Los Angeles, he became a star infielder and outfielder for the Brooklyn Dodgers (1947–56). Largely responsible for the acceptance of black athletes in professional sports, he led the Dodgers to six National League pennants and one World Series, in 1955. He was Rookie of the Year in 1947, and league batting champion and Most Valuable Player in 1949.

Robinson, Joan V(iolet), *née* **Maurice** (1903–83) Economist, born in Camberley, Surrey, SE England, UK. She studied at Cambridge, and taught there (1931–71), in 1965 succeeding her husband **(Edward) Austin (Gossidge) Robinson** (1897–1993) as professor of economics. She was one of the most influential economic theorists of her time, playing a leading role in the 1930s in the development of theories of imperfect competition, and in the post-war period as a leader of the Cambridge school, which developed macro-economic theories of growth and distribution, based on the work of Keynes.

Robinson, Mary, *née* **Bourke** (1944–) Constitutional lawyer, academic, civil rights campaigner, politician, and president of the Irish Republic (1990–7), born in Ballina, Mayo, W Ireland. Born into a Roman Catholic family, she graduated in law from Trinity College, Dublin, and furthered her legal studies at Harvard University. Appointed Trinity College Professor of Constitutional and Criminal Law in 1969 at 25 years of age, she was elected to the Senate or upper house of the Dáil Eireann (the Irish parliament) in the same year. As a barrister she has been responsible for landmark legal cases, particularly in relation to the rights of women and minority groups. In 1976 she joined the Irish Labour Party but left in protest against the Anglo-Irish Agreement (1985), which she argued did not represent the rights of Unionists in Northern Ireland. In 1990 she became the first woman to hold the office of President of the Republic and the first successful candidate to be nominated from outside the two largest parties in the state. During her term of presidency, she elevated what was a figurehead role into a means of highlighting the needs of the disadvantaged. In 1997 she became the UN High Commissioner for Human Rights, in which role she expanded the UN system of monitoring and exposing the abuse of economic, social, civil, and political rights on a global scale. She retired from the post in 2002.

Robinson, Sir Robert (1886–1975) Chemist, born near Chesterfield, Derbyshire, C England, UK. He studied at Manchester University, and taught at Sydney, Liverpool, St Andrews, Manchester, London, and Oxford universities, becoming Waynflete professor at Oxford (1930–55). He is particularly noted for his work on plant pigments, alkaloids, and other natural products, and in the development of penicillin. Knighted in 1939, he was president of the Royal Society (1945–50) and was awarded the Nobel Prize for Chemistry in 1947.

Robinson, Sugar Ray, originally **Walker Smith** (1921–89) Professional boxer, born in Detroit, Michigan, USA. He turned professional in 1940 and was never knocked out in 201 contests. Holder of the world welterweight title (1946–51) and the world middleweight title (1950–1), he lost the middleweight title to Randolph Turpin in 1951 but soon regained it. He was a professional boxer for 20 years but bore few, if any, visible signs of his calling. Very popular in Europe, he travelled in considerable style with a large entourage.

roble beech A tree similar to the beech, and replacing that genus in the S hemisphere; also called **southern beech**. It differs chiefly by having nuts in threes, enclosed in a spiny or scaly case. (Genus: *Nothofagus*, 35 species. Family: Fagaceae.)

robotics (cybernetics) The application of automatic machines (*robots*) to perform tasks traditionally done by humans. Robots are widely used in industry to perform simple repetitive tasks accurately and without tiring, and to work in environments which are dangerous to human operators. They can be programmed to carry out many different activities, which is what makes them different from simple automatic handling devices. They can be used as sensors, equipped for artificial vision, touch, and temperature sensing. Many are capable of simple decision-making without the intervention of the operator, by using computer programs which have been developed from an expert's knowledge of the tasks. If the robots are in human form, they are called *androids*.

robotics (dance) *street dance*

Rob Roy (Gaelic 'Red Robert'), nickname of **Robert MacGregor** or **Campbell** (1671–1734) Highland outlaw, born in Buchanan, Stirling, C Scotland, UK. Initially he was a grazier, but by 1712 he was in debt to James Graham, 1st Duke of Montrose, and began a life of briganding, chiefly at the expense of Montrose. He was distrusted by both sides during the Jacobite rebellion (1715), stealing from both without favour. After the rebellion he continued to raid Montrose, and was eventually captured and imprisoned in London. He was pardoned in 1727 while facing deportation. His life was romanticized in the novel by Sir Walter Scott.

Robson, Dame Flora (McKenzie) (1902–84) Actress, born in South Shields, Durham, NE England, UK. She studied at the Royal Academy of Dramatic Art, London, and first appeared at the Shaftesbury Theatre, London, in 1921. She gained fame mainly in historical roles in plays and films, such as Queen Elizabeth in *Fire over England* (1931), and Thérèse Raquin in *Guilty* (1944). She consolidated her reputation with memorable stage performances in Shaw's *Captain Brassbound's Conversion* (1948) and Ibsen's *Ghosts* (1958). She appeared in more than 60 films, and was created a dame in 1960.

Rochas, Marcel [rosha] (1902–55) Fashion designer, born in Paris, France. He set up a couture house in Paris in 1925, launching his first fragrances in 1931, and the sheepskin jacket in 1942. He set up a range of companies in perfumes and fashion during the late 1940s. The couture house closed upon his death in 1955, but his wife Hélène took over the perfume department until she left the company in 1989.

Rochdale 53°38N 2°09W, pop (2001e) 205 200. Town in Greater Manchester, NW England, UK; on the R Roch, 16 km/10 mi NE of Manchester; railway; textiles (especially cotton), engineering; Co-operative Society founded here in 1844; football league team, Rochdale.

Roche limit [rosh] The lowest orbit at which a satellite can withstand tides raised within it by its parent planet. French mathematician Edouard Roche (1820–83) studied rotating liquid masses, and noted in 1848 that, if a moon orbited close enough to its parent planet, the stresses would exceed the strength of rock, tearing the satellite apart. This mechanism could explain the presence of rings around some planets.

Rochester (UK), ancient **Durobrivae** 51°24N 0°30E, pop (2000e) 25 500. Town in the Medway Towns urban area and Rochester upon Medway district, Kent, SE England, UK; W of Chatham; an important early settlement at a ford over the R Medway; railway; 12th-c cathedral; 11th-c castle; Gad's Hill nearby, the home of Charles Dickens.

Rochester (USA) 43°10N 77°37W, pop (2000e) 219 800. Seat of Monroe Co, W New York, USA; port on Genesee R, 10 km/6 mi from L Ontario; first settled, 1811; city status, 1834; airfield; railway; university (1850); optical and photographic instruments, machines and tools; International Museum of Photography, Rochester Museum, Memorial Art Gallery; Lilac Festival (May).

rochet [rochit] A white, full-length, linen robe. It is worn by bishops, especially of the Anglican Communion, on ceremonial occasions.

rock A naturally occurring material which comprises the solid Earth. Rocks are an assemblage of minerals, and are classified according to origin.

rock ape *Barbary ape*

rock art *Palaeolithic / Paleolithic art*

rock crawler A secondarily wingless, mainly nocturnal insect found in cold habitats above the tree line and around glaciers; body poorly pigmented with a thin flexible cuticle. (Order: Grylloblattaria, c.13 species.)

rock crystal *quartz*

rock dove A pigeon native to Europe and Asia (*Columba livia*); grey with metallic neck feathers; inhabits cliffs and fields; eats seeds, grass, and snails; nests on cliffs (or buildings). It is the ancestor of all domestic and town-dwelling pigeons.

Rockefeller, John D(avison) [rokuhfeler] (1839–1937) Industrialist and philanthropist, born in Richford, New York, USA. After high school he went into the business world, and showed a talent for organization. In 1875 he founded with his brother

William Rockefeller (1841–1922) the Standard Oil Company, securing control of the US oil trade. In the late 19th-c his power came under strong public criticism. He withdrew from active business in 1897, and devoted the rest of his life to philanthropy. He gave over $500 million in aid of medical research, universities, and churches, and established in 1913 the Rockefeller Foundation 'to promote the well-being of mankind'. One of his sons, **John D Rockefeller Jr** (1874–1960) built the Rockefeller Center.

Rockefeller Center A complex of 14 skyscrapers commissioned by John D Rockefeller Jr (1874–1960) and built (1931–40) in Manhattan, New York City. The centre now consists of 21 buildings housing offices, restaurants, shops, cinemas, broadcasting stations, and the Radio City Music Hall.

rocket A self-propelling device in which the fuel substances needed to produce the propulsion are carried internally. The term most commonly refers to space vehicles, although it can also apply to distress rockets and fireworks. In addition, rockets are used to power missiles, and for supersonic and assisted-take-off aeroplane propulsion. Rockets work by burning fuel inside a combustion chamber. Both the fuel and the oxygen (*oxidant*) needed to burn it are carried inside the rocket itself. When the fuel is burnt, a large volume of hot gas is produced, which exerts great pressure on the inside surface. The upward pressure is much greater than the downward pressure, because the gases are allowed to escape through a nozzle at the bottom. The stronger pressure at the top results in an upward force (*thrust*) that makes the rocket rise. The force and the upward movement continue until all the fuel is exhausted. **Solid fuel rockets** commonly use a mixture of nitrocellulose and nitroglycerine as the fuel source. The more efficient **liquid fuel rockets** use kerosene (fuel) and liquid oxygen (oxidant). Other means of propulsion, such as nuclear furnaces, are being developed. No single rocket is powerful enough to lift itself into orbit. A space-launcher is made up of several rockets creating a multi-stage (*step*) rocket. Once the fuel for one stage is exhausted, that stage is dumped, and the next stage is ignited. The rocket launcher becomes progressively lighter and faster as it climbs into space. One of the largest rockets was the Saturn V Moon rocket (a three-stage rocket) which weighed 2700 tonnes at launch.

Rockhampton 23°22S 150°32E, pop (2000e) 65 600. City in Queensland, Australia, on the Fitzroy R; railway; air link and hydrofoil service to Great Keppel I; university (1992); centre of Australia's largest beef-producing area; to the W, area around Emerald, Anakie, Rubyvale, Sapphire, and Willows rich in gemstones; Rocky Round-up rodeo (Apr); cooeeing contest (Aug) at nearby Cooee Bay.

Rockingham, Charles Watson Wentworth, 2nd Marquess of (1730–82) British statesman and prime minister (1765–6, 1782). Created Earl of Malton in 1750, he served as gentleman of the bedchamber to George II and George III. As leader of a prominent Whig Opposition group, he was called upon to form a ministry in 1765. He repealed the Stamp Act, affecting the American colonies, then court intrigues caused his resignation. He opposed Britain's war against the colonists. His was the most consistent Opposition Whig group to George III's government in the 1760s and 1770s, and leading spokesmen, such as Fox and Burke, were adherents. He died soon after taking office as prime minister for the second time.

Rock Island 41°30N 90°34W, pop (2000e) 39 700. Seat of Rock Island Co, NW Illinois, USA; at junction of the Rock and Mississippi rivers; 125 km/78 mi NW of Peoria; first settled by Sauk and Fox Indians and named in 1841; Black Hawk lived here; Chicago and Rock Island Railroad built the first bridge across the Mississippi (1856); agricultural machinery, timber; Hauberg Indian Museum.

rock music A type of popular music, originally called **rock and roll**, which spread throughout the USA and Europe in the 1950s. It began as a basically simple musical style, dominated by a strong dance beat and by the use of the electric guitar. It developed out of country and western, and more particularly from rhythm and blues – a style which previously had been played almost exclusively by US black artists. The term 'rock and roll' was popularized by Cleveland disc jockey Alan Freed, who was also the first person to play rhythm and blues music to a predominantly white radio audience. The music gained widespread popularity during the late 1950s, when major artists included Bill Haley, Elvis Presley, and Chuck Berry. Primarily aimed at and enjoyed by a young audience, it became an important symbol of teenage rebellion. During the 1960s the format was expanded considerably by such artists as Bob Dylan and Jimi Hendrix, and by bands such as the Rolling Stones and the Beatles. Then and since, the music has taken on a variety of outside influences, and groups have frequently expanded on the basic rock instrumentation of electric guitars, electric bass, vocals, and drums. Over the period, rock music has diversified into a distinct series of subgenres, such as **hard rock**, in the late 1960s and early 1970s, and **punk rock** in the late 1970s – most of which have been characterized not only by musical differences but by their own associated features in dress, lifestyle, and (from the 1980s onwards) video publicity.

rock rabbit *hyrax; pika*

rockrose A small evergreen shrub, mostly native to the Mediterranean region and parts of Asia; leaves opposite, lance-shaped to oblong; flowers 5-petalled, white, yellow, or red. Some species are grown in gardens. (Genus: *Helianthemum*, 100 species. Family: Cistaceae.)

rock salt *halite*

Rocky Mountain goat A wild goat (*Oreamnos americanus*) native to the mountains of North America; back legs shorter than front legs; thick shaggy white coat and short backward-curved horns; also known as **mountain goat**, **goat antelope**, or **antelope goat**.

Rocky Mountains or **Rockies** Major mountain system of W North America, extending from C New Mexico generally NNW through the USA, into W Canada and N Alaska and reaching the Bering Strait N of the Arctic Circle; about 4800 km/3000 mi long; forms the continental divide, separating the Pacific drainage from the Atlantic and Arctic; highest point in the USA Mt Elbert (4399 m/14 432 ft), in Canada Mt Robson (3954 m/12 972 ft); principal pass the South Pass (Wyoming), followed by the Oregon Trail; divided into the Southern, Middle, Northern, and Arctic sections; important source of mineral wealth; several national parks, including Rocky Mountain, Grand Teton, Yellowstone, Glacier (Montana), Banff, Jasper, Yoho, Kootenay, Glacier (British Columbia), Northern Yukon, Gates of the Arctic.

Rocky Mountain sheep *bighorn*

Rocky Mountain spotted fever *typhus*

Rococo [rokohkoh] (Fr *rocaille*, 'rock-work') In art history, the period following the late Baroque in European art and design. It flourished especially in France and S Germany c.1700–50, until superseded by the Neoclassical taste spreading from Rome. Whereas Baroque was dramatic and powerfully theatrical, Rococo sought effects of charm and delicacy on a small scale – surface effects rather than bold masses. It was therefore most successful as a style of interior decoration, exemplified in the designs of Pierre Lepautre (c.1648–1716), Gilles-Marie Oppenord (1672–1742), Nicolas Pineau (1684–1754), and Juste Aurèle Meissonier (c.1693–1750). The greatest Rococo painter was Watteau.

Roddenberry, Gene, popular name of **Eugene Wesley Roddenberry** (1921–91) Writer, and film and television producer, born in El Paso, Texas, USA. He joined the Army Air Corps and served as a bomber pilot (1941–6) and as a crash investigator (1946–9). As an airline pilot (1949–53), he survived an air-crash in the Syrian desert. He moved to Los Angeles, joined the police, wrote scripts in his spare time for *Dragnet*, and became a full-time writer, contributing to several series including *Highway Patrol* and *Dr Kildare*. Always interested in science-fiction, he is best known as the creator and producer of *Star Trek*.

Roddick, Dame Anita (Lucia) (1943–) Retail entrepreneur, born in Brighton, East Sussex, SE England, UK. She worked in her Italian parents' ice-cream parlour, trained as a drama teacher, and became intrigued by the idea of selling cosmetics in much the same way as a greengrocer would sell vegetables. In 1976 she opened a small shop in a back street of Brighton selling beauty products made from natural products, not tested on animals, and supplied in refillable containers. Her growing commitment to ecology and the Third World brought the Body Shop chain a profit of £6 million in the 1980s. By the late 1990s its share value had plunged from £38 million to £3·4 million. However, with new management and plans to expand into online shopping, confidence in its profitability was restored. Among her many awards are the International Banksia Environmental Award (1993) and the Botwinick Prize in Business Ethics (1994). She and her husband resigned as co-chairs in 2002, but retained seats on the board. She launched her own publishing company in 2003, and was made a dame later that year.

rodent A mammal of worldwide order Rodentia (3 suborders, 30 families, 1702 species); successful in most environments; 40% of all living mammal species are rodents; eats a wide range of food; chisel-like upper and lower incisor teeth grow continuously, kept short by gnawing; suborders are Myomorpha (**mouse-like rodents**, 1137 species), Sciuromorpha (**squirrel-like rodents**, 377 species), and Hystricomorpha (**porcupine-like rodents**, 188 species, sometimes called Caviomorpha or **cavy-like rodents**).

rodeo A US sport, consisting mainly of competitive riding and a range of skills which derive from cowboy ranching practices. The events include bronco riding with and without saddle, bull riding, steer wrestling, calf roping, and team roping. In bronco riding, for example, the cowboy must stay on a wild bucking horse for a set time holding with only one hand, points being awarded for style to the horse and rider.

Rodgers, (Charles) Richard (1902–79) Composer, born in New York City, USA. He left Columbia University to study composition at the Institute of Musical Art (now the Juilliard School, New York City). With the lyricist **Lorenz Hart** (1895–1942) his first professional success was the *Garrick Gaieties* (1925). Other successes included *Babes in Arms* (1937), with the songs 'The Lady Is a Tramp' and 'My Funny Valentine'; *The Boys from Syracuse* (1938), with 'Falling in Love with Love'; and *Pal Joey* 1940, with 'Bewitched, Bothered and Bewildered'. After Hart's death (1943) he collaborated in a spectacular series of hit musicals with Oscar Hammerstein II, especially *Oklahoma!* (1943, Pulitzer). Other successes were *South Pacific* (1949, Pulitzer), *The King and I* (1951), and *The Sound of Music* (1959).

Rodin, (René François) Auguste [rohdĩ] (1840–1917) Sculptor, born in Paris, France. He trained in Paris and Brussels, and began to produce sculptures which, with their varying surfaces and finishes, resembled the Impressionist painters' effects of light and shade. The great 'La Porte de l'enfer' (The Gate of Hell) was commissioned for the Musée des Arts Décoratifs in 1880, and during the next 30 years he was mainly engaged on the 186 figures for these bronze doors. He also worked on the monument 'Les Bourgeois de Calais' (1884–6, New York City, The Burghers of Calais), which was finally dedicated in 1895. Among his other works is 'Le Penseur' (1904, The Thinker), in front of the Panthéon in Paris.

Rodman, Dennis (Keith), nickname **The Worm** (1961–) Eccentric, abrasive basketball player, born in Trenton, New Jersey, USA. He started his professional career with the Detroit Pistons, winning two championships (1989–90) with them before joining the Chicago Bulls, winning consecutive championships in 1996–8. He led the NBA in rebounding for seven consecutive seasons (1992–8). He signed for the LA Lakers in 1998, but was waived by the club after less than three months. He is the author of *Bad As I Wanna Be* (1996) and *Walk On the Wild Side* (1997).

Rodnina, Irina [rodneena] (1949–) Figure skater, born in Moscow, Russia. She won the pairs title at three Olympics – 1972 (with Alexei Ulanov), 1976, and 1980 (both with Alexandr Zaitsev) – and won four world titles with Ulanov (1969–72) and six with Zaitsev (1973–8). During the same years she won the corresponding European titles. She married Zaitsev in 1975, retired in 1980, and trained to be an astronaut.

Rodrigo, Joaquín [rodreegoh] (1902–99) Composer, born in Sagunto, E Spain. Although blind from the age of three, he studied music with Dukas in Paris (1927–33), and travelled widely before settling in Madrid in 1939. He is best known for his compositions for guitar, and following the successful first performance of his work *Concierto de Aranjuez* in Barcelona (1940), he became generally regarded as the leading post-Civil War Spanish composer.

Rodrigues Island [rohdreegez] 19°45S 63°20E, pop (2000e) 42 900. Island in the Indian Ocean, E of Mauritius; part of the Mascarene Is; a dependency of Mauritius; rises to 396 m/1299 ft at Mt Limon; chief town, Port Mathurin; fishing, subsistence agriculture; labour supply to Mauritius.

rods and cones Photoreceptor cells of the vertebrate retina, so called because of their shapes. Rods are sensitive to dim light (*scotopic*) and function at twilight. Cones are sensitive to bright light (*photopic*) and function in daylight. Nocturnal animals usually have more rods than cones. Many mammals have two types of cone, but humans and apes have three.

roe deer A small true deer (*Capreolus capreolus*) native to Europe and Asia; the smallest European deer (shoulder height, 75 cm/30 in); short upright antlers with three tines; virtually no tail; white rump; inhabits open woodland edges.

Roentgen, Wilhelm Konrad von *Röntgen*

Rogation Days In the Christian Church, the three days before Ascension Day, once observed with fasting, processions, and prayers to God for a successful harvest (**rogations**, Lat *rogare*, 'to ask').

Rogers, Bruce (1870–1957) Typographer and book designer, born in Linnwood, Indiana, USA. Trained as an artist, in 1895 he moved to Boston to the Riverside Press, and from 1900 worked in their new limited editions department. Among his typeface designs are the Montaigne (1901) and the Centaur (1915). He became adviser to the Cambridge University Press, UK (1916), the Harvard University Press (1919–34), and the Oxford University Press, where he designed the Oxford Lectern Bible (1935).

Rogers, Carl R(ansom) (1902–87) Psychotherapist, born in Oak Park, Illinois, USA. He studied psychology at Columbia University Teachers College (1931), taught at Chicago University (1945–57), and produced the book *Client-centered Therapy* (1951). This form of psychotherapy led to open therapy sessions and encounter groups in which patients talk out their problems under the supervision of a passive therapist. He was also a notable pioneer in carrying out systematic evaluations of the efficacy of psychotherapy. He later became resident fellow at the Western Behavioral Science Institute (1964–8) and the Center for Studies of the Person, both at La Jolla, CA (1968–87).

Rogers, Ginger, originally **Virginia Katherine McMath** (1911–95) Film actress and dancer, born in Independence, Missouri, USA. She made her professional debut at age 14 with Eddie Foy's vaudeville troupe, and by 1928 was appearing with her first husband, **Jack Pepper**, as a vaudeville song-and-dance team. She made her screen debut in *Young Man in Manhattan* (1930). She and Fred Astaire were not given star billing when they first danced together in *Flying Down to Rio* (1933), but they stole the picture and went on to make nine other films. She won an Oscar for best actress in *Kitty Foyle* (1940). Appearing in films and nightclubs until the mid-1960s, she found a new public when she took over the lead in such musicals as *Hello, Dolly!* and *Mame*. She was a cousin of the film actress, Rita Hayworth.

Roget, Peter Mark [rozhay] (1779–1869) Physician and scholar, creator of *Roget's Thesaurus*, born in London, UK. He studied medicine at Edinburgh, became physician to the Manchester

Infirmary (1804), physician to the Northern Dispensary, London (1808), and Fullerian professor of physiology at the Royal Institution (1833–6). He was also secretary of the Royal Society (1827–49), and an original member of the Senate of London University. He is best known for his *Thesaurus of English Words and Phrases* (1852), which he wrote after his retirement from medical practice.

Röhm, Ernst [roem], also spelled **Roehm** (1887–1934) Nazi leader, born in Munich, SE Germany. He became an early supporter of Hitler, and the organizer and commander of the stormtroopers ('Brownshirts' and 'Blackshirts'). He became state commissar of Bavaria, but in 1934 his plans to increase the power of this force led to his execution on Hitler's orders.

role A part played by an actor. In social psychology, the term is extended to refer to the part played by an individual in a given set of social circumstances (eg the role of 'mother' or 'leader'). **Role-playing** is the active performance of lines of action in a particular social setting; also, the conscious adoption of such lines of action, in situations of pretence, deception, or simulation. Role-playing as simulation may be used as a training or therapeutic method for improving social skills of a professional (eg interviewing) or non-professional kind. It has also been employed as a research method, where subjects playing the role of themselves, a prescribed character, or 'everyman', overtly act out or passively imagine participation in a scenario. **Role-conflict** may arise when someone tries to play two roles governed by incompatible normative expectations – for example, a clash between work and family duties, such as when a policeman is required to arrest his own son.

Rolfe, Frederick William (Serafino Austin Lewis Mary), pseudonym **Baron Corvo** (1860–1913) Novelist and essayist, born in London, UK. A convert to Roman Catholicism, his life was shattered by his rejection from the novitiate for the Roman priesthood at the Scots College in Rome; but it prompted his most famous work, *Hadrian the Seventh* (1904), in which a self-modelled priest is unexpectedly chosen for the papacy. His other major work is *The Desire and Pursuit of the Whole*, published posthumously in 1934.

rolfing A system of deep massage, developed by Dr Ida Rolf (1896–1979), and also known as **structural integration**. It was designed to break down abnormal connective tissue formed as the result of defective posture, and thereby allow readjustment. A course of treatment commences with the patient being photographed from front, back, and sides to detect abnormal posture and muscle tension. During the course of 10 one-hour treatment sessions the therapist uses deep massage applied with elbows, knuckles, hands, and fingers to realign the body structures. Some patients report pain and discomfort during treatment, but may be up to half an inch taller if they persevere to the end of the course.

Rolland, Romain [rolã] (1866–1944) Writer, born in Clamecy, C France. He studied in Paris and Rome, and in 1910 became professor of the history of music at the Sorbonne. He resigned in 1912 to devote himself to writing, published several biographies and a 10-volume novel, *Jean-Christophe* (1904–12), and in 1915 was awarded the Nobel Prize for Literature. He lived in Switzerland until 1938, completing another novel cycle, several plays, and many pieces of music criticism. On his return to France he became a mouthpiece of the opposition to Fascism and the Nazis, and his later works contain much political and social writing.

roller A crow-like bird of the widespread Old World family Coraciidae (11 species); usually blue and brown; inhabits woodland or open country; eats insects and small vertebrates; nests in hole; somersaults in flight when displaying (hence its name). The name is also used for the **cuckoo-roller** (Family: Leptosomatidae) and the **ground-roller** (Family: Brachypteraciidae). It is also a breed of canary.

roller skating A pastime first seen in Liège, Belgium, in 1760. The modern four-wheeled skate was introduced by the US inventor James L Plymton in 1863. As a sport it developed in the late 19th-c, and competitions exist as for ice skating: individual, pairs, dancing, and speed skating. Blade-type skates are now replacing the corner-wheel model.

Rolling Stones, The Rock group, members **Mick Jagger** (1943–) vocals, **Keith Richards** (1943–) guitar, **Bill Wyman** (1941–) bass, **Charlie Watts** (1942–) drums, **Ron Wood** (1947–) guitar, former member **Brian Jones** (1944–69) guitar, one of the longest-running and most successful popular music groups to emerge in the 1960s. They first performed together in 1962. At first, they were very much in the shadow of The Beatles, but their less boyish, more rebellious style together with their more aggressive blues-based music soon won them a large following. Although their uninhibited life styles and overtly sexual lyrics often hit the headlines, it was the excellence of their compositions (usually by Jagger and Richards) that ensured their continuing success. Among their early hits were 'The Last Time' and 'Satisfaction'. Later albums include *Exile on Main Street* (1972), *Voodoo Lounge* (1994), and *Bridges to Babylon* (1997).

Rollins, Sonny, popular name of **Theodore Walter Rollins** (1929–) Jazz saxophonist and composer, born in New York City, USA. He learned to play piano, alto saxophone, and tenor saxophone while at school, and early on worked and recorded with major bebop figures such as Charlie Parker and Miles Davis. From the mid-1950s he emerged as an important voice in the 'hard bop' movement. His use of calypso themes reflects his roots in the Virgin Is, and he is considered one of the most powerful improvisers on tenor and soprano saxophones.

Rollo, originally **Hrolf** (c.860–c.932) Viking leader and first duke of Normandy. As leader of the Norman pirates settled at the mouth of the Seine, he attacked (910) Paris and Chartres. He secured from Charles III of France in 911 a large district on condition that he defend it against attack, be baptized, and become Charles's vassal. This grant was the nucleus of the Duchy of Normandy, and Rollo was baptized (912) as Robert. Rollo's direct descendants included William the Conqueror, king of England.

Rolls, C(harles) S(tewart) (1877–1910) Motorist and aeronaut, born in London, UK. He studied at Cambridge, and from 1895 experimented with the earliest motor cars, forming a partnership with Henry Royce in 1906 for their production. In 1906 he crossed the English Channel by balloon, and in 1910 made the first return crossing by aeroplane. Soon afterwards, he died in a flying accident, the first British pilot to do so.

Rolls-Royce A major British firm of car engine and aero-engine manufacturers, founded in 1906. In the 1970s the firm was split into two separate companies, following financial problems caused by the high cost of aero-engine research and development. The aero-engine side of the business passed into British government ownership, while Rolls-Royce (Cars) remained a separate commercial enterprise. In 1987 the aero-engine business was returned by the government to private ownership as a fully commercial company. In 1998 Rolls-Royce Cars was bought by the German automobile company, Volkswagen.

ROM [rom] Acronym for **read-only memory**, a type of computer memory, usually integrated circuits, which can only be read from; the data is fixed during the manufacture of the chip. ROM is used where the data does not have to be altered; the data also remains intact even if the electrical power is removed.

Rom A travelling people whose origins lie in the subcontintent of India, now concentrated in S Europe, but found throughout the world; popularly called **Gypsies**, but not by the people themselves. Their language, Romani, is derived from Sanskrit, and varies from country to country. Many speak the national language of the country where they live, or a combination of Romani and the local language. They have also adopted the religion of the country where they live, but have their own baptismal, marriage, and burial practices. Because of the negative connotations of the word Gypsy, 'Traveller' is generally the preferred term in Britain. There are an estimated 9–12 million Rom today, worldwide.

Romains, Jules [romĩ], pseudonym of **Louis Henri Jean Farigoule** (1885–1972) Writer, born in Saint-Julien-Chapteuil, SE France. He studied at Paris, and became a teacher, but established his name with his poems *La Vie unanime* (1908, The Unanimous Life), and brought about the Unanimist school, devoted to a belief in universal brotherhood and group consciousness. He became a full-time writer from 1919, and remained prominent in French literature, his best-known works being the comedy *Knock, ou le triomphe de la médecine* (1923, Dr Knock, or the Triumph of Medicine) and the cycle of novels, *Les Hommes de bonne volonté* (27 vols, 1932–46, Men of Good Will), covering the early 20th-c era of French life.

Roman architecture A form of classical architecture in which the clear, expressive use of the column and horizontals by the Greeks was replaced by a plastic use of rounded forms such as the arch, dome, and vault. There is greater reliance on the wall, combined with a more decorative use of architectural orders. The development of concrete used in conjunction with brick, along with a great deal of engineering skill, allowed the construction of buildings such as the Pantheon, Rome (100–125), with a 43 m/141 ft dome, and the Colosseum, Rome (72–80). Domestic buildings included the *domus*, a single-storey urban house based around an atrium; the *insula*, a multi-storey urban tenement block; and the *villa*, an often luxurious rural residence that reaches its apogee in Hadrian's Villa, Tivoli (AD 123). Other typically Roman buildings include the triumphal arch, basilica palace, and the complicated planning of the *thermae*, or baths.

Roman art Historically the most important artistic tradition in the ancient world, if not in all Western history, which has seen a whole series of classical (ie Roman) revivals from the early Middle Ages down to the 18th-c. Roman artists owed a strong debt to Hellenistic Greek art, especially in painting and sculpture, and many classical Greek statues survive only as Roman copies. However, in portraiture, especially busts, and in reliefs (eg those on Trajan's column and on triumphal arches), Roman sculptors were highly original, and set standards that were keenly pursued from the Renaissance to the 18th-c. Not much painting has survived, but murals in Roman houses featured scenes from Homer and Ovid in landscape settings.

Roman Catholicism The doctrine, worship, and life of the Roman Catholic Church (over 1080 million members worldwide in 2004). A direct line of succession is claimed from the earliest Christian communities, centring on the city of Rome, where St Peter (claimed as the first bishop of Rome) was martyred and St Paul witnessed. After the conversion of the Emperor Constantine (4th-c), Roman bishops acquired something of the authority and power of the emperor. Surviving the fall of Rome in the 5th-c, the Church was the only effective agency of civilization in Europe, and after the 11th-c schism with the Byzantine or Eastern Church, it was the dominant force in the Western world, the Holy Roman Empire. The Protestant Reformation of the 16th-c inspired revival, and the need to restate doctrine in an unambiguous form and to purge the church and clergy of abuses and corruption was recognized. The most dramatic reforms were enacted by the two Vatican Councils of the 19th-c and 20th-c. The Second Vatican Council (1962–5) signalled a new era, with a new ecumenical spirit pervading the Church. Although the doctrines of the faith remained largely untouched, there was a new openness to other Christian denominations – indeed, other world religions. Great emphasis was placed on the Church as the 'people of God', with the laity being given a much more active part in liturgy (eg the Mass being said in the vernacular instead of Latin).

Doctrine is declared by the pope, or by a General Council with the approval of the pope, and is summarized in the Nicene Creed. Scripture is authoritative, and authoritatively interpreted by the *magisterium* or teaching office of the Church. The tradition of the Church is accepted as authoritative, special importance being attributed to the early church fathers and to the mediaeval scholastics, notably St Thomas Aquinas. Principal doctrines are similar to those of mainstream Protestant and Orthdox Churches – God as Trinity, creation, redemption, the person and work of Jesus Christ, and the place of the Holy Spirit – the chief doctrinal differences being the role of the Church in salvation, and its sacramental theology. Modern liturgies reflect a cross-section of historical inheritance, cultural environment, and social factors. Ancient traditional practices such as the veneration of the Virgin Mary and the Saints, or the Stations of the Cross, are still regarded as valuable aids to devotion. At the other extreme, Roman Catholic priests in South America, preaching liberation theology, have assumed a political role, for which they have been rebuked by Rome.

The hierarchy of the Church includes cardinals, bishops, priests, and several minor orders. Many religious orders, male and female, exist within the Church. The vast and complex organization of the Church is controlled by the Vatican, an independent state in Rome which, under the direction of the pope, implements Church policy, and administers property and finance. In predominantly Catholic countries, the Church maintains a degree of political influence, and extends canon law into the realm of civil law, notably on moral issues (eg birth control).

romance (Mediaeval Lat *romanice* 'in the Romanic tongue') A literary genre which may be traced back to late Classical times, with Longus' *Daphnis and Chloe* and Apuleius's *Golden Ass* (both 2nd-c AD). The romance proper, as a tale (in verse or prose) of courtly love or pastoral idyll, flourished in late mediaeval and Renaissance Europe. There were three main sources: the Classical (Alexander, Troy, Thebes); Arthurian legend; and 'the matter of France' (Charlemagne and his court). The Renaissance romance drew also on pastoral sources, as in Sidney's *Arcadia* (1595). The romance was symbolically engulfed by the novel in Cervantes's *Don Quixote* (1605, 1615). But the modern 'romance' novel maintains a loyal (mainly female) readership, as is proved by the spectacular sales and borrowings of books by authors such as Catherine Cookson and Barbara Cartland.

Romance languages The languages which developed from the 'vulgar' or spoken form of Latin used throughout the Roman Empire. The major ones are Italian, French, Spanish, Portuguese, and Romanian, all of which are official languages in their respective states. There are also several other varieties, such as Sardinian, Rhaetian (dialectal variants in N Italy and Switzerland), and Catalan, used mainly in NE Spain. Colonialism has dispersed the Romance languages throughout the world, so that over 700 million people now speak a Romance language or a creole based on one. French is spoken by c.72 million as a mother-tongue in France, Canada, Belgium, Switzerland, Luxembourg, Monaco, and many parts of Africa, Oceania, and the Americas, and is used as a second language by a further 200 million. Spanish is spoken by over 270 million people in Spain, most of the countries of Central and South America, and by rapidly increasing numbers in the USA. Portuguese is spoken by c.175 million people, mainly in Brazil, and also in Portugal and parts of Africa. Italian is spoken by c.63 million in Italy and adjoining localities, as well as in parts of N Africa and the Americas.

Roman Curia (Lat *curia*, 'court') An organization in the Vatican (Rome) which administers the affairs of the Roman Catholic Church under the authority of the pope. It is comprised of congregations (administrative), tribunals (judicial), and offices (ministerial), all as defined in canon law.

Romanesque architecture The form of architecture prevalent in W Europe 10th–12th-c AD, so called because of the Roman elements – columns and round arches – which are used in un-Roman ways to decorate apses, facades, towers, and naves with many tiers of arcades. The use of rib vaults signified the introduction of Gothic architectural forms. Its greatest monuments are huge vaulted churches richly decorated with sculpture, such as at Santiago de Compostela and Durham.

Romania

□ International Airport ∴ World heritage site

Roumania, or **Rumania**, official name **Republic of Romania**, Romanian **Republica România** Local name România

Timezone GMT +2

Area 237 500 km²/91 675 sq mi

Population total (2002e) 21 667 000

Status Republic

Date of independence 1918

Capital Bucharest

Languages Romanian (official), with French, Hungarian, and German widely spoken

Ethnic groups Romanian (89%), Hungarian (7%), German (2%), Ukrainian, Serb, Croat, Russian, Turk, and Gypsy (2%)

Religions Eastern Orthodox Christian (80%), Roman Catholic (6%), Calvinist, Lutheran, Baptist (4%)

Physical features Carpathian Mts form the heart of the country; highest peak, Negoiul, 2548 m/8359 ft; crossed by many rivers; c.3500 glacial ponds, lakes, and coastal lagoons; over 25% of land forested.

Climate Continental, with cold, snowy winters and warm summers; winters can be severe; mildest along the Black Sea coast; average annual temperatures range from 7°C (N), to 11°C (S), -3°C (Jan), 24°C (Jul); average annual rainfall 579 mm/22·8 in.

Currency 1 Leu (plural lei) = 100 bani

Economy Gradual change from agricultural to industrial economy (since World War 2); state owns nearly 37% of farm land, mainly organized as collectives and state farms; wheat, maize, sugar beet, fruit, potatoes; livestock; oil, natural gas; iron and steel, metallurgy, engineering, chemicals, textiles, electronics, timber; tourism.

GDP (2002e) $169·3 bn, per capita $7600

Human Development Index (2002) 0·775

History Formed from the unification of Moldavia and Wallachia, 1862; monarchy created, 1866; Transylvania, Bessarabia, and Bucovina united with Romania, 1918; support given to Germany in World War 2; occupied by Soviet forces, 1944; monarchy abolished and People's Republic declared, 1947; Socialist Republic declared, 1965; increasingly independent from the USSR from the 1960s; leading political force was the Romanian Communist Party, led by dictator Nicolae Ceauşescu; popular uprising due to violent repression of protest led to the overthrow of the Ceauşescu regime, 1989; new constitution, 1991; governed by a President, Prime Minister, Chamber of Deputies, and Senate.

Republic

Head of State

1947–8 Mihai Sadoveanu *Interim*
1948–52 Constantin I Parhon
1952–8 Petru Groza
1958–61 Ion Georghe Maurer
1961–5 Georghe Gheorghiu-Dej
1965–7 Chivu Stoica
1967–89 Nicolae Ceau·sescu
1989–96 Ion Iliescu
1996–2000 Emil Constantinescu
2000– Ion Iliescu

Head of Government

1980–3 Ilie Verdet
1983–9 Constantin Dascalescu
1989–91 Petre Roman
1991–2 Theodor Stolojan
1992–6 Nicolae Vacaroiu
1996–8 Victor Ciorbea
1998–9 Radu Vasile
1999–2000 Mugur Isarescu
2000– Adrian Nastase

roman fleuve [rohmã floev] (Fr 'river-novel') A term used for a series of novels, linked by common characters or preoccupations. Examples are Zola's Rougon–Macquart series (1871–93), the seven parts of Proust's *A la recherche du temps perdu* (1913–27), Galsworthy's *The Forsyte Saga* (1906–28), and Anthony Powell's 12-volume *A Dance to the Music of Time* (1951–76).

Roman history **The Monarchy** (753–509 BC). Founded, according to tradition, in 753 BC, Rome was initially ruled by kings, of whom Romulus was the first and Tarquinius Superbus the seventh and last. Expelled in 509 BC because of his tyrannical ways, he left the Romans with a long-abiding hatred of monarchy.

The Republic (509–31 BC). Brought into being with the overthrow of the monarchy, the Republican system of government was designed to prevent a tyrant ever ruling Rome again. Executive power was entrusted to two annually elected officials (*consuls*); their advisory council, the Senate, an ex-officio body of magistrates, provided the necessary elements of experience and continuity. The system brought stability, and Rome grew rapidly from a small city-state into an empire. The Punic Wars brought the W Mediterranean under her control, while the campaigns against the rulers of the Hellenistic world added Macedon, Greece, Asia Minor, and the Levant. But the system which had served the city-state so well could not cope with the government of this Empire. The Republic perished at Actium in 31 BC after decades of civil war in which great warlords such as Caesar, Pompey, Antony, and Octavian fought for supreme power.

The Empire (31 BC–AD 476 in the W, AD 1453 in the E). Cobbled together out of the wreckage of the Republic, the Roman Empire was the creation of one man, the first emperor, Augustus, who gave it its official name *Principate* (ie rule of the first citizen, or *princeps*), and the constitutional and administrative framework which lasted until the 3rd-c. Abroad, too, Augustus's arrangements affected the nature of the Empire permanently – the unbridled expansionism of Republican days was abandoned, and territorial limits were set – the Rhine and Danube in Europe, the Euphrates in Asia. Subsequent modifications were few; Britain (43), Dacia, and Arabia (both annexed by Trajan in 106) were the only significant later additions.

From the outset, the Rhine–Danube frontier was the hardest to hold, with the tribes across the rivers exerting a relentless pressure upon the Roman defences. Rome managed to contain this pressure for several centuries, but only at an increasing cost to herself. The area saw a steady military build-up and ultimately constant fighting. The foundation in the 3rd-c of a new imperial capital (Nicomedia) nearer this frontier shows how the Empire's centre of gravity had shifted from Rome and Italy to the N and E. This was the point where the very integrity of the Empire was threatened; and it was here that Rome's defences in the end were breached. In the 5th-c, hordes of trans-riverine tribesmen (eg Huns, Vandals, Visigoths, Ostrogoths) poured into the W provinces carrying all before them. In 476 with their deposition of the last emperor, Romulus Augustulus, they marked symbolically their destruction of the W half of the Empire. The E provinces, however, proved more resilient; here the barbarian challenge was contained for another thousand years, until the E capital Constantinople fell to the Ottoman Turks in 1453.

Romani The language of the Rom, of Indo-Aryan origin, spoken by c.5–8 million, especially in a wide range of dialects worldwide; earlier spelled **Romany**. Dialects of Romani have taken on features of the languages with which they have come into contact in various parts of the world. It is essentially a spoken language, with a rich oral literature, and is also widely used as an argot, when Rom groups come into contact with the local communities.

Romania *p.1315*

Romanian *Romance languages*

Romanist The name given by art historians to those Dutch and Flemish artists who, in the 16th-c, travelled to Italy to see the works of the great Renaissance masters. Thus Jan Gossaert (called Mabuse) went to Italy in 1508, taking back to Antwerp the decorative details of the Renaissance and new subjects including the classical nude.

romanization The use of the Roman alphabet to replace a language's writing system constructed on a different principle. This procedure has been very common in language planning, especially in countries where the native script is non-alphabetic in character, as in Chinese logographic writing or the Japanese katakana syllabary. Romanized versions also exist for several alphabetic systems, such as Arabic and Hindi.

Romanization In antiquity, the process whereby the subject peoples of W Europe adopted the language and customs of the Romans. At first involuntary, under the Empire it became a deliberate government policy. Roman-style towns were built in the less developed provinces, and the provincial aristocracy were encouraged to learn Latin and participate in local government. The prizes could be, in the first instance, the award of Roman citizenship and later even enrolment into the Roman Senate itself.

Roman Law The corpus of Roman Law starts with the primitive code, the Twelve Tables (450 BC), and ends with Justinian's complex codification (AD c.530). In the intervening centuries Rome grew from a tiny city-state into a vast world empire and exchanged a Republican form of government for a monarchical one. Roman law reflects these changes: under the empire, the emperor himself gradually became the sole source of law, his pronouncements (*edicta*), written opinions on legal points (*rescripta*), and even instructions to his officials (*mandata*) all being legally binding. The collective name for these enactments is 'constitutions'. Older forms of law-making withered away, as the bodies formerly responsible (eg the people's assemblies (*comitia*) and the Senate) became obsolete or radically altered.

Roman numerals The Roman symbols for numbers, which have a fixed value, and do not use the concept of place-value. The symbols generally used are I = 1, V = 5, X = 10, L = 50, C = 100, D = 500, and M = 1000 (the symbols L and D were later developments). In general, symbols were placed in decreasing order of size, eg XVI = 16. A symbol may be repeated once, twice, or three times (eg XVIII = 18), but not four times, this being avoided by altering the normal order of the symbols, so that 19 = XIX not XVIIII. Some minor variations are found, eg today IIII is sometimes used on clock-faces instead of IV.

Romanovs [**roh**manofs] The second (and last) Russian royal dynasty (1613–1917). The name Romanov was adopted in the 16th-c by a family of boyars that traced its origins back to the 14th-c. The first Romanov tsar (Mikhail) was elected in 1613 after the Time of Troubles. The Romanovs ruled as absolute autocrats, allowing no constitutional or legal checks on their political power. The marriage of Nicholas II to Princess Alexandra of Hesse brought haemophilia into the family; their son, Alexey (1904–18), was afflicted with the disease. The dynasty ended with the abdication of Nicholas II in February 1917, and his execution and that of his immediate family by Bolshevik

Roman religion

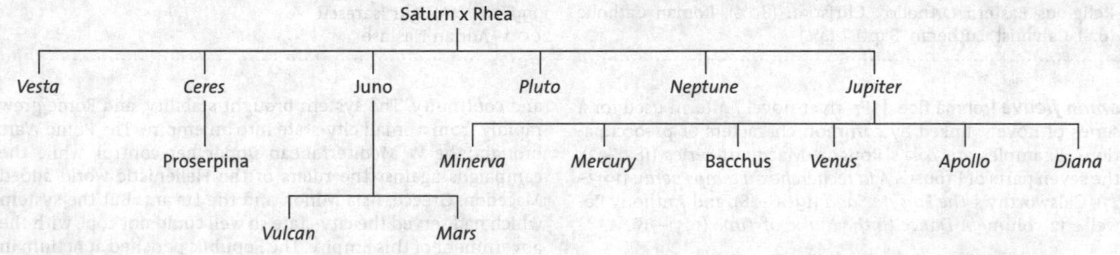

The 12 major gods of Olympus are shown in italic type. Bacchus in some accounts supplants Vesta. Pluto and Prosperpina are gods of the underworld.

The first Romans were farmers and lived in a world full of *numen*, a powerful spiritual force behind appearances waiting to be revealed, and *genius*, the spirit of an ancestor, or a locality. Etruscan and Italic deities were absorbed, and a priestly college was established, presided over by the *pontifex maximus*. By Cicero's time the diversity of cults had been organized into uniformity throughout most of Italy. Augustus took the title of *pontifex* for himself, and reaffirmed the ancient worship. The Romans believed that all peoples worshipped the same gods under different names (eg Mercury = Hermes), and so had no difficulty in absorbing Greek mythology, having nothing comparable themselves. After Augustus's death, the worship of the emperor became a religious duty, but increasingly exotic foreign cults flourished. When Constantine accepted Christianity in AD 312, the ancient Roman religion became 'paganism', ie the practices of country people.

guards in July 1918. In 1998, under the orders of President Boris Yeltsin, their presumed remains were exhumed and laid to rest on an island in St Petersburg.

Roman religion *p.1316*

Roman roads *see panel*

Romans, Letter to the A New Testament book, often considered the most significant of the works of the apostle Paul. Although Paul did not establish the Church in Rome, he wrote to it (perhaps c.55–8) to present his understanding of salvation for both Gentiles and Jews, and to warn against libertine and legalistic interpretations of the Christian message. Chapters 1–8 set out his understanding of justification and salvation; Chapters 9–11 address the problem of Israel's unbelief; Chapters 12–16 deal with Christian living and community relationships.

Romanticism (literature) A large-scale movement of the mind in the late 18th/early 19th-c, which affected the whole of human understanding and experience. The Renaissance made humanity the measure of the universe; Romanticism placed the individual at the centre of his/her own world. This was partly the work of philosophers, from the solipsist Berkeley and the sceptical Hume to Kant, with his dynamic model of the mind; but it was the imaginative writers of the time who effectively authorized and liberated the subjective impulse. Among the more important writers associated with Romanticism are, in England, Wordsworth, Coleridge, Blake, Keats, Shelley, Scott, and Byron; in Germany, Goethe, Herder, Heine, and Schiller; in France, Rousseau, Lamartine, Vigny, and Hugo; and in the USA, Edgar Allen Poe. But there are few writers who bear no trace of this profound revolution in thought and feeling, which is still discernible as one of the major tributaries of the modern age.

Roman roads

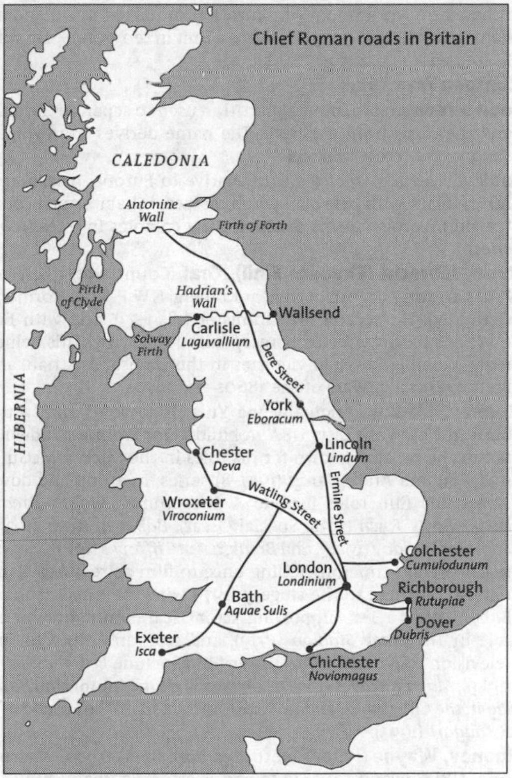

A network of over 80 000 km/50 000 mi of usually straight roads radiating from ancient Rome. Built primarily for military purposes, the roads also served an important commercial function. Main routes were constructed on an earth footing with a layer of small stones in mortar above, on top of which was a hard filling surfaced with stone slabs. The first roads were built with a slope and ditches, allowing water to drain away. The Appian Way, built in the 3rd-c BC and linking Rome with present-day Capua, was the first great Roman road. The Aurelian Way connected Rome with present-day Pisa, while the Flaminian Way served as the main northern route.

Romanticism (music) Music particularly of the period c.1810–1910, in which subjective emotion is felt to take precedence over objective detachment, content over form, colour over line, and the lyrical and poetic over the architectonic. The Romantic period in music saw the growth of the modern symphony orchestra, an increased and more integral use of chromaticism, a general expansion of the inherited genres of opera, symphony, concerto, etc, and the emergence of new genres (the concert overture and symphonic poem) in which composers could express a response to literature and the other arts. National styles, based to some extent on a new awareness of a country's folk heritage, began to assert themselves, as in Czechoslovakia and Russia. The works of the major Romantic composers form the staple repertory of modern concert halls and opera houses.

Romanticism (visual arts) As in literature, an attitude of mind, rather than a style. Between c.1760 and c.1850 the range of subjects greatly expanded. Some were chosen for their heightened emotional qualities, such as the death-bed scenes by Greuze, David, and West, or horrific disasters, such as 'The Raft of the Medusa' (1819) by Géricault. Others were chosen for their exotic appeal, as with Delacroix's 'Algerian Women' (1834). Its features include: a cult of nostalgia, a yearning for 'long ago and far away'; Egyptian, Greek and mediaeval revivals in architecture and the decorative arts; and the treatment of lost causes: the Jacobites, the Huguenots, the Cavaliers. Leading romantics in Britain include Turner and Constable; in Germany, Caspar David Friedrich (1774–1840); in Spain, Goya.

Romany *Rom; Romani*

Romberg, Sigmund (1887–1951) Composer of operettas, born in Nagykanizsa, W Hungary. He trained in Vienna as an engineer, also studying violin and composition. He settled in the USA in 1909, and in New York City introduced the use of dance bands in restaurants. Of more than 70 works, his most famous were *Blossom Time* (1921), *The Student Prince* (1924), *The Desert Song* (1926), and *The New Moon* (1928).

Rome, Ital **Roma** 41°53N 12°30E, pop (2000e) 2 820 000. Capital city of Italy, Lazio region, WC Italy; on the R Tiber, 27 km/17 mi from the Tyrrhenian Sea (E); on the left bank are the Seven Hills of Rome – the Capitoline (50 m/165 ft), Quirinal (52 m/172 ft), Viminal (56 m/185 ft), Esquiline (53 m/175 ft), Palatine (51 m/168 ft), Aventine (46 m/152 ft), and Caelian (50 m/165 ft) – on which the ancient city was built during the 8th-c BC; centre of the Roman Empire; sacked by Germanic tribes, 5th-c; ecclesiastical centre from 6th-c; Vatican City on W bank; capital of unified Italy, 1871; two airports (Fiumicino, Ciampino); railway; metro; university (1303); important centre of fashion and film (Cinecittá), television and publishing; headquarters of many cultural and research institutions; oil refining, chemicals, pharmaceuticals, fertilizers, iron and steel, glass, cement, engineering, textiles, brewing, foodstuffs; centre of Rome is a world heritage site; a major tourist city; Palazzo Venezia (15th-c), Forum Romanum (AD 113), with relics of ancient Rome (Arch of Titus, Via Sacra, Curia, Arch of Septimius Severus), Colosseum (from AD 75), Baths of Caracalla (217), Arch of Constantine (312), Pantheon (27 BC), Trevi Fountain (1762), Galleria Borghese; replica of London's Globe Theatre (2003); several Renaissance palaces; numerous churches, notably St Peter's (in the Vatican), St John Lateran (Rome's cathedral), San Lorenzo and San Paolo outside the Walls, Santa Maria Maggiore; Sistine Chapel in Vatican Museum; spring festival (Mar–Apr); numerous religious feasts and celebrations.

Rome, Treaties of *EURATOM; European Community*

Rømer, Ole (Christensen) [roemer] (1644–1710) Astronomer, born in Århus, NC Denmark. While working at the Royal Observatory in Paris (1672–81) he used eclipses of Jupiter's satellites to make the first determination of the velocity of light (1675), which he calculated to be 225 000 km per sec (140 000 mi per sec). 20th-c measurements give the speed as 299 793 km per sec (186 282 mi per sec).

Rommel, Erwin (Johannes Eugen) (1891–1944) German field marshal, born in Heidenheim, S Germany. He studied at Tübingen, fought in World War 1, taught at Dresden Military Academy, and became an early Nazi sympathizer. He commanded Hitler's headquarters guard during the early occupations, and led a Panzer division during the 1940 invasion of France. He then commanded the Afrika Korps, where he achieved major successes. Eventually driven into retreat by a strongly reinforced Eighth Army, he was withdrawn, a sick man, from North Africa, and appointed to an Army Corps command in France. Returning home wounded in 1944, he condoned the plot against Hitler's life. After its discovery, he committed suicide.

Romney, George [romnee, ruhmnee] (1734–1802) Painter, born in Dalton-in-Furness, Lancashire, NW England, UK. From 1757 he set up as a portrait painter, leaving his family and moving to London in 1762. Apart from two visits to France, and two years residence in Italy (1773–5), he stayed in Cavendish Square, where his reputation rivalled that of Reynolds. His many pictures of Lady Hamilton are particularly well known.

Romulus and Remus [romyulus, reemus] In Roman legend, the twin sons of Mars and the Vestal Virgin Rhea Silvia; an example of an invented myth, to explain the name of the city. They were thrown into the Tiber, which carried them to the Palatine, where they were suckled by a she-wolf. In building the wall of Rome, Remus made fun of the work and was killed by Romulus or one of his followers. Having founded Rome, Romulus was later carried off in a thunderstorm.

Romulus Augustulus [romyulus awguhstyulus] (5th-c AD) *Augustulus*

Ronaldo (Luiz Nazario de Lima) [ronaldoh], nickname **Ro-Ro** (1976–) Footballer, born in Itaguai, Brazil. A forward, he played for Cruzeiro, Brazil, then PSV Eindhoven and Barcelona, moving to Inter Milan in 1997 and Real Madrid in 2002. While at Barcelona he scored a Spanish league record of 34 goals in a season, his team also winning the European Cup Winners' Cup and the Spanish cup final. He has been FIFA World Footballer of the Year three times (1996, 1997, 2002) and European Player of the Year twice (1997, 2002). By the beginning of 2004 he had won 70 caps playing for Brazil. He won the Golden Boot Award for the 2002 World Cup's leading scorer, with eight goals.

Ronay, Egon [ronay, eegon] (1920–) Gastronome and writer, born in Hungary. He studied law at Budapest, and trained as a chef at home and in London before becoming manager of the family group of restaurants in Hungary. He emigrated to England in 1946 and opened his own restaurant in London (1952–5). He founded the annual *Egon Ronay's Guide to Hotels and Restaurants* in 1956, and subsequently similar guides to pubs, ski resorts, and various other places of interest to tourists in Britain and Europe.

roncey *cob*

Ronda 36°46N 5°12W, pop (2000e) 34 200. Picturesque town in Málaga province, Andalusia, S Spain, on R Guadalevin; railway; famous for its school of bullfighters; clothes, wine, leather, soap; Fiesta of La Reconquista (May), fiesta and fair (Sep).

rondeau [rondoh] (Fr *rond* 'round') An Old French verse form of 13 or 15 (usually octosyllabic) lines, in three stanzas, using only two rhymes. It was popular in 16th-c France, and among the French Romantics (eg de Musset), and was imported into England in the late 19th-c (eg by Dobson, Swinburne).

rondo A musical structure in which restatements of the initial theme are separated by contrasting episodes, eg on the pattern A–B–A–C–A–B–A, perhaps with an introduction and a coda. In the **sonata rondo**, the 'B' theme of this scheme is stated first in a related key, returning in the home key, and the 'C' theme may be replaced by development.

Ronsard, Pierre de [rõsah(r)] (1524–85) Renaissance poet, born in La Possonnière, C France. He trained as a page, but became deaf, and took up writing, studying for seven years at the Collège de Coqueret, and becoming a leader of the *Pléiade* group. His early works include *Odes* (1550) and *Amours* (1552), and he later wrote two bitter reflections on the political and economic state of the country. He was highly successful in his lifetime, but his fame suffered an eclipse after his death until the growth of the Romantic movement in the 19th-c.

Röntgen, Wilhelm Konrad von [roentguhn], also spelled **Roentgen** (1845–1923) Physicist, born in Lennep, W Germany. He studied at Zürich, and became professor of physics at Strasbourg (1876–9), Giessen (1879–88), Würzburg (1888–1900), and Munich (1900–20). In 1895 he discovered the electromagnetic rays which he called *X-rays*, for which he received the first Nobel Prize for Physics in 1901.

röntgen or **roentgen** [rontguhn, -juhn] The unit of exposure to ionizing radiation; symbol *R*; named after Wilhelm Röntgen. It is based on the amount of ionization produced in a standard volume of air by X-rays; classed as a unit in temporary use with SI units, $1\ R = 2{\cdot}58 \times 10^{-4}$ C/kg.

Röntgen rays *X-rays*

rood screen An ornamental partition used to separate the altar and the choir from the nave. The name derives from Anglo-Saxon *rood*, 'cross, crucifix'.

rook A crow (*Corvus frugilegus*) native to Europe, Asia, and N Africa; black with pale bare patch on face; inhabits open country; omnivorous; forms dense nesting colonies in trees (*rookeries*).

Roon, Albrecht (Theodor Emil), Graf (Count) **von** (1803–79) Prussian army officer, born near Kolberg, NW Poland (formerly Germany). He became war minister (1859–73), and with Bismarck's support effectively reorganized the army. This helped make possible Prussian victories in the Danish, Austrian, and Franco-Prussian Wars of the 1860s and 1870s.

Rooney, Mickey, originally **Joe Yule, Jr** (1920–) Film actor, born in New York City, USA. A child actor from a vaudeville family, he became known for his roles in the Mickey McGuire (1927–33) and Andy Hardy (1937–8) series. In an up-and-down career, his film roles include *A Midsummer Night's Dream* (1935), *Boy's Town* (1938, Special Oscar), *Babes in Arms* (1939), *Summer Holiday* (1948), and *Breakfast at Tiffany's* (1961). He was married eight times, including once to film actress Ava Gardner. He returned to the stage in 1979 with the musical *Sugar Babes*, gained a Best Supporting Actor Oscar nomination for his role in *The Black Stallion* (1979), and won an Emmy for his television role in *Bill* (1982). Later films include *Erik the Viking* (1989), *Making Waves* (1994), *Long Road Home* (1996), and *Babe: Pig in the City* (1998), and he wrote and acted in *The Legend of O B Taggart* (1995).

Rooney, Wayne (1985–) Footballer, born in Liverpool, Merseyside, NW England, UK. He joined Everton Football Club as a youth and first played for England in the under-15 team. A talented forward, he made his premiership debut with Everton in 2002 and scored his first goal for the club a few days before his 17th birthday. In 2003 he became the youngest ever senior England international (17 yrs 111 days) when he debuted as a substitute in a friendly match against Australia. His first full appearance was against Turkey (Apr 2003) in a successful qualifying match for the Euro 2004 competition, and in a later round of the same competition he became England's youngest goal scorer. He was voted BBC Young Sports Personality of the Year in 2002.

Roosevelt, (Anna) Eleanor [rohzuhvelt, roozvelt] (1884–1962) Diplomat and humanitarian, born in New York City, USA, the niece of Theodore Roosevelt and the wife of Franklin D Roosevelt, her distant cousin, whom she married in 1905. She took up extensive political work after her husband's infirmity from polio in 1921, and proved herself an invaluable adviser to him while he was president (1933–45). She became a symbol of what First Ladies could do to promote social and political causes. She acquired an independent voice with her newspaper column 'My Day', and in 1941 was appointed assistant director of the office of civilian defence. After her husband's death in 1945 she extended the scope of her activities, and was a delegate to the UN Assembly (1946), US representative at the General Assembly (1946–52), and chair of the UN Human Rights Commission (1947–51).

Roosevelt, Franklin D(elano) [rohzuhvelt, roozvelt], nickname **FDR** (1882–1945) US statesman and 32nd president (1933–45), born in Hyde Park, New York, USA. He became a lawyer (1907), a New York State senator (1910–13), and assistant secretary of the navy (1913–20). He was Democratic candidate for the vice-presidency in 1920, and Governor of New York (1928–32), although stricken with paralysis (polio) in 1921. As president, he met the economic crisis with his 'New Deal' for national recovery (1933), and became the only president to be re-elected three times. He strove in vain to ward off war, modified the USA's neutrality to favour the Allies, and was brought in by Japan's action at Pearl Harbor (1941). He met with Churchill and Stalin at Teheran (1943) and Yalta (1945), but died at Warm Springs, GA, where he had long gone for treatment, three weeks before the German surrender.

Roosevelt, Theodore [rohzuhvelt, roozvelt], known as **Teddy Roosevelt** (1858–1919) US Republican statesman and 26th president (1901–9), born in New York City, USA. He studied at Harvard, and became leader of the New York legislature (1884). In 1898 he raised a volunteer cavalry ('Roosevelt's Roughriders') in the Cuban War, and came back to be Governor of New York State (1898–1900). Elected vice-president in 1900, he became president on the death (by assassination) of McKinley, and was elected in 1904 in his own right. He was awarded the Nobel Peace Prize in 1906 for mediating the end of the Russo–Japanese War. An expansionist, he insisted on a strong navy and the regulation of trusts and monopolies, promoted the construction of the Panama Canal, and introduced a 'Square Deal' policy for social reform. As Progressive candidate for the presidency in 1912, he was defeated by Wilson. He worked vigorously during World War 1 pressing for America's intervention.

Root, Elihu (1845–1937) Jurist and statesman, born in Clinton, New York, USA. He studied law at New York University, and practised in New York City. He became US secretary of war (1899–1904), and secretary of state (1905–9), and was awarded the Nobel Prize for Peace in 1912 for his promotion of international arbitration. He participated in the founding of the League of Nations.

root (botany) The part of a plant's axis which usually lies underground, absorbing water and nutrients, and anchoring the plant in the soil; also commonly serving as a storage organ. It originates as the *radicle*, the embryonic root of the seed, and develops in one of two basic ways, either by repeated branching of the radicle to form a mass of fibrous **lateral roots** or by forming a central **taproot** with relatively few laterals. The tip of the root bears a cap, the *calyptra*, a continuously growing layer of cells which protect the root as it pushes through the soil. Immediately behind the calyptra is a region bearing **root hairs** – single-celled structures mainly responsible for the absorption of water from the soil. Behind this region the root may develop lateral branches which extend the root system. Like the stem, the root has a vascular system to conduct water and nutrients to and from it, but in roots the vascular tissue usually forms a solid rather than hollow cylinder which better resists the tensions that would otherwise uproot the plant. Unlike stems, roots generally lack buds and green tissue.

Roots can be modified in various ways to enhance or add to their functions. Swollen taproots act as storage organs; contractile roots help to pull rhizomes or corms deeper into the soil. **Pneumatophores** are specialized breathing roots developed in swampy, oxygen-poor ground. Roots which develop above ground are called **aerial roots**, and occur in many plants. They grow from stems or leaves, and absorb moisture direct from the atmosphere. Other types of aerial root include **buttress** or **prop roots**, which help support the stem or trunk, and **climbing** and **adhesive** roots, which help to elevate the plant. In epiphytes, the aerial roots are often green and capable of photosynthesis. A common phenomenon is the formation of symbiotic associations between plant roots and micro-organisms such as nitrogen-fixing bacteria and mycorrhizal fungi, which enhance the absorbing abilities of the roots.

root (linguistics) The basic element (*morpheme*) of a word, to which affixes can be added to give derived forms. For example, from the root *kind*, we may derive *un-kind*, *kind-ly*, *kind-ness*, etc. The root carries the core meaning of the word, and prefixes modify that meaning in regular ways. In addition, the suffixes carry grammatical information, marking the form's part of speech, as in *kind-ly* (adjective), *kind-ness* (noun). Roots in highly inflected languages normally cannot stand alone. A root to which other elements have been added, so that the form can serve as the basis for inflections, is known as a **stem**. For example, Latin *am-* 'love' is a root, to which *-av-* can be added to form the perfect stem *amav-*; this is then inflected for person and number (*amavi* 'I have loved', *amavimus* 'We have loved', etc).

root nodule A small, tumour-like swelling on the roots of some plants caused by the invasion of benign micro-organisms which are able to fix atmospheric nitrogen into nitrates to the benefit of the host in return for sugars. An example is the nitrogen-fixing bacterium *Rhizobium*, associated with all members of the pea family Leguminosae.

rope A length of thick fibre used to secure objects together. The fibres are twisted or plaited for added strength, and can be natural (eg hemp, sisal, flax, jute, cotton) or synthetic (eg nylon, polyester). Synthetic fibre ropes are lighter and stronger, but they can be stretched more. Heavy ropes, such as those used to tie large ships to jetties, may have a diameter of up to 25 cm/10 in, though most are much thinner. Wire ropes are also used as cables on suspension bridges.

Roraima, Mount [roriyma] 5°12N 60°43W. Peak at the junction of the Brazil, Guyana, and Venezuela borders, South America; 442 km/275 mi SE of Ciudad Bolivar (Venezuela) in the Serra de Pacaraima; highest peak (2875 m/9432 ft) in the Guiana Highlands; a giant table mountain, total area 67 sq km/26 sq mi.

ro-ro [rohroh] A term derived from 'roll on, roll off', a vessel designed to permit vehicles to drive on and off the ship under their own power. Access to the vessel is normally made through the bow or stern doors.

Røros Mining town on the Glomma R in Norway; founded in 1644 after the discovery of large deposits of copper in the region; old miners' village, with unpainted timber houses; 18th-c church; a world heritage site.

rorqual [raw(r)kwal] A baleen whale of worldwide family Balaenopteridae (6 species); throat has 10–100 longitudinal furrows, allowing it to expand when feeding; small dorsal fin near tail; female larger than male; comprises **blue**, **sei**, **fin**, **minke**, **Bryde's**, and **humpback** whales.

Rorschach, Hermann [raw(r)shahkh] (1884–1922) Psychiatrist and neurologist, born in Zürich, N Switzerland. He devised a diagnostic procedure for mental disorders based upon the patient's interpretation of a series of standardized ink blots (the *Rorschach test*). His work received little attention until after his death.

Rorty, Richard (McKay) (1931–) Philosopher, born in New York City, USA. He studied at Chicago and Yale universities, and taught at Yale, Wellesley College, and Princeton, before becoming professor of humanities at Virginia University from 1982. In

1979 he published the controversial *Philosophy and the Mirror of Nature*, which mounted a forceful and dramatic attack on the foundationalist, metaphysical aspirations of traditional philosophy. He later became influential in literary criticism, social theory, and intellectual history generally, with works such as *Contingency, Irony and Solidarity* (1988).

Rosa, Salvator [rohza] (1615–73) Painter, born near Naples, SW Italy. He became famous in Rome for his talents as painter, etcher, actor, and poet, but he made powerful enemies by his satires, and withdrew to Florence, returning to Rome after nine years. He owes his reputation mainly to his landscapes of wild and savage scenes.

Rosario [rosarioh] 33°00S 60°40W, pop (2000e) 1 214 000. Chief city in Santa Fe province, and third largest in Argentina; on the R Paraná, NW of Buenos Aires; Argentina's largest inland port, founded in 1725; airport; railway; university (1968); distribution centre and export outlet for local agricultural provinces; steel, machinery, cars, food processing; racecourse; golf club, boat club, aero club in the fashionable suburb of Fisherton; museums, cathedral, Municipal Palace (1896), Monument of the Flag (1957).

rosary A form of religious meditation, found in several religions, in which a sequence of prayers is recited using a string of beads or a knotted cord, each bead or knot representing one prayer in the sequence. In Christianity, it most commonly refers to the Rosary of the Blessed Virgin Mary, one of the most popular of Roman Catholic devotions. This is a sequence of one Our Father, ten Hail Marys, and one Glory Be to the Father (a *decade*), repeated fifteen times (in the full version) or five times (in the more commonly used shorter version), each decade being associated with a particular 'mystery' or meditation on an aspect of the life of Christ or the Virgin Mary. It probably dates from the 13th-c.

Roscius [roshius], in full **Quintus Roscius Gallus** (c.134–62 BC) Roman comic actor, a slave by birth. He became the greatest comic actor in Rome, and was freed from slavery by the dictator, Sulla. He gave Cicero lessons in elocution, and was defended by him in a lawsuit.

Roscommon, Ir **Ros Comáin** pop (2000e) 53 000; area 2463 sq km/951 sq mi. County in Connacht province, WC Ireland; bounded E by R Shannon and watered by R Suck; capital, Roscommon, pop (2000e) 1500; 13th-c abbey and castle, formerly a wool town; agriculture, cattle; numerous lakes.

Rose, Pete(r Edward) (1942–) Baseball player and manager, born in Cincinnati, Ohio, USA. He surpassed Ty Cobb's 57-year-old record of 4191 base hits in 1985, and was the National League's Most Valuable Player in 1973. In his career (1963–86), spent mainly with the Cincinnati Reds, he had a record 4256 base hits. He was banned from baseball while Cincinnati manager in 1989 after an investigation into alleged gambling offences which resulted in a prison sentence.

rose A member of a genus of well-known shrubs or scrambling perennials, nearly all native to the N hemisphere. So-called climbing roses do not climb in a true sense, but grow up through other vegetation or similar supports, and are prevented from slipping back by the tough, often hooked, prickles on the stems. The leaves are pinnate, with three or (usually) more oval, toothed leaflets; they are semi-evergreen, many retaining at least some leaves throughout the winter. The flowers of wild species are 5-petalled, flat or shallowly dish-shaped, white or yellow to red or purple, and often fragrant. Many garden roses have larger flowers with more numerous, less spreading petals, reaching an extreme in the tight, many-petalled blooms of cabbage roses. Cultivated forms also show a greater range of colours than wild plants. The orange, red, or black fruit (*hip* or *hep*) consists of a fleshy receptacle expanded to enclose the dry *achenes* or true fruits within, the whole structure often being crowned with the persistent sepals. The hips are attractive to birds and animals, and are a rich source of vitamin C. The bright red growths resembling balls of thread often found on roses (called *robins' pincushions*) are galls caused by the gall-wasp Cynips.

Prized for centuries for their beauty and as a source of perfume, roses are probably the world's most widely cultivated ornamental plants, with many wild species being taken directly into gardens or playing an important role in the development of garden forms. They are very hardy, tolerate most growing conditions, and provide a profusion of forms and colours. Exactly when they were first brought into cultivation is uncertain, but they were being grown in China and probably elsewhere c.5000 BC. Several distinct types of rose such as cluster-flowered bush roses (*floribundas*) have been developed by horticulturists, and there are now over 20 000 named cultivars, with several hundred more produced each year by the flourishing rose-breeding industry. The rose has been extensively used as both a decorative and a heraldic symbol, for example by the Royal Houses of York and Lancaster, and is the national emblem of England. (Genus: *Rosa*, 250 species. Family: Rosaceae.)

Roseanne, popular name of **Roseanne Barr** (1952–) Actor and producer, born in Salt Lake City, Utah, USA. After an unsettled youth, and a period during the early 1980s as a stand-up comedy performer, she made a breakthrough into television, hosting a number of specials and series, and becoming especially known for her realistic, unglamorized sitcom *Roseanne* (1988–97). Her film credits include *She-Devil* (1989), *The Final Nightmare* (1991), and *Blue in the Face* (1995). She has also written two autobiographical books, *Roseanne: My Life as a Woman* (1989) and *My Lives* (1994).

Roseau [rozoh], formerly **Charlotte Town** 15°18N 61°23W, pop (2000e) 15 000. Seaport and capital town of Dominica, Windward Is; on SW coast; cathedral (1841); trade in tropical fruit and vegetables; thermal springs nearby; Victoria Memorial Museum; badly damaged by hurricane, 1979.

rosebay willow-herb An erect perennial species of willow-herb (*Epilobium angustifolium*), growing to 120 cm/4 ft, native to Europe, Asia, and North America; creeping, spreading roots; leaves in whorls of three; flowers in long spikes, 2–3 cm/¾–1¼ in diameter, with four narrow, dark purple sepals and four paler, spoon-shaped, notched petals, on a slender, purplish ovary-tube; capsule with numerous white-plumed seeds; also known as **fireweed**, from its ability to rapidly colonize ground recently cleared by burning. It is sometimes cultivated for ornament, but is also an aggressive weed. (Family: Onagraceae.)

Rosebery, Archibald Philip Primrose, 5th Earl of (1847–1929) British statesman and prime minister (1894–5), born in London, UK. He studied at Oxford, succeeded to the earldom in 1868, and after holding various educational and political posts, became foreign secretary (1886, 1892–4) under Gladstone, whom he succeeded as premier for a brief period before the Liberals lost the election of 1895. He was noted for his racehorse stables, and in his later years as a biographer of British statesmen.

rosella An Australian parrot, related to the budgerigar; inhabits woodland and open country; can be an agricultural pest. (Genus: *Platycercus*, 8 species.)

rosemary A dense, aromatic, evergreen shrub (*Rosmarinus officialis*), growing to 2 m/6½ ft, native to the Mediterranean, typical of dry scrub; leaves narrow, dark green above, white beneath, margins inrolled; flowers pale blue, 2-lipped, upper slightly hooded, lower 3-lobed, spreading. It is widely cultivated for ornament and as a culinary herb. (Family: Labiatae.)

Rosenberg [rohzenberg] Alleged spies: **Julius Rosenberg** (1918–53) and **Ethel Rosenberg** (1915–53), husband and wife, both born in New York City, USA. They were part of a transatlantic spy ring uncovered after the trial of Klaus Fuchs in Britain. Julius was an engineer with the US Army Signal Corps, and Ethel's brother, David Greenglass, worked at the nuclear research station at Los Alamos. They were convicted of passing on atomic secrets through an intermediary to the Soviet vice-consul. Greenglass turned witness for the prosecution and saved his life. The Rosenbergs were sentenced to death in 1951 and, despite numerous appeals from many West European countries and three stays of execution, were executed at Sing Sing prison, NY. There was great controversy over the case, as many people felt that they were the victims of the witch-hunt atmosphere in the USA in the early 1950s.

rose of Jericho A much-branched annual (*Anastatica hierochuntica*), growing to 15 cm/6 in, native to N Africa and W Asia; flowers small, white, cross-shaped. When the plant dies in the dry season, the spreading branches curve inwards, forming a basket-like ball which blows about like a tumbleweed, only expanding and releasing seeds from the pods when wetted by rain. (Family: Cruciferae.)

rose of Sharon A semi-evergreen shrub (*Hypericum calycinum*) native to SE Europe and W Asia; rhizomatous; stems to 60 cm/2 ft, slender; leaves elliptical; flowers 7–8 cm/2¾–3 in diameter, 5-petalled, pale yellow with darker stamens. It is widely planted for ornament and ground cover. (Family: Guttifereae.)

Roses, Wars of the (1455–85) A series of civil wars in England, UK, which started during the weak monarchy of Henry VI; named from the emblems of the two rival branches of the House of Plantagenet, York (white rose) and Lancaster (red rose) – a symbolism which was propagated by the Tudor dynasty (1485–1603), which united the two roses. The wars began when Richard, Duke of York, claimed the protectorship of the crown after the king's mental breakdown (1453–4), and ended with Henry Tudor's defeat of Richard III at Bosworth (1485). The armies were small, and the warfare intermittent, although marked by brutal executions. The wars were not purely dynastic in origin, but were escalated by the gentry and by aristocratic feuds, notably between the Nevilles and the Percies, and by the unstable 'bastard feudal' system, in which relations among landed elites were increasingly based upon self-interest – a system that the Tudors sought to control.

Rose Theatre A London playhouse built c.1587 by Philip Henslowe on land he had leased on the S bank of the Thames, with a capacity of 2500 spectators. Rebuilt in 1592, the Rose was where Marlowe's plays were first performed, as well as some of the early plays of Shakespeare. The theatre was pulled down c.1606. In 1989, the foundations of this theatre were discovered in good preservation, giving an invaluable insight into Elizabethan stagecraft.

Rosetta Stone A black basalt slab with a trilingual inscription in Greek and Egyptian hieroglyphic and demotic found in 1799 at Raschid, near Alexandria, on the Rosetta branch of the R Nile. Cross-correlation by Thomas Young and, particularly, Jean François Champollion allowed hieroglyphs to be deciphered for the first time, and provided the key to the Ancient Egyptian language. It is now in the British Museum.

rose window A round window with mullions or tracery radiating outwards from the centre. It is commonly associated with Gothic architecture, and is also known as a **wheel window**.

rosewood A high-quality wood scented like roses, because of the presence of aromatic gum. It is obtained from various trees of the genus *Dalbergia*, native to the tropics and subtropics, which have pinnate leaves and pea-flowers. (Family: Leguminosae.)

Rosh Hashanah [rosh hashahna, hashanah] The Jewish New Year (1 Tishri), which falls in September or October. During the New Year's Day service, a ram's horn is blown as a call to repentance and spiritual renewal.

Rosicrucianism [rohzikrooshnizm] An esoteric movement which spread across Europe in the early 17th-c. In 1614–15 two pamphlets appeared in Germany and were attributed to Christian Rosenkreutz (1378–1484), who claimed to possess occult powers based on scientific and alchemical knowledge he had brought from the East. He founded the Order of the Rosy Cross, and the pamphlets invited men of learning to join. No trace of the Order has been found, but many occult organizations claim Rosicrucian origins.

rosin A resin obtained as the residue from the distillation of turpentine, melting point c.120°C; also called **colophony**. Its colour varies from colourless to dark brown. It is used as a flux in soldering.

Roskilde [rohskilduh] 55°39N 12°07E, pop (2000e) 51 000. Port and ancient town at S end of Roskilde Fjord, Zealand, Denmark; capital of Denmark, 10th-c–1443; Peace of Roskilde (1658), by which Denmark lost land E of The Sound to Sweden; railway; university (1970); engineering, foodstuffs, distilling, tanning; triple-towered cathedral (12th-c); Viking Ships museum.

Ross, Sir James Clark (1800–62) Polar explorer, born in London, UK. He discovered the north magnetic pole in 1831, then commanded an expedition to the Antarctic seas (1839–43), where the *Ross Barrier, Sea*, and *Island* are named after him. He was knighted in 1843.

Ross, Jonathan (1960–) British television and radio presenter, born in London, UK. He began as a researcher for Channel 4 and soon co-founded his own production company, Channel X, to produce *The Last Resort* (1987), an innovative chat-show series. His prolific career as a presenter includes BBC TV's long-running *Film Night* (from 1999) and *It's Only TV...But I Like It* (from 1999). In 2000 he joined the panel of the sports quiz show *They Think It's All Over*, and also began a Saturday morning show for Radio 2, receiving the 2002 Sony Radio Award. His talk-show *Friday Night With Jonathan Ross* (2001–) won the British Comedy Award for best comedy entertainment programme in 2003.

Ross, Nick, popular name of **Nicholas David Ross** (1947–) British broadcaster and journalist. He studied at Queen's University, Belfast, and joined the BBC in Northern Ireland in 1971. Moving to London, he became a reporter on such programmes as *World At One*, *Today*, and *Newsdesk*, becoming nationally known for his investigative reporting in *Call Nick Ross* (from 1987). He has also presented a wide range of news and discussion television programmes, notably *Crimewatch UK* (from 1984) and *Westminster with Nick Ross* (from 1994). He has also been much involved in work on social issues, such as medical ethics, crime, and road safety.

Ross, Sir Ronald (1857–1932) Physician, born in Almora, NE India. He studied medicine at St Bartholomew's Hospital, London, then joined the Indian Medical Service (1881–99). He became professor of tropical medicine at Liverpool, and directed the Ross Institute for Tropical Diseases from 1926. He received the 1902 Nobel Prize for Physiology or Medicine for his work on the life cycle of the malaria parasite, discovered by Laveran, and laid the foundation for combatting the disease.

Rossby waves Planetary-scale waves of westerly wind flow, found at high altitudes and based on the jet stream; named after the Swedish-American meteorologist C G Rossby (1898–1957). Occurring in both hemispheres, three to six waves complete the westerly circuit around the Earth. They result from a combination of the rotation of the Earth (planetary vorticity) and the variation with latitude of the Coriolis force, balanced by relative vorticity (the rotation of air associated with the clockwise spinning of an anticyclone and anticlockwise spinning of a depression or cyclone in the N hemisphere). In the N hemisphere a westerly moving wind, with zero initial vorticity, will be deflected northwards. As latitude increases, the relative vorticity becomes negative (*anticyclonic*), and the air is deflected back towards the Equator to a position where the vorticity becomes positive (*cyclonic*), and the air is deflected polewards once more.

Ross Dependency Land area 413 500 sq km/159 600 sq mi; permanent shelf ice area 337 000 sq km/130 000 sq mi. Antarctic territory administered by New Zealand (since 1923), including all the land between 160°E and 150°W and S of 60°S; no permanent inhabitants; scientific stations near L Vanda and at Scott Base on Ross I.

Rossellini, Roberto [roseleenee] (1906–77) Film director, born in Rome, Italy. His first independent film was *Roma, città aperta* (1945, Rome, Open City), made while it was still under

German occupation, often with hidden cameras in a style which came to be known as 'neo-Realism'. It was followed by *Paisà* (1946, Paisan) and *Germania, anno zero* (1947, Germany, Year Zero). Later films on spiritual themes, and his liaison with Ingrid Bergman, were condemned by the Catholic Church in the USA, but another war-time story, *Il generale della Rovere* (1959, General della Rovere), restored his popularity. He later produced several television documentaries on historical figures, such as Louis XIV and Socrates.

Rossetti, Christina (Georgina) [rozetee] (1830–94) Poet, born in London, UK, the sister of Dante Gabriel Rossetti. A devout Anglican, and influenced by the Oxford Movement, she wrote mainly religious poetry, such as *Goblin Market and Other Poems* (1862). By the 1880s, recurrent bouts of illness had made her an invalid, but she continued to write, later works including *A Pageant and Other Poems* (1881) and *The Face of the Deep* (1892). Her work displays the influence of the Pre-Raphaelite artistic movement, which her brother helped to found.

Rossetti, Dante Gabriel [rozetee] (1828–82) Poet and painter, born in London, UK, the brother of Christina Rossetti. He trained at the Royal Academy in London, and helped to form the Pre-Raphaelite Brotherhood (c.1850), which aimed to return to pre-Renaissance art forms involving vivid colour and detail. His early work was on religious themes, such as 'The Annunciation' (1850, Tate, London); his later manner became more secular, and more ornate in style. The death of his wife in 1862, and adverse criticism of his poetry, turned him into a recluse, but *Ballads and Sonnets* (1881) contains some of his best work.

Rossini, Gioacchino (Antonio) [roseenee] (1792–1868) Composer, born in Pesaro, E Italy. He studied in Bologna, and began to write comic operas. Among his early successes were *Tancredi* (1813) and *L'Italiana in Algeri* (1813, The Italian Girl in Algiers), and in 1816 he produced his masterpiece, *Il Barbiere di Siviglia* (The Barber of Seville). As director of the Italian Theatre in Paris (1823), he adapted several of his works to French taste, and wrote *Guillaume Tell* (1829, William Tell). In 1836 he retired to Bologna and took charge of the Liceo, which he raised to a high position in the world of music. The revolutionary disturbances in 1847 drove him to Florence, and he returned in 1855 to Paris. Later works include his *Stabat Mater* (1841) and the *Petite messe solennelle* (1863). His overtures in particular have continued to be highly popular items in concert programmes.

Rosslare [roslair], Ir **Ros Láir** 52°17N 6°23W, pop (2000e) 850. Port town in Wexford county, Leinster, SE Ireland; on St George's Channel, 8 km/5 mi SE of Wexford; ferry links with Fishguard and Milford Haven.

Ross Sea Extension of the Pacific Ocean between Marie Byrd Land and Victoria Land in New Zealand's territory of Antarctica; S arm covered by the Ross Ice Shelf; McMurdo Sound (W) generally ice-free in late summer, an important base point for exploration; main islands, Roosevelt (E) and Ross (W); active volcano (Mt Erebus) on Ross I.

Rostand, Edmond [rostã] (1868–1918) Poet and playwright, born in Marseille, S France. After some early poetry, he achieved international and enduring fame with his play, *Cyrano de Bergerac* (1897, filmed 1950, 1990), the story of the gifted nobleman who felt no-one could love him because of his enormous nose. This was followed by several other verse-plays, such as *L'Aiglon* (1900, The Eaglet) and *Chantecler* (1910).

Rostock or **Rostock-Warnemünde** 54°04N 12°09E, pop (2000e) 258 000. Industrial port and capital of Rostock county, N Germany; at the mouth of R Warnow, on the Baltic Sea; founded, 12th-c; former Hanseatic League port; badly bombed in World War 2, rebuilt in the 1950s; chief cargo port of former East Germany; railway; rail ferry to Denmark; university (1419); shipyard, marine engineering, fish processing, electronics; navigation museum, 15th-c town hall.

Rostov-na-Donu [rostof na donoo], Eng **Rostov-on-Don** 47°15N 39°45E, pop (2000e) 1 020 000. Port capital of Rostovskaya oblast, SE European Russia; on R Don, 46 km/29 mi from its entrance into the Sea of Azov; major grain-exporting centre in the 19th-c; access to the Volga–Don canal; airport; railway; university (1917); farm machinery, machine tools, aircraft, shipbuilding, clothing, leather, foodstuffs, wine.

Rostropovich, Mstislav Leopoldovich [rostropohvich] (1927–) Cellist and composer, born in Baku, Azerbaijan (formerly USSR). He studied at the Moscow Conservatory (1943–8), where he later became professor of cello (1956). In 1975, while in the USA, he and his wife decided not to return to the USSR, and he became musical director and conductor of the National Symphony Orchestra, Washington, DC (1977–94). He formed a close friendship with Benjamin Britten, who wrote several cello works for him. He was made an honorary knight in 1987. His wife is the soprano, **Galina Vishnevskaya** (1926–).

Rota [rohta] pop (2000e) 2850; area 85 sq km/33 sq mi. One of the three major islands in the N Mariana Is, W Pacific, 51 km/32 mi NE of Guam; length, 18 km/11 mi; airport; sugar cane, sugar refining; site of ancient stone columns.

Rotary International *service club*

rotation *crop rotation*

Rotblat, Joseph (1908–) Physicist and anti-nuclear weapons activist, born in Warsaw, Poland. Educated in Poland, he moved to Liverpool University in 1939, then participated in the atomic bomb project in the USA. After the war, he became a British citizen, working first at Liverpool (1945–9) then at St Bartholomew's Hospital, London (1950–76), and devoted himself to the peaceful application of nuclear physics, chiefly in relation to medicine. In 1955 he joined a group of scientists arguing for an end to nuclear weapons, and helped to found the annual series of conferences on arms control in Pugwash, Nova Scotia, in 1957 (the Pugwash Conferences), acting first as secretary-general (1957–73) and later as president (from 1988). His books include *Science and World Affairs* (1962), *Scientists in the Quest for Peace* (1972), and *A World at the Crossroads* (1994). He received the Nobel Peace Prize, along with the Conferences, in 1995.

Roth, Henry (1906–95) Novelist, born of Jewish parents in Tysmenytsya, W Ukraine (formerly Tysmenica, Austria–Hungary), and taken to New York City in 1907. He was educated at the City College there, and worked as a precision metal grinder in New York and Boston. From 1946 he lived in Maine and New Mexico. His only novel, *Call It Sleep* (1934), is a classic treatment of Jewish immigrant life and childhood.

Roth, Philip (Milton) (1933–) Novelist, born in Newark, New Jersey, USA. He studied at the University of Chicago, and taught there for a while. His first book *Goodbye, Columbus* (1959), consisted of a novella and five short stories, and gained him the National Book Award in 1960. Jewish-American life in particular, and modern American society in general, are the subjects of his subsequent comedies of manners, which include *Letting Go* (1962), the notorious 'masturbation' novel *Portnoy's Complaint* (1969), and *My Life as a Man* (1974). Later novels record the history of a central character Nathan Zuckerman, in the trilogy *Zuckerman Bound* (1989), while fact and fiction are elaborately interwoven in *The Facts: a Novelist's Autobiography* (1988) and *Deceptions* (1990). Other books include *Operation Shylock: A Confession* (1993), *American Pastoral* (1998, Pulitzer), and *The Human Stain* (2000, PEN/Faulkner Award; filmed 2003). He was married to the actress Claire Bloom (dissolved, 1995).

Rotherham [rotheram] 53°26N 1°20W, pop (2001e) 248 200. Town in South Yorkshire, N England, UK; on the R Don, 9 km/5 mi NE of Sheffield; railway; coal, iron, steel, machinery, brassware, glass; late Gothic All Saints Church, Chantry Chapel of Our Lady (1383).

Rothermere, Viscount *Harmsworth, Harold Sydney*

Rothko, Mark, originally **Marcus Rothkowitz** (1903–70) Painter, born in Dvinsk, Russia (now Daugavpils, Latvia). His family emigrated to the USA in 1913. He studied for a while at Yale, then travelled the USA until settling in New York City in 1925, where he took up painting. Largely self-taught as an artist, he held his first one-man show in 1933. During the 1940s he was influenced by Surrealism, but by the early 1950s he had evolved his own peaceful and meditative form of abstract expressionism, staining huge canvases with rectangular blocks of pure colour, very different from the busy patterns of Jackson Pollock and others.

Rothschild, Meyer (Amschel), Eng [**rothschiyld**], Ger [**rohtshilt**] (1743–1812) Financier, the founder of a Jewish banking dynasty, the House of Rothschild, born in Frankfurt, WC Germany. The family name comes from the 'red shield' (Ger *roter schild*) hung on the wall of an ancestor's dwelling. Having studied as a rabbi, he became the financial adviser to the Landgrave of Hesse-Kassel, Wilhain IX. The house transmitted money from the English government to Wellington in Spain, paid the British subsidies to Continental princes, and negotiated loans for Denmark (1804–12). His five sons continued the firm, establishing branches in other countries, and negotiated many of the great government loans of the 19th-c. His grandson, **Lionel** (1808–79), became the first Jew to sit in the British House of Commons (1848). He lent the British government £4 million in 1875 to buy the Suez Canal shares. His son **Nathan** (1840–1915) in his turn was the first British Jewish peer; it was to his son, **Lionel Walter** (1868–1937), the second baron and distinguished scientist and scholar, that the Balfour Declaration for the founding of a Jewish homeland in the British mandated territory of Palestine was addressed in 1917.

rotifer [rohtifer] A microscopic aquatic animal with an unsegmented body typically covered by a horny layer which may be thickened into plates; lacks a muscular body wall; swims by means of a ring of beating hair-like structures (*cilia*) that resembles a spinning wheel; group contains c.1800 species; also known as **wheel animalcules**. (Phylum: Rotifera.)

Rotorua [rohtorooa] 38°07S 176°17E, pop (2000e) 58 000. Health resort in North Island, New Zealand; in a region of thermal springs, geysers, and boiling mud; Whakarewarewa (Maori village); Maori arts and crafts centre.

rotten borough The name given to certain British parliamentary boroughs before the Great Reform Act of 1832. These had few voters, had lost their original economic function, and were usually controlled by a landowner or by the Crown. Elections were rarely, if ever, contested. Examples were Gatton, Dunwich, and Old Sarum. Most rotten boroughs were disfranchised by the Reform Act of 1832.

Rotterdam 51°55N 4°30E, pop (2000e) 617 000. Industrial city and chief port of The Netherlands, in South Holland province, W Netherlands; at the junction of the R Rotte with the Nieuwe Maas, 24 km/15 mi from the North Sea; major commercial centre of NW Europe since the 14th-c; city centre almost completely destroyed by German bombing, 1940; Europort harbour area inaugurated, 1966; approach channel deepened in 1984; railway; underground; university (1973); shipbuilding (largest shipyard in Europe), ship repairing, machinery, rolling stock, bicycles, engineering, oil refining, petrochemicals (largest plant on the Continent of Europe), foodstuffs, electronics, computers, clothing; birthplace of Erasmus; restored Groote Kerk, several museums; philharmonic orchestra.

rottweiler [rotviyler] A German breed of dog, developed around the Alpine town of Rottweil to protect and herd cattle; agile, with heavy muscular body and neck; powerful muzzle and short soft ears; short black and tan coat; tail docked short; popular guard dogs; attracted adverse publicity in the late 1980s, following reports of several fatal attacks on children.

Rouault, Georges (Henri) [roo-oh] (1871–1958) Painter and engraver, born in Paris, France. He was apprenticed to a stained-glass designer in 1885, and retained the art's glowing colours, outlined with black, in his paintings of clowns, prostitutes, and biblical characters. He joined the Fauves c.1904, and held his first one-man show in 1910. During the two World Wars he worked on a series of religious engravings, and also designed ballet sets and tapestries.

Roubaix [roobay] 50°42N 3°10E, pop (2000e) 103 000. Industrial and commercial town in Nord department, NW France; on the Belgian border, 11 km/7 mi NE of Lille; chartered in 1469; centre of N France textile industry; textile machinery, clothing, carpets, plastics, rubber products; 15th-c Gothic Church of St-Martin.

Roubillac, Louis François [roobeeyak], also spelled **Roubiliac** (1702–62) Sculptor, born in Lyon, SC France. He studied in Paris, and settled in London (c.1730). His statue of Handel for Vauxhall Gardens (1738) first made him popular, and he completed statues of Newton, at Cambridge (1755), Shakespeare (1758, British Museum), and others.

Rouen [rooã], Lat **Rotomagus** 49°27N 1°04E, pop (2000e) 108 000. River-port and capital of Seine-Maritime department, NW France; on right bank of R Seine, 86 km/53 mi NW of Paris; fifth largest port in France; former capital of Upper Normandy; scene of trial and burning of Joan of Arc, 1431; badly damaged in World War 2, but reconstructed largely as a Ville Musée (museum town); road and rail junction; university (1967); cotton, paper, petrochemicals, electronics, lubricants; birthplace of Flaubert; restored Gothic Cathedral (13th–16th-c); 14th-c Abbey Church of St-Ouen; Palais de Justice; Gros Horloge (clock tower).

Rouget de Lisle, Claude Joseph [roozhay duh leel] (1760–1836) French army officer, born in Lons-le-Saunier, EC France. He wrote and composed the *Marseillaise* when stationed in 1792 as captain of engineers at Strasbourg. Its original name was 'Chant de guerre de l'armée du Rhin' (War Song of the Rhine Army), but it became known in Paris when it was sung by volunteers from Marseille during the French Revolution.

roughage *dietary fibre*

Rough Riders The nickname for the First US Volunteer Cavalry Regiment, commanded during the Spanish–American War (1898) by Colonel Leonard Wood (1860–1927) and Lieutenant-Colonel Theodore Roosevelt. The Rough Riders' 'charge' up San Juan Hill in Cuba (1 Jul 1898) was actually carried out on foot.

roulette A casino game played with a spinning wheel and ball. The wheel is divided into 37 segments numbered 0–36, but not in numerical order (some wheels have a 38th segment numbered 00). All numbers are alternately either red or black except the 0. Punters bet, before and during the spin of the wheel (until the croupier stops all betting with the call 'Rien ne va plus'), on the landing place of the ball after the wheel has stopped spinning. Bets take various forms. They can be on a single number, any two numbers, three numbers, and so on. Bets can also be placed as to whether the winning number will be odd or even, or red or black.

Roumania *Romania*

rouncy *cob*

rounders An outdoor bat-and-ball game from which baseball probably derived. Very popular in England, the first reference to rounders was in 1744. Each team consists of nine players, and the object, after hitting the ball, is to run around the outside of three posts before reaching the fourth and thus scoring a rounder.

Roundheads *Cavaliers*

roundworm infestation A condition in which roundworms (*nematodes*) live within the body of their hosts, many without causing disease. In humans the most common disease-inducing worms include (1) those that inhabit the intestine, such as *Ascaris*, threadworms, whipworms, *Strongyloides*, and hookworms, the commonest cause of anaemia in the tropics; (2) worms such as *Filaria* that dwell in human tissues and are conveyed to humans by insect bites, producing diseases such as Bancroftian filariasis and river blindness; and (3) worms that cause disease in animals and are occasionally passed to humans, such as *Toxocara canis*, a common worm in dogs, which may affect children in close contact with affected puppies.

roup [roop] The name used for several diseases of poultry; one is characterized by swellings under the tail; another by the production of pus from the nostrils.

Rous, (Francis) Peyton [rows] (1879–1970) Pathologist, born in Baltimore, Maryland, USA. He studied medicine at Johns Hopkins University, then worked at the Rockefeller Institute for

Medical Research to the age of 90, studying cancer. He devised culture methods for viruses and cancerous cells. The **Rous chicken sarcoma**, which he discovered in 1911, remains the best-known example (as well as the first) of a cancer produced by a virus. He shared the 1966 Nobel Prize for Physiology or Medicine.

Rousseau, Henri Julien Félix [roosoh], known as **le Douanier** ('the Customs Officer') (1844–1910) Primitive painter, born in Laval, NW France. He worked for many years as a minor customs official, hence his nickname. Retiring in 1885, he spent his time painting and copying at the Louvre, and exhibited for several years at the Salon des Indépendants. He produced painstaking portraits, exotic imaginary landscapes, and dreams, such as 'Sleeping Gypsy' (1897, New York City).

Rousseau, Jean-Jacques [roosoh] (1712–78) Political philosopher, educationist, and essayist, born in Geneva, SW Switzerland. Largely self-taught, he carried on a variety of menial occupations, until after he moved to Paris in 1741, where he came to know Diderot and the *encyclopédistes*. In 1754 he wrote *Discours sur l'origine de l'inégalité et les fondements parmi les hommes* (1755, Discourse on the Origin and Foundations of Inequality Amongst Men), emphasizing the natural goodness of human beings, and the corrupting influences of institutionalized life. He later moved to Luxembourg (1757), where he wrote his masterpiece, *Du contrat social* (1762, The Social Contract), a great influence on French revolutionary thought, introducing the slogan 'Liberty, Equality, Fraternity'. The same year he published his major work on education, *Emile*, in novel form, but its views on monarchy and governmental institutions forced him to flee to Switzerland, and then England, at the invitation of David Hume. There he wrote most of his *Confessions* (published posthumously, 1782). He returned to Paris in 1767, where he continued to write, but gradually became insane.

Rousseau, (Pierre Etienne) Théodore [roosoh] (1812–67) Landscape painter, born in Paris, France. He studied the old masters in the Louvre, and by 1833 had begun sketching in the Forest of Fontainebleau. His 'Forest of Compiègne' (1834) was bought by the Duc d'Orléans, but some 12 years of discouragement followed. During the 1840s he settled at Barbizon, where he worked with a group of other painters, becoming leader of the Barbizon school. From the 1850s his work became increasingly accepted.

Routledge, George [rowtlej] (1812–88) Publisher, born in Brampton, Cumbria, NW England, UK. He went to London in 1833, and started up as a bookseller (1836) and publisher (1843). He later took his two brothers-in-law, W H and Frederick Warne (1825–1901), into partnership.

Roux, (Pierre Paul) Emile [roo] (1853–1933) Bacteriologist, born in Confolens, C France. He studied at Clermont-Ferrand, became assistant to Pasteur, and was appointed his successor (1905–18). In 1894 he helped to discover diphtheria antitoxin, and also worked on rabies and anthrax.

Rovaniemi [rovanyaymee] 66°29N 25°40E, pop (2000e) 34 800. Capital city of Lapp province, Finland; 160 km/99 mi N of Oulu, just S of the Arctic Circle; established, 1929; airfield; railway; river access to the Baltic; centre for timber trade; largely destroyed by fire (1944–5), and rebuilt by Alvar Aalto, who laid out the main streets in the design of a reindeer's antlers.

rove beetle An elongate, dark- or metallic-coloured beetle, usually with short, truncated wing cases; most are predators on other insects, some feed on fungal spores; common in leaf litter and damp habitats. (Order: Coleoptera. Family: Staphylinidae, c.30 000 species.)

rovings Loose assemblages of fibres produced at intermediate stages of the conversion of slivers (the untwisted strands produced by a combing machine) into yarns. Modern spinning methods often convert slivers directly into yarns.

Rovno [rovno], Polish **Rowne**, Ger **Rowno** 50°39N 26°10E, pop (2000e) 236 000. Capital city of Rovenskaya oblast, Ukraine, on R Uste; formerly in Poland; railway; machinery, metalwork, chemicals, flax, clothing; wooden Church of the Assumption (1756).

rowan [rohan] A slender deciduous tree (*Sorbus aucuparia*), growing to 20 m/65 ft, native to Europe; leaves pinnate with 5–8 pairs of toothed leaflets; flowers creamy, in large clusters; berries red, rarely yellow; also called **mountain ash**. It is often planted as a street or garden tree, together with several pink- or white-flowered species from Asia. (Family: Rosaceae.)

Rowe, Nicholas [roh] (1674–1718) Poet and playwright, born in Little Barford, Bedfordshire, SC England, UK. He studied at Westminster, and became a lawyer, but from 1692 devoted himself to literature. Three of his plays became very popular: *Tamerlane* (1702), *The Fair Penitent* (1703), and *Jane Shore* (1714). The name of his character Lothario (in *The Fair Penitent*) is still used to describe a fashionable rake. He was the first to publish a critical edition of Shakespeare (1709–10). In 1715 he was appointed poet laureate and a surveyor of customs in London.

rowing A sport or pastime in which a boat is propelled by oars as opposed to mechanical means. If there is only one rower with two oars it is known as **sculling**. Rowing involves two or more people, each rower having one oar. The sport dates from ancient times, but as an organized sport it can be traced to 1715, when the first rowing of the Doggetts Coat and Badge race took place on the R Thames. Famous races include the Oxford and Cambridge Boat Race (began 1829), and the Diamond Sculls and Grand Challenge Cup, both contested at the Henley Royal Regatta every year. Harvard and Yale universities first raced in 1851. The international body is the Fédération Internationale des Sociétés d'Aviron (FISA). Rowing has been part of the Olympics since 1900 (for men) and 1976 (for women).

Rowland, Tiny, originally **Rowland W Furhop** (1917–98) Financier, born in India. He joined Lonrho (London and Rhodesian Mining and Land Company) in 1961, and became chief executive and managing director. In 1983 he became chairman of *The Observer* newspaper, which he sold to *The Guardian* in 1993. He stepped down from Lonrho in 1994, following a bitter battle for control of the company with German property tycoon Dieter Bock.

Rowlandson, Thomas (1756–1827) Caricaturist, born in London, UK. He studied in London and Paris, then travelled widely in Britain, and became a specialist in humorous watercolours commenting on the social scene. Some of his best-known works are his illustrations to the 'Dr Syntax' series (1812–21) and 'The English Dance of Death' (1815–16).

Rowley, Thomas [rohlee] *Chatterton, Thomas*

Rowling, J(oanne) K(athleen) (1965–) British writer, born in Chipping Sodbury, Gloucestershire, W England, UK. She grew up in Chepstow, Gwent, and studied at Exeter University. She taught English as a foreign language in Portugal, where she married and later divorced Jorge Arantes. Returning to Scotland, she continued to teach, while writing the first of her enormously succcessful children's books, *Harry Potter and the Philosopher's Stone* (1997; filmed 2001, US title *Harry Potter and the Sorcerer's Stone*), about a boy and his adventures at Hogwarts, a magic school for wizards. It was followed by *Harry Potter and the Chamber of Secrets* (1998; filmed 2002) and *Harry Potter and the Prisoner of Azkaban* (1999). The first three books in the series (seven are planned in all) sold over 35 million copies worldwide, while the fourth, *Harry Potter and the Goblet of Fire* (2000), achieved a record pre-publication sale of 2 million copies. The long awaited *Harry Potter and the Order of the Phoenix* (2003), became the fastest-selling book ever, with sales reaching 250 million worldwide (Nov 2003). Her many awards include the British Book Awards' Children's Book of the Year, and the Whitbread Children's Book of the Year.

Rowntree Foundation A charity founded by Joseph Rowntree, a Quaker chocolate manufacturer. His York factory provided excellent facilities and he pursued enlightened employment policies. In 1904, he moved much of his wealth to the trusts that bear his name. The *Joseph Rowntree Village Trust* (est. 1904) administered New Earswick, Rowntree's model village. The *Jo-*

seph Rowntree Memorial Trust (1959) was renamed the *Joseph Rowntree Foundation* in 1990, and is the UK's largest independent social policy research and development charity.

Royal Academy of Arts A British academy founded in 1768 under royal patronage, with the aim of holding annual exhibitions (which are still held) to raise the status of artists, and to foster the development of a national school of history painting to rival the great schools of the continent. The Academy's first president was Sir Joshua Reynolds. Its premises are at Burlington House, London, UK.

Royal Academy of Dramatic Art (RADA) A London theatre school founded in 1904 by Beerbohm Tree, and granted its Royal Charter in 1920. The leading drama school in the country, it is located in Chenies Street. George Bernard Shaw bequeathed to the Royal Academy a third part of his royalties while his copyright lasts. Major refurbishment of its Malet Street premises began in 1997, and was completed in 2001.

Royal Academy of Music A London conservatory founded in 1822, opened in 1823, and granted its royal charter in 1830. It moved to its present location in Marylebone, London in 1912.

Royal Air Force (RAF) Britain's air force, established 1 April 1918, combining the existing forces of the Royal Flying Corps and the Royal Naval Air Service. Vital to Britain's survival in two World Wars, today the RAF comprises three Commands: Strike, Support, and RAF Germany. Responsibility for operating Britain's nuclear deterrent was transferred from the RAF's bomber squadrons to the Royal Navy's *Polaris* submarine force in 1969.

Royal Albert Hall, popularly known as the **Albert Hall** Concert hall built (1867–71) in memory of Prince Albert, consort of Queen Victoria of Great Britain, located S of Kensington Gardens, London, UK. Designed by British army engineer, Major General H Y D Scott, the hall is an oval arena with a domed roof constructed of iron and glass. The brick exterior is decorated with a terracotta relief depicting the development of the arts and sciences. With seating for c.8000 people, the hall is used for many events, including the popular Promenade Concerts performed there since 1941. The South Porch extension, part of a major refurbishment project, opened in 2003.

Royal and Ancient Golf Club of St Andrews (R & A) The ruling body of the game of golf in the eyes of most countries (the USA being a notable exception). Golf was played at St Andrews in the 16th-c, and the R & A was formed on 14 May 1754 when 22 noblemen formed themselves into the Society of St Andrews Golfers. In 1834 the club adopted its present name.

royal antelope A dwarf antelope (*Neotragus pygmaeus*) native to W Africa; the smallest known antelope (shoulder height, 25 cm/10 in – so small that local people call it *king of the hares*, hence *royal*); reddish-brown; male with very short horns; female without horns; nocturnal.

royal assent A legal stage through which a bill has to pass in the UK before it becomes law. Because the legislature in the UK is the Monarch-in-Parliament, after a bill has passed through both Houses of Parliament, the monarch's assent is required in order that it may become law. This approval is a formality; it has never been withheld in modern times.

Royal Astronomical Society A society founded in 1820 in London, UK for the encouragement and promotion of astronomy and geophysics. Its main functions are to publish the results of research, to maintain as complete a library as possible, and to meet regularly for discussion. It received a Royal Charter in 1831.

Royal Australian Air Force (RAAF) Australia's air force, established in 1921, formed from the wartime Australian Flying Corps. Poorly equipped with donated British government aircraft, it was under threat of being divided between the army and the navy until 1932. Its strength in the mid-1920s was 1200 men and 128 aircraft, but in the late 1930s it was expanded and improved, and by the mid-1980s it had 22 000 personnel. The RAAF saw service in all theatres of World War 2.

Royal Australian Navy (RAN) Australia's Navy, established in 1911, formed from the naval forces of the Australian colonies at Federation (1901). Based on the British Royal Navy, it had an early success in 1914 in sinking the German raider *Emden*, and saw action in the Atlantic, Mediterranean, and the Pacific. In the inter-war years, it was greatly reduced in size: by 1939, it had only 5440 personnel; but by 1945 this figure had increased to 42 600. After the war, the RAN was reorganized around two aircraft carriers, but its Fleet Air Arm was disbanded. It saw action in E Asia and off Vietnam.

Royal Ballet, The Britain's largest and most prestigious ballet company. In 1931, Ninette de Valois and Lilian Baylis organized the Vic–Wells Ballet at the Sadler's Wells Theatre in London, later known as the Sadler's Wells Ballet. In 1946 the main body of dancers transferred to the Royal Opera House in Covent Garden, retaining the Sadler's Wells Theatre Ballet and the Sadler's Wells School under the direction of Peggy van Praagh. In 1956 these companies fused as one large company renamed The Royal Ballet. The company was under the directorship of Anthony Dowell between 1986 and 2001. In 1990 the touring company of the Royal Ballet found a permanent home in Birmingham and became the Birmingham Royal Ballet, and in 1994 the company, Dance Bites, was established to create new works for the Royal Ballet.

Royal British Legion An organization for all ex-servicemen and women, and serving members of HM Forces. Formed in 1921 as the British Legion, it was granted the Royal prefix in 1971. Its aim is to provide social and welfare services for its members and to perpetuate the memory of those who died in the service of their country. It provides poppies from its own factory for the Remembrance (or Poppy Day) Appeal each November.

Royal Canadian Mounted Police *Mounties; police*

Royal College of Music A London conservatory founded by royal charter in 1883 and opened that year. It moved to its present location in Prince Consort Road in 1894.

Royal Commission In the UK, a body appointed by the sovereign on the prime minister's recommendation to investigate and report on the operation of laws which it is proposed to change. It may also deal with social, educational, or other matters about which the government wishes to make general, long-term policy decisions.

Royal Court Theatre Theatre in Sloane Square, London, UK, founded in 1888. A grade II listed building, it was closed in 1996 for major refurbishment and reopened in early 2000. The theatre is known for its support of the works of new writers and as a platform for emerging talent.

Royal Family, British *Anne, Princess; Charles, Prince; Diana, Princess; Edinburgh, Duke of; Edward, Prince; Elizabeth II; Gloucester, Duke of; Kent, Duke of; Margaret, Princess; York, Duke of*

royal fern A perennial fern (*Osmunda regalis*) with thick rhizomes forming large clumps, native to wet or boggy places throughout temperate regions; fronds to 3 m/10 ft, bi-pinnate; fertile fronds with small upper leaflets bearing numerous brown sporangia. (Family: Osmundaceae.)

royal garden parties In the UK, four summer gatherings held in June/July by the Queen, three in the grounds of Buckingham Palace, and the other at the Palace of Holyroodhouse, Edinburgh. Up to 10 000 people are invited to each party, to which formal or national dress must be worn.

Royal Geographical Society A society founded in London in 1830 for the 'advancement of geographical science'. Membership is open to all who are interested in the subject, and the society has been responsible for a number of scientific expeditions.

Royal Greenwich Observatory An observatory founded by Charles II of England and built by Christopher Wren in 1675 to improve navigation and time-keeping. Its first director and Astronomer Royal was John Flamsteed. Its role in the preparation of calendars, the *Nautical Almanac* (first published in 1767), Astronomical Ephemeris, and time-keeping was of major importance until the mid-20th-c. The observatory was responsible for the testing of the marine chronometers constructed by John Harrison (1736, 1749, 1763) that eventually solved the problem of measuring longitude when at sea. Its transit circle began operation in 1851 for the accurate measurement of time; and the International Meridian Conference at Washington in 1884 agreed to take the axis of this telescope as the prime meridian of longitude, separating the eastern hemisphere from the western hemisphere, and the starting point for international time zones. Its scientific activities moved in 1948 to Herstmonceux, East Sussex, and the Old Greenwich Observatory is now a museum and planetarium. Its headquarters moved to Cambridge in 1990. It was closed in 1998, and the Nautical Almanac Office moved to the Rutherford Appleton Laboratory in Oxfordshire.

Royal Horticultural Society A society founded in the UK in 1804 'for the improvement of horticulture'; it received its Royal Charter in 1809. An experimental garden is maintained at Wisley, Surrey; shows and competitions, most notably the Chelsea Flower Show, are held annually.

royal household In the UK, the collective term for those departments which serve members of the royal family in matters of day-to-day administration. In mediaeval times no distinction existed between the sovereign's ministers and personal servants; a survival of this earlier fusion of posts is to be found today in the titles of government Whips, such as Treasurer of the Household and Comptroller of the Household.

Royal Institution In the UK, a learned scientific society founded in 1799 by the physicist, Count Rumford. Its laboratories became Britain's first research centre, used in the 19th-c by Sir Humphry Davy and Michael Faraday. Lectures are still given at its headquarters in Albemarle Street, London, notably the Christmas lectures for young people.

royal jelly A highly nutritious substance produced by the salivary glands of the worker bees to nourish the queen bee and those larvae that are destined to become queens. There are many anecdotal reports of its beneficial effects on humans, both as a general 'tonic' and also as a means of alleviating a range of complaints, such as rheumatoid arthritis and chronic fatigue syndrome. Analysis has shown that royal jelly contains c.20 amino acids and various vitamins, including vitamin B complex and vitamin C, with trace elements such as potassium, chromium, manganese, and nickel. There are no toxic constituents, but neither are there any unique substances present for the miraculous effects claimed by distributors and devotees. Although it is usually taken in the form of a rather expensive dietary supplement, royal jelly has also been incorporated into some cosmetic products, where it is claimed to have a rejuvenating action on the skin.

Royal Marines (RM) Britain's Marine force, which can trace its origin to the Lord High Admiral's Regiment first raised in 1664. The title *Royal Marines* was conferred in 1800. The first RM Commando units were raised in 1942.

Royal Military Academy, popularly known as **Sandhurst** Military academy situated in Sandhurst, Berkshire, England, UK. It developed from the Royal Military Academy (founded 1799) at Woolwich, London, and the Royal Military College which was established (1802) by royal warrant at Great Marlow, and moved to Sandhurst in 1812. The present academy was formed in 1947.

Royal Mint The British government department responsible for manufacturing metal coins. The London mint probably dates from AD 825, and since the mid-16th-c it has enjoyed a legal monopoly of coinage. It is now situated in Llantrisant, S Wales, 7 km/4 mi outside Pontypridd.

Royal National Lifeboat Institution (RNLI) In the UK, a rescue organization manned by volunteers and financed by voluntary contributions, founded by Sir William Hillary (1771–1847) in 1824 as the Royal National Institution for the Preservation of Life from Shipwreck, changing to its present name in 1854. The modern RNLI operates over 200 lifeboat stations and maintains over 250 active vessels. The offshore boats are powerful self-righting craft, carrying advanced safety equipment.

Royal Navy (RN) The naval branch of the British armed forces. A national English Navy is as old as Saxon times, but the Royal Navy as such originates in the time of Henry VIII, when a Navy Board and the title of Lord High Admiral were established. The primary instrument of British imperial expansion in the 18th-c and 19th-c, it reached the peak of its global power at the end of World War 2, when it had more than 500 warships. A fraction of that size today, the RN has been responsible for the operation of Britain's nuclear deterrent since 1969.

Royal Observatory, Edinburgh An observatory at Edinburgh, EC Scotland, UK, founded in 1818. A pioneer of new techniques in astronomy, it houses the UK Astronomy Technology Centre, responsible for developing instrumentation for UK astronomers.

Royal Ocean Racing Club A prestigious club founded in London, UK, in 1925 to encourage long-distance yacht-racing and the development of sailing vessels in which speed and seaworthiness are combined. Candidates for full membership must have a good background of racing experience and have completed not less than 500 miles of racing offshore, including at least two overnight races, within the previous five years.

Royal Opera House The home of the Royal Ballet and the Royal Opera in Bow Street, London, UK. Three successive buildings have occupied the site since the Theatre Royal opened there in 1732. The present building, by Edward Middleton Barry (1830–80), opened in 1858. It was closed for refurbishment, 1997–9.

royal prerogative The set of powers, most of which are ill-defined, remaining within the preserve of the British monarch. These include the power to declare war, make treaties, appoint judges, pardon criminals and, most significantly, dissolve Parliament. In practice all these powers are taken on the advice of, and in effect made by, the prime minister and other government ministers.

Royal Scottish Society for the Prevention to Children *NSPCC*

Royal Shakespeare Company An English theatre company based in Stratford-upon-Avon, Warwickshire and London, UK which has as a primary objective the regular production of Shakespeare's plays. It was developed out of the Shakespeare Memorial Theatre by Peter Hall between 1960 and 1968. Under his leadership and then that of Trevor Nunn, a major international reputation was established by the early 1970s. Adrian Noble took over as artistic director in 1999. In 2001 he proposed a major restructuring of the company (involving shorter runs of plays, flexible actor contracts, a variety of working spaces, and an acting academy) and a radical redevelopment of the theatre sites. The ensuing controversy led to his resignation in 2002 (taking effect from 2003), and he was succeeded by Michael Boyd.

Royal Society (RS) In the UK, a prestigious scientific institution – the oldest in the world to have enjoyed continuous existence. The inaugural meeting was held in Gresham College, London in 1660, and in 1662 Charles II granted a charter to the Royal Society of London for the Promotion of Natural Knowledge. Isaac Newton was its president, 1703–27.

Royal Society for Nature Conservation, also known as **The Wildlife Trusts** A British conservation society which co-ordinates the work of county naturalist trusts and urban wildlife groups. It was founded in 1912 as the Society for the Promotion of Nature Reserves. Together, it manages over 2000 reserves.

Royal Society for the Prevention of Cruelty to Animals *RSPCA*

Royal Society for the Protection of Birds *RSPB*

Royal Television Society (RTS) A society formed in 1927 in London, UK for the furthering of the "new scientific medium of television". Granted its royal title in 1966, the society now represents over 4000 members from the broadcasting industry, with regional centres in the UK, Ireland and North America.

Each runs its own programme of lectures, workshops, masterclasses, awards, and social events.

Royal Victorian Order An order of knighthood instituted in 1896 by Queen Victoria, designed to reward distinguished service to the sovereign. There are five classes: Knights and Dames Grand Cross (GCVO), Knights and Dames Commander (KCVO/DCVO), Commanders (CVO), Lieutenants (LVO), and Members (MVO). The motto is 'Victoria' and the ribbon blue with red and white edges.

Royce, Sir (Frederick) Henry (1863–1933) Engineer, born in Alwalton, Cambridgeshire, EC England, UK. He began as a railway apprentice, but became interested in electricity and motor engineering, founding the firm of Royce Ltd in Manchester (1884). He made his first car in 1904, and his meeting with C S Rolls in that year led to the formation of Rolls–Royce, Ltd (1906). He was created a baronet in 1930.

Rozeanu, Angelica [roziahnoo], *née* **Adelstein** (1921–) Table tennis player, born in Romania. She won 12 world titles between 1950 and 1956, including the singles title a record six times in succession (1950–5), and was a member of the Romanian Corbillon Cup winning team (1950–1, 1953, 1955–6). She was made a Master of Sport, and appointed to the Romanian Olympic Commission. Upon her retirement in 1960, she emigrated to Israel.

RR Lyrae variable A type of variable star, all with approximately the same luminosity. This gives a key to finding distances in space, because the identification of an RR Lyrae is the key to its absolute luminosity; by comparing this to the observed magnitude, the distance is inferred.

RSI *repetitive strain injury*

RSPB In the UK, an abbreviation of **Royal Society for the Protection of Birds**, a society originally formed to protest against the killing of birds for their plumage. It is now one of the major conservation bodies, owning over 100 nature reserves.

RSPCA In the UK, an abbreviation of **Royal Society for the Prevention of Cruelty to Animals**, the main animal welfare society, founded in 1824, supported by voluntary contributions. Its 230 inspectors investigate complaints, and where necessary institute legal proceedings. In the USA there are several animal societies. The oldest is the **American Society for the Prevention of Cruelty to Animals** (1866), but the **Animal Protection Society of America** (1968) has a larger membership.

Ruapehu, Mount [rooapayhoo] 39°18S 175°40E. Active volcano and highest peak on North Island, New Zealand; rises to 2797 m/9176 ft in Tongariro National Park; last eruptions, 1995–6, 1999.

rubber A resilient, elastic substance obtained from a variety of unrelated, latex-producing, tropical trees. These include Ceará rubber (*Manihot glaziovii*), Panama rubber (*Castilla elastica*), and indiarubber (*Ficus elastica*), but easily the most important source is Parà rubber (*Hevea braziliensis*), an evergreen tree native to Brazil. Raw rubber, or **caoutchouc**, is obtained from the milky latex exuded by the trees as a response to injury; exactly why they produce latex is not known. The latex is collected by making a series of spiral cuts halfway around the circumference of the trunk, severing the lactifers which run just beneath the bark, and allowing the fluid to flow down the cuts and collect in cups. The cuts heal quickly, and must be re-opened every day or so, these later cuts often yielding a greater quantity of latex than the initial ones. Alternatively, the cuts can be treated with a chemical which inhibits coagulation, prolonging the flow. A tree can yield 280 g/10 oz of latex before the flow stops. The tapping process begins when the trees are 5–7 years old, and continues throughout their lives (up to 30 years), with periodic breaks to allow the trees to recover. The alkaline latex is congealed using acid, pressed, and sometimes smoked, before undergoing various industrial treatments and manufacture into final products.

Initially, Parà rubber was collected solely from wild trees in Brazil, but from c.1900 they were introduced as plantation trees to other tropical countries, notably Malaysia, which has become the world's largest producer. **Synthetic rubbers**, made by the polymerization of isoprene or substituted butadienes, exceed natural rubber in the quantity used. **Styrene butadiene rubber** (SBR), containing c.25% styrene and 75% butadiene, is one of the most important forms in current use.

rubber plant / tree *indiarubber tree; rubber*

Rubbia, Carlo (1934–) Physicist, born in Gorizia, NE Italy. He studied at Pisa, Rome, and Columbia universities, and from 1960 headed the proton–antiproton collider team at CERN, Geneva. In 1972 he became professor of physics at Harvard, and in 1989–93 was director-general of CERN, after which he continued his research at CERN. He shared the Nobel Prize for Physics in 1984 with Simon van der Meer (1925–) for their work leading to the discovery of the W and Z sub-atomic particles.

Rubbra, Edmund (1901–86) Composer, born in Northampton, Northamptonshire, C England, UK. He studied at Reading and London, and developed an interest in the polyphonic music of the 16th–17th-c. He wrote 11 symphonies, chamber, choral and orchestral music, songs, and solo instrumental works. He taught at Oxford (1947–68), and became professor of composition at the Guildhall School of Music (1961–74).

rubella A highly infectious disease, caused by a virus, that affects older children and young adults; also called **German measles**. Although a trivial short-lived illness, limited to fever and a rash, it is important because women who are infected in the first 18 weeks of pregnancy are likely to have children with congenital abnormalities such as deafness, blindness, and brain damage. A vaccine to prevent the disease is available, and is given to infants and children.

Rubénisme A movement in French painting in the late 17th-c. There was a famous quarrel in the French Academy about which was more important – colour or design. The design party appealed to the example of Poussin (and were called *Poussinistes*); the colourists (who won) referred to Rubens. Among artists themselves, the greatest *Rubéniste* was Watteau.

Rubens, Bernice (Ruth) (1928–) Novelist and director of documentary films, born in Cardiff, S Wales, UK. She studied at the University of Wales, later becoming a Fellow of University College, Cardiff. She was a film-maker of distinction before she chose a full-time writing career, beginning with *Set on Edge* (1960). Later novels include *The Elected Member* (1970, Booker Prize), *Brothers* (1987), *Yesterday in the Back Lane* (1995), *I, Dreyfus* (1998), and *Nine Lives* (2002).

Rubens, (Peter Paul) [roobenz] (1577–1640) Painter, born in Siegen, WC Germany. He was educated at Antwerp, and was intended for the law, but began to study art, travelling to Venice in 1600. He entered the service of the Duke of Mantua, and was sent to Spain as a diplomat (1605). There he executed many portraits and works on historical subjects. He then travelled in Italy, producing work much influenced by the Italian Renaissance, and in 1608 settled in Antwerp, becoming court painter to the Archduke Albert. His triptych 'The Descent from the Cross' (1611–14) in Antwerp Cathedral is one of his early masterpieces. He became a prolific and renowned painter, and in 1622 was invited to France by Marie de Médicis, for whom he painted 21 large subjects on her life and regency (Louvre). He was sent on a diplomatic mission to Philip IV of Spain (1628), and there executed some 40 works. The following year he became envoy to Charles I of England, where his paintings included 'Peace and War' (National Gallery, London). He was knighted by both Charles I and Philip IV. In 1630 he retired to Steen, where he engaged in landscape painting.

rubidium–strontium dating A method of radiometric dating for rocks more than 10 million years old. It uses the fact that the radioactive isotope rubidium-87 decays with a known half-life to yield strontium-87, and hence the amount of each isotope in a rock or mineral can be used to determine its age.

Rubik's Cube A mathematical puzzle named after its inventor, Hungarian architect Ernö Rubik (1944–). A coloured cube is divided into 26 small incomplete cubes (*cubelets*), of which 6 are centres which can only turn in place, 8 are corners, and 12 are edges; the last 20 can all be shifted in position. There are c.$4{\cdot}3 \times 10^{22}$ combinations, but only one possible way of getting all six sides to form a different colour. Patented in 1975, it became a world craze in the late 1970s.

Rubin, Robert E [**roo**bin] (1938–) US statesman, born in New York City, USA. Educated at Harvard, Yale, and the London School of Economics, he became a lawyer, and joined the firm of Goldman, Sachs & Co in New York City (1966–93, co-chairman, 1990–2). He then joined the White House as assistant to the president for economic policy (1993–5), directing the activities of the National Economic Council. He became secretary of the Treasury in 1995, and was reappointed to this post in Clinton's 1997 administration.

Rubinstein, Artur [**roo**binstiyn] (1887–1982) Pianist, born in Łódź, C Poland. He made public appearances from the age of six, and his European debut in Berlin at 13. He studied at the Warsaw Conservatory, then in Berlin, and moved to the USA during World War 2, becoming a US citizen in 1946. He continued to perform there with enormous success, making over 200 recordings.

Rubinstein, Helena [**roo**binstiyn] (1870–1965) Beautician and business executive, born in Kraków, S Poland. She attended medical school in Kraków, then moved in the 1890s to Australia, where she opened the country's first beauty salon in Melbourne (1902). Her face cream, formulated according to a family recipe, made her fortune. She studied with European dermatologists, and opened salons in London (1908) and Paris (1912). In 1915 she emigrated to New York City and launched an international business empire. She set cosmetic trends, introducing waterproof mascara, foundation make-up, and all-day spa treatments, stressing the scientific preparation of her products and the instruction of clients in their use. Her success was spiced by a 50-year feud with arch-rival Elizabeth Arden. Her many philanthropies included the endowment of a contemporary art museum in Israel and a medical research foundation.

Rublyov or **Rublev, Andrey** [rub**lyof**] (c.1360–c.1430) Painter, born in Russia. Little is known about his life or works, but he is generally regarded as the greatest of Russian icon painters. He became a monk and was an assistant to the Greek painter Theothanes, with whom he worked in Moscow from 1405. He painted icons in the Cathedral of the Annunciation in the Kremlin, Moscow, and also murals, such as in the Cathedral of the Dormition at Vladimir and at Moscow. In 1422 he returned to Troitsky-Sergieva, where he is traditionally believed to have produced his most famous work, the icon of the Old Testament Trinity, represented by three graceful angels.

Ruby, Jack L, originally **Jacob Rubenstein** (1911–67) Assassin, born in Chicago, Illinois, USA. He came from a broken home, and engaged in petty crimes, served in the air force (1943–6), and operated nightclubs and dance halls in Dallas, TX. Two days after the assassination of President John F Kennedy, he shot and killed Lee Harvey Oswald, the alleged assassin of the president. Despite many attempts to link Ruby to some conspiracy, it is generally believed that he acted on his own. He was sentenced to death in 1964, but died while awaiting a second trial.

ruby A gem variety of corundum, coloured deep crimson to pale red by the presence of minor impurities of chromium. The best specimens come from Myanmar, Sri Lanka, and Thailand.

rudbeckia A biennial or perennial, native to North America; large flower-heads, characterized by the conspicuous conical receptacle in the centre, giving rise to the alternative name of **coneflower**; outer ray florets red, yellow, or orange. It is often grown as an ornamental. (Genus: *Rudbeckia*, 15 species. Family: Compositae.)

rudd Freshwater fish (*Scardinius erythrophthalmus*) widespread in European rivers and lakes, ranging E to the Caspian region; length up to 40 cm/16 in; greenish-brown on back, sides yellow, fins reddish; feeds on invertebrates as well as on some plant material; popular with anglers. (Family: Cyprinidae.)

Rudolf I (1218–91) German king (1273–91), the founder of the Habsburg sovereign and imperial dynasty, born in Schloss Limburg, EC Germany. He increased his possessions by inheritance and marriage until he was the most powerful prince in Swabia. Chosen king by the electors, he was recognized by the pope in 1274.

Rudolf, Lake *Turkana, Lake*

rue A small aromatic evergreen shrub (*Ruta graveolens*) with acrid scent and taste, native to the Balkans; leaves bluish-green, divided into wedge-shaped, slightly rounded segments; flowers with 4–5 rather dirty yellow petals curved up at the tips. It is cultivated as a culinary and medicinal herb. (Family: Rutaceae.)

ruff A sandpiper (*Philomachus pugnax*) native to Europe, Asia, and Africa; inhabits open country near water; breeding male with naked face and large ruff of feathers around neck; males display communally. The name is sometimes used for the male, with the female called **reeve**.

Rugby 52°23N 1°15W, pop (2000e) 60 700. Town in Warwickshire, C England, UK; on R Avon, 17 km/10 mi E of Coventry; famous boys' public school (1567) where the game of rugby football originated; railway; engineering, cement, light industry.

rugby 7s Rugby 7s is a shortened and faster verson of the traditional 15-a-side rugby team game. Teams of seven compete for two seven-minute halves with the emphasis on speed and mobility. Sevens originated in 1883 in the Scottish Borders town of Melrose, when a local butcher, Ned Haig, seeking to shore up his financially failing rugby club, came up with the idea for a tournament. Unable to fit in several full-length 15-a-side games in one afternoon, he proposed shorter games with fewer players. Seven a-side rugby was little more than a training exercise in preparation for the traditional game, but that changed when the Hong Kong 7s event was set up in 1976; the establishing of the Rugby World Cup Sevens competition in 1993 firmly cemented Rugby 7s's position as a world-class sport in its own right. It was introduced as a Commonweath Games event in Kuala Lumpur in 1998.

rugby football *football, Rugby League; football, Rugby Union*

Ruggles, Carl (1876–1971) Composer, born in Marion, Massachusetts, USA. He was the founder of the Winona Symphony Orchestra, MA (1912), and taught composition at Miami University (1938–43). His radical modernity and individuality met largely with incomprehension, and in later years he concentrated on painting. He destroyed many of his early works, but the best-known and longest of those which survive is the 17-minute orchestral *Sun-treader* (1926–31).

Ruhr, River [roor] River in Germany; rises N of Winterberg; flows W to the R Rhine at Duisburg; length 213 km/132 mi; navigable length 41 km/25 mi (head of navigation at Witten); its valley is an important mining and industrial area, cities include Essen, Bochum, Duisburg, Gelsenkirchen, Dortmund.

Ruiz, Nevado del [roo**ees**] 4°53N 75°22W. Active Andean volcanic peak in WC Colombia; rises to 5399 m/17 713 ft in the Cordillera Central; 32 km/20 mi SE of Manizales; thermal springs, NW; erupted in 1985, causing flood and mudslide, with loss of many lives; Parque de los Nevados (National Park) includes snow-capped peaks of El Ruiz, Santa Isabel, El Cisne and Tolima.

ruler Someone who exercises supreme authority or control over a state. The term was traditionally used with reference to individuals who have a hereditary right to rule (eg kings, queens, shahs), but is now also applied to the leaders of elected governments (eg presidents, prime ministers) and to those who have seized power (eg dictators, military juntas). In many instances, different notions of 'rule' co-exist, as in the case of the UK, where both the monarch and the political party in government can be said to 'rule'.

rum A spirit distilled either from sugar cane, freshly crushed, or from the fermentation of molasses, a by-product of the West Indian sugar-cane industry. The British navy gave rum a special status in alcoholic beverages by providing a daily tot to all serving sailors. It is drunk wherever sugar cane is grown, but the most notable varieties come from the West Indies.

Rumania *Romania*

rumba A dance of Cuban origin which became popular as a ballroom dance in the USA and Europe in the 1930s. Its distinctive rhythm, often played on maracas or bongos, is the *tresillo*, a bar of eight quavers/eighth-notes divided 3 + 3 + 2.

Rumford, Count *Thompson, Benjamin*

ruminant A mammal of suborder Ruminantia, comprising the *traguloids* (chevrotains) and *pecorans* (other deer, giraffes, and Bovidae), and suborder Tylopoda (the camel family); an artiodactyl; many-chambered stomach breaks down coarse plant material; camels and chevrotains have three chambers; pecorans have four – the *rumen* (or *paunch*), *reticulum* (or *honeycomb bag*), *omasum* (*manyplies*, or *psalterium*), and *abomasum* (or *reed*); swallows much food quickly, then moves to a place of safety where it regurgitates mouthfuls (*cud*), chews them thoroughly, then reswallows; also known as a **cud-chewer**.

rummy A large family of domestic card games. In one popular version, each player has seven cards, and the object is to form them into two hands, one of three cards and one of four (or one hand of seven) by taking and discarding cards from the pack. The hand obtained must be three (or four) cards of the same denomination, or a sequence of three (or four) cards of the same suit. A variation popular in the USA is **gin rummy**, in which hands (of three or four) are laid face upwards, and can be added to by players in certain circumstances during the game. Points are deducted according to which cards are left in the hand when one of the players wins the game by disposing of all his or her cards.

Rump Parliament The members of the British Long Parliament who were left after Pride's Purge of conservative and moderate 'presbyterian' elements (Dec 1648). It numbered about 60, but by-elections brought it up to 125 by 1652. It ordered the execution of Charles I (1649), and abolished the monarchy and the House of Lords, establishing the Commonwealth in its place. When it fell out with the army, Cromwell dismissed it (Apr 1653). It was recalled in 1659 with the fall of the Protectorate, and dissolved itself in 1660.

Rum Rebellion In Australian history, an uprising in Sydney which deposed the governor of New South Wales, Captain William Bligh (1808). Led by John Macarthur, a former army officer, and Major George Johnston, the Rebellion occurred because of personal antagonisms, and Bligh's attempt to end the use of rum as a currency. Bligh returned to England but was not reinstated as governor; Johnston was court-martialled and dismissed from the army; and Macarthur, on going to Britain, was forbidden to return to Australia until 1817.

Rumsfeld, Donald (1932–) US Republican politician, born in Chicago, Illinois, USA. He studied at Princeton University, graduating in 1954, then served in the US Navy. He served three terms in the House of Representives (1962–9), then joined the Nixon administration as an assistant to the president (1969–72). He was chief-of-staff under Gerald Ford (1974–5), who also appointed him defence secretary (1975–7). He then became president and chief executive officer for the pharmaceutical firm G D Searle & Co (1977–85), held posts in various business corporations, and for a time was Ronald Reagan's special ambassador to the Middle East (1983–4). Appointed defence secretary (2001–) by George W Bush, he was responsible for the US campaign during the Iraq War (2003). He was awarded the Presidential Medal of Freedom in 1977.

Runcie (of Cuddesdon), Robert (Alexander Kennedy) Runcie, Baron [ruhnsee] (1921–2000) Archbishop of Canterbury (1980–91), born in Crosby, Lancashire, NW England, UK. He studied at Oxford and Cambridge, served in the Scots Guards during World War 2, and was ordained in 1951. He was Bishop of St Albans for 10 years before becoming Archbishop of Canterbury. His period as archbishop was marked by a papal visit to Canterbury, the war with Argentina, ongoing controversies over homosexuality and women in the Church, and his highly acclaimed chairmanship of the Lambeth Conference in 1987. His books include *Windows onto God* (1983) and *The Unity we Seek* (1989). He was created a life peer in 1991.

Rundstedt, (Karl Rudolf) Gerd von [rundshtet] (1875–1953) German field marshal, born in Aschersleben, EC Germany. He served in World War 1, and in the early 1930s became military commander of Berlin. In 1939 he directed the attacks on Poland and France. Checked in the Ukraine in 1941, he was relieved of his command, but in 1942 was given a new command in France. He was recalled after the success of the 1944 Allied invasion, but returned to direct the Ardennes offensive. War crimes proceedings against him were dropped on the grounds of his ill health.

Runeberg, Johan Ludvig [roonuhberg] (1804–77) Finnish poet, writing in Swedish, born in Jakobstad, W Finland. His first poems appeared in 1830, and he became known for his epic poems, notably *Elgskyttarne* (1832, The Moose Hunters) and *Hanna* (1836). His major work is the verse romance based on Scandinavian legend, *King Fjalar* (1844). One of his poems became Finland's national anthem.

runes The letters of the earliest Teutonic alphabet; widely known as the *futhark*, from the names of its first six symbols (*f, u, th, a, r, k*). Used mainly by the Scandinavians and the Anglo-Saxons, it comprised 24 basic symbols, though there was considerable regional variation both in the overall number of symbols and the symbol shapes used. Runes are preserved in c.4000 inscriptions and a few manuscripts, dating from the 3rd-c AD. Their derivation is uncertain, but the letters show some resemblance to the Roman alphabet, and they may have developed through the need to adapt the Roman characters to the style of carving prevalent in N Europe at the time.

runner In botany, a lateral shoot which grows along the ground, rooting at the tip or at the nodes to form new plants. Typical of rosette plants, runners are often markedly different from the normal shoots.

runner bean A twining perennial (*Phaseolus coccineus*) growing to 5 m/16 ft, native to tropical America; leaves with three broadly oval leaflets; pea-flowers scarlet or less commonly white, in stalked clusters from the leaf axils; pods up to 40 cm/16 in long, rough, containing large red, kidney-shaped seeds, veined like marble, purple-black. It is a common garden vegetable, widely cultivated for the edible young pods. Dwarf, non-climbing varieties are also grown. (Family: Leguminosae.)

running *athletics; cross-country running*

Runnymede A meadow on the S bank of the R Thames, Surrey, SE England, UK; 7 km/4 mi SE of Windsor, near Egham; here, or on Magna Carta Island in the river, King John signed the Magna Carta (1215); Commonwealth Air Forces war memorial (1953), Kennedy memorial; owned by the National Trust since 1931.

Runyon, (Alfred) Damon (1884–1946) Writer and journalist, born in Manhattan, Kansas, USA. After service in the Spanish–American War (1898) he turned to journalism and sports reporting for the *New York American*, and then to feature-writing with syndicated columns. His short stories, written in a racy style with liberal use of American slang and jargon, and depicting life in underworld New York City and on Broadway, won him enormous popularity. His famous collection, *Guys and Dolls* (1931), was the basis of a successful musical (1950) and film (1955). Other books include *Blue Plate Special* (1934) and *Take it Easy* (1938). From 1941 he worked as a film producer.

Rupert, Prince, also known as **Rupert of the Rhine** (1619–82) Royalist commander in the English Civil War, born in Prague, Czech Republic, the third son of the Elector Palatine Frederick V and Elizabeth, the daughter of James I of England. A notable cavalry leader, he won several victories in the major battles of the war, but was defeated at Marston Moor (1644), and after his surrender of Bristol he was dismissed by Charles I. Banished by parliament, he led the small Royalist fleet until it was routed by Blake (1650). He escaped to the West Indies, returning to Europe in 1653, and lived in Germany until the Restoration.

rupture *hernia*

Rusedski, Greg [ruzetskee] (1973–) Tennis player, born in Montreal, Quebec, SE Canada. A prominent junior player in Canada, winning six junior titles (1985–90), he then turned professional, winning tournaments at Newport (1993), Seoul (1995), and Beijing (1996). He became a British subject in 1995, and the first British player to finish in the world's top 50 since John Lloyd in 1985. A left-handed player, known for his very fast serves, he progressed with alacrity, moving ahead of Tim Henman to become British Number 1 in 1997. By the end of the 1999 Wimbledon Championships he was ranked 10th in the world listings, four places behind Henman. A variety of injuries kept him off the circuit for much of 2002–3.

rush A densely tufted annual or evergreen perennial; cosmopolitan, but typically found in cold and wet places; leaves narrow, flat, channelled, or cylindrical and pointed; flowers with six perianth-segments, brownish, in dense heads, sometimes borne laterally below tip of stem. (Genus: *Juncus*, 300 species. Family: Juncaceae.)

Rush, Geoffrey (1951–) Actor, born in Toowoomba, Queensland, NE Australia. He trained at the Lecoq School in Paris, and was known for 25 years predominantly as a theatre actor in Australia, working with the Queensland, Sydney, and Melbourne Theatre Companies, and particularly remembered for his role in Gogol's *Diary of a Madman*. He became known internationally for his role as David Helfgott in the 1996 film *Shine*, for which he won, in 1997, the Academy, Golden Globe, BAFTA, and Australian Film Institute Awards for Best Actor, as well as critics awards in New York, Los Angeles, and Boston. In 1999 he won a BAFTA for Best Supporting Actor for his role in *Shakespeare in Love*. Later films include *Mystery Men* (1999) and *Ned Kelly* (2003).

Rush, Ian (1961–) Footballer, born in St Asaph, Denbighshire, NC Wales, UK. After playing one season with Chester, he moved to Liverpool in 1981, and scored heavily (110 goals in 182 league matches). He won all the major honours in British football, and the European Cup Medal in 1984. He played for Juventus (1986–8) before returning to Liverpool, joined Leeds United in 1996, moving to Newcastle United (1997–8), to Wrexham as coach (1998–2000), and then to Sydney Olympic (Australia). He was a regular member of the Welsh international team from 1980, gaining 73 caps with Wales.

Rush–Bagot Convention (1817) An agreement between the USA and Britain to demilitarize the Great Lakes by limiting the number, tonnage, and armament of ships on each side. The convention ended the threat of a Great Lakes arms race, but complete disarmament on the US/Canada border did not follow until decades later. The parties involved were acting US secretary of state Robert Rush, and British minister to the USA Charles Bagot.

Rushdie, (Ahmed) Salman (1947–) Writer, born in Mumbai (Bombay), W India, of Muslim parents. He emigrated to Britain in 1965, and studied at Cambridge. He worked as an actor and an advertising copywriter before becoming a writer, producing his first novel, *Grimus*, in 1975. He became widely known after the publication of his second novel, *Midnight's Children* (1981, Booker, James Tait Black prizes), a fantasia of Indian history in the 20th-c. This was followed in 1983 by *Shame*, set in Pakistan. *The Satanic Verses* (1988, Whitbread) caused worldwide controversy because of its treatment of Islam from a secular point of view, and in 1989 he was forced to go into hiding because of a sentence of death (*fatwa*) passed on him by Ayatollah Khomeini of Iran for blasphemy (officially lifted in 1998). His later books include a novel for children, *Haroun and the Sea of Stories* (1990), a book of essays, *Imaginary Homelands* (1991), and the novels *East, West* (1994), *The Moor's Last Sigh* (1995, Whitbread), *The Ground Beneath Her Feet* (1999), and *Fury* (2001). He was involved in the stage adaptation of *Midnight's Children* which premiered in London in 2003.

Rushmore, Mount 43°53N 103°28W. Mountain in W South Dakota, USA, in the Black Hills, SW of Rapid City; a national memorial; height 1943 m/6375 ft; famous for the gigantic sculptures of four past US presidents (Washington, Jefferson, Roosevelt, Lincoln); each head 18 m/60 ft high; constructed 1927–41 under the direction of Gutzon Borglum.

Rusk, (David) Dean (1909–94) US secretary of state (1961–9), born in Cherokee Co, Georgia, USA. He studied at Davidson College and at Oxford, and in 1934 was appointed associate professor of government at Mills College, Oakland, CA. After World War 2, he held various governmental posts: special assistant to the secretary of war (1946–7), assistant secretary of state for UN affairs, deputy under-secretary of state, and assistant secretary for Far Eastern Affairs (1950–1). In 1952 he was appointed president of the Rockefeller Foundation, and from 1961 was secretary of state under Kennedy, in which capacity he played a major role in handling the Cuban crisis of 1962. He retained the post under the Johnson administration, retiring in 1969. After leaving public service, he became professor of international law at the University of Georgia.

Ruska, Ernst (1906–88) Physicist, born in Heidelberg, SWC Germany. He studied high voltage and vacuum methods at Munich and Berlin, and from 1928 worked on the development of the electron microscope. His transmission electron microscope achieved magnifications of up to $10^6\times$, compared with $2000\times$ for a good optical microscope, and its commercial availability (from 1938 onwards) revolutionized biology. He was awarded the 1986 Nobel Prize for Physics.

Ruskin, John (1819–1900) Writer and art theorist, born in London, UK. He studied at Oxford, and after graduating met Turner, and championed his painting in his first critical work, *Modern Painters* (1843–60). This book, along with *The Seven Lamps of Architecture* (1848) and *The Stones of Venice* (1851–3), made him the most influential critic of the day, and his social, political, and economic criticism gave him the status of a moral guide or prophet. *Unto This Last* (1860) is said to have influenced Gandhi in its defence of individual craftsmanship against the mass production that followed the Industrial Revolution. He became professor of fine art at Oxford in 1870, and founded several educational institutions. His last work was an unfinished autobiography, *Praeterita* (1886–8).

Russell, Bertrand (Arthur William) Russell, 3rd Earl (1872–1970) Philosopher, mathematician, prolific writer and controversial public figure, born in Trelleck, Monmouthshire. He studied at Cambridge, where he became a fellow of Trinity College in 1895. Concerned to defend the objectivity of mathematics, he pointed out a contradiction in Frege's system, and published his own *Principles of Mathematics* (1903), which argued that the whole of mathematics could be derived from logic, and the monumental *Principia mathematica* (with Whitehead, 1910–13), which worked this out in a complete formal system. Russell's famous 'theory of types' and 'theory of descriptions' belong to this same pre-World War 1 period. Politics became his dominant concern during the War, and his active pacifism caused the loss of his Trinity fellowship in 1916 and his imprisonment in 1918, during which he wrote his *Introduction to Mathematical Philosophy* (1919). He then made his living by lecturing and journalism, and became a celebrated controversialist. He visited the Soviet Union, where he met Lenin, Trotsky, and Gorky; he also taught in Beijing (1920–1). In 1927, with his second wife, Dora, he founded and ran a progressive school near Petersfield. In 1931 he succeeded his elder brother as 3rd Earl Russell. His second divorce (1934) and re-marriage (1936) helped to make controversial his book *Marriage and Morals* (1932); and his lectureship at City College, New York was terminated in 1940 after complaints that he was an 'enemy of religion and morality'. The rise of fascism led him to renounce his pacifism in 1939; his fellowship at Trinity was restored in 1944, and he returned to England after World War 2 to be honoured with an Order of Merit, and to give the first BBC Reith Lectures in 1949. He was awarded the Nobel Prize for Literature in 1950. He had meanwhile continued publishing important philosophical work, mainly in epistemology, and in 1945 published the best-selling *History of Western Philosophy*. He also wrote a stream of provocative, popular works on social, moral, and religious questions, such as *Why I am not a Christian* (1957). After 1949 he became a leading figure in the cause of nuclear disarmament, and in 1961 was again imprisoned after a demonstration in Whitehall. The last major publications were his three volumes of *Autobiography* (1967–9).

Russell, Henry Norris (1877–1957) Astronomer, born in Oyster Bay, New York, USA. He graduated from Princeton with the highest grade then recorded, earned his doctorate there, then worked at Cambridge (1900–5). He returned to Princeton, became director of the Observatory (1908), and was appointed professor of astronomy in 1911. Independently of Hertzsprung, he discovered the relationship between stellar absolute magnitude and spectral type, and represented the results in the Hertzsprung–Russell diagram, first published in 1913.

Russell, Jack, popular name of **John Russell** (1795–1883) Clergyman, born in Dartmouth, Devon, SW England, UK. He studied at Oxford, became curate of Swymbridge near Barnstaple (1832–80), and master of foxhounds. He developed the West Country smooth-haired, short-legged terrier, since named after him.

Russell, (Ernestine) Jane (Geraldine) (1921–) Film actress, born in Bemidji, Minnesota, USA. Discovered by Howard Hughes, she made her first film, *Outlaw*, in 1940, but because of censorship problems it was not released until 1946. Known for her striking looks, she became one of the leading Hollywood sex symbols of the 1950s, her other films including *Paleface* (1948), *Gentlemen Prefer Blondes* (1953), *Waco* (1966), and *Darker Than Amber* (1970).

Russell (of Kingston Russell), John Russell, 1st Earl, known as **Lord John Russell** (1792–1878) British statesman and prime minister (1846–52, 1865–6), born in London, UK. He studied at Edinburgh, and became an MP in 1813. He was home secretary (1835–9) and secretary for war (1839–41), and became Liberal prime minister after the Conservative Party split over the repeal of the Corn Laws (1846). In Aberdeen's coalition of 1852 he was foreign secretary and Leader of the House of Commons. He lost popularity over alleged incompetent management of the Crimean War, and retired (1855), but became foreign secretary again in the second Palmerston administration (1859), and was made an earl in 1861. On Palmerston's death, he again became premier, resigning in 1866.

Russell, Ken, popular name of **Henry Kenneth Alfred Russell** (1927–) Film director, born in Southampton, Hampshire, S England, UK. In 1955 he made some documentary shorts which earned him a freelance assignment with BBC Television, for whom he produced experimental studies of Debussy, Isadora Duncan, Delius, and Richard Strauss, which gradually abandoned naturalism. He turned to feature films with *Women in Love* (1969), but continued with musically inspired themes in *The Music Lovers* (1971) and *Mahler* (1974). Other productions include *The Devils* (1971), *Savage Messiah* (1972), *Gothic* (1987), and *The Rainbow* (1989), and for television *Lady Chatterley* (1993) and *Treasure Island* (1995).

Russell, Pee Wee, popular name of **Charles Ellsworth Russell** (1906–69) Jazz clarinet player, born in Maple Wood, Missouri, USA. He travelled the American Midwest with bands from age 16. In 1925, he worked in St Louis with Frankie Trumbauer (1901–56) and Bix Beiderbecke, and thereafter was associated with their coterie of Chicago-based Dixielanders. As part of the entrepreneurial troupe of Eddie Condon (1905–73) for nearly two decades, he played frequently at Nick's famous Dixieland bar in Greenwich Village, in concerts at Carnegie Hall, and on network radio broadcasts. In the 1960s, he was discovered by a younger audience. He played with Thelonious Monk at the Newport Jazz Festival in 1963, fronted a pianoless quartet, and recorded with a large orchestra (*The Spirit of '67* in 1967).

Russell, William, Lord (1639–83) English Whig politician. He studied at Cambridge, travelled in Europe, and at the Restoration became an MP. A supporter of Shaftesbury, and a leading member of the movement to exclude James II from the succession, he was arrested with others for participation in the Rye House Plot (1683), found guilty by a packed jury, and beheaded.

Russell, Willy, popular name of **William Martin Russell** (1947–) Playwright, born in Whiston, Lancashire, NW England, UK. He gained popularity with his cheerful but sharp portrayal of Liverpudlian life in such comedies as *Stags and Hens* (1978) and such musicals as *John, Paul, George, Ringo and Bert* (1974). Among his best-known plays are *Educating Rita* (1979), *Blood Brothers* (1983), and *Shirley Valentine* (1986).

Russell's viper A viper (*Vipera russelli*) found from India to Java and on Komodo I; powerful venom; probably responsible for more human deaths from snakebite than any other species (mainly because it is common near habitation).

Russia *pp.1332–3*

Russian *Russian literature; Slavic languages*

Russian art The art associated with Russia, which flourished under Byzantine influence down to the 18th-c, as seen in the 11th-c cathedral of Sta Sophia at Kiev, with its cupolas and mosaics by Greek artists. Since the 18th-c, W European influences have predominated. In the early 20th-c, Russian artists contributed to the abstract movement.

Russian blue A breed of domestic cat; *foreign short-haired* variety; thick blue-grey coat, each hair often with a silver tip; large thin ears and green eyes; also known as an **Archangel cat**.

Russian Civil War (1918–22) A war which took place in Russia following the October 1917 Revolution. Anti-Bolshevik forces (Whites) led by tsarist generals mounted a series of military and political campaigns against the new Soviet regime, supported by the intervention of allied troops and the governments of Britain, France, the USA, and Japan. They were opposed by the Soviet Red Army, created by Trotsky, which successfully fought back against the Whites between 1918 and 1922. There were five main theatres of war: the Caucasus and S Russia; Ukraine; the Baltic provinces; the Far North; and Siberia. After the end of World War 1 the military justification for allied intervention disappeared. The Red Army, which generally enjoyed more popular support than the Whites, gradually defeated the counter-revolutionary forces on all fronts, and established Soviet military and political power throughout the whole of Russia and its borderlands, with the exception of Poland, Finland, and the Baltic states, which received their independence.

Russian history There are six major periods of Russian history; the *Kievan* (9th–13th-c), *Mongol* (13th–15th-c), *Muscovite* (15th–17th-c), *Imperial* (18th–19th-c), *Soviet* (20th-c), and *Post-Soviet*. After the Mongol domination, the Moscow Grand Princes became rulers of an independent Muscovite state supported by the service-nobility (*dvoryanstvo*) and the Orthodox Church. During Peter I's reign (1682–1725) the Russian Empire was established, stretching from Europe to the Pacific. In the Imperial period, the basis of the mainly agricultural economy was serfdom, half of the peasantry being owned by feudal landlords. After serfdom was abolished in 1861, the economy gradually began to industrialize along capitalist lines. Throughout the 19th-c a revolutionary movement constantly challenged the autocratic state. This, combined with increasing industrial and rural unrest led to the revolutions of 1905 and 1917, the collapse of the empire, and the formation of the first Soviet government under Lenin.

After the Civil War, the Union of Soviet Socialist Republics (the Soviet Union) was founded in 1922. The mid-20th-c was dominated by the dictatorship of Stalin, which involved forced industrialization and mass political terror. Stalin's excesses were later officially condemned. Soviet expansion into Poland, the Baltic states, and the Balkans continued during 1940. Despite the Nazi–Soviet Pact (Aug 1939), Russia was invaded by Hitler in 1941. In the face of German forces surging towards Moscow, Stalin effected a 'scorched-earth' policy. The siege of Leningrad inflicted 1 250 000 Russian deaths. The Battle of Stalingrad (Aug 1942–Jan 1943) was the turning point of the war on the Eastern front. By April 1945, Soviet troops had

Russia

□ International Airport ∴ World heritage site

official name **Russian Federation**, formerly (1917–91) the **Russian SFSR (Soviet Federal Socialist Republic)**, Russ **Rossiyskaya**

Local name Rossiyskaya (Rossiyskaya Federatsiya)

Timezone GMT ranges from +2 to +12

Area 17 075 400 km²/6 591 100 sq mi

Population total (2002e) 143 673 000

Status Republic

Date of independence 1991

Capital Moscow

Languages Russian (official), and c.100 different languages

Ethnic groups Russian (82%), Tatar (3%), Ukrainian (3%)

Religions Christian (Russian Orthodox 25%), non-religious (60%), Muslim

Physical features Occupying much of E Europe and N Asia; consists of c.75% of the area of the former USSR and over 50% of its population; vast plains dominate the W half; Ural Mts separate the E European Plain (W) from the W Siberian Lowlands (E); E of the R Yenisey lies the C Siberian Plateau; N Siberian Plain further E; Caucasus on S frontier; Lena, Ob, Severnaya Dvina, Pechora, Yenisey, Indigirka, and Kolyma rivers flow to the Arctic Ocean; Amur, Argun, and rivers of the Kamchatka Peninsula flow to the Pacific Ocean; Caspian Sea basin includes the Volga and Ural rivers; over 20 000 lakes, the largest being the Caspian Sea, L Taymyr, L Baikal.

Climate Half of country covered by snow for 6 months of year; coldest region, NE Siberia, average annual temperature -46°C (Jan), 16°C (Jul); summers in rest of country generally short and hot; average annual temperature -18–9°C (Jan), 16–24°C (Jul) in Moscow; average annual rainfall 500–750 mm/20–30 in.

Currency Rouble (R)

Economy Oil fields in W Siberia (provide 50% of country's petroleum); series of 5-year plans since 1928 promoted industry; heavy-industry products include chemicals, construction materials, machine tool, and steel-making; mining, major producer of iron ore, manganese, natural gas, nickel, and platinum, also coal, copper, gold, zinc, tin, lead; agriculture, primarily wheat, fruit, vegetables, tobacco, cotton, sugar beet; textiles; timber.

GDP (2002e) $1·409 tn, per capita $9700

Human Development Index (2002) 0·781

History Conquered by Mongols in 13th-c; Ivan IV (the Terrible) became first ruler to be crowned Tsar, 1547; Time of Trouble, 1604–13; under Peter the Great, territory expanded to the Baltic Sea and St Petersburg founded as capital, 1703; Napoleon invasion failed, 1812; Crimean War, 1853–6; emancipation of the serfs, 1861; assassination of Alexander II, 1881; Balkan War with Turkey, 1877–8; Russo-Japanese War, 1904–5; establishment of a parlia-

reached Berlin. Around 20 million Soviet citizens were killed in the war. In the Cold War that followed, Soviet foreign policy was pursued against the USA and its allies. Khrushchev challenged the personality cult of Stalin (1956), but took Russia to the brink of nuclear war in the Cuban Missile crisis (1962). In the mid-to-late-1980s, a programme of economic and political restructuring (*perestroika*) was introduced by President Gorbachev. By 1990, this process led to demands for independence from several Soviet republics, to the demise of the Communist Party of the Soviet Union, and (following the failed coup of 1991) to the break-up of the Soviet Union and its replacement by the Commonwealth of Independent States.

Russian literature The development of Russian literature was delayed until the 18th-c. Before this time there was a rich and varied oral tradition of folk tales and *byliny* or epic songs, supplemented from the 16th-c by historically-based material. Some Western influence was relayed via Poland in the 17th-c, but it was French classicism which provided the real stimulus for the philologist Mikhail Lomonosov (1711–65), the poet Gavriil Derzhavin (1743–1816), the fables of Ivan Krylov (1769–1844), and the dramatist Aleksandr Griboedov (1795–1829). Aleksandr Pushkin (1799–1837) transcended all influences to become a major figure in both prose and verse; the Byronic novel in verse, *Evgeny Onegin* (1828), is his most characteristic work. The legacy of Pushkin has been divided between Romanticism and the Realism which has haunted Russian literature. The poet Mikhail Lermontov (1814–41) was drawn to both; as was the novelist Nikolai Gogol (1809–52), perceiving like Dickens the fantastic side of ordinary life. The novels of Ivan Turgenev (1818–83) and Ivan Goncharov (1812–91) reflected social problems, as was urged by the influential critics Vissarion Belinsky (1811–48) ment (Duma) with limited powers, 1906; Russia allied with Britain and France, World War I; revolution overthrew Nicholas II, Bolsheviks (Communists) seized power under the dictatorship of Lenin, 1917; Russia forced to withdraw from War; renamed the Russian Soviet Federated Socialist Republic, 1918, and Moscow reinstated as capital; Russia became part of the Union of Soviet Socialist Republics (USSR), 1922; death of Lenin, 1924; Trotsky deported in 1928, by which time Stalin acquiring dictatorial power; USSR fought with the Allies against Germany in World War II; from 1946 development of the Cold War between East and West; troops intervened in Afghanistan, 1979; radical reform of the system under the leadership of Gorbachev, 1985–91; first contested elections in Soviet history held, and the end of the Cold War announced, 1989; troops withdrawn from Afghanistan, 1989; USSR dissolved, 1991; Russian Republic became independent and a founder member of the Commonwealth of Independent States, 1991; war in Chechnya, 1994–6; further invasion of Chechnya, 1999–; governed by a president, prime minister, and Federal Assembly, consisting of a State *Duma* and a Federation Council.

Soviet Union
Head of State
1917 Lev Borisovich Kamenev
1917–19 Yakov Mikhailovich Sverlov
1919–46 Mikhail Ivanovich Kalinin
1946–53 Nikolai Mikhailovich Shvernik
1953–60 Kliment Yefremovich Voroshilov
1960–4 Leonid Ilyich Brezhnev
1964–5 Anastas Ivanovich Mikoyan
1965–77 Nikolai Viktorovich Podgorny
1977–82 Leonid Ilyich Brezhnev
1982–3 Vasily Vasiliyevich Kuznetsov *Acting*
1983–4 Yuri Vladimirovich Andropov
1984 Vasily Vasiliyevich Kuznetsov *Acting*
1984–5 Konstantin Ustinovich Chernenko
1985 Vasily Vasiliyevich Kuznetsov *Acting*
1985–8 Andrei Andreevich Gromyko
1988–90 Mikhail Sergeyevich Gorbachev

Executive President
1990–1 Mikhail Sergeyevich Gorbachev

Russian Federation
Head of State
1991–9 Boris Yeltsin
1999– Vladimir Putin

Head of Government
1991–2 Yegor Gaidar *Acting*
1992–8 Viktor Chernomyrdin *Interim*
1998 Sergei Kiriyenko
1998–9 Yevgeny Primakov
1999 Sergey Stepashin
1999–2000 Vladimir Putin
2000–4 Mikhail Kasyanov
2004 Victor Khristenko *Acting*
2004– Mikhail Fradkov

and Nikolai Chernyshevsky (1828–89). Meanwhile, poets such as Fyodor Tyuchev (1803–73) and Afanasi Fet (1820–92) ignored the Realist initiative, as did Nikolai Leskov (1831–95) with his stories of the exotic and grotesque.

Leo Tolstoy (1828–1910) and Fyodor Dostoevsky (1821–81) evade these categorizations. Tolstoy's *War and Peace* (1863–9) and Dostoevsky's *Crime and Punishment* (1866) simultaneously explore the materiality and the mystery of human experience. The stories and plays of Anton Chekhov (1860–1904) are also too subtle for simple classification. In the 20th-c, the Symbolists Aleksandr Blok (1880–1921) and Andrei Bely (1880–1934), followed by the Acmeists Anna Akhmatova (1888–1966) and Osip Mandelstam (1891–1938), and the Futurists Vladimir Mayakovsky (1894–1930) and Viktor Khlebnikov (1885–1922), reclaimed the world of poetry: but post-revolutionary Russia has generally been hostile to such work, as it was to the poems and novels of Boris Pasternak (1890–1960). The official socialist Realism privileged the materialist fiction of Maxim Gorky (1868–1936) and Mikhail Sholokhov (1905–84). Much literature circulated unpublished (*samizdat*) or was published abroad (*tamizdat*) by such writers as Aleksandr Solzhenitsyn (1918–), Joseph Brodsky (1940–96), and Irina Ratushinskaya (1954–).

Russian Orthodox Church A Church originating from missionary activity of the see of Constantinople of the Orthodox Church, with a community organized at Kiev in the 9th-c. In 988, Christianity was declared (by Vladimir) the official faith; in the 14th-c Moscow became the see of the metropolitan; and in the 15th-c the Church declared itself autonomous. It existed in a state of tension with the emperor, and after the Revolution of 1917, was separated from the state and suffered some persecution. Gaining some recognition as a result of support of the authorities in World War 2, it was largely controlled by government agencies. It reflected the Byzantine or Greek tradition until the 19th-c, when a new translation of the Bible was approved, and in the 20th-c there was some revival of interest on the part of the intelligentsia, conscious of the role the Church had played in Russian art and culture. The contemporary Russian Church retains fidelity in doctrine and liturgy to its Orthodox inheritance, but is also developing its national character.

Russian Revolution (1917) The revolution which overthrew the Russian imperialist regime and set up the first Marxist proletarian state. Mass demonstrations of revolutionary workers and soldiers in Petrograd led to the abdication of Nicholas II and the overthrow of the imperial government in February 1917. There followed a period of power-sharing between a provisional government and the Petrograd Soviet, known as 'dual power'. Lenin's Bolsheviks refused to collaborate, and in October led an insurgency of armed workers, soldiers, and sailors, seizing political power and establishing the first Soviet government. Under the Treaty of Brest-Litovsk (March 3, 1918), Russia gave up the Baltic states, Finland, Poland, and the Ukraine. Opposition to Russia losing these territories led to the Red Terror, in which counter-revolutionaries (Whites) were arrested and executed. The Red Army defeated White Russian forces in 1921. With Lenin's Russian Communist party in full control, strikes and peasant uprisings were suppressed. In December 1922, the Union of Soviet Socialist Republics (USSR) was officially established.

Russian Space Agency An agency established by decree in February 1992 to administer the civilian and commercial space programme of the Russian Federation. It is based on the principal assets and ongoing projects of the former Soviet space programme, most of which were carried out within Russian territory. Key space assets in other now-dependent states are available on a commercial basis, eg Baikonur Cosmodrome in Kazakhstan, and Yuzhnoye Research and Production Association (launch vehicle production) in Ukraine. Earlier the Soviet space programme had been a dominant element in the exploration of space since the launch of Sputnik in 1957. Military and civilian programmes were administered by a complex organization whose characteristic secrecy increasingly diminished in the 1980s as the programme took on an international emphasis. Traditional civilian co-operative programmes were managed through the Soviet Academy of Sciences. The Russian Space Agency now resembles more the structure of NASA and the European Space Agency. It has some facilities under its direct control, co-ordinates activities with other (now private) enterprises, and works closely with the Russian Academy of Sciences. Three principal launch sites (cosmodromes) are Biakonur (or Tyuratam), Plesetsk, and Kaputstin Yar, which in the past have launched about 100 spacecraft per year. The mission control facility is located in Kaliningrad (near Moscow). Ongoing projects include the Mir space station, the Granat high-energy astronomy mission (with France), several other large international astronomy missions, and with the US and other partners, the International Space Station.

Russian State Library The national library and depository of Russia, and one of the most extensive libraries in the world, known as the **Lenin Library** until 1992. When it was established in Moscow in 1917, confiscated private collections formed the bulk of its holdings. It now houses over 28 million books and periodicals.

Russian wolfhound *borzoi*

Russo–Finnish War (1939–40) A war between the USSR and Finland during the winter of 1939–40 (the **Winter War**). Soviet forces invaded Finland in order to secure Finnish territory from which to defend Leningrad against German attack. In spite of courageous Finnish resistance and early Russian bungling, Finland capitulated (Mar 1940) and was forced to cede territory to the Soviet Union. When Germany invaded the Soviet Union in 1941, the Finns sought to regain their territories by fighting on the side of the Axis powers, but capitulated to the Soviet Union in 1944.

Russo–Japanese War (1904–5) A war between the Russian Empire and Japan over rival territorial claims and imperial ambitions in N China and Korea. It was a series of military and naval disasters for Russia; it had little popular support, and was marked by ineffectual command and political confusion. The war ended in Japanese victory with the Treaty of Portsmouth (1905). Russia lost a number of areas, including the S half of Sakhalin and Dongbei. The 1905 revolution broke out in Russia soon after the end of the war. The victory was important to Japan since it had for the first time defeated a Western power at sea and on land.

Russo–Turkish Wars A series of wars between the Russian and Ottoman Empires from the 17th-c to the 19th-c, principally for domination of the Black Sea and adjacent regions. From the mid-18th-c they also involved national liberation struggles of the Slavonic and Orthodox peoples of the Balkans from Ottoman rule. As a result of the wars (the last in 1877–8), many areas gained their independence or were incorporated into the Russian Empire.

rust The product of corrosion, especially of iron-containing materials. It consists mainly of iron(III) oxide (Fe_2O_3) or hydrated forms.

rust fungus A parasitic fungus that occurs as a thread-like network (*mycelium*) between cells of the host plant; includes the genus *Puccinia*, containing over 4000 species, some of which are parasites of commercial cereal crops. (Subdivision: Basidiomycetes. Order: Uredinales.)

Rutanzige, Lake *Edward, Lake*

Ruth, Babe, popular name of **George Herman Ruth**, nicknames **the Babe**, **the Bambino**, **the Sultan of Swat** (1895–1948) Baseball player, born in Baltimore, Maryland, USA. He started his career as a pitcher with the Boston Red Sox in 1914, joined the New York Yankees as an outfielder in 1920, and hit a record 54 home runs in that season. He bettered the record to 60 in 1927, a figure which stood until 1961. In the 1926 World Series he became the first man to hit three home runs in one game. When he retired in 1935 he had hit 714 home runs, a figure not bettered until 1974, and 94 wins and a 2·28 earned-run average as a pitcher, establishing him as the most versatile player in baseball history. Yankee Stadium is affectionately known as 'The House that Ruth Built' because of the increased income he brought to the club during his career. *The Babe Ruth Story* was filmed in 1948, and *The Babe* in 1991.

Ruth, Book of A book of the Hebrew Bible/Old Testament, presenting a popular story ostensibly set in the time of Israel's tribal judges, but named after its central character, Ruth. Ruth's mother-in-law, Naomi, arranges a levirate marriage of Ruth to Boaz, the rich kinsman of Naomi's deceased husband, upon their return to Judah from Moab; Ruth became the mother of Obed, grandfather of David. Usually dated c.5th–4th-c BC, it is significant for its liberal attitudes to non-Israelites and mixed marriages, since Ruth was a Moabite.

Rutherford (of Nelson), Ernest Rutherford, 1st Baron (1871–1937) Physicist, a pioneer of subatomic physics, born near Nelson, New Zealand. He studied at Christchurch University, moved to Cambridge, UK (1895), and in 1898 became professor of physics at McGill, Canada, where with Frederick Soddy he proposed that radioactivity results from the disintegration of atoms (1903). In 1907 he became professor at Manchester, developing the modern concept of the atom, and in 1911 propounded his theory of atomic structure. In 1919 he became professor at Cambridge and director of the Cavendish Laboratory. He received the Nobel Prize for Chemistry in 1908, was knighted in 1914, and made a peer in 1931.

Rutherford, Dame Margaret (1892–1972) Theatre and film actress, born in London, UK. She made her stage debut in 1925 at the Old Vic theatre, and gained fame as a character actress and comedienne, her gallery of eccentrics including 'Miss Prism' in *The Importance of Being Earnest* (stage 1939, film 1952) and 'Miss Whitchurch' in *The Happiest Days of Your Life* (stage 1948, film 1950). She also scored a success as Agatha Christie's 'Miss Marple' in a series of films from 1962. She won an Oscar for her role in *The VIPs* in 1964, and was created a dame in 1967.

Ruthwell Cross A runic stone cross at Ruthwell, near Dumfries, S Scotland, UK, dating from the 7th-c. It is carved with scenes from the New Testament and stands 5 m/18 ft high.

rutile [**roo**tiyl, -teel] A titanium dioxide (TiO_2) mineral, usually red-brown to black due to impurities of iron oxide, widespread in igneous and metamorphic rocks and in veins with quartz. It is a source of titanium and is also used as a gemstone.

Rutland County in the UK, known as the smallest in England, incorporated into Leicestershire in 1974, then made a unitary authority in 1997. It has given its name to a reservoir, Rutland Water.

Ruysdael, Jacob van [**roys**dahl], also spelled **Ruïsdael** (c.1628–82) Landscape painter, born in Haarlem, The Netherlands. He became a member of the Haarlem painters' guild (1648), and moved to Amsterdam (c.1657), thereafter travelling in Holland and Germany. His best works are country landscapes, and he also excelled in cloud effects, particularly in his seascapes.

Ruyter, Michiel Adriaanszoon de [**roy**ter] (1607–76) Dutch naval commander, born in Flushing, The Netherlands. He went to sea at nine, and by 1635 had become a merchant captain. In the Dutch Wars with England he had considerable success as a naval commander, defeating the English in the 'Four Days' Battle' off Dunkirk (1666), and destroying much of the English fleet at Medway (1667), and the larger Anglo-French fleets at Solebay (1672) and off Ostend and Kijkduin (1673), thus preventing an English invasion of the Dutch Republic. In 1675 he sailed for the Mediterranean to help the Spaniards against the French, but was mortally wounded in a battle in the Bay of Catania, off Sicily.

Rwanda *p.1335*

Ryan, Elizabeth (1892–1979) Tennis player, born in Anaheim, California, USA. She won 19 Wimbledon titles (12 doubles and seven mixed doubles), a record which stood from 1934 until 1979, when it was surpassed by Billie Jean King. Six of her women's doubles titles were with Suzanne Lenglen.

Ryan, Meg (1963–) Film actress, born in Fairfield, Connecticut, USA. After roles on stage and in television soaps, she appeared in *Top Gun* (1985), and became well known for her performance in *When Harry Met Sally* (1989). Later films include *Sleepless in Seattle* (1993), *French Kiss* (1995), which she also co-produced, *City of Angels* (1998), *Proof of Life* (2000), and *In the Cut* (2003).

Ryan, (Lynn) Nolan (1947–) Baseball player, born in Refugio, Texas, USA. He is regarded as one of the fastest pitchers ever seen in major league baseball, one of his pitches being timed at 162·3 kph/100·9 mph. He started his career with the New York Mets in 1966, then played for the California Angels, the Houston Astros and in 1993 was with the Texas Rangers when he retired after an unprecedented 27 seasons. He compiled more strikeouts (5714) and no-hitters (seven) than any player in baseball history. His season total of 383 strikeouts in 1973 is also an all-time record.

Rwanda

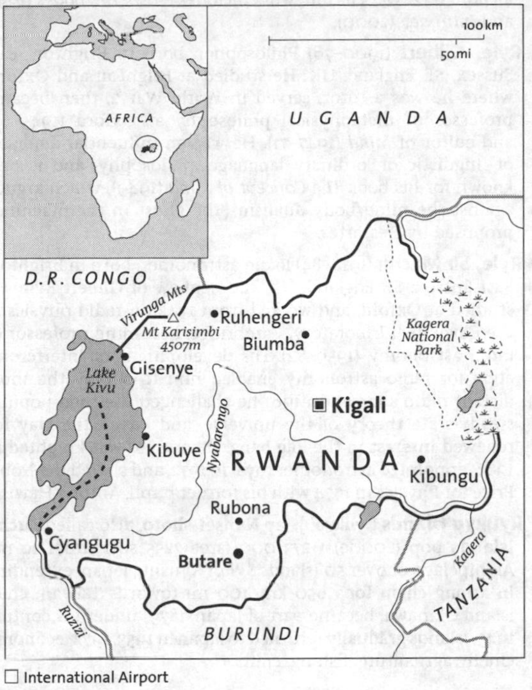

[rooanda], official name **Republic of Rwanda**

Local name Rwanda

Timezone GMT +2

Area 26 338 km²/10 169 sq mi

Population total (2002e) 7 398 000

Status Republic

Date of independence 1962

Capital Kigali

Languages French, Kinyarwanda, and English (official), with Kiswahili widely used in commerce

Ethnic groups Hutu (84%), Tutsi (14%), Pygmoid Twa (1%)

Religions Christian (65%), local indigenous beliefs (25%), Muslim (9%)

Physical features Landlocked in C Africa; mountainous, with many of the highest mountains formed by volcanoes; highest point Karisimbi, 4507 m/14 787 ft, in the Virunga range; W third drains into L Kivu and then the R Congo, remainder drains towards the R Nile; L Kivu and R Ruzizi form W border as part of Africa's Great Rift Valley.

Climate Tropical climate, influenced by high altitude; average annual temperature 19°C (Jan), 21°C (Jul) in Kigali; average annual rainfall 1000 mm/40 in in Kigali; two wet seasons (Oct–Dec, Mar–May); highest rainfall in the W, decreasing in the C uplands and to the N and E.

Currency 1 Rwanda Franc (RF) = 100 centimes

Economy Based largely on agriculture; coffee, tea, pyrethrum, maize, beans, livestock; minerals; plastic goods, textiles.

GDP (2002e) $8·92 bn, per capita $1200

Human Development Index (2002) 0·403

History In the 16th-c the Tutsi tribe moved into the country and took over from the Hutu, forming a monarchy; German protectorate, 1899; mandated with Burundi to Belgium as the Territory of Ruanda-Urundi, 1919; United Nations Trust Territory administered by Belgium, after World War 2; unrest in 1959 led to a Hutu revolt and the overthrow of Tutsi rule; independence, 1962; military coup, 1973; return to civilian rule, 1980; rebellion by (mainly Tutsi) Rwandan Patriotic Front, 1990; new constitution, 1991; peace accord with rebels, 1993; unprecedented outbreak of inter-ethnic violence, with over half a million deaths, 1994; governed by a President, Prime Minister, Council of Ministers, and National Development Council; elections scheduled for 1999, but transitional government rule extended to 2003; new elections, Aug 2003.

Head of State
1973–94 Juvenal Habyarimana
1994–5 Théodore Sindikubwabo *Interim*
1995–2000 Pasteur Bizimunga
2000– Paul Kagame

Head of Government
1991–2 Sylvestre Nsanzimana
1992–3 Dismas Nsengiyaremye
1993–4 Agathe Uwilingiymana
1994–5 Jean Kambanda *Acting*
1995–2000 Pierre-Celestin Rwigyema
2000– Bernard Makuza

Ryazan [ryazan] 54°37N 39°43E, pop (2000e) 524 000. Capital city of Ryazanskaya oblast, Russia; on R Oka, 192 km/119 mi SE of Moscow; founded, 1095; former capital of a principality; railway; cellulose, clothing, footwear, oil refining, chemicals.

Ryde 50°44N 1°10W, pop (2000e) 21 300. Resort town in Isle of Wight, S England, UK; on NE coast of the island, 11 km/7 mi SW of Portsmouth; railway; ferry link with the mainland from Fishbourne to the W; transport equipment, tourism; Quarr Abbey (1132).

Ryder, Albert (Pinkham) (1847–1917) Romantic painter, born in the whaling town of New Bedford, Massachusetts, USA, and always deeply attached to the sea. He worked slowly, producing only 165 pictures in a personal but richly imaginative style, as in 'Siegfried and the Rhine Maidens' (1888–91, National Gallery of Art, Washington, DC).

Ryder (of Warsaw), Sue Ryder, Baroness (1923–2000) Philanthropist, born in Leeds, West Yorkshire, N England, UK. Educated at Benenden School in Kent, she nursed in occupied Europe in World War 2. As a result of her experiences there, she established the Sue Ryder Foundation, begun at Cavendish, Suffolk, in 1953, which now comprises 80 centres worldwide, offering residential care for the sick and disabled. In some countries projects function under the auspices of the Ryder–Cheshire Foundation, which linked her work with that of her husband, Leonard Cheshire. She was created a life peer in 1979.

Ryder, Winona [winohna] (1971–) Film actress, born in Winona, Michigan, USA. She attended the American Conservatory Theatre in San Francisco, and made her film debut in *Lucas* (1986), and went on to star in *Beetlejuice* (1988), *Edward Scissorhands* (1990), and *Mermaids* (1990). She received a Best Supporting Actress Oscar nomination for *The Age of Innocence* (1993), and a Best Actress nomination for her role as Jo in *Little Women* (1995). Later films include *Looking For Richard* (1996), *Girl, Interrupted* (1999), *Autumn in New York* (2000), and *Lost Souls* (2000).

Ryder Cup A golf tournament played every 2 years between professional male golfers from the USA and Europe. First played at Worcester, MA, in 1927, the Cup was donated by English businessman Samuel Ryder (1859–1936), who suggested the idea of a regular international competition between the USA and Great Britain. The Great Britain team became a European team in 1979.

rye A cereal (*Secale cereale*) resembling barley, but with longer, narrower ears. It succeeds on poor soils, and is cultivated mainly in cold regions such as parts of North America and E Europe. It is used to make black bread, crispbreads, alcohol, and straw for hats and thatching. It is also planted for animal forage and, in the USA, for stabilizing soil. (Family: Gramineae.)

Rye House Plot An alleged plot by Whigs (Apr 1683) to murder Charles II of England and James, Duke of York, at Rye House near Hoddesdon, Hertfordshire, SE England, UK; a counter-part to the alleged Popish Plot of 1678. It was foiled by the early departure of the royal pair from Newmarket. The conspirators were betrayed and captured; two of them, Algernon Sidney and William, Lord Russell, were executed.

rye whisky / whiskey A whisky distilled from the fermentation of rye, popular in the S USA. Most other whiskies (but not bourbon) are made from barley.

Rykov, Alexey Ivanovich [reekof] (1881–1938) Russian revolutionary and politician, born in Saratov, W Russia. He studied at Kazan University. He helped organize the October Revolution in Petrograd (1917), and was appointed People's Commissar for Internal Affairs in the first Soviet government. He held a number of senior government and party posts (1919–37), becoming a member of the Politburo (1919–29). In 1928, with Bukharin and others, he led the 'right opposition' against Stalin's economic policies. In 1937 he was arrested for alleged anti-Party activities, and shot some months later.

Rylance, Mark (1960–) Actor and director, born in Kent, SE England, UK. Brought up in Milwaukee, WI, he trained as an actor at the Royal Academy of Dramatic Art and with the Chrysalis Theatre School, London. He was given his first job in 1980 at the Glasgow Citizens Theatre, and went on to work for many of Britain's leading theatre companies. In 1994 he received an Olivier Award for Best Actor in Thelma Holt's production of *Much Ado About Nothing*. In 1995 he was appointed artistic director of Shakespeare's Globe Theatre in London. Performances at the Globe include *Two Gentlemen of Verona* (1996), *Henry V* (1997), *Anthony and Cleopatra* (1999, playing Cleopatra), *Hamlet* (2000), *Twelfth Night* (2002, playing Olivia), and *Richard II* (2003). His film work includes *Prospero's Books* (1991) and *Intimacy* (2000).

Ryle, Gilbert (1900–76) Philosopher, born in Brighton, East Sussex, SE England, UK. He studied at Brighton and Oxford, where he was a tutor, served in World War 2, then became professor of metaphysical philosophy at Oxford (1945–68) and editor of *Mind* (1947–71). He was an influential defender of linguistic or 'ordinary language' philosophy, and is best known for his book *The Concept of Mind* (1949), which argued against the mind/body dualism ('the ghost in the machine') proposed by Descartes.

Ryle, Sir Martin (1918–84) Radio astronomer, born in Brighton, East Sussex, SE England, UK, the nephew of Gilbert Ryle. He studied at Oxford, and worked from 1945 on radio physics at the Cavendish Laboratory, Cambridge, becoming professor of radio astronomy (1959–82). His development of interferometers for radio astronomy enabled him to survey the most distant radio sources. In 1961 he challenged the then-popular steady-state theory of the universe, and paved the way for renewed interest in the 'big bang' theory. He was knighted in 1966, appointed astronomer royal in 1972, and shared the Nobel Prize for Physics in 1974 with his former pupil, Antony Hewish.

Ryukyu Islands [ryukyoo], Jap **Nansei-shoto**, also called **Luchu Islands** pop (2000e) 1 273 000; area 2255 sq km/871 sq mi. Archipelago of over 50 islands SW of Kyushu, Japan, extending in a long chain for c.650 km/400 mi towards Taiwan; chief island Okinawa; became part of Japan, 1879; under US control, 1945; islands gradually returned to Japan in 1953, 1972; economy chiefly agriculture, fishing, crafts.

S

Saar, River [zah(r)], Fr **Sarre** River in France and Germany; rises in the Vosges, flows N through NE France and NW across the German border to the R Moselle just above Trier; length 240 km/150 mi; navigable length 120 km/75 mi; its valley is a noted wine area.

Saarbrücken [zah(r)brükn], Fr **Sarrebruck** 49°15N 6°58E, pop (2000e) 198 000. Capital of Saarland province, SW Germany; on the R Saar, 62 km/38 mi SE of Trier; economic and cultural centre of Saarland; railway; university (1948); ironworks, metal products, coal, oil products, rubber, machine tools, electrical engineering, optical equipment; collegiate Church of St Arnual (13th–14th-c); noted for its trade fairs.

Saarinen, Eero (1910–61) Architect and furniture designer, born in Kirkkonummi, S Finland. He went to the USA in 1923 with his architect father Eliel Saarinen (1873–1950), then studied sculpture in Paris (1929–30) and architecture at Yale (1930–4). He became a US citizen in 1940. His designs for Expressionist modern buildings include the Trans-World Airlines Kennedy Terminal, New York City (1956–62).

Saatchi & Saatchi [sahchee] Advertisers: **Charles Saatchi** (1943–) and **Maurice Saatchi** (1946–), born in Iraq. They immigrated to England with their father in 1947, and set up their advertising agency in 1970. They quickly gained fame with advertisements such as a pregnant man to promote contraception, and were engaged by the Conservative Party in 1978 to create election posters and slogans. They bought out three US agencies in the 1980s to become the world's largest agency, but suffered badly in the stock market crash at the end of the decade. In 1995, following a controversial share option package, chairman Maurice Saatchi left the company, and with his brother set up a new agency, M&C Saatchi. Maurice was made a Lord in 1996 and became a shadow Treasury spokesman. In 2003 he was appointed co-chairman of the Conservative Party led by Michael Howard.

Sabah [sabah], formerly **North Borneo** pop (2000e) 1 829 000; area 73 711 sq km/28 452 sq mi. State in E Malaysia, on the N tip of Borneo; bounded SW by Brunei, W by the South China Sea, E by the Sulu Sea, and S by Kalimantan (Indonesia); highest peak, Mt Kinabalu, 4094 m/13 432 ft; watered by the R Kinabatangan; British protectorate, 1882; member of the Federation of Malaysia, 1963; capital, Kota Kinabalu; copper, oil, timber, copra, rice, rubber.

Sabbath or **Shabbat** (Heb 'cessation', 'rest') The seventh day of the week, which in Jewish belief is designated a day of rest and cessation from labour, beginning just before sunset on Fridays. The laws of Sabbath observance derive from a short ban found in the Pentateuch (*Ex* 20.8–11; 31.12–17) and from God's own rest in the Genesis creation account. Rabbinic regulations specify 39 forbidden activities, which are then further elaborated, but in more liberal Reform Judaism the Sabbath is mainly a day of worship.

Sabin, Albert (Bruce) [saybin] (1906–93) Microbiologist, born in Białystok, NE Poland. He moved to the USA in 1921, and became a US citizen in 1930. He studied at New York University, then held a research post at the Rockefeller Institute, New York City, and became professor of research paediatrics at the University of Cincinatti (1946–60, then emeritus). He later held research consultancy posts at the University of South Carolina (1974–82) and the Fogarty International Center, MD (1984–6). He is best known for his research into a live virus as a polio vaccine, which works by causing a harmless infection of the intestinal tract, stimulating immunity to natural infection without causing disease. This replaced the Salk vaccine, as it gives longer-lasting immunity, and may be given orally.

Sabines [sabiynz] A people of ancient Italy, inhabiting the mountainous country NE of Rome. Often at war with the Romans, they were ultimately conquered and absorbed by them.

sable An Asian marten (*Martes zibellina*) with a thick and silky winter coat valuable to the fur trade (summer coat shorter and coarse); inhabits high forests, usually near streams. The fur of the **American pine marten** (*Martes americana*) is known as *American sable* or *Hudson Bay sable*.

sable antelope A horse-like antelope native to Africa S of the Sahara (*Hippotragus niger*); black with pale underparts (young are reddish-brown); long curved horns (length in male, over 1 m/3¼ ft); inhabits woodland.

Sabra and Chatila Palestinian refugee camps on the outskirts of Beirut, Lebanon, developed in the 1950s and 1960s. They were the scene of a massacre of Palestinians by Christian Phalangists in 1983.

Sabratha Phoenician colony founded in the 8th-c BC on the NW coast of present-day Libya. The city was incorporated in Roman Africa in the 2nd-c BC. Now a world heritage site, the ruins of Sabratha include a reconstructed theatre facing the sea.

sabretooth A fossil cat, often referred to as **sabretooth tiger**, but not closely related to the tiger; upper canine teeth enlarged, sabre-like, adapted for efficient stabbing action; jaw modified to give extra wide gape; body size up to that of lion; became extinct in the late Pleistocene epoch. (Genus: *Smilodon*. Family: Felidae.)

saccades [sakaydz] The jerky flicking of the eye from one point to another, in contrast with its slow drifts. They may be either voluntary (as in reading) or involuntary, and their study can provide important information about the nature of the reading process and other visual activities.

saccharin [sakarin] $C_7H_5NO_3S$, melting point 229°C. A white solid which has more than 400 times the sweetening power of sucrose. The normal form of the artificial sweetener is its sodium salt. Many people find that it leaves a bitter aftertaste.

Sacco and Vanzetti [sakoh, vanzetee] **Nicola Sacco** (1891–1927) and **Bartolomeo Vanzetti** (1888–1927) Political radicals, the chief figures in an American *cause célèbre* which had worldwide reverberations. Accused of a payroll murder and robbery in Massachusetts in 1920, they were found guilty, and seven years later were executed in spite of conflicting and circumstantial evidence, and the confession of another man to the crime. Both had been anarchists, and the suspicion that this had provoked deliberate injustice aroused an international outcry.

Sachs, Hans [zaks] (1494–1576) Poet, playwright, and composer, born in Nuremberg, SC Germany. He was trained as a shoemaker, and travelled through Germany (1511–16) practising his craft and frequenting the schools of the *Meistersinger* ('mastersingers', professional songwriters). He wrote over 6300 pieces, some celebrating the Reformation, others dealing with common life and manners in a vigorous, humorous style. His life and work were celebrated by Wagner in his opera dedicated to Sachs, *Die Meistersinger von Nürnberg* (1868, The Meistersinger of Nuremberg).

Sachs, Nelly (Leonie) [zaks] (1891–1970) Poet and playwright, born in Berlin, Germany. Of Jewish descent, she fled from Nazi Germany in 1940, settled in Stockholm, and took Swedish nationality. Her best-known play is *Eli: ein Mysterienspiel vom Leiden Israels* (1951, Eli: a Mystery Play of the Sufferings of Israel). She shared with S Y Agnon the Nobel Prize for Literature in 1966.

sackbut *trombone*

Sacks, Oliver (Wolf) (1933–) Neurologist, born in London, UK. Educated at Oxford, he trained as a doctor at Middlesex Hospital, London, then studied neurology at the University of California, Los Angeles. After taking up an appointment in New York City, he worked with a group of patients who had contracted a form of sleeping sickness, and became internationally known following his account of the tragically brief cure they experienced after receiving treatment with L-dopa, *Awakenings* (1973; filmed, 1990). His insights into unusual syndromes, along with an appealing literary style, resulted in a series of best-selling books, such as *The Man who Mistook his Wife for a Hat* (1986), *An Anthropologist on Mars* (1995), and *The Island of the Colorblind* (1998).

Sackville, Thomas, 1st Earl of Dorset (1536–1608) English statesman and poet, born in Buckhurst, Sussex, England, UK. He became a lawyer and entered parliament (1558), then collaborated with Thomas Norton (1532–84) in the tragedy *Gorboduc* (1561), the first English play in blank verse. Knighted in 1567, he later became a diplomat in Europe, Lord High Treasurer (1599), and an earl (1604).

Sackville-West, Vita, popular name of **Victoria Mary Sackville-West** (1892–1962) Poet and novelist, born at Knole, Kent, SE England, UK. Educated privately, she started writing as a child. Her work expresses her closeness to the countryside where she lived, notably in the long poem, 'The Land' (1926). Her best-known novels are *The Edwardians* (1930) and *All Passion Spent* (1931). In 1913 she married diplomat and critic Harold Nicolson (1886–1968), a marriage which endured despite their homosexual affairs. *Passenger to Teheran* (1926) records their years in Persia. Her friendship with Virginia Woolf occasioned the latter's *Orlando* (1928). She wrote a weekly gardening column for *The Observer* for many years.

sacrament A Christian rite understood as an outward and visible sign of an internal and spiritual grace. Orthodox and Roman Catholic Churches recognize seven sacraments: baptism, confirmation, the Eucharist (Mass), penance, extreme unction, holy orders (ordination), and matrimony. Protestant Churches recognize only baptism and the Eucharist (Communion) as sacraments.

Sacramento 38°35N 121°29W, pop (2000e) 407 000. Capital of state and seat of Sacramento Co, C California, USA, on the E bank of the Sacramento R; settled, 1839; expanded rapidly after gold discovered nearby, 1848; state capital, 1854; airport; railway; university (1947); food processing, high technology; professional team, Kings (basketball); Roman Corinthian State Capitol (1860) in Capitol Park; Crocker Art Gallery; Sutter's Fort (1840, now restored) contains a museum of Indian and pioneer relics.

Sacramento River Longest river in California, USA; rises in the Klamath Mts; flows 615 km/382 mi S to Suisin Bay; major tributaries the Pit, Feather, American; navigable as far as Red Bluff (412 km/256 mi) for small craft; Sacramento the principal port; joins with the San Joaquin to form the basis of the immense Central Valley Project for flood-control, irrigation, and hydroelectricity, using several dams and reservoirs.

Sacré Coeur Cathedral [sakray koer], Fr **Basilique du Sacré Coeur**, Eng **Church of the Sacred Heart** Roman Catholic church in the Montmartre district of Paris, France. Designed by Paul Abadie in Romano-Byzantine style (1876–1912), it was consecrated in 1919. A popular tourist venue, the interior contains one of the world's largest mosaics, depicting Christ with outstretched arms.

sacred ibis An ibis (*Threskiornis aethiopicus*) native to Africa S of the Sahara, S Arabia, and Aldabra (formerly also Egypt); white with dark head and neck; soft dark plumes on tail; eats fish and insects; nests in tree or on ground.

sacrum A triangular-shaped bone at the lower end of the vertebral column, formed by fusion of the five sacral vertebrae. In humans standing upright, it lies almost horizontally, articulating with the two hip bones to complete the ring of bone known as the *pelvis*, and with the rest of the vertebral column at the fifth lumbar vertebra. The sacrum gives attachment to the muscles of the back and the buttock.

Sadat, (Mohammed) Anwar el- [sadat] (1918–81) Egyptian statesman and president (1970–81), born in the Tala district, N Egypt. He trained for the army in Cairo, and in 1952 was a member of the Free Officers who executed the coup which deposed King Farouk. After becoming president, he temporarily assumed the post of prime minister (1973–4), after which he sought settlement of the conflict with Israel. He recovered the Suez Canal Zone from Israel and established close relations with the USA. He met the Israeli premier in Jerusalem (1977) and at Camp David, USA, in 1978, and the same year he and Begin were jointly awarded the Nobel Peace Prize. Sadat's initiative led to the signing of a peace treaty between Israel and Egypt in 1979. Following bitter criticism by other Arab statesmen and hard-line Muslims, he was assassinated in Cairo by extremists.

Saddam Hussein *Hussein, Saddam*

saddleback A bird restricted to isolated pockets in New Zealand (*Creadion carunculatus*); dark with orange-brown band across back; long legs and tail; long curved bill; fold of skin on each cheek; weak flier; inhabits forests; eats insects; related to the huia. (Family: Callaeidae.)

saddle-bill stork *jabiru*

Sadducees [sadyuseez] A major party within Judaism (c.2nd-c BC–AD 70), the name probably deriving from the priest Zadok, whose descendants held priestly office from Solomon's times. They were mainly aristocrats, associated with the Jerusalem priesthood (including the high priest among their number), and influential in Israel's political and socio-economic life. Josephus suggests that they differed from the Pharisees by their denials of the legal force of oral traditions, of bodily resurrection, and of divine determinism.

Sade, Marquis de [sahd], popular name of **Donatien Alphonse François, comte** (Count) **de Sade** (1740–1814) Writer, born in Paris, France. He studied at Paris, served in the army, and was in 1772 condemned to death at Aix for his cruelty and sexual perversions. He escaped, but was later imprisoned at Vincennes (1777) and in the Bastille (1784), where he wrote *Les 120 Journées de Sodome* (c.1784, The 120 Days of Sodom). After his release (1790), he wrote the licentious novels *Justine* (1791), *La Philosophie dans le boudoir* (1795, Philosophy in the Bedroom), and *Juliette* (1797). He died insane, his name providing the language with the word *sadism*.

Sadler's Wells Theatre A popular London dance and opera theatre, so-called because in 1683 Richard Sadler discovered a medicinal well in his garden and established a music house there. Light entertainment was provided, and the theatre became famous for pantomimes, harlequinades, and burlesques. In the 19th-c it fell into disrepair, but in 1931 was reopened under Lilian Baylis and became one of the leading theatres in London for the production of ballet and opera. In 1946 the ballet company transferred to the Royal Opera House, Covent Garden, where it eventually became the Royal Ballet. Ballet productions continued to be staged at Sadler's Wells and the company was eventually named the Sadler's Wells Royal Ballet. The old theatre was demolished in 1966 and a new building was opened in 1998, with Stephen Remington as director.

Sado [sahdoh] area 856 sq km/330 sq mi. Island in Chubu region, Japan; in the East Sea (Sea of Japan), 48 km/30 mi W of Niigata, off N Honshu; 56 km/35 mi long, 19 km/12 mi wide; mountainous, with a central plain; rises to 1173 m/3848 ft (N); chief town and port, Ryotsu; farming, fishing, timber.

sadomasochism Sexual behaviour in which gratification is based on the infliction (**sadism**) or receipt (**masochism**) of pain or humiliation; often abbreviated as **SM**. An example would be a couple in which one partner has heightened sexual arousal from beating his or her partner, while the other derives pleasure from the experience of being beaten.

Safavids [safahweedz] A Persian dynasty (1501–1736) which laid down the foundations of the modern Iranian state. It made Shiism the official religion, and saw a flowering of the arts.

safety film Also termed **non-flam**: photographic film with its emulsion coated on a cellulose triacetate or polyester base, which is slow burning and of low inflammability. The contrast is with the highly dangerous cellulose nitrate used before 1950.

safety lamp A device used by miners to detect explosive methane gas in mines (*firedamp*), invented in 1815 by Sir Humphry Davy. Any methane present would cause a change in the appearance of the flame, but a double layer of wire gauze surrounding it prevented the gas igniting. Flame lamps have now been almost entirely replaced by lamps powered by electricity.

safflower An annual growing to 1 m/3¼ ft (*Carthamus tinctorius*); leaves elliptical, finely spiny-toothed around the margin; flower heads thistle-like, up to 3 cm/1¼ in across, the florets bright red-orange. It is probably native to W Asia, but is no longer known in the wild. It has a long history of cultivation, formerly as a dye plant, but now mainly for the seeds, which yield a useful oil. (Family: Compositae.)

saffron An autumn-flowering species of crocus (*Crocus sativus*), native to S Europe and Asia, with lilac flowers. The large, 3-branched, bright orange stigmas are a source of saffron, used as a food dye and as flavouring. (Family: Iridaceae.)

Safire, William [safiyr] (1929–) Journalist, born in New York City, USA. A former public relations writer, and a speechwriter and special assistant to President Nixon, he became a Washington-based columnist for the *New York Times* in 1973. He won the Pulitzer Prize for commentary in 1978, and went on to become a national figure known for his weekly column devoted to language matters.

saga (Old Norse 'saying') A mediaeval Icelandic or Scandinavian prose narrative, transcribed from oral tradition after 1100, and later composed in writing. There are several cycles, such as the Norwegian *Sverris saga*, the Orkney *Orkneyinga saga*, the Danish *Knytlinga saga*, and the Icelandic *Hrafnkels saga*. The term is also more generally used of any extended narrative, in fact or fiction: Galsworthy's *Forsyte Saga*, or the Watergate saga.

Sagan, Carl (Edward) [saygn] (1934–96) Astronomer and writer, born in New York City, USA. He studied at the universities of Chicago and California (Berkeley), taught at Berkeley, Stanford, Harvard, and the Smithsonian Institution, and became professor of astronomy and space science at Cornell (1970). As director of the Laboratory for Planetary Studies there, he was closely associated with the NASA programme of Solar System exploration from its inception and was involved in the Mariner, Viking, and Voyager spacecraft missions to the planets. He investigated the origin of life on Earth and the possibility of extraterrestrial intelligence by the use of radio astronomy techniques. Through such books as *Cosmic Connection* (1973) and a television programme, *Cosmos*, he did much to popularize this aspect of science.

Sagan, Françoise [sagã], pseudonym of **Françoise Quoirez** (1935–) Novelist, born in Paris, France. Educated privately, at the age of 18 she wrote, in only four weeks, the best-selling *Bonjour tristesse* (1954, Good Morning Sadness), followed by *Un Certain Sourire* (1956, A Certain Smile). Both novels are direct testaments of adolescent wisdom and precocity, written with the economy of a remarkable literary style. Her many later novels, including *Aimez-vous Brahms?* (1959, Do You Like Brahms?, filmed in 1961 as *Goodbye Again*), have had a mixed critical reception. She has also written several plays, and a ballet, *La Chamade* (1966). In 1993 appeared *Oeuvres*, a volume of collected works.

Sagarmatha National park and world heritage area in Nepal; encompasses the peak of Mt Everest – Sagarmatha (Nepalese, 'whose head touches the sky') – and six other mountains over 7000 m/23 000 ft; established to protect the flora and fauna of the area, and the culture of the Sherpas who inhabit the region.

sage An aromatic shrub (*Salvia officinalis*) growing to 0·5 m/1½ ft, native to S Europe; young stems square; leaves oblong, stalked, wrinkled, velvety, in opposite pairs; flowers 1–2 cm/0·4–0·8 in, purplish, 2-lipped, the upper lip hooded. It is widely cultivated as a culinary and medicinal herb. Purple-leaved and variegated forms are grown as ornamentals. (Family: Labiatae.)

sagebrush The name applied to certain North American species of *Artemisia*, including **big sagebrush** (*Artemisia tridentata*), a much-branched aromatic shrub growing to 3 m/10 ft; leaves wedge-shaped, 3-toothed at the tips, silvery hairy; flower-heads small, greenish, and inconspicuous; also called **sagebush**. The pollen is a common cause of hay fever during late summer. (Genus: *Artemisia*. Family: Compositae.)

sagebush *sagebrush*

sage grouse A grouse native to W North America (*Centrocercus urophasianus*); lives in drier areas than other grouse, inhabiting sagebrush plains; eats sagebrush leaves; males display at traditional sites (strutting grounds).

Sagitta [sajita] (Lat 'arrow') The third-smallest constellation, lying in the Milky Way near Cygnus.

Sagittarius [sajitairius] (Lat 'archer') A S constellation of the zodiac, lying between Scorpius and Capricornus, and containing numerous star clusters and nebulae. It lies in the direction of the centre of our Galaxy, although the view is obscured by intervening clouds of dust a few kiloparsec away. Radio and infrared radiation from the Galactic centre can penetrate this dust, providing information on conditions there.

sago palm A small tree with large feathery leaves, native to SE Asia and the Pacific. The trunk contains large starch reserves to fuel a single great burst of flowering by the mature tree, after which it dies. Sago, a primary source of carbohydrate in the tropics, is obtained from the pith of trunks cut when the first flowers appear. (Genus: *Metroxylon*, 15 species. Family: Palmae.)

saguaro [sagwahroh] The largest of the cacti (*Carnegiea gigantea*), slow-growing, reaching 21 m/70 ft, with a thick stem and candelabra-like branches and white flowers; found only in Arizona, S California, and the Sonoran desert in Mexico. (Family: Cactaceae.)

Sagunto [sagoontoh], Arabic **Murviedro** (to 1877), ancient **Saguntum** 39°42N 0°18W, pop (2000e) 56 000. Town in Valencia province, E Spain; on R Palancia, 25 km/15 mi N of Valencia; Costa del Azahar to the N; steel, fruit, linen, brandy; Roman theatre, fortress, Church of St Mary.

Sahara Desert (Arabic 'wilderness') Desert in N Africa; the largest desert in the world, area 7·7 million sq km/3 million sq mi; average width, 1440 km/895 mi across N Africa from the Atlantic to the Libyan Desert, in which it continues unbroken to the Nile, and beyond that in the Nubian Desert to the Red Sea; covers parts of Morocco, Algeria, Tunisia, Libya, Egypt, Sudan, Chad, Niger, Mali, Mauritania, and Western Sahara; includes the Ahaggar and Tibesti Mts; parts of the Atlas Mts in the NW; areas of drift sand (*erg*), rock (*hamada*), or gravel and pebbles (*areg*); wind erosion intense; only small amounts of unpredictable rain, usually brief, heavy thunderstorms; scattered outlets of surface water at oases, where agriculture is possible; generally void of vegetation, apart from areas of stunted scrub; climate arid since the glacial epoch, when the region was relatively humid with a park savannah vegetation; camel caravans follow routes marked by oases; oil exploration near the Algeria–Libya frontier; phosphates in Morocco and Western Sahara; first crossed by Europeans in the 1820s.

sahel [sahel] A vegetation zone intermediate between desert and savannah conditions where rainfall is irregular and unpredictable. The vegetation is a transitional scrubland. The name is most commonly applied to the area S of the Sahara (**the Sahel**), including parts of Mauritania, Chad, Mali, Senegal, Burkina Faso, and Niger. The area frequently suffers from drought and famine.

Said, Edward W(adi) [saeed] (1935–2003) Writer and political commentator, born in Jerusalem, Israel. He studied at Cairo, Princeton, and Harvard universities, then joined the English department at Columbia. He became one of the major Palestinian spokesmen in the debate on the future of the Middle East, and took part in the 1988 gathering that declared the existence of an independent Palestinian state. He is best known for his writings on 'Orientalism'.

saiga [sayga] A goat-antelope native to Asia (*Saiga tatarica*); thick pale brown coat with longer hairs down throat; eyes protruding; nose grotesquely swollen with large downward-facing nostrils at tip; male with short yellow horns; inhabits cold steppelands.

Saigon *Ho Chi Minh City*

Sailer, Toni (Anton) [ziyler] (1935–) Alpine skier, born in Kitzbühel, W Austria. In 1956, he became the first man to win all three Olympic skiing titles (downhill, slalom, giant slalom). He was the world combined champion (1956, 1958) and the world downhill and giant slalom champion (1958). He later became an actor and singer, a hotel owner, and an investor in a textile business.

sailfish Large agile billfish (*Istiophorus platypterus*) widely distributed in open ocean surface waters; length up to 3·5 m/11½ ft; blue-grey above, underside silver; easily recognized by long tall dorsal fin; feeds on fish and squid; highly prized as excellent sport fish, and also taken commercially in some areas. (Family: Istiophoridae.)

sailing A term used to describe the sport or pastime of travelling over water in a suitable craft, especially one with sails. Sailing takes many forms. As a pastime, most use is made of small single- or double-sailed dinghies, often fitted with an outboard motor or auxiliary engine used when there is no wind; but large ocean-going yachts may be 25 m/80 ft or more in length. Several classes of racing yacht are recognized in Olympic and major international competitions.

sailing rig The system of sails and masts used on a boat. In a **lateen rig**, a large triangular sail is attached to a long tapering spar, resulting in an adaptable rig that can be secured at a variety of angles. Probably originating in Mesopotamia, it was adopted by the Egyptians, and later found throughout the Mediterranean. The Barbary Coast pirates of North Africa used it until the early 19th-c, and it can still sometimes be seen in Arab dhows. In a **fore-and-aft rig**, the sails are set in a fore-and-aft line, and are usually triangular, though sometimes quadrilateral. This rig is very much more efficient and manageable than the square rig, giving better performance to windward. In a **square rig**, the sails are bent on to spars which are hung on the mast at the middle, thus usually making a square angle to the ship's fore-and-aft line.

Saimaa [siymah] Lake system extending over the Finnish Lake Plateau, SE Finland; total area 4400 sq km/1700 sq mi; fifth largest lake system in Europe; timber floating; important communications system; L Saimaa area, 1300 sq km/500 sq mi; maximum depth 100 m/325 ft; linked to an inlet of the Gulf of Finland by the Saimaa Canal (60 km/37 mi).

sainfoin [sanfoyn] A perennial growing to 80 cm/30 in (*Onobrychis viciifolia*), possibly native to C Europe; leaves pinnate with 6–14 pairs of oblong-oval leaflets; pea-flowers bright pink veined with purple, up to 50 in each long-stalked, spike-like inflorescence arising from the leaf axils; pods 1-seeded, covered with a net-like pattern of ridges and tubercles. It is widely cultivated for fodder. (Family: Leguminosae.)

saint In Roman Catholic and Orthodox teaching, a man or woman recognized as being in heaven because of their special qualities. In the New Testament, all Christian believers are referred to as saints, but in the 2nd-c, veneration of saints (often martyrs) began, and individual saints were eventually looked to for intercession and devotion. The practice of veneration was forbidden by 16th-c Reformers, but continued in the Orthodox and Roman Catholic Churches. An elaborate procedure is required before canonization may proceed.

St Albans [awlbnz], Lat **Verulamium** 51°46N 0°21W, pop (2001e) 129 000. Town in Hertfordshire, SE England, UK; on R Ver, 40 km/25 mi NW of London; named after the first Christian martyr to be executed in Britain; Magna Carta drafted here; royal charter (1553); city status (1887); agricultural research station; railway; agricultural trade, micro-electronics, printing; cathedral (1115, founded as Benedictine abbey, 793); Roman theatre; museum with Iron Age and Roman exhibits.

St Andrews 56°20N 2°48W, pop (2000e) 15 400. Town in Fife, E Scotland, UK; on S side of St Andrews Bay, 17 km/11 mi SE of Dundee; university (oldest in Scotland, founded 1412); textiles; tourism; St Andrews Royal and Ancient Golf Club, West Port (city gate, built 1589, restored 1843), remains of castle (1200) and cathedral (12th–13th-c); repertory theatre; arts centre; golf week (Apr); British Amateur Golf Championships (Jun).

St Anthony's fire *ergotism*

St Anton am Arlberg 47°08N 9°52E, pop (2000e) 2400. Winter sports resort in the Lechtal Alps (Arlberg massif), Vorarlberg, W Austria; cableway facilities on Valluga, Galzig, Brandkreuz, and Kapall; major skiing centre.

St Bartholomew's Day Massacre (24 Aug 1572) The slaughter of French Huguenots in Paris, ordered by King Charles IX and connived at by the queen mother, Catherine de' Medici, to coincide with celebrations for the marriage of Marguerite de Valois and Henry of Navarre (18 Aug). An attempted assassination of the Huguenot leader Admiral Coligny failed (22 Aug), but mass butchery of Huguenots followed.

St Basil's Cathedral Part of the Historical Museum in Moscow. It was built (1555–61) on the orders of Tsar Ivan IV to celebrate his victory over the Tatar state of Kazan. Originally the Cathedral of the Intercession of the Virgin, the present title was adopted after 1588, when a chapel was added to house the remains of the ascetic Basil the Blessed. Eight chapels cluster round the principal church, and the assortment of spires and domes, together with the brightly painted exterior, create an exuberant, fairy-tale effect.

St Bernard The heaviest breed of dog (up to 100 kg/220 lb), developed at the Hospice of St Bernard in Switzerland to track people lost in the mountain snow; orange-brown and white; large with broad head, deep muzzle, pendulous ears; two forms: *smooth-haired* and *rough-haired*; also known as **Great St Bernard**.

St Bernard's Passes Two transalpine frontier passes: the **Great St Bernard**, which crosses the Pennine Alps between Martigny in Switzerland and Aosta in Italy, and the **Little St Bernard**, which crosses the Graian Alps between Aosta and Bourg St Maurice in France. St Bernard of Menthon founded hospices in both passes in the 10th-c.

St Catharines 43°10N 79°15W, pop (2000e) 144 500. City in SE Ontario, Canada, S of Toronto; founded, 1784; railway; at entrance to Welland Ship Canal; university (1964); heart of Canada's fruit belt and major wine-growing region; light and heavy industry; Royal Canadian Henley Regatta (Aug); Niagara Grape and Wine Festival (Sept).

St Christopher-Nevis *St Kitts-Nevis*

St Croix [saynt kroy], formerly **Santa Cruz** pop (2000e) 56 200; area 218 sq km/84 sq mi. Largest of the three main US Virgin Is, Lesser Antilles, Caribbean, 120 km/75 mi E of Puerto Rico; main towns, Christiansted (former capital of the Danish West Indies) and Frederiksted; tourism, oil refining, alumina, textiles, pharmaceuticals, rum, fragrances.

St-Cyr, Ecole de [aykol duh sī seer] A French military academy founded by Napoleon at Fontainebleau, but transferred to St-Cyr in 1808. The school was moved to Coetquidan in Brittany after World War 2, but retained the name of its former home. A new military school was opened in 1966. The buildings that it occupied at St-Cyr were the former premises of a school for the daughters of impoverished noblemen established by Louis XIV and Madame de Maintenon in 1687.

St David's, Welsh **Tyddewi** 51°54N 5°16W, pop (2000e) 1860. Village city in Pembrokeshire, SW Wales, UK; 25 km/15 mi NW of Milford Haven on St Bride's Bay; episcopal seat; 12th-c cathedral honours the 6th-c Welsh patron saint, Dewi (David); mediaeval place of pilgrimage; smallest cathedral seat in UK; city status, 1994.

St-Denis (France) [sĩ duhnee] 48°56N 2°21E, pop (2000e) 95 000. Modern industrial town and railway centre in Seine-Saint-Denis department, NC France; N suburb of Paris; paints and varnishes, cars and aeronautical equipment; 12th-c Gothic Basilica of St-Denis, with tombs of several French monarchs.

St-Denis (Réunion) [sĩ duhnee] 20°52S 55°27E, pop (2000e) 145 000. Capital of Réunion, on the N coast; airport; commerce, administration, tourism, agricultural trade.

Saint-Denis, Michel (Jacques Duchesne) [sĩ duhnee] (1897–1971) Theatre director, actor, and teacher, born in Beauvais, N France. In 1931 he founded the Compagnie des Quinze, and directed numerous influential productions. When this company disbanded, he settled in England, founding with George Devine and others the London Theatre Studio (1936). His influence on British theatre continued with his work for the Old Vic (1947–52) and later with the Royal Shakespeare Company, where he became a director in 1962. He was appointed director of the Comédie de l'Est in 1952.

St Denis, Ruth, originally **Ruth Dennis** (1879–1968) Dancer, director, choreographer, and teacher, born in Somerville, New Jersey, USA. She formed the *Denishawn* partnership with Ted Shawn, and became known, first in Europe, for exotic, colourful, Oriental dances such as *Rhada* (1906). She married Shawn in 1914, and founded a school and company with him in 1915, which was frequented by many Hollywood stars. Fusing all manner of dance forms together, the company toured the USA until it folded in 1931, when the couple separated. She continued to dance into her 80s.

Sainte-Beuve, Charles Augustin [sĩt boev] (1804–69) Literary critic, born in Boulogne, NW France. He studied at Paris, trained in medicine, then turned to writing. He produced several volumes of poetry, and in the *Revue de Paris* (1829) began his *Causeries*, longer critical articles on French literature. His major works include several books of 'portraits' of literary contemporaries. His single novel, *Volupté*, appeared in 1835. In 1840 he became keeper of the Mazarin Library, and in 1848 professor of French literature at Liège. Nominated a senator in 1865, his speeches in favour of liberty of thought earned him great popularity.

St Elias, Mount [eliyas] 60°17N 140°55W. Mountain in St Elias Mts, on the Yukon–Alaska border, USA; rises to 5489 m/18 008 ft; second highest peak in the USA.

St Elmo's fire A blue-green-coloured electrical discharge which occurs during thunderstorm weather around the masts of ships, weather-vanes, and aircraft wing tips. It is especially common in the Doldrums.

St-Etienne [sĩtaytyen] 45°27N 4°22E, pop (2000e) 208 000. Manufacturing town and capital of Loire department, SW France; on the Central Plateau, 51 km/32 mi SW of Lyon; railway; university; school of mining (1816); food processing, electronics, firearms, chemicals; centre of metallurgical industry since 16th-c.

Saint-Exupéry, Antoine (Marie Roger) de [sĩt egzüpayree] (1900–44) Airman and writer, born in Lyon, SC France. A commercial and wartime pilot, his philosophy of 'heroic action' is found in such novels as *Vol de nuit* (1931, Night Flight). He is also known for his popular children's fable for adults, *Le Petit Prince* (1943, The Little Prince). He was declared missing after a flight to North Africa in World War 2, and the wreckage of his plane was found off the coast of France in 1999.

St Gallen [sankt galen], Fr **St Gall** [sĩ gal] 47°25N 9°23E, pop (2000e) 77 000. Ancient abbey town and capital of St Gallen canton, NE Switzerland; in a high valley in the Pre-Alps, 62 km/38 mi E of Zürich; developed around the abbey founded by St Gall, 7th-c; major educational institution until 11th-c, with world-famous library; a world heritage site; university; commerce, textiles, engineering, tourism; cathedral and abbey library (18th-c); Olma agriculture and milk industries fair, Spring and Leisure Fair (Apr).

St George's 12°03N 61°45W, pop (2000e) 8460. Port and capital town of Grenada, on SW coast; airport; founded as French settlement in 1650; port trade; tourism.

St George's Channel Stretch of sea between the SE of Ireland (W) and Wales (E), connecting the Atlantic Ocean with the Irish Sea; at its narrowest between Carnsore Point (Ireland) and St David's Head (Wales), 74 km/46 mi across.

St Germain-en-Laye [sĩ zhairmĩ ã lay] 48°54N 2°05E, pop (2001e) 37 600. Historic city in NC France; bordering the Marly le Roi forest; founded, 1020; birthplace of Louis XIV, Charles IX, Claude Debussy, and the Alain family; famous chateau built by Louis VI (1124) contains the National Antiquities Museum; Priory Museum; former Claude Debussy House now a museum.

St Gotthard Pass [gotah(r)d] 46°34N 8°31E. Mountain pass and tunnel (road and rail, 15 km/10 mi) between Andermatt and Airolo, over the St Gotthard massif in the Lepontine Alps, SC Switzerland; height, 2108 m/6916 ft; 11 people lost their lives and 128 were reported missing when two trucks collided and caught fire in the tunnel, causing part of the roof to collapse, Oct 2001 (re-opened, Dec); pass open between June and October; St Gotthard Hospice (14th-c).

St Helena *p.1342*

St Helens 53°28N 2°44W, pop (2001e) 176 800. Industrial town in Merseyside, NW England, UK; 18 km/11 mi E of Liverpool; railway; coal, engineering, textiles, glass.

St Helens, Mount 46°12N 122°12W. Volcano in SW Washington, USA, in the Cascade Range; rises to 2549 m/8363 ft; erupted 18 May 1980, causing damage amounting to $2·5 thousand million; a large area in the W states affected by volcanic ash; 100 people were killed and 276 homes destroyed.

St Ives 50°12N 5°29W, pop (2000e) 10 800. Resort town in Cornwall, SW England, UK; 12 km/7 mi NE of Penzance; railway; tourism, water sports, fishing; festival of music and the arts (Sep).

St James's Palace Until the mid-19th-c, one of the principal royal palaces in London, UK. Only parts of the original Tudor palace built for Henry VIII remain (notably the gatehouse and the chapel royal), and much of the building dates from the 18th-c.

Saint John (Canada) 45°16N 66°03W, pop (2000e) 84 000. Seaport in S New Brunswick, Canada, on Bay of Fundy at mouth of St John R; harbour ice-free all year; French fort, 1631–5; taken by British, 1758; many United Empire Loyalist immigrants after American Revolution; largely destroyed by fire, 1877; airfield; railway; shipbuilding, steel, pulp; Old Courthouse (1830), Trinity Church (rebuilt 1877), Chubb's Corner (1878), New Brunswick Museum, Martello Tower (1812), Fort Howe (1778); Reversing Falls (water falls in opposite directions over a rocky ledge according to the tide).

Saint John (US Virgin Is) pop (2000e) 3030; area 52 sq km/20 sq mi. Smallest of the three main US Virgin Is, Lesser Antilles, Caribbean, 8 km/5 mi E of St Thomas; contains the Virgin Is National Park, established in 1956, area 71 sq km/27 sq mi.

St John Ambulance Brigade A worldwide charitable organization that provides medical and nursing help to the aged, sick, and injured. It derives its inspiration from the Hospitallers, a military and religious order founded in the 11th-c (the Knights of Saint John of Jerusalem).

Saint John's 47°34N 52°41W, pop (2000e) 107 600. Port and provincial capital of Newfoundland, Canada, SE of the island; Cabot landed here, 1497; British possession, 1583; held by the

St Helena

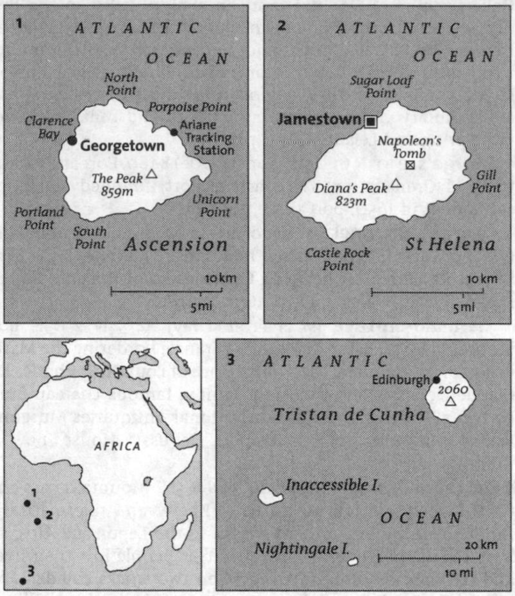

☐ International Airport

[heleena] (UK British Dependent territory)

Timezone GMT

Area 122 km²/47 sq mi

Population total (2000e) 7200

Capital Jamestown (on St Helena Island)

Physical features Volcanic group of islands in the S Atlantic, 1920 km/1200 mi from the SW coast of Africa; includes St Helena, Ascension, Gough I, Inaccessible I, Nightingale I, and Tristan da Cunha; rugged, volcanic terrain; highest point, Diana's Peak, 823 m/2700 ft.

Climate Tropical marine; mild, tempered by SE 'trade' winds.

Currency 1 St Helena Pound (£) = 100 pence

Economy Fish (mostly tuna); agriculture, coffee; postage stamps; heavily subsidized by the UK.

GDP (1998e) $18 mn, per capita $2500

History Discovered by the Portuguese on St Helena's feast day, 1502; annexed by the Dutch, 1633; annexed by the East India Company, 1659; Napolean exiled here, 1815–21; Ascension and Tristan da Cunha made dependencies, 1922; evacuated between 1961–3, following volcanic eruption; governed by an executive council and 12-member elected Legislative Council.

French, taken by the British, 1762; airport; railway; university (1925); two cathedrals; shipbuilding, fish processing, timber; Signal Hill (where first wireless message received by Marconi, 1901), Colonial Building (1850).

St John's wort An annual or perennial, sometimes a shrub, native throughout temperate regions and tropical mountains; leaves gland-dotted, opposite or whorled, very narrow to oval; flowers often large and showy, yellow, 5-petalled with numerous stamens; fruit a capsule or berry. (Genus: *Hypericum*, 400 species. Family: Guttifereae.)

Saint-Just, Louis (Antoine Léon Florelle) de [sī zhüst] (1767–94) French revolutionary, born in Decize, C France. He studied at Soissons and Reims, then studied law, and while in Paris began to write poetry and essays, notably *L'Esprit de la révolution* (1791, Spirit of the Revolution). He was elected to the National Convention (1792), attracted notice by his fierce tirades against the king, and as a devoted follower of Robespierre was sent on diplomatic and military missions. He joined the Committee of Public Safety (1793), contributing to the destruction of Danton and Hébert, became president of the Convention (1794), and sponsored the radical Ventôse Laws, redistributing property to the poor. He was guillotined with Robespierre in the Thermidorian Reaction.

St Kilda 57°49N 8°34W. A group of small volcanic islands in the Atlantic Ocean, 100 km/62 mi W of Scotland, UK; abandoned in 1930, having been inhabited for 2000 years; cliffs (over 400 m/1400 ft) colonized by over a million sea birds; a world heritage site.

St Kitts-Nevis *p.1343*

Saint-Laurent, Yves (Henri Donat Mathieu) [sī lohrã] (1936–) Fashion designer, born in Oran, N Algeria. He studied in Paris, graduating in modern languages, and was employed by Dior in 1955 after winning an International Wool Secretariat design competition. On Dior's death in 1957, he took over the house. In 1962 he opened his own house, and launched the first of his 160 Rive Gauche boutiques (1966), selling ready-to-wear clothes, a trend which many other designers were to follow. He also creates costumes for theatre, ballet, and films, and in 1985 was awarded a Best Fashion Designer Oscar.

St Lawrence River, Fr **St Laurent** A principal river of North America, in E Canada, the chief outlet for the Great Lakes; issues from NE end of L Ontario and flows NE to the Gulf of St Lawrence N of the Gaspé Peninsula; forms part of border between Canada and USA; total length 1197 km/744 mi; Thousand Islands rapids in Ontario used for hydroelectric power; several lakes along its course; major tourist area; tidal below Quebec, and increases gradually in width to c.145 km/90 mi; principal cities on its banks include Kingston, Montreal, Trois-Rivières, Quebec; formerly navigable for ocean-going vessels only as far as Montreal; St Lawrence Seaway (1955–9) between L Ontario and Montreal now allows passage to Great Lakes; often partly unnavigable in winter months.

St Lawrence Seaway A system of canals, locks and dredged waterways providing a navigable channel from the Atlantic and the Gulf of St Lawrence to all of the Great Lakes. In 1954 the Canadian and US governments co-operated on a project to establish a shipping lane 8 m/27 ft deep along the St Lawrence R; this was completed in 1959. The Welland Ship Canal is generally considered to be part of the present-day seaway.

Saint Leger, Barry [**sel**injer, saynt **le**jer] (1737–89) British army colonel, who fought in the American Revolution. He is best known as the founder of the Classic horse race at Doncaster, South Yorkshire. First run in 1776, it was named after him in 1778 (always with the latter pronunciation).

St Leger *Classics*

St-Lô [sī **loh**], ancient **Briovera**, later **Laudus** 49°07N 1°05W, pop (2000e) 23 900. Market town and capital of Manche department, NW France, 54 km/34 mi W of Caen; fortified by Charlemagne; almost completely destroyed in World War 2, but mediaeval part of town largely preserved; railway; horse breeding; 14th–15th-c Church of Notre-Dame (restored), Romanesque Church of Ste-Croix (restored).

St-Louis (Senegal) [sī **looee**] 16°01N 16°30W, pop (2000e) 136 000. Seaport capital of Saint-Louis region, Senegal; on a small island at the mouth of the R Sénégal, 177 km/110 mi NE of Dakar; built in 1658 on Sor I as a French trading company fort, and prospered with the slave trade; capital of French West Africa, 1895–1902; airfield; railway terminal; transportation point for surrounding area, fishing.

St Louis (USA) [saynt **loo**is] 38°37N 90°12W, pop (2000e) 241 000. City and port in E Missouri, USA, on the Mississippi R; settled by the French, 1764; under Spanish control, 1770–1800; ceded to the USA, 1804; city status, 1822; railway; three universities (1818, 1853, 1960); largest city in the state; busiest inland port on the Mississippi; a major land transport hub; aircraft, spacecraft, machinery, metal and food products, chemicals, beer, fur trade, livestock, grain; professional teams, Cardinals (baseball), Blues (ice hockey); Gateway Arch (a giant steel

St Kitts-Nevis

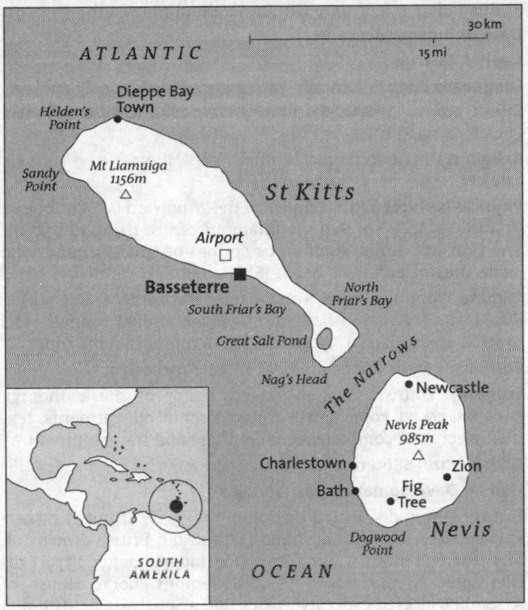

☐ International Airport

official name **Federation of St Kitts and Nevis**, with **Christopher** a former alternative for **Kitts**

Local name Saint Christopher (Kitts) and Nevis

Timezone GMT −4

Area 269 km^2/104 sq mi

Population total (2002e) 46 200

Status Independent state within the Commonwealth

Date of independence 1983

Capital Basseterre

Languages English (official), with creole-English widely spoken

Ethnic groups Black African descent (94%), mulatto (3%), White (1%)

Religions Christian (Anglican 36%, Methodist 32%, other Protestant 8%, Roman Catholic 11%)

Physical features Located in the N Leeward Is, E Caribbean; comprises the islands of St Christopher (St Kitts), Nevis, and Sombrero; volcanic origin with mountain ranges rising to 1156 m/3793 ft at Mt Liamuiga; Nevis dominated by a central peak rising to 985 m/3232 ft.

Climate Tropical, warm climate; average annual temperature 26°C; average annual rainfall 1375 mm/54 in; low humidity, modified by sea winds; hurricanes possible (Jul-Oct).

Currency 1 East Caribbean Dollar (EC$) = 100 cents

Economy Sugar and its products (supply 60% of total exports); copra, cotton, electrical appliances, footwear, garments, tourism.

GDP (2002e) $339 mn, per capita $8800

Human Development Index (2002) 0·814

History St Kitts was the first British colony in the W Indies, 1623; control disputed between France and Britain, 17th-18th-c; ceded to Britain, 1783; St Kitts and Nevis united, 1882; area gained full internal self-government, 1967; Anguilla declared itself independent from the control of St Kitts, which led to British troops intervention, 1969; island reverted to being a British dependent territory, 1971, and was formally separated from St Kitts-Nevis, 1980; independence of St Kitts-Nevis, 1983; British monarch represented by a Governor-General; governed by a Prime Minister and two legislative chambers; island of Nevis has its own legislature (the Nevis Island Assembly), and executive, which has exclusive responsibility for the island's internal administration; Nevis I voted in favour of secession, 1997.

Head of State

(British monarch represented by Governor-General)
1983–96 Sir Clement Athelston Arrindell
1996– Sir Cuthbert Montroville Sebastian

Head of Government

1983–95 Kennedy Alphonse Simmonds
1995– Denzil Douglas

arch on the river bank, 192 m/630 ft high, symbolizing the city as the gateway to the West); Art Museum, Science Center, Missouri Botanical Garden, Goldenrod Showboat, Sports Hall of Fame; Ragtime and Jazz Festival (Jun), Veiled Prophet Fair (Jul).

St Lucia *p.1344*

St-Malo [sĩ mahloh] 48°39N 2°00W, pop (2000e) 51 600. Old port in Ille-et-Vilaine department, W France; at mouth of R Rance; badly damaged in World War 2; boatbuilding, fishing, electrical products, tourism; birthplace of Chateaubriand; tidal power station nearby.

St Mark's Cathedral, Ital **San Marco** A church constructed in 1063–71 on the site of a 9th-c shrine which housed the relics of St Mark, in Venice. It is built on a Byzantine Greek-cross plan, and is surmounted by five mosaic-covered domes. The richly decorated interior is faced with marble and mosaic. It became a cathedral in 1807.

St Michael and St George, Most Distinguished Order of In the UK, an order of chivalry for those who have held high office or rendered distinguished service abroad or in foreign affairs; in practice most members belong to the diplomatic service. There are three classes: Knights and Dames Grand Cross (GCMG), Knights and Dames Commanders (KCMG/DCMG), and Companions (CMG). The motto is *Auspicium melioris aevi* (Lat 'a pledge of better times'), and the ribbon has equal stripes: blue, scarlet, blue.

St Moritz [morits], Ger **Sankt Moritz**, Fr **Saint** [sĩ] **Moritz**, Romansch **San Murezzan** 46°30N 9°51E, pop (2000e) 5700. Resort town in Graubünden canton, SE Switzerland, in the Upper Engadine valley; altitude 1853 m/6079 ft; railway; spa; winter sports resort, home of the 1928 and 1948 Winter Olympics; facilities include a high ski-jump and the Cresta Run (bobsledding); Schiefer Turm.

St-Nazaire [sĩ nazair] 47°17N 2°12W, pop (2000e) 69 100. Seaport and industrial town in Loire-Atlantique department, W France; on right bank of R Loire at its mouth, 53 km/33 mi WNW of Nantes; thought to occupy site of Roman Carbilo; developed as deep-water port for Nantes in 19th-c; major debarkation port for American Expeditionary Force in World War 1; German submarine base in World War 2, in which the town was largely destroyed; shipbuilding, marine engineering, steel, fertilizers, brewing, food canning.

St Paul 44°57N 93°06W, pop (2000e) 287 200. Capital of state in Ramsey Co, SE Minnesota, USA; a port on the Mississippi River E of its twin city Minneapolis; founded, 1840; capital of Minnesota Territory, 1849; city status, 1854; state capital, 1858; railway; university (1854); major industrial and commercial centre for a vast agricultural region; computers, electrical equipment, motor vehicles, chemicals, beer; State Capitol, modelled after St Peter's in Rome, with the largest unsupported marble dome in the world; Winter Carnival (Feb), Festival of Nations (Apr).

saintpaulia *African violet*

St Paul's Cathedral A Baroque cathedral on Ludgate Hill, London, UK, built by Wren between 1675 and 1710 to replace the mediaeval cathedral destroyed by the Fire of London in 1666. It is surmounted by a central lantern dome which still dominates the C London skyline.

St Lucia

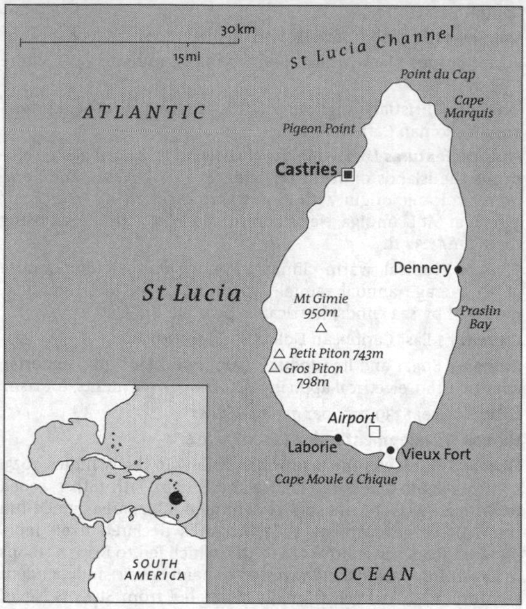

☐ International Airport

[loosha]

Local name Saint Lucia

Timezone GMT −4

Area 616 km^2/238 sq mi

Population total (2002e) 160 000

Status Independent state within the Commonwealth

Date of independence 1979

Capital Castries

Languages English (official), with French patois widely spoken

Ethnic groups African descent (90%), mixed (6%), East Indian (3%), Caucasian (1%)

Religions Christian (Roman Catholic 90%, Protestant 7%, Anglican 3%)

Physical features Second largest of the Windward Is, E Caribbean. Volcanic island; forested mountainous centre rising to 950 m/3117 ft at Mt Gimie; sulphurous springs of Qualibou and twin peaks of Gros and Petit Pitons (SW).

Climate Tropical climate; average temperature 26°C; wet season (Jun–Dec), dry season (Jan–Apr); average annual rainfall 1500 mm/60 in (lowlands), 3500 mm/138 in (mountainous zone).

Currency 1 East Caribbean Dollar (EC$) = 100 cents

Economy Tourism (fastest-growing sector of the economy); bananas, cocoa, copra, citrus fruits, coconut oil; garments, textiles, electronic components; oil refining and transshipment.

GDP (2002e) $866 mn, per capita $5400

Human Development Index (2002) 0·772

History Reputedly visited by Columbus, 1502; disputed ownership between England and France, 17th-18th-c; British Crown Colony, 1814; full internal autonomy, 1967; independence, 1979; British monarch represented by a Governor-General; House of Assembly, elected every five years, and a Senate; constitutional amendment approved (Jul 2003) to replace oath of allegiance to Queen Elizabeth II with an oath to St Lucia and its people.

Head of State
(British monarch represented by Governor-General)
1997– Perlette Louisy

Head of Government
1997– Kenny Anthony

St Peter's Basilica The largest Christian church, started in 1506 in Rome on the site of the 4th-c basilica built by Emperor Constantine. The present building was designed by Bramante on a Greek cross plan. This was adopted by successive architects, including Raphael and Michelangelo, but in 1605 Maderna was instructed to extend the nave, thereby changing the plan to that of a Latin cross. The immense dome, designed by Michelangelo and completed by Giacomo della Porta and Domenico Fontana, has a diameter of 42 m/137 ft.

St Petersburg, Russ **Sankt Peterburg**, formerly **Petrograd** (1914–24), **Leningrad** (1924–91) 59°55N 30°25E, pop (2000e) 4 994 000. Seaport in NW European Russia; on the R Neva and its islands, at the head of the Gulf of Finland; largest Russian Baltic port (frozen, Jan–Apr) and second largest Russian city; former capital of the Russian Empire (1712–1918); founded by Peter the Great, 1703; leading centre in the October Revolution, 1917; scene of a major siege by Germany in World War 2 (1941–4), in which nearly a million died; airport; railway junction; university (1819); Academy of Sciences (1726); nuclear power equipment, ships, tractors, machine tools, precision optical instruments, solar research; famous for its 18th–19th-c architecture and many bridges over the Neva; Winter Palace (1754–62, rebuilt 1839) now part of the State Hermitage Museum, St Isaac Cathedral (19th-c), Kazan Cathedral (1801–11), Fortress of Peter and Paul (1703), St Nicholas Navy Cathedral (1753–62); over 60 museums; White Nights art festival (Jun).

St Pierre et Miquelon [sĩ pyair ay meeklõ] pop (2000e) 7000; area 240 sq km/93 sq mi. Two islands comprising a French overseas department in the N Atlantic Ocean, S of Newfoundland; main town, St Pierre; settled by Breton and Basque fishermen, 16th–17th-c; disputed between UK and France, 19th-c; confirmed as French territory, 1946; fishing, tourism.

St-Quentin [sĩ kãtĩ] 49°51N 3°17E, pop (2000e) 65 000. Industrial town in Aisne department, N France, on R Somme; railway; centre of woollen industry in Middle Ages; canal link to Belgium and N Germany; surrounded by battlefields throughout World War 1; chemicals, metalworks, electrical products, textiles; 12th–15th-c basilica, late-Gothic town hall, museum of entomology.

Saint-Saëns, (Charles) Camille [sĩ sãs] (1835–1921) Composer and music critic, born in Paris, France. He began to compose at five, and studied at the Paris Conservatoire, writing his first symphony in 1853. He was a distinguished pianist and organist, and in 1871 helped to found the Société Nationale de Musique. He wrote four further symphonies, 13 operas, of which the best known is *Samson et Dalila* (1877), and the popular *Carnaval des animaux* (1886, Carnival of the Animals). He also wrote piano, violin, and cello concertos, church music (including his *Messe solennelle*, 1855), chamber music, and songs.

St-Savin sur Gartempe, Church of [sĩ savĩ sür gah(r)tãmp] An abbey church in St-Savin, W France; a world heritage monument. The original building, which was founded in 811 by Charlemagne over the tomb of the hermit St Savinus, was soon destroyed. The present building dates from the 11th-c, and is noted for its life-sized murals depicting biblical scenes.

Saint-Simon, Claude Henri de Rouvroy, comte de (Count of) [sĩ seemõ] (1760–1825) Social reformer, the founder of French Socialism, born in Paris, France. He served in the American War of Independence, and during the French Revolution was imprisoned as an aristocrat. Lavish expenditure reduced him to poverty, and he turned to writing. His writing was a reaction against the savagery of the revolutionary period, and proclaimed a brotherhood of man in which science and technology would become a new spiritual authority. His books include *Du*

St Vincent

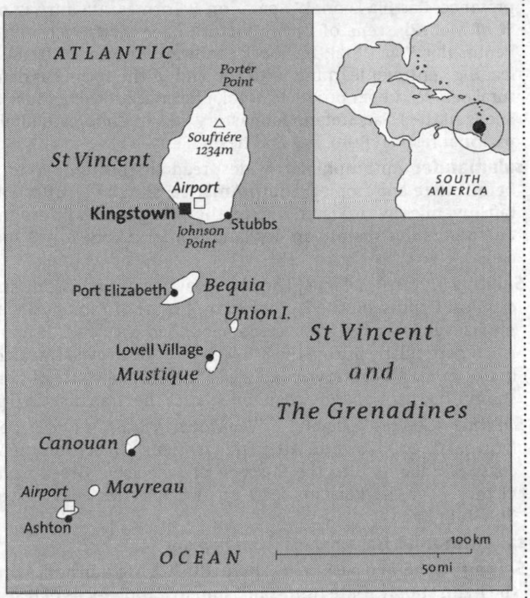

☐ International Airport

official name **Saint Vincent and the Grenadines**

Local name Saint Vincent and the Grenadines

Timezone GMT −4

Area 390 km²/150 sq mi

Population total (2002e) 113 000

Status Independent state within the Commonwealth

Date of independence 1979

Capital Kingstown

Languages English (official), with French patois widely spoken

Ethnic groups Black African descent (82%), mixed (14%), White, Asian, and Amerindian minorities

Religions Christian (Anglican 42%, Methodist 21%, Roman Catholic 12%)

Physical features Island group of the Windward Is, E Caribbean, comprising the island of St Vincent and the N Grenadine Is; St Vincent volcanic in origin; highest peak, Soufrière, active volcano 1234 m/4048 ft (N), most recent eruption, 1979.

Climate Tropical climate, average annual temperature, 25°C; average annual rainfall 1500 mm/60 in (coast), 3800 mm/150 in (interior).

Currency 1 East Caribbean Dollar (EC$) = 100 cents

Economy Based on agriculture; bananas, arrowroot (world's largest producer), coconuts, spices, sugar cane; food processing, textiles; tourism.

GDP (2002e) $339 mn, per capita $2900

Human Development Index (2002) 0·733

History Visited by Columbus, 1498; British control in 1763; part of West Indies Federation, 1958–62; achieved internal self-government, 1969; independence, 1979; British sovereign represented by a Governor-General; a Prime Minister leads a unicameral National Assembly.

Head of State
(British monarch represented by Governor-General)
1996–2002 Charles Antrobus
2002– Sir Freddy Ballantyne

Head of Government
2000–1 Arnhim Eustace
2001– Ralph Gonsalves

système industriel (1821, On the Industrial System) and *Nouveau christianisme* (1825, New Christianity). In his later years, he relied on family and friends to survive, and lost an eye following an attempted suicide in 1823.

Saint-Simon, Louis de Rouvroy, duc de (Duke of) [sĩ seemõ] (1675–1755) Writer, born in Paris, France. After some time in the army, he joined the court of Louis XIV, and from the 1690s kept a journal, published as his *Mémoires* (1752), giving impressions and descriptions of court life up to 1723.

Saints, the *Clapham Sect*

St Swithin's Day *Swithin, St*

St Thomas pop (2000e) 53 600; area 72 sq km/28 sq mi. One of the three main US Virgin Is, Lesser Antilles, Caribbean, 64 km/40 mi N of St Croix; length, 21 km/13 mi; rises to 474 m/1555 ft at Crown Mt; capital, Charlotte Amalie; airport; tourism, rum distilling; Coral World underwater observatory.

St-Tropez [sĩ trohpay] 43°16N 6°39E, pop (2000e) 6100. Fashionable resort on the Mediterranean coast, SE France, SW of Cannes; former small fishing port now frequented by yachtsmen, artists, and tourists.

St Valentine's Day (14 Feb) A day on which special greetings cards (**valentine cards** or **valentines**) are sent, usually anonymously, to a person or people to whom one feels attracted. The saint ostensibly commemorated on this day was an obscure 3rd-c Roman priest, and none of the traditions connected with 14 February have anything to do with him. There is a traditional English belief that birds choose their mates on this day.

St Vincent *see panel*

St Vincent, Cape, Port **Cabo de São Vicente** 37°01N 8°59W. Rocky headland 60 m/200 ft above sea-level on the Atlantic coast, Portugal; SW extremity of Portugal and of continental Europe; in the 12th-c a ship bearing the body of St Vincent came ashore here; scene of a British naval victory over the Spanish fleet in 1797.

St Vitus' dance *chorea*

Saipan [siypan] pop (2000e) 48 300; area 122 sq km/47 sq mi. Largest of the N Mariana Is, W Pacific, 240 km/150 mi NE of Guam; length 23 km/14 mi; barrier reef protects a wide lagoon off the W coast; loss of Saipan in June 1944, bringing Tokyo within range of US bombers, was a serious blow to Japan in World War 2, and brought down the Tojo government; airport; tourism, copra, tropical fruit.

saithe [sayth] Commercially important codfish (*Pollachius virens*) widely distributed in inshore waters of the N Atlantic; length up to 1·2 m/4 ft; dark green on back, sides and underside silvery-grey; feeds on other fishes and crustaceans; popular with sea anglers; also called **coalfish**, **coley**, or **pollock**. (Family: Gadidae.)

Saka Era [sahka] An era of dating in India calculated from AD 78. Possibly founded by Kaniska, it was certainly used early in the 2nd-c AD by Western Satraps, rulers in W India, and was also present in Sanskrit inscriptions in SE Asia. It has been used alongside Gregorian dates by the Indian Government since 1957.

Sakai [sakaee] 34°35N 135°28E, pop (2000e) 825 000. Second largest city in Osaka prefecture, SC Honshu, Japan, on E shore of Osaka-wan Bay; important self-governing port, 14th–15th-c, but overtaken by Osaka in 16th-c, and now silted up; two universities; chemicals, fertilizers, aluminium products, machinery; early 5th-c imperial tomb.

saké [sakay] A Japanese rice wine, brewed in Japan for centuries, and very popular in winter. The drink has sweeter and drier varieties, and special, first-, and second-class grades. It is generally warmed in small bottles and drunk from small cups. Leaving your cup full means you have had enough. Saké is also presented to Shinto shrines, especially at New Year.

Sakhalin [sakaleen], Jap **Karafuto** area 74 066 sq km/28 589 sq mi. Island in the Sea of Okhotsk, E Russia, separated from the Russian mainland (W) by the Tatar Strait, and from Japan (S) by La Pérouse Strait; length 942 km/585 mi; maximum width

160 km/100 mi; highest point 1609 m/5279 ft; first Russian visit, 1644; colonized by the Japanese, 18th-c; ceded to Russia in exchange for the Kuril Is, 1875; became Russia's most notorious penal colony; Japan gained control of S area, 1905; ceded to the USSR, 1945; two parallel mountain ranges run N–S; agriculture in the C and S; severe climate, annual mean temperature near freezing point; largely forested; oil, coal, timber, paper, dairy farming.

Sakharov, Andrey [sakarof] (1921–89) Physicist, born in Moscow, Russia. He studied in Moscow, joined the nuclear weapons research group (1948), and is usually credited with a critical role in developing the Soviet hydrogen bomb. He became a full member of the Academy of Sciences in 1953. In 1958 he openly opposed nuclear weapon tests, thereafter supporting East–West co-operation and human rights, and in 1975 was awarded the Nobel Peace Prize. Exiled to Nizhni Novgorod (formerly Gorky) in 1980 as a leading dissident, he lived under poor conditions until released in 1986 and restored to favour. He was elected to the Congress of People's Deputies in 1989.

Sakhmet or **Sekmet** [sakmet] An ancient Egyptian goddess of Memphis, depicted with the head of a lioness; her name means 'powerful'. She is associated with savage cruelty, in particular towards the enemies of the Pharaoh.

Saki *Munro, H H*

saki [sakee] A New World monkey; coat long, especially around face; tail long; broad mouth turns downwards at sides, producing a sad expression; lives in groups of up to 10 along river banks or forest edges. (Genus: *Pithecia*, 4 species.)

Sakigake and Suisei project [sakeegakay, sooisay] The first Japanese interplanetary spacecraft, launched to intercept Halley's comet. *Sakigake* ('forerunner') was launched (Jan 1985) as a test spacecraft for *Suisei* ('comet', launched Aug 1985). They were instrumented to measure solar wind interaction and the hydrogen cloud of the comet. They made successful encounters (11 and 8 Mar 1986 respectively) at substantially greater distances from the nucleus than other spacecraft in the 'Halley Armada' (VEGA and Giotto). They were built and operated by the Institute for Space and Astronautical Science.

salad burnet *burnet*

Saladin [saladin], in full **Salah al-Din Yussuf ibn Ayub** (1137–93) Sultan of Egypt and Syria, the leader of the Muslims against the crusaders in Palestine, born in Tekrit, Mesopotamia. He entered the service of Nur al-din, Emir of Syria, and on his death (1174) proclaimed himself sultan, asserted his authority over Mesopotamia, and received the homage of the Seljuk princes of Asia Minor. His remaining years were occupied in wars with the Christians, whom he defeated near Tiberias in 1187, recapturing almost all their fortified places in Syria. The Third Crusade, headed by the kings of France and England, captured Acre in 1191, and he was defeated.

Salado, River [salathoh], Span (**Río**) River forming part of a C Argentine system; rises as the Bermejo in W La Rioja province, flowing S then SE to join the R Colorado 240 km/150 mi W of Bahía Blanca; lower course sometimes called the Curacó; total length, 1200 km/750 mi; this river must be distinguished from the **R Salado del Norte**, NC Argentina, which rises in the Andes, and flows 2000 km/1250 mi SE to the Paraná at Santa Fe.

Salam, Abdus (1926–96) Theoretical physicist, born in Jhang Maghiana, C Pakistan. He studied at Punjab University and Cambridge, and became professor of mathematics at the Government College of Lahore and at Punjab University (1951–4). He lectured at Cambridge (1954–6), and became professor of theoretical physics at Imperial College, London (1957), and founder-director of the International Centre for Theoretical Physics in Trieste (1964), renamed the Abdus Salam International Centre for Theoretical Physics following his death. In 1979 he shared the Nobel Prize for Physics with Steven Weinberg and Sheldon Glashow for their theory combining both the weak nuclear force and electromagnetic interactions between elementary particles; their predictions were confirmed experimentally in the 1970s and 1980s.

Salamanca [salamangka], ancient **Helmantica** or **Salmantica** 40°58N 5°39W, pop (2000e) 165 000. Capital of Salamanca province, Castilla-León, W Spain; on R Tormes, 212 km/132 mi W of Madrid; scene of British victory over the French in the Peninsular War (1812); bishopric; railway; university (1218), a leading centre of learning until the end of the 16th-c; agricultural centre, rubber products, wool, pharmaceuticals; House of Shells (15th-c), San Stefano monastery, old and new cathedrals; patronal festival (Jun), fair and fiesta (Sep).

salamander An amphibian widespread in the temperate N hemisphere and tropical South America; slim body with long tail; juveniles live in water, with feather-like gills and fin around tail; adults live mainly on dry land. (Order: Urodela, 358 species.)

Salamis (Cyprus) [salamis] The principal city of prehistoric and classical Cyprus, on the E coast 8 km/5 mi N of Famagusta, its mediaeval and modern successor. Founded c.1075 BC, it flourished particularly during the 8th–4th-c BC. Destroyed by earthquake in AD 332–42, it was rebuilt as the Christian city of Constantia, but permanently abandoned after the Arab raids in 647.

Salamis (Greece) [salamis] or **Koulouri** 37°58N 23°30E, pop (2000e) 22 100. Town in Attica department, Greece, on the W coast of Salamis I; to the E, scene of a decisive Greek naval victory over the Persians, 480 BC; local ferries; Navy Week (Jun–Jul).

sal ammoniac [sal amohniak] *ammonium*

Salang Tunnel and pass in the Hindu Kush, E Afghanistan; along the main supply route from Tajikistan to Kabul; focus of resistance activity by the Mujahideen guerrillas against the Soviet troops and the Afghan Army during the occupation of Afghanistan (1979–89).

Salazar, António de Oliviera [salazah(r)] (1889–1970) Portuguese dictator (1932–68), born near Coimbra, C Portugal, where he studied law, and taught economics. In 1928 he became minister of finance, with extensive powers. As premier, he introduced a new, authoritarian regime, the *Estado Novo* ('New State'). He was also minister of war (1936–44) and of foreign affairs (1936–47) during the delicate period of the Spanish Civil War, in which he supported Franco. He maintained Portuguese neutrality during World War 2. He retired following a stroke in 1968.

Salcantay, Nevado [nayvahdoh salkantiy] 13°18S 72°35W. Andean peak in SC Peru, 72 km/45 mi NW of Cuzco; highest point in the Cordillera Vilcabamba at 6271 m/20 574 ft; Machu Picchu to the N.

Salchow, (Karl Emil Julius) Ulrich [salkoh] (1877–1949) Swedish figure skater, born in Copenhagen, Denmark. The first man to win an Olympic gold medal for this sport (1908), he was a record 10 times world champion (1901–5, 1906–11) and nine times European title holder between 1898 and 1913. He was the originator of a type of jump performed in the free-style element of figure skating, and since named after him.

Sale (Australia) 38°06S 147°06E, pop (2000e) 15 300. City in SE Victoria, Australia; railway; supply centre for the Bass Strait oil fields; Omega Navigation Tower (427 m/1400 ft), the highest building in Australia; oil and natural gas display; regional arts centre; tourism.

Sale (UK) 53°26N 2°19W, pop (2000e) 57 100. Town in Greater Manchester, NW England, UK; 8 km/5 mi SW of Manchester; railway; engineering.

Salem (Massachusetts) [saylem] 42°31N 70°53W, pop (2000e) 40 400. Seat of Essex Co, NE Massachusetts, USA; residential suburb of Boston on Massachusetts Bay; settled, 1626; developed as port serving East Indies trade; 20 people executed as witches here, 1692; railway; birthplace of Nathaniel Hawthorne; Witch Museum, Salem Maritime National Historic Site, Pioneer Village.

Salem (Oregon) [saylem] 44°56N 123°02W, pop (2000e) 136 900. State capital in Marion Co, NW Oregon, USA; on the Willamette R; founded by Methodist missionaries, 1841; capital of Oregon

Territory, 1851; state capital, 1859; railway; university (1842); food processing, high technology equipment, metal goods.

Salerno [salairnoh] 40°40N 14°46E, pop (2000e) 162 000. Industrial town and capital of Salerno province, Campania, SW Italy; 50 km/31 mi SE of Naples, on a bay of the Tyrrhenian Sea; founded by the Romans, 197 BC; one of the earliest universities in Europe, a notable school of medicine (10th-c, closed 1812); scene of major World War 2 fighting, after Allied landing (1943); archbishopric; railway; new university (1970); milling, engineering, cement, textiles; cathedral (11th-c); Castello di Arechi.

Sales, Francis of *Francis of Sales, St*

sales tax A tax levied on goods sold, usually a percentage of the price. It is levied in the USA by most states, at differing rates, and on most products. The retail price quoted may include the sales tax element.

Salford [sawlferd] 53°30N 2°16W, pop (2001e) 216 100. City in Greater Manchester, NW England, UK; on the R Irwell and Manchester Ship Canal, W of Manchester; chartered in 1230; designated a city in 1926; university (1967); railway; docks for Manchester; textiles, electrical engineering, chemicals, clothing; Roman Catholic cathedral (1848); Peel Park Museum; art gallery.

Salians *Franks*

Salic Law In normal usage, a rule of succession to the throne barring women, and men whose royal descent is only through females. The principle was established in France from 1316, partly by ingeniously invoking the law-code of the Salian Franks, issued c.511 and given definitive form c.798 – Salic Law (Lat *Lex Salica*) in its original sense.

salicylic acid [salisilik] A drug first prepared from an extract of meadowsweet (*Spirea ulmaria* – hence the word *aspirin*), and in 1838 from an extract of willow bark; its salt, *sodium salicylate*, was first used therapeutically for rheumatic pains and feverish cold in 1875. It was superseded in 1899 by the more potent *acetylsalicylic acid* (aspirin).

Salieri, Antonio [salyayree] (1750–1825) Composer, born in Verona, NE Italy. He arrived in Vienna at 16, and worked there for the rest of his life, becoming court composer (1774) and *Hofkapellmeister* (1788). He wrote over 40 operas, an oratorio, and Masses, and became a famous rival of Mozart.

Salinger, J(erome) D(avid) [salinjer] (1919–) Novelist and short-story writer, born in New York City, USA. Educated at public schools, he studied for a while at New York and Columbia universities, and after serving in the army in World War 2 devoted himself to writing. He graduated from popular magazines to the *New Yorker*, but his fame rests on *The Catcher in the Rye* (1951), his only and enduringly popular novel (which sells 250 000 copies annually). Its hero plays truant from boarding-school and goes to New York, where he tries in vain to lose his virginity. Written in a slick and slangy first-person narrative, it provoked a hostile response from some critics, but this did not prevent it becoming a college set text. His small collections of short stories include *Franny and Zooey* (1961), and two long short stories, *Raise High the Roof Beam, Carpenters* and *Seymour: an Introduction* (1963). He has become a recluse in his later years, living in New Hampshire, but allowed publication of *Hapworth 16, 1924* (first published in 1965) as a novella in 1997.

salinity The saltiness of seawater, ie the total amount of dissolved substances in seawater, usually reported in parts per thousand (‰), grams of solute per kilogram of seawater. The average salinity of ocean water is about 35‰.

Salisbury (Rhodesia) [sawlzbree] *Harare*

Salisbury (UK) [sawlzbree], sometimes called **New Sarum** 51°05N 1°48W, pop (2001e) 114 600. City in Wiltshire, S England, UK; at the junction of the Avon, Nadder, Bourne, and Wylye Rivers, 34 km/21 mi NW of Southampton; Old Sarum (3 km/1¾ mi N), Iron Age hill fort, later the centre of settlement, but abandoned when New Sarum was founded in 1220 (though continued to return two members to parliament until the passing of the Reform Bill, 1832); Duke of Buckingham beheaded here in 1483, when Salisbury was the headquarters of Richard III; railway; engineering, tourism, agricultural trade; 13th-c cathedral, with the highest spire in Britain, contains one of four copies of the Magna Carta; Churches of St Thomas (15th-c), St Martin (13th–15th-c) and St Edmund (1407).

Salisbury, Marquess of [sawlzbree] *Cecil, Robert*

Salisbury Plain [sawlzbree] A chalk plateau of open downs in Wiltshire, S England, UK, rising to an average of 140 m/450 ft and covering some 77 700 ha/192 000 acres. Much of the area is now either under cultivation or used for army training, but it remains remarkable for its prehistoric sites, particularly Stonehenge.

Salish [saylish] North American Indian groups, part of the Plateau Indian culture, speaking a language of the Algonkian–Wakashan family; also called **Flatheads**. They originally settled between the Rocky Mts and the Cascade Mts in present-day British Columbia, Washington, Idaho, and Montana. Today they are mostly settled on small reservations, working as farmers and labourers. They are also known as **interior Salish**, to distinguish them from the culturally different **coastal Salish**.

saliva A secretory product of insect and terrestrial vertebrate salivary glands. In the latter it is a clear, often sticky solution of salts and proteins. It includes *mucin*, which binds food together and lubricates the throat to facilitate swallowing, and sometimes (eg in humans) the enzyme *α-amylase* (*ptyalin*), which aids starch digestion. Anti-coagulants are often present in the saliva of blood-sucking insects.

salivary glands Glands which secrete saliva, consisting of an excreting part (the *alveoli* or *acini*), and ducts which transport the saliva to the oral cavity. In humans there are three pairs of large glands (*parotid*, *submandibular*, and *sublingual*) and numerous small glands (in the palate, tongue, lips, and cheeks) which open directly onto the surface of the oral mucous membrane. The secretion of saliva is under the control of both the parasympathetic and sympathetic nervous systems.

Salk, Jonas (Edward) [sawlk] (1914–95) Virologist, discoverer of the first vaccine against poliomyelitis, born in New York City, USA. He studied at New York University College of Medicine, worked on an influenza vaccine at Michigan (1942–4), and later became director of virus research (1947–9) and professor (1949–54) at Pittsburgh. In 1953–4 he prepared inactivated poliomyelitis vaccine, given by injections, which (after some controversy) was successfully tested. He was a founding director of the Salk Institute, CA, in 1975.

sallow Any of several species of willow with broad, greyish leaves, and catkins (the 'pussy willows' of hedgerows) appearing before the leaves. (Family: Salicaceae.)

salmon Large, anadromous (ascending rivers to breed) fish (*Salmo salar*), widespread and locally common in the N Atlantic (**Atlantic salmon**) and in NW North America (**Pacific salmon**); length up to 1·5 m/5 ft; adults undertake extensive migrations at sea, feeding on a variety of fishes and crustaceans, returning to the headwaters of freshwater rivers to breed; greatly prized as game fish, and also taken commercially at sea; with the trouts and chars, comprise the very important family, Salmonidae.

Salmonella [salmonela] A genus of rod-shaped, typically motile bacteria that can grow with or without oxygen. Two species cause typhoid and paratyphoid fever respectively; other species cause food poisoning. The main source of infection is contaminated meat, particularly poultry. Acute vomiting and diarrhoea occur 12–24 hours after eating contaminated food. (Kingdom: Monera. Family: Enterobacteriaceae.)

Salome [salohmee] (1st-c) The traditional name of the daughter of Herodias. She danced before Herod Antipas (*Mark* 6.17–28), and was offered a reward. At her mother's instigation, she was given the head of John the Baptist. However, the incident is not recorded in the historical account by Josephus.

Salon [salõ] In France, an exhibition of art by members of the French Royal Academy, originating in 1667 and held then in the

Salon d'Apollon of the Louvre Palace, Paris; held annually since the time of the French Revolution. In the 19th-c the selection jury refused to hang many of the Impressionist and Postimpressionist painters, whose work was then shown (1863 and 1883) in the **Salon des Refusés**. The **Salon des Indépendents** is an annual art exhibition first held in Paris in 1884. In recent years, the term has come to be applied to other kinds of exhibition, such as the book-fair, **Salon du Livre**.

Salonga [salongga] area 36 560 sq km/14 112 sq mi. National park in Democratic Republic of Congo; a world heritage site; established in 1970; main rivers include the Salonga, Lomela, and Luilaka.

Salonica *Thessaloníki*

Salote Tupou III [salohtay] (1900–65) Queen of Tonga, who succeeded her father, King George Tupou II, in 1918. She is remembered in Britain for her colourful and engaging presence during her visit for the coronation of Elizabeth II in 1953.

salp *tunicate*

salsa A type of popular dance music of Cuban–Puerto Rican origin, taken to the E USA in the 1940s and 1950s, since when it has both merged with jazz and absorbed other influences such as rock, while retaining its distinctive rhythm. From the late 1980s it became absorbed into world popular music. The word originated as a culinary term, describing a spicy sauce.

salsify A plant, usually biennial (*Tragopogon porrifolius*), growing to 125 cm/50 in, native to the Mediterranean region; cylindrical taproot; leaves grass-like; flower-heads solitary, violet-purple, surrounded by about eight bracts; fruit with a large feathery parachute of hairs. It is widely grown for its edible fleshy root, and sometimes as an ornamental. (Family: Compositae.)

SALT [sawlt] Acronym for **Strategic Arms Limitation Talks**, held between the USA and USSR. There were two rounds of talks. The first began in Helsinki in 1969, designed to place a numerical limit on intercontinental nuclear weapons in the hope of slowing down the arms race. An agreement (SALT 1) was reached in 1974. After this there was a hardening of attitudes in the West against the intentions of the USSR, largely because of its refusal to allow on-site verification and its other international activities (eg the invasion of Afghanistan). In consequence, SALT 2 (1979) was not ratified by the US Senate, which felt it set dangerous precedents for SALT 3, and it was withdrawn. Both sides have, however, kept to the limitations set. With the end of the Cold War, the USA and Russia moved to reduce rather than merely limit nuclear weapons and the focus shifted to the Strategic Arms Reduction Talks (START).

salt An ionic compound derivable in principle from the reaction of an acid with a base. Most salts are solids at normal temperatures, and dissolve in water to release positive and negative ions (cations and anions). Common salt is sodium chloride (NaCl), obtained from mineral deposits or the evaporation of salt waters. Salt monopolies have been economically important throughout history.

Salta [salta] 24°46S 65°28W, pop (2000e) 416 400. Capital of Salta province, NW Argentina; on the R Arias, in the Lerma valley; altitude 1190 m/3904 ft; founded, 1582; site of battle in which Spanish royalists were defeated (1813); airport; railway; university (1967); commercial and trade centre for extensive farming, timber, stock-raising, and mining area; cathedral contains venerated Christian images sent from Spain in 1592, and thought to have caused a miracle in September 1692, when an earthquake ceased on their being carried through the streets; large parade held (Sep) in celebration of this event.

Saltillo [salteeyoh] 25°30N 101°00W, pop (2000e) 530 000. Resort capital of Coahuila state, N Mexico, 85 km/53 mi SW of Monterrey; altitude 1609 m/5279 ft; founded, 1575; railway; university (1867, refounded 1957); agricultural trade, textiles, ceramics, coal mining; cathedral (18th-c); fiestas (Oct).

Salt Lake City 40°45N 111°53W, pop (2000e) 181 700. State capital in Salt Lake County, N Utah, USA; on the Jordan R, near the S end of the Great Salt Lake; settled by Mormons, 1847; expanded as centre on route to California gold mines; world centre of the Mormon Church (60% of the population are Mormons); railway; university (1850); processing centre for irrigated agricultural region; aerospace components, electronic equipment, processed foods, agricultural chemicals; silver, lead, and copper smelting plants; professional team, Utah Jazz (basketball); Temple Square, Trolley Square, Salt Lake Art Center, Utah Museum of Fine Arts, Pioneer Memorial Museum, Hansen Planetarium, Utah Museum of Natural History; Utah Arts Festival (Jun).

saltpetre *potassium*

saltwort A prickly, much-branched annual (*Salsola kali*), native to the N hemisphere; stems red-striped; leaves narrow, very succulent, spine-tipped; flowers tiny, green. It is salt-tolerant, growing on sandy shores. (Family: Chenopodiaceae.)

saluki [salookee] The fastest breed of dog (speeds recorded up to 69 kmh/43 mph), developed in Arabia to hunt in the desert with Bedouin; oldest of the greyhound group; resembles the greyhound, with long hair on ears, tail, and backs of legs (a smooth-haired form also exists); also known as **Arabian hound** or **gazelle hound**.

Salut, Iles du [eel dü salü] Island archipelago c.13 km/8 mi off the coast of French Guiana, NE South America; includes Ile Royale, Ile Saint Joseph, and Ile du Diable (Devil's I); housed notorious French penal colonies from 1898; last prisoners left in 1953; political prisoners on Devil's I included Alfred Dreyfus; hotel on Ile Royale is the warders' former mess hall.

Salvador [salvadaw(r)], also known as **Bahia** 12°58S 38°29W, pop (2000e) 2 364 000. Port capital of Bahia state, NE Brazil, on the Atlantic coast SE of Recife; European discovery, 1501; founded 1549, capital of Brazil until 1763; airfield; railway; university (1946); trade in sugar, tropical fruit, cocoa, sisal, soya beans, gemstones; tobacco, food processing, oil refining, petrochemicals, tourism; most of the city's churches and the fortifications date from the 17th–18th-c; older parts of the upper city are a national monument and world heritage site; government palace, city library (1811), fort of Santo Antônio da Barra (1580); carnival (Nov–Jan); the most African city in W hemisphere (former centre of slave trade), especially in local food, dress, music.

Salvador, El *El Salvador*

salvage Compensation paid by the owner to someone (the **salvor**) who voluntarily saves life or maritime property (a ship or its cargo) from loss or damage. The service must be rendered at sea or in tidal waters. A salvor may claim an award in the courts, where he or she has acted voluntarily. Salvage may also be the subject of prior agreement between the salvor and the property owner. The rules apply equally to aircraft, but no award of salvage can be made unless the aircraft was over the sea or tidal waters at the time the help was given. The award covers services given to save life, or the wreck of or cargo from aircraft.

Salvarsan *arsenicals*

Salvation Army A non-sectarian Christian organization founded in the East End of London by William Booth in 1865, dedicated to minister to the poor and needy. It retains a military-style structure and evangelical atmosphere, and its members, both men and women, wear distinctive uniform. In 2004 it was working in some 110 countries.

salvia A member of a large genus of tropical and temperate annual or perennial herbs and shrubs; stems square; leaves in opposite pairs; flowers 2-lipped, the upper often hooded. The flower shape and colour are closely geared to pollinators. The New World species, pollinated by birds, typically are red, and have flowers with long straight tubes. In other species the flowers range from cream to red, mauve, or blue, are often curved, and are pollinated by long-tongued bees. Popular garden plants include the scarlet-flowered annual *Salvia splendens*. Some are aromatic herbs. (Genus: *Salvia*, 700 species. Family: Labiatae.)

sal volatile [sal volatilee] *ammonium*

Salween, River *Thanlwin, River*

Salyut (Russ 'salute') **space station** [salyoot] The first-generation Soviet space station, capable of docking with the Soyuz crew ferry and Progress resupply vehicle; it provided 100 m³/3500 cu ft of living space for up to five cosmonauts. Two versions have been flown in a programme spanning 1971 to the present, aimed at accumulating data on long-duration space-flight experience and biomedical experiments, Earth remote sensing, and microgravity science. The first station was flown in 1971, the last (Salyut 7) in 1982. The station's orbit eventually decayed, with the vehicle re-entering the atmosphere and burning up. Crews have accumulated many hundred days of flight experience. A notably dangerous repair mission was undertaken to Salyut 7 in 1985, by V Dzhanibekov and V Savinykh, after the station seriously malfunctioned between crew occupancies.

Salzburg [**zahl**tsboorg] 47°25N 13°03E, pop (2000e) 150 000. Capital of Salzburg state, C Austria; on the R Salzach; Old Town between the left bank of the river and the Mönchsberg ridge; railway; university (re-opened 1962); archbishopric; textiles, brewing, metallurgy; cathedral (1614–28), St Peter's Church (1130–43), Franciscan Church, Kollegienkirche (1694–1707), town hall (originally 1407); fortress of Hohensalzburg (1077) dominates the town; a focal point for the international tourist trade; birthplace of Mozart, a fame reflected in the Mozarteum (musical academy) and the Mozart Festival (Jan); Easter Festival, Salzburg Festival (Jul–Aug).

Salzburg Alps [**zahl**tsboorg] A division of the Eastern Alps along the Austro-German border S of Salzburg; highest peaks are the Hochkönig (2938 m/9639 ft) in Austria, and the Watzmann (2713 m/8901 ft) in Germany.

Salzkammergut [**zalts**kamergut] E Alpine region in C Austria; popular tourist area with many lakes; mountains include Dachstein and Totes Gebirge; towns include Gmunden, Hallstatt, Bad Aussee; name originally applied to a salt-mining area around Bad Ischl.

Samara [sa**mah**ra], formerly (1935–91) **Kuybyshev** 53°10N 50°10E, pop (2000e) 1 250 000. River-port in EC European Russia; on the R Volga where it meets the R Samara; founded as a fortress, 1586; Soviet government transferred here in World War 2, 1941–3; airport; railway; university (1969); machines, metalworking, oil refining, foodstuffs.

Samaranch, Juan Antonio [sama**ranch**] (1920–) Seventh president of the International Olympic Committee (IOC), born in Barcelona, Spain. He was elected to the IOC in 1966, and elected president in 1980. He received much criticism following allegations of corruption within the IOC in 1998–9 over the bids of various cities to host the Olympics, but he is also credited with ensuring the financial success of the IOC through sponsorship deals and television rights at competitive levels. On his retirement as president of the IOC in 2001, he was conferred with the title of honorary life president.

Samaria [sa**mair**ia] The site in C Palestine of the ancient capital of the N kingdom of the Hebrews, Israel. Destroyed by the Assyrians c.722 BC, Herod the Great rebuilt and enlarged it in the 20s BC. It remained a flourishing Greek-style city throughout the Roman period. It is now in the Israeli-occupied West Bank.

Samaritans **1** A sect of Jewish origin, living in Samaria, the N territory of Israel, who apparently were not deported in the Assyrian conquest of c.721 BC and who were in tension with the Jews of Judea during the rebuilding of Jerusalem after the return from exile and well into New Testament times. Jews criticized them for their mixed ancestry, their building of a rival temple on Mt Gerizim, and their schism from true Judaism. A small remnant survives today.
2 A group founded in London in 1953 by an Anglican priest, Chad Varah (1911–), providing a telephone counselling service to support those who are depressed or contemplating suicide. It is named after the 'Good Samaritan' in the parable of Jesus. By 2004 there were 203 branches in the UK and Ireland operated by some 21 000 volunteers. A free, confidential, and anonymous service is offered 24 hours a day.

Samarkand [samah(r)**kand**] 39°40N 66°57E, pop (2000e) 430 300. Capital city of Samarkandskaya oblast, Uzbekistan; a major industrial, scientific, and cultural centre situated in the fertile Zeravshan valley; on Chinese northern Silk Road from 2nd-c BC; conquered by Chinese army, 42 BC; Abbasid capital, 9th–10th-c; Chinese influence, 12th-c; known as the city of Timur (1333–1405), after the Tatar conqueror; ruled by the Uzbeks, 16th–19th-c; it is a world heritage site; airfield; railway; university (1933); solar research, fruit, wine, furniture, porcelain, clothing, foodstuffs, sheepskins, silk, cotton; Gur Amir mausoleum.

samba A Brazilian dance which existed in various rural and urban forms, always accompanied by singing, before it was taken up as a ballroom dance in the 1930s. Lively, syncopated rhythms are a dominant feature.

Samhain [**sow**uhn] One of the Celtic quarterly feasts. It was celebrated on 1 November to mark the beginning of winter when, it was believed, the way to the 'other world' was opened and the dead could return to communicate with the living. There are many tales of mysterious happenings at Samhain.

samizdat [sam**iz**dat] (Russian *sam*, 'self' + *izdatelstvo*, 'publishing') Privately circulated editions of book-length and shorter texts not authorized for publication by the State censorship in the former USSR, and usually reproduced from typescript. The publishing of such work abroad was known as **tamizdat** (Russian *tam*, 'there').

Samoa *p.1350*

Samoa (American) *American Samoa*

Samos [**say**mos] pop (2000e) 43 800; area 476 sq km/184 sq mi. Wooded island in the E Aegean Sea, Greece, separated from W coast of Turkey by a strait only 2 km/1¼ mi wide; rises to 1440 m/4724 ft in the W; birthplace of Pythagoras; site of the Heraion; commerce, wine, tourism.

Samothrace [**sam**ohthrays], Gr **Samothráki** pop (2000e) 4250; area 178 sq km/69 sq mi. Greek island in the NE Aegean Sea, 40 km/25 mi from the mainland; rises to 1600 m/5249 ft; noted for its sanctuary of the Great Gods, and for the 'Victory of Samothrace' sculpture (Louvre, Paris).

Samoyed (anthropology) *Nenets*

Samoyed (zoology) [**sam**oyed] An active spitz breed of dog, developed in Siberia; medium-sized with an extremely thick coat of straight pale hairs; tail carried over back only when alert, loosely curled.

samphire A fleshy, much-branched perennial (*Crithmum maritimum*), growing to 30 cm/12 in, native to coastal areas of Europe, the Mediterranean, and the Black Sea; leaves divided into narrow linear segments, circular in cross-section; flowers yellowish, in umbels 3–6 cm/1¼–2½ in across. The fleshy leaves are sometimes made into a pickle. (Family: Umbelliferae.)

Sampras, Pete (1971–) Tennis player, born in Washington, District of Columbia, USA. He turned professional in 1988, and went on to become the youngest men's US Open champion (1990), a title he subsequently won in 1993, 1995, 1996, and 2002. The most successful player of his generation, his other notable achievements include the Association of Tennis Professionals Tour World Championship title (1991, 1994, 1996–7), Wimbledon singles title (1993–5, 1997–2000), and he also reached Number 1 in the world rankings in seven successive years (1993–2000). In 2000 he set a new milestone by winning his seventh Wimbledon singles, in the process setting a new world record of 13 Grand Slam titles. He announced his retirement in 2003. He started the fund-raising 'Aces for Charity' (participants give $100 to charity for every ace served) in 1997.

Samson (c.11th-c BC?) Biblical character, a legendary hero of the tribe of Dan, purportedly the last of Israel's tribal leaders ('judges') prior to Samuel and the establishment of the monarchy under Saul. Stories (*Jud* 13–16) tell of his great strength, his battles against the Philistines, his 20-year rule, and his fatal infatuation with Delilah. When she cut his hair, breaking his

Samoa

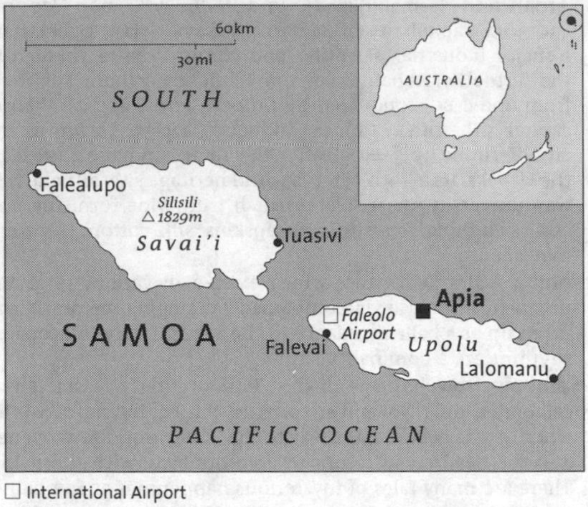

(Western) [samoha], formerly (to 1997) **Western Samoa**, official name **The Independent State of Samoa**

Local name Samoa i Sisifo (Samoan)

Timezone GMT −11

Area 2842 km²/1097 sq mi

Population total (2002e) 178 000

Status Independent state within the Commonwealth

Date of independence 1962

Capital Apia

Languages Samoan and English (official)

Ethnic groups Polynesian, with Pacific Islanders, Euronesian, Chinese, and European minorities

Religions Christian (99%) (Protestant 70%, Roman Catholic 20%, other 9%)

Physical features Two large (Upolu, Savai'i) and seven small islands in the South Pacific Ocean, 2600 km/1600 mi NE of Auckland, New Zealand; formed from ranges of extinct volcanoes, rising to 1829 m/6001 ft on Savai'i; last volcanic activity, 1905–11; thick tropical vegetation; several coral reefs along coast.

Climate Tropical climate; cool, dry season (May–Nov), average temperature 22°C; rainy season (Dec–Apr) with temperatures reaching 36°C; average annual rainfall, 2775 mm/109 in; frequent hurricanes.

Currency 1 Tala (WS$) = 100 sene

Economy Largely agricultural subsistence economy; taro, yams, breadfruit, pawpaws, coconuts, cocoa, bananas; tourism increasing; internal transportation system depends largely on roads and ferries; charter air service operates between the two main islands.

GDP (2002e) $1 bn, per capita $5600

Human Development Index (2002) 0·715

History Visited by the Dutch, 1772; 1889 commission divided Samoa between Germany (which acquired Western Samoa) and the US (which acquired Tutuila and adjacent small islands, now known as American Samoa); New Zealand granted a League of Nations mandate for Samoa, 1919; UN Trust Territory under New Zealand, 1946; independence, 1962; became a member of the Commonwealth, 1970; governed by a Monarch as Head of State for life, a Prime Minister, and a 47-member Legislative Assembly (Fono).

Head of State (O le Ao O le Malo)
1963– Malietoa Tanumafili II

Head of Government
1982 Tupuola Taisi Efi
1982–6 Tofilau Eti
1986–8 Va'ai Kolone
1988–98 Tofilau Eti Alesana
1998– Tuila'epa Sa'ilele Malielegaoi

Nazirite vow, he lost his strength, and was held by the Philistines until his hair grew back and he pulled down their temple upon them.

Samsova, Galina (1937–) Ballet dancer and director, born in Russia. She studied at the State Ballet School, Kiev, joined the Kiev Opera House (1956–60), and became principal dancer with the National Ballet of Canada (1961–4), the London Festival Ballet (1964–73), the New London Ballet (1973–8), and Sadlers Wells Royal Ballet (1980–90, also as a teacher). In 1991 she was appointed artistic director of the Scottish Ballet.

Samudragupta [samudragupta] (?–c.380) North Indian emperor with a reputation as a warrior, poet, and musician. He epitomized the ideal king of the golden age of Hindu history.

Samuel (Heb probably 'name of God') (11th-c BC) Biblical character, the last of the judges and first of the prophets, the son of Elkanah and his wife Hannah. He was an Ephraimite who was dedicated to the priesthood as a child by a Nazirite vow. After the defeat of Israel and loss of the Ark of the Covenant to the Philistines, he tried to keep the tribal confederation together, moving in a circuit among Israel's shrines. He presided, apparently reluctantly, over Saul's election as the first king of Israel, but later criticized Saul for assuming priestly prerogatives and disobeying divine instructions given to him. Samuel finally anointed David as Saul's successor, rather than Saul's own son, Jonathan.

Samuel, Books of Two books of the Old Testament, which were one in the Hebrew Bible and probably were also once combined with *Kings*; also called **1** and **2 Kings**, in some Catholic versions. They present a narrative of Israel's history from the time of the prophet Samuel and Israel's first king Saul (*1 Sam*) to the story of David's accession and reign (*2 Sam*). They are probably a compilation from several, partially-overlapping sources, with a late editing after the Exile.

Samuel Johnson Prize Literary prize established in 1999 to celebrate the variety and originality of contemporary non-fiction published in the UK. Sponsored anonymously by a British businessman, the annual prize is worth £30 000 to the winner, with the other shortlisted authors receiving £2500 each. The prize is open to works in the areas of current affairs, history, politics, science, sport, travel, biography, autobiography, and the arts.

Samuelson, Paul (Anthony) (1915–) Economist and journalist, born in Gary, Indiana, USA. He studied at Chicago and Harvard universities, and became professor at the Massachusetts Institute of Technology (1940–85). His classic publication, *Foundations of Economic Analysis* (1947), is a treatise on his work in economic theory, for which he was awarded the Nobel Prize for Economics in 1970.

Samuelsson, Bengt (Ingemar) (1934–) Biochemist, born in Halmstad, SW Sweden. He studied at Stockholm University, where he became a professor in 1967. He shared the 1982 Nobel Prize for Physiology or Medicine for discoveries concerning prostaglandins and related substances.

samurai [samuriy] Japanese warrior-gentry. After 1192 the Kamakura elaborated a military feudal system: knights (*samurai*) held land from lords (*daimyo*) for military service. Educated in Chinese Confucian ethics, they were expected to display such virtues as frugality, incorruptibility, loyalty, self-sacrifice, and valour, and to avoid dishonour by ritual suicide. They became involved in administration under the Tokugawas (17th–19th-c), and began to move from the land into castle-towns. Shinto bushido developed from samurai ethics under the later Tokugawas, influencing the Japanese army's officer class pre-1945. Samurai legends were popular in Kabuki theatre, and are enjoyed in Japanese films today.

San *Khoisan*

Sana [sanah] 15°27N 44°12E, pop (2000e) 638 400. Political capital of Republic of Yemen; former capital of North Yemen; on a high plateau of the Arabian peninsula, altitude 2170 m/7119 ft; c.65 km/40 mi inland from al-Hudaydah, its port on the Red Sea; walled city, a world heritage site; university (1970); textiles, cement; Great Mosque, museum of S Arabian antiquities.

San Andreas Fault A major fault in the Earth's crust running for about 950 km/600 mi through NW California to the Colorado Desert. It marks the boundary between the Pacific and American crustal plates, which are slipping past each other at an average rate of 1 cm/³⁄₈ in a year. Sudden movements can cause earthquakes, the most notable of which devastated San Francisco in 1906. Serious movement also occurred in 1989, 1993, and 1994.

San Andrés-Providencia [san andrays provithensia] pop (2000e) 47 600; area 44 sq km/17 sq mi. Intendencies of Colombia, comprising two small islands and seven groups of coral reefs and cays in the Caribbean; 480 km/300 mi N of Colombia; largest island, San Andrés; Providencia (also called Old Providence), 80 km/50 mi NE of San Andrés; San Andrés was the headquarters of pirate Henry Morgan in 17th-c; part of Columbia since 1822; a duty-free zone; important international airline stopover; coconuts, vegetable oil, tourism.

San Antonio 29°25N 98°30W, pop (2000e) 1 144 600. Seat of Bexar Co, SC Texas, USA, on the San Antonio R; eighth largest city in the USA; settled by the Spanish, 1718; captured by the Texans in the Texas Revolution, 1835; scene of the Mexican attack on the Alamo, 1836; five different flags flown during the city's history (Spain, Mexico, Republic of Texas, Confederate States of America, USA); airport; railway; two universities (1852, 1869); military aviation centre; industrial, trade, and financial centre for a large agricultural area; processed foods, aircraft, electronic equipment, building materials, chemicals, wood products, clothing, machinery; educational, artistic, and cultural centre; tourism; professional team, Spurs (basketball); the Alamo, Paseo del Rio (the Spanish Governor's palace), Museum of Art, Institute of Texan Cultures, Tower of the Americas (229 m/750 ft high); Fiesta San Antonio (Apr), Folklife Festival (Aug).

sanction In international law, penalties imposed by one state against another in an attempt to force compliance with international law or the fulfilment of treaty obligations. Aside from war, two kinds of sanctions are recognized. *Retorsion* is a lawful act designed to injure another state, such as the withdrawal of economic aid. *Reprisals* are acts ordinarily illegal, but which in classical international law are made lawful on account of a prior unlawful act committed by the other state. The UN Security Council has power to authorize and enforce sanctions against states by its members, though the UN Charter has created doubts about the rights of individual states to legally impose sanctions, especially in the form of reprisals.

Sand, George [sã, zhaw(r)zh], pseudonym of **(Amandine) Aurore (Lucile) Dudevant**, *née* **Dupin** (1804–76) Novelist, journalist, and feminist, born in Paris, France. She left her husband (Baron Dudevant) and family in 1831, and returned to Paris to take up literature, becoming the companion of those poets, artists, philosophers, and politicians whose work she found inspiring. After 1848 she settled at Nohant, where she spent the rest of her life in literary and political activity, varied by travel. Her first novel, *Indiana* (1832), was followed by over 100 books, the most successful being those describing rustic life, such as *François le champi* (1848), which sparked Marcel's discovery of his vocation as a writer in Proust's *A la recherche du temps perdu*. She also wrote plays, autobiographical works (notably about her open relationships with de Musset and Chopin), and letters. Her protest against social conventions and class restrictions can be found in novels such as *Consuelo* (1842–3).

sand Grains of rock and mineral with sizes between 63 μm and 2 mm (0·0025–0·079 in), formed by the physical weathering of rocks, and composed of resistant minerals (usually quartz) not destroyed during weathering. **Black sand**, containing volcanic rock, and **coral sand** also occur. Accumulations of sand can be formed by the action of waves on coastal beaches, and by the wind in deserts. Quartz-rich sand is used as an industrial source of silica for glassmaking and in cement.

sandalwood A hemiparasitic tree (*Santalum album*) native to SE Asia; leaves opposite, oval; flowers rather inconspicuous, red, with 4-lobed bells. A fragrant timber is obtained from the white outer wood, used for carvings, incense, and joss sticks. Sandal oil is made from the yellow heartwood, and the roots are used for perfume and soap. (Family: Santalaceae.)

Sanday, Edgar *Faure, Edgar*

Sandburg, Carl (August) (1878–1967) Poet, born in Galesburg, Illinois, USA. After trying various jobs, fighting in the Spanish–American War, and graduating from Lombard College, he became a journalist in Chicago, and started to write for *Poetry*. His work reflects industrial America, and includes *Chicago Poems* (1915) and *Good Morning, America* (1928). His *Complete Poems* gained him the Pulitzer Prize in 1950. Interested in American folksongs, he published a collection in *The American Songbag* (1927). His popular two-part biography, *Abraham Lincoln: the Prairie Years* (1926) and *Abraham Lincoln: the War Years* (1939), was awarded the Pulitzer Prize in history (1940).

sand dollar A flattened, disk-like sea urchin found burrowing in soft sediments of shallow tropical and temperate seas; tubular feet arranged in a petal-like pattern on the upper body surface, serving a respiratory function; c.130 living species. (Class: Echinoidea. Order: Clypeasteroida.)

sand dune A heaped accumulation of wind-driven sand with a shape determined by the speed and direction of the wind. Dunes slowly migrate with the wind direction, as sand particles are blown up the gentle slope and fall down the steep slope. They are characteristic of sandy deserts, such as the Sahara.

sanderling A pale sandpiper (*Calidris alba*) native to the N hemisphere; inhabits tundra and (in winter) coasts; eats minute crustaceans; follows edges of breaking waves on shore.

sandfly A small, hairy fly commonly found in moist, shady habitats; some feed by sucking blood of vertebrates, including humans; may act as carriers of diseases, such as leishmaniasis. (Order: Diptera. Families: Psychodidae and Phlebotamidae.)

sandgrouse A bird native to Africa, Asia, and S Europe; resembles a plump pigeon; inhabits open country; eats seeds, shoots, and insects; males transport drinking water to chicks by saturating feathers on underparts. (Family: Pteroclididae, 16 species.)

sand hopper A semiterrestrial crustacean, with a flattened body, capable of vigorous jumping; often abundant along the sea shore, feeding on detritus; also known as a **beach flea**. (Class: Malacostraca. Order: Amphipoda)

Sandhurst *Royal Military Academy, Sandhurst*

San Diego [san deeaygoh] 32°43N 117°09W, pop (2000e) 1 223 400. Seaport seat of San Diego Co, SW California, USA, on the E shore of San Diego Bay, just N of the Mexico border; sixth largest city in the USA; first permanent white settlement in California; naval and marine base; airport; railway; four universities; shipbuilding, food processing, aerospace industries, tourism; cultural, convention, and research centre; professional teams, Padres (baseball), Chargers (football); early 19th-c adobe buildings in the Old Town district; San Diego de Alcalá mission (established 1769 by Junípero Serra and now restored), the first mission in California; Serra Museum; Cabrillo National Monument; aquatic park, zoo.

Sandino, Augusto César [sandeenoh] (1895–1934) Nicaraguan revolutionary, born in Niquinohome (or La Victoria), W Nicaragua. He led guerrilla resistance to USA occupation forces after 1926, and was later murdered, on the orders of Somoza, near

Managua. The Nicaraguan revolutionaries of 1979 (later known as *Sandinistas*) took him as their principal hero.

Sandjak of Novi Pazar, Serbo-Croat **Sandžak**, Turkish **Sancak** Historical province of the Ottoman Empire, comprising 8000 sq km/3000 sq mi on both sides of the border between Serbia and Montenegro. Under Ottoman rule before 1912, the region was garrisoned by Austria–Hungary from 1879 to 1908 in order to keep Serbia and Montenegro apart. Conquered by and partitioned between Serbia and Montenegro (1912), it was absorbed into the Yugoslav state in 1918. Reconstituted as a potential federal unit by the communist-led Partisans 1943–5, Sandjak was instead divided again between Montenegro and Serbia at the end of World War 2. By 1992 it was a potential flashpoint in the wars of Yugoslav succession, with more than half of its 400 000 population composed of Slav Muslims.

sand lizard A lizard of the family Lacertidae, native to Europe and W Asia (*Lacerta agilis*); brown or green with small dark rings and two pale lines along back; inhabits heathland and sandy areas; eats mainly insects. The name is also used for some other species in this family (eg of genus *Psammodromus*).

Sandown 50°39N 1°09W, pop (2000e) 17 200 (with Shanklin). Town in Isle of Wight, S England, UK; on Sandown Bay, S of Ryde and N of Shanklin; home of the poet Swinburne; railway; boatbuilding, electrical goods, tourism.

sandpiper A wading bird, widespread, mostly native to the N hemisphere, migrating to the S during the N winter; long legs and bill; inhabits swamps or coasts; eats invertebrates and some berries. The name is sometimes restricted to only some species in this family. (Family: Scolopacidae, c.86 species.)

sand spurrey A slender, sprawling annual or biennial (*Spergula rubra*), native to much of the temperate N hemisphere, especially on light, lime-free soils; narrow, opposite leaves; silver-brown leaf-like projections; flowers pink, 5-petalled. (Family: Caryophyllaceae.)

sandstone A sedimentary rock composed of grains of sand (usually quartz) cemented together by a matrix, usually silica or calcium carbonate. It may be formed through deposition by water in marine or freshwater environments, or by wind action (as dunes). It is quarried as a building stone.

Sandwich, John Montagu, 4th Earl of (1718–92) British politician, remembered as the inventor of *sandwiches*, which he supposedly devised in order to eat while playing around the clock at a gaming-table. He was First Lord of the Admiralty under both Henry Pelham and Lord North (1748–51, 1771–82), and was frequently attacked for corruption and incompetence. The Sandwich (Hawaiian) Is were name after him by Captain Cook.

Sandwich Island *Efate*

San Francisco 37°47N 122°25W, pop (2000e) 776 700. City co-extensive with San Francisco Co, W California, USA; bounded W by the Pacific Ocean, N by the Golden Gate, E by San Francisco Bay; built on a series of hills; connected to Marin Co (N) by the Golden Gate Bridge and to Oakland (E) by the Transbay Bridge; Golden Gate Bridge is one of the longest single-span suspension bridges in the world (1280 m/4200 ft, excluding the approaches); mission and pueblo founded by the Spanish, 1776 (named Yerba Buena); Mexican control, 1821; taken by the US Navy, 1846; renamed San Francisco, 1848; grew rapidly after the discovery of gold nearby; from the 1860s developed as a commercial and fishing port; terminus of the first transcontinental railway, 1869; devastated by earthquake and fire, 1906; several areas seriously damaged by earthquake, 1989; tram (cable-car); railway; airport; four universities, including Berkeley (1868) and Stanford (1891); financial and insurance centre of W coast; trade in fruit, cotton, mineral ores; fishing, textiles, printing, plastic and rubber products, shipbuilding, aircraft and missile parts; major tourist, cultural, and convention centre; professional teams, Giants (baseball), 49ers (football); largest Chinatown in the USA; Mission Dolores (1782), Cow Palace (shows, exhibitions, conventions, circuses), Museum of Art, Civic Center complex at City Hall, Fisherman's Wharf, Nob Hill mansions; Alcatraz I in San Francisco Bay, site of the first lighthouse on the California coast and of a Federal prison (1934–63).

Sangay [sangiy] 2°00S 78°20W. Active Andean volcano, EC Ecuador; rises to 5230 m/17 159 ft; Sangay National Park established in 1975; area 2770 sq km/1069 sq mi; a world heritage site.

Sanger, Frederick (1918–) Biochemist, born in Rendcombe, Gloucestershire, SWC England, UK. He studied in Cambridge, and worked there throughout his career, after 1951 at the Medical Research Council Unit. By the mid-1950s he had secured a notable success through experimental work which revealed the full sequence of the 51 amino acids in insulin, for which he was awarded the Nobel Prize for Chemistry in 1958. He then worked on the problems of the nucleic acids, and devised new methods to elucidate molecular structures for these also. His Nobel Prize for Chemistry in 1980 made him the first to receive two such awards.

Sanger, Margaret (Louise), *née* **Higgins** (1879–1966) Social reformer and founder of the birth control movement, born in Corning, New York, USA. Educated at Claverack College, she became a trained nurse. Appalled by the high rates of infant and maternal mortality in a poor area of New York City, she published a radical feminist magazine, *The Woman Rebel* (1914), with advice on contraception. She started the first US birth-control clinic in New York City in 1916, but was charged with creating a 'public nuisance', and imprisoned for 30 days. After a world tour, she founded the American Birth Control League in 1921. Her many books include *What Every Mother Should Know* (1917) and *My Fight for Birth Control* (1931).

sangha [sangga] The community of *bhikkus* – those who have formally committed themselves to pursuing the Buddhist way of life and to living in accord with the set of rules known as the Patimokkha. It began with the first disciples of Buddha, and remains influential and widespread today.

Sanhedrin [sanhedrin] (Gr 'council', also called by Josephus the *gerousia*, Gr 'senate') A Jewish council of elders meeting in Jerusalem, which during the Graeco-Roman period acquired internal administrative and judicial functions over Palestinian Jews, despite foreign domination. Convened by the high priest, its membership numbered 71, although local courts with this designation outside Jerusalem had fewer members (usually 23 or just 3) and more limited jurisdiction. After the fall of Jerusalem in AD 70, the Jerusalem Sanhedrin was effectively replaced by a new court of sages at Jabneh.

sanicle A perennial (*Sanicula europaea*) growing to 60 cm/2 ft, native to woods in Europe, Asia, and Africa; leaves mostly basal, glossy and dark green, divided into 5–7 wedge-shaped lobes with toothed margins; flowers white or pink, in dense rounded umbels; fruit thickly covered with hooked bristles. (Family: Umbelliferae.)

San Joaquin River [san wakeen] River in C California, USA, in the S part of the Central Valley; rises in the Sierra Nevada; joins the Sacramento R just above Suisin Bay; 510 km/317 mi long; major tributaries the Fresno, Merced, Mariposa; connected with the Sacramento R in the Central Valley Project to increase irrigation, flood-control, and hydroelectricity.

San Jorge, Golfo [san khorkhay], Eng **Gulf of St George** Broad inlet of the Atlantic in S Argentina; extends 235 km/146 mi N–S between Cabo Dos Bahías (N), where there is a penguin rookery, and Cabo Tres Puntas (S); 160 km/100 mi W–E; port of Comodoro Rivadavia on W shore.

San José (Costa Rica) [san hohzay] 9°59N 84°04W, pop (2000e) 355 900. Capital city of Costa Rica, on the Pan-American Highway, in a broad fertile valley of the Meseta Central; altitude 1150 m/3773 ft; founded, 1737; capital, 1823; laid out in regular grid pattern; airport; railway; university (1940); coffee, tobacco, food processing, flowers, footwear, chemicals, electronics; cathedral, national theatre, national museum.

San Jose (USA) [san hohzay] 37°10N 121°53W, pop (2000e) 894 900. Seat of Santa Clara Co, W California, USA, in the fertile

Santa Clara Valley, at head of San Francisco Bay; first city in the state, 1777; state capital, 1849–51; railway; university; electronics, food processing, high technology, guided missiles.

San Juan [san **hwan**] 18°29N 66°08W, pop (2000e) 422 000. Seaport capital of Puerto Rico, E Caribbean; on an island linked to the N coast of the mainland by a bridge; founded, 1510; birthplace of Ricardo E Alegría; airport; two universities (1912, 1950); cigars, tobacco, sugar, clothing, tourism; El Morro (1591, old Spanish fortress), cathedral (16th-c), Church of San José (16th-c), La Fortaleza (1533–40), Castillo de San Cristóbal (old fortress).

Sankara [sangkara, shangkara] (?700–?750) Hindu philosopher and theologian, born in Kalati, Kerala, SE India. The author of commentaries on the Hindu Scriptures, and founder of monastic centres in different parts of India, he is the most famous exponent of *Advaita* (the Vedanta school of Hindu philosophy), and the source of the main currents of modern Hindu thought. In this approach, Brahma alone has true existence, and the goal of the self is to become one with the Divine. His views were strongly opposed by Ramanuja and his successors.

Sankey, Ira David *Moody, Dwight Lyman*

Sankt Gallen *St Gallen / St Moritz* (under **Saint**)

San Lorenzo An early Olmec ceremonial centre in Veracruz province, Mexico. Occupied from c.1500 BC, it flourished c.1200–900 BC until succeeded by La Venta. On a partly artificial plateau c.50 m/160 ft high and 1·25 km/0·8 mi long stood c.200 houses with a population of c.1000 sustained by maize agriculture, hunting, and fishing. The site is notable for its sculpture, which includes colossal basalt heads up to 2·3 m/8 ft high and 20 tonnes weight.

San Luis Potosí [san looees potosee] 22°10N 101°00W, pop (2000e) 633 000. Capital of San Luis Potosí state, NC Mexico, NW of Mexico City; altitude 1877 m/6158 ft; founded as a Franciscan mission; seat of the Juárez government, 1863; railway; university (1826); mining centre; refining of silver and arsenic, footwear, clothing; cathedral, Casa de la Cultura, Palacio de Gobierno (1770), Church of San Francisco.

San Marino (city) [san mareenoh] 43°56N 12°26E, pop (2000e) 2500. Capital city of San Marino, C Italy, on Monte Titano; accessible only by road; surrounded by three enclosures of walls, including many gateways, towers, and ramparts; basilica, St Francis's Church, governor's palace.

San Marino *see panel*

San Martín, José de [san mah(r)teen] (1778–1850) South American patriot, born in Yapeyú, Argentina. He played a major role in winning independence from Spain for Argentina, Chile, and Peru. In 1817 he led an army across the Andes into Chile, defeating the Spanish at Chacubuco (1817) and Maipó (1818). He then captured Lima, and became Protector of Peru (1821), but resigned the following year after failing to reach an agreement with Bolívar, and died an exile in France.

San Miguel de Tucumán or **Tucumán** [san meegel thay tukuman] pop (2000e) 563 400. Capital of Tucumán province, NW Argentina; on the R Salí; busiest city in N Argentina; founded, 1565; many colonial buildings; site of defeat of Spanish royalists in 1812; two universities (1914, 1965); airport; railway; sugar refining, tourism; cathedral.

San Pedro Sula [soola] 15°26N 88°01W, pop (2000e) 404 000. Industrial centre of Honduras, and capital of Cortés department; second largest city in Honduras; airport; railway; trade in bananas, coffee, sugar, timber; textiles, zinc roofing, furniture, cement, plastics, steel rolling.

San Salvador [san salvadaw(r)] 13°40N 89°18W, pop (2000e) 591 300. Capital city of El Salvador, on the R Acelhuate; altitude, 680 m/2230 ft; founded, 1525; destroyed by earthquake, 1854; capital, 1839; railway; food processing, textiles, commerce; cathedral; International Industrial Fair (Nov, every two years).

San Salvador de Jujuy or **Jujuy** [san salvathor thay khookhooee] 24°10S 65°48W, pop (2000e) 138 500. Resort capital of Jujuy province, N Argentina; on the R Grande de Jujuy; founded, 1561, and again in 1575, after destruction by Indians; hot springs at Termas de Reyes (19 km/12 mi); airport; railway; agricultural, trade, mining, and timber centre; fishing, tourism, hydroelectricity; cathedral (18th-c), government house, Palacio de Tribunales.

San Marino

(state) [san mareenoh], official name **Most Serene Republic of San Marino**, Ital **Serenissima Repubblica di San Marino**

Local name San Marino (*see map, p.793*)

Timezone GMT +1

Area 61 km²/23 sq mi

Population total (2002e) 27 700

Status Republic

Capital San Marino

Language Italian (official)

Ethnic groups Sanmarinesi (San Marino citizens) (87%), Italian (12%)

Religion Roman Catholic (95%)

Physical features Landlocked in C Italy; smallest republic in the world, land boundaries, 34 km/21 mi; ruggedly mountainous, centred on the limestone ridges of Monte Titano, 793 m/2602 ft and the valley of the R Ausa.

Climate Temperate climate, with cool winters, warm summers; average annual temperatures -6°C (Jan), 26°C (Jul); moderate rainfall; average annual rainfall 880 mm/35 in.

Currency 1 euro = 100 cents (previous to February 2002, 1 Italian Lira (L, Lit)/1 San Marino Lira = 100 centesimi).

Economy Wheat, grapes, cheese, livestock; postage stamps, tourism, textiles, pottery; chemicals, paints, wine.

GDP (2001e) $940 mn, per capita $34 600

History Founded by a 4th-c Christian saint as a refuge against religious persecution; treaty of friendship with the Kingdom of Italy, preserving independence, 1862; in World War 2, followed Italy and declared war on Britain, 1940; declared neutrality shortly before Italian surrender, 1943; governed by an elected unicameral Parliament (the Grand and General Council) a Congress of State; parliament elects two of its members every six months to act as Captains-Regent (Capitani Reggenti), with the functions of Head of State.

Head of State/Government (Captains-Regent)
2001 Luigi Lonfernini/Fabio Berardi
2001–2 Alberto Cecchetti/Gino Giovagnoli
2002– Antonio Lazzaro Volpinari/Giovanni Francesco Ugolini

Secretary of State
1986–2002 Gabriele Gatti
2002– Fiorenzo Stolfi

sans-culottes [sã külot] (Fr, literally 'without breeches') A term first applied to the extreme republicans of Paris during the French Revolution, who wore long trousers instead of the knee breeches worn by the upper classes. It was later used to describe the mass of the working populace in French towns at the time of the Revolution, but more specifically to small-time Parisian shopkeepers, craftsmen, wage-earners, and unemployed who were politically active. Their demands for food controls and democratic government made them temporary allies of the Jacobins. The term *enragés* was applied to the extreme faction of the *sans-culottes*.

San Sebastián, Span [san sayvastyan], Basque **Donostia** 43°17N 1°58W, pop (2000e) 172 000. Fortified Basque seaport, fashionable resort, and capital of Guipúzcoa province, N Spain; on R Urumea, 469 km/291 mi N of Madrid; bishopric; airport; railway; seaport trade, fisheries, electronics, gloves, dairy produce; Church of St Mary (18th-c), Mount Urgel Park; Tamborada (Jan), Semana Grande (Aug).

sansevieria [sansiveeria] *mother-in-law's-tongue*

Sanskrit The name given to the early forms of Indo-Aryan, at c.1000 BC, in which the sacred Hindu texts known as the Vedas were written. Their grammatical form and pronunciation have been scrupulously preserved as a matter of religious observance. Sanskrit proved to be the key to the reconstruction of Indo-European in the 19th-c.

Sanskrit literature *Indian literature*

Sanskrit theatre / theater The classical Indian dramatic tradition which has a rich literature, written in Sanskrit, best exemplified by the plays of Bhasa, Sudraka, and Kalidasa. It was an aristocratic form of theatre with elaborate conventions governing all aspects of its stagecraft, recorded by Bharata around the 2nd-c BC. It had a history of over 1000 years of performance, then declined after the Mohammedan invasion of N India in the 11th-c. Its influence is still strong in some of the traditional styles of dance and drama popular in modern India.

Sansom, William (Norman Trevor) (1912–76) Writer, born in London, UK; in his youth he studied and travelled in Europe. His first collection of stories, *Fireman Flower and Other Stories*, appeared in 1944. His many novels include the much acclaimed *The Body* (1949). In addition to many collections of stories, he also wrote travel books, children's stories, essays, and songs. He was a friend of the writer Henry Green (1905–73), serving with him in the London Fire Service during World War 2.

Sansovino, Jacopo [sansoveenoh], originally **Jacopo Tatti** (1486–1570) Sculptor and architect, born in Florence, NC Italy. He was a pupil of Andrea Contucci Sansovino, from whom he took his name, and was responsible for bringing the High Renaissance style of his native Florence to Venice. From 1529 he was chief architect in Venice, where he is noted for several buildings, notably the Library of St Mark's (1540s). His early sculptures include the 'Bacchus' (c.1514, Bargello, Florence), and the 'Madonna del Parto' (c.1519, S Agostino, Rome); later works include the two monumental statues, 'Mars' and 'Neptune' (1554–6, Doge's Palace, Venice).

Sans Souci [sã soosee] A Rococo palace built (1745–7) at Potsdam, EC Germany, for Frederick II of Prussia, who collaborated with his architect, Georg Wenzeslaus von Knobelsdorff (1699–1753), on its design. It has been preserved in its original state, and houses several picture galleries.

Santa Ana 14°00N 79°31W, pop (2000e) 286 000. Capital city of Santa Ana department, NW El Salvador; 55 km/34 mi NW of San Salvador, on NE slopes of Santa Ana volcano; second largest city in the country; business centre of W El Salvador; railway; on the Pan-American Highway; coffee, sugar cane; cathedral, Church of El Calvario.

Santa Anna, Antonio López de (1797–1876) Mexican soldier, president (1833–6, 1846–7, 1853–5), and dictator (1839, 1841–5), born in Jalapa, E Mexico. Following the Texas revolt (1836), he defeated Texan forces at the Alamo, but was then routed at San Jacinto R, and imprisoned for eight months. He was recalled from exile in 1846 to be president during the war with the USA, and was twice defeated in the field. He was again recalled by a revolution in 1853, and appointed president for life, but in 1855 he was driven from the country. In 1867, after the death of Maximilian, he tried to effect a landing, but was captured and sentenced to death, then allowed to retire to New York. He returned at the amnesty of 1872.

Santa Barbara 34°25N 119°42W, pop (2000e) 92 300. Resort seat of Santa Barbara Co, SW California, USA, on the Pacific Ocean; founded, 1782; railway; university (1891); oil, aerospace, electronics; tourism; Vandenburg air force base nearby; Santa Barbara Mission (established 1786, present building completed 1820); many buildings with Spanish architecture.

Santa Claus A name derived from *Sinte Klaas*, a Dutch dialect form of St Nicholas, the patron saint of children, on the eve of whose feast day (6 Dec) presents were traditionally given to children, as if from the saint. Belief in Santa Claus, also known as **Father Christmas**, is fostered by adults, but confined to children. Santa Claus lives at the North Pole, dresses in a red fur-lined robe, or suit and bonnet, travels in a sleigh pulled by reindeer and, now on Christmas Eve, goes down chimneys to distribute gifts by placing them in stockings which are specially left out. Countries vary greatly in the way they act out these traditions.

Santa Cruz [kroos] or **Santa Cruz de la Sierra** 17°45S 63°14W, pop (2000e) 678 700. City in Santa Cruz department, E Bolivia; founded in 1561 by Spanish; airport; railway; university (1880); oil refining, gas fields; sugar cane, coffee, rice, tobacco, soya, maize, sugar refining; gas pipeline to Yacuiba; cathedral; carnival (before Lent).

Santa Cruz de Tenerife [santa krooth thay tenereefay] 28°28N 16°15W, pop (2000e) 192 000. Seaport and capital of Santa Cruz de Tenerife province, Canary Is, on N coast of Tenerife I; airport; oil refinery, wine, tobacco, pharmaceuticals, beer, pottery, tourism, agricultural trade; carnival (Feb), Festival of Spain (Apr–May), spring festival (May), Fiesta of La Virgen del Carmen (Jul).

Santa Fe (Argentina) [santa **fay**] 31°38S 60°43W, pop (2000e) 494 200. River-port capital of Santa Fe province, NEC Argentina; at the mouth of the R Salado, and linked to the R Paraná by a short canal; founded, 1573, but present site not occupied until 1660; airfield; railway; two universities (1919, 1959); rail, shipping, commercial, industrial, and agricultural centre; cathedral; Jesuit La Merced Church (1660–1754), Casa de Gobierno, San Francisco Church (1680), Museo Histórico Provincial.

Santa Fe (USA) [santa **fay**] 35°41N 105°57W, pop (2000e) 62 200. State capital in Santa Fe Co, NC New Mexico, USA; at the foot of the Sangre de Cristo Mts; the oldest seat of government in the USA; founded by the Spanish, 1609; centre of Spanish–Indian trade for over 200 years; after Mexican independence (1821), centre of trade with the USA; occupied by US troops, 1846; territorial capital, 1851; railway; administrative and tourist centre; noted for Indian wares; Palace of the Governors (1610), San Miguel Church (1636), Cathedral of St Francis, Museum of International Folk Art; Indian Market (Aug), Santa Fe Fiesta (Sept).

Santa Fe Trail [santa **fay**] A trading route from W Missouri through Kansas and Colorado to Santa Fe in New Mexico. The trail was pioneered by William Becknell in 1821, the year of Mexico's independence from Spanish rule. It remained a commercially important route for over 50 years, but declined after the Santa Fe railway was opened in 1880.

Santa Marta [santa **mah(r)**ta] 11°18N 74°10W, pop (2000e) 201 500. Caribbean port in N Colombia; at mouth of R Manzanares; 96 km/60 mi E of Barranquilla, to which it is linked by road and bridge (1974); founded by Rodrigo de Bastidas, 1525; Simón Bolívar died here, 1830; airport; railway; oil terminal; trade in bananas, coffee, cocoa; leading seaside resort.

Santa Monica 34°01N 118°29W, pop (2000e) 84 100. Residential city in Los Angeles Co, SW California, USA; on the Pacific Ocean in Santa Monica Bay; 24 km/15 mi W of Los Angeles; railway; airport; many museums and galleries; international film festival; a fashionable resort with famous pier (512 m/1679 ft long); aircraft industry, plastics, cosmetics.

Santander [santandair] 43°27N 3°51W, pop (2000e) 192 000. Seaport, resort, and capital of Santander province, N Spain; 393 km/244 mi N of Madrid; bishopric; airport; railway; car ferries to Plymouth, Gijón; university (1972); paper, glass, soap, chemicals, brewing, textiles, shipbuilding, fish processing; royal palace, cathedral (13th-c), prehistory museum; Fiesta of Santiago (Jul–Aug), Semana Grande (Aug).

Santander, Francisco de Paula [santandair] (1792–1840) Colombian statesman, born in Rosario de Cúcuta, New Granada (modern Colombia). He took part in the Spanish-American Wars of Independence, acted as vice-president of Grancolombia (1821–7) during Bolívar's campaigns, and was president of New Granada in 1832–7.

Santarém (Brazil) [santarem] 2°26S 54°41W, pop (2000e) 279 800. River-port in Pará state, N Brazil, at the junction of the Tapajós and Amazon Rivers; founded, 1661; third largest town on the Amazon; airfield; commerce, jute, gold, bauxite, timber, oil seed, textiles.

Santarém (Portugal) [santarã], ancient **Scalabis** or **Praesidium Julium** 39°12N 8°42W, pop (2000e) 23 500. Walled capital of

Santarém district, C Portugal, 69 km/43 mi NE of Lisbon; railway; olive oil, wine, fruit, horse breeding, tourism; Seminario (1676), Churches of Santa Clara (13th-c), Senhorã da Graça, São João de Alporão, Torre das Cabeças; festival of São José (Mar), music festival (Apr), festival of flowers (May), agricultural show (Jun), food festival (Oct).

Santa Rosa de Copán *Copán*

Santa Sophia *Hagia Sophia*

Santayana, George [santayahna], originally **Jorge Augustín Nicolás Ruiz de Santayana** (1863–1952) Philosopher, poet, and novelist, born in Madrid, Spain. He moved to Boston in 1872, and was educated at Harvard, where he became professor of philosophy (1907–12), while retaining his Spanish nationality. His writing career began as a poet with *Sonnets and Other Verses* (1894), but he later became known as a philosopher and stylist, in such works as *The Life of Reason* (5 vols, 1905–6), *Realms of Being* (4 vols, 1927–40), *Platonism and the Spiritual Life* (1927), and his novel *The Last Puritan* (1935). He moved to Europe in 1912, stayed in Oxford during World War 1, then settled in Rome.

Santer, Jacques [sãtair] (1937–) Statesman, prime minister of Luxembourg (1984–95), and president of the European Commission (1995– 9), born in Wasserbillig, E Luxembourg. He studied law at the universities of Strasbourg and Paris, and attended the Institute of Political Science in Paris. Entering politics, he became secretary to the Christian Social People's Party (1966–72), secretary-general (1972–4), and president (1974–82). In 1975 he became a member of the European Parliament, and in 1984 was elected Luxembourg's prime minister, serving three successive terms in office. He became president of the European Commission as a compromise choice, after Britain vetoed the selection of Belgian prime minister Jean-Luc Dehaene. He resigned in 1999, along with the entire Commission, following the publication of a damning report on corruption and maladministration within the European bureaucracy. In the same year he was elected to the European Parliament.

Santiago [santyahgoh], **Gran Santiago**, or **Santiago de Chile** 33°27S 70°38W, pop (2000e) 6 037 000. Capital of Chile, crossed E–W by R Mapocho; founded, 1541; capital, 1818; often damaged by floods, fires, and earthquakes; commercial centre; over half Chile's manufacturing located here; airport, 56 km/32 mi NW; railway; metro; three universities (1738, 1888, 1947); cathedral; textiles, food processing, metals, shoes; Avenida O'Higgins (the Alameda) stretches for more than 3 km/1¾ mi, lined with ornamental gardens and statues; Santa Lucía Hill, site of first fort; Palacio de la Moneda, Parque O'Higgins, Parque Forestal; several museums and churches; conical hill of San Cristóbal to the NE forms Parque Metropolitano, ascended by funicular railway and chair lift.

Santiago (de los Caballeros) [santyahgoh] 19°30N 70°42W, pop (2000e) 565 900. City in C Santiago province, Dominican Republic; second largest city in country; airfield; most important trading, distributing, and processing centre in N; in fertile Cibao agricultural region; cigarettes, pharmaceuticals, rum; scene of decisive battle of Dominican struggle for independence (1844); cathedral, fort.

Santiago de Compostela [santyahgoh thay kompostayla], ancient **Campus Stellae**, Eng **Compostella** 42°52N 8°37W, pop (2000e) 106 000. City in La Coruña province, Galicia, NW Spain, on R Sar; former capital of the Kingdom of Galicia; world-famous place of pilgrimage in the Middle Ages (shrine of St James); airport; railway; university (1501); the old town is a world heritage site; linen, paper, soap, brandy, silverwork; cathedral (11th–12th-c); Fiesta of Santiago Apostol (Jul).

Santiago de Cuba [santyahgoh thay kooba] 20°00N 75°49W, pop (2000e) 433 500. Seaport capital of Santiago de Cuba province, SE Cuba, on S coast; Cuba's second largest city; founded, 1514; formerly capital of the republic; scene of events in Spanish-American War of 1898, when town surrendered to US forces; scene of Castro's 1953 revolution; rail terminus; university (1947); trade in coffee, tobacco, sugar; cathedral (1528); Museum of Colonial Art; San Pedro de la Roca Castle, a world heritage site; Festival de Caribe (Apr); carnival (Jul).

Santiago del Estero [santyahgoh thel estayroh] 27°48S 64°15W, pop (2000e) 224 700. Capital of Santiago del Estero province, N Argentina; on the R Dulce; the oldest Argentine town, founded in 1553 by settlers from Peru; university; railway; airfield; agricultural trade and lumbering centre; cathedral; Gothic Church of San Francisco (founded, 1565), Museo Arqueológico; convent of Santo Domingo contains one of two copies of the Holy Shroud of Turin.

Santo Domingo, formerly (1936–61) **Ciudad Trujillo** 19°30N 70°42W, pop (2000e) 2 710 000. Capital city of Dominican Republic; on right bank of R Ozama; founded, 1496; airport; harbour; highway junction; university (1538); Renaissance cathedral (1514–40), Alcazar castle (1514).

Santorini [santoreenee], Gr **Santorin**, ancient **Thera** or **Thíra** pop (2000e) 7600; area 75 sq km/29 sq mi. Island in the S Cyclades c.140 km/87 mi N of Crete. The last great eruption of its volcano (c.1470 BC), in an explosion four times more powerful than Krakatoa, has been held responsible (probably mistakenly) for the rapid decline of Minoan civilization. The excavated site displays notable wall paintings and 3-storeyed houses.

Santos [santohs] 23°56S 46°22W, pop (2000e) 561 800. Port in São Paulo state, SE Brazil; 63 km/39 mi SE of São Paulo and 5 km/3 mi from the Atlantic coast, on an island; founded in 1534; railway; the most important Brazilian port, handling over 40% of all imports, and about half of all exports; major industrial area around the steelworks, oil refinery and hydroelectric plant at Cubatão, known locally as the Valley of Death because of chemical factory pollution; railway.

São Francisco, River [sõw franseeskoh] (Port **Río**) River in E Brazil; rises in the Serra de Canastra, flows NE, NW, then SE to enter the Atlantic 96 km/60 mi NE of Aracajú; length 2900 km/1800 mi; main route of access into the interior of E Brazil; hydroelectricity at several points.

Saône, River [sohn], ancient **Arar** River in E France rising in the Mts Faucilles (Vosges); flows SW then S to meet the R Rhône at Lyon; length 480 km/298 mi; linked by canal to the Loire, Seine, Marne, Meuse, Moselle, and Rhine.

São Paulo [sõw powloh] 23°33S 46°39W, pop (2000e) 12 834 000. Capital of São Paulo state, SE Brazil, on the R Tietê; founded by Jesuits, 1554; international (Guarulhas) and local (Congonhas) airports; railway; three universities (1934, 1952, 1970); developed since the 19th-c to become the leading commercial and industrial centre in South America; fastest-growing South American city; pharmaceuticals, machine tools, furniture, steel, vehicles, chemicals, food processing; neo-Gothic cathedral, Museum of Art, Museum of Brazilian Art, Iparinga Monument, the Anhembi (one of world's largest exhibition halls), Butantã Institute (with snake farm).

São Tiago [sõw tyahgoh] or **Santiago** 14°55N 23°31W; pop (2000e) 166 900; area 991 sq km/382 sq mi. Largest island in Cape Verde, in the Sotavento group; rises to 1320 m/4331 ft at Antonia Peak; chief town, Praia; fine beaches at Gamboa, Prainha, Quebra-Canela; Ribeira Grande, 15th-c colonial capital; airport; coffee, sugar, oranges.

São Tomé and Príncipe *p.1356*

sapi-utan or **sapi-outan** *anoa*

sapodilla plum *chicle*

saponification The hydrolysis of a fat (glyceride) in a basic solution, yielding glycerol and the salts of the fatty acids (soaps). The reaction is an example of an ester hydrolysis.

Sapor II *Shapur II*

Sapper, pseudonym of **Herman Cyril McNeile** (1888–1937) Novelist, born in Bodmin, Cornwall, SW England, UK. He trained as a soldier before achieving fame as the creator of 'Bulldog' Drummond, the aggressively patriotic hero of a series of thrillers written between 1920 and 1937. *The Final Count* (1926) is a typical example.

São Tomé and Príncipe

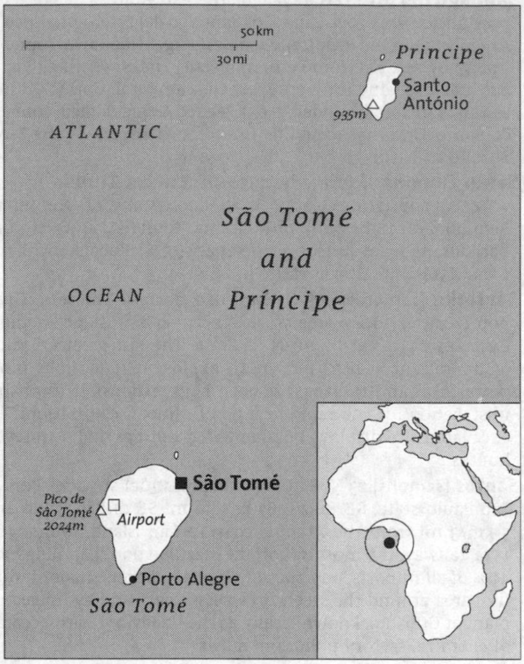

□ International Airport

[sõw tomay, preensipe], Port **São Tomé e Príncipe**, official name **Democratic Republic of São Tomé and Príncipe**

Local name São Tomé e Príncipe
Timezone GMT
Area 1001 km^2/387 sq mi
Population total (2002e) 147 000
Status Democratic republic
Date of independence 1975
Capital São Tomé
Languages Portuguese (official), with a number of creoles spoken
Ethnic groups Portuguese-African descent, African minority
Religions Roman Catholic (80%), Seventh Day Adventist, and Evangelical Protestant
Physical features Equatorial volcanic islands in the Gulf of Guinea, off the coast of Equatorial Guinea, W Africa; comprise São Tomé, Príncipe, and several smaller islands; São Tomé (area 845 km^2/326 sq mi), greatest height, 2024 m/6640 ft, Pico de São Tomé in central volcanic uplands; heavily forested.
Climate Tropical climate; average annual temperature 27°C (coast), 20°C (mountains); rainy season (Oct–May); annual average rainfall 500–1000 mm/20–40 in.
Currency 1 Dobra (Db) = 100 centimos
Economy Based on agriculture (employs c.70% of population); cocoa, copra, palm kernels, coffee, wine, fishing; restructured economy since 1985, with greater involvement in commerce, banking, and tourism.
GDP (2002e) $200 mn, per capita $1200
Human Development Index (2002) 0·632
History Visited by the Portuguese, 1469–72; Portuguese colony, 1522; resistance to Portuguese rule led to riots in 1953, and the formation of an overseas liberation movement based in Gabon; independence, 1975; sole legal party was the Movement for the Liberation of São Tomé and Príncipe, until new constitution in 1990 approved multi-party democratic system; bloodless coup by army rebels (Jul 2003) when President Fradique de Menezes was visiting Nigeria; he returned when agreement to restore democratic rule was reached; governed by a President, a Prime Minister, and a National Assembly.

Head of State
1975–91 Manuel Pinto da Costa
1991–2001 Miguel Trovoada
2001– Fradique de Menezes

Head of Government
1994–5 Carlos da Graça
1995–6 Armindo Vaz d'Almeida
1996–9 Raul Bragança Neto
1999–2001 Guilherme Posser da Costa
2001–2 Evaristo de Carvalho
2002 Gabriel Costa
2002– Maria das Neves de Sousa

sapphire A gem variety of corundum, coloured by the addition of minor amounts of impurity. It occurs in a variety of colours (except red, when it is termed *ruby*), but blue is the most valuable.

Sappho [safoh] (c.610–c.580 BC) Greek poet, born in Lesbos, Greece. The most celebrated female poet of antiquity, she wrote lyrics unsurpassed for depth of feeling, passion, and grace. Only two of her odes are extant in full, but many fragments have been found in Egypt. She is said to have plunged into the sea from the Leucadian rock because Phaon did not return her love, but this event seems to have no historical foundation. Tradition also represents her poetry as a celebration of lesbian love, but this too has been disputed. She wrote in a great many metres, one of which, the **Sapphic**, is named after her. She influenced many later writers, among them Catullus, Ovid, and Swinburne.

Sapporo [sapohroh] 43°05N 141°21E, pop (2000e) 1 724 000. Capital of Hokkaido prefecture, WC Hokkaido, Japan; founded, 1871; railway; subway; university (1876); winter sports, timber, brewing, flour, electronics, agricultural machinery; Ainu museum; Snow Festival with snow sculpture (Jan–Feb); scene of 1972 Winter Olympics; Sapporo Dome Stadium (2001).

saprophyte [saprohfiyt] A plant which feeds on the products of decay. It includes many fungi. A few flowering plants are saprophytic; they have reduced leaves, lack chlorophyll, and form symbiotic associations with mycorrhizal fungi which aid in the breakdown of dead tissue on which the plant feeds.

sapsucker A woodpecker, native to North America and the Caribbean; inhabits woodland; eats sap, insects, berries, and nuts; juvenile plumage differs from adult. (Genus: *Sphyrapicus*, 2 species.)

Saqqarah [sakara] The large necropolis of Memphis in Egypt, where several pharaohs and many noble Egyptians were buried. The most famous surviving monument is the stepped pyramid of Zozer (c.2630 BC). Designed by Imhotep, it marked a radical advance in pyramid design.

sarabande A 16th-c dance of Spanish or Latin-American origin in triple time. In a different form and slower tempo it became a standard movement of the Baroque suite, where a long note on the second beat is a distinctive feature.

Saragossa [saragosa], Span **Zaragoza**, ancient **Salduba** 41°39N 0°53W, pop (2000e) 594 000. Industrial city and capital of Saragossa province, Aragón, NEC Spain; on R Ebro, 325 km/202 mi NE of Madrid; scene of a long siege against the French in the Peninsular War (1808–9); archbishopric; airport; railway; university (1553); iron and steel, machinery, chemicals, textiles, soap, paper, foodstuffs, plastics, glass; El Pilar and La Seo cathedrals, 16th-c Exchange, Aljafarería Moorish palace; Fiesta of Our Lady of Pilar (Oct), spring festival (May).

Sarah or **Sarai** (Heb 'princess') Biblical character, the wife and half-sister of Abraham, who is portrayed (*Gen* 12–23) as having accompanied him from Ur to Canaan. On account of her beauty, she posed as Abraham's sister before Pharaoh in Egypt and Abimelech in Gerar, since their desire for her might have endangered her husband's life. Long barren, she is said to have eventually given birth to Isaac in her old age as God promised. She is said to have died at age 127 in Kiriath-arba.

Sarajevo [sarayayvoh] 43°52N 18°26E, pop (2000e) 400 000. Capital of Bosnia and Herzegovina; on R Miljacka; governed by Austria, 1878–1918; scene of the assassination of Archduke Francis Ferdinand and his wife (28 Jun 1914); under siege and badly damaged in civil war, 1992–3; airport; railway; university (1946); vehicles, brewing, engineering, chemicals, carpets, tobacco; educational and cultural centre; site of 1984 Winter Olympic Games; old town, Husref Bey mosque, Imperial mosque, two cathedrals; song festival (Apr), International Festival of Military Music (Jun), slivovitz and wine fair (Oct).

Saramago, José [saramahgoh] (1922–) Writer, born in Azinhaga, Portugal. A former technician, journalist and translator, since 1979 he has worked as a writer, publishing plays, short stories, novels, poems, libretti, diaries, and travelogues. He gained an international reputation in the 1980s with his satirical novel, *Memorial do Convento* (1982) , later works including *O Año da Morte de Ricardo Reis* (1984, The Year of the Death of Ricardo Reis), *O Evangelho Segundo Jesus Christo* (1991, The Gospel According to Jesus Christ), and *Todos os Nomes* (1997, All the Names). He was awarded the Nobel Prize for Literature in 1998.

Sarandon, Susan [sarandon], originally **Susan Abigail Tomalin** (1946–) Film actress, born in New York City, USA. Educated at the Catholic University of America, Washington, she began her screen career in *Joe* (1970), and became well known after her role in *The Rocky Horror Picture Show* (1975). Later films include *The Witches of Eastwick* (1987), *Thelma and Louise* (1991), *Dead Man Walking* (1995, Oscar), *Earthly Possessions* (1999), and *Igby Goes Down* (2003). A commitment to political activism brought her into the public eye in 1993, when she and co-star Tim Robbins interrupted the Academy Awards ceremony in order to draw attention to the situation of HIV-positive Haitian refugees.

Saransk [saransk] 54°12N 45°10E, pop (2000e) 318 000. Capital city of Mordovskaya, C European Russia, on R Insar; founded as a fortress, 1641; railway; university (1957); foodstuffs, electrical engineering, machinery, chemicals, clothing; Church of John the Apostle (1693).

Sarapis *Serapis*

Saratoga, Battle of [saratohga] (Oct 1777) One of the most important engagements of the US War of Independence. Actually fought near modern Schuylerville, NY, the battle brought the defeat of a large British army under John Burgoyne by American continental troops and militia under Horatio Gates. The outcome ended British plans to cut New England off from the rest of the states, and encouraged French intervention on the American side.

Saratov [saratof] 51°30N 45°55E, pop (2000e) 905 000. River-port capital of Saratovskaya oblast, E European Russia, on R Volga; founded as a fortress, 1590; airport; railway; university (1909); oil refining, chemicals, clothing, leatherwork, precision instruments; Troitskii Cathedral (1689–95).

Sarawak [sarahwak] pop (2000e) 2 076 000; area 124 449 sq km/ 48 037 sq mi. State in E Malaysia, on NW coast of Borneo; bounded S by Kalimantan (Indonesia), N by the South China Sea and NE by Brunei and Sabah; flat, narrow coastal strip, belt of foothills, and highly mountainous forested interior; highest peak, Mt Murud (2423 m/7949 ft); watered by the R Rajang; given by the Sultan of Brunei to James Brooke, the 'white raja' in 1841, and governed by the Brooke family until World War 2; British protectorate, 1888; Crown Colony, 1946; capital, Kuching; oil, rice, sago, rubber, pepper, fishing; national park around Mt Mulu.

Sarcodina [sah(r)kodiyna] A subphylum of protozoans, all of which possess some kind of pseudopodia; most are free-living in aquatic habitats or soil; cell body typically naked, sometimes with a shell (*test*); reproduces by splitting in two (*binary fission*); often produces resistant cysts to aid dispersal and avoid adverse conditions.

sarcoidosis [sah(r)koydohsis An uncommon, multi-system, chronic inflammatory disorder of unknown cause. Immature cells accumulate to form lumps (*granulomas*) in any organ in the body. The clinical features depend on which organs are affected; for example skin, eyes, lungs, or heart. The granulomas tend to resolve spontaneously but may leave scarring, causing permanent organ damage.

sarcoma [sah(r)kohma] A malignant tumour in connective tissue, bone, or muscle. Sarcomas are much less common than are **carcinomas**, which arise from the lining tissues of the skin and internal organs.

Sardanapalus [sah(r)danapalus] (7th-c BC) Legendary Assyrian king, notorious for his effeminacy and sensual lifestyle. He probably represents an amalgam of at least three Assyrian rulers, one of them being Assurbanipal.

sardine *pilchard*

Sardinia, Ital **Sardegna** pop (2000e) 1 644 000; area 24 000 sq km/9300 sq mi. Region and island of Italy; settled by Phoenicians; formed part of Kingdom of Sardinia, 18th-c; capital and chief port, Cagliari (airport); main towns, Nuoro, Sassari, Carbonia, Oristano, Iglesias; length 272 km/169 mi; width 144 km/ 89 mi; second largest island in the Mediterranean; largely hilly, rising to 1835 m/6020 ft in the Monti del Gennargentu; well-wooded C and N; mineral-bearing SW; fertile alluvial plain of Campidano; corn, wine, olives, cereals, citrus fruits, vegetables, tobacco, pastoral farming; sea salt, mining (zinc, lead, manganese, coal), cement, sugar refining, coral, basket making, food processing, petrochemicals, tourism.

Sardinia, Kingdom of An Italian kingdom created 1718–20 through the Duchy of Savoy's acquisition of Sardinia, in compensation for the loss of Sicily. Despite its name, the kingdom's heart remained Savoy/Piedmont. In the mid-19th-c, Sardinia/ Piedmont emerged as the chief driving force behind the move towards Italian unity. In 1861, Victor Emmanuel II of Sardinia became the first King of Italy.

Sardinian *Romance languages*

Sardis [sah(r)dis] The capital of Lydia and the political centre of Asia Minor in the pre-Hellenistic period. A flourishing city in Roman imperial times, it contained one of the largest and richest Jewish communities in the entire empire.

sardonyx [sah(r)doniks] A white and brown variety of onyx.

Sardou, Victorien [sah(r)doo] (1831–1908) Playwright, born in Paris, France. His first efforts were failures, but after his marriage he met the actress **Virginie Déjazet** (1798–1875), for whom he wrote several plays, and his work became widely known in Europe and the USA. His plays include *Les Pattes de monde* (1860, trans A Scrap of Paper), *La Tosca* (1887), on which Puccini's opera is based, and over 60 others, many written for Sarah Bernhardt.

Sargasso Sea [sah(r)gasoh] Sluggish area of the Atlantic Ocean, between the Azores and the West Indies within the 'Horse Latitudes'; a still sea, located at the centre of clockwise-moving warm surface currents, allowing great biological activity; abundance of surface gulfweed; breeding ground for eels which migrate to Europe.

Sargent, John Singer [sah(r)jnt] (1856–1925) Painter, born in Florence, NC Italy. He studied at Florence and Paris, where he first gained recognition, but most of his work was done in England, where he became the most fashionable portait painter of his age. He had to leave Paris following a furore about his decolleté portrait 'Madame Gautreau' (1885), and he travelled much to the USA, where he became a US citizen in 1876. As well as portaits, he worked on decorative paintings for public buildings, such as 'The Evolution of Religion' (1890–1910) for Boston Public Library.

Sargent, Sir (Harold) Malcolm (Watts) [sah(r)jnt] (1895–1967) Conductor, born in Ashford, Kent, SE England, UK. Originally an organist, he first appeared as a conductor when his *Impression on a Windy Day* was performed at a Promenade Concert in 1921. He conducted the Royal Choral Society from 1928, the Liverpool Philharmonic Orchestra (1942–8), and the BBC Symphony Orchestra (1950–7). From 1948 he was in charge of the London Promenade Concerts. His sense of occasion and unfailing panache won him great popularity at home and abroad. He was knighted in 1947.

Sark, Fr **Sercq** pop (2000e) 640; area 4 sq km/1½ sq mi. Smallest of the four main Channel Islands, lying between Guernsey and the Cotentin Peninsula, France; consists of Great and Little Sark, connected by an isthmus; separate parliament (the Chief Pleas); Seigneurie of Sark established by Elizabeth I; ruler known as the Seigneur (male) or Dame (female); no cars allowed on the island.

Sarmatia [sah(r)maysha] In Roman times, the area to the N of the Black Sea and the middle and lower Danube occupied by the Sarmatians, a nomadic people closely related to the Scythians. Although never conquered by Rome, Sarmatia did not escape Roman control altogether: many Sarmatian chieftains were clients of Rome and ruled in her interest.

saros [sahros] The natural cycle over which sequences of lunar and solar eclipses repeat themselves. The period is 6585·32 days (c.18 years): over this cycle the Earth, Sun, and Moon return to the same relative positions. An eclipse in one saros occurs about 8 hours later and 115° of longitude further West in the next cycle. This predictability was apparently known to the Maya, and to the builders of Stonehenge.

Saroyan, William [saroyan] (1908–81) Writer, born in Fresno, California, USA. He left school at 15, and began writing short stories in the late 1920s. His first volume, *The Daring Young Man on the Flying Trapeze* (1934), was a great success, and was followed by a number of highly original novels and plays. He was awarded (but declined) the Pulitzer Prize for his play *The Time of Your Life* (1939). Among later works are the novel *The Human Comedy* (1943) and the memoir *Places Where I've Done Time* (1975).

Sarpedon [sah(r)peedn] In the *Iliad*, a son of Zeus, who led the Lycian troops on the Trojan side, and made an important speech on the duties of a warrior. He was killed by Patroclus, and carried off by Sleep and Death to Lycia.

Sarraute, Nathalie [saroht], *née* **Nathalie Ilyanova Tcherniak** (1902–99) Writer, born in Ivanova, W Russia. Her parents settled in France when she was a child, and she studied at the Sorbonne, at Oxford, and in Berlin before becoming a member of the French bar (1926–41). Her first book was a collection of sketches on bourgeois life, *Tropismes* (1939, Tropisms), in which she rejected traditional plot development. Known and widely translated as the leading theorist of the *nouveau roman* ('new novel'), she developed her views in such novels as *Portrait d'un Inconnu* (1947, Portrait of a Man Unknown), *Le Planétarium* (1959, The Planetarium), and *Les Fruits d'or* (1963, The Golden Fruits). Later works include *Collected Plays* (1981), *Tu ne t'aimes pas* (1989, You Don't Love Yourself), and *ICI* (1995).

sarrusophone [saroozofohn] A musical instrument made of brass in various sizes, with a double reed. It was designed by a French bandmaster, W Sarrus, in 1856 as a substitute for oboes and bassoons in military bands, but enjoyed only brief success.

SARS Acronym for **severe acute respiratory syndrome**, a highly contagious viral infection first recorded in November 2002 in Guandong province, China, which subsequently began to spread around the world through air travel. By the end of 2003 the virus had killed 818 people worldwide and infected over 8000, with China and Hong Kong most affected. Known symptoms are similar to those of influenza, including high fever, headache, dry cough, and shortness of breath, and may progress to pneumonia. The incubation period is thought to be between two to seven days. The World Health Organization (WHO) announced that SARS was a new strain of coronavirus, the family of viruses that are a cause of the common cold, and this was later confirmed. The rapid spread of the disease prompted the WHO to issue a global alert advising the wearing of face masks in public areas, restricted air travel, the screening of air passengers to detect any rise in body temperature, and the isolation of infected patients. Efforts to develop a safe and effective human vaccine against the disease are ongoing.

sarsaparilla [sasparila] A climbing, prickly perennial, native to tropical and subtropical regions; leaves leathery, 3-veined; flowers greenish or yellowish, six perianth-segments; berries red or black. The dried roots, especially of *Smilax americana* species, yield a tonic drink, as well as a drug used to treat rheumatism. In the 19th-c US West it was used as a beverage flavouring. (Genus: *Smilax*, 350 species. Family: Smilacaceae.)

Sarto, Andrea del [sah(r)toh], originally **Andrea d'Agnolo**, or **Andrea Vannucchi** (1486–1531) Painter, born in Florence, NC Italy, the son of a tailor (It *sarto* 'tailor'). He was engaged by the Servites to paint a series of frescoes for their Church of the Annunciation (1509–14), and a second series was next painted for the Recollets. Many of his most celebrated pictures are in Florence.

Sartre, Jean-Paul [sahtr] (1905–80) Existentialist philosopher and writer, born in Paris, France. He taught philosophy at Le Havre, Paris, and Berlin, was imprisoned in Germany (1941), and after his release joined the resistance in Paris. In 1945 he emerged as the leading light of the left-bank intellectual life of Paris. His name is synonymous with existentialism, a philosophy which seeks the freedom of the individual human being, and which he shared with his companion, Simone de Beauvoir. His novels include the trilogy, *Les Chemins de la liberté* (1945–9, Paths of Freedom), and he also wrote (especially after the war) a large number of plays, such as *Huis clos* (1944, trans In Camera/No Exit) and *Le Diable et le bon Dieu* (1951, trans Lucifer and the Lord). His philosophy is presented in *L'Etre et le néant* (1943, Being and Nothingness). In 1964 he published his autobiography *Les Mots* (Words), and was awarded (but declined) the Nobel Prize for Literature. In the later 1960s he became heavily involved in opposition to US policies in Vietnam, and supported student rebellion in 1968.

SAS Abbreviation of **Special Air Service**, a British army unit specializing in clandestine and anti-terrorist operations. First formed in 1941 as a special commando unit to parachute behind enemy lines, the SAS (motto 'Who Dares Wins') was revived as a regular unit of the British Army in 1952 for special operations. Its work is highly secret, but it served with distinction during the Falklands campaign (1982) and the Gulf War (1991).

sashimi [sasheemee] Japanese sliced raw fish, considered a delicacy, and served in many special restaurants. Popular are tuna, sea bream, flatfish, squid, octopus, and shellfish. They are eaten with a seasoning of soy sauce and *wasabi*, green mustard. Slices of raw fish on small portions of boiled seasoned rice are called *sushi*.

Saskatchewan [saskachuan] pop (2000e) 1 108 000; area 652 380 sq km/251 883 sq mi. Province in W Canada; bounded S by the USA; fertile plain in S two-thirds; N third is in the Canadian Shield; rises to 1392 m/4567 ft in the Cypress Hills (SW); many lakes, largest Athabasca (NW), Reindeer (NE), Wollaston (NE); several rivers; capital, Regina; other chief towns, Saskatoon, Moose Jaw, Prince Albert, Yorkton; wheat (about two-thirds of Canada's production), barley, cattle, dairy farming, oil, natural gas, potash (largest fields in the world), timber; important fur-trading region at end of 17th-c; Hudson's Bay Company land, acquired by Canada in 1869 to become part of Northwest Territories; railway arrived, 1882–3; land and treaty disputes led to North-West Rebellion, 1885; province of Canada, 1905; governed by a Lieutenant-Governor and an elected 66-member Legislative Assembly.

Saskatchewan River [saskachuan] River in S Canada, formed in Saskatchewan, 48 km/30 mi E of Prince Albert, by two headstreams which rise in the Rocky Mts of W Alberta; flows E into L Winnipeg; length 1300 km/800 mi.

Saskatoon [saskatoon] 52°10N 106°40W, pop (2000e) 207 800. Town in C Saskatchewan, Canada, on the S Saskatchewan R; settled in 1882 as a temperance colony; developed in early 1900s with settlers from the USA; airfield; railway; university (1907); centre of large grain-growing area; light and heavy industry, oil-related industries, meat packing, flour milling; the Western Development Museum, Memorial Art Gallery; Pioneer Days and Saskachimo Exposition (Jul).

Sasquatch *Bigfoot*

sassaby *topi*

sassafras [sasafras] A name applied to several different plants. True sassafras (*Sassafras albidum*), is a large shrub or tree, growing to 30 m/100 ft, native to E North America; aromatic foliage; inconspicuous greenish flowers; blue-grey, berry-like fruits. **Oil of sassafras**, chiefly a flavouring, is distilled from the bark, twigs, and roots. Infusion of the bark is medicinal. (Family: Lauraceae.)

Sassanids [sasanidz] The aggressive Persian dynasty that overthrew the Parthian Empire in AD 224 and became Rome's fiercest challenger in the E. They were driven from Mesopotamia by the Arabs in AD 636.

Sassari [sasahree] 40°43N 8°34E, pop (2000e) 123 000. Capital town of Sassari province, Sardinia, Italy, 176 km/109 mi NW of Cagliari; archbishopric; university (1562); centre of agricultural trade; food processing, cheese, tobacco; cathedral (begun 12th-c); Cavalcata Sarda (traditional costumes) (May) on feast of the Assumption; Fiera dell'artigieneto, a biennial crafts fair (May).

Sassoon, Siegfried (Loraine) [sasoon] (1886–1967) Poet and novelist, born in Brenchley, Kent, SE England, UK. World War 1, in which he served, gave him a hatred of war, fiercely expressed in his *Counterattack* (1918) and *Satirical Poems* (1926). He also wrote several semi-autobiographical works, such as *Memoirs of a Fox-Hunting Man* (1928). His later poetry was increasingly devotional, and he became a Catholic in 1957.

SAT 1 In the United States an abbreviation for **Scholastic Aptitude Test**, a general examination of verbal and mathematical skills not related to specific course work, taken by high-school pupils wishing to attend university. The test claims to be objective, but has been criticized for being culturally biased towards the middle class.

2 In England and Wales the term is an abbreviation for **Standard Assessment Task**, a test administered to children at the ages of 7, 11, 14, and 16 to discover what level of the national curriculum they have reached.

Satan *Devil*

Satanism The worship of Satan or other figures of demonology. It may include the perversion of religious rituals (eg the black Mass), the practice of witchcraft, and other practices associated with the occult. There was a revival of Satanism in the 19th-c, and instances of it are still to be found.

satellite 1 A spacecraft orbiting the Earth or other heavenly body. The first artificial satellite was Sputnik 1, launched by the USSR on 4 October 1957, and there are now more than 3000 satellites orbiting the Earth for remote sensing, military surveillance, communications, and space astronomy. Geostationary satellites orbit at 35 900 km/22 300 mi above Earth, taking 24 hours to orbit, so they appear in almost the same part of our sky at all times. They are important for communications, especially satellite television, since fixed dishes can be used at ground stations.

2 The moons of the planets in our Solar System. Jupiter and Saturn have extensive systems. Ganymede (Jupiter) is the biggest, exceeding the size of Mercury and Pluto.

satellite DNA A type of DNA, in which short base-pair sequences are repeated many times, and localized in the centromeric region of chromosomes. It may be involved in the pairing of the centromere regions during meiosis. Centromeric satellite DNA is to be distinguished from **micro-satellite DNA** which, although also composed of repetitive units of DNA sequence, is distributed throughout the length of chromosomes. The pattern of micro-satellite DNA repeat sequences is essentially unique for each individual, and forms the basis of DNA fingerprint identity analysis.

satellite television Television transmission using super-high-frequency beam linkage by way of an artificial satellite followed in its elliptical terrestrial orbit; commenced in 1962 with Telstar. Shortly after, satellites in fixed geostationary orbit above the Equator were introduced, providing continuous communication without tracking. Initially this was between large ground stations, but in the 1970s direct broadcasting from satellite (DBS) was developed experimentally. Programmes were relayed at sufficient power to serve domestic TV receivers within a specific territory, known as the 'footprint', using small individual dish antennae of 60 cm/23 in diameter or less. Several commercial DBS services were provided in the USA during the 1980s, and in Europe from 1989.

sati or **suttee** [satee] A custom which led Indian widows to burn themselves alive on their husbands' funeral pyres. It was a voluntary act, but one often committed under pressure from the family, who sought prestige or property left to the wife. It was prohibited during Mughal times, and suppressed by the British in 1828.

Satie, Erik (Alfred Leslie) [satee] (1866–1925) Composer, born in Honfleur, NW France. He worked as a cafe pianist, and studied erratically in Paris, not beginning to compose seriously until after he was 40. He wrote ballets, lyric dramas, and whimsical pieces which were in violent revolt against musical orthodoxy, and influenced Debussy, Ravel, and others.

satin spar A fibrous, massive form of gypsum, used for ornamental carving.

satinwood A deciduous tree (*Chloroxylon swietenia*) growing to 30 m/100 ft, native to S India and Sri Lanka; leaves to 60 cm/2 ft, pinnate with 10–20 pairs of asymmetric leaflets; flowers 5-petalled, creamy-white, in clusters. It provides very hard, heavy, yellow wood, valued for its satin-like lustre. (Family: Flindersiaceae.)

satire A literary genre whose double derivation, from Latin *satura* 'mixture' and the parodic satyr play, underlines its complex form and motive. The motive includes the exposure of folly and the castigation of vice, with the Latin satirists Horace and Juvenal representing these two extremes. But satire is also both festive and fictive, and the works of Rabelais and Swift, the plays of Ben Jonson and Molière, and the novels of Dickens are much more than the sum of their moral exhortations. Among modern novelists, Evelyn Waugh, Achebe, and Rushdie are noted for their use of satire. Satire has colonized all literary forms, and in doing so has tended to expose formal conventions themselves. This excess of consciousness explains the overlap between satire, parody, and irony.

satisficing [satisfiysing] In economics, an alternative theory to the view that human activities can be seen as choosing between known alternatives with the aim of maximizing something, usually profits for firms or utility for individuals. Satisficing argues that uncertainty makes maximizing very difficult, and risk-aversion may make it undesirable. Instead, activities proceed by trial and error. Any policy, such as price-setting, is continued as long as it produces results which are up to some customary acceptable level, ie are satisfactory. If the results fall below this level, trial and error starts again. Thinking on these lines owes much to the US economist Herbert Simon, who was awarded the Nobel Prize for Economics in 1978.

satrapy [satrapee] The chief territorial sub-division of the Achaemenid Empire, administered by a satrap (literally, a 'protector of the kingdom'). About 20 in number, the most westerly was Ionia and the most easterly Gandhara.

satsuma [satsooma] A citrus fruit (*Citrus reticulata*); a variety of mandarin with an easily detachable rind. (Family: Rutaceae.)

Satu Mare [satu maray] 47°48N 22°52E, pop (2000e) 138 000. Resort town and capital of Satu Mare county, NW Romania, on R

Someș; airfield; railway junction; tourism, grain, livestock, timber, wine trade, mining equipment, rolling stock, electric motors, textiles, food processing.

saturated In chemistry, a term describing a hydrocarbon containing no multiple bonds. The name derives from the fact that these compounds contain the maximum amount of hydrogen for their carbon content. Alkanes are saturated hydrocarbons; alkenes and alkynes are **unsaturated**.

saturated fatty acids *polyunsaturated fatty acids*

Saturn (astronomy) The sixth planet from the Sun, notable for its ring system – first seen by Galileo in 1610, and first explained by Huygens in 1656. It has 31 known moons, the largest of which, Titan, has a dense atmosphere. Its main characteristics are: mass $5{\cdot}68 \times 10^{26}$ kg; mean density 0·69 g/cm^3; equatorial radius 60 268 km/37 449 mi; polar radius 54 364 km/33 780 mi; rotational period (equatorial) 10 h 14 m; orbital period 29·5 years; inclination of equator 26·7°; mean distance from the Sun 9·54 AU. Like Jupiter, it is a hydrogen/helium planet with a presumed innermost core of rocky composition and several Earth masses, an outer core of metallic hydrogen and helium, a liquid mantle of hydrogen/helium, and an atmosphere about 1000 km/600 mi deep. Also, like Jupiter, it is believed to have several cloud layers: solid ammonia (the highest), ammonium hydrosulphide, water ice, and water-ammonia. It is less colourful than Jupiter, and less vividly banded, possibly due to greater obscuration by ammonia clouds. It has less obvious discrete features such as vortices, but Voyager images do reveal definite structure within the bands of clouds. The rings were observed by Voyager to have particle sizes ranging up to several metres. Their infrared signature suggests that they are made of water ice – possibly created by break-up of a moon or captured comet whose orbit decayed inside the Roche limit. The rings show a complex structure including several divisions and innumerable 'ringlets'. The moons, except Titan, are low in density, indicating that they are mainly composed of ices, but still with some 'rocky' material which comprises the core. Most are locked in synchronous orbits about Saturn. They have all been subject to meteoritic bombardment, and exhibit cratered surfaces.

Saturn (mythology) or **Saturnus** A Roman god; either Etruscan in origin, or, as legend has it, a genuine importation of the Greek Cronus. At his festival (**Saturnalia**, 17 Dec, and for some days after) the social order in the household was turned upside down: servants and slaves had temporary liberty while their masters waited on them at table; there were wild parties, and presents were exchanged.

saturniid moth [saterneeid] A moth of the family Saturniidae; large, with wingspan up to 30 cm/12 in; conspicuous eyespots and banded markings present on wings; pupal cocoons of some species used for production of silk; c.1300 species, including the *atlas* and *emperor moths*. (Order: Lepidoptera.)

satyagraha [satyagrahha] (Hindi: 'truth-force') Gandhi's philosophy of non-violent resistance to evil. It was conceived in South Africa in response to laws discriminating against Asians (1906), and used in campaigns against British rule in India. The approach involved fasting, economic boycotts, hand-spinning, and hand-weaving.

satyr In Greek mythology, a minor deity associated with Dionysus; usually depicted with goat-like ears, tail, and legs. Rural, wild and lustful, the satyrs were said to be the brothers of the nymphs.

satyriasis [satiriyasis] Pathological exaggerated sexual drive or excitement in a male. Some individuals have an associated psychiatric disorder. Treatment has included behavioural approaches, psychoanalytic therapies, and the use of female hormones in extreme cases. The corresponding drive in females is known as **nymphomania**.

satyrid butterfly [sateerid] A group of butterflies now included in the family Nymphalidae; wings mostly brown or orange-black, with eyespots; adults generally shade-loving; caterpillars mostly feeding on grasses and sedges. (Order: Lepidoptera.)

sauce A seasoned liquid served with or over a food; it may be hot or cold, savoury or sweet. Cold sauces may be formed from a mixture (eg vinaigrette), an emulsification (eg mayonnaise), or a purée (eg any fruit sauce). For hot sauces the liquid used may be stock, milk, or water, and the thickening agent may be a blend of melted butter and flour (as in the classic béchamel and velouté sauces), egg yolks and cream, a starch thickener (eg cornflour, arrowroot), butter (eg hollandaise), or, in 'new' cookery, a purée of vegetables.

Saudi Arabia *p.1361*

sauerkraut [sowerkrowt] A popular German food, produced by layering alternately shredded white cabbage and salt in a wooden box. Air is expelled by placing a weight on top. The cabbage salt layers are left for 3–4 weeks to ferment.

Saul [sawl] (11th-c BC) Biblical character, the first king to be elected by the Israelites. He conquered the Philistines, Ammonites, and Amalekites, became jealous of David, his son-in-law, and was ultimately engaged in a feud with the priestly class. Eventually, Samuel secretly anointed David king, and Saul fell in battle with the Philistines on Mt Gilboa.

Saul of Tarsus *Paul, St*

Sault Sainte Marie [soo saynt maree], Fr [soh sĩt maree] 46°32N 84°20W, pop (2000e) 91 300. Town in SW Ontario, Canada, on N shore of St Mary's R, linking L Huron and L Superior; opposite Sault Ste Marie, Michigan, connected by an international bridge; fort, 1751, taken by the British, 1762; Soo canals link L Superior (183 m/600 ft) and L Huron (177 m/581 ft); airport; railway; steel, lumber, paper, agricultural trade, tourism.

Saunders, Jennifer (1958–) British comedy writer and actress. Trained at the Central School of Speech and Drama, London, she teamed up with Dawn French in a comedy act, taking it from clubs to theatre (*An Evening with French and Saunders*, 1989), and making a successful breakthrough into television with 'The Comic Strip Presents ...' (1990), 'Girls on Top' and five series of 'French and Saunders'. She became internationally known following the success of her comedy series *Absolutely Fabulous* (1993–5, 2001; Emmy, 1993), starring herself and Joanna Lumley, which generated a US version in 1995. In 1999 she teamed up again with French in the series *Let Them Eat Cake*.

Saurischia [sawriskia] The reptile-hipped dinosaurs; characterized by a forward pointing pubis bone in the pelvic girdle, as in modern reptiles. They comprise two main groups: the Theropoda, including the two-legged flesh-eaters such as *Tyrannosaurus*; and the giant plant-eating forms belonging to the Sauropodomorpha, including *Diplodocus*.

saury [sawree] Agile, slender-bodied fish, widespread and locally common in temperate ocean surface waters; head pointed or forming a narrow beak; feeds on other fishes and crustaceans; includes the Atlantic skipper, *Scomberesox saurus*; body length up to 45 cm/18 in. (Family: Scomberosocidae, 2 genera, 4 species.)

sausage A cylindrical portion of minced meat, usually blended with breadcrumbs and herbs, and enclosed in an edible casing. Originally, the casing came from prepared animal intestine; today it is made from edible carbohydrate polymers. Sausages may be wet (requiring cooking) or dry (ready to eat), as in frankfurters and salami respectively.

sausage dog *dachshund*

Saussure, Ferdinand de [sohsür] (1857–1913) Linguist, the founder of modern linguistics, born in Geneva, SW Switzerland. He taught historical linguistics at Paris (1881–91), and became professor of Indo-European linguistics and Sanskrit (1901–13) and of general linguistics (1907–13) at Geneva. The work by which he is best known, the *Cours de linguistique générale* (1916, Course in General Linguistics) was compiled from the lecture notes of his students after his death. His focus on language as an 'underlying system' inspired a great deal of later semiology and structuralism.

Savage, Michael Joseph (1872–1940) New Zealand statesman and prime minister (1935–40), born in Benalla, Victoria, SE Australia. He emigrated to New Zealand in 1907. An MP from 1919,

Saudi Arabia

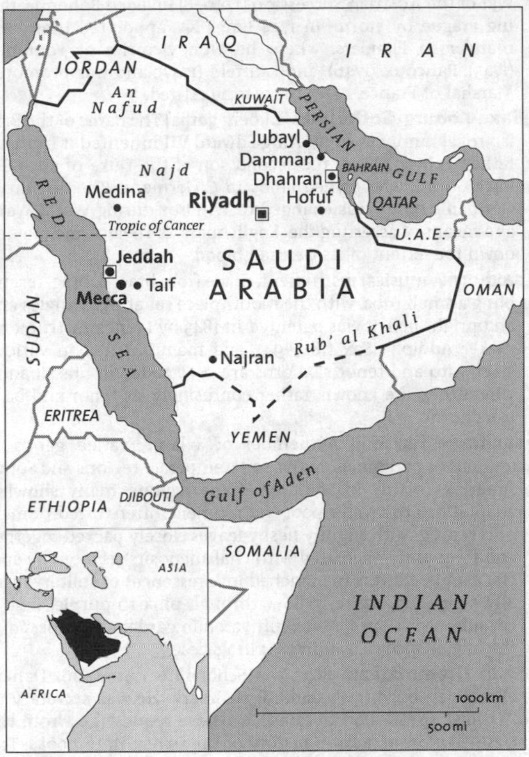

☐ International Airport — — Boundary awaiting demarcation

[sowdee araybia], official name **Kingdom of Saudi Arabia**, Arabic **Al-Mamlaka al-Arabiya as-Saudiya**

Local name al-'Arabīyah as-Sa'ūdīyah (Arabic)

Timezone GMT +3

Area 2 331 000 km²/899 766 sq mi

Population total (2002e) 23 370 000

Status Kingdom

Capital Riyadh (Ar-Riy-ad)

Language Arabic (official)

Ethnic groups Arab (90%), Afro-Asian (10%)

Religions Muslim (Sunni 85%, Shi'ite 15%), small Christian minority

Physical features Comprises four-fifths of the Arabian peninsula; Red Sea coastal plain bounded E by mountains; highlands in SW contain Jebel Abha, Saudi Arabia's highest peak, 3133m/10 279 ft; Arabian peninsula slopes gently N and E towards oil-rich al-Hasa plain on the Persian Gulf; interior comprises two extensive areas of sand desert, the An Nafud (N)and Rub' al-Khali (the Great Sandy Desert) (S); salt flats numerous in E lowlands; large network of wadis drains NE; 95% of land is arid or semi-arid desert.

Climate Hot, dry climate; average temperatures 21°C (N), 26°C (S), rise to 50°C in the interior; night frosts common in N and highlands; Red Sea coast hot and humid; average annual temperatures 14°C (Jan), 33°C (Jul) in Riyadh; average annual rainfall 100 mm/0·4 in.

Currency 1 Saudi Arabian Riyal (SAR, SRls) = 100 halalah

Economy Oil discovered in 1930s; now the world's leading oil exporter (reserves account for c.25% of world's known supply); rapidly-developing construction industry; large areas opened up for cultivation in 1980s; agriculture; wheat, dates, livestock; pilgrimage trade.

GDP (2002e) $268·9 bn, per capita $11 400

Human Development Index (2002) 0·759

History Famed as the birthplace of Islam, a centre of pilgrimage to the holy cities of Mecca, Medina, and Jedda; modern state founded by Ibn Saud who by 1932 united the four tribal provinces of Hejaz (NW), Asir (SW), Najd (C), and al-Hasa (E); governed as an absolute monarchy based on Islamic law and Arab Bedouin tradition; King (official title: Custodian of the Two Holy Mosques (Mecca and Medina)) is Head of State and Prime Minister, assisted by a Council of Ministers; there is no parliament; royal decree, 1992, provided for the creation of a Consultative Council.

Head of State/Government (Monarch)
Family name: al-Saud

1932–53 Abdulaziz ibn Abdur-Rahman ibn Saud
1953–64 Saud IV ibn Abdulaziz
1964–75 Faisal II ibn Abdulaziz
1975–82 Khalid (II) ibn Abdulaziz
1982–96 Fahd ibn Abdul-Aziz
1996 Abdullah ibn Abdul Aziz *Acting*
1996– Fahd ibn Abdul-Aziz

he became leader of the Labour Party in 1933 and then prime minister. As leader of the first Labour government, he presided over a notable set of social reforms. He died in office.

Savannah 32°05N 81°06W, pop (2000e) 131 500. Seat of Chatham Co, E Georgia, USA; port near the mouth of the Savannah R; founded, 1733; during the War of Independence, held by the British, 1778–82; captured by Sherman during the Civil War, 1864; airfield; railway; trade in tobacco, cotton, sugar, clay, woodpulp; chemicals, petroleum, rubber, plastics, paper products; fisheries; railway engineering; naval stores centre; city's historic district designated a national historic landmark; St Patrick's Festival (Mar).

savannah The grassland region of the tropics and subtropics, located between areas of tropical rainforest and desert. The length of the arid season prevents widespread tree growth; the scattered trees which do exist, such as acacia and baobab, are adapted to reduced precipitation levels. Fires, both natural and as a result of human activity, help to promote and maintain grassland.

Savery, Thomas (c.1650–1715) Engineer, born in Shilstone, Devon, SW England, UK. He developed and patented a device for pumping water out of mines (1698), using steam pressure admitted to a closed chamber containing water. When the steam had forced the water to a higher level, the steam was condensed, creating a vacuum which drew up more water from below through a valve, refilling the closed chamber for the process to be repeated. This was the first practical steam engine, and he manufactured several until he joined with Newcomen to help develop Newcomen's more efficient and practical steam piston engine.

Save the Children Fund In the UK, the largest international children's charity, founded in 1919, and having as its president the Princess Royal. It is concerned with the rescue of children from disaster and the longer-term welfare of children in need. Together with the US **Save the Children Federation**, it is a member of the **International Save the Children Alliance**.

Savile, Jimmy [savil], popular name of **Sir James Wilson Vincent Savile** (1926–) Television and radio personality, born in Leeds, West Yorkshire, N England, UK. A former miner, he achieved fame as a radio disc-jockey and television personality, with regular appearances on *Top of the Pops* from 1963. On television he began to host *Jim'll Fix It* in 1975, helping to realize the dreams of ordinary people. His flamboyant style contrasts with his other role as a voluntary helper at Leeds Infirmary and elsewhere; he has used his nationwide prominence and popularity to raise huge sums of money for deserving causes (such as £12 million to rebuild the National Spinal Injuries Centre at Stoke Mandeville). He has written two volumes of autobiography, *As It Happens* (1975) and *Love Is an Uphill Thing* (1976). He was knighted in 1990.

saving That part of income which is not spent on consumption. In economics, the marginal propensity to save is that proportion of additional income which is not consumed. High saving permits rapid economic growth, as in Japan or Taiwan. If saving is low, there can be little investment, and growth will be slow, as in many less developed countries or the USA. While high savings are necessary for growth, they are not sufficient. If there is little investment, high individual willingness to save will produce low aggregate incomes through lack of demand.

savings and loan associations *building society*

Savonarola, Girolamo [savonarohla] (1452–98) Religious and political reformer, born in Ferrara, NE Italy. He became a Dominican at Bologna in 1474, and after an initial failure, came to be recognized as an inspiring preacher. He was vicar-general of the Dominicans in Tuscany (1493), and his preaching began to point towards a political revolution as the means of restoring religion and morality. When a republic was established in Florence (1494), he was its guiding spirit, fostering a Christian commonwealth, with stringent laws governing the repression of vice and frivolity. His denunciations of the abuses of Church and government leaders made him many enemies, including Pope Alexander VI, who summoned him to Rome (1495) to answer a charge of heresy. He disregarded the order, was excommunicated in 1497, and burned in Florence.

savory Either of two related species with square stems, opposite paired leaves, and 2-lipped purplish or white flowers in whorls forming loose spikes. **Summer savory** (*Satureja hortensis*) is a slender, bushy annual native to the Mediterranean. **Winter savory** (*Satureja montana*) is a woody perennial native to S Europe. Both are grown as culinary herbs. (Genus: *Satureja*. Family: Labiatae.)

Savoy, House of Rulers of the duchy of Savoy, a transalpine area in present-day Switzerland and France, from the 11th-c to the 19th-c. Its heyday in European politics was from the mid-14th-c to the mid-15th-c; thereafter it was hemmed in by French and Spanish monarchies. It suffered in the Italian Wars of the 16th-c, the Thirty Years' War, and the Napoleonic Wars.

saw, musical A common handsaw used as a musical instrument by pressing it towards the thigh and drawing a violin bow across the straight edge. The pitch is controlled by the curve of the blade, and it is usually imbued with a heavy vibrato by movements of the hand or leg.

saw-bill *merganser*

Sawchuk, Terry, popular name of **Terrance (Gordon) Sawchuck** (1929–70) Ice hockey player, born in Winnipeg, Manitoba, C Canada. One of the game's greatest goaltenders, he started his career with the Detroit Red Wings in 1950, and later played for the Boston Bruins, Toronto Maple Leafs, Los Angeles Kings, and New York Rangers. His 103 shutouts are a National Hockey League record. He appeared in 971 games (1950–70), a record for a goaltender. He was largely responsible for the crouched stance subsequently adopted by other goaltenders.

sawfish A very large and distinctive ray, with a greatly prolonged snout, armed on each side with a regular row of strong blunt teeth; the saw is used to delve in soft sediments for food; widespread in tropical seas, and may be common in shallow estuaries ranging into fresh water; largest species is *Pristis pectinata*; length up to 7·5 m/25 ft. (Family: Pristidae, 1 genus.)

sawfly A wasp-like insect which lacks a constricted waist; egg-laying tube large, saw-like, and used for depositing eggs deep into plant tissues; larvae caterpillar-like, feeding on, or boring into, plant stems, leaves, or wood. (Order: Hymenoptera. Suborder: Symphyta.)

Saxby, Joseph *Dolmetsch, Carl*

Saxe, (Hermann) Maurice, comte de (Count of), usually called **Marshal de Saxe** (1696–1750) Marshal of France, born in Goslar, C Germany, the illegitimate son of Augustus II, King of Poland, formerly Elector of Saxony. He served in the French army in the War of the Polish Succession (1733–8), and in the War of the Austrian Succession (1740–8) invaded Bohemia, taking Prague by storm. In 1744 Louis XV appointed him commander in Flanders, where he won victories at Fontenoy (1745), Raucoux (1746), and Lauffeld (1747), and was promoted Marshal of France. After the war he retired.

Saxe-Coburg-Gotha [saks **koh**berg **go**tha] The name of the British royal family, 1901–17. King Edward VII inherited it from his father, Prince Albert, the second son of the Duke of Saxe-Coburg-Gotha, who owned lands in C Germany. The obviously Germanic name was changed to Windsor during World War 1 as a means of asserting the 'Englishness' of royalty and playing down the extent of its German blood.

saxhorn A musical instrument, made from brass tubing, resembling a small tuba, with the mouthpiece set at right angles and an upright bell. It was patented in 1843 by French instrument-maker Adolphe Sax (1814–94), and manufactured in various sizes. Alto and tenor saxhorns are used today in brass bands, where they are known, rather confusingly, as tenor and baritone horns.

saxifrage [**sak**sifrij] A member of a large, varied genus of annuals or perennials, native to N temperate regions and South America, mainly in arctic or alpine regions, many showing adaptations to a water-poor environment; often tufted, domed, or creeping, with slightly fleshy leaves closely packed together and frequently encrusted with chalk deposits secreted by special glands; flowers in branched inflorescences or solitary, usually 5-petalled, white, yellow, through pink to purple; fruit a capsule. Many species are cultivated in gardens. (Genus: *Saxifraga*, 370 species. Family: Saxifragaceae.)

Saxo Grammaticus (Lat 'the Scholar') (c.1140–1206) Danish chronicler, born in Zealand, E Denmark. He was secretary to Archbishop Absalon of Lund, at whose request he wrote the *Gesta Danorum*, a Latin history of the Danes, in 16 books. The work is partly legendary and partly historical.

Saxons A Germanic people from the N Danish plain. Under pressure from the migrating Franks they spread from their home-lands into Italy and the Friesian lands, engaging in piracy (3rd–5th-c). With the Angles and Jutes, they formed the bulk of the invaders who in the two centuries following the Roman withdrawal from Britain (409) conquered and colonized most of what became Anglo-Saxon England. They were especially prominent in Essex, Sussex, and Wessex. Charlemagne established Christianity over his empire in the 9th-c, and rulers of the Saxon duchy – Saxony – formed a German royal dynasty in the 10th-c. After the 12th-c, Saxony was dissolved and the name transferred to another region of Germany.

Saxony A German ducal and electoral state which experienced many changes of fortune. Prominent from the 9th–11th-c, it was reduced by Emperor Frederick I to two small areas on the R Elbe (1180–1422). Dynastic alliances enlarged the Saxon state on the Middle Elbe in the 15th-c. Frederick the Wise adopted Lutheranism (1524), establishing Saxony's Protestant leadership, and despite family divisions, it grew prosperous in the 16th-c. The reign of John George I (1611–56) marked its steady eclipse by Brandenburg, and new duchies (eg Hanover) were formed out of Lower Saxony. Under the Catholic elector Frederick Augustus (r.1694–1733), Saxony's prestige improved with the acquisition of the Polish crown, but his namesake became a client of Napoleon, only to lose two-fifths of his territory at the Congress of Vienna (1815). Saxony was merged in the North German Confederation (1866) and the German Second Reich (1871).

saxophone A single-reed musical instrument, made of metal with a wide conical bore. It was patented in 1846 by French instrument-maker Adolphe Sax (1814–94), and made in a variety of sizes and pitches, the most frequently used being the alto and tenor instruments. These are usually joined by the soprano and baritone instruments to form the saxophone quartet; bass and contrabass sizes are also in use. A favourite in jazz and dance bands of the 20th-c, the saxophone has been used occasionally in orchestral music.

Sayan Mountains [sayan] Mountain range mainly in S Siberian Russia, and extending into N Mongolia; E Sayan Mts stretch 1100 km/680 mi SE from the lower R Yenisey, forming the boundary between Russia and Mongolia in the E; highest peak, Munku-Sardyk (3491 m/11 453 ft); W Sayan Mts lie entirely within Russia, stretching 640 km/400 mi NE from the Altay Mts; gold, coal, graphite, silver, lead; lumbering, hunting, agriculture.

Sayers, Dorothy L(eigh) (1893–1957) Writer, born in Oxford, Oxfordshire, SC England, UK. She studied at Oxford, and became a celebrated writer of detective stories. Beginning with *Whose Body?* (1923) and *Clouds of Witness* (1926), she related the adventures of her hero Lord Peter Wimsey in various accurately observed milieux – such as advertising in *Murder Must Advertise* (1933) and bell-ringing in *The Nine Tailors* (1934). She then earned a reputation as a leading Christian apologist with her plays, radio broadcasts, and essays.

SBS Abbreviation of **Special Boat Service**, the naval arm of British Military Special Forces responsible for all non-conventional maritime operations. Resourced from the Royal Marines, the SBS has seen action in the Falklands War of 1982 and the Gulf War of 1991. It provided the blueprint for the formation of the American SEALS (Sea, Air, Land teams).

scabbardfish *ribbonfish*

scabies [skaybeez] A common but harmless itchy skin infestation with a mite (*Sarcoptes scabei*), which burrows below the skin surface. It spreads from person to person by direct contact. Superimposed streptococcal infection is common in the tropical countries.

scabious A perennial growing to 70 cm/27 in (*Scabiosa columbaria*), native to Europe, W Asia, and N Africa; leaves pinnately lobed, in opposite pairs; flowers bluish-lilac, with five unequal petals, in heads 1·5–3·5 cm/½–1½ in across. The flowers around the rim of the head have much larger petals than those in the centre. It is cultivated along with other similar species for ornament. (Family: Dipsacaceae.)

Scafell Pike [skawfel], also spelled **Scawfell** 54°28N 3°12W. Mountain in Lake District of Cumbria, NW England, UK; highest peak in England, rising to 977 m/3205 ft in the Cumbrian Mts, W of Ambleside.

scalar In mathematics, a physical quantity which can be represented by a real number, having magnitude but not direction, such as mass, time, and temperature. Any real number may be considered to be a scalar, in contrast with complex numbers, which may be considered to be vectors.

Scalawags A derogatory term for white Southerners who co-operated with occupying forces during the era of Reconstruction following the American Civil War. Many Scalawags had never favoured secession, and some were principled opponents of slavery.

scald *burn*

scale In music, the notes forming the basic vocabulary of a melodic or harmonic system, arranged in a succession of upward or downward steps. Since stepwise movement is common in most types of music, the practising of scales forms a basic part of an instrumentalist's training. The important scales in Western music include the *major* and *minor* scales, the *pentatonic* scale, the *whole tone* scale, and the *chromatic* scale.

scale insect A plant-sucking bug; wingless adult females usually protected by a scale-like wax covering secreted over the body; males non-feeding, with one pair of wings; less than 8 mm/⅓ in long; newly hatched larvae (*crawlers*) dispersed by wind; c.4000 species, including many pests of economically important plants. (Order: Homoptera. Family: Coccidae.)

scales Small bony or horny plates which form the body covering of fishes and reptiles. The scales covering the wings of some insects, such as butterflies and moths, are modified cuticular hairs.

Scalfaro, Oscar (Luigi) [skalfahroh] (1918–) Italian politician and president (1992–9), born in Novara, Piedmont, Italy. He was a leader of the Azione Cattolica (Catholic Action) movement, a member of the Constituent Assembly (1946), then a deputy. He served as minister for transport (1966–8, 1972), education (1972–3), and the interior (1983–7), before becoming president.

Scaliger, Julius Caesar [skalijer], originally **Benedetto Bordone** (1484–1558) Humanist scholar, born in Riva, N Italy. He studied medicine at Padua, became a French citizen in 1528, and settled in Agen, where he wrote learned works on grammar, philosophy, botany, zoology, and literary criticism. Titles include *De plantis* (1556) and his best-known work, *Poetice* (1561). His third son, **Joseph Justus Scaliger** (1540–1609), became one of the most erudite scholars of his day, best known for his *Opus de emendatione temporum* (1583), a study of earlier methods of calculating time.

scallop A marine bivalve mollusc with unequal shell valves; lives unattached to a substrate, and is able to swim by clapping its valves together; margin of its mantle provided with a ring of tentacles and numerous eyes; fished commercially for human consumption. (Class: Pelecypoda. Order: Ostreoida.)

scaly anteater *pangolin*

scaly-tailed squirrel A squirrel-like rodent; inhabits woodland in C Africa; not a true squirrel; base of tail with large scales on undersurface; six species resemble flying squirrels, with a membrane supported by long rod of cartilage projecting from each elbow. (Family: Anomaluridae, 7 species.)

scaly-weaver *weaverbird*

scampi The Italian culinary term for large Gulf shrimps or Dublin Bay prawns, usually fried in batter.

Scanderbeg *Skanderbeg*

Scandinavian languages The languages of the N Germanic branch of Indo-European, including Norwegian (c.5 million in Norway and the USA), Swedish (c.9 million in Sweden, Finland, and the USA), Danish (c.5 million in Denmark, Germany, and the USA), Icelandic (c.0·25 million in Iceland and the USA), and Faroese (c.40 000 in the Faroe Is). These languages are mutually intelligible to varying degrees, though there are substantial differences between the *continental* varieties as a group (Swedish, Danish, Norwegian), and the *insular* varieties (Icelandic, Faroese). Their status as separate languages rests on the political independence of their speech communities.

Scandinavian literature *Danish / Icelandic / Norwegian / Swedish literature*

scanner An input device in a computer system which scans documents and transfers a map of the document into the memory of the computer. The document is represented by an array of pixels, with the number of pixels per square inch of document signifying the quality of the scanner. Low-quality scanners scan only black and white at 300 pixels per inch; high-quality ones scan in full colour at 1200 pixels per inch. In each element of the array a value is stored to represent the colour and brightness of that pixel. Most scanners are accompanied by software which can analyse the page image, pick out blocks of text, and convert the image into a text string. This software allows text documents to be input quickly and converted to textual strings by the software, ready for use in a word processor or a desk-top publishing system. Full colour pictures can also be read and processed by imaging software.

scanning The exploration of a picture area along a systematic series of lines, providing information in sequential form. In video, the camera image scanned by a set of horizontal lines is reproduced on the screen of a cathode ray tube in the same fashion. For TV broadcasting, two sets of interlaced alternate scanning lines are employed, giving a total picture coverage of 525 lines 30 times a second for American NTSC and 625 lines 25 times a second for European PAL. Optical scanning at a much slower rate is also employed for the transmission of facsimile documents and pictures over land lines, and for the electronic preparation of colour separations in graphic arts, and the exposure system in laser printers using electrophotography.

scanning probe microscopy A general term for a variety of microscope techniques in which a sample surface is studied using a probe tip which scans relative to the sample surface. The *scanning tunnelling microscope* (STM) uses an electron tunnelling current to image a conducting surface. The *atomic force microscope* (AFM) measures the force on the tip to map a conducting or non-conducting surface. Magnetic and electrical surface properties can be characterized using coated tips, for example in *scanning electrical potential microscopy* (SEPM) which uses a platinum-coated probe to simultaneously map the surface and its charge. The *scanning near-field optical microscope* (SNOM), creates optical images with a resolution of tens of nanometres using light from a fine fibre scanning the surface, evading the diffraction limit applicable to normal microscopes because the light leaves the fibre very close to the sample surface. The applications of scanning probe microscopy are limitless, ranging from checking semiconductor wafers and optical disks during manufacture, to observing cells, proteins, bacteria, and viruses in situ.

Scapa Flow The area of open water in the Orkney Is, NE Scotland, UK, surrounded by the islands of Mainland, Hoy, Flotta, S Ronaldsay, and Burray. It was a British naval base in World Wars 1 and 2. In 1919 the German naval fleet was scuttled there.

scapegoat In ancient Jewish ritual (*Lev* 16), on the Day of Atonement and after the sacrifices of a bull and a goat as sin-offerings, a second goat (the 'scapegoat') was released into the wilderness 'to Azazel', possibly a desert demon, symbolizing how the people's sins were removed. The high priest cast lots to determine the respective fates of the two goats. Today the term is more generally applied to one who takes the blame for another.

Scaphopoda [skafopoda] *tusk shell*

scapula A triangular bone on each side of the body over the upper part of the back (second to seventh ribs); also called the **shoulder-blade**. With the clavicle it forms the *pectoral girdle*. Its only point of attachment to the axial skeleton is indirectly via the clavicle. It sits within a bed of muscles which connect it to the thorax, vertebral column, and upper limb. Its position on the chest wall therefore depends on the interplay of the activities of the various muscles attached to it. It moves in conjunction with the shoulder joint to increase the total range of movement of the upper limb.

scarab beetle A dung beetle that has specialized forelegs for forming dung into a ball and rolling it into an underground chamber for feeding larvae. The scarab was symbolic in ancient Egypt of resurrection and immortality. Amulets and stamp seals were often made in the shape of the beetle, and worn either in pendants or rings. (Order: Coleoptera. Family: Scarabeidae.)

Scarborough [skah(r)bruh] 54°17N 0°24W, pop (2001e) 106 200. Coastal resort town in North Yorkshire, N England, UK; on the North Sea 25 km/15 mi N of Bridlington; a Roman signal station in the 4th-c; England's oldest spa town; railway; electrics, foodstuffs, fishing, tourism; castle (12th-c), museum of regional archaeology; football league team, Scarborough.

Scardino, Marjorie (Morris) [skah(r)deenoh] (1947–) Businesswoman, born in Texas, USA. She trained as a lawyer at George Washington and San Francisco Universities, joined a Georgia law firm, and later founded the *Georgia Gazette*. She then became president of the Economist Newspaper Group in New York (1985–92), and its chief executive in London (1992–6). She joined the Pearson group as its chief executive in 1997, the first woman to head one of the UK's top 100 companies, and was named businesswoman of the year in 1998. She became chair of the company in 1999.

Scarfe, Gerald (1936–) Cartoonist, born in London, UK. His cartoons, based on extreme distortion in the tradition of Gillray (eg Mick Jagger's lips are drawn larger than the rest of his face), have appeared in *Punch*, *Private Eye*, and elsewhere, especially *The Sunday Times* since 1967. Appointed artist to the *New Yorker* from 1993, he has also worked as a theatrical designer and animated film director, notably with *Hercules* (1997). An exhibition of his work, *Heroes and Villains*, was held at the National Portrait Gallery in 2003. He is married to actress Jane Asher.

Scargill, Arthur (1938–) Trade unionist, born in Leeds, West Yorkshire, N England, UK. He became president of the National Union of Mineworkers in 1981, and a member of the Trades Union Congress General Council. He is primarily known for his strong, Socialist defence of British miners that has often brought his union into conflict with the government, most particularly during the miners' strike (1984–5), and when British Coal announced the closure of most deep-mine collieries in 1992.

Scarlatti, (Pietro) Alessandro (Gaspare) [skah(r)latee] (1660–1725) Composer, born in Palermo, Sicily, S Italy. He produced his first opera in Rome (1679), where he became *maestro di cappella* to Queen Christina of Sweden. He was musical director at the court in Naples (1683–1702, 1709–25), and became a leading figure in Italian opera. He reputedly wrote over 100 operas, of which 40 survive complete, the most famous being *Tigrane* (1715). He also wrote 10 Masses, c.700 cantatas, and oratorios, motets, and madrigals.

Scarlatti, (Giuseppe) Domenico [skah(r)latee] (1685–1757) Composer, born in Naples, SW Italy, the son of Alessandro Scarlatti. From 1711 he was *maestro di cappella* in Rome to the Queen of Poland, for whom he composed several operas, and he also served in Lisbon and Madrid. As choirmaster of St Peter's, Rome (1714–19), he wrote much church music. He was a skilled harpsichordist, and is mainly remembered for the 555 sonatas written for this instrument.

scarlet fever An acute infectious disease of children caused by haemolytic streptococci. A sore throat is followed by a generalized red rash. It responds rapidly to antibiotics, but complications include middle-ear infection, rheumatic fever, glomerulonephritis, and Sydenham's chorea.

scarlet pimpernel *pimpernel*

Scarron, Paul [skarõ] (1610–60) Writer, born in Paris, France. During his 20s the onset of paralysis forced him to take up writing for a living, and he produced many sonnets, madrigals, songs, epistles, and satires. He is best known for his realistic novel, *Le Roman comique* (1651–7, The Comic Novel). In 1652 he married Françoise d'Aubigné (later, Madame de Maintenon).

scat singing Wordless or meaningless improvisatory jazz singing, often imitating rapid instrumental solos. It was made popular by Louis Armstrong, Ella Fitzgerald, Cab Calloway, Sarah Vaughan, and many others, and in turn had an influence on the development of instrumental jazz improvisation. Louis Armstrong's 'Heebie Jeebies' (1926) was the first recorded example; dubious legend has it that he dropped the song-sheet or forgot the words.

scattering In physics, the redirection of a beam of light or sound, or a stream of particles resulting from collisions. An approaching beam is directed on to a target material which scatters it into a detector. Scattering experiments are an important source of information in atomic, nuclear, particle, and solid state physics.

Scawfell *Scafell Pike*

scepticism / skepticism A philosophical tradition which casts doubt on the possibility of human knowledge, either in general or in some particular sphere. Pyrrho is usually credited as the founder, and from 280–80 BC it was the official philosophy of the Academy.

Schacht, (Horace Greely) Hjalmar [shahkht] (1877–1970) Financier, born in Tinglev, SW Denmark (formerly Germany). In 1923 he became president of the Reichsbank, and founded a new currency which ended the inflation of the mark. He was minister of economics (1934–7), but in 1939 was dismissed from his bank office for disagreeing with Hitler over rearmament expenditure. Interned by the Nazis, he was acquitted at Nuremberg. In 1953 he set up his own bank in Düsseldorf.

Schaffhausen [shafhowzn], Fr **Schaffhouse** 47°42N 8°38E, pop (2000e) 36 000. Industrial town and capital of Schaffhausen canton, NE Switzerland; on the R Rhine, 37 km/23 mi N of Zürich; well-preserved mediaeval town; railway; engineering, iron and steel works, chemicals, aluminium smelting; falls and rapids nearby; Kastel Munot (1564–85), Minster (1087–1150).

Scharnhorst, Gerhard Johann David von [shah(r)nhaw(r)st] (1755–1813) Prussian general and military reformer, born in Bordenau, NC Germany. He worked with Gneisenau to reform the Prussian army after its defeat by Napoleon, served as chief-of-staff to Blücher, and was fatally wounded fighting the French at Lützen.

Schawlow, Arthur (Leonard) [showloh] (1921–99) Physicist, born in Mount Vernon, New York, USA. He studied at Toronto and Columbia universities, worked at Bell Telephone Laboratories (1951–61), then became professor at Stanford, CA. With his brother-in-law, Charles Townes, he devised the laser in 1958, although the first working model was made by Maiman in 1960. He shared the 1981 Nobel Prize for Physics for his work in spectroscopy.

Scheel, Walter [shayl] (1919–) West German statesman and president (1974–9), born in Solingen, C Germany. After serving in the *Luftwaffe* in World War 2 he went into business, joined the Free Democratic Party, and was elected to the Bundestag in 1953. He was minister for economic co-operation (1961–6) and foreign minister (1969–74), and in 1970 negotiated treaties with the USSR and Poland.

scheelite [sheeliyt] A mineral calcium tungstate ($CaWO_4$) occurring in hydrothermal veins and pegmatites. It is an important ore of tungsten.

Schelde or **Scheldt, River** [skelduh, skelt], Fr **Escaut** River rising in Aisne department, N France; flows N and NE through Belgium to Antwerp, then NW to meet the North Sea through two estuaries (East and West Schelde) in The Netherlands; length 435 km/270 mi; connected by canal to several other N European rivers.

Scheler, Max [shayler] (1874–1928) Philosopher and social theorist, born in Munich, SE Germany. He taught at the universities of Jena (1900–6), Munich (1907–10), Cologne (1919–27), and Frankfurt (1928). Influenced by Husserl, he developed a distinctive version of phenomenology which he set out in his major work, *Der Formalismus in der Ethik und die materiale Wertethik* (1921, Formalism in Ethics and the Material Value Ethics). He also did influential work in the sociology of knowledge. Other works include *Die Sinngesetze des emotionalen Lebens* (1923, trans The Nature of Sympathy) and *Die Stellung des Menschen im Kosmos* (1928, trans Man's Place in Nature), a work of philosophical anthropology, with a pantheistic view of how God is realized in history and in the world.

Schelling, Friedrich (Wilhelm Joseph) von [sheling] (1775–1854) Philosopher, born in Leonberg, SW Germany. He studied at Tübingen and Leipzig, became professor at Jena (1798–1803), Würzburg (1803–8), and Erlangen (1820–7), and from 1806 was secretary of the Royal Academy at Munich. He moved to a chair at Berlin in 1841. His early work, influenced by Fichte and Kant, culminated in his *System des transzendentalen Idealismus* (1800, System of Transcendental Idealism), which argued that only in art can the mind become fully aware of itself, and he was an important influence on Coleridge and on Romanticism generally.

scherzo [skairtsoh] A lively musical piece, though not necessarily a 'joke', as the Italian name suggests. Haydn and Beethoven established it as an alternative to the minuet (whose metre and structure it took over) in the classical symphony and sonata.

Schiaparelli, Elsa [skyaparelee] (1890–1973) Fashion designer, born in Rome, Italy. After studying philosophy, she lived in the USA, working as a film script writer, then went to Paris in 1920. She designed and wore a black sweater knitted with a white bow, as a result of which she received orders from a US store, which started her in business. Her designs were inventive and sensational, and she was noted for her use of colour, including 'shocking pink', and her original use of traditional fabrics. She featured zippers and buttons, and made outrageous hats.

Schiaparelli, Giovanni (Virginio) [skyaparelee] (1835–1910) Astronomer, born in Savigliano, NW Italy. He studied at Berlin and at Pulkova, Russia, and became director of Brera Observatory, Milan. He discovered the link between meteor showers and comets, observed double stars, discovered the asteroid Hesperia, and termed vague linear features on Mars as 'canali' (1877).

Schick Test A test of the susceptibility to diphtheria, in which a small amount of diphtheria toxin is injected into the skin. A localized reaction indicates susceptibility, when immunization may be desirable. The test is named after the Austrian paediatrician, Bela Schick (1877–1967).

Schiele, Egon [sheeluh] (1890–1918) Painter, born in Tulln, NE Austria. He studied at the Vienna Academy of Fine Arts in 1906, met Klimt in 1907, and developed a powerful form of Expressionism in which figures, often naked and emaciated and drawn with hard outlines, fill the canvas with awkward, anguished gestures. In 1912 he was arrested, and some of his work was destroyed by the police. He died in the influenza epidemic of 1918.

Schiller, (Johann Christoph) Friedrich (von) [shiler] (1759–1805) Historian, playwright, and poet, born in Marbach, SW Germany. He attended a military academy, and became an army surgeon in Stuttgart, where he began to write *Sturm und Drang* ('storm and stress') verse and plays. The revolutionary appeal of his first play, *Die Räuber* (1781, The Robbers), made it an instant success. He later settled in Dresden, where his works included the poem *An die Freude* (Ode to Joy, later set to music by Beethoven in his Choral Symphony). He became professor of history at Jena in 1788, where he developed a close friendship with Goethe. His last decade was highly productive, including the dramatic trilogy, *Wallenstein* (1796–9), the greatest German historical drama *Maria Stuart* (1800), and *Wilhelm Tell* (1804).

Schinkel, Karl Friedrich [shingkl] (1781–1841) Architect, born in Neuruppin, NE Germany. He studied at Berlin and in Italy, became state architect of Prussia (1815), and director of public works (1830). He designed a wide range of buildings, in Classical style, and introduced new streets and squares in Berlin. He also became known as a painter, illustrator, and furniture and stage designer.

schipperke [shiperkee, skiperkee] A breed of dog, developed in Belgium, originally used as a watchdog on barges; small, lively; erect pointed ears, pointed muzzle, no tail; thick, usually black, coat; also known as **little boatman**, **little captain**, or **little corporal**.

schist [shist] A medium-grade regional metamorphic rock characterized by a foliated texture, resulting from the alignment and segregation of layers of mica minerals.

schistosomiasis [skistosomiyasis] A common cause of illness in tropical countries, resulting from infestation with one of three species of the genus *Schistosoma*, a fluke; also known as **bilharziasis**. These penetrate the skin of people bathing in contaminated water. Once inside the body, they spread in the blood and cause disease of the lungs, liver, brain, and kidney. Clinical features include pneumonia, liver failure, fits, and coma. The flukes lay eggs in the kidney, which are passed out in the urine. They hatch in the water and the larvae grow and develop inside snails. Reducing the number of snails is one strategy for controlling the disease.

schizophrenia A major psychiatric disorder characterized by an alteration of thinking and perception, including a loss of contact with reality. In addition there may be a basic change in personality and a loss of normal emotional responsiveness. Schizophrenic patients often feel that their unexpressed thoughts are known to others and can be influenced by external forces. Trivial events and objects take on inappropriately significant meaning. There may be considerable withdrawal. The causes are not fully understood, but there is a major genetic component and a well-established higher incidence in winter-born children. Brain damage, either at birth or subsequently, may produce a schizophrenia-like picture, and social stresses are thought to be of particular significance in the relapse of this condition. Management includes prevention (by minimizing social stresses), prophylactic drug treatment, treatment of acute illness (usually with anti-psychotic drugs), skilful counselling concerning the impact of the illness for the sufferers, and rehabilitation.

Schlegel, August Wilhelm von [shlaygl] (1767–1845) Poet and critic, born in Hanover, NC Germany, the brother of Friedrich von Schlegel (1772–1829). He studied theology at Göttingen, but soon turned to literature, settling in Jena, where he became professor of literature and fine art (1798). He then lectured at Berlin (1801–4), and from 1818 until his death was professor of literature at Bonn. He is famous for his translations of Shakespeare and other authors, and for founding Sanskrit studies in Germany. He was a leading figure of the Romantic movement.

Schleiermacher, Friedrich (Ernst Daniel) [shliyermahkher] (1768–1834) Theologian and philosopher, born in Wrocław, SW Poland (formerly Breslau, Prussia). He studied at Halle, became a preacher in Berlin (1796), and was professor at Halle (1804–6) and Berlin (from 1810). He was a leader of the movement which led to the union in 1817 of the Lutheran and Reformed Churches in Prussia. His most important work is *Der Christliche Glaube* (1821–2, The Christian Faith), and he also wrote on Christian ethics, a life of Jesus, sermons, and letters. He is generally held to be the founder of modern Protestant theology.

Schlesinger, Arthur M(eier), Jr [shlezinjer] (1917–) Historian, born in Columbus, Ohio, USA, the son of Arthur M Schlesinger. He studied at Harvard and Cambridge, and was professor of history at Harvard (1954–61) before becoming special assistant to President Kennedy (1961–3). His publications include *The Age of Jackson* (1945) and *A Thousand Days: John F Kennedy in the White House* (1965) (both Pulitzer Prizes). He later became professor of humanities at the City University of New York (1966–95, now emeritus) and president of the American Institute of Arts and Letters (1981).

Schlesinger, John [shlezinjer] (1926–2003) Film director, born in London, UK. He directed art documentary films for television, and made his first feature film of contemporary social realism, *A Kind of Loving*, in 1962, followed by *Billy Liar* (1963). His interpretation of Hardy's *Far from the Madding Crowd* (1967), the downbeat urban *Midnight Cowboy* (1969, Oscar), and the sensitive *Sunday, Bloody Sunday* (1971) showed his width of range. Later productions in the USA explored political responsibilities, such as *Day of the Locust* (1975), *Marathon Man* (1976), and *Yanks* (1979). Films of the 1980s include *Honky Tonk Freeway* (1980), *Believers* (1987), and *Madame Sousatzka* (1989), and for television *An Englishman Abroad* (1983). Later titles include *Pacific Heights* (1990), *The Innocent* (1993), *Cold Comfort Farm* (TV, 1996), and *The Next Best Thing* (2000). He also directed for stage and opera.

Schleswig [shlezvig] A breed of heavy horse, developed in Germany; height, 15·2–16 hands/1·5–1·6 m/5 ft 2 in–5 ft 4 in; usually pale brown with yellow mane; body long and deep; short powerful legs; also known as **Schleswig heavy draught**.

Schleswig-Holstein [shlezvig holshtiyn] pop (2000e) 2 700 000; area 15 721 sq km/6068 sq mi. Northernmost province of Germany, bounded N by Denmark; includes the North Frisian Is; capital, Kiel; chief towns include Lübeck, Flensburg; coast includes an extensive swimming and sailing resort area; shipbuilding, machinery, foodstuffs, electrical engineering; focus of a dispute between Denmark and Prussia in the 19th-c, leading to war (1863) and annexation by Prussia (1866).

Schlick, Moritz [shlik] (1882–1936) Philosopher, one of the leaders of the Vienna Circle of logical positivists, born in Berlin, Germany. He studied physics at Heidelberg, Lausanne, and Berlin, taught at Rostock and Kiel, and from 1922 was professor of inductive sciences at Vienna. An early exponent of Einstein's relativity theories, his major works include *Allgemeine Erkenntnislehre* (1918, General Theory of Knowledge) and *Fragen der Ethik* (1930, Problems of Ethics). He was shot down on the steps of the university by a deranged student.

Schlieffen, Alfred, Graf von (Count of) [shleefn] (1833–1913) Prussian field marshal, born in Berlin, Germany. He entered the army in 1854, and rose to become chief of general staff (1891–1905). He advocated the plan, which bears his name (1895), on which German tactics were unsuccessfully based in World War 1. He envisaged a German breakthrough in Belgium and the defeat of France within six weeks by a major right-wheel flanking movement through The Netherlands, cutting off Paris from the sea, holding off the Russians meanwhile with secondary forces.

Schliemann, Heinrich [shleeman] (1822–90) Archaeologist, born in Neubukow, N Germany. After a successful business career, he retired early to realize his ambition of finding the site of the Homeric poems by excavating the tell at Hisarlik in Asia Minor, the traditional site of Troy. From 1871 he discovered nine superimposed city sites, one containing a considerable treasure (found 1873) which he over-hastily identified as Priam's. He also excavated several other Greek sites, including Mycenae (1876) and Tiryns (1884).

schlieren photography [shleeren] A means of forming a photographic image of density variations in a transparent fluid. It relies on the refraction of incident light due to variations in the fluid density, and is used in the analysis of wind tunnel experiments to show the flow and pressure patterns round an object.

Schmidt, Helmut (Heinrich Waldemar) [shmit] (1918–) West German statesman and chancellor (1974–82), born in Hamburg, N Germany. After service in World War 2, he studied at Hamburg, joined the Social Democratic Party in 1946, and became a member of the Bundestag in 1953. He was minister of defence (1969–72), and of finance (1972–4), in which role he created a firm basis for Germany's continued economic growth. He succeeded Brandt as chancellor, describing his aim as the 'political unification of Europe in partnership with the United States'.

Schmidt telescope [shmit] An astronomical instrument invented in 1930 by Bernhard Schmidt (1879–1935), which uses a correcting plate in the optical path to achieve distortion-free images over a wide field. It is used to make photographic sky surveys.

schnauzer [shnowtser] A German breed of dog; terrier-like with thick wiry coat; marked eyebrows, moustache, and beard; top of head flat, with short pendulous ears; three forms: **giant** (bred to herd sheep and cattle), **standard**, and **miniature** (both used as rat-catchers).

Schneider Trophy [shniyder] A flying trophy for seaplanes presented by French armaments magnate Jacques Schneider in 1913. After being won outright by Great Britain in 1931 the contest ceased, but the races were revived in the 1980s.

Schnitzler, Arthur [shnitsler] (1862–1931) Playwright and novelist, born in Vienna, Austria. He was a physician before he turned playwright, writing highly psychological, light-heartedly short plays and novels. They include his one-act play cycles *Anatol* (1893) and *Reigen* (1900, Merry-go-round, filmed as *La Ronde*, 1950). An exponent of *fin-de-siecle* Viennese life with its sexual repressions and social duplicity, he draws a picture of human deceit and of the inferior role of women in society.

Schoenberg, Arnold [shoenberg], also spelled **Schönberg** (1874–1951) Composer, born in Vienna, Austria. He was largely self-taught, and in his 20s lived by orchestrating operettas while composing such early works as the string sextet *Verklärte Nacht* (1899, Transfigured Night). His search for a personal musical style emerged in these works, which were not well received: his *Chamber Symphony* caused a riot at its first performance in 1907 through its abandonment of the traditional concept of tonality. He became known for his concept of '12-note' or 'serial' music, used in most of his later works. At the end of World War 1 he taught in Vienna and Berlin, until exiled by the Nazi government in 1933. He settled in California, and took US nationality in 1941.

scholastic aptitude test *SAT 1*

scholasticism The Catholic philosophical tradition dominant in the mediaeval universities of the 12th–14th-c in Western Europe. Anselm spoke of 'faith seeking understanding', and the philosophy was generally used in the service of theology; it often took the form of a recovery and interpretation of Greek philosophy, particularly the work of Aristotle. The Renaissance humanists gave the 'schoolmen' a bad name, accusing them of sterile logic-chopping and a rigid reliance on authority; but in fact important and original work was done in such areas as logic, theories of language and meaning, metaphysics, and political theory. Thomas Aquinas made the central contribution ('Thomism'), but Anselm, Abelard, Duns Scotus, Suárez, and William of Ockham are also major figures.

Scholes, Myron S (1941–) US economist. He studied at the University of Chicago (1962), went on to gain a PhD from MIT (1968), and joined the faculty at Stanford University in 1983. He shared the 1997 Nobel Prize in Economics for his contribution to a new method of determining the value of derivatives.

Schönberg, Arnold *Schoenberg, Arnold*

Schönbrunn Palace [shoenbrun] A Baroque palace in Vienna, Austria, designed (1696–1730) by Fischer von Erlach for Emperor Leopold I, and converted by Nikolaus Pacassi for Maria Theresa's use in the 1740s. Although the palace is used for state receptions, some rooms are open to the public.

school (art) In art history, very broadly the art of one country (eg 'the French school') or more specifically one city (eg 'the Fiorentine school' or 'Avignon school'). Connoisseurs like to distinguish a master's autograph work from that of his followers or assistants by referring to the latter as 'school' works, and this type of classification has proved useful to the art trade. The term is, however, often used very imprecisely.

school (education) A place where learning can take place, usually classified according to whether it is for primary or secondary age pupils. Schools and schoolmasters were noted by Arabs to be in every Chinese town by 851; and primary and secondary schools were established in all 1000 sub-prefectures of China by 1107. The term can also denote a grouping of subjects, such as a 'humanities school'. In the USA it is widely used in the sense of a college dealing with a specific discipline within a university, such as Columbia University's School of Journalism.

School of the Air A two-way radio educational service for Australian children living in isolated areas; begun in South Australia in 1951 to supplement correspondence teaching and reduce feelings of isolation. The Aussat satellite (launched in 1985) was partly intended to improve the technical quality of broadcasts.

schooner A sailing vessel with more than one mast, each fore-and-aft-rigged. The masts are usually of equal height, but when two-masted the forward one is often shorter.

Schopenhauer, Arthur [shohpenhower] (1788–1860) Philosopher, born in Gdańsk, N Poland (formerly Danzig, Germany). He studied at Göttingen and Berlin, and reacted strongly against the German idealist tradition of Hegel, Fichte, and Schelling. He taught at Berlin (1820), where he boldly held his lectures at the same times as Hegel, but he failed to attract students. He then lived in retirement as a scholar at Frankfurt. His chief work, *Die Welt als Wille und Vorstellung* (1819, The World as Will and Idea), emphasizes the central role of human will as the creative, primary factor in understanding. His conception of the will as a blind, irrational force led him to a rejection of Enlightenment doctrines and to pessimism. He eventually attracted attention with a collection of diverse essays and aphoristic writings, published under the title of *Parerga und Paralipomena* (1851), and subsequently influenced not only existentialism and other philosophical movements, but a range of writers and artists, such as Wagner, Tolstoy, Proust, and Mann.

Schreiner, Olive (Emilie Albertina) [shriyner], pseudonym **Ralph Iron** (1855–1920) Writer, born in Wittebergen, South Africa. Largely self-educated, she went to England (1881–9), working as a governess, while she wrote her successful *The Story of an African Farm* (1883), the first sustained, imaginative work in English to come from Africa. In her later work she became a passionate propagandist for women's rights, pro-Boer loyalty, and pacifism, as in *Woman and Labour* (1911).

Schröder, Gerhard [shroeder] (1944–) German statesman and chancellor (1998–), born in Mossenberg, Germany. He studied at Göttingen, qualified as a lawyer, and was a member of the German federal parliament as a social democrat (1980–6). He served as minister president of Lower Saxony (1990–8), and defeated Helmut Kohl to become chancellor of the Federal Republic of Germany in 1998, he won a second term in 2002.

Schrödinger, Erwin [shroedinger] (1887–1961) Physicist, born in Vienna, Austria. He taught at Stuttgart, Wrocław, Poland (formerly Breslau, Prussia), Zürich, Berlin, Oxford (1933–8), and Dublin (1940–56), after which he retired to Vienna. His celebrated wave equation (1926), describing the behaviour of matter as waves, is as important to science at the subatomic level as Newton's laws of motion are to mechanics in the normal-size world. A versatile scientist, he also made significant contributions to molecular biology, and philosophy. He shared the Nobel Prize for Physics in 1933. His books include *What is Life?* (1946) and *Science and Man* (1958).

Schrödinger's equation [shroedinger] A fundamental equation of quantum mechanics. It describes the evolution in space and time of the wavefunction of a quantum system, given the forces acting on it. For simple atoms, solutions obtained using approximation techniques give good agreement with experiments.

Schubert, Franz (Peter) [shoobert] (1797–1828) Composer, born in Vienna, Austria. At 11 he became a member of the chapel choir at the imperial court, and with little formal training began to compose. From 1817 he lived precariously as a composer and teacher, until he formed an association with the operatic baritone, **Johann Michael Vogl** (1768–1840), with whom he founded the successful 'Schubertiads' – private and public accompanied recitals of his songs – which made them known throughout Vienna. His major works include the Trout Piano Quintet (1819), his C major symphony (1825), and his B minor symphony (1822), known as the 'Unfinished'. He is particularly remembered as the greatest exponent of German songs (*Lieder*), which number c.600. He also wrote a great deal of choral and chamber music.

Schuller, Gunther (1925–) Composer, French hornist, educator, and jazz scholar, born in New York City, New York, USA. He became first chair of the Metropolitan Opera Orchestra at age 19. He left that post to pursue composition and teach at Yale (1964–6), and was president of the New England Conservatory (1966–77). Meanwhile, he taught at Tanglewood in the summer and directed the music school there (1974–84). A prolific composer, his mature work uses 12-tone technique often inflected by his involvement in jazz. His prose writings include the classic 1968 study *Early Jazz*.

Schultz, Theodore (William) [shults] (1902–98) Economist, born in Arlington, South Dakota, USA. He studied at South Dakota State College and Wisconsin University, then taught at Iowa State College (1930–43) and the University of Chicago (1943–72), and served as consultant and adviser to US and UN agencies and private foundations. He shared the 1979 Nobel Prize for Economics for his work stressing the importance of the human factor in agriculture.

Schulz, Charles (Monroe) (1922–2000) Strip cartoonist, the creator of *Peanuts*, born in Minneapolis, Minnesota, USA. Learning cartooning from a correspondence course, he worked as a freelancer for a religious magazine and the *Saturday Evening Post* (1947). He submitted a sample strip about children entitled *Li'l Folks* to many newspapers before United Features accepted it, retitling it *Peanuts* (1950). It became one of the world's most successful strips, and has been adapted for television and stage. Schulz based the Charlie Brown character on himself.

Schumacher, Michael [**shoo**maker] (1969–) Motor-racing driver, born in Hürth-Hermuhlheim, Germany. He began racing karts at the age of five, became German and European Senior Kart champion in 1987, moved up to Formula Ford (1988) and Formula Three (1989), and won the German F3 Championship in 1990. He made his F1 debut with Jordan in 1990, but was immediately given a place in the Benetton team, with whom he became world champion in 1994 and 1995. He joined the (unusually) struggling Ferrari team in 1996, and achieved second place in the 1997 championship, but lost this position following an enquiry into a driving incident in which his car hit Villeneuve's. In 1999, while in contention for the driver's championship, he suffered a broken leg at the British Grand Prix at Silverstone, which ended his challenge for the season. He won the world championship for Ferrari three years in succession (2000–2), gaining a record sixth title in 2003.

Schuman, Robert [**shoo**man] (1886–1963) French statesman and prime minister (1947–8), born in Luxembourg. He held several government posts after World War 2, and as foreign minister (1948–52) proposed the *Schuman plan* (1950) for pooling the coal and steel resources of West Europe, which came to fruition in the European Coal and Steel Community. He was president of the EEC Assembly (1958–60).

Schumann, Clara (Josephine) [**shoo**man], *née* **Wieck** (1819–96) Pianist and composer, born in Leipzig, EC Germany. She gave her first concert at 11, and published four of her Polonaises the following year. Her compositions include chamber music, songs, and many piano works, including a concerto. She married Robert Schumann in 1840, and from 1878 was principal piano teacher in the Conservatory at Frankfurt.

Schumann, Elisabeth [**shoo**man] (1885–1952) Operatic soprano and *Lieder* singer, born in Merseburg, EC Germany. She made her debut in Hamburg in 1909, and in 1919 was engaged by Richard Strauss for the Vienna State Opera, and sang in his and Mozart's operas all over the world, making her London debut in 1924. She later concentrated more on *Lieder* by such composers as Schubert, Hugo Wolf, and Richard Strauss. She left Austria in 1936, and became a US citizen in 1944.

Schumann, Robert (Alexander) [**shoo**man] (1810–56) Composer, born in Zwickau, E Germany. He studied law at Leipzig, then turned to music, and particularly the piano, but after injuring a finger in 1832, he gave up performing for writing and composing. He produced a large number of compositions, until 1840 almost all for the piano. He then married Clara, the daughter of his piano teacher, Friedrich Wieck, after much opposition from her father, and under her influence began to write orchestral works, notably his A minor piano concerto (1845) and four symphonies. He also wrote chamber music and a large number of songs (*Lieder*), in addition to his continuing piano compositions. In 1843 he was appointed professor at the new Leipzig Conservatory, but mental illness caused him soon to leave, and he moved to Dresden, then Düsseldorf (1850), where he attempted suicide (1854). He died in a sanatorium in Endenich (now part of Bonn).

Schuman Plan A plan to unify Europe formulated in 1950 by the French foreign minister, Robert Schuman. He proposed that W European countries should allow their coal and steel industries to be run by a common authority, with free movement of capital and labour. This plan, which had been drafted by Jean Monet, became effective in 1952 with the formation of the European Coal and Steel Community, the first step towards the creation of a European Community.

Schuschnigg, Kurt von [**shush**nik] (1897–1977) Austrian statesman and chancellor (1934–8), born in Riva, N Italy (formerly Austria–Hungary). He served in World War 1, practised law, was elected a Christian Socialist Deputy (1927), and became minister of justice (1932) and of education (1933). His attempt to prevent Hitler occupying Austria led to his imprisonment until 1945. He then lived in the USA, where he became professor of political science at St Louis University (1948–67), before returning to Austria (1967), and writing *Im Kampf gegen Hitler* (1969, trans The Brutal Takeover).

Schuyler Mansion [**skiy**ler] Mansion house in Albany, E New York, USA, the former home of Major General Philip John Schuyler, patriot of the American Revolution. Designed and built by him in 1762, it was acquired by the state of New York in 1911, and restored and opened to the public as a historic monument in 1917.

Schwann, Theodor [shvahn] (1810–82) Physiologist, born in Neuss, W Germany. He studied medicine at Berlin University, and became professor at Louvain (1838) and Liège (1848). He discovered the enzyme pepsin, investigated muscle contraction, demonstrated the role of micro-organisms in putrefaction, and extended the cell theory (previously applied to plants) to animal tissues, thus founding modern histology.

Schwartz, Melvin [**shvaw(r)ts**] (1932–) Physicist, born in New York City, New York, USA. He studied at Columbia, then worked at Brookhaven National Laboratory (1956–8), taught at Columbia (1958–66), and moved to Stanford as a physics professor (1966–83). In 1970 he founded a company, Digital Pathways, to produce security systems for computers, and in 1983 left academic work to devote himself to this company. He shared the 1988 Nobel Prize for Physics for his work on neutrinos, and in 1991 returned to the Brookhaven National Laboratory to resume his work with high-energy and nuclear physics.

Schwarzenberg, Felix (Ludwig Johann Friedrich) [**shvah(r)t**senberg] (1800–52) Austrian statesman, born in Krumau, N Austria. During the 1848 Revolution, he was made prime minister, and created a centralized, absolutist, imperial state. He then sought Russian military aid to suppress the Hungarian rebellion (1849), and demonstrated Austrian superiority over Prussia at the Olmütz Convention (1850). His bold initiatives temporarily restored Habsburg domination of European affairs.

Schwarzenegger, Arnold [**shwaw(r)t**seneger] (1947–) US film actor, born near Graz, SE Austria. He took up body-building at the age of 14, winning several Mr Universe and Mr Olympia titles, then starred in a body-building documentary, *Pumping Iron* (1977). He had various small film roles before he was cast in *Stay Hungry* (1976), for which he received a Golden Globe as best newcomer. In the 1980s he became established as the leading figure in a new genre of muscular action films, beginning with *Conan the Barbarian* (1982) and *Conan the Destroyer* (1984), which became increasingly technological and violent with *The Terminator* (1984) and *Total Recall* (1990). Later films include the comedy *Twins* (1988), *Terminator 2: Judgment Day* (1991), *Last Action Hero* (1992), *Batman and Robin* (1997), and *Terminator 3: Rise of the Machines* (2003). He became an American citizen in 1983. A staunch public supporter of the US Republican Party, in 2003 he successfully ran for governor of California.

Schwarzkopf, (Olga Maria) Elisabeth (Friederike) [**shvah(r)t**skopf] (1915–) Soprano, born in Janotschin, C Poland. She studied at Berlin, where she made her debut in 1938, and sang in the Vienna State Opera (1944–8) and at Covent Garden (1949–52). She first specialized in coloratura roles, and later appeared more as a lyric soprano, especially in recitals of *Lieder*.

Schwarzkopf, H Norman [**shvah(r)t**skopf], nickname **Stormin' Norman** (1934–) US army officer, born in Trenton, NJ. He trained at West Point, served in Vietnam, and advanced through the ranks to general. He commanded US and allied forces against Iraq during 'Operation Desert Storm' in 1991, and then retired from the army.

Schwarzschild, Karl [**shvah(r)t**sshild] (1873–1916) Theoretical astrophysicist, born in Frankfurt, WC Germany. He computed exact solutions of Einstein's field equations in general relativity – work which led directly to modern research on black holes.

The *Schwarzschild radius* is the critical radius at which an object becomes a black hole if collapsed or compressed indefinitely. At this radius the escape velocity is the speed of light. Its value is 9 mm/0·35 in for Earth, 3 km/1·9 mi for the Sun.

Schweitzer, Albert [shviytser] (1875–1965) Medical missionary, theologian, musician, and philosopher, born in Kaysersberg, NE France (formerly Germany). He studied at Strasbourg, Paris, and Berlin, and in 1896 made his famous decision that he would live for science and art until he was 30, then devote his life to serving humanity. He became a curate at Strasbourg (1899), taught at the university (1902), and was appointed principal of the theological college (1903). His religious writing includes *Von Reimarus zu Wrede* (1906, trans The Quest of the Historical Jesus), and major works on St Paul. True to his vow, despite his international reputation in music and theology, he began to study medicine in 1905, and after qualifying (1913), set out with his newly-married wife to set up a hospital to fight leprosy and sleeping sickness at Lambaréné, French Equatorial Africa, where he remained for the rest of his life, apart from fund-raising visits and occasional lectures in Europe. He was awarded the Nobel Peace Prize in 1952.

Schwerin [shvayreen] 53°37N 11°22E, pop (2000e) 132 000. Capital of Schwerin county, N Germany; surrounded by 11 lakes, SW of Rostock; former capital of Mecklenburg state; railway; marine engineering, power cables, sewing machines, plastics, hydraulic products, pharmaceuticals, food processing, tourism; palace, 13th-c Gothic cathedral, art museum.

Schwimmer, David [shwimer] (1966–) Actor and director, born in New York City, USA. He studied theatre and speech at Northwestern University, then co-founded Chicago's Lookingglass Theatre Company, where he has directed a number of productions. He played several small roles in television series, eventually becoming well known for his role as Ross Geller in the acclaimed television series *Friends* (1994–2004). Roles in feature films include *Crossing the Bridge* (1992), *The Pallbearer* (1996), *Kissing a Fool* (1998), and *Uprising* (2001).

Schwitters, Kurt [shviterz] (1887–1948) Artist, born in Hanover, NC Germany. He studied at the Dresden Academy, and painted abstract pictures before joining the Dadaists. His best-known contribution to the movement was 'Merz', a name he gave to a form of collage using such everyday detritus, such as broken glass, tram tickets, and scraps of paper picked up in the street. From 1920 onwards he slowly built from bits and pieces of rubbish a three-dimensional construction which he called his 'Merzbau', and which filled the house before being destroyed in an air raid in 1943. In 1937 he fled from Nazi Germany to Norway, then in 1940 to England.

Schwyz [shveets] 47°02N 8°39E, pop (2000e) 13 300. Capital town of Schwyz canton, C Switzerland, 35 km/22 mi E of Lucerne; the town and canton gave their name to the whole country; the flag of Schwyz (white cross on a red ground) has become the national flag; railway; tourism; Church of St Martin (18th-c), town hall (1642–3), museum.

sciatica [siyatika] Pain in the distribution of the sciatic nerve (ie over the buttocks and the back of the leg as far as the foot). It is commonly due to pressure on the lumbosacral nerve roots of the sciatic nerve, resulting from the prolapse of an intervertebral disc.

science *philosophy of science*

science fiction Fiction that focuses on the technical possibilities and human effects of scientific advance. Mary Shelley's *Frankenstein* (1818) is a precursor, though the first novelist to explore this theme systematically was Jules Verne, with four novels (1863–73) including *20 000 Leagues under the Sea* (1870). H G Wells brought more scientific rigour to his five novels at the end of the century, which include *The Time Machine* (1895) and *The First Men in the Moon* (1901). In 1926 there was the first publication of Hugo Gernsback's journal *Amazing Stories*, which established the popularity of 'SF' as a genre; but major authors, such as Ray Bradbury (*Fahrenheit 451*, 1954), Arthur C Clarke (*Childhood's End*, 1954), and Isaac Asimov (*Foundation Trilogy*, 1957–63), did not emerge until after World War 2. Other important works from this period are Walter M Miller's *A Canticle for Leibowitz* (1960), Frank Herbert's *Dune* (1965), and Kurt Vonnegut's *Slaughterhouse Five* (1969). There is now a 'new wave' of science fiction writers, including J G Ballard, Brian Aldiss, Michael Moorcock, and Thomas Disch; and a specialist sub-genre of computer SF, pioneered by William Gibson.

Science Museum A museum in S Kensington, London, UK, housing the most important British collection of scientific and technological exhibits. The collection was separated from the Victoria and Albert Museum in 1909, and has since expanded.

science park A concentration of scientific and high technology industries and businesses on one site. This allows individual businesses to co-operate and make use of products and ideas developed at the site. The term includes research parks established by universities to promote academic and business links in science, and technology parks designed for the commercial exploitation of high technology. Science parks began in the USA in the 1930s. In the UK the first were started in the late 1970s (eg the Cambridge Science Park).

Scientology® (Latin, *scio* 'know' + Greek *logos* 'study') An applied religious philosophy and non-denominational religion, founded in the USA by L Ron Hubbard in 1952. The Church of Scientology was formed by Scientologists in 1954. It holds man to be an intrinsically spiritual being of unlimited ability and beneficence, its goal the achievement of complete certainty of one's spiritual existence and relationship to the Supreme Being. A central technique is **Dianetics**® (Greek *dia* 'through' + *nous* 'soul'), a spiritual healing technology aimed at the improvement of mental ability and the alleviation of psychosomatic ills.

Scilly, Isles of [silee] pop (2001e) 2200; area 16 sq km/6 sq mi. A group of c.140 islands and islets 40–60 km/25–35 mi SW of Land's End, Cornwall, SW England; administered by Duchy of Cornwall; includes the five inhabited islands of St Mary's (chief town, Hugh Town), St Martin's, Tresco, St Agnes, Bryher; tourism, horticulture (early vegetables and flowers), agriculture; Bronze Age settlements.

scintillation counter A device for detecting the passage of charged particles, using materials such as sodium iodide, or special plastics which emit light (**scintillate**) when charged particles pass through them. The light pulses are recorded using photomultipliers. The technique is an important means of timing the passage of particles in particle physics experiments.

Scipio Africanus [skipioh], in full **Publius Cornelius Scipio Africanus**, also called **Scipio Africanus Major** (236–c.183 BC) Innovative Roman general of the Second Punic War, whose victory at Ilipa (206 BC) forced the Carthaginians out of Spain, and whose defeat of Hannibal at Zama (202 BC) broke the power of Carthage altogether. Honoured for this with the title **Africanus**, he remained in the forefront of affairs until forced into retirement by his political enemies of the 180s.

Scipio Aemilianus [skipioh aymiliahnus], in full **Scipio Aemilianus Publius Cornelius**, also called **Scipio Africanus Minor** (185–129 BC) Roman statesman, general, and orator, the adopted grandson of Scipio Africanus Major. He is famous primarily for the sack of Carthage in the Third Punic War (146 BC), the destruction of Numantia (133 BC), and his patronage of the arts. Members of the so-called *Scipionic circle* included the historian Polybius, the Stoic Panaetius, the poet Lucilius, and the playwright Terence. His opposition to the reforms of the Gracchi may have been the cause of his sudden death, possibly by poison.

scirocco *Sirocco*

scissorbill *skimmer*

Scofield, (David) Paul [skohfeeld] (1922–) Actor, born in Hurstpierpoint, West Sussex, England, UK. He studied at the Croydon Repertory School and the London Mask Theatre before making his professional debut in 1940. At Stratford-upon-Avon in the

1940s, he began to distinguish himself in Shakespearian roles, and later starred in Peter Brook's production of *King Lear* (1962, subsequently filmed) and in *Othello* (National Theatre, 1980). His Sir Thomas More in Bolt's *A Man For All Seasons* (Globe Theatre, London, 1960, filmed 1966) remains one of the great performances in post-war British theatre, and work in plays by contemporary playwrights, such as Hampton's *Savages* (1973) and Shaffer's *Amadeus* (1979), give evidence of his range and versatility. Later film credits include *Quiz Show* (1995) and *The Crucible* (1996). He was made a Companion of Honour in 2001.

scoliosis [skoliohsis] *vertebral column*

Scopes Trial (1925) A trial of a high-school teacher, John Thomas Scopes, in Tennessee, who instructed his biology students in the evolutionary theory of creation in violation of a Tennessee state law mandating that only the literal account of the creation as told in the Book of Genesis should be taught. He was arrested and charged with violating the statute. The trial was broadcast on the radio and became a media event. Many accepted the view that monkeys and humans had common ancestors, and so the Scopes case was sometimes called the 'Monkey Trial'. Scopes was found guilty and paid a small fine of $100, and the Tennessee law remained in effect until 1967.

scops owl A typical owl of widespread genus *Otus* (c.40 species); an Old World species, often called **scops owl**, with the New World species called **screech owl**; inhabits woodland or dry open country; eats insects (occasionally small birds).

scorpion A terrestrial arthropod; body typically elongate, up to 18 cm/7 in long, including a long tail bearing a conspicuous terminal sting; venom of some forms dangerous to humans; most are nocturnal predators of other arthropods; c.1200 species, mostly tropical in distribution. (Class: Arachnida. Order: Scorpiones.)

scorpionfish Robust, bottom-living, marine fish with well-developed fin and body spines, frequently armed with venom glands; strong cryptic coloration; widespread in tropical to cool temperate seas; includes the W Atlantic *Scorpaena plumieri*, common on shallow reefs and hard bottoms; length up to 40 cm/16 in. (Family: Scorpaenidae, 11 genera.)

scorpion fly A slender, winged insect that typically inhabits moist forests; mouthparts forming a long snout; feeding on nectar or preying on other insects; two pairs of similar, membranous wings; male holds end of abdomen upturned, resembling the tail of a scorpion; larvae caterpillar-like. (Order: Mecoptera, c.450 species.)

Scorpius (Lat 'scorpion') One of the few constellations that really does look like the object it is named after; often wrongly called **Scorpio**. It is in the S sky, in a very rich part of the Milky Way, with many good clusters as well as Scorpius X-1, the first X-ray source discovered outside our Solar System. It is a constellation of the zodiac, lying between Libra and Sagittarius. The brightest star is Antares, a huge supergiant some 500 times the Sun's diameter, near the end of its evolution; distance: 185 parsec.

Scorsese, Martin [skaw(r)sayzee] (1942–) Film director, writer, and producer, born in Flushing, Long Island, New York, USA. He studied film at New York University, then made commercials and worked as a film editor before returning to direction with *Boxcar Bertha* (1972). Considered one of the foremost directors of his generation, his work has sought to illuminate masculine aggression and sexual inequality, and he has frequently questioned traditional American values. His many films include *Alice Doesn't Live Here Anymore* (1974), *Taxi Driver* (1976), *Raging Bull* (1980), the controversial *The Last Temptation of Christ* (1988), *GoodFellas* (1990, BAFTA best film and director), *The Age of Innocence* (1993), *Kundun* (1997), *Bringing Out the Dead* (1999), and *Gangs of New York* (2002, Golden Globe, best director; Oscar nomination). In 2004 he was honoured with the Directors Guild of America's lifetime achievement award.

Scotch whisky A spirit distilled from malted barley, either *single malt*, the product of one distillery (c.40 varieties of Island, Highland, Lowland, and Speyside malts), or *blended* whiskies. Grain whisky, distilled from barley and maize (corn) in continuous stills, is now used as the base for much of the blended whisky. About 85% of the whisky made in Scotland is exported.

Scotland

□ International Airport

Area 78 742 km²/30 394 sq mi
Population total (2001e) 5 062 000
Status Constituent part of the United Kingdom
Capital Edinburgh
Languages English, Scots Gaelic (Gallic) (known or used by c.80 000 residents)
Physical features Comprises the N part of the UK, and includes the island groups of Outer and Inner Hebrides, Orkney and

Scotland *see panel*

Scotland Yard, officially **New Scotland Yard** The headquarters and administration departments of the Metropolitan Police, situated at Westminster in London, UK, although the title is often used synonymously to indicate the Criminal Investigation Department (CID). Originally a part of the precincts of the old Whitehall Palace, its name derives from lodgings made over to the kings of Scotland. New Scotland Yard, designed by Norman Shaw, became the police headquarters in 1890. In 1967 Scotland Yard moved to its present buildings on Broadway and Victoria Street.

Scott, George C(ampbell) (1927–99) Stage and film actor, born in Wise, Virginia, USA. He grew up in Detroit and served in the US Marine Corps (1945–9). After starting at the School of Journalism at the University of Missouri, he changed to English and drama and began to act in student shows (1949–53). He spent the next four years holding odd jobs as he worked in small theatre companies in Toledo, Ohio, Washington, DC, and Ontario, Canada. His New York stage debut in the 1957 Shakespeare

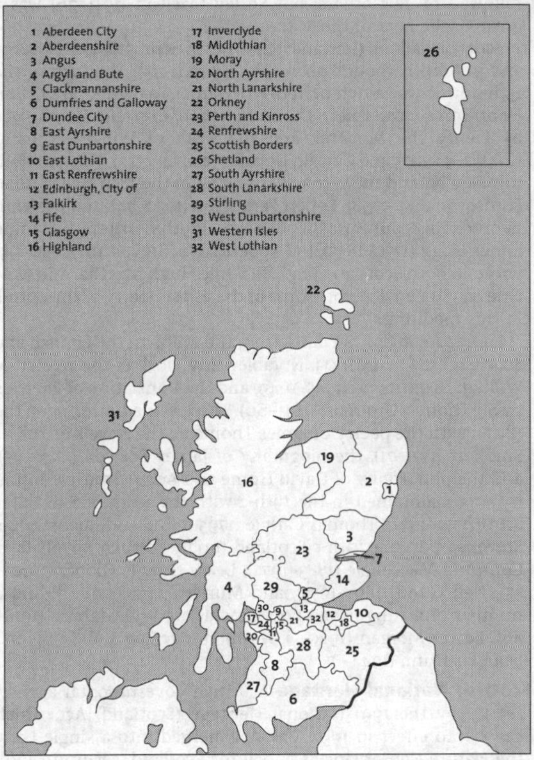

Shetland; divided into Southern Uplands, rising to 843 m/2766 ft at Merrick; Central Lowlands (most densely populated area); and Northern Highlands, divided by the fault line following the Great Glen, and rising to 1344 m/4409 ft at Ben Nevis; W coast heavily indented; several wide estuaries on E coast, primarily Firths of Forth, Tay and Moray; many freshwater lochs in the interior, largest being Loch Lomond, 70 km²/27 sq mi, and deepest Loch Morar, 310 m/1020 ft.

Economy Based on coal, but all heavy industry declined through the 1980s, with closure of many pits; oil services on E coast; tourism, especially in Highlands; shipbuilding, steel, whisky, textiles, agriculture, forestry.

History Roman attempts to limit incursions of N tribes marked by Antonine Wall and Hadrian's Wall; beginnings of unification, 9th-c; wars between England and Scotland in Middle Ages; Scottish independence declared by Robert Bruce, recognized 1328; Stuart succession, 14th-c; crowns of Scotland and England united, 1603; parliaments united under Act of Union, 1707; unsuccessful Jacobite rebellions, 1715 and 1745; devolution proposal rejected, 1979; vote for Scottish parliament, 1997; in 1974, divided into 12 regions (including three islands councils); local government reorganization, 1996, replaced this two-tier system by a single tier of 29 mainland councils, plus the three islands councils; successful referendum for Scottish parliament, 1997; devolved Scottish parliament, 1999.

Name / Area (km² / sq mi) / Population total (2000e) / Admin centre
Aberdeen City / 186 / 72 / 221 000 / Aberdeen
Aberdeenshire / 6318 / 2439 / 227 000 / Aberdeen
Angus / 2181 / 842 / 113 000 / Forfar
Argyll and Bute / 6930 / 2675 / 92 000 / Lochgilphead
Clackmannanshire / 157 / 61 / 49 000 / Alloa
Dumfries and Galloway / 6439 / 2485 / 150 000 / Dumfries
Dundee City / 65 / 25 / 156 000 / Dundee
East Ayrshire / 1252 / 483 / 126 000 / Kilmarnock
East Dunbartonshire / 172 / 66 / 112 000 / Kirkintilloch
East Lothian / 6778 / 2616 / 87 000 / Haddington
East Renfrewshire / 173 / 67 / 88 000 / Giffnock
Edinburgh, City of / 262 / 101 / 448 000 / Edinburgh
Falkirk / 229 / 115 / 145 000 / Falkirk
Fife / 1323 / 511 / 134 000 / Glenrothes
Glasow, City of / 175 / 68 / 633 000 / Glasgow
Highland / 25 284 / 9953 / 210 000 / Inverness
Inverclyde / 162 / 63 / 91 000 / Greenock
Midlothian / 356 / 137 / 81 000 / Dalkeith
Moray / 2238 / 864 / 87 000 / Elgin
North Ayrshire / 884 / 341 / 141 000 / Irvine
North Lanarkshire / 474 / 183 / 331 000 / Motherwell
Orkney / 992 / 383 / 20 000 / Kirkwall
Perth and Kinross / 5311 / 2050 / 132 000 / Perth
Renfrewshire / 261 / 101 / 179 000 / Paisley
Scottish Borders / 4734 / 1827 / 107 000 / Newton St Boswells
Shetland / 1438 / 555 / 23 000 / Lerwick
South Ayrshire / 1202 / 464 / 116 000 / Ayr
South Lanarkshire / 1771 / 684 / 311 000 / Hamilton
Stirling / 2196 / 848 / 83 000 / Stirling
West Dunbartonshire / 161 / 63 / 99 000 / Dunbarton

Festival brought him such praise that he was soon taking leading roles in stage plays and films, and starred in an admired television series, *East Side, West Side* (1963–4). He made his film debut in *The Hanging Tree* (1959), and other early roles included *The Hustler* (1961) and *Dr Strangelove* (1963). His most celebrated film role was in *Patton* (1970), for which he received an Oscar for best actor, but he refused to accept it after denouncing the Academy Awards as a 'meat parade'. In 1971 he also refused the Emmy Award as best actor in a TV production of Arthur Miller's *The Price* (1970). Intense as an actor and in person, he was particularly known for his portrayal of 'angry men', but he also played comic and warm-hearted characters. He directed two films, *Rage* (1972) and *The Savage is Loose* (1974), and occasionally returned to the theatre to take on stage roles. Later films included *Dick Tracy* (1989), *Malice* (1993), and *Country Justice* (1997).

Scott, Sir George Gilbert (1811–78) Architect, born in Gawcott, Buckinghamshire, SC England, UK. He studied in London, and influenced by Pugin became the leading practical architect of the British Gothic revival, responsible for the building or restoration of many ecclesiastical and civil buildings, such as the Albert Memorial (1862–3), St Pancras Station and Hotel in London (1865), and Glasgow University (1865). He became professor of architecture at the Royal Academy in 1868, and was knighted in 1872.

Scott, Paul (Mark) (1920–78) Novelist, born in London, UK. He studied in London, then served with the Indian army in India and Malaya (1943–6), and worked as a literary agent until 1960. His reputation is based on four novels collectively known as *The Raj Quartet* (1966–74), comprising *The Jewel in the Crown* (1966), *The Day of the Scorpion* (1968), *The Towers of Silence* (1972), and *A Division of the Spoils* (1974), in which he gave an exhaustive account of the British withdrawal from India. This quartet was adapted for the Granada television series *The Jewel in the Crown* (1982). He received the Booker Prize for his last novel, *Staying On* (1977).

Scott, Sir Peter (Markham) (1909–89) Artist, ornithologist, and broadcaster, born in London, UK, the son of Robert Falcon Scott. An Olympic sportsman (dinghy sailing), he served in the navy in World War 2. He began to exhibit his paintings of bird scenes in 1933, and after the war led several ornithological expeditions (Iceland, 1951, 1953; Australasia and the Pacific, 1956–7). His writing and television programmes helped to popularize natural history, and he received a knighthood in 1973.

Scott, R(obert) F(alcon) (1868–1912) Antarctic explorer, born in Devonport, Devon, SW England, UK. He joined the navy in 1881, and commanded the National Antarctic Expedition (1901–4) which explored the Ross Sea area, and discovered King Edward VII Land. In 1910 he led a second expedition to the South Pole (17 Jan 1912), only to discover that the Norwegian expedition under Amundsen had beaten them by a month. All members of his party died, their bodies and diaries being found by a search party eight months later. He was posthumously knighted, and the Scott Polar Research Institute at Cambridge was founded in his memory.

Scott, Ronnie, born **Ronald Schatt** (1927–96) Jazz saxophonist and night club owner, born in London, UK. After visiting New York as a member of the band aboard the *Queen Mary*, he returned to England and disseminated the modern bebop style. He had been a soloist in several great European jazz orchestras, as well as a leader in his own right. In 1959 he opened a club in London's Soho district, and this quickly became an international jazz centre.

Scott, Sir Walter (1771–1832) Novelist and poet, born in Edinburgh, EC Scotland, UK. He studied in Edinburgh, trained as a lawyer (1792), and began to write ballads in 1796, though his first major publication did not appear until 1802: *The Border Minstrelsy*. His ballads made him the most popular author of the day, and were followed by other romances, such as *The Lady of the Lake* (1810). He then turned to historical novels, all published anonymously, which fall into three groups: those set in the background of Scottish history, from *Waverley* (1814) to *A Legend of Montrose* (1819); a group which takes up themes from the Middle Ages and Reformation times, from *Ivanhoe* (1819) to *The Talisman* (1825); and his remaining books, from *Woodstock* (1826) until his death. His last years were spent in immense labours for his publishers, much of it hack editorial work, in an attempt to recover from bankruptcy following the collapse of his publishing ventures in 1826. His journal is an important record of this period of his life. He was created a baronet in 1820.

Scottish Ballet A company which began life as Western Theatre Ballet in Bristol in 1957, founded by **Elizabeth West** (1927–62) and **Peter Darrell** (1928–87). In 1969 it divided into two: most dancers went to Scotland to form the Scottish Theatre Ballet (since 1974 the Scottish Ballet), and some went to Manchester to form the Northern Ballet. Many new works have been created by Darrell, such as *Tales of Hoffmann* (1972).

Scottish Borders pop (2000e) 106 100; area 4672 sq km/ 1804 sq mi. Council in SE Scotland, UK, formerly the region of **Borders**; bounded NE by the North Sea, SE by England; crossed E–W by Southern Uplands; rivers include the Tweed and Teviot; capital Newtown St Boswells, near Melrose; other chief towns, Hawick, Peebles, Galashiels; livestock, forestry, textiles; Melrose Abbey (12th-c), Abbotsford (home of Walter Scott), Dryburgh Abbey; Muirfoot, Lammermuir, and Pentland Hills.

Scottish Environment Protection Agency *Environment Agency*

Scottish Gaelic [galik] A Celtic language spoken in Scotland, chiefly in the NW mainland and in the Western Isles, where it is an official regional language; also called **Scots Gaelic** (or simply **Gaelic**) and sometimes **Erse**. It developed from Irish Gaelic, which was brought to Scotland by immigrants from the 6th-c. A standard written language did not develop until the Bible translation of 1801. Currently spoken by c.80 000 people, its numbers are declining, though there is an enthusiastic revivalist movement. It may also still be heard in Cape Breton I, Nova Scotia, where many Scots Gaels emigrated in the 18th-c.

Scottish literature Scottish literature may be divided into that written in Gaelic, in Scots, and in English. Though there are some manuscripts from the 12th-c, little early Gaelic literature survives in Scotland, despite the claim by James Macpherson (1736–96) to have reconstructed the poems of the ancient bard Ossian; and there is hardly any trace of the great bardic families that preserved the oral tradition. It was not until the mid-18th-c that Alexander MacDonald published poetry in Gaelic, to be followed by few others; but Sorley Maclean (1911–96) was a great Gaelic poet of the 20th-c.

Scots or 'Lallans' (lowlands) first survives in 13th-c minstrelsy, and in John Barbour's poem *The Bruce* (1375). The turn of the 15th–16th-c was a rich period, with James I's own *King's Quair*, Henryson's masterpiece *The Testament of Cresseid*, *The Wallace* by Henry the Minstrel, and the work of William Dunbar (c.1460–c.1520), and Gawain Douglas (c.1474–1522). The oral tradition lay behind the vernacular revival in the 18th-c with Allan Ramsey (c.1685–1758), Robert Fergusson (1750–74), and pre-eminently Robert Burns (1759–96). Several 19th-c writers, including James Hogg (1770–1835) and Robert Louis Stevenson (1850–94) wrote in both Scots and English; while Hugh MacDiarmid (C M Grieve, 1892–1978) wrote some of the finest poetry of the 20th-c in this medium.

Literature in English dates from the union of the English and Scottish crowns in 1603. Notable early work is the poetry of William Drummond (1585–1649) and the translation of Rabelais by Sir Thomas Urquhart (1611–60). There was a flowering in the 18th-c with the poetry of James Thomson, the novels of Tobias Smollett (1721–71), the biography of James Boswell (1740–95), and the philosophy of David Hume and Adam Smith. Centrality was maintained in the 19th-c with the work of Sir Walter Scott (1771–1832), Thomas Carlyle (1795–1881), and Robert Louis Stevenson. In the 20th-c Scotland produced such novelists as Compton Mackenzie (1883–1972), Lewis Grassic Gibbon (1901–35), Neil Gunn (1891–1973), and Muriel Spark (1918–); and a number of distinguished poets, including W S Graham (1918–86), Edwin Morgan (1920–), Norman MacCaig (1910–96), and Douglas Dunn (1942–).

Scottish National Heritage A British governmental agency, set up by the 1991 National Heritage (Scotland) Act, which came into effect in 1992. The Act merged into a single body the Nature Conservancy Council for Scotland, set up in 1991, with the Countryside Commission for Scotland.

Scottish National Party (SNP) A political party formed in 1928 as the National Party of Scotland, which merged with the Scottish Party in 1933. It first won a seat at a by-election in 1945. Its greatest success was in the 1974 general election, when it took nearly a third of Scottish votes and won 11 seats. In the 1992 general election it won three seats, all in the NE of Scotland, and in 1997 it won six, principally in rural areas. In the 1999 elections to the Scottish Parliament, and aided by the proportional system, the party won 35 of the 129 seats and took 29% of the votes. Its principal policy aim is independence for Scotland from the UK.

Scottish Parliament A legislative body tracing its origins to the groups of advisors to Scottish monarchs in the 12th-c. Following the uniting of the crowns of Scotland and England in the persons of James VI (Scotland) and I (England), Scotland retained its parliament unil 1707, when the Act of Union was passed bringing together the Scottish and English parliaments as the British parliament meeting in Westminister. The Scottish parliament was re-established as a result of the 1997 referendum, at which almost two-thirds of those participating voted for the establishment of such a body with tax-raising powers. It reassembled in 1999, meeting in the Church of Scotland Assembly Rooms while waiting for a new parliament to be built at Holyrood (both in Edinburgh). It has responsibility for all matters apart from basic economic policy, defence, social security, foreign policy, immigration and nationality, and employment, which are reserved to the British (Westminister) parliament. The parliament is made up of 129 MSPs (Members of the Scottish Parliament) elected to 4-year terms through a combination of first-past-the-post single member constituency contests, with additional members elected proportionally via regional lists. One MSP is elected by the parliament to serve as presiding officer (a post first held by Lord Steel). The political leader of the parliament and head of the Scottish Executive is known as the first minister, a post first held by Donald Dewar, then by Henry McLeish (2000–1) and Jack McConnell (2001–). The first election resulted in a distribution of seats for Labour (56), Scottish National Party (35), Conservatives (18), and Liberal Democrats (17), with 3 others elected; the result was the UK's first coalition government at national level since World War 2, in a Labour administration which included the Liberal Democrats. Following Labour's success in the 2003 election, a second coalition deal was agreed with the Liberal Democrats.

Scottish reel A form of stepping dance performed to music in 4/4 time and showing French aristocratic connections. It was originally performed in circles as in 'round reels' (such as threesome, foursome, fivesome, sixsome, and eightsome reels) and later in lines, 'longwise' forms in which dancers weave in and out among one another, several at a time. The feet are in balletic positions with the weight on the balls of the feet. Typical steps include the slip step, travelling step, and pas de basque. In highland reels, men's costume is the kilt; women wear dresses with a tartan sash. Similar dance forms appear in Ireland and Scandinavia.

Scottish terrier A breed of dog; long body with very short legs; short erect tail; long head, with eyebrows, moustache, and beard; short erect ears; coat black, thick and wiry, almost reaching the ground; also known as **Scottie**. The coarser-haired form is called the **Aberdeen terrier**.

Scottish universities The universities of Scotland: St Andrews (founded 1411, chartered 1413); Glasgow (founded 1451, chartered 1453), Aberdeen (founded 1494, chartered 1496), Edinburgh (founded and chartered 1582), Strathclyde (founded as a college 1796, chartered 1964), Heriot Watt (founded as a college 1821, chartered 1966), Dundee (founded as a college 1881, chartered 1967), Stirling (founded and chartered 1967), Paisley (founded as a college 1897, chartered 1992), Robert Gordon (founded as a college 1903, chartered 1992), Caledonia (founded as a college 1875, chartered 1993), and Napier (founded as a college 1964, chartered 1993).

Scott Report An official report, published in the UK in 1996, criticizing government ministers' complicity in arms sales to Iraq, contravening a UN embargo. It censured the government for its handling of the *Matrix Churchill* affair, and called for reform. Sir Richard Scott, then a member of the English Court of Appeal, found in his inquiry (1995–6) that ministers had misled parliament and the public, but exonerated them from conspiracy. It examined the controversial question of the extent to which governments and agencies of government in England and Wales may be immune from disclosing relevant information to a court of law. The Crown, government departments, and all other public bodies which are agencies of the Crown, are entitled to Public Interest Immunity, formerly known as Crown Privilege, for reasons such as national security. During the Iran–Iraq war (1980–8), government guidance prohibited the sale of lethal weapons to these countries, and three directors of Matrix Churchill were prosecuted for exporting machinery capable of being assembled by Iraq into lethal weapons. In 1992, Alan Clark, a senior member of the Conservative government, revealed that evidence which affected the defence and would have prevented the prosecution, had not been produced by the government, which had claimed immunity, whereupon the prosecution collapsed. As a result, Public Interest Immunity is used more sparingly, and the government is committed to more openness in disclosing information.

scouting The practice of teaching the young to become good citizens and leaders, based on the principles laid down by Robert Baden-Powell, founder of the Boy Scout movement in 1908. Scouts are taught to do duty to God, their country, and other people. The Scout Association operates in over 100 nations, and has over 14 million members, classified into *Beaver Scouts* (aged 6–8), *Cub Scouts* (aged 8–11), *Scouts* (11–16), and *Venture Scouts* (16–29). Their motto is 'Be prepared'. The corresponding association for girls, known as *Girl Scouts* or *Girl Guides*, was founded in 1910 by Baden-Powell and his sister, Agnes. In the UK, its four classes of membership are *Rainbow Guides* (aged 5–7), *Brownie Guides* (aged 7–10), *Guides* (10–16), and *Ranger Guides* (14–20); in the USA, the groups are *Brownies* (7–8), *Juniors* (9–11), *Cadettes* (12–14), and *Seniors* (15–17). There are around 7 million Guides throughout the world.

scrambling *moto-cross*

scrambling circuit A circuit or device used to protect the security of voice, data, or video signals in communication systems. The original signal is coded by the scrambler before transmission, and reconstituted into its original form at the receiver. The technique prevents unauthorized personnel gaining access to the signals during transmission.

scramjet A special ramjet designed for operation at very high speeds (c.6–25 times the speed of sound) where the performance of a conventional ramjet becomes impracticable. In principle, the engine is similar in operation to a conventional ramjet, but the gases flowing through the combustion chamber move at supersonic rather than subsonic speed. In March 2004, a NASA scramjet reached Mach 7 (7700 km/h, 4780 mph).

scrapie [**skray**pee] A progressive degenerative disease of the central nervous system of sheep and goats worldwide. Symptoms may not appear until two years after infection. There are two forms of the disease: in one, there is uncontrollable itching, the animal scraping itself against objects (hence the name); in the other, there is drowsiness, trembling of the head and neck, and paralysis of the legs. The animals usually die within six months of the first symptoms appearing. The causal agent is widely accepted as one of the slow or unconventional viruses. Some individuals show a genetic susceptibility to the disease.

screamer A bird native to South America; large body, longish fleshy legs, small head, and chicken-like bill; angle of wing with sharp spur; found near water; eats water plants; swims and flies well; related to ducks and geese. (Family: Anhimidae, 3 species.)

scree Loose, angular fragments of rock debris, formed by the action of rain and frost, which accumulate on hill slopes; also termed **talus**.

screech owl *barn owl; scops owl*

screen In photography, the surface on which an image is displayed – reflective for front projection, translucent for back projection. Reflection characteristics should suit the viewing conditions: the picture on a diffuse matt white screen can be viewed over a wide angle, whereas a metallized or glass-beaded surface reflects much more light but only over a narrow angle. In the cinema theatre, the screen is perforated with a pattern of small holes so that sound from loudspeakers behind is not seriously attenuated.

screening A system which prevents the pick-up or transmission of stray electrical signals; also known as **shielding**. In coaxial cable links between aerials and televisions, the outer metal webbing screens the signal-carrying inner wire. Grids in the front of microwave ovens shield users from harmful microwaves. Conducting enclosures and meshes shield electrical signals. Enclosures of ferromagnetic material, typically iron, shield magnetic fields. A *Faraday cage* is an earthed wire mesh cage used for electrostatic screening.

screening tests Investigations that are carried out on apparently well persons in order to identify unrecognized disease. Screening is undertaken for a number of reasons. It may be done in epidemiological research to determine the incidence and prevalence of a disease. It may be carried out in order to protect the public, especially against communicable disease. *Prescriptive* screening is carried out solely for the benefit of the individual, to detect disease at an early stage in its development; included in this category are mammography surveys to detect carcinoma of the breast, regular cervical smears to detect cervical cancer, blood pressure measurement, chest radiography, and the biochemical analysis of blood.

screen-process printing A form of printing in which ink is forced through the mesh of a screen (originally – but less frequently today – made of silk). The image to be communicated is the uninked area of the printing substrate (normally paper), created by hand or photomechanical transfer on the screen. Screen-process is used for a wide range of commercial printed work in which large areas of solid colour are required, such as posters and showcards. It is also widely used in the decoration of fabrics.

screw pine A member of a large genus of evergreen trees and shrubs, native to Old World tropics, superficially resembling palms; stems supported by aerial roots; leaves sword-shaped; flowers small, in a spadix protected by a sheathing spathe; fruit pineapple-shaped, starchy, in some species edible like breadfruit. (Genus: *Pandanus*, 600 species. Family: Pandanaceae.)

screwworm The larval stage of a fly found in North and South America. The larvae are parasitic on the tissues of mammals, including humans, excavating a cavity in the skin, and feeding on living and dead tissues. It can cause serious damage, and occasionally death. (Order: Diptera. Family: Calliphoridae.)

Scriabin, Alexander Nikolayevich [skryahbyin] (1872–1915) Composer and pianist, born in Moscow, Russia. He studied at the Moscow Conservatory, and became professor of the pianoforte (1898–1904). His compositions include three symphonies, two tone poems, and 10 sonatas. After 1900 his involvement with theosophy influenced several of his compositions, such as *Prometheus* (1910), which was performed to the accompaniment of coloured lights.

scribe In general, a writer of documents or copyist; more specifically, in post-exilic and pre-rabbinic Judaism, a class of experts on the Jewish law (the *sopherim*). Although Ezra was both a priest and a scribe, a class of lay Torah scholars eventually arose, who not only preserved and interpreted Biblical laws, but by New Testament times were also involved with courts of justice. Most were Pharisees. They were also attested in Judaism outside of Palestine.

Scribner, Charles, originally **Charles Scrivener** (1821–71) Publisher, born in New York City, USA. He graduated from Princeton in 1840, and in 1846 founded with Isaac Baker (d.1850) the New York publishing firm of Baker & Scribner, which was called Charles Scribner's Sons from 1878. He founded *Scribner's Monthly* (1870–81), which later became *Scribner's Magazine* (1887–1939). His three sons continued the business.

scrofula [skrofyula] Tuberculosis of the lymph nodes of the neck, with abscess formation and ulceration of the overlying skin. Now a rare condition, it was formerly known as 'the King's evil', because of the popular belief that the sovereign's touch would cure it.

scrotum The pouch which in most male mammals holds the testes. It is necessary for normal germ cell production because the temperature of the deeper part of the body is high enough to damage the developing germ cells. Some mammals however, notably the elephant, have testes which remain within the abdominal cavity and do not descend to lie superficially in a scrotum.

scrub bird A bird native to Australia; small with strong legs, stout sharp bill, and broad fan-shaped tail; inhabits wet woodland; eats insects (occasionally small vertebrates); feeds on ground; seldom flies. (Family: Atrichornithidae, 2 species.)

scrub-fowl *megapode*

scuba diving A form of underwater swimming with the aid of a *s*elf-*c*ontained *u*nderwater *b*reathing *a*pparatus (abbreviated as *scuba*), or *aqualung*. The first such device was developed by French naval officer Jacques Yves Cousteau and engineer Emil Gagnan in 1943. The Confédération Mondiale des Activités Subaquatique (World Underwater Federation) was founded in 1959.

sculling *rowing*

sculpin *bullhead*

Sculptor A small, faint S constellation, but including several galaxies.

sculpture Traditionally, modelling in a soft material such as clay or wax, the result sometimes being cast in metal, or carving from some hard material such as stone or wood. In the 20th-c there was much work done by joining together prefabricated pieces, a technique known as *assemblage*. Early Greek bronzes were cast from wooden models, using the 'lost wax' process, but most Renaissance and modern bronzes are cast from clay originals. An alternative process involves firing the clay model in a kiln, to produce a terracotta. Stone carving has been characterized by its greatest practitioners, notably Michelangelo, as a process of releasing from the block a formal idea conceived by the artist as already existing in the stone. Tools include saws, a variety of chisels, drills, and – for finishing – rasps and abrasives. Throughout history and in all cultures, sculpture has been coloured, but since the Renaissance the preference has been for displaying the natural surface of the material used. Marble, the most prestigious stone, has normally been given a high polish.

scumbling A technique in painting whereby one colour is dragged or rubbed across another to give a rich, rough texture. Unlike a glaze, which is transparent, a scumble is opaque, and the effect depends upon allowing the underneath layer to show through in irregular patches.

scurvy A nutritional disorder which results from a lack of vitamin C. Bleeding occurs into the skin, around teeth and bones, and into the joints.

scurvy-grass A N temperate annual or perennial; leaves oval to kidney-shaped, fleshy, forming a rosette; flowers white, cross-shaped. The sharp-tasting leaves, rich in vitamin C, were used by 17th-c sailors to combat scurvy. (Genus: *Cochlearia*, 25 species. Family: Cruciferae.)

Scutari, Lake [skutahree], Albanian **Ligen i Shkodrës**, Serbo-Croatian **Skadarsko Jezero**, ancient **Lacus Labeatis** Lake in SW Yugoslavia and NW Albania; largest lake in the Balkans; town of Shkodër on SW shore; area 370 sq km/143 sq mi; underwater springs.

Scutum (Lat 'shield') A small S constellation in the Milky Way.

Scylla [sila] In Greek mythology, a sea-monster usually located in the Straits of Messina opposite to Charybdis. Originally a woman, she was changed by Circe or Amphitrite into a snake with six heads; in the *Odyssey* she snatched six men from Odysseus's ships.

Scyphozoa [skiyfozoha] A class of jellyfish with gastric tentacles derived from the stomach wall (*endoderm*) and 4-radial body symmetry; polyp stage of life-cycle reduced or absent. (Phylum: Cnidaria.)

Scythians [sithianz] In Graeco-Roman times a nomadic people of the Russian steppes who migrated to the area N of the Black Sea in the 8th-c BC, displacing the Cimmerians who previously lived there. They were well known to the Greeks, with whom they traded corn for luxury goods. Highly skilled metal workers, the tombs of their kings and chieftains contain exquisite gold and silver artefacts, often inlaid with enamel and precious stones.

SDI Abbreviation of **Strategic Defense Initiative**, the proposal first made by President Reagan in 1983 (dubbed by the press 'Star Wars') that the US should develop the technologies for a defensive layered 'shield' of weapons based primarily in space, able to shoot down incoming ballistic missiles. The proposal was controversial – not least because the technologies it would need to perfect, such as directed energy, might ultimately be used for offensive as well as defensive purposes.

SDP *Social Democratic Party*

sea A part of an ocean which is generally shallower and defined by somewhat loosely drawn boundaries related to the surrounding landmasses. *Epicontinental* seas, such as the North Sea and the China Sea, lie over part of a continental shelf. *Landlocked* seas, such as the Mediterranean, are isolated from the oceans except by narrow channels. Large inland lakes may also be called seas, such as the Caspian Sea. (*see p.1375*)

sea, law of the A branch of international law developed through custom, the 1958 Geneva Conventions, and the 1982 UN Convention on the Law of the Sea (still not ratified by many principal states). Several institutions were created by the Convention, including the International Tribunal for the Law of the

Largest Seas

Name	Area* km²	sq mi
Coral Sea	4 791 000	1 850 200
Arabian Sea	3 863 000	1 492 000
S China (Nan) Sea	3 685 000	1 423 000
Caribbean Sea	2 515 000	971 000
Mediterranean Sea	2 510 000	967 000
Bering Sea	2 304 000	890 000
Bay of Bengal	2 172 000	839 000
Sea of Okhotsk	1 590 000	614 000
Gulf of Mexico	1 543 000	596 000
Gulf of Guinea	1 533 000	592 000
Barents Sea	1 405 000	542 000
Norwegian Sea	1 383 000	534 000
Gulf of Alaska	1 327 000	512 000
Hudson Bay	1 232 000	476 000
Greenland Sea	1 205 000	465 000
Arafura Sea	1 037 000	400 000
Philippine Sea	1 036 000	400 000
Sea of Japan	978 000	378 000
E Siberian Sea	901 000	348 000
Kara Sea	883 000	341 000
E China Sea	664 000	256 000
Andaman Sea	565 000	218 000
North Sea	520 000	201 000
Black Sea	508 000	196 000
Red Sea	453 000	175 000
Baltic Sea	414 000	160 000
Celebes Sea	280 000	110 000
Persian Gulf	240 000	93 600
St Lawrence Gulf	238 300	92 000

Oceans are excluded. *Areas are rounded to nearest 1000 km²/sq mi.

Sea, for settling disputes. It divides the sea into three zones. *Internal waters* include ports, rivers, lakes, and canals. *Territorial waters* include the width of sea adjacent to a coastal state, which legally belongs to that state. The width was traditionally 5 km/3 mi, measured from the low water line, although many states now claim a greater width. Foreign ships have a right of innocent passage through territorial waters; this does not extend to foreign aircraft in the airspace above the waters. Outside the territorial waters are the *high seas*, which may be used freely by all shipping. Many states claim exclusive economic zones extending beyond territorial waters; for example, exclusive fishery rights extending for 320 km/200 mi are now claimed by most coastal states. In consequence of its membership of the EU, the UK has assumed certain obligations affecting shipping – for example, collectively with other member states to counteract disruption of bulk cargoes by other countries.

sea anemone [anemonee] A typically solitary, marine coelenterate with a cylindrical body attached at its base to a substrate, and bearing a circle of tentacles at the top around its mouth; some species form colonies; c.800 species known, from the inter-tidal zone to abyssal depths. (Phylum: Cnidaria. Order: Actiniaria.)

sea bass Any of a large number of fishes of the order Perciformes (Family: Serranidae), length up to 1·8 m/6 ft. Especially popular amongst anglers and fished commercially in some areas; found in inshore waters along the Pacific coast of North America; best known are the Striped Bass (*Roccus saxatilis*, also known as *Morone saxatilis*), Giant Sea Bass (*Stereolepis gigas*), Kelp Bass (*Paralabrax clathratus*), Barred Sand Bass (*Paralabrax nebulifer*), and Spotted Sand Bass (*Paralabrax maculatofasciatus*).

Seaborg, Glenn T(heodore) (1912–99) Nuclear chemist, born in Ishpeming, Michigan, USA. He studied at the University of California at Los Angeles and Berkeley, becoming professor of chemistry at Berkeley in 1945, and was part of the team which discovered the transuranic elements plutonium (1940), americium, and curium (1944). By bombarding the last two with alpha rays he produced the elements berkelium and californium in 1950. He shared the 1951 Nobel Prize for Chemistry with Edwin McMillan (1907–91), and later became chairman of the US Atomic Energy Commission (1961–71). The 106th element was named seaborgium in his honour in 1994 – the first chemist to have an element named after him in his lifetime.

sea bream Any of several deep-bodied fish widespread in tropical to temperate seas; includes European *Pagellus bogaraveo*, ranging from the Mediterranean to Norway; length up to 50 cm/20 in; head bluntly rounded; pinkish-red, with a large dark spot above the pectoral fin; popular with anglers, and commercially fished in some areas; also called **porgy**. (Family: Sparidae.)

sea buckthorn A thorny, deciduous, suckering shrub (*Hippophae rhamnoides*), growing to 3 m/10 ft, native mainly to the coasts of Europe and Asia; leaves up to 8 cm/3 in, narrow, covered with minute silvery scales; flowers tiny, green, appearing before leaves; males and females on separate plants; berries bright orange. It is sometimes planted as a dune stabilizer. (Family: Eleagnaceae.)

sea butterfly A planktonic marine snail, with a reduced or absent shell; found in open oceanic waters; feeds mainly on other invertebrates; possesses lateral fins used in active swimming; also known as a **pteropod**. (Class: Gastropoda. Order: Gymnosomata.)

sea canary *beluga* (mammal)

sea cow A term used for any mammal of the order Sirenia (manatees and the dugong); formerly used also for the walrus and the hippopotamus.

sea cucumber A typically sausage-shaped, soft-bodied marine invertebrate (echinoderm); mouth at one end surrounded by up to 30 tentacles, anus at the other end; skin leathery, containing minute bony structures (*ossicles*); found on or in the seabed, from shallow water to the deep sea. (Class: Holothuroidea.)

sea-dog *skimmer*

sea duck *diving duck*

sea eagle A fish-eating eagle of genus *Haliaeetus* (8 species), found on coasts. Other species of *Haliaeetus* (especially those found near fresh water) are called **fish eagles**, though they do eat other vertebrates as well as fish.

sea elephant *elephant seal*

sea fan A branching form of coral found in colonies mostly in warm shallow waters around coral reefs; body supported by a skeleton formed from horny protein-like material; growth typically 2-dimensional, producing a fan-like colony. (Phylum: Cnidaria. Order: Gorgonacea.)

sea-floor spreading The movement of oceanic crustal plates away from a central mid-oceanic ridge, where new crust is formed by basaltic igneous rock intruded into the fissures as the plates move apart. All the major ocean basins contain a mid-ocean ridge, and the age of the ocean floor increases away from its axis.

sea gooseberry *ctenophore*

seagull *gull*

sea hare A herbivorous marine mollusc, typically found on seaweed in shallow water; shell small, more or less internal; can expel coloured ink from its mantle when irritated. (Class: Gastropoda. Order: Anaspidacea.)

sea holly A stiff perennial growing to 60 cm/2 ft (*Eryngium maritimum*), a coastal plant of sandy and shingle shores, native to Europe, N Africa, and SW Asia; holly-like leaves bluish-green, spiny-tipped; flowers bluish-white, in dense globular heads 1·5–3 cm/½–1¼ in across, surrounded by spiny bracts; fruit covered in hooked bristles. The young tops of the roots are sometimes eaten as a vegetable. (Family: Umbelliferae.)

sea horse A distinctive small fish, widely distributed and usually found concealed amongst algae and other marine growths; body with segmented armour and slender prehensile tail, length 4–30 cm/1½–12 in; snout prolonged into a horse-like head; swims upright in water, using delicate membranous fins; feeds on small planktonic organisms; male develops the eggs and bears the young. (Genus: *Hippocampus*. Family: Syngnathidae.)

sea ice Ice formed from freezing sea water. At high latitudes in the Arctic and Antarctic, the temperature may drop low enough for sea water to freeze (on average, at −1·9°C). As ice forms, dissolved salts are excluded from the ice structure, increasing the salinity of the surround water, and producing sea ice with a lower salinity than the water from which it formed. Eventually all of the salt is excluded from the sea ice, leaving fresh water ice. Icebergs are distinct from sea ice, and represent large pieces of glaciers which have broken off at the coast and drifted out to sea.

seakale A perennial (*Crambe maritima*) native to the Atlantic coasts of Europe; fleshy root; large, bluish, cabbage-like leaves; white, cross-shaped flowers. The forced, blanched shoots are eaten as a vegetable. (Family: Cruciferae.)

seal (communications) A blob of wax, or other adhesive substance, bearing an impression, and attached to a document as evidence of its authenticity; also the engraved or carved object (the *matrix* or *die*) used to make the impression. The study of seals, which are found from the oldest times, is known as **sigillography**, and is particularly useful in historical studies as a means of identifying, dating, and validating documents.

seal (zoology) A marine mammal of the family Phocidae, called the **true seal**, **earless seal**, or **hair seal** (19 species); has fur and a thick layer of blubber; no external ears; cannot turn rear flippers forwards; moves on land by shuffling body horizontally along the ground; in water swims with up and down strokes of hind flippers; group of young called a 'pod'.

sea lavender A perennial with a deep tap-root (*Limonium vulgare*), native to salt marshes in Europe and North America. It has a much-branched flowering stem, bearing rows of numerous small, lilac, slightly papery flowers. It is very salt-tolerant, able to withstand periodic immersion by high tides. (Family: Plumbaginaceae.)

sea leopard *leopard seal*

sea lettuce A green seaweed (*Ulva lactuca*) in which the body (*thallus*) is sheet-like and only two cells thick; found on rocks in the intertidal zone and in estuaries. (Class: Chlorophyceae. Order: Ulvales.)

sea level datum *Ordnance Datum*

sea lily *crinoid*

sea-lion A marine mammal of the family Otariidae, called **eared seals** (14 species); resembles the true seal, but has small external ears and, on land, turns long hind flippers forwards under its body, and moves rapidly with body raised from the ground; swims mainly using forelimbs; spends more time on land than true seals; some (**fur seals**) have a thick undercoat of soft fur, and have been hunted commercially.

SEALS *SBS*

Sealyham terrier [seeliam] A breed of dog, developed in the 19th-c on the Sealyham estate, Haverfordwest, Wales, by John Owen Tucker Edwardes, who tried to breed the most vicious terrier possible; long body with short legs; short erect tail; long head with eyebrows, moustache, and beard; short pendulous ears; thick pale wiry coat.

Seaman, David (Andrew) (1963–) Footballer, born in Rotherham, South Yorkshire, N England, UK. A goalkeeper, he played for Peterborough, Birmingham, and Queens Park Rangers, before joining Arsenal in 1989. He established himself as the England goalkeeper under Terry Venables, playing in the teams for Euro 96, World Cup (1998, 2002), and Euro 2000, and by the end of the 2003 season had won 75 caps. He moved to Manchester City for the 2003–4 season but retired in 2004.

seamount An undersea mountain which by definition must rise at least 1000 m/3300 ft above the surrounding sea floor, and whose summit must be more than 200 m/660 ft beneath the surface of the ocean (shallower features are **oceanic banks**). Though found in all ocean basins, the majority of seamounts are located in the Pacific Ocean, with more than 10 000 already discovered. Most are believed to be extinct volcanoes. A special class of seamounts, termed **guyots**, are flat on top, and considered to be the remains of sunken islands or oceanic banks. Most coral atolls are thought to lie on top of seamounts which have subsided from the surface in tropical seas.

sea mouse A marine annelid worm with a flattened body covered with bristles that conceal lines of dorsal scales; body oval shaped, bearing paddle-like lobes (*parapodia*) along both sides; found in shallow coastal waters. (Class: Polychaeta. Order: Phyllodocida.)

seance A meeting of one or more persons, generally with a spiritualist medium, for the purpose of contacting the deceased. A seance, sometimes referred to as a 'sitting', may involve apparently paranormal phenomena associated with mental mediumship, such as the medium supposedly receiving communications from deceased people, or the apparent control of the medium by an alleged spirit (a *spirit guide* or *control*). Seances may also involve physical mediumship, such as materializations, and some psychokinetic activity (raps, movement of objects, etc). They are also frequently associated with the fraudulent production of phenomena of this kind.

sea otter A mammal native to N Pacific coasts (*Enhydra lutris*); lives mostly in the water; thick insulating coat; broader body than freshwater otters; front feet small, not webbed; eats mainly shellfish; floats on its back with a stone on its chest, and breaks prey open on the stone; formerly near extinction, and now protected in some areas. (Family: Mustelidae.)

sea pen A type of coral found in colonies embedded in soft substrates on the sea bed; colony comprises a main axial individual (*polyp*) bearing secondary polyps on side branches; often supported by a horny skeleton. (Phylum: Cnidaria. Order: Pennatulacea.)

Sea Peoples An assortment of marauders, probably from the Mycenaean world, who destroyed the Hittite empire in Anatolia c.1200 BC, and penetrated as far S as Egypt before being checked and dispersed. The Achaeans may have been among the invaders.

sea perch Small, deep-bodied fish (*Morone americana*) found in fresh, brackish, and coastal marine waters of the W North Atlantic; length up to 35 cm/14 in; silver with greenish-grey upper surface; valuable commercially, and a good sport fish for anglers. (Family: Serranidae.)

sea pie *oystercatcher*

sea pink *thrift*

seaplane An aircraft capable of taking off and landing upon water using a specially shaped body or floats. Seaplanes, first developed in the USA, were designed to take advantage of the sea as a runway. The most famous seaplanes were those that took part in the Schneider Trophy races of the late 1920s and early 1930s, when the trophy was finally won by a British Supermarine S6B at a speed of 655 kph/407 mph. Large seaplanes, known as 'flying boats', were used as passenger and cargo aircraft in the 1930s, especially on trans-Pacific routes; they were also used in World War 2 for anti-submarine and rescue duties. Examples include the Pan Am Clippers, Catalina, Dornier, and Sunderland flying boats, as well as one of the world's largest aircraft, the 8-engined wooden HK-1, known as 'Spruce Goose', built by Howard Hughes in 1940, but which flew only once.

search engine A resource on the World Wide Web, accessible via a browser, which helps a user to find sites and information. Search engines (eg Altavista, Lycos, Infoseek, Google) continually traverse the Web, following links that are built into documents, and building up indexes of material – for example, recovering titles, headings, and subheadings, important words, and the first few lines from documents. Manipulation of the indexes is carried out using standard techniques of information retrieval, and the continual traversal ensures that the indexes are routinely updated. The indexes enable search engines to locate many of the documents related to a particular search topic. However, most searches retrieve large numbers of irrelevant documents, within which relevant 'hits' can be lost, and a great deal of effort is currently being devoted to finding ways of improving search results.

Search for Extraterrestrial Intelligence (SETI) A research programme, originally managed by NASA's Ames Research Center, aimed at using large radio telescopes to detect artificially generated radio signals coming from interstellar space. The hypothesis that intelligent life may exist elsewhere in the galaxy is based on telescopic and spacecraft evidence that organic molecules are common in space, and on the hypothesis that planetary formation is a common by-product of star formation. The search is conducted in the quiet region of the electromagnetic spectrum – the 'microwave window' between 1000 and 10 000 mHz frequency. First proposed in 1959, a new programme was initiated at the world's largest radio telescope at Arecibo, Puerto Rico, on 12 October 1992 – the 500th anniversary of Columbus's landing in North America. It was based on the increasing power of available radio telescopes and on advanced electronics able to search millions of frequency bands each second. The NASA-supported programme was cancelled by the US Congress in October 1993, but work has continued under private sponsorship. In May 1999 the SETI@home project was set up which harnesses the power of millions of home computers to analyse signals picked up by Serendip IV, a detector placed on the Arecibo radio telescope. When the participants' computers are idle, a programme analyzes the data which is then sent automatically to researchers at the University of California at Berkeley. Over one million people worldwide are currently involved in the project.

Searle, Ronald (William Fordham) [serl] (1920–) Artist, born in Cambridge, Cambridgeshire, EC England, UK. He served in World War 2, and the drawings he made during his three years' imprisonment by the Japanese helped to establish his reputation as a serious artist. After the war he became widely known as the creator of the macabre schoolgirls of 'St Trinian's'. He settled in France in 1961. He also designed animated films, such as *Dick Deadeye* (1975), and produced the animated sequences for *Those Magnificent Men in Their Flying Machines* (1965).

sea robin *gurnard*

Sears Tower The national headquarters of Sears, Roebuck and Co in Chicago, Illinois, USA; the second tallest office building in the world (as of 2004). Built in 1970–4, architects Skidmore Owings & Merrill, it has 110 storeys and reaches a height of 443 m/1454 ft.

seascape painting A genre of painting which flourished in the Netherlands in the 17th-c, reflecting the importance of overseas trade for the Dutch economy. A later master was Turner, whose stormy seas (eg 'Calais Pier', 1803, National Gallery, London) and shipwrecks (eg 'Wreck of a Transport Ship', c.1810, Gulbenkian Foundation, Lisbon) are among the highest achievements of 19th-c English art.

seasickness *travel sickness* 1

sea slug A marine slug-like mollusc, often brightly coloured and of an elaborate shape, with various projections (*papillae*) along its body; shell absent; mostly carnivorous, but most species have a specialized diet. (Class: Gastropoda. Order: Nudibranchia.)

sea snake A venomous snake of family Hydrophiidae (50 species), sometimes included in family Elapidae; inhabits warm coastal waters in the Pacific and Indian oceans; small head, thick body, tail flattened from side to side; eats fish and fish eggs; venom very powerful; most give birth to live young in the water, and spend entire life at sea. Species of genus *Laticauda* are called *sea kraits*; these lay eggs, and are often found on land.

seasonal affective disorder (SAD) A form of 'winter depression', due to lack of light, which is accompanied by fatigue and lethargy, with a craving for carbohydrates which often results in weight gain. Up to 10% of the population may be affected to some extent during the winter months, since light affects the body's biological rhythms through hormonal and neurochemical messenger substances released by the pineal gland. The best cure for SAD is natural sunlight, but sitting for 4–6 hours per day in front of a high intensity artificial 'light box' will relieve symptoms for 80% of the patients within five days. The minimal light intensity necessary to influence the pineal gland is c.2500 lux, whereas indoor lighting usually emits only approximately 500 lux.

Seaspeak A variety of English, developed in the 1980s, used for international communications at sea. It is restricted in its expressive capacity to a relatively small set of messages, and is intended to forestall difficulties and misunderstandings which might arise from the multiplicity of languages spoken by the world's sailors.

sea spider A long-legged, small-bodied marine arthropod, found on the seabed from the intertidal zone to deep sea; most are predators, sucking juices from soft-bodied prey such as sea anemones and seaweeds; contains c.1000 species. (Subphylum: Chelicerata. Class: Pycnogonida.)

sea squirt *tunicate*

sea star *starfish*

SEATO *South East Asia Treaty Organization*

Seattle [seeatl] 47°36N 122°20W, pop (2000e) 563 400. Seat of King Co, WC Washington, USA; on the E shore of Puget Sound; transportation, industrial, commercial, financial, and cultural centre of the Pacific NW; founded, 1851; developed rapidly as a seaport after the 1897 Alaskan gold rush and the opening of the Panama Canal; main port serving Alaska; airport; railway; monorail; two universities (1861, 1892); aircraft, shipbuilding, food canning; trade in grain, timber, fruit, fish; close to scenic and recreational areas; Space Needle, a tower 183 m/600 ft high with a revolving restaurant and observation deck; Seattle Art Museum; professional teams, Mariners (baseball), SuperSonics (basketball), Seahawks (football).

sea urchin A typically hollow, globular, marine invertebrate (echinoderm); body formed by fused skeletal plates bearing movable spines; anus usually on upper surface, mouth on lower surface; complex jaw apparatus known as 'Aristotle's lantern'; feeds by scavenging, grazing, or ingesting sediment; contains c.5000 fossil and 950 living species, including sand dollars and heart urchins. (Phylum: Echinodermata. Class: Echinoidea.)

seaweed A common name for any large marine alga belonging to families Chlorophyceae (**green seaweeds**), Phaeophyceae (**brown seaweeds**), and Rhodophyceae (**red seaweeds**).

sebaceous glands *skin*

Sebald, W(infried) G(eorg) [zaybalt] (1944–2001) Novelist, born in Germany. He studied German literature and language in Freiburg, Switzerland, and in Manchester. An original and innovative writer, his major themes were journeys and the lives of writers who are also travellers, with each narrative haunted by visions of destruction. *The Emigrants* (1996), his first novel to appear in English, is the evocation of an exiled painter whose parents perished in the Nazi death camps. *The Rings of Saturn* (1998) is the account of a walking trip through Suffolk, while *Vertigo* (1999) comprises four narratives of travels from England to Vienna and Italy. His final novel, *Austerlitz* (2001), won *The Independent* Foreign Fiction Prize. He was professor of European Literature at the University of East Anglia.

Sebastian, St (?–288) Roman martyr, a native of Narbonne, S France. He was a captain of the praetorian guard, and secretly a Christian. When his belief was discovered, Diocletian ordered his death by arrows; but the archers did not quite kill him, and he was nursed back to life. When he upbraided the tyrant for his cruelty, he was beaten to death with rods. Feast day 20 January.

Sebastiano del Piombo [pyomboh] *Piombo, Sebastiano del*

Sebastopol [sebastopol], Russ **Sevastopol** 44°36N 33°31E, pop (2000e) 358 000. Port in Krymskaya (Crimean) oblast, Ukraine; on the SW shore of a peninsula separating the Sea of Azov from the Black Sea; founded, 1783; besieged by the British and French for nearly a year (1854) in the Crimean War; rail terminus; naval base; seaside resort; health resorts nearby; bricks, tiles, food products, textiles, shoes.

seborrhoea [sebuhreea] Excessively oily skin due to overactive *sebaceous glands*, the glands in the skin that secrete a natural oil called *sebum*. The skin appears shiny and can feel greasy and unpleasant. *Seborrheic dermatitis* may develop – reddened, flaky patches of skin, usually appearing on the scalp and producing dandruff as the scales are shed.

SECAM [seekam] Acronym for **Séquentiel Couleur à Mémoire**, a coding system for colour television developed in France in the 1960s and later adopted in the USSR, Eastern Europe, and some Middle East countries. The two colour difference signals are not phase-separated, but transmitted on alternate lines of the picture. A delay line in the receiver allows them to be combined at the final stage, although at some sacrifice of colour definition.

Secession, Right of A US constitutional doctrine that individual states enjoyed the right to leave (or secede from) the Federal Union. Espoused by the South before the Civil War, the doctrine was discredited during that conflict.

Secombe, Sir Harry (Donald) [seekm] (1921–2001) Comedian, singer, and media personality, born in Swansea, SC Wales, UK. A choir boy and office worker, he made his stage debut in 1946 before becoming a regular on the radio show *Variety Bandbox* (1947). An exuberant comic, he was a member of *The Goons* (1951–9), a radio show whose lunacy had a wide-reaching influence. Besides countless variety shows, his stage appearances include *Humpty Dumpty* (1959), *Pickwick* (1963), and *The Four Musketeers* (1967), and his films include *Oliver!* (1968) and *Song of Norway* (1970). As a writer he contributed regularly to *Punch*, and his fiction includes *Twice Brightly* (1974), *Katy and the Nurgla* (1978), and *The Nurgla's Magic Tear* (1990). A professional singer with dozens of albums to his credit, he hosted the religious television series *Highway* (1983–93). He was knighted in 1981, and a volume of autobiography, *Arias and Raspberries*, appeared in 1989.

second Base SI unit of time; symbol *s*; defined as the duration of 9 192 631 770 periods of the radiation corresponding to the transition between the two hyperfine levels of the ground state of the caesium-133 atom. Formerly defined as 1/86 400 of the mean solar day, the atomic definition is now the basis of universal time.

secondary education The phase of education following the primary stage, beginning in most countries at the age of 11 or 12. Usually the style of education moves towards more specialized work in key subjects, or fields of study taught by specialist teachers. Secondary education usually ends at some point between the age of 15 and 19, this varying in different countries, and culminates in most cases in some kind of public-leaving examination or award. In some countries secondary education is not universally available. Its organization is also varied, sometimes within the same country, and may involve either a single secondary school or a break and a move to a senior school at the age of 14, 15, or 16.

secondary emission The emission of electrons from the surface of a material because of its bombardment with electrons. The emitted electrons have a spectrum of energies ranging up to that of the incident electrons. Metals emit fewer secondary electrons than insulators. The effect is exploited in photomultipliers.

secondary modern school A school in those parts of the UK which operate a selective system. Intake consists of those children who were not successful in gaining entry to a grammar school, or who did not wish to attend it.

secondary store *backing store*

second-generation computers *computer generations*

second messenger In physiology, a term used to describe intermediate factors (eg nucleotides, phospholipids, calcium ions) present within the cell wall or interior. When activated by a variety of neurotransmitters or hormones (the **first messengers**) they initiate a sequence of events leading ultimately to a cellular response (such as contraction, relaxation, secretion, or a change in electrical activity).

second sight A Celtic folklore term for paranormal ability, most frequently used to refer to precognitive extrasensory perception abilities. Second sight is often regarded as an unwanted gift, as anyone possessing it does not have control over what they will 'see', and thus may obtain unpleasant information, such as concerning an impending illness or death.

second-strike capability *strategic capability*

Second World *Three Worlds theory*

Second World War *World War 2*

Secretariat American racehorse. He set record times for the Kentucky Derby (1 min 59·4 s for 1¼ mi, 1973) and Belmont Stakes (2 min 24 s for 1½ mi, 1973). That year he became the first horse for 25 years to win the Triple Crown.

Secretariat, UN *United Nations*

secretary In its most widely used sense, a person who carries out general clerical duties in an office, such as typing and filing; now often replaced by such a term as **administrative assistant**. In business, it refers to the legally required position of **Company Secretary**, whose responsibilities include ensuring that the company complies with the provisions of legislation (such as the Companies Acts in the UK), and other regulations. In trade unions, it refers to the most senior full-time employee. In government, it is used for the person who administers a department of state, either the elected minister (the 'secretary of state') or a permanent civil servant. In the USA, Secretaries (eg Secretary of Defense) are the most senior officers of the administration, appointed by the president.

secretary bird A large, ground-dwelling bird of prey (*Sagittarius serpentarius*) native to S Africa; long stilt-like legs; head with an untidy crest of long feathers (resembling pens held behind the ear of a secretary); inhabits grassland; eats small ground-living animals; walks up to 30 km/20 mi a day; soaring flight; nests in trees. (Family: Sagittariidae.)

secretary of state The title of most UK government ministers who preside over a department, as distinct from junior ministers. It has increasingly replaced the title of *minister*, although formally there is now little to distinguish them except that secretaries of state are normally in charge of larger departments. In the USA, the term refers to the head of the state department in charge of foreign affairs, a senior member of the administration.

secretion The process by which material is taken up (eg from the blood) or produced by a cell and expelled to serve a purpose elsewhere in the body. The term also refers to the specific substance (eg a hormone or neurotransmitter) expelled by the cell or organism.

secret service *intelligence service*

sect A separately organized group, usually religious, which rejects established religious or political authorities, and claims to adhere to the authentic elements of the wider tradition from which it has separated itself. It is distinctive and exclusive, claiming to possess true belief, correct ritual, and warranted standards of conduct. Membership is voluntary, but the sect accepts or rejects persons on the basis of some test of worthiness, and membership takes precedence over all other allegiances.

section (pathology) A thin slice of material mounted for inspection under a microscope. The technique is chiefly used in biology and medical pathology.

section (technology) A term used to describe a two-dimensional view in an architectural or engineering drawing, which reveals the internal structure of the subject of the drawing. The object is drawn as if cut through by an imaginary plane with the part between the observer and the cutting plane removed. The angle at which the plane cuts the object is chosen to reveal the desired detail.

secular Christianity A mid-20th-c theology which acknowledged the secularization of W civilization and sought to present a 'religionless' Christianity, with the emphasis on human freedom and responsibility, and divine transcendence understood historically rather than metaphysically.

secure accommodation A type of secure residential establishment, community home, or registered childrens' home, or unit within an otherwise open establishment, used to detain young people in Scotland, England, and Wales who have a history of absconding, are likely to continue to abscond, and are liable to harm themselves or others if they continue to do so. First set up in 1964, it is a comparatively little used disposal, and requires the order of a court or a children's hearing before implementation, other than in an emergency situation. Young people who have been sentenced by a criminal court to a period of detention for a serious offence may also be placed there as as alternative to a young offender institution. The court must believe that the protection of the public justifies the security requirement.

securities A general term for financial assets, such as stocks, shares, and bonds. Securities are pledged by a borrower to a lender as a collateral for a loan. Should the loan not be repaid, the lender has the right to take the security in place of the repayment. A security may be a document which demonstrates its holder's right to a share in a company's equity or to the ownership of one of its bonds.

Securities and Exchange Commission (SEC) A body set up in 1934 in the USA during the Great Depression to regulate and control the issue of shares by corporations. It ensures that statements about the stocks being sold are accurate, and generally regulates the way US stock markets operate.

Securities and Investments Board (SIB) An agency set up in 1985 to regulate the activities of investment business in the UK. It has power, under the Financial Services Act (1986), to oversee the activities of various self-regulatory organizations which have been set up to control aspects of the UK's financial markets. These include the Investment Management Regulatory Board (IMRO), dealing with investment managers; the Financial Intermediaries, Managers and Brokers Regulatory Association (FIMBRA), covering independent life assurance and unit trust salesmen and brokers; the Life Assurance and Unit Trust Companies (LAUTRO); and the Securities Association, monitoring some 700 firms, including investment banks, provincial stockbrokers, and securities dealers. The SIB can subpoena documents and witnesses, and initiate prosecutions. It has no powers in relation to takeovers or insider dealing.

Security Council *United Nations*

sedative A drug used to calm anxious patients without actually causing sleep; however, many sedatives in larger doses can be used as sleeping agents. *Phenobarbitone* was previously the most commonly used sedative, but it has been replaced for this purpose by drugs such as the safer *benzodiazepines* (eg diazepam). Sedatives used in the 19th-c include bromides, chloral hydrate, and paraldehyde.

Seddon, Richard John, nickname **King Dick** (1845–1906) New Zealand statesman and prime minister (1893–1906), born in Eccleston, Lancashire, NW England, UK. He settled in New Zealand in 1866 and entered parliament in 1879. As prime minister he led a Liberal Party government remembered for its social legislation, such as the introduction of old-age pensions. He died at sea, while returning to New Zealand from Australia.

sedge A name applied to many members of the family Cyperaceae but especially to two plants. *Carex* is a huge genus, found almost everywhere, but especially common in alpine and marshy, subarctic habitats, where it forms an important and characteristic part of the vegetation. It is mostly a rhizomatous perennial; tufts of grass-like leaves; stems triangular in cross-section; flowers tiny, lacking perianth; males and females usually in separate spikes which resemble those of grasses; characteristic fruit oval, 3-sided, beaked. (Genus: *Carex*, 1500–2000 species). *Cladium mariscus* is similar to *Carex*, but has keeled, saw-edged leaves, and is a dominant plant of fens and swamps throughout warmer regions. (Family: Cyperaceae.)

sedimentary rock Consolidated deposits composed of material laid down by water, wind, ice, or gravity, or by chemical precipitation. They are generally classified into three groups: *Clastic rocks* are made up of fragments of pre-existing rocks or minerals, and bound together by a cementing medium which is formed after deposition, eg shales, sandstones, and conglomerates. *Organic rocks* are composed largely of the remains of living organisms, eg coal and fossiliferous limestone. *Inorganic rocks* are formed by chemical precipitation from supersaturated solutions, eg some limestones and evaporite deposits.

sedimentation The process of deposition of rock fragments suspended in water on to the floor of an ocean, sea, lake, or river floodplain. The unconsolidated sediment may become compacted, dewatered, and cemented together by processes collectively known as *diagenesis*, ultimately forming a sedimentary rock.

Seebeck effect *thermoelectric effects*

seed The mature, fertilized ovule of a plant, containing the embryo and a food store to sustain the seedling during germination, enclosed within a protective coat, the *testa*. In gymnosperms the seeds lie exposed on the cone scales; in flowering plants they are protected within the ovary. Some seeds are very large and are produced in small numbers (eg the coconut); others are very small and are produced in prodigious numbers (eg the orchid). Seeds, aided by the fruit, offer a means of dispersal, and in annuals a means of surviving harsh seasons. Some seeds germinate immediately after dispersal, but others remain dormant until exposed to specific conditions, such as low temperatures or high light intensities.

seed fern An extinct group of plants occurring as fossils from the Devonian to Triassic periods. They had fern-like fronds, but woody stems and seed-like structures reminiscent of seed plants. They were formerly considered potential ancestors (now discounted) of flowering plants, but are possibly ancestral to cycads and two fossil gymnosperm groups, Bennettitales and Caytoniales. (Order Pteridospermales.)

seed-leaf *cotyledons*

seed plant Any plant reproducing by seeds. All flowering plants and gymnosperms are included. In some classifications these together form the division Spermatophyta.

Seeger, Pete(r) (1919–) Folk-singer and songwriter, born in New York City, USA. He studied sociology at Harvard before becoming a professional musician in the late 1930s. In 1940, along with Woody Guthrie, he formed the Almanac Singers, and started the 'protest' movement in contemporary folk-music. His later group, the Weavers, carried on this tradition. A popular solo artist, his left-wing politics caused him to be blacklisted for many years. His best-known songs include 'Where Have All the Flowers Gone?', 'If I Had a Hammer', and 'Little Boxes'.

Seghers, Hercules [**say**gerz] (c.1589–c.1635) Painter, born in Haarlem, The Netherlands. He may have studied in Amsterdam. He was author of some of the grandest and most romantic mountain landscapes of the 17th-c (influencing Rembrandt, who collected his work), yet fewer than 15 pictures survive. Most of his works are original and powerful etchings, but even these are rare. He was last recorded in 1633, living in The Hague.

segmented worm *annelid*

Segovia [seg**oh**via] 40°57N 4°10W, pop (2000e) 55 000. Capital of Segovia province, Castilla-León, NWC Spain, 87 km/54 mi NW of Madrid; altitude c.1000 m/3000 ft; bishopric; railway; wool, thread, pottery, cement, flour, fertilizers, rubber, chemicals; Roman aqueduct and old town, a world heritage site; cathedral (16th-c), Moorish citadel, El Parral monastery, Churches of St Martin and St Esteban.

Segovia, Andrés [segohvia] (1894–1987) Guitarist, born in Linares, SC Spain. Largely self-taught, he gave his first concert in 1909, and quickly gained an international reputation. Influenced by the Spanish nationalist composers, he evolved a revolutionary guitar technique permitting the performance of a wide range of music, and many modern composers wrote works for him. He was created Marquis of Salobrena by royal decree in 1981.

Segrè, Emilio (Gino) [segray] (1905–89) Physicist, born in Tivoli, WC Italy. He studied at Rome University, becoming an assistant professor in 1932. Appointed director of physics at Palermo (1936), he was dismissed by the Fascist government while on a tour of America, where he remained (1938). He joined the University of California, Berkeley, and became a US citizen in 1944. He helped to develop the atomic bomb at Los Alamos, and shared the 1959 Nobel Prize for Physics with Owen Chamberlain for the discovery of the antiproton (1955).

segregation The cultural, political, organizational, and typically geographical separation of one group of people from another. It is often based on perceived ethnic or racial divisions, an extreme example being apartheid (literally 'separateness') in S Africa, where physical segregation between whites and blacks was most apparent (eg in public transport, washrooms, housing, sport). It also characterized the period of black slavery in the USA, generally being associated with the exploitation of poorer ethnic groups by a politically dominant elite.

Seiber, Mátyás [shiyber] (1905–60) Composer, born in Budapest, Hungary. He studied at Budapest under Kodály, became professor of jazz (1928–33) at Frankfurt, and in 1935 settled in Britain as a teacher. He gained only belated recognition as a composer, his works including chamber music, piano pieces, and songs. He was killed in a motor accident in South Africa.

seiche [saysh] An oscillation or sloshing of water in a partially confined body of water such as a bay or an estuary. The period of time required for the oscillation is determined by the physical size and shape of the basin.

Seifert, Jaroslav [siyfert] (1901–86) Poet, born in Prague, Czech Republic. His first collection was *Mêsto v slzáck* (1921, City of Tears). Later works include *Zhasnête světla* (1938, Put Out The Lights), and the appearance of the post-war volume *Přílba hlíny* (1945, A Helmet of Earth) established him as the national poet. He refused all compromise after the Communist takeover in 1948, and *Morový sloup* (1977, trans The Prague Column) had to be published abroad. He was awarded the Nobel Prize for Literature in 1984.

Seikan Tunnel [saykan] A Japanese rail tunnel beneath the Tsugara Strait, linking Tappi Saki, Honshu, with Fukushima, Hokkaido; constructed 1972–88; longest railway tunnel in Japan, length 54 km/34 mi.

Seine, River [sen] River in NC France, rising in the Langres plateau, 30 km/19 mi NW of Dijon; flows NW through the limestone Champagne Pouilleuse, W and S across the fertile dairy country of Brie, then NW past Paris and Rouen to Normandy; estuary discharges into the English Channel S of Cap de la Hève; length 776 km/482 mi; third longest river in France; several canal links to other major rivers.

Seinfeld, Jerry [siynfeld] (1954–) Comedian, actor, and writer, born in Brooklyn, New York City, USA. He studied at Queen's College, then began working in Manhattan comedy clubs, eventually becoming MC at the Comic Strip. He later starred in his own television special *Jerry Seinfield's Stand-up Confidential* (1987) and went on to become a household name with his successful long-running sit-com series *Seinfeld* (1990–9). He continues his career as a touring stand-up comedian and is a regular television host. His book of comic observations, *SeinLanguage* (1993), became a best-seller.

seismic wave A shock wave propagated through the Earth as a result of an earthquake. There are four types of wave. *P* (compressional) and *S* (transverse) waves both have high frequency, and are transmitted through the Earth, but only *P* waves can travel through fluid zones. *L* waves are transverse, have low frequency, and are confined to the upper part of the crust. *Rayleigh* waves develop close to the epicentre, and are responsible for the rolling movement of the Earth's surface during an earthquake.

seismic zone A belt of intense earthquake activity which occurs at the boundaries between crustal plates.

seismograph The data collected by a **seismometer**, an instrument that records and measures the arrival of seismic waves from distant earthquakes, or from movement caused by explosions in the Earth's crust. The first seismograph was Chinese, in AD 132.

seismology The study of earthquakes and the propagation of seismic waves through the Earth. By studying the velocity of seismic waves, the structure of the Earth and the discontinuities which define its core, mantle, and crust have been discovered. By using artificial explosions to generate shock waves, the structure of the underlying rocks can be determined, and applied to the exploration for oil and gas.

seismometer *seismograph*

sei whale [say] A rorqual found in open oceans worldwide, except in polar regions (*Balaenoptera borealis*); length, up to 20 m/65 ft; dark grey with white underparts; streamlined, with a flat head; eats minute crustaceans and some small fish.

Sejanus [sejaynus] (?–31) Prefect of the Praetorian Guard (14–31), and all-powerful at Rome after the Emperor Tiberius's retirement to Capri (26). He systematically eliminated possible successors to Tiberius, such as Agrippina's sons, so that he himself might wield supreme power after Tiberius's death as regent for his young grandson Gemellus. His plans, however, were made known to Tiberius, and his fall from grace was sudden and spectacular.

Sekmet *Sakhmet*

Sekondi-Takoradi 4°59N 1°43W, pop (2000e) 134 000. Major seaport and capital of Western region, S Ghana; on the Gulf of Guinea, 180 km/112 mi WSW of Accra; founded by the Dutch, 16th-c; Sekondi expanded after construction of railway to Tarkwa (1898–1903), and merged with Takoradi, 1946; important supply base during World War 2; railway repair, cigarettes, boatbuilding, foodstuffs, trade in minerals.

seladang *gaur*

selaginella [selajinela] A member of a large genus of mostly tropical spore-bearing plants related to clubmosses and quillworts; long, regularly branched stems with numerous small leaves in four ranks, either all alike or with the upper two small and the lower two larger and spreading; sporangia arranged in cone-like strobili. It is one of the few living members of the ancient Class Lycopsida. (Genus: *Selaginella*, 700 species. Family: Selaginellaceae.)

Selangor [saylanggaw(r)] pop (2000e) 2 461 000; area 7997 sq km/3087 sq mi. State in W Peninsular Malaysia, on the Strait of Malacca; British protectorate, 1874; separated from federal territory of Wilayah Persekutuan, 1981; capital, Shah Alam; rubber, tin, commerce.

Selcraig, Alexander *Selkirk, Alexander*

Selden, John (1584–1654) Historian and antiquary, born in Salvington, West Sussex, S England, UK. He studied at Oxford and London, became a lawyer (1612), entered parliament in 1623, and in 1628 helped to draw up the Petition of Rights, for which he was imprisoned until 1634. He entered the Long Parliament in 1640, but after the execution of Charles I he took little part in public matters. His best-known book, *Table Talk*, was published after his death (1689).

select committee Members of a legislature whose task is to inquire into matters that come within its competence, usually as prescribed by the legislature or government. Two main types may be distinguished: *ad hoc*, which normally ceases to exist when its task is completed; and *permanent* or *standing*, which normally lasts for an electoral term and which investigates particular policy areas or the actions of government departments. Select committees vary in their power and influence across political systems; membership is usually based on party composition in the legislature. An example is the Senate committee set up to investigate the Watergate affair.

selection (Australian history) *free selection*

selective school *comprehensive school; grammar school; grant maintained school*

selective service *conscription*

Selene [seleenee] In Greek mythology, the goddess of the Moon. There seems to have been no cult among the Greeks, but the Moon was important in witchcraft. She was depicted as a charioteer (the head of one of her horses may be seen among the Elgin Marbles).

selenium [seleenium] Se, element 34. A metalloid in the oxygen group, found as a minor constituent of sulphide ores, and mainly produced from the residue of copper refinement. Its chemistry is similar to that of sulphur, with main oxidation states −2, +2, +4, and +6. *Hydrogen selenide* (H_2Se) has a particularly obnoxious smell and is very toxic. Mainly important for its electrical properties, selenium can be used to convert light to electric current (in photocells) and alternating current to direct current (in rectifiers).

selenium cell [seleenium] An early photoconductive light-sensitive detector, consisting of a thin film of selenium between suitable electrodes. The conductivity of the selenium increases with the increasing intensity of light falling on it.

Seles, Monica [selesh] (1973–) Tennis player, born in Novi Sad, Union of Serbia and Montenegro (formerly Yugoslavia). In 1990 she became the youngest woman to win a 'Grand Slam' singles title in the 20th-c, winning the French Championship at 16 years 169 days (a record broken by Hingis in 1997). She was also the youngest player to win the Australian Open in 1991, and before she reached 18 she had won three out of four Grand Slam singles titles. In 1993 she was unable to play for some months following an incident on court in which she was stabbed by a deranged fan of Steffi Graf. Though seldom the same force subsequently, she won the 1996 Australian Open title. She became a US citizen in 1994.

Seleucids [seloosidz] The Greek dynasty descended from Alexander the Great's general, Seleucus. The main beneficiaries of Alexander's Persian conquests, initially the Seleucids ruled a vast empire stretching from Asia Minor to NW India. By the time Rome suppressed them in 63 BC, all that was left was their Syrian heartland.

Seleucus I Nicator ('Conqueror') [silookus, niykayter] (c.358–281 BC) Macedonian general of Alexander the Great, and founder of the Seleucid dynasty. He rose from being satrap of Babylonia (321 BC) to being the ruler of an empire which stretched from Asia Minor to India. To hold his unwieldy empire together, he founded a new, more central capital at Antioch in N Syria (300 BC).

self-determination A doctrine dating back to the 18th-c that cultural communities and national groupings have the right to determine their own destiny, including political independence and the right to self-rule. The principle that each nation has the right to fashion its own state is incorporated in the United Nations Charter, and is a major plank in anti-colonialism.

self-heal A perennial (*Prunella vulgaris*), often purple- or bronze-tinged, native to the temperate N hemisphere and Australia; stems growing to 30 cm/12 in, square, erect or spreading; leaves oval, in opposite pairs; flowers 2-lipped, violet-blue, in crowded whorls forming a dense terminal spike. It is an old medicinal herb. (Family: Labiatae.)

self-help group An organization formed by people with a common problem, or difficult situation, to enable them to help each other, such as Alcoholics Anonymous. Support is provided at meetings and by individual contacts, which are especially valuable for those (such as single parents) who are coping on their own. Specially structured recovery programmes of this kind called **twelve-step programs** have become highly popular in the USA.

self / not-self The mechanism by which the immune system of the body is able to recognize the body's own cells and cell-products (**self**) as distinct from foreign material (**not-self**). It does not respond to self material, but makes an immune response to not-self, leading to its destruction or rejection. During early prenatal life the immune system is not capable of making this distinction: all living material is self, but in most mammals a stage of immune competence is achieved before birth. Disease of the immune system may lead to self material being misidentified as not-self, and the body may then mount an immune response to its own tissues, as in rheumatoid arthritis.

self-regulatory organization (SRO) A body which manages its own affairs and has its own rules of conduct, eliminating the need for government legislation. Lloyd's and the London Stock Exchange are two such bodies. From time to time the government may threaten to introduce legislation to ensure public control, usually if some adverse event has taken place. These bodies then modify their own rules to guard against any repetition of the problem.

Selfridge, Harry Gordon (c.1864–1947) Businessman, born in Ripon, Wisconsin, USA. Educated privately, he joined a trading firm in Chicago and brought new ideas and great organizing ability into the business, being made a junior partner in 1892. While visiting London in 1906 he bought a site in Oxford St, and built upon it the large store which now bears his name (opened 1909). He became a British citizen in 1937.

Seljuqs / Seljuks A family of Turkish mercenary soldiers that rose to prominence and conquered much of Asia Minor in the 11th–12th-c. They were converted to the Muslim faith, and became established as sultans in the area of present-day Syria and E Turkey. Their decline in the 13th-c was brought on by Mongol pressure from the E and their defeat at Kösedagh (1243).

Selkirk, Alexander, also spelled **Selcraig** (1676–1721) Sailor whose story suggested that of Defoe's *Robinson Crusoe*, born in Largo, Fife, E Scotland, UK. He joined the South Sea buccaneers, quarrelled with his captain, and at his own request was put ashore on Juan Fernández I, off the coast of Chile (1704). He lived there alone until 1709, when he was discovered and brought back to Britain. He returned to Largo in 1712, before returning to a life at sea.

Sellafield, formerly **Windscale** 54°38N 3°30W. Nuclear power plant in Cumbria, NW England; on the Irish Sea coast, W of Gosforth; processes nuclear waste; nearby Calder Hall gas-cooled, moderated nuclear reactors, operational 1956–2003.

Sellars, Peter (1957–) Stage director, born in Pittsburgh, Pennsylvania, USA. He studied at Harvard, became director of the Boston Shakespeare Company (1983–4), and directed the American National Theater at the Kennedy Center in Washington, DC (1984–6), where his radical staging of Sophocles' *Ajax* divided audiences and critics. He is internationally recognized as a daringly innovative director of opera, setting his productions in the cultural landscape of 20th-c America. Later productions include *Mathias der Maler* (1995), *Theodora* (1996), and *Nixon in China* (2000). He is professor of World Arts and Cultures at the University of California, Los Angeles, USA.

Sellers, Peter (1925–80) Actor and comedian, born in Southsea, Hampshire, S England, UK. After a spell as a stand-up comic and impressionist, he moved into radio. His meeting with Spike Milligan heralded *The Goon Show* (1951–9), which revolutionized British radio comedy. He made his film debut in 1951, and became one of the stalwarts of British film comedy, appearing in *The Ladykillers* (1955), *I'm All Right Jack* (1959), and *Only Two Can Play* (1962). *Lolita* (1962) and *Dr Strangelove* (1963) established his international reputation, and his popularity was unrivalled as the incompetent Inspector Clouseau in a series of films that began with *The Pink Panther* (1963) and extended beyond his death to *The Trail of the Pink Panther* (1982). He received an Oscar nomination for *Being There* (1980).

Selous Game Reserve [suhloo] A game reserve established upon the Rufiji R system, C Tanzania, in 1905; still largely unexplored; noted for the variety of its scenery and wildlife; a world heritage site.

Selous mongoose *meerkat*

Selten, Reinhard [zelten] (1930–) Economist, born in Wrocław, SW Poland (formerly Breslau, Prussia). He studied mathematics at Frankfurt-am-Main, and later worked at universities in California, Berlin, and Bielefeld before moving to the Rheinische Friedrich-Wilhelms University in Bonn in 1984. He shared the Nobel Prize for Economics in 1994 for his contribution to the analysis of equilibria in the theory of non-co-operative games.

selva The Portuguese term for the tropical rainforest of the Amazon Basin. Its use has been extended to cover similar vegetation types elsewhere.

Selwyn-Lloyd, (John) Selwyn (Brooke) Lloyd, Baron [selwin loyd] (1904–78) British statesman, born in Liverpool, Merseyside, NW England, UK. He studied at Cambridge, became a barrister, and practised in Liverpool. He entered local government, served in World War 2, and became a Conservative MP in 1945. He was appointed minister of state (1951), supply (1954–5), and defence (1955), and as foreign secretary (1955–60) he defended Eden's policy on Suez. He later became Chancellor of the Exchequer, introducing the 'pay pause' (1960–2), Lord Privy Seal and Leader of the House (1963–4), and Speaker of the House of Commons (1971–6). He was created a life peer in 1976.

Selznick, David O(liver) (1902–65) Cinema mogul, born in Pittsburgh, Pennsylvania, USA. He worked for his father in film distribution and promotion, and as a story editor and associate producer at MGM and Paramount. He was appointed vice-president in charge of production at RKO when the studio created such films as *King Kong* (1933). In 1936 he formed his own company, producing *A Star Is Born* (1937) and his greatest achievement, the enduring screen adaptation of *Gone With the Wind* (1939), for which he received an Oscar. Among the stars he created was **Jennifer Jones** (1919–), who also appeared in his last co-production, *A Farewell to Arms* (1957), and to whom he was married from 1949 until his death.

semantics The study of the meaning system of a language. The word *meaning* has itself many meanings, and semantic approaches vary widely. In one view, meaning is the relationship between language and the external world (*referential* or *denotative* meaning), and semantics enquires into the precise relationship between a word and the concept it stands for. In another, it involves the mental state of the speaker, as reflected in a range of personal and emotional overtones (*affective* or *connotative* meaning). In a third, it refers to the social context in which language is used, and from which it derives part of its significance (*contextual* meaning). In a fourth, it refers to the sense relations which link words and phrases, by which we know, for example, that some words have the 'same' meaning (eg *car, automobile*), some have 'opposite' meaning (eg *single, married*), and some have an 'included' meaning (eg *banana*, included within *fruit*). Within linguistics, it is useful to distinguish between *lexical* meaning (the 'dictionary meaning' of a word), and *structural* meaning, which a form derives from its position and function in the grammatical system of the language. A considerable part of the present-day subject is devoted to the study of the meanings of expressions in terms of formal systems of analysis, or calculi (**formal semantics**).

semaphore A code and signalling apparatus for visual communication. It consists of one or two mechanically-operated arms attached to an upright post, or two hand-held flags at arm's length, which are moved in a vertical plane to a sequence of positions. Each position represents a different letter of the alphabet, numeral, or punctuation feature. The system was widely used in visual telegraphy, especially at sea, before the advent of electricity. Old-style railway signals are a simple form of semaphore, with a single arm having two positions to indicate 'stop' or 'go'.

Semarang [samarahng] 6°58S 110°29E, pop (2000e) 1 588 000. Fishing port and capital of Java Tengah province, C Java, Indonesia; large Chinese population; airfield; railway; university (1960); shipbuilding, fishing, textiles, trade in coffee, sugar, rubber; Gedung Batu cave, Mudu war memorial, Klinteng Sam Poo Kong temple.

Semele [semilee] In Greek mythology, the daughter of Cadmus, and mother by Zeus of Dionysus. She asked Zeus to appear in his glory before her, and was consumed in fire, but it made her son immortal. Semele is probably related to the Phrygian goddess Zemelo.

semen Yellow-white fluid ejaculated from the penis at orgasm. It consists of spermatozoa and the seminal plasma, the secretions from the accessory sex glands (seminal vesicles, prostate, urethral, and bulbo-urethral glands). The secretions assist in the nourishment and motility of the spermatozoa. Fructose is their main source of energy, and prostaglandins facilitate their transport in the female reproductive tract by increasing the motility of the uterus.

semicircular canals *vestibular apparatus*

semiconductor A substance whose electrical conductivity is between that of an insulator and a conductor at room temperature. The conductivity can be made to vary with temperature and the impurities in the semiconductor crystal. In **intrinsic** semiconductors, usually made from pure crystals of germanium or silicon (known as semi-metals), conductivity rises with temperature. The conductivity of **extrinsic** semiconductors depends on introducing impurities into intrinsic semiconductors – a process known as 'doping'. If arsenic or phosphorus is added (which have more electrons than the silicon) the semiconductor becomes known as an **n-type** (a negative carrier of electricity). If silicon is doped with elements such as boron or aluminium (which have fewer electrons in their atoms than silicon), a **p-type** (positive) semiconductor is created, containing conductive holes. Typical semiconductor devices such as diodes and transistors (combinations of p- and n-types) have different arrangements of impurities. Gallium arsenide is the newest and fastest type of semiconductor, and has replaced silicon in many microchips.

semiconductor diode A simple diode consisting of a positive/negative junction made of a semiconductor material such as silicon. An electric current flows when a forward bias is applied to the junction; reverse bias produces only a small leakage current until breakdown voltage is reached. Semiconductor diodes are used to rectify alternating currents and as voltage limiters, and have replaced thermionic valve diodes in most applications.

semiconductor laser A tiny laser, about the size of a grain of salt, crucial to optical fibre communications and compact disk players. Light emission results from the passage of electrical current through a 'sandwich' of layers of semiconductor materials. A simple version of the device was first demonstrated in 1962. Optical communications rely on near-infrared lasers operating at wavelengths between one and two microns. The first semiconductor laser to operate at blue wavelengths was demonstrated in 1995, and the first ultraviolet one in 1996, offering greater storage capacity for optical data storage systems. Quantum cascade lasers, invented in 1994, offer greater laser power compared to conventional semiconductor lasers.

semi-diurnal tide A tidal cycle with two high and two low tides per lunar day; also known as a **semi-daily tide**. The two high tides are of nearly equal height, and the two low tides nearly equal.

Seminole [seminohl] A Muskogean-speaking North American Indian group of SE USA, descended from Creeks who settled in Florida in the late 18th-c, many intermarrying with runaway Negro slaves. They fought whites encroaching on their territory, eventually surrendering to US troops in the 1820s and 1830s, and moved to reservations in Oklahoma, now numbering c.12 000 (2000 census).

semiology *semiotics*

semi-opera A stage entertainment of the Restoration period with spoken dialogue, in which music played an incidental but substantial role, often in self-contained masques. Purcell's *The Fairy Queen* (1692) is an outstanding example.

semiotics The study of signs, sign systems, and the social production of meaning, also known as **semiology**. It is a multidisciplinary area of study, which derives from the pioneering work on language by the Swiss linguist Ferdinand de Saussure and the US philosopher C S Peirce. A fundamental notion is the arbitrary nature of communication systems (written and spoken language, gestures, dress, etc). Meaning is largely produced by relationships and differences between individual signs, organized in codes, rather than by simple reference to external reality. Although inherently unstable, such systems are regulated by convention, the source and purpose of which are found in a given culture. The field is often divided into three main branches: *syntax*, the study of how linguistic items can be transformed into other linguistic items; *semantics*, the study of meaning and reference; and *pragmatics*, the study of how context affects linguistic interpretation.

Semipalatinsk [semipalatinsk], formerly **Semipalatka** 50°26N 80°16E, pop (2000e) 356 000. River-port capital of Semipalatinskaya oblast, Kazakhstan, on R Irtysh; founded as a fortress, 1718; airport; railway; wool textiles, clothing, footwear, foodstuffs, ship repairing, meat packing.

semi-precious stones *gemstones*

Semiramis [semiramis] (9th-c BC) Semi-legendary Queen of Assyria, the daughter of the goddess Derceto, and wife of Ninus, with whom she is supposed to have founded Babylon. The historical germ of the story seems to be the three years' regency of Sammu-ramat (811–808 BC), widow of Shamshi-Adad V, but the details are legendary, derived from Ctesias and the Greek historians, with elements of the Astarte myth.

Semites A group of peoples found in SW Asia. In antiquity they included the Ammonites, Amorites, Assyrians, Babylonians, Canaanites, and Phoenicians; today the most prominent Semitic peoples are the Jews and the Arabs.

Semitic alphabets The writing systems of the Semitic languages spoken in the Middle East, in which only consonants are registered, the vowels being optionally marked by diacritics. The earliest known alphabet was North Semitic, developed from the second millennium BC in Palestine and Syria. This became the model for the Hebrew, Arabic, and Phoenician alphabets.

Semitic languages *Afro-Asiatic languages*

Semmelweiss, Ignaz Philipp [zemelviys] (1818–65) Physician, born in Buda, NC Hungary. He studied at the universities of Pest and Vienna. As assistant in the obstetric clinic at Vienna (from 1844) he sought a reason for the heavy mortality rate of women suffering 'childbed' or puerperal fever. His findings showed that the infection was carried by medical students from one patient to another, so he introduced antisepsis by the washing of their hands in a chlorinated lime. Although this dramatically reduced the mortality rate, his views were not accepted until after his death, when Joseph Lister applauded his findings. Ironically he died from an infection of his hand, caused as a result of an operation he performed.

semolina A heated solution of the flour of hard durum wheat. It is used to make pasta and milk puddings.

Sen, Amartya (Kumar) (1933–) Economist, born in Bengal, E India. He studied at Calcutta and Cambridge universities, and became a fellow of Trinity College, Cambridge (1957–63). He held professorial posts at New Delhi University (1963–71), the London School of Economics (1971–7), and Oxford (1977–88), then moved to Harvard. In 1988 he was appointed Master of Trinity College. Noted for his work on the nature of poverty, famine, and social choice, his 1981 book, *Poverty and Famines: An Essay on Entitlement and Deprivation*, challenged the prevailing wisdom that declining food supply is the most important cause of famine. He concluded that there are social and economic factors at work which limit the economic opportunities of certain groups and so cause starvation. He was awarded the 1998 Nobel Prize for Economics for his contributions to welfare economics.

Senanayake, Don Stephen [senaniykee] (1884–1952) First prime minister of Sri Lanka (1947–52), born in Colombo, W Sri Lanka. He studied in Colombo, then worked on his father's rubber estate. Entering the Legislative Council in 1922, he founded the co-operative society movement in 1923, and was elected to the State Council in 1931, where he was minister of agriculture for 15 years. Following independence, he became prime minister, as well as minister of defence and external affairs.

Senate (Roman) An advisory body, first to the kings, then the consuls, finally the emperor. Initially composed of heads of families of the patrician class, by the end of the Republic it was made up of ex-magistrates, and its resolutions had come to have the force of law.

Senate (USA) One of the two houses of the US Congress, consisting of two senators from each State (100 in all), chosen by the people to serve for six years; a third are chosen every two years. It has powers of 'advice and consent' on presidential treaties and appointments. Much of its work is done through committees rather than on the floor. It is presided over by the US vice-president, who can cast the deciding vote if there is a tie.

Sendai [sendaee] 38°16N 140°52E, pop (2000e) 952 000. Capital of Miyagi prefecture, NE Honshu, Japan, on W Ishinomaki-wan Bay; airport; railway; university (1907); rice, commerce, food processing, pottery, metal products; base for tours to local hot springs and spas; Miyagi Stadium (2001); Tanabata, or Star Festival (Aug).

Sendero Luminoso [sendairoh loominohsoh] (Span 'Shining Path') A rural guerrilla movement of uncompromisingly revolutionary character, which began operating in the Peruvian C Andes (though capable, also, of mounting terrorist actions in cities) from 1980 onwards.

Seneca, Lucius Annaeus [seneka], known as **the Elder** (c.55 BC–c.AD 40) Roman rhetorician, born in Córdoba, S Spain. Besides a history of Rome, now lost, he wrote several works on oratory. Parts of his *Colores controversiae* and *Suasoriae* have survived.

Seneca, Lucius Annaeus [seneka], known as **Seneca the Younger** (c.5 BC–AD 65) Roman philosopher, statesman, and writer, born in Córdoba, S Spain, the son of Seneca (the Elder). Banished to Corsica (41–9) by Claudius, on a charge of adultery, he was recalled by Agrippina, who entrusted him with the education of her son, Nero. Made consul by Nero in 57, his high moral aims gradually incurred the emperor's displeasure, and he withdrew from public life. Drawn into conspiracy, he was condemned, and committed suicide in Rome. The publication of his *Tenne Tragedies* in 1581 was important in the evolution of Elizabethan drama, which took from them the five-act division, as well as the horrors and the rhetoric. He is most notable for his prose works on natural science, philosophy, and letters, marked by an epigrammatic style.

Seneca [seneka] An Iroquois-speaking North American Indian group, who settled in present-day W New York State and E Ohio. A member of the Iroquois League, they expanded through warfare in the 17th-c. They supported the British during the American Revolution, which led to the destruction of their villages by US troops, and their settlement on reservations in 1797.

Senefelder, Aloys [zaynefelder, alohis] (1771–1834) Inventor, born in Prague, Czech Republic. He became an actor and playwright and, while trying to engrave printing plates to publish his plays, accidentally discovered the technique of lithography by using a grease pencil on limestone (1796). After various trials he opened an establishment of his own in Offenbach-am-Main, and later in Munich to train others in the process.

Sénégal, River River in W Africa; rises in the Fouta Djallon massif (Guinea), and flows N and NW, forming the N frontier of Senegal with Mauritania; enters the Atlantic Ocean at Saint-Louis; upper course above Bafoulabé known as the R Bafing; navigable as far as Bafing at high water; length including the Bafing, 1635 km/1016 mi.

Senegal *p.1384*

Senegal

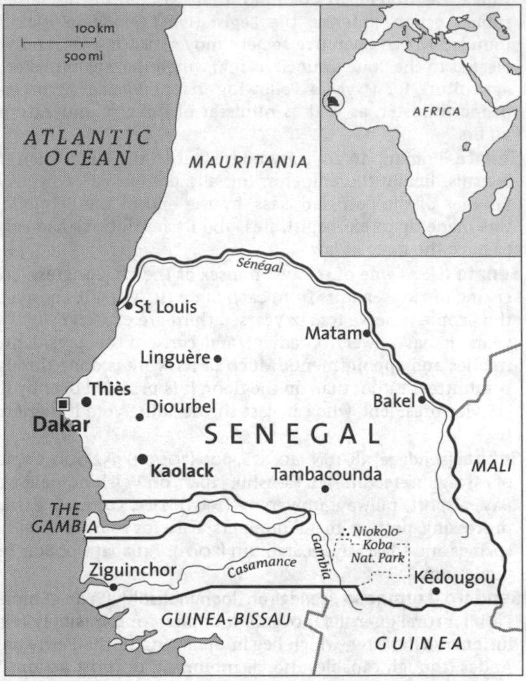

□ International Airport ∴ World heritage site

[senegawl], **Sénégal**, official name **Republic of Senegal**, Fr **République du Sénégal**

Local name Sénégal (French)

Timezone GMT

Area 196 790 km²/75 729 sq mi

Population total (2002e) 9 905 000

Status Republic

Date of independence 1960

Capital Dakar

Languages French (official), with various ethnic languages spoken

Ethnic groups Wolof (36%), Serer (19%), Fulani (13%), Toucouleur (9%), Diola (9%), Mandingo (9%), European and Lebanese (1%)

Religions Sunni Muslim (91%), Roman Catholic (5%), local beliefs (3%)

Physical features Located in W Africa; extensive low-lying basin of savannah and semi-desert vegetation to the N; sand dunes along coastline; dunes and mangrove forests in S, where land rises to around 500 m/1640 ft; lowland savannah and semi-desert regions of N drain into R Sénégal, which forms the N and NE boundary with Mauritania and Mali.

Climate Tropical climate; rainy season (Jun–Sep); high humidity levels and high night-time temperatures, especially on the coast. Average temperature, 22–8°C; average annual rainfall 541 mm/21 in at Dakar.

Currency 1 CFA Franc (CFAFr) = 100 centimes

Economy Agriculture (employs c.75% of workforce); groundnuts, cotton, sugar, millet, sorghum, maize, livestock; minerals, iron ore, gold; oil, natural gas; fishing, timber; textiles, chemicals; shipbuilding and repairing; tourism; maritime disaster (Sep 2002) when Senegalese ferry capsized killing 1200 people.

GDP (2002e) $15·64 bn, per capita $1500

Human Development Index (2002) 0·431

History Part of the Mali Empire, 14th–15th-c; French established a fort at Saint-Louis, 1658; incorporated as a territory within French West Africa, 1902; autonomous state within the French community, 1958; joined with French Sudan as independent Federation of Mali, 1959; withdrew in 1960 to become a separate independent republic; joined with The Gambia to form the Confederation of Senegambia, 1982–9; Confederation collapsed, 1989, following violent clashes between Senegalese and Mauritanians; governed by a President (elected for a 5-year term), Prime Minister, a Senate and National Assembly.

Head of State
1981–2000 Abdou Diouf
2000– Abdoulaye Wade

Head of Government
1991–8 Habib Thiam
1998–2000 Mamadou Lamine Loum
2000–1 Moustapha Niasse
2001–2 Madior Boyé
2002– Idressa Seck

Senegambia, Confederation of [senegambia] An association between The Gambia and Senegal, begun in 1982, designed to integrate military, economic, communications, and foreign policies, and to establish joint institutions while preserving independence and sovereignty. It proved to be of limited value, and was ended by mutual agreement in 1989.

senescence A series of changes in the body which are related to increasing mortality with increasing age. Modern views hold that it is essentially a continuing and increasing failure of adaptability to environmental variations. When the range of environments to which the body can adapt is less than the minimum range normally experienced, death results. In the past, many causes of this decreased adaptability have been suggested, but modern theory suggests that it is due ultimately to errors in the replication of DNA in cell division and/or errors in the production of proteins and enzymes by cells. These errors accumulate as a result of mutation in the hereditary material as the individual becomes older.

Senghor, Léopold Sédar [sãgaw(r)] (1906–2001) Senegalese statesman and first president (1960–80), born in Joal, W Senegal. He became a teacher, writer, and politician, a member of the French Constituent Assembly in 1945, deputy for Senegal in the French National Assembly (1948–58), and president following his country's independence. He also won several literary awards as a poet, and was the first black African to join the French literary institute, the Academie Francaise.

senile dementia *dementia*

Senna, Ayrton, in full **Ayrton Senna da Silva** (1960–94) Motor racing driver, born in São Paulo, Brazil. He began racing karts when he was four, moved to Formula Three racing in Britain in 1981, and joined a Formula One team in 1984. In a career marked by an aggressive competitiveness and rivalry (especially with Alain Prost), he became World Formula One champion 1988, 1990, and 1991, and had 41 Grand Prix victories (second only to Alain Prost). He also built up a major business in São Paulo marketing a range of Senna products. He was killed during the 1994 San Marino Grand Prix.

senna A drug obtained from the pods and dried leaves of certain species of *Cassia*, a large group of trees and shrubs native to Africa and Arabia, and often cultivated elsewhere; it is one of the most widely grown species. A source of **Alexandrian senna** is *Cassia acutifolia*, a shrub growing to 90 cm/3 ft or more, native to Egypt, and from the Sudan to Nigeria; leaves with 3–7 pairs of oval leaflets; flowers 5-petalled, yellow veined with red in long clusters. (Genus: *Cassia*. Family: Leguminosae.)

Sennacherib [senakerib] (8th–7th-c BC) King of Assyria (704–681 BC), the son of Sargon II and grandfather of Assurbanipal. He was an able ruler, whose fame rests mainly on his conquest of Babylon (689 BC) and his rebuilding of Nineveh. He figures prominently in the Bible, because of his attack on Jerusalem.

Sennett, Mack, originally **Michael** or **Mikall Sinnott** (1880–1960) Film director, producer, and actor, born in Richmond, Quebec, SE Canada. He worked as a comic in burlesque companies, and from 1908 in silent films. He later formed his own company, and made hundreds of shorts, establishing a whole generation of players and a tradition of knockabout slapstick under the name of Keystone Komics (1912) and later the Sennett Bathing Beauties (1920). He was given a special Academy Award in 1937 for his long contribution to film comedy.

sensitive plant A perennial, prickly-stemmed herb (*Mimosa pudica*), growing to 90 cm/3 ft, native to South America; a common weed in tropical areas, and in cooler climates often cultivated as a novelty in hothouses; leaves divided into narrow leaflets. It is exceedingly sensitive, exhibiting nastic movement, closing up at night. This response can also be triggered at greater speed by a shock stimulus such as a touch or shake. The exact mechanism is unknown, although signals passed through the phloem may cause changes in water potential in the cells of the leaflet stalk, or perhaps involve contractile proteins. The movement may be a means of reducing transpiration or a protective response to grazing animals. After a while the leaflets return to their original position. (Family: Leguminosae.)

sentence In law, the decision of a court imposed on a person convicted of a crime, such as a fine, a period of imprisonment, a period of supervision, the death sentence in certain jurisdictions, or an absolute discharge. Penal policy as reflected in sentences aims variously at deterrence, denunciation, prevention of further crime, punishment, and rehabilitation. Probation, although a final disposal, does not class as a conviction, being the equivalent of an absolute discharge. The courts have wide discretionary powers of sentencing all crimes except murder and treason. Normally, an attempt to commit a crime carries the same sentence as the crime itself, but in practice attempts are usually punished less severely, as less harm has been done.

Seoul or **Sŏul** [sohl] 37°30N 127°00E, pop (2000e) 11 670 000. Special city (with provincial status) and capital of Korea, in the Han river valley; founded, 14th-c; called Hanyang until the 20th-c; seat of the Yi dynasty government 1392–1910; seized by Japanese, 1592–3; liberated by Chinese, 1593; centre of rebellions, 19th-c; badly damaged in Korean War; held, lost, and recaptured by South Korean/US forces, 1950–1; airport (Kimpo); railway; 17 universities; engineering, textiles, tanning, food processing; Kyongbok-kung Palace (14th-c, rebuilt 1867), including National Museum and National Folk Museum; Ch'angdŏkung palace (1405, rebuilt 1611); Toksu-kung palace, including Museum of Modern Art; Chongmyo (ancestral tablets of Yi dynasty), Namdaemun (Great South Gate, reconstructed 1448), Pagoda Park, Seoul Grand Park, Seoul Land (Korean version of Disneyland); location of 1988 Olympic Games; Seoul World Cup Stadium (2001), built for World Cup (soccer) events in 2002.

sepal [sepl] One of the outermost whorl of flower parts, collectively termed the *calyx*. Usually green, free, or sometimes fused together, they protect the flower in bud. They sometimes assume other roles, such as becoming enlarged and brightly coloured, and acting as petals.

separate property *community property*

separation, judicial An order granted by a court in the UK where either marriage partner presents a petition supported by one of the facts necessary for a divorce. The parties remain married, however. Parties to a marriage may live apart by private agreement without a court order, though the formal order of separation means that neither party can be accused of desertion and the parties are freed from marital obligations. In England and Wales, the grounds for separation are the same as those for divorce, and the courts have the same powers with regard to financial orders and children. In the USA, legal separation also changes the parties' financial obligations to each other, especially in community property jurisdictions.

separation of powers A political doctrine, associated with the 18th-c philosopher Montesquieu, who argued that, to avoid tyranny, the three branches of government (legislature, executive, and judiciary) should be separated as far as possible, and their relationships governed by checks and balances. The US Constitution is a practical example of an attempt at separation of powers. Parliamentary systems such as that of the UK do not have a complete separation, as the heads of the executive (ie government ministers) sit as members of the legislature, as does the Lord Chancellor. Nonetheless, most systems claim independence of the judiciary.

separatism The demand by a particular group or area for separation from the territorial and political sovereignty of the state of which they are a part. Examples of separatist movements are the Basques in Spain and the Tamils in Sri Lanka. Separatism is associated with claims for the right to self-determination, and is often connected with discrimination against minorities.

sepek takraw (Malay 'kick', Thai 'rattan ball') A three-a-side court game played on a badminton court with a ball made from the rattan palm. The ball is propelled over the centre net (which is lower than in badminton) by players using any part of the body other than their arms or hands. It is popular in SE Asia, particularly the Philippines, Malaysia, and Thailand.

Sephardim [sefah(r)dim] Descendants of Jews who lived in Spain and Portugal before 1492, but who were then expelled for not accepting Christianity, and became refugees in N Africa, Turkey, and Italy. Subsequently they migrated to N Europe and the Americas, where during the 16th–17th-c they kept distinct from other Jews (especially those from C Europe), considering themselves innately and culturally superior. They preserved their own rituals, customs, dialect (Ladino), and pronunciation of Hebrew.

sepiolite *meerschaum*

septicaemia / septicemia [septiseemia] The occurrence and multiplication of bacteria in the blood stream; more commonly known as **blood poisoning**. It may arise as a feature of generalized infections such as typhoid, or as a complication of localized infections such as pneumonia or osteomyelitis due to a range of different bacteria. Affected individuals are extremely unwell with a high fever. If untreated, the condition progresses rapidly to septic shock and death.

***Septoria* diseases** [septawria] Two related diseases of wheat causing yield loss by reducing the photosynthetic capacity of the leaves (**Septoria leaf blotch**) or ears (**Septoria glume blotch**). Both diseases are spread by the splash of spores from infected tissues, and are more serious on shorter-stemmed varieties. Both may be controlled by fungicidal sprays, but the timing is critical. Some varieties show partial resistance. (*Septoria tritici = Mycosphaerella graminicola* (leaf blotch) and *Septoria nodorum = Leptosphaeria nodorum* (glume blotch). Order: Ascomycetes.)

Septuagesima [septyuajesima] In the Western Christian Church, the third Sunday before Lent, apparently so called by analogy with *Quinquagesima* which is two Sundays later. (Lat *septuagesimus*, 'seventieth'.)

Septuagint [septyuajint] A translation into Greek of the Hebrew Bible, obtaining its name (meaning 'translation of the 70') from a legend in the *Letter of Aristeas* (2nd-c BC) about its composition as the work of 72 scholars, six from each of the 12 tribes of Israel. The translation was begun c.3rd-c BC to meet the need of Greek-speaking Jews in the Diaspora, but work progressed by several stages over about a century. It has a different order of books from that in the Hebrew canon, and contains some works not in that canon. When it was adopted by Christians as their preferred version of the Old Testament, it lost favour among the Jews.

sequence (mathematics) In mathematics, an ordered set of numbers such that the nth term can always be written as a function of n. In an arithmetic sequence, where a is the first term and d the common difference, the nth term is $a + (n-1)d$. A

Serbia and Montenegro, Union of

□ International Airport

formerly (1992–2003) **Federal Republic of Yugoslavia**

Local name Srbija i Crna Gora

Timezone GMT +2

Area 102 173 km²/39 438 sq mi

Population total (2003e) 10 600 000

Status Federal Republic

Date of independence 27 April 1992 (as Federal Republic of Yugoslavia); proposal to replace Yugoslavia by a Union of Serbia and Montenegro agreed in April 2002, formally implemented in February 2003.

Capital Belgrade (also capital of Serbia); judicial capital at Podgorica (capital of Montenegro)

Languages Serbian, with Albanian and Hungarian also spoken

Ethnic groups Serbian (63%), Albanian (16%), Montenegrin (5%), other (16%)

Religions Serbian Orthodox (65%), Muslim (19%), Roman Catholic (4%), other Christian (12%)

Physical features Mountainous country with fertile valleys; Mt Durmitor (Montenegro) rises to 2522 m/8274 ft; Adriatic fringed by the Dinaric Alps; fertile Danubian plain in NE Serbia; chief river, R Danube, also the Tisza, Drava, Sava, and Morava; limestone karst plateaux in W along coast.

Climate Moderate, continental climate; average annual temperatures 0°C (Jan), 22°C (Jul) in Belgrade; average annual rainfall 610 mm/24 in.

Currency (Serbia) the dinar of 100 paras, (Montenegro) the euro (from 2002)

Economy Badly affected by the 1990s war and sanctions imposed during the Milosevic era; stabilization measures introduced since 2000; corn, wheat, tobacco, sugar beets, livestock; mining and manufacturing industries; food processing, wine, wood and metal products, oil refining; exports of textiles, leather goods, chemicals, machinery; natural resources of copper, coal, timber, iron, lead, zinc, bauxite, limestone.

GDP (2002e) $23·15 bn, per capita $2200

History Federal Republic of Yugoslavia declared, 1992, consisting of two of the six republics that made up former Yugoslavia (see separate entry), Montenegro and Serbia; fighting between ethnic groups in Bosnia continued until 1995, when peace accord signed in Dayton, Ohio; conflict in Kosovo between Serbia and ethnic Albanian resistance movement (Kosovo Liberation Army), 1997; escalation of conflict (early 1999) led to Serbian incursions into Kosovo and displacement of Kosovar Albanians; NATO airstrikes campaign against Yugoslav targets (Mar); President Milosovic accepted peace terms (Jun), with deployment of NATO troops into Kosovo and the departure of Serb forces; Milosevic ousted after elections, 2000, and arrested for crimes against humanity, 2001; new accord, leading to a Union of Serbia and Montenegro, 2002; new constitution (2003) recognizes a President elected for a 4-year term, Prime Minister, cabinet, and 126-member unicameral parliament (91 Serbian, 35 Montenegrin); union arrangement to remain in place for a minimum of three years after which a referendum will decide its future.

Republic of Yugoslavia
National Assembly – President
1953–80 Josip Broz Tito

Collective Presidency
1980 Lazar Kolisevski
1980–1 Cvijetin Mijatović
1981–2 Serghei Kraigher
1982–3 Petar Stambolić
1983–4 Mika Spiljak
1984–5 Veselin Duranović
1985–6 Radovan Vlajković
1986–7 Sinan Hasani
1987–8 Lazar Mojsov
1988–9 Raif Dizdarević
1989–90 Janez Drnovsek
1990–1 Borisav Jovic
1991–2 Stipe Mesic

series is the sum of the terms in a sequence. Thus the exponential series is $1 + \frac{x}{1!} + \frac{x^2}{2!} + \frac{x^3}{3!} + \frac{x^4}{4!} + ...$

sequence (music) **1** From c.850 to c.1000, a non-biblical Latin text added to a long portion of chant originally sung to one syllable at the end of the Alleluia; later, a similar syllabic chant specially composed. All but four sequences (they include the *Dies irae* of the Requiem Mass) were banned from the liturgy in the 16th-c, but the *Stabat mater* was later admitted.
2 A musical phrase immediately repeated at a different pitch. The opening of Beethoven's Fifth Symphony furnishes a familiar example.

Sequoia (California) [**sek**woya] National park in E California, USA, in the Sierra Nevada, E of Fresno; contains the enormous, ancient sequoia trees; area 1631 sq km/630 sq mi.

Sequoia or **Sequoyah** (Cherokee) [**sekwoy**a], also known as **George Gist** or **Guest** (c.1770–1843) Cherokee Indian leader, born in Taskigi, North Carolina, USA. Probably the son of Nathaniel Gist, a British trader, and a Cherokee mother, he was a major figure behind the decision of the Cherokee to adopt as much as possible of the white culture, while retaining their own identity. He personally invented an alphabet for their language. The sequoia (coast redwood) was named after him.

sequoia [**sekwoy**a] *coast redwood*

seraphim [**ser**afim] Heavenly beings mentioned in Jewish Scriptures only in the vision in *Isa* 6, where they are described as having six wings and being stationed above the throne of God, chanting refrains announcing the holiness of God. The origin of the term is uncertain. They are similar to the cherubim in *Ezek* 1.

Serapis [se**ray**pis, **ser**apis] A compound deity, combining the names and aspects of two Egyptian gods, Osiris and Apis, to which were further added features of major Greek gods, such as Zeus and Dionysus. The god was introduced to Alexandria by

Federal Republic of Yugoslavia
1992–3 Dobrica Cosic
1993 Milos Radulovic *Acting*
1993–7 Zoran Lilic
1997–2000 Slobodan Milosevic
2000–3 Vojislav Kostunica

Head of Government (Prime Minister)
1929–32 Petar Zivkovic
1932 Vojislav Marinković
1932–4 Milan Srskić
1934 Nikola Uzunović
1934–5 Bogoljub Jevtić
1935–9 Milan Stojadinović
1939–41 Dragisa Cvetković
1941 Dusan Simović

Government in exile
1942 Slobodan Jovanović
1943 Milos Trifunović
1943–4 Bozidar Purić
1944–5 Ivan Subasić
1945 Drago Marusić

Home government
1941–4 Milan Nedić
1943–63 Josip Broz Tito
1963–7 Petar Stambolić
1967–9 Mika Spiljak
1969–71 Mitja Ribicic
1971–7 Dzemal Bijedić
1977–82 Veselin Duranović
1982–6 Milca Planinć
1986–9 Branko Mikulić
1989–92 Ante Marković

Federal Republic of Yugoslavia
1991–3 Milan Panić
1993–8 Radoje Kontić
1998–2000 Momir Bulatovic
2000–1 Zoran Zizic
2001– Dragisa Pesic

Union of Serbia and Montenegro (from Feb 2003)

Head of state and government
2003– Svetozar Marovic

Serbia head of state
appointment pending

Serbia head of government
2003 Zoran Djindjic
2003 Zoran Zivkovic

Montenegro head of state
2003– Filip Vujanovic

Montenegro head of government
2003– Milo Djukanovic

Ptolemy I in an attempt to unite Greeks and Egyptians in common worship.

Serbia [serbia], formerly spelled **Servia**, Serbo-Croatian **Srbija** pop (2000e) 10 530 000; area 88 361 sq km/34 107 sq mi. Mountainous republic in the Union of Serbia and Montenegro (former federation of Yugoslavia); land rises to the Dinaric Alps (W) and Stara Planina (E); Serbian state founded, 6th-c; overrun by Turks, 1389; kingdom, 1882; incorporated into Yugoslavia, including the autonomous regions of Vojvodina (N) and Kosovo (S), 1918; constituent republic, 1946; capital, Belgrade; chief towns include Niš, Priština, Prizren, Kragujevac, Leskovac; continuing unrest from the 1980s in Kosovo between the Albanian majority and Serbian minority, causing many Serbs to leave the region; confrontation with Croatia over disputed border areas and status of Serbian minority, leading to civil war, 1991; UN sanctions imposed in an effort to alleviate conflict in former Yugoslav republics, 1992; part of new Federal Republic of Yugoslavia, 1992; fighting continued in Bosnia until 1995, when a peace agreement established a Bosnian-Serb republic alongside a Muslim-Croat Federation; confrontation with NATO over Serbian intervention in Kosovo, March 1999, followed by airstrikes against military targets throughout Serbia; part of Union of Serbia and Montenegro, 2002; wheat, maize, vines, livestock, coal, copper.

Serbia and Montnegro, Union of *see panel*

serenade Originally, music to be played or sung in the evening, especially for courting. The term is now most widely applied to works for full or string orchestra in several movements, which are lighter in style and less ambitious than a symphony.

Serengeti [serenggetee] area 14 763 sq km/5698 sq mi. National park in N Tanzania; a world heritage site; established in 1951; average elevation c.1500 m/5000 ft; noted for its wildlife, especially wildebeeste, gazelle, zebra, impala, buffalo, topi, eland, kongoni, giraffe, elephant, hyena, and lion; famous for the mass migratory treks of the grass-eating animals and their predators as they follow the rains to new grazing grounds.

serfdom The condition of peasants lacking personal freedom, especially of movement and the disposal of property, and liable to uncertain or arbitrary obligations; an intermediate position between slavery and freedom. In general, they were attached to the land, and denied freedom of movement or freedom to marry without permission of their lord. They were obliged to work on their lord's fields, to contribute a proportion of their own produce, to surrender part of their land on death, and submit to the justice and penalties administered by their lord in the manorial court. The lord had obligations to his serfs (unlike slaves), most notably to provide military protection and justice. Serfdom was hereditary. In Britain, an acute shortage of manpower as a result of the Black Death led to the substitution of wages for labour services, and peasants' agitation for further improvements. Post-mediaeval references to serfdom in W Europe normally have scant social reality; but in E Europe serfdom persisted – in Russia until 1861.

sergeant at arms In the UK, the officer of the House of Commons responsible for maintaining order and for internal administration. Appointed by the sovereign on the recommendation of the house, he also has certain ceremonial functions, particularly that of carrying the Speaker's mace in procession to the Chair at the beginning of the day's business.

serialism A method of composing music in which a series (or 'row' or 'set') of different notes is used, in accordance with certain strict practices, as the basis of a whole work. The most common type is 12-note serialism, in which the 12 pitches of the chromatic scale are re-ordered to form one of a possible 479 001 600 different series. This can then be presented vertically as chords, or horizontally as melodic lines, or as a mixture of both; it can be used backwards (*retrograde*), or with the intervals inverted (*inversion*), or in both retrograde and inversion; it can also be transposed to any other pitch. Thus, 48 versions of a single series are possible, and these provide all the pitch material for the composition. Schoenberg arrived at 12-note serialism in 1923, as a means of structuring atonal music; his method was adopted, in very different ways, by his pupils Berg and Webern. Some later composers, notably Boulez, Nono, and Stockhausen, have applied serial methods to such other elements of composition as rhythm, dynamics, and articulation.

serial killing A class of murder which, although known to have existed for centuries, became increasingly prominent during the latter part of the 20th-c. Serial killing involves a succession of at least two but usually more murders committed as discrete episodes over a substantial period of time, often months or years. This is in contrast to a mass murder or mass killing, where a number of people are killed over a short period of time, such as a few hours, as part of a single continuous act. Serial killers are typically males acting alone, though there are examples of female killers and of killers working together. Frequently psychologically disturbed, but not usually insane, the manner and form of killing will often reveal a deranged personality. Infamous serial killers include Ted Bundy, Andrei Chikatilo, Jack the Ripper, and Frederick and Rosemary West.

seriema [seriema] A ground-dwelling bird, inhabiting grassland and scrub in the New World tropics; long legs and neck; tuft of feathers between eyes; poor flier; eats insects, small vertebrates, leaves, seeds, and fruit; also known as the **cariama**. (Family: Cariamidae, 2 species.)

series (mathematics) *sequence* (mathematics)

serin *canary*

serjeanty [sah(r)juhntee] or **sergeantry** The name for a wide range of tenures in mediaeval times, by which men held land on condition of performing some definite personal service, other than knight-service, to the superior lord. The services demanded were weighty or frivolous, but the distinction made in England between grand and petty serjeanties is an invention of legal antiquarians.

Sermon on the Mount or **Plain** A collection of Jesus's ethical teaching, depicted in *Matt* 5–7 as preached on a mountain early in Jesus's ministry, but in *Luke* 6.20–49 as on a 'plain'. Matthew's version is longer, and contains the Beatitudes, teaching about true adherence to God's law, instruction on love of enemies, the Lord's Prayer, admonitions about material anxieties, the Golden Rule, and exhortations to observe what is taught.

serology [serolojee] A branch of medicine which specializes in the analysis of serum. In particular it looks for evidence of infection, by the detection of antibodies or micro-organisms.

Serote, Mongane Wally [serohtay] (1944–) Poet and novelist, born in Sophiatown, NE South Africa. An influential figure in the 'politics of culture' in South Africa, he became one of the 'township poets' of the 1970s, whose angry verse broke a decade of African creative silence. His first volume of verse, *Yakhal 'inkomo* (1972), was followed by four others, and in 1981 he published a novel, *To Every Birth Its Blood*. He lived in exile for much of the 1970s and 1980s, and after his return to South Africa in 1990 headed the Department of Art and Culture of the African National Congress.

serotine bat [serotiyn] A bat found from Europe to SE Asia and N Africa (*Eptesicus serotinus*); brown with pale tips to the hairs; slow flying; eats mainly large moths and beetles. (Family: Vespertilionidae.)

serotonin [serotohnin] A widely distributed chemical substance (a monoamine), particularly found in the blood, brain, and certain cells of the gut; it is also known as **5-hydroxytryptamine (5-HT)**. It is synthesized from the amino acid *tryptophan*, plays an important part in haemostasis, and probably also acts as a neurotransmitter in the central nervous system. It is involved in sleep, emotional disposition (mood), prolactin secretion, and circadian rhythms.

serow [seroh] A goat-antelope, native to SE Asia; thick dark coat; long pointed ears and short, slightly curved, horns; two species: **mainland serow** (*Capricornis sumatrensis*) and **Japanese**, **Formosa**, or **Taiwanese serow** (*Capricornis crispus*).

Serpens (Lat 'serpent') A constellation of the equatorial region of the sky. It is unique, because it is bisected (by Ophiuchus) into two distinct sections: **Serpens Caput** ('head') and **Serpens Cauda** ('body').

serpent *snake*

serpentine A hydrous magnesium silicate ($Mg_3Si_2O_5(OH)_4$) occurring in altered basic and ultrabasic igneous rocks by the decomposition of olivine and pyroxene. There are two main forms: **chrysotile** (an asbestos variety) and **antigorite**. It is soft, green to black, and used in decorative carving.

SERPS *pension*

serpulid [serpyulid] A tube-building bristleworm; reduced head, bearing a crown of gills; body retractable inside a calcareous tube; aperture closed by a flap (*operculum*); found in the intertidal zone in shallow waters. (Phylum: Annelida. Class: Polychaeta.)

sertão [sertõw] The remote underdeveloped backlands and semi-arid plateau of NE Brazil. It is a major area of drought (eg in the late 19th-c). There is a discontinuous vegetation cover of thorn scrub, as well as sandy saline soils and rock pavement. The economy is based on semi-nomadic subsistence cattle-rearing.

Sertoli cells [sertohlee] Cells of the seminiferous tubules of the testis which act to provide the optimal environment for the development of the spermatozoa. They play an important role in the development and maintenance of the blood–testis barrier.

serum The residue of any animal liquid after the separation and removal of the more solid components. It is specifically used to refer to human blood serum, which is a clear, yellowish fluid separated from clotted blood plasma. Serum containing appropriate antibodies is used in the protection against specific diseases (eg typhoid, tetanus).

serum sickness The repeated administration of an antigenic substance (a foreign protein), such as in immunization, which sometimes gives rise to an acute severe reaction. These reactions include fever, urticaria, arthritis, and inflammation of the heart and kidneys.

serval [servl] A nocturnal member of the cat family (*Felis serval*), native to S Africa; slender, with long neck and short tail; pale with small or large dark spots (small-spotted type formerly called **servaline cat**); occasionally black; solitary; inhabits savannah near streams; eats rodents, birds, and small antelopes.

Servetus, Michael [servaytus] (1511–53) Theologian and physician, born in Tudela, N Spain. He studied law, worked largely in France and Switzerland, and while studying medicine at Paris discovered the pulmonary circulation of the blood. In his theological writings he denied the Trinity and the divinity of Christ, and angered both Catholics and Protestants. He escaped the Inquisition, but was burnt by Calvin in Geneva for heresy.

service club A group of men and women organized to perform voluntary community service. The first such club, for business and professional men, was formed in 1905 by US lawyer Paul Harris (1868–1947) in Chicago, IL, using the name *Rotary* (because the meetings took place at each member's office in turn). This grew into Rotary International, whose motto 'Service above Self' embodies the ideals of all service clubs, and which is now a worldwide organization. Women were admitted for the first time in 1987. *Kiwanis International* began in 1915 in Detroit, MI, and the *International Association of Lions Clubs* was formed in Dallas, TX, in 1917; there are many others. All sponsor a wide range of community projects.

service industry An industry which does not manufacture a product, but provides a service. It is a fast-growing sector in most Western nations, representing a higher proportion of gross domestic product and employment than manufacturing industry. Activities range from banking and other financial services to tourism, hotels, and catering. The expression 'post-industrial society' refers to a situation where relatively few people are engaged in manufacturing.

service tree The name given to two species of *Sorbus*, native to Europe, both deciduous trees with white flowers in large, flat clusters. The true service tree (*Sorbus domestica*) has pinnate leaves with 6–10 pairs of toothed leaflets, and reddish-brown berries 2–3 cm/$\frac{3}{4}$–$1\frac{1}{4}$ in, edible when over-ripe. The wild service tree or **chequerberry** (*Sorbus torminalis*) has lobed leaves and brown berries 1–2 cm/0·4–0·8 in, used for preserves and drinks. (Family: Rosaceae.)

Servile Wars The collective name for the official attempts to suppress the slave uprisings of the late 2nd-c and early 1st-c BC in Sicily and S Italy. The most serious was the revolt led by Spartacus, in which tens of thousands of slaves were involved. It took the Romans two years to suppress it (73–71 BC).

servo system A system controlled by a servomechanism: a high-power output device is controlled with a command signal from a low-input device. The servomotor corrects the difference between demanded output and actual output using feedback, which results in an amplification of effort. Power-assisted braking or steering are servo systems. Microscopic devices (micromachines) are now being used as actuators in servo systems. They move many things a tiny amount (such as microflaps on an aircraft wing), giving a combined effect equivalent to moving something much bigger a large amount.

sesame [sesamee] An annual (*Sesamum indicum*) growing to 60 cm/2 ft, probably native to SE Asia; leaves opposite and usually lobed below, alternate above; flowers c.3 cm/1¼ in long, white, usually marked with purple or yellow, solitary in the leaf axils; fruit an oblong capsule. It is cultivated in warmer countries for its seeds, which are used for baking and as a source of oil in margarine, soap manufacture, and cosmetics. (Family: Pedaliaceae.)

Sessions, Roger (Huntingdon) (1896–1985) Composer, born in New York City, USA. He studied at Harvard and Yale universities, and also under Ernest Bloch, then spent some time in Europe. He later taught in the USA, working at the universities of Princeton (1935–45, 1953–65) and California, Berkeley (1945–52), and at the Juilliard School, New York City (from 1965). His compositions include eight symphonies, a violin concerto, piano and chamber music, two operas, and a Concerto for Orchestra (1981, Pulitzer).

Set or **Seth** An ancient Egyptian god, depicted with the head of an animal with a long muzzle. The brother and enemy of Osiris, he was associated with evil forces and rebellion.

set In mathematics, a well defined class of elements, ie a class where it is possible to tell exactly whether any one element does or does not belong to it. We can have the set of all even numbers, as every number is either even or not even, but we cannot have the set of all large numbers, as we do not know what is meant by 'large'. The **empty set** $\varnothing$ is the set with no elements. The **universal set** $\mathscr{E}$ or $\mathscr{U}$ is the set of all elements, and the complement A' of a set A is the set of all elements in $\mathscr{E}$ which are not in A. However, universal sets must also be defined carefully, else paradoxes result; one cannot speak of the set of all sets, for example. To do so would admit Russell's paradox (based on the set of all sets that are not members of themselves) which destroyed Frege's attempt to base all mathematics on logic. The **intersection** of two sets A and B (written $A \cap B$) is the set of all elements in both A and B. The **union** of two sets A and B (written $A \cup B$) is the set of all elements in either A or B or both.

set-aside policy An agricultural policy designed to reduce surplus production, by requiring the withdrawal of land from production in exchange for specific payments or guarantees. It has been used extensively in the USA and also in Europe within the EU's Common Agriculture Policy. While it is a logical response to overproduction, it has the negative effect of a further intensification on the productive land.

Seth, Vikram (1952–) Novelist, poet, and travel-writer, born in Calcutta, E India. He studied at Oxford, Stanford, and Nanjing universities. In 1983 he won the Thomas Cook Travel Book award for *From Heaven Lake*, an account of his journey through Sinkiang and Tibet to Nepal. His novel *A Suitable Boy* (1993), one of the longest works of fiction in English, examines the lives of four families against the background of a turbulent post-independence India. His other writing includes the poetry collections *Mappings* (1980) and *Beastly Tales from Here and There* (1992), and the novel *An Equal Music* (1999).

SETI *Search for Extraterrestrial Intelligence*

Seton, St Elizabeth Ann [seetn], *née* **Bayley** (1774–1821) The first native-born saint of the USA, born in New York City. She married into a wealthy trading family, and in 1797 founded the Society for the Relief of Poor Widows with Small Children. In 1803 she was widowed herself, with five children. She converted to Catholicism, founded a Catholic elementary school in Baltimore, and in 1809 founded the USA's first religious order, the Sisters of Charity. She was beatified by Pope John XXIII in 1963, and canonized in 1975. Feast day 4 January.

setter A long-haired sporting dog which belongs to one of several breeds performing the same function as a pointer; probably developed by breeding spaniels with pointers.

Settlement, Act of An important British statute of 1701 which determined the succession of the English throne after the death of Queen Anne and her heirs, if any. It excluded the Catholic Stuarts from the succession, which was to pass to the Protestant Electress Sophia of Hanover, descendant through the female line of James I. Future monarchs were to be communicant members of the Church of England, and were not permitted to leave the country without the consent of parliament. The House of Hanover, which ruled Britain (1714–1901), owed its claim to this Act.

Setúbal [setoobal] 38°31N 8°54W, pop (2000e) 83 000. Industrial seaport and capital of Setúbal district, S Portugal; at the mouth of R Sado, 32 km/20 mi SE of Lisbon; railway; cement, car parts, domestic appliances, steel, ship repair, fish canning, salt, wine; Santiago fair (Jul–Aug).

Seurat, Georges (Pierre) [soerah] (1859–91) Artist, born in Paris, France. He studied and set up a studio in Paris, where he became known for such works as 'Une Baignade, Asnières' (Bathers at Asnières, 1883–4, National Gallery, London), and 'Un Dimanche d'été à la Grande-Jatte' (Sunday Afternoon on the Grande Jatte, 1884–6, Chicago), painted in a Divisionist style. His colour theories were influential, but his main achievement was the marrying of an Impressionist palette to Classical composition.

Seuss, Dr, pseudonym of **Theodor Seuss Geisel**, other pseudonyms **Theo LeSieg** and **Rosetta Stone** (1904–91) Writer and illustrator of children's books, born in Springfield, Massachusetts, USA. He studied at Dartmouth College, NH, did postgraduate work at Oxford and the Sorbonne, worked as an illustrator and humorist for US periodicals, then became a writer and animator in Hollywood, settling in La Jolla, CA. He wrote the screenplay for the award-winning animated cartoon *Gerald McBoing Boing* (1950). His famous series of 'Beginner Books' started with *The Cat in the Hat* (1957) and *Yertle the Turtle* (1958). By 1970, 30 million copies had been sold in the USA, and Seuss had become synonymous with learning to read. His books for adults include *You're Only Old Once!* (1986) and *Oh, the Places You'll Go!* (1990).

Seven against Thebes In Greek legend, seven champions who attacked Thebes to deprive Eteocles of his kingship. They were led by his brother Polynices; the other six were Tydeus, Adrastus (or Eteoklos), Capaneus, Hippomedon, Parthenopaeus, and Amphiarus. They were defeated by another seven champions at the seven gates of Thebes; all were killed in battle, except for Amphiarus, whom the Earth swallowed alive, and Adrastus, who escaped. Later the sons of the Seven, the Epigoni, led by Adrastus, succeeded in destroying the city.

Seven Days' Battles (26 Jun–2 Jul 1862) The final conflict in the Peninsular Campaign during the American Civil War, fought below Richmond between the York and James Rivers. The battles began with a Southern offensive intended to drive the Union forces off the Peninsula, but ended with a Confederate withdrawal.

seven deadly sins The fundamental vices thought, in Christian tradition, to underlie all sinful actions. They are pride, covetousness, lust, envy, gluttony, anger, and sloth.

Seven Sisters *Pleiades* (astronomy)

Seven Sleepers of Ephesus In mediaeval legend, seven persecuted Christians who fled into a cave at the time of the Emperor Decius (AD 250); they slept for 200 years, emerging in 447 at the time of Theodosius II. The story was thought to confirm the resurrection of Christ.

seven whistler *whimbrel*

Seven Wise Men of Greece Seven men famed in antiquity for their wisdom. The lists vary, but Solon of Athens, Thales of Miletus, Bias of Priene, and Pittacus of Mytilene are common to all of them. These and all the others mentioned belonged to the period 620–550 BC.

Seven Wonders of the Ancient World The most renowned artificial structures of the ancient world: the Pyramids of Egypt; the Hanging Gardens of Babylon; the Tomb of Mausolus at Halicarnassus; the Temple of Artemis at Ephesus; the Colossus of Rhodes; the Statue of Zeus at Olympia; and the Pharos of Alexandria.

Seven Years' War (1756–63) A major European conflict rooted in the rivalry between Austria and Prussia and the imminent colonial struggle between Britain and France in the New World and the Far East. Hostilities in North America (1754) pre-dated the Diplomatic Revolution in Europe (1756), which created two opposing power blocs: Austria, France, Russia, Sweden, and Saxony against Prussia, Britain, and Portugal. British maritime superiority countered Franco-Spanish naval power, and prevented a French invasion. The European war, precipitated by Prussia's seizure of Saxony, was marked by many notable pitched land battles. Saved from total defeat when Russia switched sides, Frederick II of Prussia retained Silesia in 1763.

severe acute respiratory syndrome *SARS*

severe combined immunodeficiency (SCI) A type of immune deficiency resulting from failure of the thymus to develop, and thus to produce lymphocytes, key cells in the body's immune response. Babies born with this condition have little ability to withstand infection, and rarely survive beyond infancy; but some success has been obtained with thymic transplantation.

Severini, Gino [severeenee] (1883–1966) Artist, born in Cortona, C Italy. He studied in Rome and Paris, and signed the first Futurist manifesto in 1910. After 1914 he reverted to a more representational style, which he used in fresco and mosaic work, particularly in a number of Swiss and Italian churches. From 1940 onwards he adopted a decorative Cubist manner.

Severn, River River in SE Wales and W England, UK; rises on Plynlimon, C Wales; flows NE and E to Shrewsbury, then SE and S through Worcester and Gloucester; wide estuary into the Bristol Channel; navigable to Gloucester; length 354 km/220 mi; known for the **Severn bore** (tidal wave c.2 m/6 ft); railway tunnel (completed 1885); **Severn Bridge**, suspension bridge carrying M4 motorway, links Aust in Somerset with Beachley on the Monmouthshire border (988 m/3241 ft) completed 1966; **Severn Bridge II** (456 m/1496 ft) completed 1996.

Severnaya Zemlya [sayvernaya zemlya], formerly **Zemlya Imperatora**, Eng **North Land** or **Nicholas II Land** area 37 000 sq km/14 300 sq mi. Uninhabited archipelago in the Arctic Ocean, N of the Taymyr Peninsula, Russia; separates the Laptev Sea (E) from the Kara Sea (W); glaciers on the larger islands.

Severus, Lucius Septimius [seveerus] (c.146–211) Roman emperor (193–211), the founder of the Severan dynasty (193–235), and the first Roman emperor to be born in Africa (at Leptis Magna, of Romanized Punic stock). Declared emperor by the army in 193, he spent the early years of his reign securing his position against his rivals. Once established, he proved to be an able administrator, effecting many reforms, and showing a particularly close interest in the army and the law. His final years were spent in Britain, trying unsuccessfully to restore order in the N of the province.

Sévigné, Madame de [sayveenyay], *née* **Marie de Rabutin-Chantal** (1626–96) Writer, born in Paris, France. She was a member of French court society, and after the marriage of her daughter in 1669 she began a series of letters, lasting over 25 years, recounting the inner history of her time in great detail, and in a natural, colloquial style. The letters were published posthumously (1725).

Seville [sevil], Span **Sevilla**, ancient **Hispalis** 37°23N 6°00W, pop (2000e) 667 000. River-port and capital of Seville province, Andalusia, SW Spain; on R Guadalquivir, 538 km/334 mi SW of Madrid; Moorish cultural centre, 8th–13th-c; trading centre with the Americas, 16th-c; archbishopric; airport; railway; university (1502); tourism, furniture, olives, agricultural machinery, chemicals; birthplace of Velásquez and Murillo; cathedral (15th-c), largest Gothic church in the world, with tomb of Columbus; Moorish citadel and Archivo de Indias, a world heritage site; Maria Luisa Park, fine arts museum, Pilate's House, Palace of St Telmo; Scipio's Roman settlement of Italica, 7 km/4 mi NW; April fair, Festival of Spain (autumn), Fiesta of La Virgen de los Reyes (Aug), St Miguel fair (Sep).

Sèvres porcelain [sevr] The French royal porcelain factory, founded at Vincennes c.1740 and moved to Sèvres in 1756. It produced luxury soft-paste porcelain and from c.1769 hard-paste. Early Sèvres included beautiful figures in white unglazed 'biscuit' ware, but the factory's speciality was items with exquisitely painted panels reserved in richly coloured plain grounds with elaborate gilding.

sewage Waste matter, especially human excrement, carried away from houses by special conduits (**sewers**). The use of water-borne sewage disposal became established in the 1870s, the sewers being linked either directly to the sea through an outfall, if a suitable one was available, or to a **sewage farm**. A sewage farm uses beds of sand to grow and support a gelatinous bacterial film which develops as the true filter, removing almost all solids. Other precipitation treatments remove substances in solution, to allow the effluent water to be reused for drinking, if need be.

Seward Peninsula Peninsula in Alaska, USA, separating Kotzebue Sound (N) and Norton Sound (S); the most W point of the North American continent.

Sewell, Anna [syooel] (1820–78) Novelist, born in Great Yarmouth, Norfolk, E England, UK. An invalid for most of her life, she wrote *Black Beauty* (1877), the story of a horse, written as a plea for the more humane treatment of animals. It is perhaps the most famous fictional work about horses (filmed, 1946, 1971, 1994).

sewellel [sewelel] *mountain beaver*

Sexagesima [seksajesima] In the Western Christian Church, the second Sunday before Lent, apparently so called by analogy with *Quinquagesima*, the following Sunday. (Lat *sexagesimus*, 'sixtieth').

sex chromosome A chromosome represented differently in the sexes, and responsible for the genetic determination of the sex of an individual. The sex carrying a homologous pair of sex chromosomes (XX) is *homogametic*; the sex with a dissimilar pair (XY) or unpaired (X) sex chromosome is *heterogametic*. All gametes of the homogametic sex carry one X-chromosome. Half of the gametes produced by the heterogametic sex carry an X-chromosome and the other half a Y-chromosome, or no sex chromosome at all. In humans, the female is the homogametic sex and the male is the heterogametic sex.

sex discrimination Unfavourable treatment, whether direct or indirect, or victimization of a person because of sex or marital status. In many jurisdictions, dismissal on the grounds of pregnancy, or discrimination when taking on staff or affording access to promotion is also unlawful, as is victimization of someone claiming discrimination. European Communities law calls for member states to apply the principle that men and women shall receive equal pay for equal work. In England and Wales, the relevant Acts are the Sex Discrimination Acts of 1975 and 1986. Also, under the Equal Pay Act (1976), women doing broadly similar or the same work as men qualify for equal pay and conditions of employment. Action for a breach may be taken in an industrial tribunal or, where employment is not involved, in the civil courts.

sex hormones Steroid hormones produced and secreted mainly by the gonads and also by the adrenal glands, necessary for sexual development and the control of reproductive function. In humans the most important are certain androgens (testosterone and dihydrotestosterone) found predominantly in males, and progestogens (progesterone) and certain oestrogens (oestradiol, oestrone, and oestriol) found predominantly in females. They probably act on the brain to influence sexual and other behaviour.

sexism A set of preconceived assumptions about the 'proper' roles, attitudes, and characteristics (especially physical) that men and women should have, typically working to the advantage of men over women; for example, the assumption that 'a woman's place is in the home', or that men are 'naturally aggressive'. Sexism can be identified by behaviour, speech, and the written word, and is criticized most strongly by feminists.

sex linkage Genes carried on the X and Y chromosomes, and the characteristics they control; also called **X linkage**. In mammals females have two X chromosomes and males an X and a Y chromosome. Women transmit one X chromosome to either sons or daughters, while men pass their X chromosome only to their daughters. A characteristic feature of X-linked inheritance is thus the absence of male-to-male transmission. Most X-linked diseases in humans are inherited as recessives, with the males the affected sex (eg haemophilia, Duchenne muscular dystrophy). As there are only a few functional genes on the Y chromosomes in humans, the terms *sex linkage* and *X linkage* have become synonymous.

Sextans (Lat 'sextant') A very faint equatorial constellation between Leo and Hydra.

sextant An optical instrument for measuring angular distances; in particular, the elevation of the Sun above the horizon at noon, for determining latitude. The observer views the horizon through a telescope, and simultaneously (through a mirror attached to an arm on a graduated arc) the Sun. The mirror can be moved over the arc to produce a coincidence of the Sun-image and the horizon. For land use, an artificial horizon is provided by a pool of mercury; in aircraft, a bubble-level horizon is used.

sex therapy Treatment for sexual problems of psychological origin, which may arise as a result of a mental reaction to physical illness by the affected individual or partner, or to psychological attitudes themselves, either of which imperil normal sexual relations. An assessment of the individual or couple's problem is followed by simple counselling or, in the event of failure, by referral to specially trained sex therapists, who generally advise a graduated programme of tasks which the couple pursue at home. Emphasis is placed on the need for mutual understanding of each other's problems, and the need for mutual communication.

Sextus Empiricus [empirikus] (early 3rd-c) Greek philosopher and physician, active at Alexandria and Athens, who is the main source of information for the Sceptical school of philosophy. Little is known of his life, but his extant writings, *Outlines of Pyrrhonism* and *Against the Dogmatists*, had an enormous influence when they were rediscovered and published in Latin translations in the 1560s.

sexually transmitted diseases *AIDS; gonorrhoea; syphilis; venereal disease*

sexual topics *dyspareunia; incest; masturbation; Oedipus; paedophilia; sadomasochism; satyriasis; transsexual; vaginismus; voyeurism*

Seychelles *see panel*

Seyfert, Carl (Keenan) [sayfert] (1911–60) US astronomer, who first drew attention (1943) to the existence of galaxies with brilliant nuclei, now known as **Seyfert galaxies**, which are related to quasars.

Seymour, Jane [seemoor] (c.1509–37) Third queen of Henry VIII, the mother of Edward VI, and the sister of Protector Somerset. She was a lady-in-waiting to Henry's first two wives, and married him 11 days after the execution of Anne Boleyn. She died soon after the birth of her son, later Edward VI.

Sezession [setsesyohn] (Ger 'secession') The name adopted by a number of groups of modern artists in Germany between c.1890 and World War 1, who seceded from the orthodox academic bodies to form their own exhibiting societies. The Munich *Sezession* was founded in 1882, Vienna in 1897, Berlin in 1899.

Seychelles

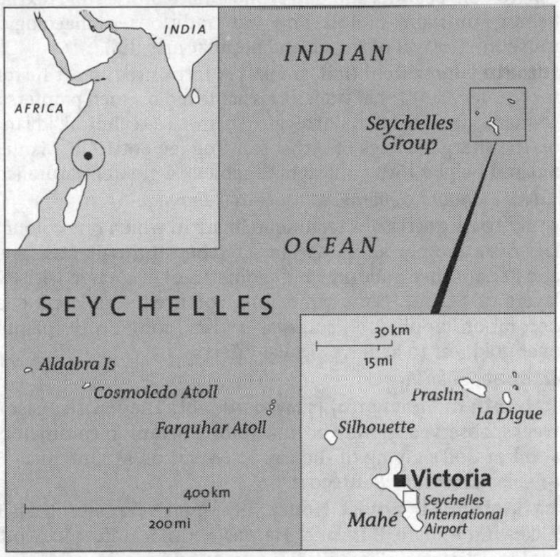

[sayshelz], official name **Republic of Seychelles**

Local name Seychelles

Timezone GMT +4

Area 455 km²/175 sq mi

Population total (2002e) 83 400

Status Republic

Date of independence 1976

Capital Victoria (on Mahé Island)

Languages Creole French (official since 1981), and English

Ethnic groups Seychellois (Asian, African, and European admixtures), Malagasy (3%), Chinese (2%), English (1%)

Religions Roman Catholic (95%)

Physical features Island group in SW Indian Ocean, N of Madagascar, comprising 115 islands; main islands include Mahé (largest), Praslin, and La Digue; islands fall into two main groups, a compact group of 41 mountainous islands rising steeply from the sea, highest point 906 m/2972 ft on Mahé; and a group of low-lying coralline islands and atolls to the SW, flat, waterless and mostly uninhabited.

Climate Tropical climate; average annual temperature 27°C (Jan), 26°C (Jul); wet humid season (Dec–May); average annual rainfall 2375 mm/93·5 in.

Currency 1 Seychelles Rupee (SR) = 100 cents

Economy Agriculture; fruit, vegetables, livestock, cinnamon, copra; brewing, plastics, steel fabricated goods, fishing; tourism.

GDP (2002e) $626 mn, per capita $7800

Human Development Index (2002) 0·811

History Colonized by the French, 1768; captured by Britain, 1794; incorporated as a dependency of Mauritius, 1814; separate Crown Colony, 1903; independent republic within the Commonwealth, 1976; constitution, 1979, established a one-party state; governed by a President, elected for a 5-year term, a Council of Ministers, and a unicameral National Assembly; legislation legalizing the activity of opposition parties adopted, 1991.

Head of State/Government
1977–2004 France-Albert René
2004– James Michel

Sfax [sfaks] 34°45N 10°43E, pop (2000e) 303 000. Seaport and capital of Sfax governorate, E Tunisia, 240 km/150 mi SE of Tunis; chief port and second largest city of Tunisia; built on the site of Roman and Phoenician settlements; occupied by

Sicilians (12th-c) and Spaniards (16th-c); also a base for Barbary pirates; modern city built after 1895; airfield; railway; trade in esparto, oil, peanuts and dates; phosphate processing, textiles, fishing; museum of folk arts and traditions, archaeological museum; festival of music and popular arts (Jul).

sfumato [sfumahtoh] (Ital 'smoke') A term used in art history for the very soft tonal transitions achieved by such painters as Leonardo da Vinci and Correggio. This was a technical advance on the sharp outlines of 15th-c painting (eg Botticelli, Mantegna) and helped 16th-c masters to achieve a greater naturalism.

SGML *Standard Generalized Mark-up Language*

sgraffito or **graffito** A technique in art in which one colour is laid over another and a design scratched through. Mediaeval and Renaissance buildings were sometimes decorated with two layers of plaster – one white, one coloured – and scratched decoration applied. Mediaeval artists sometimes painted over gold leaf to achieve similar effects.

Shabbat *Sabbath*

Shabuoth or **Shavuot(h)** [shavoo-oth, -ot] The Jewish Feast of Weeks, observed in May or June (6 or 7 Sivan) in commemoration of God's giving of the Law to Moses on Mount Sinai (*Ex* 19); also known as **Pentecost**.

Shackleton, Sir Ernest Henry (1874–1922) Explorer, born in Kilkea, Co Kildare, E Ireland. He was a junior officer in Scott's National Antarctic Expedition (1901–3), and nearly reached the South Pole in his own expedition of 1909. In 1915 his ship *Endurance* was crushed in the ice, and he and five others made a perilous journey of 1300 km/800 mi to bring relief for the crew. Knighted in 1909, he died at South Georgia during a fourth expedition.

shad Small, herring-like fish (*Alosa sapidissima*) native to the Atlantic seaboard of North America but now widespread on the Pacific coast also; adults live in coastal marine waters migrating into fresh water to breed; live in large schools feeding mainly on plankton; length up to 75 cm/30 in; silver with greenish-blue upper surface. (Family: Clupeidae.)

shaddock A citrus fruit (*Citrus grandis*) resembling grapefruit, 10–25 cm/4–10 in diameter; globose or pear-shaped, with greenish-yellow rind and sweet pink or yellow pulp. It is grown mainly in the tropics. (Family: Rutaceae.)

shadow-mask tube A cathode-ray tube for the display of colour video images. Electron beams from three separate guns modulated by the red, green, and blue signals are deflected by the scanning system through holes in the shadow-mask plate to fall on minute phosphor dots of the appropriate colour comprising the screen. These dots glow according to the intensity of the beam reaching them and, being too small to be seen individually, appear as additive colour hues. In most tubes the phosphor dots are arranged as triads in delta formation, but vertical stripes in groups of three are also employed, when the shadow-mask plate becomes a grille.

shadow puppets Puppets which are manipulated in performance so as to cast a shadow on a screen. There are two major traditions. In one, the sticks operating the two-dimensional figures are worked from below, as with Balinese and Javanese shadow theatre. In the other, the sticks are operated from behind, at right angles to the screen, and the puppets are pressed close to its surface, as with Chinese and Turkish shadow theatre.

Shadwell, Thomas (c.1642–92) Playwright, born in Brandon, Norfolk, E England, UK. He studied at Cambridge, became a lawyer, and found success with his first satirical comedy, *The Sullen Lovers* (1668), and such later 'comedies of manners' as *Epsom-Wells* (1672). He carried on a literary feud with Dryden, whom he satirized, and who attacked him in turn in *MacFlecknoe* (1684) and other poems. He succeeded Dryden as poet laureate in 1689.

Shaftesbury, Anthony Ashley Cooper, 1st Earl of [shahftsbree] (1621–83) English statesman, born in Wimborne St Giles, Dorset, S England, UK. He studied at Oxford, became a member of the Short Parliament (1640) and of the Barebones Parliament (1653), and was made one of Cromwell's Council of State, but from 1655 was in Opposition. At the Restoration he became a baron and Chancellor of the Exchequer (1661–72), a member of the Cabal (1667), an earl (1672), and Lord Chancellor (1672–3). He was dismissed in 1673, and led the opposition to the succession of James, Duke of York (later James II). Charged with treason in 1681, he was acquitted, but fled to Holland in 1682.

Shaftesbury, Anthony Ashley Cooper, 3rd Earl of [shahftsbree] (1671–1713) Philosopher, born in London, UK, the grandson of the 1st Earl of Shaftesbury. He studied in London and Winchester, and entered parliament in 1695, but ill health drove him from politics to literature. He is best known for his essays, collected as *Characteristics of Men, Manners, Opinions, Times* (1711). He was one of the leading English deists, with a considerable influence in Europe. He succeeded to the earldom in 1699, and in 1711 moved to Naples.

Shaftesbury, Anthony Ashley Cooper, 7th Earl of [shahftsbree] (1801–85) Factory reformer and philanthropist, born in London, UK. He studied at Oxford, entered parliament in 1826, and became the main spokesman of the factory reform movement. He piloted successive factory acts (1847, 1859) through parliament, prohibiting employment of women and children in the coal mines (1842), providing for care of the insane (1845), establishing a 10-hour day for factory workers (1847), providing lodging houses for the poor (1851) and rudimentary schooling for waifs. A leader of the evangelical movement within the Church of England, he succeeded to his earldom in 1851.

shaft graves Two groups of royal tombs at the W end of the citadel of Mycenae, Greece, the most notable discovered in 1876 by Heinrich Schliemann. They consist of six wooden-roofed, rock-cut, rectangular chambers c.4·5 m/15 ft by 6·4 m/21 ft, each with between two and five spectacular burials of the 16th-c BC, with gold death masks, jewellery, drinking vessels, and weapons. They were claimed (erroneously) by Schliemann as the graves of Homer's Agamemnon and Clytemnestra.

shag *cormorant*

Shah Jahan [jahahn] (1592–1666) Mughal emperor of India (1628–58), born in Lahore, NE Pakistan. His reign saw two wars in the Deccan (1636, 1655), the subjugation of Bijapur and Golconda (1636), and attacks on the Uzbegs and Persians. A ruthless but able ruler, the magnificence of his court was unequalled. His buildings included the Taj Mahal (1632–54), the tomb of his beloved third wife, **Mumtaz Mahal** (1592–1631). From 1658 he was held prisoner by his son Aurangzeb.

Shaka [shahka] (c.1788–1828) African ruler, born near Melmoth, KwaZulu Natal, E South Africa. He was a highly successful military ruler, who intensified the centralization of Zulu power, adapted the weapons and tactics of local warfare, and set about the incorporation of neighbouring peoples. The rise of the Zulu kingdom under Shaka was associated with a series of wars and population movements known as the *difaqane*. He was killed by his half-brother Dingane. He remains an enigmatic and contentious figure, the subject of novels and films, and his career is a much debated issue in South African history.

Shakers The popular name for members of the United Society for Believers in Christ's Second Appearing, founded in England under the leadership of Ann Lee, a psychic visionary, who led them to America in 1774. They believed that Christ had appeared with Ann Lee. Communitarian and pacifist, their ecstatic dancing gave rise to their popular name. They were known for their furniture and other designs. Their acceptance of strict celibacy has led to their decline, and in 1992 the Canterbury Shaker Valley community ceased to exist following the death of the last Shaker sister there, Ethel Hudson, aged 96. By 2000 only the Sabbathday Lake Shaker community remained active, with a total of seven members.

Shakespeare, William (1564–1616) Playwright, actor, and poet, the greatest English writer, born in Stratford-upon-Avon, Warwickshire, C England, UK, the son of **John Shakespeare**, a glover, and **Mary Arden**, of farming stock. Much uncertainty sur-

Shakespeare: The Plays

Early comedies	*Written*	*Well-known characters*
The Comedy of Errors	1590–94	Antipholus, Dromio, Adriana
Love's Labour's Lost	1590–94	Armado, Berowne, Costard
The Two Gentlemen of Verona	1592–3	Proteus, Valentine, Julia, Sylvia
The Taming of the Shrew	1592	Petruchio, Katharina, Sly
Histories		
Henry VI Part I (with other authors)	1589–90	Henry, Talbot, Joan of Arc
Henry VI Part II	1590–91	Henry, Margaret, Jack Cade
Henry VI Part III	1590–91	Henry, Margaret, Richard of Gloucester
Edward III (with other authors)	1590–5	Edward, Philippa, Prince Edward, Countess of Salibury
Richard III	1592–3	Richard, Margaret, Clarence, Anne
King John	1595–7	John, Constance, Arthur, Bastard
Richard II	1595	Richard, John of Gaunt, Bolingbroke
Henry IV Part I	1596	Henry, Hal, Hotspur, Falstaff
Henry IV Part II	1597	Henry, Hal, Falstaff, Mistress Quickly
Henry V	1599	Henry (formerly Hal), Pistol, Nym, Katherine
Henry VIII (with John Fletcher)	1613	Henry, Katherine, Wolsey
Middle comedies		
A Midsummer Night's Dream	1595	Oberon, Titania, Puck, Bottom
The Merchant of Venice	1596–8	Bassanio, Portia, Shylock, Jessica
The Merry Wives of Windsor	1597	Falstaff, Mistress Quickly, Shallow
As You Like It	1599	Rosalind, Orlando, Touchstone, Jaques
Twelfth Night	1600–2	Orsino, Olivia, Viola, Malvolio, Feste, Sir Andrew Aguecheek
Dark comedies		
Much Ado About Nothing	1598	Beatrice, Benedick, Dogberry, Verges
All's Well That Ends Well	1602–3	Bertram, Helena, Parolles
Measure for Measure	1604–5	Duke, Angelo, Isabella, Mariana
Tragedies		
Romeo and Juliet	1595–6	Romeo, Juliet, Mercutio, the Nurse
Hamlet	1600–1	Hamlet, Ophelia, the Ghost, the Grave-Digger
Othello	1604	Othello, Desdemona, Iago, Cassio
King Lear	1605–6	Lear, Cordelia, the Fool, Kent, Edgar/Poor Tom
Macbeth	1605–6	Macbeth, Lady Macbeth, Banquo, the Three Witches
Greek and Roman plays		
Titus Andronicus	1590–94	Andronicus, Aaron, Lavinia
Julius Caesar	1599	Caesar, Brutus, Cassius, Antony
Troilus and Cressida	1601–2	Troilus, Cressida, Pandarus
Timon of Athens (with Thomas Middleton)	1605–9	Timon, Apemantus
Antony and Cleopatra	1606–7	Antony, Cleopatra, Enobarbus
Coriolanus	1607–8	Coriolanus, Volumnia, Menenius
Late plays		
Pericles (with George Wilkins)	1607–8	Pericles, Marina
Cymbeline	1609–10	Innogen, Iachimo, Posthumus
The Winter's Tale	1611	Leontes, Perdita, Florizel, Autolycus
The Tempest	1613	Prospero, Miranda, Ferdinand, Ariel, Caliban
The Two Noble Kinsmen (with John Fletcher)	1613	Arcite, Palamon, Emilia, Theseus

rounds his early life. He was the eldest of three sons, and there were four daughters. He was educated at the local grammar school, and married **Anne Hathaway**, from a local farming family, in 1582, who bore him a daughter, Susanna, in 1583, and twins Hamnet and Judith in 1585. He moved to London, possibly in 1591, and became an actor. During 1592–4, when the theatres were closed for the plague, he wrote his poems 'Venus and Adonis' and 'The Rape of Lucrece'. His sonnets, known by 1598, though not published until 1609, fall into two groups: 1 to 126 are addressed to a fair young man, and 127 to 154 to a 'dark lady' who holds both the young man and the poet in thrall. Who these people are has provided an exercise in detection for numerous critics. The first evidence of his association with the stage is in 1594, when he was acting with the Lord Chamberlain's company of players, later 'the King's Men'. When the company built the Globe Theatre south of the Thames in 1599, he became a partner, living modestly at a house in Silver St until c.1606, then moving near the Globe. He returned to Stratford c.1610, living as a country gentleman at his house, New Place. His will was made in March 1616, a few months before he died, and he was buried at Stratford. The modern era of Shakespeare scholarship has been marked by an enormous amount of investigation into the authorship, text, and chronology of the plays, including detailed studies of the age in which he lived, and of the Elizabethan stage. Authorship is still a controversial subject for certain plays, such as *Titus Andronicus*, *Two Noble Kinsmen*, *Henry VI*, part I, as is Shakespeare's part in *Timon of Athens*, *Pericles*, *Henry VIII*, and (the latest proposed addition to the canon) *Edward III*. This has involved detailed studies of the various editions of the plays, in particular the different quarto editions, and the first collected works, the First Folio of 1623. It is conventional to group the plays into early, middle, and late periods, and to distinguish comedies, tragedies, and histories, recognizing other groups that do not fall neatly into these categories.

shale Sedimentary rock predominantly formed from consolidated and compacted clay deposits. It has a characteristic fissility along the bedding planes (ie it splits easily along closely-spaced parallel surfaces) because of the orientation of the platy clay minerals. Oil shale contains sufficient decayed organic matter that an oil can be extracted from it by destructive distillation.

Shalimar Gardens A celebrated garden designed by the Mughal emperor Jahangir for his wife, Nur Jahan, in 1616. The garden is laid out on four terraces by Dal Lake, in Kashmir, India.

shallot [shalot] A variety of onion with clusters of small, oval bulbs, widely grown as a vegetable.

Shalyapin, Fyodor (Ivanovich) [shalyapeen], often spelled **Chaliapin** (1873–1938) Bass, born near Kazan, W Russia. He was largely self-taught, but after a short period of study in Tbilisi (1892–3) he made his way as an opera singer, becoming well known through the roles he sang with the Marmontov Company after 1896. Among his most famous roles was that of Boris Godunov in Musorgsky's opera. He left Russia in 1921, and died in Paris.

shaman [shayman, shahman] A person thought to possess special powers to communicate with and influence the spirits by dissociating his soul from his body. The spirits assist him in performing his duties, which include discovering the cause of illness, famine, and any other misfortune, and prescribing an appropriate cure. Shamans are found among Siberian and Asian peoples; similar practitioners are found in many other religions, under other names.

Shamir, Yitzhak [shameer], originally **Yitzhak Jazernicki** (1915–) Zionist leader and prime minister of Israel (1983–4, 1986–92), born in Ruzinoy, E Poland. He studied law at Warsaw University and at the Hebrew University of Jerusalem, and in his 20s became a founder member of the Israel Freedom Fighters, a terrorist group later known as the Stern Gang. He was arrested by the British in 1941 and exiled to Eritrea in 1946, but given asylum in France. He returned to the new state of Israel (1948), and entered the Knesset (1973–96). He was foreign minister (1980–3), before taking over the leadership of the right-wing Likud Party, and becoming prime minister. From 1984 he shared an uneasy coalition with the Labour leader Shimon Peres, and was re-elected in 1988, but lost his position when Labour under Rabin won the 1992 election.

shamisen A Japanese lute, with a long, slender neck and three silk or nylon strings which are plucked with an ivory plectrum. It is used principally to accompany singing.

Shammai [shamiy] (c.1st-c BC–AD 1st-c) Jewish scholar and Pharisaic leader, apparently a native of Jerusalem. He was the head of a famous school of Torah scholars, whose interpretation of the Law was often in conflict with the equally famous school led by Hillel. Relatively little is known of Shammai himself, except that his legal judgments were often considered severe and literalistic, compared to Hillel's. Both are often referred to in Mishnah.

shamrock The name applied to several different plants with leaves divided into three leaflets, including **wood sorrel** (*Oxalis acetosella*) and various species of **clover** (*Trifolium species*). Although adopted as the national emblem of Ireland, and worn each year on 17 March to commemorate St Patrick, its true botanical identity remains uncertain, although many regard **lesser trefoil** (*Trifolium dubium*) a likely candidate. It is a slender annual growing to 25 cm/10 in; flowers yellow, up to 15 clustered in tiny stalked heads up to 9 mm/0·35 in across, petals later turning dark brown; native to Europe, N Africa, and the W African islands (Macaronesia). (Family: Leguminosae.)

Shan A Tai-speaking people, the second largest minority group in Myanmar (formerly Burma). Originating in SW China (early rice culture), they were forced S by the Mongols between the 10th-c and 13th-c, and ruled Burma during the 13th–16th-c. Buddhists, with a strong identity, they are mainly concentrated in Shan state, constituting half of its population of over 3 million. Most are rice farmers.

Shang or **Yin dynasty** (1523–1028 BC) The earliest historical Chinese dynasty (the dates are disputed). Evidence is found in the Zhou and Han periods, and in 200 000 Shang period oracle bones which yield detail of daily life, as well as royal and ministerial chronologies. Its capital (from 1300 BC) was at Anyang, N of the Yellow River. The culture included kingship, law, priests, slavery, and proto-feudalism. There was solar measurement, astronomical records, and a 12-month calendar. Its characteristics are shared with contemporary cultures in Crete, Greece, the Indus, and Upper Mesopotamia.

Shanghai 31°13N 121°25E; pop (2000e) 9 158 000, administrative region 13 876 000; municipality area 5800 sq km/2239 sq mi. Port in E China, on the Yellow Sea, on Huangpu and Wusong Rivers; largest city in China; developed in the Yuan period as a cotton centre; trading centre in the 17th–18th-c; opened to foreign trade, 1842, and developed as the principal centre for European influence in China; by the 1940s, world's fifth largest port; Japanese occupation, 1937–45; power centre of Jiang Qing in the Cultural Revolution, 1966–76; two airports; two airfields; rail and sea links to other cities; university (1895) and several other higher education institutions; oil refining, shipbuilding, engineering, chemicals, pharmaceuticals, textiles, paper, publishing; People's Park, People's Square, Jade Buddha Temple (1882), Industrial Exhibition Hall, Museum of Natural History, Songjiang County Square Pagoda and Dragon Wall (11th-c), Longhua Temple (c.7th-c); Yu Yuan (Garden of Happiness), 1577, the basis for 'willow pattern' chinaware.

Shankar, Ravi [shangkah(r)] (1920–) Sitarist, born in Benares, N India. He is widely regarded as India's most important musician, not only because of his virtuoso playing, but also as a teacher and composer. After years of intensive musical study, he set up schools of Indian music, founded the National Orchestra of India, and in the mid-1950s became the first Indian instrumentalist to undertake an international tour. He found himself in demand in the West as a performer and teacher in all areas of music – from the Edinburgh International Festival to the jazz and rock worlds. George Harrison of the Beatles was one of his pupils. He has written several film scores, the most notable being for Satyajit Ray's trilogy, *Apu*.

Shanklin *Sandown*

Shankly, Bill, popular name of **William Shankly** (1913–81) Footballer and manager, born in Scotland, UK. As a player he won an FA Cup Medal with Preston North End, and five Scotland caps. As a post-war manager he found success with Liverpool (1959–74), after unremarkable spells with Carlisle, Grimsby, Workington, and Huddersfield. He created a team which was not only highly successful in Britain and Europe, but which encouraged individual expression and communicated great exhilaration to the spectators.

Shannon, Ir **Rineanna** 52°42N 8°57W, pop (2000e) 8000. Town in Clare county, Munster, W Ireland; W of Limerick near R Shannon; duty-free airport; gateway to Ireland for transatlantic visitors; electronics; boat show rally (Jul).

Shannon, River River in Ireland, rising in Co Cavan, Ulster, and flowing c.385 km/240 mi SW through L Allen, L Ree, and L Derg to Limerick Bay; navigable for most of its length; hydroelectric power at Ardnacrusha.

SHAPE *NATO*

Shapur or **Sapor II** [shapoor], known as **the Great** (309–79) King of Persia (309–79). He was declared king at his birth by the Persian nobility, and ruled with the help of regents until the age of 16. Under him the Sassanian empire reached its zenith. He successfully challenged Roman control of the Middle East, forcing Jovian to cede five provinces to him (363), and establishing Persian control over Armenia.

sharecropping A US agricultural practice by which short-term tenants (usually black) worked land for landlords (usually white) for a percentage of the crop raised. As much a means of labour and racial control as of economic production, sharecropping provided the economic basis of post-slavery white supremacy.

sharefarming A form of tenure in which the landlord provides the land, fixed equipment, and often a proportion of the variable inputs, in exchange for an agreed proportion of the final crop. It has been popular in some continental European countries, such as France, and also in the USA and New Zealand.

shares Certificates of part ownership of a company, which represent equal amounts of money invested in the company. The **shareholders** provide the original capital for the company and are its residual owners. They are entitled to any profits made, either as dividends or as a capital distribution if the company is sold or wound up. If the company makes losses they may lose their money, hence the term **risk capital**, though if the company has limited liability they cannot lose more than they put in. Shareholders normally elect the company's directors, though it is possible to have some non-voting shares, or limits on the votes one shareholder can exercise. Shares have normally been paper certificates, but electronic share registers are now possible. Shares without a register, or **bearer shares**, are possible (though not legal in some countries). Shares can be traded on stock exchanges in many countries, at prices which often change rapidly, and are regarded as relatively risky investments.

Sharia [shareea] The sacred law of Islam, embracing all aspects of a Muslim's life. It has four sources: the *Qur'an*, the *sunna* or 'practice' of the Prophet Mohammed, *ijma* or 'consensus of opinion', and *qiyas* or 'reasoning by analogy'. Four Sunni schools of law are recognized under Sharia.

Sharif, Omar [shareef], originally **Michael Shalhouz** (1932–) Film actor, born in Alexandria, N Egypt. He made his Egyptian film debut in 1953, becoming a top male star in the country, before attracting international attention for his role in *Lawrence of Arabia* (1962). Later films include *Doctor Zhivago* (1965, Golden Globe), *Funny Girl* (1968), *The Tamarind Seed* (1974), *Return to Eden* (1982), and *The Mirror Has Two Faces* (1996), and he appeared in the 1996 television production of *Gulliver's Travels*. He has published an autobiography, *The Eternal Male* (1977), and is also renowned as a bridge player. In 2003, he received the Venice Film Festival's Golden Lion award for his achievement in film.

Sharjah [shah(r)ja], or **Shariqah** pop (2000e) 385 900; area 2600 sq km/1000 sq mi. Third largest of the United Arab Emirates, NE of Dubai; capital, Ash Sharjah; offshore oil production began in 1974; natural gas, ship and vehicle repairing, cement, paper bags, steel products, paint.

shark Any of a large group of active, predatory, cartilaginous fishes belonging to 19 separate families: Alopiidae (thresher sharks), Carcharhinidae (blue sharks, white sharks), Cetorhinidae (basking sharks), Chlamydoselachidae (frilled sharks), Dalatiidae (dwarf sharks), Echinorhinidae (bramble sharks), Heterodontidae (Port Jackson sharks), Hexanchidae (cow sharks), Lamnidae (mackerel sharks), Mitsukurinidae (goblin sharks), Odontaspidae (sand sharks), Orectolobidae (wobbegongs), Oxynotidae, Pseudotriakidae, Rhincodontidae (whale sharks), Scyliorhinidae (dogfishes, catsharks), Sphyrnidae (hammerhead sharks), Squalidae (dogfishes), Triakidae (leopard sharks).

shark-sucker *remora*

Sharman, Helen (Patricia) (1963–) Britain's first astronaut, born in Sheffield, South Yorkshire, N England, UK. She studied chemistry at Sheffield University, then worked in electrical engineering and confectionery research. In 1989 she responded to an advertisement asking for trainee astronauts, and was eventually selected from over 13,000 applicants to be the British member of the Russian scientific space mission, Project Juno (May 1991), spending eight days in space. She has since become well known as a lecturer and broadcaster in science education; her book *The Space Place* appeared in 1997.

Sharon, Ariel [sharon] (1928–) Prime minister of Israel (2001–) and soldier, born in Kfar Maalal, a communal farm in W Palestine, the son of Russian immigrant parents. In 1942 he joined the Jewish military underground organization, the Haganah, fought in the Arab–Israeli War of 1948–9, and went on to a series of command positions, notably in the Yom Kippur War (Oct 1973). His political career began when he won a seat in the Knesset (1973–4), and served for right-wing parties in various government posts for the next two decades. He was minister of defence (1981–3) during the war in Lebanon, but was forced to resign when he was found indirectly responsible for the massacre of civilians at refugee camps in Lebanon. Re-elected to the Knesset (1999), he served as chairman of the Likud following the resignation of Benjamin Netanyahu. In 2001, after months of failed peace negotiations by Ehud Barak, an Israeli public voted Sharon their next leader. He won a second term in 2003.

Sharp, Cecil (James) (1859–1924) Collector of folk songs and dances, born in London, UK. He studied at Cambridge, became a lawyer, then turned to music. He published several collections of British and US folk material, and in 1911 founded the Folk-Dance Society. His work is commemorated by Cecil Sharp House, London, the headquarters of the society.

Sharpe, Tom, popular name of **Thomas Ridley Sharpe** (1928–) Novelist, born in London, UK. He studied at Cambridge and did his National Service in the Marines before going to South Africa in 1951, from where he was deported in 1961. He was a lecturer in history at the Cambridge College of Arts and Technology (1963–71) before turning to full-time writing, beginning with *Riotous Assembly* (1971). Later novels include *Indecent Exposure* (1973), *Porterhouse Blue* (1974), a series introducing the character of Wilt (from 1976), and *The Midden* (1996).

Sharpe, William F (1934–) Economist, born in Cambridge, Massachusetts, USA. He taught at Washington, Irvine, and Stanford (from 1970) universities. He shared the 1990 Nobel Prize for Economics for his contributions to the corporate finance field, particularly his studies in financial decision-making under uncertainty.

Sharpeville [shah(r)pvil] 26°40S 27°52E, pop (2000e) 143 000. Black African industrial township in South Africa, S of Johannesburg; scene of the Sharpeville massacre (1960); centre of the Sharpeville Students National Resistance Movement; inauguration of the new constitution took place here in December 1996.

Sharpeville massacre (21 Mar 1960) A major incident in the black African township of Sharpeville in Transvaal province, South Africa, when police opened fire on a crowd demonstrating against the laws restricting non-white movements and requiring non-whites to carry identification (the *pass laws*); 69 people were killed and 180 wounded. The anti-pass-law campaign had been called by both the African National Congress (ANC) and the rival Pan-African Congress (PAC). The massacre produced an international outcry, and made black nationalism in South Africa increasingly radical. The ANC formed a fighting wing, the *Umkhonte We Sizwe* ('Spear of the Nation'), and both the ANC and PAC were banned. Later in the year South Africa became a republic, and was refused re-admission to the Commonwealth.

Sharpless, Barry K (1941–) Chemist, born in Philadelphia, Pennsylvania, USA. He studied at Dartmouth College and Stanford University, later joining the Scripps Research Institute at La Jolla, CA. He shared the 2001 Nobel Prize for Chemistry for work on chirally catalysed hydrogenation reactions.

Shastri, Lal (Bahadur) [shastree] (1904–66) Indian statesman and prime minister (1964–6), born in Mughalsarai, Uttar Pradesh, NC India. He joined the independence movement at 16, and was often imprisoned by the British. He excelled as a Congress Party official, and in Nehru's cabinet became minister of transport (1957), commerce (1958), and home affairs (1960). He succeeded Nehru as premier, but died in office from a heart attack, the day after signing a 'no war' agreement with Pakistan.

Shatner, William (1931–) Actor and writer, born in Montreal, Quebec, SE Canada. Educated at McGill University, he became a stage actor in Canada and New York, from 1956 obtaining roles in films and television series. He became internationally known following the cult success of the *Star Trek* television series (1966–9), in which he played Captain James T(iberius) Kirk. He reprised the role in several feature film sequels, directing as well as acting in *Star Trek V: The Final Frontier* (1989). Later film appearances include *Starfleet Academy* (1997) and *Free Enterprise* (1998). He has also written a number of science-fiction books, starting with *Tek War, Tek Lab* (1989). Other books include *Star Trek Preserver* (2000).

Shatt al-Arab [**shat** al **a**rab] Tidal river formed by the union of the Tigris and Euphrates Rivers, SE Iraq; flows 192 km/119 mi SE through marshland to enter the Persian Gulf; part of the Iraq–Iran border in its lower course; wide delta, containing the world's largest date-palm groves; navigable for ocean-going vessels as far as Basra; international commission in 1935 gave control to Iraq, but disputes over navigational rights continued; Iran–Iraq boundary settled by Algiers agreement, 1975; claimed by Saddam Hussein as primary reason for invading Iran in 1980.

Shavuot(h) *Shabuoth*

Shaw, Anna Howard (1847–1919) Suffragist, born in Newcastle upon Tyne, Tyne and Wear, NE England, UK. Her family emigrated to the USA in 1851, and in 1880 she became the first woman to be ordained as a Methodist preacher. In 1886 she graduated from Boston University as a doctor, but decided to devote herself entirely to the cause of women's suffrage. An eloquent, powerful lecturer, she campaigned widely. She was president of the National American Woman Suffrage Association (1904–15), and head of the Women's Committee of the Council of National Defense during World War 1. She published her autobiography, *The Story of a Pioneer*, in 1915.

Shaw, Artie, originally **Arthur Jacob Arshawsky** (1910–) Clarinet player and bandleader, born in New York City, USA. He turned professional in 1925, and gained popularity during the 1930s, becoming internationally known after recording 'Begin the Beguine' (Cole Porter). Other hits include 'Stardust' (1940) and 'Moonglow' (1941). Although a gifted jazz musician, his public appearances were erratic, and died away during the 1950s. He wrote an autobiography, *The Trouble with Cinderella* in 1952. He married eight times, always to a well-known beauty, including actresses Lana Turner, Ava Gardner, and Evelyn Keyes. He quit music altogether in 1955.

Shaw, Fiona (1958–) Actress, born in Cork, Co Cork, S Ireland. After studying philosophy at University College, Cork, she trained as an actor at the Royal Academy of Dramatic Art, graduating with the Bancroft Gold Medal. Throughout her career she has worked consistently with the Royal Shakespeare Company. She often collaborates with the director Deborah Warner, most notably with *Richard II* (1995), in which her playing of the title role provoked both enormous criticism and rapturous praise. Film work includes *My Left Foot* (1988), *London Kills Me* (1991), *Three Men and a Little Lady* (1996), *Butcher Boy* (1996), and *The Last September* (1999).

Shaw, George Bernard (1856–1950) Playwright, essayist, and pamphleteer, born in Dublin, Ireland. In 1876 he left office-work in Ireland and moved to London, UK. In 1882 he turned to socialism, joined the committee of the Fabian Society, and became known as a journalist, writing music and drama criticism, and publishing critical essays. He began to write plays in 1885, and among his early successes were *Arms and the Man* (1894), *Candida* (1897), and *The Devil's Disciple* (1897). There followed *Man and Superman* (1905), *Major Barbara* (1905), *The Doctor's Dilemma* (1906), and several others, displaying an increasing range of subject matter. Later plays include the 'religious pantomime' *Androcles and the Lion* (1912), and the 'anti-romantic' comedy *Pygmalion* (1913), adapted as the musical play *My Fair Lady*, in 1956 (filmed, 1964). After World War 1 followed *Heartbreak House* (1919), *Back to Methuselah* (1921), and *Saint Joan* (1923). He wrote over 40 plays, and continued to write them even in his 90s. He was also passionately interested in the question of spelling reform, wrote most of his own work in shorthand, and left money in his will for the devising of a new English alphabet on phonetic principles (which came to be called *Shavian*). In 1925 he was awarded the Nobel Prize for Literature.

Shaw, (Richard) Norman (1831–1912) Architect, born in Edinburgh, EC Scotland, UK. He studied in London, where he practised. He was a leader of the trend away from Victorian style back to traditional Georgian design, as in New Scotland Yard (1888) and the Piccadilly Hotel (1905).

Shawnee [shaw**nee**] North American Algonkin Indians who originally settled in Ohio, but who were pushed out of the area by the Iroquois. Defeated in 1794 by US forces at the Battle of Fallen Timbers, they were divided up into three sections and settled in Oklahoma.

Shearer, Alan (1970–) England footballer, born in Newcastle-upon Tyne, Tyne & Wear, NE England, UK. He played for Southampton (1988–92), then transferred to Blackburn Rovers (1992–6) at a then record British fee of £3·2 million. He transferred to Newcastle United in 1996 for a world record fee of £15 million. By June 1997 he had a tally of 213 league goals. He joined the England squad in 1992, becoming captain in 1996, and by mid-2000 (when he announced his retirement) had won 62 caps. He was named 1994 Footballer of the Year and 1995 Professional Footballers' Association Player of the Year. In April 2002 he achieved his 200th goal for Newcastle United. In 2003 he received the Domestic Player of the Decade award, presented by the FA Premier League to mark the first 10 years of the Premiership.

Shearing, George (Albert) (1919–) Jazz pianist, bandleader, and composer, born in London, UK. Blind from birth, he had some success touring and on radio in Britain, before moving to the USA in the late 1940s. There he gained worldwide fame through his recordings and his lush 'locked hands' style of piano-playing. His compositions include 'Lullaby of Birdland' and 'September in the Rain'.

shear modulus A measure of a material's resistance to twisting; symbol *G*, units Pa (pascal); also called the **modulus of rigidity** or **torsion modulus**. A higher *G* value means that the material is harder to twist. It is defined as shear stress divided by shear strain, and is applicable only to solids. For example, for steel $G = 0{\cdot}8 \times 10^{11}$Pa.

shearwater A petrel with a long slender bill; plumage dark above, dark or pale beneath. Some species with long wings and tail are found over the open ocean, and fish in flight; species with shorter wings and tail fish while swimming near coasts. The name is also used for skimmers.

sheathbill A white, pigeon-like shorebird, native to the Antarctic and sub-Antarctic; short, stout bill with horny cover at base; the only native Antarctic bird without webbed feet; flies reluctantly but well; eats shore animals and seaweed; often scavenges in penguin colonies. (Family: Chionididae, 2 species.)

Sheba, Queen of [**shee**ba] (c.10th-c BC) Monarch mentioned in the Bible (1 *Kings* 10 and 2 *Chron* 9), perhaps from SW Arabia (modern Yemen), although placed by some in N Arabia. She is said to have journeyed to Jerusalem to test the wisdom of Solomon and to exchange gifts, though this may imply a trade pact. The story depicts the splendour of Solomon's court.

Sheene, Barry (Stephen Frank) (1950–2003) Motorcycle racer, born in East London, UK. He made his professional debut at age 18 and went on to win the British (1970) and European (1973) 750 cc titles. With Suzuki he won two successive 500 cc World Championships (1976, 1977). In 1982 he was seriously injured in a practice race at Silverstone and surgeons rebuilt his legs using metal plates held together by 27 screws. He later retired to Australia (1987), where he became a popular TV commentator for motorsports, and was inducted into the Motorcycle Hall of Fame in 2001.

sheep A grazing mammal of family Bovidae; may be classified as an antelope; eight species in genus *Ovis* (seven wild species and the domestic sheep, *Ovis aries*); male with large spiralling horns; female with small horns (females of some domestic breeds and the European mouflon are hornless); wild sheep have a coarse outer coat and a fleecy underlayer which grows only in winter; domesticated breeds have only the underlayer, which is thick and grows continuously (presumably as a result of selective breeding); mouflon domesticated 10 000–11 000 years ago in Middle East; male called a *ram* or *tup*, female a *ewe*, young a *lamb*.

sheepdog Any working dog used to guard sheep from wild animals or to assist in herding; also any dog belonging to a breed formerly used for this purpose.

sheep–goat effect In parapsychology, an experimental effect in which those who accept the possibility of paranormal effects ('sheep') tend to produce better results under laboratory test conditions than those who do not ('goats').

sheep ked A small, wingless fly that is an external parasite on sheep; feeds by sucking blood; a pest of economic importance that causes staining of the wool. (Order: Diptera. Family: Hippoboscidae.)

sheet lightning *lightning*

Sheffield 53°23N 1°30W, urban area pop (2001e) 513 200. City in South Yorkshire, N England, UK; on the R Don; separated from Manchester to the W by the High Peak of Derbyshire; developed as a cutlery-manufacturing town in the early 18th-c and as a steel town in the 19th-c; city status in 1893; major rebuilding after World War 2 bombing; university (1905); Sheffield Hallam University (1992, formerly Sheffield Polytechnic); railway; steels, engineering, tool-making, cutlery, silverware, glass, optical instruments; cathedral (12th-c); Mappin Art Gallery; Crucible Theatre; Abbeydale industrial hamlet; Cutlers' Hall (1832); football league teams, Sheffield United (Blades), Sheffield Wednesday (Owls).

Sheffield plate An imitation silver plate made from copper sheet rolled between sheets of silver, discovered c.1742 by a Sheffield cutler, Thomas Boulsover (1706–88). This technique was exploited commercially by Matthew Boulton in Birmingham.

Sheffield Shield A silver trophy purchased from a donation of £150 by Lord Sheffield to promote Australian cricket. It has been the object of annual cricket competitions between the colonies (to 1900) and the states (after 1900) since 1892–3.

Shekinah [shekiyna] (Heb 'dwelling', 'residence') God's special 'presence' with his people, Israel; in rabbinic works, his immanence, often associated with particular locations where he consecrated a place or object, as with the burning bush at Sinai or the Tabernacle in the wilderness. The motifs of light and glory are frequently linked with it. Some later Jewish philosophers considered it a created entity or intermediary figure distinct from God.

Shelburne, William Petty Fitzmaurice, 2nd Earl of (1737–1805) British statesman and prime minister (1782–3), born in Dublin, Ireland. He studied at Oxford, entered parliament, succeeded to his earldom in 1761, and became President of the Board of Trade (1763) and secretary of state (1766). Made premier on the death of Rockingham, he resigned when outvoted by the coalition between Fox and North. In 1784 he was made Marquess of Lansdowne.

sheldgoose A South American goose of the genus *Chloephaga* (5 species); eats grass (4 species) or seaweed (the **kelp goose**, *Chloephaga hybrida*); nests on ground. (Subfamily: Anatinae. Tribe: Tadornini.)

sheldrake *shelduck*

shelduck A goose-like duck, native to the Old World (except the far N); eats grass, water weeds, and invertebrates; nests in burrows or holes; also known as a **sheldrake**. (Genus: *Tadorna*, 7 species. Subfamily: Anatinae. Tribe: Tadornini).

shelf *continental margin*

shell The mineralized outer covering of a variety of invertebrate animals, such as molluscs and brachiopods; usually containing a large amount of calcium. The calcareous shell of a bird's egg is a secondary egg membrane secreted by the genital duct of the mother bird.

shellac A resin generally obtained from a secretion from the insect *Tachardia lacca*. Solutions of shellac are used as varnishes and French polish.

Shelley, Mary (Wollstonecraft), *née* **Godwin** (1797–1851) Writer, born in London, UK, the daughter of William Godwin and Mary Wollstonecraft. She eloped with Percy Bysshe Shelley in 1814, and married him two years later. She wrote several novels, notably *Frankenstein, or the Modern Prometheus* (1818), *Valperga* (1923), *The Last Man* (1926), and the autobiographical *Lodore* (1835), as well as travel books, and journals, and edited Shelley's poems and other works (1823) after his death.

Shelley, Percy Bysshe [bish] (1792–1822) Poet and political thinker, born at Field Place, near Horsham, West Sussex, S England, UK. He studied at Oxford, but was expelled for his pamphlet, *The Necessity of Atheism* (1811). He eloped to Scotland with Harriet Westbrook, married her and settled in Keswick, where he was influenced by William Godwin, and wrote his revolutionary poem *Queen Mab* (1813). He formed a liaison with Godwin's daughter, Mary, with whom he eloped (1814), and whom he married in 1816 after learning that Harriet had committed suicide. From 1818 he lived in Italy, touring with his family and friends. There he met Byron, and wrote the bulk of his poetry, including odes, lyrics, and the verse drama *Prometheus Unbound* (1818–19). During this tour, he was drowned in the Bay of Spezia near Livorno.

shellfish An informal name for edible molluscs and crustaceans collectively; includes groups such as shrimps, crabs, lobsters, clams, bivalves, whelks, and mussels.

Shelter (National Campaign for the Homeless) In the UK, a charity founded in 1966 to provide help for the homeless and to campaign on their behalf. Its income comes principally from donations.

Sheltie *Shetland pony; Shetland sheepdog*

Shem Biblical character, the eldest son of Noah, the brother of Ham and Japeth. He is said to have escaped the flood with his father and brothers, and to have lived 600 years. His descendants are listed (in *Gen* 10), and he is depicted as the legendary father of 'Semitic' peoples, meant to include the Hebrews.

Shema [shemah] (Heb 'hear') A well-known ancient Jewish prayer, traced at least to the 2nd-c AD, incorporating the words of *Deut* 6.4–9, 11.13–21 and *Num* 15.37–41, and beginning 'Hear, O Israel: the Lord our God, the Lord is one'. It introduces the Jewish morning and evening prayers, preceding the Amidah and itself preceded by two benedictions. It may be recited in any language and affirms belief in the oneness of God.

Shenandoah River [shenuhndohuh] River in West Virginia and Virginia, USA; formed at the junction of the North Fork and South Fork Rivers; flows 88 km/55 mi NE to meet the Potomac R near Harper's Ferry; Shenandoah National Park (775 sq km/300 sq mi).

Shenyang [shuhnyahng], formerly **Mukden** 41°50N 123°26E, pop (2000e) 5 206 000, administrative region 6 060 000. Capital of Liaoning province, NE China; largest industrial city in NE China; trading centre for nomads, 11th-c; capital of Manchu, later Qing dynasty, 1625–44; invasion by Japanese (1931), leading to the establishment of Manchukuo, occupied by Nationalists, 1945; taken by Communists, 1948; renamed, 1949; railway; airfield; university; electrical equipment, engineering, chemicals, textiles, food processing; Imperial Palace (1625–36), Dongling (tomb of Nurhachi, founder of Manchu state), Beiling (tomb of Nurhachi's son and heir, Abukai).

she-oak An evergreen, somewhat weeping tree (*Casuarina stricta*), growing to 18 m/60 ft, native to SE Australia and Tasmania; slender, cylindrical, grooved and jointed stems and branches; leaves reduced to whorls of scales sheathing each joint; flowers also very reduced, males in spikes, females in clusters which resemble cones in fruit. The curious structure and reduction of the various organs are adaptations to the very dry conditions in which the tree grows. (Family: Casuarinaceae.)

Shepard, Alan (Bartlett), Jr (1923–98) Astronaut, the first American in space, born in East Derry, New Hampshire, USA. He trained at the US Naval Academy (1945), and from 1947 flew jet aircraft on test and training missions. One of the original seven NASA astronauts, on 5 May 1961, 23 days after Yuri Gagarin's historic orbit of the Earth, he was launched in Freedom 7 by a Redstone rocket vehicle, on a ballistic sub-orbital trajectory to a height of 116 mi, landing 302 mi downrange after a 15-min flight. He was director of astronaut training at NASA (1965–74), and commanded the Apollo 14 lunar mission in 1971.

Shepard, Sam, popular name of **Samuel Shepard Rogers** (1943–) Playwright and actor, born in Fort Sheridan, Illinois, USA. He studied agriculture, but joined a touring group and moved to New York City (1963), where his first plays were produced by Theater Genesis. He was resident playwright at the Magic Theater, San Francisco, from 1974. His works include *The Tooth of Crime* (1972), *Killer's Head* (1975), *Curse of the Starving Class* (1976), and *Buried Child* (1980, Pulitzer). He returned to acting later in the 1970s. Other works include the plays *A Lie of the Mind* (1985), which was very successful in the USA, *States of Shock* (1988), and *Simpatico* (1994), and the screenplay *Paris, Texas* (1984). His film appearances include *The Pelican Brief* (1993). His book of short stories, *Cruising Paradise*, appeared in 1996.

Shepherd, Cybill (1950–) Film actress, born in Memphis, Tennessee, USA. She was a successful model before her critically acclaimed film debut in *The Last Picture Show* (1971), following this with *The Heartbreak Kid* (1973) and *Taxi Driver* (1976). She also starred with Bruce Willis in the long-running television series *Moonlighting* (1985–9). Later films include *Once Upon a Crime* (1992) and *Married To It* (1993), and the television sitcom *Cybill* (1995–98).

shepherd moons Small natural moons whose gravitational fields serve to confine narrow rings around some of the outer planets. For example, the 'F' Ring of Saturn discovered by Pioneer 11 is a ribbon c.100 km/60 mi wide; its 'braided' structure was observed by Voyager spacecraft, which also discovered moons Pandora and Prometheus near the ring edges. Uranus's Epsilon Ring is similarly bounded by Ophelia and Cordelia. Shepherd moons are believed to control other narrow rings around these planets, but they have not yet been discovered; analogously, small moons within the rings are believed responsible for gaps observed in the rings.

Shepherd of Hermas, The A popular 2nd-c Christian work purportedly from Hermas, a Roman slave who was freed and became a merchant. The work is divided into visions, mandates, and similitudes (or parables), and is called 'The Shepherd' after the angel of repentance who appears in one of the visions. Its strong moral earnestness and stress on the need for penitence after baptism appealed to parts of the early Church, which for a time considered it 'inspired', but ultimately distinguished it from the New Testament canon.

shepherd's purse A small annual weed (*Capsella bursa-pastoris*) 3–40 cm/1¼–15 in, found almost everywhere; a rosette of oblong, lobed, or entire leaves and white, cross-shaped flowers; capsules heart-shaped, reminiscent of an old-style peasant's purse. (Family: Cruciferae.)

Shepparton 36°25S 145°26E, pop (2000e) 27 900. City in N Victoria, Australia, in the fertile Goulburn Valley; railway; grain, fruit, wool, wine, food processing; Arts Centre; International Village, featuring worldwide tourist information.

Sher, Sir Antony [shair] (1949–) Actor, writer, and painter, born in Cape Town, SW South Africa. He moved to England in 1968 and studied at the Webber-Douglas Academy of Dramatic Art. He appeared in plays at the Royal Court Theatre, including David Hare's *Teeth 'n' Smiles* in 1975, and joined the Royal Shakespeare Company in 1982. His Fool in *King Lear* was the first of his innovative creations of Shakespearian characters. An exciting actor to watch, in his role as *Richard III* (1984) he used crutches, and as Shylock in *The Merchant of Venice* (1987) and as Macbeth (1999) he was a powerful stage presence. He has appeared occasionally in television drama, notably in *The History Man* (1981), and his films include *Mrs Brown* (1997) and *Shakespeare in Love* (1998). His books include *The Year of the King* (1985), an account of his work on *Richard III*, *Woza Shakespeare!* (1996, with Gregory Doran), and the novels *The Indoor Boy* (1991) and *Cheap Lives* (1995). He was knighted in 2000. An autobiography, *Beside Myself*, appeared in 2001.

sherardizing [sherah(r)diyzing] A steel protection process named after English inventor Sherard Osborn Cowper-Coles (1866–1935). A steel object is heated in finely divided zinc dust to just below the melting point of the zinc. An amalgam forms, so that the outermost layer of the finished product is pure zinc, which grades into an adherent iron/zinc alloy. It is very corrosion resistant, and good for surface painting.

Sheraton, Thomas (1751–1806) Cabinet-maker, born in Stockton-on-Tees, Durham, NE England, UK. He settled in London c.1790, wrote a *Cabinetmaker and Upholsterer's Drawing Book* (1794), and produced a range of Neoclassical designs which had a wide influence on contemporary taste in furniture.

Sheridan, Philip H(enry) (1831–88) US general, born in Albany, New York, USA. He trained at West Point, and commanded a Union division at the beginning of the Civil War, taking part in many campaigns. In 1864 he was given command of the Army of the Shenandoah, turning the valley into a barren waste and defeating General Lee. He had a further victory at Five Forks in 1865, and was active in the final battle which led to Lee's surrender.

Sheridan, Richard Brinsley (Butler) (1751–1816) Playwright, born in Dublin, Ireland. He studied at Harrow, turned immediately to writing, and settled in London. In 1775 appeared the highly successful comedy of manners, *The Rivals*, and this was followed by several other comedies and farces, notably *The School for Scandal* (1777). He became manager of Drury Lane Theatre in 1778, and a Whig MP (1780–1812). He proved to be a great parliamentary orator, and held various junior offices. The extravagances of his second wife, and the burning down of his theatre in 1809, caused him grave financial hardship, and he died in poverty.

sheriff Originally, the monarch's representative in the English shires responsible for legal, administrative, and military matters. Since the Middle Ages the office has largely declined in importance in England and Wales, and the sheriff's duties are now largely ceremonial and administrative. The sheriff (commonly known as **High Sheriff**) acts as the returning officer during parliamentary elections in county constituencies. In Scotland, however, since 1825, sheriffs have been legally qualified judges with a wide civil and criminal jurisdiction. They are appointed from solicitors and advocates of at least 10 years' standing, and sit in the **Sheriff Court**. In criminal matters they can sit with a jury or alone, if the offence is a summary one, and in civil cases they sit singly. Appeal from the decision of a sheriff goes to the High Court of Justiciary in criminal cases and to the sheriff-principal and thence to the Court of Session in civil matters. In the USA, sheriffs are generally elected in each of the 3000 or more counties. They are responsible for law enforcement principally in rural areas, though many of their duties have been transferred to local or state police. In addition to their law enforcement duties, they serve the function of a court officer executing court orders and holding prisoners.

Sheringham, Teddy (1966–) Footballer, born in Highams Park, NC Greater London, UK. A forward, he played for Millwall, Aldershot, Nottingham Forest, and Tottenham Hotspur, signing for Manchester United in 1997, and returning to Tottenham in 2001. He won two Player of the Year awards during the 2000–1 season, and was an England team member in the 2002 World Cup campaign, winning 51 caps by the end of the

2003 season. He joined Portsmouth FC for the start of the 2003–4 season.

Sherman, William Tecumseh (1820–91) US general, born in Lancaster, Ohio, USA. Trained at West Point, he became a general in the Union army during the Civil War. His most famous campaign was in 1864, when he captured Atlanta, and commenced his famous 'March to the Sea', with 65 000 men, which divided the Confederate forces. After capturing Savannah, he moved N through the Carolinas, gaining further victories which helped to bring forward the Confederate surrender.

Sherpa A mountain people of Sikkim State and Nepal, India. Related to Tibetans, they share their culture and language. They are famous as mountain traders and porters in the Himalayas.

Sherrington, Sir Charles Scott (1857–1952) Physiologist, born in London, UK. He studied at Cambridge and Berlin, taught at London University, where he became professor of pathology (1891–5), and was then professor of physiology at Liverpool (1895–1913) and Oxford (1913–35). His research on the nervous system constituted a landmark in modern physiology. His 1904 publication *The Integrative Action of the Nervous System* was the first to recognize the role of the nervous system in coordinating the activities of all the cells of the body. He also conducted research into infectious diseases including cholera, malaria, and sleeping sickness, and served on government committees investigating the lighting of factories, the effects of alcohol, and foot-and-mouth disease. Knighted in 1922, he shared the Nobel Prize for Physiology or Medicine in 1932.

sherry A white wine (usually a blend of younger and older wines), fortified with brandy; named after Jerez de la Frontera in the Andalusian region of Spain, the centre of excellence for sherry. There are several types: *fino* is dry, light-coloured, of a high quality, and usually drunk young; *amontillado* is darker and moderately dry; *oloroso* is fuller and dark, the sweetest available.

Sherwood Forest An area of heath and woodland, mainly in Nottinghamshire, C England, UK, where mediaeval kings hunted deer. It is famed for being the home of Robin Hood. In 2002 it was designated a national nature reserve.

Shetland, also called **The Shetlands**, formerly **Zetland** pop (2000e) 23 100; area 1433 sq km/553 sq mi. Group of c.100 islands off coast of NE Scotland, UK; 80 km/50 mi NE of Orkney Is; c.20 inhabited; chief islands, Mainland, Unst, Yell, Fetlar, Whalsay; low-lying, highest point Ronas Hill in N Mainland (450 m/1476 ft); capital, Lerwick, on Mainland; annexed by Norway in 9th-c; annexed by Scotland, 1472; target of first German air-raid on Britain in World War 2 (Nov 1939); cattle and sheep raising, knitwear, fishing, oil services at Lerwick and Sandwick, oil terminal at Sullom Voe; small Shetland ponies, well-known for their strength and hardiness; several prehistoric remains, especially Staneydale Temple (W Mainland), Neolithic or early Bronze Age hall; Jarlshof (S Mainland), remains of three villages occupied from Bronze Age to Vikings; Mousa Broch (Iron Age, on Mousa).

Shetland pony The strongest of all breeds of horse (can pull twice its own weight), developed on the Scottish Shetland and Orkney Is; height, 9 hands/0·9 m/3 ft; stocky, with short legs; long mane and tail; also known as **Sheltie** or **Shelty**. The taller and more slender **American Shetland pony** was developed in the USA from Shetland stock.

Shetland sheepdog A type of sheepdog developed in the Shetland Is, Scotland; resembles a small collie with a thick coat; also known as a **Sheltie**, or **Shelty**.

Shevardnadze, Eduard Amvrosiyevich [shevernadze] (1928–) Georgian head of state (1992–2003) and former Soviet statesman, born in Mamati, W Georgia. He studied at the Kutaisi Pedagogical Institute, joined the Communist Party of the Soviet Union in 1948, and worked in the Komsomol Youth League during the 1950s and the Georgian interior ministry during the 1960s, where he gained a reputation as an opponent of corruption. He became Party chief in 1972, and introduced agricultural experiments. In 1978 he was inducted into the Politburo as a candidate member, and in 1985 was promoted by the new Soviet leader, Mikhail Gorbachev, to full Politburo status and appointed foreign minister. He resigned in 1990, expressing concern over some of Gorbachev's decisions and warning of dictatorship. He helped defeat the attempted coup in August 1991, and was briefly foreign minister again at the end of that year. He then returned to Georgia, which had become an independent republic following the break-up of the Soviet Union (1991), and was elected Chairman of the State Council in December 1992, but was unable to prevent the country's slide into civil war. Stability was eventually restored, and he was elected president in 1995 and 2000. But growing public discontent mounted after allegations of irregularities in the parliamentary elections of November 2003 and forced his resignation later that month.

shiatsu [sheeatsoo] (Jap 'finger pressure') A form of massage in which pressure is applied to acupuncture points and meridians using the fingers, thumbs, and sometimes elbows, knees, hands, and feet. The diagnosis of energy imbalance or blockage is made according to the principles of traditional Chinese medicine, but with an emphasis on abdominal diagnosis to select the points and meridians for treatment. The massage is designed to release blockages and balance the flow of energy, and healing energy may also be transmitted from the practitioner to the patient during a shiatsu treatment.

shield A geological term for a large region of stable continental crust, usually Precambrian in age and forming the core of a continental land mass. It is predominantly composed of metamorphic and igneous rocks.

shield bug A typically shield-shaped true bug; adults mostly feed on plants, sometimes as predators; c.5000 species, including some pests of economically important crops. (Order: Heteroptera. Family; Pentatomidae.)

shielding *screening*

shifting cultivation A system of agriculture found in areas of tropical rainforest; also known as **swidden cultivation**. It is a response to loss of soil fertility and vegetation regeneration which occurs after a few years' cultivation, forcing farmers to move to new areas. *Slash and burn* describes the method of vegetation clearance. In some regions people move on to completely new areas. Elsewhere they live in a permanent settlement and practise a form of land rotation known as *bush and fallow*, in which vegetation is allowed to regenerate in areas where soil fertility is exhausted. It is then recultivated.

Shih-chia-chuang *Shijiazhuang*

Shih Tzu [shee tsoo] A toy breed of dog of Tibetan or Chinese origin; similar to the Pekinese in shape; muzzle short but not flat; thick straight coat, especially on head, where hair cascades from top to cover eyes and ears.

Shiites [sheeiyts] A minority division, representing c.10% of Islam, which holds that legitimacy derives from the descendants of the Prophet Mohammed. Shiites believe that Mohammed's rightful successor was the fourth caliph Ali ibn Abi Taleb who, as cousin and son-in-law, was the Prophet's closest male relation. As the *shia* or party of Ali, the Shiites venerate his lineal descendants as infallible *imams*. Shiism has a distinct school of Islamic law. Three main groups are distinguished: the Zaydis of Yemen; the Ismailis of India and East Africa; and the Imamis, or 'twelvers', who recognize twelve *imams*, the last of which disappeared in the 9th-c and whose return as the *mahdi* is expected to usher in an age of justice. The Imamis are the largest group, and are found in Iran, where Shiism is the state religion of the Islamic Republic. Large communities are also to be found in Iraq and Lebanon.

Shijiazhuang or **Shih-chia-chuang** [shoejiahjwahng] 38°04N 114°28E, pop (2000e) 1 550 000, administrative region 3 038 000. Capital of Hebei province, N China; a major railway junction; mining (coal, iron ore, limestone, marble), cotton-growing, textiles, dyeing, printing; China's largest pharmaceutical plant; Longcang Temple stela (Sui dynasty, 590–618), Zhuanlunzang pavilion (10th-c); to the N, 6th-c Buddhist monastery of Longxing Si, containing 10th-c bronze statue of Guanyin, Goddess of Mercy (22 m/72 ft high, with 42 arms).

shikki [shikee] Japanese lacquerware, also known as *nurimono*. Lac, a natural varnish from lacquer trees, is applied to wooden cups, trays, tables, and many other items. Hardwearing, a good insulator and shiny, it is well suited to traditional art and craft objects, though often expensive. It is still widely used in homes and restaurants for traditional food boxes, soup bowls, chopsticks, etc.

Shikoku [shikohkoo] pop (2000e) 4 330 000; area 18 795 sq km/ 7255 sq mi. Smallest of the four main islands of Japan; S of Honshu and E of Kyushu; bounded N by the Seto Naikai Sea, S by the Pacific Ocean; subtropical climate; mountainous and wooded interior; chief towns, Matsuyama, Takamatsu; rice, wheat, tobacco, soya beans, orchards, copper, camphor.

Shilluk An E Sudanic-speaking people living along the Nile S of Khartoum in the Sudan Republic. They are farmers, with many cattle, and organized into a kingdom under the *reth* or king, the prototype of the 'divine kingship' in ethnographic studies.

Shiloh [shiyloh] The site of an ancient city in C Palestine about 14 km/9 mi N of Bethel; noted as the central sanctuary of the tribes of Israel during the conquest and settlement of Palestine under the tribal judges. It also sheltered the Ark of the Covenant, and was thus a strong unifying force amongst the tribes. It was destroyed c.1050 BC, when the Ark was captured by the Philistines, and the priesthood then moved to Nob.

Shiloh, Battle of [shiyloh] (1862) An engagement in the American Civil War in SW Tennessee between Union forces under General Grant and Confederate forces under Albert Sidney Johnston (1803–62); also called the **Battle of Pittsburg Landing**. Losses were heavy on both sides, with 13 000 Union and 11 000 Confederate casualties.

Shilton, Peter (1949–) Footballer, born in Leicester, Leicestershire, C England, UK. Starting his career with Leicester City at the age of 16, he also played for Stoke City, Nottingham Forest, Southampton, and Derby County. He made his international debut for England in 1970, and became the first England goalkeeper to gain 100 caps. He has won all the major honours in the game, including League championship and European Cup medals. On his retirement he had gained a record 125 caps.

shingles A condition arising from the re-activation of the chickenpox virus which lies latent in the ganglia of sensory somatic nerves; also known as **herpes zoster**. It causes pain and a blister-like (vesicular) rash over the segmental distribution of the affected nerve. Common sites are the trunk, the cornea of the eye, and the adjacent skin above the eye.

Shinkansen [shingkansen] The Japanese New Tokaido Line, a standard gauge line from Tokyo to Osaka for high speed trains (commonly known as **bullet trains**). Completed in 1964, the network has been extended from Aomori in the North to Hakasa in the South. It uses a fully computerized seat reservation system, like airlines. It provides an excellent service, and has been commercially successful, unlike many of the old lines.

Shinto [shintoh] The indigenous religion of Japan, 'the way of the spirits', so named in the 8th-c to distinguish it from Buddhism, from which it subsequently incorporated many features. It emerged from the nature-worship of Japanese folk religions, and this is reflected in ceremonies appealing to the mysterious powers of nature (*kami*) for benevolent treatment and protection. By the 8th-c, divine origins were ascribed to the imperial family and the Japanese islands, and in time these became the basis for State Shintoism and its loyalty and obedience to the Emperor. Shinto influenced the development of bushido under the Tokugawa shogunate. In the 19th-c it was divided into Shrine (*jinga*) Shinto and Sectarian (*kyoho*) Shinto, with the former regarded as a 'state cult' and the latter officially recognized as a religion but ineligible for state support. In 1945, State Shinto lost its official status. There were over 2·7 million Shintoists in 2004.

shinty A twelve-a-side stick-and-ball game originating in Ireland more than 1500 years ago, taken to Scotland, and now popular in the Scottish Highlands. The playing field is up to 155 m/170 yd long and 73 m/80 yd wide with two goals, known as *hails*, at each end. The object is to score goals by using the *caman* (stick) to propel the ball.

Shinwell, Emmanuel Shinwell, Baron, popularly known as **Manny Shinwell** (1884–1986) British statesman, born in London, UK. A 'street-corner socialist' in Glasgow, he became a Labour MP in 1922, held junior office in the interwar Labour governments, and in the post-war Labour government was minister of fuel and power responsible for nationalizing the mines (1946), secretary of state for war (1947), and minister of defence (1950–1). Well known for his party political belligerence, in his later years he mellowed into a back-bench 'elder statesman'. He was awarded a life peerage in 1970. He wrote several autobiographical works, including *I've Lived Through It All* (1973).

ship A sea-going vessel of considerable size. The Egyptians built river boats around 3000 BC, but at the time of Queen Hatshepsut (c.1500 BC) an expedition to E Africa was mounted using vessels of about 20 m/60 ft in length. These are the first sea-going ships of which there are reliable pictorial records; they were steered by oars over the stern. Great strides were made in ship design by the Phoenicians, who traded throughout the Mediterranean, but they left no pictorial records. Chinese ships were making voyages of over a year by the 1st-c AD. The stern-mounted rudder was in use by AD 100 (Europe, 12th-c), and multiple-masted ships with water-tight bulkheads before 200 (Europe, 15th–18th-c). Greeks and Romans built galleys relying on oars for manoeuvrability and much of their propulsion, a square sail coming into use when the wind was favourable. Roman merchant vessels 28–56 m/90–180 ft long were propelled by a large square sail hung from a single mast, with a smaller sail mounted on a bowsprit to improve steering qualities; they were steered with two oars or sweeps mounted on the stern. Viking ships varied in length from 20 m/70 ft to 40 m/120 ft, were propelled by a large square-rigged sail and oars, and steered with a massive sweep hung over the starboard side well aft. By the 15th-c the Portuguese had developed the lateen-rigged caravel into a three- or four-masted ocean-going craft. Out of this grew the carrack, where lateen sails gradually gave way to square sails and the forecastle developed a pronounced overlap at the stem. The stern-mounted rudder appears to have come into general use at about this time. In China, during this period, ships of up to 1500 tons were in use, including ironclads armed with cannon (documented from 1371). In Europe, the square rig increased in complexity and refinement until the last decade of the 19th-c. US influence dates from 1845, with the clipper ship. Their ships were generally larger than the British, and very often faster. The ultimate refinement in sail came with the British-built tea clippers, such as the *Cutty Sark*. These ships were immediately made obsolescent by the opening of the Suez Canal (1869) because they could not navigate in this area of light and fickle winds.

In 1802 the first viable steamship, the *Charlotte Dundas*, was used as a tug on the Forth–Clyde canal. The first steamship to cross the Atlantic was the US-built *Savannah*, but she steamed for only 3½ days out of her 25-day passage, sailing for the rest of the time. The first continuous steam crossing of the Atlantic was achieved by the British-owned packet vessel, the 700-tonne *Sirius*, in 1838. Brunel's *Great Britain* (1844) was the first screw-propelled, double-bottomed, iron-hulled transatlantic passenger ship. High pressure steam in 1860 heralded the end of the sailing ship's supremacy. Steam turbines were demonstrated at the Spithead Review in 1897, and powered the *Mauretania* when she took the Blue Riband in 1907. The diesel engine, patented in 1892, won ocean-going acceptance in the 5000-gross-tonne *Selandia* in 1912; but these engines, though cheaper to run and occupying less space, could not provide the power nor the reliability needed for passenger vessels until the late 1970s. In 1968 the Queen Elizabeth 2 was built with steam turbines, but in 1987 she was re-engined using diesel-electric propulsion, gaining power and speed with lower fuel costs. (In 1991, only 2·8% of the world's ships were steam-powered, but this represented 16·8% of world tonnage.) Nuclear-fuelled vessels provide analternative means of generating the heat to provide steam to drive turbines. This method is used in government vessels such as ice-breakers, aircraft carriers, and missile-carrying submarines, but it has proved to be uneconomical for merchant vessels. In the 1970s very large tankers were built, powered by steam turbines. When fully laden they displace 600 000 tonnes, but steam at a relatively modest speed of 15 knots. Future developments will see no great overall increase in ship size, but there will be faster container ships and many large cruise ships, all diesel-engined.

Shipley, Jenny (1952–) New Zealand politician and prime minister (1997–9), born in Gore, New Zealand. She studied at Christchurch Teachers College, worked as a primary school teacher, then entered politics, becoming an MP for the (conservative) National Party in 1987. Her ministerial portfolios included social welfare (1990–3), health (1993–6), women's affairs (1990–6, 1997), and transport (1997). She became the country's first woman prime minister following the retirement of Jim Bolger, but lost office in the 1999 elections.

Shipman, Harold (Frederick) (1946–2004) Doctor and serial murderer, born in Nottingham, Nottinghamshire, England, UK. He studied at Leeds University (1965–70), worked at Pontefract General Infirmary, then became a GP in Todmorden. Fined for making out drug prescriptions to himself (to feed a pethadine addiction), he received treatment, and became a GP again in Hyde, Greater Manchester. After falling out with his partners, he set up his own practice. Arrested in 1998, he was sentenced to life imprisonment in January 2000 for the murder of 15 of his elderly patients by injecting them with diamorphine. A public inquiry reported in July 2002 that there had been 215 victims in all, dating from 1975, with another 45 likely, and a further 38 uncertain, making him Britain's worst ever serial killer. All the killings were carried out by injecting drugs, usually at a patient's home, but sometimes at his own surgery. No clear conclusion was reached about his motivation. He committed suicide in prison

ship money An English tax on maritime areas to support royal naval forces, abuse of which brought discredit to Charles I. The tax, dating from mediaeval times, had been collected without difficulty under James I. Charles I's extension of the tax to inland shires in 1635 caused opposition. The proposal to make it permanent in 1636 provoked refusals to pay by John Hampden and others; it was outlawed in 1641.

Ship of Cheops [keeops] An ancient Egyptian funeral ship found dismantled at Giza in 1954 in one of five boat pits (the last still unexcavated) around the Pyramid of Cheops (2551–2528 BC). Perfectly preserved by airless conditions, it comprised 1224 pieces of timber laid in 13 layers, together with ropes, baskets, and matting. Reconstructed, the ship measures 44 m/143 ft long with a beam of 6 m/19 ft. Carrying six pairs of oars 6·5–8·5 m/21–28 ft long, and a cabin amidships, it displaces 45 tonnes.

Shipton, Eric (Earle) (1907–77) British mountaineer. He spent many years climbing in E and C Africa, and obtained much of his knowledge of the East during his terms as consul-general in Kashgar (1940–2, 1946–8) and Kunming (1949–51). Between 1933 and 1951 he either led or was a member of five expeditions to Mt Everest, and helped pave the way for the successful Hunt–Hillary expedition of 1953.

shipworm A typically marine bivalve mollusc; body elongate, with reduced shell plates used to burrow into submerged wood such as ship hulls. (Class: Pelecypoda. Family: Teredinidae.)

Shirakawa, Hideki (1936–) Chemist, born in Tokyo, Japan. He studied at the Tokyo Institute of Technology (1966), and became professor of chemistry at the University of Tsukuba (1979). He shared the 2000 Nobel Prize for Chemistry with Alan J Heeger and Alan G MacDiarmid for their discovery and development of conductive polymers.

Shiraz [sheeraz] 29°38N 52°34E, pop (2000e) 1 171 000. Capital city of Shiraz district, Fars, SW Iran; 184 km/114 mi NE of Bushehr, its port on the Persian Gulf; capital of Persia, 1750–79; fifth largest city in Iran; airfield; university (1945); noted for its wines, rugs, hand-woven textiles, silverwork, mosaics.

shire The largest breed of horse, developed in England from war-horses used to carry knights in armour; used for farm work; height, 17–18 hands/1·7–1·8 m/5 ft 8 in–6 ft; black or brown and white; convex face; long legs with hair covering hooves.

Shiva [sheeva] One of the three principal deities of the Hindu triad (*Trimurti*) – a god of contrasting features: creation and destruction, good and evil, fertility and asceticism. He is the original Lord of the Dance (*Nataraja*) and his principal symbolic representation is a phallic emblem denoting procreation.

Shivaji [shivahjee] (c.1627–80) Founder of the Maratha Empire in W India, born at Shivner, Poona. He campaigned against the Mughals, and was enthroned as an independent ruler in 1674. Renowned as a military leader, social reformer, and advocate of religious tolerance, his last years were made difficult by internal problems and pressure from outside enemies.

Shkodër [shkohder], Ital **Scutari**, ancient **Scodra** 42°05N 19°30E, pop (2000e) 93 500. Market town and capital of Shkodër district, NW Albania, between the R Drin and L Scutari; former capital of Albania; railway; ferrous metallurgy, foodstuffs, tobacco, cement, leather, wood products; citadel (14th-c), cathedral.

shochu [shohchoo] Japanese alcoholic spirits, distilled from potatoes, colourless, but with a certain odour. It is cheaper than saké, and traditionally a rough drink for labourers and poor people. It was popularized in the 1980s.

shock A term used by the lay public to denote the psychological state of fear or grief that follows a sudden accident, calamity, or bereavement. Its medical use refers to a clinical state in which the blood pressure and circulation is insufficient to maintain the functioning of the brain or other organs. This may arise because of loss of blood, because of inadequate pumping of blood by the heart, or because the capacity of the blood vessels to hold a normal amount of blood is suddenly increased. Serious bleeding following trauma leads to shock because the normal response of blood vessels to contract after blood loss is unable to compensate for the loss of blood volume. Acute heart failure arising from a myocardial infarct may result in failure to maintain the necessary blood pressure. Septicaemia sometimes causes the abnormal dilation of blood vessels, and so lowers the blood pressure.

Shockley, William B(radford) (1910–89) Physicist, born in London, UK. He studied at the California Institute of Technology and Harvard, began work with Bell Telephone Laboratories in 1936, and became professor of engineering at Stanford in 1963. During World War 2 he directed US research on antisubmarine warfare. In 1947 he helped devise the point-contact transistor. He then devised the junction transistor, which heralded a revolution in radio, TV, and computer circuitry. He shared the Nobel Prize for Physics in 1956 with John Bardeen and Walter Brattain. In his later years Shockley provoked outrage with his racist comments and sterilization schemes for people of low IQ.

shock therapy A term sometimes used as a synonym for *electroconvulsive therapy*, but also for *electrosleep*, in which a weak rhythmically-repeated pulse of unidirectional electric current is applied to the brain for the treatment of anxiety, insomnia, and a variety of other medical conditions with a psychological component (eg bronchial asthma and duodenal ulceration). Because the term is ambiguous, psychiatrists often recommend its avoidance.

shock wave A moving, large-amplitude compression wave across which density, temperature, and pressure change abruptly. It is caused by a violent disturbance or supersonic motion. An explosion will produce a pressure shock wave in the surrounding air. A thunderclap is a shock wave caused by the rapid heating of air by lightning. A heavy impact on a solid will cause a stress shock wave. Shock waves cause a non-linear response in the medium.

shoddy Products made from reprocessed old wool. Strictly the term applies only to the loose fibre, but it is commonly used to describe the products made from shoddy. In popular use, the word has acquired a pejorative sense.

shoebill A large, grey, stork-like bird with a large head (*Balaeniceps rex*); bill extremely wide and deep, shaped like a broad shoe; inhabits marshes in C Africa; nocturnal; eats small vertebrates, molluscs, and carrion; also known as the **shoe-billed stork** or **whale-headed stork**. (Family: Balaenicipidae.)

Shoemaker, Willie, popular name of **William Lee Shoemaker**, nickname **the Shoe** (1931–2003) Racing jockey and trainer, born in Fabens, Texas, USA. Only 149·8 cm/4 ft 11 in tall, and weighing 43 kg/95 lb, he won more races than any other jockey – 8833 winners between 1949 and his retirement in 1989. In 1953 he rode a world record 485 winners in one season. He was severely injured in a car accident in 1991, but survived to become a trainer.

Shoemaker–Levy 9 [shoomaker-leevee] The name given to a comet (estimated to have been c.2 km/1·2 mi in diameter) which crashed into the planet Jupiter in 1994; jointly discovered by US astronomer Carolyn (Spellman) Shoemaker (1929–), her husband, astrogeologist Eugene (Merle) Shoemaker (1928–97), and amateur astronomer David Levy (1948–) at Palomar Observatory, CA. Over 20 fragments made spectacular impacts into the planet during the period 16–22 July, leaving dark markings observable by telescopes on Earth.

shofar or **shophar** [shohfah(r)] A Hebrew term for a ram's horn, blown as a musical instrument; mentioned in the Bible as to be sounded particularly at the Jewish New Year (Rosh Hashanah) and at the close of the Day of Atonement (Yom Kippur), but also used at war or for announcing important events. In modern times in Israel it has also been blown on Friday afternoons to announce the Sabbath.

shogi [shohgee] A Japanese form of chess, believed to have originated in India. Played on a squared board, the pieces have different powers; the object is to checkmate the king. Each player has 20 pieces.

shogun [shohgn] A Japanese general, the head of a system of government which dates from 1192, when a military leader received the title *seii-tai-shogun* ('Barbarian Quelling Generalissimo') from the Emperor. Most important were the Kamakura shogunate (1192–1333) and the Tokugawa shogunate (1603–1868), who ruled as military dictators, the emperor remaining a figurehead, without power. In principle, the shoguns' rule strictly regulated and controlled life down to the smallest detail. The system ended in 1868.

Sholem Aleichem [alaykhem], also spelled **Sholom** or **Shalom** (Hebrew, 'peace unto you'), pseudonym of **Solomon J Rabinowitz** (1859–1916) Writer, born in Pereyaslev, C Ukraine. After working as a rabbi, he devoted himself to writing and Yiddish culture. The pogroms of 1905 drove him to the USA, where he attempted to establish himself as a playwright for the Yiddish theatre in New York City. His short stories and plays portray Jewish life in Russia in the late 19th-c with vividness, humour, and sympathy, and were first widely introduced to a non-Jewish public in 1943 in Maurice Samuel's *The World of Sholom Aleichem*. The popular musical *Fiddler on the Roof* is based on the stories of Aleichem.

Sholes, Christopher Latham [shohlz] (1819–90) Inventor, born near Mooresburg, Pennsylvania, USA. An apprentice printer at first, he later worked as a newspaper editor and government official. His best-known invention is the typewriter, which he developed with fellow inventors Carlos Glidden and Samuel Soulé in 1867. A patent was granted in 1868, which Sholes sold to the Remington Arms Company, who then marketed the first Remington Typewriter in 1874.

Sholokhov, Mikhail Alexandrovich [sholokhof] (1905–84) Novelist, born near Veshenskaya, SW Russia. After serving in the Red Army (1920), he became a writer, best known for his novel tetralogy *Tikhy Don* (1928–40, And Quiet Flows the Don, trans 1960), and other novels of Cossack life. He received the Nobel Prize for Literature in 1965.

Shona [shona] A cluster of Bantu-speaking agricultural peoples of E Zimbabwe, who include the Manyika, Kalanga, and Haranga. A powerful state during the 13th–15th-c, with their capital at Great Zimbabwe, they resisted encroachment of white pioneers in the 1890s, but were ruthlessly suppressed. Their members dominate ZANU, the ruling party of Zimbabwe.

shooting The use of firearms for pleasure, hunting, sport, or in battle. The first reference to the gun was in 1326, and it soon became the chief weapon of war. It developed as a sport in the 15th-c, the first shooting club being formed in Lucerne, Switzerland, in 1466. Competitive shooting takes many forms and uses different types of weapon. The most popular weapons are the standard pistol, small bore rifle, full bore rifle, air rifle, and air pistol. All events involve shooting at targets, either still or moving, as in clay-pigeon shooting. In the UK, hunting for game is very popular among the aristocracy, particularly grouse shooting, which has a specifically defined season (12 Aug to 10 Dec). Several tournaments are held, such as those organized by the National Rifle Association (founded, 1871) in the USA.

shooting star *meteor*

shop stewards Workers appointed by their fellows within a trade union to represent them on matters relevant to their pay and conditions. In some instances the post is a full-time job, but often in very small firms, very little time will be spent in these matters. It is estimated that there are over 200 000 union representatives in the UK.

Short, Clare (1946–) British stateswoman. She studied at Keele and Leeds universities, and after working as a civil servant and in local community organizations, became an MP in 1983. She was the opposition spokesperson on employment (1985–8), social security (1988–91), environmental protection (1992–3), and women (1993–5), then joined the shadow cabinet (1995), and was spokesperson on transport (1995–6) and overseas development (1996–7). She served as secretary of state for international development in Tony Blair's Labour government from 1997 until her resignation in 2003.

Short, Nigel (1965–) Chess player, born in Atherton, Lancashire, NW England, UK. He won the British Championship in 1977, became an international master in 1980, and in 1984 was the UK's youngest ever grandmaster. In 1993 he beat Jan Timmen to become the first UK grandmaster to qualify for a World Championship match, but was defeated by Gary Kasparov. He resigned from FIDE (the international chess organization) in 1993 and with Kasparov formed the Professional Chess Association.

shorthand A method of writing at speed to take verbatim records of speech, also known as **stenography**. Shorthand systems variously use symbols which are abbreviations of words (as in *speedwriting*), representations of speech sounds, or arbitrary symbols which the user has to memorize. It has been much used in commerce and industry, and in courts of law, for taking records of the proceedings of meetings, and for the dictation of correspondence. The use of shorthand was popular in Ancient Greece and Rome, came into fashion in England in the 16th-c, and was further popularized by the need for written commercial records with the advent of the Industrial Revolution. However, in recent years, its popularity has lessened with the advent of dictating machines permitting audio playback to the typist.

shorthorn A type of domestic cattle with short horns. In 18th-c England, Charles and Robert Colling improved the type, leading to such breeds as the **Durham** (the *shorthorn* of the American ranchers) and the **Teeswater**. In 19th-c England, Thomas Bates developed the **dairy shorthorn**. Other breeds are the **northern dairy shorthorn**, **whitebred shorthorn**, **beef shorthorn**, and the (often hornless) **Lincoln red**.

short-sightedness *eye*

short story A prose fiction of not more than some 10 000 words. Beyond this lie the similarly imprecise categories 'long short story', 'novella', and 'short novel'. There are many rudimentary forms of short story, including myths, fables, legends, and parables, and the mediaeval *fabliau* was a clear progenitor. Boccaccio and Chaucer were masters of the art, as were such Chinese writers as Tao Qian (4th–5th-c). But the modern short story began in the mid-19th-c with Edgar Allan Poe, and was confirmed as a major genre by Maupassant in France and Turgenev and Chekhov in Russia. Many important 20th-c writers (eg Kafka, who wrote nearly 80 short stories using a remarkable variety of length, style, theme, and technique) favoured the form on account of its concentration and atmospheric potential.

Short Take-Off and Landing *STOL*

Shoshoni [shohshohnee] North American Indians who once lived in California, Nevada, Utah, and Wyoming, speaking a Uto-Aztecan language. Shoshoni were semi-nomadic hunter-gatherers; Wind River and N Shoshoni acquired horses and hunted the buffalo, culturally resembling Plains Indians. The Comanche split from the Wind River group and became feared raiders in the SW. They now live mainly on reservations.

Shostakovich, Dmitri Dmitriyevich [shostakohvich] (1906–75) Composer, born in St Petersburg, NW Russia. He studied at the Conservatory there, and composed his first symphony in 1925. His music was at first highly successful, but his operas and ballets were later criticized by government and press for a failure to observe the principles of 'Soviet realism'. He was reinstated by his fifth symphony (1937), and subsequently composed prolifically in all forms. He wrote 15 symphonies, as well as violin, piano, and cello concertos, chamber music, and choral works.

shotgun A smooth-bore weapon firing cartridges filled with small lead or steel pellets (*shot*), which spread in flight to broaden their destructive effects; widely used by farmers and sportsmen. Single-barrelled, pump-action, multiple-round shotguns have a military application for close-in defence.

shot put An athletics field event in which the contestant throws a heavy metal ball for distance. The shot weighs 7·3 kg/16 lb for men and 3·6 kg/8 lb 13 oz for women. It is cupped with the hand and released, after the athlete has spun around the throwing circle, with the arm extended. The thrower must not leave the 2·1 m/7 ft diameter circle. In competition six throws are allowed. The current world record for men is 23·12 m/75 ft 10 in, achieved by Randy Barnes (1966–) of the USA in 1990 in Los Angeles, CA; for women it is 22·63 m/74 ft 3 in, achieved by Natalya Lisovskaya (1962–) of Russia in 1987 in Moscow.

shou *red deer*

shoulder Commonly used to refer to the rounded region at the top of the arm passing towards the neck and upper back; more specifically, in anatomy, the ball and socket joint between the humerus and the scapula. It is an extremely mobile joint, at the expense of some stability. When dislocation occurs, it tends to be a downward and forward movement of the humerus with respect to the scapula.

shove-halfpenny; shovelboard *shuffleboard*

shoveller / shoveler A dabbling duck, native to South America (1 species), S Africa (1 species), Australia and New Zealand (1 species), and the N hemisphere (1 species); nests in reed beds; also known as the **spoonbill**. (Genus: *Anas*, 4 species.)

Showa Tenno ('Emperor') **Hirohito** [shoha tenoh hirohheetoh] (1901–89) Emperor of Japan (1926–89), the 124th in direct lineage, born in Tokyo, Japan. His reign was marked by rapid militarization and aggressive wars against China (1931–2, 1937–45) and against the USA and Britain (1941–5), which ended with the two atomic bombs on Hiroshima and Nagasaki. Under US occupation, in 1946 Hirohito renounced his legendary divinity and most of his powers to become a democratic constitutional monarch.

showboat A paddle-wheel river steamer complete with theatre and its own repertory company. They were mainly used along the Mississippi in the 19th-c.

show jumping Horse jumping over a course containing a variety of strategically placed fences. Most competitions involve all competitors having one attempt at clearing the fences. Those who clear the fences and incur no penalty points are then involved in a 'jump-off' against the clock, where speed as well as accuracy is important. Points are incurred for knocking down a fence, or for refusing to jump a fence.

show trials Originally a series of trials held in Moscow in the late 1930s under Stalin. It refers to any political trial where the accused make a public confession of their 'crimes', although their guilt is often open to doubt. The process tries to justify political repression by allowing the state to point to the use of 'fair' procedures in dealing with opponents of the regime.

shoyu [shohyoo] Japanese soy sauce, made from soya beans, wheat, salt, and water. It is dark brown in colour, with a different taste from Chinese soy sauce, added to many dishes as flavouring. Soya bean paste (*miso*) is used in many foods, such as *miso-shiru* (bean paste soup).

Shrapnel, Henry (1761–1842) British artillery officer, who retired from active service as a lieutenant-general in 1825. In c.1793 he invented the *shrapnel shell*, an anti-personnel device which exploded while in flight, scattering lethal lead shot and other material.

shrew A widespread mammal of family Soricidae (246 species); an insectivore; mouse-like with a longer pointed snout and small eyes; ears often hidden in fur; often lives near water; some have a venomous bite. The name is also used for several other small mammals, and for the 15 species of African **elephant shrews** (Order: Macroscelidea).

Shrewsbury [shrohzbree, shroozbree], Anglo-Saxon **Scrobesbyrig** 52°43N 2°45W, pop (2000e) 63 200. County town of Shropshire, WC England, UK; on the R Severn, 63 km/39 mi NW of Birmingham; Roman city of Uriconium to the E; headquarters of Edward I during the struggle for Wales; site of Battle of Shrewsbury (1403); railway; engineering, agricultural trade, market gardening; Church of St Mary, abbey church, Rowley's mansion (1618), castle (11th-c); Shropshire and W Midland agricultural show (May), National Ploughing Championships (Oct); football league team, Shrewsbury Town (Shrews).

shrike A bird mainly of the Old World, especially Africa; strong bill with hooked tip; grasping, clawed feet; eats insects and small mammals; often hangs prey from thorns or twigs. The **red-backed shrike** (*Lanius collurio*) is also called the **butcherbird**. The name *shrike* is also used for many birds of other families. (Family: Laniidae, c.72 species.)

shrimp An aquatic crustacean; females typically carry eggs on abdominal legs until ready to hatch into swimming larvae (*zoeae*); many species are of considerable economic importance as food; some are cultured commercially. (Class: Malacostraca. Order: Decapoda.)

shrimp plant A bushy perennial (*Beloperone guttata*) growing to 1 m/3¼ ft, native to Mexico, named for the flower spikes which fancifully resemble crustacea; stems arching; leaves oval, in pairs; flowers hooded, white, almost hidden by broadly oval, overlapping pinkish bracts. (Family: Acanthaceae.)

Shropshire, sometimes abbreviated **Salop** pop (2001e) 283 200; area 3490 sq km/1347 sq mi. County in WC England, UK; bounded W by Powys and Wrexham in Wales; drained by the R Severn; county town, Shrewsbury; chief towns include Telford, Oswestry, Wellington, Ludlow; Wrekin a unitary authority from 1998; agriculture (especially dairy farming, cattle, sheep, cereals), engineering; Ironbridge Gorge open-air museum.

Shroud of Turin *Holy Shroud*

Shrove Tuesday In the UK, the day before the beginning of Lent, so called because traditionally on that day Christians went to confession and were 'shriven' (absolved from their sins). Shrove Tuesday is often known as **Pancake Day** from the custom of making pancakes on that day, and is called **Fastnacht** in Germany, **Carnival** in Italy, and **Mardi Gras** in the Americas.

shrub A woody perennial plant, usually differentiated from a *tree* by being smaller and having a trunk which produces branches at or near the base; but the distinction is far from clear-cut, and some large shrubs are essentially small trees. Many shrubs are very small, and woody only at the very base, and can easily be mistaken for herbs; but they do not die back to ground level in winter.

shuffleboard A game in which discs are sent moving by hand or with an implement along a board or court, so that they come to a halt within a predetermined area. It was popular as an aristocratic game in England in the Middle Ages, often played on boards of some length. Today, a version of the game, also called **shovelboard**, is a popular deck sport aboard ship. Wooden discs, usually c.15 cm/6 in diameter, are pushed along the deck with long-handled drivers and into a scoring area. This version was later adapted to playing on land, and the National Shuffleboard Association was founded in 1931. Another version of the game, known as **shove-halfpenny**, is played on a small board in English pubs, where coins or small discs must be pushed so as to stop between narrowly ruled lines.

Shull, Clifford G(lenwood) (1915–2001) Physicist, born in Pittsburgh, Pennsylvania, USA. He studied at New York University, later moving to Oak Ridge National Laboratory (1946–55) and to MIT. He shared the Nobel Prize for Physics in 1994 for his work in the field of neutron scattering.

Shultz, George P(ratt) (1920–) US statesman, born in New York City, USA. He studied at Princeton and the Massachusetts Institute of Technology, then taught at MIT and Chicago, where he became dean of the Graduate School of Business. He was named secretary of labour by President Nixon (1969), and went on to hold a number of high governmental posts before returning to private life in 1974. In 1982 President Reagan made him secretary of state, a post he retained for the rest of the Reagan presidency.

Shute, Nevil, pseudonym of **Nevil Shute Norway** (1899–1960) Writer, born in London, UK. He studied at Oxford, became an aeronautical engineer, and began to write novels in 1926. After World War 2, he emigrated to Australia, which became the setting for most of his later books, notably *A Town Like Alice* (1949) and *On the Beach* (1957), which were both made into successful films. He published his autobiography, *Slide Rule*, in 1954.

shuttle 1 In spinning, a spindle-shaped device holding a bobbin, used to carry the crosswise threads (*weft*) through the lengthwise threads (*warp*) during weaving. Few modern weaving machines employ shuttles.
2 *space shuttle*

Shwe Dagon Pagoda An important Buddhist pilgrimage site in Yangon (Rangoon), Myanmar. It consists of a magnificent gold-plated shrine (*stupa*) 98 m/326 ft high. Its tip is set with many thousands of diamonds, rubies, and sapphires. Tradition holds that the Shwe Dagon houses eight of the Buddha's hairs, and that a pagoda has occupied this site for over 2000 years.

Shwezigon Pagoda A pagoda erected in the 11th-c near Pagan, Myanmar, as a reliquary shrine for a tooth and a bone of the Buddha. It is the centre of one of Myanmar's most popular yearly festivals.

sial [siyal] The silica and alumina-rich upper part of the Earth's crust which makes up the bulk of the continents and overlies the sima.

Sialkot [syalkoht] 32°29N 74°35E, pop (2000e) 494 000. City in Punjab province, E Pakistan, E of the R Chenab; railway; rubber goods, ceramics, cutlery, surgical instruments; ancient fort, mausoleum of Sikh apostle Nanak.

Siam *Thailand*

siamang [siyamang] A gibbon (*Hylobates syndactylus*) native to Malaysia and Sumatra; the largest gibbon (armspan of 1·5 m/5 ft); long black coat; web of skin joining second and third toes; throat with large red balloon-like vocal sac (inflates just before calling).

Siamese cat A domestic cat of the *foreign short-haired* variety; many breeds, some called **Siamese** in Britain, **short-hair** in the USA; lean, with a triangular face and blue eyes; coat pale with darker *points* (ie face, legs, and tail); many named after the dark colour (eg **red point Siamese** or **red colorpoint short-hair**).

Siamese twins A fault in embryological development in which identical twins are born physically joined together. The deformity ranges from one in which the twins may merely share one umbilical cord to one in which heads or trunks are joined together and cannot be separated. The name derives from the first twins in whom the condition was recognized in modern times, Chang and Eng (1811–74), born in Siam (modern Thailand).

Sian *Xian*

Sian Ka'an [syan kahn] A reserve covering over 5000 sq km/1900 sq mi in the Yucatán Peninsula, Mexico; a world heritage area. In addition to the flora and fauna of the region, the reserve also protects 20 Maya archaeological sites and the way of life of c.800 descendants of the Maya Indians.

Sibelius, Jean (Julius Christian) [sibaylius] (1865–1957) Composer, born in Tavastehus, S Finland. He turned from law to music, studying at the Helsinki Conservatory, Berlin, and Vienna. A passionate nationalist, he wrote a series of symphonic poems based on episodes in the Finnish epic *Kalevala*. From 1897 a state grant enabled him to devote himself entirely to composition, and his seven symphonies (he destroyed his eighth), symphonic poems – notably *Finlandia* (1899) – and violin concerto won great international as well as national popularity.

Siberia area c.7 511 000 sq km/2 900 000 sq mi. Vast geographic region of Asiatic Russia, comprising the N third of Asia; from the Ural Mts (W) to the Pacific Ocean (E), and from the Arctic Ocean (N) to the Kazakhstan steppes and the Chinese and Mongolian frontiers (S); Arctic islands include Severnaya Zemlya, New Siberian Is, Wrangel I; off the Pacific coast are Sakhalin, the Aleutian Is, and the Kuril Is; **W Siberian Lowlands** stretch over 1500 km/1000 mi from the Ural Mts (W) to the R Yenisey (E); **C Siberian Plateau** lies between the R Yenisey (W) and the R Lena (E); **E Siberian Highlands**, including the Altay Mts, rise to 4506 m/14 783 ft at Gora Belukha; c.155 000 rivers, notably the Ob, Yenisey, Lena; extreme continental climate; average winter temperatures generally below −18°C; January temperatures in NE average −51°C; summer temperatures relatively high, average 15–18°C (Jul), in coldest winter areas; precipitation generally low; tundra extends c.320 km/200 mi inland along the Arctic coast; coal, timber, gold, iron, nickel, dairying, grain, cattle, reindeer, maize, sorghum, soya beans, hydroelectric power; chief cities (Novosibirsk, Omsk, Krasnoyarsk, Irkutsk, Khabarovsk, Vladivostok) lie on the Trans-Siberian Railway; used as a penal colony and place of exile for political prisoners; vast areas occupied by counter-revolutionary armies, after the 1917 Revolution, overthrown by Soviet forces in 1922; dramatic economic development under the 5-year plans, relying heavily on forced labour and population resettlement to establish mining, industrial, and agricultural installations; historical territory of Siberia now divided into three planning regions: West Siberia, East Siberia, and Russian Far East.

Siberian argali *argali*

Siberian husky A friendly, medium-sized Arctic spitz breed of dog developed in Siberia; coat thick, soft, white with grey or tan; tail carried in single curve over back, or relaxed when at rest.

Siberian Plateau, Central, Russ **Sredne Sibirskoye Ploskogorye** Upland region in E Siberian Russia, between the R Yenisey (W) and the R Lena (E); average height, 300–800 m/1000–2500 ft.

Siberut [siberoot] area 500 sq km/200 sq mi. Island 140 km/87 mi off the W coast of Sumatra, Indonesia; a nature and 'traditional use' reserve area protecting the dwarf gibbon, pig-tailed langur, Mentawi leaf monkey, and Mentawi macaque; air connections with Padang.

Sibyl or **Sibylla** In Roman legend, a prophetess who uttered mysterious wisdom. Aeneas met the Cumaean Sibyl, who was inspired by Apollo and whose prophecies were written on leaves; she had been given a thousand years of life, and eventually shrank to a tiny creature hung up in a bottle. Later there were said to be 10 Sibyls, and because of Virgil's Fourth Eclogue, they became famous in Christian art, as in the Sistine Chapel. The **Sybilline Books** were nine books of prophecy offered by the Sybil to Tarquinus Priscus, who refused to pay her price; she destroyed three, and came again, with the same result; she destroyed three more, and then Tarquin bought the remainder for the price originally asked.

Sicilian Vespers The wholesale massacre of the French in Sicily which began the Sicilian revolt against Charles of Anjou, King of Naples–Sicily, and a war ending in 1302. It was so called because the first killings occurred during a riot in a church outside Palermo at vespers (evensong) on Easter Monday, 1282. Verdi wrote an opera, *The Sicilian Vespers* (1855), in which he combined the religious theme of the event with the opportunities for characteristic spectacle and ballet.

Sicily, Ital **Sicilia** pop (2000e) 5 000 000; area 25 708 sq km/ 9923 sq mi. Largest and most populous island in the Mediterranean, separated from the mainland of Italy by the narrow Strait of Messina; length 288 km/179 mi; width 192 km/119 mi; settled by the Greeks, 8th-c BC; province of Rome, 2nd-c BC; Norman conquest, 11th-c; conquest by Aragon, 1282; Kingdom of the Two Sicilies, 1815; conquest by Garibaldi, 1860, and unification with Italy; capital, Palermo; other chief towns, Trapani, Messina, Catania, Syracuse; mountainous, average height 450 m/1450 ft; Monti Nebrodi (N) rise to nearly 2000 m/ 6500 ft; large earthquake zone on E coast, culminating in Mt Etna (3390 m/11 122 ft), highest point; an under-developed area, with considerable poverty; intensive vegetable growing, fruit, wine in fertile coastal areas; arable and pastoral farming in dry interior; fishing, salt extraction, petrochemicals, food processing, potash, asphalt, marble, tourism.

Sickert, Walter (Richard) (1860–1942) Artist, born in Munich, SE Germany. After three years on the English stage, he turned to art, studying in London and Paris, where he met Degas, and used his techniques to illustrate music-hall interiors and London life. The Camden Town Group (later the London Group) was formed under his leadership (c.1910), and he became a major influence on later English painters.

sickle cell disease An inherited chemical abnormality of haemoglobin (the oxygen-carrying pigment in red blood cells), affecting people from sub-Saharan Africa. It is caused by the inheritance of an abnormal gene. If the gene is inherited from only one parent, there are few symptoms (*sickle cell trait*), but the gene can still be passed on to the next generation. Individuals who inherit abnormal genes from both parents suffer the full-blown disease. The red cells contain haemoglobin S instead of the normal haemoglobin A. As a result they become sickle-shaped in place of their normal bi-concave circular form, making them more fragile and less flexible; they do not survive long in circulation, leading to chronic anaemia. This is punctuated by a series of crises, often precipitated by infections, in which red cells block small blood vessels, preventing oxygen supply to the tissues.

Siddons, Sarah, *née* **Kemble** (1755–1831) Actress, born in Brecon, Powys, E Wales, UK, the sister of John Kemble (1757–1823). She was a member of the theatre company run by her father, Roger Kemble, from her earliest childhood, and in 1773 married her fellow actor, **William Siddons** (1744–1808). She gained a great reputation in the provinces, and after playing at Drury Lane in 1782 became the unquestioned queen of tragedy, renowned for her beauty, dignity, and rich, resonant voice.

side drum A shallow drum with a skin at each end, the upper one struck with a pair of wooden sticks, the lower fitted with *snares* (strings of metal or gut) which, when engaged, give the tone a rasping edge. It is used in orchestras, dance bands, and military bands, and is worn slightly to one side when marching (hence the name).

sidereal day *day*

sidereal time Time measured by considering the rotation of the Earth relative to the distant stars (rather than to the Sun, which is the basis of civil time).

sidewinder A snake which moves by pushing its head forward onto the ground, then winding the body forwards and sideways until it lies stretched out to one side; meanwhile the head is moved forward again. Repeating this behaviour allows the snake to move rapidly over soft sand. Sidewinding is used by several species, especially vipers (eg the horned viper), but no species uses it all the time. *Crotalus cerastes* (the North American horned rattlesnake) usually uses sidewinding, and is commonly called the **sidewinder**.

Sidgwick, Henry (1838–1900) Philosopher, born in Skipton, North Yorkshire, N England, UK. He studied at Cambridge, where he became a fellow of Trinity College (1859) and professor of moral philosophy (1883). His best-known work, *Methods of Ethics* (1874), develops the utilitarian theories of John Stuart Mill. He was also active in promoting higher education for women, notably in the founding of Newnham College, Cambridge, in 1880. His wife, Eleanor Balfour (the sister of A J Balfour), was its principal from 1892 to 1910. In 1882 he was a founder and the first president of the Society for Psychical Research.

Sidi bel Abbès [sidee bel abes] 35°15N 0°39W, pop (2000e) 250 800. Chief town of Sidi bel Abbès department, N Algeria, N Africa; 56 km/35 mi S of Oran; originally a walled town, and a military post under French occupation; headquarters of the French Foreign Legion until 1962; railway; cereals, wine, machinery.

Siding Spring Observatory An observatory in the Warrumbungle Mts of New South Wales, Australia, administered by the Australian National University. It is the site of the 3·9 m/ 150 in Anglo-Australian Telescope, the 1·2 m/48 in UK Schmidt Telescope, and telescopes of the Australian National University.

Sidmouth (of Sidmouth), Henry Addington, 1st Viscount [sidmuhth] (1757–1844) British statesman and prime minister (1801–4), born in London, UK. He studied at Oxford, left law for politics, and became an MP in 1783. He was Speaker of the House (1789–1801) when, upon Pitt's resignation, he was invited to form a Tory ministry. His administration negotiated the Peace of Amiens (1802), which held for barely a year. His government ended in 1804, when he was created a viscount. He later became home secretary under Liverpool (1812–21), unpopular for coercive measures such as the Six Acts of 1819.

Sidney, Algernon (1622–83) English politician, born in Penshurst, Kent, SE England, UK. He became a cavalry officer in the English Civil War on the parliamentary side, and was wounded at Marston Moor (1644). In 1645 he entered parliament, and served as governor in several cities. An extreme Republican, he resented Cromwell's usurpation of power, and retired to Penshurst (1653–9). After the Restoration he lived on the European mainland, but in 1677 was pardoned and returned to England. In 1683 he was implicated on very little evidence in the Rye House Plot, and beheaded.

Sidney, Sir Philip (1554–86) Poet, statesman, soldier, and courtier, born in Penshurst, Kent, SE England, UK. He studied at Oxford, and perhaps also at Cambridge, then travelled in Europe (1572–5). He gained Elizabeth I's displeasure when he advised her against a projected marriage plan, and in 1580 left the court. Knighted in 1583, he was sent to Holland to assist in the struggle against Spain, and was fatally wounded at Zutphen. His literary work, written in 1578–82, was not published until after his death. It includes the unfinished pastoral romance, *Arcadia*, the *Defence of Poesie*, and a sonnet cycle, *Astrophel and Stella*, considered one of the finest Elizabethan examples of this genre. In his *Defence of Poesie* (1595), he wrote the most notable work of Elizabethan literary criticism, upholding the superiority of poetry as a means of teaching virtue. He is also known for the patronage he bestowed on poets, as shown by the dedications in Spenser's *The Sheepheardes Calendar* (1579) and in over 40 works by English and European authors.

Sidon [siydon] 33°32N 35°22E, pop (2000e) 31 000. Seaport capital of W Lebanon, on the Mediterranean Sea, 35 km/22 mi N of Tyre, at the centre of a well-watered coastal plain; founded in the third millennium BC; once noted for its glass and purple dyes; railway; oil refining; Crusader castle; ruins of Phoenician Temple of Echmoun nearby.

Siegfried Line [zeegfreed] Name given by the Allies in World War 2 to a 600 km/373 mi line of defensive fortifications constructed in 1936–40 along Germany's borders with France, Luxembourg, Belgium, and S Netherlands. It provided respite to retreating German forces in 1944, but was breached by the Allies in 1945, and largely dismantled after the war. All remains were demolished during 2003 to mark the 40th anniversary of the Franco-German friendship treaty (1963).

Sielmann, Heinz [zeelman] (1917–) Naturalist and nature film photographer, born in Königsberg, Prussia (now Kaliningrad, Russia). He began to make films in 1938, and won the German Oscar for documentary films three years running (1953–5). He evolved techniques enabling him to film the inside of animal lairs and birds' nests, which revolutionized the study of animal behaviour.

Siemens, (Ernst) Werner von [zeemens] (1816–92) Electrical engineer, born in Lenthe, NC Germany (formerly Prussia), the brother of William (Wilhelm) Siemens. In 1834 he entered the Prussian artillery, and in 1844 took charge of the artillery workshops at Berlin. He developed the telegraphic system in Prussia, founded a telegraph manufacturing firm (Siemens & Halske) in 1847, devised several forms of galvanometer, and determined the electrical resistance of different substances. He also built the first electric motor used in the electrification of railway lines (1878), which was demonstrated at the Berlin Fair the following year. He was ennobled in 1888.

siemens [seemnz] SI unit of electrical conductance; symbol *S*; defined as 1 divided by resistance as measured in ohms.

Siena [syayna], ancient **Suene Julia** 43°19N 11°19E, pop (2000e) 64 500. Capital town of Siena province, Tuscany, C Italy; 70 km/43 mi S of Florence; founded by the Etruscans; centre of the Ghibelline faction and a rival of Florence, 12th-c; influential centre of mediaeval art; archbishopric; university (1240); major tourist city; glass, textiles, bricks, confectionery, crafts, cultural activities; cathedral (12th–14th-c); town hall (13th-c) with tower, Torre del Mangia (14th-c); Palazzo Buonsignori (14th-c), Church of San Domenico (13th–15th-c), Baptistery San Giovanni (12th-c), house of St Catherine; Palio parade and horse race (Jul–Aug).

Sienese School A school of art which flourished in Siena in the 14th-c and early 15th-c. Great artists included Duccio, Martini, and the Lorenzetti brothers. Sienese art is more charming and decorative than that of Florence, less dramatic, and has deep roots in the Gothic and Byzantine traditions.

Sienkiewicz, Henryk (Adam Alexander Pius) [shengkyayvich] (1846–1916) Novelist, born in Wola Okrzejska, E Poland. He studied at Warsaw, travelled in the USA, and in the 1870s began to write articles, short stories, and novels. His major work was a war trilogy about 17th-c Poland, beginning with *Ogniem i mieczem* (1884, With Fire and Sword), but his most widely known book is the story of Rome under Nero, *Quo Vadis?* (1896), several times filmed, notably in 1951 by Mervyn Le Roy (1900–87). He received the Nobel Prize for Literature in 1905.

Sierra Club A US private, non-profit conservation organization. It was founded by the US naturalist and writer, John Muir (1838–1914) in 1892.

Sierra Leone *p.1407*

Sierra Nevada (Spain) [syera nayvahtha] Mountain range in Andalusia, S Spain, rising to 3478 m/11 411 ft at Mulhacén, the highest peak in continental Spain.

Sierra Nevada (USA) [syera nevahda] Mountain range in W USA, mainly in E California; extends NW–SE for 725 km/450 mi between the Cascade and Coastal Ranges; highest point in the USA outside Alaska, Mt Whitney (4418 m/14 495 ft); contains Yosemite, Sequoia and Kings Canyon national parks.

Sierra Nevada de Mérida [syeruh nayvahthuh thay mayreethuh] Mountain range in W Venezuela; a spur of the Andes; length, 500 km/300 mi; width, 50–80 km/30–50 mi; rises to 5007 m/16 427 ft at Pico Bolívar, highest peak in Venezuela; world's highest and longest cable railway runs to Pico Espejo (4765 m/15 633 ft), built by French in 1958.

sievert [seevert] In radioactivity, the SI unit of dose equivalent, equal to absorbed dose multiplied by the relative biological effectiveness; symbol *Sv*; because it takes account of different radiations' ability to cause biological damage, *Sv* is used in radiation safety measurements.

Sieyès, Emmanuel Joseph, comte de (Count of) [syayes], also known as **Abbé Sieyès** (1748–1836) French political theorist and clergyman, born in Fréjus, SE France. His pamphlet, *Qu'est-ce que le tiers-état?* (1789, What is the Third Estate?) stimulated bourgeois awareness and won him great popularity. He became a member of the National Convention, and later served on the Committee of Public Safety (1795) and in the Directory. In 1799, he helped to organize the revolution of 18th Brumaire, becoming a member of the Consulate. When Napoleon assumed supreme power, his authority waned, and he withdrew to his estates. He was exiled at the Restoration (1815), and lived in Brussels until 1830, returning after the July Revolution to Paris.

sifaka [sifaka] A leaping lemur; long silky hair and long tail; variable in colour (usually white with dark patches); small gliding membranes from arms to sides of body; can leap 10 m/33 ft between trees; eats leaves. (Genus: *Propithecus*, 2 species.)

sigillography *seal* (communications)

Sigiriya An ancient city in C Sri Lanka – also the rock which towers 180 m/600 ft above it; a world heritage site. The rock is surmounted by a palace built in the 5th-c by King Kasyapa I. Sigiriya is renowned not only for the grandeur of its ruins, but also for the frescoes adorning the W cliffs of the rock.

Sigismund (1368–1437) Holy Roman Emperor (1433–7), probably born in Nuremberg, SC Germany, the son of Charles IV. He became King of Hungary (1387), Germany (1411), and Bohemia (1419). In 1396 he was defeated by the Ottoman Turks at Nicopolis, but later conquered Bosnia, Herzegovina, and Serbia. As emperor, he induced the Pope to call the Council of Constance to end the Hussite schism (1414), but made no effort to uphold the safe conduct he had granted to John Huss to attend the Council, and permitted him to be burned. As a result, his succession in Bohemia was opposed by the Hussites.

sign Something that stands for something else, which it may or may not resemble, the relationship often being agreed by convention; for example, an arrow indicates direction, and greying hair the ageing process. In semiotics a sign comprises a *signifier* (its physical appearance, sound, etc) and a *signified* (the mental concept it evokes). Each sign's meaning is determined partly by its differential relationship with other signs in the same code, partly by its relationship with the thing it stands for. *Signification* is the process by which signs acquire meaning in a specific cultural context.

Signac, Paul [seenyak] (1863–1935) Artist, born in Paris, France. He exhibited in 1884 with the Impressionists, and was later involved in the neo-Impressionist movement. With Seurat he developed Divisionism (but using mosaic-like patches of pure colour rather than Seurat's pointillist dots), mainly in seascapes. In his writing he sought to establish a scientific basis for his theories.

signal detection theory An approach to the detection of physical signals, developed in communication engineering, but widely applied in experimental psychology. The theory holds that, when attempting to detect differences between sources of stimulation, responses are governed by two factors: the observer's sensitivity and the observer's decision criteria. It provides rigorous methods and mathematical tools for measuring both factors.

Sierra Leone

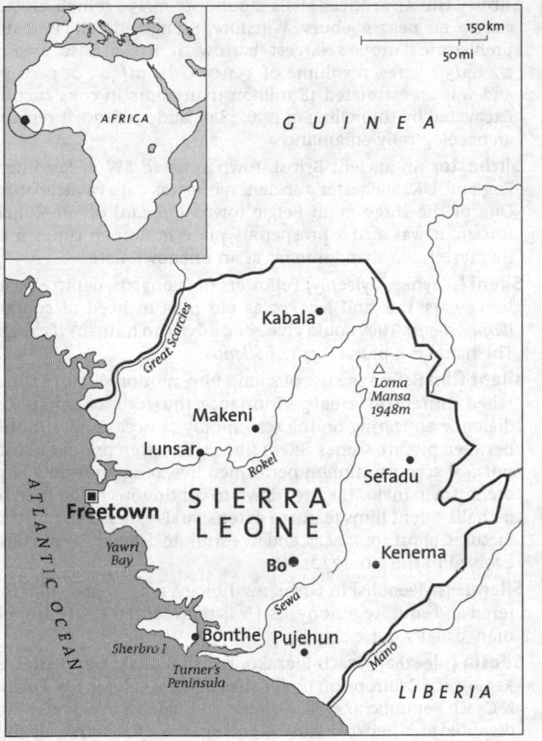

□ International Airport

[syera leeohn], official name **Republic of Sierra Leone**

Local name Sierra Leone

Timezone GMT

Area 71 740 km²/27 692 sq mi

Population total (2002e) 4 823 000

Status Republic

Date of independence 1961

Capital Freetown

Languages English (official), with Krio widely spoken

Ethnic groups African origin (99%) (including Mendes, Temnes, Limbas, Korankos, and Lokos)

Religions Local beliefs (30%), Sunni Muslim (60%), Christian (Protestant 6%, Roman Catholic 2%)

Physical features Low narrow coastal plain in W Africa; rises to an average height of 500 m/1600 ft in the Loma Mts (E), highest point, Loma Mansa, 1948 m/6391 ft; Tingi Mts rise to 1853 m/6079 ft (SE); principal rivers include the Great Scarcies, Rokel, Gbangbaia, Jong, and Sewa.

Climate Equatorial climate; temperatures uniformly high throughout the year; average annual temperature 27°C; rainy season (May–Oct); highest rainfall on coast; average annual rainfall 3436 mm/135 in at Freetown.

Currency 1 Leone (Le) = 100 cents

Economy Mining (most important sector of the economy); diamonds (represent c.60% of exports); bauxite, gold, titanium, iron ore, and other mineral and metal ores; subsistence agriculture (employs over 70% of population); rice, coffee, cocoa, citrus fruits; timber; food processing.

GDP (2002e) $2·826 bn, per capita $500

Human Development Index (2002) 0·275

History First visited by Portuguese navigators and British slave traders; land bought from local chiefs by English philanthropists who established settlements for freed slaves, 1780s; British Crown Colony, 1808, hinterland declared a British protectorate, 1896; independence declared within the Commonwealth as a constitutional monarchy, 1961; period of military rule, 1967–8; became a republic, 1971; established as a one-party state, 1978; new constitution, 1991, allowing for multi-party politics, and interim government formed until general elections; interrupted by military coup in 1992, House of Representatives dissolved, and Supreme Council of State (SCS) and Civilian Council of State Secretaries (Cabinet) established; further military coup, 1997, overturned 1998; renewed fighting in early 1999, followed by Lomé (Togo) peace agreement (Jul) and establishment of UN peacekeeping force; UN troops attacked and abducted by rebels (Apr 2000), leading to UK-sponsored military assistance plan within the country, and arrival of UN reinforcements; peace declared, 2002.

Head of State/Government

1971 Christopher Okero Cole
1971–85 Siaka Probin Stevens
1985–92 Joseph Saidu Momoh
1992–6 Valentine Strasser
1996 *Military rule*
1996–7 Ahmad Tejan Kabbah
1997–8 Johnny Paul Koroma
1998– Ahmad Tejan Kabbah

sign language A communication system in which manual signs are used to express a corresponding range of meanings to those conveyed by spoken or written language. There are several different kinds of sign language. The most widely used are those which have developed naturally in a deaf community, such as the American, British, French, and Swedish Sign Languages. Contrary to popular belief, such languages are not mutually intelligible, as they use different signs and rules of sentence structure. There are also several systems which have been devised by educators and linguists for working with language-handicapped populations, such as Seeing Essential English (1966), the Paget-Gorman Sign System (1951), and Cued Speech (1966). The study of sign languages has been traced back to the work of Abbé Charles Michel de l'Epée (1712–89), who in 1775 developed a sign language for use in a Paris school for the deaf. The manual alphabet (finger-spelling) is also included under the general heading of sign language.

Signorelli, Luca [seenyawrelee], also known as **Luca da Cortona** (c.1441–1523) Painter, born in Cortona, C Italy. He painted many frescoes at Loreto, Rome, Florence, Siena, Cortona, and Orvieto, where the cathedral contains his greatest work, the frescoes of 'The Preaching of Anti-Christ' and 'The Last Judgment' (1500–4). He was one of the painters summoned by the Pope in 1508 to adorn the Vatican, and dismissed to make way for Raphael.

Sigurd [seegoord] In Norse mythology, the son of Sigmund the Volsung, who kills Fafnir the dragon and wins Brunhild. He marries Gudrun, having forgotten Brunhild, and is killed by Gudrun's brother Gutthorm. Virtually the same story is told of **Siegfried [zeegfreed]** in German legends.

Sihanouk, Prince Norodom [seeanook] (1922–) Cambodian leader, born in Phnom Penh, Cambodia. He was King of Cambodia (1941–55), chief of state (1960–70, and of the Khmer Republic 1975–6), prime minister on several occasions between 1952 and 1968, president of the government in exile (1970–5, 1982–91), president (1991–3), and once again king (1993–). He studied in Vietnam and Paris, was elected king in 1941, and negotiated the country's independence from France (1949–53). He abdicated in 1955 in favour of his father, in order to become an elected leader under the new constitution. As prime minister, and from 1960 head of state, he steered a neutralist course during the Vietnam War. In 1970 he was deposed in a right-wing military coup led by Lon Nol, fled to Beijing, and formed a joint resistance front with Pol Pot which successfully overthrew Lon Nol in 1975. Re-appointed head of state, he was ousted a year later by the Communist Khmer Rouge leadership. In 1982 he was elected president of the new government-in-exile. He returned to Cambodia in November 1991 as president of the Supreme National Council, after the signing of a peace treaty ended 13 years of civil war, and was crowned king under the new constitution in 1993.

sika [**see**ka] A true deer (*Cervus nippon*) native to E Asia (introduced in New Zealand and UK); brown (with pale spots in summer) with white rump; white spot halfway down rear leg; long antlers; can interbreed with the red deer to produce fertile offspring; also known as **Japanese deer**.

Sikhism [**seek**izm] A religion founded by the Guru Nanak (1469–1539) in the Punjab area of N India. Under his leadership and that of his nine successors Sikhism prospered. It combines aspects of Hinduism and Islam, and is called a religion of the gurus, seeking union with God through worship and service. God is the true Guru, and his divine word has come to humanity through the 10 historical gurus. The line ended in 1708, since when the Sikh community is called guru. The Adi Granth, their sacred scripture, is also called a guru. The Sikh understanding of life is closely related to Punjab identity. There were some 24 million Sikhs in 2004.

Sikh Wars [seek] Two campaigns (1845–6, 1848–9) between the British and the Sikhs which led to the British conquest and annexation of the Punjab, NW India (Mar 1849).

Sikkim [**sik**im] pop (2001e) 540 500; area 7300 sq km/2817 sq mi. State in NE India, in the E Himalayas; bounded W by Nepal, N by China, and E by China and Bhutan; ruled by Namgyal dynasty, 14th-c until 1975; part of British Empire, 1866–1947; protectorate of India, 1950; voted to become a state, 1975; capital, Gangtok; governed by a 32-member Assembly; Mt Kangchenjunga on Nepal border; inhabited mostly by Lepchas, Bhutias, and Nepalis; state religion, Mahayana Buddhism, but many of the population are Hindu; rice, maize, millet, cardamom, soybean, fruit, tea; cigarettes, copper, zinc, lead, watches, carpets, woodwork, silverwork.

Sikorski, Władysław (Eugeniusz) [si**kaw(r)**skee] (1881–1943) Polish general, statesman, and prime minister (1922–3), born in Galicia (part of modern Poland). He studied at Kraków and Lvóv, fought in the Russian–Polish War (1920–1), became commander-in-chief (1921), and premier. After Piłsudski's coup (1926) he retired and wrote a military history in Paris. He returned to Poland in 1938, but on being refused a command, fled to France, becoming commander of the Free Polish forces, and from 1940 was premier of the Polish government in exile in London. He was killed in an air crash. A national hero, his body was returned to Poland in 1993, and given a state funeral.

Sikorsky, Igor (Ivan) [si**kaw(r)**skee] (1889–1972) Aeronautical engineer, the inventor of the helicopter, born in Kiev, Ukraine. He began experimenting with building helicopters in 1909, but shelved his work due to lack of experience and money, and turned to aircraft. He built and flew the first four-engined aeroplane in 1913. He emigrated to the USA in 1919, and became a US citizen in 1928. He founded the Sikorsky Aero Engineering Corporation (1923), merging the company into the United Aircraft Corporation. The recipient of the highest awards and medals for aviation, he built several flying-boats, including the *American Clipper* (1931), and in 1939 developed the first successful helicopter, the VS-300.

silage A fodder made from grass, maize, or other leafy material and preserved by its own partial fermentation in an airtight tower-silo, silage pit or, more commonly, in a large airtight roll baled and sealed in plastic sheeting. Silages are usually made for the winter housing period for stock and to allow excess grass growth in the spring and summer to be preserved. Initial fermentation creates organic and amino acids, which act as preservatives. Silage is fed mainly to beef and dairy cattle, but can be fed to other ruminants.

Silbury Hill An artificial chalk mound, 40 m/130 ft high, erected c.2700 BC near Avebury, Wiltshire, S England, UK. Probably prehistoric Europe's largest barrow, it has a base area of 2·2 ha/5·4 acres, a volume of 354 000 cu m/463 000 cu yd, and was an estimated 18 million man-hours in construction. Excavated by tunnelling in 1776, 1849, and 1968–70, it remains archaeologically enigmatic.

Silchester An ancient British town situated SW of Reading, S England, UK. Silchester's ancient name was Calleva Atrebatum. One of the three main Belgic towns (*oppida*) of pre-Roman Britain, it was also a prosperous place in Roman times until its mysterious abandonment at an unknown date.

Sileni [si**lay**nee, sy**lee**niy] Followers of Dionysus, depicted with horse ears, tail, and legs, or as old men in need of support (*Papposileni*). They could give good advice to humans if caught. The name is a plural form of *Silenus*.

silent film Before the use of sound film, motion pictures which relied entirely on visual performance, the words of any spoken dialogue appearing on the screen only as occasional subtitles between picture scenes. Silent films were often presented with musical accompaniment performed live, ranging from a large orchestra in major theatres down to continuous piano in smaller halls. Silent films featured extensive slapstick comedy, trick pictures, short romances, and five-minute dramas. Sound films evolved in the late 1920s.

Silenus [sy**lee**nuhs] In Greek mythology, a demi-god, who fostered and educated Dionysus. He is represented as a festive old man, usually quite drunk.

Silesia [si**lee**zha], Czech **Slezsko**, Polish **Śląsk**, Ger **Schlesien** Region of EC Europe on both banks of the R Oder in SW Poland, N Czech Republic, and SE Germany; bounded S by Sudetes Mts; disputed area between Austria and Prussia, 17th–18th-c; divided into Upper and Lower Silesia, 1919; greater part granted to Poland, 1945; a largely industrial region, including the coal-mining and metal industries of Katowice and nearby cities.

silhouette A technique of paper cut-out picture popularized by French finance minister Etienne de Silhouette (1709–67) and used for cheap miniature portraits until the rise of photography in the mid-19th-c. The term is often extended to cover any type of dark image against a light background, or light on dark, as in Greek vase-painting.

silica Silicon dioxide (SiO_2), the main constituent of the Earth's crust, occurring in nature as pure minerals or combined with other elements in silicate minerals. The crystalline forms of silica are quartz, tridymite, and cristobalite, which are progressively higher temperature phases, and the cryptocrystalline varieties termed chalcedony. Amorphous silica is found naturally in opal, and may be produced by the rapid cooling of molten silica; it is used in the production of glass and cement.

silicate minerals A group of minerals constituting about 95% of the Earth's crust, and containing silicon and oxygen combined with one or more other elements. Structurally they are all based on SiO_4, the tetrahedron, and most are complex polymeric structures of tetrahedra. They are classified according to the degree of polymerization, from silicates containing isolated SiO_4 groups (eg olivines, garnets) to rings (eg beryl) to chain silicates (eg pyroxenes (single chains) and amphiboles (double chains)), sheets (eg micas, clays), and three-dimensional frameworks (eg quartz, feldspars).

silicon Si, element 14, melting point 1410°C. A grey solid nonmetal, the second most common element in the crust of the Earth, 26% by weight. It is the second element in the carbon group, and like carbon it forms mainly covalent compounds, with a valence of 4. It does not occur uncombined in nature. In addition to a large number of minerals which are essentially SiO_2, it occurs in many alumino-silicates. Very pure silicon is widely used in electronic devices. It is also doped with controlled amounts of aluminium, phosphorus, and other elem-

Silk Road

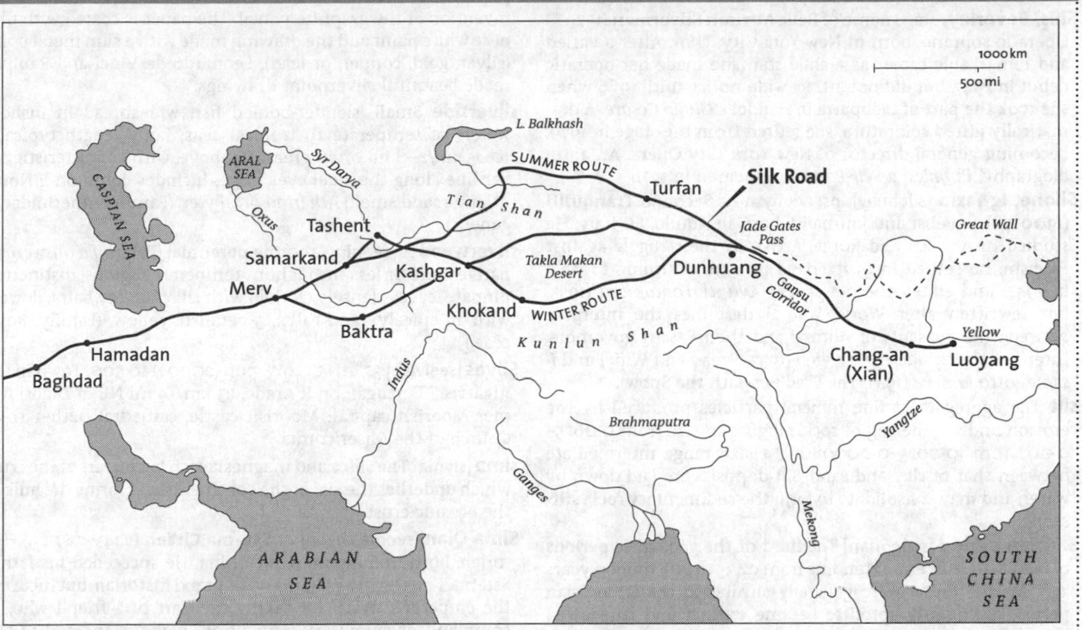

Ancient trade route from E China to C Asia and Europe. From the 2nd-c AD, the best-known route ran from Xian through the Hexi Corridor to the E Mediterranean coast. During the Sui dynasty (581–618), a route further N ended at Istanbul. In exchange for silk, China received grapes, cotton, chestnuts, lucerne, and pomegranates; Chinese techniques for silkworm breeding, iron-smelting, paper making, and irrigation spread W. The route also brought Buddhism to China. The silk trade had a serious economic impact on the Roman Empire. Payment was in precious metals, and by AD 10 China's gold reserves exceeded those of much later mediaeval Europe. The situation possibly contributed to the fall of Rome.

ents to alter its conductivity. Silicates are the main constituents of brick, stone, cement, and glass.

silicon carbide SiC. A compound produced by fusing a mixture of carbon and silica; also known as **carborundum**. It has several crystalline modifications, all of which are high-melting and hard, and is used mainly as an abrasive.

silicon chip A very small slice of silicon, a few millimetres square, on which many electronic circuits containing many components are built; also called an **integrated circuit**. Silicon chips are reliable and cheap to produce in large numbers (although the manufacturing process is very complex), and they are now used in computers, calculators, many modern programmed household appliances, and in most electronic applications. They have been a major factor in the microminiaturization of devices: a computer which once filled a large room can now be made on one small silicon chip.

silicone An open-chain or cyclic polymer containing the repeating unit $-SiR_2-O-$, where R– is an alkyl group. Odourless, colourless, insoluble in and unreactive with water, and having high flashpoints, silicones are used in high-temperature lubricants, hydraulic fluids, and varnishes.

Silicon Valley Santa Clara County, W California, USA, between Palo Alto and San José; a world centre since the 1970s for electronics, computing, and database systems.

silicosis [silikohsis] An industrial disease of occupations such as coal mining, stone dressing, and sand blasting, and of the ceramics industry. It is caused by inhalation of fine particles of silica which induce scarring of the lungs.

silk A very fine fibre obtained from the cocoons of silkworms. Japan and China provide most of the high-quality cultivated silk. The fabrics are renowned for their lustre, drape, and handle. The rearing of silkworms (**sericulture**) originated in China before 1100 BC; major finds have been uncovered in 2nd-c BC tombs. The secret of silk manufacture passed to Japan at an early date, but not to Europe until the early modern period. Previously it was believed to grow on trees, or to be taken from a great horned worm.

silk-cotton tree *kapok tree*

Silk Road *see panel*

silk-screen *screen-process printing*

silkworm The larva of the common silk moth, *Bombyx mori*, that spins the silk cocoon from which commercial silk is derived; larvae feed on mulberry leaves. The cocoon is unwound mechanically, after softening, and each may contain up to 3 km/2 mi of silk. The domesticated silkworm is no longer found in the wild. (Order: Lepidoptera. Family: Bombycidae.)

silky-flycatcher *flycatcher*

silky terrier A toy breed of dog developed from terriers (including the Yorkshire terrier) in Australia; short legs, erect ears; long, straight, silky, brown and blue-grey coat (hair 12–15 cm/5–6 in long).

sill A sheet-like body of igneous rock that has been intruded between layers of sedimentary rock, and shows a conformable relationship with the bedding planes. It is usually composed of medium-grained rock, typically dolerite. Examples include the Palisades Sill in New Jersey, USA, and the Whin Sill in N England.

Sillitoe, Alan [silitoh] (1928–) Novelist, born in Nottingham, Nottinghamshire, C England, UK. Before serving in the Royal Air Force, he worked in a bicycle factory for several years, which provided the subject for his first and most popular novel, *Saturday Night and Sunday Morning* (1958). Later novels include *A Tree on Fire* (1967), *A Start in Life* (1970), *Life Goes On* (1985), *Leonard's War* (1991), *Snowstop* (1993), and *The German Numbers Woman* (1999). His story *The Loneliness of the Long Distance Runner* (1959) was filmed in 1962. He has also written a number of books of poetry, and books for children, several starring the character 'Marmalade Jim'. An autobiography, *Life Without Armour*, appeared in 1995.

Sills, Beverley, stage name of **Belle Miriam Silverman** (1929–) Operatic soprano, born in New York City, USA. After a varied and remarkable career as a child star, she made her operatic debut in 1947, but did not attract wide notice until 1966 when she took the part of Cleopatra in Handel's *Giulio Cesare*. A dramatically gifted coloratura, she retired from the stage in 1979, becoming general director of New York City Opera. An autobiography, *Bubbles: a Self-Portrait*, appeared in 1976.

Silone, Ignazio [siloh**nay**], pseudonym of **Secondo Tranquilli** (1900–78) Novelist and journalist, born in Aquilo, EC Italy. He studied in Abruzzi and Rome. Active in the struggle against Fascism, he settled in Switzerland in 1931, returning to Italy in 1944, and edited the newspaper *Avanti*. *Fontamara* (1933, but rewritten after World War 2) describes the interplay between the peasants of Abruzzi and their Fascist governors. Later novels include *Pane e vino* (1937, Bread and Wine) and *Il seme sotto la neve* (1941, The Seed Beneath the Snow).

silt The aggregate of fine mineral particles produced by the erosion and weathering of rock, ranging in size from 0·0625–0·002 mm (0·0025–0·00008 in), a size range intermediate between that of clay and sand. Silt deposits are laid down by water, and may consolidate to form the sedimentary rock, **siltstone**.

Silurian period [siyl**oo**rian] The third of the geological periods of the Palaeozoic era, extending from c.435 to 408 million years ago. Marine fauna were generally similar to the Ordovician period, although graptolites became extinct and true-jawed fish evolved. The earliest land plants appeared.

Silvanus or **Sylvanus** [sil**vay**nus, sil**vah**nus] In Roman religion, the god of uncultivated land, especially woodland; he was therefore strange, and dangerous, like Pan. The name is possibly a synonym of Faunus.

silver Ag (Lat *argentum*), element 47, melting point 961°C. A lustrous transition metal, relatively rare, but occurring uncombined in nature, known and used since ancient times. It also occurs as a sulphide (Ag_2S), particularly along with those of other elements; a major source is the sludge from copper refinement. Of all elements, it is the best conductor of electricity. Long used extensively in coinage, it has now become too expensive for that purpose. Much used in jewellery and medals, it requires regular cleaning, as the surface becomes coated with Ag_2S. Its compounds, which normally show oxidation state +1 (especially AgBr), are used in photography; surfaces of AgBr, after activation by light, are easily reduced to Ag.

silver birch A slender, elegant, short-lived species of birch (*Betula pendula*) reaching 15–18 m/50–60 ft, with distinctive silvery-white bark. Native to Europe, usually in colder regions, it is often planted for ornament. (Family: Betulaceae.)

silver fir An evergreen conifer native to the temperate N hemisphere; foliage often silvery or bluish; needles leathery, leaving distinctive circular scars when shed; cones breaking up to release seeds when ripe. Widely grown for timber and as ornamentals; its resin yields *Canada balsam*. It is sensitive to polluted air, and does not thrive in or near industrial areas. (Genus: *Abies*, 50 species. Family: Pinaceae.)

silverfish A tapering, primitively wingless insect covered with silvery white scales; tail 3-pronged; commonly found in houses; active at night, moves swiftly; feeds on a variety of plant and animal matter. (Order: Thysanura. Family: Lepismatidae.)

silver fox *red fox*

silver Persian *chinchilla cat*

silver plate A term applied to goods made of silver of sterling standard (an alloy with 925 parts of silver out of every 1000, the rest usually being copper), established by law in England in the 13th-c. Hallmarking was introduced from 1300. It should not be confused with the various 19th-c techniques of **silver plating**, which involved a thin skin of sterling silver applied to base metal.

silverpoint A technique used by artists for drawing on paper, popular in the Renaissance, but afterwards superseded by the invention of the graphite pencil. The paper is coated with Chinese white paint and the drawing made with a slim metal point (silver, gold, copper, or lead). Leonardo da Vinci and Raphael made beautiful silverpoint drawings.

silverside Small, slender-bodied fish widespread in inshore waters of temperate to tropical seas; body length typically 10–15 cm/4–6 in; often greenish above, with characteristic silver line along the side; eyes large; includes common E North Atlantic sand smelt, *Atherina presbyter*. (Family: Atherinidae, 8 genera.)

silverweed A creeping, rooting perennial (*Potentilla answerina*) native more or less throughout temperate regions; distinctive, pinnate leaves, densely clothed with silky, silvery hairs; flowers with an epicalyx and calyx, 5-petalled, yellow. (Family: Rosaceae.)

Silves [**seel**vish] 37°11N 8°26W, pop (2000e) 10 500. Town in the Algarve, S Portugal; on R Arade, 23 km/14 mi NE of Lagos; former Moorish capital; Moorish castle, cathedral (12th–13th-c), Church of the Misericordia.

sima [**siy**ma] The silica and magnesia-rich lower part of the crust which underlies the sial of the continents and forms the bulk of the oceanic crust.

Sima Qian [seema chyan] or **Ssu-ma Ch'ien** (c.145–c.87 BC) Historian, born in Lung-men, EC China. He succeeded his father Ssu-ma T'an (?–110 BC) in 110 BC as grand historian, but incurred the emperor's wrath for taking the part of a friend who, in command of a military expedition, had surrendered to the enemy. Imprisoned and destined for execution, he was castrated instead, perhaps to enable him to complete his work. He is chiefly remembered for the *Shih Chi*, the first history of China compiled as dynastic histories, in which annals of the principal events are supplemented by princely and other biographies, as well as notes on economic and institutional history. Many of his observations, such as the names of many Shang kings, have been confirmed by 20th-c archaeology, and his work, with its central concept of cyclical growth and decay, is of major significance.

Simbirsk [sim**birsk**], formerly **Ulyanovsk** (1924–91) 54°19N 48°22E, pop (2000e) 665 000. River-port in WC European Russia; founded as a fortress, 1648; airfield; railway; machinery, metalworking, leatherwork, footwear, vodka; birthplace of Lenin; renamed after his family name, Ulyanov; Palace of Books (1847).

Simenon, Georges (Joseph Christian) [seemen**õ**] (1903–89) Master of the crime novel, born in Liège, E Belgium. He began as a journalist, then moved to Paris in 1922, where he wrote serious psychological novels as well as detective stories. He was one of the most prolific authors of his day, producing over 500 novels under a variety of pseudonyms. He revolutionized detective fiction with his tough, morbidly psychological Inspector Maigret series, beginning in 1933, which has provided several films and television series. Autobiographical writings include *When I Was Old* (trans 1971) and *Intimate Memoirs* (trans 1984).

Simeon, tribe of One of the 12 tribes of ancient Israel, purportedly descended from Jacob's second son by Leah. Its territory was in the S extremity of Palestine, S of Judah, into which it seems to have been nearly absorbed.

Simeon Stylites, St [stiy**liy**teez] (387–459) The earliest of the Christian ascetic 'pillar' saints. After living nine years in a Syrian monastery without leaving his cell, he became revered as a miracle-worker. To separate himself from the people, c.420 he established himself on top of a pillar c.20 m/70 ft high at Telanessa, near Antioch, where he spent the rest of his life preaching to crowds. He had many imitators, known as *stylites*. Feast day 5 January (W), September (E).

Simien National park situated in a region of mountains and severe erosion in N Ethiopia; established in 1969 to protect threatened native species such as the lion-maned gelada baboon, and the Ethiopian ibex; a world heritage site.

simile *metaphor*

Simla [**simla**] 31°07N 77°09E. Hill station in Himachal Pradesh state, N India; NE of Chandigarh, to which it is linked by rail; altitude c.2200 m/7100 ft; established in 1819 as former summer capital of British India; grain, timber, handicrafts.

Simmons, Jean (1929–) Film actress, born in London, UK. She made her first film appearance in *Give Up The Moon* (1942), and had minor parts in a number of British films before going to Hollywood in 1950, where she became a leading star of the following decade. Her films include *The Robe* (1953), *Guys and Dolls* (1955), *The Big Country* (1958), *Spartacus* (1960), and *How to Make an American Quilt* (1995). During the 1980s she appeared in several television productions, including *The Thorn Birds* (1983) and *Great Expectations* (1989).

Simnel, Lambert (c.1475–c.1535) Pretender to the throne, the son of a joiner. Exploited by Roger Simon, a priest from Oxford, because of his resemblance to Edward IV, he was coached to impersonate one of his sons imprisoned in the Tower. He was set up in Ireland in 1487 as, first, a son of Edward IV, and then as the Duke of Clarence's son, Edward, Earl of Warwick (1475–99). He had some success among Yorkist adherents, and was crowned at Dublin as Edward VI, but after landing in Lancashire with 2000 German mercenaries he was defeated at Stoke Field, Nottinghamshire. After imprisonment, he was supposedly employed in the royal kitchens.

Simon, Claude (Eugène Henri) [seemõ] (1913–) Novelist, born in Tananarive, C Madagascar. He was educated at Paris, Oxford, and Cambridge universities, fought in World War 2, and later earned a living producing wine at Salses. His novels include *Le Vent* (1957, The Wind), *L'Herbe* (1958, The Grass), and – part of a four-volume cycle – *La Route des Flandres* (1960, The Flanders Road). He received the Nobel Prize for Literature in 1985.

Simon, Herbert (Alexander) (1916–2001) Economist, born in Milwaukee, Wisconsin, USA. He studied at the University of Chicago, then held chairs at Illinois Institute of Technology (1946–9) and Carnegie–Mellon University (from 1949). A man of wide talents, who wrote on psychology and computers as well as on economics and political science, he was awarded the Nobel Prize for Economics in 1978. His pioneering study, *Administrative Behavior* (1947), rejects the conventional theory of the firm as an omnisciently rational profit-maximizing entrepreneur, and asserts that decision-makers must be content with a satisfactory alternative.

Simon (of Stackpole Elidor), John (Allsebrook) Simon, 1st Viscount (1873–1954) British statesman and lawyer, born in Manchester, Greater Manchester, NW England, UK. He studied at Edinburgh and Oxford, entered parliament in 1906, and was knighted in 1910. He was attorney general (1913–15) and home secretary (1915–16), before resigning from the cabinet for his opposition to conscription. Deserting the Liberals to form the Liberal National Party, he supported MacDonald's coalition governments and became foreign secretary (1931–5), home secretary in the Conservative government (1935–7), Chancellor of the Exchequer (1937–40), and Lord Chancellor in Churchill's wartime coalition (1940–5). He was created a viscount in 1940.

Simon, (Marvin) Neil (1927–) Playwright, born in New York City, USA. His prolific career began with revue sketches written with his brother. His first Broadway Show, *Catch a Star!*, opened in 1955, and a series of long-running successes followed in the 1960s, including *Barefoot in the Park* (1963) and *The Odd Couple* (1965). His later work includes *The Sunshine Boys* (1972), *California Suite* (1976), *Biloxi Blues* (1985, Tony), *Rumors: a Farce* (1990), *Lost in Yonkers* (1991, Pulitzer, Tony), *London Suite* (1995), and *Rewrites: a Memoir* (1996). He has also written the film scripts for several of his stage plays.

Simon, Paul (1941–) Singer, songwriter, and guitarist, born in Newark, New Jersey, USA. He teamed up with Art Garfunkel at the age of 15 when they were known as Tom and Jerry, but he also pursued a solo career, under various pseudonyms, before 'The Sound Of Silence' (1965) brought them their first major success as a duo, Simon and Garfunkel. In 1968 the film *The Graduate* became one of the first major films to use rock music in its soundtrack, using songs written by Simon (notably, 'Mrs Robinson', which became a hit), and they had a major success with the album *Bridge Over Troubled Water* (1970). After splitting from Garfunkel, he returned to a solo career, releasing his album *Paul Simon* in 1972. *Graceland* (1986), which featured the work of several African musicians, was one of the most successful albums of the 1980s. There have been occasional reunion concerts with Garfunkel. Simon's musical *The Capeman* was an expensive flop on Broadway in 1998. An album, *You're the One*, appeared in 2000, and he was inducted into the Rock and Roll Hall of Fame in 2001.

Simond, Paul Louis [seemõ] (1858–1947) Bacteriologist, born in Beaufort-sur-Gervanne, Drôme, France. He studied medicine at Bordeaux, and later joined the Pasteur Institute in Paris (1895–7) where he worked with Yersin, discoverer of the plague bacillus (1894). Simond's subsequent work showed that plague is primarily a disease of rats spread by rat fleas which transmit the disease to humans.

Simone, Nina [simohn], stage name of **Eunice Kathleen Waymon** (1933–2003) Jazz singer, pianist, and songwriter, born in Tryon, North Carolina, USA. She moved to Philadelphia at 17, and supported herself teaching piano and accompanying singers. Her first record (1958) included two hits, a melodramatic 'I Loves You Porgy', and a lilting 'My Baby Just Cares for Me'. She used her smoky contralto voice to great dramatic effect singing protest songs in the 1960s, and she could turn concert audiences into clenched-fist activists with 'Mississippi Goddam', a tough song about racism. She also sought out poetic songs for her repertoire, and set poetry to music, memorably with African-American poets in 'Compensation' by Paul Laurence Dunbar and 'Backlash Blues', and 'Young, Gifted and Black' by Langston Hughes. She was arrested (1978) for withholding taxes in 1971–3 in protest at her government's undeclared war in Vietnam.

Simon Magus [maygus], Eng **Simon the Magician** (1st-c) Practitioner of magic arts, who appears in Samaria c.37, well known for his sorceries. With Peter's condemnation of his offer to buy the gift of the Holy Ghost, and Simon's submission, the narrative of *Acts* (8.9–24) leaves him. Later Christian authors bring him to Rome and make him the author of heresies. The term *simony* derives from his name.

Simon Peter *Peter, St*

simony [simonee] The practice of giving or acquiring some sacred object, spiritual gift, or religious office for money, or carrying on a trade in such matters. The practice was most notorious in the mediaeval trade in indulgences.

simple harmonic motion A periodic motion in which the restoring influence acting towards the rest position is proportional to the displacement from rest, as in a pendulum undergoing small swings. Simple harmonic motion is much easier to analyze than general periodic motion; the latter can be broken down into simple harmonic components.

Simplon Pass, Ital **Passa del Sempione** Mountain pass between Brig, Switzerland, and Domodossola, Italy, over the S Bernese Alps; height, 2006 m/6581 ft; built on the orders of Napoleon, 1801–5; opening of the rail tunnel (20 km/12 mi) in 1906 has made the road route less important.

Simpson, Sir James Young (1811–70) Obstetrician, born in Bathgate, West Lothian, EC Scotland, UK. He trained in Edinburgh, where he became professor of midwifery in 1840. He introduced chloroform as an anaesthetic (1847), and was the first to use it as an anaesthetic in labour. He was created a baronet in 1866.

Simpson, N(orman) F(rederick) (1919–) Playwright, born in London, UK. He worked in a bank and served in the Intelligence Corps in World War 2 before becoming an adult education lecturer. The success of *A Resounding Tinkle*, a zany disruption of middle-class normality, in a competition organized by *The*

Observer in 1957 brought him to prominence. His absurdist approach is also seen in *One-Way Pendulum* (1959). Written during the brief popularity of the Theatre of the Absurd in Britain, his work belongs to a comic tradition illustrated by *The Goon Show* and *Monty Python*.

Simpson, O(renthal) J(ames) (1947–) Player of American football, born in San Francisco, California, USA. He joined the Buffalo Bills in 1968, and led the League as top rusher four times (1972–6). He rushed for a record 2002 yards in 1973, and in 1975 had a then record 23 touchdowns in one season. He became a successful broadcaster, and there was widespread shock in the USA when in 1994 he was arrested on a charge of murdering his ex-wife and her male friend. His court case achieved unprecedented media publicity in 1995, the jury acquitting him later that year. In 1997 a civil trial jury found him responsible for the murders and damages were awarded against him.

Simpson, Thomas (1710–61) Mathematician, born in Nuneaton, Warwickshire, C England, UK. He became professor of mathematics at Woolwich (1743), and published a long series of works (1737–57) on algebra, trigonometry, chance, and other topics.

Simpson Desert Desert in SE Northern Territory and SW Queensland, C Australia; mostly scrubland and sand dunes; area c.77 000 sq km/30 000 sq mi; first crossed in 1939 by Cecil Madigan; Queensland region contains a national park (c.5550 sq km/2150 sq mi).

simulator A mechanical, electromechanical, or computer device for producing a realistic representation of an event or system. It is used where the real thing is very expensive and inaccessible, and to train operators (eg aircraft pilots) in safety. In an aircraft simulator, the visual and movement responses that a pilot would experience in flight are reproduced by computer graphics and mechanical movement of the simulated flight deck. Computers are also used to simulate complex phenomena where there are many variables, such as in atmospheric circulation studies.

simultaneity *special relativity*

simultaneous linear equations Two or more equations that are true at the same time. Two simultaneous equations in two unknowns, such as $x + y = 5$, $x - y = 3$, in general have one pair of solutions, here $x = 4$, $y = 1$. However, they may have an infinite number of solutions, such as $x + 2y = 3$ and $2x + 4y = 6$, which are satisfied by all numbers of the form $x = k$, $y = \frac{1}{2}(3 - k)$. They may also have no solutions, as with $x + 2y = 4$ and $x + 2y = 5$. Similarly, n equations in n unknowns may have one unique set of solutions, no solutions, or an infinite number of solutions.

sin A religious term signifying purposeful disobedience to the known will of God or an action offensive to God. It is a factor in many religions, though it is represented in a wide variety of ways. The Hebrew Bible represents sin as a constant element in the experience of Israel. There is an emphasis upon human responsibility for sin, and this is carried over into Christian doctrine, where it is joined with the idea of the inevitability of sin in the concept of **original sin**. Islam identifies two types of sin: inadvertent or accidental sins and wilful transgressions. Unlike Christianity, Islam does not have a concept of original sin.

Sinai [siyniy] pop (2000e) 246 300; area 60 174 sq km/23 227 sq mi. Desert peninsula and governorate in NE Egypt; bounded by Israel and Gulf of Aqaba (E) and Egypt and Gulf of Suez (W); N coastal plain rises S to mountains reaching 2637 m/8651 ft at Mt Catherine, Egypt's highest point, and Mt Sinai, 2286 m/7500 ft; capital, al-Arish; oil, manganese; some livestock and agriculture in irrigated areas; a battlefield since ancient times; taken by Israel, 1967; returned to Egypt following the peace agreement, 1984; tourist resorts in S include Sharm el-Sheikh, Dahab, Ras Muhammad, Nuweiba.

Sinai, Mount [siyniy] Mountain of uncertain location, traditionally placed among the granite mountains of the S Sinai peninsula, but sometimes located in Arabia E of the Gulf of Aqaba; also called **Horeb** in the Hebrew Bible. According to the Book of Exodus, this is where God revealed himself to Moses, and made a covenant with Israel by giving Moses the Ten Commandments on tablets of stone.

Sinanthropus [sinanthropus] *Zhoukoudian*

Sinatra, Frank, popular name of **Francis Albert Sinatra** (1915–98) Singer and film actor, born in Hoboken, New Jersey, USA. Now widely recognized as one of the greatest singers of popular songs, he became known in the 1940s. With the Tommy Dorsey orchestra (1940–2) his hit records included 'I'll Never Smile Again' and 'Without A Song', and he starred on radio and in movies, most notably *Anchors Aweigh* (1945). Then his appeal diminished. He was all but forgotten by 1953, when his memorable acting in the movie *From Here to Eternity* won an Oscar and revived his career. Several choice roles in films followed, such as *High Society* (1956) and *The Manchurian Candidate* (1962), and his revival as an actor led to new opportunities as a singer. He produced his masterworks in a series of recordings (1956–65), especially the albums *Songs for Swinging Lovers* (1956), *Come Fly With Me* (1959), and the recordings 'That's Life' (1966), and 'My Way' (1969). His personal life always proved noteworthy, with turbulent marriages to Ava Gardner and Mia Farrow, among others, and alleged Mafia connections.

Sinclair, Upton (Beall) (1878–1968) Novelist and social reformer, born in Baltimore, Maryland, USA. He studied at New York and Columbia universities, and became a journalist. He horrified the world with his exposure of meat-packing conditions in Chicago in his novel *The Jungle* (1906). Later novels such as *Metropolis* (1908), *Oil!* (1927), and *Boston* (1928) were increasingly moulded by his socialist beliefs. For many years prominent in Californian politics, he attempted to found a communistic community in Englewood, NJ (1907). He also wrote a monumental 11-volume series about 'Lanny Budd', starting with *World's End* (1940) and including *Dragon's Teeth* (1942, Pulitzer).

Sind pop (2000e) 31 112 000; area 140 914 sq km/54 393 sq mi. Province in SE Pakistan; bounded E and S by India and SW by the Arabian Sea; capital, Karachi; fertile, low-lying and generally flat land dissected by the R Indus; invaded by Alexander the Great, 325 BC; arrival of Islam, 8th-c; part of the Chandragupta Ganges Empire and the Delhi Empire; under British rule, 1843; autonomous province, 1937; province of Pakistan, 1947; agricultural economy; rice, cotton, barley, oilseed; irrigation from the Sukkur Barrage (N).

sinfonietta An orchestral piece, usually in several movements but on a smaller scale, and normally for smaller forces, than a symphony; a well-known example is Janáček's *Sinfonietta* (1926). The term is also used for a chamber orchestra, such as the London Sinfonietta (founded 1968).

Singapore *p.1413*

Singapore City 1°20N 103°50E. Seaport capital of Singapore, on SE coast of Singapore I; one of the world's busiest ports; third largest oil refining centre; distribution base for many international companies; first container port in SE Asia, 1972; airport; railway; two universities (1953, 1964); Tiger Balm Gardens, St Andrew's Cathedral, Sultan Mosque, Monkey God Temple, Poh Toh Temple, Siang Lin-Si Temple, House of Jade, national museum, botanical gardens.

Singer, Isaac Bashevis (1904–91) Yiddish writer, born in Radzymin, E Poland (then part of tsarist Russia). He studied in Warsaw, emigrating to the USA in 1935, where he worked as a journalist for the *Jewish Daily Forward*. He became a US citizen in 1943. He set his novels and short stories among the Jews of Poland, Germany, and America, combining a deep psychological insight with dramatic and visual impact. His novels include *The Family Moskat* (1950), *The Manor* (1967), *The Estate* (1970), and *Enemies: a Love Story* (1972), and he also wrote short stories and stories for children. He was awarded the Nobel Prize for Literature in 1978.

Singer, Isaac M(erritt) (1811–75) Inventor and manufacturer of sewing machines, born in Pittstown, New York, USA. He patented a rock drill in 1839, a carving machine in 1849, and at Boston in 1852 an improved single-thread, chain-stitch

Singapore

☐ International Airport

official name **Republic of Singapore**

Local name Singapore

Timezone GMT +8

Area 618 km²/238 sq mi

Population total (2002e) 4 000 000

Status Republic

Date of independence 1965

Capital Singapore City

Languages English, Malay, Chinese, and Tamil (official)

Ethnic groups Chinese (77%), Malay (15%), Indian (6%)

Religions Chinese population mainly Buddhists, Malay mainly Muslim, also Taoist, Christian, and Hindu minorities

Physical features Located at the S tip of the Malay Peninsula, SE Asia; consists of the island of Singapore and c.50 adjacent islets; linked to Malaysia by a causeway across the Johor Strait; Singapore Island is low-lying, rising to 177 m/581 ft at Bukit Timah; Selatar River drains N-E; deep-water harbour (SE).

Climate Equatorial climate; high humidity; no clearly defined seasons; average annual temperature range, 21–34°C; average annual rainfall, 2438 mm/96 in.

Currency 1 Singapore Dollar/Ringgit (S$) = 100 cents

Economy Major transshipment centre (one of world's largest ports); oil refining; rubber, food processing, chemicals, electronics; ship repair; financial services; fishing; tourism (affected by the SARS outbreak, 2003).

GDP (2002e) $112·4 bn, per capita $25 200

Human Development Index (2002) 0·885

History Originally part of the Sumatran Srivijaya kingdom; leased by the British East India Company, on the advice of Sir Stamford Raffles, from the Sultan of Johore, 1819; Singapore, Malacca, and Penang incorporated as the Straits Settlements, 1826; British Crown Colony, 1867; occupied by the Japanese, 1942–5; self-government, 1959; part of the Federation of Malaya from 1963 until its establishment as an independent state in 1965; governed by a President, a Prime Minister, and a unicameral Parliament.

Head of State
1959–70 Yusof bin Ishak
1970–81 Benjamin Henry Sheares
1981–5 Chengara Veetil Devan Nair
1985–93 Wee Kim Wee
1993–9 Ong Teng Cheong
1999– Sellapan Ramanathan Nathan

Head of Government
1959–90 Lee Kuan Yew
1990– Goh Chok Tong

sewing machine, incorporating some features of Elias Howe's machine. His company quickly became the largest producer of sewing machines in the world.

Singer, Peter (Albert David) (1946–) Philosopher, born in Melbourne, Victoria, SE Australia. He was educated at the universities of Melbourne and Oxford, then taught at New York University before becoming professor of philosophy at Monash University in 1977, where he is associated with the Centre for Human Bioethics. His writing focuses on ethics, particularly in relation to animals and the environment. Also known also as a political activist, his best known works, *Animal Liberation* (1977) and *Practical Ethics* (1979), were still exercising influence in the 1990s.

singing One of the oldest of human activities, which, in the sense of inflected pitch, may well have preceded speech as a form of human communication. In Western art music, it has usually been allied to words (especially poetry), but this is by no means the case in many ethnic communities, or even in some Western folk traditions (eg Irish keening). The training of choirs was important in the mediaeval and Renaissance church, but it was with the development of opera in the 17th-c that the highly trained solo singer, especially the soprano and the castrato, came into prominence. Singing treatises of the period tend to concern themselves with matters of notation and vocal embellishments, and it was not until the 19th-c that teachers began to set down methods of voice production. The 20th-c witnessed a reaction against a too scientific and 'cultured' approach to vocal training, and a return to more natural methods of voice production.

single-cell proteins *novel proteins*

Single European Market A market created by the removal of internal trade barriers within the European Community during the 1980s. The Single European Act was introduced in 1985 to help speed up the process of implementing a single European market. The European Parliament was given greater voice and influence, and member states agreed to adopt common policies and standards on matters ranging from taxation and employment to health and the environment. In addition, the Court of First Instance was established to hear appeals on European Community rulings brought by individuals, organizations, or corporations, and each member state undertook to bring its economic and monetary policies in line with its neighbours, using the European Monetary System as a model.

Single Integrated Operational Plan *SIOP*

single lens reflex (SLR) A popular and versatile design of camera, with a surface-silvered mirror behind the lens angled at 45° to reflect the image onto a focusing screen. The camera lens is used both for the viewfinder system and for taking the photograph. Focusing is precise, and framing is free from parallax, so that 'what you see is what you get' in the picture. The spring-loaded mirror lifts out of the way before exposure. Most cameras have an 'instant return' mirror feature in that the mirror drops back after exposure, giving a brief interruption of viewing. The screen image is reversed left to right, but this is corrected by a pentaprism so the viewfinder image is seen as correct. The lens is kept at full aperture to assist viewing and focusing, and the iris diaphragm closes down its preset value as the mirror rises, to give the correct exposure, and re-opens afterwards.

Singspiel [zingshpeel] A German opera with spoken dialogue. Mozart's *Die Zauberflöte* (The Magic Flute) is a famous example.

Sinhalese [singgaleez] The dominant ethnic group (74%) of Sri Lanka, descended from N Indians who came to the area in the 5th-c BC. Predominantly Buddhist, they have an occupational caste system.

Sining *Xining*

Sinitic languages *Chinese*

Sinn Féin [shin fayn] (Gaelic 'Ourselves Alone') An Irish political party founded in 1900 by Arthur Griffith in support of Irish independence from Britain. By the end of World War 1 it had become the main Irish nationalist party. It formed a separate assembly from the UK parliament, and succeeded in creating the Irish Free State (1922). Following the Anglo-Irish Treaty, it split to form the two main Irish parties, and in 1970 it split again into official and provisional wings. It has remained active in Northern Ireland, and has close contacts with the Irish Republican Army. Sinn Féin obtained a high profile for its role in relation to the IRA ceasefire (1994), but conflict with the UK government over its attitude to the resumption of the IRA campaign (1996) led to its being excluded from all-party talks on the future of Northern Ireland that year. The party was eventually invited to join the talks following the resumption of the IRA ceasefire (1997), and in 1999 took its place in the Northern Ireland Assembly, with Seamus Mallon as the Catholic deputy leader of the new government.

Sino–Japanese War **1** (1894–5) A longstanding conflict between Chinese and Japanese interests in Korea, which resulted in war during the late Qing period. China suffered a humiliating defeat, and by the Treaty of Shimonoseki (1895) recognized Korean independence and ceded Taiwan, the Liaodong Peninsula, and the Pescadores to Japan.
2 (1937–45) The Sino–Japanese War proper broke out in 1937 with the Japanese invasion of Tianjin and Beijing, but this was only the ultimate phase of Japan's territorial designs on China. Manchuria had already been occupied and a puppet state created in 1932. Nanjing was invaded in December 1937, and most of N China was soon under Japanese control. There was an invasion force of 1·2 million, up to 6 million Chinese military casualties by 1941, 4 million civilian casualties, and 40 million refugees. Jiang Jieshi moved his capital to Chongqing in W China, and some resistance continued with Western assistance. From December 1941, US intervention became the major factor in the Pacific War, which ended with Japan's surrender in 1945.

Sinope [siynohpee] The outermost natural satellite of Jupiter, discovered in 1914; distance from the planet 23 700 000 km/ 14 727 000 mi; orbital period 758 days; diameter 36 km/22 mi.

sinopia [seenohpia] (Ital 'red ochre') A term used not only for the reddish-brown pigment itself, but also for the underdrawings made by fresco painters using this substance. Modern conservation has brought to light the hidden *sinopie* underneath many Renaissance frescoes.

Sino–Tibetan languages A family of languages spoken in China, Tibet, and Myanmar (Burma). Alongside their similarities with each other, they display similarities with other neighbouring language groups, so their classification is tentative. There are some 300 languages in the family, the main ones being Tibetan, Burmese, and the eight major varieties of Chinese.

sintering One of the techniques of powder metallurgy. Metal parts are made by forming a shape in metal powder and then holding it for several hours just below the melting point of the metal, or (if an alloy) at that of the higher melting component. It is an economical process for making small parts, and is necessary for metal which has so high a melting point that it cannot easily be cast. It can produce porous structures, advantageous in lubrication.

Sintra [seentra], formerly **Cintra** 38°48N 9°22W, pop (2000e) 20 600. Small resort town in Lisbon district, C Portugal, 10 km/ 6 mi N of Estoril; former summer residence of the Portuguese royal family; railway; agricultural centre, tourism; National Palace (14th–15th-c), Moorish castle, Pena palace; São Pedro fair (Jun).

sinus [siynuhs] In anatomy, a space within the head or elsewhere in the body. The air-filled **paranasal sinuses** all communicate with the nasal cavity, at the front of the face, and are lined with respiratory epithelium. Their purpose is to lighten the skull and also act as resonance chambers in the production of sounds. (A change in the quality of the voice during a cold results from these sinuses becoming infected, and filling with fluid, thus affecting their resonating properties.) The blood-filled **intracranial sinuses** are generally found between the layers of the outer membrane which surrounds the brain (the *dura mater*), and drain venous blood from the brain to the internal jugular vein. The term *sinus* is also used in pathology to refer to an abnormal, blind-ended opening on an epithelial surface.

sinusitis [siynyusiytis] Infection of the lining of one or more sinuses around the nose and in the bones of the face, which sometimes arises from infection of the upper respiratory passages (eg common cold). It results in severe pain over the sinus, headache, and fever.

Sion (Jerusalem) [ziyon] *Zion*

Sion (Switzerland) [syõ], Ger **Sitten** 46°14N 7°22E, pop (2000e) 26 500. Capital town of Valais canton, SW Switzerland, 80 km/ 50 mi S of Bern; bishopric since the 6th-c; railway; market town for wine, fruit, and vegetables of the Rhône valley; brewing; former cathedral (10th–13th-c), 17th-c town hall, Church of Notre-Dame (12th–13th-c), bishop's fortress (1294); Internal Music Festival (Jul–Aug).

SIOP Abbreviation of **Single Integrated Operational Plan**, the all-embracing military plan, the subject of continual updating according to policy, for the deployment and use of US nuclear forces.

Sioux [soo] or **Dakota** A cluster of Siouan-speaking North American Indian groups belonging to the Plains Indian culture. Having moved from further N into present-day N and S Dakota, they acquired horses, fought wars against other Indian groups, and hunted the buffalo. They were later involved in clashes with advancing white settlers and prospectors, and were finally defeated at Wounded Knee (1890). They now number c.108 000 (2000 census), living mostly on reservations.

Sioux Falls [soo] 43°33N 96°44W, pop (2000e) 154 000. Seat of Minnehaha Co, SE South Dakota, USA, on Big Sioux R; largest city in the state; established, 1857; city status, 1883; airfield; railway; industrial and commercial centre in a livestock farming region; meat processing; sandstone quarries.

siphon / syphon A means of transferring liquid from one level to a lower level, relying on a liquid-filled tube, the siphon, that first raises the liquid from the upper level before depositing it in the lower level. Liquid moves through the tube under the influence of gravity at a rate proportional to the difference in levels.

Siphonaptera [siyfonaptera] *flea*

Sipuncula [sipunkyula] *peanut worm*

Siqueiros, David Alfaro [sikayros] (1896–1974) Mural painter, born in Chihuahua, N Mexico. He helped to launch the review *El Machete* in Mexico City in 1922, and was imprisoned for revolutionary activities (1930). He was later expelled from the USA, and during the 1930s worked in South America. One of the principal figures in 20th-c Mexican mural painting, he was notable for his experiments with modern synthetic materials.

Siraj-ud-Daula [siraj ud dowla], originally **Mirza Muhammad** (c.1732–57) Ruler of Bengal under the nominal suzerainty of the Mughal empire. He came into conflict with the British over their fortification of Calcutta, and marched on the city in 1756. The British surrender led to the infamous Black Hole, for which he was held responsible. Following the recapture of Calcutta, the British under Clive joined forces with his general, Mir Jafar, and defeated him at Plassey in 1757. He fled to Murshidabad, but was captured and executed.

siren A salamander native to SE North America; dark, eel-like body; length, up to 90 cm/36 in; no hind legs; tiny front legs; feathery gills; spends life in muddy pools; burrows in mud during drought; covering of slime becomes dry and paper-like; can rest like this for two months. (Family: Sirenidae, 3 species.)

Sirens In Greek mythology, deceitful creatures, half-woman and half-bird, who lured sailors to death by their singing. Odysseus was able to sail past their rocky island by stopping the ears of his crew with wax; and by having himself bound to the mast, was restrained when he heard their song. In later legends they drown themselves after this defeat.

si-rex [siyreks] *rex*

Sirhan, (Bishara) Sirhan [sirhahn] (c.1943–) Assassin of Senator Robert Kennedy, born in Palestine. He was a refugee whose family settled in Pasadena, CA, in 1956, having fled from Israeli bombings in Beirut. When Robert Kennedy, who was running for the presidential nomination in 1968, took an overtly pro-Israeli stance in order to gain Jewish votes, Sirhan was enraged and shot him. At his trial, he said that Kennedy's repeated promises of arms for Israel 'burned him up'. He was found guilty of premeditated murder of the first degree, and the death penalty was recommended. Senator Edward Kennedy's plea for lenience led to this sentence being commuted to life imprisonment.

Sirius [sirius] The brightest star in our sky, and ninth nearest, at 2·6 parsec; also known as the **dog star**. It has a faint companion star, which was the first white dwarf star to be recognized as such.

Sirocco / Scirocco [sirokoh] A wind similar to the Khamsin in origin, blowing from the Sahara Desert. As it crosses the Mediterranean Sea it picks up moisture, and arrives in S Europe as a moist, oppressive, warm wind.

Sirte, Gulf of [seertay], Arabic **Khalij Surt** Gulf in the Mediterranean Sea off the coast of N Libya, between Misratah (W) and Benghazi (E); access to the Gulf waters is an area of dispute between Libya and the USA.

siskin A finch, found worldwide; eats seeds and insects. (Genus: *Carduelis*, 16 species, or *Serinus*, 2 species. Family: Fringillidae.)

Sisley, Alfred [seeslay] (1839–99) Impressionist painter and etcher, born in Paris, France, of English ancestry. After training in Paris, he painted landscapes almost exclusively, particularly in the valleys of the Seine, Loire, and Thames, and was noted for his subtle treatment of skies. His works began to sell only after his death.

Sistine Chapel [sisteen] A chapel in the Vatican, built in 1475–81 for Pope Sixtus IV. It is remarkable for a series of frescoes executed on its ceiling and altar wall by Michelangelo. It is the scene of papal elections and the home of the Sistine Choir.

Sisyphus [sisifus] In Greek mythology, a Corinthian king who was a famous trickster; in one story he catches and binds Thanatos (Death). In the Underworld he was condemned to roll a large stone up a hill from which it always rolled down again.

sitar [sitah(r)] A large Indian lute, with a gourd resonator and a long fretted neck. It originated in Persia in the Middle Ages. The modern concert sitar, used in Indian classical music, is about 122 cm/4 ft long, with usually seven strings plucked with a wire plectrum. In addition, about 12 sympathetic strings vibrate freely when the main strings are sounded.

sitatunga [sitatungga] A spiral-horned antelope (*Tragelaphus spekei*) native to Africa S of the Sahara; shaggy, slightly oily coat; brown with small white patches and lines; hooves long and splayed; inhabits wet areas; swims well; may hide under water with only nostrils showing.

Sites of Special Scientific Interest (SSSIs) Areas designated by English Nature for the purposes of conservation, including some of the UK's best examples of particular wildlife habitats, interesting geological or physiographical features, and habitats for rare plants and animals. In return for compensation, management agreements may be made between English Nature and site landowners to protect them. Nevertheless, many have been lost or damaged. In 2004 there were over 4000 such sites in England (c.7% of the land), and over 1000 in Wales (c.11% of the land).

Sitka National park on W Baranof I, SE Alaska, USA; Indian stockade, totem poles, Russian blockhouse; established, 1910; scene of last stand of Tlingit Indians against the Russians, 1804; town and naval base of Sitka nearby.

Sitting Bull, Sioux name **Tatanka Iyotake** (1834–90) Warrior and chief of the Dakota Sioux, born near Grand River, South Dakota, USA. He was a leader in the Sioux War (1876–7), and led the defeat of Custer and his men at the Little Bighorn (1876). He escaped to Canada, but surrendered in 1881. After touring with Buffalo Bill's Wild West Show, he returned to his people, and was present in 1890 when the army suppressed the 'ghost dance' messianic religious movement. He was killed during the army's action.

Sitwell, Dame Edith (Louisa) (1887–1964) Poet and critic, born in Scarborough, North Yorkshire, N England, UK, the sister of Osbert and Sacheverell Sitwell. She first attracted notice through editing an annual anthology of new poetry, *Wheels* (1916–21), which encouraged Modernist writers, notably Pound and T S Eliot, as well as Wilfred Owen. Her recital of some of her own poems under the title *Façade* (1922), to music by William Walton, was given a stormy public reception in London on account of its lack of any clear meaning. She became a Catholic in 1955, after which her works reflect a deeper religious symbolism, as in *The Outcasts* (1962). She was created a dame in 1954. Her autobiography, *Taken Care Of*, was published posthumously in 1965.

Sitwell, Sir (Francis) Osbert (Sacheverell) (1892–1969) Writer, born in London, UK, the brother of Edith and Sacheverell Sitwell. He was educated at Eton, served in World War 1, began writing poetry, and acquired notoriety with his satirical novel of the Scarborough social scene, *Before the Bombardment* (1927). He is best known for his five-volume autobiographical series, beginning with *Left Hand: Right Hand* (1944). Other collections of essays include *Penny Foolish* (1935) and *Pound Wise* (1963). He became a baronet in 1942.

Sitwell, Sir Sacheverell [sasheverel] (1897–1988) Poet and art critic, born in Scarborough, North Yorkshire, N England, UK, the brother of Edith and Osbert Sitwell. He was educated at Eton, served in the army, then travelled in Spain and Italy, where he began to write books on art and architecture, such as *Southern Baroque Art* (1924). His many volumes of poetry cover a period of over 30 years, from *The People's Palace* (1918) to *An Indian Summer* (1982). He became a baronet on the death of his brother, Osbert, in 1969.

SI units *units* (scientific)

Six, Les [lay sees] A group of composers united for about six years after 1917 to further the cause of modern French music. It comprised Georges Auric, Louis Durey, Arthur Honegger, Darius Milhaud, Francis Poulenc, and Germaine Tailleferre (1892–1983).

Six Day War *Arab–Israeli Wars*

sixth-form college A college in the UK for pupils over the age of 16 and up to 18 or 19, which often takes pupils from feeder schools catering for 11- to 16-year-olds. It specializes in A-level work, but other forms of examination and qualification may also be offered.

Sizewell Nuclear power station in Suffolk, E England; gas-cooled, graphite-moderated reactors came into operation in 1966; site of the first UK pressurized light-water-moderated and cooled reactor (**Sizewell B**).

Sjælland [shelahn] area 7500 sq km/2900 sq mi. Group of islands in Danish territorial waters, between Jutland and S Sweden; includes Zealand (Sjælland), on which Copenhagen is located, Møn, Samsø, Amager, and Saltholm.

ska The Jamaican popular music of the early 1960s, drawing on American rhythm and blues and 'jump' music, and Jamaica's own 'mento', a form of calypso. Ska records were first produced by such sound-system operators as Clement 'Sir Coxone' Dodd and Duke Reid, and featured artists including Alton Ellis, Delroy Wilson, and Prince Buster and the Skatalites. Ska with a slower beat became 'rocksteady' in the later 1960s. A UK ska revival in the 1970s was driven by 'two-tone' bands such as the Specials (or the Special AKA), Madness, and Bad Manners.

Skagerrak [skagerak] Arm of the Atlantic Ocean linking the North Sea with the Baltic Sea by way of the Kattegat; bounded (N) by Norway and (S) by Denmark; main arm, Oslo Fjord; 240 km/150 mi long and 135 km/84 mi wide.

skaldic poetry (Old Norse *skaldr* 'poet') Poetry composed and recited by recognized individuals in Iceland and the Scandinavian countries between 800 and 1100. After this time, written versions made the *skaldr* redundant. Its complex verse-forms, diction, and imagery are described by Snorri Sturluson in the *Prose Edda*.

Skalkottas, Nikos or **Nikolaus** [skalkotas] (1904–49) Composer, born in Khalkis, Greece. He studied at the Athens Conservatory and in Berlin, where he was a pupil of Weill and Schoenberg, then earned his living as an orchestral violinist in Athens. His works, dating mostly from the period 1935–45, show a complex use of serial techniques, and exploit Greek and Balkan folk elements, but were not much performed until after his death.

Skanda [skahnda] The Hindu god of War, the 'Attacker'. He is also responsible for the demons who bring diseases.

Skanderbeg [skanderbek], nickname of **George Castriota** or **Kastrioti** (1405–68) Albanian patriot, the son of a prince of Emathia. Carried away by Ottoman Turks at the age of seven, he was brought up a Muslim, and became a favourite commander of Sultan Murad II (ruled 1421–51), who gave him his nickname, a combination of *Iskander* ('Alexander') and the rank of Bey. In 1443 he changed sides, renounced Islam, and drove the Turks from Albania. For 20 years he maintained Albanian independence, but after his death opposition to the Turks collapsed.

Skara Brae [skahra bray] An exceptionally preserved Neolithic village of c.3100–2500 BC on the Bay of Skaill, Orkney, NE Scotland, UK, exposed below sand dunes by storms in 1850. It supported a population of c.30–40, and comprises a tight cluster of nine squarish stone huts, turf-roofed, and with alleys between, furnished internally with stone-slabbed dressers, cupboards, box beds, hearths, water tanks, and latrines. A world heritage site.

skate Any of several bottom-living rays of the family Rajidae; includes the large European species, *Raja batis*, found in deeper offshore waters from the Arctic to the Mediterranean; length up to 2·5 m/8 ft; upper surface greenish-brown with lighter patches; fished commercially along with other species such as the smaller thornback ray *Raja clavata*, length up to 85 cm/34 in.

skateboarding Riding on land on a single flexible board, longer and wider than the foot, fixed with four small wheels on the underside. It is possible to achieve speeds of over 100 kph/60 mph. It developed as an alternative to surfing, and became very popular in the USA during the 1960s and in the UK during the 1970s and late 1980s.

skating *ice hockey; ice skating; roller skating*

Skegness [skegnes] 53°10N 0°21E, pop (2000e) 19 000. Resort town in E Lincolnshire, EC England, UK; on the North Sea coast, 30 km/19 mi NE of Boston; railway; engineering, tourism; bird reserve just S of the town.

skeleton *see panel*

Skeleton Coast area 16 390 sq km/6326 sq mi. National park in NW Namibia; established in 1971; runs along the Atlantic Ocean coast between Walvis Bay and the Angolan frontier.

Skelton, John (c.1460–1529) Satirical poet, born in Norfolk, E England, UK. He studied at Oxford and Cambridge universities, was tutor to Prince Henry (the future Henry VIII), took holy orders in 1498, and became rector of Diss in 1502, but seems to have been suspended in 1511 for having a concubine or wife. He had produced some translations and elegies in 1489, but began

skeleton

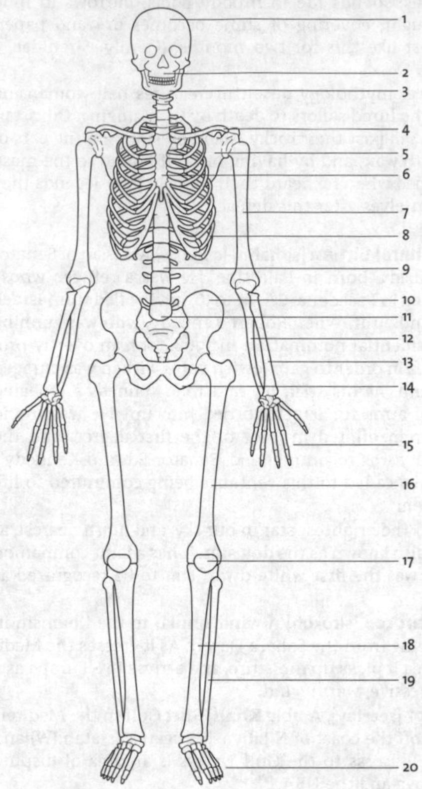

1 skull, displaying the frontal bone, and the front parts of the parietal and temporal bones.
2 maxilla
3 mandible
4 clavicle
5 scapula (obscured in this view by the upper ribs).
6 sternum
7 humerus
8 ribs
9 vertebral column, displaying (from above to below) cervical, thoracic, lumber, sacral and coccygeal vertebrae.
10 illium
11 sacrum
12 ulna
13 radius
14 coccyx
15 bones of the hand, comprising the eight carpels, the five metacarpels, the three phalanges in each finger, and the two phalanges in the thumb.
16 femur
17 patella
18 tibia
19 fibula
20 bones of the foot, comprising the seven tarsals, the five metatarsals, the two phalanges in the big toe, and the three phalanges in the other toes.

The hardened tissues forming the supporting framework of plants and animals. In vertebrates it usually refers to the assembly and arrangement of bones. The **appendicular skeleton** comprises the bones of the limbs and the pelvic and pectoral girdles, while the **axial skeleton** comprises the bones of the vertebral column, skull, ribs, and sternum. A total of 208 bones are usually recognized in the skeleton: skull (22), ears (6), vertebrae (26), vertebral ribs (24), sternum (3), throat (1), pectoral girdle (4), arms (60), hips (2), legs (60). Medical problems affecting the skeleton include fracture, osteoarthritis, Paget's disease, and scoliosis.

to write satirical vernacular poetry, overflowing with grotesque words and images and unrestrained joviality, as in *The Bowge of Courte* (c.1499), *Colyn Cloute* (1522), and *Why come ye nat to courte* (1522). His favourite metre, with short lines based on the rhythms of natural speech and quick, recurring rhymes, is known as *skeltonic*.

skepticism *scepticism*

sketch In art, a term with two meanings: **1** A rough preliminary drawing in which the artist tries out his ideas.
2 A drawing (in any medium, including paint) of a deliberately spontaneous and 'unfinished' appearance, but considered as an end in itself. Sketches of the first sort were normally destroyed by the artist on completion of the picture; but with the rise of collecting in the 16th-c they were sought after, which greatly encouraged the production of sketches of the second sort.

sketchphone A system, linked to the telephone network, by which line drawings and sketches can be transmitted long distances to suitable receiving equipment. An electronic touch-sensitive screen sends sketches via a computer and the telephone line to a receiver.

Skiathos [skeeathos] area 48 sq km/18 sq mi. Island of the N Dodecanese, Greece, in the W Aegean Sea, 4 km/2½ mi from the mainland; chief town, Skiathos; a popular holiday resort.

Skiddaw [skidaw] 54°40N 3°08W. Mountain in the Lake District of Cumbria, NW England, UK; rises to 928 m/3045 ft E of Bassenthwaite.

Skien [shee-en] 59°14N 9°37E, pop (2000e) 50 000. Ancient town and river-port capital of Telemark county, SE Norway; on the Skiensalv (river); railway; copper, iron ore, heavy industry.

skiffle A type of popular music of the 1950s in which the washboard provided a distinctive timbre. It emanated from the USA, but the best-known singer was the Scot, Lonnie Donegan.

skiing The art of propelling oneself along on snow while standing on skis, and with the aid of poles, named from the Norwegian word *ski*, 'snow shoe'. Very popular as a pastime and as a sport, the earliest reference to skiing dates from c.2500 BC. Competitive skiing takes two forms. **Alpine skiing** consists of the downhill and slaloms (zig-zag courses through markers), which are races against the clock. **Nordic skiing** incorporates cross-country skiing, the biathlon, and ski jumping. Other forms include **ski-flying** (hang-gliding on skis) and **skijoring** (being towed behind a vehicle or horse), as well as several free-style varieties.

skimmer A bird inhabiting tropical fresh waters and coasts in America, Africa, India, and SE Asia; related to the tern; lower bill longer and narrower than upper; catches fish by flying low with lower bill cutting water surface; also known as the **shearwater**, **sea-dog**, or **scissorbill**. (Family: Rhynchopidae, 3 species.)

skin The tough, pliable, waterproof covering of the body, blending with the mucous membranes of the mouth, nose, eyelids, and urogenital and anal openings. It is the largest single organ in the body – approximately 1·8 sq m/19·4 sq ft in the adult human and 1–2 mm/0·04–0·08 in thick. As well as a surface covering, it is also a sensory organ providing sensitivity to touch, pressure, changes in temperature, and painful stimuli. Its waterproofing function prevents fluid loss from the body, but it also has an absorptive function when certain drugs, vitamins, and hormones are applied to it in a suitable form. It is usually loosely applied to underlying tissues, so that it is easily displaced. When subjected to continuous friction, it responds by increasing the thickness of its superficial layers. When wounded, it responds by increased growth and repair. Skin is composed of a superficial layer (the *epidermis*) and a deeper layer (the *dermis*). The epidermis consists of many cell layers, the deeper ones actively proliferating, with the cells produced gradually passing towards the surface (becoming keratinized as they do so), to be ultimately shed as the skin rubs against clothing and other surfaces. The epidermis contains many sensory nerve endings, but no blood vessels. It is firmly anchored to the underlying dermis by epidermal pegs and reciprocal projections from the dermis. The dermis is the deeper interlacing feltwork of collagen and elastic fibres containing blood and lymphatic vessels, nerves and sensory nerve endings, a small amount of fat, hair follicles, sweat and sebaceous glands, and smooth muscle. It is firmly anchored to the subcutaneous connective tissue. Skin colour, largely under genetic control, depends on the presence of pigment (*melanin*) and the vascularity of the dermis. In response to sunlight, skin increases its degree of pigmentation, making it appear darker. Some areas show a constant deeper pigmentation – the external genitalia, the perianal region, the armpit (axilla), and the areola of the breast.

skin cancer *keratosis; melanoma*

skin-diving A form of underwater swimming, popularized in the 1930s. Until the advent of the scuba, skin-divers used only goggles, face mask, flippers, and a short breathing tube, or *snorkel*.

skin effect For alternating current, an effect whereby the bulk of the current is carried along the outer edge of the conductor; contrasts with direct current, where the current is spread evenly across the diameter of the conductor. It is caused by induced eddy currents in the core of the conductor, which oppose the applied current primarily in the interior. The skin effect is more noticeable at high frequencies. An implication is that carriers of high frequency current need only be hollow tubes instead of solid rods or wires.

skink A lizard of the family Scincidae (1275 species), worldwide in tropical and temperate regions; usually with a long thin body and short legs (some species without legs); head often with large flat scales; tongue broad, rounded; many species burrow; most eat invertebrates; large species eat plants.

Skinner, B(urrhus) F(rederic) (1904–90) Psychologist, born in Susquehanna, Pennsylvania, USA. He studied at Harvard, teaching there (1931–6, 1947–74, then emeritus) and also at Minnesota University (1936–45). A leading behaviourist, he was a proponent of operant conditioning, and the inventor of the *Skinner box* for facilitating experimental observations. His main scientific works include *The Behavior of Organisms* (1938) and *Verbal Behavior* (1957), but his social and political views have reached a wider public through *Walden Two* (1948) and *Beyond Freedom and Dignity* (1971).

skipjack Small species of tuna fish (*Katsuwonus pelamis*) widespread in offshore waters of tropical to temperate seas; locally abundant and very important in commercial tuna fisheries, as well as being excellent sport fish; body length up to about 1 m/3¼ ft; upper surface blue, sides silver with darker longitudinal banding. (Family: Scombridae.)

skipper A butterfly with relatively short wings and a large head and body; antennae often club-shaped, and widely separated at base; caterpillars commonly feed on grasses. (Order: Lepidoptera. Family: Hesperiidae, c.3100 species.)

Skiros [skeeros] pop (2000e) 3000; area 209 sq km/81 sq mi. Largest island of the N Dodecanese, Greece, in the Aegean Sea; length 36 km/22 mi; maximum width 14 km/9 mi; handicrafts, particularly hand-weaving and furniture; tourism.

skittles A game played in several different forms, all of which have the same objective: to knock down nine pins with a ball. It is especially known in the UK, where popular forms are **alley skittles**, played in long alleys, and **table skittles**, played indoors and on a specially constructed table with a swivelled ball attached to a mast by means of a chain. The pins are much smaller than those used in ten-pin bowling, and are replaced on their spots manually (instead of mechanically, as in bowling).

Skopje [skopye], or **Skoplje**, Turkish **Usküp**, ancient **Scupi** 42°00N 21°28E, pop (2000e) 587 000. Industrial capital of the Former Yugoslav Republic of Macedonia, on R Vardar, 320 km/200 mi SE of Belgrade; capital of Serbia, 14th-c; largely destroyed by earthquake, 1963; airport; railway; university (1949); flour, brewing, tobacco, cement, carpets; old town and bazaar, ethnographic museum, Daut Pasha Hammam (Turkish bath-house, 1489), Mustapha Pasha mosque, museum of contemporary art; trade fair (Jun), international tobacco and machinery fair (Sep).

Skorzeny, Otto [skaw(r)**tsay**nee] (1908–75) Soldier, born in Vienna, Austria. He joined the Nazi Party in 1930, was mobilized into the SS, and fought in France, Serbia, and Russia (1939–43). He was noted for his commando-style operations in World War 2. He freed Mussolini from internment in a mountain hotel on the Gran Sasso Range (1943), and abducted Horthy, the Regent of Hungary (1944), but failed to capture Tito. During the German counter-offensive in the Ardennes (1944), he carried out widespread sabotage behind Allied lines. He was tried at Nuremberg as a war criminal, but was acquitted (1947).

Skou, Jens C [skoh] (1918–) Chemist, born in Lemvig, W Denmark. He studied at Aarhus University, where he went on to teach. He shared the 1997 Nobel Prize for Chemistry for the discovery of an ion-transporting enzyme, Na+, K+-ATPase.

Skraelings [**skray**lingz] (Old Norse *skraelingr* 'pitiful wretch') The name given by the Vikings to the native peoples – principally Beothuk Indians and Inuit – they encountered in Greenland and North America. *Skraelingsland* was Labrador.

skua A large, gull-like seabird; widespread; usually dark plumage, fleshy band (*cere*) at base of bill; central tail feathers longest; chases other seabirds until they disgorge food; undertakes long migrations; also known as the **jaeger** or **bonxie**. (Family: Stercorariidae, 7 species.)

skull The skeleton of the head and face, composed of many individual bones closely fitted together. It consists of a large cranium, the cavity of which encloses the brain; and the facial skeleton, the bones of the face, which complete the walls of the *orbits* (eye sockets), nasal cavity, and roof of the mouth. The lower jaw (*mandible*) may also be included as part of the skull. At birth and in the young child, the skull bones are separable, though with difficulty; with increasing age the joints between the bones may become ossified. In the young, this greater elasticity reduces the risk of fracture, and at birth allows 'moulding' of the skull by the mother's birth canal.

The skull articulates with the upper part of the vertebral column. The top of the skull is relatively smooth and rounded, while the underside is irregular, having many openings for the passage of nerves and vessels. It functions to protect the brain, to provide bony support for the openings of the digestive and respiratory tracts (mouth and nose respectively), and to house and protect the eyeballs (within the orbital cavities) and the organs of hearing and balance (within the temporal bone). The major bony parts (the number present is shown in parentheses) are the *frontal* (1), *parietal* (2), *occipital* (1), *temporal* (2), *maxillary* (2), *ethmoid* (1), and *zygomatic* (2) bones.

skull-cap A very widespread perennial; stem square; leaves in opposite pairs; flowers 2-lipped, often with upturned tube; calyx with distinctive helmet-shaped dorsal flange. Many species have brightly coloured flowers, and are cultivated for ornament. Others are medicinal, used for nerve tonics. (Genus: *Scutellaria*, 300 species. Family: Labiatae.)

skunk A mammal of family Mustelidae, native to the New World; long black and white coat; squirts foul-smelling fluid as defence; eats insects, vegetation, small vertebrates; nine species in genera *Mephitis* (**striped** and **hooded skunks**, or (in USA) **polecats**, **wood-pussies**, **essence pedlars**, **pikets**, or **PKs**), *Spilogale* (**spotted skunks**), and *Conepatus* (**hog-nosed skunks**).

Skyamsen *Thunderbird*

skydiving Falling from an aircraft and freefalling down to a height of 600 m/2000 ft, when the parachute must be opened, before gliding to the ground. During the free fall, the parachutist can perform a wide range of stunts. In team events, members form different kinds of pattern by holding hands. The sport is often called simply **freefalling**.

Skye Island in Highland, W Scotland, UK; largest island of the Inner Hebrides, area 1665 sq km/643 sq mi; Skye and Lochalsh district pop (2000e) 12 300; separated from mainland (E) by the Sound of Sleat; Skye Bridge completed, 1995; Cuillin Hills in SW, rising to 1008 m/3307 ft at Sgurr Alasdair; much indented by sea lochs; chief towns, Portree, Broadford, Dunvegan; ferry links from Uig to Lochmaddy (North Uist) and Tarbert (Harris); also Armadale–Mallaig and Kyleakin–Kyle of Lochalsh; Dunvegan castle, Kilmuir croft museum, Clan Donald centre at Ardvasar, Dunsgiath castle, Skye water mill and black house (W of Dunvegan); crofting, fishing, sheep, cattle, tourism.

Skye terrier A small terrier developed in Britain; long body with very short legs and long tail; long straight coat reaching the ground; long hair on head (covering eyes), ears, and tail; may be aggressive to strangers.

Skylab project The first US space station, launched on a Saturn V vehicle in May 1973, based on technology and equipment inherited from the Apollo Project. The laboratory/habitat was built within the empty third stage Saturn V fuel tank (prior to launch). It was operated in low Earth orbit for 171 days by three successive three-man crews. The longest staytime in space was 84 days for the third crew. It was used for a variety of in-orbit experiments and for Earth observations. After the last crew completed its mission, the station was left unattended until atmospheric re-entry in July 1979. It was the source of worldwide attention during its final days because there were fears of debris impacting Earth's surface (some pieces were in fact recovered from the Australian desert). Notable also were the emergency repairs effected by the first crew, after the station's micrometeoroid and heat shield was torn off during the launch.

skylark A lark native to the Old World N hemisphere; inhabits grassland, farmland, salt marshes, and sand dunes; sings during ascending and descending fluttering flight. (Genus: *Alauda*, 2 species.)

skyscraper A multi-storey building of great height, typically using a steel frame and curtain wall construction, the floors being accessed via high-speed lifts. It was William Le Baron Jenney's 10-storey Home Insurance Company Building in Chicago (1885) that first made use of steel-girder construction, the term 'skyscraper' being introduced at the end of the 19th-c. At 451·9 m/1483 ft, the Petronas Twin Towers (1996) was the world's tallest building at the beginning of 2004, but several taller buildings are scheduled, such as the Freedom Building, designed to replace the World Trade Center. Perhaps the most famous skyscrapers are those of the 1920s, such as the Empire State Building (1930–1) and the Chrysler Building (1928–30), both in New York City.

Slade, Felix (1790–1868) Antiquary and art collector, born in Halsteads, Yorkshire, N England, UK. He bequeathed his engravings and Venetian glass to the British Museum, and founded art professorships at Oxford, Cambridge, and the Slade School of Art, London, which is named after him.

slander In English law, a defamatory statement made in some transient form – sounds (not necessarily words) or gestures. The term is not recognized by all jurisdictions (eg in Scotland, where such statements are part of the general law against defamation).

slash and burn cultivation *shifting cultivation*

slate A fine-grained metamorphic rock having a perfect cleavage because of the parallel alignment of mica crystals. This is the result of directed stress during the low-grade regional metamorphism of shale or mudstone. Split into thin sheets it is used for roofing, being durable and light. Well-known occurrences are in N Wales and the Vosges, France.

slave-making ant A parasitic ant, the workers of which raid the nests of other ant species and carry off the pupae. These pupae are reared as slaves to feed their captors and care for the captors' larvae. (Order: Hymenoptera. Family: Formicidae.)

slavery A system of social inequality in which some people are treated as items of property belonging to other individuals or social groups. There have been different types and conditions of slavery. At one extreme, slaves might be worked to death, as in the Greek mining camps of the 5th-c and 4th-c BC. At the other, slaves were used less as chattels and more as servants, working in households, and to an extent even administering them, and acting as tutors to young children.

slave trade A trade in Africa which started in ancient times. Slaves were sent across the Sahara and were traded in the Mediterranean by Phoenicians; Graeco-Roman traders in the Red Sea and beyond traded slaves from E Africa to Egypt and the Middle East. These trades continued in mediaeval times, but the scale of the trade built up with the arrival of the Portuguese in Africa and the development of the labour-intensive plantation system in the W African islands of São Tomé and Principe, Brazil, the Caribbean, the southern American colonies, and later the Indian Ocean islands and South and East Africa. The Portuguese dominated the trade in the 16th-c, the Dutch in the early 17th-c, while the late 17th-c was a period of intense competition with the French, British, Danes, and Swedes joining the early practitioners. The trade reached its peak in the second half of the 18th-c, and from this period the E African slave trade became more significant, particularly during the period of Omani power up to the 1860s. The British abolished the slave trade in 1807, and the institution of slavery in 1833. They then instituted Royal Naval anti-slaver squadrons on the coasts of W and E Africa. There have been various estimates of the number of slaves removed from Africa, the most reliable figure being c.12·5 million between 1650 and 1850. Many other people must have lost their lives in the wars stimulated by the trade, and the total drain meant that at the very least the African population remained static for over two centuries.

Slavic or **Slavonic languages** The NE branch of the Indo-European languages, normally divided into **South Slavic** (eg Bulgarian), **West Slavic** (eg Polish), and **East Slavic** (eg Russian). All of the main languages have official status and a standard form. There are written records of Old Church Slavonic from the 9th-c, and its modern form, Church Slavonic, is used as a liturgical language in the Eastern Orthodox Church. The Baltic and Slavic languages between them have c.300 million mother-tongue speakers, more than half of whom speak Russian. Russian is spoken by c.150 million people as a mother-tongue, and by a further 120 million as a second language, throughout the republics of the former USSR. Polish is spoken by c.44 million in Poland and surrounding areas, as well as by emigrants in several parts of the world, such as the UK and USA. Serbian (7·5 million) and Croatian (4·8 million) are spoken chiefly in Yugoslavia and Croatia, respectively. Czech is spoken in the Czech Republic by c.12 million; Slovak in Slovakia by c.5 million. All the East Slavic languages, and some others, are still written in Cyrillic script.

Slavic religion An animistic religion, with themes from hunting, fishing, and agriculture, common to Slavic regions, being practised certainly up to the 14th-c, with traces surviving into the 20th-c. Local deities and supreme gods were worshipped, but there were no temple centres or any organized priestly caste.

Slavs The largest group of European peoples sharing a common ethnic and linguistic origin, consisting of Russians, Ukrainians, Byelorussians, Poles, Czechs, Slovaks, Bulgarians, Serbs, Croats, Montenegrins, and Macedonians. The ancient Slavs, inhabiting C and E Europe, were first mentioned in 2nd-c AD sources. After Christianity was introduced to the Slavs during the 9th-c and 10th-c, the Eastern and Western Churches were separated in 1054. The Serbs, Macedonians, Bulgarians, and most Belorussians, Russians, and Ukrainians joined the Orthodox Church. Until 1912, the Ottoman Empire included parts of present-day Bosnia and Herzegovina, Bulgaria, Croatia, the Former Yugoslav Republic of Macedonia, Serbia and Montenegro, and Slovenia. Many Slavs were forced to convert to Islam, mostly in Bosnia and S Bulgaria. After World War 2, the Slav nations were largely ruled by socialist governments, most of which were overthrown in 1989–91. Ancient national and religious conflicts resurfaced after the death of Tito.

sleep An unconscious state where the subject shows little responsiveness to the external world. There are two phases of sleep which alternate throughout the night. In deep sleep, the brain activity (EEG) shows slow delta waves (**slow wave sleep**, or **SWS**). This is interrupted every 90 minutes or so by 30 minutes of **rapid eye movement** (**REM**) **sleep**. Here the muscles are completely relaxed, but the closed eyes show rapid movements. The brain activity is that of wakefulness, but the subject does not respond to stimuli. Dreaming occurs in REM sleep, and perhaps also in SWS. The sleep cycle is controlled by the reciprocal activity of nerve cells in the brain stem. Sleep is restorative. Growth hormone, which promotes cell division, is secreted during SWS.

sleep apnoea/apnea [apneea] The periodic reduction or cessation of breathing during sleep due to narrowing of the upper airways. It is caused by relaxation of the muscles of the soft palate and uvula, allowing the soft tissues of these structures to partially occlude the airway and also to vibrate, producing snoring. The condition leads to disturbed sleep and daytime drowsiness, and has been associated with higher rates of accidents in affected individuals. It has also been associated with higher rates of cardiovascular disease, but this is not substantiated by clear evidence.

sleeping sickness *trypanosomiasis*

sleep-walking or **somnambulism** A state in which a sleeping individual rises from the bed and walks about for a variable period. It is unrelated to dream activity, and occurs particularly when an individual is subject to stress. It is most common in children, and in most cases stops by the time the child reaches puberty. There are few long-term consequences, and the most important component of management is ensuring that the sleep-walker has a safe environment (eg blocking off access to a flight of stairs).

sleet A form of precipitation found in near-freezing surface air. In the UK the term is used for partially melted snow which reaches the ground, or a mixture of snow and rain. In the USA it describes raindrops which have frozen into ice pellets, and then partially thawed before reaching the ground.

slepton *supersymmetry*

slide A still picture transparency mounted for projection. Large slides 82·5 mm/3¼ in square, often hand-drawn, were used in magic lanterns, but the modern form is a colour photograph 36 × 24 mm in a standard mount 50 mm/2 in square. One of the most popular formats for photography, slides are widely used as illustrations in educational and commercial presentations, in audio-visual shows, and as inserts in television news and current affairs programmes.

slide projector A projector which shows an enlarged image of a slide transparency on a screen. Up to 80 standard slides loaded in straight or circular feed trays can be automatically selected one at a time by remote control or signals from a magnetic tape. To avoid the brief dark interval between successive pictures, slide projectors are often used in pairs so that one image dissolves smoothly into the next; several pairs may be grouped for elaborate multi-image presentation.

slide rat *pika*

Sliema [sleema] 35°55N 14°31E, pop (2000e) 14 500. Residential and resort town on N coast of main island of Malta, across Marsamxett Harbour from Valletta; largest town in Malta; casino, water-sports facilities, yacht repair yard; boat to Comino.

Sligo (county) [**sliygoh**], Ir **Sligeach** pop (2000e) 55 000; area 1795 sq km/693 sq mi. County in Connacht province, W Ireland; bounded N by the Atlantic Ocean; watered by R Moy; Ox Mts to the W; capital, Sligo; cattle, dairy farming, coal; associated with W B Yeats.

Sligo (town) [**sliygoh**] 54°17N 8°28W, pop (2000e) 18 000. Seaport capital of Sligo county, Connacht, W Ireland; at head of Sligo Bay where it meets R Garrogue; railway; technical college; fishing, textiles, food processing; megalithic stones at nearby Carrowmore; Yeats international summer school and language school; Gaelic cultural activities (summer).

Slovak Republic

☐ International Airport

or **Slovakia**, Slovak **Slovenská Republika**

Local name Slovenská republiká

Timezone GMT +1

Area 49 035 km^2/18 927 sq mi

Population total (2002e) 5 383 000

Status Republic

Date of independence 1993

Capital Bratislava

Languages Slovak (official), with Czech and Hungarian widely spoken

Ethnic groups Slovak (87%), Hungarian (11%), Czech (1%), with German, Polish, and Ukrainian minorities

Religions Roman Catholic (70%), Protestant (6%)

Physical features Dominated by the Carpathian Mountains, consisting of a system of E–W ranges separated by valleys and basins; ranges include the Low Tatras of the Inner Carpathians, 1829 m/6000 ft, and the highest point, Gerlachovsky, 2655 m/8711 ft in the Tatra Mts (N); main rivers include the Danube, Vah, Hron; National parks at Pieniny, Low and High Tatra.

Climate Continental climate; warm humid summers, cold dry winters; snow remains on the mountains for 130 days of the year; average annual temperature -4°C (Jan), 18°C (Jul) in Bratislava; average annual rainfall 500–650 mm/20–30 in.

Currency 1 Slovak koruna = 100 halers

Economy Agricultural region, especially cereals, wine, fruit; steel production in Košice; heavy industry suffering since previously dependent on state subsidies.

GDP (2002e) $67·34 bn, per capita $12 400

Human Development Index (2002) 0·835

History Settled in 5th–6th-c by Slavs; part of Great Moravia, 9th-c; part of Magyar Empire from 10th-c; became part of Kingdom of Hungary, 11th-c; united with Czech lands to form the separate state of Czechoslovakia, 1918; under German control, 1938–9; Slovakia became a separate republic under German influence, 1939; Czechoslovakia regained its independence, 1945; under Communist rule following 1948 coup; attempt at liberalization by Dubček terminated by intervention of Warsaw Pact troops, 1968; from 1960s, Slovaks revived efforts to gain recognition for Slovak rights; fall from power of Communist party, 1989; 1992 agreement to divide Czechoslovakia into its constituent republics led to declaration of independence of Slovak Republic, 1993; governed by a President, Prime Minister, Council of Ministers, and National Council; also known as Slovakia.

Head of State
1993–8 Michal Kovac
1999– Rudolf Schuster

Head of Government
1993–4 Vladimir Mečiar
1994–7 Jozef Moravcik
1997–8 Vladimir Mečiar
1998– Mikulás Dzurinda

Slim (of Yarralumia and of Bishopston), William (Joseph) Slim, 1st Viscount (1891–1970) British field marshal, born in Bristol, SW England, UK. Educated in Birmingham, he joined the army at the outbreak of World War 1, and served in Gallipoli and Mesopotamia. In World War 2, his greatest achievement was to lead his reorganized forces, the famous 14th 'Forgotten Army', to victory over the Japanese in Burma. He was Chief of the Imperial General Staff (1948–52), and a highly successful Governor-General of Australia (1953–60). Knighted in 1944, he became a viscount in 1960.

slime mould A primitive micro-organism resembling a fungus, but with an amoeba-like colony stage in its life-cycle; some are cellular, some plasmodial (lacking walls between cells). (Class: Myxomycota.)

slipped disc *prolapsed intervertebral disc*

slipper gloxinia *gloxinia*

slippery elm A species of elm (*Ulmus rubra*) native to North America. The slippery inner bark contains a sticky juice used in medicines. (Family: Ulmaceae.)

Sloane, Sir Hans (1660–1753) Physician, born in Killyleagh, Co Down, SE Northern Ireland, UK. He studied in London and in France, and settled in London as a physician, but spent 1685–6 in Jamaica, collecting a herbarium of 800 species. His museum and library of 50 000 volumes and 3560 manuscripts formed the nucleus of the British Museum.

sloe *blackthorn*

sloop A single-masted, fore-and-aft rigged sailing vessel with only one headsail. In the 18th-c, the term was also used for any small naval vessel. In World War 2, it referred to an anti-submarine vessel superior to a corvette in speed and equipment.

sloth A South American mammal of family Megalonychidae (**two-toed sloths**, 2 species) or of family Bradypodidae (**three-toed sloths**, 3 species); two-toed sloths actually have two fingers (all sloths have three toes); an edentate; eats leaves; hangs upside down in trees using huge claws; round head, shaggy coat (which hides ears), no tail; grooves on hairs may contain blue-green algae which assist camouflage.

sloth bear A bear native to S India and Sri Lanka (*Melursus ursinus*); long black shaggy coat with pale snout and yellow crescent on chest; long front claws; can close nostrils; eats mainly bees and termites.

slotted ring *Cambridge ring*

Slough [slow] 51°31N 0°36W, pop (2001e) 119 100. Town and unitary authority (from 1998) in S England, UK; NE of Windsor, 30 km/18½ mi W of C London; railway; paints, pharmaceuticals, electronics, plastics, aircraft parts, vehicle parts, foodstuffs; London Heathrow airport nearby.

Slovakia *Slovak Republic*

Slovak literature *Czech and Slovak literature*

Slovak Republic *see panel*

Slovenes A Slavonic people, concentrated in the NW corner of the Balkan peninsula; overwhelmingly Roman Catholic. Before 1918, the majority of Slovenes were subjects of the Habsburg Empire; thereafter they formed one of the peoples of Yugoslavia until the achievement of an independent republic of Slo-

Slovenia

□ International Airport

[slohveenia], Slovene **Slovenija**

Local name Slovenija

Timezone GMT +1

Area 20 251 km²/7817 sq mi

Population total (2002e) 1 948 000

Status Republic

Date of independence 1991

Capital Ljubljana

Languages Slovene, Croatian

Ethnic group Slovene (90%)

Religions Roman Catholic, Protestant, some Eastern Orthodox

Physical features Mountainous republic between Austria and Croatia; Slovenian Alps (NW) rise to 2863 m/9393 ft at Triglav in the Julian Alps (Julijske Alpe); rivers include Sava, Savinja, and Drava; chief port, Koper.

Climate Continental climate; more Mediterranean in W; average annual temperature -1°C (Jan), 19°C (Jul) in Ljubljana; average annual rainfall 1600 mm/63 in.

Currency (1991) 1 Slovene Tolar = 100 paras

Economy Agriculture; maize, wheat, sugar beet, potatoes, livestock, wine, timber, lignite; textiles; large iron and steel plants; vehicles; coal, lead, mercury mining in W.

GDP (2002e) $37·06 bn, per capita $19 200

Human Development Index (2002) 0·879

History Settled by Slovenes, 6th-8th-c; later controlled by Slavs and Franks; part of the Austro-Hungarian Empire until 1918; people's republic within Yugoslavia, 1946; declaration of full sovereignty, 1990; declaration of independence from Yugoslavia as the Republic of Slovenia, 1991, opposed by central government, brief period of fighting upon the intervention of the federal army who withdrew in Aug 1991; tricameral legislature replaced by a bicameral National Assembly, consisting of a Chamber of Deputies and a State Council.

Head of State

1991–2002 Milan Kučan

2002– Janez Drnovšek

Head of Government

1991–2 Lojze Peterle

1992–2000 Janez Drnovšek

2000 Andrej Bajuk

2000–2 Janez Drnovšek

2002– Anton Rop

venia in 1991; c.100 000 continue to inhabit Italy and c.80 000 Austria.

Slovenia *see panel*

Slovo, Joe [slohvoh] (1926–95) South African political leader, born in Lithuania. He moved to South Africa as a child, and became one of the most influential white South Africans associated with the national liberation movement. He qualified as a lawyer, and became an active member of the Communist Party in the 1940s. He left the country in June 1963, and continued to work for the Communist Party and the African National Congress (ANC). He held high office in both organizations, and also served as chief-of-staff of Umkhonto we Sizwe, the armed wing of the ANC (1985–7). He returned to South Africa in 1990, and played a major role in the negotiations for a new dispensation. In 1994 he was appointed minister for housing in Mandela's first cabinet.

slow-worm A legless lizard (*Anguis fragilis*) native to Europe, NW Africa, and SW Asia; grey or brown; female with darker line along side; long tail may be shed, but never grows back to full length; eats worms and slugs; also known as **blindworm** – a name additionally used for skinks of genus *Typhlosaurus*. (Family: Anguidae.)

SLR *single lens reflex*

slug (zoology) A terrestrial snail with an elongate body and usually a small external shell, or no shell at all; typically two pairs of tentacles on its head, the upper pair bearing the eyes; common in moist environments. (Class: Gastropoda. Subclass: Pulmonata.)

slump *depression* (economics); *recession*

slurry *manure*

Sluter, Claus or **Claes** [slooter] (c.1350–c.1405) Sculptor, probably born in Haarlem, The Netherlands. He went to Dijon under the patronage of Philip the Bold of Burgundy. His chief works are the porch sculptures of the Carthusian house of Champmol near Dijon, and the tomb of Philip the Bold.

Smalley, Richard E (1943–) Chemist, born in Akron, Ohio, USA. He studied at Princeton University, then moved to Rice University, Houston, in 1976. He shared the Nobel Prize for Chemistry in 1996 for his contribution to the discovery of fullerenes (1985).

smallpox An ancient and highly infectious viral disease. It gives rise to characteristic blister-like skin lesions and carries a high mortality. As a result of a World Health Organization programme including vaccination, smallpox was declared in 1979 to have been completely eradicated. The virus is kept under laboratory conditions in two centres, one in Russia, the other in the USA.

Smalltalk The first object-oriented computer programming language, developed at Xerox PARC.

smart bomb *bomb*

smart card A plastic card, similar to a credit card, which has a micro-computer embedded in the card rather than a magnetic strip. The micro-computer has contacts which can be used for input and output, and the card can be used to process information held in the memory. Current uses for the card include identification, holding medical data in case of emergency, building up credits in reward schemes, and storing credits to use in telephone boxes, buses, and underground railways. An emerging use for the smart card is as a substitute for cash (*electronic cash*). At a terminal in a bank a credit can be read on to the card. When used as cash at participating retailers, the credit on the buyer's card is reduced while the credit on the retailer's card is increased. When the credit eventually becomes close to nothing, it can be increased again at the bank terminal, just like withdrawing cash at an automated teller machine.

smart material A substance which responds in a specific mechanical way to a given trigger. The trigger can be a change in pressure, temperature, electric field, or magnetic field. The response can be a change in size, shape, rigidity, transparency, colour, or electric potential. *Shape memory alloys* (SMA) are metals which return to their manufactured shape when they are heated. Spacecraft aerials, for example, have been made from SMAs; these unfurl when an electric current passes through them. *Smart crystals*, which produce electric signals when they are deformed, are used as sensors; others change colour with temperature and can be used for warnings. *Smart ceramics* expand or contract in response to an electric signal; these are being used as synthetic muscles. *Smart liquids* which set when exposed to a magnetic field can be used to dampen vibrations in machines, or as protection in earthquake areas.

smelt Slender-bodied marine and freshwater fish belonging to either the N hemisphere family Osmeridae or the Australasian family Retropinnidae; several species migrate into fresh water to breed; includes the European smelt, *Osmerus eperlanus* (length up to 30 cm/12 in), found in coastal waters and rivers from Biscay to Norway.

smelting Obtaining a metal from its ore by heating, using fuel which will simultaneously remove other components of the ore (such as the oxygen of oxides), and a flux to promote the removal of impurities. Copper was probably the first metal to be obtained from an ore, and tin, lead, and silver were also smelted in early times. Charcoal was the universal fuel and reducing agent until the use of coke in the 18th-c. Forced draughts were used in classical times, leading eventually to the blast furnace. There are many variants of the fuel combustion forms of smelting, and electrical methods are also employed, as in the case of aluminium.

Smetana, Bedřich [**smet**ana] (1824–84) Composer, born in Litomyšl, C Czech Republic (formerly Bohemia, Austrian Empire). He studied in Prague, and in 1848 opened a music school with the financial support of Liszt. He became conductor of the Philharmonic Orchestra in Göteborg, Sweden, in 1856. Returning to Prague in 1861, he was instrumental in establishing the national opera house. His compositions, intensely national in character, include nine operas, notably *Prodaná nevěsta* (1866, The Bartered Bride), and many chamber and orchestral works, including the series of symphonic poems *Má vlast* (1874–9, My Country). Overwork destroyed his health, and in 1874 he became deaf, though he continued to compose until a mental breakdown in 1883.

smew A small bird, a species of merganser (*Mergus albellus*) native to the N Old World; untidy crest on back of head; male white with black back and tail, black patch below eye and on back of head; female mainly brown; inhabits fresh or sheltered coastal waters.

Smiles, Samuel (1812–1904) Writer and social reformer, born in Haddington, East Lothian, E Scotland, UK. He studied at Edinburgh, and settled as a surgeon in Leeds, but left medicine for journalism, editing the *Leeds Times* (1838–42), and becoming involved in railway companies until 1866. His main work was a guide to self-improvement, *Self-Help* (1859), with its short lives of great men and the admonition 'Do thou likewise'. He also wrote many biographical and moral books.

Smiley, Jane (1952–) Novelist, born in Los Angeles, California, USA. She grew up in St Louis, and studied at Vassar and the University of Iowa, where she attended the writers' workshop. An early short story, *Lily*, won the O Henry Award, later appearing in a collection *The Age of Grief* (1987). Many of her stories are set on farms. *A Thousand Acres* (1992), a modern retelling of the *King Lear* story set in a farming community in Iowa, won a Pulitzer Prize and the National Book Critics Award. *Moo* (1995) is a satire on the American agribusiness. Later novels include *Horse Heaven* (2000) and *Good Faith* (2003).

Smith, Adam (1723–90) Economist and philosopher, born in Kirkcaldy, Fife, E Scotland, UK. He studied at Glasgow and Oxford, lectured in Edinburgh, and became professor of logic at Glasgow (1751), but took up the chair of moral philosophy the following year. In 1776 he moved to London, where he published *An Inquiry into the Nature and Causes of the Wealth of Nations* (1776), the first major work of political economy. This examined in detail the consequences of economic freedom, such as division of labour, the function of markets, and the international implications of a *laissez-faire* economy. His appointment as commissioner of customs in 1778 took him back to Edinburgh.

Smith, Bessie, nickname **Empress of the Blues** (c.1895–1937) Blues singer, born in Chattanooga, Tennessee, USA. Raised in poverty in the US South, she ran away as a teenager with Ma Rainey's Rabbit Foot Minstrels, a black revue. She began her career in the modest circuit of vaudeville tents and small theatres, but her magnificent voice, blues-based repertoire, and vivacious stage presence soon gained her recognition as one of the outstanding African-American artistes of her day. She made a series of recordings throughout the 1920s, accompanied by leading jazz musicians, including Louis Armstrong, and these are regarded as classic blues statements. She starred in the 1929 film, *St Louis Blues*.

Smith, Delia (1941–) Television chef and writer, born in Woking, Surrey, SE England, UK. She left school aged 16 years and worked as a hairdresser, travel agent, dishwasher, and waitress before learning to cook in a London restaurant. She was a columnist for the *Sunday Mirror* magazine (1969) and the *Evening Standard* (1972–84). In 1973 she published her first cookery book, *How to Cheat at Cooking*, and her popularity increased with the many highly successful television series that followed. An inspirational cook, her cookbook *Delia Smith's Christmas* (1990) has sold over five million copies. Later best-selling books include *Summer Collection* (1993), *Winter Collection* (1995), and *How to Cook* (1999). A new series of books, *The Delia Collection*, began in 2003. The adjective and noun **Delia** was included in the 2001 edition of the *Collins English Dictionary* after its lexicographers found it had passed into everyday use.

Smith, Dodie, in full **Dorothy Gladys Smith**, pseudonym **C L Anthony** (1896–1990) Playwright, novelist, and theatre producer, born in Whitefield, Greater Manchester, NW England, UK. Educated in London, she studied at the Royal Academy of Drama and Art. She started as an actress, but turned to writing, producing such successful plays as *Dear Octopus* (1938). She is also known for her children's book *The Hundred and One Dalmatians* (1956), made into a popular Disney cartoon film (1961) and revived as a 'live' action film (1996).

Smith, Florence Margaret *Smith, Stevie*

Smith, Frederick Edwin *Birkenhead, Earl of*

Smith, Ian (Douglas) (1919–) Rhodesian politician and prime minister (1964–79), born in Selukwe, C Zimbabwe (formerly Rhodesia). He studied in Rhodesia and South Africa, fought in World War 2, and became an MP in 1948. In 1961 he was a founder of the Rhodesian Front, dedicated to immediate independence without African majority rule. As premier, he unilaterally declared independence (UDI, 1965), which resulted in the imposition of increasingly severe economic sanctions by the UN at Britain's request. After an intensive guerrilla war, he created an 'internal settlement', and Muzorewa's caretaker government made him a member of the Transitional Executive Council of 1978–9 to prepare for the transfer of power. The internal settlement was overturned by the Lancaster House Agreement, and he was elected an MP under Mugabe's government, where he continued to be a vigorous opponent of the one-party state.

Smith, John (1580–1631) Adventurer, born in Willoughby, Lincolnshire, EC England, UK. He fought in France and Hungary, where he was captured by the Turks and sold as a slave. After escaping to Russia, he joined an expedition to colonize Virginia (1607), and was saved from death by Pocahontas. His energy in dealing with the Indians led to his being elected president of the colony (1608–9). He wrote valuable accounts of his travels, and produced several important maps.

Smith, John (1938–94) British politician, born in Dalmally, Argyll and Bute, W Scotland, UK. He studied at Glasgow University, was called to the Scottish bar in 1967, and made a QC in 1983. He became a Labour MP in 1970, held junior government posts under Harold Wilson, and in 1978 was appointed secretary of trade and industry by James Callaghan. From 1979 he was Opposition Front Bench spokesman on trade, energy, and employment, consolidating his reputation on becoming shadow Chancellor of the Exchequer in 1988. A heart attack in the same year seemed to threaten his career, but he made a full recovery in 1989, and succeeded Neil Kinnock as Labour leader after the 1992 general election. A highly respected figure, his unexpected death after a further heart attack in 1994 caused an unusually strong sense of national loss.

Smith, Joseph (1805–44) Founder of the Church of Jesus Christ of Latter-day Saints (the Mormons), born in Sharon, Vermont, USA. He received his first 'call' as a prophet at Manchester, New York, in 1820. Later he was told of a sacred religious record on golden plates, with two stones which should help to translate it, and in 1827 this was delivered into his hands. In the *Book of Mormon* (1830), Christ is said to have appeared and established his Church in the New World. Smith claimed to have received authority from St John the Baptist and the apostles to be the instrument of the Church's re-establishment. Despite ridicule and hostility, the new Church rapidly gained converts. He founded Nauvoo, IL, in 1840, becoming mayor. Violence followed events surrounding his announcement as a candidate for the US presidency. He was imprisoned for conspiracy, and killed by a mob which broke into a jail in Carthage, IL, where he and his brother Hyram were awaiting trial.

Smith, Maggie, popular name of **Dame Margaret Natalie Smith** (1934–) Actress, born in Ilford, E Greater London, UK. A student at the Oxford Playhouse School, she made her stage debut with the Oxford University Dramatic Society in 1952, and appeared in New York City as one of the *New Faces of '56*. Gaining increasing critical esteem for her performances, she joined the National Theatre, where she played in *Othello* (1963), *Hay Fever* (1966), and *The Three Sisters* (1970), among others. Her film debut in 1958 was followed by such films as *The VIPs* (1963), *The Pumpkin Eater* (1964), and *The Prime of Miss Jean Brodie* (1969, Oscar). Later stage work includes *Virginia* (1980), *Lettice and Lovage* (1988, Tony), and *The Lady in the Van* (1999). She received an Oscar for her role in *California Suite* (1978), and BAFTA awards for her roles in *A Private Function* (1984), *A Room With a View* (1986), and *The Lonely Passion of Judith Hearne* (1987). Later film appearances include *The First Wives Club* (1996), *Tea with Mussolini* (1998), and *Gosford Park* (2001). In 2003 she won an Emmy for her role in the TV mini-series *My House in Umbria*. She was created a dame in 1990.

Smith, Ozzie, popular name of **Osborne Earl Smith**, nickname **the Wizard of Oz** (1954–) Baseball player, born in Mobile, Alabama, USA. In a career that began in 1978, he established himself as a fielding shortstop, playing for the San Diego Padres and the St Louis Cardinals. He was inducted into the baseball Hall of Fame in 2002.

Smith, Stevie, pseudonym of **Florence Margaret Smith** (1902–71) Poet and novelist, born in Hull, NE England, UK. Educated in London, she worked in publishing, then began to write herself. In 1935 she took her first collection of poems to a publisher, who rejected them and advised her to try a novel. The result was *Novel on Yellow Paper* (1936), a largely autobiographical monologue in a humorous conversational style. Her first book of poetry, *A Good Time Was Had By All*, was published in 1937, and she gradually acquired a reputation as an eccentrically humorous poet on serious themes. Later books include *Not Waving but Drowning* (1957), *The Frog Prince* (1966), and *Scorpion* (1972).

Smith, Vernon L Economist, born in Wichitaw, Kansas, USA. He studied at the California Institute of Technology, University of Kansas, and Harvard University, later joining the Interdisciplinary Center for Economic Science in Fairfax, VA. He shared the 2002 Nobel Prize for Economics for having established laboratory experiments as a tool in empirical economic analysis, especially in the study of alternative market mechanisms.

Smith, Will, popular name of **Willard Christopher Smith Jr** (1968–) Film actor and rapper, born in Philadelphia, Pennsylvania, USA. He began rapping at the age of 12, became known as the 'Fresh Prince', and formed a successful duo with 'Jazzy Jeff' Townes. His first major film role was in *Six Degrees of Separation* (1993), and later films include *Independence Day* (1996), *Men in Black* (1997, sequel 2002), *Wild Wild West* (1999), *Ali* (2001), a biography of the boxer Muhammad Ali, and *Bad Boys II* (2003). He continues to combine successful careers as an actor and recording artist.

Smithfield An area just outside the walls of the City of London, UK, in former times the scene of tournaments, trials, fairs, and cattle markets. The main London meat market was located here in the mid-19th-c.

Smithsonian Institution A foundation for the promotion of knowledge, endowed in 1826 by the English scientist James Smithson (1765–1829), established by Act of Congress in 1846, and opened in Washington, DC in 1855. It administers a number of art, history, and science museums, scientific research centres, and is the parent organization of several autonomous artistic and academic establishments.

smog A form of air pollution with several sources. In Britain before the mid-20th-c, the smogs of industrial cities were a form of radiation fog, in which soot and smoke acted as condensation nuclei, and gases such as sulphur dioxide (SO_2) and carbon monoxide (CO) were unable to escape. Such a smog (Dec 1952) was responsible for the deaths of more than 4000 people in London, which led to the Clean Air Act of 1956. At lower latitudes, photochemical smogs (*heat hazes*) occur. Emissions of hydrocarbons and oxides of nitrogen from industrial processes and vehicle exhausts react with sunlight.

smoked foods The preservation of food using the ancient method of exposing it over a period of time to wood smoke. The preservation is achieved partly through drying and partly through the effects of chemicals in the smoke.

smoke tree A deciduous shrub growing to c.3 m/10 ft (*Cotinus coggyria*), native to S Europe and Asia; leaves rounded, widest above the middle, turning bronzy-purple in autumn; flowers 4–6-petalled, tiny, purplish, eventually fading pink, in plume-like inflorescences, at a distance reminiscent of smoke. (Family: Anacardiaceae.)

smoking The practice of inhaling the fumes from burning tobacco leaves, generally using cigarettes, cigars, or pipes, introduced into Europe from the Americas by early explorers. The practice is habit-forming, and is known to be a causative factor in the development of several diseases, notably lung cancer, throat cancer, coronary heart disease, and respiratory conditions such as bronchitis and emphysema. The risk increases with the number of cigarettes smoked per day. In several countries, there have been anti-smoking advertising campaigns and a ban on the press and television advertising of tobacco products; cigarette packets and press advertisements also carry government health warnings.

Smolensk [smolensk] 54°49N 32°04E, pop (2000e) 348 000. River-port capital of Smolenskaya oblast, WC European Russia, on the upper Dnepr R; first mentioned, 9th-c; part of Russia, 1654; severely damaged in World War 2; railway; linen textiles, flax, fertilizers, engineering; Cathedral of the Assumption (12th-c).

Smollett, Tobias (George) (1721–71) Novelist, born in Cardross, Argyll and Bute, W Scotland, UK. He studied medicine at Glasgow University, served on the Cartagena expedition in 1741, and settled in London as a surgeon in 1744. He turned to writing, achieving success with his first works, the picaresque novels *The Adventures of Roderick Random* (1748) and *The Adventures of Peregrine Pickle* (1751). He spent several years in journal editing, translating, and writing historical and travel works. He retired to Italy in 1768, and completed his masterpiece, *The Expedition of Humphry Clinker* (1771), just before he died.

smooth snake A harmless European snake (*Coronella austriaca*) of family Colubridae; scales smooth, not ridged; side of head with dark horizontal line; inhabits dry heathland or open woodland; eats mainly lizards, also some small snakes and mammals.

smut fungus A fungus that is a parasite of plants, especially grasses, including cereals and sugar cane; fungus body (*mycelium*) grows within host tissues and forms masses of black, soot-like spores on the surface of the infected plant. (Subdivision: Basidiomycetes. Order: Ustilaginales.)

Smuts, Jan (Christiaan) (1870–1950) South African general, statesman, and prime minister (1919–24, 1939–48), born in Malmesbury, Cape Colony, SW South Africa. He studied at Cambridge, became a lawyer, fought in the second Boer War (1899–1902), and entered the House of Assembly in 1907. He held several cabinet posts, led campaigns against the Germans in South West Africa and Tanganyika, was a member of the Imperial War Cabinet in World War 1, and succeeded Botha as premier. He was a significant figure at Versailles, and was instrumental in the founding of the League of Nations in 1919. As minister of justice under Hertzog, his coalition with the Nationalists in 1934 produced the United Party, and he became premier again in 1939.

Smyrna *Izmir*

Smythe, Pat(ricia), married name **Koechlin** (1928–96) Show jumper, born in Switzerland. She won the European championship four times on *Flanagan* (1957, 1961–3), and in 1956 was the first woman to ride in the Olympic Games, winning a bronze medal in the team event. She won the Queen Elizabeth II Cup on *Mr Pollard* in 1958. She rode very little after her marriage in 1963.

Smythson, Robert (c.1535–1614) English architect. Trained as a mason, his first recorded work was at Longleat (1568), which he may have designed. His masterpiece was Wollaton Hall, Nottingham (1580–8), a mock mediaeval castle, made up of classical and Flemish Mannerist elements. He developed a new vertical plan, with the great hall set transversely, which revolutionized the spatial possibilities of contemporary buildings. He settled in Wollaton, which has led the nearby country houses, Worksop Manor, Balborough (1585), and Hardwick Hall, Derbyshire (1591–7) to be attributed to him.

Snagge, John (Derrick Mordaunt) (1904–96) British broadcaster. He studied at Oxford, and joined the BBC as an assistant station director in 1924. He became an announcer in 1928, worked in outside broadcasts (1933–9), then held a series of senior posts in programme presentation, retiring from the BBC in 1965. He provided the commentary on the Oxford and Cambridge Boat Race for half a century (1931–80). More than anyone else, his voice came to represent the traditional values of the BBC.

snail A common name for many types of gastropod mollusc, but sometimes used more specifically for members of the subclass Pulmonata; predominantly terrestrial or freshwater forms; usually possess a spirally coiled external shell, without an operculum closing off the shell aperture; mantle cavity modified as a vascularized lung for air breathing; includes pond snails and garden snails. (Class: Gastropoda.)

snail kite A true kite found from Florida to South America (*Rostrhamus sociabilis*); lives near freshwater marshes; eats only snails of genus *Pomacea*; upper bill long, slender and sickle-shaped, used for extracting snail from shell; also known as **everglades kite**.

snake A reptile believed to have evolved c.135 million years ago, either from burrowing lizards or from a group of swimming marine lizards; also known as **serpent**; c.2400 living species, found worldwide except in very cold regions and on some islands; characterized by having separate jaw bones connected by ligaments; these bones can move apart, allowing prey much wider than the snake's head to be swallowed; eats animals (or eggs); cannot chew (swallows prey whole, digestive juices dissolving bones and teeth); long cylindrical scaly body; no limbs or eyelids; no obvious ears; skin moulted several times each year; internal organs modified to fit into the thin body; kidneys lie one behind the other, not side by side; left lung absent or small (except in pythons and boas); c.300 venomous species, which inject less than half their venom with each bite; more than 50 species dangerous to humans; 30 000–40 000 people die each year from snakebite. (Suborder: Serpentes or Ophidia. Order: Squamata.)

snake bird *darter*

snakefly A predatory insect characterized by an elongation of the thorax that produces a snake-like neck; adults have two pairs of similar wings with complex veins; usually found on or under bark; feeds on insects. (Order: Neuroptera. Family: Raphidiidae.)

snake-necked turtle A side-necked turtle, native to South America and Australasia; very long slender neck; lives in or near fresh water; usually carnivorous; called *tortoise* in Australia; also known as **long-necked turtle**. (Family: Chelidae, 36 species.)

snake plant *mother-in-law's-tongue*

Snake River River in NW USA; rises in NW Wyoming; flows through Idaho (via the Snake R Plain), along part of the Oregon–Idaho and Washington–Idaho borders, into Washington, joining the Columbia R near Pasco; length c.1600 km/1000 mi; major tributaries the Bruneau, Boise, Owyhee, Grande Ronde, Clearwater, Palouse; contains several gorges, the largest being Hell's Canyon; used for irrigation and hydroelectricity.

snake's head *fritillary* (botany)

snapdragon A short-lived, slightly bushy perennial (*Antirrhinum majus*), growing to 80 cm/30 in, native to Europe; lower leaves opposite, upper alternate; flowers strongly zygomorphic, the tube with two lips, the lower 3-lobed, with a projection (the *palate*) closing the tube and forming a landing platform for bumble-bees, the only insects with sufficient weight and strength to part the lips and reach the nectar within. The flowers of the wild plants are reddish-purple, with cultivars in a range of colours. It is cultivated as an ornamental annual. (Family: Scrophulariaceae.)

snapper Deep-bodied fish of the family Lutjanidae (4 genera, 300 species), widespread and locally common in tropical seas; name derives from the long conical front teeth and highly mobile jaws; some species are a valuable food fish; includes the common tropical Atlantic **grey snapper**, *Lutjanus griseus*. The name is also used for some of the large family Sparidae, with similar canine-like front teeth.

snapping turtle A reptile native to North and Central America; large head which cannot be withdrawn into shell; strong hooked jaws; long tail; inhabits fresh water; eats animals that live in (or enter) water; two species: **snapping turtle** (*Chelydra serpentina*) and **alligator snapping turtle** (*Macroclemys temminckii*). (Family: Chelydridae.)

snare drum *side drum*

Snead, Sam(uel Jackson), nickname **Slammin' Sam** (1912–2002) Golfer, born in Hot Springs, Virginia, USA. He was the winner of a record 81 tournaments on the US Professional Golfers Association Tour between 1936 and 1965. Professional since 1934, he is credited with 135 victories worldwide. He won the (British) Open in 1946, and was three-times winner of the US PGA Championship (1942, 1949, 1951) and the US Masters (1949, 1952, 1954). His six Senior Championships (1964–5, 1967, 1970, 1972–3) are a record.

Snell's law *refraction*

Śniardwy [shnyah(r)dvee] area 114 sq km/44 sq mi. Lake in Suwałki voivodship, NE Poland; largest lake in Poland; greatest depth 23 m/77 ft.

snipe A sandpiper, found worldwide; mottled brown plumage; shortish legs and long straight bill; inhabits mainly marshes and mountain meadows; small groups called 'wisps'. (Genus: *Gallinago*, 17 species, or *Coenocorypha*, 1 species.)

snooker A popular indoor game played with cues on a standard English billiards table by two (sometimes four) players. 22 balls are placed at specific positions on the table: one white, 15 reds, and six coloured balls (yellow, green, brown, blue, pink, and black). The object is to use the cue to hit the white ball to sink ('pot') the other balls in any of six pockets around the table. The coloured balls have an ascending points value of 2–7, while each red is worth one point. After potting a red, the successful player must then attempt to pot a coloured ball, after which a further red is played; this sequence (known as a 'break') continues until a foul is played or a ball not potted. Reds stay in the pocket when potted. The colours return to their fixed positions (if possible) after being potted, unless there are no reds left; they must then be potted in ascending order, and stay off the table. The game ends when the black is finally potted; and the winner is the player with most points. Snooker was invented by army officers serving in the Devonshire Regiment in India in 1875, who developed it from Black Pool. The game was named by one of the officers, Neville Chamberlain. It is now one of the most popular television sports.

Snorri Sturluson *Sturluson, Snorri*

Snow, C(harles) P(ercy) Snow, Baron (1905–80) Novelist and physicist, born in Leicester, Leicestershire, C England, UK. He studied at Leicester and at Cambridge, where he became a fellow of Christ's College (1930–50). He was the author of a cycle of successful novels portraying English life from 1920 onwards, starting with *Strangers and Brothers* (1940), and including *The Masters* (1951), *The New Men* (1954), and *Corridors of Power* (1964). His controversial *The Two Cultures and the Scientific Revolution* (1959) discussed the dichotomy between science and literature, and his belief in closer contact between them. He married the novelist Pamela Hansford Johnson in 1950, was knighted in 1957, and became a life peer in 1964.

Snow, Peter (John) (1938–) Broadcaster and writer, born in Dublin, Ireland. He studied at Oxford, joined the army, then became a newscaster and reporter for ITN (1962–6), and a diplomatic and defence correspondent (1966–79), joining the BBC as presenter of *Newsnight* in 1979. He has also become known as the co-presenter of the general elections from 1974, increasingly identified with the 'swingometer' coverage of the results as they are announced. His books include a biography of Saddam Hussein (1972).

snow A type of solid precipitation which forms at temperatures below the freezing point of water. At very cold temperatures, single ice crystals may fall as snow. At higher temperatures, ice crystals aggregate into geometrical forms called **snow flakes**. Close to freezing point, snow may turn to sleet as it begins to thaw. Snow fall is measured by depth (in millimetres or inches). To convert this to equivalent precipitation it is important to know the density of the fallen snow, which varies with meteorological conditions; as a rough guide, 150 mm (6 in) of moist snow is equivalent to 25 mm (1 in) of rain, as is also 760 mm (30 in) of dry snow. The deepest snowfall in the USA over a 12-month period was 31 102 mm (1224·5 in) at Paradise, Mt Rainier, WA, in 1971–2, while the deepest snow in England was 1524 mm (60 in) in Teesdale, Durham, in 1947.

snowball tree *guelder rose*

snowboarding A popular recreation and sport that developed in the 1970s, using a single board (a relative of the skateboard) on snow. Snowboarders claim it offers more flexibility than skiing for off-piste snowboarding as well as the opportunity for acrobatic tricks. Snowboarding is an official sport of the Winter Olympics for both men and women, with slalom racing and acrobatic displays in a specially built 'half-pipe'.

snow bunting A species of bunting (*Plectrophenax nivalis*) native to the northern N hemisphere; in winter white with black back; in summer brown head and back, white underparts; inhabits open stony country or (in winter) coasts; eats seeds and insects.

Snowdon, Welsh **Yr Wyddfa** 53°04N 4°05W. Mountain with five peaks rising to 1085 m/3560 ft in Gwynedd, NW Wales, UK; highest peak in England and Wales; centre of Snowdonia National Park (area 2188 sq km/845 sq mi, established 1951); tourism; rack railway from Llanberis to main peak.

Snowdon, Antony Armstrong-Jones, 1st Earl of (1930–) Photographer and designer, born in London, UK. He studied at Cambridge, and married Princess Margaret in 1960 (divorced 1978). A freelance photojournalist since 1951, he designed the Aviary of the London Zoo in 1965, and in recent years has devoted much effort to presenting the conditions of the handicapped, both in photographic studies and in television documentaries. In 2003 he published *Snowdon on Russia*, a book of photographs taken over many years visiting the country, with an accompanying exhibition in London.

snowdrop A bulb often flowering in late winter (*Galanthus nivalis*) native to Europe and W Asia; leaves strap-shaped, very narrow, bluish-green; flowers on long stalks, solitary, drooping, white; three outer perianth-segments spreading; three inner smaller, with green spot at base of apical notch. (Family: Amaryllidaceae.)

snow goose A goose native to North America and from E Siberia to Japan (*Anser coerulescens*). There are two races: **greater** and **lesser**. The lesser has two colour phases, the darker being called the **blue goose**; sometimes described as 3 species.

snow leopard A rare big cat (*Panthera uncia*) native to the mountains of SC Asia, living near the snow line; thick pale grey coat with dark rings (sometimes enclosing small spots); inhabits meadows, rocks, and (in winter) forests; eats goats, sheep, deer, smaller mammals, birds; also known as **ounce**.

snow sheep *bighorn*

snowshoe hare A nocturnal North American hare (*Lepus americanus*) with a coat which is brown in summer, white in winter; inhabits coniferous forests; populations undergo large fluctuations in numbers over 8–10-year periods; also known as **snowshoe rabbit** or **varying hare**.

Snowy Mountains Scheme A massive construction project in SE Australia carried out 1949–72, but first proposed in 1881. The object of the scheme was to divert the Snowy R inland into the Murrumbidgee R to provide hydroelectricity and irrigation. It consists of 16 storage dams, 7 power stations, 80 km/50 mi of aqueducts, and 145 km/90 mi of tunnels.

snowy owl A typical owl native to the northern N hemisphere (*Nyctea scandiaca*); plumage mainly white; inhabits tundra, marshes, and Arctic islands; hunts during day; eats mammals and birds up to the size of Arctic hares and ducks; nests on ground.

snuff Any drug prepared as a fine powder which is administered by sniffing; it is absorbed through the nasal mucous membranes. More commonly, snuff is synonymous with tobacco snuff, taken for its nicotine content. Tobacco snuff was used by some American Indian tribes and later adopted by Europeans. In the 17th-c, snuff-taking was adopted in parts of Asia where smoking was illegal. It reached the peak of popularity in the French court in the 18th-c, but its use was brought to an end by the French Revolution. Snuff is rarely used nowadays.

Snyder, Gary (Sherman) (1930–) Poet, born in San Francisco, California, USA. He studied at Reed College, OR, Indiana University, and the University of California, Berkeley, then tried various jobs before beginning to write. He is associated with the Beat poets. From the outset he identified with the natural world and the values of simple living and hard physical work. Since 1965 he has lived mainly in Japan, writing poems which bring together American and Eastern culture. His later works include *Turtle Island* (1975, Pulitzer) and *Mountains and Rivers Without End* (1996), a poem cycle some thirty years in the writing. In

1999 appeared *The Gary Snyder Reader: Prose, Poetry, and Translations 1952–1998*.

Snyders, Frans (1579–1657) Painter, born in Antwerp, N Belgium. He specialized in still-life and animals, often assisting Rubens and other painters. He became court painter to the Governor of the Low Countries, for whom he painted some of his finest hunting scenes.

Soane, Sir John (1753–1837) Architect, born in Goring, Oxfordshire, SC England, UK. He trained in London, visited Italy (1777–80), held several government posts, and became professor of architecture at the Royal Academy (1806). His designs include the Bank of England (1792–1833, now rebuilt), and Dulwich Picture Gallery (1811–14). His house at Lincoln's Inn Fields has become a museum.

soap The salt of a fatty acid, usually stearic (octadecanoic) or palmitic (hexadecanoic) acids. Soaps appear to have originated in prehistoric Germany, where fats were hydrolysed by natural alkali from wood ashes. Soaps are ionic detergents, and commercial soaps for washing are normally sodium or potassium salts. Hard water causes the calcium or magnesium salt to precipitate. Insoluble calcium soaps are, however, used as lubricants.

soapstone *talc*

soapwort A perennial with creeping stolons and erect leafy stems (*Saponaria officinalis*), native to Europe and Asia; flowers 2·5 cm/1 in diameter, fragrant; calyx tubular, often reddish; five petals, spreading, pale pink, each with two scales at the base. (Family: Caryophyllaceae.)

Sobers, Gary [sohberz], popular name of **Sir Garfield St Aubrun Sobers** (1936–) Cricketer, born in Barbados. A great West Indian all-rounder, he is the only man to score 8000 Test runs and take 200 wickets. During his career (1953–74) he scored 28 315 runs in first-class cricket (average 54·87) and took 1043 wickets (average 27·74). Against Pakistan at Kingston in 1958 he scored a Test cricket world record 365 not out, which stood until 1994. Playing for Nottinghamshire against Glamorgan at Swansea in 1968, he scored a record 36 runs in one (six-ball) over. He retired in 1974, and was knighted the following year.

Sobukwe, Robert Mangaliso [sohbookway] (1924–78) African nationalist leader, born in Graaff-Reinet, S South Africa. He was the co-founder and first president of the Pan African Congress, the main rival to the African National Congress (ANC) as opponent of the apartheid regime. His political involvement began while he was at the University of Fort Hare, when he joined the ANC Youth League. In 1958 he broke with the ANC on 'Africanist' grounds, advocating African political self-sufficiency, and hostile to alliance with leftists of other races. He was jailed in 1960, and detained on Robben I (1963–9) under legislation (nicknamed the 'Sobukwe clause') used only against him. After his release from prison, he lived a further nine years under house arrest and stringent restrictions.

soca [sohka] Caribbean (originally Trinidadian) dance music, developed in the 1970s from calypso; the word may be a portmanteau of *soul* and *calypso*. Soca is generally faster than calypso, with a more varied instrumentation. Its first performers included Lord Shorty (real name Garfield Blackman, 1941– , later known as Ras Shorty) and calypsonians such as Mighty Shadow (real name Winston Bailey, born late 1930s), and Maestro (real name Cecil Hume, 1945–78). **Parang soca** is a popular fusion with **parang**, a Trinidadian Christmas music, and **chutney soca** adds Indian flavourings.

soccer *football, Association*

soccerene *buckminsterfullerene*

Sochi [sochee] 43°35N 39°46E, pop (2000e) 338 000. Seaport in Krasnodarskiy kray, S European Russia; founded as a spa, 1896; stretches for over 30 km/19 mi along the E shore of the Black Sea; airport; railway; important holiday and health resort; fortress ruins (1838).

Social and Liberal Democratic Party (SLDP) *Liberal Party* (UK)

social anthropology *anthropology*

social behaviourism A school of thought in social psychology which argues that all observable social action is in response to the hidden needs, desires, or beliefs of the deeper 'self'. These ideas were given particular prominence through the work of social psychologist George Herbert Mead (1863–1931).

social chapter The chapter of the Maastricht Treaty of 1991 dealing with the labour market and social security. This was agreed by 11 of the then 12 members of the European Community (now European Union). The chapter's provisions arose from a programme suggested by the Social Affairs Commissioner of the EC. This concerned health and safety at work, conditions of employment, part-time and temporary workers, freedom of movement within the EC, the treatment of immigrant workers, and social security. The UK government did not sign the chapter in 1991, because of concerns that it would harm the economy by increasing rigidities in the labour market, but later did so.

social cognition In psychology, the processes through which the social world is perceived, understood, and reasoned about. Theorists who write about these processes tend to stress the impact of thinking on social action.

social contract or **social compact** The voluntary, unwritten agreement between a society's members to act in a mutually responsible manner, accepting the authority of the state which in turn guarantees and upholds certain moral principles. The philosophy maintains that greater efforts should be made to secure more equality for all sections of society. How far government should interfere with market forces to achieve this would be the subject of consensus within a nation. This philosophy was first propounded by Hobbes, Locke, and Rousseau, and has been an important feature of much liberal political theory in recent years. The concept was also seen in the UK in 1975, when the Labour government under Wilson arrived at a consensus with the Trades Union Council on the broad social and economic policies that the government should pursue. However, in 1978 no agreement could be reached, and the system lapsed.

Social Credit A monetary theory proposed by C H Douglas in Canada in 1924. It involved increasing consumer purchasing power by means of a state-backed 'credit'. It was embraced most notably by William Aberhart of Alberta, whose Social Credit Party held provincial office from 1935 to 1971. Social Credit political movements were also consequential in British Columbia, New Zealand, and Quebec (*Créditistes*).

Social Darwinism A school of thought which developed within 19th-c sociology based on the belief that social evolution depended on society adapting most efficiently to its environment. The associated 'eugenics movement' argued that Western society had developed because of the superior abilities of whites compared with other 'racial' groups.

social democracy A section of the socialist movement which emerged in the late 19th-c after the break-up of the First International, and which advocates achieving social change through reformist rather than revolutionary means. Social democrats accept and work through existing state structures, although such movements may contain radical left-wing sections. Some political parties that adopted the social democratic label in the latter part of the 20th-c were, however, moderate centrist parties.

Social Democratic Party (SDP) A UK political party formed in 1981 by a 'gang of four', comprising David Owen, Shirley Williams, Roy Jenkins, and Bill Rogers (1928–). They broke away from the Labour Party primarily over disagreements on policy and the degree of influence exerted on Party policy by the trade unions. Although espousing socialist principles, the Party was a moderate centrist one. The SDP formed an electoral pact with the Liberals in 1981, but despite some early electoral successes failed to break the two-party 'mould' of British politics. It merged with the Liberal Party in 1988, becoming the **Social and Liberal Democrats** (later known as the **Liberal Demo-**

crats), although a rump, led by David Owen, continued as the SDP until 1990.

social engineering A term used (often critically) to describe the techniques dominant social groups may use to manipulate the subordinate population. It is typically applied to policies of government that lack democratic accountability; for example, many criticized the manipulative family planning programmes of the Indian government during the 1970s.

Social Gospel An early 20th-c movement in the USA concerned with the application of Christian principles to the social and political order in the service of the Kingdom of God. Among its most prominent leaders were Washington Gladden (1836–1918), Walter Rauschenbusch (1861–1918), and Shailer Matthews (1863–1941).

social history History which concentrates upon the interaction of groups and upon the nature of social structures in the past. Once undervalued, both as a descriptive subject concerned with unearthing the minutiae of everyday life and as a less analytical appendage to economic history, social history has developed rapidly since the 1960s. It has incorporated social science methods, particularly in analyzing the importance of class and status in understanding the process of social change. While much social history has concentrated upon the history of the lower orders, usually neglected in political history, increasing attention has been paid since the early 1960s to the analysis of the middle classes and the aristocracy as social groups. The insights of social history have also begun to broaden the scope of political history, such that the distinction between the two disciplines has become blurred.

socialism A wide-ranging political doctrine which first emerged in Europe during industrialization in the 18th-c. Most socialists would agree that social and economic relationships play a major part in determining human possibilities, and that the unequal ownership of the means of production under capitalism creates an unequal and conflictive society. The removal of property employed in the production process, or some means of counterbalancing its power, it is held, will produce a more equal society where individuals enjoy greater freedom and are able to realize their potential more fully. A socialist society will thus bring about a greater degree of equality in living standards. Possibly the major division within socialism is between those who believe that to bring it about revolution is necessary, and those who believe change can be achieved through reforms within the confines of democratic politics. There are also differences as to how far capitalist production needs to be eradicated to bring about a socialist society, and more socialists now opt for social democracy or market socialism.

Socialist Labor Party The longest-lasting socialist party in the USA. It nominated its first presidential candidate in 1892 and has existed ever since.

Socialist Party (UK) *Militant Tendency*

Socialist Realism In literature and art, the officially approved style of the former Soviet Union and of other socialist states, intended to appeal to the masses, and typically representing ordinary workers going about their mundane tasks. It produced armies of writers, artists, and composers (the 'engineers of human souls', in Stalin's words) who were dedicated to the propaganda of social realism as a reaction to 'bourgeois' realism. The Hungarian Marxist critic Georg Lukács was a major proponent, and Russian self-exile Andrei Sinyavsky (1925–97) a noted antagonist. The novels of Mikhail Sholokhov may be cited, but few writers could exactly fulfil a prescription for what Trotsky called 'the literature of the future'.

Socialist Revolutionary (SR) Party A neo-populist revolutionary party in Russia, founded in 1902 and led by Victor Chernov (1873–1952). The SR's radical agrarian programme envisaged the uncompensated redistribution and 'socialization' of the land among a communally organized peasantry. Their 'fighting detachments' carried out a number of spectacular political assassinations between 1902 and 1918. In 1917 Chernov was minister of agriculture under Kerensky in the provisional government.

social medicine *community medicine*

social mobility The way individuals or groups move from one status or class position to another, either higher ('upward' social mobility) or lower ('downward' social mobility), within the social hierarchy. It is typically measured in terms of movement across a range of pre-existing positions which enjoy unequal access to material and cultural 'goods'. One can improve one's access to such goods, and so be upwardly mobile in a number of ways, most importantly by education, marriage, or occupation. Entire social groups may also be mobile, by using their resources to enhance their position: for example, occupational groups may improve their status by 'professionalizing' their expertise.

social movement Any significant social or political force which aims to bring about change, but which has only the minimum of organization and operates through self-generating and independent action, such as the women's movement. These movements have played a significant part in many important social and political changes. They sometimes produce more organized forms of action, in the form of political parties and pressure groups, as for example has been the case with the green movement.

social psychology The study of the behaviour of groups of individuals. Social psychologists might record anything from fine-grained details of the body posture and gaze direction of an individual, in an attempt to understand non-verbal communication, to large-scale characteristics of crowd behaviour. They are also concerned with concepts that necessarily involve more than one individual, such as leadership, friendship, and persuasion.

social realism A term current in art criticism since World War 2, referring to pictures which treat 'real life' subjects in a way that challenges the values of 'bourgeois' society. Courbet's 'Stonebreakers' (1849) may have been the first great social realist picture. In the 20th-c the term was applied to the US Ashcan School, and in Europe to Italian artist Renato Guttoso (1912–87).

social science A general term designating a number of disciplines, such as sociology, economics, political science, and geography, which have explored various aspects of society – such as social structure, the market, power, and spatial relations – through methods which are conventionally understood to be 'scientific'. Research involves data collection and analysis in order to test hypotheses or models. Mathematical analyses are now commonplace in some areas, such as demography and social mobility studies. Nevertheless, there is still debate over whether these disciplines can be truly 'scientific', given that they are measuring patterns of human behaviour rather than the organic or inanimate material of the natural and physical sciences.

social security In the USA, a tax on wages and salaries imposed to pay for retirement benefits, disability insurance, and hospital insurance. The tax is an important part of all Federal revenues (around 40%), and is the equivalent of British national insurance. In the UK, social security refers to the provision of financial aid by the state to reduce poverty. It comprises a wide range of benefits (covering such matters as housing and family allowances) which are available to those in need. More broadly, social security is a system of financial maintenance organized by governments to protect individuals against loss of earnings resulting from sickness, unemployment, and old age, and to give support to families with children. The term also covers social insurance and social assistance schemes. With social security receipts accounting for a quarter of GDP in some countries, governments have raised insurance contributions and reduced benefits while boosting the importance of occupational and personal insurance. Most developing countries and former communist countries lack either the money or the administrative infrastructure for social security systems.

social stratification A system of social inequality in which social groups occupy different positions (or *strata*) based on their unequal access to and ownership of material, political, and cultural (eg educational) resources. Social stratification is never a random process, but a product of economic and social relations that 'allocate' people to specific positions within a structured social hierarchy.

social studies A range of disciplines within the arts, humanities, and social sciences, including sociology, history, economics, and geography, whose principal concern is the study of various aspects of society. With the development of more sophisticated and scientific analyses, the term is less favoured today and more likely to be replaced by **social sciences**.

social system The structured pattern of social relationships which together have a systemic character. A society has a social system inasmuch as change in some aspects of society will bring change in other parts. There have been different types of social system prevailing in different periods of history, such as feudalism, capitalism, and socialism. Sociologists have also distinguished 'traditional' from 'modern' social systems, but there is considerable debate over the exact meaning of these two terms.

social work A term which is usually understood to refer to the occupational activities of the social-work profession, ie the provision of social services to the 'needy', including counselling, care, and the general administration of the benefits of the state. Social work has its origins in late 19th-c charitable organizations which provided assistance to hospital staff and helped distribute poor relief.

society *class; consumer / post-industrial society*

Society Islands, Fr **Archipel de la Société** pop (2000e) 193 000; area 1535 sq km/592 sq mi. One of the five archipelagoes of French Polynesia, comprising the Windward Is (including Tahiti) and the Leeward Is; two clusters of volcanic and coral islands in a 720 km/450 mi chain stretching NW–SE; visited by Captain Cook in 1769, and named by him after the Royal Society; French protectorate, 1844; French colony, 1897; capital, Papeete (Tahiti); phosphates, copra, vanilla, mother-of-pearl.

Socinus, Laelius [sosiynus], Ital **Lelio (Francesco Maria) Sozini** (1525–62) Protestant reformer, born in Siena, C Italy. He trained as a lawyer at Padua, then turned to biblical studies. He travelled widely in Europe, settling in Zürich (1548). His anti-Trinitarian views were developed by his nephew into a doctrine known as *Socinianism*.

sociobiology The integrated study of the biological basis of social behaviour, based on the assumption that all behaviour is adaptive. Emphasis is placed on social systems as ecological adaptations, and explanations are given in terms of evolutionary theory.

sociogram *sociometry*

sociolinguistics The study of the relationships between language and the society which uses it. The subject has a wide range, encompassing the analysis of all the varieties used in a community, and the contexts in which they are appropriate. This includes the use of standard and non-standard forms, and the attitudes towards them of different groups; the language of different social class and caste groups; the differences between male and female speech; and the character of multilingual societies, particularly the social functions assigned to the languages by bilingual members of the community. The subject sometimes includes such societally-based studies as dialectology and ethnolinguistics.

sociology The study of patterned social behaviour which constitutes a social system or society, a term originally coined by French social theorist Auguste Comte. Sociologists explore the way in which social structures are continually modified as a result of social interaction, and thereby seek to explain the development of new institutions or new types of society. Modern sociology has a number of key theoretical approaches which try to account for social structure and social change. While they differ in very important respects, they all share the belief that they can 'get behind' the surface appearance of everyday life, to reveal its complexity and interest. Any aspect of society can be examined sociologically, but there have emerged certain areas of study that have gained most attention, such as crime, the family, gender, the media, science and technology, medicine, and systems of inequality.

sociometry A technique for mapping social networks. The networks are based on respondents ranking those people they find more and those less desirable; the technique can be used by psychologists to build a theory of association between people. A graphical representation of a network of social relationships is known as a **sociogram**.

sockeye Species of salmon (*Oncorhynchus nerka*), widespread in the N Pacific Ocean and adjacent rivers; length up to 80 cm/ 32 in; feeds mainly on crustaceans during life at sea; migrates into fresh water to breed, the adults dying after spawning; an important commercial species along the American seaboard; also known as **red salmon**. (Family: Salmonidae.)

Socrates [sokrateez] (469–399 BC) Greek philosopher, born in Athens, Greece. Little is known of his early life. By Plato's account, he devoted his last 30 years to convincing the Athenians that their opinions about moral matters could not bear the weight of critical scrutiny. His technique, the *Socratic method*, was to ask for definitions of such morally significant concepts as piety and justice, and to elicit contradictions from the responses, thus exposing the ignorance of the responder and motivating deeper enquiry into the concepts. His profession to know none of the answers himself is ironic: he most probably held the doctrines that human excellence is a kind of knowledge; thus, that all wrongdoing is based on ignorance, that no one desires bad things; and that it is worse to do injustice than to suffer it. He was tried on charges of impiety and corruption of youth by zealous defenders of a restored democracy in Athens. Found guilty, he was put to death by drinking hemlock. His personality and his doctrines were immortalized in Plato's dialogues; his influence on Western philosophy is incalculable.

soda *sodium*

soda bread A type of bread which uses sodium bicarbonate to provide the necessary carbon dioxide. In contrast to yeast-risen bread, it is easier and quicker to prepare.

Soddy, Frederick (1877–1956) Radiochemist, born in Eastbourne, East Sussex, SE England, UK. He studied in Wales and at Oxford, and held posts at Montreal, Glasgow, Aberdeen, and Oxford, where he was professor of chemistry (1919–36). In 1913 he discovered forms of the same element with identical chemical qualities but different atomic weights (which he called *isotopes*), for which he received the Nobel Prize for Chemistry in 1921.

Soderbergh, Steven [sohderberg] (1963–) Director and screenwriter, born in Atlanta, Georgia, USA. He gained recognition with his directorial debut, *sex, lies, and videotape* (1989), which was nominated for an Academy Award and won the Palme d'Or at Cannes. Later films include *Kafka* (1991), *The Limey* (1999), *Erin Brockovich* (2000), *Traffic* (2000, Oscar, Best Director), and *Full Frontal* (2003).

Södertälje [soedertelye], formerly **Tälje** 59°11N 17°39E, pop (2000e) 85 000. Industrial town in Stockholm county, SE Sweden; suburb of Stockholm on the Södertälje Canal (1807–19); originally a Viking trading station set between L Mälar and the Baltic Sea.

sodium Na (Lat *natrium*), element 11, melting point 97·8°C. A very soft and reactive alkali metal, not found free in nature, but always in the form of one of its salts, in which it shows oxidation state +1. These occur in salt deposits, but **sodium chloride** (common salt, or NaCl) can also be extracted from ocean water, of which it makes up about 3·5%. The metal is obtained by electrolysis of molten NaCl, and is a very strong reducing agent, widely used in organic reactions and for the production of **sodium cyanide** (NaCN) and **sodium cyanamide** (Na_2CN_2), used in metallurgy and fertilizers. **Sodium carbonate** and

bicarbonate (Na_2CO_3 and $NaHCO_3$), also called *washing so*[…] and *baking soda*, are important industrial chemicals, as […]s **sodium hydroxide** (NaOH), also called *caustic soda* or [l]*ye*, used in soap making.

Sodom and Gomorrah [sodom, gomohra] Two of five 'cities of the plain' in ancient Palestine, perhaps now submerged under the S end of the Dead Sea or located to the SE of the Dead Sea. In *Gen* 18–19 the people were legendary for their wickedness, especially their sexual perversity. The stories tell how Lot and his family were warned to flee from their home in Sodom just before the city was destroyed by 'brimstone and fire' as a divine judgment.

Soekarno, Achmad *Sukarno*

Sofia [sofeea], Bulgarian **Sofiya**, Lat **Serdica** 42°40N 23°18E, pop (2000e) 1 223 000. Capital of Bulgaria since 1878, situated on a plateau in W Bulgaria; Roman town 1st–4th-c; under Byzantine rule 6th–9th-c; under Turkish rule 1382–1878; airport (Vrazhdebna); railway; university (1888); steel, machinery, electronics, food processing, chemicals, museums, theatres, opera house, observatory; Alexander Nevsky memorial cathedral; 4th-c St George Rotunda; 6th-c Church of St Sofia; Boyana Church; Sofia Musical Weeks (May–Jun); chorus festivals; international book fair.

softball A smaller version of baseball, played using a diamond-shaped infield with bases 60 ft (18·3 m) apart. The object, as in baseball, is to score runs by completing a circuit of the diamond before being put out. The principal differences between the two sports are that the softball field is smaller, the ball is bigger, the pitcher throws the ball underarm, and the game lasts seven innings (not nine). Slow-pitch softball is played ten (not nine) a side.

soft-shelled turtle A reptile native to E USA, Africa, and S Asia; small shell covered by leathery skin (without horny plates); nostrils on end of narrow projection; three claws on each foot; inhabits fresh water (occasionally estuaries). (Family: Trionychidae. Order: Chelonia, 22 species.) The SE Asian *Carettochelys insculpta* (Family: Carettochelyidae) is called the **pig-nosed softshell turtle**.

soft systems methodology A technique for looking at organizational systems to see whether they function in the optimum manner needed to achieve the objectives of the organization. It is an approach taken when there seem to be some difficulties in the existing business system, but the problems involved are complex, fuzzy, or not well understood. A soft systems study is often the first step in carrying out a systems analysis and design on an organization, prior to introducing replacement computer-based systems.

software The suite of all computer programs, including operating system, compilers, packages, and user programs, which enable a particular computer centre to operate. The notion is contrasted with the **hardware** and the **liveware**. **Software engineering** is a methodology for developing computer software with the objective of ensuring that the software is efficient, does the job for which it is intended, and is produced within cost and on time. The intention is that software design and production should be akin to the design and production of other engineering products. A **software house** is an organization devoted primarily to the production of computer software either for a manufacturer, for a computer user, or for direct sale.

Sogne Fjord [songnuh fyaw(r)d], Norwegian **Sognefjorden** Inlet of Norwegian Sea, Sogn og Fjordane county, W coast of Norway; extends E inland 204 km/127 mi; largest Norwegian fjord; average width, 5 km/3 mi; maximum depth, 1245 m/4085 ft.

SOHO *Solar and Heliospheric Observatory project*

soil The top layer of the Earth's surface, comprising a mixture of fine weathered rock particles and organic matter. The finest particles form clay; the less fine, silt; and the coarsest, sand. Provided moisture is available, soils generally support vegetation, and provide a habitat for a wide range of soil flora and fauna.

soil management The application of scientific management to agricultural land, including the maintenance of soil structures, the supply of nutrients, and the control of soil pollution and erosion. Many farmers now use a policy of reduced tillage to conserve their fertile topsoil. Good physical conditions in the soil are achieved by the maintenance and balance of organic matter through crop rotation and fertilization. *Cover crops* may be planted to protect the soil during winter; *green manure crops* are grown solely to be ploughed into the ground and serve to increase the organic matter content of the soil. Further nutrients are supplied through the manuring of the soil with animal waste, compost, and chemical or organic fertilizer. The maintenance of specific soil acidities is important in order to encourage the adaptation of high-yielding crops to different soils. Soil pollution is now recognized to have adverse effects on plant growth and on animal and human health. It is caused by the presence of toxic compounds, chemicals, salts, radioactive materials, or disease-causing agents that enter the soil through industrial waste and pesticides. By careful soil management some of these toxins may decompose and eventually disappear.

soil profile A vertical section through the soil revealing four basic soil horizons: the surface layer, or **topsoil**, which contains organic material; an **upper subsoil**, rich in nutrients but containing little organic matter; a **lower subsoil** of partly weathered mineral material; and the **bedrock** material from which the upper layers may have been derived.

soil science The study of soil, its information, and its management as a medium for plant growth. It includes both the physical management of soil, through cultivation, drainage, and irrigation, and the chemical management of soil, through the control of nutrient status, acidity, and salinity.

soja *soya bean*

Soka Gakkai [sohka gakiy] (Jap 'value-creating society') An association of lay Buddhists of the Nichiren school, founded in Japan in 1937 by Tsunesaburo Makiguchi and Josei Toda. Claiming over 12 million followers in 2004, it is highly organized, and dedicated to the promotion of Nichiren beliefs. It sponsors its own political party and operates its own schools and a university.

Solar and Heliospheric Observatory (SOHO) project A co-operative project between the European Space Agency and NASA to study the Sun from its deep core to its outer corona, and also to study the solar wind. SOHO was launched by an Atlas vehicle in December 1995, and subsequently inserted into a 'halo' orbit around the L1 Lagrangian point, located about 1·5 million km/900 000 mi sunward from the Earth. From this vantage point, SOHO has continuously monitored the Sun, the heliosphere, and the solar wind particles.

solar cell A device for converting light directly into electrical power. It exploits the photovoltaic effect in junctions between semiconductor materials. Commercial cells using single crystals of silicon are efficient (converting c.14% of incident energy to electricity) but expensive; other materials are cheaper, such as germanium arsenide and amorphous silicon, but less efficient. The cells are arranged in arrays in series and parallel to give the desired voltage and current. A single silicon cell, 10 cm/4 in in diameter, has an output voltage of about 0·6 V and an output power of about 0·4 W. Solar cells are used to provide electrical power in remote places, such as buoys and space satellites.

solar constant The total radiation falling on the Earth from the Sun; symbol *S*, value 1365 W/m^2 (watts per metre squared). A better term is **total solar irradiance**, more fully the sum over the entire spectrum of the Sun's irradiance at all wavelengths incident on top of the Earth's atmosphere at an Earth–Sun distance of 1 Astronomical Unit. The total solar irradiance continually changes by as much as 1% and is therefore not constant, though the term *solar constant* remains in use by meteorologists and climatologists.

solar day *day*

solar flare A violent release of energy in the vicinity of an active region on the Sun, emitting energetic particles, X-rays, and radio waves. It causes notable auroral displays in our upper atmosphere.

solar neutrino problem The discrepancy between the number of neutrinos that are expected to emanate from the Sun due to the nuclear processes that power it, and the number reaching Earth from the Sun, which is too small. The problem was first noted by US physicist Raymond Davis, whose neutrino detection experiment began running in 1967. Despite a variety of experiments since, the discrepancy remains. Revision of models of the Sun, or of the understanding of neutrinos, may be necessary to resolve the problem.

solar power Energy radiating from the Sun, exploited in a number of ways to provide energy for heat and electricity generation. **Solar panels** or **collectors** (a black metal absorber) can be used to extract heat from the warmth of sunshine to heat water or air in pipes contained in or beneath the panels. In some arid countries, panels are used to power stills for evaporating saline water, condensing the vapour and collecting it as freshwater. Collectors can also be focused onto a small area of water to heat it, producing steam for electricity generation. The use of solar energy is constrained by the need for sufficient sunshine, the supply of which is unpredictable at temperate latitudes. However, in many developing countries it has great potential, especially as it is a renewable energy resource. By the early 1980s, solar collectors were producing energy equivalent to 0·01% of the world's total oil consumption.

solar prominence Flame-like clouds of matter in the solar chromosphere, sometimes triggered by solar flares, reaching heights of 1 000 000 km/600 000 mi at extremes. They are visible using special instruments such as the coronagraph, or during a total eclipse.

Solar System The Sun and its associated, gravitationally bound, system of nine planets, their 101 numbered satellites (March 2004), the c.75 000 numbered asteroids, the comets, and interplanetary dust. The planets – Mercury, Venus, Earth, Mars (the four 'inner planets'), Jupiter, Saturn, Uranus, Neptune (the four outer 'gas giants') and Pluto – and asteroids orbit approximately in the plane of the Sun's equator, and rotate about the Sun in the same direction (counter-clockwise when viewed from a N polar direction). There is systematic variation in the character of the planets: the inner planets are comparatively small and dense, and are composed of high-temperature condensates (chiefly iron and metal silicates), while the four outer planets are much larger, and mainly composed of low-temperature condensates (chiefly gases and ices); Pluto is unique and poorly known. The asteroids also show systematic variation of properties with distance from the Sun. The comets – made of ices and dust – lie at greatest distance from the Sun in a shell known as the *Oort Cloud*, and are only tenuously bound gravitationally. Much information has also been derived from the study of meteorites which originate from asteroids. It is thought that the planetary system was formed 4·6 thousand million years ago as a by-product of the Sun's formation, which resulted from the gravitational collapse of an accumulation of gas and dust in this region of the Milky Way galaxy. Many more satelites and asteroids await confirmation.

solar time Time measured by considering the rotation of the Earth relative to the Sun. **Mean solar time** is established by reference to the mean Sun, and was established as the fundamental measure of clock time before it was realized that the Earth has variable rotation. **Apparent solar time** is time shown by a sundial. The difference between the two can amount to 16·4 min (early November).

solar wind A stream of charged particles (*plasma*) emanating from the upper atmosphere (corona) of the Sun and expanding continuously into the interplanetary medium with a velocity of 300–800 km/s (200–500 mi/s). Most of the flow appears to originate in the Sun's polar regions. The solar magnetic field is embedded in radially outflowing plasma, and due to the Sun's rotation forms a spiral pattern like a rotating garden water sprinkler. The plasma interacts dynamically with planetary environments as it flows by them, notably by shaping the magnetospheres of those planets with magnetic fields. It is a highly dynamic phenomenon, influenced by such factors as solar flares and X-ray bursts.

solar year *tropical year*

solder An alloy which will melt easily at a moderate temperature, and so provide a bond between two metal surfaces. It usually consists of tin and lead, when used for joining copper, brass, or iron with tin-plate. As distinct from **welding**, soldering only fills in interstices in the juxtaposed metals, and does not fuse into them.

soldier beetle An elongate beetle; wing cases usually parallel-sided; adults commonly found on flowers and vegetation; larvae typically predatory, found in soil, leaf litter, and under bark; adults feed on nectar, pollen, or as predators. (Order: Coleoptera. Family: Cantharidae, c.5000 species.)

sole Any of the flatfish in the family Soleidae, widespread in shallow continental shelf waters of tropical to temperate seas; includes the common European sole, or **Dover sole** (*Solea solea*), distributed from the Mediterranean to Norway; length up to 50 cm/20 in; both eyes on right side of body; very popular food fish, taken commercially mainly by trawl. The name is also used elsewhere for flatfish belonging to other families.

Solemn League and Covenant An alliance between the English Parliament and the Scottish Covenanters against Charles I, agreed in September 1643. Parliament promised £30 000 a month to the Scots and the introduction of full Presbyterianism in England; the Scots agreed to provide an army to the hard-pressed parliamentarians to fight Charles. The pact facilitated parliamentary victory in the first Civil War, but although it was part of the bargain, Presbyterianism was never fully implemented in England.

solenodon [soleenodon] A mammal native to Cuba (*Solenodon cubanus*), and to Haiti and the Dominican Republic (*Solenodon paradoxurus*); an insectivore, resembling a very large shrew (length, up to 33 cm/13 in), with longer legs; has a venomous bite; inhabits forests; eats plants and small vertebrates. (Family: Solenodontidae, 2 species.)

solenoid A coil of wire, usually cylindrical, partially surrounding a movable iron core. When a current flows in the coil, a magnetic field is produced which makes the core move. A solenoid converts electrical energy into mechanical energy, as in operating a switch or circuit breaker.

Solent, the A channel separating the I of Wight from mainland England; a major shipping route from Southampton; yacht racing.

sol-fa, tonic *tonic sol-fa*

solfeggio [solfejioh] *solmization*

solicitor A lawyer whose responsibilities involve giving legal advice to clients. In order to practise, solicitors in the UK require a practising certificate from the appropriate Law Society. Solicitors have a right to appear for clients in the lower courts, but may not act as advocates in the Supreme Court or House of Lords unless they have the appropriate advocacy qualification. Most are concerned with advice on criminal law, family law, landlord and tenant law, and debt disputes. Solicitors also instruct barristers or advocates appearing for a client in either the lower or superior courts. The distinction between solicitors and barristers does not exist in the USA. A hybrid lawyer, termed a **solicitor advocate**, who can appear in the superior courts, was introduced in Scotland in 1993.

solicitor general In the UK, one of the government's law officers, who is a member of the House of Commons and junior to the attorney general. There is also a solicitor general for Scotland, who holds a similar position.

solid A dense form of matter characterized by its ability to transmit twisting forces and its inability to flow; virtually incompressible; tends to retain shape when stressed; described as rigid, the atoms generally not being free to move from point to point. Solids are divided into *crystals*, comprising ordered arrays of atoms; *amorphous solids*, which are disordered arrays; and *polymers* and *rubbers*, which comprise long chain-like molecules.

Solidarity (Polish *Solidarność*). An organization established in Poland (1980) as the National Committee of Solidarity to co-ordinate the activities of the emerging independent trade union following protracted industrial unrest, notably in the Lenin shipyard in Gdańsk. Its first president was Lech Wałęsa. It organized a number of strikes in early 1981 for improved wages and conditions, and became a force for major political reform. It attempted to seek reconciliation with the Polish government through proposing a council for national consensus, but suffered continuous harassment and was rendered largely ineffective by the declaration of martial law (Dec 1981) and by being made illegal. It remained underground, but came back into the political arena in mid-1988. Following its successes in the 1989 elections, Solidarity entered into a coalition government with the Communists, with one of its members (Tadeusz Mazowiecki) eventually becoming prime minister. Jerzy Buzek, who became prime minister in 1997, was also a member. In 1997, 36 organizations (parties, societies, trade unions) formed the coalition known as Solidarity Election Action (AWS), and in December 1999 the Solidarity congress transferred its voting rights within the coalition to the Solidarity Electoral Action Social Movement.

solid-state device A device in which an electric signal flows through a solid material rather than a vacuum. Most of the components (transistors, resistors, capacitors, and diodes), are made from a single solid piece of semiconductor material, such as silicon. They are much smaller and lighter than the traditional vacuum tubes and electrical components, and use less power, last longer, are more dependable, and cost less. Even smaller devices are being created using nanotechnology – placing individual atoms exactly, and making wires which are only a single atom thick.

solid-state physics The study of all properties of matter in the solid state; a sub-branch of condensed matter physics, which includes liquids and solids. Traditionally it focuses on crystal structure, more recently embracing more complex systems such as alloys, ceramics, amorphous solids, and surfaces.

Solihull [**solihuhl**] 52°25N 1°45W, pop (2001e) 199 500. Town in West Midlands, C England, UK; a suburb of SE Birmingham; National Exhibition Centre; Birmingham airport nearby; railway; vehicles, packaging, machinery.

soliloquy A stage device whereby a character talks aloud but alone, as it were confiding in the audience. The soliloquies of Richard III and Hamlet are famous examples in Shakespeare. The soliloquy is rare today in the theatre, but may be found in T S Eliot's *Murder in the Cathedral* (1935) and Robert Bolt's *A Man for All Seasons* (1954). A soliloquy shares similarities with the interior monologue or 'voice-over' in film.

Solingen [**zohlingn**] 51°10N 7°05E, pop (2000e) 168 000. Industrial city in Düsseldorf district, W Germany; in the Ruhr valley, 22 km/14 mi SE of Düsseldorf; badly bombed in World War 2; cutlery, chemicals, petrochemicals, hardware.

solipsism In philosophy, the theory that 'I' alone exist and that the 'outside world' exists only in my consciousness. However implausible, the thesis proves hard to refute from within theories such as Descartes', which make introspection and immediate experience the ultimate source of factual knowledge.

solitaire An extinct dodo-like bird. The name is also used for the **Hawaiian honeycreeper** (*Viridonia sagittirostris*) and New World thrushes of the genera *Myadestes* (7 species) and *Entomodestes* (2 species).

soliton A moving, solitary, stable wave having a well-defined position and constant amplitude; they can be observed in water in shallow channels, such as tidal bore waves. Solitons may provide a description of fundamental particles.

solmization A system for learning and recalling music by fitting syllables to pitches in a scale. The one used in Western music is attributed to Guido d'Arezzo (11th-c), who fitted the initial syllables of the first six lines of a Latin hymn to the notes of the hexachord to make *ut* (later changed to *do*), *re*, *mi*, *fa*, *sol*, *la*; *si* was added later. Textless singing exercises using these syllables are called *solfeggio*, in France *solfège*.

solo One of the family of trick-taking card games, similar to bridge. Players have to declare how many tricks they will win before each game. Tricks are won as in whist, but with the difference that the declarer plays without a partner (hence the name), and there is an auction.

Solomon (Hebrew Bible) (10th-c BC) King of Israel, the second son of David and Bathsheba. His outwardly splendid reign (described in 1 *Kings* 1–11 and 2 *Chron* 1–10) saw the expansion of the kingdom and the building of the great Temple in Jerusalem. But high taxation and alliances with heathen courts bred discontent, which later brought the disruption of the kingdom under his son, Rehoboam. Solomon was credited with extraordinary wisdom, and became a legendary figure in Judaism, so that his name became attached to several biblical and extra-canonical writings.

Solomon (music), professional name of **Solomon Cutner** (1902–88) Pianist, born in London, UK. After appearing with great success as a child prodigy, he retired for further study, and won a high reputation as a performer of the works of Beethoven, Brahms, and some of the modern composers. He did not tour as extensively as most players, and was forced to retire after a stroke in 1965.

Solomon, John (William) (1931–) British croquet player. He made his international debut against New Zealand in 1950 at age 19, and never missed an England Test Match between 1950 and 1973. He won a record 10 Open Croquet Championships (1953, 1956, 1959, 1961, 1963–8), the Men's Championship 10 times between 1951 and 1972, the Open Doubles Championship 10 times (all with Edmond Cotter) between 1954 and 1969, and the Mixed Doubles title once (with Freda Oddie) in 1954. He was winner of the President's Cup a record nine times.

Solomon, Psalms of A book of the Old Testament Pseudepigrapha, consisting of 18 psalms, probably written c.1st-c BC in response to the Roman occupation of Jerusalem. It expresses hopes for a Jewish state free of foreign domination, brought about by a messianic deliverer. It is traditionally considered the work of a Pharisee, but this is uncertain, and is significant for its expression of Jewish messianic expectations at this time.

Solomon Islands *p.1432*

Solomon Sea *Coral Sea*

Solomon's seal A perennial growing to 80 cm/30 in (*Polygonatum multiflorum*), native to Europe and Asia; rhizomatous; stems arching; leaves 5–12 cm/2–4¾ in, oval, in two rows; flowers white, bell-shaped, hanging in clusters beneath the stem. (Family: Liliaceae.)

Solon [**sohlon**] (7th–6th-c BC) Athenian statesman, law-giver, and poet. As chief archon, he enacted many economic, constitutional, and legal reforms, and paved the way for the development of democracy at Athens, and her emergence as a great trading state. Enslavement for debt was abolished, a new currency instituted, and citizenship granted to foreign craftsmen settling in Athens. Wealth rather than birth was made the criterion for participation in political life, and Draco's inhumane legal code was largely repealed.

Solow, Robert (Merton) [**soloh**] (1924–) Economist, born in New York City, USA. He studied at Harvard, and became professor at the Massachusetts Institute of Technology in 1958. He was awarded the 1987 Nobel Prize for Economics for his 'study of the factors which permit production growth and increased welfare'.

solstice An event when the Sun is at its furthest point from the Equator, resulting in the longest day and shortest night (the **summer solstice**) in one hemisphere and the shortest day and longest night (the **winter solstice**) in the other hemisphere. In the N hemisphere, the summer solstice is on 21 or 22 June and the winter solstice on 21 or 22 December. Solstices occur

Solomon Islands

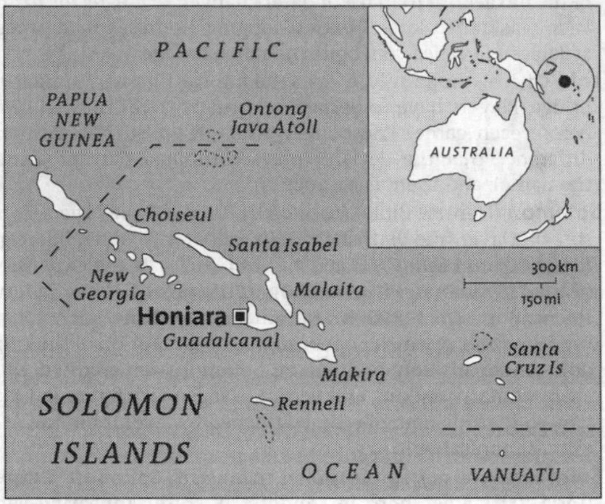

☐ International Airport

Local name Solomon Islands
Timezone GMT +11
Land area 27 556 km²/10 637 sq mi
Population total (2002e) 439 000
Status Independent state within the Commonwealth
Date of independence 1978
Capital Honiara
Languages English (official), with pidgin English and c.80 local languages also spoken
Ethnic groups Melanesian (93%), Polynesian (4%), Micronesian (1·5%), European (1%), Chinese (0·5%)
Religions Christian (95%) (Protestant 41%, Anglican 34%, Roman Catholic 19%)
Physical features Archipelago of several hundred islands in the SW Pacific Ocean, stretching c.1400 km/870 mi, between Papua New Guinea (NW) and Vanuatu (SE); six main islands, Choiseul, Guadalcanal, Malaita, New Georgia, San Cristobal (now Makira), Santa Isabel; highest point, Mt Makarakomburu, 2477 m/8126 ft, on Guadalcanal (largest island); large islands have forested mountain ranges and coastal belts; Anuta, Fataka, and Tikopia islands are volcanic; Tikopia and Anuta struck by Cyclone Zoë (Dec 2002).
Climate Equatorial climate; high humidity; average annual temperature 27°C; maximum rainfall Nov–Apr; average annual rainfall, c.3500 mm/138 in; periodic cyclones.
Currency 1 Solomon Islands Dollar (SI$) = 100 cents
Economy Based on agriculture; forestry, livestock, fisheries, taro, rice, bananas, yams, copra, oil palm, rice; milling, fish processing; crafts.
GDP (2001e) $800 mn, per capita $1700
Human Development Index (2002) 0·622
History Visited by the Spanish, 1568; S Solomon Is placed under British protection, 1893; outer islands (Santa Cruz group) added to the protectorate, 1899; scene of fierce fighting in World War 2; achieved internal self-government, 1976; independence, 1978; British monarch represented by a Governor-General; Prime Minister leads a unicameral National Parliament; fighting between two rival militias led to military coup (Jun 2000) and the resignation of Bartholomew Ulufa'alu; peace treaty brokered by Australia (Oct 2000); continued ethnic unrest, with departure of prime minister Kemakeza from the capital and arrival of Australian-led peace-keeping force (Jul 2003).
Head of State
(British monarch represented by Governor-General)
1999– Sir John Ini Lapli
Head of Government
1978–82 Peter Kenilorea
1982–4 Solomon Mamaloni
1984–6 Peter Kenilorea
1986–9 Ezekiel Alebua
1989–93 Solomon Mamaloni
1993–4 Frances Billy Hilly
1994–7 Solomon Mamaloni
1997–2000 Bartholomew Ulufa'alu
2000–2001 Manasseh Sogavare
2001– Sir Allan Kemakeza

because the Earth's axis is inclined to the plane of its orbit around the Sun.

Solti, Sir Georg [sholtee] (1912–97) Conductor, born in Budapest, Hungary. World War 2 forced him to give up his post as conductor of the Budapest Opera, and he worked in Switzerland until 1946, when he became director at the Munich Staatsoper (until 1952), at Frankfurt (1952–61), and Covent Garden, London (1961–71). He conducted the Chicago Symphony Orchestra (1969–91) and the London Philharmonic (1979–83, then emeritus), and later became artistic director of the Salzburg Easter Festival (1992–3). He was granted an honorary knighthood in 1971, and took British nationality in 1972.

solubility The extent to which one substance (the *solute*) dissolves in another (the *solvent*). It is expressed in many ways, generally as the mass or number of moles of solute which dissolve in a unit volume of solvent.

solution A uniform phase, generally liquid, containing more than one component. When one component is present in excess, it is called the **solvent**; minor components are called **solutes**. Many alloys are solid solutions, in which the various metal atoms are randomly dispersed through the structure.

Solutrian [solyutreean] In European prehistory, a short division of the Upper Palaeolithic Age, named after the site at La Solutré, Saône et Loire, C France, discovered in 1866. Its finely-made, bifacial stone tools date to c.19000–18000 BC.

Solvay process or **ammonia–soda process** A technique for the production of sodium carbonate (an important industrial alkali), devised in 1865 by Belgian chemist Ernest Solvay (1838–1922), and improved by Ludwig Mond in 1870. Sodium chloride is treated with ammonia and then with carbon dioxide. This produces sodium bicarbonate (which is heated to give the desired sodium carbonate) and ammonium chloride, which is treated with lime to recover the ammonia for recycling.

solvent The major component of a solution. Water is often described as the 'universal solvent', but the term is also applied specifically to volatile organic materials such as acetone and ethyl acetate, used in paints and adhesives.

Solway Firth Inlet of the Irish Sea, separating Cumbria, England, from Dumfries and Galloway, Scotland; estuary of Esk and Eden Rivers; length c.65 km/40 mi; width at mouth, c.40 km/25 mi; noted for its salmon fisheries.

Solzhenitsyn, Alexander (Isayevich) [solzhenitsin] (1918–) Writer, born in Kislovodsk, SW Russia. Educated at Rostov in mathematics and physics, he fought in World War 2, and was imprisoned (1945–53) for unfavourable comment on Stalin's conduct of the war. On his release, he became a teacher, and started to write. His first novel (trans titles), *One Day in the Life of Ivan Denisovich* (1962), set in a prison camp, was acclaimed both in the USSR and the West; but his subsequent denunciation of Soviet censorship led to the banning of his later, semi-autobiographical novels, *Cancer Ward* (1968) and *The First Circle* (1968). He was expelled from the Soviet Writers' Union in 1969, and awarded the Nobel Prize for Literature in 1970 (received in 1974). His later books include *The Gulag Archipelago* (1973–8), a factual account of the Stalinist terror, for which he was arrested and exiled (1974), and *Invisible Allies* (1996). He lived in the USA,

Somalia

[sohmahleeuh], official name **Somali Democratic Republic**, Arabic **Jamhuriyadda Dimugradiga Somaliya**

Local name Somaliya

Timezone GMT +3

Area 637 357 km²/246 201 sq mi

Population total (2002e) 7 753 000

Status Republic

Date of independence 1960

Capital Mogadishu

Languages Somali, Arabic (official)

Ethnic groups Somali (85%), Bantu (15%), with Arab, European, and Asian minorities

Religions Sunni Muslim (99%), small Christian minority

Physical features Occupies the E Horn of Africa, where dry coastal plain broadens to the S, and rises inland to a plateau c.1000 m/ 3300 ft; forested mountains on the Gulf of Aden coast rise to 2416 m/7926 ft at Mt Shimbiris; main rivers, Jubba and Webi Shabeelle.

Climate Predominantly arid; average daily maximum temperatures 28–32°C in Mogadishu; average annual rainfall 490 mm/ 19·3 in; heavier rainfall (Apr–Sep) on E coast; serious, persistent threat of drought.

Currency 1 Somali Shilling (SoSh) = 100 cents

Economy Agriculture (c.50% nomadic people raising cattle, sheep, goats, camels); khat (qat), bananas, sugar, spices, cotton, rice, citrus fruits, tobacco, iron ore; textiles; fishing.

GDP (2001e) $4·27 bn, per capita $600

History Settled by Muslims, 7th-c; Italian, French, and British interests after the opening of the Suez Canal, 1869; after World War 2, Somalia formed by the amalgamation of Italian and British protectorates; independence, 1960; from the 1960s, territorial conflict with Ethiopia over Ogaden which has a large Somali population; military coup, 1969; peace agreement with Ethiopia, 1989; governed by a President, Council of Ministers, and People's Assembly; new constitution approved, 1990; NW region seceded as Somaliland Republic, 1991; civil war, 1991–2, forced UN troops to intervene to safeguard food supplies for starving population, 1992; gradual withdrawal of forces, 1993-5; National Salvation Council formed, 1997; further peace accord, signed in Cairo by 26 of the country's 28 factions, 1997, but discord ongoing into 2000; transitional government formed, 2000; peace agreement, Jan 2004

Head of State

1980–91 Mohammed Siad Barre
1991–2000 Ali Mahdi Muhammed *Interim*
2000– Abdiqassim Salad Hassan (elected by the parliament-in-exile)

Head of Government

1991–8 Umar Arteh Ghalib
1998–2000 Hussein Mohamed Aidid
2000–1 Ali Khalif Galaid
2001–3 Hasan Abshir Farah
2003– Abdi Yusuf Mohammed

where he became a US citizen in 1974 and in 1975 an honorary fellow of the Hoover Institution on War, Revolution, and Peace. He was awarded the Templeton Prize for Progress in Religion in 1983, and the Russian State Literature Prize in 1990. He returned to Russia in 1994, and the following year published *The Russian Question at the End of the Twentieth Century*.

Somali [somahlee] A Cushitic-speaking people of Somalia and parts of Kenya, Ethiopia, and Djibouti. Roughly two-thirds are transhumant herders (the Samaal) living inland, with farmers and traders along the coast (the Saab). Divided into many traditionally autonomous groups, they have a powerful sense of cultural unity based largely on Islam and the Somali language.

Somalia *see panel*

Somaliland Republic *Somalia*

somatic gene therapy The notion that a particular gene might be inserted into the body (somatic) cells of individuals who are born with a defective or absent gene. The therapeutic gene may be delivered directly to the body 'in vivo'. Alternatively, an 'ex vivo' procedure may be used where cells are first removed, genetically modified and corrected, then returned to the patient. In principle, any accessible somatic cells such as those from bone marrow, muscle, and liver can be subjected to one or other of these procedures. Although having great promise, technical difficulties with regard to efficiency in gene delivery and function are delaying its introduction into clinical medicine. However, steady progress is being made with many clinical trials around the world.

somatids [sohmatidz] Ultramicroscopic particles claimed to be present in the blood of animals, including human beings. These are said to be living and reproducing subcellular bodies, with a distinct life-cycle affected by the presence of disease, toxins, or degenerative conditions (eg cancer, AIDS). Their existence was proposed in the 1950s by French biologist Gaston Naessens, who claimed that the examination of somatids made it possible to predict the development of disease before it actually occurs.

somatomedins [sohmatohmedinz] A group of related chemical substances (peptides) with similarities to insulin, present in the plasma of vertebrates, which mediate the growth-promoting actions of somatotrophin (growth hormone). They are synthesized and released mainly by the liver into the blood, and stimulate protein synthesis and cell replication in individual tissues or organs.

somatostatin [sohmatohstatin] Hormone-like polypeptide identified in the brain (hypothalamus), pancreas (D-cells in the islets of Langerhans), stomach (mucosal D-cells), and small and large intestines. It generally has an inhibitory action: *hypothalamic* somatostatin (a neurohormone) inhibits growth hormone and thyroid-stimulating hormone secretion from the front lobe of the pituitary; *pancreatic* somatostatin (a paracrine) inhibits insulin and glucagon release.

somatotrophin *growth hormone*

Somers (of Evesham), John Somers, Baron [suhmerz] (1651–1716) English statesman, born in Worcester, Hereford and Worcester, WC England, UK. He studied at Oxford, and became a lawyer (1676) and a Whig MP (1689). He helped to draft the Declaration of Rights (1689), and after the Revolution of 1688 held several posts under William III, culminating as Lord Chancellor (1697). William's most trusted minister, he was the object of frequent attacks, which led to his impeachment (and acquittal) in 1701. He was president of the Privy Council under Anne (1708–14).

Somerset [suhmerset] pop (2001e) 498 100; area 3451 sq km/1332 sq mi. County of SW England, UK; bounded N by the Bristol Channel; uplands in the W include Exmoor and the Brendon and Quantock Hills; Mendip Hills in NE, Blackdown Hills in S; county town, Taunton; chief towns include Bridgwater and Yeovil; N Somerset, and Bath & NE Somerset, separate unitary authorities from 1996; agriculture (especially dairy farming), tourism, light engineering, beverages (especially cider), footwear, food processing; Cheddar Gorge, Wookey Hole limestone caves.

Somme, River [som] River in N France, rising near St-Quentin; flows SW then NW and W to the English Channel near Saint-Valéry-sur-Somme; length 245 km/152 mi; linked by canals to the waterways of the industrial N; scene of some of the worst fighting in World War 1 (1916).

Somme, Battle of the [som] (1916) A major British offensive against German troops in NW France (1 Jul–19 Nov) which developed into the bloodiest battle in world history, with more than a million casualties. It was launched by British commander-in-chief, Douglas Haig. When the attack was abandoned, the Allies had advanced 10 miles from previous positions. The battle formed part of the war of attrition on the Western Front.

somnambulism *sleep-walking*

Somnath, Temple of [sumnaht] A famous Shiva temple in SW Gujarat, India. Its fabled wealth attracted the attention of Mahmud of Ghazni, who sacked it in 1024, removing its jewels together with (according to tradition) its wonderful gates. The event helped to create a tradition of Muslim intolerance and ferocity among N Indian Hindus.

Somoza (García), Anastasio [somohza] (1896–1956) Nicaraguan dictator, born in San Marcos, W Nicaragua. He studied in the USA. As chief of the National Guard, he established himself in supreme power in the early 1930s, and retained power until assassinated. His sons **Luis Somoza Debayle** (1923–67) and **Anastasio Somoza Debayle** (1925–80) continued dynastic control of Nicaragua until the 1979 revolution.

sonar Acronym for **sound navigation and ranging**, a means of detecting underwater vessels and objects, shoals of fish, and seabed features. The device emits pulsed bursts of sound underwater and listens for reflected echoes (**active sonar**), or simply listens for and interprets the sounds that a target, such as a submarine, may itself make (**passive sonar**).

sonata A musical composition, usually for keyboard (harpsichord, piano, organ) or for another instrument with keyboard. The main Baroque type, however, was the trio sonata for two solo instruments (usually violins) and continuo, exemplified in works by Corelli, Purcell, and Handel. These were normally in four or more movements, but the 550 or so keyboard sonatas of Domenico Scarlatti are nearly all single-movement works of a type much cultivated in Italy and Spain. The classical sonatas of Haydn, Mozart, and Beethoven are nearly all in three or four movements, with the first usually in what has become known as 'sonata form', and the last often a sonata rondo. This overall plan was adopted by many 19th–20th-c composers, including Schubert, Chopin, Brahms, Shostakovitch, and Prokofiev. Others (such as Liszt), have occasionally united the different movements into a single structure, or rejected the traditional form altogether.

sonatina A sonata of modest proportions, often not difficult to play.

Sonderbund [zonderbunt] A political and military league of seven Swiss Catholic cantons (Uri, Schwyz, Unterwalden, Zug, Fribourg, Lucerne, Valais), formed in 1845 to resist liberal plans for centralization. The 25-day Sonderbund War (1847) ended with the government's defeat of the Sonderbund, and the creation of a Federal State (1848).

Sondheim, Stephen (Joshua) [sondhiym] (1930–) Composer and lyricist, born in New York City, USA. He studied with Oscar Hammerstein II and Milton Babbitt, and wrote incidental music for *Girls of Summer* (1956), before earning his first success with the lyrics for Bernstein's *West Side Story* (1957) and Jule Styne's *Gypsy* (1959). His own highly successful musicals, including *A Funny Thing Happened on the Way to the Forum* (1962), *Follies* (1971), *A Little Night Music* (1972), *Sweeney Todd* (1979), and *Sunday in the Park with George* (1984, Pulitzer), have contributed greatly to the revival of the musical in the USA. Later works include *Assassins* (1991) and *Passion* (1994).

song Quite apart from liturgical song (for which a special nomenclature exists), folksong, popular music, and the indigenous music of non-Western cultures, there remains a vast corpus of song which defies any brief survey or classification. Mediaeval vernacular song, at least as it has reached us, was unaccompanied monody, sung mainly to courtly, amatory, sometimes religious texts. Renaissance song was largely polyphonic, reaching its highest point of development in the Italian and English madrigal. The earliest important repertories of solo song with notated accompaniment are from the early 17th-c – those of Monteverdi, and other Italian monodists, and the lute-songs of Dowland and his English contemporaries. The main type of small-scale solo vocal music of the Baroque period was the cantata, perfected by Alessandro Scarlatti and Handel. The development of the piano in the late 18th-c made possible the rich flowering of Romantic song, especially in Germany, while a special contribution of later composers (such as Mahler and Britten) has been the song cycle with orchestra.

songbird A bird of the passerine sub-order Oscines. This sub-order includes most birds renowned for their singing ability.

song cycle A sequence of separate songs united by some common theme or narrative thread. The earliest was perhaps Beethoven's *An die ferne Geliebte* (1816, To the Distant Beloved); later examples include Schubert's *Die Winterreise* (The Winter Journey), and Mahler's *Kindertotenlieder* (Songs on the Death of Children).

Song or **Sung dynasty** **1** (960–1279) A Chinese dynasty established by Taizu (r.960–76), which re-unified China after post-Tang confusion. It boasts no epic figures, though important reforms were attempted by Wang Anshi (1021–86). The period is famed for its art, literature, and historical writing, besides important agrarian, financial, industrial, scientific, and technological progress. Examples include the emergence of the world's earliest mechanical industry (water-power), the production of coke, and the development of the camera obscura, mariner's compass, movable type, spinning wheel, and water clock. Among warfare innovations was the cannon (1259). There were two dynastic phases: the Northern Song (960–1126) had its capital at Kaifeng on the Yellow River; later all N China was lost, and the Southern Song relocated to Hangzhou, S of the Yangtze. The dynasty fell to the Mongols under Kublai Khan.
2 A name often applied to the highly influential family of T V Soong. (*See* **Song Ziwen**.)

Songhai [songgiy] A W African state which rose to power in the region formerly dominated by Mali in the second half of the 15th-c, commanding the trade routes of the Sahara, the great market at Timbuktu, and the area W to Senegal. It declined as a result of the Portuguese re-orientation of trade routes, and was attacked by Moroccan forces in the 1590s. Songhai peoples still control much of the Saharan caravan trade.

Song of Solomon, Song of Songs, or **Canticles** A book of the Hebrew Bible/Old Testament, probably a collection of love songs, although sometimes considered a single poem or drama. The absence of explicit religious content, and the presence of erotic allusions, caused some 2nd-c rabbis to question its canonical status, but allegorical religious interpretation made it acceptable in most Christian and Jewish circles. Although the poems may be quite ancient, the collection is usually dated c.3rd-c BC on linguistic grounds.

Song of the Three Young Men Part of the Old Testament Apocrypha, or in Catholic versions an extension of the Book of Daniel inserted between what would be 3.23 and 24 in other texts; one of several additions to Daniel found in Greek and Latin versions, but not in Hebrew. It tells of three Jewish captives in Babylon who are cast into a fiery furnace for refusing to worship an idol, and it presents a hymn of thanksgiving and praise that is today known as the *Benedicite* in Catholic worship. Its date is uncertain, but is often put c.2nd–1st-c BC.

song thrush A thrush native to Europe (N Africa during winter) and NE Asia (*Turdus philomelos*); similar to the mistle thrush, but wing feathers an even brown; inhabits woodland, hedgerows, and gardens; eats snails by breaking the shells against a rock (called its *anvil*).

Song Ziwen [sung tseewen], also spelled **Sung Tsu-wen** or **Soong Tse-ven**, abbreviated as **Soong, T V** (1894–1971) Chinese diplomat and financier, born in Shanghai, E China. He studied at Harvard. His sister **Song Qingling** (c.1892–1981) married Sun Yatsen, and through this Song became closely associated with the Nationalist Party. He provided the financial stability which made possible the 1926 Northern Expedition that reunited China under the Nationalists. A second sister, **Song Meiling** (1897–2003) married Jiang Jieshi in 1927. Song served as finance minister of the new government until 1931. When the Nationalist government was overthrown in 1949, he moved to the USA. A film made in Hong Kong, *The Soong Sisters*, was released in 1997.

sonic boom A pressure shock wave created by aircraft travelling at supersonic speeds. The shock wave is produced continually, and travels outwards from the aircraft. Where it meets the ground it is perceived as a loud bang. Its intensity at ground level depends on aircraft height, flight pattern, and weather, and may be sufficient to cause damage to buildings. A sonic boom was also produced when the British car *ThrustSSC* broke the land speed sound barrier in 1997.

sonnet (Ital *sonnetto* 'little song') A poem of 14 lines, usually in iambic pentameter, and with a structural balance between the first 8 lines (*octave*) and the last 6 (*sestet*). A variety of rhyme schemes may be employed. Introduced in 13th-c Italy, the sonnet was established by Petrarch as a major form of love poetry, and was adapted in French and English vernacular literature in the late 16th-c. Sydney, Spenser, and Shakespeare wrote outstanding sonnets, a tradition that was continued by Donne, Milton, Keats, Wordsworth, Baudelaire, and Mallarmé. The sonnet has remained one of the most popular and adaptable of all poetic forms. Among recent distinguished poets who have composed sonnets are Dylan Thomas, Robert Lowell, and Seamus Heaney.

Son of Man A term found in Jewish and Christian literature, most strikingly in the New Testament Gospels as a frequent self-designation of Jesus. The term's significance is debated: in Aramaic it is an idiomatic reference to 'man' in general, and possibly also a circumlocution for 'I'; in *Dan* 7 it is associated with the righteous ones who are exalted at the end of the age and given dominion; in 1 *Enoch* 48 it apparently describes a heavenly messianic figure who will exercise judgment in the End times.

Sons of Liberty An organization in the American Revolution that provided popular leadership in the resistance movement against Britain. Composed mainly of artisans, small traders, and dissident intellectuals, it operated as an organized intercolonial group in 1765–6. Thereafter, the men who had taken part continued to provide popular leadership. The term was also used to describe all Americans involved in the revolutionary movement.

Soong Meiling / Tse-ven *Song Ziwen*

sooty shearwater *muttonbird*

Soper, Donald (Oliver) Soper, Baron [sohper] (1903–98) Methodist minister, born in London, UK. Widely known for his open-air speaking on London's Tower Hill, he became superintendent of the West London Mission in 1936, and wrote many books on Christianity and social questions, and particularly on international issues from the pacifist angle. He was made a life peer in 1965, and was still preaching at Tower Hill on his 90th birthday.

sopherim *scribe*

Sophia Alexeyevna [sohfeea aleksayevna] (1657–1704) Regent of Russia (1682–9), born in Moscow, Russia, the daughter of Tsar Alexey I Mihailovitch and his first wife, Maria Miloslavskaya. On the death of her brother, Tsar Fyodor Alexeyevich (1682), she opposed the accession of her half-brother, Peter (the future Peter the Great), and took advantage of a popular uprising in Moscow to press the candidature of her mentally deficient brother, Ivan. A compromise was reached whereby both Ivan (V) and Peter were proclaimed joint tsars, with Sophia as regent. Supported by leading boyars, she became the *de facto* ruler of Russia. A faction of the nobility succeeded in removing her from power in 1689, and (apart from a failed attempt to regain power in 1698) she spent the rest of her life in a convent in Moscow.

Sophists [sofists] Itinerant teachers (literally 'experts') in 5th-c Greece who, for a fee, offered professional training in rhetoric and other skills to aspiring public figures and men of affairs. They are vividly portrayed in the dialogues of Plato, usually as dialectical opponents of Socrates and as somewhat irresponsible, if accomplished, performers who imparted their techniques in a moral vacuum. Their admirers, by contrast, have hailed them as leaders of a 5th-c humanist enlightenment. The best known Sophists are Protagoras, Hippias, Gorgias, and Prodicus.

Sophocles [sofokleez] (c.496–406 BC) Greek tragic playwright, born in Colonus Hippius. He wrote 123 plays, of which only seven survive, all written after his victory over Aeschylus in a dramatic contest in 468 BC: *Ajax*, *Electra*, *Women of Trachis*, *Philoctetes*, and his three major plays *Oedipus Rex*, *Oedipus at Colonus*, and *Antigone*. His introduction of a third actor, taking further the innovations of Aeschylus, allowed greater complexity of plot and a greater depth of character in Greek drama. He played an important part in Athenian public life, and assisted Pericles in the war against the Samians (440 BC).

Sophonias [sofoniyas] *Zephaniah, Book of*

Sopot [sopot], Ger **Zoppot** 54°27N 18°01E, pop (2000e) 53 500. Resort town in Gdańsk voivodship, N Poland, between wooded slopes and the Bay of Gdańsk; part of the *Tri-City* with Gdańsk and Gdynia; railway; hydrotherapy treatment centre, open-air opera, racecourse; international song festival.

Sopwith, Sir Thomas (Octave Murdoch) (1888–1989) Aircraft designer and sportsman, born in London, UK. He won a prize for the longest flight across the English Channel in 1910, and founded the Sopwith Aviation Co in 1912, building many of the aircraft used in World War 1, such as the Sopwith Camel. Chairman of the Hawker-Siddeley Group from 1935, and president from 1963, he was knighted in 1953.

sorbic acid A permitted food preservative which can inhibit the growth of moulds. Such preservatives are known as *antimycotic*. Sorbic acid is obtained from the unripe fruits of the mountain ash.

Sorbonne [saw(r)bon] *Paris, University of*

Sorbs *Wends*

sorcery *witchcraft*

Sorel, Georges (1847–1922) Social philosopher, born in Cherbourg, NW France. He was trained as an engineer, and worked in the government department of bridges and roads (1870–92).

He became interested in philosophy and social theory when he was 40, and left his job for study. His best-known work is *Réflexions sur la violence* (1908, Reflections on Violence), in which he argued that serious political opposition must also resort to violence, and that Socialism would only be achieved by confrontation and revolution.

sorghum [saw(r)guhm] A cereal resembling maize (corn) in general appearance, but with dense heads of small grains. The most important is *Sorghum vulgare*, also called **kaffir corn** or **guinea corn**, cultivated as a staple food in much of Africa and parts of Asia, and in America and Australia for animal feed. One variety yields sugar in the same way as sugar cane. (Genus: *Sorghum*, 60 species. Family: Gramineae.)

sororate *levirate*

sorority *fraternity and sorority*

Soros, George [sawros] (1930–) Financier and philanthropist, born in Budapest, Hungary. A member of a prosperous Jewish family, he spent much of World War 2 in hiding from the Nazis. He moved to London in 1947, studied at the London School of Economics, joined the merchant bank Singer & Friedlander, and in 1956 went to New York City, working as a financial analyst. In 1969 he set up the Quantum and Quota groups of hedge funds, which grew rapidly from his daring speculations, and in 1979 he began to establish a network of Soros Foundations, mainly in C and E Europe, to advance opportunities in education and business. After the fall of communism in 1989, he dispersed over $2 billion of his personal fortune to promote the market economy throughout the former communist countries of C and E Europe. In 1992 his currency speculation earned him about $1 billion (£625 million) after betting that the British government would be forced to devalue sterling and leave the European Exchange Rate Mechanism. In 2000 the Soros funds were badly affected by misguided speculations on internet and telecommunications stocks that failed to pay off. He published *The Crisis of Global Capitalism* in 1998.

sorrel Any of several species of dock, native to Europe, usually with spear-shaped, acid-tasting leaves used as vegetables or in salads. (Genus: *Rumex*. Family: Polygonaceae.)

sort and merge A computer package designed to sort or re-sort files of computer data, and to combine two distinct files into a single sorted file. Such a package was in constant use when business computing was dominated by batch processing and the use of magnetic tape; but since these have been replaced, to a large extent, by on-line processing and the use of magnetic disk, the use of sort and merge has reduced.

sorus [sawruhs] A plant structure formed from a number of sporangia. It is usually associated with ferns, where they are arranged in distinctive patterns on the undersides of the fronds, but they are also found in some algae and fungi. The lid-like flap of tissue covering and protecting the sorus in some ferns is known as the **indusium**.

Sosigenes of Alexandria [sosijeneez] (1st-c BC) Astronomer and mathematician who advised Julius Caesar on calendar reform. He recommended a year of 365·25 days, and inserted an extra 67 days into the year 46 BC to bring the months back in register with the seasons.

Sotheby, John [suhthebee] (1740–1807) Auctioneer and antiquarian. He was the nephew of Samuel Baker, who founded the first sale room in Britain exclusively for books, manuscripts, and prints at Covent Garden in 1744. He became a director of the firm (1780–1800), then known as Leigh & Sotheby, which was transferred to the Strand in 1803.

Sotho–Tswana A cluster of Sotho-speaking peoples of Botswana, Lesotho, the Transvaal, Orange Free State, and N Cape. The pre-colonial social organization of all these peoples was very similar, which distinguishes them from the other main S African group of Bantu-speakers, the Nguni. The main sub-groupings are the various Tswana groups, traditionally independent chiefdoms; the S Sotho of Lesotho and the Orange Free State, who were united in a single political unit in the early 19th-c; and the Pedi and other N Sotho peoples of the N Transvaal.

Soto *Zen Buddhism*

Soto, Hernando / Fernando de *de Soto, Fernando*

Soufflot, Jacques Germain [soofloh] (1713–80) Architect, born in Irancy, France. He trained in Italy (1731–8), and became the leading French exponent of Neoclassicism. He designed the Panthéon and the Ecole de Droit in Paris, the Hôtel Dien in Lyon, and the Cathedral in Rennes.

Sŏul *Seoul*

soul (music) A strongly emotional type of popular music which followed on from rhythm and blues in the 1960s, and drew on other types of pop music. It is associated primarily with black US singers, such as Aretha Franklin (1942–).

soul (religion) Usually, the principle of life, the ultimate identity of a person, or the immortal constituent of the self. The concept derives from Plato, for whom it was a metaphysical entity, ultimately incorruptible and eternal. In Christian thought, the concept became fused with the idea of the resurrection of the body. There are links with the concept of *atman* in Hindu and Buddhist thought.

Soult, Nicolas Jean de Dieu [soolt] (1769–1851) French marshal, born in Saint-Amans-la-Bastide, S France. Created marshal of France by Napoleon in 1804, he led the French armies in the Peninsular War (1808–14) until defeated at Toulouse (1814). A skilled opportunist, he turned Royalist after Napoleon's abdication, but joined him in the Hundred Days, acting as his chief-of-staff at Waterloo. Exiled at the Second Restoration (1815) until 1819, he was gradually restored to all his honours, and presided over three ministries of Louis Philippe (1832–4, 1839–40, 1840–7), and once again professed himself to be a republican when Louis was overthrown in 1848.

Sound, The, Danish **Øresund** Strait between Zealand I, Denmark, and S Sweden, connecting the Kattegat with the Baltic Sea; width of narrowest section, 6 km/4 mi; a bridge connecting Copenhagen to Malmö in Sweden was opened in 2000.

sound A wave motion comprising a sequence of pressure pulses passing through some medium, typically air. The source of sound is a mechanical oscillator in the medium, such as a vibrating guitar string or a loudspeaker cone in air. It can be detected aurally, or using microphones or transducers. The speed of sound in air is 332 m/s; in fresh water at 20°C, it is 1482 m/s.

sound barrier *aerodynamics*

sound film Cinema pictures with synchronized sound. In 1926, 16-in gramophone discs running at 33 rpm (revolutions per minute) were linked to the film projector, but this was quickly replaced by integral sound-on-film systems. A photographic sound record is printed by the side of the picture as a continuous track in which sound modulations are represented by variations of either its density or its width. During projection the track passes a narrow illuminated slit, varying the transmitted light received by a photocell to produce electrical signals which are amplified to loudspeakers behind the screen. To record high frequencies it was necessary to increase the filming rate from 16 to 24 frames a second, and for projection up to 48 frames a second. By 1930, sound film had become universal in cinemas, although the variable density system of modulation gradually disappeared. Improvements in the quality of photographic sound recording and reproduction have continued, with noise reduction, extended frequency range, and stereophonic presentation, and the use of digital sound representation is envisaged.

sound intensity level Symbol L_I, units db (decibel); noise level relative to the faintest audible sound, which is rated as 0 db. It is related to sound intensity I, units W/m^2, the power per unit area of the sound wave. $L_I = 10 \log(I/I_0)$, where I_0 is taken to be 10^{-12} W/m^2, the sound intensity corresponding to 0 db. A whisper has a typical sound intensity level of 20 db; a conversation of 50 db; a busy street of 70 db; heavy machinery of 90 db; and jet aircraft of 120 db.

sound law A regular series of changes in the sound system of a language, during a period of its history. The Great Vowel Shift in English, which took place around the end of the 14th-c, provides an example: the pronunciation of several vowels altered markedly in the direction of their modern forms. For example, Middle English *gōs* (pronounced with a vowel similar to that in *toast*) became Modern *goose*, and *gēs* (similar to the vowel in *lace*) became *geese*. In English, the nature of such changes can often be deduced from the spelling, which is less prone to change, and tends to preserve the values of an earlier period of pronunciation.

sound navigation and ranging *sonar*

sound recording The conversion of sound into a storage medium from which it can later be reproduced. At first, the process was conducted entirely acoustically: sound signals were stored by direct mechanical conversion into grooves in a cylinder or disc, and reproduced using a phonograph or gramophone. In **digital recording**, which became dominant in the 1980s, the signal converted into corresponding electrical vibrations is sampled (up to 30 000 times a second), and the information represented and recorded numerically. With the *compact disk*, these digits are then directly decoded in the reproducing device, giving a recording that suffers no distortion as a result of the transmission process. Standard recording practice is to use a microphone array, the amplified electrical signal levels being balanced by recording engineers in a mixing console, and recorded digitally on a multi-track tape recorder. After dubbing and editing, copies are made from the master tape in several ways. For records, the tape drives an analogue disc-cutting machine acting on a lacquer-coated aluminium master; this leads to a nickel stamper from which multiple plastic pressings are made. For tapes, copies are made using a bank of cassette tape recorders. For digital compact disks, a laser inscribes a photoresist-coated master with a spiral track of pits and plateaux.

sour cherry *cherry*

sour sop A small evergreen tree (*Annona muricata*), growing to c.5 m/16 ft, native to Central America; leaves pinnate; flowers fleshy with six green and yellow petals; fruit 25 cm/10 in, heart-shaped, green, covered with fleshy spines, containing numerous seeds buried in white, fragrant pulp. It is widely cultivated in the tropics for the fruit, used for flavouring drinks. (Family: Annonaceae.)

Sousa, John Philip [**sooz**a] (1854–1932) Composer and bandmaster, born in Washington, District of Columbia, USA. His early training as a conductor was gained with theatre orchestras, and in 1880 he became conductor of the US Marine Band. His own band, formed 12 years later, won an international reputation. As well as more than 100 popular marches, including 'The Stars and Stripes Forever' (1896) and 'The Liberty Bell' (1893), he composed 10 comic operas, the most successful of which was *El Capitan* (1896). He also invented the *sousaphone*.

sousaphone [**soo**zafohn] A musical instrument resembling a tuba, but with the tubing encircling the player's body. It was designed by John Philip Sousa to be played while marching, and was first made in 1898.

souslik [**soos**lik] or **suslik** [**suhs**lik] A squirrel native to Asia, Europe, and North America; coat may be striped or spotted; inhabits open country; lives in burrows; some species called *gophers*; also known as **ground squirrel**. (Genus: *Spermophilus*, 32 species.)

Sousse [soos] 35°50N 10°38E, pop (2000e) 109 000. Port and capital of Sousse governorate, NE Tunisia, 115 km/71 mi SE of Tunis; founded by the Phoenicians, 9th-c BC; destroyed by the Vandals, AD 434; railway; tourism, crafts, clothing, ceramics, carpets; Mosque Zakak, the Great Mosque (850), Hanafite Mosque, Ribat fortress (9th-c); festival of music and popular arts (Apr–May), Aoussou Festival (Jul–Aug).

South Africa *p.1438*

South African Native National Congress *African National Congress*

South America The fourth largest continent, extending c.7500 km/5000 mi from 12°25N to 56°S; area c.18 million sq km/7 million sq mi; linked to North America (NW) by the isthmus of Panama; bounded N by the Caribbean Sea, E by the Atlantic Ocean, and W by the Pacific Ocean; includes Argentina, Bolivia, Brazil, Chile, Colombia, Ecuador, Guyana, Paraguay, Peru, Suriname, Uruguay, and Venezuela; outlying islands include the Falkland Is, Galápagos Is, and Tierra del Fuego; the Andes run almost the full W length, rising to 6969 m/22 834 ft at Aconcagua; largest lake, Titicaca; major river basins, the Orinoco, Paraná, and Amazon (containing the world's largest tropical rainforest); considerable evidence of early Indian kingdoms, notably the Incas, destroyed by Spanish and Portuguese invaders during the 16th-c; most countries achieved independence following wars in the early 19th-c. (*see panel p.1439*)

Southampton, Lat **Clausentum**, Anglo-Saxon **Hamwih** 50°55N 1°25W, pop (2001e) 217 500. Port city and (from 1997) unitary authority in Hampshire, S England, UK; on Southampton Water, at the mouth of the Test and Itchen Rivers; major UK port handling container traffic and passenger ships; four tides daily; site of both Roman and Saxon settlements; *Mayflower* set sail from here en route to Plymouth and North America in 1620; *Titanic* sailed from here on her disastrous maiden voyage (1912); city status (1964); railway; ferries to the I of Wight and N Europe; university (1952); marine engineering, petrochemicals, cables, electrical goods; St Michael's Church (1070); 15th-c Guildhall; 14th-c wool house now housing a maritime museum; *Mayflower* memorial; football league team, Southampton (Saints).

Southampton, Henry Wriothesley, 3rd Earl of [**roths**lee] (1573–1624) Courtier, born in Cowdray, Sussex, S England, UK. He was known as a patron of poets, notably of Shakespeare, who dedicated to him both *Venus and Adonis* (1593) and *The Rape of Lucrece* (1594). Some scholars have maintained that Southampton is the patron and friend described in Shakespeare's sonnets. He became involved in the rebellion of Essex (1600), and was imprisoned, but released by James I. He died while in charge of English volunteers against Spain in Holland.

South Australia pop (2000e) 1 548 000; area 984 000 sq km/379 900 sq mi. State in S Australia; established as a British Crown Colony, 1836; became a state, 1901; included most of Northern Territory, 1863–1901; composed of seven statistical divisions; bordered S by the Great Australian Bight and the Southern Ocean; largely desert, notably the Great Victoria Desert and Nullarbor Plain; fertile land in the SE corner irrigated by the Murray R; coastline dissected by the Spencer and St Vincent Gulfs; dry salt lakes inland (Eyre, Torrens, Gairdner, Frome); the Gawler Ranges in the S, Flinders and Mt Lofty Ranges in the E; highest point, Mt Woodroffe (1440 m/4724 ft); Murray R enters the ocean in the SE; Woomera Prohibited Area (weapons-testing range) extends across the Great Victoria Desert into Western Australia; 9600 km/6000 mi-long Dingo Fence protects S grazing sheep from wild dogs (possession of a dingo is illegal in this state); capital, Adelaide; principal towns Whyalla, Mount Gambier, Port Pirie, Port Augusta; wheat, barley, fruit, wool, meat, wine, oil refining, natural gas; copper, silver, lead mining; supplies 95% of world's opals; oranges and other citrus fruit in irrigated orchards along the Murray R; almost half of Australia's wine produced from the Barossa Valley N of Adelaide; state holidays Labour Day (Oct), Proclamation Day (Dec).

South Carolina pop (2000e) 4 012 000; area 80 580 sq km/31 113 sq mi. State in SE USA, divided into 46 counties; the 'Palmetto State'; settled by the French at Port Royal, 1562; included in the Carolina grant in 1663, but returned to the Crown in 1729; brought under American control after the battle of Guilford Courthouse, 1781; eighth of the original 13 states to ratify the Constitution, 1788; the first state to secede from the Union, 1860; Confederate forces attacked Fort Sumter 12 Apr 1861, starting the Civil War; slavery abolished, 1865; re-admitted to the Union, 1868; capital, Columbia; other chief cities, Charleston, Greenville, Spartanburg; bounded E and SE by the Atlantic Ocean; rivers include the Pee Dee, Edisto, Savannah (forms most of Georgia border), Wateree, and Congaree, the

South Africa

□ International Airport

official name **Republic of South Africa**, Afrikaans **Republiek van Suid-Afrika**

Local name South Africa

Timezone GMT +2

Area 1 233 404 km^2/476 094 sq mi

Population total (2002e) 45 172 000

Status Republic

Date of independence 1961

Capitals Cape Town (legislative); Pretoria (administrative); Bloemfontein (judicial)

Languages (co-official) Afrikaans, English, Ndebele, Pedi, Sotho, Swazi, Tsonga, Tswana, Venda, Xhosa, Zulu

Ethnic groups Black African (70%), White (18%), Asian (3%), Coloured (9%)

Religions Christian (most whites and Coloureds and c.60% Africans), traditional beliefs, Hindu, Muslim, and Jewish minorities

Physical features Occupies the S extremity of the African plateau; fringed by fold mountains and a lowland coastal margin to the W, E, and S; N interior comprises the Kalahari Basin, scrub grassland, and arid desert; Great Escarpment rises E to 3482 m/11 424 ft at Thabana Ntlenyana; Orange R flows W to meet the Atlantic; chief tributaries, Vaal and Caledon rivers.

Climate Subtropical in E; average annual temperature 4°C (Jan), 17°C (Jul) in Cape Town; average annual rainfall 1008 mm/39·7 in Durban; dry moistureless climate on W coast; desert region further N, annual average rainfall less than 30 mm/1·2 in.

Currency 1 Rand (R) = 100 cents

Economy Industrial growth as a result of 19th-c gold (c.50% of export income) and diamond discoveries; grain, wool, sugar, tobacco, cotton, citrus fruit, dairy products, livestock, fishing; motor vehicles, machinery, chemicals, fertilizers, textiles, clothes, metal products, electronics, computers, tourism.

GDP (2002e) $427·7 bn, per capita $10 000

Human Development Index (2002) 0·695

History Originally inhabited by Khoisan tribes; Portuguese reached the Cape of Good Hope in late 15th-c; settled by Dutch, 1652; arrival of British, 1795; British annexation of the Cape, 1806; Great Trek by Boers NE across the Orange R to Natal, 1836; first Boer republic founded, 1839; Natal annexed by the British in 1843, but the Boer republics of Transvaal (founded 1852) and Orange Free State (1854) were recognized; Zulu War, 1879; South African Wars, 1880–1, 1899–1902; Transvaal, Natal, Orange Free State, and Cape Province joined as the Union of South Africa, a dominion of the British Empire, 1910; sovereign state within the Commonwealth, 1931–61; independent republic, 1961; independence granted by South Africa to Transkei (1976), Bophuthatswana (1977), Venda (1979) and Ciskei (1981), not recognized internationally; politics dominated by treatment of non-White majority following the apartheid (racial segregation) policy after 1948; continuing racial violence and strikes led to a state of emergency in 1986, and several countries imposed economic and cultural sanctions; progressive dismantling of apartheid system by F W de Klerk from 1990; Black Nationalist leader Nelson Mandela freed after more than 27 years in prison, and the African National Congress unbanned, 1990; readmitted into international sport, USA lifted trade and investment sanctions, 1991; most remaining apartheid legislation abolished, 1991; new constitution, 1996; governed by a President, Cabinet, National Assembly and Senate; elections in May 1994 brought victory to the ANC.

Head of State/Government
1961–7 Charles Robberts Swart
1967 Theophilus Ebenhaezer Dönges
1967–8 Jozua François Naudé
1968–75 Jacobus Johannes Fouché
1975–8 Nicolaas Diederichs
1978–9 Balthazar Johannes Vorster
1979–84 Marais Viljoen
1984–89 Pieter Willem ('P W') Botha
1989–94 Frederick Willem de Klerk
1994–9 Nelson Rolihlahla Mandela
1999– Thabo Mbeki

South African Provinces
Name / Area (km^2 / sq mi) / State capital
Eastern Cape / 170 616 / 65 858 / Bisho
Mpumalanga / 81 816 / 31 581 / Nelspruit
KwaZulu Natal / 91 481 / 35 312 / Pietermaritzburg (Ulundi)
North-West / 118 710 / 45 822 / Mmabatho
Northern Cape / 363 389 / 140 268 / Kimberley
Limpopo / 119 606 / 46 168 / Pietersburg
Free State / 129 437 / 49 963 / Bloemfontein
Gauteng / 18 760 / 7241 / Johannesburg (Pretoria)
Western Cape / 129 386 / 49 943 / Cape Town

latter two joining to form the Santee; Blue Ridge Mts in the extreme NW; highest point Mt Sassafras (1085 m/3560 ft); flat and (in the S) swampy coastland, cut by numerous rivers and creeks to form the Sea Islands, a major tourist centre; ground rises inland towards the rolling Piedmont, the agricultural and manufacturing centre; reservoirs at L Murray, L Marion, and L Moultrie; textiles and clothing, using the large cotton crop; lumber, chemicals, machinery, foodstuffs; tobacco, soybeans, poultry, cattle, dairy products, peaches, peanuts, sweet potatoes, corn; fishing.

South China Sea area c.3 685 000 sq km/1 423 000 sq mi. W arm of the Pacific Ocean, bounded by Taiwan (N), the Philippines (E), Borneo (SE), and the SE Asian coast (NW, W, SW); subject to violent typhoons; main arms, Gulfs of Tongkin and Kompong; shallow in SE, c.60 m/200 ft; deep basin in

South America

NE, reaching 5490 m/18 012 ft; numerous island groups and coral reefs; major fishing region.

Southcott, Joanna (c.1750–1814) Religious fanatic, born in Dorset, S England, UK. In c.1792 she declared herself to be the woman (predicted in *Rev* 12) who would give birth to the second Prince of Peace. She went to London, where she obtained a great following, but died soon after the predicted date of the birth. Her followers, who believed she would rise again, were still to be found at the beginning of the 20th-c.

South Dakota [dakohta] pop (2000e) 754 800; area 199 723 sq km/77 116 sq mi. State in NC USA, divided into 66 counties; the 'Sunshine State' or 'Coyote State'; part of the USA as a result of the Louisiana Purchase, 1803; included in Dakota Territory, 1861; population swelled when gold was discovered in the Black Hills, 1874; separated from North Dakota and became the 40th state of the Union, 1889; capital, Pierre; other chief cities, Sioux Falls, Rapid City, Aberdeen; crossed by the Missouri and Big Sioux Rivers; the Bois de Sioux and Minnesota Rivers form part of the E border; the Black Hills rise in the SW corner of the state; highest point, Mt Harney Peak (2207 m/7241 ft); W of Missouri R is a semi-arid, treeless plain, one-third owned by Sioux Indians; severe erosion has formed the barren Bad Lands, where there are many ancient marine and land fossils; E of the R Missouri are rich, fertile plains; cattle, wheat, hogs, dairy products, corn, soybeans, oats; meat packing, food processing; town of Lead in the Black Hills is the nation's leading gold-mining centre; second largest gold and beryllium producer in the USA; Mt Rushmore (in the Black Hills); Indian reservations at Crow Creek, Rosebud, Pine Ridge, Cheyenne.

South Downs Way Long-distance footpath following the South Downs of East and West Sussex, S England, UK; stretches from Eastbourne to Harting; length 130 km/80 mi.

South East Asia Treaty Organization (SEATO) An organization founded mainly to provide collective defence in the case of an attack by external aggressors against any one of the eight signatories to the treaty: Australia, France, New Zealand, Pakistan, the Philippines, Thailand, UK, and USA. A further purpose was economic co-operation. SEATO's headquarters is in Bangkok. By 1992 it was inactive.

Southend [sowth**end**], in full **Southend-on-Sea** 51°33N 0°43E, pop (2001e) 160 300. Resort town and unitary authority (from 1998), Essex, SE England, UK; on the R Thames estuary, 57 km/35 mi E of London; famous pier, 2 km/1¼ mi long; railway; airfield; 12th-c Prittlewell Priory museum; football league team, Southend United (Shrimpers).

Southern Alps Mountain range in WC South Island, New Zealand; length c.320 km/200 mi NE–SW; contains New Zealand's highest peaks, Mt Cook (3764 m/12 349 ft), Mt Tasman (3497 m/11 472 ft), and Mt Dampier (3440 m/11 286 ft); 19 named peaks exceed 3000 m/10 000 ft; only two mountain passes (Haast Pass and Arthur's Pass) allow E–W travel; popular area for mountain-climbing and skiing.

Southern Cross *Crux*

Southern Ocean *Antarctic Ocean*

southernwood An aromatic shrub (*Artemisia abrotanum*) growing to 1 m/3¼ ft; leaves finely divided with narrow thread-like lobes, grey-haired beneath; flower-heads globular, 3–4 mm/0·12–0·16 in across; florets dull yellow. Of uncertain origin, it is widely grown as an ornamental. Its sweetly aromatic leaves are used for flavouring. (Family: Compositae.)

Southey, Robert [suhthee] (1774–1843) Writer, born in Bristol, SW England, UK. He studed at Oxford, left without a degree, then studied law and settled in Keswick, where he was associated with Wordsworth and Coleridge. Originally a radical in politics, his views mellowed, and in 1809 he began to contribute to the Tory *Quarterly Review*. His literary output was considerable, and many of his short poems are familiar, such as 'Inchcape Rock' and 'After Blenheim'. Although made poet laureate in 1813, his prose became more widely known than his poetry, and included a life of Nelson, a naval history, and his letters.

South Georgia 54°30S 37°00W; area c.3750 sq km/1450 sq mi. Barren, mountainous, snow-covered island in the S Atlantic, about 500 km/300 mi E of the Falkland Is; a British Overseas Territory administered from the Falkland Is; length, 160 km/100 mi; discovered by the London merchant De la Roche, 1675; landing by Captain Cook, 1775; British annexation, 1908 and 1917; invaded by Argentina and recaptured by Britain, April 1982; only village, Grytviken; research stations maintained here and on the neighbouring Bird I; sealing and whaling centre until 1965; burial place of Ernest Shackleton.

South Glamorgan pop (2000e) 419 200; area 416 sq km/161 sq mi. Former county in S Wales, UK; created in 1974, and replaced in 1996 by Cardiff and Vale of Glamorgan counties.

South India, Church of A Church inaugurated in 1947 in Chennai (Madras), India, from the merger of Anglicans, Methodists, and United Churches. It reflected a common desire for missionary and social work as well as worship, and tries in its organization to preserve the traditions of each of its constituent traditions. It is governed by a General Synod, with bishops, presbyters, and deacons, and significant lay participation.

South Island pop (2000e) 1 065 000; area 153 978 sq km/59 435 sq mi. The larger and southernmost of the two main islands of New Zealand; separated from North Island by the Cook Strait, and from Stewart I (S) by the Foveaux Strait; fertile plains on coast give way to mountains; Southern Alps run through the centre, containing Mt Cook (3764 m/12 349 ft), highest point in New Zealand; Westland to the W, a narrow forested strip; Canterbury Plain to the E, largest area of flat lowland; numerous bays and fjords to the SW; chief towns include Christchurch, Invercargill, Dunedin, Nelson; tobacco, hops, coal, cement, timber, greenstone, sheep, pottery, fruit, tourism.

South Korea *Korea*

South Orkney Islands, Span **Orcadas del Sur** area 620 sq km/239 sq mi. Group of islands in the S Atlantic, NE of the Graham Peninsula; main islands Coronation, Signy, Laurie, Inaccessible; used by British and US whalers since 1821; barren and uninhabited, apart from scientific research; claimed by Argentina.

South Pacific Commission *Pacific Community*

South Pacific Forum An organization founded in 1971 to provide a setting where the heads of government of independent and self-governing Pacific island states could meet to discuss their common political concerns with each other and with Australia and New Zealand; also known as the **Pacific Islands Forum**. It had 16 members in 2004. Its executive arm is the **South Pacific Bureau for Economic Co-operation**.

South Pole *Poles*

Southport 53°39N 3°01W, pop (2000e) 89 700. Coastal resort town in Merseyside, NW England, UK; on the Irish Sea, S of the R Ribble estuary, 25 km/15 mi N of Liverpool; the original 'garden city'; a notable golfing area (Birkdale); railway; chemicals, engineering; annual flower show.

South Sandwich Islands 56°18S–59°25S 26°15W. Group of small, uninhabited islands in the S Atlantic, c.720 km/450 mi SE of South Georgia; a British Overseas Territory administered from the Falkland Is; discovered by Captain Cook, 1775; annexed by Britain, 1908 and 1917.

South Sea Bubble A financial crisis in Britain (1720) arising out of speculation mania generated by Parliament's approval of the South Sea Company's proposal to take over three-fifths of the National Debt. This led to gross over-speculation, as several other spurious companies began to offer shares. Many investors were ruined in the aftermath, but Robert Walpole's plan for stock transfer retrieved the situation and made his reputation. The South Sea Company continued its existence until 1856.

South Shetland Islands area 4622 sq km/1784 sq mi. Group of mountainous islands in the S Atlantic, NW of the Graham Peninsula, c.880 km/550 mi SE of Cape Horn; main islands King George, Elephant, Clarence, Gibbs, Nelson, Livingston, Greenwich, Snow, Deception, Smith; discovered in 1819; occasionally used for scientific bases.

Southwark [suhtherk] 51°30N 0°06W, pop (2001e) 244 900. Borough of C Greater London, UK; S of the R Thames; includes the suburbs of Bermondsey, Southwark, Camberwell; formerly famous for its inns and Elizabethan theatres (site of Globe Theatre); railway; 13th-c Southwark Cathedral, Dulwich College (1621), Guy's Hospital (1721), Imperial War Museum, Shakespeare's Globe, Tate Modern.

Southwell, Robert (1561–95) Poet and martyr, born in Horsham, Norfolk, E England, UK. He studied at Douai and Rome, and was ordained as a Jesuit in 1584. He travelled to England as a missionary in 1586, aiding persecuted Catholics, but was betrayed, tortured, and executed. Beatified in 1929, he is known for his devotional lyrics (such as 'The Burning Babe'), and for several prose treatises and epistles.

Southwest Africa *Namibia*

Southwest Africa People's Organization (SWAPO) A nationalist organization in Southwest Africa (Namibia), which opened a guerrilla campaign against South African rule in Namibia in 1969. South Africa had acquired the mandate to the German colony of Southwest Africa after World War 1, and had refused to hand it over to the United Nations trusteeship council after World War 2, attempting instead to integrate it into South Africa. The South Africans tried to create an internal settlement in Namibia, but without UN support. Front-line states and the Organization of African Unity gave their support to SWAPO, and Angola provided it with bases for its liberation movement. South Africa attempted to destabilize Angola by supporting a dissident movement, UNITA, within that state. The Angola regime was supported by Cuban forces. At the end of 1988, an international agreement was reached in Geneva linking arrangements for the future independence of Namibia with the withdrawal of Cuban troops from Angola, and the cessation of South African attacks on that country and its support for the UNITA rebels.

Southwest Indians North American Indian groups living in the SW states of Arizona, New Mexico, Utah, Colorado, and Texas, and in Mexico. Historically, some of the tribes came to the area from Middle America, such as the Pueblo (including the Hopi and Zuni), introducing many aspects of Middle American culture, while others migrated from the NE, such as the Athapascan-speaking Navajos and Apaches. Many prehistoric remains provide evidence of early settlement, dating back to possibly 10 000 years ago. Farming spread to the area from Mexico, and probably for more than 1000 years many groups have been living in permanent settlements, growing crops and producing basketry, weavings, and other crafts. Contact with whites since the 16th-c has been disruptive, and today most Indians are poor, depending for their survival on outside aid. The largest Indian groups in North America currently live in the area.

South Yorkshire *Yorkshire, South*

Soutine, Chaim [sooteen, khiym] (1893–1943) Artist, born in Smilovich, C Belarus. He studied at Vilnius, and went to Paris in 1911, where he became known for his paintings of carcases, and for his series of 'Choirboys' (1927). After his death he was recognized as a leading Expressionist painter.

sovereign A British gold coin originally worth £1, but since the abolition of the gold standard worth considerably more. Until recently, sovereigns were minted only on special occasions, but now they can be purchased, their price varying with the price of gold. New coins are called *Britannias*.

sovereignty The capacity to determine conduct within the territory of a nation-state without external legal constraint. Sovereign powers may be exercised by a legislature, as in the UK. Where legal limits are placed upon the organs of government by the constitution, as in the USA, sovereignty is claimed to reside with the people.

soviet Originally, a workers' council established in Russia after the 1905 revolution. They re-appeared as workers' and soldiers' councils, important instruments of the 1917 revolution. Members of soviets were elected by popular vote, and lower soviets could not control higher ones. The highest was the Supreme Soviet, the legislative body of the USSR.

Soviet space programme A dominant element in the exploration of space after the launch of Sputnik in 1957 until the demise of the Soviet Union in 1990. It was formally replaced by the Russian Space Agency in 1992.

Soviet Union, official name **Union of Soviet Socialist Republics (USSR)**, Russ **Soyuz Sovyetskikh Sotsialisticheskikh Republik** (Cyrillic alphabet, **CCCP**) pop (1990) 290 122 000; area 22 402 076 sq km/8 647 201 sq mi. Former federation of 15 republics, comprising most of E Europe and N and C Asia, which until its dissolution (1991) jointly formed the world's largest sovereign state; capital, Moscow; ethnic groups included Russian (52%), Ukrainian (16%), and over 100 others; chief religion, Russian Orthodox (18%), with 70% atheist; official language, Russian; unit of currency, the rouble of 100 kopeks; Union Republics were usually known as **Soviet Socialist Republics (SSR)**; there were in addition 20 **Autonomous Soviet Socialist Republics (ASSR)**, and several smaller divisions (6 *krays*, 123 *oblasts*, 8 *autonomous oblasts*, 10 *autonomous okrugs*); formed in 1922 following the October Revolution (1917) and the subsequent Civil War; first Soviet government headed by Lenin; vigorous socialist reform begun by Stalin in the 1920s, including the collectivization of agriculture and rapid industrialization; territories extended in the W after World War 2, with a corridor of communist-dominated countries between USSR and W Europe; period of Cold War following World War 2; intervention to suppress Hungarian uprising (1956) and Czech programme of liberalization (1968); invasion of Afghanistan, 1979–88; series of disarmament agreements in 1980s, with new approach to international relations under Gorbachev; constitutional reforms implemented in 1989 instituted a new Congress of the USSR People's Deputies, with 2250 members; competition was introduced for some seats; the Congress elected from its ranks a 542-member Supreme Soviet, which acted as the effective legislature, and like the previous (larger) Supreme Soviet consisted of the Council of the Union and the Council of Nationalities; the Republics had their own Supreme Soviets, Presidiums, and Council of Ministers; major internal changes in 1991, following the emerging independence of several republics and the reduced role of the Communist Party; failure of an attempted coup (19–22 Aug 1991), with resistance led by Yeltsin, resulted in the process of radical reform, liberalization, and recognition of independence movements in the constituent republics; recognition of Estonia, Latvia, and Lithuania (1990–1) was followed by the abolition of the Communist Party and ultimately the country's dissolution (December 1991); most of the constituent republics then formed the Commonwealth of Independent States.

sow *pig*

Soweto [sohwetoh] 26°15S 27°52E, pop (2000e) 1 073 000. Black African township in NE South Africa; the name derives from the official title of South-West Township; linked by rail (8 km/5 mi) to industrial W Johannesburg; resistance to the teaching of Afrikaans in schools led to student riots in June 1976, when several hundred people were killed.

sow thistle The name for several species of the genus *Sonchus*, annuals or perennials from Europe, Asia, and Africa; stems exuding a white latex when broken; leaves often spiny-margined, the stem leaves clasping with two rounded ear-like lobes at the base; large, yellow dandelion-like flower-heads. They are not true thistles, which tend to have stiffer and much sharper spines. (Genus: *Sonchus*. Family: Compositae.)

soya bean A bushy, reddish-haired annual (*Glycine max*), growing to 2 m/6½ ft; leaves with three large oval leaflets; pea-flowers rather inconspicuous; violet, pink, or white, in small clusters in the leaf axils; pods up to 8 cm/3 in long, hairy; also called **soja** or **soy bean**. It is of unknown origin, but has a long history of cultivation in E Asia, and many varieties are now widely grown in both the Old and New World. The edible seeds (**soya beans**), which are rich in protein, are eaten as a vegetable and used in the production of artificial meat, to make flour, and to yield an oil employed in margarine and cooking oils. There are also numerous industrial uses, such as in enamels, paints, varnishes, lubricants, and rubber substitutes. The plants also provide a valuable food for livestock. (Family: Leguminosae.)

Soyinka, Wole [soyingka, wolay], popular name of **Akinwande Oluwole Soyinka** (1934–) Writer, born near Abeokuta, SW Nigeria. He studied at Ibadan and Leeds, and became a play-reader at the Royal Court Theatre, where his first play, *The Invention*, was performed in 1955. After returning to Ibadan in 1959, he founded two theatre companies, and built up a new Nigerian drama, in English but using the words, music, and dance of the traditional Yoruba festivals. His writing is deeply concerned with the tension between old and new in modern Africa. His poetic collection *A Shuttle in the Crypt* (1972) appeared after his release in 1969 from two years of political detention. His first novel *The Interpreters* (1965), was called the first really modern African novel. *The Open Sore of a Continent*, his personal examination of the Nigerian crisis, appeared in 1996. Later work includes *The Burden of Memory, the Muse of Forgiveness* (1998) and a verse collection, *Samarkand & Other Markets I Have Known* (2002). He became professor of comparative literature at Ife in 1972, and professor of African studies and theatre at Cornell University in 1988. He was awarded the Nobel Prize for Literature in 1986.

Soyuz (Russ 'union') spacecraft A Soviet basic space capsule, consisting of three modules (orbiter, descent, and instrumentation), and carrying a crew of one to three. It has been flown on several dozen missions, and is capable of precision targeting to soft-land in C Asia (contrasting with the US ocean-recovery technique). It has been used to ferry crew to and from Salyut and, later, Mir space stations with which docking takes place. The first flight was in 1967, when its pilot, V Komarov, was killed in a landing accident. Soyuz 19 docked with the Apollo spacecraft in Earth orbit after its rendezvous (Jul 1975). There was a notable launch accident (Sep 1983) in which the crew of Soyuz T-10A ejected to safety as the launch vehicle exploded. The Soyuz spacecraft is being used for crew return and transfer to the International Space Station.

Spaak, Paul Henri (1899–1972) Belgian statesman and prime minister (1938–9, 1946, 1947–9), born in Schaerbeek, C Belgium. He became the first Socialist premier of his country, and foreign minister with the government-in-exile during World War 2, and in 1946 president of the first General Assembly of the United Nations. After his later periods as premier, he was again foreign minister (1954–7, 1961–8), in which role he became one of the founding fathers of the EEC, and secretary-general of NATO (1957–61).

spacecraft Vehicles designed to operate in the vacuum–weightlessness–high radiation environment of space; used to convey human crew, to acquire scientific data, to conduct utilitarian operations (eg telecommunications and synoptic weather observations), and to conduct research (eg microgravity experiments). The first spacecraft (Sputnik 1) was launched by the USSR in 1957 (4 Oct). They require highly reliable automated command and control, attitude stabilization, thermal control, radio telemetry, and data processing systems. Specialized spacecraft have been designed to be controllable on re-entry into the Earth's atmosphere (eg the NASA Space Shuttle), and to operate in atmospheres of other planets (eg Soviet Venera and US Pioneer atmospheric entry probes).

space exploration Imagined for centuries, the era began with the first artificial satellite (Sputnik, 1957, Soviet Union) and the first manned flight (Gagarin, 1961, Soviet Union), with subsequent rapidly evolving capabilities in Earth orbit and Solar System exploration (initiated by Mariner 2, 1962, USA). It has been an arena of intense international competition and, recently, co-operation. The utilitarian uses of space – communications and meteorology – are now taken for granted; astronomy and Earth remote-sensing capabilities provide a new perspective on the universe and our own planet. Solar System exploration has provided reconnaissance as far as Neptune, in-depth exploration of Mars and Venus, and detailed study of the Moon; the study of comets and asteroids is less advanced. Human activity has been demonstrated even to the point of crewed lunar landings (Apollo programme, 1969–72) and continuing space station occupancy (Skylab, Salyut, Mir, International), but remains dangerous and costly. Launch vehicle advances have achieved a re-usable crewed orbiter (US space shuttle), but inexpensive, reliable transportation is still in the future. The Soviet Union was a dominant participant from the beginning but later Russian exploration effort has been blunted by economic disruption. The USA has retained its dominance, with Europe and Japan increasingly influential; China launched its first spacecraft capable of carrying a human in 1999. In the USA the scientific exploration of space has developed a multi-disciplinary emphasis on the study of the origin and distribution of life in the universe. The rate at which future human exploration proceeds beyond low earth orbit into deep space will be limited by space physiological effects and by the costliness of launch vehicles.

Spacelab A research facility flown in the cargo bay of the NASA space shuttle; designed, built, and financed by the European Space Agency. It had flown four times by the end of 1985. It consists of a pressurized experiment module for scientist-astronaut activities, and one or more pallets upon which telescopes and Earth remote-sensing experiments are mounted.

space law A branch of international law which deals with rights in outer space. Terrestrial airspace is generally considered by states both in international agreements and their municipal laws to be synonymous with the earth's atmosphere. There is increasing interest in the use of the upper atmosphere and orbital zones for the purposes of communications. Foreign aircraft have no right to fly over the territory or territorial waters of another state. In practice, states enter into bilateral agreements with other states whereby each grants the other rights in air space. The rules relating to aircraft do not apply to artificial satellites in outer space. The Outer Space Treaty of 1967 provides that outer space may be used by all states. The United Nations Committee on the Peaceful Uses of Outer Space (COPUOS) elaborates rules on space law, which include the allocation and control of radio frequencies, the legality of the use of reconnaissance satellites, and the definition and delimitation of outer space. The military use of outer space is also dealt with. There has recently been international pressure to decrease US control of the international satellite industry.

space mine A proposed munition of warfare in space; a spacecraft loaded with explosive which can be directed to detonate against a target spacecraft.

space physiology and medicine The branch of medicine devoted to understanding the effects of space flight on human physiology and to assuring the health of astronauts. The observed effects of weightlessness include motion sickness, cardiovascular deconditioning, red blood cell mass loss, and bone mineral loss. Exercise, diet, biofeedback, and drug therapy have been used as countermeasures with some success. Radiation protection is a matter of concern for long-duration missions; and medical care during flights is also an issue. Long-duration flight experience has mainly been accumulated by the USSR on Salyut and Mir space stations – 366 days in the case of Mir cosmonauts (1977–8). The minimum round trip flight duration for a manned Mars mission would be about one year for a two-week stay at the planet, but current planning by NASA envisions missions of c.three-year total duration with c.500 days spent on the Martian surface.

space shuttle A re-usable crewed launch vehicle. The first-generation US shuttle launched in April 1981, managed by NASA's Johnson and Marshall Space Centers. The first Soviet shuttle, *Buran*, was launched in November 1988 for a single test flight without crew, using the Energiya booster. The European Space Agency shuttle Hermes programme was cancelled after several years' development. The US shuttle carries up to seven crew, and is capable of launching a 24 400-kg/53 700-lb payload into low Earth orbit; missions are up to 14 days' duration. It comprises a delta-winged lifting body orbiter with main engines, a jettisonable external fuel tank, and two auxiliary solid rocket boosters. The fleet comprises four vehicles: *Columbia*, *Discovery*, *Atlantis*, and *Endeavour*. It has been successfully used to launch numerous science and applications satellites and onboard experiments, to carry the Spacelab module, and to retrieve spacecraft from orbit. The *Challenger* explosion on the 25th flight (28 Jan 1986) 73 sec after launch caused the loss of the crew. The first reflight took place in September 1988, and a replacement orbiter, *Endeavour*, became operational in May 1992. A disaster on re-entry in February 2003 destroyed *Columbia* with loss of the crew, causing indefinite postponement of the space programme.

space station A long-lived crewed spacecraft in low Earth orbit; examples are the US Skylab and the Russian (formerly Soviet) Mir. It is used for the accumulation of long-duration flight experience and related biomedical research, for astronomy, for Earth observations, and for microgravity experiments. The US space station programme underwent a major redesign in 1993 to incorporate substantial participation by Russia. The first launches to begin the construction of this International Space Station were carried out in 1998 and the first crew arrived in 2000.

Space Telescope *Hubble Space Telescope*

space–time A fundamental concept in the special and general theories of relativity. Einstein showed that a complete description of relative motion required equations including time as well as the three spatial dimensions. The form in which time is expressed gives it the mathematical property of a fourth coordinate, or dimension. Space–time is the single entity which unifies both space and time into a four-dimensional structure. In the general theory, Einstein showed that this 'fabric of the universe' becomes curved in the presence of matter, and this enabled him to give an elegant account of gravitation which has replaced Newton's theory.

space tourism *Tito, Dennis*

Spacey, Kevin [spaysee], stage name of **Kevin Spacey Fowler** (1959–) Film and theatre actor, born in South Orange, NJ, USA. He studied drama at the Juilliard School for two years, and after various roles on US stage and in television he moved into films. During the 1990s *The Usual Suspects* (1995) and *Se7en* (1995) catapulted him into international stardom. Later films include *LA Confidential* (1997), *American Beauty* (1999, Oscar), *The Shipping News* (2001), and *The Life of David Gale* (2002). His theatre work includes roles in *Lost in Yonkers* (1991) and *The Iceman Cometh* (1998). In 2003 he was appointed artistic director of the Old Vic Theatre, London.

spadefoot toad A frog native to Europe, Asia, and North America; sharp projections (*spades*) on hind feet; burrows in dry sandy areas; breeds rapidly in temporary pools; in desert pools some tadpoles grow up to 18 cm/7 in long, and eat smaller tadpoles. (Family: Pelobatidae, 54 species.)

spadix [spaydiks] A specialized type of inflorescence in which the usually tiny flowers are crowded on a fleshy, cylindrical axis, generally enveloped by a large bract – the *spathe*. It is typical of, but not confined to, the arum family Araceae.

spaghetti *pasta*

spaghetti Western A motion picture drama following the themes and settings of the American 'Western', but cheaply produced by European companies on locations in Spain and Italy. The first of this genre was *A Fistful of Dollars* (1964, *Per un pugno di dollari*), a German–Spanish–Italian co-production directed by Sergio Leone and starring Clint Eastwood, both of whom repeated their success during the following 10 years.

spagyrik [spajeerik] A system of diagnosis and treatment, first developed in Germany, based on the analysis of body fluids to detect disease and give information about a patient's general pattern of health. Blood and/or urine samples are heated, distilled, and recombined as a clear liquid, which is allowed to crystallize on a glass slide. The pattern of the crystals is said to give information about health and disease, and even to give early warning of disease processes before conventional tests can detect any abnormality. The liquid from the recombination process is used as a form of treatment, being given back to the patient in small doses to stimulate the immune system.

Spain *p.1444*

spandrel A triangular space on the wall of a building, defined by the curve of an arch, a vertical line drawn up from the side of the arch, and a horizontal line through its apex. Particularly in 20th-c architecture, it refers to an infill panel below a window, often of a different material to the rest of the wall.

spaniel A sporting dog belonging to one of several breeds originally developed to assist hunters; bred to retrieve game, especially birds; usually small, affectionate, with long pendulous ears; now popular pets.

Spanish *Romance languages; Spanish literature*

Spanish–American War (1898) A brief conflict growing out of US intervention in the Cuban revolution for independence, effectively ended by the destruction of the Spanish fleet. The war resulted in Cuban independence under US suzerainty, and the US acquisition of Puerto Rico and the Philippines.

Spanish–American Wars of Independence (1810–26) Wars fought in South America, following Napoleon's invasion of Spain (1808): reformers in the major South American colonies set up semi-independent governments (1810), which were rejected both by royalists in the colonies and by the Spanish king, Ferdinand VII, when restored in 1814. The ensuing wars were fought in two main theatres: Venezuela, New Granada and Quito, where Simón Bolívar was the leading patriot general; and Argentina and Chile, from where General José de San Martín mounted an invasion of the Viceroyalty of Peru, still held by Spain (1820–1). The final liberation of Peru was effected in 1824 by Bolívar. The last Spanish garrisons in South America, at Callao (Peru) and on the island of Chiloé (Chile), surrendered to the patriots in 1826.

Spanish Armada A fleet of 130 Spanish ships, commanded by the Duke of Medina Sidonia, carrying 20 000 soldiers and 8500 sailors, sent by Philip II of Spain to invade England in 1588. The invasion was in retaliation for English support of Protestant rebels in the Netherlands, the execution of Mary, Queen of Scots (1587), and raids on Spanish shipping, such as Drake's at Cádiz (1587); Philip's aim was to gain control of the English Channel. The fleet, delayed by storms and hampered by orders to rendezvous with Spanish forces in the Netherlands, anchored off Calais on 6 August. The following night the English sent fireships into the anchorage, causing the Spanish fleet to scatter. The next day the Spanish fleet was routed by English attacks commanded by Charles Howard off Gravelines (28–29 Jul); 44 ships were lost in battles and during the flight home around Scotland and Ireland under heavy storms. Although a victory for the English, counter-armadas were unsuccessful, and the war lasted until 1604.

Spanish art The art associated with Spain, which has flourished in the Peninsula since prehistoric times. The Roman occupation (218 BC–AD 414) saw extensive building, but most of this has perished. After the Muslim invasion of 711, Córdoba became the centre of an artistically splendid culture which exerted a deep influence on later Christian art. A recognizable national tradition began in the 9th-c with the Mozarabic style (ie the art of Spanish Christians under Muslim rule). From the 11th-c, richly decorated Romanesque cathedrals were built, such as at Santiago de Compostela. The great period in painting and sculpture began in the late 16th-c, when a powerfully emotional realism emerged in response to Counter-Reformation ideals. Major painters included El Greco, Velázquez, and Zurbarán; sculptors included Juan Martínez Montañés (1568–1649) and Alonso Cano (1601–67). The most important later masters were Goya and Picasso.

Spain

☐ International Airport

Span **España**, ancient **Iberia**, Lat **Hispania**, official name **Kingdom of Spain**, Span **Reino de España**

Local name España (Spanish)

Timezone GMT +1

Area 504 750 km^2/194 833 sq mi

Population total (2002e) 40 998 000

Status Kingdom

Capital Madrid

Languages Spanish (official) with Catalan, Galician, and Basque also spoken in their respective regions

Ethnic groups Spanish (Castilian, Valencian, Andalusian, Asturian) (73%), Catalan (16%), Galician (8%), Basque (2%)

Religions Roman Catholic (99%), other Christian (including Anglican, Baptist, Evangelical, Mormon, Jehovah's Witnesses) and Muslim minorities

Physical features Located in SW Europe, occupying four-fifths of the Iberian peninsula; includes the Canary Is, Balearic Is, several islands off the coast of N Africa, as well as the Presidios of Ceuta and Melilla in N Morocco; mostly a furrowed C plateau (the Meseta, average height 700 m/2300 ft) crossed by mountains; Andalusian or Baetic Mts (SE) rise to 3478 m/11 411 ft at Mulhacén; Pyrénées (N) rise to 3404 m/11 168 ft at Pico de Aneto; rivers run E-W, notably the Tagus, Ebro, Guadiana, Miñho, Duero, Guadalquivir, Segura, Júcar.

Climate Continental climate in the Meseta and Ebro Basin, with hot summers, cold winters, low rainfall; highest rainfall in the mountains; S Mediterranean coast has warmest winter temperatures on European mainland; average annual temperatures 5°C (Jan), 25°C (Jul) in Madrid; average annual rainfall 419 mm/16·5 in.

Currency 1 euro = 100 cents (previous to February 2002, 1 Peseta (Pta, Pa) = 100 céntimos).

Economy Traditional agricultural economy gradually being supplemented by varied industries; textiles, iron, steel, shipbuilding, electrical appliances, cars, wine; forestry; fishing; tourism; zinc and other mineral ores; cereals, olives, almonds, pomegranates; member of EC, 1986.

GDP (2002e) $850·7 bn, per capita $21 200

Human Development Index (2002) 0·913

History Early inhabitants included Iberians, Celts, Phoenicians, Greeks, and Romans; Muslim domination from the 8th-c; Christian reconquest completed by 1492; a monarchy since the unification of the Kingdoms of Castile, León, Aragón, and Navarre, largely achieved by 1572; 16th-c exploration of the New World, and the growth of the Spanish Empire; period of decline after the Revolt of the Netherlands, 1581, and the defeat of the Spanish Armada, 1588; War of the Spanish Succession, 1701–14; Peninsular War against Napoleon, 1808–14; war with the USA in 1898 led to the loss of Cuba, Puerto Rico, and remaining Pacific possessions; dictatorship under Primo de Rivera (1923–30), followed by exile of the King and establishment of the Second Republic, 1931; military revolt headed by Franco in 1936 led to civil war and a Fascist dictatorship; Prince Juan Carlos of Bourbon nominated to succeed Franco in 1969; acceded, 1975; terrorist bombings at Madrid railway stations, Mar 2004; under 1978 constitution, the Kingdom of Spain is a constitutional monarchy; Monarch appoints the Prime Minister; governed by a bicameral Parliament (Cortes Generales) comprising a Congress of Deputies and a Senate; moved towards local government autonomy with the creation of 17 self-governing regions.

Second Republic
President
1931–6 Niceto Alcalá Zamora y Torres
1936 Diego Martínez Barrio *Acting*

Civil War
1936–9 Manuel Azaña y Díez
1936–9 Miguel Cabanellas Ferrer

Nationalist Government
Chief of State
1936–75 Francisco Franco Bahamonde

Kingdom of Spain
Head of State (Monarch)
1975– Juan Carlos I

Head of Government
1976–81 Adolfo Suárez
1981–2 Calvo Sotelo
1982–96 Felipe González Márquez
1996–2004 José Maria Aznar
2004– José Luis Rodríguez Zapatero

Spanish bayonet A species of yucca (*Yucca aloifolia*). It is often grown as an indoor novelty, resembling a short log which puts forth leaves when watered. (Family: Agavaceae.)

Spanish chestnut *sweet chestnut*

Spanish Civil War (1936–9) The conflict between supporters and opponents of the Spanish Republic (1931–6). The 'Republicans' included moderates, socialists, communists, Catalan and Basque regionalists, and anarchists. The 'Nationalist' insurgents included monarchists, Carlists, conservative Catholics, and fascist Falangists. The armed forces were divided. Both sides attracted foreign assistance: the Republic from the USSR and the International Brigades; the Nationalists from fascist Italy and Nazi Germany. The Nationalist victory was due to the balance of foreign aid; to 'non-intervention' on the part of the Western democracies; and to greater internal unity, achieved under the leadership of General Franco.

The war took the course of a slow Nationalist advance. The Nationalists initially (Jul 1936) seized much of NW Spain and part of the SW, then (autumn 1936) advanced upon but failed to capture Madrid. They captured Málaga (Mar 1937) and the N coast (Mar–Oct 1937); advanced to the Mediterranean, cutting

Republican Spain in two (Apr 1938); overran Catalonia (Dec 1938–Feb 1939); and finally occupied Madrid and SE Spain (Mar 1939). Some 400 000 were killed in the war, and there were a further 100 000 executions of Republicans from 1939 to 1943. Many towns (such as Guernica) were destroyed.

Spanish fly A slender, metallic-green beetle which exudes acrid yellow fluid from its joints; larvae eat honey of ground-dwelling bees; wing cases formerly collected as a source of blistering agent (*cantharidin*) and as a counter-irritant; more popularly (but completely spuriously), used as an aphrodisiac, where its high toxicity has led to many cases of fatal poisoning. (Order: Coleoptera. Family: Meloidae.)

Spanish literature Spanish literature begins with the *Cantar de Mio Cid* (c.1140, Song of my Cid), one of the few popular epics to survive in written form. The 14th-c miscellany *Libro de buen amor* (The Book of Good Love) by Juan Ruiz is a more self-conscious work; but real sophistication had to await the absorption of classical and Italian influences in the 16th–17th-c. The mystical writings of St Teresa (1515–82) and St John of the Cross (1542–91) sounded a distinctive note, and Garcilaso de la Vega (1503–36) and Luis de León (1527–91) began the long tradition of Spanish love poetry, secular and religious. The Golden Age of Spanish literature continues with the satires of Francisco de Quevedo (1580–1645) and the numerous plays of Lope de Vega and Pedro Calderón (1600–81). But the greatest single work is Miguel de Cervantes' complex masterpiece *Don Quixote* (1605–15), an essential reference point in world fiction. Scientific and political thought occupied the 18th-c. A short-lived Romantic movement much influenced by Byron and Scott gave way to a rich Realist tradition in fiction, the most important writer being Benito Pérez Galdós (1843–1920), with over 80 novels on Spanish life and history. The 'Generation of '98', including Pío Baroja (1872–1956) and novelist and social critic Miguel de Unamuno (1864–1936) provided new perspectives; as did the poets Juan Ramón Jiménez (1881–1958; Nobel Prize, 1956) and Antonio Machado (1875–1939). Two other notable poets fell victims to Franco in the Spanish Civil War, Federico García Lorca (1899–1936) and Miguel Hernández (1910–42). Perhaps Spanish literature has not recovered since that time; but meanwhile a number of Spanish-American writers have become dominant figures in world literature.

Spanish Main The mainland area of Spanish South America, known until the 19th-c for its pirates. It extends from Panama to the Orinoco R estuary in Venezuela.

Spanish moss A plant (*Tillandsia usneoides*), an epiphyte, related to pineapple, native to warm parts of America. The roots are present in the seedlings only; the mature plants are anchored by winding around tree branches and hanging in grey festoons. It is able to survive very dry conditions. The slender stems are covered with scaly hairs which absorb water directly from the atmosphere. Greenish, 3-petalled flowers are occasionally produced. It is used to stuff upholstery, hence its alternative name, **vegetable horsehair**. (Family: Bromeliaceae.)

Spanish Riding School A school of classical horsemanship situated in Vienna, founded in the late 16th-c. The school is famous for its Lipizzaner horses, bred especially for *haute école* (Fr 'high school') riding, and originally imported from Spain.

Spanish Succession, War of the (1701–13) A conflict fought in several theatres – the Netherlands, Germany, Spain, the Mediterranean, and the Atlantic – between the Grand Alliance (headed by Britain, the Dutch, and the Habsburg emperor) and Louis XIV of France, supported by Spain. Hostilities arose after the death of the last Habsburg King of Spain, Charles II; attempts to negotiate compromise Partition Treaties (1698, 1700) failed. The war was concluded by the Treaties of Utrecht.

Spanish Town 17°59N 76°58W, pop (2000e) 99 000. Capital city of St Catherine parish, Middlesex county, S Jamaica; on the R Cobre, 18 km/11 mi W of Kingston; second largest city in Jamaica; capital, 1535–1872; railway; serves a rich agricultural area; cathedral (1655), ruins of the King's House (1762), court house (1819), folk museum, White Marl Arawak museum.

Spark, Dame Muriel (Sarah), *née* **Camberg** (1918–) Writer, born in Edinburgh, EC Scotland, UK. Educated in Edinburgh, she became editor of *Poetry Review* (1947–9), and published poetry, short stories, and critical biographies, including works on Wordsworth, Mary Shelley, and Emily Brontë. She is best known for her novels, notably *Memento Mori* (1959), *The Ballad of Peckham Rye* (1960), and especially *The Prime of Miss Jean Brodie* (1961, filmed 1969). Other books include *The Mandelbaum Gate* (1965, James Tait Black), *The Driver's Seat* (1970, filmed 1974), *A Far Cry from Kensington* (1988), and *Reality and Dreams* (1996), as well as her stories, collected in 1986, and *The Young Man Who Discovered the Secret of Life and Other Stories* (1999). An autobiography, *Curriculum Vitae*, appeared in 1992. She lives in Italy, and was made a dame in 1993.

spark ignition engine An internal combustion engine which initiates the combustion of its air/fuel mixture by means of a spark, usually generated by a sparking plug. This type of engine is most commonly found in motor cars.

sparrow A small songbird, native to the Old World, with some introduced in the New World and Australasia; plumage usually brown/grey; inhabits open country and habitation. The name is also used for some buntings, accentors, and estrildid 'finches'. (Family: Ploceidae, c.37 species; but some authorities place the sparrow in a separate family Passeridae.)

sparrowhawk A hawk (Genus: *Accipiter*, 24 species), native to the Old World, and to Central and South America; inhabits scrub and woodland; eats birds, other small vertebrates, and insects. The name was formerly used for *Falco sparverius*, a New World falcon.

sparrow-weaver *weaverbird*

Sparta (Greece) **[spah(r)ta]**, Gr **Spartí** 37°05N 22°25E, pop (2000e) 16 200. Capital town of Lakonia department, S Greece; on the R Evrotas, 50 km/31 mi SW of Athens; refounded on an ancient site in 1834; trade in fruit and olive oil; carnival (Feb).

Sparta (Greek history) **[spah(r)ta]** One of the two leading city-states of ancient Greece, the other being Athens. Initially, Sparta's political and cultural development was entirely normal, but this situation changed with the revolt (c.650 BC) of Messenia, a territory crucial to her viability as a state. The need to suppress the revolt and prevent a similar recurrence led to a series of military and social reforms, traditionally associated with Lycurgus, which effectively arrested her development. While Athens went on to develop a radical democracy, acquire an overseas empire, and become a cultural pace-setter, militaristic Sparta remained backward, inward-looking, and utterly philistine. Her defeat of Athens in 404 BC put her centre stage, but she played her role so badly that the other city-states combined against her. Thebes delivered the final blow at Leuctra in 371 BC.

Spartacists A left-wing revolutionary faction (the *Spartakusbund*), led by Rosa Luxemburg and Karl Liebknecht (1871–1919) in 1917, which supported the Russian Revolution, and advocated ending the war and a German socialist revolution. In his publications, Liebknecht called on the modern 'wage slave' to revolt as the Roman gladiator Spartacus had done. In 1918 the Spartacists became the German communist party. Luxemburg and Liebknecht were murdered in disturbances in Berlin during the period following the Kaiser's abdication in 1918.There was a further Spartacist rising in the Ruhr in 1920.

Spartacus **[spah(r)takus]** (?–71 BC) Thracian-born slave and gladiator at Capua, who led the most serious slave uprising in the history of Rome (73–71 BC). With a huge army of slaves and dispossessed, he inflicted numerous defeats on the Roman armies sent against him, until defeated and killed by Crassus. His supporters were crucified wholesale, their bodies left hanging along the Appian Way to act as a deterrent to other would-be rebels.

Spartakiad **[spah(r)takiad]** Sporting games held every four years in the former Soviet Union, until 1979 for nationals only. They were named after the ancient Greek city of Sparta, which placed great emphasis on physical fitness.

spasm A sudden intense contraction of a muscle due to stimulation by the nerve that supplies it.

spastic *cerebral palsy*

spathe [spayth] A large sheathing bract which surrounds the specialized inflorescence called a *spadix*. The spathe is often brightly coloured.

spatial filtering *optics*

SP betting An illegal but popular system in Australia for making off-course betting on horse races. Up to the 1960s many hotels and barbers offered SP ('starting price') betting, but since that time, competition from the government-run Totalisator Agency Boards (TABS) and large-scale illegal bookmaking rings have made SP betting a thing of the past.

Speaker The officer who presides over a legislative chamber. The post originated in 14th-c England, where one member of the House of Commons was designated to speak to the king. In the UK, the Speaker presides over the House of Commons, maintains order, and interprets its rules and practice. He or she is a constituency MP elected by fellow members, but must sever party connections and be entirely impartial. Most Commonwealth countries have similar officers, although seldom is the office so detached from party political affairs, and in some instances speakers are notably partisan. In the US House of Representatives, the Speaker is a leader of the majority party, and expected to assist in securing the passage of his or her party's legislation.

Spearman, Charles Edward (1863–1945) British psychologist, born in London, UK. He studied in Leipzig, then returned to London, where he became professor of mind and logic at University College. He was a pioneer of the statistical technique of factor analysis, and played a considerable role in the early development of intelligence testing.

spearmint *mint*

Spears, Britney (Jean) (1981–) Pop singer and actress, born in Kentwood, Louisiana, USA. She began competing in talent shows at an early age and attended the Professional Performing Arts School in New York City during school vacations. At age 11 she joined the cast of the popular TV show *The All New Mickey Mouse Club*, and later signed a development deal with Jive Records. The title track of her first album, *Baby One More Time* (1999), became a Number 1 hit. Later albums include *Britney* (2001) and *In the Zone* (2003). She made her film debut in *Crossroads* (2002).

spear thistle A biennial thistle (*Cirsium vulgare*), growing to 150 cm/5 ft or more, native to Europe, W Asia, and N Africa; stems spiny-winged; leaves lobed, margins with long stout spines; flower-heads to 4 cm/1½ in across, reddish-purple; fruits with a parachute of feathery hairs aiding dispersal by the wind. It is believed to be the thistle adopted as the national emblem of Scotland. (Family: Compositae.)

Special Air Service *SAS*

Special Boat Service *SBS*

Special Branch A branch of the British police force principally responsible for investigating offences against public order, including terrorism, sedition, treason, and contravention of the Official Secrets Act. It was formed in 1883 following a series of bomb attacks on mainland Britain by Irish Nationalists. It has a role in information-gathering and the surveillance of subversive organizations.

Special Drawing Rights (SDRs) Rights which can be exercised by members of the International Monetary Fund to draw on a pool of mixed currencies (US dollar, British pound, Japanese yen, French franc, German mark) set up by the Fund for use in emergencies. The facility is available to solve temporary balance of payments problems.

special education The provision of education to children who have special educational needs. They may be pupils who suffer from some kind of physical or mental disability, who have learning or emotional difficulties, or whose needs cannot otherwise be catered for within the normal provision. In many cases the pattern is to provide special schools, but the trend in some countries has been for such children to be taught in ordinary schools.

special effects Trick shots in motion pictures and video, forming two main groups: those achieved entirely in front of the camera, and those in which the recorded image is modified. Among the former are the many ways in which the area photographed is extended, by scenes painted on glass or miniature sets built in perspective; scale models shot in slow motion represent trains, liners, and spaceships while animated models, shot frame-by-frame, bring fantastic creatures to life. A frequent need for image combination is to show live actors performing against a different background, which may be an actual distant location, a model, or even a drawing. An early technique was back-projection, now replaced by the more efficient reflex front projection. In another method the actors are shot against a large uniform blue backing, to be combined with the background later, using travelling mattes for film and chromakey for video. Two or more camera images must often be combined in dissolves, wipes, and split screen effects; in film all these need optical printing at the laboratory after photography, but in video they can be made directly, either during shooting or in videotape editing. Vision mixers and computer-generated imagery provide vast scope for image manipulation effects which are completely beyond those possible on film.

speciality fibres Textile fibres obtained mainly from the goat and camel families, such as cashmere, mohair, vicuna, camel, alpaca, and angora (rabbit). They are relatively rare and expensive.

Special Operations Executive (SOE) An organization set up with British war cabinet approval in July 1940 in response to Churchill's directive to 'set Europe ablaze'; it later also operated in the Far East. It promoted and co-ordinated resistance activity in enemy-occupied territory until the end of World War 2.

special relativity A system of mechanics applicable at high velocities (approaching the velocity of light) in the absence of gravitation; a generalization of Newtonian mechanics, due almost entirely to Albert Einstein (1905). Its fundamental postulates are that the velocity of light c is the same for all observers, no matter how they are moving; that the laws of physics are the same in all inertial frames; and that all such frames are equivalent. On this basis, no object may have a velocity in excess of the velocity of light; and two events which appear simultaneous to one observer need not be so for another. The system gives laws of mechanics which reproduce those of 'common sense' Newtonian mechanics at low velocities, and is well supported experimentally, especially in particle physics. Generalized special relativity, incorporating gravitation, is called **general relativity**. The constancy of the velocity of light is supported experimentally (eg the Michelson–Morley experiment), and implied by Maxwell's equations of electromagnetism, which express the velocity of light in terms of simple fundamental electric and magnetic constants. Newtonian mechanics is impossible to reconcile with this, since it produces velocity addition rules which fail for light and Maxwell's equations. Einstein's solution (1905) was to insist that the velocity of light really is the same for all observers, and that the form of Maxwell's equations is the same for all. This then implied that the rules of mechanics needed to be rewritten. The new system of mechanics derived by Einstein is consistent only if old notions of basic quantities such as mass, energy, space, and time are modified; it also incorporates a velocity addition rule. Special relativistic mechanics is fully supported by observation.

species A group of organisms, minerals, or other entities formally recognized as distinct from other groups. In biology, the species is a group of actually or potentially interbreeding natural populations, reproductively isolated from other similar groups such that exchange of genetic material cannot occur (the **species barrier**). Most species cannot interbreed with others; those that can, typically produce infertile offspring. This biological concept of the species cannot be applied to fossils, or to organisms that do not reproduce sexually. These species are defined on a comparative morphological basis.

specific dynamic action A transient rise in resting metabolic rate following the consumption of a meal. Also known as *diet-induced thermogenesis* or the *thermic* effect of food, its exact role in energy metabolism is poorly understood.

specific gravity *relative density*

specific heat capacity *heat capacity*

specific performance In law, a court order directed to a person in breach of a contractual obligation, ordering that he or she carry out the contract as agreed; known as a *specific implement* in Scottish law. The court may refuse to grant the order, where damages are an adequate remedy or the order could not be enforced. Specific performance may however be a suitable remedy for a breach of contract to sell (or buy) land, and in the US is considered a remedy in equity, not law.

speckle interferometry A technique used in optical and infrared astronomy to produce high-resolution images. It processes numerous short exposures in a way which removes the effects of erratic motions (twinkling) caused by turbulence in the Earth's atmosphere.

speckle pattern A granular image formed where a laser beam strikes an unpolished surface. It is a form of interference pattern present only with laser light – a consequence of laser light's unique (coherence) properties.

spectacled bear The only bear native to the S hemisphere (*Tremarctos ornatus*); inhabits forests in W foothills of the Andes; small (shoulder height, 75 cm/30 in); dark with pale rings around eyes; builds platforms in trees from broken branches; eats mainly plants; also known as **Andean bear**.

spectacles A frame which supports lenses held in front of each eye, designed to correct abnormalities of refraction, such as long or short sight, and *astigmatism* (asymmetry of the cornea). Convex lenses help those who are long-sighted; concave lenses those who are short-sighted. **Bifocal spectacles** have lenses where the upper and lower parts have different curvatures, enabling the wearer to focus on distant and near objects respectively.

Spector, Phil (1940–) Record producer, born in New York City, USA. In the 1960s he developed a distinctive 'wall of sound' style using echo-effects and other innovative recording techniques; hits by such groups as the Ronettes (with his wife Ronnie Spector), the Crystals, and Darlene Love made him a millionaire in his early 20s. The Righteous Brothers' 'You've Lost That Loving Feeling' was his last major single success, in 1965. Later he worked with the Beatles and with ex-Beatles John Lennon and George Harrison. His *Christmas Album* remains a festive classic.

spectroscopy The study of energy levels in atoms or molecules, usually using absorbed or emitted electromagnetic radiation. Inner atomic electrons give spectra in the X-ray region; outer atomic electrons give visible light spectra; the rotation and vibration of molecules give infrared spectra; the precession of nuclear magnetic moments gives radio-wave spectra. Many types of spectroscopy exist, often used to identify the structure of an unknown substance or to detect the presence of known substances.

spectrum The distribution of electromagnetic energy as a function of wavelength or frequency. A common example is the spectrum of white light dispersed by a prism to produce a rainbow of constituent colours; the rainbow is the spectrum of sunlight refracted through raindrops. For white light the colours are red, orange, yellow, green, blue, and violet in order of decreasing wavelength. All objects with temperatures above absolute zero emit electromagnetic radiation by virtue of their warmth alone; this *black body radiation* is emitted at progressively shorter wavelengths as temperature is increased. The universe (3K) sends us microwaves; objects at room temperature (295K) infrared rays; the Sun (6000K) yellow light; and the solar corona (1 million K) X-rays. Individual atoms can emit and absorb radiation only at particular wavelengths corresponding to the transitions between energy levels in the atom. The spectrum of a given atom (or element) therefore consists of a series of emission or absorption lines. A familiar example is sodium, used in low pressure street lights, where almost all the energy emerges as a pair of lines in the yellow part of the spectrum. The device for displaying a spectrum is called a **spectrograph**. By analyzing the spectrum of a substance, its chemical composition can be deduced.

speech pathology The study and treatment of all forms of clinically abnormal linguistic behaviour; also known as **(speech and) language pathology**. In several countries (eg the USA), the designation **speech pathologist** applies to professionals concerned with the treatment of language-handicapped people; in others (eg the UK) the equivalent profession is that of **speech and language therapist**.

speech therapy *speech pathology*

Speed, John (1552–1629) Antiquary and cartographer, born in Cheshire, NWC England, UK. He began as a tailor, but his considerable historical learning brought him patronage, and he was able to publish his 54 *Maps of England and Wales* (1608–10) and other works.

speed (pharmacology) *amphetamine*

speed (photography) A rating of the sensitivity of a photographic material on a recognized numerical scale. Previously, ASA (in which doubling the sensitivity doubles the rating number), and DIN (a German industrial standard, where doubling sensitivity adds 3° to the rating) were used, now combined in an International Standards scale in a form such as ISO 200/24°. The arithmetic Exposure Index (EI) rating refers to speed values used in practice for non-standard processing or treatment of a material.

speed (physics) The rate of change of distance with time; symbol v, units m/s; a scalar quantity. Speed is the magnitude of velocity, but unlike velocity specifies no direction.

speed of light *velocity of light*

speedometer An instrument fitted in a vehicle to show its speed. Usually a cable from the vehicle road-drive rotates a magnet, which induces an eddy current in a non-magnetic conductor attached to a pointer. The interaction of the permanent magnet and the induced fields turns the pointer against a restoring spring.

speedway A form of motorcycle racing on machines with no brakes and only one gear. The most popular form is on an oval track, and involving four riders at one time. Other forms include **long track racing** and **ice speedway**. The sport originated in the USA in 1902.

speedwell An annual or perennial, some agricultural weeds, native to N temperate regions; stems creeping or erect; leaves opposite, lance-shaped or oval, often toothed; flowers solitary or in spikes, blue or white, with a short tube and four petals, upper largest, lower smallest. (Genus: *Veronica*, 300 species. Family: Scrophulariaceae.)

Speenhamland system [speenuhmland] The most famous of many local expedients in Britain to improve the operation of the old poor laws at a time of crisis. The name was taken from the Berkshire parish whose magistrates in 1795 introduced scales of relief for labourers dependent both on the prevailing price of bread and the size of labourers' families. The principles spread to many S and E parishes in the early 19th-c. It was criticized by some political economists for encouraging the poor to breed!

Speer, Albert [shpeer] (1905–81) Architect and Nazi government official, born in Mannheim, SWC Germany. He joined the Nazi Party in 1931, became Hitler's chief architect in 1934, and was minister of armaments in 1942. Always more concerned with technology and administration than ideology, he openly opposed Hitler in the final months of the war, and was the only Nazi leader at Nuremberg to admit responsibility for the regime's actions. He was imprisoned for 20 years in Spandau, Berlin, and after his release in 1966 became a writer.

Speke, John Hanning (1827–64) Explorer, born in Bideford, Devon, SW England, UK. He served in India, and in 1856 went with Burton to search for the equatorial lakes of Africa. They discovered L Tanganyika (1858), then Speke travelled on alone, finding the lake he named Victoria, and saw in it the headwaters of the Nile. Back in England, his claims to have discovered the source of the Nile were doubted, and so a second expedition set out (1860–3). On his return, his claims were again challenged, and he was about to defend his discovery when he was killed in a shooting accident.

speleology / spelaeology The scientific exploration and study of caves and other underground features, surveying their extent, physical history and structure, and natural history. When cave-exploring is taken up as a hobby, it is known as **spelunking** (US) or **potholing** (UK), where people descend through access points (potholes) to follow the course of underground rivers and streams.

spelling reform A movement to regularize a language's spelling system. In English, for example, the spelling system is widely perceived as being irregular, because of a relatively small but frequently used number of striking inconsistencies between sounds and letters. The irregularity was famously illustrated by George Bernard Shaw's mischievous spelling of *fish* as *ghoti* – *f* as in *rough*, *i* as in *women*, *sh* as in *patient*! Such variations in spelling patterns (one sound represented by several letters or letter-sequences; one letter representing several sounds) result from the disparate historical sources of English words, which have at various periods been influenced by Anglo-Saxon, Old Norse, Latin, Norman French, and Greek, each with its own conflicting spelling conventions.

The retention of such disparity has largely resulted from the conservatism forced on the written language by the needs of the printing press for continuity in spelling practices. This has led to calls for reform of the spelling system – sometimes for the complete replacement of existing symbols (as in Shaw's proposal for a new alphabet), more usually for a 'standardizing system', in which the existing alphabet is used in a way which more consistently reflects the correspondence between sound and symbol. Several dozen proposals were fully worked out in the course of the 20th-c. The main aim is to ease reading and spelling problems for learners and users of the language. The vested interests of the publishing world, allied to general public tolerance and conservatism, have so far militated against the widespread adoption of any new standardizing system.

spelunking *speleology*

Spence, Sir Basil (Urwin) (1907–76) Architect, born in Mumbai (Bombay), W India. He studied at Edinburgh and London, and gradually emerged as the leading post-war British architect, with his fresh approach to new university buildings, the pavilion for the Festival of Britain (1951), and most famously the new Coventry Cathedral (1951), which boldly merged new and traditional structural methods. He was professor of architecture at Leeds (1955–6) and at the Royal Academy (1961–8). He was knighted in 1960.

Spence, Michael A(ndrew) (1943–) Economist, born in Montclair, New Jersey, USA. He taught at Stanford University (1973–6) and Harvard (1971–3, 1976–90) before returning to Stanford as dean of the business school (1990). His principal contributions include work on the economics of information and in the dynamic aspects of competition. He shared the Nobel Prize for Economics in 2001 for the analysis of markets with asymmetric information.

Spencer, Herbert (1820–1903) Evolutionary philosopher, born in Derby, Derbyshire, C England, UK. He became a civil engineer for a railway in 1837, but engaged extensively in journalism. A firm (pre-Darwinian) believer in evolution, his main work is the nine-volume *System of Synthetic Philosophy* (1862–93), which brought together biology, psychology, sociology, and ethics. He was a leading advocate of 'Social Darwinism'.

Spencer, Sir Stanley (1891–1959) Artist, born in Cookham, Windsor and Maidenhead, S England, UK. He studied in London, then lived and worked mainly at Cookham. During 1926–33 he executed murals (using his war experiences) in the Oratory of All Souls, Burghclere. He produced many purely realistic landscapes, but his main works interpret the Bible in terms of everyday life, such as 'Resurrection: Port Glasgow' (1950, Tate, London). He was knighted in 1959.

Spencer-Churchill, Baroness *Churchill, Winston*

Spender, Sir Stephen (Harold) (1909–95) Poet and critic, born in London, UK. He studied at Oxford, and became one of the group of modern poets with Auden and Day-Lewis in the 1930s. His many poetic works include *Poems from Spain* (1939), *Ruins and Visions* (1942), and *The Generous Days* (1971). His *Collected Poems, 1928–85* were published in 1985. He was co-editor of *Horizon* (1939–41) and *Encounter* (1953–67), co-founder of *Index on Censorship* in 1971, and professor of English at University College London (1970–7). He was knighted in 1983.

Spengler, Oswald [shpenggler] (1880–1936) Philosopher of history, born in Blankenburg, C Germany. He studied at Halle, Munich, and Berlin, and taught mathematics before devoting himself entirely to the morbidly prophetic *Der Untergang des Abendlandes* (2 vols, 1918–22, The Decline of the West), which argues that all cultures are subject to the same cycle of growth and decay in accordance with predetermined 'historical destiny'. His views greatly encouraged the Nazis, though he never became one himself.

Spenser, Edmund (?1552–99) Poet, born in London, UK. He studied at Cambridge, and obtained a place in Leicester's household, which led to a friendship with Sir Philip Sidney and a circle of wits (the *Areopagus*). His first original work was a sequence of pastoral poems, *The Shepheards Calendar* (1579), which heralded the English literary Golden Age. In 1580 he became secretary to the lord deputy in Ireland, and for his services was given Kilcolman Castle, Co Cork, where he settled in 1586. Here he began his major work, *The Faerie Queene*, using a nine-line verse pattern which later came to be called the *Spenserian stanza*. The first three books, dedicated to Elizabeth I (the fairy queen, Gloriana), were published in 1590, and the second three in 1596, but the poem was left unfinished at his death.

sperm The male gamete of animals: also called **spermatozoa**. It is typically a small motile cell which locates and penetrates the female gamete (*ovum*). It contains little cytoplasm.

spermaceti [spermaseetee] A waxy oil found in the head of sperm whales (almost 2000 l/440 UK galls/530 US galls per whale in *Physeter catodon*); solidifies in air; function unclear; formerly used as a lubricant, and in ointments and candles; name (mistakenly) means 'whale's sperm'.

sperm bank The storage of human sperm for long periods in a frozen state, with a view to future use in artificial insemination. In this way young men receiving treatment for malignant disease which may lead to sterility can preserve their procreative ability. Infertile couples may use stored donor spermatozoa, selected as being of above-average quality with regard to motility and numbers.

sperm whale A toothed whale, widespread in tropical and temperate seas; eats mainly squid; bulbous head contains spermaceti organ; three species: **sperm whale** or **cachalot** (*Physeter catodon*), the largest toothed mammal (length up to 20 m/65 ft), grey-black, head up to one-third length of body; **pygmy sperm whale** (*Kogia breviceps*), length 3·4 m/11 ft, and **dwarf sperm whale** (*Kogia simus*), length 2·5 m/8 ft, both with head one-sixth length of body. (Family: Physeteridae.)

Speyer Cathedral [shpiyer] Romanesque cathedral founded by Conrad II (c.990–1039) in 1060 at Speyer, SW Germany. The church, which is noted for its royal tombs and crypt, has required reconstruction on several occasions, most recently after World War 2. It is a world heritage site.

Spey, River River in NE Scotland, UK; rises near Corrieyairack Pass, SE of Fort Augustus; flows NE into Spey Bay, to the E of

Lossiemouth; noted for its salmon fishing; length 171 km/ 106 mi; in lower reaches, the fastest-flowing river in Britain.

sphalerite [sfaleriyt] A zinc sulphide (ZnS) mineral, also known as **zinc blende**. Colourless when pure, it often contains iron, which darkens its colour. It occurs in hydrothermal veins, usually associated with galena and silver minerals. It is the principal ore of zinc.

sphere In mathematics, the locus in space of all points equidistant from a fixed point (the centre). The distance of each point from the centre is the radius *r* of the sphere. The surface area of a sphere is $4\pi r^2$; the volume of a sphere is $\frac{4}{3}\pi r^3$. Archimedes discovered that the surface area of a sphere is equal to the curved surface area of the cylinder circumscribing the sphere, and asked that this should be commemorated on his tombstone. When Cicero was serving in Syracuse 200 years after the death of Archimedes, he discovered a tomb which he recognized as that of Archimedes, because it displayed the diagram.

sphinx [sfingks] In ancient Greece a mythological monster with a human head and a recumbent animal body (usually a lion's); sometimes it was winged and had female breasts. Originating in the East, probably Egypt, it is found throughout the Levant and E Mediterranean. In Greek mythology, it was associated particularly with Thebes, where, until the time of Oedipus, it devoured all who could not answer its riddle: What goes on four legs in the morning, two at noon, and three in the evening? (Answer: Man.)

sphygmomanometer [sfigmomanomiter] A device for measuring blood pressure. An inflatable rubber cuff is placed round a limb (usually the arm), and inflated until the pulse (heard through a stethoscope) can no longer be detected. The cuff is then slowly deflated until the sound of the pulse can be heard again. The first sound heard reflects the pressure of blood in the arteries as the heart actively contracts (*systole*). As the deflation of the cuff continues, a second sound is heard, reflecting the resting pressure (*diastole*) within the arteries. The pressure is read off either electronically or direct from a column of mercury.

Spica [spiyka] *Virgo*

spice A pungent-tasting plant used to flavour or preserve food. The term is used particularly when referring to hard parts, such as dry fruits and seeds, but it can include parts such as flower buds.

Spice Girls, The British pop singing group, with members **Victoria ('Vicki') Addams**, known as 'Posh Spice' (1975–), born in Hertfordshire; **Melanie Jayne Chisholm**, or 'Mel(anie) C', known as 'Sporty Spice' (1975–), born in Liverpool, **Melanie Janine Brown**, or 'Mel(anie) B', known as 'Scary Spice' (1975 –), born in Yorkshire; **Emma Lee Bunton**, or 'Emma', known as 'Baby Spice' (1976–), born in Finchley, N London; and **Geri Estelle Halliwell**, or 'Geri', known as 'Ginger Spice' (1972–), born in Watford, Hertfordshire. From earlier careers as dancers, singers, or models, they came together in 1996, their first record, 'Wannabe!', becoming a number 1 hit in the UK. Later hits were 'Say You'll Be There' (1996), '2 Become 1' (1996), and 'Who Do You Think You Are' (1997). The group made a feature film, *Spiceworld – the Movie*, in 1997. Geri left the group in 1998, and was appointed Goodwill Ambassador for the UN Population Fund later that year. All remaining members have since gone on to release solo singles. Victoria married footballer David Beckham in 1999. In 2000 they made pop history by becoming the first female group to have had nine number 1 singles when their double A-sided 'Holler Holler/Let Love Lead the Way' went straight to number 1 in the charts.

Spice Islands *Moluccas*

spider A predatory, terrestrial arthropod; body divided into head (*prosoma*) and abdomen (*opisthosoma*) joined by slender waist; prosoma with 2–8 simple eyes, a pair of fangs (*chelicerae*) used to inject poison into prey, and four pairs of slender legs; opisthosoma bears respiratory organs (both lungs and tracheae) and usually three pairs of silk-spinning organs (*spinnerets*). Spider silk is used to make webs, traps, homes, and funnels, to wrap prey, and in dispersal (as small spiders on silk threads can be carried by the wind). (Class: Arachnida. Order: Araneae, c.35 000 species.)

spider crab A slow-moving crab with a small slender body and long legs; leg span up to 4 m/13 ft in the giant species; body and appendages often covered with growths of seaweed, sponges, or hydroids for camouflage. (Class: Malacostraca. Order: Decapoda.)

spider mite A small, reddish mite that sucks at the undersides of leaves and can cause great destruction of economically important crops, such as tomatoes and beans. (Order: Acari. Family: Tetranychidae.)

spider monkey A New World monkey; slender with extremely long legs and tail; thumbs small or absent; may swing from trees using fingers as hooks, but usually walks along tops of branches. (Genus: *Ateles*, 4 species.)

spider plant A fleshy-rooted perennial (*Chlorophytum comosum*) native to S Africa; leaves tufted, narrow, curved; inflorescence to 60 cm/2 ft, branched, bearing white flowers and tufts of leaves which root on contact with the soil, forming new plants. A cultivar with cream-striped leaves is widely grown as a house plant. (Family: Liliaceae.)

spider wasp A slender, solitary wasp; long-legged adult females usually run over ground to catch spiders; these are paralysed, and an egg is laid on each spider, which is usually left in a burrow or cup-shaped nest made of mud. (Order: Hymenoptera. Family: Pompilidae.)

Spielberg, Steven [speelberg] (1947–) Film-maker, born in Cincinnati, Ohio, USA. An amateur film-maker as a child, he became one of the youngest television directors at Universal Studios. A highly praised television film, *Duel* (1972), brought him the opportunity to direct for the cinema, and a string of hits have made him the most commercially successful director of all time. His films have explored primeval fears, as in *Jaws* (1975, three Oscars), or expressed childlike wonder at the marvels of this world and beyond, as in *Close Encounters of the Third Kind* (1977, two Oscars) and *ET* (1982, four Oscars). Later films include literary adaptations, such as *The Color Purple* (1985) and *Empire of the Sun* (1987), as well as the continuing adventures of his dare-devil hero, Indiana Jones, in such films as *Raiders of the Lost Ark* (1981, five Oscars) and *Indiana Jones and the Temple of Doom* (1984, Oscar). Imaginative fantasy is dominant in his version of Peter Pan, *Hook* (1991), *Jurassic Park* (1993, three Oscars), and its sequel *The Lost World: Jurassic Park* (1997). *Schindler's List* (1993, seven Oscars) also received the 1994 BAFTA award for best director and best film, and *Saving Private Ryan* (1998) won him an Oscar for best director. His company (Amblin Entertainment, founded in 1982) has produced several other successful films, notably *Back to the Future* (1985) and its two sequels, and *Who Framed Roger Rabbit* (1988). In 1994 Spielberg formed a new studio, Dreamworks SKG, followed in 1995 by Dreamworks Interactive, to produce interactive games, videos, and teaching material. In 2001 he completed the science fiction film *AI: Artificial Intelligence*, a project begun by the late Stanley Kubrick. That same year he was awarded an honorary British knighthood. In 2004 he was honoured with the Directors Guild of America lifetime achievement award.

spikelet A structure peculiar to the inflorescence of grasses, consisting of one or several reduced flowers enclosed in a series of small bracts. The spikelets can be arranged in several ways to form the inflorescence.

Spillane, Mickey [spilayn], pseudonym of **Frank Morrison Spillane** (1918–) Detective fiction writer, born in New York City, USA. During the late 1940s and early 1950s, under his pseudonym, he wrote a series of successful novels featuring detective Mike Hammer. *The Girl Hunters* (1962) was made into a film for which Spillane both wrote the script and acted as Hammer. In later novels he introduced the character Tiger Mann. His work contained elements of violence, sadism, and sexual immorality which some readers found disturbing, but his literary style and forceful main characters gained popular appeal, and the mixture translated readily to film. Later novels include *The Last Cop Out* (1973), *The Day the Sea Rolled Back* (1981), and *The Killing Man* (1990).

spin A vector attribute of subatomic particles, having a precise meaning only in quantum theory, but modelled on classical mechanical spin; symbol *S*; units ($h/2\pi$), where *h* is Planck's constant (but usually values are stated with units omitted). It may thus be thought of as referring to a particle spinning on its axis, with a higher spin number corresponding to a faster rotation. In the quantum case, only certain values of spin are possible. Electrons and protons have spin ½; photons have spin 1.

spina bifida [spiyna bifida] A congenital defect of one or more vertebrae, in which the arch of a vertebra fails to develop. The condition varies in severity. In *spina bifida occulta*, the spinal cord and its covering membrane (*meninges*) are undisplaced and covered by skin; there are no adverse effects. In more serious cases, a *meningocele* or *myelomeningocele* may develop, in which the meninges, or meninges and spinal cord, protrude out of the back; the unprotected spinal cord is then vulnerable to damage. The defect usually affects the lower back, and damage to the spinal cord results in paralysis of the lower limbs. The cause is unknown, but it may be related to a deficiency of folic acid in the developing fetus, and pregnant women are sometimes given folic acid supplements to prevent the condition. Antenatal diagnosis can be made by detecting an abnormal protein (*alfa-foetoprotein*) in amniotic fluid, or by ultrasonography.

spinach beet *beet*

spinal cord That part of the vertebrate central nervous system contained within and protected by the vertebral column, continuous above with the medulla oblongata of the brain. It is essentially a long, thick cable formed by thousands of parallel-running axons (*white matter*) surrounding a central H-shaped core of cell bodies (*grey matter*). It has a minute central canal (containing cerebrospinal fluid) which is continuous with the ventricles of the brain. In the human adult it is approximately 45 cm/18 in long, and extends down as far as the second lumbar vertebra. The end tapers to a pointed tip. The front (*ventral*) horns of the grey matter contain the cell bodies of the neurones that supply voluntary muscles; their axons form the ventral roots of the spinal nerves. The rear (*dorsal*) horns of the grey matter consist of cell bodies concerned with the processing of sensory information, which enters the spinal cord through the dorsal roots. Between the ventral and dorsal horns on each side, in the thoracic and upper lumbar segments of the cord, a lateral horn projects which contains the cell bodies of neurones of the sympathetic part of the autonomic nervous system, and the sacral part of the cord gives rise to the pelvic parasympathetic outflow. The peripheral white part of the spinal cord consists of axons arranged in tracts that convey information to or from the brain, or between different segments of the spinal cord. In humans, 31 pairs of spinal nerves arise from the spinal cord, formed from the ventral (motor) and dorsal (sensory) nerve roots.

spindle tree A small deciduous tree or shrub (*Euonymus europaeus*), growing to 6 m/20 ft, native to Europe and W Asia; leaves narrowly oval, pointed, toothed; flowers in clusters of 3–8, greenish with four narrow petals; fruit a pink, 4-lobed capsule 1–1·5 cm/0·4–0·6 in, splitting to reveal seeds with fleshy orange arils. (Family: Celastraceae.)

spin doctors *agenda setting*

spine *vertebral column*

spinel [spinel] The name given to a group of minerals which are double oxides of divalent and trivalent metals. Its principal members are *chromite* ($FeCr_2O_4$), the chief source of chromium, *magnetite* (Fe_3O_4), and *spinel* ($MgAl_2O_4$), which may be valuable as a gemstone, particularly when coloured red because of minor impurities. They occur as accessory minerals in igneous and metamorphic rocks.

spinet A keyboard instrument resembling a harpsichord, but with a single set of strings running diagonally to the keyboard. It was particularly popular in 17th-c England.

spin glass A dilute mixture of a magnetic material in some other substance, often a metal (eg weak alloys of iron in gold, or manganese in copper), in which the magnetic component is randomly dispersed. It shows no long-range magnetic ordering, but is characterized by a sharp peak in magnetic susceptibility as temperature increases, which is thought to indicate a phase transition.

spinifex A coarse, spiny-leaved grass, native to E Asia and Australasia. The spikelets have long, spiny bracts, and are massed to form globular heads which break off and act as tumbleweeds before breaking up. (Genus: *Spinifex*, 3 species. Family: Gramineae.)

Spinks, Leon (1953–) Boxer, born in the USA. He won a gold medal in the light heavyweight division at the 1976 Olympic Games, and went on to briefly hold the world heavyweight title in a split decision over Muhammad Ali in 1978. His brother **Michael Spinks** also won the heavyweight title (1983), making them the only brothers to hold world boxing titles.

spinning The conversion of fibres into yarns. Two main types of yarn were traditionally produced: in *woollen* yarns, the fibres are randomly arranged; in *worsted* types, the fibres lie parallel to the length of the yarn. In the 18th-c, the process was the earliest to be mechanized, initially using cotton. New methods, such as friction and rotor spinning, are now very important and are far removed from the early hand methods using the distaff and, later (from 11th-c China) the spinning wheel.

Spinoza, Baruch or **Benedictus de** [spinohza] (1632–77) Philosopher and theologian, born in Amsterdam, The Netherlands, into a Jewish emigré family from Portugal. His deep interest in optics, the new astronomy, and Cartesian philosophy made him unpopular, and he was expelled from the Jewish community in 1656. He became the leader of a small philosophical circle and made a living grinding and polishing lenses. His major works include the *Tractatus theologico-politicus* (1670), published anonymously in 1670 but banned in 1674 for its controversial views on the Bible and Christian theology, and his *Ethica*, published posthumously in 1677, a complete, deductive, metaphysical system, intended to be a proof of what is good for human beings derived with mathematical certainty from axioms, theorems, and definitions. He rejected Cartesian dualism in favour of a pantheistic God who has matter and mind as two of his attributes and is the ultimate substance and explanation of the world. He is regarded, along with Descartes and Leibniz, as one of the great Rationalist thinkers of the 18th-c.

spin resonance *magnetic resonance*

spin statistics *Bose–Einstein statistics; Fermi–Dirac statistics*

spiny anteater *echidna*

spiny lobster A lobster-like marine crustacean with a well-developed abdomen but without conspicuous pincers (*chelipeds*); antennae often very long; commonly exploited for food; known as **crawfish** in North America. (Class: Malacostraca. Order: Decapoda.)

spiracle An external opening of the respiratory system of insects. The system comprises flexible tubes (*tracheae*) and air sacs that penetrate throughout the insect's body. Air enters the tracheae through 10 pairs of spiracles arranged along body segments.

spiraea / spirea [spiyreea] A deciduous, sometimes suckering shrub, native to the temperate N hemisphere; leaves narrow to broadly oval, entire, toothed or lobed; flowers 5-petalled, white or pink, in dense clusters. It is a popular ornamental. (Genus: *Spiraea*, 100 species. Family: Rosaceae.)

spirit control *seance*

spiritism *spiritualism*

spirits Alcoholic beverages produced by distilling ethanol from a fermentation of mash from various sources, such as barley for whisky, sugar cane for rum, and potatoes for vodka. Many are flavoured to give a distinct taste, such as by the use of the juniper berry for gin. Others are blended with wines to produce such drinks as port, a blend of brandy and wine.

spiritualism An organized religion which believes that spirits of the deceased survive bodily death and communicate with the living, usually via a medium by means of messages, or apparently paranormal physical effects. While many different cultures, past and present, believe in *spiritism* (the ability of spirits of the deceased to communicate with the living), spiritualism is primarily a Western religion, most commonly found in North America and in Europe, arising in the mid-1800s. It attempts to distinguish itself from other spiritist beliefs by taking a 'scientific' approach; spiritualists query whether communicating spirits are who they claim to be by posing questions which could only be answered by the spirit of the deceased and by the person asking the question. Spiritualists believe in God, and feel that through communications with the deceased they may come to better understand the laws of God. They welcome members from different religious faiths. Spiritualism is frequently criticized for having at least some members who use trickery to produce its phenomena.

spirochaete [spiyrohkeet] A motile, spiral-shaped bacterium. Some spirochaetes are free-living in aquatic habitats; others inhabit the intestinal tract and genital areas of animals. They include the causative agents of such diseases as syphilis and relapsing fever. (Kingdom: Monera. Family: Spirochaetaceae.)

Spirogyra [spiyrojiyra] A genus of filament-like green algae found in fresh water; chloroplast a spiral, ribbon-like band extending along the cell; sexual reproduction involves conjugation between two filaments, and results in the formation of a resistant zygote. (Class: Chlorophyceae. Order: Zygnematales.)

spiroplasm A motile, spiral-shaped mycoplasm, parasitic in insects and plants. It includes the causative agent of yellow disease in plants. (Kingdom: Monera. Class: Mollicutes.)

spit A ridge of sand and gravel stretching out along a coastline, deposited by longshore drift and often forming a lagoon on the landward side. A spit which links an island to the mainland is termed a **tombolo**.

Spitalfields An area in the East End of London, UK, which flourished as a centre of silk-weaving from the late 17th-c (when Huguenot weavers settled there) until the late 19th-c. It lies on the site of a 12th-c spittle-house, or hospital, from which its name derives.

Spitsbergen *Svalbard*

spittlebug *froghopper*

Spitz, Mark (Andrew) (1950–) Swimmer, born in Modesto, California, USA. He trained at the Santa Clara Swim Club, and studied at Indiana University (1972). He won two gold medals at the Mexico City Olympic Games (1968) in team events. His outstanding achievement came at the Munich Olympic Games (1972), when he became the first athlete to win seven gold medals at one Games, four of which were for individual events. He turned professional in 1972, and also appeared in several films.

spitz [spits] (Ger 'pointed') A dog belonging to a group of breeds, characterized by a curled tail usually held over the back, pointed ears and muzzle, and (usually) a thick coat.

spleen A soft, delicate, relatively mobile organ which is responsible for clearing the body of bacteria, protozoa, and non-living particles; the destruction of red blood cells; and the metabolism of iron, fats, and proteins. It is situated under cover of the rib-cage on the left side of the body towards the midline to the rear. It cannot normally be felt from outside unless enlarged to three times its normal size. It receives a large blood supply from the aorta, and acts as a reservoir from which blood can be returned to the general circulation when required. It can be ruptured by severe blows to the lower left part of the thoracic cage. Because of its large blood supply, it bleeds profusely, and therefore has to be removed quickly, otherwise the abdominal cavity soon fills with blood and death may result. In adults, the loss of the spleen does not usually cause any ill effects.

spleenwort A member of a large and widespread genus of perennial ferns, found especially in the temperate N hemisphere; fronds entire, pinnate or bi-pinnate, often leathery; sori oval, oblong, or narrow. Some species are viviparous, budding tiny plantlets on the fronds which detach and form new plants. (Genus: *Asplenium*, 650 species. Family: Polypodiaceae.)

Split, Ital **Spalato** 43°31N 16°28E, pop (2000e) 195 000. Seaport and city in W Croatia; largest town on the Croatian Adriatic coast; airport; railway; car ferries to Italy and Turkey; university (1974); shipyards, coal, fishing, tourism; Diocletian's palace (3rd-c), a world heritage site; cathedral; summer festival of drama and music (Jun–Aug), festival of light music (Jul).

Spock, Benjamin (McLane), popular name **Dr Spock** (1903–98) Paediatrician, born in New Haven, Connecticut, USA. He studied at Yale (where he became a star oarsman and rowed in the 1924 Olympics) and Columbia University. He qualified as a doctor, having trained in both paediatrics and psychiatry, and started a practice in Manhattan in 1933. His book, *The Common Sense Book of Baby and Child Care* (1946), urging parents to adopt a more flexible and understanding attitude to childcare, made his name a household word, and sold more than 50 million copies (later called *Dr Spock's Baby and Child Care*). He resigned from his psychiatry and child development work at Western Reserve, Cleveland, OH (1955–67), to devote himself to pacifism, and was a People's Party candidate for the US presidency in 1972 and the vice-presidency in 1976. In 1994 he published *A Better World for Our Children*.

Spode, Josiah [spohd] (1755–1827) Potter, born in Stoke-on-Trent, Staffordshire, C England, UK. After working as a china retailer in London, he inherited the pottery founded c.1770 by his father, **Josiah Spode** (1733–97). The business flourished under his direction, and was renowned for transfer-printed earthenware, stoneware, and superbly decorated bone-china. In 1806 he was appointed potter to the Prince of Wales. In 1833 the factory was acquired by William Taylor Copeland and Thomas Garrett, and in c.1845 it introduced Parian porcelain figures, which resembled marble.

Spohr, Louis [shpohr], originally **Ludwig Spohr** (1784–1859) Composer, violinist, and conductor, born in Brunswick, NC Germany. Largely self-taught, he became court conductor at Kassel (1822–57), and is remembered chiefly as a composer for the violin, for which he wrote 17 concertos. He also composed nine symphonies, 11 operas, and other choral and chamber works.

spoils system The US practice of filling public offices on the basis of loyalty to the party in power: 'to the victors belong the spoils'. It was said to have originated with De Witt Clinton, governor of New York (1817–23). In common use during the 19th-c, it was in disrepute thereafter as a result of civil service reforms. However, it is still practised to some extent.

Spokane [spohkan] 47°40N 117°24W, pop (2000e) 195 600. Seat of Spokane Co, E Washington, USA, on the Spokane R; founded, 1872; city status, 1891; airfield; railway; university (1887); commercial centre for inland farming, forestry, and mining areas (the 'Inland Empire'); art centre; museum; Episcopal and Roman Catholic Cathedrals.

Spoleto [spolaytoh], Lat **Spoletium** 42°44N 12°44E, pop (2000e) 20 000. Town in Perugia province, Umbria, C Italy, 96 km/ 60 mi NE of Rome; textiles, tourism; cathedral (11th-c), San Salvatore basilica (4th-c), Roman theatre, amphitheatre, bridge, triumphal arch; Festival of Two Worlds (music, drama, art, Jun–Jul).

spondylosis [spondilohsis] Degeneration of the vertebral bodies and of the joints between them. It especially affects the cervical and lumbar vertebrae (ie the spine in the neck and lower back).

sponge A multicellular animal with a body that lacks organization into tissues and organs; body perforated by a complex system of internal canals through which flagellate cells propel water; water typically enters body via pores (*ostia*), and leaves via larger pores (*oscula*); feeds by filtering food from water within the canal system; body often supported by a skeleton of mineralized tiny pointed structures (*spicules*) or organic fibres; mostly marine, found from intertidal zone to deep sea; sometimes in fresh water. (Phylum: Porifera.)

spontaneous generation The concept that life can arise spontaneously from non-living matter by natural processes without the intervention of supernatural powers; also known as **abiogenesis**.

spontaneous symmetry breaking In physical systems, the reduction of symmetry in an unpredictable way as a system changes to one of lower energy. For example, when a ferromagnetic material such as iron is cooled to below its Curie temperature its atoms align, representing a state of reduced energy and symmetry. It is an important principle in particle physics, especially in the prediction of masses of W and Z particles in weak interaction theory.

spoonbill An ibis-like bird, native to Old World (Genus: *Platalea*, 5 species) or Central and South America (*Ajaia ajaja*); bill straight and broadly flattened at tip; eats aquatic animals and plants or insects. (Family: Threskiornithidae.)

Spooner, William Archibald (1844–1930) Anglican clergyman and educationist, dean (1876–89) and warden (1903–24) of New College, Oxford. As an albino he suffered all his life from weak eyesight, but surmounted his disabilities with heroism, and earned a reputation for kindness. His name is associated with a nervous tendency to transpose initial letters or half-syllables in speech, the *spoonerism* (eg 'a half-warmed fish' for 'a half-formed wish').

spoonworm An unsegmented, soft-bodied marine worm; body cylindrical or sac-like, bearing an extendable tube (*proboscis*) used for food collection and respiration, and spines that assist in burrowing or anchorage. (Phylum: Echiura, c.140 species.)

sporangium [sporanjium] The organ in which spores are formed in certain types of plant. In algae and fungi they are unicellular; in bryophytes and ferns they are multicellular.

spore A plant reproductive cell which is capable of developing into a new individual, either directly or after fusion with another spore. Spores typically function as a means of dispersal, and sometimes also as a resistant stage allowing the organism to survive periods of adverse conditions. A spore does not contain an embryo, and is thus distinct from a **seed**.

sporophyte [spohrofiyt] The asexual (spore-producing or *diploid*) generation in the life cycle of a plant, produced by the fusion of two haploid gametes. In ferns and flowering plants it is the dominant part of the life cycle, being more specialized than the gametophyte, and capable of surviving in a wider range of conditions. In bryophytes it is the minor generation, at least partly reliant on the gametophyte for survival.

Sporozoa [sporozoha] A class of parasitic protozoans found in animal hosts. Reproduction typically involves an alternation between asexual (*multiple fission*) and sexual phases; sexual reproduction results in the formation of resistant cysts containing infective stages; several species cause serious diseases in humans and domesticated animals. (Phylum: Apicomplexa.)

sporting dog A dog belonging to a group of breeds developed to assist in field sports; includes pointers, setters, retrievers, spaniels (these four also called **gundogs**); used occasionally to include terriers and hounds.

Sports, Book of A statement by James I of England in 1618, declaring which sports could be legally performed on Sundays after divine services. It was re-issued in 1633 and declared from pulpits. It provoked refusals from tender consciences, deprivations from livings, and pamphleteer Prynne's remark, 'so many paces in the dance; so many paces to hell'.

sports injuries Damage to the body occurring during the course of physical activity and exercise, including bruises, fractures, sprains, and repetitive strain injuries. They may occur due to trauma or overuse. Minor injuries can be treated with rest, ice, compression, and elevation; more serious injuries require medical attention. Injuries can be prevented by the appropriate use of protective equipment when engaged in sporting activities, such as shin pads for football, gumshields for boxing, and helmets for horse-riding.

sports medicine The medical care of sportsmen and sportswomen. It involves the care and prevention of soft tissue injuries (eg strains and torn ligaments), injuries of overuse (eg inflammation in and around tendons as a result of repetitive movements), fractures from accidents or from excessive stress to bones, and trauma to the brain, as occurs in boxing. It is also concerned with methods of rehabilitation, the study of factors that improve performance, such as diet, training, and cardiorespiratory function, the effect of mechanical stresses, and the psychology of competition. The effects and detection of body-building drugs and other banned substances in professional sport is a growing aspect of the discipline.

spots (photography) *luminaires*

sprain Injury to a joint without fracture or displacement of bones. It is usually the result of a twisting movement, in which ligaments and tendons are torn.

sprat Small, slender-bodied fish (*Sprattus sprattus*) widespread and locally common in large shoals in coastal waters from Norway to the Mediterranean; length up to 15 cm/6 in; silver with upper surface green; support important commercial fisheries, being sold fresh or canned; young fish sold as whitebait. (Family: Clupeidae.)

spreadsheet A computer program which allows data, numbers, or text to be entered and presented in a rectangular matrix. Data can be manipulated in a variety of different ways defined by the user; for example, columns or rows of numbers can be added, interchanged, or multiplied by constants. Spreadsheets provide a powerful and relatively simple means of analyzing financial and other numeric data, and are widely used in the commercial world.

Spring, Dick, popular name of **Richard Spring** (1950–) Irish statesman. He studied at Trinity College Dublin, and was called to the bar in 1975. He became a member of the Dáil in 1981, and quickly rose to be leader of the Labour Party (1981–97) and deputy prime minister (1982–7, 1993–7). He was minister of state in the departments of justice (1981–2), the environment (1982–3), and energy (1983–7), and became well known abroad following his appointment as minister for foreign affairs (1993–7). He remains an MP.

Spring and Autumn Annals, Chin **Chunqiu** or **Ch'un-ch'iu** The earliest known Chinese historical writing. Traditionally edited by Confucius (d.479 BC) it may be from that century. The work succinctly narrates events in NE China from 722 to 481 BC. The text is obscure, and explanatary commentaries elaborate the meaning.

springbok or **springbuck** A gazelle (*Antidorcas marsupialis*) native to S Africa; reddish-brown with white rump and thick dark line along side; both sexes with short lyre-shaped horns with inturned tips; inhabits dry open country; may leap 3·5 m/11½ ft into the air when alarmed.

Springboks The name used by South African sports teams, particularly in cricket and rugby. Adopted by the first South African rugby team touring Great Britain (1906–7, captain Paul Roos), the 1912 team adopted the tradition of taking springbok heads with them to present to teams who beat them. The name's association with apartheid led to many teams, including cricket (which adopted the name Proteas), dropping it in the post-apartheid era. It was retained by rugby union, with the permission of President Mandela, following its victory in the 1995 World Cup.

Springer, Jerry, popular name of **Gerald N Springer** (1944–) Television presenter, lawyer, and politican, born in London, England, UK. His parents fled Nazi Germany to London, and in 1949 they emigrated to Queens, New York. He studied political science at Tulane University (1965) and law at Northwestern University (1968), then practised law in Cincinnati, where he became a member of the city council (1971–7) and was elected mayor (1977–81). Also pursuing a career in broadcasting, he was news anchor for WLWT-TV in Cincinnati (1982–

3), and has hosted the controversial *Jerry Springer Show* since 1991. A show about his life, *Jerry Springer – The Opera*, opened in London's West End in 2003 and won the Evening Standard Theatre Award for best musical.

springer spaniel A medium-sized spaniel with thick coat; ears shorter and more highly set than in cocker spaniels; two breeds, white and brown (or black) **English springer spaniel**, and older, shorter-eared, white and red-brown **Welsh spaniel** or **Welsh springer spaniel**.

Springfield, Dusty, originally **Mary O'Brien** (1939–99) Pop singer, born in London, UK. She was originally part of The Springfields, a vocal/guitar trio singing folk and country music. Her debut solo single 'I Only Want To Be With You' (1964) was a UK hit, and marked a move towards a Motown-influenced style; it was the first record to be played on BBC's television show 'Top Of The Pops'. Her debut album, *A Girl Called Dusty* (1964), reached number 6 in the charts. Her career declined following a move to the USA in the 1970s, but in 1987 she achieved a successful comeback as guest vocalist on The Pet Shop Boys' hit single 'What Have I Done To Deserve This', and a later album, *Reputations* (1990), reached number 18 in the UK music charts. She acquired something of a cult following, as part of the renewed interest in music of the 1960s.

Springfield (Illinois) 39°48N 89°39W, pop (2000e) 111 500. Capital of state in Sangamon Co, C Illinois, USA; settled, 1818; city status, 1840; home and burial place of President Lincoln; railway; major commercial centre; electrical equipment, machinery, chemicals.

Springfield (Massachusetts) 42°06N 72°35W, pop (2000e) 152 100. Seat of Hampden Co, SW Massachusetts, USA, on the Connecticut R; railway; machinery, metal and paper products; game of basketball devised at Springfield College; Springfield Armoury (1794–1968), basketball hall of fame; Eastern States Expo (Sep).

Springfield (Missouri) 37°13N 93°17W, pop (2000e) 148 000. Seat of Greene Co, SW Missouri, USA; established, 1829; railway; university; industrial, trade and shipping centre; dairy products, livestock, poultry, fruit; clothing, furniture, typewriters; tourist centre for Ozark Mts; Museum of the Ozarks.

springhaas [**spring**hahs] A nocturnal squirrel-like rodent (*Pedetes capensis*), native to S Africa; superficially resembles a small kangaroo (length, less than 1 m/3¼ ft) with bushy black-tipped tail; inhabits open sandy country; digs burrows; also known as **springhare** or **jumping hare**. (Family: Pedetidae.)

Springsteen, Bruce (1949–) Rock singer and guitarist, born in Freehold, New Jersey, USA. In 1973, having travelled with obscure bands such as Doctor Zoom and the Sonic Boom, he signed with Columbia Records and released his first recording amid unprecedented hype, being featured on the front covers of both *Time* and *Newsweek* in the same week. In the event, his ascent to stardom was more gradual, and more merited. In 1976, he released a hit in 'Born to Run', a raucous song, roughly sung, with memorable, streetwise images in the lyric. Other hits with similar virtues followed, and by the mid-1980s he had become one of the world's most popular white rock stars. His albums include *The River* (1980), *The Ghost of Tom Joad* (1995), and *The Rising* (2002).

springtail A blind, primitively wingless insect often extremely abundant in soils or leaf litter; leaps by means of a forked spring organ folded up on underside of abdomen. (Order: Collembola, c.2000 species.)

spring tide An especially large tidal range occurring twice monthly, produced by the tidal forces of the Sun and Moon acting in conjunction. These maximum monthly tides occur during new and full Moon, and have nothing to do with the spring season. The term 'spring' comes from German *gespringen* ('to jump up'), which reflects the higher than normal nature of these tides.

spruce An evergreen conifer native to the temperate N hemisphere, especially E Asia; leaves needle-like, leaving persistent, peg-like bases on shoot when shed; cones pendulous, ripe after one year. It is a widespread forestry tree, grown for timber and for its turpentine-yielding resin. (Genus: *Picea*, 50 species. Family: Pinaceae.)

sprue *malabsorption*

sprung rhythm A term invented by the poet Gerard Manley Hopkins to describe a rhythm founded on stress rather than syllable count, most notably used in 'The Windhover'. Novel in the late 19th-c, this in fact relates back to Old English and Welsh alliterative verse. The rediscovery of this form of poetic composition has had a far reaching influence, notably on poets of the 20th-c, particularly T S Eliot, Dylan Thomas, and Ted Hughes.

spurge A member of a large worldwide genus of diverse, latex-producing plants, annuals or perennials, sometimes shrubs. Some from arid regions look like cacti, having independently evolved similar adaptations to drought, and when not in flower can be distinguished from cacti only by the presence of latex. Its distinctive flower, called a *cyathium*, is in fact a condensed and reduced inflorescence represented by a single ovary (the female flower), several stamens (the male flowers), four large glands, and a ring of perianth-like, often brightly coloured bracts. (Genus: *Euphorbia*, 2000 species. Family: Euphorbiaceae.)

spurrey *corn spurrey; sand spurrey*

Sputnik [**sput**nik] (Russ 'travelling companion') The world's first artificial satellite. **Sputnik 1** was launched by the USSR (4 Oct 1957) from Tyuratam launch site; weight 84 kg/185 lb; battery powered; it transmitted a radio signal for 21 days. **Sputnik 2** was launched in November 1957; weight 508 kg/1120 lb; it carried the dog 'Laika', killed by injection after 7 days of returning biomedical data.

sputtering The ejection of atoms from the surface of a metal, caused by the impact of ions. It may be used to produce ultra-clean metal surfaces by knocking off contaminant atoms, or as a source of metal atoms in the vacuum deposition of thin metal films, for example in the preparation of samples for scanning electron microscopy. Magnon sputtering uses magnetic fields to enhance a plasma at the target material which is then deposited as a thin film.

spy story A specialized form of fiction which centres on the hazards and excitements of espionage. Spying has a long history; there is a spy's guide in Chinese from the 6th-c BC, and a recognizable spy novel *Sa Kno* by the Chinese author Lo Kra-Chung (1260–1341). But the modern spy story begins with the works of William le Queux (1864–1927) and Erskine Childers (eg *The Riddle of the Sands*, 1903). Conrad contributed *The Secret Agent* (1907) to the genre, and two novels by John Buchan have become classics: *The Thirty-Nine Steps* (1915) and *Greenmantle* (1916). Between the wars Somerset Maugham, Eric Ambler, and Graham Greene wrote authentic and unsensational spy stories; then Ian Fleming's James Bond glamorized the enterprise in book and film. But the novels of John le Carré (eg *The Spy who Came in from the Cold*, 1963), Len Deighton (eg *Funeral in Berlin*, 1964), and Frederick Forsyth (eg *The Odessa File*, 1972) have returned to a more realistic not to say cynical presentation of espionage.

squall A sudden increase in wind speed. For at least one minute, minimum velocity must increase by at least 8 m/s (26 ft/s), and reach 11 m/s (36 ft/s) before declining rapidly.

squall-line A narrow line of thunderstorms which may extend for hundreds of kilometres ahead of a cold front, though only a few kilometres wide. It is associated with thunderstorms, gale force winds, and a sudden drop in temperature.

Square Deal The popular name for the domestic policies of US President Theodore Roosevelt, especially the enforcement of the Anti-trust Acts. The term was coined by him during a speaking tour in the summer of 1902.

squark *supersymmetry*

squash (botany) Any of several species of the cucumber family (*Cucurbita maxima / mixta / moschata / pepo*), native to America; all trailing or climbing vines with tendrils; large, yellow, funnel-shaped flowers; fruits of various shapes and colours. Cultivated for their fruits, they are divided into two types: **summer squashes**, derived from marrow, are eaten before becoming ripe and fibrous; **winter squashes**, derived from four species including marrow and pumpkin, are eaten ripe and can be stored through winter. (Family: Cucurbitaceae.)

squash rackets (UK) / **squash racquets** (US) A popular indoor racket-and-ball court game, usually called **squash**. It developed from rackets at Harrow school in c.1850, but with a softer ball. It is played by two players on an enclosed court 32 ft (9·75 m) long by 21 ft (6·4 m) wide. Each hits the ball against a front wall alternately. The object is to play a winning shot by forcing your opponent to fail to return the ball before the second bounce. Popular as a means of keeping fit, it is a strenuous game that requires players to be in good physical condition.

squeak rabbit *pika*

squeezed light Light in which either phase or amplitude has been reduced ('squeezed') at the expense of the other, according to the limits imposed by quantum theory. It is a quantum effect that cannot be explained by classical optics, and can be generated in certain non-linear optical effects. First produced in 1985 by Dick Slusher and Bernard Yurke, squeezed light can be exploited in precise optical measurements requiring low levels of optical noise.

squid A carnivorous marine mollusc with a streamlined body bearing fins towards the back; shell reduced to an internal cartilaginous rod; eight arms and two tentacles around mouth, used to catch prey; active swimmers; found in coastal and oceanic waters. (Class: Cephalopoda. Order: Teuthoidea.)

squill A perennial native to Europe, Asia, and S Africa; small bulb; narrow leaves; flowers star- or bell-shaped, sometimes drooping, blue or purple. **Spring squill** (*Scilla verna*) produces flowers and leaves in the spring; **autumn squill** (*Scilla autumnalis*) produces flowers later in the year, before the leaves appear. (Genus: *Scilla*, 80 species. Family: Liliaceae.)

squint A defect in the alignment of the eyes, most commonly affecting movement in the horizontal plane; also known as **strabismus**. It is usually congenital, and may be associated with an abnormality in focusing (*refractive error*). In adults, it arises from weakness of one or more of the muscles that move the eyeball, and occurs in several diseases.

squirrel A rodent of family Sciuridae (267 species), virtually worldwide except Australasia; fine fur and bushy tail; most eat seeds; range from small tree-dwelling squirrels to cat-sized ground-dwelling squirrels (including prairie dogs and marmots); ground squirrels live in extensive burrows, and may hibernate for up to nine months.

squirrel monkey A New World monkey; small, lively, with long black-tipped tail; white face with black tip to muzzle; coat short, greyish; inhabits woodland near riverbanks; troops may contain up to 100 individuals. (Genus: *Saimiri*, 2 species.)

squirting cucumber A roughly hairy, spreading or trailing perennial (*Ecballium elaterium*), native to the Mediterranean; leaves heart-shaped, slightly lobed; flowers yellow; fruit 2·5–5 cm/1–2 in long, oval. When the ripe fruit is touched or falls, the seeds and a watery liquid are forcibly ejected in a jet through the hole formed by the stalk. (Family: Cucurbitaceae.)

Sri Jayawardenapura-Kotte [sree jiyahwah(r)dnapoora] 6°55N 79°52E, pop (2000e) 122 000. Capital of Sri Lanka since 1983; located in an E suburb of Colombo; relocation ongoing during the 1990s.

Sri Lanka *p.1455*

Srinagar [sreenagah(r)] 34°08N 74°50E, pop (2000e) 700 000. Summer capital of Jammu–Kashmir state, N India, in the Vale of Kashmir, on R Jhelum; founded, 6th-c; capital status, 1948; birthplace of Sheikh Mohammed Abdullah; airfield; shawls (cashmeres), silks, woollens, carpets; Buddhist ruins, mosque (1623).

SS Abbreviation of **Schutzstaffel** (Ger 'protective squad'), a Nazi organization founded in Germany in 1925 as Hitler's personal bodyguard. From 1929 it was transformed and expanded by Himmler into an elite force. Within the Third Reich it became an independent organization, controlling a dominant repressive apparatus, and responsible for concentration camps and racial policy. It formed its own armed detachments, which after 1939 became the *Waffen* ('armed') SS. During World War 2 it became an alternative army, an autonomous power within the Third Reich, and the principal agent of racial extermination policy.

stabilizers (economics) The factors in a modern economic system which help to keep the economy stable, avoiding the worst effects of trade cycle fluctuations. They mainly relate to fiscal policy, in that tax receipts will change with rises or falls in incomes (**automatic stabilizers**). Payments such as unemployment benefit and various other means-tested benefits also rise as incomes fall, and fall as incomes rise. The government can also help stabilize the economy with positive steps, such as public works to alleviate recession, and changes in tax rates.

stabilizers (shipping) A device which limits rolling in a ship, usually in the form of movable fins. They were first fitted successfully in the P & O liner *Chusan* in 1950. An older form fitted in the Italian liner *Conti de Savoia* in 1932 was claimed to be successful, but it was never fitted in other vessels.

Staël, Madame de [stahl], popular name of **Anne Louise Germaine Necker, Baroness of Staël-Holstein** (1766–1817) Writer, born in Paris, France, the daughter of the financier, Jacques Necker. Both before and after the French Revolution, her *salon* became a centre of political discussion. In 1803 she was forced to leave Paris, and visited Weimar, Berlin, and Vienna, returning to France at intervals. She wrote novels, plays, essays, historical and critical works, and political memoirs, becoming known with her *Lettres* (1788, Letters) on Rousseau, and achieving European fame with her romantic novel, *Corinne* (1807). Her major work, *De L'Allemagne* (1810, On Germany), was published in London in 1813.

staffage [stafahj] In art history, a French term referring to the small figures and animals which provide interest in a landscape. In the 17th-c it was common for a landscape painter to employ a specialist to add the staffage.

Stafford 52°48N 2°07W, pop (2001e) 120 700. County town of Staffordshire, C England, UK; railway; engineering, chemicals, electrical goods, footwear, timber; 11th-c castle, destroyed in the Civil War; Churches of St Mary and St Chad, 18th-c William Salt library, Shire Hall, Borough Hall, Guildhall; birthplace of Izaak Walton; Shugborough (6 km/4 mi E), the ancestral home of the Earls of Lichfield.

Staffordshire pop (2001e) 806 700; area 2716 sq km/1049 sq mi. County in C England, UK; in the basin of the R Trent; county town, Stafford; chief towns include Stoke-on-Trent (new unitary authority, 1997), Newcastle-under-Lyme, Burton-upon-Trent; agriculture, coal, pottery, brewing; Potteries, Vale of Trent, Cannock Chase.

Staffordshire bull terrier A medium-sized terrier developed in Britain as a fighting dog or guard dog; thick-set muscular body with a short coat, broad head, long muzzle, soft ears.

stag beetle A large, dark-coloured beetle; males up to 66 mm/2½ in long, typically with large, antler-like processes on head, formed from mandibles; larvae fleshy, living in rotting wood; adults feed on liquids and sap. (Order: Coleoptera. Family: Lucanidae, c.1200 species.)

stage That part of a theatre where the performance is presented. The relationship established between performers and audience by the position of the stage is of fundamental importance to any theatrical event.

stagecoach A type of horse-drawn coach that appeared c.1640 offering carriage to the public on predetermined routes and stages, usually running between provincial towns and London. With the introduction by the Post Office of mail coaches in the 1780s, new standards of time-keeping and efficiency were forced upon the privately-owned stagecoach lines. The coming of the railways in the 1830s and 1840s quickly ended the dominating role of stagecoaches within public transport, although

Sri Lanka

☐ International Airport

[sree **langka**], formerly **Ceylon**, official name **Democratic Socialist Republic of Sri Lanka**

Local name Sri Lanka

Timezone GMT +5·5

Area 65 610 km²/25 325 sq mi

Population total (2002e) 18 870 000

Status Republic

Date of independence 1972

Capital Sri-Jayawardenapura (since 1983); (former capital, Colombo)

Languages Sinhala, Tamil (official), English also spoken

Ethnic groups Sinhalese (74%), Tamil (18%), Muslim (7%), Burgher, Malay, and Veddha (1%)

Religions Buddhist (69%), Hindu (15%), Christian (8%), Muslim (8%)

Physical features Island state in the Indian Ocean; separated from the Indian sub-continent by the Palk Strait, linked by a series of coral islands known as Adam's Bridge; low-lying areas in N and S, surrounding SC uplands; highest peak, Pidurutalagala, 2524 m/8281 ft; coastal plain fringed by sandy beaches and lagoons; c.50% of land is tropical monsoon forest or open woodland.

Climate Equatorial, tropical climate; modified temperatures in interior according to altitude; average annual temperature 27°C in Sri-Jayawardenapura; average annual rainfall 2527 mm/99·5 in; greatest rainfall on SW coast and in the mountains; monsoon season (Dec–Feb) in NE, dry, semi-arid for rest of year; severe flooding in SC districts (May 2003) with 200 000 made homeless.

Currency 1 Sri Lanka Rupee (SLR, SLRs) = 100 cents

Economy Agriculture (employs 52% of labour force); rice, rubber, tea, coconuts, spices, sugar cane; timber, fishing; graphite, coal, precious and semi-precious stones; electricity produced largely by water power; textiles, chemicals, paper.

GDP (2002e) $73·7 bn, per capita $3700

Human Development Index (2002) 0·741

History Visited by the Portuguese, 1505; taken by the Dutch, 1658; British occupation, 1796; British colony, 1802; Tamil labourers brought in from S India during colonial rule, to work on coffee and tea plantations; Dominion status, 1948; changed former name of Ceylon and became the independent republic of Sri Lanka, 1972; acute political tension between the Buddhist Sinhalese majority and the Hindu Tamil minority, who wish to establish an independent state in the N and E (Liberation Tigers of Tamil Eelam, LTTE); considerable increase in racial violence in the area during the 1980s; state of emergency declared, 1983; ceasefire agreed, 1994, but conflict soon resumed; President Kumaratunga wounded in bomb attack at election rally (1999), but re-elected; suicide attack by Tamil Tigers on international airport (2001); ceasefire agreed (Dec 2001) with mediation by Norway; conflict ongoing; ceasefire and a political agreement reached between government and rebels in late 2002 raised hopes for a lasting peace; Tamil Tigers issued power-sharing proposals (Nov 2003); political crisis after suspension of parliament (Nov 2003); Tamil Tigers leadership split (Mar 2004); fresh elections (Apr 2004).

Head of State
1989–93 Ranasinghe Premadasa
1993–4 Dingiri Banda Wijedunga
1994– Chandrika Bandaranaike Kumaratunga

Head of Government
1989–93 Dingiri Banda Wijedunga
1993–4 Ranil Wickremasinghe
1994 Chandrika Bandaranaike Kumaratunga
1994–2000 Sirimavo R D Bandaranaike
2000–1 Ratnasiri Wickremanayake
2001– Ranil Wickremesinghe

in some isolated parts of Britain their use continued until the 1870s. In the USA, the first mail stagecoaches ran between Boston and New York in 1784, but the main period of their use was from 1800 to 1840, by which time all the principal cities as far W as Pittsburgh were connected by several stagecoach lines. However, the stagecoach in the USA never achieved the importance that river travel did, and by 1850 with the coming of the railroad they ceased to be of importance, except in some isolated areas in the West.

stagflation An economic situation in which there is continuing inflation in spite of depressed economic conditions and high unemployment. Prior to the 1970s economists had thought that while inflation and stagnation were both unpleasant, they were at least alternatives; after the 1973–4 oil crisis they discovered that inflation and stagnation could coexist. This was very embarrassing for believers in demand management, as raising demand might worsen inflation while cutting demand would worsen unemployment. Supply-side economists would argue that this showed how necessary their policies were.

staghound *deerhound*

stag's horn fern A type of fern (*Platycerium bifurcatum*), an epiphyte, native to Australia. Its sterile fronds are rounded, and braced against the tree to form the mantle, giving anchorage and support. Its fertile fronds are long, branched like antlers, and bear numerous sporangia, giving a suede-like appearance to the underside. (Family: Polypodiaceae.)

stained glass Pieces of different coloured glass mounted in lead framing to form a pictorial image. It was introduced from Byzantine art for the windows of European buildings in the late 12th-c, and flourished most splendidly in Western Romanesque and Gothic churches. It remained popular throughout the mediaeval period, and was enthusiastically revived in the 19th-c (eg by Burne-Jones, Matisse, Rouault) and later in the USA by Louis Comfort Tiffany (1848–1933). In the Middle Ages the glass itself was often coloured by the addition of metal oxides during the glass-making process, or by the layering of coloured glass over uncoloured glass (*flashing*); but from the 16th-c the technique of painting in enamel on the glass became more common.

stainless steels A group of steels which resist rusting and chemical attack through the addition of nickel and chromium. They are used to make utensils, cutlery, and chemical reaction vessels.

stakeholder economy *New Labour*

Stakhanovism [stak**a**novizm] An economic system in the former USSR designed to raise productivity through incentives. It was named after the first worker to receive an award, coalminer Alexei Grigorievich Stakhanov (1906–77), who in 1935 reorganized his team's workload to achieve major gains in production. The movement lasted only until 1939.

stalactites and stalagmites Icicle-like deposits of limestone formed by precipitation from slowly dripping water from the ceilings of caves. **Stalactites** grow from the ceiling, while **stalagmites** form on the floor and grow upwards at a rate of less than half a millimetre per year.

Stalin, Joseph (1879–1953) Georgian Marxist revolutionary and later virtual dictator of the USSR (1928–53), born in Gori, C Georgia, the son of a cobbler and ex-serf. He studied at Tiflis Orthodox Theological Seminary, from which he was expelled in 1899. After joining a Georgian Social Democratic organization (1898), he became active in the revolutionary underground, and was twice exiled to Siberia (1902, 1913). As a leading Bolshevik he played an active role in the October Revolution (1917), and became people's commissar for nationalities in the first Soviet government and a member of the Communist Party Politburo. In 1922 he became general secretary of the Party Central Committee, a post he held until his death, and also occupied other key positions which enabled him to build up enormous personal power in the party and government apparatus. After Lenin's death (1924) he pursued a policy of building 'socialism in one country', and gradually isolated and disgraced his political rivals, notably Trotsky. In 1928 he launched the campaign for the collectivization of agriculture during which millions of peasants perished, and the first 5-year plan for the forced industrialization of the economy. Between 1934 and 1938 he inaugurated a massive purge of the party, government, armed forces, and intelligentsia in which millions of so-called 'enemies of the people' were imprisoned, exiled, or shot. In 1938 he signed the Non-Aggression Pact with Hitler which bought the Soviet Union two years respite from involvement in World War 2. After the German invasion (1941), the USSR became a member of the Grand Alliance, and Stalin, as war leader, assumed the title of *generalissimo*. He took part in the conferences of Tehran, Yalta, and Potsdam which resulted in Soviet military and political control over the liberated countries of post-war E and C Europe. From 1945 until his death he resumed his repressive measures at home, and conducted foreign policies which contributed to the Cold War between the Soviet Union and the West. He was posthumously denounced by Khrushchev at the 20th Party Congress (1956) for crimes against the Party and for building a 'cult of personality'. Under Gorbachev many of Stalin's victims were rehabilitated, and the whole phenomenon of 'Stalinism' officially condemned by the Soviet authorities. While many regard Stalin as a brutal dictator possibly equalled only by Hitler in the scale of the terror he wreaked, others question whether the Soviet Union would have survived to win victories in World War 2 under a more liberal leader.

Stalingrad, Battle of (1942–3) One of the great battles of World War 2 and a landmark in military history, fought between Nazi German and Soviet troops in and around Stalingrad (now Volgograd) on the R Volga during the winter of 1942–3. In September 1942 a German army exceeding 500 000 men and commanded by General Friedrich von Paulus began an all-out attack on the port of Stalingrad, which was defended by Soviet divisions under General Vasily Chuikov. In November two Soviet forces, advancing in a pincer movement, encircled the Germans, who were routed. The Germans alone suffered over 300 000 casualties, many of whom were taken as prisoners-of-war. The city was almost totally destroyed. The Red Army remained on the offensive for the remainder of the war. The battle is regarded as a major turning-point in the Allied victory over Germany.

Stalinism A label used pejoratively outside the former USSR to refer to the nature of the Soviet regime when Stalin began to assume power during and after his struggle to succeed Lenin, following the latter's death in 1924; it continued until his own death in 1953. It refers to a monolithic system, tightly disciplined and bureaucratic, with the party hierarchy having a monopoly of political and economic power. It also encompasses the total subservience of society and culture to political ends, suppression of political opponents, terrorism, and the acceptance of dogmas in the communist movement of Stalin's time. The process of de-Stalinization began with Khrushchev's 'secret speech' to the 20th Party Congress in 1956.

Stallone, Sylvester [stal**oh**n] (1946–) Film actor, director, and writer, born in New York City, USA. He studied drama at the University of Miami, and suddenly became known through the success of his first film *Rocky* (1976, 2 Oscars), which he also wrote. Later films established him as an action-film hero, notably the *Rocky* sequels (1979, 1982, 1985, 1990), *First Blood* (1981), *Rambo* and its sequels (1985, 1988), whose title added a word to the language, and *Cliffhanger* (1992). Other films include *Assassins* (1995), *Judge Dredd* (1995), *Daylight* (1996), *The Hunter* (1997), and *Get Carter* (2000). He wrote and directed the Rocky sequels, *Paradise Alley* (1978), and *Staying Alive* (1983, which he also produced), and has written the screenplays for several of his other films.

stamen The male organ of a flower, consisting of a stalk-like *filament* bearing sac-like *anthers* containing pollen; collectively forming the *andrecium* or third whorl of a flower. The number and arrangement is often diagnostic for plant families.

Stamitz, Johann (Wenzel Anton) [sht**a**mits] (1717–57) Violinist and composer, born in Havlíčkův Brod, C Czech Republic. He became concert master at the Mannheim court in 1745, where he developed sonata form, and trained the orchestra to a level of perfection unrivalled in Europe. His works include 74 symphonies, several concertos, chamber music, and a Mass. He founded a school of symphonists which had a profound influence on Mozart.

stammering *stuttering*

Stamp Act A British Act passed in 1765 by the administration of George Grenville (1712–70), which levied a direct tax on all papers required in discharging official business in the American colonies. It was the first direct tax levied without the consent of the colonial assemblies, and it caused much discontent in the colonies, six of which petitioned against it. The Act was withdrawn by the Rockingham government in 1766.

standard form In mathematics, a number in the form $A \times 10^n$, where $1 \leq A < 10$ and n is an integer, positive or negative. This is useful for very large numbers, eg $3\,000\,000\,000 = 3 \times 10^9$, and very small numbers, eg $0{\cdot}000\,000\,003 = 3 \times 10^{-9}$.

Standard Generalized Mark-up Language (SGML) A standard for coding documents so that they can be stored in a document database and presented on an output medium in the correct form for that medium. For example, if the output were to be printed it would appear in one form; if it were to be presented on a computer screen it would be in a different form; but in each case the presentation would be what was appropriate for that document. A development in the 1990s for generating World Wide Web pages is the **HyperText Mark-up Language (HTML)**.

standard language The variety of a language which has greatest social and political prestige within a speech community. It cuts across regional differences in usage, and tends to have a levelling effect on regional variation on account of its social and political power-base. It functions as a linguistically 'neutral' norm for use in the media and education, and is the variety usually employed in religious, legal, and literary style.

standard of living The level of welfare achieved by a nation or group; usually measured in terms of food, clothing, housing, and other material benefits. There has been a considerable long-term rise in living standards in the West, particularly since 1945; but the same has not been true of the poorer developing nations. A simple measure for comparative purposes is gross national product per head of population. This shows a very fast rate of growth in W Europe, the USA, Japan, and some newly industrialized countries, and a very wide gap between the richest nations and the poorest.

Standard Positioning Service *Global Positioning System*

standard time The officially established local time adopted by a region or country, + or − so many hours from Greenwich Mean Time. The Earth can be divided into 24 time zones each based on sections of 15° of longitude. In each of these, standard time is calculated from the position of the Sun at a central point within the zone. In practice, to avoid unnecessary complications in countries which span more than 15° of longitude, zones may be larger. Some countries have more than one time zone; for example in the USA there are seven standard time zones and in continental Europe two (+1 hour and +2 hours from GMT). Zones differ generally by a whole hour, although there are a few cases of half-hour zones (eg South Australia, India).

standing crop *biomass*

standing wave *wave motion*

Standish, Myles (c.1584–1656) Colonist, probably born in Ormskirk, Lancashire, NW England, UK. After serving in Holland, he sailed with the *Mayflower* in 1620, and became military head of the first American settlement at Plymouth, and treasurer of the colony (1644–9).

Stanford, Sir Charles (Villiers) (1852–1924) Composer, born in Dublin, Ireland. He studied at Cambridge, Leipzig, and Berlin, and became organist at Trinity College (1872–93), professor in the Royal College of Music (1883), and professor of music at Cambridge (1887). He wrote several major choral works, six operas, seven symphonies, and a great deal of chamber music, songs, and English Church music. He was knighted in 1901.

Stanhope, James Stanhope, 1st Earl [stanuhp] (1675–1721) British soldier and statesman, born in Paris, France. He entered parliament as a Whig in 1701, and commanded in Spain during the War of the Spanish Succession (1701–13). He was secretary of state for foreign affairs under George I, and became his chief minister in 1717.

Stanislavsky [stanislavskee], originally **Konstantin Sergeyevich Alexeyev** (1863–1938) Actor, theatre director, theoretician, and teacher, born in Moscow, Russia. As a talented amateur actor, he co-founded the Moscow Society of Art and Literature (1888), and in 1898 helped to found the Moscow Arts Theatre. His work with this influential company, and his teaching on acting, proved to be a major contribution to 20th-c theatre. His system remains the basis of much Western actor-training and practice, and his theories and methods are recorded in his many books, among them *My Life in Art* (1924), *An Actor Prepares* (1926), and *Building a Character* (1950).

Stanisław I Leszczyński [stanislav leshinskee] (1677–1766) King of Poland (1704–9, 1733–5), born in Lvov (Lwow), W Ukraine (formerly Poland). After his election in 1704, he was driven out by Peter the Great, under the influence of Charles XII of Sweden. Re-elected in 1733, he lost the War of the Polish Succession, and formally abdicated in 1736, receiving the Duchies of Lorraine and Bar.

Stanisław II Poniatowski [stanislav, ponyatofskee] (1732–98) Last king of Poland (1764–95), born in Wołczyn, SC Poland. He travelled to St Petersburg in 1757, and became a favourite of the future empress, Catherine II. Through her influence he was elected king, but was unable to stop the partitions of Poland (1772, 1793). Despite the rebellion of Kosciusko, the country was partitioned again in 1795, and he abdicated.

Stanley 51°45S 57°56W, pop (2000e) 1600. Port and capital of the Falkland Is, on the E coast of East Falkland; airport (Mt Pleasant), with links to the UK and to airstrips throughout the colony; whaling, wool trade, service industries.

Stanley, Mount Mountain in the Ruwenzori range on the frontier between Democratic Republic of Congo and Uganda; height of Margherita Peak 5110 m/16 765 ft; highest point in Democratic Republic of Congo and Uganda; first ascent, by the Duke of Abruzzi's expedition, 1906.

Stanley, Sir Henry Morton, originally **John Rowlands** (1841–1904) Explorer and journalist, born in Denbigh, Denbighshire, NC Wales, UK. Abandoned as a child in a workhouse, in 1859 he went as cabin boy to New Orleans, where he was adopted by a merchant who bestowed his own name on the young man. In 1867 he joined the *New York Herald*, and as its special correspondent he travelled to Abyssinia and Spain. Instructed to 'find Livingstone' in Africa (1869), he left Zanzibar for Tanganyika (1871) and encountered Livingstone at Ujiji. In 1874 Stanley led a second expedition which explored L Tanganyika, and traced the Congo to the sea. On a third expedition (1879), he founded the Congo Free State, and a further expedition went to the aid of Emin Pasha in the Sudan (1887–9). He became a US citizen in 1885, but returned to Britain (1890), re-naturalized in 1892, and became an MP (1895–1900). He was knighted in 1899.

Stanley Cup An end-of-season ice hockey series between the winners of the two conferences in the National Hockey League (NHL) in the USA and Canada. It was first presented in 1893 by Lord Stanley of Preston, then Governor-General of Canada.

Stanleyville *Kisangani*

Stannaries Former tin-mining districts of Cornwall, SW England, UK, lying within the lands of the Duchy of Cornwall. In ancient times the tin miners of the Stannaries held special privileges, including the right to send representatives to the Stannary Parliament and to administer their own courts.

Stanton, Elizabeth, *née* **Cady** (1815–1902) Social reformer and women's suffrage leader, born in Johnstown, New York, USA. She studied at Troy (New York) Female Seminary, and became involved in the anti-slavery and temperance movements. At her wedding in 1840 to the abolitionist Henry B Stanton, she insisted on dropping the word 'obey' from the marriage vows. In 1848, with Lucretia Mott, she organized the first women's rights convention at Seneca Falls, NY, which launched the women's suffrage movement. With Susan B Anthony she founded the National Woman Suffrage Movement in 1869.

stapelia [stapeelia] A perennial native to arid areas of tropical and S Africa, superficially resembling cacti, and similarly drought-adapted; fleshy, green stems swollen with water-storage tissue; leaves reduced to deciduous scales. The large carrion flowers, with five petals surrounding an inner, horned ring, are mottled red or maroon, and produce an overpowering smell of rotten meat. (Genus: *Stapelia*, 75 species. Family: Asclepiadaceae.)

Staphylococcus [stafilohkokus] A spherical bacterium c.1 micron in diameter, commonly occurring in clusters, and requiring oxygen for growth. It is found on the mucous membranes and skin of humans and other animals. It can cause superficial abscesses, and chronic to fatal systemic infections. (Kingdom: Monera. Family: Micrococcaceae.)

Staples, The *Farne Islands*

star (astronomy) A sphere of matter held together entirely by its own gravitational field, and generating energy by means of nuclear fusion reactions in its deep interior. The important distinguishing feature of a star is the presence of a natural nuclear reactor in its core, where the pressure of the overlying mass of material is sufficient to cause nuclear reactions, the principal one of which is the conversion of hydrogen to helium.

The Nearest Stars

Star	*Distance (light years)*
Proxima Centauri	4·24
Alpha Centauri A	4·34
Alpha Centauri B	4·34
Barnard's Star	5·97
Wolf 359 (CN Leonis)	7·80
Lalande 21185	8·19
UV Ceti A	8·55
UV Ceti B	8·55
Sirius A	8·67
Sirius B	8·67
Ross 154	9·52
Ross 248 (HH Andromedae)	10·37
Epsilon Eridani	10·63
Ross 128 (FI Virginis)	10·79
L 789-6	11·12
GX Andromedae	11·22
GQ Andromedae	11·22
61 Cygnus A	11·22
61 Cygnus B	11·22
HD 173739	11·25
Epsilon Indi	11·25
Tau Ceti	11·41

About 0·5% of the mass becomes electromagnetic radiation. The minimum mass needed to make a star is c. 7% the mass of the Sun; the maximum about 100 times as great as the Sun.

star (computing) A topology for a computer network in which one computer occupies the role of a central node and all the remaining computers are linked solely to that central node. Communication between any two of the computers must pass through the central node.

starch $(C_6H_{10}O_5)_n$. A carbohydrate; a condensation polymer of glucose, and isomeric with cellulose, found as a reserve material in living cells. Partial hydrolysis gives amylose (an oligomer) and maltose (a dimer). Its non-food uses include adhesives, pill fillers, and paper sizing.

Star Chamber, Court of the The royal prerogative court in Britain for hearing subjects' petitions and grievances, of uncertain date but increasingly prominent under the Tudors and early Stuarts. It consisted of privy councillors and two chief justices, who dealt swiftly and efficiently with cases, particularly those involving public order. Charles I used it against government opponents, such as John Bastwick (1593–1654) and William Prynne, punished in 1637 for penning anti-episcopal tracts. Such actions made the Court of the Star Chamber notorious among the parliamentary classes for its oppressive methods, and in 1641 the Long Parliament abolished it.

star cluster A group of stars physically associated in space. Loosely packed, open clusters in a galactic plane contain a few dozen to a few hundred stars and are young. Dense, globular clusters are found scattered in a halo around galaxies. They are spherical, have hundreds of thousands of stars, and are very old, of similar age to the Galaxy itself.

Star Festival *Tanabata*

starfish A typically 5-armed, star-shaped marine invertebrate (echinoderm); arms merge gradually into a central body disc; more than five arms often present; most species omnivorous, feeding as scavengers or predators; can digest prey externally; contains c.1500 living species, from intertidal zone to deep sea; also called **sea star**. (Phylum: Echinodermata. Subclass: Asteroidea.)

stargazer Heavy-bodied, bottom-living marine fish of the family Uranoscopidae (3 genera); distinguished by a large vertical mouth and tiny eyes placed on top of a robust flattened head; fins well developed, gill cover bearing a strong poison spine; powerful electric organs located behind the eyes; widespread in tropical to temperate seas, typically living buried in soft sediments.

Stari Ras Former Serbian city located near the present-day town of Novi Pazar in Yugoslavia; a world heritage site. It became the first capital of independent Serbia in the 12th-c, but little now remains of the city save the 13th-c monastery of Sopocani, founded by King Uros I.

starling A songbird, native to the Old World, with some introduced to the Americas; plumage often with metallic sheen, usually dark but sometimes colourful; inhabits woodland, open country; omnivorous; gregarious; flocks often a major nuisance on city buildings and large structures (eg the Forth Bridge, Scotland). The name is also used for the **military starling** (*Leistes militaris*), an American oriole. (Family: Sturnidae, 92 species.)

Star of Bethlehem A star mentioned in *Matt* 2.1–12, depicted as heralding Jesus's birth and guiding Magi from the East to the birthplace in Bethlehem. Although sometimes considered a comet (Halley's comet c.11 BC), a supernova, or a conjunction of Jupiter and Saturn in the constellation Pisces (c.7 BC), it is doubtful that these can explain the sustained presence or movement that is described. An even more spectacular planet pairing occurred on the night of June 17 in 2 BC when Venus, the brightest planet of all, passed directly in front of Jupiter and the two seemed to merge. Legends about the births of Mithridates and Alexander Severus also allege the presence of special stars.

star-of-Bethlehem A perennial with a small bulb (*Ornithogalum umbellatum*), native to S Europe and the Mediterranean region; leaves narrow, grooved, with a white stripe down the centre; flowers 1·5–2 cm/0·6–0·8 in diameter; six narrow petals, white with a green stripe on the back. (Family: Liliaceae.)

Star of David or **Magen David** ('Shield of David') A six-pointed star, consisting of two crossed equilateral triangles, which in the last two centuries has come particularly to symbolize Jewry, although it is a very ancient symbol. It appears on Israel's national flag today as a blue design against white. It has also symbolized the Zionist movement, and a red version signifies the society in Israel that corresponds to the Red Cross.

Starr, Kenneth (1946–) Lawyer, born in Vernon, Texas, USA. He graduated in 1968 from George Washington University, Washington, DC, and rose rapidly as a Republican lawyer, becoming the youngest-ever judge on the US Court of Appeal in 1983, and solicitor general under President George Bush. He became nationally known as the Independent Prosecutor chosen to investigate the alleged misdeeds of President Clinton, first with reference to the Whitewater scandal, then in relation to Paula Jones and Monica Lewinsky. The 'Starr Report' into the latter appeared in the autumn of 1998, and he himself gave evidence before the House judiciary committee set up to consider impeachment. He became a symbol of the cultural tensions within the USA during the late 1990s. To his supporters, he was the dedicated prosecutor pursuing the truth against a president who, Starr believed, had betrayed his trust. Among the defenders of Clinton, Starr was regarded as an out-of-control prosecutor engaged in a political vendetta. These irreconcilable positions reflected the way the Clinton scandals and the resulting impeachment case had polarized American opinion.

Starr, Ringo, originally **Richard Starkey** (1940–) Drummer, singer, songwriter, and actor, born in Liverpool, Merseyside, NW England, UK. He replaced Pete Best as the Beatles' drummer, and following the group's break-up in 1970 embarked on a solo career with the albums *Sentimental Journey* (1970), *Beaucoups of Blues* (1971), and *Ringo* (1973). He continued to record into the 1980s, with albums such as *Stop and Smell the Roses* (1981), then built up his 'All Starrs' band, which toured from 1989 onwards. His wry, deadpan humour was a major feature of the Beatles' films, and he continued as an actor as early as 1968, in *Candy*, following this with *The Magic Christian* (1969). Later films include *Blindman* (1972), *That'll Be The Day* (1973), *Lisztomania* (1975), *Stardust* (1975), and *Alice Through the Looking Glass* (1985), and in 1973 he produced the horror spoof, *Son of*

Dracula. He later became more involved with general show-business concerns, but joined the remaining Beatles in producing their anthology in 1995.

Star-Spangled Banner *national anthem*

star system The process of building up an individual leading actor or actress in motion pictures as an internationally recognized personality, which took root in Hollywood before 1920 and developed with the power of the major studios. The studios combined worldwide publicity with tight control of the artistes, who were their 'property' and their best guarantee of box-office success.

START [stah(r)t] Acronym for **Strategic Arms Reduction Talks**, held between the USA and USSR in 1982 and 1983, adjourned, then resumed at the end of the decade between Presidents Reagan and Bush and General Secretary Gorbachev. While the early talks had become bogged down in disputes over the types and numbers of nuclear missiles and warheads which should be included in agreements, the later talks were more successful. **START 1** (the first **Strategic Arms Reduction Treaty**) was signed in 1991, and aimed to cut the overall number of nuclear warheads held by the two super-powers by between 25% and 30%. This was the first agreement to reduce, rather than merely limit, the growth in numbers of nuclear weapons. In December 1992, a second treaty (**START 2**) was agreed between Presidents Bush and Yeltsin. In this, the USA and Russia agreed to cut by two-thirds their stocks of long range, land-based missiles with multiple warheads. The treaty was ratified by the USA in 1996 and by Russia in 2000, opening the way forward for talks on a **START 3**.

Star Trek US science-fiction television series which has achieved cult status since its birth in 1963. Creator Gene Roddenberry imbued the series with a liberal, almost philosophical quality which set it apart from the sci-fi dramas of an earlier television age. Although only 72 episodes were made before its withdrawal by NBC because of poor ratings in 1969, the adventures of the starship *Enterprise*, boldly going where no man had gone before, and led by Captain James T Kirk (William Shatner) and the half-Vulcan/half-human Mr Spock (Leonard Nimoy) inspired great loyalty and affection among thousands of fans (*Trekkers* or *Trekkies*). During the 1990s three further TV series were produced: *Star Trek: The Next Generation* and *Deep Space Nine*, with Captain Jean Luc Picard (Patrick Stewart); and *Star Trek: Voyager*, with Captain Kathryn Janeway (Kate Mulgrew). A new 'prequel' series entitled *Enterprise* appeared in 2002 and starred Scott Bakula as Captain Jonathan Archer. The original series has been repeated all over the world, and by 2003 there had been 10 *Star Trek* feature films.

Star Wars *SDI*

Stasi *German reunification*

state (politics) A form of political association which in the main enjoys the unique right of being able to use legitimate coercion over a particular territory. The rights and duties of office holders of the state are set down in law, including constitutional law. Many regard it as the means for achieving national unity, and throughout history several writers have attributed a mission or wider purpose to the state over and above its individual parts. Liberals tend to see it simply as an expression of the views of individuals within society. Marxists, on the other hand, see the state as an instrument of class rule. In practice, it is difficult to define precisely what constitutes the state, unless it is simply seen as a set of public rules and offices, and there is considerable disagreement over what it is and should be.

State Department The oldest department of the US government, established by the fourth Act of Congress (Jul 1789), responsible to the president for the conduct of foreign affairs. It is headed by a secretary of state, and is regarded as the most senior department of government.

Staten Island [statn] pop (2000e) 443 700; area 153 sq km/ 59 sq mi. Borough of New York City, USA, co-extensive with Richmond Co; an island separated from New Jersey by Kill van Kull and Arthur Kill Channels, and from Long Island by the Narrows; oil refining, shipbuilding, paper, printing; first settled in 1641; named by early Dutch settlers after the *Staaten* or States General of 17th-c Holland.

states' rights A US Constitutional doctrine that the separate states enjoy areas of self-control which cannot be breached by the federal government. The doctrine flourished among white Southerners between Reconstruction and the Civil Rights Movement, and amounted to a code term for white supremacy.

statice [**sta**tisee] A biennial native to the Mediterranean (*Limonium sinuatum*); leafy, winged stem; distinctive rosette of wavy-edged leaves; flowers papery, various colours, in one-sided spikes. It is often grown for the everlasting flowers used in dried decorations. (Family: Plumbaginaceae.)

static electricity Electric charge which does not flow. Objects can acquire a static charge by rubbing against one another (eg by combing hair or rubbing a toy balloon on wool), which transfers electrons from one object to the other. High voltages can be produced; a static build-up can cause dangerous sparks.

statics *disequilibrium*

Stations of the Cross A popular form of devotion in the Roman Catholic and some Anglican Churches. It consists of meditating on a series of 14 pictures or carvings recalling the passion of Christ from his condemnation to his burial.

statistical linguistics *mathematical linguistics*

statistical mechanics A branch of physics which provides a link between large-scale phenomena involving many atoms or molecules, and the microscopic properties and interactions of individual atoms and molecules. Observable macroscopic properties correspond to the combination of the average value of some attribute (eg velocity) for a single atom with the distribution of that attribute over the entire collection of particles. The subject is essential in understanding such domains as critical phenomena and the thermodynamic properties of solids.

Statistical Package for the Social Sciences (SPSS) A computer package available on mainframes, minicomputers, and personal computers for the performance of statistical analyses on large sets of data.

statistics The branch of mathematics which deals with the collection and analysis of numerical data. From an analysis of the data, a statistician will produce numbers giving information. Numbers commonly found useful are those representative of a set of data – 'averages', such as *mean*, *median*, and *mode*, and those indicating variation in the data, describing the spread or dispersion, such as *range* and *standard deviation*.

Statue of Liberty *Liberty, Statue of*

status The social position a person occupies, and the rank or esteem it enjoys. Systems of social stratification may be based on a strong status order, as in traditional caste systems, or status may be just one dimension of a more complex social hierarchy.

statute A particular law passed by a legislature, such as an act of parliament, or a bill passed by the US Congress and signed by the president. A statute has a short title by which it is generally known, eg the Housing Act (1985). In the UK, the statute must have the consent of both Houses of Parliament and the sovereign.

statute of limitations *limitation of actions*

Staudinger, Hermann [shtowdinger] (1881–1965) Chemist, born in Worms, SWC Germany. He studied at Halle, and became professor at Freiburg (1926–40), then research director (1940–51). He was awarded the Nobel Prize for Chemistry in 1953 for his research in macro-molecular chemistry, which contributed to the development of plastics.

Stauffenberg, Claus, Graf von (Count of) [**shtowfnberg**] (1907–44) German soldier, born in Jettingen, SC Germany. Initially welcoming the advent to power of Hitler, he quickly became alienated by Nazi brutality. He was a colonel on the German general staff in 1944, and placed the bomb in the unsuccessful attempt to assassinate Hitler at Rastenburg (20 Jul 1944). He was shot next day.

Stavanger [stavanger] 58°58N 5°45E, pop (2000e) 103 000. Seaport capital of Rogaland county, SW Norway; on a S branch of the Bokn Fjord, 304 km/189 mi SW of Oslo; founded, c.8th-c; airport; rail terminus; important North Sea oil centre; oil refinery, fish-canning, shipyards, oil-rig construction; St Swithin's Cathedral (12th-c).

Stavisky, (Serge) Alexandre [staviskee] (?1886–1934) Swindler, born in Kiev, Ukraine. He went to Paris in 1900 and was naturalized in 1914. He floated a series of fraudulent companies, and in 1933 was discovered to be handling bonds to the value of more than 500 million francs on behalf of the municipal pawnshop in Bayonne. He fled to Chamonix, and probably committed suicide; but in the meantime the affair had revealed widespread corruption in the government, business, the judiciary, and the police, and precipitated the fall (1934) of the prime minister, Camille Chautemps.

Steadman, Alison (1946–) Actress, born in Liverpool, Merseyside, NW England, UK. She trained at East 15 Theatre School (1966–9). Major roles include *Abigail's Party* (1977, Best Actress, Evening Standard Awards), and *The Rise and Fall of Little Voice* (1992, Best Actress, Olivier Awards). Film and television work includes *The Singing Detective* (1986, TV), *Clockwise* (1986), *Shirley Valentine* (1989), *Pride and Prejudice* (1995, TV), and *Fat Friends* (TV, 2000–4).

steady-state theory One of two rival theories of cosmology (the other is the 'big bang'), proposed in 1948. It asserts that 'things are as they are because they were as they were'. The universe is infinitely old, and contains the same density of material (on average) at all points and at all times. In order to compensate for the observed expansion of the universe, it is thus necessary to postulate the continuous spontaneous creation of matter. From the mid-1960s this model fell out of favour.

steam The vapour phase of water (H_2O); also called **live steam**, to distinguish it from **dead steam**, visible droplets of recondensed vapour.

steam engine An external combustion engine, in which the engine's working fluid (steam) is generated in a boiler outside the engine. The steam is brought into the engine by valves, and through its pressure and expansive properties a piston is made to oscillate within a cylinder. This oscillatory motion is then converted into rotary motion by means of a crankshaft mechanism.

steamship *ship*

stearic acid [steearik] $C_{17}H_{35}COOH$, IUPAC **octadecanoic acid**, melting point 71°C. A waxy solid, the commonest of the fatty acids obtained from the saponification of animal fat. It is used in soap and candle manufacture.

stearin(e) [steearin] The name used to describe fats derived from stearic acid, and also for a mixture of stearic and palmitic acids used in candle manufacture.

steatite [steeuhtiyt] *talc*

Steel (of Aikwood), David (Martin Scott), Lord (1938–) British politician, born in Kirkcaldy, Fife, E Scotland, UK. He studied in Kenya and at Edinburgh, and became an MP in 1965. He sponsored a controversial bill to reform the laws on abortion (1966–7), and was active in the anti-apartheid movement. He became Liberal chief whip (1970–5) before succeeding Jeremy Thorpe as Liberal leader (1976–88). In 1981 he led the party into an alliance with the Social Democratic Party, the two parties successfully merging in 1987–8. He was knighted in 1990, and created a life peer in 1997. In 1999 he was elected as a founding member of the Scottish Parliament, and its first presiding officer.

steel The chief alloy of iron, and the most used of all metals. It consists of iron hardened by the presence of a small proportion of carbon. It was made in small amounts in ancient times by heating cast-iron to reduce surface carbon, and was later made in crucibles in small quantities for tools. Steel production began in China before the 6th-c AD. Western large-scale manufacture for constructional purposes began with the Bessemer process (1856 onwards). Most steel used today is a simple **carbon steel**, but there exist many special steels formed by the addition of other metals, such as high alloy steels for tools, and **stainless steel** (with nickel and chromium).

steel band An ensemble, native to Trinidad, consisting mainly of steel drums – tuned percussion instruments made from used oildrums. Some steel bands are highly accomplished at playing arrangements of Western classics, as well as West Indian music for Carnival and other community festivities.

Steel, Danielle (Fernande Schuelein) (1947–) Writer, born in New York City, USA. She studied in New York and at the Lycée Français in Paris, then enrolled at the Parsons School of Design in New York, later working in public relations and advertising. A best-selling writer of romantic fiction, she achieved success with her fourth novel, *The Promise* (1978), and now has over 125 million books in print worldwide. She has also published several works of non-fiction, including *Having a Baby* (1984) and *His Bright Light* (1998), as well as a book of poetry, *Love: Poems* (1981), and the Max and Martha series of children's books (1989).

Steele, Sir Richard (1672–1729) Essayist, playwright, and politician, born in Dublin, Ireland. He studied at Oxford, and joined the army, but gave it up to become a writer. He wrote three successful comedies, and in 1707 became editor of the *London Gazette*. He is best known for the satirical, political, and moral essays which formed much of the content of the new periodicals the *Tatler* (1709–11), which he founded, and the *Spectator* (1711–12), which he co-founded with Addison. He supported the House of Hanover, and was rewarded by George I with the appointment of supervisor of Drury Lane Theatre, and a knighthood (1715).

steel engraving In printmaking, a technique of engraving introduced in the 19th-c, in which steel plates were introduced to cope with the enormous demand for reproductions of popular pictures. These were harder and longer-lasting than the traditional copper plates; but they proved almost impossible to cut, so as an alternative copper plates were given a steel facing by the simple process of electrolysis.

Steen, Jan (Havickszoon) [stayn] (1626–79) Painter, born in Leyden, The Netherlands. He joined the Leyden guild of painters in 1648, lived in The Hague until 1654, then became a brewer at Delft and an innkeeper at Leyden. His best works were genre pictures of social and domestic scenes depicting the everyday life of ordinary folk, as in 'The Music Lesson' (National Gallery, London).

steenbok or **steinbok** A dwarf antelope native to Africa S of the Sahara (*Raphicerus campestris*); reddish-brown with white underparts; large ears with white insides; short vertical horns; inhabits grass or scrubland; when threatened, lies flat and relies on camouflage.

steeplechase **1** A form of National Hunt horse racing in which the horses have to negotiate fixed fences normally 3–4 ft (0·9–1·2 m) high. The first steeplechase was in Ireland in 1752, when a Mr O'Calloghan and a Mr Blake matched their horses to race over 4½ mi (7·2 km) across country between Buttevant Church and St Mary's, Doneraile. The world's most famous steeplechase is the Grand National.
2 A track athletics event over 3000 m. The competitors have to negotiate 28 hurdles and seven water jumps. Each obstacle is 3 ft (0·9 m) high.

Stefan, Josef (1835–93) Physicist, born in St Peter, S Austria. He studied at Vienna, where he spent his career. His work in experimental physics was wide-ranging, but his fame rests on his research on thermal radiation, begun in 1879. He found empirically a law describing radiant heat loss from a hot surface (**Stefan's law** or **Stefan–Boltzmann law**), and used it to make the first satisfactory estimate of the Sun's surface temperature. Attempts by others to find a theoretical basis for Stefan's law led to major advances in physics, and eventually to Planck's quantum theory of 1900.

Stegodon [stegodon] An extinct, elephant-like mammal known from the Pliocene epoch of India; upper tusks long and very closely placed together; lower tusks only vestiges; only two cheek teeth present at a time. (Order: Proboscidea.)

Stegosaurus [stegosawrus] A large dinosaur attaining a length of 9 m/30 ft; characterized by two rows of plates along back from skull to tail; four-legged, but forelimbs shorter than hindlimbs; known from the Upper Jurassic period of Colorado. (Order: Ornithischia.)

Steichen, Edward (Jean) [stiykhn] (1879–1973) Photographer, born in Luxembourg. His family moved to the USA in 1882, and he studied art in Milwaukee (1894–8). He was a member of The Linked Ring in England, and in 1902 helped Alfred Stieglitz to found the American Photo-Secession Group. In World War 1 he served as commander of the photographic division of the US army, and in the 1920s achieved success with his 'New Realism' fashion and portrait photography. He was head of US Naval Film Services during World War 2, and director of photography at the New York Museum of Modern Art (1945–62), organizing the world-famous exhibition *The Family of Man* in 1955.

Steig, William [stiyg] (1907–2003) Artist, cartoonist, and writer, born in Brooklyn, New York City, New York, USA. He studied in New York at City College (1923–5) and the National Academy of Design (1925–9). In 1930 he began to make wood sculptures and to work as a free-lance artist, notably for the *New Yorker*. He later began writing as well as illustrating children's books, many of them classics of the genre, such as *Sylvester and the Magic Pebble* (1969). Dreamworks based the film *Shrek* (2001) on his book of the same name.

Steiger, Rod(ney Stephen) [stiyger] (1925–2002) Film actor, born in Westhampton, New York, USA. He trained at the Actors' Studio in New York City, emerging as an exponent of the Method, and made his Broadway debut in 1951 in *Night Music*. He became known following his first major role, in *On the Waterfront* (1954), and went on to star in a variety of demanding roles. His many other films include *Al Capone* (1958), *Dr Zhivago* (1965), *The Pawnbroker* (1965), *In the Heat of the Night* (1967, Oscar, Golden Globe), *American Gothic* (1988), *The Specialist* (1994), *Mars Attacks!* (1995), and *End of Days* (1999).

Stein, Gertrude [stiyn] (1874–1946) Writer, born in Allegheny, Pennsylvania, USA. She studied psychology and medicine at Radcliffe College and Johns Hopkins University, but settled in Paris, where she was absorbed into the world of experimental art and letters. Her main works include *Three Lives* (1908), *Tender Buttons* (1914), in which she tried to apply the theories of Cubist art to writing, and her most widely-read but lighthearted book, *The Autobiography of Alice B Toklas* (1933). She was revered as a critic in Paris, and her home became a salon for artists and writers between the two World Wars.

Stein, (Heinrich Friedrich) Karl, Freiherr (Baron) **von** [shtiyn] (1757–1831) Prussian statesman, born in Nassau, WC Germany. He studied law at Göttingen, and entered the service of Prussia in 1780, becoming secretary for trade (1804–7). As chief minister (1807–8), he carried out important reforms in the army, economy, and both national and local government. In 1812 he went to St Petersburg, and built up the coalition against Napoleon. He was later adviser to Alexander I (1812–15), then retired to Kappenberg in Westphalia.

Stein, Peter [shtiyn] (1937–) Theatre director, born in Berlin, Germany. From his very first production in 1967, he became established as a leading avant-garde director in Germany. Since 1970, he has been responsible for a series of collective creations at the Berlin Schaubuhne, where over a long rehearsal period the political and social context of a play is woven into an ensemble presentation.

Steinbeck, John (Ernst) [stiynbek], pseudonym **Amnesia Glasscock** (1902–68) Novelist, born in Salinas, California, USA. He studied marine biology at Stanford, but did not take a degree, and worked at various jobs before deciding to become a writer. His first successful novel was *Tortilla Flat* (1935), but his best-known work and the high point of his career was *The Grapes of Wrath* (1939), a novel about a poor farming family moving in the Depression from Oklahoma to what they hope will be a better life in California; it was made into a classic film by John Ford in 1940. It led to much-needed agricultural reform, and won for Steinbeck the 1940 Pulitzer Prize. His other works include *Of Mice and Men* (1937), *The Moon is Down* (1942), *East of Eden* (1952), and *The Winter of our Discontent* (1961). He was awarded the Nobel Prize for Literature in 1962.

steinbok *steenbok*

Steiner, (Francis) George [stiyner] (1929–) Critic and scholar, born in Paris, France. He studied there and at Chicago, Harvard, and Oxford universities. He worked at the Institute for Advanced Study at Princeton (1956–8), then taught at Cambridge, where he became a fellow of Churchill College in 1969. He was appointed professor of English and comparative literature at Geneva (1974–94, now emeritus), and at Oxford (1994–5), where he became a fellow of St Anne's College. One of the leading exponents of comparative literature, his publications include *The Death of Tragedy* (1961), *Language and Silence* (1967), *After Babel* (1975), and *Antigones* (1984). *Real Presences* (1989) challenges the demoralizing consequences of deconstructive thought. Later books include *Proofs and Three Parables* (1992) and *The Deeps of the Sea and Other Fiction* (1996), and a memoir, *Errata: an examined life* (1998). In 2003 appeared his Charles Eliot Norton lectures as *Lessons of the Masters*.

Steiner, Rudolf [shtiyner] (1861–1925) Social philosopher, the founder of anthroposophy, born in Kraljevec, NW Croatia. He studied science and mathematics, and edited Goethe's scientific papers, before coming temporarily under the spell of the theosophists. In 1912 he propounded his own approach, establishing his first 'school of spiritual science', or *Goetheanum*, in Dornach, Switzerland. His aim was to integrate the psychological and practical dimensions of life into an educational, ecological, and therapeutic basis for spiritual and physical development. Many schools and research institutions arose from his ideas, notably the Rudolf Steiner Schools, focusing on the development of the whole personality of the child. Several are for children with special needs.

Steinway, Henry (Engelhard) [stiynway], originally **Heinrich Engelhardt Steinweg** (1797–1871) Piano-maker, born in Wolfshagen, NC Germany. He fought at Waterloo, and in 1835 established a piano factory in Brunswick. In 1850 he transferred the business to the USA, where he introduced many innovations into the instrument, such as a cast-iron frame.

stele [steelee, -liy] (plural **stelai**) In ancient Greece, a carved or inscribed upright rectangular stone which could be used as a gravestone, a boundary marker on property, or a permanent display board for public laws and documents.

stellar evolution The sequence of events and changes covering the entire life-cycle of a star. The principal stage of evolution is the nuclear burning of hydrogen to form helium, with a consequential release of energy. Eventually the hydrogen in the core is exhausted, and the star becomes a red giant. In the final stages of evolution there are several paths, depending on the mass of the star: the formation of a white dwarf (stars like our Sun), a neutron star (a few solar masses), or a supernova (tens of solar masses).

stellar populations Groups of stars crudely classified by their age and location within a galaxy. **Population I** stars are young (up to a few thousand million years), found in spiral arms, whereas **Population II** are older and distributed throughout the Galaxy, but predominantly in the halo and central bulge. Even at a quite superficial level the two populations are readily distinguished: I has brilliant blue supergiants, whereas in II red giants and faint dwarf stars predominate. The chemical evolution of a galaxy means that the I stars are much richer in the heavier elements synthesized in stellar explosions than the ancient II stars, which formed before heavy elements were abundant.

stem (botany) The main axis of a plant, usually but not always above ground, and bearing the buds, leaves, and reproductive organs. It is formed from the apical end of the embryonic axis lying above the cotyledons in the seed, developing into the *plumule* or embryonic shoot. This may form one or several stems, often branched to display the leaves to best advantage for photosynthesis. The stem contains a vascular system: this conducts water and nutrients from the roots to the leaves, and the products of photosynthesis from the leaves to all other parts of the plant. In woody species, the stem is strengthened with additional supporting tissues, and protected by bark and cork layers. Stems may show various modifications, and assume new or additional functions, sometimes taking over from other organs. Thus, runners and rhizomes are stems which grow horizontally above and below ground respectively, giving rise to new plants at intervals; bulbs, corms, and tubers are stems modified to form storage organs that live from one growing season to the next, initiating new growth each year; and the stems of cacti store water. Green stems can photosynthesize, functioning as leaves, and may even be flattened and leaf-like in appearance. Stems can also act as climbing organs, either the whole stem twining or the tips only being modified to form tendrils.

stem (linguistics) *root* (linguistics)

Stendhal [stendahl], pseudonym of **Marie-Henri Beyle** (1783–1842) Writer, born in Grenoble, E France. He was a soldier under Napoleon, settled in Paris in 1821, and after the 1830 revolution was appointed consul at Trieste and Civitavecchia. He wrote biographies, and critical works on music, art, and literature, but was best known for his novels, notably *Le Rouge et le noir* (1830, Scarlet and Black) and *La Chartreuse de Parme* (1839, The Charterhouse of Parma). He is also known for his treatise *De l'Amour* (1827, On Love), and for his autobiographical works, especially his *Journal* (1888).

Sten gun The standard submachine-gun of the British Army from 1942 onwards. The gun was cheap, rugged, and manufactured in large quantities. Its name derives from its designers Stephard and Turpin, and the Enfield factory where it was made.

Stenmark, Ingemar (1956–) Skier, born in Tärnaby, W Sweden, 100 mi S of the Arctic Circle. One of the greatest slalom/giant slalom racers, he won both events at the 1980 Olympics with a 8 cm/3 in metal plate in his ankle following an accident the previous year. Between 1974 and 1989 he won a record 86 World Cup races, including a record 13 in the 1979 season. Overall champion three times (1976–8), he won 15 slalom/giant slalom titles and five world titles. He retired in 1989, and now lives in Monte Carlo.

Steno, Nicolaus [steenoh], Lat name of **Niels Steensen** (1638–86) Anatomist and geologist, born in Copenhagen, Denmark. He studied anatomy in Amsterdam, where he discovered the duct of the parotid gland and explained the function of the ovaries. He settled in Florence in 1665, as physician to the duke. Although brought up a strict Lutheran, he then became a Catholic, and in 1677 was made a bishop and apostolic vicar to N Germany. He was the first to explain the structure of the Earth's crust.

stenography *shorthand*

stenotype *palantype*

step dance A social and often competitive form of dance relying on rhythmically complex footwork using parts of the foot, heel, and toe beats, often performed in clogs. It has been maintained through folk festivals both as a social and an exhibition dance. The structure is part fixed and part improvised in performance.

stephanotis [stefanohtis] A twining, evergreen perennial (*Stephanotis floribunda*), native to Madagascar; a clustered waxy flower; stems to 3 m/10 ft or more; leaves glossy, oblong-elliptical; flowers in axillary clusters, tubular with five spreading lobes, white, strongly fragrant; also called **Madagascar jasmine**. (Family: Asclepiadaceae.)

Stephen (c.1090–1154) Last Norman king of England (1135–54), the son of Stephen-Henry, Count of Blois, and Adela, the daughter of William the Conqueror. He had sworn to accept Henry I's daughter, Empress Matilda, as queen, but seized the English crown and was recognized as Duke of Normandy on Henry's death in 1135. Though defeated and captured at the Battle of Lincoln (Feb 1141), he was released nine months later after Matilda's supporters had been routed at Winchester. But Matilda strengthened her grip on the West Country; David I of Scotland annexed the N English counties by 1141; and Matilda's husband, Count Geoffrey of Anjou, conquered Normandy by 1144–5. Stephen was also repeatedly challenged by baronial rebellions, and after 18 years of virtually continuous warfare, he was forced in 1153 to accept Matilda's son, the future Henry II, as his lawful successor. His reputation as the classic incompetent king of English mediaeval history is nevertheless undeserved. He was remarkably tenacious in seeking to uphold royal rights, and his war strategy was basically sound. His inability to defend the Norman empire was due largely to the sheer weight of his military burdens, especially the major offensives of the Scots in the N and the Angevins in the S.

Stephen I, St (c.975–1038) The first king and spiritual patron of Hungary (997–1038). He formed Pannonia and Dacia into a regular kingdom, organized Christianity, and introduced many social and economic reforms. Married to a German princess, he encouraged German immigration. He received from Pope Sylvester II the title of 'Apostolic King' and, according to tradition, St Stephen's Crown, now a Hungarian national treasure. He was canonized in 1083. Feast day 16 August.

Stephen, St (1st-c) The first Christian martyr (*Acts* 6–7). He was one of the seven chosen to manage the finances and alms of the early Church, and was possibly one of the Hellenists. Charged by the Jewish authorities for speaking against the Temple and the Law, he was tried by the Sanhedrin, and stoned to death by the crowds in Jerusalem. Feast day 26 December.

Stephen, Sir Ninian (Martin) (1923–) Judge, born in England, UK. His schooling was undertaken in Edinburgh, London, and Switzerland, before he moved to Melbourne as a teenager. He studied law at the University of Melbourne, served in World War 2, and became a QC in 1966. He was a justice of the Victoria Supreme Court (1970–2) and the High Court of Australia (1972–82). Appointed Governor-General of Australia in 1982, he retired from the position in 1989, when Prime Minister Bob Hawke made him Australia's first ambassador for the environment, a non-political role from which he retired in 1991. He was knighted in 1972. His interest in human rights prompted his appointment as judge on the International Criminal Tribunals for Yugoslavia in 1993 and for Rwanda in 1995.

Stephenson, George (1781–1848) Railway engineer, born in Wylam, Northumberland, NE England, UK. He worked in a colliery, received a rudimentary education at night school, and in 1812 became engine-wright at Killingworth where he constructed his first locomotive (1814). He is best remembered for the *Rocket*, an engine running at 58 km/36 mi an hour, built in collaboration with his son Robert for the Rainhill Trials of 1829. He worked as an engineer for several railway companies, and became a widely used consultant. The modern railway gauge in Britain derives from that at Killingworth.

Stephenson, Robert (1803–59) Civil engineer, born in Willington Quay, Northumberland, NE England, UK, the son of George Stephenson. He studied at Newcastle upon Tyne and Edinburgh, assisted his father in surveying the Stockton and Darlington Railway, worked as a mining engineer in Colombia, then managed his father's locomotive engine-works at Newcastle. In collaboration with his father, he designed the famous engine the *Rocket* for the Rainhill Trials of 1829. He attained independent fame through his tubular design for the Britannia Bridge over the Menai Straits in Wales (1846–9), and for bridges at Conwy, Newcastle upon Tyne, Montreal (Canada), and elsewhere. He became an MP in 1847.

Stephenson, Sir William, known as **Intrepid** (1896–1989) Secret intelligence chief, born in Point Douglas, near Winnipeg, Manitoba, C Canada, of Scottish descent. Educated in Winnipeg, he became involved in British secret intelligence through visits to Germany to buy steel in the early 1930s. His information on Enigma, the German cipher machine, led to MI6's acquisition of a prototype in 1939. In 1940 he was appointed British intelligence chief in North and South America, representing the interests of MI5, MI6, and Special Operations Executive. The novelist Ian Fleming, a member of his wartime staff, is said to have adopted Stephenson as a model for the character 'M' in the James Bond books.

steppe The extensive grassland, treeless region of Eurasia. It extends from the Ukraine through SE European and C Asian Russia to the Manchurian plains. Large areas of steppe are important for wheat growing (eg in the Ukraine).

steradian [**steray**dian] SI unit of solid angle; symbol *sr*; an area drawn on the surface of a sphere equal to the square of the radius of the sphere subtends a solid angle of 1 steradian at the centre of the sphere; the total area of a sphere subtends a solid angle of 4π sr at the centre.

stereochemistry The study of the spatial relationships between atoms in molecules, especially the configuration of the atoms bonded to a central atom and the occurrence of geometrical and optical isomers.

stereolithography *lithography*

stereophonic sound The recording and transmission of sound which, when reproduced, appears to the listener to come from different directions and to reproduce a sound field similar to that where the sound was originally recorded. It normally uses two microphones, and two loudspeakers to reproduce the sound which has been recorded on two separate channels. Two-track stereo tape recordings appeared in 1954; the first single-groove, two-track stereo records were made in 1957; and FM stereo broadcasts began in 1961.

stereoscopic photography, also termed **3-D** (three-dimensional) **films** The recording and presentation of paired images to give the viewer an impression of solidity and depth. The basic system, developed from 1845, is to photograph the scene with two cameras whose lenses are 65 mm/2½ in apart, the normal separation of human eyes, and view the results in a device which allows each eye to see only its appropriate right-eye or left-eye record. Twin lens cameras produce pairs of colour transparencies to be mounted for individual viewing, or shown to a large audience on two projectors each fitted with a polarizing filter orientated at right angles to the other. The two pictures are superimposed on a metallized screen, and the viewers wear spectacles with corresponding polarizing filters so that each eye sees only the correct image. 3-D cinematography is similarly based on recording right-eye and left-eye views, either on separate strips or side by side on one wide film. An early form of cinema presentation used anaglyph prints, but current practice for colour film is polarized projection and viewing. Holographic methods for both still and moving monochrome pictures are gaining in importance for scientific and technical applications.

sterilization **1** A surgical operation to render the individual unable to conceive. In the male the simplest procedure is to sever each vas deferens (the tube that carries sperm from the testicles to the penis) in the groin, a procedure known as *vasectomy*. In the female, the approach is to sever or obliterate the uterine tubes. In either case, access of sperm to the ova is blocked.
2 *asepsis*

Sterkfontein [**sterk**fontayn] A valley near Krugersdorp, Transvaal, South Africa, containing limestone caverns with important early hominid remains. The Sterkfontein site itself has yielded many specimens of *Australopithecus africanus* (2·4–2·8 million years ago) and *Homo habilis* (1·5–2·0 mya). The nearby sites of Kromdraai (2+ mya) and Swartkrans (1·0–2·0 mya) contain remains of *Australopithecus robustus*.

sterling The name of the currency of Britain, usually used to distinguish the British pound from other currencies (**pound sterling**). The name derives from the Norman coin known as a *steorling*, which had a star on one face. The **sterling area** was the name given to countries which kept their reserves in sterling – mainly the British Commonwealth nations. Sterling is no longer a reserve currency, this role having been adopted by the US dollar.

Stern, Howard (1954–) Radio disc-jockey and television talk-show host, born in New York City, USA. He studied at Boston University, where he became involved with college radio, then took various deejay jobs, eventually basing himself in New York City (from 1982). He has built a reputation as a 'shock jock', developing a flamboyant style and explicit programme content, in various 'Howard Stern' shows on radio and television during the 1990s, which has brought him fines and controversy as well as a huge public audience. His best-selling book *Private Parts* (1993) was later issued as a recording and filmed (both 1997).

Stern, Otto [**sh**tern] (1888–1969) Physicist, born in Zary, W Poland (formerly Sorau, Germany). He studied at the University of Breslau (now Wrocław), and taught at several German universities before emigrating to the USA in 1933, and becoming professor of physics at the Carnegie Technical Institute at Pittsburgh (1933–45). In 1920 he carried out an experiment with **Walter Gerlach** (1889–1979), demonstrating that certain atoms have a quantized magnetic moment, which provided major evidence in favour of quantum theory. He became a US citizen in 1939, and was awarded the Nobel Prize for Physics in 1943.

Sternberg, Josef von [**shtern**berg], originally **Jonas Stern** (1894–1969) Film director, born in Vienna, Austria. He worked in silent films in Hollywood in the 1920s as scriptwriter, cameraman, and director, but went to Germany to make his most famous film *Der blaue Engel* (1930, The Blue Angel) with Marlene Dietrich. This was followed by six more Hollywood features in which she starred, the last being *The Devil is a Woman* (1935). His autocratic methods and aloof personality made him unpopular in the studios, and his later career was erratic. His last film, *The Saga of Anatahan* (1953), was made in Japan.

Sternberg, Sir Sigmund (1921–) Businessman and religious ecumenist, born in Budapest, Hungary. Brought up in the Orthodox Jewish tradition in Hungary, he left the country for England in 1939. He became a worker in the scrap metal industry, and within a few years created the Sternberg group of companies. In the mid-1960s he became well known for his involvement in community work. He was made chairman of the International Council of Christians and Jews in 1979, and in the 1990s set up the Three Faiths Forum (including Muslims). He was knighted in 1976, appointed a Papal Knight in 1985, and awarded the Templeton Prize for Progress in Religion in 1998 for his interfaith work worldwide.

Sterne, Laurence (1713–68) Novelist, born in Clonmel, Co Tipperary, SC Ireland. He studied at Cambridge, was ordained in 1738, and appointed to a living in Yorkshire. In 1759 he wrote the first two volumes of his eccentric and influential comic novel *The Life and Opinions of Tristram Shandy*, which was very well received in London, the remaining volumes appearing between 1761 and 1767. From 1762 he lived mainly abroad for health reasons, publishing *A Sentimental Journey through France and Italy* in 1768. His *Letters from Yorick to Eliza* (1775–9) contained his correspondence with a young married woman to whom he was devoted.

sternum An elongated, almost flat bone lying in the midline of the front wall of the thorax; also known as the **breastbone**. It articulates with the clavicle (providing the only point of attachment of the upper limb and pectoral girdle to the axial skeleton) and the ribs, and overlies a large proportion of the heart, thereby affording it some protection.

steroid Any of several natural products, including many hormones, bile acids, and the *sterols*, derived from the non-glyceride portion of fats, the best known of which is cholesterol. The molecule contains the cyclopentanoperhydrophenanthrene nucleus. Steroids are responsible for maintaining many vital functions, including sexual characteristics, salt and water balance, and muscle and bone mass.

stethoscope A medical instrument used for detecting sounds within the body, invented by French physician René Laënnec in 1816.The first stethoscopes consisted of simple tubes or cones made of paper or wood. Modern instruments consist of a bell or diaphragm made of metal or plastic that is placed on the patient's body to pick up and amplify sound and conduct it via a flexible Y-shaped rubber tube to earpieces placed in the ears of the examiner. Normal and abnormal sounds can be detected from heart, lungs, and bowels.

Stevenage [**steev**nij] 51°55N 0°14W, pop (2001e) 79 700. Town in Hertfordshire, SE England, UK; 45 km/28 mi N of London; the first 'new town', 1946; railway; wide range of light industries.

Stevens, Wallace (1879–1955) Poet, born in Reading, Pennsylvania, USA. He studied at Harvard, became a journalist and lawyer, then joined an insurance company at Hartford, where he lived until his death. For many years he wrote abstruse and philosophical verse, and was over 40 when his first volume, *Harmonium* (1923), was published. His *Collected Poems* appeared in 1954. He is now regarded as a major if idiosyncratic poet in the Symbolist tradition.

Stevenson, Adlai (Ewing) [**ad**liy] (1900–65) US politician and lawyer, born in Los Angeles, California, USA. He studied at Princeton, and practised law in Chicago. He took part in several European missions for the State Department (1943–5), and was elected Democratic Governor of Illinois (1948). He helped to found the UN (1946), stood twice against Eisenhower as presidential candidate (1952, 1956), and was the US delegate to the UN (1961–5).

Stevenson, Juliet (1956–) Actress, born in London, UK. After graduating from the Royal Academy of Dramatic Art she joined the Royal Shakespeare Company, where she was made an associate artist in 1988. Other theatre work includes *Death and the Maiden* (1992, Olivier Award, Best Actress). She is well known to a wider audience through her work in film and television, including *The Mallens* (1978, TV), *Drowning by Numbers* (1988), *Truly Madly Deeply* (1991, Evening Standard British Film Awards, Best Actress), an adaptation of *Emma* (1996), *Cider With Rosie* (1998, TV), and *Mona Lisa Smile* (2003).

Stevenson, Robert Louis (Balfour) (1850–94) Writer, born in Edinburgh, EC Scotland, UK. He studied at Edinburgh, became a lawyer (1875), then turned to writing travel sketches, essays, and short stories for magazines. The romantic adventure story *Treasure Island* (1883) brought him fame, and entered him on a course of romantic fiction which included *Kidnapped* (1886), *The Strange Case of Dr Jekyll and Mr Hyde* (1886), *The Master of Ballantrae* (1889), and the unfinished *Weir of Hermiston* (1896), considered his masterpiece. In 1888 he settled for health reasons at Vailima, Samoa.

Stevenson screen A shelter for meteorological instruments, particularly thermometers, providing protection from solar radiation. It is a white, wooden box with louvred sides to give ventilation. The thermometers within the screen should be 1·25 m/4·1 ft above the ground to avoid strong temperature gradients at ground level, and to give comparability from screen to screen. It was invented by Thomas Stevenson (1818–87), the father of Robert Louis Stevenson.

Stewart, Alec (James) (1963–) Cricketer, born in Merton, Greater London. He began playing for Surrey in 1981, made his Test debut in 1990, and by the end of the 2003 season had played in a record 133 Tests, scoring 8463 runs and 15 centuries, and making 273 dismissals (a wicket-keeping record). Undaunted by his already weighty responsibilities as opening batsman and wicketkeeper, he took over as England captain (1998–9), leading them to their first win in a five-test series for 12 years (1998). He announced his retirement from international and county cricket in 2003.

Stewart, Dugald (1753–1828) Philosopher, born in Edinburgh, EC Scotland, UK. He studied at Edinburgh, where his father was professor of mathematics, and at Glasgow under Thomas Reid. He succeeded to his father's chair in 1775, then was professor of moral philosophy at Edinburgh (1758–1810). Much influenced by Reid's 'common sense' philosophy, he became the leader of the Scottish school. A prolific author, his major work was *Elements of the Philosophy of the Human Mind* (3 vols, 1792, 1814, 1827). A large monument on Calton Hill, Edinburgh, attests to his fame at the time of his death.

Stewart, Sir Jackie, popular name of **John (Young) Stewart** (1939–) Motor-racing driver, born in Milton, West Dunbartonshire, W Scotland, UK. He started in 99 races, and won 27 world championship races between 1965 and 1973, a record until surpassed by Alain Prost in 1987. He was world champion in 1969 (driving a Matra), 1971, and 1973 (both Tyrrell). He retired at the end of 1973, and took up a career in broadcasting. He is also expert at clay pigeon shooting, and has come close to Olympic selection. Since 1996 he has been chairman of Stewart Grand Prix. He received a knighthood in 2001.

Stewart, James (Maitland) (1908–97) Film star, born in Indiana, Pennsylvania, USA. An architecture student at Princeton University, he started in films in 1935, establishing a character of honesty and integrity in *You Can't Take It With You* (1938), *Destry Rides Again* (1939), and the comedy *The Philadelphia Story* (1940, Oscar), and *It's a Wonderful Life* (1946). He served with distinction in the US air force during World War 2, and returned to make a series of outstanding Westerns (1950–5) and two successes for Hitchcock, *Rear Window* (1954) and *Vertigo* (1958). His later work continued to provide a wide range of character roles, including *Fool's Parade* (1971) and *Right of Way* (1982). He received an American Film Institute Life Achievement Award in 1980, and an honorary Oscar in 1985.

Stewart, J(ohn) I(nnes) M(ackintosh), pseudonym **Michael Innes** (1906–94) Critic, and writer of detective fiction, born in Edinburgh, EC Scotland, UK. He studied at Oxford, and taught English at Leeds, Adelaide, and Belfast universities before returning to Oxford in 1949. Under his own name he wrote several novels and critical studies, notably *Eight Modern Writers* (1963). He was better known for his prolific work as Michael Innes, beginning with *Death at the President's Lodging* (1936, in USA as *Seven Suspects*), featuring the policeman hero John Appleby. Later books include *The Secret Vanguard* (1940), *A Private View* (1952), and *A Family Affair.*

Stewart, Patrick (1940–) Actor and playwright, born in Mirfield, West Yorkshire, N England, UK. He trained at Bristol Old Vic Theatre School, then worked in various repertory companies, joining the Royal Shakespeare Company in 1966. He has performed a wide range of theatre, film, and television roles, but is best known for his role as Captain Jean-Luc Picard in the follow-up series of *Star Trek: The Next Generation* (1987). Later films include *Star Trek: First Contact* (1996), *Star Trek: Insurrection* (1998), and *X-Men* (2000; sequel 2003). Later stage roles include *Othello* (1997) and *Who's Afraid of Virginia Woolf?* (2001).

Stewart, Rod(erick David) (1945–) Singer and songwriter, born in London, UK. After singing with various groups in the mid-1960s, he began a career as a soloist, then joined The Faces (1969–75) while continuing to record on his own. In 1971 he simultaneously topped the UK and US music charts with the album *Every Picture Tells A Story* and the single 'Maggie May'. His numerous hit songs include 'Sailing' (1975), which has become the unofficial British Navy anthem after being used as the signature tune of the 1976 BBC television documentary, 'Sailor'. Later albums include *Blondes Have More Fun* (1978), *Every Beat of My Heart* (1986), *Unplugged and Seated* (1993), *When We Were The New Boys* (1998), and *As Time Goes By* (2003).

Stewart Island pop (2000e) 700; area 1735 sq km/670 sq mi. Island of New Zealand, to the S of South Island, across the Foveaux Strait; highest point, Mt Anglem (977 m/3205 ft); a refuge for animal and bird life; largely uninhabited; small settlement of Oban on Halfmoon Bay; accessible by plane or ferry from Bluff, S of Invercargill; fishing.

Stewarts *Stuarts*

stibine [stibeen] SbH_3. A highly poisonous gas formed by the reduction of antimony compounds.

stibnite An antimony sulphide (Sb_2S_3) mineral found in low-temperature hydrothermal veins, lead-grey in colour, often occurring as long prismatic crystals. It is the chief ore of antimony.

stick insect A large twig-like insect with an elongate body and legs; resemblance to twig enhanced by habit of swaying from side to side; up to 30 cm/12 in long; feeding on leaves; also known as **walking sticks**. (Order: Phasmida. Family: Phasmatidae, c.2000 species.)

stickleback Small marine or freshwater fish of the family Gasterosteidae (5 genera), common throughout the N hemisphere; body typically elongate with a number of strong dorsal spines; mouth small and protruding; male builds nest, and guards developing eggs; includes the familiar and ubiquitous **3-spine stickleback** (*Gasterosteus aculeatus*), found in streams and lakes as well as shallow marine habitats; length up to 6 cm/ 2½ in.

Stieglitz, Alfred [**steeg**lits] (1864–1946) Photographer, born in Hoboken, New Jersey, USA. He studied engineering and photography in Berlin, and travelled extensively in Europe before returning to New York City in 1890. He founded the American Photo-Secession Group with Edward Steichen in 1902, and consistently influenced the development of creative photography as an art form through his magazine *Camera Work* (1903–17) and his gallery of modern art in New York City. His polemical writings and his own creative work established him as a major figure in photographic art.

Stiernhielm, Georg [**styern**yelm] (1598–1672) Poet, born in Vika, C Sweden. He studied at Uppsala and in Germany. Ennobled by Gustavus Adolphus, he became the favourite court poet of Queen Christina. Besides much lyric poetry, he wrote a didactic allegorical poem, *Hercules* (1647). He has come to be known as 'the father of Swedish poetry'.

stifftail A diving duck, native to the New World, S Europe, Africa, W Asia, and Australasia; long, stiff, tail feathers; inhabits fresh waters; mainly nocturnal. (Tribe: Oxyurini, especially Genus: *Oxyura*, 6 species. Subfamily: Anatinae.)

Stigler, George J(oseph) (1911–91) Economist, born in Renton, Washington, USA. He studied at Chicago University, held professorships at Minnesota, Brown, and Columbia, and taught at the University of Chicago from 1958. His books include *The Theory of Price* (1946) and *The Economist as Preacher* (1983). He was awarded the Nobel Prize for Economics in 1982 for his work on market forces and regulatory legislation.

Stiglitz, Joseph E (1942–) Economist, born in Gary, Indiana, USA. He completed his PhD from the Massachusetts Institute of Technology at age 24, and went on to teach at several universities before settling at Princeton (1979). He is known best by other economists for his highly technical analysis of the competitive process. He shared the Nobel Prize for Economics in 2001 for the analysis of markets with asymmetric information.

stigma In flowering plants, the part of the carpel receptive to pollen. Sticky secretions, corrugated surfaces, or hairs may help collect and retain pollen grains. Those of wind-pollinated flowers are often feathery, to increase the contact area, while those of insect-pollinated flowers are often borne on elongated styles which present the stigma in the appropriate position to pick up pollen from the insect's body. The stigma, and often the style, may through physiological means operate a complex compatibility system which accepts only pollen of the correct type.

stigmata [**stig**mata, stig**mah**ta] Marks or wounds appearing on the human body, similar to those of the crucified Jesus. They may be temporary (related to ecstasy or revelation) or permanent, and are alleged to be a sign of miraculous participation in Christ's passion.

stilbestrol / stilboestrol *DES*

Stilicho, Flavius [**stil**ikoh] (?–408) Roman general, half-Roman, half-Vandal, who was virtual ruler of the West Roman empire (395–408) under the feeble Emperor Honorius. His greatest achievements were his victories over Alaric and the Visigoths in N Italy at Pollentia (402) and Verona (403).

still life In art, the representation of objects such as books, candles, cooking utensils, musical instruments, fruit, flowers, etc. Still life was painted in antiquity; in W Europe it flourished above all in the Netherlands in the 17th-c. Some still lifes are obviously symbolic; others seem to be demonstrations of painterly skill.

stilt A long-legged wading bird, especially *Himantopus himantopus* (from warm regions worldwide, with many names for different races); also the **banded** or **red-breasted stilt** (*Cladorhynchus leucocephala*), from Australia and New Zealand. (Family: Recurvirostridae, 2 species.)

Stilwell, Joseph W(arren), nickname **Vinegar Joe** (1883–1946) US general, born in Palatka, Florida, USA. He trained at West Point in 1904, became an authority on Chinese life and an expert Chinese speaker, and was military attaché to the US Embassy in Beijing (1932–9). In 1942 he commanded US forces in China, Burma, and India. Recalled after a dispute with Jiang Jieshi in 1944, he commanded the US 10th Army in the Pacific until the end of the War.

Stimson, Henry L(ewis) (1867–1930) US statesman, born in New York City, USA. He studied at Yale and Harvard, and was called to the bar in 1891. He became US attorney for the New York southern district in 1906, secretary of war under Taft (1911–13), Governor-General of the Philippines (1927–9), and Hoover's secretary of state (1929–33). The *Stimson doctrine* denounced Japanese aggression in Manchuria (1931). Recalled by Franklin D Roosevelt as secretary of war (1940–5), his influence was decisive in leading Truman to use the atomic bomb against Japan (1945).

stimulants Drugs such as amphetamine, which produce feelings of wakefulness, alertness, elation, and an increased capacity to concentrate. Caffeine is a mild stimulant. Contrary to popular belief, alcohol is not a stimulant.

stimulated emission *laser*

Sting, originally **Gordon Matthew Sumner** (1951–) Singer, songwriter, and actor, born in Newcastle upon Tyne, Tyne and Wear, NE England, UK. Former vocalist and lyricist of The Police, his first film role came in *Quadrophenia* (1978), and his first solo hit song was 'Spread A Little Happiness' (1982), taken from the soundtrack of the television film *Brimstone and Treacle*, in which he also starred. His debut album, *The Dream of the Blue Turtles* (1985), topped both the UK and US music charts. Later albums include *Soul Cages* (1991), which reached number 1 in the UK music charts, *Mercury Falling* (1996), and *Sacred Love* (2003). Later films include *Dune* (1984) and *Lock, Stock and Two Smoking Barrels* (1999). He has been much associated with campaigns to do with the environment and with Amnesty International.

stinging nettle A perennial with creeping rhizomes (*Urtica dioica*) often forming large patches, native or introduced throughout temperate regions; leaves heart-shaped, toothed; flowers tiny, green, in drooping spikes; males and females on separate plants. The whole plant is covered in stinging hairs acting like hypodermic syringes, each with a bulbous base containing acid, and a brittle, needle-like tip. When touched, the tip pierces the skin and breaks off, while pressure on the base injects acid, causing a sting and subsequent rash. Wilting or cooking removes the ability to sting. The leaves are used as a vegetable and for tea; the stems yield tough fibres for cloth. (Family: Urticaceae.)

stingray Any of several bottom-living rays (Families: Dasyatidae, Potamotrygonidae, Urolophidae) in which the tail is whip-like and armed with one or more sharp poison spines; includes the large European stingray, *Dasyatis pastinaca*, common in shallow inshore waters from the North Sea to the Mediterranean; body length up to 2·5 m/8 ft.

stinkhorn The fruiting body of some fungi of the order Phallales; body initially phallus-like, with a white stem and swollen ovoid cap; cap dissolves into putrid slime, containing spores that are dispersed by flies attracted over great distances by the fetid odour. (Subdivision: *Basidiomycetes*.)

stipendiary magistrate A salaried and legally qualified magistrate in England and Wales. Such magistrates may sit alone when trying cases, unlike lay magistrates, and are found in London (**metropolitan stipendiary magistrates**) and other large towns. In Scotland, stipendiary magistrates are appointed by the local authority from among qualified lawyers, and sit in certain district courts as an alternative to one or more JPs.

Stirling 56°07N 3°57W, pop (2000e) 30 300. City and capital of Stirling council, C Scotland, UK, on S bank of R Forth, 34 km/21 mi NE of Glasgow; city status granted 2002; railway; university (1967); machinery, textiles, brick making, coachbuilding; Stirling castle (12th-c), former residence of Scottish kings; ruins of Cambuskenneth Abbey (1147), scene of Bruce's parliament (1326); Church of the Holy Rude (1414), MacRobert Arts Centre, Smith Art Gallery and Museum; Wallace Monument (1870), 2 km/1¼ mi NE; Stirling Festival (May).

Stirling Range Mountain range in SW Western Australia; extends 64 km/40 mi parallel with SW coast; rises to 1109 m/3638 ft at Bluff Knoll.

stitchwort Either of two species of bluish-green perennials with brittle stems native to woodlands in Europe, N Africa, and Asia Minor; leaves paired, narrow, rather grass-like; flowers white, 5-petalled. The **greater stitchwort** (*Stellaria holostea*) has flowers 2–3 cm/¾–1¼ in diameter, petals divided to halfway. The **lesser stitchwort** (*Stellaria graminea*) has flowers 0·5–1·2 cm/⅕–½ in in diameter, with petals divided to more than halfway. (Genus: *Stellaria*. Family: Caryophyllaceae.)

stoat A mammal of family Mustelidae, native to Europe, Asia, and North America (*Mustela erminea*); in summer, resembles a large weasel (length, 50 cm/20 in) with black tip to tail; winter coat (*ermine*) white, with black tail tip; inhabits woodland and tundra; eats mainly rabbits.

stochastic processes *random processes*

stock An annual or perennial, growing to 80 cm/30 in, native to Europe and Asia; slightly woody stems; leaves greyish; flowers in spikes, purple, red or white, cross-shaped, often double in cultivars. It includes **garden stock** or **gilliflower** (*Matthiola incana*) and **night-scented stock** (*Matthiola bicornis*). (Genus: *Matthiola*, 55 species. Family: Cruciferae.)

stock-car racing A type of motor racing which takes different forms in the USA and UK. In the USA, highly supercharged production cars race around banked concreted tracks. In the UK, 'bangers' (old cars) race against each other on a round or oval track with the intention of being the last car still moving at the end of the race. Several 'rough' tactics amongst drivers are allowed, in the hope of eliminating a fellow driver.

stock exchange An institution through which stocks, shares, and bonds are traded under standard rules. Originally a stock exchange would have a single building where deals were arranged in person; nowadays trading is normally by telephone and computer networks. Many major cities in the West have a stock exchange, Wall Street in New York City being the largest, and there are important stock exchanges in Tokyo, Hong Kong, and Frankfurt. The London Stock Exchange, located in the City of London near the Bank of England, deals in some 7000 securities. Until 1986, business was carried out on 'the floor of the House', ie in the Stock Exchange itself. Individuals and institutions wishing to buy or sell securities would contact a *stockbroker*, who would place the order with a *jobber* (a trader on the floor). 27 October 1986 was the date of the 'Big Bang' when the distinction between brokers and jobbers was abolished, as were minimum commission scales; and a computerized system was introduced for share trading. Firms are now brokers/dealers; they may buy and sell on their own account as well as act as agents for others. The London Stock Exchange has some 5000 individual members and over 300 member firms.

Stock Exchange Automated Quotations (SEAQ) A system introduced in 1986 in the London stock market for trading securities. It is a computerized market-making activity which enables member firms to buy and sell and quote prices for specific securities. The prices are therefore known to all continuously.

Stockhausen, Karlheinz [shtokhowzn] (1928–) Composer, born in Mödrath, W Germany. He studied at Cologne and Bonn, joined the *musique concrète* group in Paris, and experimented with compositions based on electronic sounds. In 1953 he helped to found the electronic music studio at Cologne, and became director there (1963–77), later becoming professor of composition at the Hochschule für Musik in Cologne (1971–77). He has written orchestral, choral, and instrumental works, including some which combine electronic and normal sonorities, such as *Kontakte* (1960), and parts of a huge operatic cycle, *Licht* (Light). In 1991 he commenced a project to produce his complete works on CD.

Stockholm 59°20N 18°03E, pop (2000e) 709 000. Seaport and capital of Sweden; on a group of islands and the adjacent mainland, where L Mälar joins the Saltsjö, an arm of the Baltic Sea; largest city in Sweden; founded, 1255; important trading centre of the Hanseatic League; capital, 1436; bishopric; airport; railway; underground railway; university (1878); metalworking, engineering, textiles, foodstuffs, brewing, tourism; royal palace (18th-c), German church (17th-c), national museum, Drottningholm Palace (royal family residence).

Stockholm syndrome The unnaturally close relationship that occasionally develops between a hostage of a criminal or terrorist and his or her captor. It was first described in a woman held hostage in a bank in Sweden who remained faithful to the thief during his imprisonment.

stock market The system of buying and selling stocks and shares; also, a building in which these transactions take place (the **stock exchange**). A stock market 'crash' refers to a situation when the prices of stocks fall dramatically, resulting in many bankruptcies. The most famous case was the Wall Street crash of 1929; a less dramatic crash also occurred in October 1987 in most world stock markets.

Stockport 53°25N 2°10W, pop (2001e) 284 500. Town in Greater Manchester, NW England, UK; at junction of the Tame and Goyt Rivers which join to form the R Mersey, 10 km/6 mi SE of Manchester; birthplace of Joan Bakewell; railway; Manchester airport nearby; electronics, computers, aerospace, textiles (especially cotton), printing, engineering, foodstuffs; football league team, Stockport County.

stocks In economics, a term used in two main senses, both of which refer to amounts at a given moment; opposed to **flows**, which refer to changes over time. **1** Stocks of goods (or **inventories**), are raw materials, fuels, or unsold products in store at a given date.

2 The term is also used to mean financial assets: in the UK, for example, government debt is called **government stock**, and is traded on the stock exchange; in the USA, company shares are called **common stocks**.

Stockton *Macmillan, Harold*

Stockton-on-Tees 54°34N 1°19W, pop (2000e) 90 000. Town in NE England, UK, on the R Tees estuary; unitary authority, 1996 (pop (2000e) 180 000); developed with the opening of the Stockton–Darlington railway in 1825; ship repairing, engineering, chemicals.

Stoicism A philosophical movement which flourished in the Hellenistic Roman period from c.320 BC–AD 200 alongside and in competition with Epicureanism and Scepticism. The **Stoics**, named after the 'Painted Stoa' (colonnade) where they met, believed in a rational, materialistic, and deterministic universe in which virtue consisted in understanding natural necessity and then cheerfully accepting it; the individual soul is literally a part of the larger cosmos, into which it is absorbed.

The major figures in its formulation were the founder, Zeno of Citium, and the two succeeding heads of the School, Cleanthes and Chrysippus. It accorded well with the ethos of Rome, and was later taken up by such figures as Seneca and Epictetus.

Stoke-on-Trent 53°00N 2°10W, pop (2001e) 240 600. Industrial city and (from 1997) unitary authority in Staffordshire, C England, UK; part of the Potteries urban area; on the R Trent, 217 km/135 mi NW of London; an amalgam (1910) of the former Tunstall, Burslem, Hanley, Stoke-on-Trent, Fenton, and Longton municipal authorities; railway; University of Keele (1962) nearby; Staffordshire University (1992, formerly Polytechnic); clayware (largest producer in the world), coal, steel, chemicals, engineering, rubber, paper; birthplace of Josiah Wedgwood and Arnold Bennett; Wedgwood museum at Barlaston (7 km/4 mi S); Alton Towers theme park nearby; football league teams, Stoke City (Potters), Port Vale.

Stoker, Bram, popular name of **Abraham Stoker** (1847–1912) Writer, born in Dublin, Ireland. Educated at Dublin, he studied law and science, and partnered Henry Irving in running the Lyceum Theatre from 1878. Among several books, he is chiefly remembered for the classic horror tale *Dracula* (1897), which has occasioned a whole series of film adaptations, notably *Nosferatu* (Murnau, 1921), *Dracula* (Hammer Films, 1958), and *Bram Stoker's Dracula* (Coppola, 1993). Other novels include *The Mystery of the Sea* (1902) and *The Lady of the Shroud* (1909).

Stoker, Richard (1938–) Composer, pianist, artist, and writer, born in Castleford, West Yorkshire, N England, UK. He studied at the Royal Academy of Music with Lennox Berkeley, and in Paris with Nadia Boulanger. A professor at the Royal Academy (1963–87), his varied compositions include the opera *Johnson Preserv'd* (1967), works for piano and organ, string quartets, film and stage scores, and many choral works. He edited *Composer Magazine* (1969–80), and his books include poetry, novels, short stories (collected, 1997), and two volumes of autobiography, *Open Window – Open Door* (1985) and *Between the Lines* (1991).

Stokes' law In physics, a law expressing the viscous drag force F acting on a spherical object of radius r moving with velocity v through a fluid of viscosity η as $F = 6\pi\eta v$; stated in 1845 by British physicist George Stokes (1819–1903). It determines the terminal velocity of small raindrops, or small bubbles in water.

Stokowski, Leopold [stokofskee], originally **Antoni Stanislaw Boleslawowicz** (1882–1977) Conductor, born in London, UK. He studied at the Royal College of Music, London, and built up an international reputation as conductor of the Philadelphia Symphony Orchestra (1912–36), the New York Philharmonic (1946–50), and the Houston Symphony Orchestra (1955–60). He made three films with the Philadelphia Orchestra, including Walt Disney's *Fantasia* (1940). In 1962 he founded the American Symphony Orchestra in New York City.

STOL [estol] Acronym used for a fixed-wing aircraft specially designed for **Short Take-Off and Landing**. These aircraft usually accomplish their function by special aerodynamic devices providing high lift. The ability to have short take-offs is highly dependent on the aircraft being able to perform well at low forward speeds, and until World War 2 this was not a major problem because of the generally low speeds employed. The war brought a need for slow-speed STOL observation aircraft, of which the Fieseler Fi 156 Storch was the most famous.

stolon A long shoot which bends under its own weight to the ground, and roots at the tip or at the nodes to form new plants.

Stolypin, Peter Arkadyevich [stolipin] (1862–1911) Russian statesman and prime minister (1906–11), born in Dresden, E Germany. He studied at St Petersburg, and after service in the ministry of the interior (from 1884), became governor of Saratov province (1903–6), where he ruthlessly put down local peasant uprisings and helped to suppress the revolutionary upheavals of 1905. As premier, he introduced a series of agrarian reforms, which had only limited success. In 1907 he suspended the second Duma, and arbitrarily limited the franchise. He was assassinated in Kiev.

stomach A digestive pouch between the oesophagus and the duodenum, which stores food, secretes gastric juice (that kills ingested bacteria and initiates protein digestion) and, by wave-like contractions, churns and releases its contents into the duodenum at a controlled rate. Its size and position in humans is related to body build, but varies within the same individual with posture (standing, lying down) and contents (empty, full). It is divided into the *cardiac* region around the *cardiac orifice* (where the oesophagus opens into it), the *fundus* (the region above the level of the cardiac orifice), the *body*, and the *pylorus*, which opens into the duodenum at the *pyloric orifice*. Its most fixed parts are the cardiac and pyloric orifices, the latter remaining closed except for the periodic release of the stomach contents into the duodenum. Medical problems affecting the stomach include gastric and peptic ulcers, gastritis, and stomach cancer.

stomach cancer A cancer arising in the lining of the stomach. It usually affects people in late middle-age, and tends not to be recognized until a late stage, when it has invaded through the stomach wall and infiltrated adjacent organs. It also spreads in the blood to the liver. Presentation is with weight loss, upper abdominal pain, and nausea. The lesion may obstruct the passage of food through the stomach, leading to vomiting, or may bleed slowly over a long period, leading to anaemia. Surgical treatment requires the removal of all or part of the stomach, but the prognosis is poor.

stomata In plants, pores concentrated on the lower leaf surface through which gases and water vapour enter and leave the leaf. They are bounded by *guard cells*, which bend when swollen with water and open the stoma, or straighten when dehydrated and close it, preventing further water loss from the leaf.

Stone, Oliver (1946–) Film director and screenwriter, born in New York City, New York, USA. Dropping out of Yale in 1965, he taught English and history in Saigon, Vietnam, as a civilian. He returned to Vietnam with the US Army (1967–8) and was wounded in combat. He studied at the film school of New York University and had written numerous unfilmed scripts before he made his directorial debut with the Canadian horror film *Seizure* (1973). He won an Oscar for *Midnight Express* (1978), but subsequent screenplays were for mostly forgettable action films. He then wrote and directed two highly regarded films, *Salvador* (1986) and *Platoon* (1987); the latter won him Oscars for best director and best picture. He received another Oscar for *Born On The Fourth Of July* (1989). He produced and directed a series of commercially successful but often edgy films, the most controversial being *JFK* (1991), his highly partisan account of the assassination of President Kennedy. Later films include *Nixon* (1995), *Beyond Borders* (2000) and *Alexander* (2004).

Stone, Sir (John) Richard (Nicholas) (1913–91) Economist, born in London, UK. He changed from law to economics at Cambridge under Keynes, spent three years in the City of London, and during World War 2 was a government economist. He became director of the Department of Applied Economics at Cambridge (1945–55) and was appointed professor of economics (1955–80). He was awarded the 1984 Nobel Prize for Economics for his development of the complex models on which world-wide standardized national income accounts are based.

Stone Age *Three Age System*

stonebass *wreckfish*

stone carving *sculpture*

stonechat A thrush (*Saxicola torquata*) native to most of the Old World, male with dark head, white neck spots and pale reddish breast; inhabits open country; eats insects, grain, and berries; often perches on bush, fence, etc.

stone circles Circular or near-circular rings of prehistoric standing stones found, particularly in Britain and Ireland, in the Late Neolithic and Early Bronze Age. About 900 examples survive, some as much as 400 m/1300 ft in diameter. They most probably functioned as temples in which celestial events, the passing of the seasons, and the fertility of the land and people could be celebrated.

stonecrop A member of a large genus of succulents, mostly perennials, native to N temperate regions; leaves very narrow to almost circular, but always fleshy; flowers 5-petalled, starry, mainly white, yellow, or red. (Genus: *Sedum*, 300 species. Family: Crassulaceae.)

stone curlew *thick-knee*

stonefish Grotesque fish found in shallow inshore waters of the Indo-Pacific region, especially around coral reefs; body strongly camouflaged in shape and colour; length 30–60 cm/12–24 in; dorsal fin armed with sharp poison spines that can inflict extremely painful stings. (Genus: *Synanceia*. Family: Synanceiidae.)

stonefly A primitive, winged insect typically found among stones along river banks; adults are poor fliers that run and hide when disturbed; larvae usually aquatic in running water. (Order: Plecoptera, c.2000 species.)

Stonehenge A prehistoric monument near Amesbury, Wiltshire, S England, UK, 130 km/80 mi W of London; a world heritage site. It was constructed in three major phases within the Middle–Late Neolithic period: 2950–2900 BC, a circular ditch with low inner and outer banks, c.110 m/360 ft in diameter, and a circle of pits known as 'Aubrey Holes' which perhaps held timber posts; 2900–2400 BC, posts were set up inside the earthwork, and cremations were placed in the Aubrey Holes; the third phase, 2550–1600 BC, is that of the surviving stone monument, when a 30 m/100 ft diameter lintelled circle and inner horseshoe of 80 dressed sarsen (sandstone) blocks, each weighing 20–50 tonnes, were erected, and bluestones from South Wales were set up in a circle and horseshoe. Alignment on the midsummer sunrise/midwinter sunset implies prehistoric use for seasonal festivals, but the association with the druids dates only from 1905, and has no historical basis. The theory, proposed in 1921 by British petrographer Herbert Thomas, that the pillars had been transported by land on wooden rollers from South Wales to Salisbury Plain has now been superseded by the view that they were carried to the area by glaciers.

Stone Mountain Memorial A memorial carving on the exposed face of Stone Mountain in NW Georgia, USA. The work, which was completed in 1972, depicts Confederate leaders Jefferson Davis, Robert E Lee, and 'Stonewall' Jackson. It was executed by sculptors Gutzon Borglum, Augustus Lukeman, and Walter Kirtland Hancock, who worked on it in succession over a period of 50 years.

stone-plover *plover*

stoneware A type of ceramic midway between pottery and porcelain, made of clay and a fusible stone. It is fired to a point where partial vitrification renders it impervious to liquids, but unlike porcelain it is seldom more than slightly translucent.

Stooges, The Three Comedy trio. Originally the **Horwitz** (later **Howard**) brothers, **Samuel** (b.1895), **Moses** (b.1897), and **Jerome** (Jerry) (b.1911), they were known by their respective nicknames of Shemp, Moe, and Curly (with the bald head). They first played knockabout humour in association with comedy star Ted Healy, who called them The Southern Gentlemen. Moe, Shemp, and Ted's real-life valet, Ken Lackey, comprised the original trio of Stooges. (Curly, then only 19 years old, was considered the 'baby' of the group and his mother refused to let him travel far from home). Lackey left in 1928 and various replacements were tried until another vaudeville comic, **Larry Fine** (originally **Feinberg**, with the wild wavy hair) joined Moe and Shemp. The trio appeared with Healy in the feature-length film *Soup to Nuts* in 1930, marking the big-screen debut of the Stooges. Shemp then left to pursue his own career and was replaced by Curly. They then parted from Healy, and as Larry, Curly and Moe they made 191 short films and 13 feature films for Columbia, all characterized by anarchic knockabout humour, with sound effects perfectly synchronized with their blows. There were further personnel changes: Shemp returned, replacing Curly (d.1952), and in turn was replaced by **Joe Besser**. There was less interest in the act during the early 1950s, but when several of their films were released for television towards the end of the decade, they once again became acclaimed. **Joe de Rita** (b.1909) replaced Joe Besser as the new Curly, and the new trio appeared in the successful burlesque *Have Rocket, Will Travel* (1959), followed by *Snow White and the Three Stooges* (1961). In their final form, billed as Larry, Moe, and Curly Joe, they made 12 features before their retirement. Moe and Larry died in 1975, and Joe de Rita in 1993.

stoolball An 11-a-side bat-and-ball game resembling cricket and rounders. The batter defends his wicket, a 1 ft (30 cm) square wooden board 4 ft 8 in (1·4 m) from the ground, which the underarm bowler attempts to hit. Runs are scored in a similar way to cricket. The bat is wooden, but similar in shape to a tennis racket.

Stopes, Marie (Charlotte Carmichael) [stohps] (1880–1958) Pioneer advocate of birth control, suffragette, and palaeontologist, born in Edinburgh, EC Scotland, UK. She studied at London and Munich, and became the first female science lecturer at Manchester (1904). Alarmed at the unscientific way in which men and women embarked upon married life, she wrote a number of books on the subject, of which *Married Love* (1918), in which birth control is mentioned, caused a storm of controversy. She later founded the first birth control clinic, in London (1921). She wrote over 70 books, including *Contraception: its Theory, History and Practice* (1923) and *Sex and Religion* (1929).

stop–go policy A government economic policy in which action taken to boost the economy (**go**) results in inflation or exchange rate problems. Action is then taken to cure these problems, which results in a slow-down of the economy (**stop**). The phrase was particularly applied to the incomes policies tried out in many countries without much success in the 1960s.

Stoppard, Miriam, *née* **Stern** (1937–) British physician, writer, and broadcaster. She studied at London and Durham, specializing in dermatology, then worked in industry (1968–77) before becoming a writer and broadcaster. She is well known for her television series, especially *Miriam Stoppard's Health and Beauty Show* (from 1988), and among her books are *The Baby and Child Medical Handbook* (1984), *The Magic of Sex* (1991), *The Menopause* (1994), *Conception, Pregnancy and Birth* (2000), and *Defying Age* (2003). She married Tom Stoppard in 1972 (divorced, 1992).

Stoppard, Sir Tom, originally **Tomas Straussler** (1937–) Playwright, born in Zlín, SE Czech Republic of Czech parents. He lived in Singapore, moving with his family to England in 1946, where he was educated. In 1960 he went to London as a freelance journalist and theatre critic, and wrote radio plays. He made his name with *Rosencrantz and Guildenstern Are Dead* (1967, Tony). Other plays include the philosophical satire *Jumpers* (1972), *Travesties* (1974, Tony), *The Real Thing* (1982, Tony), *Hapgood* (1988), *Arcadia* (1993), *Indian Ink* (1995), and *The Invention of Love* (1997). He has also written a novel, *Lord Malquist and Mr Moon* (1966), as well as several short stories. His television plays include *Professional Foul* (1977) and *Squaring the Circle* (1984), and his screenplays include *Empire of the Sun* (1987) and *Shakespeare in Love* (1998). He was married to Miriam Stoppard (divorced, 1992). He received a knighthood in 1997.

storax An aromatic gum obtained by making incisions in the trunk of sweet gums (Genus: *Liquidambar*) and the storax tree (*Styrax offinale*), a small deciduous tree with drooping clusters of 3–6 white flowers, native to the Mediterranean region.

Storey, David (Malcolm) (1933–) Novelist and playwright, born in Wakefield, West Yorkshire, N England, UK. He studied at the Slade School of Art, London. The action of *This Sporting Life* (1960), his first novel, is set in the world of rugby league, and the characters of his play *The Changing Room* (1972) are footballers. The play *Life Class* (1974), is set in an art college. Other novels, such as *Saville* (1976, Booker), use autobiographical material from his Yorkshire mining country background, as does the play *In Celebration* (1969). Later plays include *Early*

Days (1980) and *The March on Russia* (1989). His *Collected Poems* appeared in 1992.

stork A large bird, native to warm regions worldwide; long legs, neck, and long stout bill; flies with neck and legs outstretched; inhabits forest, dry country, or water margins; eats invertebrates, small vertebrates, or carrion. The **white stork** (*Ciconia ciconia*) is the stork of fable, a summer visitor to Europe, which prefers to nest on buildings; its numbers in N Europe diminished in the 20th-c. (Family: Ciconiidae, 17 species.)

storksbill An annual or perennial native to temperate regions; leaves divided into two rows of leaflets; flowers white, pink, or purple; fruit with a long point resembling a bird's beak. Changes in humidity cause the beak of ripe fruits to twist and untwist like a corkscrew, helping to embed the seed in the soil. (Genus: *Erodium*, 90 species. Family: Geraniaceae.)

Storm, (Hans) Theodor Woldsen [shtorm] (1817–88) Writer, born in Husum, N Germany. He trained as a lawyer, wrote a volume of poems (1857), and became known for his novellas, notably *Der Schimmelreiter* (1888, The Rider on the White Horse). His idea was that literature should stem from true emotion; much of his work is therefore nostalgically lyrical.

storm An intense meteorological disturbance, categorized on the Beaufort scale as force 10 (storm) or force 11 (violent storm). Wind speeds range from 25–32 m/s (55–72 mph).

storm-cock *mistle thrush*

Störmer, Horst L(udwig) (1949–) Physicist, born in Frankfurt-am-Main, WC Germany. He graduated from Stuttgart University in 1977, joined Columbia University, NY, and shared the 1998 Nobel Prize for Physics for his contribution to the discovery of a new form of quantum fluid with fractionally charged excitations.

Stormont A suburb of Belfast, NE Northern Ireland, UK, in which are situated Parliament House (built in 1932 to house the parliament of Northern Ireland, then the home of the Northern Ireland Assembly), Stormont House, and Stormont Castle.

storm petrel A petrel, worldwide, found at sea unless breeding; eats plankton snatched from sea surface; nests in burrows. Some (subfamily: Oceanitinae) 'walk' across the water surface in flight; others (subfamily: Hydrobatinae) swoop over the water. Many make long migrations. (Family: Hydrobatidae, 22 species.)

storm surge A localized rise in sea level produced by on-shore winds and reduced atmospheric pressure caused by large storms. Much of the flood damage produced by hurricanes, typhoons, and other major storms is the result of storm surge. Along the coasts of India and China these surges have resulted in death tolls of hundreds of thousands. One of the most devastating surges in recent history occurred in the North Sea during the winter of 1953, causing the sea level to rise more than 3 m/10 ft along the coast of The Netherlands.

Stornoway 58°12N 6°23W, pop (2000e) 8490. Port capital of Western Isles, NW Scotland, UK, on E coast of Lewis; airfield; fishing, oil supply services, tweeds, knitwear, tourism; An Lanntair art gallery, Museum nan Eilean Steornabhagh.

Stoss or **Stozz, Veit** [shtohs] (c.1447–1533) Woodcarver and sculptor, born in Nuremberg, SC Germany. He worked mainly in Kraków (1477–96), where he carved the high altar of the Marjacki Church. Back in Nuremberg, he worked for 30 years in various churches, including the church of St Lorenz, which contains his 'Annunciation'.

stout *beer*

Stowe, Harriet (Elizabeth) Beecher [stoh], *née* **Beecher** (1811–96) Novelist, born in Litchfield, Connecticut, USA. Brought up with puritanical strictness, she studied then taught at her sister's school. In 1836 she married a theological professor, with whom she lived in poverty until the immediate success and scandal of her first novel *Uncle Tom's Cabin* (1852), which was prompted by the passing of the Fugitive Slave Law. Making extensive tours in Europe (1853, 1856 and 1859), she formed important literary friendships, and wrote a host of other books, including *Dred: A Tale of the Great Dismal Swamp* (1856), *The Minister's Wooing* (1859), and *Old Town Folks* (1869).

Strabane [straban], Ir **An Srath Ban** 54°49N 7°27W, pop (2000e) 12 000. Market town in Strabane district, Tyrone, W Northern Ireland, UK; administrative centre of the district of Strabane, pop (2000e) 37 500; on the Mourne and Finn Rivers, where they meet to form the R Foyle; Irish border town; textiles, engineering, salmon fishing.

strabismus *squint*

Strabo [strayboh] (Gr 'squint-eyed') (c.64 BC–c.AD 23) Geographer and historian, born in Amaseia, Pontus. He spent his life in travel and study, was at Corinth in 29 BC, explored the Nile in 24 BC, and seems to have settled at Rome after AD 14. Of his great historical work in 47 books, *Historical Studies*, only a few fragments survive; but his *Geographica* in 17 books has come down almost complete, and is of great value for the results of his own extensive observation. He makes copious use of his predecessors, Eratosthenes, Polybius, Aristotle, Thucydides, and many writers now lost.

Strachey, (Giles) Lytton [straychee] (1880–1932) Biographer and critic, born in London, UK. He studied at Cambridge, lived in London, and became a member of the Bloomsbury Group of writers and artists. He began his writing career as a critic, but turned to biography, creating a literary bombshell with his *Eminent Victorians* (1918), an iconoclastic challenge to the self-assured, monumental studies previously typical of this genre. Later works included *Queen Victoria* (1921) and *Elizabeth and Essex* (1928). His approach to biography was revolutionary, and marked a turning-point in the genre. His method was to be selective, irreverent, and witty, as well as accurately perceptive. It set the tone for generations of biographers to come.

Stradivari or **Stradivarius, Antonio** [stradivahrius] (c.1644–1737) Violin maker, born in Cremona, N Italy. He experimented with the design of string instruments, and assisted by his two sons perfected the Cremona type of violin. It is thought that he made over a thousand violins, violas, and violoncellos between 1666 and his death; about 650 of these still exist.

Strafford, Thomas Wentworth, 1st Earl of (1593–1641) English statesman, born in London, UK. He studied at Cambridge, was knighted in 1611, and in 1614 succeeded to his baronetcy and became MP for Yorkshire. He acted with the Opposition (1625–8), but after being appointed president of the North and Baron Wentworth (1628), he supported Charles I. In 1632 he became lord deputy of Ireland, where he imposed firm rule. In 1639 he was made the king's principal adviser, and Earl of Strafford. His suppression of the rebellion in Scotland failed, and he was impeached by the Long Parliament. Despite a famous defence at Westminster, he was executed on Tower Hill.

straight line In geometry, a line such that, if *P*,*Q*,*R* are any three points on this line, the gradient of *PQ* is equal to the gradient of *QR*. In Cartesian geometry, the equation of a straight line can be written in the form $ax + by + c = 0$.

strain The fractional change in the dimensions of some object subjected to stress, expressed as a number. For force acting along the axis of a rod, **linear strain** is the change in length divided by the original length. **Volume strain** is the fractional change in volume for an object pressured on all sides. **Shear strain** measures the effectiveness of a twisting force.

Straits Settlements The name given to the former British crown colony which consisted of Singapore, Malacca, the Dindings, Penang, and Province Wellesley. All became part of Malaysia in 1963, and Singapore became independent in 1965.

strangeness In particle physics, an internal additive quantum number conserved in strong and electromagnetic interactions, but not in weak interactions; symbol *S*. It was introduced during the 1930s to explain 'strange' reactions observed in cosmic ray experiments. Strange quarks are those having strangeness $S = -1$; strange particles contain at least one strange quark.

Strangford Lough Inlet of the North Channel, E Northern Ireland, UK, separated from the sea (E) by the Ards peninsula;

length, 27 km/17 mi; width, 6 km/4 mi; entrance c.1 km/¾ mi wide, 8 km/5 mi long; contains several islands.

strangler fig *fig*

Stranraer [stranrah(r)] 54°54N 5°02W, pop (2000e) 10 100. Port in Dumfries and Galloway, SW Scotland, UK; at the head of Loch Ryan; railway; ferries to N Ireland; footwear, metal products, transport equipment; Wigtown district museum.

Strasberg, Lee, originally **Israel Strassberg** (1901–82) Actor, director, and teacher, born in Budanov, W Ukraine (formerly Budzanow, Austria). He emigrated to the USA in 1909, and gained a reputation with the Theater Guild of New York. In 1931 he was involved in the formation of the Group Theater, with which he worked as a teacher, evolving a technique (influenced by Stanislavsky) which became known everywhere as 'method acting'. He exercised great influence as a director of the Actor's Studio (1949–82), his pupils including Marlon Brando, Anne Bancroft, and Paul Newman.

Strasbourg [strazberg], Fr [strazboor], Ger **Strassburg** [shtrasboork], ancient **Argentoratum** 48°35N 7°42E, pop (2000e) 264 000. Industrial and commercial city, and capital of Bas-Rhin department, NE France; on the R Ill, W of its junction with the R Rhine; sixth largest city in France; important transportation centre and largest river-port in France; part of a bishopric since 1003; free imperial city in 13th-c; ceded to France, 1697; taken by Germany, 1871; returned to France, 1918; railway junction; university (founded 1537); trade in minerals, building materials, petroleum products, grain; iron and steel, metalworking, engineering, furniture, foodstuffs, paper, textiles, tanning; seat of the Council of Europe, European Parliament, European Commission of Human Rights, and European Science Foundation; printing developed here by Gutenberg; tourist centre of Alsace; congress and conference centre; Gothic cathedral (begun 1015, with noted 14th-c astronomical clock), Château des Rohan (1728–42), old town hall, Palais de l'Europe (1972–7), La Petite France (16th-c quarter of old Strasbourg); international music festival (Jun).

Strategic Arms Limitation Treaty *SALT*

Strategic Arms Reduction Talks *START*

strategic capability The capability of states with long-range missiles or aircraft to make war or carry out reprisals. It is divided into a number of categories depending on the ability or otherwise of a state to respond to an attack, and whether it can destroy an adversary's strategic military installations or its civilian industries and cities. A **first-strike capability** defines the state's capacity to launch an initial attack. In a **pre-emptive strike**, the intention is to disarm an enemy by 'getting in first', thereby reducing or removing one's vulnerability to attack. A **second-strike capability** is the capacity to survive a first attack with sufficient resources intact to be able to inflict unacceptably high damage on an aggressor. Such a capability relies on having appropriate early warning systems of an attack, and the holding of missiles in underground silos and on submarines. It is this second-strike capability which underpins the doctrine of Mutually Assured Destruction (MAD) and the concept of deterrence.

Strategic Defense Initiative *SDI*

strategic studies The academic study of the military, political, economic, social, and technological factors which affect the relations between nations. As distinct from military science, which from ancient times has concerned itself with the deployment of personnel and material in war, strategic studies looks at the continuous process of military relations between nations in war and peace, and has risen to particular prominence in the age of nuclear weapons.

Stratford-upon-Avon 52°12N 1°41W, pop (2001e) 111 500. Town in Warwickshire, C England, UK; on the R Avon, 13 km/8 mi SW of Warwick; birthplace of William Shakespeare; railway; tourism, engineering, boatbuilding, textiles; Royal Shakespeare Theatre (season Apr–Jan); Anne Hathaway's Cottage; Holy Trinity Church (where Shakespeare and his wife are buried); Shakespeare's birthday and St George's Day (23 Apr); Mop Fair (12 Oct).

Strathclyde [strathkliyd] pop (2000e) 2 293 000; area 13 537 sq km/5225 sq mi. Former region in W and C Scotland, UK, established in 1975, and replaced in 1996 by 10 local councils: Argyll and Bute, West Dunbartonshire, East Dunbartonshire, Renfrewshire, Inverclyde, City of Glasgow, East Renfrewshire, North Ayrshire, East Ayrshire, South Ayrshire.

stratification A geological term for the formation of layers in sedimentary rock in which breaks in the deposition or changes in the nature of the deposited material define visible bedding planes. The term is also used in describing sequences of lava flows.

stratigraphy A branch of geology concerned with the study of sequences of layers of rock, usually sedimentary. It aims to unravel changes in their depositional environment, and to correlate rocks of the same age in different places by their rock type and fossil content. *(see panel)*

Strato or **Straton of Lampsacus** [straytoh, strayton] (?–c.270 BC) Greek philosopher, the successor to Theophrastus as the third head of the Peripatetic School which Aristotle founded. His writings are lost, but he seems to have worked mainly to revise Aristotle's physical doctrines. He had an original theory about the void, its distribution explaining differences in the weights of objects. He also denied any role to teleological, and hence theological, explanations in nature.

stratocumulus clouds [stratohkyoomyuluhs] Low layer clouds with a distinct cumulus or rounded shape; layers of cloud are rolled into rounded forms. They are white or grey in colour, and are found at c.500–2000 m/1600–6500 ft. Cloud symbol: Sc.

stratosphere The layer of the Earth's atmosphere at a height of c.15–50 km/10–30 mi, separated from the troposphere below by the tropopause, and from the mesosphere above by the stratopause. A stable layer, unaffected by the weather, it has a gradually increasing temperature with height from about −50°C to around 0°C. It contains the ozone layer.

Stratton, Charles (Sherwood), nickname **General Tom Thumb** (1838–83) Midget showman, born in Bridgeport, Connecticut, USA. He stopped growing at six months of age, and stayed 63 cm/25 in until his teens, eventually reaching 101 cm/40 in. Barnum displayed him in his museum, from the age of five, under the name of General Tom Thumb, and he became famous throughout the USA and Europe. In 1863 his marriage

The Stratigraphical Column

The sequence of rock layers was established by stratigraphers during the 19th-c.

Holocene	Charles Lyell	1833
Pleistocene	Charles Lyell	1839
Pliocene	Charles Lyell	1833
Miocene	Charles Lyell	1833
Oligocene	Heinrich Ernst Beyrich	1854
Eocene	Charles Lyell	1833
Palaeocene	Wilhelm Philipp Schimper	1874
Cretaceous	Jesan Baptiste Julien d'Omalius d'Halloy	1822
Jurassic	Alexander von Humboldt	1799
Triassic	Friedrich August von Alberti	1834
Permian	Roderick Impey Murchison	1841
Carboniferous	William David Conybeare William Phillips	1822
Devonian	Roderick Impey Murchison Adam Sedgwick	1839
Silurian	Roderick Impey Murchison	1835
Ordovician	Charles Lapworth	1879
Cambrian	Adam Sedgwick	1835

to **Lavinia Warren** (1841–1919), also a midget, was widely publicized.

stratus clouds [stratuhs] The lowest layer of clouds in the atmosphere. They are composed of water droplets, and result in dull, overcast, and often drizzly conditions associated with the warm sector of a depression. They are found up to c.500 m/1600 ft, above which other stratiform clouds (eg altostratus, nimbostratus clouds) form.

Strauss, Johann [strows], known as **the Elder** (1804–49) Violinist, conductor, and composer, born in Vienna, Austria. He founded with Josef Lanner (1801–43) the Viennese Waltz tradition, and toured widely in Europe with his own orchestra. He composed several marches, notably the *Radetzky March* (1848), and numerous waltzes. His younger sons **Eduard Strauss** (1835–1916), and **Josef Strauss** (1827–70) were both conductors, and Josef and his eldest son **Johann** became known as composers of waltzes.

Strauss, Johann [strows], known as **the Younger** (1825–99) Violinist, conductor, and composer, born in Vienna, Austria, the eldest son of Johann Strauss (the Elder). He studied law, but turned to music, touring with his own orchestra. He wrote over 400 waltzes, notably *An der schönen blauen Donau* (1867, trans The Blue Danube) and *Geschichten aus dem Wienerwald* (1868, Tales from the Vienna Woods), as well as polkas, marches, several operettas, including *Die Fledermaus* (1874, The Bat), and a favourite concert piece, *Perpetuum Mobile*.

Strauss, Richard [strows] (1864–1949) Composer, born in Munich, SE Germany. He studied at Munich and Berlin, and conducted at Meiningen, Munich, Weimar, Bayreuth, and Berlin. He is best known for his symphonic poems, such as *Till Eulenspiegels lustige Streiche* (1894–5, Till Eulenspiegel's Merry Pranks) and *Also sprach Zarathustra* (1895–6, Thus Spoke Zarathustra), and his operas, notably *Der Rosenkavalier* (1911) and *Ariadne auf Naxos* (1912, Ariadne on Naxos). He also wrote concertos, songs, and several small-scale orchestral works.

Stravinsky, Igor (Fyodorovich) [stravinskee] (1882–1971) Composer, born near St Petersburg, NW Russia. He studied law, but turned to musical composition under Rimsky-Korsakov. He became famous with his music for the Diaghilev ballets *The Firebird* (1910), *Petrushka* (1911), and *The Rite of Spring* (1913). Essentially an experimenter, after World War 1 he devoted himself to Neoclassicism, as in his ballet *Pulcinella* (1920) based on Pergolesi, the opera-oratorio *Oedipus Rex* (1927), and the choral *Symphony of Psalms* (1930). He settled in France (1934) and finally in the USA, where he became a US citizen (1945). Other major compositions include the *Symphony in C major* (1940), the opera *The Rake's Progress* (1951), and such later work as *Requiem Canticles* (1966), in which he adopted serialism.

Straw, Jack, popular name of **John Whitaker Straw** (1946–) British statesman. He studied at Leeds University, became president of the National Union of Students (1969–71), and was called to the bar in 1972. He became a member of Islington Council (1971–8), and was elected an MP in 1979. After holding several junior posts, he became the opposition spokesman on Treasury and economic affairs (1981–3) and the environment (1983–7), then joined the shadow cabinet, and was spokesman on education (1987–92), environment and local government (1992–3), local government (1993–4), and home affairs (1994–7). He became home secretary in the 1997 Labour government, and secretary of state for foreign and commonwealth affairs in 2001.

strawberry A perennial with arching runners rooting at nodes to form new plants, native to North and South America, Europe (N as far as Ireland), and Asia; leaves in a basal rosette, with three toothed leaflets; flowers 5-petalled, white; fruit consisting of swollen, fleshy, red receptacle bearing brown, dry, achenes (the 'seeds') on the surface. The **wild strawberry** (*Fragaria vesca*) has fruits 2 cm/¾ in long. The **alpine strawberry** is a variety with few or no runners. The **garden strawberry** (*Fragaria × ananassa*) is a larger-fruited hybrid first raised in 18th-c France. The **hautbois strawberry** (*Fragaria moschata*) has purplish, musky fruits. (Genus: *Fragaria*, 15 species. Family: Rosaceae.)

strawberry finch *avadavat*

strawberry tree An evergreen shrub or small tree (*Arbutus unedo*), native to the Mediterranean and W Europe north to Ireland; leaves reddish, leathery; flowers white, bell-shaped, in drooping clusters; fruits red, spherical, covered with soft warts. (Family: Ericaceae.)

streaming Putting children into higher or lower groups according to their general ability, as opposed to teaching them in *mixed ability* (also known as 'heterogeneous') groups, or *mixed age* (also called 'vertical' or 'family') groups. If this is done on the basis of their competence in a particular subject, the process is known as **setting**. In the USA the equivalent term is **tracking**.

streamlining A condition of fluid flow such that no turbulence occurs. Streamlining refers to the design of the shape of machinery or apparatus (eg automobiles, aircraft) so that turbulence is reduced to a minimum. It may also refer to the design of fixed structures which stand in an air or liquid stream where it is desired to reduce turbulence.

stream of consciousness A term introduced by William James in his *Principles of Psychology* (1890) to describe the continuous, random activity of the mind. It has been adopted by writers and critics to refer to the techniques used to register this inner experience in writing and may be traced back to John Locke's notion of 'the association of ideas', used for a similar purpose by Sterne in *Tristram Shandy* (1760–7). Notable early exponents were James Joyce in *Ulysses* (1922) and Dorothy Richardson (1873–1957) in her 12-volume *Pilgrimage* (1915–67). Virginia Woolf (*Mrs Dalloway*, 1925; *The Waves*, 1931) and William Faulkner (*The Sound and The Fury* 1931) are two of the most distinguished exponents of the stream-of-consciousness method.

Streep, Meryl (Louise) (1949–) Actress, born in Summit, New Jersey, USA. She studied at Vassar College and Yale Drama School, making her New York stage debut in 1969, and her film debut in 1977. *Kramer vs. Kramer* (1979, Oscar) established her as a first-rank star, and she has since consistently underlined her range, showing sensitivity and a facility with accents in a series of acclaimed characterizations, including *The French Lieutenant's Woman* (1981, BAFTA best actress), *Sophie's Choice* (1982, Oscar), *Silkwood* (1983), *Out of Africa* (1985), *Cry in the Dark* (1989), and *Postcards From the Edge* (1990). Later films include *Death Becomes Her* (1993), *Bridges of Madison County* (1995), *Dancing at Lughnasa* (1998), *The Hours* (2002), and *Adaptation* (2002, Oscar nomination).

street dance Forms of competitive dance that started in the early 1970s among gangs of youths in New York City, such as the Zulu Kings (showing African links) and the Rock Steady Crew. The dance movement known as 'King Tut' uses head and arm movements typical of Egyptian dance. **Break dancing** was part of the Bronx graffiti art and rapping culture. It aims to develop control and co-ordination to perform acrobatic and athletic feats either solo, with a partner, or in a group to demonstrate superiority over rival gangs. Dancers spin the body on the head, back, and hands, performing aerial dives and fast footwork. 'The Turtle' and 'the Beetle Crawl' are typical patterns. **Body popping** is a jerky articulation of isolated parts of the body creating a chain of movement that ripples, for example, in 'the Wave'. In contrast there are also smooth gliding movements. References to birds or snakes are found. **Robotics** is a form where mime and puppet movements are important. A mechanical effect is created by tense muscles in a stiff body; the movements are small and sharp.

street hockey A form of hockey played on roller skates, popular in the USA, and now becoming so in the UK. It is so named because children used to play on the street, but it is now generally played on enclosed areas, such as playgrounds.

Street-Porter, Janet (1946–) British television executive, presenter, and journalist. A columnist and fashion writer for leading magazines and newspapers, she entered independent television in 1975 as a presenter, moving on to devise such programmes as *Get Fresh* for ITV and *Bliss* and *Network 7* for Channel 4. She joined the BBC as head of Youth and Entertainment Features (1988–94) and was appointed managing director of the cable channel Live TV for the Mirror Group (1994–5). In 1996 she became director and co-founder of Screaming Productions, and was appointed editor of the *Independent on Sunday* (1999–2001), becoming its editor-at-large in 2001. She received the BAFTA Award for originality in 1988.

Strehler, Giorgio [**stray**ler] (1921–97) Theatre director, born in Trieste, NE Italy. A pioneer and figurehead in post-World War 2 theatre, he became artistic director of Milan's Piccolo Teatro, which he established with Paolo Grassi in 1947, and a leading force in the Theatre de l'Europe (a united European venture). Notable among more than 200 productions are his revisions of plays by Goldoni and Shakespeare, and his 'dialectical' renderings of Brecht.

Streicher, Julius [**shtriy**kher] (1885–1946) Nazi journalist, and politician born in Fleinhausen, SC Germany. He was associated with Hitler in the early days of Nazism, founding the Nuremberg branch of the party, taking part in the 1923 Munich putsch. A ruthless persecutor of the Jews, he incited anti-Semitism through the newspaper *Der Stürmer*, which he founded and edited (1923–45). He was hanged at Nuremberg as a war criminal.

Streisand, Barbra [**striy**sand], originally **Barbara Joan Streisand** (1942–) Singer, actress, and director, born in New York City, USA. Starting as a nightclub singer, stage and television appearances brought her the lead in the Broadway show *Funny Girl* (1964), which she repeated in the 1968 film version to win an Oscar. Later films include *Hello Dolly* (1969), *The Way We Were* (1973), *A Star Is Born* (1976), which she produced, *Yentl* (1983), which she co-scripted, composed, directed and starred in, *Prince of Tides* (1991), which she co-produced and directed, and *The Mirror Has Two Faces* (1996). A multi-talented entertainer, her 1965 television special, *My Name is Barbra*, won five Emmy Awards, and she has been the recipient of numerous Grammy Awards, including three as best female vocalist (1964, 1965, 1978). Later albums include *Concert Highlights* (1995) and *Higher Ground* (1997). She has maintained parallel careers as a recording artist and film actress.

strength (physics) *tensile strength*

Streptococcus [streptoh**ko**kus] A spherical to ovoid bacterium which occurs in chains. It tolerates oxygen, but does not use it in metabolism. Some species are useful in dairy fermentations; others are found in animal intestinal tracts and may be disease-causing. It includes the causative agents of scarlet fever and pneumonia. (Kingdom: Monera. Family: Streptococcaceae.)

streptomycin [streptom**iy**sin] An antibiotic discovered in 1944 which became the first clinically effective drug for the treatment of tuberculosis. Side-effects occur quite frequently, most commonly deafness. Although drug resistance developed during its first years of use, it is still occasionally used in a cocktail of several drugs for treating tuberculosis. It is also used in the treatment of unusual infections not responsive to safer antibiotics, such as plague.

Stresemann, Gustav [**shtray**zeman] (1878–1929) German statesman and chancellor (1923), born in Berlin, Germany. Entering the Reichstag in 1907 as a National Liberal, he became leader of the Party, and later founded and led its successor, the German People's Party. He was briefly chancellor of the new German (Weimar) Republic, then minister of foreign affairs (1923–9). He pursued a policy of conciliation, helped to negotiate the Locarno Pact (1925), and secured the entry of Germany into the League of Nations (1926). He shared the Nobel Peace Prize in 1926.

stress (accent) *accent 2*

stress (physics) A force per unit area which acts on an object, attempting to deform it. A force *F* applied along the axis of a bar of cross section *A* produces a **linear stress** of *F/A*, units Pa (pascal). Such a force is involved in attempts to pull apart layers of atoms (**tensile stress**) or to push them together (**compressive stress**). A twisting force causes **shear stress**, which tries to slide layers of atoms over one another.

stress (psychology) In psychology, effects arising when certain external circumstances (**stressors**) lead to stereotyped non-specific behaviours from a person (the **stress response**). Stressors may be physical (noise, heat) or psychological (bereavement, unemployment), but their effect depends on their interpretation by the recipient. The stress response, physiologically, consists of cortical desynchronization and release of stress hormones; behavioural symptoms include attentional selectivity, memory loss, and autonomic activity (eg sweating). Coping strategies include denial (denying that the stressing circumstances exist) and intellectualizing (giving a rational evaluation of the situation).

stress analysis A means of predicting and monitoring stress within a structure. Stress is a measure of the deforming force applied to a body. The two main types are *normal* or *direct stress* (such as pulling (tension) or pressing (compression)) and *shear*, which is a sideways stress. Stress concentrates at points where the material changes shape. The more severe the change in shape, the higher will be the stress concentration. Engineers use computers to help calculate the stresses in a particular structure under operating loads. **Photoelastic stress analysis** is a means by which the stresses can be made visible. A clear plastic model is made of the structure to be tested. Loads are applied, then the structure is viewed through polarized filters. Stress changes the photoelastic properties of the plastic, creating a pattern of coloured fringes. Maximum points of stress show up as the brightest spots in this pattern.

Stretton, Hugh (1924–) Writer and academic, born in Melbourne, Victoria, SE Australia. He studied at Oxford and Princeton universities, became a fellow of Balliol College, Oxford (1948–54), and held teaching posts in history (1954–68) and economics (1968–89, then visiting fellow) at the University of Adelaide. His books include *The Political Sciences* (1969), *Ideas for Australian Cities* (1970), and *Political Essays* (1987). An important social theorist with a strong concern for social justice, he was one of the first people to look at the problems of urban Australia, and has criticized many of the trends in contemporary Australian society.

strict liability A legal principle found, in certain circumstances, in both criminal and civil law which places liability for an act or occurrence and its consequences on the person actually responsible for the act, despite that person having no wilful intent to commit the act, nor being reckless or even negligent in relation to the act's occurrence; sometimes termed **absolute liability**. In criminal law, strict liability is normally only found in regulatory offences, such as food hygiene regulations and road traffic offences, and is imposed by statute. Normally, the penalty for a strict liability crime is a fine. Where strict liability exists in tort (or delict), unless the person can rely on certain very limited defences, he or she will be liable for all the injury or damage directly consequent to the act; for example, a pharmacist who honestly and without negligence supplied drugs on a forged prescription has been convicted.

strike (economics) A form of industrial action, where a group of workers stop work in protest at some action by their employer, or because of a failure of collective bargaining to achieve the desired results. An **official strike** is one which has been formally agreed by a majority of members of the union, whereas an **unofficial strike** occurs where action has been taken by employees without the formal support of the union, as set out in its constitution. Since the passing of the Trade Union Act (1984), unions in the UK have to hold a secret ballot of members before strike action is formally declared.

strike (geology) *dip and strike*

Strindberg, (Johan) August (1849–1912) Playwright, born in Stockholm, Sweden. He studied at Uppsala, and settled in Stockholm as a writer. He first achieved fame with the novel *Röda* *rummet* (1879, The Red Room), followed by several plays. He travelled in France, Switzerland, and Denmark, then published his *Giftas I* and *II* (1884–6), collections of short stories, which led to his recall to Sweden (1884) to stand trial for alleged blasphemy. His plays *Fadren* (1887, The Father) and *Fröken Julie* (1888, Miss Julie) brought him to the forefront as the exponent of naturalistic drama. Later plays were more symbolic in form and religious in theme. His final 'chamber plays' were written for the *Intimate Theatre*, which he founded in 1907.

string instrument A musical instrument in which the sound is produced by the vibrations of one or more taut strings made from gut, metal, or (more recently) nylon. The vibrations are produced either by drawing a bow across the strings, or by plucking or striking the strings. The number of strings and their tuning have varied, but the difficulty of bowing one inner string without touching its neighbours, obviated to some extent by the use of a curved bridge, means that bowed instruments have usually had fewer strings than plucked ones, and rarely more than six. The bowed string instruments of the modern orchestra – violin, viola, cello, and double bass – all have four strings (some double basses have five). Many plucked instruments are fitted with keyboards; others are played with sticks or hammers, or are plucked or strummed with fingers or plectra. The strings themselves are in some cases *stopped* (usually by pressure from the player's fingers) to produce different pitches: others are played *open* (ie unstopped). In the former case, the fingerboard is often *fretted* (ie fitted with raised strips of metal, gut, or wood) to facilitate note-finding and to produce a clear sound. A large number of non-bowed string instruments are folk instruments, the only one commonly found in the modern orchestra being the harp. Bowed string instruments such as the violin may be plucked as well, a technique known as *pizzicato*.

string quartet An ensemble of two violins, viola, and cello; also, a piece of music for such an ensemble. Since the mid-18th-c the string quartet has been regarded as the most satisfying medium for serious chamber music. The first important composer of string quartets was Haydn, who established the four-movement structure and wrote some of the earliest masterpieces in the form. The other Viennese masters, Mozart, Beethoven and Schubert, also cultivated it with particular distinction and originality; notable among later examples are those of Bartók and Shostakovitch.

stringy-bark *gum tree*

strobilus [strobiylus] A cone-shaped group of leaves or leaf-like structures bearing sporangia and found in spore-bearing vascular plants. In gymnosperms it has become the woody cone, and is still recognizable in some primitive flowering plants, such as magnolia.

strobo-flash Photographic recording of a moving object by a series of very brief exposures at regular intervals, as by sequential electronic flash lighting during the open period of the camera shutter. In cinematography, strobe-lighting with electronic flash synchronized to the camera frame rate produces sharp images of fast-moving objects.

stroboscope A device for producing a succession of short pulses of light, usually using light from a mercury arc lamp. The pulse frequency is variable, with several thousand flashes per second possible. In photography, it may be used to produce several images of a moving object in a single picture.

Stroessner, Alfredo [stresner] (1912–) Paraguayan dictator, born in Encarnación, Paraguay. He took up a military career, fighting in the Chaco War, and became president in 1954. He was re-elected at regular intervals, but forced to stand down after a coup in 1989. He now lives in Brazil.

Stroheim, Erich von [strohhiym], originally **Erich Oswald Stroheim** (1886–1957) Film director and actor, born in Vienna, Austria. He served in the Austrian army, and held a variety of jobs before moving to the USA in 1914. He made his film debut in small parts in D W Griffith's films, also working as an assistant to the director in *Intolerance* (1916). His first success as film director was with *Blind Husbands* (1919), followed by the classic film *Greed* (1923), and he had box-office hits with *The Merry Widow* (1925) and *The Wedding March* (1928). Later he returned to film acting, often playing the roles of German officers, such as Rommel in *Desert Fox* (1951).

stroke A sudden interference with the blood supply to the brain which results in the death of nerve tissue followed by varying degrees of disability of speech, sight, understanding, movement, or sensation, depending on the part of the brain affected. Typically, death of nerve cells on one side of the brain leads to paralysis on the opposite side of the body. If the part of the brain that controls vital functions is affected, death is the result. It may be caused by the rupture of an artery, by the clotting of blood within an artery (*thrombosis*), or by an embolism.

Strong, Sir Roy (Colin) (1935–) Art historian and museum director, born in London, UK. He studied at Queen Mary College, London, and at the Warburg Institute, and became assistant keeper at the National Portrait Gallery, London in 1959, and its director in 1967. He was director of the Victoria and Albert Museum (1974–87), has produced numerous books, and wrote and presented the BBC television series *Royal Gardens* (1992). He was knighted in 1982.

strong interaction The strong short-range force binding together protons and neutrons in atomic nuclei, and quarks in protons and neutrons; also called **strong nuclear force**. It is independent of and stronger than electromagnetic force, and governs nuclear fission, fusion, and alpha decay. The widely accepted theory of strong force is quantum chromodynamics.

strong nuclear force *strong interaction*

strontium Sr, element 38, melting point 769°C. A very reactive metal, similar to calcium, both being alkaline earth elements. Not found uncombined, its main sources are the sulphate and the carbonate, $SrSO_4$ and $SrCO_3$. Its main importance is that it will replace calcium in most crystals, and this is particularly serious since one isotope, strontium-90, is an important product of nuclear fission, with a half-life of 28 years.

structuralism A theory which attempts to define the general properties of cultural systems, including language, mythology, art, and social organization; the approach derives from the work of the Swiss linguist Ferdinand de Saussure and the French anthropologist Claude Lévi-Strauss. The fundamental thesis is that individual terms or phenomena can be understood only in relationship to other elements of the same system, and that each system is built up using a limited set of contrasts or oppositions. Some structuralists believe that this reflects innate characteristics of the human mind, while others believe that the repetitive form taken by cultural structures has to do with the constraints imposed upon any medium of communication, which has to encode, decode, and transmit messages. The impact of structuralism on literary criticism has been especially significant, since by redefining the relationship between language and world as cultural rather than natural, structuralism undermines traditional conceptions of meaning, and (as Roland Barthes has shown) exposes the ideology built into our assumptions and values.

Structured Query Language (SQL) A query language, developed by IBM, which has now become an international standard for framing queries to a relational database. The language has been extended to incorporate the definition of a database structure.

structured systems design methodology A set of techniques and formal procedures for analyzing some aspect of an organization's information processing, and designing a new computer-based system to take its place. In the UK a common structured design methodology is known as Information Engineering. Another is Structured Systems Analysis and Design Methodology (SSADM), an approach developed by the UK government's Central Computing and Telecommunications Agency for use in the development of new computer-based systems in government departments.

structure plan A requirement of UK planning law. Each planning authority has to produce a structure plan which is approved by the secretary of state for the environment. It forms the basis for policies of development (eg land use, traffic management) in the authority's area. Development proposals for farming and forestry are not included. Once approved, a plan may be renewed after five years, but most last for longer.

Struve [shtroovuh] A distinguished astronomical dynasty. **Friedrich Georg Wilhelm von Struve** (1793–1864), born in Germany, became director of the Dorpat Observatory, Estonia, in 1818; his son, **Otto W Struve** (1819–1905) became director of Pulkova Observatory in 1861. The latter's elder son, **Karl Hermann Struve** (1854–1920) became director of the Berlin Observatory in 1904, while his younger son, **Gustav Wilhelm Ludwig Struve** (1858–1920) became director of Kharkov Observatory in 1894. The latter's son, **Otto Struve** (1897–1963) fought with the Imperial Russian army, and emigrated to the USA in 1921, becoming a US citizen. He founded then directed the McDonald Observatory (1939–47), and became the first director of the US National Radio Astronomy Observatory (1959–62). Members of four generations of the family received the gold medal of the Royal Astronomical Society, a feat unique in the history of astronomy.

strychnine A poisonous alkaloid present in members of the genus *Strychnos*, thorny trees or climbing shrubs with hook-like tendrils, native to the tropics. *Strychnos nux vomica* was introduced into Germany in the 16th-c as a rat poison (and is still used for this purpose). Although strychnine became widely used in medicine in the 18th-c, it has no justifiable clinical use. Accidental poisonings occasionally occur; death results from asphyxia. Strychnine has been used by drug dealers to bulk out supplies of heroin, since both drugs are white powders that share a similar bitter taste. (Genus: *Strychnos*, 200 species. Family: Loganiaceae.)

Stuart (Australia) *Alice Springs*

Stuart or **Stewart, Prince Charles Edward (Louis Philip Casimir),** known as **the Young Pretender** and **Bonnie Prince Charlie** (1720–88) Claimant to the British crown, born in Rome, Italy, the son of James Francis Edward Stuart. Educated in Rome, he became the focus of Jacobite hopes. In 1744 he went to France to head the planned invasion of England, but after the defeat of the French fleet he was unable to leave for over a year. He landed with seven followers at Eriskay in the Hebrides (Jul 1745) and raised his father's standard at Glenfinnan. The clansmen flocked to him, Edinburgh surrendered, and he kept court at Holyrood. Victorious at Prestonpans, he invaded England, but turned back at Derby for lack of evident English support, and was routed by the Duke of Cumberland at Culloden Moor (1746). The rising was ruthlessly suppressed, and he was hunted for five months. With the help of Flora Macdonald and other islanders he crossed from Benbecula to Portree, disguised as her maid. He landed in Brittany, then lived in France and Italy, where (after his father's death in 1766) he assumed the title of Charles III of Great Britain.

Stuart or **Stewart, Prince James (Francis Edward),** also known as **the Old Pretender** (1688–1766) Claimant to the British throne, born in London, UK, the only son of James II of England and his second wife, Mary of Modena. As a baby he was conveyed to St Germain, and proclaimed successor on his father's death (1701). After failing to land in Scotland in 1708, he served with the French in the Low Countries. In 1715 he landed at Peterhead during the Jacobite rising, but left Scotland some weeks later. Thereafter he lived mainly in Rome.

Stuart, Gilbert (Charles) (1755–1828) Painter, born in North Kingstown, Rhode Island, USA. He travelled to Edinburgh in 1772, returned a year later, and began to paint portraits at Newport. In 1775 he went to London, where he studied under Benjamin West and became a fashionable portrait painter in the manner of Reynolds. In 1792 he returned to America, and as the leading portraitist painted nearly 1000 portraits, including those of Washington, Jefferson, Madison, and John Adams.

Stuart, John McDouall (1815–66) Explorer, born in Dysart, Fife, E Scotland, UK. He accompanied Captain Charles Sturt's Australian expedition (1844–6), made six expeditions into the interior (1858–62), and in 1860 crossed Australia from south to north. *Mt Stuart* is named after him.

Stuarts, earlier spelled **Stewarts** A Scottish royal family, commencing with Robert II (r.1371–90), which succeeded to the English throne in 1603 with the accession of James VI and I, the cousin of Elizabeth I, and the great-grandson of Henry VIII's sister, Margaret. As English monarchs the family's fortunes were mixed. James I (1603–25) and Charles II (1649–85) were both successful politicians (although the latter spent his first 11 years as king in exile). But Charles I (1625–49) and James II (1685–8) were not, and both lost their thrones. The Stuart line ended in 1714 with the death of Queen Anne, although pretenders laid claim to the throne and invaded Britain in support of their claims as late as 1745.

Stubai Alps [shtoobiy], Ger **Stubaier Alpen** Mountain range of the E Alps in Tirol state, W Austria, rising to 3507 m/11 506 ft at Zuckerhütl; numerous glaciers.

Stubbs, George (1724–1806) Anatomist, painter, and engraver, born in Liverpool, Merseyside, NW England, UK. He studied at York, and in 1754 travelled in Italy and Morocco. In 1766 he published his monumental *Anatomy of the Horse*, illustrated by his own engravings. He was best known for his sporting pictures, and excelled in painting horses.

stucco [stukoh] A good quality plaster often used in classical architecture for low relief ornamental carvings and mouldings. It is also employed as an inexpensive render which can replace or resemble stone.

Studenica Monastery [stooduhnitsa] The most notable of the Serbian monasteries, founded in 1183 near Uscé, Serbia. The complex, a world heritage site, includes several churches noted for their mediaeval frescoes. Those which decorate the Church of the Virgin prefigure developments in Western art generally associated with late 13th-c Italy.

Students for a Democratic Society (SDS) A radical splinter group of the movement opposed to US involvement in Vietnam, founded at Columbia University, New York City, and advocating social disruption and violence. Although the movement spread to over 200 universities, it was subject to factionalism. Two of its members were given punitive sentences in the Chicago Conspiracy Trial of 1969.

study skills The ability to study effectively. Many schools and colleges offer courses in study skills. Topics covered usually include effective reading (how to skim, scan, slow down at important stages, make notes, use an index), information gathering and the proper use of library and resource centre facilities, revision techniques, and understanding one's own learning strategies.

stump-jump plough An Australian-designed plough (patented 1881) with shears that work independently of each other, allowing the cultivation of land with roots or large stones. Ordinary ploughs break under such conditions. The stump-jump plough was used to open up the mallee lands of SE Australia.

stupa [stoopa] An Indian cairn or mound originally constructed over the ashes of an emperor or some other great person, such as the Buddha. Later they were used to house the ashes of Buddhist monks and holy relics.

sturgeon Any of a group of large primitive fish found in fresh and marine waters of the N hemisphere; body elongate, armed with rows of heavy bony scales; head tapering, underside of mouth with long barbels; tail asymmetrical, the upper lobe long; body length 1–5 m/3–16 ft; several species support important commercial fisheries; eggs sold as caviar; danger of commercial extinction in the Caspian region, due to poaching. (Family: *Acipenseridae*, 4 genera, 25 species.)

Sturluson, Snorri [sturluson] (1179–1241) Icelandic poet, statesman, and historian. In 1215 he was elected law-speaker of the island, but after becoming involved in a plan for Norway to rule Iceland, he incurred the ill-will of the Norwegian king, Haakon

IV (reigned 1217–63), who had him murdered. His main works were the *Prose Edda*, a literary fund of ancient Icelandic saga and mythology, and *Heimskringla* (The Circle of the World), a series of sagas of the Norwegian kings down to 1177.

Sturm und Drang **[shtoorm unt drang]** (Ger 'storm and stress') A revolutionary literary movement in late-18th-c Germany, which rejected classical values in favour of subjective feeling and artistic creativity. An important tributary of the Romantic movement, it influenced Goethe, Schiller, and Herder.

Sturt, Charles (1795–1869) Explorer, born in Bengal, India. He went as an army captain to Australia, and headed three important expeditions (1828–45), discovering the Darling (1828) and the lower Murray Rivers (1830). Blinded by hardship and exposure, he received in 1851 a pension from the first South Australian parliament.

stuttering A disorder of fluency in the use of language; also called **stammering**. There is difficulty in controlling the rhythm and timing of speech, and a failure to communicate easily, rapidly, and continuously. Individual sounds may be abnormally repeated, lengthened, or fail to be released. Symptoms range from mild to severe. The cause is unknown, but several physiological, genetic, and psychological factors have been implicated. A large number of treatments are available (some of which, often advertised in the popular press, can make exaggerated claims for success). Approaches used in speech therapy include the teaching of new techniques of speech production (eg slowed speech), the use of acoustic devices to be worn by the stutterer to facilitate fluent speech, and the training of new attitudes to the task of becoming part of the everyday speech community.

Stuttgart **[shtutgah(r)t]** 48°47N 9°12E, pop (2000e) 588 000. Capital of Baden-Württemberg province, SW Germany; on the R Neckar, 61 km/38 mi SE of Karlsruhe; founded, 10th-c; former capital of the kingdom of Württemberg; former seat of the Reichstag National Assembly; badly bombed in World War 2; railway, airport; two universities (1967); notable mineral springs; cars, electrical equipment, paint, telecommunications, engineering, precision equipment, foodstuffs, textiles, paper, publishing; major fruit and wine area; birthplace of Hegel; castle (originally 13th-c, much rebuilt), palace (18th-c), St Leonard's Church (15th-c), Stiftskirche (12th-c), Liederhall; Spring Festival (Apr), Stuttgart Ballet Week (May), Lichterfest (Jul), Cannstatt Folk Festival (Sep).

Stuyvesant, Peter **[stiyvesant]** (1592–1672) Dutch administrator, born in Scherpenzeel, The Netherlands. He became Governor of Curaçao, and from 1646 directed the New Netherland colony. He proved a vigorous but arbitrary ruler, a rigid sabbatarian, and an opponent of political and religious freedom, but did much for the commercial prosperity of New Amsterdam until his reluctant surrender to the English in 1664.

stye A localized infection in a gland or around a hair follicle in the eyelid. It causes a small, painful swelling in the eyelid, and is best treated by an appropriate antibiotic.

style (botany) In flowering plants, the upper part of the carpel, separating the ovary and stigma. It may be elongated in order to better present the stigma to receive pollen. In more primitive flowers the styles (like the carpels) are generally separate; in more advanced flowers they are often fused. It sometimes persists after fertilization, and aids in seed dispersal, as with the plume-like styles of clematis, which catch the wind.

stylistics The systematic study of style, using the principles and procedures of linguistics. 'Style' here includes a range of senses, from the features of language which identify an individual (as in 'Shakespeare's style') to those which identify major occupational groups within a community (as in 'legal style', 'scientific style'). Stylistic studies also encompass the social role a speaker or writer is playing (eg 'being a lawyer, preacher'), the particular medium of communication selected (eg public lecture, newspaper article), and the degree of social closeness or distance between the participants (leading to differing degrees of formality or casualness in usage). In all cases, stylistics focuses upon the *choices* that are available to the language user. **Literary stylistics**, accordingly, studies the linguistic choices made by authors in the various genres of literature (novel, short story, poetry, etc). In **stylometry** or **stylostatistics**, a quantitative analysis is made of a text, to determine its statistical structure. Such studies are particularly important in plotting historical changes in style, or in investigating questions of disputed authorship.

Stylites, Simeon *Simeon Stylites, St*

stylometry *stylistics*

stylops A small parasitic insect which uses bees or other insects as host; males with fan-like hindwings and reduced forewings; females typically larva-like and wingless. (Order: Strepsiptera. Family: Stylopidae.)

Styne, Jule (1905–94) Songwriter, born in London, UK. He began composing background music for films in 1937, and wrote his first songs for the film *Hit Parade of 1941*. For three decades he wrote dozens of memorable melodies for films and Broadway musicals, among them 'Diamonds are a Girl's Best Friend' for *Gentlemen Prefer Blondes* (1949), 'Three Coins in the Fountain' (1954, Oscar), 'Everything's Coming up Roses', 'Small World', and 'Together' for *Gypsy* (1959), and 'People' and 'Don't Rain on My Parade' for *Funny Girl* (1964).

styrene C_6H_5–$CH=CH_2$, boiling point 145°C, **phenylethene** or **vinylbenzene**. A colourless liquid, which undergoes addition polymerization to a glassy resin called **polystyrene**. 'Expanded' polystyrene, made porous with trapped gas, is widely used as a thermally-insulating packing material.

styrene butadiene rubber *rubber*

Styx [stiks] In Greek mythology, a principal river of the Underworld; the name means 'hateful'. It was so terrible that even the gods in Homer swore by it. In Virgil's *Aeneid* the souls of the dead are ferried across it by Charon. It was also the name of a river in Arcadia, which passes through a gloomy gorge.

Suárez, Francisco **[swahreth]**, known as **Doctor Eximus** ('Exceptional Doctor') (1548–1617) Philosopher and theologian, born in Granada, S Spain. He entered the Society of Jesus in 1564, was ordained in 1572, taught theology at Segovia, Valladolid, Rome, Alcalá, Salamanca, and Coimbra, and is often rated as the greatest of scholastic philosophers after Aquinas. His main works were the *Disputationes metaphysicae* (1597, Metaphysical Disputations), the *Tractatus de legibus ac Deo legislatore* (1612, Treatise on Law and on God the Law-giver) which foreshadows the modern doctrine of international law, and the *Defensio fidei Catholicae* (1613, Defence of the Catholic Faith) condemning the divine-right theories of kingship of James VI and I.

subatomic particles A general term for all particles smaller than atoms. It refers to electrons, protons, and neutrons, which directly constitute atoms, and to other particles including composite particles, resonances, and fundamental particles. They are classified by mass, spin, charge, and other properties. All subatomic particles are either bosons (force particles) or fermions (matter particles).

subconscious *unconscious*

subduction zone A region in which one crustal plate of the Earth is forced down (**subducted**) beneath another, and moves down into the mantle where it is eventually assimilated. Present-day subduction zones occur around the margins of the Pacific Ocean at the sites of deep ocean trenches, and are associated with earthquake and volcanic activity and the formation of island arcs such as Japan and the Aleutian Is.

sublimation (chemistry) Passing directly from solid to vapour without an intermediate liquid phase. Substances which sublime at normal pressures include solid carbon dioxide ('dry ice') and iodine.

sublimation (psychiatry) The psychological process in which unacceptable drives and behaviours are channelled unconsciously into socially acceptable patterns of behaviour. The benefits are both the unconscious avoidance of the anxiety associated with unacceptable actions, and the positive rewards associated with socially acceptable and valued behaviour. An example would be a young man with strong aggression who takes up competitive sports (eg football or the martial arts), and succeeds in these. Society approves of his sporting prowess and he avoids unacceptable aggressive actions.

subliminal advertising Advertising designed to be imperceptible to the conscious mind of audiences. It mostly involves split-second projections of brand names or commands ('Eat Popcorn'), screened in the cinema or on television, or sound messages at frequencies beyond the range of human hearing. In the late 1950s the alleged use of such 'sub-threshold effects' for commercial ends caused alarm in the USA and UK. In particular, Vance Packard's book, *The Hidden Persuaders*, brought the issue to the notice of an anxious general public. Subliminal advertising is now banned in most countries, though its actual extent and effectiveness are still disputed.

subliminal perception Literally, perception that is below the threshold (of awareness). Evidence for subliminal perception comes from laboratory experiments where the presence of a briefly presented stimulus, which an observer is unable to report, can influence the speed or accuracy of processing of subsequent stimuli.

submachine-gun A small-arm midway in size between a pistol and a rifle, capable of firing a burst of automatic fire. First developed practically around 1918, it was used extensively during World War 2 (the British Sten gun and German MP 38 being typical weapons), but it has been replaced in most modern armies by the assault rifle.

submarine A vessel capable of remaining submerged for a considerable period of time. Submarines as originally conceived were strictly speaking 'submersibles'; a World War 2 U-boat, for example, would typically have spent 85% of her time on the surface. The longest known submerged patrol was steamed in 1982–3 by HM Submarine *Warspite* lasting 111 days in the S Atlantic, during which she covered 30 804 nautical miles (57 085 km). Such endurance comes from the installation of a nuclear reactor which supplies the heat to produce steam for the turbines. Since the advent of nuclear-armed, submarine-launched ballistic missiles, such as Polaris and Trident, submarines have become the most powerfully armed and strategically important of all warships, playing two distinct roles. They can act as an attack vessel, armed with torpedoes and missiles to attack other ships (including other submarines) at sea; and they can act as a floating platform for long-range missiles. **Ballistic missile submarines** (SSBNs) carrying submarine-launched ballistic missiles (SLBMs), are now exclusively nuclear-powered, and are operated by the US, Russian, British, French, and Chinese navies.

submarine canyon An underwater canyon which typically cuts the continental margin, and may lead across the continental rise as far as the abyssal plains. These canyons serve as channels for the transport of shallow water sediments from the continental shelf to the deep sea. Turbidity currents are suspected as the most likely mechanisms for the transportation of these sediments.

Subotica [soobotitsa], Hung **Szabadka** 46°04N 19°41E, pop (2000e) 101 000. Largest town in the autonomous province of Vojvodina, NW Serbia; railway; fruit trade, foodstuffs, chemicals; Palic health resort nearby; Duzijanca traditional harvest festival (Jul).

subpoena [suhpeena] (Lat 'under penalty') An order to a person to attend court to give evidence (*subpoena ad testificandum*) or produce relevant documents (*subpoena duces tecum*). Failure to comply with the order is a contempt of court. It is used in a number of jurisdictions, but not in Scots law. Subpoenas to attend court in England and Wales have been largely supplanted by summonses.

subsistence agriculture A form of farming where the land provides most of the necessities of life – food, fuel, and shelter. Tools and other items which cannot be generated in this way are acquired through trading surplus commodities.

substance P A chemical substance (a peptide) found throughout the body, particularly high concentrations occurring in the gut, spinal cord, and brain. Its physiological role is unclear: it possibly acts as a neurotransmitter for neurones conveying sensory information from peripheral pain receptors to the central nervous system.

substitution reaction A chemical reaction in which one group in a molecule is replaced by another. A typical example is the formation of an alcohol from an alkyl halide: $OH^- + RCl \rightarrow ROH + Cl^-$

succession (botany) *vegetation succession*

succinic acid [suhksinik] $HOOC–CH_2–CH_2–COOH$, IUPAC **butanedioic acid**, melting point 188°C. A colourless solid, occurring in sugar cane, and also formed during fermentation. Important derivatives include the cyclic anhydride, used in resins, and the imide, used as a disinfectant.

Succoth *Sukkoth*

succubus [suhkyubuhs] *incubus*

succulent A plant in which the stems and leaves are fleshy and swollen with water-storage tissues; common in arid regions and other places where water is present, but not easily available. Succulents often have adaptations to reduce water-loss, such as thick, waxy cuticles and reduced or inrolled leaves. Examples are cacti, houseleeks, and many bromeliads.

Suchow *Suzhou*

sucker A shoot growing from a root, usually at some distance from the parent and eventually developing its own root system and becoming independent of the parent plant. Many trees produce suckers freely, and can eventually form small groves in this way.

sucking fish *remora*

Suckling, Sir John (1609–41) Poet and playwright, born in Whitton, Middlesex, SE England, UK. He studied at Cambridge, then lived splendidly at court, but involvement in political intrigue on behalf of the Royalist party led him to flee the country, and he died (it is said by Aubrey, by his own hand) in Paris. His plays (such as *Aglaura*, 1637) are austere, but his lyrics, influenced by Donne and Herbert, are highly acclaimed. They were published in *Fragmenta aurea* (1646). Contemporary sources describe him as a wit and gamester, and he is credited with having invented the game of cribbage.

Sucre [sookray], originally **Charcas**, also known as **Ciudad Blanca** 19°05S 65°15W, pop (2000e) 133 100. Judicial and legal capital of Bolivia, and capital of Chuquisaca department; altitude 2790 m/9153 ft; founded 1538; revolutionary centre against Spain in 18th-c; airfield; railway; university (1624); oil refining, cement, agricultural centre; colonial Legislative Palace (Casa de Libertad, where Declaration of Independence signed), Santo Domingo (Palace of Justice), 17th-c cathedral and museum, Churches of San Miguel and San Francisco.

Sucre, Antonio José de [sookray] (1793–1830) South American soldier–patriot, born in Cumaná, Venezuela. He was Bolívar's lieutenant, defeated the Spaniards at Ayacucho (1824), and became the first president (1826) of Bolivia. He resigned in 1828, took service with Colombia, and won the Battle of Tarqui (1829) against Peru. He was assassinated near Paslò.

sucrose [sookrohs] $C_{12}H_{22}O_{11}$, the best-known sugar – a disaccharide made up of a glucose molecule joined to a fructose molecule. It is digested in the small intestine to produce equal proportions of the monosaccharides glucose and fructose, which are then absorbed. Sucrose is the sugar of table sugar, icing sugar, and castor sugar, and may be obtained from either sugar beet or sugar cane. Western diets derive c.17% of their energy from sucrose. While expert committees disagree about a recommended value for daily intakes of sugar for adults, there is general agreement that for children exposure to frequent intakes of sugar predisposes to dental caries.

Sudan *p.1477*

Sudbury 46°30N 81°01W, pop (2000e) 104 000. Town in N Ontario, Canada; developed after arrival of railway, 1883; city, 1930; railway; university (1960); mining (nickel, copper, cobalt,

Sudan

□ International Airport — — Border in dispute

[soodan], official name **Republic of Sudan**, Arabic **Jamhuryat es-Sudan**

Local name As-Sūdān (Arabic)

Timezone GMT +2

Area 2 505 870 km²/967 243 sq mi

Population total (2002e) 37 090 000

Status Republic

Date of independence 1956

Capital Khartoum

Languages Arabic (official), local languages, including Darfurian, Nilotic, and Nilo-Hamitic, are also spoken

Ethnic groups Black (52%), Arab (39%), Beja (6%)

Religions Muslim (Sunni 70%), traditional animist beliefs (20%), Christian (5%)

Physical features Largest country on the African continent, astride the middle reaches of the R Nile; E edge formed by Nubian Highlands and an escarpment rising c.2000 m/6500 ft on the Red Sea; Imatong Mts (S) rise to 3187 m/10 456 ft at Kinyeti, highest point in Sudan; Darfur Massif in the W; White Nile flows N to meet the Blue Nile at Khartoum.

Climate Tropical, continental; desert conditions in NW, with temperatures rarely falling below 24°C; hottest months (Jul–Aug); sandstorms common; average annual temperature 23°C (Jan), 32°C (Jul) in Khartoum; average annual rainfall 157 mm/6·2 in.

Currency Sudanese dinar = 100 piastres

Economy Dominated by agriculture (employs c.75% of population); commercial farming (N) and livestock farming (S); large-scale irrigation schemes, fed by dams; major famines, especially 1984–5, 1990–1; gum arabic (80% of world supply); reserves of copper, lead, iron ore, chromite, manganese, gold; development hindered by poor transport system.

GDP (2002e) $52·9 bn, per capita $1400

Human Development Index (2002) 0·499

History Christianized in 6th-c; Muslim conversion from 13th–c; Egyptian control of N Sudan, early 19th-c; Mahdi unified W and C tribes in a revolution, 1881; fall of Khartoum, 1885; combined British-Egyptian offensive, 1898, leading to a jointly administered condominium; independence, 1956; period of military rule following coup in 1985; drought and N-S rivalry have contributed to years of instability and several coups; a transitional constitution of 1987 provided for a President, Prime Minister, Council of Ministers, and a Legislative Assembly; military coup, 1989, suspended constitution and dissolved National Assembly which was replaced by a Revolutionary Command Council; subsequent civil war between government and rebel Sudanese People's Liberation Army (SPLM); national constitutional conference to discuss reform, 1992; peace talks begun, 1993; new constitution, 1998; peace talks with SPLM continuing into 2004.

Chief of State

1956–8 *Council of State*
1958–64 Ibrahim Abboud
1964–5 *Council of Sovereignty*
1965–9 Ismail al-Azhari
1969–85 (Nemery) Gaafar Mohamad al-Nimeiri (President from 1971)

Chairman – Transitional Military Council

1985–6 Abd al-Rahman Siwar al-Dahab

Chairman – Supreme Council

1986–9 Ahmad al-Mirghani
1989–93 Omar Hassan Ahmed al-Bashir

Head of State/Government

1993– Omar Hassan Ahmad al-Bashir

platinum, palladium), smelting, refining, pulp, paper, tourism, fishing, hunting; Canada Centennial Numismatic Park.

sudden infant death syndrome (SIDS) The sudden, unexpected death of an infant for which no adequate cause can be found on clinical or post-mortem examination; also known as **cot death**. Typically an apparently healthy infant is put to bed in the evening and is found to be dead in the night or early morning. Several causes may be responsible, but all remain speculative. Current theories include the cessation of breathing (*apnoea*) as a result of an unusually prolonged spell of respiratory irregularity that to lesser degrees affects many newborn or immature infants; an exaggerated neural response to the drawing up of a small amount of stomach contents into the respiratory tract; obstruction to the airways as a result of temporary closure of the structures below the pharynx; increased vulnerability to toxins of respiratory bacteria that are normally harmless; the presence of harmful chemicals in mattresses; and disturbance of body temperature control related to a cold environment or to excessive covering with bedding. SIDS is more common among infants of parents who smoke. The incidence has decreased since 1992, when parents were advised to put infants to sleep on their back or side rather than on their stomach.

Sudeten or **Sudetenland** [soodaytenland] Mountainous territory on Polish–Czech border, comprising the Sudetic Mts rising to 1603 m/5259 ft at Sněžka; during World War 2, the name also applied to the parts of Bohemia and Moravia invaded by German-speaking people; occupied by Germany in 1938, and restored to Czechoslovakia in 1945.

Sue, Eugène [sü], pseudonym of **Marie Joseph Sue** (1804–57) Novelist, born in Paris, France. He served as a surgeon in Spain (1823) and at Navarino Bay (1827) and wrote a vast number of Byronic novels, idealizing the poor, such as *Les Mystères de Paris* (1843, The Mysteries of Paris), which was a major influence on Hugo. A republican deputy, he was driven into exile in 1851.

Sue Ryder Homes *Cheshire, Leonard*

Suetonius [swetohnius], in full **Gaius Suetonius Tranquillus** (75–160) Roman biographer and antiquarian. He became Hadrian's secretary, a post he lost when he was compromised in a court intrigue. He then devoted himself to writing, his best-known work being *De vita Caesarum* (The Lives of the [First

Twelve] Caesars), remarkable for its terseness, elegance, and impartiality. Only fragments survive of his other writings.

Suez [sooiz], Arabic **al-Suweis** 29°59N 32°33E, pop (2000e) 469 800. Seaport capital of Suez governorate, E Egypt; on Gulf of Suez, Red Sea, at S end of Suez Canal, 129 km/80 mi E of Cairo; railway; oil refining and storage, fertilizers, shipping services.

Suez Canal *see panel*

Suez Crisis A political crisis focused on the Suez Canal in 1956. When Egypt's President Nasser bought armaments from the Soviet block, the USA withdrew its support for the building of the Aswan Dam, whose financing collapsed. To remedy this, Nasser nationalized the Suez Canal, so that Canal revenues might pay for the Dam. Given the strategic interests of Britain and France in the Canal, they sought first to overturn Nasser's decision by appeal to the International Court, which instead confirmed the legality of the Egyptian government's move; thereafter, Britain and France worked to overthrow Nasser himself. Excluding the USA from their planning, they colluded with Israel to provoke a conflict which would serve as a pretext for Anglo-French intervention. Israel invaded the Sinai in October 1956, followed by French and British forces in the cities of the Canal Zone. Diplomatic action by the USA and the USSR forced Britain and France to withdraw, and Israel to relinquish the Sinai.

suffix *affix*

Suffolk [suhfuhk] pop (2001e) 668 500; area 3797 sq km/1466 sq mi. County of E England, UK; bounded E by the North Sea; county town, Ipswich; chief towns include Lowestoft, Felixstowe, Bury St Edmunds; engineering, fishing, high technology, agriculture (wheat, barley, sugar beet), food processing, horse breeding; Sizewell, Sutton Hoo ship burial.

Suffolk punch A heavy breed of horse developed in England; height, 16 hands/1·6 m/5 ft 4 in; plain brown; large powerful body with short, strong legs; traditionally a popular farm horse.

suffragette A woman identified with the late 19th–early 20th-c movement in the UK and USA to secure voting rights for women. The vote was won after the end of World War 1 in 1918, though it was limited to those women of 30 years of age or over. There were many men and women opponents of female suffrage, and in England it was not until 1929 that women over 21 achieved the right to vote.

Sufism Islamic mysticism which represents a move away from the legalistic approach in Islam to a more personal relationship with God. The word comes from Arabic *suf* 'wool', because the early story-tellers from whom Sufism evolved wore woollen garments. Sufis aim to lose themselves in the ultimate reality of the Divinity by a variety of mystical paths, including the constant repetition of the *dhikr* or 'mentioning (of God)'.

Sugar Act (1764) The first piece in the programme of imperial reform that led to American independence. It attempted for the first time to raise colonial revenue without reference to the colonial assemblies. The colonials responded with protest, but not outright resistance, and the Act was sporadically enforced until the complete breakdown of British–American relations.

sugar beet *beet*

sugar cane A bamboo-like grass but with soft canes 3–8 m/10–26 ft high, 3·5–5 cm/$1\frac{1}{2}$–2 in diameter; white to yellowish-green, red, or purplish; cultivated in tropical and sub-tropical environments; long thought to be sterile, but now known to be fertile, with several vigorous high-yielding hybrids available. The cane is cut, chopped, and soaked in water to extract the sugar (*sucrose*); the sugary solution is filtered, clarified, and dried. As the drying process develops, sucrose crystallizes out, leaving *molasses* behind. The raw sugar is brown, and can be further purified to yield white sugar. Contrary to popular belief, there are no nutritional differences between white and brown sugar. (*Saccharum officinarum*. Family: Gramineae.)

sugar palm A tree growing to 12 m/40 ft, native to Malaysia (*Arenga sacchifera*); leaves 1–1·5 m/$3\frac{1}{4}$–5 ft, feathery, silver beneath; also called **gomuti palm**. When mature, inflorescences form successively from the tip to the base of the trunk, which dies in corresponding stages. Sugar is obtained from the copious sap collected when the young inflorescences are cut. (Family: Palmae.)

sugars A group of sweet-tasting carbohydrates, chemically classified into single-unit (*monosaccharide*) and double-unit (*disaccharide*) types. Most people take *sugar* to mean *sucrose*; however, many other sugars are present in our diet, although in smaller amounts than sucrose. These include *lactose*, the sugar of milk, and free *glucose* and *fructose* in fruits and honey. Free glucose is only half as sweet as sucrose, while free fructose is about 70% more sweet.

Suharto [soohah(r)toh] (1921–) Indonesian soldier, statesman, and president (1968–98), born in Kemusu, Java. As is common in Java, he used only his given name. Educated for service in the Dutch colonial army, in 1943 he was given command of the Japanese-sponsored Indonesian army, and in 1965 he became Indonesia's chief of the army staff. The policies of President Sukarno led to a threat of civil war in 1965 and 1966, and Suharto assumed executive power in 1967, ordering the mass arrest and internment of alleged Communists. He became titular president in 1968, thereafter being re-elected to office every five years, but was forced to step down in 1998 following an economic crisis and civil disturbance.

suicide The act of deliberate self-destruction. Up to 1961 in the UK, attempted suicide was considered to be a crime, and it is still illegal in some US states. Since then it has been accepted as

Suez Canal

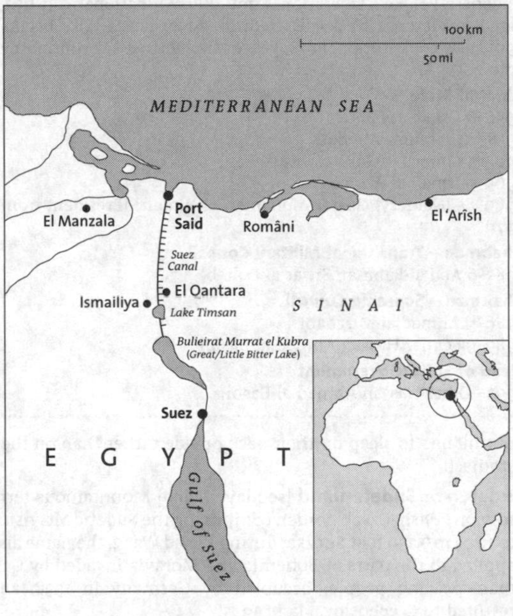

Canal connecting the Mediterranean and Red Seas, in NE Egypt; built by Ferdinand de Lesseps, 1859–69; length 184 km/114 mi, including 11 km/7 mi of approaches to Suez (S end) and Port Said (N end); minimum width, 60 m/197 ft; minimum draught, 16 m/52 ft; passes through L Timsah, and the Great and Little Bitter Lakes; by 1882 Convention, open to vessels of any nation (except in wartime); controlled by British, 1882–1956; nationalized by Egypt, 1956; blocked by Egypt during war with Israel, 1967; re-opened, 1975; a major international waterway, and a substantial Egyptian economic asset.

a terminal symptom of a mental illness or abnormal mental state. It is a recognized complication of severe depressive illness or psychosis in which the individual suffers from inconsolable moods of despair, guilt, and self-blame. In other cases death results unintentionally from a conscious attempt to manipulate a situation, or from an impulse to obtain redress of circumstances which cause distress. Such individuals do not wish to die, but have misjudged the full effect of the act or of the lack of help. This especially applies to the act of self-poisoning, where the majority of persons do not die, and usually live to regret their attempt. Such acts, sometimes referred to as **parasuicide**, do however increase the risk of later successful suicide. In some societies, suicide in certain circumstances is socially acceptable (eg as an obligation following the death of a master or a spouse) and in ancient Greece and Rome, it was offered to the privileged as an alternative to execution. Recent years have seen the emergence of such groups as the Hemlock Society in the USA, and other societies which represent the 'right to die'.

Sui dynasty [swee] (581–618) A two-reign dynasty which began the second great imperial phase of Chinese history (590–907). After the post-Han (from 220) period of disunion, the crown was seized by Yang Jian, who took the reign name Wendi (590–604). He was followed by Yang Guang (Yangdi, 604–18). The Sui conquered the S and reunited China (590). They rebuilt the two Yellow River capitals Changan (Xian) and Luoyang, and built a third at Yangzhou on the Yangtze. They facilitated communication between the two great river basins by building the Grand Canal. They also improved administration, and instituted a strict legal code. The dynasty fell to Northern insurrection, and was replaced by the great Tang dynasty in 618.

suite In Baroque music, a set of dances, all in the same key, perhaps preceded by a prelude; the terms *partita* and *ordre* are also used. By c.1700 the standard dances were the allemande, courante, sarabande, and gigue, with additional dances (if any) placed between the last two. Since the 19th-c the term has been used for a sequence of separate but connected pieces (as in Holst's *The Planets*) and for an orchestral selection from an opera, ballet, or other long work.

Sukarno or **Soekarno, (Achmed)** [sukah(r)noh] (1902–70) Indonesian statesman, and first president of Indonesia (1945–66), born in Surabaya, Java. As is common in Java, he used only his given name. He formed the Indonesia National Party in 1927, was imprisoned by the Dutch in Bandung (1929–31), and lived in exile until 1942, when he was made leader during the Japanese occupation. He became president when Indonesia was granted independence in 1945. His popularity waned as the country suffered increasing internal chaos and poverty, while his government laid themselves open to charges of corruption. An abortive Communist coup (1965) led to student riots and a takeover by the army, his powers gradually devolving onto General Suharto. Sukarno finally retired in 1968.

Sukhothai [sukotiy] 17°00N 99°51E. Ancient ruined city of Thailand, 440 km/273 mi N of Bangkok; founded in the mid-13th-c when the nation of Thailand came into being; former capital of the Thai-Khmer state; now a historical park.

sukiyaki [sukeeyakee] A Japanese beef dish. Traditionally Buddhism avoided meat, but Westerners introduced meat eating after 1868, and *sukiyaki* was an adaptation to Japanese taste. Thinly sliced beef is cooked with suet in an iron pan in the middle of the table. Sauce is added, made of *shoyu*, beaten raw egg, sugar, and *mirin* (a type of sweet saké).

Sukkoth or **Succoth** [suhkohth, -koht] The Jewish Feast of Tabernacles or Booths, celebrated in September or October (15–21 Tishri) as a festival of thanksgiving. Booths, or light temporary shelters (*Sukkot*), are constructed in homes or gardens and in synagogues, in memory of the huts or tents used by the Israelites in the desert after leaving Egypt (*Ex* 13).

Sukkur [sukoor], also **Sakhar** 27°42N 68°54E, pop (2000e) 315 000. City in Sind province, Pakistan; on E bank of R Indus, 360 km/224 mi NE of Karachi; Sukkur (Lloyd) Barrage built 1928–32 (dam 58 m/190 ft high), with seven canals irrigating 18 million sq km/7 million sq mi; railway junction; textiles, vegetable oils, flour milling.

Sulaiman or **Suleyman I** [sülayman], known as **the Magnificent** (1494–1566) Ottoman Sultan (1520–66). He added to his dominions by conquest Belgrade, Budapest, Rhodes, Tabriz, Baghdad, Aden, and Algiers. His fleets dominated the Mediterranean, though he failed to capture Malta. His system of laws regulating land tenure earned him the name *Kanuni* ('lawgiver'), and he was a great patron of arts and architecture. He died during the siege of Szigeth in his war with Austria.

Sulawesi [sulawaysee] pop (2000e) 14 715 000. Island in Indonesia, off E Borneo; mountainous and forested; rice, tuna, maize, kapok, copra; nickel, coal, asphalt, mica, sulphur, salt; divided into four provinces; **Sulawesi Selatan**, **South Sulawesi**, formerly **South Celebes**, pop (2000e) 8 205 000, area 27 686 sq km/10 687 sq mi, capital Ujung Pandang; **Sulawesi Tengah**, **Central Sulawesi**, formerly **Central Celebes**, pop (2000e) 2 011 000; area 69 726 sq km/26 914 sq mi, capital Palu; **Sulawesi Tenggara**, **South-East Sulawesi**, formerly **South-East Celebes**, pop (2000e) 1 586 000, area 72 781 sq km/28 093 sq mi, capital Kendari; **Sulawesi Utara**, **North Sulawesi**, formerly **North Celebes**, pop (2000e) 2 913 000, area 19 023 sq km/7343 sq mi, capital Manado; includes the Sangir Is.

Suleyman *Sulaiman*

sulfur *sulphur*

Sulla, Lucius Cornelius, nickname **Felix** ('Lucky') (138–78 BC) Roman politician of the late Republic, whose bitter feud with Marius, begun in Africa in 107 BC during the Jugurthine War, twice plunged Rome into civil war in the 80s BC. In 88 BC he chose to lead his army against the state rather than surrender to Marius his command of the war against Mithridates, and on returning to Rome (83 BC) used his forces to defeat the Marians and secure his own (illegal) position. Appointed 'Dictator' in 82 BC, he set about reforming the state, and enacted a number of measures to boost the authority of the Senate. These did not long survive his sudden retirement in 79 BC, but his reform of criminal jurisdiction lasted into the empire.

Sullivan, Sir Arthur (Seymour) (1842–1900) Composer, born in London, UK. He studied in London and Leipzig, and became an organist in London. His association with the theatre started in 1867, and from 1871 he was known for his collaboration with W S Gilbert in such comic operas as *HMS Pinafore* (1878) and *The Pirates of Penzance* (1879). He also composed a grand opera, *Ivanhoe* (1891), cantatas, ballads, a *Te Deum*, and hymn tunes. He was knighted in 1883.

Sullivan, Jim, popular name of **James Sullivan** (1903–77) Rugby league player, born in Cardiff, S Wales, UK. He played rugby union for Cardiff before joining Wigan rugby league club in 1921. His all-time records include 2867 goals in a career, 22 in one match against Flimby and Fothergill in 1925, and 928 senior appearances. His total of 6022 points was surpassed by Neil Fox in 1978. Player-coach of Wigan in 1932, he retired in 1946, and later coached Rochdale Hornets and St Helens. He was one of the first players elected to the Rugby Hall of Fame in 1988.

Sullivan, Louis (Henry) (1856–1924) Architect, born in Boston, Massachusetts, USA. He studied in Paris and in 1886 won the New Exposition building contract (1886) with **Dankmar Adler** (1844–1900). He was one of the first to design skyscrapers, such as the Wainwright building in St Louis (1890–1). His experimental, functional skeleton constructions of skyscrapers and office blocks, particularly the Stock Exchange, Chicago, earned him the title 'the father of Modernism', and greatly influenced other architects.

Sully, Maximilien de Béthune, duc de (Duke of) [sülee] (1560–1641) Huguenot soldier, financier, and statesman who became Henry IV's chief minister, born in Rosny, NC France. He fought in the later stages of the Wars of Religion (1574–98) and was wounded at Ivry (1590). Instrumental in arranging Henry's marriage to Marie de Médicis (1600), he became the king's trusted counsellor. His major achievement was the restoration of the economy after the civil wars. In 1606 he was created duke, but after Henry's assassination (1610) was forced to retire to his estates.

Sully-Prudhomme [sülee prüdom], pseudonym of **René François Armand Prudhomme** (1839–1907) Poet, born in Paris, France. He studied science, then developed an interest in philosophy which underlies most of his poetical works. His early *Stances et poèmes* (1865) was widely praised, and among his later important works were the didactic poems *La Justice* (1878, Justice) and *Le Bonheur* (1888, Happiness). A leader of the Parnassian movement, which tried to restore elegance and control to poetry in reaction against Romanticism, he received the first Nobel Prize for Literature in 1901.

sulphonamides / sulfonamides [suhlfonamiydz] The first drugs to be used for the prevention and cure of bacterial infections in humans; their introduction in the late 1930s resulted in a sharp decline in deaths from infectious diseases. The therapeutic value of Prontosil (a dye), the first of many sulphonamides, was discovered in 1938 by Gerhard Domagk. Some resistance developed through overuse (eg the mass prophylactic use of sulphadiazine in military personnel during World War 2), and they were generally superseded by penicillin; but they are still important in the treatment of some infections.

sulphur / sulfur S, element 16, a non-metal occurring in nature in yellow molecular crystals of S_8, also called **brimstone**. The molecular structure is that of a puckered ring. The solid melts at 113°C and boils at 440°C. The viscosity of liquid sulphur increases on heating, as the rings are converted to chains of indefinite length. Gaseous sulphur above the boiling point contains substantial S_2, analogous to O_2. Many other different forms have been identified. In addition to the free element, sulphur is also recovered from many sulphide ores. It shows a great variety of oxidation states, the most common being −2, +4, and +6, giving rise to compounds called **sulphides**, **sulphites**, and **sulphates**. By far the most important use is oxidation to sulphuric acid.

sulphur-bottom whale *blue whale*

sulphuric / sulfuric acid H_2SO_4, boiling point 330°C. A strong dibasic acid, a colourless oily liquid, formerly known as **oil of vitriol** or simply **vitriol**. It is one of the most important industrial chemicals, produced by the catalytic oxidation of sulphur dioxide, produced by the oxidation of sulphur or by the roasting of sulphide ores. It is used in the production of almost all other acids, and in the manufacture of fertilizers, fabrics, dyestuffs, and detergents.

Sulston, Sir John E (1942–) British microbiologist. He studied at the University of Cambridge, later joining the Sanger Centre in Cambridge. He shared the 2002 Nobel Prize for Physiology or Medicine for discoveries concerning the genetic regulation of organ development and programmed cell death. He was knighted in 2001.

sultan A sovereign of a Muslim state. From the 11th-c, the title was increasingly used by local Islamic rulers throughout the Middle East and beyond. The first sultan of the Ottoman Empire was Osman I (r.1299–1326), and the title continued to be used in Turkey until 1922. Famous Indian sultanates between the 13th-c and 16th-c include those of Delhi (1206–1526), Bengal (1336–1576), Kashmir (1346–1589), Gujarat (1391–1583), Jaunpur (1394–1479), Malwa (1401–1526), and Khandesh (1370–1526). Other areas which recognized sultanates include Egypt, Morocco, the Philippines, Indonesia, Malaysia (former Malay States, notably Kedah, Kelantan, Malacca, Johore, Pahang, Perak, Selangor, and Trengganu), Yemen (to 1967), the Maldives (to 1968), Nigeria (Sokoto, 1804–1981), and Tanzania (to 1964). The title is still used in some countries, such as Oman and Brunei.

sumac or **sumach** [soomak] Any of several species of a genus which includes poison ivy and the turpentine tree, many causing skin damage or dermatitis. The best known is **stag's horn sumac** (*Rhus typhina*), a suckering shrub native to North America; twigs velvety-hairy; leaves pinnate; flowers in conical clusters, males green, females reddish. (Genus: *Rhus*. Family: Anacardiaceae.)

Sumatra [sumahtra], Indonesian **Sumatera** pop (2000e) 43 369 000; area 473 606 sq km/182 812 sq mi. Island in W Indonesia, S of the Malay Peninsula; 1760 km/1094 mi long and 400 km/250 mi wide; includes the Riau archipelago (E) and the Mentawi Is (W); centre of Buddhist kingdom of Srivijaya, 7th–13th-c; possibly visited by Marco Polo, 13th-c; separatist movement followed Indonesian independence, 1949; growing civil unrest in Aceh province in support of independence, 1999; major cities include Medan, Jambi, Padang, Pekanbaru, Banda Aceh; Bukit Barisan range (W) rises to 3805 m/12 483 ft at Gunung Kerinci; Batanghari, longest river in Sumatra; swamp and marshland in SE (a third of the island); flash floods cause devastation and casualties in northern Medan area (Nov 2003); oil, tin, bauxite, gold, natural gas; rubber, coffee, tea, pepper.

Sumer [soomer] The name given to the part of Lower Mesopotamia between Babylon and the Persian Gulf. It is the place where the world's first urban civilization evolved; among the greatest of Sumerian city-states were Eridu, Ur, and Uruk. Surviving art forms date from c.2500 BC, and include the stone statues of Gudea and many coloured bas-reliefs.

Sumerian and Assyrian architecture One of the earliest instances of architecture, dating from the 4th millennium BC, located on the Euphrates delta on the Persian Gulf. It is characterized by the use of brick arches, domes, and vaults, typically decorated with a surface geometrical pattern of red, black, and brown mosaics, as at the ziggurat temple of Warka (c.2900–2340 BC). It was later adapted by the Assyrians in N Mesopotamia for buildings such as the vast 23-acre Palace of Saragon at Khorsabad (c.722–705 BC).

summary trial A trial in a court of summary jurisdiction, in England and Wales in the magistrates' court, and in Scotland in either the Sheriff Court without a jury or in district courts. Many offences are classified as 'summary' and this usually determines the venue. A number of offences may be tried on either a summary or indictable basis and certain ones such as theft are regularly tried in courts of summary jurisdiction. The decision about mode of trial largely rests with the prosecutor, although in England and Wales the defence have a right in certain circumstances to demand a trial on indictment before a jury. Such a right does not exist in Scotland. In certain cases an accused charged with a summary offence may be tried before a jury either in the Crown Court (in England and Wales) or the Sheriff Court (in Scotland). A number of indictable offences such as murder or rape must be tried in the Crown Court (in England and Wales) or the High Court (in Scotland). Magistrates may try offenders summarily or may commit them to a higher court for trial.

summer cypress A bushy annual (*Kochia scoparia*), growing to 1 m/3¼ ft or more, native to Europe and Asia; leaves very narrow, pale green; flowers tiny, green. The colour and habit are slightly reminiscent of cypress trees. Cultivars with leaves turning deep russet-red in autumn are sometimes called **burning bush**. (Family: Chenopodiaceae.)

summer-grape *grapevine*

Summers, Anne (Fairhurst) (1945–) Academic, journalist, and bureaucrat, born in Deniliquin, New South Wales, SE Australia. She studied at the universities of Adelaide, Sydney, and New South Wales. Her influential book *Damned Whores and God's Police* (1975) was a ground-breaking study of the role of women in Australian history. She worked as a journalist for various newspapers, then became a 'femocrat' (1983–6) as head of the Office of the Status of Women in the Department of Prime Minister and Cabinet. She returned to journalism in 1986, and in 1987 became editor-in-chief of the American feminist magazine *Ms*, and its editor-at-large (1990–2). She was adviser on women's affairs to Paul Keating in 1992, returning again to journalism as editor of the *Sydney Morning Herald* and (until 1997) *The Age*'s colour supplement.

Summer Time *Daylight Saving Time*

summit diplomacy A term first used in the 1950s for negotiations between heads of state and governments with the intention of resolving disagreements; also known as **summitry**. It was regarded as a means of circumnavigating what was viewed as less effective traditional diplomacy. Since the 1960s it has been applied to any special meeting between national leaders, usually following lengthy diplomatic negotiations, with a symbolic and formal content.

sumo wrestling A Japanese national sport steeped in history and tradition. Competition takes place in a 12 ft (3·66 m) diameter circle, the object being to force one's opponent out of the ring or to the ground. Sumo wrestlers are very large and eat vast amounts of food to increase their weight and body size.

Sumy [**soo**mee] 50°55N 34°49E, pop (2000e) 295 000. Capital city of Sumskaya oblast, NE Ukraine, on R Psel; founded, 1652; airfield; railway; wool textiles, clothing, fertilizers, foodstuffs.

Sun The central object of our Solar System and the nearest star to the Earth. Its basic characteristics are: mass $1{\cdot}99 \times 10^{30}$ kg; radius 696 000 km/432 500 mi; mean density 1·4 g/cm^3; mean rotation period 25·4 days; luminosity $3{\cdot}85 \times 10^{24}$ J/s. Its average distance from Earth is 150 million km/93 million mi, and on account of this proximity it is studied more than any other star. The source of its energy is nuclear reactions in the central core (temperature 15 million K, relative density 155) extending to a quarter of the solar radius and including half the mass. Our Sun is nearly 5000 million years old, and is about halfway through its expected life-cycle. Every second it annihilates 5 million tonnes of matter, to maintain power output of 39×10^{26} watts of energy.

sun bear The smallest bear (length, 1·3 m/4 ft), native to SE Asia (*Helarctos malayanus*); short black coat with pale snout and yellow crescent on chest; inhabits tropical forest; climbs well; eats honey, insects, small vertebrates, fruit; also known as **honey bear**, **Malay bear**, or **bruang**.

sunbird A small songbird, native to the Old World tropics and the Middle East; slender curved bill and tubular tongue; inhabits woodland (drab species) or open country (bright, often iridescent, species); eats nectar, fruit, and insects. Unrelated birds of the genus *Neodrepanis* (Family: Philepittidae) are called **false sunbirds** or **sunbird-asities**. (Family: Nectariniidae, 106 species.)

sunbittern A long-legged water bird (*Eurypyga helias*), native to Central and South America; slim head, sharp pointed bill, rounded wings and tail, mottled plumage; inhabits edges of streams in woodland; eats fish and aquatic invertebrates. (Family: Eurypygidae.)

sunburn Damage to the skin caused by strong sunlight, especially in people with fair complexions. Short exposure results in redness and itch. More prolonged exposure causes pain, swelling of the skin, and blistering, accompanied by fever, headache, and nausea. Serious overexposure can cause skin cancers.

Sunda Islands [**soon**da] Island group in Indonesia, comprising the **Greater Sunda Is** of Java, Sumatra, Borneo, and Sulawesi, with their small adjacent islands, and **Nusa Tenggara**, formerly the **Lesser Sunda Is** of Bali, Lombok, Sumba, Sumbawa, Flores, and Timor, with their small islands.

Sun Dance An annual summer ceremony of the Plains Indians of North America. Originally it may have been a rite of thanksgiving to the supreme being for those things of nature upon which life depends, but it developed regional variations and additional features. It served as a source of power and spiritual achievement, a rite of initiation, and as a means of group affirmation and renewal. Participants are subject to a demanding discipline including ceremonial dancing while gazing at the Sun. The rite is a proclamation of death and rebirth, and involves vows and self-offering.

Sundance Kid, popular name of **Harry Longabaugh** or **Langbaugh** (1867–?1909) Outlaw, born in Phoenixville, Pennsylvania, USA. He was imprisoned in Sundance gaol for horse stealing (1887–9), after which he began life as an outlaw. He teamed up with Butch Cassidy, and drifted throughout North and South America robbing banks, trains, and mines. His date and place of death is uncertain, but it is generally held that he was fatally shot by a cavalry unit in Bolivia.

Sundanese A people from the highlands of W Java, Indonesia, but now also living in other parts of Java and Sumatra. One of three main groups on the island, they converted to Islam in the 16th-c. They are culturally similar to other Javanese, but have a distinctive language.

Sundarbans National park in India and Bangladesh; area c.10 000 sq km/3900 sq mi; established in 1973 to protect the mangrove habitat of the Ganges delta and its wildlife, particularly India's largest surviving population of tigers; a world heritage site.

Sunday The day of the week set aside by the Christian religion for divine worship, mainly in commemoration of Christ's resurrection. Already in New Testament times it replaced the Jewish Sabbath, when Paul and the Christians of Troas gathered on the first day of the week to 'break bread' (*Acts* 20), and it is called 'the Lord's day' (*Rev* 1). In 1971 the UK ratified the recommendation of the International Standardization Organization that Monday replace Sunday as the first day of the week.

Sunday School Classes for the religious education of children, usually linked to worship services, in Protestant Churches. They derive from the Sunday charity school, instituted in London in 1780, for the basic education of children of the poor.

Sunday trading The opening of shops for trading on a Sunday. In England and Wales, as a result of a 20-year sustained campaign, the Shops Act (1950), which prohibited Sunday opening ('Keep Sunday Special'), was repealed by the Sunday Trading Act (1994). The Employment Rights Act (1996) contains regulations controlling Sunday trading. Larger shops may now open on a Sunday for a continuous period of six hours between 10 am and 6 pm, and small shops may open at any time. Some establishments, such as DIY stores and garden centres, may open on Sundays regardless of size. A shop worker may opt out of doing shop work on Sunday, and may not be dismissed for refusing Sunday work.

Sunderland, formerly **Wearmouth** 54°55N 1°23W, pop (2001e) 280 800. Port city in Tyne and Wear, NE England, UK; at the mouth of the R Wear, 16 km/10 mi SE of Newcastle upon Tyne; site of monastery (674); city status, 1992; railway; University of Sunderland (1992, formerly Polytechnic); shipbuilding, ship repair, chemicals, glass, vehicles, coal trade; museum, art gallery; football league team, Sunderland (Black Cats).

sundew A carnivorous plant, usually a small perennial, native in most tropical and temperate regions, especially Australasia and S Africa; leaves spoon- or paddle-shaped, covered with long, red hairs; flowers 5-petalled, in slender spikes. The long hairs of the leaves are tentacle-like, being mobile and ending in a spherical gland which secretes a sticky substance. Insects attracted to the glistening drops are caught, and their struggles cause the surrounding hairs to bend inwards, preventing escape. The leaf itself may also bend over to enfold the prey. The glands then secrete enzymes, and the plant digests the prey before the leaf and hairs unfold. (Genus: *Drosera*, 100 species. Family: Droseraceae.)

sundial A device for showing the passage of time by the shadow cast on a graduated scale by a *gnomon* (some solid object, such as a rod or triangular plate attached to the dial). The earliest-known sundial dates from c.300 BC. With the development of Greek mathematics very elaborate dials were made. The study revived in the Middle Ages: many types were devised, and the theory of dialling was much studied until dials were gradually outmoded by clocks in the 17th–18th-c.

Sundsvall [**suns**val] 62°22N 17°20E, pop (2000e) 98 200. Seaport and commercial town in SE Västernorrland county, E Sweden, on the Gulf of Bothnia; important trading centre from the 6th-c; charter, 1624; railway; woodworking, papermaking, oil port.

sunfish Large and very distinctive fish (*Mola mola*) widespread in open waters of tropical to temperate seas; body compressed, almost circular; length typically 1–2 m/3¾–6½ ft, but up to 4 m/13 ft; mouth small, teeth fused into a sharp beak; dorsal and anal fins tall, posteriorly positioned, tail fin absent; also called **trunkfish**. (Family: Molidae.)

sunflower A large annual (*Helianthus annuus*) growing to 3 m/10 ft, a native of North America; stem stout, usually unbranched, bearing broadly oval to heart-shaped leaves; usually a solitary drooping flower-head up to 30 cm/12 in across; outer ray florets golden yellow. It is a popular garden ornamental. Several varieties are cultivated for the edible and rich oil-yielding seeds. (Family: *Compositae*.)

Sung dynasty *Song 1*

sungrabe *finfoot*

Sung Tsu-wen *Song Ziwen*

Sun Microsystems A major company in the information technology field, specializing in the provision of hardware and software for the Internet and the World Wide Web. The company has developed, and currently markets, the JAVA programming language.

Sunnism [**sunizm**] The orthodox version of Islam, which bases its legitimacy on the sayings and actions, or *sunnah*, of the Prophet Mohammed. Sunnis represent c.85% of Muslims in the world. They are divided into four legal schools whose differences lie in their interpretation of the sources of Islamic law – the Qur'an, the sayings of the Prophet, and interpretive sciences.

sun rose An evergreen shrub native to the Mediterranean region; leaves opposite, very narrow to oval or oblong; flowers large, white, or pink, with five distinctive crumpled petals. (Genus: *Cistus*, 20 species. Family: Cistaceae.)

sunscreen The use of barrier creams to reduce the penetration of ultraviolet rays to the skin. A number of substances are used, including para-aminobenzoic acid and zinc.

sun spider A long-legged, predatory arthropod found mostly in deserts and arid habitats; fangs (*chelicerae*) massive; other mouthparts (*pedipalps*) leg-like; first pair of legs slender, used as feelers; also known as **wind scorpions**. (Class: Arachnida. Order: Solpugida, c.900 species.)

sunspot An apparently dark region on the solar photosphere. Sunspots have a temperature of 4000K in the central part, termed the *umbra*, compared to 6000K for the photosphere generally, so appear dark by contrast. The lighter, outer part of the spot, the *penumbra*, has a temperature of c.5500K. Sunspots are caused by an intense magnetic field erupting from within the Sun, and follow a cycle of growth and decay over c.11 years.

sunstroke *heat stroke*

Sun Temple A richly sculptured Hindu temple built in the 13th-c at Konarak, Orissa, India. The temple itself represents seven horses pulling the splendid chariot of Surya, the Sun-god. It was known as the Black Pagoda to sailors of old, who navigated by it.

Sun Yixian [sun yeeshan], or **Sun Yatsen**, originally **Sun Wen** (1866–1925) Founder and early leader of China's Nationalist Party, born in Xiang-shan, Guangdong, SE China. He was educated in Hawaii and in Hong Kong, where he trained as a doctor. Alarmed by the weakness and decay of his country, he founded the Society for the Revival of China, and sprang to fame when, on a visit to London, he was kidnapped by the Chinese legation and released through the intervention of the Foreign Office. He then helped to organize risings in S China. He returned to China after the 1911 Wuhan rising, realized that he would not be widely acceptable as president, and voluntarily handed over the office to Yuan Shikai. After the assassination of his follower, Sung Chiao-jen, civil war ensued (1913), and he set up a separate government at Guangzhou (Canton). He was widely accepted as the true leader of the nation.

Super Bowl The annual championship of American football's National Football League, played in January between the champions of the American Football Conference and the champions of the National Football Conference. Held at a neutral ground, it was first played in 1967. The most successful teams are Dallas Cowboys and San Francisco 49ers, with five championships each.

superconducting quantum interference device (SQUID) A ring of superconducting material employing Josephson junctions, used for the accurate measurement of minute magnetic fields. It relies on an interaction between the field under test and the current around the ring. It can be used to measure low temperatures and to monitor brain activity.

superconductivity The property of zero electrical resistance, accompanied by the expulsion of magnetic fields (the Meissner effect), exhibited by certain metals, alloys, and compounds when cooled to below some critical temperature, typically less than −260°C. Both effects must be present for true superconductivity. An electrical current established in a superconducting ring of material will continue indefinitely while the low temperature is maintained. A superconducting material subjected to a current larger than some critical current, or to a magnetic field larger than some critical field, will cease to be superconducting. Superconductivity was first observed by Heike Kamerlingh-Onnes in 1911, using mercury. Some metals, such as copper and gold, do not become superconducting; platinum becomes superconducting only when powdered. High temperature superconductivity, for temperatures in excess of −250°C, was first observed in 1986 by physicists K Alexander Müller (1927–) and Georg Bednorz, using a ceramic of copper oxide containing barium and lanthanum. Similar effects have been observed in other ceramics, some of which superconduct at temperatures greater than −150°C. The phenomenon of high temperature superconductivity is poorly understood; but devices such as magnetometers which use high-temperature superconductors are available commercially. Superconductivity at temperatures of c.30K has been observed in fullerenes to which certain metals have been added. Superconductors are currently used in large magnets, such as those required by nuclear magnetic resonance spectrometers and particle accelerators.

supercooling The cooling of certain liquids, a condition which occurs in many processes, natural and industrial, below a temperature considered their freezing point. When this is done the condition is unstable, and the supercooled liquid will, if disturbed, change into the solid phase stable at that temperature. These supercooling conditions occur in the formation of ice crystals in clouds, the freezing of surface water in lakes, and freeze drying. The passage from supercooled water to ice is usually brought about by some nucleus, such as a dust particle. Certain substances can, however, persist in a supercooled state, notably glasses, which although to all intents and purposes permanent solids, are considered to be supercooled liquids.

super-ego *ego*

superfluidity The property of zero resistance to flow (ie zero viscosity), exhibited by liquid helium at temperatures below −271°C. Superfluid helium exhibits unusual properties, including the ability to creep out of a container apparently in defiance of gravity, and the inability to be set spinning in the way a solid object can. Superfluidity is an example of quantum behaviour directly observable on a large scale. The superfluidity of helium-4 at 2·19 K was discovered in 1938 by Piotr Kapitza; that of helium-3 at 3 mK by David Lee, Douglas Osheroff, and Robert Richardson in 1972. Superfluid helium-3 is of great interest as a test bed of quantum effects in condensed matter.

supergiant A rare type of star, very massive, and the most luminous known. Examples include Betelgeuse and Rigel (in Orion), Antares, and Deneb. They are 10–60 solar masses, 10 000 times or more brighter than the Sun, and thus visible at great distances.

supergravity A speculative quantum theory incorporating gravity, electromagnetic force, and nuclear force. It is a gauge theory based on supersymmetry, postulating gravitons and gravitinos as carriers of the gravitational force. Theoretically attractive, it lacks experimental support.

superheavy elements Elements having an atomic number (number of protons, Z) greater than 112. Superheavy elements do not occur in nature, and it was once believed impossible to create them via collisions between smaller nuclei. In fact, several new elements have been created by exactly this method. The heaviest naturally occurring atom is uranium, Z=92. Elements having a greater atomic number were created artificially by Edwin McMillan, Glenn Seaborg, and others. By 1994 the heaviest element known was meitnerium, Z=109. In 1999 scientists at Dubna, Russia, collided a calcium isotope into a plutonium target to create element 114. Also in 1999, a team at the Lawrence Berkeley National Laboratory in California claimed discovery of elements 116 and 118 by bombarding a lead target with krypton ions (though the claim for 118 was retracted in 2001). It is not known if there is a maximum atomic number beyond which an element cannot be created.

superheterodyne [sooperheterodiyn] The most common technique used in radio reception. The incoming radio-frequency signal is converted into a lower intermediate frequency by mixing it with a signal generated inside the receiver, called the *local oscillator*. This intermediate frequency is easier to amplify and manipulate than the initial radio frequencies.

Superior, Lake Largest of the Great Lakes, and the largest freshwater lake in the world; part of US–Canadian boundary; length 563 km/350 mi; breadth 257 km/160 mi; maximum depth 405 m/1329 ft; area 82 103 sq km/31 692 sq mi, 35% in Canada; connected with L Huron (SE) via St Marys R (the Soo canals); several islands, including Isle Royale (a US national park); transport of minerals (especially iron ore), grain.

supernatural *paranormal*

supernova A rare and spectacular explosion resulting in the destruction of a star. There are two main types. **Type II supernovae** occur at the endpoint of the evolution of a massive star, when the hydrogen fuel in the star core has all been converted to helium. The star therefore cools, and contracts. This is a runaway process, because as the star shrinks, the gravitational force at the surface increases, resulting in an intensification of inwards forces. In stars of a few solar masses, the central core implodes in less than one second, and this triggers an instantaneous nuclear explosion of all the unprocessed material outside the core. At the centre a neutron star, pulsar, or black hole is the endpoint. The exploded atmosphere is blasted into space at about one-tenth the speed of light, and the remnant can be detected for hundreds of years on account of its radio emission. Light emission from it is temporarily 100 million times brighter than the Sun, and the star can be seen for up to two years. **Type I supernovae** are divided into three classes: Type Ia are thought to occur in binary star systems in which gas from one star falls into a white dwarf companion, increasing its mass so that it collapses and explodes. Types Ib and Ic are thought to be due to the collapse of evolved stars that have lost some or all of their outer layers, and have more in common with Type II. Well-known examples are the supernovae of 4 July 1054 (Crab Nebula, Type II, recorded only in China), 1604 (seen by Kepler, Type Ia), and 1987 in the Large Magellanic Cloud (Type II). Supernovae are intrinsically rare; none have been sighted within our Milky Way since the invention of the telescope.

superovulation syndrome A condition which occasionally results when infertile women are given human gonadotrophic hormone and/or the synthetic drug clomiphene to stimulate ovulation. Several ova may be released simultaneously and then fertilized, with consequential multiple births.

superphosphates Fertilizers containing phosphate as the $H_2PO_4^{2-}$ ion. They are so called because, for a given weight, $Ca(H_2PO_4)_2$ contains more phosphorus than does $CaHPO_4$.

superposition *interference*

Superrealism *Photorealism*

supersonic In fluid mechanics, fluid flow which is faster than the velocity of sound in that fluid, either in the case of an object moving through the fluid, or a fluid moving around a stationary object. Supersonic aircraft fly faster than the speed of sound in air.

superstition A derogatory description of any behaviour, usually traditional in origin, that has lost its rationale though still betraying a fear of the unknown. Examples would be: 'touching wood' when mentioning one's good fortune, a hidden reference to the cross on which Christ was crucified; or regarding the sight of a magpie as a bad omen when setting out on a journey. In Ancient Roman religion, *superstition* referred to an act or attitude of excessive piety; the term was later applied by Christian clergy to religious or quasi-religious acts which they regarded as pagan or corrupt, such as calendar customs or ringing church bells to avert thunderstorms. Some groups or professions (such as actors and sailors) are especially prone to superstitions, almost certainly because their occupations are insecure.

superstrings A speculative quantum theory, embracing all the forces of nature, which may avoid the difficulties encountered by early unification schemes involving gravity; proposed by British physicist Michael Green and US physicist John Schwartz in 1984. It is based on a fundamental extended submicroscopic string in place of the usual point particle, plus supersymmetry. It is consistent only in 10 dimensions, and has no experimental support.

supersymmetry In particle physics, a symmetry relation linking particles of different (ie integer and half-integer) spins. Theories incorporating supersymmetry predict particles that are partners to observed particles, having the same mass but different spin. No such supersymmetric partners (squark, slepton, photino, and others) have been observed.

supination [soopinayshn] A movement of the forearm in which the palm of the hand is brought to face forwards, so that the thumb is directed away from the body. In this position the radius and ulna lie parallel to each other. It is a much more powerful movement than pronation, and as most people are right-handed, this accounts for the right-hand thread on screws and other such phenomena.

supply and demand An economic concept which states that the price of an article (or 'good') will move to the level where the quantity demanded by purchasers equals the quantity that suppliers are willing to sell.

supply-side economics The view that the main contribution of policy to promoting the growth of incomes is through measures to improve the supply of goods and services and the working of markets. This may take the form of removing private agreements on restrictive practices, or reforming government regulations or excessive taxes which impede efficiency. The approach contrasts with the Keynesian view, which puts more weight on managing the economy so as to increase demand. Supply-side views had considerable influence on policy in the UK and USA during the 1980s.

supportive psychotherapy An approach in which an attempt is made to reinforce the patient's defences, thus allowing the suppression of disturbing psychological material. There is no attempt to probe emotional conflicts in any depth. The technique is used in situations where the symptoms are relatively trivial and therefore not meriting detailed investigation, or with patients who are too fragile to achieve greater insight without major and possibly permanent decompensation (psychological breakdown with the possible development of a psychosis). The technique emphasizes reassurance, counselling, re-education, persuasion and suggestion. It is often carried out by non-medical members of a psychiatric team, such as nursing staff.

supralittoral zone *benthic environments*

suprarenal glands *adrenal glands*

Suprematism A form of modern art based on four simple shapes: rectangle, circle, triangle, and cross. The movement was started in Russia c.1913 by Kazimir Malevich (1878–1935), who demonstrated the aesthetic purity of it all by painting a white square on a white ground.

Supreme Court In the USA, the highest federal court established under the constitution, members of which are appointed by the president with the advice and consent of the Senate. In addition to its jurisdiction relating to appeals, the court also exercises oversight of the constitution through the power of judicial review of the acts of state, federal legislatures, and the executive.

Supreme Headquarters Allied Expeditionary Force (SHAEF) An organization formally established (13 Feb 1944) in the UK in World War 2 under General Eisenhower, with Air Chief Marshal Tedder as deputy supreme commander, to mount the Allied invasion of occupied Europe and strike at the heart of Germany. It was wound up at the end of the war.

Supreme Soviet *soviet*

Surabaya [soorabahya] or **Surabaja** 7°14S 112°45E, pop (2000e) 2 930 000. Industrial seaport capital of Java Timor province, E Java, Indonesia, at mouth of R Kali Mas; Indonesia's second largest city; port facilities at Tanjung Perak; important trading centre since the 14th-c; airfield; railway; university (1954); naval base; oil refining, textiles, glass, footwear, tobacco, rubber.

Surat [soorat] 21°12N 72°55E, pop (2000e) 1 757 000. Port in Gujarat, W India, on the Gulf of Cambay, 240 km/150 mi N of Mumbai; rich trading centre of Mughal Empire, 17th–18th-c; first English trading post in India, 1612; headquarters of British East India Company until 1687; railway; university (1967); textiles, engineering; noted for its sari thread work and diamond cutting.

Sûreté [süruhtay], in full **Sûreté nationale** (Fr 'National Security') One of four police forces existing in France, which are largely independent of each other. Founded in the early 19th-c, the *Sûreté* is under the control of the minister of the interior, and is responsible for criminal investigations, corresponding roughly to the CID in Britain and the FBI in the USA.

surf Wind-generated waves that have broken upon encountering shallow water. In common usage, the term refers to the entire range of waves in shallow water from breakers to swash, but scientifically it is used specifically for the turbulent walls of water (*bores*) formed by breaking waves. As waves formed offshore travel into shallow water, their steepness increases to a critical point where they become unstable and 'break'. This typically occurs in water depth of about 1·3 times the wave height. Once a wave has broken, the water particles move laterally towards the shore, and are known as surf.

surface active agent *surfactant*

surface physics The study of the electronic and structural properties of the surface of matter, ie the outermost layer of atoms. Surface properties are important in several domains, including catalysis, corrosion, the emission of electrons from surfaces, optical properties, and friction. Surface layers formed at the interface of two solids are also important, as in semiconductor devices. Experiments rely on such techniques as electron diffraction, atomic force microscopy, and field ion microscopy.

surface printing A term sometimes used for those techniques of printmaking which do not involve cutting, etching, or scraping the block or plate. The main techniques are lithography and monotype, but the term is sometimes extended to include screen-printing.

surface structure *deep structure*

surface tension A property of the surface of a liquid. It provides the apparent 'skin' present on liquids that holds oil in droplets and allows some pond insects to walk on water. It is a tensioning force due to the inward attraction of molecules at the surface, since such molecules are attracted more by other liquid molecules than by the gas molecules above. Symbol γ, units N/m (newtons per metre); for water at 20°C in air, $\gamma = \cdot 073$ N/m. Surface tension for a given liquid depends on the gas at the surface, and decreases with temperature. Because of surface tension, liquid surfaces appear elastic, as observed in bubbles and soap films.

surfactant Any substance that strongly influences the surface properties of a material; also called a **surface active agent**. It is often applied to soaps and detergents, whose cleaning powers depend on the surfactant's ability to increase the spreading and wetting power of water. Surfactants are also important in lubrication and water repellent coatings.

surgeonfish Any of the family Acanthuridae of colourful, deep-bodied fish widespread in tropical seas, especially in the Indo-Pacific; name refers to the sharp movable spine on sides of tail which can be erected for defence; body length typically 10–40 cm/4–16 in; teeth specialized for scraping algae from coral surfaces; also called **tang**.

surgery The branch of medicine which treats diseases and conditions by operating on the patient. The use of the hands for the treatment of disease dates from prehistoric times. Trephining the skull to allow the escape of disease from the body was a very early procedure, and practised along with the splinting of fractures, the lancing of abscesses, and the application of pressure for bleeding. Obstacles to the development of surgery were pain, infection, and shock, which could not be controlled until the 20th-c. Consequently, early surgical operations were limited to those near the surface of the body, such as hernia repair, removal of bladder stones, and amputation. With modern anaesthesia, all parts of the body have become accessible, beginning with the removal of the appendix for appendicitis, and leading to the repair of perforated peptic ulcers, the removal of part of the lungs for cancer, neurosurgery, the replacement of blocked blood vessels to the heart, and organ transplantation. The development of artificial body parts and their substitution for worn-out tissues such as the replacement of hip joints and the aorta is also a remarkable modern development.

suricate *meerkat*

Suriname *p.1485*

Surrealism (Fr 'over' or 'intense' realism) An important movement in modern art and literature which flourished between the World Wars, mainly in France. The first Surrealist manifesto of André Breton (1924) proposed the subversion of 19th-c Realism by the three related means of humour, dream, and counter-logic (the absurd). This initiative was taken up by many artists and writers, and the term is now used to describe the heightened or distorted perception and registration of reality, by whatever means. The basic idea was to free the artist from the demands of logic, and to penetrate beyond everyday consciousness to the 'super-reality' that lies behind. Freud's theory of the subconscious was appealed to, and many pictures by Dali, Magritte, and Tanguy seek to recreate the fantasy world of dreams. Objects are taken out of their normal context, their scale drastically changed, or they are represented as made of an inappropriate material, such as Dali's melting watches. Other leading Surrealists include Ernst, Chirico, and Arp, and its influence is clear in many works by Picasso and Klee. In literature, the movement is illustrated by the poetry of Aragon and Eluard, the plays of Ionesco and Beckett, and the novels of Genet and Burroughs. Luis Buñuel guaranteed its impact on the cinema. Advertising since c.1960 has been indebted to the images of Surrealism, usually rendered by trick photography.

Surrey pop (2001e) 1 059 000; area 1679 sq km/648 sq mi. County in SE England, UK; partly in Greater London urban area; drained by the Thames, Mole, and Wey Rivers; crossed E–W by the North Downs, rising to 294 m/964 ft at Leith Hill; administrative centre, Kingston-upon-Thames; chief towns include Guildford, Reigate, Leatherhead, Staines, Woking; largely residential; agriculture, light industry; Box Hill, Leith Hill, Runnymede, Royal Botanic Gardens (Kew), North Downs.

Surrey, Henry Howard, Earl of (c.1517–47) Courtier and poet, born in Hunsdon, Hertfordshire, SE England, UK. In 1532 he accompanied Henry VIII to France, was knighted in 1541, and served in Scotland, France, and Flanders. On his return in 1546, he was condemned and beheaded on the charge of treasonably

Suriname

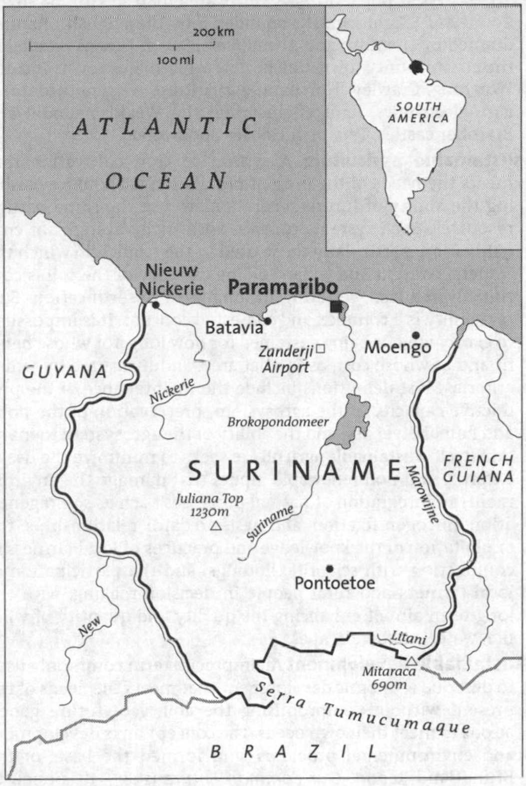

□ International Airport

[soorinam], also **Surinam**, official name **Republic of Suriname, Republiek Suriname**

Local name Suriname

Timezone GMT −3

Area 163 265 km^2/63 020 sq mi

Population total (2002e) 436 000

Status Republic

Date of independence 1975

Capital Paramaribo

Languages Dutch (official), Hindi and Javanese (native languages), Sranan Tongo, Chinese and Spanish also spoken

Ethnic groups Indo-Pakistan (37%), Creole (31%), Javanese (15%), Amerindian (3%), Chinese (2%), European (1%)

Religions Hindu (27%), Protestant (25%), Roman Catholic (23%), Muslim (20%), indigenous beliefs (5%)

Physical features Located in NE South America; N natural regions, range from coastal lowland through savannah to mountainous upland; coastal strip covered by swamp; highland interior (S) overgrown with dense tropical forest; highest point, Juliana Top, 1230 m/4035 ft, in SC; seven major rivers including Marowijne (E), Corantijn (W), Suriname.

Climate Equatorial tropical, uniformly hot and humid; two rainy seasons (May-Jul, Nov-Jan); average annual temperatures 22–33°C in Paramaribo; average monthly rainfall 310 mm/12·2 in (N), 67 mm/2·6 in (S).

Currency 1 Suriname Guilder/Florin (SGld, F) = 100 cents

Economy Based on agriculture and mining, but hindered by lack of foreign exchange; bauxite mining (provides c.80% of export income); sugar cane, rice, citrus fruits, coffee, bananas, oil palms, cacao, fishing; vast timber resources.

GDP (2002e) $1·469 bn, per capita $3400

Human Development Index (2002) 0·756

History Sighted by Columbus, 1498; first settled by the British, 1651; taken by the states of Zeeland, 1667; captured by the British, 1799; restored to the Netherlands, 1814 and remained part of Netherland West Indies as Dutch Guiana; independence as the Republic of Suriname, 1975; emigration of c.40% of population to the Netherlands, following independence; military coup, 1980; ban on political activities lifted, 1985; 1987 constitution provides for a National Assembly, and a President elected by the Assembly.

Head of State (President)
1988–90 Ramsewak Shankar
1990–1 Johan Kraag
1991–6 Ronald Venetiaan
1996–2000 Jules Wijdenbosch
2000– Ronald Ventiaan

Head of Government (Vice-President)
1988–90 Henck Arron
1990–1 Jules Wijdenbosch
1991–6 Jules Adjodhia
1996–2000 Pretaapnarain Radhakishun
2000– Jules Ajodhia

quartering the royal arms and advising his sister to become the king's mistress. He was then barely 30. He is remembered for his graceful and polished love poetry, influenced by the Italian tradition, in which he pioneered the use of blank verse (in his translation of Virgil's *Aeneid*) and the Elizabethan sonnet form.

Surrey, Earl of *Howard, Henry*

surrogate mother An arrangement whereby a woman agrees to bear a child for someone else and to hand over that child at birth to another person or persons, who are known as the *commissioning parents*. In England and Wales, for example, legislation provides that parental responsibility is given up in favour of the commissioning parents, and when they are married, a *parental order* may be made. This order provides for the child to be treated in law as the child of the parties to the marriage, provided certain conditions are met. If such conditions are not fulfilled, or if the parents are not married, then a *Section 8 order* may be made. Adoption procedures are sometimes used when the surrogacy agreement has gone wrong and the parties are in dispute.

Surtees, John (1934–) Motor-racing driver and motor-cyclist, born in Westerham, Kent, SE England, UK, the only man to win world titles on both two and four wheels. He won the 350 cc motor cycling world title in 1958–60, and the 500 cc title in 1956 and 1958–60 (all on an MV Augusta). He then turned to car racing, and won the 1964 world title driving a Ferrari. He later became a racing car manufacturer.

Surtsey Island [sertsee] area 1·9 sq km/0·7 sq mi. Volcanic island off S coast of Iceland; one of the Westman Is; erupted and formed in 1963; now a nature reserve.

surveillance TV Closed circuit television with many security applications, from supervising customer areas in supermarkets to continuous remote monitoring of several unattended locations from a central office. Small monochrome cameras sensitive to low light levels are fitted with wide-angle lenses for maximum coverage from a fixed viewpoint or one which can be varied by remote control. A time-lapse videotape recorder may be operated frame-by-frame at specified intervals or triggered by a movement detector.

surveying The accurate measurement and collection of data, such as relief, for a given area in order to make a map, or to record changes in the characteristics of the Earth's surface over time. It has traditionally been based on fieldwork, using equipment such as chains, plane tables, and theodolites, used to measure the distance, elevation, and angle of an object from an observation point. The use of aerial photographs and satellite imagery as a basis for mapping is increasing. **Geodetic surveying** is the measurement of the size and shape of the Earth, and the determination of the position of places on its surface.

Surveyor programme A series of robotic soft-lander missions to the Moon undertaken by NASA (May 1966–Jan 1968) in preparation for the manned Apollo landings. It was highly successful, with five of the seven spacecraft landing as planned. Surface material properties were measured at landing sites, and panoramic images returned. Chemistry measurements on later missions (5 and 6) demonstrated the basaltic character of Moon rocks long before the Apollo samples were returned. The camera and scoop of Surveyor 3 were recovered by Apollo 12 astronauts from the Ocean of Storms landing site. The series was managed and operated by NASA's Jet Propulsion Laboratory.

Surya [soorya] The Sun-god in Hindu mythology. He was the son of Indra, the pre-eminent god of the Rig-Veda.

Susa [sooza] The Greek name for **Shushan**, in antiquity, the main city of Elam and the capital of the Achaemenid Empire under Darius I and his successors. It is the site of the world's best preserved ziggurat.

Susanna, Book of A book of the Old Testament Apocrypha, or Chapter 13 of the Book of Daniel in Catholic versions of the Bible; an addition to the Book of Daniel of uncertain date or provenance. It tells of how the beautiful Jewess Susanna is wrongfully accused in Babylon of adultery and is condemned to death, but is rescued by Daniel. The artful narrative commends lessons of Jewish morality and faith in God.

suslik *souslik*

Suslov, Mikhail Andreyevich [suslof] (1902–82) Soviet politician, born in Shakhovskoye, W Russia. He joined the Communist Party in 1921, and was a member of the Central Committee from 1941 until his death. An ideologist of the Stalinist school, he became a ruthless and strongly doctrinaire administrator. Very different from Khrushchev in temperament and political outlook, he opposed Khrushchev's 'de-Stalinization' measures, economic reforms, and foreign policy, and was instrumental in unseating him in 1964.

suspended sentence A sentence of imprisonment which is not activated immediately, but may be imposed should the offender commit a further offence during the period of suspension, in addition to any penalty the later court imposes. Used in England and Wales for a number of years, suspended sentences may operate in conjunction with supervision by a probation officer. If the suspended sentence is for a prison term of more than six months, the court may make a *suspended sentence supervision order*. Suspended sentences are not available in all jurisdictions (eg in Scotland).

suspension A mixture in which particles (of solid or liquid) are dispersed through another phase (liquid or gas) without dissolving in it. Suspensions are not indefinitely stable, and will eventually settle into separate phases.

Sussex Former county of England, UK; divided into East Sussex and West Sussex in 1974, West Sussex gaining part of S Surrey.

Sussex, East pop (2001e) 492 300; area 1795 sq km/693 sq mi. County of SE England, UK; bounded S by the English Channel; South Downs parallel to the coast, part of the Weald to the N; drained by the R Ouse; county town, Lewes; chief towns include Brighton, Eastbourne, Bexhill, Hastings; Brighton and Hove a unitary authority (from 1997); agriculture (cereals, fruit, vegetables), electronics, furniture, service industries; major tourist area on S coast; Beachy Head, Ashdown Forest, the Weald, Romney Marsh; castles at Bodiam, Hastings, Lewes, Pevensey; site of Battle of Hastings.

Sussex, Kingdom of A kingdom of the Anglo-Saxon heptarchy (seven kingdoms), situated between Kent and Wessex, and founded probably by c.500. The South Saxons remained heathen until St Wilfred, Bishop of York, led (681–6) the Christian conversion of the people. After its reduction to a dependency of Mercia in the late 8th-c, it never regained the status of a kingdom, and was annexed to Wessex in the 9th-c.

Sussex, West pop (2001e) 753 600; area 1989 sq km/768 sq mi. County of S England, UK; bounded S by the English Channel; drained by the Adur and Arun Rivers; South Downs parallel to the coast; county town, Chichester; other major towns include Worthing, Crawley, Horsham; agriculture, horticulture, tourism, electronics, light engineering; the Weald, Arundel and Bramber castles, Petworth House, Goodwood.

sustainable agriculture A system of crop cultivation that meets the needs of the present population without jeopardizing the ability of future generations to use the same natural resources. Such systems contrast with many systems of crop cultivation, particularly those used in the tropics, in which the mineral content and water-holding capacity of the soil is continually reduced, resulting in long-term desertification. Sustainability is a complex and contested concept; it is impossible to clarify what is being sustained for how long, for whose benefit and at whose cost, over what area, and measured by which criteria. Most definitions include the maintenance of the productive capacity of the agrosystem; preservation of the floral and faunal diversity; and the ability of the agrosystem to maintain itself. Sustainable agriculture seeks to minimize the use of external and non-renewable inputs that damage the environment; an integration of natural processes such as soil regeneration, nitrogen fixation, and pest–predator relationships; the exploitation of the knowledge and practices of local farmers in conjunction with scientific findings; and the participation of local farmers and rural people in decision-making, with the long-term aim of enhancing the quality and quantity of wildlife, water, and landscapes.

sustainable development An imprecise term commonly used to describe economic development that meets the needs of the present without compromising the ability of future generations to meet their own needs. The concept links development and environmental problems, and formed the basis of the Brundtland Report, *Our Common Future* (1987). It is open to criticism: development is usually accepted as synonymous with economic growth, which may be contradictory to sustainability and environmental protection.

Sutcliffe, Peter, known as **the Yorkshire Ripper** (1946–) Convicted murderer, born in Bingley, West Yorkshire, N England, UK. Employed at one time as a gravedigger, he shocked his workmates with his unnatural interest in corpses. He murdered 13 women over five years in N England and the Midlands. Many of his victims were prostitutes, the first being Wilma McCann, whose body was found in 1975. A lorry driver at the time, he was interviewed by the police on several occasions, before a routine check on a car registration led to his arrest in 1981. He identified himself as the murderer, was tried and found guilty of 13 murders and seven attempted murders, and given a life sentence on each account. He has twice been assaulted in Broadmoor, where he is now held.

Sutherland, Donald (1934–) Film actor, born in St John, New Brunswick, E Canada. He studied at the University of Toronto, and for a time at the Royal Academy of Dramatic Art, London. An actor of enormous versatility, he became known for his role in *The Dirty Dozen* (1967), following this with *M*A*S*H* (1970) and *Klute* (1971). Among his later films are *Ordinary People* (1980), *Backdraft* (1991), *A Time To Kill* (1996), *Instinct* (1999), *Space Cowboys* (2000), and *Uprising* (2001).

Sutherland, Graham (Vivian) (1903–80) Artist, born in London, UK. He studied at London, worked mainly as an etcher until 1930, then made his reputation as a painter of Romantic, mainly abstract landscapes. He was an official war artist (1941–5), and later produced several memorable portraits, including 'Maugham' (1949), and 'Beaverbrook' (1951). His 'Churchill' (1955) did not find favour with Lady Churchill and was never seen by the public. He also designed ceramics, posters, and textiles. His large tapestry, 'Christ in Majesty', was hung in the new Coventry Cathedral in 1962.

Sutherland, Dame Joan (1926–) Operatic soprano, born in Sydney, New South Wales, SE Australia. She made her debut at Sydney in 1947, moved to London in 1951, and joined the Royal Opera, becoming resident soprano at Covent Garden. She gained international fame in 1959 with her roles in Donizetti's *Lucia di Lammermoor* and Handel's *Samson*. She has sung regularly in opera houses and concert halls all over the world, and in 1965 returned to Australia for a triumphant tour with her own company. In 1954 she married the conductor **Richard Bonynge** (1930–), and was made a dame in 1979. In 1990 she gave her final performance at the Sydney Opera House.

Sutlej, River [sutlej] River of Asia; the longest of the five rivers of the Punjab; rises in Tibet (Xizang), and flows NW as the **Xiangquan He**; enters India, meandering through the Himalayas, and flows SW to its confluence with the R Chenab E of Alipur; combined stream flows SW for 81 km/50 mi to meet the Indus; length 1370 km/850 mi; used for irrigation and hydroelectric power, particularly at the Bhakara Dam, India.

Sutro, Adolph [sutro] (1830–98) US businessman, born in Aachen, W Germany. In 1850 he arrived in New York City, the next year moving to San Francisco, where he established a trading business. In 1859 he founded a metallurgical works in Nevada, building the Sutro Tunnel for the draining and ventilation of mines in the Comstock Lode. In 1879 he returned to San Francisco, where he became a major landowner, and mayor (1894–6). His book collection became the Sutro Library in San Francisco.

suttee *sati*

Sutton Hoo ship burial The grave of an Anglo-Saxon king, probably Raedwald of East Anglia (c.600–624/5), discovered beneath a barrow on the R Deben near Woodbridge, E England in 1939. Amidships in a 40-oar open rowing boat (4·25 m/14 ft in beam and 27 m/89 ft long) stood a wooden burial chamber containing silver plate, gold jewellery, and coins, weapons, and domestic equipment (now in the British Museum). It is the richest single archaeological find ever made in Britain.

Suva [soova] 18°08S 178°25E, pop (2000e) 81 100. Chief port and capital of Fiji, on SE coast of Viti Levu I; overlooked by Colo-i-suva Forest Park; city since 1953; university (1968); copra processing, soap, edible oil, handicrafts, steel rolling mill, tourism.

Suva Convention *Lomé Convention*

Suwon [soowuhn] or **Suweon** 37°16N 126°59E, pop (2000e) 722 000. Industrial capital of Kyonggi province, NW Korea; 48 km/30 mi S of Seoul; subway from Seoul; agricultural college; reconstructed fortress walls and gates; Korean Folk Village nearby; Suwon World Cup Stadium (2001).

Suzhou [soojoh] or **Suchow** 31°21N 120°40E, pop (2000e) 983 800, administrative region 6 292 000. City in Jiangsu province, E China, on the banks of the Grand Canal; first settled c.1000 BC; capital, Kingdom of Wu, 518 BC; railway; silk, light industry, chemicals, electronics, handicrafts; over 150 ornamental gardens (a world heritage site), including Canglang (Surging Wave) pavilion (c.1044), Shizilin (Lion Grove, 1350), and Wangshi Yuan (Garden of the Master of the Nets, 12th-c); Huqiu (Tiger Hill) artificial hill (height 36 m/118 ft), built by the King of Wu as a tomb for his father.

Suzman, Helen, *née* **Gavronsky** (1917–) South African politician, born in Germiston, Transvaal, NE South Africa. She studied at Witwatersrand University, then became a lecturer there (1944–52). Deeply concerned about the apartheid system erected by the National Party under Daniel Malan, she joined the Opposition, and was elected to parliament in 1953. She gradually gained the respect of the black community and, for years the sole MP of the Progressive Party, proved to be a fierce opponent of apartheid. In 1978 she received the UN Human Rights Award, and later served as president of the South African Institute of Race Relations (1991–3). The Helen Suzman Foundation seeks to promote liberal democracy in southern Africa.

Svalbard [svalbah(r)d] pop (2000e) 3400; area 62 000 sq km/23 900 sq mi. Island group in the Arctic Ocean, c.650 km/400 mi N of the Norwegian mainland; four large and several smaller islands; chief islands, Spitsbergen, Nordaustlandet, Edgeøya, Barentsøya, Prins Karls Forland; discovered, 1596; formerly an important whaling centre; incorporated in Norway, 1925; two-thirds of the population are former Soviet citizens; administrative centre, Longyearbyen; coal, phosphate, asbestos, iron ore, galena, sphalerite, chalcopyrite, limestone dolerite, anhydrite.

Svedberg, Theodor [svayberg], Swed **The Svedberg** [te svedberj] (1884–1971) Physical chemist, born in Fleräng, E Sweden. He studied at Uppsala, where he spent his whole career. In 1924 he described his ultracentrifuge, in which a solution can be spun at very high speed, generating centrifugal forces many thousand times that of gravity, and used it to develop methods for separating proteins. He was awarded the Nobel Prize for Chemistry in 1926.

Sverdlovsk [sverdlofsk] *Yekaterinburg*

Sveshtari tomb [sveshtahree] A 3rd-c BC tomb, located near the village of Sveshtari in N Bulgaria; a world heritage site. The tomb, which was discovered in 1982, is noted for the 10 caryatids and the frieze decorating the burial chamber.

Svevo, Italo [zvayvoh], pseudonym of **Ettore Schmitz** (1861–1928) Novelist, born in Trieste, NE Italy. He worked as a bank clerk, then turned to writing, encouraged by James Joyce, who taught him English. He had a considerable success with *La coscienza di Zeno* (1923, The Confessions of Zeno), a psychological study of inner conflicts.

Swabia, Ger **Schwaben** A SW mediaeval German duchy, extending from the R Rhine in the W to the Alps in the S, Bavaria in the E, and Franconia in the N, containing the cities of Strasbourg, Constance, and Augsburg. The Peasants' War of 1524–5 began here, because landlords and peasants were at odds, imperial authority was increasing, and Lutheran doctrines were spreading.

Swabian League An alliance of 22 imperial German cities, clerical lords, and princes, with a league of knights of Swabia (1488), to support the Holy Roman Empire and to check the threats of Wittelsbach, the dukes of Bavaria, and Swiss rebels against the Habsburgs. It was active in suppressing rebellions in 1523–5, but declined because of religious divisions caused by the Reformation.

Swahili [swaheelee] A cluster of Bantu-speaking peoples of the coast and islands of E Africa, ethnically and culturally an amalgam of African groups and Arab immigrants entering the area continually since ancient times. By the 10th-c, they controlled the trade of E Africa and the Indian Ocean; from the 12th-c they built large and distinctive mosques, forts, and palaces; and by the 15th-c they were at the height of their power as a trading nation. The Swahili language probably replaced Arabic from about the 13th-c, and is today spoken by c.30 million as a lingua franca throughout E Africa.

swallow A small songbird, found worldwide; dark blue/green above, pale below; tail long, forked; inhabits open country near fresh water; eats small insects caught in flight; temperate populations migrate; nests in holes or mud nests on cliffs, buildings, etc. The name is also used for several unrelated birds. (Family: Hirundinidae, 57 species.)

swallowtail butterfly A large, colourful butterfly in which hindwings are extended into slender tails; adults and larvae usually distasteful to predators. (Order: Lepidoptera. Family: Papilionidae.)

Swammerdam, Jan [svamerdam] (1637–80) Naturalist, born in Amsterdam, The Netherlands. He trained in medicine, then turned to the study of insects, devising a classification which laid the foundations of entomology. He first observed red blood corpuscles (1658), and discovered the valves in the lymph vessels and the glands in the Amphibia named after him.

swamp A permanently flooded area of land with thick vegetation of reeds or trees. **Mangrove swamps** are common along river mouths in tropical and subtropical areas. In the Carboniferous period, marine swamps were common, and are the origin of present-day coal deposits.

swamp cypress A deciduous or semi-evergreen conifer, native to the SE USA and Mexico; leaves awl-shaped, soft; also called **bald cypress**. In swampy ground the root system of *Taxodium distichum* produces woody, hollow 'knees', which project into the air and are believed to act as pneumatophores. (Genus: *Taxodium*, 3 species. Family: Taxodiaceae.)

swamp hawk *marsh harrier*

swan A large water-bird of the duck family; found worldwide; usually white; neck very long; male called *cob*, female *pen*. (Tribe: Anserini. Genera: *Cygnus*, 10 species, and *Coscoroba*, 2 species. Subfamily: Anserinae.)

Swan Hill 35°23S 142°37E, pop (2000e) 10 300. Town in N Victoria, Australia, on the Murray R; railway; airfield; sheep farming, fruit growing, wine; Pioneer Settlement (open-air museum); Clockworld (collection of over 500 clocks and watches from the past 300 years).

Swan River Major watercourse of SW Australia; rises as the Avon R in the hills near Corrigin; flows past Perth, entering the Indian Ocean at Fremantle; receives the Helena and Canning Rivers; length (including the Avon) 386 km/240 mi; the Swan River Settlement (1829) was the first colonial settlement in Western Australia; Swanland is a fertile region producing wheat, fruit, wine, wool, timber.

Swanscombe skull The partial skull (rear vault) of an archaic form of *Homo sapiens* found at Swanscombe near London in 1935–6, and 1955. Its possible age is 250 000 years.

Swansea, Welsh **Abertawe** 51°38N 3°57W, pop (2001e) 223 300. Port city and (from 1996) unitary authority (pop (2000e) 233 000) in SC Wales, UK; on the Bristol Channel at the mouth of the R Tawe where it enters Swansea Bay; chartered, 1158–84; airfield; railway; university college (1920); national vehicle licensing centre; trade in coal, oil, ores; Norman castle, Royal Institution of South Wales (1835), Guildhall, industrial and maritime museum, marina; Swansea Music Festival (Oct); football league team, Swansea City (Swans).

swastika [swostika] A symbol consisting of a cross with its four arms bent at right angles, either clockwise or anticlockwise. Found in ancient Hindu, Mexican, Buddhist, and other traditions, possibly representing the Sun, it is now politically and culturally tainted since its appropriation by the Nazi Party as its official emblem. The name derives from the Sanskrit *svasti + ka*, meaning a mystical cross used to denote good luck.

Swazi A Bantu-speaking agricultural and pastoral people living in Swaziland and adjoining parts of S Africa. They are one of the Nguni cluster of peoples, and were formed into a kingdom in the early 19th-c. Swaziland, independent since 1968, is governed by traditional Swazi institutions, with the king as head of state.

Swaziland *p.1489*

sweat A dilute solution of salts (mainly sodium chloride) and other small molecules (eg urea, lactic acid, and ammonia) actively secreted by sweat (*sudoriferous*) glands present in the skin of mammals. It provides a mechanism for the excretion of salt and nitrogen. Evaporation of sweat from the skin surface involves heat loss; sweating is thus particularly important in humans with respect to temperature regulation.

sweat lodge A rite of purification, spiritual and physical, widely found among North American Indians, especially among C and SW tribes. The leader conducts the participants into a specially constructed lodge, where they are seated around a mound of heated stones. Prayers and songs are offered as the leader pours heated water over the stones. It is believed that gods and spirits are present, prompting spontaneous individual and collective prayers.

swede A biennial vegetable (*Brassica napus*, variety *napobrassica*), related to rape, with a taproot and stem base forming a fleshy tuber. In its second (sometimes first) year, the tubers 'bolt', producing tall stems and numerous yellow cross-shaped flowers. (Family: Cruciferae.)

Sweden *p.1490*

Swedenborg, Emanuel [sweednbaw(r)g], originally **Emanuel Swedberg** (1688–1772) Mystic and scientist, born in Stockholm, Sweden. He studied at Uppsala, travelled in Europe, and on his return was appointed assessor in the college of mines. He wrote books on algebra, navigation, astronomy, and chemistry, and in 1734 published his monumental *Opera philosophica et mineralia* (Philosophical and Logical Works), a mixture of metallurgy and metaphysical speculation on the creation of the world. Curious dreams convinced him that he had direct access to the spiritual world. He communicated his spiritual explorations in *Heavenly Arcana* (1749–56), and spent the rest of his life in Amsterdam, Stockholm, and London, expounding his doctrines in such works as *The New Jerusalem* (1758). In 1787 his followers (known as *Swedenborgians*) formed the Church of the New Jerusalem.

Swedish *Germanic / Scandinavian languages; Swedish literature*

Swedish literature The translation of the Bible by the brothers Petri (1526–41) provides the earliest work. Classical influences dominated the 17th-c, and English and French the 18th-c, until the Realistic poetry of Karl Bellman (1740–95), Thomas Thorild (1759–1808), and Johan Kellgren (1751–95). The writing of Emanuel Swedenborg (1688–1772) ranged from science to mysticism. The verse dramas of Per Atterbom (1790–1835) brought Romanticism to Sweden, and epic works by the Finn Johan Runeberg (1804–77) were also popular. The novel took root by the mid-19th-c, with the versatile Karl Almqvist (1793–1866) and the early feminist Fredrika Bremer (1810–65). The obsessive themes of August Strindberg (1849–1912) produced both novels and plays. Poets Gustav Fröding (1860–1911) and Eric Karlfeldt (1864–1931) reacted in the 1890s against Naturalism. The early 20th-c brought the pessimistic novels of Hjalmar Söderberg (1869–1941) and the fantasy fiction of Hjalmar Bergman (1883–1931); also the adventurous poets Gunnar Ekelof (1907–68) and Harry Martinson (1904–78). Post-war literature has dwelt on spiritual impoverishment, with the documentary novel significantly popular (Per Sundman, 1922–92). Meanwhile, following the example of Selma Lagerlöf (1858–1940; Nobel Prize, 1909), a number of Swedish writers such as Astrid Lindgren (1917–2002) and Tove Jansson (1914–2001) have written successful books for children.

Sweet, Henry (1845–1912) Philologist, born in London, UK. He became reader in phonetics at Oxford, where he pioneered Anglo-Saxon studies. His works include Old and Middle English texts, primers, and dictionaries, and a historical English grammar. He was the probable source for Professor Higgins in Shaw's *Pygmalion* (1913).

sweet alyssum [alisuhm] A low, bushy annual or perennial (*Lobularia maritima*) native to the Mediterranean; leaves narrow; flowers very numerous, white or blue, cross-shaped. It is one of the most popular garden bedding plants, grown as a hardy annual, and often referred to simply as 'alyssum'. (Family: Cruciferae.)

sweet bay An evergreen shrub or tree (*Laurus nobilis*), growing to 20 m/65 ft, but often less, native to the Mediterranean; leathery leaves lance-shaped, wavy-edged; male and female flowers yellow or white, 4-lobed; berry black; often referred to simply as **bay**. It is the 'laurel' of poets and victors in classical times, and is now a popular pot herb. (Family: Lauraceae.)

sweet briar *eglantine*

sweet cherry *cherry*

sweet chestnut A deciduous tree (*Castanea sativa*) growing to 30 m/100 ft, native to the Mediterranean and W Asia, and cultivated and naturalized elsewhere; leaves oblong, toothed, glossy; long catkins have green female flowers below yellow males; nuts shiny, brown, three enclosed in a densely spiny case; also called **Spanish chestnut**. The nuts are the familiar roast chesnuts. (Family: Fagaceae.)

sweet cicely A perennial (*Myrrhis odorata*) growing to 2 m/6½ ft, smelling strongly of aniseed, native to Europe; leaves divided, leaflets with oval toothed segments, leaf stalks sheathing; flowers tiny, white, in umbels 1–5 cm/0·4–2 in across, petals

Swaziland

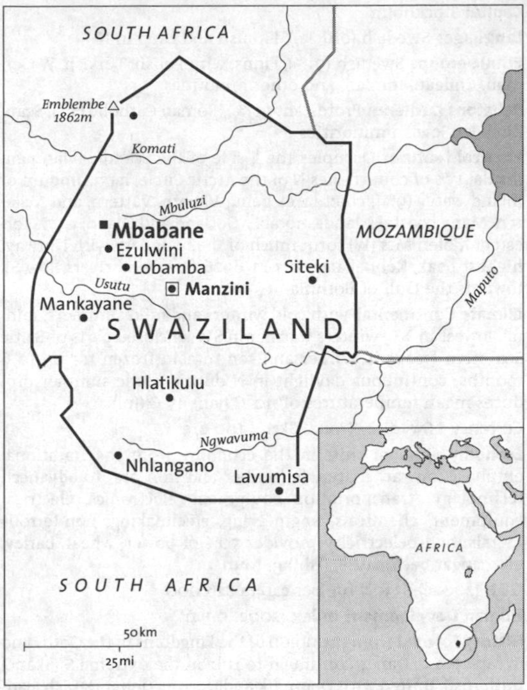

☐ International Airport

[swahzeeland], official name **Kingdom of Swaziland**

Local name Swaziland

Timezone GMT +2

Area 17 363 km^2/6702 sq mi

Population total (2002e) 1 124 000

Status Kingdom

Date of independence 1968

Capital Mbabane

Languages English and Siswati (official)

Ethnic groups Swazi (97%), European (3%)

Religions Christian (Roman Catholic, Anglican, Methodist, and Evangelical Lutheran) (57%), traditional animist beliefs (40%)

Physical features Landlocked, in SE Africa; divided into four topographical regions, mountainous Highveld (W), highest point Emblembe, 1862 m/6109 ft; heavily populated Middleveld (C), descending to 600–700 m/2000–2300 ft; rolling, bush-covered Lowveld (E), irrigated by river systems; Lubombo escarpment, covering 90% of the territory; main rivers, Komati, Usutu, Mbuluzi, flow W–E.

Climate Temperate; tropical in W, with relatively little rain, 500–890 mm/20–35 in; susceptible to drought; subtropical and drier in C; average annual temperature 15°C (Jul), 22°C (Jan) in Mbabane; average annual rainfall 1402 mm/55 in; rainy season (Nov–Mar).

Currency 1 Lilangeni (plural Emalangeni) (Li, E) = 100 cents

Economy Agriculture (employs 70% of population); maize, groundnuts, beans, sorghum, cotton, tobacco, pineapples, citrus; sugar refining, several hydroelectric schemes; asbestos, iron ore, coal, textiles, cement, paper, chemicals.

GDP (2002e) $5·542 bn, per capita $4800

Human Development Index (2002) 0·577

History Arrival of Swazi in the area, early 19th-c; boundaries with the Transvaal decided, and independence guaranteed, 1881; British agreed to Transvaal administration, 1894; British High Commission territory, 1903; independence as a constitutional monarchy within the Commonwealth, 1968; all political parties are banned under 1978 constitution; governed by a bicameral Parliament consisting of a National Assembly and a Senate; the King has considerable executive power, appointing a Cabinet and Prime Minister.

Head of State (Monarch)
1899–1982 Sobhuza II (Chief from 1921)
1983 Dzeliwe *Queen Regent*
1983–6 Ntombi *Queen Regent*
1986– Mswati III

Head of Government
1978–9 Prince Maphevu Dlamini
1979–83 Prince Mbandla Dlamini
1983–6 Prince Bhekimpi Dlamini
1986–9 Sotsha Dlamini
1989–93 Obed Dlamini *Acting*
1993–6 Jameson Mbilini Dlamini
1996–2003 Sibusiso Barnabus Dlamini
2003– Absalom Themba Dlamini

unequal; also called **garden myrrh**. It is cultivated as a seasoning. (Family: Umbelliferae.)

sweet corn *maize*

sweeteners *additives*

sweet gale *bog myrtle*

sweet gum A deciduous tree native to North America, Asia Minor, and China; leaves 5-lobed, turning bright red in autumn; male and female flowers tiny, in separate, globular heads. It yields storax, a fragrant amber-coloured gum used in adhesives and perfumes. (Genus: *Liquidambar*, 6 species. Family: Styracaceae.)

sweet pea An annual climber (*Lathyrus odoratus*), a native of S Italy and Sicily, but widely grown as an ornamental; stems broadly winged, growing to 2 m/6½ ft or more; leaves divided with two oblong–oval, fine-pointed leaflets and branched tendrils; flowers up to 3·5 cm/1½ in, sweetly scented, borne in the upper leaf axils. The wild plants are purple-flowered, but following many years of intensive plant breeding, cultivars now exist in a wide range or combination of colours. (Family: Leguminosae.)

sweet potato A tuberous perennial with trailing or climbing stems (*Ipomoea batatas*); leaves oval to heart-shaped; flowers large, purple, funnel-shaped. Its origin is obscure. It is unknown in the wild, but numerous different strains are cultivated throughout warm regions as a staple food. The edible tubers, sometimes wrongly called *yams*, resemble large potatoes, but may have white, yellow, to red or purple, sweet-tasting flesh. (Family: Convolvulaceae.)

sweet sop *custard apple*

sweet violet A species of violet (*Viola odorata*) lacking stems but with creeping stolons, native to Europe, Asia Minor, and N Africa. Its strongly-scented flowers are distilled for perfume and for flavourings. However, the scent rapidly becomes undetectable, because of the dulling effect on the nose of the chemical, iodine. (Family: Violaceae.)

sweet william A biennial (*Dianthus barbatus*) native to S Europe; leaves elliptical, in opposite pairs, sheathing stem; flowers in dense, compact heads, epicalyx of four long scales, calyx cylindrical; five petals, dark red or pink, in garden forms also white, and often spotted or barred. (Family: Caryophyllaceae.)

Sweyn or **Svein** [svayn], known as **Forkbeard** (?–1014) King of Denmark (c.985–1014) and England (1013–14), the son of Harold Blue-tooth, and the father of Canute. He first attacked England in 994, and had broken the back of English resistance by 1012. During his final campaign in 1013, he established mastery over the whole country and was recognized as king, while Ethelred the Unready withdrew to exile in Normandy.

swidden cultivation *shifting cultivation*

Sweden

☐ International Airport

Swed **Sverige**, official name **Kingdom of Sweden**, Swed **Konungariket Sverige**

Local name Sverige (Swedish)

Timezone GMT +1

Area 411 479 km²/158 830 sq mi

Population total (2002e) 8 925 000

Status Kingdom

Capital Stockholm

Languages Swedish (official), Finnish and Lapp in N

Ethnic groups Swedish (91%), Finns, with Polish, Turkish, W German, Chilean, Iranian, and other minorities

Religions Lutheran Protestant (93%), Roman Catholic (2%), Scandinavian Jewish minorities

Physical features Occupies the E side of the Scandinavian peninsula; 15% of country lies N of the Arctic Circle; large amount of inland water (9%); chief lakes being Vänern, Vättern, and Mälaren. Many coastal islands, notably Gotland and Öland; c.57% forested; Kjölen Mts (W) form much of the boundary with Norway; highest peak, Kebnekaise, 2111 m/6926 ft; several rivers flow SE towards the Gulf of Bothnia.

Climate Continental, with cold winters and mild summers; rainfall lowest in NE; winters warmer in SW; enclosed parts of Baltic Sea often freeze in winter and can remain frozen for up to 6 months; continuous daylight in N during Arctic summer produces mean temperatures of -10°C (Jan), 15°C (Jul).

Currency 1 Swedish Krona (Skr) = 100 øre

Economy Gradual shift in the economy from the traditional emphasis on raw materials (timber and iron ore) to advanced technology; transportation equipment, electronics, electrical equipment, chemicals, engineering, steelmaking, non-ferrous metals; hydroelectricity provides 70% of power; wheat, barley, oats, sugar beet, cattle, fishing; tourism.

GDP (2002e) $230·7 bn, per capita $26 000

Human Development Index (2002) 0·941

History Formed from the union of the kingdoms of the Goths and Svears, 7th-c; Danes continued to rule in the extreme S (Skåne) until 1658; united with Denmark and Norway under Danish leadership, 1389; union ended in 1527, following revolt led by Gustavus Vasa; Sweden acquired Norway from Denmark, 1814; union with Norway dissolved, 1905; a neutral country since 1814; Social Democratic Party controlled government, 1932–76 and returned to power, 1982; a representative and parliamentary democracy, with a Monarch as Head of State; governed by a Prime Minister and a unicameral Parliament (Riksdag) elected every three years; joined European Union, 1995; Swedish Foreign Minister Anna Lindh murdered, Sep 2003.

Head of State (Monarch)
1973– Carl XVI Gustaf

Head of Government
1978–9 Ola Ullsten
1979–82 Thorbjörn Fälldin
1982–6 (Sven) Olof Palme
1986–91 Ingvar Carlsson
1991–4 Carl Bildt
1994–6 Ingvar Carlsson
1996– Goran Persson

Swift, Graham (1949–) Novelist and short-story writer, born in London, UK. He studied at Cambridge and York universities, and published his first novel, *The Sweet Shop Owner*, in 1980. Later books include *The Shuttlecock* (1981), *Ever After* (1992), *Last Orders* (1996, Booker), and *The Light of Day* (2003). He has also written two collections of stories (1982, 1985).

Swift, Jonathan (1667–1745) Clergyman and satirist, born in Dublin, Ireland. He studied at Dublin, then moved to England, where he became secretary to the diplomat, Sir William Temple. During a visit to Ireland, he was ordained in the Anglican Church (1695). He wrote several poems, then turned to prose satire, exposing religious and intellectual complacency in *A Tale of a Tub* (1704), and produced a wide range of political and religious essays and pamphlets. He was made Dean of St Patrick's, Dublin, at the fall of the Tory ministry in 1714, and afterwards visited London only twice. His world-famous satire, *Gulliver's Travels*, appeared (anonymously, like all his works) in 1726. In later years he wrote a great deal of light verse, and several essays on such topics as language and manners. He also progressively identified himself with Irish causes, in such works as *The Drapier's Letter* (1724) and the savagely ironic *A Modest Proposal* (1729).

swift A swallow-like bird of the worldwide family Apodidae (**true swifts**, 78 species) or the SE Asian family Hemiprocnidae (**crested swifts**, 4 species); small feet; lands only on near-vertical surfaces; spends most of its life flying; eats insects caught in the air; may even copulate in flight. The name is also used for the **swift parakeet** (Family: Psittacidae).

swiftlet A small *true swift* (Family: Apodidae), native to the Indian Ocean, S Asia, and the W Pacific; nests in caves (or buildings). Some species use echolocation. Birds' nest soup is made from the saliva-rich nests of three species of the genus *Aerodramus*. (Tribe: Collocaliini, 15 species.)

swift moth A medium to large moth with wings typically rounded at tip; wings coupled in flight by overlapping lobe of forewing; females scatter eggs on vegetation; caterpillars feed on roots or in wood. (Order: Lepidoptera. Family: Hepialidae.)

swimming The act of propelling oneself through water without any mechanical aids. One of the oldest pastimes, the earliest reference to it as a sport is in Japan in 36 BC. There are four primary strokes: the *breast stroke*, developed in the 16th-c, and the *front crawl* (freestyle), *backstroke*, and *butterfly*, developed in the 20th-c. In competitions there are also relays, involving four swimmers, and medley races, which are a combination of all four strokes. In major events the pool is normally 50 m/55 yd long and divided into eight lanes. Race lengths range from 50 m/55 yd to 1500 m/1640 yd.

Swinburne, Algernon Charles (1837–1909) Poet and critic, born in London, UK. He studied at Oxford, and became associated with the Pre-Raphaelite Brotherhood. Leaving without a degree, he travelled in Europe, and throughout his life spent a great deal of time in Northumberland, which he called the 'crowning county' of England. He achieved success with his play *Atalanta in Calydon* (1865), and the first of his series of *Poems and Ballads* (1866) took the public by storm. Other works include *Songs before Sunrise* (1871) and *Essays and Studies* (1875). In 1879, after a breakdown caused by alcoholism, he submitted to the care of a friend, **Theodore Watts-Dunton** (1832–1914), and lived in semi-seclusion for the rest of his life, publishing over 20 books of poetry, drama, and prose, including critical studies of Shakespeare, Hugo, and Ben Jonson.

Swindon 51°34N 1°47W, pop (2001e) 180 100. Old market town in Thamesdown (unitary authority from 1997), Wiltshire, S England, UK; 113 km/70 mi W of London; developed into a modern industrial town with the arrival of the Great Western Railway in the 19th-c; railway; railway engineering, vehicle parts, pharmaceuticals, electronics, clothing; Great Western Railway museum (1962); 9 km/5 mi E is the White Horse of Uffington; football league team, Swindon Town (Robins).

swine *pig*

swine fever The name used for two highly contagious viral infections of pigs. An infection of the intestines is called *hog cholera*, and an infection of the lungs is called *swine plague*.

swing music A term originally used to describe most forms of jazz-based popular music, but from the 1930s it was applied more specifically to 'big-band' dance music with a propulsive rhythm and strong solo instrumental lines, with or without the improvisatory element that is an essential of jazz. Like most American popular music, it was developed by black musicians such as Fletcher Henderson and Don Redman (1900–64), and exploited to great commercial profit by whites. The best known band leaders were Benny Goodman, Duke Ellington, Count Basie, and Glenn Miller.

Swiss cheese plant *monstera*

Swiss Guards The papal police corps, originally instituted by Pope Julius II (r.1503–13) and recruited from the mercenaries of the cantons of the Swiss confederacy, whose reputation as infantrymen was established after their victories over the Burgundian cavalry in 1476. As mercenaries, they fought in various European armies from the 15th-c until the 19th-c. Recruited from the Catholic cantons of central Switzerland, the Swiss guard at the Vatican is dressed in dark blue, yellow, and red uniforms, reputedly designed by Michelangelo.

Swiss lake dwellings Prehistoric settlements around the Swiss lakes, first identified in 1854 at Obermeilen, L Constance, by Swiss archaeologist Ferdinand Keller (1800–81), when abnormally low water revealed extensive timber piling. Over 200 comparable Neolithic sites preserved by waterlogging were subsequently revealed (1860–75). Thought by Keller to have been built on platforms over open water in the manner of the Pacific Is, the houses are now known merely to have been sited on the marshy lake edge.

Swithin or **Swithun, St** (?–862) English saint and theologian. He was adviser to King Egbert, and in 852 he was made Bishop of Winchester, where he died. When in 971 the monks exhumed his body to bury it in the rebuilt cathedral, the removal, which was to have taken place on 15 July, is said to have been delayed by violent rains – hence the current belief that if it rains on that day, it will rain for 40 days more. Feast day 15 July.

Switzerland *p.1492*

Sword-Brothers *Livonian Knights*

sword dance A ceremonial form of dance. In Scotland individuals or groups perform jigs over crossed swords placed on the floor. In England the dancers are linked by metal or wooden swords held in the hand, and perform intertwining figures without breaking the circle. The dance ends with all swords locked in a knot or rose and the simulated ritual decapitation of the leader. *Longsword* is a slow version found in S Yorkshire, and *Rapper* a fast form found in N Yorkshire.

swordfish Large, agile, and very distinctive fish (*Ziphias gladius*) found worldwide in temperate and warm temperate seas; length up to 5 m/16 ft; upper jaw prolonged into a flattened blade or 'sword', teeth absent; dorsal fin tall; feeds mainly on small fish and squid; exploited commercially in many areas. (Family: Xiphiidae.)

swordtail Small, colourful, freshwater fish (*Xiphophorus helleri*) native to streams and swamps of Central America; length up to c.12 cm/5 in; green with orange side stripe; lower edge of tail fin in male prolonged to form the 'sword'; a popular aquarium fish, with many varieties produced by selective breeding. (Family: Poeciliidae.)

Sybaris [**si**baris] An ancient Greek city under the toe of Italy whose citizens were notorious for their wealth and luxurious lifestyle – whence the term **sybarite**. It was obliterated in 510 BC by the neighbouring town of Croton, and never refounded.

sycamore A spreading deciduous tree (*Acer pseudoplatanus*), growing to 35 m/115 ft, native to C and S Europe and W Asia; leaves 10–15 cm/4–6 in, palmately divided into five toothed lobes; flowers yellowish, lacking petals, in pendulous clusters; winged seeds fused in pairs. It is widely planted for shelter and ornament, seeding and spreading freely. (Family: Aceraceae.)

Sydenham's chorea [**sid**nuhmz ko**ree**a] Irregular, jerking, and unpredictable movements of the limbs, and sometimes of the whole body, arising as a complication of streptococcal infections such as rheumatic fever and scarlet fever; girls are especially affected. It is named after English physician Thomas Sydenham (1624–89).

Sydney 33°55S 151°10E, pop (2000e) 3 909 000. Port and state capital of New South Wales, Australia, on the shore of Port Jackson; largest city in Australia; Sydney statistical division comprises 44 municipalities and shires; founded as the first British settlement, 1788; airport; railway; five universities (1850, 1949, 1964, 1989, 1990); two cathedrals; two major harbours (Sydney, Port Botany Container Terminal); commercial, cultural, and financial centre; coal, electronics, oil refining, metal products, machinery, brewing, chemicals, paper, clothing, food processing; trade in wool, grain; Sydney Harbour Bridge (1932); Sydney Opera House on Bennelong Point peninsula (1973); State Parliament House; art gallery (1871); The Rocks (heritage area); Darling Harbour; Chinatown; National Maritime Museum; Festival of Sydney (Jan); Sydney Royal Easter Show; Sydney Cup Week (horse racing) (Apr); location of Olympic Games in 2000.

Sydney Harbour Bridge One of Australia's best-known landmarks, and the widest and heaviest arch bridge in the world, built 1923–32; length of main arch 503 m/1651 ft; highest point 134 m/440 ft above sea-level. The bridge provides a rail and road link across the harbour. It was finally paid for by tolls in 1985. A harbour tunnel was opened in 1992.

Sydney Opera House Australia's best-known contemporary building. Its imaginative design came from an international competition, won in 1956 by the Danish architect Joern Utzon (1918–). Because no building with its features had been built before, costs mounted enormously (from the original A$7·5 million), and in the political controversy Utzon resigned in 1966. Completed in 1973, it cost over A$100 million, much of this coming from a New South Wales government lottery.

Switzerland

□ International Airport

Fr **La Suisse**, Ger **Schweiz**, Ital **Svizzera**, ancient **Helvetia**, official name **Swiss Confederation**, Fr **Confédération Suisse**, Ger **Schweizerische Eidgenossenschaft**, Ital **Confederazione Svizzera**

Local names Schweiz (German), La Suisse (French), Svizzera (Italian)

Timezone GMT +1

Area 41 228 km^2/15 914 sq mi

Population total (2002e) 7 282 000

Status Confederation

Date of independence 1291

Capital Bern (Berne)

Languages German, French, Italian, Romansch (official), Spanish and Turkish also spoken

Ethnic groups (of Swiss nationals) German (74%), French (20%), Italian (4%), Romansch (1%)

Religions Christian (Roman Catholic 49%, Protestant 48%), Jewish minority

Physical features Landlocked, with Alps running roughly E–W in the S; highest peak, Dufourspitze, 4634 m/15 203 ft; Pre-Alps (NW) average 2000 m/6500 ft; sparsely-forested Jura Mts run SW–NW; mean altitude of C plateau, 580 m/1900 ft, fringed with great lakes; chief rivers, Rhine, Rhône, Inn, and tributaries of the Po; c.3000 sq km/1160 sq mi of glaciers, notably the Aletsch.

Climate Temperate climate, subject to Atlantic, Mediterranean and E and C European influences; warm summers, with considerable rainfall; perennial snow cover above 300m/9842 ft; average annual temperature 0°C (Jan), 19°C (Jul) in Bern; average annual rainfall 1000 mm/40 in; the Föhn (warm wind) noticeable late winter and spring in the Alps.

Currency 1 Swiss Franc (SFr, SwF) = 100 centimes

Economy Increased specialization and development in high-technology products; machinery, precision instruments, watches, drugs, chemicals, textiles; a major financial centre; headquarters of many international organizations; all-year tourist area; dairy farming, wheat, potatoes, sugar beet, grapes, apples.

GDP (2002e) $233·4 bn, per capita $32 000

Human Development Index (2002) 0·928

History Part of the Holy Roman Empire, 10th-c; Swiss Confederation created, 1291; expanded during 14th-c; centre of the Reformation, 16th-c; Swiss independence and neutrality recognized under the Treaty of Westphalia, 1648; conquered by Napoleon, who instituted the Helvetian Republic, 1798; organized as a confederation of cantons in 1815; federal constitution, 1848; Red Cross founded, 1863; neutral in both World Wars; helped form European Free Trade Association, 1960; Jura became 23rd canton of Switzerland, 1979; became a full member of the UN, 2002; bicameral Federal Association comprising of a Council of States (Ständerat) and a National Council (Nationalrat); President elected yearly by Federal Council.

Head of State/Government
1996 Jean-Pascal Delamuraz
1997 Arnold Koller
1998 Flavio Cotti
1999 Ruth Dreifuss
2000 Adolf Ogi
2001 Moritz Leuenberger
2002 Kaspar Villiger
2003 Pascal Couchepin
2004 Joseph Deiss

syenite [siyeniyt] A coarse-grained igneous rock containing feldspar and hornblende as essential minerals, with some biotite.

Sykes–Picot Agreement [siyks peekoh] A secret agreement concluded in 1916 by diplomat Sir Mark Sykes (for Britain) and Georges Picot (for France) partitioning the Ottoman Empire after the war. France was to be the dominant power in Syria and Lebanon, and Britain in Transjordan, Iraq, and N Palestine. The rest of Palestine was to be under international control, and an Arab state was to be established. Russia, it emerged later, was also party to the agreement.

syllabary A writing system in which the basic units (*graphemes*) correspond to syllables, normally representing a sequence of consonant and vowel. An example is found in Japanese *kana*, where the graphemes correspond to such spoken sequences as *ka*, *ga*, and *no*. This system is modelled on the spoken language, Japanese being a language which has no true consonant clusters. Consequently, borrowings from English are regularly restructured to break up any consonant clusters into strings of consonant + vowel, eg *spry* would typically appear as 'saparai'.

syllogism In logic, a deductive argument containing two premisses and a conclusion derived from them. **Categorical syllogisms** contain subject–predicate sentences, as in 'Some dogs are chihuahuas; all chihuahaus are small; *therefore* some dogs are small'. **Hypothetical syllogisms** contain conditional sentences: 'If roses are red, then violets are blue; if violets are blue, then carnations are pink; *therefore* if roses are red, then carnations are pink'.

Sylt [zilt, zült] Largest of the North Frisian Is, off the Schleswig-Holstein coast; area 99 sqkm/38 sq mi; length 37 km/23 mi; popular summer resort.

Sylvanus *Silvanus*

Sylvester II, originally **Gerbert of Aurillac** (c.940–1003) Pope (999–1003), born in Aurillac, SC France. Renowned for his achievements in chemistry, mathematics, and philosophy, he is said to have introduced Arabic numerals and to have invented clocks. He became Abbot of Bobbio (982) and Archbishop of Ravenna (988). As pope, he upheld the primacy of Rome against the separatist tendencies of the French Church.

symbiosis [simbiohsis] A general term for the living together of two dissimilar organisms, usually to their mutual benefit. It is commonly used to describe all the different types of relationship between the members of two different and interacting species, including parasitism, mutualism, commensalism and inquilinism. It is sometimes used in a restricted sense for those mutualistic relationships in which each interacting species derives benefit from the association.

symbol Something which, by convention, stands for something else. A symbol is a variety of sign, whose form and meaning are often arbitrary, and agreed upon by the community using it (eg black or white as the colour of mourning). With scientific symbols (such as in chemistry) that agreement is universal, formal, and fixed. However, most symbols, such as words themselves, are less rigidly constrained, allowing scope for differing interpretations. This is particularly so in literature, where writers often create their own symbols.

symbolic interactionism A sociological theory which explains patterns of behaviour according to the meanings and symbols that people share in everyday interaction. The theory was developed by the Chicago school of sociologists in the 1930s, and emphasizes that a mutual understanding between people depends on their continually monitoring, checking, and negotiating the meaning of what they say and how they behave.

symbolic logic *mathematical logic*

Symbolism In general terms, the belief that ideas or emotions may be objectified in terms which make them communicable, whether in words, music, graphics, or plastic forms. In the West, this belief may be traced back to Plato; it was elaborated by the Neoplatonists and by Swedenborg, and is clearly active in much Romantic poetry (especially Coleridge, Shelley, and Blake) and in the writings of Poe. The systematic invocation of a transcendental world in poetry was practised by several French poets in the mid-19th-c (eg Rimbaud, Verlaine, and Mallarmé), who came to be known as Symbolists. Their influence on subsequent art, literature, and aesthetic theory has been far-reaching. The modern novel as well as poetry and drama is often heavily symbolic; the visual arts and the cinema likewise employ sophisticated 'coding' techniques.

Symbolists A group of mid-19th-c French poets, including Baudelaire, Mallarmé, Verlaine, and Rimbaud. Their general aim was to invoke rather than to describe reality, by subliminal means. A Symbolist manifesto was published in 1886 by Jean Moréas (1856–1910), and the ideas were ably expounded by Arthur Symons in *The Symbolist Movement in Literature* (1899). In art, there was a reaction against Realism and Impressionism; leading artists included Denis, Puvis de Chavannes, and Redon.

symmetry Any aspect of a system that is the same after some operation. For example, a square rotated by 90° is indistinguishable from the original, and so has symmetry under rotation by 90°. A circle is symmetric under any rotation about its centre. In physical systems, symmetry is related to conservation laws, and is expressed mathematically using group theory.

symmetry breaking *spontaneous symmetry breaking*

sympathetic nervous system *autonomic nervous system*

symphonic poem A single-movement orchestral work in which a composer seeks to express the emotional, pictorial, or narrative content of a poem, story, painting, etc. It was developed by Liszt from the programmatic concert overture and taken up by other Romantic composers, including Smetana, Franck, and Strauss. Strauss preferred the term *Tondichtung* ('tone poem').

symphony An orchestral work originating in the 18th-c, although the term had been used earlier with different meanings. The classical symphony of Haydn, Mozart, Beethoven, and Schubert was mostly in four movements: a fast movement in sonata form; a slow movement; a minuet or scherzo; and a finale, often in sonata form like the first movement. In the 19th c the structure was varied a good deal, and programmatic or descriptive intentions were often present, as in the five-movement *Symphonie fantastique* of Berlioz. The example of Beethoven's Ninth Symphony, which used solo singers and chorus, was followed by many composers, including Mahler. Sibelius's structural innovations led eventually to a single-movement symphony (No. 7, composed in 1924), while other composers (eg Shostakovich) have either modified the Romantic structure to serve their expressive purposes or, like Stravinsky, sought to restore the older symphonic styles.

Symplegades [simplaygadeez] In Greek mythology, the Clashing Rocks, situated at the entrance to the Black Sea, through which the *Argo* had to pass.

synagogue (Gr 'congregation', 'meeting') The local Jewish institution for instruction in the Torah and worship, but not infringing on the ritual or sacrificial roles of the Jerusalem priesthood. In antiquity, it was the local religious focal point of individual Jewish communities, both in Palestine and in cities of the Diaspora. Congregations were usually governed by a body of elders, who exercised certain disciplinary functions. While the term *synagogue* applied to the congregation, eventually it was also used of the buildings in which the people met, and in great cities such as Alexandria these could be quite elaborate. After the destruction of Jerusalem and the Temple in AD 70, the institution of the synagogue gained even greater importance as the major religious institution in Jewish life. Rabbis became leaders of synagogues in this later period. In Orthodox synagogues, men and women have traditionally separated; but in non-Orthodox synagogues, they now sit together.

synapse [siynaps] The specialized junction between two neurones, present in the nervous system of all animals. Nerve impulses at the axon terminals of one neurone are transmitted across the junction either chemically (by neurotransmitters) or electrically (by local currents) to influence the excitability of the other neurone.

synchronous transmission A protocol for the transmission of data between computers, in which the communications clocks of the two computers are first synchronized and the data is then sent in one continuous burst.

synchrony *diachrony*

synchrotron A machine for accelerating subatomic particles, usually protons or electrons. The particles are guided through an evacuated pipe in a circular path by magnets, accelerated by radio-frequency (rf) electric fields. In a large machine, each pulse of particles may make tens of thousands of revolutions, being accelerated at each pass through the rf source. Magnetic field and rf frequency increase in a synchronized way with increasing particle velocity to maintain a circular path. Machines vary in size up to several kilometres diameter. They are a major experimental tool in particle physics.

synchrotron radiation X-ray radiation emitted by charged particles travelling around a synchrotron. Accelerating electrical charges emit electromagnetic radiation, so by the same mechanism charged particles moving in a circle emit radiation. Thought at one time merely a radiation hazard associated with accelerators, synchrotron radiation has become one of the most powerful research tools available for the study of condensed matter and biological systems, using X-ray diffraction, microscopy, and spectroscopy; custom-built synchrotrons produce very bright, well collimated beams no more than a few millimetres across.

syncline A geological fold structure in the form of a trough or inverted arch, produced by the downfolding of stratified rocks. It is the opposite of an anticline.

syncope [singkopee] *fainting*

sync pulse In motion pictures, signals linked to the camera frame rate recorded on the separate sound magnetic tape for subsequent matching to the picture. In a television signal, sync pulses are included at the end of every line and after each field period to ensure correct operation of transmission, recording, and receiving equipment.

syndicalism A revolutionary socialist doctrine that emphasized workers taking power by seizing the factories in which they worked; developed in the 1890s, and common in France, Italy, and Spain in the early 20th-c. The state was to be replaced by worker-controlled units of production. Often a general strike was advocated as part of the strategy. By 1914 it had lost its political force. The name, deriving from *syndicat* (Fr 'trade union'), has also been applied to various non-revolutionary doctrines supporting worker control.

Synge, (Edmund) J(ohn) M(illington) [sing] (1871–1909) Playwright, born near Dublin, Ireland. A key figure in the Irish Literary Revival, he was educated at Dublin, studied music in Europe, then turned to writing. He lived for a while among the people of the Aran Is, who provided the material for his plays, notably the elegiac *Riders to the Sea* (1904) and the subversive *The Playboy of the Western World* (1907). He had a profound influence on the next generation of Irish playwrights and was a director of the Abbey Theatre from 1904.

synodic period The average time taken by a planet to return to the same position in its orbit relative to the Earth. For the Moon this is 29·53 days, the interval between successive new Moons.

synonym A word which is similar enough in meaning to another word for it to be usable as a substitute in some contexts, such as *illuminate* and *light*. An **antonym** is a word which has the opposite meaning to another, such as *light* and *dark*. A **hyponym** is a word whose meaning is included within that of another, such as *horse* and *animal*. The study of sense relations of this kind is part of the subject of semantics.

synoptic gospels A term applied to three New Testament Gospels (Matthew, Mark, Luke), so called because of the striking amount of common material that they contain. Most of Mark's Gospel, for example, is reproduced in Matthew and Luke, and the correspondence often extends to the order of passages and wording, although differences also exist. The precise way in which the works are interrelated is known as the 'synoptic problem', for which many competing solutions have been offered. John's Gospel presents a strikingly different portrayal of Jesus.

synovitis [siynoviytis] Inflammation of the synovial membranes that enclose tendons or cover surfaces within and around the joints. It arises from persistent injury (eg from sports), or from bacterial or immunological inflammation, when it takes the form of arthritis.

synroc [sinrok] An artificial ceramic material used to store high-level radioactive waste. The waste is added to mixed powdered metal oxides from which the ceramic is formed by heat and compression. Radioactive waste atoms displace some host atoms, and so are chemically bound into a material similar in type to natural ceramic. It is under development as an alternative to storage using glass.

syntax In linguistics, the study of sentence structure; alternatively, the study of how words can be combined into larger grammatical units. A syntax for a language specifies a set of grammatical categories (such as verb, noun phrase, and sentence) and a set of rules which define the ways in which these categories relate to each other.

synthesizer An electronic apparatus for generating musical sounds, usually fitted with one or more keyboards and loudspeakers. One of the earliest and best known was developed in 1964 by Robert A Moog (1934–). Like many of those which followed, it could produce only one sound at a time, but since 1975 newer 'polyphonic' types have been developed, including digital ones based on microprocessors, which are not limited in this respect.

synthetic chemistry The study of the preparation of chemical compounds. It is generally divided into organic and inorganic chemistry, and is particularly important in the pharmaceutical industry.

synthetic elements In chemistry, isotopes (generally radioactive) made by nuclear reactions. All isotopes of all actinide elements are synthetic.

synthetic language *analytic language*

Synthetism A term sometimes used by art critics to refer to the Symbolist artists, to distinguish them from the Symbolist poets. It is also sometimes applied to the *Nabis*.

syphilis [sifilis] A chronic sexually transmitted disease caused by *Treponema pallidum*. Initially, a primary lesion (a *chancre*) develops on the genitals or anus, followed several weeks later by features of a generalized infection, with fever and a rash. The condition may then remain dormant for years. Nodules (*gumma*) then form in the skin and mucous membranes, and these may break down to form large ulcers. Thereafter the cardiovascular and nervous systems become affected, resulting in damage to the heart valves, swelling of the aorta (*aneurysm*), and a combination of inco-ordination, loss of sensation, and dementia known as *generalized paralysis of the insane*.

syphon *siphon*

Syracuse (Italy) [siyrakyooz, sirakyooz], Ital **Siracusa** 37°04N 15°18E, pop (2000e) 122 000. Seaport capital of Siracusa province, Sicily, S Italy; 53 km/33 mi SE of Catania; founded by Greek settlers, 734 BC; leading cultural centre, 5th-c BC; taken by the Romans, 212 BC; archbishopric; railway; food processing, paper making, construction, petrochemicals, tourism; birthplace of Archimedes, Theocritus; cathedral (640), Greek theatre (3rd-c BC), Roman amphitheatre, temples, aqueducts.

Syracuse (USA) [sirakyooz] 43°03N 76°09W, pop (2000e) 147 300. Seat of Onondaga Co, C New York, USA; 19 km/12 mi S of W end of L Oneida; developed in association with salt works during the 1780s and later at the junction of the Erie and Oswego Canals; city status, 1848; airfield; railway; university (1870); electrical equipment.

Syria *p.1495*

Syriac *Aramaic*

syringa [siringga] *lilac; mock orange*

Syrinx [siringks] In Greek mythology, a nymph pursued by Pan. She called on the Earth to help, and so sank down into it and became a reed-bed. Pan cut some of the reeds, and made the panpipes.

syrinx [siringks] The voice-producing organ of birds; situated in the windpipe where this divides into two. It has vibrating membranes, a reverberating capsule (*tympanum*), and various muscles. The structure and position of the syrinx has been used in bird classification to indicate the relationships of groups.

system Any biological, mechanical, or organizational entity which carries out a specific function, receiving inputs from its surroundings and sending outputs to its surroundings. It follows that any system is a part of a wider system, which in turn is part of a wider system, and so on. In computing, the word is used to refer to a part of the information processing of an organization which might be appropriate for implementation by a computer, such as the handling of a payroll or the handling of bills and invoices. Today, **systems analysts** are just as concerned about the human organizational systems as the clerical processing systems.

systematics The classification of organisms into a hierarchical series of groups which emphasizes their presumed evolutionary interrelationships. The main categories of modern classifications are (in order of increasing generality) species, genus, family, order, class, phylum (animals), division (plants), and kingdom.

systemic lupus erythematosus (SLE) [loopus erithematohsus] A chronic multi-system inflammatory disease affecting connective tissue throughout the body, ten times more common in women. The exact cause is unknown, but it is characterized by the presence of several auto-antibodies in the blood; onset is around 20–40 years, and is gradually progressive. The disease is aggravated by sunlight and some drugs. Typical features include a facial rash with a 'butterfly' distribution across the cheeks and nose, arthritis affecting small joints, kidney failure, anaemia, fluid round the heart and lungs, fever, weight loss, and fatigue. It is treated with steroids and immunosuppressive drugs.

systemic sclerosis [sklerohsis] A rare generalized disease of connective tissue throughout the body, thought to have an auto-immune cause; also known as **scleroderma**. The skin becomes

Syria

□ International Airport

Arabic **Suriya**, official name **Syrian Arab Republic**, Arabic **Al-Jumhuriyah al-Arabiyah as-Suriyah**

Local name as-Suriyah (Arabic)

Timezone GMT +2

Area 185 180 km^2/71 479 sq mi

Population total (2002e) 17 156 000

Status Republic

Date of independence 1946

Capital Damascus

Languages Arabic (official), Kurdish, Armenian, Aramaic, and Circassian also spoken

Ethnic groups Arab (90%), Kurd, Armenian, Turkish, Circassian, and Assyrian

Religions Muslim (Sunni Muslim 74%, Alawite, Druse, and other sects 16%), Christian (10%)

Physical features Narrow Mediterranean coastal plain; Jabal al Nusayriyah mountain range rises to c.1500 m/5000 ft; steep drop (E) to Orontes R valley; Anti-Lebanon range (SW) rises to 2814 m/9232 ft at Mt Hermon; open steppe and desert to the E.

Climate Coastal Mediterranean, hot, dry summers, mild, wet winters; desert or semi-desert climate in 60% of country; annual rainfall below 200 mm/8 in; Khamsin wind causes temperatures to rise to 43–9°C; average annual temperatures 7°C (Jan), 27°C (Jul) in Damascus.

Currency 1 Syrian pound (LS, Syr £)= 100 piastres

Economy Oil (most important source of export revenue since 1974); Euphrates dam project (begun 1978) presently supplies 97% of domestic electricity; intended to increase arable land by 6400 km^2/500 sq mi; food processing; textiles; tobacco; cement.

GDP (2002e) $63·48 bn, per capita $3700

Human Development Index (2002) 0·691

History Part of Phoenician Empire; Islam introduced in 7th-c; conquered by Turks, 11th-c; part of Ottoman Empire, 1517; brief period of independence in 1920, then made a French mandate; independence, 1946; merged with Egypt to form United Arab Republic, 1958; re-established itself as independent state under present name, 1961; Golan Heights region seized by Israel, 1967; after outbreak of civil war in Lebanon (1975), Syrian troops sent to restore order, and became much involved in the region's power struggle; breaking of diplomatic relations with Great Britain, 1986; condemned Iraqi invasion of Kuwait and sent allied forces troops in Gulf War in 1990, restoring relations; accepted US proposals for terms of an Arab-Israeli peace conference, 1991; governed by a president, prime minister, and 250-member People's Council.

Head of State
1971–2000 Hafez al-Assad
2000– Bashar al-Assad

Head of Government
1971–2 Abdel Rahman Khleifawi
1972–6 Mahmoud bin Saleh al-Ayoubi
1976–8 Abdul Rahman Khleifawi
1978–80 Mohammed Ali al-Halabi
1980–7 Abdel Rauof al-Kasm
1987–2000 Mahmoud Zubi
2000–3 Muhammad Mustafa Miro
2003– Muhammad Naji al-Utri

progressively thickened and shiny, and adheres to underlying tissues. Joints become painful and stiff. The alimentary tract, lungs, and heart may also be involved.

systems analysis In computing, generally used to refer to the techniques involved in the intimate understanding, design, and optimization of computer systems. **Systems analysts** are responsible for the precise definition and implementation of a computer system in business, research, and other contexts. **Systems design** is the process of designing a new computer system to replace an existing manual system or an inappropriate computer system.

systems building *prefabrication*

systole [sistolee] Phases of the cardiac cycle when the atria (**atrial systole**) contract to force blood into the ventricles, and then the ventricles (**ventricular systole**) contract forcibly, ejecting the blood into the aorta (from the left ventricle) and pulmonary trunk (from the right ventricle).

syzygy [sizijee] An astronomical situation which occurs when the Sun, Earth, and Moon or a planet are roughly in a straight line. Eclipses are likely when the Moon is at syzygy.

Szczecin [shchecheen], Ger **Stettin** 53°25N 14°32E, pop (2000e) 419 000. Industrial river-port capital of Szczecin voivodship, NW Poland; on R Oder 60 km/37 mi from the Baltic Sea; largest Baltic trading port; urban status, 1243; member of the Hanseatic League, 1360; Prussian rule, 1720–1945; badly damaged in World War 2; ceded to Poland, 1945; contains area of Międzyodrze, 5 km/3 mi of docks, canals, and transshipment facilities; airfield; railway; maritime college; medical academy; technical university (1946); shipbuilding, yacht-building, synthetic fibres, cranes, iron, tools, deep-sea fishing, fish processing; St James's Cathedral, castle (16th-c), 13th–14th-c city walls.

Szeged [seged] 46°16N 20°10E, pop (2000e) 171 000. River-port capital of Csongrád county, S Hungary, on R Tisza; railway; university (1872, refounded 1921); biological centre of the Hungarian Academy of Sciences; railway; timber and salt trade, chemicals, hemp, salami, red pepper; cultural centre of the S Alföld; medicinal baths; castle (1242), votive church; open-air arts festival (Jul–Aug).

Székely [saykel] A Magyar-speaking people, since the 11th-c inhabiting the SE Transylvanian region of post-1918 Romania; generally believed to be of ethnically Turkic descent. In both the interwar and the contemporary periods, the position of the Székely has given rise to disputes between the Romanian and Hungarian states.

Székesfehérvár [saykeshfeheervah(r)], Ger **Stuhlweissenburg**, ancient **Alba Regia** 47°15N 18°25E, pop (2000e) 106 000. Capital of Fejér county, WC Hungary; ancient capital of Hungarian kingdom; badly damaged in World War 2; market centre for tobacco, wine, fruit; light metal works; cathedral, episcopal palace, Garden of Ruins with remains of 11th-c royal cathedral.

Szell, George [sel] (1897–1970) Conductor and pianist, born in Budapest, Hungary. A child prodigy, he was educated at the Vienna State Academy, and made his debut as a conductor in Berlin (1914), later conducting many of the world's major orchestras. He settled in the USA in 1939, and from 1946 was musical director and conductor of the Cleveland Symphony Orchestra.

Szewinska, Irena [shevinska], *née* **Kirszenstein** (1946–) Athlete, born in St Petersburg, NW Russia. She established herself at the 1964 Olympics with a silver medal in the long jump, and a gold in Poland's relay squad. She set world records at 100 m and 200 m in 1965, won three gold medals at the European Championships in 1966, and took the Olympic 200 m title in 1968 in world record time. She later won bronze medals at the 1971 European Championships and the 1972 Olympics. She then stepped up to 400 m, and in 1976 won the Olympic title in a new world record 49·28 sec. She appeared in her fifth Olympics at Moscow in 1980.

Szilard, Leo [silah(r)d] (1898–1964) Physicist, born in Budapest, Hungary. He studied at Budapest and Berlin universities, fleeing from Germany in 1933. He worked first in London, then in 1938 emigrated to the USA, where he began work on nuclear physics at Columbia University. In 1934 he had taken a patent on nuclear fission as an energy source, and on hearing of Otto Hahn and Lise Meitner's fission of uranium (1938), he approached Einstein in order to write together to President Roosevelt, warning him of the possibility of atomic bombs. He was a central figure in the Manhattan Project, and after the War became a strong proponent of the peaceful uses of atomic energy.

Szombathely [sombot-hay], Ger **Steinamanger**, ancient **Sabaria** 47°14N 16°38E, pop (2000e) 83 300. Capital of Vas county, W Hungary, on R Gyöngyös; bishopric; railway; chemicals, textiles, timber; cathedral, 14th-c Franciscan church, 17th-c Dominican church, Garden of Ruins with excavations of 4th-c imperial palace.

Szymborska, Wislawa [simbaw(r)ska] (1923–) Poet and critic, born in Bnin (now part of Kornik), WC Poland. She moved to Kraków in 1931, where she studied literature and sociology at the Jagiellonian University (1945–8), and then worked for a Polish literary magazine (1953–81). Her first collections of poetry appeared in 1952 and 1954, but were subject to the censorship of the era, and she now recognizes only her work published after 1957. English-language collections include *People on a Bridge* (1990), *View with a Grain of Sand* (1995), *Sounds, Feelings, Thoughts* (1996), and *Poems, New and Collected* (1998). She is also known for her translations from French poetry. She received the Nobel Prize for Literature in 1996.

t

Tabari, al- [tabahree], in full **Abu Jafar Mohammed Ben Jarir al-Tabari** (839–923) Historian, born in Amol, Persia. He travelled throughout the Middle East collecting scholarly material, and wrote a major commentary on the Qur'an, and a history of the world from creation until the early 10th-c. His work provided a basis for later historical and religious studies.

Tabarley, Eric (1931–98) French yachtsman. He was twice winner of the single-handed trans-Atlantic race – in 1964 in *Pen Duick II*, and in 1976 in *Pen Duick VI*.

tabasco sauce [tabaskoh] A red sauce rich in chillies and hot red peppers, originating in the Mexican state of Tabasco. It is made from the fruit of the plant *Capsicum frutescens*, and is used to flavour soups, stews, and other hot dishes.

Tabernacle A movable sanctuary or tent; in early Israelite religion, the shelter for the Ark of the Covenant during the desert wanderings and conquest of Canaan, eventually replaced by Solomon's Temple. Elaborate instructions for its construction and furnishing are given in the Book of Exodus, but many consider these to derive from a later priestly source.

Tabernacles, Feast of *Sukkoth*

tablature A system of musical notation tailored to a particular instrument or group of instruments and indicating the keys, frets, etc to be used rather than the pitch to be sounded. German organ tablature used mainly letters in conjunction with rhythmic signs; lute tablatures used letters or numerals on lines representing the strings of the instrument. The only instruments for which tablature is normally used today are the ukulele and the guitar: the notation conveys a diagrammatic indication of finger-placings.

Table Mountain 33°58S 18°25E. Mountain in SW South Africa; height 1086 m/3563 ft; a flat-topped central massif flanked on either side by the Lion's Head and Devil's Peak; often shrouded in cloud, known as the 'Tablecloth'; Kirstenbosch national botanical gardens on E slopes; Cape Town at the foot.

table tennis An indoor bat-and-ball game played by two or four players on a table measuring 9 ft (2·75 m) by 5 ft (1·52 m). The centre of the table has a net 6 in (15·25 cm) high stretched across it. The ball must be hit over the net and into the opposing half of the table. The object is to force one's opponent to make an error and thus not return the ball successfully. In doubles, the players must hit the ball alternately and in order. The winner is the first to reach 11 points with at least a two-point lead. The exact origins of the game are uncertain, but it is thought to have been first played in the 1880s. Known as **ping pong** in the early part of the 20th-c, it is very popular in China and Korea.

taboo A prohibited form of conduct; from a Polynesian word, *tapu*. A wide variety of actions may be *tapu*: a chief's *tapu* may prevent him being allowed to carry burdens; children may be prohibited from touching sea-going canoes, or men's weapons, or from eating certain foods. Breaching a *tapu* may result directly in sickness or death, or may provoke physical punishment. Captain Cook recorded the term during his voyages in the Pacific, and noted the right of the chiefs to declare places or objects *tapu* to commoners. The term became part of English usage during the early 19th-c, and is now used more generally, especially with reference to any subject-matter (eg death, politics) or language (eg swearing, obscenity) which people on occasion avoid.

tabor A small double-headed side drum with snares, known from mediaeval times. It was often played with one stick, the player at the same time blowing a three-holed pipe to accompany dancing.

Tabriz [tabreez], ancient **Tauris** 38°05N 46°18E, pop (2000e) 1 373 000. Capital city of Tabriz district, NW Iran; fourth largest city in Iran; often severely damaged by earthquakes; airport; railway; university (1949); industrial and commercial centre; carpets; ruined 15th-c Blue Mosque and citadel.

Tachisme *action painting*

tachometer [takometer] An instrument for measuring the speed of rotation. There are many methods; a typical modern device rotates a magnet near a non-magnetic conductor, exerting a force through the field produced by eddy currents. It is widely used to monitor the driving practices of lorry-drivers and bus-drivers.

tachycardia An abnormally fast heart rate. It may arise due to a normal physiological process, such as during exercise, the ingestion of drugs such as caffeine and amphetamine, or generalized disorders such as serious infections or hyperthyroidism. It may also be due to specific disorders of the heart that disrupt the normal electrical pathways of the heart muscle, in which case the heart rate may be irregular. Extremely rapid heart rates do not allow time for adequate pumping of the blood at each beat and result in heart failure.

tachyon [takyon] A hypothetical elementary particle having imaginary mass (ie m^2 less than 0), and able to travel faster than the velocity of light without violating special relativity. Observable effects are predicted, but have not been seen.

Tacitus [tasitus], in full **Publius** or **Gaius Cornelius Tacitus** (c.55–120) Roman historian. He studied rhetoric at Rome, became a praetor, and established a great reputation as an orator, becoming consul in 97. His major works are two historical studies, the 12-volume *Historiae* (Histories), of which only the first four books survive whole, and the *Annales* (Annals), of possibly 18 books, of which only eight have been completely preserved. His concise and vivid prose style was a major influence on later writers, such as Gibbon.

Tacoma [takohma] 47°14N 122°26W, pop (2000e) 193 600. Port seat of Pierce Co, WC Washington, USA, on Commencement Bay; settled, 1868; city status, 1875; railway; university (1888); air force base; major NW Pacific container port exporting timber, fruit, tallow, agricultural machinery; boatbuilding, chemicals, food processing, metalwork, wood, paper products; state historical society; tourist centre; Chinese museums, Museum of Glass (opened 2002), Fort Nisqually; daffodil festival.

tactical voting The act of casting a vote in an election for a candidate with the best chance of defeating another candidate who would otherwise be the most likely to win. This generally occurs where the candidate of one's choice is highly unlikely to be successful, or where preventing a particular candidate from being elected is of greater importance.

Tadmur or **Tadmor,** ancient **Palmyra** 34°36N 38°15E, pop (2000e) 28 000. Ancient city in Hims governorate, C Syria, a world heritage site; 208 km/129 mi NE of Damascus; financial capital of the E world, 1st–2nd-c; on ancient caravan route from Persian Gulf to Mediterranean Sea; rail terminus; many examples of Hellenistic art and architecture; numerous temples, including Temple of Bêl; Monumental Arch; several tombs on hill slopes (E).

tadpole The larva of an amphibian, especially a frog or toad; largest 25 cm/10 in long; usually a short spherical body, feathery gills, large tail; most eat microscopic plants; with age, gills and tail shrink, legs appear, and larvae become carnivorous; also known as **pollywog**, or **porwiggle** (from Old English *tade poll*, 'toad head', Middle English *pollwyggle*, 'head wiggle').

tadpole shrimp A primitive freshwater crustacean found in temporary pools in arid regions; shield-shaped carapace covers head and thorax; abdomen slender, with many segments; feeds on detritus or as a predator; c.11 living species. (Class: Branchiopoda. Order: Notostraca.)

Taegu or **Daegu** [tiygoo] 35°52N 128°36E, pop (2000e) 2 448 000. City with provincial status in SE Korea; largest inland city after Seoul; railway; university (1946); market town at centre of apple-growing area; textiles; Haeinsa temple (802) with the Tripitaka Koreana, a set of 80 000 wooden printing blocks engraved with Buddhist scripture (13th-c); Tonghwasa Temple nearby (17th-c); Daegu World Cup Stadium (2001).

Taejon or **Daejeon** [tiyjon] 36°20N 127°26E, pop (2000e) 1 167 000. Capital of Ch'ungch'ongnam province, C Korea; badly damaged in Korean War; railway; university (1952); agricultural centre; Yusong Hot Springs (W); Kyeryongsan national park (W); Daejeon World Cup Stadium (2001).

taekwondo [tiykwondoh] A martial art developed in Korea by General Choi Hong Hi. It officially became part of Korean tradition and culture in 1955, and is now popular as a sport. The International Taekwondo Federation was founded in 1966.

Taft, William Howard (1857–1930) US statesman and 27th president (1909–13), born in Cincinnati, Ohio, USA. He studied at Yale, became a lawyer, solicitor general (1890), the first civil governor of the Philippines (1901), and secretary of war (1904–8). During his presidency he secured an agreement with Canada which meant relatively free trade but the Canadian electorate rejected it in 1911. He became professor of law at Yale in 1913, and later served as Chief Justice of the USA (1921–30). His split with Theodore Roosevelt over the political direction of the party led to the breakup of the Republicans in 1912 and Taft's defeat.

Taganrog [taganrok] 47°14N 38°55E, pop (2000e) 293 000. Seaport in Rostovskaya oblast, S European Russia; on NE shore of the Gulf of Taganrog of the Sea of Azov; founded as a fortress and naval base, 1698; rail terminus; metallurgy, machines, foodstuffs, shipyards, leatherwork; birthplace of Chekhov.

Tagore, Rabindranath [tagaw(r)] (1861–1941) Poet and philosopher, born in Kolkata (formerly Calcutta), E India. He is best known for his poetic works, notably *Gitanjali* (1912, Song Offering), and his short stories, such as *Galpaguccha* (1912, A Bunch of Stories), but he also wrote plays (such as *Chitra*, 1896) and novels (such as *Binodini*, 1902). In 1901 he founded near Bolpur the Santiniketan, a communal school to blend Eastern and Western philosophical and educational systems. He received the Nobel Prize for Literature in 1913, the first Asian to do so, and was knighted in 1915 – an honour which he resigned in 1919 as a protest against British policy in the Punjab.

Tagus, River [tayguhs], Span **Río Tajo**, Port **Río Tejo** River rising in the Sierra de Albarracín, Spain; flows 785 km/488 mi SW to the Portuguese border, which it follows for 44 km/27 mi; below Vila Franca de Xira, opens out into the Tagus estuary at Lisbon Bay; 229 sq km/88 sq mi of the estuary given reserve status in 1976; length, 1007 km/626 mi; navigable, 212 km/132 mi to Abrantes.

Tahiti [taheetee], Fr **Archipel de Tahiti** [taeetee] 17°37S 149°27W; pop (2000e) 164 000; area 1042 sq km/402 sq mi. Largest island of French Polynesia, S Pacific Ocean, belonging to the Windward group of the Society Is; length, 48 km/30 mi; French colony, 1880; capital, Papeete; rises to 2237 m/7339 ft in the volcanic peak of Mt Orohena; vanilla, coconuts, copra, sugar cane, tourism; home of Gauguin (1891–3).

tahr [tah(r)] A S Asian goat-antelope; thick coat except on head; short curved horns; inhabits steep, tree-covered hillsides; three species: **Himalayan tahr** (introduced in New Zealand), **Nilgiri tahr**, and **Arabian tahr**. (Genus: *Hemitragus*.)

Tai [tiy] National park in Guiglo and Sassandra departments, SW Côte d'Ivoire; area 3300 sq km/1300 sq mi; established in 1972; a world heritage site.

Tai, Mount [tiy], Chin **Taishan** The most revered of China's five sacred mountains, and a key geological, religious, and cultural site in Shandong province; a world heritage site. Evidence of settlement dates back 400 000 years, and the area is rich in fossils, medicinal plants, ancient ruins, and temples.

tai chi chuan [tiy chee chwan] A Chinese martial art said to date from the 13th-c, when a Taoist monk, Chang San Feng, observed a fight between a snake and a crane and devised a series of postures based on the movements of these animals from which the present forms are developed. The foundation of the art is the practice of 'the form', a series of 108 movements in a slow, continuous sequence, which is used as a method of meditation to harmonize the mind, body, and spirit. Each posture has several fighting applications, and weapon forms are also practised using the broad sword, straight-edged sword, and spear, which help to develop speed, stamina, and power. Studies have demonstrated beneficial effects for those suffering from anxiety, high blood pressure, and heart problems, and in the long term practitioners show a lower incidence of atheroma, osteoporosis, and spinal problems when compared with a matched control group.

Taif, at- [at tiyf] 21°05N 40°27E, pop (2000e) 473 000. Summer resort town in Mecca province, WC Saudi Arabia; 64 km/40 mi ESE of Mecca; on a high plateau at an altitude of 1158 m/3799 ft; the unofficial seat of government during the summer; airfield; centre of fruit-growing district (grapes, apricots, pomegranates).

taiga [tiyga] A Russian term for the open coniferous forest zone intermediate between the boreal forest and tundra regions. Sometimes it is used synonymously with the term *boreal*, though in the taiga the vegetation canopy is more open, with occasional stands of deciduous trees. Open areas are usually poorly drained muskeg.

Tailang *Mon*

tailorbird An Old World warbler (Family: Sylviidae) native to India and SE Asia; inhabits forest and cultivation; eats insects and nectar; nest formed by folding a large leaf and 'sewing' the edges together with separate stitches of wool, silk, or spider's web. (Genus: *Orthotomus*, 9 species.)

Taimyr, Lake *Taymyr, Lake*

Tainan or **T'ai-nan** [tiynahn] 23°01N 120°14E, pop (2000e) 745 000. Independent municipality and oldest city in Taiwan, on SW coast of Taiwan I; capital, 1684–7; university (1971); agricultural trade, fish market, crafts; oldest Confucian temple in Taiwan (1665), Yi T'sai castle (1874).

Taine, Hippolyte (Adolphe) [ten] (1828–93) Critic, historian, and positivist philosopher, born in Vouziers, NE France. He studied at Paris, turned to writing, and made a reputation with his critical works, followed by several philosophical studies in which he attempted to explain moral qualities and artistic excellence in purely descriptive, quasi-scientific terms. His greatest work, *Les Origines de la France contemporaine* (1875–94, The Origins of Contemporary France), constituted a strong attack on the men and the motives of the Revolution.

taipan [tiypan] A venomous snake (*Oxyuranus scutellatus*), native to NE Australia and New Guinea; one of the world's most deadly snakes; the largest Australian snake (length up to 4 m/13 ft); aggressive (but rare); brown with paler head; eats mainly small mammals. The Australian **fierce snake** (*Parademansia microlepidota*) is sometimes placed in genus *Oxyuranus* and called **desert taipan**. (Family: Elapidae.)

Taiwan

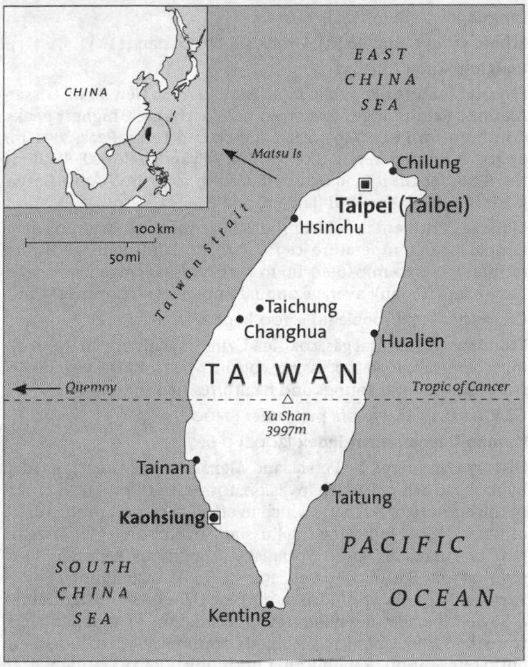

☐ International Airport

[tiywan], official name **Republic of China**, formerly **Formosa**

Local name T'aiwan

Timezone GMT +8

Area 36 000 km^2/13 896 sq mi

Population total (2002e) 22 457 000

Status Republic

Date of independence 1949

Capital Taipei

Languages Mandarin Chinese (official), various dialects including Taiwanese and Hakka also spoken

Ethnic groups Han Chinese (98%), small (Polynesian) aboriginal minority

Religions Taoist, Buddhist, Christian (Protestant and Roman Catholic)

Physical features Consists of Taiwan I and several smaller islands c.130 km/80 mi off the SE coast of mainland China; mountain range runs N–S, covering two-thirds of the island; highest peak, Yu Shan 3997 m/13 113 ft; low-lying land mainly in the W; crossed by the Tropic of Cancer.

Climate Tropical monsoon-type climate; hot, humid summers, mild, short winters; wet season (May–Sep); typhoons common (Jul–Sep); average daily temperature 12–19°C (Jan), 24–33°C (Jul) in Taibei; average annual rainfall 2500 mm/98 in.

Currency 1 New Taiwan Dollar (NT$) = 100 cents

Economy Progressed from agriculture to industry since 1950s; high technology, textiles, electronics, plastics, petrochemicals, machinery; natural gas, limestone, marble, asbestos; sugar, bananas, pineapples, citrus fruits, vegetables, tea, fish; affected by SARS outbreak, 2003.

GDP (2001e) $386 bn, per capita $17 200

History Taiwan (Formosa) visited by the Portuguese, 1590; conquered by Manchus, 17th-c; ceded to Japan following Sino-Japanese War, 1895; returned to China, 1945; Nationalist government moved to Taiwan by Jiang Jieshi (Chang Kai-shek); government still maintains claim to legal jurisdiction over mainland China and continues to designate itself as the Republic of China; protected by US naval forces during Korean War, 1950–3; signed mutual defence pact with USA, 1954–79; end of state of civil war with People's Republic of China declared by President Lee Teng-hui, 1991; governed by a President, who appoints a premier; elections held for a reformed National Assembly, 1991.

Head of State

1950–75 Chiang Kai-shek
1975–8 Yen Chia-kan
1978–88 Chiang Ching-kuo
1988–2000 Lee Teng-hui
2000– Chen Shui-bian

Head of Government

1972–8 Chiang Ching-kuo
1978–84 Sun Yun-suan
1984–9 Yu Kuo-hwa
1989–90 Lee Huan
1990–3 Hau Pei tsun
1993–6 Lien Chan
1997–2000 Vincent Siew
2000 Tang Fei
2000–2 Chang Chun-hsiung
2002– Yu Shyi-kun

Taipei or **Taibei** [tiybay], also **T'ai-pei** 25°05N 121°32E, pop (2000e) 2 934 000. Capital of Taiwan, at the NW end of the island; one of the fastest-growing cities in Asia; occupied by the Japanese, 1895–1945; seat of the Nationalist Government, 1949; airport; airfield; railway; three universities (1927, 1928, 1946); textiles, plastics, electronics, foodstuffs, shipbuilding, machinery, crafts; National Palace Museum, Zhong Zheng Memorial Hall, Long Shan (Dragon Mountain) Temple (1740, rebuilt several times).

Taiping Rebellion (1850–64) A major uprising against the Qing dynasty in China. Hong Xiuquan (1814–64), a Hakka schoolmaster and failed Confucian scholar, became a Christian in 1837, and saw himself as the younger brother of Christ, with a divine mission. By 1850 he had recruited 10 000 members of his God Worshippers League, and in 1851 declared himself Heavenly King of the Heavenly Kingdom of Great Peace (*Taiping Tian Guo*). After taking several cities, Nanjing was made his capital in 1853. A counter-attack was led by the Confucian Zeng Guofan, other provincial leaders, and General Gordon. Nanjing fell in 1864, and the Taipings were eliminated. Hong, a figurehead since 1856, committed suicide. The Taiping beliefs (they made property communal, promoted sex equality, and were against caste) appeared heroic to 20th-c revolutionaries, and the rebellion contributed to the collapse of the Qing dynasty.

Tairov, Alexander Yakovlevich [taeerof], originally **Alexander Kornblit** (1885–1950) Theatre director and actor, born in Rovno, SW Ukraine. He acted in Kiev, St Petersburg, Riga, and Simbirsk (1905–13), then directed at the Free Theatre in Moscow, before founding the Moscow Chamber Theatre with his wife in 1914. He remained director of this theatre until shortly before his death, pioneering a 'synthetic theatre' of abstract balletic movement which aspired to the emotional precision of music. His *Notes of a Director* appeared in 1921.

Taiwan *see panel*

Taiyuan or **T'ai-yüan** [tiyyüan] 37°50N 112°30E, pop (2000e) 2 287 000, administrative region 2 819 000. Capital of Shanxi province, NEC China; founded during W Zhou dynasty (11th–8th-c BC); capital of Hunnish kingdom, AD 304; development promoted by the West in late 19th-c; railway; coal, iron, steel, chemicals, textiles; Shanxi Museum; c.25 km/15 mi SE, Jinci temples from the N Wei dynasty.

Taizé [tayzay] An ecumenical community founded near Lyon, France, by members of the French Reformed Church in 1940. Members observe a rule similar to most monastic orders. Their

Tajikistan

[tajikistahn], official name **Republic of Tajikistan**, also spelled **Tadzhikistan**, Tajik **Jumhurii Tojikistan**

Local name Tojikiston

Timezone GMT +3

Area 143 100 km^2/55 200 sq mi

Population total (2002e) 6 327 000

Status Republic

Date of independence 1991

Capital Dushanbe

Languages Tajik (official), Russian

Ethnic groups Tajik (64%), Uzbek (24%), Russian (1.1%)

Religion Sunni Muslim

Physical features Republic in SE Middle Asia; Tien Shan, Gissar-Alai, and Pamir ranges cover over 90% of the area; highest peaks, Communism Peak, 7495 m/24 590 ft, and Lenin Peak, 7134 m/23 405 ft, located in N part of Pamirs; R Pyandzh flows E–W along the S border till it is joined by R Valksh to form R Amu Darya; lakes include L Kara-Kul (largest) and L Sarez.

Climate Continental; subtropical valley areas, hot, dry summers; annual mean temperature -0·9°C (Jan), 27°C (Jul); average annual rainfall 150–250 mm/6–10 in; in highlands, average mean temperature -3°C (Jan); average annual rainfall 60–80 mm/2–3 in.

Currency 1 Tajik rouble (R) = 100 kopecs

Economy Oil, natural gas, coal, lead, zinc, machinery, metalworking, chemicals, food processing; cotton, wheat, maize, vegetables, fruit; hot mineral springs and health resorts.

GDP (2002e) $8·476 bn, per capita $1300

Human Development Index (2002) 0·667

History Conquered by Persia, and Alexander the Great; invaded by Arabs in 8th-c; Turkish invasion, 10th-c; until mid 18th-c, part of the emirate of Bukhara, which in effect became a protectorate of Russia, 1868; following the Russian Revolution (1917), became part of Turkestan Soviet Socialist Autonomous Republic, 1918; scene of the Basmachi revolt, 1922–3; Tajik Autonomous Soviet Socialist Republic created as part of the Uzbek SSR, 1924; became a Soviet Socialist Republic, 1929; declaration of independence from the Soviet Union, 1991; joined Commonwealth of Independent States, 1991; Republican Communist Party remained in power until civil war, 1992; governed by a president, prime minister, and Supreme Assembly.

Head of State
1992– Imamoli Rakhmanov

Head of Government
1996–9 Yahya Azimov
1999– Akil Akilov

aim is the promotion of Christian unity, particularly between Protestants and Catholics. They provide a popular retreat and mission to the young. The community has also become known for its haunting liturgical music.

Taizhong or **T'ai-chung** [tiychung] 24°09N 120°40E, pop (2000e) 839 000. Independent municipality and third largest city in Taiwan; economic, cultural, and commercial centre of C Taiwan; agricultural trade; designated an export processing zone.

Tajikistan *see panel*

Taj Mahal [tahj mahahl] A renowned monument to love constructed (1632–54) at Agra in Uttar Pradesh, India, as a mausoleum for Mumtaz Mahal, the favourite wife of Shah Jahan. Built of white marble and inlaid with semi-precious stones and mosaic work, it is a masterpiece of Mughal architecture, and a world heritage site. A huge central dome surrounded by four smaller domes surmounts the main structure, which is flanked by four slim minarets. The whole is mirrored in an ornamental pool.

takahe [takahee] A large, rare, flightless rail (*Notornis mantelli*), native to New Zealand; green back, blue head, neck, and breast; stout red bill; inhabits high valleys in the Murchison Mts; eats coarse vegetation, especially snow-grass.

take all A parasitic disease (*Gauemannomyces graminis*) which attacks the roots of wheat, barley, and rye, causing severe losses when susceptible crops are grown successively on the same land. The disease blocks the phloem vessels in the roots, causing death (*take all*) or premature ripening (*whiteheads*) of the crop. The disease favours light alkaline soils and above-average rainfall in winter. The best means of control is cultural: using a two-year break from wheat and/or barley; preventing build-up by avoiding more than three years of continuous wheat or barley; and avoiding wheat after barley. Fungicidal control is largely ineffective, but levels of infection may fall if susceptible crops are grown for many years on the same land (*take all decline*), possibly due to the development of soil antagonists. (Order: Ascomycetes.)

Talamanca Range–La Amistad Reserve A reserve on the Costa Rican border with Panama; area 50 000 sq km/19 000 sq mi; stretches from the Pacific to the Atlantic, encompassing a wide range of ecosystems, and providing a unique habitat for many species; a world heritage area.

talapoin [talapoyn] The smallest Old World monkey, from W Africa (*Miopithecus talapoin*); greenish with pale underparts; round head and long tail; partly webbed hands and feet; swims well; inhabits forest near water; also known as **pygmy guenon**.

Talas River, Battle of (751) A major battle near Tashkent in Turkestan, in which the Arabs defeated the Chinese, whose power had extended W since the 2nd-c BC (Han Period), but especially since the 7th-c (early Tang). The W spread of Chinese suzerainty was halted; Islam replaced Buddhism as Asia's dominant religion; and Chinese prisoners may have spread knowledge of papermaking, porcelain, and other technological advances to the West.

Talbot, William Henry Fox (1800–77) Pioneer of photography, born in Melbury Abbas, Dorset, S England, UK. He studied at Cambridge, and became an MP (1833). In 1838 he succeeded in making photographic prints on silver chloride paper, which he termed 'photogenic drawing', and he later developed and patented the Calotype process.

talc A hydrous magnesium silicate mineral ($Mg_3Si_4O_{10}(OH)_2$), formed in metamorphic rocks as light-grey soft masses; also known as **steatite** or **soapstone**. It may be associated with serpentine. There are large deposits in Austria and India. It is used in cosmetics (talcum powder) and in the paper, paint, rubber, and textile industries. It may also be carved for ornaments.

Talca [talka] 35°25S 71°39W, pop (2000e) 208 800. Capital of Maule region, C Chile; S of Santiago; founded, 1692; destroyed by earthquake, 1742 and 1928, then completely rebuilt; Chilean independence declared here, 1818; railway; major wine-producing area; O'Higgins Museum.

Talcahuano [talka-hwanoh] 36°40S 73°10W, pop (2000e) 282 000. Port in Bío-Bío region, C Chile; on a peninsula, 12 km/7 mi from Concepción; best harbour in Chile, containing main naval base and dry docks; railway; steel, using iron ore from N Chile.

Taliban / Taleban [taliban] (Persian 'students of religion') An Islamic revolutionary movement in Afghanistan, founded in 1995 by a group of young men of conservative views who emerged from religious schools and who had known only war against the Soviet occupiers (1979–89). They organized an unofficial army which, during the civil war that followed the Soviet withdrawal, was able to capture Kabul in 1996 and to take control of most of the country. Using harsh measures, they introduced a strictly conservative Islamic government with uncompromising observance of Muslim *sharia* (law). Men were forced to grow beards and wear black; women were forbidden to work outside the home or receive education, and were made to wear heavy veiling (the *burqa*). In October 2001, the Taliban government refused to give up Osama bin Laden, following his suspected involvement in the World Trade Center terrorist attack the previous month, provoking a US-led military attack on Afghanistan, and the removal of their regime.

Ta-lien *Dalian*

Taliesin [talyesin] (6th-c) Welsh bard, possibly mythical, said to have flourished in the ancient Welsh territories of N Britain. He is known only from a collection of poems, *The Book of Taliesin*, transcribed in the late 13th-c. His name is given in the 9th-c *Historia Britonum* of Nennius.

talipes [talipeez] *club foot*

tallage A manorial obligation in the form of a tax, paid by villeins in Britain in return for protection; also a tax paid on the ancient demesne lands of the crown (ie recorded in the Domesday Book as royal lands in 1066), even if subsequently granted away as fiefs. Included within the royal demesne were the chartered towns, which resisted the collection of tallage. London especially resisted the collection of the tax, and in 1332 Parliament protested the imposition of a tallage. It was frequently levied to pay for military campaigns before 1340, when Parliament abolished it, and substituted subsidies and aids.

Tallahassee [talahasee] (Muskogean 'town-old') 30°27N 84°17W, pop (2000e) 150 600. Capital of state in Leon Co, NW Florida, USA; originally a settlement of Apalachee Indians; state capital, 1824; ordinance of secession from the Union adopted here, 1861; railway; two universities (1857, 1887); government and trade centre; wood products, processed foods.

Talleyrand (-Périgord), Charles Maurice de [talayrã] (1754–1838) French statesman, born in Paris, France. Educated for the Church, he was ordained (1779), appointed Bishop of Autun (1788), elected to the States General, and made president of the Assembly (1790). He lived in exile in England and the USA until after the fall of Robespierre. As foreign minister under the Directory (1797–1807), he helped to consolidate Napoleon's position as consul (1802) and emperor (1804). Alarmed by Napoleon's ambitions, he resigned in 1807, becoming leader of the anti-Napoleonic faction. He became foreign minister under Louis XVIII, representing France with great skill at the Congress of Vienna (1814–15). He then lived largely in retirement, but was Louis Philippe's chief adviser at the July Revolution, and was appointed French ambassador to England (1830–4).

Tallien, Jean Lambert [talyĩ] (1767–1820) French revolutionary politician, born in Paris, France. As president of the Convention (1794), he was denounced by Robespierre, but conspired with Barras and Fouché to bring about Robespierre's downfall. He became a member of the Council of Five Hundred under the Directory (1795–9), and accompanied Napoleon to Egypt (1798).

Tallinn [talin], formerly Ger **Revel** or **Reval** (to 1917) 59°22N 24°48E, pop (2000e) 456 000. Seaport capital of Estonia, on S coast of the Gulf of Finland; member of the Hanseatic League; taken by Russia, 1710; capital of independent Estonia, 1918–40; occupied by Germany in World War 2; airfield; railway; extensive military and naval installations; major transportation junction; electric motors, shipbuilding, superphosphates, shale gas; citadel (13th-c), former Governor's Palace (1767–73), Toomkirik (cathedral, 13th–15th-c); old town a world heritage site.

Tallis, Thomas (c.1505–85) English musician, 'the father of English cathedral music'. One of the greatest contrapuntists of the English School, an adaptation of his plainsong responses, and his setting of the Canticles in D Minor, are still in use. He wrote much church music, including a motet in 40 parts, *Spem in alium*. In 1575 Elizabeth I granted him, with Byrd, a monopoly for printing music and music paper in England.

Talmud [talmud] (Heb 'study') An authoritative, influential compilation of rabbinic traditions and discussions about Jewish life and Laws, including worship, diet, purity, and social welfare. After the Mishnah of Rabbi Judah was compiled (c.200), it became itself an object of study by Jewish scholars in Palestine and Babylon; their commentary on it (the *Gemara*), together with the Mishnah, constitutes the Talmud, of which there were two versions: the Jerusalem or Palestinian Talmud (c.4th-c) and the longer Babylonian Talmud (c.500).

talus *scree*

Tamale [tamale] 9°26N 0°49W, pop (2000e) 197 000. Capital of Northern region, Ghana; 430 km/267 mi N of Accra; airfield; educational centre; cotton, groundnuts, civil engineering.

tamandua [tamandooa] *anteater*

tamaraw or **tamarau** *water buffalo*

tamarin [tamarin] A marmoset of genus *Saguinus* (10 species); lower canine teeth longer than incisors; eats fruit and small animals; also known as **long-tusked marmoset**. The name is also used for *Leontopithecus rosalia* (**golden lion tamarin**, **golden marmoset**, or **lion-headed marmoset**).

tamarisk A slender shrub or tree, native to the Mediterranean and Asia; deciduous small twigs with scaly leaves giving a feathery appearance; flowers in spikes, 4–5 petals, pink or white. It is salt tolerant, and often grows in sandy soils and near the sea. (Genus: *Tamarix*, 54 species. Family: Tamaricaceae.)

Tambo, Oliver (1917–93) South African politician, born in Bizana, E South Africa. He studied at Fort Hare University, and began a teacher's diploma course, but was expelled for organizing a student protest. In 1944 he joined the African National Congress (ANC), and was appointed vice-president of its youth league. He attempted to join the priesthood, but in 1956 was imprisoned, and released the following year. When the ANC was banned in 1960, he left South Africa to set up an external wing. With the continued imprisonment (until 1990) of Nelson Mandela, he became acting ANC president in 1967, and president in 1977. He returned to South Africa in 1990.

tambourine A small frame drum fitted with jingles, and covered on one side with parchment or plastic. It may be shaken, tapped with the fingertips, stroked with a moistened thumb, etc to produce various effects, mostly while accompanying dancing.

Tambov [tambof] 52°44N 41°28E, pop (2000e) 333 000. Capital city of Tambovskaya oblast, SC European Russia, on a tributary of the R Oka; founded as a fortress, 1636; airfield; railway; synthetic resins and plastics, clothing, engineering.

Tamburlaine *Timur*

Tamerlane *Timur*

Tamil A Dravidian-speaking people of S India and Sri Lanka, living as traders and seafarers. Predominantly Hindu, they were instrumental in diffusing Indian culture to many parts of SE Asia in the 11th-c. Many migrated in the 19th-c as labourers to Fiji, West Indies, Mauritius, South Africa, and SE Asia. Tamil is now the major Dravidian language of S India, with written records dating from the 3rd-c BC.

Tamil Nadu [tamil nahdoo], formerly **Madras** pop (2001e) 62 110 800; area 130 069 sq km/50 207 sq mi. State in S India, bounded E and S by the Bay of Bengal; Sri Lanka to the S; part of the Chola Empire, 10th–13th-c; first British trading settlement, 1611; largely under British control by 1801; boundaries of Mysore state altered in 1956 and 1960; renamed Tamil Nadu, 1968; capital, Chennai (Madras); governed by a 63-member Legislative Council and a 234-member Legislative Assembly; most S point, Cape Comorin; several hill ranges and rivers; population mainly Hindu (c.90%); rice, maize, pulses, millets, sugar cane, cotton, oilseed, tobacco, coffee, tea, rubber, pepper; coal, chromite, bauxite, limestone, manganese; textiles, tanning, machinery, tyres, forestry.

Tamil Tigers A Tamil separatist guerrilla movement in Sri Lanka. It emerged from the youth movements of the early 1970s, protesting against the second-class status of Sri Lanka's minority Tamils, who represent 18% of its predominantly Singhalese population. By the mid-1980s, the 'Tigers' had several well-trained and well-equipped armies of liberation, with training and staging bases in the S Indian state of Tamil Nadu. They demanded *Tamil Eelam*, an independent homeland in the N and E of Sri Lanka. Most powerful among them are the Liberation Tigers of Tamil Eelam, led by Vellupillai Prabhakaran, having gained by 1986 control of much of the N Jaffna Peninsula. Their relations with the Indian government deteriorated from 1987, when Rajiv Gandhi's peace accord with President Jayawardene brought the Indian army into Sri Lanka (*for recent events, see* **Sri Lanka**).

Tammany Hall The most powerful of the four Democratic Party Committees in New York City; originally a club (the Society of Tammany) founded in 1789, which in the late 19th-c and early 20th-c was notorious for its political corruption. During the selection process for presidential candidates, it generally controlled the votes of the other New York City representatives. However, as formal party control of political activity weakened, so did that of the City committees.

Tammerfors *Tampere*

Tammuz or **Thammuz** [tamuz] A Babylonian god of vegetation who was beloved by Ishtar (in Syria by Astarte). He returns from the dead and dies again each year.

tamoxifen [tamoksifen] A drug used in the treatment of breast cancer, first developed by the British pharmaceutical company ICI. In the 1980s it was shown to be helpful in the treatment of about half of all breast cancer cases. It works by blocking the action of the female sex hormone oestrogen on cancers whose growth is linked to oestrogen levels. Some new studies have shown that tamoxifen given prophylactically may also prevent, or at least delay, the development of, breast cancer in some women.

Tampa 27°57N 82°27W, pop (2000e) 303 400. Seat of Hillsborough Co, W Florida, USA; a port on the NE coast of Tampa Bay; developed around a military post, 1824; later a cigar-making centre, then a resort; airport; railway; university (1931); processing and shipping centre for citrus fruit and phosphates; brewing, printing and publishing, electrical equipment, food products (mainly shrimp), fabricated metals, chemicals, cigars; professional team, Buccaneers (football); David Falk and Tampa Theatres, Museum of Science and Industry, Tampa Museum, Busch Gardens; Gasparilla Festival (Feb).

Tampere [tampere], Swed **Tammerfors** 61°32N 23°45E, pop (2000e) 177 700. City in Häme province, SW Finland; on the Tammerkoski rapids by L Näsijärvi, c.160 km/100 mi NW of Helsinki; second largest city in Finland; established, 1779; developed as industrial centre in 19th-c; airfield; railway; boat trips to Virrat; university (1966); technological institute (1965); hydroelectricity; footwear, leather, textiles, metal, timber products; cathedral (20th-c); Theatre Summer (Aug).

Tampico [tampeekoh] 22°18N 97°52W, pop (2000e) 327 000. Seaport in Tamaulipas state, NE Mexico, on the Gulf of Mexico; airport; railway; oil refining, oil products, boatbuilding, timber, fishing, fish processing.

tam-tam *gong*

Tana, Lake, Amharic **Tana Hāyk** Lake in NWC Ethiopia; area 3600 sq km/1400 sq mi; altitude 1830 m/6000 ft; source of the Blue Nile; notable for its 40 monasteries on islands in the lake.

Tanabata A Japanese festival (7 Jul, but in some places 7 Aug) dedicated to the two stars Vega and Altair – two lovers (in the Chinese folk-tale) allowed to meet only once a year on that night; also called **Star Festival**.

tanager [tanajer] A songbird, native to the New World tropics; plumage usually brightly coloured; wings short, rounded; usually inhabits woodland; eats fruit, insects, seeds, and nectar. (Family: Thraupidae, c.239 species.)

Tanaka, Koichi (1959–) Chemist, born in Toyama, N Honshu, Japan. He studied at Tohoku University (BEng 1983), later joining the Shimadzu Corporation. He shared the 2002 Nobel Prize for Chemistry for the development of soft desorption ionization methods for mass spectrometric analyses of biological macromolecules.

Tananarive *Antananarivo*

Tancred [tangkred] (c.1076–1112) Norman crusader, the grandson of Robert Guiscard. He went on the First Crusade, distinguished himself in the sieges of Nicaea, Tarsus, Antioch, Jerusalem, and Ascalon, and was given the principality of Tiberias (1099). He also ruled at Edessa and Antioch.

tang *surgeonfish*

Tanga [tangga] 6°10S 35°40E, pop (2000e) 250 000. Seaport capital of Tanga region, NE Tanzania; on the Indian Ocean opposite Pemba I; formerly the starting point for caravans heading into the interior; occupied by the British, 1916; Tanzania's second largest port; centre of an agricultural area; tourism, sisal, cocoa, clothing, seafoods, fruit, coconut oil, tea.

Tanganyika, Lake [tangganyeeka] Freshwater lake in EC Africa; mostly along the Tanzania–Democratic Republic of Congo frontier, with smaller sections within the Zambian (S) and Burundian (NW) frontiers; length, 645 km/400 mi NNW–SSE; the longest, deepest (over 1400 m/4600 ft) and second largest lake (after L Victoria) in Africa; second only to L Baikal (Russia) in depth; width, 25–80 km/15–50 mi; altitude, 772 m/2533 ft; main ports are at Kigoma (Tanzania), Kalémié (Democratic Republic of Congo), and Bujumbura (Burundi); European discovery in 1858 by John Speke and Richard Burton; small-scale naval warfare took place on the lake between British and German forces in 1915–16.

Tang or **T'ang dynasty** (618–907) A major Chinese dynasty, when China's power and culture dazzled virtually all Asia. The capital at Changan (modern Xian) and other cities became industrial and commercial centres. The dynasty, established by Gaozu (Kao-tsu, r.618–26), had two outstanding emperors: Taizong (T'ai-tsung, r.626–49) and Xuanzong (Hsüan-tsung, r.712–55). The Tang dynasty is generally regarded as the golden age of Chinese poetry (49 000 poems by 2200 poets survive). It was also a major period for printing, porcelain, technology (eg gunpowder), medicine, education, and science. Confucianism was established, but religious toleration was practised. Later years saw military defeat in Turkestan by Islam (751) and internal weakening after the rebellion of An Lushan (755–7). Fifty years of chaos followed the final collapse.

tangent A line (usually a straight line) which touches a curve at a point P with the same gradient as the curve at P. It is sometimes convenient to think of a tangent meeting a curve at two (or more) coincident points. The tangent to a circle at a point P is perpendicular to the radius of the circle through P.

tangerine A citrus fruit (*Citrus reticulata*); a variety of mandarin with bright orange rind. (Family: Rutaceae.)

Tangier or **Tangiers** [tanjeer(z)], ancient **Tingis** 35°48N 5°45W, pop (2000e) 365 000. Seaport capital of Nord-Ouest province, N Morocco; at W end of the Strait of Gibraltar, an important strategic position at entrance to the Mediterranean; held by the Vandals, Byzantines, and Arabs; occupied by the Portuguese in 1471, and later by the Spanish, English, and Moors; established as an international zone, 1923; Spanish occupation in World War 2; part of Morocco, 1959; free port status restored, 1962; airport; railway; university (1971); textiles, cigarettes, fishing, tourism; royal summer residence; kasbah fortress, Dar Shorfa Palace; Caves of Hercules on coast to the W.

Tangshan or **T'angshan** 39°37N 118°05E, pop (2000e) 1 692 000, administrative region 6 855 000. City in E Hebei province, N China; SE of Beijing; devastated by major earthquake, 1976; railway; coal mining, heavy industry.

Tanguy, Yves [tãgee] (1900–55) Artist, born in Paris, France. Mainly self-taught, he began to paint in 1922, joining the Surrealists in 1926. He worked in Africa from 1930, and moved to the USA in 1939, where he became a US citizen. All his pictures are at the same time Surrealist and nonfigurative, being peopled with numerous small objects or organisms, whose meaning and identity, as in the landscape of another planet, are unknown.

Tanizaki, Junichiro [tanizakee] (1886–1965) Novelist, born in Tokyo, Japan. He became known in the West only after the translation in 1957 of his long novel *Sasameyuki* (1943–8, trans The Makioka Sisters), a notable example of descriptive realism. Among his later novels are *Kagi* (1960, The Key) and *Futen rojin nikki* (1962, Diary of a Mad Old Man). He also translated Murasaki's *The Tale of Genji* (1010) into modern Japanese.

tank An armoured fighting vehicle, typically equipped with tracks enabling it to manoeuvre across broken ground, and armed by a high velocity gun in a rotating turret. The first practical tanks were devised and used in action in 1916 by the British. In the years before 1939, they were developed into fast-moving, hard-hitting machines capable of independent action. This had a great impact on warfare, amply demonstrated by the success of the German Panzer divisions and the *blitzkrieg* concept (1939–42). Huge armoured battles continued to be fought on the E and W Fronts, and the tank emerged as the most important land weapon of World War 2. Even in the nuclear age, tanks and tank forces remain the most important part of a modern land force. The vehicles show a great deal of electronic sophistication, equipped with advanced night vision devices, laser range-finders, and fire control computers.

tanker A vessel designed to carry liquid in bulk in a number of tanks, each of which is an integral part of the hull structure. The vessel with the largest gross tonnage is the Norwegian-registered oil tanker *Jahre Viking* of 260 851 gross tonnes and a deadweight capacity of 564 739 tonnes. Previously known as the *Seawise Giant*, she is the largest ship ever built.

Tannaim [tanaeem] (Aramaic 'teachers', 'transmitters of oral tradition') Early sages and teachers of Judaism (mainly AD 10–220) who were instrumental in the emerging rabbinic movement by their study of the Jewish Law (Torah) and formulation of the nucleus of the Mishnah and midrashim. Followers of Hillel and Shammai are often considered the first Tannaim.

Tannhäuser [tanhoyzer] The name of both a legendary German knight and a 13th-c *minnesinger* or minstrel, conflated in a popular ballad. It tells of a man who seeks forgiveness for a life of pleasure, but, being refused absolution by the pope, returns to his former ways. The story is the subject of an opera by Richard Wagner, produced in 1845, and of Swinburne's 'Laus veneris'.

tanning The process of turning raw animal hide or skin into a permanent, durable, flexible form. Cleaned skin is soaked in solutions of vegetable extracts containing tannins (eg oak bark) or, since the 19th-c, chrome salts.

tannins A mixture of derivatives of polyhydroxybenzoic acid from various plants, notably tea. They are water-soluble, with a bitter and astringent taste, and have long been used in the tanning of leather and in dyeing.

Tantalus [tantalus] In Greek mythology, a son of Zeus and Pluto. As king of Sipylos in Lydia, he committed terrible crimes. He stole the food of the gods, so becoming immortal, and served them his son Pelops in a dish. For this he was punished in the Underworld; he sits in a pool which recedes when he bends to drink, and the grapes over his head elude his grasp.

tantra [tantra] A type of Hindu or Buddhist ritual text, and the practice of its instruction. Tantras may include texts describing spells, magical formulas, mantras, meditative practices, and rituals to be performed. The practice of Tantra requires instruction by a guru.

Tanzania *p.1504*

Taoism or **Daoism** [towizm] Chinese philosophical tradition, initially based on the ideas of 'Laozi' (Lao-tzu, ?6th-c BC) and Zhuangzi (Chuang-tzu, 369–286 BC). The *Tao* is the 'way' governing all human existence, which in Taoist terms (unlike the human-interrelational harmony of Confucianism) lies in harmony between the individual and the natural world. Appropriate conduct arises from such harmony. From these origins as a life-philosophy, Taoism developed (1st-c BC) as a cult, its idealized dream-world readily absorbing primitive mystical and shamanistic beliefs. Rapid expansion occurred from the 3rd-c AD, and headquarters were established in Jiangxi province from 748 to 1927. Favoured as a court religion under the Sui and Tang dynasties (590–906), Taoism came into conflict with Buddhism, and the latter was suppressed (845). In 1281, Taoism itself was suppressed by Kublai Khan, and many books destroyed, but rose again to favour under Ming emperors (1368–1644). It has been important in its close connections with alchemy, its influence on Chan Buddhism, and its impact on Chinese writers and painters.

tape recorder Equipment for storing sound and other information on magnetic tape; also used to play back these recordings. The sound to be recorded is turned into an electrical signal by a microphone, and fed to the recording head. Magnetic tape passes over this head, and a record of the original sound is imprinted in magnetic signals on the tape. Electrical signals from a radio or other source can also be recorded on tape. Tape recorders are widely used in the recording and broadcasting industry, and in home entertainment. Portable tape recorders are popular with those who like to take their music with them.

tapestry A heavy decorative textile, hand-woven with multicolour pictorial designs, and often of large size. Oriental in origin, tapestries were used for wall hangings, furniture, and floor coverings. Imitation tapestry fabrics are made on jacquard looms. The Middle Ages is the period of greatest renown for tapestry weaving, with France, Belgium, and Holland excelling at the craft. Some tapestries were not woven but were embroidered – the Bayeux Tapestry being a famous example.

tapeworm A parasitic flatworm; adults commonly found in intestines of vertebrates; body typically comprises an attached head (*scolex*) and a chain of segments (*proglottids*) produced by budding; life-cycle usually includes a larval stage found in a different intermediate host that is eaten by the final host. (Phylum: Platyhelminthes. Class: Cestoda.)

tapeworm infestation A condition in which tapeworms (*cestodes*) live within the body of their hosts. The largest is *Taenia saginata* (beef tapeworm), which lives in the intestine and may be several metres in length. It does not cause serious disease in humans, but the knowledge of its presence may distress the patient. Other tapeworms include *Taenia solium*, which affects pigs and causes hydatid disease in humans, and smaller worms which affect dogs, cats, sheep, and fish. The fish tapeworm is common in Scandinavia, Africa, and Asia, and causes a form of anaemia similar to that arising from vitamin B_{12} deficiency.

tapioca [tapiohka] A starchy preparation derived from the root crop cassava. The flour of the cassava is low in protein, which is

Tanzania

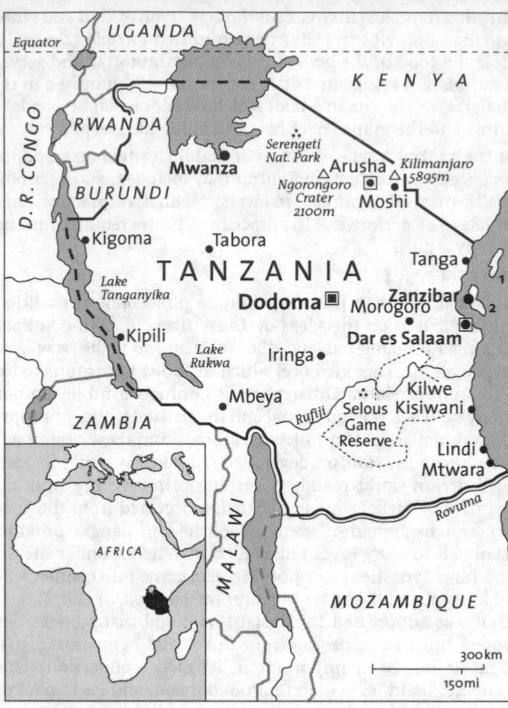

□ International Airport ∴ World heritage site 1 *Pemba* 2 *Zanzibar*

[tanzaneea], official name **United Republic of Tanzania**

Local name Tanzania

Timezone GMT +3

Area 945 087 km²/364 900 sq mi

Population total (2002e) 34 902 000

Status Republic

Date of independence 1961

Capital Dodoma (formerly Dar es Salaam)

Languages Swahili and English (official), various tribal languages

Ethnic groups Bantu (99%) (including Nyamwezi and Sukuma 21%, Swahili 9%, Hehet and Bena 6%, Makonde 6%, Haya 6%), Arab, Asian, and European minorities

Religions Mainland: Christian (34%), Muslim (33%), traditional animist beliefs (33%); Zanzibar: Muslim (96%), Hindu (4%)

Physical features Largest E African country, just S of the Equator; includes the islands of Zanzibar, Pemba, and Mafia; coast fringed by long sandy beaches protected by coral reefs; rises towards a C plateau, average elevation 1000 m/3300 ft; Rift Valley branches round L Victoria (N), several high volcanic peaks, notably Mt Kilimanjaro, 5895 m/19 340 ft; extensive Serengeti Plain to the W; other main lakes, L Tanganyika and L Rukwa.

Climate Tropical; hot, humid climate on coast and offshore islands; average temperatures 27°C (Jan), 23°C (Jul); average annual rainfall 1000 mm/40 in; hot and dry on C plateau, average annual rainfall 250 mm/10 in; semi-temperate conditions above 1500 m/5000 ft.

Currency 1 Tanzanian Shilling (TSh) = 100 cents

Economy Agriculture; rice, sorghum, coffee, sugar, cloves (most of world's market), coconuts, tobacco, cotton; reserves of iron, coal, tin, gypsum, salt, phosphate, gold, diamonds, oil; tourism.

GDP (2002e) $20·42 bn, per capita $600

Human Development Index (2002) 0·440

History Swahili culture developed, 10th–15th-c; Zanzibar became the capital of the Omani empire in 1840s; became a British protectorate, 1890; German East Africa established, 1891; British mandate to administer Tanganyika, 1919; first E African country to gain independence and become a member of the Commonwealth, 1961; republic, 1962; Zanzibar given independence as a constitutional monarchy with Sultan as Head of State; Sultan overthrown, 1964, and Act of Union between Zanzibar and Tanganyika led to the United Republic of Tanzania; a one-party state following 1965 constitution; legislation passed allowing for opposition parties, 1991, following a unanimous vote for a multi-party system; governed by a President, Cabinet, and National Assembly.

Head of State
1964–85 Julius Kambarage Nyerere
1985–95 Ndugu Ali Hassan Mwinyi
1995– Benjamin Mkapa

Head of Government
1964–77 Rashid M Kawawa (Vice President to 1972)
1977–80 Edward M Sokoine
1980–3 Cleopa D Msuya
1983–4 Edward M Sokoine
1984–5 Salim A Salim
1985–90 Joseph S Warioba
1990–4 John Malecela
1994–5 Cleopa Msuya
1995– Frederick Sumaye

readily removed by washing in water. Tapioca is used in puddings and as a thickening agent in liquid food.

tapir [tayper] A nocturnal mammal native to Central and South America and SE Asia; resembles a small, smooth-skinned, hornless rhinoceros, with a short smooth coat, and a snout extended as a short trunk; the only perissodactyl with four toes on front feet; inhabits woodland; young with pale horizontal stripes and spots. (Family: Tapiridae, 4 species.)

tar The liquid product of heating coal in the absence of air (**coal tar**). It contains many important substances, extractable by solvents or further distillation, and useful in the chemical industry (benzene, phenol, pyridine, etc). **Wood tar** is the first product of the destructive distillation of wood. Further distillation yields *creosote* and a variety of organic compounds depending on the wood; for example, resinous woods yield turpentine. The residue is *pitch*.

Tara A prehistoric hillfort, 40 km/23 mi NW of Dublin, E Ireland, the supposed site of St Patrick's conversion of Lóegaire in the 5th-c, and the traditional seat of the kings of Ireland from pre-Christian times to the death of Maél Sechnaill II of Meath in 1022. Archaeologically its earthworks are poorly known, apart from the Mound of the Hostages, a megalithic passage grave of the early 3rd millennium BC.

tarantella [tarantela] A lively folk dance that first appeared in the 17th-c in S Italy, named after the seaport of Taranto. It was said to cure (or in some legends to be induced by) the bite of the tarantula. Chopin, Liszt, and other composers used the dance in rapid 6/8 time in the form of a *perpetuum mobile*, proceeding throughout in notes of the same value.

Tarantino, Quentin (Jerome) [taranteenoh] (1963–) Film director, producer, actor, and screenwriter, born in Knoxville, Tennessee, USA. He wrote his first screenplay, *True Romance* (1987, released 1993) while working at Video Archives, Manhattan Beach. Lacking the finance to direct the project himself, he sold his script, and also that of *Natural Born Killers* (released 1994), thus enabling him to start production of *Reservoir Dogs* (1992), in which he was director, screenwriter, and actor. The success of this film, and its successor *Pulp Fiction* (1994; Cannes Palme d'Or; Oscar for Best Original Screenplay), in which he had the same roles, brought him celebrity status. He then acted in several films, such as *Desperado* (1995), before returning to production (while continuing as an actor) with *Four Rooms*

(1995) and *Jackie Brown* (1998). He wrote and directed *Kill Bill*, a film shown in two parts (Volumes 1 and 2), in 2003.

tarantula Any of the large hairy spiders of the family Therophosidae; rather sluggish spiders with a strong bite which may be venomous; hairs can cause rash when handled. The name is also used for a large, hairy species of wolf spider (family: Lycosidae), found in Italy. (Order: Araneae.)

Tarawa 1°30N 173°00E, pop (2000e) 31 000. Capital town of Kiribati, on Tarawa atoll in the Gilbert Is, C Pacific Ocean; airport; copra, mother-of-pearl; scene of US–Japanese battle in 1943.

Tarbes [tah(r)b], ancient **Bigorra** 43°15N 0°03E, pop (2000e) 52 600. Industrial and commercial city, and capital of Hautes-Pyrénées department, S France; on left bank of R Adour, 37 km/23 mi SE of Pau; originally a Roman settlement; ancient capital of province of Bigorre; road and rail junction; firearms, furniture, footwear, agricultural trade; 12th–14th-c cathedral, national stud farm (Les Haras, 1806), Jardin Mussey.

Tardigrada [tah(r)digrada] *water bear*

tare *vetch*

targum [tah(r)gum] (Heb 'translation') An Aramaic translation of the Hebrew Scriptures or parts thereof, probably originally composed orally (c.1st-c BC) when the Torah was read aloud in the synagogues, since most Jews of the time understood Aramaic rather than Hebrew, but then written in the rabbinic period. The translations sometimes betray early rabbinic ideology. Best known is the *Targum Onkelos*.

tariff A tax on goods entering a country. Tariffs may be intended mainly to raise revenue, particularly in less developed countries. A revenue tariff will be most effective at a moderate level; if it is too high, goods will simply be smuggled. Tariffs may be aimed at reducing imports in general. If the balance of trade needs to be improved, tariffs are an inefficient method, as they do nothing to help exports, and devaluation would be better. Alternatively, tariffs may be designed to promote the domestic production of the goods concerned. Tariffs generally harm other countries, are the subject of various international agreements, including the World Trade Organization, and are entrusted to supranational institutions such as the EU.

Tarim Basin, Chin **Talimu Pendi** Largest inland basin in China; area 530 000 sq km/205 000 sq mi; bounded by Kunlun and Altun Shan Ranges (S) and Tian Shan Range (N); desert and salt lakes in centre, including largest desert in China, Takla Makan (area 327 000 sq km/126 000 sq mi); dominated by China, from 2nd-c AD; disputed between Chinese and Tibetans, 7th-c; rich in salt and non-ferrous metals; nuclear testing takes place in the region.

Tarim He or **Talimu He** River in NW China, in N Tarim Basin; largest inland river in China; fed by glaciers and melting snow from the Tian Shan Mts (N); a frequently changing river course; length 2179 km/1354 mi.

Tarkenton, Fran(cis Asbury) (1940–) Player of American football, born in Richmond, Virginia, USA. He studied at the University of Georgia, where he led his team to victory in the Orange Bowl (1960). He joined the National Football League (NFL) Minnesota Vikings (1961) as starting quarterback, was traded to the New York Giants (1967), then rejoined the Vikings (1972). His career totals of 47 003 yds passing, 3686 passes completed, and 342 touchdown passes were all NFL records at the time of his retirement in 1978. He was elected to the Hall of Fame in 1986. He later worked as a football commentator and business consultant.

Tarlton or **Tarleton, Richard** (?–1588) English clown of humble origin and rudimentary education, who first performed with the Earl of Leicester's Men, but joined the Queen Elizabeth's Men on the formation of that company in 1583. He became the most famous and skilful popular entertainer of his age, especially in his improvization of doggerel verse and in the dramatic jigs which were a regular feature of the playhouses. He has been identified with Spenser's 'Pleasant Willy' and Shakespeare's Yorick.

taro [taroh] A perennial (*Colocasia esculenta*) native to SE Asia; leaves large, oval, with long stalk attached near centre of blade; spathe pale yellow; also called **dasheen**. It is cultivated commercially in the tropics for its large corms, rich in easily digested starch suitable for invalids and infants. The corms must first be boiled to remove poisonous calcium oxalate crystals. (Family: Araceae.)

tarot [taroh] A pack of playing cards used chiefly in fortune-telling. It consists of 22 picture cards of the *major arcana* (*arcana* 'secret') and the 56 cards in suits of the *minor arcana*. There are four suits: staves (or wands), cups, swords, and coins. The oldest cards date from 15th-c Italy. There are many theories about their origin and symbolism: their design was influenced by occult features, introduced in the late 19th-c. Some designs relate to ancient religions, such as the Hindu deities, the sacred Book of Days used by Aztec priests, and the Book of Thoth, the Egyptian God of Wisdom and the Occult.

tarpan A wild horse native to the steppes of SE Europe; thought to be a *plateau type* ancestor of modern domestic breeds; grey-brown with dark stripe along spine, occasionally with stripes on front legs; stiff, erect mane; wild tarpan hunted to extinction for food in 1879 (last captive individual died in 1919); subsequently tarpan-like horses were bred selectively to 'restore' the type.

Tarpeia [tah(r)peea] According to a Roman legend, a Roman woman who betrayed the Capitol to the Sabines, in return for 'what they wore on their left arms' (meaning gold rings and bracelets). In their disgust, they threw their shields on her and crushed her to death. Her name was given to the Tarpeian Rock, from which criminals were thrown to their deaths.

tarpon Large fish (*Tarpon atlanticus*) widespread in open waters of the Atlantic Ocean, and greatly prized as a sport fish; length up to 2·4 m/8 ft; mouth oblique, lower jaw prolonged; dorsal fin small with long posterior fin ray; larvae live in shallow inshore waters and brackish marshes. (Family: Megalopidae.)

Tarquinius Superbus, Lucius [tah(r)kwinius sooperbus] (6th-c BC) Tyrannical king of Rome, possibly of Etruscan extraction, whose overthrow (510 BC) marked the end of monarchy at Rome, and the beginning of the Republic. Most of the details about his life are probably fictional.

tarragon An aromatic perennial (*Artemisia dracunculus*) growing to 120 cm/4 ft, native to Asia; leaves narrowly lance-shaped, the basal ones 3-lobed at the apex; flower-heads globular, 3 mm/0·12 in across, yellowish, drooping in lax panicles. It is widely cultivated as a culinary herb, and for seasoning vinegar. (Family: Compositae.)

Tarragona [taragona], Lat **Tarraco** 41°05N 1°17E, pop (2000e) 112 000. Port and capital of Tarragona province, Catalonia, NE Spain; 534 km/332 mi NE of Madrid; archbishopric; airport; railway; agricultural trade, chemicals, vegetable oils; Roman aqueduct and amphitheatre, cathedral (12th–13th-c), archaeological museum; Fiesta of St Magin (Aug), Fiesta of Santa Tecia (Sep). The archaeological excavations a world heritage site.

Tarrant, Chris(topher John) (1946–) British television presenter, writer, and producer. He studied English at Birmingham University, and obtained his first job in television as a newsreader with ATV in Birmingham. He went on to make his name with programmes for Independent Television, such as *Tiswas* (1974), *OTT* (1981), and *Tarrant on Television* (from 1989), and he began to host Capital Radio's breakfast show in 1987. In 1998 he became a household name as presenter of the TV quiz show *Who Wants to be a Millionaire*. His many awards include the 2001 Sony Radio Academy's gold award in recognition of his services to the industry.

tarsier [tah(r)sier] A nocturnal primate native to Indonesia and the Philippines; large eyes, long hind legs; long naked tail with tuft of hairs at the tip; leaps between branches; inhabits woodland. (Family: Tarsiidae, 3 species.)

Tarski, Alfred (1902–83) Logician and mathematician, born in Warsaw, Poland. He studied at Warsaw, and taught there until 1939, when he emigrated to the USA, teaching at the University of California, Berkeley (1942–68). He made contributions to many branches of pure mathematics and mathematical logic, but is most remembered for his definition of 'truth' in formal logical languages.

Tarsus [tah(r)suhs] 36°52N 34°52E, pop (2000e) 176 000. Town in Içel province, S Turkey, on W bank of R Pamuk; important ancient city of Asia Minor; birthplace of St Paul; railway; agricultural trade centre.

tartan A fabric of a twill structure, made from variously coloured warp and weft yarns, using checkered designs which are almost always symmetrical. Tartans are mainly associated with the Scottish clans, in a tradition of dress dating from the 17th-c.

Tartar *Tatar*

tartaric acid [tah(r)tarik] IUPAC **2,3-dihydroxybutanedioic acid**, $C_4H_6O_6$. A compound with three stereo-isomers: a pair of mirror images, and one in which one half of the molecule is the mirror image of the other, called **meso-tartaric acid**. One isomer, and its potassium and calcium salts, is found widely in plants. Potassium hydrogen tartrate is used as an acid in baking powder, and is called **cream of tartar**. **Tartar emetic** is a double salt of potassium and antimony.

Tartarus [tah(r)tarus] In Greek mythology, the name of the part of the Underworld where those who offended the gods were punished. The Titans were thrust down there after their rebellion, and infamous criminals were tortured.

tartrazine An artificial yellow colouring (E102) permitted for use in foods. It has been associated with hypersensitivity reactions among urticaria sufferers and asthmatics. The prevalence of true tartrazine sensitivity is about 1 in 10 000, while the self-diagnosed sensitivity is 7%.

Tarutao [tahrutow] area 1400 sq km/540 sq mi. Marine national park in Thailand; a group of 51 islands 30 km/19 mi off the W coast, near the Thailand–Malaysia frontier, N of the Langkawi Is.

Tashkent [tashkent] 41°16N 69°13E, pop (2000e) 2 457 000. Capital city of Uzbekistan, in the foothills of the Tien Shan Mts; oldest city of C Asia, known in the 1st-c BC; Chinese influence, 7th-c AD; Chinese–Arab conflict, 8th-c; taken by Russia, 1865; virtually rebuilt after earthquake damage, 1966; airport; railway; university (1920); solar research, chemicals, heavy engineering, clothing, footwear, textiles, cotton; venue for international conferences; Islamic centres of Kukeldash (c.17th-c) and Barakkhana (c.15th–16th-c).

Tasman, Abel Janszoon [tazmn] (1603–c.59) Navigator, born near Groningen, The Netherlands. He was sent in quest of the 'Great South Land' by **Antony van Diemen** (1593–1645), Governor-General of Batavia, and in 1642 discovered the area he named Van Diemen's Land (now Tasmania) and New Zealand, followed by Tonga and Fiji (1643). He made a second voyage (1644) to the Gulf of Carpentaria and the NW coast of Australia.

Tasmania, formerly **Van Diemen's Land** (to 1856) pop (2000e) 501 000; area 67 800 sq km/26 200 sq mi. Island state of Australia, separated from the mainland by the Bass Strait; includes the main island of Tasmania, and several smaller islands, notably King I (1099 sq km/424 sq mi), Flinders I (1374 sq km/530 sq mi), Bruny I (362 sq km/140 sq mi); discovered by Abel Tasman, 1642; first European settlement, 1803 (a British dependency of New South Wales); Port Arthur was the largest penal colony in Australia; became a separate colony, 1825; now divided into four statistical divisions; the smallest of Australia's states; mountainous interior, with a Central Plateau rising to 1617 m/5305 ft at Mt Ossa; a temperate maritime climate influenced by the westerly 'Roaring Forties' winds; the most fertile regions along the NW and E coasts and along the river valleys; capital, Hobart; chief towns Devonport, Launceston, Burnie-Somerset, Queenstown, New Norfolk; sheep, cattle, pigs, cereals, apples, hogs, wood, paper, chemicals, machinery, textiles; mining of tin, copper, zinc, lead, silver, gold, coal; abundant hydroelectric power; first Aborigines to settle here crossed the land bridge now replaced by the Bass Strait 25 000 years ago; tourism; Western Tasmania Wilderness National Parks; numerous unique plants and animals, notably the thylacine (now feared to be extinct) and the Tasmanian devil, both carnivorous marsupials; state holidays Labour Day (Mar), Bank Holiday (Apr).

Tasmanian devil An Australian carnivorous marsupial (*Sarcophilus harrisii*); the largest dasyure (length, up to 1·1 m/3·6 ft); bear-like in shape, with large powerful head and long bushy tail; dark with pale throat, pale patches on sides, pale muzzle; eats mainly carrion (including fur and bones), also kills snakes, birds, etc.

Tasmanian tiger / wolf *thylacine*

Tasman Sea [tazmn] Part of the Pacific Ocean separating E Australia and Tasmania from New Zealand; linked to the Indian Ocean by the Bass Strait; shallow, narrow continental shelf off Australia, sinking to depths of 4570 m/14 990 ft in the Tasman abyssal plain; named for the Dutch explorer Abel Tasman.

TASS *ITAR-TASS*

Tassili N'Ajjer [tasilee najair] National park in E Algeria, N Africa; NE of the Ahaggar (Hoggar) Mts; area 1000 sq km/400 sq mi; established in 1972; a sandstone plateau contains many prehistoric cave paintings of animals and people.

Tasso, Torquato (1544–95) Poet, born in Sorrento, SW Italy. He studied law and philosophy at Padua, where he published his first work, a romantic poem, *Rinaldo*. After joining the court of the Duke of Ferrara, he wrote his epic masterpiece on the capture of Jerusalem during the first crusade, *Gerusalemme Liberata* (1581, Jerusalem Liberated). He later rewrote his work, in response to criticisms, as *Gerusalemme Conquistata* (1593, Jerusalem Conquered). He died in Rome, where he was to have been crowned as poet laureate.

taste buds Small sensory organs located on the tongue and palate, which recognize four primary tastes: sweet, sour, salt, and bitter. Some parts of the mouth are more sensitive to certain tastes; for example, the tip of the tongue is sensitive to salt and sweet stimuli, the back to bitter stimuli, and the edges to sour and salt.

tatami [tatahmee] Traditional Japanese floor matting. Layers of bound rushes are set in a rectangular framework and covered with smooth mats edged with narrow strips of dark cloth. Tatami are standard size, equivalent to one sleeping space, and rooms are described as '6 mat, 8 mat' etc. Shoes are never worn on tatami.

Tatar or **Tartar** A Turkic-speaking people living in Russia. Sunni Muslims since the 14th-c, they were a highly stratified mediaeval society. Traditionally farmers and pastoralists, in the 18th–19th-c, they became important as political agents, traders, teachers, and administrators in the Russian Empire.

Tate, Ellalice *Hibbert, Eleanor*

Tate, Sir Henry (1819–99) Sugar magnate, art patron, and philanthropist, born in Chorley, Lancashire, NW England, UK. He patented a method for cutting up sugar loaves (1872), came to London (1880), and rapidly made a large fortune from 'Tate's cube sugar'. At Park Hill, Streatham, he formed a valuable collection of works by contemporary masters, which he offered to the nation on condition that the government should find a site for a gallery which he would build. The building was erected on ground formerly occupied by Millbank penitentiary (demolished, 1893) and opened (1897) as the National Gallery of British Art (later known as the *Tate Gallery*).

Tate, James (Vincent) (1943–) Poet, born in Kansas City, Missouri, USA. He studied at the University of Missouri (1963–4), Kansas State (1965 BA), and the University of Iowa (1967 MFA). He taught at several universities, including Columbia (1969–71) and the University of Massachusetts, Amherst (1971). He is known for his preoccupation with the use of language, seen in such books as *The Lost Pilot* (1967) and *Constant Defender* (1983). In 1992 he won the Pulitzer Prize for his *Selected Poems* (1991), and his later works include *Shroud of the Gnome* (1997).

Tate, Nahum [nayuhm] (1652–1715) Poet and playwright, born in Dublin, Ireland. He studied at Dublin, and moved to London, where his first play was staged in 1678. He is known for his 'improved' versions of Shakespeare's tragedies, substituting happy endings to suit the popular taste, and with Dryden's help he wrote a second part to that poet's *Absalom and Achitophel* (1682). In collaboration with **Nicholas Brady** (1659–1726) he compiled a metrical version of the psalms. He became poet laureate in 1692.

Tate Gallery A London gallery housing the nation's chief collection of British art and modern foreign art. It was opened in 1897 as a branch of the National Gallery, but became administratively autonomous in 1915, and fully independent in 1955. The Tate Modern gallery, on the site of the former Bankside power station, London, opened in May 2000. There is also a Tate Gallery at the Albert Dock development in Liverpool.

Tati, Jacques [tatee], popular name of **Jacques Tatischeff** (1908–82) Actor and film director, born in Le Pecq, NC France. He began in music hall, directed his first film in 1931, then wrote, directed, and acted in slapstick film comedies. After *Jour de fête* (1947, trans The Big Day), directed and written by himself, he made his reputation as the greatest film comedian of the post-war period, notably in *Les vacances de Monsieur Hulot* (1953, Mr Hulot's Holiday), *Mon oncle* (1958, My Uncle), and *Trafic* (1971) in which he presented the pipe-smoking, lugubrious Hulot, forever beset by physical mishaps and confrontations with modern technology.

Tatra Mountains [tahtra], Czech **Tatry** Mountain group in C Carpathian Mts, comprising the **High Tatra** (*Vysoké Tatry*) and **Low Tatra** (*Nízke Tatry*); highest group, of the Carpathians, rising to 2655 m/8711 ft at Gerlachovský Štít; High Tatra National Park, area 500 sq km/200 sq mi, established in 1948.

Tatum, Art(hur) [taytm] (1910–56) Jazz pianist, born in Toledo, Ohio, USA. Nearly blind, he learned violin and then piano at Cousino School for the Blind and the Toledo School of Music. A professional musician from his teens, and largely self-taught, he became the first supreme keyboard jazz virtuoso. Moving to New York City in 1932, he made solo recordings and club appearances, becoming known for his technique, drive, and improvisational powers. The most influential of the swing-style pianists, he continued to work in the idiom until his death.

Ta-t'ung *Datong*

Taung skull The partial skull and brain cast of a young *Australopithecus africanus*, found at Taung, S Africa, in 1924. This was the first discovery of these small-brained early hominids.

Taunton [tawntn] 51°01N 3°06W, pop (2000e) 55 700. County town in Somerset, SW England, UK; on the R Tone, in the Vale of Taunton Deane; founded in 705; rebellion of Perkin Warbeck ended here (1497); Duke of Monmouth crowned king here (1685); 12th-c castle hall, where Bloody Assizes held (1685); railway; cider, textiles, leather, optical instruments, light engineering; Somerset county museum.

Taupo, Lake [towpoh] area 606 sq km/234 sq mi. Lake in C North Island, New Zealand, filling an old volcanic crater; length 40 km/25 mi, width 27 km/17 mi; largest New Zealand lake; used as a reservoir, and also for fishing and water sports; town of Taupo in NE; location of a geothermal power scheme; thermal pools at Tokaanu.

tauraco *turaco*

Taurus [tawrus] (Lat 'bull') A prominent N constellation of the zodiac, including the Pleiades and Hyades clusters and the Crab Nebula. It lies between Aries and Gemini. Its brightest star is the red giant Aldebaran, one of the few stars whose diameter has been measured directly, at about 45 times the Sun's diameter; distance: 20 parsec.

Taurus Mountains [tawrus], Turkish **Toros Dağlari** Mountain chain of S Turkey, extending in a curve from L Eğridir roughly parallel to the Mediterranean coast as far as the R Seyhan; highest peak, Ala Dağlari (3910 m/12 828 ft); its NW extension across the R Seyhan is called the **Anti-Taurus**; in the SE are the Cilician Gates, an important pass in ancient times; chromium, copper, silver, zinc, iron, arsenic.

tautomerism [tawtomerizm] In chemistry, the existence of a rapidly established equilibrium between two isomers which differ only in the location of one or more hydrogen atoms.

Tavener, Sir John (Kenneth) (1944–) Composer, born in London, UK. He studied at the Royal Academy of Music, London (1961–5), and has been professor of music at Trinity College of Music since 1969. His music is predominantly religious, and includes the cantata *The Whale* (1966), *Ultimos ritos* (1972, Last Rites) for soloists, chorus, and orchestra, and a sacred opera *Therese* (1979). In 1994 he co-published *Ikons: Meditations in Words and Music*. He was converted to the Russian Orthodox faith in 1976. His *Song for Athene* (1993), written to commemorate the death of a family friend, Athene Hariades, in a cycling accident, became nationally known when it was chosen as part of the funeral ceremony for Princess Diana in 1997. His choral work, *A New Beginning*, was premiered during the Millennium Dome New Year celebrations, and among later works are *The Veil of the Temple* (2003). He was knighted in 1999.

tawny owl A typical owl (*Strix aluco*) native to Europe, Asia, and N Africa; mottled brown with black eyes and no ear tufts; inhabits woodland and habitation (occasionally open country); eats small vertebrates and insects. The name is also used for the **tawny fish owl** and **tawny-browed owl**.

taxation The means by which a government raises money to finance its activities. **Direct taxes** are paid by individuals (eg income tax, national insurance contributions) and companies (eg corporation tax). **Indirect taxes** are those levied on goods and services (eg value-added tax, sales tax). Taxation rules frequently change, in response to government policy and needs, and changes are generally announced in a budget statement. In the past, tax has been levied on many things, including windows and jockeys.

tax-haven A country where tax rates are particularly low. Companies or individuals may choose to reside there to avoid paying high rates of tax in their own home country. The Isle of Man, the Channel Is, and some West Indian countries are current examples.

Taxila [taksila] The chief city of the Achaemenid satrapy of Gandhara, now a major archaeological site covering 65 sq km/25 sq mi in Punjab, Pakistan; a world heritage area. Excavations have revealed three distinct cities, the earliest dating from c.400 BC; the second was occupied successively by Bactrian Greeks, Scythians, Parthians, and Kushans; the third was founded c.130 and flourished for over five centuries.

taxis [taksis] A directed movement or orientation reaction of an organism to a stimulus. Taxis is usually used with a prefix to indicate the nature of the stimulus, for example *chemotaxis* (for a chemical stimulus), *phototaxis* (for a light stimulus), and *thermotaxis* (for a temperature stimulus). Movement towards the stimulus is a **positive taxis**, movement away from stimulus a **negative taxis**, so that an animal that moves towards the source of a light is 'positively phototactic'.

taxol A substance which occurs naturally in the bark of the evergreen Pacific yew tree (*Taxus brevifolia*), and which has shown promising activity against certain forms of cancer, including cancer of the lung, ovary, head, and neck. When first isolated in the 1960s there were problems with using it due to severe toxicity, but these have now been partly overcome. Taxol works by disrupting cell division and interfering with the separation of the nuclear chromosome. It requires the bark of 12 000 trees to produce 2·5 kg of taxol, and strenuous efforts are being made to synthesize it artificially.

taxonomy The theory and practice of describing, naming, and classifying organisms. It is divided into **alpha taxonomy**, the description and designation of species typically on the basis of morphological characters; **beta taxonomy**, the arrangement of species into hierarchical systems of higher categories; and **gamma taxonomy**, the study of the evolutionary relationships between groups (*taxa*) and of variation within and between populations.

Tay, River Longest river in Scotland, UK; length 192 km/119 mi; rises on Ben Lui in the Grampians; flows NE, E, then SE to enter the Firth of Tay, extending 40 km/25 mi NE to the North Sea at

Buddon Ness; crossed at Dundee by the Tay Bridge; noted for its salmon fishing.

Taylor, Elizabeth (Rosemond) (1932–) Film star, born in London, UK. In 1939 she moved with her family to Los Angeles, where her charm took the eye of the Hollywood film world, and she made her screen debut in 1942 at the age of 10. As a child star she made a number of films, including *National Velvet* (1944). She was first seen as an adult in *Father of the Bride* (1950). Her later films included *Cat on a Hot Tin Roof* (1958), *Butterfield 8* (1960, Oscar), and *Cleopatra* (1962), which provided the background to her well-publicized romance with Richard Burton. With Burton she made several more films, including *Who's Afraid of Virginia Woolf?* (1966, Oscar). Later films include *The Mirror Crack'd* (1980) and *Young Toscanini* (1988). There was a break in her acting career in the 1980s, while she received treatment for alcohol addiction, and in the 1990s her private life continued to capture the headlines. In 1985 she founded the American Foundation for AIDS Research. She has been married eight times: **Nicky Hilton Jr** (1950–1), actor **Michael Wilding** (1952–7), film producer **Mike Todd** (1957–8), **Eddie Fisher** (1959–64), **Richard Burton** (1964–74, 1975–6), US senator **John W Warner** (1976–82), and **Larry Fortensky** (1991–6). In 1999 she received a BAFTA Fellowship award for her lifetime achievements in film, and in 2003 announced her retirement. She became a dame in 1999.

Taylor, Frederick W(inslow) (1856–1915) Engineer, born in Philadelphia, Pennsylvania, USA. Employed in the Midvale steelworks in Philadelphia (1878–90), he became chief engineer in 1889, and introduced time-and-motion study as an aid to efficient management. From 1893 he worked as an independent consultant in what he called 'scientific management', and applied its principles successfully to both small and large-scale businesses. He published *The Principles of Scientific Management* (1911).

Taylor (of Gosforth), Sir Peter Murray Taylor, Baron (1930–97) British judge. He studied at Cambridge, was called to the bar in 1954, and became a QC (1967), a High Court judge (1980–7), a Lord Justice of Appeal (1987–92), and Lord Chief Justice of England (1992–6). In 1989 he was chairman of the Hillsborough football stadium Disaster Inquiry leading to the Taylor Report. He was knighted in 1980, and made a life peer in 1992.

Taylor, Zachary (1784–1850) US general, statesman, and 12th president (1849–50), born in Montebello, Virginia, USA. He joined the army in 1808, fought against the Indians, and in 1840 was given command of the army in the SW. In the Mexican War (1846–8) he captured Matamoros, and won a major victory at Buena Vista, though heavily outnumbered. He emerged from the War as a hero, and was given the Whig presidential nomination. The main issue of his presidency was the status of the new territories and the extension of slavery there, but he died only 16 months after taking office.

Taymyr or **Taimyr, Lake** [tiymeer] area 4560 sq km/1760 sq mi. Lake in N Siberian Russia, on the N Taymyr Peninsula; length, 250 km/155 mi; maximum depth, 26 m/85 ft; frozen over (Sep–Jun); coal deposits nearby.

Tay-Sachs disease [tay-zaks] A rare inherited disorder in which an abnormal accumulation of lipid occurs in the brain, because the enzyme for breaking it down is absent. Clinical features usually appear in infancy with blindness, paralysis, mental retardation, and eventually death. It is most common in descendants of C and E European (Ashkenazi) Jews. The condition is named after British ophthalmologist Warren Tay (1843–1927), who first described characteristic cherry-red spots in the retinae of affected children, and US neurologist Bernard Sachs (1858–1944).

Tayside pop (2000e) 405 000; area 7493 sq km/2893 sq mi. Former region in E Scotland, UK, created in 1975 and replaced in 1996 by Angus, Perth and Kinross, and Dundee City councils.

Tbilisi [tbileesee], formerly **Tiflis** (to 1936) 41°43N 44°48E, pop (2000e) 1 250 000. Capital city of Georgia; on the R Kura, between the Greater and Lesser Caucasus; founded, 5th-c; ancient trading point between Europe and India; airport; railway junction; university (1918); machinery, film making, printing, publishing, foodstuffs, wine, silk, electrical equipment, locomotives, plastics; ruins of Narikala (4th–17th-c), Anchiskhati Church (6th-c), Sioni Cathedral (6th–7th-c).

TBS (Transmission Based Signalling) *train protection systems*

TBVC states Abbreviation used for the four former 'independent homelands' within South Africa: Transkei, Bopuphatswana, Venda, and Ciskei. Established by South Africa in 1976, 1977, 1979, and 1981 respectively, they were not given international recognition, on the grounds that this would have implied acceptance of the policy of apartheid. Following the South African elections of 1994, the homelands were incorporated into the new South African provinces.

Tchad *Chad*

Tchaikovsky or **Tschaikovsky, Piotr Ilyich** [chiykofskee] (1840–93) Composer, born in Kamsko-Votkinsk, W Russia. He began as a civil servant, joined the St Petersburg Conservatory in 1862, and moved to Moscow in 1865. There he became known for his operas, Second Symphony, and First Piano Concerto. After an unsuccessful marriage, he retired to the country to devote himself to composition, making occasional visits abroad. Among his greatest works are the ballets *Swan Lake* (1876–7), *The Sleeping Beauty* (1890), and *The Nutcracker* (1892), the last three of his six symphonies, two piano concertos, the *1812 Overture*, and several tone poems, notably *Romeo and Juliet* and *Capriccio Italien*.

Tchogha Zanbil [chohga] The site in SW Iran of a religious centre built in the 13th-c BC by King Untash Napirisha; a world heritage site. The city comprises three palaces, five underground tombs, ten temples, and a ziggurat. For 600 years it was inhabited only by priests.

tea A small evergreen tree (*Camellia sinensis*) growing to c.4 m/13 ft in the wild, but only a small shrub in cultivation; leaves leathery, toothed and pointed; flowers 5-petalled, white, fragrant; native to Myanmar and Assam, but cultivated in Tibet and China for social drinking and meditation from early times, and subsequently the Arab world and Japan (9th-c); India, Japan, and Sri Lanka are now also major producers. Tea was introduced into Europe c.1610, with the beginning of trade between Europe and the Far East. Cultivated plants are pruned to encourage new growth. The shoot tips with the first two leaves are picked, allowed to wither, then rolled, fermented, and dried; when infused with boiling water they make the well-known beverage containing the stimulants tannin and caffeine. The popularity of tea-drinking in 8th–9th-c China may have influenced the contemporary development of porcelain. (Family: Theaceae.)

tea ceremony *chanoyu*

Teacher of Righteousness The religious leader and founder of the Qumran community, probably in the mid-2nd-c BC; apparently a Zadokite priest who opposed the Hasmoneans, assuming the role of Jewish high priest, and led his followers into exile near the Dead Sea. His identity is otherwise unknown, but this title is applied to him in the Damascus Document and various Qumran commentaries, because of his role in guiding the community in their interpretation of the Torah.

teachers' college *college of education*

Teagarden, Jack, popular name of **Weldon Leo Teagarden** (1905–64) Jazz trombonist and singer, born in Vernon, Texas, USA. He started playing professionally at 10. In 1928 he worked his way to Chicago, and supported himself playing in the Ben Pollack orchestra until 1933. He moved to New York as a featured soloist in Paul Whiteman's orchestra (1933–8) and set a new standard for jazz trombone, smooth but forceful, in numerous recordings. His first recorded vocal, 'A Hundred Years from Today' was a hit in 1933. Big, sleepy-eyed, and rural, he donned a tuxedo when he led his own orchestra (1939–46). He joined Louis Armstrong's All Stars (1947–51), then formed small bands for concert tours and played with local musicians in club dates.

teak A large evergreen tree (*Tectona grandis*), growing to 45 m/150 ft, native to S India and SE Asia; leaves up to 45 cm/18 in, oval, opposite; flowers small, white, 5-lobed bells. It is a source of high-quality, durable, water-resistant timber. Extremely heavy, teak sinks in water unless thoroughly dried, so the trees are killed by having a girdle of bark cut near the base, and are left for up to two years before felling. (Family: Verbenaceae.)

teal A small dabbling duck (Genus: *Anas*, 16 species), found worldwide; eats water-weeds and invertebrates. The name is also used for the perching ducks *Nettapus coromandelianus*, *Callonetta leucophrys*, and *Amazonetta brasiliensis*. (Subfamily: Anatinae.)

Teamsters' Union The **International Brotherhood of Teamsters, Chauffeurs, Warehousemen and Helpers of America**, the largest US labour union, with over 1·5 million members working in such diverse fields as transport, warehousing, health care, office management, and construction, as well as many who work in the bakery, dairy, brewery, and food-processing industries. Founded in 1903, it was expelled from the AFL/CIO in 1957 for corruption, but was re-affiliated in 1987. It carries out a normal range of union activities on behalf of its members, and has considerable power in some industrial sectors. Its headquarters is in Washington, DC.

Te Anau, Lake [tee anow] area 344 sq km/133 sq mi. Lake in SW South Island, New Zealand, on E edge of Fiordland national park; second largest lake in New Zealand, and largest on South I; length 61 km/38 mi; width 9·7 km/6 mi; glow-worm caves in the W; water sports.

Teapot Dome Scandal A US government scandal during the Harding administration in the early 1920s involving the lease of land for oil exploration in California, and especially at Teapot Dome, Wyoming. The attorney general was forced to resign, after refusing access to files. Following other resignations, criminal proceedings were introduced, and secretary of the interior Albert B Fall received a prison sentence.

teasel A large, stiff, and prickly biennial (*Dipsacus fullonum*), growing to 2 m/6½ ft, native to Europe and the Mediterranean; stem angled; rosette leaves oblong to elliptical, dying after the first year; stem leaves narrower, paired, fused at base to form water-filled cups; flowers tiny, white or mauve, in heads the size and shape of an egg, surrounded by curved, prickly bracts. The heads of the cultivated **fuller's teasel** (subspecies *sativus*) have stiff bracts used for raising the nap on cloth; the bracts of the wild plant (subspecies *fullonum*) are too flexible. (Family: Dipsacaceae.)

Tebbit (of Chingford), Norman (Beresford) Tebbit, Baron (1931–) British statesman, born in Enfield, N Greater London, UK. He left school at 16, worked as a journalist, and after national service in the RAF became an airline pilot, later heading the British Airline Pilots' Association. He became a Conservative MP in 1970, serving in Margaret Thatcher's governments as employment secretary (1981–3) and secretary for trade and industry (1983–5). His career was interrupted in 1984 when both he and his wife were badly hurt in the IRA bombing of the Grand Hotel in Brighton. In 1985 he became Chancellor of the Duchy of Lancaster and also chairman of the party. In 1987, there were open disagreements between him and Mrs Thatcher over the handling of the general election campaign, and shortly after the Conservative victory he retired to the back-benches. Noted for a vigorous style of rhetoric, he is remembered for his 'on your bike' speech (recommending a course of action to the unemployed) to the Conservative Party conference in 1981. He was made a life peer in 1992.

Technicolor The trademark of a colour cinematography process internationally dominant between 1935 and 1955. Shooting involved special three-strip cameras and multiple release prints by photo-mechanical dye-transfer. Even after the introduction of colour negative in 1953, dye-transfer printing continued to the mid-1970s.

technocracy A label meaning 'rule by experts', used in describing a supposed shift in 'real' power from elected governments to technical specialists. The term was in vogue in the 1930s and again in the 1960s when economic, social, and strategic defence planning was adopted in some Western industrial societies, and the role of experts in decision-making was enhanced. As a consequence of this shift, 'the end of ideology' was hailed in some quarters.

technology The use of tools, machines, materials, techniques, and sources of power to make work easier and more productive. Industrial technology began 200 years ago with the introduction of power-driven machines, the growth of factories, and the mass production of goods. Whereas science is concerned with understanding how and why things happen, technology deals with making things happen; it can be subdivided into many specializations, such as medical, military, and nuclear. Technology has helped people to gain control over nature, and so build a civilized world. Undesirable side-effects include increased pollution and loss of jobs as a result of automation.

tectonics The study of the structure of the Earth's crust, particularly such processes as the movement of rocks during folding and faulting.

Tecumseh [tekumsuh], originally **Tecumtha** (c.1768–1813) Indian chief of the Shawnees, born in Old Piqua, Ohio, USA. He joined his brother, 'The Prophet', in a rising against the whites, suppressed at Tippecanoe by William Harrison in 1811. Passing into the English service, he commanded the Indian allies in the War of 1812 as brigadier-general. He fell fighting at the Thames in Canada (1813).

Tedder (of Glenguin), Arthur William Tedder, Baron (1890–1967) British marshal of the Royal Air Force, born in Glenguin, Scotland, UK. During World War 2 he directed research and development at the Air Ministry, served as commander-in-chief (RAF) in the Middle East Air Force, moved on to the Mediterranean theatre (1943), and became deputy supreme commander of the Allied Expeditionary Force under Eisenhower (1943–5). He was appointed air marshal in 1945, and created a baron in 1946.

Tees, River [teez] River of NE England, UK; rises on Cross Fell, Cumbria and flows 128 km/79 mi SE through Co Durham and along the North Yorkshire border, then develops into a broad estuary that meets the North Sea below Middlesbrough; passes through heavily industrialized **Teesside**, linked to R Tyne as part of UK's first regional water grid system supplying water to industrial NE; upper river valley known as **Teesdale**.

Teesside Urban area surrounding the R Tees estuary in NE England, UK; includes Stockton-on-Tees, Redcar, Thornaby, Middlesbrough; formed in 1967; railway; airport (Middleton St George).

teeth Small, bone-like structures of the jaws used for the biting and chewing of food. They are firmly anchored in the alveolar bone of the jaws, and project from the gums. The number, arrangement, and type of teeth varies between different animals. Some animals have two sets (eg most mammals); others have several rows which gradually move forwards as others are lost (eg sharks). Each tooth consists of a core of *pulp* surrounded by *dentine*, which is covered in its upper part by *enamel* and in its lower part by *cement* (essentially bone). The *crown* is the enamel-covered part that projects beyond the gums; it may have one or more projections called *cusps*. The surfaces of the crowns form the *occlusal surfaces*, which meet when the upper and lower teeth are brought together. The cement-covered part of the tooth is the *root*, and is firmly attached to the bone of the alveolar socket by the peridontal membrane. The pulp and dentine have an extensive blood and nerve supply. In many mammals, different types of teeth can be identified: *incisors* for cutting, *canines* for cutting and tearing, and *premolars* and *molars* for grinding. In humans the first set of teeth (*deciduous* or *milk* teeth) usually appears between 6 and 24 months of age, there being 20 deciduous teeth in all (2 incisors, 1 canine, and 2 molars in each half-jaw). These gradually become replaced (from about age 6) by the *permanent* teeth, with the addition of 3 more teeth in each half-jaw giving a total

Human Teeth

	Eruption	Shedding
Milk		
incisor 1	6 months	6–7 years
incisor 2	8 months	7–8 years
canine 1	18 months	10–12 years
molar 1	1 year	9–11 years
molar 2	2 years	10–12 years
Permanent		
incisor 1	7–8 years	
incisor 2	8–9 years	
canine 1	10–12 years	
premolar 1	10–11 years	
premolar 2	11–12 years	
molar 1	6–7 years	
molar 2	12 years	
molar 3	17–21 years	

Note: the lower teeth usually appear before the upper equivalent teeth.

complement of 32 (2 incisors, 1 canine, 2 premolars, 3 molars in each half-jaw). The third molar is often referred to as the *wisdom tooth*, because of its time of eruption. Not all of the teeth may appear.

tefillin [tefileen] Jewish phylacteries or frontlets, consisting of two black leather cubes with leather straps, bound over the forehead and left arm, and worn by adult Jewish males during morning prayers, except on sabbaths and festivals. The cubes contain scriptural texts (such as *Deut* 6.4–9, 11.13–21; *Ex* 13.1–16), and the explanation of their use is traced to Biblical commandments about the words of the Law being a 'sign upon your arm or frontlets between your eyes'. They are not worn by Reform Jews.

Tegucigalpa [taygoosigalpa] 14°05N 87°14W, pop (2000e) 817 000. Capital city of Honduras; founded as a mining centre, 1524; comprises two distinct towns, the almost flat Comayagüela and the hilly Tegucigalpa, separated by the R Choluteca; altitude 975 m/3200 ft; capital, 1880; airport; university (1847); textiles, sugar, wood products, plastics, chemicals, metal and electrical products; some silver, lead, zinc mining; 18th-c cathedral, 18th-c Church of Virgen de los Dolores; devastated by hurricane Mitch in 1998.

Tehran or **Teheran** [tairahn] 35°44N 51°30E, pop (2000e) 8 317 000. Capital city of Iran, in Tehran province, N Iran; altitude 1200–1700 m/4000–5500 ft; superseded Esfahan as capital of Persia, 1788; largely rebuilt after 1925; airport; road and rail junction; six universities (oldest, 1935); carpets, textiles, tanning, chemicals, glass, car assembly; Niavaran, Golestan, Marmar, Saadabad, and Baharstan Palaces; Shahyad Tower, symbol of modern Iran.

Tehran Conference [tairahn] The first inter-allied conference of World War 2, attended by Stalin, Roosevelt, and Churchill in 1943. The subjects discussed were the co-ordination of Allied landings in France with the Soviet offensive against Germany, Russian entry in the war against Japan, and the establishment of a post-war international organization. Failure to agree on the future government of Poland foreshadowed the start of the Cold War.

Teilhard de Chardin, Pierre [tayah duh shah(r)dĩ] (1881–1955) Geologist, palaeontologist, Jesuit priest, and philosopher, born in Sarcenat, C France. He lectured in pure science at the Jesuit College in Cairo, was ordained in 1911, and in 1918 became professor of geology at the Institut Catholique in Paris. He went on palaeontological expeditions in China and C Asia, but his unorthodox ideas led to a ban on his teaching and publishing. Nevertheless, his work in Cenozoic geology and palaeontology became known, and he was awarded academic distinctions. His major work, *Le Phénomène humain* (written 1938–40, The Phenomenon of Humanity) was posthumously published. Based on his scientific thinking, it argues that humanity is in a continuous process of evolution towards a perfect spiritual state. From 1951 he lived in the USA.

Te Kanawa, Dame Kiri [tay kahnawa] (1944–) Operatic soprano, born in Gisborne, New Zealand. After winning many awards in New Zealand and Australia she moved to London, where she made her debut with the Royal Opera Company in 1970. She has since taken a wide range of leading roles, and in 1981 sang at the wedding of the Prince and Princess of Wales. She was made a dame in 1982 and has produced many non-classical recordings. In 1989 she published *Land of the Long White Cloud: Maori Myths and Legends*.

tektite A rounded, flat, and glassy meteorite ranging in diameter from submillimetre size up to c.10 cm/4 in.

Tel Aviv–Yafo 32°05N 34°46E, pop (2000e) 444 000. Twin cities in Tel Aviv district, W Israel, a commercial port on the Mediterranean Sea; Israel's largest conurbation; Tel Aviv founded in 1909 as a garden suburb of Yafo (Jaffa), the most ancient port in Israel and today an artists' centre; former capital (to 1950) of Israel; airport; railway; two universities (1953, 1974); commercial centre (Israeli stock exchange), food processing, textiles, chemicals; Franciscan monastery of St Peter (1654).

telebanking A system which enables banking transactions to be carried out via a communications network. This could be over interactive cable television, with provision for the user to send signals to the bank, but is more commonly by telephone through a viewdata system or an interactive computer link.

telecine [teleesinee] Equipment for converting motion picture film to video for broadcast television or videotape recording. In the flying spot system, a continuously moving film is scanned by a spot of light generated on a cathode ray tube. The transmitted light is then converted to red, green, and blue signals by a beam-splitting optical system and three photo-multiplier tubes. Developments in digital scanning allow special effects to be introduced during transfer.

Telecom Gold An electronic mail service offered by the UK telephone agency, British Telecom.

telecommunications The transmission of data-carrying signals, often between two widely separated points; it includes radio, telegraphy, telephones, television, and computer networks. Telecommunications in the modern sense began in the 19th-c: the Great Western Railway telegraph lines from Paddington to Slough, England, opened in 1843; telephones for commercial use were installed in Boston and Cambridge, MA, in 1877; radio telegraphy became a commercial success after Marconi founded the Wireless, Telegraph and Signal Co in London in 1897. During the 20th-c, first radio (from the 1920s) and then television (from the 1950s) became important for communication over distance. In 1962 the US Telstar 1 satellite was launched to relay communications signals; however, this had a low orbit, and so could be used for only a short part of each day. Now large numbers of *geostationary* satellites provide day-long international links for telephony and television transmissions, carried by high frequency radio waves (microwaves). The use of optical fibre links in telephone cables enables hundreds of simultaneous conversations to be transmitted.

teleconferencing The connection of several locations by television links to provide continuous intercommunication of sound and sight. In some applications, the picture is presented as a rapidly changing series of stills, rather than in continuous motion, in order to reduce the bandwidth required in transmission.

telegraphy Communication at a distance of written, printed, or pictorial matter, by the transmission of electrical signals along wires. Modern examples of this are telex and fax. In **radiotelegraphy** the message is carried by radio waves rather than along a wire.

telekinesis *psychokinesis*

Tel el-Amarna [**tel** el **amah(r)**na] The ancient Akhetaten ('the horizon of Aten'), a short-lived Egyptian city on the E bank of the R Nile, c.250 km/150 mi S of Cairo. Founded c.1350 BC by the heretic pharoah Akhenaten as both a royal residence and administrative capital, it was abandoned on his death, and subsequently demolished. Notable finds are the cuneiform Amarna tablets, c.300 diplomatic documents discovered in 1887; and the celebrated painted bust of Akhenaten's queen, Nefertiti, found 1911–12 and now in Berlin.

Telemachus [tel**e**makus] In the *Odyssey*, the son of Odysseus and Penelope. He sets out to find his father, visiting Nestor and Menelaus. Later he helps Odysseus fight Penelope's suitors.

Telemann, Georg Philipp [**tay**leman] (1681–1767) Composer, born in Magdeburg, EC Germany. He studied at Leipzig, and taught himself music by learning to play a wide range of instruments and studying the scores of the masters. He held several posts as *Kapellmeister*, notably at Frankfurt (1712–21), and became musical director of the Johanneum at Hamburg from 1721 until his death. A prolific composer, his works include church music, 46 passions, over 40 operas, oratorios, many songs, and a large body of instrumental music.

telemarketing A marketing system which uses the telephone, handling responses to advertisements which carry telephone numbers. The telephone operators receive calls, take orders, or arrange for brochures to be sent. It also involves making calls to prospective clients on behalf of marketing outlets, to generate leads, orders, or interest.

teleological argument *design, argument from*

teleology **1** The theory that some phenomena or events can best be explained by reference to the forward ends, purposes, or aims to which they are directed, rather than by prior causes; it is usually contrasted with *mechanism*. This applies particularly to human behaviour and to that of living organisms (eg a cat stalking a mouse).

2 In ethics, teleological theories such as utilitarianism claim that actions should be judged by the goodness or badness of their *consequences* not by their supposed intrinsic properties; they are usually contrasted with deontological theories, like those of Kant.

3 In theology, the teleological argument is the argument from design.

teleost [**tel**iost, **tee**liost] Any of a large group of ray-finned fishes (Actinopterygii) in which the tail is symmetrical, without an upturned body axis; comprises the great majority of extant species of true bony fishes, exhibiting rich diversity, and found in all marine and freshwater habitats.

telephone A device for transmitting speech sounds over a distance. In 1876 Alexander Graham Bell was granted a patent to develop such an instrument, and his induction receiver, along with Thomas Edison's carbon transmitter, form the basis of the modern telephone. In the mouthpiece, a carbon microphone translates sound vibrations into a varied electric current which is relayed through wires to the receiver, where it is converted back into sound waves by a diaphragm and an electromagnet. Amplifiers (repeaters) placed at intervals along a line make long-distance telephoning possible, and vacuum-tube amplifiers with long-life expectancy make transatlantic cable-laying economically viable. Today, communications satellites and computerized call-routing systems transmit millions of simultaneous calls worldwide. Modern telephone instruments are largely electronic, with keypads replacing dials, and the addition of such 'smart' features as last-number recall. Developments of the 1990s included the growth in use of cordless telephones, the worldwide introduction of mobile phones, and the first digital videophones.

telephoto lens A camera lens of long focal length but comparatively short overall dimensions, giving increased magnification for a limited angle of view. In 35 mm still cameras, focal lengths of 100–300 mm are usual, but for special purposes such as news work, sports, and natural history 500–1000 mm may be employed. It is sometimes confused with a *long focus* lens which, while of long focal length, may not be of telephoto design.

telerecording The transfer of a video programme to motion picture film. Since the interval between successive video frames is very short, a film camera with extremely rapid movement from one frame to the next is essential. Direct photography of a shadow-mask colour video display is not satisfactory, and a three-tube system is preferred, in which separate cathode-ray screens for the three colour components are optically combined in register when photographed on colour negative film. For high definition recordings, three colour separations can be recorded by electron beam as successive frames on black-and-white film, printed in combination to produce a colour negative. In another method, red, green, and blue laser beams modulated by the video information are combined by a rotating mirror optical system to scan colour negative film directly, exposing each frame as a series of fine horizontal lines.

telescope An optical instrument for producing magnified images of distant objects. Telescopes came into widespread use in Europe at the beginning of the 17th-c, but may have been known earlier. The earliest known devices were made c.1608 by Lippershey and Galileo. Astronomical telescopes produce an inverted image, but give a larger field of view and higher magnification than terrestrial (upright image) telescopes. **Refracting telescopes** use a lens to bring light rays to a focus, a technique first applied to astronomy by Galileo. In its modern form, with lenses corrected for chromatic aberration, this telescope is still in use, especially among amateurs. **Reflecting telescopes** use a mirror to bring the light rays to a focus, a technique first applied to astronomy by Newton, who recognized its merits in overcoming the false colours of lenses. Herschel developed techniques for casting large primary mirrors (1783). The largest telescopes today are all reflectors. For special purposes, such as photography, there may be a combination of mirror and lens, as in the Schmidt camera. **Radio telescopes** collect and analyse cosmic radio emission from celestial sources. The basic type consists of a steerable, paraboloidal collecting dish with a central detector connected to amplifiers. Radio-source structure can be displayed through an image analysis system to produce a picture similar to a photograph. A **radio interferometer** is a group of steerable antennae which send to a common receiver the interference responses characteristic of the source. Telescopes for other types of radiation (eg infrared, ultraviolet, X-rays) are also used, sometimes above the Earth's atmosphere.

Telescopium [tele**skoh**pium] (Lat 'telescope') A small, faint S constellation delineated by Lacaille in honour of the astronomical telescope.

teleshopping A system for shopping from home, using a communications network such as the Internet or a public videotex system; also called **on-line shopping**. A list of food and goods available to the shopper is displayed on the computer or television screen, and these can be ordered directly over the communications link.

Telesto [tel**es**toh] The 13th natural satellite of Saturn, discovered in 1980, moving along the same orbit as Tethys; distance from the planet 295 000 km/183 000 mi; diameter 30 km/19 mi.

Teletex A service, provided by a posts, telegraph and telephones authority, which offers computer-based facilities such as electronic mail to a subscriber.

teletext An information service of alpha-numerical data and simple diagrams transmitted as individual pages in digitally coded form in the field-blanking intervals of a TV broadcast signal. The constantly updated results, typically news headlines, football scores, weather maps, etc, can be displayed on any domestic receiver equipped with a decoder and page-selection keyboard. In the UK, the services Ceefax (BBC) and Oracle (IBA) were introduced in the 1970s.

teletype An old form of keyboard printer-based terminal used for linking into a computer. Teletypes were slow and unreliable, and came to be replaced by a combination of visual display unit and (where hard copy is required) attached printer.

television The transmission and reproduction of moving pictures and associated sound by electronic means; developed in the late 19th-c and early 20th-c, with the first pictures presented by Baird in 1926. The image of a scene in a TV camera using a vidicon tube is analysed by scanning along a series of horizontal lines, the variations of brightness along each line being converted into a train of electrical signals for transmission or recording. Cameras using solid-state sensors such as charge-coupled device arrays read out the image information by sequential interrogation of each pixel. At the receiver the picture is reconstituted on the fluorescent screen of a cathode-ray tube by an electron beam scanning a precisely similar pattern, the brightness of each point depending on the beam intensity controlled by the incoming signal. The number of scanning lines and the picture frequency vary in different systems, the American standard having 525 lines with 30 pictures per second (pps) and the European 625 lines at 25 pps. In both cases one complete picture, or *frame*, is scanned in two sets of alternate lines, termed *fields*, which are interlaced to reduce flicker in the receiver image. As scanning returns from the end of one line to the start of the next, there is a brief period without picture information, *horizontal blanking*; similarly after each completed field there is the vertical interval, *field blanking*, while scanning returns from bottom to top. Synchronizing pulses at precise time intervals are inserted in these periods to ensure correct scanning in the receiver. For terrestrial broadcasting the complete vision signal modulates a radio wave in one of the ultra-high-frequency (UHF) bands between 470 and 890 mHz as a carrier, while the corresponding sound (audio) signal has its own carrier at a slightly higher frequency. High-definition TV systems with more than 1000 scanning lines will be transmitted via satellite using the super-high-frequency (SHF) band, 11·7 to 12·5 gHz.

television camera *camera*

telex An international telegraphic system in which telephone lines transmit printed messages, using devices which convert typed words into electrical signals and vice versa (*teleprinters*); the name is a contraction of 'teletypewriter exchange service'. Subscribers to the service have their own call sign and number. The system is relatively cheap, and has been much used by commercial organizations, but has largely been overtaken by fax and e-mail.

Telford 52°42N 2°28W. A new town in Shropshire, WC England, UK, designated in 1963, comprising three previous urban areas: **Telford Dawley**, pop (2000e) 30 600; **Telford North**, pop (2000e) 56 700; **Telford South**, pop (2000e) 24 900; Telford and Wrekin a unitary authority in 1998; on the R Severn SE of Shrewsbury, 55 km/34 mi NW of Birmingham; originally designated as Dawley New Town; railway; electronics, plastics, vehicles, metal products.

Telford, Thomas (1757–1834) Engineer, born near Langholm, Dumfries and Galloway, SW Scotland, UK. He began as a stonemason, taught himself architecture, and in 1787 became surveyor of public works for Shropshire. He planned the Ellesmere (1793–1805) and Caledonian (1803–23) canals, the road from London to Holyhead, with the Menai Suspension Bridge (1826), and built in all over 1000 mi of road and 1200 bridges, as well as harbours, docks, and other buildings.

Tell, Wilhelm, Eng **William Tell** (13th–14th-c) Legendary Swiss patriot of Bürglen in Uri, a famous crossbow marksman, reputedly the saviour of his native district from the oppressions of Austria. According to tradition, he was compelled by the tyrannical Austrian governor to shoot an apple off his own son's head from a distance of 80 paces. Later, Tell slew the tyrant, and so initiated the movement which secured the independence of Switzerland. Similar tales are found in the folklore of many countries, and Tell's existence is disputed. His name first occurs in a chronicle of 1470.

tell An Arabic 'mound' or 'hill', equivalent to Persian *tepe*, Turkish *hüyük*; in archaeological usage, an artificial mound formed through the long-term accumulation of mud brick from houses successively levelled and rebuilt. Most common in the Near East, Anatolia, and the Balkans, tells can stand 30 m/100 ft high, and yield evidence of occupation over several millennia.

Teller, Edward (1908–2003) Physicist, born in Budapest, Hungary. He studied at Karlsruhe, Munich, and Göttingen universities, and under Niels Bohr at Copenhagen. He left Germany in 1933, moving to the USA in 1935. He contributed profoundly to the modern explanation of solar energy, anticipating the theory behind thermonuclear explosions. He was a member of the team under Fermi that produced the first nuclear chain reaction (1941), and worked on the atomic bomb project at Los Alamos (1943–5). He favoured immediate development of a thermonuclear weapon, but had to wait until 1950 for Truman to give approval, and the first H-bomb was tested in 1952. He was director of the Livermore Laboratory, CA (1958–60), and professor of physics at California, Berkeley (1963). He supported the use of nuclear power for peaceful means, including the use of nuclear devices to excavate large areas for harbours, canals, and mining.

Tellus *Gaea*

telomere The part of a chromosome further from the centromere in eucaryotes, containing G-rich repetitive DNA. Without telomeres chromosomes are unstable, and can combine with other chromosomes to give ring structures. Telomeres generally decrease in length during the ageing process, probably because of the loss of activity of the enzyme telomerase.

Tel Quel [tel kel] A French journal of cultural criticism, founded in 1960 by French writer Philippe Sollers (1936–). It provided a platform for many radical interventions in the overlapping fields of art, literature, philosophy, politics, semiotics, and psychoanalysis by such writers as Barthes, Derrida, Foucault, Kristeva, and Todorov. It ceased publication in 1982.

Telugu [teluhgoo] The Dravidian language associated particularly with the state of Andhra Pradesh in S India. It has some 73 million speakers.

Tema [tema] 5°41N 0°00W, pop (2000e) 144 000. Seaport in Greater Accra region, S Ghana, E of Accra; railway; largest artificial harbour in Africa (1962); civil engineering, metal smelting, oil refining, chemicals.

tembadau *banteng*

Tempe [tempee] 33°25N 111°56W, pop (2000e) 158 600. Health resort in Maricopa Co, SC Arizona, USA; settled, 1872; railway; university (1885); Fiesta Bowl (Jan).

tempera [tempera] A method of painting with powdered pigment mixed with egg-yolk and water, usually on specially prepared wooden panels. This technique was normal in the Middle Ages, and was not generally superseded until oil painting became popular in the late 15th-c.

temperament A tuning system for keyboard and fretted string instruments in which some of the 'pure' intervals of 'just intonation' (the tuning derived from the natural harmonic series) are made slightly larger or smaller (ie 'tempered') in order to accommodate polyphony and a wide range of modulation. In **equal temperament**, which became universally employed in the 19th-c, the octave is divided into 12 equal semitones, the only pure interval being the octave itself. Earlier tuning systems had sought various compromises between purity of interval, variety of key, and flexibility of modulation.

temperance movement A response to the social evils caused by the alcoholism so widespread in the 18th-c and 19th-c. Temperance societies were organized first in the USA, then in Britain and Scandinavia. The original aim was to moderate drinking, but prohibition became the goal. Federal prohibition became a reality in the USA in 1919, but was repealed in 1933.

temperature Measurement related to heat flow between objects. Heat will be transferred between objects having different temperatures. It is measured using thermometers, thermocouples, and pyrometers, and is controlled using thermostats.

The Kelvin temperature scale is used in physics (an SI unit), fixed by the triple point of water, 273·16 K. Other temperature scales include the Celsius (°C), also called Centigrade, Fahrenheit (°F) and Rankine (°R).

temperature inversion A meteorological phenomenon which results when a layer of warm air traps cooler air below – the reverse of the normal state of affairs, where air temperature decreases with increasing altitude. A surface temperature inversion occurs when radiation fog develops. Inversions also occur at higher altitudes, such as when a warm air mass overrides a colder one along a warm front. Inversions may result in significant air pollution, as pollutants are trapped below the warm air until the inversion clears.

Templars The Poor Knights of Christ and of the Temple of Solomon; an international religious–military order, whose members were subject to monastic vows. The order was founded c.1120 chiefly to protect pilgrims to the Holy Land; its name derives from the location of its headquarters – near the site of the Jewish Temple in Jerusalem. It developed into a great army, acquiring wealth and property, and was suppressed by Pope Clement V in 1312.

Temple A group of buildings, including the 12th-c Temple church, in Fleet St, London, UK. They were established on land once owned by the Knights Templar, and have housed the offices of the Inner and Middle Temples for centuries. The 12th-c Temple in Paris was also Templar property. It later became a royal prison, and was demolished in 1811.

Temple, Jerusalem The central shrine of Jewish worship and its priesthood since its establishment under Solomon. It was first destroyed by Nebuchadnezzar in c.587 BC, but rebuilt later in the 6th-c BC after the return from exile. Extended on an elaborate scale by Herod the Great, beginning c.20 BC, it was barely renewed before its destruction under Titus during the Jewish revolt of AD 70. Still unrestored today, its site is now partly occupied by the Muslim mosque, the Dome of the Rock, built in the late 7th-c.

Temple, Shirley, married name **Black** (1928–) Child film star, born in Santa Monica, California, USA. Precociously talented, she appeared in a series of short films from the age of three-and-a-half, and graduated to full stardom with a leading role in *Little Miss Marker* (1934). An unspoilt personality who sang, danced, and did impressions, she captivated Depression-era audiences, becoming a world favourite in such films as *Curly Top* (1935) and *Dimples* (1936). She received an honorary Academy Award in 1934. Retiring from the screen, she became a Republican, was appointed US representative to the UN General Assembly in 1969, was Ambassador to Ghana (1974–6), White House chief of protocol (1976–7), and Ambassador to Czechoslovakia (1989–93).

Temple, Sir William (1628–99) Diplomat and essayist, born in London, UK. He studied at Cambridge, became a diplomat in 1655, was made ambassador at The Hague, and negotiated the Triple Alliance (1668) against France. He was made a baronet, and in 1677 helped to bring about the marriage of the Prince of Orange to the Princess Mary, daughter of James, Duke of York (later James II). After the 1688 revolution he declined a political post to devote himself to literature, living in retirement at Moor Park, Surrey. His essay style was a major influence on 18th-c writers, including Swift, who was his secretary.

Temple, William (1881–1944) Anglican clergyman, born in Exeter, Devon, SW England, UK. He studied at Oxford, was ordained in 1908, and became Bishop of Manchester (1921–9), Archbishop of York (1929–42), and Archbishop of Canterbury (1942–4). An outspoken advocate of social reform, he crusaded against usury, slums, dishonesty, and the aberrations of the profit motive. He was also a leader in the reform of Church structures and in the ecumenical movement.

temple A building in the ancient world used as a sanctuary for the gods. Temples had rather different functions from modern churches. They were not places where people gathered together indoors for communal worship; their main purpose was to provide, quite literally, a dwelling place for the gods. Thus all temples, whether big or small, were for the most part no more than a repository for the cult statue(s) of the god(s) to whom they had been dedicated. The dark, unlit room in which the statue(s) stood was called the *naos* (Greek) or *cella* (Latin); the main altar for sacrifice was outside the building. Thus most religious activity was external to the temple rather than inside it. Graeco-Roman temples were sometimes also used as storage places for state treasures and important documents. The Parthenon at Athens not only housed the cult statue of Athena Parthenos; it also contained the national treasury.

Temple Bar A site at the junction of the Strand and Fleet St, London, UK, where from 1301 a gateway marked the boundary of the Cities of London and Westminster. The original gateway was replaced in 1672 by one designed by Wren; in 1878 this was in turn replaced by a statue of a griffin.

Temple of Heaven A group of buildings in Beijing, in which the emperors formerly conducted their devotions. The complex was laid out in 1406–20, and is regarded as a masterpiece of traditional Chinese architecture.

Temple of the Tooth The Dalada Maligawa, an important Buddhist pilgrimage site in Kandy, Sri Lanka. The shrine was built to house one of the Buddha's teeth, which is believed to have been conveyed to Sri Lanka in 1590.

Templeton, Sir John Marks (1912–) Businessman and philanthropist, born in Winchester, Tennessee, USA. He studied at Yale and Oxford, started on Wall Street in 1937, and went on to found several major investment funds. A Presbyterian elder, he is widely known for the establishment in 1972 of the *Templeton Prize for Progress in Religion*, the world's largest money award (exceeding $1 million in 1992). He was knighted in 1987.

Templeton Prize A prize for progress in religion, awarded annually by the Templeton Foundation, New York City. It was created in 1972 by US businessman John Marks Templeton to recognize achievements in spirituality – a category he felt was overlooked by the Nobel awards. It is the world's largest money award, annually adjusted to ensure that no other annual award exceeds it; its total passed $1 million dollars for the first time in 1992. Its aim is to increase sensitivity to the diversity of religious thought and work. Prizewinners, who may belong to any religious tradition, are chosen for their achievements of a spiritual nature that specifically increase human love or understanding of God. Its first recipient was Mother Teresa in 1973.

tempura [tempura] Japanese fritters, probably originating with the Portuguese in 16th-c Japan. They are served crisp, with diluted soy sauce mixed with grated radish to balance the oil.

Ten, the A group of American painters from New York and Boston who exhibited together during 1898–1919. Originally members of the Society of American Artists, they felt its exhibitions were too large and conservative, and left to form their own group. Most of the Ten had studied in Paris and were greatly influenced by French Impressionism. The members were: Frank Benson (1862–1951), Joseph R De Camp (1858–1923), Thomas Dewing (1851–1938), Childe Hassam (1859–1935), Willard L Metcalf (1858–1925), Robert Reid (1862–1929), Edward E Simmons (1852–1931), Edmund Tarbell (1862–1938), John Henry Twachtman (1853–1902), and J Alden Weir (1852–1919). William Merritt Chase (1849–1916) replaced Twachtman upon his death (1902). Their contribution to modern art was in helping to establish a tradition of setting up exhibiting organizations independent of official bodies, foreshadowing The Eight and the Armory Show.

tenant farming A form of tenure where a farmer pays rent to a landlord for the use of a farm's land and buildings. Tenants usually own their own stock and working capital. However, there are legal constraints on the development and use of agricultural land whether it is owner-occupied or tenanted land.

tench Freshwater fish (*Tinca tinca*) native to slow rivers and lakes of Europe and W Asia, but now more widespread; length up to 60 cm/2 ft; body stout, fins rounded; mouth with pair of thin barbels; dark green to brown; fished commercially in some areas, and popular with anglers. (Family: Cyprinidae.)

Ten Commandments or **Decalogue** The fundamental laws of the Jews; in the Bible, said to have been given to Moses on Mt Sinai. They describe the general religious and moral requirements for the Jewish people, and set the terms of God's covenant with them, although often phrased as universal principles. Slightly variant forms of the 'ethical' decalogue are found in *Ex* 20 and *Deut* 5, but a 'cultic' variant appears in *Ex* 34.14–26 (covering major Jewish feasts and offerings). A further tradition declares that God inscribed them on two tablets of stone which were then deposited in the Ark of the Covenant (*Deut* 9). The well-known 'ethical' decalogue contains the commands: (1) the God of Israel shall be acknowledged as one and unique, (2) worship of images is prohibited, (3) misuse of the Lord's name is prohibited, (4) the Sabbath must be observed, (5) one's parents must be honoured, (6–10) murder, adultery, theft, false testimony, and coveting one's neighbour's goods are prohibited. This numbering varies, however, in some Jewish and Christian circles.

tendinitis Inflammation of a tendon, the fibrous cord attaching a muscle to a bone. It results in pain over the affected area, particularly on movement. It is often cause by repetitive strain on the tendon, and can be alleviated by rest.

tendon An extremely strong fibrous cord or sheet of connective tissue (bundles of collagen fibres), continuously attaching muscle to bone or cartilage. When tendon fibres pass across or around bony surfaces, they may develop either a surrounding (*synovial*) sheath or a (*sesamoid*) bone within them in order to reduce friction. Occasionally the sheath becomes inflamed (*tenosynovitis*), and movement may be painful. The two layers of the sheath may then be heard rubbing against one another, producing a creaking noise (*crepitus*). Sometimes a tendon may appear as a thin sheet of dense connective tissue, in which case it is known as an *aponeurosis*.

tendril An organ with which climbing plants attach themselves to supports; derived from modified leaves, branches, or inflorescences. Most tendrils coil around the support; others end in sticky, sucker-like pads; a few are negatively phototropic, and grow into dark cracks in the support.

tenebrism In art history, the realistic and strongly-shadowed style adopted by certain Spanish and Neapolitan painters in the early 17th-c. The **tenebristi** were not an organized group, but were all influenced by the dramatic style of Caravaggio.

Tenerife *Canary Islands*

Teng Hsiao-p'ing *Deng Xiaoping*

Teniers, David [teneerz], known as **the Elder** (1582–1649) Baroque genre painter, born in Antwerp, N Belgium, about whom little is known. He probably studied in Italy under Rubens, became a master in the Antwerp guild (1606), and an art dealer in the 1630s. Primarily a painter of religious scenes, some paintings by his son were formerly attributed to him.

Ten Lost Tribes of Israel Ten tribes of Israel taken captive by Assyria in 721 BC and merged (hence 'lost') with the Assyrians. They are alleged by British Israelites to be the ancestors of the British and American peoples, but this theory is largely discredited.

Tennant Creek 19°31S 134°15E, pop (2000e) 3800. Town in Northern Territory, Australia, between Darwin and Alice Springs; airfield; an important gold mining centre since the 1930s; also bismuth, copper, silver; 114 km/70 mi S are the Devil's Marbles, an outcrop of weathered round granite boulders in a scenic reserve; Goldrush festival in May.

Tennessee pop (2000e) 5 689 300; area 109 149 sq km/ 42 144 sq mi. State in SEC USA, divided into 95 counties; the 'Volunteer State'; ceded by France, 1763; explored by Daniel Boone, 1769; temporary state of Franklin formed in 1784, after the War of Independence; Federal government created the Territory South of the Ohio (1790); admitted as the 16th state to the Union, 1796; seceded, 1861; the scene of many battles during the Civil War, including Shiloh, Chattanooga, Stone River; slavery abolished, 1865; re-admitted to the Union, 1866; Ku Klux Klan founded at Pulaski, 1866; capital, Nashville–Davidson; other chief cities, Memphis, Knoxville, Chattanooga; Mississippi R follows the W border; Holston and French Broad Rivers form the Tennessee R; highest point Clingmans Dome (2025 m/ 6644 ft); in the E lie the Great Smoky Mts, Cumberland Plateau, narrow river valleys, and heavily forested foothills, which severely restrict farming; fertile 'bluegrass' country in the C, ideal for livestock and dairy farming; in the W is a rich floodplain where most of the state's cotton is grown; many lakes created by the Tennessee Valley Authority's damming of the Tennessee and Cumberland Rivers; tobacco, soybeans, hay, cotton; cattle and dairy products; chemicals, processed foods, textiles, electrical equipment; coal, cement; nation's largest producer of zinc and pyrites; several popular tourist areas.

Tennessee River River in SE USA; formed near Knoxville, Tennessee, by the confluence of the French Broad and Holston Rivers; forms part of the Alabama–Mississippi border; flows into Kentucky to join the Ohio R at Paducah; length (including the French Broad) 1398 km/869 mi; major tributaries the Little Tennessee, Clinch, Hiwasee, Elk, Duck; used for irrigation, flood-control, and hydroelectric power (controlled by the **Tennessee Valley Authority**, a government agency established in 1933).

Tennessee walking horse A breed of horse developed in the USA for riding; all descended from one stallion called Black Allan; height, 15–16 hands/1·5–1·6 m/5–5 ft 4 in; uniform colour; tail held erect at base; unusually smooth fast walk, unique to the breed.

Tenniel, Sir John [teneel] (1820–1914) Artist, born in London, UK. Self-trained, he became known as a *Punch* cartoonist (from 1851) and book illustrator, notably in his work for *Alice's Adventures in Wonderland* (1865) and *Through the Looking-glass* (1872). He was knighted in 1893.

tennis *see panel, p.1515*

Tennis Court Oath (1789) A dramatic incident which took place in the first stage of the French Revolution. An oath was taken in a tennis court at Versailles by representatives of the Third Estate of the French Assembly, or Estates General, who had been locked out of their assembly place. Declaring themselves (as opposed to the nobles and clergy) to be the National Assembly, the deputies swore never to separate until a constitution was established for France. The new constitution abolished the *ancien régime*, nationalized the church's lands, and divided the country into departments to be ruled by elected assemblies.

tennis elbow Pain in the external aspect of the elbow following repetitive trauma, such as may occur in playing tennis. It may result from small tears in the muscles in the region.

Tennyson, Alfred Tennyson, 1st Baron [tenison], known as **Alfred, Lord Tennyson** (1809–92) Poet, born in Somersby, Lincolnshire, E England, UK. He studied at Cambridge, and published his first poetry in 1829, but it was not well received; a revised volume in 1842 established his reputation, including such major poems as 'The Lady of Shallott' and 'The Lotus-eaters'. His major poetic achievement was the elegy mourning the death of his friend Arthur Hallam, 'In Memoriam' (1850); and in the same year he succeeded Wordsworth as poet laureate. In 1855 he wrote *Maud: a Monodrama*, and 1859–85 published a series of poems on the Arthurian theme, *Idylls of the King* (1859). In the 1870s he wrote several plays, and continued to write poetry until his death. In his later years, he was acclaimed by the whole nation, and he was created a baron in 1884.

Tenochtitlan [tenochtit**lahn**] The island capital of L Texcoco, now beneath Mexico City, from which the Aztecs dominated Mexico from c.1344–5 to the Spanish Conquest in 1519. About 13 sq km/5 sq mi in area, it had c.60 000 houses and a population of c.200 000.

ten-pin bowling *bowling*

tenrec [**ten**rek] A mammal of family Tenrecidae (31 species), native to Madagascar; an insectivore; species can resemble hedgehogs, moonrats (but lack tails), shrews, or moles; female

tennis

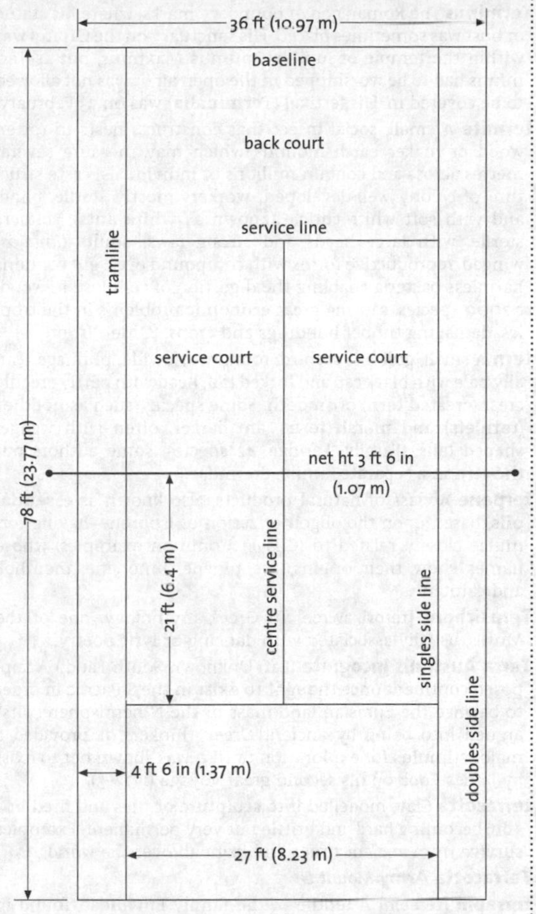

A racket-and-ball game for two or four players developed from real tennis; also known as **lawn tennis**. It is played on a rectangular court measuring 78 ft (23·77 m) long by 27 ft (8·23 m) wide for singles, or 36 ft (10·97 m) wide for doubles. A net 3 ft (0·9 m) high at the centre is stretched across the width of the court. Playing surface varies, and can be grass, clay, shale, concrete, wood, or other suitable artificial materials. The object is to play winning strokes by forcing one's opponent(s) to fail to return the ball successfully over the net. In doubles, players may hit the ball in any order, but must serve in rotation. The most famous lawn tennis championship is the All England Championships at Wimbledon each year. 'Field Tennis' was played in the 18th-c, but the game similar to the modern game was introduced by Major Walter Clopton Wingfield at a Christmas party at Nantclywd, Wales, in 1873. His game was called *sphairistike*.

of the hedgehog-like **common tenrec** (*Tenrec ecaudatus*) has up to 29 nipples.

Tenrikyo [tenreekyoh] (Jap 'teaching of heavenly truth') A Japanese faith-healing movement founded in 1838 by a female shaman Nakayama Miki (1798–1887). Her birthplace, Tenri, near the ancient capital of Nara, is the chief religious centre of this missionary sect.

tensile strength The stretching stress at which a material breaks; symbol σ, units Pa (pascal). For metals this is greater when the metal is cold-worked or stretched into wires. For stresses slightly less than tensile strength, most materials undergo plastic deformation. For steel piano wire and cast iron, tensile strengths are 2×10^9 and 2×10^8 Pa, respectively.

tenure A teacher's right to permanency of appointment, usually gained after successful completion of a probationary period. The concept became a contentious political issue in the UK when the government abolished it for university teachers appointed after the 1988 Education Bill had been introduced in Parliament. In US universities, tenure is still granted, though less frequently than in the past, and the practice is controversial.

Ten Years' War (1868–78) The name usually given to the unsuccessful Cuban insurrection against Spanish colonial rule. The rebels accepted their defeat in the Pact of Zanjón (Feb 1878).

Tenzing Norgay, known as **Sherpa Tenzing** (1914–86) Mountaineer, born in Tsa-chu, near Makalu, E Nepal. He made his first climb as a porter with a British expedition in 1935, and later climbed many of the Himalayan peaks. In 1953 he succeeded in reaching the Everest summit with Edmund Hillary, for which he was awarded the George Medal. He later became head of the Institute of Mountaineering at Darjeeling.

Teotihuacán [tayoteewakahn] A great city, 30 km/20 mi NE of Mexico City, flourishing c.450–650 with a population of c.125 000–200 000, but destroyed and burnt in c.700; a world heritage site. Fully urbanized, its N–S street grid covers 20 sq km/8 sq mi and contained 5000 buildings. Major monuments include the 70 m/220 ft-high Pyramid of the Sun, the Pyramid of the Moon, and the *Ciudadela* or royal palace, with its temple of Quetzalcoatl.

tepal *perianth*

teratorn A condor-like vulture with a wingspan exceeding 4 m/13 ft; the largest flying bird ever to have lived, now extinct; known from Pleistocene fossils from a Californian tar pit. (Genus: *Teratornia*.)

Terborch or **Terburg, Gerard** [terbaw(r)kh] (1617–81) Painter, born in Zwolle, The Netherlands. He studied at Haarlem, and travelled widely in Europe, before settling at Deventer in 1654, where he became burgomaster. He worked mostly on a small scale, producing genre pictures and fashionable portraits, but is best known for his painting of 'The Peace of Munster' (1648, National Gallery, London).

Terbrugghen, Hendrik [tairbrookhen] (c.1588–1629) Painter, born in Deventer, The Netherlands. He studied at Utrecht, and was until c.1615 in Italy, where he came under the influence of Caravaggio. He excelled in chiaroscuro effects and in the faithful representation of physiognomical details and drapery, as in his 'Jacob and Laban' (1627, National Gallery, London).

terebinth *turpentine tree*

Terence, in full **Publius Terentius Afer** (c.190–159 BC) Latin comic poet, born in Carthage, N Africa. He became the slave of a Roman senator, who gave him an education in Rome and freed him. His successful first play, *Andria* (166 BC, The Andrian Girl), introduced him to Roman society, where his chief patrons were Laelius and the younger Scipio. His surviving six comedies are Greek in origin and scene, directly based on Menander. Many of his conventions were later used by European playwrights.

Terengganu [terenggahnoo] pop (2000e) 936 000; area 12 928 sq km/4990 sq mi. State in NE Peninsular Malaysia; formerly a fief of Malacca and then of Johor, before coming under the rule of Thailand; ceded to Britain, 1909; capital, Kuala Terengganu; fishing, offshore oil.

Teresa of Ávila, St (1515–82) Saint and mystic, born in Ávila, C Spain. She entered a Carmelite convent there in 1535, and became famous for her ascetic religious exercises and sanctity. In 1562, with assistance from John of the Cross, she re-established the ancient Carmelite rule, with additional observances. Her many writings include an autobiography, *The Way of Perfection*, and the mystical work, *The Interior Castle*. She was canonized in 1622; feast day 15 October.

Teresa (of Calcutta), Mother, originally **Agnes Gonxha Bojaxhiu** (1910–97) Christian missionary in India, born in Skopje, Yugoslavia (formerly Albania). She went to India in 1928, and taught at a convent school in Calcutta, taking her final vows in 1937. She became principal of the school, but in 1948 left the convent to work alone in the slums. After medical training in Paris, she opened some classrooms for destitute children in Calcutta. She was gradually joined by other nuns, and her House for the Dying was opened in 1952. Her sisterhood, the Missionaries of Charity, started in 1950, and in 1957 she started work with lepers and in many disaster areas of the world. She was awarded the Pope John XXIII Peace Prize (1971), the inaugural Templeton Prize for Progress in Religion (1973), and the Nobel Peace Prize (1979). In 2003 she was beatified by Pope John Paul II in a ceremony in St Peter's Square timed to coincide with the celebrations for his silver jubilee.

Teresa of Lisieux *Theresa of Lisieux*

Tereshkova, Valentina [tereshkova] (1937–) Cosmonaut and the first woman to fly in space, born in Maslennikovo, W Russia. She worked in a textile factory, qualified as a sports parachutist, and entered training as a cosmonaut in 1962, becoming a solo crew member of the three-day Vostok 6 flight launched on 16 June 1963. She was made a hero of the Soviet Union, and became a member of the Central Committee of the Soviet Communist Party in 1971. Since 1992 she has been chairman of the Russian Association of International Co-operation.

Terfel, Bryn [tervel, brin], originally **Bryn Terfel Jones** (1965–) Bass baritone, born in Pant-glas, Caernarfonshire, Wales, UK. He studied at the Guildhall School of Music and Drama, and became popularly known after winning the Lieder Prize in the Cardiff Singer of the World competition in 1989. He has since appeared at many of the world's leading opera houses, his roles including Leporello in *Don Giovanni* at the Salzburg Festival (1994–6), *Figaro* at the New York Metropolitan Opera (1994), Nick Shadow in *The Rake's Progress* at the Welsh National Opera (1996), and the title roles in *Don Giovanni* (2002) and *Falstaff* (2003) at Covent Garden, London. In 1993 he received the Newcomer of the Year International Classic Music Award.

Terkel, Studs, popular name of **Louis Terkel** (1912–) Writer and oral historian, born in New York City, USA. He went to Law School in Chicago, acted in radio soap operas, became a disc jockey, radio commentator, and television host, and travelled worldwide conducting interviews with the famous and the anonymous. Described by J K Galbraith as 'a national resource', his publications include *Giants of Jazz* (1957), *Working* (1974), *The Good War: an Oral History of World War Two* (1984, Pulitzer), *My American Century* (1997), and *Will the Circle be Unbroken?* (2002).

term or **terminal figure** A sculptured head, or head and shoulders, on a pillar which tapers towards its base. Such figures have become popular as garden ornaments since the Renaissance. The term is very similar to a **herm**, so-called because in Greece the god Hermes was frequently represented in this way.

term bank A large computerized databank of terminology, cross-referenced for the same items in a range of languages. The provision of such resources followed the 20th-c explosion in technical terminology, which led to an urgent need to standardize usage between different languages, and to register and correlate differences where they exist. The European Union has its own version in the European Automatic Dictionary, on-line via Euronet.

Terme [tairmay] The national museum of Rome, containing one of the world's most important collections of Greek and Roman art. It is housed in the ancient Diocletian Baths.

terminal *computer terminal*

terminal velocity The greatest velocity an object will reach when allowed to fall through some fluid (usually air or water). Terminal velocity is attained when the resistive forces due to the medium, which increase with velocity, are equal and opposite to the accelerating force acting in the direction of motion. Its value depends on the fluid and on the object's shape, density, and surface roughness.

Terminus The Roman god of boundary marks, where his statue or bust was sometimes placed. His sanctuary on the Capitol was within the temple of Jupiter Optimus Maximus, but as Terminus had to be worshipped in the open air, it was not allowed to be covered in. His festival (**Terminalia**) was on 23 February.

termite A small, social insect that constructs nests in rotten wood or makes earth mounds which may measure several metres across and contain millions of individuals: caste structure of colony well-developed; workers mostly sterile, blind, and with soft white cuticle (known as **white ants**); soldiers sterile, with large heads and strong jaws; adults (*imagos*) winged, reproductive forms with compound eyes; gut contains harmless bacteria enabling the digestion of cellulose in wood; c.2000 species, causing great economic problems in the tropics, damaging timber buildings and crops. (Order: Isoptera.)

tern A small, gull-like seabird, found worldwide; plumage usually pale with black cap and forked tail; head with partly erectile crest (**crested tern**) or smooth. Some species, such as **noddies** (**ternlets**) and **marsh terns**, are darker, often with wedge-shaped tails. (Family: Laridae, 42 species; some authors put the tern in a separate family, Sternidae.)

terpene A class of natural products, also known as **essential oils**, based upon the oligomerization of isoprene, having formulae closely related to $(C_5H_8)_n$. Common examples, whose names show their origins, are pinene, limonene, menthol, and carotene.

Terpsichore [terpsikawree] In Greek mythology, one of the Muses, usually associated with dancing or lyric poetry.

Terra Australis Incognita (Lat 'Unknown South Land') A supposed continent once thought to exist in the S Pacific in order to balance the Eurasian land-mass of the N hemisphere. First argued into being by ancient Greek thinkers, it provided a major stimulus for exploration until it was shown not to exist by James Cook on his second great voyage (1772–5).

terracotta Clay, modelled into sculpture or tiles and fired in a kiln, becoming hard and brittle but very permanent. Examples survive from ancient times and from all over the world.

Terracotta Army *Mount Li*

terrapin [terapin] A reptile of the family Emydidae, found in fresh or brackish water or on land; hind feet may be enlarged to assist with swimming; some species eat small animals when young, plants when adult; also known as **pond turtle**. The name is sometimes used only for some of the pond turtle species. (Order: Chelonia.)

terrier A small hardy domestic dog, bred for hunting (especially foxes); originally sent into burrows after prey; traditionally aggressive, tenacious, fearless; many modern breeds.

Territorial Army, in full **Territorial and Voluntary Reserve Army (TAVRA)** A British reserve military force, first formed in 1908 by amalgamating the old volunteer and yeomanry regiments in a new force of part-time soldiers, each battalion of which was attached to a battalion of the regular army. The 'Terriers' (known as the Territorial Force to 1920, the Territorials thereafter) fought with distinction in the two world wars. They receive continuous training on a part-time basis, and are assigned to UK field forces prepared to be sent as a direct reinforcement to the British Army of the Rhine, or to act in home defence. The **Voluntary Reserve** consists of ex-regular soldiers who commit themselves to reserve service for a fixed period and have a legal obligation to serve when requested by the government.

territory In US history, political status prior to the attainment of statehood, held in two stages. In the first, an 'unorganized territory' was ruled by a judge; in the second, an 'organized' territory could elect its own legislature and non-voting delegate to Congress. Hawaii and Alaska lost their territorial status in the mid-20th-c, when they became US states, and the Virgin Is, Guam, and American Samoa still have this classification.

terrorism Coercive and violent behaviour undertaken to achieve or promote a particular political objective or cause, often involving the overthrow of established order. Terrorist activity is designed to induce fear through its indiscriminate, arbitrary, and unpredictable acts of violence, often against members of the population at large. It may be 'official', as under Stalin, or 'unofficial', as employed by various opposition or underground movements. Such movements are usually minority groups who feel there are no other means available to them of achieving their objectives. Terrorism may be confined to a specific territory or may have an international dimension, manifest in hijackings and hostage-taking, as witnessed in the suicide terrorist attacks on 11 September 2001 when hijacked passenger aircraft were deliberately flown into the twin towers of the World Trade Center, New York City, and the Pentagon, Washington DC. **Bioterrorism** is the use of organic agents such as micro-organisms and viruses which cause disease and death in humans.

Terry, Dame (Alice) Ellen (1847–1928) Actress, born in Coventry, West Midlands, C England, UK, a member of a large family of actors. She appeared on stage at eight, from 1862 played in Bristol and, after a short-lived marriage and retirement, established herself as the leading Shakespearean actress in London, dominating the English and US theatre (1878–1902) in partnership with Henry Irving. In 1903 she went into theatre management, and toured and lectured widely. She was made a dame in 1925.

Terry-Thomas, originally **Thomas Terry Hoar Stevens** (1911–90) Film actor, born in Finchley, NW Greater London, UK. He began his career as Thomas Terry in music hall and radio before changing his name to Terry Thomas, afterwards adding the hyphen for comic effect. He was the gap-toothed villain in dozens of post-World War 2 comedies, satirizing and eventually personifying the upper-class bounder in such films as *I'm All Right Jack* (1959), *School for Scoundrels* (1960), and *Those Magnificent Men In Their Flying Machines* (1965).

Tertiaries Members of the Third Order of religious life. Normally, these are lay people striving after Christian perfection in life in the world under the guidance of a religious Order, such as the Franciscans or Dominicans. A **Regular Tertiary** is a member of a community bound by vows.

tertiary education Post-secondary education. It is often used to refer to further and higher education, but in the UK it can also refer to attendance at a **tertiary college**, which is a college for all those over 16 wishing to pursue academic or vocational courses.

Tertiary period The earlier of the two geological periods of the Cenozoic era, extending from c.65 to 2 million years ago. It is divided into five epochs: the Palaeocene, Eocene, Oligocene, Miocene, and Pliocene. Early Tertiary times are marked by great mountain-building episodes (Alps, Himalayas, Andes, Rockies) and the diversification of mammals.

Tertullian [tertulian], in full **Quintus Septimus Florens Tertullianus** (c.160–220) Christian theologian, born in Carthage. He lived for some time at Rome, was converted (c.196), and then returned to Carthage. His opposition to worldliness in the Church culminated in his becoming a leader of the Montanist sect (c.207). The first to produce major Christian works in Latin, he thus exercised a profound influence on the development of ecclesiastical language. He wrote books against heathens, Jews, and heretics, as well as several practical and ascetic treatises.

Teruel [terooel], ancient **Turba** 40°22N 1°08W, pop (2000e) 29 000. Capital of Teruel province, Aragón, EC Spain; on R Turia, 302 km/188 mi from Madrid; bishopric; railway; clothes, woollens, soap, leather, flour, wood products, foodstuffs; cathedral (16th-c), Los Arcos aqueduct, Church of St Peter; the town's Mudéjar architecture, a mixture of Christian and Islamic influences, is a world heritage site.

terza rima [tertsa reema] (Ital 'third rhyme') An Italian verse form, where the rhyme dovetails the three-line stanzas, ending with aba, bcb, cdc, etc. It is used by Dante in the *Divina commedia*, and also by Petrarch and Boccaccio. Chaucer used it for part of *A Complaint to his Lady*, but it was Sir Thomas Wyatt who pioneered its use in England. Other poets who have employed it are Byron, Shelley, Browning and, more recently, Auden.

Tesla, Nikola [tesla] (1856–1943) Physicist and electrical engineer, born in Smiljan, W Croatia. He studied at Graz, Prague, and Paris, emigrating to the USA in 1884. He left the Edison Works at Menlo Park to concentrate on his own inventions, and in 1885 sold the patent rights to his system of alternating-current dynamos, transformers, and motors to George Westinghouse. His inventions included electric bulbs and the high-frequency coil which now bears his name. The unit of magnetic induction is named after him.

tesla SI unit of magnetic flux density; symbol *T*; defined as a magnetic flux of 1 weber per square metre; named after Nikola Tesla.

tessera *mosaic*

tessitura [tessitoora] That part of a vocal compass in which the most demanding passages in a piece of music are concentrated. An aria, operatic role, etc may be said to demand a high tessitura, without containing any exceptionally high notes.

Test Act A British Act passed in 1673 by a parliament anxious to curb Catholic influence at Charles II's court. Every office holder had to take Oaths of Supremacy and Allegiance, and to take Communion according to the rites of the Church of England. A declaration against the doctrine of transubstantiation also had to be made. The passage of the Act necessitated the resignation of the king's brother, James, Duke of York, as Lord High Admiral. The Act remained in force until 1828.

testament literature A loose genre of writings found in the Old Testament Pseudepigrapha, stemming from post-exilic times, which purportedly gives the last words or 'testaments' of significant figures from Israel's history. Although often ethical in nature, testaments also include visions of the future. In their present form, some may reflect Christian and not just Jewish interests. Most notable are the *Testaments of the 12 Patriarchs*, the *Testament of Moses*, the *Testament of Adam*, and the *Testament of Job*.

testing *achievement / criterion-referenced / norm-referenced / objective test; continuous assessment; SAT*

testis (plural **testes**) The essential reproductive gland (*gonad*) of male animals, producing spermatozoa; also known as the **testicle**. In vertebrates the Leydig cells of the testis also synthesize and secrete sex hormones (*androgens*). In mammals (eg humans), there are usually two, lying suspended within the scrotum, oval and flattened in shape. Each testis is divided into a number of wedge-shaped small lobes, containing a convoluted seminiferous tube (from which the spermatozoa arise). The spermatozoa pass from this tube into a straight seminiferous tube, then into the rete testis and to the highly convoluted *epididymis* (a duct c.6 m/20 ft long in men). Between the seminiferous tubes are groups of glandular Leydig cells (the *interstitial cells*) which produce *testosterone*, essential for the development and maintenance of male sexual characteristics.

testosterone [testosterohn] The male sex hormone, produced in the testes, and responsible for the development of the primary sex organs, secondary sex characteristics (eg facial hair), and sexual behaviour.

test-tube baby The lay term to indicate ***in vitro* fertilization and embryo replacement (IVF)**. The procedure is indicated in infertility, notably when there is damage to the uterine tubes that is not amenable to repair, but it is also used for other causes of infertility. Such women are given drugs that stimulate ovulation. Several ova are then retrieved from the surface of the ovaries by a technique known as *laparoscopy* and placed in a suitable culture medium to which spermatozoa are added. About 40 hours later the ova are examined to confirm that fertilization has occurred, after which the fertilized ovum (4–8 cells in size) is transferred to the uterus via the vagina and cervix. Successful pregnancy occurs in about 10–20% of cases.

tetanus [tetanuhs] A disease resulting from infection with *Clostridium tetani*, which exists in the soil and in the gut of humans and other animals; also known as **lockjaw**. It especially affects farmers and gardeners. Infection enters the body through wounds in the skin caused by a nail or splinter. The bacteria produce a toxin which affects motor nerve cells in the spinal cord, and induces convulsions and muscle spasms. The disease can be prevented by active vaccination, and treated by antitoxin and penicillin.

tetany A state of neuromuscular hyperexcitability, usually associated with low blood calcium levels, but also induced by the toxin produced by the *clostridium tetani* bacteria. It leads to muscle cramps, high blood pressure, convulsions, and spasm of the larynx, which may result in life-threatening obstruction of the airway. There are two classic clinical signs of tetany: *Chvostek's sign* is a facial twitch elicited by tapping the facial nerve on the side of the jaw, *Trousseau's sign* is a rigid position of the hands with flexion at the joints of the wrist and between hand and fingers, and extension of the finger joints, produced by placing pressure around the upper arm.

Tethys [teethis] The third natural satellite of Saturn, discovered in 1684; distance from the planet 295 000 km/183 000 mi; diameter 1060 km/660 mi; orbital period 1·888 days. Two other satellites, Calypso and Telesto, move along the same orbit.

Tétouan or **Tetuán** [taytwahn] 35°34N 5°22W, pop (2000e) 291 000. City in Nord-Ouest province, NE Morocco; 60 km/37 mi SE of Tangier; settled by Moorish exiles from Spain, 15th-c; captured by Spanish, 1860; airfield; textiles, leather, soap, tiles; trade in agriculture and livestock; Medina a world heritage site.

tetra Any of many small colourful freshwater fish (Family: Characidae), from South and Central America; popular with aquarists; length typically 3–10 cm/1¼ in; body rather carp-like, but lacking barbels and with well-developed jaw teeth.

tetracyclines [tetrasiyklinz] A class of antibiotics obtained from *Streptomyces*, a genus of organisms intermediate between bacteria and fungi, active against a broad spectrum of infections. The first to be produced was chlortetracycline (aureomycin, now superseded) in 1948.

tetraethyl lead $Pb(C_2H_5)_4$. An organometallic compound made by the reaction of lead chloride with a Grignard reagent, used as an additive to petrol to control 'knocking'. Its hazardous properties and those of its decomposition products are leading to its progressive disuse.

Tetragrammaton *Yahweh*

Tetzel, Johann (c.1465–1519) Monk, born in Pirna, E Germany. He became a Dominican in 1489, and was appointed in 1516 to preach an indulgence in favour of contributors to the building fund of St Peter's in Rome. This he did with great ostentation, thereby provoking the Wittenberg theses of Luther, and his own reply.

Teutonic Knights Members of the Order of St Mary of the Teutons, a religious-military order founded c.1190 and inspired by crusading ideals. By the 14th-c they controlled the E Baltic lands of the Livonian Knights, Prussia, and E Pomerania. In 1410 the Poles and Lithuanians routed the Order at Tannenberg. The Order was dissolved in Germany in 1809, but re-established in Austria in 1834. Its habit was a white robe with a black cross.

tex *count* (textiles)

Texas pop (2000e) 20 851 800; area 691 003 sq km/266 807 sq mi. State in SW USA, divided into 254 counties; the 'Lone Star State'; second largest state in the USA; first settled by the Spanish in the late 1600s; first American settlement, 1821; American rebellion after request for separate statehood turned down by Mexico, 1835; declared independence, defeated by Santa Anna at the Alamo, 1836; Mexican army then defeated by Sam Houston at San Jacinto, 1836; independence of Texas recognized; admitted to the Union as the 28th state, 1845; US–Mexican War, with Mexican defeats at Palo Alto and Resaca de la Palma, 1846–8; joined the Confederate states in the Civil War (the only state not to be overrun by Union troops); re-admitted to the Union, 1870; discovery of extensive oil deposits (1901) transformed the economy; capital, Austin; other chief cities, Houston, Dallas, San Antonio, El Paso, Fort Worth; bounded SE by the Gulf of Mexico, SW by Mexico; rivers include the Red, Sabine, Trinity, Brazos, Colorado; Rio Grande forms the state's entire international border with Mexico; Davis and Guadalupe Mts in the extreme W; highest point, Guadalupe Peak (2667 m/8750 ft); much of the E hilly, forested country with cypress swamps, cotton and rice cultivation, extensive oil fields; Gulf coastal plains around Houston heavily industrialized; tourism and heavy industry in the drier S coastal region; intensive agriculture in the irrigated lower Rio Grande valley, producing citrus fruits and winter vegetables; richest agricultural land in the C and N (the Blackland prairies); SC plains and Edwards Plateau have vast wheat and cotton farms and cattle ranches; far N dry, barren, mountainous; nation's leading producer of oil and natural gas; chemicals, processed foods, machinery, fabricated metals; major producer of cattle, sheep, cotton; wheat, sorghum, dairy produce, rice, vegetables, fishing; large Spanish-speaking population.

textlinguistics The study of the structure of linguistic texts (spoken or written), in which the texts are seen as having a specific communicative function, such as road signs, poems, or conversations. Analyses are made of the way the elements of a text cohere, and how its content is structured, from such points of view as grammar, vocabulary, pronunciation, and graphic layout.

textual criticism A scholarly procedure devoted to establishing the authenticity and accuracy of literary texts; unlike other forms of criticism, not interpretive or evaluative in character. It involves the scrutiny of manuscripts where they exist, the collation of different readings (*recension*), and where evidence is incomplete or inconclusive, the practice of emendation. The method was first applied to biblical texts in the 19th-c, but is now used even on the works of modern authors (such as Joyce and Proust).

Thabana Ntlenyana, Mount [tabana ntlenyana] or **Mount Thadentsonyane** 29°28S 29°16E. Mountain in E Lesotho, in the Drakensberg Mts; highest peak in Lesotho, 3482 m/11 424 ft, and also in Africa S of Mt Kilimanjaro.

Thackeray, William Makepeace (1811–63) Novelist, born in Kolkata (formerly Calcutta), E India. He studied at Cambridge, left without taking a degree, and visited Germany (1830–1), where he met Goethe. In line for a large inheritance, he turned to journalism, bought the *National Standard* (1833), and lost his fortune a year later. He first attracted attention as a writer with his work in *Punch* (1842), in which he exploited the view of society as seen by a footman, and the great theme of English snobbery. Most of his major novels were all published as monthly serials: *Vanity Fair* (1847–8), *Pendennis* (1848), and *The Newcomes* (1853–5) – *Henry Esmond* (1852) being the exception. He travelled widely as a lecturer in Europe, and in 1860 became the first editor of *The Cornhill Magazine*, where much of his later work appeared.

Thaddeus, St *Jude, St*

Thai [tiy] The official language of Thailand, spoken by c.30 million people, with much dialectal variation. Its relationship with other language groups in neighbouring China and the Pacific is not clear. There is written evidence of the language from the 13th-c.

Thailand *p.1519*

thalamus *diencephalon*

thalassaemia / thalassemia [thalaseemia] An inherited disease of the blood in which there is defective production of haemoglobin (the oxygen-carrying pigment in red blood cells), resulting in anaemia. It occurs in people of SE Asian and Mediterranean origin. There are two types, *alpha* and *beta thalassaemia*, both caused by the inheritance of an abnormal gene. If the gene is from only one parent, symptoms are mild (*thalassaemia minor*), but the gene can still be passed on to the next generation. Individuals who inherit abnormal genes from both

Thailand

[tiyland], Thai **Muang Thai**, formerly **Siam**, official name **Kingdom of Thailand**

Local name Muang Thai

Timezone GMT +7

Area 513 115 km²/198 062 sq mi

Population total (2002e) 63 430 000

Status Kingdom

Capital Bangkok (Krung Thep)

Languages Thai (official), Malay and English also spoken

Ethnic groups Thai (75%), Chinese (14%), Khmer and Mon minorities

Religions Theravada Buddhist (95%), Muslim, Hindu, Sikh and Christian (4%)

Physical features Agricultural region dominated by the floodplain of the Chao Phraya R; NE plateau rises above 300 m/1000 ft and covers a third of the country; mountainous N region rising to 2595 m/8514 ft at Doi Inthanon; narrow, low-lying S region separates the Andaman Sea from the Gulf of Thailand; covered in tropical rainforest, except sparsely vegetated Khorat plateau (NE).

Climate Equatorial climate in the S; tropical monsoon climate in the N and C; high temperatures and humidity; wet season (Jun–Oct); average annual temperature 26°C (Jan), 28°C (Jul) in Bangkok; average annual rainfall 1400 mm/55 in.

Currency 1 Baht (B) – 100 satang

Economy Agriculture; rice, maize, bananas, pineapple, sugar cane, rubber, teak; textiles, electronics, cement, chemicals, food processing, tourism; tin (world's third largest supplier), tungsten (world's second largest supplier), manganese, antimony, lead, zinc, copper, natural gas.

GDP (2002e) $445·8 bn, per capita $7000

Human Development Index (2002) 0·762

History Evidence of Bronze Age communities, 4000 BC; Thai nation founded, 13th-c; only country in S and SE Asia to have escaped colonization by a European power; revolution brought end to absolute monarchical rule, 1932; followed by periods of military rule interspersed with brief periods of democratic government; 1991 constitution (with amendments) provides for a National Legislative Assembly comprising a House of Representatives, an elected Senate, and a cabinet headed by a Prime Minister; King is Head of State.

Head of State (Monarch)

1946– Bhumibol Adulyadej (Rama IX)

Head of Government

1976–7 Thanin Kraivichien
1977–80 Kriangsak Chammanard
1980–8 Prem Tinsulanonda
1988–91 Chatichai Choonhavan
1991–2 Anand Panyarachun *Military Junta*
1992 Suchinda Kraprayoon
1992–5 Chuan Leekpai
1995–6 Banharn Silpa-Archa
1996–7 Chavalit Yongchaiyudh
1997–2001 Chuan Leekpai
2001– Thaksin Shinawatra

parents suffer serious or fatal disease (*thalassaemia major*). The alpha type results in fetal death and stillbirth; the beta type leads to severe anaemia from childhood. The bone marrow and spleen expand to try to compensate by producing more red blood cells, and this leads to skeletal abnormalities, especially of the skull and face. Treatment is with repeated blood transfusions, but this may damage the liver and heart.

Thaleia *Thalia*

Thales [thayleez] (c.620–c.555 BC) Greek natural philosopher, traditionally regarded as the first philosopher, born in Miletus. His mercantile journeys took him to Egypt and Babylon, where he acquired land-surveying and astronomical techniques, and is said to have predicted the solar eclipse in 585 BC. None of his writings survive, but Aristotle attributes to him the doctrine that water is the original substance from which all things are derived.

Thalia or **Thaleia** [thaliya] In Greek mythology, the Muse of comedy and idyllic poetry.

thalidomide A sedative introduced in West Germany in 1956, in the UK in 1958, and subsequently in some other countries. It became widely used because of its particular safety (even massive overdoses are not lethal). However, it was recognized as a teratogen (causing congenital abnormalities) and withdrawn; approximately 20% of babies whose mothers had taken thalidomide during early pregnancy suffered absence of limbs or part of limbs. It has been estimated to be responsible for 10 000 cases of deformity. Since this disaster, all drugs and other chemicals with which humans come into contact have been required to prove lack of teratogenic potential before they can be marketed. Thalidomide has recently been shown to be a powerful anti-cancer agent because it blocks the growth of blood vessels that feed tumours.

Thallophyta [thalofita] A collective name formerly used for all lower plant-like organisms that lack differentiation into root, stem, and leaf; sometimes treated as a subkingdom of plants comprising the eucaryotic algae and fungi; also known as **Thallobionta**.

thallus The body of a plant which is not differentiated into stem, leaves, and roots. It is usually flattened, and may also be branched.

Thames, River [temz], Lat **Tamesis** River rising in the Cotswold Hills, SE Gloucestershire, England, UK; flows 352 km/219 mi E and SE through Oxfordshire, the former county of Berkshire, Surrey, and Greater London; approaches the North Sea in a long, wide estuary between Essex (N) and Kent (S); navigable as far as London by large ships; chief tributaries, the Cherwell, Thame, Lea, Colne, Roding, Kennet, Mole, Wey, and Medway Rivers; upper part beyond Oxford often called R Isis; joined by Grand Union Canal near Brentford; known as the *Pool of London* by London Bridge; two embankments built at London, from Blackfriars Bridge to Westminster (1864) and from Westminster Bridge to Vauxhall (1866); Thames Conservancy Board established in 1857; administration of the river below Teddington given to the Port of London Authority in 1908; tidal barrier built across approach to London to reduce risk of floods (completed 1983).

Thanet, Isle of Urban area in E Kent, SE England, UK, originally an island; contains the towns of Margate, Broadstairs, and Ramsgate; railway.

Thanksgiving Day A day set apart for a public acknowledgment of God's goodness and mercy; in Canada the second Monday in October, and in the USA the fourth Thursday of November, both public holidays. The occasion dates from 1621, when the new American settlers celebrated their first harvest. It gradually spread throughout the USA, and has been observed nationally since 1863. In modern times, the day is especially important for family reunions.

Thanlwin, River, formerly **Salween** River in SE Asia, rising in SW China; flows generally S through Myanmar, forming part of Myanmar–Thailand border, to enter the Gulf of Martaban, an inlet of the Andaman Sea; because of rapids, navigable only to Kamamaung (120 km/75 mi from mouth); length 2815 km/1750 mi.

Thant, U [oo tant] (1909–74) Burmese diplomat, born in Pantanaw, S Myanmar (formerly Burma). He studied at Yangon, and was a teacher who took up government work when Burma became independent in 1948, becoming the country's UN representative in 1957. As secretary-general of the UN (1962–71), he played a major diplomatic role during the Cuban crisis (1962). He also formulated a plan to end the Congolese Civil War (1962), and mobilized a UN peace-keeping force in Cyprus (1964).

Thar Desert [tah] or **(Great) Indian Desert** area c.320 000 sq km/125 000 sq mi. Arid region in NW India and E Pakistan, S Asia; 800 km/500 mi long and 400 km/250 mi wide; between the Indus and the Sutlej Rivers (W) and the Aravalli Range (E); bounded S by the Rann of Kutch; crossed by irrigation canals in N and W, largest the Rajasthan Canal.

Tharp, Twyla (1942 –) Dancer, choreographer, and director, born in Portland, Indiana, USA. She studied with Graham, Cunningham, and Paul Taylor, and danced with Taylor (1963–5). Since then she has choreographed and danced with her own group, The Twyla Tharp Dance Foundation, and made new work for various other ballet and modern dance companies. Flippant, throwaway movement, and an amusing edge to her works, disguises meticulous structure and comment on current social issues, as in *Push Comes to Shove* (1976). Later works include *In the Upper Room* (1987) and *The Elements* (1996). She formed her own company, Tharp!, in 1996.

Thatcher (of Kesteven), Margaret (Hilda) Thatcher, Baroness, *née* **Roberts** (1925–) British stateswoman and prime minister (1979–90), born in Grantham, Lincolnshire, EC England, UK. She studied at Oxford, and worked as a research chemist (1947–51). She married **Denis Thatcher** (1915–2003) in 1951, studied law, and was called to the bar in 1954. Elected as Conservative MP for Finchley in 1959, she joined the shadow cabinet in 1967. She became secretary of state for education and science (1970–4), joint shadow Chancellor (1974–5), and in 1975 replaced Edward Heath as Leader of the Conservative Party to become the first woman party leader in British politics. Under her leadership, the Conservative Party moved towards a more 'right wing' position, and British politics and society became more polarized than at any time since World War 2. Her government instituted the privatization of nationalized industries and national utilities, tried to institute a market in state-provided health care and education, and reduced the role of local government as a provider of services. She was re-elected in 1983 with a large majority, despite the worst unemployment figures for 50 years, aided by the tide of popular feeling following the Falklands War, and disarray in the Opposition parties. She was elected for a third term of office in 1987, and by 1988 had become the longest serving premier of the 20th-c. Her personal political philosophy was popularly referred to as *Thatcherism*, characterized by the resolution to persevere with policies despite objections from critics and doubts from her supporters. She resigned (Nov 1990) as a result of the controversy and infighting which followed her opposition to full monetary and economic union with Europe. Created a life peer in 1992, she continues to put forward her views on politics in speeches given throughout the world and through the establishment of a Foundation named after her. She published her memoirs, *Margaret Thatcher: the Downing Street Years*, in 1993, and later books include *Statecraft* (2002).

Thatta monuments A group of monuments in Thatta, former capital of Sind in present-day Pakistan; a world heritage site. During the 14th–18th-c the city flourished as a centre of Islamic arts. Its monuments include the 17th-c Great Mosque built by Shah Jahan, and graves in the 'City of Mausoleums', a vast necropolis covering 15 sq km/6 sq mi.

Thaw, John (Edward) (1942–2002) Actor, born in Manchester, Greater Manchester, NW England, UK. He studied at the Royal Academy of Dramatic Art in London, and went on to a prolific career in television, theatre, and films. Best known for his television work, which included *The Sweeney* (1974–8), *Inspector Morse* (1987–2000), *Kavanagh QC* (1995–2000), *Goodnight Mr Tom* (1999), and *The Glass* (2001), he won a number of BAFTA awards and was honoured with a fellowship in 2001. He married actress Sheila Hancock in 1973.

theatre / theater Derived from the Greek for 'seeing place', the term originally signified the area occupied by spectators. It now describes the whole building and the social art form it houses. Since the Renaissance, scenic illusion has played a dominant role in the history of Western theatre, as is evident in the development of the proscenium. However, throughout the 20th-c, with film and television appropriating this pictorial tradition, theatre rediscovered the efficacy of open stages, emblematic staging, and the direct presentational styles of such popular forms as *commedia dell'arte*, boulevard theatre, or mummers' plays. In this respect, for modern Western theatre the influence of the ancient and sophisticated traditions of, for example, Chinese, Indian, and Japanese theatre has been strong.

Theatre, the The earliest of the London playhouses. It was erected on a leased plot in the parish of St Leonhard's, Shoreditch, London in 1576 by James Burbage, the son of a carpenter and travelling player. A circular wooden building with three galleries around an open yard, it was also used for the display of fencing and other physical spectacles. With the ground lease due to expire in 1598, Burbage's sons Richard and Cuthbert dismantled the building a week before the expiry date and removed it piecemeal to land leased on the other side of the Thames in Southwark, not far from the Rose, where it was built as the Globe.

Theatre de Complicite [komplisitay] An innovative international touring theatre company based in London, co-founded in 1983 by Simon McBurney (1957–), Annabel Arden (1959–), and Marcello Magni. Arising initially from the clown-based training of Jacques Lecoq, the company's work has always had strong physical and comedic elements, but it was its application of these principles to classic texts and literary adaptations that initially defined its style. The company continues to innovate, combining electronic media, image and music, and site-specific performance to create surprising, disruptive theatre. Productions include *The Visit* (1989), *The Winter's Tale* (1992), *Mnemonic* (1999), *The Noise of Time* (2000), *The Elephant Vanishes* (2003), and *Measure for Measure* (2004).

theatre / theater in the round, also called **arena theatre** A theatre in which the auditorium surrounds a central stage and both performer and audience share the same acoustic space. Also known as an **arena stage**, the form demands that the actors project in all directions simultaneously.

Theatre Workshop An English theatre company founded in Manchester by Joan Littlewood in 1945. From 1953 onwards it was based in London at the Theatre Royal, Stratford East, and is best remembered for its vigorous ensemble acting exemplified by such shows as *The Hostage* and *Oh, What a Lovely War* (1963).

Thebe [theebee] A tiny natural satellite of Jupiter, discovered in 1979 by Voyager 2; distance from the planet 222 000 km/ 138 000 mi; diameter 100 km/60 mi.

Thebes (Egypt) [theebz] The ancient capital of Upper Egypt, and the location of many magnificent pharaonic temples and tombs, such as Tutankhamen's; a world heritage site. It was situated on the R Nile, where the town of Luxor now stands – a major tourist centre from as far back as Roman times.

Thebes (Greece) [theebz] In ancient Greece, the most powerful city-state in Boeotia. Although prominent in Greek legend (the Oedipus cycle is based there), in historical times it was rarely able to rival Athens and Sparta. Only under the brilliant Epaminondas in the 370s BC did it succeed briefly in being the leading power in Greece. It is now the capital town of Boeotia department, SE Greece, 52 km/32 mi NNW of Athens; pop (2000e) 20 000, a market town for a rich agricultural region.

theft The taking or appropriation of property belonging to another person without consent, with the intention of permanently depriving that person of the property. Borrowing is not theft, but such temporary appropriation may in certain jurisdictions sometimes be the subject of other criminal sanctions. For example, in the UK the temporary taking of a motor-car without the owner's consent is a statutory criminal offence, known as *aggravated vehicle taking* and *joyriding* in most US jurisdictions. Most US jurisdictions divide theft into **petty theft** (usually involving thefts of property worth less than $400) and **grand theft** (all other property). In the United Kingdom, theft involving the use of force may amount to robbery.

thegn or **thane** [thayn] (Old English 'one who serves') In Anglo-Saxon England, a member of the noble class. Until the Norman Conquest, thegns were indispensable to effective royal control of the localities. From 1066, most of them lost lands, status, and political influence to Norman barons and knights. Some even entered the service of the Byzantine emperor.

theine [theein] *caffeine*

theism Belief in a single divine being, transcendent and personal, who created the world and, although involved with and related to the creation, is distinct from it. It is a feature of Jewish and Islamic as well as Christian faith, and is contrasted with both deism and pantheism.

theme park An entertainment centre based on a particular theme, the most popular being wildlife parks. Many are also amusement parks. The first theme park was Disneyland, in Anaheim, CA, opened in 1955, based on the Walt Disney cartoon characters.

Themis [themis] In Greek mythology, the goddess of established law and justice (really a personification). As a consort of Zeus, she is the mother of the Horae and the Moerae.

Themistocles [themistokleez] (c.523–c.458 BC) Athenian general, visionary politician, and hero of Salamis. By persuading the Athenians to develop Piraeus as a port (493 BC), and to use their rich silver deposits to build a fleet (483 BC), he not only made possible their great naval victory at Salamis (480 BC), but also laid the foundations of their maritime empire. He fell from favour c.470 BC, and was ostracized. After many adventures, he served the Persian king in Asia Minor as the Governor of Magnesia.

Theocritus [theeokritus] (c.310–250 BC) Greek pastoral poet, probably born in Syracuse. He was brought up in Cos, and lived for a time at the court of Ptolemy Philadelphus in Alexandria. About 30 of his poems survive, though the authenticity of some have been disputed. His short poems dealing with pastoral subjects, and representing a single scene, came to be called 'idylls' (*eidullia*). Tennyson was deeply influenced by him, as were the pastoral poets of the Renaissance.

theodicy [theeodisee] The defence and vindication of God, defined as both omnipotent and good in the light of evil in the world. The term was first used by Leibniz in 1710.

theodolite [theeodoliyt] An optical surveying instrument for measuring vertical or (more importantly) horizontal angles. It is a small telescope, with cross wires, movable over horizontal and vertical graduated circular scales. It is usually seen mounted on a stable tripod.

Theodora (c.500–47) Byzantine empress (527–47). She was an actress, dancer, and prostitute who became mistress, then wife, of Justinian (525). A woman of great intelligence and courage, she played a major role throughout his long and distinguished reign, and probably saved his throne during the Nika riots by her intervention (532).

Theodorakis, Mikis [thayodorahkees] (1925–) Composer, born in Khios, Greece. He studied at the Paris Conservatoire, and in 1959 his ballet *Antigone* was produced at Covent Garden. On his return to Greece he became intensely critical of the musical and artistic establishment. When the right-wing government took power in 1967, he was imprisoned and his music banned, but he was released in 1970, after worldwide appeals. His prolific musical output includes oratorios, ballets, song cycles, and music for film scores, the best known of which is *Zorba the Greek* (1965).

Theodore of Mopsuestia (c.350–428) Christian theologian, born in Antioch, S Turkey (formerly Syria). He was made Bishop of Mopsuestia in Cilicia in 392. He wrote commentaries (mostly now lost) on almost all the books of Scripture, adopting a literal meaning in preference to the use of allegorical interpretation. As the teacher of Nestorius, he was perhaps the founder of Nestorianism, and his views on the Incarnation were condemned by the fifth ecumenical council in 553.

Theodoric or **Theoderic** [theeodorik], known as **the Great** (?–526) King of the Ostrogoths (471–526), who invaded Italy in 489, defeating the barbarian ruler, Odoacer. His long reign secured for Italy tranquillity and prosperity, the Goths and the Romans continuing as distinct nations, each with its own tribunals and laws. He established his capital at Ravenna.

Theodosian Code [theeodohshan] A codification of the law promulgated throughout the Roman Empire in 438 by the Emperor Theodosius II (401–50). Its 16 books summarized all the laws that had been enacted since the beginning of the reign of Constantine the Great (312).

Theodosius I [theeodohshus], known as **the Great** (c.346–95) Roman emperor of the East (379–95). Made emperor because of his military abilities, he solved the long-standing Gothic problem by allowing the Goths to settle S of the Danube as allies of Rome. His title comes from his vigorous championship of orthodox Christianity.

Theodosius II [theeodohshus] (401–50) Roman emperor (408–50), the grandson of Theodosius I and, like him, a staunch champion of orthodox Christianity. He is chiefly remembered for his codification of the Roman law in 438.

theology Literally, the science of the divine, or of discourse about God. In Christianity, it is understood as the systematic critical clarification of the historical beliefs of the Church. It has been divided into **natural theology**, that which can be known about God from nature or by reason alone, and **revealed theology**, that which can only be known through the self-disclosure of God.

Theophrastus [theeohfrastus] (c.372–286 BC) Greek philosopher, born in Eresus, Lesbos, Greece. At Athens he studied under Aristotle, becoming his close friend, and head of the Peripatetic school after his death. He was responsible for preserving many of Aristotle's works, along with many fragments of the Presocratics. Among his own works which have survived are two books on plants, and *Charactēres*, describing 30 moral types based on studies by Aristotle.

theorbo [theeaw(r)boh] A large lute with six strings above a fretted fingerboard, and seven or eight additional bass strings which are not stopped and have a separate pegbox. It was widely used in the 17th-c as a continuo instrument.

theorem A proposition proved by logical deduction from one or more initial premises. Although geometrical theorems are the most widely known, theorems exist in all branches of mathematics. A simple theorem which is proved and then used towards the proof of another theorem is known as a *lemma*. If the theorem is 'statement *p* implies statement *q*', the *converse* is 'statement *q* implies statement *p*'. The converse of a theorem is not always true. For example, if two triangles are congruent, they are equal in area, but two triangles that are equal in area are not necessarily congruent.

theosophy [theeosofee] Any system of philosophical or theological thought based on the direct and immediate experience of the divine. It has been used to describe any developed system of mystical thought and practice, and especially the principles of the Theosophical Society founded in 1875 by Madame Blavatsky (1831–91) and H S Olcott (1832–1907) in New York City.

Thera [theera] *Santorini*

Therapsida [therapsida] An order of fossil reptiles including the direct ancestors of the mammals; known mainly from the Permian and Triassic periods; many with well-differentiated dentitions; some with a secondary palate, and mammal-like limbs, but only one middle-ear bone. (Subclass: Synapsida.)

Theravada [theravahda] The form of Buddhism commonly found in S Asia (Sri Lanka, Myanmar, Thailand, Cambodia, and Laos). Its doctrines remain essentially as they were in the 3rd-c BC, and it is generally distinguished from the later **Mahayana** ('greater vehicle') Buddhism in its rejection of the theory of bodhisattvas.

Theresa, Mother *Teresa, Mother*

Theresa of Lisieux, St [leesyoe], originally **(Marie Françoise) Thérèse Martin**, also known as **the Little Flower** and **St Theresa of the Child Jesus** (1873–97) Saint, born in Alençon, NE France. An intensely religious child, she entered the Carmelite convent of Lisieux in Normandy at the age of 15, where she remained until her death from tuberculosis nine years later. During her last years she wrote an account of her life which was published posthumously as *Histoire d'une âme* (1898, Story of a Soul), showing how the most ordinary person can attain sainthood by following her 'little way' of simple, childlike Christianity. She was canonized in 1925, and in 1947 associated with Joan of Arc as patron saint of France. She was made a doctor of the Church in 1997. Feast day 1 October.

therm *British thermal unit*

thermae [thermiy] The elaborate public bathing complexes that were a standard feature of urban life under the Roman Empire. Functioning very much as community centres, the larger thermal establishments contained far more than changing rooms and hot and cold baths. Among other facilities on offer there might be exercise grounds (*palaestrae*), clubrooms, lecture theatres, and libraries.

thermal conduction The transfer of heat through a substance without bulk movement of the substance; thermal conductivity symbol *k*, units W/(m.K) (watts per metre.kelvin). Heat transfer through poor conductors is via the thermal vibrations of atoms. Metals are good conductors, and heat transfer is via conduction electrons in the free electron gas; metals typically conduct heat a thousand times better than non-metals such as glass or wood.

thermal efficiency In thermodynamics, the ratio of useful work derived from a heat engine to the heat absorbed by it; symbol *e*, a number between 0 and 1. It represents a theoretical maximum possible efficiency. For car engines, $e = 0{\cdot}5$; for coal-fired power stations, $e = 0{\cdot}4$ (approximate values).

thermal equilibrium In thermodynamics, a characteristic of two systems when heat ceases to flow between them. Quantities such as pressure and temperature, which are monitors of thermal variations, cease to change. For example, a cup of coffee allowed to reach thermal equilibrium will be the same temperature as the surrounding room, and the same temperature throughout the coffee.

thermal expansion The increase in size observed in most materials when heated. The expansion results from the increased thermal motion of atoms. The change in the length of a solid rod equals the product of its starting length, the change in temperature, and α, the coefficient of expansion. For copper, $\alpha = 1{\cdot}7 \times 10^{-5}/°C$.

thermal insulation Shielding whose function is to reduce heat flow. Heat loss by conduction is stemmed using layers of material having low thermal conductivity. Loss by convection is reduced by preventing the movement of fluids around the object. Loss by heat radiation is reduced using reflective coatings.

thermal noise In electronic circuits, a background signal due to thermal effects which partially masks the true signal. It is caused by the random thermal motion of conduction electrons in resistive components, and decreases with reduced temperature and resistance. It is one source of audio amplifier hiss.

thermal printer A type of printer which generally uses thermally sensitive paper and produces characters using a set of electrically heated wires. Although thermal printers are relatively inexpensive, the special paper they use is not.

thermic lance A torch-like cutting device for resistant steel and alloys, which depends on the fact that iron will burn in oxygen. A main nozzle for a jet of oxygen has a subsidiary nozzle for acetylene, which serves only to preheat the metal to the temperature at which it will begin to burn in the stream of oxygen. Thereafter the oxygen stream is sufficient to maintain the burning of the steel.

Thermidor coup [thermidaw(r)] The *coup d'état* of 26–27 July 1794 (8–9 Thermidor Year II, which gave its name to the group), when Robespierre and his Jacobin supporters were overthrown, ending the most radical phase of the French Revolution. Among the instigators of Thermidor were such former Jacobins as Joseph Fouché and Paul Barras who, with members of the Convention, set about dismantling the machinery of the Reign of Terror.

thermionics The study of the processes involved in thermionic emission, ie the emission of electrons from a metal surface caused by applying heat to that surface. Normally such electrons would return to the metal, but in devices such as thermionic valves and electron guns they are drawn away by a positively charged anode to give a useful beam of electrons. The effect was discovered by Thomas Edison in 1883.

thermionic valve An electronic device (an *electron tube*) containing two or more electrodes, which are used to regulate the flow of electrons in an electric current. A heated cathode emits electrons which are attracted to a positively-biased anode, and the electron flow is controlled by varying the voltage on intermediate electrodes called *control grids*. The simplest type is the diode used in rectifying circuits. Thermionic valves were used in all types of electronic circuit, but have now almost entirely been replaced by semiconductor devices such as the transistor.

thermistor A temperature sensor constructed from semiconductor material whose electrical resistance falls rapidly as the temperature rises; an abbreviation of **thermal resistor**. It is made from cobalt, nickel, and magnesium oxides mixed with finely divided copper. Thermistors are used in electronic circuits measuring or controlling temperature, in wave-guides to measure the transmitted power, and in time-delay circuits.

thermite A mixture of aluminium and iron oxide which, if ignited, undergoes a fierce chemical reaction producing a high temperature (c.2400°C) and yielding molten iron (or other metal if another oxide is used). The process was devised in 1895 by German chemist Hans Goldschmidt (1861–1923). It is useful for the preparation of intractable metals, or in welding, and has been used for incendiary bombs.

thermochemistry The study of the energy changes accompanying chemical reactions. Such energies have precise values for precisely defined reactants and products. Thermochemical methods are widely used in determining the energy value of foods.

thermocline The depth in the ocean where temperature decreases rapidly. In many ocean areas, including all of the tropics, a permanent thermocline begins at approximately 100 m/325 ft depth. This is just below the surface layer mixed by the wind, where sea surface temperatures may range as high as 28°C. The thermocline may extend to depths of 1000 m/3250 ft or more, where temperatures may be as low as 2°C. In some ocean areas, such as the N Atlantic, seasonal warming may produce a shallow 'seasonal thermocline' above the deeper permanent thermocline.

thermocouple A type of thermometer that allows the direct electronic monitoring of temperature. A temperature-dependent potential difference exists across the junction between two different metals (the *contact potential*). If one such junction is placed in the sample, and the other held at constant temperature, the potential difference between the two junctions is a measure of the sample temperature.

thermodynamics The study of heat and heat-related phenomena, based on four fundamental laws.

Zeroth Law If two systems are in thermodynamic equilibrium with a third, they will be in thermodynamic equilibrium with one another. For example, two objects left to stand a while in a still room will be the same temperature as the room and therefore as each other.

First Law The sum of the energy changes occurring in some isolated process is zero, which is equivalent to the statement that total energy is conserved. For example, a battery may be used to raise the temperature of some water electrically, in which case chemical energy from the battery is converted into heat; but the total energy of the complete system before and after the circuit is switched on is the same.

Second Law A law giving direction to thermodynamic processes in time, and thus forbidding some which would otherwise be allowed by the First Law. It may be expressed in several equivalent ways. **1** No heat engine can have a thermal efficiency of 100%, ie it is impossible to convert heat totally into mechanical work; for example, car engines and power stations can never be 100% efficient, no matter how well they are built. **2** No process may have as its only outcome the transfer of heat from a cold object to a hot one; for example, a refrigerator requires power to make an object at room temperature cold, whereas a cold object will warm up to room temperature on its own. **3** A system will always finish in the state which can be realized in the greatest number of ways; for example, a drop of ink in water will finish up dispersed evenly through the water since this corresponds to the greatest number of arrangements of ink and water atoms. **4** For a closed system, entropy is either constant or increasing.

Third Law Absolute zero can never be reached.

Before the 19th-c, it was generally assumed that heat was a material substance, termed *caloric*. Hot objects were thought to contain more caloric than cold ones, and an object's supply of caloric was limited. The modern conception, that heat is a form of energy, and that heat flow is energy transfer, was originally due to Count Rumford in 1798. Conservation of energy was first understood by Sadi Carnot in 1830, James Joule in 1843, and others. Joule used a system of falling weights to drive paddles immersed in water, thereby raising its temperature and establishing the equivalence of mechanical energy and heat (1845). The idea that all forms of energy are equivalent comes from Hermann von Helmholtz. Lord Kelvin proposed the absolute thermodynamic temperature scale (1845), which now bears his name. The second law of thermodynamics is due to him (1851) and Rudolf Clausius (1850). Kelvin developed the notion that mechanical energy gradually dissipates into heat energy, an idea developed by Clausius into the concept of entropy. Classical thermodynamics, which is independent of the microscopic detail of systems, stems largely from their work. Expressing the thermodynamic properties of systems on the assumption that they are composed of large numbers of distinct atoms is termed *statistical mechanics*.

thermoelectric effects A general expression for temperature-dependent electrical properties of matter. Thermocouples use a potential difference resulting from the difference in temperature between two junctions of dissimilar metals (the **Seebeck effect**, discovered in 1821 by German physicist Thomas Seebeck 1770–1831). The **Peltier effect** (discovered in 1834 by French physicist Jean Peltier (1785–1845)) is the reverse of the Seebeck effect, and may be used to make refrigerators having no moving parts, essentially by operating a thermocouple in reverse.

thermogenesis *specific dynamic action*

thermography A detection technique which converts invisible heat energy into a visible picture. Objects radiate varying amounts of infrared (IR) heat energy, depending on their temperature. Inside a thermograph, a solid-state detector 'sees' the IR, even in the dark or smoke. TV-style pictures show temperatures by variations in brightness or colour. In printing, thermography simulates the effect produced by printing using a steel die engraving. The image is printed with adhesive ink, then dusted with powdered resin. Heat fuses the resin and ink to produce a raised, embossed effect image.

thermohaline circulation Marine circulation caused by differences in the temperature and salinity of sea water. These differences are caused by heating or cooling, evaporation or precipitation, and freezing and thawing, and result in density differences in surface sea water. An increase in salinity or a decrease in temperature produces an increase in density, and conversely a decrease in salinity or an increase in temperature produces a decrease in density. Though the density differences appear small (1·02–1·07 g/cm^3), they produce a vertical circulation. When the density of surface water is greater than that of the water below it, it sinks, pushing less dense water aside, until it reaches a level where the water below is denser. Here it spreads laterally. The result is an ocean made up of layers of water with the most dense on the bottom and those of progressively lower densities lying above. The oceans for the most part are vertically stratified in this manner. The water layers having characteristic temperatures and salinities are known as *water masses* or *water types*.

The thermohaline circulation differs from the wind-driven surface water circulation pattern, which is arranged in latitudinal belts following climatic zones. The well-mixed surface layer and the thermocline zone are the zones which experience the greatest changes in physical properties. Below the base of the main ocean thermocline (about 1000 m/3250 ft), variations in physical properties tend to be much smaller. This deep thermohaline circulation is almost completely unconnected with the surface circulation except around Antarctica, where the Antarctic Circumpolar Current extends from the surface to the bottom, and forms the main link between the three major ocean basins. In fact, most deep water masses are formed at high latitudes, the bottom waters of all oceans coming from the Antarctic.

thermoluminescence dating A method of dating ancient pottery by measuring the energy accumulated in the crystal lattice of its inclusions of quartz, through the breakdown over time of naturally occurring uranium. The technique is now increasingly extended to burnt flint, calcite, and sediments.

thermometer A device for measuring temperature. In household alcohol and mercury thermometers, heat causes the liquid in a reservoir to expand, forcing some of the liquid up a graduated tube. The graduations are fixed by calibration against known markers of chosen temperature scale. The first reliable mercury-in-glass thermometer was invented by Gabriel Fahrenheit in 1714.

thermonuclear bomb *hydrogen bomb*

thermoplastic A class of resin which softens and hardens reversibly on heating and cooling any number of times.

Thermopylae [thermopilee] A pass between mountains and sea in C Greece. The failure of the Greeks to hold it in 480 BC enabled the Persians to invade Attica, capture Athens, and sack the Acropolis.

thermoset A class of resin which sets irreversibly on heating. Examples include epoxy resins such as Araldite.

thermosphere The upper atmospheric layer above the mesopause (c.80 km/50 mi, separating the mesosphere from the thermosphere) in which atmospheric densities are very low. The lower part is composed mainly of nitrogen (N_2) and oxygen in molecular (O_2) and atomic (O) forms, whereas above 200 km/125 mi atomic oxygen predominates over N_2 and N. Temperatures increase with altitude because of the absorption of ultraviolet radiation by atomic oxygen. The term **ionosphere** is also used for the atmosphere above 80 km/50 mi.

Theroux, Paul (Edward) [theroo] (1941–) Novelist and travel writer, born in Medford, Massachusetts, USA. He studied at the University of Maine (1959–60), the University of Massachusetts (1963 BA), and Syracuse University (1963). He was a lecturer in English in Malawi as a member of the Peace Corps (1963–5) but was expelled on a charge of spying. He continued to teach in Uganda (1965–8) and in Singapore (1968–71), then settled in London. He wrote of the expatriate life, and won critical praise for his travel accounts, such as *The Great Railway Bazaar: By Train Through Asia* (1975) and *The Old Patagonian Express* (1979) – a genre which continued with *Travelling the World* (1990) and other books. His novels include *Waldo* (1969), *Saint Jack* (1973, filmed 1979), *Picture Palace* (1978, Whitbread), the highly acclaimed *The Mosquito Coast* (1981, James Tait Black, filmed 1987), *Chicago Loop* (1990), *The Pillars of Hercules* (1995), *Kowloon Tong* (1997), and *Sir Vidia's Shadow* (1998). He has also written short stories, plays, children's books, reviews, and works of criticism – notably, an appraisal of his teacher and mentor in *V S Naipaul: An Introduction to His Works* (1972).

Theseus [theesyoos] A legendary king and national hero of Athens, who features in the story of Oedipus, Procrustes, the Argonauts, and others. With Ariadne's help he killed the Minotaur; he conquered the Amazons, and married their queen, Hippolyta; later, he married Phaedra.

Thessalonians, Letters to the New Testament writings of Paul to the church he founded in the capital of the Roman province of Macedonia, although his authorship of the second letter is disputed. In the first letter (perhaps AD c.50), he defends his earlier ministry in Thessalonica against Jewish propaganda, appears gratified at their perseverance despite persecution, and instructs them about ethical matters and Christ's second coming. The second letter is similar, but emphasizes the persecution of the community, and tries to dampen a fanaticism based on the belief that the Day of the Lord had already arrived, leading to idleness.

Thessaloníki [thesaloneekee], also **Salonika** or **Salonica** 40°38N 22°58E, pop (2000e) 1 021 000. Seaport and capital of Salonica department, Greece; second largest city of Greece; founded, 315 BC; capital of Roman Macedonia, 148 BC; held by Turkey, 1430–1912; base for Allied operations in World War 1; airport; railway; ferry to mainland and islands; two universities (1925, 1957); textiles, metal products, chemicals, cigarettes, agricultural trade, tourism; Arch of Galerius (297), 5th-c Basilica of Ayia Paraskevi, 9th-c Basilica of Ayios Dimitrios; carnival (Feb), Navy Week (Jun–Jul), international trade fair (Sep), song festival and film festival (Sep).

Thessaly [thesalee], Gr **Thessalía** pop (2000e) 764 000; area 14 037 sq km/5418 sq mi. Fertile agricultural region of E Greece, bounded W by the Pindus Mts, and E by the Aegean Sea; annexed by Greece, 1881; capital, Larisa; famed in ancient times for its horses; major cereal region in Greece.

Thetis [thetis] In Greek mythology, a nereid destined to bear a son greater than his father. This was the secret known to Prometheus. She was married to Peleus, and was the mother of Achilles.

thiamine A water-soluble vitamin (B_1) which acts as an enzyme co-factor in the oxidation of glucose. A deficiency leads to beriberi, a disease once common, especially in SE Asia, where polished rice, low in vitamin B_1, was the staple food. Thiamine is more rapidly degraded in the cooking process when the medium is alkaline; thus, the use of soda in the boiling of vegetables reduces thiamine concentrations.

thiazole [thiyazohl] C_3H_3NS, boiling point 117°C. A five-membered ring compound; a colourless liquid, the basis for a range of dyestuffs. This ring system occurs in vitamin B_1 (*thiamine*).

thickhead A songbird, native to E India, SE Asia, and Australia; rounded head and strong bill, inhabits forest and scrubland; eats insects; relatively inactive and unafraid of humans; also known as **whistler**. (Family: Pachycephalidae, 46 species.)

thick-knee A plover-like bird, widespread; legs with swollen ankles (not knees!); plumage mottled; eyes large, yellow; inhabits dry pebbled areas or water margins; eats invertebrates; mainly nocturnal; also known as the **stone curlew**, **stone plover**, **Norfolk plover**, **dikkop**, **willaroo**, or **goggle-eye**. (Family: Burhinidae, 9 species.)

Thiers, (Louis) Adolphe [tyair] (1797–1877) French statesman, historian, and first president of the Third Republic (1871–3), born in Marseille, S France. He studied at Aix, and became a lawyer and journalist. He held several posts in the government of Louis-Philippe, and was twice prime minister (1836, 1839). He supported Napoleon in 1848, but was arrested and banished at the coup of 1851, only to re-enter the Chamber in 1863 as a critic of Napoleon's policies. After the collapse of the Second Empire, he became chief of the executive power in the provisional government, suppressed the Paris Commune, and was elected president. Defeated by a coalition of monarchists, he resigned in 1873. His most ambitious literary work was the 20-volume *L'histoire du consulat et de l'empire* (1845–62, History of the Consulate and the Empire).

Thiès [tyes] 14°49N 16°52W, pop (2000e) 233 000. Capital of Thiès region, Senegal, 55 km/34 mi E of Dakar; airfield; railway junction; African cultural and craft centre noted for its tapestries; aluminium, cotton, phosphates, cement, asbestos.

Thimphu [thimpoo] or **Thimbu**, also **Tashi Chho Dzong** 27°32N 89°43E; pop (2000e) town, 14 400; Official capital of Bhutan, C Asia, on R Raidak; founded, 1581; fortified town, a major monastery; capital since 1962; air strip; rice, wheat, maize, timber; Tashi Chho Dzong castle.

thin films Fine layers of material formed by deposition on some substrate, varying in thickness from single atom layers, about 10^{-10} m, to 10^{-6} m. They are used as samples in analytic techniques such as transmission electron microscopy and neutron diffraction. The materials in a thin film configuration can have structures distinct from those in the bulk state, and the structure of the film material can be controlled by the production method. A number of novel effects (such as the quantum Hall effect) are observed in thin films, often because the electrons are constrained to move in a plane. Commercial uses include reflective coatings on compact discs, anti-reflective coatings on lenses, and the production of electronic components and integrated circuits. They are formed using a variety of techniques, such as vacuum deposition, molecular beam epitaxy, electroplating, and others.

Thingvellir [theengvetlir] 64°15N 21°06W. National shrine of Iceland, 52 km/32 mi E of Reykjavík at the N end of Thingvalla Water; the Icelandic *Althing*, oldest parliament in the world, was founded here in 930; focal point of the country until 1880; a national cemetery.

Thíra [theera] *Santorini*

third-generation computers *computer generations*

third stream A type of music which aims to combine the styles of Western art music with those of jazz or various ethnic traditions. Among composers associated with it are André Hodeir (1921–), John Lewis (1920–2001), and Günther Schuller (1925–).

Third World *Three Worlds theory*

Thirteen Colonies The American provinces that revolted against British rule and declared independence in 1776. From N to S they were New Hampshire, Massachusetts, Rhode Island, Connecticut, New York, New Jersey, Pennsylvania, Delaware, Maryland, Virginia, North Carolina, South Carolina, and Georgia. Fourteen states actually declared independence, because Vermont separated from New York at the same time. In imperial terms the Thirteen Colonies had been less important to British statesmen than the sugar-producing islands of the West Indies.

thirty-eighth parallel The boundary line proposed for the partition of Korea at the Potsdam Conference in 1945, after the defeat of Japan (which had annexed Korea in 1910). In 1948 the communist state of North Korea was proclaimed (but not recognized by the Western powers). Since the Korean War, the 38th parallel again forms the line of division between North and South Korea.

Thirty-nine Articles A set of doctrinal formulations for the Church of England, issued after several earlier efforts under Elizabeth I in 1563 (but without Article 29 about 'eating the body', in order to appease the Romanists), and finally adopted as a whole by the Convocation of 1571. They do not comprise a creed, but rather a general Anglican view on a series of contentious matters in order to maintain the unity of the Anglican churches and Anglican Communion. Some articles are ambiguous in wording, but they are generally opposed to both extreme Romanist and extreme Anabaptist views. They concern matters such as the presence of Christ in the Eucharist, the authority of Scriptures and the Councils, and the doctrine of predestination. Church of England clergy have been required since 1865 to affirm these principles in general terms.

Thirty Tyrants The Spartan-backed clique which seized power in Athens towards the end of the Peloponnesian War (404 BC), overthrew the democracy, and instituted a reign of terror. They were overthrown in 403 BC and democracy was restored.

Thirty Years' War (1618–48) A complex phase, specifically German in origin, of a long and intermittent power struggle between the kings of France and the Habsburg rulers of the Holy Roman Empire and Spain (1491–1715). The background was complicated by the developing confrontation between militant Calvinism and re-invigorated, post-Tridentine Catholicism; also by the underlying constitutional conflict between the Holy Roman Emperor and the German princes, illustrated in the Bohemian Revolt (1618). With the Elector Frederick V's defeat (1620) and intervention by other powers (eg Sweden, Transylvania, Denmark, France), the conflict intensified, spreading to other theatres. Isolated as Spain collapsed, the emperor opened negotiations (1643–8) which ended the German war at the Peace of Westphalia.

thistle The name applied to several spiny plants of the daisy family, Compositae, many belonging to the genera *Cirsium* and *Carduus*. All have leaves with spiny margins, flower-heads often almost globular, solitary or in clusters, surrounded by overlapping, usually spine-tipped bracts; florets reddish, purple, or white; the national emblem of Scotland. (Family: Compositae.)

Thistle, Most Ancient and Most Noble Order of the A Scottish order of chivalry, probably instituted in the late 15th-c by James III of Scotland, and the personal gift of the sovereign. There are 16 knights under the sovereign (though there may be additional members). The motto of the order is *Nemo me impune lacessit* (Lat 'No-one provokes me with impunity'); the ribbon is dark green.

Thomas, St (1st-c) A disciple of Jesus Christ, listed as one of the 12 apostles in the Gospels, but most prominent in John's Gospel, where he is also called **Didymus** ('the Twin'), and where he is portrayed as doubting the resurrection until he touches the wounds of the risen Christ (*John* 20). Early church traditions describe him subsequently as a missionary to the Parthians or a martyr in India. Many later apocryphal works bear his name, such as the *Gospel of Thomas*, *Acts of Thomas*, and *Apocalypse of Thomas*. He is the patron saint of Portugal. Feast day 21 December.

Thomas, Clarence (1948–) Jurist, born in Savannah, Georgia, USA. He studied at Yale, and in 1992 was named by President Bush as the second black American to sit in the Supreme Court, succeeding Thurgood Marshall. His Senate confirmation hearings attracted widespread attention due to allegations of sexual misconduct brought by a former colleague, Anita Hill. Thomas was confirmed, but a number of women sought Congressional and Senate seats in the campaign of 1992 in protest.

Thomas, D(onald) M(ichael) (1935–) Novelist, poet, and translator, born in Redruth, Cornwall, SW England, UK. He studied at Oxford, and went on to work as a teacher and lecturer. His early collections, *Personal and Possessive* (1964), *Two Voices* (1968), and *Logan Stone* (1971), feature erotic poems, science fiction ballads, and Cornish lyrics. His controversial novel *The White Hotel* (1981) brought him greater public recognition. Other novels include his first, *The Flute Player* (1979), *Lying Together* (1990), and *Flying into Love* (1992). He has also translated major literary works from Russian. *Memories and Hallucinations* (1988) is a volume of autobiography. His *Charlotte: the Final Journey* (2000) is a continuation of Charlotte Brontë's *Jane Eyre*.

Thomas, Dylan (Marlais) (1914–53) Poet, born in Swansea, SC Wales, UK. He worked as a journalist, and established himself with the publication of *Eighteen Poems* in 1934. He married Caitlin Macnamara (1913–94) in 1936, and published *Twenty-Five Poems* the same year. His *Collected Poems* appeared in 1953, and he then produced his best-known work, the radio 'play for voices', *Under Milk Wood* (published in 1954). He also wrote an unfinished novel, *Adventures in the Skin Trade* (1955), and several collections of short stories, many of which were written originally for radio. All his work, whether in verse or prose, shows rhythmic drive and verbal flamboyance. He became an alcoholic in later years, and died on a lecture-tour of the USA.

Thomas, (Philip) Edward, pseudonym **Edward Eastaway** (1878–1917) Poet and critic, born in London, UK. He studied at Oxford, and became a hack writer of reviews, critical studies, and topographical works. Not until 1914, encouraged by Robert Frost, did he realize his potential as a poet, writing most of his work during active service between 1915 and his death. He died in action at Arras, just before the publication of *Poems* (1917), under his pseudonym. He also wrote a novel, and several books about the English countryside.

Thomas, Sir George (Alan) (1881–1972) Badminton player, born in Istanbul, NW Turkey. He was the winner of a record 21 All-England titles between 1903 and 1928, including the singles four times (1920–3). In 1934 he was elected president of the International Badminton Federation, a post he held for 21 years, and in 1939 presented a Cup (the *Thomas Cup*) to be contested by national teams. He represented England for 27 years at badminton, was also an international competitor at lawn tennis and chess, and was twice British chess champion.

Thomas, R(onald) S(tuart) (1913–2000) Poet, born in Cardiff, S Wales, UK. He studied at the University of Wales, was ordained in 1936, and became a rector in the Church of Wales (1942–78). He published his first volume, *The Stones of the Field* in 1946, and came to attention outside Wales with *Song at the Year's Turning* (1955). *Selected Poems, 1946–68* appeared in 1973. His work deals with pastoral themes and the nature of God, coupled with an intense love of Wales and its people, evoked by nature imagery. *Later Poems, 1972–1982* appeared in 1983, and subsequent volumes include *The Echoes Return Slow* (1988), *Counterpoint* (1990), and *No Truth with the Furies* (1995). His *Autobiographies* was published in 1997.

Thomas, Terry *Terry-Thomas*

Thomas (à) Becket *Becket, Thomas*

Thomas à Kempis *Kempis, Thomas à*

Thomas Aquinas *Aquinas, St Thomas*

Thomism [tohmizm] In Christian philosophical theology, the name given to the doctrines of Thomas Aquinas, and to later schools claiming descent from him.

Thompson, Sir Benjamin, Graf (Count) **von Rumford,** known as **Count Rumford** (1753–1814) Administrator and scientist, born in Woburn, Massachusetts, USA. He married in 1772, and joined the army, but during the Revolution left his family and fled to England (1776), possibly because he was politically suspect. After the peace he was knighted. In 1784 he entered the service of Bavaria, where he carried out military, social, and economic reforms, for which he was made head of the Bavarian war department and a count of the Holy Roman empire. Always an enthusiastic amateur scientist, he first showed the relation between heat and work, a concept fundamental to modern physics. In 1799 he returned to London and, with Sir Joseph Banks, founded the Royal Institution.

Thompson, Daley, popular name of **Francis Morgan Thompson** (1958–) Athlete, born in London, UK. An outstanding decathlete, his first major honour was in the 1978 Commonwealth Games, which he retained in 1982 and 1986. He was world champion (1983), European champion (1982, 1986), and Olympic champion (1980, 1984). He broke the world record four times between 1980 and 1984. Having suffered from injuries, he announced his retirement in 1992.

Thompson, Emma (1959–) Actress, born in London, UK. She studied at Cambridge and made her stage debut with the Footlights while still a student. She played opposite Robert Lindsay in *Me and My Girl* (1983), going on to appear on BBC TV's *Fortunes of War* for which she won a BAFTA award. In 1989 she appeared in the film of *Henry V*, directed by Kenneth Branagh whom she married the same year (divorced, 1996). On stage, she appeared in Branagh's production of *Look Back in Anger* (1989), *A Midsummer Night's Dream* (1990), and *King Lear* (1990). With Branagh she went on to make the films *Dead Again* (1991) and *Much Ado About Nothing* (1993). Other films include *Howard's End* (1992, Oscar, BAFTA), *Remains of the Day* (1993), *In the Name of the Father* (1994), *Primary Colors* (1998), and *Love Actually* (2003). She wrote the screenplay for *Sense and Sensibility* (1996) which won an Oscar for best adapted screenplay. In 1997 she starred in *The Winter Guest* in which she played opposite her real-life mother, the actress Phyllida Law.

Thompson, Francis (1859–1907) Poet, born in Preston, Lancashire, NW England, UK. He studied for the priesthood, turned to medicine, but failed to graduate. He was rescued from poverty, ill health, and opium addiction by Wilfrid and Alice Meynell, to whom he had sent some poems for Meynell's magazine *Merry England*. His later work was mainly religious in theme; it includes the well-known 'The Hound of Heaven'.

Thompson, John T(alafierro) (1860–1940) US soldier and inventor, born in Newport, Kentucky, USA. He graduated in 1882 at the Military Academy, and in 1918 originated the Thompson submachine gun, which came to be known as the *Tommy gun* – a ·45 calibre gun weighing 10 lb. It was first used for military purposes by the US Marines in Nicaragua in 1925.

Thomsen, Christian Jörgensen (1788–1865) Archaeologist, born in Copenhagen, Denmark. He worked for his wealthy businessman father, and collected antiquities from an early age. In 1816 he was appointed secretary of the Royal Commission for the Preservation of Antiquities, and during his work there he classified specimens into three groups representing chronologically successive ages. He is credited with developing the three-part system of prehistory, named as the Stone, Bronze, and Iron Ages, described in *Ledetraad til Nordisk Oldkyndighed* (1836, A Guide to Northern Antiquities).

Thomson, Sir George (Paget) (1892–1975) Physicist, born in Cambridge, Cambridgeshire, EC England, UK, the son of Sir Joseph Thomson. He studied there, and became a fellow of Trinity College. He was professor at Aberdeen (1922) and at Imperial College, London (1930), Master of Corpus Christi, Cambridge (1952–62), and scientific adviser to the UN Security Council (1946–7). For his contributions to electrical science he was awarded the Faraday Medal by the Institution of Electrical Engineers (1960). He shared the 1937 Nobel Prize for Physics for his discovery of electron diffraction by crystals, and was knighted in 1943.

Thomson, James (1700–48) Poet, born in Ednam, Scottish Borders, SE Scotland, UK. Educated at Edinburgh for the ministry, he abandoned his studies and turned to writing in London (1725). He is best known for his four-part work, *The Seasons* (1730), the first major nature poem in English, and for his ode 'Rule, Britannia' from *Alfred, a Masque* (1740), and the Spenserian allegory *The Castle of Indolence* (1748).

Thomson, Sir J(oseph) J(ohn) (1856–1940) Physicist, born in Cheetham Hill, Greater Manchester, NW England, UK. He studied at Cambridge, where he became professor of experimental physics in 1884. He showed in 1897 that cathode rays were rapidly-moving particles, and by measuring their speed and specific charge deduced that these 'corpuscles' (electrons) must be nearly a 2000th smaller in mass than the lightest known atomic particle, the hydrogen ion. He received the Nobel Prize for Physics in 1906, and was knighted in 1908. Through his work, the Cavendish Laboratory became a major research institution.

Thomson (of Fleet), Roy (Herbert) Thomson, Baron (1894–1976) Newspaper and television magnate, born in Toronto, Ontario, SE Canada. He held a variety of jobs, and became prosperous after setting up his own radio transmitter at North Bay (1931), founding what later became the NBC network. He started other radio stations, and bought many Canadian and US newspapers. He settled in Edinburgh on acquiring his first British paper, *The Scotsman* (1952), bought the Kemsley newspapers in 1959 (including *The Sunday Times*, to which he added the first colour supplement in 1962), and in 1966 took over *The Times*. Other business interests included Scottish Television and North Sea oil. He was created a peer in 1964.

Thomson, Tom, popular name of **Thomas John Thomson** (1877–1917) Painter, born in Claremont, Ontario, SE Canada. He worked as an engraver and designer-illustrator before turning to art in 1906. He spent a great deal of time working in Algonquin Park, Ontario, producing many sketches and some larger canvases, such as 'The West Wind' (1917, Toronto). He was found drowned near Wapomeo I, leaving a mystery about the manner of his death which to some extent has obscured his artistic accomplishments.

Thomson, Virgil (1896–1989) Composer and critic, born in Kansas City, Missouri, USA. He studied at Harvard and in Paris, where he came under the influence of several French composers, in particular the group known as *Les Six*. He set some of the writings of Gertrude Stein to music, and wrote operas – notably, *Four Saints in Three Acts* (1934), first performed by a black cast, and *The Mother of Us All* (1947) – as well as symphonies, ballets, and choral, chamber, and film music. He was also music critic of the *New York Herald Tribune* (1940–54).

Thomson, Sir William *Kelvin, 1st Baron*

't Hooft, Gerardus [tohft] (1945–) Physicist, born in Den Helder, The Netherlands. He studied at the University of Utrecht, where he became professor (1977), and carried out research under Martinus Veltman into gauge theories in particle physics, black holes, and other aspects of quantum physics. He shared the 1999 Nobel Prize for Physics for his role in elucidating the quantum structure of electroweak interactions.

Thor In Norse mythology, the god of thunder, son of Odin and Frigga; also known as **the Hurler**. His hammer is called Miolnir. In the stories, much is made of his appetite for food and drink. He is the strongest of the gods, and protects them. At Ragnarok he will fight with the World Serpent, kill it, and then die.

thoracic duct The main lymphatic duct of the body, draining the whole of the body (except the right side of the head, neck, and thorax, and right upper limb) into the junction of the left internal jugular and sub-clavian veins. In particular, it conveys lymph containing absorbed fat from the intestine to the general circulation.

thorax That part of the body between the neck and the abdomen enclosed by the thoracic part of the vertebral column, the ribs, and the sternum, and separated from the abdomen by the diaphragm; also known as the **thoracic cage** or **chest**. Roughly cone-shaped, it surrounds and protects the lungs, heart, and great vessels, and also contains the oesophagus, thymus gland, and thoracic duct. It provides support against the elastic pull of the lungs, which would otherwise collapse. The thorax is able to change its shape (and thus volume) by moving its bony parts with respect to each other in respiration, as well as by contracting the diaphragm. The breast sits on the upper part of the front of the thorax.

Thoreau, Henry (David) [thoroh] (1817–62) Essayist and poet, born in Concord, Massachusetts, USA. He studied at Harvard, became a teacher, and c.1839 began his walks and studies of nature which became his major occupation. Although he sometimes lived at the family home of his friend and mentor Ralph Waldo Emerson, from 1845–7 he lived in a shanty he built himself in the woods by Walden Pond, near Concord, where his writings included the American classic *Walden, or Life in the Woods* (1854). After his death, several books were published, based on his daily journal (from 1835) of his walks and observations, such as *Summer* (1884) and *Winter* (1887). He is also known for his social criticism, his championing of individual civil liberties – his essay *On the Duty of Civil Disobedience* (1849) influenced Gandhi – and his connections with Transcendentalism.

thorn-apple An evil-smelling annual weed (*Datura stramonium*) found throughout most of the N hemisphere; up to 1 m/3¼ ft high; leaves coarsely toothed; flowers trumpet-shaped, white to blue; fruit a spiny, ovoid capsule containing poisonous seeds; also called **jimson weed**, possibly after Jamestown, VA, the site of early records of its narcotic effects on humans. (Family: Solanaceae.)

thornbill A warbler, native to Australia and New Guinea; inhabits woodland, scrub, and savannah; eats insects and seeds; also known as the **thornbill warbler**. The name is also used for eight species of hummingbird. (Genus: *Acanthiza*, 12 species. Family: Acanthizidae.)

Thorndike, E(dward) L(ee) (1874–1949) Psychologist, born in Williamsburg, Massachusetts, USA. He studied at Wesleyan University and Harvard, and became professor at Teachers College, Columbia (1904–40), where he worked on educational psychology and the psychology of animal learning. As a result of studying animal intelligence, he formulated his famous 'law of effect', which states that a given behaviour is learned by trial-and-error, and is more likely to occur if its consequences are satisfying. His works include *Psychology of Learning* (1914) and *The Measurement of Intelligence* (1926).

Thorndike, Dame (Agnes) Sybil (1882–1976) Actress, born in Gainsborough, Lincolnshire, EC England, UK. She trained as a pianist, but turned to the stage, making her debut in 1904, and joining a repertory company in Manchester. In 1924 she played the title role in the first English performance of Shaw's *Saint Joan*, and during World War 2 was a notable member of the Old Vic Company. She married the actor Lewis Casson in 1908, and was made a dame in 1931.

Thornhill, Sir James (1675–1734) Baroque painter, born in Melcombe Regis, Dorset, S England, UK. He executed paintings for the dome of St Paul's, Blenheim, Hampton Court, and Greenwich Hospital, and founded a drawing school, where Hogarth (who became his son-in-law) was one of his pupils. In 1718 he was made history painter to the king. Knighted in 1720, he became an MP in 1722.

thorny devil *moloch* (zoology)

thoroughbred The fastest breed of horse (over 65 kph/40 mph), developed in England for racing; height, 16 hands/1·6 m/5 ft 4 in; elegant, athletic, highly-strung; all descended from three Arab stallions of the early 18th-c – the Darley Arabian, the Godolphin Barb, and the Byerley Turk; also known as **English thoroughbred** or **racehorse**.

Thorpe, Ian, known as **The Thorpedo** (1982–) Swimmer, born in Paddington, Sydney, Australia. In the 1998 World Championships he became the youngest male world champion in history by winning the 400 m freestyle. At the Pan Pacific Championships in 1999 he smashed four world records in four days. He won four gold medals at the Kuala Lumpur 1998 Commonwealth Games, and two gold medals at the 1998 World Swimming Championships. At the 2000 Sydney Olympics he won five medals (including three gold), and at the 2001 World Championships in Japan he won six gold medals. At the 2002 Manchester Commonweath Games he won a total of seven medals (six gold and a silver), and at the 2003 World Championships in Barcelona won gold medals in the 200 m and 400 m freestyle. His individual world records include the 200 m freestyle (1:44.06), the 400 m freestyle (3:40.17), and the 800 m freestyle (7:39.16).

Thorpe, (John) Jeremy (1929–) British politician, born in London, UK. He studied at Oxford, became a barrister in 1954, and a Liberal MP in 1959. Elected leader of the Liberal Party in 1967, he resigned the leadership in 1976 following a series of allegations of a previous homosexual relationship with Norman Scott. In 1979, shortly after losing his seat in the general election, he was acquitted of charges of conspiracy and incitement to murder Mr Scott.

Thorvaldsen, Bertel [torvalsn] (c.1768–1844) Neoclassical sculptor, born in Copenhagen, Denmark. He studied at Copenhagen and Rome, working in both places. His best-known pieces include 'Christ and the Twelve Apostles', the reliefs 'Night and Morning', the 'Dying Lion' at Lucerne, and the Cambridge statue of Byron. All the works in his possession he bequeathed, with the bulk of his fortune, to his country.

Thoth [thoht, toht] An ancient Egyptian Moon-god, sometimes depicted with the head of an ibis, sometimes as a baboon. He wears a crown showing the Moon's disc. The god of words, magic, and scribes, in the Underworld he records the souls of the dead. He is usually identified with Hermes.

Thothmes III *Thutmose III*

thought experiment In physics, an experiment visualized but not performed because it is too difficult, but which nonetheless may demonstrate important principles; also called a **gedanken-experiment**. The classic example is Einstein's analysis of experiments performed in free-falling or accelerating lifts to demonstrate the equivalence principle.

Thousand, Expedition of the (1860) A military campaign led by Garibaldi, originally involving 1146 men, which formed a crucial stage in the Italian Risorgimento. Sailing from Genoa, they arrived in Sicily, and quickly defeated Neapolitan forces. Assisted by a local popular rising, they seized Sicily, crossed to the mainland, and four months later had liberated the Kingdom of Naples.

Thrace [thrays], Gr **Thráki** pop (2000e) 353 000; area 8578 sq km/3311 sq mi. NE region of Greece, bounded N by Bulgaria, E by Turkey, and S by the Aegean Sea; in classical times, part of an area associated with the worship of Dionysus; area now divided between Turkey, Greece, and Bulgaria; capital, Komotini; region of fertile plains, producing corn, wine, rice, and tobacco.

threadfin Any of the tropical marine and estuarine fish in the family Polynemidae (3 genera); long free pectoral fin rays which serve in part as sensitive feelers, and from which they derive their name; body length may reach over 1·5 m/5 ft; several are valuable food fish.

Three Age System The chronological division of Old World prehistory into three ages of **Stone**, **Bronze**, and **Iron**. Rooted in classical ideas about the past, the scheme owes its archaeological exploitation to a Dane, Christian Jürgensen Thomsen (1788–1865), who adopted it in 1819 to classify the collections of the new National Museum in Copenhagen. It became widely influential a generation later with the English publication of Thomsen's *Ledetraad til Nordisk Oldkyndighed* (1836, A Guide to Northern Antiquities), and his pupil Jens Worsaae's *Danmarks*

Oldtid (1843, trans Primaeval Antiquities of Denmark). The subdivision of the Stone Age into the **Palaeolithic** (**Old Stone Age**), characterized by chipped stone, and the **Neolithic** (**New Stone Age**), characterized by polished stone tools, stems from the English archaeologist Sir John Lubbock's *Prehistoric Times* (1865). The term **Mesolithic** (**Middle Stone Age**), covering the five millennia following the end of the last glaciation, also dates from then. The term **Chalcolithic** for the **Copper** or earliest Bronze Age belongs to more recent times.

three-body problem *many body theory*

three-day event A combined training competition, also known as **horse trials**, comprising the three main equestrian disciplines: dressage, showjumping, and cross-country.

three-D (3-D) films *stereoscopic photography*

Three Emperors' League, Ger ***Dreikaiserbund*** An entente (1873, renewed 1881 and 1884) between emperors William I of Germany, Francis Joseph of Austria–Hungary, and Alexander II of Russia. It was designed by Bismarck to protect Germany by isolating France and stabilizing SE Europe. Largely superseded by the Dual Alliance (1879) of Germany and Austria–Hungary, it lapsed in 1887.

Three Worlds theory A theory that sees the world as being divided into three main blocs of countries, defined by their economic status. These are the developed capitalist economies (the **First World**), the developed communist countries (the **Second World**), and underdeveloped countries (the **Third World**), covering most of Latin America and recently independent African and Asian states. The Third World countries tend to adopt a position of neutrality, thereby dividing the world politically in three. The large number and diversity of Third World nations makes an adequate definition impossible: the concept includes the oil-rich countries alongside the poorest countries. Some (including the United Nations) recognize a 'Fourth World', of the 25 poorest nations. The collapse of the Communist states after 1989 makes the typology somewhat redundant, although the term *Third World* is likely to persist due to its extensive usage.

thresher shark Large and very distinctive surface-living shark (*Alopias vulpinus*), widespread in tropical to temperate seas; easily recognized by the remarkably long upper lobe of tail fin which may exceed half its body length; tail lobe used to round up shoals of fish by thrashing the water surface; body length up to 6 m/20 ft. (Family: Alopiidae.)

threshold In psychology, the physically measured value of stimulation at which an observer's response changes from one category to another. The smallest amount of stimulation required for detection is the **absolute threshold**; the smallest detectable difference between sources of stimulation is the **difference threshold**.

thrift A densely tufted perennial (*Armeria maritima*), woody at base, native to Europe; leaves grass-like, bluish-green; flowers pink, scented, in long-stalked, hemispherical heads; also called **sea pink**. It is a mainly coastal plant, occasionally found inland. (Family: Plumbaginaceae.)

thrip A minute insect in which the wings, when present, are slender with a long fringe of hairs; mouthparts specialized for piercing and sucking; feeds on plant juices, fungi, pollen, and body juices of insects. (Order: Thysanoptera, c.5000 species.)

Throckmorton, Sir Nicholas (1515–71) English diplomat. He fought at Pinkie (1547), was knighted in 1547, and became ambassador to France and Scotland. In 1569 he was imprisoned for promoting the scheme to marry Mary, Queen of Scots, to the Duke of Norfolk, but soon released. His daughter, **Elizabeth Throckmorton**, married Sir Walter Raleigh. His nephew, **Francis Throckmorton** (1554–84) was executed for planning a conspiracy to overthrow Elizabeth I.

thrombophlebitis *phlebitis*

thrombosis [throm**boh**sis] The formation of a blood clot within a blood vessel, resulting in a partial or complete blockage. Its basis is the formation of the protein, fibrin, which is formed from a soluble precursor, fibrinogen. Fibrin forms a mesh in which platelets and red blood cells are trapped, and produces a plug to the flow of blood. The conversion of fibrinogen to fibrin is activated by a complex series of enzymes which include 13 coagulation factors and requires calcium ions. The process is initiated by contact of the blood with damaged blood vessels and tissues and often occurs on a patch of atherosclerosis. Thrombosis may occur within any artery or vein in the body. Myocardial infarction or stroke result when the coronary or cerebral arteries are blocked. Thrombosis within veins, particularly in the legs, may break off and give rise to an embolus.

thrush (disease) *candidiasis*

thrush (ornithology) A medium-sized songbird, widespread, inhabiting diverse regions from tropical rainforests to deserts; often feeds on ground; eats fruit and invertebrates. Some species are called **chats**. (Family: Turdidae, c.300 species.)

ThrustSSC British jet-powered car, driven by Andrew Green, which broke the world land speed record at the Black Rock site, Great Basin, USA, in 1997, and became the first car to travel at supersonic speed. It achieved a speed of 1227·95 kph/763·035 mph (Mach 1·020).

Thucydides [thyoo**sid**ideez] **1** (c.460–c.400 BC) Athenian aristocratic historian of the Peloponnesian War. Though scrupulously accurate in his narrative of events, he is not altogether unprejudiced. Exiled for 20 years by the democracy for military incompetence in the N Aegean (424 BC), he is consistently critical of the democratic system and its leaders in the war years. **2** (5th-c BC) Athenian politician, son-in-law of Cimon, and leader of the opposition to Pericles until ostracized in 443 BC. He was probably a relative of Thucydides, the historian.

Thuggee [**thuh**gee] An Indian cult which combined robbery and ritual murder (usually by strangling) in the name of Kali (the Hindu goddess of destruction). Under British governor-general Lord Bentinck (1833–5), and his agent Captain William Sleeman, vigorous steps were taken to eradicate the problem.

thuja [**thoo**ja] *arbor vitae*

Thule [**thyoo**lee] 77°30N 69°29W. Eskimo settlement in NW Greenland; on coast of Hayes Halvø peninsula; founded as a Danish trading post in 1910; Danish–US airforce base nearby; scientific installations; name also given by the ancients to the most northerly land of Europe, an island described c.310 BC by the Greek navigator, Pytheas.

Thumb, General Tom *Stratton, Charles*

Thummim *Urim and Thummim*

Thun [toon], Fr **Thoune** 46°46N 7°38E, pop (2000e) 40 000. Town in Bern canton, W Switzerland, on the R Aare near L Thun; gateway to the Bernese Oberland; railway junction; engineering, watches, cheese; castle (1191).

Thunder Bay 48°27N 89°12W, pop (2000e) 127 700. Resort and port in S Ontario, Canada, on NW shore of L Superior; created in 1970 by the union of Fort William and Port Arthur; airfield; railway; university (1965); grain storage and shipping point; shipbuilding, paper, pulp, vehicles; Centennial Park.

Thunderbird or **Skyamsen** A totem figure in NW American Indian religion. Lightning flashes from its eye and it feeds on killer whales. The chief of the Thunderbirds was Golden Eagle (Keneun).

thunderstorm A storm of heavy rain, thunder, and lightning which occurs when cumulonimbus clouds develop in unstable, humid conditions. As air rises, condensation releases latent heat, and this increases the available energy, reinforcing the rising tendency of the air. Above the level at which condensation occurs, supercooled water droplets coalesce to form precipitation-sized droplets. As rain falls, instability decreases, the cloud ceases to grow, and precipitation soon stops. However, a series of cumulonimbus clouds may allow storms to continue. During a thunderstorm, an electric charge builds up at the base of the cloud, and when large enough, is discharged in the form of lightning. Thunderstorms are often associated with the passage of a cold front during a depression, and with intense heating and moisture availability at low latitudes.

Thurber, James (Grover) (1894–1961) Writer and cartoonist, born in Columbus, Ohio, USA. He studied at Ohio State University, and was a clerk in Washington, DC, and at the US embassy in Paris before embarking on a career in journalism. In the early 1920s he reported for various papers in the USA and Europe, and in 1927 was appointed managing editor of the *New Yorker*. His popular drawings first appeared in *Is Sex Necessary?* (1929), which he co-authored. A plethora of books followed, often combining humorous essays with characteristic doodles, and a number of short stories, including most memorably *The Secret Life of Walter Mitty*.

Thuringia [thuringia] A historic area of Germany, including the Harz Mts and Thuringian Forest, a march or frontier region against the Slavs. Controlled by various dynasties, from the 10th-c Dukes of Saxony to the House of Wettin (1265), it was divided between Saxony, Hesse-Kassel, and others 1485–1920, and is now a province within united Germany.

Thuringian Forest, Ger **Thüringer Wald** Region of forest land covering about two-thirds of the county of Suhl in S Germany between the Weisse Elster (E) and R Werra (W); formerly included in the German state of Thuringia, becoming part of East Germany in 1945; popular tourist region; winter sports resort at Oberhof.

Thurso 58°35N 3°32W, pop (2000e) 8690. Port town in Highland, N Scotland, UK; on N coast, at head of R Thurso, 30 km/19 mi NW of Wick; N terminus of railway system; car ferry service to Orkney from Scrabster; St Peter's Church (17th-c), Thurso Folk Museum.

Thutmose III [thutmohsuh], also **Thothmes** or **Tuthmosis** (?–1450 BC) Egyptian pharoah (c.1504–1450 BC). He was one of the greatest of Egyptian rulers, who re-established Egyptian control over Syria and Nubia, and ornamented his kingdom with revenues from these conquests. He built the temple of Amon at Karnak, and erected many obelisks, including 'Cleopatra's Needle'. In the early years of his reign, power lay in the hands of Hatshepsut, the sister/wife of Thutmose II.

Thyestes [thiyesteez] In Greek mythology, a son of Pelops, who inherited the curse upon that house. His brother Atreus set before him a dish made of the flesh of Thyestes' children. Later, he became the father of Aegisthus.

thylacine [thiylasiyn] An Australian marsupial, probably extinct since the 1930s; length, up to 1·6 m/5¼ ft; dog-like, with long thick tail; sandy brown with dark vertical stripes over back and hindquarters; could sit upright on hind legs and tail like a kangaroo; female with short backward-facing pouch covering four teats; when last known, was nocturnal in the Tasmanian mountains; ate wallabies, smaller marsupials, birds, and (since European settlement) sheep; also known as the **Tasmanian wolf** or **tiger**. (Family: Thylacinidae.)

thyme A small spreading aromatic shrub, often only a few cm high, native to Europe and Asia; leaves small, narrow, in opposite pairs; flowers 2-lipped, usually pink or mauve, in crowded whorls forming spikes or heads. It is widely cultivated as a culinary herb, with variegated forms as ornamentals. It is a large genus, with numerous narrowly defined species and hybrids, many with distinctive scents and tastes. The best known are **common thyme** (*Thymus vulgaris*), **lemon thyme** (*Thymus citriodora*), and **carroway thyme** (*Thymus herba-barona*). (Genus: *Thymus*, c.400 species. Family: Labiatae.)

thymine [thiymeen] $C_5H_6N_2O_2$, 5-methyluracil. One of the pyrimidine bases in DNA, usually paired with adenine.

thymus A lymphoid gland of vertebrates, which in mammals lies in the upper part of the chest close to the great vessels and the heart, its shape and size being determined by the surrounding structures. In humans, its size shows great individual variation at any given age; it is present at birth (average weight 13 g/0·5 oz), and continues to grow until puberty (average weight in the adolescent 37 g/1·3 oz), after which it gradually regresses. The thymus appears to have a special relation to cells of the immune system. Its presence is essential in the newborn for the development of lymphoid tissue and immunological competence. In adults it is concerned with lymphocyte production, of which only a few are released into the circulation, the remainder being destroyed within the gland itself. In early life, precursor cells migrate from bone marrow into the thymus, where they mature to become T-lymphocytes (*T-cells*) responsible for cellular immunity.

thyratron An electronic valve filled with a gas (usually mercury vapour or an inert gas) at low pressure. It is used for switching, and as a controlled rectifier in applications such as welding. Such valves are now being replaced by semiconductor devices.

thyristor [thiyrister] A semiconductor device that acts as a switch; also often called a **silicon-controlled rectifier (SCR)**. It is made of a sandwich of p-n-p-n semiconductor material. A flow of current is initiated by a signal, and the current then becomes independent of the signal. This flow will stop only if the voltage across the thyristor is reversed. A **triac** is a thyristor which, once triggered, remains on until the voltage across it falls to zero. Thyristors are replacing gas-filled electronic valves.

thyrocalcitonin *calcitonin*

thyroid gland An endocrine gland of vertebrates situated in the region of the neck, overlying the lower part of the larynx and the upper part of the trachea. Because of its attachment to the larynx, it moves upward on swallowing. In humans its size varies with age, sex, and general nutrition, increasing slightly in women during menstruation and pregnancy. The thyroid secretes thyroid hormone and calcitonin (from C-cells). Unlike other endocrine glands, it maintains a large store of hormone.

thyroid hormone A collective term for iodine-containing amine hormones secreted from vertebrate thyroid glands. In humans and other mammals, the principle hormones are thyroxine (T_4) and trilodothyronine (T_3), which have important roles in fetal development and throughout life in the control of metabolism. Their synthesis and release is controlled by *thyroid-stimulating hormone* (TSH), a glycoprotein hormone produced in the front lobe of the pituitary gland of vertebrates, also known as *thyrotrophin*. In amphibian tadpoles, thyroid hormone is essential for metamorphosis.

thyrotrophin *thyroid hormone*

Thysanoptera [thiysanoptera] *thrip*

Tiahuanaco [teeawanahkoh] An ancient urban and ceremonial settlement covering 4 sq km/1·5 sq mi near the S end of L Titicaca, Bolivia. At an altitude of 3842 m/12 600 ft, it was occupied c.1500 BC–AD 1200, flourishing particularly AD c.500–1000 with a population of c.30 000. The ceremonial core, covering 50 ha/125 acres, is notable for the Akapana, a stone platform-mound 200 m/660 ft square and 15 m/50 ft high.

Tiananmen Square [tianahnmen] or **T'ien-an-men Square** The largest public square in the world, covering 40 ha/98 acres and lying S of the Ming Tiananmen ('Gate of Heavenly Peace') leading into the Forbidden City in C Beijing. It has long been the venue of mass manifestations (eg in the May Fourth Movement, 1919) and it was here that the People's Republic was proclaimed in September 1949. In 1966, during the Cultural Revolution, Mao Zedong addressed rallies of over a million Red Guards in the square. In June 1989, it was the scene of mass protests by students and others against the Chinese government, crushed by troops of the Chinese Army with an undisclosed number of dead. To the S stands a 36 m/120 ft marble monument to the People's Heroes.

tiang *topi*

Tianjin, Tientsin, or **T'ien-chin** [tianjin] 39°08N 117°12E; pop (2000e) 6 528 000; administrative region 9 136 000; municipality area 4000 sq km/1500 sq mi. Port city in E China; 50 km/31 mi W of Bohai Gulf on Hai He R; on Grand Canal; China's largest artificial harbour, built during Japanese occupation (1937–45), completed 1952; founded in Warring States period (403–221 BC); developed in Middle Ages as a grain port; attacked by British and French in 1860; massacre of foreigners, 1870; badly damaged by earthquake, 1976; railway; airport; two universities; designated a special economic zone; iron and steel, consumer goods, carpets; Tianjin Art Museum, Industrial Exhibition Hall, many European-style buildings and Victorian mansions.

Tian Shan or **T'ien Shan** Mountain range in C Asia, on border of Russia and China; separates Tarim (N) and Dzungarian (S) Basins; contains glaciers up to 70 km/40 mi long; length, 2500 km/1500 mi; passes at Shengli Daban and Qijiaojing; higher in W, rising to 7439 m/24 406 ft at Tomur (Pobedy) peak; contains rich deposits of coal, rock salt, and metals; dense forests on N slopes; mainly grassland in S.

Tiber, River [**tiy**ber], Ital **Tevere**, ancient **Tiberis** Third longest river of Italy, rising in the Etruscan Apennines on Monte Fumaiolo; length 405 km/252 mi; flows S and SW past Rome to enter the Tyrrhenian Sea near Ostia; two mouths, the Fiumara (silted up) and the Fiumicino, kept navigable by canalization.

Tiberias [tiy**bee**rias], Hebrew **Tevarya** 32°48N 35°32E, pop (2000e) 44 000. Holiday resort town in Northern district, N Israel, on W shore of L Tiberias; named after the Roman emperor, Tiberius; medicinal hot springs known since ancient times; one of the four holy cities of the Jews; Jewish settlement re-established in 1922; Monastery of St Peter.

Tiberias, Lake or **Sea of Galilee** [tiy**bee**rias], Hebrew **Yam Kinneret**, ancient **Sea of Chinnereth** area 166 sq km/64 sq mi. Lake in Northern district, NE Israel, in the Jordan valley; 210 m/689 ft below sea-level; length 22·5 km/14 mi; width 12 km/7½ mi; maximum depth 46 m/150 ft; fed and drained by the R Jordan; Israel's largest reservoir, with water piped as far as the Negev; many centres around the lake of historic and scriptural interest, especially connected with the life of Jesus; first kibbutz founded to the S in 1909.

Tiberius [tiy**bee**rius], in full **Tiberius Julius Caesar Augustus** (42 BC–AD 37) Roman emperor (14–37), the son of Livia, and stepson and successor of the Emperor Augustus. Deeply conservative by nature, he was content to continue Augustus's policies and simply consolidate his achievements. Despite the soundness of his administration and foreign policy, politically his reign was a disaster. The suspicious death of his heir Germanicus (19) was followed by the excesses of his chief henchman, the praetorian prefect Sejanus, and the reign of terror that followed Sejanus's downfall (d.31) made him an object of universal loathing. Few mourned when he died on Capri, the island retreat that had been his home since 26.

Tibesti Mountains [tee**bes**tee] Mountain range in NC Africa, largely in NW Chad, partly in Libya and Sudan; area 100 000 sq km/38 600 sq mi, length 480 km/300 mi; highest mountain group in Sahara; highest peak, Emi Koussi (3415 m/11 204 ft); spectacular rock formations created by wind erosion.

Tibet, Chin **Xizang** [shitsang] pop (2000e) 2 448 000; area 1 221 600 sq km/471 500 sq mi. Designated by Chinese as an autonomous region in SW China; S and W border includes Bhutan, India, and Nepal; in the Tibet Plateau, average altitude 4000 m/13 000 ft; Himalayas in the S, on borders with India, Nepal, and Bhutan, rising to 8848 m/29 028 ft at Mt Everest; Kunlun Shan range in the N; major farming area in S valleys; several rivers and lakes (largest salt-water lake, Nam Co, NW of Lhasa); capital, Lhasa; wheat, peas, rape seed; sheep, yak and goat raising, forestry, medicinal musk, caterpillar fungus, textiles; mining of chromium, iron, copper, lead, zinc, borax, salt, mica, gypsum; Tibetans originated in China, c.2500 BC; dominated N China, 4th-c AD; N Tibet conquered by Sui dynasty, 6th-c; first King of Tibet, 630; Tibetan–Chinese royal marriage link in 641, with introduction of Buddhism and Chinese culture; Tangut Tibetans conquered W China, 990, and established rich civilization, but overrun by Mongols, 1227; ruled by Mongols, 1279–1368; dominant religion Lamaism (Tibetan Buddhism) from 7th-c; semi-independent from 14th-c; Chinese protectorate, following defeat by Qing army, 1720; dispute with Britain caused by defeat of Nepal by Chinese army from Tibet, 1791; total separation of China and Tibet demanded by Britain, 1912, rejected by China; Chinese ethnic penetration during World War 2; invaded by China, 1950, against Indian protests, and full control asserted after 1959 revolt, with suspected atrocities; declared an autonomous region of China in 1965; Dalai Lama given refuge in India; most monasteries and temples now closed or officially declared historical monuments, but many people still worship daily; thought to be fewer than 1000 monks now in Tibet, compared to over 100 000 monks in 2500 monasteries prior to 1959; further uprising in 1993.

Tibetan One of the major languages in the Sino-Tibetan group. During the occupation of Tibet by China, Chinese was promoted officially at the expense of Tibetan, but there are probably 3–4 million speakers. Written records, mainly to do with the Buddhist religion, date from the 8th-c. The writing is horizontal, under the influence of Sanskrit.

Tibetan art The art associated with Tibet, which for a thousand years has reflected the intense spirituality and mysticism of Lamaism. Wall-paintings and banners, Buddhist sculpture in stone, wood, metal, and ivory, as well as tombs and stupas, were produced by anonymous craftsmen following age-old rules.

Tibet Plateau or **Qinghai–Tibet Plateau**, Chinese **Xizang Gaoyuan** Plateau in W and SW China; includes Xizang, Qinghai, W Sichuan, and SW Gansu; average altitude, 4000 m/13 000 ft, highest plateau in the world ('the roof of the world'); area 2·3 million sq km/0·9 million sq mi; bounded S by the Himalayas, N by Kunlun Shan and Qilian Shan Ranges, W by Karakoram Range, and E by Hengduan Shan Range; several internal ranges separate basins, valleys, and lakes; source of many rivers of E, SE, and S Asia, including the Yangtze, Yellow, Mekong, Thanlwin (Salween), Indus, Brahmaputra, and Tarim; major farming region in S, with warm, humid climate; C and N are cold and dry, with ice and snow for six months each year; uplift continues at over 10 mm/0·4 in per year.

tibia *leg*

Tibullus, Albius [tibulus] (c.54–19 BC) Latin poet, considered by Quintilian to be the greatest elegiac writer. He fought in Aquitania, but withdrew from military life and became a member of a literary circle in Rome. The heroine of his first book of love poetry was the wife of an officer absent on service in Cilicia; of his second, a fashionable courtesan. The other works under his name are probably by several authors.

tic An involuntary non-rhythmic motor movement or vocal production which serves no apparent purpose. It may occur as the result of a neurological lesion, and most famously in *Gilles de la Tourette syndrome*, where the patient may suddenly utter a sound like a bark, or swear without provocation or intention to do so.

tick A large mite specialized as a blood-feeding, external parasite of terrestrial vertebrates; fangs modified for cutting skin; cuticle typically elastic, stretching to accommodate blood meal; can transmit diseases of humans and domesticated animals. (Order: Acari. Family: Ixodidae.)

tickbird *oxpecker*

ticket of leave A pass issued to convicts in Australia as a reward for good behaviour; it was a form of parole which could be issued after 4, 6, or 8 years depending on whether the sentence was for 7, 14 years, or life, respectively. About 30% of convicts received tickets of leave by 1840.

tidal wave The extremely long-period waves driven by the forces producing the tides. The term is often popularly but incorrectly used to refer to tsunamis, which are not related to tides.

tide The regular, periodic rise and fall of the surface of the sea. The tides are produced by differences in gravitational forces acting on different points on the Earth's surface, and affect all bodies of water to some extent. These so-called tidal forces are produced primarily by the Sun and Moon. The Sun's tidal forces are only about half as strong as those of the Moon, due to the Sun's greater distance from the Earth. The position of the Sun, Moon, and other celestial bodies with respect to the Earth produces variations in the timing and magnitude of the tides.

T'ien-ching *Tianjin*

Tientsin *Tianjin*

Tiepolo, Giovanni Battista [tyaypoloh] (1696–1770) Artist, born in Venice, NE Italy. The last of the great Venetian painters, he became renowned as a decorator of buildings throughout Europe. Examples of his work can be found in the ceiling paintings of the Würzburg and Madrid palaces, where his imaginary skies are filled with floating, gesticulating, Baroque figures, apparently unbounded by the structure of the buildings.

Tiergarten [teergah(r)tn] A park covering 255 ha/630 acres in Berlin, Germany. Originally a royal hunting ground, it was landscaped in the 18th-c and opened to the public. The park was re-established, after being severely damaged during World War 2 and the bitter winter that followed, when many trees were cut for fuel.

Tierra del Fuego [tyera thel fwaygoh] pop (2000e) 78 200; area 78 746 sq km/28 473 sq mi. Island group at the extreme S of South America; E side (about one third) belongs to Argentina (National Territory), remainder belongs to Chile; boundary agreed in 1881; bounded by the Magellan Strait (N), Atlantic Ocean (E), Pacific Ocean (W), and Beagle Channel (S); highest point Monte Darwin (2438 m/7999 ft); Cape Horn southernmost point; discovered by Magellan 1520; capital (Argentina) Ushuaia, southernmost town in the world on Isla Grande de Tierra del Fuego; capital (on Chile mainland), Punta Arenas; sheep, timber, fishing, oil, natural gas; dispute over islands at E end of Beagle Channel, resolved in 1985 in favour of Chile.

tiger A member of the cat family (*Panthera tigris*) native to S and SE Asia; reddish-brown with dark vertical stripes (occasional individuals almost white with pale stripes and blue eyes); inhabits diverse habitats, often near water; swims well; hunts by sight and sound; eats mainly large mammals; several subspecies: **Bengal**, **Indochinese**, **Chinese**, **Sumatran**, **Siberian** (the largest known cat), and possibly extinct **Caspian**, **Bali**, and **Javan** tigers.

tiger beetle An active, brightly-coloured beetle found in open, sunny habitats; larvae typically live in burrows; both larvae and adults feed mainly on small insects. (Order: Coleoptera. Family: Carabidae.)

tiger cat A common name sometimes used for medium-sized spotted wild cats (eg ocelot, margay, serval, and Central American *little spotted cat*). The name is also used for a domestic cat with tabby coloration.

tiger fish Large, predatory, freshwater fish with strong, fang-like teeth, widespread in rivers and lakes of Africa; length up to 1·8 m/6 ft; powerful and much prized as a sport fish. The name is also used for several fish in other families that are predatory with strong teeth, or have conspicuous striped coloration. (Genus: *Hydrocynus*. Family: Characidae.)

tiger heron *heron*

tiger-moth A medium-sized, typically colourful moth; caterpillar larvae usually hairy, known as **woolly bears**; may be an important pest causing damage to tree foliage; many produce sound using a vibrating organ on side of body. (Order: Lepidoptera. Family: Arctiidae.)

tiger shark Large and very dangerous shark (*Galeocerda cuvier*) widely distributed in tropical and warm temperate seas; length up to 5 m/16 ft; grey to brown, with darker vertical stripes and patches, the pattern becoming indistinct in large specimens. (Family: Carcharhinidae.)

tigon [tiygn] *liger*

Tigray or **Tigre** [teegray] pop (2000e) 3 671 000; area 64 921 sq km/40 575 sq mi. Region in NE Ethiopia and Eritrea; mountainous W half, with peaks including Mokada (2295 m/7529 ft); low-lying E half, with large section below sea-level at centre of Danakil Depression; capital, Mekele; one of the areas most severely affected by the drought in the 1980s, and a centre of resistance to the government; Tigray people are Semitic-speaking, mostly nomadic herders in the N, agriculturalists in the S.

tigrillo *ocelot*

Tigris, River [tiygris], Arabic **Shatt Dijla**, Turkish **Dicle** River in SE Turkey and Iraq; rises in EC Turkey, and flows generally SE through Iraq; joins the Euphrates 64 km/40 mi NW of Basra to form the Shatt al-Arab; length 1850 km/1150 mi; navigable to Baghdad for shallow-draft vessels; several dams used for flood control and irrigation; ancient transportation route, with several ancient cities along its banks, eg Nineveh, Seleucia, Ashur, Calah.

Tijuana [teehwahna] 32°32N 117°02W, pop (2000e) 894 000. Border town in NW Baja California Norte, NW Mexico; on the Pacific Ocean at the frontier with California, USA; airfield; tourist town with casinos and nightclubs; horse racing, dog racing, bullfights.

Tikal [teekahl] An ancient Mayan city in the Petén rainforest of N Guatemala, settled by 250 BC, at its peak in the 7th–8th-c AD, but abruptly abandoned c.900. In area 16 sq km/6 sq mi, it contained an estimated 3000 buildings with a population of c.20–30 000. Monuments include palaces, plazas, ten reservoirs, and six temple pyramids, the largest 70 m/229 ft high. It is a world heritage site.

Tilburg [tilberkh] 51°31N 5°06E, pop (2000e) 168 000. Industrial city in North Brabant province, S Netherlands; on the Wilhelmina Canal, 54 km/34 mi SE of Rotterdam; railway; woollens, metalworking; major business and cultural centre in the S; capital of Dutch Catholicism.

Tilbury 51°28N 0°23E, pop (2000e) 12 100. Town in Essex, SE England, UK; on the R Thames estuary, E of London; railway; major port and docks for London and the SE.

till or **boulder clay** A geological term for sediment or drift consisting of an unstratified and unsorted deposit of clay, sand, gravel, and boulders left behind after the retreat of glaciers and ice-sheets. **Tillite** is till which has consolidated into solid rock.

Tillett, Ben(jamin) (1860–1943) Trade union leader, born in Bristol, SW England, UK. He worked as a brickmaker, bootmaker, and sailor, and achieved prominence as leader of the great dockers' strike (1889), and of the transport workers' strike in London (1911). He later became a Labour MP (1917–24, 1929–31).

Till Eulenspiegel *Eulenspiegel, Till*

Tilley, Vesta, stage name of **Matilda Alice, Lady de Frece**, *née* **Powles** (1864–1952) Music-hall entertainer, born in Worcester, Hereford and Worcester, WC England, UK. She first appeared as 'The Great Little Tilley', aged four, in Nottingham, adopted her professional name, and became a celebrated male impersonator. Her many popular songs included 'Burlington Bertie' and 'Following in Father's Footsteps'. She retired in 1920.

Tillich, Paul (Johannes) [tilikh] (1886–1965) Protestant theologian and philosopher, born in Starzeddel, E Germany. He became a Lutheran pastor (1912) and served as military chaplain in the German army in World War 1. He taught at Berlin (1919–24) and held professorships at Marburg (1924–5), Dresden (1925–8), Leipzig (1928–9), and Frankfurt (1929–33). An early critic of Hitler, in 1933 he was barred from German universities, and moved to the USA, teaching at the Union Theological Seminary in New York City (1933–55), Harvard Divinity School (1955–62), and Chicago Divinity School (1962–5), and becoming a US citizen in 1940. His influence is characterized by an attempt to mediate between traditional Christian culture and the secular orientation of modern society. His main scholarly work was *Systematic Theology* (3 vols, 1951, 1957, 1963), and his popular books included *The Courage to Be* (1952) and *Dynamics of Faith* (1957).

Tilly, Johann Tserclaes, Graf (Count) **von** (1559–1632) Flemish soldier, born in Tilly, SC Belgium. He successfully commanded the forces of the Catholic League in the Thirty Years' War, gaining decisive victories at the White Mountain and Prague (1620). Created a count of the Holy Roman Empire, he defeated Denmark at Lütter (1626). His destruction of Magdeburg (1631) branded him a brutal soldier, and he was routed by Gustav II Adolf at Breitenfeld in Saxony (1631). He was fatally wounded crossing into Bavaria.

timber line The boundary above which trees occur but do not achieve full growth. Between the timber line and the tree line, the trees are stunted and dwarfed.

timber wolf *wolf*

timbre The sound quality of a voice or musical instrument, which depends on the prominence or otherwise of upper harmonics (*partials*) in the notes produced. The timbre of a flute or recorder, for example, is weak in upper harmonics compared with that of the much brighter violin or trumpet. The 'clanging' sound of a bell results from the number and strength of upper partials which are not concordant with the fundamental.

Timbuktu [tim**buhk**too], Fr **Tombouctou** 16°49N 2°59W, pop (2000e) 32 000. Town in Gao region, N Mali, 690 km/429 mi NE of Bamako; settled in the 11th-c; a chief centre of Muslim learning; declined after conquest by Morocco, 16th-c; taken by the French, 1893; airfield; adjoining town of Kabara serves as a port on the R Niger; tourism, salt, power plant; Djinguereber Mosque (13th-c), Sankore Mosque (14th-c), Sidi Yahya Mosque (15th-c).

time That which distinguishes sequential events from simultaneous events; symbol t, units s (second); the fourth dimension, in addition to the three spatial dimensions. It allows the assignment of cause and effect, and, according to our perception, the assignment of past, present, and future. In Newtonian mechanics, time is absolute, meaning that a second as measured by one observer is the same as a second measured by any other observer in the universe. Relativity explains that this view of the nature of time is false. In thermodynamic systems, the directionality of time derives from entropy. Time directionality in particle physics was first seen in 1998 via the properties of particles called *kaons*.

time and motion study The technique of job analysis to discover how tasks are actually carried out; more usually known now as **work study** or **industrial engineering**. Its aim is to find the most efficient way of performing a task, both in terms of time and effort, in order to raise productivity. When used as a basis for wage negotiations, it can lead to industrial disputes.

time code A series of digitally coded signals appearing sequentially on the magnetic tape of a video or audio recording, and sometimes on film, to provide specific identification for each frame in editing and post-production. In its simplest form it denotes Hours, Minutes, Seconds, and Frames, which may be selected as 24, 25, or 30 per second.

time dilation The slowing of time for objects moving at velocities close to the velocity of light, as perceived by a stationary observer. If observer A watches the clock held by observer B as B moves past, A will see B's clock as running slowly. In turn, B will see A's clock as running slowly. The symmetry is consistent with the principle that no observer is 'more at rest' than any other. Time dilation is observed in particle physics where moving unstable particles appear to decay more slowly than identical stationary particles.

time-lapse photography A series of photographs taken at regular intervals from the same viewpoint to record the development of a subject, for example, plant growth, cloud formation, metallic corrosion, or traffic flow. When filmed as successive single frames, subsequent projection at normal speed provides a rapid presentation of slow changes. A similar technique is available in video cameras.

Time of Troubles, also known as the **Time of the Five Dmitris** A period of intense social and political turmoil in Russia (1598–1613), involving a series of successive crises, civil wars, famines, Cossack and peasant revolts, foreign invasions, and widespread material destruction. In 1591 the legitimate heir of Ivan the Terrible, Dmitri, was murdered, possibly on the orders of Boris Godunov. Subsequently, four pretenders assumed his name. The first appeared in Poland c.1600. Enlisting the support of Lithuanians and Poles, he invaded Russia and was crowned tsar in 1605. He was killed in an insurrection by the boyars, and in 1607 another Dmitri appeared, aided by the Poles and identified by the late tsar Dmitri's widow, the Polish noblewoman Marina Mniszech, as her legitimate husband and tsar of Russia. In 1610 he too was killed, and in 1612 a man claiming to be Dmitri's son was put to death. Another, also claiming to be Dmitri's son, was beheaded in 1613. The period ended with a national uprising against the invading Poles, and the election of the boyar Michael Romanov, first of the Romanov line, as tsar. The political turmoil and power struggles following the collapse of communism in the early 1990s was also referred to by the Russian people as 'The Time of Troubles'.

time-sharing (computing) A means of providing simultaneous access by several users to the same computer. Each user, in turn, is assigned full use of the central processing unit for a very small duration, making it appear that each user has continuous access.

time-sharing (leisure) The joint ownership of holiday accommodation by a consortium. Depending upon the number of shares acquired, each share holder is entitled to a specific period of use. A register of time-share owners exists, enabling them to exchange their accommodation for another during their holiday entitlement period.

Times Square The area in New York City formed by the intersection of Broadway, 42nd Street, and 7th Avenue, and at the centre of the city's theatre district. It takes its name from the Times Tower, built in 1904 to house the offices of the *New York Times*.

Timgad The former Roman city of Thaugadi in NE Algeria; a world heritage site. Founded by the Emperor Trajan in AD 100, and abandoned after the 5th-c, it is a noted example of Roman planning. The site has been extensively restored, and archaeological work still continues.

Timişoara [timish**wah**ra], Hung **Temesvár** 45°45N 21°15E, pop (2000e) 319 000. Capital of Timiş county, W Romania, on the Bega Canal; ceded to Romania, 1919; violent suppression of a pro-Hungarian demonstration there in December 1989, with many civilians killed, sparked a more general uprising against the Ceauşescu regime; railway; university (1962); technical university (1920); fine arts academy; electrical engineering, textiles, chemicals, pharmaceuticals, food processing, footwear, metal; two cathedrals; Hunyadi Castle (15th-c).

Timor [**tee**maw(r)] pop (2000e) 1 905 000; area 33 912 sq km/13 090 sq mi. Mountainous island in SE Asia, in the Sunda group, NW of Australia; divided between Portugal and Holland, 1859; **West Timor** (former Dutch Timor) included in Indonesia at independence, administered as part of the province of Nusa Tenggara Timur; capital, Kupang; coffee, coconuts, maize; former Portuguese territory of **East Timor** granted full independence, 2002 (*see* **East Timor**).

Timor Sea [**tee**maw(r)] Part of the Pacific Ocean, SE of Timor, Indonesia, and NW of Northern Territory, Australia; lies over a wide continental shelf, with depths down to 110 m/360 ft, but deepens off Timor.

Timoshenko, Semyon Konstantinovich [timoh**sheng**koh] (1895–1970) Russian general, born in Furmanka, S Ukraine. He joined the Tsarist army in 1915, and in the Revolution took part in the defence of Tsaritsyn. In 1940 he smashed Finnish resistance during the Russo-Finnish War, then commanded in the Ukraine, but failed to stop the German advance (1942). He also served as People's Commissar of Defence, improving the system of army training. He retired in 1960.

Timothy, Letters to Two of the Pastoral Letters in the New Testament, for which Pauline authorship is often disputed today. Both letters are purportedly addressed to Paul's close companion Timothy (*Acts* 16.1; 1 *Thess* 3.2), but mostly concern questions of church order and discipline, and problems with false teachers who seemingly were spreading gnostic and Jewish speculations. The second letter, however, does make several references to Paul's personal experiences and circumstances.

timpani [**tim**panee] (singular **timpano**) Drums made from large copper bowls (hence the English name **kettledrum**), with heads of calfskin or plastic, which can be tuned to various pitches by means of hand-screws or, in modern instruments, pedals. They are normally played with two felt-headed sticks, but other types may be specified. As military instruments, two timpani were carried on horseback at either side of the rider. Since the 17th-c they have been regular members of the orchestral percussion section.

Timur [ti**moor**], known as **Timur Lenk** (Turkish 'Timur the Lame'), English **Tamerlane** or **Tamburlaine** (1336–1405) Tatar conqueror, born near Samarkand, SE Uzbekistan. In 1369 he ascended the throne of Samarkand, subdued nearly all Persia, Georgia, and the Tatar empire, and conquered all the states between the Indus and the lower Ganges (1398). He won Damascus and Syria from the Mameluke sovereigns of Egypt, then defeated the Turks at Angora (1402), taking Sultan Bayezit prisoner. His death, while taking a 200 000 army to conquer Ming China, made possible the reopening of Chinese W trade routes, and a Persian trade mission to China (1409).

tin Sn (Lat *stannum*), element 50, melting point 232°C, density 7·3 g/cm³. A white metal in the carbon group of elements, occurring in nature mainly as the oxide (SnO_2), and isolated by reduction with carbon. The metal forms a very strongly adhering oxide coat, and is therefore not corroded easily. Tin is used as a plating for other metals because of its corrosion resistance. Tin compounds are less widely used than the metal. Common oxidation states of tin are +2 and +4.

tinamou [**ti**namoo] A partridge-like bird, native to the New World tropics; inhabits woodland, scrub, or grassland; eats plant material, insects, and (occasionally) mice; eggs incubated by male. (Family: Tinamidae, c.50 species.)

Tinbergen, Jan [**tin**bergen] (1903–94) Dutch economist, born in The Hague, The Netherlands, the brother of Nikolaas Tinbergen. He studied at Leyden. His major contribution was the econometric modelling of cyclical movements in socio-economic growth. He was director of the Central Planning Bureau in The Netherlands (1945–55), then professor of development planning at the Netherlands School of Economics (1955–73), and also worked with developing countries. In 1969 he shared the first Nobel Prize for Economics. There are Tinbergen Institutes for economic research in Amsterdam and Rotterdam.

Tinbergen, Nikolaas [**tin**bergen] (1907–88) Ethologist, born in The Hague, The Netherlands, the brother of Jan Tinbergen. He graduated in zoology at Leyden, and later taught there, and from 1947 at Oxford. His major concern was with the patterns of animal behaviour in nature, showing that many are stereotyped. His research covered several species, in relation to camouflage, learning behaviour, courtship, and aggression, and he also studied autism in children. He shared the Nobel Prize for Physiology or Medicine in 1973.

Tindale *Tyndale, William*

tineid moth [**tin**eeid] A small, drab moth of the family Tineidae; caterpillars mainly feed on dried organic matter; c.3500 species, including the clothes moths, which cause damage to carpets and clothes, and other pests of stored products. (Order: Lepidoptera.)

Tinian [**tin**ian] pop (2000e) 2500; area 101 sq km/39 sq mi. One of the N Mariana Is, W Pacific, 5 km/3 mi SW of Saipan; length 18 km/11 mi; four long runways built by the USA during World War 2; plaque commemorates the launching of the Hiroshima bombing mission in 1945; site of ancient stone columns.

tinnitus [**tin**itus] A ringing or hissing sound heard within the ear, which may arise from almost any disorder of the ear or its nerve supply. When the cause is simple, such as excessive wax in the external ear, the condition is easily remedied; in other cases, the disorder is usually intractable.

Tin Pan Alley A nickname coined towards the end of the 19th-c for the popular music-publishing centre of New York City situated on 28th Street and 6th Avenue, and later on Broadway near 49th Street. In the UK it can refer to the area around Denmark Street in Soho, London.

tinplate A thin steel sheet coated with tin by dipping or electrolytic deposition. It is used for light robust containers and protective constructions. First tried out in the late 17th-c, it was not used to any extent until the invention of canning in the early 19th-c, since when it has attained worldwide industrial importance.

Tintoretto [tinto**ret**oh], originally **Jacopo Robusti** (1518–94) Venetian painter, probably born in Venice, NE Italy, the son of a dyer (Ital *tintore*). Except for visits to Mantua (1580, 1590–3), he lived all his life in Venice, painting portraits and biblical subjects in which he attempted (according to a contemporary critic) to combine the energetic drawing of Michelangelo with the glowing colour of Titian. His most spectacular works are sacred murals painted for religious confraternities, especially the 50 or so canvases decorating the Church and Scuola of S Rocco. The Scuola contains a vast iconographical scheme from the Old and New Testaments, including the 'Crucifixion' (1565) and 'Annunciation' (1583–7). Other major works include 'The Last Supper' (1547, Venice), 'The Last Judgment' (c.1560, Venice), and the 'Paradiso', famous for its great size (1588, Venice). Three of his seven children also became painters, including **Marietta** (1560–90), known as **la Tintoretta**.

Tipasa A village on the N coast of Algeria, standing on the ruins of the ancient city of Tipasa; a world heritage site. The original settlement, founded in the 5th-c BC, passed through many hands, from Phoenician to Roman, before it was abandoned in the 5th-c.

Tipperary [tipuh**rair**ee], Ir **Thiobrad Arann** County in Munster province, SC Ireland; divided into **North Riding** (pop (2000e) 58 500; area 1996 sq km/770 sq mi) and **South Riding** (pop (2000e) 76 000; area 2258 sq km/872 sq mi); watered by R Suir; Silvermine Mts (N), Galty Mts (S), Slieve Ardagh Hills (W); capital, Clonmel; rich dairy-farming area; centre for horse and greyhound breeding; festival of Irish and modern music and dance at Tipperary town (Jun).

Tippett, Sir Michael (Kemp) (1905–98) Composer, born in London, UK. He studied at the Royal College of Music, London, and became director of music at Morley College (1940–51). His oratorio, *A Child of Our Time* (1941), reflecting the problems of the 1930s and 1940s, won him wide recognition. A convinced pacifist, he was imprisoned for three months as a conscientious objector during World War 2. He scored a considerable success with his operas *The Midsummer Marriage* (1952) and *King Priam* (1961), and among his other works are four symphonies, a piano concerto, and string quartets. His books include *Music of the Angels* (1980), *Those Twentieth Century Blues* (1991), and *Tippett on Music* (1995). He was knighted in 1966, and received the Order of Merit in 1983.

Tippoo Sultán [ti**poo**], also known as **Tippoo Sahib** (1749–99) Sultan of Mysore (1782–99), born in Devanhalli, S India, the son of Haidar Ali. He continued his father's policy of opposing British rule, and in 1789 invaded the British-protected state of Travancore. In the ensuing war (1790–2) he was defeated by Cornwallis, and had to cede half his kingdom. After recommencing hostilities in 1799, he was killed during the siege of Seringapatam.

Tiranë [tee**rah**na], Ital **Tirana** 41°20N 19°50E, pop (2000e) 277 200. Capital town of Albania and of Tiranë district; in a valley in the foothills of the Kruja-Dajti Mts, 40 km/25 mi from the Adriatic Sea; founded by Turks in the early 17th-c; made capital in 1920; residential area built by the Italians (1939–43); industrial area to the W; university (1957); railway; airport (Rinas); textiles, foodstuffs, footwear, metalworking, ceramics, glass, engineering, wood products, distilling, building materials, furniture; coal mines nearby.

tire *tyre*

Tiresias [tiy**ree**zias] In Greek mythology, a blind Theban prophet, who takes a prominent part in Sophocles' plays about Oedipus and Antigone. Later legends account for his wisdom by saying that he had experienced the life of both sexes.

Tirol or **Tyrol** [ti**rohl**] pop (2000e) 656 300; area 12 647 sq km/4882 sq mi. Federal state of W Austria, bounded by Germany to the N and Italy to the S; drained by the R Inn; lakes include the Achensee, Walchsee, Tristacher See, Schwarzsee; capital, Innsbruck; hydroelectric power (Zillertal, Kaunertal), agriculture, forestry, powder metallurgy, diesel engines, vehicles, optical instruments; leading state for tourism, especially winter sports (eg at Kitzbühel).

Tirol Alps *Bavarian Alps*

Tirpitz, Alfred (Friedrich) von [teerpits] (1849–1930) German admiral, born in Kostrzyn, W Poland (formerly Küstrin, Prussia). He joined the Prussian navy in 1865, was ennobled in 1900, and rose to be Lord High Admiral (1911). As secretary of state for the imperial navy (1897–1916), he raised a fleet to challenge British supremacy of the seas, and acted as its commander (1914–16). He advocated unrestricted submarine warfare, and resigned when this policy was opposed. He later sat in the Reichstag, then retired to Ebenhausen.

Tirso de Molina [teersoh, moleena], pseudonym of **Gabriel Téllez** (c.1571–1648) Playwright, born in Madrid, Spain. Educated at Alcalá, he became prior of the monastery of Soria. A disciple of his contemporary, Lope de Vega, he wrote many comedies and religious plays, but is best known for his treatment of the Don Juan legend in *El burlador de Sevilla* (1635, The Seducer of Seville).

Tirthankara [teertangkara] (Sanskrit, 'ford-maker') A title used by Jains of the 24 great heroes of their tradition who, by their teaching and example, taught them the way to cross the stream from the bondage of physical existence to freedom from rebirth. They are also called *Jina*, 'conqueror', from which Jains take their name.

Tiruchchirappalli [tiroochirapahlee] or **Trichinopoly** [trikinopolee] 10°45N 78°45E, pop (2000e) 835 000. City in Tamil Nadu, S India, on the Kaveri R; airfield; railway; educational, religious, and commercial centre, noted for its gold, silver, and brass working; fort, shrine of Sringam, monument to Shiva.

Tiryns [teerinz] An ancient Greek town in the Argolid near Mycenae, famous for the remains of its fortified Bronze Age palace. Large parts of its Cyclopean walls still stand.

Tissot, James Joseph Jacques [teesoh] (1836–1902) Painter, born in Nantes, W France. He trained in Paris, where he was influenced by Degas, then in the 1870s settled in London, painting highly accomplished scenes of Victorian life. As a result of a visit to Palestine in 1886, he produced a series of the life of Christ in water-colour.

tissue A group or layer of similarly specialized cells, or cells and associated fibres, which have specific functions. Most animals are composed of some or all of the following types of tissue. **Epithelial tissue** consists of cells only, and covers all internal and external surfaces. **Connective tissue** (eg fat) consists of cells and fibres, and tends to have a passive role, supporting or joining the more functionally active tissues. **Skeletal tissue** (eg bone, cartilage) is modified connective tissue, in which the cells and fibres lie in a rigid matrix. **Muscular tissue** consists of fibres arranged in particular patterns, and is responsible for producing movements at joints (*skeletal muscle*), peristaltic contractions of the alimentary tract (*smooth muscle*), and the regular beating of the heart (*cardiac muscle*). **Nervous tissue** is composed of cells, some of which have long processes (*axons* or *dendrites*), specialized to convey and transmit information from one part of the body to another.

tissue fluid *interstitial fluid*

Tisza, River [tisa], Czech **Tisa**, Russian **Tissa** Longest tributary of the R Danube in E Europe; rises in the W Ukrainian Carpathian Mts and flows S into the Great Plain of Hungary, where it is used for irrigation and hydroelectricity; major land reclamation schemes along its course; enters the Danube SW of Belgrade; length 962 km/598 mi; navigable for 780 km/485 mi.

tit A small, lively, acrobatic songbird, native to the N hemisphere and Africa; inhabits woodland and habitation; in the wild, eats insects and seeds; also known as the **titmouse** or **typical tit**; includes the **chickadees** of North America. The name is also used for the **long-tailed tit** (Family: Aegithalidae), the **penduline tit** (Family: Remizidae), and numerous other birds of diverse groups. (Family: Paridae, 46 species.)

Titan (astronomy) [tiytn] Saturn's largest satellite, discovered in 1655 by Huygens; distance from the planet 1 222 000 km/759 000 mi; diameter 5150 km/3200 mi; orbital period 15·945 days. It is the second-largest moon in the Solar System, and the only satellite with a substantial atmosphere, principally composed of nitrogen and methane with a surface pressure greater than Earth's atmosphere. It was approached closely by Voyager 1, but global haze cover prevented observation of the surface.

Titan (mythology) [tiytn] In Greek mythology, a member of the older generation of gods, the children of Uranus and Gaia. After Zeus and the Olympians took power, the Titans made war on them; but they were defeated and imprisoned in Tartarus. One or two, notably Prometheus, helped Zeus. The Titans may represent memories of pre-Greek Mediterranean gods.

Titania (astronomy) The largest satellite of Uranus, discovered in 1787 by W Herschel; distance from the planet 436 000 km/271 000 mi; diameter 1580 km/980 mi, orbital period 8·7 days. It has an icy, cratered surface, with extensive scarps.

Titania (mythology) In Greek mythology, a female Titan, identified with the Moon. In Shakespeare's *A Midsummer Night's Dream* she is the queen of the fairies, who is tricked into falling in love with Bottom the weaver.

Titanic [tiytanik] British 46 329-gross-tonnes passenger liner, belonging to White Star Line, which collided with an iceberg in the N Atlantic on her maiden voyage in April 1912. Lifeboat capacity was inadequate, and just over 700 people were saved, while 1500 went down with the ship. The vessel was rediscovered in 1985, explored, and photographed on the seabed. As she was found to be broken into two unequal pieces, each severely damaged, it is unlikely that she will ever be raised. The task is not impossible, but it would be prohibitively expensive. An Oscar-winning film of the tragedy, directed by James Cameron, was released in 1997.

titanium Ti, element 22, melting point 1660°C. A lustrous, white metal, with a relatively low density of 4·5 g/cm^3. It is found widely distributed in nature, never uncombined, and usually as an oxide (TiO_2). The metal, produced by magnesium reduction, is used in some alloys, especially for aircraft. Its compounds usually show oxidation states +3 and +4. The dioxide is a particularly important white pigment in paints.

titanothere [tiytanotheer] A medium to large plant-eating mammal; known as fossils from the early Tertiary period of North America and E Asia; some stood 2·5 m/8 ft at the shoulder; often with paired nasal horns; includes *Brontotherium*. (Order: Perissodactyla.)

Titchmarsh, Alan (Fred) (1949–) Gardener, broadcaster, and writer, born in Ilkley, West Yorkshire, N England, UK. He became an apprentice gardener for Ilkley Urban District Council (1964–8), then joined the Royal Botanic Gardens at Kew (1972–4). He began presenting radio and television programmes for the BBC, and became a household name for his expert advice on gardening matters. In 1996 he began presenting the popular radio series, *Gardener's World*, and fronted TV 's *Ground Force* (1997–2003). A regular contributor to magazines and newspapers, his books include *Gardening Techniques* (1981), *Alan Titchmarsh's Complete Book of Gardening* (1999), and *How To Be a Gardener* (2002). He has also written novels, including *The Last Lighthouse Keeper* (1999), and an autobiography, *Trowel and Error* (2002).

tithes Offerings of a proportion (literally 'the tenth part') of one's property or produce to God, often given to the priesthood of temples; customary among peoples since ancient times. In Jewish Law, instructions regarding tithes were listed in *Lev* 27, and were subsequently elaborated in the Talmud. Taxes of this description were used to support Christian clergy in Europe from mediaeval times, and in England from the 10th-c, until greater secularization after the Reformation brought increased opposition. Civil tithes were replaced in England by a rent charge in 1836, and even this was abolished in 1936.

titi or **tee-tee** [**tee**tee] A New World monkey of genus *Callicebus* (3 species); thick coat and long tail; moves slowly; characteristically crouches on a branch with all four feet together, tail hanging vertically. The name is also used for short-tusked marmosets of genus *Callithrix* (3 species).

Titian [**tish**an], Ital **Tiziano Vecellio** (c.1490–1576) Venetian painter, born in Pieve di Cadore, NE Italy. Trained in the studio of Giovanni Bellini, he assisted Giorgione with the paintings on the Fondaco dei Tedeschi (1508). His early paintings display Giorgione's influence, and his own revolutionary style is not apparent until after c.1516, in such works as 'The Assumption of the Virgin' (1516–18, Venice). For the Duke of Ferrara he painted three great mythological subjects, 'The Feast of Venus' (c.1515–18), 'The Bacchanal' (c.1518, both Prado, Madrid), and the richly-coloured 'Bacchus and Ariadne' (c.1523, National Gallery, London). From 1530, he also painted many pictures for Emperor Charles V, and this period includes his 'Ecce Homo' (1543, Vienna). He later executed a series of works on mythological scenes for Philip of Spain, and in his last years painted several religious and mythological subjects, such as 'The Fall of Man' (c.1570, Madrid) and 'Christ Crowned with Thorns' (c.1570, Munich). He is widely acclaimed as the greatest of the Venetian painters.

Titicaca, Lake [teeteekakuh] Lake in SE Peru and W Bolivia; largest lake in South America (area 8290 sq km/3200 sq mi) and highest large lake in world (3812 m/12 506 ft); major transportation artery between Peru and Bolivia; length 177 km/110 mi; width 56 km/35 mi; maximum depth 475 m/1558 ft; two parts, L Chucuito (Lago Mayor) and L Huinamarca (Lago Minor), connected by Strait of Tiquina; freight ferries run from Guaqui (Bolivia) to Puno (Peru); mining centre, Matilde, on NE shore; hunting and fishing resort; base for Bolivian Yacht Club; contains 36 islands, including Isla del Sol and Isla de la Luna (also known as Coati) with archaeological remains; on SW shore is Copacabana, a place of recreation for the Royal Inca family, famous for its sanctuary and 17th-c temple (Franciscan monastery) with statue of Virgin de Candelaria (1576), place of pilgrimage; ruins of ancient centre of Tiwanaku empire nearby is a world heritage site.

Titius-Bode law *Bode's law*

title A word used before someone's name to show an acquired or inherited rank or honour, a person's sex (*Mr, Mrs, Ms*) or occupation (*Doctor, Colonel*), or some other attainment (eg *Dr* for a PhD degree).

titmouse *tit*

Tito [**tee**toh], known as **Marshal Tito**, originally **Josip Broz** (1892–1980) Yugoslav statesman and president (1953–80), born in Kumrovec, NW Croatia. In World War 1 he served with the Austro-Hungarian army, was taken prisoner by the Russians, and became a Communist. He was imprisoned for conspiring against the regime in Yugoslavia (1928–9), and became secretary of the Communist Party in 1937. In 1941 he organized partisan forces against the Axis conquerors, and after the war became the country's first Communist prime minister (1945), consolidating his position with the presidency in 1953. He broke with Stalin and the Cominform in 1948, developing Yugoslavia's independent style of Communism (**Titoism**), and played a leading role in the association of nonaligned countries. His marriage to a Serb symbolized his attempts to unify the two conflicting national groups within Yugoslavia. Some believe that unity was never viable, however, and that Tito's rule encouraged nationalism – which erupted in civil war in the 1990s.

Tito, Dennis (1941–) American multimillionaire businessman. Before moving into a highly successful business career, he was a rocket scientist at the US space agency NASA's jet propulsion laboratory in Pasadena, CA. On 28 April 2001, he made history as the world's first 'space tourist', having completed nine months training for the mission at a military base near Moscow. Paying a reputed $20 million (£14 million) to the Russians, he boarded a Soyuz spacecraft, along with two Russian cosmonauts, and was launched from the Baikonur cosmodrome in Kazakhstan for his 6-day stay aboard the International Space Station. His return flight landed successfully in the Kazakhstan desert on 6 May 2001.

Titograd *Podgorica*

titration A technique for finding the volume of one solution chemically equivalent to a given volume of another, usually by adding the first solution slowly until equivalence is reached. This can be detected by the addition of a small amount of an indicator material.

Titus [**tiy**tus], in full **Titus Flavius Vespasianus** (39–81) Roman emperor (79–81), the elder son and successor of Vespasian. Popular with the Romans for his generosity, charm, and military prowess, he is execrated in Jewish tradition for his destruction of Jerusalem (70) and suppression of the Jewish Revolt. His brief reign was marred by many natural calamities, notably the eruption of Vesuvius (79). He completed the Colosseum, begun by his father.

Titus, St [**tiy**tus] (1st-c) In the New Testament, a Gentile companion of the apostle Paul. He is not mentioned in Acts, but is referred to in Galatians 2 and 2 Corinthians 8.6. Ecclesiastical tradition makes him the first Bishop of Crete. The purported Letter of Paul to Titus gives advice on the way the churches there should be organized. Feast day 6 February (W), 23 August (E).

Titus, Letter to One of the Pastoral Letters in the New Testament, for which Pauline authorship is usually disputed today. The letter addresses problems of church order and false (gnostic?) teachers, with specific instructions about the importance of sound doctrine, the selection of elders and bishops, family and social relationships, and submission to rulers and authorities.

Tiv An agricultural people of C Nigeria, living along the Benue R. An egalitarian people, they are organized according to kinship ties. Much of their traditional culture is still intact, and they have expanded into neighbouring groups. They speak a Niger–Congo language.

Tiwi [**tee**wee] The Aboriginal inhabitants of Melville and Bathurst Islands, off Darwin, Northern Territory, Australia. Cut off from the mainland for 5000 or more years, the Tiwi developed a distinctive culture, best known today for its colourful *pukamuni* funeral poles, and also for new art media such as fabric painting.

Tlaloc [**tla**lok] The Aztec god of rain, to whom children were sacrificed in time of drought. The features of his face are formed of serpents, representing the lightning.

Tlapanek *Hokan languages*

Tlemcen [tlem**sen**], ancient **Pomaria** 34°53N 1°21W, pop (2000e) 333 700. Chief town of Tlemcen department, NW Algeria, N Africa; 113 km/70 mi SW of Oran; capital of major Moroccan dynasties (12th–16th-c); despite French occupation from 1842, a well-preserved Muslim culture; railway; agriculture, carpets; leather, olive oil, tourism; Almovarid Great Mosque (1135), Grand Mosque, Museum of Bel Hassane.

Tlingit A North American Indian group of the Pacific NW coast (from Prince William Sound to S Alaska), who lived mainly by fishing and hunting, c.14 000 (1990 census). They are famed for their art, including Chilkat blankets woven from cedar bark and goat hair, and subtly coloured wood sculptures.

TNT (explosive) The abbreviation for **trinitrotoluene**, $C_7H_5N_3O_6$. A high explosive made by the nitration of toluene with nitric and sulphuric acids; a solid melting at 82°C. Used for filling shells and bombs, it is one of the most effective and easiest to handle of the military high explosives.

TNT (transport) *Abeles*

toad *frog*

toadfish Robust, bottom-living fish of the family Batrachoididae (6 genera), found in inshore waters of tropical to temperate seas; body typically elongate, tapering to a small tail, dorsal and anal fins long; eyes placed on top of flattened head, mouth large with strong teeth; some species have powerful poison spines.

toadflax An annual or perennial, native to the N hemisphere, especially the Mediterranean region; leaves opposite, alternate or whorled; flowers in a variety of colour combinations, strongly zygomorphic; tube spurred and 2-lipped, the lower lip 3-lobed with a projection (the *palate*) closing the tube, so that pollinators must part the lips to reach nectar held in the spur. (Genus: *Linaria*, 150 species. Family: Scrophulariaceae.)

toadstool An informal name for many typically umbrella-shaped fungal fruiting bodies, especially those that are poisonous or inedible.

Toamasina, also **Tamatave** 18°10S 49°23E, pop (2000e) 195 000. Port on the E coast of Madagascar, on the Indian Ocean, 367 km/228 mi NE of Antananarivo; Madagascar's main port, and a popular tourist resort; airfield; railway; surrounded by sugar-cane plantations; Ivoloina Gardens nearby.

tobacco An annual or shrubby perennial, native to warm parts of the New World and Australasia; large leaves; tubular flowers, greenish, yellow, pink, or reddish. The dried, slightly fermented leaves of various species, principally *Nicotiana tabacum*, are used for smoking, chewing, and snuff, and contain the powerful alkaloid *nicotine* which is both poisonous and addictive. (Genus: *Nicotiana*, 66 species. Family: Solanaceae.)

Tobago [tobaygoh] pop (2000e) 48 000; area 300 sq km/116 sq mi. Island in the W Caribbean; part of the Republic of Trinidad and Tobago; chief town, Scarborough; united with Trinidad in 1889; airport; luxury hotel-conference centre at Rocky Point; tourist complex at Minster Point.

Tobin, James [tohbin] (1918–2002) Economist, born in Urbana-Champaign, Illinois, USA. He studied at Harvard and, following wartime service in the US navy, went on to teach there. In 1955 he became a professor at Yale, later serving as a member of President Kennedy's Council of Economic Advisors (1961–2). His research activities extended, developed, and refined Keynesian ideas concerning money demand, inflation, consumption, and saving, and elaborate on the roles of monetary and fiscal policies. In 1981 he was awarded the Nobel Prize for Economics, primarily for his 'portfolio selection theory' of investment.

Tobit or **Tobias, Book of** [tohbit] A book of the Old Testament Apocrypha, or deuterocanonical book in Catholic Bibles; named after its hero, Tobit, written perhaps c.3rd–2nd-c BC by an unknown author. This popular legend is set in 8th-c BC Nineveh, from where Tobit's son (Tobias) is sent to Media, accompanied by the angel Raphael, to reclaim money deposited there by his father. He also learns magic formulas to heal his father's blindness and to exorcize a demon from his future wife, Sarah. The characters exemplify aspects of Jewish piety.

tobogganing *bobsledding*

Tobruk or **Tubruq** [tubruk] 32°06N 23°56E, pop (2000e) 142 000. Seaport in Darnah province, N Libya, on the Mediterranean coastline; occupied by the Italians, 1911; important battle site in World War 2; taken by Australians (Jan 1941), then changed hands several times until finally taken by the British (late 1942); naval ship repair.

Toby jug A pottery jug in the form of a seated figure, usually a stout man smoking a pipe and wearing a tricorn hat which forms the pouring lip. Such jugs seem to have been introduced in N Staffordshire c.1770. Makers included Ralph Wood (1748–95) and Enoch Wood (1759–1840).

Toc H A Christian fellowship founded in 1915 as a club for British soldiers serving in Belgium. Its name derives from its location in Talbot House (named after Lt Gilbert Talbot (1891–1915)), the initials of which were 'pronounced' by army signallers as 'Toc H'. The club is non-sectarian, and now engages in a wide range of social work in the English-speaking world.

Tocharian or **Tokharian** An extinct Indo-European language, formerly spoken in the N part of Chinese Turkestan during the first millennium AD. Documents dating from the 7th-c were discovered only in the 1890s, and translated a decade later. The language was written in a syllabic script, and is largely preserved in commercial documents and Buddhist religious texts.

tocopherols A small group of compounds having antioxidant properties; α-tocopherol (vitamin E) is the most active, inhibiting rancidity in oils rich in polyunsaturated fatty acids. It is widely distributed in foods, but its highest concentrations are found in vegetable oils. In the body, it serves the same function, preserving the integrity of membranes rich in the polyunsaturated fatty acids. Vitamin E deficiency in humans is extremely rare.

Tocqueville, Alexis (Charles Henri Maurice Clérel) de [tokveel] (1805–59) Historian and political scientist, born in Verneuil, NC France. He became a lawyer (1825), and in 1831 went to the USA to report on the prison system. On his return, he published a penetrating political study, *De la Démocratie en Amerique* (1835, Democracy in America), which gave him a European reputation. The book is required reading on political science courses in the USA. He became a member of the Chamber of Deputies in 1839, and in 1849 was vice-president of the Assembly and briefly minister of foreign affairs. After Louis Napoleon's coup, he retired to his estate, where he wrote the first volume of *L'Ancien Régime et la Révolution* (1856, The Old Regime and the Revolution). He died before it could be completed.

Todai [tohdiy] The Japanese abbreviation of *Tokyo Daigaku*, Tokyo University, founded in 1877, an amalgamation of older institutions. It is Japan's leading 'national' (ie state) university. Entrance is strictly on merit, by examination. Many Todai graduates go into large companies or government ministries.

Todaiji [tohdiyjee] Buddhist shrine at Nara, Japan. Founded in 743, it contains a huge Buddha, 16 m/53 ft high, made of 450 000 kg/1 million lb of bronze, on a base 20 m/68 ft across. (The Buddha has been rebuilt.) It also houses the Shosoin, a museum of 10 000 precious objects from China, India, Persia, and Japan.

Todd, Mike, popular name of **Michael Todd**, originally **Avrom Hirsch Goldbogen** (1909–58) Showman, born in Minneapolis, Minnesota, USA. The son of a poor rabbi, he made his first fortune at 14 in sales promotion. In 1927 he went to Hollywood, staged a real 'Flame Dance' spectacle at the Chicago World Fair in 1933, and produced plays, musical comedies, and films, including a jazz version of Gilbert and Sullivan, called *The Hot Mikado* (1939), and an up-dated *Hamlet* (1945). He sponsored the three-dimensional TODD-AO wide-screen process with his film *Around the World in Eighty Days* (1956, Oscar). He married the film actress Elizabeth Taylor in 1957, but was killed in an aircrash the following year.

tog A unit for measuring the 'warmth' rating in bedding textiles. The tog rating is a measure of thermal resistance: the higher the value, the better its performance.

Togliatti *Tolyatti*

Togo, Heihachiro, Koshaku (Marquess) [tohgoh] (1847–1934) Japanese admiral, born in Kagoshima, S Japan. He trained at Greenwich, served against China (1894), and as commander during the war with Russia (1904–5), bombarded Port Arthur and defeated the Russian fleet at Tsushima (1905). He was ennobled in 1907.

Togo *p.1537*

Tojo, Hideki [tohjoh] (1885–1948) Japanese general, statesman, and prime minister (1941–4), born in Tokyo, Japan. He attended military college, became military attaché in Germany (1919), served in Manchuria as chief-of-staff (1937–40), and during World War 2 was minister of war (1940–1) and premier. Convinced Japan must fight the USA, he planned the war strategy originating with the attack on Pearl Harbor, seeing Japan as a liberating force in Asia against Western domination. Arrested in 1945, he attempted to commit suicide, but was hanged as a war criminal.

tokamak [tokamak] A machine used in nuclear fusion research. A helical system of magnetic fields confines the plasma of reactive charged particles in a hollow doughnut-ring-shaped chamber, where it is then heated by passing an electric current

Togo

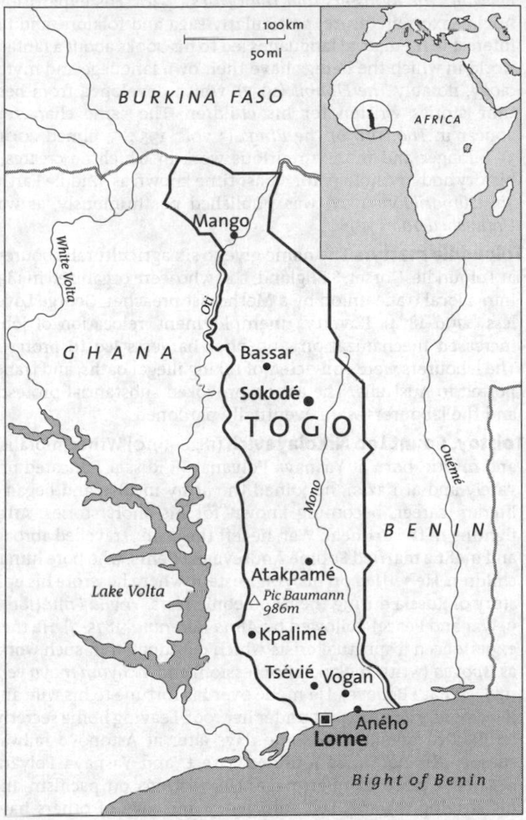

□ International Airport

[tohgoh], official name **Republic of Togo**, Fr **République Togolaise**
Local name République Togolaise (French)
Timezone GMT
Area 56 790 km^2/21 921 sq mi
Population total (2002e) 5 286 000
Status Republic
Date of independence 1960
Capital Lomé
Languages French (official), local languages (Ewe, mostly in S, 47%), Hamitic people in N, mostly Voltaic speaking)
Ethnic groups Ewe (35%), Kabyè (22%), Mina (6%), with c.34 other ethnic groups, European and Syrian-Lebanese minorities
Religions Traditional animist beliefs (50%), Christian (35%), Muslim (10%)
Physical features Located in W Africa; land rises from the lagoon coast of the Gulf of Guinea, past low-lying plains to the Atakora Mts running NE–SW in the N; highest peak, Pic Baumann, 986 m/3235 ft; flat plains in NW; main rivers, Oti, Mono.
Climate Tropical, high temperatures and humidity; wet seasons (Mar–Jul, Oct–Nov); single rainy season in N (Jul–Sep); average annual temperature 27°C (Jan), 24°C (Jul) in Lomé; average annual rainfall 875 mm/34 in; dry Saharan Harmattan blows from NE (Oct–Apr).
Currency 1 CFA Franc (CFAFr) = 100 centimes.
Economy Largely agricultural economy; coffee, cocoa, cotton, cassava, maize, rice, timber; phosphates, bauxite, limestone, iron ore, marble; cement, steel, oil refining, food processing, crafts, textiles, beverages.
GDP (2002e) $7·594 bn, per capita $1400
Human Development Index (2002) 0·493
History Formerly part of the Kingdom of Togoland; German protectorate, 1884–1914; mandate of the League of Nations in 1922, divided between France (French Togo) and Britain (part of British Gold Coast); trusteeships of the United Nations, 1946; French Togo became an autonomous republic within the French Union, 1956; British Togoland voted to join the Gold Coast (Ghana), 1957; independence, 1960; military coups in 1963, 1967; return to civilian rule, 1980; National Conference, 1990, elected an interim Supreme Republican Council to supervise parliamentary elections in 1992; now governed by a president, prime minister, and 81-member National Assembly, elected for five years.
Head of State
1960–3 Sylvanus Olympio
1963–7 Nicolas Grunitzky
1967– Gnassingbé Eyadéma
Head of Government
1991–4 Joseph Kokou Koffigoh
1994–6 Edem Kodjo
1996–9 Kwasi Klutse
1999–2000 Koffi Eugene Adoboli
2000–2 Messan Agbeyome Kodjo
2002– Koffi Sama

through it, and additional methods using radio-frequency fields and ion beams, to temperatures in excess of 10^8°C.

tokay gecko [tohkay gekoh] A large gecko (*Gekko gekko*) (length, almost 30 cm/12 in), native to India and SE Asia; mottled coloration; nocturnal; eats insects and small vertebrates; common in houses; male calls 'gekk-ho' loudly (all geckos named after this call); also known as **common gecko**.

Tokelau [tohkelow], formerly **Union Islands** 8–10°S 171–173°W; pop (2000e) 1000; area 10·1 sq km/3·9 sq mi. Island territory under New Zealand administration, consisting of three small atolls (Atafu, Nukunonu, Fakaofo) in the S Pacific Ocean, c.3500 km/2200 mi N of New Zealand; chief settlement, Nukunonu; timezone GMT −11; ethnic group, Polynesian; chief languages, Tokelauan, English; inhabitants are citizens of New Zealand; Western Samoa and New Zealand currencies in use; each atoll consists of low-lying, scrub-covered, reef-bound islets encircling a lagoon; hot and humid climate, tempered by trade winds; British protectorate in 1889; annexed in 1916, and included with the Gilbert and Ellice Islands Colony; returned to separate status in 1925, under administrative control of New Zealand, but substantially self-governing at local level; copra, coconuts, breadfruit, pawpaw, bananas, pigs, fowl; principal revenue earners are copra, stamps, souvenir coins, and handicrafts.

token economy A system whereby residents or members of an institution (eg psychiatric hospital, school, custody centre) can earn *tokens* in exchange for socially approved or co-operative behaviour. They then use the tokens to 'buy' chosen goods or privileges.

token ring A form of computer local area network, developed by IBM and using a ring topology, in which a token is passed around the computers on the ring. If the token is free then a computer may attach a message to the token and transmit it. If the token is not free then the computer must wait until the token comes round again.

Tokharian *Tocharian*

tokonama [tokonahma] A Japanese alcove, in Japanese-style houses the place for scroll paintings, flower arrangements, and art objects, especially at New Year. At home or in a restaurant the most honoured place for the guest is next to the tokonama.

Tok Pisin [tok pizhin] An English-based pidgin, spoken by c.750 000 people in Papua New Guinea, and heavily influenced by local Papuan languages. It is now spoken by some as a mother-tongue, and has thus become a creole.

Tokugawa, Ieyasu [tokugahwa] (1542–1616) The third of the three great historical unifiers of Japan, after Nobunaga and Hideyoshi, a noble born in Okazaki, E Japan. Civil war followed Hideyoshi's death, and Tokugawa took power after the Battle of Sekigahara (1600), founding the Tokugawa shogunate (1603–1868). In 1605 he transferred the title to his son, thus achieving dynastic continuity while retaining effective control. He completed Edo Castle (the present Tokyo Imperial Palace) as his headquarters, and instituted an all-pervading centralized control of Japanese life, whose effects are still felt. He was buried in a sumptuous tomb at Mt Nikko, and a cult followed, with Ieyasu shrines all over Japan.

Tokugawa shogunate [tokugahwa] The last and most powerful of the Japanese shogunates (1603–1868), established by Ieyasu Tokugawa at Edo (modern Tokyo). Tokugawa power was cemented through ruthless domination of *daimyo* (noble) lands and lifestyles. Western commercial contacts were developed, important poetry and the great ukiyo-e art were produced, and there was rapid educational advance. Nevertheless, a series of diplomatic reversals after 1853, in which Japan was unable through technological backwardness to resist Western demands for trading rights led to samurai-inspired civil war from 1865, and the restoration of imperial authority in 1868.

Tokyo 35°40N 139°45E, pop (2000e) 8 184 000 (metropolitan district). Seaport capital of Japan, Kanto region, E Honshu; on N shore of Tokyo-wan bay, on R Sumida; founded as village of Edo, 12th-c; headquarters of the Tokugawa shogunate, 1603; imperial capital, 1868; severe earthquake damage, 1923; heavily bombed in World War 2; airport; railway; over 100 universities; shipbuilding, engineering, chemicals, textiles, electrical goods, vehicles, financial services, information technology; dense population and traffic congestion; Tokyo Tower (1958), National Museum of Western Art, Tokyo National Museum, Tokyo Metropolitan Art Museum, Ginza shopping district, 17th-c Imperial Palace, Meiji Shrine, Sensaii Temple, Yasukuni Shrine; Disneyland (1983), 10 km/6 mi SE.

Toledo (Spain) [tolay<u>th</u>o], Lat **Toletum** 39°50N 4°02W, pop (2000e) 61 000. Capital of Toledo province, Castilla-La Mancha, C Spain; on R Tagus, 71 km/44 mi SW of Madrid; former capital of Visigothic kingdom of Castile and of Spain; railway; tourism, metalwork, silk, artwork, confectionery; noted for its swords and knives; Moorish citadel, cathedral (13th–17th-c), El Greco's house, Churches of St Thomas and St Romanus, Santa Cruz museum; archbishop is primate of Roman Catholic province of Spain; old city is a world heritage site; Fiesta of Olivio (Apr–May), fiesta and fair (Aug).

Toledo (USA) [toleedoh] 41°39N 83°33W, pop (2000e) 313 600. Seat of Lucas Co, NW Ohio, USA; port at the mouth of the Maumee R, at the W end of L Erie; formed by the union of two settlements, 1833; involved in the 'Toledo War' (1835–6), a boundary dispute between Ohio and Michigan; railway; university (1872); vehicles, glass and fabricated metal products, machinery, oil products; trade in coal and grain; one of the country's largest rail centres; Museum of Art, Zoological Gardens, Crosby Gardens, Fort Meigs State Memorial, Bluebird Passenger Train.

tolerance In medicine, a diminishing effect when certain drugs are given continuously. Several mechanisms are responsible, which include a change in the wall of the cell membranes that bind the drug, or a change in the way the drug is degraded in the body. *Immunological tolerance* represents the inherent or acquired failure of the immune system to distinguish between self and not-self, preventing an immunological reaction to foreign protein or organ graft.

Tolkien, J(ohn) R(onald) R(euel) [tolkeen] (1892–1973) Philologist and writer, born in Bloemfontein, EC South Africa. He studied in Birmingham and at Oxford, where he became professor of Anglo-Saxon (1925–45) and Merton professor of English language and literature (1945–59). His scholarly works include *Beowulf: The Monsters and the Critics* (1936). His expertise in Anglo-Saxon literature, particularly saga and folklore, and his interest in mediaeval languages led to his books about a fantasy world in which the beings have their own language and mythology, notably *The Hobbit* (1937), which developed from bedtime stories written for his children. The same characters appear in *The Lord of the Rings* (3 vols, 1954–5, filmed 2001–3), a longer and more ambitious work in which he creates a history and mythology for a past time known as 'Middle Earth'. *The Silmarillion* (1977) was published posthumously, as was *Unfinished Tales* (1980).

Tolpuddle martyrs The name give to six agricultural labourers at Tolpuddle, Dorset, S England, UK, who were organized in 1833 into a local trade union by a Methodist preacher, George Loveless (1796–1874). Poverty, unemployment, relocation of jobs, increased mechanization, and poor harvests led to protests. The labourers were convicted of taking illegal oaths, and transported to Australia. The action provoked substantial protests, and the labourers were eventually pardoned.

Tolstoy, Count Leo Nikolayevich (1828–1910) Writer, moralist, and mystic, born at Yasnaya Polyana, SE Russia. Educated privately and at Kazan, he joined the army in 1851, and began a literary career, becoming known for his short stories. After fighting in the Crimean War, he left the army, travelled abroad, and in 1862 married Sophie Andreyevna Behrs, who bore him 13 children. He settled on his Volga estate, where he wrote his epic story of Russia during the Napoleonic Wars, *Voyna i mir* (1865–9, War and Peace), followed by *Anna Karenina* (1875–7). He then experienced a spiritual crisis which culminated in such works as *Ispoved* (written 1879, A Confession) and *V chyom moya vera* (1883, What I Believe). He made over his fortune to his wife and lived poorly as a peasant under her roof. Leaving home secretly, he died of pneumonia some days later at Astopovo railway station. His doctrines founded a sect, and Yasnaya Polyana became a place of pilgrimage. His writings on pacifism and his striving towards self-sufficiency and love of others have attracted adherents (including Gandhi) beyond Russia itself, and he remained a formative influence on pacifist movements in the 20th-c.

Toltecs [tolteks] A people (or peoples) who controlled most of C Mexico between AD c.900 and AD 1150; the last such dominant culture prior to the Aztecs. Their capital was at Tula, 80 km/50 mi N of Mexico City. The most impressive Toltec ruins are at Chichen Itzá in Yucatán, where a branch of the culture survived beyond the fall of its C Mexican hegemony.

Toluca or **Toluca de Lerdo** [tolooka] 19°17N 99°39W, pop (2000e) 587 000. Capital of México state, C Mexico, 66 km/41 mi W of Mexico City; altitude 2675 m/8776 ft; founded, 1535; university (1956); textiles, pottery, food processing; Churches of Tercer Orden and Vera Cruz, Convent of Carmen, Museo de Bellas Artes, Palacio de Gobierno, Museo del Arte Popular.

toluene [tolyooeen] $C_6H_5CH_3$, IUPAC **methylbenzene**, boiling point 111°C. A colourless liquid with a characteristic odour, widely used as an organic solvent, being substantially less toxic than benzene. It is obtained from coal tar, and is the starting point for many organic syntheses.

Tolyatti or **Togliatti** [tolyatee], formerly **Stavropol** (to 1964) 53°32N 49°24E, pop (2000e) 650 000. Town in Samarskaya oblast, Russia, on the Samara reservoir; founded, 1738; relocated in the mid-1950s when it was flooded by the reservoir of the nearby hydroelectric power plant; rail terminus; synthetic rubber, fertilizers, machinery, foodstuffs.

Tomar [tumah(r)] 39°36N 8°25W, pop (2000e) 13 800. Town in Santarém district, C Portugal, on R Nabão; railway; textiles, paper, cork, distilling; Convent of Christ, a world heritage site; Church of São João Baptista; festival of the Tabuleiros (Jul, even-numbered years).

tomatillo An annual native to tropical America (*Physalis ixocarpa*); flowers bright yellow with dark basal spots; berry 5 cm/2 in, yellow to purple, often bursting through the bladdery calyx. It is a locally important food crop. (Family: Solanaceae.)

tomato A bushy annual (*Lycopersicon esculentum*) native to Pacific South America, but now cultivated on a commercial scale throughout the world; leaves pinnate with toothed or lobed leaflets; flowers in short sprays (*trusses*), yellow, with five reflexed petals; berry bright red, fleshy, edible; originally called **love apple** and regarded as an aphrodisiac. The plants are resistant to pests such as greenfly, probably as a result of naturally produced chemicals in the sap. (Family: Solanaceae.)

Tombaugh, Clyde W(illiam) [tombow] (1906–97) Astronomer, born in Streator, Illinois, USA. Too poor to attend college, he built his own 9-in (23 cm) telescope, and became an assistant at the Lowell Observatory, Arizona, where he discovered Pluto (1930) and galactic star clusters. He became astronomer at the Aberdeen Ballistics Laboratories in New Mexico, and taught at New Mexico State University (from 1961).

tombolo [tombohloh] *spit*

Tommy gun *submachine-gun; Thompson, John T*

tomography [tohmografee] A technique using X-rays or ultrasound to produce an image of structures in the body.

Tompion, Thomas (c.1639–1713) Clockmaker, born in Northill, Bedfordshire, SC England, UK, acknowledged as the greatest English maker. He was admitted to the London Clockmakers' Company in 1671, and became Master of the Company in 1703. In 1676 he was appointed clockmaker to the newly-opened Royal Observatory. His craftsmanship and scientific knowledge enabled him to make watches, table clocks, and long-case clocks with greatly improved time-keeping. He made one of the first English watches equipped with a balance spring (1675), and patented the cylinder escapement (1695).

Tomsk 56°30N 85°05E, pop (2000e) 501 000. River-port capital of Tomskaya oblast, WC Siberian Russia, on R Tom; founded, 1604; major Siberian trade centre until bypassed by the Trans-Siberian railway in the 1890s; airfield; railway; university (1888); machinery, metalworking, chemicals, pharmaceuticals.

Tom Thumb *Stratton, Charles*

tomtit *bluetit; great tit*

tom-tom A cylindrical, double-headed, high-pitched drum, played with sticks in sets of two or more in Western dance bands and jazz groups.

tonality The property of music which is written 'in a key', ie with a particular pitch as a point of aural reference (usually firmly established at the beginning and end) towards which other key centres gravitate. The theoretical corner-stones of tonality are the diatonic major and minor scales, in which pitches are related to a **tonic**, or key note, so that the intervals between any two degrees of the scale remain the same whichever note serves as the tonic. Tonality admits only two modes (major and minor), but each of these may be expressed in 12 possible keys, related to each other in a kind of hierarchical system based on the number of diatonic notes they have in common. Tonality gradually replaced modality in the 16th–17th-c, and served as the main structural basis for musical work of the next 250 years. It became threatened in the late 19th-c when the level of chromaticism (ie the use of notes foreign to the diatonic scale) began to weaken the aural perception of a tonic, and in the 20th-c several alternatives to tonality were proposed.

Tone, (Theobald) Wolfe (1763–98) Irish nationalist, born in Dublin, Ireland. A Protestant, he studied at Dublin, was called to the bar in 1789, acted as secretary of the Catholic Committee, and helped to organize the Society of United Irishmen (most of whose members were Protestants), who aimed for political freedom for Ireland and the end of British rule. Tone had to flee to the USA and to France (1795). He induced France to invade Ireland on two occasions, and was captured during the second expedition. He was tried in Dublin and condemned to be hanged, but committed suicide.

tone In music, **1** the interval (equal to two semitones) between, for example, the first two notes of a diatonic scale, or *doh* and *ray* in tonic sol-fa.
2 The timbre of a voice or instrument.
3 US usage for *note* (pitch) in such contexts as '12-tone music', 'tone cluster', and 'tone row'.

tone cluster *note-cluster; tone 3*

tone language A language in which the pitch level (**tone**) carried by a word is an essential signal of its meaning. In one variety of Chinese, for example, the word *ma* means 'mother' with a level tone, and 'horse' with a falling-rising tone.

tone poem *symphonic poem*

tong *triad*

Tonga *p.1540*

Tongariro [tonggareeroo] 39°08S 175°42E; area 765 sq km/295 sq mi. Active volcano rising to 1968 m/6457 ft in Tongariro national park in CSW North Island, New Zealand; park also contains the active volcanoes of Ruapehu and Ngauruhoe; winter skiing resort; many historical Maori sites; park established in 1887.

Tongeren [tongeren], Fr **Tongres** 50°47N 5°28E, pop (2000e) 29 900. Rural market town in S Limburg province, E Belgium, on R Jeker; oldest town in Belgium, founded 1st-c AD; basilica of Our Lady.

Tongres [tõgr] *Tongeren*

tongue A highly mobile, muscular structure vital for the digestive functions of chewing, taste, and swallowing. In humans it is also important in speech, being essential for the production of all vowels and most consonants. It consists of a free front part within the mouth (horizontal at rest), containing numerous taste buds, and a more fixed back part in the oropharynx, which has accumulations of lymphoid tissue associated with it (the *lingual tonsil*). The two parts are separated by a V-shaped furrow on the upper surface, with its apex directed backwards. A pit at the apex marks the site of origin of the thyroglossal duct (which in the embryo gives rise to the thyroid gland). The upper surface (*dorsum*) of the front part is covered with various types of *papillae*, most of which are studded with taste buds. The mucous membrane covering the tongue is continuous with that of the floor of the mouth and the oropharynx. The muscles of the tongue are grouped into those which change its shape (the *intrinsic muscles*) and those which change its position within the mouth (the *extrinsic muscles*).

tongue worm A simple, worm-like arthropod that lives as an internal parasite in the lungs and nasal passages of reptiles, birds, and mammals; feeds on blood. (Subphylum: Pentastomida, c.55 species.)

tonic sol-fa A system of musical notation devised by John Curwen, who based it on the solmization system of Guido d'Arezzo, anglicizing the pitch names to *doh, ray, me, fah, soh, la, te*. These could be abbreviated to their initial letters, and furnished with other signs to indicate note-lengths, rests, and octave transposition. An ability to read the notation requires training in sol-fa, which is gained through singing exercises in the schoolroom with the help of a scale-chart, or 'modulator'.

toning Chemically converting a black-and-white photograph to another colour. Examples include changing the black metallic silver of the image to silver sulphide for sepia tones, or to iron or copper compounds for blue or red-brown respectively. A wide range of other hues can be obtained by bleaching the silver image and redeveloping with colour couplers.

Tonkin or **Tongking, Gulf of** [tongkin] Gulf in Indo-China, situated E of Vietnam and W of Hainan I, China; an inlet of the South China Sea.

Tonkin Gulf Resolution (1964) A resolution adopted by the US Congress after alleged attacks by North Vietnamese torpedo boats on US destroyers in the Gulf of Tonkin. It empowered the president to take 'all necessary steps, including the use of armed force' to assist a member of the Southeast Asia Treaty Organization seeking aid 'in defense of its freedom'. It became

Tonga

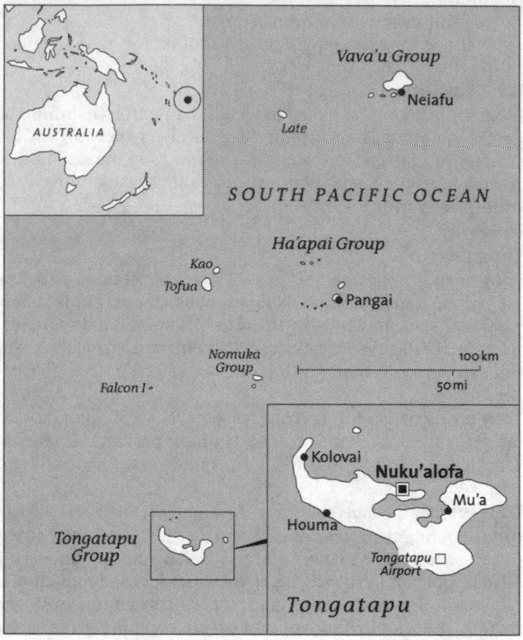

official name **Kingdom of Tonga**, Tongan **Pule'anga Fakatu'i 'o Tonga**, formerly **Friendly Islands**

Local name Tonga

Timezone GMT +13

Area 646 km²/249 sq mi

Population total (2002e) 101 000

Status Independent kingdom within the Commonwealth

Date of independence 1970

Capital Nuku'alofa

Languages Tongan and English (official)

Ethnic groups Tongan (98%), other Polynesian, European minorities

Religions Christian (Free Wesleyan Methodists 47%, Roman Catholic 14%, Mormon 9%, Anglican minorities)

Physical features Island group in the SW Pacific Ocean, 2250 km/1400 mi NE of New Zealand; consists of 169 islands, 36 inhabited, divided into three main groups, Ha'apai, Tongatapu, and Vava'u; Tongatapu, largest island, inhabited by two-thirds of the population; W islands mainly volcanic, some still active; highest point, extinct volcano of Kao, 1014 m/3327 ft.

Climate Semi-tropical; average annual temperature 26°C (Jan), 21°C (Jul) in Nuku'alofa; average annual rainfall 1750 mm/69 in; occasional hurricanes in summer months.

Currency 1 Pa'anga/Tongan Dollar (T$) = 100 seniti

Economy Largely based on agriculture; copra, coconuts, bananas, watermelons, yams, taro, cassava, groundnuts, rice, maize, tobacco, sugar cane; tourism and cottage handicrafts are small but growing industries.

GDP (2001e) $236 mn, per capita $2200

History Early settlers were Polynesians; visited by Dutch, early 17th-c; visited by the British explorer, James Cook, 1773; Methodist missionaries converted most of population to Christianity during early 19th-c; Chief Taufa'ahau united the islands and declared himself the first Monarch of Tonga, 1845; became a British protectorate, 1900, under its own monarchy; independence, 1970; governed by a Sovereign, a Privy Council, and a unicameral Legislative Assembly of Cabinet members, nobles, and elected people's representatives.

Head of State (Monarch)
1918–65 Salote Tupou III
1965– Taufa'ahau Tupou IV

Head of Government (Prime Minister)
1970–91 Fatafehi Tu'ipelehake
1991–2000 Baron Vaea
2000– Ulukalala Lavaka Ata

the legal underpinning for the US position during the Vietnam War.

Tonlé Sap [tonlay sap], Eng **Great Lake** Freshwater lake in WC Cambodia, in a depression on the Cambodian Plain, where it acts as a natural flood reservoir; area 2850 sq km/1100 sq mi during the dry season; linked to the Mekong R by the Tonlé Sap R, confluence at Phnom Penh; seasonal reversal of the river, flowing towards the Mekong in the dry season, and away from it in the wet season; height raised by c.9 m/29 ft and area almost tripled during the wet season; important communications route; fishing.

tonnage and poundage British mediaeval customs duties: tonnage was collected on tuns of imported wine; poundage at a rate of 3d (old pence) per £ of the value of imports. From the reign of Henry V, Parliament granted the taxes for life to monarchs, with the exception of Charles I in 1625 (who collected them anyway). They were incorporated into the civil list in 1697.

tonne *kilogram*

tonsillitis Acute or chronic inflammation of the tonsils, usually due to infection with streptococci. The condition usually responds to treatment with antibiotics. Removal of the tonsils (**tonsillectomy**) is now rarely required, and only for repeated or serious infection.

tonsils Accumulations of lymphoid tissue found at the entrance to the respiratory and digestive tracts. Four such regions can be identified on each side of the body. The **palatine tonsils** (also referred to simply as 'the tonsils') are found at the sides of the entrance to the oropharynx. The **lingual tonsils** are under the epithelium of the back part of the tongue (again in the proximity of the oropharynx). The **tubal tonsils** are in the nasopharynx, associated with the opening of the auditory tube. The **pharyngeal tonsils** are situated close to the base of the skull above the auditory tube behind the nasal cavity; they are also known as the **adenoids**). The four pairs of tonsils form a protective ring of tissue whose primary function is to combat airborn infections entering the body.

tonsure The shaving of all or part of the head, to denote clerical or monastic status. It is still compulsory for certain monks and priests.

Tony An annual award for theatrical achievement in New York City; named after US actress and director Antoinette Perry (1888–1946). It recognizes several categories within plays and musicals, including acting, direction, music, choreography, and design, as well as best play, best musical, and best revival.

Tooke, John Horne [tuk], originally **John Horne** (1736–1812) Radical politician, born in London, UK. He studied at Cambridge, and became a lawyer, and in 1760 a vicar. In 1771 he formed the Constitutional Society, supporting the American colonists and parliamentary reform. His spirited opposition to an enclosure bill procured him the favour of the rich Mr Tooke of Purley in Surrey, which led to his new surname and *The Diversions of Purley* (1786), written while in prison for supporting the US cause. He was tried for high treason in 1794, acquitted, and became an MP in 1801.

tool Any implement which is used to carry out a task. Early man made the first axes by sharpening flint. Stone tools were replaced from around 4000 BC by bronze and then iron tools, which were later used to build instruments and simple machines. The Industrial Revolution saw the introduction of machine tools, and mass production of goods became a possibility. Modern tools are now available for almost any task, often powered by electricity, and varying enormously in size, from the vast grabs used in the building industry to the sensitive handling tools used in the nuclear industry. New tools have had to be developed to allow scientists to move and accurately place individual atoms. These include advanced computer graphics, virtual reality, and feedback devices so that scientists can 'see' and 'feel' the atoms.

Toole, John Kennedy (1937–69) Novelist, born in New Orleans, Louisiana, USA. His novel *A Confederacy of Dunces* (1980), published 11 years after he committed suicide, won critical acclaim, and was awarded the 1981 Pulitzer Prize. *The Neon Bible* was published in 1989.

tooth *teeth*

toothwort A parasitic perennial (*Lathraea squamaria*), native to Europe and Asia; stem white; flowers tinged dull purple, forming a 1-sided spike. It closely resembles the broomrapes, but is parasitic on roots of trees and shrubs, especially elm and hazel. (Family: Scrophulariaceae.)

Toowoomba 27°35S 151°54E, pop (2000e) 89 500. City in Queensland, Australia, 130 km/80 mi W of Brisbane; airfield; railway; university (1989); commercial centre for the rich agricultural Darling Downs area; trading in meat, wool, wheat, dairy produce; engineering, food processing, iron, clothing, agricultural machinery; Early Settlers Museum; St Matthew's Church (1859); Carnival of Flowers (Sep).

topaz An aluminium silicate mineral ($Al_2SiO_4(OH,F)_2$), occurring in acid igneous rocks, pegmatites, and veins, with a colour range including colourless, yellow, and blue. It may be used as a gemstone.

top-down processing *bottom up / top-down processing*

tope [tohp] Slender-bodied, grey shark (*Galeorhinus galeus*) common in inshore waters of the E North Atlantic; related species found around Australia; length up to c.2 m/6½ ft; feeds mainly on bottom-living fish. (Family: Carcharhinidae.)

Topeka [topeeka] 39°03N 95°40W, pop (2000e) 122 400. Capital of state in Shawnee Co, E Kansas, USA, on Kansas R; settled by anti-slavery colonists, 1854; capital, 1861; railway; university (1865); marketing and processing centre for agricultural products, particularly cattle and wheat; railway engineering; important centre for psychiatric research and therapy.

topi [tohpee] An African ox-antelope (*Damaliscus lunatus*) with a long face; lyre-shaped horns ringed with ridges; coat with large dark patches on rich chestnut-red; inhabits grassland; fastest of all hoofed mammals (over 70 kph/40 mph); also known as **bastard hartebeest**, **sassaby**, **tsessebi**, **tiang**, **tiangs damalisc**, or **korrigum**.

top minnow *killifish*

topography The study of the physical characteristics of the Earth's surface (eg relief, soils, vegetation). A topographical map portrays information such as elevation and gradient through the use of symbols and special shading to show contours and spot heights.

topology A generalization of geometry which studies the properties of shapes and space that are independent of distance. The usual map of the London Underground is an example of a topological diagram, for it shows the lines joining various stations, yet is not to scale. Topology developed very widely in the 20th-c, and can perhaps now best be described as the study of continuity. In many branches of mathematics, topological information is of the most basic kind. The topology of a space determines what kind of functions it can have defined upon it, what other spaces it might be found in, and so forth. For this reason, topology is often used in applied mathematics to explain some of the fundamental properties of matter and of dynamical systems.

tor A mound of weathered, well-jointed, resistant, bare rocks. The rock is usually crystalline, and is exposed when surrounding and overlying rocks are stripped away by agents of erosion, such as frost action and chemical weathering. Examples include the granite tors of Dartmoor, UK. Similar features in the tropics are known as **kopjes**.

Torah [tohra] (Heb 'instruction') The Jewish Law, most narrowly considered the Priestly Code found in the Pentateuch and said to have been given to Moses by God. The term was also often applied to the Pentateuch as a whole; and as the importance of the Prophets and Writings grew, it was sometimes used to describe them all as divinely revealed instructions and traditions. This written Torah was eventually supplemented in Pharisaic and rabbinic tradition by the Oral Torah, not a fixed revelation but an elucidation and application of the Written Torah by sages of various periods.

Torbay 50°28N 3°30W, pop (2001e) 129 700. Unitary authority (from 1998) in Devon, SW England, UK, formed in 1968; includes the resort towns of Torquay, Paignton, and Brixham; railway; tourism, horticulture, electronics.

Torfaen [to(r)viyn] pop (2000e) 91 500; area 126 sq km/49 sq mi. County (unitary authority from 1996) in SE Wales, UK; administrative centre, Pontypool; other chief town, Cwmbran.

Tories The British political party which emerged in 1679–80 as the group opposed to the exclusion of James, Duke of York, from succession to the throne. The name was taken from 17th-c Irish outlaws who plundered and killed English settlers. The party developed after the Glorious Revolution of 1688 as the supporters of the divine right of monarchy, and had particular support from the country squirearchy and most sections of the Anglican church. It opposed religious toleration for Catholics and Dissenters. The Tories enjoyed periods of power in the reign of Queen Anne, but the party went into decline after the Hanoverian succession, when some of its supporters became Jacobites. It is generally agreed to have revived under the younger Pitt as the leading opposition to French Revolutionary ideology in the 1790s, and Lord Liverpool became the first prime minister to acknowledge the title 'Tory' in the early 19th-c. Toryism developed into Conservatism under Peel, but survived as a nickname for the Conservatives.

torii [tohree] A Shinto gateway in Japan, the traditional arch at the entrance to the sacred grounds of Shinto shrines, generally orange-red in colour, but sometimes unpainted, giving the name of the deity. At shrines of the harvest god, or the fox deity (*Inari*), those wanting good fortune may donate torii with their names. A famous torii is found on the Inland Sea off Miyajima.

tormentil [taw(r)mentil] Any of various species of *Potentilla*, with 4-petalled, yellow flowers. (Family: Rosaceae.)

tornado A column of air rotating rapidly (up to 100 m/s, c.225 mph) around a very low pressure centre. Over the Great Plains of the USA they may develop from squall-line thunderstorms, and are common in spring and early summer. The mechanism of formation is not fully understood, but they are associated with low pressure systems, and resemble a dark funnel extending from the cloud base to the ground. Although short-lived, lasting 1–2 hours and usually only a few hundred metres in diameter, they can be very destructive in restricted areas. A tornado is also known as a **twister** in the USA.

Tornio, River, Swed **Torneälv** River in N and NE Sweden; issues from L Torneträsk in NW Sweden; flows SE and S, forming part of the Swedish–Finnish border in its lower course; enters the Gulf of Bothnia at Tornio; length 566 km/352 mi.

Toronto 43°42N 79°25W, pop (2000e) 711 100, (metropolitan area) 3 358 000. Capital of Ontario province, Canada, on N shore of L Ontario, at the mouth of the Don R; largest city in Canada; French fort, 1749; occupied by the British, 1759; settled by United Empire Loyalist migrants from the American Revolution, 1793; named York; capital of Upper Canada, 1796; city and modern name, 1834; capital of Ontario, 1867; ice-free harbour (Apr–Nov); two airports; railway; subway; two universities (1827, 1959); leading commercial and cultural centre; diverse industries, such as meat packing, petroleum and metal products, machinery, clothing, food processing, publishing, trade in coal and grain; economy hit by SARS epidemic (2003); professional teams, Blue Jays (baseball – winners of World Series in 1992), Maple Leafs (ice hockey), Argonauts (football); several theatres, ballet, Toronto Symphony Orchestra; O'Keefe Centre, home of the Canadian Opera Company; Art Gallery of Ontario, Sigmund Samuel Canadiana Gallery; Osgoode Hall (1828); old City Hall (1891–9) with 91 m/298 ft-high clocktower; Fort York (1793, restored 1934); Ontario Centennial Centre of Science and Technology; Canadian National Exhibition, Skydome; Horse Show, Dog Show (Aug–Sep), Royal Agricultural Winter Fair (Nov).

torpedo A munition of naval warfare, in essence a guided underwater missile, equipped with a motor to propel it through the water and an explosive charge fused to detonate on impact with its target. The first practical torpedo dates from the middle of the 19th-c. In modern warfare, guided torpedoes are a key anti-submarine weapon, equipped with sonar-seeking heads which identify and track underwater sounds, and computerized systems to guide them towards the source of noise.

torpedo ray *electric ray*

Torquay [taw(r)kee] 50°28N 3°30W, pop (2000e) 61 300. Resort town in Torbay unitary authority, Devon, SW England, UK; 30 km/19 mi S of Exeter; centre for recreational sailing; railway; Torr Abbey (12th-c), Kent's Cavern; regatta (Aug); football league team, Torquay United (Gulls).

torque In mechanics, the ability of a force to cause rotation. Torque equals the product of the force with the perpendicular distance between the rotation axis and the line of action of the force; symbol Γ; units Nm (newton.metre).

Torquemada, Tomás de [taw(r)kaymahtha] (1420–98) First inquisitor-general of Spain, born in Valladolid, NWC Spain. He was Dominican prior at Segovia (1452–74), and persuaded Ferdinand and Isabella to ask the pope to sanction the institution of the 'Holy Office' of the Inquisition. As grand inquisitor from 1483, he displayed great cruelty, and was responsible for an estimated 2000 burnings.

torr Unit of pressure; symbol *torr*; named after Evangelista Torricelli; defined via atmospheric pressure, a standard atmosphere having a pressure of 760 torr by definition; 1 torr equals the pressure of a column of mercury 1 mm high (to within one part in 7×10^6); 1 torr = 133·3 Pa (pascal, SI unit); still commonly used in vacuum physics.

Torrens, Lake Salt lake in SC South Australia, W of the Flinders Ranges; 240 km/150 mi long; 65 km/40 mi wide; area 5775 sq km/2229 sq mi.

Torreón [torayohn] 25°34N 103°25W, pop (2000e) 553 000. Town in Coahuila state, N Mexico, on the R Nazas; railway; cotton, wheat.

Torres Strait [torez] Channel between the Coral Sea (E) and the Arafura Sea (W), to the N of Cape York, Queensland, Australia; c.130 km/80 mi wide; discovered by Spanish explorer Luis Vaez de Torres, 1606; contains **Torres Strait Islands**, which may be remains of a land bridge linking Asia and Australia; annexed by Queensland in 19th-c; inhabited by Polynesians, Melanesians, Aborigines, pop (2000e) 6800; pearl culture, fishing; much emigration to Australia.

Torricelli, Evangelista [torichelee] (1608–47) Physicist and mathematician, born in Faenza, NEC Italy. He moved to Rome in 1627, where he devoted himself to mathematics, became Galileo's amanuensis (1641), and succeeded him as professor at the Florentine Academy. He discovered the effect of atmospheric pressure on water in a suction pump, and gave the first description of a barometer, or **Torricellian tube** (1643).

Tórshavn [tors-hown], also **Thorshavn** 62°02N 6°47W, pop (2000e) 16 300. Seaport capital of the Faeroe Is; on SE coast of Strømø I; commerce and fishing.

torsion The application of twisting force. **Torsional forces** cause shear strain. **Torsion pendulums** rely on a flat disc suspended horizontally by a wire attached centrally, so that the disc twists first one way then the other. **Torsion balances** measure forces by detecting the degree of twist.

tort A wrong (mediaeval Lat *tortum* 'wrong') which harms someone else, actionable in the civil courts of England and Wales. The usual remedies are damages and/or an injunction. In some instances, the tort may be 'waived', and the defendant required to account for profits gained through the wrong. The law of tort, as well as protecting individual rights to property damage and personal injury caused by negligence, also protects other interests, such as reputation (defamation), title to property (trespass), enjoyment to property (nuisance), and commercial interests (conspiracy). Inducing a breach of contract is also a tort, though breach of contract, another civil wrong, is not so classified. The term is also used in the USA. **Delict** is the analogous term in Scots law.

Tortelier, Paul [taw(r)telyay] (1914–90) Cellist, born in Paris, France. He studied at the Paris Conservatoire, and made his debut there in 1931. Before World War 2 he played in orchestras in Monte Carlo and Boston, then achieved worldwide recognition as one of the leading soloists on his instrument. His son **Yan Pascal Tortelier** (1947–) and daughter **Maria de la Pau Tortelier** (1950–) are highly gifted players of the violin and piano respectively.

tortoise A land-dwelling reptile of order Chelonia; feet short, round, with short claws; toes not webbed; used especially for 41 species of family Testudinidae; native to tropical and subtropical regions (except Australasia); usually vegetarian.

tortoise beetle A flattened beetle in which the sides of the body are expanded to give a tortoiseshell-like appearance; larvae feed on plants and typically conceal themselves beneath faeces and cast skins. (Order: Coleoptera. Family: Chrysomelidae.)

tortoiseshell butterfly A colourful butterfly; wings reddish with dark patches, and with blue patches on both wings or on hindwings; forelegs reduced, non-functional; eggs ribbed; caterpillars with spikes. (Order: Lepidoptera. Family: Nymphalidae.)

tortoiseshell cat A British short-haired domestic cat; mottled coat of black, dark red, and light red (with no white); difficult to produce; almost always female (males rare and sterile); also known as **calimanco** or **calico cat** or **clouded tiger**. The name (often shortened to **tortie**) is also used for other breeds with mottled markings.

torture In law, the infliction of severe physical or mental suffering, whether for punishment, intimidation, or to extract a confession for a crime. The Universal Declaration of Human Rights (1948) prohibits the use of torture, and it has been universally condemned. Since the early 19th-c, the use of torture in all European countries has been banned, but it is still widely used in many parts of the world. Modern techniques include not only the traditional methods of inflicting physical pain, but psychological and pharmacological methods, such as the suppression of the body's natural pain inhibitors. International campaigns against torture are led by Amnesty International, and there are conventions which specifically outlaw its practice and provide for sanctions to enforce these, such as the United Nations Charter to the Convention Against Torture (1984). In most developed countries, confessions from suspects which have been extracted under torture are excluded from court proceedings without considering whether or not they may be true, and they are not admissible as evidence in court.

Toruń [toroon], Ger **Thorn** 53°01N 18°35E, pop (2000e) 205 000. Industrial river port and capital of Toruń voivodship, NC Poland, on R Vistula; railway; university (1945); synthetic fibres, electronics, wool, fertilizer; founded in 1231 by the Teutonic Knights; birthplace of Copernicus; Church of St John (13th-c), palace of the bishops of Kujawy (1693), castle (13th-c), ethnographical museum, burghers' manor (15th-c); mediaeval town, a world heritage site; annual Polish theatre festival.

torus *Joint European Torus*

Torvill and Dean Figure skaters **Jayne Torvill** (1957–) and **Christopher Dean** (1958–), both from Nottingham, Nottinghamshire, C England, UK. They were world ice dance champions (1981–4) and Olympic champions (1984). Their highly acclaimed performances included an interpretation of music from Ravel's *Bolero*, and the musical, *Barnum*, which was choreographed by British actor Michael Crawford. At the height of their success, they received a record total of 136 perfect 'sixes' (the highest award a judge can give in ice-skating). They retired from competitive skating in 1984, and became professional, producing their own ice show. They returned to national and international competition when the competitions were declared open to professionals in 1993 and competed in the 1994 European Championships, where they won the gold medal, and the 1994 Winter Olympics, when they won the bronze medal.

Toscanini, Arturo [toskaneenee] (1867–1957) Conductor, born in Parma, N Italy. He studied cello at Parma and Milan, and while playing at Rio de Janeiro in 1886 was suddenly called upon to replace the conductor, presenting a triumphant performance of *Aida*. He later conducted at La Scala, Milan (1898–1908), the Metropolitan Opera House, New York (1908–15), the New York Philharmonic (1926–36), and the Bayreuth (1930–1) and Salzburg (1934–7) festivals. He also brought into being the National Broadcasting Orchestra of America (1937–53).

Tosefta or **Tosephta** [tohsefta] (Aramaic 'supplement') A large collection of rabbinic, extra-Mishnaic traditions and discussions which expand and supplement the teachings of the Mishnah, but are usually considered of lesser authority. The material is arranged topically, with headings similar to those of the Mishnah. In its present form, it was perhaps compiled AD c.4th–5th-c, but some of the traditions were much earlier.

Toshodaishi [tohshohdiyshee] Buddhist shrine at Nara, Japan. Founded in the 8th-c by Ganjin, a Chinese monk (and containing an important contemporary lacquered bust), its Golden Hall is one of the finest examples of Tang Chinese building.

total art *Gesamtkunstwerk*

totalitarianism In its modern form, a political concept first used to describe the USSR's communist regime and Italy and Germany's fascist regimes during the period between the two World Wars. It is difficult to distinguish empirically from related concepts such as authoritarianism and dictatorship, but certain common features can be identified. These relate to the use of power and the means of government employed by the leadership, which claims exclusive rights to govern, usually on behalf of the party and its ideology. Furthermore, all aspects of social, political, industrial, military, and economic life are controlled or permeated by the state apparatus. Political opposition is suppressed, and decision-making is highly centralized. It is thus the conceptual opposite of **democracy**.

Totalizator A method of placing bets at horse race or greyhound meetings, commonly known as the **Tote**. All money invested is returned to winning punters, less expenses and taxes. Totalizator betting was first tried at Newmarket and Carlisle on 2 July 1928.

total solar irradiance *solar constant*

totem A word of North American Indian origin, widely used by social anthropologists and others to describe an animal or plant to which a particular clan or tribe has a special attachment. Some Australian Aboriginal tribes, for example, have the kangaroo as a totem, others the witchetty grub. Sometimes the totem may not be eaten; sometimes it must be eaten on special ritual occasions. The totem symbolizes the group and its solidarity, as flags and other emblems do for modern Western societies. Attachment to the totem, or **totemism**, has been regarded as a key aspect of primitive religion, notably by the French sociologist Emile Durkheim in *The Elementary Forms of Religious Life* (1912).

totem pole An elaborately carved pole about 20 m/65 ft high, erected in front of houses, made by Pacific NW Coast American Indians. Totem poles depict the guardian spirits of kin groups and their leaders, and confer prestige upon their owners.

toucan A largish bird with an enormous bill, native to the New World tropics; brightly coloured; bare coloured skin around eye; long tail; inhabits woodland; eats seeds, fruit, invertebrates, and small vertebrates. (Family: Ramphastidae, 42 species.)

touch-me-not *balsam*

touch screen A form of screen on a computer display which can sense any point at which it is touched and communicate the coordinates of that point to the computer. This is used in situations where the computer can display a set of options and the operator touches the screen at the option which is to be selected.

toughness A measure of a material's resistance to the propagation of cracks. A material is tough if it is difficult to tear or shatter. Glass is brittle because of the presence of many tiny cracks, but fibre-glass is tough, since embedding glass fibres in resin prevents the spread of cracks.

Toulon [toolõ], Lat **Tilio Martius** 43°10N 5°55E, pop (2000e) 176 000. Fortified naval port and capital of Var department, SE France; on Mediterranean Sea, 70 km/43 mi SE of Marseille; most important naval port in France; major naval station in World War 1; French fleet scuttled here in 1942, to prevent German capture; railway; episcopal see; shipbuilding, oil refining, armaments, chemicals, textiles; Gothic Cathedral of Ste-Marie-Majeure (11th–12th-c), naval museum, opera house, zoo.

Toulouse [toolooz], ancient **Tolosa** 43°37N 1°27E, pop (2000e) 376 000. Capital city of Haute-Garonne department, S France; on R Garonne and Canal du Midi, 213 km/132 mi SE of Bordeaux; capital of former province of Languedoc; fourth largest city in France; road and rail junction; archbishopric; university (1229); Catholic Institute of Toulouse (1877); cultural and economic centre of S France; electronics, aircraft, armaments, textiles, chemicals; Church of St-Sernin (11th–12th-c), Gothic Church of the Jacobins (1216), cathedral (11th–17th-c), observatory, botanical gardens; known as 'the red city' because of its numerous brick buildings.

Toulouse-Lautrec (-Monfa), Henri (Marie Raymond) de [toolooz lohtrek] (1864–1901) Painter and lithographer, born in Albi, S France. Physically frail, at the age of 14 he broke both his legs, which then ceased to grow. From 1882 he studied in Paris, and in 1884 settled in Montmartre, where he painted and drew the cabaret stars, prostitutes, barmaids, clowns, and actors of that society, as in 'The Bar' (1898, Zürich) and 'At the Moulin Rouge' (1892, Chicago). He also depicted fashionable society, such as 'At the Races' (1899, Albi), and produced several portraits. His alcoholism brought a complete breakdown, forcing him into a sanatorium (1899), but he recovered to resume his hectic life. Over 600 of his works are in the Musée Lautrec at Albi.

touraco *turaco*

Touraine [tooren] Former province in C France, now occupying the department of Indre-et-Loire and part of Vienne; became part of France, 1641; known for its Huguenot silk-weaving trade; chief town, Tours.

Tour de France [toor duh frãs] The world's most gruelling bicycle race, first held in 1903. Riders have to cover approximately 4800 km/3000 mi of French countryside during a three-week period each July. About 10 million people watch the race each year.

Tourette's syndrome A rare disorder of unknown cause characterized by repetitive muscle movements and vocal outbursts. Muscular tics usually affect the face and take the form of grimacing and blinking. They are accompanied by loud vocalizations, which may include grunts and noises, or uncontrollable use of obscenities and short phrases. The tics are made worse by emotional stress and are absent during sleep. It occurs most often in boys, and typically begins around 7–8 years of age. Although not serious, the condition can be extremely disruptive to life, especially to schooling, and highly embarrassing in adults.

tourist industry The sector providing services for holiday makers. Tourism has become the major global economic activity, surpassing even the trade in oil and manufactured goods. For developed and underdeveloped countries alike, it has become a major source of foreign exchange earnings, a creator of employment, and a contributor to government revenues. In labour terms, it is probably the major source of employment in countries such as Italy, France, Spain, and the UK. In the second half of the 20th-c the emergence of specialist tour operators who organize package holidays by purchasing transport, accommodation, and related services, and selling them at a single price, brought foreign holidays within the price-range of a new and growing group of consumers. Technological advances in the airline business made long-haul holiday travel a growing sector in international tourism. An important submarket within the tourist industry caters for the business traveller who attends conferences at quality conventions and exhibition centres in virtually every city and beauty-spot in the world, offering a much higher expenditure per visit. In 2000 this market was estimated to generate over US$ 110 billion in revenue globally. For many developing countries tourism has become one of the major features of economic and social development; in countries such as India and Thailand tourism is the prime source of foreign exchange revenue. However, the benefits of tourism may be outweighed by the damage done to local communities and the environment, and the repatriation of profits by foreign investors. Increasingly, the development of **ecotourism** or **green tourism** has become linked to the concept of sustainability without degrading or depleting the resources which made development possible. 2002 was recognized by the UN as the International Year of Ecotourism.

tourmaline [toormaleen] A complex borosilicate mineral containing sodium, calcium, iron, magnesium, and other metals, found in igneous and metamorphic rocks. It forms hard, dense, prismatic crystals, and may be used as a gemstone.

Tournai [toornay], Flemish **Doornik**, ancient **Tornacum** 49°52N 5°24E, pop (2000e) 68 800. Administrative and cultural town in W Hainaut province, W Belgium, on the R Scheldt, 22 km/14 mi E of Lille; bishopric; second oldest town in Belgium, founded 275 AD; railway; cement, machinery, foodstuffs, textiles (especially carpets), tourism; cathedral (11th–12th-c, restored 19th-c) is a world heritage site.

Tourneur, Cyril [terner] (c.1575–1626) English playwright. He published several poems, but is known for his two plays, *The Revenger's Tragedy* (1607, sometimes assigned to Webster or Middleton), and *The Atheist's Tragedy* (1611).

Tours [toor], ancient **Caesarodunum** or **Turoni** 47°22N 0°40E, pop (2000e) 135 000. Industrial and commercial city, and capital of Indre-et-Loire department, WC France; between Loire and Cher Rivers, 206 km/128 mi SW of Paris; episcopal see, 3rd-c; grew up around tomb of St Martin (died in 397), becoming a place of pilgrimage and centre of healing; Huguenot silk industry in 15th–16th-c; airport; road and rail junction; university (1970); metallurgy, plastics, electronics, wine, tourism; birthplace of Balzac; cathedral (12th–16th-c), several silk museums, museum of Touraine wines, art museum.

Toussaint l'Ouverture [toosĩ loovertür], originally **François Dominique Toussaint** (1746–1803) Revolutionary leader, born a slave in Haiti (formerly St Domingue). In 1791, he joined the insurgents, and by 1797 was effective ruler of the former colony. He drove out British and Spanish expeditions, restored order, and aimed at independence. Napoleon sent a new expedition to Saint Domingue, and proclaimed the re-establishment of slavery. Toussaint was eventually arrested, and died in a French prison. His nickname comes from his bravery in once making a breach in the ranks of the enemy.

Tower Bridge The easternmost bridge on the R Thames, London, UK. The bridge can open to allow large ships in and out of the Pool of London. It was designed by Sir Horace Jones (1819–87) and Sir John Wolfe Barry (1836–1918), and opened in 1894.

Tower of London A palace-fortress started by William I as a wooden fortification in 1067 and replaced by him with one in stone (c.1077–97). Successive Norman, Plantagenet, and Tudor monarchs added to it until Edward I completed the outer wall, extending to around 7 ha/18 acres. The keep or White Tower is one of the earliest fortifications on such a scale in W Europe, begun by William I in 1078. The Armour Collection, one of the world's greatest, was started by Henry VIII and increased by Charles II. From 1300 to 1810 the Tower housed the Royal Mint, and in 1303 the crown jewels were moved there for safe keeping. From the 12th-c to the 20th-c the Tower served as a state prison. The ancient Ceremony of the Keys still takes place at the Tower every night, conducted by the Chief Yeoman Warden, the sentries, and the Tower guards.

Townes, Charles H(ard) (1915–) Physicist, born in Greenville, South Carolina, USA. He worked at Bell Telephone Laboratories, taught at Columbia University, and became professor of physics at Massachusetts Institute of Technology (1961–7) and at California, Berkeley (1967). He shared the 1964 Nobel Prize for Physics with Alexander Prokhorov and Nikolay Basov for his work on the development of the maser, and later the laser.

town gas *gas 2*

town hall clock *moschatel*

Townsend, Sue (1946–) Novelist and playwright, born in Leicester, Leicestershire, C England, UK. She made her name through a series of novels introducing the character of Adrian Mole, beginning with *The Secret Diary of Adrian Mole Aged 13¾* (1982), later books including *The Cappuccino Years* (1999). Her plays include *Bazaar and Rummage* (1982) and *The Queen and I* (1992). A novel, *Number 10*, appeared in 2003.

Townshend (of Rainham), Charles Townshend, 2nd Viscount [townzend], known as **Turnip Townshend** (1674–1738) British statesman, born in Raynham, Norfolk, E England, UK. He studied at Cambridge, succeeded his father as viscount (1687), was made secretary of state by George I (1714–16, 1721–30), and became a leading figure in the Whig ministry with his brother-in-law, Robert Walpole. After a resignation engineered by Walpole, he acquired his nickname for his interest in agricultural improvement, and his proposal to use turnips in crop rotation.

Townshend Acts (1767) Taxes imposed by the British parliament on five categories of goods imported into the American colonies, after successful colonial resistance to the Stamp Act (1765). The Townshend Taxes likewise met resistance, and four categories were repealed in 1770. The fifth, on tea, remained in effect until the Boston Tea Party. The Acts are named after the British chancellor of the exchequer, Charles Townshend (1725–67), who sponsored them.

Townsville 19°13S 146°48E, pop (2000e) 96 500. Industrial port and resort in Queensland, Australia, on Cleveland Bay; founded, 1864; largest city in tropical Australia; headquarters of the Great Barrier Reef Marine Park Authority and the Australian Institute of Marine Science; airport; railway; university (1970); army and air-force bases; copper, lead, nickel, cobalt and silver mining, food processing, engineering; trade in beef, wool, sugar; Townsville Pacific Festival (Jun); Magnetic I a tourist centre.

toxaemia / toxemia of pregnancy *eclampsia*

toxicology The study of the adverse effects of chemicals on living systems. Toxicology allows prediction of the risks likely to be associated with a particular chemical or drug. The modern science was founded in the 19th-c by French chemist Mathieu Orfila (1787–1853).

toxic shock syndrome A sudden collapse with shock and falling blood pressure, which results from toxins released into the blood stream by infection with staphylococci. A rare occurrence, it has been mainly associated with the use by women of superabsorbent tampons, the infection originating in the vagina.

toxin A poison produced by a micro-organism, which causes certain diseases or disorders. Botulinum toxin from the bacterium *Clostridium botulinum* is one of the most powerful, deadly toxins known. Toxins from *Salmonella typhi* cause typhoid fever; toxins from *Pasteurella pestis* cause bubonic plague; toxins from *Shigella dysenteriae* cause dysentery. Toxins can also be secreted by plants and animals.

toxocariasis [toksohkariyasis] Human infection with *Toxocara canis*, a roundworm carried by dogs. Infection is acquired by eating dirt contaminated with roundworm eggs. The larvae migrate around the body causing disease in a variety of organs, notably the eye leading to blindness.

toxoplasmosis [toksohplazmohsis] A disease caused by the protozoan *Toxoplasma gondi*, acquired by eating infected meat, or by contact with contaminated cat faeces. It is often harmless, but may cause serious disease in the immuno-compromized individuals, such as those with AIDS. The infection is passed to the fetus during pregnancy, resulting in abortion or congenital toxoplasmosis in the child, with blindness and brain damage.

toy dog *non-sporting dog*

Toynbee, Arnold (Joseph) [toynbee] (1889–1975) Historian, born in London, UK. He studied at Oxford, served in the Foreign Office in both World Wars, and attended the Paris peace conferences (1919 and 1946). He was professor of modern Greek and Byzantine history at London (1919–24) and director of the Royal Institute of International Affairs, London (1925–55). His major work was the multi-volume *Study of History* (1933–61).

Toynbee, Polly, popular name of **Mary Louisa Toynbee** (1946–) British journalist and broadcaster. She studied at Oxford, becoming a reporter with *The Observer* (1968–71) and editor on *The Washington Monthly* (1971–2), rejoining *The Observer* as a feature writer (1972–7). She then became a columnist on *The Guardian* (1977–88), BBC social affairs editor (1988–95), and associate editor and columnist on *The Independent* (from 1995).

Toynbee Hall The first university settlement (institutions through which universities provide support to deprived inner city communities), founded in E London in 1885. It was named after the social reformer and economist Arnold Toynbee (1852–83), who dedicated himself to improving the quality of life of the urban poor.

TPWS (Train Protection and Warning System) *train protection systems*

trabeated construction *post and lintel*

trace elements *nutrients*

tracer bullet A bullet containing a charge of chemical compound (such as phosphorus) which glows brightly as it flies through the air, indicating in darkness or through the fog of war the 'trace' of the bullet's path, and thus its efficacy in reaching the target. It can be fired by a variety of weapons from small side-arms to fighter aircraft cannons.

tracery The ornamental stone pattern work used in the upper part of a window, screen, panel, or other building element. It is usually associated with Gothic architecture, although the term was first used in 17th-c England. There are two main types: the simpler **plate tracery**, giving emphasis to the spaces in between, and the more complicated **bar tracery**, used extensively in Gothic churches. Various stylistic sub-divisions include *geometrical*, *intersecting*, *panel*, and *reticulated*.

trachea [trakeea] A tube connecting the larynx with the principal bronchi; also known as the **windpipe**. Lined by respiratory (columnar ciliated) epithelium, it has an external fibrous membrane which encloses hoops of cartilage (open at the back) that prevent the trachea from collapsing. During breathing the trachea stretches longitudinally (up to 2 cm/0·8 in). In the human adult it is 9–15 cm/3·5–6 in long. In cases of respiratory distress the trachea can be surgically opened between the cartilage rings within the lower part of the neck to provide a passage for air (**tracheostomy**).

trachoma [trakohma] An eye infection caused by the bacterium *Chlamydia trachomatis*. It is endemic in developing countries, and the world's leading preventable cause of blindness. The bacterium is passed between children and affects the eyelid, causing inflammation. Repeated infection leads to scarring, and eventually the eyelashes turn inwards, irritating and damaging the surface of the eye, and resulting in profound vision loss.

track and field *athletics*

Tractarianism *Oxford Movement*

tractor A self-propelled vehicle found on farms or similar places of work, and normally used for towing and powering various agricultural machines. Tractors do not usually have a frame or springs, but use the engine and transmission housing to provide structural rigidity, with the tyres to provide cushioning. There are two major types of tractors: the **wheel tractor** and the **tracklayer tractor**, known as a **caterpillar**. Wheel tractors are used for planting, cultivating, and harvesting crops; the spacing of the wheels enables them to be driven between rows of crops. Caterpillar tractors are driven on two endless tracks; they are used for heavy jobs such as land clearing and for work on soft or rugged land.

Tracy, Spencer (Bonadventure) (1900–67) Film actor, born in Milwaukee, Wisconsin, USA. Trained at the American Academy of Dramatic Arts, he made his Broadway debut in 1923 and his feature film debut in 1930. Initially typecast as a tough guy and gangster, he became one of Hollywood's finest actors of the 1940s and 1950s. Nominated nine times for an Oscar, he was the only actor ever to receive two consecutive awards, with *Captains Courageous* (1937) and *Boys' Town* (1938). A lifelong personal and professional association with Katharine Hepburn resulted in them co-starring in nine films, including his final performance in *Guess Who's Coming to Dinner* (1967).

trade association *employers' association*

trade cycle *business cycle*

trademark A symbol placed on an article to show that it has been made by a certain company. When the mark is registered, its unauthorized use is illegal. It is an important marketing device, aimed at creating a strong brand image for a product. In the USA, trademarks often include the sign ®, signifying that the mark has been registered.

trade rat *pack rat*

tradescantia [tradeskantia] A succulent perennial with jointed, often trailing stems, native to the New World; leaves alternate, oval, stalkless; flowers 3-petalled, often white or blue, in small terminal clusters; named after John Tradescant the Younger, botanist and gardener to Charles I of England. Several species and cultivars, especially those with variegated leaves, are grown as house plants. (Genus: *Tradescantia*, 60 species. Family: Commelinaceae.)

Trades Union Congress (TUC) A voluntary association of trade unions in the UK, founded in 1868. In 2003 there were 71 affiliated unions, representing over 6·7 million members. The role of the TUC is to develop systematic relations with the government and the Confederation of British Industry, to represent the interests of its members on national councils and commissions, and to help settle disputes between members. It also has representation on the Council of ACAS (the Advisory, Conciliation and Arbitration Service). It meets annually in September to decide policy, and representation at the Conference is based on one delegate per 5000 members. There is a separate Scottish Trades Union Congress.

trade union An association of people, often in the same type of business, trade, or profession, who have joined together to protect their interests and improve their pay, working conditions, and security of employment; also known in the USA as a **labor union**. In the UK, the trade union movement developed in the early years of the 19th-c, growing rapidly after the repeal of the Combination Acts (declaring unions illegal) in 1824–5. The Grand National Consolidated Trade Union claimed a million members. In 1834, six Dorset farmworkers were sentenced to transportation to Australia after attempting to press for higher wages; these have become famous as the 'Tolpuddle Martyrs'. Since then, unions have played an important role in industrial relations. They have developed in all Western nations over the last 150 years. In the UK there are almost 100 such bodies, half of them supporting the Labour Party. They are often organized into branches, with local 'shop' representation in the form of a *shop steward*. Trade unions aim to achieve their objectives through collective bargaining, supported when necessary by industrial action. Many unions also have wider political objectives and seek to influence government economic and social policies through national representative organizations such as (in the UK) the Trades Union Congress. The Transport and General Workers Union (TGWU) is Britain's largest trade union, with c.1·4 million members drawn from many industries and trades. In the 1930s, the Congress of Industrial Organizations (CIO) was formed in the USA as a means of providing union membership for unskilled workers, such as in the steel and automobile industries. It merged with the American Federation of Labor in 1955.

trade winds Winds blowing from areas of high pressure, centred on the Tropics of Cancer (23·5°N) and Capricorn (23·5°S), towards the Intertropical Convergence Zone at the Equator. In the N hemisphere the trade winds blow from the NE, whereas in the S hemisphere they blow from the SE. The winds blow stronger over the oceans than over land.

traditional Chinese medicine (TCM) A system of medicine based on Taoist principles and texts, dating back more than 2000 years. It views health as a state in which the mind, body, and spirit are in harmony, and there is a perfect balance of yin and yang energy. Disease is due to an imbalance of energy, blockage of energy flow, and the influence of internal or external 'perverse energies', which are described according to the climatic conditions that they resemble (eg wind, heat, and damp). Diagnosis is based on a detailed history and clinical examination which emphasizes close inspection of the tongue, and feeling the varied qualities of the pulses at different sites in the body. Treatment is given using various techniques such as acupuncture, moxibustion, shiatsu, herbal remedies, and dietary advice.

traditional dance Dances which are handed on from generation to generation and are based on local customs and practices. **Ceremonial dances** are found in many countries, and are performed at particular times of the year and in a performer/audience context; **social dances** are performed at any time of the year, and are participatory and recreational in context. In England, for example, the main forms of ceremonial dance are *morris* and *sword*, though *hobby horse* and *horn dances* also exist. Regional differences are evident, but all involve visits from one place to another with the purpose of bringing good luck, and contain some kind of disguise which should not be broken. The origins are uncertain, but similarities with other rituals can be traced worldwide and back to pre-Christian times. Social forms are *country dancing* and *step dancing*. The dances of 16th-c country folk are generally seen as the first examples of this informal and neighbourly dance style. Lines, circles, and square sets are common patterns, and the steps are based on simple walking and skipping. Cecil Sharp was the most influential figure in the revival of interest in traditional dances at the beginning of the 20th-c and in the establishment of the English Folk Dance and Song Society. In Scotland, the main form is social dancing, but with the elegance of the French court. The indigenous dance is the reel. Country dances progress in two long lines, in male/female couples. There are also square dances such as the quadrille, and circle dances such as the Circassian circle. The dances take place to traditional tunes, formerly played on the fiddle, and now also on the accordion. They are promoted by the Royal Scottish Country Dance Society. In Ireland, early forms of traditional dance share the European history of country and court dance. Jigs and reels are typical, resembling English and Scottish stepping. The competitive high stepping form is a creation of the 20th-c. Arms are held stiffly to the sides; the body is erect; there is rapid, complex rhythmic use of the feet; and the knees are sharply lifted. This style achieved world-wide popularity in the mid-1990s through the show *Riverdance*.

Trafalgar, Battle of (21 Oct 1805) The most famous naval engagement of the Napoleonic Wars, which destroyed Napoleon's hopes of invading England and established British naval supremacy for a century. Fought off Cape Trafalgar, Spain, between the British and Franco-Spanish fleets, the British triumph was marred by the death of Nelson at the moment of victory.

traffic lights A set of coloured lights at a road junction whose function is to control the flow of traffic on main-road intersections. First used in the USA in 1914, traffic lights, suspended above or set alongside roads, have been adopted universally and follow a uniform pattern, using combinations of green, amber, and red (with countries showing some variation in the timing of amber). Today, the signalling systems are for the most part computerized. The fixed-time system is most widely used, and is set to favour traffic on main roads. A system that sets the cycle lengths of the signal changes can be operated to vary during the day to accommodate changing traffic patterns. Advanced traffic control systems operate on a continuously varying signal plan devised by a computer in the light of closely monitored traffic conditions relayed from traffic detectors on or under the street.

tragedy In Western tradition, a play which presents the occurrence and the effects of a great misfortune suffered by an individual, and reverberating in society. Earlier, this required a great person as protagonist, but modern writers have attempted to confer tragic status on ordinary people. The fundamental purpose of tragedy (reminding us of its origins in religious ritual) was claimed by Aristotle to be 'the awakening of pity and fear', of a sense of wonder and awe at human potential, including the potential for suffering; it makes or implies an assertion of human value in the face of a hostile universe.

Not all cultures have produced tragedy; indeed, it has only three great 'moments' in Western history – in ancient Greece, in early 17th-c England, and in later 17th-c France. Elizabethan tragedy began with very simple materials, in the 'revenge' tradition deriving from the Roman dramatist Seneca; but Marlowe's *Dr Faustus* (c.1590) already shows a man facing the heights and depths of his own nature, while Shakespeare's greatest tragedies (*Hamlet*, *Othello*, *King Lear*, *Macbeth*, 1600–6) take us through suffering and madness to the very brink of being, where the 'bare forked animal' struggles for meaning on the 'sterile promontory' of this world. In France, the tragedies of Corneille (*Le Cid*, 1636) and more especially Racine (*Andromaque*, 1667; *Phèdre*, 1677) reincarnated with their grave alexandrines the severe beauty of Greek drama. Since this time tragic vision and utterance have been complicated (some would say denied) by the mass misfortunes and partial consolations of the modern world; see the complementary arguments in Nietzche's *The Birth of Tragedy* (1872) and George Steiner's *The Death of Tragedy* (1961). But plays such as Arthur Miller's *Death of a Salesman* (1949) are tragedies for our time; and one should not overlook the tragic dimension achieved by opera (Verdi) and cinema. Some novels, such as Hardy's *The Mayor of Casterbridge* (1886) can be described as tragedies; others, such as Melville's *Moby Dick* (1851) have recognizably tragic protagonists.

tragi-comedy A form of drama which allows the mixture of tragic and comic elements. Decried by Neoclassical critics, it was defended by Dr Johnson in his *Preface to Shakespeare* (1765) as 'exhibiting the true state of sublunary nature'. Much modern drama (eg Beckett's *Waiting for Godot*, 1953 and Brendan Behan's *The Quare Fellow*, 1954) exploits ambiguous and incongruous emotions in the spirit of tragi-comedy.

tragopan A pheasant, native to SE Asia; inhabits woodland; nests in tree. (Genus: *Tragopan*, 5 species.)

Traherne, Thomas [trahern] (c.1637–74) Mystical writer, born in Hereford, Hereford and Worcester, WC England, UK. He studied at Oxford, and was ordained rector at Credenhill. The manuscripts of his *Poetical Works* (1903) and *Centuries of Meditations*

(1908) were discovered by chance on a London street bookstall in 1896.

train protection systems Systems of railway signalling designed to prevent train collisions and derailments. The most basic form is the **Automatic Warning System (AWS)**, which works by sounding a warning in the driver's cab if the line ahead is not clear. If the driver fails to acknowledge the warning by pressing a button, the brakes are automatically applied. Its effectiveness is not foolproof because frequent sounding can lead to driver desensitization, and the warning can be easily overriden. AWS is now supplemented by a **Driver Reminder Appliance (DRA)**, a device set by the driver whenever the train stops at a red signal. The train will not restart until the device is reset, which should remind the driver to check that the signal has cleared. Electronic technology has brought the development of more sophisticated systems, known collectively as **Automatic Train Protection (ATP)**. These systems monitor the speed of the train and calculate a safe speed based on a number of factors. If this calculated speed, indicated on the cab display, is exceeded by more than a set margin, automatic braking is applied until the train slows down sufficiently. The driver cannot override the system, and thus the system should eliminate most 'signals passed at danger' (SPADs), which have been factors in several collisions. The **Train Protection and Warning System (TPWS)** incorporates the existing AWS but provides a higher degree of protection. The system can initiate emergency braking if a train is either about to pass a red signal or has exceeded the maximum permitted speed. The driver cannot override the system. TPWS has been designed to enable simple installation to existing track and trains; however, it does not monitor the train continuously, and thus gives less complete protection than ATP. In the UK, AWS has been standard for many years; DRA fitment was completed at the end of 1998; ATP was 80% operational by the end of 1999, but full implementation to European standards is not expected until 2010; TPWS became fully operational in 2003. Other systems include **Automatic Train Control (ATC)**, used for example on the Docklands Light Railway in London, which dispenses with the need for a driver; 'trainstop' systems, such as that used on the London Underground, which automatically stop a train when it passes a red signal; and **Transmission Based Signalling (TBS)**, a new generation of signalling which uses radio transmission and in-cab signalling display.

Trajan [trayjn], in full **Marcus Ulpius Trajanus** (c.53–117) Roman emperor (98–117), selected as successor by the aged Nerva for his military skills. He was the first emperor after Augustus to expand the Roman empire significantly, adding Dacia and Arabia (AD 106). The wealth from Dacia's gold mines enabled him to launch an ambitious building programme, especially in Rome, where he constructed a new forum, library, and aqueduct. A sensitive but firm ruler, he was one of Rome's most popular emperors.

Tralee [tralee], Ir **Tráighlí** 52°16N 9°42W, pop (2000e) 18 000. Capital of Kerry county, Munster, SW Ireland; NE of Slieve Mish Mts; connected to the Atlantic Ocean by a canal; railway; technical college; agricultural trade, bacon-curing, tourism; St Patrick's Week festival (Mar); Rose of Tralee festival (Sep), with street dancing and singing.

tram A passenger vehicle normally propelled by an electric motor fed from overhead lines, designed to run on rails set into public roads; in the USA known as a **trolley car**. The tram is still a major means of transport in several US and European cities (eg New Orleans, Cologne); in the UK there is a tourist service in Blackpool, and in the 1990s new services began in Manchester and Sheffield. In general, the improvement of road surfaces through the abandonment of cobbles and the improvement of self contained motor transport has meant that the tram has been unable to compete without subsidy.

trampolining The art of performing acrobatics on a sprung canvas sheet stretched across a frame, first used at the turn of the 20th-c as a circus attraction. The name derives from Spanish *trampolin* 'springboard'. It was developed into a sport following the design of a prototype modern trampoline by American diving and tumbling champion George Nissen in 1936. It became an Olympic sport in Sydney in 2000.

tranquillizer *benzodiazepines*

transactional analysis A method of psychotherapy in which the parent, child, or adult component of any interaction is analysed in addition to considering the unconscious pattern of a patient's actions. The purpose is to unravel emotional problems and to highlight the specific strategies an individual uses in social communication. The technique was developed by psychiatrist Eric Berne (1910–70) from the late-1940s, in his view as a way of more quickly attaining treatment objectives compared with traditional psychoanalysis. It has become a significant component of professional and managerial training in recent decades.

transactionalism In social anthropology, the theory that social relationships are negotiated by participants and maintained by the exchange of goods, services, and information. Transactionalism is opposed to a *structural* approach, which views the social system as an organic entity that transcends and outlives individual action.

transaction processing A form of computer processing of data, through the use of a terminal, in which the operation is carried out as a sequence of transactions. At each transaction the computer poses a question via the terminal, and the terminal operator gives a response. For example, to book an airline seat the computer asks which flight, then which class, then whether smoking or non-smoking, etc. The terminal operator responds. At the end of the questions the seat to be booked has been specified and a ticket can be issued.

Transalpine Gaul *Gaul*

Transcaucasia Region extending S from the Greater Caucasus to the Turkish and Iranian frontiers, between the Black Sea (W) and the Caspian Sea (E); comprises the republics of Georgia, Azerbaijan, and Armenia, which in 1922–36 formed the Transcaucasian SFSR; chief towns include Kutaisi, Batumi, Tbilisi, Gyandzha, Baku.

transcellular fluid A component of extracellular fluid, separated from the rest of the fluid by a layer of cells (eg an epithelium). Important examples are cerebrospinal fluid, the fluids inside the eye, the synovial fluid of joints, and the contents of the gastro-intestinal tract.

transcendentalism **1** In philosophy, the theory, particularly associated with Kant, that the world of experience is conditioned by and logically dependent on the organizing structure of principles and concepts common to all rational minds. **2** A religious or mystical belief in a world or state of being beyond the reach of human apprehension and experience. **3** A philosophical and literary movement in 19th-c New England as a reaction against 18th-c rationalism, led by Emerson and Thoreau. Influenced by Romanticism and German Idealism, it exalted the ideals of self-knowledge, self-reverence, and individual autonomy, and asserted the presence of the divine in nature as well as in the individual.

transcendental meditation (TM) A meditation technique taught by Maharishi Mahesh Yogi, based in part on Hindu meditation. It has been widely practised in the West since the 1960s, when he 'converted' the Beatles. Its practitioners are taught to meditate for 20 minutes twice a day as a means of reducing stress, achieving relaxation, and increasing self-understanding.

transcription (genetics) The making of a complementary RNA copy of a gene in the DNA. Transcription requires the DNA or chromatin to be in an open configuration, allowing the binding of specific proteins (**transcription factors**) to the promoter of the gene being transcribed. Transcription is carried out by enzymes known as *RNA polymerases*.

transcutaneous electrical nerve stimulation (TENS) A method of pain relief, especially for localized pain, in which a surface electrode is applied to the skin and a low-frequency pulsed electrical current is applied. The electrode may be applied over specific acupuncture points, but the method is generally less effective than acupuncture itself, though the mechanism of action is thought to be similar. TENS has also been used for obstetric analgesia and post-operative pain relief. There is no evidence for its efficacy in non-painful conditions, though it has been tried for the treatment of asthma and depression using appropriate acupuncture points.

Transdanubia, Hung **Dunántúl** Geographical region in Hungary, lying W of the R Danube and extending to the Hungarian Alps and S to the R Drava; occupies a third of Hungary; hilly and fertile region, noted for livestock and wine production.

transducer Any device which converts one form of energy into another. A microphone is an acoustic transducer, converting sound waves into electrical signals. Electromechanical transducers convert electrical signals into mechanical oscillations, as in piezo-electric ultrasound generators.

transept The part of a cruciform-planned church that projects out at right angles to the main body of the building, usually between nave and chancel.

transfer (of training) The effect of performing one task on the subsequent performance of another. Performance on the subsequent task may be improved, in comparison with a control group (**positive transfer**); or it may be inhibited (**negative transfer**). It is important to take account of unwanted transfer effects in the design of experiments involving several different treatments of the same subjects.

transference In psychiatry, the unconscious attachment of feelings originally associated with significant early figures in one's life (eg parents) to others (particularly to the psychotherapist). In psychotherapy this allows for the exploration of a patient's early difficulties which have remained unresolved. The term was coined by Freud in 1895.

transfer pricing The price charged when an article is passed from one part or department of a company to another. There are difficulties when the transfer is across national frontiers, as in the case of transnational companies, since the company may avoid taxes in a high-tax country by under-pricing exports from it and over-pricing imports to it, thus shifting profits to countries with lower tax rates.

Transfiguration An event described in the synoptic gospels when Jesus was temporarily changed in appearance on a mountain in front of his disciples Peter, James, and John, so that his clothes became 'gleaming white' (*Mark* 9.2–3) and his face 'shone' (*Luke* 9.28–9; *Matt* 17.2). The revelation of glory is described as accompanied by an appearance of Elijah and Moses, and a heavenly voice similar to that at Jesus's baptism. Feast day 6 August.

transformational grammar *generative grammar*

transformer A device, with no moving parts, which transfers an alternating current (AC) from one circuit (called the *primary winding*) to one or more other circuits (*secondary winding*) by electromagnetic induction, usually with a change in voltage. There is no electrical connection between the two circuits. It is often used for converting the high voltage from AC power supplies to the normal domestic supply voltage.

transgenic Descriptive of an artificial organism containing extra copies or foreign DNA from the same or unrelated species. Transgenic organisms are made in the laboratory by inserting the DNA into zygotes or cells using various technologies, and then allowing them to develop normally. Genetically modified crops are examples of transgenic plants. The pigs developed for human heart transplants are transgenic for specific human proteins.

transhumance The transfer of livestock, usually cattle and sheep, between winter and summer pastures. It is characteristic of some mountainous regions, where whole families may move with their flocks up to the high-altitude pastures. It may also occur in arctic regions, where livestock are moved to more northerly pastures for the summer.

transistor A solid-state device, made from a sandwich of semiconductors, usually germanium or silicon, with different electrical characteristics (p- and n-type). A p-type (positive) semiconductor is made by adding impurities such as boron or aluminium. An n-type (negative) semiconductor is made by adding arsenic or phosphorous. Transistors can be used as amplifiers or rectifiers. Small, robust, and safe (since they need low voltage), and needing little power to operate, transistors have replaced thermionic valves in television, radio, and computers, and have revolutionized the construction of electronic circuits.

transit circle *meridian circle*

transit instrument An astronomical instrument for observing the passage of a body over the meridian of the observer. The earliest was developed in 1689 by Danish astronomer Ole Roemer (1644–1710). Generally, a telescope is mounted on a fixed horizontal axis so as to sweep the meridian in a vertical plane. It is used for such purposes as correcting clocks, by recording a fixed local time (eg noon) by observation. Since the difference in time between noon at some place and noon at Greenwich is a measure of its longitude, the instrument can also be used as a means of determining longitude.

transition In genetics, a type of mutation caused by the substitution in DNA or RNA of one purine by the other, or of one pyrimidine by the other. It may be brought about by mutagens such as nitrous acid, hydroxylamine, and the base analogues.

transition elements Chemical elements in which an incomplete electron shell other than the valence level is being filled. They are all metals, and include the elements with atomic numbers 21 (scandium) to 29 (copper) and their groups. They have similar chemistries, and most show oxidation states +2 and +3 commonly. They typically form coloured, paramagnetic compounds and a large range of co-ordination compounds.

transition state In a chemical reaction, an unstable arrangement of atoms characteristic of the highest energy through which the atoms must pass during the reaction.

transit time In nutrition, the time taken for an ingested marker to move along a specified region of the gut. Whole gut transit time measures mouth to anus velocity. Velocities may also be measured separately through the small and large bowels.

Transkei [tranzkiy] Former independent black homeland in SE South Africa; between the Kei and Mtamvuna Rivers on the Indian Ocean; capital, Umtata; traditional territory of the Xhosa; self-government, 1963; granted independence by South Africa (not recognized internationally), 1976; bloodless military coup, 1987; incorporated into Eastern Cape province in the South African constitution of 1994.

translation (genetics) The making of a protein from a messenger RNA which takes place on a ribosome in the cytoplasm of the cell. Each three nucleotide bases of the mRNA represent a specific amino acid which are joined together in succession.

translation (language) The conversion of one language into another; often used specifically with reference to written texts, as opposed to the **interpretation** of spoken language. There are various types of translation: **word-for-word translation**, in which each word is found an equivalent, carrying over the grammatical and lexical features of the original, often makes little sense, because it breaks the structural rules of the target language; for example, Welsh *Mae hi yn bwrw hen wragedd a ffyn* would translate as 'Is she in rain old women and sticks'. **Literal translation** adheres to the linguistic structure of the original, but transposes it into the appropriate grammatical conventions of the target language; the above example would give 'She is raining old women and sticks'. **Free translation** translates the 'sense' of the text, relaxing the shackles of strict linguistic equivalence, and seeks an idiomatic equivalent for the Welsh expression, giving something like 'It is raining cats and dogs'.

transliteration The written representation of a word in the closest corresponding characters of a different language. The process is commonly seen at work in loan-words, as in the

Welsh *bws* from 'bus', and in the writing of proper names, as in *Tchaikovsky* and *Moscow* from Russian Cyrillic characters.

translocation In genetics, the transfer of a segment of one chromosome to another. Translocations are frequently reciprocal.

transmembrane potential *membrane potential*

transmission The system fitted to an engine that transmits the power generated by the engine to the point at which it is required. Normally this system is composed of mechanical components such as gears, shafts, clutches, and chains, but other methods using hydraulic and electrical means can also be used.

transmutation In nuclear physics, the conversion of one nuclide to another, either by natural radioactive decay or by collision with other nuclei or particles. Loosely, one element can thus be transmuted into another. Alchemy failed, since it attempted to manipulate only chemical properties, not the nucleus, which is what controls the element's type. The first artificial transmutation was achieved by Ernest Rutherford, who in 1919 turned nitrogen into oxygen.

transnational corporations Large corporate enterprises whose activities spread across a number of nations, via subsidiaries, holding companies, etc; sometimes used interchangeably with **multinational corporations**. It also implies that these firms have no obvious 'national' economy with which they are most closely associated. Hence, at times, these corporations may act in ways which appear to go against the interests of their 'home' economy, such as closing some factories as part of a global restructuring programme.

transpiration The loss of water vapour from a plant. It mainly occurs from leaves via the stomata, which partially control the process by opening and closing in response to humidity changes in the air. The process cools and prevents damage to the leaves in hot weather, and helps draw water up from the roots to other parts of the plant.

transplantation The transfer of an organ or tissue from one person to another. Unless the recipient is an identical twin, such a graft sets up an immunological reaction of variable severity which may destroy the transplanted tissue. This reaction results from the introduction of foreign protein to the recipient. It may be partially or completely controlled by the use of immunosuppressive drugs, and is less severe in closely related persons. Tissues that have been transplanted successfully (since the 1960s) are bone marrow, undertaken for leukaemia, and the kidney, liver, heart, and lungs, carried out for severe organ failure. In recent years, limbs have been transplanted successfully. Tissue for transplantation may be obtained from living donors or from suitable cadavers. The cornea in front of the eye has also been transplanted since the 1930s, but is a special case as it does not set up any immunological reaction in the host. Corneas can be stored in banks, and used to treat blindness when this results from damage to the front of the eyes, for example from cataracts.

transportation Sentence of banishment from England for those convicted of certain offences, introduced in 1597. Increasingly large numbers of English convicts were shipped to North America in the 17th-c and 18th-c as the number of crimes for which transportation could be applied was greatly expanded; but in 1788, after the US War of Independence, the inflow was stopped. As a result, the British government turned their attention to Australia, and from the first British settlement (1788) to 1820, convicts were the largest single group in the population; 162 000 convicts (137 000 males and 25 000 females) were transported to Australia from 1788 to 1868, mainly in New South Wales (1788–1840), Van Dieman's Land, (1803–52) and Western Australia (1850–68). Most of the convicts were young, poorly-educated urban-dwellers convicted of some form of theft. A number of those who arrived before 1820 became wealthy; others, especially those at Port Arthur or Norfolk I, lived and died under a savage and inhuman rule. But the typical fate of most convicts was assignment to private service, usually with a conditional pardon or ticket of leave which amounted to freedom in Australia but not permission to return to Britain.

transposing instrument A musical instrument which sounds at a higher or lower pitch than that at which its music is notated. There are various practical and historical reasons for this, the main one being to regularize the fingering of wind instruments, so that a player can change from one size (and pitch) of an instrument to another, without having to adopt a different fingering system. In the modern orchestra the main transposing instruments are as follows (sound level above/below written pitch is shown in parentheses): piccolo (one octave above), cor anglais (a perfect 5th below), clarinet in A (a minor 3rd below), clarinet in B♭ (a major 2nd below), horn in F (a perfect 5th below), trumpet in B♭ (a major 2nd below), celesta (one octave above), and double bass (one octave below).

Transputer A one-chip computer developed in the UK by Inmos Ltd, which has been designed specifically to allow parallel processing involving large numbers of Transputers working together. This technique can provide very fast, powerful computers, and systems have been designed which include more than 1000 Transputers. A special language, OCCAM, has been developed for the Transputer.

transsexual A person who has changed behaviour, physical appearance, and body (by surgery and/or the consumption of hormones) to that of the opposite sex. It is a form of gender alteration in which anatomically normal individuals realize that they are physically normal, but wish to convert to the opposite sex.

Trans-Siberian Railway *p.1550*

transubstantiation The Roman Catholic doctrine of the Eucharist (Mass), affirming the belief that the bread and wine used in the sacrament are converted into the body and blood of Christ, who is therefore truly present. The doctrine, rejected by 16th-c Reformers, was reaffirmed by the Council of Trent.

transuranic elements [tranzyur**a**nik] *actinides*

Transvaal [tranz**vahl**] Former province in South Africa; settled by the Boers after the Great Trek of 1836; independence, 1852, recognized by Britain; known as the South African Republic; annexed by Britain, 1877; Boer rebellion in 1880–1 led to restoration of the republic; annexed as a British colony, 1900; self-government, 1906; joined Union of South Africa, 1910; in the 1994 constitution, divided into Northern Province and Mpumalanga.

transverse stage An open stage in a theatre positioned in the middle of the auditorium but stretching from wall to wall, dividing the audience into two groups facing each other across the acting area.

transverse wave *wave motion*

transvestism The recurrent practice of dressing in the clothes of the opposite sex, normally for sexual excitement. It usually begins in adolescence.

Transylvania [transil**vay**nia], Hung **Erdély**, Ger **Siebenbürgen** Geographical region and province of N and C Romania, separated from Wallachia and Moldova by the Carpathian Mts; a former Hungarian principality that became part of the Austro-Hungarian Empire; incorporated into Romania, 1918; part of the region ceded to Hungary by Hitler in World War 2; chief towns, Cluj-Napoca and Brașov.

Transylvania Company An American land company organized in 1775. It bought the site of original white settlements in Kentucky from the Indians, in defiance of British policy that all lands in the W belonged to the Crown. The company collapsed during the American Revolution.

Transylvanian Alps or **Southern Carpathian Mountains**, Romanian **Carpatii Meridionali** Mountain range in C Romania; a S branch of the E European Carpathian Mts; highest peak, Negoiul (2548 m/8359 ft); includes the national park of Retezat, area 130 sq km/50 sq mi, established in 1935.

trapdoor spider A spider that lives in a silk-lined tube constructed in a burrow in the ground, closed off by a silk lid; passing insects are attacked and pulled into the tube with great

Trans-Siberian Railway

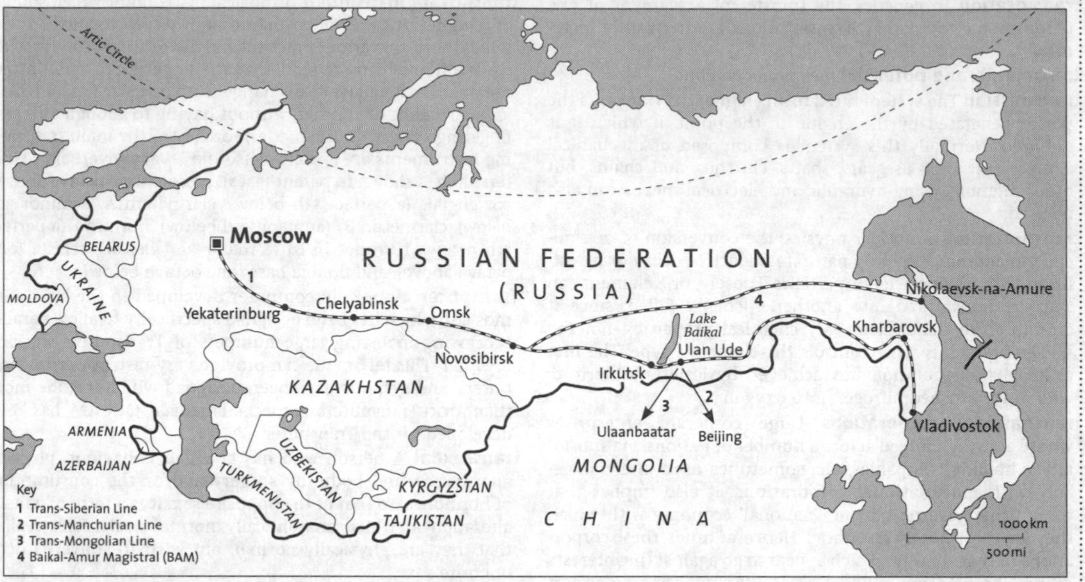

An important rail route extending across Siberia, originally between terminals at Chelyabinsk in the Urals and Vladivostok on the Pacific. It was constructed 1891–1905, with an extension around L Baykal completed in 1916. The line, which has played a major role in the development of Siberia, is now largely electrified; the journey from Moscow to Vladivostok (9311 km/5786 mi) takes 7 days. During the 1960s and 1970s a more northerly parallel line was built from N of L Baikal to Nikolaevsk-na-Amure: the Baikal–Amur Magistral (BAM).

speed; found in Africa, the Americas, and Australia. (Order: Araneae.)

trapezium rule In mathematics, an approximate method for finding the value of an integral. Regarding the integral as the area of a region between a curve and the *x*-axis, this region is divided into *n* trapezia, width *h*, each of which has area $\frac{1}{2}h(y_r + y_{r+1})$. The area of the whole region is $\frac{1}{2}h[y_0 + 2(y_1 + y_2 + ...) + y_n]$.

Trapido, Barbara (1942–) Novelist, born in Cape Town, South Africa. Disenchanted with the South African political situation, she emigrated to the UK in 1963. Her novels are influenced by the satirical wit of Shakespeare's comedies and by the dialogue of Jane Austen, and include *Brother of the More Famous Jack* (1982, Whitbread), *Noah's Ark* (1984), *Temples of Delight* (1990), *Juggling* (1994), and *The Travelling Hornplayer* (1999). The autobiographical novel *Frankie & Stankie* appeared in 2003. She now lives in Oxford.

Trappists The popular name of the Cistercians of the More Strict Observance, centred on the monastery of La Trappe, France, until 1892. The Order continues throughout the world, devoted to divine office, and noted for its austerity (eg perpetual silence, and abstention from meat, fish, and eggs).

trap shooting *clay pigeon shooting*

Trás-os-Montes [**trash ush mõtsh**] ('beyond the mountains') area 10 784 sq km/4163 sq mi. Mountain area and former province of NE Portugal, bounded N and E by Spain; population concentrated in the fertile valleys, growing grapes and fruit; sheep and goats graze on the bare upland plateaux.

Traun, Lake [trown], Ger **Traunsee** or **Gmundner See** Lake in Reutte district, Tirol, C Austria; area 24·5 km/15 mi; length 12 km/7 mi; width 3 km/1¾ mi; maximum depth 191 m/627 ft; summer resorts include Gmunden, Traunkirchen, Ebensee, Rindbach; water sports.

travelator *escalator*

traveller's tree An evergreen tree (*Ravenala madagascariensis*) somewhat resembling a palm, native to Madagascar, and widely cultivated in the tropics; leaves grow to 3 m/10 ft, in two ranks, giving a fan-like appearance. The sheathing stalks form the trunk, and collect considerable quantities of drinkable water. (Family: Strelitziaceae.)

travelling matte An image combination process in cinematography for superimposing foreground action on a separately photographed background scene by printing at the laboratory. A matte, a strip of film with opaque silhouettes of the foreground, is used to reserve this area when printing the background, and the foreground action is inserted into this space at a second printing using a complementary matte. In video special effects, a corresponding result is obtained by 'keying'.

travel sickness 1 Nausea and vomiting induced by the motion of ships, cars, and aeroplanes in some healthy individuals; also called **motion sickness**. The motion disturbs the function of the balance apparatus in the inner ear, and causes a reflex stimulation of the vomiting centre in the brain stem. Psychological factors play a part in some people.
2 A short attack of diarrhoea commonly affecting those who visit foreign countries. It sometimes arises due to food poisoning, but may be a result of ingesting unfamiliar food and water, or harmless (non-pathogenic) bacteria to which the traveller is not accustomed.

Traven, B [trayvn], pseudonym of **Albert Otto Max Frege** (?1882/90–1969) Writer of adventure stories, who claimed he was born in Chicago, Illinois, USA, but was probably born in 1882 in Zwiebodzin, W Poland (formerly Germany). He wrote *Der Shatz der Sierra Madre* (1935, The Treasure of the Sierra Madre), on which the celebrated film by John Huston is based. Little is known about his background, but he lived in Mexico during the 1930s and later. Most of his novels were first published in Germany, such as *Das Todenschiff* (1926, The Death Ship) and *Die Rebellion der Gehenklen* (1936, The Rebellion of the Hanged). He probably used several different names, including **(Benick) Traven Torsvan**, **Ret Marut**, and **Hal Groves**, under which name he died.

Travers, Ben(jamin) (1886–1980) Playwright, born in London, UK. He became famous for the farces which played in the Aldwych Theatre, London, continuously from 1922 until 1933. His later work was not so successful, although he was still writing in his 90s, and his last play, *The Bed Before Yesterday* was first produced in 1975.

travertine [travertin] A type of limestone formed by precipitation from springs or streams rich in dissolved calcium carbonate. When porous and spongy in appearance, it may be termed *calc tufa*. It is extensively mined in Tuscany, Italy, and used as a paving stone.

Travolta, John [travolta] (1954–) Film actor, born in Englewood, New Jersey, USA He made his debut in an off-Broadway production of *Rain* (1972), then joined the Broadway cast of *Grease*, and became well known for his role in the TV series *Welcome Back Koter*. International fame came with the box-office hit films *Saturday Night Fever* (1977), *Grease* (1978), and *Staying Alive* (1983). Later films include *Pulp Fiction* (1994), *Get Shorty* (1995, Golden Globe), *Michael* (1997), *Battlefield Earth* (2000), and *Basic* (2003).

trawler A vessel designed to drag a large bag-shaped net along or near the bottom of the sea to catch fish. Modern trawlers equipped with echo-sounder fish-finders and refrigeration to preserve their catch may be as big as 4000 gross tonnes.

treacle A product obtained from molasses, used to sweeten and darken cakes and puddings. During the refining process, the molasses darkens from a richly golden syrup to a black treacle, also known as **blackstrap molasses** in the USA.

treason The crime of betrayal of a state or failing to pay proper allegiance to a government or monarch. In the USA, treason is defined and limited in Article III, section (3) of the Constitution, and conviction requires the testimony of at least two witnesses or a confession in open court as well as wrongful intent and an overt act. In the UK the law on treason is governed by the Treason Act (1351), which was redefined in 1795, and comprises a large number of unlawful activities, including plotting the sovereign's death, levying war against the monarch in his or her realm (*insurrection*), insulting a monarch (*lèse-majesté*), spying, and acting on behalf of an enemy in wartime. Disloyalty is essential to the crime – the person who commits treason must owe allegiance to the Crown. This includes British subjects, but persons other than British subjects may owe this allegiance. An alien who has accepted the protection of the Crown may also commit treason. The punishment for acts of treason may either be capital punishment or prolonged imprisonment.

treasury In business and accounting, the function of managing finance, especially its provision and use. It includes the provision of capital, borrowing, the short-term deposit of surplus funds, and foreign exchange dealing. In UK government terms, the **Treasury** is the name of the department responsible for managing the nation's finances, headed by the Chancellor of the Exchequer, who is responsible to the prime minister (the First Lord of the Treasury). It operates through the central bank to manage the government's monetary policy. In the USA, it is known as the **Department of Treasury**, and elsewhere usually as the **Ministry of Finance**.

treasury bills Bills sold at a discount over a three-month period by the Bank of England on behalf of the government. The bills are issued to discount houses at below their face value, and are redeemed at face value, the difference (as a percentage) being the *discount rate*. These bills are frequently used by the government as a form of short-term borrowing.

treaty ports *Opium Wars*

Trebizond, Turkish **Trabzon** A city on the Black Sea coast of present-day Turkey, former capital of a Christian empire (1204–1461), founded by Alexius Comnenus. It was the outpost of Greek culture in Asia Minor until the Greek defeat by the Turks in 1922.

Tree, Sir Herbert (Draper) Beerbohm (1853–1917) Actor-manager, born in London, UK, the half-brother of Max Beerbohm. After a commercial education in Germany, he became an actor, took over the Haymarket Theatre (1887), and built His Majesty's Theatre (1897), where he rivalled Irving's productions at the Lyceum. He founded the Royal Academy of Dramatic Art in 1904, and scored a great success with the first production of Shaw's *Pygmalion* in 1914.

tree A large, perennial plant with a single, woody, self-supporting stem (the *trunk* or *bole*) extending to a considerable height above the ground before branching to form the leafy *crown*. Trees exhibit a wide variety of shapes, from very narrow, columnar forms to wide-spreading ones, and may be evergreen or deciduous. They occur in many different plant families. Dicotyledonous and gymnosperm trees grow in height by extension of the shoots, and in girth by the addition of internal tissue layers; monocotyledonous trees achieve their full girth as seedlings, and subsequently increase in height only. A few other groups, such as the so-called tree-ferns, produce arborescent or tree-like forms.

treecreeper Either of two families of songbirds of the N hemisphere: the **treecreeper** (US **creeper**) (Family: Certhiidae, 6 species); and the **Australian treecreeper** (Family: Climacteridae, 6 species), native to Australia and New Guinea; inhabits woodland; eats insects caught on trees and (Australian treecreepers) on ground.

tree-dating *dendrochronology*

tree duck *whistling duck*

tree fern The name applied to members of two fern families in which the woody rhizome forms a trunk-like stem reaching 25 m/80 ft, and is covered with the scars of old frond-bases, the current fronds forming a crown. It is native to much of the tropics and subtropics, and is the characteristic plant of various regions. The very slender, superficially palm-like habit makes it a popular ornamental. (Families: Cyatheaceae, Dicksoniaceae.)

tree frog A frog adapted to live in trees; flat with sucker-like discs on fingers and toes; two families: **true tree frogs** (Hylidae, 637 species) and **Old World tree frogs** (Rhacophoridaea, 184 species). The name is also used for some frogs in other families.

treehopper A small, hopping insect that feeds by sucking the sap of trees and shrubs; nymphs often gregarious; many produce honeydew and are attended by ants; mainly in warm dry regions. (Order: Homoptera. Family: Membracidae, c.2500 species.)

tree kangaroo A kangaroo of genus *Dendrolagus* (7 species); hind legs not longer than front legs; hands and feet with long claws; hair on neck grows forwards and sheds water when head held low; inhabits rainforests; may jump to ground from heights of 18 m/60 ft; eats leaves and fruit.

tree of heaven A fast-growing deciduous tree (*Ailanthus altissima*) to 20–30 m/65–100 ft, native to China, and widely planted elsewhere for ornament, shade, and as a soil stabilizer; leaves pinnate, with 13–25, 2–4-toothed leaflets, red when young; flowers in large clusters, starry, greenish-white, strong-smelling; fruit with an elongated wing. (Family: Simaroubaceae.)

tree shrew A small SE Asian mammal, rodent-like with a long tail and long thin shrew-like muzzle; tail bushy or with tufted tip; lives in trees and on ground; eats insects and fruit; formerly classified as insectivores or as primates; resembles ancestral mammals of 220 million years ago. (Order: Scandentia. Family: Tupaiidae, 16 species.)

tree snake Any snake which spends much of its life in trees. The term is applied to many unrelated species, but within the family Colubridae some species of genus *Boiga* may be called **brown tree snakes**, and species of *Dendrelaphis* may be called **green tree snakes**.

trefoil A member of either of two groups of plants belonging to the pea family, Leguminosae. Genus *Trifolium* comprises yellow-flowered species of clovers. Genus *Lotus* includes a widely distributed group of annual or perennial herbs, occurring in Europe, Asia, Africa, North America, and Australia; leaves divided into five leaflets; pea-like flowers, small, often yellow or reddish-coloured; pods long, many-seeded.

Trekkies *Star Trek*

Tremain, Rose (1943–) [tremayn] Novelist and short-story writer, born in London, UK. She studied at the Sorbonne and the University of East Anglia, and published her first novel, *Sadler's Birthday*, in 1976. Later novels include *The Cupboard* (1981), *Restoration* (1989), *Sacred Country* (1992, James Tait Black), *Music and Silence* (1999), and *The Colour* (2003). Her books of short stories include *Evangelista's Fan* (1994), and she has also written for children.

Trematoda [trematohda] A class of parasitic flatworms; body flattened and covered with a horny layer (*cuticle*); one or more attachment organs present; gut well developed, often with large intestinal cavity for storing and digesting food, and without an anus; contains c.8000 species, including the monogenetic and digenetic flukes. (Phylum: Platyhelminthes.)

Tremblay, Michel [trãblay] (1942–) Playwright, born in Montreal, Quebec, SE Canada. His first play, *Le Train* (1959), won a Radio-Canada award. *Les Belles-Soeurs* (1968, The Sisters-in-law) is written in the street language, *joual*. Many consider *Le Vrai Monde* (1987, The Real World), his 19th play written in as many years, his most important work to date. A new departure was his opera *Nelligan* (1990), with music by André Gagnon.

Tremiti Islands (Ital **Isole**) pop (2000e) 350; area 3 sq km/ 1·16 sq mi. Rocky limestone archipelago in Puglia, S Italy, in the Adriatic Sea; chief islands, San Domino, San Nicola, Caprara; popular area for scuba diving.

tremor Involuntary shaking movements affecting any part of the body, but usually most obvious in the hands. It may be due to a variety of disorders including thyrotoxicosis, alcohol withdrawal, and Parkinson's disease, which produces a characteristic 'pill rolling' tremor. Some people have a natural fine tremor, known as *benign essential tremor* that is not related to an underlying disease process.

Trenchard (of Wolfeton), Hugh Montague Trenchard, 1st Viscount (1873–1956) British marshal of the Royal Air Force, born in Taunton, Somerset, SW England, UK. He joined the army in 1893, served in India, South Africa, and West Africa, and developed an interest in aviation. He commanded the Royal Flying Corps in World War 1, helped to establish the RAF (1918), and became the first chief of air staff (1918–29). As commissioner of the London Metropolitan Police (1931–5), he founded the police college at Hendon. He became a peer in 1930.

trench mouth Severe and often recurring infection of the teeth and surrounding tissues. It is due to inadequate cleaning of the teeth, which allows plaque and bacteria to build up and invade the gums and bones supporting them. Repeated infections in the bone leads to permanent holes, ultimately resulting in the teeth loosening and falling out, and painful abscesses developing.

trench warfare Fighting from long narrow ditches in which troops stood and were relatively sheltered from enemy fire. Trenches were used in the Crimean War, and on a far larger scale in World War 1. After the first Battle of the Marne (1914) the retreating Germans dug themselves in N of the R Aisne, setting the pattern for trench warfare on the Western Front. Thousands of miles of parellel trenches were dug, linked by intricate systems of communications and protected by barbed wire. A network of trenches were dug along battlefield fronts stretching from the North Sea to Switzerland, creating a stalemate in the fighting. To break it, various new weapons were introduced: hand-grenades, poison gas, trench mortars, and artillery barrage. Not until 1918, with an improved version of the tank (invented in 1915), was it possible to press forward over the trenches. Advances in land weaponry have made trench warfare obsolete.

Trent, Council of (1545–63) A Council of the Roman Catholic Church, held at Trento, Italy. It was called to combat Protestantism and to reform the discipline of the Church, and as such spear-headed the Counter-Reformation by clarifying many points of doctrine and practice.

Trent, River River rising S of Biddulph in N Staffordshire, C England, UK; flows 275 km/171 mi SE, then E and NE through Derbyshire and Nottinghamshire to meet the Humber estuary near Whitton; linked by canal to many Midland industrial towns.

Trent Affair (1861) An incident between the USA and Britain in which the USS *San Jacinto* removed two officials of the Confederate States from the British ship *Trent*. The issue provoked considerable British anger until the Confederate officials were released by the American secretary of state.

Trento, Ger **Trent** 46°04N 11°08E, pop (2000e) 100 000. Capital town of Trento province, Trentino-Alto Adige, N Italy, on the left bank of the R Adige; archbishopric; railway; electrical goods, chemicals, cement, lumber, cultural activities, wine; cathedral (11th–13th-c), Castello del Buon Consiglio (13th-c), Church of Santa Maria Maggiore (16th-c), where the Council of Trent met (1544–63); Film Festival (Apr).

Trenton 40°14N 74°46W, pop (2000e) 85 400. State capital of New Jersey in Mercer Co, W New Jersey, USA, on the E bank of the Delaware R; settled by English Quakers in the 1670s; city status, 1792; scene of a British defeat by George Washington, 1776; monument (47 m/154 ft) marks the battle site; railway; manufactured steel, machinery, ceramics; research and development centre; State House complex; William Trent House.

trepanning One of the earliest surgical operations: the removal of a rectangle or disc of bone from the vault of the skull, commonly to alleviate pressure on the brain caused by skull fracture; also known as **trephination**. Prehistoric instances are known from Europe, the Pacific, North and South America (notably a skull from Cuzco with seven healed holes), Africa, and Asia. The instrument involved (now called a **trephine**) is still commonly used in neurosurgical operations.

trephination *trepanning*

trespass Unlawful entry onto the property of another. It includes entry below the land (eg mining) and within a reasonable distance above the land (eg shooting a bullet). Historically, the notion includes any unlawful act which interferes with another's property or rights. Despite the widely posted notice, trespassers can be sued, not prosecuted, although trespass may sometimes constitute a crime; for example, squatters may be criminally liable. In Britain, the Criminal Justice and Public Order Act (1994) created new offences of **aggravated trespass** and **collective trespass**, mainly as a reaction to hunt saboteurs and New Age travellers.

Tretyakov Gallery [tretyakof] One of the world's largest art galleries, located in Moscow, and housing exhibits of Russian painting and sculpture from the 11th-c to the present. The museum building was designed by Viktor M Vasnetsov (1848–1926) and erected in 1901–2; the gallery passed into state ownership in 1918. Because of lack of space to house the 50 000 exhibits, a new gallery is presently under construction.

Treurnicht, Andries Petrus [troyernikht] (1921–93) South African politician, born in Piketberg, SW South Africa. He studied theology at the universities of Cape Town and Stellenbosch, and was elected to parliament in 1971. He became Transvaal provincial National Party leader in 1978, and held a succession of posts in the cabinets of P W Botha from 1979. He and his colleagues resigned from the party in 1982 to form the new, right-wing Conservative Party (CP). The CP, which has pressed for a return to traditional apartheid values and effective partitioning of the country, had secured the support of more than a quarter of the white electorate by the turn of the decade.

Trevelyan, G(eorge) M(acaulay) [trevelyan] (1876–1962) Historian, born in Welcombe, Warwickshire, C England, UK. He studied at Cambridge, served in World War 1, and became professor of modern history at Cambridge (1927–40). He is best known as a pioneer social historian. His *English Social History* (1944) was a companion volume to his *History of England* (1926).

Trèves *Trier*

Trevithick, Richard [**trevithik**] (1771–1833) Engineer and inventor, born in Illogan, Cornwall, SW England, UK. He became a mining engineer at Penzance, and between 1796 and 1801 invented a steam carriage which ran between Camborne and Tuckingmill, and which in 1803 was run from Leather Lane to Paddington by Oxford St. He later went to Peru and Costa Rica (1816–27), where his engines were introduced into the silver mines.

triad The Western name given to a Chinese secret society (because of the importance of the triangle, representing the harmony of Earth, Heaven, and Man, in the initiation ceremonies). These societies originated in response to Qing suppression of Ming loyalists in the later 17th-c, and were active in the Taiping Rebellion (1850–64) and the 1911 revolution. Triads are now reputedly prominent in organized crime, especially international drug trafficking. They have similarities with the Chinese protection associations (*tongs*) which developed in the USA in the second half of the 19th-c, and which led to a period of clashes between rival Chinese gangs in some US cities.

triangle (mathematics) A plane figure bounded by three straight lines (*sides*). If all three are equal, the triangle is said to be *equilateral*; if two are equal, it is said to be *isosceles*. The sum of the angles of a triangle was proved by the Greeks to be equal to two right angles. If the largest angle in a triangle is less than a right angle, the triangle is called *scalene*; if the largest angle is greater than a right angle the triangle is *obtuse-angled*; if the largest angle is a right angle, the triangle is called *right-angled*, and the subject of Pythagoras's theorem. A *spherical* triangle is one drawn on the surface of a sphere, much used in navigation. In such a triangle, the angle-sum is not two right angles; in particular, a spherical triangle with two vertices on the equator and one at a pole can have an angle sum of three right angles.

triangle (music) A musical instrument of great antiquity, made from a steel rod in the form of a triangle, with one corner left open. It is struck with a short metal beater to produce a high, silvery sound of indefinite pitch.

Triangulum (Lat 'triangle') A small but distinctive N constellation between Aries and Andromeda. It includes the notable spiral galaxy M33. There is also a prominent S constellation **Triangulum Australe** ('southern triangle').

Trianon, Grand / Petit *Versailles*

Triassic period [**triyasik**] The earliest of the periods of the Mesozoic era, extending from c.248 to 213 million years ago. It was characterized by the first appearance of dinosaurs and small mammals. Plant life was mainly primitive gymnosperms, with ferns and conifers dominant.

triathlon A three-part sporting event consisting of sea swimming (3·8 km/2·4 mi), cycling (180 km/112 mi), and marathon running (42·2 km/26·2 mi). The events take place in sequence on a single occasion.

tribe A term sometimes used to describe ethnic minorities which formerly enjoyed political autonomy, but which have been incorporated into a nation state. In practice, it is usually applied only to such groupings in Third World countries, and its use carries a denigrating implication that the 'tribe' is backward, and that its political aspirations, if any, are illegitimate.

tribes of Israel *Israel, tribes of*

tribology [**triybolojee**] The study of phenomena involving the sliding of one surface over another. It includes friction, lubrication, and wear.

tribunal An official body exercising functions of a quasi-judicial nature. In the UK, tribunals frequently deal with matters where the citizen is in conflict with a government department. They tend to be specialized, governing such issues as employment rights, social security, mental health, and taxation. The proceedings of a tribunal may be subject to judicial review. Tribunals exist outside the ordinary courts of law, but their decisions are subject to judicial control under the doctrine of *ultra vires* and error of law.

tribunes In late Republican Rome, 10 annually elected officials whose function was to defend the lives and property of ordinary citizens. The office was part of the the hierarchy of offices (the *cursus honorum*), coming between the quaestorship and praetorship.

Triceratops [**triyseratops**] The largest ceratopsian dinosaur, known from the Cretaceous period of North America; heavily built, reaching 9 m/30 ft in length; four-legged; bony frill at back of skull relatively short; paired nasal horns above eyes well developed; plant-eating; probably lived in herds. (Order: Ornithischia.)

Trichina [**trikiyna**] A small roundworm (*Trichinella spiralis*), parasitic in the human small intestine; infection usually results from eating raw or undercooked pork. (Phylum: Nematoda.)

Trichinopoly [**trikinopolee**] *Tiruchchirappalli*

trichinosis A foodborne disease caused by a microscopic parasite, *Trichinella spiralis*, acquired by eating the undercooked meat of infected animals, usually pork. The parasites spread throughout the body and become embedded in muscles, forming cysts, and provoking an inflammatory reaction. This leads to muscle pain and weakness accompanied by fever, profuse sweating, a rash, and swelling around the eyes. Involvement of the heart muscle can lead to cardiac failure and death. Prevention is by ensuring that food, particularly pork products, is properly cooked.

trichomoniasis [**trikomoniyasis**] Infestation of the mucous membrane of the vagina with a flagellated protozoan. It causes irritation and vaginal discharge, and may be passed to the male urethra during sexual contact.

trick or treat *Hallowe'en*

Trident missile The US Navy's third-generation submarine-launched ballistic missile (SLBM) system, following on from the earlier Polaris and Poseidon missiles. The first version, Trident C-4, became operational in 1980. The larger Trident D-5 was tested with the US Navy in 1989, and entered service with the British Royal Navy in the mid-1990s. The missile has a very long range (11 000 km/7000 mi), and carries up to 14 individually targetable re-entry vehicles (MIRVs). A stellar-inertial navigation system gives it accuracy equivalent to its land-based counterparts, even though it is launched from a moving platform.

Trier [**treer**], Fr **Trèves**, Eng **Treves** [**treevz**], ancient **Augusta Treverorum** 49°45N 6°39E, pop (2000e) 101 000. River-port capital of Trier district, W Germany; on the R Moselle near the Luxembourg border; one of Germany's oldest towns; bishopric since the 4th-c; railway, university (1970); Roman Catholic Theological College; centre of wine production and trade; birthplace of Marx; Porta Nigra (2nd-c), cathedral (4th-c, 11th–12th-c), and Roman basilica, world heritage sites.

Trieste [**tree-est**] 45°39N 13°47E, pop (2000e) 255 000. Seaport and capital town of Trieste province, Friuli-Venezia Giulia, NE Italy, on the Adriatic coast; largest port in the Adriatic; capital of Free Territory of Trieste, established by the United Nations in 1947, divided in 1954 between Italy and Yugoslavia; airport; railway; university (1938); shipbuilding and repairing, oil refining, spirits and liqueurs, banking and finance, medical research, pharmaceuticals; birthplace of Italo Svevo; town hall (1876), Cathedral of San Giusto (14th-c), Church of Sant'Antonio (1849), castle (14th–17th-c), Roman theatre; International Trade Fair (Jun–Jul).

triggerfish Deep-bodied fish with a spiny first dorsal fin; large front spine, locked in upright position by a second smaller spine, and serving to wedge the fish in rock crevices away from predators; body strongly compressed, teeth well-developed, pelvic fins absent. (Family: Balistidae, 5 genera.)

Triglav [**treeglaf**] 46°21N 13°50E. Mountain in NW Slovenia; highest peak in the Julian Alps, rising to 2863 m/9393 ft.

triglyceride The major chemical compound found in dietary fats and in the storage fat in adipose tissue. A glycerol molecule ($C_3H_8O_3$) combines with three fatty acids, mostly of chain length 14–20.

trigonometry The branch of mathematics mainly concerned with relating the sides and angles of a triangle, based on triangles being similar if they have one right angle and one other angle equal. The **trigonometric functions** can be defined as the ratio of sides of a right-angled triangle, the commonest being

$$\text{sine} = \frac{\text{opposite}}{\text{hypotenuse}},\ \text{cosine} = \frac{\text{adjacent}}{\text{hypotenuse}},\ \text{tangent} = \frac{\text{opposite}}{\text{adjacent}}.$$

The most useful results for triangles that do not contain a right angle are the sine formula

$$\frac{a}{\sin A} = \frac{b}{\sin B} = \frac{c}{\sin C}$$

and the cosine formula $a^2 = b^2 + c^2 - 2bc \cos A$.

Trikhonís, Lake [treekhonees] area 96 513 sq km/37 254 sq mi. Largest lake in Greece, 16 km/10 mi NE of Missolonghi; length 19 km/12 mi; width 4·8 km/3 mi.

trilobite An extinct primitive marine arthropod, characterized by two grooves along its body producing a tri-lobed appearance; diverse and widespread from the Cambrian to the Permian periods; ranged from minute to 1 m/3 ft long; mostly living on sea bottom; sometimes planktonic. (Phylum: Arthropoda. Class: Trilobita, c.4000 species.)

trimaran [triymaran] A vessel with a narrow hull and large outriggers or floats giving the appearance of a three-hulled craft. The design gives great stability, thus permitting a large sail area which produces relatively high speed. It is mainly used for yachts.

Trimble, David (1944–) Northern Ireland politician, born in Bangor, NE Northern Ireland. He studied at Queens University, Belfast, was called to the bar, then became a lecturer at Belfast. He was elected MP for Upper Bann in 1990, and leader of the Ulster Unionist Party in 1995. He came to prominence for his role in the peace negotiations of the mid-1990s, and shared the 1998 Nobel Peace Prize with John Hume for his efforts. He became first minister of the new Northern Ireland Assembly in 1998, and retained this position when devolution became a reality in December 1999. He narrowly defeated a challenge to his leadership of the Ulster Unionists in 2000, coming mainly from Unionists unsure of or opposing the Good Friday Agreement. He broke with Unionist tradition by meeting leaders of Sinn Féin while maintaining criticism of their links with the IRA. He also attempted to remove the Orange Order's block vote within the Unionist party. He resigned in July 2001 following a lack of progress on the issue of arms decommissioning by the IRA, but was re-elected first minister in November.

Trimurti [trimoortee] (Sanskrit, 'having three forms') The Hindu triad, manifesting the cosmic functions of the Supreme Being, as represented by Brahma, Vishnu, and Shiva. Brahma is the balance between the opposing principles of preservation and destruction, symbolized by Vishnu and Shiva respectively.

Trincomalee or **Trinkomali** [tringkomalee] 8°44N 81°13E, pop (2000e) 55 000. Seaport capital of Trincomalee district, Sri Lanka; 257 km/160 mi NE of Colombo on Koddiyar Bay, at the mouth of the R Mahaweli; one of the earliest Tamil settlements; taken by the British, 1795; principal British naval base during World War 2 after the fall of Singapore; notable deep-water harbour; exports dried fish and coconuts; ruins of Temple of a Thousand Columns (3rd-c BC), Hindu temple, Fort Fredrick.

Trinidad and Tobago *p.1555*

trinitrotoluene [triyniytrotolyooeen] *TNT* (explosive)

Trinity A distinctively Christian doctrine that God exists in three persons, Father, Son, and Holy Spirit. The unity of God is maintained by insisting that the three persons or modes of existence of God are of one substance. The doctrine arose in the early Church because strictly monotheistic Jews nevertheless affirmed the divinity of Christ (the Son) and the presence of God in the Church through the Holy Spirit. The functions of the persons of the Trinity, and the relationship between them, have been the subject of much controversy (eg the split between Eastern and Western Churches on the *Filioque* clause), but the trinitarian concept is reflected in most Christian worship.

Trinity House The lighthouse authority for England and Wales, the Channel Islands, and Gibraltar. It is one of the principal pilotage authorities, and also supervises the maintenance of navigation marks carried out by local harbour authorities. Its pilotage role is undergoing a fundamental change, with control being gradually devolved to local port management.

Trinity Sunday In the Christian Church, the Sunday after Whitsunday, observed in honour of the Trinity. It was introduced by Pope John XXII in 1334 to mark the end of the feast days commemorating the life of Christ.

trio 1 An ensemble of three singers or instrumentalists, or a piece of music for such an ensemble. The **string trio** is normally composed of violin, viola, and cello; in the **piano trio**, a piano replaces the viola. Haydn, Mozart, and Beethoven are among those who wrote for both these ensembles.
2 The central section of a minuet or scherzo, which in the earliest examples often employed a three-part texture.

triode An electronic valve having three electrodes; a positive anode, an electron-emitting cathode, and a negatively biased control grid. A triode controls the flow of electrons from the cathode to the anode. It can be used as an amplifier or oscillator.

tripack Originally a combination of three photographic emulsion layers coated on two or three supports to produce colour separation negatives by a single exposure in the camera. It is now entirely replaced by **integral tripack** having the three or more emulsions on a single base.

tripe The fore-stomach of a ruminant, used as food – both the rumen (**plain tripe**) and the reticulum (**honeycomb tripe**). In France and the UK it is traditionally stewed with onions, vegetables, and herbs, although recipes differ.

Triple Alliance A diplomatic term for an alliance of three powers. Examples include the Anglo–Dutch–Swedish Alliance of 1668, the Anglo–Dutch–French Alliance of 1717, and the Austro–German–Italian Alliance of 1882.

Triple Alliance, War of the or **Paraguayan War** (1864–70) A devastating war fought by Paraguay against the combined forces of Brazil, Argentina, and Uruguay (the **Triple Alliance**), and provoked by the ambitions of the Paraguayan dictator Francisco Solano López (1826–70). The eventual victory of the Allies (most of the troops were provided by Brazil) was achieved at the cost of reducing the male population of Paraguay by nine-tenths.

Triple Crown A term used in many sports to describe the winning of three major events. In British horse racing it is the Derby, 2000 Guineas, and St Leger; in US racing, the Kentucky Derby, Preakness Stakes, and Belmont Stakes. In British Rugby Union it is the beating of the other three Home countries in the International Championship.

Triple Entente A series of agreements between Britain and France (1904) and Britain and Russia (1907) initially to resolve outstanding colonial differences. It aligned Britain to France and Russia, who had concluded a military alliance in 1893–4. In 1914, the Triple Entente became a military alliance.

triple glazing Three layers of glass separated by air spaces to give improved thermal or acoustic insulation. As with double glazing, the spaces may be permanently sealed or openable, the former being the most common and efficient. The insulation from triple glazing is significantly greater than from double glazing.

triple jump An athletics field event in which competitors execute a jump in three phases for distance, beginning after a run-up at a take-off board and finishing in a sandpit. The athlete takes off and lands on the same foot, then takes a stride to land on the other, and ends with a two-footed jump. The rules governing fair jumps and measurement are the same as for the long jump. In competition, six jumps are allowed. The event was formerly called the **hop, step, and jump**. The current world record for men is 18·29 m/60 ft 0¼ in, achieved by Jonathan Edwards (1966–) of Great Britain, in 1995 at Gothenburg, Sweden; for women, it is 15·50 m/50 ft 10¼ in, achieved by Inessa Kravets (1966–) of Ukraine, in 1995 at Gothenburg, Sweden.

Trinidad and Tobago

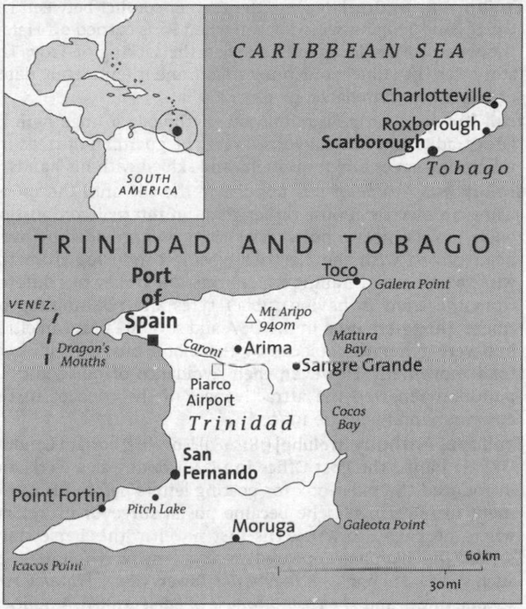

official name **Republic of Trinidad and Tobago**

Local name Trinidad and Tobago

Timezone GMT −4

Area 5128 km^2/1979 sq mi

Population total (2002e) 1 304 000

Status Independent republic within the Commonwealth

Date of independence 1962

Capital Port of Spain

Languages English (official), Hindi, French, Spanish

Ethnic groups African (43%), East Indian (40%), mixed (14%), Chinese (1%)

Religions Christian (Roman Catholic 34%, Protestant 29%), Hindu (25%), Muslim (6%)

Physical features Southernmost islands of the Lesser Antilles, SE Caribbean; Trinidad, area 4828 km^2/1864 sq mi, traversed by three mountain ranges (N, C and S), rising to 940 m/3084 ft at El Cerro del Aripo; drained by Caroni, Ortoire and Oropuche rivers; Tobago, area 300 km^2/116 sq mi, Main Ridge extends along most of island, rising to 576 m/1890 ft.

Climate Tropical, hot and humid; average annual temperature 29°C; dry season (Jan–May); wet season (Jun–Dec); average annual rainfall 1270 mm/50 in (SW Trinidad), 2540 mm/100 in (Tobago mountains).

Currency 1 Trinidad and Tobago Dollar (TT$) = 100 cents

Economy Oil and gas (main industries); industrial complex, W coast of Trinidad; cement, oil refining, petrochemicals; cocoa, coffee, fruit; tourism.

GDP (2002e) $11·07 bn, per capita $10 000

Human Development Index (2002) 0·805

History Trinidad visited by Columbus in 1498; settled by Spain in 16th-c, and acquired by Britain in 1797; Tobago captured by French, 1781, and acquired by Britain, 1802; Tobago became a British colony, 1814; Trinidad and Tobago united as British Crown Colony, 1899; independent member of the Commonwealth, 1962; republic, 1976, governed by a President and bicameral Parliament, comprising a Senate and House of Representatives; also a 15-member Tobago House of Assembly.

Head of State
1976–87 Ellis Emmanuel Clarke
1987–97 Noor Mohammed Hassanali
1997–2003 Arthur Napoleon Raymond Robinson
2003– Max Richards

Head of Government
1962–81 Eric Williams
1981–6 George Chambers
1986–91 Arthur Napoleon Raymond Robinson
1991–5 Patrick Manning
1995–2001 Basdeo Panday
2001– Patrick Manning

Tripoli (Lebanon) [**trip**olee], Arabic **Trablous**, Gr **Tripolis**, ancient **Oea** 34°27N 35°50E, pop (2000e) 219 000. Seaport capital of Tripoli division, NW Lebanon; second largest city in Lebanon; trade centre for N Lebanon and NW Syria; mostly occupied by Sunni Muslims; two Palestinian refugee camps nearby; railway; port trade, oil refining; Tower of the Lion, 12th-c Crusader Castle of St Gilles, 13th-c Mamelukes' Grand Mosque.

Tripoli (Libya) [**trip**olee], Arabic **Tarabulus** or **Tarabulus al-Gharb**, ancient **Oea** 32°54N 13°11E, pop (2000e) 808 000. Seaport capital of Libya; on the Mediterranean coast, 345 km/214 mi SW of Malta; founded by the Phoenicians, and later developed by the Romans; important Axis base in World War 2; bombed (1941–2) and occupied by the British (1943); bombed by US Air Force in response to alleged terrorist activities, 1986; airport; railway; university (1973); olive oil, fruit, fish, textiles; arch of Marcus Aurelius (1st-c BC); old city partly surrounded by Byzantine and mediaeval walls.

Tripolitania [tripoli**tay**nia] Region of N Africa, lying between Tunis and Cyrenaica; former province of W Libya; under Turkish control from the 16th-c until 1911; under Italian control until 1943; British control until 1952.

Tripp, Linda *Lewinsky, Monica*

triptych *altarpiece*

Tripura [**trip**ura] pop (2001e) 3 191 200; area 10 477 sq km/4044 sq mi. State in E India, bounded N, W and S by Bangladesh; became a state of India, 1949; status changed to union territory, 1956; reverted to a state, 1972; capital, Agartala; governed by a 60-member Legislative Assembly; mostly hilly and forested; tribal shifting cultivation gradually being replaced by modern farming methods; rice, wheat, tea, cotton, jute, oilseed, sugar cane; food processing, steel, handicrafts.

trireme [**triy**reem] A Mediterranean war galley of Greek origin propelled by three banks of oars. Speeds of up to nine knots are claimed for short distances. It was fitted with a square sail for use with a favourable wind, and also a strong projection fixed to the bow below the waterline, used to ram other ships.

Tristan da Cunha [tristan da **kun**ya] 37°15S 12°30W; pop (2000e) 370; area 110 sq km/42 sq mi. Small volcanic island in the S Atlantic, about midway between S Africa and South America; volcanic cone rises to 2060 m/6758 ft; three uninhabited islands nearby; inhabitants are the descendants of a British garrison established in 1816 during Napoleon's exile in St Helena; became a dependency of St Helena, 1922; chief settlement, Edinburgh; islanders evacuated in 1961 after a volcanic eruption, but returned in 1963; fishing, (crayfish), crafts, postage stamps.

Tristram or **Tristan** [**tris**tram] In the Arthurian legends, a knight who was sent to woo Iseult the Fair (Isolde) on behalf of his uncle, King Mark of Cornwall. He fell in love with her himself, then fled to Brittany, where he married Iseult of the White Hands.

triticale [triti**kay**lee] An artificial hybrid (*Triticosecale*), derived from wheat (*Triticum*) and rye (*Secale*), giving yields and grain quality approaching those of wheat in cold climates where only rye could be grown previously. The cultivation of triticale is expanding rapidly in Poland and Russia, though little cultivated elsewhere. It is well adapted to hot dry climates. (Family: Gramineae.)

tritium [tritium] A heavy isotope of hydrogen, in which the nucleus comprises one proton and two neutrons rather than a single proton (as for common hydrogen). It is radioactive, with a half-life of 12·3 years. It does not occur naturally, but is formed in nuclear reactions, and is an important ingredient of nuclear fusion reactions and hydrogen bombs.

Triton (astronomy) [triytn] The principal natural satellite of Neptune, discovered in 1846; distance from the planet 355 000 km/221 000 mi; diameter 2705 km/1681 mi, orbital period 5·9 days. Uniquely, for a large moon, its orbit is retrograde about Neptune. The encounter by Voyager 2 (Aug 1989) showed that it has a thin atmosphere of nitrogen, with a surface pressure of 10 microbar. There is a darker pinkish hemisphere and a lighter bluish-white hemisphere, both with a complex geological history including impacts, flooding, melting, faulting, and collapse. There are signs of current nitrogen volcanism. It is similar in size and character to the planet Pluto, and was probably once an independent body that was captured.

Triton (mythology) [triytn] In Greek mythology, the son of Poseidon and Amphitrite. He is depicted in art as a fish from the waist down, and blowing a conch-shell. The beings of similar form (*mermen*) who serve Poseidon are often referred to as Tritons.

triton shell [triytn] A large marine snail found in the Indo-Pacific region; one of the world's largest snails, length up to 36 cm/14 in; shells used as ceremonial trumpets by Pacific islanders. (Class: Gastropoda. Order: Mesogastropoda.)

triumphal arch A free-standing gateway of purely aesthetic and symbolic function, usually monumental in proportion, built of stone, and with ornate surface decoration. It was first used in Rome in the 2nd-c BC, but the most famous example is the Arc de Triomphe, Paris (1806–35), architect J F Chalgrin.

triumvirate Literally Lat, 'a group of three men'; in ancient Rome **1** the name given to any publicly appointed administrative board of three; **2 First Triumvirate** the name commonly, though incorrectly, applied to the unofficial coalition between Caesar, Pompey, and Crassus in 60 BC; **3 Second Triumvirate** the name given to the joint rule from 43 BC of Antonius, Octavian (Augustus), and Lepidus.

Trivandrum or **Trivandram** [trivandruhm] 8°31N 77°00E, pop (2000e) 970 000. Capital of Kerala state, SW India; 1255 km/780 mi SE of Mumbai; on the Malabar coast; airfield; railway; university (1937); commercial and cultural centre; textiles, soap, copra, coir ropes; noted for its wood and ivory carving; early 18th-c temple to Vishnu.

trivium *quadrivium*

Trobriand Islander A Melanesian people of the scattered Trobriand Is, off New Guinea; cultivators, and famous for their ceremonial gift exchange system, the *kula*. They were studied by Malinowski from 1915, and their way of life described in several monographs, including *Argonauts of the Western Pacific* (1922).

trogon [trohgn] A bird native to the New World tropics, Africa, and SE Asia; plumage soft, brightly coloured; tail long; inhabits woodland; eats insects, spiders, fruit, and (occasionally) small vertebrates. (Family: Trogonidae, c.40 species.)

Troilus [trohilus, troylus] In Greek legend, a prince of Troy, the son of Priam and Hecuba, who was killed by Achilles. In mediaeval stories, he is the lover of Cressida.

Trojan asteroids Asteroids which have orbits very similar to Jupiter, positioned 60° ahead or behind the planet, where they are trapped in a stable configuration. Nearly 500 are known. They are named after the heroes of the *Iliad*.

Trojan Horse A huge wooden horse, according to legend left behind on the beach by the Greeks, who had pretended to give up the siege of Troy. Told by Sinon that it was an offering to Athena, the Trojans broke down their city wall to bring it inside. At night, warriors emerged and captured the city.

Trojan War In Greek legend, the 10-year conflict between the Greeks and Trojans, which began when Paris carried off Helen, the wife of Menelaus, and ended in the sacking of Troy. The story was the subject of Homer's *Iliad*, and is tentatively dated on the basis of archaeology to c.1260 BC.

troll [trohl] In early Scandinavian mythology a huge ogre, in later tradition a mischievous dwarf, the guardian of treasure, inhabiting caves and mountains and skilled with his hands.

trolley bus A type of bus popular in the UK until the 1960s, using an electric motor rather than an internal combustion engine as its motive power. Electricity was provided by overhead cables, with the electricity being conducted from the wires by means of trailing wiper arms. The trolley bus differed from the tram in having rubber tyres and not running on tracks. They were used in the USA and several European cities, but were generally replaced by the motor bus, with its freer road movement. However, their avoidance of noise and air pollution renewed the attractiveness of the concept in the environmentally-aware 1990s.

Trollope, Anthony [troluhp] (1815–82) Novelist, born in London, UK. He joined the Post Office in 1834, working as a clerk, and introduced the pillar-box for posting letters before his retirement in 1867. In 1841 he became postal surveyor in Ireland, where he began to write. His first novel in the 'Barsetshire' series, *The Warden*, appeared in 1855, and was followed by such successful books as *Barchester Towers* (1857), *Framley Parsonage* (1861), and *The Last Chronicle of Barset* (1867). A political series followed, known as the 'Palliser' novels (after the central character), including *Phineas Finn* (1869) and *The Eustace Diamonds* (1873). Among his later novels were *The Way We Live Now* (1875) and *Mr Scarborough's Family* (1883). His revealing autobiography, written in 1875–6, was published in 1883.

Trollope, Joanna (1943–) Writer and novelist, born in Gloucestershire, SWC England, UK, a descendant of Anthony Trollope. She studied at Oxford, then became an English teacher and freelance writer for various leading magazines and newspapers. Her novels include *Eliza Stanhope* (1978), *A Village Affair* (1989), *The Rector's Wife* (1991), *Marrying the Mistress* (2000), *Girl From the South* (2002), and *Brother and Sister* (2004). She has also written novels as **Caroline Harvey**, including *Legacy of Love* (1992) and *The Brass Dolphin* (1999).

trombone A musical instrument made from brass tubing, mainly cylindrical, which expands to a bell at one end and is fitted with a cup-shaped mouthpiece at the other. A slide is used to vary the length, and therefore the fundamental pitch, of the instrument, which is made in various sizes. Its history dates back to the 15th-c; until c.1700 it was known as the **sackbut**. It was much used in the 17th–18th-c for church music and for supernatural scenes in opera, and in the 19th-c it became a regular member of the symphony orchestra. Trombones are prominent also in jazz groups, and in brass, dance, and military bands.

Tromp, Maarten (Harpertszoon) (1598–1653) Dutch admiral, born in Brielle, The Netherlands. In 1639 he defeated a superior Spanish fleet off Gravelines, and won the Battle of the Downs later that year. Knighted by Louis XIII of France (1640) and by Charles I of England (1642), he then fought the French pirates based on Dunkirk, while his encounter with Blake in 1652 started the first Anglo-Dutch War. Victorious off Dover, he was defeated by a superior English fleet off Portland, and finally off Terhejide, near Schevingen, where he was killed.

trompe l'oeil [trōp loeec] (Fr 'deceive the eye') A painting which may have little aesthetic value, but which is cleverly designed to trick the spectator into thinking the objects represented are really there. According to Pliny, the ancient Greek painter Zeuxis painted grapes which birds tried to peck.

Tromsø [tromsoe] 69°42N 19°00E, pop (2000e) 54 000. Seaport capital of Troms county, N Norway; on a small island between South Kvaløy and the mainland; founded, 13th-c; charter, 1794;

largest town in N Norway; base for expeditions to the Arctic; bishopric; university (1972); fishing, fish processing, sealing; observatory for the study of the aurora borealis; Tromsdalen church (1975), Tromsø museum.

Trondheim [trondhiym], formerly **Nidarøs** 63°36N 10°23E, pop (2000e) 145 000. Seaport and capital of Sør-Trøndelag county, C Norway, at the mouth of the R Nidelv (Nea), on S shore of Trondheim Fjord; former capital of Norway during the Viking period; occupied by the Germans, 1940–5; bishopric; airport; railway; university (1968); shipbuilding, fishing, trade in timber; cathedral (1066–93), royal palace (18th-c), Church of Our Lady (13th-c).

Troödos Mountains [trohuhthos] Mountain range in C Cyprus; rises to 1951 m/6400 ft at Mt Olympus, highest peak on the island.

Troon 55°32N 4°40W, pop (2000e) 14 400. Town and golf resort in South Ayrshire, W Scotland, UK; at N end of Ayr Bay, 9 km/6 mi N of Ayr; railway; boatbuilding.

Trooping the Colour In the UK, originally the display of the regimental standard to the troops; now usually taken to refer to the annual ceremony on Horse Guards Parade, London, when the monarch reviews one of the five battalions of the Guards regiment and its flag, or **colour**, is presented. The ceremony takes place to mark the monarch's official birthday, and is currently in June.

tropical rainforest *rainforest*

tropical year or **solar year** The time taken for the Earth to complete one revolution round the Sun relative to the vernal equinox: 365·24219 mean solar days.

tropic bird A marine bird, native to tropical seas worldwide; plumage white or pink with black line through eye; wings slender, pointed; central tail feathers very long (may be longer than body); catches fish and squid by plunging into water; on land, is unable to stand. (Family: Phaethontidae, 3 species.)

tropics A climatic zone located between the Tropics of Cancer (23·5°N) and Capricorn (23·5°S). The N tropic is so called because the Sun at the summer solstice (when it is vertically over that tropic) enters the zodiacal sign of Cancer; the S tropic is named for a similar reason. A number of different climates are recognized, based on the seasonal distribution of precipitation; there is no satisfactory single definition. Temperatures are generally high, such as a mean monthly temperature greater than 20°C. In the *humid* tropics mean annual rainfall is above 2000 mm/c.80 in, and only one month of the year has less than 50 mm/c.2 in. Rainforest is the characteristic vegetation. In a tropical *wet–dry* climate, there is greater seasonality; mean annual rainfall is greater than 1000 mm/c.40 in, with at least five wet months, each receiving more than 50 mm/c.2 in. Savannah is the characteristic vegetation.

tropism [trohpizm] A plant response by directional movement towards (**positive tropism**) or away from (**negative tropism**) a sustained external stimulus. It is attained by unequal growth of the sides of the organ stimulated by growth hormones. **Phototropism** is a response to light; **geotropism** to gravity; and **chemotropism** to chemicals.

troposphere The lowest layer of the Earth's atmosphere, within which the weather is active because of the continual motion of the air and a steadily decreasing temperature with height. The upper boundary of the troposphere (the **tropopause**) is located at a temperature inversion: warmer air in the stratosphere overlies the troposphere, and effectively forms a barrier to convection. The height of the tropopause is correlated with sea level temperature, season, and daily changes in surface pressure; it is at c.8–16 km/5–10 mi, generally higher at the Equator than at the Poles, and also higher at the Poles in summer than in winter.

Trotsky, Leon, pseudonym of **Lev Davidovich Bronstein** (1879–1940) Russian Jewish revolutionary, born in Yanovka, S Ukraine. He studied at Odessa, and in 1898 was arrested as a Marxist and exiled to Siberia. He escaped in 1902, joined Lenin in London, and in the abortive 1905 revolution was president of the St Petersburg Soviet. He then worked as a revolutionary journalist in the West, returning to Russia in 1917, when he joined the Bolsheviks and played a major role in the October Revolution. In the Civil War he was commissar for war, and created the Red Army. After Lenin's death (1924) his influence began to decline. He was ousted from the party by Stalin, who opposed his theory of 'permanent revolution', exiled to C Asia (1927), and expelled from the Soviet Union (1929). He continued to agitate as an exile, and was sentenced to death in his absence by a Soviet court in 1937. He finally found asylum in Mexico, but was assassinated by Ramón Mercader, a Spanish Communist. The Soviet government denied any responsibility and Mercader was convicted and imprisoned.

Trotskyism A development of Marxist thought by Leon Trotsky. Essentially a theory of permanent revolution, Trotskyism stressed the internationalism of socialism, avoided co-existence, and encouraged revolutionary movements abroad; this conflicted with Stalin's ideas of 'socialism in one country'. Trotskyism has since inspired other extreme left-wing revolutionary movements but they are factionally divided, and have little support.

troubadours [troobadoor] (Provençal, 'inventor') Court poet-musicians (some known by name, such as Guillaume d'Acquitaine) who flourished in the S of France 1100–1350. They wrote (in the S dialect *langue d'oc*) mainly love poems, and had an important influence on the development of the European lyric. They included Bernart de Ventadorn (c.1130–90) and Arnaut Daniel (c.1150–c.1200). Their equivalent in the N (writing in the N dialect *langue d'oil*) were the **trouvères**, who also wrote *chansons de geste*. Among the best known were Blondel de Nesle (12th-c) and Adam de la Halle (c.1250–88).

trout Any of several species of the family Salmonidae, existing in two forms: the **brown trout**, confined to fresh water, and the migratory and much larger **sea trout**; includes the European trout (*Salmo trutta*), found in marine and adjacent freshwaters from Norway to the Mediterranean, Black Sea, and Caspian Sea; an excellent food fish, very popular with anglers, and also farmed commercially.

trout lily *dog's tooth violet*

trouvères [troovair] *troubadours*

Trowbridge [trohbrij] 51°20N 2°13W, pop (2000e) 30 800. County town of Wiltshire, S England, UK; 12 km/7 mi SE of Bath; railway; foodstuffs; brewing, clothing, printing, dairy products.

Troy, Turkish **Truva**, also ancient **Ilium** Ancient ruined city in Çanakkale province, W Turkey; the archaeological site lies S of the Dardanelles, near Hisarlik; in Greek legend it was besieged by a confederation of Greek armies for 10 years (Trojan War), as recounted by Homer in the *Iliad*; from the Stone Age to Roman times, over a period of 4000 years, the city was rebuilt on the same site nine times; excavated by Heinrich Schliemann in the 1870s, the occupation level known as Troy VIIa is thought to be the city of the Greek legend. Walls 5·4 m/18 ft thick were discovered in 1993.

Troyes [trwah], ancient **Augustobona Tricassium** 48°19N 4°03E, pop (2000e) 63 500. Capital city of Aube department, NEC France; on channel of the R Seine, 150 km/93 mi SE of Paris; bishopric, 4th-c; capital of old province of Champagne; railway; centre of hosiery trade; textiles, machinery, foodstuffs; cathedral (13th–16th-c), Church of St-Urbain (13th-c), Church of Ste-Madeleine (16th-c), former Abbey of St-Loup, with famous library, Musée des Beaux-Arts, hosiery museum.

Trucial States The former name of the United Arab Emirates of Abu Dhabi, Ajman, Dubai, al-Fujairah, Ras al-Khaimah, Sharja, and Umm al-Qaiwain on the Persian Gulf and Gulf of Oman. The name derives from a truce signed between the ruling sheiks and Great Britain in 1820. In 1892 they accepted British protection.

truck gardening *market gardening*

Trudeau, Pierre (Elliott) [troodoh] (1919–2000) Canadian statesman and prime minister (1968–79, 1980–4), born in Montreal, Quebec, SE Canada. He studied at Montreal, Harvard, and London universities, became a lawyer, helped to found the political magazine *Cité Libre* (1950), and was professor of law at Montreal (1961–5). Elected an MP in 1965, he became minister of justice (1967), an outspoken critic of separatism for Quebec, and in 1968 succeeded Pearson as federal leader of the Liberal Party and prime minister. His term of office saw the October Crisis (1970) in Quebec, the introduction of the Official Languages Act, federalist victory during the Quebec Referendum (1980), and the introduction of Canada's constitution (1982). He resigned as leader of the Liberal Party and from public life in 1984.

Trueman, Freddy, popular name of **Frederick Sewards Trueman** (1931–) Cricketer and broadcaster, born in Stainton, South Yorkshire, N England, UK. Educated at Maltby Secondary School, he became an apprentice bricklayer before developing into the first genuinely fast bowler in post-war English cricket. A Yorkshire player for 19 years (1949–68), he played in 67 Tests for England between 1952 and 1965, and took a record number of 307 wickets, three times taking 10 wickets in a match. In his first-class career he took 2304 wickets, and made three centuries. A bluff and forthright Yorkshireman, he has worked as a cricket writer and commentator since he retired.

Truffaut, François [troofoh] (1932–84) Film critic and director, born in Paris, France. His first career, as a critic from 1953, led to his *auteur* ('author') concept of film-making. In 1959 he made his first feature as director/actor/co-scriptwriter, *Les Quatre Cents Coups* (The 400 Blows), an autobiographical study of a troubled adolescent, effectively launching the French *Nouvelle Vague* ('New Wave') movement. This was followed by *Tirez sur le pianiste* (1960, Shoot the Pianist), *Jules et Jim* (1962), and *Fahrenheit 451* (1966), in all of which he was also co-scriptwriter. Several of his films contain autobiographical elements, relating to an unhappy childhood and turbulent youth. He continued actively at work throughout the 1970s, notably with *La Nuit américaine* (1972, trans Day for Night), for which he received an Oscar, and *Le Dernier Métro* (1980, The Last Metro), which was a major commercial success. He acted in several of his films, and also in *Close Encounters of the Third Kind* (1977). He returned from colour photography to his first love of black-and-white in his final film, *Vivement Dimanche* (1983, Lively Sunday), a tongue-in-cheek evocation of the work of one of his idols – Hitchcock.

truffle The underground fruiting body of fungi belonging to the genus *Tuber*; often found in soils under beech woods; may be fleshy or waxy; remains closed and has no active dispersal mechanism for spores; much sought after as a delicacy. (Subdivision: Ascomycetes. Order: Tuberales.)

Trujillo [trooheelyoh] 8°06S 79°00W, pop (2000e) 635 000. Capital of La Libertad department, NW Peru; founded by Pizarro, 1536; airfield; university (1824); cathedral, several convents, monasteries, and colonial churches, neighbouring archaeological sites.

Trujillo (Molina), Rafael Leonidas [trooheelyoh] (1891–1961) Dictator of the Dominican Republic (1930–61), born in San Cristóbal, S Dominican Republic. He rose to prominence as commander of the police. His regime was both highly repressive and highly corrupt, and he was assassinated in Santo Domingo, a city he had renamed Ciudad Trujillo.

Truk or **Chuuk** pop (2000e) 66 700 area 127 sq km/49 sq mi. One of the Federated States of Micronesia, W Pacific, comprising 11 high volcanic islands in the Chuuk lagoon and numerous outlying atolls; capital, Weno (formerly Moen); more than 60 ships of the Japanese wartime fleet lie sunk at various depths in the lagoon, one of the largest in the world.

Truman, Harry S (1884–1972) US statesman and 33rd president (1945–53), born in Lamar, Missouri, USA. Elected as a Democrat to the US Senate in 1934, he was chairman of a special committee investigating defence. Made vice-president in 1944, he became president on the death of Roosevelt, and was re-elected in 1948 in a surprise victory over Thomas E Dewey. His decisions included the dropping of two atom bombs on Japan, the post-war loan to Britain, and the sending of US troops to South Korea. He promoted the policy of giving military and economic aid to countries threatened by Communist interference (the **Truman Doctrine**). At home he introduced a 'Fair Deal' of economic reform.

trumpet A musical instrument made from cylindrical brass (or other metal) tubing, fitted with a cup-shaped mouthpiece, and widening at the other end to a flared bell. It was traditionally used for signalling, and since the 17th-c as an orchestral and solo instrument. Until the 19th-c it was restricted to the notes of the harmonic series, many trumpeters of Bach's time specializing in the high *clarino* register. The fundamental pitch could be altered by fitting 'crooks' (pieces of tubing) of various lengths; since about 1830, trumpets have been fitted with valves to perform the same function more easily. The modern trumpet has three valves and is a transposing instrument pitched in B♭.

trumpet creeper *trumpet vine*

trumpeter A plump, ground-living bird, native to tropical South America; plumage mainly black with short tail; neck slender and legs long; flies reluctantly; inhabits rainforests; eats fruit and insects. (Family: Psophiidae, 3 species.)

trumpet vine A deciduous climber native to E Asia and E North America; stems clinging by aerial roots; leaves pinnate; flowers orange-scarlet, trumpet-shaped with five unequal lobes; also called a **trumpet creeper**. It is a popular ornamental. (Genus: *Campsis*, 2 species. Family: Bignoniaceae.)

trunkfish Small and bizarre fish whose body is encased in rigid and often ornate case-like armour of small polygonal plates; includes *Lactophrys trigonus*, found around reefs and sea grass beds of the W Atlantic; length up to 40 cm/16 in; fins small and membranous, eyes prominent. (Family: Ostraciontidae.)

Truro 50°16N 5°03W, pop (2000e) 20 700. City and county town of Cornwall, SW England, UK; on R Truro, 20 km/12 mi SW of St Austell; Royal Institution of Cornwall; railway; foodstuffs, engineering, seaweed fertilizer, pottery; cathedral (1880–1910), Pendennis Castle (1543).

trust An arrangement whereby a person (the **trustee**) holds property for the benefit of another (the **beneficiary**). The terms of the settlement or will creating the trust are binding on the trustees, insofar as they are possible and lawful. Some trusts are created by operation of law. A trustee in breach of trust is liable for the damage suffered. Trust law is considered to be the most significant contribution of English equity to jurisprudence.

Trusteeship *Trust Territory*

Trusteeship Council *United Nations*

Trust Territory A non-self-governing area, the administration of which is supervised by the United Nations under Article 75, established after World War 2. The origins of the system lay in the need to administer colonial territories taken from powers defeated in World War 1. Trusteeship Agreements are entered into between the administering country, whose task is to prepare the people for independence and encourage the development of human rights, and the United Nations. Most such areas are now independent, with the exception of a small number of Pacific islands.

Truth, Sojourner, originally **Isabella Van Wagener** (c.1797–1883) Evangelist, abolitionist, feminist, and reformer, born a slave in Ulster County, New York, USA. After years of abuse, a new master, Isaac Van Wagener, set her free. From him she took her surname, and became an ardent evangelist. In 1843 she felt called by God to change her name to Sojourner Truth, and to fight against slavery and for women's suffrage. Preaching widely across the USA, she drew large crowds, was appointed counsellor to the freedmen of Washington by Abraham Lincoln, and continued to promote black civil rights until her retirement in 1875.

Truth and Reconciliation Commission A committee established in South Africa in 1995 to investigate the abuses of the apartheid era. Its hearings, under the chairmanship of Archbishop Desmond Tutu, achieved an international profile, though the value of the exercise as a means of achieving better race relations was frequently questioned within the country. Its report was published in 1998.

Truth or Consequences, or **Truth or C.**, formerly **Hot Springs** (to 1950) 33°08N 107°16W, pop (2000e) 7300. Town in Sierra Co, SW New Mexico, USA, on the Rio Grande; the new name was adopted by a citizens' vote, following the offer made by the presenter of a famous radio programme that if the town adopted the name of his show he would hold a yearly fiesta with the programme presented from there.

trypanosomiasis [tripanohsomiyasis] Any of several diseases caused by infection with trypanosomes, protozoa that infest domestic and wild animals and are transmitted to humans by insect vectors. **African trypanosomiasis** is transmitted by bites from tsetse flies and is common across Africa; it is also known as **sleeping sickness**. Initial symptoms are high fever, fatigue, headache, and joint pain; as the disease develops it leads to anaemia, and kidney and liver failure; finally the patient is overcome by extreme drowsiness followed by coma and death. **American trypanosomiasis** is transmitted by blood-sucking bugs, and occurs widely in South and Central America; also known as **Chagas' disease**, after the Brazilian physician Carlos Chagas (1879–1934). Young children are commonly affected with fever. Acute symptoms include fever, rash, and enlargement of the spleen and lymph nodes. Chronic disease may follow with heart arrhythmias and enlarged intestines.

tsaine *banteng*

tsar or **czar** The title used by the rulers of Russia from 1547 to 1721; derived from the Latin *Caesar*. It remained in common use until the Revolution (1917), although the official title of the ruler from 1721 until 1917 was *Emperor*.

Tsavo [tsahvoh] National park in SE Kenya, established in 1948; area 20 800 sq km/8000 sq mi; home of many African herd animals, as well as of the lion, hippopotamus, and rhinoceros.

Tschaikovsky, Piotr Ilyich *Tchaikovsky*

Tseng Kuo-fan *Zeng Guofan*

tsessebi *topi*

tsetse fly [tetsee, tseetsee] A small biting fly found in tropical Africa; mouthparts form a needle-like proboscis; feeds on blood of vertebrates; of great medical and veterinary importance as the carrier of sleeping sickness (in humans) and nagana (in cattle); serious epidemics in the early 20th-c, and recurrent outbreaks since; a major impediment to the use of horses and draught oxen in the early European exploration of Africa. (Order: Diptera. Family: Glossinidae.)

Tsinan *Jinan*

Tsingtao *Qingdao*

Tsiolkovsky, Konstantin Eduardovich [tseeolkofskee] (1857–1935) Russian physicist and rocketry pioneer, born in Izhevsk, W Russia. Self-educated, and handicapped by deafness from the age of 10, his visionary ideas on the use of rockets for space exploration were published in 1903. From 1911 he developed the basic theory of rocketry and multi-stage rocket technology (1929). Much earlier (1881), unaware of Maxwell's work, he independently developed the kinetic theory of gases.

Tsui, Daniel C [tsooee] (1939–) Physicist, born in Henan, C China. He graduated from the University of Chicago in 1967, joined Princeton University, and shared the 1998 Nobel Prize for Physics for his contribution to the discovery of a new form of quantum fluid with fractionally charged excitations.

tsunami [tsunahmee] Long-period ocean waves produced by movements of the sea floor associated with earthquakes, volcanic explosions, or landslides. Tsunamis may cross entire ocean basins at speeds as great as 800 km/500 mi per hour, and strike coastal regions with devastating force. Thousands of lives have been lost in regions of the Pacific subject to destructive tsunamis, which may reach heights in excess of 30 m/100 ft. They are also referred to as **seismic sea waves**, and in popular (but not technical oceanographic) use as **tidal waves**.

tsutsugamushi fever [tsutsugamushee] An infectious disease caused by a rickettsia, a bacterium that is spread to humans through the bites of *Leptotrombidium* mites that usually live in the ground, but can also infest humans. The disease was first recognized on Honshu I in Japan, but also occurs in SE Asia, Indonesia, India, and Nepal. It tends to affect people walking in mountainous or forested areas, the mite's natural habitat, and is most common in mild weather in autumn or in early spring when the mites are most active. A swollen, reddened area appears at the site of a bite, accompanied by headaches, fatigue, and a high fever. The bitten area later ulcerates and forms a characteristic black scab. If untreated by antibiotics, complications such as pneumonia, hepatitis, and cerebral haemorrhage can occur, and the disease is frequently fatal.

Tsvetayeva, Marina Ivanova [tsvetiyuhva], married name **Efron** (1892–1941) Poet, born in Moscow, Russia. Strongly anti-Bolshevik, she was allowed to emigrate in 1922, and wrote and published most of her poetry abroad, such as *Vyorsty* (1922, Miles), and *Posle Rossii 1922–25* (1928, After Russia). She returned to the USSR in 1939. After the execution of her husband and the arrest of her daughter, she committed suicide in Yelabuga.

Tswana *Sotho–Tswana*

Tuamotu Archipelago [towmohtoo] 135–143°W 14–23°S; pop (2000e) 13 500; area 826 sq km/319 sq mi. Island group of French Polynesia, E of the Society Is; consists of two parallel ranges of 78 atolls; largest group of coral atolls in the world; chief islands include Rangiroa, Hao, Fakarava; area used for nuclear testing by the French since 1962.

Tuareg [twahreg] A Berber pastoral people of the C Sahara and the N Sahel zone of W Africa. A traditionally highly-stratified feudal society, in the past they were caravan traders and feared raiders. Many died during the severe drought of the 1970s.

tuatara [tooatahra] A rare lizard-like reptile (*Sphenodon punctatus*), native to islands off the coast of New Zealand; the only remaining member of the order Rhyncocephalia; primitive in form (resembling extinct species); green or orange-brown; length, up to 65 cm/26 in; male with crest of tooth-like spines along back; nocturnal; digs burrow or shares burrow of a nesting petrel; eats invertebrates, small vertebrates, birds' eggs.

Tuatha de Danann [tooaha day donan] A legendary race of wise beings who arrived in Ireland c.1500 BC, and became the ancient gods of the Irish; the name means 'the people of the goddess Danu'. They were conquered by the Milesians, and retreated into tumuli near the R Boyne. In historical terms, they seem to preserve a memory of the pre-Celtic population of Ireland.

tuba A musical instrument made from brass tubing curved elliptically, with usually three valves, a mouthpiece set at right angles, and a wide bell pointing upwards. It is the largest and lowest in pitch of all brass instruments, and succeeded the ophicleide as the bass of the orchestral brass section in the mid-19th-c. It is made in various sizes, some of which are known by other names.

tubenose A marine bird found worldwide; musk-like odour; nostrils long and tubular on long, grooved, hooked bill; also known as **petrel**. Its stomach contains oil which is used to feed its young, or which may be vomited as a defence. The order includes albatrosses, fulmars, shearwaters, and various petrels. (Order: Procellariiformes, or Tubinares.)

tuber An underground organ storing food for the next season's growth. **Stem tubers** are distinguished by the presence of buds or 'eyes'; **root tubers** bear no buds.

tuberculosis (TB) A chronic debilitating disease almost always caused in humans by *Mycobacterium tuberculosis*, characterized by deposits of infected granules (*tubercles*) throughout the body. It thrives in overcrowded and deprived conditions, and was the scourge of poor communities in the 19th-c. It remains a major health problem in the developing world, and is re-emerging in the West as a significant infectious threat. In 1998 the World Health Organization reported that TB is killing more people worldwide than any other infectious disease. People with suppressed immune systems, such as AIDS patients, are especially vulnerable. The micro-organisms are spread in the air, and enter the body via the respiratory tract, initially establishing a primary infection in the lung. This infection is not always accompanied by symptoms, and may only become apparent on a chest X-ray as a lesion in the lung with associated enlarged lymph nodes. Over months and years, the lesion gradually enlarges due to reinfection or periodic reactivation of the initial infection. This results in the destruction of lung tissue and the formation of a cavity, producing cough, haemoptysis, and shortness of breath. General symptoms include fever and weight loss, which may be profound. The infection may spread locally, causing pneumonia, or elsewhere in the body to affect almost any organ, such as the lining of the brain (*tuberculous meningitis*), the kidneys (*renal tuberculosis*), or the bones and joints. Occasionally, infection spreads in the blood and deposits tubercles throughout the body (*military tuberculosis*). Treatment requires long courses of powerful antibiotics. However, new strains of antibiotic-resistant micro-organisms are emerging, causing considerable concern.

Tubifex [tyoobifeks] A genus of freshwater annelid worms, found part buried in mud on river beds in low oxygen conditions; red in colour because of haemoglobin in blood; feed by extracting organic material from mud; commonly used to feed aquarium fishes. (Class: Oligochaeta. Order: Haplotaxida.)

Tübingen [tübingen] 48°32N 9°04E, pop (2000e) 82 600. Capital of Tübingen district, SW Germany; on R Neckar, 27 km/17 mi S of Stuttgart; railway; university (1477); publishing, paper, textiles, machinery.

Tubman, Harriet, *née* **Ross** (c.1820–1913) Slavery abolitionist, born in Dorchester Co, Maryland, USA. She escaped from slavery in Maryland (1849) and went north via the 'Underground Railway', a network of secret safe-houses. She returned to the South frequently to escort escaping slaves through this route, becoming known as 'the Moses of her People'. She devoted her life to the abolitionist cause.

Tubruq *Tobruk*

Tubuai Islands [toobwiy] or **Austral Islands**, Fr **Iles Tubuai** pop (2000e) 8900; area 137 sq km/53 sq mi. Volcanic island group of French Polynesia, 528 km/328 mi S of the Society Is; comprises a 1300 km/800 mi chain of volcanic islands and reefs; chief islands, Rimatara, Rurutu, Tubuai, Raivaevae, Rapa; chief settlement, Mataura (Tubuai); coffee, copra.

tubular bells A set of metal tubes tuned to different pitches and suspended in a large frame. They are struck with a short mallet to produce bell sounds in orchestral and operatic music.

Tubulidentata [tyubulidentahta] The smallest extant order of mammals comprising a single species, the aardvark (Orycteropodidae); characterized by the absence of tooth enamel, each tooth having tubular pulp cavities surrounded by hexagonal dentine prisms.

TUC *Trades Union Congress*

Tucana [tookahna] (Lat 'toucan') A faint S constellation, which includes the prominent Small Magellanic Cloud and the notable globular cluster 47 Tuc.

Tucker, Albert Lee (1914–99) Painter, born in Melbourne, Victoria, SE Australia. Educated in Melbourne, he received no formal art training. He was known as a pioneer of Surrealism in Australia, and for his Expressionist and nightmarish images. His painting 'Victory Girls' (1943), part of the series 'Images of Modern Evil', is typical of his enraged indictment of a corrupt, debased society, a view which he defended in writing of a polemical nature in the magazine *Angry Penguins* during the 1940s. He was also known for his paintings of harsh Australian landscape as well as for his self-portraits. He left Australia in 1947, working and exhibiting in Japan, Europe, and the USA, returning in 1960. An important retrospective of his work was mounted by the Australian National Gallery in 1990.

Tucson [tooson] 32°13N 110°58W, pop (2000e) 486 700. Seat of Pima Co, SE Arizona, USA, on the Santa Cruz R; the Spanish founded the Presidio of San Augustín de Tuguison in 1776 near the site of the San Xavier del Brac Indian Mission (1700); ceded to the USA, 1853; city status, 1883; state capital, 1867–77; airport; railway; university (1885); electronic, optical and research industries; processing and distributing centre for cotton, livestock, and nearby mines; major tourist and health resort; Davis-Monthan Air Force Base nearby; Tucson Festival (Apr).

Tucumán *San Miguel de Tucumán*

Tudjman, Franjo [tujman] (1922–99) Croatian president (1990–9), born in Veliko Trgvoisaeem Zagorie, NW Croatia. A member of the military (1945–61), he left to pursue an academic career. He founded and directed the Institute of the Worker's Movement in Zagreb (1961–7) and also served as professor of politics at Zagreb University (1962–7). Because of his views, he was expelled from the ruling Communist Party in 1967 and also lost his university post. He was jailed for two years in 1972 and again for three in 1981 following Tito's death. In 1989 he founded the Croatian Democratic Union and became its president. Under his leadership, Croatia achieved full sovereignty, and he became a major figure in Balkan politics in the mid-1990s following the break-up of Yugoslavia.

Tudor, Owen *Catherine of Valois*

Tudors A N Wales gentry family, one of whose scions married a Plantagenet in the early 15th-c. Elevated to the peerage in the mid-15th-c, they ruled England from 1485 to 1603. The dynasty began when Henry, 2nd Earl of Richmond and son of Margaret Beaufort (a Lancastrian claimant to the crown) overthrew Richard III in 1485. It ended with the death of Elizabeth I in 1603.

tuff *pyroclastic rock*

tug of war An athletic event of strength involving two teams who pull against each other from opposite ends of a long thick rope. A team normally consists of eight members. With sheer strength and determination they have to pull their opponents over a predetermined mark. Ancient Chinese and Egyptians participated in similar events. The modern rules were drawn up by the New York Athletic Club in 1879. It was part of the Olympic programme 1900–28.

tui [tooee] A honeyeater (*Prosthemadera novaeseelandiae*) native to the New Zealand area; dark plumage with small knot of white feathers on throat, and collar of delicate white filaments; inhabits forest and habitation; eats insects, fruit, and nectar; also known as **parson bird**.

Tuileries [tweeleree(z)] Formal gardens laid out in the 17th-c by Le Nôtre in Paris. They are all that remain of the former Tuileries Palace built for Catherine de' Medici in the 16th-c, and destroyed by fire in 1871.

Tukhachevsky, Mikhail Nikolayevich [tookachefskee] (1893–1937) Russian soldier and politician, born near Slednevo, W Russia. He served in the Tsarist Army in World War 1, but became a member of the Communist Party in 1918. He commanded Bolshevik forces against the Poles in the Russo-Polish War (1920), against the White Russians (1919–20), and during the Kulak uprising of 1921. He served on the commission on military invention (1922), and was chief of armaments (1931). He is renowned for his work on tactical doctrine, notably on tank warfare. Appointed to the Military Soviet in 1934, he was created Marshal of the Soviet Union in 1935, but was later executed for treason during Stalin's purge of Red Army officers.

Tula (Mexico) **[toola]** An ancient Meso-American city, c.65 km/40 mi NW of Mexico City, from which the Toltecs dominated C Mexico c.900–1150 AD. It was 14 sq km/5½ sq mi in area and at its height had a population of c.30–40 000. It developed from AD c.750, and was destroyed c.1168. Within its overall grid of houses and courtyards lies a central plaza containing temple pyramids, colonnaded meeting halls, and a ballcourt.

Tula (Russia) **[toola]** 54°11N 37°38E, pop (2000e) 541 000. Industrial capital town of Tulskaya oblast, NC European Russia; on R Upa, 193 km/120 mi S of Moscow; Imperial Small Arms Factory founded here by Peter the Great, 1712; railway; airfield; metallurgy, machinery, chemicals, biscuits; Uspenskii Cathedral (1762–4).

tularaemia / tularemia A disease caused by infection with *Francisella tularensis*. The bacterium normally infects game animals but can remain alive for weeks in soil and water, and is highly infectious. It is acquired by humans by inhalation, direct skin contact, in the bites of ticks that infest wildlife, or by ingestion of contaminated meat and water. Hunters and trappers are most often affected. The clinical features depend on the method of entry into the body, and include fatigue, fever, swollen lymph nodes, pneumonia, skin ulcers, and gastro-enteritis. Infection may spread throughout the body, and the disease is fatal if untreated, in c.10% of cases. The organism has recently been the subject of considerable research because of its potential as a biological warfare agent.

tulip A bulb native to Europe and Asia, especially the steppe regions with cold winters and hot dry summers; stems erect; leaves narrow to oval, sometimes wavy; flowers solitary, occasionally 2–6, in a variety of shapes and colours but usually large and showy, with six rounded or pointed, in some forms fringed perianth-segments or tepals. A popular ornamental for centuries, a huge industry is built around several thousand named cultivars, especially in Holland, the country foremost in breeding tulips. (Genus: *Tulipa*, 100 species. Family: Liliaceae.)

tulip tree A deciduous tree (*Liriodendron tulipifera*) reaching 35 m/115 ft, native to North America; leaves 4-lobed with a squared apex; flowers with six greenish-yellow petals, resembling the tulip in size and shape, hence the name. It is a valuable timber tree, known commercially as **Canary** or **American whitewood**, and also called **tulip poplar** in North America. (Family: Magnoliaceae.)

Tull, Jethro (1674–1741) Agriculturist, born in Basildon, West Berkshire, S England, UK. He studied at Oxford, and became a lawyer, but turned to farming. He introduced several new farming methods, including the invention of a seed drill which planted seeds in rows (1701).

Tullamore [tuhl**a**maw(r)], Ir **Tulach Mhór** 53°16N 7°30W, pop (2000e) 9600. Capital of Offaly county, Leinster, C Ireland; road junction on the Grand Canal, W of Dublin; railway; agricultural trade, spinning, distilling; abbey nearby at Durrow founded by St Columba.

Tulsa [**tuhl**sa] 36°10N 95°55W, pop (2000e) 393 000. Seat of Tulsa Co, NE Oklahoma, USA; port on the Arkansas R; settled as a Creek Indian village in the 1830s; developed in the 1880s with the coming of the railway; airport; university (1894); major national centre of the petroleum industry; oil refining, petrochemicals, aerospace industry, metal goods; Gilcrease Institute of Art; May Festival, Great Labour Day Raft Race.

tumbleweed The name given to various bushy plants which, at the end of the growing season, break off at ground level and are blown and rolled considerable distances by the wind, simultaneously scattering their seeds. They are mainly found in dry, open country most suitable for this method of dispersal.

tumour A swelling of any kind in any part of the body. The literal definition refers to swellings of any origin, including infections and cysts. However the term is more often used to refer to benign or malignant growths (*neoplasms*). Benign growths occur locally and have well defined margins. Malignant growths (*cancer*) invade surrounding tissues and also spread to other areas of the body via the blood and lymphatic systems (*metastasis*).

tuna Any of several large, fast-swimming, predatory, fish (especially the *Thunnus* species) found in surface ocean waters; belong with the mackerels to the family Scombridae; body characteristically spindle-shaped and adapted for power and speed; many heavily exploited commercially.

Tunbridge Wells or **Royal Tunbridge Wells** 51°08N 0°16E, pop (2000e) 60 300. Spa town in Kent, SE England; 50 km/31 mi SE of London; iron-rich springs discovered in 1606; fashionable health resort in 17th–18th-c; 'Royal' since 1909, a legacy of visits made by Queen Victoria; railway; light industry, printing.

tundra The treeless vegetation zone found polewards of the taiga of North America, Europe, and Asia. Often underlain by permafrost, the vegetation is dominated by mosses, lichens, herbaceous perennials, dwarf shrubs, and grasses. The growing season is short, but warm enough for snow to melt and the active layer of permafrost to thaw. The resulting boggy depressions provide breeding ground for mosquitoes.

tungro *rice blast*

tungsten W (from Ger *wolfram*), element 74, density 20 g/cm^3, melting point 3410°C. A grey metal, difficult to work, occurring mainly with other elements in oxide ores, from which it can be recovered by carbon reduction. The metal is used extensively for lamp filaments, because of its high melting point and general lack of reactivity. Compounds mainly show the oxidation states +4 and +6. **Tungsten carbide** (WC), is very hard, and is used in cutting and grinding tools.

Tungurahua [tungur**ah**wa] 1°26S 78°26W. Andean volcano in C Ecuador; 30 km/19 mi SE of Ambato; rises to 5016 m/16 456 ft; spa town of Baños at N foot; dormant, though emits vapours from time to time; erupted in 1886, devastating Baños.

Tunguska, River River in N Russia; comprises two tributaries of the R Yenisey, known as the Lower and Stony Tunguska; greatest length 3200 km/2000 mi.

Tunguska event An explosion of enormous force low in the atmosphere over the Siberian wilderness area of Tunguska R valley (30 Jun 1908). This naturally occurring event is thought to have resulted from the impact of a small comet nucleus or asteroid. Equivalent to about a 2-megaton atomic bomb explosion, it levelled 3000 sq km/1200 sq mi of forest. No meteoritic debris was recovered, suggesting that the impactor was of low strength and perhaps made of volatile materials.

tunicate [**tyoo**nikuht] A marine invertebrate chordate; may be solitary or in colonies, base-attached or free-swimming; adult body enclosed in leathery tunic (*test*); water drawn into a branchial sac via an inhalant siphon; food particles then trapped by mucus and water expelled from an exhalant siphon; larval stage possesses a notochord, dorsal nerve cord, and posterior tail; c.1250 species, including sea squirts, salps, and larvaceans. (Phylum: Chordata. Subphylum: Tunicata.)

tuning fork A two-pronged metal instrument, invented in 1711 by English trumpeter John Shore (c.1662–1752), which is made to vibrate and then pressed down on a wooden surface to produce a note (virtually free from upper harmonics) to which voices or instruments can adjust their pitch.

Tunis [**tyoo**nis] 36°50N 10°13E, pop (2000e) 778 000. Seaport capital of Tunisia, 240 km/150 mi from Sicily; in a strategic position on the Mediterranean; Phoenician origin, later dominated by Carthage; capital status, 1236; captured by Turks, 1533; gained notoriety as a pirate base; occupied by French, 1881; airport; railway; university (1960); chemicals, textiles, tourism; Great Mosque of Zitouna (9th-c), Dar Ben Abdullah (19th-c house), Museum of Islamic Art, Palace of Dar Hussein, Dar Ben Abdullah Museum, Dar Lasram Museum, Bardo National Museum; Medina of Tunis is a world heritage site; film festival of Carthage (Oct).

Tunisia *p.1562*

Tunja [**toon**kha] 5°33N 73°23W, pop (2000e) 121 500. Capital of Boyacá department, EC Colombia; in arid mountainous area, altitude 2819 m/9249 ft; university (1953); one of the oldest cities in Colombia, seat of the Zipa (one of the two Chibcha kings); refounded as a Spanish city, 1539; decisive battle of Boyacá fought 16 km/10 mi to the S, 1818; Church of Santo Domingo (begun 1594), Santa Clara Chapel (1580), Parque Bosque de la Republica, Casa del Fundador Suárez Rendón (1540–3, now a museum).

tunnel An artificial underground passage constructed for a variety of purposes, such as roads, railways, canals, mining, or conducting water. Tunnels are constructed either by cutting away the material above and then covering the tunnel over (the *cut and cover* method), or by driving through the ground using hand tools, a tunnelling shield, or rock drills as appropri-

Tunisia

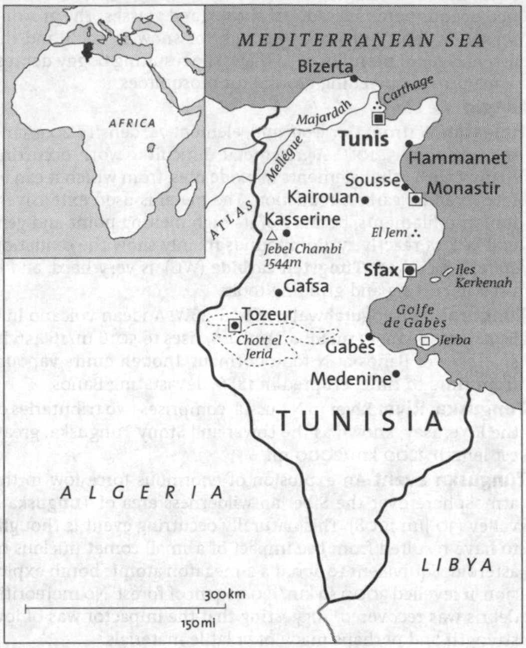

□ International Airport ∴ World heritage site

[tyoonizia], official name **Republic of Tunisia**, Arabic **al-Jumhuria at-Tunisia**

Local names Tunis (Arabic), Tunisie (French)
Timezone GMT +1
Area 164 150 km²/63 362 sq mi
Population total (2002e) 9 764 000
Status Republic
Date of independence 1956

Capital Tunis
Languages Arabic (official), French and Berber widely spoken
Ethnic groups Arab (98%), European (1%), small Jewish minority
Religions Sunni Muslim (98%), Christian (1%), small Jewish minority

Physical features Located in N Africa, on Mediterranean coast; Atlas Mts (NW) rise to 1544 m/5065 ft at Jebel Chambi; Majardah river valley is the most fertile area (N); from Tabussah range, land descends across a plateau to the Saharan desert (S) and a coastal plain (E).

Climate Mediterranean in N, with hot, dry summers, mild, rainy winters; extreme desert-continental conditions in S, with little rainfall; average annual temperature 9°C (Jan), 26°C (Jul); average annual rainfall 400 mm/15·7 in.

Currency 1 Tunisian Dinar (TD, D) = 1000 millimes

Economy Agriculture (employs c.50% of population, but of declining importance); wheat, barley, grapes; olive oil (world's fourth largest producer); phosphates (fifth largest producer).

GDP (2002e) $67·13 bn, per capita $6800

Human Development Index (2002) 0·722

History Ruled by Phoenicians, Carthaginians, Romans, Byzantines, Arabs, Spanish, and Turks; under the control of the Ottoman Empire, 1574; French protectorate, 1881; gained internal self-government in 1955; independence, 1956; monarchy abolished and republic declared, 1957; executive power held by President, who appoints the Prime Minister and Council of Ministers; unicameral legislature, National Assembly, elected every five years; new constitution, 2002.

Head of State
1957–87 Habib Bourguiba
1987– Zine al-Abidine bin Ali

Head of Government
1970–80 Hadi Nouira
1980–6 Mohammed Mezali
1986–7 Rashid Sfar
1987 Zine al-Abidine bin Ali
1987–9 Hadi Baccouche
1989–99 Hamed Karoui
1999– Mohammed Ghannouchi

ate. In soft ground, some form of tunnel lining is required, and this is put in place either as the tunnel advances or immediately afterwards. The longest tunnel in the world is the Delaware Aqueduct in New York (169 km/105 mi), which is used for water supply.

tunnel diode A heavily doped semiconductor junction diode, with a very thin junction region. Breakdown occurs at very low reverse voltages, and there is no region of high reverse resistance. It has a negative resistance over part of its operating region, and is used in high frequency amplifiers and oscillators.

tunnelling *quantum tunnelling*

Tunnicliffe, Charles Frederick (1901–79) Bird artist, born in Langley, Cheshire, NWC England, UK. He won a scholarship to the Royal College of Art. He illustrated Henry Williamson's *Tarka the Otter* (1927) and *Salar the Salmon* (1935) with his own wood-engravings, provided innumerable illustrations for the Royal Society for the Protection of Birds, and published six books of his own, including *Shorelands Summer Diary* (1952), *My Country Book* (1945), and *Bird Portraiture* (1945). A collection of his work is now based at Oriel Môn, Llangefni, Anglesey, NW Wales.

tunny *tuna*

Tuonela [toouhnayla] In the Finnish poem *Kalevala*, the name of a dark river in the Far North, which borders the Other World. To visit Tuonela is the object of the shaman in his trance, when he tries to accompany the spirits of the dead.

tup *sheep*

Tupamaros [toopamahros] An Uruguayan urban guerrilla movement founded by Raúl Sendic in 1963, named after the 18th-c Peruvian Indian rebel, Túpac Amaru. The movement was suppressed by the military-controlled government of 1972–85.

tupelo [tyoopeloh] A deciduous tree (*Nyssa sylvatica*) native to the swamps of E North America; leaves turning bright scarlet in autumn; inconspicuous flowers, small, greenish; males and females on separate trees; edible fruit 1–2 cm/0·4–0·8 in, oval, blue-black; also called **black gum** and **pepperidge**. It is cultivated mainly for ornament. (Family: Nyssaceae.)

Tupolev, Andrey Nikolayevich [toopolef] (1888–1972) Aircraft designer, born in Moscow, Russia. From 1922 he headed the design office of the central aerohydrodynamics institute in Moscow, producing over 100 types of aircraft, and in 1955 he built the first Soviet civil jet, the Tu-104. In 1968 he completed the first test flight of a supersonic passenger aircraft, the Tu-144.

Tupungato, Cerro [tupungahtoh] 33°22S 69°50W. Mountain on the border between Argentina and Chile, rising to 6800 m/22 309 ft; c.80 km/50 mi SE of Cerro Aconcagua.

tur *goat*

turaco [toorakoh] A large African bird, inhabiting woodland and dry scrub; eats fruit and insects; tail long; head usually with crest; also known as the **touraco**, **tauraco**, (in S Africa) **lourie** or **loerie**, and (in W Africa) **plantain-eater**. The woodland species are brightly-coloured (some colours produced by pigments being found only in this family); the scrubland species (also called **go-away birds**) are duller. (Family: Musophagidae, 24 species.)

turbidity current A current composed of sediment particles suspended in water that may flow down slope underwater at a velocity measured in tens of knots. It is thought to be an important agent in transporting shallow marine sediments to the deep sea, carving out a submarine canyon in the process. As these turbidity currents lose speed on the low gradients of the continental rise and abyssal plains, they leave sedimentary deposits known as *turbidities*.

turbine A balanced wheel having at its rim a large number of small radiating blades of aerofoil cross section. When an axial flow of fluid is made to pass over the blades, the turbine rotates about its shaft. The shaft's rotation can then be used for useful external work. If the fluid is steam, the engine is called a **steam turbine**; if water, a **water turbine**. In a **turbo-jet** aircraft, the gas turbine engine is arranged so that the thrust is derived directly from the rearward expulsion of exhaust gases. In a **turbo-prop** aircraft, the exhaust gases drive a turbine fixed to a propeller; the use of the propeller increases the efficiency of propulsion at low speeds over that of a jet.

turbo-jet; turbo-prop *turbine*

turbot European flatfish (*Scophthalmus maximus*) widespread on gravel bottoms of inshore waters of the E North Atlantic; length up to 1 m/3¼ ft; light brown with darker spots and patches; feeds mainly on small fishes; excellent food fish taken commercially by trawl and line; also popular with sea anglers. (Family: Scophthalmidae.)

turbulence In fluid flow, a flow in which pressure and velocity change constantly and erratically. Common examples are wind and water swirling around obstructions. Flow along pipes becomes turbulent at sufficiently high flow rates.

Turenne, Henri de la Tour d'Auvergne, vicomte de (Viscount of) [türen] (1611–75) French marshal, born in Sedan, France, son of the Protestant Duc de Bouillon, and grandson of William I (the Silent). He learned soldiering from his uncles, the Princes of Orange, and in the Thirty Years' War fought with distinction for the armies of the Protestant alliance. He captured Breisach (1638) and Turin (1640), and for the conquest of Roussillon from the Spaniards (1642) was made Marshal of France (1643). In the civil wars of the Frondes, he joined the *frondeurs* at first, but then switched sides; his campaigning (1652–3) saved the young King Louis XIV and Mazarin's government. In the Franco-Spanish war he conquered much of the Spanish Netherlands after defeating Condé at the Battle of the Dunes (1658). He won lasting fame for his campaigns in the United Provinces during the Dutch War (1672–5), but advancing along the Rhine he was killed at Sasbach.

Turgenev, Ivan (Sergeyevich) [toorgyaynyef] (1818–83) Novelist, born in Orel, W Russia. He studied at St Petersburg and Berlin universities, and joined the Russian civil service in 1841, but in 1843 abandoned this to take up literature. His first studies of peasant life, *Sportsman's Sketches* (1852, trans title), made his reputation, but earned governmental ill favour. He was banished for two years to his country estates, and then lived mainly in Germany and France. His greatest novel, *Fathers and Sons* (1862, trans title), was badly received in Russia, but a particular success in England. He also wrote poetry, plays (of which *A Month in the Country* (1855) is the best known), short stories, and tales of the supernatural.

Turgot, Anne Robert Jacques [toorgoh] (1727–81) French statesman and economist, born in Paris, France. Educated at the seminary of Saint-Sulpice, he renounced the Church for the law, became a magistrate in the *Parlement* of Paris, and was promoted to intendant at Limoges (1761–74), where he carried out reforms. Here he published his best-known work, *Réflexions sur la formation et la distribution des richesses* (1766, Reflections on the Formation and Distribution of Wealth). Appointed comptroller-general of finance by Louis XVI (1774), he embarked on a comprehensive scheme of national economic reform, but the opposition of the privileged classes to his Six Edicts led to his overthrow (1776), and he died forgotten, his reforms abandoned.

Turin [tyoorin], Ital **Torino**, ancient **Augusta Taurinorum** 45°04N 7°40E, pop (2000e) 991 000. Capital city of Turin province, Piedmont, NW Italy, on left bank of R Po; founded by the Taurini; Roman colony under Augustus; capital of Kingdom of Sardinia, 1720; centre of the 19th-c Risorgimento; capital of the Kingdom of Italy until 1861–5; airport; railway; archbishopric; university (1404); iron, steel, cars, machinery, rolling stock, underwater defence systems, textiles, vermouths, confectionery, coffee, insurance and banking, printing and publishing; Porta Palatina (Roman city gate) (1st-c AD), cathedral (15th-c), Palazzo Reale (1646–58), Palazzo Carignano (1680), Palazzo Madama (13th-c); carnival (Feb), biennial International Motor Show and Industrial Vehicle Show.

Turin, Shroud of *Holy Shroud*

Turing, Alan (Mathison) [tooring] (1912–54) Mathematician, born in London, UK. He studied at Cambridge and Princeton, worked in cryptography during World War 2, then joined the National Physical Laboratory (1945) and the computing laboratory at Manchester (1948). He provided a precise mathematical characterization of computability, and introduced the theoretical notion of an idealized computer (since called a **Turing machine**), laying the foundation for the field of artificial intelligence. He committed suicide after being prosecuted for homosexuality.

Turkana, Lake [toorkahna], formerly **Lake Rudolf** (to 1979) area 6405 sq km/2472 sq mi. Lake in NW Kenya and Ethiopia, E Africa, 400 km/250 mi N of Nairobi; N extremity extends into Ethiopia; length 290 km/180 mi; width 56 km/35 mi; depth c.70 m/230 ft; the lake is surrounded by extensive Plio-Pleistocene deposits covering the last 3–4 million years. Within these, Richard Leakey and his associates have recovered many important hominid fossils, many from the periods 2·3–2·6 and 1·4–1·9 million years ago (mya). Major localities on the E side of the lake include Ileret and Koobi Fora, with fossils of *Australopithecus boisei*, *Homo habilis*, *Homo rudolfensis*, and *Homo erectus*. On the W side there have been major discoveries at Lomekwi – the 2·6 million-year-old cranium of *Australopithecus aethiopicus* (an early robust australopithecine) – and at Nariokotome, with the virtually complete skeleton of a *Homo erectus* youth dated to 1·6 mya.

Turkestan Historical area of C Asia occupying parts of modern Kazakhstan, Kyrgyzstan, Tajikistan, Turkmenistan, Uzbekistan, and Xinjiang, including the great trading centres of Samarkand and Tashkent. Traversed by the E–W Silk Road, and thus of great economic importance to China, it attracted repeated Chinese strategic interest from the 2nd-c BC onwards. Conquered by the Tang dynasty (657) it was later taken by the Arabs (751) and the Mongols (1211–21). E Turkestan was overrun by the Kiangxi Emperor's forces (from 1715) and again under the Qianlong Emperor (1755–9), when it was annexed to China as Xinjiang ('new dominion').

Turkey *p.1564*

turkey A large pheasant-like bird, native to C and S North America; head naked; male with pendulous fold of skin at base of bill, and prominent spur on each leg; inhabits mixed woodland; omnivorous; plumage dark, mottled (domestic populations paler); domesticated in 16th-c; a popular poultry bird, especially in the USA at Thanksgiving and the UK at Christmas. (Family: Meleagrididae, 2 species.)

Turkish *Altaic*

Turkish cat A breed of long-haired domestic cat from the area around L Van, Turkey; thick white coat with reddish-brown markings on head and reddish-brown tail; enjoys swimming; also known as **Van cat** or **swimming cat**.

Turkmenistan *p.1565*

Turks and Caicos Islands *p.1566*

Turku [toorkoo], Swed **Åbo** 60°27N 22°15E, pop (2000e) 163 000. Seaport and capital of Turku-Pori province, SW Finland; on Aurajoki (river) near its mouth on the Gulf of Bothnia; third largest city in Finland; established, 11th-c; capital of Finland until 1812; peace between Sweden and Russia signed here,

Turkey

□ International Airport

Turkish **Türkiye**, official name **Republic of Turkey**, Turkish **Türkiye Cumhuriyeti**

Local name Türkiye Cumhuriyeti

Timezone GMT +2

Area 779 452 km²/300 868 sq mi

Population total (2002e) 69 359 000

Status Republic

Capital Ankara

Languages Turkish (Türkçe) (official), Kurdish and Arabic; Greek, Armenian, and Yiddish minorities

Ethnic groups Turkish (85%), Kurd (12%)

Religions Sunni Muslim (98%), Greek Orthodox, Armenian, and Jewish minorities

Physical features Lying partly in Europe and partly in Asia, W area (Thrace), E area (Anatolia); Turkish Straits (Dardanelles, Sea of Marmara, Bosporus) connect the Black Sea (NE) and Mediterranean Sea (SW); mountainous area, Taurus Mts, cover the entire S part of Anatolia; highest peak Mt Ararat, 5165 m/16 945 ft; earthquake region (major disasters in the NW, Aug and Nov 1999, E in May 2003); sources of rivers Euphrates and Tigris in E.

Climate Mediterranean climate on Aegean and Mediterranean coasts, with hot, dry summers, warm, wet winters; mean temperature 19°C (Jul); average annual temperatures 0·3°C (Jan), 23°C (Jul) in Ankara; average annual rainfall 723 mm/28 in.

Currency 1 Turkish Lira (TL) = 100 kurus

Economy Agriculture (employs c.50% of workforce); cotton, tobacco, fruits, nuts, livestock; minerals, textiles, glass, and cement; many Turks find work elsewhere in Europe, especially Germany.

GDP (2002e) $489·7 bn, per capita $7300

Human Development Index (2002) 0·742

History Seljuk sultanate replaced by the Ottoman in NW Asia Minor in 13th-c; Turkish invasion of Europe, first in Balkans, 1375; fall of Constantinople, 1453; empire at its peak under Sulaiman the Magnificent, 16th-c; Young Turks seized power, 1908; Balkan War, 1912–13; allied with Germany during World War 1; Republic followed Young Turk revolution, led by Kemal Atatürk, 1923; policy of westernization and economic development; neutral throughout most of World War 2, then sided with Allies; military coups in 1960 and 1980; strained relations with Greece, and invasion of Cyprus, 1974; aided the allied forces during the Gulf War, 1991; constitution provides for a single-chamber National Assembly; a President appoints a Prime Minister and a Council of Ministers.

Head of State

1982–9 Kenan Evren
1989–93 Turgut Özal
1993–2000 Süleyman Demirel
2000– Ahmet Necdet Sezer

Head of Government

1980–3 Bülent Ulusu
1983–9 Turgut Özal
1989–91 Yildirim Akbulut
1991 Mesut Yilmaz
1991–3 Süleyman Demirel
1993–6 Tansu Çiller
1996 Mesut Yilmaz
1996–7 Necmettin Erbakan
1997–9 Mesut Yilmaz
1999–2002 Bulent Ecevit
2002–3 Abdullah Gul *Acting*
2003– Recep Tayyip Erdogan

1743; airport; railway; ferries to Sweden and Åland Is; two universities (Swedish 1918, Finnish 1920); shipbuilding, engineering, foodstuffs, textiles; Rantasipi Congress Centre; music festival (Aug).

turmeric [termerik] A perennial native to India (*Curcuma longa*), related to ginger and East Indian arrowroot; rhizomatous; stem to c.1 m/3¾ ft; flowers with a yellow lip, borne in a dense spike with white and pink bracts. It is cultivated for the fleshy, aromatic rhizomes, ground to provide the distinctive smell and colour of curry powder. It also produces a yellow dye. (Family: Zingiberaceae.)

Turnbull, Malcolm (Bligh) (1954–) Merchant banker, lawyer, and republican, born in Sydney, New South Wales, SE Australia. He studied at the universities of Sydney and Oxford, where he was Rhodes Scholar for New South Wales in 1978. He worked as a political correspondent for various newspapers and radio stations before being admitted to the bar in 1980. He set up his own law firm in 1986, and became known for successfully defending Peter Wright in the *Spycatcher* trial, publishing his account of the case in 1988. A prominent advocate of an Australian Republic, in 1993 he was appointed chairman of the Republic Advisory Committee.

Turner, J(oseph) M(allord) W(illiam) (1775–1851) Landscape artist and watercolourist, born in London, UK. After little formal education, he entered the Royal Academy at 14, and soon began to exhibit. He travelled widely in Britain, making architectural drawings in the cathedral cities, and spent three years in collaboration with Girtin producing watercolours. He then took to oils, his early works including 'Frosty Morning' (1813) and 'Crossing the Brook' (1815). After his first visit to Italy (1819), his work showed several literary influences, as in 'Ulysses Deriding Polyphemus' (1829). His second visit (1829) marks the beginning of his last great artistic period, including 'The Fighting Téméraire' (1839) and 'Rain, Steam and Speed' (1844, Tate, London). His revolution in art foreshadowed Impressionism, and found a timely champion in John Ruskin, whose writing helped to turn the critical tide in Turner's favour. Turner bequeathed 300 of his paintings and 20 000 watercolours and drawings to the nation. He led a secretive private life, never married, and died in a temporary lodging in Chelsea, under the assumed name of Booth.

Turner, Kathleen (1954–) Actress, born in Springfield, Missouri, USA. She made her film debut in *Body Heat* (1981), and went on to star in such popular films as *Romancing the Stone* (1984),

Turkmenistan

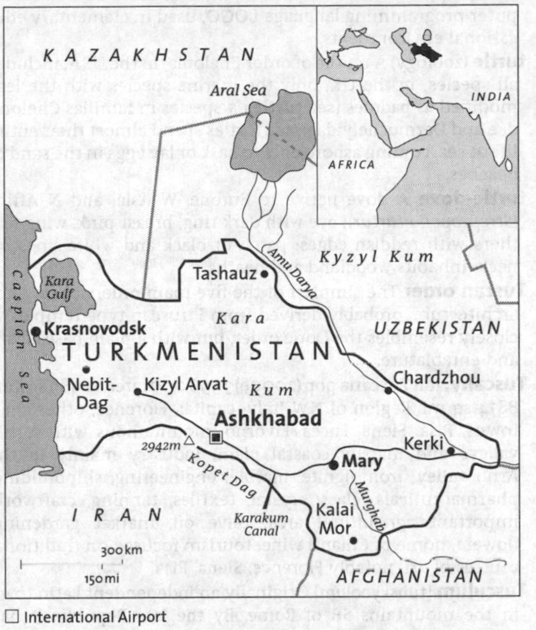

[terkmeni**stahn**], official name **Republic of Turkmenistan**, formerly **Turkmenia**, Turkmen **Türkmenistan Jumhuriyäti**

Local name Turkmenostan

Timezone GMT +5

Area 488 100 km^2/188 400 sq mi

Population total (2002e) 4 946 000

Status Republic

Date of independence 1991

Capital Ashkhabad (Ashgabad)

Languages Turkmenian (official), other Turkic languages, Russian

Ethnic groups Turkmen (72%), Russian (10%), Uzbek, Kazakh, Ukrainian minorities

Religion Sunni Muslim

Physical features Kara Kum (Black Sands) desert, area 310 800 km^2/120 000 sq mi, covers c.80% of the country; Turan Plain covers four-fifths of Turkmenistan; foothills in the S; Kopet Dag mountain range is volcanic; other foothills are spurs of the Kugitangtau and Pamir-Alay ranges; Rivers Amu Darya and Murghab.

Climate Continental, great variation of temperatures; temperatures range from 50°C (Jul) in Kara Kum, to -33°C (Jan) in the Kushka; in the mountains; average annual rainfall 120–250 mm/ 5–10 in.

Currency Manat = 100 gapik

Economy Mineral resources of oil, natural gas, sulphur, potassium, and salt; oil, gas extraction (main industries); textiles; cotton production; agriculture; raising of Karakul sheep, Turkoman horses, and camels.

GDP (2002e) $31·34 bn, per capita $6700

Human Development Index (2002) 0·741

History Part of the ancient Persian empire; ruled by Seljuk Turks, 11th-c; conquered by Genghis Khan and the Mongols, 13th-c; Uzbeks invaded, 15th-c; divided into two: one part belonged to the Khanate of Khiva (which became part of the Russian empire), and the other to the Khanate of Bukhara; Turkistan Autonomous Soviet Socialist Republic formed, 1922; full Soviet Socialist Republic, 1924; declared sovereignty, 1990; independence and membership of Commonwealth of Independent States, 1991; governed by a President, who is both head of state and government, and parliament (*Majlis*).

Head of State/Government
1991– Saparmurad Niyazov

Prizzi's Honor (1985), and *War Of The Roses* (1989). She received a Best Actress Oscar nomination for her role in *Peggy Sue Got Married* (1986), and provided the husky voice for Jessica Rabbit in the film *'Who Framed Roger Rabbit?'* (1988). Later films include *Serial Mom* (1994) and *The Real Blonde* (1998). She also earned critical acclaim for her performance on Broadway in *Indiscretions* (1995) and also for her West End debut as Mrs Robinson in *The Graduate* (2000).

Turner, Nat (1800–31) Slave leader, born in Southampton Co, Virginia, USA. The son of an African native, he became a religious fanatic, believing that God had chosen him to lead his people out of bondage. He mounted the only sustained slave revolt in US history (1831), but was captured, tried, and hanged. A number of books have been written about the incident, notably the controversial *The Confessions of Nat Turner* (1967) by William Styron.

Turner, Tina, originally **Annie Mae Bullock** (1939–) Singer, born in Nutbush, Tennessee, USA. She achieved considerable success in the rhythm-and-blues vocal duo, Ike and Tina Turner, before their marriage and professional partnership was officially dissolved in 1976. Her first solo single, 'Let's Stay Together' (1983), reached number 6 in the UK music charts. Other hit singles include 'What's Love Got To Do With It?' (1984) and 'Private Dancer' (1985). She appeared in the film *Mad Max: Beyond Thunderdrome* (1985), and recorded the title song for the James Bond film *Goldeneye* (1996). Her autobiography *I Tina* (1989) was filmed as *What's Love Got To Do With It* (1993).

Turner Prize Britain's most prestigious prize for contemporary art, awarded to a British artist under 50 for an outstanding exhibition in the previous year. An initiative of the Tate Gallery, London, it was first awarded in 1984, and has since attracted considerable controversy for its choice of winners, regularly forcing a public debate on the question of 'Is it art?'.

turnip An annual or biennial vegetable (*Brassica rapa*), 1 m/$3\frac{1}{4}$ ft high; bright green, deeply-lobed leaves; yellow, cross-shaped flowers. The cultivated turnip (subspecies *rapa*) has an edible tuberous taproot, and is widely grown as a vegetable and for fodder. The wild turnip (subspecies *moestris*) lacks a swollen taproot. (Family: Cruciferae.)

turnkey system A method of acquiring a system of computer hardware and software as a whole from a single supplier. Buying a turnkey system removes the need for carrying out a full systems analysis and design exercise.

turnover tax A tax levied at several stages in the progression from materials to finished goods, or when certain services are provided. For example, a miller pays turnover tax on wheat from the farmer; the baker pays it on the flour; and the customer pays it on the bread. Unlike value-added tax, there is no credit for tax paid at earlier stages.

turnpike A gate across a road to stop the passage of vehicles or persons until a toll is paid. The roads were known as **turnpike roads**, and were common during the 18th–19th-c. The tolls collected were used both for the upkeep of the road and as profit for the shareholders.

turnstone Either of two species of sandpiper, genus *Arenaria*: the **ruddy turnstone** (*Arenaria interpres*), found worldwide on coasts; also the **black turnstone** (*Arenaria melanocephala*), found on the W coast of North America; turns stones and sea-

Turks and Caicos Islands

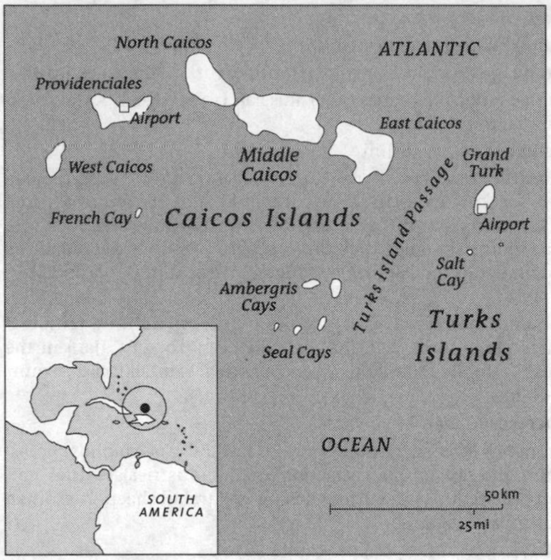

[kaykos]

Timezone GMT –5

Area 500 km^2/200 sq mi

Population total (2003e) 19 350

Capital Cockburn Town

Physical features Two island groups comprising c.30 islands and cays, forming the SE archipelago of the Bahamas chain, W Atlantic Ocean; Turk I and Caicos I are separated by 35 km/ 22 mi; only 6 of the other islands are inhabited.

Climate Subtropical climate; average annual temperatures 24–7°C (Jan), 29–32°C (Jul); average annual rainfall 525 mm/21 in; occasional hurricanes.

Currency 1 US Dollar ($, US$) = 100 cents

Economy Tourism is a rapidly expanding industry; corn, beans, fishing, fish processing.

GDP (2000e) $231 mn, per capita $9600

History Visited by the Spanish, 1512; linked formally to the Bahamas, 1765; transferred to Jamaica, 1848; British Crown Colony, 1972; internal self-government, 1976; British sovereign represented by a Governor, who presides over a Council.

weed with short bill, seeking invertebrates; also eats carrion. (Family: Scolopacidae.)

turpentine tree A deciduous shrub or small tree (*Pistacia terebinthus*), growing to 10 m/30 ft, native to the Mediterranean region and SW Asia; leaves leathery, pinnate with 3–9 leaflets; flowers tiny, in axillary plumes; fruits coral-red; also called **terebinth**. It produces a resin which yields turpentine. (Family: Anacardiaceae.)

Turpin, Dick, popular name of **Richard Turpin** (1706–39) Robber, born in Hempstead, Essex, SE England, UK. He was a butcher's apprentice, smuggler, housebreaker, highwayman, and horse thief. He entered into partnership with Tom King, whom he accidently killed while firing at a constable (or innkeeper). He was hanged at York for horse stealing. The legendary ride from London to York, attributed to him, was probably actually carried out by 'Swift John Nevison' (1639–84), who in 1676 is said to have robbed a sailor at Gadshill at 4 am, and to have established an 'alibi' by reaching York at 7.45 pm.

turquoise A hydrated aluminium phosphate mineral formed by the surface alteration of aluminium-rich rock, with bright-blue to green-blue masses or veins, opaque with a waxy lustre. It is valued as a semi-precious stone.

turtle (computing) An electromechanical computer drawing device. The precise movements of the turtle are sent to it by the computer. The device is normally associated with the computer programming language LOGO, used in elementary educational environments.

turtle (zoology) A reptile of order Chelonia; in the USA, includes all species; in the UK, only the marine species with the legs modified as paddles (**sea turtles**, 7 species in families Cheloniidae and Dermochelyidae); sea turtles spend almost their entire life at sea, coming ashore only to bask or lay eggs in the sand of beaches.

turtle-dove A dove native to Europe, W Asia, and N Africa (*Streptopelia turtur*); eye with dark ring; breast pink, wing feathers with reddish edges; patch of black and white lines on neck; inhabits woodland and heaths.

Tuscan order The simplest of the five main orders of classical architecture, probably derived from Etruscan-type temples. It closely resembles the Doric order, but with a plain base, shaft, and entablature.

Tuscany, Ital **Toscana** pop (2000e) 3 596 000; area 22 989 sq km/ 8874 sq mi. Region of NW Italy; capital, Florence; other chief towns, Pisa, Siena, Lucca, Livorno; mountainous with fertile valleys and marshy coastal plain; industry mainly in the Arno valley; iron, lignite, marble; engineering, shipbuilding, pharmaceuticals, glass, crystal, textiles, tanning, craftwork; important agricultural area; olive oil, market gardening, flowers; home of Chianti wine; tourism focused on traditional centres of art, notably Florence, Siena, Pisa.

Tusculum [tuh**sk**yoolum] Originally an independent Latin town in the mountains SE of Rome. By the late Republic it had become a fashionable country retreat for wealthy Romans. Both Cicero and Lucullus had villas there.

Tuskeegee Institute US institution dedicated to black education. It was founded by Booker T Washington in 1881, and since then has specialized in vocational and technical education.

tusk shell A marine, bottom-living mollusc found partly embedded in sediment from shallow water to abyssal depths; body bilaterally symmetrical, within a curved, tubular shell open at both ends; foot protrusible, often used for burrowing; head poorly developed, but with a tube (*proboscis*) for catching protozoan prey. (Class: Scaphopoda.)

Tussaud, Marie [tuh**saw**d], Fr [tüsoh], *née* **Grosholtz** (1761–1850) Modeller in wax, born in Strasbourg, NE France. She was apprenticed to her uncle, Dr Curtius, in Paris, and inherited his wax museums after his death. After the Revolution, she attended the guillotine to take death masks from the severed heads. She toured Britain with her life-size portrait waxworks, and in 1835 set up a permanent exhibition in Baker St, London. It was burnt down in 1925, and re-opened in Marylebone Rd in 1928. The exhibition still contains her own handiwork, notably images of Marie Antoinette, Napoleon, and Burke and Hare in the Chamber of Horrors.

tussock moth A medium-sized moth in which the proboscis is usually absent; wings often white with darker markings; caterpillars often brightly coloured and hairy; hairs commonly woven into walls of pupal cocoon. (Order: Lepidoptera. Family: Lymantriidae.)

Tutankhamen or **Tut'ankhamun** [tootan**kah**men, tootangka**moon**] (14th-c BC) Egyptian pharaoh of the 18th dynasty (1361–1352 BC), the undistinguished son-in-law of the heretic pharaoh, Akhenaton. He came to the throne at the age of 12, and is famous only for his magnificent tomb at Thebes, which was discovered intact in 1922 by Lord Carnarvon and Howard Carter.

Tuthmosis *Thutmose III*

Tutin, Dame Dorothy [tyoo**tin**] (1931–2001) Actress, born in London, UK. She trained at the Royal Academy of Dramatic Art, London, and made her acting debut in 1950. She toured Russia with the Shakespeare Memorial Theatre (1958), made her first appearance in a contemporary play in *The Devils* (1961), and subsequently played many leading roles in classical and modern plays, including Queen Victoria in *Portrait of a Queen*

Tuvalu

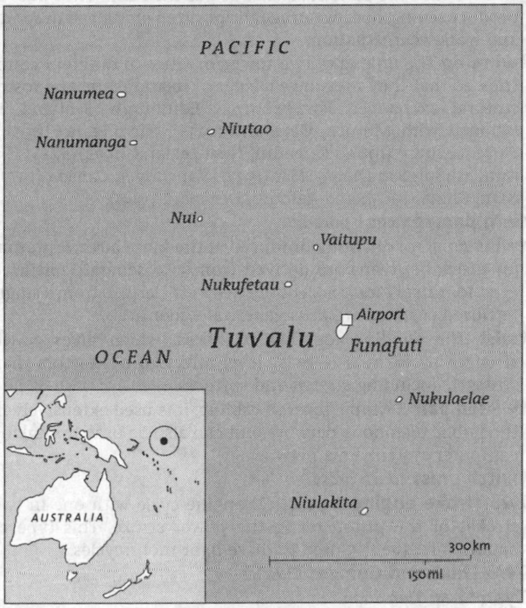

[toovaloo], formerly **Ellice Is** (to 1976)
Local name Tuvalu
Timezone GMT +12
Area 26 km^2/10 sq mi
Population total (2002e) 10 900
Status Independent state within the Commonwealth
Date of independence 1978
Capital Funafuti (Fongafale)
Languages Tuvaluan, English
Ethnic group Polynesian (96%)
Religions Christian (Protestant Church of Tuvalu, Roman Catholic, Baha'i) (97%), small Muslim minority
Physical features Island group in the SW Pacific, 1050 km/650 mi off Fiji; comprises nine low-lying coral atolls, running NW–SE in a chain 580 km/360 mi long; consists of the islands of Funafuti, Nukufetau, Nukulaelae, Nanumea, Niutao, Nanumanga, Nui, Vaitupu, and Niulakita; all low-lying, highest point, 4·6 m/15 ft, on Niulakita.
Climate Hot, humid climate; average annual temperatures 29°C (Jan), 27°C (Jul) in Funafuti; average annual rainfall 3535 mm/139 in.
Currency 1 Australian Dollar ($A) = 100 cents
Economy Subsistence economy; agriculture, coconuts, copra, tropical fruit; fish; handcrafted products, postage stamps.
GDP (2002e) $12·2 mn, per capita $1100
History Invaded by Samoans, 16th-c; British protectorate, as the Ellice Is, 1892; administered as a colony jointly with Gilbert Is (now Kiribati), 1915; American soldiers occupied the Ellice Islands during World War 2, to counter the advance of the Japanese in 1942; separate constitution, following 1974 referendum; independence as a constitutional monarchy within the Commonwealth, 1978; Tuvalu Trust Fund set up by Britain, Australia, New Zealand, and South Korea, 1987; British monarch represented by a Governor-General; governed by a Prime Minister, Cabinet, and unicameral Parliament.
Head of State
(British monarch represented by Governor-General)
1998–2003 Sir Tomasi Puapua
2003– Sir Faimala Luka
Head of Government
2001 Lagitupu Tuilimu *Acting*
2001 Faimalaga Luka
2001–2 Koloa Talake
2002– Saufatu Sopoanga

(1965). She received a Variety Club of Great Britain Award for her role in the film *Savage Messiah* (1972). Later films included *The Shooting Party* (1984), *Alive and Kicking* (1997), and *Maybe Next Year* (1998). In 1999 she appeared in *The Gin Game* at the Savoy. She was made a dame in 1999.

Tutsi *Hutu and Tutsi*

Tutu, Desmond (Mpilo) (1931–) Anglican clergyman, born in Klerksdorp, N South Africa. He studied at the universities of South Africa and London, was briefly a schoolteacher, then became an Anglican parish priest (1960). He rapidly rose to become Bishop of Lesotho (1977), secretary-general of the South African Council of Churches (1979), the first black Bishop of Johannesburg (1984), and Archbishop of Cape Town (1986), retiring in 1996. A critic of the apartheid system, he repeatedly risked imprisonment for his advocacy of the imposition of punitive sanctions against South Africa by the international community. He condemned the use of violence by opponents of apartheid, seeking instead a peaceful, negotiated reconciliation between the black and white communities. He was awarded the Nobel Prize for Peace in 1984, and was appointed chair of the Truth and Reconciliation Commission in 1995.

Tutuola, Amos [tutwohla] (1920–97) Novelist, born in Abeokuta, SW Nigeria. He was celebrated in the West as the author of *The Palm-Wine Drinkard* (1952), a transcription in pidgin English prose of an oral tale of his own invention. Later novels in the same manner included *My Life in the Bush of Ghosts* (1954), *The Brave African Huntress* (1958), *Ajaiyi and His Inherited Poverty* (1967), and *The Wild Hunter in the Bush of Ghosts* (1989).

Tuvalu *see panel*

TVA (Tennessee Valley Authority) *Tennessee River*

Twain, Mark, pseudonym of **Samuel Langhorne Clemens** (1835–1910) Writer, journalist, and lecturer, born in Florida, Missouri, USA. A printer (1847–57) and later a Mississippi river-boat pilot (1857–61), he adopted his name from a well-known call used when sounding the river shallows ('Mark twain!' meaning 'by the mark two fathoms'). He edited for two years the Virginia City *Territorial Enterprise*, and in 1864 moved to San Francisco as a reporter. In 1867 he visited France, Italy, and Palestine, gathering material for his *The Innocents Abroad* (1869), which established his reputation as a humorist. On his return to America, he settled in the East, and in 1870 married **Olivia Langdon** (d.1904), the daughter of a wealthy New York coal merchant. In 1871 they moved to Hartford, CT, where they built a distinctive house (now open to the public) at the centre of a community of artists, known as Nook Farm. His two greatest masterpieces, *The Adventures of Tom Sawyer* (1876) and *The Adventures of Huckleberry Finn* (1884), drawn from his own boyhood experiences, are firmly established among the world's classics; other favourites are *A Tramp Abroad* (1880) and *A Connecticut Yankee in King Arthur's Court* (1889). Widely known as a lecturer, he developed a great popular following. Financial speculations led to the loss of most of his earnings by 1894, and he embarked on a world lecture tour to restore some of his wealth. In his later years, he was greatly honoured (especially in England), but following the death of his wife and of two of his daughters, his writing took on a darker, pessimistic character, as seen in his autobiography (1924).

twayblade An orchid (*Listera ovata*) native to cool and arctic regions of Europe and Asia; stem with one pair of broad, oval leaves; flowers green with a yellowish 2-lobed lip. Any insect visiting the flower triggers an explosion of sticky liquid which sets in 2–3 seconds, glueing the pollen grains to the insect's head. (Family: Orchidaceae.)

Tweed, River River in SE Scotland and NE England, UK, rises at Tweed's Well; flows generally E, forming part of the border between England and Scotland; enters the North Sea at Berwick-upon-Tweed; length, 155 km/96 mi.

tweed A coarse, heavy, wool, outerwear fabric, first made in S Scotland, manufactured in several distinctive weave patterns. Often mistakenly associated with the R Tweed, the name originates from *tweel*, a Scottish word for twill fabrics. Its manufacture in the I of Harris was developed c.1850 by Lady Dunmore, who encouraged its use amongst the British aristocracy. Traditional tweeds have a 'country' look, but modern designs are often multi-coloured and lighter weight.

Tweed Ring US 19th-c political scandal. Led by the state senator William Magear 'Boss' Tweed (1823–78), the ring ruled New York City in the 1860s and 1870s, before being exposed by the *New York Times* in 1871. During its power the city government suffered vast amounts of fraud, extortion, and theft. Its headquarters, Tammany Hall, became synonymous with urban corruption and machine politics.

Twelfth Night The evening of 5 January, the last evening of the 12 days of the traditional Christmas festival. It was formerly marked by particularly boisterous and anarchic festivities before the return to sober normality on **Twelfth Day** (Epiphany, 6 Jan).

Twelve, the *apostle*

twelve-step program *self-help group*

Twelve Tables Drawn up by a commission of 10 men in 451–450 BC, the first attempt by the Romans to codify their laws. Produced under pressure from the plebeians, their publication (on 12 tablets) was intended to curb the power of the patricians. Although the original tablets themselves do not survive, quotations from them in ancient authors indicate that they contained rulings from all branches of the law as it existed at that time.

twelve-tone music Music based on the 12 notes of the chromatic scale arranged in a predetermined order.

Twenty-one Demands A series of demands presented by Japan to China in 1915, which included recognition of Japanese control of Manchuria, Shandong, Inner Mongolia, SE China and the Yangzi Valley; imposition of Japanese advisers in the Chinese administration; and compulsory purchase of 50% of its munitions from Japan. President Yuan Shikai accepted them as the basis of a treaty, but the resulting popular patriotic protest movement gave impetus to the rise of Chinese nationalism.

Twickenham Rugby Union football ground in W London, UK. Opened in 1910, it has been the venue for almost all England internationals since then, as well as for the Rugby Football Union (RFU) Cup Final since 1972 and for the Oxford *v* Cambridge University match. The headquarters of the RFU, it was extensively remodelled in the 1980s and 1990s, and staged the 1991 World Cup Final. Capacity: 78 000.

Twiggy, professional name of **Lesley Lawson**, *née* **Hornby** (1949–) Fashion model, actress, and singer, born in London, UK. She became a modelling superstar almost overnight at the age of 17, and was a symbol of the 'swinging sixties' in London's Carnaby Street. She has made numerous appearances on television, and her films include *The Boy Friend* (1971), *The Blues Brothers* (1981), and *Madame Sousatzka* (1989). In 2001 she was briefly co-presenter of ITV's popular *This Morning* programme.

twilight The interval of time shortly after sunset or just before sunrise. **Civil twilight** begins or ends when the Sun is 6° below the local horizon; **nautical twilight** 12° below the horizon, and **astronomical twilight** 18° below the horizon.

twilight sleep Originally, the use of morphine and hyoscine to induce tranquility and reduce the pain during uterine contractions in labour. This drug regime is now rarely employed.

twill A type of woven fabric characterized by a pattern of diagonal lines. Many variations are possible, such as *herringbone* twills, where the pattern zigzags across the cloth. Twill weaves produce strong, hard-wearing fabrics, often employed in sports and work-wear situations.

twinning The linking of two towns or cities in different countries, so that they may have a 'special relationship' and foster cultural exchanges. For example, Edinburgh, Scotland, is twinned with Munich, Germany (1954); Nice, France (1958); Florence, Italy (1964); Dunedin, New Zealand (1974); Kiev, Ukraine (1989); San Diego, USA (1977); Vancouver, Canada (1977); Xian, China (1985); and Aalborg, Denmark (1991).

twin paradox *clock paradox*

twins A pair of offspring produced at the same birth. **Fraternal** (or *dizygotic*) twins are derived from two separate fertilized eggs. **Identical** (or *monozygotic*) twins are derived from a single fertilized egg, and are thus genetically identical.

twist The winding together of fibres, which gives added strength to yarns. The twist level affects other factors than strength, including stretch and softness.

twisted pair A simple form of cabling. It is used extensively in the public telephone network, but can also be used for linking computer systems in a network.

twitch grass *couch grass*

two-stroke engine A practical engine cycle with one in two strokes of the piston being the power stroke. This type of engine is frequently used to drive light motorcycles.

Two Thousand Guineas *Classics*

Tyan Shan *Tian Shan*

Tyche [tiykee, tiykay] The Greek goddess of chance or luck, prominent in the Hellenistic period. She is depicted as blind, or, with a wall, as the luck of a city.

Tyler, Anne, married name **Anne Modarressi** (1941–) Writer, born in Minneapolis, Minnesota, USA. She studied at Duke and Columbia universities, then worked as a Russian bibliographer at Duke (1962–3), and as a library assistant at McGill University, Montreal (1964–5). She settled in Baltimore and began to write short stories and novels concerned with the themes of loneliness, isolation, and human interactions. Among her best-known works are *The Accidental Tourist* (1985; filmed, 1988) and *Breathing Lessons* (1989, Pulitzer). Later novels include *A Patchwork Planet* (1998), *Back When We Were Grownups* (2001), and *The Amateur Marriage* (2004).

Tyler, John (1790–1862) US statesman and 10th president (1841–5), born in Charles City Co, Virginia, USA. He became a lawyer, a member of the state legislature (1811–16), Governor of Virginia (1825–7), and a senator (1827–36). Elected vice-president in 1840, he became president on the death of Harrison in 1841, only a month after his inauguration. His administration was marked by the annexation of Texas. He later remained active in politics, adhering to the Confederate cause until his death.

Tyler, Wat (?–1381) English leader of the Peasants' Revolt (1381). The rebels of Kent, after taking Rochester Castle, chose him as captain, and marched to Canterbury and London. At the Smithfield conference with Richard II blows were exchanged, and Tyler was wounded by the Mayor of London, William Walworth (d.1385). He was taken to St Bartholomew's Hospital, where Walworth had him dragged out and beheaded.

Tynan, Kenneth [tiynan] (1927–80) Theatre critic, born in Birmingham, West Midlands, C England, UK. He read English at Oxford, where he became deeply involved in the theatre. As drama critic for several publications, notably *The Observer* (1954–63), he was one of the first to champion John Osborne and the other new playwrights of the time. He became literary manager of the National Theatre (1963–9), an editor in films and television, and achieved further fame with his controversial revue *Oh! Calcutta* (1969). He fought for the removal of theatrical censorship and campaigned for greater freedom in sexual attitudes.

Tyndale or **Tindale, William** [tindayl] (?–1536) Translator of the Bible, probably born in Slymbridge, Gloucestershire, SWC England, UK. He studied at Oxford, and became a chaplain and tutor, sympathetic to humanist learning. In 1524 he went to Hamburg and Wittenberg, and in 1525 to Cologne, where he completed his translation of the English New Testament. In 1531 he moved to Antwerp, where he continued to work on an Old Testament translation, but before it was finished he was seized, accused of heresy, imprisoned, and executed. His work became the basis of most later English translations of the Bible, and much influenced the Authorised Version of 1611.

Tyne, River [tiyn] River of NE England, UK; formed by confluence of North Tyne and South Tyne, NW of Hexham, Northumberland; flows 48 km/30 mi E through Tyne and Wear to meet the North Sea between Tynemouth and South Shields; South Tyne rises on Cross Fell, E Cumbria; North Tyne rises in the Cheviot Hills, and is dammed to form Kielder Water reservoir; linked to R Tees as part of regional water grid system; navigable 13 km/8 mi above Newcastle; serves the industrial towns of Newcastle, Jarrow, Gateshead, Wallsend, and South Shields.

Tyne and Wear [weer] pop (2001e) 1 076 000; area 540 sq km/208 sq mi. County of NE England, UK, created in 1974; bounded E by the North Sea; drained by the Tyne and Wear Rivers; administrative centre, Newcastle upon Tyne; chief towns include Gateshead, Jarrow, Wallsend, Sunderland; a highly industrialized area, especially since the Industrial Revolution; suffered serious decline following the Great Depression, especially in shipbuilding; now designated a special development area, with considerable diversification of industries; shipbuilding, engineering, coal mining, chemicals; metropolitan council abolished in 1986.

Tyneside Urban area in Tyne and Wear, NE England, UK; includes Newcastle upon Tyne, Gateshead, Jarrow, Felling, Hebburn, Newburn, Longbenton–Killingworth, Wallsend, and North and South Shields; airport (Woolsington); railway; The Baltic, a centre for contemporary art, was opened in Gateshead in 2002.

typesetting The preparation of type (text matter) for printing. The invention of movable type in the West in the 15th-c revolutionized book production. Individual metal characters or *sorts* were arranged by hand by *compositors* (who selected the capital letters from the *upper case* and the smaller letters from the *lower case*, giving rise to our modern terminology). It was not until the late 19th-c that *hot metal* processes, chiefly *Linotype* and *Monotype*, automated the process of assembling type by using keyboards that controlled the casing, from molten metal (hence the name 'hot metal'), of complete lines of type or *slugs* (Linotype) or of individual characters arranged in lines (Monotype) with the spacing correctly adjusted. For offset lithography, the dominant form of printing today, type images are produced on photosensitive paper or film by a computer-controlled phototypesetting machine. The instructions about typeface and size, layout, and so on are usually keyed in on a separate computer.

typewriter A hand-operated machine for producing printed letters and other symbols on paper. Traditionally, characters mounted on rods are made to hit an inked ribbon against paper by pressing on keys; the paper is automatically moved when a key is struck. William Burt patented the notion (he called it a 'typographer') in 1829, and some very slow machines were built around that time; but the prototype of the machine we know today was built by Christopher Sholes in 1867, and developed by the Remington firm soon after. Later developments include electric typewriters, in which the keys need only to be touched; the 'golf-ball' typewriter, using replaceable spheres with additional symbols and typefaces; and electronic typewriters, with memory, screen, fast printing, and many of the editing and storage features of word processors.

typhoid fever An infectious disease caused by *Salmonella typhi*, also known as **enteric fever**. It is acquired by ingesting food or liquids contaminated with faeces from an infected person, and is often spread in water supplies or during food preparation. Clinical features include a high fever, drowsiness, aches, diarrhoea, and an abdominal rash, progressing to delirium and coma. Following recovery, some people become chronic carriers of the disease, and continue to excrete the bacteria in their stools. Prevention is by careful sanitation and good standards of food hygiene. Immunization is desirable for people travelling to areas of the world, such as the Indian subcontinent, where the infection is endemic.

typhoon *hurricane*

typhus Any of several illnesses caused by infection with a strain of *Rickettsia*; also known as **spotted fever**. Louse-borne typhus is caused by *Rickettsia prowazeki*. It is common in overcrowded conditions and results in a severe illness with headache, prostration, and a measles-like rash. Flea-borne typhus is caused by *Rickettsia mooneri*, and results in a milder illness. Tick-borne typhus fever (**Rocky Mountain spotted fever**) is caused by *Rickettsia rickettsii*. It occurs in the USA and South America and is similar to the louse-borne disorder. Several other species cause similar infections in South Africa, Australia, and India. A specific serological test, the Weil–Felix reaction, is the basis of diagnosis. The infections respond to the appropriate antibiotic.

typical owl *owl*

typography The design of letterforms for use as typefaces, and the selection of typefaces for typeset documents. Typefaces are designed and used for a multitude of purposes (eg books, newspapers, stationery, handbills) and for use on various kinds of typesetting equipment, in both print and non-print media (such as film and television). Many typefaces in use today are called after the printers who originally cut them, such as Baskerville and Caslon, although the exact forms may have changed to suit modern typesetting and printing requirements. New typefaces are, however, still being designed: Times New Roman, designed by Stanley Morison in 1932 for the redesigned *Times* newspaper, has been called the most important type design of the 20th-c, and one of the most eminent typographers is Hermann Zapf, whose designs include the widely used Palatino and Optima. Helvetica, designed for the Haas type foundry in Switzerland, has become one of the most popular sans serif typefaces today. The selection of a typeface by a designer or typographer is based on a number of considerations. It is chosen for its appeal, its appropriateness, and its legibility with reference to the job in hand. Typefaces can vary immensely in their appearance. They can be divided into two major classes: the *serif* faces, with short cross-strokes at the ends of the letters, and the *sans-serif* faces, which lack these cross-strokes. Within these classes, typefaces vary in the size of their *x-height*, the style of the serif, their weight (or 'blackness'), the angle of the curves, and so on, all of which affect both the appearance of the text on a page and how long the printed document will be.

Tyr [teer] The Norse god of battle, who guards the other gods. He was the only one brave enough to place his hand in the mouth of the wolf Fenrir as a pledge. When the wolf realized that it was caught, it bit off the hand.

tyramine [tiyramin] A chemical compound derived from the amino acid *tyrosine*, which occurs in foods such as cheese and wine, sometimes in large quantities. Normally tyramine is degraded by the enzyme monoamine oxidase (MAO). If MAO is reduced, as occurs with certain antidepressants, tyramine accumulates, leading to an elevation in blood pressure. Migraine headaches may be associated with excess amine production aggravated by a high intake of tyramine.

Tyrannosaurus rex [tiranosawrus reks] The largest terrestrial flesh-eating animal of all time; known from the Cretaceous period; a dinosaur reaching 12 m/40 ft in length; skull massive with short, deep jaws bearing dagger-like teeth; tail heavy and muscular; forelimbs tiny, each with only two fingers; slow-moving, with a top speed of about 4 kph/2½ mph; probably a scavenger rather than an active hunter. (Order: Saurischia.)

tyrant In Greek city-states of the 7th-c and 6th-c BC, a neutral term, possibly of Lydian origin, simply describing an absolute ruler who had seized power illegally. Only later (5th-c BC) did it acquire its present meaning – a cruel and oppressive ruler.

Tyre [tiyr], Arabic **Sour** 33°12N 35°11E, pop (2000e) 17 500. Mediterranean fishing port, SW Lebanon; railway; ancient city was the most important commercial centre in the E Mediterranean, noted for silk, glass, and Tyrean purple dye; excavations since 1947 have uncovered remains of Crusader, Arab, Byzantine, and Graeco-Roman cities; several Roman remains, including one of the largest hippodromes of the Roman period; a world heritage site.

tyre / tire A circular cushion fixed to the rim of a wheel, which absorbs variations in the road surface, so providing an easier ride to the vehicle. Most tyres are *pneumatic*, being flexible tubes stiffened by high-pressure air. Depending upon the type of tyre, this pneumatic stiffening may or may not be provided by a thin inner tube. The tyre is composed of the *tread*, which comes into contact with the road surface, and the *body* or *carcase*. Most tyres are made of a combination of rubber compounded with other chemicals and fabric, usually nylon or polyester. The inventor of the pneumatic tyre was Robert William Thomson, who patented a design for application to coaches in 1845. In spite of this, solid rubber tyres were used extensively until 1888, when John Boyd Dunlop successfully applied the pneumatic tyre to the bicycle, and tyres assumed a recognizably modern form.

Tyrol *Tirol*

Tyrone [tiyrohn], Ir **Tir Eoghain** pop (2000e) 166 700; area 3136 sq km/1210 sq mi. County in W Northern Ireland, UK, consisting of four districts (Cookstown, Dungannon, Omagh, Strabane); bounded E by Lough Neagh, and NW and S by the Republic of Ireland along the R Foyle; hilly, with the Sperrin Mts rising (N) to 683 m/2241 ft at Mt Sawel; county town, Omagh; other chief towns, Dungannon, Cookstown, Strabane; oats, potatoes, flax, turnips, sheep, cattle.

Tyrrhenian Sea [tiyreenian] Arm of the Mediterranean Sea; bounded by the Italian Peninsula, Sicily, Sardinia, and Corsica; major ports, Naples and Palermo.

Tyson, Mike, popular name of **Michael (Gerald) Tyson** (1966–) Boxer, born in New York City, USA. The National Golden Gloves heavyweight champion in 1984, he turned professional the following year. A lethal puncher, he beat 15 of his first 25 opponents by knockouts in the first round. He beat Trevor Berbick (1952–) for the World Boxing Council version of the world heavyweight title in 1986 to become the youngest heavyweight champion (20 years 145 days), and added the World Boxing Association title in 1987, when he beat James Smith (1954–). Later that year he became the first undisputed champion since 1978, when he beat Tony Tucker (1958–). He won 41 of 42 decisions before losing the title in 1990. In 1992 he was jailed following a trial for rape, and released in 1995. He regained the WBC heavyweight title in 1996, then vacated it soon afterwards. In 1998 he was found guilty of assaulting a fellow motorist in a traffic incident. In June 2002 he unsuccessfully fought Lennox Lewis for the heavyweight title.

Tyumen [tyoomayn] 57°11N 65°29E, pop (2000e) 493 000. Capital city of Tyumenskaya oblast, SW Siberian Russia, on R Tura; founded, 1585; first settled Russian town E of the Ural Mts; formerly an important centre of trade with China; railway junction; university; cotton textiles, clothing, machine tools and instruments, oil refining.

Tz'u-hsi *Ci-xi*

Tzu-po *Zibo*

U

U and non-U Terms coined by English linguist Alan Ross (1907–80) in an effort to capture the essentials of class-based variation in English usage. Though a gross distinction, both socially and linguistically, it does highlight an important intersection of social class and language use in British English. Markers of **upper-class** (U) and **non-upper-class** (non-U) usage can be features of pronunciation and grammar, styles of greeting in correspondence, and (most prolifically) vocabulary, such as U *luncheon* and *pudding* for non-U *dinner* and *sweet*. The contentiousness of the notion becomes apparent on considering the intermediate gradations in usage which go unremarked – the third term *lunch* for most people of professional status, and the use of *pudding* by non-U speakers from many dialectal backgrounds.

Ubangi, River [oobanggee], Fr **Oubangui** Major tributary of R Congo, in N and WC Africa; follows frontier between Central African Republic and Democratic Republic of Congo to join R Congo 97 km/60 mi SW of Mbandaka, length 1060 km/660 mi; including longest headstream (R Uele), 2250 km/1400 mi.

U-boat An abbreviation of *Unterseeboot* (Ger 'submarine'). The German Navy launched large-scale submarine offensives in both World Wars, and each time the U-boats came close to victory.

Ucayali, River [ookiyalee] River in E Peru; one of the Amazon's main headstreams, formed by the union of the Apurímac and Urubamba Rivers; flows c.1600 km/1000 mi N, joining the R Marañón to form the Amazon 88 km/55 mi SW of Iquitos; navigable by small craft.

Uccello, Paolo [oocheloh], originally **Paolo di Dono** (1397–1475) Painter, born in Pratovecchio, NC Italy. He trained under Ghiberti, worked in Venice as a mosaicist (1425–31), then settled in Florence. He applied the principles of perspective to his paintings, as seen in 'The Flood' (1447–8, Florence), where his use of perspective and foreshortening gives a sternly realistic effect.

ud [ood] An Arabian lute, known since the 7th-c, with usually five courses of strings, played with a plectrum or with the fingers of both hands. It is the ancestor of the European lute.

udad *aoudad*

Udall, Nicholas [yoodal] (1504–56) Playwright, born in Southampton, Hampshire, S England, UK. He studied at Oxford, and became (c.1534) headmaster of Eton. His dismissal in 1541 for indecent offences did not affect his standing at court, and Edward VI appointed him prebendary of Windsor. He made many classical translations, but is chiefly remembered as the attributed author of the first significant verse comedy in English, *Ralph Roister Doister* (c.1553, printed 1566).

Udine [oodeenay] 46°04N 13°14E, pop (2000e) 101 000. Industrial town and capital of Udine province, Friuli-Venezia Giulia, NE Italy, 61 km/38 mi NW of Trieste; important road and rail junction; suffered severe bombing in World War 2; archbishopric; railway; brewing, furniture, freight distribution, textiles, leather, chemicals; castle (16th-c), cathedral (1236), town hall (15th-c).

UEFA (Union of European Football Associations) [yooayfa] A football organization founded in 1954 by the representatives of the association football governing bodies of 30 European nations, and in 2004 consisted of 52 member associations. UEFA is responsible for organizing the three major European club tournaments: the Champions' Cup, the Cup Winners' Cup, and the UEFA Cup. They also run their own European Championship, a World Cup style of competition for national teams.

Ufa [oofa] 54°45N 55°58E, pop (2000e) 1 092 000. Capital city of Bashkirskaya, E European Russia; in the Ural Mts, on the R Ufa, at its confluence with the Dema and Zilim Rivers; founded as a fortress, 1586; birthplace of Sergei Aksakov; airport; railway; university (1957); clothing, cotton textiles, oil refining, chemicals.

Uffizi [oofeetsee] A museum in Florence, NC Italy, housing one of the world's greatest collections of works by Italian masters. The Renaissance palace, designed by Vasari in 1560, was opened to the public by the Medici family in the 17th c.

Uganda *p.1572*

Uganda Martyrs A group of 22 African youths, converted to Roman Catholicism, killed for their faith in Uganda between 1885 and 1887. Canonized in 1964, they were among many Christians put to death in that period of persecution.

Ugarit [oogareet] A flourishing Canaanite city on the coast of N Syria opposite Cyprus, which in the late Bronze Age (c.1450–1200 BC) enjoyed wide contacts with the Egyptians, the Hittites, and the Mycenaeans. It was destroyed by the Sea Peoples c.1200 BC.

UHT milk An abbreviation of **ultra-high-temperature milk**; milk heated to a temperature of 132°C for one second, and subsequently packed in an airtight container. It will then have a shelf-life of six months at room temperature.

Uighurs [weegoorz] One of China's national minorities, mostly settled in Xinjiang. Of Turkic origin, they conquered Mongolia in AD 745 and held equal status in Tang China until 840, when they moved their power centre to Turfan (modern Turpan), where they still reside. They developed their own script, which was used as a written language by the Mongols. They adopted Manichaeism in 763, and influenced its spread in China until its suppression in 843. They were brought into the Chinese empire in the 18th-c.

Ujung Pandang [oojoong pandang], formerly **Makassar** or **Macassar** (to 1973) 5°09S 119°28E, pop (2000e) 1 108 000. Seaport capital of Sulawesi Selatan province, Indonesia; in SW corner of Sulawesi I; important trade centre of E Indonesia, established by the Dutch in 1607; free port, 1848; airfield; university (1956); coffee, rubber, copra, resin, spices.

UK Athletics The governing body for athletics in England and Wales. It was set up following the financial demise of the British Athletic Federation in 1998. Its headquarters is in Birmingham and ex-athlete David Moorcroft became its first chief executive.

ukiyo-e [ookeeyoh ay] (Jap 'pictures of the floating world') In Japanese painting and printmaking, a movement that flourished in the 16th–19th-c. Stressing aesthetics, style, and contempt for ugliness, favourite themes included theatrical subjects, actors, prostitutes, and landscapes. Colour was added, along with Dutch-influenced perspective, by Masonobu (1686–1764). The coloured landscape woodcuts of Hokusai and Hiroshige influenced 19th-c French artists. Later, Kiyochika (1847–1915) fused the genre with Western techniques, including light and shade.

Uganda

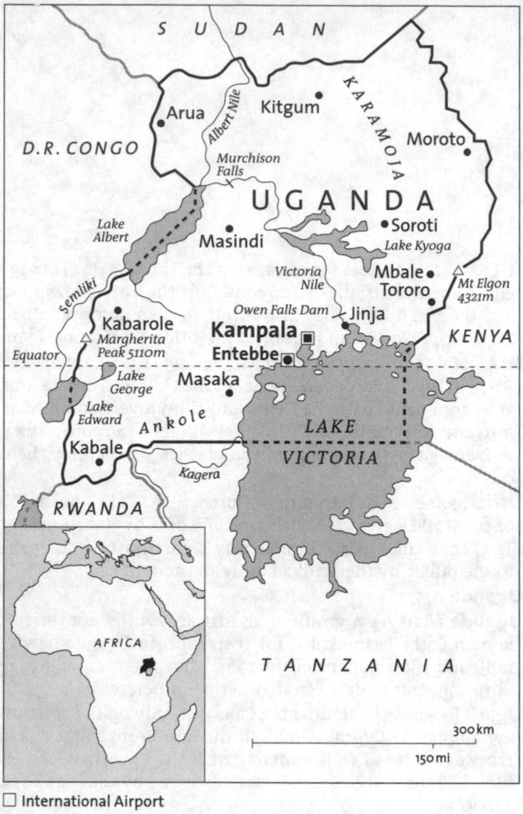

[yooganda], official name **Republic of Uganda**

Local name Uganda (Swahili)

Timezone GMT +3

Area 241 038 km^2/93 040 sq mi

Population total (2002e) 24 378 000

Status Republic

Date of independence 1962

Capital Kampala

Languages English (official), Swahili, Luganda (Ganda), Ateso, and Luo are also spoken

Ethnic groups Bantu, with Nilotic and Hamitic minorities

Religions Christian (66%) (Roman Catholic 33%, Protestant 33%), traditional animist beliefs (18%), Muslim (6%)

Physical features Landlocked country in E Africa, mainly plateau, height 1200 m/4000 ft; dry savannah or semi-desert in the N; fertile L Victoria basin; highest point in Uganda and Zaïre, Margherita Peak, 5110 m/16 765 ft; main lakes, Victoria (SE), George and Edward (SW), Albert (W), Kwania and Kyoga (C), Bisina (formerly L Salisbury) (E); main rivers are the upper reaches of R Nile, the Victoria Nile, and the Albert Nile.

Climate Tropical climate; temperatures rarely rise above 29°C, or fall below 15°C (S); average annual temperature 23°C (Jan), 21°C (Jul); average annual rainfall 1150 mm/45 in.

Currency 1 Uganda Shilling = 100 cents

Economy Agriculture; coffee (over 90% of exports), tea, sugar, cotton; bananas, plantains, cassavas, potatoes, sweet potatoes, maize, sorghum.

GDP (2002) $30·49 bn, per capita $1200

Human Development Index (1998) 0·444

History Visited by Arab traders, 1840s; explored by Speke, 1860s; granted to the British East Africa Company, 1888; Kingdom of Buganda became a British protectorate, 1893; other territory included by 1903; independence, 1962; Dr Milton Obote assumed all powers, 1966; coup led by General Idi Amin Dada, 1971; Amin's regime overthrown, 1979; further coup in 1985, overthrew Obote; National Resistance Movement captured Kampala, 1986, and Museveni became president; elections to Constituent Assembly, 1994; new constitution, 1995; peace deal signed (Dec 2002) between government and the rebel Uganda National Rescue Front (UNRF II).

Head of State
1981–5 (Apollo) Milton Obote
1985–6 *Military Council* (Tito Okello Lutwa)
1986– Yoweri Kaguta Museveni

Head of Government
1985–6 Abraham N Waliggo
1986–91 Samson B Kisekka
1991–4 George Cosmas Adyebo
1994–9 Kintu Musoke
1999– Apollo Nsimbabi

Ukraine *p.1573*

ukulele [yookuhlaylee] A Hawaiian musical instrument, resembling a small guitar, with four gut or nylon strings that are strummed with the fingernails and fingertips. It was for many years a favourite instrument in the USA for popular music, especially as an accompaniment to a solo singer.

Ulaanbaatar [**oo**lahn **bah**taw(r)], formerly **Ulan Bator**, **Urga** (to 1924) 47°54N 106°52E, pop (2000e) 674 000. Capital of Mongolia, in Selenge county, C Mongolia, surrounded by the Khenti Mts; founded as Urga in 1639, centre of Lamaistic religion in Mongolia; trading centre on caravan routes between Russia and China, 18th-c; capital, 1921; university (1942); meat processing, carpets, brewing, wood processing, veterinary medicine, mining, foodstuffs.

Ulanova, Galina Sergeyevna [oo**lah**nova] (1910–98) Ballerina, born in St Petersburg, NW Russia. She studied at the Mariinski Theatre School, and made her debut at the Kirov Theatre in St Petersburg in 1928. After 1944 she was prima ballerina of the Bolshoi Theatre, Moscow, with which she had first appeared in 1935. She became the leading ballerina of the Soviet Union, and was four times a Stalin Prize winner. She appeared in several films made by the Moscow State Ballet Company, and in 1957 was awarded the Lenin Prize. She gave her final performance in 1962, and continued to teach at the Bolshoi.

Ulan-Ude [oolan ooday], formerly **Verkhneudinsk** (to 1934) 51°45N 107°40E, pop (2000e) 358 000. Capital city of Buryatskaya, SE Siberian Russia; on R Selenga, 75 km/47 mi E of L Baikal; founded, 1666; airfield; railway junction; meat processing, machinery, metalwork, boatbuilding, woodwork; Odigitrievskii Cathedral (1741–85).

Ulbricht, Walter (Ernst Karl) [ulbrikht] (1893–1973) East German statesman, chairman of the Council of State (1960–73), born in Leipzig, EC Germany. At first a cabinet-maker, he entered politics in 1912, and in 1928 became Communist deputy for Potsdam. He left Germany on Hitler's rise in 1933, spending most of his exile in the Soviet Union. In 1945 he returned as head of the German Communist Party, and became deputy premier of the German Democratic Republic and general secretary of the Communist Party in 1950. He was largely responsible for the 'sovietization' of East Germany, and built the Berlin wall in 1961. He retired as general secretary in 1971, but retained his position as head of state until his death.

ulcer A break in the surface of the skin or mucous membrane, which may be acute in onset and short-lived or persistent. They

Ukraine

☐ International Airport

[yookrayn], official name **Republic of Ukraine**, Ukrainian **Ukrayina**

Local name Ukraina

Timezone GMT +2

Area 603 700 km²/233 028 sq mi

Population total (2002e) 48 120 000

Status Republic

Date of independence 1991

Capital Kiev

Languages Ukrainian (official), Russian

Ethnic groups Ukrainian (73%), Russian (22%), Moldovan, Bulgarian, and Polish minorities

Religions Orthodox (Autocephalous and Russian) (76%), Roman Catholic (14%), Jewish (2%), Baptist, Mennonite, Protestant, and Muslim (8%)

Physical features Most fertile area of former USSR, consisting largely of black soil steppes, forming a substantial part of the East European Plain; borders the Black Sea and Sea of Azov (S); Carpathian Mts, 2061 m/6762 ft at Mt Goverla (SW); Crimean Mts (S); main rivers, Dnepr, Yuzhny, Bug; Donets coalfield, area 25 900 km²/10 000 sq mi.

Climate Moderate, mild winters, hot summers (SW); average annual temperatures -3°C (Jan), 23°C (Jul); average annual rainfall in Crimea 400–610 mm/16–24 in.

Currency 1 hryvna = 100 kopijka

Economy Important industrial bases for iron and steel manufacture, chemical and engineering bases; ship-building on Black Sea; agriculture (was the USSR's major wheat producer); wheat, corn, rye, potatoes, cotton, flax, sugar beet; coal and salt deposits in Donets basin.

GDP (2002) $218 bn, (2002) per capita $4500

Human Development Index (1998) 0·748

History Conquered by Mongols, 1240; dominated by Poland, 13–16th-c; applied to Moscow for help fighting Poland in return for sovereignty, 1654; declared independence from Russia in 1918, after Russian Revolution; became a member of the USSR, 1922; suffered devastation during World War 2; Chernobyl the site of the world's worst nuclear accident, 1986; declared independence, 1991; ongoing disputes with Russia over control of the Black Sea Fleet and status of the Crimea; introduction of border controls and new currency, 1993, in contravention of CIS agreements; new constitution, 1996; governed by a President and Supreme Council.

Head of State
1991–4 Leonid M Kravchuk
1994– Leonid Kuchma

Head of Government
1990–2 Vitold P Fokin
1992–3 Leonid Kuchma
1993 Yukhim Zvagilsky
1994–5 Vitalii Masol
1995–6 Yevhenii Marchuk
1996–7 Pavlo Lazarenko
1997 Vasyl Durdynets
1997–9 Valery Pustovoytenko
1999–2001 Viktor Yushchenko
2001–2 Anatoly Kinakh
2002– Viktor Yanukovich

may be caused by trauma (physical or chemical), infection, inadequate blood supply, or auto-immune disease. Ulcers may also occur in the mouth and gastro-intestinal tract.

Uleåborg *Oulu*

Ulfilas or **Wulfila** [ulfilas, wulfila] (c.311–83) Gothic translator of the Bible. Consecrated a missionary bishop to his fellow countrymen by Eusebius of Nicomedia in 341, after seven years' labour he was forced to migrate with his converts across the Danube. He devised the Gothic alphabet, and carried out the first translation of the Bible into a Germanic language (c.350).

Ullapool [uhlapool] 57°54N 5°10W, pop (2000e) 1360. Port town in Highland, NW Scotland, UK; on E shore of Loch Broom; ferry service to Stornoway, I of Lewis; tourist resort; fishing, fish processing; Ullapool museum.

Ullmann, Liv (Johanne) (1939–) Actress, born in Tokyo, Japan. She studied acting at the Webber-Douglas School in London before beginning her career with a repertory company in Stavanger. Her screen image was largely defined through a long association with the Swedish director Ingmar Bergman, in which she laid bare the inner turmoil of women experiencing various emotional crises. Their films together include *Persona* (1966), *Viskningar och rop* (1972, Cries and Whispers), *Ansikte mot Ansikte* (1975, Face to Face), and *Höstsonaten* (1978, Autumn Sonata), and he wrote the script for her later film *Private Confessions* (1996). She has worked extensively for the charity UNICEF, and written two autobiographical works, *Changing* (1977) and *Choices* (1984). In 1999 she directed *Faithless*.

Ullswater Lake in the Lake District of Cumbria, NW England, UK; SW of Penrith; second largest lake in England; length 12 km/7 mi; width 1 km/¾ mi; depth 64 m/210 ft.

Ulm [oolm] 48°24N 10°00E, pop (2000e) 114 000. Industrial and commercial city in Baden-Württemberg province, S Germany; on R Danube, 72 km/45 mi SE of Stuttgart; scene of Napoleon's defeat of Austria, 1805; railway; university (1967); cars, transport equipment, electrical engineering, textiles, leatherwork; birthplace of Einstein; Gothic Minster (1377–1529), with the world's highest spire (161 m/528 ft).

Ulm, Charles (Thomas Philippe) (1898–1934) Pioneer aviator, born in Melbourne, Victoria, SE Australia. He met Charles Kingsford Smith, and joined him in several aviation adventures and an unsuccessful business venture (1927–31). He carried the first airmail between Australia, New Zealand, and New Guinea (1934). In December the same year, investigating the possibilities of regular airmail flights across the Pacific, he set out from

California with two companions in his new twin-engine aircraft, but vanished without trace somewhere over the Hawaiian Is.

ulna *arm*

Ulster [uhlster] pop (2000e) 232 300; area 8012 sq km/3093 sq mi. Province in Ireland, comprising counties of Cavan, Donegal, and Monaghan; Donegal separated by part of Connacht, lying W of Northern Ireland; Cavan and Monaghan lie to the S of Northern Ireland; chief towns include Donegal, Letterkenny, Cavan, and Monaghan; a former kingdom; land confiscated by the English Crown, and distributed to Protestant English and Scots settlers in the 17th-c; partitioned in 1921 into the present-day division. The name continues to be used as an alternative for **Northern Ireland**.

Ulster Plantation The settlement of English and Scottish Protestants in Ulster during the reign of James I (ruled 1603–25); the direct cause of three centuries of conflict between the North and the South, Catholics and Protestants, and Ireland and England. The English Reformation under Henry VIII had given rise in England to increased fears of foreign, Catholic invasion, and control of Ireland became even more important. Henry VIII put down a rebellion (1534–7), confiscated land, and established a Protestant 'Church of Ireland' (1537). The Irish rebelled three times during the reign of Elizabeth I and were brutally suppressed. Under James I, Ulster was settled by thousands of English and Scottish Protestants, and many of the Catholic Irish were driven off their lands. The policy led to rebellions by the native Irish and the Anglo-Irish aristocracy (1563–9, 1580–3, 1598–1603). Another Irish rebellion, begun in 1641 in reaction to the hated rule of Charles I's deputy, Thomas Wentworth, Earl of Strafford, was crushed (1649–50) by Oliver Cromwell, in which possibly two-thirds of the Irish Catholics died. More land was confiscated, often given to absentee landlords, and more Protestants settled in Ireland. Successive generations of Ulster Protestants have wanted to remain part of Britain, throughout the establishment of the Irish Free State (1922) and the Irish Republic (1949), and up to the present day. Ulster Roman Catholics constitute two-fifths of the population and, along with many in the Republic, oppose partition.

Ultra A British security classification (the very highest) given during World War 2 to intelligence gathered from the breaking of the key German military codes used with their 'Enigma' encryption device. 'Ultra' intelligence was available to the British high command from the outset of the war, and was of crucial importance during the Battle of Britain and the Battle of the Atlantic.

Ultramontanism [uhltramon**tay**nizm] Literally, 'beyond the mountains'; a movement, deriving from France, asserting the centralization of the authority and power of the Roman Catholic Church in Rome and the pope. It gained impetus after the French Revolution (1789), and reached its high point with the First Vatican Council (1870) and the declaration of papal infallibility.

ultrasound Sound of a frequency greater than 20 000 Hz; inaudible to humans, but certain animals such as dogs and bats can hear some ultrasonic signals. Pulses of very high frequency sound are reflected back to different extents by different materials (eg the tissues of the human body). If such a 'sonar' device is connected to a computer, accurate representations of the structure of the material can be made (in the medical case, with relatively little danger of injury to the patient). It is produced and detected using high-frequency transducers. Ultrasound is therefore widely used in medical scanning (eg in the examination of a fetus) and in certain surgical procedures (acoustic surgery). It is also used in engineering as a means of crack detection, eg in railway lines and pressure vessels. The study of ultrasound is **ultrasonics**.

ultraviolet astronomy The detection and analysis of radiation from celestial sources in the wavelength range 50–320 nm. The hottest stars emit most of their radiation in this waveband, which is accessible only from rockets and satellites. Extensive spectrographic studies of active galaxies and quasars, as well as of stars and the interstellar medium, have been carried out using the International Ultraviolet Explorer (a UK–NASA–European Space Agency satellite) in the 120–300 nm range.

ultraviolet radiation Electromagnetic radiation of wavelength a little shorter than visible light, between $3{\cdot}9 \times 10^{-7}$ m and 10^{-8} m; discovered in 1801 by German physicist Johann Ritter (1776–1810). Invisible to the naked eye, it causes fluorescence in some substances. It is produced by electron transitions in atoms, such as in mercury discharge lamps. Ultraviolet radiation from the Sun causes tanning of the skin.

Ulugh Beg [**ooloog bayg**] (1394–1449) Ruler of the Timurid empire (1447–9). A grandson of Tamerlane, he made his name particularly as an astronomer. He founded an observatory at Samarkand, compiled astronomical tables, and corrected errors made by Ptolemy of Alexandria, whose figures were still in use. He also wrote poetry and history. After a brief reign, he was overthrown and slain by a rebellious son in 1449.

Uluru [oolooroo] National park in Northern Territory, C Australia; area c.1325 sq km/500 sq mi; contains the Olgas, a series of steep-sided rock domes, and Ayers Rock; an area of continuing cultural and religious significance to the Aboriginal people; a world heritage site.

Ulvaeus, Bjorn *Abba*

Ulysses *Odysseus*

Ulysses project A joint ESA–NASA space exploration mission to observe the Sun and solar wind from a high solar latitude perspective. It required the spacecraft to fly on a trajectory which passes over the poles of the Sun, using a boost from Jupiter's gravity field. The spacecraft was launched using the NASA shuttle in 1990, and flew by Jupiter in 1992, where its trajectory was bent steeply out of the ecliptic to return over the Sun's S polar region (1994) and N polar region (1995) at a distance of about 1 Astronomical Unit. Originally named the 'International Solar Polar Mission', it was planned as a two-spacecraft mission, before the cancellation of the NASA spacecraft. Ulysses observations have provided a detailed characterization of the solar corona, the solar wind, the heliospheric magnetic field, solar energetic particles, galactic cosmic rays, solar radio bursts, and plasma waves. The spacecraft is in the process of making a second orbit of the Sun.

U-matic The trade name for the first helical-scan videotape cassette recorder introduced by Sony in 1970, initially for the professional non-broadcast market. It uses ¾-in (19 mm) tape at a speed of 9·53 cm/3¾ in per second in a large cassette 221 × 140 × 32 mm with a playing time of up to 1 hour. It is widely used for all forms of industrial video production, and its extended high-band form, known as BVU or U-format SP, can provide the quality required for broadcast television standards.

Umayyad Mosque [umi**yad**] The great mosque at Damascus in Syria, built (705–15) on the site of a Christian church to John the Baptist, and believed to incorporate the reliquary shrine of the saint's head.

Umayyads [umi**yadz**] A Damascus-based dynasty, founded by the Muslim general Muawiya ibn Abi-Sufyan (c.605–80), which ruled until 750. It replaced the era of the four Medina-based caliphs, of whom the last, Ali, was murdered in 661.

umbel A type of inflorescence, typical of the carrot family Umbelliferae, in which all the flower-stalks arise from the top of the stem, the outermost stalks longest, giving a flat-topped, umbrella-shaped cluster of flowers.

Umberto I (1844–1900) King of Italy (1878–1900), born in Turin, NW Italy. He fought in the war against Austria (1866), and as king brought Italy into the Triple Alliance with Germany and Austria (1882). He supported Italian colonialism in Africa, but his popularity declined after Italy's defeat by the Ethiopians at Adowa in 1896. He was assassinated at Monza.

Umberto II [um**bair**toh] (1904–83) Last king of Italy (1946), born in Racconigi, NW Italy. He succeeded to the throne after the abdication of his father, Victor Emmanuel III, but himself abdicated a month later, after a national referendum had declared for a republic. He left Italy, and in 1947 he and his descendants were banished from Italy. He then lived in Portugal.

umbilical cord A solid flexible cord which connects the developing fetus of the placental mammals (eg humans and dogs) to the placenta within the uterus. When first formed, it is comparatively short, but it increases in length as the fetus and amniotic cavity enlarge (the average length in humans is 60 cm/24 in.) It allows the fetus to float freely in the fluid of the uterus (the *amniotic fluid*) and through the umbilical blood vessels it contains, to obtain nutrition from the placenta, as well as to eliminate waste products, by the flow and return of blood through the vessels within it. At birth it is severed close to the infant's front abdominal wall, leaving a scar (the **umbilicus** or *navel*).

umbra *sunspot*

umbrella bird A large cotinga; males with dark plumage and umbrella-like crest covering head and bill; breast with inflatable air sac and pendant feathered fold of skin; call is like a bull bellowing. (Genus: *Cephalopterus*, 3 species.)

Umbria [umbria] pop (2000e) 822 000; area 8456 sq km/3265 sq mi. Region of C Italy; capital, Perugia; other chief towns, Foligno and Terni; L Trasimeno, largest lake in the Italian peninsula; prosperous farming region (corn, olives, wine, sugar beet, tobacco, market gardening, sheep farming); industry around Terni, Narni, and Foligno (chemicals, metalworking); textiles, crafts, and confectionery in Perugia and Spoleto; tourism; Umbrian school of painting during the Renaissance (eg Raphael); Basilica of St Francis in Assisi severely damaged by earthquake, 1997 is a world heritage site.

Umbriel [uhmbriel] The third-largest satellite of Uranus, discovered in 1851, distance from the planet 266 000 km/165 000 mi; diameter 1170 km/730 mi; orbital period 4·1 days.

Umeå [ümayaw] 63°50N 20°15E, pop (2000e) 97 000. Seaport and capital of Västerbotten county, N Sweden; on the Gulf of Bothnia at the mouth of the R Ume; seat of the Provincial Appeal Court; railway; university (1963); woodworking.

Umm al-Qaiwain [oom al kiywiyn] pop (2000e) 41 900; area 750 sq km/290 sq mi. Member state of the United Arab Emirates, between Sharjah and Ras al-Khaimah; capital, Umm al-Qaiwain; fishing, light industry; agriculture concentrated in the fertile enclave of Falaj al-Mualla.

Un-American Activities Committee A committee of the House of Representatives established in 1938 to consider the loyalty of federal government employees. Supposedly concerned with identifying Communists, it was notorious for harassing individuals whose political opinions offended committee members. Its name was later changed to the International Security Committee, and it was abolished in 1975.

Unamuno (y Jugo), Miguel de [oonamoonoh] (1864–1936) Philosopher and writer, born in Bilbao, N Spain. He studied at Bilbao and Madrid, became professor of Greek at Salamanca University (1892), and a writer of mystical philosophy, historical studies, essays, travel books, and austere poetry. His main philosophical work is *Del sentimiento trágico de la vida en los hombres y en los pueblos* (1913, The Tragic Sense of Life in Men and Peoples). He was exiled as a republican in 1924, but reinstated in 1931. As rector of Salamanca, he defied the forces of Franco in the Civil War.

uncertainty principle *Heisenberg uncertainty principle*

unconscious When used psychoanalytically, the collection of feelings, drives, memories, and emotional conflicts which individuals are not aware of, but which influence their mental processes and behaviour, such as dreams and slips of the tongue indicating true feelings. In contrast, the **subconscious** is used colloquially to describe memories about which an individual is only dimly aware, but which can be recalled if focused upon.

underground A complete railway system designed to operate underground in tunnels or tubes, also known as the **tube**, **subway**, or **metro**. Traction is supplied almost exclusively by electric motor. Undergrounds are usually built where the provision of normal surface or overhead railways is not possible, usually because of congestion or other environmental considerations. Due to their high cost of construction, undergrounds are normally used only for passenger traffic within large cities. In London in 1863 the Metropolitan Railway subway system was opened using steam locomotives. The first practical underground railway was the City and South London Railway, which opened for traffic in 1890, and the idea rapidly spread around the world thereafter. The world's largest system (in terms of number of stations, 468) is the New York City subway (383 km/238 mi). London Underground in 2000 had 392 km/244 mi of track, with 274 stations, following the completion of the Jubilee Line extension in 1999.

underground economy *black economy*

Underground Railroad A network of safe houses, hiding places, and routes to aid escaped American slaves to reach freedom in the N or Canada. Never formally organized, it was active as early as 1786, but was most widespread and active after 1830. One of the major means of resistance to slavery, estimates suggest that it helped at least 50 000 runaways.

Underhill, Evelyn (1875–1941) Anglican mystical poet and writer, born in Wolverhampton, West Midlands, C England, UK. She studied at King's College, London, and became lecturer on the philosophy of religion at Manchester College, Oxford. She led religious retreats, was a religious counsellor, and wrote numerous books on mysticism, including *The Life of the Spirit* (1922), volumes of verse, and four novels. Her *Mysticism* (1911) became a standard work.

underpainting In art, preliminary layers of paint, often monochrome, establishing the balance of light and shade in a picture before the application of coloured glazes and impasto. This method was normal for most painters until the late 19th-c.

underpopulation *overpopulation*

underwater camera A conventional camera in a pressure-resistant housing, for use in water down to considerable depths. External controls are linked to the camera controls for operation. The camera lens views through a flat window or dome port made of clear glass or plastic. The flat port gives pincushion distortion of the image, and the focal length of the lens is increased by a factor of 1·33 due to the refractive index of water being greater than that of air. Alternatively, a sealed camera body is used with special lenses designed only for underwater use, with the water in contact with the front element.

underwing moth A moth with rather narrow wings; at rest, hindwings concealed beneath usually drab forewings; during flight hindwings revealed, often with flashes of bright colours. (Order: Lepidoptera. Family: Noctuidae.)

underwriter In business or insurance, a person or company that guarantees payment if a certain event should occur. In insurance, the underwriter pays in the event of fire or theft. In finance, an underwriter of a share issue guarantees that they will buy at a pre-arranged price any shares not 'taken up' (ie bought) by others. A premium is charged for this service.

Undset, Sigrid [oonset] (1882–1949) Norwegian novelist, born in Kalundborg, C Denmark. She worked in an office for 10 years, then turned to writing. Her major novels were *Kristin Lavransdatter* (1920–2), a 14th-c trilogy, followed by a series *Olav Audunssön* (4 vols, 1925–7). She became a Catholic in 1924, which influenced her later work, most of which had contemporary settings. She was awarded the Nobel Prize for Literature in 1928. An ardent anti-Nazi, her works were blacklisted in Germany during the Nazi period.

undue influence In law, improper pressure used by one person who abuses a position of influence or power upon another, in relation to some transaction, for example, by a beneficiary under a will upon the testator. A gift (or contract) may be set aside where there has been undue influence applied by the donee (or one contracting party) to the donor (or other contracting party). Certain relationships (eg between solicitor and client, parent and child, religious leader and follower) carry the presumption of undue influence, so that the burden of disproof lies on the stronger party.

undulant fever *brucellosis*

unemployment A situtation where a person able and willing to do work is not employed. Unemployment may be due to several possible causes, none of which are mutually exclusive. **Demand-deficiency** or **Keynesian unemployment** is where there is simply insufficient demand. In **classical unemployment**, the lowest pay that workers will accept is above what employers think their labour is worth. **Frictional unemployment** is where workers and employers exist whose offers are mutually acceptable, but who are looking for and have not yet located each other. **Mismatch** occurs when the vacant jobs and unemployed workers differ in skill or location. All these causes may operate at once, in varying proportions. Possible cures include expanding effective demand, lowering wages, improving the mechanics of matching workers and vacancies, and assisting mobility and the acquisition of skills. Unemployment is endemic in industrial societies, though the rates vary widely between countries and over time. In developing countries, population expansion, out-of-date forms of land tenure, and the mechanization of agriculture have driven many people off the land to join a growing number of urban unemployed. In socialist countries which followed an ideology of central planning or statist economics, unemployment soared with the collapse of communism from zero levels to over 50 per cent.

UNESCO [yooneskoh] Acronym for **United Nations Educational, Scientific and Cultural Organization**, founded in 1946 with the objective of contributing to peace and security by promoting collaboration among nations through education, science, and culture. It has a general conference, executive board, and secretariat, with headquarters in Paris. In the mid-1980s, there emerged serious concern among the non-communist industrialized countries over the organization's administrative inefficiency and its allegedly inappropriate political aims. In consequence the USA left at the end of 1984, which had a major impact on UNESCO's finances. The UK and Singapore subsequently withdrew, and Yugoslavia was suspended in 1992, but the UK rejoined in 1997, newly constituted Yugoslavia (now Serbia and Montenegro) in 2000, and the USA in 2003. In 2004 there were 190 member states and 6 associate members.

Ungaretti, Giuseppe [unggaretee] (1888–1970) Poet, born in Alexandria, N Egypt. He studied at Paris, and fought in the Italian army in World War 1, where he began to write poetry, first published as *Il porto sepolto* (1916, The Buried Port). He became professor of Italian literature at São Paulo, Brazil (1936–42) and at Rome (1942–58). His poems, characterized by symbolism, compressed imagery, and modern verse structure, became the foundation of the *hermetic* movement (from *ermetico* 'obscure', a term used by a critic of his work).

Ungaro, Emanuel (Maffeolti) [unggaroh] (1933–) Fashion designer, born in Aix-en-Provence, SE France, of Italian parents. He trained to join the family tailoring business, but went instead to Paris in 1955, worked for a small tailoring firm, and later joined Balenciaga. In 1965 he opened his own house, with Sonia Knapp designing his fabrics. Initially featuring rigid lines, his styles later softened. In 1968 he produced his first ready-to-wear lines.

Ungava–Quebec Crater *Chubb Crater*

ungulate A mammal in which toes end in hooves rather than claws; includes *artiodactyls* (**even-toed ungulates**) and *perissodactyls* (**odd-toed ungulates**); also the **primitive ungulates** (elephant, hyrax, aardvark); usually large and herbivorous.

unicameral system A legislature which has only one chamber. This uncommon system tends to be found in countries with relatively small populations, where there would be problems in maintaining a dual system of representation. New Zealand, Israel, and Denmark are examples.

UNICEF The **United Nations Children's Fund**, formerly known as the **United Nations International Children's Emergency Fund**, established in 1946 to provide help for children left destitute after Word War 2, and now concerned with children in need everywhere. It was given a permanent role within the UN in 1953. In 2004, UNICEF was supporting programmes in over 158 countries in relation to child health, nutrition, water and sanitation, or education, and also providing emergency aid in many parts of the world. Funded entirely by voluntary contributions from the general public and governments, and with national committees in most industrialized countries, it is unique in the UN system.

unicorn A fabulous creature, a horse with a single horn on its forehead; probably based on stories of the rhinoceros. In mediaeval legend it could be captured only by a virgin putting its head in her lap.

Unidad Popular [oonithath populah(r)] (Span 'People's Unity') A coalition of six left-wing political parties in Chile (Communists, Socialists, Radicals, and three minor groups) formed to support the presidential candidacy and government (1970–3) of Dr Salvador Allende.

Unification Church *Moonies*

uniformitarianism In geology, the principle that geological processes controlling the evolution of the Earth's crust were of the same kind throughout geological time as they are today. First formulated by British geologist James Hutton, it contrasts with the earlier theory of **catastrophism**, which postulated that the history of the Earth has to be explained by events radically different from anything going on at the present day.

Uniformity, Acts of A series of acts passed by the English parliament in 1549, 1552, 1559, and 1662. They sought to impose religious uniformity by requiring the use of the Church of England liturgy as contained in the Book of Common Prayer (various editions, 1549–1662). The act of 1552 penalized Catholic recusants; that of 1662 excluded dissenting Protestant clergy, who formed themselves into Nonconformist groups. The Toleration Act (1689) brought some improvement in England, but until the 19th-c Nonconformists were debarred from holding political office.

Uniform Resource Locator *World Wide Web*

union (economics) *trade union*

union (mathematics) *set*

Union, Acts of The Acts which joined England in legislative union with Scotland (1707) and Ireland (1800). The 1707 Act brought 45 Scottish MPs to join the new House of Commons of Great Britain, and 16 peers became members of the House of Lords. The Scottish legal system remained separate. The 1800 Act created the United Kingdom of Great Britain and Ireland, which came into effect in 1801, and lasted until 1922. This was brought about after the collapse of the Irish rebellion (1798) in order to increase British security in the French wars. The Irish parliament was abolished; 100 Irish MPs were added to the UK House of Commons, and 32 Peers to the Lords. The Churches of England and Ireland were united.

Union Islands *Tokelau*

Unionist *Conservative Party*

Union Movement A party formed by Sir Oswald Mosley in 1948 as a successor to his New Party (1931) and the British Union of Fascists (1932). It put up a handful of candidates 1959–66, failing to secure a significant number of votes. The party's main plank was opposition to immigration, but it also included a call to unite Europe into a vast market to buy and sell from Africa. Mosley gave up the leadership in 1966, and the movement went into decline, dying out by the end of the 1960s.

Union of European Football Associations *UEFA*

Union of Soviet Socialist Republics *Soviet Union*

Uniramia [yooniraymia] A group of arthropods characterized by their 1-branched (*uniramous*) limbs, and by jaws that bite transversely at the tip; comprises the insects (Insecta), centipedes (Chilopoda), millipedes (Diplopoda), and velvet worms (Onychophora); sometimes treated as a separate phylum at the arthropodan level of organization.

Unitarians A religious group which, although in many ways akin to Christianity, rejects the doctrines of the Trinity and

United Arab Emirates

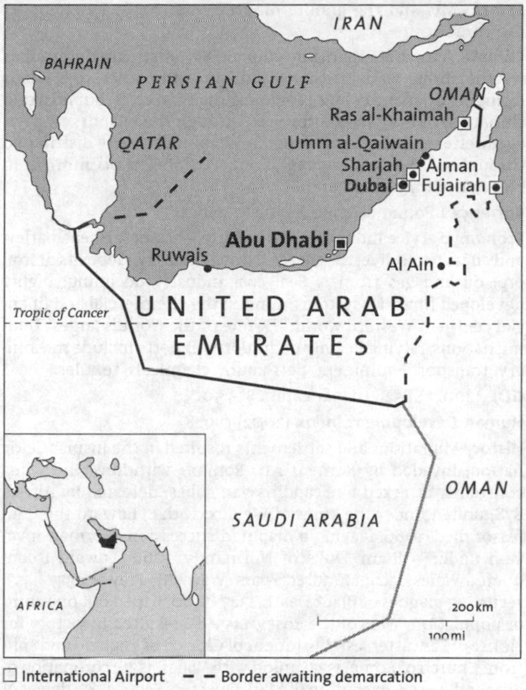

Arabic **al-Arabiyah al-Muttahida**, formerly **Trucial States**

Local name Ittih-ad al-Im arat al-'Arab-iyah

Timezone GMT +4

Area 83 600 km^2/32 300 sq mi

Population total (2002e) 3 550 000

Status Federation of autonomous emirates

Date of independence 1971

Capital Abu Dhabi

Languages Arabic (official), English, Farsi, Urdu, and Hindi also spoken

Ethnic groups Emirian (19%), other Arab (23%), S Asian (50%)

Religions Muslim (Sunni 80%, Shi'ite 16%), Christian (4%), small Hindu minority

Physical features Seven states in EC Arabian peninsula on S shore (Trucial Coast) of the Persian Gulf; al-Fujairah has a coastline along the Gulf of Oman; salt marshes predominate on coast; barren desert and gravel plain inland; Hajar Mts in al-Fujairah rise to over 1000 m/3000 ft in E.

Climate Hot, dry desert climate, extreme summer temperatures exceeding 40°C and limited rainfall; frequent sandstorms; average annual temperatures 23°C (Jan), 42°C (Jul) in Dubai; average annual rainfall 60 mm/2·4 in.

Currency 1 United Arab Emirates Dirham (DH) = 100 fils

Economy Based on oil and gas (main producers, Abu Dhabi, Dubai); important commercial and trading centre; saline water supplies have restricted agriculture to oases and irrigated valleys of Hajar Mts; vegetables, fruits, dates, dairy farming; tourism.

GDP (2002) $53.97 bn, per capita $22 100

Human Development Index (2002) 0·812

History Originally peopled by sea-faring tribes, converted to Islam in 7th-c; Mecca conquered by powerful sheikdom of Carmathians; upon its collapse piracy common, area known as the Pirate Coast; Portuguese explorers arrived, 16th-c; British East India Company arrived, 17th-c; British attacked the coastal ports, 1819–20 and exacted a pledge to renounce piracy in the General Treaty, 1820; became known as Trucial Coast after signing of Treaty of Maritime Peace in Perpetuity, 1853; administered by British India, 1873–1947, and thereafter by London Foreign Office; Trucial States Council formed, 1960; federated and became United Arab Emirates, 1971, comprising seven emirates: Abu Dhabi, Ajman, Dubai, al-Fujairah, Ras al-Khaimah, Sharjah, and Umm al-Qaiwain; Ras al-Khaimah joined federation, 1972; governed by Supreme Council of the seven emirate rulers (each of whom is an absolute Monarch in own state).

Head of State

1971– Zayed bin Sultan al-Nahyan

Head of Government

1971–9 Maktoum bin Rashid al-Maktoum
1979–90 Rashid bin Said al-Maktoum
1990– Maktoum bin Rashid al-Maktoum

the divinity of Christ. As an organized group, it dates back to the 16th-c Protestant Reformation, first in parts of S Europe, and from the 18th-c in Britain and America.

Unitas, Johnny [yoonitas], popular name of **John Constantine Unitas** (1933–2002) Player of American football, born in Pittsburgh, Pennsylvania, USA. A quarter-back, he signed for the Baltimore Colts in 1956. Two years later he led them to a championship victory against the New York Giants in overtime. The game was broadcast live in the USA, and helped American football to its big television breakthrough. He was voted the league's Most Valuable Player in 1959, 1964, and 1967. In 1973 he joined the San Diego Chargers, but was injured after only three games, and retired. He was elected to the Hall of Fame in 1979.

United Arab Emirates *see panel*

United Church of Canada A Church established in Canada in 1925 through the union of the Presbyterian, Congregational, and Methodist Churches in Canada. Although its system of government was to be presbyterian in character, a minority of Presbyterian congregations refused to join, and continued as the Presbyterian Church in Canada. In 1968 there was a further merger, with the Canadian branch of the Evangelical United Brethren Church.

United Church of Christ A Christian denomination formed in the USA in 1961 (after 20 years of negotiations) by the union of the Congregational and Christian Churches with the Evangelical and Reformed Church. Envisioned as an ecumenical Protestant Church, it allows for variation in local organization and in the interpretation of doctrine, but continues to reflect its Reformed theological background.

United Fronts Two attempts to promote co-operation between the Chinese Communist and Nationalist Parties in the face of Japanese aggression. In Dec 1936, the Xian incident ended with an anti-Japanese alliance between the two Parties, and after the outbreak of the Sino–Japanese War (1937) the Communist Party initiated a second united front. Clashes between Nationalist and Communist forces led to its virtual disintegration by 1941.

United Gold Coast Convention A nationalist party formed in the Gold Coast (later, Ghana) in 1947. Kwame Nkrumah became secretary-general in 1948, but it was soon apparent that he was at odds with the leadership, since he desired to promote a more radical approach. In 1949 he formed the Convention People's Party, which led Ghana to independence in 1957.

United Irishmen, Society of A society formed in Belfast in 1791 by Protestant lawyer Wolfe Tone, which supported the French Revolution and espoused both religious equality and parliamentary reform. Its early support was primarily located in Ulster. As agitation increased, so United Irishmen became increasingly associated with support for Catholicism. The Society was instrumental in organizing French support for the

United Kingdom (UK)

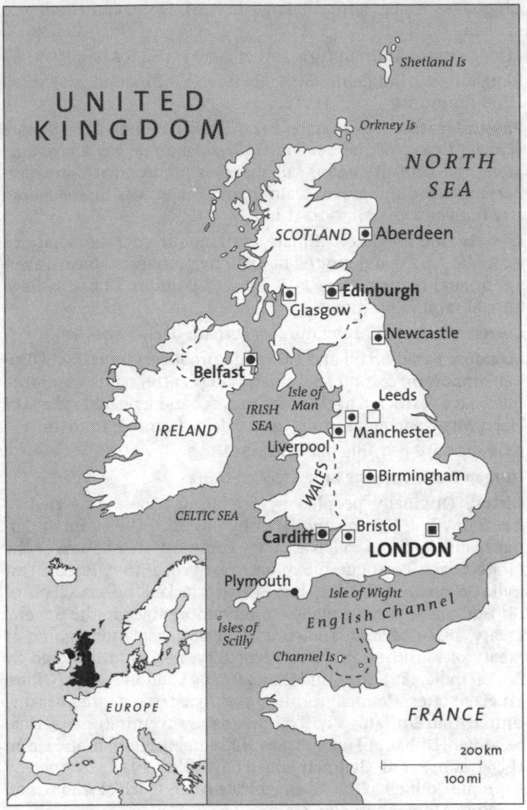

☐ International Airport

also **United Kingdom of Great Britain and Northern Ireland**

Local names United Kingdom of Great Britain and Northern Ireland, Great Britain, Britain

Timezone GMT

Area 244 755 km^2/94 500 sq mi

Population total (2002e) 60 178 000

Status Kingdom

Capital London

Languages English, Irish Gaelic, Scots Gaelic (Gallic), Welsh

Ethnic groups English (81·5%), Scottish (9·5%), Irish (2·4%), Welsh (1·9%), West Indian, Asian, and African (2%), Arabic, Turkish, and Greek minorities

Religions Christian (90%) (Anglican 63%, Roman Catholic 14%, Presbyterian 4%, Methodist 3%, Baptist 1%, Orthodox 1%, other 6%), Muslim (3%), Sikh (1%), Hindu (1%), Jewish (1%), other (1%)

Physical features Varied landscape, comprising the mountainous Lake District in NW, rocky moors in SW, hilly downs of S and SE, and the low, marshy fenlands of C and E; Cheviot Hills separate Scotland and England; highest point, Ben Nevis in Scotland, 1342 m/4406 ft; the Pennines form a ridge down the middle of England, from Lake District to C; highest point in England and Wales, Mt Snowdon in Wales, 1085 m/3560 ft; in N Ireland, the Sperrin Mts and the granite Mourne Mts rise to heights over 610 m/2000 ft.

Climate Temperate maritime climate; SW airstream determines weather, bringing depressions (causing wet weather) or N winds (bringing drier and colder); some regional diversity, but no world climate systems' boundaries pass through the islands; on average, wetter and slightly warmer in W; rainfall evenly distributed throughout the year; average annual rainfall 1600 mm/60 in (W), 800 mm/30 in (C and E).

Currency 1 Pound Sterling (£) = 100 pence

Economy Service industries; agriculture, potatoes, wheat, barley, and sugar beets; livestock; large fishing industry; deposits of iron ore; oil and gas from N Sea; coal industry declining; highly developed financial systems; London the commercial and financial centre of Western world; UK one of the world's largest trading nations, relying heavily on imports; exports include machinery, transport equipment, petroleum, chemicals, textiles.

GDP (2002) $1·528 tn, per capita $25 500

Human Development Index (2002) 0·928

History Migrations and settlements resulted in the insular Celtic nation; invaded by Rome, 1 AD; Romans withdrew, the 5th-c; constantly attacked by Scandinavian tribes; defeated by Alfred, 878; united under the kings of Wessex, 10th-c; Edward the Confessor died, 1066, leaving a disputed succession; Norman invasion under William, Duke of Normandy, 1066; Edward I conquered Wales, 1301; Hundred Years' War with France, 1337–1453; recurring plagues of Black Death, 1347–1400, wiped out one-third of population; Wars of the Roses, 1455–85, resulted in victory for House of Lancaster; establishment of Church of England and split from Church of Rome, 1533; union with Wales, 1536; coronation of Elizabeth I, 1558; execution of Mary Queen of Scots, 1587; defeat of the Spanish Armada, 1588; English Civil War, 1642–6 and 1648–9; execution of Charles I, 1649; England and Scotland joined by the Act of Union, 1707; 1714–60, development of parliamentary government under Hanoverian kings; revolt of the American colonies, 1775–81. Ireland officially joined to Great Britain, 1801; World War 1, 1914–18; became the United Kingdom of Great Britain and Northern Ireland following the establishment of the Irish Free State, 1922; General Strike, 1926; abdication of Edward VIII, 1936; World War 2, 1939–45; National Health system implemented, 1948; Indian independence, 1947; joined EC, 1973; Falklands War with Argentina, 1982; involvement in Gulf War, 1991; involvement in Iraq War (2003); a kingdom with the Monarch as Head of State; governed by a bicameral Parliament, comprising an elected 659-member House of Commons and a House of Lords; a Cabinet is appointed by the Prime Minister.

Head of State (Monarch)

1952– Elizabeth II

Head of Government

1951–5 Winston Leonard Spencer Churchill *Con*
1955–7 (Robert) Anthony Eden, 1st Earl of Avon *Con*
1957–63 (Maurice) Harold Macmillan, 1st Earl of Stockton *Con*
1963–4 Alexander Frederick (Alec) Douglas-Home, Baron Home of the Hirsel *Con*
1964–70 (James) Harold Wilson, Baron Wilson *Lab*
1970–4 Edward Richard George Heath *Con*
1974–6 (James) Harold Wilson, Baron Wilson *Lab*
1976–9 (Leonard) James Callaghan, Baron Callaghan *Lab*
1979–90 Margaret Hilda Thatcher *Con*
1990–7 John Major *Con*
1997– Anthony Charles Lynton (Tony) Blair *Lab*
Con Conservative *Lab* Labour *Lib* Liberal

unsuccessful Irish rebellion of 1798, and afterwards went into decline.

United Kingdom (UK) *see panel*

United Kingdom Atomic Energy Authority An authority set up by the Atomic Energy Authority Act in 1954, which has prime responsibility for research and the development of nuclear power in the UK on behalf of the government. It conducts research into new reactor systems, including safety and environmental issues, and provides support for the UK nuclear industry.

United Nations (UN) An organization formed to maintain world peace and foster international co-operation, formally established on 24 October 1945 with 51 founder countries. Its permanent headquarters are in New York. The UN Charter, which was drafted during the war by the USA, UK, and USSR, remains virtually unaltered despite the growth in membership and activities. There are six 'principal organs'. The **General Assembly** is the plenary body which controls much of the UN's work, supervises the subsidiary organs, sets priorities, and debates major issues of international affairs. The 15-member **Security Council** is dominated by the five permanent members (China, France, Russia, UK, and USA) who each have the power of veto over any resolutions; the remaining 10 are elected for 2-year periods. The primary role of the Council is to maintain international peace and security; its decisions, unlike those of the General Assembly, are binding on all other members. It is empowered to order mandatory sanctions, call for ceasefires, and establish peacekeeping forces (these forces were awarded the Nobel Peace Prize in 1988). The use of the veto has prevented it from intervening in a number of disputes, such as Vietnam. The **Secretariat**, under the secretary-general, employs some 25 000 (from 160 countries) worldwide. The staff are answerable only to the UN, not national governments, and are engaged in considerable diplomatic work. The secretary-general is often a significant person in international diplomacy and is able to take independent initiatives. The **International Court of Justice** consists of 15 judges appointed by the Council and the Assembly. As only states can bring issues before it, its jurisdiction depends on the consent of the states who are a party to a dispute. It also offers advisory opinions to various organs of the UN. The **International Criminal Court** (ICC), consisting of 18 judges elected by the States Parties, was inaugurated in 2003. The **Economic and Social Council** is elected by the General Assembly; it supervises the work of various committees, commissions, and expert bodies in the economic and social area, and co-ordinates the work of UN specialized agencies. The **Trusteeship Council** (suspended at the end of 1994) oversaw the transition of Trust Territories to self-government.

In addition to the organs established under the Charter, there is a range of subsidiary agencies, many with their own constitutions and membership, and some pre-dating the UN. The main agencies are the **Food and Agriculture Organization**, the **Intergovernmental Maritime Consultative Organization**, the **International Atomic Energy Authority**, the **International Bank for Reconstruction and Development** ('World Bank'), the **International Civil Aviation Organization**, the **International Development Association**, the **International Finance Corporation**, the **International Fund for Agricultural Development**, the **International Labour Organization**, the **International Monetary Fund**, the **United Nations Educational, Scientific and Cultural Organization**, the **Universal Postal Union**, the **International Telecommunication Union**, the **World Meterological Organization**, and the **World Health Organization**.

The UN had 191 members in 2004. It is generally seen as a forum where states pursue their national interest, rather than as an institution of world government, but it is not without considerable impact. Jointly, with secretary-general Kofi Annan, it was awarded the Nobel Peace Prize in 2001.

United Nations Agencies *United Nations*

United Nations Conference on Trade and Development (UNCTAD) An organ of the UN, established by the 1964 General Assembly, which meets irregularly to consider ways of increasing international trade and promoting economic development. Its executive board meets annually. It provides the main forum through which underdeveloped countries can put their views to the major economic powers.

United Nations Educational, Scientific and Cultural Organization *UNESCO*

United Provinces of the Netherlands Seven sovereign states of the Dutch Republic (Holland, Zeeland, Gelderland, Utrecht, Friesland, Groningen and Overyssel), roughly comprising the present kingdom of The Netherlands, but originally part of the Burgundian lands until they achieved independence from the

United Nations Membership

Grouped according to year of entry.

1945	Argentina, Australia, Belgium, Belorussian SSR (Belarus, 1991). Bolivia, Brazil, Canada, Chile, China (Taiwan to 1971), Colombia, Costa Rica, Cuba, Czechoslovakia (to 1993). Denmark, Dominican Republic, Ecuador, Egypt, El Salvador, Ethiopia, France, Greece, Guatemala, Haiti, Honduras, India, Iran, Iraq, Lebanon, Liberia, Luxembourg, Mexico, Netherlands, New Zealand, Nicaragua, Norway, Panama, Paraguay, Peru, Philippines, Poland, Saudi Arabia, South Africa, Syria, Turkey, Ukrainian SSR (Ukraine, 1991), UK, Uruguay, USA, USSR, Venezuela, Yugoslavia (Serbia and Montenegro, 2002)
1946	Afghanistan, Iceland, Sweden, Thailand
1947	Pakistan, Yemen (N)
1948	Burma (Myanmar, 1989)
1949	Israel
1950	Indonesia
1955	Albania, Austria, Bulgaria, Ceylon (Sri Lanka, 1970), Finland, Hungary, Ireland, Italy, Jordan, Kampuchea (Cambodia), Laos, Libya, Nepal, Portugal, Romania, Spain
1956	Japan, Morocco, Sudan, Tunisia
1957	Ghana, Malaya (Malaysia, 1963)
1958	Guinea
1960	Cameroon, Central African Republic, Chad, Congo, Córe d'Ivoire (formerly Ivory Coast), Cyprus, Dahomey (Benin, 1975), Gabon, Madagascar, Mali, Niger, Nigeria, Senegal, Somalia, Togo, Upper Volta (Burkina Faso, 1984), Zaïre
1961	Mauritania, Mongolia, Sierra Leone, Tanganyika (within Tanzania, 1964)
1962	Algeria, Burundi, Jamaica, Rwanda, Trinidad and Tobago, Uganda
1963	Kenya, Kuwait, Zanzibar (within Tanzania, 1964)
1964	Malawi, Malta, Tanzania, Zambia
1965	Maldives, Singapore, The Gambia
1966	Barbados, Botswana, Guyana, Lesotho
1967	Yemen (S, to 1990)
1968	Equatorial Guinea, Mauritius, Swaziland
1970	Fiji
1971	Bahrain, Bhutan, China (Peoples' Republic), Oman, Qatar, United Arab Emirates
1973	Bahamas, German Democratic Republic (within GFR, 1990) German Federal Republic
1974	Bangladesh, Grenada, Guinea-Bissau
1975	Cape Verde, Comoros, Mozambique, Papua New Guinea, São Tomé and Principe, Suriname
1976	Angola, Seychelles, Western Samoa
1977	Djibouti, Vietnam
1978	Dominica, Solomon Islands
1979	St Lucia
1980	St Vincent and the Grenadines, Zimbabwe
1981	Antigua and Barbuda, Belize, Vanuatu
1983	St Christopher and Nevis
1984	Brunei
1990	Liechtenstein, Namibia, Yemen (formerly N Yemen and S Yemen)
1991	Estonia, Federated States of Micronesia, Latvia, Lithuania, Marshall Islands, N Korea, Russia (formerly USSR), S Korea
1992	Armenia, Azerbaijan, Bosnia-Herzegovina, Croatia, Georgia, Kazakhstan, Kyrgysztan, Moldova, San Marino, Slovenia, Tajikistan, Turkmenistan, Uzbekistan
1993	Andorra, Czech Republic, Eritrea, Former Yugoslav Republic of Macedonia, Monaco, Slovak Republic
1995	Belau
1999	Nauru, Tonga, Kiribati
2000	Tuvalu
2002	East Timor, Switzerland

United States of America (USA)

also called **United States**, and often **America**

Local names: United States, America

Timezone GMT −5 (E coast) to −8 (Pacific coast)

Area 9 160 454 km²/3 535 935 sq mi

Population total (2002e) 287 602 000

Status Federal republic

Date of independence 1776

Capital Washington, DC.

Languages English, large Spanish-speaking minority

Ethnic groups European origin (including 9% Hispanic) (89·3%), African American (12·1%), Asian and Pacific (2·9%), Native American, Aleut, and Inuit (0·9%)

Religions Christian (70%) (Protestant 61%, Roman Catholic 25%), atheist (7%), other (5%), Jewish (2%)

Physical features Includes the separate states of Alaska (GMT −9) and Hawaii (GMT −10). E Atlantic coastal plain is backed by the Appalachian Mts from the Great Lakes to Alabama, a series of parallel ranges including the Allegheny, Blue Ridge, and Catskill Mts; plain broadens out (S) towards the Gulf of Mexico and into the Florida peninsula; Gulf Plains stretch N to meet the Great Plains from which they are separated by the Ozark Mts; further W, Rocky Mts rise to over 4500 m/14 750 ft; highest point in US, Mt McKinley, Alaska, 6194 m/20 321 ft; Death Valley, -86 m/-282 ft, is the lowest point; drainage N is into the St Lawrence R or the Great Lakes; in the E, the Hudson, Delaware, Potomac, and other rivers flow E to the Atlantic Ocean; central plains drained by the great Red River–Missouri–Mississippi system and by other rivers flowing into the Gulf of Mexico; main rivers in W, Columbia and Colorado; deserts cover much of Texas, New Mexico, Arizona, Utah, Nevada.

Climate Climate varies from conditions found in hot, tropical deserts (SW), to those typical of Arctic continental regions on the northern Pacific Coast; continental climate on High Plains, with summer dust storms and winter blizzards; temperate continental on Central Plains; continental Mid West and the Great Lakes, with very cold winters; cool temperate in N Appalachians, warm temperate in S; subtropical to warm temperate on the Gulf Coast, with plentiful rainfall and frequent hurricanes and tornadoes; temperate maritime on the Atlantic coast, with heavy snowfall in N; cool temperate in New England, with warm summers and severe winters; mean annual temperatures range from 29°C in Florida, to -13°C in Alaska; average annual temperatures in Chicago, -3°C (Jan), 24°C (Jul); in Arizona, 11°C (Jan), 32°C (Jul); average annual rainfall in Alabama, 1640 mm/65 in, in Arizona, 180 mm/7 in; hot and humid in Hawaii, with average annual rainfall 1524–5080 mm/60–200 in.

Currency 1 US Dollar ($, US$) = 100 cents

Economy One of the world's most productive industrial nations; highly diversified economy; vast mineral and agricultural resources; major exporter of grains, cereals, potatoes, sugar, fruit; livestock farming of beef, veal, pork; chief exports include aircraft, cars, machinery, chemicals, military equipment, non-fuel minerals; advanced system of communications and transportation; leader in space-exploration programme of the 1970s.

Spanish crown (1568–1609). The republic declined in the 18th-c, collapsing during the Revolutionary Wars (1795).

United Service Organizations (USO) An association of agencies, such as the YMCA, the YWCA, and the Salvation Army, whose aims are to care for the recreational needs of the Armed Forces. It was founded in the USA in 1941.

United States military academies Federal training institutions for people who want to become officers in the US armed forces.The **United States Air Force (USAF) Academy** was formed by Act of Congress in 1948, and is located near Colorado Springs, CO. The **United States Military Academy** was founded in 1802, and is now at West Point on the Hudson R, NY. The **United States Naval Academy** was founded in 1845, and is at

GDP (2002) $10·45 tn, per capita $36 300

Human Development Index (1998)0·939

History First settled by groups who migrated from Asia across the Bering Straits over 25 000 years ago; explored by the Norse in 9th-c; and by the Spanish in 16th-c, who settled in Florida and Mexico; in the 17th-c, settlements by the British, French, Dutch, Germans, and Swedes; many Black Africans introduced as slaves to work on the plantations; British control during 18th-c after defeat of French in Seven Years' War; revolt of the English-speaking colonies in the War of Independence, 1775–83, resulted in the creation of the United States of America; Louisiana sold to the USA by France in 1803 (the Louisiana Purchase) and the westward movement of settlers began; Florida ceded by Spain in 1819, and further Spanish states joined the Union, 1821–53; 11 Southern states left the Union over the slavery issue and formed the Confederacy, 1860–1; Civil War, 1861–5, ended in victory for the North, and the Southern states later rejoined the Union; Alaska purchased from Russia, 1867; Hawaiian islands annexed, 1898; several other islands formally associated with the USA, such as Puerto Rico, American Samoa, and Guam; in the 19th-c, arrival of millions of immigrants from Europe and the Far East; more recent arrival of large numbers of Spanish-speaking people, mainly from Mexico and the West Indies; entered World War 1 on the side of the Allies, 1917, and again in World War 2 in 1941; became the chief world power opposed to communism, a policy which led to involvement in the Korean War (1950–3) and Vietnam (1956–75); campaign for Black civil rights developed, 1960s, and eventually led to Civil Rights Act (1964); invasion of Grenada, 1983; mid 1980s rapprochement of US and USSR; invasion of Panama, 1989; involvement in Gulf War, 1991; military intervention in Somalia, 1993; following the Al-Qaeda attack on the World Trade Center in New York (11 Sep 2001), and earlier terrorist attacks (notably, the 1998 bomb attacks on US embassies in Kenya and Tanzania, and the bombing of the USS *Cole* warship in the port of Aden, Yemen in 2000), the USA led the successful campaign to remove the Taliban from power in Afghanistan; further campaign against international terrorism, 2002; Iraq's apparent failure to comply with a UN resolution to eliminate its weapons of mass destruction led to invasion by US-led military coalition forces and the removal of Saddam Hussein (Mar–Apr 2003), with the US presence in Iraq scheduled to remain until mid-2004; ongoing terrorist threats against the USA, both within the country and abroad, brought unprecedented levels of security throughout 2003–4. Congress consists of 435-member House of Representatives, and a 100-member Senate; President elected every 4 years by a college of state representatives, appoints an executive Cabinet responsible to Congress; divided into 50 federal states and the District of Columbia; each state having its own two-body legislature and governor.

Head of State/Government (President)
Vice President in parentheses

1945–53 Harry S Truman (33rd) *Dem No Vice President 1945–9* (Alben W Barkley, 1949–53)

1953–61 Dwight David Eisenhower (34th) *Rep* (Richard Milhous Nixon)

1961–3 John Fitzgerald Kennedy (35th) *Dem* (Lyndon Baines Johnson)

1963–9 Lyndon Baines Johnson (36th) *Dem No Vice President 1963–5* (Hubert Horatio Humphrey, 1965–9)

1969–74 Richard Milhous Nixon (37th) *Rep* (Spiro Theodore Agnew, 1969–73) *No Vice President Oct–Dec 1973* (Gerald Rudolph Ford, 1973–4)

Annapolis, MD. In each of these institutions, there are about 4400 officer cadets in training; women have been admitted since 1976. The **United States Coast Guard (USCG) Academy** was founded in 1876, and has been located at New London, CT, since 1936. This has a complement of 850 male and female cadets.

United States of America (USA) *p.1580–82*

United States Trust Territory of the Pacific Islands 1–22°N 142–172°E; pop (1990e), before devolution, 40 000; sea area 7·5 million sq km/3 million sq mi; land area 1854 sq km/716 sq mi. Group of c.2000 islands in the W Pacific Ocean, N of Papua New Guinea; until 1990, comprised the Commonwealth of the N Mariana Is, Federated States of Micronesia, Republic of Belau, and the Marshall Is; population mostly Micronesian, with some

cont... United States of America

1974–7 Gerald Rudolph Ford (38th) *Rep No Vice President Aug–Dec 1974* (Nelson Aldrich Rockefeller, 1974–7)
1977–81 James Earl (Jimmy) Carter (39th) *Dem* (Walter Frederick Mondale)
1981–9 Ronald Wilson Reagan (40th) *Rep* (George Herbert Walker Bush)
1989–92 George Herbert Walker Bush (41st) *Rep* (J Danforth Quayle)
1992–2001 William Jefferson Clinton (42nd) *Dem* (Alfred Gore)
2001– George (W) Bush (43rd) *Rep* (Dick Cheney)
Dem Democrat *Rep* Republican

American States Timezones: two sets of figures indicate that different zones operate in a state; the second figure refers to Summer Time (Apr–Oct, approximately):
2 Aleutian/Hawaii Standard Time : 3 Alaska Standard Time : 4 Pacific Standard Time : 5 Mountain Standard Time : 6 Central Standard Time : 7 Eastern Standard Time

Name / Area (km² / sq mi) / Capital / Time Zone / Population Figures (2000e) / Nickname(s)
Alabama (AL)/ 133 911 / 51 705 / Montgomery / 7/8 / 4 387 000 / Camellia State, Heart of Dixie, Yellowhammer
Alaska (AK) / 1 518 748 / 586 412 / Juneau / 3/4 / 624 000 / Mainland State, The Last Frontier, The Great Land
Arizona (AZ) / 295 249 / 114 000 / Phoenix / 5 / 4 893 000 / Apache State, Grand Canyon State
Arkansas (AR) / 137 403 / 53 187 / Little Rock / 6/7 / 2 564 000 / Bear State, Land of Opportunity
California (CA) / 411 033 / 158 706 / Sacramento / 4/5 / 33 609 000 / Golden State
Colorado (CO) / 269 585 / 104 091 / Denver / 5/6 / 4 145 000 / Centennial State
Connecticut (CT) / 12 996 / 5 018 / Hartford / 7/8 / 3 292 000 / Nutmeg State, Constitution State, The Insurance State
Delaware (DE) / 5 296 / 2 045 / Dover / 7/8 / 763 000 / Diamond State, First State, Blue Hen State
District of Columbia (DC) / 173·5 / 670 / Washington / 7/8 / 516 000
Florida (FL) / 151 934 / 58 664 / Tallahassee / 6/7, 7/8 / 15 323 000 / Everglade State, Sunshine State, Peninsular State
Georgia (GA) / 152 571 / 58 910 / Atlanta / 7/8 / 7 944 000 / Empire State of the South, Peach State
Hawaii (HI) / 16 759 / 6 471 / Honolulu / 2 / 1 181 000 / Aloha State
Idaho (ID) / 216 422 / 83 564 / Boise / 4/5, 5/6 / 1 273 000 / Gem State
Illinois (IL) / 145 928 / 56 345 / Springfield / 6/7 / 12 189 000 / Prairie State, Land of Lincoln
Indiana (IN) / 93 716 / 36 185 / Indianapolis / 6/7, 7/8 / 5 979 000 / Hoosier State
Iowa (IA) / 145 747 / 56 275 / Des Moines / 6/7 / 2 878 000 / Hawkeye State, Corn State
Kansas (KS) / 213 089 / 82 277 / Topeka / 5/6, 6/7 / 2 670 000 / Sunflower State, Jayhawker State
Kentucky (KY) / 104 658 / 40 410 / Frankfort / 6/7, 7/8 / 3 989 000 / Bluegrass State
Louisiana (LA) / 123 673 / 47 752 / Baton Rouge / 6/7 / 4 381 000 / Pelican State, Sugar State, Creole State
Maine (ME) / 86 153 / 33 265 / Augusta / 7/8 / 1 258 000 / Pine Tree State, Lumber State
Maryland (MD) / 27 090 / 10 460 / Annapolis / 7/8 / 5 213 000 / Old Line State, Free State
Massachusetts (MA) / 21 455 / 8 284 / Boston / 7/8 / 6 206 000 / Bay State, Old Colony
Michigan (MI) / 151 579 / 58 527 / Lansing / 6/7, 7/8 / 9 903 000 / Wolverine State, Great Lake State
Minnesota (MN) / 218 593 / 84 402 / St Paul / 6/7 / 4 823 000 / Gopher State, North Star State
Mississippi (MS) / 123 510 / 47 689 / Jackson / 6/7 / 2 785 000 / Magnolia State
Missouri (MO) / 180 508 / 69 697 / Jefferson City / 6/7 / 5 501 000 / Bullion State, Show Me State
Montana (MT) / 380 834 / 147 046 / Helena / 5/6 / 886 000 / Treasure State, Big Sky Country
Nebraska (NE) / 200 342 / 77 352 / Lincoln / 5/6, 6/7 / 1 671 000 / Cornhusker State, Beef State
Nevada (NV) / 286 341 / 110 561 / Carson City / 4/5 / 1 878 000 / Silver State, Sagebrush State
New Hampshire (NH) / 24 032 / 9 279 / Concord / 7/8 / 1 217 000 / Granite State
New Jersey (NJ) / 20 167 / 7 787 / Trenton / 7/8 / 8 192 000 / Garden State
New Mexico (NM) / 314 914 / 121 593 / Santa Fe / 5/6 / 1 747 000 / Sunshine State, Land of Enchantment
New York (NY) / 127 185 / 49 108 / Albany / 7/8 / 18 233 000 / Empire State
North Carolina (NC) / 136 407 / 52 699 / Raleigh / 7/8 7 758 000 / Old North State, Tar Heel State
North Dakota (ND) / 180 180 / 69 567 / Bismarck / 5/6, 6/7 / 630 000 / Flickertail State, Sioux State
Ohio (OH) / 107 040 / 41 330 / Columbus / 7/8 / 11 279 000 / Buckeye State
Oklahoma (OK) / 181 083 / 69 919 / Oklahoma City / 6/7 / 3 378 000 / Sooner State
Oregon (OR) / 251 409 / 97 073 / Salem / 4/5 / 3 349 000 / Sunset State, Beaver State
Pennsylvania (PA) / 117 343 / 45 308 / Harrisburg / 7/8 / 11 982 000 / Keystone State
Rhode Island (RI) / 3139 / 1212 / Providence / 7/8 / 994 000 / Little Rhody, Plantation State, Ocean State
South Carolina (SC) / 80 579 / 31 113 / Columbia / 7/8 / 3 932 000 / Palmetto State
South Dakota (SD) / 199 723 / 77 116 / Pierre / 5/6, 6/7 / 735 000 / Sunshine State, Coyote State
Tennessee (TN) / 109 149 / 42 144 / Nashville / 6/7, 7/8 / 5 533 000 / Volunteer State
Texas (TX) / 691 003 / 266 807 / Austin / 5/6, 6/7 / 20 385 000 / Lone Star State
Utah (UT) / 219 880 / 84 899 / Salt Lake City / 5/6 / 2 169 000 / Mormon State, Beehive State
Vermont (VT) / 24 899 / 9614 / Montpelier / 7/8 / 597 000 / Green Mountain State
Virginia (VA) / 105 582 / 40 767 / Richmond / 7/8 / 6 955 000 / Old Dominion State, Mother of Presidents
Washington (WA) / 176 473 / 68 139 / Olympia / 4/5 / 5 825 000 / Evergreen State, Chinook State
West Virginia (WV) / 62 758 / 24 232 / Charleston / 7/8 / 1 802 000 / Panhandle State, Mountain State
Wisconsin (WI) / 145 431 / 56 153 / Madison / 6/7 / 5 227 000 / Badger State, America's Dairyland
Wyoming (WY) / 253 315 / 97 809 / Cheyenne / 5/6 / 479 000 / Equality State

Polynesian; official language, English; islands mainly of volcanic origin, few rising above 120 m/400 ft; administered by Japan in the inter-war years; placed under UN trusteeship, 1947; Commonwealth of the N Mariana Is established in political union with the USA, 1975; each of the other territories negotiating a status of free association with the USA, 1986; trust status ended, 1990, and for Belau, 1994; economy based on agriculture, fisheries, tourism; coconuts, sugar cane, cassava, yams, copra, fish processing.

United States Virgin Islands *Virgin Islands, United States*

unities In literature, the dimensions of time, place, and action, requiring a play to consist of one plot unfolding in one place within one day. Neoclassical critics made into strict rules what had been offered as guidelines in Aristotle's *Poetics*. In 17th-c France Corneille and Racine wrote tragedies modelled on Greek examples and followed the strict French convention that required the action to take place in one day in one location. It was later rejected by Hugo and others in the turbulent period of French Romanticism. Dr Johnson rejected the unities in his *Preface to Shakespeare* (1765).

units (scientific) Most quantities in science are expressed using the International System of units, abbreviated to **SI units** (Le Système International d'Unités), introduced in 1960 by the General Conference on Weights and Measures (*Conférence Générale des Poids et Mesures*). The most fundamental are called **base units**: the metre, kilogram, second, ampere, kelvin, candela, and mole. All quantities of interest can be expressed in terms of these units. Certain combinations which appear often are called **derived units** and have special names, eg the newton, which is defined as $m.kg/s^2$. From 1995 the radian and steradian are also classed as derived units (previously, they were called **supplementary units**). Many other units exist, either for historical reasons or because they are more convenient in some special application than the corresponding SI unit; examples are the parsec, a length unit used in astronomy, and calories, which are used in measurements of the energy content of food. Other systems of units have been used: these include the old FPS British system, based on foot, pound, and second; the CGS system, based on centimetre, gram, and second; and the MKSA system, based on metre, kilogram, second, and ampere. SI units are an extension of MKSA units.

unit trust A form of investment. The trust buys shares in a number of companies, and offers the public an opportunity to buy a unit of the portfolio. It is a means of spreading risk. There are over 1000 unit trusts in the UK, catering for the general investor and for special situations.

Universal Declaration of Human Rights An international declaration, adopted in 1948 by the General Assembly of the UN. It declares that all human beings are born free and equal in dignity and rights without discrimination of race, colour, sex, language, political opinion, or religion. The Declaration is not legally binding, but it has greatly influenced the activities of the UN, affecting both national and international law, and has widely influenced debate on human rights. The International Covenants on Civil and Political Rights and on Economic, Social and Cultural Rights (both 1966) bind countries which have signed them. The 1948 Declaration and these two Covenants are sometimes known as the **International Bill of Rights**. The United Nations has set up a Commission on Human Rights, which investigates widespread violations of human rights. In addition, the Human Rights Committee, which was set up in 1977, has the power to look into complaints from individuals about breaches of the 1966 Covenants on civil and political rights. There are also various regional conventions, such as the European Convention on Human Rights. Humanitarian law regulating war crimes has followed a separate course. Various tribunals have, since World War 2, rounded up senior war criminals, such as the Nuremberg Tribunal (1945–6) and the International War Crimes Tribunal against former Yugoslav and Rwandan nationals (set up by the UN Security Council). In 1998, a UN conference agreed on a treaty setting up a permanent International Criminal Court. The US opposes this court, but 58 of the 60 countries necessary to establish the Court have formally signed the treaty.

universalism The religious belief that all people will be saved. It implies rejection of the traditional Christian belief in hell. A feature of much contemporary Protestant theology, it is motivated by moral doubts concerning eternal punishment, and by a recognition of the validity of other non-Christian world faiths.

Universal Postal Union *United Nations*

universals (linguistics) Features or rules claimed to be common to all languages. They are important to the theories of Chomsky and others who argue that the capacity of children to learn language so efficiently depends in part at least on their innate knowldge of such universals.

universals (philosophy) The general or abstract properties applicable to all the individuals of a certain kind or class (eg 'redness', 'courage', 'motherhood'). Unlike the *particulars* which exemplify them, universals have no location in space or time. Realists (eg Plato), nominalists (eg William of Ockham), and conceptualists (eg Berkeley) have disagreed about what kind of status to ascribe to them, regarding them respectively as separately existing entities, just names, and ideas existing only in minds.

universal time (UT) The precise system of time measurement used for all practical purposes. Formerly based on *mean solar time*, it has since 1972 been based on *international atomic time*, a uniform time derived from the frequencies of selected transitions within atoms.

universe In modern astronomy, everything that is in the cosmos and that can affect us by means of physical forces. The definition excludes anything that is in principle undetectable physically, such as regions of space–time that were, are, or will be irreversibly cut off from our own space–time.

university An institution of higher education which offers study at degree level. Courses may be taken leading to bachelor, master, or doctoral level. Both academic and vocational courses are followed, leading to qualifications in such professions as medicine, teaching, engineering, and the law, sometimes in conjunction with professional bodies. Research is given a high priority. The earliest European universities are Bologna (10th-c), Paris (1170), Oxford (1249), and Cambridge (1284). The first Chinese university was established in 124 BC; by AD 200 it had 3000 students, following 7-year degrees.

univocalic [yoonivoh**kal**ik] A written composition that makes use of only one vowel, in all its words. The opening couplet from a 16-line poem by C C Bombaugh, written in 1890, illustrates the nature of the task: 'No monk too good to rob, or cog, or plot./No fool so gross to bolt Scotch scollops hot...'

Unix An operating system developed by AT&T Laboratories in the USA which has become widely adopted, particularly in educational centres, and is seen as a suitable operating system to form the basis of open systems interconnection. The Open Software Foundation is seeking to develop Unix as a standard operating system for this purpose.

Unknown Soldier or **Warrior** An unnamed soldier, taken as representative of all those who died in World War 1, whose grave is a memorial to all war dead. Several countries have such a memorial: in France beneath the Arc de Triomphe; in the UK in Westminster Abbey; in the USA in Arlington National Cemetery.

Unleavened Bread, Feast of *Passover*

Unrepresented Nations and Peoples' Organization A body established in 1991 to represent ethnic and minority groups unrecognized by the United Nations, with the aim of defending the right of self-determination of oppressed peoples. The founding charter was signed by representatives of Armenia, Estonia, Georgia, Latvia, the Kurds, Tibet, Turkestan, the Volga, the Crimea, the Albanian Greek minority, North American Indians, Australian Aborigines, West Irians, West Papuans, Philippines Cordillera minorities, and Taiwan non-Chinese. Later representatives included Rwanda, East Timor, Tuvush (Russia), Inkeri (Russia), Komi (Russia) Mapuche (Peru), Ogoni (Nigeria), Sandzak (Yugoslavia), Udmurt Kenesh, (Russia), Nagaland (Myanmar), Stifelsen Skanelans (Sweden), Khalistan (India), and Karen (Myanmar). The body had 52 members in 2004. Six former members (Armenia, Belau, Estonia, Georgia, Latvia, East Timor) have been admitted to the UN having gained full independence.

Unser, Al (1939–) Motor-racing driver, born in Albuquerque, New Mexico, USA. He won the Indianapolis 500 four times (1970–1, 1978, 1987), beating his brother, **Bobby** (1934–), who won the race in 1968, 1975, and 1981. His son, **Al Unser, Jr**

(1962–), also became a champion auto racer and was twice winner of the Indianapolis 500 (1992, 1994).

Unsworth, Barry (Forster) (1930–) British novelist. He studied at Manchester University and later became writer in residence at the University of Liverpool (1984–5) and Lund University, Sweden (1988–). His works include *The Greeks Have a Word for It* (1967), *Mooncranker's Gift* (1973), *Pascali's Island* (1980, filmed 1988), *Sacred Hunger* (1992, co-winner Booker Prize), and *Losing Nelson* (1999). *The Songs of the Kings* appeared in 2003.

Unter den Linden [unter den lindn] A boulevard running between Marx–Engels Platz and the Brandenburg Gate, in the heart of present-day Berlin, Germany. Formerly a stately avenue lined with lime trees and historic buildings, much of its character was destroyed during World War 2.

Untersee [unterzay] *Zeller See*

untouchables *caste*

Upanishads [oopanishadz] The last section of the Hindu scriptures (the Veda), composed in Sanskrit between 800 and 400 BC. The name, meaning 'to sit near', refers to the secret transmission of these teachings by gurus.

upas tree [yoopas] An evergreen tree (*Antiaris toxicaria*) native to Malaysia; leaves oblong; flowers tiny, green, in globose heads. The milky latex is used to make a powerful arrow-poison. In the 18th-c, misunderstanding led to the belief that poisonous emanations from the tree killed all life for miles around. (Family: Moraceae.)

Updike, John (Hoyer) (1932–) Writer, born in Shillington, Pennsylvania, USA. He studied at Harvard and Oxford, then wrote poetry, stories, and criticism for the *New Yorker* magazine. His novels explore human relationships in contemporary US society, and include *Rabbit, Run* (1960), *Rabbit is Rich* (1981, Pulitzer), *The Witches of Eastwick* (1984, filmed 1987), *Roger's Version* (1986), *Rabbit at Rest* (1990, Pulitzer), and *Seek My Face* (2003). He has also published several collections of short stories, selected in *Forty Stories* (1987), and a memoir, *Self-Consciousness* (1989).

Upham, Charles Hazlitt [uhpam] (1908–94) New Zealand soldier, born in Christchurch, New Zealand. For valour in Crete (1941) and N Africa (1942) during World War 2, he became the only combatant soldier ever awarded the Victoria Cross and Bar.

Up-Helly-Aa [uhp heli ah] A festival held annually in Lerwick in the Shetland Islands, UK, on the last Tuesday in January, ending in the burning of a replica Viking longship. It probably originated in a Celtic midwinter fire festival.

Upjohn, Richard (1802–78) Architect, born in Shaftesbury, Dorset, S England, UK. Apprenticed to a cabinet-maker, he emigrated in 1829 and became an architect in Boston (1934–8). His first and best-known major building was Trinity Church, New York City (1839–46), which definitively linked the Protestant Episcopal Church with the Gothic Revival style. He designed many residences and public buildings, and his later ecclesiastical architecture incorporated Romanesque and Italianate forms. He was a founder and first president (1857–76) of the American Institute of Architects.

Upper Volta *Burkina Faso*

Uppsala [upsala] 59°55N 17°38E, pop (2000e) 179 000. Capital city of Uppsala county, E Sweden, 64 km/40 mi NW of Stockholm; archbishopric; railway; educational centre, with university (1477) and many other academic institutions; engineering, pharmaceuticals, printing; cathedral (13th–15th-c), with tombs of Gustavus Vasa and other kings; castle (16th-c).

Upsilon Andromedae The first star other than the Sun known to have a multiple-planet system. The existence of three planets around the star was confirmed in 1999. All the planets are much larger and heavier than the Earth, with masses up to about five times that of Jupiter. Upsilon Andromedae is somewhat hotter, bigger, and brighter than the Sun, and also younger, with an estimated age of 2·6 billion years. It lies 44 light years away and is faintly visible to the naked eye at 4th magnitude.

Ur [oor] An ancient Sumerian city-state lying to the SE of Babylon; the early home of the Jewish patriarch Abraham. It was at its zenith in the third millennium BC, when twice it became the capital of Sumer. Destroyed by Elam c.2000 BC, the city recovered but never attained its former greatness. It was finally abandoned in the 4th-c BC.

uraemia / uremia [yooreemia] A rise in the concentration of urea in the blood, one of the first chemical abnormalities to be detected in kidney failure. It produces a characteristic lemon yellow tinge to the skin. The term now encompasses all the many chemical abnormalities that occur in the blood in the course of kidney failure.

Uralic languages A family of languages descended from an ancestor spoken in the region of the N Ural Mts over 7000 years ago. Although some have been written since the 13th-c, Uralic languages are now in decline, largely because of the propagation of Russian in their place. The major languages are Finnish, Estonian, and Lapp, with an isolated member, Magyar, in Hungary. Numerous minor languages are scattered through N Russia.

Ural Mountains [yooral(z)] or **The Urals**, Russ **Uralskiy Khrebet** Mountain range in Russia, forming the traditional boundary between Europe and Asia, and separating the E European Plain (W) from the W Siberian Lowlands (E); extends 1750 km/1100 mi S from Novaya Zemlya in the Arctic Ocean to the N Kazakhstan border; low, parallel N–S ridges, generally 200–1000 m/700–3300 ft high; N Urals contain the highest peak, Mt Narodnaya (1894 m/6214 ft); C Urals form a plateau, crossed by several transport routes, including the Trans-Siberian Railway; S Urals consist of several parallel ranges, reaching a maximum width of 150–200 km/100–125 mi; heavily forested; rich mineral deposits; oil, iron ore, coal, copper, manganese, gold, aluminium, potash, bauxite, asbestos, zinc, lead, silver, nickel, gemstones; industrialized area in the S; cities include Magnitogorsk, Yekaterinburg (Sverdlovsk).

Urania [yooraynia] In Greek mythology, the Muse of astronomy.

uraninite *pitchblende*

uranium U, element 92, density 19 g/cm^3, melting point 1132°C. The heaviest of the naturally occurring elements, it has no stable isotopes, but the commonest (^{238}U) has a half-life of more than 10^9 years. Once used as a yellow glass pigment, uranium compounds are now used almost exclusively for conversion to plutonium in nuclear fuel applications.

uranium–lead dating A method of radiometric dating for old rocks, using the fact that the radioactive isotope uranium-238 decays with a known half-life to give lead-206, and another isotope of uranium, uranium-235, decays to give lead-207. The amount of each isotope in a rock can be used to determine its absolute age.

Uranus (astronomy) [yooranuhs, yuraynuhs] The seventh planet from the Sun, discovered by William Herschel in 1781; a smaller 'gas giant' than Jupiter or Saturn, and a near-twin to Neptune. It is accompanied by 17 known moons and a faint ring system. It has the following characteristics: mass $8{\cdot}7 \times 10^{25}$ kg; radius 25 559 km/15 882 mi; mean density 1·3 g/cm^3; rotational period 17·2 h (retrograde); orbital period 84·01 years; eccentricity of orbit 0·047; inclination of equator 98°; mean distance from the Sun $2{\cdot}87 \times 10^9$ km/$1{\cdot}78 \times 10^9$ mi. Composed mainly of hydrogen and helium, like Jupiter and Saturn, Uranus has a larger percentage of ammonia and methane. Its interior lacks sharp compositional boundaries, but has a rock-rich core, ice-rich mantle, and deep atmosphere. Its low temperature allows condensation of methane clouds (methane gas in the upper atmosphere absorbs red light and accounts for the planet's greenish hue), with ammonia and water clouds also likely at lower levels. It is highly unusual in having a rotation axis tilted so that the poles lie almost in the ecliptic, and its equatorial plane with rings and moons lies almost perpendicular to the ecliptic. It was observed at close range for the first time by Voyager 2 in 1986.

Little contrast was observed in the clouds, which do show evidence of a banded structure. There is no significant internal heat souce; the circulation is driven primarily by an unusual distribution of solar heat input and rapid rotation. The temperatures at the poles and the equator are similar, indicating some dynamical means of redistributing heat deposited at the poles. Voyager discovered two new rings to add to the nine already observed telescopically. The rings are very dark, narrow, widely separated, and slightly eccentric. There are five major moons (Miranda, Ariel, Umbriel, Titania, Oberon) in synchronous rotation; 10 additional small moons were discovered by Voyager, and others have since been observed, making 27 in all (as of 2004).

Uranus (mythology) [yooranuhs, yuraynuhs] or **Ouranus** In Greek mythology, the earliest sky-god, who was the father of the Titans. A very insubstantial figure, not the subject of worship or of art, he was displaced by Cronus. He is equivalent to Roman **Caelus**, 'the heavens'.

Urartu [urah(r)too] A state which flourished from the 9th-c to the 7th-c BC in the mountains of E Turkey around L Van. Abutting onto the territory of the Assyrians, then at the height of their power, Urartu was often engaged in hostilities with them.

Urban II, originally **Odo of Lagery** (1042–99) Pope (1088–99), born in Châtillon-sur-Marne, NE France. He became a monk at Cluny, and was made Cardinal Bishop of Ostia in 1078. As pope, he introduced ecclesiastical reforms, drove foreign armies from Italy, and launched the first Crusade. He was beatified in 1881.

Urban VI, originally **Bartolomeo Prignano** (c.1318–89) Pope (1378–89), born in Naples, SW Italy. He was Archbishop of Acerenza (1363), then of Bari (1377), and became papal chancellor for Pope Gregory XI, whom he was elected to succeed (Apr 1378). His choice appeased the Romans, who wanted an end to the French-dominated papacy at Avignon (begun 1309), but once pope he became hostile to the French cardinals, who declared his election null and void and elected the French cardinal Robert of Geneva (later antipope Clement VII (Sep 1378)). This action began the Western Schism that split the Roman church for almost 40 years (1378–1417). Urban may have died by poisoning.

urbanization The demographic process whereby an increasing proportion of the population of a region or country live in urban areas, particularly a country's largest urban settlement. It is characterisitic of economically advancing nations, where it is occurring at a much faster rate than it did historically in the developed (Western) world. Urbanization is linked to industrialization, though large urban areas did of course exist before the Industrial Revolution (eg in Asia).

Urdu *Indo-Aryan languages*

urea [yureea] $H_2N–CO–NH_2$, melting point 135°C. A colourless solid, manufactured by heating ammonia and carbon dioxide under pressure: $2NH_3 + CO_2 \rightarrow H_2NCONH_2 + H_2O$; also called **carbamide**. Although excreted in the urine of mammals, it is used as an animal feed additive as well as a fertilizer. It is the starting material for urea resins.

urea formaldehyde resin A plastic made by the co-polymerization of urea with formaldehyde. Its main outlets are in adhesives, and as a thermosetting resin for moulding. It is also used for plastic foam formation.

Ure Smith, Sydney George [yoor] (1887–1949) Artist, editor, and publisher, born in London, UK. He arrived in Australia as an infant in 1888, and was educated in Melbourne and Sydney. His etchings appeared in a number of volumes, including *The Charm of Sydney* (1918) and *Old Colonial Byways* (1928). He published the seminal journal *Art in Australia* (1916–39), founded his own publishing house (1939), and was active in promoting the contemporary arts in Australia through a variety of periodicals and books.

urethritis [yoorethriytis] Inflammation of the urethra, caused by one of several organisms such as *Neisseria gonorrhoeae* and *Chlamydia*. The symptoms include a burning sensation on passing urine, and frequency of urination.

Urey, Harold (Clayton) [yooree] (1893–1981) Chemist and pioneer in the study of the Solar System, born in Walkerton, Indiana, USA. He studied at the universities of Montana, California, and Copenhagen, then taught at Johns Hopkins (1924–9), Columbia (1929–45), and Chicago (1945–58). He was director of war research in the atomic bomb project at Columbia (1940–5). In 1932 he isolated heavy water and discovered deuterium, for which he was awarded the Nobel Prize for Chemistry in 1934. His work on lunar and planetary formation laid the scientific foundation for space-age exploration of the Solar System.

Urfé, Honoré d' [ürfay] (1568–1625) Writer, born in Marseille, S France. He was the author of the pastoral romance, *Astrée* (1610–27), set on the banks of the Lignon, describing the lives of shepherds and shepherdesses whose chief interest was love. It is regarded as the first French novel.

uric acid [yoorik] An acid derived from purine, $C_5H_4N_4O_3$; like urea, used by animals as a means of excreting nitrogen. Deposits of crystals of uric acid and its salts in the body cause pain in gout and rheumatism.

Urim and Thummim [oorim, thuhmim] Objects of uncertain description, kept in the breastplate and vestments of the Israelite high priest. They were apparently used to discern God's answer to 'yes'-or-'no' questions put to him, and served either as gemstones catching the light (if *urim* means 'lights') or as flat markers used in casting lots (if *urim* means 'curse' and *thummim* means 'perfect').

urinary stones The formation of calculi within the kidneys, ureters, and bladder. They commonly consist of salts of calcium, magnesium, ammonium phosphate, carbonate, and oxalate. They tend to form when the urine becomes too concentrated, for example in dehydration. Other factors associated with their formation include high dietary calcium and oxalate intake, and familial factors. Uric acid stones are found in gout, and cystine stones in a rare metabolic disease, cystinuria. Stones may irritate the urinary tract, producing bleeding, and may also predispose to kidney infection. When in the ureter, stones cause intense pain in the back and flanks; often they are passed out spontaneously, but shock waves may be used to break them up (*lithotripsy*).

urinary system The physiological system involved in the production, storage, and excretion of urine. In mammals it consists of a pair of kidneys each connected to a muscular sac (the *bladder*) by a narrow fibromuscular tube (the *ureter*); a single *urethra* leaves the bladder to the exterior. Urine produced by the kidneys is temporarily stored in the bladder, then expelled via the urethra.

urine A liquid or semi-solid solution produced by the kidneys in vertebrates (eg humans), Malpighian tubules in some invertebrates (eg insects), and nephridia in most invertebrates (eg annelids, molluscs). It consists of water, the end-products of metabolism (eg urea, uric acid, hydrogen ions), dietary constituents taken in excess (eg salts, vitamins), and foreign substances (eg drugs), or their derivatives. The volume and composition of urine is species-, diet-, and environment-specific, as well as being influenced by the state of health and the degree of physical activity. The expulsion of urine from the bladder is referred to as *micturition*.

Uris, Leon (Marcus) [yooris] (1924–2003) Novelist, born in Baltimore, Maryland, USA. He dropped out of high school and joined the Marine Corps, taking part in battles in the Pacific. *Battle Cry* (1956) uses the experience to telling effect, but *Exodus* (1958) remains his best-known book. Depicting the early years of struggle to defend the state of Israel, it was made into a highly successful film. Other novels included *QB VII* (1970), *Trinity* (1976), *The Haj* (1984), *Mitla Pass* (1989), and *A God in Ruins* (1999). *O'Hara's Choice* (2003) was published posthumously.

URL *World Wide Web*

Urnes Stave Church [oornuhs] A 12th-c church constructed of wooden staves in Urnes, Sogn og Fjordane county, Norway. The

Uruguay

☐ International Airport

[yooruhgwiy], official name **Oriental Republic of Uruguay**, Span **República Oriental del Uruguay**

Local name Uruguay

Timezone GMT −3

Area 176 215 km^2/68 018 sq mi

Population total (2002e) 3 383 000

Status Republic

Date of independence 1828

Capital Montevideo

Language Spanish (official)

Ethnic groups European (mainly Spanish, Italian) (90%), mestizo (8%)

Religions Roman Catholic (60%), Protestant (2%), Jewish (2%), unaffiliated (30%)

Physical features Located in E South America; grass covered plains (S) rise to a high, sandy plateau, traversed SE and NW by the Cuchilla Grande and Cuchilla de Haedo, rising to 501 m/ 1644 ft at Cerro Mirados; R Negro flows SW to meet the R Uruguay on the Argentine frontier.

Climate Temperate, with warm summers, mild winters; average annual temperature 10°C (Jul), 22°C (Jan) in Montevideo; average annual rainfall 978 mm/38 in; rainy season (Apr–May), occasional droughts.

Currency 1 New Uruguayan Peso (NUr$, UrugN$) = 100 centésimos

Economy Traditionally based on livestock and agriculture; meat, wool, fish, wheat, barley, maize, rice; naturally-occurring minerals include granite and marble; hydroelectric power, food processing and packing, light engineering, cement, textiles, leather, steel.

GDP (2002) $26·82 bn, per capita $7900

Human Development Index (2002) 0·831

History Originally occupied by Charrúas Indians; visited by the Spanish, 1516; part of the Spanish Viceroyalty of Río de la Plata, 1726; province of Brazil, 1814–25; independence as the Eastern Republic of Uruguay, 1828; unrest caused by Tupamaro guerrillas in late 1960s and early 1970s; military rule until 1985; a President is advised by a Council of Ministers; bicameral legislature consists of a Senate and Chamber of Deputies.

Head of State/Government

1966–7 Alberto Heber Usher
1967 Oscar Daniel Gestido
1967–72 Jorge Pacheco Areco
1972–6 Juan María Bordaberry Arocena
1976–81 Aparicio Méndez
1981–5 Gregorio Conrado Alvarez Armelino
1985–90 Julio María Sanguinetti Cairolo
1990–4 Luis Alberto Lacalle Herrera
1995–2000 Julio María Sanguinetti Cairolo
2000– Jorge Luis Batlle Ibáñez

church, considered to be the finest of its kind, is a world heritage monument.

Ursa Major [ersa mayjer] (Lat 'great bear') A huge and conspicuous constellation, the third-largest, containing the Plough asterism. It is mentioned extensively in literature from the earliest times, and is one of the two constellations (the other being Orion) that most people in the N hemisphere can locate without difficulty. It contains the wide double star Mizar and Alcor, spiral galaxies, and a notable planetary nebula.

Ursa Minor [ersa miyner] (Lat 'little bear') The constellation around the N celestial pole. Its brightest star is Polaris.

Ursula, St (fl.4th-c) Legendary saint and martyr. She is especially honoured in Cologne, where she is said to have been slain with some 11 000 virgins by a horde of Huns on her journey home from a pilgrimage to Rome. The legend was very popular in the Middle Ages, and was given strength when a burial ground, believed to be that of the slain virgins, was found near the Church of St Ursula in Cologne in 1106. She became the patron saint of many educational institutes, particularly the teaching order of the Ursulines. Feast day 21 October.

Ursulines Worldwide congregations of sisters engaged in the education of girls. The principal and oldest congregation was founded in 1535 by St Angela Merici as the Company of St Ursula, after the 4th-c legendary saint and martyr.

urticaria [ertikairia] An allergic reaction affecting the skin, resulting in the formation of red, itching weals and blisters; also known as **nettle rash** or **hives**. It can be provided by direct contact with an irritant, or occur as part of a generalized allergic response to an allergen.

Uruguay, River (Span **Río**), Port **Rio Uruguai** South American river; rises in S Brazil and flows W, SW, and S along the Brazil–Argentina and Uruguay–Argentina borders, joining the R Paraná above Buenos Aires to form the R Plate; length c.1600 km/ 1000 mi; navigable only in its lower course; main ports, Concepción del Uruguay (Argentina) and Paysandú (Uruguay).

Uruguay *see panel*

Uruk [ooruk] One of the greatest city-states of Sumer, lying to the NW of Ur. The home of the legendary Gilgamesh, it is also the site of the earliest writing ever found. Although it came under the domination of Ur c.2100 BC, it outlasted its powerful neighbour, surviving well into the Parthian period (3rd-c AD).

Ürümqi [urumchee], **Urumchi**, or **Wulumuqi**, also spelled **Wu-lu-mu-ch'i** $43^\circ 43$N $87^\circ 38$E, pop (2000e) 1 357 000, administrative region 1 439 000. Capital of Xinjiang Uighur autonomous region, NW China; railway; airfield; eight universities; two medical schools; agricultural college (1952); steel, oil, chemicals, textiles, farm machinery; communist base in 1930s and 1940s.

urus [yoorus] *aurochs*

USA *United States of America*

Usama bin Laden *Osama bin Laden*

USA Track and Field In the USA, the body which oversees amateur athletics, formed in 1888; formerly known as the **Ama-**

teur Athletics Association of the United States and (until 1992) the **Athletics Congress**. Its headquarters is in Indianapolis, IN.

Usborne, Mount 51°35S 58°57W. Mountain on the island of East Falkland, c.65 km/40 mi W of Stanley; highest point in the Falkland Is, rising to 705 m/2313 ft.

USENET Originally, a term referring to a network of computers all running the Unix operating system and each communicating with the others. Since the advent of the Internet it has come to mean the worldwide set of all newsgroups. A *newsgroup* is a set of computer sites which are able to send electronic messages to and receive electronic messages from all the other members in the group, just by reference to the group. A member of the group may be linked to the Internet, but does not have to be.

Usher *Ussher*

US Marines or **US Marine Corps** World-famous fighting force, created by Congress in 1798, which served with distinction in the Pacific in World War 2 and during the Korean and Vietnam Wars. Marines are traditionally known as 'leathernecks', from the leather collars on the early uniforms.

Uspallata [uspayahta] 32°50S 70°04W. Pass in the Andes between Mendoza (Argentina) and Santiago (Chile); at the foot of Aconcagua; rises to 3900 m/12 795 ft; statue of Christ of the Andes (Cruz del Paramillo) at 3050 m/10 000 ft erected in 1904 to commemorate peaceful boundary settlements.

Ussher or **Usher, James** (1581–1656) Bishop and biblical scholar, born in Dublin, Ireland. He studied at Dublin, was ordained in 1601, and became a professor of divinity (1607–21), Bishop of Meath (1620), and Archbishop of Armagh (1625). He settled in England after 1640, and though loyal to the throne was treated with favour by Cromwell. His major work was the *Annales veteris et novi testamenti* (1650–4, Annals of the Old and New Testament), which gave a long-accepted chronology of Scripture, and fixed the Creation at occurring in 4004 BC.

USSR *Soviet Union*

Ustinov *Izhevsk*

Ustinov, Sir Peter (Alexander) [yustinof] (1921–2004) Actor and playwright, born in London, UK of White Russian parents. He first appeared on the stage in 1938, and after army service in World War 2 worked in films as an actor, writer, and producer, and in broadcasting as a satirical comedian. A prolific playwright, his works include *The Love of Four Colonels* (1951), *Romanoff and Juliet* (1956), and *Overheard* (1981). He made over 50 films, including *Spartacus* (1961, Oscar, Best Supporting Actor), *Topkapi* (1965, Oscar, Best Supporting Actor), *Death on the Nile* (1978), *Appointment with Death* (1988), *Lorenzo's Oil* (1992), and *The Bachelor* (1999), and in his later years established a considerable reputation as a raconteur and as an ambassador for UNICEF. He was knighted in 1990.

Ust-Kamenogorsk [oostkamyinogaw(r)sk] 50°00N 82°36E, pop (2000e) 343 000. River-port capital of Vostochno Kazakhstanskaya oblast, Kazakhstan, on R Irtysh; founded as a fortress, 1720; airfield; railway; machinery, metallurgy; zinc, copper, lead.

Usumacinta, River [oosumaseenta] River in Guatemala and Mexico, formed by the meeting of the Pasión and Chixoy Rivers on the border; follows a winding course NW to enter the Gulf of Mexico at Frontera; length (with the Chixoy, which rises in Guatemala) c.965 km/600 mi navigable for 480 km/300 mi.

US War of Independence *American Revolution*

Utah [yootaw] pop (2000e) 2 223 200; area 219 880 sq km/84 899 sq mi. State in W USA, divided into 29 counties; the 'Beehive State'; first white exploration by the Spanish, 1540; acquired by the USA through the Treaty of Guadalupe Hidalgo, 1848; arrival of the Mormons, 1847; Utah Territory organized, 1850; several petitions for statehood denied because of the Mormons' practice of polygamy; antagonism between Mormon Church and Federal law over this issue led to the 'Utah War', 1857–8; joined the Union as the 45th state, 1896; capital, Salt Lake City; other chief cities, Provo and Ogden; rivers include the Colorado and Green; contains the Great Salt Lake in the NW, the largest salt-water lake in the country (2590 sq km/1000 sq mi); L Utah is a freshwater lake S of Great Salt Lake; the Wasatch Range, part of the Rocky Mts, runs N–S through the state; the Uinta Mts in the NE; highest point, Kings Peak (4123 m/13 527 ft); mountainous and sparsely inhabited E region dissected by deep canyons; major cities (containing four-fifths of the population) lie along W foothills of the Wasatch Range; the Great Basin further W; the arid Great Salt Lake Desert in the NW; cattle, sheep, poultry, hay, wheat, barley, sugar-beet; copper, petroleum, coal; aerospace research, machinery, transportation equipment, electronic components, fabricated metals, processed foods; tourism (Arches, Bryce Canyon, Glen Canyon National Recreation Area, Zion National Park).

Utamaro, (Kitagawa) [ootamahroh], originally **Kitagawa Nebsuyoshi** (1753–1806) Painter and engraver, born in Tokyo, Japan. Trained in Edo (modern Tokyo), he came to specialize in portraits of court ladies in which the gracefulness of face, figure, and flowing robes was depicted with a precise detail and personally developed use of close-up which brought him great contemporary success. He also painted flowers, birds, and fish, and carried the technique of the *ukiyo-e* or 'popular school' to its highest artistic level.

uterine tubes A pair of long ducts passing outwards from the upper part of the uterus towards the ovary; also known as the **Fallopian tubes**. Each tube has a funnel-shaped lateral end (the *infundibulum*) with projecting finger-like processes (the *fimbriae*, one of which is connected to the ovary), an expanded region the *ampulla*), and a narrow part (the *isthmus*). The infundibulum collects the ovum released from the ovary and conveys it towards the uterus. Fertilization occurs within the ampullary part of the tube.

uterus [yooteruhs] A pear-shaped, thick-walled muscular organ of females which projects upwards and forwards above the bladder from the upper part of the vagina; also known as the **womb**. It consists of a *fundus* (the region of the body above the level of entrance of the uterine tubes), a *body*, and the *cervix* (separated from the body by a slight narrowing). The lower end of the cervix is surrounded by and opens into the upper part of the vagina. At birth the uterus is mainly an abdominal organ, the cervix being relatively large and not distinct from the body. It grows slowly until just before puberty, when its growth is rapid for a time. In old age the uterine wall becomes harder and more fibrous than in the younger woman. The pregnant uterus increases rapidly in size and weight as it rises into the abdomen. In the human female, the nonpregnant uterus is c.7·5 cm/3 in in length and weighs 40 g/1·4 oz. During pregnancy it increases in size to become c.30 cm/12 in in length and can weigh as much as 1 kg/2·2 lb by the eighth month. Immediately after childbirth it contracts, so that by the end of the eighth week it is back to its normal size (this process is known as *involution*). The epithelial lining (*endometrium*) is influenced by oestrogens and progestagens produced by the ovary. If implantation does not follow ovulation, the superficial layers of the endometrium are shed in response to hormonal changes, causing the menstrual flow.

Uther Pendragon [yoother pendragn] In the Arthurian legends, a king of Britain, who was the father of King Arthur by Ygraine, the wife of Duke Gorlois of Cornwall.

Utica [yootika] 43°06N 75°14W, pop (2000e) 60 700. Seat of Oneida Co, C New York, USA, on the Mohawk R; railway; Munson–Williams–Proctor Institute (art); Utica Eisteddfod; dairy farming, textiles.

utilitarianism In ethics, the theory that all actions are to be judged by their consequences for the general welfare; 'the greatest happiness of the greatest number' is the sole criterion of moral choice. The classical exponents of the theory are Bentham, the Mills (James and J S), and Sidgwick, and it flourished particularly in the 19th-c.

Uzbekistan

□ International Airport

[uzbekistahn], official name **Republic of Uzbekistan**, Uzbek **Ozbekistan Jumhuriyäti**

Local name Ozbekiston Republikasy

Timezone GMT +5

Area 447 400 km²/172 696 sq mi

Population total (2002e) 25 484 000

Status Republic

Date of independence 1991

Capital Tashkent

Language Uzbek

Ethnic groups Uzbek (71%), Russian (8%), Tajik (5%), Kazakh (4%)

Religion Sunni Muslim

Physical features Located in C and N Middle Asia; four-fifths of area is flat, sandy plain/desert (W); Turan Plain (NW) rises near the Aral Sea to 90 m/300 ft above sea level; delta of major river R Amu Darya forms alluvial plain over C Kara-Kalpak; Sultan-Uizdag Mts rise to 500 m/1600 ft; Kyzyl Kum broken by hills in SE; lowest point, Mynbulak, -12 m/-39 ft; Pskem Mts in E rise to 4299 m/14 104 ft at Beshtor Peak.

Climate Dry and continental; average annual temperatures in S, -12°C (Jan), 32–40°C (Jul); low rainfall.

Currency 1 Som = 100 tiyin

Economy Deposits of coal, natural gas, oil, gold, lead, copper, and zinc; third largest cotton-growing area in the world; silk, wool; agriculture dependent on irrigated land; abundant orchards and vineyards; industry powered hydroelectrically.

GDP (2002) $66·06 bn, per capita $2600

Human Development Index (2002) 0·727

History Conquered by Alexander the Great, 4th-c BC; invaded by Mongols under Genghis Khan, 13th-c; Genghis Khan's grandson, Shibaqan, inherited the area; converted to Islam in 14th-c, under the ruler of Kipchak, Uzbek; became part of Tamerlane the Great's empire, 16th-c; conquered by Russia, mid-19th-c; became the Uzbek Republic in 1924, and Uzbekistan Soviet Socialist Republic in 1925; declared independence, 1991, joined CIS in 1991; governed by a President, Prime Minister, and 250-member Supreme Assembly; new constitution adopted, 1992; proposal for a bicameral legislature approved, 2002.

Head of State
1991– Islam A Karimov

Head of Government
1995–2003 Otkir Sultonov
2003– Shavkat Mirziyoev

utility In computing, a term used for a computer program which carries out a specific function needed by a computer centre, but which is not sufficiently extensive to justify the development of a computer package. Normally a function such as sort and merge is provided as a utility.

Utopia (Gr 'nowhere') A name for a fictional republic, invented by Sir Thomas More in *Utopia* (1516); hence, any imaginary (and by implication, unattainable) ideal state. Later works include Samuel Butler's *Erewhon* (= Nowhere), 1872; William Morris's *News from Nowhere* (1891); and Aldous Huxley's *Island* (1962). The term **dystopia** refers to the reverse, a nightmare state such as in Orwell's *Nineteen Eighty-Four* (1949).

utopianism A general term to describe a political philosophy distinguished by its belief in an ideal future state of global social harmony. Its supporters work to establish the basis for the **utopia** of the future. It has taken many forms, such as Owenism, anarchism, and other radical forms of social collectivism.

Utrecht [yootrekt], Dutch **[ootrekht]**, Lat **Trajectum ad Rhenum** 52°06N 5°07E, pop (2000e) 244 000. Capital of Utrecht province, W Netherlands; on R Kromme Rijn and the Amsterdam–Rhine Canal, 32 km/20 mi SE of Amsterdam; NE end of the Randstad conurbation; political and cultural centre; Union of Utrecht (1579); Treaties of Utrecht (1713–14); archbishopric; railway; university (1634); steel rolling, machinery, building materials, pharmaceuticals, chemicals, fertilizers, electrical products, foodstuffs, textiles, furniture, tourism; Cathedral of St Michael (1254), Maliebaan (1636), Paushuize (1523, Pope's House), several museums and old churches; centre for trade fairs.

Utrecht, Treaties of (1713–14) The peace settlement ending the War of the Spanish Succession, a series of agreements between France, Spain, Britain, Holland, and the League of Augsburg, including the Treaties of Rastadt and Baden. The Bourbons made considerable concessions in terms of territory and dynastic claims, but Louis XIV's grandson, Philip V, retained the throne of Spain.

Utrecht School A group of Dutch painters who went to Rome early in the 17th-c and were deeply influenced by Caravaggio. The most important were Dirck van Baburen (c.1595–1624), Gerrit van Honthorst, and Hendrik Terbrugghen.

Utrillo, Maurice [ootreeloh] (1883–1955) Painter, born in Paris, France, the illegitimate son of Suzanne Valadon. Despite acute alcoholism, he was a prolific artist, producing picture-postcard views of the streets of Paris, particularly old Montmartre.

Uttar Pradesh [ootar pradaysh] pop (2001e) 166 052 900; area 294 413 sq km/113 643 sq mi. State in NC India, bounded N by Nepal and China; known as the Bengal Presidency until 1833, then divided into provinces of Agra and Oudh; under one administration, 1877; called United Provinces of Agra and Oudh, 1902; renamed as United Provinces, 1935; adopted present name in 1950; capital, Lucknow; governed by a 108-member Legislative Council and a 426-member Legislative Assembly; official language, Hindi; crossed by several rivers and canals; largest producer of foodgrains in India; sugar, edible oils, textiles, leather, paper, chemicals, handloom weaving; coal, copper, limestone, bauxite, silica, phosphorite, pyrophyllite.

Uttley, Alison, *née* **Alice Jane Taylor** (1884–1976) Writer of children's stories, born at Castle Top Farm, near Cromford, Derbyshire, C England, UK. She was widowed in 1930, and turned to writing to support herself and her young son. *The Country Child* (1931) was followed by a series of books, mainly for children, which revealed her knowledge of the countryside. Many were in the Beatrix Potter tradition, featuring much-loved characters such as 'Little Grey Rabbit' and 'Sam Pig'. They were illustrated by C F Tunnicliffe.

U2 [yoo too] Irish rock band made up of **Bono** (real name Paul Hewson, 1960– , vocals), **the Edge** (real name David Evans, 1961– , guitar), **Adam Clayton** (1960– , bass), and **Larry Mullen** (1961– , drums). Formed in Dublin in 1976, the group found huge international success in the 1980s and 1990s, particularly as a live 'stadium' band, with a grandiose and portentous style, allied to earnest ethical and political concerns; Bono in particular has campaigned actively on human-rights issues. They were the subjects of the documentary film *Rattle and Hum* (1988).

Utzon, Jørn (1918–) Architect, designer of the Sydney Opera House, born in Copenhagen, Denmark. He studied at the Royal Danish Academy. In 1956 he won an international competition with his imaginative design for the Opera House but project costs escalated and in the ensuing controversy he resigned (1966). His other buildings include the Bank Melhi (Teheran), the Kuwait House of Parliament, Bagsvaerd Church (Copenhagen), and Paustian's House of Furniture (Copenhagen). In 1966 he won the competition for the design of the Zürich Schausspielhaus. He has received many design awards, including the 2003 Pritzker Architecture Prize for his work on Sydney Opera House.

uvula [yoovyula] The conical, midline muscular extension of the soft palate, of variable length in humans (5–20 mm/0·2–0·8 in). It is elevated in swallowing, and is occasionally used in the production of speech sounds (eg the French 'uvular r').

Uxmal [ooshmahl] An ancient Mayan city, 80 km/50 mi S of Merida in the Yucatan peninsula, Mexico. Covering 60 ha/160 acres it flourished AD c.600–1000, and was finally abandoned c.1450. Its ceremonial buildings are a notable feature – particularly the Temple of the Magician on its huge pyramid, and the so-called Governor's Palace, erected on a triple terrace.

Uzbekistan *p.1588*

Vaal River [vahl] River in South Africa; length 1200 km/750 mi; a major tributary of the Orange R which it joins SW of Kimberley; rises close to the Swaziland frontier; flows W and then SW along the border between Eastern Transvaal and Free State; dammed at Bloemhof.

Vaasa [vahsa], Swed **Vasa**, formerly **Nikolainkaupunki** 63°06N 21°38E, pop (2000e) 55 000. Seaport and capital of Vaasa province, SW Finland; on the Gulf of Bothnia, 352 km/219 mi NW of Helsinki; established, 1606; destroyed by fire, 1852; rebuilt on present site c.1860; airfield; railway; shortest ferry route between Finland and Sweden; ship repairing, metal products, textiles; Vaasa Festival (Jun), Stundars Feast (Jul).

Vac [vats] 47°49N 19°10E, pop (2000e) 34 300. River port and summer resort town in Pest county, NC Hungary; on R Danube, 32 km/20 mi N of Budapest; bishopric; railway; textiles, footwear, cement, distilling, tools; cathedral, triumphal arch.

vaccination The induction of immunity against infectious agents. The name is derived from *vaccinia* or cowpox – the virus that was administered by Edward Jenner in 1792 to protect against smallpox. This was the first time the technique had been used in the West, though the Chinese had discovered the importance of inoculation against smallpox in the 16th-c. It involves the introduction into the body of a small quantity of living or dead micro-organisms, or proteins (antigens) derived from them. This sensitizes the body to recognize the micro-organism as foreign and to mount an effective immune response against it in the event of a future infection, thereby preventing the development of the disease. Vaccines have been used successfully to protect against a variety of infectious diseases, including tuberculosis, poliomyelitis, tetanus, diphtheria, measles, mumps, and rubella. Smallpox has now been eradicated by a worldwide vaccination programme. In 1998 controversy arose in the UK when British surgeon Andrew Wakefield (1957–) suggested a link between the MMR (measles–mumps–rubella) vaccine and autism, but other studies have so far not confirmed the link, and the three-in-one procedure continues to be widely used worldwide.

vacuum Any space in which no matter is present. In the laboratory, near vacuum is achieved by pumping out air from an enclosed chamber. Vacua of between 10^{-4} and 10^{-10} Pa are needed in many experiments if results are not to be affected by unwanted gas atoms. Many physics experiments and standard techniques are only possible due to modern high vacuum technology. A perfect vacuum can never be attained; the closest is interstellar space.

vacuum deposition A technique for producing thin films of materials. Atoms of a material are evolved from a heated source in the vacuum chamber, and allowed to strike the surface of the substrate to be coated. The technique is used to provide the aluminium coating on compact disks; and printed circuit boards are made by depositing a metal film through a mask.

vacuum technology A technology which produces and uses pressures from a thousand to one million million times less than the atmosphere. Thin coatings (metal or non-metal) are made by evaporation in a vacuum, and used in optical instruments or the electronics industry. The technology is used to provide vacuums inside television tubes, X-ray tubes, particle accelerators, and for dehydration at low temperatures ('freeze drying').

Vadim, Roger [vadim], originally **Roger Vadim Plemiannikov** (1928–2000) Film director, born in Paris, France. His sensational *Et Dieu créa la femme* (1956, And God Created Woman), starring his wife Brigitte Bardot as a sex-kitten, was a massive box-office success, and paved the way for further sex-symbol presentations of his later wives, Annette Stroyberg in *Les Liaisons dangereuses* (1959, Dangerous Liaisons), Jane Fonda in *Barbarella* (1968), and his lover, Catherine Deneuve, in *La Vice et la vertue* (1962, Vice and Virtue). His later US productions include *Night Games* (1979) and *Surprise Party* (1983).

Vaduz [vahdoots] 47°08N 9°32E, pop (2000e) 5500. Capital of Liechtenstein, in the R Rhine valley; metalworking, engineering, tourism, agricultural trade; 12th-c castle (rebuilt, 20th-c), Red House, Prince's picture gallery, state art collection, postal museum.

vagina A variable-sized fibro-muscular tube, open at its lower end, which communicates at its upper end with the cavity of the uterus. At its lower end the vagina opens into the *vestibule* or pudendal cleft between the *labia minora*. In virgins this opening is partly closed by a thin crescent-fold (the *hymen*). In the human female the vagina is directed upwards and backwards making an angle of 90° with the axis of the cervix.

vaginismus A spasm of the muscles surrounding the entry of the vagina, preventing entry of the penis (or an inanimate object). This can be treated by counselling, which includes educational explanation concerning sexual intercourse, combined with the use of behavioural techniques.

vagus [vayguhs] The 10th cranial nerve, arising from the medulla oblongata and forming the main part of the cranial parasympathetic outflow. It descends in the neck, supplying the muscles of the larynx and pharynx, and then passes through the thorax into the abdomen. In the thorax it supplies the oesophagus, trachea, lungs, heart, and great vessels, while in the abdomen it supplies the stomach, the small and part of the large intestine, the pancreas, and the liver. The vagus nerve carries out a wide range of regulatory functions, for example decreasing heart rate and stimulating gastric acid secretion.

Váh, River River in the Slovak Republic, rising on slopes of the Low Tatra as two headstreams; flows S to meet R Danube at Komárno; length 392 km/244 mi.

Vakhtangov, Evgeny Bagrationovich [vakhtangof] (1883–1923) Theatre director, actor, and teacher, born in Vladikavkaz, Armenia. He became an actor with The Moscow Art Theatre in 1911, and from 1920 was head of the Third Studio, which after 1926 became the Vakhtangov Theatre. In all aspects of his work he made a synthesis of Stanislavsky's and Meyerhold's methods, stressing the expressiveness of the actor. His concept of 'fantastic realism' informed his finest and most influential productions, notably Anski's *The Dybbuk*, staged for the Habima Theatre in 1922.

Val Camonica A world heritage site in Lombardy, N Italy, where 130 000 rock engravings dating from the 7th-c BC to the 1st-c AD have been exposed. The carvings have proved to be an important record for reconstructing the economic and cultural life of the Bronze Age.

valence or **valency** [**vay**lens, **vay**lensee] The combining power of an atom expressed either as (1) the **covalence**, or net number of bonds an atom makes, weighting double bonds as two, etc, or (2) the **electrovalence**, essentially equivalent to the oxidation state. Valence electrons are those furthest from the nucleus of an atom, and are those involved in chemical change.

Valencia (Spain) [va**len**sia], Span [va**len**thia] pop (2000e) 3 881 000; area 23 260 sq km/8978 sq mi. Autonomous region of E Spain, occupying a narrow coastal area from the Ebro delta to R Segura; a former Moorish kingdom, under Spanish rule from 1238; C plateau cut by several rivers; includes tourist resorts on the Costa Blanca and Costa del Azahar; chief town, Valencia, pop (2000e) 763 000, on R Turia; third largest city in Spain; archbishopric; airport; railway; car ferries to Balearics and Canary Is; university (1500); tourism, wine, fruit, chemicals, shipyards, textiles, vehicles, ironwork, silk; ceramics museum, fine arts museum, Serranos military towers (14th-c), cathedral (13th–15th-c); Fiesta of La Virgen de los Desamparados (May), St James fair (Jul).

Valencia (Venezuela) [va**len**sia] 10°11N 67°59W, pop (2000e) 1 093 000. Capital of Carabobo state, N Venezuela; on R Cabriales, near L Valencia; third largest city in Venezuela, founded, 1555; airport; university (1852); noted for its oranges; agricultural trade; Plaza de Toros (second largest in Americas, after Mexico); cathedral (1580, but remodelled-18th-c) containing Virgen del Socorro (1550); Valencia fair (Nov), parade of Virgen del Socorro, Valencia week (Mar).

valentine (card) *St Valentine's Day*

Valentino [valen**tee**noh], popular name of **Valentino Garavani** (1933–) Fashion designer, born in Rome, Italy. He studied fashion in Milan and Paris, then worked for Dessès and Laroche in Paris. He opened his own house in Rome in 1959, but achieved worldwide recognition with his 1962 show in Florence.

Valentino, Rudolph [valen**tee**noh] (1895–1926) Film actor, born in Castellaneta, SE Italy. He studied agriculture, but emigrated to the USA in 1913, and first appeared on the stage as a dancer. In 1919 he made his screen debut, but his first leading role was as Julio in *The Four Horsemen of the Apocalypse* (1921), which made him a star. His performances in such films as *The Sheik* (1921), *Blood and Sand* (1922), *The Eagle* (1925), and *The Son of the Sheik* (1926) established him as the leading 'screen lover' of the 1920s. He became ill and died of a perforated ulcer at the height of his fame, and his body lay in state, attracting crowds, riots, and suicide attempts by his fans.

Vale of Glamorgan, Welsh **Bro Morgannwg** pop (2001e) 119 300; area 337 sq km/130 sq mi. County (unitary authority from 1996) in S Wales, UK; administrative centre, Barry; agriculture, engineering, light industry; tourism at Barry I.

Valera, Eamon de *de Valera, Eamon*

valerian A perennial herb native to Europe, Asia. Valerian (*Valeriana officinalis*) has pinnate leaves; toothed leaflets; flowers 5 mm/0·2 in diameter, pink, in dense terminal heads; the corolla tube 5-lobed, pouched at base; fruits with a parachute of feathery hairs. The related and similar **red valerian** (*Centranthus ruber*) has undivided, oval leaves and red or white spurred flowers. (Family: Valerianaceae.)

Valéry, (Ambroise) Paul (Toussaint Jules) [vala**yree**] (1871–1945) Poet and critic, born in Sète, S France. He settled in Paris in 1892, and after writing a great deal of poetry relapsed into a 20 years' silence, taken up with mathematics and philosophical speculations, later published as *Cahiers* (29 vols, 1957–60). He emerged in 1917 with a new Symbolist poetic outlook and technique in *La Jeune Parque* (1917, The Young Fate) and *Les Charmes* (1922). One of his aphorisms was: 'A poem is never finished, only abandoned' – an axiom which applies also to encyclopedias.

Valetta *Valletta*

Valhalla [val**ha**la] In Norse mythology, a great hall built by Odin to house warriors who die bravely in battle. Every night they get drunk, and every day fight to the death and rise again. After this intensive training they will form an army to help the gods in the Last Battle.

Valium *benzodiazepines*

Valkyries [val**kee**reez, **val**kireez] (Old Norse 'choosers of the slain') In Norse and German mythology, the Maidens of Odin. They rode out with the Wild Hunt, or appeared as swans, in order to collect warriors killed in battle for Valhalla.

Valladolid [valyado**leeth**] 41°38N 4°43W, pop (2000e) 333 000. Capital of Valladolid province, Castilla-León, NWC Spain; on R Pisuerga, 193 km/120 mi NE of Madrid; archbishopric; airport; railway; university (1346); vehicles, cement, ironwork, flour, leather goods; Columbus died here; cathedral (16th-c), Cervantes museum, Santa Cruz College; International Film Week (Apr), fair and fiesta (Sep), Festival of Spain (Oct–Nov).

Valle d'Aosta [va**lay** da**os**ta], Fr **Val d'Aoste** pop (2000e) 117 000; area 3263 sq km/1259 sq mi. Autonomous region of NW Italy (1948), bounded W by France and N by Switzerland; tourism, wine-growing, livestock, textiles, food processing; crafts, especially wood and marble; population mostly French-speaking; an important valley since ancient times, being the access route to the Great and Little St Bernard Passes through the Alps.

Vallée de Mai [va**lay** duh **me**] Nature reserve on Praslin I in the Seychelles; a world heritage area. It is noted as the unique habitat of the coco-de-mer palm: 4000 trees, many of them over 800 years old, grow in the reserve.

Valles Marineris [**val**ez mari**nair**is] A vast, complex system of interconnected canyons stretching for c.4000 km/2500 mi around Mars; located just S of the equator, and extending from near the summit of a region of extensive volcanism ('Tharsis') to the E until it merges with a region characterized as 'chaotic' terrain. Generally the canyons are over 3 km/1½ mi deep and over 100 km/60 mi wide; in the central section they are over 7 km/4 mi deep and 600 km/350 mi wide. There are giant landslides in places along their steep walls. They were discovered by Mariner 9 orbiter in 1972, and studied in detail by Viking orbiters.

Valletta or **Valetta** [va**le**ta] 35°54N 14°32E, pop (2000e) 107 000. Capital of Malta, on a peninsula between the Grand Harbour and the Marsamxett Harbour; a world heritage site; founded by the Knights of St John, 1566; airport (Luqa); university (1769); dockyards, yachting centre, transshipment centre, tourism; Palace of the Grand Masters, St John's cathedral (16th-c), National Museum of Fine Arts.

valley An elongated trough in the Earth's surface, most commonly formed by the erosional action of rivers over a long period of time. It may also be carved out by a glacier, in which case it is U-shaped rather than (as in a river valley) V-shaped. Extensional movements of the Earth's crust may produce large rift valleys by faulting.

Valley Forge National historical park in Chester Co, Pennsylvania, USA, 7 km/4 mi SE of Phoenixville, on the R Schuylkill; winter headquarters of George Washington, 1777–8; renowned for the endurance and loyalty shown by the troops during the severe winter.

Valley of the Kings A remote limestone wadi on the W bank of the R Nile at Luxor, 650 km/400 mi S of Cairo: its Arabic name is *Wadi Biban el Moluk* ('The Valley of the Gates of the Kings'). Cut into its walls are the tombs of the Egyptian kings of the New Kingdom (XVIII–XX Dynasties, 1550–1070 BC), their families, and retainers. Those of Rameses VI, Horemheb, Amenhotep II, Tuthmosis III, Seti I, and Tutankhamun are of particular note.

Valois, Dame Ninette de [**val**wah], originally **Edris Stannus** (1898–2001) Dancer, born in Blessington, Co Wicklow, E Ireland. She first appeared in pantomime at the Lyceum in 1914, and made a European tour with Diaghilev (1923–5). She became director of ballet at the Abbey Theatre, Dublin, and in 1931 founded the Sadler's Wells Ballet (now the Royal Ballet), continuing as its artistic director until 1963. She was regarded as the pioneer of British ballet, both in her own choreography – such as *The Rake's Progress* (1935) and *Checkmate* (1937) – and in the development of a school and two major companies. She was created a dame in 1951 and made a Companion of Honour in 1982.

Valois [valwah] A ruling dynasty of France from the accession of Philip VI, Count of Valois (1328), to the death of Henry III (1589). The succession was maintained in the direct male line from the 14th-c until Louis XII of the Orleans branch assumed the crown (1498). The last three Valois kings – Francis II (1559–60), Charles IX (1560–74), and Henry III (1574–89) – were all childless.

Valparaíso [valparaeesoh] 33°03S 71°07W, pop (2000e) 333 900. Port and capital of Valparaíso region, C Chile; seat of Chilean parliament; Chile's main port and a major commercial centre; lower and upper areas, connected by winding roads and funicular railways; founded, 1536; most old buildings destroyed by earthquakes; railway; cathedral; Naval Academy; two universities (1926, 1928); chemicals, textiles, sugar, clothing, vegetable oils; funicular railway runs from the Plaza Aduana to the Paseo Veintiuno de Mayo terrace on Cerro Artillería, giving panoramic view; firework display on the bay at New Year.

value-added The value which is added to the materials and components bought in by a company. It is the sum of wages, interest payments, depreciation, and profits.

value added network (VAN) A computer network which provides additional facilities other than simple data communication. For example, the Prestel network enables users to access the computers of other organizations, such as banks and building societies, in a meaningful way.

valve *thermionic valve*

vampire In Slavic and Greek folklore a dead person of either sex whose body does not decompose after burial as expected. This is an indication of incomplete funeral rites, lack of baptism, or dying in a state of sin. Vampires, like other ghosts or returning spirits, seek to take living people with them into the after-life. Typically, they rise at night to prey on and suck the blood of the living. Like other ghosts too, vampires are repelled by crucifixes, garlic, and daylight; they can be destroyed by being beheaded or pierced through the heart with a wooden stake. Bram Stoker's *Dracula* (1897) popularized and distorted the myth. *Dracula* was made into a very popular film in 1931 by Tod Browning, with Bela Lugosi in the title role, and several retellings and variations of the original story have since been made for both cinema and televison.

vampire bat A bat of family Desmodontidae, native to the New World tropics; sharp pointed incisor teeth; no tail; flies low over ground; drinks blood; lands near resting animal and walks to it using wings and legs; may trim hair or feathers with teeth; makes shallow incision with incisors (prey usually not disturbed) and laps blood; tongue has grooves to carry blood to mouth; bat's saliva prevents blood clotting, and wound may bleed for eight hours; feeding may take two hours; at least 20 ml of blood drunk per night. There are three species: the **common** or **great vampire** (*Desmodus rotundus*), the **white-winged vampire** (*Diaemus youngi*), and the **hairy-legged vampire** (*Diphylla ecaudata*). Bats of the family Megadermatidae, and some species of *Phyllostomidae*, are called **false vampires** (they do not drink blood).

Van, Lake, Turkish **Van Gölü** area 3173 sq km/1225 sq mi. Salt lake in mountainous E Anatolia, Turkey; largest lake in the country; length, 120 km/75 mi; width, 80 km/50 mi; ferry service; salt extraction, fishing; home of the ancient Armenian civilization.

vanadium [vanaydium] V, element 23, density 6·1 g/cm^3, melting point 1890°C. A metal, not occurring free in nature, and often replacing phosphorus as an impurity in phosphate rocks. The main uses for the metal are in steel production, usually in combination with chromium. Its compounds show many colours and oxidation states, +2, +3, +4, and +5 all being easily prepared. The stability of the +5 state accounts for its interchangeability with phosphorus.

Van Allen, James (Alfred) (1914–) Physicist and pioneer in space physics, born in Mt Pleasant, Iowa, USA. He studied at Iowa Weslyan College and the University of Iowa, and became director of high altitude research at Johns Hopkins University in 1946, where he used captured German V-2 rockets to carry instruments into the upper atmosphere. He became professor of physics at Iowa in 1951, and was involved in the design and building of the instruments of the USA's first satellite, Explorer I (1958). Using data from this and later satellite observations, he showed the existence of two zones of radiation around the Earth (*Van Allen radiation belts*).

Van Allen radiation belts Two rings of high-energy-charged particles surrounding the Earth, probably originating in the Sun and trapped by the Earth's magnetic field. The lower, more energetic belt is at c.300 km/185 mi from the Earth's surface; the outer belt at c.16 000 km/10 000 mi. They were discovered in 1958 by physicist James Van Allen from satellite data.

Vanbrugh, Sir John [vanbruh] (1664–1726) Playwright and Baroque architect, born in London, UK. He became a leading spirit in society life, scored a success with his comedies *The Relapse* (1696) and *The Provok'd Wife* (1697), and became a theatre manager with Congreve. As architect, he designed Castle Howard, Yorkshire (1699–1726), and Blenheim Palace (1705–20). He became comptroller of royal works in 1714, and was knighted the same year.

Van Buren, Martin (1782–1862) US statesman and eighth president (1837–41), born in Kinderhook, New York, USA. Called to the bar in 1803, he practised in Kinderhook, was elected to the state Senate (1812–16), and became state attorney general (1816–19). In 1821 he entered the US Senate as a Democrat, and was elected Governor of New York in 1828. He supported Andrew Jackson for the presidency, and in 1829 became secretary of state. In 1832 he was elected vice-president, and in 1836 president. His four years of office were darkened by financial panic, but he did what he could to lighten it by forcing a measure for a treasury independent of private banks. He was strictly neutral during the Canadian rebellion of 1837.

Vance, Cyrus (Roberts) (1917–2002) Lawyer and public official, born in Clarksburg, West Virginia, USA. He studied at Yale, became a lawyer, and entered government in 1957. He joined the Kennedy administration in 1960, becoming secretary of the army in 1962. President Johnson appointed him deputy secretary of defence (1963), but he later resigned (1969) and returned to private law practice. He was appointed secretary of state (1977) by President Carter, and is remembered for his work as a peace negotiator, notably towards an arms-limitation treaty with the Soviet Union. He worked with Lord Owen for the UN Security Council as the secretary-general's representative during the Yugoslavian conflict, and was instrumental in drawing up the unsuccessful Vance–Owen peace initiative (1992–3).

Vancouver, George (1757–98) Navigator and explorer, born in King's Lynn, Norfolk, E England, UK. He sailed with James Cook on his second and third voyages, was promoted captain (1794), and did survey work in Australia and New Zealand. He is best known for the extent and precision of his survey of the Pacific coast of North America, from San Francisco to S Alaska (1791–4).

Vancouver 49°13N 123°06W, pop (2000e) 528 600; (Greater Vancouver) 1 468 000. Seaport in SW British Columbia, Canada, opposite Vancouver I, between Burrard Inlet (N) and Fraser R (S); third largest city in Canada; settled c.1875, named Granville; reached by railway, 1886; city and modern name, 1886; airport; railway; two universities (1908, 1963); shipbuilding, fishing, oil refining, distilling, brewing, timber, trucks and trailers, machinery, tourism; professional teams, Vancouver Canucks (ice hockey), BC Lions (football); Stanley Park, with zoo, aquarium, and totem poles; Vancouver Art Gallery, Vancouver Symphony Orchestra, Vancouver Opera, H R MacMillan Planetarium, Maritime Museum, Museum of Anthropology; Grouse Mountain and Mount Seymour ski runs; Chinatowns, second largest Chinese community in North America; Sea Festival (Jul), Pacific National Exhibition (Aug).

Vandals A Germanic people, originally perhaps from the Baltic area, who settled in the Danube valley in the 4th-c. Pushed W by the Huns, they invaded Gaul (406), crossed into Spain, conquered Roman Africa (429–39), and sacked Rome (455). The Byzantine general Belisarius reconquered N Africa in 533–4. The modern word *vandalism* derives from their name.

Van de Graaff, Robert J(emison) (1901–67) Physicist, born in Tuscaloosa, Alabama, USA. An engineering graduate, he studied physics at the Sorbonne and Oxford, where he devised an improved type of electrostatic generator (later called the *Van de Graaff generator*). At the Massachusetts Institute of Technology, he developed this into the *Van de Graaff accelerator*, which became a major tool of atomic and nuclear physicists.

Van de Graaff generator A machine for producing high electrostatic potential differences, invented by Robert Van de Graaff in 1931. An electric charge deposited by electrical discharge onto a moving rubber loop is transported to the interior of a hollow metal dome, where it is transferred to the dome and stored. Potential differences of several million volts may be obtained. The device provided an early type of particle accelerator.

Vanderbilt, Cornelius, known as **Commodore** (1794–1877) Financier, born on Staten Island, New York, USA. From a poor family, he left school at 11, and at 16 bought a boat and ferried passengers and goods between Staten Island and New York City. By 40 he had become the owner of steamers running to Boston and up the Hudson R. In 1849, during the Gold Rush, he established a route by L Nicaragua to California, and during the Crimean War a line of steamships to Le Havre. In 1862 he sold his ships and entered on a great career of railroad financing, gradually obtaining a controlling interest in a large number of railways. He endowed Vanderbilt University in Nashville, TN.

Vanderbilt, Harold S(tirling) (1884–1970) Industrialist, born in Oakdale, New York. USA. He developed the current scoring system for contract bridge while playing aboard the SS *Finland* in 1925, on a journey from Los Angeles to Havana. He also invented the first unified bidding system and presented the Vanderbilt Cup.

van der Goes, Hugo [khoos] (c.1440–82) Painter, probably born in Ghent, NW Belgium. Dean of the painters' guild at Ghent (1473–5), he painted the magnificent Portinari Altarpiece containing 'The Adoration of the Shepherds' (c.1475, now in the Uffizi Gallery) for the S Maria Nuova Hospital in Florence, and many other notable works. He spent the last years of his life in the monastery of Soignies, near Brussels.

van der Post, Sir Laurens (Jan) [post] (1906–96) Writer and philosopher, born in Philippolis, C South Africa. He served with the commandos in World War 2, and was captured by the Japanese. On his return to South Africa he made several voyages of exploration to the interior. He wrote novels, but was best known for his books in the mixed genre of travel, anthropology, and metaphysical speculation. These include *Venture to the Interior* (1951), *The Lost World of the Kalahari* (1958), and *The Voice of the Thunder* (1993). *The Seed and the Sower* (1963) was filmed as *Merry Christmas, Mr Lawrence* (1983). A volume of autobiography, *The Admiral's Baby*, was completed in 1996. The influence of Jung is pervasive in his work. He was knighted in 1981.

van der Waals, Johannes Diderik [wahlz] (1837–1923) Physicist, born in Leyden, The Netherlands. Largely self-taught, he studied at Leyden Universiy, and became professor at Amsterdam (1877–1908). He extended the classical 'ideal' gas laws (of Robert Boyle and Jacques Charles) to describe real gases, deriving the *van der Waals equation of state* (1873). This work led others to liquefy a range of common gases, and also provided new basic concepts for physical chemistry. He also investigated the weak attractive forces (*van der Waals forces*) between molecules. He was awarded the Nobel Prize for Physics in 1910.

van der Waals interaction [van der wahlz] A weak electrostatic interaction between neutral atoms that decreases with distance r between atoms as r^{-6}; discovered by Johannes van der Waals in 1873. It results from the electric dipoles on atoms, which are either permanent or temporarily induced. It is responsible for the liquefaction of helium and other noble gases. These interactions are strongest between polarizable molecules, generally those containing atoms of high atomic number or having multiple bonds.

Van Diemen's Land *Tasmania*

van Dyck, Sir Anthony [diyk] (1599–1641) Painter, one of the great masters of portraiture, born in Antwerp, N Belgium. He worked under Rubens, who greatly influenced his style, visited England in 1620, and from 1621 travelled widely in Italy, where he painted portraits and religious subjects. By 1627 he was back in Antwerp, and in 1632 went to London, where he was knighted by Charles I, and made painter-in-ordinary. His work greatly influenced the British school of portraiture in the 18th-c. His paintings of the royal family and other notables of the time left a thoroughly romantic glimpse of the Stuart monarchy.

Van Dyke, Dick (1925–) Popular entertainer, born in West Plains, Missouri, USA. A radio announcer in the US air force during World War 2, he later toured with the nightclub act *The Merry Mutes*, and as half of 'Eric and Van'. He acted as master of ceremonies on such television programmes as *The Morning Show* (1955) and *Flair* (1960). His Broadway debut in 1959 was followed by *Bye, Bye Birdie* (1960–1), which won him a Tony award, and which he repeated on film in 1963. His television series, *The Dick Van Dyke Show* (1961–6), was one of the most popular in the history of the medium, and won him Emmies in 1962, 1964, and 1965. His film career includes *Mary Poppins* (1964) and *Chitty, Chitty, Bang, Bang* (1968), and he returned to the screen as Fletcher in *Dick Tracy* (1990).

Vane, Sir Henry (1613–62) English statesman, born in Hadlow, Kent, SE England, UK. He studied at Oxford, travelled in Europe, became a Puritan, and sailed for New England (1635), where he was Governor of Massachusetts; but his advocacy of toleration lost him popularity, and he returned in 1637. He entered parliament, became joint treasurer of the navy, and was knighted (1640). He helped to impeach Strafford, promoted the Solemn League and Covenant, and was a strong supporter of the Parliamentary cause in the Civil War. During the Commonwealth he was appointed one of the Council of State (1649–53), but he opposed Cromwell's becoming Lord Protector in 1653, and retired from politics. On Cromwell's death he returned to public life (1659), opposed the Restoration, and was imprisoned and executed.

Vänern, Lake [venern] area 5585 sq km/2156 sq mi. Lake in SW Sweden; length, 146 km/91 mi; maximum depth, 98 m/321 ft; largest lake in Sweden; chief towns on its banks, Karlstad, Vänersborg, Lidköping, Mariestad.

van Gogh, Vincent (Willem) [hokh], Br Eng [gof], US Eng [goh] (1853–90) Painter, born in Groot-Zundert, The Netherlands. At 16 he worked in an art dealer's, then as a teacher, and became an evangelist at Le Borinage (1878–80). In 1881 he went to Brussels to study art, and settled at The Hague, where he produced his early drawings and watercolours. At Nuenen he painted his first masterpiece, a domestic scene of peasant poverty, 'The Potato Eaters' (1885, Amsterdam). He studied in Paris (1886–8), where he developed his individual style of brushwork and a more colourful palette. At Arles, the Provençal landscape gave him many of his best subjects, such as 'Sunflowers' (1888, Tate, London) and 'The Bridge' (1888, Cologne). He showed increasing signs of mental disturbance (after a quarrel with Gauguin, he cut off part of his own ear), and was placed in an asylum at St Rémy (1889–90). He then stayed at Auvers-sur Oise, where at the scene of his last painting 'Cornfields with Flight of Birds' (1890, Amsterdam) he shot himself, and died two days later. One of the pioneers of Expressionism, he used colour primarily for its emotive appeal, and profoundly influenced the Fauves and other experimenters of 20th-c art.

vanilla An evergreen climbing orchid (*Vanilla planifolia*), native to Central America. The large green flowers are followed by

Vanuatu

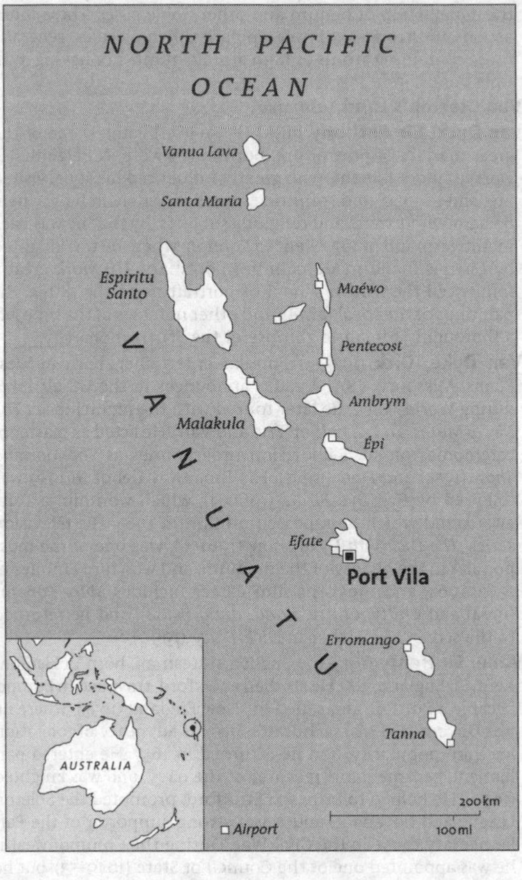

[vanooahtoo], official name **Republic of Vanuatu**, formerly **New Hebrides**

Local name Ripablik Blong Vanuatu
Timezone GMT +11
Area 14 763 km^2/5698 sq mi
Population total (2002e) 207 000
Status Independent republic within the Commonwealth
Date of independence 1980
Capital Port Vila (on Efate Island)
Languages Bislama, English, and French (official)
Ethnic groups Melanesian (95%), Micronesian, Polynesian, and European minorities
Religions Christian (70%) (Presbyterian 40%, Roman Catholic 15%, Anglican 15%), indigenous beliefs (8%), other (15%)
Physical features Mountainous, volcanic Y-shaped island chain in SW Pacific Ocean, 400 km/250 mi NE of New Caledonia; consisting of 12 islands and 60 islets; two-thirds of population occupy the 4 main islands of Efate, Espiritu Santo, Malekula, and Tanna; highest peak, rises to 1888 m/6194 ft, on Espiritu Santo; islands comprise raised coral beaches fringed by reefs; several active volcanoes.
Climate Tropical, high temperatures; hot and rainy season (Nov–Apr) when cyclones may occur; average annual temperatures, 27°C (Jan), 22°C (Jul) in Vila; average annual rainfall 2310 mm/91 in.
Currency 1 Vatu (VT) = 100 centimes
Economy Agriculture; subsistence farming and plantations; yams, breadfruit, taro, copra, beef, cocoa, coffee, timber; manganese, fish processing, foodstuffs, crafts; tourism rapidly increasing, especially from cruise ships.
GDP (2002) $663 mn, per capita $2900
Human Development Index (2002) 0·542
History Visited by the Spanish, 1606; charted and named the New Hebrides by British explorer James Cook, 1774; under Anglo-French administration as the condominium of the New Hebrides, 1906; escaped Japanese occupation during World War 2; independence as the Republic of Vanuatu, 1980; governed by a President, Prime Minister, Cabinet, and representative Assembly.
Head of State
1999– John Bernard Bani
Head of Government
1999–2001 Barak Sope
2001– Edward Natapei

slender pods up to 15 cm/6 in long, which turn black when dried and contain the essence *vanillin*, used as flavouring. (Family: Orchidaceae.)

vanitas A type of still-life picture, produced mainly in Leyden in the 17th-c, in which symbolic objects such as skulls, hourglasses, and old books are arranged to remind us that life is short and uncertain. The name comes from the Bible (*Eccles* 1.2): *vanitas vanitatum* ('vanity of vanities').

van Meegeren, Han or **Henricus** [maygeren] (1889–1947) Artist and forger, born in Deventer, The Netherlands. In 1945 he was accused of selling art treasures to the Germans. To clear himself, he confessed to having forged the pictures, and also the famous 'Supper at Emmaus', which had been 'discovered' in 1937, and accepted by the majority of experts as by Vermeer. His fakes were subjected to a detailed scientific examination, and in 1947 their maker was sentenced to 12 months' imprisonment for forgery, and died a few weeks later.

Vannes [van], ancient **Dariorigum** 47°40N 2°47W, pop (2000e) 50 600. Port and capital of Morbihan department, NW France; on Gulf of Morbihan, 107 km/66 mi WNW of Nantes; railway; animal feedstuffs, chicken and turkey processing, textiles, shipbuilding, petfoods; picturesque Old Town, Château Gaillard (Brittany's first parliament building), Cathedral of St-Pierre (13th–19th-c).

van Nistelrooy, Ruud [nistelroy], properly **Rutgerus van Nistelrooy** (1976–) Footballer, born in Oss, SE Netherlands. He began his professional career as a forward with Den Bosch (1993–7) and SC Herenveen (1997–8), then signed for PSV Eindhoven. He moved to Manchester United Football Club for a British record transfer fee of £19 million in 2001. Domestic honours include Dutch league champion (2000–1), Player of the Year and Golden Boot Award 1999 and 2000 (Netherlands), and Professional Footballers' Association Player of the Year for 2002 (England). By 2004 he had gained 29 international caps.

van't Hoff, Jacobus Henricus *Hoff, Jacobus Henricus van't*

Vanua Levu [vanooa layvoo] area 5556 sq km/2145 sq mi. Mountainous volcanic island in SW Pacific Ocean; second largest of the Fiji Is, 32 km/20 mi NE of Viti Levu; length 176 km/109 mi; chief town, Labasa; coconut plantations; sugar, copra, gold, tourism; Great Sea Reef the third longest barrier reef in the world; severely damaged by Cyclone Ami (Jan 2003).

Vanuatu *see panel*

Van Vleck, John H(asbrouck) (1899–1980) Physicist, born in Middletown, Connecticut, USA. He studied at Wisconsin and Harvard, and taught at Minnesota (1923–8), where he expanded Dirac's quantum mechanics to explain the electric and magnetic properties of atoms. His classic treatise, *The Theory of Electric and Magnetic Susceptibilities* (1932), earned him the title 'the father of modern magnetism'. He promoted the union of physics and chemistry, applying his discoveries to chemical bonding in crystals. Returning to Harvard (1934–69), he used his theory in studies of magnetic resonance and in the development of computer memory systems. He shared the 1977 Nobel Prize for Physics.

vapour pressure The pressure exerted by the gas (vapour) surrounding a solid or liquid. A solid or liquid is always surrounded by a vapour of the same substance in equilibrium with it. For example, at room temperature, the vapour pressure of water is c.0·2% of atmospheric pressure. Vapour pressure increases with temperature.

Varanasi *Benares*

Vargas, Getúlio (Dornelles) [vah(r)gas] (1883–1954) President of Brazil (1930–45, 1951–4), born in São Borja, Brazil. He was elected a Federal deputy in 1923, and in 1930 seized power by revolution. His government did much to unify Brazil. From 1937, when he dissolved Congress and suppressed all political parties and trade unions, he governed as a mild dictator. In 1945 he was ousted by popular clamour for a democratic constitution, but under this was voted back to office (1950). Four years later, in the face of mounting opposition, he committed suicide in Rio de Janeiro.

Vargas Llosa, Mario *Llosa, Mario Vargas*

variable star Any star with a luminosity that is not constant. The variation can be regular or irregular. Stars may vary in their apparent magnitude for several reasons. In an *eclipsing binary*, the pair of stars periodically eclipse, as seen from the Earth, and the apparent magnitude of the pair falls when one member is concealed from view. Also, many stars *pulsate*, and the change in size and surface temperature leads to a consequential change in luminosity. The principal types are Cepheid variables, RR Lyrae stars, and the long-period Mira variables.

variance In mathematics, a measure of the spread or dispersion from the mean of a set of scores. If $\bar{x}$ is the mean of the scores $x_1, x_2, x_3, \ldots x_n$, the variance s_x^2 is given by

$$\frac{1}{n}\sum_{i=1}^{n}(x_i - m_x)^2.$$

The standard deviation is the square root of the variance. The **covariance** s_{xy} of a sample of n pairs of scores $(x_i y_i)$ is

$$\frac{1}{n}\sum_{i=1}^{n}(x_i - m_x)(y_i - m_y).$$

This measures the association between the two variables x and y.

variations (music) A type of musical composition in which a theme is presented a number of times in different guises or with fresh embellishments. The theme itself may be the composer's own (eg Haydn's *Variations in F minor* for piano), or someone else's (eg Brahms's *Variations on a Theme of Paganini*), or a folksong (eg Delius's *Brigg Fair*). Elgar's *Enigma Variations* (on an original theme) are musical portraits of himself and friends 'pictured within'.

varicose veins Distended veins which result from obstruction to the flow of blood within them or incompetence of their valves. They may occur anywhere in the body, but the veins in the legs are most often affected. Prolonged standing and familial factors contribute to their development. When severe, they lead to pain, swelling and ulcers of the affected leg, and may require surgical removal.

varifocal lens A lens whose design allows focal length to be varied to change image size. Unlike a zoom lens, sharp focus is not maintained during this operation, and some refocusing is necessary afterwards. Some camera lenses are varifocal to give an improved performance at the expense of operating speed. 'Zoom' lenses for slide projectors are varifocal, and not true zooms.

Varna, formerly **Stalin** (1949–56), Lat **Odessus** 43°13N 27°56E, pop (2000e) 298 400. Resort and capital of Varna province, E Bulgaria; in a bay of the Black Sea, 469 km/291 mi E of Sofia; site of the defeat, by the Turks, of the Polish King Vladislav Varnenchik (1444); third largest town and largest harbour in Bulgaria; airport; railway; shipbuilding, chemical industry, power production, food processing, tourism; Roman thermae and baths; gold hoard (3500–3000 BC) discovered in the Varna necropolis (1972); museums, theatre, art gallery, opera house; Summer International Music and Ballet Festivals.

varnish A liquid which dries to a hard protective transparent or decorative film, consisting of a solution of gums in oil with a thinner such as turpentine. **Spirit varnishes** have resins (such as, notably, shellac) dissolved in alcohol (industrial or methylated spirit). Modern varieties have polymers such as polyurethane in solvents. The ancient Japanese and Chinese lacquers consisted simply of the exudation of certain trees, with colours added.

varnish tree *lacquer tree*

Varro, Marcus Terentius (116–27 BC) Roman scholar and writer, born in Reate. He studied at Athens, fought under Pompey, and in the Civil War was legate in Spain. Pardoned by Caesar, he was appointed public librarian (47 BC), but under the second triumvirate Antony placed his name on the list of the proscribed. His property was restored by Augustus. He wrote over 600 works, covering a wide range of subject matter, but only one on agriculture and part of his book on Latin survive.

varve dating A method of dating the ages of Pleistocene shales, by counting the layers (**varves**) found in the fine lake sediments deposited by the water flowing from glaciers. The layered arrangement arises from the alternation of fine and coarser material from winter to summer.

varying hare *snowshoe hare*

Vasa (Finland) *Vaasa*

Vasa (Sweden) A royal dynasty that provided all Swedish monarchs from 1523 to 1818, with only two exceptions. It was founded by Gustavus I (r.1523–60), who led the country's conversion to the Lutheran Reformation and ousted foreign powers. Great military leaders Gustavus II Adolphus (r.1611–32) and Charles XII (r.1682–1718) made Sweden into a major European power before the latter's defeat by the Russians at Poltava (1709).

Vasarely, Viktor [voshoraylee] (1908–97) Painter, born in Pecs, S Hungary. He began as a medical student in Budapest before studying art (1928–9) at the 'Budapest Bauhaus' (the Mühely Academy), moving to Paris in 1930. His particular kind of geometrical–abstract painting, which he began to practise c.1947, pioneered the visually disturbing effects that were later called Op Art. He also experimented with kinetic art.

Vasari, Giorgio [vazahree] (1511–74) Art historian, born in Arezzo, NC Italy. He studied under Andrea del Sarto, and lived mostly at Florence and Rome. He was an architect and painter, best known for his design of the Uffizi in Florence, but today his fame rests on *The Lives of the Most Eminent Italian Architects, Painters, and Sculptors* (1550, trans title), which remains the major source of information on its subject.

vascular plant Any plant possessing xylem and phloem, distinct conducting tissues which together make up the vascular system; they include flowering plants, gymnosperms, ferns, clubmosses, and horsetails, and in some classifications form the Division Tracheophyta. Additional differences between vascular plants and the non-vascular bryophytes and algae are the presence of stomata, and the sporophyte as the dominant generation. The lack of fossil links between tracheophytes and the mosses and algae is cited as evidence that these groups evolved separately.

vascular tissue The conducting tissues, both xylem and phloem, which transport water, minerals, and sap through a plant, and help provide internal support. It forms thin strands called **vascular bundles**, with xylem to the inside and phloem to the outside, separated by a cambium layer which provides for secondary growth of the conducting tissues. These bundles are scattered throughout the stem or arranged in a ring. In trees and shrubs the bundles eventually join to form a band.

vasectomy *sterilization* 1

vasoactive intestinal polypeptide (VIP) A chemical substance (a 28-amino-acid polypeptide) first discovered in pig intestine and later found in other mammals. It is thought to be a NANC type of neurotransmitter regulating blood flow, glandular and intestinal secretions, and smooth muscle relaxation (especially in the airways). It is present in high concentration in the human penis, where it may be involved in erection.

vasopressin *antidiuretic hormone*

vassal A freeman who had acknowledged the lordship of a superior by giving homage and swearing fealty, normally in return for a fief. Obligations existed on both sides. The lord's default, especially in giving protection, rendered the relationship void, as did the disobedient vassal's withholding of military assistance and general support.

VAT Acronym for **value-added tax**, an indirect tax levied on products or services as a percentage of their value. The customer pays VAT in addition to the normal price. The seller pays VAT on the value of sales, less VAT on purchased inputs. VAT is used in many countries; in the UK it was introduced in 1973, replacing purchase tax. Some goods, such as food in the UK, or businesses below a minimum turnover, are exempt.

Vatican City, Ital **Stato della Città del Vaticano** pop c.1000; area 44 ha/109 acres. Papal sovereign state in Rome, on the W bank of the R Tiber; created in 1929 by the Lateran Treaty; timezone GMT +1; includes St Peter's, the Vatican Palace and Museum, several buildings in Rome, and the pope's summer villa at Castel Gandolfo; three entrances, in the care of the Pontifical Swiss Guard ('The Bronze Doors', at the end of the right-hand colonnade; the Arch of Charlemagne, or 'Arch of the Bells'; and the Via di Porta Angelica); contains several great museums and works of art; major library; the city issues its own stamps, and formerly its own coinage; it adopted the euro in 2002.

Vatican Councils Two councils of the Roman Catholic Church. The **First Vatican Council** (1869–70) was called by Pope Pius IX to deal with doctrine, discipline and canon law, foreign missions, and the relationship between Church and state. It is best remembered for the decree on papal infallibility (1870) and the triumph of the Ultramontanists. The **Second Vatican Council** (1962–5) was called by Pope John XXIII, with the task of renewing religious life and bringing up-to-date the belief, structure, and discipline of the Church (*aggiornamento*). Its reforms in liturgy and its ecumenical tendencies have had far-reaching effects throughout the Christian world.

Vättern, Lake [vetern], also **Vetter** or **Wetter** area 1912 sq km/738 sq mi. Lake in S Sweden, E of L Vänern; extends 130 km/81 mi from Askersund (N) to Jönköping (S); maximum width 30 km/19 mi; Sweden's second largest lake; connected with the Baltic by the Göta Canal.

Vauban, Sebastien le Prestre de [vohbã] (1633–1707) French soldier and military engineer, born in Saint Léger, EC France. After serving in the Frondes (1651), he joined the government forces in 1653, and by 1658 was chief engineer under Turenne, serving with him at the siege of Lille (1667). He brought about a revolution in siege warfare and fortification; he directed siege operations throughout Louis XIV's campaigns, and surrounded the kingdom with a cordon of fortresses (1667–88). He was created Marshal of France in 1703.

vaudeville In the USA, a variety show tradition stemming from the family entertainments created by Tony Pastor from 1881 onwards. In France, the term was originally used for the dumb shows with songs of the Paris fairs, and later for the light satirical songs popular in 18th-c theatres. The 'vaudeville finale', in which each character sang a verse in turn, was used in comic operas such as Mozart's *Die Entführung aus dem Serail* (The Seraglio). Vaudeville developed its own stars, such as the comedian W C Fields (1880–1946) and the 'black-face' artist Lew Dockstader (1856–1923). It died out in the USA during the early 1930s with the advent of radio and sound film.

Vaughan, Henry [vawn] (1622–95) Religious poet, born in Newton-by-Usk, S Wales, UK. He studied at Oxford and London, became a doctor, and settled near Brecon. His best-known works are the pious meditations *Silex scintillans* (1650, enlarged 1655) and the prose devotions *The Mount of Olives* (1652). He also published elegies, translations, and other pieces, all within the tradition of metaphysical poetry. Of these, 'The Retreat' is considered his masterpiece, with its images of light and colour and its use of natural phenomena as emblems of spiritual states. He styled himself 'Henry Vaughan, Silurist', a reference to his homeland in the Welsh borderland, which was once occupied by the ancient British Silures.

Vaughan, Michael (1974–) Cricketer, born in Eccles, Manchester, NW England, UK. A batsman and bowler, he played county cricket for Yorkshire and made his Test debut for England against South Africa at Johannesburg in 1999. He scored his maiden Test century against Pakistan at Old Trafford in 2001, but a knee injury kept him out of action for the rest of the summer. Returning to form in 2002, he became a prolific scorer for England. In 2003 he was named captain of England's one-day team, and then appointed Test captain after Nasser Hussain stepped down.

Vaughan, Sarah (Lois) [vawn], nickname **Sassie** (1924–90) Jazz singer and pianist, born in Newark, New Jersey, USA. As a child she sang Gospels in church and studied the organ. Winning a talent competition in 1942, she came to the attention of singer Billy Eckstine, and through him of Earl Hines, who promptly hired her as a singer and pianist. In 1944 she made her first recording with 'I'll Wait and Pray', the following year launching out on a solo career. By the early 1950s she was internationally acclaimed for her vibrato, range, and expression. Her most notable hits include 'It's Magic', 'Send in the Clowns', and 'I Cried for You'.

Vaughan Williams, Ralph [vawn] (1872–1958) Composer, born in Down Ampney, Gloucestershire, SWC England, UK. He studied at Cambridge, London, Berlin, and Paris, but remained unaffected by continental European influence, and developed a national style of music deriving from English choral tradition, especially of the Tudor period, and folksong. Notable in his early orchestral music is the *Fantasia on a Theme of Thomas Tallis* (1910) for strings. He composed nine symphonies, the ballet *Job* (1930), the opera *The Pilgrim's Progress* (1948–9), and numerous choral works, songs, and hymns. He also wrote for the stage, as in his music for *The Wasps* (1909), and for films, such as *Scott of the Antarctic* (1948).

vault An arched covering over any building; usually built of stone or brick, and sometimes imitated in wood or plaster. Various configurations exist, including the barrel, cross, domical, fan, and rib vaults.

Vavilov, Nikolay Ivanovich [vavilof] (1887–1943) Plant geneticist, born in Moscow, Russia. He studied at Cambridge and at the John Innes Horticultural Institute, London. He was appointed by Lenin to direct Soviet agricultural research as director of the All Union Academy of Agricultural Sciences (1920). He established 400 research institutes and built up a collection of 26 000 varieties of wheat. This led him to formulate the principle of diversity, which postulates that, geographically, the centre of greatest diversity represents the origin of a cultivated plant. His international reputation was challenged by the politico-scientific 'theories' of Lysenko, who denounced him at a genetics conference (1937) and gradually usurped his position. Vavilov was arrested as a 'British spy' in 1940, and is thought to have died of starvation in a Siberian labour camp.

VDU *visual display unit*

Veblen, Thorstein (Bunde) [veblen] (1857–1929) Economist and social scientist, born in Cato, Wisconsin, USA. He studied at Carleton College, Johns Hopkins University, and Yale, and taught at the universities of Chicago (1892), Stanford (1906), and Missouri (1911). He then left academic life, and worked as a writer of literary and political articles in New York City. His best-known work is *The Theory of the Leisure Class* (1899), in which he attempted to apply an evolutionary approach to the study of economics.

vector (mathematics) In mathematics, a quantity having magnitude and direction. Vector quantities include position (showing the position of one point relative to another), displacement (the distance in a certain direction), velocity, acceleration, force, and momentum. They contrast with the *scalar* quantities of distance, time, mass, energy, etc, which have magnitude only. Vectors can also be defined in a more abstract form, as an ordered set of numbers subject to certain laws of composition. This set will often be displayed as the entries in a matrix, eg

$$\begin{bmatrix} 3 \\ 4 \end{bmatrix}$$

or (3 4). Addition of two vectors is then defined by

$$\begin{bmatrix} a \\ b \end{bmatrix} + \begin{bmatrix} c \\ d \end{bmatrix} = \begin{bmatrix} a+c \\ b+d \end{bmatrix}.$$

The number of entries is called the *dimension* of the vector, and vectors so defined can have any number of dimensions.

vector (medicine) An organism, commonly an arthropod, which acts as an intermediary agent in transferring a pathogenic micro-organism from one host to another. Examples are ticks in typhus, mosquitoes in yellow fever and malaria, and sandflies in leishmaniasis.

vector graphics A form of producing drawings by computer, in which lines are generated on the screen of a computer terminal in order to build up a specialized drawing. Such a drawing is also suitable for output to an X–Y plotter.

vector potential *magnetic vector potential*

Veda [vayda] The 'sacred knowledge' of the Hindus, dating from c.1500 BC, contained in the four collections called the *Vedas*, the *Brahmanas* appended to them, and the *Aranyakas* and *Upanishads* which serve as an epilogue or conclusion. Originally the Veda consisted of the **Rig-veda** (sacred songs or hymns of praise), **Sama-veda** (melodies and chants used by priests during sacrifices), and **Yajur-veda** (sacrificial formulae); to which was later added the **Athara-veda** (spells, charms, and exorcistic chants). The Aranyakas and Upanishads deny that ritual sacrifice is the only means to liberation, and introduce monistic doctrine. They were eventually understood as the fulfilment of Vedic aspirations, and are called the *Vedanta* ('the conclusion of the Veda').

Vedanta (Sanskrit 'conclusion of the Veda') Originally the teachings of the Upanishads; later, a trend in Indian philosophy advocating the identity of the individual self, *atman*, with a transindividual super-self, *brahman*, an undifferentiated being-and-consciousness considered the single source of cognition and action. Later elaborations include the non-dualistic (*Advaita*) version of Shankara (8th-c) and the strongly theistic version of Ramanuja (11th-c).

Vedic Age [vaydik] A period in the history of India (1500–600 BC) which began with the migration of Indo-European tribes (Indo-Aryans) to N India. It was a period of transition from nomadic pastoralism to settled village communities, with cattle the major form of wealth. There was religious worship of personified forces of nature and abstract divinities, centred on a ritual of sacrifice.

veduta [vaydoota] (Ital 'view') In art, a painting of a place, usually a city. Canaletto's views of Venice are well-known, especially in England, as they were bought by 18th-c Grand Tourists rather as we might buy coloured postcards today, and can be seen in most galleries and country houses.

Veeck, Bill, popular name of **William Louis Veeck Jr** (1914–86) Baseball executive, born in Chicago, Illinois, USA, the son of William Veeck who owned the Chicago Cubs (1919–33). He lost a leg in World War 2. He became the owner of the Cleveland Indians (1947–9), St Louis Browns (1951–3), and Chicago White Sox (1959–61, 1976–80). In 1947 he signed Larry Doby (1924–) as the first African-American to play in the American League. He was elected to the baseball Hall of Fame in 1991.

V-effect *alienation-effect*

Vega [vayga] *Lyra*

Vega (Carpio), Lope (Félix) de [vayga] (1562–1635) Playwright and poet, born in Madrid, Spain. He studied at Alcalá, served in the Armada (1588), and became secretary to the Duke of Alba (1590) and Duke of Sessa (1605). He joined a religious order in 1610, took orders in 1614, and became an officer of the Inquisition. He died poor, for his large income from his dramas and other sources was almost entirely devoted to charity and church. He excelled in the writing of sonnets and *canciones* (songs) and first made his mark as a ballad writer, notably in the *Arcadia*, a pastoral on the Duke of Alva, and *Dragoneta*, celebrating the death of Drake, both published in 1598, though written some years earlier. After 1588 he produced a wide range of historical and contemporary dramas – about 2000 plays and dramatic pieces, of which over 400 still survive. Several deal with historical or quasi-historical topics, such as *Alcalda de Zalamea*; others deal with everyday life, the most characteristic being the 'cloak and dagger plays', such as *Maestro de Danzar*, *Azero de Madrid*, and *Noche de San Juan*. He also wrote a wide range of works in other genres, such as the epic *Jerusalén conquistada* (1609), the religious pastoral *Pastores de Belén* (1612), and the prose drama *Dorotea* (1632). The most influential dramatist of the Golden Age of Spanish literature, he established a pattern that was to characterize the dramas of his age: to disregard the Aristotelian unities of time and place, to divide the play into three acts, and to use colloquial language where appropriate.

vegan *vegetarianism*

VEGA project [vayga] A highly successful Soviet mission to Venus and Halley's Comet undertaken 1984–6; the name is an acronym based on the Russian equivalents for 'Venus' and 'Halley'. Two spacecraft each deployed a lander and a balloon at Venus (Jun 1985), then used a Venus gravity assist to fly on to intercept Halley's Comet (6 and 9 Mar 1986), Vega 2 passing within 8900 km/5530 mi of its nucleus. The mission carried an ambitious science payload, highly international in scope; all elements of the mission were boldly undertaken in public view, and proved to be highly successful. The balloons were deployed at 54 km/34 mi altitude and tracked for two days by an international network of antennas, including NASA's Deep Space Network (DSN) – a notable example of international co-operation. Likewise for the Halley flyby, the VEGA Project supplied optical navigation data, and DSN supplied radio tracking inputs to the European Space Agency's Giotto Project. This provided the first close-up view of the comet's nucleus, and the first measurements of gas and dust properties. The spacecraft were severely battered by the 75 km/s (50 mi/s) impact of Halley dust, becoming non-operational.

Vegemite The registered trade name for a popular Australian spread for sliced bread. First produced in 1923 under the name 'Parwill', vegemite is a concentrated yeast based on vegetable extract, now owned by the multi-national Kraft Corporation.

vegetable In a broad sense, anything of or concerning plants; but commonly referring to a plant or its parts, other than fruits and sometimes seeds, used for food. The term is often qualified by reference to the particular parts eaten (eg leaf vegetable, root vegetable). A number of foods often called vegetables are actually fruits, such as the tomato.

vegetable horsehair *Spanish moss*

vegetarianism The practice of eating a diet devoid of meat. People who follow a diet containing dairy products and eggs are known as **ovo-lacto-vegetarians**. Those who shun all animal foods are known as **vegans**. People become vegetarians for a variety of ethical, ecological, and religious reasons. The vegetarian diet may be healthier than that of the omnivore, since it is likely to contain less fat, more fibre, and more antioxidant micronutrients. There are few nutritional disadvantages in being vegetarian, the only possible problem being in the low levels and low availability of iron in vegetable foods. Veganism may, however, pose problems, with low dietary intakes of available calcium, iron, and zinc, and little or no dietary intake of vitamin B_{12}, which is not found in higher plants. Vegans overcome the latter problem by taking vitamin B_{12} tablets, or by eating fermented foods where the bacteria provide the B_{12}.

vegetation succession The sequential development of plant communities occupying one site over a period of time. For example, a pond is gradually colonized by floating aquatic vegetation. With the infilling of sediments the water becomes shallower, and rooted plants (eg reeds and sedges) become established. Eventually the pond dries out, and shrubs and trees colonize the site.

vegetative reproduction Any means by which a plant reproduces itself without forming seeds or spores. In single-celled algae and fungi, it is achieved by simple cell division. Many bryophytes produce detachable buds called *gemmae*. Higher plants, especially flowering plants, may increase by a variety of means, such as bulbils, tubers, stolons, and runners. Fragments of stems or roots may break off and grow into new plants, as in many perennial weeds. Some plants, including fern species, bud off small plantlets along the edges of their leaves or in the leaf axils, a process called *vivipary*. Some species (eg blackberries) reproduce entirely in one or more of these ways, never producing viable seeds; All new plants produced by these means are *clones*, ie with a genetic make-up identical to that of the parent. A successful plant can thus produce offspring equally well-adapted to similar conditions. The process is also used in horticulture, allowing mass production of plants with desirable traits which might be lost in breeding.

Veil, Simone (-Annie) [vayl], *née* **Jacob** (1927–) Administrator and public official, born in Nice, SE France. At the age of 13, she was deported to Auschwitz. She studied law, and worked for the French Ministry of Justice (1957–65), later becoming minister of health (1974–9), and minister of social affairs (1993–5). A popular campaigner for women's rights, she was elected the first president of the European Parliament (1979–82).

vein A vessel usually conveying deoxygenated blood from tissues back to the heart. **Deep veins** accompany arteries; **superficial veins** lie in the subcutaneous tissue, and often appear as blue channels just below the skin (eg at the wrist and on the forearm). Blood flow in veins is slower and at a lower pressure than in arteries; consequently veins are usually larger than their corresponding arteries and their walls are thinner. When empty, veins collapse. In most veins valves are present, formed by endothelial folds strengthened by fibrous and elastic tissue. The valves are arranged to prevent flow back to the periphery, and so help to support a column of blood in veins where there is an upward flow (eg the veins of the legs). Incompetence of the valves in leg veins leads to **varicose veins**, which can become painful and require surgical removal.

Vejle [**viy**luh] 55°43N 9°30E, pop (2000e) 52 900. Seaport and manufacturing town, capital of Vejle county, E Jutland, Denmark, at head of Vejle Fjord; railway; engineering, foodstuffs; 13th-c St Nicholas's Church; 28 km/17 mi W is Billund, with Legoland®, a miniature town built of Lego® plastic bricks; 14 km/9 mi NW is Jelling, with 10th-c burial mounds of King Gorm and Queen Thyra.

Vela [**vee**la] (Lat 'sails') A S constellation in the Milky Way whose four brightest stars form a near quadrilateral. It includes the Vela pulsar, which emits optical flashes and spins 11 times per second.

Velázquez, Diego (Rodriguez de Silva) [velathketh] (1599–1660) Painter, born in Seville, SW Spain. He studied in Seville, where he set up his own studio in 1618. His early works were domestic genre pieces, of which 'Old Woman Cooking Eggs' (1618, Edinburgh) is typical. He moved to Madrid in 1823, and on the advice of Rubens, visited Italy (1629–31), which transformed his sombre, naturalistic style into a more colourful approach, influenced by Titian. He then devoted himself to court portraits, executing several of the royal family and other personalities. He is best known for his three late masterpieces, 'Las meninas' (1655, The Maids of Honour, Madrid), 'Las Hilanderas' (c.1657, The Tapestry Weavers, Madrid), and 'Venus and Cupid', known as 'The Rokeby Venus' (c.1658, National Gallery, London). He was knighted in 1659.

Velde, Henry (Clemens) van de [**vel**duh] (1863–1957) Architect, designer, and teacher, one of the originators of the Art Nouveau style, born in Antwerp, N Belgium. He started as a painter before pioneering the modern functional style of architecture. A disciple of William Morris and John Ruskin in the Arts and Crafts movement, he founded (with his pupil Walter Gropius) the Deutscher Werkbund movement in Germany in 1906, and was a director of the Weimar School of Arts and Crafts from which the Bauhaus sprang.

Velde, Willem van de [**vel**duh], known as **the Elder** (c.1611–93) Painter of maritime scenes, born in Leyden, The Netherlands. In 1657 he went to England, and painted large pictures of sea battles in indian ink and black paint for Charles II and James II. His second son, **Adriaen van de Velde** (1636–72), was a landscape painter.

veld(t) [velt] The undulating plateau grassland of S Africa, primarily in Zimbabwe and the Republic of South Africa. It can be divided into the **high veld** (over 1500 m/c.5000 ft), **middle veld** (900–1500 m/c.3 000–5000 ft) and **low veld** (under 900 m/c.3000 ft). The nature of the veld also changes from bush veld to grass veld or sand veld.

Veliko Turnovo [**vel**ikuh **toor**novuh] 43°04N 25°39E, pop (2000e) 60 400. Capital of Veliko Turnovo province, NEC Bulgaria; on the R Yantra, 240 km/150 mi NE of Sofia; airport; railway; university; capital of the Second Bulgarian Kingdom (1187–1393); Tsarevets Hill with its fortress walls, patriarch's palace, royal palace and defensive tower, Forty Martyrs Church (1230), National Revival Museum.

Velingrad 42°01N 23°59E, pop (2000e) 23 200. Spa town in Pazardzik province, S Bulgaria, in the Rhodope Mts; a well-known therapeutic centre, with 70 thermal springs; railway.

vellum *parchment*

velocity For *linear motion*, the rate of change of distance with time in a given direction; velocity v, units m/s. For *rotational motion*, it is the rate of change of angle with time; **angular velocity** ω, units radian/s. Both are vector quantities.

velocity of light A universal constant, the same value for all observers and all types of electromagnetic radiation; symbol c, approximate value $2{\cdot}998 \times 10^8$ m/s (roughly 186 000 mi/s). First determined in 1676 by Danish scientist Olaf Rømer (1644–1710) using astronomical observations, it is expressed in electromagnetic quantities via Maxwell's equations. The speed of light is now defined to be 299 792 458 m/s which thus fixes the length of the metre in terms of the second.

Veltman, Martinus (J G) (1931–) Physicist, born in The Netherlands. He studied at the University of Utrecht, and became a fellow at CERN, Geneva, then professor of physics at Utrecht (1966) and at the University of Michigan (1981), where he is now professor emeritus. He carried out pioneering research on the renormalizability of gauge theories in particle physics, and shared the 1999 Nobel Prize for Physics for his role in elucidating the quantum structure of electroweak interactions.

Velvet Underground US rock band, formed in 1966, originally with **Lou Reed** (1944– , vocals, songwriter), **John Cale** (1940– , vocals, various instruments, songwriter), **Sterling Morrison** (bass guitar), **Maureen Tucker** (drums), and (slightly later) **Nico** (1940– , vocals). They were associated with Andy Warhol, and joined his Exploding Plastic Inevitable rock revue. Their albums *The Velvet Underground and Nico* (1967) and *White Heat/White Light* (1968), redolent of hard drugs and deviant sex, had little success when first released but have since become rock classics, with a huge and continuing influence on later artists. After the band broke up in 1970, Lou Reed and John Cale pursued successful solo careers.

velvet worm A primitive terrestrial arthropod; body cylindrical, segmented, length up to 150 mm/6 in; head with a pair of antennae and a pair of jaws; legs lobe-like; c.70 species,

Venezuela

[venezwayla], official name **Republic of Venezuela**, Span **República de Venezuela**

Local name República de Venezuela

Timezone GMT −4

Area 912 050 km²/352 051 sq mi

Population total (2002e) 25 093 000

Status Republic

Date of independence 1830

Capital Caracas

Languages Spanish (official), Italian, c.25 Indian languages also spoken in the interior

Ethnic groups Mestizo (69%), European (20%), African origin (9%), Indian (2%)

Religions Roman Catholic (92%), Protestant (2%)

Physical features Occupies most of the N coast of South America; Guiana Highlands (SE) cover almost half the country; Venezuelan Highlands in the W and along the coast, highest point, Pico Bolívar 5007 m/16 411 ft; vast grasslands (Llanos) in the Orinoco basin; chief river, Orinoco; largest lake in South America, L Maracaibo, 21 486 km²/8296 sq mi; highest waterfall in the world, Angel Falls 979 m/3212 ft.

Climate Tropical, generally hot and humid; average annual temperatures 18°C (Jan), 21°C (Jul) in Caracas; one rainy season (Apr–Oct); average annual rainfall 833 mm/33 in.

Currency 1 Bolívar (B) = 100 céntimos

Economy Since 1920s, based on oil from Maracaibo (now provides over 90% of export revenue); aluminium (second-highest source of revenue); iron ore, gold, diamonds; only 4% of the land is under permanent cultivation; beef and dairy farming; coffee, cocoa, cotton, rice, tobacco, sugar.

GDP (2002) $131·7 bn, per capita $5400

Human Development Index (2002) 0·770

History Originally inhabited by Caribs and Arawaks; seen by Columbus, 1498; Spanish settlers, 1520; frequent revolts against Spanish colonial rule; independence movement under Simón Bolívar, leading to the establishment of the State of Gran Colombia (Colombia, Ecuador, Venezuela), 1821; independent republic, 1830; short-lived military coup, April 2002; governed by an elected bicameral National Congress, comprising a Senate and a Chamber of Deputies; a President is advised by a Council of Ministers.

Head of State/Government
1959–64 Romulo Betancourt
1964–9 Raul Leoni
1969–74 Rafael Caldera Rodriguez
1974–9 Carlos Andrés Pérez
1979–84 Luis Herrera Campins
1984–9 Jaime Lusinchi
1989–93 Carlos Andrés Pérez
1993 Ramon José Velásquez *Interim*
1994–8 Rafael Caldera Rodríguez
1998–2002 Hugo Chavez Fríaz
2002 Pedro Carmona *Transitional*
2002– Hugo Chavez Fríaz

mostly nocturnal and feeding on small invertebrates. (Phylum: Arthropoda. Subphylum: Onychophora.)

Venables, Terry, popular name of **Terence Frederick Venables** (1943–) Football player, manager, and coach, born in London, UK. He began his career with Chelsea (1958–66), then joined Tottenham Hotspur (1966–8) and Queens Park Rangers (1968–73). As a manager, he took Crystal Palace from the third division to the top of the first division (1976–80), then managed Queens Park Rangers (1980–4), Barcelona (1984–7) – who won the Spanish Championship in 1984 – and Tottenham Hotspur (1987–93), where he was also chief executive (1991–3) until a much publicized conflict with club chairman Alan Sugar. Venables later became the English national team coach (1994–6), and then coach to the Australian national soccer team. He returned to English football when he took over as coach at Middlesbrough in 2000, followed by an eight-month spell as manager of Leeds United in 2002–3. He was co-author of the 1970s TV detective series, Hazell, and his other writing includes a volume of autobiography (1994) and *The Best Game in the World* (1996).

Venda [venda] Former independent black homeland in NE South Africa; self-government, 1973; granted independence by South Africa (not recognized internationally), 1979; bloodless military coup, 1990; incorporated into Northern Province in the South African constitution of 1994.

Vendée, Wars of the [vãday] French counter-revolutionary insurrections in the W provinces against the central government in Paris. The brutal rising in La Vendée (1793), when priests and nobles encouraged the conservative peasantry to rebel against the Convention's conscription and anticlerical policies, was a precedent for other provincial revolts in 1795, 1799, 1815, and 1832.

Vendôme, Louis Joseph, duc de (Duke of) [vãdohm] (1654–1712) French general, born in Paris, France, the great-grandson of Henry IV. He fought in the Dutch campaign of 1672, and in the War of the League of Augsburg (1689–97). He commanded in Italy and Flanders during the War of the Spanish Succession (1701–13), was victorious at Cassano (1705) and Calcinato (1706), but was defeated at Oudenaarde by Marlborough (1708), and recalled after the loss of Lille. Sent to Spain in 1710 to aid Philip V, he recaptured Madrid, and defeated the English at Brihuega and the Austrians at Villaviciosa.

Venera Programme [venaira] A highly successful evolutionary series of Soviet space missions to Venus, 1961–83 (plus VEGA landers and balloons of 1985). Its highlights include: the first successful atmospheric entry probe (Venera 4, 1967); the first complete descent to the surface (Venera 5, 1969); the first science measurements on the surface (Venera 7, 1970); the first TV pictures from the surface (Venera 9, 1975); the first chemical analysis of the soil (Venera 13, 1981); the first high resolution images of the surface from orbit using radar to penetrate clouds (Venera 15/16, 1983); and the first balloons deployed and tracked in the atmosphere (VEGA, 1985).

venereal disease (VD) A range of infectious diseases usually transmitted by sexual contact and occasionally in other ways. Examples include AIDS, hepatitis B and C virus infection, syphilis, gonorrhoea, herpes, and chancroid.

Venetian School The art associated with Venice, beginning with the building of the Basilica of St Mark in the 11th-c, with its rich mosaics and proud Byzantine domes. Painting developed from the 14th-c onwards and became one of the greatest traditions in Renaissance Europe. Leading masters included Bellini, Giorgione, Titian, Veronese, and Tintoretto. In contrast to Florence, Venice fostered a painterly and atmospheric approach based on colour and tone rather than on outline. The Baroque period saw the building of magnificent churches such as Sta Maria della Salute, and the 18th-c saw a final flowering in painting, with G B Tiepolo, Canaletto, and Guardi.

Venezuela *p.1599*

Venice, Ital **Venezia**, Lat **Venetia** 45°26N 12°20E, pop (2000e) 317 000. Seaport capital of Venice province, Veneto, NE Italy, on the Gulf of Venice, at the head of the Adriatic Sea; 4 km/2 mi from the Italian mainland in a salt-water lagoon, separated from the Adriatic by narrow spits of land; built on 118 small islands, and crossed by more than 150 canals, notably the Grand Canal, the main traffic artery; the houses and palaces are built on piles; connects with the mainland by a road and rail causeway, and by ferries; important art collections; airport; railway; shipbuilding, freight, commerce, lace, textiles, glass, crafts; a major tourist area; St Mark's Church (remodelled 11th-c) and Campanile (97 m/319 ft-high bell-tower, rebuilt 1905–12), Doge's Palace (14th–15th-c), Bridge of Sighs (c.1595), Church of Saints John and Paul (13th-c), La Fenice opera house (re-opened 2003); Venetian Carnival (Feb–Mar), Gondola Race (Sep), Festival of Modern Art (Sep); birthplace of Marco Polo, Vivaldi, Goldoni, Canaletto, Tintoretto; fresh anxiety since the 1980s over the risk to the city from flooding and pollution; the Moses Project designed to prevent tidal flooding is launched, 2003 (planned completion 2010); Venice and the lagoon are world heritage sites.

Venn diagram In mathematics, a diagram illustrating the relations between sets, devised by the British logician, John Venn (1834–1923). For example, the diagram shows that Set *A* is a subset of *B*, and *B* does not contain any elements of *C*, ie *B* and *C* are disjoint.

ventricles **1** The chambers of the heart which eject blood into the pulmonary trunk (right ventricle) or the aorta (left ventricle).
2 The spaces within the brain where cerebrospinal fluid (CSF) is produced. There are four ventricles (the remains of the original hollow part of the neural tube of the embryo), below which a central canal extends into the spinal cord. Apertures in the system allow CSF to escape into the subarachnoid space. Any blockage or acute narrowing traps CSF within the ventricles, leading eventually to their enlargement (*hydrocephalus*).

Ventris, Michael (George Francis) (1922–56) Linguist, born in Wheathampstead, Hertfordshire, SE England, UK. As a teenager he heard Arthur Evans lecture on the undeciphered Minoan scripts found on tablets excavated at palace sites in Crete (Linear B), and determined to solve the puzzle. Although an architect by training, after World War 2 he devoted much of his time to analysis of the texts, and in 1952 announced that the language of Linear B was early Greek, a conclusion later confirmed by other scholars. He was killed in a road accident shortly before the publication of his joint work with John Chadwick (1920–98), *Documents in Mycenaean Greek*.

Ventura Publisher® [**ventyoora**] A desk-top publishing package developed by Xerox for the preparation of large textual documents such as scientific papers and books.

Venturi tube [**ventooree**] A device for measuring the amount of fluid flowing in a tube; named after the Italian physicist Giovanni Battista Venturi (1746–1822). The tube is constricted to form a throat, and pressure is measured on either side, the pressure difference indicating the rate of flow. Devices of this kind are also used in engine carburettors.

venue *jurisdiction* 2

Venus (astronomy) The second planet from the Sun, attaining the greatest brilliancy in the night sky, outshining all the stars, hence its poetic names 'morning/evening star'. There are no natural satellites. It has the following characteristics: mass $4{\cdot}87 \times 10^{24}$ kg; radius 6052 km/3760 mi; mean density 5·2 g/cm^3; equatorial gravity 887 cm/s^2; rotational period 243 days (retrograde); orbital period 224·7 days; obliquity 0°; orbital eccentricity 0·007; mean distance from the Sun $108{\cdot}2 \times 10^6$ km/$67{\cdot}2 \times 10^6$ mi. It approaches nearer to the Earth than any other planet, and is a near twin to Earth in size and density, but with a radically different atmosphere of mainly carbon dioxide, 90 times denser than our own, and with surface temperatures near 460°C. It is completely shrouded in clouds and haze layers of sulphuric acid composition. The thick atmosphere and cloud cover create a greenhouse effect that maintains high temperatures, even though clouds reflect a large fraction of incident sunlight. There is no observable magnetic field.

The surface was mapped at sub-kilometre resolution by the Magellan spacecraft in 1990–2. About 85% consists of volcanic plains (mostly at low elevations) marked by thousands of individual volcanic constructs and (unlike most other solid planetary surfaces) relatively few (c.900) impact craters. The most extensive plains are flood lavas, within which are found shield volcanoes, cones, and domes of up to c.90 km/60 mi diameter. Some features appear unique to Venus, and have been given descriptive names: *coronae* are complex volcano-tectonic features whose morphology suggests they result from mantle plumes; *arachnoids* have inner concentric and outer radial ridges and fractures; *pancake domes* are almost perfectly circular, with steep sides and heights of a few hundred metres. The surface is evidently very young (200–700 million years). Surface features are disrupted by tectonic activity, and deformation occurs over a wide variety of styles and scales (up to 1000 km/600 mi). There is no evidence for Earth-like plate tectonics, though some features do resemble terrestrial subduction trenches. Reconstruction of the planetary history by interpretation of the Magellan geological observations and the earlier Pioneer and Venera atmospheric composition measurements is a process expected to continue for many years.

Venus (mythology) Originally an obscure Italian deity of the vegetable garden, she was identified with Aphrodite, and, as the Roman goddess of love, took over the latter's mythology and attributes.

Venus's fly trap A small carnivorous perennial (*Dionaea muscipula*), native only to the pine barrens of SE USA; leaves forming a rosette; flowers white, 5-petalled, in slender spikes up to 15 cm/6 in high. Each leaf is divided into a lower, winged portion and an upper portion (the trap) formed by two hemispherical lobes each bearing three trigger hairs and fringed with teeth. Stimulation of these hairs by an insect causes the lobes to snap shut, the teeth crossing to trap the prey. When the lobes are tightly squeezed together, red glands on the inner surface secrete enzymes, and the plant digests the prey before the leaf re-opens. (Family: Droseraceae.)

Venus's girdle A ribbon-like comb jelly; body flattened; main tentacles reduced; secondary tentacles present in grooves near mouth. (Phylum: Ctenophora.)

Veracruz [vayrakroos] 19°11N 96°10W, pop (2000e) 394 000. Seaport in Veracruz state, E Mexico, on the Gulf of Mexico; site of Cortés landing, 1519; airport; railway; principal port of entry for Mexico; textiles, chemicals, iron and steel, soap, sisal, trade in coffee, vanilla, tobacco; Palacio Municipal (17th-c), Castle of San Juan de Ulúa (1565), Baluarte de Santiago fort, city museum.

verbena *lemon verbena; vervain*

Verde, Cape *Cap Vert*

Verdi, Giuseppe (Fortunino Francesco) [vairdee] (1813–1901) Composer of dramatic opera, born in Le Roncole, N Italy. Of humble, rural origin, his early musical education was subsidized by locals who admired his talent. He studied at La Scala, Milan, and began to write operas, achieving his first major success with *Nabucco* (1842). *Rigoletto* (1851), *Il Trovatore* (1853), and *La Traviata* (1853) established him as the leading operatic composer of the day. His spectacular *Aïda* was commissioned for the new opera house in Cairo, built in celebration of the Suez Canal (1871). Apart from the *Requiem* (1874), there was then a lull in output until, in his old age, he produced *Otello* (1887) and *Falstaff* (1893). An enthusiastic nationalist in his youth, he came to find active participation in politics not to his taste, and he resigned his deputyship in the first Italian parliament (1860). Later in life he became a senator.

verdigris [verdigree] Basic copper carbonate, approximately $Cu_3(CO_3)_2(OH)_2$, formed in the atmospheric corrosion of copper surfaces. It is green in colour.

Verdun *World War 1*

Vereeniging, Peace of [verayniging] (1902) The peace treaty which ended the Boer War, signed at Pretoria. The Boers won three important concessions: an amnesty for those who had risen in revolt within the Cape Colony; a promise that the British would deny the franchise to Africans until after the Boer republics were returned to representative government; and additional financial support for reconstruction. The Peace ensured that there would be no significant change in the political relationship of whites and blacks in South Africa.

Vergil *Virgil*

Vergina [vairgeena] Ancient Aigai, Greece, the first capital of Macedonia. It is notable archaeologically for the excavation in 1977 of the reputed grave of Philip of Macedon, the father of Alexander the Great. Below a burial mound 110 m/360 ft diameter and 14 m/46 ft high lay a spectacular vaulted tomb with a painted stucco facade; finds included weapons, armour, drinking vessels, furniture, and a gold casket holding cremated bones and a gold wreath of acorns and oak leaves.

verificationism In philosophy, the criterion of significance applied by logical positivists. A statement or principle was said to be meaningful only if it was analytic (when its truth follows from its meaning, as in 'bachelors are unmarried men' or '4 + 4 = 8') or if it could in principle be verified by empirical observation. The effect, and the intention, was to discriminate in favour of science, logic, and mathematics and against metaphysics, theology, and normative ethics.

Verlaine, Paul (Marie) [verlen] (1844–96) Poet, born in Metz, NE France. Educated in Paris, he joined the civil service, but mixed with the leading Parnassian writers, and achieved success with his second book of poetry, *Fêtes galantes* (1869). In 1872 he left his family to travel with the young poet Rimbaud, but their friendship ended in Brussels (1873) when Verlaine, drunk and desolate at Rimbaud's intention to leave, shot him in the wrist. While in prison for two years, he wrote *Romances sans paroles* (1874, Songs Without Words). He became a Catholic, then taught French in England, where he wrote *Sagesse* (1881, Wisdom), which contains perhaps his finest lyrics. In 1877 he returned to France, where he wrote critical studies, notably *Les Poètes maudits* (1884, The Accursed Poets), short stories, and sacred and profane verse.

Vermeer, Jan [vermayr] (1632–75) Painter, born in Delft, The Netherlands. He married in 1653, and that year was admitted master painter to the Guild of St Luke, which he served as headman. He gained some recognition in his lifetime in Holland, but made little effort to sell; as a result, his art was forgotten until 19th-c researchers re-established his reputation. He painted small detailed domestic interiors, notable for their use of perspective and treatment of the various tones of daylight. Forty of his paintings are known, among them the 'Allegory of Painting' (c.1665, Vienna) and 'Woman Reading a Letter' (c.1662, Amsterdam).

vermiculite [vermikyuliyt] A group of clay minerals formed by the alteration of micas. They consist of porous and flaky particles which expand to about 20 times their volume when heated, producing low-density, thermally insulating, and inert material used in plaster, insulation, and packing material, and as a medium for raising plants from seed.

vermilion *mercury* (chemistry)

Vermont [vermont] pop (2000e) 608 800; area 24 899 sq km/ 9614 sq mi. New England state in NE USA, divided into 14 counties; the 'Green Mountain State'; explored by Champlain, 1609; first settlement established at Fort Dummer, 1724; 14th state admitted to the Union, 1791; capital, Montpelier; largest town, Burlington; the Green Mts run N–S through the C; rivers drain W from the mountains into L Champlain which forms much of the W border, and E into the Connecticut R which forms much of the E border; highest point, Mt Mansfield (1339 m/4393 ft); forestry and timber products, arable farming, grazing, dairy products, maple syrup (largest producer in USA), marble and granite.

vermouth A fortified red or white wine. Pure alcohol is used for the fortification, up to the same alcohol level as sherry, and various herbs and spices are added for flavour. *Martini* is a popular cocktail of gin (or vodka) and vermouth.

vernal equinox *equinox*

Verne, Jules (1828–1905) Writer, born in Nantes, W France. He studied law at Paris, then turned to literature. From 1848 he wrote opera libretti, then in 1863 developed a new vein in fiction, exaggerating and anticipating the possibilities of science. His best-known books are *Voyage au centre de la terre* (1864, Journey to the Centre of the Earth), *Vingt mille lieues sous les mers* (1870, Twenty Thousand Leagues under the Sea), and *Voyage autour du monde en quatre-vingts jours* (1873, Around the World in Eighty Days). Several successful films have been made from his novels. He greatly influenced the early science fiction of H G Wells.

Vernon, Edward, nickname **Old Grog** (1684–1757) British admiral. He joined the navy in 1700, and also became an MP (1727–41). In 1739, during the War of Jenkins' Ear, he was sent to harry the Spaniards in the Antilles, and his capture of Portobello made him a national hero. During the Jacobite rebellion of 1745 his masterly disposition in the Channel successfully kept the standby Gallic reinforcements in their ports. He received his nickname from his grogram coat, and in 1740 ordered the dilution of navy rum with water, the mixture being thereafter known as 'grog'.

Verona [verohna] 45°26N 11°00E, pop (2000e) 264 000. Capital town of Verona province, Veneto, N Italy, on the R Adige c.80 km/50 mi from Venice; important communications centre; railway; agricultural market centre; chemicals, engineering, freight distribution, antiques, shoes, textiles, paper, furniture, tourism; many Roman and mediaeval remains; birthplace of Catullus; cathedral (12th–15th-c), Church of San Giorgio in Braida (16th-c), Castel Vecchio (1354–5), Church of San Zeno Maggiore (11th–12th-c); agricultural livestock fair (Mar), operatic festival in the Roman amphitheatre (Jul–Aug). A world heritage site.

Veronese, Paolo [vayronayzay], originally **Paolo Caliari** (c.1528–88) Venetian decorative painter, born in Verona, N Italy. He worked at Verona and Mantua, then settled in Venice (1555), where he came to rank with Titian and Tintoretto. The Church of San Sebastiano in Venice contains many pictures of the period before his visit to Rome (1560). His major paintings include 'The Marriage Feast at Cana' (1562–3, Louvre), 'The Adoration of the Magi' (1573, National Gallery, London), and 'Feast in the House of the Levi' (1573, Venice), which brought him before the Inquisition for trivializing religious subjects.

Verrazano-Narrows Bridge A major steel suspension bridge across the entrance to New York harbour, connecting Staten I with Brooklyn; constructed in 1959–64; length of main span 1298 m/4260 ft; Narrows named after the Italian explorer, Giovanni da Verrazano (1485–1528).

Verrocchio, Andrea del [verohkioh], originally **Andrea del Cione** (c.1435–88) Sculptor, painter, and goldsmith, born in Florence, NC Italy. Of the paintings ascribed to him, only the 'Baptism' (1474/5) in the Uffizi is certain, and this was completed by Leonardo da Vinci, whom he taught. He is best known for his equestrian statue of Colleoni at Venice.

verruca [vuhrooka] *wart*

Versace, Gianni [versachee] (1946–97) Fashion designer, born in Reggio di Calabria, S Italy. He moved to Milan, and in 1973 began freelance designing for the Italian labels Genny, Callaghan, and Complice, before launching his own ready-to-wear collection in 1978. He became known for his glamorous styles, producing a range of siren dresses that became his trademark, and often using innovative materials and techniques, such as his use of aluminium mesh, or of 'neo-couture' laser technology to fuse leather and rubber. He worked with the top supermodels, and his designs had enormous appeal among the stars of film and pop music. He was shot dead by an assassin outside his home in Miami Beach, Florida.

Versailles [vairsiy] A chateau built for Louis XIII at the village of Versailles, 23 km/14 mi SW of Paris in the 17th-c, and transformed under Louis XIV to create a palace, unequalled in its display of wealth, in which to house the entire court. Later extensions were the Grand Trianon (a smaller residence in the palace grounds) and the Petit Trianon (added by Louis XV). The palace was ransacked during the French Revolution, but has been restored to its original state, and is now a world heritage site. It has been the scene of several peace treaties, notably at the end of the American War of Independence (1783), the Franco-Prussian War (1871), and World War 1 (1919).

Versailles, Treaty of [vairsiy] A peace treaty drawn up in 1919 between Germany and the Allied powers at Paris within the overall framework of the Versailles peace settlement (1919–23). Of the 434 articles, the most controversial was article 231 assigning to Germany and her allies responsibility for causing World War 1, and establishing liability for severe reparation payments. Germany lost all overseas colonies; considerable territory to Poland in the E, almost all of Western Prussia; and Alsace-Lorraine to France. The terms of the treaty caused great hardship and resentment in Germany, helping to pave the way for the rise of Nazism. Many of the terms were broken by Hitler in the years following his rise to power in 1933. The Rhineland was demilitarized and occupied by Allied troops, and German armed forces were strictly limited. Germany had to abolish compulsory military service and stop almost all war production. The treaty also established the League of Nations and the International Labour Organization.

verse A single line of poetry, a stanza, or poetry in general (as in the phrase 'English verse'). **Versification** refers to the technical characteristics of a given poetic form, and also to the exploitation of these by a given poet. *Verse* also has a special use in biblical contexts, where it refers to a traditional division of the text of a chapter.

Vert, Cap *Cap Vert*

vertebra *vertebral column*

vertebral column The backbone of all vertebrates: a series of bony elements (**vertebrae**) separated by **intervertebral discs**, and held together by ligaments and muscles. The amount of movement between adjacent vertebrae is small, but when added together the vertebral column is extremely mobile. In the majority of vertebrates, the column lies horizontally, being supported by hindlimbs and forelimbs. In humans, however, it is held erect and supported by the hindlimbs only. It carries and supports the thorax, and gives attachment to many muscles; it surrounds and protects the spinal cord from mechanical trauma; it acts as a shock absorber (by virtue of its curvatures and the presence of the intervertebral discs); and it can transmit forces from one part of the body to another. In humans, it is 72–75 cm/28–30 in long (c.40% of an individual's height) and consists of 7 cervical, 12 thoracic, 5 lumbar, 5 fused sacral, and 4 fused coccygeal vertebrae. At birth it presents a single C-shaped curvature (concave forward) which acquires secondary curvatures in the opposite direction in both the lumbar and cervical regions. The cervical curvature develops in order to keep the head erect, while the lumbar curvature is associated with the development of standing and walking.

The intervertebral disc is responsible for c.25% of the length of the vertebral column. Each disc consists of a central gelatinous core surrounded by rings of fibrous tissue. During the course of the day the discs gradually lose water and become thinner; consequently at the end of the day an individual is not as tall as first thing in the morning (the difference may be as large as 2 cm/0·8 in. Similarly, with increasing age the discs also lose water, so that an individual's height may decrease in later life.

The mobility of the vertebral column is determined and controlled by the interplay between the geometry of the bony elements and the arrangement of the soft tissue elements (disc, ligaments, and muscles). An abnormal sideways bending of the vertebral column (*scoliosis*) may be present in as many as 15% of the population, but is of clinical significance in only 0·5%; it is more common in females than in males. In the majority of cases the underlying cause of the scoliosis is unknown, but factors include weakness of the back muscles and disease of the spine.

Vertebrata *Chordata*

vertical integration A business situation where a company expands by buying up its suppliers or its customers, thus controlling all the processes of production, from raw materials through to the sale of the final product. The advantages for a company are that, since it owns its suppliers or customers, the profits made by them are kept in the firm. In addition, owning suppliers should ensure delivery of the materials and components they produce, and owning customers guarantees a market for the firm's products. The major disadvantage is that management may not have expertise in all stages. An example of vertical integration is the oil industry, where all stages can be owned, from oil wells, through tankers and refineries, to petrol stations.

Vertical Take-Off and Landing *VTOL*

vertigo An abnormal sensation of movement, either of the body in space, or of other objects around it; affected individuals complain of feeling dizzy or giddy. It is usually a symptom of disorders such as infections that affect the balance apparatus located in the inner ear.

Verulamium [veryulaymium] A Belgic town in Roman Britain which stood on the site of present-day St Albans. Completely destroyed in the Revolt of Boadicea (Boudicca) in AD 60, it was later rebuilt and became a focal point for the Romanization of the province.

vervain A tough-stemmed perennial (*Verbena officinalis*), growing to 60 cm/2 ft, native to Europe, Asia, and N Africa; leaves opposite, pinnately lobed; flowers 4 mm/0·16 in, lilac, in slender spikes. (Family: Verbenaceae.)

vervet monkey A guenon (*Cercopithecus aethiops*) native to Africa S of the Sahara; yellow-brown with a black face surrounded by white whiskers; inhabits grassland near trees; adult male with blue scrotum; many geographical variations, including the *grass monkey*, *grivet monkey*, and *green monkey*.

Verwoerd, Hendrik (Frensch) [fervoort] (1901–66) South African statesman and prime minister (1958–66), born in Amsterdam, The Netherlands. He studied at Stellenbosch, where he became professor of applied psychology (1927) and sociology (1933), and edited the nationalist *Die Transvaler* (1938–48). Elected senator in 1948, he became minister of native affairs

(1950), and introduced most of the apartheid legislation with the support of the premier, Johannes Strijdom, whom he succeeded. His administration was marked by further development and ruthless application of the highly controversial apartheid policy, an attempt on his life (1960), and the establishment of South Africa as a republic (1961). He was assassinated in Cape Town.

Very, Edward Wilson [veeree] (1847–1910) US ordnance expert and inventor. He served in the US navy (1867–85), became an admiral, and in 1877 invented chemical flares (*Very lights*) for signalling at night.

Very Large Array The world's most elaborate full synthesis radio telescope at Socorro, NM, consisting of 27 antennae each 25 m/81 ft in diameter, arranged on rail tracks forming a Y pattern up to 36 km/22 mi across. It is used to investigate the structure of gaseous nebulae in our Galaxy, and of remote radio galaxies and quasars.

very large scale integration (VLSI) A technique of manufacturing integrated circuits with a very high number of individual components. It is usually defined to refer to integrated circuits containing more than 100 000 components in one chip. VLSI is the successor to LSI (*large scale integration*), which involved only thousands of gates on a single chip, and which followed immediately from the invention of the silicon chip.

Vesalius, Andreas [vezaylius], Lat name of **Andries van Wesel** (1514–64) Anatomist, born in Brussels, Belgium. He studied at Louvain, Padua, and Paris universities, and became professor at Padua, Bologna, and Basel. His major work was the *De humani corporis fabrica libri septem* (1543, Seven Books on the Structure of the Human Body), which greatly advanced the science of anatomy with its detailed descriptions and drawings. He was sentenced to death by the Inquisition for his new approach, which involved dissection of the human body, but the sentence was commuted to a pilgrimage to Jerusalem.

Vespasian [vespayzhn], in full **Titus Flavius Vespasianus** (9–79) Roman emperor (69–79), the founder of the Flavian dynasty (69–96). Declared emperor by the troops in the East, where he was engaged in putting down the Jewish Revolt, he ended the civil wars that had been raging since Nero's overthrow, put the state on a sound financial footing, and restored discipline to the army. Among his many lavish building projects was the Colosseum. He was succeeded by his son, Titus.

Vespers The evening hour of the divine office of the Western Church. In monastic, cathedral, and collegiate churches in the Roman Catholic Church it is sung daily between 3 and 6 pm.

Vespucci, Amerigo [vespoochee] (1454–1512) Explorer, born in Florence, NC Italy. He promoted a voyage to the New World in the track of Columbus, sailed with its commander (1499), and explored the coast of Venezuela. In 1505 he was naturalized in Spain, and from 1508 was pilot-major of the kingdom. His name was given to America through an inaccurate account of his travels published in Lorraine (1507), in which he is represented as having discovered and reached the mainland in 1497.

Vesta (astronomy) The fourth asteroid discovered (1807) by Wilhelm Olbers; diameter 580 km/369 mi. It is the only asteroid that can ever be seen with the unaided eye, mainly on account of its high reflectivity.

Vesta (mythology) Roman goddess of the hearth. Her sacred fire, and a shrine containing sacred objects, were kept in a round building, and tended by the **Vestal Virgins**.

Vestal Virgins In ancient Rome, the aristocratic, virgin priestesses of Vesta, the goddess of the hearth. They tended the sacred flame which burned perpetually in the Temple of Vesta near the forum.

Vesterålen or **Vesteraalen** [vesterolen] Island group in the Norwegian Sea, off the NW coast of Norway, SW of Narvik, just N of the Lofoten group; principal islands Hinnøy, Langøya, Andøya, Hadseløy; fishing, fish processing.

vestibular apparatus [vestibyuler] The part of the internal ear concerned with balance, consisting of a series of spaces and tubes within the temporal bone of the skull. It contains the *saccule* and *utricle*, which convey information regarding head position by responding to linear and tilting movements, and three *semicircular canals*, which convey information about rotatory and angular movements of the head. Hair-like processes project into a jelly-like mass containing numerous crystalline bodies (the *otoliths*). Under the influence of gravity the otoliths move and stimulate the hair cells, thereby conveying information regarding head position. The nerve impulses generated by the hair cells enter the brain through the vestibulo-cochlear nerve, and evoke reflex movements of the eyes, trunk, and limbs, as well as the conscious sensation of head movement.

vestigial organ [vestijial] A degenerate or imperfectly formed organ that has been reduced in structure or functional significance during the course of evolution or development. The human appendix and the wings of an ostrich are regarded as vestigial structures.

vestments Special and distinctive garments worn by clergy in religious worship and liturgy. In the Christian Church, they include the *alb*, a long white garment reaching to the ankles; the *amice*, formerly a neckcloth, a linen square worn round the back to protect the other vestments; the *cassock*, a long black gown worn under other vestments; the *chasuble*, an outer sleeveless vestment worn by a priest or bishop when celebrating Holy Communion; the *cope*, a costly embroidered vestment, semi-circular in shape, worn by bishops and priests on special occasions; the *stole*, a folded and narrow vestment worn over both shoulders; and the *surplice*, of white linen, worn by choir and servers as well as clergy.

Vestris, Madame, popular name of **Lucia Elizabeth Vestris** or **Mathews**, *née* **Bartolozzi** (1797–1856) Actress, born in London, UK. At 16 she married the dancer Armand Vestris (1787–1825), the son of Auguste Vestris (1760–1842), but they separated two years later, and she went on the stage in Paris. She appeared at Drury Lane in 1820, becoming famous in a wide range of roles. She was lessee of the Olympic Theatre for nine years, and later managed Covent Garden and the Lyceum.

Vesuvius [vesoovius], Ital **Vesuvio** 40°49N 14°26E. Active volcano in Campania, SW Italy, 15 km/9 mi SE of Naples; height 1277 m/4190 ft; crater circumference, 1400 m/4593 ft, depth 216 m/709 ft; first recorded eruption AD 79, overwhelming Pompeii, Herculaneum, and Stabiae; eruptions at long intervals until 1631, more regular activity since; last eruption, 1944; fruit and vines grow on lower slopes.

vetch A member of a large group of annuals or perennials, often climbing or scrambling, native to N temperate regions and South America; also called **tare**; leaves pinnate with 2–many, often narrow leaflets, usually terminating in a tendril, which is sometimes branched; pea-flowers solitary or in small or long spike-like inflorescences arising from the leaf axils; pods flattened, splitting lengthwise into two valves. It is generally of little economic importance, and sometimes an agricultural pest. One form of common vetch (*Vicia sativa*), a purple-flowered annual native to Europe, N Africa, and parts of Asia, is widely cultivated for animal forage. (Genus: *Vicia*, 140 species. Family: Leguminosae.)

Veterans' Day A public holiday in the USA (Nov 11), held to honour veterans of all wars; originally instituted as **Armistice Day** after World War 1, by which name it was known until 1954.

veterinary science The science concerned with the diseases of animals, especially their treatment or their avoidance. It is applied primarily to domesticated animals, or to captive animals in zoos. Most countries have a national veterinary association, such as the **British Veterinary Association (BVA)** and the **American Veterinary Medical Association (AVMA)**. Many of these have large groups forming separate but affiliated associations devoted to species such as horses, or groups of species such as small (ie companion) animals. Internationally veterinary matters are dealt with by the **World Veterinary Association (WVA)**, founded in 1863. The international aspects of companion animal veterinary medicine come under the **World**

Small Animal Veterinary Association (WSAVA), founded in 1958.

Vézelay church [vayzelay] The 12th-c abbey church of St Madeleine, a world heritage monument at Vézelay, C France. It is noted both as a masterpiece of Romanesque architecture and as the start of one of the main pilgrimage routes to Santiago de Compostela in Spain.

Vézère Valley [vayzair] A stretch of the Vézère R valley in S France, of great archaeological importance; a world heritage site. Its yield of flint tools and fossilized remains has been formative in the modern understanding of the Old Stone Age. The grottoes are also noted for their wall paintings and engravings.

VHS (**Video Home Service**) The trade name for a videotape cassette recorder introduced in 1975 by JVC/Matsushita for the domestic market, and widely adopted by other manufacturers. It uses ½ in (12·7 mm) tape at a speed of 2·34 cm/⅔ in per second in a cassette 189 × 104 × 25 mm/7½ × 4 × 1 in. It has a playing time of up to 4 hours, and has proved to be the most internationally popular home VTR system. A smaller cassette (VHS-C) is used for camcorders. **Super-VHS** is an improved version with separate luminance and chrominance signals, using metal particle tape to give higher picture definition and colour quality.

Viagra® Trade-name of an anti-impotence drug developed by the Pfizer Corporation in the USA, made available in 1998. Its action, increasing blood flow to the male genitals, was first noted as part of research into treatment for heart disease.

Vian, Boris [veeã] (1920–59) Playwright, novelist, and poet, born in Ville d'Avray, NC France. A Bohemian with a heart condition, he dabbled in many things – acting, jazz, engineering, anarchism, pornography – and excelled in fiction. A tragi-comic writer, he won a cult following for such novels as *L'Ecume des jours* (1947, trans Froth on the Daydream) and *L'Arrache-coeur* (1953, trans Heartsnatcher).

Vianney, Jean-Baptiste-Marie, St [veeanee], Fr [veeanay], known as **the Curé d'Ars** (1786–1859) Roman Catholic clergyman, born in Dardilly, SC France. He was ordained a priest (1815) and entered service at Écully. He became priest of Ars in 1818, gaining renown as a holy confessor, gifted with supernatural powers, who was subjected to attacks by the devil. Ars consequently became a place of pilgrimage. He was canonized as the patron saint of parish priests in 1925. Feast day 4 August.

Viaud, Louis Marie Julien [veeoh], pseudonym **Pierre Loti** (1850–1923) Writer and French naval officer, born in Rochefort, W France. He entered the navy in 1869, and served in the East, retiring as captain in 1910. His first novel, *Aziyadé* (1879), quickly gained the respect of critics and public alike. He continued to write throughout his naval career, using experiences and observations on his voyages as source material for his books. His best-known novel is *Pêcheur d'Islande* (1886, Fisherman of Iceland), a descriptive study of Breton fisher life in Icelandic waters. Other works include *Rarahu*, published in 1882 as *Le Mariage de Loti* (The Marriage of Loti) – a pseudonym he received from the women of the South Sea Islands.

Viborg [veebaw(r)] 56°28N 9°25E, pop (2000e) 30 000. Ancient city and capital of Viborg county, NC Jutland, Denmark; railway; engineering, distilling, textiles; 12th-c Gothic cathedral (restored 1864–76).

vibraphone A musical instrument resembling a xylophone, but with metal bars and resonators that are fitted with electrically operated vanes. These rapidly open and close to produce a vibrating, tremolo effect, but the mechanism may be switched off if required. The instrument is usually played with soft beaters, and since the 1920s has frequently been used in jazz, dance, and orchestral music.

vibration *oscillation*

Vibrio A genus of straight or curved, rod-shaped bacteria, typically with flagella at one end. They can grow in the presence or absence of oxygen, and are found in aquatic environments and animal intestines. They include the causative agent of cholera. (Kingdom: Monera. Family: Vibrionaceae.)

viburnum *guelder rose*

vicar (Lat *vicarius*, 'substitute') Literally, one who takes the place of another; for example, the pope is said to be the Vicar of Christ. In Anglican Churches, the term applies technically to the priest acting for the rector, but is widely used for any parish priest or minister.

Vicente, Gil [veesentay] (c.1470–c.1537) Portuguese playwright and poet. He accompanied the court, writing many plays and entertainments in both Spanish and Portuguese. He wrote on religious, national, and social themes, as well as farces, and pastoral and romantic plays, all with great lyricism and a predominantly comical spirit. Among his best-known works are *Inferno*, *Purgatório*, and *Glória*, and the farces *Inês Pereira* and *Juiz da Beira*.

Vicenza [vichentsa], ancient **Vicetia** 45°33N 11°33E, pop (2000e) 113 000. Capital town of Vicenza province, Veneto, NE Italy; 35 km/22 mi NW of Padua; railway junction; textiles, carpets, iron and steel, papermaking, gold jewellery; home of Palladio; Basilica Palladiana (1549–1614), Teatro Olimpico (1580), La Rotonda (1550–1606), cathedral (15th-c).

viceroy The governor of a colony or province, acting in the name and by the authority of the supreme ruler, the monarch. Following the Indian Mutiny in 1857, India was brought directly under the British government (1858), who sent a viceroy to act as governor under a London-based secretary of state within the Cabinet. Lord Louis Mountbatten became the last Viceroy of India in March 1947.

Vichy [veeshee] The informal name of the French political regime between 1940 and 1945; officially **l'Etat Français** ('the French State'). Established at the spa town of Vichy following Germany's defeat of France (1940), its head of state was Marshal Philippe Pétain, and its other dominant political figure Pierre Laval, prime minister from 1942. Although a client regime of Germany, Vichy succeeded in maintaining a degree of autonomy, which was centred on the cult of Pétain, then 84 years old. At first comprising 55 per cent of France's land area, Vichy France abolished the constitution and dissolved the Third Republic. It issued a new constitution establishing an autocratic state. French Jews were excluded from most areas of society. From 1942 to 1944 Vichy police helped the Germans to deport to the camps 76 000 Jews, many of whom had escaped to France; only 3 per cent survived. The Vichy government was never recognized by the Allies, and it collapsed when Germany surrendered in 1945.

Vickers test *hardness*

Vickrey, William (1914–96) Economist, born in Victoria, British Columbia, SW Canada. He studied at Yale, then moved to Columbia University, where he stayed throughout his career. He shared the Nobel Prize for Economics in 1996 for his work in analyzing the consequences of incomplete financial information.

Vicksburg 32°21N 90°53W, pop (2000e) 26 400. Seat of Warren Co, W Mississippi, USA; port on the Mississippi R; settled, 1791; captured by Union forces during the Civil War (1863) after a long siege – the **Vicksburg Campaign** gave control of the Mississippi to the North, splitting the Confederacy on a N–S axis; national cemetery nearby, where c.13 000 unknown Union troops are buried, brought from all over the South.

Vicky, pseudonym of **Victor Weisz** (1913–66) Political cartoonist, born in Berlin, Germany. He emigrated to Britain in 1935, worked with several newspapers, and established himself as the leading left-wing political cartoonist of the period. His collections include *Vicky's World* (1959).

Vico, Giambattista [veekoh] (1668–1744) Historical philosopher, born in Naples, SW Italy. He studied law, but devoted himself to literature, history, and philosophy, becoming in 1699 professor of rhetoric at Naples. In his *Scienza nuova* (1725, New Science), now recognized as a landmark in European intellectual history, he attempted to systematize the humanities into a single human science in a cyclical theory of the growth and decline of societies. Though his historicist philosophy of history was largely neglected in the 18th-c, it undoubtedly influenced many later scholars, including Goethe and Marx.

Victor Emmanuel II (1820–78) First king of Italy (1861–78), born in Turin, NW Italy. As king of Sardinia from 1849, he appointed Cavour as his chief minister (1852). He fought against Austria (1859), winning victories at Montebello, Magenta, and Solferino, and gaining Lombardy. In 1860 Modena, Parma, the Romagna, and Tuscany were peacefully annexed, Sicily and Naples were added by Garibaldi, and Savoy and Nice were ceded to France. Proclaimed King of Italy at Turin, he fought on the side of Prussia in the Austro–Prussian War (1866), and after the fall of the French empire (1870) he entered and annexed Rome.

Victor Emmanuel III (1869–1947) King of Italy (1900–46), born in Naples, SW Italy. He initially ruled as a constitutional monarch, but defied parliamentary majorities by bringing Italy into World War 1 on the side of the Allies in 1915, and in 1922 when he offered Mussolini the premiership. The Fascist government then reduced him to a figurehead. He played an important part in effecting Mussolini's fall (1943), but was irremediably tarnished by his association with Fascism. Having relinquished power to his son, he abdicated in 1946.

Victoria (Australia) pop (2000e) 4 689 000; area 227 600 sq km/ 87 900 sq mi. State in SE Australia; named by Captain Cook, 1770; Melbourne settled, 1835; separated from New South Wales, 1851; gold discovered at Ballarat, 1851; bordered S by the Bass Strait and SW by the Southern Ocean; second smallest state; E is the Great Dividing Range, known in this region as the Australian Alps; highest point Mt Bogong (1986 m/6516 ft); about 36% of the land occupied by forest; SW region known as Gippsland; several inland lakes, mostly very saline; irrigation storages include L Eildon on the Goulburn R and L Hume on the Murray; contains 25% of the Australian population concentrated into 3% of the land; capital, Melbourne; principal cities, Geelong, Ballarat, Bendigo; produces about a fifth of Australia's agricultural output of wheat, oats, barley, maize, tobacco, hops, fodder crops, citrus fruits, grapes, apples, vegetables, wool, hides, mutton, lamb, dairy products; timber, coal mining (Latrobe Valley one of the world's largest deposits of brown coal), motor parts; oil and natural gas fields in the Gippsland Basin and Bass Strait; state holiday Labour Day (Mar).

Victoria (Canada) 48°25N 123°22W, pop (2000e) 79 800. Capital of British Columbia, Canada, at SE end of Vancouver I, on the Juan de Fuca Strait; founded as fur-trading post, 1843; colonial capital, 1866; provincial capital, 1871; airfield; railway; university (1963); shipbuilding, timber, fish canning, computer software, tourism; Parliament Buildings (1893–7), Empress Hotel (1906–8), Thunderbird Park (unique collection of totem poles), Butchart Gardens; Commonwealth Games (1994).

Victoria (Seychelles) 4°37S 55°28E, pop (2000e) 25 400. Seaport capital of the Seychelles, Indian Ocean; situated on the NE coast of Mahé I; trade in copra, vanilla, cinnamon, tortoiseshell, guano.

Victoria, in full **Alexandrina Victoria** (1819–1901) Queen of Great Britain (1837–1901) and (from 1876) Empress of India, born in London, UK, the only child of George III's fourth son, Edward, and Victoria Maria Louisa of Saxe-Coburg, sister of Leopold, King of the Belgians. Taught by Lord Melbourne, her first prime minister, she had a clear grasp of constitutional principles and the scope of her own prerogative, which she resolutely exercised in 1839 by setting aside the precedent which decreed dismissal of the current ladies of the bedchamber, thus causing Peel not to take up office as prime minister. In 1840 she married Prince Albert of Saxe-Coburg and Gotha, and had four sons and five daughters. Strongly influenced by her husband, with whom she worked in closest harmony, after his death (1861) she went into lengthy seclusion, neglecting many duties, which brought her unpopularity and motivated a republican movement. But with her recognition as Empress of India, and the celebratory golden (1887) and diamond (1897) jubilees, she rose high in her subjects' favour, and increased the prestige of the monarchy. She had strong preferences for certain prime ministers (notably Melbourne and Disraeli) over others (notably Peel and Gladstone), but following the advice of Albert did not press these beyond the bounds of constitutional propriety. At various points in her long reign she exercised some influence over foreign affairs, and the marriages of her children had important diplomatic, as well as dynastic implications in Europe. She died at Cowes, Isle of Wight, England, UK, and was succeeded by her son as Edward VII. Her reign, the longest in English history, saw advances in industry, science (Darwin's theory of evolution), communications (the telegraph, popular press), and other forms of technology; the building of the railways and the London Underground, sewers, and power distribution networks; bridges and other engineering feats; a vast number of inventions; a greatly expanded empire; unequal growth of wealth, with class differences to the fore; tremendous poverty; increase in urban populations, with the growth of great cities like Manchester, Leeds, and Birmingham; increased literacy; and great civic works, often funded by industrial philanthropists.

Victoria, Tomás Luis de, Ital **Vittoria, Tommaso Ludovico da** (c.1548–1611) Composer, born in Ávila, C Spain. He studied music in Rome, and at Loyola's Collegium Germanicum was appointed chaplain and (in 1573) choirmaster. In 1578 he was made chaplain at San Girolamo della Carità, and c.1585 returned to Spain as chaplain to the widowed Empress Maria in Madrid, where he was choirmaster until his death. He wrote only religious music, his 180 works including several books of motets and over 20 Masses.

Victoria, Lake area 69 500 sq km/26 827 sq mi. Lake in E Africa, bounded S by Tanzania, NW by Uganda, and NE by Kenya; largest lake on the African continent; altitude 1300 m/4265 ft; 400 km/250 mi long; 240 km/150 mi wide; contains several islands, notably the Sese archipelago; level raised by the Owen Falls Dam, 1954; main lakeside ports, Kisumu (Kenya) and Mwanza (Tanzania); European discovery by John Speke, 1858; extensively explored by Stanley, 1875; originally called Ukewere, renamed in honour of Queen Victoria.

Victoria and Albert Museum A museum of fine and applied arts, opened in London, UK in 1852 as the Museum of Manufactures, and later renamed the Museum of Ornamental Art. Articles bought from the Great Exhibition (1851) formed the core of the original display. In 1899, when Queen Victoria laid the foundation stone of the present building, she requested that it be renamed the Victoria and Albert. In 2002 the museum celebrated its 150th anniversary. It is currently undergoing a major redevelopment programme and five new galleries were opened in 2003.

Victoria Cross (VC) In the UK, the highest military decoration, instituted by Queen Victoria in 1856 and awarded 'for conspicuous bravery in the face of the enemy'. Since 1902 it can be conferred posthumously; in 1920 women became eligible, but no woman has yet received it. The medal is inscribed 'For valour'; the ribbon is crimson.

Victoria Desert *Great Victoria Desert*

Victoria Falls, indigenous name **Mosi oa Tunya** ('the smoke that thunders') Waterfalls on the Zambezi R, on the Zambia–Zimbabwe frontier, SC Africa; height, 61–108 m/200–354 ft; width, 1688 m/5538 ft; comprises five main falls (Eastern Cataract, Rainbow Falls, Devil's Cataract, Horseshoe Falls, Main Falls); European discovery by Livingstone, 1855; named after Queen Victoria; facing towns of Livingstone (Zambia) and Victoria Falls (Zimbabwe); major tourist attraction.

Victoria Island Island in Northwest Territories, Canada, in the Arctic Ocean; area 217 290 sq km/83 874 sq mi; 515 km/320 mi long; 274–595 km/170–370 mi wide; deeply indented; discovered 1838; named for Queen Victoria; sparse population.

Victoria Nile Upper reach of River Nile in NW Uganda; flows generally NW from the N end of L Victoria to enter L Kyoga, then in a NW arc into the Kabalega national park, passing the

Kabalega (Murchison) Falls; ends in a swampy delta at the NE end of L Albert; length 420 km/260 mi.

Victoria Peak 22°18N 114°08E. Principal peak on Hong Kong Island, SE Asia; height, 554 m/1818 ft; named after Queen Victoria; Peak Tramway (opened 1888) takes tourists to the summit for notable views of the city and harbour.

***Victory*, HMS** Nelson's flagship at the battle of Trafalgar (1805). Originally laid down in 1759, but not completed until 1778, she was the seventh vessel in the Royal Navy to bear the name. She is now in permanent dry dock, but still flies the white ensign as flagship to the commander-in-chief, Portsmouth.

vicuña [vikunya] A wild member of the camel family (*Vicugna vicugna*), native to high grassland in the C Andes; resembles a llama, but smaller, more slender, and more graceful; produces the finest wool in the world; the only living artiodactyl in which the lower incisor teeth grow continuously.

Vidal, (Eugene Luther) Gore [vidal], pseudonym **Edgar Box** (1925–) Novelist, playwright, and essayist, born in West Point, New York, USA. He joined the US Army Reserve Corps, which gave him the material for his first critically-acclaimed novel, *Williwaw* (1946), published when he was just 19. His later novels include several satirical comedies, such as *Myra Breckenridge* (1968) and *Duluth* (1983), and the historical trilogy, *Burr* (1973), *1876* (1976), and *Lincoln* (1984). His fictional history of America reached the 20th-c with *Empire* (1987) and *Hollywood* (1989). Other novels include *Live From Golgotha* (1992) and *The Smithsonian Institution* (1999). He has also written short stories, plays (notably *Visit to a Small Planet*, 1956), film scripts, essays, reviews, and a volume of memoirs, *Screening History* (1992), and been active in several other media, including politics, television, and publishing.

video Strictly, that part of the television signal which carries the picture information, as distinct from the audio signal carrying the sound; but by extension the term has become generally accepted to cover the electronic recording and reproduction of combined picture and sound, especially in its non-broadcast application. As a noun, a 'video' is an abbreviation for a videotape recorder, a videotape cassette, or the recorded programme itself.

videocassette recorder (VCR) *videotape recorder*

videoconferencing The use of computer networks and virtual reality to enable groups in separate locations to conduct a conference with the impression that they are all in the same room. The use of computer networks to establish the videoconference allows the participants to have shared access to computer files and computer programs throughout the conference.

video disk A reproduction medium in which both picture and sound are recorded as an extremely fine spiral or concentric tracks on a flat circular disk. A series of pits in a reflective surface is optically scanned with a helium-neon or diode laser, and the reflected beam read by a photo–diode to produce the signal. A 30 cm/12 in diameter disk can contain an hour's programme, and by recording exactly two fields per rotation throughout the spiral, single-frame still pictures can be shown. Unlike videotape, access from one part of the programme to another can be very rapid.

video games *electronic games*

videogram A complete programme recorded as a videotape cassette or video disk for distribution by sale or hire.

videotape A high-quality magnetic coating on a flexible polyester base for recording and reproducing video signals. The original formulae using dispersions of ferric oxide were improved by the addition of cobalt; further developments with chrome dioxide, metal-particle dispersions, and metal-evaporated coatings allowed increased information packing on narrower and thinner strips. Videotape has been made in widths of 2 in (50·8 mm, now obsolete), 1 in (25·4 mm), ¾ in (19 mm), ½ in (12·7 mm), ⅓ in (8 mm), and ¼ in (6·3 mm); the latter two widths are used for domestic applications. Overall thickness has been reduced from 30–35 μ to 13–16 μ, and metal-evaporated types are as thin as 10 μ.

videotape recorder (VTR) A device for recording the picture and sound signals from a television camera on magnetic tape; also called a **videocassette recorder (VCR)**. To obtain a writing speed sufficient for the very high frequencies of a television signal, the recording head must travel rapidly across the moving magnetic tape. In early VTR machines, tape 2-in wide ran at 15-in/s past a rotating drum with four heads, producing quadruplex transverse tracks across its width; sound and control signals were recorded longitudinally on the two edges. This became the standard in television broadcasting from 1956 to the 1980s. Modern VTRs use narrower tape with helical scanning, each diagonal track recording a single TV field, with audio and control on the edges. The first helical-scan system meeting broadcast TV standards was the C format with 1-in tape running from reel to reel; but for the less critical home video market cheaper and more convenient handling was needed. The easily-loaded cassettes of the U-matic system provided this, rapidly followed by several other systems, including Betamax and VHS, all incompatible; U-matic was preferred for professional production and VHS for domestic use. In the 1980s two more helical systems for high-quality production and broadcast were introduced, Betacam in 1981 and M-II in 1986; both use ½-in tape with component recording of the luminance and compressed chrominance signals on separate adjacent tracks. In 1987–8, digital recording on videotape (DVTR) became available in the D1 and D2 formats, and soon after, the first digital recorders using solid-state storage chips.

videotex An interactive information service using a telephone link between the user and a central computer; formerly called **viewdata**. An example is Prestel, run by British Telecom in the UK. It can be used for home banking, armchair shopping, ticket ordering, and other such functions. The service is different from **teletext**, which is a non-interactive system transmitted along with television signals.

videowall A rectangular grouping of a number of separate video monitor screens, from 3 × 3 units upwards. They can be programmed for the display of individual single, multiple, or combination images with a sound track from videotape or disk recordings.

Vidor, King (Wallis) [veedaw(r)] (1894–1982) Film director, born in Galveston, Texas, USA. A cinema projectionist and freelance newsreel cameraman, he made his debut as a director in 1913. In Hollywood from 1915, he worked on a variety of film-related jobs before directing a feature film, *The Turn of the Road* (1919). A successful mounting of *Peg o' My Heart* (1922) brought him a long-term contract with MGM. Interested in the everyday struggles of the average American, his many films include *The Big Parade* (1925), *The Crowd* (1928), and *Our Daily Bread* (1934). He also directed Westerns, melodramas, and historical epics such as *Solomon and Sheba* (1959). Nominated five times for an Oscar, he received an honorary award in 1979.

Vienna, Ger **Wien** 48°13N 16°22E, pop (2000e) 1 597 000. Capital city and a state of Austria; at the foot of the Wienerwald on the R Danube; C area surrounded by the monumental buildings and gardens of the Ringstrasse, developed 1859–88; badly damaged in World War 2, and occupied by the Allies (1945–55); to the NE extends a circuit of inner suburban districts; UNO-City, conference and office complex (opened 1979), with the offices of the United Nations agencies based in Vienna; archbishopric; university of technology (1815); university (1873–84); Spanish Riding School; refugees arriving in Austria are initially housed at the Traiskirchen camp amidst the Panonian vineyards near the city; metal products, precision instruments, electrical goods, engines, gearboxes, textiles, furniture; major tourist city, with several theatres, museums, concert halls, parks; associations with many composers in 18th–19th-c; Gothic St Stephen's Cathedral, St Peter's Church, Baroque Schottenkirche (12th-c, rebuilt 1638–48), former Bohemian Court Chancery, Gothic Church of Maria am Gestade, Romanesque Ruprechtskirche (12th–13th-c), Franciscan church (1603–11), Maria Theresa monument (1887), Palais Trautson (High Baroque architecture),

Neo-Gothic town hall (1872–83), Baroque Palace of Schönbrunn, Opera House, Burgtheater; International Trade Fair (spring, autumn); Vienna Festival (May–Jun), 'Viennale' film festival (Oct).

Vienna, Congress of (1814–15) A European assembly convened at the instigation of the four victorious powers (Austria, Britain, Prussia, and Russia) to redefine the territorial map of Europe after the defeat of Napoleon. Dominated by the Austrian chancellor Metternich, its guiding principle was the notion of legitimacy, ie the restoration and strengthening of the hereditary rulers of Europe. The Hapsburgs regained control of Lombardy, Venetia, Tuscany, Parma, and Tyrol; Prussia gained parts of Saxony as well as regaining much of Westphalia and the Rhineland; Denmark lost Norway to Sweden; the new kingdom of The Netherlands was formed; the pope was restored to the Vatican and the Papal States; the German Confederation was established; and the kingdom of Poland was restored, but as part of the Romanov Russian empire. The negotiators were concerned to create a balance of power and to avoid alienating any major state; they incurred posterity's criticism for ignoring nationalism and perpetuating autocracy.

Vienna Circle A group of philosophers, scientists, and mathematicians centred on Vienna University in the 1920s and 1930s. It was founded by Schlick, and had among its associates Gödel, Neurath, and Carnap. It became an international focus for logical positivism, and when the Circle itself dissolved with the rise of Nazism most of its members emigrated to the USA.

Vientiane [vyentyan], Lao **Viangchan** 17°59N 102°38E, pop (2000e) 560 000. Capital city of Laos, SE Asia; port on R Mekong, close to the Thailand frontier (W); airport; university (1958); brewing, textiles, cigarettes, detergents, matches, timber products; maize, rice, livestock; national museum, national library; Nam Ngum Dam (N), That Luang Temple (16th-c).

Vierzehnheiligen [feertsaynhiyligen] (Ger 'Fourteen Saints') A pilgrimage church near Bamberg, SEC Germany. A masterpiece of South German Rococo architecture, it was built in 1743–72 by Balthasar Neumann (1687–1753). It conceals a complex interior plan – a cross-shape made up of six overlapping ovals – within a conventional and straight-sided exterior.

Viet Cong or **Vietcong** ('Vietnamese Communists') The name given by the South Vietnamese government in 1959 to all the guerrilla forces that fought them during the Vietnam War. In 1960 they formed the National Liberation Front.

Viet Minh or **Vietminh** The abbreviation of **Viet Nam Doc Lap Dong Minh** ('League for the Independence of Vietnam'), a politico-military organization formed by Ho Chi-minh in 1941. It included nationalists and communists, and aimed at liberating Vietnam from the Japanese and gaining independence from France. In 1945 it formed a government in Hanoi, and its army defeated the French at Dien Bien Phu in 1954.

Vietnam *p.1608*

Vietnamese An Austro-Asiatic language, spoken in Vietnam, Laos, and Cambodia by over 50 million people. 1000 years of political and linguistic domination by China (until the 10th-c) has resulted in little being known of early Vietnamese, and there are no known early writings. A Latin-based alphabet, called *Quoc-ngu* (national language) was introduced in the 17th-c.

Vietnam War (1946–75) Hostilities between communist North Vietnam and non-communist South Vietnam, and others, also known as the **First** and **Second Indo-Chinese Wars**. The first began in 1946 after the breakdown of negotiations between France and the communist-dominated Viet Minh under Ho Chi-minh. France deployed 420 000 troops to support the 200 000 Vietnamese army, but suffered defeat at Dien Bien Phu in 1954. The subsequent Geneva settlement left North Vietnam under communist rule, and the South governed first by the emperor Bao Dai (until 1955) and then by Ngo Dinh Diem's regime. (The elections planned at Geneva never took place.) From 1961, under President Kennedy, US aid and numbers of 'military advisers' increased considerably, to help contain what the Americans feared as the 'domino effect' of Asian communism. Using the Tonkin Gulf Resolution (1964) as his authority, President Johnson ordered bombardment of the North in 1965. By 1968 over 500 000 US troops were involved. The Tet offensive of February 1968 led to Johnson's withdrawal from politics, and negotiations with North Vietnam. The USA extended the war into Cambodia and Laos, but failure in the field and opposition at home forced President Nixon to withdraw in 1973. The North's victory was completed with the capture of Saigon in 1975 (renamed Ho Chi Minh City). The USA suffered 200 000 casualties, with 58 000 killed or missing.

viewdata *videotex*

Vignola, Giacomo (Barozzi) da [veenyohla] (1507–73) Architect, born in Vignola, N Italy. He studied at Bologna, and became the leading Mannerist architect of his day in Rome. His designs include the Villa di Papa Giulio for Pope Julius III, and the Palazzo Farnese in Piacenza. He also designed the Church of the Gesú in Rome, which with its cruciform plan and side chapels had a great influence on French and Italian church architecture.

Vigny, Alfred Victor, comte de (Count of) [veenyee] (1797–1863) Romantic writer, born in Loches, WC France. He served in the army (1814–28), then turned to writing. His best-known works include the historical novel *Cinq-Mars* (1826), a volume of exhortatory tales *Stello* (1832), and the Romantic drama *Chatterton* (1835). Several other works, including his journal and the philosophical poems, *Les Destinées* (1864, Destinies), were published after his death.

Vigo [veegoh] 42°12N 8°41W, pop (2000e) 278 000. Naval and commercial port in Pontevedra province, Galicia, NW Spain; Spain's chief port for transatlantic traffic; airport; boat services to the Canary Is; shipbuilding, metallurgy; watersports; Castle of St Sebastian, Castro Castle; Fiesta of La Virgen del Monte Carmel (Jul), Pilgrimage to Monte de Santa Tecia (Aug).

Viking project The first successful landing mission to Mars (Jul 1976), planned to search for evidence of life on Mars, and consisting of two highly instrumented orbiter-lander spacecraft. It was launched on Titan-Centaur vehicles in 1975, with the first landing (20 Jul 1976) on Chryse Planitia and the second (3 Sep 1976) on Utopia Planitia. Although evidence for life was not found, data from other lander and orbiter experiments have provided the basis for continuing intensive research on Martian evolution and climate. Orbiters and landers continued to return imaging and other data for several years after the primary project was completed. The project was managed by NASA's Langley Research Center, and operated from the Jet Propulsion Laboratory.

Vikings Raiders, traders, and settlers from Norway, Sweden, and Denmark, who between the late 8th-c and the mid-11th-c conquered and colonized large parts of Britain (from 787), Normandy, and Russia; attacked Spain, Morocco, and Italy; traded with Byzantium, Persia, and India; discovered and occupied Iceland and Greenland; and reached the coast of North America (c.1000). As sea-borne raiders they gained a deserved reputation for brutality and destructiveness, but as merchants and settlers they played an influential and positive role in the development of mediaeval Europe. Their earliest overseas settlements were in the Orkney and Shetland Is, which remained united to the Norwegian crown until 1472. They lacked experience as rulers, however, and they eventually exhausted their power. The settlers brought to Britain and Ireland art, new farming methods, shipbuilding technology, merchant skills, a new language, the jury system, and numerous place names (usually ending in *-by*). The hallmark of their legacy in Iceland was the great mediaeval sagas.

Vila [veela], also **Port-Vila** 17°45S 168°18E, pop (2000e) 24 600. Port and capital town of Vanuatu, on the SW coast of Efate I; airport; meat canning, agricultural trade.

Vila Real [veela rayal] 41°17N 7°45W, pop (2000e) 15 300. Capital of Vila Real district, N Portugal; on R Corgo, 77 km/48 mi NE of Oporto; airfield; olive oil, pottery, tanning, textiles; Mateus

Vietnam

official name **Socialist Republic of Vietnam**, Vietnamese **Cong Hoa Xa Hoi Chu Nghia Viet Nam**

Local name Công Hòa Xã Hôi Chu Nghĩa Viêt Nam (Vietnamese)

Timezone GMT +7

Area 329 566 km²/127 212 sq mi

Population total (2002e) 79 939 000

Status Socialist republic

Date of independence 1976

Capital Hanoi

Languages Vietnamese (official), French, Chinese, English, Khmer

Ethnic groups Vietnamese (85–90%), Chinese (3%), various minorities include Khmer, Cham, Hmong, Nung, and Tay

Religions Buddhist (principal), Taoist, Confucian, Muslim, Roman Catholic, Hoa Hoa, Cao Dai, Protestant, and animist beliefs

Physical features Occupies a narrow strip along the coast of the Gulf of Tongking and the S China Sea on Indochinese peninsula in SE Asia; highest peak Fan si Pan, 3143 m/10 312 ft; Mekong R delta (S) and Red R delta (N) linked by narrow coastal plain; heavily forested mountains and plateaux.

Climate Tropical, monsoon climate; sub-tropical in N; average annual temperatures 17°C (Jan), 29°C (Jul) in Hanoi; average annual rainfall 1830 mm/72 in; typhoons and flooding frequent in N and SW;

Currency 1 Dông = 10 hao = 100 xu

Economy Agriculture (employs over 70% of the workforce); however, natural disasters, war, and political unrest have adversely affected economy; Vietnam War brought depopulation of the countryside and considerable destruction of forest and farmland; exports include coal, minerals, rice, rubber, sugar cane.

GDP (2002) $183·8 bn, per capita $2300

Human Development Index (2002) 0·688

History Under the influence of China for many centuries; regions of Tongking (N), Annam (C), and Cochin-China (S) united as Vietnamese Empire, 1802; French protectorates established in Cochin-China, 1867, and in Annam and Tongking, 1884; formed the French Indo-Chinese Union with Cambodia and Laos, 1887; occupied by the Japanese in World War 2; communist Viet-Minh League under Ho Chi-minh formed after the War, not recognized by France; Indo-Chinese war, resulting in French withdrawal, 1946–54; 1954 armistice divided the country between the communist 'Democratic Republic' in the N, and the 'state' of Vietnam in the S; civil war led to US intervention on the side of S Vietnam, 1965; fall of Saigon, 1975; reunification as the Socialist Republic of Vietnam, 1976; large numbers of refugees tried to find homes in the W in the late 1970s; Hanoi invaded neighbouring Cambodia, overthrowing hostile Khmer Rouge government, 1978; Chinese responded with invasion of Vietnam in 1979 - greatly increased the number trying to leave the country by sea (Vietnamese boat people); in 1984, Hanoi agreed to talks with US about whereabouts of missing US servicemen; limited troop withdrawals from Laos and Cambodia, 1989; Vietnam supported Cambodian peace agreement, 1991; new constitution, 1992, replaced Council of Ministers with a Prime Minister and a Cabinet.

Head of State
1976–80 Ton Duc Thang
1980–1 Nguyen Hun Tho *Acting*
1981–7 Truongh Chinh
1987–92 Vo Chi Cong
1992–7 Le Duc Anh
1997– Tran Duc Luong

Head of Government
1976–87 Pham Van Dong
1987–8 Pham Hung
1988 Vo Van Kiet *Acting*
1988–91 Do Muoi
1991–7 Vo Van Kiet
1997– Phan Van Khai

General Secretary
1960–80 Le Duan
1986 Truong Chinh
1986–91 Nguyen Van Linh
1991–7 Do Muoi
1997–2001 Le Kha Phieu
2001– Nong Duc Manh

wine produced nearby; cathedral, Church of São Pedro (16th-c), Mateus Villa, Roman sanctuary of Panoias 5 km/3 mi SE.

Villa, Pancho [veeyah], also known as **Francisco Villa**, originally **Doroteo Arango** (1878–1923) Mexican revolutionary, born in Hacienda de Río Grande, Mexico. He lived his early life as a fugitive before joining Francisco Madero's successful uprising against the Mexican dictator, Porfirio Díaz (1909). He fled to the USA in 1912, and after the assassination of Madero the following year formed the 'Division del Norte' (Division of the North). Together with **Venustiano Carranza** (1859–1920), he led a successful revolt against the regime of Victoriano Huerta (1914), but the two leaders became rivals, and Villa was forced to flee to the mountains. He agreed to retire from politics, and was pardoned (1920), but was later assassinated.

Villahermosa [veelya-airmohsa] 18°00N 92°53W, pop (2000e) 470 000. River-port capital of Tabasco state, SE Mexico, on the R Grijalva; university (1958); agricultural trade, distilling, sugar refining; Centro de Investigaciones de las Culturas Olmecas; Mayan brick-built ruins of Comacalco to the NW.

Villa-Lobos, Heitor [veela lohbush] (1887–1959) Composer and conductor, born in Rio de Janeiro, Brazil. He studied at Rio and travelled widely in Brazil, collecting material on folk music. His many compositions include 12 symphonies, as well as operas, large-scale symphonic poems, concerti, and ballets. He is also known for the nine suites *Bachianas Brasileiras* (1930–45), in which he treats Brazilian style melodies in the manner of Bach. In 1932 he became director of musical education for Brazil.

Villars, Claude Louis Hector, duc de (Duke of) [veelah(r)] (1653–1734) French marshal under Louis XIV, born in Moulins, C France. He fought in the third Dutch War (1672–8), and in the War of the Spanish Succession (1701–13) inflicted heavy losses on Marlborough at Malplaquet (1709). In 1711 he headed the last army France could raise, and defeated the British and Dutch at Denain (1712). He later became the principal adviser on military affairs, and fought again in his 80s at the outbreak of the War of the Polish Succession (1733–8).

Villas-Boas Brothers A family of brothers – **Orlando Villas-Boas** (1916–2002), **Claudio Villas-Boas** (1918–98), and **Leonardo Villas-Boas** (1920–61) – who devoted their lives to the care and welfare of the Amerindians living around the Xingu R, Matto Grosso, Brazil, previously unknown tribes whom they met during a military expedition to the interior in 1943. They were awarded the Founder's Gold Medal of the Royal Geographical Society (1967), and were twice nominated for the Nobel Peace Prize.

Villehardouin, Geoffroi de [veelah(r)dwĩ] (c.1160–c.1213) French mediaeval chronicler, born near Bar-sur-Aube, EC France. He was marshal of Champagne, and took part in the Fourth Crusade. His unfinished *Histoire de l'empire de Constantinople* described the events from 1198 to 1207, including the capture and sack of Constantinople in 1204.

villein [vilayn] (Old Fr 'village dweller') In mediaeval England, a legally unfree peasant or serf, who was tied to the manor, liable to arbitrary obligations, including labour services on the lord's estate (*demesne*), denied control over goods and property, and wholly bound to the lord's jurisdiction. In practice, custom often mitigated the main disabilities. Underlying economic forces (notably the underpopulation caused by the Black Death), rather than the Peasants' Revolt, effectively ended villeinage in the 15th-c.

Villeneuve, Jacques [veelnoev] (1971–) Motor-racing driver, born in Quebec, SE Canada. His father, Giles Villeneuve, also a racing driver, moved the family to Monaco in 1978, but at the age of 17 Jacques returned to Quebec to begin his racing career. In 1994, in his first season on the Indy Car circuit, he was named Rookie of the Year, and in 1995 became the youngest driver to win the PPG Indy Car World Series title. He joined Formula One in 1996, driving for the Williams-Renault team, finished second in the World Driver's Championship, and won the Championship in 1997.

Villeneuve, Pierre (Charles Jean Baptiste Sylvestre) de [veelnoev] (1763–1806) French admiral, born in Valensole, SW France. He commanded the rear division of the French navy at the Battle of the Nile (1798, also known as the Battle of Aboukir Bay), and saved his vessel and four others. In 1805 he was in charge of the French fleet at Trafalgar, where he was taken prisoner. Released in 1806, he committed suicide in Rennes, during his return journey to Paris to face Napoleon.

Villiers de L'Isle Adam, comte (Count) **(Philippe) Auguste (Mathias)** [veelyay duh leel adã] (1838–89) Writer, born in St-Brieuc, NW France. He was a Breton count who claimed descent from the Knights of Malta. A pioneer of the Symbolist movement, his work includes much poetry, but he is best known for his prose style. He wrote short stories, such as *Contes cruels* (1883, Cruel Tales), and novels such as *Isis* (1862), on the Ideal, and *L'Eve future* (1886), a satire on the materialism of modern science. His plays include *La Révolte* (1870, The Revolt) and his masterpiece, *Axel* (1885). A Catholic aristocrat, he lived for a while with the monks of Solesmes.

Villon, François [veeyõ], pseudonym of **François de Montcorbier** or **François des Loges** (1431–c.1465) Poet, born in Paris, France, one of the greatest lyric poets of his day. While at university in Paris, he had to flee after fatally wounding a priest in a street brawl (1455). He joined a criminal organization, the 'Brotherhood of the Coquille', and wrote some of his ballades in its secret jargon. Pardoned in 1456, he returned to Paris and there wrote 'Le Lais' (The Legacy, also known as 'Le Petit Testament'), followed by his long poetic sequence, 'Le Grand Testament' (1461). The latter incorporates a number of ballads in *jargon* and *jobelin*, the slang of the day, and *rondeaux* – 13-line poems with a double rhythm pattern. Among these are some of his best-known poems, including the 'Ballade des dames du temps jadis', with its famous incantation, 'Mais ou sont les neiges d'antan?'. Throughout this period, he is known to have taken part in several crimes, and in 1463 received a death sentence, commuted to banishment. He left Paris, and nothing further is known of him.

Vilnius [veelnius], formerly **Wilno** (1920–39), also **Vilna** 54°40N 25°19E, pop (2000e) 585 000. Capital city of Lithuania, on R Vilnya; one of the largest industrial centres of the Baltic region; formerly part of Poland; ceded to Russia, 1795; occupied by Germany in World War 2; airport; railway junction; university (1579); machinery, metalworking, chemicals, foodstuffs, textiles; cathedral (1777–1801), Gediminas Castle.

Vimy Ridge [veemee] An escarpment 8 km/5 mi NE of Arras (Pas-de-Calais), a strongly held part of the German defence line on the Western Front in World War 1. It was successfully stormed during the Battle of Arras by the Canadian Corps of the British 1st Army (1917). This feat of arms had great symbolic significance in establishing Canada's identity as an independent nation.

Viña del Mar [veenya thel mah(r)] 33°02S 71°35W, pop (2000e) 351 900. Seaside town in Valparaíso region, C Chile; 9 km/5 mi from Valparaíso city; residential suburb and popular South American resort; railway; Sporting Club, with racecourse and playing fields; golf, casino, sports stadium, Laguna Sausalito (artificial lake), Salinas golf course, Cerro Castillo (presidential summer palace), Quinta Vergara (gardens, in which the Palacio Vergara houses the Museo de Bellas Artes and the Academia de Bellas Artes); Teatro Municipal; festival of El Roto (Jan); international musical festival (Feb).

Vincent de Beauvais [vĩsã duh bohvay], Lat **Vincentius Bellovacensis** (c.1190–c.1264) French Dominican priest and encyclopedist, who compiled, under the patronage of Louis IX, the *Speculum majus* (Great Mirror). Its three parts, on natural, doctrinal, and historical subjects, were supplemented by a section on morals in the 14th-c, written by an unknown author.

Vincent de Paul, St (c.1580–1660) Priest and philanthropist, born in Pouy, SW France. Ordained in 1600, he was captured by corsairs in 1605, and sold into slavery at Tunis, but after persuading his master to return to the Christian faith, escaped to France in 1607. He formed associations for helping the sick, became almoner-general of the galleys (1619), and in 1625 founded the Congregation of Priests of the Missions (or *Lazarists*, from their priory of St Lazare) and in 1634 the Sisterhood of Charity. He was canonized in 1737. Feast day 27 September.

Vincentians *Lazarists*

Vinci, Leonardo da *Leonardo da Vinci*

vine *climbing plant; grapevine*

vinegar A sour liquid used as a food preservative or domestic flavour enhancer. It derives from the oxidization of alcohol by bacteria, the ethanol being converted to acetic acid. There is a wide range of vinegars, with different colours and aromas, determined by the source of the alcohol used, eg red wine, white wine, cider, malt.

vinegar eel A small roundworm, length 1–2 mm/0·04–0·08 in, found in fermenting vinegar; feeds on yeasts. (Phylum: Nematoda.)

Viner, Charles [viyner] (1678–1756) Legal scholar, born in Salisbury, Wiltshire, S England, UK. He studied law at Oxford, but never qualified and never practised, yet he produced a massive *Abridgment of Law and Equity* of the law of England in 23 volumes (1741–56). He left most of his considerable estate to Oxford University to enable it to found the Vinerian Scholarships and the Vinerian chair of English law, first held by Sir William Blackstone.

vine snake A tree snake of family Colubridae; name used especially for New World species of genus *Oxybelis* and S Asian species of genus *Dryophis*; green or brown with pointed snout; length, up to 2 m/6½ ft, but thickness only 10–15 mm/0·4–0·6 in; resembles forest vines; eats juvenile birds and lizards.

Vingt, les [lay vĩ] A group of 20 modern painters, including Ensor, founded in Brussels in 1884. For 10 years they held exhibitions where pictures by leading Postimpressionists such as Seurat, Gauguin, Cézanne, and van Gogh were shown.

vingt-et-un *pontoon*

Vínland [veenland] A generalized Norse name meaning 'Berry Land' or 'Vine Land', applied to the E coast of North America from the time of its first sighting by the Viking Leif Eriksson AD c.985. Though the 'Vinland Map', purportedly of the 1440s, is a 20th-c forgery, accounts of the Norse discovery of America in Icelandic sagas are confirmed by archaeological evidence.

Vinson Massif Highest peak in Antarctica, rising to 4897 m/16 066 ft in the Ellsworth Mts.

vinyl An important organic chemical grouping (CH_2=CH–). The double bond lends itself to polymerization, so that many types of polymer are based on it, their nature depending on the substituents.

viola A bowed string instrument, in all essential respects like a violin but slightly larger and tuned a fifth lower.

viola da gamba Strictly speaking, any member of the viol family – bowed string instruments held upright on the knees, or between the legs, of the player; more generally, the bass instrument of that family, loosely resembling a cello but with sloping shoulders, a flat back, six strings, and a fretted fingerboard like a guitar's.

violet An annual or perennial native to most temperate regions, many being alpine species; leaves often heart-shaped; zygomorphic flowers 5-petalled with a backward projecting spur, blue, yellow, white, or these colours combined, sometimes fragrant. It includes the species and varieties commonly known as **pansies**. (*Viola*, 500 species. Family: Violaceae.)

violin The most widespread of all bowed string instruments, and one of the most important instruments in Western music since the 17th-c. The four-string violin was developed in the 16th-c from earlier three-string types, and reached its highest point of perfection between 1650 and 1730 in the hands of Stradivari and the Amati and Guarneri families. Later modifications have included the lengthening of the fingerboard, and the provision of a chin rest; steel and nylon have largely replaced gut as the main material for the strings. The other regular members of the violin family are the viola, cello, and double bass.

Viollet-le-Duc, Eugène (Emmanuel) [vyohlay luh dük] (1814–79) Architect and archaeologist, born in Paris, France. He studied in France and Italy, and in 1840 directed the restoration of Ste Chapelle, Paris. His other restorations included the cathedrals of Notre Dame, Amiens, and Laon, and the Château de Pierrefonds.

violoncello *cello*

viper A venomous snake of family Viperidae (187 species), worldwide except Australia; most give birth to live young; thick body; head usually triangular, broad (due to poison glands and associated muscles at sides); fangs attached to front of upper jaw, folding flat against roof of mouth; venom destroys blood cells and vessels, and causes internal bleeding.

viper's bugloss [byooglos] A stout, erect, bristly biennial (*Echium vulgare*), growing to c.1 m/3¼ ft, native to Europe and W Asia; leaves 15 cm/6 in, lance-shaped to oblong, rough; a large panicle formed by the basal stalked inflorescence of numerous coiled cymes, with flowers all on one side; flowers funnel-shaped, pink in bud, opening blue. (Family: Boraginaceae.)

Virgil or **Vergil,** in full **Publius Vergilius Maro** (70–19 BC) Latin poet, born in Andes, near Mantua. He studied rhetoric and philosophy in Rome, and became one of the endowed court poets who gathered round the minister and patron, Maecenas. His *Eclogues* (37 BC) were received with great enthusiasm. Soon afterwards he withdrew to Campania, where he wrote the *Georgics* or *Art of Husbandry* (36–29 BC), and for the rest of his life worked at the request of the emperor on the *Aeneid*, an epic poem in 12 books modelled on the epics of Homer, which relates the wanderings of the Trojan hero Aeneas after the fall of Troy. When this was almost completed, he travelled in Greece and Asia, but fell ill, and died in Brundisium. His wish that the poem (unfinished at his death) should be burned was not respected. His works, written mainly in hexameter verse, have exerted an immense influence on later classical and post-classical writers, among them Dante, Milton, and Dryden.

virginals A keyboard instrument with a mechanism similar to that of the harpsichord, but with strings set at right angles to the keys (as in the clavichord). No fully convincing explanation of the name has been advanced. The instrument was widely used from the 15th-c to the 17th-c, when it was superseded by the spinet.

Virgin Birth The Christian belief that Jesus Christ had no human father, but was conceived through the power of the Holy Spirit without his mother, Mary, losing her virginity.

Virginia pop (2000e) 7 078 500; area 105 582 sq km/40 767 sq mi. State in E USA, divided into 95 counties and 41 independent cities; 'Old Dominion'; bounded E by Maryland, Chesapeake Bay, and the Atlantic Ocean; first permanent British settlement in America (at Jamestown, 1607); named after Elizabeth I (the 'Virgin Queen'); one of the first colonies to move for independence; scene of the British surrender at Yorktown, 1781; 10th of the original 13 states to ratify the Constitution, 1788; scene of several major battles in the Civil War (Richmond was the Confederacy capital); re-admitted to the Union, 1870; capital, Richmond; other chief cities, Norfolk, Virginia Beach, Newport News; Potomac R follows the Maryland state border; Rappahannock, York, and James Rivers cross the state to Chesapeake Bay; Blue Ridge Mts in the W; highest point Mt Rogers (1743 m/5718 ft); flat and swampy coastal area (the Tidewater region); to the W, land rises into the rolling, fertile Piedmont, interrupted further W by the Blue Ridge Mts; W of these lies a series of beautiful valleys (the Valley of Virginia), notably the Shenandoah; tobacco (chief agricultural crop), dairy produce, cattle, hay, corn, peanuts, sweet potatoes, apples; chemicals, tobacco products (Richmond), electrical equipment, ships (on the shores of Hampton Roads channel); coal mining (in the SW); scenic mountains, valleys, and shores, as well as the area's history, make tourism a major state industry.

Virginia Beach 36°51N 75°59W, pop (2000e) 425 300. Independent city, SE Virginia, USA, on the Atlantic Ocean; a major summer resort; naval air station; railway; Cape Henry Memorial (site of English landing in 1607); Marine Science Museum.

Virginia creeper Either of two species of very similar deciduous climbers with sucker-bearing tendrils, tiny green flowers, and bright red autumn foliage, both widely grown as ornamentals. *Parthenocissus quinquefolia*, native to E North America, has palmate leaves with five pointed leaflets; *Parthenocissus tricuspidata* native to China and Japan, has 3-lobed leaves. (Family: Vitaceae.)

Virginia Resolutions *Kentucky and Virginia Resolutions*

Virgin Islands, British *p.1611*

Virgin Islands, United States *p.1611*

Virgo (Lat 'virgin') A constellation of the zodiac, which contains an abundance of faint galaxies as well as the first quasar to be recognized as such, 3C 273, and one of the largest galaxies known, M87. Its brightest star is Spica, a spectroscopic binary; distance 80·4 parsec. Virgo lies on the celestial equator, between Leo and Libra.

viroid A fragment of infectious nucleic acid that resembles a virus; typically consisting of a small loop of ribonucleic acid not enclosed within a protein shell (*capsid*). It includes the causative agents of some plant diseases, such as hop stunt.

virtual image *optics*

Virgin Islands, British

(UK British Overseas Territory) (*see map, right*)

Timezone GMT –4

Area 153 km²/59 sq mi

Population total (2000e) 19 600

Capital Road Town (on Tortola Island)

Physical features Island group at the NW end of the Lesser Antilles chain, E Caribbean, NE of Puerto Rico; comprises 4 large islands (Tortola, Virgin Gorda, Anegada, Jost Van Dyke) and over 30 islets and cays; only 16 inhabited; hilly terrain, except for flat coral island of Anegada; highest point, Sage Mt, 540 m/1772 ft, on Tortola I.

Climate Subtropical climate; average annual temperatures 17–28°C (Jan), 26–31°C (Jul); average annual rainfall 1 270 mm/50 in.

Currency 1 US Dollar (US$) = 100 cents

Economy Tourism (accounts for 50% of national income); construction and stone extraction; rum, paint, gravel, livestock, coconuts, sugar cane, fruit and vegetables, fish.

History Tortola colonized by British planters, 1666; constitutional government, 1774; part of the Leeward Is, 1872; separate Crown Colony, 1956; governor represents the British sovereign; Executive Council and Legislative Council.

virtual particle A term used to describe any particle appearing as an intermediary in a subatomic particle reaction. Virtual particles borrow energy according to the Heisenberg uncertainty principle, and in so doing temporarily violate the mass-energy conservation law. For example, an electron and a positron may interact via a virtual photon – an unphysical photon which has borrowed energy to become temporarily heavy. No virtual particle is directly observable, but they are needed to describe particle reactions in quantum field theory.

virtual reality A computing technique in which the computer user sees only a computer output screen, and all the movements and sounds from the user are recorded by the computer. This allows the computer to simulate another environment in which users might well believe they are wholly involved. Virtual reality is used in a wide range of contexts, such as flight simulators for training pilots, videoconferencing suites (where the participants are separated by long distances but can imagine that they are all in the same room), and computer games.

Virunga [virungga] National park in the Kivu region of NW Democratic Republic of Congo; environments include marshy deltas, savannah, volcanic landscapes, and snow-covered mountains; noted for its wild mammals, particularly its gorilla colonies; a world heritage site.

virus The smallest infectious particle, 10–300 nm in diameter. Viruses infect other micro-organisms such as bacteria, fungi, and algae, as well as higher plants and animals. The genetic material of each virus is present as a molecule of either ribonucleic acid or deoxyribonucleic acid, encased inside a protein shell (*capsid*). Complex viruses have an outer envelope surrounding the capsid. Viruses replicate only in living cells, their nucleic acid directing the host cell to synthesize material required for producing more virus. Virus particles can survive in a dried, crystalline, and metabolically inert state. The study of viruses is known as **virology**. A metaphorical extension of the notion is found in computing.

virus yellows A complex aphid-transmitted disease of sugar beet, caused by barley yellows virus (*BYV*) and/or barley mild yellows virus (*BMYV*). These viruses cause yellowing of the leaves and blockage of the phloem vessels so that sugars cannot be translocated to the roots, resulting in severe loss of yield, especially if infection starts early in the growing season. It may be controlled by insecticidal sprays, but these must be applied before the insect vectors first arrive. (Order: Viruses.)

Virgin Islands, United States

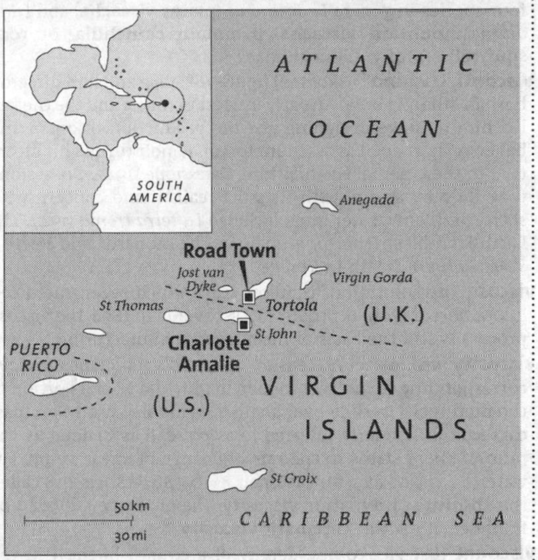

□ International Airport

official name **Virgin Islands of the United States**, formerly **Danish West Indies** (to 1917)

Local name US Virgin Islands

Timezone GMT –4

Area 342 km²/132 sq mi

Population total (2000e) 121 000 (St Croix 53 900, St Thomas 51 400, St John 2900)

Status Territory

Capital Charlotte Amalie (on St Thomas Island)

Languages English (official), with Spanish and Creole widely spoken

Ethnic groups West Indian, French, Hispanic

Religion Protestant

Physical features Nine islands and 75 islets in the Lesser Antilles, Caribbean Sea; three main inhabited islands, St Croix, St Thomas, and St John; volcanic origin, mostly hilly or rugged and mountainous; highest peak, Crown Mt, 474 m/1555 ft on St Thomas.

Climate Subtropical climate; average annual temperatures 21–9°C (Dec–Mar), 24–31°C (Jun–Sep); low humidity; rainy season (May–Nov); subject to severe droughts, floods and earthquakes.

Currency 1 US Dollar (US$) = 100 cents

Economy Tourism (chief industry); St Croix industries include oil and alumina products, clocks and watches, textiles, rum, fragrances, petrochemicals; vegetables, fruit, sorghum.

GDP (2002) 2·4 bn, per capita 19 000

History Originally inhabited by Ciboney Indians, followed by Arawak Indians, then Caribs; discovered by Columbus in 1493; Denmark colonized St Thomas and St John, 1665 and 1718, and bought St Croix from France, 1733; purchased by US, 1917; now an unincorporated territory of the US; a Governor heads a unicameral legislature.

Head of State/Government

1991–97 Bailey Olter

1997– Jacob Nena

Visayan Islands [visiyan] area 61 991 sq km/23 928 sq mi. Island group in the C Philippines; N of Mindanao I, S of Luzon I; bounded by the Sulu Sea (W) and Philippine Sea (E); chief islands include Cebu, Bohol, Panay, Leyte, Samar, Negros, Masbate; sugar, coconuts.

viscacha [vis**ka**cha] A cavy-like rodent from South America; resembles a large chinchilla; lives among rocks or in burrows; four species in genera *Lagostomus* (**plains viscacha**) and *Lagidium* (**mountain viscacha**, **mountain chinchilla**, or **rock squirrel**). (Family: Chinchillidae.)

Visconti, Luchino [vis**kon**tee] (1906–76) Stage and film director, born in Milan, N Italy. An early interest in music and the theatre led him to stage designing and the production of opera and ballet. A short spell as assistant to Jean Renoir turned his attention to the cinema. His first film, *Ossessione* (1942, Obsession), took Italy by storm, with its strict realism and concern with social problems. Later films included *La terra trema* (1947, The Earth Trembles), *Il gattopardo* (1963, The Leopard), and *Morte a Venezia* (1971, Death in Venice).

viscose The solution of cellulose from which regenerated cellulose fibre (rayon) is produced. Discovered in 1892, the viscose process is still the basis of most rayon manufacturing.

viscosity [vis**kos**itee] A measure of a fluid's reluctance to flow, corresponding to internal friction in the fluid as one portion of the fluid seeks to slide over another; symbol η, units Pa.s (pascal.second); formerly referred to as *poise*. It is defined as the ratio of shear stress to the rate of change of shear strain. For water, η = 0·001 Pa.s; for castor oil, η = 0·986 Pa.s. η is also called the **absolute** or **dynamic viscosity**. The quantity η divided by fluid density is the **kinematic viscosity**.

viscount (Lat *vice-comes* 'deputy of a count') In the UK, the second lowest rank of the peerage, often the second title of an earl or marquess bestowed as a courtesy title on his eldest son.

Vishinsky *Vyshinsky, Andrei*

Vishnu [**vish**noo] A major Hindu deity, second in the triad (*Trimurti*) of gods manifesting the cosmic functions of the Supreme Being. The preserver of the universe and the embodiment of goodness and mercy, he is believed to have assumed visible form in nine descents (*avataras*), three in non-human form, one in hybrid form, and five in human form, of which his appearances as Rama and Krishna are the most important.

visible record computer (VRC) An old form of computer in which the files of data to be processed are held as cards with a magnetic strip on one edge. The magnetic strip holds the data which the computer is to read and process. The card also has printing on it, which provides users with a visible record of the data being processed. Although there are still some visible record computers in operation, they are now uncommon.

visibles *invisibles*

Visigoths A Germanic people, forming one of the two great Gothic tribes, who fled from the Huns in 376 into the Roman Empire, and eventually founded the Visigothic kingdom, embracing at its height in the 7th-c Portugal, virtually all Spain, and part of S Gaul. It was extinguished by the Arab conquest of 711.

vision The process by which organisms form an internal representation of the external environment on the basis of the pattern of light available to them. The crucial requirement is for a light-sensitive receptor. Higher animals have many such *photoreceptors* (about 230 million in each eye in humans) making up a photoreceptive surface, the *retina*. For anything more than crude light detection, an *image* is essential; this constitutes an orderly representation on the retina of the spatial array of objects in the environment. Information from the retina passes up the 1 million fibres of the optic nerve to the occipital cortex, the first of many brain regions devoted to vision. The way in which the brain encodes basic visual features such as colour, edges, and movement is becoming increasingly understood, but very little is known of how these features are interpreted to enable us to recognize objects.

vision mixer Equipment used in video production for the selection of programme material from several sources – multiple cameras, telecine, slide scanner, videotape recorder – with facilities for transition effects between scenes and for image combination at the time of shooting and in post-production editing. The term also refers to the technician who operates the equipment under the director or editor.

Vistula, River [**vis**tyula], Pol **Wisa** Longest river in Poland; rises in the Carpathians in SW Poland and flows NE, N, and NW for 1047 km/651 mi to meet the Baltic Sea at Gdańsk; navigable for 941 km/585 mi; linked by canal to E and W Europe; dammed at Goczałkowice.

Visual Basic A high-level computer programming language, and the development software to suppport it, enabling programmers to create user-interactive programs very quickly. Developed by Microsoft, it provides visual programming facilities (the ability to create code by manipulating icons) as well as more traditional text-based programming methods.

visual display unit (VDU) The screen attached to a computer. Most VDUs are based on cathode-ray-tube technology similar to that used in television sets, and both single colour and full colour versions are used. An increasing number of VDUs are being based on liquid crystal displays, particularly in portable computer applications.

vitalism The doctrine that the difference between living organisms and inanimate bodies cannot be fully explained solely in material or physico-chemical terms. Organisms have additional, non-material, vital elements, which may or may not be capable of existing apart from their hosts. Bergson and Driesch were two of the best-known exponents.

vitamins Organic substance present in minute quantities in natural foods that are essential for health, classified as either **water soluble** or **fat soluble**. Fat soluble vitamins include A (retinol), D (cholecalciferol), K (phytomenadione), and E (α-tocopherol). Water soluble vitamins include C (ascorbic acid), B1 (thiamine), B2 (riboflavin), B6 (pyridoxine), and B12 (cyanocobalamin), as well as nicotinic acid, folic acid, pantothenic acid, and biotin. Their absence from the diet or presence in insufficient amounts results in specific abnormalities, due to the derangement of particular metabolic processes: these include eye disease (A), rickets and osteomalacia (D), haemorrhagic problems (K), scurvy (C), beriberi (B1), and anaemia (B12). (*see panel p.1613*)

Vitebsk [**vee**tyepsk] 55°10N 30°14E, pop (2000e) 364 200. River-port capital of Vitebskaya oblast, NE Belarus, on R Zapadnaya Dvina; founded, 11th-c; airfield; railway; agricultural trade, wool textiles, footwear, machine tools.

Viti Levu [veetee **lay**voo] area 10 429 sq km/4026 sq mi. Largest and most important island of Fiji, SW Pacific Ocean, separated from Vanua Levu, 32 km/20 mi NE, by the Koro Sea; length 144 km/89 mi; width 104 km/65 mi; mountainous interior, rising to 1324 m/4344 ft at Tomaniivi (Mt Victoria); lower reaches of main rivers provide fertile alluvial flats; capital, Suva; airport; gold mining, sugar milling, tourism; experimental irrigated rice projects near Suva; Colo-i-suva Forest Park.

Vitosha or **Vitosa** [vee**tosh**a] 42°40N 23°15E. Mountain, 20 km/12 mi E of Sofia; one of W Bulgaria's winter resorts; altitude 1810 m/5938 ft; notable ski facilities.

vitriol *sulphuric acid*

Vitruvius [vi**troo**vius], in full **Marcus Vitruvius Pollio** (1st-c) Roman architect and military engineer. He was in the service of Augustus, and wrote the 10-volume *De architectura* (On Architecture), the only Roman treatise on architecture still extant.

Vittoria, Tommasso Ludovica da *Victoria, Tomás Luis de*

Vittoria [vee**toh**ria], Span **Vitoria** 42°51N 2°40W, pop (2000e) 208 000. Basque capital of Alava province, N Spain, 351 km/218 mi N of Madrid; scene of French defeat in the Peninsular War (1813); bishopric; airport; railway; vehicles, steel, electronics, explosives, arms, machinery, furniture, sugar refining; Church of St Peter, old and new cathedrals; Fiesta of St Prudence (Apr), La Virgen Blanca fair (Aug), pilgrimage to Olarizu (Sep), autumn music festival.

Vittorino da Feltre [vitoreenoh da **fel**tray], originally **Vittorino dei Ramboldini** (c.1378–1446) Educationist, born at Feltre, NE Italy. He studied and taught at Padua, and in 1423 was sum-

The Main Types Of Vitamin

Fat soluble vitamins

Vitamin	*Chemical name*	*Precursor*	*Main symptom of deficiency*	*Dietary source*
A	retinol	β-carotene	xerophthalmia (eye disease)	retinol: milk, butter, cheese, egg yolk, liver, and fatty fish carotene: green vegetables, yellow and red fruits and vegetables, especially carrots
D	cholecalciferol	UV-activated 7-dehydro-cholesterol	rickets, osteomalacia	liver oils of fatty fish, margarine, some fortified milks, and breakfast cereals
K	phytomenadione		haemorrhagic problems	green leafy vegetables and liver
E	α tocopherol		extremely rare in humans	vegetable oils

Water soluble vitamins

Vitamin	*Chemical name*	*Main symptom of deficiency*	*Dietary source*
C	ascorbic acid	scurvy	citrus fruits, potatoes, green leafy vegetables
B-vitamins			
B_1	thiamine	beriberi	seeds and grains; widely distributed
B_2	riboflavin	failure to thrive	liver, milk, cheese, yeast, leafy vegetables
–	nicotinic acid	pellagra	meat, fish, wholemeal cereals, pulses
B_6	pyridoxine	dermatitis; neurological disorders	cereals, liver, meat, fruits, leafy vegetables
B_{12}	cyanocobalamin	anaemia	meat, milk, liver, egg yolk
–	folic acid	anaemia	liver, green vegetables, nuts
–	pantothenic acid	dermatitis	widespread
–	biotin	dermatitis	liver, kidney, yeast extracts

moned to Mantua as tutor to the children of the Marchese Gonzaga. There he founded a school for both rich and poor children (1425), in which he devised new methods of instruction, introducing a wide curriculum, and integrating the development of mind and body through the study of the Classics and Christianity.

Vivaldi, Antonio (Lucio) [vivaldee] (1678–1741) Violinist and composer, born in Venice, NE Italy. He was ordained in 1703, but gave up officiating, and was attached to the Conservatory of the Ospedale della Pietà at Venice (1703–40). The 12 concertos of *L'Estro Armonico* (1712) gave him a European reputation, and *The Four Seasons* (1725), an early example of programme music, proved highly popular. He also wrote many operas, sacred music, and over 450 concertos. Though he was a major influence on the development of the solo concerto, he was largely forgotten after his death; and only after Bach transcribed many of his concertos for the keyboard did they come to be increasingly played.

Vivekananda [vivaykananda], also known as **Swami Vivekananda**, originally **Narendranath Datta** or **Dutt** (1862–1902) Hindu philosopher, born in Calcutta, E India. He studied in a Western-style university, and first joined the Brahmo Samaj, attracted by its policy of social reform. Later, he met Ramakrishna and became his leading disciple, establishing the headquarters of the Ramakrishna Order at Belur Math on the Ganges, near Calcutta. He attempted to combine Indian spirituality with Western materialism, and became the main force behind the Vedanta movement in the West.

Viverridae [viveridee] A family of small to medium-sized carnivores native to the S Old World; 72 species; long thin body, long tail, pointed muzzle, short legs; coat often spotted or banded; most secrete pungent fluid from glands near tail; inhabit woodland or dense undergrowth; eat small vertebrates, invertebrates, eggs, fruit, carrion.

Vivés, Juan Luis [veevays], Lat **Ludovicus Vives** (1492–1540) Philospher and humanist, born in Valencia, E Spain. He studied at Paris but, disliking scholasticism, went to Louvain, where he became professor of humanities (1519). He dedicated his edition of St Augustine's *Civitas Dei* to Henry VIII, who summoned him to England in 1523 as tutor to Princess Mary. His writings include *Adversus Pseudodialecticos* (1570, Against the Pseudo-Dialecticians), and several other works on educational theory and practice. Imprisoned in 1527 for opposing Henry's divorce, he then lived mostly at Bruges.

viviparity [viviparitee] In animals, the production of live young rather than eggs. The embryos grow within the mother's body, which provides nourishment via a placenta or similar structure. Viviparity occurs in placental mammals and some other animals. In plants, it refers to the production of seeds that germinate within the fruit while still attached to the parent plant.

vivisection The practice of dissecting live animals for experimental purposes. Research includes experiments which look for the effects of new drugs, food additives, cosmetics, and a wide range of chemicals on the body tissue and behaviour of such animals as guinea pigs, rabbits, rats, and monkeys, as an alternative to using human subjects. Such research is now strictly controlled by legislation in most Western nations, but nonetheless provokes considerable public opposition in some countries, including the use of violence against scientists and research organizations by animal rights extremists.

Vlaanderen [vlanderen] *Flanders*

Vladimir I, St, in full **Vladimis Svyatoslavich**, known as **the Great** (956–1015) First Christian sovereign of Russia (980–1015), the son of Svyatoslav, Grand Prince of Kiev (d.972). He became Prince of Novgorod in 970, and in 980 seized Kiev from his brother after his father's death. He consolidated the Russian realm from the Baltic to the Ukraine, extending its dominions into Lithuania, Galicia, and Livonia, with Kiev as his capital. He made a pact with Byzantine Emperor Basil II (c.987), accepting Christianity and marrying the emperor's sister. He then ordered the conversion to Christianity of his subjects, punishing those who resisted. Feast day 27 September.

Vladivostok [vladi**vos**tok] 43°10N 131°53E, pop (2000e) 645 000. Seaport capital of Primorskiy kray, Russia, on the East Sea (Sea of Japan); chief Russian port on the Pacific Ocean (kept open in winter by ice-breakers); base for fishing and whaling fleets; founded, 1860; terminus of the Trans-Siberian Railway; university (1920); naval base; shipbuilding and repairing, precision instruments, foodstuffs, building materials.

Vlaminck, Maurice de [vla**mĩk**] (1876–1958) Artist, born in Paris, France. He was largely self-taught, worked with Derain, and came to be influenced by van Gogh. By 1905 he was one of the leaders of the Fauves, using typically brilliant colour, then painted more Realist landscapes under the influence of Cézanne (1908–14), and later developed a more sombre Expressionism.

Vlissingen *Flushing*

Vlorë or **Vlora** [**vlor**uh], Ital **Valona**, ancient **Aulon** 40°27N 19°30E, pop (2000e) 84 300. Seaport and capital of Vlorë district, SW Albania, on the Bay of Vlorë, 112 km/69 mi SW of Tiranë; a 5th-c bishopric; independence proclaimed here in 1912; railway; well-protected harbour; fishing, olive oil processing.

VLSI *very large scale integration*

Vltava, River [**vuhl**tava], Ger **Moldau** River in the Czech Republic, formed in the Bohemian Forest by the junction of two headstreams; flows SE and N to meet the R Elbe near Mělník; length 427 km/265 mi; navigable for c.80 km/50 mi; major source of hydroelectricity.

VOA *Voice of America*

vocal cords Two muscular folds in the larynx, behind the Adam's apple. They are very flexible, and are brought together to impede the airflow during speech, when they vibrate and produce voice, used in the articulation of vowels and many consonants. They are also used to vary the pitch of the voice (generally, the faster the vibration, the higher the pitch) and are also involved in the production of several distinctive tones of voice. When they are completely open, the air flows freely, as in whispering and the pronunciation of 'h'.

vocational education Education which is aimed at the preparation of students for their present or future employment. Often undertaken in colleges of further education, it can also take place on the job in the workplace itself. A wide range of vocational qualifications is usually available, some from chartered award-giving institutions, others from professional organizations. In addition, pre-vocational education is available for pupils of school age who wish to acquire work experience and explore the nature of different careers before making their choice.

vodka A colourless spirit produced from potatoes, the national alcoholic drink of Poland and Russia. It is almost tasteless, and is thus used in many mixed drinks, such as the 'Bloody Mary' (vodka and tomato juice). It is best served chilled.

Vogel, Hans-Jochen [**fohgl**] (1926–) German politician. He was successor to Schmidt as leader of the Social Democratic Party (SPD), and the Party's nominee for the chancellorship of West Germany in 1983. A former minister of housing and town planning (1972–4) and minister of justice (1974–81), he also served briefly as governing Mayor of West Berlin (1981). He replaced Brandt to become SPD chairman (1987–91).

Voice of America (VOA) The external broadcasting service of the US government, founded in 1942. By 2000, the VOA was broadcasting worldwide in English and 52 other languages (including six to the former USSR and 10 to Africa) from three stations in the USA, and 15 overseas relay stations.

voiceprint A visual representation of the features of a person's voice, as analysed using acoustic techniques (usually the sound spectrograph). Voiceprinting was devised in the 1960s, on analogy with fingerprinting, and the claim was made that a voiceprint is unique to the individual. Although introduced as evidence in some court cases (chiefly in the USA), the technique has remained controversial, but more sophisticated approaches are now being developed following electronic and computational advances.

Voight, Jon(athan) [**voyt**] (1938–) Film actor, born in Yonkers, New York, USA. He gained recognition for his role in *Midnight Cowboy* (1969, Oscar nomination) and became a leading actor during the 1970s. Among his many films are *Deliverance* (1972), *Coming Home* (1978, Best Actor Oscar), *Runaway Train* (1985, Oscar nomination), *Mission: Impossible* (1996), *Uprising* (2001), and *Holes* (2003). In 2001 he appeared with his daughter, actress Angelina Jolie, in *Lara Croft: Tomb Raider*.

Volans [**voh**lanz] (Lat 'flying fish') A tiny and inconspicuous S constellation near the Large Magellanic Cloud.

volcano A vent or fissure in the Earth's crust where molten lava is erupted onto the surface. The shape of a volcano depends on the composition of the lava. Lower-temperature, viscous, silica-rich lava forms steep-sided cones interbedded with ash, such as Mt Fuji, Japan. Less viscous, silica-poor, basaltic lavas form gentle slopes, as found in Iceland. Most volcanoes are confined to the zones along boundaries between crustal plates, and are closely associated with earthquakes, as in the circum-Pacific 'ring of fire'; but there are notable exceptions, such as the Hawaiian Is, which have formed on a 'hot spot' in the Earth's crust. The scientific study of volcanoes is known as **vulcanology**.

Volcano Islands Group of Japanese islands in the W Pacific Ocean; includes Iwo Jima, Kita Iwo, and Minami Iwo; administered by the USA, 1945–68; returned to Japan in 1968; sulphur, sugar.

Volcanus *Vulcan*

vole A mouse-like rodent native to Asia, Europe, and North America; most species with large head, blunt snout, and short tail; eats grass, seeds and insects; population numbers rise and fall drastically every few years; closely related to lemmings. (Tribe: Microtini, 96 species.)

Volga, River, ancient **Rha** Longest river of Europe, in C European Russia; rises in the Valdai Hills, and flows generally SE to enter the Caspian Sea, forming a broad delta below Astrakhan; length, 3531 km/2194 mi; principal navigable waterway in Russia; linked by canal to the Baltic, White Sea, Sea of Azov, and Black Sea; many reservoirs on its course; important source of hydroelectric power and irrigation.

Volgograd [**vol**gograd], formerly **Tsaritsyn** (to 1925), **Stalingrad** (1925–61) 48°45N 44°30E, pop (2000e) 1 200 000. Capital city of Volgogradskaya oblast, SE European Russia, on R Volga; E terminus of the Volga–Don Canal; founded 1589; largely destroyed in World War 2; airport; railway; aluminium, oil, oil refining, clothing, footwear, leatherwork, tractors, foodstuffs.

volleyball A court game, usually played indoors by two teams of six-a-side. Players hit a large ball with their hands or arms over a raised net in the hope of forcing an error, points are scored scored by the serving team. Invented in 1895 by William G Morgan at the YMCA, Holyoke, MA, it was originally known as *mintonette*.

Volstead, Andrew J [**vol**sted] (1860–1947) US politician, born in Goodhue Co, Minnesota, USA. He practised law, and entered Congress as a Republican in 1903. He was the author of the Farmers' Co-operative Marketing Act, but is best known for the Prohibition Act of 1919, named after him, which forbade the manufacture and sale of intoxicant liquors. This Act, passed over President Wilson's veto, was in force until 1933.

Volsungasaga [**vol**sungasahga] A 13th-c German epic deriving in part from the Norse *Edda*. It tells the story of the dynasty of the Volsungs, which is linked to that of the Nibelungs.

volt SI unit of electrical potential difference; symbol *V*; named after Alessandro Volta; if the power dissipated between two points along a wire carrying a current of 1 amp is 1 watt, then the potential difference between the two points equals 1 volt. In

1990 the Josephson constant, K_{J-90}, became the international standard of voltage measurement.

Volta, River River in Ghana, formed by junction of Black Volta and White Volta Rivers as they enter L Volta; flows S to enter the Gulf of Guinea at Ada; dammed at Akosombo to form L Volta (area 8500 sq km/3300 sq mi); Volta River Scheme designed to supply power, improve navigation, and help develop bauxite deposits; length including L Volta c.480 km/300 mi.

Volta, Alessandro (Giuseppe Antonio Anastasio) [**vol**ta] (1745–1827) Physicist, born in Como, N Italy. He invented the electrophorus, a device to generate static electricity (1775), discovered methane gas (1778), and was appointed professor of natural philosophy at Pavia (1778–1804). Inspired by the work of his friend Luigi Galvani, Volta found that electric current is generated when two dissimilar metals come into contact, and developed the first electric battery (1800), providing future researchers with a constant source of current electricity. His name is given to the unit of electric potential, the volt.

voltage *potential difference*

Voltaire [vol**tair**], pseudonym of **François Marie Arouet** (1694–1778) Writer, the embodiment of the 18th-c Enlightenment, born in Paris, France. Educated by the Jesuits in Paris, he studied law, then turned to writing. For lampooning the Duc d'Orléans he was imprisoned in the Bastille (1717–18), where he rewrote his tragedy *Oedipe*. This brought him fame, but he gained enemies at court, and was forced to go into exile in England (1726–9). Back in France, he wrote plays, poetry, historical and scientific treatises, and his *Lettres philosophiques* (1733, Philosophical Letters). He regained favour at court, becoming royal historiographer, then moved to Berlin at the invitation of Frederick the Great (1750–3). In 1755 he settled near Geneva, where he wrote the satirical short story, *Candide* (1759). From 1762 he produced a range of anti-religious writings and the *Dictionnaire philosophique* (1764). Always concerned over cases of injustice, he took a particular interest in the affair of Jean Calas, whose innocence he helped to establish. In 1778 he returned as a celebrity to Paris. His ideas were an important influence on the intellectual climate leading to the French Revolution.

voltmeter An instrument used for measuring potential difference or electromotive force between points in a circuit. Most voltmeters consist of an ammeter connected in line with a high resistance, and calibrated in volts. The current flowing is proportional to the potential difference, although the presence of the measuring instrument reduces the potential difference.

Voluntary Reserve *Territorial Army*

Voluntary Service Overseas (VSO) A British charity founded in 1958 to send skilled volunteers to work for two-year periods in developing countries. The host government provides a living allowance and accommodation; VSO provides briefing, air fare, and a grant.

Volvox A genus of freshwater green algae commonly occurring in spherical colonies (*coenobia*) of more than 500 cells; cells flagellate, usually containing a single cup-shaped chloroplast. (Class: Chlorophyceae. Order: Volvocales.)

von Braun, Wernher *Braun, Wernher von*

V-1 The abbreviation of *Vergeltungswaffe-1* (Ger 'revenge weapon 1'); small, winged, pilotless aircraft powered by a pulse jet motor, developed by the Luftwaffe. They carried a tonne of high explosive several hundred miles at a speed of c.800 kph/500 mph, slow enough for some to be intercepted by gunfire and high speed aircraft. Between 1944 and 1945, 5823 were launched against Britain. From the noise of their motors, they were also known as **buzz-bombs**.

von Klitzing, Klaus (1943–) Physicist, born in Sroda, WC Poland (formerly Schroda, Germany). He studied at Brunswick and Würzburg, became professor at Munich in 1980, and in 1985 was appointed director of the Max Planck Institute, Stuttgart. In 1977 he presented a paper on two-dimensional electronic behaviour in which the quantum Hall effect was clearly seen, but few realized its significance, and he came to appreciate what had occurred only in 1980. He was awarded the 1985 Nobel Prize for Physics.

von Klitzing constant A constant which forms the international standard of resistance measurement; symbol R_K, defined as h/e^2, where h is Planck's constant and e is the electron charge; derived from the quantized Hall effect by Klaus von Klitzing; R_K is measured experimentally; an internationally agreed exact value of R_{K-90} = 25 812·807 Ω (ohms) became the basis of the standard for resistance measurement in 1990.

Vonnegut, Kurt (Jr) [**von**eguht] (1922–) Novelist, born in Indianapolis, Indiana, USA. He studied at Cornell, and served in the US Air Force in World War 2. Afterwards he studied anthropology at Chicago University, and worked as a reporter and public relations writer. His novels are satirical fantasies, usually cast in the form of science fiction, as in *Player Piano* (1952), *Cat's Cradle* (1963), and *Galapagos* (1985). He is best known for *Slaughterhouse-Five* (1969), based on his experiences as a prisoner-of-war at the destruction of Dresden in 1945. Later novels include *Breakfast of Champions* (1973; filmed 1999), *Jailbird* (1979), *Deadeye Dick* (1982), *Hocus Pocus* (1990), and *Timequake* (1997). A volume of essays and speeches, *Fates Worse Than Death*, appeared in 1991.

Von Neumann, John [**noy**man], originally **Johann von Neumann** (1903–57) Mathematician, born in Budapest, Hungary. He escaped from Hungary during the Communist regime (1919), studied at Berlin and Zürich, and emigrated to the USA in 1933, to join the Institute for Advanced Study, Princeton. Equally at home in pure and applied mathematics, he wrote a major work on quantum mechanics (1932), which led him to a new axiomatic foundation for set theory, and participated in the atomic bomb project at Los Alamos during World War 2, providing a mathematical treatment of shock waves. His mathematical work on high-speed calculations for H-bomb development contributed to the development of computers, and he also introduced game theory (1944), which was a major influence on economics.

voodoo The popular religion of Haiti, also found in the West Indies and parts of South America. A blending of Roman Catholicism with W African religion, its followers attend both the church and the voodoo temple, where a voodoo priest or priestess leads a ritual invoking of the spirits of the voodoo world through magical diagrams, songs, and prayer. The spirits possess the members in trance.

Voortrekkers *Afrikaners; Great Trek*

Voronezh [vo**ron**yesh] 51°40N 39°10E, pop (2000e) 888 000. River port capital of Voronezhskaya oblast, EC European Russia, on R Voronezh; founded as a fortress, 1586; airport; railway; university (1918); agricultural trade, excavators, synthetic rubber, foodstuffs, atomic power generation.

Voroshilov, Kliment Yefremovich [voro**shee**lof] (1881–1969) Soviet marshal, statesman, and president (1953–60), born near Dnepropetrovsk, EC Ukraine. He joined the Russian Social Democratic Labour Party in 1903, but political agitation soon brought about his exile to Siberia, where he remained a fugitive until 1914. He played a military rather than a political role in the 1917 Revolution, and as commissar for defence (1925–40) was responsible for the modernization of the Red Army. He was removed from office after the failure to prevent the German siege of Leningrad, but stayed active in the Party, and became head of state after Stalin's death.

Voroshilovgrad *Lugansk*

Vorster, John [**faw(r)**ster], originally **Balthazar Johannes Vorster** (1915–83) South African statesman, prime minister (1966–78), and president (1978–9), born in Jamestown, SC South Africa. He studied at Stellenbosch, became a lawyer, and joined an extreme Afrikaner movement. In 1953 he became a Nationalist MP, and was minister of justice under Verwoerd (1961), whom he succeeded, maintaining the policy of apartheid. In 1978, after a scandal over the misappropriation of government funds, he resigned for health reasons, and was elected president, but stood down from this position nine months later when an investigating Commission found him jointly responsible.

vortex A rotational form of fluid flow. Lines of flow are curved, and may even form closed loops. Examples of vortices are whirlpools, tornadoes, and the circulating eddies caused by obstructions in rivers.

Vorticism A modern art movement started in England in 1913, partly inspired by the Futurists. Leading members included Wyndham Lewis, C R W Nevinson, and Henri Gaudier-Brzeska. Two issues were published of a journal, *Blast* (1914), and an exhibition was held (1915), after which the movement petered out.

Vortigern [vaw(r)tijern] (fl.425–50) Semi-legendary British king who, according to Bede, recruited Germanic mercenaries led by Hengist and Horsa to help fight off the Picts after the final withdrawal of the Roman administration from Britain (409). Tradition has it that the revolt of these troops opened the way for the Germanic conquests and settlements in England.

Vosges Mountains [vohzh], ancient **Vosegus** area 7425 sq km/ 2866 sq mi. Range of hills in NE France near the Franco-German frontier; separated from the Jura (S) by the Belfort Gap; thickly-wooded hills, several rivers descending to the Rhine and the Central Plateau; highest point, Ballon de Guebwiller (1423 m/ 4669 ft); length, 250 km/155 mi; skiing and rock climbing.

Vostok (scientific station) 78°27S 106°51E. Russian scientific station in Antarctica; lowest temperature ever recorded on Earth (−88·3°C) measured here; South Geomagnetic Pole (1985) nearby.

Vostok (spacecraft) [vostok] ('East') **spacecraft** The first generation of Soviet crewed spacecraft, carrying a single person. Vostok 1 carried the first human into space (12 Apr 1961) – Yuri Gagarin, who orbited Earth once on a flight of 118 min. Crew were recovered over land after ejection from the capsule at 7000 m/23 000 ft altitude after re-entry. The last Vostok flight carried Valentina Tereshkova, the first woman to fly in space (Vostok 6, 16 Jun 1963). **Voskhod** ('Sunrise') was an intermediate-generation Soviet-crewed spacecraft following Vostok and preceding Soyuz; it made only two flights, in 1964 and 1965.

voting *franchise* (politics)

voucher scheme A scheme for giving parents a voucher equivalent in value to the average cost of a child's education, which they are then entitled to spend at a school of their choice. This may be either a local authority school or a private fee-paying school, where they might have to top up the fee. The system has been tried on an experimental basis in the USA, and is favoured by some politicians in the UK.

Vought, Chance (Milton) [vawt] (1890–1930) Aircraft designer and manufacturer, born in New York City, USA. He was taught to fly by the Wright brothers, and was chief engineer of the Wright company until forming his own firm in 1917. Among his famous designs were the Vought–Wright Model V military biplane (1916), the Vought VE-7 (1919), the Vought UO-1 military observation plane (1922–5), and the FU-1 single-seat high-altitude supercharged fighter (1925).

vow A solemn promise made on a religious occasion. Examples include the marriage vows, the vows made by monks and nuns (now usually of poverty, chastity, and obedience), and vows made to saints in times of crisis.

vowel One of the two main categories of speech sound (the other being **consonant**). Phonetically, a vowel is a sound produced when the air flows freely through the mouth without constriction from the pharynx, tongue, or lips – an **oral vowel**; it may also flow partly through the nose (a **nasal vowel**). Vowel quality is determined by the shape of the lips and the position of the tongue. Phonologically, a vowel is defined by its function in the structure of a syllable: it forms the nucleus of the syllable, and (unlike a consonant) can stand alone (as in such words as *I* and *a* in English).

Voyager project A multiple outer-planet flyby mission undertaken by NASA to make the first detailed exploration beyond Mars, and designed to take advantage of a rare (every 175 years) celestial alignment of Jupiter, Saturn, Uranus, and Neptune. Twin spacecraft in the Mariner series were launched on Titan-Centaur vehicles in 1977. They flew through the Jovian system (Mar, Jul 1979) and, with a boost from Jupiter's gravity, flew on to Saturn (encounters Nov 1980, Aug 1981). Following the Saturn flyby, Voyager 1's trajectory is taking it upward out of the ecliptic. In February 1998 it overtook the Pioneer 10 probe (launched 1972) to become the most distant man-made object in space, and in November 2003, at 8 bn mi/13·5 bn km from Earth, it was about to leave the Solar System and begin its transition into interstellar space; Voyager 2 used Saturn's gravity to fly on to the historic encounters with Uranus (Jan 1986) and Neptune (Aug 1989). The spacecraft, powered by radioisotope thermo-electric generators, were built and are operated by NASA's Jet Propulsion Laboratory. They may send back data about the outermost reaches of the Solar System until well into the 21st-c.

voyeurism A repeated tendency to observe others engaging in intimate, including sexual, behaviour. Sexual excitement often occurs in anticipation of the voyeuristic act, which may be accompanied by masturbation.

Voysey, Charles (Francis Annesley) [voyzee] (1857–1941) Architect and designer, born in London, UK. A disciple of John Ruskin and William Morris, he designed traditional country houses influenced by the Arts and Crafts Movement, with accentuated gables, chimney stacks, buttresses, and long sloping roofs. He was also an important designer of wallpaper, textiles, furniture, and metalwork.

Voznesensky, Andrey Andreyevich [vozhneshenskee] (1933–) Poet, born in Moscow, Russia. Educated as an architect, he published his first two collections *Mozaika* and *Parabola* in 1960. His best-known volume *Antimiry* (Antiworlds) appeared in 1964, and the more difficult poems of *Soblazn* (Temptation) in 1979. The rock musical *Avos*, based on one of his poems, was produced in Moscow in 1981. In 1990 appeared *Epitaph for Vysotsky*.

VSEPR Abbreviation of **valence shell electron pair repulsion**, a simple but effective method for predicting the configuration of bonded atoms about a central one in terms of the pairs of valence electrons on the central atom. For example, water, where the oxygen atom has two bonds and two lone pairs, has four pairs, and is thus an essentially tetrahedral arrangement, resulting in an H–O–H angle of less than 110°, while O=C=O, with no lone pairs on C, is linear.

VSO *Voluntary Service Overseas*

VTOL [veetol] Acronym used for a fixed-wing aircraft specially designed for **Vertical Take-Off and Landing**. The most successful aircraft of this type is the Hawker Siddeley Harrier, which can deflect the thrust from its jet engine from the vertical to the horizontal while in flight. Since the early 1950s the USA has built a series of propeller-driven aircraft of various configurations, some of which stood on their tails and took off vertically, such as the Convair XFY-1.

V-2 The abbreviation of *Vergeltungswaffe-2* (Ger 'revenge weapon 2'); a guided ballistic missile developed by the German army, which began rocket experiments under the direction of Wernher von Braun in 1937. Because of its very high speed, it could not be intercepted by gun or aircraft. It was unstoppable, but wildly inaccurate. Between September 1944 and March 1945, 1054 fell on Britain.

Vuillard, (Jean) Edouard [vweeyah(r)] (1868–1940) Painter and printmaker, born in Cuiseaux, E France. One of the later Impressionists, a member of *Les Nabis*, he was influenced by Gauguin and the vogue for Japanese painting. He executed mainly flower pieces and simple interiors, painted with a great sense of light and colour, and is also known for his textiles, wallpapers, and decorative work in public buildings.

Vulcan, also **Vulcanus** or **Volcanus** The Roman god of fire, especially destructive fire and volcanic activity, sometimes called **Mulciber**. He was identified with the Greek Hephaestus, and later given his attributes, such as metal-working.

vulcanite or **ebonite** A hard black material made by the vulcanization of rubber with a high proportion of sulphur (2:1). It was important as an insulator before the coming of modern synthetics.

vulcanization The modification of the properties of rubber by chemical treatment, originally and still mainly (except for certain synthetic rubbers) with sulphur. Other chemicals may speed the vulcanization process or serve as extenders. The technique, which originated with Charles Goodyear in 1839, improves tensile strength, elasticity, and abrasion resistance.

vulcanology *volcano*

Vulgate [vuhlgayt] The Latin translation of the Christian Bible, originating with Jerome (c.405), who attempted to provide an authoritative alternative to the confusing array of Old Latin versions in his day. From c.7th-c, it emerged in Western Christianity as the favourite Latin version (*vulgate* meaning the 'common' edition), but was itself revised and corrupted through the centuries. In 1546 the Council of Trent recognized it as the official Latin text of the Roman Catholic Church.

Vulpecula [vulpekyula] (Lat 'little fox') A small N constellation in the Milky Way in which the first pulsar was discovered in 1967.

vulture A bird of prey specialized to feed on carrion; head often lacking long feathers. There are two groups. **Old World vultures** (Family: Accipitridae, 14 species) evolved over 20 million years ago; formerly worldwide but now absent from the Americas; no sense of smell. **New World** or **cathartid vultures** (Family: Cathartidae, 7 species) evolved more recently; formerly present in the Old World but now restricted to the Americas.

Vygotsky, Lev Semenovich [vigotskee] (1896–1934) Psychologist, born in Orsha, E Belarus. Originally a teacher and literary scholar with interests in creativity, he took up a scientific post at the Institute of Psychology in Moscow in 1924. He examined contemporary psychology, notably behaviourism and introspectionism, attempting to establish a Marxist view that thought originates in interactions, which themselves are influenced by social history. His writings, such as *Thought and Language* (1934–62) and *Mind in Society* (1978), have had a major influence on Soviet and (since the 1960s) Western psychology, particularly on specialists in child development.

Vyshinsky, Andrey Yanuaryevich [vishinskee] (1883–1954) Russian jurist and politician, born in Odessa, S Ukraine. He studied law at Moscow, joined the Communist Party in 1920, and became professor of criminal law and attorney general (1923–5). He gained worldwide notoriety as an aggressive and vengeful advocate. He was the public prosecutor at the state trials (1936–8) which removed Stalin's rivals, and later became the Soviet delegate to the UN (1945–9, 1953–4), and foreign minister (1949–53).

W

WAAC; WAAF *women's services*

WAC *women's services*

Wace, Robert [ways] (12th-c) Anglo-Norman poet, born in Jersey, Channel Is. He studied in Paris, and was a Canon of Bayeux (1160–70). He wrote several verse lives of the saints, a Norman-French version of Geoffrey of Monmouth's *Historia regum Britanniae* entitled the *Roman de Brut* (1155), and the *Roman de Rou* (1160–74), an epic of the exploits of the Dukes of Normandy.

Waddington, C(onrad) H(al) (1905–75) Embryologist and geneticist, born in Evesham, Hereford and Worcester, WC England, UK. He studied at Cambridge, and became professor of animal genetics at Edinburgh (1947–70). He introduced important concepts into evolutionary theory, envisaging a mechanism by which Lamarckianism could be incorporated into orthodox Darwinian genetics. He wrote a standard textbook, *Principles of Embryology* (1956), and also helped to popularize science in such general books as *The Ethical Animal* (1960).

wadi [wodee] A desert ravine or steep-sided gorge formed during flash floods, but generally containing water only during rainy seasons.

Wafd The name of the Egyptian nationalist party which derived from a delegation (*wafd*) sent under the nationalist leader Saad Zaghlul to the British High Commissioner in Cairo in 1919 to demand Egyptian independence. The Wafd played a leading role in Egyptian politics until the revolution in 1952. The 'New Wafd' became an opposition party in 1984, but was unable to regain its former influence.

Wagga Wagga 35°07S 147°24E, pop (2000e) 59 000. Town in New South Wales, Australia; at the centre of a rich agricultural area W of Canberra; railway; airfield; Charles Sturt University (1989).

Wagner, Otto [vahgner] (1841–1918) Architect and teacher, born in Penzing, NE Austria. Professor at the Vienna Academy (1894–1912), he was the founder of the Vienna School. Though for many years a classical revivalist, he became an important advocate of purely functional architecture, notably through his book *Modern Architecture* (1895). His most influential work, produced at the end of his career, includes several stations in Vienna, and the Vienna Postal Savings Bank (1904–6), regarded as the first example of modern architecture in the 20th-c.

Wagner, (Wilhelm) Richard [vahgner] (1813–83) Composer, born in Leipzig, EC Germany. His early efforts at composition were unsuccessful, and in Paris (1839–42) he made a living by journalism and hack operatic arrangements. His *Rienzi* (1842) was a great success at Dresden, and he was appointed *Kapellmeister*, but his next operas, including *Tannhäuser* (1845), were failures. Deeply implicated in the revolutionary movement, he fled from Saxony (1848), moving to Paris and Zürich. The poem of the *Ring* cycle was finished in 1852, and in 1853 he began to write *Das Rheingold* (The Rhinegold), followed by *Die Walküre* (1856, The Valkyries) and the first two acts of *Siegfried* (1857). In 1861 he was allowed to return to Germany, but still lacked recognition and support, and had to flee from Vienna to avoid imprisonment for debt. In 1864 he was saved from ruin by the eccentric young King of Bavaria, Ludwig II, who became a fanatical admirer of his work, and offered him every facility at Munich. His first wife, Minna, having died in 1866, Wagner then married Cosima von Bülow, the wife of his musical director, after her divorce. *Die Meistersinger* was completed in 1867, and *Götterdämmerung* in 1874. To fulfil his ambition to give a complete performance of the *Ring* (*Die Walküre, Siegfried, Götterdämmerung*, with *Das Rheingold* as introduction), he started the now famous theatre at Bayreuth, which opened in 1876. *Parsifal*, his last opera, was staged in 1882, a year before his sudden death from a heart attack, in Venice. His son **Siegfried Wagner** (1869–1930) was director of the Bayreuth theatre from 1909. His grandson **Wieland Wagner** (1917–66) took over the directorship in 1951, and revolutionized the production of the operas, stressing their universality as opposed to their purely German significance. Wieland's brother **Wolfgang Wagner** (1919–) became artistic director at Bayreuth in 1966.

wagtail A small, ground-dwelling songbird, found worldwide; plumage usually bold, black-and-white, yellow, or green (dull species are called **pipits**); long tail which wags vertically; inhabits open country; eats mainly insects. The name is also used for two New World flycatchers and one fantail. (Family: Motacillidae, 48 species.)

Wahhabis [wahabeez] An Islamic movement which derives from Mohammed ibn Abd al-Wahhab (1703–92), a religious reformer from Uyaina near Riyadh, and Mohammed ibn Saud, the ancestor of the present rulers of Saudi Arabia. The alliance was to lead to the unification in the 18th-c of most of the peninsula under the Saudi banner. The modern reunification of the kingdom was carried out 1902–32 by King Abd al-Aziz, otherwise known as 'Ibn Saud'. Arabs call the followers of Abd al-Wahhab *muwahhidun* or 'unitarians' rather than *Wahhabis*, which is an anglicism. The movement maintains that legal decisions must be based exclusively on the Qur'an and the *Sunna*. The original Wahhabis banned music, dancing, poetry, silk, gold, and jewellery, and in the 20th-c the *ikhwan* ('brotherhood') attacked telecommunications as innovations not sanctioned by God.

Waikato, River [wiykatoh] River in North Island, New Zealand; length 425 km/264 mi from its source, the Upper Waikato R; longest river in New Zealand; rises in L Taupo then flows NW to enter the Tasman Sea S of Manukau Harbour; source of hydroelectric power.

Waikiki Beach [wiykeekee] Resort beach in SE Honolulu on the Pacific island of Oahu, Hawaii state, USA; surfing popular on the reef; concerts and hula shows featured at the Kapiolani Park.

Wain, John (Barrington) [wayn] (1925–94) Writer and critic, born in Stoke-on-Trent, Staffordshire, C England, UK. He studied at Oxford, and lectured in English at Reading (1947–55) before becoming a freelance writer. His novels include *Hurry on Down* (1953) and *The Contenders* (1958), tilting at post-war British social values as viewed by a provincial. He also wrote poetry (*Poems, 1949–79* appeared in 1981), plays, and several books of literary criticism, notably *Preliminary Essays* (1957). He was professor of poetry at Oxford (1973–8). Later books include *Lizzie's Floating Shop* (1981), *Young Shoulders* (1982, Whitbread), and *Comedies* (1990). He also produced two volumes of autobiography, *Sprightly Running* (1982) and *Dear Shadows* (1986).

Waismann, Friedrich [viysman] (1896–1959) Philosopher, born in Vienna, Austria. He became a prominent member of the Vienna Circle, along with Carnap and Schlick, and later taught at Cambridge and Oxford. He argued that most empirical concepts have an 'open texture', in that we cannot completely foresee all the possible conditions in which they might properly be used, and therefore even empirical statements cannot be fully verified by observation. His main philosophical works include *The Principles of Linguistic Philosophy* (1965) and *How I See Philosophy* (1968).

Waitangi, Treaty of [wiytangee] A compact signed by Maori representatives and Governor William Hobson at Waitangi (6 Feb 1840) on the occasion of the British annexation of New Zealand. The legal force of the Treaty, and the obligations it imposed of protecting Maori interests in land, were subsequently denied by a settler-controlled government and judiciary, but this interpretation was reversed in the 1980s. In 1975 a tribunal was set up to hear Maori claims concerning breaches of the Treaty.

Waitangi Day [wiytangee] The national day of New Zealand (6 Feb), commemorating the Treaty of Waitangi made between Britain and the Maori chiefs in 1840.

Waite, Terry [wayt], popular name of **Terence (Hardy) Waite** (1939–) Consultant and former hostage, born in Bollington, Cheshire, NWC England, UK. After several posts as an adviser and administrator for various Church projects, including periods in Africa, in 1980 he became Adviser to the Archbishop of Canterbury on Anglican Communion Affairs. As the Archbishop's special envoy (from 1980), he was particularly involved in negotiations to secure the release of hostages held in the Middle East; between 1982 and the end of 1986, 14 hostages, for whom he was interceding, were released. He was himself kidnapped in Beirut in January 1987 while involved in secret negotiations to win the release of hostages held in Lebanon, and not released until November 1991. A volume of memoirs, *Taken on Trust*, was published in 1993.

Waitz, Grete [viyts], *née* **Andersen** (1953–) Athlete, born in Oslo, Norway. Formerly a track champion at 3000 m, at which she set world records in 1975 and 1976, she was later one of the world's leading female road athletes. The world marathon champion in 1983, and the Olympic silver medallist in 1984, she four times set world best times for the marathon. She won the London Marathon in 1983 and 1986, and the New York marathon a record nine times between 1978 and 1988. She has also been the women's cross-country champion five times (1978–81, 1983).

Wajda, Andrzej [viyda] (1926–) Film director, born in Suwałki, NE Poland. He studied art at the Krakow Academy of Fine Arts, then enrolled in the Łódź film school (1950). His first feature film, *Pokolenie* (1954, A Generation), dealt with the effects of the war on disillusioned Polish youth. He is best known outside Poland for *Czlowiek z marmary* (1977, Man of Marble), dealing with the Stalinist era, and *Czlowiek z zelaza* (1981, Man of Iron, Palme d'Or), which uses film made during the rise of the Solidarity trade union. His works range from romantic comedy to epic, including literary adaptations (such as *Crime and Punishment*, 1984) and World War 2 dramas, such as *Korczak* (1990) and *Holy Week* (1996). He has also worked in television and the theatre. He received an Honorary Award at the 2000 Oscar ceremony.

Wakefield 53°42N 1°29W, pop (2001e) 315 200. Administrative centre of West Yorkshire, N England, UK, on the R Calder, 13 km/8 mi S of Leeds; a woollen centre since the 16th-c; railway; textiles, chemicals, mining machinery, machine tools; site of Battle of Wakefield (1460) in Wars of the Roses.

Wakefield, Edward Gibbon (1796–1862) Originator of subsidized emigration from Britain, born in London, UK. He was imprisoned for tricking an heiress into marriage, and was inspired by the plight of his fellow prisoners to write *A Letter from Sydney* (1829), in which he proposed the sale of small units of crown land in the colonies to subsidize colonization by the poor from Britain (rather than convicts). His proposals (later called *Wakefield settlements*) were adopted in 1831, and in the South Australia Act of 1834. He influenced the South Australian Association (1836), formed the New Zealand Association (1837), and inspired the Durham Report (1839) on colonial affairs in Canada. He emigrated to New Zealand in 1853, and was a member of the General Assembly until a breakdown forced his retirement.

Wakefield settlements Settlements of British migrants founded and organized according to Edward Gibbon Wakefield's ideas of 'systematic colonization'. He proposed (1829) that the revenue from the sale of crown land should be used to finance the migration of suitable workers and their families. The aim was to maintain traditional standards of order and refinement by transplanting a cross-section of English society, and restricting land ownership to the wealthy. The settlements were Adelaide, in Australia; and Wellington, Wanganui, New Plymouth, Nelson, Otago, and Canterbury in New Zealand.

Wake Islands 19°18N 166°36E; pop (2000e) 200; area 10 sq km/4 sq mi. Horseshoe-shaped coral atoll enclosing three islands (Wake, Wilkes, Peale) in C Pacific Ocean, 1200 km/750 mi N of Kwajalein, Marshall Is; annexed by USA, 1898; seaplane base opened, 1935; important for trans-Pacific air flights; under control of US Air Force since 1972.

Waksman, Selman A(braham) [waksman] (1888–1973) Biochemist, born in Priluka (Pryluky), WC Ukraine. He became a US citizen in 1916, and studied at Rutgers University, where he ultimately became professor of soil microbiology in 1930. His research into the breaking down of organic substances by micro-organisms and into antibiotics led to his discovery of streptomycin (1943), the first agent active against tuberculosis, for which he was awarded the Nobel Prize for Physiology or Medicine in 1952.

Walachia *Moldavia and Wallachia*

Walburga, Walpurga, or **Walpurgis, St** *Walpurga*

Walcott, Derek (Alton) [wolkot] (1930–) Poet and playwright, born in Castries, St Lucia, West Indies. He studied at the University of the West Indies, Jamaica, and has lived mostly in Trindad, where he founded the Trindad Theatre Workshop in 1959. He produced three early but assured volumes, *In A Green Night* (1962), *The Castaway* (1965), and *The Gulf* (1969). Later works include *Collected Poems 1948–84* (1986), the epic *Omeros* (1990), *Selected Poetry* (1993), and *The Bounty* (1997). *What the Twilight Says: Essays* appeared in 1998. He was awarded the Nobel Prize for Literature in 1992.

Waldenses or **Waldensians** A small Christian community originating in a reform movement initiated by Peter Waldo at Lyon, France, in the 12th-c. They rejected the authority of the pope, prayers for the dead, and veneration of the saints. Excommunicated and persecuted, they survived through the Middle Ages. After the Reformation, as Protestants, they continued mainly in N Italy, with missions in South America.

Waldheim, Kurt [valthiym] (1918–) Austrian statesman and president (1986–92), born near Vienna. He served on the Russian front, but was wounded and discharged (1942), then studied at Vienna, and entered the Austrian foreign service (1945). He became minister and then ambassador to Canada (1955–60), director of political affairs at the ministry (1960–4), Austrian representative at the UN (1964–8, 1970–1), foreign minister (1968–70), and UN secretary-general (1972–81). His presidential candidature was controversial, because of claims that he had lied about his wartime activities and been involved in anti-Jewish and other atrocities while serving as a lieutenant in the Wehrmacht (1942–5), but he denied the allegations and, despite international pressure, continued successfully with his campaign. In June 1991, amid continuing controversy, he decided not to stand again for president after serving his term.

Waler A breed of horse, developed in the 19th-c in Australia, especially New South Wales (hence the name); a riding horse, developed by cross-breeding various imported breeds; strong with good stamina.

Wales

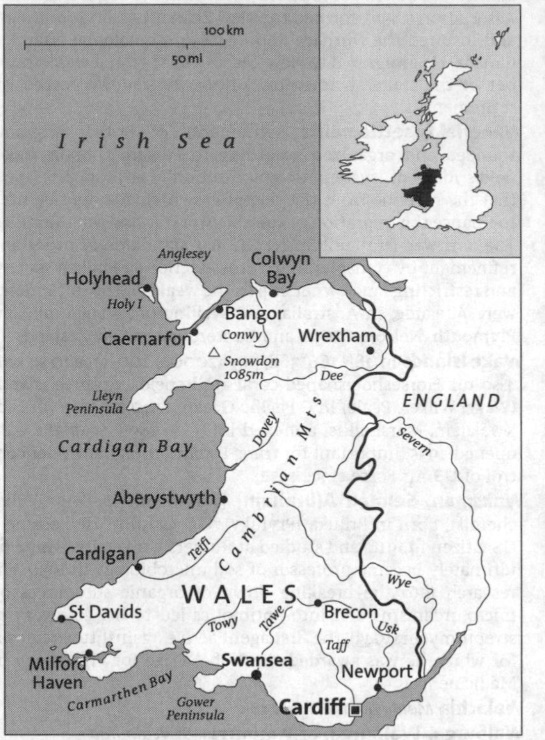

□ International Airport

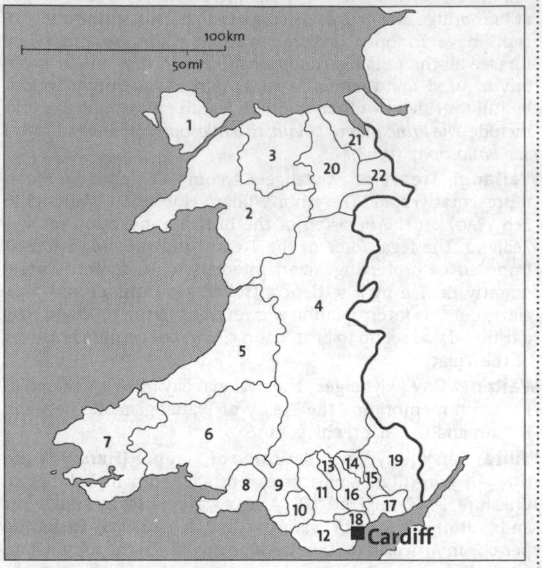

1 Anglesey
2 Gwynedd
3 Conwy
4 Powys
5 Cardiganshire
6 Carmarthenshire
7 Pembrokeshire
8 Swansea
9 Neath & Port Talbot
10 Bridgend
11 Rhondda Cynon Taff
12 Vale of Glamorgan
13 Merthyr Tydfil
14 Blaenau Gwent
15 Torfaen
16 Caerphilly
17 Newport
18 Cardiff
19 Monmouthshire
20 Denbighshire
21 Flintshire
22 Wrexham

Welsh **Cymru [kuhmree]** (UK)

Local name Cymru (Welsh)

Area 20 761 km²/8014 sq mi

Population total (2001e) 2 903 100

Status Principality (Constituent part of the United Kingdom)

Capital Cardiff

Languages English, Welsh

Physical features Situated on the W coast of the UK, divided into 8 counties since 1974; includes the island of Anglesey off the NW coast; land rises to 1085 m/3560 ft at Snowdon (NW), also Cambrian Mts (C); Brecon Beacons (S); drained by the Severn, Clwyd, Dee, Conwy, Dovey, Taff, Towy, and Wye rivers.

Economy Coal; slate, lead, steel; industrialized S valleys and coastal plain; tourism in N and NW; ferries to Ireland at Holyhead, Fishguard; important source of water for England.

History Rhodri Mawr united Wales against Saxons, Norse, and Danes, 9th-c; Edward I of England established authority over Wales, building several castles, 12th–13th-c; Edward I's son created first Prince of Wales, 1301; 14th-c revolt under Owen Glendower; politically united with England by Act of Union, 1535; centre of Non-conformist religion since 18th-c; University of Wales, 1893, with constituent colleges; political nationalist movement (Plaid Cymru) returned first MP, 1966; Welsh television channel; 1979 referendum opposed devolution; successful referendum for devolved Welsh Assembly, 1997; Welsh Assembly, 1999.

Name / Area (km² / sq mi) / Population total (2000e) / Admin centre

Conwy / 1130 / 436 / 111 800 / Colwyn Bay
Anglesey / 719 / 277 / 67 900 / Llangefni
Blaenau Gwent / 109 / 42 / 74 000 / Ebbw Vale
Bridgend / 246 / 95 / 132 200 / Bridgend
Caerphilly / 729 / 108 / 172 700 / Hengoed
Cardiff / 139 / 54 / 312 100 / Cardiff
Cardiganshire / 1797 / 694 / 70 400 / Aberystwyth
Carmarthenshire / 2398 / 926 / 170 700 / Carmarthen
Denbighshire / 844 / 326 / 92 200 / Ruthin
Flintshire / 437 / 169 / 146 800 / Mold
Gwynedd / 3869 / 1494 / 119 200 / Caernarfon
Merthyr Tydfil / 111 / 43 / 60 100 Merthyr Tydfil
Monmouthshire / 851/ 328 / 85 000 / Cwmbran
Neath and Port Talbot / 442 / 171 / 141 500 / Port Talbot
Newport / 191 / 74 / 138 800 / Newport
Pembrokeshire / 1590 / 614 / 114 700 / Haverfordwest
Powys / 5204 / 2009 / 123 200 / Llandrindod Wells
Rhondda, Cynon Taff / 424 / 164 / 241 400 / Cardiff (temporary)
Swansea / 378 / 164 / 233 000 / Swansea
Torfaen / 12649 / 91 500 / Pontypool
Vale of Glamorgan / 337 / 130 / 120 300 / Barry
Wrexham / 499 / 130 / 124 600 / Wrexham

Wales *see panel*

Wales, Princess of *Diana, Princess of Wales*

Wałęsa, Lech [vawensa] (1943–) Polish president (1990–5) and former trade unionist, born in Popowo, N Poland. A Gdańsk shipyard worker, he became leader of the independent trade union, Solidarity, which openly challenged the Polish government's economic and social policies. He held negotiations with the leading figures in the Church and State, but was detained by the authorities when martial law was declared in 1981. He was released in 1982, and was awarded the Nobel Peace Prize in 1983. He continued to be a prominent figure in Polish politics, and was much involved in the negotiations which led to Solidarity being involved in government in 1989. When the constitution was amended (1990) to allow free presidential elections, Wałęsa gained a landslide victory. He was defeated by Alexander Kwasniewski in 1995.

Walker, Alice (Malsenior) (1944–) Novelist and poet, born in Eatonville, Georgia, USA. She studied at Spelman College, Atlanta, and Sarah Lawrence College, then worked as a social worker, teacher, and lecturer. An accomplished poet, she is best known for her novels, notably *The Color Purple* (1982, Pulitzer), later made into a successful film, which tells the story of two black sisters in the segregated world of the Deep South. Later novels include *Possessing the Secret of Joy* (1992) and *By the Light of My Father's Smile* (1998). She has also written volumes of short stories and essays, including *You Can't Keep a Good Woman Down* (1981) and *In Search of My Mother's Garden* (1983).

Walker, John E (1941–) Chemist, born in Halifax, West Yorkshire. He studied at Oxford, then worked at the Molecular Biology Laboratory in Cambridge. He shared the 1997 Nobel Prize for Chemistry for his contribution towards the elucidation of the enzymatic mechanism underlying the synthesis of adenosine triphosphate.

walking Either a leisurely pursuit, or a competitive sport, also known as **race walking**. As a sport, both road and track race walking are popular. The rules governing the use of the feet are strict: one foot must be touching the ground at all times, and the lead leg must be straight as it passes under the torso. It has been an Olympic event since 1956, over distances of 20 km (12·4 mi) and 50 km (31 mi). **Fell walking** is a popular form of leisure activity in the UK.

walking stick *stick insect*

Walkley Award Annual awards in recognition of excellence in Australian journalism, established in 1956 by Sir William Gaston Walkley, founder of Ampol Petroleum in Australia. The prestigious awards now cover more than 30 categories. In 2000 the federal council of the Media, Entertainment and Arts Alliance formally established the Walkley Foundation for Journalism.

wallaby *kangaroo*

Wallace, Alfred Russel (1823–1913) Naturalist, born in Usk, Monmouthshire, SE Wales, UK. He travelled and collected plant samples in the Amazon (1842–52) and the Malay Archipelago (1854–62), and propounded a theory of evolution by natural selection independently of Darwin. His memoir, sent to Darwin in 1858 from the Moluccas, formed an important part of the Linnaean Society meeting which first promulgated the theory, modifying and hastening the publication of Darwin's *The Origin of Species*. Wallace contributed greatly to the scientific foundations of zoogeography, including his proposal for the evolutionary distinction between the fauna of Australia and Asia (**Wallace's line**).

Wallace, (Richard Horatio) Edgar (1875–1932) Writer of crime novels, born in London, UK. He served in the army in South Africa, where he later (1899) became a journalist, and in 1905 published his first success, the adventure story *The Four Just Men*. He wrote over 170 novels and plays, and is best remembered for his crime novels, such as *The Clue of the Twisted Candle*. He later became a film scriptwriter. His autobiography, *People*, appeared in 1926.

Wallace, Lew(is) (1827–1905) Writer and soldier, born in Brookville, Indiana, USA. He served in the Mexican War (1846–8) and with distinction as a major-general in the Federal army in the American Civil War (1861–5). Governor of New Mexico (1878–81) and minister to Turkey (1881–5), he was author of several novels, including the remarkably successful religious novel *Ben Hur* (1880), which has twice formed the subject of a spectacular film.

Wallace, Sir William (c.1270–1305) Scottish knight and champion of the independence of Scotland, probably born in Elderslie, Renfrewshire, W Scotland, UK. He routed the English army at Stirling Bridge (1297), and was knighted. He was given control of the government of Scotland as 'Guardian' in the name of the Scottish king imprisoned by Edward I of England, but was defeated by Edward at Falkirk (1298). He was eventually captured near Glasgow (1305), and executed in London. Many legends soon collected around him due to his immense popular appeal as a national figure resisting foreign oppression, and these were the subject of the Oscar-winning film, *Braveheart* (1995).

Wallachia [wolaykia] *Moldavia and Wallachia*

wallaroo A kangaroo with a shaggy coat and naked muzzle; two species: the solitary **wallaroo**, **euro**, or **hill kangaroo** (*Macropus robustus*) from rocky hill regions, and the **antilopine wallaroo** (*Macropus antilopinus*), which occurs in groups ('mobs') on N Australian grassland.

wallcreeper A nuthatch-like bird (*Tichodroma muraria*), native to S Europe and Asia; blue-grey with broad red and white wings; bill long, slender, curved; inhabits rocky areas of high mountains; eats insects and spiders. (Family: Tichodromadidae.)

Wallenstein or **Waldstein, Albrecht (Wenzel Eusebius), Herzog von** (Duke of) [wolenstiyn], Ger [valenshtiyn] (1583–1634) Bohemian general, born in Heřmanice, NW Czech Republic. During the Thirty Years' War he became commander of the imperial armies and won a series of victories (1625–9), gaining the titles of Duke of Mecklenburg and 'General of the Baltic and Oceanic Seas'. His ambition led to his dismissal in 1630, but he was reinstated to defend the empire against Swedish attack. He recovered Bohemia, but was defeated by Gustav II Adolf at Lützen (1632), and was again dismissed. His intrigues led to an imperial proclamation of treason, resulting in his assassination at Eger by Irish mercenaries.

Waller, Edmund (1606–87) Poet and politician, born in Coleshill, Buckinghamshire, SC England, UK. He studied at Cambridge, became an MP in 1621, and was a member of the Long Parliament in 1640. In 1643 he plunged into a conspiracy (**Waller's plot**) against parliament, was arrested, and banished, but returned to England in 1651. His collected poems were published in 1645, among them his well-known pieces, 'On a Girdle' and 'Go, lovely Rose!'. Waller was one of the first poets to write in heroic couplets in English, a form that was to prevail for some 200 years.

Waller, Fats, popular name of **Thomas Wright Waller** (1904–43) Jazz pianist, organist, singer, and songwriter, born in New York City, USA. He performed with such ebullience, frequently parodying songs and styles, that it was sometimes hard for audiences to see him as more than a buffoon. A brilliant piano player in the stride tradition, he was a natural songwriter, as seen in such hits as 'Ain't Misbehavin'' (1929) and 'Keeping Out of Mischief Now' (1932). He is rumoured to have written many more standards, among them 'On the Sunny Side of the Street', and then sold the rights for quick cash. He died of pneumonia on his way to Kansas City from Los Angeles, while entertaining soldiers at training camps.

walleye Large, freshwater fish (*Stizostedion vitreum*) related to the zander, found in rivers and lakes of E North America; length up to 90 cm/3 ft; feeds mainly on small fishes and crustaceans; an excellent food fish and sport fish. (Family: Percidae.)

wallflower A perennial reaching 20–60 cm/8–24 in (*Cheiranthus cheiri*), native to the E Mediterranean; stem slightly woody at base; leaves lance-shaped, crowded on stem; flowers yellow to orange-red, fragrant. Cultivars have a wide colour range and are grown as biennials. (Family: Cruciferae.)

Wallis, Sir Barnes (Neville) (1887–1979) Aeronautical engineer and inventor, born in Ripley, Derbyshire, C England, UK. He trained as a marine engineer, and became a designer in the airship department of Vickers, where he designed the R100. His many successes include the design of the Wellington Bomber, the bombs which destroyed the German warship Tirpitz and V-rocket sites, and the 'bouncing bombs' which destroyed the Mohne and Eder dams. He later became chief of aeronautical research at the British Aircraft Corporation, Weybridge (1945–71), and in the 1950s designed the first swing-wing aircraft. He was knighted in 1968.

Wallis, John (1616–1703) The leading English mathematician before Isaac Newton, born in Ashford, Kent, SE England, UK.

He studied at Cambridge, and took orders, but in 1649 became professor of geometry at Oxford. His *Arithmetica infinitorum* (1655, The Arithmetic of Infinitesimals) was a stimulus for Newton's work on calculus and the binomial theorem. He also wrote on proportion, mechanics, grammar, logic, decipherment (he deciphered encrypted messages intercepted from Royalist supporters), theology, and the teaching of the deaf. He was one of the founders of the Royal Society.

Wallis and Futuna Islands, official name **Territory of the Wallis and Futuna Islands** pop (2000e) 15 300; area 274 sq km/106 sq mi. Island group in the SC Pacific Ocean, NE of Fiji; a French overseas territory comprising the Wallis Is and the Hooru Is, 230 km/140 mi apart; capital, Matu Utu on Uvéa; chief ethnic group, Polynesian; chief religion, Roman Catholicism; unit of currency, the euro; Wallis Is (area 159 sq km/61 sq mi) include Uvéa, rising to 145 m/476 ft at Mt Lulu, ringed by low-lying coral reefs; Hooru Is (115 sq km/44 sq mi) include Futuna and Alofi, mountainous and volcanic; Futuna rises to 765 m/2510 ft at Mt Puke; Alofi is uninhabited; warm and damp climate, with a cyclone season (Oct–Mar); French protectorate, 1842; overseas territory of France, 1961; governed by an administrator, assisted by an elected 20-member Territorial Assembly; subsistence farming, fishing, copra, yams, taro roots, bananas, timber.

Wallonia French-speaking region of S Belgium; pop (2000e) 3 246 000. Walloons (36% of Belgian population); dividing line with Flanders to the N; many towns renowned for their art treasures (Tournai, Huy, Namur, Liège); steel, engineering.

Walloon *Fleming and Walloon*

Wall Street A street in New York City, USA, where the New York Stock Exchange and other major financial institutions are located. The road follows what once was the walled N boundary of the original Dutch colony.

walnut A deciduous, spreading tree (*Juglans regia*), growing to 30 m/100 ft, native to the Balkans, and widely planted and naturalized elsewhere; leaves pinnate with 7–9 pairs of elliptical leaflets; male flowers in catkins on old wood, females in clusters on new wood; fruit 4–5 cm/1½–2 in, smooth, green. The wrinkled woody seed is the familiar walnut. The timber is used commercially, especially for furniture. (Family: Juglandaceae.)

Walpole, Horace or **Horatio, 4th Earl of Orford** (1717–97) Writer, born in London, UK, the youngest son of Sir Robert Walpole. At Cambridge he had the poet Thomas Gray as a friend, with whom he embarked on the 'Grand Tour' of Europe (1739). He returned to England in 1741, and entered parliament for an undistinguished career. After his father's death he purchased a small villa which he gradually 'gothicized' (1753–76) into the stuccoed and battlemented pseudo-castle of Strawberry Hill, and where he established a private press. His house brought about a Gothic architectural revival, and his *The Castle of Otranto* (1764) initiated a vogue for Gothic romances. His literary reputation rests chiefly upon his letters, which deal, in the most vivacious way, with party politics, foreign affairs, literature, art, and gossip. His firsthand accounts in them of such events as the Jacobite trials after the 1745 Rising and the Gordon Riots are invaluable.

Walpole, Sir Hugh (Seymour) (1884–1941) Writer, born in Auckland, New Zealand. He studied at Durham and Cambridge universities, became a teacher, then an author. His many novels were very popular during his lifetime, and include *The Secret City* (1919), *The Cathedral* (1922), and the four-volume family saga, *The Herries Chronicle* (1930–3). He was knighted in 1937.

Walpole, Sir Robert, 1st Earl of Orford (1676–1745) English statesman, and leading minister (1721–42) of George I and George II, born in Houghton, Norfolk, E England, UK. He studied at Cambridge, became a Whig MP in 1701, and was made secretary for war (1708) and treasurer of the Navy (1710). Sent to the Tower for alleged corruption during the Tory government (1712), he was recalled by George I, and made a privy councillor and (1715) Chancellor of the Exchequer. After the collapse of the South Sea Scheme, he again became chancellor (1721), and was widely recognized as 'prime minister', a title (unknown to the Constitution) which he hotly repudiated. A shrewd manipulator of men, he took trouble to consult backbench MPs, and followed policies of low taxation designed to win their favour. He was regarded as indispensible by both George I and George II. His popularity began to wane in the 1730s over the Excise Scheme and also over his determination to avoid foreign wars. He did not fully recover from the outbreak of a war he had opposed in 1739, and resigned in 1742. His period in office is widely held to have increased the influence of the House of Commons in the Constitution. He was knighted in 1725, and created an earl in 1742.

Walpurga, Walburga, or **Walpurgis, St** [valpoorga] (c.710–c.777) Abbess and missionary, born in Wessex, England. She joined St Boniface on his mission to Germany, and became Abbess of Heidenheim, where she died. Her relics were transferred (c.870) to Eichstätt. **Walpurgisnacht** (the eve of St Walpurgis, 30 Apr) arises because popular superstition coincidentally regards the night before the day of the transfer of her remains (1 May) as one when large numbers of witches fly. Feast day 25 February.

walrus A marine mammal (*Odobenus rosmarus*) of family Odobenidae; resembles a large sea-lion with a broad bristly snout; canine teeth enormous, forming tusks; skin with little hair; inhabits coastal Arctic waters; eats mainly clams.

Walsingham, Sir Francis [wolsingam] (c.1530–90) English statesman, born in Chislehurst, Kent, SE England, UK. He studied at Cambridge, became a diplomat, and was made a secretary of state to Elizabeth I (1573–90), a member of the Privy Council, and knighted. A Puritan sympathizer, and a strong opponent of the Catholics, he developed a complex system of espionage at home and abroad, enabling him to reveal the plots of Throckmorton and Babington against the Queen, and was one of the commissioners to try Mary at Fotheringay. In his last months he increasingly took up religious meditation.

Walter, Bruno [valter], originally **Bruno Walter Schlesinger** (1876–1962) Conductor, born in Berlin, Germany. As a teenager, he conducted at Cologne, then worked with Mahler in Hamburg and Vienna. He was in charge of Munich Opera (1913–22), and from 1919 was chief conductor of the Berlin Philharmonic. International tours won him a great British and American reputation. Driven from both Germany and Austria by the Nazis, he settled in the USA, where he became chief conductor of the New York Philharmonic in 1951.

Walter, Hubert (c.1140–1205) English clergyman and statesman. He became Bishop of Salisbury (1189), and accompanied Richard I on the Third Crusade (1190–3). Appointed Archbishop of Canterbury in 1193, he played key roles in raising the ransom to secure Richard's release from captivity, and in containing the rebellion of the king's brother, John. At the end of 1193, he became justiciar of England, and was responsible for all the business of government until his resignation in 1198. On John's accession (1199), he became chancellor, and was consulted on important matters of state. He was the first English statesman to tax revenue for secular purposes.

Walter, Harriet (Mary) (1956–) British actress. After training at the London Academy of Music and Drama she gained early experience with the Joint Stock touring theatre company, Paine's Plough (touring), and the Duke's Playhouse, Lancaster. She has frequently worked with the Royal Shakespeare Company, becoming an associate artist in 1987. Her films include *Sense and Sensibility* (1996), *Bedrooms and Hallways* (1998), *Onegin* (1999), *Villa des Roses* (2002), and *Bright Young Things* (2003). Her Shakespearian stage roles include Lady Macbeth (1999) and Beatrice (2002). She is an associate artist with Peter Hall's Cannon's Mouth theatre company.

Walter, John (1739–1812) Printer and newspaper publisher, born in London, UK. In 1784 he acquired a printing office in Blackfriars, London, the nucleus of the later Printing House Square buildings, and in 1785 founded *The Daily Universal Register* newspaper, which in 1788 was renamed *The Times*. His son, **John** (1776–1847) managed the paper from 1802 to 1847, followed by his grandson.

Walther von der Vogelweide [valter fon der **fohg**lviyduh] (c.1170–1230) German lyric poet. In 1190–8 he was in high favour at the court of Austria, and was later at Mainz and Magdeburg. In 1204 he outshone his rivals in the great contest at the Wartburg. He first sided with the Guelphs, but made friends with the victorious Hohenstaufen, Frederick II, who gave him a small estate. He wrote political, religious, and didactic poems, and a wide range of love poems.

Walton, Izaak (1593–1683) Writer, born in Stafford, Staffordshire, C England, UK. In 1621 he settled in London as an ironmonger, but left the city for Staffordshire during the Civil War, and after the Restoration lived in Winchester. Best known for his treatise on fishing and country life, *The Compleat Angler* (1653), he also wrote several biographies.

Walton, Sir William (Turner) (1902–83) Composer, born in Oldham, Lancashire, NW England, UK. He studied at Oxford, where he wrote his first compositions, and became known through his instrumental setting of poems by Edith Sitwell, *Façade* (1923). His works include two symphonies, concertos for violin, viola, and cello, the biblical cantata *Belshazzar's Feast* (1931), and the opera *Troilus and Cressida* (1954). He is also known for his film music, notably for Olivier's *Henry V*, *Hamlet*, and *Richard III*. He was knighted in 1951.

waltz A dance in triple time, originating in Austria and S Germany, which supplanted the minuet and the *Deutsche* (German Dance) to become the most popular ballroom dance in 19th-c Europe – despite the initial shock caused by the requirement that the man should grasp his female partner at the waist. Austrian composer and violinist Joseph Lanner (1801–43) and the Strauss family established the style in Vienna, its most distinctive musical feature being an accompaniment of a low note on the first beat, and a repeated chord in the inner parts on the second and third. The *English* or *Boston* waltz carries a more even emphasis on all three beats. The modern waltz uses a slower tempo.

Walvis Bay [**wol**vis], Afrikaans **Walvisbaai** 22°59S 14°31E, pop (2000e) 35 000. Seaport in WC Namibia; on the Atlantic Ocean coast, 275 km/171 mi WSW of Windhoek; Walvis Bay enclave (area 1124 sq km/434 sq mi) formerly administered by South Africa as part of Cape Province; annexed by the Dutch, 1792; taken by Britain, 1878; incorporated into Cape Colony, 1884; a South African enclave after Namibian independence; transferred to Namibia, 1994; airfield; railway terminus; handles most of Namibia's trade; fishing.

wampum [**wom**puhm] Beads used as a form of exchange, mnemonic devices, and guarantees of promises by certain Iroquois-speaking North American Indian groups, and later in trade with Europeans. They were made of bits of seashells cut, drilled, and strung into belts or strands.

Wanamaker, Sam [**won**amayker] (1919–93) Actor and director, born in Chicago, Illinois, USA. He studied at Drake University, IA, then trained at Goodman Theatre, Chicago, worked with summer stock companies in Chicago as an actor and director, and made his London debut in 1952. In 1957, he was appointed director of the New Shakespeare Theatre, Liverpool, and in 1959 joined the Shakespeare Memorial Theatre company at Stratford-upon-Avon. He produced or directed several works at Covent Garden and elsewhere in the 1960s and 1970s, including the Shakespeare Birthday Celebrations in 1974. He worked both as director and actor in films and television, his appearances included *Spiral Staircase* (1974), *Private Benjamin* (1980), *Superman IV* (1986), and *Baby Boom* (1988). In 1970 he founded the Globe Theatre Trust, a project to build a replica of Shakespeare's Globe Theatre near its original site on Bankside in London; it was officially opened in 1997.

wandering Jew A species of tradescantia (*Tradescantia fluminensis*) with variegated leaves. It is a popular house plant. (Family: Commelinaceae.)

Wandering Jew A character in Christian legend who taunted Christ as he carried his cross, and was condemned to wander the Earth until the end of the world or until Christ's second coming. Various Jews, notably Ahasuerus of Hamburg in 1602, have been identified with the character, who has been seen as a symbol of the Diaspora of the Jewish people.

wandering sailor A species of tradescantia (*Tradescantia blossfeldiana*), with leaves maroon on undersides. It is a popular house plant. (Family: Commelinaceae.)

Wanganui, River [wanga**noo**ee] River in W North Island, New Zealand; rises NW of L Taupo, then flows S to enter the Tasman Sea 195 km/121 mi N of Wellington; length 290 km/180 mi; longest navigable river in New Zealand; paddle-boats visit a local winery; town of Wanganui near the mouth, pop (2000e) 46 000, an outdoor resort area and agricultural centre.

Wang Jingwei [wang jingway] (1883–1944) Associate of the revolutionary and Nationalist leader Sun Yixian (Sun Yatsen), born in Guangzhou (Canton), SE China. He studied in Japan, where he joined Sun's Revolutionary Party, and from 1917 became his personal assistant. In 1927 he was appointed head of the new Nationalist government at Wuhan, and in 1932 became titular head of the Nationalist Party. In 1938, after the outbreak of war with Japan, he offered to co-operate with the Japanese, and in 1940 became head of a puppet regime ruling the occupied areas.

Wankel engine [**vang**kl] A particular form of internal combustion engine whose piston rotates about a horizontal axis in a specially shaped combustion chamber, rather than oscillating within a cylinder, as in a conventional internal combustion engine. Although not the only type of rotary piston engine, the Wankel engine has been mass-produced for use in motor cars, and is the best-known example. Particular problems related to sealing and reliability have been overcome, but to date it has not achieved widespread application. It is named after its designer, German engineer Felix Wankel (1902–88).

wapiti [**wop**itee] *red deer*

war A military conflict between two or more states, or, in the case of civil war, between different groups within a state. International war is subject to international law, and wars can be either lawful or unlawful. There have been a series of treaties since the 18th-c covering the conduct of war, largely designed to prevent 'unnecessary suffering', or action that has no military advantage. The most influential theoretician of war until the advent of nuclear warfare was the Prussian general Carl von Clausewitz, whose major publication *On War* (1833) maintained that 'war is nothing but a continuation of political intercourse with the admixture of other means'. The use of more overtly ideological wars and modern weapons have made it more difficult to regulate the conduct of war (eg greater difficulty in protecting civilians from aerial bombardment). Today the main source of international law on war or the use of force is the United Nations Charter, notably article 2(4). Distinctions are also now drawn between **conventional warfare**, which does not involve the use of nuclear weapons, **nuclear warfare**, **chemical warfare**, and **biological warfare**. A **guerrilla war** is conducted by non-regular forces, often avoiding direct engagement, designed to make a state ungovernable prior to a seizure of power.

Warbeck, Perkin (c.1474–99) Pretender to the English throne, born in Tournai, W Belgium. In 1492 he was persuaded by enemies of Henry VII to impersonate Richard, Duke of York, the younger of the two sons of Edward IV who had been murdered in the Tower of London (1483). With the promise of support from many quarters in England, Ireland, Scotland, and on the European mainland, he made two unsuccessful attempts to invade England (1495–6), and was captured at Beaulieu during a third attempt (1497). Imprisoned in the Tower, he was executed after trying to escape.

warble fly A small, robust fly; larvae live as parasites under the skin of mammals, feeding on fluids exuding from tissues, and causing swellings (*warbles*) under the skin; some species important as pests of domesticated animals. (Order: Diptera. Family: Oestridae, c.60 species.)

warbler A songbird of the families Sylviidae (**Old World warblers**, 350 species), Parulidae (**American warblers** or **wood warblers**, 114 species), Acanthizidae (**Australian warblers**, 65 species), or Maluridae (**Australian wren-warblers**, 26 species). The name is also used for the **warbler-finch** (one of Darwin's finches).

Ward, Artemus *Browne, Charles Farrar*

Ward, Dame Barbara (Mary), Baroness Jackson of Lodsworth (1914–81) Journalist, economist, and conservationist, born in York, North Yorkshire, N England, UK. She studied at Oxford, became foreign editor of *The Economist*, and was a prolific and popular writer on politics, economics, and ecology. Her books include *The International Share Out* (1936), *Spaceship Earth* (1966), and *Only One Earth* (1972). She was created a dame in 1974, and became a life peer in 1976.

Ward, Judith (Minna) (1949–) Victim of a miscarriage of justice. She was convicted and jailed for life in 1974 in England for the M62 coach-bombing by the IRA in which 12 people died. She served 18 years before having her conviction quashed by the Court of Appeal in 1992, on the basis that there had been a substantial miscarriage of justice in relation to forensic evidence.

wardship proceedings Proceedings whereby the custody of a person under the age of 18 living in England and Wales, or an English subject living outside the jurisdiction of the English courts, is transferred to the Family Division of the High Court, who are thereafter empowered to make decisions in respect of the child. The child's welfare is the primary consideration. Proceedings can be initiated by a variety of individuals, but they must have some relationship to the child (eg parents, foster parents, or the local authority). Being made a **ward of court** results in all major decisions in a child's life being subject to the approval of the court. These include marrying, leaving the court's jurisdiction, adoption, psychiatric examination, blood tests, nontherapeutic medical treatment, and abortion. The wardship may be ended by a court order or on the child becoming 18. Since the Children Act (1989), the use of wardship proceedings is less necessary. Its more valuable features are incorporated into the act, and wardship and local authority care are incompatible. In most cases, the child's interests are not best served by wardship proceedings; a contact order or similar order under section 8 of the Children Act would be favoured. However, in exceptional cases, for instance where there is a foreign element or where abortion is involved, wardship procecedings are still used. Wardship proceedings do not exist in all jurisdictions (eg Scotland).

warez [wairz] Illegally copied or pirated software. This is usually computer application software, but may be any pirated digital media. Typically, a website devoted to warez downloads might contain software, music files, and copyrighted images. There is a tendency among the distributors of warez to append a 'z' to any word to denote its illegal provenance. Thus there are websites containing 'tunez', 'filez', or 'crackz'.

warfarin [waw(r)farin] An anticoagulant, sometimes used therapeutically to dissolve blood clots. It is a member of the *coumarin* class of anticoagulants. Coumarins were discovered in the 1920s, following the observation that cattle feeding on a certain type of hay – later found to contain dicoumarol – were prone to prolonged bleeding when injured, as well as to spontaneous haemorrhages. The name warfarin is an acronym of the original patent holder, Wisconsin Alumni Research Foundation, plus the suffix *arin* (from coumarin). Warfarin is also used as a rat poison: rats accumulate the poison and eventually die from internal haemorrhage. However, colonies of rats have recently become resistant to warfarin. Accidental poisoning with warfarin can be treated with vitamin K.

Warhol, Andy [waw(r)hohl], originally **Andrew Warhola** (1927–87) Pop artist and film-maker, born in Pittsburgh, Pennsylvania, USA. He studied art in New York City, and worked as a commercial designer before becoming a pioneer of 'Pop Art' (1961), with brightly coloured exact reproductions of familiar everyday objects, such as the famous soup-can label. His first films, such as the three-hour silent observation of a sleeping man, *Sleep* (1963), developed into technically more complex work, though still without plot, as seen in *Chelsea Girls* (1966). After 1968, when he was shot and seriously wounded by one of his starlets, control of his films was passed to others. Later films with which he was associated include *Flesh for Frankenstein* (1973) and *Blood for Dracula* (1974). He also turned to portrait painting in the 1970s. The Andy Warhol Museum opened in Pittsburgh in 1994.

Warlock, Peter, pseudonym of **Philip Arnold Heseltine** (1894–1930) Musicologist and composer, born in London, UK. Largely self-taught, in 1920 he founded *The Sackbut*, a spirited musical periodical. His works include the song cycle *The Curlew* (1920–2), the orchestral suite *Capriol* (1926), many songs, often in the Elizabethan manner, and choral works.

warlords Chinese provincial military rulers who engaged in a bitter power struggle and civil war after the death of Yuan Shikai in 1916. They were partially subdued by the Northern Expedition of Jiang Jieshi in 1927, though substantial local power remained. Chinese warlordism may be traced back to the 5th-c BC. The term has more recently been used for local military leaders in Afghanistan, Angola, Bosnia, and Somalia.

Warlpiri The dominant language of the central desert of Australia. Warlpiri country was colonized by cattle stations (ranches) during the early 20th-c. Resistance culminated in the Coniston massacre of 1928, after which many Warlpiri sought work looking after cattle. Some cattle stations are now Aboriginal-owned. The principle Warlpiri settlement is Yuendumu, NW of Alice Springs.

warm bloodedness *homoiothermy*

Warne, Shane, popular name of **Shane Keith Warne** (1969–) Cricketer, born in Melbourne, Victoria, SE Australia. A hugely charismatic leg-spinner, his mix of acute spin and control has made him highly effective, particularly against England. His total of 501 wickets (average 25·51) in 108 Tests up to March 2004 made him the first spin bowler to take 500 Test wickets. He was man-of-the-match in the semi-final and final of the 1999 World Cup, and in 2000 was named as one of Wisden's Five Cricketers of the Century. In 2003 he received a one-year ban for drug-related offences.

Warner, Jack, originally **Jack Leonard Eichelbaum** (1892–1978) Film mogul, born in London, Ontario, SE Canada. In partnership with his older brothers **Harry** (1881–1958), **Albert** (1884–1967), and **Sam** (1887–1927), after a period in film exhibition and distribution, he moved into production and set up studios in 1923. The Warners were the first to introduce sound into their films, and the success of *The Jazz Singer* (1927) led to great expansion in both cinema ownership and studio resources, until the US Anti-Trust Laws in the 1950s forced them to dispose of their theatres. Jack had always been the one most directly concerned with actual film creation, and he continued to supervise major productions such as *My Fair Lady* (1964) and *Camelot* (1967), but when he became the last surviving brother, he sold his interest and the name to the Canadian company, Seven Arts.

Warnock (of Weeke), (Helen) Mary Warnock, Baroness, *née* **Wilson** (1924–) Philosopher and educationist. She studied at Oxford, and became a fellow and tutor in philosophy at St Hugh's College, Oxford (1949–66, 1976–84). She has taken part in and chaired several important committees of inquiry: special education (1974–8), animal experiments (1979–85), human fertilization (1982–4, regarding *in-vitro* fertilization and human embryo experiments), higher education (1984), teaching quality (1990), and bioethics (1992–4). She was made a life peer in 1985.

War of 1812 (1812–14) A war between Britain and the USA, declared by the latter on the basis of British conduct towards neutral US shipping during the Napoleonic Wars. Expectations of conquest were also important. Fought at sea, along the Canadian border, in Chesapeake Bay, and on the lower Mississippi, it brought the British capture and burning of Washington, DC, and the bombardment of Baltimore. US victories in several sea duels and at New Orleans (fought after the Treaty of Ghent had restored peace) became central elements in the US military self-image.

War of Independence, US *American Revolution*

War of the Pacific (1879–83) A war fought by Chile with Peru and Bolivia (in alliance since 1873) and arising out of Chilean grievances in the Atacama desert, then Bolivian-held. Chile won command of the sea in the early months of the war, and sent large expeditions to Peru, occupying the capital, Lima (Jan 1881). Peace treaties with Peru (1883) and Bolivia (1904) gave Chile large territorial gains.

warranty *condition*

Warren, Earl (1891–1974) US Republican politician and judge, born in Los Angeles, California, USA. He studied at the University of California, practised law, and served successively in California as state attorney general and governor (1943–53). He was then appointed chief justice of the US Supreme Court (1953–69). He led a number of notably liberal decisions, such as ending segregation in schools (*Brown* v. *Board of Education of Topeka*, 1954), guaranteeing the right to counsel in criminal cases, and protecting accused persons from police abuses. He headed the Commission which investigated the assassination of President John F Kennedy (1963–4) and concluded that the killing was not part of a domestic or foreign conspiracy.

Warren, Robert Penn (1905–89) Writer and poet, born in Guthrie, Kentucky, USA. He studied at Vanderbilt, Berkeley, and Yale universities, and was a Rhodes scholar at Oxford. He became professor of English at Louisiana, Minnesota, and Yale. Recipient of two Pulitzer Prizes (for fiction in 1947, for poetry in 1958), he established an international reputation with his political novel, *All the King's Men* (1943, Pulitzer, filmed 1949). Other works include *Night Rider* (1939), *Wilderness* (1961), and *Meet Me in the Green Glen* (1971). He also published some volumes of short stories, and verse including *Rumour Verified* (1981).

Warrington 53°24N 2°37W, pop (2001e) 191 100. Town in Cheshire, NWC England, UK; on the R Mersey, 25 km/15 mi SW of Manchester; designated a 'new town' in 1968; unitary authority from 1998; railway; engineering, brewing, distilling, tanning, wire, chemicals, soap.

Warsaw, Polish **Warszawa** 52°15N 21°00E, pop (2000e) 1 665 000. River-port capital of Poland, on R Vistula, on the Mazovian plain; city centre is a world heritage site; established, 13th-c; capital of the Duchy of Mazovia, 1413; capital of Poland, 1596; occupied by Germany in both World Wars; Jewish ghetto established in 1940, with uprising and death of most residents in 1943; largely destroyed in World War 2; post-war reconstruction of the mediaeval old town followed the pre-war street pattern; airport; railway; Polish Academy of Sciences; two universities (1818, 1945); steel, metallurgy, machinery, electrical engineering, clothing, food processing, pharmaceuticals, printing; restored 14th-c Cathedral of St John, royal castle, Adam Mickiewicz museum of literature, Łazienkowski Palace; international book fair (May), folk fair (May), modern music festival (Sep), international Chopin piano competitions (every 5 years), jazz festival (Oct).

Warsaw Ghetto The Nazi-enforced Jewish quarter of Warsaw, established in 1940 following the German occupation of Poland in World War 2. Some 500 000 Jews were isolated in a ghetto of less than 2·6 sq km (1 sq mi), through which Poles were allowed to pass. Between July and October 1942 more than 300 000 were sent to concentration camps, most of them to Treblinka, where they died in the gas chambers. In reprisal for a Jewish uprising (Feb 1943) in the ghetto, German troops killed an estimated 40 000 of the Jews who had survived the battle. When Warsaw was liberated (Jan 1945) by Soviet troops, only about 200 Jews remained.

Warsaw Pact The countries which signed the East European Mutual Assistance Treaty in Warsaw in 1955: Albania, Bulgaria, Czechoslovakia, East Germany, Hungary, Poland, Romania, and the USSR. Albania withdrew in 1968. The pact established a unified military command for the armed forces of all the signatories. All members were committed to giving immediate assistance to any other party attacked in Europe. It was a communist response, in part, to the formation of NATO by the West, and was formally dissolved in 1991.

Warsaw uprising (Aug–Oct 1944) A Polish insurrection in which the Poles tried to expel the German army before the Soviet forces occupied the city. As the Red Army advanced, Soviet contacts in Warsaw encouraged the underground Polish Home Army, supported by the exiled Polish government in London, to stage an uprising. Polish resistance troops led by General Tadeusz Komorowski gained control of the city against a weak German garrison. Heavy German air raids lasting 63 days preceded a strong German counter-attack. The Soviet army under the Polish-born field marshal Konstantin Rokossovsky (1896–1968), encamped on the outskirts of Warsaw, failed to give help to the insurgents or allow Western allies to airlift supplies to the Poles. Supplies ran out and the Poles surrendered. German forces then systematically deported the population of Warsaw, including the main body of Poles that supported the Polish government in exile, and razed the city. Up to 180 000 people died in the uprising. The Red Army resumed its advance into Poland and occupied Warsaw, establishing a communist provisional government (1 Jan 1945) and assuring Soviet control over Poland.

warships Vessels designed for use in wartime. Navies of the world still employ a vast range of warships, but the use of highly sophisticated guided-missile weaponry has made their roles less easily defined than those of the World War 2 period. The role of minesweepers has changed subtly to 'mine countermeasure', whereas the traditional aircraft carrier is still common, although probably at the limit of development. The US navy has recommissioned battleships, while Russia has redesigned and revived the battle-cruiser. Modern submarines remain submerged for over three months when neccessary, and can perform a diversity of roles. The term *cruiser* is now used mainly for guided-missile vessels packing awesome fire power. The role of the destroyer is mainly offensive in the hunter-killer context, whereas frigates are mainly general-purpose defence vessels.

wart A small benign overgrowth in the outer layer of the skin, arising from a virus infection; also known as a **verruca**. Warts are common in children, and unpredictable in occurrence, recurrence, and spontaneous disappearance.

wart disease A disease (*Synchytrium endobioticum*) causing excessive cell division in the tubers of potatoes, resulting in the growth of soft warty tissues which destroy their economic value. It caused much concern when first observed in Europe in 1910, but it was subsequently noticed that certain varieties were immune, and legislation was passed requiring that only immune varieties should be grown in infected areas. All new European varieties are now officially tested, and only those showing immunity are released for cultivation. (Order: Chytridiales.)

warthog A wild pig native to Africa S of the Sahara (*Phacochoerus aethiopicus*); sparse covering of shaggy hair, especially on shoulders; face broad, flattened, with four wart-like knobs of thickened skin, large curved tusks; inhabits open country.

wart snake A snake of family Acrochordidae (2 species), found from India to Australia; specialized for life in fresh water (almost helpless on land); rough scales produce a 'warty' skin; also known as **water snake**. Some experts include these species in the family Colubridae, and call the 37 species of rough-skinned Asian snakes in this family **wart snakes**.

Warwick [worik] 52°17N 1°34W, pop (2001e) 126 000. County town of Warwickshire, C England, UK; on the N bank of the R Avon, 15 km/9 mi SW of Coventry; founded in 914 and partly destroyed by fire in 1694; university (1965); railway; agriculture, engineering, carpets, tourism; 14th-c Warwick Castle, Lord Leycester hospital (1383); annual Mop Fair.

Warwick, Dionne [worik], originally **Warrick** (1940–) Popular and soul singer, born in East Orange, New Jersey, USA. She sang in a gospel trio before recording her first hit songs on Scepter, including 'Walk On By' (1964) and 'I Say a Little Prayer' (1967). After a lull in her career in the 1970s, her album *Dionne* (1979) sold a million copies. She went on to release the albums *Heartbreaker* (1982) and *How Many Times Can We Say Goodbye?* (1983).

Warwick, Richard Neville, Earl [worik], also known as **Warwick the Kingmaker** (1428–71) English soldier and politician, who exercised great power during the first phase of the Wars of the Roses. Created Earl of Warwick in 1450, he championed the Yorkist cause. In 1460 he defeated and captured Henry VI at Northampton, had his cousin, Edward of York, proclaimed king as Edward IV (1461), and then destroyed the Lancastrian army at Towton. When Edward tried to assert his independence, Warwick joined the Lancastrians, forced the king to flee to Holland, and restored Henry VI to the throne (1470). He was defeated and killed by Edward IV at the Battle of Barnet.

Warwickshire [woriksheer] pop (2001e) 505 900; area 1981 sq km/765 sq mi. County of C England, UK; drained by R Avon; county town, Warwick; chief towns include Nuneaton, Royal Leamington Spa, Rugby, Stratford-upon-Avon; agriculture, tourism, engineering, textiles; castles at Kenilworth and Warwick; Shakespeare industry at Stratford; annual Mop Fairs.

Wasa [vahsa] A four-masted Swedish warship of 1628 which foundered on her maiden voyage due to poor stability, with a loss of 50 personnel. She was salvaged in 1961 and preserved in dry dock in Stockholm. She is the best surviving example of a 17th-c ship.

Wash, The Shallow inlet of the North Sea on E coast of England; between Norfolk (S) and Lincolnshire (W and N); receives the Welland, Witham, Nene, and Ouse Rivers; bounded by a low marshy coast.

Washington (DC) 38°54N 77°02W, pop (2000e) 572 000. Capital of the USA, co-extensive with the District of Columbia; situated between Maryland and Virginia, on the E bank of the Potomac R, at its junction with the Anacostia R; the US legislative, administrative, and judicial centre: the Federal Government provides most of the city's employment; site chosen in 1790 by George Washington, planned by Pierre L'Enfant; occupied by the Federal Government, 1800; sacked and burned by the British, 1814; centre of government, justice, and law enforcement; two airports (Reagan National, Dulles); railway; five universities; professional teams, Bullets (basketball), Capitals (ice hockey), Redskins (football); the International Spy Museum opened in 2002.

Washington (state) pop (2000e) 5 894 100; area 176 473 sq km/68 139 sq mi. State in NW USA, divided into 39 counties; the 'Evergreen State'; first settled in the late 18th-c, part of Oregon Territory, a prosperous fur-trading area; Britain and the USA quarrelled over the region until the international boundary was fixed by treaty to lie along the 49th parallel, 1846; became a territory, 1853; joined the Union as the 42nd state, 1889; after arrival of the railway (1887), developed through lumbering and fishing; Seattle an important outfitting point during the Alaskan gold rush, 1897–9; capital, Olympia; other chief cities, Seattle, Tacoma, Edmonds, Bellingham; bounded N by Canada (British Columbia), NW by the Strait of Juan de Fuca, W by the Pacific Ocean; rivers include the Columbia, Snake, Okanogan, Sanpoil, Yakima; Olympic Peninsula with the Olympic Mts in the NW (Mt Olympus 2428 m/7966 ft); Puget Sound to the E, extending c.160 km/100 mi inland, with numerous bays and islands; Cascade Range runs N–S through the middle of the state; mountainous and forested country in the W; dry and arid land in the E; highest point Mt Rainier (4395 m/14 419 ft); Mt Saint Helens volcano in the S (erupted May 1980); North Cascades National Park; apples (nation's largest crop), wheat, livestock, dairy produce; aircraft, aerospace, oil refining, food processing; mining (wide range of minerals); major tourist area; substantial Indian population and several reservations.

Washington, Booker T(aliaferro) (1856–1915) Black leader and educationist, born in Franklin Co, Virginia, USA. After emancipation (1865), he studied at Hampton Institute, Virginia, and Washington, DC, becoming a teacher, writer, and speaker on black problems. In 1881 he was appointed principal of the newly opened Tuskegee Institute, Alabama, and built it up into a major centre of black education. He was the foremost black leader in late 19th-c USA, winning white support by his acceptance of the separation of blacks and whites. He was strongly criticized by Du Bois, and his policies were repudiated by the 20th-c civil rights movement.

Washington, George (1732–99) Commander of American forces and first president of the USA (1789–97), born in Bridges Creek, Virginia, USA. His family originated from Washington, near Durham, England, where their Old Hall still stands. He had an informal education, worked as a surveyor, and first fought in the campaigns of the French and Indian War (1754–63). He then managed the family estate at Mount Vernon, VA, becoming active in politics, and represented Virginia in the first (1774) and second (1775) Continental Congresses. He was given command of the American forces, where he displayed great powers as a strategist and leader of men. Following reverses in the New York area, he retreated through New Jersey, inflicting notable defeats on the enemy at Trenton and Princeton (1777). He suffered defeats at the Brandywine and Germantown, but held his army together through the winter of 1777–8 at Valley Forge. After the alliance with France (1778), he forced the surrender of Cornwallis at Yorktown in 1781. He then retired to Mount Vernon, and sought to secure a strong government by constitutional means. In 1787 he presided over the Constitutional Convention, and became president, remaining neutral while political parties were formed, but eventually joining the Federalist Party. He retired in 1797.

Washington Monument A marble column in honour of George Washington, designed by Robert Mills (1781–1855) and erected (1848–84) in Washington, District of Columbia, USA. The tower, which is 169 m/555 ft high, incorporates many blocks of stone bearing inscriptions from the states, foreign governments, or organizations who donated them. Its lengthy period of construction was caused by a shortage of funds.

wasp The common name of several different types of solitary and social insects of the order Hymenoptera, including spider wasps, digger wasps, ichneumons, woodwasps, potter wasps, gall wasps, and hornets. Social wasps (mainly in the family Vespidae) are usually banded black and yellow; females inflict painful stings; some produce nests of paper-like material; larvae fed on masticated paste of arthropod prey. Solitary wasps usually provision their nest with paralyzed prey to feed the larvae.

Wasserman, August Paul von [vaserman] (1866–1925) Bacteriologist, born in Bamberg, SEC Germany. He studied medicine at Erlangen, Vienna, Munich, and Strasbourg universities, and worked in bacteriology at the Robert Koch Institute in Berlin from 1890. He discovered a blood-serum test for syphilis in 1906 (the **Wasserman reaction**).

waste disposal The disposal of waste from domestic, industrial, and agricultural sources; a major environmental concern. Methods commonly used include burial in landfill sites and at sea, incineration (sometimes for power generation), and the production of refuse-derived fuel pellets which can be used as an energy source. Care is needed with the disposal of toxic and hazardous substances to ensure that pollution of water, air, and land is avoided, and to prevent the build-up of methane, an inflammable gas. It is possible to recover this landfill gas as an energy source. An alternative to the disposal of some waste is recycling (eg of paper and glass).

watch A small timepiece for wear or in the pocket. Watches have been made ever since the invention of the mainspring (c.1500) which Peter Henlein, a locksmith in Nuremberg, used to replace weights in driving clocks. Like clocks they needed a means of maintaining a constant speed as the mainspring ran down. The earliest means was the *fusee* (a cord wound round a conical barrel). From c.1670 the spring-maintained balance became general. In recent times electrical movements have been much used, a small battery replacing the mainspring as a source of energy. Timing methods include a tiny, electrically driven tuning fork, and the vibration of a quartz crystal. Sometimes the traditional analogue display (by rotation of hands) is replaced by a digital display using a liquid crystal display (LCD) face.

water H_2O. The commonest molecular compound on Earth; a liquid, freezing to ice at 0°C and boiling to steam at 100°C. It covers about 70% of the Earth's surface, and dissolves almost everything to some extent. However, it is a poor solvent for substances which are found in solution as molecules (eg oxygen, methane). It is essential to life, and occurs in all living organisms. It is strongly hydrogen-bonded in the liquid phase, and co-ordinates to dissolved ions. Unusually, the solid is less dense than the liquid; this results in ice floating, and accounts for the destructiveness of continued freezing and thawing. Water containing substantial concentrations of calcium and magnesium ions is called 'hard', and is 'softened' by replacing these ions with sodium or potassium, which do not form insoluble products with soaps.

water avens *avens*

water bear A microscopic animal possibly related to the arthropods; body short, bearing four pairs of stumpy legs usually armed with claws; mouthparts elongated for piercing; c.400 species, found in surface water-films on mosses, lichens, algae, plant litter, and soil. (Phylum: Tardigrada.)

water beetle A dark, shiny beetle up to 40 mm/1½ in long; silvery in appearance underwater because of air layer trapped on the underside of body and wing cases; larvae feed on snails; adults usually plant feeders; abundant in the tropics. (Order: Coleoptera. Family: Hydrophilidae, c.2000 species.)

water birth A technique in which a mother gives birth to her baby while seated in a pool of warm water. The pool contains water at 35–37°C to a depth of 38–40 cm, allowing the level to reach the armpits when seated, and the mother-to-be usually enters the water when her cervix is 5–7 cm dilated. The technique was pioneered in the 1960s by Dr Igor Tjarkousky, then developed by Dr Michel Odent at Pithivier Hospital in France. The reduced requirement for analgesia, reduced duration of labour, reduced incidence of tears in the vagina, reduced need for episiotomy, and reduced incidence of fetal distress are well documented. Some psychotherapists also believe that the birth of a baby into a warm and quiet environment avoids the trauma of delivery, and thus reduces the incidence of psychological problems in later life.

water boatman A predatory aquatic bug that swims upside-down in water, using its paddle-like hindlegs; forelegs used to grasp prey; worldwide. (Order: Heteroptera. Family: Notonectidae, c.200 species.)

water buck A grazing antelope native to Africa S of the Sahara (*Kobus ellipsiprymnus*); large with shaggy brown or grey coat; male with long erect horns ringed with ridges; inhabits savannah and woodland near water; two forms: **common waterbuck** and **defassa waterbuck**.

water buffalo A SE Asian member of the cattle family; lives near water; often wallows; closely related to the anoa; two species: *Bubalis bubalis* (**Asian water buffalo**, **wild water buffalo**, **Asiatic buffalo**, **carabao**, or **arni** – widely domesticated), and *Bubalis mindorensis* (**tamaraw** or **tamarau**).

water chestnut A free-floating aquatic annual (*Trapa natans*), native to warm parts of Europe, Asia, and Africa, and introduced elsewhere; roots green; leaves in rosettes, blade rhomboid, stalk with an air chamber; flowers white, 4-petalled; fruits woody, triangular with 2–4 spiny horns. Fast-growing, it forms thick, floating mats which can block waterways. The fruit, rich in starch and fat, forms a staple food in much of Asia. The water chestnuts sold in Europe are often storage organs of the sedge *Cyperus esculentus*. (Family: Trapaceae.)

watercolour Any form of painting in which the pigment is mixed with a water-soluble medium such as gum arabic. Watercolour was used in ancient Egypt and China, and mediaeval manuscripts were illuminated with water-based paint. However, gouache and tempera are not regarded as 'pure' watercolour, which relies on transparent washes on special heavy paper, usually white or light-tinted. The great masters of 'pure' watercolour were all English, including Girtin, Cotman, and Turner.

watercress A semi-aquatic perennial (*Nasturtium officinale*), native to Europe and Asia; hollow stems creeping, rooting; leaves pinnate; flowers small, white, cross-shaped. It has been cultivated since the 19th-c as a vitamin-C-rich salad plant. Its peppery tasting leaves stay green in the autumn. (Family: Cruciferae.)

water-crowfoot An aquatic species of buttercup, growing in still or slow-moving water. Its leaves are of two kinds, either or both of which may be present, depending on the species: *submerged* leaves are finely divided and filamentous; *floating* leaves are circular or lobed. The predominantly white flowers project above the water. (Genus: *Ranunculus*. Subgenus: *Batrachium*, c.30 species. Family: Ranunculaceae.)

water deer A deer native to China and Korea (*Hydropotes inermis*), and introduced in UK and France; the only true deer without antlers; canine teeth of male form long downward pointing tusks; inhabits marshland; eats water plants; also known as **Chinese water deer**.

waterfall A sudden interruption in the course of a river or stream where water falls more or less vertically, in some cases for a considerable distance, such as over the edge of a plateau or where overhanging softer rock has been eroded away. The spectacular Niagara Falls and Victoria Falls are probably the best-known, but are not among the world's highest waterfalls. (*see panel*)

water fern *azolla*

water flea A small aquatic crustacean; characterized by a jerky swimming motion using large antennae for propulsion; body short; head free; trunk enclosed by a bivalved carapace; often reproduces by parthenogenesis; c.450 species, most fresh water but a few marine. (Class: Branchiopoda. Order: Cladocera.)

Waterford (city) 52°15N 7°06W, pop (2000e) 42 000. Seaport, county borough, and capital of Co Waterford, Munster, S Ireland; on R Suir at its mouth on Waterford harbour; railway; technical college; shipyards, food processing, footwear, paper; noted for its glass and crystal; remains of city walls, cathedral (1793), Blackfriars priory (1226); light opera festival (Sep).

Waterford (county), Ir **Phort Láirge** pop (2000e) 92 000; area 1839 sq km/710 sq mi. County in Munster province, S Ireland; bounded S by Atlantic Ocean, with coastal inlets at Youghal,

Highest Waterfalls

Name	Height m	ft	Location
Angel (upper fall)	807	2 648	Venezuela
Itatinga	628	2 060	Brazil
Cuquenan	610	2 000	Guyana/Venezuela
Ormeli	563	1 847	Norway
Tysse	533	1 749	Norway
Pilao	524	1 719	Brazil
Ribbon	491	1 612	USA
Vestre Mardola	468	1 535	Norway
Roraima	457	1 500	Guyana
Cleve-Garth	450	1 476	New Zealand

Distances are given for individual leaps.

Dungarvan, Tramore, and Waterford; Knockmealdown Mts in the W; watered by Suir and Barrow Rivers; apple growing, cattle, glass making; popular resorts such as Tramore on S coast.

waterfowl Aquatic birds, especially ducks, geese, and swans; also known as **wildfowl**. The name *waterfowl* is often used for populations kept in captivity; *wildfowl* for wild birds, especially those hunted. Some other water birds (eg waders) may also be included.

water gas A gas produced by passing steam over hot coke to give hydrogen and carbon monoxide: $H_2O + C \rightarrow CO + H_2$. This process yields a gas of high energy content, but it is endothermic, and is thus often made concurrently with producer gas, so that the reaction is spontaneous. The resulting 'semiwater gas' has a lower energy content.

Watergate (1972–4) A political scandal that led to the first resignation of a president in US history (Richard Nixon, in office 1968–74). The actual 'Watergate' is a hotel and office complex in Washington, DC, where the Democratic Party had its headquarters. During the presidential campaign of 1972, a team of burglars was caught inside Democratic headquarters, and their connections were traced to the White House and to the Committee to Re-elect the President. Investigations by the Washington Post, a grand jury, and two special prosecutors revealed that high officials who were very close to President Nixon were implicated, and that Nixon himself was aware of illegal measures to cover up that implication. A number of officials were eventually imprisoned. Nixon himself left office when it became clear that he was likely to be impeached and removed. He was later pardoned by President Ford.

water glass A concentrated aqueous solution of sodium silicate (Na_2SiO_3), which sets to a hard, transparent layer, and is used as a waterproofing agent and a preservative.

Waterhouse, Alfred (1830–1905) Architect, born in Liverpool, Merseyside, NW England, UK. He studied at Manchester, where he designed the town hall and assize courts, then built the romanesque Natural History Museum in London (1873–81). He also designed many educational buildings, and from his great use of red bricks came the name *red-brick university*.

water hyacinth A free-floating perennial aquatic plant (*Eichhornia speciosa*), native to South America, and introduced elsewhere; roots purple; leaves in rosettes, blade circular, stalk inflated and bladder-like; flowers c.4 cm/1½ in long, funnel-shaped, violet, in short dense inflorescence. It grows and spreads rapidly, blocks waterways, reservoirs, etc, and is probably the world's most troublesome aquatic weed. (Family: Pontederiaceae.)

waterlily An aquatic perennial found in still or very slow-moving water in many parts of the world; large, floating, or slightly emergent leaves and flowers; leaves heart-shaped or rounded; flowers bowl-shaped with numerous petals and stamens. (Genera: *Nymphaea, Nuphar.* Family: Nymphaeaceae.)

Waterloo, Battle of (18 Jun 1815) The final defeat of Napoleon, ending the French Wars and the emperor's last bid for power in the Hundred Days, fought near the Belgian village of Waterloo. A hard-fought battle, in which Blücher's Prussian force arrived at the climax to support Wellington's mixed Allied force; a number of crucial blunders by the French contributed to their defeat.

Waterloo Cup *bowls; coursing*

water louse A freshwater crustacean found in stagnant or slow-flowing water containing rotting plants; abdominal segments fused; adult females carry developing young in brood pouch on underside of thorax; feeds on decaying vegetation. (Class: Malacostraca. Order: Isopoda.)

water-melon A trailing vine (*Citrullus lanatus*) with tendrils, native to the Mediterranean, Africa, and tropical Asia; leaves deeply palmately-lobed; male and female flowers yellow, c.3 cm/1¼ in diameter, funnel-shaped; fruit up to 60 cm/2 ft long, ovoid, rind dark green, leathery; black seeds embedded in red flesh. It is cultivated for fruit, especially in the USA. (Family: Cucurbitaceae.)

water milfoil A submerged aquatic perennial, found almost everywhere; stems rooted or free-floating, leaves feathery, in whorls; flowers small, in slender spikes above water, reddish or yellowish, males 4-petalled, females without petals. Some species are used as aquarium plants. (Genus: *Myriophyllum*, 45 species. Family: Halagoraceae.)

water moccasin *cottonmouth*

water opossum *yapok*

water polo Developed in Britain in 1869, and played by teams of seven-a-side in a swimming pool. The object is to score goals by propelling the ball into the opposing team's goal at the end of the pool. Originally known as 'football in water', it is now an Olympic event.

water rat A term used generally for many unrelated rats which inhabit the edge of water bodies; some species modified to a semi-aquatic lifestyle, with webbed hind feet and waterproof fur. The name is sometimes used for the water vole.

water scorpion An aquatic bug that lives submerged, breathing through a tubular tail that reaches the surface; lies in wait for prey, which is grasped with forelegs; c.200 species, found in still or slow-moving waters. (Order: Heteroptera. Family: Nepidae.)

water skiing Recreational and competitive sport in which persons, either barefoot or mounted on special skis made from wood, plastic, or reinforced fibreglass, are towed across the surface of the water by fast-moving motorboats. The sport was invented in 1922 in the USA, and the first national skiing tournament was held at Long Island, New York in 1939. International competitions, including the prestigious World Cup, are governed by the International Water Ski Federation.

water snake *grass snake; wart snake*

water spider The only spider that lives permanently submerged; builds a bell-shaped retreat which it fills with air carried down on hindlegs; breathing by means of air film over body surface; feeds mainly on crustaceans; bite venomous, causing vomiting and fever. (Order: Araneae. Family: Agelenidae.)

water-spout The marine equivalent of a tornado; a rapidly rotating funnel of air which extends from the cloud base to the water surface, picking up water. Condensation also occurs within the vortex. When a water-spout reaches land, its water content is rapidly released.

water table The surface below which the ground is saturated with water. The position of the water table varies with the topography and amount of rainfall; where it intersects the surface, springs are formed.

water turkey *darter*

water vole A vole of genus *Arvicola*; three species: *Arvicola richardsoni* of NW North America, *Arvicola sapidus* from Europe, and *Arvicola terrestris* from Europe and Asia; most individuals burrow into banks of streams and ponds, but some live away from water; also known as **bank vole**.

Watford 51°40N 0°25W, pop (2002e) 84 405. Residential town in Greater London urban area and Watford district, Hertfordshire, SE England, UK; 30 km/19 mi NW of central London; R Gade is to the W, R Colne is to the E; malting and wool production (13th–14th-c); 18th-c silk spinning industry, the last mill closed in 1881; Grand Union Canal passes through Cassiobury Park; railway; thriving commerce and industry; electronics, engineering, printing; historic market (founded, 1170); Watford Football Club (Hornets), Rugby Club (Saracens); Palace Theatre (1911), museum, leisure centre; Rainbow Festival (Jul).

Watling Street *Roman roads*

Watson, James D(ewey) (1928–) Geneticist, born in Chicago, Illinois, USA. He studied at Chicago and Indiana universities, worked in Copenhagen, then went to Cambridge, where with Crick and Wilkins he helped discover the molecular structure of DNA, sharing with them the 1962 Nobel Prize for Physiology or Medicine. He became professor of biology at Harvard in 1961, and director (1968–94) then president (1994–) of the Cold

Spring Harbor Laboratory at Long Island, NY. He was awarded an honorary knighthood in 2001.

Watson, John B(roadus) (1878–1958) Psychologist, born in Greenville, South Carolina, USA. He studied at Chicago, and became professor of psychology at Johns Hopkins University (1908–20), where he established an animal research laboratory. He became known for his behaviourist approach, which he later applied to human behaviour. In 1921 he entered advertising, and wrote several general books on psychology.

Watson, Russell (1974–) Tenor, born in Salford, Greater Manchester, NW England, UK. He left school at 16, began work in an engineering factory, and in his spare time sang in local working men's clubs. His performance one night of Puccini's aria 'Nessun dorma' received a standing ovation, and he decided to become a professional singer (1996). His debut album, *The Voice* (2000), topped the UK classical chart for many months. Later albums include *Encore* (2001) and *Reprise* (2002).

Watson, Tom, popular name of **Thomas (Sturges) Watson** (1949–) Golfer, born in Kansas City, Missouri, USA. He turned professional in 1971, and has since won 32 tournaments on the US tour. He has won the (British) Open five times (1975, 1977, 1980, 1982–3), the US Open (1982), and the US Masters (1977, 1981).

Watson-Watt, Sir Robert Alexander (1892–1973) Physicist who developed the radio location of aircraft, born in Brechin, Angus, E Scotland, UK. He studied at St Andrews University, taught at Dundee University, and in 1917 worked in the Meteorological Office, designing devices to locate thunderstorms, and investigating the ionosphere (a term he invented in 1926). He became head of the radio section of the National Physical Laboratory (1935), where he began work on locating aircraft. His work led to the development of radar (Radio Detection and Ranging) which played a vital role in the defence of Britain against German air raids in 1940. He was knighted in 1942.

Watt, James (1736–1819) Inventor, born in Greenock, Inverclyde, WC Scotland, UK. He went to Glasgow in 1754 to learn the trade of mathematical-instrument maker, and there, after a year in London, he set up in business. He was employed on surveys for several canals, improved harbours and rivers, and by 1759 was studying steam as a motive force. In 1763–4, in the course of repairing a working model of the Newcomen engine, he found he could greatly improve its efficiency by using a separate steam condenser. After other improvements, he went into partnership with Matthew Boulton, and the new engine was manufactured at Birmingham in 1774. Several other inventions followed, including the double-acting engine, parallel motion linkage, the centrifugal governor for automatic speed control, and the pressure gauge. The term *horse-power* was first used by him, and the SI unit of power is named after him.

watt SI unit of power; symbol *W*; named after James Watt; the production of 1 joule of energy per second corresponds to a power of 1 watt; commonly used as **kilowatts** (*kW*, 10^3 W) or **megawatts** (*MW*, 10^6 W).

Watteau, (Jean) Antoine [vatoh] (1684–1721) Rococo painter, born in Valenciennes, N France. In 1702 he went to study in Paris, where he worked as a scene painter and a copyist. His early canvases were mostly military scenes, but it was the mythological 'L'Embarquement pour l'île de Cythère' (1717, Embarkation for the island of Cythera) which won him membership of the Academy. He is also known for his 'Fêtes galantes' (Scenes of Gallantry) – quasi-pastoral idylls in court dress which became fashionable in high society.

wattle Any of a large group of mainly trees or shrubs, native to many tropical and subtropical areas, but notably Australia where (together with the eucalypts) they form the dominant tree vegetation. The leaves are divided into numerous tiny leaflets or, in many species, reduced in the adult form to a flattened leaf-stalk (*phyllode*) resembling a leaf-blade. The flowers are mostly yellow, very small but numerous, in rounded or catkin-like clusters. Many species are planted as shade trees and for ornament. The foliage may be used as fodder for livestock. Many are useful timber trees, producing very hard tough wood. The bark and pods are employed for tanning. Some yield gum arabic. Several species are widely cultivated for stabilizing sandy soils. Commonly cultivated species include the **blue-leaved wattle** (*Acacia cyanophylla*) from W Australia, a small tree growing to 10 m/30 ft; leaf stalks bluish-green, up to 30 cm/12 in long, often pendulous; flowers in heads to 1·5 cm/0·6 in across, arranged in long leafy clusters; pods brown, constricted between the seeds. Also common is the **silver wattle** (*Acacia dealbata*) from SE Australia and Tasmania, a tree growing to 30 m/100 ft; leaves finely divided with 20–50 pairs of narrow leaflets, silvery-white when young; flowers deep yellow, fragrant, in rounded heads. It is the 'mimosa' of florists. (Genus: *Acacia*, 1200 species. Family: Leguminosae.)

wattle and daub A framework of interlaced twigs and rods plastered with mud or clay. The walls of timber-framed houses were often made of wattle and daub. If protected from the weather by good overhanging eaves to the roof, these walls can last for hundreds of years.

wattmeter An instrument for measuring electric power. Many types are used, the most common being the **electrodynamic wattmeter** which depends on the interaction of fields in two sets of coils. The **thermal wattmeter** depends on the heating effect of the current, and the **electrostatic wattmeter** is employed for calibration and standardization purposes.

Watts, George Frederick (1817–1904) Painter, born in London, UK. He studied in London, and first attracted notice by his cartoon of 'Caractacus' (1843) in the competition for murals for the new Houses of Parliament. He became known for his penetrating portraits of notabilities, 150 of which he presented to the National Portrait Gallery in 1904. He also executed some sculpture, notably 'Physical Energy' in Kensington Gardens, London.

Watts Towers A group of sculptures incorporating metal, stone, cement, tiles, glass, and waste materials, in the Watts district of Los Angeles, California, USA. The towers were completed in 1954, having been constructed over a period of 35 years by Simon Rodin (1879–1965).

Waugh, Evelyn (Arthur St John) [waw] (1903–66) Writer, born in London, UK. He studied at Oxford, and quickly established a reputation with such stylistically brilliant satirical novels as *Decline and Fall* (1928), *Vile Bodies* (1930), *A Handful of Dust* (1934), and *Scoop* (1938). He became a Catholic in 1930, and his later books display a more serious attitude, as seen in the religious theme of *Brideshead Revisited* (1945), a nostalgic evocation of student days at Oxford, which was made into a successful television series. His 'sword of honour' trilogy, in which he analyses the eternal struggle between good and evil and a civilization's fight against barbarism, contains *Men at Arms* (1952), *Officers and Gentlemen* (1955), and *Unconditional Surrender* (1961). His diaries were published in 1976, and his letters in 1980.

WAV [wav] *digital media*

wave (oceanography) In oceanography, a disturbance moving under or along the surface of the water. Most ocean surface waves are generated by the wind blowing over the surface of the sea, imparting energy to the water. The speed with which these waves travel is determined by their wavelength and/or the depth of the water through which they are moving. The height of wind-generated ocean surface waves is determined by the wind *velocity*, the length of time the wind blows over the water (*duration*), and the distance it blows over the water (*fetch*). Waves can be transmitted over thousands of miles of ocean, often losing little energy until they break upon a shore.

wave (physics) *wave motion*

wavefunction In quantum mechanics, a wave expression containing all possible information about a quantum system, such as electrons in atoms. The square of the wavefunction is related

wave motion

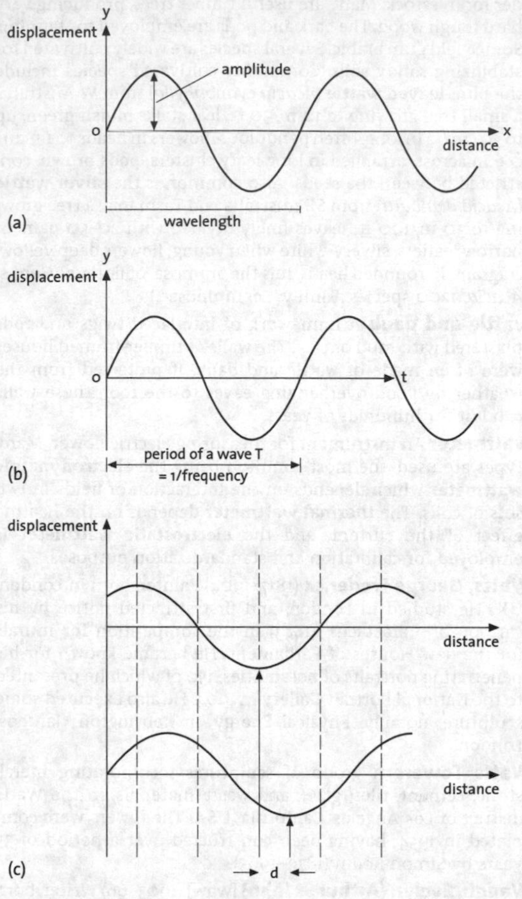

A disturbance from equilibrium which propagates in time from one place to another. Many phenomena are governed by waves, such as electromagnetic waves, quantum matter waves for electrons, seismic waves, and vibration. **Longitudinal waves** occur when the displacement is in the same direction as the wave propagation (eg sound waves). **Transverse waves** correspond to a displacement perpendicular to the direction of wave propagation (eg ripples on water). **Standing waves** (also called **stationary waves**) result from interference between waves travelling in opposite directions (eg on a guitar string, where waves run along the string, reflected from end to end). For standing waves, the ratio of the instantaneous value of displacement at one point to that at another does not change. **Periodic waves** (ie waves produced by some regular repeating motion) are described by amplitude A, frequency f or period T, and wavelength λ; wave velocity $v = f\lambda$ m/s. **Sine waves** may be expressed as $y = A\sin 2\pi(ft - x/\lambda)$. Complicated periodic waves can be expressed as sums of sine waves using Fourier analysis.

to the outcome of physical observation. Variation of wavefunction in space and time is described by Schrödinger's equation.

wavelength The distance between two successive peaks of a wave along the direction of propagation; symbol λ, units m (metres). The wavelength of light is 390–780 nm; the wavelength of sound, 16 mm–16 m.

Wavell, Archibald Percival Wavell, 1st Earl [wayvl] (1883–1950) British field marshal, born in Winchester, Hampshire, S England, UK. He trained at Sandhurst Military Academy, served in South Africa and India, became Allenby's chief-of-staff in Palestine, and in 1939 was given the Middle East command. He defeated the Italians in N Africa, but failed against Rommel, and in 1941 was transferred to India, where he became viceroy, and was made field marshal and viscount (1943). He was later created an earl (1947), and held the posts of Constable of the Tower (1948) and Lord-Lieutenant of London (1949).

wave motion *see panel*

wavenumber *wavelength*

wave-particle duality The principle that subatomic particles also exhibit wave-like properties, whereas electromagnetic waves also exhibit particle-like properties. The former can be illustrated by interference as observed in electron and neutron diffraction; the latter in the Compton and photoelectric effects.

Wave Rock Unique rock formation in SC Western Australia, near the town of Hyden; estimated to be 2700 million years old; wave-shaped granite formation eroded by water and wind.

wax A substance of a firm but plastic solid consistency, with a low coefficient of friction, and water-repellant. There are two main kinds. **Mineral waxes**, notably **paraffin wax**, are hydrocarbons of high molecular weight with a microcrystalline structure. **Plant** and **animal waxes** are esters of fatty acids, which fulfil a mainly protective function (as **beeswax** in the honeycomb). There are also synthetic organic substances of the same general chemical composition as these natural waxes. Beeswax has a long history as a preferred material for candles and polishes, and (since it can be finely worked sculpturally) as a medium for modelling, such as in wax museums and anatomical models.

waxbill A songbird of the weaver-finch family; native to Africa, Arabia, and S Asia to N Australia (introduced elsewhere); inhabits open woodland and scrub; eats seeds and insects. The name is sometimes used for the entire family. (Family: Estrildidae, 17 species.)

wax flower *wax plant*

wax moth A small moth that feeds on the wax and combs of honeybees. It fills the tunnels inside the hive with silk. (Order: Lepidoptera. Family: Pyralidae.)

wax plant An evergreen climbing perennial (*Hoya carnosa*) reaching 6 m/20 ft or more, native to Australia; leaves elliptical, glossy and rather fleshy; flowers in drooping heads, fragrant, 5-petalled, waxy-white with red centre; also called **wax flower**. (Family: Asclepiadaceae.)

waxwing A songbird of the N hemisphere; grey-brown with black tail; head with crest; some individuals with red, wax-like tips to some wing feathers; inhabits woodland and gardens; eats berries and insects. (Family: Bombicillidae, 3 species.)

wayfaring tree A deciduous, star-shaped, hairy shrub or small tree (*Viburnum lantana*), growing to 6 m/20 ft, native to Europe, typically a plant of chalk soils; leaves ovoid, toothed, rough-textured; flowers 5-petalled, white, in rounded clusters 6–10 cm/2½–4 in across; fruit berry-like, red becoming black when ripe. (Family: Caprifoliaceae.)

Wayland In Norse, German, and Old English legends, a clever inventor, also known as **Wayland the Smith**. He is lame, having been maimed by King Nidud. Many heroes carry swords made by him; his 'Smithy' is a dolmen on the Berkshire Downs, UK.

Wayne, Anthony, known as **Mad Anthony** (1745–96) Revolutionary soldier, born in Easttown, Pennsylvania, USA. In 1776 he raised a volunteer regiment, and in Canada covered the retreat of the provincial forces at Three Rivers. He commanded at Ticonderoga until 1777, when he joined Washington in New Jersey. He fought bravely at Brandywine (1777), led the attack at Germantown, captured supplies for the army at Valley Forge, carried Stony Point, and saved Lafayette in Virginia (1781). In 1793 he led an expedition against the Indians.

Wayne, John, originally **Marion Michael Morrison**, nickname **the Duke** (1907–79) Film actor, born in Winterset, Iowa, USA. After a succession of small parts in low-budget films and serials, he achieved stardom as the Ringo Kid in *Stagecoach* (1939). He went on to make over 80 films, typically starring as a tough but warm-hearted gunfighter or lawman. Classics of the Western genre include *She Wore a Yellow Ribbon* (1949), *The Man who Shot Liberty Vallance* (1962), and *True Grit* (1969, Oscar). Later films include urban cop thrillers such as *McQ* (1974) and *Brannigan* (1975). He also directed *The Alamo* (1960) and *The Green Berets* (1968). His final performance was in *The Shootist* (1976), portraying a legendary gunfighter dying of cancer – a poignant film, as he fought against this disease himself.

weak interaction The feeble short-range force responsible for radioactive beta decay, characterized by the presence of a particle called the neutrino; also known as **weak nuclear force**. It is mediated by W and Z particles. Weak force is the only force exhibiting a handedness.

weak nuclear force *weak interaction*

Weald, The [weeld] Area in Kent, Surrey, and Sussex, SE England, UK, between North and South Downs; fertile agricultural area; fruit, vegetables, hops, sheep; former extensive woodlands, providing charcoal for iron industry in Middle Ages; often refers strictly to area in Kent SW of the greensand ridge from Hythe through Ashford to Westerham.

weapons of mass destruction (WMD) Weapons which are capable of a high level of physical destruction or which can be used to kill large numbers of people. They include nuclear, biological, chemical (NBC), and radiological weapons. Nuclear weapons include atomic and hydrogen bombs. Biological weapons include the use of such diseases as anthrax, botulinum toxin, ricin, plague, and smallpox. Chemical weapons include the use of mustard gas, sarin, VX, soman, and tabun. Radiological weapons are so-called 'dirty' bombs containing radioactive material. In arms control usage, the term excludes devices which transport or propel such weapons, as long as they are clearly separate from the weapons. The notion achieved worldwide prominence in 2003–4 in relation to the international campaign to find and eliminate weapons of mass destruction in Iraq.

weasel A small carnivorous mammal with a long thin body, short legs, and small head; tail usually half length of body; brown with pale underparts (may be all white in winter). The name is also used for the **North African striped weasel** (*Poecilictis libyca*), **African striped weasel** (*Poecilogale albinucha*), and **Patagonian weasel** (*Lyncodon patagonicus*). (Genus: *Mustela*, 9 species. Family: Mustelidae.)

weather The atmospheric processes operating at a location at a particular time: for example, day-to-day conditions of temperature, precipitation, atmospheric pressure, and wind; the scientific study of weather is *meteorology*. A location's range of weather conditions is determined by its climate. Weather differs from climate in that it is concerned with short-term meteorological events, whereas climate encompasses all the weather characteristics of a place, and is concerned with the long-term behaviour of atmospheric processes. **Weather forecasting** is the prediction of future weather conditions, and is usually restricted to the immediate future (up to 3 days or so, but with decreasing confidence up to 10 days). The degree of success in forecasting is dependent on location; some regions (eg NW Europe) experience complex weather patterns, others (eg desert regions) experience more consistent weather patterns. Weather records were kept in China as early as 1216 BC.

weather balloon *radiosonde balloon*

weather satellite A satellite used to record global weather patterns. It contains several remote sensing instruments, and measurements are made of atmospheric energy fluxes, atmospheric and surface temperatures, cloud cover, and amounts of water vapour. Weather satellites are generally in polar, near-polar, or geostationary orbit. In polar orbit (eg NOAA 14) they are c.500–1500 km/300–900 mi above the Earth, and their paths cross the Equator at approximately 90°, with each orbit crossing over or near to the Poles about every 90 minutes. Geostationary satellites (eg GEOS) remain in the same position relative to the Earth at all times, at an altitude of about 35 400 km/22 000 mi. Satellite observations allow access to remote areas of the Earth for which surface meteorological data are lacking.

Weaver, James B(aird) (1833–1912) Politician, born in Dayton, Ohio, USA. Admitted to the bar in 1856, he practised law in Bloomfield, IA, then fought in the Civil War as a Unionist. He joined the Greenback Party, serving in the US House of Representatives (1879–81, 1885–9), and ran unsuccessfully for the presidency as Greenback candidate (1880). Later prominent in the rise of the People's Party which stood for continued wide circulation of paper money as a mechanism for economic growth, he was elected party president (1892), but failed in his bid for the presidency as a Populist candidate (1892).

Weaver, Sigourney, originally **Susan Alexandra Weaver** (1949–) Motion-picture actress, born in New York City, USA. She completed a university education at Stanford and Yale universities before embarking on a film career. Her big break came when she was cast as astronaut Ripley in the film *Aliens* (1979), a part originally written for a man. Later films include *Eyewitness* (1981), *Ghostbusters* (1984), the three *Aliens* sequels (1986, 1992, 1997), *The Ice Storm* (1997), *Galaxy Quest* (1999), and *Holes* (2003).

weaver *weaverbird*

weaverbird A finch-like songbird, also known as **weaver**. The family includes the **true weaver**, **buffalo-weaver**, **sparrow-weaver**, and **scaly-weaver**. Many (not all) species weave nests suspended from branches. The group sometimes includes **weaver-finches**.

weaver-finch A finch-like bird, also known as the **estrildid finch** or (sometimes) the **waxbill**; native to the Old World tropics; eats grass seeds, fruit, and insects. (Family: Estrildidae, c.130 species.)

weaving An ancient craft in which fabric is produced by interlacing *warp* (lengthwise) and *weft* (crosswise) threads on machines called *looms*. Hand looms are known from very early times. They developed little until the flying shuttle was invented by John Kay in 1733, followed later in the century by Cartwright's power loom (1785). Today's modern weaving machines have dispensed with shuttles; 'bullets', 'rapiers', water jets, and air jets now carry the weft across the warp, with 1000 picks per minute being possible on some machines.

Webb Social reformers, historians, and economists: **Sidney James Webb** (1859–1947) and **(Martha) Beatrice Webb**, *née* **Potter** (1858–1943), married in 1892. He was born and studied in London, UK, became a lawyer, and joined the Fabian Society, where he wrote many powerful tracts. She was born in Standish, Gloucestershire, SWC England, and became involved with the social problems of the time. After their marriage they began a joint life of service to Socialism and trade unionism, publishing their classic *History of Trade Unionism* (1894), *English Local Government* (9 vols, 1906–29), and other works. They also started the *New Statesman* (1913). Sidney became an MP (1922), President of the Board of Trade (1924), dominions and colonial secretary (1929–30), and colonial secretary (1930–1), and was created Baron Passfield in 1929.

Webb, James E(dwin) (1906–92) US official and administrator of NASA during its programme to land a man on the Moon, born in Tally Ho, North Carolina, USA. He became head of Bureau of the Budget under President Truman (1946–9), and later his under-secretary of state (1949–52). He was chosen by President Kennedy in 1961 to create in NASA an agency capable of successfully undertaking the Apollo Project, and retired from NASA in 1968, a year before the Apollo 11 landing.

Webb, Karrie (1974–) Golfer, born in Ayr, Queensland, NE Australia. In 1996 she became the first woman to break the $1 million prize-money barrier while playing on the US Ladies' PGA tour, and was named 'Rookie of the Year'. She won the Women's British Open title in 1995, the youngest ever winner, and won it again in 1997 and 2002. Other major tournament titles include the Australian Ladies' Masters (1998, 1999, 2000),

Du Maurier Classic (1999), US Women's Open (2000, 2001), and the LPGA title (2001).

Webb, Sidney James *Webb*

Webber, Andrew Lloyd *Lloyd Webber, Andrew*

Weber, Carl (Maria Friedrich) von [vayber] (1786–1826) Composer and pianist, born in Eutin, N Germany. Nurtured by his family for music, he began to compose, and became conductor of the opera at Wrocław, Poland (formerly Breslau, Prussia) (1804)). In 1813 he settled in Prague as opera *Kapellmeister*, and about 1816 was invited by the King of Saxony to direct the German opera at Dresden. He is known as the founder of German Romantic opera, notably in *Der Freischütz* (1821, The Freeshooter), *Euryanthe* (1823), and *Oberon* (1826), and he also wrote several orchestral works, as well as piano, chamber, and church music, and many songs.

Weber, Ernst (Heinrich) [vayber] (1795–1878) Physiologist, born in Wittenberg, EC Germany. He became professor of anatomy (1818) and of physiology (1840) at Leipzig, where he devised a method of determining the sensitivity of the skin, introducing the concept of the 'just noticeable difference'. His findings were expressed mathematically by Fechner (the *Weber–Fechner Law of the Increase of Stimuli*).

Weber, Max [vayber] (1864–1920) Sociologist and economist, born in Erfurt, C Germany. He studied at Heidelberg and Berlin universities, and held posts at Berlin (1893), Freiberg (1894), Heidelberg (1897), and Munich (1919). His best known work is *Die protestantische Ethik und der Geist des Kapitalismus* (1904, The Protestant Ethic and the Spirit of Capitalism), which was a major influence on sociological theory. He helped to draft the constitution for the Weimar Republic (1919).

weber [vayber] SI unit of magnetic flux; symbol *Wb*; named after German scientist Wilhelm Weber (1804–91); defined as the amount of flux which, when allowed to decrease steadily to zero in 1 second, will produce 1 volt of electromotive force in the loop of wire through which the flux passes.

Webern, Anton (Friedrich Ernst von) [vaybern] (1883–1945) Composer, born in Vienna, Austria. He studied under Schoenberg, and became one of his first musical disciples, making wide use of 12-tone techniques, which led to several hostile demonstrations when his works were first performed. For a while he worked as a conductor and tutor in various cities, before settling in Mödling in 1918. His works, which include a symphony, cantatas, several short orchestral pieces, chamber music, a concerto for nine instruments, and songs, have profoundly influenced many later composers. The Nazis banned his music, and he worked as a proofreader during World War 2. He was accidentally shot dead by a US soldier near Salzburg.

webspinner A small, slender insect commonly found in tropical forests, inhabiting extensive galleries or tunnels of silk constructed under bark, and in soil, litter, or moss. (Order: Embioptera, c.200 species.)

Webster, Daniel (1782–1852) US orator, lawyer, and statesman, born in Salisbury, New Hampshire, USA. He studied at Dartmouth, Salisbury, and Boston, and was admitted to the bar in 1805. A prominent lawyer of the US Supreme Court, and a leading orator, he was a congressman (1813–17, 1823–7), senator (1827–41, 1845–50), and secretary of state (1841–4, 1850–2). He is best remembered for the *Webster–Ashburton Treaty* of 1842 between Britain and the USA, which established the present-day boundaries between NE USA and Canada.

Webster, John (c.1580–c.1625) English playwright. Little is known of him, though he is supposed to have been at one time clerk of St Andrews, Holborn. He collaborated with several other writers, especially Thomas Dekker, but is best known for his two tragedies, *The White Devil* (1612) and *The Duchess of Malfi* (1623), which have been staged more often than any plays of his time, apart from those of Shakespeare.

Webster, Noah (1758–1843) Lexicographer, born in Hartford, Connecticut, USA. He studied at Yale, and became a lawyer, but preferred teaching. He achieved fame with the first part (later known as 'Webster's Spelling Book') of *A Grammatical Institute of the English Language* (1783). Political articles and pamphlets, lecturing, and journalism occupied him until 1798, when he retired to literary life. He is best known for his work in lexicography, notably the *American Dictionary of the English Language* (2 vols, 1828), which was a major influence on US dictionary practice.

Webster–Ashburton Treaty (1842) An agreement between Britain and the USA which established the present-day boundary between NE USA and Canada. Among specific issues were disputed territory between Maine and New Brunswick and at the N end of Lake Champlain, navigation rights on the St John's R, and control of the Mesabi iron deposits. The treaty also established provisions for joint US/British action against the African slave trade. The parties involved were US secretary of state Daniel Webster and Alexander Baring, Baron Ashburton (1774–1848).

Weddell Sea Arm of the Atlantic Ocean, SE of Argentina; bounded by the Antarctic Peninsula (W), Coats Land (E), and S Orkney and Sandwich Is (N); ice shelves cover the S extent; named after James Weddell (1787–1834), who claimed to have discovered the sea in 1823.

Wedekind, Frank [vaydekint] (1864–1918) Playwright, born in Hanover, NC Germany. He worked in business and journalism, before becoming a cabaret performer, playwright, and producer. He is best known for his unconventional tragedies, in which he anticipated the Theatre of the Absurd: *Erdgeist* (1895, Earth Spirit), *Frühlings Erwachen* (1891, Spring Awakening), and *Die Büchse der Pandora* (1903, Pandora's Box).

Wedgwood, Dame Cicely (Veronica) (1910–97) Historian, born in Stocksfield, Northumberland, NE England, UK. She studied at Oxford, and became a specialist in 17th-c history, writing such biographies as *Oliver Cromwell* (1939) and *William the Silent* (1944, James Tait Black). She also wrote several general works, such as *The Thirty Years' War* (1938). She was created a dame in 1968.

Wedgwood, Josiah (1730–95) Potter, born in Burslem, Staffordshire, C England, UK. He worked in the family pottery business, became a partner of Thomas Whieldon in 1754, and began to devise improved wares. In 1759 he opened a factory at Burslem, and a decade later opened one near Hanley, which he called 'Etruria'. Inspired by antique models, he invented unglazed black basalt ware and blue jasper ware with raised designs in white. From 1768 to 1780 he was in partnership with **Thomas Bentley** (1730–80), who introduced advanced marketing techniques to the firm. Wedgwood's concern over social welfare led him to build a village for his workmen at Etruria.

Weeks, Feast of *Shabuoth*

Weelkes, Thomas (c.1575–1623) Madrigal composer, probably born in Elsted, Surrey, SE England, UK. He became organist at Winchester College (1597) and Chichester Cathedral (1602). Nearly 100 of his madrigals have survived, as well as some instrumental music, and fragments of his sacred music.

weeping willow Any of several species of willow, all making quite large trees, with the smaller branches pendulous, often reaching the ground. Many are ornamentals, and arose in cultivation. One of the most common is **golden weeping willow**, *Salix × chrysocoma*. (Family: Salicaceae.)

weever Bottom-dwelling fish with powerful poison spines on first dorsal fin and gill covers; eyes large and placed on top of head, mouth oblique; typically lives partly buried in sandy bottoms feeding on small fishes and crustaceans. (Genus: *Trachinus*. Family: Trachinidae.)

weevil A robust beetle with a characteristic snout on the front of the head; wing cases often sculptured and toughened; antennae club-like, with elbow joint; species include many important pests such as the grain weevil and cotton boll weevil. (Order: Coleoptera. Family: Curculionidae, c.60 000 species.)

Wegener, Alfred (Lothar) [vaygener] (1880–1930) Explorer and geophysicist, originator of the theory of continental drift, born in Berlin, Germany. He was professor of meteorology at Hamburg (1919), and of geophysics and meteorology at Graz

(1924). His theory is named after him (**Wegener's hypothesis**), and is the subject of his main publications. His ideas first met with great hostility, but by the 1960s plate tectonics was established as a major tenet of modern geophysics. He died during his fourth expedition to Greenland.

Weigel, Helene [viygl] (1900–71) Actress-manager, born in Vienna, Austria. She married Bertolt Brecht in 1929, and became a leading exponent of his work, particularly in *Die Mutter* (1932, The Mother) and *Mutter Courage und ihre Kinder* (1949, Mother Courage and her Children). She took control of the Berliner Ensemble after Brecht's death in 1956, and was instrumental in furthering his influence through the international tours she managed and in which she starred.

weigela [wiyjeela] A small deciduous shrub native to E Asia; leaves opposite, oval, finely toothed; flowers trumpet-shaped, 5-lobed, pink or crimson, in clusters. It is widely grown as an ornamental. (Genus: *Weigela*, 12 species. Family: Caprifoliaceae.)

weight The downwards force on an object due to the gravitational attraction of the Earth; symbol G, units N (newton); distinct from mass. The weight of an object of mass 1 kg is 9·81 N, using $G = mg$, where m is mass and g is acceleration due to gravity, $g = 9{\cdot}81\ \mathrm{m/s^2}$. Weight decreases with altitude.

weight for height A measure used in nutrition studies to enable the weight of people to be compared. Direct comparisons of weight are invalid, since a six-foot person will weigh more than a five-foot person; thus weights are usually adjusted to correct for height. The most commonly used method is to divide weight in kilograms by the square of height in metres, yielding a figure known as the **body mass index**.

weightlifting A test of strength by lifting weights attached to both ends of a metal pole (*barbell*). Weightlifting formed part of the Ancient Olympic Games, and in the 19th-c was a popular attraction at many of the leading circuses. It was introduced as a sport c.1850, and held its first world championship in 1891. Competitors have to make two successful lifts: the *snatch*, taking the bar directly above the head, and the *clean and jerk*, taking the bar onto the chest then above the head with outstretched arms. The aggregate weight of the two lifts gives a lifter's total, and competitors gradually increase the weight attempted for their next lifts. Another form of weightlifting is **powerlifting**, which calls for sheer strength as opposed to technique. This takes three forms: the *squat*, *dead lift*, and *bench press*. Weight training is increasingly popular amongst keep-fit enthusiasts, as well as top sportsmen and sportswomen.

Weil, Simone [vayl] (1909–43) Philosophical writer and mystic, born in Paris, France. She taught philosophy in several schools, interspersing this with periods of manual labour to experience the working-class life. In 1936 she served in the Republican forces in the Spanish Civil War. In 1941 she settled in Marseille, where she developed a deep mystical feeling for the Catholic faith, yet a profound reluctance to join an organized religion. She escaped to the USA in 1942 and worked for the Free French in London, before dying from voluntary starvation in an attempt to identify with her compatriots suffering in France. Her posthumously published works include *La Pesanteur et la grâce* (1946, Gravity and Grace) and *Attente de Dieu* (1950, Waiting for God).

Weill, Kurt [viyl] (1900–50) Composer, born in Dessau, EC Germany. He studied and worked at Berlin, became a composer of instrumental works, then collaborated with Brecht, achieving fame with *Die Dreigroschenoper* (1928, The Threepenny Opera), its best-known song, 'Mack the Knife', becoming an international classic. A refugee from the Nazis, he settled with his actress wife Lotte Lenya in the USA in 1935. His Broadway works included *Knickerbocker Holiday* (1938) and *Lady in the Dark* (1941), and he also wrote the 'folk opera' *Down in the Valley* (1948), which used traditional Kentucky tunes. His later operas and musical comedies, all of which contain an element of social criticism, did not repeat the success of the first.

Weil's disease [viyl] An infectious disease caused by *Leptospira icterohaemorrhagiae*, also known as **leptospirosis**. The microorganism is carried by rodents, and is contracted by humans from their urine. People bathing in canals or stagnant fresh water pools are vulnerable to infection through cuts or abrasions in the skin. The disease causes a flu-like illness, followed by kidney and liver damage, and there is a mortality of c.20%. It is named after German physician Adolf Weil (1848–1916), who first described the condition in 1886.

Weimar [viymah(r)] 50°59N 11°20E, pop (2000e) 67 100. City in Weimar district, S Germany, on R Ilm; railway; colleges of technology, music, and architecture; farm machinery, chemicals; associations with Schiller, Goethe, Liszt; former concentration camp of Buchenwald nearby; Goethe National Museum, Liszt Museum, observatory, Weimar Castle, Belvedere Castle (18th-c).

Weimar Republic [viymah(r)] The name by which the German federal republic of 1919–33 is known. In 1919 a National Constituent Assembly met at Weimar, on the R Elbe, and drew up a constitution for the new republic. The government moved from Weimar to Berlin in 1920. The period was one of great instability, economic crises, and artistic achievements. Unable to meet reparation costs drawn up at Versailles, Germany's currency collapsed and the German people suffered large financial losses as well as the loss of continental territories and all overseas colonies. The Nazi and Communist parties took advantage of a nation in chaos and set about disrupting the republic. Following parliamentary (*Reichstag*) elections in September 1930 the Nazis became the second-largest party, and in the July 1932 elections, the largest, exploiting anti-communist fears and anti-semitic prejudice. The Weimar period made Berlin renowned for its avant-garde art, theatre, and music, all of which were suppressed after the Nazis came to power. In 1933, two months after becoming chancellor, Hitler passed an Enabling Act suspending the Weimar constitution. On Hindenburg's death in 1934, Hitler declared himself president and proclaimed the Third Reich.

Weinberger, Caspar (Willard) [wiynberger] (1917–) US statesman, born in San Francisco, California, USA. After military service (1941–5) he worked as a lawyer, before entering politics as a member of the California state legislature in 1952. He was state finance director of California during Ronald Reagan's governorship (1968–9). He served in the Nixon and Ford administrations, then became secretary of defense after Reagan's election victory in 1980. Briefed to supervise a major military build-up, he developed such high-profile projects as the Strategic Defense Initiative. A 'hawk' on East–West issues, he opposed detente, resigned his office in 1987, and returned to private life. He was awarded an honorary knighthood in 1988 for his services to Britain, notably during the Falklands War (1982).

Weinberg–Salam theory *Glashow–Weinberg–Salam theory*

Weissmuller, Johnny [wiyzmuhler], popular name of **(Peter) John** (originally **Jonas**) **Weissmuller** (1904–84) Swimmer and film-star, born in Freidorf, W Romania. His family emigrated to the USA in 1908. In 1922 he made history by becoming the first person to swim 100 m in under one minute, and he won the 100 m freestyle at the 1924 and 1928 Olympics, and the 400 m in 1928. After turning professional in 1932, he became a swimsuit model for a clothing firm. His name is most widely known for his starring role in 12 Tarzan films, made between 1932 and 1948. He is credited with inventing the King of the Jungle's celebrated yodelling call (actually a combination of recorded animal cries).

Weizmann, Chaim (Azriel) [viytsman, khiym] (1874–1952) Jewish statesman and president of Israel (1949–52), born near Pinsk, SW Belarus. He studied in Germany and Switzerland, then lectured on chemistry at Geneva and Manchester universities. He helped to secure the Balfour Declaration of 1917, and became president of the Zionist Organization (1920–30, 1935–46) and of the Jewish Agency (from 1929). He played a major role in the establishment of the state of Israel (1948), and was its first president.

Weizsäcker, Carl Friedrich von [viyseker] (1912–) Physicist, born in Kiel, N Germany. He joined the Max Planck Institute (1945–57), where he later became director (1970), and was professor of philosophy at the University of Hamburg (1957–69). His several key discoveries in modern nuclear physics, along with his application of this field to astrophysics, caused him to question the estrangement of religion and science and led to his investigation of Christianity's obligation to technology. He was joint recipient of the Templeton Prize for Progress in Religion in 1989.

Welch, Raquel, originally **Raquel Tejada** (1940–) Actress, born in Chicago, Illinois, USA. She entered beauty contests as a teenager, and worked as a model, waitress, and television weathergirl before making her film debut in 1964. Launched as a sex symbol after her scantily clad appearance in *One Million Years* BC (1966), she was rarely challenged by later roles, though for her role in *The Three Musketeers* (1973) she received a Best Actress Golden Globe Award. Absent from the cinema since 1979, she continues to be regarded as one of the world's great beauties, and her career has included nightclub entertaining, the Broadway musical *Woman of the Year* (1982), and the publication of a *Total Beauty and Fitness Programme* (1984).

weld A biennial, native to Europe, W Asia, and N Africa (*Reseda luteola*); leaves narrow, wavy; first year rosette dense; stem in second year growing to 1·5 m/5 ft; flowers small, yellowish, 4-petalled, in long spike, three petals divided into three or more lobes; fruit a 3-lobed capsule; also called **dyer's rocket**. It was once cultivated as a source of bright yellow dye. (Family: Resedaceae.)

Weldon, Fay, originally **Franklin**, *neé* **Birkinshaw** (1933–) Writer, born in Alvechurch, Worcestershire, WC England, UK. She studied at the University of St Andrews, and worked as an advertising copywriter before becoming a full-time author, writing novels, short stories, and television plays. Her work deals with contemporary feminist themes, as in *Female Friends* (1975) and *Puffball* (1980), and caustic satires of male-dominated society, as in *The Hearts and Lives Of Men* (1987) and *Darcy's Utopia* (1989). Later books include *Wicked Women* (1995), *Big Girls Don't Cry* (1998), and *Mantrapped* (2004).

Welensky, Sir Roy [welenskee] (1907–91) Rhodesian statesman, born in Harare (formerly Salisbury), Zimbabwe (formerly Southern Rhodesia). A railway worker and trade unionist, he was elected to the Legislative Council of Northern Rhodesia (now Zambia) in 1938, knighted in 1953, and from 1956 to its break-up in 1963 was prime minister of the Federation of Rhodesia and Nyasaland (now Malawi). His handling of the constitutional crisis in 1959 aroused much controversy.

welfare economics The branch of economics concerned with how economies should be run (in contrast to **positive economics**, which concerns how they actually work). Welfare economics considers the criteria which should decide what goods and services are produced, what methods should be used to produce them, and how purchasing power should be allocated to individuals. It also studies how far such criteria can be satisfied by markets, and how far their application need involve government regulation or taxation. Modern welfare economics is based on the work of Pareto.

welfare state A system of government whereby the state assumes responsibility for protecting and promoting the welfare of its citizens in such areas as health, income maintenance, unemployment, and pensions. Although earlier origins can be found, the development of modern welfare states was significantly influenced by the Beveridge Report of 1942, and a comprehensive system was established in the UK following World War 2, funded out of national insurance contributions and taxation. Such systems may be universal in coverage or subject to some form of means testing. Critics on the political right of the system claim that welfare provision decreases self-reliance and freedom of choice. In recent years the principal challenge to the welfare state has been that politically acceptable tax levels are too low to sustain its costs, resulting in benefit deregulation and the contracting-out of services.

Welland, Colin (Williams) (1934–) Actor and playwright, born in Liverpool, Merseyside, NW England, UK. He studied at Goldsmiths' College, London, worked as an art teacher, and began his career as an actor in Manchester in 1962. As a dramatist, he has written both for film and television. In 1970, 1973, and 1974 he was voted best TV playwright in Britain. His work for television has included *Roll on Four O'Clock* (1970), *Kisses at Fifty* (1973), and *Bambino Mio* (1994). His screenplays include *Chariots of Fire* (1981) and *Twice in a Lifetime* (1987).

Welland Ship Canal Canal in Ontario, E Canada, linking L Erie and L Ontario, bypassing Niagara Falls; first canal opened, 1829; modern canal, 1932; modernized and expanded, 1972; length 61 km/38 mi; can be used by vessels up to 223 m/732 ft in length.

Welles, (George) Orson (1915–85) Director, producer, writer, and actor, born in Kenosha, Wisconsin, USA. He appeared at the Gate Theatre, Dublin, in 1931, returned to America, became a radio producer in 1934, and founded the Mercury Theatre in 1937. In 1938 his radio production of H G Wells's *War of the Worlds* was so realistic that it caused panic in the USA. In 1941 he wrote, produced, directed, and acted in the film *Citizen Kane*, a revolutionary landmark in cinema technique, with its use of sound, deep-focus photography, and out-of-sequence storytelling. His later work includes his individual film versions of *Macbeth* (1948) and his Falstaff film, *Chimes at Midnight* (1966), along with a variety of memorable film roles, the most celebrated being that of Harry Lime in *The Third Man* (1949). He also appeared on stage in Shakespeare's *Othello* (1951) and in his own adaptation of Melville's *Moby Dick* (1955).

Wellesley, Arthur *Wellington, 1st Duke of*

Wellesley (of Norragh), Richard (Colley) Wellesley, 1st Marquess (1760–1842) British administrator, born in Dangan, Co Meath, E Ireland, the brother of Arthur Wellesley, Duke of Wellington. He became an MP (1784), a Lord of the Treasury (1786), a marquess (1799), and governor-general of India (1797–1805). Under his administration British rule in India became supreme: the influence of France was extinguished, and the power of the princes reduced by the crushing of Tippoo Sahib (1799) and the Marathas (1803). After his return to England, he became ambassador to Madrid (1805), foreign minister (1809), and Lord-Lieutenant of Ireland (1821, 1833).

Wellesz, Egon (Joseph) [veles] (1885–1974) Composer and musicologist, born in Vienna, Austria. He studied under Schoenberg, and became professor of musical history at Vienna (1930–8). Exiled from Austria by the Nazis, he became a research fellow then lecturer and reader in music (1944–56) at Oxford. His works include six operas, nine symphonies, and much choral and chamber music.

Wellington 41°17S 174°47E, pop (2000e) 355 000. Capital city and seat of government of New Zealand, on S coast of North Island; founded, 1840; capital, 1865; airport; railway; ferry to South Island; university (1899); vehicles, footwear, chemicals, soap, metal products, trade in dairy produce, meat; Government Building, Parliament Buildings (1922, 1980), General Assembly Library (1897), War Memorial Museum, St Paul's Cathedral (1866), Michael Fowler Centre, national art gallery, national museum.

Wellington, Arthur Wellesley, 1st Duke of (1769–1852) British general, statesman, and prime minister (1828–30), born in Dublin, Ireland, the brother of Richard Wellesley. He joined the army in 1787, was sent to India with his regiment, and there defeated Tippoo Sahib, became governor of Mysore, and broke the power of the Marathas. Knighted in 1804, he became an MP (1806), and Irish secretary (1807). He defeated the Danes during the Copenhagen expedition (1807), and in the Peninsular War drove the French out of Portugal and Spain, gaining victories at Talavera (1809), Salamanca (1812), and Toulouse (1814). For his role in this campaign he was given many honours, and created Duke of Wellington. After Napoleon's escape from Elba, he routed the French at Waterloo (1815). He supported Liverpool's government, and joined it as master-general of the Ordnance (1818). He also became constable of the Tower (1826) and army commander-in-chief (1827). His period as prime minister significantly weakened the Tory Party, which split over the question of Catholic emancipation, and was further weakened by disagreements over trade and reform. Wellington's opposition to parliamentary reform brought down his government, which was succeeded by the Whigs. He was foreign secretary under Peel (1834–5), and retired from public life in 1846.

wellingtonia *mammoth tree*

Wells, H(erbert) G(eorge) (1866–1946) Writer, born in Bromley, S Greater London, UK. He was apprenticed to a draper, tried teaching, studied biology in London, then made his mark in journalism and literature. He played a vital part in disseminating the progressive ideas which characterized the first part of the 20th-c. He achieved fame with scientific fantasies such as *The Time Machine* (1895) and *War of the Worlds* (1898), and wrote a range of comic social novels which proved highly popular, notably *Kipps* (1905) and *The History of Mr Polly* (1910). Both kinds of novel made successful (sometimes classic) early films. A member of the Fabian Society, he was often engaged in public controversy, and wrote several socio-political works dealing with the role of science and the need for world peace, such as *The Outline of History* (1920) and *The Work, Wealth and Happiness of Mankind* (1932).

wels Large, nocturnal, freshwater catfish (*Silurus glanis*) found in large rivers and lakes of E Europe; length up to 3 m/10 ft; body devoid of scales, mouth with long barbels, anal fin long; feeds on fish and other aquatic vertebrates; fished commercially in some areas using traps and lines, and also farmed. (Family: Siluridae.)

Welsh The Celtic language spoken in Wales, assigned equal status with English in all legal and administrative affairs. Of all the extant Celtic languages, Welsh enjoys the most vibrant literary scene, which continues a tradition dating from the epic poem *Taliesin* (c.6th-c), and the prose tales of the *Mabinogi*, preserved in mediaeval manuscripts recording an oral tradition many centuries older. Its high point is the annual, week-long, high-culture festival, the National Eisteddfod, which has become the focal point of Welsh identity for many. A development of equal importance, particularly for the majority who have no commitment to high culture, is the establishment of a Welsh-language television channel, which has broadened the range of information and entertainment sources in the media. There are now c.580 000 speakers of Welsh.

Welsh, Irvine (1957–) Writer, born in Leith, Edinburgh, EC Scotland, UK. He left school at 16 and held various jobs before taking a business course at Heriot-Watt University in Edinburgh (1988–90). He became known with his controversial first novel, *Trainspotting* (1993; filmed 1996), and later books include *Marabou Stork Nightmares* (1995), *Filth* (1998), and *Porno* (2002). His short story collections include *The Acid House* (1994) and *Ecstasy: Three Tales of Chemical Romance* (1996).

Welsh Assembly, properly **National Assembly for Wales** A legislative body established under the 1998 Government of Wales Act, following a 1997 referendum at which just over half of those voting were in favour. The Assembly was formally opened in 1999, taking over the powers and authority previously exercised by the secretary-of-state for Wales. Broadly these include responsibility for secondary legislation in all policy areas except foreign affairs, defence, broadcasting, the emergency services and the justice system, and the exchequer function. The Assembly receives its revenue through a block grant from the Westminister parliament, which retains responsibility for primary legislation. A presiding officer elected by the 60 members oversees the Assembly (a post first held by Lord Dafydd Elis Thomas). The political leader of the Assembly is the first secretary, and Labour's Alun Michael (1943–) was the first to hold the position, until forced to resign in 2000 (to be followed by Rhodri Morgan). The first secretary appoints a cabinet made up of Assembly secretaries, each of whom is responsible for a policy area. Elections for the Assembly are held every four years with 40 members being elected from single-member constituencies and a further 20 by the Additional Member System (AMS), a form of proportional representation. The first election resulted in the formation of a minority Labour administration (28 seats), ahead of Plaid Cymru (17), the Conservatives (9), and Liberal Democrats (6). Labour increased their position (30 seats) in the 2003 election.

Welsh cob *Welsh pony*

Welsh corgi *corgi*

Welsh literature The *cynfeirdd* or early poets produced a rich literature in Welsh from the late 6th-c, many poems being attributed to Aneirin and Taliesin from that period. This poetry survives in the 'Four Books of Wales', dating from the 12th–14th-c, which also contain the mediaeval prose tales comprising the *Mabinogion*, a conscious synthesis of Arthurian and native materials. The mediaeval court poets (or *Gogynfeirdd*) constituted the bardic schools, and drew up the rules of Welsh versification, while Dafydd ap Gwilym (flourished 1340–70) developed the simpler *cywyddau* or lyrical code. The first formal Eisteddfod was held in the 15th-c; and the Bible was translated into Welsh by 1588. From this point the anglicization of Welsh culture led to a gradual decline. A late great work in Welsh was Ellis Wynne's prose *Gweledigaetheu y Bardd Cwsc* (1703, Visions of the Sleeping Bard). There was still a vigorous tradition of ballad and folk-song, and religious fervour occasioned a revival in the 18th-c, with the lyrics of Williams Pantycelyn (1717–91) and many fine Methodist hymns, although Methodism inhibited the development of prose fiction. Antiquarian interest also played its part, inspired by Lewis Morris (1701–65), although 19th-c poets such as John Blackwell (1797–1840) and John Ceiriog Hughes (1832–87) tended to avoid the traditional metres. A 20th-c revival was prompted by the example of Sir John Morris-Jones (1864–1929); important figures include T(homas) Gwynn Jones (1871–1949) and T(homas) H(erbert) Parry-Williams (1887–1975), and there were several popular poets, notably Cynan (Albert Evans-Jones, 1895–1970). Meanwhile, many Welsh writers have contributed to English literature, including the three Powys brothers (John Cowper, 1872–1964; Llewelyn, 1884–1939, Theodore Francis, 1875–1953), and the poets Dylan Thomas (1914–53) and R S Thomas (1913–2000).

Welsh Nationalist Party *Plaid Cymru*

Welsh pony A breed of horse divided by size and appearance: Section A (**Welsh mountain pony**), height up to 12 hands/1·2 m/4 ft; Section B (resembling Section A but 12–13½ hands/1·2–1·4 m/4–4 ft 6 in high); Section C (resembling a small Welsh cob, up to 13½ hands/1·4 m/4 ft 6 in high); Section D is the **Welsh cob**; round, short-legged, usually grey; a popular child's pony. The **American Welsh pony** in the USA is a breed descended from Welsh animals.

Welsh poppy A perennial growing to 60 cm/2 ft (*Mecanopsis cambrica*), native to W Europe, an isolated, westernmost species of an otherwise Asian genus; leaves pale green, divided into lobed segments; flowers 5–7 cm/2–2¾ in diameter, 4-petalled; fruit an elliptical capsule; producing yellow latex. (Family: Papaveraceae.)

Welty, Eudora (Alice) (1909–2001) Writer, born in Jackson, Mississippi, USA. She studied at Mississippi State College for Women, the University of Wisconsin, and Columbia's Graduate School of Business (1930–1), then worked for newspapers and a radio station in Mississippi, as a publicity agent for the Works Progress Administration (WPA), and lectured at several colleges, living most of her life in Jackson. She has been praised for her finely tuned Southern 'Gothic' novels, such as *The Optimist's Daughter* (1972, Pulitzer), and the keen sense of local place in her short fiction, as seen in *The Collected Stories of Eudora Welty* (1980).

welwitschia [welwichia] A peculiar gymnosperm (*Welwitschia mirabilis*) found only in the deserts of SW Africa, where most of the moisture comes from sea fogs. Its turnip-like stem produces just two strap-shaped leaves several metres long, which grow throughout the plant's life of over a century, becoming torn and ragged. (Family: Gnetaceae.)

Welwyn Garden City [welin] 51°48N 0°13W, pop (2000e) 41 900. Town in Hertfordshire, SE England, UK; 10 km/6 mi NE of St Albans; founded in 1919 by Ebenezer Howard; designated a 'new town' in 1948; railway; chemicals, plastics, pharmaceuticals, food processing.

Wembley Stadium One of the most famous football stadiums in the world, built in Wembley in NE London in 1923 for the British Empire Exhibition of 1924–5. Designed by Sir John Simpson and Maxwell Ayrton, it had a capacity of 120 000, now reduced to 92 000. It was used for a wide range of other occasions, such as greyhound racing, hockey matches, speedway racing, pop concerts, and religious meetings. It was demolished in 2003 to make way for a new national stadium, designed by the architect Norman Foster, on the same site, and scheduled for completion in 2006.

Wenceslaus or **Wenceslas, St** [wenseslas], known as **Good King Wenceslas** (c.903–35) Duke and patron of Bohemia, born in Stochov, W Czech Republic. He received a Christian education, and after the death of his father (c.924) encouraged Christianity in Bohemia, against the wishes of his mother. Probably at her instigation, and because he had put his duchy under the protection of Germany, he was murdered by his brother, Boleslaw. He became the patron saint of Bohemia and Czechoslovakia. Feast day 28 September.

Wendi [wendee], also spelled **Wen-ti** (541–604) First emperor of the Chinese Sui dynasty. As **Yang Jian**, a northerner having close family ties both to the Han nobility and the N Zhou dynasty (557–80), he slaughtered a king and 59 princes to seize the throne, ruling as Wendi ('cultured emperor', 590–604). His lands were around Changan (Xian), which he kept as the imperial capital. Conquering S China with 518 000 men, he then secured Annam's submission (603). Anti-intellectual, he opposed Confucianism but favoured Buddhism. He simplified administration, demanded total obedience to severe laws, and stopped officials working in their home areas. He was murdered by his son and successor, Yang Guang (Yangdi).

Wends A C European people, of Slavic origins, who settled in Lusatia in the 9th-c, in a region around modern Dresden; also known as **Sorbs** or **Lusatians**. They were conquered by the Germans in the 10th-c, and by the Poles and again by the Germans in the 11th-c. In 1815 much of the region eventually became part of Prussia. Small numbers of Sorbian (or Wendish) speakers remain in modern S Germany.

wentletrap A marine snail from the Indo-Pacific region; usually colourless shell with a highly sculptured surface and regularly spaced ribs. (Class: Gastropoda. Order: Mesogastropoda.)

Wentworth, Thomas *Strafford, Earl of*

Wentworth, W(illiam) C(harles) (1790–1872) Australian politician and landowner, born on Norfolk I, New South Wales, SE Australia. He took part in the expedition which explored the Blue Mts in 1813, then studied at Cambridge and became a lawyer. He was a staunch protagonist of self-government for Australia, which he made the policy of his newspaper, *The Australian* (established 1824), and he was elected to the Legislative Council in 1842. He retired to England in 1862.

Wenzel, Hanni [ventsl] (1956–) Alpine skier, born in Staubirnen, Germany. At the 1980 Olympics she won the gold medal in the slalom and giant slalom, and the silver in the downhill. Her total of four Olympic medals (including a bronze in 1976) is a record for any skier. She was combined world champion and overall World Cup winner in 1980.

werewolf In traditional belief, a person assuming the form of a wolf, usually involuntarily and temporarily. There are traces of the belief in Ancient Greek religion, and it existed in much of Europe, but especially in the Balkans. It seems to be related to some kind of initiation rite, in which youths wore animal skins.

Wergeland, Henrik Arnold [vergeland] (1808–45) Poet, playwright, and patriot, born in Kristiansand, S Norway. He is best known for his poetry, notably his Creation epic, *Skabelsen, Mennesket, og Messias* (1830, Creation, Humanity, and Messiah), and for such narrative poems as *Den Engelske Lods* (1844, The English Pilot). A leader of the cause of Norwegian nationalism, he became Norway's national poet.

Wesak [wesahk] A Buddhist festival held in May to celebrate the birth, enlightenment, and death of the Buddha.

Weser, River [vayzer], ancient **Visurgis** Major river in Germany, formed by the confluence of the Werra and Fulda Rivers at Münden in Lower Saxony; flows generally N to the North Sea forming an estuary at Wesermünde; length 440 km/273 mi; connected to the Rhine and Elbe by the Mittelland Canal.

Wesker, Arnold (1932–) Playwright, born in London, UK, of a Russian father and Hungarian mother. His working-class Jewish family background, and his varied attempts at earning a living, are important ingredients of his plays, such as *The Kitchen* (1959) and *Chips with Everything* (1962). His use of a working-class setting rather than the drawing rooms of polite comedy was influential in the development of 'kitchen sink' drama. The Kahn family trilogy, *Chicken Soup with Barley*, *Roots*, and *I'm Talking About Jerusalem* (1959–60), echo the march of events, before and after World War 2, in a left-wing family. Later plays include *The Friends* (1970), *Caritas* (1981), *Little Old Lady* (1988), *Tokyo* (1994), *Longitude* (2002), and a series of monologues for women. He is also known for founding the theatre project Centre 42 (1961–70). His collected plays were published in 1989–90, and a collection of stories, *The King's Daughters*, in 1996.

Wesley, John (1703–91) Evangelist and founder of Methodism, born in Epworth, Lincolnshire, EC England, UK. He studied at Oxford, was ordained deacon (1725) and priest (1728), and in 1726 became a fellow at Oxford and lecturer in Greek. Influenced by the spiritual writings of William Law, he became leader of a small group which had gathered round his brother Charles, nicknamed the Methodists, a name later adopted by John for the adherents of the great evangelical movement which was its outgrowth. On their father's death, the brothers went as missionaries to Georgia (1735–8), but the mission proved a failure. In 1738, at a meeting in London, during the reading of Luther's preface to the Epistle to the Romans, he experienced an assurance of salvation which convinced him that he must bring the same assurance to others; but his zeal alarmed most of the parish clergy, who closed their pulpits against him. This drove him into the open air at Bristol (1739), where he founded the first Methodist Chapel, and then the Foundry at Moorfields, London, which became their headquarters. His life was frequently in danger, but he outlived all persecution, and the itineraries of his old age were triumphal processions throughout the country. He was a prolific writer, producing grammars, histories, biographies, collections of hymns, his own sermons and journals, and a magazine.

Wesley, Samuel (1766–1837) Organist and composer, born in Bristol, SW England, UK, the nephew of John Wesley. One of the most famous organists of his day, he was an ardent enthusiast of J S Bach. Though a Roman Catholic (to the displeasure of his father and uncle), he wrote also for the Anglican Liturgy, leaving a number of fine motets and anthems, including *In exitu Israel*.

Wessex A kingdom of the Anglo-Saxon heptarchy (seven kingdoms), with its main centres at Winchester and Hamwic (Southampton). Under Alfred (871–99), Wessex – by then incorporating Kent and Sussex – was the only English kingdom to withstand the onslaughts of the Danes. Alfred's successors reconquered the Danelaw, and had united all England under a single monarchy by 954. In the novels of Thomas Hardy, Wessex is used to mean the SW counties of England, mainly Dorsetshire.

West, Benjamin (1738–1820) Painter, born in Springfield, Pennsylvania, USA. He showed early promise as an artist, was sent on a sponsored visit to Italy, and on his return journey settled in London (1763) as a portrait painter. He was subsequently patronized by George III for 40 years, and was a founder of the Royal Academy (1768), and its president (from 1792). The representation of modern instead of classical costume in his best-known picture, 'The Death of General Wolfe' (c.1771, several versions), was an innovation in English historical painting.

West, Frederick (1941–95) and **Rosemary West** (1953–) Serial murderers: Frederick, a builder born in Much Marcle, Herefordshire, WC England, UK, and his wife Rosemary, born in Devon, SW England, UK. In 1994 they were accused of killing 10 women, among them the former wife and a daughter of Frederick West, following the discovery of numerous bodies buried in their garden and house at 25 Cromwell Street, Gloucester, England. In 1995 Frederick was found hanged in his Birmingham prison cell while awaiting trial. Rosemary was convicted of 10 murders and sentenced to life imprisonment, and in 1996 the Court of Appeal refused her permission to appeal against her conviction. The house at Cromwell Street was demolished, and in 1997 became the site of a landscaped garden.

West, Mae (1893–1980) Actress, born in New York City, USA. A child performer, she spent some years in vaudeville and on Broadway before her first film, *Night After Night* (1932). Throughout the 1930s a series of racy comedies, often with her own dialogue-script, all celebrating the sexually emancipated woman, although under much pressure from censorship. She subsequently returned to the stage and nightclubs, but made two late character appearances in *Myra Breckenridge* (1970) and *Sextette* (1978), before her death from a stroke in Los Angeles. Her name was given to a pneumatic lifejacket which, when inflated, was considered to give the wearer the generous bosom for which she was noted.

West, Nathanael, pseudonym of **Nathan Wallenstein Weinstein** (1903–40) Novelist, born in New York City, USA. He studied at Brown University, then went to Paris, where he associated with Surrealist writers, and wrote his first novel. He returned to New York City and wrote four short fantasy novels, of which the best known are *Miss Lonelyhearts* (1933) and *The Day of the Locust* (1939), a satire on Hollywood. He was killed, along with his wife, in a traffic accident.

West, Dame Rebecca, pseudonym of **Cicily Isabel Andrews**, *née* **Fairfield** (1892–1983) Novelist and critic, born in London, UK. Educated in Edinburgh, she was for a short time on the stage, and took her name from the character she played in Ibsen's *Kosmersholm*. She is best known for her studies arising out of the Nuremberg war trials: *The Meaning of Treason* (1949) and *A Train of Powder* (1955). Her novels include *The Judge* (1922), *The Thinking Reed* (1936), and *The Birds Fall Down* (1966). Her long association with H G Wells produced a son, the critic and author **Anthony West** (1914–87). She was created a dame in 1959.

West Bank pop (2000e) 1 662 000; region of the Middle East W of the R Jordan and the Dead Sea; comprises the Jordanian governorates of Jerusalem, Hebron, and Nablus; part of the former mandate of Palestine, administered by Jordan, 1949–67; seized by Israel in the 1967 War, and remained under Israeli occupation, administered as the district of Judea-Samaria, where numerous settlements have been built; area includes Old (East) Jerusalem, as well as Bethlehem, Jericho, Hebron, and Nablus; scene of the uprising (*Intifada*) against the Israelis (1987–91), during which time schools and many shops were closed; some areas returned to the Palestine National Authority (Jericho and Hebron), with others being the focus of intense negotiations between the Palestinians and Israel.

West Bengal [benggawl] pop (2001e) 80 221 200; area 87 853 sq km/33 911 sq mi. State in NE India, bounded NW by Nepal, E by Bangladesh, and S by the Bay of Bengal; crossed by many rivers; created in 1947, when the former province of Bengal was divided between the new state of West Bengal and the Muslim majority districts of East Bengal (now Bangladesh); capital, Kolkata (Calcutta); governed by a 295-member Legislative Assembly; rice, foodgrains, oilseed, jute; coal, aluminium, steel, fertilizer; extensive rail network.

West Berlin *Berlin*

westerlies The prevailing winds found at mid-latitudes, between 30° and 60°N and S of the Equator. In the N hemisphere the prevailing direction is from the SW; in the S hemisphere it is from the NW. Westerlies in the S hemisphere are stronger because there is a smaller land mass, and are known as the **Roaring Forties**, from the latitudes at which they occur.

Western A novel or film concerned with the opening up and civilizing of the American West; an epic theme featuring hunters and trackers, cowboys and Indians, horses, stagecoach and railroad, the cavalry, lawmen, women, the California goldrush, and dogs. Fenimore Cooper established a model in *The Pioneers* (1823), basing his Leatherstocking on the exploits of Daniel Boone. Davy Crockett and Kit Carson were similarly fictionalized; and journalist E Z C Judson (1828–86; pseudonym Ned Buntline) promoted Buffalo Bill Cody to mythic status as 'the *beau ideal* of the plains' in dime novels (from 1860), for which Prentiss Ingraham (1843–1904) later wrote over 200 Buffalo Bill stories. Cody's Wild West Show (from 1882) was a by-product. The railroad robbery by Butch Cassidy and his Wild Bunch in 1900 occasioned Edwin S Porter's film *The Great Train Robbery* (1903), beginning the great tradition of Western films, such as *Stagecoach* (1939), *High Noon* (1952), *Shane* (1953), and *Butch Cassidy and the Sundance Kid* (1969). The Western film has drawn on 20th-c Western fiction by such writers as Zane Grey (1872–1939), and C E Mulford, creator of Hopalong Cassidy.

Western Australia pop (2000e) 1 754 000; area 2 525 500 sq km/975 000 sq mi. State in W Australia; Dutchman Dirk Hartog landed here in 1616, and Englishman William Dampier in 1688; Britain's first non-convict settlement on the Swan R, 1829; governed at first by New South Wales; separate colony, 1890; now comprises nine statistical divisions; bounded S by the Great Australian Bight, W by the Indian Ocean and N by the Timor Sea; a third of the total area of Australia; over 90% occupied by the Great Plateau (mean altitude 600 m/2000 ft above sea-level); highest point, Mt Meharry (1245 m/4085 ft); Great Sandy Desert, Gibson Desert, Great Victoria Desert, Nullarbor Plain in the E; near the border with Northern Territory is Wolf Crater, the world's second largest meteorite crater; many dry salt lakes in the interior (notably L Lefroy and L McLeod); several archipelagoes off the coast; principal rivers the Swan, Avon, Blackwood, Gascoyne, Drysdale, Murchison, Ashburton, Fitzroy; capital, Perth; principal towns, Port Hedland, Busselton, Albany, Kalgoorlie, Carnarvon, Bunbury, Geraldton, Broome; major producer of diamonds from the Kimberley region; export of crayfish tails, fishing, forestry, wheat, sheep, wine, agricultural machinery; gold, iron ore, nickel, uranium, bauxite, mineral sands, superphosphates, oil and natural gas; state holidays Labour Day (Mar), Foundation Day (Jun); significant tourist industry, having many beaches, golf courses, cultural and historical attractions.

Western Cape One of the nine new provinces established by the South African constitution of 1994, in SW South Africa; several mountain ranges along the Great Escarpment; capital, Cape Town (also legislative capital of South Africa); pop (2000e) 4 332 000; area 129 386 sq km/49 943 sq mi; chief languages, Afrikaans (63%), English (20%), Xhosa; tourism (Table Mountain, Robben I, Cape of Good Hope, Cape Agulhas); South Africa's richest province; business services, textiles, publishing, wines, sheep, wheat, fishing.

Western European Union An organization of 10 W European nations, founded in 1954 to co-ordinate defence and other policies, replacing the defunct European Defence Community, and reactivated in the 1980s; its members include Belgium, France, Germany, Greece, Italy, Luxembourg, The Netherlands, Portugal, Spain, and the UK. It contains a Council of Ministers, a representative assembly in the Consultative Assembly of the Council of Europe, and a Standing Armaments Committee which works in co-operation with NATO. Several E European countries are linked to it under the heading of Associate Partners. Its headquarters is in Brussels.

Western Sahara

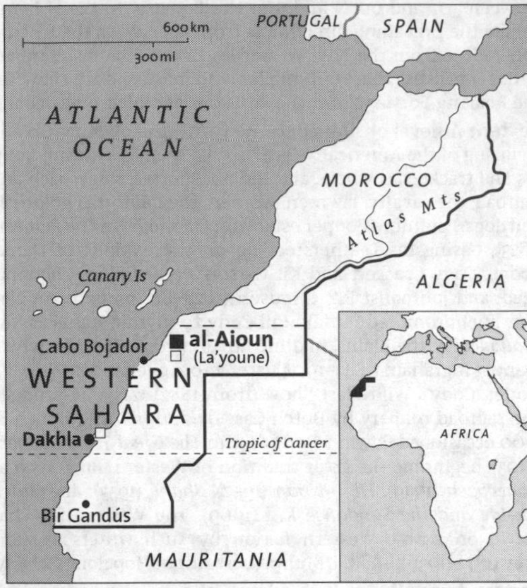

Timezone GMT

Area 252 126 km²/97 321 sq mi

Population total (2000e) 244 900

Status Under dispute, still officially part of Morocco

Capital al-Aioun

Languages Arabic (Hassaniya and Moroccan), French, Berber dialects, Spanish

Ethnic groups Mainly of Arab and Berber descent

Religion Sunni Muslim

Physical features Located in NW Africa, between Morocco (N), Mauritania (S), and Atlantic Ocean (E); low, flat terrain rising to small mountains in S and NE.

Climate Hot, dry desert; limited rainfall; fog and heavy dew produced by cold offshore currents.

Currency 1 Moroccan Dirham (DH) = 100 Moroccan francs

Economy Limited by low rainfall and few natural resources; fishing and phosphate mining are main sources of income.

GDP Not available

History Spanish province known as Spanish Sahara (Western Sahara) since 1884; partitioned by Morocco and Mauritania after its Spanish status ended in 1975; independence proclaimed in 1976, as Saharan Arab Democratic Republic (SADR); Morocco refused to withdraw its claim to the region, resulting in fighting between Morocco and Polisario guerrillas; Mauritania withdrew its claim after signing a peace treaty with the Polisario Front, 1979; SADR admitted to the Organization of African Unity, 1982; UN-supervised talks to decide the region's future, 1990; Polisario guerrilla warfare stopped under UN ceasefire, 1991; renewed fighting, 1993; agreement to UN proposal for a referendum, 1994, but implementation postponed in 1996.

Main SADR government leaders

Head of State

1982– Mohammed Abdelazziz

Head of Government

1999– Bouchraya Hamoudi Bayoune

Officially administered by the Moroccan government.

Western Isles pop (2000e) 29 500; area 2898 sq km/1119 sq mi. Administrative region in W Scotland, UK; group of islands off the W coast (Outer Hebrides), separated from the mainland by the Minch and Little Minch; bounded W by the Atlantic Ocean; main islands, Lewis, North Uist, Benbecula, South Uist, Barra; c.210 km/130 mi N–S; capital, Stornoway, on Lewis; fishing, cattle, sheep, Harris tweed; name often used to refer to both Inner and Outer Hebrides.

Western Reserve Territory in NW Ohio successfully claimed by the state of Connecticut in 1786, during the final settlement of interstate boundary disputes that dated from the colonial era. Connecticut's claim thereafter was to simple ownership, not to jurisdiction. The matter was resolved in 1800, when Connecticut agreed to have the territory added to Ohio.

Western Sahara *see panel*

Western Samoa *Samoa*

Western Wall The only surviving part of the Second Temple of Jerusalem and, as such, the most sacred of Jewish sites. Traditionally a place of prayer and lamentation during the dispersion of the Jews, it was formerly often referred to as the **Wailing Wall**.

West Germany *Germany*

West Glamorgan pop (2000e) 374 700; area 817 sq km/315 sq mi. Former county in SC Wales, UK; created in 1974, and replaced in 1996 by Swansea, and Neath and Port Talbot, unitary authorities.

West Highland Way Long-distance footpath in Scotland, UK; stretching from Milngavie near Glasgow to Fort William; length 158 km/98 mi; opened in 1980.

West Highland white terrier A small, muscular terrier developed in Scotland; thick coat of straight white hair; rounded head; short, pointed, erect ears.

West Indies Federation (1958–1962) An unsuccessful attempt to establish a single government for the English-speaking West Indies. After the Federation failed, the countries of the English-speaking Caribbean slowly gained their independence.

Westinghouse, George (1846–1914) Engineer, born in Central Bridge, New York, USA. In 1863 he invented an air-brake for railways, and founded a company (now a corporation) for the manufacture of this and other appliances. He was a pioneer in the use of alternating current for distributing electric power, and founded the Westinghouse Electrical Co in 1886.

West Irian *Irian Jaya*

Westland area 1175 sq km/454 sq mi. National park, E South Island, New Zealand; joins the Mt Cook National Park along the main divide of the Southern Alps; glaciers, mountains, lakes, forest; established in 1961; a world heritage site.

Westman Islands, Icelandic **Vestmannaeyjar** pop (2000e) 5560; area 21 sq km/8 sq mi. Group of 15 islands and 30 reefs off the S coast of Iceland; includes the volcanic island of Heimaey which erupted in 1973; island of Surtsey was formed during eruptions in 1963–6; fish processing.

Westmeath [westmeeth], Ir **na h-Iarmhidhe** pop (2000e) 63 000; area 1764 sq km/681 sq mi. County in Leinster province, C Ireland; bounded on SW by R Shannon; crossed by the Royal Canal; capital, Mullingar; cattle, agriculture.

West Midlands pop (2001e) 5 267 300; area 899 sq km/347 sq mi. County of C England, UK; adminstrative centre, Birmingham; other chief towns include Wolverhampton, West Bromwich, Coventry, Walsall; vehicles, aircraft, engineering; metropolitan council abolished in 1986.

Westminster, City of 51°30N 0°09W, pop (2001e) 181 300. Borough of C Greater London, UK; N of the R Thames; includes Hyde Park, St James's Park, Green Park and the suburbs of Paddington, Westminster, and Marylebone; administrative centre of the UK; Statutes of Westminster (1275, 1285, 1290) laid the foundations of English law; includes the major tourist area from Westminster Bridge through Trafalgar Square to the West End.

Westminster, Palace of *Houses of Parliament*

Westminster, Statutes of Part of a comprehensive legislative programme undertaken by Edward I to reform English law and administration. The first Statute (1275) was concerned mainly with codes of law, notably compulsory trial by jury; the second (1285) covered many fields of law, and facilitated the creation of entailed estates; the third (1290) protected lords' feudal incidents.

Westminster Abbey The collegiate church of St Peter in Westminster, London, UK. There was probably a monastic settlement on this site from the 8th-c. The first recorded abbey church, consecrated in 1065, was replaced from 1245 by the present building in early English Gothic style. The monastery was dissolved in 1540. Westminster Abbey has a special importance in English history, serving as a coronation church and national shrine, with many memorials to those who have shaped the country's history and culture.

Westminster Assembly A body of clerics (120) and laymen (30) convened by the English Long Parliament in 1643 to arrange a religious settlement to replace the Church of England. Dominated by Presbyterians, it produced a directory of public worship to replace the Prayer Book, and the Westminster Confession of Faith. Its influence declined when the power of the army, which favoured toleration, increased after 1648.

Westminster Confession of Faith The main Presbyterian Confession of Faith, adopted by the Westminster Assembly, England, in 1643. It sets forth the main doctrines of the Christian faith from a Calvinistic perspective, and became the major confessional influence among Reformed Churches of the English-speaking world.

Westmorland Former county of NW England, UK; part of Cumbria since 1974.

Weston-super-Mare 51°21N 2°59W, pop (2002e) 73 400. Resort town in N Somerset, SW England, UK; located 28 km/17 mi SW of Bristol, on the Bristol Channel; flourished as a seaside resort in 19th-c; railway; plastics, engineering; Grand Pier (1904), Winter Gardens and Pavilion (1927).

Westphalia A NW German principality, first settled by Saxons c.700, given to the Archbishop of Cologne (1180), and later forming part of the Lower Rhine–Westphalian Circle of the Empire (1512). In 1803–6 it was divided between Brandenburg-Prussia and neighbouring states. Although the name was coined for Napoleon's satellite kingdom (1807), the princes regained possession (1814–15).

West Point A US military academy founded by Act of Congress in 1802 at the West Point military station on the Hudson R in the state of New York.

West Sussex *Sussex, West*

West Virginia pop (2000e) 1 808 300; area 62 758 sq km/ 24 232 sq mi. State in E USA, divided into 55 counties; the 'Mountain State'; part of Virginia until the Civil War, when the area remained loyal to the Union, and split from Confederate East Virginia, 1861; 35th state admitted to the Union as West Virginia, 1863; capital, Charleston; other chief cities, Huntington, Wheeling, Parkersburg, Morgantown; Ohio R follows the Ohio state border, with several tributaries; Potomac R forms part of the N border; Allegheny Mts dominate the E; highest point, Mt Spruce Knob (1481 m/4859 ft); a rugged, hilly state, most of which is in the Allegheny Plateau; 65% forested; some cattle, dairy products, apples, eggs, corn, tobacco; nation's leading producer of bituminous coal; major producer of natural gas; also stone, cement, salt, oil; glass, chemicals, metals, machinery; both summer and winter tourism.

wet rot A type of timber decay caused by the cellar fungus, *Coniophora puteana*; found only in wood with a high moisture content.

Wexford (county), Ir **Loch Garman** pop (2000e) 103 000; area 2352 sq km/908 sq mi. County in Leinster province, SE Ireland; bounded by St George's Channel and Atlantic Ocean with bays at Wexford, Waterford, and Bannow; Wicklow Mts (N), Blackstairs Mts (W); watered by R Barrow and R Slaney; capital, Wexford; main seaport, Rosslare; rich farmland (cattle) and resort area.

Wexford (town) 52°20N 6°27W, pop (2000e) 16 000. Capital of Wexford county, Leinster, SE Ireland; at mouth of R Slaney where it meets Wexford harbour; railway; machinery, motor vehicles, brewing, cheese, textiles; opera festival (Oct).

Weyden, Rogier van der [viydn] (c.1400–64) Religious painter, born in Tournai, W Belgium. He studied in Tournai, and by 1436 was official painter to the city of Brussels. Little is known of his life, and even his identity has been disputed. He executed many portraits and altarpieces, and among his best-known works are 'The Descent from the Cross' (c.1435–40, Madrid) and the 'Last Judgment' altarpiece (c.1450, Beaune).

Weyl, Hermann [viyl] (1885–1955) Mathematician, born in Elmshorn, N Germany. He studied at Göttingen under David Hilbert, and became professor at Zürich (1913) and Göttingen (1930). Refusing to stay in Nazi Germany, he went to Princeton in 1933. He made important contributions to the theory of Riemann surfaces, the representation theory of Lie groups, the mathematical foundations of relativity and quantum mechanics, and the philosophy of mathematics. His book *Symmetry* (1952) is a largely non-technical account of the relation between group theory and symmetry in pattern and design.

whale An aquatic mammal of worldwide order Cetacea (79 species); evolved from four-legged land mammals; spends entire life in water; resembles fish in shape (although tail blades – *flukes* – are horizontal, not vertical); breathes air through opening(s) on top of head; has insulating layer of oily blubber under skin; two major groups: **toothed whales** (5 families with 69 species, including the sperm whale, killer whale, dolphin, and porpoise); eat mainly fish and squid; locate prey using sonar; single breathing opening; larger **baleen whales** (3 families with 10 species, including rorquals, grey whales, and right whales); sieve plankton using baleen plates; double breathing openings; once hunted extensively.

whalebone *baleen*

whale-headed stork *shoebill*

whale shark The largest of all fishes (*Rhincodon typus*), widely distributed in surface waters of tropical seas; length up to 18 m/ 60 ft; weight up to 20 tonnes; feeds mainly on small planktonic organisms. (Family: Rhincodontidae.)

whaling The hunting of whales for oil, meat, and blubber, which has resulted in a serious decline in whale populations and the near-extinction of several species. Whaling began in the 10th-c in the Bay of Biscay, but in the last two centuries it has been concentrated in Arctic and Antarctic waters. Overexploitation reached a peak in the Arctic in the 1930s, and in the Antarctic in the 1960s. The International Whaling Commission, established in 1946, exists to regulate the industry, but overfishing continues. A moratorium on commercial whaling was set up in 1986, but not all countries have agreed to it, and several have used loopholes, which allow the killing of whales for scientific research, in order to continue whaling.

Wharton, Edith (Newbold), *née* **Jones** (1862–1937) Novelist and short-story writer, born in New York City, USA. Educated at home and in Europe, she formed a durable friendship with Henry James, who did much to encourage and influence her work. Her tragedy *The House of Mirth* (1905) established her as a major novelist. Other works include *The Age of Innocence* (1920, Pulitzer), and her best-known novel, *Ethan Frome* (1911). Her autobiography, *A Backwards Glance*, appeared in 1934.

wheat A cereal second only to rice in importance, originating in the Middle East but cultivated throughout temperate regions of the world; its inflorescence is a dense, cylindrical head. There are numerous species and cultivars with different growth properties and yielding different qualities of flour, such as **bread wheat** (*Triticum aestivum*) and **durum wheat** (*Triticum durum*) from which pasta is made. Wheat is the cereal most suitable for making bread, because of the presence of the elastic protein gluten. (Genus: *Triticum*, 20 species. Family: Gramineae.)

wheatear A thrush native to the N hemisphere and S Africa; inhabits open country, especially dry stony areas; eats insects and seeds. The name is a corruption of 'white arse' (after white rump). (Genus: *Oenanthe*, 20 species.)

Wheatley, Dennis (Yates) (1897–1977) Novelist, born in London, UK. He inherited the family wine business, but sold up in 1931 to concentrate on novel writing. He produced an enormously popular mix of satanism and historical fiction. Indicative titles in a lurid oeuvre are *The Devil Rides Out* (1935), *The Scarlet Impostor* (1942), and *The Sultan's Daughter* (1963). His three-volume autobiography was published posthumously (1978–80).

Wheatstone, Sir Charles (1802–75) Physicist, born in Gloucester, Gloucestershire, SWC England, UK. He became professor of experimental philosophy at London (1834), known for his experiments in sound. He invented the concertina (1829), took out a patent for an electric telegraph (1837), explained the principle of the stereoscope (1838), and invented a sound magnifier for which he introduced the term *microphone*. **Wheatstone's bridge**, a device for the comparison of electrical resistances, was brought to notice (though not invented) by him. He was knighted in 1868.

wheel One of the most important innovations in human material culture, allowing continuous rotary motion, and the continuous conversion of rotary motion into linear motion, and vice versa. The earliest wheels are found c.3500 BC; the earliest with spokes c.2000 BC. The first were sections of tree trunks, but later types were built up of planks joined and cut to shape. Other improvements were the separate axle, the reinforced hub, which could be lubricated, and the metal tyre, which strengthened the rim.

wheel animalcule *rotifer*

Wheeler, Sir (Robert Eric) Mortimer (1890–1976) Archaeologist, born in Glasgow, W Scotland, UK. He studied at London University, and became director of the National Museum of Wales (1920), and keeper of the London Museum (1926–44). He carried out notable excavations in Britain at Verulamium (St Albans) and Maiden Castle, and was director-general of archaeology in India (1944–7), working to particular effect at Mohenjo-daro and Harappa. He then became professor of the archaeology of the Roman provinces at the newly founded Institute of Archaeology in London (1948–55). Knighted in 1952, he was well known for spirited popular accounts of his subject, in books and on television. His works include *Archaeology from the Earth* (1954) and the autobiographical *Still Digging* (1955).

wheel window *rose window*

whelk A marine snail with a spirally coiled external shell; aperture closed off by a chitinous covering (*operculum*) once head and body are drawn inside; single gill present in mantle cavity; most species are carnivores or scavengers. (Class: Gastropoda. Order: Neogastropoda.)

Whichcote, Benjamin (1609–83) Philosopher and theologian, born in Stoke, Shropshire, WC England, UK. He was a student at Cambridge, a fellow of Emmanuel College in 1633, and was ordained and appointed Sunday Afternoon Lecturer in Trinity Church (1636–56). He became provost of King's College in 1644, but lost the post at the Restoration in 1660 by order of Charles II. He published nothing in his lifetime, but is regarded as the spiritual founder of the 'Cambridge Platonists'.

Whicker, Alan (Donald) [wiker] (1925–) British broadcaster and journalist, born in Cairo, Egypt. He served with the Army Film Unit in World War 2, and was a war correspondent in Korea before joining the BBC (1957–68). He worked on the *Tonight* programme (1957–65) and began his *Whicker's World* documentary series in 1958. Television's most travelled man, he has allowed viewers to eavesdrop on the lives of the rich and famous as well as discovering the exotic and extraordinary aspects of everyday lives in all parts of the world. Consistently in the top-10 ratings, he has received numerous awards including election to the Royal Television Society's Hall of Fame in 1993. Among his books are *Some Rise By Sin* (1949) and the autobiographies *Within Whicker's World* (1982) and *Whicker's World: Take 2* (2001). He returned to the battlefields of his youth to film *Whicker's War* (2004) for Channel 4.

whidah *whydah*

Whig Party (USA) One of two major US political parties during the decades prior to the Civil War. The name was adopted in 1834 to signify opposition to 'King' Andrew Jackson (president, 1829–37). The Whigs stood for greater governmental intervention in the economy than did the Democrats, who followed Jackson, but both parties agreed on the necessity of keeping the slavery issue out of politics. The Whigs collapsed in 1854, precisely because the slavery issue could no longer be contained.

Whigs (UK) A British political party which emerged in 1679–80 as the group agitating for the exclusion of James, Duke of York, on the grounds of his Catholicism. The name was probably a contraction of 'Whiggamores' – militant Scottish Presbyterians. The party benefited from the political changes of the Revolution of 1688 and, during its long period of dominance in British politics after 1714, drew much strength from defending 'the principles of 1688', which included limited monarchy and the importance of parliament. Whiggery is better seen as a general set of beliefs along these lines, rather than as a unified party. Most of its leaders were great landowners who used political patronage to create family-based groupings in parliament. The party was supported by many in the moneyed and commercial classes, and by Nonconformists who looked to the Whigs (usually mistakenly) to provide religious toleration. Whig fortunes waned in the late 18th-c, and Whigs became leading members of the new Liberal party from the mid-19th-c.

whimbrel A curlew (*Numenius phaeopus*) which breeds in the N hemisphere on tundra and moors; migrates to muddy and sandy shores in the S hemisphere; striped head; eats insects, berries, and shore invertebrates, especially crabs; also known as the **seven whistler**. *Numenius minutus*, found from Asia to Australasia, is sometimes called the **little whimbrel**.

whinchat A bird of the thrush family Murcicapidae, native to Europe, N Africa, and W Asia (*Saxicola rubetra*); mottled above, pale beneath, with light 'eyebrow' line; inhabits moors and grassland; other species of *Saxicola* also sometimes called whinchats.

whip A party official in a legislative chamber responsible for ensuring that members attend and vote in accordance with party policy; the name derives from the jargon of hunting, a 'whipper in'. Success will depend upon the extent of party cohesiveness and discipline that can be exercised. In the UK, the term is also the title of a weekly document detailing forthcoming parliamentary business.

whipbird An Australian babbler; plumage dark, soft; tail long; bill sharp; head with crest; lives near ground in woodland and scrub; eats insects and spiders; nests in dense undergrowth. (Genus: *Psophodes*, 2 species.)

whippet A small slender breed of dog developed in Britain by cross-breeding small greyhounds with terriers; resembles greyhound but slightly deeper body; occasionally used for racing or hunting rabbits.

Whipple, George H(oyt) (1878–1976) Pathologist, born in Ashland, New Hampshire, USA. He studied at Yale and Johns Hopkins universities, worked at California (1914–21), and became professor of pathology at Rochester in 1921. While at California he researched the effect of diet on haemoglobin production in dogs, discovering that raw liver could restore depleted levels. He shared the 1934 Nobel Prize for Physiology or Medicine with George Minot and William Murphy, who applied his discoveries to humans.

whip-poor-will A North American bird (a goatsucker, *Caprimulgus vociferus*); inhabits open woodland. *Caprimulgus noctitherus* is sometimes called the **Puerto Rican whip-poor-will**.

whip scorpion A nocturnal, predatory arthropod; body scorpion-like, up to 75 mm/3 in long, ending in a long whip-like tail; feeds on insects and small amphibians; usually found under stones and bark in the tropics and subtropics. (Class: Arachnida. Order: Uropygi, c.85 species.)

whip snake Any long thin snake resembling a whip. In the family Colubridae the name is used especially for some species of the genus *Coluber* (from Europe and North America) and North American species in the genus *Masticophis*.

whirligig A dark, shiny beetle that lives in groups on the surface of ponds; fast-moving, typically swimming in small circles using paddle-like middle and hind legs; eyes divided for vision above and below water surface; feeds on insects at water surface. (Order: Coleoptera. Family: Gyrinidae.)

whirlwind A column of air rotating rapidly around a localized centre of low pressure. It is caused by local surface heating, which results in instability and convectional uprising.

whiskey *whisky*

Whiskey Rebellion (1794) An insurrection of farmers in W Pennsylvania, USA, against the excise tax imposed by the federal government on whisky, which they made in large quantities from their crops of grain. The rebellion was suppressed by government forces led by Henry Lee (1756–1818) and Alexander Hamilton.

whisk fern A member of a group of only 10 living species plus various fossil forms, considered the most primitive of vascular plants and possible ancestors of the ferns. They are epiphytic or grow in rock crevices, and have rhizoids but no true roots. The slender, green stems are regularly forked and have a primitive, poorly defined vascular tissue. Leaf-like appendages are tiny, the fertile ones bearing spores. Fossil forms date mainly from the Devonian period, the most famous being *Rhynia*. (Class: Psilophyta.)

whisky (Ireland/US **whiskey**) A spirit distilled from fermented grain, such as barley, rye, wheat, or (in US bourbon) corn; the main spirit produced and consumed in Ireland and Scotland. Whiskies can be single malt, a product of a single distillate, or a blend of several batches, often from several different distilleries.

whist A non-gambling card game, normally played with four people in pairs. Each player receives 13 cards, and the object is to win more tricks than the opposing pair. Trumps are decided before each game, and at **whist drives** trumps are normally played in the following order; hearts, clubs, diamonds, spades. A round of 'no trumps' is also common.

Whistler, James (Abbott) McNeill (1834–1903) Artist, born in Lowell, Massachusetts, USA. He studied for the army, then left the USA to take up art in Paris, and later in London, where his work was controversially received. He is best known for his evening scenes ('nocturnes'), such as 'Old Battersea Bridge' (c.1872–5, Tate, London), and for the famous portrait of his mother (1871–2, Musée d'Orsay). He also became known for his etchings and lithographs, especially those dealing with the London riverside.

Whistler, Rex (John) (1905–44) British artist. He studied at London, and excelled in the rendering of 18th-c life, ornament, and architecture, particularly in book illustration, murals, and designs for the theatre and ballet. Fine examples of his work, including a large mural, are preserved at Plas Newydd, Anglesey.

whistler (ornithology) *thickhead*

whistler (zoology) *mountain beaver*

whistling duck A small, slender duck, widespread in the tropics; dives for food; feeds at night; eats invertebrates and plant material; some species nest in hollow trees; also known as **tree duck**. (Tribe: Dendrocygnini, 8 species.)

Whitbread Book Awards British book prizes, established in 1973. The awards were initially given in four categories (novel, first novel, poetry, and biography) to works by writers who must have been resident in Great Britain or Ireland for at least six months per year for the preceding three years. Category winners are also eligible to become the Whitbread Book of the Year, which is announced two weeks later. Since 1996 the Whitbread Children's Book of the Year has been announced as a separate award. The total prize fund is £50 000: each of the category award winners receives £5000, and the overall winner receives a further £25 000.

Whitby, Synod of A meeting in Britain in 663/4 when, before Oswi, King of Northumbria, the differences in organization between Roman and Celtic Christianity were debated. Roman concepts of church order prevailed, with the result that the two Christian traditions in Britain were eventually united in their acceptance of the authority and practices of Rome.

White, Alan *Oasis*

White, Gilbert (1720–93) Clergyman and naturalist, born in Selborne, Hampshire, S England, UK. He studied at Oxford, where he became a fellow of Oriel College. He was ordained in 1751, and from 1755 lived uneventfully as curate in Selborne, where he kept a journal containing observations made in his garden. His letters on the subject, written over a period of 20 years, were published as *The Natural History and Antiquities of Selborne* (1789). It has become an English classic: an inspirational naturalist's handbook, it has never been out of print.

White, Patrick (Victor Martindale) (1912–90) Writer, born in London, UK of Australian parents. His youth was spent partly in Australia, and partly in England, where he studied at Cambridge. His first novel, *Happy Valley*, appeared in 1939, and after service as an intelligence officer in World War 2 he returned to Australia, where he wrote several novels, short stories, and plays, achieving international success with *The Tree of Man* (1954), an epic of pioneer Australia, and *Voss* (1957), a novel on a similar scale. A poetic writer of great intensity and some wit, he wrote of great visionaries as well as the sordidness of the everyday. He received the Nobel Prize for Literature in 1973. His autobiographical *Flaws in the Glass* was published in 1981, and he later became vocal on such issues as Aboriginal affairs and the environment.

White, T(erence) H(anbury) (1906–64) Novelist, born in Mumbai (Bombay), W India. He studied at Cambridge, and taught at Stowe School, England (1930–6), where he wrote his first success, *England Have My Bones* (1936). With the exception of the largely autobiographical *The Goshawk* (1951), his best work was in the form of legend and fantasy, especially his sequence of novels about King Arthur, *The Once and Future King* (1958), beginning with *The Sword in the Stone* (1937). His King Arthur novels were adapted for the stage as a musical, *Camelot* (1959), by Alan J Lerner and Frederick Loewe.

white ant *termite*

White Australia Policy The unofficial national policy of Australia from 1901 to the late 1960s, designed to exclude non-European migrants; it was particularly aimed at Asians, Pacific Islanders, and Africans who, it was feared, might come to dominate Europeans. The trade union movement supported the policy on the grounds that it excluded workers who might undermine union wage rates. In the 1950s and 1960s, the Colombo Plan (1950) brought Asian students to Australia, and their presence helped to reduce racial prejudice in the major urban areas. In the late 1960s, the policy was progressively dismantled, and race was replaced as a basis for admission by other criteria such as educational and technical qualifications.

whitebait Small silvery fish found abundantly in shallow coastal waters and estuaries; includes the S African *Atherina breviceps*, and in the N Atlantic the small first-year herrings, *Clupea harengus*, and young sprats, *Sprattus sprattus*.

whitebeam A spreading, deciduous tree or shrub (*Sorbus aria*), native to Europe; leaves oval, shallowly lobed or toothed, white-woolly beneath; flowers white, in clusters; berries red. Cultivars with white-flecked berries and purple twigs are common street trees. (Family: Rosaceae.)

white bryony A perennial with a large, white, tuber-like base (*Bryonia dioica*), native to Europe, W Asia, and N Africa; stems long, slender, climbing by tendrils; leaves palmately 3–5-lobed, toothed; flowers greenish-white, 5-petalled, males 12–18 mm/$\frac{1}{2}$–$\frac{3}{4}$ in diameter, females smaller, on separate plants; berry 5–8 mm/0·2–0·3 in diameter, changing from green through white and orange to red. (Family: Cucurbitaceae.)

White Canons *Premonstratensians*

white cedar A species of *arbor vitae* (*Thuja occidentalis*), native to E North America, which provides white or yellowish timber. (Family: Cupressaceae.)

white currant *red currant*

white dwarf A small, dim star in the final stages of its evolution. The masses of known white dwarfs do not exceed 1·4 solar masses. They are defunct stars, collapsed to about the diameter of the Earth, at which stage they stabilize, with their electrons forming a degenerate gas, the pressure of which is sufficient to balance gravitational force.

white-eye A small songbird, native to Old World tropical regions; white ring around eye; tongue-tip brush-like; inhabits woodland edges and scrub; eats soft fruit, nectar, insects, and spiders. The name is also used for some pochards. (Family: Zosteropidae, c.85 species.)

Whitefield, George [**whitfeeld**] (1714–70) Methodist evangelist, born in Gloucester, Gloucestershire, SWC England, UK. Associated with the Wesleys at Oxford and on their mission to Georgia, he became an enthusiastic evangelist. He founded no distinct sect, but had many adherents in Wales and Scotland, who formed the Calvinistic Methodists. The Countess of Huntingdon appointed him her chaplain, and built and endowed many chapels for him. He made several visits to America, where he founded an orphanage, and played an important role in the Great Awakening.

whitefish Any of a small group of freshwater and brackish-water fishes widespread in lakes and large rivers of the N hemisphere; some populations are migratory, others remain in fresh water; species include the vendace, cisco, and houting. (Genus: *Coregonus*. Family: Salmonidae.)

whitefly A small, sap-sucking bug; adults active fliers; bodies and wings covered with a waxy, white powder; immature stages immobile, typically found on underside of leaves; commonly produces honeydew, and attended by ants. (Order: Homoptera. Family: Aleyrodidae, c.1200 species.)

White Friars *Carmelites*

Whitehall A wide thoroughfare lying between Parliament and Trafalgar Squares in London, UK, and by association the offices of central government which line it. All that remains of the Palace of Whitehall, from which the street takes its name, is the 17th-c banqueting house designed by Inigo Jones.

Whitehead, A(lfred) N(orth) (1861–1947) Mathematician and Idealist philosopher, born in Ramsgate, Kent, SE England, UK. He studied at Cambridge, where he was senior lecturer in mathematics until 1910. He then taught at London (1910–14), becoming professor of applied mathematics at Imperial College (1914–24), and was then professor of philosophy at Harvard (1924–37). He collaborated with his former pupil, Bertrand Russell, in writing the *Principia mathematica* (1910–13). His best known philosophical works are *The Concept of Nature* (1920) and *Process and Reality* (1929). Other more popular works include *Adventures of Ideas* (1933) and *Modes of Thought* (1938). He received the Order of Merit in 1945.

Whitehorse 60°41N 135°08W, pop (2000e) 20 000. Capital of Yukon territory, NW Canada; on the R Lewes; founded during Klondike gold rush, 1900; mining, government, fur-trapping, tourism.

White Horse, Vale of the Site in Oxfordshire, SC England, UK, of a stylized representation of a horse, carved on the chalk hillside about 3000 years ago. A 1990–5 study revealed that deep trenches were dug in the shape of the horse, then filled with chalk quarried from the hill above the site. Perhaps originally a cult object for the local Celtic tribe, the Belgae, it has inspired many imitations.

White House The official residence of the US president, situated on Pennsylvania Avenue in Washington, District of Columbia, USA. The 132-room Neoclassical mansion was built (1793–1801) from the designs of James Hoban (1762–1831), who also supervised its reconstruction (1814–29) after it was burnt down by the British in 1814. Major restoration work was carried out in 1948–52 after the building was discovered to be in danger of collapse.

Whitelaw, Billie (1932–) Actress, born in Coventry, West Midlands, C England, UK. She made her London debut in Feydeau's *Hotel Paradiso* in 1956, then joined the National Theatre (1964) and the Royal Shakespeare Company (1971). A noted interpreter of Samuel Beckett's work, her performances include *Play* (1964), Mouth in *Not I* (1973), and *Footfalls* (1976). She has appeared in a wide range of other classical and modern parts, and received several awards. She has also had a varied film career, appearing in such films as *Frenzy* (1972), *The Omen* (1976), *Water Babies* (1978), *The Krays* (1990), and *Jane Eyre* (1996). Work for television includes the BBC drama series *Born to Run* (1997), and *Merlin* (1998). Her autobiography, *Billie Whitelaw...Who He?*, was published in 1995.

Whitelaw, William (Stephen Ian) Whitelaw, 1st Viscount, popularly known as **Willie Whitelaw** (1918–99) British statesman, born in Nairn, Highland, N Scotland, UK. He studied at Cambridge, served in World War 2, and became a Conservative MP in 1955. After a number of junior posts, and several years as Chief Whip (1964–70), he became Leader of the House of Commons (1970–2), secretary of state for Northern Ireland (1972–3) and for employment (1973–4), and home secretary (1979–83). Made a viscount in 1983, he was Leader of the House of Lords until 1988, when he retired following a stroke.

Whiteman, Paul (1890–1967) Jazz bandleader, born in Denver, Colorado, USA. He became famous in the 1920s as a pioneer of 'sweet-style' as opposed to traditional jazz. His band employed such exponents of true jazz as Bix Beiderbecke, the trumpeter, and Whiteman became popularly regarded as the inventor of jazz itself, rather than of a deviation from earlier jazz style. He was responsible for Gershwin's experiments in symphonic jazz, commissioning *Rhapsody in Blue* for a concert in New York City in 1924.

White Nile or **Bahr El Ablad** Upper reach of R Nile in S and E Sudan; a continuation of the Albert Nile, which crosses into SE Sudan from NE Uganda at Nimule; flows generally N to Khartoum, where it is joined from the E by the Blue Nile, forming the R Nile proper; length 1900 km/1180 mi.

whiteout A condition which occurs when there is a scattering of light between the base of low cloud and a bright snow surface, making it difficult to locate the horizon. The term is also used for blizzard conditions in which it is difficult to determine direction.

white paper In the UK, a government publication printed for the information of parliament, setting out the government's policy and legislative intentions in a specific area, such as the annual Expenditure White Paper. Such a statement of policy is not bulky enough to need the protective covers of a blue book. Depending upon the area in question, different degrees of scope exist for consultation and discussion before the proposals are put into effect. White papers are often preceded by green papers (so called because they have green covers), which are consultative documents designed to elicit public debate. White papers are also available to the public.

Whiteread, Rachel (1963–) Artist and sculptor, born in London, UK. She studied at Brighton Polytechnic and the Slade School of Art in London, and became known for her casts of ordinary domestic objects, such as wardrobes and baths. In 1993 she captured the public imagination with her life-sized cement cast of a three-storey terraced house in East London. The project gained her the Turner Prize and was demolished soon afterwards. Later work includes a plastercast *Untitled (Room 101)* (2003) on view in the Victoria and Albert Museum.

White Russia *Belarus*

White Russians The name collectively given to counter-revolutionary forces led by ex-tsarist officers, which fought unsuccessfully against the Bolshevik Red Army during the Russian Civil War (1918–22). The name was derived from the royalist opponents of the French Revolution, known as the Whites, because they adopted the white flag of the French Bourbon dynasty. The White Russians were weakened by their own internal quarrels and by their refusal to grant land reforms in the areas under their control. The Whites were supported by the military intervention of British, American, French, and Japanese troops; when these withdrew, White resistance to the Red Army collapsed.

White Sands An area of white gypsum sand dunes in S New Mexico, USA, designated a national monument in 1933. It is surrounded by a missile testing range. The first nuclear explosion took place here in July 1945.

White Sea, Russian **Beloye More** area c.95 000 sq km/36 670 sq mi. Arm of the Arctic Ocean and inlet of the Barents Sea, NW European Russia; port of Belmorsk connected to St Petersburg on the Baltic by a 225 km/140 mi-long canal system, completed in 1933; ice-breakers keep some sea channels open in winter; herring and cod fishing.

white shark Large and extremely aggressive shark (*Carcharodon carcharias*), considered the most dangerous of all sharks; widespread in tropical to temperate seas, mostly in open waters but occasionally inshore; length up to 6 m/20 ft; grey to brown above, underside white; teeth large and finely serrated; feeds on a variety of fish and on other sharks, dolphins, and seals; many attacks on humans are by white sharks. (Family: Lamnidae.)

whitethroat Either of two species of Old World warbler, native to Europe, Africa, and S Asia: the **whitethroat** (*Silvia communis*); and the **lesser whitethroat** (*Silvia curruca*), which includes **small** and **Hume's whitethroats**); inhabits open woodland; eats insects and fruit. (Genus: *Silvia*.)

Whitewater scandal A series of allegations of financial misconduct levelled against Bill and Hillary Clinton, relating to a commercial land development in the 1980s. Whitewater was the name of an Arkansas property development corporation in which (at the time) Governor Clinton and his wife (a member of a local law firm) were partners. The allegations surfaced in the media following Clinton's inauguration as president in 1993, but despite probes by the Senate and a special prosecutor, the Clintons were never charged with wrongdoing.

white whale *beluga* (mammal)

Whitgift, John (c.1530–1604) Anglican clergyman, born in Grimsby, North East Lincolnshire, EC England, UK. He studied at Cambridge, was ordained in 1560, and rose to be Dean of Lincoln (1571), Bishop of Worcester (1577), Archbishop of Canterbury (1583), and a privy councillor (1586). He attended Elizabeth I in her last moments, and crowned James I. He was a champion of conformity, and vindicated the Anglican position against the Puritans.

whiting European codfish (*Merlangius merlangus*) widely distributed in shallow shelf waters from N Norway to the Black Sea; length up to 70 cm/28 in. (Family: Gadidae.) The name is also used for a popular food and game fish of the W North Atlantic (*Menticirrhus saxatilis*. Family: Sciaenidae.)

Whiting, John (Robert) (1917–63) Playwright, born in Salisbury, Wiltshire, S England, UK. He trained at the Royal Academy of Dramatic Art, London, becoming an actor before emerging as a playwright, with such early plays as *Saint's Day* (1951) and *A Penny for a Song* (1956). His best-known work was *The Devils* (1961), a dramatization of Huxley's *The Devils of Loudon*, commissioned by the Royal Shakespeare Company, which achieved great success, despite (or because of) its harrowing torture scenes.

Whitlam, (Edward) Gough [gof] (1916–) Australian statesman and prime minister (1972–5), born in Melbourne, Victoria, SE Australia. He studied at Canberra and Sydney universities, and became a lawyer. He was elected a Labor MP in 1952, and became leader of the Australian Labor Party in 1967. The first Labor prime minister in 23 years, he ended conscription, relaxed the policy on non-white immigrants, and increased federal government involvement in welfare, education, and the arts. He was dismissed by the governor-general, Sir John Kerr, after the Opposition blocked his money bills in the upper house of the Senate – the first time the crown had so acted against an elected prime minister. The ALP lost the ensuing election, and he resigned as an MP in 1978 to take up a university appointment at Canberra. A flamboyant, erudite figure who remains controversial, his book *The Whitlam Government* was published in 1985, and an account of his activities since leaving politics, *Abiding Interests*, in 1997.

Whitman, Walt(er) (1819–92) Poet, born in Long Island, New York, USA. He worked in offices and as a teacher, then took up journalism (1848–54). An outstanding proponent of free verse, his major poetic work was *Leaves of Grass* (1855), originally a small folio of 95 pages, which grew in succeeding editions to over 400 pages. Many of the poems in it are now considered American classics, such as 'When Lilacs Last in the Courtyard Bloom'd', and 'O Captain! My Captain!'. During the Civil War he became a volunteer nurse – a bitter experience which forms much of the subject matter of his later prose works, notably *Democratic Vistas* (1871) and *Specimen Days and Collect* (1882). He was a major influence on later US poets.

Whitney, Eli (1765–1825) Inventor, born in Westborough, Massachusetts, USA. He studied at Yale, and went to Georgia as a teacher. He found a patron in Mrs Nathanael Greene, the widow of a general, stayed on her plantation, read law, and set to work to invent a cotton-gin (patented in 1793) for separating cotton fibre from the seeds. His machine was pirated, and unsuccessful lawsuits in defence of his rights took up all his profits, plus the $50 000 voted him by the state of South Carolina. In 1798 he obtained a government contract for the manufacture of firearms, and made a fortune in this business, developing a new system of mass-production.

Whitsunday or **Whit Sunday** In the Christian Church, the seventh Sunday after Easter, commemorating the day of Pentecost. The name Whit ('white') Sunday derives from the white robes traditionally worn by those baptized on this day.

Whittier, John Greenleaf (1807–92) Quaker poet and abolitionist, born near Haverhill, Massachusetts, USA. Largely self-educated, he embarked on a career as a writer and journalist, publishing a collection of poems and stories, *Legends of New England*, in 1831. In 1840 he settled at Amesbury, where he devoted himself to the cause of emancipation. His later works include *In War Time* (1864) and *At Sundown* (1892). In his day he was considered second only to Longfellow.

Whittington, Dick, popular name of **Richard Whittington** (c.1358–1423) English merchant, supposed to have been the youngest son of Sir William Whittington of Pauntley in Gloucestershire, SWC England, UK, on whose death he set out at 13 for London, where he found work as an apprentice. He became an alderman and sheriff, and thrice Lord Mayor of London (1397–9, 1406–7, 1419–20). The legend of his cat is an accepted part of English folklore.

Whittle, Sir Frank (1907–96) Aviator and inventor of the British jet engine, born in Coventry, West Midlands, C England, UK. He entered the RAF as a boy apprentice, became a fighter pilot (1928) and a test pilot (1931–2), then went to Cambridge to read science (1934–7). He had been considering jet propulsion since joining the RAF, and patented a turbo-jet engine in 1930, but received no government support for his ideas until the outbreak of war. His engine successfully powered an aircraft flight in 1941, and by 1944 was in service with the RAF. He was knighted in 1948.

Whitworth, Kathy, popular name of **Kathrynne Ann Whitworth** (1939–) Golfer, born in Monahans, Texas, USA. The most successful woman golfer to date, she has won all the women's major events on the US circuit except the US Open. She turned professional in 1958, and won the US Ladies Professional Golf

Association Championship three times: in 1967, 1971, and 1975. She was the leading money-winner eight times between 1965 and 1973 and won a record 88 LPGA titles.

WHO *United Nations*

whooping cough An acute severe bronchitis caused by *Bordetella pertussis*, mainly affecting children; also known as **pertussis**. It is characterized by a series of violent coughs followed by a deep inspiration (the 'whoop'). It is highly infectious and spread by infected droplets produced by the cough. Diagnosis is by swabs from the nasopharynx, and the bacteriological culture of the causative micro-organism. The condition carries a high mortality in infants, and active immunization is highly desirable.

whooping crane A crane native to North America (*Grus americana*); breeds in Canada; migrates to Gulf of Mexico; plumage white; face red; extremely rare (only 18 birds known in 1969, but this had increased to 377 in a 1998 survey).

whortleberry *bilberry; cowberry*

Whovian *Doctor Who*

whydah [widuh] A songbird of the genus *Vidua* (8 species), with uncertain relationships, treated variously as a weaver-finch or weaverbird, and sometimes put in a separate family Viduidae; finch-like; male with very long tail; lays eggs in nests of (other) weaver-finches; young reared by 'foster' parents; also known as **whidah** or **widow finch**. Some species are called **combassous**, **indigo birds**, or **indigo finches**. The name (as well as **widow bird**) is also used for some weaverbirds of the genus *Euplectes*.

Whymper, Edward (1840–1911) Wood-engraver and mountaineer, the first to climb the Matterhorn, born in London, UK. He was trained as an artist on wood, but became better known for his mountaineering than for his book illustrations. In the period 1860–9 he conquered several hitherto unscaled peaks of the Alps, including the Matterhorn (1865), when four of his party fell to their death. He later travelled in Greenland, the Andes, and Canada.

Wichita [wichitaw] 37°42N 97°20W, pop (2000e) 344 300. Seat of Sedgwick Co, S Kansas, USA, on the Arkansas R; settled, 1866; named after an Indian tribe; city status, 1870; largest city in Kansas; airport; railway; two universities (1892, 1898); chief commercial and industrial centre in S Kansas; aircraft, chemical and petroleum products, railway engineering, food processing (grain and meat); world's largest producer of general aviation aircraft; Cow Town (1870s replica); Wichita River Festival (May).

Wicklow, Ir **Cill Mhantáin**, nickname **the Garden of Ireland** pop (2000e) 98 000; area 2025 sq km/782 sq mi. County in Leinster province, E Ireland; bounded E by Irish Sea; watered by Slaney, Liffey, and Avoca Rivers; Wicklow Mts (W); capital, Wicklow (pop (2000e) 5300); agriculture; resort towns (eg Bray).

Widdecombe, Ann (Noreen) [widikum] (1947–) British stateswoman, born in Bath, SW England, UK. She studied at Birmingham University and Oxford, and stood unsuccessfully in the 1979 and 1983 general elections before being elected as Conservative MP for Maidstone in 1987. She became minister-of-state for employment (1994–5) and at the Home Office (1995–7), then shadow secretary for health (1998–9) and shadow home secretary (1999–2001). Her somewhat idiosyncratic approach to politics has given her a cult status amongst some groups. She also attracted publicity when she converted from Anglicanism to Roman Catholicism over the issue of women priests.

wide-angle lens A lens that has a wide field angle of view or coverage compared with the standard lens fitted to the camera. Its focal length is less than the diagonal of the film format in use. The standard lens has a field angle of c.52°, and coverage of 55–65°, 65–80°, and 80–110° is given by **semi wide-angle**, **wide-angle**, and **extreme wide-angle** lenses respectively.

wide area network (WAN) *local area network*

wide-screen cinema For more than 50 years the proportions of the cinema screen were comparatively square, 4 × 3, aspect ratio (AR) 1·33:1. But following public interest in Cinerama, 20th-Century Fox in 1953 introduced CinemaScope, whose double-width format, 2·35:1 proved popular. Enlarged screens were installed in many theatres, but in some there was insufficient proscenium width, and in these the screen height was reduced to give a wide-screen appearance with AR between 1·65:1 and 1·85:1. Several systems using film gauges wider than 35 mm were tried, but of these only 70 mm prints, AR 2·2:1, have continued. The IMAX and OPTIMAX systems, using a very large frame on 70 mm, provide the widest screen presentation, but can be seen at only about 100 purpose-built theatres throughout the world. All regular feature films are now wide-screen, but television has retained the former 4 × 3 proportion, so there is some loss of picture when they are shown in video. High-definition television in the 1990s adopted a wider format.

widgeon *wigeon*

Widor, Charles Marie (Jean Albert) [weedaw(r)] (1844–1937) Composer, born in Lyon, SC France. He was organist at Lyon and (1870) at St Sulpice, Paris, and became professor of organ (1890) and composition (1896) at the Paris Conservatoire. He composed 10 symphonies for the organ, as well as a ballet, chamber music, and other orchestral works, and is probably best known for his Toccata, a favourite for weddings.

widow bird / finch *whydah*

Wieland, Christoph Martin [veelant] (1733–1813) Writer, born near Biberach, S Germany. After several early devotional works, he made the first German translation of Shakespeare (1762–6), and wrote a number of popular romances, notably *Agathon* (1766–7). After holding a professorship at Erfurt, he was called to Weimar to train the grand-duchess's sons, where he lived until his death. During this time he translated many classical authors, and wrote his best-known work, the heroic poem 'Oberon' (1780).

Wieliczka salt mine [vyelitska] A salt mine in S Poland which has been worked for over 500 years, and which is still in operation; a world heritage site. Apart from its antiquity and immense size, the mine is noted for its museum of salt mining techniques and equipment, and for its subterranean architecture and sculptures.

Wieman, Carl E (1951–) Physicist, born in Corvallis, Oregon, USA. He studied at the Massachusetts Institute of Technology, and at Stanford and Chicago universities, and went on to work at the National Institute of Standards and Technology at the University of Colorado. He shared the 2001 Nobel Prize for Physics for the achievement of Bose–Einstein condensation in dilute gases of alkali atoms, and for early fundamental studies of the properties of the condensates.

Wien [veen] *Vienna*

Wien, Wilhelm (Carl Werner Otto Fritz Franz) [veen] (1864–1928) Physicist, born in Gaffken, Germany. He studied at Göttingen and Berlin, worked as assistant to Helmholtz, and later was professor at Würzburg (1900–20) and then at Munich. In the early 1890s he studied thermal radiation, and by 1896 had developed **Wien's formula** describing the distribution of energy in a radiation spectrum as a function of wavelength and temperature. The formula's accuracy reduces as wavelength increases, and it was this failure which inspired Planck to devise the quantum theory, which revolutionized physics in 1900. Wien was awarded the Nobel Prize for Physics in 1911.

Wiener, Norbert [weener] (1894–1964) Mathematical logician, the founder of cybernetics, born in Columbia, Missouri, USA. A child prodigy, he entered university at 11, studied at Harvard, Cornell, Cambridge, and Göttingen universities, and became professor of mathematics at the Massachusetts Institute of Technology (1932–60). During World War 2 he worked on guided missiles, and his study of the handling of information by electronic devices, based on the feedback principle, encouraged comparison between these and human mental processes in *Cybernetics* (1948) and other works.

Wiesbaden [veezbahdn] 50°05N 8°15E, pop (2000e) 267 000. Capital city of Hesse province, WC Germany; on the R Rhine, 32 km/20 mi W of Frankfurt am Main; railway; chemicals, cement, hydraulics, tools; popular health resort; a traditional wine centre, most of the large German Sekt (sparkling wine) cellars are in this area.

Wieschaus, Eric F(rancis) [**vee**shows] (1947–) Developmental biologist, born in South Bend, Iowa, USA. He studied at Yale University, where he became professor of biology, then moved to Princeton. He shared the Nobel Prize for Physiology or Medicine in 1995 for his research into how genes control early development of the human embryo. Using the fruit fly, his contribution, in collaboration with Nuesslein-Volhard, was to identify a number of genes which determine the body plan and formation of body segments.

Wies pilgrimage church [vees] An 18th-c church in Wies, Germany, founded in 1330 to house a miraculously weeping statue of Jesus, and soon the centre of a religious cult. The present building, a masterpiece of Bavarian religious Baroque, was designed by Dominikus Zimmermann (1685–1766); it is a world heritage site.

Wigan 53°33N 2°38W, pop (2001e) 301 400. Town in Greater Manchester, NW England, UK; 27 km/17 mi NE of Liverpool, on R Douglas and the Leeds–Liverpool Canal; a borough since 1246; railway; engineering, cotton, foodstuffs, packaging; Wigan Pier, now a museum, made famous by George Orwell, in *The Road to Wigan Pier* (1932); football league team, Wigan Athletic (Latics).

wigeon or **widgeon** A dabbling duck of the genus *Anas*: the **European wigeon** (*Anas penelope*), from Eurasia and N Africa (some reach North America); the **North American wigeon** or **baldpate** (*Anas americana*), some of which reach Europe; and the **Chiloë wigeon** (*Anas sibilatrix*), from South America.

Wiggin, Kate Douglas, *née* **Smith** (1856–1923) Novelist and kindergarten educator, born in Philadelphia, Pennsylvania, USA. She led the kindergarten movement in the USA with the opening of the first free kindergarten on the W coast, but she is best remembered for her children's novels, notably *Rebecca of Sunnybrook Farm* (1903). Other titles include the 'Penelope' exploits, *The Birds' Christmas Carol* (1888), and *Mother Carey's Chickens* (1911).

Wight, Isle of, Lat **Vectis** pop (2001e) 132 700; area 381 sq km/ 147 sq mi. Island county off the S coast of England, UK, a unitary authority from 1995; in the mouth of Southampton Water, separated from Hampshire by the Solent and Spithead; an irregular range of chalk hills running E–W ends at the imposing cliffs of the vertical sandstone Needles near Alum Bay; drained by the R Medina; county town, Newport; chief towns include Cowes, Ryde, Sandown, Shanklin, Ventnor; ferry services from Portsmouth, Southampton, Lymington; tourism, agriculture, hovercraft and boat building, electronics; yachting (especially Cowes Regatta Week); Osborne House.

Wightman Cup An annual lawn tennis competition involving professional women's teams from the USA and UK. It was first held in 1923, and named after the former US player Hazel Wightman (*née* Hotchkiss) (1886–1974). It was scrapped in 1992, due to the overwhelming superiority of the Americans, and consequent lack of commercial support.

Wigman, Mary, originally **Marie Wiegmann** (1886–1973) Dancer, choreographer, and teacher, born in Hanover, NC Germany. Her career as Germany's most influential and creative modern dancer began after World War 1, when she toured extensively and opened a school in Dresden in 1920. The school became the focal point of the *Neue Künstlerische Tanz* ('new artistic dance'), also known as *Ausdruckstanz* ('expressive dance'), a theatrical dance form not based on classical techniques. Her activities were reduced during World War 2, but in 1945 she started work again in Leipzig and Berlin. Through her schools and her highly dramatic performances she provided the focus for the development of a performance form of European modern dance.

Wilberforce, William (1759–1833) British politician, evangelist, and philanthropist, born in Hull, NE England, UK. He studied at Cambridge, became an MP (1780), and in 1788 began the movement which resulted in the abolition of the slave trade in the British West Indies in 1807. He next sought to secure the abolition of all slaves, but declining health compelled him in 1825 to retire from parliament. He died in London, one month before the passing of the Slavery Abolition Act. He was a lifelong friend of the Younger Pitt, and he supported Pitt's attacks in the 1790s on those radical political reformers who drew their inspiration from the French Revolution and Thomas Paine, though he remained a political independent. His evangelical beliefs led him to urge the aristocracy to practise 'real Christianity', and to give a moral lead to the poor, and he promoted many schemes for the welfare of the community.

Wilbur, Richard (Purdy) (1921–) Poet, born in New York City, USA. He studied at Amherst and Harvard universities, and taught at many institutions, notably at Wesleyan University (1957–77). Based in Cummington, MA, he has won acclaim for his translations as well as for his own lyrical poetry, as in *New and Collected Poems* (1988). Later works include *The Pig in the Spigot* (2000). He is widely known for his often performed translations of Molière, and for his lyrics to the musical, *Candide* (1956). He received the Pultizer Prize for *Things of This World* in 1956, and was named poet laureate of the USA in 1987.

Wilbye, John (1574–1638) Madrigal composer, born in Diss, Norfolk, E England, UK. He was a farmer, who became a household musician at Hengrave Hall in Essex (c.1593–1628). He is known for only 66 madrigals, but these are renowned for his careful setting of literary texts, and for several translations of Italian poems.

wild boar A wild ancestor (*Sus scrofa*) of the domestic pig, native to Europe, NW Africa, and S Asia; thick dark hair; male with tusks; domesticated in SE Asia 5–10 000 years ago.

wild cat A member of the cat family (*Felis silvestris*), found from N Europe to Africa and India; ancestor of the domestic cat, but larger, with a shorter, thicker tail; inhabits forest, scrubland, and open country; eats small rodents and birds. The name is also used for any member of the family other than the domestic cat.

wild cherry *gean*

Wilde, Oscar (Fingal O'Flahertie Wills) (1854–1900) Writer, born in Dublin, Ireland, the son of Sir William Wilde. He studied at Trinity College, Dublin, and at Oxford, and established himself among the social and literary circles in London. He was celebrated for his wit and flamboyant manner, and became a leading member of the 'art for art's sake' movement. His early work included *Poems* (1881), the novel *The Picture of Dorian Gray* (1891), and several comic plays, notably *Lady Windermere's Fan* (1892) and *The Importance of Being Earnest* (1895). *The Ballad of Reading Gaol* (1898) and *De profundis* (1905) reflect two years' hard labour for homosexual practices revealed during his abortive libel action (1895) against the Marquess of Queensberry, who had objected to Wilde's association with his son. He married **Constance Lloyd** (1858–98) in 1884, and had two sons, Cyril (1885–1915) and Vyvyan (1886–1967) for whom he wrote the classic children's fairy stories *The Happy Prince and Other Tales* (1888). He died an exile in Paris, having adopted the name of **Sebastian Melmoth**.

wildebeest [**wil**duhbeest, **vil**duhbeest] An African grazing antelope; sturdy, with a large convex face; short horns spread sideways with upturned tips; long mane; long fringe of hairs along throat; tail almost reaching ground; inhabits grassland; two species: *Connochaetes taurinusa* (**blue wildebeest** or **brindled gnu** – includes **Cookson's wildebeest** and **white-bearded wildebeest**), and *Connochaetes gnou* (**black wildebeest** or **white-tailed gnu**); also known as **gnu**.

Wilder, Billy, originally **Samuel Wilder** (1906–2002) Film director, born in Sucha, Poland (formerly Austria). A law student at Vienna University, he worked as a journalist and crime reporter. He wrote for several German films from 1929, but as a Jew was forced to leave in 1933, and moved to Hollywood, working initially as a screenwriter. He started as a director in 1942 with *The Major and the Minor*, and continued for some 40 years with a wide variety of productions, which he often co-produced and scripted, including *Double Indemnity* (1944), *The Lost Weekend* (1945, Oscar), *Stalag 17* (1953), *Sunset Boulevard* (1950), and *The Apartment* (1960, Oscar). Many of his later productions were in Europe, such as *The Private Life of Sherlock Holmes* (1970) in England, and *Fedora* (1978) in Germany. He received the American Film Institute Life Achievement Award in 1986.

Wilder, Gene, originally **Jerome Silberman** (1935–) Film actor, writer, and director, born in Milwaukee, Wisconsin, USA, the son of Russian immigrants. He trained in England at the Bristol Old Vic, taught fencing as a professional, then joined the Actors' Studio. He made his film debut in a small role in *Bonnie and Clyde* (1967), and received a Best Supporting Actor Oscar nomination for *The Producers* (1968). He developed an appealing, vulnerable, somewhat nervous screen persona, as seen in *Blazing Saddles* (1974), *Young Frankenstein* (1974, which he also co-wrote and directed), *Stir Crazy* (1982), and other films. Known also as a screenwriter and director, he returned to the stage in 1996, starring in the London production of *Laughter on the 23rd Floor*.

Wilder, Thornton (Niven) (1897–1975) Writer, born in Madison, Wisconsin, USA. He studied at Yale, then taught literature and classics at the University of Chicago (1930–7). His first novel, *The Cabala*, appeared in 1926, and was followed by *The Bridge of San Luis Rey* (1927, Pulitzer). Other titles include *The Woman of Andros* (1930) and *The Ides of March* (1948). As a playwright, he is best-remembered for *Our Town* (1938) and *The Skin of Our Teeth* (1942), both Pulitzer Prizes. His later plays include *The Matchmaker* (1954), on which the successful musical *Hello Dolly* (1964) was based.

Wilderness, Battle of (1755) A conflict in Western Pennsylvania, in which Indians and French troops decimated a large British army under General Edward Braddock. Washington, who commanded the American auxiliaries, emerged from that fight with a considerable military reputation.

Wilderness Campaign (1864) An indecisive conflict in the American Civil War between the Union army under General Grant and the Confederate army under General Lee, fought in the Wilderness area of Virginia. It was the first test of Grant's strategy of relentless pressure on Lee, regardless of his own losses.

Wilderness Road The early route across the S Appalachian Mts, from the Holston R through Cumberland Gap to Boonesborough on the Kentucky R. It was constructed in 1775 by a party led by Daniel Boone under the sponsorship of Richard Henderson, founder of the Transylvania Company.

wildfowl *waterfowl*

wildlife refuge An area set aside for the protection and conservation of wildlife (eg Serengeti National Park, Tanzania, and Australia's Great Barrier Reef). Ideally, it should be a wilderness area large enough to sustain its plant and animal population. With increased global pressure for land, wildlife refuges may also need to serve a purpose; for example, the Indonesian government has foregone timber revenues from a new rainforest park in Sulawesi, but in doing so has protected the catchment area of rice farmers downstream of the reserve.

Wildlife Trusts *Royal Society for Nature Conservation*

wild ox *aurochs*

Wiles, Andrew (John) (1953–) Mathematician, born in Cambridge, Cambridgeshire, EC England, UK. He studied at Clare College, Cambridge, and joined Princeton University in 1980. In 1993 he announced that he had solved one of mathematics' oldest mysteries, Fermat's last theorem – a problem which had intrigued him since childhood. His proof makes use of the Taniyama-Weil conjecture, a problem in number theory dealing with the nature of elliptic curves. In 1986 US mathematician Kenneth A Ribet had shown that, if this conjecture could be solved, a proof of Fermat's theorem would follow. Inspired by Ribet's work, Wiles devoted seven years to solving a special case of the conjecture, and by 1994 it had been accepted that a proof of the theorem had indeed been found.

Wilfrid or **Wilfrith, St** (634–709) Monk and bishop, born in Northumbria. He trained at Lindisfarne, and upheld the replacement of Celtic by Roman religious practices at the Synod of Whitby (664). As Bishop of York (c.665), he was involved in controversy over the organization of the Church in Britain, and was the first churchman to appeal to Rome to settle the issue. He built a monastery at Hexham and at Ripon, introduced the Benedictine Rule, and was one of the first Anglo-Saxons to despatch missionaries to Germany. Feast day 12 October.

Wilhelm, (James) Hoyt (1923–2002) Baseball pitcher, born in Huntersville, North Carolina, USA. During World War 2 he distinguished himself in combat during the Battle of the Bulge (1944). During his 21-year career in baseball (1952–72), mostly as a reliever for the New York Giants and Chicago White Sox, he appeared in more games (1070) than any other pitcher. A right-handed knuckleballer, he was elected to the Baseball Hall of Fame in 1985.

Wilhelmina (Helena Pauline Maria) [wiluh**mee**na] (1880–1962) Queen of The Netherlands (1890–1948), born in The Hague, The Netherlands. She succeeded her father William III at the age of 10, her mother acting as regent until 1898. An upholder of constitutional monarchy, she especially won the admiration of her people during World War 2. Though compelled to seek refuge in Britain, she steadfastly encouraged Dutch resistance to the German occupation. In 1948, she abdicated in favour of her daughter Juliana, and assumed the title of Princess of The Netherlands.

Wiliamowitz-Moellendorff, (Emmo Friedrich Wichard) Ulrich von [vilyamovits **moe**lendaw(r)f] (1848–1931) Classical scholar, born in Poznan, WC Poland (formerly Posen, Prussia). He studied at Bonn and Berlin, and was appointed professor of Greek at Greifswald (1876), Göttingen (1883), and Berlin (1897–1922). His many works include books on Homer, Callimachus, Aeschylus, Euripides, Pindar, Sappho, Simonides, Aristotle, and Plato.

Wilkes, John (1727–97) British politician and journalist, born in London, UK. He studied at Leyden, became an MP (1757), and attacked the ministry in his weekly journal, *North Briton* (1762–3). He was imprisoned, released, then expelled from the house for libel. Re-elected on several occasions, and repeatedly expelled, he came to be seen as a champion of liberty, and an upholder of press freedom. In 1774 he became Lord Mayor of London, and in the same year finally gained admission to parliament, where he remained until his retirement.

Wilkes Land Area of Antarctica between Queen Mary Land (W) and Terre Adélie, lying mostly between 105° and 135°E; includes the Australian scientific station at Casey (established 1961).

Wilkie, Sir David (1785–1841) Painter, born in Cults, Fife, E Scotland, UK. He studied at Edinburgh and London, where he settled after the success of his 'Pitlessie Fair' (1804, Edinburgh) and 'The Village Politicians' (1806, London). His fame mainly rests on his genre painting, but he also painted portraits, and in his later years sought to emulate the richness of colouring of the old masters, choosing more elevated subjects. He was made painter-in-ordinary to the king in 1830, and was knighted in 1835.

Wilkins, Sir George (Hubert) (1888–1958) Polar explorer and pioneer aviator, born at Mt Bryan East, South Australia. He was part of an expedition to the Arctic (1913–18), then flew from England to Australia (1919), explored the Antarctic with Shackleton (1921–2), and made a pioneer flight from Alaska to Spitsbergen over polar ice (1928). In 1931 he failed to reach the North Pole in the submarine *Nautilus*. He was knighted in 1928.

Wilkins, Maurice (Hugh Frederick) (1916–) Biophysicist, born in Pongaroa, New Zealand. He studied at Birmingham and Cambridge universities, carried out wartime research into uranium isotope separation in California, then joined the Medical Research Council's Biophysics Research Unit at King's College, London in 1946, becoming deputy-director (1955) and director (1970–2). His X-ray diffraction studies of DNA helped Crick and

Watson determine its structure, and he shared with them the Nobel Prize for Physiology or Medicine in 1962.

Wilkins, Roy (1910–81) Journalist and civil rights leader, born in St Louis, Missouri, USA. He edited an African-American weekly, the *St Paul Appeal*, before joining the staff of the *Kansas City Call*, a leading black weekly. In 1931 he served as executive assistant secretary of the National Association for the Advancement of Colored People, became editor of the organization's newspaper, *Crisis* (1934–49), and was then appointed as executive secretary, retiring in 1977. He was considered one of the most articulate spokesmen for the more moderate wing of the civil rights movement.

Wilkinson, Sir Geoffrey (1921–96) Inorganic chemist, born in Todmorden, West Yorkshire, N England, UK. He studied at Imperial College, London, where he returned in 1956 after war work in Canada and the USA. While at Harvard in 1952, he showed that ferrocene has a molecule with an iron atom sandwiched between two carbon rings; since then, thousands of such *metallocenes* have been made and studied. He shared the Nobel Prize for Chemistry in 1973, and was knighted in 1976.

Wilkinson, Jonny (1979–) Rugby Union player, born in Surrey, SE England, UK He played cricket and tennis for Hampshire Schools before deciding on a career in rugby, signing as a fly-half for Newcastle Falcons. Called up to the England first-team squad, his debut against Ireland (1998) as a substitute late in the game made him England's youngest player of the 20th-c. In the 1999 Five Nations competition he scored all of England's points against Ireland with seven penalties, a record-equalling achievement, and in the inaugural 2000 Six Nations campaign he established a new championship points tally. In the 2003 World Cup, he scored all England's points in the 24–7 semi-final win over France, and in the final against Australia secured his country's victory with a drop-goal in the last minutes of extra time. He was voted the International Rugby Players' Association player of the year in 2003, and also won the BBC Sports Personality of the Year Award.

will (law) A document in which a person (the *testator* or *testatrix*) sets out the way in which his or her property (the *estate*) is to be distributed by executors to beneficiaries after death. In order to be valid, a will must comply with certain requirements (which vary between jurisdictions): for example, in the UK it must be signed in the presence of two witnesses, both of whom are present at the same time. A will can be altered by codicil, or destroyed by the testator. It is automatically revoked on marriage or divorce. A will may be challenged on various grounds, including the ground that it has not been properly executed. A dependant (eg a spouse) can expect to receive reasonable financial provision under a will, and can apply to the court if this is not provided. If a person dies without making a will (dies *intestate*), statutory rules in some jurisdictions govern the distribution of property (*intestate succession*). A **holographic will**, recognized in Scotland and many US jurisdictions, is a handwritten will to which different legal requirements apply.

will (philosophy) *free will*

Willandra Lakes A world heritage site covering c.6000 sq km/ 2300 sq mi in the Murray R Basin in New South Wales, Australia. The region contains an extensive system of Pleistocene freshwater lake sites, and provides a remarkable 'fossil landscape', generally unmodified since the end of the Pleistocene ice age. Certain archaeological discoveries made here have been dated at 30 000–40 000 years BC.

Willard, Emma, *née* **Hart** (1787–1870) Pioneer of higher education for women, born in Berlin, Connecticut, USA. In 1814 she opened Middlebury Female Seminary, offering an unprecedented range of subjects, in order to prepare women for college. Unsuccessful in gaining funding for her school, she moved to Troy, NY (1821), where she received financial help. The school (now called the Emma Willard School) developed quickly, and her campaigns paved the way for co-education.

willaroo *thick-knee*

Willem-Alexander [wilem], in full **Willem-Alexander, Prince of Orange-Nassau, jonkheer van Amsberg** (1967–) Prince of the Netherlands, born in Utrecht, W Netherlands, the eldest son of Queen Beatrix of The Netherlands and Prince Claus von Amsberg. After an education in The Netherlands and Britain he was commissioned into the navy, and in 1987–93 studied history at the University of Leiden. He regularly represents the Queen at official functions at home and abroad. In 2002 he married Argentinian Maxima Zorreguieta, a former New York investment banker. Their daughter, Catharina-Amalia Beatrix Carmen Victoria, second in line to the Dutch throne, was born in 2003.

Willemstad [vilemstaht] 12°12N 68°56W, pop (2000e) 53 000. Capital town of the Netherlands Antilles, on SW coast of Curaçao I; established by the Dutch as a trading centre, mid-17th-c; airport; free port; oil refining (handling Venezuelan oil), ship repair, financial services, tourism; inner city and harbour, a world heritage site.

Willendorf [vilendaw(r)f] A prehistoric site near Krems, lower Austria, with Gravettian occupation dated c.32–28 000 BC. It is celebrated for the 'Willendorf Venus', a large-bellied, heavy-breasted limestone statuette, 11 cm/4⅜ in high, its limbs under-emphasized but the buttocks enlarged. Painted with red ochre, it presumably served as a fertility or house goddess.

William I (of England), known as **the Conquerer** (c.1028–87) Duke of Normandy (1035–87) and the first Norman king of England (1066–87), the illegitimate son of Duke Robert of Normandy. Edward the Confessor, who had been brought up in Normandy, most probably designated him as future King of England in 1051. When Harold Godwinson, despite an apparent oath to uphold William's claims, took the throne as Harold II, William invaded with the support of the papacy, defeated and killed Harold at the Battle of Hastings, and was crowned king on Christmas Day, 1066. The key to effective control was military conquest backed up by aristocratic colonization, so that by the time of the Domesday Book (1086), the leaders of Anglo-Saxon society S of the Tees had been almost entirely replaced by a new ruling class of Normans, Bretons, and Flemings, who were closely tied to William by feudal bonds. He died near Paris in an accident on horseback, while defending Normandy's S border.

William I (of Germany), Ger **Wilhelm** (1797–1888) King of Prussia (1861–88) and first German emperor (1871–88), born in Berlin, Germany, the second son of Frederick William III. His use of force during the 1848 revolution made him unpopular, and he was forced to leave Prussia temporarily for London. As king he consolidated the throne and strengthened the army, placing Bismarck at the head of the ministry. He was victorious against Denmark (1864), Austria (1866), and France (1871), and was then proclaimed emperor. The rapid rise of Socialism in Germany led to severe repressive measures, and he survived several attempts at assassination.

William I (of the Netherlands), **Prince of Orange**, known as **William the Silent** (1533–84) First of the hereditary stadtholders (governors) of the United Provinces of the Netherlands (1572–84), born in Dillenburg, WC Germany. He joined the aristocratic protest to the oppressive policies of Philip II of Spain, and in 1568 took up arms against the Spanish crown. After initial reverses, he began the recovery of the coastal towns with the help of the Sea Beggars, and became stadtholder of the Northern provinces, united in the Union of Utrecht (1579). He was assassinated in Delft by a Spanish agent. His byname comes from his ability to keep secret Henry II's scheme to massacre all the Protestants of France and The Netherlands, confided to him when he was a French hostage in 1559.

William I (of Scotland), known as **William the Lion** (c.1142–1214) King of Scots (1165–1214), the brother and successor of Malcolm IV. In 1173–4 he invaded Northumberland during the rebellion against Henry II, but was captured at Alnwick, and by the Treaty of Falaise (1174) recognized Henry as the feudal superior of Scotland. Despite his difficulties with England, he made Scotland a much stronger kingdom. In 1189 Scottish independence was restored, and in 1192 Celestine III declared the Scottish Church free of all external authority save the pope's.

William II (of England), known as **William Rufus** (c.1056–1100) King of England (1087–1100), the second surviving son of William the Conqueror. His main goal was the recovery of Normandy from his elder brother Robert Curthose. From 1096, when Robert relinquished the struggle and departed on the First Crusade, William ruled the duchy as *de facto* duke. He also led expeditions to Wales (1095, 1097), conquered Carlisle and the surrounding district (1092), and after the death of Malcolm III he exercised a controlling influence over Scottish affairs. Contemporaries condemned his government of England as arbitrary and ruthless. He exploited his rights over the Church and the nobility beyond the limits of custom, and quarrelled with Anselm, Archbishop of Canterbury. His personal conduct outraged the moral standards of the time, for he was most probably a homosexual. He was killed by an arrow while hunting in the New Forest. It has been supposed that he was murdered on the orders of his younger brother, who succeeded him as Henry I, but his death was almost certainly accidental.

William II (of Germany), Ger **Wilhelm**, known as **Kaiser Wilhelm** (1859–1941) German emperor and king of Prussia (1888–1918), born in Potsdam, EC Germany, the eldest son of Frederick III (1831–88) and Victoria (the daughter of Britain's Queen Victoria), and grandson of Emperor William I. He dismissed Bismarck (1890), and began a long period of personal rule, displaying a bellicose attitude in international affairs. He pledged full support to Austria–Hungary after the assassination of Archduke Francis Ferdinand at Sarajevo (1914), but then made apparent efforts to prevent the escalation of the resulting international crisis. During the war he became a mere figurehead, and when the German armies collapsed, and US President Wilson refused to negotiate while he remained in power, he abdicated and fled the country. He settled at Doorn, in The Netherlands, living as a country gentleman. He lived to see the resurgence of German military might in the Nazi period, dying in June 1941. Hitler admired him greatly (as much for his anti-semitism as for his militarism), and had him buried with full military honours.

William III (of Great Britain), known as **William of Orange** (1650–1702) Stadtholder of the United Provinces (1672–1702) and king of Great Britain (1689–1702), born in The Hague, The Netherlands, the son of William II of Orange by Mary, the eldest daughter of Charles I of England. In 1677 he married his cousin, **Mary** (1662–94), the daughter of James II by Anne Hyde. Invited to redress the grievances of the country, he landed at Torbay in 1688 with an English and Dutch army, and forced James II to flee. William and Mary were proclaimed rulers early the following year. He defeated James's supporters at Killiecrankie (1689) and at the Boyne (1690), then concentrated on the War of the League of Augsburg against France (1689–97), in which he was finally successful. In later years, he had to withstand much parliamentary opposition to his proposals, and there were many assassination plots. He died in London, childless, the crown passing to Mary's sister, Anne.

William IV, known as **the Sailor King** (1765–1837) King of Great Britain and Ireland, and king of Hanover (1830–7), born in London, UK, the third son of George III, and before his accession known as **Duke of Clarence**. He entered the navy in 1779, saw service in the USA and the West Indies, became admiral in 1811, and Lord High Admiral in 1827–8. His elder brother having died, he succeeded George IV in 1830. Widely believed to have Whig leanings at his accession, he developed Tory sympathies, and did much to obstruct the passing of the first Reform Act (1832). He was the last monarch to use prerogative powers to dismiss a ministry with a parliamentary majority when he sacked Melbourne in 1834 and invited the Tories to form a government. He was succeeded by his niece, Victoria.

William of Malmesbury [mahmzbree] (c.1090–c.1143) English chronicler and Benedictine monk, the librarian of Malmesbury Abbey, Wiltshire, S England, UK. The emphasis he placed on the importance of documentary material and non-written sources, including architectural and other kinds of visual evidence, gives him a key place in the development of historical method. His main works are: *Gesta regum anglorum*, a general history of England from the coming of the Anglo-Saxons; *Gesta pontificum anglorum*, an ecclesiastical history of England from the Conversion; and *Historia novella*, a contemporary narrative of English affairs from c.1125 to 1142.

William of Ockham or **Occam** [okam], known as **the Venerable Inceptor** (c.1285–c.1349) Scholastic philosopher, born in Ockham, Surrey, SE England, UK. He entered the Franciscan order, and studied theology at Oxford, but because of his controversial views he left technically still an 'undergraduate' – hence his nickname. Summoned to Avignon (1324) to respond to charges of heresy, he became involved in a dispute between the Franciscans and Pope John XXII over apostolic poverty. He fled to Bavaria in 1328, where he remained until 1347, writing treatises on papal versus civil authority. His best-known philosophical contributions are his successful defence of nominalism against realism, and his deployment in theology of the rule of ontological economy, 'entities are not to be multiplied beyond necessity', so frequently and to such effect that it came to be known as **Ockham's razor**.

William of Tyre (c.1130–86) Chronicler and clergyman, born in Palestine of French parents. Educated at Paris and Bologna, he entered the service of the kings of Jerusalem, and was appointed Archbishop of Tyre in 1175. His main work, *Historia rerum in partibus transmarinis gestarum* (History of Deeds in Foreign Parts), deals with the history of Palestine from 614 to 1184, and is especially valuable to the historian of the 12th-c Crusades.

William of Wykeham or **Wickham** [wikam] (1324–1404) English statesman and clergyman, born in Wickham, Hampshire, S England, UK, the son perhaps of a serf, who rose to become the chief adviser of Edward III. He was appointed Keeper of the Privy Seal (1363), Bishop of Winchester (1367), and was twice Chancellor of England (1367–71, 1389–91). He founded New College, Oxford, and Winchester College to provide education for 70 poor scholars, both of which were fully established by the 1390s.

Williams, Betty *Corrigan, Mairead*

Williams, (George) Emlyn (1905–87) Playwright and actor, born in Pen-y-ffordd, Flintshire, NE Wales, UK. He studied at Oxford, joined a repertory company in 1927, and achieved success as a playwright with *A Murder Has Been Arranged* (1930) and the psychological thriller, *Night Must Fall* (1935). He appeared in many London and Broadway productions, featured in several films, and gave widely acclaimed readings from the works of Dickens, Dylan Thomas, and Munro (Saki). He wrote the autobiographical *George* (1961) and *Emlyn* (1973), as well as *Beyond Belief* (1967), and a novel, *Headlong* (1980).

Williams, Hank, popular name of **Hiram King Williams** (1923–53) Singer and guitarist, born in Mount Olive West, Alabama, USA. He began recording for the MGM label (1947) and produced many hit records, notably 'Lovesick Blues' (1949), 'Your Cheatin' Heart', and 'Hey, Good Lookin''. He joined the Grand Ole Opry in Nashville (1949), and gained international fame as a performer of both country and western and popular music. His untimely death from a heart attack may have been due to drug and alcohol abuse. His son, **Hank Williams Jr** (1949–), continues as a successful country singer and songwriter.

Williams, Jody (1950–) US activist, born in Putney, Vermont, USA, the campaign coordinator for the International Campaign to Ban Landmines. She shared the 1997 Nobel Peace Prize along with the organization for their work towards the banning and clearing of anti-personnel mines.

Williams, John (Christopher) (1942–) Guitarist, born in Melbourne, Victoria, SE Australia. Resident in England since 1952, he trained at the Accademia Musicale Chigiana di Siena, Italy, and the Royal College of Music, London, studied with Segovia, and made his professional debut in 1958. He has since taught at colleges in London and Manchester. His musical sympathies are wide-ranging, from renaissance to jazz. Several modern composers have written works for him, and he founded a jazz and popular music group known as Sky (1979–84). He later formed the contemporary music group Attacca.

Williams, John (Towner) (1932–) Film composer and conductor, born in New York City, New York, USA. He is the leading screen composer of his generation, his early films including *Superman* (1978) and the *Star Wars* and *Indiana Jones* series. In 1980 he became conductor of the Boston Pops, retiring from that post in 1992 to devote his time to composing. Later scores include *A.I. Artificial Intelligence* (2001), *Harry Potter and the Philosopher's Stone* (2001), and *Star Wars Episode II* (2002).

Williams, J(ohn) P(eter) R(hys) (1949–) Rugby union player and physician, born in Bridgend, S Wales, UK. He was an excellent tennis player as a junior, representing Wales, and winning the Wimbledon Junior Championship (1966). He studied medicine at St Mary's, London, and became consultant in trauma and orthopaedic surgery at the Princess of Wales Hospital, Bridgend (1986). He played rugby for London Welsh and Bridgend, as well as for Wales (captain, 1978) and the British Lions (tours of New Zealand in 1971, South Africa in 1974). When he retired in 1982 he was the most-capped Welshman with 55 caps. He was later a Welsh national selector, team manager at Bridgend RFC, and was still playing junior rugby at the age of 50. He published his autobiography, *JPR*, in 1979.

Williams, Mary Lou, born **Mary Elfrieda Scruggs** (1910–81) Jazz pianist, arranger, and composer, born in Atlanta, Georgia, USA. She left high school to become a touring show pianist. Her first important period as a performer and arranger was during the 1930s with the Kansas City-based Andy Kirk and his Clouds of Joy. Her outstanding qualities as an arranger brought her work from Duke Ellington (for whom she arranged the well-known 'Trumpets No End'), Earl Hines, and Benny Goodman, among others.

Williams, Robbie (1974–) Pop singer, born in Stoke-on-Trent, Staffordshire, C England, UK. At age 16 he joined British boy band *Take That* (1991), leaving four years later to pursue a solo career. His albums include *Life Thru a Lens* (1997), *Sing When You're Winning* (2000), his tribute album to Frank Sinatra, *Swing When You're Winning* (2001), and *Escapology* (2002). Among his hit singles to reach Number 1 in the UK charts are 'Millennium' (1998), 'Rock DJ' (2000), and 'Eternity/The Road to Mandalay' (2001). He also works on behalf of the children's charity UNICEF.

Williams, Robin (1952–) Film actor and entertainer, born in Chicago, Illinois, USA. He studied acting at the Juilliard School in New York City, then settled in San Francisco and developed a nightclub act. He starred in the television comedy series *Mork and Mindy* (1978–82), made his film debut in *Popeye* (1981), and became known for his versatile and energetic performances. He earned an Oscar nomination and a Golden Globe Award for *Good Morning Vietnam* (1987), another Oscar nomination for *Dead Poets Society* (1989), and a Best Supporting Actor Oscar for *Good Will Hunting* (1997). Other films include *Awakenings* (1990), *Hook* (1991), *Mrs Doubtfire* (1993), *The Birdcage* (1996), *Get Bruce* (1999), and *The Final Cut* (2004). He provided the voice of the genie in *Aladdin* (1991), and the voice of Dr Know in *Artificial Intelligence: AI* (2001). He has also continued to perform as a stand-up comic entertainer.

Williams, Roger (c.1604–83) Colonist who founded Rhode Island, born in London, UK. He studied at Cambridge, took Anglican orders, became an extreme Puritan, and emigrated to New England in 1630. He refused to join the congregation at Boston, and moved to Salem, where he was persecuted and banished. He then purchased lands from the Indians, and founded the city of Providence (1636), allowing full religious toleration. In 1643 and 1651 he travelled to England to procure a charter for his colony, and became its first president (1654–8).

Williams, Rowan (1950–) Anglican clergyman, born in Swansea, SC Wales, UK. He studied theology at Christ's College, Cambridge, and after research at Oxford returned to Cambridge in 1977, where he spent nine years in academic and parochial work. He was professor of divinity at Oxford (1986–92), and was consecrated Bishop of Monmouth in 1992, becoming Archbishop of Wales in 2000. In 2002 he succeeded George Carey as Archbishop of Canterbury. He has written a number of books on the history of theology and spirituality.

Williams (of Crosby), Shirley (Vivien Teresa Brittain) Williams, Baroness, *née* **Catlin** (1930–) British stateswoman, born in London, UK, the daughter of Vera Brittain. She studied at Oxford, and worked as a journalist. Secretary of the Fabian Society (1960–4), she became a Labour MP in 1964. After many junior positions, she was made secretary of state for prices and consumer protection (1974–6), and for education and science (1976–9). She lost her seat in 1979, as a member of the so-called 'Gang of Four', became a co-founder of the Social Democratic Party in 1981, and the party's first elected MP later that year. She lost her seat in the 1983 general election, but remained as the SDP's president (1982–7). Her first husband (1955–74) was the philosopher, Bernard Williams. After her second marriage, to Harvard professor of politics, Richard Neustadt, she moved to the USA, where she became professor of electoral politics at Harvard. She was made a life peer in 1993, and in 2000 she became leader of the Liberal Democrats in the House of Lords.

Williams, Serena (1981–) Tennis player, born in Saginaw, Michigan, USA, the sister of Venus Williams. Coached by her father, her achievements include the US Open singles title in 1999. She partnered her sister to gain doubles titles in the US Open (1999), French Open (1999), Wimbledon (2000, 2002), and Australian Open (2001, 2003). Further successes include singles titles at the French Open (2002), Wimbledon (2002, 2003), the US Open (2002), and the Australian Open (2003). At the beginning of 2004 she had a world ranking of Number 3.

Williams, Tennessee, pseudonym of **Thomas Lanier Williams** (1911–83) Playwright, born in Columbus, Mississippi, USA. He studied at Columbia University and the universities of Missouri and Iowa, then worked at a wide range of theatrical jobs until he achieved success with *The Glass Menagerie* (1944). His other plays, almost all set in the Deep South against a background of decadence and degradation, include *A Streetcar Named Desire* (1947, Pulitzer), *Cat on a Hot Tin Roof* (1955, Pulitzer), *Suddenly Last Summer* (1958), *Sweet Bird of Youth* (1959), and *The Night of the Iguana* (1961). In addition to his plays, he wrote short stories, essays, poetry, memoirs, and two novels, *The Roman Spring of Mrs Stone* (1950) and *Moise and the World of Reason* (1975). He published a volume of autobiography, *Memoirs*, in 1975. He was in ill health in his later years, following a breakdown in 1969, and although he wrote some further plays in the 1970s, they were unsuccessful.

Williams, Venus (1980–) Tennis player, born in Lynwood, California, USA. Coached by her father, she became the dominant female player of 2000, that year winning the Wimbledon singles title, the US Open, and Olympic gold in Sydney. She also won the Wimbledon doubles title, partnered by her younger sister, Serena Williams. She retained the Wimbledon and the US Open singles titles in 2001, but in 2003 was defeated by her sister in the Wimbledon singles final. She was the first African-American to reach the Number 1 ranking in either the men's or women's game. At the beginning of 2004 she had a world ranking of Number 11.

Williams, William Carlos (1883–1963) Poet and novelist, born in Rutherford, New Jersey, USA. He studied in Geneva and at Pennsylvania University, and became a doctor. His poems, from *Spring and All* (1923), commanded attention and were collected in two volumes (1950–1). He is especially known for his 'personal epic' poem, *Paterson* (5 vols, 1946–58). He also wrote plays, essays, a trilogy of novels, and criticism, including *In the American Grain* (1925). He was awarded a posthumous

Pulitzer Prize for *Pictures from Brueghel, and Other Poems* (1962).

Williamsburg 37°17N 76°43W, pop (2000e) 12 000. Independent city and capital of James City Co, SE Virginia, USA, between the York and James Rivers; settled, 1633 (as Middle Plantation, renamed 1699); state capital, 1699–1780; Colonial Williamsburg is a major building restoration scheme; College of William and Mary (1693).

Williamson, Malcolm (Benjamin Graham Christopher) (1931–2003) Composer, born in Sydney, New South Wales, SE Australia. He moved to England in 1953, and began his career as a solo pianist and organist. His compositions include the opera *Our Man in Havana* (1963), the chamber opera *The Red Sea* (1972), and the operatic sequence *The Brilliant and the Dark* (1969). He also wrote seven symphonies, concertos for piano, organ, violin, and harp, several works for television and films, a great deal of vocal, choral, organ, and piano music, and 'cassations' (mini-operas), which often involve the audience. He was made Master of the Queen's Musick in 1975, and was associated with several choirs and music societies.

Willis, Bruce (1955–) Film actor, born in West Germany. He grew up in New Jersey from the age of two, took up acting in the mid-1970s, and got some small parts in film and television. After moving to Los Angeles, he became widely known for his role as David Addison in the television series *Moonlighting* (1985–9). He made his film debut in *Blind Date* (1987), and achieved star status following his role in the first of the *Die Hard* series (1988, 1990, 1995). Later films include *Pulp Fiction* (1994), *Armageddon* (1998), *The Sixth Sense* (1999), *Bandits* (2001), and *Tears of the Sun* (2003). He was married to actress Demi Moore (1987–98).

will o' the wisp *ignis fatuus*

willow A member of a large genus of mostly N temperate deciduous trees and shrubs; leaves oval or lance-shaped; flowers in separate male and female catkins; seeds plumed with silky hairs for wind dispersal. Willows show a wide range of form, from low, creeping arctic species to large trees, many growing in or near water. They are a source of withies for basketwork, and cricket bats. The bark contains salicin, an original source of aspirin. Some species are ornamental, with brightly-coloured winter twigs. Numerous natural hybrids are known. (Genus: *Salix*, 500 species. Family: Salicaceae.)

willow-herb A member of a somewhat variable genus of mostly perennials, native throughout temperate and arctic regions; narrow to lance-shaped leaves in pairs; flowers with four rose, purple, sometimes white petals on top of a long, cylindrical, purplish ovary; fruit a capsule containing numerous white-plumed seeds. (Genus: *Epilobium*, 215 species. Family: Onagraceae.)

willow pattern A decorative scene used on pottery table-wares, showing a Chinese landscape, with buildings, and figures crossing a bridge, carried out in blue transfer-printing on white. Purportedly first engraved by Thomas Minton for Thomas Turner at Caughley c.1780, it was subsequently produced by many factories, notably Spode.

Wills, Helen (Newington), married names **Moody** and **Roark** (1905–98) Tennis player, born in Berkeley, California, USA. A great baseline player, she won the Wimbledon singles title eight times in nine attempts (1927–30, 1932–3, 1935, 1938). Between 1927 and 1932 she won all the major singles championships (except the Australian) without losing a set. In all, she won 31 Grand Slam events.

Willstätter, Richard [vilshteter] (1872–1942) Organic chemist, born in Karlsruhe, SW Germany. He studied at Munich University, and became professor at Zürich (1905–12). He did notable work on natural product chemistry, especially on plant pigments (for which he was awarded the Nobel Prize for Chemistry in 1915) and on medicinal chemicals, and he developed effective gas masks in World War 1. He became professor at Munich in 1916, but increasing anti-Semitism made his position difficult, and he resigned his chair in 1925 in protest. The rise of Nazi power forced him to flee, and he reached Switzerland in 1939.

Wilmington 39°45N 75°33W, pop (2000e) 72 700. Seat of New Castle Co, N Delaware, USA; a port at the confluence of Brandywine Creek, the Christina R, and the Delaware R; founded by the Swedes as Fort Christina, 1638; taken by the British and renamed Willington, 1731; renamed Wilmington, 1739; city status, 1832; largest city in the state; airfield; railway; chemicals ('the chemical capital of the world'), explosives, automobiles; shipyards, railway engineering; home of several large corporations; State House complex, Winterthur Museum, Hagley Museum.

Wilmot Proviso (1846) A motion introduced in the US Congress by David Wilmot (Democrat, Pennsylvania) to forbid the expansion of slavery into territory acquired during the Mexican War. It passed the House of Representatives but not the Senate, where the South and the North had equal strength. The debate was a major step in the politicization of the slavery issue.

Wilson, Sir Angus (Frank Johnstone) (1913–91) Writer, born in Bexhill, East Sussex, SE England, UK. He studied at Oxford, began writing in 1946, and rapidly established a reputation with his short stories, *The Wrong Set* (1949). His works include the novels *Hemlock and After* (1952), *Anglo-Saxon Attitudes* (1956), which were both best-sellers, and a family chronicle, *The Old Men at the Zoo* (1961), *Late Call* (1965), and *No Laughing Matter* (1967), as well as the play *The Mulberry Bush* (1955) and two further volumes of short stories. He was professor of English literature at East Anglia (1966–78), was knighted in 1980, and moved to France. His *Collected Stories* were published in 1987.

Wilson, Brian *Beach Boys, The*

Wilson, Carl *Beach Boys, The*

Wilson, C(harles) T(homson) R(ees) (1869–1959) Physicist, born in Glencorse, Midlothian, EC Scotland, UK. He studied at Manchester and Cambridge universities, where he became professor of natural philosophy (1925–34). While studying cloud formation as a meteorologist, he developed the device called the **Wilson cloud chamber**. He made use of X-rays to investigate cloud formation due to the presence of ionized particles, and his finding that the radiation left a trail of water droplets in the chamber led to the wide use of the chamber in nuclear physics. He shared the 1927 Nobel Prize of Physics.

Wilson, Colin (Henry) (1931–) Novelist and writer on philosophy, sociology, and the occult, born in Leicester, Leicestershire, C England, UK. He left school at 16, held various jobs, and served briefly in the Royal Air Force before writing his best-seller *The Outsider* (1956), a study of modern alienation. A prolific author, he has written many books and novels, including *Ritual in the Dark* (1960), *The Mind Parasites* (1966), *The Occult* (1971), *Poltergeist!* (1981), *Written in Blood* (1989), *Spider World: The Magician* (1992), and *From Atlantis to the Sphinx* (1996). *The Essential Colin Wilson* appeared in 1984. His psychic interests brought him status as a cult figure in the 1980s, and in 1999 he published *Alien Dawn*, an investigation into reports of alien visitations and other strange phenomena.

Wilson, Colin St John (1922–) British architect. He studied at Cambridge (1940–2) and at London University's School of Architecture (1946–9). He returned to Cambridge as a lecturer (1955–69), became professor of architecture (1975–89, now emeritus), and was made a fellow of Pembroke College in 1977. His many design projects include the extension to the British Museum (1973–9) and the new British Library (1962–97) in Euston Road, London.

Wilson, Dennis *Beach Boys, The*

Wilson, Edmund (1895–1972) Literary and social critic, born in Red Bank, New Jersey, USA. He studied at Princeton University, and became a journalist with *Vanity Fair*, associate editor of the *New Republic* (1926–31), and chief book reviewer for the *New Yorker*. An early critical success was his study of the Symbolist movement, *Axel's Castle* (1931). He was a prolific and wide-ranging author, producing several studies on aesthetic, social, and political themes, as well as verse, plays, and travel books.

His historical works include *In Patriotic Gore* (1962), on the literature from the period of the American Civil War, and *The Scrolls from the Dead Sea* (1955), a contentious account for which he learned Hebrew. His third marriage (of four) was to novelist Mary McCarthy.

Wilson, Edward O(sborne) (1929–) Biologist, born in Birmingham, Alabama, USA. He studied at the University of Alabama, then at Harvard, where he joined the faculty in 1956. His early work was in entomology, but his conclusions (eg on the behaviour of competing populations of different species) were extended to other species including the human, notably in his book *Sociobiology: the New Synthesis* (1975). This book virtually founded the subject of sociobiology, and stimulated much discussion and some contention. He also wrote *On Human Nature* (1978, Pulitzer). In 1990 he was awarded Sweden's Crafoord Prize.

Wilson (of Rievaulx), (James) Harold Wilson, Baron (1916–95) British statesman and prime minister (1964–70, 1974–6), born in Huddersfield, West Yorkshire, N England, UK. He studied at Oxford, where he became a lecturer in economics in 1937. A Labour MP in 1945, he became President of the Board of Trade (1947–51), and the principal Opposition spokesman on economic affairs. An able and hard-hitting debater, in 1963 he succeeded Gaitskell as leader of the Labour Party, becoming prime minister in 1964. His economic plans were badly affected by a balance of payments crisis, leading to severe restrictive measures. He was also faced with the problem of Rhodesian independence, opposition to Britain's proposed entry into the European Economic Community, and an increasing conflict between the two wings of the Labour Party. Following his third general election victory, he resigned suddenly as Labour Party leader in 1976. Knighted in 1976, he became a life peer in 1983.

Wilson (of Libya and of Stowlangtoft), Henry Maitland Wilson, Baron (1881–1964) British field marshal, born in London, UK. He trained at Sandhurst Military Academy, fought in South Africa and in World War 1, and at the outbreak of World War 2 was appointed commander of British troops in Egypt. He led the initial British advance in Libya (1940–1) and the unsuccessful Greek campaign (1941), and became commander-in-chief, Middle East (1943), and supreme allied commander in the Mediterranean theatre (1944). He headed the British Joint Staff Mission in Washington (1945–7), and was raised to the peerage in 1946.

Wilson, (Charles) Kemmons (1913–2003) Hotelier, born in Osceola, Arkansas, USA. The owner of a slot-machine business and a small cinema chain, he became dissatisfied with family holiday accommodation, and devised the Holiday Inn motel, opening the first one in Memphis in 1952. He went international in 1960, and by 1978 had built the world's largest lodging chain. He retired in 1979.

Wilson, Richard (1714–82) Landscape painter, born in Penygroes, Powys, E Wales, UK. He began as a portrait painter, but after a visit to Italy (1752–6) turned to landscapes. In London in 1760 he exhibited his 'Niobe', and was recognized as one of the leading painters of his time. In 1776 he became librarian to the Royal Academy.

Wilson, Richard (1936–) Actor and director, born in Greenock, Inverclyde, WC Scotland, UK. He trained at the Royal Academy of Dramatic Art, London, and became well known as a theatre actor and director during the 1980s. His first television role was in 1972, in the series *My Good Woman*, other appearances including *Crown Court* (1973–84) and *Only When I Laugh* (1979–82). His film work includes roles in *A Passage to India* (1984), *Fellow Traveller* (1990), and *The Man Who Knew Too Little* (1997), but it was his characterization of Victor Meldrew in several series of *One Foot in the Grave* (1990–2000, BAFTAs in 1991 and 1993) that made him a national figure, his exasperated 'I don't believe it!' becoming a national catch-phrase. He was elected Rector of Glasgow University in 1996.

Wilson, Robert (1941–) Epic theatre-maker, director, and designer, born in Waco, Texas, USA. America's most flamboyant post-modern creator of theatrical spectacle, his early training was as a painter in Texas, Paris, and New York City. In contrast with traditional theatre, he mixes a combination of movement, contemporary music, and exciting imagery, often in very long performances. His work includes *The Life and Times of Sigmund Freud* (1969), *A Letter for Queen Victoria* (1974), and *The CIVIL WarS* (begun in 1984), one of the most ambitious theatrical events ever proposed. Later productions include *Orlando* (1993), *Monsters of Grace* (1998), *Wings on a Rock* (1999), and *Scourge of Hyacinth* (1999).

Wilson, (Thomas) Woodrow (1856–1924) US statesman and 28th president (1913–21), born in Staunton, Virginia, USA. He studied at Princeton and Johns Hopkins universities, became a lawyer and university professor, and was president of Princeton, and Governor of New Jersey (1911). Elected Democratic president in 1912 and 1916, his administration, ending in his physical breakdown, is memorable for the Prohibition and women's suffrage amendments to the constitution, disputes with Mexico, America's participation (from April 1917 onwards) in World War 1, his peace plan proposals (the 'fourteen points'), and his championship of the League of Nations. His health declined as the US Senate was debating the Treaty of Versailles; the treaty was defeated after his stroke in October 1919. He received the Nobel Peace Prize in 1919.

Wiltshire pop (2001e) 433 000; area 3481 sq km/1344 sq mi. County of S England, UK; chalk downland of Salisbury Plain at the centre of the county; drained by the Avon and Kennet Rivers; county town, Trowbridge; chief towns include Salisbury, Swindon, Chippenham; Thamesdown a unitary authority from 1997; agriculture, engineering, clothing, brewing; many ancient prehistoric remains, such as Stonehenge, Avebury, Silbury Hill; Marlborough Downs, Savernake Forest, Longleat House, Wilton House.

Wimbledon Residential district in Merton borough, S Greater London, UK; Wimbledon Common; headquarters of the All England Tennis Club; annual lawn tennis championships (Jun–Jul).

wimp *dark matter*

WIMP interface *graphic user interface*

Winchester, Lat **Venta Belgarum**, Anglo-Saxon **Wintanceaster** 51°04N 1°19W, pop (2001e) 107 200. City and county town in Hampshire, S England, UK; on the R Itchen, 105 km/65 mi SW of London; Roman settlement the fifth largest in Britain; capital of Wessex in 519, and capital of England in 827; William the Conqueror crowned here as well as in London; Domesday Book compiled here; from the 14th-c the city declined into a small provincial town; railway; engineering; burial place of St Swithin; longest Gothic cathedral N of the Alps (11th–16th-c); Winchester College (1382), oldest public school in England; 12th-c St Cross Hospital; 13th-c castle hall, containing a mediaeval 'replica' of Arthur's Round Table; Southern Cathedrals Festival (Jul).

Winchester disk A small, solid, rotatable disk, coated with magnetizable material, used as a computer storage medium for microcomputers. The disk is housed in a hermetically sealed unit, and is rotated rapidly while in use. In comparison with floppy disks of similar size, a Winchester disk can store considerably more data (typically up to 50 gigabytes), and since it rotates much more rapidly than floppy disks, data can be written to and read from the disk more rapidly.

Winckelmann, Johann (Joachim) [vingkelman] (1717–68) Archaeologist and art historian, born in NEC Stendal, Germany. He studied theology and medicine at Halle and Jena universities, in 1748 turned to the history of art, and became librarian to a cardinal in Rome (1755). His works include the pioneering study, *Geschichte der Kunst des Alterthums* (1764, History of the Art of Antiquity), and in 1763 he became superintendent of Roman antiquities. He was murdered in Trieste.

wind The movement of air along the pressure gradient from areas of high to lower pressure; one of the basic elements of weather. Pressure gradients develop through the unequal cooling or heating of a layer of atmosphere. The steeper the gradient, the stronger the wind. Wind direction is also determined by the Coriolis force and by surface friction. The Coriolis force opposes the force of the pressure gradient and, at high altitudes where the frictional effect of the Earth's surface is absent, exactly balances the pressure gradient, producing a geostrophic wind. In the N hemisphere the Coriolis force deflects wind to the right, and in the S hemisphere to the left. At low altitudes, the frictional force of the Earth's surface reduces the influence of the Coriolis force, diverting the wind towards the centre of the low pressure area. As one of the basic elements of weather, there are many local names for different winds.

wind chill An effect of wind decreasing the apparent temperature felt by a human body. Strong winds increase the heat loss from exposed flesh, and so at low temperatures may induce hypothermia at a higher air temperature than would occur in calm conditions. The wind chill equivalent temperature relates air temperature to wind speed. For example, an air temperature of −18°C with no wind would be equivalent to −38°C at 7 m/23 ft/s.

Windermere (lake) Largest lake in England, in the Lake District of Cumbria, NW England, UK; extending 18 km/11 mi S from Ambleside; linked to Morecambe Bay by the R Leven; largest island, Belle Isle; remains of 13th-c chapel on Ladyholme.

Windermere (town) 54°23N 2°54W, pop (2000e) 8380. Lakeside resort town in Cumbria, NW England, UK; 11 km/7 mi NW of Kendal, on L Windermere; railway; major tourist centre; 15th-c Church of St Martin; Rydal Mount (10 km/6 mi NW), Wordsworth's home from 1813 to 1850; Brantwood, home of Ruskin.

Windhoek [vinthuk] 22°34S 17°06E, pop (2000e) 200 000. Capital of Namibia, 1450 km/900 mi N of Cape Town, South Africa; altitude, 1650 m/5413 ft; occupied by South African forces, 1915; capital of German South-West Africa, 1922; airport; railway; administration, meat canning, diamonds, copper, sheepskins (karakul); cathedral.

wind instrument *aerophone*

windmill A mill worked by the action of wind on sails. Windmills have been used principally for grinding corn, cleansing (*fulling*) cloth, and for drainage. There are three types: **post mills**, where the mill itself revolves on a central post to face the wind, and **tower mills** (built of brick) and **smock mills** (built of timber), where only the cap revolves. Windmills were in common use until the end of the 19th-c, when they were largely superseded by the advent of steam power.

windows A form of graphic user interface in which the computer presents on a screen a set of sub-screens, each sub-screen corresponding to a different program running in the computer. The sub-screens (windows) can be moved about, placed one on top of another, or temporarily shrunk in order to minimize the amount of information presented on the screen at any time, and to allow different programs to pass files between them. For example, in a windows environment the output from a spreadsheet can be passed to a desk-top publishing system for incorporation into a technical report. *Windows* is also the name of a registered trade mark of a multitasking operating environment for the IBM PC marketed by Microsoft.

windpipe *trachea*

Windscale *Sellafield*

wind scorpion *sun spider*

wind shear A meteorological term applied to the rate of change of wind velocity. As it changes with height it is known as the **vertical wind shear**. The amount of shear depends on the temperature structure of the air.

Windsor (Canada) 42°18N 83°00W, pop (2000e) 214 200. Town in S Ontario, Canada, on Detroit R, opposite Detroit, MI; founded, 1835; rapid industrial growth in 19th-c; connected to Detroit by bridge and tunnel; railway; university (1857); vehicles, food processing, pharmaceuticals, paints, salt, distilling; Hiram Walker Historical Museum; Point Pelee National Park to the S (area 15·5 sq km/6 sq mi, established 1918), notable for birds and butterflies.

Windsor (UK) 51°30N 0°38W, pop (2000e) 33 800. Town linked with Eton in Windsor and Maidenhead unitary authority, S England, UK; W of London, on R Thames; railway; Windsor Castle, Eton College (1440); Legoland theme park nearby; Royal Windsor Horse Show (May); horse racing at Royal Ascot (Jun); Eton wall game on St Andrew's Day (30 Nov).

Windsor, Duke and Duchess of *Edward VIII*

Windsor, Lady Louise *Edward, Prince*

Windsor, House of The name of the British royal family since 1917. This unequivocally English name resulted from a Declaration by George V, a member of the House of Saxe-Coburg-Gotha. It was felt that a Germanic surname for the British monarchy was inappropriate during a war against Germany.

Windsor Castle The largest of England's castles, situated on the R Thames at Windsor, S England, UK. It was founded by William I and first used as a royal residence by Henry I. The process of converting Windsor from a fortress into a palace began in the 16th-c. The castle stands on the edge of Windsor Great Park, formerly a royal hunting ground. The principal changes to the castle were made in the early 19th-c, when George IV commissioned Sir Jeffry Wyatville as his architect; he built the machicolated walls and several towers, raised the massive Round Tower, giving the castle its outline, and remodelled the State Apartments, adding the Waterloo Chamber. This section was severely damaged by fire in 1992. Restoration work was completed in 1997 and the castle re-opened to the public at the end of that year.

wind tunnel *aerodynamics*

wind-up power Self-contained energy which stores human energy in a mechanical device and releases it in a controlled fashion over a period of time, much as in a traditional clock. Pioneered by British inventor Trevor Baylis to power his wind-up radio (1993) and Freeplay's torch (launched in 1998), it works on the principle that a spring inside the device is wound up by hand, releasing power as it unwinds (a wind-up time of 25 seconds allows a play-back time of 30 minutes). Using a new technology, clockwork generators are fitted with a special spring called a *tensator*, which is also found in seatbelt retractors and builders' rulers. Also known as a *constant force spring*, a tensator delivers its stored mechanical energy more evenly than the coiled springs used in ordinary clockwork. Driving a small dynamo through a gear chain, the tensator is capable of powering the devices. Wind-up technology is currently being developed further in landmine detection, laptop computers, global positioning systems, coolers to keep medical supplies at the correct temperature, and water chlorinators to purify water.

Windward Islands (Caribbean) Island group of the Lesser Antilles in the Caribbean Sea; S of the Leeward Is, from Martinique (N) to Grenada (S), excluding Trinidad and Tobago; so called because of their exposure to the prevailing NE trade winds; formerly the name of a British colony comprising Dominica, St Lucia, St Vincent, and Grenada.

Windward Islands (French Polynesia), Fr **Iles du Vent** pop (2000e) 164 000. Island group of the Society Is, French Polynesia; comprises Tahiti, Moorea, and the smaller Mehetia, Tetiaroa, and Tubuai Manu Is; capital, Papeete; coconuts, tourism.

wine The alcoholic beverage produced from the fermentation of grapes or other fruits. The alcohol content varies from 7% to 13%, but is usually 12%, the point at which fermentation stops. A wine's taste is determined by the type of grape used, the soil in which it is grown, and the local climate. It may be white, red, or rosé, dry or sweet, still or sparkling. White wine can be made from red (or black) grapes as well as white (or green): the final colour depends on whether the skins are left to ferment with the juice. Sweet wine is taken from the vat before fermentation has finished, while some sugar remains; dry wine is left to ferment until all the sugar has been converted to alcohol. Sparkling wine is produced by bottling it before the fermentation process is completed, so that fermentation continues in the bottle. Fermentation is stopped by the addition of alcohol (eg brandy) to produce fortified wines (eg sherry and port).

Known since ancient times, viniculture was taken to Italy by the Greeks, and by the Romans to Gaul (modern France). France has long been regarded as the producer of the greatest wines, in Bordeaux (claret) and Burgundy. France and Italy are the leading growers and producers, with Spain and Germany also traditional winemaking centres. The 20th-c saw the development of vineyards all over the world, and in the 1980s other European countries (eg Bulgaria) began to produce large quantities of wine for export. Following the devastation of European vineyards by the phylloxera insect in the 19th-c, most grapes in Europe are grown on cuttings grafted on to American root stock (which is resistant to phylloxera). In California and Australia, winemaking has developed as an industry; all processes, from the delivery of the grape to the packing of filled bottles for transportation, can be carried out in factory surroundings, to produce all qualities of wine from basic to excellent.

Winfrey, Oprah (Gail) [winfree] (1954–) Television talk-show host, actor, and producer, born in Kosciusko, Mississippi, USA. After an unsettled childhood, she moved to Nashville and studied at Tennessee State University, beginning work as a radio reporter. She hosted her first TV chat-show in Baltimore in 1978, moving to Chicago in 1984, where she launched the highly successful *Oprah Winfrey Show* (3 Emmies) in 1986. She then moved into management, establishing Harpo Productions in Chicago. Her film work includes *The Color Purple* (1985, Oscar nomination), *Throw Momma From the Train* (1987), and *Beloved* (1998). She is also well-known for her exercise and dieting programmes, and as an activist in support of children's rights. In 2002 she received the inaugural Bob Hope Humanitarian Award.

Wingate, Orde (Charles) (1903–44) British general, born in Naini Tal, NE India. He trained at Woolwich, was commisioned in 1922, and served in the Sudan (1928–33) and Palestine (1936–9), where he helped create a Jewish defence force. In the Burma theatre (1942) he organized the Chindits – specially trained jungle-fighters drawn from British, Ghurka, and Burmese forces, who were supplied by air, and thrust far behind the enemy lines. He helped Frank Merrill train a similar group of US troops.

winkle *periwinkle* (zoology)

Winkler, Hans-Günther [vingkler] (1926–) Show jumper, born in Wuppertal-Barmen, W Germany. He is the only man to have won five Olympic gold medals at show jumping: the team golds in 1956, 1960, 1964, and 1972, and the individual title on *Halla* in 1956. On the same horse he won the individual world title in 1954 and 1955. He made his international debut in Spain in 1952, and later became (West German) team captain.

Winnipeg 49°53N 97°10W, pop (2000e) 691 000. Capital of Manitoba province, C Canada, on the Red R where it meets the Assiniboine R; established 1738 as Fort Rouge; fur-trading post, 1806; modern name, 1873; expansion after arrival of railway, 1881; severely damaged by flood, 1950; airport; universities (1877, 1967); meat packing, fur trading, textiles, machinery, aircraft parts; professional teams, Winnipeg Jets (ice hockey), Winnipeg Blue Bombers (football); railway memorial; Centennial Arts Centre (concert hall, planetarium, museum), Civic Auditorium (home of Winnipeg Symphony Orchestra), Art Gallery, Royal Winnipeg Ballet; Festival du Voyageur (Feb); Folklorama (Aug).

Winnipeg, Lake Lake in SC Manitoba province, S Canada, 64 km/40 mi NE of Winnipeg; length 386 km/240 mi; breadth 88 km/55 mi; area 24 390 sq km/9414 sq mi; drained N into Hudson Bay by the Nelson R; a remnant of the glacial L Agassiz.

Winslet, Kate (1975–) Actress, born in Reading, S England, UK. Raised in a show business family, she trained at a school for the performing arts until 1991, then secured a number of stage roles. Her breakthrough into films came with *Heavenly Creatures* (1994), and later successes include *Sense and Sensibility* (1995), *Titanic* (1997), *Iris* (2001), and *JM Barrie's Neverland* (2004). She married director Sam Mendes in 2003.

Winston, Robert (Maurice Lipson), Baron (1940–) Obstetrician, gynaecologist, and broadcaster, born in London, UK. He studied at London University's Medical College (1964) and went on to become a leading authority on reproductive medicine. His posts include head of the Department of Reproductive Medicine at Hammersmith Hospital (1978–) and professor of fertility studies at the Imperial College School of Medicine (1987–). In the 1970s he developed gynaecological microsurgery and undertook the first human tubal transplant, and in 1981 founded the National Health Service's in vitro fertilization (IVF) programme. He is well known as a television presenter of series such as *Your Life in Their Hands* (BBC, 1979–87), *Child of Our Time* (BBC, 2001–4), and *Walking With Cavemen* (2003). He was created a life peer in 1995.

Winston-Salem 36°06N 80°15W, pop (2000e) 185 800. Seat of Forsyth Co, NC North Carolina, USA; Winston founded in 1849, Salem in 1766; towns united, 1913; Wake Forest University (1834); railway; the nation's chief tobacco manufacturer; textiles, furniture; Old Salem.

winter aconite A tuberous perennial (*Eranthis hyemalis*), native to S Europe, and a popular garden ornamental. It flowers very early in spring. A ring of divided bracts forms a ruff below the bright yellow cup-shaped flower; the leaves appear after flowering. (Family: Ranunculaceae.)

wintergreen A member of a family of small evergreen perennials, native to N temperate and arctic regions; rhizomatous; leaves oval; flowers drooping, bell-shaped, 5-petalled, pink or white. Genus *Pyrola* (20 species) has alternate leaves and flowers in slender spikes; *Orthilia secunda* has alternate leaves and flowers in 1-sided spikes; *Moneses uniflora* has opposite leaves and solitary flowers. (Family: Pyrolaceae.)

Winterhalter, Franz Xaver [vinterhalter] (1806–73) Painter, born in Menzenschwand, SW Germany. He studied in Freiburg and Munich, and was appointed court painter to Grand Duke Leopold of Baden. In 1834 he went to Paris, where he became the fashionable artist of his day, painting many royal figures, such as Napoleon III and Queen Victoria.

Winter Palace *Hermitage*

Winterthur [vintertoor] 47°30N 8°45E, pop (2000e) 90 000. Town in Zürich canton, N Switzerland; near the R Töss in the Pre-Alpine region, NE of Zürich; railway junction; engineering, transport equipment, textiles; town hall (18th–19th-c).

Winter War *Russo-Finnish War*

Winthrop, John (1588–1649) English colonist, born in Edwardstone, Suffolk, E England, UK. He studied at Cambridge, became a Puritan lawyer, decided to emigrate, and while still in England was appointed governor (chief officer) of the Massachusetts Bay Company (1629), then based in England. He moved with the Company to Massachusetts the following year. Except for brief intervals he served as governor of the colony for the rest of his life.

Winton, Tim(othy John) (1960–) Writer, born in Scarborough, Perth, Western Australia, Australia. Educated at the University of Western Australia, he jointly won the Australian–Vogel award in 1981 with his first novel *An Open Swimmer*. He has won the Miles Franklin Award three times – for *Shallows* (1984), *Cloudstreet* (1991, also winner of the British Deo Gloria award), and *Dirt Music* (2001). Other novels include *The Riders* (1994) and *Blueback* (1998), and he has also published several books for children.

wipe (photography) A transition effect in motion pictures or video in which one scene is gradually replaced by the next at a boundary line moving across the picture area, sharply defined ('hard-edge') or diffuse ('soft-edge'). An expanding or contracting circular outline is termed an **iris wipe**.

wire service *news agency*

wireworm *click beetle*

Wisconsin [wiskonsin] pop (2000e) 5 363 700; area 145 431 sq km/56 153 sq mi. State in NC USA, divided into 72 counties;

the 'Badger State'; first settled by French traders, 1670; surrendered to the British, 1763; ceded to the USA, 1783 (part of the Northwest Territory); Territory of Wisconsin formed, 1836; 30th state to join the Union, 1848; bounded N by L Superior and L Michigan, E by L Michigan; capital, Madison; other chief cities, Milwaukee, Green Bay, Racine; rivers include the Mississippi (part of the W border), Menominee (part of the E border), and Wisconsin; L Winnebago lies to the E; c.26 000 sq km/ 10 000 sq mi of L Michigan lie within the state boundary; highest point, Timms Hill (595 m/1952 ft); glaciated terrain in the N and W, largely forested; over 8500 lakes; timber products, dairy products, paper, metal products, machinery, food processing, electrical equipment, transport equipment, grain, vegetables, brewing; produces more milk, butter, and cheese than any other state; over a third of the nation's cheese production; heavy industry in the Milwaukee area.

Wisdom, (Arthur) John (Terence Dibben) (1904–93) British philosopher. He studied at Cambridge, and became professor there (1952–68) and at the University of Oregon (1968–72). He was profoundly influenced by Wittgenstein, but developed a distinctive mode and style of philosophizing which represented philosophical paradoxes as revealing partial truths rather than linguistic confusions. His most important works are *Other Minds* (1952), *Philosophy and Psychoanalysis* (1953), and *Paradox and Discovery* (1965).

Wisdom, Book of *Wisdom of Solomon*

wisdom literature In the Hebrew Bible/Old Testament, a group of writings, usually including Proverbs, Ecclesiastes, the Song of Songs, and Job, although the influence of wisdom may also be found in other Biblical stories (eg Esther) and in some of the Psalms. Among the Apocrypha, it also includes Ecclesiaticus (or Sirach) and the Wisdom of Solomon. The literature is usually traced to a special class of sages in Israel who sought to draw lessons for life from general human experience rather than from revealed religious truths, although in fact their humanistic observations were increasingly integrated with a belief in Yahweh and his law.

Wisdom of Jesus, the Son of Sirach *Ecclesiasticus, Book of*

Wisdom of Solomon or **Book of Wisdom** A book of the Old Testament Apocrypha, or deuterocanonical work in the Catholic Bible, purportedly from Solomon, but usually attributed to an unknown Alexandrian Jew c.1st-c BC. Like other Jewish wisdom literature, it praises the figure of divine Wisdom against ungodliness, but is a mixture of poetry and philosophical prose rather than short aphorisms. The follies of idolatry are emphasized, and reinforced by examples from the Exodus of the contrasting fates of the faithful Israelites and idolatrous Egyptians.

Wise, Ernie *Morecambe, Eric*

Wiseman, Nicholas (Patrick Stephen), Cardinal (1802–65) Roman Catholic clergyman, born in Seville, SW Spain, of Irish parents. He was brought up at Waterford, Ireland, entered the English College at Rome, was ordained in 1825, and became rector of the College in 1828. He was made bishop, and appointed president of Oscott College, Birmingham (1840) and vicar apostolic of London district (1847–50). His appointment as the first Archbishop of Westminster and a cardinal (1850) called forth a storm of religious excitement, which led to the passing of the Ecclesiastical Titles Assumption Act. One of his best-known works was a historical novel, *Fabiola* (1854).

Wise Men *Magi* 2

wisent [veezent] *bison*

Wishart, George [wishert] (c.1513–46) Reformer and martyr, born in Pitarrow, Aberdeenshire, NE Scotland, UK. In 1538 he was a schoolmaster in Montrose, where he incurred a charge of heresy for teaching the Greek New Testament. He then spent several years in mainland Europe, returning to Scotland in 1543. He preached the Lutheran doctrine in several towns, and was arrested and burned at St Andrews. One of his converts was John Knox.

wisteria A deciduous climbing shrub from E Asia and North America; leaves pinnate with oval–oblong leaflets; pea-flowers fragrant, lilac, violet, or white, in long pendulous clusters. It is often grown for ornament, and can reach a considerable age, developing thick, gnarled stems. Commonly grown species include *Wisteria sinensis*, native to China with lilac-mauve flowers, and *Wisteria floribunda* from Japan, with blue-purple flowers. (Genus: *Wisteria*, 6 species. Family: Leguminosae.)

witan or **witenagemot** (Old English 'meeting of wise men') The council of the Anglo-Saxon kings, once regarded as the first English 'parliament'. It was not a popular or representative assembly imposing constitutional restraints on kingship, but in essence an informal advisory body of aldermen, thegns, and bishops, who gathered formally to discuss royal grants of land, church benefices, charters, aspects of taxation, defence, foreign policy, and law. It nevertheless upheld the convention that kings should take into account the views of powerful subjects. The succession of a king had usually to be acknowledged by the witan. The Norman monarchs in 1066 replaced the witan with the *curia regis*, or King's court.

witchcraft The alleged possession and exercise of magical or psychic powers, especially involving the manipulation of natural objects or events; often called *black magic* if harmful to people, *white magic* if helpful. In Africa, the power of witches is said to be innate, and people may not even know that they are witches. In Europe the Christian Church began persecuting witches in the 14th-c, alleging that witches consciously made a pact with Satan. The persecution later spread to America, and by the end of the 17th-c c.200 000 people had been executed. Contemporary witchcraft in the West sees itself as an alternative religion, celebrating gods drawn from various European pre-Christian religions, and exercising its magical powers in beneficial ways.

witch hazel A deciduous shrub or small tree, native to E Asia and E North America; flowers in short-stalked clusters, each with four long strap-shaped yellow petals, usually appearing before oval leaves. The bark yields an astringent lotion; the twigs are often used in dowsing. (Genus: *Hamamelis*, 6 species. Family: Hamamelidaceae.)

witchweed A higher plant parasite (*Striga hermonthica*) causing severe damage to the roots of sorghum, millet, sugar cane, and other tropical grain crops, and also occasionally attacking pigeon pea and other legumes. The parasite produces very large numbers of seeds, which may remain dormant in the soil for many years until stimulated to germinate by matter exuding from the roots of a susceptible crop. It is most serious in Africa and the drier parts of India, but has also been reported from North America. (Family: Scrophulariaceae.)

withdrawal syndrome Symptoms which occur when an addictive substance is no longer available to someone who has become addicted to it; they include nausea, vomiting, stomach cramps, anxiety, panic attacks, palpitations, headaches, hallucinations, sweating, shaking, and possibly convulsions. To avoid these symptoms, the treatment of drug dependency involves replacing the body's biochemical requirement for the drug with a similar but less addictive substance. Diminishing doses of the substance are given until eventually all medication can be withdrawn. To persevere with such a programme of withdrawal, an addict must be strongly motivated to stop taking the drug, and close support by counselling and other kinds of ancillary treatment such as acupuncture and psychotherapy can help to maintain the motivation.

Witt, Katerina [vit] (1965–) Figure skater, born in Karl-Marx-Stadt, E Germany. The East German champion in 1982, she won the first of six successive European titles in 1983, was world champion in 1984–5 and 1987–8, and Olympic champion in 1984 and 1988.

Witten, Edward (1951–) US physicist and mathematician. He became professor of physics at Princeton University (1980–7), then professor of natural sciences at the Institute for Advanced Study. A central figure in the study of superstrings, he has made important contributions to many areas of theoretical physics.

His work linking knot theory with quantum theory gained him the 1990 Fields Medal.

Wittenberg [vitnberg] 51°53N 12°39E, pop (2000e) 55 700. Town in Wittenberg district, EC Germany; on R Elbe, SW of Berlin; associated with the beginning of the Reformation, 1517; part of Prussia, 1814; railway; university (1817); chemical plants; 16th-c Augustinian monastery where Luther lived; Schlosskirche, to the doors of which Luther nailed his 95 theses.

Wittgenstein, Ludwig (Josef Johann) [witgenstiyn], Ger [vitgenshtiyn] (1889–1951) Philosopher, born in Vienna, Austria. He studied engineering at Berlin and Manchester, then became interested in mathematical logic, which he studied under Russell (1912–13). While serving in the Austrian army in World War 1, he wrote the *Tractatus logico-philosophicus* (1921), in which he argued that an adequate account of language must recognize that any sentence is a picture of the fact it represents, and that any thought is a sentence. He then turned temporarily away from philosophy, gave away the money he had inherited, and lived a simple ascetic life. In 1929 he began lecturing at Cambridge, submitting the *Tractatus* as his doctoral dissertation. He worked at hospitals in London and Newcastle upon Tyne during World War 2, returned to Cambridge afterwards, and resigned his chair in 1947. Between 1936 and 1949 he worked on the *Philosophische Untersuchungen* (1953, Philosophical Investigations), in which he rejected the doctrines of the *Tractatus*, claiming that linguistic meaning is a function of the *use* to which expressions are put, or the 'language games' in which they play a role. He became a naturalized British subject in 1938.

Witwatersrand [witwawterzrand], Afrikaans [vuhtvahtersrant] or **The Rand** ('white water's reef') Region centred on a ridge of gold-bearing rock in South Africa; length 100 km/60 mi; width 40 km/25 mi; Johannesburg located near its centre; the powerhouse of the South African economy, with many black townships nearby providing a reserve of labour; gold discovered in 1886 (produces about half the world's supply).

woad A biennial or perennial (*Isatis tinctoria*) with numerous yellow, cross-shaped flowers and pendulous, oblong, flattened, purplish capsules. It has been cultivated since ancient times, but is now reduced to an occasional cornfield weed. The blue dye used by Ancient Britons (and still produced until the 19th-c) is made by exposing part-dried, crushed leaves to the air. (Family: Cruciferae.)

Wobblies *Industrial Workers of the World*

Wodehouse, Sir P(elham) G(renville) [wudhows] (1881–1975) Novelist, born in Guildford, Surrey, SE England, UK. Educated in London, he worked in a bank, then became a freelance writer. He made his name with *Psmith, Journalist* (1912), *Piccadilly Jim* (1918), and other stories. His best-known works fall within his 'country house' period, involving the creation of Bertie Wooster and his 'gentleman's gentleman' Jeeves, as in *Right Ho, Jeeves* (1934), *Quick Service* (1940), and *The Mating Season* (1949). A prolific writer, he produced a succession of over 100 novels, as well as many short stories, sketches, librettos, and lyrics for the likes of Irving Berlin, Cole Porter, and George Gershwin. During World War 2 he was captured and interned in Germany, and incautiously agreed to make broadcasts for the Germans, and though they were harmless he was branded as a traitor. Eventually his name was cleared, and he then made America his home, where the climate allowed him to indulge his passion for golf. He became a US citizen in 1955, and was knighted in 1975, just weeks before his death.

Woden *Odin*

Wogan, Terry [wohgn], popular name of **Michael Terence Wogan** (1938–) Broadcaster and writer, born in Limerick, SW Ireland. He began his broadcasting career as a radio announcer in Ireland (1963) before joining the BBC (1965), where he hosted various radio programmes including *Late Night Extra* (1967–9) and *The Terry Wogan Show* (1969–72). Resident in Britain from 1969, his popularity grew when he presented Radio Two's *Breakfast Show* (1972–84). He has hosted several TV shows, including *Blankety Blank* (1977–81), *You Must Be Joking* (1981), the annual charity telethon *Children in Need*, the annual Eurovision Song Contests, and an early evening chat-show (1982–92) which became a thrice weekly fixture in 1985. He enjoyed success in the pop charts with 'The Floral Dance' (1977), and has written several books including *Banjaxed* (1979), *The Day Job* (1981), *Wogan on Wogan* (1987), and *Terry Wogan's Bumper Book of Togs* (1995). The recipient of many broadcasting 'personality of the year' awards, he returned to radio work in 1993.

Wöhler, Friedrich [voeler] (1800–82) Chemist, whose work marked a turning point for organic chemistry, born near Frankfurt, WC Germany. He studied medicine at Heidelberg, turned to chemistry, and studied with Berzelius, with whom he maintained a lifelong friendship. He taught at Berlin and Kassel, then became professor of chemistry at Göttingen (1836). He isolated aluminium (1827) and beryllium (1828), discovered calcium carbide, from which he obtained acetylene, and from 1832 worked closely with Liebig on the chemistry of the benzoyl group. His synthesis of urea from ammonium cyanate in 1828 was the first synthesis of an organic compound from an inorganic substance.

Wojtyła, Karol Jozef *John Paul II*

Wolds Way Long-distance footpath stretching from Hull to Filey, N England, UK; links with the Cleveland Way; length 115 km/71 mi.

Wolf, Hugo (Philipp Jakob) [volf] (1860–1903) Composer, born in Windischgraz, N Slovenia (formerly Austria). He studied at the Vienna Conservatory, then earned a living by teaching, conducting, and music criticism. From 1888 he composed c.300 songs, settings of poems by Goethe and others, the opera *Der Corregidor* (1895), and other works. Having lived most of his life in poverty, he became insane in 1897, and died in the asylum at Steinhof, near Vienna.

wolf A member of the dog family; two species: the **grey** (or **timber**) **wolf** (*Canis lupus*), the largest wild dog and ancestor of the domestic dog, native to forests throughout the temperate N hemisphere (distribution now patchy); and the rare **red wolf** (*Canis rufus*) of E USA. The name is sometimes used for the coyote and less closely-related dogs, such as the South American **maned wolf** (*Chrysocyon brachyurus*) and the **Falkland Island wolf** (*Dusicyon australis*).

wolf cub *scouting*

Wolfe, Charles (1791–1823) Poet, born in Dublin, Ireland. He studied at Trinity College, Dublin, and is remembered for his poem 'The Burial of Sir John Moore', which appeared anonymously in 1817 and at once caught the admiration of the public. He was ordained in 1817, and became rector of Donoughmore.

Wolfe, James (1727–59) British soldier, born in Westerham, Kent, SE England, UK. Commissioned in 1741, he fought against the Jacobites in Scotland (1745–6), and was sent to Canada during the Seven Years' War (1756–63). In 1758 he was prominent in the capture of Louisburg, and commanded in the famous capture of Quebec (1759), scaling the cliffs to defeat the French on the Plains of Abraham, where he was killed.

Wolfe, Thomas (Clayton) (1900–38) Novelist, born in Asheville, North Carolina, USA. After studying at North Carolina and Harvard universities, his writing career began abortively as a playwright, but he achieved success with his first novel, *Look Homeward, Angel* (1929). Some of his best work is to be found in the stories in *From Death to Morning* (1935). Later titles include *The Web and the Rock* (1939) and *You Can't Go Home Again* (1940) (both published posthumously). He died of a brain infection following pneumonia.

Wolfe, Tom, popular name of **Thomas Kennerly Wolfe** (1931–) Journalist, pop-critic, and novelist, born in Richmond, Virginia, USA. He studied at Washington and Yale universities, and worked as a reporter for the *Washington Post* and the *New York Herald Tribune*. A proponent of the New Journalism, his style is distinctive, clever, and narcissistic, employing eye-catching titles such as *The Electric Kool-Aid Acid Test* (1968). Much of his work previously appeared in periodicals such as the *Rolling Stone*, as did his novel, *The Bonfire of the Vanities* (1988), which became a best seller. Later books include the novel *A Man in Full* (1998) and the non-fiction *Hooking Up* (2000). He is credited with coining the phrase 'radical chic'.

Wolfenden, John (Frederick) Wolfenden, Baron [wulfenden] (1906–85) Educationist, born in Halifax, West Yorkshire, N England, UK. He studied at Oxford, where he taught philosophy (1929–34), and was then headmaster at Uppingham (1934) and Shrewsbury (1944), and Vice-Chancellor of Reading University (1950). He was best known for his government investigation of homosexuality and prostitution (the *Wolfenden Report*, 1957). Knighted in 1956, he became a life peer in 1974.

Wolfensohn, Jim, popular name of **James D Wolfensohn** (1933–) President of the World Bank, (1995–), born in Sydney, Australia. He studied at Harvard, becoming a lawyer and an officer in the Royal Australian Air Force before entering banking. He worked in Australia, London, and New York, eventually establishing an investment bank in his own name. Under his tutelage, the World Bank has sought to find ways of reducing the burden of debt on the world's poorest countries. He became a US citizen, and was awarded an honorary UK knighthood in 1995.

Wolf-Ferrari, Ermanno [volf ferahree] (1876–1948) Composer, born in Venice, NE Italy. Sent to Rome to study painting, he turned to music, and studied in Munich, returning to Venice in 1899. He became an operatic composer, his best-known works being *I quattro rusteghi* (1906, trans The School for Fathers) and *Il segreto di Susanna* (1909, Susanna's Secret). He also composed choral and chamber works, and music for organ and piano.

wolffia A tiny floating freshwater herb (*Wolffia arrhiza*) related to duckweed, consisting only of a minute green thallus 0·5–1 mm/0·02–0·04 in across, with a budding pouch from which new plants are produced. Flowers, one male and one female, concealed in a cavity, are often absent. It is the smallest flowering plant in the world. (Family: Lemnaceae.)

wolf fish Large blenny-like fish (*Anarhichas lupus*) found in moderately deep and colder waters of the N Atlantic; length up to 1·2 m/4 ft; head robust, teeth strong and pointed; body tapers to small tail fin, dorsal and anal fins long; feeds mainly on echinoderms, crustaceans, and molluscs. (Family: Anarhichadidae.)

Wölfflin, Heinrich [voelflin] (1864–1945) Art historian, born in Winterthur, N Switzerland. He studied under Jacob Burckhardt, whom he succeeded as professor of art history at Basel in 1893. He was one of the founders of modern art history, pioneering the 'scientific' method of formal analysis, based on the systematic comparison of works of art in terms of contrasting stylistic features. His approach is expounded in three books: *Renaissance and Baroque* (1888), *Classic Art* (1899), and *Principles of Art History* (1915).

wolfhound *borzoi; Irish wolfhound*

Wolfit, Sir Donald [wulfit] (1902–68) Actor-manager, born in Newark, Nottinghamshire, C England, UK. He began his stage career in 1920, formed his own company in 1937, and became known for his Shakespeare performances. During the Battle of Britain (1940) he instituted the first London season of 'Lunchtime Shakespeare'. He appeared in several films and on television, and his autobiography, *First Interval*, appeared in 1954. He was knighted in 1957.

wolfram [wulfram] *tungsten*

wolframite [wulframiyt] An iron manganese tungstate mineral ($(Fe,Mn)WO_4$), found in pegmatites and hydrothermal veins as tabular crystals or brown masses. It is the principal ore of tungsten.

Wolfram von Eschenbach [volfram fon eshenbakh] (c.1170–c.1220) Poet, born near Ansbach, SC Germany. One of the principal figures of the *Minnesang* or courtly love poetry of the chivalric age, he was a Bavarian knight who served at many courts. He is best known for his epic, *Parzival* (c.1200–10), which introduced the theme of the Holy Grail into German literature, and from which Wagner derived the libretto of his *Parsifal*.

Wolfsburg [volfsboork] 52°27N 10°49E, pop (2000e) 131 000. City in Lüneburg district, NC Germany; 24 km/15 mi NE of Brunswick, on the Mittelland and Elbe Branch Canals; founded, 1938; railway; vehicles, machinery, tools; known as the 'Volkswagen town' (site of car factory).

Wolfson, Sir Isaac (1897–1991) Businessman and philanthropist, born in Glasgow, W Scotland, UK. He quit school at 15 to become a salesman, joined Great Universal Stores as a buyer (1932), became managing director (1934), and greatly expanded the business, retiring as life-president (1987). In 1955 he set up the Wolfson Foundation for the advancement of health, education, and youth activities in the UK and the Commonwealth, and as a devout Jew was active in Jewish causes. He was made a baronet in 1962. In 1973 University College, Cambridge, was renamed *Wolfson College* after a grant from the foundation.

wolf spider A medium-to-large, hairy spider that runs over the ground to capture prey; some burrow or make funnel-shaped webs. (Order: Araneae. Family: Lycosidae, c.3000 species.)

Wollongong [wolongong] 34°25S 150°52E, pop (2000e) 192 300. Urban centre in SE New South Wales, Australia, extending 48 km/30 mi along the coast; includes the towns of Wollongong, Bulli, and Port Kembla; railway; university (1975); steel, coal, dairy farming.

Wollstonecraft, Mary [wulstonkraft], married name **Godwin** (1759–97) Feminist and educationist, born in London, UK. After working as a teacher and governess, she became a translator and literary adviser. In 1787 she published *Thoughts on the Education of Daughters*, and in 1792 she wrote *Vindication of the Rights of Woman*, advocating equality of the sexes. She was in Paris during the French Revolution where she married **Gilbert Imlay** (1754–1828), and had a daughter, Fanny. He lost interest in the relationship and she tried to kill herself twice. She recovered and eventually married William Godwin in 1797, and died of blood-poisoning in London 11 days after giving birth to a daughter, Mary (later, Mary Shelley).

Wolof [wolof] A West Atlantic-speaking agricultural people of Senegal and Gambia, traditionally grouped into a state with elaborate hierarchical distinctions. They developed a powerful empire (14th–16th-c), were involved in the European slave trade, and later worked in factories and on European trading vessels.

Wolpe, Joseph [volpay] (1915–97) Psychiatrist, born in Johannesburg, NE South Africa. He trained at the University of Witwatersrand, and later worked at Temple University, Florida. From animal experiments he concluded that behaviour was environmentally conditioned. He published *Psychotherapy by Reciprocal Inhibition* (1958), and was co-author of *Behavioural Therapy Techniques* (1966), with which he founded the field of behavioural therapy, widely used in the treatment of neurotic disorders.

Wolseley, Garnet (Joseph) Wolseley, 1st Viscount [wulzlee] (1833–1913) British field marshal, born in Golden Bridge, Ireland. He joined the army in 1852, and served in the Burmese War (1852–3), the Crimea (where he lost an eye), the Indian Mutiny (1857), and the Chinese War (1860). He put down the Red River rebellion (1870) in Canada, and commanded in the Ashanti War (1873). After other posts in India, Cyprus, South Africa, and Egypt, he led the attempted rescue of General Gordon at Khartoum. He became a baron (1882) and, after the Sudan campaign (1884–5), a viscount. As army commander-in-chief (1895–1901), he carried out several reforms, and mobilized forces for the Boer War (1899–1902).

Wolsey, Thomas, Cardinal [wulzee] (c.1475–1530) English clergyman and statesman, born in Ipswich, Suffolk, E England, UK. He studied at Oxford, was ordained in 1498, appointed chaplain to Henry VII in 1507, and became Dean of Lincoln. Under Henry VIII, he became Bishop of Lincoln, Archbishop of York (1514), and a cardinal (1515). Made Lord Chancellor (1515–29), he pursued legal and administrative reforms, and became Henry

VIII's leading adviser, in charge of the day-to-day running of government. He aimed to make England a major power in Europe, and also had ambitions to become pope, but his policy of supporting first Emperor Charles V (1523) then Francis I of France (1528) in the Habsburg–Valois conflict was unsuccessful, and high taxation caused much resentment. His despotism and personal ambition (he had begun the demolition of Christ Church cathedral in Oxford in 1525, to replace it with 'Cardinal College') contributed to the anti-clericalism of the times. When he failed to persuade the pope to grant Henry's divorce, he was impeached and his property forfeited. Arrested on a charge of high treason, he died while travelling to London.

Wolverhampton [wulverhamptn] 52°36N 2°08W, pop (2001e) 236 600. City in West Midlands, C England, UK; in the industrial 'Black Country', 20 km/12 mi NW of Birmingham; named after Wulfruna (sister of Edgar II) who endowed the first collegiate church here in 994; city status, 2000; railway; University of Wolverhampton (1992, formerly Polytechnic); metal products, locks and keys, engineering, chemicals, bicycles; 15th-c Church of St Peter; football league team, Wolverhampton Wanderers (Wolves).

wolverine A mammal of family Mustelidae, native to the N forests and tundra of Scandinavia, Asia, and North America; stocky (length, 1 m/3¼ ft), pointed muzzle, bushy tail; dark brown, often pale on face and sides; eats mainly small mammals; also known as **glutton** (*Gulo gulo*).

womb *uterus*

wombat A nocturnal Australian marsupial; length, up to 1·3 m/ 4 ft; bear-like, with a stout body, very small tail; round head, blunt muzzle with a large nose pad; pouch of female opens backwards; digs burrows; eats coarse grasses. (Family: Vombatidae, 3 species.)

Women's Institutes, National Federation of (WI) A women's voluntary organization, started in Canada in 1897 by Adelaide Hoodless to provide classes in domestic science and home-making. The WI spread to Britain in 1915, and later to other Commonwealth countries. There are now some 9200 institutes in England and Wales (but none in Scotland, which has its own **Scottish Women's Rural Institutes**).

women's liberation movement A broad cultural and political movement initiated by women to improve their social position by freeing themselves from the constraints and disadvantages of a society said to be dominated by men. 'Women's lib' has very strong roots in the USA and Europe, and has been 'politicized', especially by radical feminists who claim the continued existence of 'patriarchy' (ie male dominance) in capitalist societies; the origins of women's liberation can be traced back to the French Revolution (1789).

Women's Royal Voluntary Service (WRVS) In the UK, an organization founded in 1938 (designated Royal in 1966), made up of unpaid helpers who do community work. During World War 2 they helped mitigate the social disruptions of wartime; in peacetime their role is to supplement the social services. They pioneered the first home help scheme (1944), and run the 'Meals on Wheels' service for the housebound elderly, as well as providing voluntary workers for day centres, hospitals, playgroups, prison visiting, and rural transport.

women's services Military organizations in which women enlist for non-combatant duty. In Britain, there are separate corps for army, navy, and air force. The **Women's Royal Army Corps** (**WRAC**) was founded in 1949, directly succeeding the Auxiliary Territorial Service (ATS) within which large numbers of women had served during World War 2. It was abolished as a separate service in 1992, with a view to integrating women more fully into the main army. British women had served during World War 1 in the **Women's Auxiliary Army Corps** (**WAAC**) formed in 1917. The **Women's Royal Naval Service** (**WRNS**), popularly known as **the Wrens**, was first formed in 1917; it became part of the Royal Navy in 1993. The **Women's Royal Air Force** (**WRAF**) was formed in 1918, and later became known as the **Women's Auxiliary Air Force** (**WAAF**). In the USA, the **Women's Army Corps** (**WAC**) was established in 1948, and dissolved in 1978.

women's studies The study of the history and contemporary role of girls and women. More available in further and higher education than in schools, it is favoured by feminist groups, who feel that girls and women are disadvantaged and that the nature of this disadvantage is often not mentioned in education.

Wonder, Stevie, originally **Steveland Judkins** or **Steveland Morris** (1950–) Soul singer and instrumentalist, born in Saginaw, Michigan, USA. He was blind from birth, played the harmonica, drums, keyboards, and guitar from an early age, and was signed to Motown Records in 1961. His first album *Little Stevie Wonder: the 12-Year-Old Genius* was an immediate success. Most of his early records followed the orthodox Motown sound, but in 1971 he renegotiated his contract to gain full artistic control over his work. During the 1970s he became one of the most proficient users of synthesizer technology. His major albums include *Songs In the Key of Life* (1976), *Talking Book* (1972), *Innervisions* (1973), and *Hotter than July* (1980).

Wood, Sir Henry (Joseph) (1869–1944) Conductor, born in London, UK. He studied at the Royal Academy of Music, London, became an organist, and in 1895 helped to found the Promenade Concerts which he conducted annually until his death. He composed operettas and an oratorio, but his international reputation was gained as a conductor, first at the Queen's Hall, London, then at the Albert Hall. He was knighted in 1911.

wood The bulk of the tissue making up the trunk and branches of trees and shrubs, consisting of *xylem*. Its exact composition varies between species, affecting properties of the timber produced. For commercial purposes, it is divided into two types: **softwoods**, derived from gymnosperms, and **hardwoods**, which have a less regular grain and are derived from flowering plants – though the terms are misleading, as some softwoods are very hard and durable. As one of the most abundant elements in the world, wood has been used by humans from earliest times for fuel, building materials, and furniture, as well as in modern developments such as paper and packaging. It has been estimated that there are well over 10 000 wood products in current use.

wood alcohol *methanol*

wood avens *avens*

woodbine *honeysuckle*

wood block A percussion instrument (also known as a **Chinese block**) in the form of a hollowed rectangular or spherical block of wood, with one or more slits in the surface, which is struck with a wooden stick. Often grouped in four or five different sizes, they are frequently used in jazz and orchestral music.

Wood Buffalo National park in N Alberta and S Northwest Territories, C Canada; includes part of Buffalo L and L Claire and part of the Caribou and Birch Mts; Great Canadian Oil Sands to the S; area 44 807 sq km/17 295 sq mi; established in 1922; noted for its herds of bison; a world heritage site.

wood carving A form of sculpture found since remote prehistoric times. Wood has provided an accessible, easily-worked, and durable material. The Egyptians coated their wooden statues with stucco and painted them, a technique also used in mediaeval church art. Extraordinary heights of naturalism were reached by 15th-c sculptors in Germany, notably Veit Stoss (1447–1533), Adam Krafft (c.1455–c.1508), and Tilman Riemenschneider (1460–1531), and by Gibbons in 17th-c England. Wood proved a popular material with 20th-c sculptors, whether abstract or figurative.

woodchat A shrike native to Europe, Africa, and W Asia (*Lanius senator*); top of head and neck chestnut-brown; breast white; inhabits woodland and scrub; eats insects and small birds; also known as **woodchat shrike**.

woodchuck A marmot native to North America (*Marmota monax*); large (length, 80 cm/30 in), aggressive; may dig a den in woodland for the winter months; also known as **groundhog**.

woodcock A short-legged sandpiper, native to the Old World and E North America; mottled brown; bill long, straight, held downward during flight; inhabits woodland; eats earthworms and insect larvae. (Genus: *Scolopax*, 6 species.)

woodcreeper A bird native to the New World tropics; tail stiffened as in woodpeckers; many shapes of bill; inhabits woodland; eats insects, frogs, and snakes; also known as a **woodhewer**. (Family: Dendrocolaptidae, 47 species; sometimes placed in the family Furnariidae.)

woodcut One of the simplest and oldest methods of relief-printing. The design is gouged into the smooth surface of a block of wood, and sticky ink rolled over the top. The cutaway areas print as white patches, the rest as solid black. It therefore lends itself to crude, forceful designs with simple shapes and sharp contrasts.

wood engraving A method of printmaking from wooden blocks, which differs from woodcut in that the end rather than the side of the block is used and the wood must be very hard. The design is engraved in the wood with a burin, producing fine lines.

Woodhead, Chris(topher Anthony) (1946–) British teacher and educational administrator. He studied at Bristol and Keele universities, and became an English teacher at various schools and a tutor of English at Oxford University (1976–82). He was deputy chief education officer of the Devon (1988–90) and Cornwall (1990–1) local education authorities, and chief executive for the National Curriculum Council (1991–3) and School Curriculum and Assessment Authority (1993–4). He was appointed chief inspector for schools at the Office for Standards in Education (OFSTED) (1994–2001).

Woodhenge Prehistoric site in Wiltshire, S England, UK; 3 km/1¾ mi NE of Stonehenge, near Amesbury; discovered by aerial reconnaissance in 1926. Little visible above ground, it apparently consisted of a number of concentric ovals of wooden pillars oriented for the same ritualistic forms as were in use at Stonehenge.

woodhewer *woodcreeper*

wood-hoopoe *hoopoe*

wood-ibis *ibis*

Woodland culture A generic term for the Indian culture of the E USA as far W as the Great Plains, c.700 BC–AD 1500. Characterized archaeologically by burial mounds, cord-impressed pottery, and tobacco smoking, its main traditions are *Adena-Hopewell* (c.700 BC–AD 400), centred on S Ohio with only rudimentary horticulture, and *Mississippian* (AD c.700–1500 AD), agriculturally stronger, with an emphasis on maize, beans, squash, and the use of bows and arrows for hunting.

wood lily A perennial native to woodland in E North America (*Trillium grandiflorum*); rhizomatous; three leaves, in a single whorl near top of stem; flower solitary, terminal; three sepals, green; three petals, white turning pink. It is cultivated together with related species for ornament. (Family: Trilliaceae.)

woodlouse A terrestrial crustacean found under stones, in litter and soil; abdominal limbs modified for aerial breathing and for reproduction; thoracic legs adapted for walking; some species able to roll into a protective ball. (Order: Isopoda, c.3500 species.)

wood mouse *fieldmouse*

wood ox *anoa*

woodpecker A bird of the family Picidae (198 species), inhabiting woodland; clings to tree trunks; tail stiff and presses against tree for support (except in small **piculets** (subfamily: Picumninae, 27 species) and **wrynecks**); eats insects, fruit, nuts, young birds, and (**sapsuckers**) sap.

wood pigeon A pigeon native to Europe, N Africa, and W Asia (*Columba palumbus*); plumage dark grey with white patch on neck; inhabits woodland, cultivation, and habitation; also known as **ringdove**.

wood rat *pack rat*

woodrush A tufted perennial, sometimes with stolons, found almost everywhere; leaves grass-like, fringed with long, colourless hairs; flowers with six perianth-segments, brownish, in terminal heads. (Genus: *Luzula*, 80 species. Family: Juncaceae.)

Woods, Tiger, popular name of **Eldrick Woods** (1976–) Golfer, born in Cypress, California, USA. He studied at Stanford University and won amateur US golf titles before turning professional in 1996. He shot to fame after winning the US Masters at Augusta in 1997 – with a record score of 270 – at the age of 21, the first African-American to do so, as well as the youngest; in his first appearance at the British Open later that year he equalled the Troon course record of 64. Further successes include the 1999 and 2000 US PGA title, the US Open (2000), the Open Championhip (2000), the US Masters (2001, 2002), and the US Open (2002). In 2003 he was voted the US PGA Tour Player of Year for the fifth successive year.

wood sorrel A perennial native to Europe and temperate Asia (*Oxalis acetosella*); leaves with three heart-shaped leaflets, acid-tasting; flowers long-stalked, 1–1·6 cm/0·4–0·6 in, funnel-shaped, white or lilac. It is very shade tolerant. (Family: Oxalidaceae.)

Woodstock Small town in Ulster Co, SE New York; 16 km/10 mi NW of Kingston; tourist centre, in the foothill of the Catskill Mts; noted for its artists' colony, home of the summer school of the Art Students' League of New York since 1906, and other events in arts, crafts, and popular music. The town became world famous for the 3-day rock festival held nearby as part of the Woodstock Music and Art Fair in August 1969, which attracted (estimates vary) nearly half a million people. The largest rock festival of the 1960s, recorded in the film *Woodstock* (1970), a celebration of that decade, it is now seen as a symbol of the era of 'flower power', psychedelia, civil rights, and anti-war protest. The 'Woodstock generation' regularly recalls the event with nostalgia, and the 25th anniversary festival attracted special attention in 1994.

wood warbler *warbler*

Woodward, Bob *Bernstein, Carl*

Woodward, R(obert) B(urns) (1917–79) Organic chemist, born in Boston, Massachusetts, USA. He studied at Massachusetts Institute of Technology, and became professor of chemistry at Harvard (1953–79). In 1963, he became director of the Woodward Research Institute at Basel, which was founded in his honour. Best known for his masterly work on organic synthesis, including his synthesis of chlorophyll (1961), he was awarded the Nobel Prize for Chemistry in 1965.

woodwasp A wasp with a large egg-laying tube, and no waist separating thorax and abdomen. Some are small and parasitic (Family: Orussidae), laying eggs on the larvae of wood-boring beetles; others (Family: Siricidae) are large, and have larvae that feed on timber. (Order: Hymenoptera.)

woodwind instrument A musical instrument made principally from wood (or, in the case of the saxophone and some flutes, from metal), in which a column of air is activated by the player blowing across a mouth-hole (as in the flute or piccolo), through a duct (as in the recorder), or against a single or double reed (as in the bassoon, cor anglais, oboe, and clarinet).

woodworm *furniture beetle*

woody nightshade A scrambling woody perennial (*Solanum dulcamara*), native to Europe, Asia, and N Africa; leaves oval with 1–4 deep lobes or leaflets at the base; flowers like those of the related potato, with five purple petals, curving backwards, and a cone of yellow stamens; berries oval, green turning yellow and finally red when ripe, mildly poisonous; also called **bittersweet**. (Family: Solanaceae.)

Wookey Hole Limestone caves near the village of Wookey in Somerset, SW England, UK; on the SW slopes of the Mendip Hills near the R Axe, 22 km/14 mi SE of Weston-super-Mare; prehistoric tools found in the caves.

wool The fibre obtained from the fleeces of sheep. There are many qualities of wool, from fine soft wools obtained from the merino sheep of Australia, South Africa, and Argentina to coarse fibres which come from sheep in the cooler climates of New Zealand, Europe, and North America. Medium quality wools are used in clothing, including knitwear of the Shetland type; coarse wools are used mainly for carpets and other furnishings.

Woolf, (Adeline) Virginia, *née* **Stephen** (1882–1941) Novelist, born in London, UK, the daughter of Leslie Stephen. Educated privately, in 1912 she married Leonard Woolf, with whom she set up the Hogarth Press (1917). A leading member of the Bloomsbury Group, she made a major contribution to the development of the novel, in such works as *Mrs Dalloway* (1925), *To the Lighthouse* (1927), and *The Waves* (1931), noted for their impressionistic style, a development of the stream-of-consciousness technique. She also wrote biographies and critical essays. After mental illness, she committed suicide. Publication of her *Diary* (5 vols, 1977–84) and *Letters* (6 vols, 1975–80) further enhanced her reputation.

Woolley, Sir (Charles) Leonard (1880–1960) Archaeologist, born in London, UK. He studied at Oxford, and carried out excavations at Carchemish, al-Ubaid, and Tell el-Amarna. He subsequently directed the important excavations (1922–34) at Ur in Mesopotamia, revealing in 1926 spectacular discoveries of gold and lapis lazuli in the royal tombs. He was knighted in 1935, and wrote several popular accounts of his work, notably *Digging Up the Past* (1930).

woolly bear *carpet beetle; tiger moth*

woolly monkey A New World monkey; large round head, long grasping tail; short dense woolly coat; plain dark colour; eats fruit and some insects, if food plentiful, will eat until abdomen markedly swollen; also known as **barrigudo**. (Genus: *Lagothrix*, 2 species.)

woolly rhinoceros An extinct rhinoceros (*Coelodonta antiquitatis*), once native to Europe and N Asia; length, 3·5 m/11 ft; thick coat of long hair; snout with two horns; in old males, front horn could be 1 m/3 ft long; hunted by humans in Europe 30 000 years ago.

woolly spider monkey A rare New World monkey (*Brachyteles arachnoides*), resembling the spider monkey in having long limbs and tail, but having a thick woolly coat like the woolly monkey; thumb minute; naked face is red, especially when excited.

woolsack A large red cushion, filled with wool, upon which the Lord Chancellor sits on in the UK House of Lords. It is said to represent the authority of the Lord Chancellor, who presides over the proceedings of the House. There were originally four woolsacks, probably introduced in the reign of Edward III as symbols of England's staple trade, on which sat dignitaries who had no voice in parliamentary proceedings.

Woolworth, Frank W(infield) (1852–1919) Businessman, the founder of F W Woolworth stores, born in Rodman, New York, USA. He was a farm worker, and in 1873 became a shop-assistant. His employers backed his scheme to open 'five-and-ten cents' stores in Utica (1879), and in Lancaster, PA . The latter was a success, and in partnership with his employers, his brother, and cousin, from 1905 he began building a large chain of similar stores. At the time of his death the F W Woolworth Co controlled over 1000 stores from their headquarters in the Woolworth building in New York City. His stores started in Britain in 1910, and by the 1960s there were subsidiaries in Germany, Spain, Canada, and Mexico.

Wootton (of Abinger), Barbara Frances Wootton, Baroness (1897–1988) Social scientist, born in Cambridge, Cambridgeshire, EC England, UK. She studied at Cambridge, where she became a lecturer in economics, moving to be director of stud ies (1927–44) and professor of social studies (1948–52) at London. A frequent royal commissioner and London magistrate, she is best known for her *Testament for Social Science* (1950), in which she attempted to assimilate the social to the natural sciences. She was created a life peer in 1958.

Worcester (UK) **[wuster]**, Anglo-Saxon **Wigorna Ceaster** 52°11N 2°13W, pop (2000e) 91 600. County town of Hereford and Worcester, WC England, UK; on the R Severn, 38 km/24 mi SW of Birmingham; founded AD c.680; site of Cromwell victory in Civil War; Royal Worcester Porcelain Co established here in 1862; railway; sauce, engineering, furniture, vehicle parts, porcelain, gloves; 12th–14th-c cathedral; 11th-c Commandery founded by St Wulfstan; 18th-c Guildhall; Dyson Perrins Museum; Three Choirs Festival in rotation with Hereford and Gloucester (Sep).

Worcester porcelain [**wus**ter] Porcelain made at a factory in Worcester, England, founded in 1751 by John Wall (1708–76), and still existing. The factory produced many useful wares especially in blue and white, but is noted for its lavishly enamelled and gilded pieces of the late 18th-c, and its Regency porcelain painted with flowers and figure subjects.

word class A group of words which share several grammatical properties, such as the same kind of inflection or position in sentence structure; also known as **part of speech**. For example, the class of *nouns* consists of such words as *cat* and *table*, which have plurals in *-s*, can be preceded by the definite article, *the*, and can be used as subject and object in a sentence (*the cat/table looked nice, I see the cat/table*). The grouping of words into classes was first carried out by the Greeks, and the main classes (noun, verb, etc) have since been universally used in language description.

Worde, Wynkyn de [werd] (?–?1535) Printer, born in The Netherlands or in Alsace. He was a pupil of Caxton, and in 1491 succeeded to his stock-in-trade. He made great improvements in printing and typecutting, and was the first in England to use italic type.

word processor A computer program, normally running on a personal computer, which allows the computer to be used as a sophisticated typewriter. Documents can be held as whole documents; they can be fully edited before they are printed; and they can be repeatedly updated. A standard letter can be merged with a mailing list to produce personalized versions of the letter.

Wordsworth, Dorothy (1771–1855) Writer, born in Cockermouth, Cumbria, NW England, UK the sister of William Wordsworth, and his lifetime companion. Her *Alfoxden Journal* (1798) and *Grasmere Journals* (1800–3) show a keen sensibility and acute observation of nature in their own right, and as well as adding an important biographical perspective on her brother, gave inspiration to both him and Coleridge in their poems. In 1829 she suffered a mental breakdown from which she never fully recovered.

Wordsworth, William (1770–1850) Poet, born in Cockermouth, Cumbria, NW England, UK. Educated at Hawkshead in the Lake District and at Cambridge, he went on a walking tour through France and Switzerland (1790). Back in France in 1790, he witnessed the French Revolution, developing republican sentiments, and had an affair with a French girl, Annette Vallon, by whom he had a daughter. He returned to England at the outbreak of the war (1793), and after an unsettled period set up house at Racedown, Dorset, with his devoted sister, Dorothy. There he discovered his true vocation, that of the poet exploring the lives of humble folk living in close contact with nature. After moving to Alfoxden, Somerset (1797), he wrote with Coleridge the *Lyrical Ballads* (1798), the first manifesto of the new Romantic poetry, which opened with Coleridge's 'Ancient Mariner' and concluded with Wordsworth's 'Tintern Abbey'. After a year in Germany, he moved to Dove Cottage, Grasmere with Dorothy, married **Mary Hutchinson** in 1802, and wrote much of his best work, including his poetic autobiography, *The Prelude* (1805, published posthumously in 1850), and two books of poems (1807). Critics are inclined to mark the decline of his powers after this remarkable outpouring. He succeeded Southey as poet laureate in 1843.

work The product of force and distance; symbol W, units J (joule). Applying a force F to an object over a distance d means work $W = Fd$ is done, equal to the object's increase in kinetic energy. The rate of doing work is *power*.

workfare The proposal that income support for the non-disabled adult poor should be made conditional on performing

World (physical)

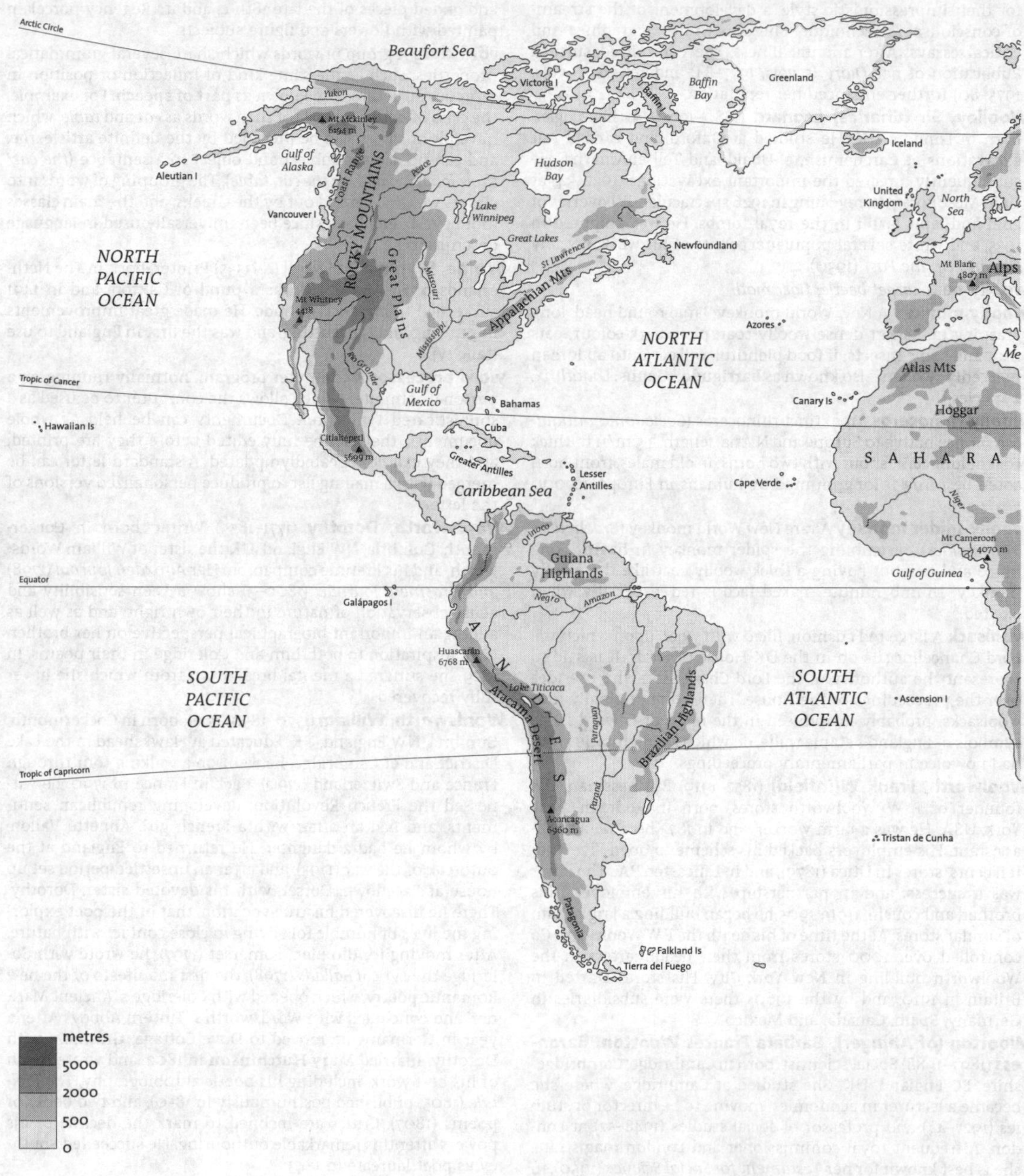
Arctic Circle
Beaufort Sea
Greenland
Victoria I
Baffin Bay
Baffin I
Yukon
Mt McKinley
6194 m
Iceland
Gulf of
Alaska
Aleutian I
Coast Range
ROCKY MOUNTAINS
Peace
Hudson
Bay
United
Kingdom
North
Sea
Lake
Winnipeg
Vancouver I
Great Lakes
Newfoundland
NORTH
PACIFIC
OCEAN
Great Plains
Missouri
St Lawrence
Mt Blanc
4807 m
Alps
Mt Whitney
4418
Appalachian Mts
Mississippi
Azores
NORTH
ATLANTIC
OCEAN
Rio Grande
Me
Atlas Mts
Tropic of Cancer
Gulf of
Mexico
Bahamas
Canary Is
Hoggar
Hawaiian Is
Cuba
Citlaltépetl
5699 m
Greater Antilles
S A H A R A
Lesser
Antilles
Cape Verde
Caribbean Sea
Niger
Orinoco
Mt Cameroon
4070 m
Guiana
Highlands
Gulf of Guinea
Equator
Galápagos I
Negro
Amazon
A
N
D
E
S
Huascarán
6768 m
SOUTH
PACIFIC
OCEAN
Lake Titicaca
SOUTH
ATLANTIC
OCEAN
Ascension I
Atacama Desert
Brazilian Highlands
Paraguay
Tropic of Capricorn
Paraná
Aconcagua
6960 m
Tristan de Cunha
Patagonia
Falkland Is
Tierra del Fuego
metres
5000
2000
500
0

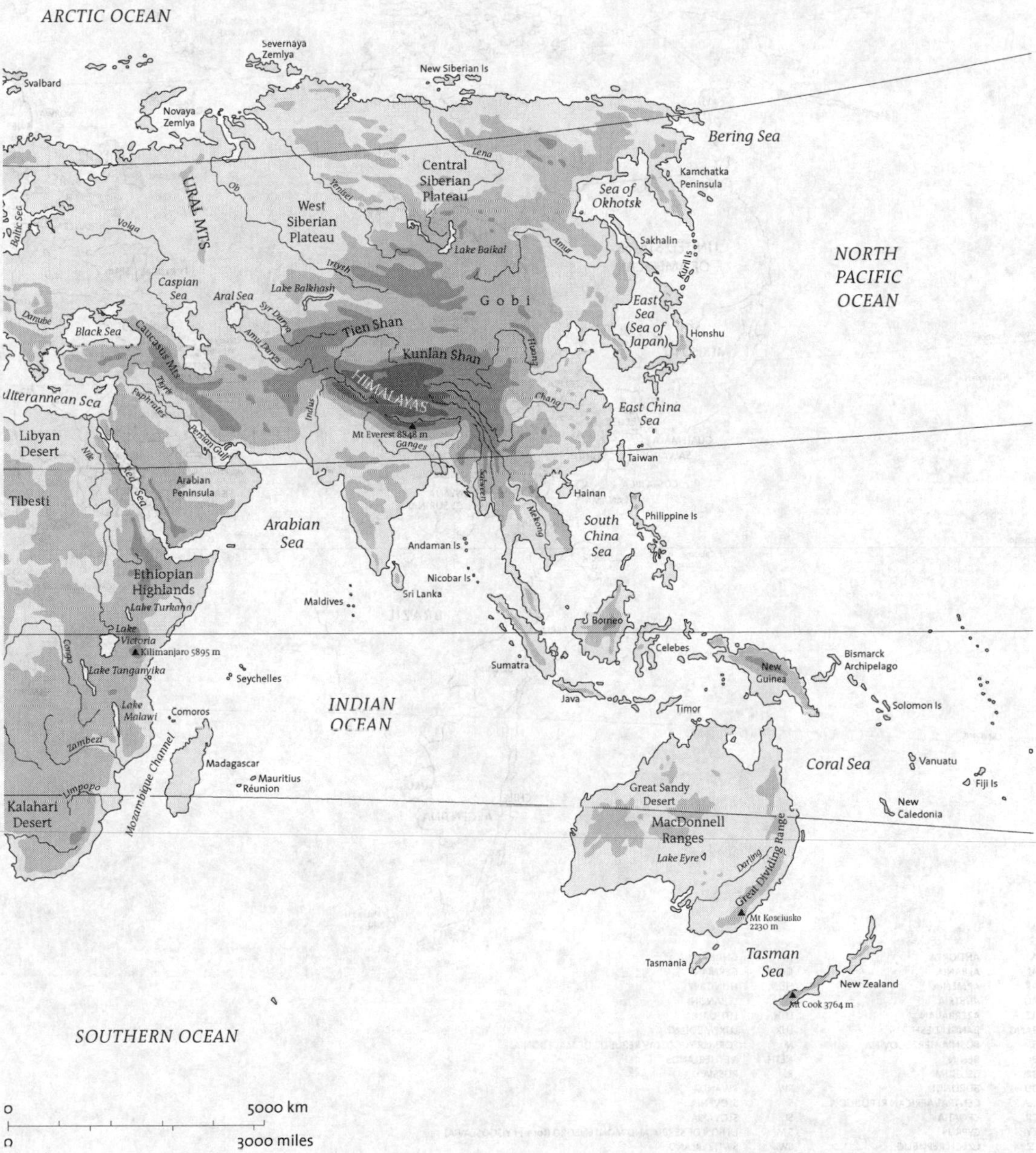
ARCTIC OCEAN
Severnaya Zemlya
Svalbard
New Siberian Is
Novaya Zemlya
Bering Sea
Lena
Central Siberian Plateau
Kamchatka Peninsula
URAL MTS
Ob
Yenisei
West Siberian Plateau
Sea of Okhotsk
Baltic Sea
Volga
Lake Baikal
Sakhalin
NORTH PACIFIC OCEAN
Amur
Kuril Is
Irtysh
Caspian Sea
Aral Sea
Lake Balkhash
Gobi
East Sea (Sea of Japan)
Danube
Syr Darya
Black Sea
Caucasus Mts
Amu Darya
Tien Shan
Honshu
Kunlun Shan
Huang
Tigris
Euphrates
HIMALAYAS
Chang
East China Sea
Indus
Persian Gulf
Mt Everest 8848 m
Libyan Desert
Nile
Ganges
Taiwan
Arabian Peninsula
Red Sea
Salween
Tibesti
Hainan
Mekong
South China Sea
Philippine Is
Arabian Sea
Andaman Is
Ethiopian Highlands
Nicobar Is
Sri Lanka
Maldives
Lake Turkana
Borneo
Lake Victoria
Kilimanjaro 5895 m
Celebes
Congo
Bismarck Archipelago
Lake Tanganyika
Sumatra
New Guinea
Seychelles
Java
Timor
Solomon Is
Lake Malawi
Comoros
INDIAN OCEAN
Zambezi
Mozambique Channel
Coral Sea
Vanuatu
Madagascar
Mauritius
Réunion
Fiji Is
Limpopo
Great Sandy Desert
New Caledonia
Kalahari Desert
MacDonnell Ranges
Great Dividing Range
Lake Eyre
Darling
Mt Kosciusko 2230 m
Tasmania
Tasman Sea
New Zealand
Mt Cook 3764 m
SOUTHERN OCEAN
0
5000 km
0
3000 miles

World (political)

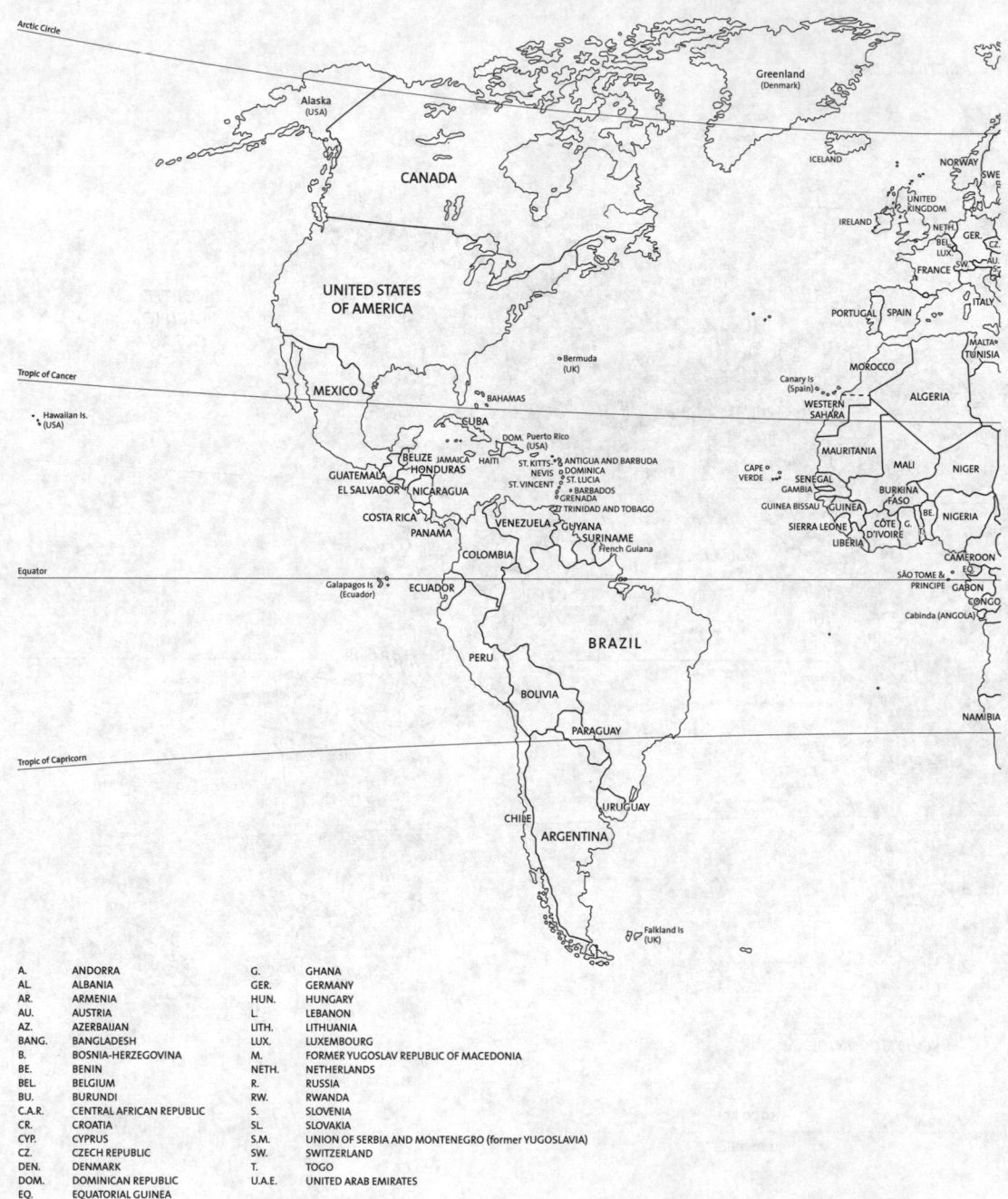

A.	ANDORRA	G.	GHANA
AL.	ALBANIA	GER.	GERMANY
AR.	ARMENIA	HUN.	HUNGARY
AU.	AUSTRIA	L.	LEBANON
AZ.	AZERBAIJAN	LITH.	LITHUANIA
BANG.	BANGLADESH	LUX.	LUXEMBOURG
B.	BOSNIA-HERZEGOVINA	M.	FORMER YUGOSLAV REPUBLIC OF MACEDONIA
BE.	BENIN	NETH.	NETHERLANDS
BEL.	BELGIUM	R.	RUSSIA
BU.	BURUNDI	RW.	RWANDA
C.A.R.	CENTRAL AFRICAN REPUBLIC	S.	SLOVENIA
CR.	CROATIA	SL.	SLOVAKIA
CYP.	CYPRUS	S.M.	UNION OF SERBIA AND MONTENEGRO (former YUGOSLAVIA)
CZ.	CZECH REPUBLIC	SW.	SWITZERLAND
DEN.	DENMARK	T.	TOGO
DOM.	DOMINICAN REPUBLIC	U.A.E.	UNITED ARAB EMIRATES
EQ.	EQUATORIAL GUINEA		

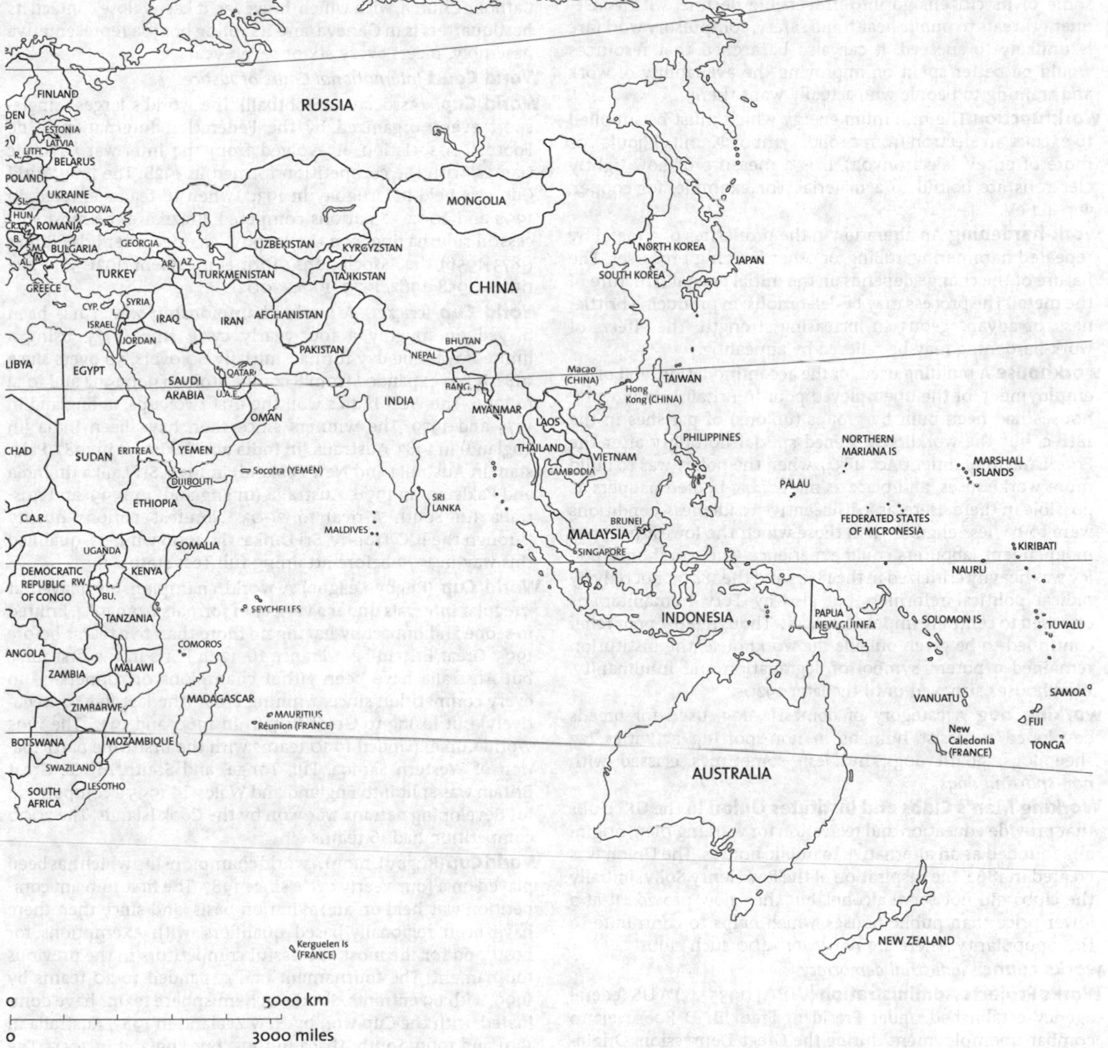
RUSSIA
FINLAND
DEN.
ESTONIA
LATVIA
LITH.
BELARUS
POLAND
UKRAINE
MOLDOVA
HUN.
ROMANIA
BULGARIA
GEORGIA
AR.
AZ.
UZBEKISTAN
KYRGYZSTAN
MONGOLIA
TURKEY
TURKMENISTAN
TAJIKISTAN
GREECE
CHINA
NORTH KOREA
JAPAN
SOUTH KOREA
CYP.
SYRIA
IRAQ
IRAN
AFGHANISTAN
ISRAEL
JORDAN
PAKISTAN
BHUTAN
NEPAL
LIBYA
EGYPT
SAUDI ARABIA
QATAR
U.A.E.
INDIA
Macao (CHINA)
Hong Kong (CHINA)
TAIWAN
BANG.
MYANMAR
LAOS
OMAN
THAILAND
VIETNAM
CAMBODIA
PHILIPPINES
NORTHERN MARIANA IS
MARSHALL ISLANDS
CHAD
SUDAN
ERITREA
YEMEN
Socotra (YEMEN)
DJIBOUTI
ETHIOPIA
SRI LANKA
PALAU
FEDERATED STATES OF MICRONESIA
C.A.R.
MALDIVES
BRUNEI
MALAYSIA
SOMALIA
UGANDA
SINGAPORE
KIRIBATI
NAURU
DEMOCRATIC REPUBLIC OF CONGO
RW.
BU.
KENYA
TANZANIA
SEYCHELLES
INDONESIA
PAPUA NEW GUINEA
SOLOMON IS
TUVALU
ANGOLA
ZAMBIA
MALAWI
COMOROS
MADAGASCAR
ZIMBABWE
MAURITIUS
Réunion (FRANCE)
SAMOA
VANUATU
FIJI
TONGA
New Caledonia (FRANCE)
BOTSWANA
MOZAMBIQUE
SWAZILAND
LESOTHO
SOUTH AFRICA
AUSTRALIA
NEW ZEALAND
Kerguelen Is (FRANCE)
0
5000 km
0
3000 miles

some type of work. The main arguments for this are that experience of work would improve people's future ability to get jobs, and the system would make it harder for people to cheat by claiming benefits while actually employed in the black economy. There are serious problems with compulsory workfare, however. Many welfare recipients are better occupied in caring for their own children or other relatives than in employment. It is also difficult to determine objectively what types of work, if any, a person can do. Unless the state is willing to see some of its citizens go into irreversible decline, with consequent threats to public health and safety, compulsory workfare is unlikely to succeed. It can also be argued that resources would be better spent on improving the availability of work and training to people who actually want them.

workfunction The minimum energy which must be supplied to extract an electron from a solid; symbol Φ, units J (joule), or more often eV (electronvolt). It is a measure of how tightly electrons are bound to a material. For example, for copper, Φ = 4·4 eV.

work-hardening An alteration in the properties of a metal by repeated hammering, rolling, or other forming processes. The nature of the change depends on the initial crystal structure of the metal. The process may be deleterious, in producing brittleness, or advantageous, in increasing strength. The effects of work-hardening may be relieved by annealing.

workhouse A building used for the accommodation, and often employment, of the unemployed poor in Britain. Many workhouses had been built by groups (unions) of parishes in the 18th-c, but the workhouse gained special notoriety after the Poor Law Amendment Act (1834), when the policy was to build more workhouses, and place as many able-bodied paupers as possible in them. Here, as a disincentive to idleness, conditions were to be 'less eligible' than those which the lowest-paid but independent labourers could experience. The workhouse policy was heavily criticized in the 1830s and the 1840s, not only by radical political reformers but also by Tory humanitarians opposed to centrally imposed policies. Though most poor relief continued to be given outside the workhouse, the institution remained a potent symbol of degradation and inhumanity. Workhouses survived until the later 1920s.

working dog A category of domestic dog, used for breeds developed to assist humans in non-sporting activities (eg sheepdogs, guard dogs, huskies); sometimes classed with *non-sporting dogs*.

Working Men's Clubs and Institutes Union In the UK, clubs that provide education and recreation for working men; originally founded as an alternative to public houses. The Union was created in 1862, the inspiration of the Rev Henry Solly; initially the clubs did not serve alcohol, but they now provide it at a lower price than public houses, which helps to contribute to their popularity. There are now over 3400 such clubs.

works council *industrial democracy*

Works Projects Administration (WPA) (1935–43) A US federal agency established under President Franklin D Roosevelt to combat unemployment during the Great Depression. Originally called the **Works Progress Administration**, it built transportation facilities, parks, and buildings. Some 8 500 000 people were employed during its history, including artists and writers as well as manual workers.

work study *time and motion study*

work-to-rule *industrial action*

world (maps) *pp.1660–3*

World Bank *IBRD*

World Chess Federation *chess*

World Commission on Environment and Development An independent body established by the UN in 1983 to formulate 'a global agenda for change'. Its purpose was to propose strategies for sustainable development by the year 2000, to promote co-operation between nations at different stages of economic development, and to consider ways by which the international community can deal with environmental concerns. Commission membership comes from 22 nations, and is chaired by Gro Harlem Brundtland. It published the Brundtland Report, *Our Common Future*, in 1987, and convened the Earth Summits in 1992 and 1997.

World Council of Churches An interdenominational council of Churches, formed in Amsterdam in 1948. Originating in the ecumenical movement of the early 20th-c, its main task is to seek the unity of the Church. It comprises most of the mainline Christian denominations with the exception of the Roman Catholic Church, with which, however, it keeps close contact. Its headquarters is in Geneva, and its ruling body, a representative Assembly, meets every six or seven years.

World Court *International Court of Justice*

World Cup (Association Football) The world's largest single-sport event, organized by the Fédération Internationale de Football Association. It evolved from the inter-war Olympic Games, with the competition formed in 1928. The first World Cup was held in Uruguay in 1930, when 16 teams entered. In 1998 and 2002, 32 nations competed. Brazil are the most successful side, having won the trophy – named after Jules Rimet (1873–1956), the Associations's former president (1921–56) – five times (1958, 1962, 1970, 1994, 2002).

World Cup (cricket) A world championship which has been played on roughly a four-yearly cycle since 1975, using a limited-over one-day format: initially 60 overs, 50 overs since 1987. It has expanded from 8 competitors to 9 in 1992 and to 12 in 1996. The West Indies won the first two cups, in England in 1975 and 1979. The winners since then have been India (in England) in 1983, Australia (in India and Pakistan) in 1987, Pakistan (in Australia and New Zealand) in 1992, Sri Lanka (in India and Pakistan) in 1996, Australia (in England) in 1999, and Australia (in South Africa) in 2003. Non-test nations qualify through the ICC Trophy. Sri Lanka, the 1996 winners, qualified this way in 1979 before attaining full Test status.

World Cup (Rugby League) A world championship played at irregular intervals under a variety of formats from 1954, limited in scope and impact by having no more than five teams before 1995. Great Britain beat France 16–12 in Paris in the first final, but Australia have been either champions or runners-up in every competition since, winning eight (the last five consecutively) but losing to Great Britain in 1960 and 1972. The 1995 World Cup expanded to 10 teams with the first-time participation of Western Samoa, Fiji, Tonga, and South Africa. Great Britain was split into England and Wales. In 1995 a competition for developing nations was won by the Cook Islands. The 2000 competition had 16 teams.

World Cup (Rugby Union) A world championship which has been played on a four-yearly cycle since 1987. The first 16-team competition was held on an invitation basis, and since then there have been regionally-based qualifiers, with exemptions for hosts and for the most successful competitors in the previous tournament. The tournament had expanded to 20 teams by 1999, with 69 entrants. Southern hemisphere teams have dominated, with the Cup won by New Zealand in 1987, Australia in 1991 and 1999, South Africa in 1995, but England in 2003. The winners receive the Webb Ellis Cup. The Women's World Cup has been played since 1991, with the US reaching all three finals. It won in 1991 but lost to England in 1994 and New Zealand in 1998.

World Federation of Trade Unions (WFTU) A leftist-oriented organization of world trade union federations, set up in 1945 by the World Trade Union Congress. The organization was initially oriented towards the Soviet Union, but with the intensification of the Cold War the democratic unions of Europe and North America broke away in 1949. They subsequently formed the International Confederation of Free Trade Unions. The largest WFTU affiliates are now in the developing nations of Asia, Latin America, and Africa, although France and Italy also have sizeable affiliates. The WFTU maintains its headquarters in Prague, Czech Republic.

World Health Organization (WHO) A specialized agency formed in 1948 within the United Nations to advance international co-operation for the improvement in health of peoples in all countries. Its headquarters are in Geneva. It is primarily concerned with the control of epidemic diseases, vaccination and other programmes, worldwide sanitation, and water supplies. A notable success has been its eradication of smallpox throughout the world. It also acts as a clearing house for information on such topics as drugs, nuclear hazards, and cancer research. There were 192 member countries in 2004.

world heritage site A site (natural or cultural) recognized by the international community (in the shape of the World Heritage Convention founded by the General Conference of UNESCO in 1972) as possessing universal value, and thus coming under a collective responsibility. A country nominates a site to the Convention, and a decision on whether to include it in the world heritage list is made by an international 21-member committee. By 2004 there were 754 sites in 129 states.

World Meteorological Organization *United Nations*

World Series America's annual baseball championship, first played in 1903 and held in October. Despite its title, only America's Major League baseball teams compete, with the winner of the American League meeting the winner of the National League over the best of seven games. The most successful side is the New York Yankees, with a record of 26 wins, the most recent in 2000.

World Small Animal Veterinary Association *veterinary science*

World's View 20°30S 28°30E. The grave of Cecil John Rhodes in Matabeleland South province, Zimbabwe, 40 km/25 mi SW of Bulawayo.

World Trade Center A complex of buildings occupying 6·5 ha/16 acres in lower Manhattan, New York City, USA. Its two 110-storey skyscrapers were the world's tallest buildings from their completion in 1973 until topped by the Sears Tower a year later. The New York landmark collapsed after two aircraft were flown deliberately at the 414 m/1360 ft towers in a terrorist attack on 11 September 2001, with a loss of life estimated (Oct 2003) to be 2752. In 2003 plans were announced for a replacement building, the Freedom Tower (architects David Childs and Daniel Libeskind), which would be the world's tallest building at 541 m/1776 ft.

World Trade Organization (WTO) A permanent body created in 1994 at the conclusion of the GATT Uruguay Round of talks to succeed GATT in monitoring international trade and resolve disputes. Equipped, unlike GATT, with strong enforcement mechanisms, it began work in 1995, with headquarters in Geneva. It meets every two years, and is overseen by a General Council. It had 146 members in 2004. A WTO summit was convened in Seattle in 1999, aimed at agreeing a new round of trade negotiations for expanding and accelerating the process of globalization and establishing tighter controls on trading policies and on the factors of production. The summit was disrupted by demonstrators concerned at the social, economic, and ecological impact of the free market system, notably on developing countries. It was reconvened in Prague in 2000.

World Veterinary Association *veterinary science*

World War 1 (1914–18) A war whose origins lay in the reaction of other great powers to the ambitions of the German Empire after 1871. The resulting political tensions divided Europe into two camps, the Triple Alliance and the Triple Entente. The assassination of the heir to the Habsburg throne, Franz Ferdinand, at Sarajevo in Bosnia (28 Jun 1914), triggered the war. Austria declared war on Serbia (28 Jul); Russia mobilized in support of Serbia (29–30 Jul); and Germany declared war on Russia (1 Aug), and on France (3 Aug). The German invasion of neutral Belgium (4 Aug) brought the British into the war on the French side. Japan joined Britain, France, and Russia under the terms of an agreement with Britain (1902, 1911), and Italy joined the Allies in May 1915. Turkey allied with Germany (Nov 1914), and they were joined by Bulgaria (Oct 1915).

Military campaigning centred on France and Belgium in W Europe, and on Poland and W Russia in E Europe. The British Expeditionary Force and French army prevented the Germans, at the first battle of Ypres, from reaching the Channel ports. By the end of 1914, a static defence line had been established from the Belgian coast to Switzerland. The Allies attempted to break the stalemate by a campaign in Gallipoli (Apr 1915–Jan 1916), but failed. On the E and SE fronts, the Central Powers occupied Poland and most of Lithuania, and Serbia was invaded. For three years, an Allied army was involved in a Macedonian campaign, and there was also fighting in Mesopotamia against Turkey. Naval competition had played a crucial role in heightening tension before 1914, but in the event, the great battle fleets of Germany and Britain did not play an important part in the war. The only significant naval encounter, at Jutland in 1916, proved indecisive.

The Allies organized a large offensive for the W front in 1916, but were forestalled by the Germans, who attacked France at Verdun (Feb–Jul). To relieve the situation, the Battle of the Somme was launched, but proved indecisive. The Germans then unleashed unrestricted submarine warfare (Jan 1917) to cripple Britain economically before the USA could come to her aid. The USA declared war (2 Apr 1917) when British food stocks were perilously low, and the German submarine menace was finally overcome by the use of convoys. Tanks were used effectively by the Allies at the Battle of Cambrai (1917). In the spring of 1918, the Germans launched a major attack in the W, but were driven back, with the USA providing an increasing number of much-needed troops. By September, the German army was in full retreat, and signified its intention to sue for peace on the basis of President Wilson's Fourteen Points. By November, when the armistice was signed, the Allies had recaptured E Belgium and nearly all French territory. Military victories in Palestine and Mesopotamia resulted in a Turkish armistice (31 Oct 1918).

Estimated combatant war losses were over 8 million: British Empire, just under 1 million; France, nearly 1·4 million; Italy, nearly ½ million; Russia, 1·7 million; USA, 115 000; Germany 1·8 million; Austria–Hungary 1·2 million, and Turkey 325 000. About double these numbers were wounded. What began as a European conflict became a world war involving 32 countries. The peace treaties that concluded the war were severe and often unenforceable, leading to the resurgence of aggressive nationalism in Germany. Despite hopes that it was 'the war to end all wars', World War 1 paved the way for the most devastating war in history.

World War 2 (1939–45) The most destructive war in history. Its origins lay in three different conflicts which merged after 1941: Germany's desire for European expansion; Japan's struggle against China; and a resulting conflict between Japanese ambitions and US interests in the Pacific. The origins of the war in Europe lay in German unwillingness to accept the frontiers laid down in 1919 by the Treaty of Versailles. After the German invasion of Czechoslovakia (Mar 1939), Britain and France pledged support to Poland. Germany concluded an alliance with Russia (Aug 1939), and then invaded Poland (1 Sep). Britain and France declared war on Germany (3 Sep), but could not prevent Poland from being overrun in four weeks. For six months there was a period of 'phoney war', when little fighting took place, but the Germans then occupied Norway and Denmark (Apr 1940), and Belgium and Holland were invaded (10 May). A combination of German tank warfare and air power brought about the surrender of Holland in four days, Belgium in three weeks, and France in seven weeks. There followed the Battle of Britain, in which Germany tried to win air supremacy over Britain, but failed. As a result, the planned invasion of Britain was postponed, and never subsequently took place. Germany launched submarine attacks against British supply routes, but then moved E and invaded Greece and Yugoslavia (Apr 1941). British military efforts were concentrated against Italy in the Mediterranean and N Africa. After early reverses for Italy, Rommel was sent to N Africa with the Afrika Corps to reinforce Italian military strength, and campaigning continued here for three years until Allied troops finally ejected German and Italian forces in mid-1943, invaded Sicily and then Italy itself, and forced Italy to make a separate peace (3 Sep 1943).

In June 1941, Germany invaded her ally Russia along a 2000 mi front, and German armies advanced in three formations: to the outskirts of Leningrad (now St Petersburg) in the N, towards Moscow in the centre, and to the Volga R in the S. After spectacular early successes, the Germans were held up by bitter Russian resistance, and by heavy winter snows and Arctic temperatures, for which they were completely unprepared. From November 1942 they were gradually driven back. Leningrad was under siege for nearly 2½ years (until Jan 1944), and about a third of its population died from starvation and disease. The Germans were finally driven out of Russia (Aug 1944). A second front was launched against Germany by the Allies (Jun 1944), through the invasion of Normandy, and Paris was liberated (25 Aug). Despite German use of flying bombs and rockets against London, the Allies advanced into Germany (Feb 1945) with the aid of American forces in ever-increasing numbers, and linked with the Russians on the R Elbe (28 Apr). The Germans surrendered unconditionally at Reims (7 May 1945).

In the Far East, Japan's desire for expansion led to her invasion of Manchuria (1931) and China proper (1937). Anglo–US warnings against Japanese policies provoked an attack on Pearl Harbor and other British and US bases (7 Dec 1941), galvanizing the USA to declare war against Japan the next day. In reply Japan's allies, Germany and Italy, declared war on the USA (11 Dec). Within four months, Japan controlled SE Asia and Burma. Not until June 1942 did naval victories in the Pacific stem the advance, and Japanese troops defended their positions grimly. Bitter fighting continued until 1945, when, with Japan on the retreat, defeated by the British in SE Asia and by the Americans in the Pacific, and having disregarded Allied demands for unconditional surrender, the USA dropped two atomic bombs on Hiroshima and Nagasaki (6 and 9 Aug). Japan then surrendered (14 Aug).

Casualty figures are not easy to obtain accurately, but approximately 3 million Russians were killed in action, 3 million died as prisoners-of-war, 8 million people died in occupied Russia, and about 3 million in unoccupied Russia. Germany suffered 3¾ million military casualties, around 6 million total casualties, and lost a million prisoners of war. Japan suffered just over 2 million military casualties and just over ¼ million civilian deaths. France lost a total of ½ million dead, and Britain and her Commonwealth just over 600 000. The USA suffered just over 300 000 casualties. It is also estimated that in the course of the German occupation of a large part of Europe, about 4 million Jews were murdered in extermination and labour camps, and an estimated 2 million more in mass murders in Eastern Europe. The long-term results of the war were the division of Germany (1945–90), the restoration to the Soviet Union of lands lost in the Versailles peace settlement (1919–21) together with the creation of communist buffer-states along the Soviet frontier with C and E Europe. Britain had accumulated a $20 billion debt, mostly to the USA through the Lend-Lease Act, while in the Far East nationalist resistance forces were to ensure the de-colonization of SE Asian countries. The USA and the Soviet Union emerged from the war as the two largest global powers, each embarking on a programme of rearmament with nuclear capability.

World Wide Fund for Nature (WWF) An international voluntary organization, founded in 1961 as the **World Wildlife Fund**, with its headquarters in Switzerland; international president, the Duke of Edinburgh. It aims to create awareness of the need for conservation of endangered wild animals, plants, and places, and promote the wise use of the world's natural resources. Examples include its campaigns to save the tiger, gorilla, and panda. It changed to its present name in 1988. In 2004 its global network was active in some 100 countries.

World Wide Web The full collection of all the computers linked to the Internet which hold documents that are mutually accessible through use of a standard protocol (the HyperText Transfer Protocol, HTTP); usually abbreviated to **Web** or **W3** and in site addresses presented as the acronym **www**. The creator of the Web, computer scientist Tim Berners-Lee, has defined it as 'the universe of network-accessible information, an embodiment of human knowledge'. It was devised in 1990 as a means of enabling high-energy physicists in different institutions to share information within their field, but it rapidly spread to other fields, and is now all-inclusive. A **Web site** is an individual computer holding documents capable of being transferred to and presented by browsers, using one of the standard formats (usually HTML or XML). Web sites are identified by a unique address, or **URL** (**Uniform Resource Locator**), with different 'pages' of data at the site distinguished by means of labels separated by forward slashes. Anything that can exist as a computer file can be made available as a Web document – text, graphics, sound, video, etc. A further necessary element of the Web is the search engine, a means of locating documents by content rather than by location. There is no theoretical limit to the size of the Web, and new sites are being added to it so rapidly that no reliable statistics are available; but growth in the late 1990s was c.40% a year. The **World Wide Web Consortium** (**W3C**) is an international industry organization, founded in 1994 to develop common protocols for the Web.

World Wildlife Fund *World Wide Fund for Nature*

worm The common name for a wide range of long-bodied, legless invertebrate animals.

wormhole A tunnel in space and time, connecting portions of the universe that are otherwise distant. Wormholes arise as solutions to the equations of Einstein's general relativity theory of gravity, but none have ever been shown to exist in nature, and they constitute a speculative area of current research. Large-scale wormholes may offer some prospect of time travel, and are beloved of science fiction writers; microscopic wormholes may be important in theories of elementary particles and quantum gravity.

worm lizard *amphisbaena*

Worms [vorms], Eng [wermz], Lat **Borbetomagus** 49°38N 8°23E, pop (2000e) 78 500. River port in Rheinhessen-Pfalz district, SWC Germany; on R Rhine, 16 km/10 mi NW of Mannheim; one of the oldest towns in Germany; capital of kingdom of Burgundy, 5th-c; scene of many Imperial Diets; badly bombed in World War 2; railway; sheeting and foils, chemicals; centre of the wine trade (notably for Liebfraumilch); cathedral (11th–12th-c).

Worms, Diet of Meetings of the estates of the German empire in 1521 and 1545, so named after the city on the R Rhine where they were held, which sealed the religious fate of 16th-c Germany. At the first, Luther was condemned, following papal declarations of heresy and excommunication (1520, 1521); at the second, an attempt to heal the religious divisions between Catholics and Lutherans failed amidst suspicion of papal intentions.

wormwood An aromatic perennial (*Artemisia absinthium*) growing to 90 cm/3 ft, native to Europe and Asia, and often introduced elsewhere; leaves deeply cut, silvery on both sides with a covering of silky hairs; flower-heads numerous, yellow, up to 3 mm/0·12 in across, drooping in a dense panicle. It is cultivated as a flavouring, and also used in the preparation of absinthe liqueur. (Family: Compositae.)

Worrall, Denis John (1935–) South African politician, born in Benoni, NE South Africa. He studied at Cape Town and Cornell universities, where he subsequently taught political science. He held a succession of academic posts and also worked as a journalist before being elected a National Party senator in 1974, and an MP in 1977. He was appointed ambassador to Australia (1982–4) and then to the UK, but on his return to South Africa in 1987 resigned from the National Party and unsuccessfully contested the general election of that year as an independent. In 1988 he established the Independent Party, and in 1989 merged with other white Opposition parties to form the reformist Democratic Party. A co-leader of this Party, he was elected to parliament in 1989.

Wörther See [voerter zay] Lake in SE Austria, W of Klagenfurt; area 18·8 sq km/7·2 sq mi; length 4 km/2½ mi width 1·5 km/0·9 mi; maximum depth 86 m/282 ft; popular for water sports; chief lakeside town, Velden; fashionable resort, Kärnten.

Worthing 50°48N 0°23W, pop (2001e) 97 500. Resort town in West Sussex, S England, UK; 17 km/10 mi W of Brighton; once a fishing village, it developed into a fashionable coastal resort after its discovery by Princess Amelia, daughter of George III; railway; electronics, engineering, plastics, furniture, horticulture; Cissbury Ring (2 km/1¼ mi N), 3rd-c fort and Neolithic flint mines.

Wotan *Odin*

wound A breach in the skin, which may also involve underlying tissues and deeper structures, usually caused by physical injury, but also by heat or chemicals. Damage to the body results from the direct effect of the injury, particularly if vital organs are involved, and also from infection of the wound with disease-causing micro-organisms.

Wounded Knee The site in South Dakota of the final defeat of Sioux Indians (29 Dec 1890). The 'battle' was in fact a massacre by US troops, suppressing ceremonies inspired by the Paiute Indian religious leader Wovoka.

woundwort An annual or perennial, found almost everywhere; square stems erect; leaves in opposite pairs; flowers 2-lipped, usually white to pink or purple with darker spots, in whorls. It had an old herbal use in salves for treating cuts; the hairy-leaved species was also used as lint. Some species produce edible tubers. (Genus: *Stachys*, 300 species. Family: Labiatae.)

Wouwerman, Philips [vowverman], also found as **Wouwermans** (c.1619–68) Painter of battle and hunting scenes, born in Haarlem, The Netherlands. His pictures are mostly small landscapes, with several figures in energetic action. His cavalry skirmishes, with a white horse generally in the foreground, were especially characteristic and popular. He had two brothers, also painters, **Peter Wouwerman** (1623–82) and **Jan Wouwerman** (1629–66), who chose similar subjects.

Wovoka (1856–1937) American Indian religious leader. He was the founder of the Ghost Dance Movement.

WPA *Works Projects Administration*

W particle A particle that carries weak nuclear force; symbol W; mass 80·4 GeV; charge +1 (W^+) or −1 (W^-); spin 1; decays to an electron or muon or tau plus corresponding neutrino. Predicted by the Glashow–Weinberg–Salam theory, it was discovered in 1983 in proton–antiproton collisions at CERN, Geneva.

WRAC *women's services*

wrack Fucus

Wrangel, Ferdinand Petrovich, Baron von [vranggl] (1794–1870) Explorer, born in Pskov, NW Russia. He travelled in Arctic waters and on Siberian coasts, and made valuable surveys and observations. The reported island in the Arctic Ocean he nearly reached in 1821 was sighted in 1849, and named after him in 1867. He was Governor of Russian lands in Alaska (1829–35) and naval minister (1855–7).

Wrangel, Pyotr Nikolayevich, Baron [vranggl] (1878–1928) Russian army officer and commander of White Russian forces during the Civil War, born in Aleksandrovsk, Lithuania. Educated at the St Petersburg Mining Institute, he entered military service in 1904 and commanded a cavalry corps during World War 1. In the Civil War, he commanded cavalry divisions and the Volunteer Army in the Ukraine, and in 1920 became commander-in-chief of the White Armies in the South. After the Red Army victory, he fled to Turkey with the remnants of his troops.

Wrangel Island [vrangl], Russ **Ostrov Vrangelya** area 5180 sq km/2000 sq mi. Tundra-covered island in the W Chukchi Sea, Russia, near the NE extremity of Asia; length, 120 km/75 mi; width, 72 km/45 mi; rises to 1097 m/3599 ft; named after F P Wrangel (Vrangel), a 19th-c Russian navigator; ceded to Russia, 1924; government Arctic station and trading post; small settlements of Chukchi and Eskimo.

wrasse [ras] Any of a large group of mostly small colourful fishes widespread in tropical to temperate seas; length typically 10–30 cm/4–12 in; includes the European **ballan wrasse** (*Labrus bergylta*) and **cuckoo wrasse** (*Labrus mixtus*), found mainly around rocky coasts feeding on crustaceans and molluscs. (Family: Labridae, 15 genera.)

wreckfish Large, heavy-bodied fish (*Polyprion americanus*) found mainly in the tropical Atlantic; length up to 2 m/6½ ft; also called **stonebass**. (Family: Serranidae.)

Wren, Sir Christopher (1632–1723) Architect, born in East Knoyle, Wiltshire, S England, UK. He studied at Oxford, became professor of astronomy at Gresham College, London (1657), and at Oxford (1661), and was one of the founders of the Royal Society. After the Great Fire of London (1666), he drew designs for rebuilding the whole city, but his scheme was never implemented. In 1669 he designed the new St Paul's (building begun 1675) and many other churches and public buildings in London, such as the Royal Exchange and Greenwich Observatory. Knighted in 1673, he held posts at Windsor Castle and Westminster Abbey, and became an MP (1685). He is buried in St Paul's.

Wren, P(ercival) C(hristopher) (1875–1941) Writer, born in Deptford, Devon, SW England, UK. He joined the Indian Educational Service in 1903, becoming principal of the Elphinstone High School, Mumbai (Bombay), in 1915. He published textbooks and a guide to the theory and practice of education, and over 30 novels, notably *Beau Geste* (1924) and *Beau Sabreur* (1926). Many of his novels are based on adventures of the French Foreign Legion, which he did not discourage readers from erroneously believing he had joined.

wren A small songbird of the New World family Troglodytidae (**wrens**, c.65 species, one extending to the N Old World); name also used for family Maluridae **Australian wrens/wren-warblers**, 26 species, including the **fairy** or **blue wrens**, **grasswrens**, and **emu-wrens**); family Xenicidae, sometimes called family Acanthisittidae (**New Zealand wrens**, 3 species); and for many small birds of other families.

wren babbler A small babbler, found from India to SE Asia; inhabits woodland; eats mainly insects, some snails, possibly seeds. (Tribe: Pomatorhinini, 22 species.)

wren-warbler *emu wren; warbler*

wrestling The sport of one man fighting against another, but without the use of fists. In most cases the object is to fell your opponent to the ground. Wrestling was contested at the Ancient Olympic Games. Many forms exist, the most popular amateur forms being **freestyle** and **Graeco-Roman**. In the latter, holds below the waist and the use of the legs are prohibited. Other forms include **Sambo**, which originated in Russia; **Sumo**, the national sport of Japan; British variations **Cumberland and Westmoreland** and **Devon and Cornwall**; **Kushti**, the national style of wrestling in Iran; **Glima**, practised in Iceland; **Schwingen**, practised in Switzerland; and **Yagli**, the national sport of Turkey. Women's wrestling has also developed in recent years: women do not compete at championship level, but do take part in professional bouts.

Wrexham [reksm], Welsh **Wrecsam** pop (2001e) 128 500; area 499 sq km/193 sq mi. County (unitary authority from 1996) in NE Wales, UK; administrative centre, Wrexham; coal, electronics, bricks, pharmaceuticals, food processing, metal goods, market; Wrexham cathedral, Church of St Giles (15th-c); football league team, Wrexham (Robins).

Wright, Frank Lloyd (1867–1959) Architect, born in Richland Center, Wisconsin, USA. He studied civil engineering at Wisconsin, and was early associated with architect Louis Sullivan. The collapse of a newly built wing led him to apply engineering principles to architecture. After setting up in practice in Chicago, he became known for low-built prairie-style residences, but soon launched into more controversial designs. An innovator in the field of open planning, he is regarded as the leading designer of modern private dwellings, planned in conformity with the natural features of the land. Among his larger works are the Imperial Hotel in Tokyo and the Guggenheim Museum of Art in New York City.

Wright, Judith (Arundell) (1915–2000) Poet, born near Armidale, New South Wales, SE Australia. She studied at Sydney, and worked in educational administration in Queensland. She was a militant environmentalist and a strong advocate of Aboriginal land rights. She is valued for the broad sympathies of *The Moving Image* (1946), in which she was one of the first white writers to recognize Aboriginal claims, and the personal lyrics of *Woman to Man* (1950). Her collections include *Collected Poems* (1971), *Four Quarters and Other Poems* (1976), *The Human Pattern* (1990), and *Collected Poems: 1942–1985* (1994). The first volume of her autobiography, *Half a Lifetime*, was published in 1999. In 1992 she became the first Australian to be awarded the Queen's Medal for Poetry.

Wright, Peter (1916–95) British intelligence officer, born in Chesterfield, Derbyshire, C England, UK. He joined the Admiralty's Research Laboratory during World War 2 as a scientific officer, and transferred to MI5 (counter-intelligence) (1955–76). Here he specialized in the invention of espionage devices and the detection of Soviet 'moles'. He bought a sheep ranch in Tasmania when he retired, and wrote his autobiography, *Spycatcher* (1987), in which he alleged that Sir Roger Hollis, the former director-general of MI5, had been a Soviet double-agent, the so-called 'Fifth Man', and that elements within MI5 had tried to overthrow the Wilson government during the mid-1960s. Attempts by the Thatcher government to suppress the book's publication and distribution for 'security reasons' were eventually unsuccessful.

Wright, Richard (Nathaniel) (1908–60) Novelist, short-story writer, and critic, born on a plantation near Natchez, Mississippi, USA. His grandparents had been slaves, his father left home when he was five, and he was brought up in poverty by various relatives. Among the first African-Americans to write about their ill-treatment by whites, his works include the short story 'The Man Who Lived Underground' (1942), and *Native Son* (1940), a best-selling novel about a black youth who accidentally kills a white girl. The latter was staged on Broadway by Orson Welles (1941), and Wright starred in a film version (1951). He is best known for his autobiographical novel, *Black Boy* (1945).

Wright, Sewall (1889–1988) Geneticist, born in Melrose, Massachusetts, USA. He studied at Harvard, worked at the US Department of Agriculture (1915–25), where he conducted experimental work in animal genetics, then became professor at the universities of Chicago (1926–54) and Wisconsin (1955–60). He is one of the founders of population genetics, and is best remembered for his concept of genetic drift, termed the **Sewall Wright effect**, which was strongly criticized at the time but is now widely accepted.

Wright brothers Aviation pioneers: **Orville Wright** (1871–1948), born in Dayton, Ohio, and **Wilbur Wright** (1867–1912), born near Millville, Indiana, USA. They were the first to fly in a powered heavier-than-air machine (17 Dec 1903), at Kitty Hawk, NC. Encouraged by this, they abandoned their cycle business and formed an aircraft production company (1909), of which Wilbur was president until his death. In 1915 Orville sold his interests in the company to devote himself to aeronautical research.

wrist The region of the upper limb between the forearm and the hand. The forearm component consists of the lower ends of the radius and ulna, articulating with one and other and with four carpel bones of the hand component. Two rows of carpel bones make an arch forming part of a tunnel (the *carpal tunnel*), which transmits nearly all the structures entering the hand (eg the long flexor tendons to the digits and the median nerve). Inflammation within the tunnel may cause compression of the median nerve (*carpal tunnel syndrome*) resulting in weakness of some of the thumb muscles, and loss of some sensation over the fingers. Similar symptoms may occur during the latter stages of pregnancy, when water retention by the body may cause enlargement of the sheaths associated with the tendons and thus compression of the median nerve. The symptoms subside when the inflammation or swelling goes.

writing systems *alphabet; cuneiform; epigraphy; graphology* **2**; *hieroglyphics; ideography; logography; pictography; syllabary*

WRNS *women's services*

Wrocław [vrotswaf], Ger **Breslau** 51°05N 17°01E, pop (2000e) 651 000. River-port capital of Wrocław voivodship, W Poland, on R Oder; capital of lower Silesia; founded, 10th-c; first Polish publications printed here, 1745; badly damaged in World War 2; airport; railway junction; technical university (1945); shipyards, metallurgy, railway carriages, electronics, chemicals, clothes; pantomime theatre established by Henryk Tomaszewski; cathedral (13th-c), Church of St Mary Magdalene (13th–14th-c), national museum; international student theatre festivals, oratorio and cantata festival, festival of jazz.

wrought iron A form of iron, of very low carbon content, once much used by blacksmiths, but now mostly replaced by steel. Pig-iron is melted with some addition of iron oxide to reduce the carbon content. As the iron becomes purer, the melting point rises and the iron becomes less fluid. It is worked around, and lumps are taken out of the furnace and hammered to remove slag, some of which remains as fibrous inclusions. Wrought iron is less brittle than cast iron. Famous wrought iron structures were the SS *Great Britain* (1856) and the Eiffel Tower (1889). It is not much used now, except for decorative purposes.

WRVS *Women's Royal Voluntary Service*

wrybill A small plover, native to New Zealand (*Anarhynchus frontalis*); bill straight when seen from side, but tip bends to right; inhabits river beds and sand flats; feeds by pointing head to right and sifting insects from surface of mud with bill.

wryneck A short-billed, uncharacteristic woodpecker, native to Europe, Asia, and Africa; mottled brown; inhabits woodland and savannah; often feeds on ground; eats mainly ants; nests in holes of other woodpeckers. (Genus: *Jynx*, 2 species. Subfamily: Jynginae.)

Wu, Empress, in full **Wu Zhao** (?625–?706) Empress of China, the only woman ever to rule China in her own name. A concubine of Emperor Taizong, she married his son, **Emperor Gaozong**, whom she dominated after his stroke (660). After his death (683) she first ruled through her own sons, then following a reign of bloody terror she seized the title *emperor* in 690 with the dynastic name Zhou (Chou). To establish legitimacy, she claimed to be Maitreya, a supposed Buddhist 'messiah', ordered public prophecy of a female monarch 700 years after Buddha, and rewrote genealogies. Highly capable, she expanded the bureaucracy and examination system, set up a personal secretariat, and dominated both Korea and Tibet. She was forced to abdicate in 705, and her family were assassinated in 710.

Wu, Chien-Shiung (1912–97) Physicist, born in Shanghai, E China. She studied at the National Centre University in China, and moved to the USA in 1936, working at the University of California, Berkeley. From 1944 she was on the staff of Columbia University, New York City. Her research was in particle physics, notably her confirmation that some physical processes (such as beta-particle emission) are not identical in a mirror-image system.

Wu Chengen [woo chengen], also spelled **Wu Ch'eng-en** (1505–82) Writer, from a merchant family, born in Huai-an, Kiangsu Province, E China. He fused popular oral traditions into *Journey to the West*, one of four great Ming period novels. Based around Xuanzang's 7th-c trip to India, it focuses on a supernatural disciple, Monkey, converted from Taoism and sent by Buddha to protect Xuanzang from demons by using a magic pin in his ear as an iron cudgel. The work lampoons traditional officialdom, and during the Cultural Revolution (1966–76) it inspired Red Guards, who identified with the intelligent, personable Monkey (his cudgel represented Mao's thoughts). Serialized on Chinese television in recent years, an English translation is entitled *Monkey*.

Wudi [woo dee], also spelled **Wu-ti** (141–86 BC) Han dynasty emperor of China (his name means 'martial emperor'). He respected Confucian scholarship, and began selecting administrators by oral examination (setting questions himself). Appointing himself head of the bureaucracy, he established (124 BC) a Confucian university for scholar-administrators. He sequestered noble lands, extended crown possessions, annexed S China, conquered Korea, Tonkin, and the SW with large armies, and invaded the Hun territories. He sent a major expedition (138–125 BC) to Bactria to ensure W trade routes, and a second expedition (101 BC, 30 000 troops) conquered Ferghana (2200 mi from Wudi's capital). These expeditions ensured Chinese control over the Tarim (later Xinjiang), and set a precedent for later spectacular Han triumphs.

Wuhan or **Wu-han** [woohan], **Han-kow**, or **Han-kou** 30°35N 114°19E, pop (2000e) 4 504 000, administrative region 7 178 000. Inland port and capital of Hubei province, EC China; at confluence of Han Shui and Yangtze Rivers; union (1950) of three municipalities of Wuchang, Hankou, Hanyang; area economically important since 4th-c; capital of later Liang dynasty, 6th-c; Hanko a major port in Ming period, 14th–17th-c; captured by Taiping rebels, 1852; capital of Guomindang government, 1925–8; seized by Japanese, 1938; now the commercial centre of C China; airfield; railway; Wuhan university (1913); Central China Engineering Institute; iron, steel, fertilizer, limestone, machine tools, cotton, fisheries; Guiyuan Buddhist Temple (c.1600), now a museum; Changjiang Bridge (first modern bridge to cross the Yangtze R, 1957); Red Hill Park in Wuchang, with Yuan dynasty pagoda (1307–15).

Wulfila *Ulfilas*

Wulumuqi *Ürümqi*

Wundt, Wilhelm (Max) [vunt] (1832–1920) Physiologist and psychologist, born in Neckarau, Mannheim, SW Germany. He taught at Heidelberg and Zürich universities, then became professor of physiology at Leipzig (1875). A distinguished experimental psychologist, he wrote on the nerves and the senses, and the relations between physiology and psychology.

Wuornos, Aileen [waw(r)nos] (1956–2002) US convicted murderer, the daughter of a child molester who hanged himself in prison. Dubbed the world's first female serial killer, she was convicted in the USA in 1992 of the murder of seven men between 1989 and 1991, and sentenced to die in the electric chair. She was executed in October 2002.

Wu Peifu [woo payfoo], also spelled **Wu P'ei-fu** (1874–1939) Major figure in the warlord struggles of China (1916–27), born in Shandong province, E China. He joined the new army created by Yuan Shikai, and after Yuan's death (1916), when Duan Qirui sought to reunite China by force, Wu and other N generals refused Duan's orders. In the civil war which followed, he was unable to sustain his government of national unity (1923), and was defeated in battle near Tientsin.

Wuppertal [vupertahl] 51°15N 7°10E, pop (2000e) 392 000. Industrial city in Düsseldorf district, W Germany; on R Wupper in the Ruhr valley, 26 km/16 mi NE of Düsseldorf; includes the former towns of Barmen, Elberfeld, and Vohwinkel; university (1972); textiles, brewing, plastics, electronics, packaging, lime, metalworking.

Würzburg [vürtsboork] 49°48N 9°57E, pop (2000e) 135 000. Industrial city in Unterfranken district, SC Germany; on R Main, 96 km/60 mi SE of Frankfurt am Main; railway; university (1582); engineering, chemicals, machine tools; centre of wine production and trade in Franconia; cathedral (11th–13th-c), St Mary's chapel (1377–1479), Old Main bridge (1473–1543), Marienberg (fortress, 13th-c); Würzburg Residence (episcopal palace built by Balthasar Neumann, 1719–44), a world heritage site.

Wüthrich, Kurt [vütrikh] (1938–) Chemist, born in Aarberg, W Switzerland. He studied at the University of Basel, later becoming affiliated to the Swiss Federal Institute of Technology in Zürich and The Scripps Research Institute in La Jolla, CA. He shared the 2002 Nobel Prize for Chemistry for his development of nuclear magnetic resonance spectroscopy for determining the three-dimensional structure of biological macromolecules in solution.

Wu Yue or **Wu Yüeh** [woo yüay], Eng **the Five Holy Mountains** Collective name for five mountains in China, regarded in Chinese legend as the gathering places of the gods; Tai Shan in Shandong province (1545 m/5069 ft), Hua Shan in Shaanxi province (2154 m/7067 ft), Song Shan in Henan province (1512 m/4961 ft), Heng Shan in Hunan province (1290 m/4232 ft), and Heng Shan in Shanxi province (2016 m/6614 ft).

www *World Wide Web*

Wyatt, James (1746–1813) Architect, born in Burton Constable, Staffordshire, C England, UK. He visited Italy for several years, and achieved fame with his Neoclassical design for the London Pantheon (1772). He became surveyor to the Board of Works (1796), restored several cathedrals, and designed many country houses. His best-known work is the Gothic revival Fonthill Abbey (1796–1807), which largely collapsed in the 1820s.

Wyatt, Sir Thomas, known as **the Elder** (1503–42) Poet and courtier, born in Allington, Kent, SE England, UK. He studied at Cambridge, was warmly received at court, knighted (1536), made high sheriff of Kent (1537), and went on several diplomatic missions. He was a student of foreign languages, translated the poems of Petrarch from the Italian, and with Surrey introduced the sonnet form into English literature. In 1557 his poems, published by Richard Tottel in *Tottel's Miscellany*, helped to establish the rondeau, lyrics with irregular speech rhythms and satires in heroic couplets, into English literature. His portrait hangs in the National Portrait Gallery, London.

Wycherley, William [wicherlee] (c.1640–1716) Playwright, born in Clive, Shropshire, WC England, UK. He studied in France and at Oxford, became a lawyer, then lived as a courtier and turned to writing. He wrote several satirical comedies, notably *The Country Wife* (1675) and *The Plain Dealer* (1677), both based on plays by Molière. He was imprisoned for debt, but was finally given a pension by James II.

Wycliffe or **Wicliffe, John** [wiklif], also spelled **Wyclif, Wycliff** (c.1330–84) Religious reformer, born near Richmond, Yorkshire, N England, UK. He studied at Oxford, where he taught philosophy, then entered the Church, becoming Rector of Lutterworth, Leicestershire, in 1374. He was sent to Bruges to treat with ambassadors from the Pope about ecclesiastical abuses, but his views were found unacceptable, and he was prosecuted. He then attacked the Church hierarchy, priestly power, and the doctrine of transubstantiation, wrote many popular tracts in English (as opposed to Latin), and issued the first English translation of the Bible (1380). His opinions were condemned, and he was forced to retire to Lutterworth, where he wrote prolifically until his death. The characteristic of his teaching was its insistence on inward religion in opposition to the formalism of the time. His followers were known as *Lollards*, and the influence of his teaching was widespread in England, in many respects anticipating the Reformation.

Wye, River **1** River rising on Plynlimon, C Wales; flows 208 km/129 mi SE and E through Powys, Hereford, and along the Monmouthshire–Gloucestershire border to meet the R Severn estuary S of Chepstow; notable for its valley scenery; fishing.
2 River rising in Buckinghamshire, SC England; flows 15 km/9 mi SE to meet the R Thames at Bourne End.
3 River rising near Buxton in Derbyshire, C England; flows 32 km/20 mi SE to join the R Derwent at Rowsley.

Wyeth, Andrew (Newell) (1917–) Painter, born in Chadds Ford, Pennsylvania, USA. He studied under his father, a book illustrator. His soberly realistic pictures, usually executed with tempera and watercolour rather than oils, typically represent poor people or rustics in landscapes from the traditional 'American scene', using off-centre compositions to give a sense of haunting unease, as in 'Christina's World' (1948, Museum of Modern Art, New York City).

Wyler, William [wiyler] (1902–81) Film director, born in Mulhouse, NE France (formerly Germany). Invited to America by his mother's cousin Carl Laemmle (1867–1939), the head of Universal Pictures, he worked there on many aspects of film-making before becoming a director of Western shorts and low budget productions. Renowned for his obsessively meticulous approach to composition, performance, and narrative structure, his many successes include *These Three* (1936), *Wuthering Heights* (1939), *The Collector* (1965), and *Funny Girl* (1968). He received Oscars for *Mrs Miniver* (1942), *The Best Years of Our Lives* (1946), and *Ben Hur* (1959). He retired in 1972, and received an American Film Institute Life Achievement Award in 1976.

Wyndham, John [windam], pseudonym of **John Wyndham Parkes Lucas Beynon Harris** (1903–69) Science-fiction writer, born in Knowle, West Midlands, C England, UK. He worked at a variety of jobs, then in the late 1920s began to write science-fiction tales for popular magazines, achieving fame with his first novel, *The Day of the Triffids* (1951). His other books include *The Kraken Wakes* (1953), *The Chrysalids* (1955), and *The Midwich Cuckoos* (1957), as well as collections of short stories, such as *The Seeds of Time* (1969).

Wynkyn de Worde *Worde, Wynkyn de*

Wyoming [wiyohming] pop (2000e) 493 800; area 253 315 sq km/ 97 809 sq mi. State in W USA, divided into 23 counties; the 'Equality State'; most of the region acquired by the USA from France in the Louisiana Purchase, 1803; Spain, Britain, and the Republic of Texas all laid claims to other parts; total American jurisdiction, 1848; Wyoming Territory established, 1868; major growth after the arrival of the railway, 1868; first territory or state to adopt women's suffrage, 1869; admitted to the Union as the 44th state, 1890; conflicts between cattle and sheep ranchers in the 1890s; contains the Wind River Indian reservation; capital, Cheyenne; other chief city, Casper; a sparsely populated state; rivers include the Snake, Yellowstone, Green, N Platte; Wind River Range in the W, Absaroka Range, Teton Mts, Bighorn Mts in the N; all form part of the Rocky Mts (largely forested); highest point Gannett Peak (4201 m/13 782 ft); eroded 'badlands' in the extreme NE; higher tablelands in the SE; in the SW, South Pass the natural gateway through the Rocky Mts; ranching and farming on the fertile Great Plains (E); cattle, sheep, sugar-beets, dairy produce, wool, hay, barley; an important mining state; oil, natural gas, sodium salts, uranium, coal, gold, silver, iron, copper; very little manufacturing (petroleum products, timber, food processing); major tourist area (hunting, fishing, rodeos); two national parks at Grand Teton and Yellowstone.

WYSIWYG [wizeewig] Acronym for **what you see is what you get**, used to refer to those computer systems, usually word processors or desk-top publishing systems, where the display on the screen exactly mimics the final result produced by the printer. In practice this result is virtually impossible to achieve.

Wyss, Johann Rudolf [vees] (1781–1830) Writer, born in Bern, Switzerland. He is best known for his completion and editing of *Der Schweizerische Robinson* (1812–13, trans The Swiss Family Robinson), written by his father, **Johann David Wyss** (1743–1818). He collected Swiss tales and folklore, and was professor of philosophy at Bern from 1806.

Wyszyński, Stefan, Cardinal [vishinskee] (1901–81) Roman Catholic clergyman, born in Zuzela, EC Poland. He studied at Włocławek and Lublin, was ordained in 1924, and became Bishop of Lublin (1946), Archbishop of Warsaw and Gniezno (1948), and a cardinal (1952). Following his indictment of the Communist campaign against the Church, he was imprisoned (1953). Freed in 1956, he agreed to a reconciliation between Church and state under the Gomułka regime, but relations remained uneasy.

wytch elm *elm*

Xanthophyceae [zanthuhfiysee-ee] *yellow-green algae*

Xavier, Francis, St *Francis Xavier, St*

Xenakis, Iannis [zenahkees] (1922–2001) Composer, born in Braila, E Romania. He studied engineering at Athens University, and worked as an architect for Le Corbusier in Paris. He did not turn to musical composition until 1954, when he wrote the orchestral piece *Metastasis*, and went on to develop a highly complex style which incorporated mathematical concepts of chance and probability (so-called *stochastic music*), as well as electronic techniques. His works are mainly instrumental and orchestral.

Xenocrates [zenokratees] (c.395–314 BC) Greek philosopher and scientist, born in Chalcedon on the Bosphorus. He was a pupil of Plato, and in 339 BC succeeded Speusippus as head of the Academy which Plato had founded. He wrote prolifically on natural science, astronomy, and philosophy, but only fragments of this output survive. He generally systematized and continued the Platonic tradition, but seems to have had a particular devotion to threefold categories, perhaps reflecting a Pythagorean influence: philosophy is subdivided into logic, ethics, and physics; reality is divided into the objects of sensation, belief, and knowledge; he distinguished gods, men, and demons; and he also probably originated the classical distinction between mind, body, and soul.

xenoglossia [zenoglosia] *glossolalia*

xenon [zenon] Xe, element 54, boiling point −107°C. The fifth of the noble gases recovered from the atmosphere, of which it makes up only 0·000009%. Like the other noble gases, it is used in gas discharge tubes. It forms the most extensive range of compounds of any noble gas, showing oxidation states of +2, +4, +6, and +8. Its fluorides, especially XeF_2, are used as fluoridating agents.

Xenophanes [zenofaneez] (c.570–c.480 BC) Greek philosopher, poet, and religious thinker, born in Colophon, Ionia (Asia Minor). He travelled extensively around the Mediterranean, perhaps spending considerable time in Sicily. He attacked traditional Greek conceptions of the gods, arguing against anthropomorphism and polytheism. He also made some bold geological speculations based on the observation of fossils.

Xenophon [zenofon] (c.435–354 BC) Greek historian, essayist, and soldier, born in Attica. A friend and pupil of Socrates, in 401 BC he served with a group of 10 000 Greek mercenaries under Persian Prince Cyrus, who was fighting against his brother, the King of Persia. After Cyrus was killed, the Greeks were isolated over 1500 km/900 mi from home. Xenophon was elected leader, and the group successfully fought their way back to the Black Sea. This heroic feat formed the basis of his major work, *Anabasis Kyrou* (The Expedition of Cyrus).

xenopus [zenopus] *clawed toad*

xerographic printer In computing, a printer which uses electrostatic techniques to provide text and/or graphics. Most photocopiers are of this type. Laser printers generally use this basic technology, which has the advantage of being silent, and capable of very high quality reproduction.

xerography [zerografee] The most widely used method of photocopying, first devised in the late 1930s by US physicist Chester F Carlson, but not developed commercially until the 1950s. A photoconductive surface is charged and exposed to the image to be copied; the charge is lost in the image areas. The secondary image so produced is developed with a charged pigment which is transferred to copy paper and fixed by heat. Using this technique, it is possible to print on both sides of the paper, vary the size of the original image, and (since the 1970s) reproduce coloured images. The name derives from the Greek words meaning 'dry writing'.

Xerxes I [zerkseez] (c.519–465 BC) Achaemenid king of Persia (486–465 BC), the son of Darius I. He is remembered in the West mainly for the failure of his forces against the Greeks in the Second Persian War at Salamis, Plataea, and Mycale.

X400 One of a series of standards, denoted by X codes, recommended by the CCITT (Comité Consultatif International de Téléphonie et de Télégraphie), covering the attachment of various terminals to public data networks. X400 is a message-handling system standard. It should enable dissimilar equipment, such as telex, word-processors and computers, to handle electronic mail.

Xhosa [khohsa] A cluster of Bantu-speaking peoples of the Transkei and Ciskei, South Africa, including the Ngqika, Gcaleka, and others who fled from Zulu armies in the early 1800s. They are mixed farmers, although many work today as migrant labourers, and are settled permanently in urban centres. Xhosa is the most widely spoken African language in South Africa.

Xia or **Hsia dynasty** [shyah] Legendary line of 17 Chinese kings from 2205–1523 BC, contemporaneous with the Egyptian Middle Kingdom. Xia historically is doubtful, though the name, always meaning 'state', appears frequently on Shang period (16th–11th-c BC) oracle bones. By tradition it is based near the Yellow River: connections with the Lungshan or later Yangshao cultures are possible. The earliest Chinese bronze dates from that period.

Xiamen, Hsia-men, or **Amoy** [shyahmuhn] 24°26N 118°07E, pop (2000e) 738 400, administrative region 1 310 000. Subtropical port city in Fujian province, SE China; on island in Taiwan Strait at mouth of Jiulong R; connected to mainland by 5 km/3 mi-long causeway (1949); founded during S Song dynasty, 1127–1279; Portuguese settlement, 1544; occupied by British, 1841, and made an open port, 1842; designated a special economic zone, 1981; new harbour; railway; airfield; university (1921); electronics, food products, textiles, building materials; centre of growing unofficial trade between China and Taiwan; 5 km/3 mi E, 10th-c Nanputuo Temple; Overseas Chinese Museum.

Xian [shyahn], also spelled **Xi'an** or **Sian** 34°16N 108°54E, pop (2000e) 3 202 000, administrative region 6 889 000. Capital of Shaanxi province, C China; location of China's oldest human remains; site of Neolithic culture; Changan area capital of China under early Zhou, Qin, early Han, Sui, and Tang dynasties; many pagodas from Tang dynasty; population had reached 2 million by early 10th-c (world's largest city to that date); railway; airport; university (1937); tourism, heavy industry, cotton, food processing, chemicals, electrical equipment, fertilizers; Ming Dynasty Drum Tower, 14th-c Bell Tower, Banpo Neolithic village (10 km/6 mi E); Mausoleum of Emperor Qin Shihuangdi (30 km/18 mi E), with terracotta warriors of

Emperor Qin, discovered 1974; Big Wild Goose pagoda (652); Great Mosque (742); Hua Qing hot springs, scene of the Xian incident (1936); Zhaoling, tomb of Tang Emperor Taizong.

Xian incident [shyahn], also spelled **Xi'an** or **Sian** (Dec 1936) An incident in which Jiang Jieshi (Chiang Kai-shek) was held hostage in Xian by one of his own commanders, the 'young marshal' Zhang Xueliang (1901–2001), who demanded an anti-Japanese united front. He was released only on the intervention of Zhou Enlai. A temporary united front of Communist and Nationalist forces resulted.

Xiaotun [shyowdun] or **Hsiao-t'un** Village near Anyang, N China. Excavations since 1927 have revealed the capital of the last 11 kings of the Shang dynasty (16th–11th-c BC), including the remains of royal, religious, and civic buildings, 11 royal tombs (with beheaded retainers), and a large number of artefacts, especially bronzes. The site was located after the 19th-c accidental discovery of oracle bones in a field.

Ximénes (de Cisneros) Francisco Jiménez, Cardinal [heemenes] (1436–1517) Clergyman and statesman, born in Torrelaguna, C Spain. He was educated at Alcalá, Salamanca, and Rome, where he obtained from the pope a nomination to the archpriestship of Uzeda (1473). The archbishop refused to admit him, and for six years imprisoned him. Released in 1479, he was named vicar-general of Cardinal Mendoza, but gave this up to enter a Franciscan monastery at Toledo (1482). Queen Isabella chose him for her confessor in 1492, and in 1495 made him Archbishop of Toledo. He was created a cardinal in 1507. On the death of Ferdinand (1516) he was appointed regent during the minority of the later Charles V. A munificent patron of religion and learning, he founded the University of Alcalá de Henares.

Xingu [sheenggoo] National park in NE Mato Grosso state, WC Brazil; crossed by branches of the Xingu R (length c.1980 km/1230 mi), a S tributary of the Amazon; created in 1961 by the Villas-Boas brothers to protect the Indian tribes, but in recent years it has suffered from property developers, and new roads now threaten the continued existence of the tribes living there.

Xinhua [shinwah] The national news agency of the People's Republic of China, with headquarters in Beijing. Founded as the communist Red China News Agency in 1931, and renamed *Hsin Hua* in 1937 (*Xinhua* since 1979), it is sometimes known nowadays as the New China News Agency.

Xining [sheening], **Hsi-ning**, or **Sining** 36°35N 101°55E, pop (2000e) 777 900, administrative region 1 212 000. Capital of Qinghai province, WC China; NW of Lanzhou; railway; airfield; chemicals, metal, leather.

Xizang *Tibet*

XML *document description language*

X-ray astronomy A general term for the study of the X-rays from cosmic sources. It needs satellite-borne instruments, because X-rays do not penetrate our atmosphere. Sources studied include Supernova remnants such as the Crab Nebula, binary stars in which transfer of mass is taking place, and active galactic nuclei.

X-ray diffraction An interference effect in which atoms in a material scatter X-rays to give a pattern of spots or concentric rings. These may be recorded, and their position and intensity used to determine the material's structure. The technique was discovered in 1912 by German physicist Max von Laue (1879–1960).

X-ray laser A source of X-rays produced by laser action; the resulting X-rays will be monochromatic (single wavelength) and coherent (in step). The first X-ray lasers compromised cylindrical arrays of wires mounted around a nuclear explosive, the explosion powering the device, or relied on massive pulses of laser light vaporizing materials such as selenium or zinc to create X-ray emitting plasmas. Bench sized X-ray lasers, first demonstrated by Jorge Rocca and colleagues in 1994, are a development of the second system, but use multiple, short, low-energy pulses of optical laser light, or electrical discharges, to energize the X-ray laser plasma. X-ray lasers, producing X-rays having wavelengths of a few tens of nanometres, can be used for X-ray microscopy, as probes for systems such as plasmas that are opaque to visible light, and to create holograms of living cells *in vivo*. X-ray lasers offer an alternative to synchrotron X-ray sources, which produce almost coherent X-rays at typically shorter wavelengths than are currently available from X-ray lasers, but require a large particle accelerator.

X-rays Invisible electromagnetic radiation having a much shorter wavelength than light, between 10^{-8} and 3×10^{-11} metres; discovered by Wilhelm Röntgen in 1895, and originally called *Röntgen rays*. They are produced by the transitions of electrons in the inner levels of excited atoms, or by the rapid deceleration of charged particles. A common means of production is by firing electrons into a tungsten target backed by a copper heat sink. X-rays are useful in medicine, since different components of the body absorb X-rays to a different extent, but enough radiation passes through the body to register on a photograhic plate beyond.

Xuanzang [shwantsang], also spelled **Hsüan-tsang** (600–64) Buddhist pilgrim, explorer, and diarist, born in Chen-lu, C China. Inspired by earlier travellers, he made an epic journey to India (629–45) for Buddhist Scriptures. He crossed the Gobi and Xinjiang, traversed modern Afghanistan, and stayed two years in the Indus valley. He visited all the major historical sites in N India, journeyed 140 mi to the S, and returned up the W coast. He returned to China carrying 150 pieces of Buddha's body, 657 books, and the recipe for making sugar. His vivid account, published in 646, is a major source on 7th-c Asia.

Xuanzong [shwantsong], also spelled **Hsüan-tsung** (685–761) Chinese Tang emperor (ruled 712–55). Of royal lineage, he eliminated the usurper Wei's family in 710, and seized the crown in 712. Known also as **Minghuang** ('brilliant emperor'), his reign displayed authentic imperial characteristics. He maintained a splendid court, reformed the coinage, initiated land registration, extended the Grand Canal, defeated the Tibetans (747), patronized leading painters and poets, and established the Academy of Letters (*Han Lin*) in 754, by which major scholars supervised all court documentation. His system lasted over 1000 years. After 745 he became obsessed with his concubine, Yang Guifei. Her protégé An Lushan rebelled in 755. Xuanzong fled, agreed to her execution, then abdicated in grief. Their love story inspired the poet Bo Juyi, and Ming period drama.

xylem [ziylem] A tissue composed of several types of conducting cells and supporting fibres which transports water and minerals up from the roots to all other parts of a plant. Located in the vascular bundles, the cells die when mature. They form the 'wood' of woody plants.

xylenes [ziyleenz] $C_6H_4(CH_3)_2$. A mixture of the three isomers of dimethylbenzene, all of which occur in coal tar, and all of which boil at c.140°C. The mixture is used as a solvent, especially in preparations for microscopy, and as a starting material for the production of phthalic acids for polymers.

xylophone A percussion instrument known in various forms since the 14th-c. The modern orchestral instrument has two rows of wooden bars arranged like a piano keyboard, with a compass of 3½–4 octaves. These are mounted over tubular resonators and played with hard wooden sticks.

X–Y plotter A form of pen recorder where one or more pens can be placed anywhere on the drawing surface. This allows complicated drawings and text to be produced.

y

yacht A sailing or power-driven vessel used for the pleasure of the owner, derived from the Dutch *jacht*, a small, fast vessel. Charles II received one as a gift from the Dutch at the conclusion of his exile in Holland in 1660. The first known yacht race was between Charles II and his brother James in 1661 from Greenwich to Gravesend and back. Yachting increased steadily in popularity throughout the 19th-c, and received a great boost from the continuing interest of Edward, Prince of Wales and other royals. The biggest growth period has been since 1960 throughout the developed world.

Yacoub, Sir Magdi (Habib) [yakoob] (1935–) Surgeon, born in Cairo, Egypt. He studied at Cairo University, taught at Chicago, and moved to Britain where he became a consultant cardiothoracic surgeon at Harefield Hospital (1969–2001) and director of medical research and education (from 1992). He was appointed professor at the National Heart and Lung Institute in 1986, and is one of the leading developers of the techniques of heart and heart–lung transplantation. He was knighted in 1992.

Yahweh [yahway] or **YHWH** The name of the God of Israel, perhaps deriving from Israel's experiences at Sinai, although also found in Biblical stories of the patriarchs. The name is usually taken to mean 'He is/will be', 'He comes to be/creates', or 'He causes to fall'. The unvocalized YHWH (known as the **Tetragrammaton**) is considered by Jews too sacred to pronounce aloud, except by the high priest in the Holy of Holies on the Day of Atonement, and is usually replaced orally by *Adonai* ('Lord') when it is read from the Bible. Christians erroneously vocalized it as *Jehovah*.

yak A member of the cattle family, native to the high Tibetan Plateau; thick shaggy brown coat; white muzzle; widely spread upturned horns; domesticated yak highly-strung and stubborn; females crossbred with male domestic cattle or zebu; hybrid offspring (a *dzo*) economically important as draught animals, but males are sterile. (*Bos mutus*; domestic form sometimes called *Bos grunniens*.)

Yakshagana [yakshagahna] A literary and theatrical tradition of Karnataka, on the W coast of India. Developed from the conventions of Sanskrit theatre, it has been influenced greatly by Kannada literature. It lacks the intricate language of hand-gestures and eye-gestures of the classical stage, but has evolved a distinctive system of symbolic make-up and costuming.

Yakut A Turkic-speaking Mongoloid people of NE Siberia, and the main group in the area. Despite the severe climate, they are sedentary cattle and reindeer herders, and fishermen, and are now fully assimilated to the Russian way of life. They call themselves *Sakha*.

yakuza [yakuza] A Japanese gangster. Like the Sicilian Mafia, Japanese organized crime has a long history. The yakuza belong to recognized groups (*boryokudan*), cultivate a pseudo-samurai loyalty, and are proud of their traditions. They are widely involved in such activities as gambling, extortion, and racketeering.

Yale University *Ivy League*

Yalow, Rosalyn S(ussman) [yaloh] (1921–) Medical physicist, born in New York City, USA. She studied at Hunter College, New York City, and the University of Illinois. From 1947 she turned her attention to nuclear medicine at the Bronx Veterans Administration Hospital. There she developed radio-immunoassay, a technique for measuring minute concentrations of active biological substances such as hormones. Director of the Berson Research Laboratory from 1973, she shared the 1977 Nobel Prize for Physiology or Medicine.

Yalta Conference A meeting at Yalta, in the Crimea, during World War 2 (4–11 Feb 1945), between the Allied leaders Churchill, Stalin, and Franklin D Roosevelt. Among matters agreed were the disarmament and partition of Germany and Austria, the Russo–Polish frontier, the establishment of the United Nations, the composition of the Polish government, and confirmation of Soviet control of E Poland. In a secret protocol it was also agreed that the Soviet Union would declare war on Japan after the war with Germany ended in return for territories lost during the Russo–Japanese War of 1905.

Yalu, River [yaloo] River forming the N border between North Korea and NE China; rises in the Changbai Shan range; flows S, W, then SW to form most of the border between North Korea and China; flows into Korea Bay; length 790 km/490 mi.

yam A tuberous perennial, native to tropical and subtropical regions; climbing aerial stems annual, twining; leaves often heart-shaped; flowers small, white or greenish, in axillary clusters. Some 60 species are important food plants, especially in SE Asia, W Africa, and South America, where they are cultivated for the starchy tubers weighing up to 9 kg/20 lb and propagated like potatoes. In recent years some species have become important as a source of a steroid-type chemical used in oral contraceptives. (Genus: *Dioscorea*. Family: Dioscoriaceae.)

Yamagata, Prince Aritomo [yamagahta] (1838–1922) Japanese general, statesman, and premier (1890–1, 1898–1900), born in Hagi, SW Japan. A disciple of the anti-Western crusader Yoshido Shoin, he was an early leader in Meiji Japan (1868), and was dominant in Japanese public life until he died. As war minister (1873) and chief-of-staff (1878), he instituted major army reforms, modelling the army on German lines, and earning the name 'father of the Japanese army'. His belief in nationalism and imperial loyalty in the army took him above party politics, and he became premier to forestall partisan government. His military reforms led to Japan's defeat of China (1895) and Russia (1905) and her emergence as a significant power. In 1915 he opposed Japan's 21 Demands on China, believing Sino-Japanese understanding was essential to allow Japan to prepare for an inevitable war against the West.

Yamamoto, Yohji [yamamohtoh] (1943–) Fashion designer, born in Tokyo, Japan. He studied at Pawat Kaio University, then helped his mother with her dress shop. He started his own company in 1972, producing his first collection in Tokyo in 1976. After some time in Paris, he opened a new headquarters in London in 1987. He designs loose, functional clothes for men and women, featuring a great deal of black, which conceal rather than emphasize the body.

Yamashita, Yasuhiro [yamashita] (1957–) Judo fighter, born in Kyushu, S Japan. He won nine consecutive Japanese titles (1977–85), the Olympic open class gold medal (1984), and four world titles: 1979, 1981, 1983, (over 95 kg class), and 1981 (open class). He retired in 1985 after 203 consecutive bouts without defeat from 1977.

Yamato period A 6th–8th-c Japanese state in the Yamato Plain near modern Kyoto, S Honshu. It arose from the proto-feudal Ancient Tomb culture (4th–6th-c), where governing groups (*uji*) were led by warriors supposedly descended from spirits (*kami*). The Yamato *uji*, 'descended' from 'Emperor Jimmu', became pre-eminent. Chinese and Korean culture penetrated, writing was adopted, adminstration improved, society stratified, and power centralized. Buddhism, introduced in 552, became dominant before 600, and many temples were built.

Yamoussoukro [yamoosookroh] 6°49N 5°17W, pop (2000e) 194 900. Capital of Côte d'Ivoire, in Bouaké department; agricultural trade, fishing, forestry, perfumes; weekend resort town, NW of Abidjan; presidential residence.

Yamuna or **Jumna, River** [yahmuna] River of NW India; rises in the Himalayas of N Uttar Pradesh; flows SW to Delhi, then generally SE to join the R Ganges; length 1370 km/850 mi; confluence with the Ganges is one of the most sacred Hindu places; Taj Mahal at Agra on its banks.

Yang, Chen Ning, known as **Frank Yang** (1922–) Physicist, born in Hofei, EC China. He gained a scholarship to Chicago in 1945, was professor at the Institute for Advanced Studies, Princeton (1955–65), and from 1965 was professor of science at New York State University Center. He became a US citizen in 1964. A researcher in particle physics, with Tsung-Dao Lee he proposed a means of testing for parity invariance in weak interactions. Mirror symmetry was subsequently found to be violated in beta decay, and the pair shared the 1957 Nobel Prize for Physics for their insights into parity.

yang *yin and yang*

Yangchow *Yangzhou*

Yangon, formerly (to 1989) **Rangoon** 16°47N 96°10E, pop (2000e) 3 445 000. Chief port and capital of Myanmar; on R Yangon; settlement around Dagon pagoda in 6th-c; capital, 1886; large Indian and Chinese population; airport (Mingaladon); railway; university (1920); oil, timber, rice; Sule and Botataung Pagodas (both over 2000 years old), Shwedagon Pagoda (height 99·4 m/326 ft), reclining Buddha Image of Chauk-Htat-Gyi Pagoda, seated Buddha Image of Koe-Htat-Gyi Pagoda, Kaba Aye (World Peace Pagoda), national museum, natural history museum.

Yangshao [yangshow] Neolithic culture of 6000–4000 BC, excavated at Yangshao, China (near the Yellow R, between Xian and Luoyang) in 1921. It is distinguished by hardstone coiled red jars with geometric black comb-pattern designs and long necks. Other artefacts include stone knives, bows, weaving, and baskets. Over 1000 similar sites, especially Banpo, have since been discovered across N China from Xinjiang to Manchuria.

Yangtze River [yangksee] or **Yangtse-kiang**, in Chinese now normally **Chang Jiang** Longest river in China and third longest in the world; length c.6300 km/3900 mi; rises in the Tanggula Shan range (source explored, early 17th-c); flows E as the Tongtian He, then S as the Jinsha Jiang, becoming the Yangtze after Yibin in S Sichuan; flows NE through the Sichuan basin, a series of gorges, and across the Hubei plain to enter the E China Sea at Shanghai; drainage area, over 1 800 000 sq km/700 000 sq mi; prone to flooding (many disasters, eg 1931); provides c.40% of China's electricity; Gezhouba Dam near Yichang one of the largest in the world; controversial Three Gorges Dam project, begun in 1994 (completion scheduled, 2009), involving creation of a 600 km lake and the relocation of over 1·2 million people; major transportation artery between E and W China throughout Chinese history, navigable for over 940 km/580 mi; bridges at Chongqing, Wuhan, and Nanjing facilitate N–S communication; densely populated river basin contains about a quarter of China's cultivated land; numerous mineral deposits; important for rice culture since Neolithic period; joined to Yellow River by Grand Canal, AD 610; political centre of China, 1127–1420; since 12th-c, area of densest urbanization, of key economic importance in China.

Yangzhou or **Yangchow** [yahngjoh] 32°25N 119°26E, pop (2000e) 508 600, administrative region 9 521 000. City in Jiangsu province, E China, on Yangtze and Hua Rivers; first settled during Spring and Autumn Period (770–476 BC); as Jiangdu, built as third capital of Sui dynasty (590–618); major communications centre after building of Grand Canal, AD 610; important Tang period (618–906) metropolis; shipbuilding centre in Yuan period (13th–14th-c); focus of salt trade from 7th-c, its great wealth making it a major arts centre, 17th–19th-c; largest multiple-purpose water control project in China (1961–75); artistic centre for crafts, lacquerware screens, jade carving and printing; Fajing Si (Tang dynasty temple), museum.

Yao (Africa) [yow] A cluster of agricultural Bantu-speaking peoples of Tanzania, Malawi, and Mozambique, organized into many small chiefdoms. They were famous 19th-c traders between the Arab-dominated coast and inland. Because of the slave trade they clashed with European colonial powers. The majority are Muslims.

Yao (Asia) A mountain village people of SE Asia, dispersed and culturally diverse. They live chiefly in China, with some also in Thailand, Vietnam, and Laos. Most are farmers who trade with people from the lowlands, although in China some are wet-rice cultivators.

Yaoundé or **Yaundé** [yaoonday] 3°51N 11°31E, pop (2000e) 1 109 000. Capital of Cameroon, W Africa; 210 km/130 mi E of Douala; established as military post by Germans in 1899; occupied by Belgian colonial troops, 1915; capital of French Cameroon, 1921; airport; railway to the coast (Douala); university (1962); football stadium (1972); tourism, sugar refining, cigarettes, oil refining.

Yap pop (2000e) 17 200; area 119 sq km/46 sq mi. One of the Federated States of Micronesia, W Pacific; comprises the four large islands of Yap, Gagil-Tomil, Map, and Rumung, with some 130 outer islands; airport; capital, Colonia; copra, tropical fruit.

yapok [yapok] A marsupial native to Central and South America (*Chironectes minimus*); slender with long legs, pointed head, long naked tail; inhabits fresh water; the only truly semiaquatic marsupial; hind feet webbed; female has watertight backward opening pouch; eats fish and large crustaceans; also known as **water opossum**. (Family: Didelphidae.)

yarn The spun thread from which woven, knitted, and other fabrics are manufactured. Yarns vary widely in their properties, depending upon fibre content, count, and the spinning process used.

Yaroslavl [yaroslafl] 57°34N 39°52E, pop (2000e) 633 000. River-port capital of Yaroslavskaya oblast, E European Russia; oldest town on the R Volga, founded c.1024; railway; university (1971); textiles, synthetic rubber, tyres, lorries, diesel engines, chemicals, leather, tobacco, oil refining; Spaso-Preobrazhenski Monastery (12th-c).

yarrow A perennial (*Achillea millefolium*) growing to 60 cm/2 ft, native to Europe and W Asia, but now widely introduced elsewhere; leaves lance-shaped in outline, finely divided; flower-heads numerous, in dense, flat-topped clusters; five outer ray florets, white or sometimes pink; also called **milfoil**. It was formerly employed extensively in herbal medicine. (Family: Compositae.)

Yates, Dornford, pseudonym of **Cecil William Mercer** (1885–1960) Novelist, born in London, UK. He studied at Oxford, and achieved great popularity with an entertaining series of fanciful escapist adventure fiction, such as *Berry and Co* (1921) and *Jonah and Co* (1922).

Yavneh [yavne] *Jabneh*

yawl *ketch*

yaws An infectious disease of tropical regions caused by the bacterium *Treponema pertenue*. The bacterium is transmitted by direct close contact with an infected person. The disease is initially confined to eruptions in the skin. Later the deep tissues and bones may be invaded, resulting in deformities and scarring.

Yayoi In Japanese archaeology, the period c.300 BC–AD 300 which follows Jomon and precedes Kofun. Chinese and Korean influences are evident. Spreading NE from Kyushu, notable features are irrigated rice cultivation, fishing, and the use of bronze and iron for weapons, tools, and bell-making. The name derives from the characteristically simple coiled pottery of the period, first identified at Yayoi, Tokyo, in 1884, which still influences the shape of saké containers.

Yeager, Chuck [yayger], popular name of **Charles Elwood Yeager** (1923–) The first pilot to break the sound barrier, born in Myra, West Virginia, USA. He trained as a fighter pilot, flying many missions in Europe, and was shot down over France. On 14 October 1947 he flew the Bell X-1 rocket research aircraft to a level speed of more than 670 mph, thus 'breaking the sound barrier'. In 1953, in the Bell X-1A, he flew at more than 2½ times the speed of sound. He later commanded the USAF Aerospace Research Pilot School, and the 4th Fighter Bomber Wing.

yeast A fungus that can occur as single cells; typically reproduces by budding or by fission; used in fermentation processes in the brewing and baking industries. (Subdivision: Ascomycetes. Order: Endomycetales.)

Yeats, W(illiam) B(utler) [yayts] (1865–1939) Poet and playwright, born near Dublin, Ireland. Educated at schools in London and Dublin, he became an art student, then turned to writing. A leader of the Irish Literary Revival, he is a major voice of modern Irish poetry in English. In 1888 he published 'The Wanderings of Oisin', a long narrative poem that established his reputation. *The Celtic Twilight*, a book of peasant legends, appeared in 1893. With his patron, Lady Gregory, he founded the Irish Literary Theatre in 1899, and was a director of the Abbey Theatre, Dublin, from 1904. He wrote nearly 30 plays, including *The Countess Cathleen* (1892), *The Land of Heart's Desire* (1894), and *Cathleen ni Houlihan* (1903). He adopted a more direct style with *Responsibilities* (1914), which also marks a switch to contemporary subjects. The symbolic system described in *A Vision* (1925) informs many of his best-known poems, which appeared in *The Tower* (1928), *The Winding Stair* (1929), and *A Full Moon in March* (1935). Much of his best poetry is inspired by personal longing, notably his unrequited love for the revolutionary Maud Gonne and for a mythical Irish Golden Age. He received the Nobel Prize for Literature in 1923, and also became a senator of the Irish Free State (1922–8). His *Collected Poems* were published in 1950.

Yekaterinburg or **Ekaterinburg** [yekatuhrinberg], formerly **Sverdlovsk** (1924–91) 56°52N 60°35E, pop (2000e) 1 365 000. Industrial capital city of Sverdlovskaya oblast, E European Russia; in the E foothills of the Ural Mts, on R Iset; founded as a military stronghold and trading centre, 1723; tsar and his family shot here, 1918; airport; on the Trans-Siberian Railway; university (1920); iron ore, gold, copper; heavy engineering, metallurgy, gem cutting, clothing, textiles, tyres, fertilizers; Museum of Mineralogy.

yellow bird's nest A plant native to N temperate regions (*Monotropa hypopitys*); a rhizomatous saprophyte; whole plant waxy, yellowish-white, completely lacking chlorophyll; stems 8–30 cm/3–12 in, slightly fleshy; leaves scale-like, clasping stem; flowers 1–1·5 cm/0·4–0·6 in, bell-shaped, 4–5 petalled. (Family: Monotropaceae.)

yellow fever A disease occurring in Africa and South America caused by a virus which infects monkeys and is transmitted to humans by mosquitoes. It is often a mild short-lived feverish illness, but may become severe, with jaundice, kidney failure, and even death.

yellowfin tuna Species of tuna fish (*Thunnus albacares*) widespread in surface waters of tropical and warm temperate seas; length up to 2 m/6½ ft; golden band along side of body, dorsal and anal fins yellow; feeds on surface fishes such as flying fish and skippers as well as on squid and crustaceans; heavily exploited commercially. (Family: Scombridae.)

yellow-green algae Aquatic algae containing the photosynthetic pigments chlorophyll *a* and *c*, and various carotenoids which produce the yellow-green colour of the chloroplasts; they vary in form from single cells to filaments; produce motile spores (*zoospores*) with a hairy forward-pointing and a naked backward-pointing flagellum. (Class: Xanthophyceae.)

yellowhammer (Ger *ammer*, 'bunting') A bird, a species of bunting (*Emberiza citronella*), native to NW regions of the Old World; black and yellow streaked plumage with chestnut rump; inhabits grass and farmland; eats seeds and insects; also known as the **yellow bunting**. The name is used in the USA for the woodpecker, *Colaptes auratus*.

Yellowknife 62°30N 114°29W, pop (2000e) 17 000. Capital of North West Territories, Canada, on NW shore of Great Slave Lake at mouth of Yellowknife R; founded, 1935; capital, 1967; gold mining.

Yellow River, Chin **Huang Ho** or **Huang He** Second longest river in China; length 5464 km/3395 mi; rises in Bayan Har Shan Range, WC China; flows NW through Inner Mongolia, then generally E or NE across the country to enter the Bo Hai Gulf S of Tianjin; series of gorges in upper reaches, used for hydroelectricity; flooding formerly a serious problem (major disasters in 1340s, 1852), so that it was known as 'China's sorrow'; now increasingly controlled by dykes; several conservancy projects on upper and middle reaches; fine loess soil of its basin established the area as the cradle of Chinese civilization; basin and tributaries provided location for capitals of all major dynasties until the 12th-c.

Yellow Sea, Chin **Hwang Hai** Inlet of the Pacific Ocean, bounded by China (N, W) and by N and S Korea (E); maximum width c.650 km/400 mi; maximum depth c.150 m/500 ft; named for its colour, because of the silt brought down by its rivers.

Yellowstone Largest US national park, and the world's first, mainly in NW Wyoming; contains over 3000 hot springs and geysers, including Old Faithful, a geyser that spurts water at regular intervals; Yellowstone and Jackson Lakes; highest point Electric Peak (3350 m/10 991 ft); area 8992 sq km/3472 sq mi.

yellow wood A member of a large genus of evergreen conifers found in the mountains of warm temperate and tropical regions of the S hemisphere; leaves variable, scaly, needle-like or large and flat; single-seeded cone becoming fleshy, brightly coloured, edible. They are important forest trees, especially in Australasia, yielding valuable timber. (Genus: *Podocarpus*, 100 species. Family: Pinaceae.)

Yeltsin, Boris (Nikolayevich) (1931–) Russian president (1991–9), born in Bukta, WC Russia. He studied at the Urals Polytechnic, and began his career in the construction industry. He joined the Communist Party of the Soviet Union in 1961, and was appointed first secretary of the Sverdlovsk region in 1976. He was inducted into the Central Committee in 1981 by Gorbachev, and briefly worked under the new secretary for the economy, Ryzhkov, before being appointed Moscow party chief in 1985. A blunt-talking reformer, he rapidly set about renovating the corrupt 'Moscow machine', and was elected a candidate member of the Politburo in 1986, but in 1987, at a Central Committee plenum, after he had bluntly criticized party conservatives for sabotaging political and economic reform (*perestroika*), he was downgraded to a lowly administrative post. He returned to public attention in 1989 by being elected to the new Congress of USSR People's Deputies, and in June 1991 he was elected president of the Russian Federation. Following the attempted coup to oust Gorbachev in August 1991, Yeltsin's political standing greatly increased when he led the protestors who defeated the coup, and following the break-up of the Soviet Union in December 1991 he remained in power as president of the Russian Federation. He continued to press for reform, but met increasing resistance from more conservative elements in the parliament. In 1993 he called for a referendum to measure his support, received a firm vote of confidence, and proposed a new constitution for Russia. Further confrontation with conservative hard liners followed, leading to his decision to suspend parliament (Sep 1993), and a subsequent conflict

Yemen

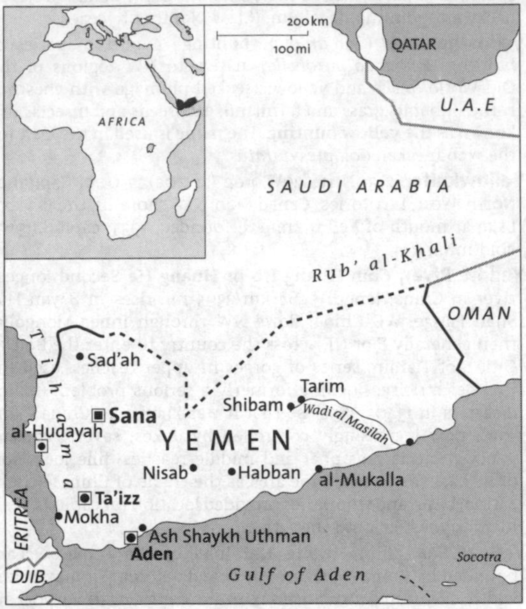

□ International Airport - - - - No defined boundary

official name **Republic of Yemen**, Arabic **al-Jumhurijah al-Yemenijah**

Local name al-Yaman (Arabic)

Timezone GMT +3

Area 531 570 km²/205 186 sq mi

Population total (2002e) 19 495 000

Status Republic

Date of independence 1967

Capitals Sana (political), Aden (commercial)

Languages Arabic (official), English

Ethnic groups Arab (96%), with Indo Pakistani, Somali, Amhara and Swahili, Persian, Jewish, and European minorities

Religions Muslim (Sunni 53%, Shiite 47%), small Christian, Hindu, and Yemeni Jew minorities

Physical features Occupies the SW corner of the Arabian peninsula; narrow coastal plain, backed by mountains rising to 3000–3500 m/10 000–11 500 ft; highlands, central plateau and maritime range of former South Yemen form the most fertile part of the country; former North Yemen is largely desert and mountainous.

Climate Hot and humid climate; lowland and desert regions in NE receive an average annual rainfall of 100 mm/4 in; hot and humid on Tihamat coastal strip with mean temperature of 29°C; mild and temperate in interior highlands, with cool winters; average annual temperatures 25°C (Jan), 32°C (Jul) in Aden; average annual rainfall, 46 mm/1·8 in.

Currency 1 Yemeni Riyal (YR, YRI) = 100 fils (former N Yemen)

Economy Based on agriculture (largely subsistence) and light industry; cotton has overtaken coffee as chief cash crop; irrigation schemes likely to increase area under cultivation; qat, a narcotic leaf, now a major enterprise; hides, vegetables, dried fish; crude- and refined-oil industry; textiles, cement, aluminium, salt.

GDP (2002) $15·07 bn, per capita $800

Human Development Index (2002) 0·479

History Part of the Minaean kingdom, 1200–650 BC; converted to Islam in 7th-c; Turkish occupation, 1538–1630 and 1872–1918; between and after Turkish rule, Yemen under the rule of the Hamid al-Din dynasty; sovereignty of Yemen acknowledged by Saudi Arabia and Britain, 1934; joined Arab League, 1945; Egypt-backed revolution in 1962, resulting in civil war; Yemen Arab Republic (North Yemen) declared, 1962; royalists defeated, 1969; neighbouring People's Republic of South Yemen established, 1967, when Britain ended 129 years of rule in Aden and the Marxist National Liberation Front took over; the People's Republic comprised Aden and 16 of the 20 protectorate states once under British control; renamed People's Democratic Republic of Yemen, 1970; negotiations to merge the two Yemens, 1979; unification proclaimed and ratified, 1990; new state called Republic of Yemen; former President of North Yemen declared President of the unified state, and former President of South Yemen became Prime Minister; supported Iraq during Gulf War, 1991; coalition government formed, 1993; governed by a president, Prime Minister, House of Representatives and Advisory Council; South Yemen declared independence as Democratic Republic of Yemen, 1994; subsequent civil war won by North Yemen.

Head of State

1990– Ali Abdullah Saleh

Head of Government

1990–4 Haider Abu Bakr al-Attas
1994–7 Abdel Aziz Abdel-Ghani
1997–8 Farag Said Ben Ghanem
1998–2001 Abdul Karim al-Iriani
2001– Abd al-Qadir Ba Jammal

involving the shelling of the Moscow parliament building (Oct), from which he emerged with his position strengthened. However, in 1995–6 opposition grew as a result of ongoing economic problems and the war in Chechnya, and although successful in the 1996 elections, continuing ill health caused him major difficulties. At the end of 1999 he surprised the world by announcing his resignation.

Yemen *see panel*

Yenisey or **Yenisei, River** [yenisay] River in C Siberian Russia; rises in the E Sayanskiy Khrebet, and flows generally N to enter the Kara Sea via a long estuary; length, 3487 km/2167 mi; navigable for five months on the upper river course, three months on the lower course; forms W boundary of the C Siberian Plateau; coal, non-ferrous metals, hydroelectric power.

yeoman A person in late mediaeval England qualified, by holding freehold land and property worth 40 shillings or more, to serve on juries and vote for knights of the shire. In the early modern period, the name is used for the better-off freeholders or tenant-farmers who were often dominant in village life and administration as churchwardens, constables, and overseers of the poor.

yeomanry A historic military expression, revived in Britain during the Napoleonic period for volunteer units of cavalry, organized on a county-by-county basis. In 1908, yeomanry regiments were absorbed by the Territorials.

Yeomen of the Guard The oldest of the four corps of the British sovereign's personal bodyguard, known also as **Beefeaters**, supposedly in tribute to their healthy appearance. They are called out for special duties only, when they wear their basically Tudor uniforms. The same uniforms are worn by the **Yeomen Warders** of the Tower of London, whose original duty was to guard the Tower, but who now attend the gates, enact the Ceremony of the Keys every night, and act as guides to the tourists.

Yerevan or **Erivan** [yerevan] 40°10N 44°31E, pop (2000e) 1 337 000. Capital city of Armenia; on R Razdan, 15 km/9 mi from the Turkish frontier; altitude of highest part, 1042 m/3419 ft; one of the world's most ancient cities; ceded to Russia, 1828; airfield; railway; university; vodka, wine, textiles, chemicals, foodstuffs, tourism; ruins of a 16th-c Turkish fortress; badly damaged by earthquake, 1988.

Yerkes Observatory [yerkeez] The observatory of the University of Chicago at Williams Bay, Wisconsin, named after its benefactor, Charles T(yson) Yerkes (1837–1905). Its main telescope is the 102-cm/40-in refractor (1897), still the world's largest refracting telescope.

Yesenin, Sergey Alexandrovich [yesaynin] (1895–1925) Poet, born in Konstantino (later renamed Yesenino in his honour), Russia. He left home at 17, and gained literary success with his first volume *Radunitsa* (1916, Mourning for the Dead). He was four times married (his third wife was Isadora Duncan), and his suicide in St Petersburg prompted a wave of imitative suicides in Russia.

yeti A supposed ape-like creature said to live at the edge of the snow-line in high valleys of the Himalayan Mts; generally described as large, covered in brown hair, and walking upright like a human; first reported in 1889; footprints of length 15–30 cm/6–12 in have been photographed, but various expeditions have failed to find it; also known as **abominable snowman**, **meti**, **temu**, **kang-mi**, **mirka**, **mi-go**, **sogpu**, or **shukpa**.

Yevtushenko, Yevgeny (Alexandrovich) [yevtushengkoh] (1933–) Poet, born in Zima, C Russia. He moved to Moscow in 1944, where he studied at the Gorky Institute of Literature. His early poetry, such as *The Third Snow* (1955, trans title), made him a spokesman for the young post-Stalin generation. His long narrative poem *Zima Junction* (1961), considering issues raised by the death of Stalin, prompted criticism, as did his *Babi Yar* (1962) which attacked anti-Semitism. In 1960 he began to travel abroad to give readings of his poetry. Three volumes of his selected poems appeared in 1987, and among later works are *Pre-morning* (1995). His first major stage piece, *Under the Skin of the Statue of Liberty*, was a huge success in 1972. Since the 1970s his artistic pursuits have widened considerably. He has written novels and other prose works, and engaged in acting, film directing, and photography. Always ready to express his beliefs, even in an unfavourable political climate, he publicly supported Solzhenitsyn when the novelist was arrested in 1974. He became a member of the Congress of People's Deputies in 1989.

yew A small evergreen tree or shrub, native to the western N hemisphere; leaves narrow, flattened, spreading in two horizontal rows; seed surrounded by a scarlet, fleshy aril. The foliage and seeds are highly poisonous, but the aril is edible, though insipid. Many were traditionally planted in walled churchyards to prevent farm stock from eating them. Popular for cemeteries, topiary, and mazes, they were once the source of the finest longbows. (Genus: *Taxus*, 10 species. Family: Taxaceae.)

Yggdrasil [igdrasil] In Norse mythology, a giant ash, the World-Tree, which supports the sky, holds the different realms of gods and men in its branches, and has its roots in the Underworld.

Yiddish A language used by E European Jews, developed from Old High German in the 9th-c, and written using the Hebrew alphabet. It flourished as a medium of literature in the 19th-c and in the first part of the 20th-c, but its literary use has diminished following the establishment of Hebrew as the official language of Israel.

yield The interest paid on a stock, share, or bond in relation to its current market value, in percentage terms. If a company pays a dividend of 20p a share, before tax is deducted, and the share price is 400p, then the dividend yield is 5%. If the share price rises to 500p, then the yield becomes 4%. These are termed **gross yields**, being before tax. More broadly, yield denotes the rate of output of any of the factors of production (ie, of land, labour, or capital).

yield point *plastic deformation*

yield stress The lowest stretching stress at which a material undergoes an irreversible plastic deformation, producing what is called a 'permanent set' in the material; symbol σ_y, units Pa (pascal). For copper, $\sigma_y = 4 \times 10^7$ Pa; for steel, 4×10^8 Pa.

yin and yang The Chinese concept that everything is explicable in terms of two complementary but opposing principles. Yang represents heaven, and is the positive, male force which is characteristically aggressive, stimulating, light, hot, and dry. Yin is seen as the negative, female force, which is characteristically cold, dark, heavy, and damp. In traditional Chinese medicine, the yang organs are the hollow organs of the stomach, gall bladder, bladder, colon, small intestine, and triple heater, and in acupuncture the yang meridians take their origin from these organs. The yin organs are solid, and include the liver, heart, spleen, lung, and kidney; they originate the yin acupuncture meridians. Yang people are active, alert, energetic, and precise, but suffer with problems of anxiety, stress, tension, irritability, and inability to relax. Yin people are calm, relaxed, peaceful, and creative, but are prone to laziness, depression, and lethargy. Food with yang characteristics include meat, eggs, cheese, brown rice, and beans, because these give warmth, energy, and strength. Yin foods include raw vegetables and salads, steamed fruit and vegetables, tropical fruits, and juices, and these characteristically have a calming and cooling effect. In good health the forces of yin and yang balance each other, but people generally have a tendency towards one or other characteristic. Representing all experience in a dynamic framework, the yin–yang concept has underpinned Chinese cyclical views of history, and was developed in a sophisticated form by Han times (3rd-c BC–AD 3rd-c).

Yinchuan or **Yinch'uan** [yinchwahn] 38°30N 106°19E, pop (2000e) 559 500, administrative region 937 000. Capital of Ningxia Hui autonomous region, N China; NE of Lanzhou; airfield; commercial centre; coal mining, wool, centre of agricultural trade; Muslims are a third of the population.

Yippies A term referring to members of the Youth International Party that was established in the USA during the mid-1960s by young, highly educated middle-class radicals who sought to create an 'alternative' American culture based on non-possessive values. They received considerable attention from the law enforcement agencies because of their alleged belief in 'free love' and use of drugs.

ylang-ylang [eelang eelang] An evergreen tree (*Cananga odorata*) growing to 25 m/80 ft, native to Malaysia and the Philippines, and cultivated elsewhere; leaves up to 20 cm/8 in long, elliptical, arranged in two rows; flowers 10 cm/4 in diameter, 6-petalled, dull yellow, fragrant. Ylang-ylang or macassar oil from the flowers is used in perfumes. (Family: Annonaceae.)

YMCA Abbreviation of **Young Men's Christian Association**, a charity founded in London in 1844 to promote the spiritual, social, and physical welfare of boys and young men. The YMCA developed rapidly in many countries, notably the USA; it is active in over 130 countries, with over 100 000 centres and 30 million people participating in its activities.

yoga In Indian religious tradition, any of various physical and contemplative techniques designed to free the superior, conscious element in a person from involvement with the inferior material world. More narrowly, Yoga is a school of Hindu philosophy which seeks to explain and justify the practices of yogic discipline.

yogurt or **yoghurt** A product, originating in the Balkans, obtained by fermenting milk with the bacteria *Lactobacillus bulgaricus* and *Streptococcus acidophilus*. This process produces lactic acid from lactose present in the milk. Yogurt may be made from full-fat, low-fat, or skimmed milk, and various sweetenings and flavourings may be added.

Yogyakarta [yagyakah(r)ta] or **Yogya** 7°48S 110°24E, pop (2000e) 547 000. Capital of Yogyakarta special territory, SC Java, Indonesia; cultural centre of Java; airfield; railway; two universities (1945, 1949); textiles, leather, railway workshops, silverwork, crafts; sultan's palace (18th-c), Soino Budoyo museum, ancient temples of Borobudur and Prambanan.

Yokohama [yohkohhahma] 35°28N 139°28E, pop (2000e) 3 325 000. Port capital of Kanagawa prefecture, C Honshu, Japan; on W shore of Tokyo-wan Bay, SW of Tokyo; second largest city in Japan, handling 15% of foreign trade; first port to be opened to foreign trade, 1859; linked to Tokyo by first Japanese railway, 1872; largely destroyed by earthquake and fire in 1923, and by bombing in 1945; railway; two universities (1949); shipbuilding, oil refining, engineering, chemicals, glass, furniture, clothes, trade in silk, rayon, fish; Foreign Cemetery, Yokohama Museum of Art, China Town, Marine Tower, Yamashita Park, Yokohama International Stadium (1997); Port Festival (May), Black Ships' Festival (Jul).

Yolngu The Aboriginal people and language of NE Arnhem Land; sometimes called **Murngin**. Three Yolngu clans were the plaintiffs in an early land rights case, the *Gove* case of 1968, against Nabalco, an aluminium mining company extracting ore on their land. The failure of the Yolgnu to secure legal recognition of their traditional title led directly to the introduction of the first Australian land rights legislation, the Aboriginal Land Rights (Northern Territory) Act of 1976. The Yolngu were the subject of W L Warner's classic anthropological study *A Black Civilization* (1937), in which he erroneously named them the Murngin.

Yom Kippur [**yohm kipoor, yom kipur**] The Day of Atonement, a Jewish holy day (10 Tishri) coming at the end of 10 days of penitence which begin on Rosh Hashanah; a day devoted to fasting, prayer, and repentance for past sins.

Yom Kippur War *Arab–Israeli Wars*

Yongle or **Yung-lo** [**yonglay**], originally **Zhu Di** (1360–1424) Third emperor (1403–24) of the Chinese Ming dynasty (1368–1644), known postumously as Chengzu, born in Nanking, EC China. The fourth son of Hongwu, he seized the crown from his nephew after much bloodshed. He moved the capital to Beijing (1421) and reconstructed the Grand Canal, developed central and local government organs, and instituted the civil service examination format which lasted to the 20th-c. He also patronized Confucianism, published the Buddhist Tripitaka, sponsored the Great Encyclopaedia (1408), and sent Zheng He to sea. He conquered the Mongols in five campaigns (dying on the fifth), annexed Annan, and enforced tribute from Borneo, Japan, Java, Korea, Siam, and SE India.

yoni [**yohnee**] *lingam*

Yonkers 40°56N 73°54W, pop (2000e) 196 100. Town in Westchester Co, SE New York, USA; a residential suburb on the Hudson R, at the N edge of Greater New York c.24 km/15 mi N of the city centre; named after the courtesy title ('Jonkheer') given to the early Dutch settler Adriaen van der Donck; railway; retailing; St Andrews golf course (first course in the USA), Hudson R Museum, Sherwood House.

York (UK), Lat **Eboracum** 53°58N 1°05W, pop (2000e) 103 000. City in North Yorkshire, N England, UK; unitary authority from 1996 (pop (2000e) 176 000); Roman settlement founded in AD 71 as capital of the Roman province of Britannia; thereafter a royal and religious centre, capital of Anglo-Saxon Northumbria; captured by the Danes (867), known as **Jorvík**; Archbishop of York bears the title Primate of England; expanded rapidly in the 19th-c as a railway centre; university (1963); railway; foodstuffs, chocolate, glass, railway coaches, scientific instruments, tourism; 14th-c city walls; York Minster (12th–15th-c), south transept badly damaged by fire in 1984, since restored; National Railway Museum; Castle Museum; Jorvik Viking Centre (1984); York Festival (Jun); football league team, York City.

York, Alvin (Cullum) (1887–1964) US soldier and popular hero, born in Pall Mall, Tennessee, USA. His fundamentalist Christian religion taught him to disapprove of war, but he resolved his doubts after joining the army in 1917. While in France, he led a small detachment against a German machine-gun emplacement, in which he killed 25 of the enemy, inducing 132 Germans to surrender. The greatest US hero of World War 1, he was awarded the Congressional Medal of Honor and returned home to a ticker-tape parade. He was a founder of the American Legion, and Gary Cooper portrayed him in the movie *Sergeant York* (1941).

York, Duke of In the UK, a title often given to the second son of the sovereign, such as Albert Frederick (later George VI), the second son of George V, and Andrew, the second son of Queen Elizabeth II.

York, House of The younger branch of the English Plantagenet dynasty, founded by Edmund of Langley, the fourth son of Edward III and first Duke of York (1385–1402), whence came three kings of England: Edward IV (1461–83), who usurped the Lancastrian King Henry VI; Edward V (1483); and Richard III (1483–5) killed at Bosworth Field, and succeeded by Henry VII, first of the Tudors.

Yorkshire, North pop (2000e) 738 300; excluding York, 605 300; area 8309 sq km/3207 sq mi. County in N England, UK, created in 1974; largest county in England, from Lancashire (W) to the North Sea (E); Pennines in the W; Vale of York, North Yorkshire Moors, Cleveland Hills in the E; R Ouse flows SE; county town, Northallerton; other chief towns Harrogate, Middlesbrough (unitary authority from 1996), Scarborough, Whitby, York (unitary authority from 1996); agriculture (cereals, dairy farming, sheep), electrical and mechanical equipment, footwear, clothing, vehicles, plastics, foodstuffs, tourism; Fylingdales radar station, Rievaulx Abbey, Yorkshire Dales national park, Castle Howard, York Minster, Fountains Abbey.

Yorkshire, South pop (2001e) 1 266 300; area 1560 sq km/602 sq mi. Area of N England, UK, created in 1974, divided into four metropolitan borough councils: Sheffield, Rotherham, Doncaster, Barnsley (administrative centre); agriculture (sheep, arable, dairy farming), coal, steel, engineering.

Yorkshire, West pop (2001e) 2 079 200; area 2039 sq km/787 sq mi. County of N England, UK; drained by the Aire and Calder Rivers; administrative centre, Wakefield; chief towns include Leeds, Bradford, Huddersfield, Halifax; metropolitan council abolished in 1986; wool textiles, coal, engineering, machinery, machine tools; Ilkley Moor, Haworth Parsonage (home of the Brontës), Peak District National Park.

Yorkshire coach horse *Cleveland bay*

Yorkshire Dales National park in North Yorkshire and Cumbria, England, UK; area 1761 sq km/680 sq mi; established in 1954; limestone scenery (eg Kilnsey Crag, Gordale Crag, Malham Cove), popular with potholers and fell walkers; three main peaks of Ingleborough, Whernside, Pen-y-Ghent; Bolton Abbey (Wharfedale), Roman fort at Bainbridge.

Yorkshire Ripper, The *Sutcliffe, Peter*

Yorkshire terrier A British toy terrier; very small, with long fine brown and blue-grey hair; coat reaches ground; head with large erect ears and very long hair; owners sometimes tie ribbons on its head.

Yorktown 37°14N 76°30W. Seat of York Co, SE Virginia, USA, at the mouth of the York R; settled, 1631; now in Colonial National Historical Park; Revolutionary troops under Washington and Rochambeau besieged British forces under Cornwallis here in 1781, until the latter surrendered; also besieged during the Civil War by Union forces under McClellan, 1862.

Yorktown Campaign (30 Aug–19 Oct 1781) The final campaign of the US War of Independence, ending with the entrapment at Yorktown, VA, of the British army under Lord Cornwallis by troops under Washington and a French fleet under Admiral de Grasse (1722–88). The defeat destroyed the political will on the English side to continue the war. It brought the fall of Lord North, prime minister since 1770, and opened the way for peace negotiations.

Yoruba [**yoruhba**] A cluster of Kwa-speaking peoples of SW Nigeria and Benin, mostly organized in culturally similar but politically autonomous kingdoms, each ruled by a king who is both political and religious head. Their dominant state in the 17th–18th-c was the kingdom of Oyo, which broke up in the early 19th-c. They are highly urbanized, Ibadan being the largest pre-colonial city in sub-Saharan Africa, and are famed for their art. Traditional religion still flourishes, although many are Muslims and Christians.

Yosemite [yohsemitee] ('grizzly bear') National park in E California, USA, in the Sierra Nevada, E of San Francisco; 11 km/7 mi-long valley full of natural granite monoliths and waterfalls; rises to 3990 m/13 090 ft in Mt Lyell; Half Dome Mt, El Capitan, Mariposa Grove; drained by the Merced R; Yosemite Falls (highest in North America), 739 m/2425 ft in two stages; area 3083 sq km/1189 sq mi.

Yoshkar Ola or **Ioshkar Ola** [yushkahrula] 56°38N 47°52E, pop (2000e) 273 000. Capital city of Mariyskaya, EC European Russia, on R Kokshaga; founded, 1578; railway; pharmaceuticals, foodstuffs, agricultural machinery.

Young, Andrew (Jackson), Jr (1932–) Civil rights activist, Protestant minister, and public official, born in New Orleans, Louisiana, USA. As a minister, he joined the Southern Christian Leadership Conference (SCLC) in 1960, and came to be one of the closest associates of Martin Luther King. As the SCLC's executive director (1964–70), he took an active role in working at desegregation. Elected as a Democrat to the US House of Representatives (1973–7), he was the first African-American to represent Georgia in Congress since 1871. In 1977 he became US representative to the UN, but was forced to resign in 1979 after it was revealed that he had met secretly with members of the PLO. He served as Mayor of Atlanta, GA (1981–9), and continued to be moderate within the African-American community.

Young, Arthur (1741–1820) Agricultural and travel writer, born in London, UK. He spent much of his life in Bradfield, Suffolk, where he rented a small farm, and carried out many agricultural experiments. In 1793 he became secretary to the Board of Agriculture. In his writings, he helped to elevate agriculture to a science, founding and editing the monthly *Annals of Agriculture* in 1784.

Young, Brigham (1801–77) Mormon leader, born in Whitingham, Vermont, USA. Converted in 1832, he became one of the 12 apostles of the Church in 1835, and its president upon the death of Joseph Smith in 1844. After the Mormons were driven from Nauvoo, he led them to Utah (1847), where they founded Salt Lake City. He was appointed Governor of Utah in 1850, but was replaced in 1857 when an army was sent to establish federal law in the territory. He established over 300 towns and settlements, had over 20 wives (estimates vary), and was the father of more than 40 children.

Young, Cy, popular name of **Denton True Young** (1867–1955) Baseball pitcher, born in Gilmore, Ohio, USA. One of the first of baseball's greats, he made his major-league debut in 1890 and played until 1911. During his career he threw 749 complete games and won 511 games, both records. National and American League's leading pitchers win the Cy Young Award every year.

Young, John (1930–) Astronaut, born in San Francisco, California, USA. He entered the US navy in 1952 and became a carrier-based fighter pilot (1955–9), a navy test pilot (1959–62), and then a NASA astronaut. He has flown in space a record six times: twice in the Gemini programme, twice in the Apollo programme (Apollos 10 and 16), and twice as commander of the space shuttle, including its first flight, STS-1, in 1981.

Young, Lester (Willis), nickname **Prez** (1909–59) Tenor saxophonist, born in Woodville, Mississippi, USA. He first played alto saxophone in a family band, but changed to tenor saxophone in 1927 and worked with a succession of bands in the mid-west, before joining the newly-formed Count Basie Orchestra in 1934 for a spell, rejoining it in 1936. The band's rise to national prominence in the late 1930s brought him recognition as an innovative soloist, whose light tone marked a break from the swing-style saxophone, and inspired such modernists as Charlie Parker. In 1944 he was drafted, disastrously, into the army, and for the rest of his life he suffered from ill-health and excessive drinking, but continued playing until his death. His nickname 'Prez', for 'President', was given to him by his close friend Billie Holiday.

Young, Simone (1961–) Conductor, born in Sydney, New South Wales, SE Australia. She studied at the Sydney Conservatorium of Music, joining the Australian Opera in 1982. In 1987 she was engaged by Cologne State Opera, first as repetiteur then as assistant conductor, and became the first woman to conduct the Vienna Volksoper, the Vienna Staatsoper, and the Paris Opera. In 1994 she made her British debut at the Royal Opera House, Covent Garden, and in 1996 her American debut at the Metropolitan Opera House, New York City. In 2001 she became musical director for Opera Australia.

Young, Thomas (1773–1829) Physicist, physician, and Egyptologist, born in Milverton, Somerset, SW England, UK. He studied medicine at London, Edinburgh, Göttingen, and Cambridge universities, then devoted himself to scientific research, becoming professor of natural philosophy to the Royal Institution (1801). His *Lectures* (1807) expounded the doctrine of interference, which established the wave theory of light. He proposed that the eye required only three basic colour receptors for full colour vision – red, green, and blue. He also did valuable work in insurance, haemodynamics, and Egyptology, and made a fundamental contribution to the deciphering of the inscriptions on the Rosetta Stone.

Younghusband, Sir Francis Edward (1863–1942) British soldier and explorer, born in Murree, N Pakistan (formerly India). He explored Manchuria in 1886, and on the way back discovered the route from Kashgar into India via the Mustagh Pass. In 1902 he went on the expedition which opened up Tibet to the Western world. British resident in Kashmir (1906–9), he wrote much on India and C Asia. He founded the World Congress of Faiths in 1936.

Young Ireland An Irish protest movement, founded in 1840, which produced *The Nation* magazine, arguing for repeal of the Act of Union. It set up an Irish Confederation in 1847, which returned several nationalists to parliament, and an unsuccessful Young Ireland rising took place in Tipperary in 1848.

Young Italy, (Ital **Giovine Italia**) An Italian patriotic organization which played an important role in the early stages of the Risorgimento, founded in Marseille (1833) by Mazzini. Designed to arouse Italian national feeling and ultimately seize power, by 1833 it possessed 60 000 members, and had committees in all leading Italian cities. It played a significant part in the revolutions of 1848.

Young Men's Christian Association *YMCA*

Young Men's / Women's Hebrew Association (YMHA/YWHA) In the USA, an organization to promote health, social activities, and Jewish culture. The first YMHA was founded in 1854, and the first independent YWHA in 1902.

young offender institution An institution in the UK where adolescent and young adult offenders between 15 and 21 may be detained either on remand or following a sentence of the court. Custodial sentences are only used in the most serious cases of violence or sexual offences, though increasingly used for persistent young offenders. These institutions replaced detention centres (formerly known as Borstal institutes) and (in England and Wales) youth custody centres in 1988. In the USA, detention centres for both male and female offenders are often known as *juvenile halls*, *youth camps*, or *youth authorities*. There are many variations in provision among different jurisdictions.

Young's modulus Linear stress divided by linear strain, a constant for a given material; symbol E, units Pa (pascal); also called the **modulus of elasticity** or the **elastic modulus**; named after Thomas Young. A high Young's modulus means that material is stiffer. For steel, $E = 2 \times 10^{11}$ Pa; for wood, E is about $0{\cdot}1 \times 10^{11}$ along the grain.

Young Turks The modernizing and westernizing reformers in the early 20th-c Ottoman Empire. With the support of disaffected army elements under Enver Pasha, they rebelled against Sultan Abd-ul-Hamid II in 1908, and deposed him in 1909. The Young Turk revolution helped precipitate Austria–Hungary's occupation of Bosnia-Herzegovina (1908), the somewhat similar Greek officers' revolt of 1909, the Italian attack on Libya (1911), and the Balkan Wars (1912–13).

Young Vic *Old Vic Theatre*

Young Women's Christian Association *YWCA*

Yourcenar, Marguerite [yersenah(r)], pseudonym of **Marguerite de Crayencour** (1903–87) Novelist and poet, born in Brussels, Belgium. Educated at home in a wealthy and cultured household, she travelled widely, and wrote a series of distinguished novels, plays, poems, and essays. Her novels, many of them historical reconstructions, include *Les Mémoires d'Hadrien* (1951, Memoirs of Hadrian) and *L'oeuvre au noir* (1968, trans The Abyss). She emigrated to the USA in 1939, was granted dual US and French nationality in 1979, and in 1980 became the first woman writer to be elected to the Académie Française.

youth court A court introduced in England and Wales in 1991 to replace the existing juvenile courts. Youth courts deal with most young offenders from the age of criminal responsibility (10 in England and Wales) up to the age of 18. The magistrates who sit in the court are empowered to impose a wide range of sentences on such young offenders, though custodial sentences have been abolished for those 12 years and younger. The court can, if it considers it appropriate, impose financial penalties on parents, and in certain circumstances on local authorities. The sentencing of young offenders has become increasingly punitive, and the Crime and Disorder Act (1998) contains radical measures designed to prevent crime and antisocial behaviour by them. These include the power of local authorities to impose a 'local child curfew scheme', and sentencing options for young offenders such as 'reparation orders', which require reparation to the victim of the crime by the accused.

youth custody centre *young offender institution*

Youth Hostels Association (YHA) *International Youth Hostel Association*

Youth International Party *Yippies*

youth training centre A type of residential establishment providing specialized child care facilities in England and Wales. In 1994, the Criminal Justice and Public Order Act introduced a new *secure training order* to deal with a small number of young persistent offenders, who it was thought were responsible for a disproportionate amount of crime. The Order gives the courts power to detain for up to two years, and comprises two parts: detention in a secure training centre, and supervision in the community.

Ypres [eepr], Flemish **Ieper** 50°51N 2°53E, pop (2000e) 35 800. Town in West Flanders province, W Belgium, close to the French border; long associated with the cloth trade; devastated in World War 1; Menin Gate (Menenpoort) memorial, graveyards, and Garden of Peace provide a place of pilgrimage; railway; textiles, textile machinery, foodstuffs, tourism; cloth hall (13th-c), St Martin's Cathedral; Festival of the Cats (May).

Ypres, Battles of (1914–17) [eepr] Major battles in World War 1, taking place in three stages. The first (30 Oct–24 Nov 1914) ended in stalement, beginning a protracted period of trench warfare on the Western Front. In the second (22 Apr–27 May 1915), the Germans used chemical warfare – chlorine gas. In the third stage (Jul–Nov 1917), after constant Allied bombardment, the Germans won the advantage, deploying mustard gas and machine-gunfire. Canadian infantrymen eventually took Passchendaele after months of bitter fighting in battlefield swamps. By the end of the battle, Allied troops had gained a mere 8 km/5 mi. More than half a million men perished.

Yrigoyen, Hipólito [eerigohzhen] *Irigoyen, Hipólito*

Ysselmeer *Ijsselmeer*

yttrium [yitrium] Y, element 39, density 4·5 g/cm^3, melting point 1522°C. A relatively rare element occurring in ores of the lanthanide elements, many of whose properties it shares. Its compounds have interesting electrical and magnetic properties. It is a constituent of many superconducting ceramics, eg $YBa_2Cu_3O_7$.

Yuan dynasty [yooan] or **Mongol dynasty** (1279–1368) A short ruling Chinese dynasty founded by Kublai Khan (1264), who took the name Yuan in 1271 and conquered the Song dynasty in 1279. The period facilitated two-way cultural diffusion, since China was part of a great empire from the Pacific to the Black Sea. There were significant developments in astronomy, medicine, shipbuilding, and technology; a vernacular literary genre evolved, with new dramatic forms; and major mathematical and geographical works were published. After Kublai's death in 1307, Yuan power rapidly declined. Civil war between Mongol princes broke out in 1328, and the dynasty was eventually overthrown by a Chinese uprising led by Zhu Yuanzhang, the first Ming emperor.

Yuan Shikai [yüan sheekiy], also spelled **Yuan Shih-k'ai** (1859–1916) Chinese soldier, statesman, and president (1912–16), born in Xiancheng, Henan, NC China. He served in the army and became imperial adviser, minister in Korea (1885–94), and Governor of Shantung (1900). Banished after the death of his patron, the Empress Dowager Ci-Xi (1908), he was recalled after the successful Wuhan nationalist rising in 1911, and became the first President of China in 1912. He lost support by procuring the murder of the parliamentary leader of the Nationalists, accepting Japan's Twenty-One Demands of 1915, and proclaiming himself emperor (1915), and was overthrown in a Japanese-backed rebellion.

Yucatán [yukatahn] pop (2000e) 1 640 000; area 38 402 sq km/ 14 823 sq mi. State in SE Mexico, on the N Yucatán peninsula, bounded N by the Gulf of Mexico; a third covered by forests; savannah vegetation in drier NW; capital, Mérida; primary world producer of henequen in early 20th-c; grain, tropical fruit, sisal, fishing, timber, sea salt, textiles, tobacco, brewing, tourism; numerous Mayan ruins, including Chichén Itzá and Uxmal; site of Indian rebellions (**Caste War of Yucatán**, 1847–1901); the name also often given to the whole peninsula, including the states of Quintana Roo and Campeche.

yucca An evergreen plant native to the USA, Mexico, and the Caribbean; somewhat palm-like in appearance, trunk short, thick; leaves sword-shaped; flowers night-scented, white, bell-shaped and hanging, in spikes, in a large pyramidal inflorescence. It forms a symbiotic association with a small moth, which lays eggs in the ovary then deliberately presses a ball of pollen onto the stigma of the flower to ensure fertilization and production of seeds, some of which form food for its larvae. Several species are grown as ornamentals. (Genus: *Yucca*, 40 species. Family: Agavaceae.)

Yugoslavia A state which arose out of the unification of Serbs, Croats, and Slovenes under one monarch in 1918. The formation of the new state did not quell long-held nationalist feelings, and in an attempt to create a sense of common patriotism King Alexander changed the kingdom's name to Yugoslavia in 1929. A period of civil war followed between Serbian royalists (Chetniks), Croatian nationalists, and Communists. Yugoslavia was occupied by Germany in World War 2, and a Federal People's Republic was established under Tito in 1945, consisting of Bosnia and Herzegovina, Croatia, Macedonia, Montenegro, Serbia, and Slovenia. Following a break with the USSR in 1948, the country followed an independent form of Communism and a general policy of non-alignment. At the end of the 1980s political disagreement between the federal republics increased. A Slovenian unilateral declaration of independence in 1990 was followed by Macedonian and Croatian declarations in 1991, considered illegal by the central government. Inter-republic talks on Yugoslavia's future followed, but confrontation between Croatia and the Serb-dominated National Army developed into civil war in 1991 (see Yugoslavian Civil War). The remaining two republics, Serbia and Montenegro, formed the Federal Republic of Yugoslavia in 1992, and the name Yugoslavia disappeared when this state changed its name to the Union of Serbia and Montenegro in 2003.

Yugoslavian Civil War (1991–5) A conflict resulting from the declaration of independence by Slovenia, Macedonia, and Croatia, considered illegal by the central Yugoslav government. The first major European conflict since World War 2, it began as a confrontation between Croatia and the Serb-dominated national army, and developed into civil war. Croatian independence was internationally recognized in 1991, but fighting continued between Croats and Muslims in Bosnia, and between Croats and Serb guerrillas in Krajina (a Serb-dominated enclave in Croatia), who wished to see the area as part of a 'Greater Serbia'. UN recognition of Bosnia-Herzegovina independence in 1992 was opposed by Serbs. UN sanctions were imposed on Yugoslavia (and suspension from the UN) following its support of Serb guerrillas in Bosnia and the Serbian policy of 'ethnic cleansing' (driving Muslims from areas shared with ethnic Serbs). Croatian-dominated Western Herzegovina proclaimed itself autonomous, raising the possibility of a 'Greater Croatia'. Continued fighting throughout 1993, despite several rounds of negotiations. Internationally sponsored plan then introduced 'safe areas' for Muslims in Bosnia, to be monitored by a UN Protection Force. Serb attacks on Sarajevo, 1994, led to NATO ultimatum, imposition of a 'no-fly' zone, and NATO bombing of Serb forces in response to attacks on safe areas, but with little military effect. In 1995, Serbs captured Muslim safe-area enclave of Srebrenica, which brought reports of major atrocities. Successful Croatian offensive in Krajina and NW Bosnia restored territorial balance in the area. Serb attack on Sarajevo led to NATO/UN attacks on Bosnian Serb targets, and Serb withdrawal. Ceasefire arranged (Oct) and a peace treaty was signed in Dayton, Ohio (Nov). Bosnia was to stay a single state, made up of the Bosnian–Croat Federation and the Bosnian Serb Republic, with a united Sarajevo, and the establishment of a NATO peace implementation force. An International Criminal Tribunal was set up by the UN Security Council in 1993 in The Hague. Teams of investigators have uncovered traces of massacres of civilians in the war-torn areas. A number of the 30 or so Bosnians, Croatians, and Serbs who have been apprehended have been tried for crimes against humanity, and sentenced to imprisonment.

Yukawa, Hideki [yukahwa] (1907–81) Physicist, born in Tokyo, Japan. He studied at Kyoto University, where he became a lecturer (1929–33), before moving to Osaka (1933–9). Professor of physics at Kyoto University (1939–50) and director of Kyoto Research Institute (1953–70), he was visiting professor at Princeton and Columbia universities (1948–53). He predicted (1935) the existence of the meson, a particle hundreds of times heavier than the electron, developed a theory of strong nuclear forces, and for his work on quantum theory and nuclear physics was awarded the Nobel Prize for Physics in 1949, the first Japanese to be so honoured.

Yukon [yookon] pop (2000e) 31 100; area 483 450 sq km/186 660 sq mi. Territory in NW Canada; boundary includes Alaska (W), Mackenzie Bay and Beaufort Sea (N); area of plateaux and mountain ranges, rising to 5950 m/19 521 ft at Mt Logan; Selwyn Mts in the E; tundra in N; drained by the Yukon R and tributaries (S), Peel and Porcupine Rivers (N); several lakes; capital, Whitehorse; other towns include Watson Lake, Dawson City; minerals (gold, silver, zinc, lead, copper), hydroelectric power; indigenous peoples include Inuit, Tlingit, and Athapaskan speaking nations; Hudson's Bay Company fur-trading post, 1842; gold prospectors from 1873; district of Northwest Territories, 1895; separate territory when Klondike gold rush at its height, 1898; governed by a 5-member Executive Council appointed from a 16-member elected Legislative Assembly.

Yukon River Major river in North America, in Yukon territory and Alaska; rises in the Rocky Mts, flows generally NW then W and SW through C Alaska, veering NW to enter the Bering Sea in a wide delta near Alakanuk; length to the head of the longest headstream (the Nisutlin) 3185 km/1979 mi; navigable to Dawson for large vessels; widens in NE Alaska into the Yukon Flats (15–30 km/10–20 mi wide for c.320 km/200 mi); ice-bound most of the year (Oct–Jun); a major transportation route during the Klondike gold rush (1897–8).

Yunupingu, Mandawuy [yunupinggoo, mandawoy] (1956–) Singer, born in Yirrkala, a former Methodist mission in NE Arnhem Land, Northern Territory, Australia. He studied education at Deakin University, and became principal of the local school, one of the first Aboriginal headmasters in the country. A member of one of the leading families in the Gumatj clans, in 1986 he established the group *Yothu Yindi* ('mother–child' in Yolngu-matha). Since then the group has achieved wide success in terms of sales, critical acclaim, and promotion of a political message. In 1993 he was made Australian of the Year, an honour also bestowed on his brother **Galarrwuy** in 1978.

Yurak *Nenets*

Yu Shan [yü shahn], Eng **Mount Morrison** Highest peak on Taiwan, and the highest in NE Asia; in the island's C range; height 3997 m/13 113 ft.

YWCA Abbreviation of **Young Women's Christian Association**, a charity formed in London in 1877 by the joining of a prayer union and a home for nurses travelling to and from the Crimean War (both established 1855). The movement spread to the USA in 1866, and a world organization was set up in 1892; it is now active in over 100 countries.

Zabaleta, Nicanor [thabalayta] (1907–93) Harpist, born in San Sebastian, N Spain. He studied in Madrid and Paris, where he made his debut in 1925. He was influential in popularizing the harp's solo repertory, and several composers wrote works for him.

Zabrze [zabuhrzhe], Ger **Hindenburg** 50°18N 18°47E, pop (2000e) 202 000. Mining and industrial city in Katowice voivodship, S Poland, W of Katowice; second largest city in upper Silesian industrial region; railway; coal mining, iron and steel, mining machinery.

Zacharias *Zechariah, Book of*

Zacynthus [zakinthus], Gr **Zákinthos** pop (2000e) 34 200; area 406 sq km/157 sq mi. Third largest of the Ionian Is, W Greece; length 40 km/25 mi; capital, Zacynthus; devastated by earthquakes in 1953; rugged W coast, hilly E coast, fertile C plain; currants, tourism.

Zadar [zadah(r)], Ital **Zara** 44°07N 15°14E, pop (2000e) 124 600. Seaport and resort town in Croatia, on the Adriatic; airfield; railway; car ferries to Ancona (Italy); conquered by Venice, 1000; passed to Austria, 1797; enclave of Italy, 1920–47; tourism, maraschino liqueur, glass, cigarettes; many Venetian buildings, Franciscan friary, cathedral, Roman remains at nearby Nin; summer festival of music.

Zadkine, Ossip [zadkeen] (1890–1967) Sculptor, born in Smolensk, W Russia. He settled in Paris in 1909, and developed an individual Cubist style, making effective use of the play of light on concave surfaces, as in 'The Three Musicians' (1926), 'Orpheus' (1940), and the war memorial in Rotterdam, entitled 'The Destroyed City' (1952).

Zadokites [zaydokiyts] Descendants of Zadok, a priest apparently of Aaronic lineage and of the family of Eleazar, who opposed the conspiracy of Abiathar against Solomon and was appointed high priest, serving in Solomon's temple. His family continued to hold this office until Jerusalem fell in 587 BC, and again later in the Second Temple period until the office became a political appointment of the occupying power under Antiochus IV (c.171 BC). The Qumran community continued to look for a renewal of the Zadokite priesthood, and described its own priestly members in these terms. Some derive 'Sadducees' from Zadokites.

Zagreb [zagreb], Ger **Agram**, Hung **Zágráb**, ancient **Andautonia** 45°48N 15°58E, pop (2000e) 724 600. Capital city of Croatia; on R Sava; Croat cultural centre; airport; railway; university (1669); electrical equipment, paper, textiles, carpets, light engineering; St Mark's Church, cathedral, ethnographical museum; trade fairs (Apr, Sep), tourism congress (Apr), international folk festival (Jul), Zagreb music and drama evenings (Jul–Sep).

Zagros Mountains [zagros] Major mountain system of W Iran, extending c.1770 km/1100 mi from the Turkish–Soviet frontier SE along the Persian Gulf; highest point, Mt Sabalan (4811 m/15 784 ft); large basins (NW), including L Urmia; series of parallel ridges separated by deep valleys (C); bare rock and sand dunes (SE); major oil fields lie along W foothills; crossed by the Trans-Iranian railway.

Zaharias, Babe *Didrikson, Babe*

Zaire *Congo, Democratic Republic of*

Zaire, River *Congo, River*

zakat [zakat] The alms tax obligatory on all Muslims to benefit the poor and needy; the third of the five 'pillars' of Islam. Traditionally, it consisted of a 2·5% annual levy on income and capital.

Zakopane [zakopane] 49°17N 19°54E, pop (2000e) 30 500. Chief town and winter sports resort in the High Tatra Mts, S Poland, S of Kraków; altitude 800–900 m/2600–3000 ft; railway; health resort, mountaineering; autumn festival, international festival of highland folklore (Sep).

Zambezi [zambeezee] or **Zambesi, River**, Port **Zambeze** River in SE Africa, flowing through Angola, Zimbabwe, Zambia, Namibia, and Mozambique; one of Africa's major rivers, length c.2700 km/1700 mi; rises in NW Zambia, and flows in a large 'S' shape generally SE; forms the Zambia–Namibia border (the Caprivi Strip); on the Zimbabwe–Zambia border are the Victoria Falls, L Kariba, and Kariba Dam; enters the Mozambique Channel as a marshy delta 210 km/130 mi NE of Beira; its middle course explored by Livingstone in the early 1850s.

Zambezi expedition [zambeezee] An official British expedition (1858–64), led by David Livingstone, to investigate the potentiality of the R Zambezi for steamship communication with the interior of Africa, in order to promote the destruction of the slave trade, its replacement by 'legitimate' commerce, and the extension of missionary activity in the region. The expedition was a failure: the Zambezi was found to be non-navigable, Livingstone's relations with his associates were difficult and helped to thwart the scientific objectives, and the earliest missionary endeavours met with disaster.

Zambia *p.1683*

Zamboanga or **Zamboanga City** [sambohangga] 6°55N 122°05E, pop (2000e) 542 000. Seaport in Zamboanga Del Sur province, W Mindanao, Philippines; founded, 1635; airfield; timber, copra, brass, tourism; Fort Pilar (17th-c); Bale Zamboanga Festival (Feb).

Zamenhof, L(azarus) L(udwig) [zamenof], pseudonym **Doktoro Esperanto** (1859–1917) Oculist and philologist, born in Białystok, NE Poland. A pioneering advocate of an international language to promote world peace, he invented Esperanto ('One who hopes') in 1887. The first international Esperanto congress was held in 1905, and although he often spoke at this and later conferences, he would not accept formal leadership of the movement.

Zamyatin, Yevgeny Ivanovich [zamyatin], also spelled **Zamiatin** (1884–1937) Writer, born in Lebedyan, W Russia. In 1914 he wrote a novella, *At the World's End*, satirizing the life of army officers, and was tried but acquitted of 'maligning the officer corps'. He lived in Newcastle upon Tyne in 1916–17, where he wrote two satires on the English, *Islanders* and *A Fisher of Men*, both set in Newcastle. Although supportive of the 1917 revolution, he was also an outspoken critic, and he was among the first writers to be hounded by the party *apparatchiks*. In 1920 he wrote *My* (We), a fantasy set in the 26th-c AD which influenced both Huxley and Orwell. It was circulated in manuscript but never published in the USSR; it prophesied Stalinism and the totalitarian state, and led to the banning of his works. His best stories are contained in *The Dragon*, first published in English

Zambia

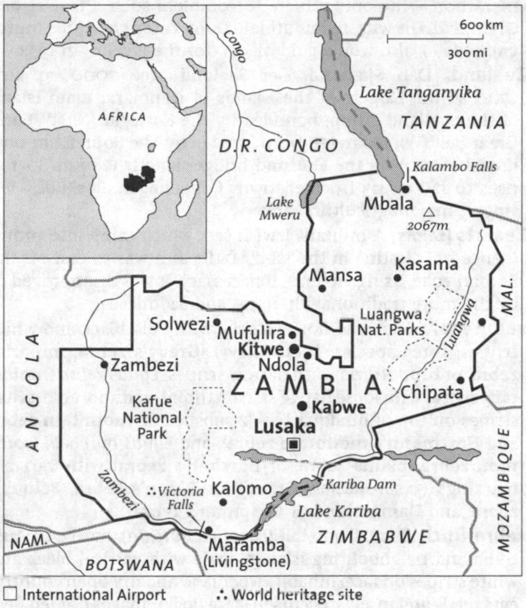

[zambia], official name **Republic of Zambia**, formerly **Northern Rhodesia** (to 1964)

Local name Zambia

Timezone GMT +2

Area 752 613 km²/290 586 sq mi

Population total (2002e) 9 959 000

Status Independent republic within the Commonwealth

Date of independence 1964

Capital Lusaka

Languages English (official), with c.70 local languages (including Tonga, Kaonde, Lunda, and Luvale) also spoken

Ethnic groups Bantu (99%), including Bemba Nyanja, Barotse, Mambwe, and Swahili peoples

Religions Christian (75%), local beliefs (23%), Muslim and Hindu (1%)

Physical features High plateau in SC Africa, altitude 1000–1400 m/3300–4600 ft; highest point, 2067 m/6781 ft, SE of Mbala; a number of rivers drain southwards to join Zambezi R in N, including R Luangwa; highest waterfall, Kalambo Falls, 221 m/726 ft; artificial L Kariba in S, 440 km²/170 sq mi.

Climate Warm temperate climate on plateau; tropical in lower valleys; although in C Africa and subequatorial, protected from very high temperatures by altitude; three distinct seasons, hot, dry (Aug–Oct), warm, wet (Nov–Apr), dry, cool (May–Jul); average annual temperatures, 21°C (Jan), 16°C (Jul) in Lusaka; average annual rainfall 840 mm/33 in.

Currency 1 Kwacha (K) = 100 ngwee

Economy Based on copper and cobalt, (provide over 50% of national income); lead, zinc, tobacco, coal; corn, tobacco, rice, sugar cane, groundnuts, cotton; sugar refining, glassware, tyres, brewing, oil refining.

GDP (2002) $8·24 bn, per capita $800

Human Development Index (2002) 0·433

History European influence followed Livingstone's discovery of the Victoria Falls, 1855; administered by the British South Africa Company under Rhodes; Northern and Southern Rhodesia declared a British sphere of influence, 1889–90; became Northern Rhodesia, 1911; British Crown Colony, 1924; joined with Southern Rhodesia and Nyasaland as the Federation of Rhodesia and Nyasaland, 1953; Federation dissolved, 1963; independence as the Republic of Zambia, 1964; governed by a President and National Assembly; new multi-party constitution adopted in 1991.

Head of State/Government (President)
1964–91 Kenneth Kaunda
1991–2002 Frederick Chiluba
2002– Levy Mwanawasa
(Vice-President)
1989–91 Malimba Masheke
1991–4 Levy Mwanawasa
1994–7 Godfrey Miyanda
1997–2001 Christon Tembo
2001– Enoch Kavindele

in 1966. With Gorky's help he was allowed to leave Russia in 1931, and he settled for exile in Paris.

zander Freshwater fish (*Stizostedion lucioperca*) found in large rivers and lakes of E Europe; length up to c.1 m/3¾ ft; greenish-grey on back, underside white; a voracious predator, feeding on a variety of other fishes; exploited commercially in some regions, and popular as a sport fish; also called **pikeperch**. (Family: Percidae.)

zang A term used in traditional Chinese medicine for the solid organs which are governed by the yin: the kidney, lung, liver, heart, and spleen. However, these organs do not correspond exactly with the corresponding anatomical Western definitions, and have functions attributed to them which are not described in Western physiology.

Zangwill, Israel (1864–1926) Writer, born in London, UK. He studied at London University, and became a journalist, as editor of the comic journal *Ariel*. He was widely known for his novels on Jewish themes, such as *Children of the Ghetto* (1892, dramatized by him in 1899) and *Ghetto Tragedies* (1893). Other works include the play *The Melting Pot* (1908), whose title became widely used as a defining label for the view of 20th-c USA which saw European immigrants being transformed into a new nation. He formed the Jewish Territorial Organization for the Settlement of the Jews Within the British Empire, of which he was president (1905–25), and was also an active supporter of the suffragettes.

Zante [zantay] *Zacynthus*

Zanuck, Darryl F(rancis) [zanuhk] (1902–79) Film producer, born in Wahoo, Nebraska, USA. He started as a scriptwriter with Warner Brothers, and soon became executive producer. He led the change to sound with *The Jazz Singer* (1927), his other notable productions of that period including *Little Caesar* (1930), *The Grapes of Wrath* (1940), and *How Green Was My Valley?* (1941). He co-founded Twentieth-Century Pictures (1933) and, after its merger with Fox Films in 1935, was controlling executive of Twentieth-Century Fox Films Corporation (president from 1965). Among his many successful titles are *The Longest Day* (1962), *Those Magnificent Men in Their Flying Machines* (1965), and *The Sound of Music* (1965). He retired in 1971.

Zanzibar (city) [zanzibah(r)] 6°10S 39°12E, pop (2000e) 203 000. Capital of Zanzibar I, Tanzania, on the W coast; airfield; cigarettes, cloves, clove oil, lime oil, crafts; Beit El Ajaib palace (1833), Dr Livingstone's residence. Stone Town, the old city and cultural heart of Zanzibar, is a world heritage site.

Zanzibar (island) [zanzibah(r)] pop (2000e) 494 000; area 1554 sq km/971 sq mi. Island region of Tanzania, including several offshore islands, such as Tumbatu (NW) and Kwale (SW); separated from the mainland by the 40 km/25 mi-wide Zanzibar Channel; length, 85 km/53 mi; width, 39 km/24 mi; highest point, 118 m/387 ft; capital, Zanzibar; populated by Bantu-speaking peoples (from the mainland), Shiraz Persians, and

Arabs; largely Islamic since the 10th-c; developed under Omani Arab rule into the commercial centre of the W Indian Ocean, 17th-c; now a world centre of clove production; mainland Zanzibari territories annexed by Germany from 1885; British protectorate, 1891; independence, 1963; ruling Sultanate overthrown in 1964, and the People's Republic of Zanzibar created; joined with Tanganyika, Zanzibar, and Pemba to form the United Republic of Tanganyika and Zanzibar, later the United Republic of Tanzania; federal regime introduced for the two regions, 1993.

Zapata, Emiliano [sapahta] (1879–1919) Mexican revolutionary, born in Anencuilio, SC Mexico. He became a sharecropper and local leader, and after the onset of the Mexican Revolution he mounted a land distribution programme in areas under his control. Along with Pancho Villa, he fought the Carranza government, and was eventually lured to his death at the Chinameca hacienda.

Zaporozhye [zapuhrozhye], formerly **Aleksandrovsk** (to 1921) 47°50N 35°10E, pop (2000e) 881 000. River-port capital of Zaporozhskaya oblast, Ukraine, on R Dnepr; founded as a fortress, 1770; airfield; railway; major industrial and energy-producing centre; iron and steel, aluminium, cars, clothing, foodstuffs, hydroelectric power.

Zapotecs A pre-Columbian Middle American Indian civilization of S Mexico (300 BC–AD 300), influenced by Olmec culture. It was centred on Monte Alban, a ceremonial site located on a high ridge in the Valley of Oaxaca.

Zappa, Frank, popular name of **Francis Vincent Zappa** (1940–93) Avant-garde rock musician and composer, born in Baltimore, Maryland, USA. He played guitar in a high school blues and rock band and briefly studied music theory in college. He led the satirical 'underground' band The Mothers of Invention (with varying line-ups) in the 1960s and 1970s, making inventive and often scabrous albums such as *Freak-Out!* (1966) and *We're Only in it for the Money* (1967, a parody of the Beatles' *Sergeant Pepper* album). Influential solo albums included *Lumpy Gravy* (1968) and *Hot Rats* (1969); and from various new groupings of Mothers came *Just Another Band from LA*, *Over-Nite Sensation*, and more. He created and scored the film *200 Motels*, and composed 'serious' music, performed by Zubin Mehta, Pierre Boulez, and others.

Zarathustra *Zoroaster*

Zaria [zaria] 11°01N 7°44E, pop (2000e) 420 000. Town in Kaduna state, SW Nigeria, 145 km/90 mi SW of Kano; founded, 16th-c; airfield; railway junction; university (1962); engineering, tanning, printing, textiles, trade in sugar, groundnuts, cotton.

Zarqa [zah(r)ka] 32°04N 36°05E, pop (2000e) 700 000. Industrial town in Amman governorate, East Bank, N Jordan; site of major industrialization programme; large phosphate reserves nearby; airfield; railway; oil refining, tanneries, thermal centre.

zarzuela [thah(r)thwayla] A type of popular Spanish opera with spoken dialogue. The name derives from the palace near Madrid (now the king's residence) where the genre was first staged in the 17th-c.

Zaslavskaya, Tatyana Ivanova [zaslavskaya] (1927–) Economist and sociologist, born in Kiev, Ukraine. She studied at Moscow University, and wrote the 'Novosibirsk Memorandum' (1983), a criticism of the Soviet economic system which was one of the factors behind policy change in Russia in the late 1980s. She joined the Communist Party in 1954, and has been a full member of the Soviet Academy of Sciences since 1981. She was personal adviser to President Gorbachev on economic and social matters. As an academic, she has been involved in the development of economic sociology.

Zatopek, Emil [zatopek] (1922–2000) Athlete and middle-distance runner, born in Kopřivnice, E Czech Republic. After many successes in Czechoslovak track events, he won the gold medal for the 10 000 m at the 1948 Olympics in London. For the next six years, despite an astonishingly laboured style, he proved himself to be the greatest long-distance runner of his time, breaking 13 world records. In the 1952 Olympics in Helsinki he achieved a remarkable golden treble: he retained his gold medal in the 10 000 m, and also won the 5000 m and the marathon – the only athlete to complete such a feat at one Olympiad. His wife, fellow athlete **Dana Zatopkova** (*née* **Ingrova**) (1922–), also won a gold medal (for the javelin) in 1952.

Zealand, Dan **Sjælland**, Ger **Seeland** area 7000 sq km/2700 sq mi. Largest of the islands of Denmark, main island of the Sjælland group; bounded by the Kattegat (N, NW) and Great Belt (W); separated from Sweden by The Sound, but now linked (2000) by the Øresund bridge; length 128 km/80 mi; rises to 126 m/413 ft; chief towns Copenhagen, Roskilde, Helsingør; major agricultural area.

Zealots [zelots] A militant Jewish sect which came into prominence in Palestine in the 1st-c AD. Its aim was to cast off the Roman yoke, using violence if necessary. It was disapproved of by the more traditional Pharisees and Sadducees.

zebra An African wild horse; stocky with bold black and white stripes; three species: *Equus grevyi* (**Grevy's zebra**, **imperial zebra**, or **hippotigris**) with narrow stripes; *Equus zebra* (**mountain zebra**) with loose flap of skin on throat, and short crosswise stripes on top of hindquarters (2 subspecies: **mountain zebra** and **Hartmann's mountain zebra**); and *Equus burchelli* (**common zebra**, **plains zebra**, or **Burchell's zebra**) with variable markings (3 subspecies: **Grant's** or **Böhm's zebra**, **Selous's zebra**, and **Damaraland** or **Chapman's zebra**).

zebra finch A small waxbill (*Poephila guttata*), native to Australia and neighbouring islands; male with vertical black and white stripes on face; inhabits woodland and dry open country; eats seeds and insects; occurs in large flocks; makes domed nest from twigs and grass; kept widely as a cage bird.

zebra fish Small, colourful fish (*Therapon jarbua*) locally common in shallow inshore waters and estuaries of the Indian Ocean and W Pacific; length up to 30 cm/1 ft; grey to silver with dark horizontal banding; a good aquarium fish, also exploited as a food fish in Japan. (Family: Theraponidae.)

zebrass An animal resulting from the mating of a male zebra and a female ass.

zebu [zeeboo] S Asian domestic cattle (introduced elsewhere); usually pale with upturned horns; fatty hump on shoulders; heavy hanging skin along throat; pendulous ears; traditionally considered sacred in India; more resistant to tropical diseases than European breeds; also known as **Brahman cattle** or **humped cattle**. (*Bos taurus*, sometimes called *Bos indicus*.)

Zebulun, tribe of [zebyoolun] One of the 12 tribes of ancient Israel, purportedly descended from the sixth son of Jacob by Leah. Its territory was in N Israel, a fertile part of later 'Galilee' between the sea of Galilee and the Mediterranean coast, but buffered on each side by other tribes; to the S it was bounded by the tribes of Issachar and Manasseh.

Zechariah or **Zacharias, Book of** [zekariya] One of 12 so-called 'minor' prophetic writings of the Hebrew Bible/Old Testament, attributed to Zechariah, writing c.520–518 BC after returning to Jerusalem from exile. It presents visions of the building of Jerusalem's Temple and of a new messianic age. Chapters 9–14, however, are often considered the work of later hands (c.3rd–5th-c BC), when the Temple rebuilding was no longer in view and when increasing disillusionment gave rise to stronger hopes for the future vindication of Israel.

Zeebrugge [zaybruguh] 51°20N 3°12E. Belgian ferry port, the scene of a major shipping disaster in March 1987, when the Townsend Thoresen ferry, *Herald of Free Enterprise*, foundered just outside the harbour, with the loss of 193 lives. The accident resulted from the main car deck doors having been left open to the sea. An official inquiry held four crew members and the ferry's operators to have been at fault in events leading to the capsize, and several recommendations to ensure future safety were made.

Zeeland [zaylant] pop (2000e) 376 000; land area 1786 sq km/689 sq mi. Province in West Netherlands, bounded on the S by Belgium and on the W by the North Sea, in the estuary area of the Rhine, Maas and Schelde Rivers; capital, Middelburg; other chief towns, Flushing, Breskens, Terneuzen; arable farming, fishing; entire area has been reclaimed from the sea by artificial dykes, and is mostly below sea-level; 'Delta Plan' intended to prevent a recurrence of the disastrous flooding of 1953, with sea and river dykes being strengthened and raised.

Zeeman, Sir Erik Christopher (1925–) British mathematician. He studied at Cambridge, and became professor of mathematics at Warwick University (1964–88). Early work developing topology and catastrophe theory produced many applications to physics, social sciences, and economics. He became principal of Hertford College, Oxford (1988–95), and was knighted in 1991.

Zeeman, Pieter (1865–1943) Physicist, born in Zonnemaire, The Netherlands. He studied at Leyden under Lorentz, became a lecturer there (1890), and was appointed professor at Amsterdam (1900), and director of the Physical Institute (1908). While at Leyden he discovered the *Zeeman effect* – when light from a source placed in a magnetic field is examined spectroscopically, a spectral line splits into several components. This discovery supported the idea of electron spin, and has helped physicists investigate atoms, and astronomers to measure the magnetic field of stars. In 1902 he shared with Lorentz the Nobel Prize for Physics.

Zeeman effect The splitting of atomic spectral lines when light-emitting atoms are subjected to strong magnetic fields; discovered in 1897 by Pieter Zeeman. It results from the interaction of the outermost atomic electron with the field, so that what was a single spectral line without the field becomes two or more lines whose frequency spacing depends on the field strength. It is a consequence of the quantum nature of electrons in atoms. Important in understanding atomic structure, historically it supported the idea of electron spin.

Zeffirelli, Franco [zefi**re**lee] (1923–) Stage, opera, and film director, born in Florence, NC Italy. He began his career as an actor and designer (1945–51), and during the 1950s produced many operas in Italy and abroad. His stage productions include *Romeo and Juliet* at the Old Vic (1960), universally acclaimed for its originality, modern relevance, and realistic setting in a recognizable Verona, and *Who's Afraid of Virginia Woolf* (1964). He has also filmed lively and spectacular versions of *The Taming of the Shrew* (1966) and *Romeo and Juliet* (1968), and *Jesus of Nazareth* (1977) for television. Later productions include *Young Toscanini* (1988), *Hamlet* (1990), *Jane Eyre* (1996), *Tea with Mussolini* (1998), and film versions of the operas *La traviata* (1983) and *Otello* (1986).

Zeiss, Carl [tsiys] (1816–88) Optician and industrialist, born in Weimar, C Germany. In 1846 he established at Jena the factory which became noted for the production of lenses, microscopes, field glasses, and other optical instruments. His business was organized on a system whereby the workers had a share in the profits.

Zeller See [**tse**ler zay] or **Untersee** [**un**terzay] Lake in N Austria, N of the Grossglockner; an arm of the Bodensee (L Constance) to which it is connected by the R Rhine; area 4·3 sq km/2¾ sq mi; length 4 km/2½ mi; width 1·5 km/0·9 mi; maximum depth 68 m/223 ft; resorts of Zell am See, Saalbach, and Kaprun have combined to form the 'Europa Sport Region'.

Zellweger, Renée (Kathleen) [**zel**weger] (1969–) Actress, born in Katy, Texas, USA. She studied English Literature at the University of Texas, Austin, where she joined an acting class. She soon gained small parts on television, and made her film debut in *My Boyfriend's Back* (1993). Her later films include *Jerry Maguire* (1996), *Nurse Betty* (2000, Golden Globe), *Bridget Jones's Diary* (2001), *Chicago* (2002), and *Cold Mountain* (2003, Oscar and BAFTA Best Supporting Actress).

zemstvo [**zem**stvoh] An organ of rural local self-government established in Russia following the emancipation of the serfs (1861). The zemstvos consisted of elected councillors, paid officials, and professional employees responsible for such matters as local education, health care, sanitation, and public welfare. Their activities were, however, severely curtailed by the bureaucratic constraints imposed by central government.

Zen Buddhism [zen **bu**dizm] A meditation school of Buddhism introduced into Japan by monks returning from China in the 12th-c. It originated in India, spreading to China, where it incorporated elements of Taoism. Zen stresses the personal experience of enlightenment based on a simple life lived close to nature, and upon methods of meditation which avoid complicated rituals and abstruse thought. In Japan, there are two main Zen bodies: **Rinzai**, introduced by Eisai (1141–1214), and **Soto**, introduced by Dogen (1200–53). Rinzai seeks spontaneous enlightenment, while Soto teaches a form of meditation in which enlightenment is a more gradual process.

zener diode [**zee**ner **diy**ohd] A semiconductor junction diode which produces a sharply increased reverse current when the reverse bias voltage reaches a certain value; named after US physicist Clarence Zener (1905–93). This effect can occur at low reverse voltages of less than 6 volts. It is repeatable and reversible, and used in voltage stabilization circuits.

Zeng Guofan [dzeng **gwoh**fan], also spelled **Tseng Kuo-fan** (1811–72) Provincial administrator, born in Hsiang-hsiang, Hunan Province, SEC China. He suppressed the Taiping Rebellion in 1864 with a S Chinese Confucian army. Seeking to regenerate China, he supported the improvements in technical and linguistic education, including US scholarships, and the development of industries such as munitions and shipbuilding. He led negotiations with the West following the Tianjin massacre (1870). The New Life Movement in the 20th-c reflected his ideals.

zenith *nadir*

Zeno of Citium [**zee**noh, **si**shium] (c.336–c.265 BC) Philosopher, the founder of the Stoic school, born in Citium, S Cyprus. He went to Athens c.315 BC, where he attended Plato's Academy and other philosophical schools, then opened his own school at the *Stoa poikile* ('painted colonnade'), from which the name of his philosophy, Stoicism, derives.

Zeno of Elea [**zee**noh, **ee**lia] (c.490–c.420 BC) Greek philosopher, a native of Elea, Italy. A favourite disciple of Parmenides, he became known for a series of paradoxes, many of which denied the possibility of spatial division or motion. The best known is 'Achilles and the Tortoise', whose conclusion is that no matter how fast Achilles runs, he cannot overtake a tortoise, if the tortoise has a head start. The rigour and dialectical nature of his arguments influenced Socrates' philosophical technique. The paradoxes were revived as serious philosophical issues by Lewis Carroll and by Bertrand Russell.

zeolites [**zee**oliyts] A group of hydrous aluminosilicate minerals containing sodium, potassium, calcium, and barium, and formed by the alteration of feldspars. They are characterized by open framework structures into which gases, ions, and molecules can easily diffuse, and hence they are used as molecular sieves and ion exchangers for water softening. They are also important catalysts for organic reactions.

Zephaniah, Benjamin [zefa**niy**a] (1958–) Poet, born in Birmingham, West Midlands, C England, UK. He spent much of his childhood in Jamaica. A popular performance poet, he has toured throughout the UK, Europe, and the Caribbean. His first book, *Pen Rhythms* (1981), was followed by *The Dread Affair* (1985), a passionate condemnation of aggression. He has also worked with several Jamaican reggae bands, including the Wailers. He has recorded his poetry in the albums *Big Boys Don't Make Girls Cry*, *Free South Africa*, and *Us and Dem*.

Zephaniah, Book of [zefa**niy**a] One of 12 so-called 'minor' prophetic writings of the Hebrew Bible/Old Testament, attributed to Zephaniah, son of Cushi and descendant of Hezekiah, active in Josiah's reign (7th-c BC), but unknown apart from this work. It strongly denounces influences from heathen cults on Jewish religion, presumably preparing for Josiah's reforms, and proclaims God's judgment on Israel's enemies, but consolation for the remnant in Jerusalem who loyally await the 'Day of the Lord'. The mediaeval Latin hymn, *Dies irae*, was inspired by Zephaniah's account of the coming day of wrath.

Zeppelin, Ferdinand (Adolf August Heinrich), Graf von (Count of) (1838–1917) German army officer, born in Konstanz, SW Germany. He served in the Franco-Prussian War, and in 1897–1900 constructed his first airship, setting up a factory for their construction at Friedrichshafen. Over 100 *zeppelins* were used in World War 1.

Zermatt [zermat] 46°01N 7°45E, pop (2000e) 4800. Fashionable skiing resort and popular mountaineering centre in the Pennine Alps, Valais canton, S Switzerland; Matterhorn rises to the SW.

zero-emission vehicle (ZEV) A type of motor vehicle with no tailpipe pollutants. During the 1980s, approaches using alternative fuels made progress towards this goal, but only specially designed vehicles powered by electricity seem likely to achieve it.

zero grazing A feeding system where freshly-cut grass is fed to cattle, which are confined to a building, yard, or paddock, rather than being allowed to graze freely where the grass is growing. Zero grazing reduces wastage caused by fouling, poaching, and selective grazing.

zero point energy In quantum mechanics, the minimum non-zero energy of a quantum state. It is the residual energy that exists even as the temperature is reduced towards absolute zero; a consequence of the uncertainty principle.

Zeta-Jones, Catherine [zeeta] (1969–) Actress and singer, born in Swansea, SC Wales, UK. She became known through her role in the BBC television series *The Darling Buds of May* (1991), and went on to feature film success with *The Mask of Zorro* (1998) and *High Fidelity* (2000). Later films include *Traffic* (2000), in which she co-starred with husband Michael Douglas (married 2000), *Chicago* (2002, BAFTA and Oscar Best Supporting Actress), and *Intolerable Cruelty* (2003).

Zeus [zyoos] In Greek mythology, the supreme god, equivalent to Jupiter. He is usually depicted with thunderbolt and eagle, and associated with the oak-tree. Many conflicting myths have arisen from his prominence in local cults; in later Greek religion, he is almost a monotheistic concept.

Zeus, statue of [zyoos] A colossal statue, wrought in ivory and gold over a core of wood, formerly located in the Temple of Zeus at Olympia. It was one of the foremost works of the great Athenian sculptor, Phidias.

Zeuxis [zyooksis] (5th-c BC) Painter, born in Heraclea, Greece. He excelled in the representation of natural objects. According to legend, his painting of a bunch of grapes was so realistic that birds tried to eat the fruit.

ZEV *zero-emission vehicle*

Zewail, Ahmed H(assan) [zuhwayl] (1946–) Chemist and physicist, born in Egypt. He studied at Alexandria and Pennsylvania universities, then moved to California, where he joined the California Institute of Technology in 1976. His research has been in the development of ultrafast lasers and electrons for studies of dynamics in chemistry and biology, and he received the 1999 Nobel Prize for Chemistry for his studies of the transition states of chemical reactions using femtosecond spectroscopy.

Zhang Guotao [jang gwohtow], also spelled **Chang Kuo-t'ao** (1897–1979) Founding member of the Chinese Communist Party, born in Jiangxi, S China. As a student he played a part in the May Fourth Movement of 1919, and in 1921 joined the new Chinese Communist Party, rising to prominence as a labour leader. He also had a leading role in the Nanchang Mutiny (1927). He opposed the elevation of Mao Zedong as leader of the Party, but his army was destroyed by Muslim forces in the NW. He defected to the Nationalists in 1938 and, when the Communists won national power in 1949, moved to Hong Kong.

Zhang Heng [jang heng], also spelled **Chang Heng** (78–139) Chinese scientist who invented the seismograph (132). He also calculated the value of π, built an armillary sphere with horizon and meridian rings, and realized natural phenomena were not caused by the supernatural. He understood the Earth was spherical, and that the Moon was lit by the Sun, revolved around the Earth, and was eclipsed by Earth's shadow. He explained the shortening/lengthening of days, and invented the grid system in cartography.

Zhang Yimou, sometimes credited as **Yi-Mou Zhang** (1951–) Film director and actor, born in Xian, C China. During the Cultural Revolution (1966–76) he was sent to work in a small village N of Xian and later to a cotton mill. He then struggled to be admitted to the Beijing Film Academy, and became one of the first group of students to be accepted after it re-opened in 1978. It was from this group that China's 'Fifth Generation' of filmmakers was born. In 1986 he started work at the Xian Film Studios, where he played the lead in Wu Tianming's *Lao jing* (1986, Old Well), for which he won the Best Actor Award at the 1987 Tokyo International Film Festival. His debut as a director came in 1987 with *Hong gao liang* (Red Sorghum), which won him critical acclaim and was also a box office success both nationally and internationally. Later films include *Yi Ge Dou Bu Neng Shao* (1999, Not One Less) and *Wo De Fu Qin Mu Qin* (2000, The Road Home).

Zhdanov *Mariupol*

Zhengzhou [juhngjoh], **Chengchow**, or **Cheng-chou** 34°35N 113°38E, pop (2000e) 2 003 000, administrative region 6 147 000. Capital of Henan province, NC China; on the Yellow R; major market and transportation centre; site of capital of Shang dynasty before 2000 BC; Shang period walled city; modern settlement since arrival of railway, 1898; railway junction; airfield; textiles, food processing, light engineering; Henan Provincial Museum; major archaeological remains.

Zhenjiang, Chen-chiang, or **Chinkiang** [juhnjiahng] 32°08N 119°30E, pop (2000e) 552 200, administrative region 2 904 000. River port in Jiangsu province, E China, at confluence of Yangtze R and Grand Canal; founded, 545 BC; a centre of Chinese Zoroastrianism, 6th–12th-c; railway; metallurgy, machinery, automobiles, ship-building, electronics, textiles, pharmaceuticals, chemicals; scenic area ('Three Hills of the Capital Gateway'); Fahaizidong (Monk Cave) and Bailongdong (White Dragon Cave); Jinshan Temple (4th-c); monastery, numerous temples, pavilions, and inscribed stone tablets on Jiao Shan Mountain (E); Dujinglou (Pavilion for Choosing Prospective Sons-in-Law), Shijianshi (Testing Swords Stone).

Zhitomir or **Jitomir** [zhitomyir] 50°18N 28°40E, pop (2000e) 293 000. Capital city of Zhitomirskaya oblast, WC Ukraine; on R Teterev, 165 km/102 mi W of Kiev; founded, 9th-c; railway junction; agricultural trade, machinery, metalworking, flax, clothing, footwear.

Zhivkov, Todor [zhivkof] (1911–98) Bulgarian statesman, prime minister (1962–71), and president (1971–89), born in Botevgrad, WC Bulgaria. He joined the (illegal) Communist Party in 1932, fought with the Bulgarian resistance in 1943, and took part in the Sofia coup that overthrew the pro-German regime in 1944. He became first secretary of the Bulgarian Communist Party in 1954, prime minister in 1962 and, as chairman of the Council of State in 1971, became effectively the president of the People's Republic. His period in office was characterized by unquestioned loyalty to the Soviet Union, and conservative policy-making, which led to mounting economic problems in the 1980s. He was eventually ousted in 1989 by the reformist Petar Mladenov in a committee-room coup and, with his health failing, was subsequently expelled from the Party, and placed under house arrest, on charges of nepotism, corruption, embezzlement of $1 million, and the dictatorial abuse of power. He was found guilty and sentenced to seven years imprisonment in 1992.

Zhou or **Chou dynasty** [joh] (1027–256 BC) The second historical Chinese dynasty. Accounts of its origins are a mixture of history and legend. It is traditionally held to have been founded by King Wu, who overthrew the last tyrannical ruler of the Shang dynasty, Zhouxin. Its capital was at Hao (near Xian) until 771 BC, and at Luoyi (near Luoyang) until its occupation by the Qin in 256 BC. A form of feudal monarchy, the Zhou saw the first flowering of Chinese historical, philosophical, and literary writing. The *Book of Songs* (*Shi Jing*) gives fuller detail on ordinary life than is known for any other ancient civilization.

Zhou Enlai [joh enliy], also spelled **Chou En-lai** (1898–1975) One of the leaders of the Communist Party of China, and prime minister of the Chinese People's Republic from its inception in 1949 until his death, born in Huaian, Kiangsu Province, E China. He was political director of the Whampoa military academy, under the command of Jiang Jieshi. In 1927 he became a member of the Politburo of the Communist Party of China, and in 1932 was appointed to succeed Mao Zedong as political commissar of the Red Army, but after 1935, following Mao's elevation, he served him faithfully, becoming the Party's chief negotiator and diplomat. As minister of foreign affairs (and concurrently prime minister) he vastly increased China's international influence. Perhaps his greatest triumph of mediation was in the Cultural Revolution in China (1966–9), when he worked to preserve national unity and the survival of government against the forces of anarchy.

Zhoukoudian or **Choukoutien** [johkohdyan] A village 55 km/34 mi SW of Beijing, where fossil human remains (originally assigned to the genus *sinanthropus* before reclassification as *Homo erectus*, and commonly known as *Peking man*) were discovered during the 1920s; a world heritage site. A wealth of other items have also been unearthed, including bead ornaments, bone implements, and imported sea shells, and are displayed in an archaeological complex. The most important Palaeolithic site in Asia, the remains are the world's oldest hominid discoveries indicating the way of life, and the earliest evidence of the deliberate use of fire for cooking.

Zhu Da [joo dah], also spelled **Chu-ta**, originally **Pa Ta Shan Jen** (c.1625–1705) Painter, and Buddhist monk, born in Nan-ch'ang, SEC China. A descendant of the Ming royal house, he entered a Buddhist monastery on the collapse of the Ming dynasty, and may have feigned madness to survive the purges of the Manchu conquerors. The individualism of his ink paintings of flowers, birds, fish, and landscapes appealed to the Japanese, and his style has become synonymous with Zen painting in Japan.

Zhu De [joo de], also spelled **Chu-teh** (1886–1976) One of the founders of the Chinese Red Army, born in Sichuan, C China. He was closely associated throughout his later career with Mao Zedong. He took part in the Nanchang Mutiny (1927), his defeated troops joining with those of Mao to found the Jiangxi Soviet. There, he and Mao evolved the idea of 'people's war', beating off attacks by vastly superior Nationalist forces until finally driven out in 1934. The Red Army then undertook the Long March, in which Zhu De was the leading commander. After the Japanese War, he was the key military strategist in the defeat of Jiang Jieshi, and from 1949 was commander-in-chief of the Chinese armed forces.

Zhu Jiang, Chu-chiang, or **Chu-kiang** [joo jiahng], Eng **Pearl River** River in S China formed by the confluence of the Xi Jiang, Bei Jiang, and Dong Jiang Rivers; forms wide estuary between Hong Kong and Macao, S of Guangzhou (Canton), flowing into the S China Sea; lengths, Xi Jiang 2197 km/1365 mi (taken as length of the Zhu Jiang itself), Bei Jiang 468 km/291 mi, Dong Jiang 523 km/325 mi; densely populated, fertile river valley; navigable as far as Wuzhou for large vessels.

Zhukov, Giorgiy Konstantinovich [zhookof] (1896–1974) Soviet marshal, born in Strelkovka, W Russia. He joined the Red Army in 1918, commanded Soviet tanks in Outer Mongolia (1939), and became army chief-of-staff (1941). He lifted the siege of Moscow, and in 1943 his counter-offensive was successful at Stalingrad. In 1944–5 he captured Warsaw, conquered Berlin, and accepted the German surrender. After the war he was commander of the Russian zone of Germany, and became minister of defence (1955), but was dismissed by Khrushchev in 1957.

Zhu Rongji [joo rongjee] (1928–) Chinese politician and prime minister (1998–). An official of the State Planning Commission in 1957, he was exiled for attacking Mao's policies, and became a farm labourer. He returned in 1962, but was purged again during the Cultural Revolution. Rehabilitated in the late 1970s, he became Mayor of Shanghai (1988–91), becoming known for his peaceful resolution of student protests there in 1989. He was appointed vice premier in 1991, and in his role as the government's chief economic policy maker (1993–8) introduced a successful austerity programme. He replaced Li Peng as premier in 1998.

Zia ul-Haq, Muhammad [zeea ul hak] (1924–88) Pakistani general and president (1978–88), born near Jullundhur, Punjab, N India. He served in Burma, Malaya, and Indonesia in World War 2, and in the wars with India (1965, 1971), rising rapidly to become general and army chief-of-staff (1976). He led a bloodless coup in 1977, imposed martial law, banned political activity, and introduced an Islamic code of law. Despite international protest, he sanctioned the hanging of former President Bhutto in 1979. He was killed in a plane crash near Bahawalpur.

Ziaur Rahman [zeeaoor ramahn] (1935–81) Bangladeshi soldier and president (1977–81). He played an important part in the emergence of the state of Bangladesh. Appointed chief of army staff after the assassination of Mujibur Rahman (1975), he became the dominant figure within the military. His government was of a military character, even after the presidential election of 1978 which confirmed his position. He survived many attempted coups, but was finally assassinated in Dhaka. His wife, **Khaleda Zia** (1945–), served as prime minister (1991–96), becoming the first woman to hold the post, and was elected again (2001–).

Zibo [tsoeboh] or **Tzu-po** 36°51N 118°01E, pop (2000e) 2 770 000, administrative region 4 287 000. City in Shandong province, E China; E of Jinan; railway; coal mining, machinery, chemicals, electrical equipment.

Zidane, Zinédine [zeedan], nickname **Zizou** (1971–) Footballer, born in Castellane, near Marseille, S France, the son of Algerian immigrant parents. He learned to play football in the streets of Marseilles, and signed as a schoolboy for Cannes FC. After a spell at Girondins de Bordeaux, he transferred to Juventus. He was a key player for his country in the 1998 FIFA World Cup Final, scoring two goals in France's 3–0 victory over Brazil, and was hailed as a national hero. He was European Footballer of the Year (1998) and FIFA World Footballer of the Year (1998, 2000, 2003). In 2001 he signed for Real Madrid for a world record transfer fee of £47·2 million.

zidovudine *AZT*

Ziegfeld, Florenz [zeegfeld] (1869–1932) Theatre manager, born in Chicago, Illinois, USA. He devised and perfected the American revue spectacle, based on the *Folies Bergères*, and his *Follies of 1907* ran for 24 editions to 1943, making his name synonymous with extravagant theatrical production. The *Follies* featured a chorus line of some of America's most beautiful women, all personally chosen to 'glorify the American girl'. He also produced a wide range of plays and other musical shows, such as *Show Boat* (1927) and *Bitter Sweet* (1929). Composers who worked with him included Irving Berlin, Gershwin, and Rogers, and the librettists Lardner and Hammerstein II.

Ziegler, Karl [zeegler] (1898–1973) Chemist, born in Helsa, C Germany. He studied at Marburg University, taught at Heidelberg and Halle, and in 1943 was appointed director of the Max Planck Carbon Research Institute at Mülheim. With Italian chemist Giulio Natta he was awarded the 1963 Nobel Prize for Chemistry for his research into long-chain polymers leading to new developments in industrial materials, such as polypropylene.

ziggurat [zigurat] A temple tower, in the shape of a mountain, found throughout ancient Sumeria and the adjacent region of Elam. It consisted of a high, pyramidal mound, constructed in stages and surmounted by a shrine. Access to the shrine was by a series of external stairways or ramps. Good examples come from Eridu, Ur, Uruk, and Choga Zanbil near Susa.

Zimbabwe

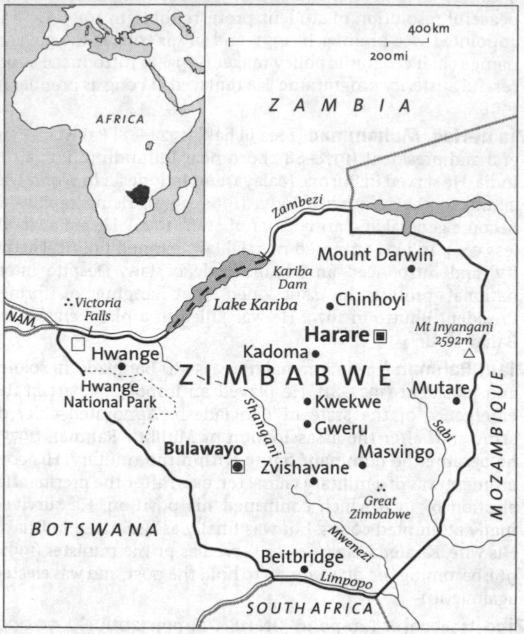

□ International Airport ∴ World heritage site

[zimbabway], official name **Republic of Zimbabwe**, formerly **Southern Rhodesia** (to 1979)

Local name Zimbabwe

Timezone GMT +2

Area 390 759 km^2/150 873 sq mi

Population total (2002e) 11 377 000

Status Independent republic within the Commonwealth

Date of independence 1980

Capital Harare

Languages English (official), Ndebele and Shona widely spoken

Ethnic groups Bantu (97%) (including Shona 71%, Ndebele 16%), European (2%)

Religions Syncretic Christian/local beliefs (50%), Christian (25%), traditional animist beliefs (24%), small Muslim minority

Physical features Landlocked country in SC Africa; mostly savannah (tropical grassland); Highveld ridge crosses SW to NE to join the Inyanga Mts on Mozambique border, highest point, Mt Inyangani, 2592 m/8504 ft; Highveld flanked by lower plateau, Middleveld; Lowveld, altitude, 300 m/1000 ft, lies NE; tropical hardwood forests (SE); chief rivers, Zambezi, Limpopo, and Sabi.

Climate Subtropical climate, strongly influenced by altitude; average annual temperature 21°C (Jan), 14°C (Jul) in Harare; average annual rainfall 828 mm/33 in; rainfall increases from SW to NE; wet season (Nov–Mar).

Currency 1 Zimbabwe Dollar (Z$) = 100 cents

Economy Agriculture (involves 70% of population), manufacturing and mining; sugar, cotton, livestock; natural resources, gold, copper, chrome, nickel, tin, asbestos; tourism to national parks; major industries in steel, textiles, vehicles, and chemicals.

GDP (2002) $26·7 bn, per capita $2100

Human Development Index (2002) 0·551

History Mediaeval Bantu kingdom during 12–16th-c, with capital at Great Zimbabwe; visited by Livingstone in the 1850s; Southern Rhodesia under British influence in the 1880s as the British South Africa Company under Cecil Rhodes; divided into Northern and Southern Rhodesia, 1911; Southern Rhodesia became a self-governing British colony, 1923; Northern and Southern Rhodesia and Nyasaland formed a multi-racial federation, 1953; independence of Nyasaland and Northern Rhodesia, 1963; opposition to the independence of Southern Rhodesia under African rule resulted in a Unilateral Declaration of Independence (UDI) by the White-dominated government, 1965; economic sanctions and internal guerrilla activity forced the government to negotiate with the main African groups: the Zimbabwe African People's Union (ZAPU), led by Joshua Nkomo, the Zimbabwe African National Union (ZANU), led by Robert Mugabe, and the United African National Council (UANC), led by Bishop Abel Muzorewa; independence as the Republic of Zimbabwe, 1980; since 1987, the post of executive President has combined the posts of Head of State and Head of Government; bicameral legislature replaced, 1990, by new single-chamber Parliament, the House of Assembly; political crisis over land redistribution, focused on white farmers, 2000 and ongoing; increasing international concern over democracy within the country, especially in relation to the election process in 2002; suspended from the Commonwealth for a year in March 2002, reaffirmed in 2003, after which Mugabe announced his country's withdrawal from the organization; sanctions extended, 2004.

Head of State/Government
1987– Robert Gabriel Mugabe

Zillertal Alps [tsilertal], Ger **Zillertaler Alpen**, Ital **Alpi Aurine** Mountain range in the E Alps of N Italy and the S Tirol of Austria; extends from the Birnlücke in the E to the Brenner in the W; the highest peak is Hochfeiler (3510 m/11 516 ft).

Zimbabwe *see panel*

Zimbabwe African National / People's Union *Patriotic Front* (Zimbabwe)

Zimmermann, Arthur [tsimerman] (1864–1940) Politician, born in Olecko, NE Poland (formerly Marggrabowa, East Prussia). After diplomatic service in China, he directed from 1904 the E division of the German foreign office, and was foreign secretary (Nov 1916–Aug 1917). In January 1917 he sent the famous **Zimmermann telegram** to the German minister in Mexico with the terms of an alliance between Mexico and Germany, by which Mexico was to attack the USA with German and Japanese assistance in return for the American states of New Mexico, Texas, and Arizona. This telegram, intercepted and decoded by British Admiralty Intelligence, finally brought the hesitant US government into the war against Germany in April 1917.

Zimmer walking frame A self-standing metal frame consisting of two double legs at the sides, joined together by a bar in front; the name derives from the US orthopaedic company which manufactures it. It is used to assist walking by elderly persons, or those with pain or weakness in the legs.

zinc Zn, element 30, density 7 g/cm^3, melting point 420°C. An active, silvery-blue metal, never occurring uncombined, but found in many minerals, especially as a sulphide. It may be recovered by roasting in air to give an oxide which is then reduced by carbon. It has been used from earliest times as an alloy with copper (*brass*), which is both stronger and less readily corroded than copper. It owes its corrosion resistance to an adherent oxide coating, and is used as a plating to protect iron (*galvanizing*). It is also used in primary batteries as an anode. In nearly all of its compounds, it has oxidation state +2. **Zinc oxide** (ZnO) is used as a pigment, filler, and mild antiseptic in cosmetics, pharmaceuticals, paints, and plastics. **Zinc sulphide** (ZnS) is used in luminous screens.

zinc blende *sphalerite*

Zinder [zinder] 13°46N 8°58E, pop (2000e) 170 000. Capital of Zinder department, SEC Niger, W Africa, 725 km/450 mi E of Niamey; on an important trade route to Kano (Nigeria); occupied by the French, 1899; colonial capital until the 1920s; airfield; tanning, food processing, power plant; market centre; Sultan's Palace (1860).

Zinjanthropus [zinjanthropus] The former name of *Australopithecus boisei*, based on a cranium found by Louis and Mary Leakey at Olduvai Gorge in 1959. It was popularly known as 'Nutcracker Man'.

Zinkernagel, Rolf M [zingkernahgel] (1944–) Immunologist, born in Basel, N Switzerland. He studied at the University of Basel and at the Australian National University, Canberra, where he worked with Peter Doherty, then became a researcher at the Institute of Experimental Immunology in Zürich. He shared the Nobel Prize for Physiology or Medicine in 1996 for his contribution to the discovery of how the immune system recognizes virus-infected cells – research which was first reported in 1974. He also shared the Paul Erlich Prize (1983) and the Albert Lasker Medical Research Award (1995) for this research.

Zinnemann, Fred [zinuhman] (1907–97) Film director, born in Vienna, Austria. He studied law at the University of Vienna (1925–7), then cinematography in Paris (1927–8). He emigrated to the USA in 1929, and began making documentary films in Hollywood, notably *That Mothers Might Live* (1938, Oscar), and *Benjy* (1951, Oscar). A recurrent theme in his films concerns the conflict of conscience and moral dilemmas of reluctant heroes, as explored in the Oscar-nominated *High Noon* (1952), and two Oscar winners, *From Here to Eternity* (1953), and *A Man For All Seasons* (1966). Other notable films included *The Sundowners* (1960) and *The Day of the Jackal* (1973).

zinnia An annual, perennial, or small shrub, distributed throughout the USA and S into South America, but predominantly Mexican; leaves in opposite pairs or whorled; chrysanthemum-like flower-heads, showy. Several are popular garden ornamentals. (Genus: *Zinnia*, 22 species. Family: Compositae.)

Zinoviev, Grigoriy Yevseyevich [zinovyef], originally **Grigoriy Yevseyevich Radomyslskiy** (1883–1936) Russian Jewish revolutionary and politician, born in Kherson province, S Ukraine. He studied at Bern University, and in 1924 was made a member of the ruling Politburo, but because of opposition to Stalin's policies was expelled from the Party (1926). Reinstated in 1928, he was again expelled in 1932, and in 1935 was arrested after the assassination of Kirov. Charged with organizing terrorist activities, he was executed following the first of Stalin's Great Purge trials in Moscow. The so-called **Zinoviev letter** urging British Communists to incite revolution in Britain contributed to the downfall of the Labour government in the 1924 general elections; fresh research reported by the Foreign Office in 1999 confirmed the view that this letter was a forgery.

Zinzendorf, Nicolaus Ludwig, Graf von (Count of) [tsintsendaw(r)f] (1700–60) Religious leader, born in Dresden, E Germany. He studied at Wittenberg, and held a government post at Dresden. He invited the persecuted Moravians to his estates, and there founded for them the colony of *Herrnhut* ('the Lord's keeping'). His zeal led to conflict with the government, and he was exiled from Saxony in 1736. Ordained at Tübingen (1734), he became Bishop of the Moravian Brethren, and wrote over 100 books.

Ziolkovsky, Konstantin Eduardovitch [zyolkofskee] (1857–1935) Engineer, born in Ijevsk, W Russia. He became a teacher in Kaluga (1892–1920), built the first wind tunnel in Russia (1891), designed large airships, and in 1903 published his first scientific paper on space flight. He continued to research designs of rocket-propelled aircraft and spacecraft, and in 1924 presented conceptual studies for manned orbital craft capable of re-entry. His outstanding work on the fundamental physics and engineering of space vehicles was recognized by the Soviet authorities, and all his works were translated into English by NASA in 1965.

Zion or **Sion** [ziyon] (Heb probably 'fortress' or 'rock') Term used in the Hebrew Bible and Jewish literature in various ways: for one of the hills in Jerusalem; for the mount on which the Temple was built; for the Temple itself; and symbolically for Jerusalem or even Israel as a whole. Today 'Mount Zion' usually denotes the SW hill in Jerusalem just S of the city wall.

Zionism The movement which sought to recover for the Jewish people their historic Palestinian homeland (the *Eretz Israel*) after centuries of dispersion. The modern movement arose in the late 19th-c with plans for Jewish colonization of Palestine, and under Theodor Herzl also developed a political programme to obtain sovereign state rights over the territory. Gaining support after World War 1, its objectives were supported by the British Balfour Declaration in 1917, as long as rights for non-Jews in Palestine were not impaired. After World War 2, the establishment of the Jewish state in 1948 received United Nations support. Zionism is still active, as a movement encouraging diaspora Jews to immigrate to and take an interest in the Jewish state.

zircon [zerkn] A zirconium silicate ($ZrSiO_4$) mineral commonly occurring in very small amounts in a wide variety of rocks. It is very hard, with a high refractive index, and is used as a gemstone. It is the principal source of zirconium.

zither A musical instrument consisting of a box strung with five fretted and about 30 open (unfretted) strings. The fretted strings are stopped by the fingers of the left hand and plucked with a plectrum worn on the right thumb; the right-hand fingers pluck the open strings. The name is also used as a generic term for a variety of instruments consisting of a string bearer with or without a separate resonator – in other words, a simple chordophone. The zither was used in China from before the 13th-c, and favoured in European Alpine societies.

Žižka, Jan [zhishka] or **Ziska, John** (c.1370–1424) Bohemian Hussite leader, born in Trocznov, Czech Republic. He fought against the Poles, Turks, and French, and soon after the murder of Huss, became chamberlain to Wenceslas IV. During the Civil War he was chosen leader of the popular party, captured Prague (1421), and erected the fortress of Tabor, his party coming to be called Taborites. Having lost both his eyes in battle, he continued to lead his troops in a series of victories, compelling Emperor Sigismund to offer the Hussites religious liberty, but he died at Przibislav before the war was over.

Zlatni Pyasăci [zlatnee pyasatsee], Eng **Golden Sands** 43°16N 28°00E. Beach resort on the Black Sea in Varna province, E Bulgaria; 17 km/10 mi NE of Varna; centre for international conferences and hydrotherapy treatment.

zodiac A zone of fixed stars, approximately 16° in width, which marks the apparent courses of the Sun, Moon, and planets (apart from Pluto) about the Earth. Early astronomers projected patterns on to this area of sky, creating 12 groupings or constellations. It is important to distinguish between constellations – rather ill-defined star groups of variable size – and *signs*, an idealized version occupying equal 30° segments. The **sidereal** zodiac moves relative to the position of the Sun at the (northern) spring equinox. The **tropical** zodiac simply takes the equinoxial position as a starting point, irrespective of the underlying constellation. Only rarely do these two zodiacs coincide. On the 21st of each month (approximately) the Sun appears to change sign in the tropical zodiac, from Aries through Taurus, Gemini, Cancer, Leo, Virgo, Libra, Scorpius (Scorpio), Sagittarius, Capricorn, Aquarius and Pisces. The disposition of the planets within the signs of the zodiac furnishes important information to the astrologer.

zodiacal light A permanent glow of light, readily visible in the tropics after sunset as a cone of light extending from the horizon. It is sunlight reflected from dust in interplanetary space.

Zoffany, John or **Johann** [tsofanee] (1734–1810) Portrait painter, born in Frankfurt (am Main), WC Germany. After studying art in Rome, he settled in London c.1758, securing royal patronage. His speciality was the conversation piece. He later lived in Florence (1772–9) and India (1783–90).

Zog I [zohg], originally **Ahmed Bey Zogu** (1895–1961) Albanian prime minister (1922–4), president (1925–8), and king (1928–39), born in Burgajet, NC Albania. He studied in Istanbul, became leader of the Nationalist Party, and formed a republican government in 1922. Forced into exile in 1924, he returned with the assistance of Yugoslavia, and became president, proclaiming himself king in 1928. After Albania was overrun by the Italians (1939), he fled to Britain, and later lived in Egypt and France. He formally abdicated in 1946.

Zohar [zohhah(r)] The main text of the Jewish Kabbalah. Discovered in Spain in the late 13th-c, it was said to be the mystical teachings of Rabbi Simeon bar Yochai and his followers, who lived in Palestine in the 2nd–3rd-c. There have always been doubts about its authenticity, but Kabbalistic tradition accepts it as genuine.

zokor *mole rat*

Zola, Emile (Edouard Charles Antoine) [zohla] (1840–1902) Novelist, born in Paris, France. He became a clerk and journalist, then began to write short stories, beginning with *Contes à Ninon* (1864, Stories for Ninon). After his first major novel, *Thérèse Raquin* (1867), he began the long series called *Les Rougon-Macquart*, a sequence of 20 books described in the subtitle as 'the natural and social history of a family under the Second Empire'. The series contains such acclaimed studies as *Nana* (1880), *Germinal* (1885), *La Terre* (1887, Earth), and *La Bête humaine* (1890, trans The Beast in Man). In 1898 he espoused the cause of Dreyfus in his open letter *J'accuse*, and was sentenced to imprisonment (1898), but escaped to England. He was given a great welcome on his return after Dreyfus had been pardoned (1899), but controversy over the affair continued to affect him until his death.

Zola, Gianfranco (1966–) Footballer, born in Oliena, Sardinia, Italy. He played for Parma, then joined Chelsea in 1996. He was also a member of the Italy national team in the Euro '96 championships, and of the Italy World Cup squad in 2002. He joined Sardinian club Cagliari for the 2003–4 season.

Zollverein [tsolferiyn] A German customs union, based on the enlarged Prussia of 1814, and officially constituted in 1834. It comprised all of Germany save the Austrian Empire, Hanover, Brunswick, Oldenburg, and three N maritime states: a total of 17 states embracing 26 million people. It represented an important stage in the German unification process.

zone plate In optics, a form of flat lens comprising alternating dark and transparent rings. Interference between light emerging from various transparent rings produces focusing. Zone plates of appropriate material are useful as lenses for microwaves and X-rays, for which glass lenses are useless.

zoogeography [zohuhjiografee] The study of the past and present geographical distribution of animals and animal communities. Hypotheses which explain these distribution patterns include dispersal (by migration or accidental transport) and separation by vicariance events (the formation of natural barriers to the spread of animals, especially by geological forces such as the spreading of the plates of the Earth's crust).

zoology The branch of biology dealing with the study of animals. It includes their anatomy, behaviour, ecology, evolution, genetics, and physiology.

zoom A visual effect in motion pictures or video, enlarging or diminishing the image as though rapidly approaching or receding. Originally made by actual camera movement, it is now provided by a **zoom lens** whose focal length, and hence its magnification, can be continuously varied. The range can be as much as 10:1, so that a single lens can function as wide-angle and telephoto. Zoom lenses are now standard for all video cameras, and are widely used in cinematography; they are sometimes fitted to portable projectors to give variable magnification for different screen sizes and distances.

zoom flash A design of electronic flash unit where the flash tube is moved backwards and forwards in its reflector behind a Fresnel lens used to spread and diffuse the light emitted on to the subject. This movement broadens or narrows the spread of light on the subject from the flash unit to suit a wide-angle or telephoto lens respectively. The action can be motorized and controlled by the focal length setting of a zoom lens on the camera. Alternatively, the flashgun coverage can be set manually to suit the lens in use.

zooplankton *plankton*

zoosemiotics [zohohsemiotiks] The science of animal communication. Combining semiotics and ethology, this interdisciplinary field seeks to understand the many complex systems of meaning employed by animals. It includes the study of acoustic, visual, and chemical systems of communication, in such domains as bird call, bee-dancing, marine echolocation, cat and dog facial expressions, primate cries, and grasshopper signals. The term was coined in 1963 by the US linguist Thomas A Sebeok (1920–2001).

Zorach, William [zawrakh] (1887–1966) Sculptor and painter, born in Eurburick-Kovno, Lithuania. His family emigrated in 1891, and settled in Cleveland, OH, where he was apprenticed to a lithographer. He moved to New York City (1907), attended the Art Students League and the National Academy of Design (1908–9) and, after study in France (1910–11), produced Fauvist style paintings. Based in New York, he focused on sculpture (1922), carving directly in stone and wood, as in 'Floating Figure' (1922). He taught at the Art Students League (1929–60), and wrote several books on sculpture.

zorilla [thoreelya] An African mammal (*Ictonyx striatus*) of family Mustelidae; long coat and long brush-like tail; black with white markings on face, long white stripes along body; superficially resembles the skunk, and may squirt foul-smelling fluid; also known as **striped polecat**.

Zorn, Anders (Leonhard) (1860–1920) Etcher, sculptor, and painter, born in Mora, C Sweden. He studied at Stockholm, travelled widely, returning to Mora in 1896. His paintings deal mainly with Swedish peasant life. He achieved European fame as an etcher, known for his series of nudes, and for his portraits.

Zoroaster [zorohaster], Greek form of **Zarathustra** (6th-c BC) Iranian prophet and founder of the ancient Parsee religion which bears his name. He had visions of Ahura Mazda, which led him to preach against polytheism. He appears as a historical person only in the earliest portion of the Avesta. As the centre of a group of chieftains, he carried on a struggle for the establishment of a holy agricultural state against Turanian and Vedic aggressors.

Zoroastrianism [zorohastrianizm] The worship of a supreme God, Ahura Mazda, in Iran during the first millennium BC. Rites of worship were performed by priests (*Magi*), and there was a body of scriptures called *Avesta*, the earliest part of which was made up of hymns attributed to a religious teacher, Zoroaster. The expansion of Islam forced Zoroastrianism out of Persia, and today it is practised by Parsees.

Zorrilla y Moral, José [thoreelya ee moral] (1817–93) Poet, born in Valladolid, NWC Spain. He studied law at Toledo and Valladolid, then devoted himself to literature in Madrid. He wrote many plays based on national legend, notably *Don Juan Tenorio* (1844), performed annually on All Saints' Day in Spanish-speaking countries.

Zouaves [zwahv] A body of troops in the French army, first raised from Algerian tribes in 1830, who dressed in flamboyant Moorish costume. During the American Civil War, several 'Zouave' style volunteer regiments were raised on the US side.

Z particle A particle that carries weak nuclear force; symbol *Z*; mass 91·2 GeV; charge zero; spin 1; decays for example to an electron plus positron, or a muon plus antimuon, or a neutrino plus antineutrino. Predicted by the Glashow–Weinberg–Salam theory, it was discovered in 1983 in proton–antiproton collisions at CERN, Geneva. The decay rate of the Z particle implies just three neutrino species in the universe.

Zrenjanin [zrenyanin], formerly **Veliki Beckerek** or **Petrovgrad** 45°22N 20°23E, pop (2000e) 142 000. River-port city in the autonomous province of Vojvodina, N Serbia; on R Begej; railway; foodstuffs, canning, machinery.

Zsigmondy, Richard (Adolf) [zigmondee] (1865–1929) Chemist, born in Vienna Austria. He studied at Munich University, carried out research at Berlin, taught at Graz, and became professor at Göttingen (1908–29). A pioneer of colloid chemistry, in 1903 he introduced the ultramicroscope, a device to assist the observation of colloidal size particles which are too small to be visible in a normal microscope. He was awarded the Nobel Prize for Chemistry in 1925.

Zuccarelli, Francesco [tsukaraylee] (1702–88) Painter, born in Pitigliano, NC Italy. He trained at Florence and Rome, and was active at Florence, but worked mainly in Venice after 1732. His pastoral landscapes, populated by shepherds and maidens and painted in a soft Rococo style, were very popular, especially in England, where he worked 1752–62 and 1765–71.

Zuccari or **Zuccaro, Taddeo** [tsukahree] (1529–66) Painter, born in Vado, N Italy. Largely self-taught, he executed several frescoes and easel pieces, especially for the Farnese family. His brother **Federigo Zuccari** (c.1543–1609) painted portraits and frescoes, visited England, and became an influential art theorist. The two brothers were leaders of the Roman late Mannerist school.

zucchini [zukeenee] *courgette*

Zuckerman (of Burnham Thorpe), Solly Zuckerman, Baron (1904–93) Zoologist, and political adviser, born in Cape Town, SW South Africa. He moved to Oxford in 1934, was a scientific adviser at Combined Operations HQ (1939–46), and became professor of anatomy at Birmingham (1946–68) and chief scientific adviser to the British government (1964–71). He carried out extensive research into primates, publishing such classic works as *The Social Life of Monkeys and Apes* (1932). He was knighted in 1956, and made a life peer in 1971. He published two volumes of autobiography, *From Apes to Warlords* (1978) and *Monkeys, Men and Missiles* (1988).

Zug [tsug] 47°10N 8°31E, pop (2000e) 22 500. Capital of Zug canton, C Switzerland; at NE end of Zuger Zee, 24 km/15 mi S of Zürich; railway junction; noted for its local kirsch; metallurgy, textiles; Gothic church (15th–16th-c).

Zugspitze [tsukshpitsuh] 47°25N 11°00E. Mountain in Germany, rising to 2962 m/9718 ft on the Wettersteingebirge of the Bavarian Alps, near the Austro-German border; highest point in Germany; hotel near the summit is one of Europe's highest atmospheric sampling stations.

Zuider Zee *Ijsselmeer*

Zukofsky, Louis [zukofskee] (1904–78) Poet, born in New York City, USA. A leading experimentalist after Pound, his poems first appeared in *An Objectivist Anthology* (1932). Later works, which experimented with sound and typography, included *All: the Collected Short Poems* (1965, 1967). He published an autobiography in 1970.

Zulu A Bantu-speaking agricultural and cattle people of Natal, South Africa; one of the Nguni group. They closely resemble the Xhosa both culturally and linguistically. The Zulu were formed into a kingdom in the early 19th-c, and became a formidable fighting force, dispersing many of the other peoples of S Africa far afield; but they were conquered by the Boers and British, and much of their territory was annexed. They have retained a strong self-identity, and are organized politically into the modern Inkatha movement under their leader Chief Mangosuthu Buthulezi. Their territory, greatly contracted, became one of the 'Homelands' of South Africa during the apartheid period: KwaZulu.

Zuni [zoonyee] A North American Indian group of the American SW, living in New Mexico and Arizona; one of the Pueblo peoples, closely resembling the Hopi and Pueblo. A peaceful agricultural people, they were defeated by the Spanish in the 17th-c. Many are assimilated to US culture, although certain traditions are still intact.

Zuo or **Tso Commentary** [zwoe], Chin **Zuo Zhuan** or **Tso Chuan** A rich narrative of the later Zhou (Chou) dynasty from 722–468 BC. It blends fact, fiction, and legend in an explanatary elaboration of the earlier *Spring and Autumn Annals*. Possibly written in the earlier 4th-c BC, it was found in a tomb in 281 AD.

Zurbarán, Francisco de [thoorbaran] (1598–1664) Religious painter, born in Fuente de Cantos, SW Spain. He spent most of his life at Seville, where his best-known work, an altarpiece, is to be found. Apart from a few portraits and still-life studies, his main subjects were monastic and historical, and he came to be called 'the Spanish Caravaggio'.

Zürich [zoorikh], Ger [tsüreekh] 47°22N 8°32E, pop (2000e) 357 000. Financial centre and capital of Zürich canton, N Switzerland; on R Limmat, at NW end of L Zürich, 96 km/60 mi NE of Bern; largest city in Switzerland; joined Swiss Confederation, 1351; important centre in the Reformation and Counter-Reformation; airport (Kloten); railway; university (1833); Swiss Federal Institute of Technology (1855); banking, finance, commerce, engineering, electrical products, textiles, tourism; Grossmünster (11th–14th-c), Fraumünster (13th-c, restored), town hall (17th-c), St Peter's Church (13th-c); International Zürich June Festival.

Zürs [tsurs] 47°09N 10°12E. Winter sports resort village in the Lechtal Alps, Vorarlberg, W Austria; altitude 1720 m/5643 ft; chairlift facilities on the Seekopf, Nördlicher, Trittkopf, and Krabachjoch mountains.

Zuse, Konrad [tsoozuh] (1910–95) Computer pioneer, born in Berlin, Germany. He studied at the Berlin Institute of Technology before joining the Henschel Aircraft Co in 1935. In the following year he began building a calculating machine in his spare time, a task which occupied him until 1945. He built a number of prototypes, the most historic of which was the Z3, the first operational general-purpose program-controlled calculator. Until 1964 he built up his own firm Zuse KG, and became an honorary professor of Göttingen University in 1966.

Zweig, Arnold [tsviyk] (1887–1968) Writer, born in Glogów, W Poland (formerly Glogau, Germany). His writing, socialistic in outlook, was coloured by his interest in Zionism, which led him to seek refuge in Palestine when exiled by the Nazis in 1934. He is best known for his pacifist novel, *Der Streit um den Sergeanten Grischa* (1928, The Case of Sergeant Grischa).

Zweig, Stefan [tsviyk] (1881–1942) Writer, born in Vienna Austria. He became known as a poet and translator, then as a biographer, short-story writer, and novelist, his work being characterized by his psychological insight into character. His best-known work was his set of historical portraits, *Sternstunden der Menschheit* (1928, trans The Tide of Fortune). He emigrated to London in 1934, and acquired British nationality, later moving to the USA and Brazil. His autobiographical *The World of Yesterday* was published posthumously in 1943.

Zwickau [tsvikow] 50°43N 12°30E, pop (2000e) 124 000. Mining and industrial city in Zwickau district, S Germany; on R Mulde, SW of Chemnitz; a free imperial city (1290–1323); railway; motor vehicles, chemicals, coal mining; birthplace of Schumann.

Zwicky, Fritz [zvikee] (1898–1974) Physicist, born in Varna, NE Bulgaria, of Swiss parents. He studied at the Swiss Federal Institute of Technology, Zürich, then took a position at the California Institute of Technology in 1925, becoming professor of astrophysics there (1942–68). He remained a Swiss citizen all his life. He researched extensively into galaxies and interstellar matter, and produced the standard catalogue on compact galaxies. In 1934 he predicted the existence of neutron stars and black holes.

Zwingli, Huldrych or **Ulrich** [tsvingglee], Lat **Ulricus Zuinglius** (1484–1531) Protestant reformer, born in Wildhaus, NE Switzerland. He studied at Bern, Vienna, and Basel, was ordained in 1506, and became a chaplain to the Swiss mercenaries. In 1518, elected preacher in the Zürich minster, he opposed the selling of indulgences, and espoused the Reformed doctrines, obtaining the support of the civil authorities. In 1524 he split with Luther over the question of the Eucharist, rejecting every form of corporeal presence. War between the cantons followed, and he was killed during a battle near Kappel.

zwitterion [tsviteriyon] A molecule containing both a positive and a negative charge simultaneously. It is the predominant form of an amino acid in solution, eg glycine NH_2–CH_2–COOH becomes $^{+}NH_3$–CH_2–COO^{-}.

Zwolle [zvoluh] 52°31N 6°06E, pop (2000e) 102 000. Capital city of Overijssel province, E Netherlands; on the Zwarte Water, which opens into the Ijsselmeer (NW); railway; canal junction; major cattle market; vehicles, machinery, foodstuffs, textiles, timber, leatherwork, chemicals, publishing, printing; St Michaelskerk (15th-c).

Zworykin, Vladimir (Kosma) [tsvorikin] (1889–1982) Physicist, born in Murom, W Russia. He studied at the St Petersburg Institute of Technology and the Collège de France in Paris, emigrated to the USA in 1919, and became a US citizen in 1924. He joined the Radio Corporation (1929), becoming director of electronic research (1946) and vice-president (1947). In 1923–4 he patented an all-electronic television system using a scanned camera-tube (the *iconoscope*), in 1929 demonstrated a cathode-ray display (the *kinescope*), and in later years contributed to the development of colour television and the electron microscope. He is regarded as 'the father of modern television'.

zydeco [ziydekoh] US dance music from SW Louisiana and W Texas, the black counterpart to white 'Cajun' music. The instrumentation usually includes piano accordion, saxophone, guitar, and washboard; there are influences from blues and, perhaps, the Carribean; and the music is fast, swinging, and syncopated. Leading performers have included singer and accordionist Clifton Chenier (1925–87), Rockin' Dopsie (born Alton Jay Rubin, 1932–93), and Queen Ida (born Ida Lewis). The word is said to be from a Creole form of *les haricots*, in the expression 'Are you getting your beans?', meaning 'Are you well?'.

zygomorphic flower A flower which is bilaterally symmetrical, so that it can be divided into equal halves in one plane only. It is often found in the more advanced plant families.

zygote [ziygoht] The fertilized egg of a plant or animal, formed by the fusion of male (*sperm*) and female (*ovum*) gametes. It is usually diploid (possessing a double chromosome set), having received a haploid chromosome set from each gamete.

Ready Reference

Measurement

Common Measures

Metric Units

		Imperial equivalent
Length		
	1 millimetre	0.03937 in
10 mm	1 centimetre	0.39 in
10 cm	1 decimetre	3.94 in
100 cm	1 metre	39.37 in
1000 m	1 kilometre	0.62 mi
Area		
	1 square millimetre	0.0016 sq in
	1 square centimetre	0.155 sq in
100 cm^2	1 square decimetre	15.5 sq in
10000 cm^2	1 square metre	10.76 sq ft
10000 m^2	1 hectare	2.47 acres
Volume		
	1 cubic centimetre	0.061 cu in
1000 cm^3	1 cubic decimetre	61.024 cu in
1000 dm^3	1 cubic metre	35.31 cu ft, 1.308 cu yds
Liquid Volume		
	1 litre $(dm)^3$	1.76 pt
100 litres	1 hectolitre	22 gal
Weight		
	1 gram	0.035 oz
1000g	1 kilogram	2.2046 lb
1000kg	1 tonne	0.0842 ton

Imperial units

		Metric equivalent
Length		
	1 inch	2.54 cm
12 in	1 foot	30.48 cm
3 ft	1 yard	0.9144 m
1760 yd	1 mile	1.6093 km
Area		
	1 square inch	6.45 cm^2
144 sq in	1 square foot	0.0929 m^2
9 sq ft	1 square yard	0.836 m^2
4840 sq yd	1 acre	0.405 ha
640 acres	1 square mile	259 ha
Volume		
	1 cubic inch	16.3871 cm^2
1728 cu in	1 cubic foot	0.028m^2
27 cu ft	1 cubic yard	0.765m^2
Liquid Volume		
	1 pint	0.571
2 pt	1 quart	1.141
4 qt	1 gallon	4.551
Weight		
	1 ounce	28.3495 g
16 oz	1 pound	0.4536 kg
14 lb	1 stone	6.35 kg
8 st	1 hundredweight	50.8 kg
20 cwt	1 ton	1.016 t

Conversion Factors

Imperial to metric

				Multiply by
Length	inches	→	millimetres	25.4
	inches	→	centimetres	2.54
	feet	→	metres	0.3048
	yards	→	metres	0.9144
	statute miles	→	kilometres	1.6093
	nautical miles	→	kilometres	1.852
Area	square inches	→	Square centimetres	6.4516
	square feet	→	square metres	0.0929
	square yards	→	square metres	0.8361
	acres	→	hectares	0.4047
	square miles	→	square kilometres	2.5899
Volume	cubic inches	→	cubic centimetres	16.3871
	cubic feet	→	cubic metres	0.0283
	cubic yards	→	cubic metres	0.7646
Capacity	UK fluid ounces	→	litres	0.0284
	US fluid ounces	→	litres	0.0296
	UK pints	→	litres	0.5682
	US pints	→	litres	0.4732
	UK gallons	→	litres	4.546
	US gallons	→	litres	3.7854
Weight	ounces (avoirdupois)	→	grams	28.3495
	ounces (troy)	→	grams	31.1035
	pounds	→	kilograms	0.4536
	tons (long)	→	tonnes	1.016

Metric to imperial

				Multiply by
Length	millimetres	→	inches	0.0394
	centimetres	→	inches	0.3937
	metres	→	feet	3.2808
	metres	→	yards	1.0936
	kilometres	→	statute miles	0.6214
	kilometres	→	nautical miles	0.54
Area	square centimetres	→	square inches	0.155
	square metres	→	square feet	10.764
	square metres	→	square yards	1.196
	hectares	→	acres	2.471
	square kilometres	→	square miles	0.386
Volume	cubic centimetres	→	cubic inches	0.061
	cubic metres	→	cubic feet	35.315
	cubic metres	→	cubic yards	1.308
Capacity	litres	→	UK fluid ounces	35.1961
	litres	→	US fluid ounces	33.8150
	litres	→	UK pints	1.7598
	litres	→	US pints	2.1134
	litres	→	UK gallons	0.2199
	litres	→	US gallons	0.2642
Weight	grams	→	ounces (avoirdupois)	0.0353
	grams	→	ounces (troy)	0.0322
	kilograms	→	pounds	2.2046
	tonnes	→	tons (long)	0.9842

Times and Distances

Air Distances

Air distances between some major cities, given in statute miles. To convert to kilometres, multiply number given by 1·6093.

* Shortest route.

	Anchorage	Beijing	Buenos Aires	Cairo	Chicago	Delhi	Hong Kong	Honolulu	Istanbul	Johannesburg	Lagos	London	Los Angeles	Mexico City	Montreal	Moscow	Nairobi	Paris	Perth	Rome	Santiago	Sydney	Tokyo	Washington
Amsterdam	4475	6566	7153	2042	4109	3985	5926	8368	1373	5606	3161	217	5559	5724	3422	1338	4148	261	9118	809	7714	1039	6006*	3854
Anchorage		4756	8329	6059	2854	8925	5063	2780	5024	1042	7587	4472	2333	3751	3100	4291	8714	4683	8368	5258	7919	8522	3443	3430
Beijing			12000	6685	7599	2368	1235	6778	4763	10108	8030	5054	6349	7912	7557	3604	8888	5108	4987	5306	13622	5689	1313	7930
Buenos Aires				7468	5587	8340	3124	8693	7783	5725	4832	6985	6140	4592	5640	8382	7427	6892	9734	6931	710	7760	13100	6097
Cairo					6135	2753	5098	9439	764	4012	2443	2187	7589	7730	5431	1790	2203	1995	7766	1329	8029	9196	6362	5859
Chigaco						8119	7827	4245	5502	8705	7065	3956	1746	1687	737	5500	8177	4140	11281	4828	5328	9324	6286	590
Delhi							2345	7888	2833	6765	5196	4169	8717	9806	7421	2698	4956	4089	5013	3679	12715	6495	3656	7841
Hong Kong								5543	5998	6728	7541	5979	7231	8794	8564	4839	7301	5987	3752	5773	3733	4586	1807	8385
Honolulu									9547	12892	10367	7252	2553	4116	4923	8802	11498	7463	7115	8150	8147	5078	3831	4822
Istanbul										4776	3207	1552	6994	7255	4795	1089	2967	1394	7846	852	10109	9883	5757	5347
Johannesburg											2854	5640	10443	10070	8322	6280	1809	5422	5564	4802	5738	7601	8535	8199
Lagos												3115	7716	7343	5595	4462	2377	2922	10209	2497	6042	11700	9130*	5472
London													5442	5703	3252	1550	4246	220	9246	898	8568	10565	6218	3672
Los Angeles														1563	2482	6992	9688	5633	9535	6340	5594	7498	5451	2294
Mexico City															2307	6700	9949	5714	11098	6601	4168	9061	7014	1871
Montreal																4393	7498	3434	12402	5431	5551	9980	6913	493
Moscow																	3951	1540	8355	1478	10118	9425	4668	4884
Nairobi																		4031	7373	3349	7547	9410	8565	7918
Paris																			12587	688	461	10150	6208*	3843
Perth																				8309	15129	2037	4925	11829
Rome																					7548	10149	6146	4495
Santiago																						13092	11049	5061
Sydney																							4640	9792
Tokyo																								6763

Flying Times

Approximate flying times between some major cities. Times quoted (in hours and minutes) are 'flying time' only. In many cases, in order to travel between two points, it is necessary to change aircraft one or more times. Time between flights has not been included.

	Anchorage	Beijing	Buenos Aires	Cairo	Chicago	Delhi	Hong Kong	Honolulu	Istanbul	Johannesburg	Lagos	London	Los Angeles	Mexico City	Montreal	Moscow	Nairobi	Paris	Perth	Rome	Santiago	Sydney	Tokyo	Washington
Amsterdam	9.00	16.50	17.45	4.20	8.35	8.15	15.15	16.42	3.15	13.15	6.40	1.05	11.15	12.27	7.40	3.15	8.15	1.10	20.35	2.20	20.50	23.05	11.40	8.55
Anchorage		11.45	10.48	13.20	5.44	16.50	11.40	5.44	12.15	19.50	14.55	8.30	6.13	10.49	7.91	12.15	17.00	9.00	17.25	12.00	19.13	16.35	7.20	7.25
Beijing			28.31	13.15	15.15	6.40	3.00	10.55	15.40	20.10	22.35	18.05	15.25	18.45	27.30	8.40	16.00	16.35	11.15	16.10	22.34	16.15	3.50	25.50
Buenos Aires				20.40	15.40	26.20	29.35	19.00	18.45	12.30	9.55	16.35	13.45	10.25	16.00	22.05	24.55	15.35	25.20	14.40	2.10	20.45	28.30	11.00
Cairo					18.40	7.00	10.55	22.50	2.00	8.55	8.20	5.35	21.00	16.47	12.35	5.25	4.55	5.05	17.10	3.25	25.10	17.20	19.40	14.20
Chigaco						20.05	17.05	9.25	12.20	21.40	14.55	8.30	5.00	5.15	2.20	12.15	17.00	9.00	23.00	11.35	17.15	21.10	12.55	1.45
Delhi							6.05	16.50	7.35	23.45	14.55	10.35	19.30	20.42	17.35	7.35	10.45	10.45	9.30	8.50	29.05	13.50	9.45	20.10
Hong Kong								13.05	17.35	14.55	22.30	16.05	15.50	19.10	23.05	18.00	12.45	16.40	8.15	15.10	19.15	10.35	4.20	24.15
Honolulu									21.05	30.25	23.40	17.15	5.15	8.35	12.50	21.00	25.45	18.05	17.25	19.13	8.35	11.50	7.05	10.55
Istanbul										16.30	8.05	3.50	14.50	15.42	10.15	4.40	7.15	3.10	15.25	2.35	21.00	18.40	14.05	11.25
Johannesburg											6.55	13.10	24.10	25.42	20.10	13.30	3.45	15.50	14.20	12.25	19.55	31.50	25.00	21.20
Lagos												6.25	17.25	19.07	13.25	10.10	6.20	7.45	25.55	6.55	24.25	28.35	18.40	14.45
London													11.00	14.35	7.00	3.45	8.30	1.05	19.30	2.25	21.55	21.55	11.50	8.10
Los Angeles														3.20	6.40	14.45	19.30	12.50	19.30	14.35	16.00	18.10	11.55	5.25
Mexico City															4.45	18.10	20.42	13.25	22.50	5.35	12.00	18.05	16.25	7.50
Montreal																10.45	15.30	6.25	26.30	8.10	14.50	24.50	18.55	2.50
Moscow																	12.50	4.00	19.40	4.10	24.05	19.40	9.25	12.30
Nairobi																		9.20	23.00	7.20	29.05	31.35	19.55	17.10
Paris																			21.40	1.55	19.45	25.05	16.45	9.25
Perth																				20.00	26.00	4.35	10.05	22.45
Rome																					18.50	23.50	17.40	12.40
Santiago																						24.30	27.55	17.40
Sydney																							9.15	23.35
Tokyo																								12.40

US Air Distances

Air distances between US cities, given in statute miles. To convert to kilometres, multiply number given by 1·6093.

	Atlanta	Boston	Chigaco	Dallas	Denver	Detroit	Houston	Kansas City	Los Angeles	Miami	Minneapolis	New Orleans	New York	Oklahoma City	Omaha	Philadelphia	Phoenix	Pittsburgh	Portland	St Louis	Salt Lake City	San Antonio	San Francisco	Seattle
Boston	946																							
Chigaco	606	867																						
Dallas	721	1555	796																					
Denver	1208	1767	901	654																				
Detroit	595	632	235	982	1135																			
Houston	689	1603	925	217	864	1095																		
Kansas City	581	1254	403	450	543	630	643																	
Los Angeles	1946	2611	1745	1246	849	1979	1379	1363																
Miami	595	1258	1197	1110	1716	1146	964	1239	2342															
Minneapolis	906	1124	334	853	693	528	1046	394	1536	1501														
New Orleans	425	1367	837	437	1067	936	305	690	1671	674	1040													
New York	760	187	740	1383	1638	509	1417	1113	2475	1090	1028	1182												
Oklahoma City	761	1505	693	181	500	911	395	312	1187	1223	694	567	1345											
Omaha	821	1282	416	585	485	651	793	152	1330	1393	282	841	1155	418										
Philadelphia	665	281	678	1294	1569	453	1324	1039	2401	1013	980	1094	94	1268	1094									
Phoenix	1587	2300	1440	879	589	1681	1015	1043	370	1972	1270	1301	2143	833	1037	2082								
Pittsburgh	526	496	412	1061	1302	201	1124	769	2136	1013	726	918	340	1010	821	267	1814							
Portland	2172	2537	1739	1637	985	1959	1834	1492	834	2700	1426	2050	2454	1484	1368	2411	1009	2148						
St Louis	484	1046	258	546	781	440	667	229	1592	1068	448	604	892	462	342	813	1262	553	1708					
Salt Lake City	1589	2105	1249	1010	381	1489	1204	919	590	2088	991	1428	1989	865	839	1932	507	1659	630	1156				
San Antonio	875	1764	1041	247	793	1215	191	697	1210	1143	1097	495	1587	407	824	1052	843	1277	1714	786	1086			
San Francisco	2139	2704	1846	1476	956	2079	1636	1498	337	2585	1589	1911	2586	1383	1433	2521	651	2253	550	1735	599	1482		
Seattle	2182	2496	1720	1670	1019	1932	1874	1489	954	2725	1399	2087	2421	1520	1368	2383	1109	2124	132	1709	689	1775	678	
Washington, DC	532	414	590	1163	1464	385	1189	927	2288	919	909	969	229	1158	1000	136	1956	184	2339	696	1839	1361	2419	2307

UK Road Distances

Road distances between British centres are given in statute miles, using routes recommended by the Automobile Association based on the quickest travelling time. To convert to kilometres, multiply number given by 1·6093.

	Birmingham	Bristol	Cambridge	Cardiff	Dover	Edinburgh	Exeter	Glasgow	Holyhead	Hull	Leeds	Liverpool	Manchester	Newcastle upon Tyne	Norwich	Nottingham	Oxford	Penzance	Plymouth	Shrewsbury	Southampton	Stranraer	York	London
Aberdeen	433	516	464	536	589	125	589	148	462	360	328	360	355	236	488	394	505	699	631	415	572	240	321	548
Birmingham		88	98	108	208	298	161	296	168	141	121	101	89	211	159	54	68	271	203	48	134	307	134	120
Bristol			171	48	206	381	83	379	251	232	212	184	172	302	233	145	74	194	125	131	76	390	226	120
Cambridge				205	124	336	250	356	260	140	148	193	161	233	63	87	100	361	292	140	131	367	157	60
Cardiff					241	401	121	399	206	252	231	204	191	322	266	165	109	231	162	110	141	409	245	155
Dover						461	244	499	370	264	272	303	291	357	173	218	146	356	287	251	152	509	281	78
Edinburgh							454	46	327	232	200	223	220	108	360	266	370	564	496	280	437	132	193	413
Exeter								454	325	306	286	258	246	376	313	219	154	109	45	205	112	464	300	200
Glasgow									325	268	220	223	218	153	380	286	368	562	494	278	434	85	213	411
Holyhead										220	165	102	122	268	305	174	239	433	365	104	305	335	191	282
Hull											60	129	99	145	151	93	190	415	346	163	257	279	38	188
Leeds												74	44	97	173	74	171	395	327	118	237	230	24	199
Liverpool													35	177	241	108	173	367	299	66	239	233	101	216
Manchester														147	185	71	160	355	286	70	277	228	71	203
Newcastle upon Tyne															257	163	260	484	416	221	327	164	90	288
Norwich																119	143	422	354	202	193	391	181	115
Nottingham																	103	328	259	86	170	297	87	131
Oxford																		264	195	121	66	380	184	56
Penzance																			77	315	223	573	409	310
Plymouth																				246	155	505	341	241
Shrewsbury																					187	288	145	163
Southampton																						446	250	80
Stranraer																							224	421
York																								212